DICTIONARY

OF THE

FRENCH AND ENGLISH

LANGUAGES

WITH MORE THAN FIFTEEN THOUSAND NEW WORDS, MEANINGS, ETC.

BY

FERDINAND E. A. GASC

NEW YORK
HENRY HOLT AND COMPANY

January, 1929

PRINTED IN THE U. S. A.

FRENCH AND ENGLISH

INDEX TO THE ABBREVIATIONS.

a., active, *actif*
abbrev., abbreviation, *abréviation*
acc., accusative, *accusatif*
acoust., acoustics, *acoustique*
adj., adjective, *adjectif*
adject., adjectively, *adjectivement*
admin., administration, *administration*
adv., adverb, *adverbe*
adverb., adverbially, *adverbialement*
affirm., affirmatively, *affirmativement*
agr., agriculture, *agriculture*
alg., algebra, *algèbre*
anat., anatomy, *anatomie*
anc., ancient, *ancien*
arch., architecture, *architecture*
arith., arithmetic, *arithmétique*
art., article, *article*
artil., artillery, *artillerie*
astr., astronomy, *astronomie*

bank., banking, *banque*
book-bind., book-binding, *reliure*
book-keep., book-keeping, *comptabilité*
bot., botany, *botanique*
brew., brewing, *terme de brasseur*
build., building, *construction*
butch., butcher's term, *boucherie*

cabinet-mak., cabinet-making, *ébénisterie*
can. law, canon law, *droit canon*
carp., carpentry, *charpenterie*
Cath. lit., Roman Catholic liturgy, *liturgie catholique*
Cath. rel., Roman Catholic religion, *religion catholique*
chem., chemistry, *chimie*
chron., chronology, *chronologie*
civ., civil, *civil*
civ. engin., civil engineering, *génie civil*
civ. law, civil law, *droit civil*
coin., coining, *monnayage*
com., commerce, *commerce*
com. nav., commercial navigation, *commerce maritime*
comp., comparative, *comparatif*
conf., confectionery, *confiserie*
conj., conjunction, *conjonction*
cook., cookery, *cuisine*
coop., cooperage, *tonnellerie*
crim. law, criminal law, *droit criminel*
cust., customs, *douanes*

dat., dative case, *datif*
def., defective, *défectif*
dem. pron., demonstrative pronoun, *pronom démonstratif*
dipl., diplomacy, *diplomatie*
dist., distillery, *distillerie*
draw., drawing, *dessin*

eccl., eccles., ecclesiastical, *ecclésiastique*
elect., electricity, *électricité*
engin., engineering, *génie civil*
Engl., English, England, *Anglais, Angleterre*
engr., engraving, *gravure*

f., feminine, *féminin*
falc., falconry, *fauconnerie*
fam., familiar, *familier*
fenc., fencing, *escrime*
feud., feudal, feudalism, *féodal, féodalité*
fig., figuratively, *au figuré*
fin., finance, *finances*
fish., fishing, *pêche*
fort., fortification, *fortification*
Fr., French, France, *Français, France*
fut., future, *futur*

geog., geography, *géographie*
geol., geology, *géologie*
geom., geometry, *géométrie*
Gr., Greek, *Grec*
gram., grammar, *grammaire*

her., heraldry, *blason*
hist., history, *histoire*
horol., horology, *horlogerie*
hort., horticulture, *horticulture*
hunt., hunting, *chasse*

imp., impersonal, *impersonnel*
ind., indicative mood, *indicatif*
inf., infinitive mood, *infinitif*
instr., instrument, *instrument*
int., interjection, *interjection*
inter., interrogatively, *interrogativement*
irr., irregular, *irrégulier*

jest., jestingly, *par plaisanterie*
Jew., Jewish, *Juif*
jewel., jewellery, *joaillerie, bijouterie*

lit., liturgy, *liturgie*
liter., literature, *littérature*
log., logic, *logique*

m., masculine, *masculin*
mach., machinery, *machines*
Mahom. rel., Mahomedan religion, *religion mahométane*
manu., manufacture, *manufacture*
mas., masonry, *maçonnerie*
math., mathematics, *mathématiques*
meas., measure, *mesure*
mech., mechanics, *mécanique*
med., medicine, *médecine*
metal., metallurgy, *métallurgie*
mil., military art, *art militaire*
mil. engin., military engineering, *génie militaire*
min., mineralogy, *minéralogie*
mus., music, *musique*
myth., mythology, *mythologie*

n., neuter, *neutre*
nat. hist., natural history, *histoire naturelle*
nav., navy, *marine*
navig., navigation, *navigation*
need., needle-work, *ouvrage à l'aiguille*
neg., negation, negatively, with a negation, *négation, négativement, avec une négation*
neut., neuter, *neutre*
nom., nominative case, *nominatif, sujet*

o., one, *un*
obj., objective case, *régime direct*
opt., optics, *optique*
o.'s, one's, *son, sa, ses*

paint., painting, *peinture*
parl., parliamentary language, *langage parlementaire*
part., participle, *participe*
pers., (said of) persons, *(des) personnes*
pers. pron., personal pronoun, *pronom personnel*
persp., perspective, *perspective*
pharm., pharmacy, *pharmacie*
philos., philosophy, *philosophie*
phys., physics, natural philosophy, *physique*
pl., plural, *pluriel*
poet., poetry, *poésie*
polit., politics, *politique*
pop., popular (vulgar), *populaire*
poss., possessive, *possessif*
post., post-office, *poste*
prep., preposition, *préposition*
pret., preterit, *prétérit*
print., printing, *imprimerie*
pron., pronoun, *pronom*

r., reflective, *réfléchi*
rail., railways, *chemins de fer*
rel., religion, *religion*
rel. order, religious order, *ordre religieux*
rel. pron., relative pronoun, *pronom relatif*
rhet., rhetoric, *rhétorique*
rid., riding, *manége*
Rom., Roman, *Romain*

s., substantive, *substantif*
school, term used in schools, *terme d'écoles*
sculp., sculpture, *sculpture*
shoot., shooting, *chasse*
sing., singular, *singulier*
spin., spinning, *filature*
stat., stationery, *papeterie*
subj., subjunctive mood, *subjonctif*
substant., substantively, *substantivement*
super., superlative, *superlatif*
surg., surgery, *chirurgie*

tech., technology, *technologie*
theat., theatres, *théâtres*
theol., theology, *théologie*

univers., universities, *universités*

V., vide, see, *voir*
v., verb, *verbe*
v.a., verb active, *verbe actif*
v.n., verb neuter, *verbe neutre*
v.r., verb reflective, *verbe réfléchi;* **verb reciprocal,** *verbe réciproque*
vers., versification, *versification*
vet., veterinary art, *art vétérinaire*

writ., writing, *écriture*

zool., zoology, *zoologie*

PLAN OF THE WORK.

† Indicates that the *gn*, *l*, or *ll*, is liquid.

‡ Means that *ch* is sounded like *k*.

' Denotes that the *h* or *o* or *y* is aspirated.

* Indicates that the *u* in *qu* is sounded as in "Aquatic."

§ Indicates that the *u* in *qu* has its pure French sound.

Qu not preceded by either of the above signs, is sounded like *q* alone: thus *quatre* is pronounced *qatre*, *qui* is pronounced *qi*, &c.

— Stands for the repetition of the leading word.

- Before final letters or syllables, shows the masculine termination, when followed by the feminine: as Curieu-x, se, *curieux*, m., *curieuse*, f.; Protec-teur, trice, *protecteur*, m., *protectrice*, f.

Words being essentially French, though used to some extent in England, will generally be found only in the French-English part, where they are reestablished by translation into their old English form, from which there never was any reason to deviate.—But all words like *boudoir*, *amateur*, *parachute*, &c., borrowed from the French and having no English equivalent in one or more senses, are duly given in the English-French part.

French words in common use, for which there is no English equivalent (as *bavaroise*, *entresol*, *feuilleton*, *bois satiné*, &c.) have been inserted, but with a definition (an accurate one) instead of an attempt at an impossible translation.

English words for which there is no French equivalent, such as 'teapoy,' 'pulled bread,' 'valentine' (letter), and a multitude of others, have been cast aside, as they can only be badly translated.

Every barbarous word from the dead languages, of which there is a good duplicate either in French or in English, has also been kept out.

Fancy denominations partaking of the nature of trade-puff advertisements, &c., have of course been deemed quite unworthy of a place in this Dictionary.

Adjectives being part of a verb, such as *Encourageant*, 'encouraging,' 'inspiriting,' from ENCOURAGER, 'to encourage,' 'to inspirit,' *Critiqué*, 'criticized,' 'censured,' from CRITIQUER, 'to criticize,' 'to censure,' &c., have been omitted whenever they have not a distinct sense from those given under the verb: it is the province of a grammar, not that of a dictionary, to conjugate verbs.

OBSERVATIONS.

§ 1. English and French words ending as mentioned below, generally differ only in their termination:—

Substantives derived from the Greek, and ending in English with **logy, sophy, graphy, pathy, tomy,** or any such way, change *y* into *ie* in French, and are feminine.

Examples:—

English.	French.
chronology,	*chronologie*, f.
philosophy,	*philosophie*, f.
geography,	*géographie*, f.
antipathy,	*antipathie*, f.
anatomy; &c.	*anatomie*, f.; &c.

Adjectives ending in English with **ic** or **ical,** generally end in French with *ique* for both genders; Adverbs formed from those adjectives, end in English with **ically** or **icly,** and in French with *iquement.*

Examples:—

English.	French.
patriotic,	*patriotique*
historic, historical,	*historique*
historically,	*historiquement*
publicly; &c.	*publiquement;* &c.

But the adjective 'public' is in French *publique* only in the feminine gender, the masculine being *public*, as in English.

Substantives ending in English with **ism,** generally end in French with *isme*, and are masculine.

Example:—

English.	French.
patriotism, &c.	*patriotisme*, m., &c.

Substantives and Adjectives ending in English with **ist,** generally end in French with *iste;* they are masculine when applied to a man, and feminine when applied to a female.

Examples:—

English.	French.
dentist,	*dentiste*, m.
pianist; &c.	*pianiste*, m.f.; &c.

Substantives ending in English with **bility** or **bleness,** generally end in French with *bilité*, and are feminine; as 'impossibility,' *impossibilité* (f.), 'instability' or 'instableness,' *instabilité* (f.), &c. So the student can easily coin for himself, if he pleases, those which, like 'palpability' and a multitude of others, are not sufficiently current to be allowed to fill, to the exclusion of far better words, whole pages in this Dictionary.

§ 2. It would be impossible to insert even in the largest dictionary all the compound nouns that may be formed in English. The following rule, about those which can be translated almost literally into French, will be useful. The order of the English nouns is to be inverted in French, and *de* or *à* placed between them:

DE, where *of, of the, made of* or *from, composed of, forming part of, coming from*, &c., may be understood;

A, where *for, used for, intended for, for the purpose of, by means of, with*, &c., may be understood.

Examples: *table* DE *cuisine* (kitchen-table), *table* A *thé* (tea-table); *robe* DE *soie* (silk-dress), *ver* A *soie* (silk-worm), *ver* DE *terre* (earth-worm); *sac* DE *papier* (paper-bag, made of paper), *sac* A *papier* (paper-bag, for putting paper in); *sucre* DE *canne* (cane-sugar), *canne* A *sucre* (sugar-cane); *moulin* A *eau* (water-mill), *chute* D'*eau* (water-fall); *boîte* A *couteaux* (knife-box); *bain* DE *pieds* (foot-bath); *huile* DE *foie* DE *morue* (cod-liver oil); *vin* DE *Bourgogne* (Burgundy wine); *confitures* DE *fraises* (strawberry jam); *train* DE *Londres* (London train); *gare* DE *Paris* (Paris terminus); &c.

There are a few exceptions, as 'salle *de* bains,' 'salle *de* danse,' 'cabinet *de* toilette,' and the like. But, with a verb, *à* is always used; as *chambre* A *coucher* (sleeping-room), *salle* A *manger* (dining-room), *papier* A *écrire* (writing-paper), *cire* A *cacheter* (sealing-wax), &c.

In a determinate sense, the article *du, de la, des,* is used instead of *de* only, and *au, à la, aux,* instead of *à* only: as, 'the street-door' (the door of *the* street), *la porte* DE LA *rue;* a 'letter-box' (for *the* letters to be sent by post), *une boîte* AUX *lettres;* &c. In speaking of made-dishes and drinks, and in the sense of 'mixed with' or 'done in' or 'composed *chiefly* (but not entirely) of,' *au, à la, aux,* are also used; as, *du café* AU *lait, une glace* A LA *creme, une tarte* AUX *confitures*, &c.—So, according to this and to the principal rule, 'a currant jam tart' is, in French, *une tarte* AUX *confitures* DE *groseilles;* &c.

Connected with the above rule are phrases of the following kind: 'silver-mounted penholder,' *porte-plume monté en argent;* 'marble-top dining-room table,' *table de salle à manger à dessus de marbre;* 'blue-striped waistcoat,' *gilet à raies bleues;* 'double-cased watch,' *montre à double boîte;* 'double-bedded room,' *chambre à deux lits;* 'a one-horse carriage,' *une voiture à un cheval;* 'a four-horse goods van,' *un fourgon de marchandises à quatre chevaux;* 'a two-storied house,' *une maison à deux étages;* 'ivory-handled knife,' *couteau à manche d'ivoire;* &c. In these examples it will be noticed that *à* is used as corresponding to the English 'with,' in the sense of 'having,' which is understood. See Gasc's *Second French Book*, pp. 75, 76, and 151.

An essential difference of construction in the two languages is this: the French people always go from the general to the particular, while the English go from the particular to the general.

Examples: 'Cod-liver oil,' *huile de foie de morue;*— 'annual general meeting,' *assemblée générale annuelle;*— Thames iron ship-building company, *compagnie de construction des bateaux en fer de la Tamise;* &c.

(Figures printed above the words: Cod(3)-liver(2) oil(1), *huile*(1) *de foie*(2) *de morue*(3); annual(3) general(2) meeting(1), *assemblée*(1) *générale*(2) *annuelle*(3); Thames(5) iron(4) ship(3)-building(2) company(1), *compagnie*(1) *de construction*(2) *des bateaux*(3) *en fer*(4) *de la Tamise*(5).)

*** After names of recipients, such as *verre* (glass), *bouteille* (bottle), *tasse* (cup), &c., DE always means 'of,' or 'made of,' and the construction is then usually the same in English and in French: as, *verre* DE *vin*, 'glass of wine,' *bouteille* D'*encre*, 'bottle of ink,' *tasse* DE *café*, 'cup of coffee'; *bouteille de grès*, 'stone bottle,' *tasse de porcelaine*, 'china cup,' &c. But, on the contrary, after the same names, A is not translated into English, and an inversion of the words must then always be made: as, *verre* A *vin*, 'wine-glass,' *bouteille* A *encre*, 'ink-bottle,' *tasse* A *café*, 'coffee-cup,' &c.

§ 3. Plural of Substantives.—Substantives generally end in the plural with *s*, in French as well as in English; as, *père*, 'father,' *pères*, 'fathers,' &c. Adjectives, in French, generally end also with *s* in the plural; as, *bon père*, 'good father,' *bons pères*, 'good fathers.'

Yet *œil*, 'eye,' makes *yeux* in the plural (except in the compounds *œil-de-bœuf*, *œil-de-chat*, &c., used in a figurative sense, plural *œils-de-bœuf*, &c., where *œils* is pluralized regularly); likewise *ciel* makes *cieux* in the plural (except when it signifies the testers of beds, the roofs of quarries, 'skies' in painting, or climates, in which senses it makes *ciels*); also *aïeul*, in the sense of 'ancestor,' makes *aïeux* in the plural, but in the sense of 'grandfather' it makes *aïeuls*, to designate both grandfathers, the paternal and the maternal (sometimes also both one's grandfather and grandmother considered together). The following, *bonhomme*, *gentilhomme*, *monsieur*, *monseigneur*, *madame*, and *mademoiselle*, make in the plural *bonshommes*, *gentilshommes*, *messieurs*, *messeigneurs*, *mesdames*, and *mesdemoiselles*.

Besides the general rule just mentioned, the following peculiar rules and exceptions are worth notice:

French Substantives and Adjectives ending in the singular with—

al change *l* into *ux* for the plural; as, *cheval*, plural *chevaux*; *royal*, plural *royaux*; &c.

Except:—

Substantives.	Plural.	Adjectives.	Plural.
aval,	avals		
bal,	bals		
bancal,	bancals	bancal,	bancals
cal,	cals	choral,	chorals
cantal,	cantals	fatal,	fatals
caracal,	caracals	final,	finals
carnaval,	carnavals	glacial,	glacials
cérémonial,	cérémonials	naval,	navals
chacal,	chacals	tribal,	tribals
choral,	chorals		
festival,	festivals		
galgal,	galgals		
narval,	narvals		
nopal	nopals		
pal,	pals		
régal,	régals		
rorqual,	rorquals		
sandal,	sandals		
serval,	servals		
val,*	vals		
verdal,	verdals		

* *Val* makes *vaux* only in the old phrase *par monts et par vaux*.

ail take *s* at the end for the plural; as, *détail*, plural *détails*; *rail*, plural *rails*; &c.

Except:—

	Plural.
aspirail,	aspiraux
bail,	baux
corail,	coraux
diguail,	diguaux
émail,	émaux
fermail,	fermaux
soupirail,	soupiraux
travail,*	travaux
vantail,	vantaux
vitrail,	vitraux

* *Travail*, in the sense of 'brake' (farriers' term), makes *travails* instead of *travaux*. *Bercail* and *Bétail* are not used in the plural.

au, eu, take *x* at the end for the plural; as, *tuyau*, plural *tuyaux*; *chapeau*, plural *chapeaux*; *nouveau*, plural *nouveaux*; *jeu*, plural *jeux*; &c.

Except:—

	Plural.
dizeau (*substantive*),	dizeaus
bleu (*adj. and subst.*),	bleus
feu (*adj.*),*	feus
landau (*substantive*),	landaus

* *But feu, subst., makes feux in the plural.*

ou take *s* at the end for the plural; as, *verrou*, plural *verrous*; *fou*, plural *fous*; *mou*, plural *mous*; &c.

Except:—

	Plural.
bijou,	bijoux
caillou,	cailloux
chou,	choux
genou,	genoux
hibou,	hiboux
joujou,	joujoux
pou,	poux

s, x, z, do not change at all for the plural; as, *bras*, plural *bras*; *divers*, plural *divers*; *noix*, plural *noix*; *sérieux*, plural *sérieux*; *nez*, plural *nez*; &c.

No Exception.

* The adjective *tout* makes *tous* in the plural masculine, and *toutes* in the plural feminine; but the substantive *tout* makes *touts* in the plural.

Words naturally invariable, and which are only accidentally employed as substantives, do not take the mark of the plural in French; thus we write *les pourquoi, les car, les si, les oui, les non, les on dit, &c.*

§ 4. Plural of Compound Substantives.—Compound substantives which have not yet passed to the state of words, that is to say, whose distinct parts are connected by a hyphen, are written in the singular or in the plural, according as the nature and particular sense of the words of which they are composed require the one or the other number. [In compound nouns, the only words susceptible, by their nature, of taking the mark of the plural, are the *substantive* and the *adjective*.] Such is the general principle, whose application will be facilitated by the following rules.

1. When a word is composed of a substantive and an adjective, both take the mark of the plural; as,

une chauve-souris,	*a bat,*	pl. *des* chauves-souris.
une basse-cour,	*a poultry-yard,*	— *des* basses-cours.

To this rule there are a few exceptions; as, une *grand'mère*, plural des *grand'mères*.

N.B.—Grand, without apostrophe, always agrees in gender and number with its substantive, but grand' is always invariable.

2. When a compound word is formed of two substantives placed immediately one after the other, both take the mark of the plural; as,

un chef-lieu,	*a county town,*	pl. *des* chefs-lieux.
un chou-fleur,	*a cauliflower,*	— *des* choux-fleurs.

The exceptions to this rule take place when there is no plurality in the idea conveyed by one or the other of the two substantives; as in un *hôtel-Dieu* (un hôtel de Dieu), a name given to the principal hospital, or infirmary, of several towns in France; plural des *hôtels-Dieu*. Also un *timbre-poste* (un timbre de la poste), a 'postage-stamp'; plural des *timbres-poste*. Also un *appui-main* (un appui pour la main), a 'maulstick'; plural des *appuis-main*. Also un *brèche-dents* (une personne qui a une brèche dans les dents), plural des *brèche-dents*.

3. When a compound word is formed of two substantives joined by a preposition, the first only generally takes the mark of the plural; as,

un arc-en-ciel,	*a rainbow,*	pl. *des* arcs-en-ciel.
un chef-d'œuvre,	*a master-piece,*	— *des* chefs-d'œuvre.

Except when there is no plurality in the idea conveyed by that first substantive; as, UN *tête-à-tête*, plural DES *tête-à-tête*. UN *coq-à-l'âne*, an unconnected, nonsensical speech, passing from one thing to another quite opposite, as from a *cock to an ass;* plural DES *coq-à-l'âne*. UN *pied-à-terre*, plural DES *pied-à-terre;* &c.

4. When a compound word is formed of a substantive joined either to a verb (though used substantively), a preposition, or an adverb, the substantive alone takes the sign of the plural, but only if there be plurality in the idea. So we write with an *s* in the plural:

un avant-coureur, *a forerunner*, pl. *des* avant-coureurs.
un contre-coup, *a counter-blow*, — *des* contre-coups.

But we write without an *s* in the plural, because the expressions are elliptical, and there is unity in the idea:

Des réveille-matin (clocks which awake in the *morning*), *alarm-clocks*.

Des contre-poison (remedies against *poison*), *counter-poisons*.

Des grippe-sou (people who gather money *sou* by *sou*, or a 'halfpenny' at a time), *money-grubbers*.

Finally, we write with an *s*, in the singular as well as in the plural, because there is always plurality in the idea:

un essuie-mains (that which wipes the *hands*) *a towel*, pl. *des* essuie-mains.

un porte-mouchettes (that which bears the *snuffers*) *a snuffer-tray*, —*des* porte-mouchettes.

un cure-dents (that which cleans the *teeth*) *a tooth-pick*, — *des* cure-dents.

un tire-bottes (that which pulls off a pair of *boots*) *a boot-jack*, — *des* tire-bottes.

un garde-côtes (a man or a vessel that guards the *coasts*) *a coast-guard*, — *des* garde-côtes.

• But we write *un* tire-bouchon (that which draws the *cork* of a bottle) *a cork-screw*, — *des* tire-bouchons (utensils which draw the *corks* of bottles).

5. When a compound substantive contains only such parts of speech as the *verb*, *preposition* or *adverb*, none of its components takes the mark of the plural; as,

un passe-passe, *a sleight of hand*, pl. *des* passe-passe.
un passe-partout, *a master-key, a pass-key*, — *des* passe-partout.

VERBAL ADJECTIVES.

Participles of verbs used as adjectives agree, in French, in gender and number with the noun or pronoun to which they refer; as,

Un homme charmant (*from* Charmer, '*to charm*').
Une femme charmante.
Des hommes charmants.
Des femmes charmantes.

Un livre bien écrit (*from* Écrire, '*to write*').
Une lettre bien écrite.
Des livres bien écrits.
Des lettres bien écrites.

NOUN-ADJECTIVES OF COLOUR.

Substantives used adjectively to express colour remain invariable, as, *Des gants* PAILLE (straw-coloured), *des robes* NOISETTE, *des rubans* CERISE: and so forth with MARRON, ORANGE, PUCE, MAUVE, CARMIN, PONCEAU, MAGENTA, and the like, which are all substantives used as adjectives. But *rose*, *violet*, *pourpre*, *blanc*, *jaune*, *bleu*, *vert*, and the like, being adjectives, take of course both gender and number.

ADJECTIVES, &C. USED SUBSTANTIVELY.

Adjectives used substantively to express the names of languages are all masculine (the substantive masculine *idiome* being understood): as, *le français*, *l'anglais*, *l'allemand*, *l'italien*, *le latin*, *le grec; parler français*, *en français*, *parler anglais*, *en anglais*, &c.

In general, adjectives, verbs, and the uninflected parts of speech taken substantively, are masculine. Examples: *le bon*, *le mauvais*, *le dormir*, *un oui*, *un non*, *un mais*, *un si*, *le pourquoi*, *le parce que*, &c.

TABLE OF

FRENCH MONEY, MEASURES AND WEIGHTS,

REDUCED TO AMERICAN MONEY, MEASURES AND WEIGHTS.

* Francs.	Centimes.	Dollars.	Cents.
Fr.	c.	$	c.
0	05	0	01
0	10	0	02
0	25	0	05
0	50	0	10
1	00	0	20
2	00	0	40
3	00	0	60
4	00	0	80
5	00	1	00
6	00	1	20
7	00	1	40
8	00	1	60
9	00	1	80
10	00	2	00
11	00	2	20
12	00	2	40
13	00	2	60
14	00	2	80
15	00	3	00
16	00	3	20
17	00	3	40
18	00	3	60
19	00	3	80
20	00	4	00

ITINERARY MEASURE.

Mètre (ten-millionth part of the arc of a meridian between the pole and the equator)		3·2808992	feet.
Décamètre	(10 metres)	32·808992	feet.
Kilomètre	(1,000 metres)	1093·633	yards.
Myriamètre	(10,000 metres)	6·2138	miles.

LONG MEASURE.

Décimètre	(10th of a metre)	3·937079	inches.
Centimètre	(100th of a metre)	0·39371	inch.
Millimètre	(1,000th of a metre)	0·03937	inch.

SUPERFICIAL MEASURE.

Are	(100 square metres)	0·098845	rood.
Hectare	(10,000 square metres)	2·471143	acres.
Centiare	(1 square metre)	1·196033	square yard.

MEASURE OF CAPACITY.

Litre	(1 cubic decimetre)	1·760773	pint.
Décalitre	(10 litres)	2·2009668	gallons.
Hectolitre	(100 litres)	22.009668 3·5317	gallons *or* cubic feet.
Kilolitre, mètre cube	(1,000 litres)	220·09668 35·3171	gallons *or* cubic feet.
Décilitre	(10th of a litre)	0·176	pint.
Centilitre	(100th of a litre)	0·0176	pint.

SOLID MEASURE.

Stère	(1 cubic metre)	1·31 cubic yard *or* 35 cubic feet, 547 cubic inches.
Décastère	(10 steres)	13·1 cubic yards, 2 feet, 21 inches.
Décistère	(10th of a stere)	3 cubic feet, 918·7 cubic inches.

WEIGHTS.

Gramme (weight of a cubic centimetre of water in its state of maximum density or 39½ Fahrenheit or 4 degrees centigrade)		15·432349	grains troy.
Décagramme	(10 grammes)	5·6438	drams avoird.
Hectogramme	(100 grammes)	3·527 3·2154	oz. avoird. *or* oz. troy.
Kilogramme	(1,000 grammes)	2·2046215 2·679227	lb. avoird. *or* lb. troy.
Quintal métrique	(50 kilogrammes)	110·231	lb. avoird.
Millier, tonneau de mer	(500 kilogrammes)	9 cwt.	94 lb. 5 oz.
Tonne	(1,000 kilogrammes)	19 cwt.	86 lb. 10 oz.
Décigramme	(10th of a gramme)	1·5432	grain.
Centigramme	(100th of a gramme)	0·1543	grain.
Milligramme	(1,000th of a gramme)	0·015432	grain.

THERMOMETER.

0°	Centigrade	Melting ice	32°	Fahrenheit.
100°	do.	Boiling water	212°	do.
0°	Réaumur	Melting ice	32°	do.
80°	do.	Boiling water	212°	do.

* The "par" of French Exchange in New York is 5 francs to the dollar. It fluctuates by eighths of centimes. Perhaps the most frequent quotation is 5.12½, which makes the franc represent $0.19512192.

FRENCH-ENGLISH.

A (*first letter of the alphabet*), *s.m.* a. *Deux* —, two a's. *Marqué à l'*—, a man of honour; a superior man; first-rate, A 1. *Ne savoir ni — ni B*, not to know A from B

A (*or* **à**, *with a grave accent*), *prep.* to; at; in; within; into; on; upon; as a, as; a; by; through; by means of; with; for; of; after; about; attending to; as to; from; under; against; after the manner of; according to; between; among; before; enough, sufficient; reason (to), occasion for; the means of; in such a way as; so as; such as; calculated to; capable of; likely (to); so far as; sold for; worth; or; and; till; good-bye till; something; anything. — *moi*, (*toi, lui*, &c.) to *or* at me; to *or* at myself; mine, my own; of mine, of my own; peculiar; to spare; my turn; (to *or* at thee *or* him, &c.). — *moi à*, my turn to; for me to. — *moi de*, my duty *or* part to; for me to. — *moi seul* or *tout seul*, alone, unassisted. — *la française*, after the French fashion. **Table — thé,** tea-table. **Machine — coudre,** sewing-machine. *C'est — qui*, they vie *or* try who. *C'était — qui passerait le premier*, they vied *or* tried who should pass first. — *qui à jouer?* whose turn is it to play? *Ils sont — jouer, — écrire*, they are playing, writing. *Il n'y a pas — hésiter*, there is no hesitating. *Cela n'est pas — craindre*, that is not to be feared

A (*without any accent*), *v.* has, gets, &c. (*V.* **Avoir**). *Robert — de l'argent*, Robert has money. *Il — du talent*, he has talent. *Robert y — été*, Robert has been there. *Il y — été*, he has been there. *Il y* —, (*imp.*) *V.* **Avoir**

Ababouiné, e, *adj.* (*nav.*) becalmed

Abaca, *s.m.* abaca, Manilla hemp

Abaisse, *s.f.* piece of rolled paste

Abaissé, e, *part. adj.* lowered, &c. (*V.* **Abaisser**); down; downcast

Abaissement, *s.m.* lowering; pulling down; falling; fall; sinking; sloping; dipping; dip; decrease, diminution, abatement; reduction; humbling, humility, humiliation; humble condition; abjection; subjection; abasement; degradation; debasement; disgrace; stooping; demeaning; depression; (*her.*) abatement; (— *de la cataracte*) couching (*in surgery*)

Abaisser, *v.a.* to lower; to let down; to let fall; to bring down, to bring lower; to cast down; to pull *or* draw down; to lessen, to diminish, to abate; to reduce; to humble; to humiliate; to subject; to abase; to degrade; to disgrace; to debase; to demean; to disparage, to depreciate; to roll; to flatten; to depress; to lop, to shorten; (*surg.*) to couch; (*nav.*) to strike; (*her.*) to abate

S'—, *v.r.* to lower oneself; to be lowered; to be laid; to bring oneself down; to go down; to descend; to decrease; to subside, to abate; to decline; to fall; to sink; to slope; to dip; to humble oneself; to stoop; to demean oneself; to cringe; to submit; to express oneself with simplicity; to fall into vulgarity [depressor

Abaisseur, *adj.m.* (*anat.*) depriment; — *s.m.*

Abait, *s.m.* (*fish.*) bait

Abaiter, *v.a.* (*fish.*) to bait [flobber-chops, chops

Abajoue, *s.f.* cheek-pouch; —**s**, *pl.* (*pers., jest.*)

Abalourdir, *v.a.* *V.* **Hébéter**

Abalourdissement, *s.m.* *V.* **Hébétement**

Abandon, *s.m.* abandonment; forsaking; leaving; desertion; forlornness; destitution; giving up *or* over; renunciation, relinquishment; surrender; neglect; negligence; carelessness, indifference; want of watchfulness; ease, unconstraint; confidence; trust; resignation; release; dereliction; depravity. *A l'*—, at random; in confusion, in disorder; at sixes and sevens; uncared for, unprotected, unprovided for; in utter neglect; (*nav.*) adrift

Abandonnataire, *s.m.f.* (*law*) relessee

Abandonné, e, *part. adj.* abandoned, deserted, &c. (*V.* **Abandonner**); forlorn; easy, careless; unbridled; depraved, shameless; — *s.m.f.* profligate, rake; reprobate; unfortunate

Abandonnement, *s.m.* abandonment; desertion; relinquishment; giving up; surrender; renunciation; resignation; profligacy

Abandonner, *v.a.* to abandon; to forsake; to desert; to leave; to give up; to renounce; to relinquish; to surrender; to deliver up; to resign; to commit; to quit; to let go; to let loose; to neglect; to fail; to give over; to release

S'—, *v.r.* to abandon oneself; to give oneself up; to give oneself; to give way; to indulge (in); to give vent (to); to be addicted (to), to take (to); to trust; to trust oneself; to throw off all constraint, to be natural; to despond; to rush on desperately; to give vent to o.'s inspiration; to be careless of o.'s personal appearance, to neglect oneself; to be careless; to lead a dissolute life; to begin to toddle; to slacken o.'s pace

Abaque, *s.m.* abacus; raised table

Abas, *s.m.* shower

Abasourdir, *v.a.* to stun, to deafen; to astound

Abat, *s.m.* shower; —**s**, *pl.* showers; offal, cats' and dogs' meat, tripes. *V.* **Abattage** *and* **Abattis**

Abatage, *s.m.* (*bad spelling*) *V.* **Abattage**

Abatant, *s.m.* (*bad spelling*) *V.* **Abattant**

Abâtardi, e, *adj.* degenerate, debased

Abâtardir, *v.a.* to debase, to corrupt

S'—, *v.r.* to degenerate [tion; degeneracy

Abâtardissement, *s.m.* debasement, corrup-

Abatée, *s.f.* (*bad spelling*) *V.* **Abattée**

Abat-faim, *s.m.* large joint [loft, loft-trap

Abat-foin, *s.m.* opening *or* trap-door of a hay-

Abatis, *s.m.* (*bad spelling*) *V.* **Abattis**

Abat-jour, *s.m.* reflector; shade; skylight; trunk-light; sun-shade, sun-blind, shutter, awning, bonnet [window, lufferboard

Abat-son, *s.m.* (*arch.*) louvre-boarding, louvre-

Abattage, *s.m.* cutting down, felling; lopping; slaughtering, slaughter, killing; (*mech.*) power, purchase; (*nav.*) heaving down, careening

Abattant, *s.m.* flap [*son* —, to cast, to fall off

Abattée, *s.f.* (*nav.*) casting, falling off. *Faire*

Abattement, *s.m.* prostration; depression, dejection, low spirits, despondency; languor, faintness; weakness; weariness; sadness; affliction

Abatteu-r, se, *s.m.f.* feller; cutter; knocker-off; slaughterman, slaughterer. *Grand — de quilles.* hard-worker; fussy person; boaster

Abattis, *s.m.* pulling down, demolition; cutting down, felling; pieces, materials, rubbish; giblets; slaughter; destruction; (*fort.*) abattis; (*hunt.*) *V.* **Abattures**
Abattoir, *s.m.* slaughter-house
Abattre, *v.a.* to bring down, to fetch down, to throw *or* knock *or* strike *or* pull *or* cut *or* blow *or* beat down, to hew *or* break down, to let down, &c.; to abate; to cut *or* knock off; to carry away; to lay; to fell; to demolish; to kill; to slaughter; to destroy; to overthrow; to put down; to prostrate; to cast down, to depress, to deject; to dishearten, to discourage; to damp; to weaken; to weary; to humble; to lower; (*nav.*) to heave down, to careen; — *v.n.* to lay down o.'s cards; (*nav.*) to cast, to swing
S'—, *v.r.* to fall down, to come down; to fall; to break down; to abate; to burst; to alight; to make a stoop (at), to come down (upon), to pounce; to be cast down *or* discouraged, to despond
Abattu, e, *part. adj.* brought down, &c. (*V.* **Abattre**); depressed, downcast, dispirited, low-spirited; low; down; languid, faint; weary; drooping; sad; afflicted [slot
Abattures, *s.f.pl.* (*hunt.*) abature, foiling, foil,
Abat-vent, *s.m.* penthouse, lean-to; garden-mat, matting, screen; weather-board; luffer-board, lufferboarding, louvre, louvre-boarding
Abat-voix, *s.m.* sounding-board [abbey
Abbatial, e, *adj. s.* abbatial, abbot's; abbacy,
Abbaye, *s.f.* abbey; abbacy. — *de Monte-à-regret,* (*pop.*) scaffold, maiden, guillotine; gallows
Abbé, *s.m.* (*obsolete*) abbé; abbot; (*modern sense*) ecclesiastic; priest; clergyman; reverend gentleman; reverend. *Monsieur l'—,* Reverend Sir, Sir. *Monsieur l'— Paul,* the Reverend Father Paul, the Reverend Mr. Paul
Abbesse, *s.f.* abbess
A B C, *s.m.* A B C, beginning, elements, rudiments; primer; spelling-book; alphabet, letters
Abcéder, *v.n.* to turn to an abscess, to gather, to come to a head; to break
Abcès, *s.m.* abscess, gathering
Abcisse, *s.f.* *V.* **Abscisse**
Abdéritain, e, Abdérite, *adj. s.* Abderite
Abdication, *s.f.* abdication; resignation; renunciation; surrender
Abdiquer, *v.a.* to abdicate; to resign; to renounce; to lay aside; to give up; to forswear; — *v.n.* to abdicate [privileges; to be abdicated
S'—, *v.r.* to abdicate *or* resign o.'s rights and
Abdomen, *s.m.* abdomen
Abdominal, e, *adj.* abdominal [abductor
Abducteur, *adj.m.* (*anat.*) abducent; — *s.m.*
Abduction, *s.f.* (*anat., log.*) abduction
Abeausir (S'), *v.r.* (*nav.*) to become *or* get fine, to appease
Abécédaire, *s.m.* spelling-book; primer; — *adj.* alphabetical; of A B C; rudimentary, elementary; beginning [(*a bird*)
Abecquement, Abèquement, *s.m.* feeding
Abecquer, Abéquer, *v.a.* to feed (*a bird*)
Abée, *s.f.* mill-dam
†Abeille, *s.f.* bee
Abencérage, *s.m.* (*hist.*) Abencerage
Aberration, *s.f.* aberration
Abêtir, *v.a.* *V.* **Hébéter;** — *v.n.,* **S'—,** *v.r.* to grow dull, to get stupid, to become besotted
Abêtissement, *s.m.* *V.* **Hébétement**
Ab hoc et ab hac, *adv.* (*Latin*) at random, confusedly [detest
Abhorrer, *v.a.* to abhor, to loathe, to hate, to
Abîme, *s.m.* abyss; hell, pit, gulf, chasm; deep; unfathomable depth; mine, treasury; mystery, enigma; ruin, perdition, destruction; misery; (*her.*) fesse-point, heart-point
Abîmer, *v.a.* to sink; to lose; to swallow up; to destroy; to ruin; to undo; to damage, to spoil; to waste; to overwhelm, to crush; to cut to pieces, to cut up [*or* ruined; to get spoilt
S'—, *v.r.* to sink; to ruin oneself; to be lost

Ab intestat, *adv.* abintestate. *Succession —,* intestate's estate, intestacy
Abject, e, *adj.* abject, mean, vile, base, low
Abjectement, *adv.* abjectly
Abjection, *s.f.* abjection, abjectness, meanness, baseness; (*theol.*) outcast
Abjuration, *s.f.* abjuration; renunciation
Abjuratoire, *adj.* abjuratory
Abjurer, *v.a.* to abjure; to forswear; to renounce, to give up, to relinquish; to quit; to
S'—, *v.r.* to be abjured, &c. [lay aside
Ablatif, *s.m.* (*gram.*) ablative, ablative case
Ablation, *s.f.* (*surg.*) ablation
Ablativo, *adv.* higgledy-piggledy
Able, *s.m.* *V.* **Ablette**
Ablégat, *s.m.* ablegate, sublegate
Ableret, *s.m.,* **Ablerette,** *s.f.* (*fish.*) purse-net
Ablette, *s.f.* whitebait, ablet, bleak
Ablier, *s.m.* (*fish.*) purse-net
Abluant, e, *adj.,* **Abluant,** *s.m.* abluent
Abluer, *v.a.* to cleanse, to wash; to revive
Ablution, *s.f.* ablution; washing
Abnégation, *s.f.* abnegation, renunciation; sacrifice; self-denial. *Faire — de,* to renounce, to set aside, to sacrifice
Aboi, *s.m.* bark, barking. *Tenir en —,* to feed with vain hopes. *Aux —s,* at bay; hard pressed; at o.'s wits' end, at *or* to o.'s last shift, at the last extremity, to extremities; in a desperate condition; driven to despair; exhausted; near its end; at the last gasp; about to give way; hard up, in distress
Aboiement, Aboiment, *s.m.* bark, barking
Abolir, *v.a.* to abolish; to do away with; to repeal; to annul; to suppress; to obliterate
S'—, *v.r.* to be abolished; to fall into disuse, to become obsolete *or* extinct
Abolissable, *adj.* abolishable
Abolissement, *s.m.* (*obsolete*) abolishment
Abolition, *s.f.* abolition; repeal; suppression
Abolition-isme, -iste. *V.* page 3, § 1
Abominable, *adj.* abominable
Abominablement, *adv.* abominably
Abomination, *s.f.* abomination. *Avoir en —,* to abominate. *Être en —,* to be abominated
Abominer, *v.a.* to abominate
A-bon-compte, *s.m.* payment in advance, advance-money, advance
Abondamment, *adv.* abundantly, copiously, plentifully; plenty; in abundance, in great quantity; amply, fully
Abondance, *s.f.* abundance, plenty, plentifulness, copiousness; affluence; richness; fulness; fluency; flow; diffuseness; heartiness; (weak) wine-and-water, washy stuff, wishy-washy, wish-wash, swipes, water bewitched (plenty of water with a little common wine, in schools). *D'—,* of plenty, &c.; (*adverb.*) extempore; off-hand
Abondant, e, *adj.* abundant, plentiful, copious; rich; teeming; ample, full; fluent, flowing; diffuse; hearty
Abonder, *v.n.* to abound; to overflow. *Il abonde dans votre sens,* he thinks as you do, he is of your opinion, he concurs entirely with you. — *dans son sens,* to be wedded to o.'s own opinion [holder
Abonné, e, *s.m.f.* subscriber; season-ticket
Abonnement, *s.m.* subscription; contract, agreement; composition; season ticket; annual ticket; (*mil.*) allowance, indemnification. *Carte d'—,* season ticket; annual ticket. — *de lecture,* subscription to a library; subscription *or* circu-
Abonner, *v.a.* to subscribe for [lating library
S'—, *v.r.* to subscribe, to become a subscriber; to contract; to compound; to take a season *or* an annual ticket
Abonnir, *v.a.n.,* **S'—,** *v.r.* to improve
Abord, *s.m.* access, approach; landing, arrival; meeting; attack; contact; resort, affluence; manner, address; first instance, first. *Au premier —,* at first view; at first. *D'—, de prime —,* first, at first, first of all, in the first place,

to begin with; at once; at first sight. *Dès l'—*, from the very first, at first, at once. *Tout d'—*, at first; at once
Abordable, *adj.* accessible, approachable
Abordage, *s.m.* landing; boarding; running foul, collision. *Aller* or *sauter à l'—, se battre à l'—*, to board an enemy's ship, to grapple. *Prendre* or *enlever à l'—*, to board
Aborder, *v.n.a.* to land, to arrive; to come; to approach; to accost; to come to; to come up to; to meet; to address; to attack; to charge; to touch; to board; to run foul of, to run into, to come into collision with, to collide with; to enter upon; to broach
Abordeur, *s.m.* (*nav.*) boarder [gines, aboriginals
Aborigène, *adj.s.* aboriginal; **—s,** *s.m.pl.* abori-
Abornement, *s.m. V.* **Délimitation**
Aborner, *v.a. V.* **Délimiter**
Aborti-f, ve, *adj.*, **Abortif,** *s.m.* abortive
Abosir (S'), *v.r.* (*nav.*) to become *or* get fine,
Abot, *s.m.* clog [to appease
Abouchement, *s.m.* conference, interview; welding, fitting; (*anat.*) anastomosis, inosculation
Aboucher, *v.a.* to bring together; to weld, to fit
S'—, *v.r.* to have an interview; to confer; to have a talk, to talk; to intrigue; (*anat.*) to in-
Abougrissement, *s.m.* stuntedness [osculate
Abouler, *v.a.n.* (*pop.*) to give, to let have; to fork out, to come down; to cut on, to come on;
Aboument, *s.m.* joining end to end [to pop in
About, *s.m.* end, butt-end
Aboutage, *s.m.* joining
Aboutement, *s.m.* joining; butt, abutment, end
Abouter, *v.a.* to place end to end, to join toge-
S'—, *v.r.* to meet at the ends [ther
Aboutir, *v.n.* to end; to be at the end (of); to border *or* abut (on); to adjoin; to open (into); to come out (into); to come (to); to lead; to meet; to join; to converge; to tend; to terminate; to have a result; to break; to bud
Aboutissant, *s.m.* abuttal, butting, butt, end. *V.* **Tenant**
Aboutissement, *s.m.* piece to lengthen; drawing to a head; breaking, suppuration; termination, end, issue, result; success, happy result [the first
Ab ovo, *adv.* (*Latin*) from the beginning, from
Aboyer, *v.n.* to bark; to snarl; to cry out (against); to long (for); to dun
Aboyeu-r, se, *s.m.f.* barker; street-news-vendor; touter, cad; snarling critic; dun; seeker, hunter; *—s.m.* (*zool.*) greenshank (*bird*)
Abrac, *s.m.* abraxas
Abracadabra, *s.m.* abracadabra
Abracadabrant, e, *adj.* (*slang*) *V.* **Mirobolant**
Abraquer, *v.a.* (*nav.*) to haul taught
Abrasion, *s.f.* (*med.*) abrasion
Abraxas, *s.m.* abraxas
Abrégé, *s.m.* abridgment, epitome, compendium, abstract, summary; brief account. *En —*, in a few words *or* lines *or* pages, shortly, briefly, concisely, summarily, compendiously; by abbreviation; abridged; on a small scale
Abrégement, *s.m.* abridging, shortening, abridgment
Abréger, *v.a.* to abridge; to epitomize; to abbreviate; to shorten; to cut shorter, to cut down. *Pour —*, to be brief
S'—, *v.r.* to become short *or* shorter
Abreuvage, Abreuvement, *s.m.* watering; soaking; steeping; priming; preparing
Abreuver, *v.a.* to water; to give to drink to, to make (...) drink; to soak; to steep; to drench; to imbibe; to imbrue; to fill; to saturate; to load; to overwhelm; to prime; to prepare
S'—, *v.r.* to drink; to soak; to quench o.'s thirst; to satiate oneself; to revel; to fill *or* cover oneself; to wallow; to bathe; to melt (into tears), to shed (abundant tears)
Abreuvoir, *s.m.* watering-place; horse-pond; trough; drinking-spot
Abrévia-teur, trice, *s.m.f.* abbreviator, abridger, epitomizer; — *adj.* abbreviating,
Abréviati-f, ve, *adj.* abbreviatory [abridging
Abréviation, *s.f.* abbreviation; contraction
Abréviativement, *adv.* by abbreviation
Abrévier, *v.a.* to abbreviate, to shorten
Abreyer, *v.a. V.* **Abrier**
Abri, *s.m.* shelter, cover; refuge; home; shadow; shade; defence; screen; protection; concealment. *A l'—*, under shelter; under cover; under the protection (of); protected (from); sheltered; secure, safe; beyond (...). *Mettre à l'—*, to shelter; to screen; to protect; to secure
Abricot, *s.m.* apricot. **— -pêche,** *s.m.* peach-
Abricoté, *s.m.* candied apricot [apricot
Abricotier, *s.m.* apricot-tree
Abrier, *v.a.* (*nav.*) to becalm, to belee
Abriter, *v.a.* to shelter; to shield, to screen; to shade; to protect; (*nav.*) to becalm, to belee
Abrivent, *s.m.* garden-mat, matting, screen; hut, shed, sentry-box [ment; abolition
Abrogation, *s.f.* abrogation; repeal; annul-
Abroger, *v.a.* to abrogate; to repeal; to annul; to abolish [fall into disuse, to grow obsolete
S'—, *v.r.* to be abrogated *or* repealed, &c.; to
Abrome, *s.m.* (*bot.*) abroma
Abrouti, e, *adj.* nipped, browsed
Abroutissement, *s.m.* damage from browsing
Abrupt, e, *adj.* abrupt; craggy, rugged
Abruptement, *adv.* abruptly; with a craggy appearance
Abrupto (Ex), *adv. adj.* ex abrupto, abruptly, suddenly, unexpectedly, on the spur of the moment; off-hand; sudden; impetuous [to besot
Abrutir, *v.a.* to brutalize, to brutify; to stupefy;
S'—, to become brutish *or* depraved; to degrade oneself; to get stupid; to be besotted
Abrutissement, *s.m.* brutishness, brutalization, sottishness [talizing, stupefying
Abrutisseu-r, se, *s.m.f. adj.* brutalizer; bru-
Abscisse, *s.f.* (*geom.*) absciss, abscissa
Abscission, *s.f.* (*surg.*) abscission
Absence, *s.f.* absence; non-attendance; absence of mind; fit of absence; inattention, inadvertence; wandering; want
Absent, e, *adj. s.* absent; away; not at home; missing, wanting; absentee
Absentéisme, *s.m.* absenteeism [away
Absenter (S'), *v.r.* to absent oneself, to stop
Abside, *s.f. V.* **Apside**
Absinthe, *s.f.* wormwood; bitters, absinthe
Absinthé, e, *adj.* absinthiated
Absinthine, *s.f.* (*chem.*) absinthine
Absolu, e, *adj.* absolute; positive; peremptory; magisterial; imperious; despotic; arbitrary; unlimited; unrestricted; unconditional; complete; full; strict
Absolument, *adv.* absolutely; positively; peremptorily; unconditionally; arbitrarily; by all means; indeed; entirely; completely; altogether; exactly; strictly [acquittal
Absolution, *s.f.* absolution; pardon; discharge;
Absolut-isme, -iste. *V.* page 3, § 1
Absolutoire, *adj.* absolutory
Absorbable, *adj.* absorbable
Absorbant, e, *adj.* absorbing; engrossing; absorbent; — *s.m.* absorbent
Absorber, *v.a.* to absorb; to imbibe; to drink in; to swallow up; to drain; to consume, to waste; to engross, to take up
S'—, *v.r.* to be absorbed *or* swallowed up, &c.
Absorption, *s.f.* absorption; consumption; dis-
Absorptivité, *s.f.* absorptivity [appearance
Absoudre, *v.a.* to absolve; to discharge, to acquit; to pardon, to forgive; to exculpate, to exonerate; to give absolution to
Absoute, *s.f.* absolution; general absolution
Abstème, *adj.* abstemious
Abstenant, e, *s.m.f.* abstainer
Abstenir (S'), *v.r.* to abstain; to refrain; to forbear; to forego [drawal, declining
Abstention, *s.f.* abstention; abstinence; with-

Abstergent, e, *adj.*, **Abstergent,** *s.m.* abstergent, detergent
Absterger, *v.a.* to absterge, to cleanse [gent
Abstersi-f, ve, *adj.*, **Abstersif,** *s.m.* abster-
Abstersion, *s.f.* abstersion [ing
Abstinence, *s.f.* abstinence; temperance; fast-
Abstinent, e, *adj.* abstinent, abstemious, sober
Abstracti-f, ve, *adj.* abstractive
Abstraction, *s.f.* abstraction. *—faite de,* setting aside; exclusive of. *Faire — de,* to abstract; to set aside. *Par —,* abstractedly
Abstractivement, *adv.* abstractedly
Abstraire, *v.a.* to abstract
Abstrait, e, *adj.* abstruse; abstracted; abstract
Abstraitement, *adv.* abstractly
Abstrus, e, *adj.* abstruse [absurdity
Absurde, *adj.m.f.*, *s.m.* absurd, preposterous;
Absurdement, *adv.* absurdly, preposterously
Absurdité, *s.f.* absurdity
Abus, *s.m.* abuse; misuse; breach; bad custom; nuisance; grievance; disorder; error; mistake, illusion. *Appel comme d'—,* appeal by writ of error
Abuser, *v.a.* to deceive, to delude; to lead away; — *v.n.* to abuse; to misuse, to make a bad use (of), to use ill; to misconstrue; to use too freely; to take advantage (of); to impose (on); to intrude, to trespass (upon); to overtax; to overtask, to overwork [mistaken
S'—, *v.r.* to deceive *or* delude oneself; to be
Abuseu-r, se, *s.m.f.* abuser; deceiver; — *adj.* deceptive, deceitful
Abusi-f, ve, *adj.* abusive; improper
Abusivement, *adv.* abusively; improperly
Abuter, *v.a.n.* to throw for first go; to aim
Abuter, Abutter, *v.a.* (*in shipbuilding*) to place end to end; — *v.n.* to abut, to butt
Abyme, *s.m.* *V.* **Abîme**
Abyssin, e, Abyssinien, ne, Abyssinique, *adj. s.* Abyssinian
Acabit, *s.m.* quality; sort, stamp, kidney
Acacia, *s.m.* acacia [demic
Académicien, ne, *s.m.f.* academician; aca-
Académie, *s.f.* academy; (*draw., paint.*) academy figure; (*obsolete*) riding-school [3, § 1
Académ-ique, -iquement, -iste. *V.* page
Académiser, *v.n.* to draw *or* paint figures
Acadien, ne, *adj. s.* Acadian [from models
†Acagnarder, *v.a.* to make lazy
S'—, *v.r.* to get lazy; to idle
Acajou, *s.m.* mahogany. — *à pommes,* cashew-nut tree. *Noix d'—,* cashew-nut
Acalèphe, *s.m.* (*zool.*) acaleph, jelly-fish
Acalifourchonné, e, *adj.* astride
Acalifourchonner (S'), *v.r.* to sit astride
Acanthacé, e, *adj.* thorny, prickly
Acanthe, *s.f.* acanthus
Acare, *s.m.* *V.* **Acarus**
Acariâtre, *adj.* peevish, cross, crabbed
Acariâtreté, *s.f.* peevishness, crabbedness
Acarides, *s.f.pl.*, **Acariens,** *s.m.pl.* acarides, acari (*cheese-mites, bird-lice, ticks,* &c.)
Acarus, *s.m.* acarus, mite, tick
Acaule, *adj.* (*bot.*) acaulous, acaulose
Accablant, e, *adj.* overwhelming; overpowering; oppressive; crushing; grievous; troublesome, annoying; sweltering, sultry
Accablement, *s.m.* heaviness; faintness, weakness, languor; extreme dejection; oppression; great pressure; crushing weight; affliction; grievousness
Accabler, *v.a.* to overwhelm; to overpower; to load; to overload; to oppress; to weigh down; to encumber; to crush down, to crush, to crush to death; to overthrow; to overcome; to stifle; to ruin; to plague; to harass; to afflict; to be too hard upon; to cast down, to depress
Accalmie, *s.f.* *V.* **Embellie**
Accaparement, *s.m.* forestalling, buying up; monopoly; engrossment
Accaparer, *v.a.* to forestall, to buy up; to monopolize; to secure, to obtain; to engross, to captivate; to seize upon
Accapareu-r, se, *s.m.f.* forestaller, monopolist, monopolizer, engrosser
†Accastillage, *s.m.* (*nav.*) upper works; fittings, ornaments, accommodation
†Accastillé, e, *adj.* (*nav.*) with upper works, furnished with upper works. *Haut —,* deep-waisted
Accéder, *v.n.* to accede; to consent; to comply; to agree; to have access; to come
Accéléra-teur, trice, *adj.* accelerating, accelerative [patch
Accélération, *s.f.* acceleration; haste; des-
Accéléré, e, *adj.* accelerated, quickened; fast; quick; — *s.m.f.* fast boat; fast coach; light van. *Pas —,* quick march *or* time *or* step. *Au pas —,* in quick time [hasten; to forward; to despatch
Accélérer, *v.a.* to accelerate; to quicken; to
Accenser, *v.a.* to annex, to join, to unite
Accent, *s.m.* accent; tone; voice; sound; cry; note; tune; song; strain; word; pronunciation; emphasis; stress; expression
Accenteur, *s.m.* (*bird*) accentor
Accentuation, *s.f.* accentuation
Accentuer, *v.a.* to accent, to accentuate; to mark with an accent; to emphasize; to lay a stress upon; to mark, to define; to fix, to determine; to make positive *or* evident; to set off. — *ses gestes,* to accompany o.'s gestures (threats) with the act
S'—, *v.r.* to be accented; to be *or* become marked *or* defined *or* fixed *or* determined; to become positive *or* evident
Acceptable, *adj.* acceptable
Acceptant, e, *s.m.f.* (*law*) accepter
Acceptation, *s.f.* acceptance
Accepter, *v.a.* to accept; to take; to receive; to admit; to consent to; to submit to, to resign oneself to, to bear; to undertake
S'—, *v.r.* to be accepted *or* taken, &c.
Accepteur, *s.m.* (*com.*) acceptor, accepter
Acception, *s.f.* respect, preference, regard, distinction; acceptation, sense, meaning
Accès, *s.m.* access; approach; admittance; fit; attack; paroxysm; burst
Accessibilité, *s.f.* accessibility
Accessible, *adj.* accessible, approachable
Accession, *s.f.* accession; consent, adhesion
Accessit, [*Latin,* "*proxime —*"] *s.m.* honourable mention
Accessoire, *adj.* accessory; minor; — *s.m.* accessory; (*theat.*) property; minor part. *Fournisseur d'—s,* property-man
Accessoirement, *adv.* accessorily
Accident, *s.m.* accident; chance; casualty; misfortune; occurrence; incident; unevenness, irregularity, undulation; varied aspect; accidental effect; accidental; (*med.*) accidental complication; case
Accidenté, e, *adj.* undulating, undulated; uneven; hilly; broken; intersected; interspersed; varied; picturesque; eventful, full of incidents; checkered [titious, fortuitous
Accidentel, le, *adj.* accidental, casual, adven-
Accidentellement, *adv.* accidentally, casually
Accise, *s.f.* *V.* **Excise** [— *adj.* cheering
Acclama-teur, trice, *s.m.f.* shouter, cheerer;
Acclamation, *s.f.* acclamation, shout, shouting, cheer, cheering, applause, plaudit, hurrah
Acclamer, *v.a.n.* to proclaim, to acclaim; to salute, to hail; to cheer, to applaud; to welcome; to respond to; to shout
Acclamper, *v.a.* (*nav.*) to clamp
Acclimatable, *adj.* acclimatizable
Acclimata-teur, trice, *s.m.f.* acclimatizer
Acclimatation, *s.f.*, **Acclimatement,** *s.m.* acclimatization [become acclimatized
Acclimater, *v.a.* to acclimatize. *S'—,* to
Accointance, *s.f.* acquaintance, connection, intimacy [quainted *or* intimate
Accointer (S'), *v.r.* to become (*or* get) ac-
Accoiser, *v.a.* (*old*) to calm, to appease, to quiet
Accolade, *s.f.* embrace, hug, kiss; accolade; (*cook., print., writ., mus.*) brace; (*jest.*) blow,

slap. *Donner l'— à*, to embrace; to dub a knight. *Recevoir l'—*, to be made a knight
Accolader, *v.a.* to bracket
Accolage, *s.m.* propping, tying up, nailing up
Accolement, *s.m.* bracketing; putting together; coupling; pathway, side
Accoler, *v.a.* to embrace; to hug; to kiss; to bracket; to put together; to couple, to join; to associate; to attach; to apply; to prop, to tie up, to nail up; to entwine, to wreathe
Accolure, *s.f.* (*agr.*) band of straw, withe, osier
Accommodable, *adj.* accommodable, that may *or* can be arranged
Accommodage, *s.m.* dressing
Accommodé, e, *part. adj* suited, &c. (*V.* **Accommoder**); favoured; well-off, well-to-do, in easy circumstances
Accommodement, *s.m.* accommodation; arrangement, settlement; agreement; composition; compromise; means of conciliation; disposition
Accommoder, *v.a.* to suit; to adapt; to accommodate; to fit up; to dress; to cook; to prepare; to trim; to arrange; to settle; to mend; to reconcile; to put in order; to dispose; to spare, to let have; to ill-use, to serve out, to give it to
S'—, *v.r.* to accommodate oneself; to agree; to come to terms; to arrange; to make a bargain; to take; to comply; to put up (with); to bear; to make shift (with); to be content *or* satisfied *or* pleased (with); to like, to relish; to settle; to take o.'s ease, to make oneself comfortable; to make free (with); to dress, to adorn oneself; to be arranged; to be dressed *or* cooked [nist
†**Accompagna-teur, trice**, *s.m.f.* accompa-
†**Accompagnement**, *s.m.* accompanying; attendance; accompaniment; appendage, accessory [to wait on; to escort; to suit, to match
†**Accompagner**, *v.a.* to accompany; to attend;
S'—, *v.r.* to accompany oneself; to be accompanied, &c.
Accompli, e, *part. adj.* accomplished; perfect; complete, completed, finished; fulfilled; performed
Accomplir, *v.a.* to accomplish; to perform; to fulfil; to complete; to finish; to achieve; to execute; to carry out; to effect; to go through; to observe, to obey
S'—, *v.r.* to be fulfilled *or* fulfilling, to be accomplished *or* accomplishing; to happen; to be past, to be spent, to pass, to elapse
Accomplissement, *s.m.* accomplishment; performance; fulfilment; completion; execution; achievement
Accon, *s.m.* flat-bottomed boat, lighter, punt
Accoquiner, *v.a. V.* **Acoquiner**
Accorage, *s.m.* propping; props
Accord, *s.m.* agreement; good understanding; union; harmony; concord; accord; accordance; consent; keeping; uniformity; tone, strain; chord; tuning; —**s**, *pl.* agreements, &c.; espousals. *D'—*, agreed; together; leagued; granted; be it so; in accordance, in conformity; in harmony; in keeping; in tune. *Demeurer* or *tomber* or *être d'—*, to agree, to be agreed, to come to an agreement; to admit. *Mettre d'—*, to make (...) agree; to reconcile; to suit; to tune. *Tenir l'—*, to keep in tune
Accordable, *adj.* reconcilable; grantable; allowable, admissible; tunable
Accordage, *s.m.* tuning
†**Accordailles**, *s.f.pl.* espousals
Accordant, e, *adj.* (*mus.*) concordant
Accordé, e, *s.m.f.* bridegroom; bride
Accordéon, *s.m.* accordion
Accorder, *v.a.* to grant; to allow; to give; to admit; to make (...) agree; to reconcile; to unite; to blend; to adjust; to tune; to betroth. *Il m'a été accordé* (or *donné*) *de*, I have been permitted to. &c. (*V.* **Donner**)
S'—, *v.r.* to agree; to coincide; to suit; to be in harmony, to harmonize; to be agreeable; to be consistent; to join, to concur; to accord; to grant to each other; to be granted; to be
Accordeu-r, se, *s.m.f.* tuner [adjusted *or* settled
Accordoir, *s.m.* tuning-hammer
Accore, *s.m.* (*nav.*) prop, shore; edge; — *adj.* (*nav.*) bluff, steep [jam, to wedge
Accorer, *v.a.* (*nav.*) to prop, to shore up; to
Accorné, e, (*her., fort.*) horned
Accort, e, *adj.* compliant, courteous, civil, amiable, affable [amiability, affability
Accortise, *s.f.* compliance, courtesy, civility,
Accostable, *adj.* (*nav.*) accessible [landing
Accoste, *s.m.* bringing *or* coming alongside;
Accosté, e, *adj.* accosted; sided; side by side (with), by the side (of), alongside (of); reached; (*her.*) accosted, coticed, cotised, cottised
Accoster, *v.a.n.* to accost, to approach, to come *or* go up to, to address, to speak to; to place by the side of *or* side by side, to join, to couple; (*nav.*) to come alongside; to land at; to reach
S'—, *v.r.* to accost each other; to come side by side; to meet; to join; to make acquaintance (with), to associate (with), to keep company (with), to frequent
Accoté, e, *adj.* inclining; leaning, resting; propped; (*her.*) accosted, coticed, cotised, cottised
Accotement, *s.m.* pathway, side-way, side; (*rail.*) outer space, bank; (*horol.*) friction
Accoter, *v.a.n.*, **S'—**, *v.r.* to rest *or* lean (sideways); to incline; to prop; (*hort.*) to dung, to mulch, to screen [railing; prop, stay, shore
Accotoir, *s.m.* arm; rest; resting-cushion;
Accouchée, *s.f.* lady *or* woman confined, lying-in woman
Accouchement, *s.m.* confinement; delivery; lying in; child-birth, labour; midwifery
Accoucher, *v.a.n.* to deliver; to be confined *or* delivered, to be in labour; to bring forth; to give birth to; to produce; to deliver oneself (of); to speak out; to make a clean breast of it. *Accouche* or *Accouchez!* out with it!
Accoucheu-r, se, *s.m.f.* accoucheur; accoucheuse, midwife
Accouder (S'), *v.r.* to lean on o.'s elbow *or* elbows, to rest o.'s elbow *or* elbows
Accoudoir, *s.m.* elbow-rest; arm; sill; rail
Accouer, *v.a.* to tie (horses) together head to tail; (*hunt.*) to pursue close, to reach
Accouple, *s.f.* leash, couple [ing; union
Accouplement, *s.m.* coupling; joining; pair-
Accoupler, *v.a.* to couple; to unite; to join; to put together; to match; to pair; to yoke
Accourcie, *s.f.* short cut; passage
Accourcir. *V.* **Raccourcir**
Accourcissement. *V.* **Raccourcissement**
Accourir, *v.n.* to run, to run up, to hasten, to hurry; to rush; to come in haste; to come up; to come; to go up; to go; to flock together
Accourse, *s.f.* gallery, passage, lobby
Accoutrement, *s.m.* accoutrement, costume, garb, dress, gear, rig [rig out
Accoutrer, *v.a.* to accoutre, to dress out, to
Accoutumance, *s.f.* custom, habit, use
Accoutumé, e, *part. adj.* accustomed; used; in the habit (of); usual, customary, wonted. *A l'—e*, as usual; usually. *Avoir* — (*de*), to have been used (to), to be accustomed (to), to be in the habit (of), to be wont (to); to use (to)
Accoutumer, *v.a.* to accustom, to use; to inure [come accustomed, to get used
S'—, *v.r.* to accustom *or* use oneself, to be-
Accouvé, e, *adj.* brooding over (the fire, &c.)
Accrédité, e, *adj.* accredited; in credit, in vogue; in high repute; well established; sanctioned, countenanced; credited; rife
Accréditer, *v.a.* to accredit; to bring into credit *or* esteem *or* vogue; to establish the credit *or* reputation *or* truth of; to spread; to

give credit to, to sanction; to confirm; to guarantee [be credited; to spread
S'—, *v.r.* to get into credit; to gain credit, to
Accréditeur, *s.m.* surety
Accrescent, e, *adj.* (*bot.*) accrescent
Accrétion, *s.f.* (*med., min.*) accretion
Accroc, *s.m.* rent; tear; hook; impediment, obstacle, hindrance, difficulty, hitch
Accroche, *s.f.* hindrance, obstacle, hitch
Accroche-cœurs, *s.m.* curl, twist, heart-breaker. *En* —, curled up, twisted up
Accrochement, *s.m.* hooking; locking; grappling; catch; stop; obstacle, difficulty, hitch; delay
Accrocher, *v.a.* to hook on; to hook; to hang up; to hang; to hitch; to catch; to get hold of; to get; to run against; to lock; to stop, to hinder; to delay; to put off; to pawn, to put up the spout; to grapple; (*pop.*) to take up, to lock up, to quod
S'—, *v.r.* to catch; to lay hold (of); to hang (on); to stick (to); to cling; to come to blows, to fight; to get locked; to grapple each other
Accrocheur, *s.m.* (*mining*) hooker-on, hitcher
Accroire, *v.a.* *Faire — à*, to make believe. *En faire — à*, to impose upon. *S'en faire* —, to overrate oneself, to be conceited
Accroissement, *s.m.* increase, extension, enlargement, growth, development; rising; addition; (*min., law*) accretion
Accroître, *v.a.n.,* **S'**—, *v.r.* to increase; to enlarge; to extend; to grow; to raise; to rise; to grow stronger; to improve; to advance; to lapse, to fall (to)
Accroupi, e, *adj.* squatting, squat, stooping, cowering down, crouching; sunk
Accroupir (S'), *v.r.* to squat; to sit squat; to cower down; to roll oneself up; to sink
Accroupissement, *s.m.* squatting, cowering
Accru, e, *part. of* **Accroître**
Accru, *s.m.* shoot
Accrue, *s.f.* increase; encroachment
†**Accueil,** *s.m.* reception; welcome; greeting; (*com.*) acceptance, honour [table
†**Accueillant, e,** *adj.* gracious, affable; hospi-
†**Accueillir,** *v.a.* to receive; to welcome; to hail; to greet; to entertain; to take up; to accept; to believe; to assail; to fall upon; to overtake, to surprise; (*com.*) to honour
Accul, *s.m.* blind alley; end of a terrier *or* burrow; (*artil.*) breeching; (*nav.*) creek
Acculée, *s.f.* (*nav.*) *V.* **Acculement**
Acculement, *s.m.* fix; (*of a cart*) trapping *or* hanging backward; (*of a horse*) jibbing; (*nav.*) rising of the floor-timbers; sternway
Acculer, *v.a.* to drive, to drive up; to drive into a corner; to drive to the last extremity; to bring to a stand; (*a cart*) to trap backward; (*hunt.*) to run home; — *v.n.* (*of carts*) to hang backward; (*nav.*) to be pooped
S'—, *v.r.* to back (against); (*of carts*) to trap *or* hang backward; (*of horses*) to jib; (*nav.*) to be pooped
Accumula-teur, trice, *s.m.f.* accumulator, hoarder; — *adj.* accumulating, hoarding
Accumulation, *s.f.* accumulation
Accumuler, *v.a.* to accumulate; to amass, to heap up; to store up; to hoard up, to hoard; to cram in
S'—, *v.r.* to accumulate, to increase
Accusable, *adj.* accusable, chargeable, impeachable
Accusa-teur, trice, *adj.* accusing; incriminating; — *s.m.f.* accuser, indicter, impeacher
Accusatif, *s.m.* (*gram.*) accusative, accusative case
Accusation, *s.f.* accusation; charge; imputation; confession; impeachment; arraignment; indictment; prosecution. *Acte d'*—, articles of impeachment; indictment, bill of indictment. *Arrêt d'*— or *de mise en* —, true bill. *Chef d'*—, *V.* **Chef.** *Chambre des mises en* —, grand jury. *Mettre en* —, to impeach; to arraign; to indict. *Prononcer la mise en* —, to find a true bill
Accusé, e, *s.m.f.* accused; culprit, prisoner; — *part. adj.* accused, &c. (*V.* **Accuser**); marked, prominent; distinct; showy [(of receipt)
Accusé, *s.m.* — *de réception*, acknowledgment
Accuser, *v.a.* to accuse; to charge; to impeach; to arraign; to indict; to prosecute; to point to the guilt of; to tell *or* go against; to blame; to reproach; to complain of; to argue; to imply; to betray; to reveal; to discover; to indicate; to show; to mark; to define; to display; to declare, to state; to call; to acknowledge; to confess; (*med.*) to complain of
Acéphale, *adj.* acephalous, without a head, headless; —**s,** *s.m.pl.* acephalans, acephala
Acérain, e, *adj.* steely [bitter
Acerbe, *adj.* acerb, rough, sour, sharp; harsh,
Acerbité, *s.f.* acerbity, sharpness; harshness
Acéré, e, *adj.* steeled; sharp-edged; sharp; pointed; keen, acute
Acérer, *v.a.* to steel; to sharpen
Acéreu-x, se, *adj.* acerous, needle-shaped
Acescence, *s.f.* acescency, acidifying
Acescent, e, *adj.* acescent
Acétabule, *s.m.* acetabulum
Acétate, *s.m.* (*chem.*) acetate
Acéteu-x, se, *adj.* (*chem.*) acetous
Acétification, *s.f.* acetification
Acétimètre, *s.m.* acetimeter, acetometer
Acétique, *adj.* (*chem.*) acetic
Achalandage, *s.m.* custom, goodwill; customers; getting custom *or* customers
Achalandé, e, *adj.* having customers, doing business; frequented. *Bien* —, with a good custom, doing a good business, driving a good trade; well frequented [to, to draw customers to
Achalander, *v.a.* to bring custom *or* customers
S'—, *v.r.* to get custom, to draw *or* attract customers; to do business; to become established
Acharné, e, *adj.* ravenous; bloodthirsty; savage; excited; enraged, rabid, infuriated, furious, mad, desperate; exasperated; bent (on); implacable, inveterate; unrelenting; unremitting; obstinate; intense; (*hunt.*) fleshed
Acharnement, *s.m.* rage, rabidness, fury, desperation; animosity; savageness; obstinacy; tenacity
Acharner, *v.a.* to set on, to set (against), to excite; to enrage; (*hunt.*) to flesh
S'—, *v.r.* to fasten oneself (upon); to set furiously (to); to be set *or* bent (upon); to fall (upon) *or* attack furiously; to become excited *or* enraged; to be implacable
Achars, Achards, *s.m.pl.* India pickles; mixed
Achat, *s.m.* purchase [pickles; piccalilli
Ache, *s.f.* (*bot.*) smallage
Achée, *s.f.* worms, gentles, bait
Achéen, ne, *adj. s.* Achean, Achæan; Achaian
Acheminement, *s.m.* step, means, way, preparation; introduction; disposition
Acheminer, *v.a.* to forward, to despatch, to send, to direct; to bring; (*rid.*) to train, to break
S'—, *v.r.* to set out; to go; to get on; to advance, to proceed, to progress; to walk; to march; to tend (to)
Achetable, *adj.* purchasable
Acheter, *v.a.* to buy, to purchase; to buy for; to bribe; to barter; to acquire; to procure; to pay for. — *à*, to buy for; to buy of *or* at *or* in
S'—, *v.r.* to buy (for) oneself; to buy for *or* of each other; to be bought *or* purchased *or* &c.
Acheteu-r, se, *s.m.f.* buyer, purchaser
Achevé, e, *part. adj.* finished, completed, complete, perfect; consummate; downright, regular, arrant, thorough; done; over; being over; broken down, on o.'s last legs, ruined; drunk, finished up; (*rid.*) thoroughly broke
Achèvement, *s.m.* finishing, completion; conclusion; finish

Achever, *v.a.* to finish, to complete; to perfect; to end; to conclude; to go on to the end, to go on, to proceed; to consummate; to crown; to give the finishing stroke to; to complete the ruin of, to ruin; to despatch, to kill; (*of time*) to serve out; (*rid.*) to break thoroughly. *Il n'acheva pas,* he said no more, he stopped
S'—, *v.r.* to be finished *or* completed; to come to an end, to end; to utterly ruin oneself; to get thoroughly drunk
Acheveu-r, se, *s.m.f.* finisher
Achillée, *s.f.* (*bot.*) millfoil, yarrow, maudlin
Achilléine, *s.f.* (*chem.*) achilleine
Achit, *s.m.* wild vine
Achoppement, *s.m.* stumbling; impediment. *Pierre d'—,* stumbling-block; obstacle; difficulty, rub, hitch
‡**Achores,** *s.m.pl.* (*med.*) scald-head
‡**Achromat-ique, -isme.** *V.* page 3, § 1
‡**Achromatiser,** *v.a.* to achromatize
‡**Achronique,** (*bad spelling*) *V.* **Acronyque**
Aciculaire, *adj.* acicular
Acide, *adj.* acid, sour, sharp; — *s.m.* acid
Acidifère, *adj.* acidiferous
Acidifiable, *adj.* acidifiable
Acidification, *s.f.* acidification
Acidifier, *v.a.,* **S'—,** *v.r.* to acidify
Acidimètre, *s.m.* acidimeter
Acidimétrie, *s.f.* acidimetry
Acidité, *s.f.* acidity, sourness, sharpness
Acidule, *adj.* acidulous, subacid [to make sourish
Aciduler, *v.a.* to acidulate, to render acidulous,
S'—, *v.r.* to become acidulous *or* sourish
Acier, *s.m.* steel. — *de cementation* or — *poule,* cemented steel, converted steel, blistered steel, blister-steel
Aciérage, *s.m.* steeling, conversion into steel
Aciération, *s.f.* formation of steel
Aciérer, *v.a.,* **S'—,** *v.r.* to turn into steel
Aciéreu-x, se, *adj.* steely
Aciérie, *s.f.* steel-works
Acineu-x, se, Aciniforme, *adj.* acinous, aciniform, grape-shaped
Acmé, *s.m.* (*med. only*) acme
Acné, *s.m.* (*med.*) acne
Acolyte, *s.m.f.* acolyte; companion, associate; confederate, pal, accomplice
Acompte, *s.m.* instalment
Acon, *s.m.* *V.* **Accon**
Aconit, *s.m.* (*bot.*) aconite, wolf's-bane, monk's-
Aconitate, *s.m.* (*chem.*) aconitate [hood
Aconitine, *s.f.* (*chem.*) aconitia, aconitine
Aconitique, *adj.* (*chem.*) aconitic
Acontias, *s.m.* (*zool.*) dart-snake
Acoquiné, e, *adj.* much in love, taken (with), caught; fond (of), attached (to)
Acoquiner, *v.a.* to allure, to entice, to captivate, to bewitch [(to), to be bewitched (with)
S'—, *v.r.* to get fond (of), to become attached
Acore, Acorus, *s.m.* (*bot.*) acorus
Acoter, Acotter, *v.a.* (*hort.*) *V.* **Accoter**
Acotylédone, *adj.* (*bot.*) acotyledonous; — *s.f.* acotyledon [*s.f.* acotyledon
Acotylédoné, e, *adj.* (*bot.*) acotyledonous; —
Acoup, *s.m.* jerk; sudden stroke *or* action; unexpected event [— *s.m.* speaking-pipe
Acoustique, *adj.* acoustic; — *s.f.* acoustics;
Acquérable, *adj.* acquirable; purchasable
Acquéreu-r, se, *s.m.f.* purchaser, buyer
Acquérir, *v.a.* to acquire; to obtain; to gain; to get; to purchase, to buy; — *v.n.* to improve
S'—, *v.r.* to acquire, to gain; to gain over; to be acquired *or* obtained, &c.
Acquêt, *s.m.* acquisition, purchase; **—s,** *pl.* common property of two married people
Acquiescement, *s.m.* acquiescence, compliance, assent [assent
Acquiescer, *v.n.* to acquiesce, to comply, to
Acquis, e, *part.adj.* acquired, &c. (*V.* **Acquérir**); accruing; added; belonging; secured, insured; devoted; admitted, received; unquestionable
cquis, *s.m.* acquirements, attainments

Acquisition, *s.f.* acquisition; purchase; conquest
Acquit, *s.m.* discharge, acquittance; satisfaction; receipt, acquittance; (*at billiards*) lead
— *-à-caution,* (*cust.*) permit. *Par manière d'—,* for form's sake, negligently, carelessly. *Pour —,* received, settled, paid. *Jouer à l'—,* to play who shall pay for the whole
Acquittable, *adj.* acquittable, to be acquitted
Acquittement, *s.m.* discharge, payment, liquidation, acquittance; acquittal
Acquitter, *v.a.* to discharge; to fulfil; to pay; to clear; to ease; to receipt; to acquit
S'—, *v.r.* to acquit oneself; to perform, to discharge, to fulfil; to execute; to deliver; to
Acre, *s.m.* acre [pay off; to be quits
Âcre, *adj.* acrid, tart, sour, sharp, bitter
Âcrement, *adv.* acridly, tartly, sourly, sharply
Âcreté, *s.f.* acridity, acrimony, tartness, sharp-
Acrimonie, *s.f.* acrimony [ness
Acrimonieu-x, se, *adj.* acrimonious
Acrobate, *s.m.f.* acrobat [winding
Acrobatique, *adj.* acrobatic; (*mech.*) lifting,
Acroléine, *s.f.* (*chem.*) acroleine
Acronyque, *adj.* (*astr.*) acronycal
Acronyquement, *adv.* acronycally
Acropole, *s.f.* acropolis
Acrostiche, *s.m. adj.* acrostic [terium
Acrotère, *s.m.* (*arch.*) acroter, acroterion, acro-
Acte, *s.m.* act; action; transaction; instrument, document; deed; title-deed; charter; indenture; agreement; certificate; note; receipt; acknowledgment; decree; decision; resolution; writ; record; bill; public discussion, debate; **—s,** *pl.* acts, &c.; registers; proceedings, transactions. — *respectueux,* notice (to o.'s parents, when of age, to give their consent to o.'s marriage). *Faire — de,* to show proof of, to show. *Faire — de présence,* to show oneself, to put in
Actée, *s.f.* (*bot.*) actæa [*or* enter an appearance
Ac-teur, trice, *s.m.f.* actor, actress, performer, player; stage-player
Acti-f, ve, *adj.* active; real; actual; effective; brisk; quick; industrious
Actif, *s.m.* assets; creditor; (*of the budget*) receipts; (*gram.*) active voice [anemone
Actinie, *s.f.* (*zool.*) actinia, animal flower, sea-
Action, *s.f.* action; act; deed; agency, operation; activity; motion; play; energy; vigour; power; effect; influence; property; vivacity; warmth; ardour; animation; life, spirit; gesture; movements; attitude; expression; subject; lawsuit, suit; prosecution; fight, battle, engagement; (*com.*) share, stock; (*jest.*) credit, reputation. *En —,* in *or* into action; acting; acted; in practice; in motion; (*mach.*) in gear. *Hors d'—,* (*mach.*) out of gear. *Par —s,* by shares;
Actionnable, *adj.* actionable [joint-stock
Actionnaire, *s.m.f.* shareholder; stockholder
Actionné, e, *adj.* sued; stirring, busy [sue
Actionner, *v.a.* to bring an action against, to
S'—, *v.r.* to stir, to bestir oneself, to be busy
Activement, *adv.* actively; vigorously
Activer, *v.a.* to quicken; to accelerate; to hasten; to forward; to expedite; to press; to urge on; to urge; to stir up; to push on; to fan; to force
S'—, *v.r.* to be quickened *or* accelerated, &c.
Activité, *s.f.* activity; action; briskness; quickness; vivacity; nimbleness; diligence; despatch, expedition; efforts; progress; spirit; vigour; employment; operation; work; active
Actuaire, *s.m.* actuary [service
Actualisation, *s.f.* adaptation to the times; actualization; actuality [actualize
Actualiser, *v.a.* to adapt to the times; to
Actualité, *s.f.* present state *or* existence; usefulness *or* interest at the present moment *or* for the time being, present usefulness, present interest; thing of the present time; passing event, thing of the day, question of the hour; ephemeral subject; actuality, reality

Actuel, le, *adj.* present; passing; of the day, of the times; modern; for the time being; actual, real; — *s.m.* present, present state, present being *or* existence
Actuellement, *adv.* at present, now, at the present time; actually, really
Acuité, *s.f.* acuteness, sharpness, keenness
Acuminé, e, *adj.* (*bot.*) acuminated
Acuponcture, Acupuncture, *s.f.* (*surg.*) acupuncture, acupuncturation
Acupression, *s.f.* (*surg.*) acupressure
Acutangle, Acutangulaire, *adj.* (*geom.*) acute-angled, acutangular
Acutangulé, e, *adj.* (*bot.*) acute-angled
Adage, *s.m.* adage, proverb, saying
Adagio, *s.m. adv.* (*mus.*) adagio
Adamantin, e, *adj.* adamantine, adamantean
Adamite, *s.m.* Adamite
Adaptable, *adj.* adaptable
Adaptation, *s.f.* adaptation
Adapter, *v.a.* to adapt; to apply; to fit; to suit
Adapteu-r, se, *s.m.f.* adapter
Addition, *s.m.f.* addition; adding up; summing up; bill, reckoning; (*print.*) side-note
Additionnel, le, *adj.* additional
Additionner, *v.a.* to add, to add up, to cast [up, to sum up
S'—, *v.r.* to be added, &c.
Adducteur, *adj.m.* (*anat.*) adducent; — *s.m.* [adductor
Adduction, *s.f.* (*anat.*) adduction
Adelphe, *adj.* (*bot.*) adelphous; **—s,** *s.m.pl.* Adelphi (*of Terence*)
Ademption, *s.f.* (*law*) ademption
Adénite, *s.f.* (*med.*) adenitis
Adénocèle, *s.f.* (*med.*) adenocele
Adent, *s.m.* (*carp.*) scarf, dovetail, tabling
Adenter, *v.a.* to scarf, to dovetail, to table
Adepte, *s.m.f.* adept
***Adéquat, e,** *adj.* (*philos.*) adequate
Adhérence, *s.f.* adherence, adhesion
Adhérent, e, *adj.*, **Adhérent,** *s.m.* adherent
Adhérer, *v.n.* to adhere, to stick *or* cling (to)
Adhési-f, ve, *adj.* (*pharm.*) adhesive; — *s.m.* adhesive substance
Adhésion, *s.f.* adhesion; compliance
Ad hoc, *adv.* (*Latin*) special; expressly, for that, to that effect *or* purpose, for *or* to the purpose; in point, to the point; positively, unequivocally [the individual
Ad hominem, *adv.* (*Latin*) personal, direct, to
Ad honores, *adv.* (*Latin*) *V.* **Honores**
Adiante, *s.m.* (*bot.*) adiantum, maiden-hair
Adieu, *adv. s.m.* good-bye; farewell; it is all over with; parting; leave. *Sans* —, I won't say good-bye; I shall see you again. *Faire ses —x*, to take o.'s leave, to say good-bye, to take o.'s farewell. — *va!* (*nav.*) about ship!
Adimain, *s.m.* Angola sheep
Adipeu-x, se, *adj.* (*anat.*) adipous, adipose, fat
Adipique, *adj.* (*chem.*) adipic
Adipocire, *s.f.* (*chem.*) adipocere
Adirer, *v.a.* (*law*) to lose, to mislay
Adition, *s.f.* (*law*) acceptance
Adive, *s.m.* (*zool.*) adive, corsac [tiguous
Adjacent, e, *adj.* adjacent, adjoining, con-
Adjectif, *s.m.*, **Adjecti-f, ve,** *adj.* adjective
Adjectivement, *adv.* adjectively
Adjectiver, *v.a.* (*gram.*) to make an adjective of, to use adjectively; (*pop.*) to abuse
Adjoindre, *v.a.* to adjoin; to add (to); to give as an assistant; to join, to unite *or* associate (with)
S'—, *v.r.* to take as an assistant; to join; to be joined *or* added; to accompany; to associate with
Adjoint, e, *adj.*, **Adjoint,** *s.m.* assistant; deputy; associate; colleague; deputy-mayor, alderman; (*gram.*) adjunct
Adjonction, *s.f.* adjunction, junction, addition, union, adjoining, joining, uniting, association; annexation
Adjudant, *s.m.* adjutant
Adjudicataire, *s.m.f.* highest bidder, purchaser; contractor; — *adj.* purchasing; contracting [awarder
Adjudica-teur, trice, *s.m.f.* adjudicator,
Adjudicati-f, ve, *adj.* adjudicating, awarding
Adjudication, *s.f.* auction; contract; award
Adjuger, *v.a.* to adjudge, to adjudicate, to award; to grant; to knock down. *Adjugé!* (*at auctions*) gone! sold! (*fam.*) done! settled!
S'—, *v.r.* to appropriate to o.'s own use; to award to oneself, to take; to take possession of; to claim for oneself; to be adjudged, &c.
Adjuration, *s.f.* adjuration; imprecation
Adjurer, *v.a.* to adjure, to call upon, to summon, to beseech, to entreat, to conjure
Adjuvant, e, *adj.*, **Adjuvant,** *s.m.* (*pharm.*) adjuvant
Ad libitum, *adv.* (*Latin*) ad libitum, at will, at pleasure, as people choose, either way, indifferently
Admettre, *v.a.* to admit; to allow of; to allow; to permit; to authorize; to receive; to accept; to adopt; to grant; to acknowledge; to recognize; to suppose; to contain
S'—, *v.r.* to be admitted, &c.
Adminicule, *s.m.* help, support; auxiliary; (*law*) circumstantial *or* presumptive evidence, presumption; **—s,** *pl.* (*on a medal*) adminicules
Administra-teur, trice, *s.m.f.* administrator, administratrix; trustee; director, directress; manager, manageress; good manager; commissioner; governor; ruler; statesman; (*of the poor*) guardian; overseer
Administrati-f, ve, *adj.* administrative
Administration, *s.f.* administration; direction; management; government; conduct; dispensation; administering; ministration, ministering; functions; tenure of office; committee; council; board; commissariat; directors; commissioners; managers; rulers; authorities; officials; offices, office; trusteeship; guardianship; (*of legal evidence*) production
Administrativement, *adv.* administratively
Administré, e, *s.m.f.* person under o.'s administration *or* jurisdiction, governed
Administrer, *v.a.* to administer, to govern, to rule, to manage, to conduct; to regulate; to dispense, to distribute; to minister; to give; to apply; to furnish; to administer the last sacraments to; (*legal evidence*, &c.) to produce, to furnish. *Droit d'—*, (*law*) letters of administration [self, to take; to give *or* &c. each other
S'—, *v.r.* to be administered, &c.; to give one-
Admirable, *adj.* admirable, wonderful; capital; very fine
Admirablement, *adv.* admirably, wonderfully
Admira-teur, trice, *s.m.f.* admirer; wonderer; — *adj.* admiring; wondering
Admirati-f, ve, *adj.* of admiration; wonderful; wondering [of admiration
Admiration, *s.f.* admiration; wonder; object
Admirer, *v.a.* to admire; to wonder at
Admissibilité, *s.f.* admissibility
Admissible, *adj.* admissible; allowable
Admission, *s.f.* admission; admittance
Admittatur, *s.m.* (*eccl.*) testimonial (*for holy*
Admixtion, *s.f.* admixture [*orders*)
Admonestation, *s.f.* admonition
Admonester, Admonéter, *v.a.* to admonish
Admoni-teur, trice, *s.m.f.* admonisher, ad-
Admonition, *s.f.* admonition [viser
Adné, e, *adj.* (*nat. hist.*) adnate
Adolescence, *s.f.* adolescence
Adolescent, e, *adj. s.* adolescent; youth, lad, stripling; young girl, lass
Adonide, *s.f.* (*bot.*) *V.* **Adonis** [adonic
Adonien, ne, Adonique, *adj.m.f.*, *s.m.* (*vers.*)
Adonis, *s.m.* Adonis, beau, exquisite; — *s.f.* (*bot.*) adonis, bird's-eye, pheasant's-eye
Adoniser, *v.a.* to dress out *or* up, to deck out
Adonné, e, *adj.* given (to), devoted, addicted
Adonner, *v.n.* (*nav.*) to veer aft, to become favourable; to rise; — *v.a.* to give up, to devote

S'—, *v.r.* to give oneself up ; to apply *or* devote oneself ; to be addicted ; to take (to); to become attached
Adoptable, *adj.* adoptable
Adoptant, e, *s.m.f.* adopter
Adopter, *v.a.* to adopt ; to admit ; to take ; to choose ; to approve, to sanction ; to pass ; to carry
Adopti-f, ve, *adj.* adoptive ; adopted ; foster
Adoption, *s.f.* adoption ; admission ; introduction ; choice ; sanction ; passing ; carrying
Adorable, *adj.* adorable ; charming, lovely ; delightful ; delicious ; exceedingly pleasant
Adorablement, *adv.* adorably
Adora-teur, trice, *s.m.f.* worshipper, adorer; admirer, lover ; — *adj.* adoring ; admiring
Adoration, *s.f.* worship, adoration
Adorer, *v.a.* to worship, to adore ; to idolize ; to be exceedingly fond of
Ados, *s.m.* (*hort.*) shelving bed
Adossé, e, *adj.* resting *or* standing (against), placed (against), having (...) at the back, supported (by) ; covered *or* protected (by) ; back to back ; (*her.*) indorsed, endorsed, addorsed
Adossement, *s.m.* backing ; position back to back
Adosser, *v.a.* to place *or* fix the back of (against), to lean *or* place with the back (against) ; to place *or* build (against) ; to strengthen backward ; to lean *or* support (against) ; to draw up (under cover of) ; to set back to back
S'—, *v.r.* to rest *or* lean *or* set o.'s back (against) ; to stand (against) ; to be sheltered (with ... behind) ; to draw up (under) ; to stand *or* sit back to back
Adouber, *v.a.* to adjust ; (*nav.*) to repair, to refit
Adouci, *s.m.* roughing down, smoothing
Adoucir, *v.a.* to soften ; to smooth ; to sweeten ; to make mild *or* milder ; to temper ; to allay, to alleviate, to assuage, to mitigate, to appease, to calm, to soothe ; to attenuate ; to break ; to ease, to render easier ; to mend ; to tame
S'—, *v.r.* to soften ; to get *or* become smooth ; to be tempered ; to become sweet ; to be allayed *or* soothed *or* alleviated *or* appeased ; to be tamed ; to become gentle *or* more gentle ; to subside ; to relent ; to cool ; (*of weather*) to get (*or* grow) mild *or* milder, to give, to break up
Adoucissage, *s.m.* roughing down, smoothing ; softening ; slight touch
Adoucissant, e, *adj.* softening, soothing ; (*med.*) emollient, demulcent
Adoucissant, *s.m.* soother ; (*med.*) emollient, demulcent
Adoucissement, *s.m.* softening ; smoothing ; sweetening ; tempering ; allaying, alleviation, assuagement, mitigation, appeasement, soothing ; ease ; relief ; consolation ; extenuation, palliation, palliative ; restriction ; abatement ; breaking up, giving ; improvement
Adoucisseu-r, se, *s.m.f.* glass-polisher, polisher
Adoué, e, *adj.* (*hunt.*) paired, coupled
Ad patres, *adv.* (*Latin*) to kingdom come, to the next world ; dead. *Aller* —, to be gathered to o.'s fathers
Adragant, *s.m.* gum tragacanth, gum-dragon, adragant
Adragant, e, *adj.* tragacanth
Ad rem, *adv.* (*Latin*) categorically, to the point, to the purpose, categorical
Adresse, *s.f.* dexterity ; skill, cleverness ; shrewdness, cunning ; artifice ; handiness ; tact ; adroitness ; address ; direction ; destination ; inquiry. *A l'— de*, addressed *or* directed to ; intended for ; pointed at. *Aller* or *être à l'— de*, to be addressed *or* directed to ; to be intended for ; to be pointed at ; to apply to ; to hit *or* strike home
Adresser, *v.a.* to address ; to direct ; to send, to forward ; to recommend ; to offer up ; to present with ; to dedicate ; to give ; to aim ; to hit ; to ask ; to make ; — *v.n.* to hit (*bien* —, to hit the mark ; *mal* —, to miss the mark)
S'—, *v.r.* to address oneself ; to apply ; to look (to) ; to appeal (to) ; to speak ; to attack, to meddle (with) ; to be addressed *or* directed. *S'— ici ! — présentement !* apply *or* inquire within ! *S'— mal*, to go *or* come to the wrong man, to mistake o.'s man. *S'— bien !* to have well chosen o.'s man indeed !
Adriatique, *adj. s.f.* Adriatic
Adroit, e, *adj.* dexterous ; skilful, clever ; ingenious ; shrewd ; artful ; handy ; neat ; adroit
Adroitement, *adv.* dexterously ; skilfully, cleverly ; artfully ; handily ; neatly, smartly ; adroitly
Adulaire, *s.f.* (*min.*) adularia, moon-stone, sun-stone
Adula-teur, trice, *adj.* adulatory ; — *s.m.f.* adulator, flatterer, fawner, sycophant
Adulation, *s.f.* adulation, flattery, sycophancy
Aduler, *v.a.* to adulate, to flatter, to fawn upon
Adulte, *s.m.f.* adult ; — *adj.* adult, grown-up, full-grown
Adultération, *s.f.* adulteration
Adultère, *s.m.* adultery ; — *s.m.f.* (*pers.*) adulterer ; adulteress ; — *adj.* adulterous, adulterate
Adultérer, *v.a.* to adulterate ; to debase ; to pervert
Adultérin, e, *adj. s.* adulterine
Adurent, e, *adj.* (*med.*) burning
Aduste, *adj.* (*med.*) adust, burnt up, hot
Adustion, *s.f.* (*surg.*) adustion, cauterization, burning
Advenir, *v.n.imp.* to happen, to occur ; to chance, to come to pass ; to befall ; to fall ; to come (of) ; to become (of) ; to fare. *Advienne que pourra*, happen *or* come what may
Adventice, Adventi-f, ve, *adj.* adventitious
Adverbe, *s.m.* adverb
Adverbial, e, *adj.* adverbial
Adverbialement, *adv.* adverbially
Adverbialiser, *v.a.* (*gram.*) to adverbialize, to make an adverb of, to use adverbially
Adversaire, *s.m.f.* adversary, opponent
Adversati-f, ve, *adj.* (*gram.*) adversative
Adverse, *adj.* adverse ; opposite. *Avocat* —, counsel on the opposite side
Adversité, *s.f.* adversity ; misfortune ; affliction
Adynamie, *s.f.* (*med.*) adynamy, debility
Adynamique, *adj.* (*med.*) adynamic
Ægagre, *s.f.* ægagrus, wild goat
Ægilops, *s.m.* (*med., bot.*) ægilops
Aérage, *s.m.* airing, ventilation. *Puits d'*—, air-shaft
Aération, *s.f.* aeration ; airing, ventilation
Aéré, e, *adj.* aired ; airy ; aerated
Aérer, *v.a.* to air, to ventilate ; (*chem.*) to aerate
Aérien, ne, *adj.* aerial ; airy ; air
Aérifère, *adj.* aeriferous
Aérification, *s.f.* aerification
Aériforme, *adj.* aeriform
Aériser, *v.a.* to aerify
Aérodynamique, *s.f.* aerodynamics
Aérograph-ie, -ique. *V.* page 3, § 1
Aérolithe, *s.m.* aerolite
Aérolog-ie, -ique. *V.* page 3, § 1
Aéromètre, *s.m.* aerometer
Aérométr-ie, -ique. *V.* page 3, § 1
Aéronaute, *s.m.f.* aeronaut
Aéronautique, *adj.* aeronautic ; — *s.f.* aeronautics
Aérostat, *s.m.* aerostat, air-balloon
Aérostatier, *s.m.* balloonist, aeronaut
Aérostation, *s.f.* aerostation
Aérostatique, *adj.* aerostatic ; — *s.f.* aerostatics
Aérostier, *s.m.* balloonist, aeronaut
Aérotherme, *adj.* hot-air, aerothermal ; — *s.m.* hot-air oven, aerothermal bakery
Æthuse, *s.f.* (*bot.*) fool's-parsley
Aétite, *s.f.* ætites, eagle-stone
Affabilité, *s.f.* affability, kindness, courtesy
Affable, *adj.* affable, kind, courteous
Affablement, *adv.* affably, kindly, courteously
Affabulation, *s.f.* moral (of a fable)
Affadir, *v.a.* to make *or* render insipid ; to cloy ; to pall ; to surfeit, to flatten ; to sicken, to turn
S'—, *v.r.* to become *or* get insipid ; to pall
Affadissement, *s.m.* cloying ; insipidity ; nauseousness
Affaibli, e, *part. adj.* weakened, &c. (*V.* **Affaiblir**) ; weak ; faint ; light
Affaiblir, *v.a.* to weaken ; to enfeeble ; to allay, to abate ; to impair ; to soften ; to lessen ; to attenuate ; to reduce ; (*of coin*) to debase ; — *v.n.* to be weakening

S'—, *v.r.* to grow *or* become *or* get weak (*or* faint), to grow weaker *or* fainter, to become enfeebled, &c.; to faint; to abate; to lower; to flag

Affaiblissement, *s.m.* weakening; enfeeblement; allaying; abatement, diminution; impairment; (*of coin*) debasement

Affainéantir, *v.a.* to make *or* render idle *or* lazy *or* slothful *or* sluggish

S'—, *v.r.* to become idle *or* lazy *or* &c., to get into idle *or* lazy *or* &c. habits

Affaire, *s.f.* affair; matter, thing; business, concern; piece of business; duty; question; point; purpose; work, piece of work; job; bargain; transaction; dealing; speculation; undertaking, enterprise; important thing; great *or* difficult matter; dispute, quarrel; difficulty, trouble, hobble, scrape; danger; need, want, occasion; circumstance, occurrence; joke; lawsuit; case; fight, battle, action, engagement; **—s,** *pl.* affairs, &c.; business, trade, commerce; engagements; things, effects; ado, fuss; public affairs; politics. *— de cœur,* matter of feeling; love affair. *— d'intérêt, — d'argent,* money matter. *— d'or,* capital business *or* bargain; splendid speculation. *— de rien,* trifling affair. *En —,* engaged in business, engaged, busy. *Pour —,* on business. *Avoir — à,* to have to deal *or* to do with. *Avoir — de,* to have occasion for, to want, to stand in need of; to have to do with. *Être à son —,* to mind o.'s business. *Être au-dessous de ses —s,* to be in a bad way. *Être au-dessus de ses —s,* to have money put by, to be beforehand with the world. *Être bien* or *mal dans ses —s,* to be in good *or* bad circumstances, to be well off *or* badly off, to be thriving *or* embarrassed. *Être dans les —s,* to be in business. *Être en —,* to be engaged in business, to be engaged *or* busy, to transact business (with). *Être l'— de* (*Être mon* or *votre,* &c. *—*), to be ...'s business; to be a thing for ... to consider; to be the thing for, to suit. *Faire —,* to conclude a business *or* a bargain, to arrange. *Faire des —s,* to do business; (*pop.*) to make much ado, to make a fuss; to bring (one) into a scrape; to quarrel (with). *Faire l'—,* to do it, to do for it, to do. *Faire l'— de* (*Faire mon* or *votre,* &c. *—*), to be the thing for, to answer ...'s purpose, to do for, to suit. *Faire une — à,* to get *or* bring into a scrape; to quarrel with. *Faire* (*bien*) *ses —s, Faire de bonnes —s,* to succeed in business, to be doing well, to drive a good trade, to thrive, to make o.'s fortune. *Faire mal ses —s, Faire de mauvaises —s,* to be unsuccessful in business, not to succeed, to be doing badly. *S'attirer* or *se faire une* (*mauvaise*) *—* or *des —s,* to get (oneself) into a scrape *or* into a quarrel, to get into hot water. *Se tirer d'—,* to get (oneself) out of a difficulty; to get off; to get on; to get over it; to make o.'s way (in the world). *Son —,* o.'s affair *or* undertaking; o.'s business *or* concern; o.'s look-out; o.'s duty; o.'s case; o.'s dispute *or* fight; the thing for one, the thing that does for one *or* suits one, the thing that answers o.'s purpose, what one wants *or* wanted; a thing for one to consider; a *or* the job for one; o.'s fortune; the thing that one deserves *or* that settles one, a thrashing, a lesson, a clincher, the death-blow, a quietus; a drop too much. *Ses —s,* o.'s affairs, o.'s business *C'est mon —,* leave it to me. *C'est juste mon —,* that just suits me. *Voilà mon —!* that is the thing for me! that is what I want! *J'en fais mon —,* I take it upon myself, I will manage it, leave it to me. *Je tiens mon —!* I have found the right thing! I have got it! I see my way! *J'ai votre —,* I have what you want. *Son — est faite,* his fortune is made; he is done for. *Son — est bonne,* he is in for it, he will catch it. *Son — est claire* or *sûre, Il est sûr de son —,* he can't escape, he will catch it for certain

Affairé, e, *adj.* busy, engaged, occupied

Affaissé, e, *adj.* sunk, sunk down, bent down, bowed down; drooping, pendant; heavy; depressed, dejected; collapsed

Affaissement, *s.m.* sinking; subsiding, subsidence; settling; giving way; weakness; depression, dejection; (*med.*) collapse

Affaisser, *v.a.* to sink; to weigh down; to weaken; to depress

S'—, *v.r.* to sink, to sink down; to subside; to settle; to give way; to fall in, to cave in; to fall; to get weak; to be depressed; to droop; to flag; to collapse; to sag; to slope [training

Affaîtage, Affaîtement, *s.m.* (*falc.*) taming,

Affaîter, *v.a.* (*falc.*) to tame, to train; (*build.*) *V.* **Enfaîter**

Affaîteur, *s.m.* (*falc.*) tamer, trainer [lowered

Affalé, e, *adj.* (*nav.*) wind-bound, embayed;

Affaler, *v.a.n.* (*nav.*) to shift, to lower, to overhaul; to drive on a lee-shore, to drive *or* drift ashore. *Affale!* lower away!

S'—, *v.r.* to be embayed, to run ashore; to slide down a rope

Affamé, e, *adj.* hungry, famished, starving, starved; greedy (of), eager (for); *— s.m.f.* starveling. *Être — de,* to be eager for, to thirst for, to long for [lure, to bait

Affamer, *v.a.* to starve, to famish; (*fish.*) to

Affanure, *s.f.* (*agr.*) wages in kind

Affe, *s.f.* (*pop.*) life. *Eau d'—,* (*pop.*) brandy

Affectation, *s.f.* affectation; affected way; appropriation, application, destination

Affecter, *v.a.* to affect; to pretend, to feign, to simulate; to assume; to love, to like, to be fond of *or* partial to, to take kindly to; to make it a point; to aim at, to aspire to, to desire; to appropriate; to apply; to intend (for), to destine (to); to assign; to give; to attach

S'—, *v.r.* to be affected, &c.; to be moved; to grieve, to take on [moving, impressive

Affecti-f, ve, *adj.* affective; affecting, pathetic,

Affection, *s.f.* affection; fondness; love; attachment; inclination; partiality, liking; ardour; (*med.*) affection, disease, complaint; touch. *Prendre en —,* to become attached to *or* fond of, to take a liking *or* a fancy to

Affectionné, e, *adj.* affectionate; loving, fond; attached; *— part.* (*followed by* de *or* par) loved, liked

Affectionnément, *adv.* affectionately, fondly

Affectionner, *v.a.* to have an affection for, to be fond of, to love; to like, to fancy, to have a liking for, to be partial to, to take kindly to; to delight in; to attach

S'—, *v.r.* to become attached (to) *or* fond (of), to take an affection (for), to take (to); to delight (in); to take a fancy (to); to attach oneself (to ...); to attach (...) to oneself; to be fond of each other

Affectueusement, *adv.* affectionately, kindly

Affectueu-x, se, *adj.* affectionate, kind

Affenage, *s.m.* foddering, feeding

Affener, *v.a.* to fodder, to feed

Affer, *v.n.* (*pop.*) to live, to enjoy life

Afférent, e, *adj.* appertaining, pertaining, belonging; coming (to), accruing (to), falling (to); (*anat.*) afferent

Affermable, *adj.* farmable; rentable; demisable

Affermage, *s.m.* farming; renting; demising

Affermer, *v.a.* to farm; to rent; to demise

S'—, *v.r.* to be farmed; to be rented

Affermi, e, *part. adj.* strengthened, &c. (*V.* **Affermir**); firm, sure, strong, solid; steady. *Mal —,* unsteady; shaky; tottering; unsafe; insecure; wavering, irresolute

Affermir, *v.a.* to strengthen; to consolidate; to make firm *or* firmer; to harden; to secure; to fasten; to fix; to confirm; to establish

S'—, *v.r.* to become (*or* grow) strong *or* firm *or* hard; to become secured *or* confirmed *or* established; to fortify oneself; to persist (in)

Affermissement, *s.m.* strengthening; consolidation; firmness; establishment

Afféron, *s.m.* tag [canting
Afféte, e, *adj.* affected, prim, finical, mincing ;
Afféterie, *s.f.* affectation ; affected ways ; mannerism ; cant [affettuoso
Affetto, Affettuoso, *adj. adv.* (*mus.*) affetto,
Affichage, *s.m.* bill-sticking *or* posting, placarding
Affiche, *s.f.* placard, bill, posting-bill, poster, board ; card ; proof, sign, mark ; boat-hook. —*s des théâtres,* play-bills. *Homme-* —, poster-bearer, boardman, sandwich-man. *Petites* —*s,* advertisement sheet, advertiser
Afficher, *v.a.* to stick up, to post up, to placard ; to make a show of ; to affect ; to put forth ; to set up ; to attract attention to, to make (...) noticed ; to publish, to expose ; to give a bad name to. *Défense d'—!* stick no bills !
S'—, *v.r.* to set up (for) ; to make oneself noticed, to attract public notice ; to expose oneself ; to be stuck up *or* &c.
Afficheur, *s.m.* bill-sticker *or* poster
Affidé, e, *adj.* confidential, devoted ; — *s.m.f.* confidential *or* secret agent, confederate, confidant
Affilage, *s.m.* setting, sharpening, whetting
Affilé, e, *adj.* sharp ; glib, nimble
Affiler, *v.a.* to set, to sharpen, to whet
Affileu-r, se, *s.m.f.* sharpener
Affiliation, *s.f.* affiliation, association
Affilié, e, *adj.* affiliated ; — *s.m.f.* affiliated member, adept ; confederate
Affilier, *v.a.* to affiliate, to receive, to admit
S'—, *v.r.* to become affiliated *or* admitted ; to associate
Affiloir, *s.m.* sharpener, hone, whetstone, steel
Affiloire, *s.f.* oilstone
Affinage, *s.m.* refining ; fining ; pointing
Affinement, *s.m.* refining ; refinement
Affiner, *v.a.* to refine ; to fine, to make finer ; to point ; to polish *or* finish the point of ; to outwit, to trick, to bilk, to cheat, to deceive ; — *v.n.* (*nav.*) to become fair, to clear up
S'—, *v.r.* to become finer, to be refined *or* fined ; (*nav.*) to become fair, to clear up
Affinerie, *s.f.* refinery, finery ; pointing-shop
Affineur, *s.m.* refiner, finer ; pointer
Affinité, *s.f.* affinity ; alliance ; connection ; relation ; congeniality ; conformity ; disposition
Affinoir, *s.m.* fine hackle
Affiquet, *s.m.* knitting-sheath ; bauble, trinket
Affirmati-f, ve, *adj.* affirmative ; positive
Affirmation, *s.f.* affirmation ; assertion ; statement
Affirmative, *s.f.* affirmative [ment
Affirmativement, *adv.* affirmatively ; in the affirmative ; positively
Affirmer, *v.a.* to affirm ; to assert ; to declare ; to state ; to assure ; to vouch ; to prove
S'—, *v.r.* to be affirmed, &c. ; to gain credit
Affixe, *s.m.* (*gram.*) affix [*or* authority
Affleurage, *s.m.* levelling ; (*carp.*) making flush ; mixing (of flour) ; mixture, mixed flour
Affleuré, e, *adj.* level ; even (with) ; (*carp.*) flush
Affleurement, *s.m.* levelling ; (*carp.*) making flush ; (*mining*) cropping out, outcrop, basset
Affleurer, *v.a.* to level, to make even ; (*carp.*) to make flush ; to be level with, to be on a level with, to come up to ; (*shipbuilding*) to fay ; to mix (*flour*) ; — *v.n.* to be level, to be on a level ; to be flush ; (*mining, geol.*) to crop out
Afflicti-f, ve, *adj.* (*law*) affecting the person, corporal ; with hard labour
Affliction, *s.f.* affliction, grief, sorrow, distress ; adversity ; calamity, misfortune, blow
Affligé, e, *part. adj.* afflicted, &c. (*V.* **Affliger**) ; of affliction, of distress
Affliger, *v.a.* to afflict ; to distress, to grieve ; to torment, to worry, to vex, to trouble ; to affect ; to mortify (*the body*)
S'—, *v.r.* to be afflicted, to be concerned, to grieve, to mourn, to fret ; to vex each other
Afflouage, *s.m.* (*nav.*) setting afloat
Afflouer, *v.a.* (*nav.*) to set afloat

Affluence, *s.f.* affluence, abundance, plenty ; concourse, crowd ; flowing, flow [affluent
Affluent, e, *adj.*, **Affluent,** *s.m.* tributary ;
Affluer, *v.n.* to flow ; to run ; to fall ; to abound, to be plentiful ; to flock, to crowd ; to resort ; to rush
Afflux, *s.m.* (*med.*) afflux ; (*fig.*) coming, arrival
Affolé, e, *adj.* desperately fond (of), mad (after), infatuated (with) ; maddened, distracted, frantic ; bewildered ; wild ; flighty ; convulsed ; flickering ; unsteady ; (*of the magnetic needle*) defective
Affolement, *s.m.* infatuation ; maddening ; madness, distractedness, distraction ; derangement ; error, defect
Affoler, *v.a.* to infatuate ; to madden ; to distract ; to bewitch ; to derange, to make defective
S'—, *v.r.* to dote (on), to become (*or* be) infatuated (with) *or* excessively fond (of) ; to become deranged *or* defective
Affolir, *v.n.*, **S'—,** *v.r.* to madden, to become *or* get *or* go mad. *Faire* —, to drive mad
Affouage, *s.m.* right of cutting wood for fuel ; keeping in fuel ; fuel [washing away
†Affouillement, *s.m.* (*build.*) undermining,
†Affouiller, *v.a.* (*build.*) to undermine, to wash away [small-bower anchor
Affourche, *s.f.* (*nav.*) small bower. *Ancre d'—,*
Affourché, e, *adj.* astride ; (*nav.*) moored across [across
Affourcher, *v.a.* to seat astride ; (*nav.*) to moor
S'—, *v.r.* to sit astride ; (*nav.*) to moor each way [fodder, forage, provender
Affourragement, *s.m.* foddering, foraging ;
Affourrager, *v.a.* to fodder, to forage
S'—, *v.r.* to take in forage
Affraîchie, *s.f.* (*nav.*) fresh gale
Affraîchir, *v.n.* (*nav.*) *V.* **Fraîchir**
Affranchi, e, *adj.* freed, enfranchised, emancipated ; paid, prepaid, post-paid, carriage-paid ; — *s.m.f.* freed man ; freed woman. *Non* —, unpaid
Affranchir, *v.a.* to free ; to set free ; to make free ; to enfranchise ; to emancipate ; to manumit ; to liberate, to discharge ; to release ; to deliver ; to give liberty to ; to relieve ; to rid ; to exempt ; to exonerate ; to dispense ; to clear ; to cleanse ; to castrate, to geld ; to spay ; to prepay, to pay the postage of ; to pay the carriage of ; (*at the end of advertisements*) all letters to be prepaid
S'—, *v.r.* to free *or* &c. oneself ; to get free ; to get rid of ; to shake off ; to break loose ; to break through ; to dispense
Affranchissement, *s.m.* enfranchisement ; emancipation ; manumission ; liberation ; discharge ; release ; deliverance, delivery ; exemption ; castration, gelding ; spaying ; prepayment, payment of postage ; postage ; prepayment of carriage [liberator ; deliverer ; gelder
Affranchisseur, *s.m.* freer ; emancipator ;
Affre, *s.f.* affright, dread, terror, horror, agony ; — *s.m.* (*pop.*) taunt, twit, jaw, jobation, blow-up
Affrètement, *s.m.* freighting, chartering
Affréter, *v.a.* to freight, to charter
Affréteur, *s.m.* freighter, charterer
Affreusement, *adv.* frightfully, horribly, horridly, terribly, dreadfully, shockingly
Affreu-x, se, *adj.* frightful, horrible, horrid, terrible, fearful, dreadful, shocking ; hideous ; ghastly ; atrocious
Affriander, *v.a.* to use *or* accustom *or* bring up to dainties, to make dainty ; to allure, to entice, to tempt ; to charm
S'—, *v.r.* to become dainty ; to be allured, &c.
Affriché, e, *adj.* (*agr.*) fallow, lying fallow
Affricher, *v.a.* (*agr.*) to let (*land*) lie fallow
S'—, *v.r.* to lie fallow
Affriolement, *s.m.* allurement, enticement
Affrioler, *v.a.* *V.* **Affriander**
Affriter, *v.a.* to season (*a frying-pan*)
Affront, *s.m.* affront, outrage, insult ; disgrace,

shame, reproach; humiliation; failure; cneck. *En avoir l'—*, *V.* **Démenti** [ders
†Affrontailles, *s.f.pl.* limits, boundaries, bor-
Affronté, e, *adj.* (*her.*) affrontee; (*carp.*) flush
Affronter, *v.a.* to affront; to face; to brave; to dare; to attack; to deceive, to cheat
Affronteu-r,se, *s.m.f.* deceiver, impostor, cheat
Affublement, *s.m.* odd dress, rig; muffling up
Affubler, *v.a.* to dress (*oddly*); to dress out *or* up; to muffle *or* wrap up; to cover
S'— (*de*), *v.r.* to put on (*an odd dress*); to muffle oneself up; to cover oneself; to be wrapped up (in); to assume
Affusion, *s.f.* (*med.*) affusion
Affût, *s.m.* hiding-place; lying in wait for game; watch; gun-carriage, carriage; stand, rest; edge. *Être à l'—*, to be upon the watch, to be watching, to lie in wait. *Homme d'—*, sharp fellow, knowing one
Affûtage, *s.m.* sharpening; set of tools; doing up *or* dressing (*of hats*); mounting (*of guns*)
Affûté, e, *adj.* sharpened; sharp
Affûteau, *s.m.* watcher
Affûter, *v.a.* to sharpen, to set; to point; to stock with tools; to mount (*a gun*) upon its carriage; (*pop.*) to chisel, to diddle
Affûtiau, *s.m.* trifle, bauble, nicknack, kickshaw; implement, utensil, tool
Afin, *conj.* — *de*, in order to, so as to, to. — *que*, in order that, so that, that, to the end that
Afistoler, *v.a.* to make fine *or* spruce, to spruce up, to trim up; to tie up, to sew up
Africain, e, *adj. s.* African; African fashion
Aga, *s.m.* aga *or* agha (*Turkish high officer*)
Agace, *s.f.* magpie
Agacement, *s.m.* setting on edge; irritation
Agacer, *v.a.* to set (*the teeth*) on edge; to irritate (*the nerves*); to torment; to plague; to provoke; to tease; to annoy; to bore; to excite; to incite; to stir up; to entice, to allure; to ogle; to set o.'s cap at
S'—, *v.r.* to be set on edge *or* irritated, &c.; to torment *or* &c. each other
Agacerie, *s.f.* enticement, allurement; enticing way; pretty way; flirtation; advance, encouragement; provocation. *Faire des —s à*, to entice, to allure, to ogle, to set o.'s cap at, to flirt with
†Agaillardir, *v.a.*, **S'—,** *v.r.* to cheer up
Agalactie, *s.f.* (*med.*) agalaxy [wood
Agalloche, *s.m.* agalloch, agallochum, aloes-
Agame, *adj.* (*bot.*) agamous; — *s.m.* agama
Agami, *s.m.* (*bird*) agami, trumpeter [(*lizard*)
Agamie, *s.f.* (*bot.*) agamy
Aganter, *v.a.* (*nav.*) *V.* **Enganter**
Agape, *s.f.* agape, love-feast
Agaric, *s.m.* (*bot.*) agaric. — *champêtre*, mushroom. — *de chêne*, touchwood
Agasse, *s.f.* magpie
Agate, *s.f.* agate [become agatized
Agatifier, Agatiser, *v.a.* to agatize. *S'—*, to
Agave, *s.f.* (*bot.*) agave, American aloe
Age (*without any accent*), *s.m.* beam (*of a plough*)
Âge (*with a circumflex accent*), *s.m.* age; years; seniority; life; time; days; period; century; generation; old age; youth. *Bas —*, *premier —*, infancy; childhood. *Jeune —*, childhood, youth. *Moyen —*, middle age; (*hist.*) middle ages. — *moyen*, middle age; average life, average of human life. *Homme d'—*, old man. — *d'homme*, man's estate, manhood; life of a man, whole life, generation. *Fleur de l'—*, prime of life. *Avant l'—*, before o.'s time, prematurely. *D'—*, of *or* &c. age; by age; by seniority; in years; old. *D'un certain —*, elderly. *En —*, in years, of age. *En bas —*, very young. *Entre deux —s*, middle-aged. *Hors d'—*, aged, old; superannuated; too old. *Être d'— à* or *en — de*, to be old enough to. *Être sur l'—*, *tirer sur l'—*, to be in years, to be growing old, to be elderly. *N'être pas de son —*, to be above o.'s years. *Quel — avez-vous?* how old are you?

Âgé, e, *adj.* aged, old
Agence, *s.f.* agency; agency business; agency office. — *d'affaires*, general agency; agency office
Agencement, *s.m.* arrangement, disposition; ordering, order; fitting; fittings; fixtures; gearing; appliances
Agencer, *v.a.* to arrange, to dispose; to order; to fit; to throw into gear, to gear; to dress up, to trim
Agenda, *s.m.* agenda, memorandum-book, diary
Agénésie, *s.f.* (*med.*) impotence [on o.'s knees
†Agenouillé, e, *adj.* kneeling, kneeling down,
†Agenouillement, *s.m.* kneeling
†Agenouiller (S'), *v.r.* to kneel down, to kneel
†Agenouilloir, *s.m.* kneeling-stool; hassock
Agent, e, *s.m.f.* agent; middleman; broker; medium. — *d'affaires*, business agent, general agent, agent, house and estate agent, scrivener, &c. — *de la force publique*, peace-officer. — *monétaire*, circulating medium. — *de police*, police-officer, policeman. *V.* **Change, Comptable,** &c.
Agérasie, *s.f.* (*med.*) green old age
Agglomération, *s.f.* agglomeration
Agglomérer, *v.a.*, **S'—,** *v.r.* to agglomerate
Agglutinant, e, *adj. s.m.* agglutinant, adhesive [sive; — *s.m.* agglutinant
Agglutinati-f, ve, *adj.* agglutinative, adhe-
Agglutination, *s.f.* agglutination
Agglutiner, *v.a.*, **S'—,** *v.r.* to agglutinate
Aggravation, *s.f.* aggravation; increase
Aggrave, *s.f.* (*can. law*) censure, admonition, threat of excommunication
Aggraver, *v.a.* to aggravate; to make worse; to increase; to make heavy; to weigh down
S'—, *v.r.* to increase, to be aggravated
Agile, *adj.* agile, nimble, quick, active
Agilement, *adv.* with agility, nimbly, quickly
Agilité, *s.f.* agility, nimbleness, quickness
Agio, *s.m.* agio, premium; stock-jobbing
Agiotage, *s.m.* stock-jobbing, jobbing
Agioter, *v.n.* to gamble in the funds, to job
Agioteu-r, se, *s.m.f.* stock-jobber, jobber; stag
Agir, *v.n.* to act; to do; to work; to operate; to behave, to deal; to exert oneself; to proceed (against; to sue). *En —*, to act, to deal, to behave. *Faire —*, to set going; to employ; to use the influence of; to bring to bear (upon). *De quoi s'agit-il?* what is the question *or* matter? what is it about? *Il s'agit* (*de ...*), it *or* the matter *or* question *or* thing *or* point is (about, to, &c. ...); (...) is concerned *or* at stake *or* the question; (...) is talked about *or* thought of. *Dont il s'agit* or *s'agissait*, in question; at issue
Agissant, e, *adj.* active; stirring, bustling
Agita-teur, trice, *s.m.f.* agitator, stirrer; — *s.m.* (*chem.*) stirring-rod, glass rod
Agitation, *s.f.* agitation; shaking; tossing; jolting; rolling; roughness; waving; wagging; stir; bustle; motion; disturbing, disturbance; restlessness; uneasiness; trouble; emotion; excitement; flutter
Agité, e, *part. adj.* agitated, &c. (*V.* **Agiter**); in agitation; in motion; restless; uneasy; fretful; fitful; rough
Agiter, *v.a.* to agitate; to put in motion; to shake; to toss; to jolt; to wave; to wag; to brandish, to flourish; to swing; to pull; to spring; to move; to stir; to disturb, to disquiet; to make uneasy; to excite; to ruffle; to debate, to discuss
S'—, *v.r.* to stir about; to bestir oneself; to toss about; to be in motion, to move; to wag; to struggle; to make oneself uneasy; to be restless *or* uneasy; to swell, to rise, to get rough; to be agitated *or* disturbed, &c.; to be waved *or* pulled *or* &c.
Agnat, *s.m.* (*law*) agnate
Agnation, *s.f.* (*law*) agnation
†Agneau, *s.m.* lamb, ram lamb, wether lamb
†Agnelage, Agnèlement, *s.m.* lambing,
†Agneler, *v.n.* to lamb, to yean [yeaning

†**Agnelet,** *s.m.* lambkin; (*old coin*) agnelet, agnel
†**Agnelin,** *s.m.* lamb's skin with the wool on
†**Agneline,** *adj.f.* of a lamb *or* teg. *Laine* —, shorn lamb's wool, teg-wool
†**Agnelle,** *s.f.* ewe-lamb
†**Agnellement,** *s.m.* lambing, yeaning
†**Agnès,** *s.f.* simple *or* innocent girl, simpleton
Agnus, Agnus Dei, *s.m.* (*Cath. rel.*) Agnus Dei, Lamb of God [castus
Agnus-castus, *s.m.* (*bot.*) chaste tree, agnus
Agonie, *s.f.* agony, death-struggles, pang, anguish, torture, great pain, distress, anxiety. *A l'*—, dying, at *or* on the point of death
Agonir, *v.a.* (*pop.*) to abuse dreadfully. — *de sottises*, to call all sorts of names [man *or* woman
Agonisant, e, *adj. s.* dying, expiring; dying
Agoniser, *v.n.* to be dying, to be at *or* on the point of death; — *v.a.* *V.* **Agonir**
Agouti, *s.m.* (*zool.*) agouti
Agra, *s.m.* agra (*Chinese scented wood*)
Agrafe, *s.f.* hook; clasp; hasp; (*build.*) cramp-iron; (*arch.*) sculptured ornament. — *et porte*, hook and eye
Agrafer, *v.a.* to hook, to clasp, to hasp, to fasten with a hook *or* clasp *or* hasp; to catch, to nab; to cage, to clap up, to quod
    S'—, *v.r.* to hook, to clasp, to cling (to), to lay hold (of); to be fastened; to fasten o.'s own
Agraire, *adj.* agrarian; of land, land [dress
Agrandir, *v.a.* to enlarge; to make larger *or* greater; to aggrandize; to magnify; to lengthen; to widen; to extend; to increase, to augment; to improve; to raise; to advance; to promote; to exalt; to elevate; to ennoble; to aggravate; to exaggerate, to amplify; to make (...) look larger *or* taller
    S'—, *v.r.* to become *or* get larger, to become greater; to enlarge; to enlarge o.'s property; to become richer; to increase o.'s power *or* credit *or* fortune; to raise *or* advance oneself, to rise; to increase; to grow; to widen; to extend; to be raised *or* exalted *or* promoted
Agrandissement, *s.m.* enlargement; aggrandizement; magnifying; increase; improvement; extension; rise; advancement; promotion, preferment; fortune; exaltation; exaggeration
Agréable, *adj. s.* agreeable, pleasant, pleasing, pleasurable; acceptable; desirable; comfortable; welcome; palatable, nice; graceful; ornamental; funny; exquisite. *Avoir pour* —, to permit, to allow; to be pleased. *Faire l'*—, to play the agreeable
Agréablement, *adv.* agreeably, pleasantly, pleasingly, pleasurably; acceptably; comfortably; luxuriously; gracefully
Agréage, *s.m.* brokerage
Agréé, *s.m.* attorney, solicitor
Agréer, *v.a.* to accept; to receive; to approve; to like; to consent to; to assent to; to admit; to allow; to rig; — *v.n.* to be agreeable; to
Agréeur, *s.m.* (*old*) *V.* **Gréeur** [please
Agrégat, *s.m.* aggregate
Agrégati-f, ve, *adj.* aggregative
Agrégation, *s.f.* aggregate, aggregation, collection, assemblage; admission, reception; fellowship; examination for a fellowship. *Concours d'*—, examination for a fellowship
Agrégé, e, *adj.* aggregate; (*bot.*) clustered [tute
Agrégé, *s.m.* fellow; assistant professor, substi-
Agréger, *v.a.* to admit, to receive; to unite, to join, to incorporate; to associate; to aggregate
Agrément, *s.m.* approbation, consent, assent; agreeableness, pleasantness, pleasingness; pleasure, gratification; amusement; charm; interest; comfort; convenience; fancy; ornament, trimmings; (*mus.*) grace; (*theat.*) divertisement. *Art d'*—, *talent d'*—, accomplishment. *Note d'*—, grace-note [adorn
Agrémenter, *v.a.* to ornament, to trim, to
Agrener, *v.a.* to feed (*game-birds*), to bait
Agréner, *v.a.* (*nav.*) to bale, to pump out
Agrès, *s.m.pl.* (*nav.*) rigging
Agresseur, *s.m.* aggressor
Agressi-f, ve, *adj.* aggressive
Agression, *s.f.* aggression
Agressivement, *adv.* aggressively
Agreste, *adj.* wild, rustic, rural
Agreyeur, *s.m.* wire-drawer
Agricole, *adj.* agricultural
Agriculteur, *s.m.* agriculturist; farmer; husbandman; — *adj.* agricultural [farming, tillage
Agriculture, *s.f.* agriculture; husbandry,
Agriffer, *v.a.* to seize with the claws; (*pop.*) *V.*
    S'—, *v.r.* to cling (with the claws) [**Griffer**
Agriministe, *s.m.f.* trimming-maker
Agrion, *s.m.* dragon-fly
Agriotte, *s.f.* *V.* **Griotte**
Agripaume, *s.f.* (*bot.*) motherwort
Agripper, *v.a.* to catch *or* lay hold of, to seize upon, to snatch, to clutch, to gripe, to grip, to grab; to hook, to fork, to crib
    S'—, *v.r.* to cling (to), to lay hold (of)
Agrolle, *s.f.* carrion crow
Agronome, *s.m.* agronomist [§ 1
Agronom-ie, -ique, -iquement. *V.* page 3,
Agrostemme, *s.f.* corn-cockle, rose-campion
Agrostide, *s.f.* agrostis, bent-grass
Agroupement, *s.m.* aggroupment
Agrouper, *v.a.* to aggroup
Aguerrir, *v.a.* to train *or* inure to war; to discipline; to inure, to harden, to accustom, to use
Aguets, *s.m.pl.* *Aux* —, in wait; on the watch *or* look-out
Agui, *s.m.* (*nav.*) girt line, sling, bowline knot
Ah, *int. s.m.* oh! ah! ha! — *çà!* now then! well
Ah-ah, *s.m.* ha-ha, sunk fence, ditch [now! why
Ahan, Ahanement, *s.m.* groan, sigh, panting; hard work, toil; pain, trouble, labour; fatigue; hard pull, great effort. *Suer d'*—, to toil and moil, to work like a slave
Ahaner, *v.n.* to groan, to sigh, to pant; to work hard, to toil, to drudge; to knock oneself up
Aheurtement, *s.m.* obstinacy, stubbornness
Aheurter (S'), *v.r.* to be obstinately bent (upon); to stick (to); to persist (in); to be obstinate *or* stubborn; to be wedded (to)
Ahi, *int.* *V.* **Aïe**
Ahuri, e, *part. adj.* confused, &c. (*V.* **Ahurir**); — *s.m.f.* giddy-head. — *de Chaillot*, mad-cap, silly fellow *or* thing
Ahurir, *v.a.* to confuse, to put out, to perplex, to flurry, to bewilder; to astound, to stun, to amaze, to dumbfound [champagne
Aï, *s.m.* (*zool.*) ai, three-toed sloth; (*wine*) Aï
Aiche, *s.m.* lob-worm, lug-worm
Aicher, *v.a.* (*fish.*) to bait
Aidant, *s.m.* aider
Aide, (*thing*) *s.f.* aid, help, assistance; succour, relief; support; chapel of ease; —**s**, *pl.* (*taxes*) aids, subsidies, excise; (*rid.*) aids; (*build.*) outrooms, small rooms, waiting-rooms, anterooms, back-rooms; (*fig.*) nooks and corners, ins and outs. *A l'*—*!* help! *A l'*— *de*, with the help *or* aid *or* assistance of, with. *Être en* — *à*, to help, to aid, to assist
Aide, (*pers.*) *s.m.f.* assistant; helper; coadjutor; under-...; (*nav.*) mate. — **-chirurgien,** *s.m.* assistant surgeon. — **-maçon,** *s.m.* bricklayer's *or* mason's labourer. — **-major,** *s.m.* (*mil.*) assistant surgeon; (*formerly*) adjutant. — **-mémoire,** *s.m.* reminder, remembrancer; memorandum-book; book of reference; handbook, manual, vademecum. — **de camp** (*pl.* —*s de camp*), *s.m.* aide-de-camp. — **de cuisine,** *s.m.f.* under-cook
Aideau, *s.m.* (*agr.*) waggon-pole (*load-prop*)
Aider, *v.a.n.* to help, to aid, to assist; to succour, to relieve; to comfort; to contribute; to shoe (*an anchor*). —*à la lettre*, to complete the sense; to partly guess the meaning; to dress up a story, to stretch
    S'—, *v.r.* to help *or* &c. oneself *or* each other (*or* one another); to avail oneself (of), to make use (of); to bestir *or* exert oneself; to act

Aïe, *int.* ay! oh! ah! ha! oh dear! gee!
Aïeul, e, *s.m.f.* grandfather; grandmother; ancestor; ancestress; **—s,** *m.pl.* grandfathers; grandfather and grandmother; **—es,** *f.pl.* grandmothers; ancestresses
Aïeux, *s.m.pl.* ancestors, forefathers [u]
Aigade, Aigaire, &c. *V.* **Aiguade,** &c. (with
Aigle, *s.m.* (*male bird*) eagle; (*pers.*) great genius, great man, master-mind, star; (*of churches*) eagle lectern, reading-desk; (*coin, orders of knighthood*) eagle; — *s.f.* (*female bird*) eagle; (*standard*) eagle; (*her., astr.*) eagle. — *royal,* (*bird*) golden eagle. *Grand* —, (*paper*) double elephant. *L'— de Meaux,* Bossuet
Aiglefin, *s.m.* sharper; (*fish*) *V.* **Èglefin**
Aiglette, *s.f.* (*her.*) eaglet
Aiglon, ne, *s.m.f.* eaglet
Aiglure, *s.f.* (*falc.*) dusky spot
Aigre, *adj.* sour, acid, tart, bitter; sharp; harsh; acrimonious; crabbed, churlish; shrill; musty; (*of metals*) crisp
Aigre, *s.m.* sourness, acidity; sharpness; mustiness; extract (*of unripe fruit, for perfumers*)
Aigre-dou-x, ce, *adj.* between sweet and sour; sourish
Aigrefin, *s.m.* sharper; (*fish*) *V.* **Ègrefin**
Aigrelet, te, *adj.* sourish, tartish
Aigrement, *adv.* sourly, sharply, harshly
Aigremoine, *s.f.* (*bot.*) agrimony
Aigret, te, *adj.* sourish, tartish
Aigrette, *s.f.* egret; tuft; plume; crest
Aigretté, e, *adj.* with an egret; tufted; crested
Aigreur, *s.f.* sourness, acidity, tartness, bitterness; sharpness; harshness; acrimony; crabbedness, churlishness; spite; (*of metals*) crispness; **—s,** *pl.* sharp things, harsh words; harshness; (*med.*) heartburn, acidity of the stomach, waterbrash
Aigrière, *s.f.* sour whey and bran, hog-wash
Aigriette, *s.f.* sour cherry
Aigrin, *s.m.* sapling (*apple or pear-tree*)
Aigrir, *v.a.n.* to make sour; to sour; to turn sour; to irritate, to embitter; to envenom; to incense, to exasperate; to aggravate, to make worse; to increase
S'—, *v.r.* to get *or* turn sour; to sour; to become irritated, &c.; to get worse; to increase; to irritate *or* &c. each other [vation
Aigrissement, *s.m.* souring; irritation; aggra-
Aigu, ë, *adj.* acute; sharp; pointed; shrill; — *s.m.* (*mus.*) sharp
Aiguade, *s.f.* (*nav.*) watering-place; water, supply of water. *Faire* —, to water, to take in fresh water [dew, dew-drops
†Aiguail, *s.m.*, **Aiguaille,** *s.f.* (*hunt.*) morning
Aiguaire, *s.f.* (*agr.*) trench
Aiguayer, *v.a.* to water; to rinse
Aigue, *s.f.* (*obsolete*) water
Aigue-marine, *s.f.* (*jewel.*) aquamarine
Aiguière, *s.f.* ewer
Aiguiérée, *s.f.* ewerful
†Aiguillade, *s.f.* goad
†Aiguillage, *s.m.* (*rail.*) pointing
†Aiguillat, *s.m.* (*zool.*) needle-fish, pipe-fish
†Aiguille, *s.f.* needle; hand; spire; index, cock; spindle; chopstick; long thin boat; (*rail.*) point, switch; (*zool.*) garfish; pipe-fish. — *à passer,* bodkin. — *à reprises,* darning-needle. — *marine,* mariner's compass *or* needle. — *de mer,* (*fish*) sea-needle, garfish; pipe-fish
†Aiguillé, e, *adj.* (*nat. hist.*) needle-shaped
†Aiguillée, *s.f.* needleful
†Aiguiller, *v.a.n.* (*rail.*) to point
†Aiguilletage, *s.m.* tagging; (*nav.*) seizing
†Aiguilleter, *v.a.* to tag; (*nav.*) to seize
†Aiguilleti-er, ère, *s.m.f.* tagger, tag-maker
†Aiguillette, *s.f.* lace-tag, tag; point; shoulder-knot, aiguillette; slice; shred; (*nav.*) knittle, lashing, aigulet
†Aiguilletti-er, ère. *V.* **Aiguilletier**
†Aiguilleur, *s.m.* (*rail.*) pointsman, switcher
†Aiguillier, *s.m.* needle-maker; needle-case
†Aiguillière, *s.f.* needle-maker; garfish-net
†Aiguillon, *s.m.* goad; sting; prickle; spur, stimulus, incentive, encouragement; (*biblical style*) thorn (*in the flesh*)
†Aiguillonné, e, *adj.* (*bot., zool.*) prickly
†Aiguillonner, *v.a.* to goad; to sting; to spur, to stimulate, to incite, to excite, to urge
†Aiguillot, *s.m.* (*nav.*) pintle [whetting
Aiguisage, Aiguisement, *s.m.* sharpening,
Aiguiser, *v.a.* to sharpen, to whet; to quicken; to point; to give a point to; to stimulate; to increase; to heighten
S'—, *v.r.* to get sharper; to be sharpened, &c.
Aiguiserie, *s.f.* sharpening-workshop
Aiguiseur, Aiguisoir, *s.m.* sharpener, whetter
Aiguité, *s.f.* acuteness
†Ail, *s.m.* garlic
Ailante, *s.m.* (*bot.*) ailanto, ailantus *or* ailanthus
Aile, *s.f.* wing; pinion; van; fan; swift; sail; aisle; brim; (*of the nose*) lateral cartilage, ala; (*horol.*) fly. — *de pigeon,* (*fig.*) powdered side-curl. *Bout d'—,* pinion; best quill. *Ne battre plus que d'une* —, to be on o.'s last legs. *Tirer de l'—,* to make wing. *Tirer pied ou — de,* to get something out of (*a person*), to make the most of (*a thing*)
Ailé, e, *adj.* winged, feathered; flying
Aileron, *s.m.* pinion; (small) wing; float-board; fin; (*arch.*) console, scroll; (*pop.*) arm
Ailette, Ailerette, *s.f.* winglet, small *or* little wing; side-lining (*of a shoe*); side-piece (*of a shirt,* &c.); (*tech.*) fly, flier; (*of old armour*) ailette [garlic
†Aillade, *s.f.* garlic sauce; bread rubbed with
†Ailler, *s.m.* quail-net
†Ailleurs, *adv.* elsewhere; somewhere else; anywhere else. *Partout* —, everywhere else. *Nulle part* —, nowhere else. *D'—,* from another place *or* cause; besides; also; in addition to which; moreover; otherwise; in other respects *or* things; on another account; on another hand; nevertheless; however; after all; it must be borne in mind; elsewhere
†Ailloli, *s.m.* garlic and olive oil sauce
Aimable, *adj.* amiable; lovable; lovely; plea-
Aimablement, *adv.* amiably [sant; civil; kind
Aimant, e, *adj.* loving, affectionate
Aimant, *s.m.* loadstone; magnet
Aimantation, *s.f.* magnetization
Aimanté, e, *adj.* magnetic. *Pierre —e,* loadstone, magnet
Aimanter, *v.a.,* **S'—,** *v.r.* to magnetize
Aimé, e, *adj.* loved, beloved
Aimer, *v.a.* to love; to be fond of; to like; to choose; to delight in; to be in love with; to admit of; to agree with, to be consistent with. — *d'amitié,* to like. — *d'amour,* to love. — *mieux, V.* **Mieux.** *J'aime à croire* (or *à penser*), I should rather think; I trust, I hope
Aimez-moi, *s.f.* (*bot.*) marsh scorpion-grass
Aine, *s.f.* groin; herring-stick
Aîné, e, *adj. s.* elder; elder brother *or* sister; eldest; eldest son *or* daughter; eldest brother *or* sister; first-born; older; oldest; senior
Aînesse, *s.f.* primogeniture; eldership; seniority. *Droit d'—,* law of primogeniture; birth-
Ainette, *s.f.* herring-stick, sprat-stick [right
Ainsi, *adv. conj.* so, thus, in this way, in that way; that is the way; likewise; therefore; so that. — *de,* so *or* thus with. — *du reste,* — *de suite,* and so on, and so forth. — *que,* as, so as, as well as, along with, like. — *soit-il!* amen! so be it! *S'il en est* —, if it is so, if so, if that is the case. *Par* —, (*local*) so, thereby, therefore
Air, *s.m.* air; wind; vent; look, appearance; mien; countenance; expression; likeness; manner, way; life, fashion; tune; song; attitude; pace; little warming *or* warm. — *de vent,* (*nav.*) point of the compass. *Bel* —, gentility, fashion. *Faux — de,* slight resemblance with. *Gens du bel —,* gentlefolks, genteel *or* fashionable people. *Grand* —, open air; majestic air, noble appearance *or*

manner; high life, fashion. *Grands —s*, great airs. *En l'—*, in the air; on high; aloft; upward, up; idle, empty; light; slight; unfounded, groundless; idly; lightly, gratuitously, at random; slightly; groundlessly; in a flutter; in confusion; upside down; in motion; about. *Entre deux —s*, in a draught. *Avoir l'—*, to look, to seem to be. *Avoir l'— de*, to look like *or* as if, to seem; to pretend. *Donner de l'— à*, to air; to ventilate. *Faire prendre l'— à*, to give an airing to, to take out. *Prendre des —s*, to give oneself airs. *Prendre l'—*, to go out in the open air; to take an airing; to breathe the fresh air. *Prendre un — de feu*, to just warm oneself a little, to have (*or* take) a warm. *Se donner des —s*, to give oneself airs, to be forward. *Se donner* or *se pousser de l'—*, (*pop.*) to take oneself off, to bolt. *Vivre de l'— du temps*, to live upon nothing, to be without means of subsistence, to starve. *Il ne fait pas d'—*, there is no air stirring

Airage, *s.m.* ventilation, airing, air

Airain, *s.m.* brass; (*poet.*) cannon; (*poet.*) bell, bells; (*poet.*) boiler, vessel; (*poet.*) steel; (*poet.*) iron. *D'—*, of brass, brass, brazen; impudent; hard, of steel, of stone, unfeeling, unpitying, merciless; dry and exceedingly hot; dry and exceedingly cold

Aire, *s.f.* area, space; thrashing-floor, barn-floor, floor; eyrie, eyry, aerie, aery, nest; (*nav.*) way (*of a ship*). *— de vent*, (*nav.*) point of the compass

Airée, *s.f.* lot of sheaves covering a barn-floor

Airelle, *s.f.* whortleberry, huckleberry; bilberry; cranberry, moorberry, cowberry

Airer, *v.n.* to build its eyrie; *— v.a. V.* **Aérer**

Ais, *s.m.* plank, board; shelf

Aisance, *s.f.* ease, easiness, facility, freedom; fulness; comfort; comforts of life; competency, easy circumstances; (*civ. law*) easement; **—s,** *pl.*, *Cabinet* or *lieux d'—s*, water-closet, privy. *Chausse d'—s*, waste-pipe. *Fosse d'—s*, cesspool. *Honnête —*, competency, small fortune

Aise, *adj.* glad, happy, pleased

Aise, *s.f.* ease, convenience; gladness, joy, pleasure; comfort. *A l'—*, at ease, at o.'s ease; easy; comfortable; easily; freely. *A son —*, at o.'s ease, at ease; easy; comfortable; comfortably; as much as one pleases; as (*or* when) one pleases; free, at home; unembarrassed; in easy circumstances, well off; well. *Mal à son —*, *mal à l'—*, uneasy; uncomfortable; embarrassed; badly off; unwell. *En prendre à son —*, to take it (*or* things) easy; to do as one pleases. *Se mettre à son —*, to take o.'s ease, to make oneself comfortable; to make oneself at home; to make free

Aisé, e, *adj.* easy; convenient, commodious; free; ready; in easy circumstances, well off. *Peu —*, straitened

Aisément, *adv.* easily; conveniently, commodiously; comfortably; freely; readily

Aissante, *s.f.*, **Aisseau,** *s.m.* (*carp.*) shingle

Aisselle, *s.f.* armpit; (*anat.*) axilla; (*bot.*) axil, axilla

Aitiologie, *s.f. V.* **Étiologie**

Ajointer, *v.a.* to join end to end, to join, to fit

Ajonc, *s.m.* furze, whin, gorse

Ajoupa, *s.m.* hut, shed

Ajouré, e, *adj.* open-work; pierced

Ajournement, *s.m.* adjournment; postponement; summons, citation

Ajourner, *v.a.* to adjourn, to put off, to defer, to postpone; to summon, to cite

S'—, *v.r.* to adjourn; to be put off, &c.

Ajoutage, *s.m.* piece joined on, addition

Ajouté, *s.m.* addition, rider

Ajouter, *v.a.* to add; to join; to superadd; to embellish. *— à la lettre*, *V.* **Aider**

S'—, *v.r.* to be added *or* joined *or* &c.

Ajoutoir, *s.m. V.* **Ajutage**

Ajus, Ajust, *s.m.* (*nav.*) hitch

Ajustage, *s.m.* adjusting; fitting; sizing

Ajustement, *s.m.* adjustment; fitting; adapting; sizing; tallying; regulation; arrangement; attire, dress; ornament; agreement; settlement; reconciliation

Ajuster, *v.a.* to adjust; to fit; to adapt; to size; to square; to tally; to tune; to arrange; to dress, to trim up; to make (...) agree; to settle; to reconcile; to aim; to aim at, to take aim at; to level; to trounce, to trim

S'—, *v.r.* to be adjusted *or* &c.; to fit; to tally; to adapt *or* suit oneself; to prepare oneself; to dress; to trick oneself out; to agree; to get reconciled; to be settled

Ajusteur, *s.m.* adjuster; fitter; mill-wright; weigher, trier, assayer

Ajustoir, *s.m.* assay-scales

Ajutage, Ajutoir, *s.m.* ajutage, adjutage, tube, spout

Alacrité, *s.f.* alacrity

Alaise, Alèse, *s.f. V.* **Alèze**

Alambic, *s.m.* alembic, still; (*fig.*) thorough investigation, careful examination

Alambiqué, e, *adj.* strained, far-fetched, over-refined, too subtle, fine-spun, wire-drawn, pretentious

Alambiquer, *v.a.n.* to puzzle; to strain, to over-refine; to subtilize

Alambiqueu-r, se, *s.m.f.* subtilizer, refiner

Alandier, *s.m.* kiln-hole

Alangui, e, *adj.* languid, languishing, enfeebled, weakened, drooping, flagging

Alanguir, *v.a.* to cause to languish, to render *or* make languid, to enfeeble, to weaken; to slacken

S'—, *v.r.* to become languid *or* languishing, to droop, to flag

Alanguissement, *s.m.* languidness, feebleness, drooping, flagging

Alarguer, *v.n.* (*nav.*) to fall off, to bear off

Alarme, *s.f.* alarm; fright; fear; uneasiness

Alarmer, *v.a.* to alarm; to frighten; to startle

S'—, *v.r.* to alarm oneself, to take alarm, to be alarmed *or* frightened

Alarmiste, *s.m.f.* alarmist

Alaterne, *s.m.* (*bot.*) alatern, buckthorn

Albain, e, *s.m.f. adj.* Alban

Albanais, e, *adj. s.* Albanian

Albâtre, *s.m.* alabaster; whiteness; fair complexion. *D'—*, of alabaster, alabaster; (*fig.*) snowy, snow-white

Albatros, *s.m.* (*bird*) albatross

Alberge, *s.f.* (*bot.*) alberge, clingstone peach

Albergier, *s.m.* (*bot.*) alberge-tree

Albicore, *s.m.* (*fish*) albicore

Albigeois, *s.m.pl.* (*hist.*) Albigenses

Albin, e, *adj.* albineous, albinous

Albina, *s.f.* albino woman *or* girl, albina

Albinisme, *s.m.* albinoism, albinism

Albinos, *s.m.f. adj.* albino

Albite, *s.f.* (*min.*) albite

Albran, Albrener. *V.* **Halbran, Halbrener**

Albuginé, e, Albugineu-x, se, *adj.* (*anat.*) albugineous, whitish

Albugo, *s.m.f.* (*med.*) albugo

Album, *s.m.* album; scrap-book; sketch-book

Albumine, *s.f.* albumen

Albuminer, *v.a.* to albumenize

Albumineu-x, se, *adj.* albuminous

Albuminurie, *s.f.* (*med.*) albuminuria

Alburno, *s.m. V.* **Burnous**

Alcade, Alcaïde, *s.m.* alcalde, alcade, alcaid

Alcaïque, *adj. s.m.* (*vers.*) alcaic

Alcalescence, *s.f.* alkalescence

Alcalescent, e, *adj.* alkalescent

Alcali, *s.m.* (*chem.*) alkali

Alcalifiable, *adj.* alkalifiable

Alcalifiant, e, *adj.* alkalifying

Alcalimètre, *s.m.* alkalimeter

Alcalimétrie, *s.f.* alkalimetry

Alcalin, e, *adj.* alkaline

Alcalinité, *s.f.* alkalinity

Alcalisation, *s.f.* alkalization

Alcaliser, *v.a.*, **S'—,** *v.r.* to alkalize, to alkalify

Alcaloïde, *s.m.* alkaloid

Alcanna, *s.f.* alkanna, alcanna, henna

Alcarazas, Alcarraza, *s.m.* alcarazza, alcarraza, water-cooler, cooler, cooling-vessel

Alcazar, *s.m.* alcazar (*Moorish palace*)
Alcée, *s.f.* (*bot.*) hollyhock
Alchimie, *s.f.* alchemy
‡†**Alchimille,** *s.f.* (*bot.*) lady's mantle
Alchimique, *adj.* alchemic
Alchimiste, *s.m.* alchemist
Alcool, *s.m.* alcohol
Alcoolat, *s.m.* (*pharm.*) spirit
Alcoolate, *s.m.* (*chem.*) alcoholate (*salt*)
Alcoolé, *s.m.* (*pharm.*) elixir
Alcoolique, *adj.* alcoholic
Alcoolisation, *s.f.* alcoholization
Alcooliser, *v.a.* to alcoholize
Alcoolisme, *s.m.* (*med.*) alcoholism
Alcoolomètre, Alcoomètre, *s.m.* alcoholometer, alcoholmeter, alcoometer
Alcoolométrie, Alcoométrie, *s.f.* alcoholometry, alcoometry
Alcoolométrique, Alcoométrique, *adj.* alcoholometrical, alcoometrical
Alcoran, *s.m. V.* **Coran**
Alcôve, *s.f.* alcove, recess
Alcyon, *s.m.* (*bird*) halcyon, kingfisher; (*polype*) alcyonium, dead man's fingers, dead man's hand
Alcyonien, ne, *adj.* halcyon, halcyonian
Alde, *s.m.* Aldine edition [Eye
Aldébaran, *s.m.* (*astr.*) Aldebaran, the Bull's
Aldée, *s.f.* (*Indian*) village
Aldéhyde, *s.m.* (*chem.*) aldehyde
Alderman, *s.m.* alderman
Aldin, e, *adj.* Aldine
Ale, *s.f.* ale
Aléatoire, *adj.* uncertain, eventual, contingent
Aléatoirement, *adv.* eventually, contingently
Alène, *s.f.* awl; (*fish*) sharp-nosed skate
Alénier, *s.m.* awl-maker
Alénois, *adj.m. V.* **Cresson**
Alentir, *v.a. V.* **Ralentir**
Alentour, *adv.* around, round, about; round it *or* them, about it *or* them. *D'*—, surrounding, neighbouring
Alentours, *s.m.pl.* surroundings; neighbourhood; environs; connections, intimates, familiars, associates, company, circle, attendants
Alépine, *s.f* bombazine
Alérion, *s.m.* (*bird*) swift; (*her.*) allerion
Alerte, *s.f.* alarm; alert; warning; — *adj.m.f.* alert, nimble, quick, active; brisk; sprightly; sharp, shrewd, wide-awake; vigilant, watchful, on the look-out; — *int.* alert! up! take care! mind! look out! *En* —, on *or* upon the alert
Alertement, *adv.* alertly, quickly, briskly
Alésage, *s.m.* drilling, boring, smoothing
Alèse, *s.f. V.* **Alèze**
Aléser, *v.a.* to drill, to bore, to smooth
Alésoir, *s.m.* drilling-bit, boring-bit, borer; polishing-tool, finishing-tool
Alester, Alestir, *v.a.* (*nav.*) to lighten (*a ship*), to buoy up (*a cable*)
  S'—, *v.r.* (*nav.*) to get ready
Alésure, *s.f.* chips, drill-shavings, scrapings
Alette, *s.f. V.* **Ailette**
Alevier, *s.m. V.* **Alevinier**
Alevin, *s.m.* fry, young fish
Alevinage, *s.m.* breeding of fish; small fish
Aleviner, *v.a.* to stock with fry
Alevinier, *s.m.* fry-pond, nurse-pond
Alexandrin, e, *adj. s.* Alexandrine; Alexandrian
Alexipharmaque, Alexitère, *adj.m.f.*, *s.m.* (*med.*) alexipharmic, alexiteric
Alezan, e, *adj.* chestnut; — *s.m.f.* chestnut horse *or* mare. — *saure, adj.* sorrel
Alèze, *s.f.* (*med.*) bed-linen, sheet; (*tech.*) plank, board (*joined to another*); osier-twig
Alfa, *s.m.* (*bot.*) *V.* **Spart**
Alfange, *s.f.* scimitar; battalion
Alfénide, *s.m.* alfenide, nickel silver, German silver, imitation silver; plated articles *or* goods *or* wares
Alfier, *s.m.* ensign, standard-bearer
Algalie, *s.f.* (*surg.*) bougie, indiarubber catheter
Alganon, *s.m.* convict-chain, chain
Algarade, *s.f.* sudden outburst of passion, insult, attack, bluster, rating, blowing-up
Algèbre, *s.f.* algebra
Algébrique, *adj.* algebraic, algebraical
Algébriquement, *adv.* algebraically
Algébriste, *s.m.* algebraist
Algérien, ne, *adj. s.* Algerian; Algerian fashion
Algide, *adj.* (*med.*) cold, algid
Algonquin, *s.m.* Algonquin, (Canadian) savage
Algor, *s.m.* (*med.*) algor
Algorithme, *s.m.* (*math.*) algorithm [catchpoll
Alguazil, *s.m.* alguazil; police spy, bumbailiff,
Algue, *s.f.* alga, weed; sea-weed; wrack, seawrack; laver; dulse; carrageen, Irish moss
Alhambra, *s.m.* Alhambra
Alibi, *s.m.* (*law*) alibi
Alibile, *adj.* (*med.*) alible [jackass
Aliboron, *s.m.* Grizzle, long-ears; donkey, ass,
Aliboufier, *s.m.* (*bot.*) styrax, storax-tree
Alicante, *s.m.* Alicant, tent (wine)
Alichon, *s.m.* float-board
Alidade, *s.f.* alidade, index, sight
Aliénabilité, *s.f.* alienability
Aliénable, *adj.* alienable, transferable
Aliénataire, *s.m.f.* alienee
Aliéna-teur, trice, *s.m.f.* alienator; alienatrix
Aliénation, *s.f.* alienation; transfer; estrangement; derangement. — *mentale*, mental alienation *or* derangement, insanity, lunacy
Aliéné, e, *adj. s.* alienated; estranged; deranged; insane, mad; lunatic. *Maison d'—s*, lunatic asylum, mad-house
Aliéner, *v.a.* to alienate; to transfer; to relinquish, to give up, to renounce; to estrange; to disaffect; to derange
  S'—, *v.r.* to alienate; to estrange oneself; to estrange; to lose; to relinquish o.'s liberty; to be alienated *or* estranged; to be lost; to become deranged
Aliéniste, *s.m. adj.* *Médecin* —, alienist, physician for lunatics
†**Aligné, e,** *part.* in a line; laid out *or* ranged in a line; formed in line, standing in a straight line; straight
†**Alignement,** *s.m.* laying out *or* standing in a line; falling into line; ranging; straight line, line, row; level; direction; (*mil.*) alignment, dressing, line; (*mil. book-keep.*) balancing of accounts; (*engin.*) alignment. —! (*mil.*) dress! *Prendre l'— de*, to trace the line of
†**Aligner,** *v.a.* to lay out in a line; to form in line *or* in a straight line; to square; to string together; to draw up; to level; (*mil.*) to dress, to draw up in a line; (*mil. book-keep.*) to balance; (*print.*) to range; (*of animals*) to serve, to line
  S'—, *v.r.* to form in line, to fall into line, to fall in, to dress; to run *or* be in a (straight) line; to keep the line; (*print.*) to range; (*pop.*) to have a set-to, to fight
†**Alignette,** *s.f.* herring-stick
†**Alignole,** *s.m.* (kind of fishing-net)
Aliment, *s.m.* food, aliment; nourishment, nutrition; feed; feeding; fuel; —**s,** *pl.* (*law*) alimony, maintenance
Alimentaire, *adj.* alimentary, feeding; of *or* for food, fit *or* used for food, used as food, food; (*med.*) dietetic. *Pension* —, maintenance; alimony; provision. *Pompe* —, donkey-engine, donkey-pump. *Provision* —, alimony *pendente lite*. *Régime* —, dietary
Alimentation, *s.f.* alimentation, feeding, feed; diet; food; supply. *Appareil* or *machine d'*—, feeding apparatus, feeder, donkey-engine
Alimenter, *v.a.* to feed; to nourish; to maintain; to sustain, to support; to supply
  S'—, *v.r.* to feed (on); to be fed, &c.
Alimenteu-x, se, *adj.* nutritive, alimental
Alinéa, *s.m.* paragraph; fresh paragraph; (*print.*) break
Alinette. *V.* **Alignette** [break
Aliquante, *adj.* (*math.*) aliquant; — *s.f.* aliquant part [part
Aliquote, *adj.* (*math.*) aliquot; — *s.f.* aliquot

Alise, *s.f.* (*bot.*) wild sorb, chess-apple
Alisé, *adj. V.* **Alizé** [tree
Alisier, *s.m.* (*bot.*) wild service-tree, chess-apple
Alisme, *s.m.*, **Alismie,** *s.f.* (*bot.*) alisma, water-
Alité, e, *adj.* laid up; bed-ridden [plantain
Aliter, *v.a.* to confine to o.'s bed, to keep in bed, to lay up; (*fish.*) to place by layers
S'—, *v.r.* to take to o.'s bed, to go to bed; to keep o.'s bed, to be confined to bed
Alizari, *s.m.* (*com.*) madder-roots
Alizarine, *s.f.* (*chem.*) alizarine
Alizarique, *adj.* (*chem.*) alizaric
Alize, *s.f. V.* **Alise**
Alizé, *adj.m.* (*nav.*) *Vents —s*, trade-winds
Alizier, *s.m. V.* **Alisier**
Alkékenge, *s.m.* alkekengi, winter-cherry
Alkermès, *s.m.* (*pharm.*) alkermes
Allah, *s.m.* Allah
Allaise, *s.f.* bar (*sand-bank in a river*)
Allaite, *s.f.* (*hunt.*) teat, dug (*of a she-wolf*)
Allaitement, *s.m.* nursing, suckling
Allaiter, *v.a.* to nurse, to suckle
Allant, *part. of* **Aller,** going, &c.; — *s.m.* goer; — *m.*, **e,** *f.*, *adj.* active, stirring, busy, bustling
Allèchement, *s.m.* allurement, enticement, bait
Allécher, *v.a.* to allure, to entice, to attract
Allée, *s.f.* passage; walk; path; lane; alley; entrance, entry; going. *— couverte*, shady walk. *—s et venues*, going (*or* coming *or* walking) in and out *or* to and fro *or* backward and forward, running about
Alléga-teur, trice, *s.m.f. adj.* alleger; alleging
Allégation, *s.f.* allegation; quotation
Allége, *s.f.* lighter; sill, window-sill; (*rail.*) tender. *Frais d'—*, (*com.*) lighterage
Allégeance, *s.f.* alleviation; relief; ease; comfort. *Serment d'—*, (*Engl. hist.*) oath of allegiance [lief; ease; mitigation; reduction
Allégement, *s.m.* lightening; alleviation; re-
Alléger, *v.a.* to lighten; to disburden, to unload; to alleviate, to allay, to relieve; to ease; to mitigate; to lessen; to reduce; (*nav.*) to lighten (*a ship*), to buoy up (*a cable*)
S'—, *v.r.* to ease oneself; to become lighter; to lessen; to be alleviated, &c.
Allégir, *v.a.* to reduce; to lighten
Allégor-ie, -ique, -iquement, -isme,
Allégoriser, *v.a.n.* to allegorize [**-iste.** *V.* p.3, §1
Allégoriseur, *s.m.* allegorizer
Allègre, *adj.* lively, sprightly, cheerful, merry; quick, nimble, brisk [ly, briskly
Allègrement, *adv.* cheerfully, merrily; quick-
Allégresse, *s.f.* mirth, joy, gladness, cheerfulness, liveliness, sprightliness, alacrity, glee; shouts of joy
Allégretto, *adv. s.m.* (*mus.*) allegretto
Allégro, *adv. s.m.* (*mus.*) allegro
Alléguer, *v.a.* to allege; to state; to plead; to produce; to adduce; to quote [wood-sorrel
Alléluia, *s.m.* hallelujah; (*bot.*) sheep's sorrel,
Allemand, e, *adj. s.* German; double-Dutch; German fashion; allemande (*dance, tune*)
Allemanderie, *s.f.* (*tech.*) finery, chafery
Aller, *s.m.* going; (*fig.*) run, course of time; (*nav.*) voyage out, outward passage; (*rail.*) single journey; down (*train*). *— et retour*, there and back; return (*ticket*); (*nav.*) voyage out and in. *Avoir l'— pour le venir*, to have o.'s labour for o.'s pains. *Donner l'— et le venir*, to box both ears. *Pis —*, *V.* **Pis-aller**
Aller, *v.n.* to go; to proceed; to repair; to leave, to depart; to get on; to go on; to move; to run; to ride; to go about; to be going; to be about; shall now, shall; will now, will; to go and; to set (to); to act; to behave; to lead; to tend, to aim; to end; to extend; to be carried; to reach; to rise; to fit; to become; to suit; to please; to match; to agree; to do; to last; to come; to amount; to be; to turn out; should, were to; to go to the watercloset; to evacuate, to be purged; to burn; to sail. *— et venir*, to go there and back; to go (*or* come *or* walk) to and fro *or* in and out *or* backward and forward, to go about. *Il va venir*, he is coming, he will be here presently. *Nous allons revenir*, we are coming back. *Je vais sortir*, I am going out. *Je vais dîner*, I am going to dine, I shall *or* will dine. *Faire —*, to set going, to put in motion; to move; to drive; to turn; to wag; to swing; to twirl, to flourish; to keep boiling; to give trouble; to humbug, to bamboozle; to purge, to open the bowels of. *Se laisser —*, *V.* **Laisser (Se).** *Allons!* let us go! come on! come! well! now! now then! very good! agreed! *Allons donc!* nonsense! pooh! indeed! come, come! now then! *Allons, bon!* well now! *Allez! va!* go! go on! begone! be off! let me tell you! depend upon it! I can tell you! I assure you! to be sure! indeed! now! come! *Va!* be it so! let it be! agreed! done! *Va pour*, let it be: let me (*or* us) have. *Comment allez-vous?* how are you? *Comment cela* (or *ça*) *va-t-il?* how do you do? how do you get on? *Je vais bien*, I am well; I am doing well; my watch is right, I am right. *Je vais* or *cela* (or *ça*) *va mieux*, I am better; I am doing better. *Cela va! Ça va!* that will do! *Et allez donc!* (*pop.*) in a trice! that's it! and no mistake! *Il y va de ..., ...* is (*or* are) at stake, ... is (*or* are) concerned. *Y —* (*with an adverb or an adverbial expression*), to go about it, to go it, to act, to deal, to proceed, to go on, to go to work, to do business; to go. *Y — (de)*, to lay, to stake, to play. *Y — de ...*, (*imp.*) ... to be at stake, ... to be concerned. *Y — par là*, to take it so. *On y va!* coming!
S'en —, *v.r.* to go (*or* get) away *or* off *or* along *or* about; to go; to run away; to escape; to be off; to make off; to come *or* drop off; to evaporate; to vanish, to disappear; to come out; to wear out *or* away *or* off; to be dying, to die; to grow old; to decline; to fade; to faint; to sink; to fall; to run out *or* over; to boil over; to be going; to be about, shall, will; to be going upon. *Allez-vous-en! va-t'en!* go away! go along! be off! *Allons-nous-en!* let us go! come along! *Faire en aller*, to drive *or* send away; to drive off; to remove. *S'en aller de la poitrine*, to be dying of consumption
Alléser, *v.a. V.* **Aléser** [hold
Alleu, *s.m.* allodium. *Franc —*, allodium; free-
Alliacé, e, *adj.* alliaceous, of garlic
Alliage, *s.m.* alloyage; alloy; alliance, union; mixture; (*arith.*) alligation. *Règle d'—*, alligation
Alliaire, *s.f.* (*bot.*) hedge-garlic
Alliance, *s.f.* alliance; marriage; match; union; covenant; confederacy, league, coalition; affinity; connection; mixture, blending, uniting, joining; combination; wedding-ring; (*jest.*) manacle, handcuff
Allié, e, *part. adj.* allied; related; connected; akin; alloyed; combined, mixed, united, joined; — *s.m.f.* ally; relation, relative; confederate; partner; associate
Allier, *v.a.* to ally; to marry; to match; to combine; to unite, to join; to mix; to alloy
S'—, *v.r.* to ally oneself; to marry, to be married; to match; to combine; to unite; to league, to band; to be mixed
Allier, *s.m.* partridge-net
Alliez, *s.m.* (*bot.*) tare
Alligator, *s.m.* alligator
Allingre, Allingue, *s.f.* weir
Allitération, *s.f.* alliteration [assessment
Allivrement, *s.m.* quota, share; taxation,
Allivrer, *v.a.* to tax, to assess
Allobroge, *s.m.* Allobroge; (*fig.*) boor
Allocation, *s.f.* grant; allowance; allocation; (*mil. admin.*) entry, item; supply, provision
Allocution, *s.f.* address, speech, allocution
Allodial, e, *adj.* allodial, freehold
Allodialité, *s.f.* free tenure, freehold
Allonge, *s.f.* piece; addition; (*of tables*) leaf; (*com.*) allonge, rider; (*of butchers*) meat-hook, hook; (*chem.*) adopter; (*nav.*) timber, futtock

Allongé, e, *adj.* lengthened; elongated; long; drawn out; stretched out, outstretched
Allongement, *s.m.* lengthening; prolongation; elongation; stretching out; delaying, delay
Allonger, *v.a.* to lengthen; to eke out; to draw, to draw out; to stretch, to stretch out; to extend; to wire-draw; to delay, to protract; to prolong; to thin *or* dilute (*a sauce*); to allonge (*a thrust*); to fetch, to deal, to hit, to strike, to give (*a blow*)
S'—, *v.r.* to lengthen; to stretch, to stretch out; to stretch oneself; to lie down *or* fall down at full length; to extend; to be lengthened, &c. [allopathic
Allopathe, *s.m.* allopathist, allopath; — *adj.*
Allopath-ie, -ique, -iquement, -iste, Allotropie, &c. *V.* page 3, § 1
Allopathiser, *v.a.n.* to allopathize
Allouable, *adj.* grantable; allowable
Allouche, Allouchier. *V.* **Alise, Alisier**
Allouer, *v.a.* to grant; to allow; to fix
Alluchon, *s.m.* cog, catch, tooth (*of a wheel*)
Allumage, *s.m.* lighting, kindling
Allume, *s.f.* brand. *Bougie d'—*, taper
Allumelle, *s.f.* charcoal furnace
Allumer, *v.a.* to light; to light up, to illuminate; to kindle, to inflame; to set on fire; to ignite; to excite; to stir up; to colour; (*pop.*) to whip; to gull; to puff
S'—, *v.r.* to light; to light up; to burn up; to kindle; to catch fire; to ignite; to be kindled; to brighten up; to blaze; to sparkle; to glare; to flare; to colour; to break out
Allumette, *s.f.* match; fusee; spill; light; lighter. — *-bougie,* — *de cire,* vesta match, vesta. — *chimique,* lucifer match, lucifer, congreve. — *de papier,* spill, pipe-light. — *pour les fumeurs,* cigar-light, fusee, &c.
Allumetti-er, ère, *s.m.f.* match-maker
Allumeu-r, se, *s.m.f.* lighter; lamp-lighter;
Allumi, *s.m.* brand [(*at auctions*) puffer
Allumière, *s.f.* match-factory; match-box
Allure, *s.f.* gait; pace; walk; carriage; manner, way, ways; demeanour; behaviour; conduct; bearing; movement, motion; direction; course; track; turn; bent; looks, appearance, aspect; (—**s,** *pl.*) intrigues; (*nav.*) trim
Allusi-f, ve, *adj.* allusive
Allusion, *s.f.* allusion; hint; innuendo. *Faire — à,* to allude to; to hint at
Alluvial, e, Alluvien, ne, *adj.* alluvial
Alluvion, *s.f.* alluvium, alluvion. *D'—*, alluvial
Alluvionnaire, *adj.* alluvial
Almadie, *s.f.* canoe, pirogue
Almageste, *s.m.* almagest
Almanach, *s.m.* almanac, calendar; directory. — *d'adresses* or *des adresses,* Post-Office directory, directory
Almandine, *s.f.* (*min.*) almandine
Almée, *s.f.* alme, almeh
Aloès, *s.m.* aloe, aloes
Aloétine, *s.f.* (*chem.*) aloetine
Aloétique, *adj.m.f., s.m.* aloetic [tion
Aloi, *s.m.* standard; quality, sort, kind; condi-
Aloïque, *adj.* aloetic
Alonge, &c. *V.* **Allonge,** &c.
Alopécie, *s.f.* (*med.*) alopecy, fox-evil
Alors, *adv.* then; at that time; now; in that case; in such a case, in such cases; therefore; by that time. *D'—*, of that time, of those times; for the time being; of old, of former times. — *que,* when, at a time when, now that. — *même que,* even when. — *comme —*, we will think about that when the time comes, we shall know what to do, all in good time
Alose, *s.f.* shad
Alosier, *s.m.*, **Alosière,** *s.f.* shad-net [sapajou
Alouate, *s.m.* (*zool.*) howler, howling-monkey,
Alouche, Alouchier. *V.* **Alise, Alisier**
Alouchi, *s.m.* alouchi (*gum*)
Alouette, *s.f.* lark; skylark. — *des prés,* titlark. *Pied-d'—*, (*bot.*) larkspur
Alourdir, *v.a.* to make heavy *or* dull, to stupefy
S'—, *v.r.* to grow heavy *or* dull
Alourdissement, *s.m.* heaviness
Aloyage, *s.m.* alloyage; pewterer's alloy
Aloyau, *s.m.* sirloin, sirloin of beef
Aloyer, *v.a.* to alloy
Alpaca, Alpaga, *s.m.* alpaca
Alpestre, *adj.* Alpine
Alpha, *s.m.* alpha
Alphabet, *s.m.* alphabet
Alphabét-ique, iquement. *V.* page 3, § 1
Alpin, e, *adj.* Alpine; mountainous, mountain
Alpiste, *s.m.* (*bot.*) alpist, canary-grass
Alque, *s.m.* *V.* **Pingouin**
Alquifoux, *s.m.* (*min.*) alquifou, potter's ore
Alsacien, ne, *adj. s.* Alsacian, Alsatian
Alsine, *s.f.* chickweed, sword-grass
Altariste, *s.m.* altarist (*in the Vatican*)
Altavelle, *s.f.* (*fish*) sting-ray, fire-flaire
Altérabilité, *s.f.* alterability, alterableness
Altérable, *adj.* alterable, changeable; corruptible, adulterable [*s.m.* (*med.*) alterative
Altérant, e, *adj.* causing thirst; — *adj.m.f.,*
Altéra-teur, trice, *adj.* altering, deteriorating; counterbalancing, weakening; — *s.m.f.* debaser; modifier
Altérati-f, ve, *adj.*, **Altératif,** *s.m.* alterative
Altération, *s.f.* alteration; change; deterioration; corruption; adulteration; debasement; impairment; injuring; misrepresentation; perversion; lessening, weakening, diminution; discomposure; faltering; thirst
Altercas, *s.m.* (*obsolete*) altercation
Altercation, *s.f.* altercation
Altère, *s.f.* *V.* **Haltère**
Altéré, e, (*part. of* **Altérer**) altered, changed, distorted, &c.; — *adj.* thirsty, dry; dried up; thirsting (for); greedy (of); longing, yearning, sighing (for); faltering, tremulous. *Être — de,* to thirst for
Alter ego, *s.m.* another self, a second self
Altérer, *v.a.* to alter, to change; to deteriorate; to adulterate; to corrupt; to falsify, to debase; to impair; to mar; to injure; to spoil; to misrepresent; to distort; to pervert; to disturb; to trouble; to discompose; to affect; to lessen, to weaken, to diminish; to make thirsty, to cause *or* excite thirst
S'—, *v.r.* to alter, to change; to be *or* become injured *or* impaired, &c.; to spoil; to be spoilt; to become distorted *or* discomposed, &c.; to lessen; to degenerate; to become worse; to falter, to tremble; to make oneself thirsty; to become *or* get thirsty
Alternance, *s.f.* alternation; succession
Alternat, *s.m.* alternateness, alternacy; rotation of crops
Alternati-f, ve, *adj.* alternate, alternative; in turn, by turns; by rotation; (*of motion*) reci-
Alternation, *s.f.* alternation [procating
Alternative, *s.f.* alternative; option, choice; alternation, interchange, succession
Alternativement, *adv.* alternately, by turns
Alterne, *adj.* alternate; reciprocal
Alterné, e, *adj.* alternate; alternating, in turns, in succession
Alterner, *v.n.a.* to alternate; to take turns; to perform alternately, to act *or* work in turn (*or* by turns); to take in turn; to fill by turns; to produce a rotation of crops
Alterquer, *v.n.* to altercate, to dispute
Altesse, *s.f.* highness
Althéa, Althée, *s.f.* marsh-mallow
Althéine, *s.f.* (*chem.*) altheine
Alti-er, ère, *adj.* haughty, proud; lofty
Altièrement, *adv.* haughtily, proudly
Altimètre, *s.m.* altimeter
Altimétr-ie, -ique. *V.* page 3, § 1
Altitude, *s.f.* altitude
Alto, *s.m.* (*mus.*) alto
Alude, *s.f.* roan, coloured sheep-skin
Aludel, *s.m.* (*chem.*) aludel, subliming-pot

Alumelle, *s.f.* (*tech., nav.*) blade
Aluminaire, *s.f.* alum-slate, alum-shale, alum-schist; — *adj.* alum
Aluminate, *s.m.* aluminate
Alumine, *s.f.* alumina [to alum
Aluminer, *v.a.* to mix with alumina *or* alum,
Alumineu-x, se, *adj.* aluminous; alumish;
Aluminière, *s.f.* alum-pit [alum
Aluminifère, *adj.* aluminiferous
Aluminique, *adj.* aluminous
Aluminite, *s.f.* aluminite
Aluminium, *s.m.* aluminium
Alun, *s.m.* alum
Alunage, *s.m.* aluming
Alunation, *s.f.* alum-making
Aluner, *v.a.* to alum
Alunerie, *s.f.* alum-works
Aluneu-x, se, *adj.* aluminous; alumish
Alunière, *s.f.* alum-pit; alum-works
Alunifère, *adj.* aluminiferous
Alunite, *s.f.* alunite, alum-stone
Alvéolaire, *adj.* alveolar
Alvéole, *s.f.m.* alveole, alveolus, cell (*in a honey-comb*), socket (*of a tooth*)
Alvéolé, e, *adj.* alveolate
Alvier, Alvinier. *V.* **Alevier,** &c.
Alvin, e, *adj.* (*med.*) alvine; — *s.m. V.* **Alevin**
Alysse, *s.f.*, **Alysson,** *s.m.* (*bot.*) madwort; gold-dust
Amabilité, *s.f.* amiability, amiableness; loveliness; kindness; politeness, civility; advances
Amadis, *s.m.* tight sleeve
Amadou, *s.m.* amadou, German tinder, tinder; touch-wood, match-wood
Amadouer, *v.a.* to coax, to wheedle, to cajole; to gain over; to appease, to quiet; to soften
S'—, *v.r.* to be coaxed, &c.; to be *or* become appeased, &c.
Amadouerie, *s.f.* German tinder factory
Amadoueu-r, se, *s.m.f.* German tinder-maker; (*fig.*) coaxer, wheedler, cajoler
Amadouvier, *s.m.* (*bot.*) agaric, touch-wood
Amaigrir, *v.a.* to make lean; to make thin, to emaciate; to thin, to lessen, to reduce, to bring down; — *v.n.*, **S'—,** *v.r.* to get (*or* grow) lean *or* thin, to waste, to fall away; to shrink
Amaigrissement, *s.m.*; growing thin, falling away, wasting, emaciation, leanness
†Amaillade, Amairade, *s.f.* trammel-net
Amalécite, *s.m.f.* Amalekite
Amalgamation, *s.f.* amalgamation
Amalgame, *s.m.* amalgam; (*fig.*) amalgamation
Amalgamer, *v.a.*, **S'—,** *v.r.* to amalgamate
Amalgameur, *s.m.* amalgamator [tion
Amandaie, *s.f.* almond-grove, almond-planta-
Amande, *s.f.* almond; kernel. — *lissée*, sugared almond. — *de terre*, rush-nut, cyperus
Amandé, e, *adj.* with almonds, amygdalate
Amandé, *s.m.* almond emulsion, milk of almonds, amygdalate
Amandier, *s.m.* almond-tree
Amant, e, *s.m.f.* paramour (*m.*); lover; suitor; sweetheart; lady-love; votary. — *de cœur*, favourite lover
Amarante, *s.f.* (*bot.*) amaranth; — *s.m.* amaranth colour, amaranth; — *adj.* amaranth-coloured, amaranthine [amaranth
Amarantine, *s.f.* (*bot.*) gomphrena, globe
†Amareilleur, *s.m.* oyster-bed keeper
Amarelle, *s.f.* (*bot.*) *V.* **Gentianelle;** — *adj.f.* *Cerise* —, morella cherry, morella
Amarescent, e, *adj.* bitterish
Amarinage, *s.m.* (*nav.*) manning (*a prize*)
Amariner, *v.a.* to man (*a naval prize*); to accustom to the sea
Amarque, *s.f.* (*nav.*) buoy [ing; anchorage
Amarrage, *s.m.* (*nav.*) mooring; seizing; lash-
Amarre, *s.f.* mooring; fast; cable; rope; line
Amarrer, *v.a.* (*nav.*) to make fast, to fasten, to moor, to secure; to hitch; to belay; to rack; to lash

Amaryllis, *s.f.* (*bot.*) amaryllis, daffodil lily
Amas, *s.m.* heap; pile; mass; hoard; store; lot; accumulation; agglomeration; cluster; drift; collection; crowd; mob
Amasser, *v.a.* to heap up; to heap; to pile up; to amass, to hoard *or* lay up; to lay by; to store up; to accumulate; to gather; to collect; to cluster; to drift
S'—, *v.r.* to gather together; to gather; to heap; to hoard; to accumulate; to collect, to assemble, to crowd; to drift; to be amassed, &c.
Amassette, *s.f.* (*paint.*) palette-knife, amassette
Amasseu-r, se, *s.m.f.* hoarder, gatherer
Amatelotage, Amatelotement, *s.m.* (*nav.*) classing, messmating
Amateloter, *v.a.* (*nav.*) to class, to mess together, to messmate
Ama-teur, trice, *s.m.f.* amateur; lover; fancier; civilian; — *adj.* (*de*) fond (of)
Amati, *s.m.* Amati violin
Amatiner, *v.a.* to rouse early, to make (...)
Amatir, *v.a.* (*tech.*) to deaden [rise early
Amaurose, *s.f.* (*med.*) amaurosis
Amaurotique, *adj. s.m.f.* (*med.*) amaurotic
Amazone, *s.f.* amazon; lady on horseback, female rider, rider; — *s.f.m.* riding-habit, habit. *Habit d'* —, riding-habit, habit
Ambages, *s.f.pl.* circumlocution, ambages
Ambassade, *s.f.* embassy
Ambassadeur, *s.m.* ambassador
Ambassadorial, e, *adj.* ambassadorial
Ambassadrice, *s.f.* ambassadress
Ambattage. *V.* **Embattage**
Ambe, *s.m.* series of two numbers
Ambesas, *s.m. V.* **Beset** [surrounding
Ambiant, e, *adj.* circumambient, ambient,
Ambidextérité, *s.f.* ambidexterity [dexter
Ambidextre, *adj. s.m.f.* ambidextrous; ambi-
Ambigu, ë, *adj.* ambiguous; obscure; doubtful
Ambigu, *s.m.* collation (*with hot and cold dishes and the dessert served together*); (*fig.*) medley, olio, compound; —, — *-comique* (*the name of a theatre in Paris*)
Ambiguïté, *s.f.* ambiguity
Ambigument, *adv.* ambiguously
Ambitieusement, *adv.* ambitiously; pretentiously, affectedly
Ambitieu-x, se, *adj. s.* ambitious; aspiring; pretentious, affected; ambitious man *or* woman
Ambition, *s.f.* ambition
Ambitionner, *v.a.* to be ambitious of *or* eager for, to aspire to, to seek after; to affect
Amble, *s.m.* amble, ambling pace. *Aller l'* —, to amble, to amble along
Ambler, *v.n.* to amble [ambling; ambler
Ambleu-r, se, Ambli-er, ère, *adj. s.*
Amblyope, *s.m.f.* (*med.*) weak-sighted person
Amblyopie, *s.f.* (*med.*) amblyopy, weakness of
Ambon, *s.m.* (*arch.*) *V.* **Jubé** [sight
Ambre, *s.m.* amber. —*gris*, ambergris
Ambré, e, *adj.* amber-scented, ambered; amber-coloured
Ambréine, *s.f.* (*chem.*) ambreine
Ambrer, *v.a.* to amber
Ambrette, *s.f.* amber-seed, musk-seed
Ambroisie, *s.f.* ambrosia [cious
Ambrosiaque, *adj.* ambrosial, fragrant, deli-
Ambrosien, ne, *adj.* Ambrosian [walk
Ambulacre, *s.m.* (*hort.*) ambulacrum, covered
Ambulance, *s.f.* movable hospital, field-hospital, temporary hospital, ambulance; medical staff of an ambulance
Ambulant, e, *adj.* walking; perambulating; ambulatory; travelling, itinerant; strolling; movable
Ambulatoire, *adj.* ambulatory, movable, itinerant; fickle, wavering, changeable
Âme, *s.f.* soul; mind; spirit; ghost; life; heart; feeling; conscience; essence; essential; core; inside, inner part; creature, fellow, person, people; (*of devices*) motto; (*of fagots*) small wood; (*of bellows*) clapper; (*of quills*) pith; (*of*

a gun) bore, inner tube; (*of violins*, &c.) sounding-post; (*of a picture*) outline, sketch; (*of a bronze cast*) plaster *or* clay model. — *damnée*, mere tool, instrument, underling. — *en peine*, tormented spirit; soul in purgatory. — *qui vive*, a living creature. *Charge d'—s*, cure of souls. *Égalité d'—*, equanimity. *Force d'—*, fortitude. *Grandeur d'—*, magnanimity. *Dans l'—*, in o.'s soul; at heart; every inch. *Avoir la mort dans l'—*, to be grieved to death. *Mettre la mort dans l'—*, to grieve to death, to be the death of. *Rendre l'—*, to give up the ghost, to die

Amé, e, *adj.* (*old*) well-beloved

Amélanche, *s.f.* (*bot.*) amelanchier-berry

Amélanchier, *s.m.* (*bot.*) amelanchier

Améliorable, *adj.* improvable; mendable

Améliora-teur, trice, *s.m.f.* improver; — *adj.* improving [ment, progress

Amélioration, *s.f.* amelioration, improve-

Améliorer, *v.a.*, **S'—,** *v.r.* to ameliorate; to improve; to better, to mend

Amen, *adv. s.m.* amen

Aménagement, *s.m.* management; disposition, arrangement, fitting, preparation

Aménager, *v.a.* to order *or* regulate the management of; to parcel out; to manage, to dispose, to arrange, to lay out, to fit up, to prepare; to do up, to do; to cut up (*a tree*); to dispose of
 S'—, *v.r.* to be parcelled out *or* managed, &c.

Amendable, *adj.* amendable, mendable; improvable; liable to a fine, finable; redeemable by a fine, compoundable

Amende, *s.f.* fine, penalty; mulct; forfeit. — *honorable*, public penance; public apology, apology, reparation, compensation, amends. *Condamner* or *mettre à l'—*, to fine

Amendement, *s.m.* amendment; improvement; manuring

Amender, *v.a.n.*, **S'—,** *v.r.* to amend; to mend; to improve; to better; —*v.a.* (*old*) to fine; (*agr.*) to manure

Amène, *adj.* gracious, affable, pleasing, pleasant

Amené, *s.m.* (*law*) warrant

Amener, *v.a.* to bring; to draw, to pull; to introduce, to bring in; to bring out *or* up *or* down; to bring over *or* about *or* forward; to fetch; to bring on, to cause, to occasion; to produce; to induce; (*at dice*) to throw; (*nav.*) to
 S'—, *v.r.* to be brought, &c. [strike, to lower

Aménité, *s.f.* amenity; pleasantness; grace

Aménorrhée, *s.f.* (*med.*) amenorrhœa

Amenuiser, *v.a.* to thin, to lessen, to reduce

Am-er, ère, *adj.* bitter; briny; sad; grievous

Amer, *s.m.* bitter; bitterness; gall; (*nav.*) landmark, sea-mark

Amèrement, *adv.* bitterly; grievously

Américain, e, *adj. s.m.f.* American; — *s.f.* American woman *or* lady *or* girl, American; American fashion; American phaeton; (*print.*) script. *Chemin de fer —*, traction railway, street railway, tramway. *Col —*, opera-tie. *Œil —*, inquisitive eye; piercing sight, good eyes; fascinating eye

Américanisation, *s.f.* americanization

Américaniser, *v.a.* to americanize. *S'—*, to become *or* be americanized, to become American

Américanisme, *s.m.* americanism

Amertume, *s.f.* bitterness; sorrow, vexation, grief, affliction [bird

Améthyste, *s.f.* amethyst; — *s.m.* humming-

Améthystin, e, *adj.* amethystine [suite

Ameublement, *s.m.* furnishing; furniture;

Ameublir, *v.a.* (*law*) to make movable; (*agr.*) to mellow [(*agr.*) mellowing

Ameublissement, *s.m.* (*law*) making movable;

Ameulonner, *v.a.* (*agr.*) to shock, to stook; to cock; to stack; to heap

Ameutement, *s.m.* training *or* forming a pack (*of hounds*); collecting, rousing; collection, mob

Ameuter, *v.a.* to train (*hounds*) to hunt together; to gather, to collect, to raise; to rouse, to excite, to stir up, to set (against)
 S'—, *v.r.* to gather *or* collect (*into a mob*); to crowd; to rise; to riot; to mutiny; to conspire

Ami, e, *s.m.f.* friend; lover; lady-love, love; companion; dear; dear boy; dear girl *or* woman; dear fellow. *Bon —*, *bonne —e*, good friend; sweetheart. *Cher —*, *chère —e*, dear friend; dear; dear boy *or* girl *or* woman; dear *or* good fellow; dear son *or* daughter *or* brother *or* sister *or* cousin *or* &c.; love. *D'—*, friendly; (*of a room, bed*) spare. *L'—!* good man! *M'amie*, (*fam.*) my dear, my darling, my love. — *de cœur*, bosom friend, sincere friend; favourite lover. — *de cour*, hollow friend, sham *or* false friend. — *de table*, trencher-friend, bottle-companion

Ami, e, *adj.* friendly (to); fond (of); beloved, favourite; propitious, favourable. — *lecteur*, kind *or* courteous reader

Amiable, *adj.* amicable, friendly, kind, courteous. *À l'—*, amicably; amicable; by private contract *or* treaty, private. — *compositeur*, compounder, arbitrator; peace-maker

Amiablement, *adv.* amicably; friendly; kindly, courteously

Amiante, *s.m.* amianthus, amianth

Amical, e, *adj.* friendly, amicable, kind

Amicalement, *adv.* in a friendly way, friendly, amicably, kindly

Amict, *s.m.* (*priest's garment*) amice, amess

Amide, *s.m.* (*chem.*) amide [amidine

Amidine, Amidone, Amidonne, *s.f.* (*chem.*)

Amidon, *s.m.* starch

Amidonner, *v.a.* to starch [works

Amidonnerie, *s.f.* starch-making; starch-

Amidonni-er, ère, *s.m.f.* starch-maker

Amie, *s.f. adj.f. V.* **Ami**; — *s.f.* (*zool.*) mud-fish

Amiénois, e, *adj. s.* of Amiens; native of

Amigdale, *s.f. V.* **Amygdale** [Amiens

Amilacé, e, *adj.* (*chem.*) amylaceous, starchy

Amincir, *v.a.* to make thin; to thin; to edge off; to reduce; to attenuate; to emaciate; to make (...) look thin
 S'—, *v.r.* to become *or* get thin; to be made thin, &c.; to make (o.'s ...) thin [thinness

Amincissement, *s.m.* making thin; thinning;

Amiral, *s.m.* admiral; guard-ship; flag-ship, admiral; (*shell*) admiral. *Grand-—*, high-admiral. *Vaisseau —*, admiral's ship, flag-ship, ad-

Amiralat, *s.m.* admiralship [miral; guard-ship

Amirale, *s.f.* admiral's wife; (*hist.*) admiral's ship *or* galley

Amirauté, *s.f.* admiralty; admiralship

Amissibilité, *s.f.* (*theol., law*) amissibility

Amissible, *adj.* (*theol., law*) amissible, liable to

Amission, *s.f.* (*theol., law*) amission, loss [be lost

Amitié, *s.f.* friendship; love; affection; amity; liking, taste; favour; pleasure; kindness; sympathy; harmony; —**s,** *pl.* regards, kind regards *or* compliments; kind attentions; caresses, marks of affection. *Prendre en —*, to take a liking to; to take a kind interest in

Amman, *s.m.* amman (*in Switzerland*)

Ammi, *s.m.* (*bot., pharm.*) bishop's-wort, ammi

Ammocète, *s.m.* (*fish*) ammocœtes

Ammodyte, *s.m.* (*zool.*) ammodyte

Ammonia-c, que, *adj.* ammoniac, ammoniacal

Ammoniacal, e, *adj.* ammoniacal

Ammoniacum, *s.m.* ammoniacum, ammoniac,

Ammoniaque, *s.f.* ammonia [gum ammoniac

Ammonite, *s.f.* (*shell*) ammonite, serpent-stone

Ammonium, *s.m.* (*chem.*) ammonium

Amnésie, *s.f.* (*med.*) amnesia, loss of memory

Amnios, *s.m.* (*anat.*) amnion, amnios

Amniotique, *adj.* amniotic

Amnistie, *s.f.* amnesty, pardon

Amnistier, *v.a.* to grant an amnesty to, to pardon; to include in the amnesty

Amodiateur, *s.m.* farmer, lessee

Amodiation, *s.f.* farming, leasing

Amodier, *v.a.* to farm out, to lease out

Amoindrir, *v.a.n.*, **S'—,** *v.r.* to lessen, to decrease, to diminish

Amoindrissement, *s.m.* diminution, de-
Amoise. *V.* **Moise** [crease, lessening; lowering
Amollir, *v.a.* to soften; to mollify; to mellow;
to weaken, to enervate, to effeminate, to unman
S'—, *v.r.* to soften; to be mollified; to flag;
to abate; to grow weak *or* enervated *or* effem-
inate; to become loose
Amollissement, *s.m.* softening; softness;
flagging; abatement; weakening, enervation,
Amome, *s.m.* (*bot.*) amomum [effeminacy
Amonceler, *v.a.* to heap up; to pile up; to
accumulate; to gather, to collect; to drift
S'—, *v.r.* to be heaped up; to be piled up; to
accumulate; to gather, to collect; to drift
Amoncellement, *s.m.* heaping up; piling up;
accumulation; gathering, collection; heap;
drift [*Vent d'—*, (*nav.*) easterly wind
Amont, *s.m. adv.* up stream, upward, up, above.
Amorçage, *s.m.* baiting; alluring; priming;
capping; beginning
Amorce, *s.f.* bait; allurement; attraction; (percussion) cap; priming; friction-tube, tube;
fuze; train of powder; powder; (*build.*) first
works, beginning, indication; (*tech.*) electro-
plating-bath. *Sans brûler une —*, without firing
Amorcement, *s.m. V.* **Amorçage** [a shot
Amorcer, *v.a.* to bait; to allure, to decoy; to
draw; to cap (*small arms*); to prime (*a cannon*);
to feed; to begin at both ends, to begin, to open,
to cut; to steep; to fetch (*a pump*); (*of a siphon*)
to fill (the tube), to exhaust (the air)
S'—, *v.r.* to be baited *or* allured *or* **&c.**
Amorçoir, *s.m.* wimble, auger
Amoroso, *adv.* (*mus.*) amoroso
Amorphe, *adj.* amorphous
Amorphie, *s.f.* amorphy, amorphism
Amortir, *v.a.* to deaden; to abate; to break;
to allay, to weaken; to soften; to reduce; to
subdue; to appease; to flatten; to slacken; to
make tender; to pay off, to liquidate; to redeem;
to sink; (*law*) to amortize; (*nav.*) to put off; —
v.n. (*nav.*) to be neaped *or* sewed, to lie dry
S'—, *v.r.* to be deadened *or* broken *or* allayed
or &c.; to abate; to slacken; to grow weak *or*
faint; to become tender
Amortissable, *adj.* redeemable
Amortissement, *s.m.* deadening; abatement;
subduing; appeasement; decline; decrease;
liquidation; redemption; sinking; (*law*) amortization; (*arch.*) finishing; pediment; (*nav.*)
lying aground. *Caisse* or *fonds d'—*, sinking-
fund
†Amouille, *s.f.* beestings, biestings, bisslings
†Amouiller, *v.n.* to be calving
Amour, *s.m.* love; passion; flame; sake; (*myth.*)
Cupid, Love; **—s,** *m.pl.* amours; loves; **—s,**
f.pl. love; delight. *— -propre*, self-love; selfishness; conceit, vanity; self-respect. *— d'enfant*,
love of a child, charming *or* darling child. *—*
d'homme, delightful man. *Faire l'—*, to court,
to make love (to), to flirt (with)
Amouraché, e, *adj.* in love, enamoured, smitten
Amouracher, *v.a.* to enamour. **S'—,** *v.r.* to
fall in love, to be enamoured *or* smitten
Amourette, *s.f.* (slight) love affair, love, amour,
intrigue, inclination; (*bot.*) quaking-grass;
(*zool.*) *V.* **Anthrène; —s,** *pl.* (*cook.*) *—s de*
veau or *de mouton*, calf's *or* sheep's marrow
Amoureusement, *adv.* lovingly; with love;
fondly; amorously; tenderly, softly, gently,
delicately; gracefully
Amoureu-x, se, *adj.* in love, enamoured;
loving; fond; amorous; of love, love; tender,
soft, delicate; graceful; *— s.m.f.* lover, follower,
sweetheart. *Devenir —*, to fall in love
Amovibilité, *s.f.* removability; uncertainty
Amovible, *adj.* at pleasure, removable; movable; held during pleasure, uncertain
Ampélite, *s.f.* ampelite, cannel coal
Amphibie, *adj.* amphibious; compliant, time-
serving; *— s.m.* amphibian, amphibious animal;
time-server, mean complier, double-dealer

Amphibole, *s.f.* (*min.*) amphibole [page 3, § 1
Amphibolog-ie, -ique, -iquement. *V.*
Amphibraque, *s.m.* (*vers.*) amphibrach
Amphictyonique, *adj.* amphictyonic
Amphictyons, *s.m.pl.* amphictyons
Amphigène, *s.m.* (*min.*) amphigene
Amphigouri, *s.m.* burlesque piece; nonsense,
rigmarole, gibberish [ludicrous
Amphigourique, *adj.* burlesque; nonsensical,
Amphigouriquement, *adv.* nonsensically
Amphimacre, *s.m.* (*vers.*) amphimacer
Amphisbène, *s.m.* (*zool.*) amphisbæna
Amphisciens, *s.m.pl.* (*astr., geog.*) amphiscians
Amphithéâtral, e, *adj.* amphitheatrical
Amphithéâtre, *s.m.* amphitheatre; first gal-
lery; lecture-room; operating *or* dissecting-
room; theatre [sea
Amphitrite, *s.f.* (*myth.*) Amphitrite; (*fig.*) the
Amphitryon, *s.m.* host; entertainer; (*myth.*)
Amphitryon [vase
Amphore, *s.f.* amphora, pitcher, jug, antique
Amphorique, *adj.* (*med.*) amphoric
Ample, *adj.* ample; full; large; wide; copious;
plentiful; hearty; spacious, roomy
Amplement, *adv.* amply; fully; largely;
widely; copiously, plentifully, abundantly;
heartily; spaciously, roomily
Ampleur, *s.f.* fulness; ampleness; largeness;
width; spaciousness, roominess
Ampliati-f, ve, *adj.* ampliating, additional
Ampliation, *s.f.* duplicate; copy; office copy;
true copy; exemplification; enlargement, ex-
tension, expansion. *Pour —*, a true copy
Amplier, *v.a.* (*law*) to defer, to put off; to defer
passing sentence on; (*nat. hist.*) to enlarge, to ex-
Amplificateur, *s.m.* amplifier [tend, to expand
Amplificati-f, ve, *adj.* (*opt.*) magnifying
Amplification, *s.f.* amplification; theme; ex-
emplification; exaggeration; (*opt.*) magnifying
Amplifier, *v.a.* to amplify; to expatiate on, to
enlarge on, to develop; to exaggerate; (*opt.*) to
Amplitude, *s.f.* amplitude [magnify
Ampoule, *s.f.* ampulla; phial; blister; bubble;
(*bot.*) bladder. *La sainte —*, (*for holy oil*) the
ampulla, the holy phial [bombastic, high-flown
Ampoulé, e, *adj.* blistered; bladdery; (*fig.*)
Ampoulette, *s.f.* peg; (*nav.*) watch-glass
Ampullacé, e, *adj.* (*nat. hist.*) ampullaceous
Ampullaire, *s.f.* ampullaria, idol-shell
Amputation, *s.f.* amputation [amputated
Amputé, e, *s.m.f.* one who has had a limb
Amputer, *v.a.* to amputate, to cut off
Amulette, *s.f.* amulet, charm
Amunitionner, *v.a.* (*mil.*) to store, to supply
Amure, *s.f.* (*nav.*) tack (*of a sail*) [(*a sail*)
Amurer, *v.a.* (*nav.*) to haul aboard the tack of
Amusable, *adj.* amusable, capable of being
amused
Amusement, *s.m.* amusement; entertainment;
sport; diversion; pleasure; fun; pastime;
trifling; sham; stop, delay, hindrance
Amuser, *v.a.* to amuse; to entertain; to divert;
to please; to gratify; to suit; to deceive, to
trifle with; to beguile; to solace; to occupy;
to idle away; to talk away; to delay, to detain
S'—, *v.r.* to amuse *or* enjoy oneself; to loiter,
to stop; to trifle o.'s time away; to waste *or*
lose o.'s time; to peddle, to potter; to play; to
sport; to make sport; to laugh (at); to be
amused *or* pleased; to take it into o.'s head, to
bethink oneself, to think (of) [bauble
Amusette, *s.f.* child's play; plaything, toy,
Amuseu-r, se, *s.m.f.* amuser, entertainer;
deceiver [sham, pretence
Amusoire, *s.f.* amusement, toy, trifle, trifling;
Amygdale, *s.f.* (*anat.*) tonsil
Amygdalin, e, *adj.*, **Amygdaline,** *s.f.*
(*pharm., chem.*) amygdaline [quinsy
Amygdalite, *s.f.* (*med.*) amygdalitis, tonsilitis,
Amygdalithe, *s.m.*, **Amygdaloïde,** *s.f.*
(*min.*) amygdaloid
Amylacé, e, *adj. V.* **Amilacé**

Amyle, *s.m.* (*chem.*) amyle, amyl
Amylène, *s.m.* (*chem.*) amylene
Amylique, *adj.* (*chem.*) amylic
An, *s.m.* year; twelvemonth; year old, year of age; —**s**, *pl.* years; years old, years of age; advanced years, old age. *Bon* —, *mal* —, one year with another. *D'un* —, of a year; perennial; yearly. *Jour de l'*—, *premier de l'*—, New-year's day. *Service du bout de l'*—, *bout de l'*—,
Ana, *s.m.* ana [anniversary of the burial service
Anabapt-isme, iste. *V.* page 3, § 1
Anabas, *s.m.* (*fish*) anabas, climbing perch
Anabase, *s.f.* (*Gr. liter.*) Anabasis
Anacarde, *s.m.* cashew-nut; marking-nut
Anacardier, *s.m.* cashew-tree
‡**Anachorète,** *s.m.* anchorite
‡**Anachorétique,** *adj.* anchoritical
‡**Anachronisme,Anacréont-ique,-isme.**
Anaconda, *s.m.* anaconda [*V.* page 3, § 1
Anafin, *s.m.* anafin (*Arabian musical instrument*)
Anagogique, *adj.* mystical
Anagrammat-ique, -iquement, -isme, -iste. *V.* page 3, § 1
Anagrammatiser, *v.a.n.* to anagrammatize
Anagramme, *s.f.* anagram
Anal, e, *adj.* (*anat.*) anal
Analectes, *s.m.pl.* analects
Analème, Analemme, *s.m.* (*astr.*) analemma
Analeptique, *adj.m.f.*, *s.m.* (*med.*) analeptic
Analog-ie, -ique, -iquement, -isme, -iste. *V.* page 3, § 1
Analogue, *adj.* analogous; similar, resembling, like, kindred; — *s.m.* analogue; fellow, like
Analyse, *s.f.* analysis; parsing *En dernière* —, in short, after all, in fine, in conclusion; in the end, ultimately [(*a flower*)
Analyser, *v.a.* to analyze; to parse; to dissect
Analyseur, *s.m.* analyzer
Analy-ste,-tique,-tiquement. *V.* page 3, § 1
Anamnestique, *adj.* (*med.*) anamnestic, com-
Anamorphose, *s.f.* anamorphosis [memorative
Ananas, *s.m.* pine-apple, pine; pine-strawberry. *Fraise* —, pine-strawberry
Anapeste, *s.m.* (*vers.*) anapest
Anapestique, *adj.* (*vers.*) anapestic
Anaphore, *s.f.* (*rhet.*) anaphora [phrodisiac
Anaphrodisiaque, *adj.m.f.*, *s.m.* (*med.*) ana-
Anarch-ie, -ique, -iquement, -iste. *V.*
Anarchiser, *v.a.* to anarchize [page 3, § 1
Anarrhique, *s.m.* wolf-fish, sea-wolf, cat-fish
Anasarque, *s.f.* anasarca, dropsy of the skin
Anastatique, *s.f.* (*bot.*) rose of Jericho, rose of the Virgin
Anastomose, *s.f.* (*anat.*) anastomosis
Anastomoser (S'), *v.r.* (*anat.*) to anastomose
Anastrophe, *s.f.* (*gram.*) anastrophe
Anathématiser, *v.a.* to anathematize
Anathème, *adj.* anathematized; — *s.m.* anathema, curse
Anatife, *s.m.* (*zool.*) barnacle (*mollusc*) [interest
Anatocisme, *s.m.* anatocism, compound
Anatom-ie, -ique, -iquement, -isme, -iste. *V.* page 3, § 1
Anatomiser, *v.a.* to anatomize; to dissect
Anatrip-sologie, -tique. *V.* page 3, § 1
Ancêtre, *s.m.f.* ancestor; ancestress
Anche, *s.f.* reed mouthpiece, reed; pipe; mill-
Anché, e, *adj.* (*her.*) curved [scuttle
Ancher, *v.a.* to reed
Anchifiure, *s.f.* worm-hole (*in a cask*)
‡**Anchilops,** *s.m.* (*med.*) anchilops
Anchois, *s.m.* anchovy. *Beurre* or *pâte d'*—, anchovy-paste
Anchoisé, e, Anchoité, e, *adj.* anchovied
‡**Anchuse,** *s.f.* (*bot.*) anchusa, orchanet, bugloss
‡**Anchusine,** *s.f.* (*chem.*) anchusine
‡**Anchusique,** *adj.* (*chem.*) anchusic
Ancien, ne, *adj.* ancient, old; old-fashioned; past; former, late, last; retired; senior
Ancien, *s.m.* ancient; senior; elder; veteran; old codger, old boy; Old Nick [formerly
Anciennement, *adv.* anciently, of old; once,
Ancienneté, *s.f.* ancientness; oldness; antiquity; age; seniority; priority. *De toute* —, from the earliest times
Ancile, *s.m.* (*Rom. hist.*) ancile
Ancipité, e, *adj.* (*bot.*) ancipital, ancipitous
Ancolie, *s.f.* (*bot.*) columbine
Ancrage, *s.m.* *V.* **Mouillage**
Ancre, *s.f.* (*nav.*) anchor; (*arch.*) brace; (*mech.*) lever; (*measure of* 10½ *gallons*) anker. *Maîtresse* —, — *de miséricorde*, — *de salut*, sheet anchor. — *de touée*, — *à jet*, (*nav.*) kedge
Ancrer, *v.n.a.* to anchor; to establish, to settle, to fix, to secure, to strengthen; (*build.*) to brace
S'—, *v.r.* to anchor *or* &c. oneself, to be anchored *or* &c., to settle oneself, to get a footing
Ancrure, *s.f.* crease
Andabate, *s.m.* andabate, gladiator
†**Andaillot,** *s.m.* (*nav.*) ring, grommet
Andain, *s.m.* (*agr.*) swath
Andalou, se, Andalous, e, *adj.* *s.* Andalusian; Andalusian horse; Andalusian fashion
Andalousite, *s.f.* (*min.*) *V.* **Macle**
Andamento, *adv.* *s.m.* (*mus.*) andamento
Andante, *adv.* *s.m.* (*mus.*) andante
Andantino, *adv.* *s.m.* (*mus.*) andantino
Andelle, *s.m.* Andelle wood, best firewood (*beech from the neighbourhood of the river Andelle, in Normandy*)
†**Andouille,** *s.f.* chitterlings, sausage; (*of tobacco*) twist, roll, pig-tail; (*pers., pop.*) poor stick. *Brouet d'*—, (*fig., pop.*) thin air, smoke
†**Andouiller,** *s.m.* antler
†**Andouillette,** *s.f.* small sausage; small roll
Andrienne, *s.f.* (*Rom. liter.*) Andria
Androgyne, *adj.* androgynous; — *s.m.* androgyne, hermaphrodite
Androïde, *s.m.* android, automaton
Andromède, *s.f.* (*astr.*, *bot.*) andromeda
Androsème, *s.m.* *Millepertuis* —, (*bot.*) tutsan
Âne, *s.m.* ass; jack-ass; donkey; dunce; — *adject.* stupid, ignorant. *À* —, on an ass, on a donkey; on asses, on donkeys; ass, donkey. — *bâté*, (*pers.*) *V.* **Bâté.** *Bonnet* or *oreilles d'*—, fool's cap. *C'est le pont aux* —*s*, it is the asses' bridge, it is the easiest thing in the world, every fool knows it. *Le coup de pied de l'*—, the kick of the ass in the fable
Anéanti, e, *part. adj.* annihilated, &c. (*V.* **Anéantir**); utterly powerless
Anéantir, *v.a.* to annihilate; to reduce to nothing; to destroy; to ruin; to astound; to thunderstrike; to prostrate; to tire out
S'—, *v.r.* to be annihilated *or* destroyed; to cease to be; to come to nothing, to be reduced to nothing; to vanish; to humble oneself
Anéantissement, *s.m.* annihilation; destruction; ruin; utter prostration, helplessness; swoon, fainting fit, unconsciousness; self-humiliation; abjection
Anecdote, *s.f.* anecdote [anecdotist
Anecdoti-er, ère, *s.m.f.* relater of anecdotes,
Anecdotique, anecdotical, of anecdotes
Ânée, *s.f.* ass's load
Anélectrique, *adj.* anelectric
Anémie, *s.f.* (*med.*) anæmia
Anémique, *adj.* (*med.*) anæmic
Anémo-graphie, -graphique, -métrie, -métrique, &c. *V.* page 3, § 1
Anémomètre, *s.m.* anemometer, wind-gauge
Anémone, *s.f.* (*bot.*) anemone, wind-flower
Anémoscope, *s.m.* anemoscope, wind-dial
Ânerie, *s.f.* stupidity; gross ignorance, ignorance; gross blunder; nonsense
Anéroïde, *s.m.* *adj.* (*phys.*) aneroid
Ânesse, *s.f.* she-ass, jenny-ass, ass
Anesthésie, *s.f.* (*med.*) anæsthesia
Anesthésique, *adj.m.f.*, *s.m.* (*med.*) anæsthetic
Aneth, *s.m.* (*bot.*) anethum, aneth, dill, fennel
Anévrismal, e, Anévrismatique, *adj.*
Anévrisme, *s.m.* (*med.*) aneurism [aneurismal
Anfractueu-x, se, *adj.* turning, winding, rugged, cragged, craggy, anfractuous, anfractuose

Anfractuosité, Anfracture, *s.f.* turning, winding, ruggedness, roughness, craggedness, cragginess, craggy part *or* portion, anfractuosity, anfractuousness, anfracture
Angade, *s.f.* little desert [service
Angarie, *s.f.* (*naval law*) compulsory transport-
Angarier, *v.a.* to compel to serve as a transport-ship; to compel, to exact service from; to worry
Ange, *s.m.* angel; angel-shot, bar-shot. — *de mer*, angel-fish. *Lit d'*—, French tent-bedstead, angel-bed. *Être aux* —, to be enraptured *or* delighted [angelot
Angélique, *s.f.* (*bot., conf.*) angelica; (*mus.*)
Angél-ique (*adj.*), **-iquement.** *V.* page 3, § 1
Angelot, *s.m.* angel-fish; (*Normandy cheese, coin, mus. instrument*) angelot
Angélus, *s.m.* (*Cath. rel.*) angelus
Angevin, e, *adj. s.* of Anjou (*formerly a province of France*) *or* of Angers (*its capital*); native of Anjou *or* of Angers, Angevin
Angine, *s.f.* (*med.*) angina, sore-throat. — *couenneuse*, diphtheria [with angina
Angineu-x, se, *adj.* (*med.*) of angina; attended
Angio-graphie, -logie, &c. *V.* page 3, § 1
Anglais, e, *adj. s.* English; British; Englishman; English boy; (*pop.*) creditor, dun; English horse; (the) English language, English; English woman *or* lady *or* girl; English fashion; ringlet; English writing; furniture binding; anglaise (*dance, tune*). *En bon* —, in plain English, Anglice; like a true Briton
Anglaiser, *v.a.* to nick (*a horse's tail*)
Angle, *s.m.* angle; corner; turning
Angles, *s.m.pl.* (*people*) Angles, Angli
Anglet, *s.m.* (*arch.*) channel
Angleu-x, se, *adj.* full of angles *or* corners
Anglican, e, *adj.* Anglican, English, of England; — *s.m.f.* churchman, Anglican
Anglicanisme, *s.m.* anglicanism
Anglicisation, *s.f.* anglicization
Angliciser, *v.a.* to anglicize [come English
S'—, *v.r.* to become *or* be anglicized, to be-
Anglicisme, *s.m.* anglicism
Anglo-, (*in compounds*) anglo-...
Anglois, *s.m.* plum-tart
Anglomane, *adj. s.m.f.* anglomaniac
Anglomanie, *s.f.* anglomania [maniac
Anglomaniser, *v.a.* to make (*one*) an anglo-
S'—, *v.r.* to become an anglomaniac
Anglo-normand, e, *adj. s.* Anglo-Norman; Anglo-Norman horse *or* mare
Anglophobe, *adj. s.m.f.* anglophobic; person affected with anglophobia, anglophobist, anglo-
Anglophobie, *s.f.* anglophobia [phobiac
Anglophobique, *adj.* anglophobic
Anglo-saxon, ne, *adj. s.* Anglo-Saxon
Angoisse, *s.f.* anguish, pang; suffering, pain; distraction, distress, affliction, trouble; anxiety;
Angoisser, *v.a.* to anguish, to distress [despair
Angola, *s.m.* angola
Angon, *s.m.* javelin; shell-fish hook
Angora, *adj.m.f., s.m.* Angora; Angora cat; Angora goat; Angora rabbit
Angousse, *s.f.* (*bot.*) dodder
Anguichure, *s.f.* (*hunt.*) horn-belt
†**Anguillade,** *s.f.* lash, lashing, cut
†**Anguille,** *s.f.* eel; (*fig.*) strip, lash; (*play*) fly the garter; (*nav.*) bilge-ways. — *de haie*, (common) snake. — *sous roche*, mystery, snake in
†**Anguiller,** *s.m.* (*nav.*) limber-hole [the grass
†**Anguillère,** *s.f.* eel-pond; eel-basket, eel-pot, eel-trap, eel-spear
†**Anguilliforme,** *adj.* anguilliform, eel-shaped
Angulaire, *adj.* angular
Angulairement, *adv.* angularly
Angulé, e, *adj.* angulated, angular [harsh
Anguleu-x, se, *adj.* angulous, angular; sharp;
Angusticlave, *s.m.* (*antiq.*) angusticlave
Angustie, *s.f.* (*med.*) stricture, contraction, narrowness [tura bark
Angusture, *s.f.* (*pharm.*) Angostura *or* Angus-

Anharmonique, *adj.* (*math.*) anharmonic
Anhélation, *s.f.* (*med.*) anhelation
Anhémie, *s.f.* *V.* **Anémie**
Anhydre, *adj.* (*chem.*) anhydrous
Anhydride, *s.m.* (*chem.*) anhydride
Anhydrite, *s.f.* (*min.*) anhydrite
Anicroche, *s.f.* difficulty, impediment, hitch
Ân-ier, ière, *s.m.f.* ass-driver
Anil, *s.m.* (*bot.*) anil
Aniline, *s.f.* (*chem.*) aniline
†**Anille,** *s.f.* crutch; ring; (*of a mill*) moline, rind, rynd; (*bot.*) tendril; (*her.*) millrind
†**Anillée,** *adj.f.* *Croix* —, (*her.*) cross moline
Animadversion, *s.f.* animadversion
Animal, e, *adj.* animal; sensual, gross; stupid
Animal, *s.m.* animal; beast, brute; creature; dolt, fool, blockhead; fellow, fish
Animalcule, *s.m.* animalcule
Animalier, *s.m.* *V.* **Animaliste**
Animalisation, *s.f.* animalization
Animaliser, *v.a.* to animalize; to animate
S'—, *v.r.* to become animalized [mals, animalist
Animaliste, *s.m.f.* painter *or* sculptor of ani-
Animalité, *s.f.* animality [animater
Anima-teur, trice, *adj.* animating; — *s.m.f.*
Animation, *s.f.* animation; movement, bustle, life; excitement, irritation, hastiness, passion
Animé, e, *part. adj.* animated, &c. (*V.* **Animer**); living; lively; gay; spirited, brisk; stirring, active, bustling, busy; bright; angry, incensed; eager, greedy; (*her.*) in action; (*her.*)
Animé, *s.f.* anime (*resin*) [anime
Animelles, *s.f.pl.* fry, lamb's fry
Animer, *v.a.* to animate; to give life to; to quicken; to brighten; to light up; to inflame; to enliven; to inspirit; to incite, to encourage; to excite; to incense, to exasperate; to inspire; to actuate; to fill; to impel
S'—, *v.r.* to become (*or* get *or* be) animated *or* excited *or* &c.; to grow *or* get warm, to warm; to bestir oneself; to brighten; to glow; to take fire, to be angry; to cheer up; to take courage; to encourage each other
Animosité, *s.f.* animosity; spite, rancour; excitement, hastiness, passion, violence
Anis, *s.m.* anise, aniseed; aniseed sugar-plum. *Graine d'*—, aniseed
Aniser, *v.a.* to flavour with aniseed
Anisette, *s.f.* anisette
Anisique, *adj.* (*chem.*) anisic
Aniterge, *s.m.* (*slang*) bum-fodder
Anker, *s.m.* (*measure*) anker
Ankylose, *s.f.* (*med.*) anchylosis, ankylosis
Ankyloser, *v.a.* (*med.*) to anchylose
S'—, *v.r.* to become anchylosed
Ankylotique, *adj.* (*med.*) anchylotic
Annal, e, *adj.* (*law*) for one year absolutely
Annales, *s.f.pl.* annals
Annaliste, *s.m.f.* annalist
Annamite, *adj. s.* Annamite
Annate, *s.f.* annates, annats, first-fruits
Anneau, *s.m.* ring; circlet; link; coil; curl, ringlet. — *brisé*, split ring
Année, *s.f.* year; twelvemonth; harvest, crop; income, rent; —**s**, *pl.* years; advanced age, old age. — *commune* or *moyenne*, one year with another. *A l'*—, by the year. *Les belles* —*s*, the prime of life. *Souhaiter la bonne* —, to wish a happy new year. *Souhait* or *compliment de bonne* —, compliments of the season
Annelé, e, *adj.* annulated; in curls, in ringlets
Anneler, *v.a.* to curl in ringlets; to ring
Annelet, *s.m.* small ring, ringlet; (*arch., her.*)
Anneleur, *s.m.* ringer [annulet
Annélides, *s.m.pl.* (*zool.*) annelides
Annelure, *s.f.* curling
Annexation, *s.f.* annexation
Annexe, *s.f.* annex; schedule, rider; chapel of ease; — *adj.* annexed
Annexer, *v.a.* to annex. *S'*—, to be annexed
Annexion, *s.f.* annexation
Annexion-isme, -iste. *V.* page 3, § 1

Annihilable, *adj.* annihilable

Annihilation, *s.f.* annihilation [hilated

Annihiler, *v.a.* to annihilate. *S'—*, to be anni-

†**Annille,** *s.f.* *V.* **Anille**

Anniversaire, *adj.m.f.*, *s.m.* anniversary

Annomination, *s.f.* annomination

Annonce, *s.f.* announcement; notice; publication; advertisement; advertising; bans; indication, sign, mark

Annoncement, *s.m.* announcement

Annoncer, *v.a.* to announce; to make known; to publish; to proclaim; to give out; to inform, to advise, to tell; to mention, to speak of; to premise; to indicate; to give indications of; to bespeak; to show; to usher in; to promise; to give hopes of; to foretell; to forebode; to advertise; to preach. *Se faire —*, to send in o.'s name

S'—, *v.r.* to present oneself; to announce its coming; to manifest itself, to make itself known; to appear; to begin; to be preceded (by); to announce to each other, to tell each other; to be announced. *S'— bien*, to promise fair, to be promising. *S'— mal*, to be unpromising

Annonceu-r, se, *s.m.f.* announcer

Annonciade, *s.f.* (*rel. order*) annunciade

Annoncia-teur, trice, *s.m.f.* announcer

Annonciation, *s.f.* announcement; Annunciation; Lady-day

Annota-teur, trice, *s.m.f.* annotator

Annotation, *s.f.* annotation

Annoter, *v.a.* to annotate

Annuaire, *s.m.* annual, year-book, calendar, almanac, directory, list. *— du commerce*, Post-Office directory [annual

Annuel, le, *adj.* annual, yearly. *Plante —le*,

Annuel, *s.m.* tax for a year; year's income; solemn feast; daily *or* weekly funeral service (*or* mass) for the first year after death

Annuellement, *adv.* annually, yearly

Annuité, *s.f.* annuity

Annulable, *adj.* defeasible; (*law*) reversible

Annulaire, *adj.* annular. *Doigt —*, ring-finger

Annulation, *s.f.*, **Annulement,** *s.m.* annulment; cancelling; repeal; abolition

Annuler, *v.a.* to annul; to nullify; to stultify; to set aside; to rescind; to repeal; to abolish; to cancel; to quash; to make void, to void; to frustrate; to render powerless

S'—, *v.r.* to be annulled, &c.

Anobli, *s.m.* newly-created nobleman

Anoblir, *v.a.* to ennoble, to confer nobility on, to raise to the peerage

S'—, *v.r.* to assume *or* purchase a title; (*fig.*) to be ennobled

Anoblissement, *s.m.* ennoblement; nobility

Anodin, e, *adj.* assuaging, soothing, anodyne; mild, gentle; unmeaning; tame; insipid; — *s.m.* anodyne

Anodonte, *s.f.* anodon, freshwater-mussel

Anomal, e, *adj.* anomalous [*V.* page 3, § 1

Anomal-ie, -isme, -istique, -istiquement

Anomie, *s.f.* anomia, beaked cockle, bowl-shell

Ânon, *s.m.* ass's foal, young ass

Anone, *s.f.* (*bot.*) anona

Ânonnement, *s.m.* faltering, stammering, stuttering, hemming and hawing; foaling

Ânonner, *v.n.a.* to falter, to stammer, to stutter, to hem and haw; to foal

Anonymat, *s.m.* anonymousness

Anonyme, *adj.* anonymous; joint-stock

Anonyme, *s.m.* anonymous person; anonymousness, anonymous. *Sous l'—*, anonymously. *Garder l'—*, not to give o.'s name, to remain anonymous

Anonymement, *adv.* anonymously

Anonymie, *s.f.* anonymousness

Anoplothère, Anoplothérion, Anoplothérium, *s.m.* (*zool.*) anoplotherium

Anordie, *s.f.* (*nav.*) north wind

Anordir, *v.n.* (*nav.*) to blow north

Anorexie, *s.f.* (*med.*) anorexy

Anormal, e, *adj.* abnormal, irregular

Anormalement, *adv.* abnormally, irregularly

Anosmie, Anosphrésie, *s.f.* (*med.*) anosmia

Anotto, *s.m.* *V.* **Roucou**

Anse, *s.f.* handle; creek, cove, bight, bay; (*pop.*) arm; (*pop.*) ear. *— de panier*, (*arch.*) surbased arch, flat arch-vault. *— du panier*, (*fig.*) servants' profits, market-penny. *Panier à deux —s*, (*fig.*) a thorn between two roses (*man walking with a female on each arm*). *Faire le panier à deux —s*, to walk with a female on each arm. *Faire le pot à deux —s*, to put o.'s arms akimbo

Ansé, e, *adj.* ansated; (*her.*) anserated

Anséatique (*bad spelling*). *V.* **Hanséatique**

Ansérine, *s.f.* (*bot.*) goose-foot

Anspect, *s.m.* (*nav.*) handspike

Antacide, *adj.m.f.*, *s.m.* (*med.*) antacid

Antagonisme, *s.m.* antagonism [gonistic

Antagoniste, *s.m.f.* antagonist; — *adj.* anta-

Antan, *s.m.* last year; olden times. *Les neiges d'—*, (*fig.*) the things of the past, the things of

Antanaclase, *s.f.* (*rhet.*) antanaclasis [old

Antarctique, *adj.* antarctic

Ante, *s.f.* (*arch.*) anta, pilaster [viously

Antécédemment, *adv.* antecedently, pre-

Antécédence, *s.f.* antecedence [previous

Antécédent, e, *adj.* antecedent, preceding,

Antécédent, *s.m.* antecedent; precedent

‡**Antéchrist,** *s.m.* Antichrist

Antédiluvien, ne, *adj.* *s.* antediluvian

Antéfixe, *s.f.* (*anc. arch.*) antefix

Antémétique, *adj.* *m.f.*, *s.m.* (*med.*) antemetic

Antenais, e, *s.m.f.* *V.* **Antenois** [lateen-yard

Antenne, *s.f.* (*zool.*) horn, feeler, antenna; (*nav.*)

Antenois, e, *s.m.f.* teg, yearling lamb, theave;

Anténuptial, e, *adj.* antenuptial [yearling

Antépénultième, *adj.m.f.*, *s.f.* antepenultimate; antepenultima, antepenult [freckles

Antéphélique, *adj.* antephelic, against

Antérieur, e, *adj.* anterior, prior, former, previous, past; fore, front, foremost

Antérieurement, *adv.* previously, before

Antériorité, *s.f.* anteriority, priority, precedence [mintic

Anthelmintique, *adj.m.f.*, *s.m.* (*med.*) anthel-

Anthère, *s.f.* (*bot.*) anther, tip [page 3, § 1

Antho-graphie, -logie, -logique. *V.*

Anthracite, *s.m.* anthracite, stone-coal

Anthrax, *s.m.* (*med.*) anthrax [(*mimic-beetle*)

Anthrène, *s.m.* (*zool.*) anthrenus musæorus

Anthropo-graphie, -graphique, -logie, -logique, -logiste, &c. *V.* page 3, § 1

Anthropomorphe, *adj.* anthropomorphous

Anthropomorphisme. *V.* page 3, § 1

Anthropomorphite, *s.m.f.* anthropomorphite

Anthropophage, *adj.* anthropophagian, anthropophagous, cannibal; — *s.m.f.* anthropophagist, anthropophagus, cannibal, man-eater

Anthropophagie, *s.f.* anthropophagy, cannibalism, man-eating [beard

Anthyllide, *s.m.* (*bot.*) kidney-vetch, Jupiter's

Anti, (*in compounds:* against) anti; (before, fore, front) ante

Antiacide. *V.* **Antacide**

Antiapoplectique, *adj.m.f.*, *s.m.* (*med.*) anti-

Antiar, *s.m.* (*bot.*) antiaris, antjar [apoplectic

Antiarine, *s.f.* (*chem.*) antiarine

Antiaristocrate, *s.m.f.* antiaristocrat

Antibiblique, *adj.* unscriptural [antibilious

Antibilieu-x, se, *adj.*, **Antibilieux,** *s.m.*

Anticatholique, *adj.* anticatholic

Antichambre, *s.f.* anteroom, antechamber. *Faire —*, to dance attendance. *Propos d'—*, gossip [choleraic

‡**Anticholérique,** *adj.m.f.*, *s.m.* (*med.*) anti-

‡**Antichrèse,** *s.f.* (*law*) antichresis (*in Roman law*), living pledge, pledge [christian

‡**Antichrétien, ne,** *adj.* antichristian; un-

‡**Antichristianisme,** *s.m.* antichristianity; antichristianism [encroachment

Anticipation, *s.f.* anticipation; advance; loan;

Anticipé, e, *part. adj.* anticipated; foregone; in advance, made in advance; premature

Anticiper, *v.a.n.* to anticipate; to forestall; to antedate; to encroach
Anticœur, *s.m.* *V.* **Avant-cœur**
Anticonstitutionnel, le, *adj.* anteconstitutional
Anticonstitutionnellement, *adv.* anticonstitutionally
Anticorrosi-f, ve, *adj.*, **Anticorrosif,** *s.m.* anticorrosive
Antidartreu-x, se, *adj.*, **Antidartreux,** *s.m.* antiherpetic
Antidate, *s.f.* antedate
Antidater, *v.a.* to antedate
Antidotaire, *s.m.* (*pharm.*) antidotarium
Antidote, *s.m.* antidote
Antidramatique, *adj.* antidramatic
Antiémétique, *adj.m.f.*, *s.m.* (*med.*) antiemetic
Antienne, *s.f.* anthem; (*fam.*) song. *V.* **Chanter**
Antiépiscopal, e, *adj.* antiepiscopal
Antiesclavagiste, *s.m.f.* abolitionist; — *adj.* antislavery
Antiévangélique, *adj.* antievangelical
Antifébrile, *adj.m.f.*, *s.m.* antifebrile
Antigoutteu-x, se, *adj.*, **Antigoutteux,** *s.m.* (*med.*) antarthritic
Antihystérique, *adj.m.f.*, *s.m.* antihysteric
Antilaiteu-x, se, *adj.* lactifuge
Antilogie, *s.f.* antilogy
Antilope, *s.f.* antelope
Antimacassar, *s.m.* antimacassar
Antiméphitique, *adj.m.f.*, *s.m.* antimephitic
Antimoine, *s.m.* antimony
Antimonarch-ique, -iste. *V.* page 3, § 1
Antimonial, e, *adj.*, **Antimonial,** *s.m.*, **Antimonié, e,** *adj.* antimonial
Antinational, e, *adj.* antinational
Antinomie, *s.f.* antinomy
Antipape, *s.m.* antipope
Antipapisme, *s.m.* antipapism, antipopery
Antipapiste, *s.m.f.* *adj.* antipapist; antipapistic
Antipather, *v.a.* (*pop.*) to dislike, to hate
Antipathie, *s.f.* antipathy
Antipathique, *adj.* antipathetic
Antipatriotique, *adj.* antipatriotic
Antipéristaltique, *adj.* antiperistaltic
Antipéristase, *s.f.* antiperistasis
Antipestilentiel, le, *adj.* antipestilential
Antiphilosophique, *adj.* antiphilosophical
Antiphlogistique, *adj.m.f.*, *s.m.* (*med.*) antiphlogistic
Antiphonaire, Antiphonier, *s.m.* antiphonary
Antiphone, *s.m.* antiphon, antiphone
Antiphon-ie, -ique, -iquement. *V.* page 3, § 1
Antiphrase, *s.f.* antiphrasis, irony
Antipied, *s.m.* (*zool.*) forefoot
Antipodal, e, *adj.* antipodal
Antipode, *s.m.* antipode; reverse
Antipoétique, *adj.* antipoetical; unpoetical
Antipopulaire, *adj.* antipopular
Antipsorique, *adj.m.f.*, *s.m.* (*med.*) antipsoric
Antiputride, *adj.* antiputrefactive, antiseptic
†**Antiquaille,** *s.f.* old curiosity, old stuff, old rubbish, old-fashioned nicknack, antiquated old thing, antiquity
Antiquaire, *s.m.f.* antiquary; curiosity dealer, antique furniture dealer, dealer in antiquities
Antique, *adj.* antique, ancient; old; antiquated, old-fashioned; former. *A l'—*, in the old style
Antique, *s.m.* (*no plural in French: a collective noun*) antiquities, ancient works of art, antique models, antiques, antique; — *s.f.* (*plural* —**s**) antique, antiquity
Antiquité, *s.f.* antiquity; ancientness; ancients. *De toute* —, from the earliest times
Antiréformiste, *s.m.f.* antireformist; — *adj.* anti-reform
Antireligieu-x, se, *adj.* antireligious; irreligious
Antirépublicain, e, *adj.* *s.* antirepublican
Antirévolutionnaire, *adj.* antirevolutionary; — *s.m.f.* antirevolutionist
Antirhumatismal, e, *adj.* (*med.*) antirheumatic
Antisciens, *s.m.pl.* (*geog.*) antiscians
Antiscorbutique, *adj.m.f.*, *s.m.* (*med.*) antiscorbutic
Antiscrofuleu-x, se, *adj.*, **Antiscrofuleux,** *s.m.* (*med.*) antiscrofulous
Antiseptique, *adj.m.f.*, *s.m.* antiseptic
Antisocial, e, *adj.* antisocial
Antispasmodique, *adj.m.f.*, *s.m.* antispasmodic
Antistrophe, *s.f.* antistrophe
Antisyphilitique, *adj.m.f.*, *s.m.* antisyphilitic
Antithèse, *s.f.* antithesis
Antithétique, *adj.* antithetic
Antitrinitaire, *s.m.f.* *adj.* antitrinitarian
Antitype, *s.m.* antitype
Antiunioniste, *s.m.f.* *adj.* antiunionist
Antivénérien, ne, *adj.* antivenereal, antisyphilitic; — *s.m.* antisyphilitic
Antofle, *s.m.* clove, mother clove
Antoiser, *v.a.* (*hort.*) to heap up (*dung*)
Antonomase, *s.f.* (*rhet.*) antonomasia
Antre, *s.m.* cave; cavern; grotto; den; lair; retreat
Anuer, *v.a.* to aim at, to take aim at
Anuité, e, *adj.* benighted, belated
Anuiter (S'), *v.r.* to be benighted, to stay till dark, to stay too late (on the road)
Anurie, *s.f.* (*med.*) anuria, anuresis
Anus, *s.m.* (*anat.*) anus
Anversois, e, *adj.* *s.* of Antwerp; Antwerper
Anvoie, *s.m.* slow-worm, blind-worm
Anxiété, *s.f.* anxiety; uneasiness, restlessness
Anxieusement, *adv.* anxiously; restlessly
Anxieu-x, se, *adj.* anxious; uneasy, restless
Aoriste, *s.m.* (*gram.*) aorist
Aorte, *s.f.* (*anat.*) aorta
Aortique, *adj.* (*anat.*) aortic, aortal
Août, *s.m.* August, the month of August; harvest-time; harvest
Aoûtement, *s.m.* ripening, maturation
Aoûter, *v.a.n.*, **S'**—, *v.r.* to ripen
Aoûteron, *s.m.* reaper, harvestman
Apache, *s.m.f.* *adj.* Apache
Apaisable, *adj.* appeasable
Apaisement, *s.m.* appeasement, pacification; reconciliation
Apaiser, *v.a.* to appease; to pacify; to calm, to still; to quiet; to lull; to assuage; to allay; to soothe; to alleviate; to quell; to subdue; to make up; to silence, to hush; to quench

S'—, *v.r.* to become (*or* be) appeased, &c.; to abate; to become (*or* get) calm *or* quiet; to fall; to cease
Apaiseur, *s.m.* appeaser; reconciler
Apalachine, *s.f.* (*bot.*) emetic holly
Apalanche, *s.f.* (*bot.*) winter-berry
Apanage, *s.m.* appanage; appendage, attribute, concomitant, lot; consequence; exclusive right
Apanager, *v.a.* to portion, to endow with an appanage
Apanagiste, *s.m.f.* possessor of an appanage, appanagist; — *adj.* having an appanage
Aparté, *s.m.* words spoken aside; — *adv.* *En* —, aside
Apathie, *s.f.* apathy, indolence, listlessness
Apathique, *adj.* apathetic, indolent, listless
Apatite, *s.f.* (*min.*) apatite
Apepsie, *s.f.* (*med.*) apepsy
Aperception, *s.f.* (*philos.*) apperception
Apercevable, *adj.* perceivable, perceptible
Apercevant, e, *adj.* (*of horses*) goggle-eyed
Apercevoir, *v.a.* to perceive, to see; to descry; to observe; to notice; to discern; to understand

S'—, *v.r.* to perceive, to see; to become *or* be aware (of); to find out; to discover; to observe; to notice; to understand; to perceive *or* see oneself; to perceive *or* see each other; to be seen, to show, to be visible
Aperçu, e, (*part. of* **Apercevoir**) perceived, &c.
Aperçu, *s.m.* glance; view; glimpse; cursory view; survey; slight notion; general idea, idea; hint; observation; sketch; outline; summary, brief account; compendium; rough estimate. *En* —, summarily. *Par* —, at a rough guess
Apériti-f, ve, *adj.* (*med.*) aperient; appetizing, relishing
Apéritif, *s.m.* (*med.*) aperient; appetizer
Apétale, *adj.* (*bot.*) apetalous
Apetisser, *v.a.n.* *V.* **Rapetisser**
A peu près. *V.* **Près** (*A peu*)
Aphanite, *s.f.* (*min.*) aphanite

Aphélie, *s.m.* (*astr.*) aphelion [apheresis
Aphérèse, *s.f.* (*gram., med., surg.*) aphæresis,
Aphlogistique, *adj.* aphlogistic, flameless
Aphone, *adj.* aphonous, without voice [voice
Aphonie, *s.f.* (*med.*) aphonia, aphony, loss of
Aphor-isme, -istique, &c. *V.* p. 8, § 1
Aphrodisiaque, *adj.m.f., s.m.* (*med.*) aphrodisiac
Aphrodite, *s.f.* aphrodite, sea-mouse
Aphthe, *s.m.* slight ulcer (*in the mouth*), aphtha; **—s,** *pl.* aphthæ; thrush
Aphtheu-x, se, *adj.* (*med.*) aphthous. *Fièvre* or *maladie —se,* (*vet.*) foot and mouth disease
Api, *s.m.* (*Pomme d'* —), (*bot.*) lady-apple; (*fig.*) ruddy cheek
Apiaire, *adj.* apiarian; **—s,** *s.m.pl.* bee tribe
Apicole, *adj.* apicultural [bee-keeper
Apiculteur, *s.m.* apiarist, apiarian, bee-master,
Apiculture, *s.f.* apiculture
Apiéceu-r, se, *s.m.f.* piece-worker, piece-hand
Apion, *s.m.* (*zool.*) clover-weevil
Apiqué, e, *adj.* (*nav.*) apeak [(*nav.*) to be apeak
Apiquer, *v.a.* (*nav.*) to peak, to top; — *v.n.*
Apitoiement, *s.m.* compassion, pity
Apitoyer, *v.a.* to move to pity, to affect, to move; to soften. *S'*—, to be moved to pity, to be affected *or* &c.; to pity, to compassionate
Apivore, *adj.* (*zool.*) apivorous [removed
Aplani, e, *part. adj.* level; flat; smooth; even;
Aplanir, *v.a* to level; to smooth; to make level *or* even; to remove. *S'*—, to become level *or* smooth *or* even *or* easy; to be made level *or* &c.; to be removed, to disappear
Aplanissement, *s.m.* levelling; smoothing; making even; smoothness; evenness; removal
Aplati, e, *part.adj.* flattened, &c. (*V.* **Aplatir**); flat
Aplatir, *v.a.* to flatten, to flat; to make *or* beat flat; to beat *or* press down; to sink; to depress; to lower, to humble; to silence, to shut up, to put *or* set down, to floor, to beat hollow; to squelch; to hush

S'—, *v.r.* to become *or* get flat, to flatten; to be flattened; to sink; to crouch; to humble oneself, to cringe

Aplatissage, *s.m.* flattening
Aplatissement, *s.m.* flattening; flatness; depression; sinking; lowering; humbling, humiliation; crouching; cringing; silencing; beating to nothing [(*instr.*), *s.m.* flatter
Aplatisseur (*pers., instr.*), **Aplatissoir**
Aplatissoire, *s f.* flatting-rollers [trawl
Aplet, *s.m.* herring-net, drift-net; long-line,
Aplomb, *s.m.* perpendicularity; uprightness; poise; equilibrium; steadiness, firmness; assurance, self-possession, coolness. *D'* —, perpendicular; perpendicularly; upright; uprightly; in equilibrium; steady, firm; steadily, firmly; (*of blows*) vigorous, smart; vigorously, smartly
Aplysie, *s.f.* (*zool.*) aplysia, sea-hare
Apnée, *s.f.* (*med.*) apnœa, suspension of breathing
Apocalypse, *s.f.* apocalypse, revelation; obscurity. *Style d'*—, obscure style. *Le cheval de l'*—, a skinny jade
Apocalyptique, *adj.* apocalyptic; obscure
Apoco, *s.m.* mere nobody, nobody, silly fellow
Apocope, *s.f.* (*gram., surg.*) apocope
Apocryphe, *adj.* apocryphal, hidden, doubtful, suspicious; fictitious, false, spurious; **—s,** *s.m.pl.* apocrypha, apocryphal writings
Apocyn, *s.m.* (*bot.*) apocynum. — *gobe-mouches,* dogbane [less; (*fish*) destitute of ventral fins
Apode, *s.m.* (*zool.*) apode; — *adj.* apodal, foot-
Apogée, *s.m.* apogee; height, acme
Apogon, *s m.* (*fish*) apogon [copying-instrument
Apographe, *s.m.* apograph, transcript, copy;
Apollinaire, *adj.* Apollinarian [butterfly
Apollon, *s.m.* (*zool.*) Apollo, crimson-ringed
Apologétique, *adj.* apologetic, apologetical; exculpatory; — *s.f.* (*theol.*) apologetics; — *s.m.* (*Tertullian's*) Apologeticus
Apologie, *s.f.* apology; justification, vindica-
Apologique, *adj.* apologetic [tion, defence
Apologiste, *s.m.* apologist

Apologue, *s.m.* apologue, fable. *Comprendre* or *entendre l'*—, (*fam.*) to know all about it; to understand
Aponévrose, *s.f.* (*anat.*) aponeurosis
Aponévrotique, *adj.* (*anat.*) aponeurotic
Apophthegme, *s.m.* apophthegm, apothegm
Apophyge, *s.f.* (*arch.*) apophyge, scape, spring
Apophyse, *s.f.* (*anat., bot.*) process, apophysis
Apoplectique, *adj. s.m.f.* apoplectic
Apoplexie, *s.f.* apoplexy. *D'*—, of apoplexy;
Apostasie, *s.f.* apostasy [apoplectic
Apostasier, *v.n.* to apostatize; — *v.a.* to re-
Apostat, *adj.m., s.m.* apostate [nounce
Apostème, *s.m.* aposteme, abscess
Apostement, *s.m.* posting, placing, putting
Aposter, *v.a.* to set to watch; to place in readiness; to place in ambush, to secrete; to post, to station, to place, to put, to set
†**Apostille,** *s.f.* postscript, marginal note, footnote; recommendation [commendation to
†**Apostiller,** *v.a.* to add a postscript *or* a re-
Apostolat, *s.m.* apostleship, apostolate
Apostolicité, *s.f.* apostolicity, apostolicalness
Apostolique, *adj.* apostolic, apostolical; papal, of the Pope, from Rome
Apostoliquement, *adv.* apostolically
Apostrophe, *s.f.* apostrophe; address; reproach; insult, attack; blow; mark, weal
Apostropher, *v.a.* to apostrophize; to address; to reproach; to fly at
Apostume, Apostumer. *V.* **Abcès, Ab-**
Apothéose, *s.f.* apotheosis [**céder**
Apothéoser, *v.a.* to apotheosize
Apothicaire, *s.m.* apothecary; dispenser. *Compte* (or *mémoire*) *d'*— exorbitant bill
Apothicairerie, *s.f. V.* **Pharmacie**
Apothicairesse, *s.f.* (*in nunneries*) dispenser
Apôtre, *s.m.* apostle; champion, advocate, preacher; (*nav.*) knight-head, bollard-timber. *Bon* —, (*ironically*) good man, good creature,
Apozème, *s.m.* (*med.*) apozem, decoction [saint
Apparaître, *v.n.* to appear; to start up; to make a short appearance, to show oneself
Apparat, *s.m.* pomp; state; show; display; pageantry; ostentation; great style; vocabulary, index. *D'*—, state; for show; ostentatious; solemn; high; great, grand; studied, set
Apparaux, *s.m.pl.* (*nav.*) apparel, furniture
†**Appareil,** *s.m.* preparation, preparative; pomp, state, show, display, pageant; sight; train; fuss; splendour; solemnity; attire, equipage, apparel; apparatus; furniture; appliance, appliances; implements; fittings; tackle; gear; machinery; organs; structure; (*surg , arch.*) dressing; (*of stones*) size; (*nav.*) purchase
†**Appareillade,** *s.f.* pairing (*of partridges*)
†**Appareillage,** *s.m.* (*nav.*) weighing, getting under weigh (*or* way); (*agr.*) pairing; matching; yoking [yoking; couple; set, team
†**Appareillement,** *s.m.* pairing; matching;
†**Appareiller,** *v.a.* to pair; to couple; to match; to yoke; to dress; to trim; to fit; to prepare; to join; — *v.n.* (*nav.*) to weigh, to get under weigh (*or* way), get under sail *or* under steam

S'—, *v.r.* to connect *or* join oneself; to associate; to bear some affinity; to couple; to match; to be matched *or* yoked; to pair

†**Appareilleur,** *s.m.* dresser; trimmer; fitter;
†**Appareilleuse,** *s.f.* procuress [gas-fitter
Apparemment, *adv.* apparently
Apparence, *s.f.* appearance; likelihood, probability; show; look; semblance; shadow; sign; trace; phenomenon. *En* —, apparently, seemingly, in appearance, in show. *Il y a* —, it seems (that); so it seems
Apparent, e, *adj.* apparent; seeming; plausible; likely; plain, evident, obvious; prominent; conspicuous; remarkable; considerable; important; eminent
Apparenté, e, *adj.* related, allied, connected; descended [ally, to marry
Apparenter, *v.a.* to connect (*by marriage*), to

S'—, *v.r.* to become related (to); to ally oneself; to marry
Apparesser, *v.a.* *V.* **Affainéantir**
Appariement, *s.m.* pairing; matching
Apparier, *v.a.*, **S'—,** *v.r.* to pair; to match
Apparieu-r, se, *s.m.f.* match-maker
Appariteur, *s.m.* apparitor; beadle; messenger; officer
Apparition, *s.f.* apparition; vision; appearance; short appearance
Apparoir, *v.n.* to appear, to be evident
Appartement, *s.m.* apartments, suite of rooms, flat; apartment, room; (*formerly, at court*) levee. *Pièce d'un* —, room, apartment
Appartenance, *s.f.* appurtenance
Appartenir, *v.n.* to belong; to appertain; to pertain; to concern; to relate; to be related (to); to be connected (with); to become, to behove; to be the business (of); to be (for); to be given (to); to be incident. *Ainsi qu'il appartiendra,* (*law*) as one may see cause. *A tous ceux qu'il appartiendra,* to all whom it may concern
S'—, *v.r.* to be o.'s own master
Appas, *s.m.pl.* attractions, charms; allurements
Appât, *s.m.* bait; allurement, enticement; inducement; temptation; hope
Appâter, *v.a.* to bait; to allure, to entice; to feed; to cram (*fowls*)
Appatronnement, *s.m.* (*agr.*) pairing; matching; yoking
Appatronner, *v.a.* (*agr.*) to pair; to match; to yoke
Appaumé, e, *adj.* (*her.*) appaume
Appauvrir, *v.a.* to impoverish, to make *or* render poor; to beggar; to weaken
S'—, *v.r.* to impoverish oneself; to become *or* be impoverished; to become (*or* grow *or* get) poor; to decay; to become weakened
Appauvrissement, *s.m.* impoverishment; beggary; diminution, waste; decay; weakening
Appeau, *s.m.* bird-call; decoy-bird, call-bird; lure, decoy, snare; (*horol.*) quarter-bell, half-hour bell
Appel, *s.m.* call; appeal; challenge; calling over; calling; call; levy; roll-call, muster. — *nominal,* (*parl.*) call of the House. *Officier d'*—, muster-master
Appelant, e, *s.m.f. adj.* decoy-bird; (*law*) appellant; appealing
Appeler, *v.a.n.* to call; to call over; to call on; to call in *or* out *or* up *or* down; to call for; to give a call; to send for; to attract; to captivate; to appeal; to name, to term; to nickname, to surname; to claim; to invite; to exhort; to summon; to challenge; to appoint; to destine, to intend *En* —, to appeal. *Faire* —, to send for
S'—, *v.r.* to be called *or* named, o.'s *or* its name to be; to call oneself; to call each other. *Comment vous appelez-vous?* what is your name? *Je m'appelle* .., my name is . . .
Appelet, *s.m.* *V.* **Aplet**
Appeleur, *s.m.* call-bird
Appellati-f, ve, *adj.* appellative
Appellation, *s.f.* calling; naming; appellation, name; appeal
Appendice, *s.m.* appendix; appendage; addition
Appendiculaire, *adj.* appendicular
Appendicule, *s.m.* appendicle
Appendiculé, e, *adj.* (*bot.*) appendiculate
Appendre, *v.a.* to hang up, to hang
Appendu, e, *adj.* suspended, hung up, hanging
Appentis, *s.m.* shed, penthouse, lean-to
Appert, *v.* *Il* —, it appears, it is evident *or* obvious
Appesantir, *v.a.* to make heavy; to weigh down; to lay heavy; to make dull, to dull, to impair
S'—, *v.r.* to become (*or* grow *or* get) heavy *or* dull; to be weighed down; to lie heavy, to press heavy, to fall heavily; to dwell (upon)
Appesantissement, *s.m.* heaviness; dulness
Appétence, *s.f.* appetence, appetency
Appéter, *v.a.* to covet, to wish for, to desire
Appétissant, e, *adj.* appetizing, exciting, inviting, tempting, relishing; desirable
Appétit, *s.m.* appetite; hunger; desire, longing; taste; relish; chives
Appiécer, *v.a.* *V.* **Rapiécer**
Appienne, *adj.f.* Appian
Applaudir, *v.a.n.* to applaud, to cheer; to praise, to commend, to approve; to rejoice (at *or* in)
S'—, *v.r.* to applaud *or* praise *or* admire oneself; to glory (in); to rejoice (at *or* in), to congratulate oneself *or* each other (on)
Applaudissement, *s.m.* applause; plaudit; cheering, cheer; praise, commendation, approbation, favour
Applaudisseu-r, se, *s.m.f.* applauder
Applicabilité, *s.f.* applicability; appositeness
Applicable, *adj.* applicable; apposite; relevant; suitable; practicable; practical
Applicage, *s.m.* applying, application
Application, *s.f.* application; applying; appliance; destination; practice; attention, care, diligence, pains; study; applique lace. *D'*—, of application; practical. — *d'Angleterre,* Honiton lace
Applique, *s.f.* inlaying; charging; fittings; bracket. *Bras d'*—, bracket
Appliqué, e, *part. adj.* applied, &c. (*V.* **Appliquer**); studious; diligent; attentive; studiously adapted; practical
Appliquer, *v.a.* to apply; to put, to lay, to lay on, to set; to stick; to fix; to affix; to appropriate; to adapt; to fit; to devote; to occupy; to give, to bestow; to administer, to hit, to strike
S'—, *v.r.* to apply *or* &c. oneself; to be applied, &c.; to apply; to set (to); to study; to make it o.'s study; to endeavour; to stick; to attribute *or* appropriate to oneself; to take to oneself
Appoggiature, *s.f.* (*mus.*) appoggiatura
Appoint, *s.m.* odd money, difference, complement, change; balance; after-payment; appoint. *D'*—, odd
Appointement, *s.m.* (*law*) appointment, decree, order, rule; —**s,** *pl.* salary, pay, allowance, emoluments, stipend; expenses, maintenance
Appointer, *v.a.* to salary, to give a salary *or* a stipend to, to put upon a salary; to point, to sharpen; to sew up, to stitch; (*mil.*) to punish (with); (*law*) to appoint, to decree; to refer (*a cause*)
Appointeur, *s.m.* reconciler; umpire, referee, judge
Appontement, *s.m.* temporary wooden bridge; (*nav.*) gangway-ladder
Apport, *s.m.* bringing, removal; material brought; quantity brought; contribution, share; share of capital; (*of marriage*) personal estate; (*law*) deposit of documents, deposit; documents deposited
Apportage, *s.m.* carriage
Apporter, *v.a.* to bring; to convey; to bring in *or* out; to bring up *or* down; to bring over; to procure; to cause; to use, to employ; to apply; to allege, to bring forward; to produce; to adduce; to bestow, to give; to raise; to show
Apportionnement, *s.m.* portioning
Apportionner, *v.a.* to portion
Apposer, *v.a.* to affix, to put, to set; to introduce
Apposition, *s.f.* affixing, putting, setting; introduction; (*gram.*) apposition
Appréciable, *adj.* appreciable; perceptible
Appréciablement, *adv.* appreciably; perceptibly
Apprécia-teur, trice, *adj. s.* appreciating; appraiser, valuer, estimator
Appréciati-f, ve, *adj.* appreciative, estimative, of estimation *or* valuation. *État* or *détail* or *devis* —, estimate
Appréciation, *s.f.* valuation, estimate; appreciation, estimation; comment
Apprécier, *v.a.* to value; to appreciate, to estimate; to appraise; to ascertain, to determine; to judge
S'—, *v.r.* to value oneself *or* each other; to be valued, &c.
Appréhender, *v.a.* to apprehend; to take up; to lay hold of, to seize; to arrest; to fear, to dread. — *au corps,* to apprehend, to take up, to arrest
Appréhensible, *adj.* apprehensible
Appréhensi-f, ve, *adj.* apprehensive
Appréhension, *s.f.* apprehension; fear, dread

Apprenable, *adj.* learnable, to be learnt
Apprendre, *v.a.* to learn; to hear; to be informed of; to understand; to teach; to train; to inform, to acquaint, to tell, to apprise, to advise, to let know
S'—, *v.r.* to be learnt; to be heard; to be taught; to be known; to tell one another
Apprenti, e, *adj.* apprenticed; articled; — *s.m.f.* apprentice; articled pupil; novice, tyro
Apprentissage, *s.m.* apprenticeship; articles; trial, experiment
Apprêt, *s.m.* preparation; cooking; dressing; stiffening; affectation
Apprêtage, *s.m.* dressing; finishing
Apprêté, e, *adj.* prepared; cooked; dressed; made; made up; studied, affected
Apprêter, *v.a.* to prepare, to get ready; to cook; to dress; to afford matter (for)
S'—, *v.r.* to prepare oneself, to prepare, to get ready; to dress; to be preparing, to be in course of preparation; to gather, to be brewing
Apprêteu-r, se, *s.m.f.* dresser
Appris, e, *part. adj.* learnt, studied, &c. (*V.* **Apprendre**); taught, bred. *Mal —,* (*adj. s.*) ill-bred, unmannerly; ill-bred *or* unmannerly [fellow *or* thing
Apprivoisable, *adj.* tamable
Apprivoisé, e, *adj.* tame; familiar; manageable, tractable, gentle; sociable [tameness
Apprivoisement, *s.m.* taming, domestication;
Apprivoiser, *v.a.* to tame, to make *or* render tame *or* familiar *or* tractable *or* sociable, to soften, to render gentle; to use *or* accustom (to)
S'—, *v.r.* to become (*or* grow *or* get) tame *or* sociable, to be tamed; to become used (to) *or* familiar (with, to)
Approba-teur, trice, *adj. s.* approbatory, approving; of approbation; approver
Approbati-f, ve, *adj.* approbative, approving; of approbation [sent
Approbation, *s.f.* approbation, approval, con-
Approbativement, *adv.* approbatively, approvingly, with approbation
Approchable, *adj.* approachable
Approchant, e, *adj. prep. adv.* bordering (upon); like, like it, somewhat like, something like, similar; approximate; near, near it, near about, about; so
Approche, *s.f.* approach; access; coming; advance; drawing near; (*print.*) space
Approcher, *v.a.n.*, **S'—,** *v.r.* to approach, to draw *or* bring near; to come *or* go *or* get near; to advance; to be coming; to be near, to be at hand; to have *or* gain access (to); to border (upon); to be like, to resemble
Approfondi, e, *adj.* deep, profound, thorough, complete, full
Approfondir, *v.a.* to deepen, to make deeper; to search into, to examine thoroughly, to examine, to investigate, to dive into, to fathom, to sift
S'—, *v.r.* to be deepened, &c.; to deepen, to become deeper; to examine oneself, to look into oneself
Approfondissement, *s.m.* deepening; fathoming; sifting; sounding; research; examination; investigation
Appropriation, *s.f.* appropriation; assimilation; fitting; cleaning; (*law*) conversion
Approprié, e, *adj.* appropriate; suitable, suited, fitted, fit; clean
Approprier, *v.a.* to appropriate, to adapt, to suit, to fit; to clean, to clean out; to put to rights
S'—, *v.r.* to appropriate to oneself, to convert to o.'s own use; to usurp; to lay claim to; to adapt *or* suit oneself; to become clean *or* tidy
Approuvable, *adj.* approvable
Approuver, *v.a.* to approve, to approve of; to like; to consent to; to sanction; to pass (*accounts*)
Approvisionnement, *s.m.* supply of provisions, supply; provision, provisions; stock; stores; storing; stocking; victualling. *Vaisseau d'—,* victualler
Approvisionner, *v.a.* to supply; to store; to stock; to cater for; to victual. *— une pièce,* (*artil.*) to serve ammunition
S'—, *v.r.* to stock oneself; to take in a supply
Approvisionneu-r, se, *s.m.f.* purveyor, provider, caterer, victualler. *— de navires,* ship-chandler [proximate; rough
Approximati-f, ve, *adj.* approximative; ap-
Approximation, *s.f.* approximation; approach; rough guess [approximately
Approximativement, *adv.* approximatively,
Approximer, *v.n.a.* to approximate, to approach
Appui, *s.m.* support; prop, stay; rest; protection; protector, supporter; rail, hand-rail; sill; buttress; fulcrum; stress, accent, emphasis; (*rid.*) appui. *Hauteur d'—,* breast-height. *Point d'—,* point of support; prop; basis; base; fulcrum. *A hauteur d'—,* breast-high. *A l'—* (*de*), in support (of), in confirmation (of), confirmative (of), corroborative (of). *Aller* or *venir à l'— de,* to support, to back, to second, to bear [out
Appui-main, *s.m.* maulstick; hand-rest
Appulse, *s.f.* (*astr.*) appulse
Appuyé, e, *part. adj.* supported, &c. (*V.* **Appuyer**); leaning, resting; reclining; recumbent; inclining; marked, significant
Appuyée, *s.f.* (*nav.*) inclination
Appuyer, *v.a.n.* to support; to prop; to stay; to lean, to rest; to press; to set, to lay, to deposit; to give; to recline; to incline; to protect; to back; to assist; to second; to countenance; to urge; to maintain; to keep up; to hang (on); to dwell; to insist; to lay a stress
S'—, *v.r.* to support oneself; to lean, to rest; to recline; to press; to urge; to rely; to depend; to trust; to dwell
Âpre, *adj.* rough; uneven; rugged; harsh; hard; sharp; sour; tart; violent; austere; eager, greedy
Âprement, *adv.* roughly; harshly; sharply; tartly; violently; eagerly, greedily
Après, *prep. adv.* after; next to; for; in; against; on, upon; at; about; behind; afterwards; then; next; after it, after him *or* her; after them; about it *or* them. *— cela,* after that; but then; after all. *— quoi,* after, afterwards, after which, after that, and then. *— que,* after, when, as soon as. *D'—,* after; from; according to; to; on, upon; following; next. *— ? Et — ?* what next? what then? what of that? well?
Après-demain, *adv. s.m.* the day after tomorrow. *— matin,* the morning after tomorrow [dinner, afternoon *or* evening
Après-dînée, *s.f.*, **Après-dîner,** *s.m.* after-
Après-midi, *s.f.m.* afternoon
Après-soupée, *s.f.*, **Après-souper,** *s.m.* after-supper, latter part of the evening
Âpreté, *s.f.* roughness; ruggedness; unevenness; harshness; sharpness; sourness; tartness, acidity; violence; asperity; austerity; eagerness; greediness [pos
A propos, *adv. prep.*, **A-propos,** *s.m. V.* **Pro-**
Apside, *s.f.* (*arch.*) apse, apsis, absis; (*astr.*) [apsis
Apte, *adj.* fit, apt; qualified
Aptère, *adj.* apterous; — *s.m.* apteran, apter
Aptéryx, *s.m.* (*bird*) apteryx
Aptitude, *s.f.* aptitude, fitness; qualification
Apurement, *s.m.* closing, auditing
Apurer, *v.a.* to audit
Apyre, *adj.* apyrous, incombustible, fire-proof
Apyrexie, *s.f.* (*med.*) apyrexia, apyrexy
***Aquafortiste,** *s.m.f.* etcher
***Aquarelle,** *s.f.* water-colour, water-colours; water-colour painting *or* drawing
***Aquarelliste,** *s.m.f.* water-colour painter
***Aquarium,** *s.m.* aquarium
***Aquatile,** *adj.* aquatile, aquatic. *Plante —,* aquatic plant, water-plant, ooze-weed
***Aqua-tinta, Aquatinte,** *s.f.* aquatint

***Aquatique,** *adj.* aquatic; water; watery
***Aqua-toffana,** *s.f.* aqua-toffana, aquetta
Aqueduc, *s.m.* aqueduct
***Aquette,** *s.f.* aquetta
Aqueu-x, se, *adj.* aqueous, watery
§Aquiculture, *s.f.* aquiculture
§Aquifère, *adj.* aquiferous
Aquilain, Aquilant, *adj.m.* brown bay; — *s.m.* brown bay horse
§Aquilaire, *s.m.* (*bot.*) aquilaria
Aquilin, e, *adj.* aquiline, hooked, Roman
Aquilon, *s.m.* north wind; cold wind, cold blast, stormy wind, wind; storm, tempest; north
Aquilonnaire, *adj.* northern, boreal
Aquosité, *s.f.* aqueousness, wateriness
Ara, *s.m.* (*bird*) macaw [*pital conveyance*)
Araba, *s.m.* araba (*Turkish carriage; field-hos-*
Arabe, *adj. s.m.f.* Arabian; Arabic; Arab; usurer, hard bargainer, screw, dun, miser, Shylock, hard-hearted wretch
Arabesque, *adj.* arabesque; — *s.f.* arabesque (*ornament, dance*); — *s.m.* arabesque style
Arabette, Arabide, *s.f.* (*bot.*) arabis, tower-mustard, wall-cress, rock-cress
Arabine, *s.f.* (*chem.*) arabine
Arabique, *adj.* Arabic; Arabian
Arabisant, *s.m.* arabist
Arabisme, *s.m.* arabism
Arable, *adj.* arable, tillable
Aracari, *s.m.* (*bird*) aracari, aricari
Aracatcha, *s.f.* (*bot.*) arracacha
Arachide, *s.f.* (*bot.*) arachis, earth-nut, pea-nut
‡Arachnide, *s.f.* (*zool.*) arachnidan
‡Arachnite, *s.f.* (*med.*) arachnitis
‡Arachnoïde, *s.f.* (*anat.*) arachnoid membrane, arachnoid; — *adj.* arachnoid; cobweb-like
Arack, *s.m.* arrack
Arada, *s.m.* (*bird*) arada, ant-catcher [fashion
Aragonais, e, *adj. s.* Aragonese; Aragonese
Aragonite, *s.f.* (*min.*) aragonite
†Araigne, *s.f.* thrush-net; hook
†Araignée, *s.f.* spider; cobweb; thrush-net; trout-net; hook; (*fort.*) araignee, arraign; (*nav.*) crow-foot. — *de mer*, *V.* **Maïa.** *Pattes d'*—, (*fig.*)
Araire, *s.m.f.* swing-plough [long thin fingers
Aralie, *s.f.* (*bot.*) aralia
Aramer, *v.a.* to tenter (*cloth*)
Arané, e, Aranéen, ne, Aranéeu-x, se, *adj.* araneous; cobweb-like, cobwebbed
Aranéides, *s.f.pl.* araneidans, weavers, retiaries
Arasement, *s.m.* levelling; last course
Araser, *v.a.* (*mas.*) to level, to make even
Arases, *s.f.pl.* (*mas.*) levelling course
Aratoire, *adj.* agricultural, farming
Araucaire, *s.m.* *V.* **Araucaria**
Araucan, *s.m.*, **Araucanien, ne,** *s.m.f. adj.* Araucanian [monkey puzzle
Araucaria, *s.m.* (*bot.*) araucaria, Chili pine,
Araucarite, *s.f.* fossil araucaria
†Arbalestrille, *s.f.* (*astr.*) Jacob's staff
Arbalète, *s.f.* cross-bow; dormouse-trap. *Attelage en* —, unicorn team. *Cheval en* —, leader in a unicorn team
Arbalétrier, *s.m.* cross-bowman; (*bird*) black swift; (*build.*) principal rafter
Arbitrage, *s.m.* arbitration
Arbitraire, *adj.* arbitrary; optional; discretionary; — *s.m.* arbitrariness, arbitrary government, despotism
Arbitrairement, *adv.* arbitrarily
Arbitral, e, *adj.* of arbitrators, by arbitration, arbitral. *Jugement* —, *sentence* —*e*, arbitrement,
Arbitralement, *adv.* by arbitration [award
Arbitre, *s.m.f.* arbitrator; arbiter; umpire; referee; ruler; disposer; (*philos.*) will. *Libre* or *franc* —, free will. *Tiers* —, umpire
Arbitrer, *v.a.* to arbitrate; to determine, to regulate, to order, to settle; to value, to estimate; to decree; to award
Arboré, e, *adj.* (*bot.*) arboreous; (*of flags*) hoisted
Arborer, *v.a.* to raise, to set up, to erect; to hoist; to proclaim, to declare oneself openly for,
Arborescence, *s.f.* arborescence [to embrace
Arborescent, e, *adj.* arborescent
Arboricole, *adj.* arboricultural
Arboriculteur, *s.m.* arboriculturist
Arboricultural, e, *adj.* arboricultural
Arboriculture, *s.f.* arboriculture
Arboriforme, *adj.* arboriform
Arborisation, *s.f.* arborization
Arboriser, *v.a.* to arborize
Arboriste, *s.m.* arborist
Arbouse, *s.f.* arbute-berry
Arbousier, *s.m.* arbute, arbutus, strawberry-tree
Arbousse, *s.f.* Astrakan water-melon
Arbre, *s.m.* tree; shaft, beam; mast. — *à pain*, bread-fruit tree, bread-tree. — *de couche*, horizontal shaft. — *de Diane*, (*chem.*) arbor Dianæ. — *de Judée*, Judas-tree. — *de plein vent*, standard tree. — *de vie*, (*bot.*) arbor vitæ, thuja. — *en espalier*, wall-tree. — *fruitier*, fruit-tree. — *vert*, evergreen. *Faire l'— fourchu*, to walk on o.'s hands with both legs in the air
Arbret, Arbrot, *s.m.* (*hunt.*) limed bush
Arbreter, *v.a.* (*hunt.*) to lime (*a bush*)
Arbrisseau, *s.m.* small tree, shrub
Arbuste, *s.m.* small shrub, shrub, bush
Arc, *s.m.* bow; arch; arc; (*of a carriage*) crane-neck perch. *Portée d'*—, *trait d'*—, bow-shot. *Tir à l'*—, archery. *En — de cercle*, semicircular. — **-boutant,** *s.m.* buttress, abutment; stay, prop, support; ringleader; (*carp.*) spur; (*nav.*) boom. — **-bouter,** *v.a.* to prop, to support, to rest, to buttress. — **-doubleau,** *s.m.* (*build.*) massive rib. — **-en-ciel,** *s.m.* rainbow. — **-en-terre,** *s.m.* inverted iris
Arcade, *s.f.* arcade; piazza; arch
Arcadien, ne, *adj. s.* Arcadian [secret
Arcane, *s.m.* arcanum, nostrum, mystery,
Arcanne, *s.f.* red chalk, red ochre, ruddle
Arcanson, *s.m.* *V.* **Colophane**
Arcasse, *s.f.* (*nav.*) stern-frame
Arcature, *s.f.* (*arch.*) arch-work
Arceau, *s.m.* arch, vault; archway; ring
‡Archa-ïque, -ïsme, -ïste. *V.* page 3, § 1
Archal, *s.m.* *Fil d'*—, wire, brass wire, iron wire
‡Archange, *s.m.* archangel [(*bot.*) archangelica
‡Archangélique, *adj.* archangelic; — *s.f.*
Arche, *s.f.* arch, arching; ark; pale of the church; (*zool.*) arca, ark-shell. — *d'alliance*, ark of the covenant. *L'— de Noé*, Noah's ark. *L'— sainte*, *l'— du Seigneur*, (*fig.*) forbidden ground
Archée, *s.f.* archeus, archæus; fire; bow-shot
Archelet, *s.m.* drill-bow; hoop (*of a net*)
‡Archéologie, *s.f.* archæology
‡Archéologique, *adj.* archæological
‡Archéologue, *s.m.* archæologist
Archer, *s.m.* archer, bowman; archeress; (*old*) police-officer, constable, bailiff; (*zool.*) archer-fish
Archère, *s.f.* archeress [(*top of a cradle*)
Archet, *s.m.* bow, fiddlestick; bow-hand; head
‡Archétype, *s.m.* archetype; — *adj.* archetypal, archetypical
Archevêché, *s.m.* archbishopric; metropolitan see, cathedral city; archiepiscopal palace, archbishop's palace *or* house *or* residence
Archevêque, *s.m.* archbishop
Archi-, (*in compounds*) arch- . . .
Archichancelier, *s.m.* archchancellor
Archidiaconal, e, *adj.* archidiaconal
Archidiaconat, Archidiaconé, *s.m.* arch-
Archidiacre, *s.m.* archdeacon [deaconry
Archidiocésain, e, *adj.* archdiocesan
Archiduc, *s.m.* archduke
Archiducal, e, *adj.* archducal
Archiduché, *s.m.* archdukedom
Archiduchesse, *s.f.* archduchess
‡Archiépiscopal, e, *adj.* archiepiscopal
‡Archiépiscopat, *s.m.* archiepiscopate
Archifou, *m.*, **Archifolle,** *f.*, *adj.* stark mad
Archiluth, *s.m.* archlute
Archimandrite, *s.m.* archimandrite
Archimillionnaire, *adj. s.* immensely rich

Archinoble, *adj.* most noble
Archipel, *s.m.* archipelago
Archipompe, *s.f.* (*nav.*) pump-well, well
Archipresbytéral, e, *adj.* archpresbyterial
Archipresbytérat, *s.m.* archpresbytery
Archiprêtre, *s.m.* archpresbyter, archpriest
Archiprêtré, *s.m.* archpresbytery
Architecte, *s.m.* architect. — *de jardins*, — *-paysagiste*, landscape-gardener
Architectonique, *adj.* architectonic; — *s.f.* architectonics
Architectonographe, *s.m.* architectonographer
Architectonograph-ie, -ique. *V.* page 3, § 1
Architectural, e, *adj.* architectural
Architecture, *s.f.* architecture
Architrave, *s.f.* (*arch.*) architrave
Architrésorier, *s.m.* archtreasurer
Architriclin, *s.m.* steward; head-man, manager; host, entertainer
Archives, *s.f.pl.* archives; records; muniment; record-office, muniment house *or* room
Archiviste, *s.m.* archivist; keeper of the records; recorder; registrar
Archivolte, *s.f.* (*arch.*) archivolt
‡**Archontat,** *s.m.* archonship
‡**Archonte,** *s.m.* archon
Archure, *s.f.* (*of mill-stones*) drum
Arçon, *s.m.* saddle-bow; bow; vine-twig. *Pistolet d'*—, horse-pistol. *Perdre* or *vider les* —*s*, to be unhorsed; to hesitate, to be confused *or* disconcerted
Arçonnage, *s.m.* bowing; (*agr.*) layering
Arçonner, *v.a.* to bow; (*agr.*) to layer
Arçonnier, *s.m.* saddle-bow maker
Arcot, *s.m.* scoria, dross
Arctation, *s.f.* (*med.*) arctation
Arctier, *s.m.* bow-maker
Arctique, *adj.* arctic
Arctitude, *s.f.* (*med.*) arctitude
Arctium, *s.m.* (*bot.*) arctium, burdock, clit-bur
Arcture, Arcturus, *s.m.* (*astr.*) Arcturus
Arcuation, *s.f.* (*med.*) arcuation
Arcure, *s.f.* arching, curving; (*hort.*) arcuation
Ardasse, *s.f.* coarse Persian silk
Ardassine, *s.f.* ardassine (*fine Persian silk*)
Ardélion, *s.m.* busybody, ardeleon
Ardemment, *adv.* ardently; hotly; fervidly, fervently; eagerly; earnestly; spiritedly; vehemently; intensely; sanguinely; passionately
Ardent, e, *adj.* ardent; burning; hot; fiery; live; fervid, fervent; eager; earnest; vehement; violent; intense; bright, shining, vivid, resplendent; glowing; sanguine; spirited; mettled, high-spirited; longing; aspiring; active; zealous; passionate; (*of the hair*) red; (*nav.*) griping
Ardent, *s.m.* *V.* **Follet (Feu)**; —**s,** *pl.* (*med.*) [carbuncle; (*pop.*) peepers
Arder, *V.* **Brûler**
Ardeur, *s.f.* ardour; burning; heat; fire; fervour; eagerness; earnestness; vehemence; intensity; spirit; mettle, fire, spiritedness; zeal; courage; love; passion
Ardez, *int.* (*old*) look! see!
†**Ardillon,** *s.m.* tongue (*of a buckle*); barb (*of a hook*)
Ardoise, *s.f.* slate
Ardoisé, e, *adj.* slated; slate-colour, slaty
Ardoiser, *v.a.* to slate
Ardoiseu-x, se, Ardoisi-er, ère, *adj.* slaty
Ardoisier, *s.m.* slate-quarrier, slate-worker
Ardoisière, *s.f.* slate-quarry
Ardre, *V.* **Brûler**
Ardu, e, *adj.* arduous, hard, difficult, steep
Arduité, *s.f.* arduousness
Are, *s.m.* are (100 *square metres, or somewhat more than* 119 *square yards English*)
Aréage, *s.m.* measuring by "ares," surveying
Arec, *s.m.* (*bot.*) areca; areca nut
Aréfaction, *s.f.* arefaction
†**Areignol,** *s.m.* *V.* **Bastude**
Arénacé, e, *adj.* arenaceous
Arénaire, *adj.* growing *or* living in sand; — *s.f.* (*bot.*) arenaria, sandwort
Arénation *s.f.* arenation
Arène, *s.f.* sand, gravel; arena; amphitheatre; lists; ring; cockpit; battle-ground; theatre, scene
Aréner, *v.n.*, **S'**—, *v.r.* to subside, to settle, to sink
Aréneu-x, se, *adj.* sandy, gravelly
Aren , *s.m.* (*bot.*) areng, gomuto palm
Aréolaire, *adj.* areolar
Aréole, *s.f.* areola; (*astr.*) halo
Aréolé, e, *adj.* areolate
Aréomètre, *s.m.* areometer
Aréomé-trie, -trique. *V.* page 3, § 1
Aréopage, *s.m.* areopagus
Aréopagite, *s.m.* areopagite
Aréopagitique, *adj.* areopagitic
Aréostyle, *s.m.* (*arch.*) areostyle
Aréotectonique, *s.f.* areotectonics (*military architecture*)
Aréotique, *adj.* (*med.*) areotic
Aréquier, *s.m.* (*bot.*) areca, cabbage-palm
Arer, *v.a.* to measure by the "are," to survey; — *v.n.* (*nav.*) to drag the anchor
Arête, *s.f.* fish-bone, bone; skeleton (*of a fish*); angle; corner; edge; ridge; sharp line; (*arch.*) arris; (*of a sword-blade*) ridge; (*bot.*) awn, beard; (*vet.*) arrest. — *de poisson*, fish-bone; (*arch.*) herring-bone work. *A vive* —, (*carp.*) sharp-edged
Arétier, *s.m.* (*arch.*) hip
Argala, *s.m.* (*bird.*) argala, adjutant
Argali, *s.m.* argali, wild sheep
Argan, Argane, *s.m.* (*bot.*) argan
Arganeau, *s.m.* convict-chain, chain; (*nav.*) ring
Argémone, *s.f.* (*bot.*) argemone, prickly poppy
Argent, *s.m.* silver; money; sum of money; cash; coin; (*her.*) argent. — *blanc*, silver coin, silver. — *fou*, world of money, deal of money. — *monnayé*, coin, money; cash. *D'*—, of silver; of money; silvery. *Faux* —, — *de chat*, — *du diable*, mica. *Point d'— point de Suisse*, nothing without paying. *Prendre pour — comptant*, to take literally, to believe too readily
Argentage, *s.m.* silvering, silver-plating
Argental, e, *adj.* argental [argentan, packfong
Argentan, *s.m.* German silver, nickel silver,
Argenté, e, *adj.* plated, silvered, silvered over; silvery, silver; (*pers.*) having some cash, in cash, flush of cash *or* of money
Argenter, *v.a.* to plate, to silver, to silver over; to bring money to, to fill the purse of
S'—, *v.r.* to be silvered over; to get money *or* cash, to fill o.'s purse
Argenterie, *s.f.* silver-plate, silver, plate
Argenteur, *s.m.* silverer, plater
Argenteu-x, se, *adj.* moneyed, warm; flush of cash *or* of money
Argentier, *s.m.* (*old*) treasurer; steward, butler; money-changer; silversmith
Argentifère, *adj.* argentiferous
Argentin, e, *adj.* silvery; ringing, clear, sonorous; Argentine
Argentine, *s.f.* (*bot.*) silver-weed; (*min.*) argentine; (*zool.*) argentine, silver-fish
Argenton, *s.m.* *V.* **Argentan**
Argenture, *s.f.* silvering, silver-plating; plated work
Argilacé, e, *adj.* argillaceous
Argile, *s.f.* clay, argil
Argileu-x, se, *adj.* clayey, argillous
Argilière, *s.f.* clay-pit
Argilifère, *adj.* argilliferous
Argilite, *s.f.* argillite
Argillacé, e, *adj.* argillaceous
Argilo-, (*in compounds*) argilo- ...
Argilolithe, *s.m.* clay-stone
Argo, *s.m.* (*myth., astr.*) Argo, the ship Argo
Argonaute, *s.m.* (*myth.*) Argonaut; (*zool.*) argonaut, paper nautilus
Argonautique, *adj.* Argonautic
Argosil, *s.m.* argosy
Argot, *s.m.* slang; (*hort.*) dead wood
Argoter, *v.a.n.* to cut the dead wood off
Argoti-er, ère, *s.m.f.* slang-talker; thief
Argotique, *adj.* slangy, slang

Argotiser, *v.n.* to talk slang
Argousier, *s.m.* (*bot.*) hippophae, sallow-thorn
Argousin, *s.m.* convict-keeper, warder; police-spy, catchpoll, bumbailiff; policeman, peeler, bobby, blue bottle, slop [draw-room
Argue, *s.f.* draw-bench, wire-drawing machine;
Arguer, *v.a.n.* to accuse; to wire-draw; to argue, to infer, to conclude; to urge
Argule, *s.m.* argulus, fish-louse, sea-louse
Argument, *s.m.* argument; arguing; conjecture; evidence, proof; theme, subject; summary
Argumentant, Argumentateur, *s.m.* arguer
Argumentation, *s.f.* argumentation, arguing
Argumenter, *v.n.* to argue; — *v.a.* to argue with [(*zool.*) argus
Argus, *s.m.* Argus; clear-sighted man; spy;
Argutie, *s.f.* quibble, quibbling, cavil, cavilling, hair-splitting
Argutieu-x, se, *adj.* quibbling, cavilling
Aria, *s.m.* (*pop.*) jumble; fuss, ado; bother, annoyance, nuisance; difficulty
Arianisme, *s.m.* Arianism
Aride, *adj.* arid, dry; barren, sterile, unfruitful
Aridité, *s.f.* aridity, dryness; barrenness, ste-
Arien, ne, *adj. s.* Arian [rility, unfruitfulness
Ariette, *s.f.* (*mus.*) arietta
†**Arille,** *s.m.* (*bot.*) aril, mace, seed-coat
Arion, *s.m.* red slug
Ariser, *v.a.* (*nav.*) to reef (*the sails*)
Aristarque, *s.m.* Aristarch
Aristo, *s.m.f.* (*pop.*) aristocrat, don, nob
Aristocrate, *adj. s.m.f.* aristocratic; aristocrat
Aristocratie, *s.f.* aristocracy [page 3, § 1
Aristocrat-ique, -iquement, -isme. *V.*
Aristocratiser, *v.a.n.* to aristocratize
Aristoloche, *s.f.* (*bot.*) aristolochia, birthwort
Aristotélicien, ne, *adj. s.* Aristotelian
Aristotélique, *adj.* Aristotelic
Aristotélisme, *s.m.* Aristotelianism
Arithmancie, *s.f.* arithmancy
Arithméticien, ne, *s.m.f.* arithmetician
Arithmétique, *adj. s.f.* arithmetical; arithmetic. *Cahier d'*—, ciphering-book
Arithmétiquement, *adv.* arithmetically
Arithmo-graphie,-graphique,-logie,&c.
Arithmomancie, *s.f.* arithmancy [*V.* p. 3, § 1
Arithmomètre, *s.m.* arithmometer, calculat-
Arizarum, *s.m.* (*bot.*) friar's cowl [ing-machine
Arlequin, *s.m.* harlequin; humbug; broken meat, scraps, leavings, hotchpotch; (*bird*) spotted redshank; (*insect*) harlequin-beetle. *Habit d'*—, (*fig.*) patchwork, medley, cento. *Manteau d'*—, (*theat.*) sides and ceiling of the proscenium
Arlequinade, *s.f.* harlequinade
Arlequine, *s.f.* harlequin's dance, tune for ditto; woman dressed as a harlequin
Arlequiné, e, *adj.* variegated, multicoloured
Arlésien, ne, *adj. s.* of Arles, Arlesian, native
Armada, *s.f.* armada (*Spanish fleet*) [of Arles
†**Armadille,** *s.f.* (*nav.*) armadilla; (*zool.*) arma-
Armand, *s.m.* arman (*horse medicine*) [dillo
Armateur, *s.m.* fitter-out; ship-owner, owner; owner *or* captain of a privateer; privateer
Armatole, *s.m.* (modern) Greek militiaman
Armature, *s.f.* fastening; binding; fencing; tressing; iron bars, stays; brace; frame-work, framing, frame; fittings; cappings; (*of a pump*) gear; (*phys.*) armature
Arme, *s.f.* weapon; arm; **—s,** *pl.* weapons; arms; armour; troops; forces; army; war, warfare; hostilities; campaign; fencing; (*her.*) arms, bearings, coat of arms, hatchment. — *blanche*, sword, bayonet, lance, side-arm. —*s savantes*, —*s spéciales*, scientific corps. — *à feu*, fire-arm. — *de jet*, — *de trait*, missile weapon, missile. *Capitaine d'*—*s*, (*nav.*) master-at-arms. *Compagnon* or *frère d'*—*s*, companion in arms, brother-in-arms, brother soldier, brother officer. *Gens d'*—*s*, (*hist.*) men-at-arms. *Homme d'*—*s*, (*hist.*) man-at-arms. *Maître d'*—*s*, fencing-master. *Place d'*—*s*, &c., *V.* **Place,** &c. *Faire* or *tirer des* —*s*, to fence. *Faire passer par les* —*s*, to shoot. *Passer* (*v.a.*) *par les* —*s*, to shoot. *Passer* (*v.n.*) *par les* —*s*, *être passé par les* —*s*, to be shot. *Passer l'*— *à gauche*, (*fig.*, *mil. slang*) to die, to kick the bucket. *Rendre les* —*s*, to lay down o.'s arms, to surrender. *Aux* —*s!* to arms! *Avec* —*s et bagage*, (*fig.*) with bag and baggage, with all o.'s traps. *Haut les* —*s!* lodge arms! *L'*— *à volonté!* slope arms! *Descendez* —*s!* ground arms! *Portez* —*s!* shoulder arms! *Reposez vos* —*s!* ground arms! — *au bras*, — *bras!* support arms! *Sous les* —*s*, under arms; prepared; (*of women*) dressed up, in full feather
Armé, e, *part. adj.* armed, &c. (*V.* **Armer**); provided; cocked, at full cock. — *en guerre*, (*nav.*) armed
Armée, *s.f.* army, force, forces, troops; host; bevy; fleet, navy. — *navale*, — *de mer*, naval forces, sea forces, navy, fleet. — *de terre*, land forces. *La grande* —, the Grand Army, Napo-
Armeline, *s.f.* ermine (*skin*) [leon's army
Armement, *s.m.* armament; arming; accoutrements; stand of arms; (*nav.*) equipment, fitting out; charging; manning; men, crew
Arménien, ne, *adj. s.* Armenian
Arménite, *s.f.* (*min.*) Armenian stone
Armer, *v.a.n.* to arm; to dub; to fortify; to strengthen; to secure; to bind; to rouse; to provoke; (*of percussion fire-arms*) to cock, to place at full cock; (*artil.*) to load; to mount; (*nav.*) to arm; to equip, to fit out; to charge; to man; to embark; to ship (*the oars*)
S'—, *v.r.* to arm oneself; to take up arms; to secure *or* strengthen oneself; to provide oneself; to provide; to summon up; to make
Armerie, *s.f.* armoury [use
Armet, *s.m.* (*old*) helmet, head-piece
Armigère, *adj.* armigerous
Armillaire, *adj.* armillary
†**Armille,** *s.f.* (*arch.*) annulet
Armillé, e, *adj.* armillate
Arminianisme, *s.m.* Arminianism
Arminien, ne, *adj. s.* Arminian
Armistice, *s.m.* armistice
Armoire, *s.f.* cupboard; wardrobe; press; closet; case, box. — *à glace*, wardrobe with plate-glass door [hatchment
Armoiries, *s.f.pl.* arms, armorial bearings;
Armoise, *s.f.* (*bot.*) artemisia, mugwort; (*silk*) *V.* **Armoisin**
Armoisin, *s.m.* armozeen *or* armozine (*silk*)
Armon, *s.m.* (*of a carriage*) futchell
Armorial, e, *adj.* armorial
Armorial, *s.m.* book of heraldry
Armoricain, e, *adj. s.* of Brittany, Armorican
Armorié, e, *adj.* with o.'s arms, with armorial bearings, blazoned, emblazoned [to emblazon
Armorier, *v.a.* to put o.'s arms on, to blazon,
Armoriste, *s.m.* armorist, blazoner; heraldic engraver [thick skin; tree-guard
Armure, *s.f.* armour; casing; coat; wrapper;
Armurerie, *s.f.* gun-making, gunsmithery; gun-trade; arm-manufactory; armoury; arms; gun-maker's shop; gunsmith's forge
Armurier, *s.m.* gun-maker; gunsmith; sword-cutler; armourer
Arnaute, *s.m.f. adj.* Arnaut (*Albanian*)
Arni, *s.m.* (*zool.*) arnee
Arnica, Arnique, *s.f.* (*bot.*) arnica
Arnicine, *s.f.* (*chem.*) arnicine
Arnotto, *s.m.* *V.* **Roucou**
Aroïdées, *s.f.pl.* (*bot.*) aroides
Aromate, *s.m.* aromatic
Aromatique, *adj.* aromatic, fragrant
Aromatisation, *s.f.* aromatization, perfuming; flavouring [perfume; to flavour
Aromatiser, *v.a.* to aromatize, to scent, to
S'—, *v.r.* to be aromatized, &c.
Aromatite, *s.f.* aromatite
Arôme, *s.m.* aroma; flavour
Aronde, *s.f.* swallow; swallow-fish; avicula.

Queue d'—, (carp.) dovetail. *A or en queue d'—*, dovetailed. *Assembler à queue d'—*, to dovetail
Arondelle, *s.f.* kind of fishing-tackle; *(nav.)* [small craft
†Arpailleur, *s.m. V.* **Orpailleur**
Arpége, Arpégement, *s.m. (mus.)* arpeggio
Arpéger, *v.n.a.* to perform arpeggios
Arpent, *s.m.* acre; two-hand saw [veying
Arpentage, *s.m.* survey; surveying; land-sur-
Arpenter, *v.a.n.* to survey; to measure; to pace; to walk fast over; to stride, to stride along
Arpenteur, *s.m.* surveyor, land-surveyor; good walker; *(zool.)* stone-curlew, whistling plover
Arpenteuse, *s.f. (adj., Chenille —)* geometer, looper *(caterpillar)*
Arpions, *s.m.pl. (pop.)* feet, trotters
Arpon, *s.m.* two-hand saw
Arqué, e, *adj.* arched, curved; bent; crooked
Arquebusade, *s.f.* arquebusade
Arquebuse, *s.f.* arquebuse, arquebus
Arquebuser, *v.a.* to shoot
Arquebuserie, *s.f. V.* **Armurerie**
Arquebusier, *s.m.* gun-maker; gunsmith; arquebusier
Arquer, *v.a.* to arch, to curve; to bend, to bend round; to make crooked; — *v.n.*, **S'—**, *v.r.* to bend, to curve; to be *(or* become) bent *or* curved [*or* crooked
Arquifoux, *s.m. V.* **Alquifoux**
Arqûre, *s.f. V.* **Arcure**
Arracacha, *s.f. V.* **Aracatcha**
Arrachage, Arrachement, *s.m.* plucking, plucking out *or* off; picking; tearing; pulling; pulling off *or* out; drawing; extraction; wrenching; wringing; digging up; weeding out; asperity, craggy part, remains; *(arch.)* toothing
Arrache-pied (D'), *adv.* without intermission, incessantly
Arracher, *v.a.* to pluck, to pluck out *or* off *or* away; to pick; to tear; to tear out *or* off *or* away; to pull; to pull off *or* out *or* up; to draw; to wrest; to wring; to snatch; to take away *or* out; to force; to extort; to get; to rescue, to save; to rouse; to detach; to dig up; to root up *or* out; to weed out; to extract; to scratch out; to gouge, to scoop out

S'—, *v.r.* to tear; to pull *or* tear out; to get off *or* away; to break away (from); to escape; to detach oneself (from); to tear oneself away; to tear *or* snatch *or* &c. o.'s ... *or* each other's ... *or* from each other; to be plucked *or* picked *or* torn *or* &c. *On se l'arrache*, they dispute who shall have him *or* it; there is a rush after it
Arracheu-r, se, *s.m.f.* drawer; puller; tearer; picker; extractor; extirpator; eradicator; digger. — *de pommes de terre, (agr.)* potato-digger, potato-raising plough
Arrachis, *s.m.* plant rooted up; fraudulent rooting up of young trees
Arrachoir, *s.m. (instr.)* rooter, digger
Arraisonner, *v.a.* to reason with; *(nav.)* to speak with [&c.; affected
Arrangé, e, *part. adj. (V.* **Arranger***)* arranged,
Arrangeant, e, *adj.* accommodating, easy to deal with, easy
Arrangement, *s.m.* arrangement; adjusting; adjustment; settling; settlement; agreement; composition; fitting up; laying out; disposition; preparation; contrivance; scheme, plan, project; measure; ordering; order; management; economy; dressing; cooking; trimming
Arranger, *v.a.* to arrange; to put *or* set in order; to put *or* set to rights; to repair, to mend; to do up; to improve; to adjust; to settle; to agree on; to accommodate; to suit; to give facilities to; to conciliate; to fit up; to lay out; to dispose; to prepare; to contrive; to plan; to order; to regulate; to manage; to make up; to dress; to cook; to trim; to spare, to let have; to ill-use, to serve out; to give it to; to trounce; to blow up; to treat

S'—, *v.r.* to put *or* place oneself; to settle oneself; to settle; to settle matters; to agree; to come to an arrangement, to come to terms; to compound; to make a bargain; to take; to arrange; to make arrangements; to take measures; to manage matters; to manage; to contrive; to put up (with); to bear; to make shift (with); to manage as one can, to do the best one can; to be pleased (with); to like, to relish; to suit *or* please oneself; to take o.'s ease, to make oneself comfortable; to make free (with); to dress; to regulate o.'s expenses *or* way of living; to come all right; to be arranged *or* put *or* placed *or* settled *or* made up *or* &c. *Arrangez-vous!* manage as you can, do the best you can, settle it as you please, that is your look-out [finisher, closer
Arrangeu-r, se, *s.m.f.* arranger; adapter;
Arraser, *v.a. V.* **Araser**
Arrentement, *s.m.* renting; lease; funding
Arrenter, *v.a.* to rent; to fund
Arrérager, *v.n.* to be in arrears
Arrérages, *s.m.pl.* arrears
Arrestation, *s.f.* apprehension; capture; arrest; custody; imprisonment. *Mettre en —*, to take into custody *or* in charge, to arrest, to apprehend
Arrêt, *s.m.* sentence; judgment; decree; decision; arrest; stopping, stoppage; stand-still; dead-lock; stop, stay; catch; rest; check; stitch; embankment, bank; *(horol.)* stop-work; **—s,** *pl. (mil., schools)* arrest, confinement. *Aux —s*, under arrest, in confinement, confined, kept in. *En —, (of a lance)* in the rest. *En —, à l'—, (of dogs)* pointing, setting. *Temps d'—*, stoppage; pause, interruption, intermission
Arrêté, *s.m.* resolution; order; decision; settlement
Arrêté, e, *part. of* **Arrêter** [tlement
Arrête-bœuf, *s.m. (bot.)* cammock, rest-harrow
Arrête-nef, *s.m. (zool.)* sucking-fish
Arrête-porte, *s.m.* door-porter; gate-stop
Arrêter, *v.a.n.* to stop; to stay; to detain, to delay; to hold *or* keep back; to pull up; to check; to hinder; to obstruct; to prevent; to suppress; to repress; to quiet, to still; to put a stop *or* an end to; to alleviate, to allay; to cease, to leave off; to stand; to bring to a stand; to arrest; to seize; to take up; to apprehend; to take into custody *or* in charge; to fasten; to engage; to secure; to book; to hire; to resolve; to determine, to decide; to arrange; to settle; to agree; to agree for *or* on; to terminate, to finish; to conclude; to decree; to appoint; to fix; to choose; to fix the attention of; to attract; to captivate; to pin; to cease talking; *(of dogs)* to point, to set; *(hort.)* to top, to nip, to trim. *Arrêtez!* stop! hold! stand! stop thief!

S'—, *v.r.* to stop; to make a stop; to stay; to make a stay; to remain; to stand; to come *or* be brought to a stand; to halt; to draw up; to cease, to leave off; to rest; to dwell (upon); to insist (upon); to consider; to mind; to notice, to take particular notice (of); to amuse oneself; to loiter; to lodge; to fix (on); to choose; to resolve, to determine, to decide; to abide (by), to stick (to); to confine oneself; to stick (at); to be embarrassed; to hesitate, to scruple; to be fastened *or* secured *or* concluded [*or* fixed *or* pinned *or* &c.
Arrêtier, *s.m.* angle
Arrêtiste, *s.m.* compiler of decrees
Arrhénatère, *s.f. (bot.)* arrhenaterum, oat-like grass, French rye-grass
Arrher, *v.a.* to give earnest money for
Arrhes, *s.f.pl.* deposit; earnest money, earnest
Arrière, *s.m.* back part; rear; *(nav.)* stern; quarter; — *prep. adj.* back; hinder, hind; behind; after; rear; *(nav.)* aft, abaft; — *adv.* behind; away! far! stand back! avaunt! away with; *(nav.)* aft, abaft; *(of the wind)* leading. *D'—, (nav.)* after. *De l'—, (nav.)* after; astern. *En —*, back; backward; behind; at the back, at *or* in the rear; behindhand; in arrears; behind o.'s back; *(nav.)* abaft; *(int.)* back! keep

back! stand back! *Avoir le vent —*, *filer vent —*, to sail before the wind. *Faire vent —*, to scud. *Se ranger de l'—*, to veer aft. *Tomber de l'—*, to fall astern. — **-ban,** *s.m.* arriere-ban; levy in mass, call of the reserve, reserve. — **-bec,** *s.m.* (*arch.*) (lower) starling, cut-water, break-water. — **-bouche,** *s.f.* (*anat.*) posterior fauces, throat. — **-boutique,** *s.f.* back-shop. — **-caution,** *s.f.* security of the bail, double security. — **-change,** *s.m.* compound interest. — **-corps,** *s.m.* back-building, back-house; recess. — **-cour,** *s.f.* back-yard, back-court. — **-dos,** *s.m.* (*arch.*) altar-screen, reredos. — **-essaim,** *s.m.* after-swarm. — **-faix,** *s.m.* *V.* **Délivre.** — **-fief,** *s.m.* mesne-fief, rere-fee. — **-fleur,** *s.f.* second blossom. — **-foin,** *s.m.* *V.* **Regain.** — **-froidure,** *s.f.* early cold. — **-garant,** *s.m.* *V.* **Arrière-caution.** — **-garde,** *s.f.* rear guard, rear; (*of a fleet*) rear division. *Vaisseau de l'—-garde,* blockship. — **-goût,** *s.m.* after-taste. — **-graisse,** *s.f.* surplus manure. — **-ligne,** *s.f.* (*mil.*) second line. — **-main,** *s.m.* back-stroke; hind-quarters. — **-neveu,** *s.m.* grand-nephew; descendant; **-x,** *pl.* descendants, latest posterity. — **-nièce,** *s.f.* grand-niece. — **-partie,** *s.f.* back. — **-pensée,** *s.f.* mental reservation; hidden thought, secret thought *or* intention. — **-petit-fils,** *s.m.* great-grand-son. — **-petite-fille,** *s.f.* great-granddaughter. — **-petits-enfants,** *s.m.pl.* great-grandchildren. — **-plan,** *s.m.* background. — **-point,** *s.m.* back-stitch. — **-pointeuse,** *s.f.* back-stitcher. — **-port,** *s.m.* (*nav.*) inner harbour, dock. — **-rang,** *s.m.* (*mil.*) rear-rank. — **-saison,** *s.f.* after-season, end of the season; end of the autumn; evening *or* decline (of life), old age. — **-train,** *s.m.* after-carriage; hind-quarters. — **-vassal,** *s.m.* undertenant. — **-vieillesse,** *s.f.* extreme old age. — **-voussure,** *s.f.* (*arch.*) back-bending

Arriéré, *s.m.* arrear, arrears

Arriéré, e, *adj.* backward, behindhand; behind o.'s time; back; due; owing; outstanding; in arrears; unexecuted, left undone; unclaimed; stale [to defer, to delay

Arriérer, *v.a.* to put off, to put *or* throw back, **S'—,** *v.r.* to stay behind; to get in arrears

Arrimage, *s.m.* stowage, stowing, trim

Arrimer, *v.a.* to stow, to trim

Arrimeur, *s.m.* stevedore

Arriser, *v.a.* (*nav.*) to reef (*the sails*)

Arrivage, *s.m.* arrival

Arrivant, e, *s.m.f.* comer

Arrivé, e, *part. adj.* arrived, come, &c. (*V.* **Arriver**); having come *or* happened; coming; happening; successful; — *s.m.f.* comer

Arrivée, *s.f.* arrival, coming; entrance; approach, access; landing; (*nav.*) falling off, lee lurch

Arriver, *v.n.* to arrive; to come; to come on; to come to; to reach; to attain; to get; to gain access; to rise; to happen; to occur; to take place; to come to pass; to befall; to chance; should, were to; to manage; to succeed; to make o.'s way in the world, to make o.'s fortune; to have done; (*nav.*) to bear up *or* down, to fall off, to veer. *Arrive que pourra, arrive qui plante,* happen *or* come what may. *Quoi qu'il arrive,* whatever may happen, in any case, at all events, happen *or* come what may

Arrobe, *s.f.* arroba (*Spanish weight*)

Arroche, *s.f.* (*bot.*) orach, French spinach

Arrogamment, *adv.* arrogantly, haughtily

Arrogance, *s.f.* arrogance, haughtiness

Arrogant, e, *adj. s.* arrogant, haughty

Arrogation, *s.f.* arrogation

Arroger (S'), *v.a.* to arrogate, to assume

Arroi, *s.m.* array, train, equipage; plight

Arrondi, e, *adj.* rounded; round; full

Arrondir, *v.a.* to round; to make round; to round off; to show the round form of; to enlarge, to aggrandize, to extend, to increase **S'—,** *v.r.* to get (*or* grow *or* become) round, to round; to show its round form; to enlarge, to extend, to increase; to increase o.'s estate [*or* wealth

Arrondissage, *s.m.* rounding

Arrondissement, *s.m.* rounding; roundness; smoothness, harmony; increase; district; ward

Arrosage, *s.m.* irrigation; watering; sprinkling

Arrosement, *s.m.* watering; sprinkling; wetting; basting; washing down; (*of shareholders*) call, calls; (*at play*) stake; paying all round

Arroser, *v.a.n.* to water; to sprinkle; to besprinkle; to bedew; to soak; to wet through; to wet; to moisten; to steep; to bathe; to drown; to irrigate; to baste; to wash down; to distribute money; to pay (*creditors*) in part, to dole out money to, to give a sop to, to silence, to quiet; to give gratuities, to fee, to tip; (*of shareholders*) to pay calls; (*at play*) to pay all round

Arroseu-r, se, *s.m.f.* waterer; — *adj.* watering

Arrosoir, *s.m.* water-pot, watering-pot; (*zool.*) [*V.* **Aspergille**

Arrow-root, *s.m.* arrow-root

Arrugie, *s.f.* (*mining*) subterranean canal, watercourse, adit, drift, level

Ars, *s.m.* (*vet.*) limb, leg [*time,* dockyard

Arsenal, *s.m.* arsenal. — *de marine,* — *mari-*

Arséniate, *s.m.* (*chem.*) arseniate

Arsenic, *s.m.* arsenic [senical

Arsenical, e, Arsénique, *adj.* (*chem.*) ar-

Arsenicaux, *s.m.pl.* (*pharm.*) arsenical compounds, arsenicals [arseniuretted

Arsénié, e, Arséniqué, e, *adj.* (*chem.*)

Arsénieu-x, se, *adj.* (*chem.*) arsenious

Arsénite, *s.m.* (*chem.*) arsenite

Arséniure, *s.m.* (*chem.*) arsenide, arseniuret

Arséniuré, e, *adj.* (*chem.*) arseniuretted

Arsin, *adj.m.* damaged by fire; — *s.m.* wood damaged by fire [guardly

†Arsouille, *s.m.f. adj.* blackguard; black-

Art, *s.m.* art; skill; science; profession; artfulness, artifice, cunning, deceit, trick, device. *D'—*, *de l'—*, of art, artistic; of skill, skilful; of science, scientific; of medical science, medical; of the profession, professional; technical; special. *Homme de l'—*, most experienced *or* skilful practitioner, best man, crack man; expert; medical man, professional man, doctor; scientific man, man of science; special man. *Faire de l'—*, to work for the love of art

Artaban, *s.m.* *Fier comme —*, *V.* **Fier,** *adj.*

Artémise, *s.f.* (*bot.*) *V.* **Armoise**

Artère, *s.f.* artery

Artérialisation, *s.f.* arterialization

Artérialiser, *v.a.* to arterialize

Artériel, le, *adj.* arterial

Artériole, *s.f.* small artery [page 3, § 1

Artério-graphie, -logie, -tomie, &c. *V.*

Artérite, *s.f.* (*med.*) arteritis

Artésien, ne, *adj.* artesian

Arthanitine, *s.f.* (*chem.*) arthanitine

Arthrite, *s.f.* (*med.*) arthritis

Arthritique, *adj.* (*med.*) arthritic, gouty

Arthrodial, e, *adj.* (*anat.*) arthrodial

Arthrodie, *s.f.* (*anat.*) arthrodia [lover; beau

Arthur, *s.m.* gay woman's lover; favourite

Artichaut, *s.m.* artichoke, globe artichoke; spiked fence [kettle

Artichautière, *s.f.* artichoke-bed; artichoke-

Article, *s.m.* article; subject, matter, thing; concern, business; head; point; item; paragraph; entry; ware; goods; (*anat.*) articulation. — *principal* or *de fond,* — *Paris,* — *Londres,* leading article. — *de Paris,* (*com.*) Paris article. *A l'— de la mort,* on (*or* at) the point of death. *Faire l'—*, to praise up *or* puff o.'s goods, to entice people into buying o.'s goods, to tout; to puff

Articlier, *s.m.* newspaper scribbler, penny-a-

Articulaire, *adj.* articular [liner

Articulation, *s.f.* articulation; joint; utterance, pronunciation; allegation, statement; enumeration [lated; uttered, &c. (*V.* **Articuler**)

Articulé, e, *adj.* jointed; articulate; articu-

Articuler, *v.a.n.* to articulate; to utter; to

pronounce; to express; to allege, to state, to assert, to set forth; to enumerate; to mark, to indicate, to show

S'—, *v.r.* to be articulated *or* jointed, to joint; to join; to stand out prominently, to show off

Artifice, *s.m.* art, contrivance; artifice; craft, deceit, sliness, cunning, guile; trick, stratagem; shuffle; fireworks. *Caisse d'—*, (*nav.*) [powder-chest

Artifi iel, le, *adj.* artificial

Artificiellement, *adv.* artificially

Artificier, *s.m.* firework-maker, pyrotechnist; firework-man; (*mil.*) fire-worker. *Maitre —*, (*mil.*) fire-master [craftily; slily

Artificieusement, *adv.* artfully, cunningly,

Artificieu-x, se, *adj.* artful, cunning, crafty; sly; shuffling; subtle, fallacious [mount, to arm

†Artiller, *v.a.* (*old*) to mount with guns, to

†Artillerie, *s.f.* artillery; ordnance, guns; gunnery [ner

†Artilleur, *s.m.* artillery-man; artillerist; gun-

Artimon, *s.m.* (*nav.*) mizzen

Artisan, e, *s.m.f.* artisan, mechanic, operative, workman; artificer; (*fig.*) architect, author, maker; cause

Artison, *s.m.* (*zool.*) wood-fretter, death-watch; moth (*dermestes, anthrenus, psocus,* &c.)

Artisonné, e, *adj.* worm-eaten; moth-eaten

Artiste, *s.m.f.* artist; artiste; actor, actress, performer, player; — *adj.* artistic. — *vétérinaire,* veterinary surgeon

Artistement, *adv.* artistically

Artistique, *adj.* artistic, of art, of artists

Artre, *s.m.* (*bird*) kingfisher

Artuson, *s.m. V.* **Artison**

Arum, *s.m.* (*bot.*) *V.* **Gouet**

Arundo, *s.f.* (*bot.*) arundo

Aruspice, *s.m.* aruspice

Aruspicine, *s.f.* aruspicy

Aryen, ne, *adj. s.* Aryan

As, *s.m.* ace; (*Roman ant.*) as

Asaret, *s.m.* (*bot.*) asarabacca, asarum

Asbeste, *s.m.* asbestus, asbestos

Asboline, *s.f.* (*chem.*) asboline

Ascaride, *s.m.* (*zool.*) ascaris [ascendency

Ascendance, *s.f.* ascending line; ascent;

Ascendant, e, *adj.* ascending; upward; ascendant

Ascendant, *s.m.* ascendency; influence; power; superiority; ruling passion; inclination; luck; ascendant

Ascenseur, *s.m.* lift, hoist

Ascension, *s.f.* ascent, rising; ascension; Ascension-day; (*mach.*) up-stroke

Ascensioniste, *s.m.f.* climber, balloonist, balloon-excursionist, ascensionist

Ascensionnel, le, *adj.* upward, up, ascensional. *Mouvement —*, (*mach.*) up-stroke; (*fig.*) upward motion [*adj.* ascetic

Ascète, Ascétique, *s.m.f.* (*pers.*), **Ascétique,**

Ascétique, *s.* (*things*); — *s.m.* ascetic work; — *s.f.* ascetic theology; ethics

Ascétisme, *s.m.* asceticism

Aschée, *s.f. V.* **Achée**

Ascidie, *s.f.* (*zool.*) ascidia

Ascidiens, *s.m.pl.* (*zool.*) ascidians

Asciens, *s.m.pl.* (*geog.*) ascians

Ascite, *s.f.* (*med.*) ascites; — *adj.* ascitic

Ascitique, *adj. s.m.f.* (*med.*) ascitic

Asclépiade, *s.m.* (*vers.*) asclepiad; — *s.f.* (*bot.*) asclepias, swallow-wort

Aselle, *s.m.* (*zool.*) wood-louse

Asexe, Asexuel, le, *adj.* (*bot.*) asexual

‡Asiarchat, *s.m.* (*hist.*) asiarchy

Asiarque, *s.m.* (*hist.*) asiarch

Asiatique, *adj. s.* Asiatic; Asiatic fashion

Asile, *s.m.* asylum; refuge; shelter; home; abode; retreat; sanctuary; protection; (*zool.*) wasp-fly. — *des pauvres,* poor-house, workhouse. *Salle d'—*, infant-school. — *-frelon,* wasp-fly

Asimine, *s.f. V.* **Corossol**

Asiminier, Asimina, *s.m. V.* **Corossolier**

Asine, *adj.f.* ass, asinine, of asses, of the ass. *Bête —*, ass. *Espèce* or *race —*, asinine species *or* race, ass species

Asoca, *s.m.* (*bot.*) asoca

Asparagine, *s.f.* (*chem.*) asparagine

Aspect, *s.m.* aspect; sight; view; point of view; prospect; look, appearance, air; face; phase; bearing

Asperge, *s.f.* asparagus

Aspergement, *s.m.* sprinkling, besprinkling

Asperger, *v.a.* to sprinkle, to besprinkle

Aspergerie, *s.f. V.* **Aspergière** [aspergeoire

Aspergès, *s.m.* aspergill, holy-water sprinkler;

Aspergière, *s.f.* asparagus-bed *or* ground

Aspergille, *s.m.* (*zool.*) aspergillum, watering-pot shell; (*bot.*) aspergillus

Aspergilliforme, *adj.* (*bot.*) aspergilliform

Aspérité, *s.f.* asperity, roughness; ruggedness, unevenness; harshness [kling

Aspersion, *s.f.* aspersion, sprinkling, besprin-

Aspersoir, *s.m.* aspergill, holy-water sprinkler; rose (*of a water-pot*)

Aspérule, *s.f.* (*bot.*) asperula, woodruff

Asphaltage, *s.m.* asphalting; asphalte

Asphalte, *s.m.* asphalt, asphaltum; asphalte

Asphalter, *v.a.* to asphalt

Asphaltique, *adj.* asphaltic

Asphaltite, *adj.* (*geog.*) Asphaltic

Asphodèle, *s.m.* (*bot.*) asphodel, daffodil

Asphyxiant, e, *part. adj.* asphyxiating, suffocating; — *s.m.* asphyxiant

Asphyxie, *s.f.* asphyxia, asphyxy, suspended animation, suffocation

Asphyxié, e, *adj.* asphyxiated, asphyxied; — *s.m.f.* person suffocated, person apparently drowned [occasion asphyxia, to suffocate

Asphyxier, *v.a.* to asphyxiate, to cause *or*

S'—, *v.r.* to destroy oneself by asphyxia, to suffocate oneself; to be suffocated

Aspic, *s.m.* (*zool.*) asp, aspic; (*anc. artil., cook.*) aspic; (*bot.*) spike, spike-lavender, aspic; (*fig.*) slanderer, backbiter

Aspidie, *s.f.* (*bot.*) shield-fern

†Aspirail, *s.m.* (*tech.*) vent-hole

Aspirant, e, *s.m.f.* aspirant; candidate; probationer; midshipman. — *de marine,* midshipman, naval cadet [exhausting

Aspira-teur, trice, *adj.* (*phys., tech.*) sucking;

Aspirateur, *s.m.* (*tech.*) aspirator; vent-hole; (*of air-pumps*) exhauster [ration

Aspirati-f, ve, *adj.* (*gram.*) aspirate; of aspi-

Aspiration, *s.f.* inspiration, inhaling; (*fig.*) aspiration, aspiring, yearning, longing; (*phys., of pumps*) exhaustion, suction; (*bot.*) suction; (*gram.*) aspiration, breathing

Aspiratoire, *adj.* aspiratory

Aspiré, e, *adj.*, **Aspirée,** *s.f.* (*gram.*) aspirate

Aspirer, *v.a.n.* to inhale, to inspire; to suck, to suck in; to draw in; to snuff in; to sniff; to exhaust; to aspirate; to aspire; to yearn, to long; to pretend; to aim [pirated

S'—, *v.r.* to be inhaled, &c.; (*gram.*) to be as-

Aspre, *s.m.* asper (*Turkish coin*)

Assabler, *v.a. V.* **Ensabler**

Assa-fœtida, *s.f.* (*pharm.*) assafœtida [sieger

†Assaillant, *s.m.* assailant; aggressor; be-

†Assaillir, *v.a.* to assail; to assault; to attack; to fall *or* come upon; to surprise; to beset

Assainir, *v.a.* to render healthy; to purify; to drain [be purified; to be drained

S'—, *v.r.* to become *or* be made healthy; to

Assainissement, *s.m.* rendering healthy; purification; draining, drainage; salubrity, healthiness; health [ment; seasoner; dressing

Assaisonnement, *s.m.* seasoning; condi-

Assaisonner, *v.a.* to season; to dress; to heighten; to set off; to temper

Assaisonneu-r, se, *s.m.f.* seasoner

Assassin, e, *s.m.f.* murderer, murderess, assassin; ruffian; — *adj.* murderous, killing. *A l'—!* murder! *Crier à l'—*, to call out murder

Assassinat, *s.m.* murder, wilful murder, assassination

Assassiner, *v.a.* to murder, to assassinate; to kill; to assault; to tire to death, to worry, to bore, to plague [ing in its own juice

Assation, *s.f.* (*pharm.*) assation, roasting, stew-

Assaut, *s.m.* assault; storm; storming; shock; attack; onset; violence; struggle; trial; alarm; fencing-match *or* bout, match, bout, round. *—d'armes,* fencing-match, fencing-bout, assault of arms. *Donner* or *livrer l'— à,* to storm. *Faire —,* (*fenc.*) to have a fencing-match, to fence. *Faire — de,* to vie in [draining, drainage
Asséchage, Assèchement, *s.m.* drying;
Assécher, *v.a.n.* to drain; to dry up; to become dry; (*nav.*) to be left dry, to appear dry
Assécution, *s.f.* (*can. law*) assecution, obtainment of a living
Asséieur, *s.m.* (*old*) assessor of taxes
Assemblage, *s.m.* assemblage; collection; rakings, lot, set; combination; mixture, jumble; union; gathering; (*carp.*) joining, scarfing, scarf, bond, tabling
Assemblée, *s.f.* assembly; meeting; convocation; call; company, party; society; congregation; fittings; (*hunt.*) meet
Assembler, *v.a.* to assemble; to collect; to get *or* bring *or* put *or* lay together; to convoke, to call together, to summon; to join; to gather; (*carp.*) to trim, to scarf, to join; (*mil.*) to muster
S'—, *v.r.* to assemble, to meet; to congregate; to come *or* get *or* gather *or* flock together; to muster
Assembleu-r, se, *s.m.f.* collector; gatherer
Asséner, *v.a.* to strike, to hit, to deal
Assentement, Assentiment, *s.m.* (*hunt.*)
Assentiment, *s.m.* assent [scent
Assentir, *v.n.* to assent; (*hunt.*) to scent
Asseoir, *v.a.* to seat; to set; to lay; to fix; to establish; to ground; to found; to settle; to pitch. *Faire —,* to make (...) sit down; to give *or* offer (...) a seat; to ask (...) to sit down; to seat; to admit
S'—, *v.r.* to sit down, to sit, to take o.'s (*or* a) seat *or* place; to be seated; to settle; to become settled; to rest; to perch; (*pop.*) to fall down. *Envoyer s'—,* (*pop.*) to knock down; to send away. *Asseyez-vous,* sit down. *Allez vous —,* go and sit down; (*pop.*) go along with you, hold your tongue, shut up
Assermenter, *v.a.* to swear in, to swear
Asserteur, *s.m.* assertor, defender
Asserti-f, ve, *adj.* assertive, dogmatical
Assertion, *s.f.* assertion; affirmation
Assertivement, *adv.* assertively, affirmatively
Assertoire, *adj.* assertory
Asservir, *v.a.* to reduce to servitude; to enslave; to subject; to subdue; to conquer; to master
S'—, *v.r.* to be enslaved *or* subjected; to make oneself a slave, to subject oneself, to submit, to be a slave
Asservissable, *adj.* conquerable
Asservissant, e, *adj.* of servitude; enslaving; slavish; coercive; fettering
Asservissement, *s.m.* servitude; slavery; inthralment; subjection; bondage
Asservisseur, *s.m.* enslaver [judge
Assesseur, *s.m.* assessor, assistant; assistant-
Assessorat, *s.m.* assessorship
Assessorial, e, *adj.* assessorial
Assette, *s.f.* adze, hatchet, hammer
Asseulé, e, *adj.* lonely, solitary [to leave alone
Asseuler, *v.a.* to abandon, to forsake, to desert,
Assez, *adv.* enough; sufficiently; su cient; long enough; often enough; commonly enough; tolerably; somewha ; rather; pretty; pretty near; so (... as); such a, such (... as). *— bien,* pretty well, well enough. *Bien —,* quite enough. *— de,* enough of, a sufficiency of, enough, sufficient, tolerable. *— joli,* rather pretty. *— mauvais,* indifferent; bad enough; somewhat uncomfortable. *— mal,* indifferently; badly enough, bad enough; somewhat uncomfortably. *— peu,* little enough, but little, indifferently; so little (as). *— semblable,* not unlike. *— souvent,* not unfrequently, often enough, pretty often. *— volontiers, d'— bon cœur,* not unwillingly, readily enough; commonly enough

Assident, e, *adj.* (*med.*) assident
Assidu, e, *adj.* assiduous; punctual; constant; diligent; attentive
Assiduité, *s.f.* assiduity; regular attendance; punctuality; constancy; diligence; application; attention
Assidûment, *adv.* assiduously; punctually; constantly; diligently; attentively
Assiégeable, *adj.* besiegeable
Assiégeant, e, *part. adj.* besieging
Assiégeant, *s.m.* besieger [crowd
Assiéger, *v.a.* to besiege; to beset; to dun; to
Assiette, *s.f.* plate; plateful; situation; site; position; proper position; state; usual *or* proper state; disposition; humour, temper; assessment; fund; level; balance; ground; (*riding*) seat; (*of a ship*) trim. *— plate,* flat plate, din-
Assiettée, *s.f.* plateful [ner-plate
†**Assignable,** *adj.* assignable
†**Assignant, e,** *s.m.f.* plaintiff
†**Assignat,** *s.m.* (*obsolete*) assignat (*paper-money*); settlement. *Legs par —,* specific legacy
†**Assignation,** *s.f.* assignation; assignment; transfer; warrant; cheque; appointment; summons, citation; writ; subpœna
†**Assigné, e,** *s.m.f.* defendant; respondent
†**Assigner,** *v.a.* to assign; to allot; to allow; to appoint; to summon, to cite; to subpœna
Assimilable, *adj.* assimilable
Assimila-teur, trice, Assimilati-f, ve, *adj.* assimilative
Assimilation, *s.f.* assimilation [pare
Assimiler, *v.a.* to assimilate; to liken, to com-
Assiminier, *s.m. V.* **Asiminier**
Assis, e, *adj.* seated, sitting; situated; placed; laid; established; resting
Assis, *s.m.* sitting. *Par — et levé,* by sitting and rising, by sitting and standing
Assise, *s.f.* (**—s,** *pl.*) (*arch.*) course; (*geol.*) layer, stratum; **—s,** *pl.* (*no sing.*) assizes, assize, sessions
Assistance, *s.f.* assistance, aid, help, succour; relief; charity; attendance; assembly; company; audience; congregation. *— publique,* public charity; relief of the poor; poor-law; poor-law board *or* commissioners
Assistant, e, *s.m.f. adj.* person present; bystander, looker-on, spectator, beholder; assistant. *Les —s,* those present, the by-standers, the spectators; the assembly, the company, the attendance, the audience; the congregation
Assister, *v.a.n.* to assist, to help, to aid, to succour; to relieve; to support; to see to; to enforce; to take part; to attend; to be present; to be (at); to stand by, to look on, to witness, to be a witness (of); to sit
Associable, *adj.* associable
Association, *s.f.* association; combination; union; confederacy; assembly; society; partnership [companion; confederate; partner
Associé, e, *s.m.f.* associate, member, fellow;
Associer, *v.a.* to associate; to admit to a share (of); to unite, to join, to combine; to take into partnership
S'—, *v.r.* to associate oneself; to associate; to keep company (with); to take a part; to share (in); to take as associate *or* associates; to take as a companion *or* partner; to admit as a member; to unite, to join, to combine; to club; to enter into partnership
Assolement, *s.m.* rotation of crops
Assoler, *v.a.* to have a rotation of crops on
Assombrir, *v.a.* to darken, to obscure; to make gloomy; to throw a gloom over; to gloom; to cloud; to sadden
S'—, *v.r.* to darken, to be darkened; to become (*or* grow *or* get) gloomy *or* cloudy *or* sad
Assommant, e, *adj.* killing; oppressive; overwhelming; dreadfully tiresome *or* dull, wearisome, exceedingly annoying *or* troublesome, plaguing, boring
Assommer, *v.a.* to knock down; to kill; to

fell; to slaughter; to murder; to beat soundly *or* unmercifully; to overwhelm; to confound, to dumbfound; to weary to death, to plague, to bore

Assommeur, *s.m.* feller; slaughterman, slaughterer; killer; fighter, bully; plague, bore

Assommoir, *s.m.* pole-axe; bludgeon, life-preserver; shillelagh; tomahawk; dead-fall, trap; dead-weight; plague, bore; dram-shop

Assompti-f, ve, *adj.* assumptive

Assomption, *s.f.* assumption

Assonah, *s.f. V.* **Sonna**

Assonnance, *s.f.* assonance

Assonnant, e, *adj.* assonant

Assorath, *s.f. V.* **Surate**

Assortiment, *s.m.* assortment; stock; set; suit; collection; match; suitableness; sorting; (*print.*) sorts; (*pop.*) cheese-scraps, hotch-potch. *Livres* (*m.pl.*) or *fonds* (*m.sing.*) *d'—*, miscellaneous stock, stock-books, books not published by the vendor. *Libraire d'—*, wholesale bookseller

Assortir, *v.a.n.*, **S'—,** *v.r.* to match; to assort; to sort; to suit; to pair; to stock, to supply

Assortissant, e, *adj.* suitable, suiting, becoming, matching, to match, to correspond

Assoter, *v.a.* to infatuate, to besot; to abash

S'—, *v.r.* to be infatuated, &c.

Assoupi, e, *adj.* drowsy; sleepy; slumbering, dozing, napping; sleeping; asleep; laid asleep; lying dormant; hushed up; appeased

Assoupir, *v.a.* to make drowsy *or* sleepy; to send to sleep; to lull; to dull; to deaden; to stop; to hush; to hush up; to calm; to still; to appease; to quell

S'—, *v.r.* to get drowsy *or* sleepy; to fall asleep; to go to sleep; to slumber, to doze; to lull; to die away; to be appeased *or* &c.

Assoupissant, e, *adj.* inducing sleep, soporific, drowsy, sleepy; dull, humdrum

Assoupissement, *s.m.* drowsiness; sleepiness; heaviness; slumber; carelessness, supineness, sloth; appeasement; hushing; (*med.*) coma

Assoupli, e, *part. adj.* made supple *or* &c., softened, supple, soft, flexible; easy; bent; broken; tractable, docile

Assouplir, *v.a.* to make (*or* render) supple *or* flexible *or* tractable; to soften; to bend; to tame; to break (*horses*, &c.)

S'—, *v.r.* to become supple *or* easy *or* &c.; to bend

Assourdir, *v.a.* to deafen; to stun the ears of; to stun; to muffle; to deaden; (*paint.*) to darken

S'—, *v.r.* to grow deaf, to become hard of hearing

Assourdissement, *s.m.* deafening; temporary deafness; deafening noise; muffling; deadening; darkening

Assouvir, *v.a.* to satiate; to glut; to gorge; to gratify

S'—, *v.r.* to be satiated *or* glutted; to satiate o.'s hunger *or* thirst; to gorge

Assouvissement, *s.m.* satiating; glutting; gorging; gratification

Assujétir, Assujettir, *v.a.* to subject; to subdue; to bring under subjection; to master, to conquer, to overcome; to bind, to tie down, to confine, to fetter; to compel, to constrain; to fix, to fasten, to make steady

S'—, *v.r.* to subject *or* tie oneself; to submit

Assujétissant, Assujettissant, e, *adj.* slavish, that ties down, restrictive, binding, constraining, confining, fettering, hard

Assujétissement, Assujettissement, *s.m.* subjection; submission; slavery; dependence; constraint, restraint; tie; exigency

Assumer, *v.a.* to assume

Assurable, *adj.* assurable, insurable

Assurance, *s.f.* assurance; certainty; reliance, trust; confidence; boldness; safety; security; promise; protestation; proof; firmness; steadiness; insurance

Assure, *s.f.* weft, woof, texture

Assuré, e, *adj.* assured; secure; safe; sure, certain; confident, bold; impudent; steady, firm; —*adj.s.* insured; policy-holder. *Mal —*, insecure, unsafe; uncertain; unsteady; shaky; tottering; faltering; feeble, weak, faint

Assurément, *adv.* assuredly, surely, to be sure; doubtless, certainly, sure enough; boldly, confidently, steadily

Assurer, *v.a.* to assure; to secure; to make sure *or* firm *or* steady; to steady; to fix; to fasten; to give boldness to, to embolden; to encourage; to compose; to assert, to affirm; to promise; to confirm; to settle; to guarantee; to insure; (*rid.*) to accustom to the bit. — *son pavillon*, (*nav.*) to fire a gun under proper colours

S'—, *v.r.* to secure; to assure oneself; to make sure (of, that); to ascertain; to rely, to trust; to be confident; to be sure, to feel assured; to secure oneself

Assureur, *s.m.* insurer, assurer, underwriter

Assurgent, e, *adj.* (*bot.*) assurgent

Assyrien, ne, *adj. s.* Assyrian

Astacites, *s.f.pl.*, **Astacolithes,** *s.m.pl.* (*fossils*) astacolites

Astarté, *s.f.* (*zool.*) astarte

Astatique, *adj.* (*phys.*) astatic

Astéisme, *s.m.* (*rhet.*) asteism

Astelle, *s.f.* (*surg.*) splint, bolster

Aster, *s.m.*, **Astère,** *s.f.* (*bot.*) aster, starwort

Astérie, *s.f.* (*min.*) asteria, cat's-eye; asterite, star-stone; (*zool.*) asterias, star-fish; (*phys.*) play of colours

Astérisme, *s.m.* asterism, star-like opalescence, play of colours

Astérisque, Astérique, *s.m.* asterisk, star

Astéroïde, *s.m.* (*astr.*) asteroid, planetoid

Asthénie, *s.f.* (*med.*) asthenia, astheny

Asthén-ique, -ologie. *V.* page 3, § 1

Asthmatique, *adj. s.* asthmatic

Asthme, *s.m.* asthma

Astic, *s.m.* glazing-stick, polisher; rotten-stone

Asticot, *s.m.* maggot, gentle, worm

Asticoter, *v.a.* to tease, to vex, to plague

Astiquer, *v.a.* to polish; to clean up, to furbish up; to dress up, to make spruce, to spruce up; to provoke; to drub

S'—, *v.r.* to dress *or* spruce oneself up; to wrangle, to spar

Astracan, Astrakan, *s.m.* (*fur*) astracan, astrakhan

Astragale, *s.m.* (*arch., artil., tech.*) astragal; (*anat.*) astragalus, ankle-bone; (*bot.*) astragalus, milk-vetch; (*gilding, paint.*) fillet

Astral, e, *adj.* astral

Astre, *s.m.* star; luminary

Astrée, *s.f.* (*astr., zool.*) astræa, astrea

Astreindre, *v.a.* to subject, to bind, to tie down; to compel, to force, to constrain, to oblige

Astriction, *s.f.* (*med.*) astriction

Astringence, *s.f.* (*med.*) astringency

Astringent, e, *adj.*, **Astringent,** *s.m.* (*med.*) astringent

Astrolabe, *s.m.* (*astr.*) astrolabe

Astrolâtre, *s.m.f.* star-worshipper

Astrol-âtrie, -ogie, -ogique, &c. *V.* page 3, § 1

Astrologue, *s.m.* astrologer

Astromètre, *s.m.* astrometer

Astronome, *s.m.* astronomer

Astronom-ie, -ique, -iquement. *V.* page 3, § 1

Astuce, *s.f.* cunning, craft, wile, guile

Astucieusement, *adv.* craftily, cunningly

Astucieu-x, se, *adj.* crafty, cunning, astute

Asturien, ne, *adj. s.* Asturian

Asyle, *s.m. V.* **Asile**

Asymétrie, *s.f.* asymmetry

Asymétrique, *adj.* asymmetrical

Asymptote, *s.f.* (*geom.*) asymptote

Asymptotique, *adj.* asymptotic, asymptotical

Atabale, *s.m.* atabal (*Moorish tabor*)

Ataghan, *s.m. V.* **Yatagan**

Ata-raxie, -xie, -xique. *V.* page 3, § 1

Atavisme, *s.m.* atavism

Atèle, *s.m.* (*zool.*) ateles, spider-monkey

Atelier, *s.m.* workshop; shop; shed; manufactory; workroom; composing-room; room; office; studio; gang; workmen, workpeople; compositors; pupils; (*fort.*) opening of trenches. *Jour d'—*, (*paint., sculp.*) best light

Atellanes, *s.f.pl.* (*hist.*) atellans
Atermoiement, *s.m.* delay of payment, composition, gaining time, delay; evasion, shift
Atermoyer, *v.a.* to delay the payment of, to put off; — *v.n.* to try to gain time, to shuffle, to shirk
S'—, *v.r.* to compound with o.'s creditors
Athée, *s.m.f.* atheist; — *adj.* atheistical
Athéisme, *s.m.* atheism
Athénée, *s.m.* athenæum
Athénien, ne, *adj.s.m.f.* Athenian; — *s.f.* antique scent-box *or* flower-vase; Athenian fashion
Athérine, *s.f.* (*fish*) atherine, sand-smelt
Athermane, Athermique, *adj.* (*phys.*) athermanous
Athérome, *s.m.* (*med.*) atheroma
Athlète, *s.m.* athlete; wrestler; champion; antagonist, combatant, adversary
Athlétique, *adj.* athletic; — *s.f.* athletics, athleticism
Athlétiquement, *adv.* athletically
Atinter, *v.a.* to trick *or* rig out
Atlante, *s.m.* (*arch.*) atlantis; — *s.f.* (*zool.*) atlanta
Atlantides, *s.f.pl.* (*astr.*) Atlantides
Atlantique, *adj. s.m.* Atlantic. *Format* —, (*print.*) broadside
Atlas, *s.m.* atlas
Atmidomètre, Atmomètre, *s.m.* atmidometer, atmometer
Atmosphère, *s.f.* atmosphere
Atmosphérique, *adj.* atmospheric
Atome, *s.m.* atom
Atom-ique, -isme, -iste, -istique. *V.* page [3, § 1
Atone, *adj.* dull, without expression, fixed, haggard, staring
Atonie, *s.f.* atony, weakness, debility, relaxation
Atonique, *adj.* (*med.*) atonic
Atourner, *v.a.* to attire, to dress out
Atours, *s.m.pl.* attire, dress; ornaments; finery. *Dame d'*—, lady of the bed-chamber
Atout, *s.m.* (*at cards*) trump; (*pop.*) knock, blow, smash; quietus; pluck
Atoxique, *adj.* without venom
Atrabilaire, *adj. s.* atrabilarian, atrabilious; morose, peevish, irritable; splenetic
Atrabile, *s.f.* atrabilis, hypochondria
Atramentaire, *adj.* atramental, inky
Âtre, *s.m.* hearth, fire-place
Atroce, *adj.* atrocious; heinous; odious; cruel; wicked; violent, excruciating; outrageous; enormous; dreadful; horrid
Atrocement, *adv.* atrociously; heinously; cruelly; wickedly; violently; outrageously; enormously; dreadfully; horridly
Atrocité, *s.f.* atrocity; heinousness; cruelty; wickedness; violence; enormity; wretched state
Atrophie, *s.f.* (*med.*) atrophy
Atrophié, e, *adj.* atrophied; wasted; withered; stunted, undeveloped
Atrophier, *v.a.* to atrophy, to waste, to wither, to stunt
S'—, *v.r.* to become atrophied, to waste away
Atropine, *s.f.* (*chem.*) atropia, atropine
Atropos, *s.m.* (*zool.*) atropos, death's-head moth
Attabale, *s.m.* *V.* **Atabale**
Attablé, e, *part.adj.* seated *or* sitting at table, at table
Attablée, *s.f.* tableful (*of people*), table (occupied by...)
Attabler, *v.a.* to set to table
S'—, *v.r.* to sit down to table, to take o.'s place at table, to sit at table
Attachant, e, *adj.* interesting, engaging; captivating; attractive; winning; taking; pleasing; endearing; lovely; confining
Attache, *s.f.* tie; tether; thong; leash; string; cord; strap; band; binder; brace; rivet; chain; clasp; buckle; fastening; bond, attachment; affection; fondness; connection; consent; (*of diamonds*) cluster; (*anat., paint., sculp.*) attachment; (*of horses*) stabling. *A l'*—, tied up. *Être d'*—, to be attached to o.'s masters, to be capable of attachment. *Mettre à l'*—, to tie up. *Prendre à l'*—, to take in (*horses*)
Attaché, e, *part. adj.* attached, &c. (*V.* **Attacher**); fond (of); bent (on), intent (on); wedded (to); sticking; clinging; cleaving; hanging; pursuing, following, dogging
Attaché, *s.m.* attaché (*of an embassy*)
Attachement, *s.m.* attachment, affection, fondness; love; regard; inclination; attention; application; zeal; tie, bond; —**s,** *pl.* (*arch.*) memoranda of work done
Attacher, *v.a.* to attach; to fasten; to tie; to bind; to connect; to join; to couple; to sew on; to nail; to pin; to button; to stick; to place; to set; to put; to apply; to give; to interest; to engage; to captivate; to attract; to allure; to win; to endear; to fix; to rivet; to occupy; to confine; to absorb
S'—, *v.r.* to attach oneself *or* to oneself; to attach; to fasten oneself; to fasten; to tie; to stick; to cling; to cleave; to pursue, to follow, to dog; to be fixed; to apply oneself, to endeavour, to strive; to set (upon); to be bent (on); to interest oneself; to gain to oneself, to win; to be wedded (to); to be (*or* become) attached *or* connected *or* &c.
Attaquable, *adj.* assailable; impeachable; objectionable; doubtful, questionable; actionable
Attaquant, *s.m.* assailant; aggressor
Attaque, *s.f.* attack; onset; assault; attempt; approach; insult; reproach; aggression; fit, stroke, touch. *D'*—, of *or* from attack; attacking; plucky, brisk; pluckily, briskly
Attaquer, *v.a.* to attack; to assail; to assault; to fall upon; to quarrel with; to reproach; to impugn; to censure; to counteract; to strike; to affect; to seize; to set to; to begin; to open; to cut into; to attempt; to strike up, to play, to sing; to spur on; to contest the validity of; to sue; to near (*a coast*)
S'—, *v.r.* to attack; to set *or* fall (upon); to challenge; to meddle (with), to interfere (with); to find fault (with); to attack each other; to be attacked *or* &c.
Attardé, e, *adj.* late, behind o.'s time, behind time, behind, behindhand, staying late *or* after the time, lingering, belated, benighted
Attarder, *v.a.* to make late, to delay, to detain
S'—, *v.r.* to make oneself late; to be late, to be belated *or* benighted; to start *or* stay late; to be out late; to keep late hours; to remain *or* stay out; to loiter; to linger
Atteindre, *v.a.n.* to reach; to attain; to get at; to strike; to hit; to touch; to hurt, to injure; to overtake; to catch; to join; to equal; to come up to; to come to; to come upon; to attack, to affect, to afflict, to seize; to infect; to charge (with)
Atteinte, *s.f.* blow, hit, stroke, injury, prejudice, hurt, harm; flaw; impression; effect; pang; breach, violation; reach; gripe; attack; fit, touch; offence; outrage; (*rid.*) attaint. *Porter* or *donner* — *à*, to injure, to prejudice, to hurt; to impair; to alter; to shake; to violate, to infringe; to commit an offence against; to be derogatory to; to lower
Attel, *s.m.* hame
Attelabe, *s.m.* (*insect*) attelabus, weevil
Attelage, *s.m.* team, set, horses; yoke, oxen; carriage, vehicle; harness; (*tech.*) draw-gear; (*rail.*) couplings
Attelé, e, *part. adj.* put to, harnessed; ready; yoked; attached; coupled; joined. — *à*, put to; drawing. — *de*, drawn by
Attelée, *s.f.* harnessing; yoking; being in harness *or* under the yoke, drawing, pull
Atteler, *v.a.* to put to, to harness; to put the horses to (a vehicle), to get ready; to yoke; to attach; to couple; to join
Attelle, *s.f.* hame; (*surg.*) splint
Attellement, *s.m.* harnessing; yoking; coupling; joining
Atteloire, *s.f.* (*of a carriage*) trace-bolt
Attenant, e, *adj.* adjoining, contiguous, next
Attenant, *prep. adv.* next to, close by
Attendant (En), waiting; in the meantime, meanwhile, in the interim, till then; till; till (...) comes *or* is ready; yet; with all that. — *que*, until, till. — *mieux*, until something better is done *or* takes place *or* happens *or* turns up

Attendre, *v.a.n.* to wait for; to wait; to stay, to stop; to tarry; to delay, to defer; to keep; to expect; to await; to hope for; to look for; to expect to catch; to be in store for; to be provided *or* ready for; to dance attendance. — *après,* to wait for; to be in want of. *Faire* —, to keep waiting; to keep waiting for; to promise. *Se faire* —, to keep one (*or* people) waiting, to be long coming, not to come, to be behind time

S'—, *v.r.* to wait for each other; to expect; to rely, to depend; to be prepared (for); to be waited for; to be expected *or* awaited. *Attendez-vous-y!* you may expect it; depend upon it; (*ironically*) I wish you may get it!

Attendri, e, *part. adj.* affected, &c. (*V.* **Attendrir**); tender; mellow; of *or* with emotion

Attendrir, *v.a.* to make tender; to affect, to move, to move to pity, to soften; to excite pity; to make mellow (*tipsy*)

S'—, *v.r.* to get (*or* become) tender; to be affected *or* moved, to be moved to pity, to feel pity; to soften, to relent; to be favourably disposed; to melt; to become mellow

Attendrissement, *s.m.* making tender; feeling, sensibility, tenderness; emotion; compassion, pity

Attendu, *prep.* considering, in consideration of, on account of. — *que,* considering that, whereas, as, inasmuch as, because, since

Attenir, *v.n.* to adjoin, to be contiguous

Attentat, *s.m.* criminal attempt, attempt; attack; crime; misdeed; deed; outrage; violation, infringement

Attentatoire, *adj.* attempting, hostile; outrageous, unlawful, criminal; in contempt (of)

Attente, *s.f.* waiting; staying, stopping; expectation, hope. *D'*—, (*adject.*) waiting; temporary

Attenter, *v.n.a.* to attempt

Attenti-f, ve, *adj.* attentive; mindful; anxious; studious; intent *or* bent (on); considerate

Attention, *s.f.* attention; care, heed; regard, considerateness; kindness; notice. *Faire* —, to pay attention, to attend, to mind, to heed; to take care; to take notice; to notice, to observe; to consider; to mark; to trouble oneself (about); to mention. — *au commandement!* (*mil.*) attention!

Attentionné, e, *adj.* showing attentions, attentive, considerate

Attentivement, *adv.* attentively, carefully, wistfully

Atténuant, e, *adj.* attenuating, attenuant; (*law*) extenuating

Atténuant, *s.m.* (*med.*) attenuant

Atténuation, *s.f.* attenuation; weakness; extenuation, mitigation, palliation

Atténuer, *v.a.* to attenuate; to weaken; to extenuate; to waste; to diminish; to deaden; to underrate; to mitigate, to palliate; to lighten

S'—, *v.r.* to be attenuated, &c.; to lessen

Atterrage, *s.m.* landing, making land; landfall, land

Atterré, e, *adj.* aground, ashore; astounded, thunderstruck

Atterrement, *s.m.* throwing down; ruin; prostration; terror

Atterrer, *v.a.* to throw *or* strike down; to overturn, to overthrow, to subvert, to crush, to destroy, to ruin; to cast down, to discourage; to overwhelm; to startle, to astound, to thunderstrike; — *v.n.* (*nav.*) to land, to make land

Atterri, e, *adj.* aground, ashore

Atterrir, *v.n.* to land, to make land; — *v.a.* to choke up, to silt

Atterrissage, *s.m.* landing, making land

Atterrissement, *s.m.* alluvium, alluvion, accretion; landing

Attestation, *s.f.* attestation, certificate; oath, affidavit

Attester, *v.a.* to attest; to testify; to vouch; to certify; to bear witness to; to witness; to affirm; to prove; to call to witness

Attic-isme, -iste. *V.* page 3, § 1

Attiédir, *v.a.* to make lukewarm; to cool, to abate; to render careless

S'—, *v.r.* to become (*or* grow) lukewarm *or* cool, to cool, to abate; to become careless *or* indifferent

Attiédissement, *s.m.* lukewarmness; coolness, abatement; indifference

Attifement, *s.m.* rigging, toggery

Attifer, *v.a.* to rig *or* dress out

Attifet, *s.m.* head-dress, head-gear; trinket

Attinter, *v.a.* (*nav.*) *V.* **Tinter**

Attique, *adj.m.f., s.m.* Attic; (*arch.*) attic; — **(L')** *s.f.* Attica

Attiquement, *adv.* in the Attic dialect; in the Attic fashion *or* style

Attirable, *adj.* attractable

†Attirail, *s.m.* implements; utensils; apparatus; gear, tackle; furniture; equipage, train, baggage, luggage, paraphernalia; stores; show, pomp

Attirant, e, *adj.* attractive, alluring, engaging

Attirer, *v.a.* to attract; to draw; to entice; to allure; to decoy; to win, to gain; to draw on; to bring on *or* over; to bring; to procure; to induce; to excite; to incite; to inspire

S'—, *v.r.* to gain, to win; to bring *or* draw on oneself; to incur; to make (*enemies*); to get into (*scrapes,* &c.); to excite; to attract; to attract each other; to be attracted *or* drawn

Attiser, *v.a.* to stir, to stir up (*the fire*); to poke (*the fire*); (*fig.*) to incense, to exasperate. — *le feu,* (*fig.*) to fan the flame

Attisoir, Attisonnoir, *s.m.* (*tech.*) poker

Attitré, e, *adj.* regular; usual, ordinary; appointed; recognized; accredited; posted; bribed, hired, hireling

Attitrer, *v.a.* to appoint, to name; to commission; to place in ambush, to keep under covert; to bribe, to hire

Attitude, *s.f.* attitude, posture

Attole, Attolon, *s.m.* cluster of small islands

Attouchement, *s.m.* touch, feeling; contact

Attrac-teur, trice, *adj.* attractile

Attracti-f, ve, *adj.* attractive

Attraction, *s.f.* attraction

Attraire, *v.a.* to attract, to allure, to entice

Attrait, *s.m.* attraction; allurement; bait; charm; taste; inclination; (*rel.*) comfort, consolation; (*tech.*) materials

Attrape, *s.f.* trick, take-in, hoax, sell, bite, catch; bait; snare, trap; (*tech.*) pincers; (*nav.*) relieving tackle

Attrape, *s.m.f.* (*in compounds, from* **Attraper,** "to catch," &c.) thing *or* animal (*m.*) *or* person (*m.f.*) that catches, &c., catcher. — **-mouches,** *s.m.* (*plant*) catchfly, fly-trap; (*bird*) fly-catcher. — **-niais,** — **-nigauds,** — **-lourdauds,** *s.m.* fool-trap, vulgar trick; clap-trap; catchpenny. — **-parterre,** *s.m.* clap-trap for the pit, clap-trap

Attraper, *v.a.* to catch; to entrap, to ensnare; to take by surprise; to overtake; to reach; to seize, to lay hold of; to overreach; to take in, to cheat; to disappoint; to play a trick to, to hoax; to chouse; to get; to obtain; to pick up; to strike; to hit; to hit off, to take off; to take; to imitate; to knock. *Attrape!* you are caught! take that! that's for your pains! it serves you right!

S'—, *v.r.* to catch *or* &c. each other; to be caught, &c.; to catch; to knock oneself; (*rid.*) to overstep, to clip

Attrapeu-r, se, *s.m.f.* catcher; hunter; deceiver, cheat, trickster, cozener

Attrapoire, *s.f.* trap, snare, pitfall; trick

Attrayant, e, *adj.* attractive, alluring, engaging

Attrempage, *s.m.* heating; annealing; tempering

Attremper, *v.a.* to heat; to anneal; to temper

Attribuable, *adj.* attributable, ascribable; imputable

Attribuer, *v.a.* to attribute; to ascribe; to impute; to attach, to assign; to grant; to confer; to award

S'—, *v.r.* to attribute to oneself; to claim as o.'s own; to assume, to take upon oneself; to be attributed, &c.

Attribut, *s.m.* attribute; quality; prerogative; privilege; symbol, emblem

Attributi-f, ve, *adj.* attributive; (*law*) relative
Attribution, *s.f.* conferring; privilege; **—s,** *pl.* functions, duties; powers; province, department; (*law*) competence
Attriquer, *v.a.* (*pop.*) to buy (*stolen goods*)
Attriqueu-r, se, *s.m.f.* (*pop.*) buyer of stolen goods, fence [afflicting
Attristant, e, *adj.* sad, sorrowful, grievous,
Attrister, *v.a.* to sadden; to damp; to gloom, to throw a gloom over; to grieve, to afflict
S'—, *v.r.* to grieve, to sorrow; to become (*or* grow) sad *or* sorrowful *or* melancholy
Attrit, e, *adj.* (*theol.*) attrite
Attrition, *s.f.* attrition
Attroupement, *s.m.* riotous *or* tumultuous assembly *or* meeting *or* crowd, crowd, multitude, gathering, mob, riot, tumult. *Loi contre les —s,*
Attrouper, *v.a.* to assemble, to gather [Riot-Act
S'—, *v.r.* to flock together; to gather in crowds, to congregate, to get together in a mob
Atypique, *adj.* atypic
Au [*contraction of* **A le,** *art.*]; (*cook.*) with; done in; preserved in; in; flavoured with; [*or simply invert, as*] *sauce — vin,* wine sauce
Aubade, *s.f.* morning serenade; blow-up
Aubain, *s.m.* alien, foreigner
Aubainage, *s.m.* escheatage
Aubaine, *s.f.* escheat (to the Crown), aubaine; (*bonne —*) windfall, godsend, prize, good fortune, good job, piece of luck *or* of good fortune, luck. *Mauvaise —,* bad job
Aube, *s.f.* dawn, daybreak; alb; paddle-board, paddle; float-board. *— mobile,* feathering paddle. *Roue à —s,* paddle-wheel. *Vapeur à —s,* paddle-wheel steamer
Aubépine, *s.f.* hawthorn, whitethorn, May
Aubère, *adj.m.f., s.m.* flea-bitten grey
Auberge, *s.f.* inn, tavern; public-house
Aubergine, *s.f.* egg-plant; egg-plant fruit, egg-apple, mad-apple [lord, host; landlady, hostess
Aubergiste, *s.m.f.* inn-keeper; publican; land-
Auberon, *s.m.* catch (*of a lock*)
Auberonnière, *s.f.* clasp (*of a lock*)
Aubète, Aubette, *s.f.* (*mil.*) orderly-room
†Aubevigne, *s.f.* (*bot.*) traveller's joy, virgin's-bower [(*a plant*) *V.* **Obier**
Aubier, *s.m.* sapwood, blea, white, alburnum;
Aubifoin, *s.m.* (*bot.*) blue-bottle, corn-flower
Aubin, *s.m.* canter-gallop, hand-canter
Aubiner, *v.n.a.* (*rid.*) to canter; (*hort.*) to earth; (*of vine*) to layer
Aubinet, *s.m.* (*nav.*) no man's land, waist-netting
Aubour, Aubours, *s.m.* (*bot.*) laburnum
Auctuaire, *s.m.* supplement
Aucuba, *s.m.* (*bot.*) aucuba
Aucun, e, *adj.* any; either; anyone; any man; no; none; not one; no one; not any; neither; not anyone; no man; (*in antiquated style*) some, some one, a few
Aucunement, *adv.* in any way, in any wise, at all; not at all, by no means, on no account, in no wise; (*in antiquated style*) in some degree, to some extent
Audace, *s.f.* audacity; boldness, daring
Audacieusement, *adv.* audaciously; boldly, daringly
Audacieu-x, se, *adj.* audacious; bold, daring
Au-deçà, Au-dedans, Au-dehors, Au-delà, Au-dessous, Au-dessus, Au-devant. *V.* **Deçà, Dedans, Dehors,** &c.
Audience, *s.f.* audience; hearing; trial; court, sitting [for hearing
Audiencer, *v.a.* to bring into court; to appoint
Audiencier, *adj.m., s.m. Huissier —,* crier, usher
Audit, *adj.m.* to *or* at the said; to *or* at the same; to *or* at ditto
Auditeur, *s.m.* hearer; auditor; (*formerly*) judge advocate, judge. *— bénévole,* favourably disposed hearer; amateur attendant (*at a course of lectures*) [cavity of the ear
Auditi-f, ve, *adj.* auditory. *Conduit — externe,*
Audition, *s.f.* hearing; auditing, audit
Auditoire, *s.m.* auditory; bar, court; audience; meeting; congregation
Auditorat, *s.m.* auditorship
Auditrice, *s.f.* hearer, auditress [St. Omer
Audomarois, e, *adj.s.* of St. Omer, native of
Auffe, *s.f.* (*bot.*) *V.* **Spart**
Auge, *s.f.* trough; manger; hod; channel, spout, bucket, ladle. *— d'écurie,* manger
Augée, *s.f.* troughful; hodful
Augeïot, *s.m.* ditch; trough; ladle
Auger, *v.a.* (*tech.*) to hollow out
Auget, *s.m.* trough; bird's trough; channel,
Augite, *s.f.* (*min.*) augite [spout, bucket
Augment, *s.m.* increase; jointure, dowry; (*Gr. gram.*) augment
Augmentable, *adj.* augmentable, increasable
Augmenta-teur, trice, *s.m.f.* augmenter; *— adj.* augmenting [*s.m.* augmentative
Augmentati-f, ve, *adj.,* **Augmentatif,**
Augmentation, *s.f.* increase, augmentation; addition; enlargement; increase of salary *or* wages *or* rent; improvement; aggravation; rise, advance
Augmenter, *v.a.n.,* **S'—,** *v.r.* to increase, to augment; to enlarge; to extend; to enhance; to better, to improve; to aggravate, to make worse; to raise the salary *or* the wages of; to raise ...'s rent; to raise; to rise
Augural, e, *adj.* augural, augurial
Augure, *s.m.* augury, omen; augur. *De bon —,* auspicious, of good omen. *De mauvais —,* ominous, portentous, of ill omen
Augurer, *v.a.n.* to augur
Auguste, *adj.* august; illustrious; noble; — *s.m.* (*used by Voltaire for* **août**) August; (*person's*
Augustement, *adv.* augustly [*name*) Augustus
Augustin, e, *s.m.f.* Augustine, Austin friar *or* nun. *Saint —,* (*print. type*) English
Augustine, *s.f.* spirit-lamp foot-warmer
Augustinien, ne, *adj. s.* Augustinian
Aujourd'hui, *adv. s.m.* to-day, this day; nowadays, now, at present; the present time, the present day. *Le jour* or *la journée d'—,* to-day. *— même,* this very day; even to this day [*of D.D.*
Aulique, *adj.* aulic; *—s.f.* thesis (*for the degree*
Au-lit, *int.* (*hunt.*) tally-ho!
Aulne, *s.m.* (*German myth.*) *Le roi des —s,* the erl-king; *—* (*bot.*) *V.* **Aune,** *s.m.*
Aulofée, Auloffe, Auloffée, *s.f.* (*nav.*) yaw to the luff, luffing, luff
Aulx (*in grammars only, not used*), *pl. of* **Ail**
†Aumaillade, *s.f.* trammel-net
†Aumailles, *s.f.pl. Bêtes —,* horned cattle
Aumône, *s.f.* alms, alms-giving, charity, benefaction, donation, gift, dole, relief, assistance; (*formerly*) fine. *Demander l'—,* to beg. *Faire l'—,* to give alms, to give to the poor, to bestow charity; to dole out, to give [visions) to the poor
Aumônée, *s.f.* distribution of bread (*or* of pro-
Aumôner, *v.n.a.* to pay a fine for the poor; to put into the poor-box; to pay, to give; to fine
Aumônerie, *s.f.* almonry; chaplaincy
Aumônier, *s.m.* almoner; chaplain; ordinary
Aumônière, *s.f.* alms-purse; almoner (*nun*)
Aumusse, Aumuce, *s.f.* hood; (*priest's garment*) almuce, aumuce [ell; measuring; measure
Aunage, *s.m.* alnage, aulnage, measuring by the
Aunaie, *s.f.* alder-grove, alder-plantation
Aune, *s.m.* alder, alder-tree; (*elf*) *V.* **Aulne**
Aune, *s.f.* ell; ell-measure; (*fig.*) measure, standard. *Tout du long de l'—,* the whole length; plenty, enough of it, excessively, with a vengeance. *Je sais ce qu'en vaut l'—,* I know it by experience, I have learnt it to my cost, I have tried it, I know what that is
Aunée, *s.f.* (*bot.*) elecampane
Auner, *v.a.* to measure by the ell; to measure; to judge of, to appreciate, to value
Auneur, *s.m.* alnager, aulnager; measurer
Auparavant, *adv.* before; previously; before now, ere now; formerly, once; in the first place; first of all, first

Auprès de, *prep.* near; close to, close by; by; next to; about; with; to; at the court of: in the presence of; in the opinion of; in the eyes of; in comparison with

Auprès, *adv.* near, close, close by; at hand, near at hand; near it, near them, close to it *or* them, by it *or* them; next to it, next to them; in comparison with it *or* them. *Tout* —, very near; close by

Auquel [*contraction of* **A lequel**]

Aura, *s.f.* (*med.*) aura

Aurade, *s.f.* (*fish*) gilt-head

Aural, e, *adj.* aural

Aurate, *s.m.* (*chem.*) aurate

Aurélie, *s.f.* (*zool.*) aurelia

Auréole, *s.f.* glory, halo, halo of glory, aureola, nimbus; crown of glory; circle; (*anat., med.*) areola

Auriculaire, *adj.* auricular; ear. *Doigt* —, ear-finger, little finger. *Témoin* —, ear-witness

Auricule, *s.f.* small ear; (*anat.*) auricle; (*plant, mollusc*) auricula

Auriculé, e, *adj.* auriculate, eared

Aurifère, *adj.* auriferous [(*of teeth*) with gold

Aurifiage, *s.m.*, **Aurification,** *s.f.* stopping

Aurifier, *v.a.* to stop (*teeth*) with gold

Aurifique, *adj.* aurific

Auriforme, *adj.* auriform, ear-shaped

†Aurillard. *V.* **Oreillard**

Aurine, *s.f.* (*chem.*) aurine

Aurique, *adj.* (*nav.*) shoulder of mutton, lateen, fore and aft; (*chem.*) auric

Auriste, *s.m.* aurist

‡Aurochs, *s.m.* (*zool.*) aurochs

Aurone, *s.f.* (*bot.*) abrotanum, southernwood

Aurore, *s.f.* dawn, dawn of day, daybreak; morning; day; east; (*astr.*) aurora; — *s.m.* gold-colour; — *adject.* gold-coloured. — *boréale*, aurora borealis, northern lights

Aurure, *s.m.* (*chem.*) auride

Auscultateur, *s.m.* auscultator; — *adj.m.* auscultating

Auscultation, *s.f.* (*med.*) auscultation

Ausculter, *v.a.* (*med.*) to auscultate

Auspice, *s.m.* auspice

Aussi, *adv. conj.* also, too, likewise; besides, moreover; therefore, so, and so, accordingly; as; as much; equally; so; so much; such; but then; then; now; indeed; either. — *bien*, as well; so well; as much; so much; any more; the more so as; as; for, because; and indeed, indeed, in fact; besides, moreover. — *peu que*, as little *or* as few as

Aussière, *s.f.* (*nav.*) hawser, warp

Aussitôt, *adv. prep.* immediately, directly; as soon as; immediately after. — *que*, as soon as; so soon as. *D'*—, so soon. — *dit*, — *fait*; — *pris*, — *pendu*, no sooner said than done, before you could say Jack Robinson

Auster, *s.m.* auster, south wind

Austère, *adj.* austere; stern, rigid, severe; strict; harsh, sharp

Austèrement, *adv.* austerely; sternly, rigidly, severely; strictly

Austérité, *s.f.* austerity; sternness, severity, rigidness; harshness, sharpness

Austral, e, *adj.* austral, southern, south

Australasien, ne, *adj. s.* Australasian

Australien, ne, *adj. s.* Australian

Austrasien, ne, *adj. s.* Austrasian

Autan, *s.m.* south wind; stormy wind, storm, blast

Autant, *adv.* as much; as many; as far; as long; as often; as loud; as well; as good; so much; so many; so far; so long; so often; so loud; the same, the like; as. *D'— mieux*, so much the better, all the better, all the more, the more, the more so, the rather, specially, especially. *D'— moins*, so much the less, all the less, the less, the less so. *D'— plus*, so much the more, all the more, the more, the more so, the rather, specially, especially. *D'— que*, forasmuch as, specially *or* especially as, more especially as, as. — *vaut*, one may as well; it is as well; quite as much. — *vaudrait*, one might as well; it would be as well

Autel, *s.m.* altar; communion table; religion worship, Church; (*astr.*) ara. — *de plume*, (*pop.*) bed, o.'s bed. *Le sacrifice de l'*—, the mass

Auteur, *s.m.* author; authoress; maker; inventor; inventress; discoverer; contriver; deviser; designer; framer; promoter; cause, source; originator; creator; founder; achiever; committer; perpetrator; spreader; informant; authority; writer; composer; painter, sculptor, engraver, artist, master; work; classic; (*pop.*) parent, papa, daddy, governor; (*law*) original vendor *or* transferrer; client. *Droit d'*—, copyright; author's share (*in a dramatic performance*)

Authenticité, *s.f.* authenticity

Authentique, *adj.* authentic; — *s.f.* original; (*old law*) authentics; judicial separation

Authentiquement, *adv.* authentically

Authentiquer, *v.a.* to authenticate

Autobiographe, *s.m.f.* autobiographer

Autobiograph-ie, -ique, -iquement. *V.* page 3, § 1

‡Autochthone, *s.m.* autochthon; — *adj.* autochthonous, autochthonic

Autoclave, *adj.* self-regulating; digesting, steaming; — *s.m.f.* digester, steamer; steam-engine. *Marmite* —, digester, steamer

Autocrate, *s.m.f.* autocrat; — *adj.* autocratic

Autocratie, *s.f.* autocracy

Autocrat-ique, -iquement. *V.* page 3, § 1

Autocratrice, *s.f.* autocratrix

Auto-da-fé, *s.m.* auto-da-fe; bonfire

Autodynamique, *adj.* autodynamic

Autographe, *adj.* autograph; autographic; — *s.m.* autograph; autographer

Autographie, *s.f.* autography

Autographier, *v.a.* to autograph

S'—, *v.r.* to be autographed

Autograph-ique, -iquement. *V.* page 3, § 1

Autographomane, *s.m.f.* autographomaniac

Automate, *s.m.* automaton; — *adj.* automatic

Automat-ique, -iquement, -isme. *V.* page 3, § 1

Automédon, *s.m.* charioteer; (*jest.*) Jehu, driver; cabby, jarvey

Automnal, e, *adj.* autumnal, autumn

Automnation, *s.f.* (*agr.*) autumnal influence

Automne, *s.m.f.* autumn; fall of the leaf, fall, yellow leaf

Automobile, Automo-teur, trice, *adj.* self-acting, self-moving; self-regulating

Autonome, *adj.* autonomous, autonomic, self-governing, self-governed, independent, free

Autonomie, *s.f.* autonomy, self-government, free government, independence, freedom

Autopsie, *s.f.* autopsy, post-mortem examination; inquest

Autor. *D'*—, *D'— et d'achar*, authoritatively; with a high hand; briskly; vigorously; irresistibly; unanswerably; authoritative; brisk; vigorous; irresistible; unanswerable

Autorisable, *adj.* authorizable

Autorisation, *s.f.* authorization; authority, consent, permission; licence; power; warrant

Autoriser, *v.a.* to authorize, to give authority to; to empower; to commission; to qualify; to license; to warrant; to justify; to legalize; to sanction; to allow

S'—, *v.r.* to assume *or* acquire *or* gain *or* get authority; to get credit; to ground *or* justify oneself on the authority (of); to think oneself warranted (by); to act on the authority (of); to be authorized *or* warranted

Autorité, *s.f.* authority; power; rule, sway; control; credit; influence; sanction; countenance, support; weight; consideration; credibility; testimony; precedent. *Faire* —, to be an authority

Autour, *s.m.* goshawk

Autour, *prep.adv.* around, round, about; around *or* about it, around *or* about them

Autourserie, *s.f.* art of training goshawks, hawking, falconry

Autoursier, *s.m.* trainer of goshawks, ostringer, hawker, falconer

Autre, *adj. pron.* other; different; else; another; further, farther; next; second; better; superior;

greater; more; other person; other fellow; other thing, other affair; other trick, &c. *Tout* —, quite different; any other. *Les —s*, the other (...); the others; others, other people. *Nul —, aucun —*, no other; no one else. *Quelque* —, some other; some one else. *Nous —s*, we; ourselves. *Vous —s*, you fellows; you; yourselves. *A d'—s!* nonsense! don't tell me! that won't do for me! tell that to the marines! I know better! *Ne pas en faire d'—s*, not to act otherwise, to do nothing else. *Il n'en fait pas d'—s, jamais d'—s*, that is the way with him, always the way with him. *Comme dit l'—* or *cet* —, as the saying is, as our friend has it

Autrefois, *adv.* formerly, in former times, once, of old, of yore; once upon a time. *D'—*, of former times; bygone

Autrement, *adv.* otherwise; differently, not in the same way (as); in other respects; else, or else; a good deal more *or* better; more, better; much, very [fashion

Autrichien, ne, *adj. s.* Austrian; Austrian

Autruche, *s.f.* ostrich; dolt, blockhead

Autrui, *s.m.* another; others, other people

Auvent, *s.m.* penthouse, lean-to; weather-board; tilt [Auvergne; Auvergnat

†**Auvergnat, e,** *adj. s.* of Auvergne; native of

Auvernat, *s.m.* auvernat (*Orleans wine, grape,*

Auverpin, *s.m.* (*fam.*) Auvergnat [*vine*)

Aux [*contraction of* **A les,** *art.*]; (*cook.*) with; done in; preserved in; in; flavoured with; [*or simply invert, as*] *soupe — choux*, cabbage soup, *tarte — confitures*, jam tart, &c.

Auxdites, *adj.f.pl.*, **Auxdits,** *adj.m.pl.* to *or* at the said; to *or* at the same, to *or* at ditto

Auxiliaire, *adj.m.f., s.m.* auxiliary; subsidiary; (*nav.*) temporary officer

Auxquelles [*contraction of* **A lesquelles**]

Auxquels [*contraction of* **A lesquels**]

Avachir (S'), *v.r.* to become (*or* get) flabby *or* loose *or* out of shape, to hang down, to flag

Aval, *s.m.* (*pl.* **—s**) (*com.*) endorsement, guarantee; foreign bill of exchange (*short-dated*)

Aval, *adv. s.m.* (*no plural*) down stream, downward,down,below. *Vent d'—*,(*nav.*) westerly wind

Avalage, *s.m.* going down stream; distance down stream; letting down into a cellar; leakage

Avalaison, *s.f.* flood, torrent; heap of alluvial stones; (*nav.*) set in westerly wind

Avalanche, *s.f.* avalanche, snow-slip

Avalasse, *s.f. V.* **Avalaison**

Avalé, e, *adj.* swallowed; let down; hanging down, falling down, flagging; sunk, sunken, fallen in; sloping off, low; gone down stream

Avalement, *s.m.* letting down, lowering; swallowing

Avaler, *v.a.n.* to swallow; to swallow down; to devour; to drink up; to endure; to brook, to pocket; to put up with; to let down; to lower; to cut off; to take off *or* down; to endorse, to guarantee; to go down stream, to follow the current, to float *or* drift down

S'—, *v.r.* to hang down; to flag; to sink, to go down, to fall in; to be swallowed, &c.; to devour each other

Avaleu-r, se, *s.m.f.* swallower; glutton. — *de frimas*, dreamer, visionary. — *de gens*, — *de charrettes* (*ferrées*), braggart, bully, fire-eater. — *de pois gris*, gormandizer, glutton, greedy gut; quack

Avalies, *s.f.pl.* skin-wool, pelt-wool, dead wools

Avaliste, *s.m.* endorser, guarantee

Avaloir, *s.m.* (*fish.*) stake-net, poke-net; (*fam.*) gullet, swallow [(*of harness*) breeching

Avaloire, *s.f.* gullet, swallow; guttler, guzzler;

Avalure, *s.f.* (*vet.*) laminitis

Avançage, *s.m.* cab-stand, stand

Avance, *s.f.* projection; seat; knee-roll (*of a saddle*), roll of the flap; lead; advance; advance-money; money in hand; work done; way in advance; first step; start; offer; gain, advantage, benefit, good; (*word marked on watches*) fast. *A l'—, d'—, en —, par —*, in advance, by anticipation, beforehand, before o.'s time, early, too fast. *Prendre l'—*, to get the start

Avancé, e, *adj.* advanced; forward; protruding; far gone; late; overripe; tainted; wiser, better, nearer; liberal. *Garde —*, advanced guard, advance-guard; outpost. *Être bien —*, to be the better *or* the wiser (for it); to have gained much (by it); to be in a pretty plight. *N'en être pas plus —*, to be none the wiser *or* the better *or* the nearer [of its turn

Avancé, *s.m.* (*law*) order to advance a cause out

Avancée, *s.f.* (*mil.*) advanced guard, advance-guard

Avancement, *s.m.* advancement; promotion; preferment; rise; improvement; progress; proficiency; forwardness

Avancer, *v.a.* to advance; to bring *or* put forward *or* forth; to bring nearer; to present, to offer; to hold out; to stretch out; to forward; to hasten, to accelerate; to push on, to get on; to urge; to force; to mature; to raise, to promote, to prefer; to help; to benefit; to shorten; to assert; to move, to play; (*of clocks*) to put forward; — *v.n.* to advance; to move *or* get *or* go *or* come *or* step forward *or* on; to pass on; to proceed; to rise; to improve, to progress, to make progress; to avail, to profit; to encroach; to protrude, to project, to jut *or* stand out; to be in advance; (*of clocks*) to gain, to be *or* go too fast. *Faire —*, to push on *or* forward; to bring on *or* up; to call. *N'— à rien*, to do no good; to be of no use; to lead to no result. *Cela m'avance bien!* what good is that to me?

S'—, *v.r.* to advance; to move *or* get *or* go *or* come *or* step forward; to proceed; to stand forward; to make progress, to progress; to move *or* go *or* get on: to rise; to go far; to engage oneself; to project; to protrude; to advance oneself, to get preferment [tion, exaction

Avanie, *s.f.* insult, affront, outrage; molesta-

Avano, *s.m.* (*fish.*) shrimp-net

Avant, *s.m.* (*nav.*) afore; (*of the ship*) head, bow, stem; — *prep. adj.* before; ere; till; above; fore, front; — *adv.* before; previously; till then; far; deep; deeply; forward; far advanced; late; till late. — *que*, — *de*, before. — *tout*, first, first of all; above all things, above all, especially. *D'—*, before, preceding; fore. *De l'—*, (*nav.*) fore; ahead. *De l'— à l'arrière*, (*nav.*) from stem to stern, fore and aft. *En —*, forward, onward, on; forth; in front; (*nav.*) ahead. *En — de*, before; in front of; in advance of. *En — marche!* (*mil.*) forward! *Plus —*, farther, further; deeper. *Aller à l'—*, (*nav.*) to have head-way. *Aller de l'—*, (*nav.*) to be under way; to go ahead. *Se ranger de l'—*, (*nav.*) to scant afore. — **-bec,** *s.m.* (*arch.*) (upper) starling; cut-water. — **-bouche,** *s.f.* (*anat.*) anterior fauces. — **-bras,** *s.m.* (*anat.*) fore-arm. — **-cale,** *s.f.* (*nav.*) launch. — **-cœur,** *s.m.* bosom; (*vet.*) anticor. — **-corps,** *s.m.* fore-building, fore-part; projecting mass, projection. — **-cour,** *s.f.* front yard, front court. — **-coureur,** *s.m.* forerunner; precursor, harbinger; premonitory symptom; (*mil.*) van-courier; *adj.* precursory, betokening, foreboding, premonitory. — **-courrier, ière,** *s.m.f.* forerunner; harbinger; (*thieves' slang*) centre-bit. — **-dernier, ière,** *adj.* last but one. — **-deux,** *s.m.* (*a dancing step*). — **-faire-droit,** *s.m.* (*law*) preventive injunction. — **-fossé,** *s.m.* (*fort.*) advance-fosse. — **-garde,** *s.f.* (*mil.*) van-guard, van; (*nav.*) van-division, van; blockship. — **-goût,** *s.m.* fore-taste; earnest; anticipation. — **-hier,** *adv. s.m.* the day before yesterday. (— *-hier soir*, the evening before last.) — **-main,** *s.m.* fore-hand stroke; fore-quarters, fore-hand; (*at cards*) lead. — **-mur,** *s.m.* screen-wall, outward wall. — **-pêche,** *s.f.* early peach. — **-pied,** *s.m.* (*anat.*) metatarsus; (*zool.*) fore-foot; (*of boots*) vamp, upper leather. — **-poignet,** *s.m.* (*anat.*)

fore-wrist, metacarpus. — **-port,** *s.m.* outer port, outer harbour; tide-dock. — **-portail,** *s.m.* fore-portal. — **-poste,** *s.m.* outpost. — **-projet,** *s.m.* rough draught, preliminary estimate. — **-propos,** *s.m.* preface, preamble, introduction, preliminary matter. — **-quart,** *s.m.* (*of clocks*) warning; warning-bell. — **-scène,** *s.f.* front of the stage, proscenium; stage-box; (*fig.*) previous events, foregone incidents, anterior part of the drama; preliminaries. — **-terrasse,** *s.f.* front terrace. — **-toit,** *s.m.* projecting roof; eaves. — **-train,** *s.m.* fore-carriage; (*of cannon*) limber; (*of a plough*) wheels, wheel; (*of a horse*) fore-quarters. — **-veille,** *s.f.* day before the eve, two days before

Avantage, *s.m.* advantage; benefit; profit; interest; superiority; odds; favour; behalf; credit; settlement; endowment; gift; gratuity; privilege; quality; pleasure; (*nav.*) weather-gage; (*rid.*) whip-hand

Avantager, *v.a.* to give an advantage *or* advantages to; to benefit; to favour; to gift; to improve the look of; to set off; to make a settlement upon, to settle upon

S'—, *v.r.* to give advantages to each other; to take advantage (of)

Avantageusement, *adv.* advantageously; profitably; favourably; eligibly; conveniently; highly, well

Avantageu-x, se, *adj.* advantageous; beneficial, profitable; useful; convenient; eligible; favourable; creditable; agreeable; commanding; prepossessing; noble; conceited, presumptuous, presuming; (*of dress*) becoming

Avare, *adj.* avaricious, miserly; stingy, niggardly; sparing; ungrateful; — *s.m.f.* miser, niggard [ringly

Avarement, *adv.* avariciously; stingily; spa-

Avariable, *adj.* damageable

Avarice, *s.f.* avarice, avariciousness; stinginess, niggardliness

Avaricieusement. *V.* **Avarement**

Avaricieu-x, se, *adj. s. V.* **Avare** [dues

Avarie, *s.f.* damage; average; loss; harbour-

Avarier, *v.a.* to damage. *S'—*, to become *or* be damaged

Avaste, *adv.* (*nav.*) avast! stop! stand away!

Avatar, *s.m.* avatar

Avé, *s.m.* ave. — *Maria*, Ave Maria

Avec, *prep. adv.* with; along with; by; in; for; of; among; towards; against; add to; besides; in spite of, notwithstanding; with it *or* them; with it *or* them on. — *cela que*, and ... besides that, and ... too, and ... withal, add to this; and then; indeed one would think (that); you don't mean to say (that). *D'—*, from

Avecque, (*old poetry*) *V.* **Avec**

Aveindre, *v.a.* to fetch, to take (from, out of)

Aveine, Avène, *s.f. V.* **Avoine**

Aveinière, Aveinerie, *s.f.* oat-field

Avelanède, *s.f.* valonia

Aveline, *s.f.* filbert, cob-nut

Avelinier, *s.m.* filbert-tree

Avénacé, e, *adj.* avenaceous

Avenant, e, *adj.* good-looking, comely, prepossessing, engaging, pleasing, agreeable, taking; happening, occurring; falling. *A l'—*, answerable (to), appropriate (to), of a piece (with), in keeping (with), to match; in proportion

Avénement, *s.m.* accession, succession, coming

Avèneron, *s.m.* wild oats

Avénière, *s.f. V.* **Aveinière**

Avenir, *v.n.* (*old*) *V.* **Advenir**

Avenir, *s.m.* future, time to come, future times, futurity; future prospects, prospects; hope, hopes, promise; chance of success; future career; after-life; future welfare *or* existence; posterity; (*law*) venire facias, notice of trial. *A l'—*, in future; henceforth, hereafter. *D'—*, *qui a de l'—*, promising, rising. *Dans l'—*, at a future time

Avent, *s.m.* advent

Aventure, *s.f.* adventure; venture; chance, accident; luck; fortune; occurrence, circumstance, occasion; event; story; intrigue; fate; lot. *Bonne —*, *la bonne —*, fortune, o.'s fortune, fortunes; destiny; prediction; luck. *Grosse —*, (*nav.*) bottomry. *A l'—*, at random; at a venture. *D'—*, *par —*, by chance, perchance, peradventure. *Mal d'—*, whitlow

Aventuré, e, *adj.* hazarded; hazardous; bold

Aventurer, *v.a.,* **S'—,** *v.r.* to adventure, to venture, to hazard, to risk

Aventureusement, *adv.* adventurously

Aventureu-x, se, *adj.* adventurous, venturous, venturesome

Aventur-ier, ière, *s.m.f.* adventurer; adventuress; — *adj. V.* **Aventureux** [turine

Aventurine, *s.f. adj.* (*min.*) aventurine, avan-

Aventuriné, e, *adj.* aventurine, avanturine

Avenu, e, *adj.* happened, occurred, done. *Non —*, not having taken place, not done; (*law*) null and void [entrance

Avenue, *s.f.* avenue, walk; way, road, passage,

Avérage, *s.m.* (*com.*) average

Avérer, *v.a.* to ascertain; to prove, to evince, to show the truth of; to confirm; to establish

S'—, *v.r.* to be ascertained *or* proved *or* &c.

Avéron, *s.m. V.* **Avèneron**

Averse, *s.f.* shower

Aversion, *s.f.* aversion; dislike

Averti, e, *part. adj.,* **Averti,** *s.m.* informed, warned, &c. (*V.* **Avertir**); (*rid.*) well trained. *Se tenir pour —*, to take it as a warning; to be on o.'s guard. *Un bon — en vaut deux*, (*proverb*) forewarned, forearmed

Avertin, *s.m.* (*disease*) avertin, sturdy, turnsick

Avertineu-x, se, *adj.* vertiginous, giddy, dizzy; whimsical, wayward; shy

Avertir, *v.a.* to inform, to let know, to tell; to advise, to give notice; to warn; to admonish. *Faire —*, to send notice, to send word

Avertissement, *s.m.* information; notice; advice; warning, caution; admonition; advertisement

Avertisseu-r, se, *s.m.f.* warner, monitor, adviser; (*theat.*) stage-wait, call-boy; — *adj.* warning, premonitory

Aveu, *s.m.* confession, avowal; admission; acknowledgment; opinion; testimony; declaration; revelation; consent, approbation; recognition, recognizance; avowed social position, character; acknowledged authorship. *Gens* or *hommes sans —*, vagrants, vagabonds

Aveuer, *v.a. V.* **Avuer**

Aveugle, *adj. s.m.f.* blind; ignorant; deluded; implicit; blind man (*or* boy) *or* woman (*or* girl), blind person; — *s.m.* (*zool.*, *serpent —*) blind-worm, slow-worm. — *-né, e*, born blind. *A l'—*, *en —*, blindly, inconsiderately

Aveuglement, *s.m.* blinding; blindness; ignorance; infatuation

Aveuglément, *adv.* blindly; implicitly

Aveugler, *v.a.* to blind; to make blind; to dazzle; to delude; to darken, to obscure, to cloud; (*nav.*) to stop, to fother (*a leak*)

S'—, *v.r.* to blind oneself; to shut o.'s eyes, to be blind, not to see; to deceive *or* flatter oneself

Aveuglette (A l'), *adv.* groping, in the dark

Avi, *s.m.* overheating, overbaking, burning

Aviceptologie, *s.f.* aviceptology, treatise on

Avicide, *s.m.* avicide [fowling *or* bird-catching

Avicule, *s.f.* (*zool.*) avicula [hungry

Avide, *adj.* greedy; eager; covetous; thirsty;

Avidement, *adv.* greedily; eagerly; covetously

Avidité, *s.f.* greediness; avidity; eagerness; covetousness; thirst; appetite, hunger

†Avignonais, e, Avignonnais, e, *adj. s.* of Avignon, Avignonese, native of Avignon

Avilir, *v.a.* to degrade; to debase; to demean; to vilify; to disgrace; to discredit; to depreciate; to disparage; to lower; to humble

S'—, *v.r.* to degrade *or* &c. oneself; to be undervalued

Avilissement, *s.m.* degradation; debasement; disgrace; discredit; depreciation; disparagement; humiliation; contempt

Aviné, e, *adj.* drunken; drunk, tipsy; given to drink; unsteady *or* shaky from drink; seasoned (with wine). *Avoir les jambes —s,* to be [reeling drunk

Aviner, *v.a.* to season (with wine)

Aviron, *s.m.* oar. — *à couple,* scull. *A —s,* oared. *A l'—,* rowing. *Aller à l'—,* to row

Avironnerie, *s.f.* oar-making *or* trade; oar-maker's shed, oar-shed, oar-shop; oars

Avironnier, *s.m.* oar-maker

Avis, *s.m.* opinion, mind; advice; piece of advice; counsel; vote; motion; intelligence, news; information; intimation; notice; warning, caution; admonition; hint; advertisement. — *au lecteur,* preface, advertisement; hint; warning; a word to the wise. *A mon —,* in my opinion. *Aller aux —,* to vote, to put it to the vote. *Changer d'—,* to alter o.'s mind. *Il m'est —, m'est —,* I rather think, I think, I have some notion *or* some idea. *Il y a jour d'—,* there is no hurry

Avisé, e, *adj.* prudent, wise, circumspect, wary, cautious; discreet; cunning; imagined, thought of; perceived; advised

Aviser, *v.a.n.* to perceive, to see; to single out; to inform; to warn, to caution; to advise; to order; to think; to consider; to reflect; to mind; to think proper; to resolve

S'—, *v.r.* to bethink oneself; to think; (it) to occur (to); to imagine; to contrive; to invent; to take it into o.'s head; to venture; to dare; to presume; to try; to notice. *Ne vous en avisez pas,* you had better not try, you had better not

Aviso, *s.m.* despatch-boat, despatch-vessel

†Avitaillement, *s.m.* victualling; provisions, [stores

†Avitailler, *v.a.* to victual, to store

S'—, *v.r.* to lay in stores; to be victualled

†Avitailleur, *s.m.* army *or* navy contractor, victualler, caterer

Avivage, *s.m.* polishing; hewing

Aviver, *v.a.* to polish; to brighten; to heighten; to sharpen; to hew; to excite, to stir; to brisk up; to enliven; to animate; to quicken

S'—, *v.r.* to be polished *or* brightened, &c.; to become sharp *or* keen; to brighten up; to [brisk up

Avives, *s.f.pl.* (*vet.*) vives

Avivoir, *s.m.* (*tool*) burnisher, polisher

Avocasser, *v.n.* to drudge at the bar, to pettifog; to quibble; to twaddle

Avocasserie, *s.f.* pettifoggery, pettifogging; cavil, cavilling, quibbling; twaddle

Avocassier, *s.m.* pettifogger; quibbler; wrangler; arguer; twaddler

Avocass-ier, ière, *adj.* pettifogging; lawyer's, of those wretched lawyers; cavilling, quibbling; wrangling; disputatious; arguing; twaddling

Avocat, *s.m.* barrister, counsel; counsellor; pleader; advocate; lawyer; defender, protector; intercessor, mediator; solicitor; (*bot.*) avocado-pear, alligator-pear. — *consultant,* chamber-counsel. — *général,* attorney-general

Avocate, *s.f.* advocate, mediatrix, interceder

Avocatier, *s.m.* avocado-pear tree

Avocatoire, *adj.* avocatory

Avocette, *s.f.* (*bird*) avocet

Avoine, *s.f.* oats. *Folle —,* wild oats

Avoinerie, *s.f.* oat-field

Avoir, *v.a.* to have; to get, to obtain; to catch; to possess; to enjoy; to be worth; to have got; to hold; to get hold of; to keep; to wear, to have on; to feel; to be; must; should; to need; to carry; to bear; to meet with; to see; to be the matter with; to ail. *J'ai vingt ans,* I am twenty years old, I am twenty. *Qu'avez-vous? Qu'est-ce que vous avez?* what is the matter with you? (*à* ...) what makes you (...)? *Je n'ai rien,* there is nothing the matter with me. *Y —,* there be, there to be; to be the matter. *Il y a,* (*imp.*) there is; there are; it is; it is now; it was; the matter is; since, ago. *Il peut y —,* there may *or* can be. *Il va y —,* there is going to be. *Qu'a-t-il? Qu'est-ce qu'il a?* what is the matter with him? *Que peut-il y —?* what can there be? what can be the matter? *Il n'y a pas à hésiter,* there is no hesitating. *Qu'y a-t-il? Qu'est-ce qu'il y a?* what is there? what is it? what is the matter? *Il y a dix ans,* ten years ago; it is now ten years; it is ten years since. *Il y a de cela dix ans,* that (*or* it) was ten years ago, it is now ten years since. *Il y a aujourd'hui un an, huit jours,* &c., this day last year, last week, &c. *Il n'a plus qu'à mourir,* nothing remains for him but to die. *Il n'y a plus qu'à mourir,* there only remains to die. *Il y en a encore,* there is still some left. *Il n'y en a plus,* there is no more left. *Il y a plus,* nay more, moreover, more than that. *Il n'y a qu'à,* it is only at *or* in; it is enough to; one has only to; if it should. *En — à* or *contre,* to be angry with; to have to complain of; to blame; to be after *or* at; to think of. *Malgré qu'on en ait, quoi qu'on en ait,* in spite of oneself; however much one may dislike it. *Il en a pour longtemps,* it will last (*or* take) him a long time. *Il n'aurait qu'à,* he might happen to, if he were to

Avoir, *s.m.* property; fortune; wealth; substance; all; gain, profit; money; credit, creditor, creditor-side. *Tout son —,* o.'s all, all one has

Avoir-du-poids, *s.m.* avoirdupois (*English weight*) [close by

Avoisinant, e, *adj.* neighbouring, adjoining,

Avoisiné, e, *adj.* with neighbours. *Être bien* (or *mal*) —, to have good (*or* bad) neighbours *or* a good (*or* a bad) neighbourhood

Avoisinement, *s.m.* nearness, proximity

Avoisiner, *v.a.* to be near; to border upon; to be adjacent *or* contiguous to, to adjoin

Avorté, e, *part. adj.* abortive; miscarried; stunted; imperfect; deformed; blasted; blighted; nipped in the bud; stopped, prevented; frustrated; baffled; failed; unsuccessful; ill-contrived [tiveness; failure

Avortement, *s.m.* abortion, miscarriage; abor-

Avorter, *v.n.* to miscarry; to slip; to be *or* prove abortive; to fail. *Faire —,* to cause *or* procure abortion; to make *or* render abortive; to nip in the bud; to blast; to blight; to stunt; to stop, to prevent; to frustrate; to baffle

Avorton, *s.m.* abortion; abortive child; scrubby fellow, runt, shrimp

Avouable, *adj.* avowable

Avoué, *s.m.* attorney, solicitor; proctor; lawyer; (*feud.*) patron, supporter

Avouer, *v.a.* to avow; to confess; to own; to acknowledge; to recognize; to admit; must say; to declare openly; to allow, to grant; to approve, to authorize; to justify

S'—, *v.r.* to avow *or* confess *or* &c. oneself; to be avowed *or* confessed, &c.; to plead (*guilty*); to make use of the name (of), to refer (to)

Avoyer, *s.m.* avoyer (*Swiss magistrate*)

Avrelon, *s.m.* (*bot.*) mountain-ash

†Avril, *s.m.* April; (*poet.*) the spring

†Avrillé, e, *adj.* (*agr.*) sown in April

†Avrillet, *s.m.* corn sown in April

Avron, *s.m.* *V.* **Avèneron**

Avuer, *v.a.* (*hunt.*) to mark down, to mark in, [to follow with the eye

Avulsion, *s.f.* avulsion

Avunculaire, *adj.* avuncular

Axe, *s.m.* axis; axle, axle-tree; trunnion

Axifère, *adj.* axiferous

Axillaire, *adj.* (*anat., bot.*) axillary

Axinite, *s.f.* (*min.*) axinite

Axiomatique, *adj.* axiomatic

Axiome, *s.m.* axiom [(*of the tiller*)

Axiomètre, Axomètre, *s.m.* (*nav.*) tell-tale

Axis, *s.m.* (*zool., anat.*) axis

Axolotl, *s.m.* (*zool.*) axolotl

Axonge, *s.f.* axunge, hog's lard; suet, tallow, [grease, fat; sandiver

Aÿ, *s.m.* (*wine*) *V.* **Aï**

Ayah, *s.f.* ayah

Ayan, *s.m.* ayan (*Turkish officer*)

Ayant-cause, *s.m.* assign

Ayant-droit, *s.m.* party entitled; party; assign
Aye, *int. V.* **Aïe**
Aye-aye, *s.m.* (*zool.*) aye-aye
Aylante, Aylanthe. *V.* **Ailante**
Aynet, *s.m. V.* **Ainette**
Ayon, *s.m.* tail-board (*of a van,* &c.)
Ayuntamiento, *s.m.* ayuntamiento (*Spanish corporation*)
Azaléa, *s.m.,* **Azalée,** *s.f.* (*bot.*) azalea
Aze, *s.m.f.* (*local*) ass. *L'— me quille,* I declare! by Jingo! I am blowed [bead-tree
‡**Azédarac, Azédarach,** *s.m.* (*bot.*) azedarach,
Azerole, *s.f.* (*bot.*) azarole
Azerolier, *s.m.* azarole-tree
Azime, *adj. V.* **Azyme**
Azimut, *s.m.* (*astr.*) azimuth
Azimutal, e, *adj.* azimuthal, azimuth; — *s.m.* azimuth compass [to whistle; to hiss
Azor, *s.m.* (*jest.*) dog; knapsack, kit. *Appeler* —,
Azotate, *s.m.* (*chem.*) azotate, nitrate
Azote, *s.m.* (*chem.*) azote, nitrogen; — *adj.* azotic, nitric
Azoter, *v.a.* (*chem.*) to azotize, to nitrogenize
Azoteu-x, se, (*chem.*) *adj.* azotous, nitrous
Azotique, *adj.* (*chem.*) azotic, nitric
Azotite, *s.m.* (*chem.*) azotite, nitrite
Aztèque, *s.m.f. adj.,* **Aztec,** *s.m.* Aztec
Azulejos, *s.m.* (*ceramics*) azulejos
Azur, *s.m.* azure, blue, sky-blue, sky-colour; smalt. *Pierre d'*—, azure-stone, lapis lazuli,
Azurage, *s.m.* azuring [lazulite
Azuré, e, *adj.* azured, azure, blue, sky-coloured
Azurer, *v.a.* to azure. **S'**—, *v.r.* to be azured
Azurin, e, *adj.* azure
Azurite, *s.f.* (*min.*) azurite, Chessy copper
Azuror, *adj.* golden blue
Azyme, *adj.* azymous, unleavened; — *s.m.* a-
Azymite, *s.m.* Azymite [zym, unleavened bread

B

B, *s.m.* b. *Être marqué au* —, to be either one-eyed (*borgne*), or squint-eyed (*bigle*), or hunchbacked (*bossu*), or lame (*boiteux*), or bandy-legged (*bancal*), or talkative (*bavard*), &c. *Les — et les F; Ne parler que par — et par F;* see **F**
Baba, *s.m.* bun; plum-cake; pound-cake
Babel, *s.f.* Tower of Babel, Babel, confusion, disorder, noise; Babylon
Babeurre, *s.m.* butter-milk
Babiche, *s.f. V.* **Barbiche**
Babiche, *s.f.,* **Babichon,** *s.m.* young *or* little barbet; King-Charles's spaniel; skye-terrier; lapdog [twaddle; barking
†**Babil,** *s.m.* prattle, chatter, tattle; empty talk,
†**Babillage,** *s.m.* prattling; chit-chat; babbling
†**Babillard, e,** *adj.* prattling, chattering, talkative; talking; babbling; indiscreet; barking; — *s.m.f.* chatterer; babbler; blabber, blab; twaddler; (*bird*) nettle-creeper
†**Babillement,** *s.m.* talkativeness, loquacity
†**Babiller,** *v.n.* to prattle, to chatter; to indulge in talk; to gossip; to blab; to twaddle; to bark
Babine, *s.f.* lip, chops [gaw, nicknack, trinket
Babiole, *s.f.* bauble, trifle; toy, plaything; gew-
Babiroussa, *s.m.* (*zool.*) babyroussa *or* babi-
Bablah, *s.m.* (*bot.*) bablah [roussa
Bâbord, *s.m.adv.* (*nav., old*) port, larboard; aport
Bâbordais, *s.m.* (*nav.*) larboard-watch
Babou, *s.f.* (*pop.*) faces, face, wry face
Babouche, *s.f.* Turkish slipper
Babouin, *s.m.* baboon; pimple (*round the lips*)
Babouin, e, *s.m.f.* roguish child, monkey, hussy
Babouine, *s.f. V.* **Babine** [levelling
Babouvisme, *s.m.* (*polit.*) Babouvism, social
Babouviste, *s.m.f.* (*polit.*) Babouvist, leveller
Babylonien, ne, *adj. s.* Babylonian
Bac, *s.m.* ferry-boat, ferry; vat, bucket, tub, trough; [*also, a slang abbreviation of* **Baccarat**]

Bacaliau, *s.m.* dried cod
Baccalauréat, *s.m.* bachelor's degree, bache-
Baccar, *s.m. V.* **Baccharis** [lorship
Baccarat, *s.m.* (*kind of game at cards*)
‡**Bacchanal,** *s.m.* uproar, row
‡**Bacchanale,** *s.f.* bacchanal, revel; wild dance
‡**Bacchanaliser,** *v.n.* to revel, to riot
‡**Bacchant,** *s.m.* Bacchant
‡**Bacchante,** *s.f.* Bacchante; bacchanalian, bacchanal; termagant [spikenard
‡**Baccharis,** *s.m.* (*bot.*) baccharis, ploughman's
Bacchie, *s.f.* red spot, red face *or* nose, grog-blossom
‡**Bacchus,** *s.m.* (*myth.*) Bacchus; (*fig.*) wine
Baccifère, *adj.* (*bot.*) bacciferous
Bacciforme, *adj.* bacciform
Baccivore, *adj.* (*zool.*) baccivorous
Bacha, *s.m. V.* **Pacha**
Bachau, *s.m.* (*jest.*) bachelor's degree. *Le moule* (or *le four*) *à* —, cramming for the bachelor's degree [degree
Bachautier, *s.m.* crammer for the bachelor's
Bâche, *s.f.* awning; top-awning; tilt; rick-cloth; tarpaulin, hide, covering; hot-bed frame; cistern, tank; drag-net; pool
Bachelette, *s.f.* maid, maiden, lass, damsel
Bachelier, *s.m.* bachelor (*univers.*); lad (*obsolete*)
Bâcher, *v.a.* to tilt, to cover [*ish irregular*)
Bachi-bozouk, *s.m.* (*mil.*) bachi-bozouk (*Turk-*
Bachique, *adj.* drinking, bacchic, convivial; merry, jolly; drunken
Bachot, *s.m.* small ferry-boat, wherry, yawl; (*jest.*) bachelor's degree (*V.* **Bachau**)
Bachotage, *s.m.* ferryman's business; passage;
Bachoteur, *s.m.* ferryman [passage-dues
Bachotier, *s.m.* crammer for the bachelor's degree [**Bachon,** *s.m.* pail, bucket, trough
Bachotte, *s.f.,* **Bachou,** *s.m.,* **Bachoue,** *s.f.,*
Bacile, *s.m.* (*bot.*) *V.* **Passe-pierre** [polite
Bacillaire, *s.m.* (*min.*) pyramidal felspar, sca-
Bacinet, *s.m. V.* **Bassinet**
Backgammon, *s.m.* backgammon
Bâclage, *s.m.* gathering of boats (*in a port*); harbour-dues; closing of a port, stopping of a river; hurrying, patching, settling; hasty work
Bâclé, e, *part. adj.* fastened, &c. (*V.* **Bâcler**); frozen over; blocked up
Bâcler, *v.a.* to fasten; to close; to stop; to chain, to bar up; to hurry over, to do in haste; to botch up; to patch up; to knock off; to despatch; to settle; to terminate, to conclude
Bacliau, *s.m. V.* **Bacaliau** [Baconian
Baconien, ne, *adj.,* **Baconiste,** *adj. s.*
Bactréole, *s.f. V.* **Bractéole**
Bactrien, ne, *adj. s.* Bactrian
Baculithe, *s.m.* (*fossil shell*) baculite
Baculométr-ie, -ique. *V.* page 3, § 1
†**Badail,** *s.m.* drag-net, dredge [broad-leaf
Badamier, *s.m.* (*bot.*) terminalia, myrobalan,
Badaud, e, *s.m.f.* lounger, idler, saunterer; ninny, simpleton, booby, gaby; gazer; cit; cockney; — *adj.* lounging, idling, sauntering; silly
Badauder, *v.n.* to lounge, to saunter, to loiter
Badauderie, *s.f.,* **Badaudage,** *s.m.,* **Badaudise,** *s.f.,* **Badaudisme,** *s.m.* lounging, sauntering; cockneyism; idle talk; foolery, silliness, simplicity
Badelaire, *s.m.* (*her.*) broad-sword
Baderne, *s.f.* (*nav.*) mat, dolphin
Badiane, *s.f.* (*bot.*) badian
Badigeon, *s.m.* stone-colour, colour; white-wash; badigeon; (*of the face, jest.*) paint, making-up
Badigeonnage, *s.m.* colouring; whitewashing
Badigeonner, *v.a.* to colour; to whitewash; to paint; to fill with badigeon
Se —, *v.r.* to paint (*o.'s face*), to make up
Badigeonneur, *s.m.* colourer, whitewasher; dauber
Badin, e, *adj.* playful, humorous, sportive; laughing; frolicsome; waggish; roguish;

jocular; droll, comical; ridiculous; — *s.m.f.* trifler; banterer; wag; joker, jester
Badinage, *s.m.* play, sport; playfulness, sportiveness; liveliness; frolicsomeness; frolics; fun, joke, joking, trifling; jocularity; lively writing; nonsense, foolery
Badinant, *s.m.* spare horse
Badine, *s.f.* switch; —**s**, *pl.* light tongs [gishly
Badinement, *adv.* playfully, sportively; wag-
Badiner, *v.n.* to play, to sport; to frolic; to trifle; to joke; to jest, to rally; to be playful *or* merry; to write *or* speak wittily; to wave *or* flutter about, to flaunt; — *v.a.* to jest with,
Badinerie, *s.f. V.* **Badinage** [to trifle with
Badois, e, *adj. s.* of Baden, Baden; Badener
†**Badouille,** *s.f.* (*pop.*) hen-pecked husband
†**Badrouille,** *s.f.* (*nav.*) swab
Bafetas, Baffetas, *s.m.* baffetas, baftas
Bafouer, *v.a.* to scoff at, to deride, to scout
Bâfre, Bâfrée, Bâfrerie, *s.f.* blow-out; guttling, stuffing, eating
Bâfrer, *v.n.* to eat greedily, to guttle, to stuff; — *v.a.* to gobble, to swallow down [guttler
Bâfreu-r, se, *s.m.f.* greedy eater, glutton,
Bagace, *s.f. V.* **Bagasse**
Bagage, *s.m.* luggage, baggage; kit. *Plier* or *trousser* —, to pack off, to go away, to cut it; to march off; to go to o.'s last home
Bagarre, *s.f.* fray, squabble, scuffle, brawl, hubbub; rush, crowd, crush; disorder, confusion; obstruction, stoppage, dead lock; hobble
Bagasse, *s.f. int.* bagasse, cane-straw, cane-trash; refuse indigo-stems; residuum of olives; (*pop.*) slut, hussy, bitch; beastly thing! confound it!
Bagassier, *s.m.* (*bot.*) bread-fruit tree
Bagatelle, *s.f.* trinket; trifle; trifling; mere nothing; bauble; toy; (*English game*) bagatelle; — *int.* not at all! pooh! stuff!
†**Bagne,** *s.m.* convict-prison *or* establishment, penitentiary, hulks; (*hort.*) mould-tub
†**Bagnolet,** *s.m.* tarpaulin
†**Bagnolette, Bagnole,** *s.f.* commode (*woman's ancient head-dress*)
Bagou, Bagout, *s.m.* gabble
Baguage, *s.m.* (*hort.*) ringing
Bague, *s.f.* ring. — *-collier*, — *-jonc*, hoop-ring. — *au doigt*, (*fig.*) clear gain; godsend; sinecure; very good thing. —*s sauves*, unhurt, unscathed, clear, safe and sound. *Jeu de —s*, roundabout, merry-go-round
Baguenaude, *s.f.* bladder-senna pod; trifle
Baguenauder, *v.n.* to trifle
Baguenauderie, *s.f.* trifling; trifle
Baguenaudier, *s.m.* bladder-senna; trifler; ring-puzzle
Baguer, *v.a.* to baste, to stitch; (*hort.*) to ring
Baguette, *s.f.* wand; rod; stick; switch; drum-stick; ramrod; chop-stick; (*paint.*) maulstick; (*chem.*) glass rod, rod; (*hort.*) high tulip; (*arch.*) baguette; —**s**, *pl.* gauntlet (*mil. punishment*). —*s à gants*, glove-stretchers. *Passer par les —s; Être passé par les —s; Faire passer par les —s;*
Baguier, *s.m.* ring-box [*V.* **Verges**
Bah, *int.* bah! pooh! foh! tut! pshaw! nonsense! indeed! you don't say so! it cannot be! never mind! nay!
Bahut, *s.m.* trunk, chest; press; (*slang*) college, school, crammer's house. *En* —, convex, bulged, barrelled [to rollic
Bahuter, *v.n.* (*pop.*) to kick up a row, to roister,
Bahuteur, *s.m.* (*pop.*) roisterer, rollicking fel-
Bahutier, *s.m.* trunk-maker [low, rollicker
Bai, e, *adj.*, **Bai,** *s.m.* bay. — *doré*, yellow-dun
Baïart, *s.m. V.* **Bayart** [trick, hoax
Baie, *s.f.* bay; bight; opening; berry; (*obsolete*)
†**Baignade,** *s.f.* bathe, bath; bathing-place
†**Baigné, e,** *part. adj.* bathed, &c. (*V.* **Baigner**); weltering; wet
†**Baigner,** *v.a.n.*, **Se** —, *v.r.* to bathe; to wash; to drench, to inundate; to cover; to steep; to water; to wet; to plunge; to dip; to imbue; to soak; to be soaked *or* steeped; to swim; to welter [bathing-woman; bath-keeper
†**Baigneu-r, se,** *s.m.f.* bather; bathing-man;
†**Baigneuse,** *s.f.* bathing-dress *or* costume; (*woman's ancient head-dress*) commode
†**Baignoir,** *s.m.* bathing-place
†**Baignoire,** *s.f.* bath, bathing-tub; (*theat.*) pit-box, pit-tier box. — *oculaire*, eye-bath, eye-cup, eye-glass. *Voiture* —, bathing-machine
†**Bail,** *s.m.* lease. *A* —, on lease [barley
†**Baillard,** *s.m.*, **Baillarge,** *s.f.* four-rowed
†**Baille,** *s.f.* (*nav.*) half-tub
†**Bâillement,** *s.m.* yawn, gape, yawning, gaping; gap; hiatus; (*a disease of birds*) gapes
†**Bâiller,** *v.n.* to yawn, to gape; to open; not to shut close; to be ajar; to be slack; to pucker
†**Bailler,** *v.a.* (*obsolete*) *V.* **Donner**
†**Bâilleu-r, se,** *s.m.f.* yawner, gaper
†**Bailleur,** *s.m.*, **Bailleresse,** *f.* lessor. — *de fonds*, money-lender; sleeping partner
†**Bailli,** *s.m.* bailiff [*London*) bailage, balliage
†**Bailliage,** *s.m.* bailiwick; (*duty on goods in*
†**Bailliag-er, ère,** *adj.* of the bailiwick
†**Baillive,** *s.f.* bailiff's wife
†**Bâillon,** *s.m.* gag; muzzle; bribe
†**Bâillonner,** *v.a.* to gag; to stop the mouth of; to muzzle; to bribe; to silence; to enslave; to wedge up (*a door*)
Bain, *s.m.* bath; bathing; bathing-place; —**s**, *pl.* baths; bathing; bathing-places; bathing-establishment; bath-room; waters. — *anglais*, sponge-bath, sponging-bath. — *complet*, bath with linen. — *simple*, bath without linen; bath in common water. — *de siége*, hip-bath. *De* —, *de —s*, bath; bathing. *Ville de —s*, watering-place. *A — de mortier*, with full mortar, bedded in mortar. — *qui chauffe*, (*fig.*) storm brewing
Bain-marie, *s.m.* [*a vessel of water, in which saucepans, &c. are placed to warm their contents*] (*cook.*) bain-marie; (*chem.*) water-bath
Baïonnette, *s.f.* bayonet. *Mettre la — au canon*, to fix bayonets. *Remettre la* —, to unfix bayonets
Baïoque, *s.f.* bajocco (*modern Roman coin*)
Bairam, *s.m.* bairam, beiram (*Turkish feast*)
Baisemain, *s.m.* kissing of hands; —**s**, *pl.* (*obsolete*) compliments, respects
Baisement, *s.m.* kissing (*of feet*)
Baiser, *v.a.* to kiss; — *s.m.* kiss; kissing; caress
Baiseu-r, se, *s.m.f.* kisser; — *adj.* kissing
Baisoter, *v.a.* to kiss about
Baisse, *s.f.* fall, decline, decrease, falling off; depression; going down; reduction. *Être en* —, to be falling
Baissé, e, *part. adj.* lowered, &c. (*V.* **Baisser**); down; downcast; hanging down; stooping. *Tête —e*, headlong
Baissement, *s.m.* lowering; stooping
Baisser, *v.a.* to lower; to let *or* put down; to bring down; to draw *or* pull down; to drop; to cast down; to hold *or* hang down; to hang; to droop; to bend; to bow; to strike; — *v.n.* to lower; to fall; to decline; to fall off; to decay; to go *or* come down; to ebb; to sink; to fail; to abate; to decrease; to lose

Se —, *v.r.* to stoop, to stoop down; to bow down; to bend; to lean over; to let down; to hang down; to lower; to be lowered, &c.
Baisser, *s.m.* lowering; dropping, falling, fall
Baissier, *s.m.* bear, operator for a fall
Baissière, *s.f.* lees (*of wine*, &c.); hollow; puddle
Baisure, *s.f.* kissing-crust
Bajoire, *s.f.* double-headed coin
Bajoue, *s.f.* cheek, chap
Bajoyer, *s.m.* side-wall; cheek, facing
Bal, *s.m.* ball; dance; dancing; ball-room. — *paré*, dress ball. — *costumé* or *travesti*, fancy dress ball, fancy ball
Balader (Se), *v.r.* (*pop.*) *V.* **Trôler**
Baladeu-r, se, *s.m.f.* (*pop.*) *V.* **Flâneur**
Baladin, e, *s.m.f.* dancer; mountebank; merry-andrew; buffoon; wag
Baladinage, *s.m.* buffoonery; nonsense

Balafo, *s.m.* banjo
Balafre, *s.f.* gash, slash, cut; scar
Balafré, e, *part.* gashed, scarred, covered with scars
Balafrer, *v.a.* to gash, to slash, to cut over the face
Balai, *s.m.* broom; brush; besom; (*pop.*) policeman, peeler, bobby, slop. — *à laver*, swab, mop. — *du ciel*, (*nav.*) sweeping wind. — *de crin*, hair-broom. — *de jonc*, carpet-broom. *Faire — neuf*, to do o.'s work well at first. *Rôtir le —*, to drudge in obscurity; to lead a wild life
Balais (Rubis), *s.m.* balas ruby
Balance, *s.f.* balance; scales, pair of scales; suspense; comparison; balance-sheet; crayfish-net; libra. — *à bascule*, weighing-machine. — *romaine*, steelyard. *Faire pencher la —*, to turn the scale
Balancé, *s.m.* (*dancing*) balance
Balancelle, *s.f.* (*nav.*) balancelle
Balancement, *s.m.* balancing; poising; poise; equilibrium; swinging; swing; swaying; sway; waving; rocking; oscillation; see-saw motion; waddling; waddle; fluctuation; hesitation; wavering; shake; libration; (*pop.*) dismissal, sack
Balancer, *v.a.n.* to balance; to poise; to weigh; to swing; to sway; to wave; to rock; to move to and fro; to counterbalance; to compensate; to counteract; to square; to be compared with; to render unsteady *or* doubtful; to oscillate; to shake; to fluctuate; to hesitate; to waver; to be doubtful; to scruple; (*pop.*) to dismiss, to give the sack; to humbug, to bamboozle
Se —, *v.r.* to swing; to sway; to rock; to wave; to nod; to waddle; to oscillate; to balance; to be balanced *or* counterbalanced; to be square; to counterbalance each other; to see-saw, to play at see-saw; to float; to hover
Balancier, *s.m.* pendulum; balance; pole, balancing-pole; beam; flier; lever; gimbal; coining-engine; stamp; (*of insects*) balancer; (*pers.*) balance-maker; scale-maker
Balancine, *s.f.* (*nav.*) lift
Balançoire, *s.f.* see-saw; swing; (*pop.*) flam, story
Balançon, *s.m.* deal battens *or* scantlings
Balandran, Balandras, *s.m.* (*old*) cloak, overcoat
Balandre, *s.f.* (*nav.*) *V.* **Bélandre**
Balane, Balanite, *s.m.* (*zool.*) balanus, balanite, acorn-shell, acorn-barnacle
Balant, *s.m.* (*nav.*) bight; swing
Balasse, *s.f.* oat-chaff mattress, chaff-bed; earthen water-cooler
Balauste, *s.f.* (*bot.*) balausta; (*pharm.*) balaustine flower
Balaustier, *s.m.* (*bot.*) balaustine, wild pomegranate-tree
Balayage, Balayement, *s.m.* sweeping
Balayer, *v.a.* to sweep; to sweep away *or* off *or* over *or* out *or* up; to brush off; to clean; to clear
Balayette, *s.f.* small broom *or* brush, whisk
Balayeu-r, se, *s.m.f.* sweeper
Balayeuse, *s.f.* (— *mécanique*) sweeping-machine, sweeper
Balayures, *s.f.pl.* sweepings. — *de mer*, seaware
Balbusard, *s.m.* *V.* **Balbuzard**
Balbutie, *s.f.*, **Balbutiement,** *s.m.* stammering, stuttering; lisping
Balbutier, *v.a.n.* to stammer, to stutter; to lisp; to hesitate
Balbuzard, *s.m.* bald-buzzard, fishing eagle
Balcon, *s.m.* balcony
Baldaquin, *s.m.* baldachin; canopy
Baleine, *s.f.* whale; whalebone; sweeping wave; ducking; movable earth
Baleiné, e, *adj.* whalebone, with whalebone
Baleineau, *s.m.* young whale, whale-calf
Baleinier, *s.m.* whaler; whalebone-cutter *or* seller. *Navire —*, whaler
Baleinière, *s.f.* whale-boat
Balestron, *s.m.* (*nav.*) sprit
Balèvre, *s.f.* lips; (*arch.*) overplus lip; (*metal.*) bur
Bâli, Bali, *s.m. adj.* *V.* **Pâli**
Balin, *s.m.* winnowing-cloth
Baline, *s.f.* packing-cloth
Balisage, *s.m* buoyage, buoying, erection of beacons; clearing
Balisaur, *s.m.* (*zool.*) balisaur
Balise, *s.f.* beacon; buoy; towing-path; canna-seed. *Droit de —*, beaconage
Balisement, *s.m.* *V.* **Balisage**
Baliser, *v.a.* to put up beacons *or* buoys in, to buoy; to clear
Baliseur, *s.m.* water-bailiff; superintendent of a towing-path; person who puts up beacons *or* buoys
Balisier, *s.m.* (*bot.*) shot, Indian shot, canna
Baliste, *s.f.* (*ancient war-engine*) ballista, balista; — *s.m.* (*zool.*) balistes, file-fish
Balistique, *s.f.* ballistics; — *adj.* ballistic
Balivage, *s.m.* staddling
Baliveau, *s.m.* staddle; scaffold-pole
Baliverne, *s.f.* idle tale *or* talk, stuff, nonsense, humbug, gammon, foolery
Baliverner, *v.n.a.* to trifle, to talk idly *or* ridiculously, to tell tales *or* idle stories; to humbug, to gammon
Baliverneu-r, se, *s.m.f.* trifler; twaddler; humbug
Ballade, *s.f.* ballad
Ballage, *s.m.* (*metal.*) balling
Ballant, *s.m.* *V.* **Balant**
Ballant, e, *adj.* swinging about, swinging; hanging down; waving to and fro; dangling; loose, slack
Ballarin, *s.m.* Hungarian hawk
Ballast, *s.m.* ballast
Ballastage, *s.m.* ballasting
Ballaster, *v.a.* to ballast
Ballastière, *s.f.* ballast-pit, ballast-hole
Balle, *s.f.* ball; bullet; shot; bale; pack; bundle; husk; chaff; boll, glume; (*of maize*) cob; (*fig.*) opportunity; turn; job; sconce, phiz, face; bob. — *au camp*, (*play*) rounders, camping. — — *au mur*, fives. — *au pot*, nine-holes, rolly-pooly. — *à la volée*, trap-ball. — *en rond*, stool-ball. — *à feu*, — *à éclairer*, (*mil.*) fire-ball, light-ball. — *de coton* (*fig.*, *pop.*) bunch of fives. — *morte*, spent ball. — *ramée*, *V.* **Boulet.** *De —*, inferior, bad, mean, paltry, of no value. *A vous la —*, this is for you; it is your turn. *Enfant de la —*, person following his (*or* her) parent's profession. *Faire —*, to act as a bullet, to strike in a lump. *Juger la —*, to foresee the end. *Prendre la — au bond*, (*fig.*) to catch (*or* seize) the opportunity. *Renvoyer la —*, (*fig.*) to give tit for tat; to retort; to turn the tables. *Se renvoyer la —*, (*fig.*) to refer to each other; to retort alternately, to bandy repartees; to turn the tables upon (*or* against) each other. *Servir la —*, (*at play*) to bowl
Baller, *v.n.* (*old*) to hop, to skip, to dance: to bow, to nod
Ballerine, *s.f.* dancer; ballet-dancer
Ballet, *s.m.* ballet
Balliste, Ballistique. *V.* **Baliste, Balistique**
Ballon, *s.m.* balloon, air-balloon; air-ball, ball; wind-bag; foot-ball; round top, swelling hill; fish-cart; (*chem.*, *pyrotechnics*, *artil.*) balloon; (*nav.*) barge of Siam, balloon; (*pop.*) bum. — *d'essai*, pilot balloon; (*fig.*) feeler
Ballonné, e, *adj.* distended, swollen, swelled
Ballonnement, *s.m.* distension, swelling; (*vet.*) hoven
Ballonner, *v.a.n.*, **Se —,** *v.r.* to distend, to swell
Ballonnier, *s.m.* foot-ball maker *or* seller; balloonist
Ballot, *s.m.* bale, package, pack; article; (*obsolete*) tub
Ballote, *s.f.* (*bot.*) ballota, black horehound
Ballotin, *s.m.* small bale
Ballottade, *s.f.* (*rid.*) ballotade
Ballottage, *s.m.* second balloting, second ballot, second voting; (*obsolete*) balloting, ballot. *Scrutin de —*, second balloting, second ballot, second voting
Ballotte, *s.f.* pail, bucket, basket; (*obsolete*) ballot, voting-ball; (*bot.*) *V.* **Ballote**
Ballottement, *s.m.* tossing; shaking
Ballotter, *v.a.* to toss, to toss *or* shake about; to send about; to bandy; to agitate, to debate; to ballot a second time; to humbug, to bamboozle, to make fun of, to trifle with; to bale up, to pack up; — *v.n.* to shake; to go to and fro

Balnéaire, *adj.* balneary, balneal, bathing, bath
Balocher, *v.n.* (*pop.*) to rollic, to roister; to sag, to dangle [funny fellow *or* girl
Balocheu-r, se, *s.m.f.* (*pop.*) rollicking fellow,
Balon, *s.m.* (*nav.*) *V.* **Ballon**
Balourd, e, *s.m.f.* dunce, dolt, numskull; — *adj.* dull, heavy, thick-headed [stupidity
Balourdise, *s.f.* stupid thing; gross blunder;
Balsamier, *s.m.* (*bot.*) balsam-tree
Balsamine, *s.f.* (*bot.*) balsam. — *des bois*, touch-me-not [(*pharm.*) balsamic
Balsamique, *adj.* balsamic; balmy; — *s.m.*
Balsamite, *s.f.* (*bot.*) costmary
Balsamodendron, *s.m.* (*bot.*) balsamodendron
Balsane. *V.* **Balzane**
Baltagi, *s.m.* baltagi (*officer in the seraglio*)
Balthazar, *s.m.* (*fam.*) feast, jollification, blow-
Baltique, *adj. s.f.* Baltic [out
Baluchon, *s.m.* (*pop.*) bundle, parcel
Balustrade, *s.f.* balustrade; fence
Balustre, *s.m.* baluster; railing [with balusters
Balustrer, *v.a.* to rail in, to fence, to surround
Balzan, e, *adj. s.* white-footed; white-footed
Balzane, *s.f.* white-foot; blaze [horse *or* mare
Bambin, e, *s.m.f.* brat, chit, young one; baby, babe
Bambochade, *s.f.* grotesque picture, caricature
Bamboche, *s.f.* puppet; dwarf, bit of a thing, runt, shrimp; frolic, prank, spree; stuff; trifle; idle story; joke; (*bot.*) bamboo; — *adj.* tipsy, tight [life; to be on the spree
Bambocher, *v.n.* to play pranks; to lead a gay
Bambocheu-r, se, *s.m.f.* gay man *or* woman,
Bambou, *s.m.* bamboo [rake; rioter; drunkard
Ban, *s.m.* ban; proclamation; beat of drum; exile, banishment; excommunication. *Au* —, under the ban. *Dispense de —s*, (marriage) licence. *Acheter des —s*, to procure a marriage licence [trite, hackneyed; mercenary
Banal, e, *adj.* common; vulgar; common-place,
Banalement, *adv.* vulgarly, trivially
Banalité, *s.f.* vulgarity; common-place
Banane, *s.f.* banana
Bananerie, *s.f.* banana-plantation
Bananier, *s.m.* banana-tree
Bananiste, *s.m.* banana-bird
Banc, *s.m.* bench; seat; pew; form; settle; bank; bed; reef; shoal; dock, bar; box; —**s**, *pl.* school-forms, school, college. — *des accusés* or *des prévenus*, dock, bar. — *du jury* or *des jurés*, jury-box. — *des témoins*, witness-box. — *de glace*, field of ice, iceberg
Bancal, e, *adj. s.* bandy-legged; bandy-legged person, bandy-legs; (*pop.*) dot-and-go-one
Bancal, *s.m.* curved sword, cavalry-sword, sabre
Bancasse, *s.f.* (*nav.*) bunk
Banche, *s.f.* reef of rocks under water
Banco, *adj.m.* (*of exchange*) banco. *Faire* —, to hold all the money staked
Bancroche, *adj. s.m.f.* bandy-legged; bandy-legged person, bandy-legs
Bandage, *s.m.* (*surg.*) bandage; truss; bandaging, application of bandages; (*of wheels*) band, hoop, tire; (*of guns*, &c.) springs
Bandagiste, *s.m.* bandage-maker; trussmaker
Bande, *s.f.* band; head-band; fillet; slip; strip; shred; bandage; belt; stripe; string; strap; girth; plate; rail; troop; company; party; gang, set, crew; shoal; flock; flight; cushion; wrapper; tire; slice; side; shore; tier; (*her.*) bend. *A la* —, (*nav.*) on the careen; lying along. *Sous* —, (*post.*) in a wrapper, as a book-parcel. *Coller sous* —, (*billiards*) to put close to the cushion; (*fig.*) to put into a fix. *Donner de la* —, (*nav.*) to lie along, to heel. *Faire — à part*, to keep apart [(*her.*) bendy
Bandé, e, *part. adj.* bandaged, &c. (*V.* **Bander**);
Bandeau, *s.m.* head-band; band; fillet; frontlet; bandage; bandage over o.'s eyes; diadem; tiara; cloud, veil, mist, darkness; (*arch.*) string-course; skirt, skirting; (*obsolete*) widow's cap. *En —x*, (*of the hair*) plain

Bandelette, *s.f.* band; fillet; string; bandlet; (*surg.*) fascia
Bander, *v.a.* to bandage; to bind up; to bind; to tie up; to stretch; to strain; to tighten; to bend; to wind up; to cock; to brace; to string; to put a bandage over; to blindfold; to line (*a sail*); — *v.n.* to be tight *or* stiff. — *les yeux à*, to blindfold, to hoodwink. — *la caisse*, to brace the drum; (*fig.*) to get away, to run away
Se —, *v.r.* to bandage oneself; to bandage (o.'s ...); to stiffen; to grow hard; to rise (against), to oppose, to league, to band together
Bandereau, *s.m.* trumpet-sling
Banderet, *s.m.* banderet (*Swiss magistrate*)
Banderole, *s.f.* banderole; streamer, pennant; shoulder-belt; musket-belt [line
Bandière, *s.f.* banner, flag. *Front de* —, front
Bandins, *s.m.pl.* (*nav.*) rails, balustrade
Bandit, *s.m.* bandit, robber, ruffian; vagabond;
Bandoir, *s.m.* (*tech.*) spring [villain
Bandoline, *s.f.* bandoline
Bandore, *s.f.* (*mus.*) bandore
Bandoulier, Bandolier, *s.m.* highwayman, robber; vagabond; worthless fellow, blackguard
Bandoulière, *s.f.* shoulder-belt; bandoleer. *En* —, slung over the shoulder
Bandure, *s.f.* (*bot.*) pitcher-plant
Bang, Banghe, Bangue, *s.m.* Indian hemp,
Banian, *s.m.* banian [bang, bangue
Bank-note, *s.f.* English bank-note
Banksia, *s.m.*, **Banksie,** *s.f.* (*bot.*) banksia, honeysuckle-tree [precincts
Banlieue, *s.f.* suburbs, outskirts; purlieus,
Banne, *s.f.* awning; tilt; canopy; tarpaulin, covering; hamper, basket; cage, hutch, corf, corve; cart; tub [light cart
Banneau, *s.m.* small hamper; pail, bucket;
Banner, *v.a.* to cover with a tilt *or* with canvas, to cover, to tilt
Banneresse, *s.f.* banneret's wife
Banneret, *s.m. adj.* banneret
Bannerette, *s.f.* small banner
Banneton, *s.m.* basket; (*fish.*) cauf
Bannette, *s.f.* small hamper; (*pop.*) apron
Banni, e, *part.* (*V.* **Bannir**); — *s.m.f.* exile
Bannière, *s.f.* banner; standard; flag, colours; streamer. *En* —, (*nav.*) flying; (*pop.*) in o.'s shirt
Bannir, *v.a.* to banish; to exile; to expel; to dismiss; to drive away; to exclude; to reject; to lay aside [ishment, liable to be banished
Bannissable, *adj.* banishable, deserving ban-
Bannissement, *s.m.* banishment, exile
Banquais, *s.m.* (*pers. or vessel*) Newfoundland fisher, (*vessel*) banker
Banque, *s.f.* bank; banking; banking business; (*among printers*) pay; pay-day; (*nav.*) Newfoundland fisher, banker; (*pop.*) juggling; dodge, trick; puff; quackery; mountebanks. *Carnet de* —, bank-book. *Livre de* —, work-book, wages-book
Banquer, *v.n.* (*nav.*) to come to a fishing-bank; to go a cod-fishing on the Newfoundland bank
Banquereau, *s.m.* (*nav.*) little bank
Banqueroute, *s.f.* bankruptcy. *Faire* —, to be a bankrupt, to become bankrupt, to break; to fail; not to pay; to break o.'s promise; to disappoint; to forfeit
Banquerouti-er, ère, *s.m.f. adj.* bankrupt
Banquet, *s.m.* banquet, feast; banqueting; (*rid.*) banquet
Banqueter, *v.n.* to banquet; to feast; to revel
Banqueteu-r, se, *s.m.f.* banqueter, feaster, reveller
Banquette, *s.f.* stuffed bench, bench, seat; window-seat; (*of roads*) foot-path, foot-way; (*of canals, bridges*) banquet; (*rail.*) step-board, foot-board; (*fort.*) banquette; (*engin.*) bank; (*of coaches*) outside. *Jouer devant* or *pour les —s*, to play to empty benches
Banquier, *s.m.* banker; (*jest.*) payer, pay-master
Banquise, *s.f.* iceberg, floe

Banquiste, *s.m.* (*pop.*) quack, mountebank; [jobber; swindler, sharper
Banse, *s.f.* hamper
Bantam, e, *s.m.f. adj.* bantam, bantam fowl
Baobab, *s.m.* (*bot.*) baobab
Bapaume, *s.f.* (*nav.*) *En* —, at a stand-still
Baphomet, *s.m.* baphomet [ducking
Baptême, *s.m.* baptism; christening; (*nav.*)
Baptiser, *v.a.* to baptize; to christen; to nickname, to dub; to put water into, to water, to dilute; to sprinkle; (*nav.*) to duck
Baptiseur, *s.m.* baptizer
Baptismal, e, *adj.* baptismal, of baptism
Baptistaire, *adj.* of baptism, baptismal; — *s.m.* certificate of baptism
Baptiste, *s.m.f.* baptist [mony of baptism
Baptistère, *s.m.* baptistery; book of the cere-
Baquet, *s.m.* tub; bucket; trough; (*pop.*) washerwoman. — *à cœur*, tap-tub
Baqueter, *v.a.* to scoop, to bale [into the tap-tub
Baquetures, *s.f.pl.* drippings of wine *or* &c.
Bar, *s.m.* handbarrow; (*fish*) basse; (*her.*) barbel
Baragouin, Baragouinage, *s.m.* gibberish; jabber; jabbering; jargon; lingo [ish
Baragouiner, *v.a.n.* to jabber; to talk gibber-
Baragouineu-r, se, *s.m.f.* jabberer
Baraque, *s.f.* hut; shed; shanty; booth; hovel; hole; wretched place; shabby house; locker
Baraquement, *s.m.* (*mil.*) hutting; huts
Baraquer, *v.a.*, **Se** —, *v.r.* (*mil.*) to hut
†**Baraquille,** *s.f.* hash-pie
Baraterie, *s.f.* (*nav.*) barratry
Barattage, *s.m.* churning
Baratte, *s.f.* churn
Baratter, *v.a.* to churn [(*a*. *h.*) outlet
Barbacane, *s.f.* (*fort.*) barbican; loop-hole;
Barbacole, *s.m.* (*obsolete*) school-master; faro (*game*)
Barbare, *adj. s.* barbarous; barbaric; barbarian
Barbarée, *s.f.* (*bot.*) winter-cress
Barbarement, *adv.* barbarously
Barbaresque, *adj.* Barbarian, of Barbary; —**s,** *s.m.pl.* Barbary nation
Barbarie, *s.f.* barbarity, barbarousness; cruelty; rudeness; gross ignorance; barbarous act
Barbariser, *v.n.a.* to barbarize
Barbarisme, *s.m.* (*gram.*) barbarism
Barbe, *s.f.* beard; barb; awn; lappet; pinner; whiskers; wattle; gills; vane, feather; rough edge; lace curtain, curtain; fur; shaving; —**s,** *pl.* (*vet.*) barbles. *A* —, with a beard; bearded; shaving. *A sa* —, to his face. — *de capucin*, chicory salad, endive. *Faire la* — *à*, to shave; (*fig.*) to cut out, to outdo. *Se faire la* —, to shave (oneself)
Barbe, *adj. s.m.* Barbary; Barbary horse, barb
Barbé, e, *adj.* (*bot., her.*) bearded
Barbeau, *s.m.* (*fish*) barbel; (*bot.*) *V.* **Bluet.** — *de mer*, gurnet; red mullet. *Bleu* —, light [blue
Barbelé, e, *adj.* barbed; spiked
Barberie, *s.f.* shaving-room
Barbet, te, *s.m.f.* water-spaniel, barbet; telltale; police-spy; (*fish*) *V.* **Rouget**
Barbette, *s.f.* (*for nuns*) stomacher; (*fort.*) barbette. *Coucher à* —, (*pop.*) to lie with a mattress on the ground
Barbeyer, *v.n.* (*nav.*) to shiver
Barbican, *s.m.* (*bird*) barbican [beard; whisker
Barbiche, *s.f.* beard on the chin, billygoat-
Barbiche, Barbichet, Barbichon, *s.m.* young water-spaniel
Barbier, *s.m.* barber; (*fish*) serranus, sea-perch
Barbifier, *v.a.* (*fam.*) to shave
†**Barbillon,** *s.m.* little barbel; wattle; barb (*of a hook or arrow*); —**s,** *pl.* (*vet.*) barbles
Barbion, *s.m.* (*bird*) bucco
Barbiton, *s.m.* (*mus.*) barbiton
Barbon, *s.m.* grey-beard; old man; dotard; (*bot.*) sweet rush. — *odorant*, lemon grass
Barbot, *s.m.* (convicts') barber; (*pop.*) duck
Barbotage, Barbotement, *s.m.* dabbling, paddling, muddling; mess; wash
Barbote, *s.f.* burbot, eel-pout
Barboter, *v.n.a.* to dabble, to paddle, to muddle; to splash the mud about; to dirty oneself; to wade; to stutter; to mutter; (*nav.*) to shiver
Barboteur, *s.m.* dabbler, paddler; tame duck
Barboteuse, *s.f.* dabbler, paddler; street-walker
Barbotière, *s.f.* duck-pond, pond; trough
Barbotine, *s.f.* (*pharm.*) semen-contra, worm-
Barbotoire, *s.f.* trough [seed
†**Barbouillage,** *s.m.* daubing; daub; scribbling; scribble; scrawl; rigmarole, twaddle
†**Barbouillée,** *s.f.* *Se moquer de la* —, to talk downright nonsense; not to care for anybody *or* anything
†**Barbouiller,** *v.a.n.* to daub; to smear, to besmear; to smudge; to blot; to soil; to make a mess *or* a muddle of; to bungle; to confuse; to turn (*the stomach*); to scribble; to scribble *or* scrawl over; to stutter; to get confused; (*med.*) to paint; (*print.*) to slur
Se —, *v.r.* to besmear o.'s face; to injure o.'s character; to cram oneself; to get fuddled; to get confused; to get cloudy
†**Barbouilleu-r, se,** *s.m.f.* dauber; scribbler; stutterer; twaddler; bungler, botcher
†**Barbouillon,** *s.m.* *V.* **Barbouilleur**
Barbu, e, *adj.* bearded
Barbu, *s.m.* (*bird*) barbet
Barbue, *s.f.* (*fish*) brill
Barcalon, *s.m.* barcalon (*Siamese prime minister*)
Barcarol, *s.m.* (Venetian) boatman
Barcarolle, *s.f.* barcarolle (*Venetian boat-song*); barge (*abusively, for* **Barquerolle**)
Barcasse, *s.f.* (*nav.*) worn-out vessel, old tub
Barce, *s.f.* (*old gunnery*) falcon
Barcelonais, e, *adj. s.* Barcelonese
Barcelonnette, *s.f.* swing-cot, cot, bassinet
Bard, *s.m.* handbarrow [port of materials
Bardage, *s.m.* carriage in a handbarrow, trans-
Bardane, *s.f.* (*bot.*) burdock, bur
Bardaque, *s.f.* earthen water-cooler
Barde, *s.m.* bard; — *s.f.* (*armour*) bard, barb; (*cook.*) thin slip (of bacon)
Bardeau, *s.m.* shingle; stave; clap-board; small raft; hinny, mule; (*bot.*) mealy-tree; (*print.*) fount-case [slips (of bacon)
Bardée, *s.f.* handbarrow-load; (*cook.*) set of
Bardelle, *s.f.* pack-saddle
Barder, *v.a.* to barb, to bard; to cover with thin slips of bacon, to lard; to cover, to bedizen; to load; to remove
Bardeur, *s.m.* handbarrow-man; stone-carrier
Bardis, *s.m.* (*nav.*) water-boards
Bardisme, *s.m.* bardism
Bardit, *s.m.* (*old*) Germanic war-song
Bardot, *s.m.* hinny; small mule, leading mule, pack-mule; drudge; butt, laughing-stock; [(*print.*) waste paper
Barége, *s.m.* barege
Barégine, *s.f.* (*chem.*) baregine
Barême, *s.m.* ready-reckoner
Baret, *s.m.* *V.* **Barrit**
Baréter, *v.n.* *V.* **Barrir**
Barfoul, *s.m.* negro-cloth [godwit
Barge, *s.f.* barge; hay-mow; wood-pile; (*bird*)
Barguette, *s.f.* ferry-boat
†**Barguignage,** *s.m.* haggling, higgling, wavering, chaffering, hesitation, dilly-dallying, dilly-dally, shilly-shallying, shilly-shally
†**Barguigner,** *v.n.* to haggle, to higgle, to chaffer, to dilly-dally, to shilly-shally
†**Barguigneu-r, se,** *s.m.f.* haggler, higgler, [chafferer
Baricaut, *s.m.* keg
Barigel, Barisel, *s.m.* (Italian) chief constable
Barigoule, *s.f.* [*kind of mushroom; a preparation of the artichoke*] *Artichaut à la* —, artichoke dressed "barigoule" fashion
Baril, *s.m.* barrel; cask; tub; keg
†**Barillage,** *s.m.* cooperage; barrels, casks
†**Barillard,** *s.m.* (*nav.*) cooper
†**Barille,** *s.f.* barilla [barrel; (*of locks*) drum
†**Barillet,** *s.m.* small barrel; casket; (*of watches*)
†**Barillon,** *s.m.* small barrel; fish-pond reservoir

Bariolage, *s.m.* medley of colours, medley, motley; variegation
Bariolé, e, *adj.* speckled, variegated, of various colours, party-coloured, medley, motley; freckled; streaked; checkered; dapple
Barioler, *v.a.* to speckle; to variegate; to make a medley of; to streak; to checker; to dapple; to intersperse; to lard
Bariolure, *s.f.* variegation; speck, spot, streak, medley, motley; mixture
Bariquaut, *s.m. V.* **Barriquaut**
Baritel, *s.m.* winding-engine. — *à chevaux,* horse-whim, whim-gin
Barium, *s.m.* (*min.*) barium, barytum
Barlong, ue, *adj.* of unequal length
Barnabite, *s.m.* Barnabite (*friar*)
Barnache, Barnacle, *s.f. V.* **Bernache**
Barologie, *s.f.* (*phys.*) barology
Baromètre, *s.m.* barometer, weather-glass. — *à cadran,* wheel-barometer
Barométr-ique, iquement. *V.* page 3, § 1
Barométrographe, *s.m.* barometrograph
Barométrographie, *s.f.* barometrography
Baron, ne, *s.m.f.* baron; baroness
Baronnage, *s.m.* baronage
Baronnet, *s.m.* baronet
Baronnial, e, *adj.* baronial
Baronnie, *s.f.* barony
Baroque, *adj.m.f., s.m.* odd, strange, whimsical, singular, uncouth; (*of pearls*) irregular
Baroscope, *s.m.* (*phys.*) baroscope
Barque, *s.f.* bark, boat; barge; ferry-boat.
Barquée, *s.f.* boat-load [*Passer la* —, (*fig.*) to die
Barquerolle, Barquette, *s.f.* small bark, barge
Barrage, *s.m.* stoppage; barrier; bar; dam; weir; toll-bar; toll; (*com.*) diaper, barrage
Barrager, *s.m.* toll-collector
Barras, *s.m.* barras
Barre, *s.f.* bar; cross-bar; tiller, helm; stroke; dash; stripe; streak; rail; pole; goal; mark; advantage; eddy of water; —**s,** *pl.* (*game*) prison-bars, prisoners' base; (*fig.*) advantage. — *de gouvernail,* helm, tiller. — *franche,* hand-tiller. *Avoir* —*s sur,* (*fig.*) to have the advantage over
Barreau, *s.m.* bar; rail; staff; splat; wire; court of justice; courts; profession of the law, law; barristers, lawyers
Barrer, *v.a.* to bar; to bar up; to fasten; to fence up; to stop up; to stop; to block up; to obstruct; to hinder; to prevent; to oppose; to thwart; to cross; to cross off; to strike out; to cancel; to annul; (*boating*) to steer
Barrette, *s.f.* cap; cardinal's cap
Barreur, *s.m.* (*boating*) coxswain
Barricade, *s.f.* barricade; stop; bar; obstruction; barring out [struct; to bar
Barricader, *v.a.* to barricade; to stop; to ob-
Se —, *v.r.* to barricade oneself; to shut oneself up; to bar out
Barrière, *s.f.* barrier; fence; gate; turnpike, toll-gate; stile; rail-fence; starting-post; list, lists; gate of Paris; low neighbourhood, back-slums; suburban public-houses *or* tea-gardens. — *de péage,* turnpike, toll-gate
Barriquaut, *s.m.* keg, small barrel *or* cask
Barrique, *s.f.* cask; hogshead
Barrir, *v.n.* (*of elephants*) to roar, to trumpet
Barrit, *s.m.* roaring *or* roar (*of the elephant*)
Barrot, *s.m.* keg of anchovies; (*nav.*) beam
Barroter, *v.a.* (*nav.*) to fill to the beams
Barrure, *s.f.* flaw, defect
Barse, *s.f.* tea-chest
Bartavelle, *s.f.* red-legged partridge
Baryte, *s.f.* (*min.*) baryta
Baryton, *s.m.* (*mus., Greek gram.*) barytone
Baryum, *s.m.* (*min.*) barytum, barium
Bas, se, *adj.* low; lower; inferior; down; shallow; short; small; petty; early; mean; vile, base, sordid; dishonourable; degrading; despicable; cringing; servile; mercenary; vulgar; cheap; poor; cloudy
Bas, *s.m.* bottom, lower part; foot; depth; extremity; end; lower end; down; small; vulgarity; lower notes; stocking, hose; — *adv.* low; low down; down; in a low tone, softly, in a whisper; silently; aside; off. *A* —, down; down with! off with! *En* —, at the bottom; at the foot; down; below; downward; downstairs. *D'en* —, *du* —, from *or* of below; lower, under, bottom. *De — en haut,* upward. *Ici-* —, here below, in this world, on earth. *Là-* —, *par là-* —, down there, below, over there, there, over the way, yonder. *Par en* —, at the bottom, in the lower part. *Plus* —, lower; lower down; below, hereafter. *Tout* —, very low, in a low voice, softly, in a whisper; quite silently; to oneself, inwardly, secretly. *Mettre* —, to lay down; to take off; to lay aside; to cast off, to cast; to bring down, to fetch down, to strike down, to shoot, to kill; to bring low; to lower; to bring forth, to drop, to slip [to pup, to kitten, to whelp, to cub, to foal, to lamb, to yean, &c.]; to cast its horns. *Mettre à* —, to pull down, to put down, to throw down, to overthrow. *Tenir* —, to keep down; to keep under
Basalte, *s.m.* (*min.*) basalt
Basaltique, *adj.* basaltic
Basane, *s.f.* sheep-skin, sheep-leather, sheep; roan; (*pers., jest., pop.*) skin, hide
Basané, e, *adj.* tawny, swarthy, sunburnt
Basaner, *v.a. V.* **Hâler**
Basanite, *s.f.* (*min.*) basanite
Bas-bleu, *s.m.* blue-stocking
Bas-Breton, *m.,* **Basse-Bretonne,** *f., adj. s.* of Lower Brittany; native of Lower Brittany; — *s.m.* (*dialect*) low Breton [*soldier*)
Baschi-bazouk *s.m.* bashi-bazouk (*Turkish*
Bas-côté, *s.m.* aisle; pathway, side-way, side-walk, side
Bascule, *s.f.* see-saw; swing; swing-gate; rocking; weighing-machine; weigh-bridge; bar, fastening, lever; spring; trap; drop; plyer; rocker; counterpoise; balance, equilibrium; well-boat. *Couteau à* —, balance-knife. *Fusil à* —, breech-loading gun. *Pont à* —, weigh-bridge. *Faire la* —, to see-saw; to swing; to rock; to trap; to balance up and down; to tip over; to weigh down
Basculer, *v.n.a. V.* **Bascule** (*Faire la*); — *v.a.* (*pop.*) to chop ...'s head off; to hang. *Être basculé,* (*pop.*) to have o.'s head chopped off; to
Bas-de-casse, *s.m.* (*print.*) lower case [swing
Bas-dessus, *s.m.* (*mus.*) low treble, second treble
Base, *s.f.* base; basis; foundation, groundwork; grounds; support; bottom; foot; stock
Baselle, *s.f.* (*bot.*) basella, Malabar nightshade, Indian spinach
Bas-Empire, *s.m.* Lower Empire
Baser, *v.a.* to base, to ground, to found, to rest, to settle, to establish, to raise, to build; to regulate [pend, to rely; to be grounded
Se —, *v.r.* to rest, to take as a basis, to de-
Bas-fond, *s.m.* low ground, lowland, hollow, valley; flat; shallow water, shallow; lower part, lowest part; lowest depth; dregs
Basilaire, *adj.* basilar, basilary
Basile, *s.m.* base slanderer, sneak
Basilic, *s.m.* (*zool.*) basilisk; (*bot.*) basil; (*ancient artil.*) basilisk; (*myth.*) basilisk, cockatrice
Basilicon, *s.m.* (*pharm.*) basilicon
Basilique, *s.f.* basilica; — *adj.* (*anat.*) basilic, basilical; —**s,** *s.f.pl.* (*hist.*) Basilic Constitu-
Basin, *s.m.* dimity [tions, Basilics
Basique, *adj.* (*chem.*) basic
Bas-métier, *s.m.* hand-frame
Bas Normand, *m.,* **Basse-Normande,** *f., adj. s.* of Lower Normandy; native of Lower Normandy; — *s.m.* (*dialect*) low Norman
Basoche, *s.f.* (*old*) corporation of lawyers
Basque, *s.f.* skirt, tail, flap (*of a coat*); — *adj. s.m.f.* Basque, Biscayan
Basquine, *s.f.* skirt (*woman's garment*)
Bas-relief, *s.m.* low relief, bas-relief

Basse, *s.f.* (*mus.*) bass, base; basist; violoncello; violoncellist; bass-voice; bass-string; bass-note; (*nav.*) shoal, sandbank, reef, ridge. — *continue*, thorough bass, continued bass. — *de viole*, bass-viol
Basse-contre, *s.f.* bass-counter, double bass
Basse-cour, *s.f.* poultry-yard; farm-yard; stable-yard; back-yard [poultry-woman
Basse-couri-er, ère, *s.m.f.* poultry-man;
Basse-fosse, *s.f.* dungeon
Basse-licier, Basse-lissier, *s.m.* low-warper
Bassement, *adv.* meanly; basely, sordidly; vulgarly, in a low style *or* way *or* condition
Bassesse, *s.f.* meanness; mean action; baseness; base action; lowness; vulgarity; humbleness, humility [legged fellow
Basset, *s.m.* basset; terrier; turnspit; short-
†**Basse-taille,** *s.f.* (*mus.*) bass, base; bass-voice; basist; (*sculp.*) flat bas-relief
Bassette, *s.f.* (*game*) basset
Basse-tube, Basse-turbe, *s.f.* bass-clarinet
Bassie, *s.f.* (*bot.*) bassia, shea-tree, butter-tree
Bassier, *s.m.* (*nav.*) heap of sand; (*mus.*) violoncellist
Bassin, *s.m.* basin; scale; pan; collection-plate, plate; reservoir; dock; haven; moat; plain, valley, hollow; river-system; (*anat.*) pelvis. — *oculaire*, eye-bath, eye-cup, eye-glass. — *à flot*, — *de port*, floating dock, wet dock. — *d'échouage*, — *de radoub*, dry dock. *Cracher au* —, (*pop.*) to contribute, to fork out
Bassinage, *s.m.* sprinkling; bathing; fomenting; warming [copper
Bassine, *s.f.* preserving-pan, skillet; pan;
Bassinée, *s.f.* panful [menting
Bassinement, *s.m.* warming; bathing; fo-
Bassiner, *v.a.* to warm (*a bed*); to bathe; to foment; (*hort.*) to sprinkle, to water
Bassinet, *s.m.* fire-pan, pan (*of a flint-lock*); socket; bassinet (*ancient head-piece*); (*bot.*) crowfoot, spearwort, butter-cup, bachelor's-button; (*anat.*) calyx. *Cracher au* —, *V.* **Bassin**
Bassinoire, *s.f.* warming-pan
Bassiste, *s.m.* (*mus.*) violoncellist
Basson, *s.m.* (*mus.*) bassoon; bassoonist
Bassoniste, *s.m.* bassoonist
Bassorine, *s.f.* (*chem.*) bassorine
Bast, Baste, *int.* pooh! foh! nonsense! bless you! never mind! well!
Baste, *s.m.* (*at cards*) basto; — *int.* (*nav.*) avast! — *pour cela*, let that pass! let it be so! well
Basterne, *s.f.* basterna [and good!
Bastide, *s.f.* blockhouse, fortlet; (*local French, in some south districts*) country-house, country-box, villa
†**Bastille,** *s.f.* bastile; fortress; fortlet; Bastille, Bastile (*State prison in Paris, destroyed in* 1789) [crenelle renverse
†**Bastillé, e,** *adj.* (*her.*) fortified with towers;
†**Bastiller,** *v.a. V.* **Embastiller**
Bastingage, *s.m.*, **Bastingue,** *s.f.* (*nav.*) barricading; netting
Bastinguer, *v.a.* (*nav.*) to barricade
Bastion, *s.m.* (*fort.*) bastion
Bastionner, *v.a.* (*fort.*) to bastion, to fortify
Bastonnade, *s.f.* bastinado, cudgelling
Bastringue, *s.m.* dancing (*at such places as public-houses or tea-gardens*), low public ball; (*pop.*) uproar, row, shindy
Bastringueuse, *s.f.* public-ball frequenter
Bastude *s.f.* (kind of fishing-net) [abdomen
Bas-ventre, *s.m.* (*anat.*) lower part of the
Bat, *s.m.* tail (*of a fish*); (*nav.*) barrel
Bât, *s.m.* pack-saddle, pannel. *Savoir où le — blesse*, to know where the shoe pinches
Bataclan, *s.m.* (*pop.*) rattle-traps, traps; tools; rest of it; uproar, row, shindy, dust
Batadoir, *s.m.* washing-board
†**Batail,** *s.m.* (*her.*) clapper (*of a bell*)
†**Bataille,** *s.f.* battle; fight; struggle, contest; battle-array; battle-piece; main body; (*game*) beggar-my-neighbour; (*tech.*) screen. *Livrer* or *donner* —, to give battle; to fight. *Livrer une* —, to fight a battle. *En* —! (*mil.*) form line! [different tincture from that of the bell
†**Bataillé, e,** *adj.* (*her.*) with a clapper of a
†**Batailler,** *v.n.* to battle, to give battle, to fight, to struggle, to dispute, to contest hard
†**Batailleu-r, se,** *adj.* combative, pugnacious, fighting, quarrelsome, disputatious, contentious; — *s.m.f.* fighter; wrangler [*V.* **Chef**
†**Bataillon,** *s.m.* battalion; host. *Chef de* —,
Bâtard, e, *s. adj.* bastard; illegitimate; natural; spurious; mongrel, of a mixed breed; inferior, smaller; similar, like, resembling, half-and-half; slip (*-door*); inclined (*writing*); —**s,** *s.m.pl.* (*fish.*) red gentles *or* worms, brandlings
Batardeau, *s.m.* cofferdam; (*fort.*) batardeau
Batardelle, *s.f.* (*nav.*) square-sterned row-galley
Bâtardière, *s.f.* nursery of grafted trees
Bâtardise, *s.f.* bastardy; spuriousness
Batate, *s.f. V.* **Patate**
Batave, *adj. s.m.f.* Batavian [drop, Rupert's-drop
Batavique, *adj. Larme* —, glass-tear, glass-
Bataycle, *s.f.* (*nav.*) stanchion
Bâté, e, *part. adj.* saddled. *Ane* —, (*fig.*) regular donkey, stupid ass, ignoramus, bumpkin, lout
Bateau, *s.m.* boat; ship; (*of a carriage*) body. — *à vapeur*, steam-boat, steamer. — *-pilote*, pilot-boat. — *-poste*, tow-boat (*towed by post-horses*); mail-boat. — *-lavoir*, — *à lessive*, — *de selle*, washerwomen's boat, washing-boat. — *à glace*, — *brise-glace*, — *-traîneau*, ice-boat. — *de passage*, passage-boat, ferry-boat, wherry. *En trois* (or *en quatre*) —*x*, at a great expense; with a great deal of fuss; with ridiculous pomp; in great state
Batelage, *s.m.* boating; boat-service; boat-dues, waterman's fare; juggling, legerdemain; buffoonery, low jests
Batelée, *s.f.* boat-load; lots, crowd
Bateler, *v.a.* to boat, to transport in a boat
Batelet, *s.m.* small boat [buffoon
Bateleu-r, se, *s.m.f.* juggler; mountebank;
Bateli-er, ère, *s.m.f.* boatman, waterman, ferryman; boatwoman
Batellerie, *s.f.* river-boats, river-navigation
Bâter, *v.a.* to saddle
Bathymétr-ie, -ique. *V.* page 3, § 1
Bâti, *s.m.* basting, tacking, basting-threads; light building; framework, framing, frame
Bâti, e, *part. adj.* built, &c. (*V.* **Bâtir**); made, shaped, formed
Bâtier, *s.m.* pack-saddle maker [ing
Batifolage, *s.m.* toying, trifling, playing, romp-
Batifoler, *v.n.* to toy, to trifle, to play, to romp
Batifoleu-r, se, *s.m.f.* trifler, romp
Bâtiment, *s.m.* building; house; edifice; structure; fabric; ship, vessel, man; boat, craft. — *-balise*, light-ship, beacon-ship. — *marchand*, — *du* (or *de*) *commerce*, merchant-vessel, me-
Bâtine, *s.f.* pillion [chantman
Bâtir, *v.a.* to build; to construct; to erect; to establish; to raise; to found; to rest; to get up; to give birth to; to arrange, to dispose; to shape, to form; to baste, to tack
Se —, *v.r.* to be building; to be built; to build for oneself; to raise
Bâtis, *s.m. V.* **Bâti,** *s.m.* [basting, tacking
Bâtissage, *s.m.* building, construction, raising;
Bâtisse, *s.f.* building, construction
Bâtisseur, *s.m.* builder; bad builder
Bâtisseuse, *s.f.* slovenly needlewoman
Batiste, *s.f.* cambric
Batogues. *V.* **Battogues**
Bâton, *s.m.* stick; cudgel; club; staff; quarter-staff; truncheon; wand; pole; (parrot's) stand; perch (*of a cage*); spindle; spoke; crosier; baton; (*in writing*) straight stroke. — *à deux bouts*, quarter-staff. — *blanc*, mere staff, no arms; no acquired fortune; no money; poverty. *A —s rompus*, by fits and starts, by bits, by snatches, interruptedly, desultorily; desultory. *Tour du* —, perquisites, profits, pickings

Bâtoniste, *s.m.* cudgel-player, single-stick player [(*of the order of French barristers*)
Bâtonnat, *s.m.* office of "bâtonnier," presidency
Bâtonnée, *s.f.* pump-draught
Bâtonner, *v.a.* to cudgel; to cancel, to strike out; to cross; to check [cat, tipcat
Bâtonnet, *s.m.* small stick; chop-stick; (*game*)
Bâtonnier, *s.m.* handle-maker; staff-bearer; wand-bearer; constable; beadle; president (*of the order of French barristers*)
‡Batrachite, *s.f.* (*min.*) batrachite, toad-stone
Batra(‡)chomyomachie. *V.* page 3, § 1
Batracien, *s.m.* (*zool.*) batrachian [striking
Battage, *s.m.* (*agr.*) thrashing; (*tech.*) beating;
Battant, *s.m.* clapper; leaf, fold; flap; trap; (*of flags*) fly; (*pers.*) beater. *A deux —s*, (*of doors*) folding
Battant, e, *adj.* beating; pelting, driving, pouring; swing (*-door*); at work, working, going, in full swing; (*of ships*) fit for battle. — *neuf*, brand-new, bran-new. *Mener* —, to drive before one
Battant-l'œil, *s.m.* morning cap
Batte, *s.f.* beater; beetle; rammer; hammer; washing-board; flat part, flat; (*harlequin's*) wooden sword *or* wand. — *à beurre*, churn-
Batte-lessive, *s.f.* (*bird*) *V.* **Lavandière** [staff
Battellement, *s.m.* projecting roof; eaves
Battement, *s.m.* beating; beat; striking; clapping; stamping; flapping; banging, bang; slamming, slam; throbbing, throb; stroke; shaking; (*of cards*) shuffling; (*in dancing*) bat-
Batte-queue, *s.m.* (*bird*) wagtail [tement
Batterie, *s.f.* battery; fight; scuffle; beating; drum-beating; park; (*abusively for* "pièces" *or* "ressort") lock (*of firearms*); hammer (*of flint-locks*); (*nav.*) broadside; tier; gun-deck; (*fig.*) battery, plan, scheme, tactics. — *de cuisine*, kitchen utensils
Batteur, *s.m.* beater; thrasher; (*hunt.*) beater-up. — *en grange*, thrasher. — *d'estrade*, scout; idle fellow, rambler; tramp. — *de fer*, fighter, swordsman. — *de pavé*, idle fellow, idler, lounger, rambler, vagabond, loafer, tramp
Batteuse, *s.f.* beater; thrashing-machine, thrasher. — *de pavé*, street-walker
Battin, *s.m.* (*bot.*) *V.* **Sparte**
Battogues, *s.m.pl.* battogues, cudgelling (*Russian punishment*); sticks
Battoir, *s.m.* battledore; beetle; beater; bat; racquet; (*pop.*) large hand, paw; (*fig.*) clapper,
Battoire, *s.f.* churn [applauder
Battologie, *s.f.* tautology, battology
Battologique, *adj.* tautological
Battre, *v.a.n.* to beat; to strike; to knock; to batter; to defeat; to subdue; to drive; to thrash; to churn; to hammer; to coin; to raise; to whip; to lash; to shuffle; to cut; to beat out; to beat up; to beat down; to beat about; to decant over and over; to go over; to search, to explore; to scour; to range; to stun; to clap; to flap; to flutter; to throb; to pant; to beat against; to bang; to patter; to wash; to shake; to be loose; to work, to be working; (*nav.*) to flag against; to flag. — *en ruine* or *en brèche*, to batter down; to run down; to nonplus. — *froid à*, to give the cold shoulder to, to look cold upon. — *le fer*, to strike the iron; to work iron; to fence
Se —, *v.r.* to fight, to have a fight; to scramble; to beat (o.'s . . .)
Battu, e, *part. adj.* beaten; fought; &c. (*V.* **Battre**); tossed; disabled; (— *de l'oiseau*) cast down; low; dejected; dispirited; (*of metals*) wrought; (*of the eyes*) heavy, dead. *Avoir les yeux —s*, to look fatigued about the eyes
Battue, *s.f.* (*hunt.*) battue, beat; (*of a horse*) tramp; (*of a fish*) mud-bed. *Faire une — dans*, to beat (*a wood*)
Batture, *s.f.* gold-lacquering; mordant, gold-size; (*nav.*) shoal, sandbank, reef, ridge; (*fish.*) shallow

Batz, *s.m.* batz (*German coin*)
Bau, *s.m.* (*nav.*) beam. *Faux* —, orlop-beam. *Maître* —, *grand* —, midship-beam
Baubi, Baubis, *s.m.* (Norman hound for hunting hares, foxes, and wild boars)
Baud, *s.m.* stag-hound, Barbary hound
Baudelaire, *s.m.* *V.* **Badelaire**
Bauder, *v.n.* (*hunt.*) to bark [frame *or* trestle
Baudet, *s.m.* donkey, ass, jackass; sawyer's
Baudir, *v.n.* (*hunt.*) to bark; — *v.a.* (*hunt.*) to excite, to cheer
†Baudreuil, *s.m.* *V.* **Baudroie** [(*old*) baldrick
Baudrier, *s.m.* shoulder-belt, cross-belt, belt;
Baudroie, *s.f.* (*fish*) angler, fishing-frog, frog-fish, toad-fish, sea-devil
Baudruche, *s.f.* goldbeater's skin
Bauge, *s.f.* lair; filth; mud; dirty hovel, filthy hole; (*squirrel's*) nest; pile (*of vine-sticks, &c.*);
Baugue, *s.f.* sea-weed [pugging mortar
Bauhine, Bauhinie, *s.f.* (*bot.*) bauhinia
Baume, *s.m.* balm, balsam; mint, balm-mint; ointment; comfort, consolation; alleviation; — *s.f.* (*local*) grotto; (*nav.*) spanker
Baumier, *s.m.* (*bot.*) balsam-tree, balm-tree
Bauque, *s.f.* *V.* **Baugue**
Bauquière, *s.f.* (*nav.*) clamp
Baux, *pl.* of **Bail**; (*nav.*) *pl.* of **Bau**
Bavard, e, *adj. s.* prattling, talkative, blabbing; prattler, talker, blab, gossip, chatterbox; twaddler
Bavardage, *s.m.* prattling, prattle, talking, talk; babbling; gossip; blabbing; tittle-tattle, scandal; talkativeness; twaddle; gibberish
Bavarder, *v.n.* to prate, to prattle, to talk, to blab, to gossip, to chatter; to twaddle
Bavarderie, *s.f.* prattle, prate, chatter; talkativeness, loquacity
Bavarois, e, *adj. s.* Bavarian; Bavarian fashion
Bavaroise, *s.f.* (drink made chiefly with tea, or milk, or coffee, or chocolate, and sweetened with some syrup) [(*of silk-worms*) first threads
Bave, *s.f.* drivel, slaver; foam; slime; spittle;
Baver, *v.n.* to drivel, to slaver, to slabber, to dribble; to foam; (*tech.*) to run down; (*pop.*) to sputter, to spout, to mouth, to hold forth
Bavette, *s.f.* feeder; bib. *Tailler des —s*, to
Baveuse, *s.f.* (*fish*) shan [gossip
Baveu-x, se, *adj.* drivelling, slavering, slabbering; foaming; slimy; slabbery; viscous; blotchy; — *s.m.f.* driveller, slaverer, slabberer. *Chairs —ses*, (*med.*) proud flesh. *Omelette —se*, soft *or* underdone omelet
Bavoché, e, *adj.* (*print.*) smeared, smeary
Bavocher, *v.a.* (*print.*) to smear [monk
Bavochure, *s.f.* (*print.*) smearing, smudge,
Bavoir, *s.m.* bib
Bavolet, *s.m.* country-woman's head-dress, rustic cap; country-lass; (*of bonnets*) curtain
Bavure, *s.f.* seam; bur; blister
Bayadère, *s.f.* bayadere
Bayard, Bayart, *s.m.* handbarrow
Bayaudier, *s.m.* *V.* **Bajoyer**
Bayer, *v.n.* to gape; to hanker (after). — *aux corneilles*, to gape in the air, to stand gaping
Bayeu-r, se, *s.m.f.* gaper; gazer; starer; idler
Bayonnais, e, *adj. s.* of Bayonne, Bayonnese,
Bayoque, *s.f.* *V.* **Baïoque** [native of Bayonne
Bazar, *s.m.* bazaar; (*pop., jest.*) blessed place; hovel; house; shop; concern; house of ill fame; traps, furniture
Bazat, Bazac, *s.m.* Jerusalem cotton, bazat
Bdellium, *s.m.* (*pharm.*) bdellium
Bdellomètre, *s.m.* (*surg.*) bdellometer
Béant, e, *adj.* gaping, yawning, wide open, open; wide; large; with widely-open mouth
Béarnais, e, *adj. s.* of Bearn, Bearnese, native of Bearn
Béat, e, *adj. s.* sanctimonious; blissful; would-be saint, bigot, hypocrite; devotee; saint
Béatification, *s.f.* beatification
Béatifier, *v.a.* to beatify
Béatifique, *adj.* beatific, beatifical, blissful

†**Béatilles,** *s.f.pl.* dainties, delicacies; nunnery fancy-works
Béatitude, *s.f.* beatitude, blessedness, bliss
Beau, Bel, *m.*, **Belle,** *f.*, *adj.* fine; beautiful; fair; handsome; pretty; nice; elegant; graceful; smart; spruce; lofty; noble; happy; glorious; splendid; illustrious; great; large; admirable; excellent; good; charming; lovely; pleasant, agreeable; useful; honourable; seemly, proper, becoming, suitable; lucky; calm, quiet; smooth; very; — *adv.* finely. *Tout —!* *V.* **Tout.** *Bel et bien*, right well; properly; soundly; in fine style; in good earnest; quite, entirely. *Bel et bon*, very fine, very good, very well; sound; positive; plain; great; capital; in plenty. *De plus belle*, more than ever; harder (*or* louder *or* faster *or* deeper *or* worse, &c.) than before *or* than ever; with renewed ardour *or* efforts; with increased vigour; again, anew, over again. *De plus — en plus —*, finer and finer; better and better; (*ironically*) worse and worse. *En —*, on the bright side; favourably; in a favourable light; under a favourable aspect; to advantage; flattered; better-looking. *Il y a — jour* or *— temps que* ..., it is a good long while since ... *Avoir* — ..., to ... in vain. *Il eut — crier*, he called out in vain, it was in vain that he called out, it was of no use (*or* it was useless) for him to call out. *Vous avez — dire, faire*, say, do what you will. *Vous avez* (or *aurez*) *— crier, on ne vous répondra pas*, you may call out as long *or* as loud as you like, you will get no answer. *L'avoir beau* or *belle*, to have a fair *or* fine opportunity. *La donner belle, le donner beau*, *V.* **Donner.** *L'échapper belle, la manquer belle*, *V.* **Échapper, Manquer.** *Faire —*, to smarten, to spruce, to make spruce; to be agreeable (to); to be a fine thing (to); to be fine weather, to be fine. *Faire le —*, to play the beau. *Se faire —*, to get handsome; to make oneself smart, to smarten up, to spruce up. *Se mettre au —*, (*of the weather*) to get fine, to clear up
Beau, *s.m.* excellence, perfection; beauty; beauties; beautiful; good things; best; fine part *or* side, fine place; fine weather, fair; fop; exquisite; beau [Beauce
Beauceron, ne, *adj. s.* of Beauce; native of
Beaucoup, *adv. s.m.* much, many; a great deal, a great many; far; highly; very; very much; very well; great. *A — près*, by far; near. *De —*, by much, by far, far
Beau-fils, *s.m.* (*with a hyphen*) stepson; (*obsolete for* "gendre") son-in-law; (*obsolete*) dandy; (*without a hyphen*) *V.* **Beau** *and* **Fils**
Beau-frère, *s.m.* brother-in-law; step-brother
Beaujolais, *s.m.* beaujolais (wine)
Beaune, *s.m.* beaune (wine)
Beau-père, *s.m.* father-in-law; step-father
Beaupré, *s.m.* (*nav.*) bowsprit
Beauté, *s.f.* beauty; fineness; handsomeness; loveliness; prettiness; comeliness; neatness; elegance; smartness; agreeableness, pleasantness; attraction; perfection; excellence
Beaux-arts, *s.m.pl.* fine arts; art [lings
Beaux-esprits, *s.m.pl.* men of wit, wits; wit-
Bébé, *s.m.* baby; baby-doll; dwarf; darling, ducky, dear [thing
Bébête, *s.f.* (*childish slang*) animal, creature,
Bec, *s.m.* beak; bill; snout; spout; nib; neb; burner, socket; lamp; rostrum; angle; point (*of land*); mouthpiece; mouth; nose; face; tongue; whistle; darling, duck. *— à —*, *V.* **Tête-à-tête.** *—jaune*, young bird; ignorance; footing. *— et ongles*, tooth and nail. *Le — dans l'eau*, in suspense. *Faire le — à*, to give (*one*) his cue. *Faire le petit —*, to mince; to turn up o.'s nose. *Passer la plume par le —*, to disappoint, to frustrate, to balk. *Se prendre de —*, to have a quarrel. — **-cornu,** *s.m.* (*obsolete*) fool, idiot. — **-courbe,** *s.m.* (*bird*) *V.* **Avocette.** — **-croisé,** *s.m.* (*bird*) cross-bill. — **-d'âne,** *s.m.* (*carp.*) paring-chisel; (*surg.*) forceps. — **-de-cane,** *s.m.* spring-lock; pick-lock. — **-de-corbin,** *s.m.* bill-head; ripping-iron; forceps; (*obsolete*) pole-axe, halberd; yeoman (of the guard). — **-de-grue,** *s.m.* (*bot.*) stork's-bill. — **-de-lièvre,** *s.m.* hare-lip; hare-lipped person. — **-en-ciseaux,** *s.m.* (*bird*) scissor-bill, cut-water. — **-en-cuiller,** *s.m.* (*bird*) spoon-bill. — **-en-scie,** *s.m.* (*bird*) goosander, merganser, smew. — **-figues,** *s.m.* *V.* **Becfigue.** — **-fin,** *s.m.* (*bird*) warbler. — **-tranchant,** *s.m.* (*bird*) *V.* **Pingouin**
Bécabunga, *s.m.* *V.* **Beccabunga**
Bécard, *s.m.* *V.* **Beccard**
Bécarde, *s.f.* (*bird*) Cayenne shrike
Bécarre, *s.m. adj.* (*mus.*) natural
Bécarriser, *v.a.* (*mus.*) to mark with a natural
Bécasse, *s.f.* woodcock; (*pers.*) idiot, goose. — *de mer*, (*fish*) snipe-fish, trumpet-fish, bellows-fish; (*bird*) curlew. *Brider la —*, (*fig.*) to catch the bird [sandpiper
Bécasseau, *s.m.* young woodcock *or* snipe;
Bécassin, Bécasson, *s.m.* (*bird*) juddock,
Bécassine, *s.f.* snipe [jack-snipe
Bécassonnier, *s.m.* water-fowl gun
Bécau, *s.m.* young snipe [lime
Beccabunga, *s.m.* (*bot.*) beccabunga, brook-
Beccard, *s.m.* male salmon; (*bird*) goosander, merganser, smew [pecker, pettychaps
Becfigue, *s.m.* (*bird*) beccafico, fig-eater, fig-
Béchamel, *s.f.* cream-sauce
Bêche, *s.f.* spade; (*zool.*) *V.* **Coupe-bourgeons.** — *de mer*, (*zool.*) beche-de-mer, trepang
Bêcher, *v.a.* to dig [bite, to slander; to bully
Bécher, *v.a.* (*pop.*) to peck, to peck at; to back-
Bêcheur, *s.m.* digger
Béchique, *adj.m.f., s.m.* (*med.*) pectoral
Bêchoir, Bêchon, Bêchot, *s.m.* (*agr.*) hoe
Bécot, *s.m.* (*pop.*) mouth; kiss
Bécoter, *v.a.*, **Se —,** *v.r.* (*pop.*) to kiss
Becque-cornu, *s.m.* (*obsolete*) fool, idiot
Becqué, e, *adj.* (*her.*) beaked
Becquée, *s.f.* beakful, billful; food
Becqueter, *v.a.* to peck; to pick [each other
Se —, *v.r.* to peck each other; to bill; to kiss
Bécune, *s.f.* (*fish*) barracuda
Bedaine, *s.f.* (*fam.*) paunch, corporation
Bédane, *s.m.* (*carp.*) paring-chisel
Bedeau, *s.m.* beadle; verger
Bédegar, Bédeguar, *s.m.* bedeguar, sweet-briar sponge, rose-gall
Bedon, *s.m.* (*pop.*) paunch, belly, corporation; fat-sides; (*obsolete*) drum
Bédouin, *s.m. adj.* Bedouin, Arab; usurer, hard bargainer, screw, dun, miser, Shylock, hard-hearted wretch
Bée, *s.m.* baa (*bleating*); — *s.f.* opening; — *adj.f.* *A gueule —*, with one end open
Béer, *v.n.* *V.* **Bayer;** — *v.a.* (*old*) to open
Beffroi, *s.m.* belfry; alarm-bell; great bell; frame, stage, cage, case
Bégaud, e, *adj.* (*pop.*) simple, silly, ignorant
Bégayement, Bégaiement, *s.m.* stammering, stuttering; lisping
Bégayer, *v.n.a.* to stammer, to stutter; to lisp
Begma, *s.m.* (*med.*) sputum
Bégone, *s.f.*, **Bégonia,** *s.m.* (*bot.*) begonia
Bégu, ë, *adj.* (*of horses*) still marking though aged, counter-marked, bishoped
Bègue, *adj. s.m.f.* stammering, stuttering; stammerer, stutterer
Bégueule, *s.f. adj.* great prude, squeamish humbug, strait-laced fool; squeamish, strait-laced [mishness, humbug
Bégueulerie, *s.f.* outrageous prudery, squea-
Béguin, e, *s.m.f.* beguin, monk; beguine, nun; bigot
Béguin, *s.m.* child's cap, cap, biggin; hood, cowl; (*pop.*) noddle, pate; whim, maggot, crotchet, hobby; fancy; love; infatuation
Béguinage, *s.m.* nunnery of beguines; conventual life; affected devotion, bigotry

Béguiner, *v.n.* to affect devotion, to play the hypocrite, to cant
Bégum, *s.f.* begum (*Indian title*)
Béhémoth, *s.m.* behemoth
Béhen, *s.m.* (*bot.*) behen [undyed serge
Beige, *adj.* (*of wool*) natural, undyed; — *s.f.*
†**Beigne,** *s.f.* (*pop.*) bunch of fives
†**Beignet,** *s.m.* fritter
Beiram, Beirem. *V.* **Bairam**
Béjaune, *s.m.* young bird, nestling, eyas, nias; youngster, novice, ninny; silliness; ignorance;
Bel, le, *adj. V.* **Beau** [footing
Bélandre, *s.f.* (*nav.*) bilander; — *s.m.* (*mil.*) hos-
Belée, *s.f.* (*nav.*) white hawser [pital conveyance
Bêlement, *s.m.* bleating
Bélemnite, *s.f.* (*fossil*) belemnite, thunderstone
Bêler, *v.n.* to bleat
Bel-esprit, *s.m.* man of wit, wit; witling
Belette, *s.f.* weasel
Belge, *adj. s.m.f.* Belgian; Belgian fashion
Bélier, *s.m.* ram; (*mil.*) battering-ram; (*poet.*) spring
Bélière, *s.f.* sheep-bell; clapper-ring; ring
Belin, *s.m. V.* **Blin**
Béliner, *v.n.* (*vet.*) to couple, to tup
Bélître, *s.m.* (*obsolete*) caitiff, rascal [shade
Belladone, *s.f.* (*bot.*) belladonna, deadly-night-
Bellâtre, *s.m.f. adj.* insipid beauty; of insipid beauty, beauish, foppish, coquettish
Belle, (*feminine of* **Beau,** *adj., which see*) — *s.f.* fair lady, handsome woman; genteel young woman; beauty; belle; mistress, sweetheart; rubber-game, rubber (*that decides the contest*), winning game, conqueror, deciding *or* odd hit (*in fencing*), deciding heat (*in racing*); fair opportunity; opportunity; revenge; —**s,** *pl.* fair sex, fair; belles; fine things; fine tricks, pretty tricks *or* pranks; fine stories. *Faire la* —, to set up for a beauty; to play the winning game *or* &c. — **-dame,** *s.f.* (*bot.*) *V.* **Arroche.** — **-de-jour,** *s.f.* (*bot.*) minor convolvulus. — **-de-nuit,** *s.f.* (*bot.*) marvel of Peru; (*pers., jest.*) night reveller, gay woman. — **d'un jour,** *s.f.* (*bot.*) day-lily. — **-fille,** *s.f.* daughter-in-law; step-daughter. — **-mère,** (*fam., obsolete,* — **-maman**) *s.f.* mother-in-law; step-mother. — **-sœur,** *s.f.* sister-in-law; step-sister. —**s-lettres,** *V.* **Lettre.** — **-tante,** *s.f.* step-aunt
Bellement, *adv.* softly, gently; nicely; finely; cleverly
Bellicant, *s.m.* (*fish*) gurnard [belligerent
Belligérant, e, *adj.,* **Belligérant,** *s.m.*
Belliqueu-x, se, *adj.* warlike, martial, bellicose; brave, courageous, valiant; quarrelsome
Bellis, *s.m.* (*bot.*) bellis, daisy
Bellissime, *adj.* extremely fine, most beautiful, most handsome; — *s.f.* (kind of pear; kind of tulip)
Bellon, *s.m.* tub; (*med.*) bellon, lead colic
Bellone, *s.f.* (*poet.*) war [*s.m.f.* pretty dear
Bellot, te, *adj.* pretty, handsome, natty; —
Bellote, *s.f.* (*bot.*) ballote oak
Belluaire, *s.m. V.* **Bestiaire;** — *adj.* belluine
Belluge, *s.f.* beluga, white sturgeon
Belluge, *s.m.,* **Bellouga, Béluca, Béluga,** *s.m.* sea-beluga, white whale
Belneau, *s.m.* dung-cart
Bel-oncle, *s.m.* step-uncle [dere
Belvéder, Belvédère, *s.m.* belvedere, belvi-
Belvisia, *s.m.,* **Belvisie,** *s.f.* (*bot.*) belvisia
Belzof, *s.m.* (*bot.*) benjamin-tree, benjamin
Bémol, *s.m. adj.* (*mus.*) flat
Bémoliser, *v.a.* (*mus.*) to mark with a flat
Ben, *s.m.* (*bot.*) ben. *Noix de* —, ben-nut
Bénar, *s.m.* truck
Bénarde, *s.f. adj.f. Serrure* —, lock opening and shutting on both sides of the door. *Clé* —,
Bénate, *s.f.* salt-case [solid key
Bénédicité, *s.m.* grace (*before meals*)
Bénédictin, e, *s.m.f. adj.* Benedictine
Bénédiction, *s.f.* blessing, benediction; consecration; thanks; plenty. *En* —, blessed. ... *que c'est une* —, famously, amazingly; dreadfully, with a vengeance [profitable spec
Bénef, *s.m.* (*pop. abbrev. of* "bénéfice") profit,
Bénéfice, *s.m.* benefit; advantage; profit; gratuity; privilege; living, benefice; relief. — *simple,* sinecure. *Représentation à* —, benefit-performance, benefit-night. *A* —, with a profit; at a premium. *Au* — *de,* for the benefit of; in aid of, in support of. *En* —, in pocket
Bénéficiable, *adj.* likely to pay
Bénéficiaire, *adj.* beneficiary. *Héritier* —, (*in law; synonymous with* "héritier sous bénéfice d'inventaire." *V.* **Inventaire**)
Bénéficiaire, *s.m.f.* beneficiary; recipient, receiver, grantee; person whose benefit it is; (*in law; synonymous with* "héritier *or* héritière sous bénéfice d'inventaire." *V.* **Inventaire**)
Bénéficial, e, *adj.* relating to livings
Bénéficiel, le, *adj.* beneficial, profitable
Bénéficier, *s.m.* beneficiary; beneficed clergyman; incumbent
Bénéficier, *v.n.* to get *or* make a profit; (*de*) to profit (by); — *v.a.* (*mining*) to work, to dig,
Se —, *v.r.* to be worked [to explore
Bénéficière, *s.f.* beneficiary
Bénéficieu-x, se, *adj.* profitable, well-paying
Benêt, *adj. s.m.* silly, simple, foolish; booby, simpleton, fool
Bénévole, *adj.* benevolent, favourably disposed, friendly, kind; gratuitous, unfounded; amateur
Bénévolement, *adv.* kindly, benevolently; gratuitously, without foundation [fashion
Bengalais, e, *adj. s.* Bengalese; Bengalese
Bengali, *s.m.* (*language*) Bengali, Bengalee; (*bird*) bengaly
Bengali, e, *adj.* Bengali, Bengalee
Béni, e, *adj.* blessed; hallowed [kindly
†**Bénignement,** *adv.* benignantly, benignly;
†**Bénignité,** *s.f.* benignity; kindness
†**Bénin,** *m.,* **Bénigne,** *f., adj.* benignant; benign; mild; gentle; placid; good-natured; kind; kind and easy
Bénir, *v.a.* to bless; to consecrate. — *la table,* to say grace (*before meals*). — *des pieds,* (*pop.*) to be hanged, to swing
Bénissable, *adj.* blessable
Bénisseu-r, se, *s.m.f.* blesser
Bénit, e, *adj.* consecrated; holy. *Eau —e; Eau —e de cour; V.* **Eau**
Bénitier, *s.m.* holy-water basin *or* pot *or* font, aspersorium; (*shell*) giant tridacna, hippopus; scollop [favourite child, darling
Benjamin, *s.m.* Benjamin, Ben, youngest boy,
Benjoin, *s.m.* benzoin, benjamin
Benne, *s.f.* hamper, basket; cage, hutch, corf, corve; grate; cart
Benoît, e, *adj.* holy, blessed; sanctimonious
Benoîte, *s.f.* (*bot.*) bennet, avens [critically
Benoîtement, *adv.* sanctimoniously, hypo-
Benzine, *s.f.* (*chem.*) benzine, benzoline, benzole
Benzoate, *s.m.* (*chem.*) benzoate
Benzoïne, *s.f.* (*chem.*) benzoine
Benzoïque, *adj.* (*chem.*) benzoic
Benzole, *s.f.* (*chem.*) benzole, benzoline, benzine
Beotien, ne, *adj. s.* Bœotian [gross ignorance
Béotisme, *s.m.* Bœotism, dulness, stupidity,
Bèque-bois, *s.m.* (*bird*) *V.* **Sittelle**
Béquée, *s.f. V.* **Becquée** [scrap
Béquet, *s.m.* small beak; pike (*fish*); patch;
Béqueter, *v.a. V.* **Becqueter**
†**Béquillard,** *s.m.* old man walking on crutches, old cripple; old codger
†**Béquille,** *s.f.* crutch; (*hort.*) spud; (*tech.*) cramp-arm; (*nav.*) shore; (*pop.*) gallows, drop
†**Béquiller,** *v.n.a.* to walk on crutches; (*hort.*) to spud; (*nav.*) to shore, to support; (*pop.*) to eat, to peck, to grub; to hang
†**Béquilleur,** *s.m.* (*pop.*) hangman, Jack Ketch
Béquot, *s.m.* young snipe
Ber, *s.m.* (*nav.*) cradle
Berbère, *adj. s.m.* of Barbary, Barbary, Barbarian; Berber; Barbary horse, barb

Berbéris, *s.m.* (*bot.*) barberry

†Bercail, *s.m.* sheep-fold, fold [wood-bird

Berce, *s.f.* (*bot.*) cow-parsnip; — *s.m.* small

Berceau, *s.m.* bassinet; cradle; arbour, bower; vault; covered walk; archery-ground; beginning, origin, source, birth, infancy, native place

Bercelonnette, *s.f. V.* **Barcelonnette**

Bercement, *s.m.* rocking; lulling; delusion, deception

Bercer, *v.a.* to rock; to swing; to dandle; to nurse; to lull; to delude; to flatter; to quiet; to bring up [lulling music

Berceuse, *s.f.* rocker; rocking-chair; lullaby;

Berche, *s.f.* (*old gunnery*) falcon

Berdin, *s.m.* vine-fretter

Béret, *s.m.* Tam o' Shanter cap, Scotch blue-bonnet (*often red, &c. in France*)

Bergamasque, *adj. s.m.f.* Bergamese; — *s.f.* bergomask (*dance, tune*)

Bergame, *s.f.* bergamot (*tapestry*)

Bergamote, *s.f.* bergamot (*pear, citron*): bergamot-box, sweetmeat-box [citrus bergamia

Bergamotier, *s.m.* (*bot.*) bergamot (*tree*),

Bergat, *s.m.* (*fish.*) bow-net

Berge, *s.f.* high *or* steep bank; bank; roadside; bluff shore, bluff; narrow barge, barge

Bergelade, *s.f.* (*agr.*) mixture of vetch and oats

Berger, *s.m.* shepherd; swain, lover. *L'heure du* —, the lovers' time, the propitious time, the happy moment; the favourable opportunity, the proper time. *L'étoile du* —, Venus, the shepherd's star [painting of pastoral life

Bergerade, *s.f.* shepherds-scene, scene *or*

Bergère, *s.f.* shepherdess; nymph, lass; sweetheart; easy chair; wagtail (*bird*); kind of ancient head-dress

Bergerette, *s.f.* young shepherdess, lass; wagtail (*bird*); honey-wine, œnomel

Bergerie, *s.f.* sheep-fold, pen; flock; pastoral; scene of pastoral life; rustic manners

Bergeron, *s.m. V.* **Bourgeron** [wagtail (*bird*)

Bergeronnette, *s.f.* young shepherdess; lass;

Bergin, *s.m.* (kind of fishing-net)

Bergot, *s.m. V.* **Bergat**

Béribéri, *s.m.* (*med.*) beriberi

Bérichet, Bérichon, Bérichot, *s.m.* wren

Béril, *s.m.* (*min.*) beryl

Berle, *s.f.* (*bot.*) water-parsnip, skirret

Berline, *s.f.* berlin (*carriage*)

Berlingot, *s.m.* single-seated berlin, brougham; kind of sugar-plum [liner, native of Berlin

Berlinois, e, *adj. s.* of Berlin, Berlinese, Ber-

Berloque, *s.f.* (*mil.*) barrack-call, dinner *or* breakfast-drum. *Battre la* —, (*fig.*) to talk at random, to wander

Berlue, *s.f.* dimness of sight; (*med.*) "muscæ volitantes." *Avoir la* —, to be dim-sighted; (*fig.*) to be blind, not to see farther than o.'s nose

Berme, *s.f.* (*of canals, and fort.*) berm, berme

Bermudien, *s.m.* (*nav.*) Bermuda-sloop

Bermudienne, *s.f.* (*bot.*) bermudiana

Bernable, *adj.* deserving to be tossed in a blanket, to be laughed at, ridiculous [nacle

Bernache, Bernacle, *s.f.* (*bird, mollusc*) bar-

Bernage, *s.m.* (*agr.*) corn and pulse (*sown in autumn for green food in the spring*)

Bernardin, e, *s.m.f.* Bernardine [pagurus

Bernard-l'ermite, *s.m.* (*zool.*) hermit-crab,

Berne, *s.f.*, **Bernement**, *s.m.*, tossing in a blanket, blanketing; chaffing. *En berne*, (*nav.*) awaft; half-mast high

Berner, *v.a.* to toss in a blanket, to blanket; to chaff, to flout, to laugh at, to make fun of, to make a fool of

Bernesque, *adj. V.* **Berniesque**

Berneu-r, se, *s.m.f.* tosser (in a blanket); chaffer, banterer; — *adj.* tossing; chaffing, bantering

Bernicle, *s.f.* (*zool.*) *V.* **Bernacle**; **—s**, *pl.* (*pop.*) trifles, trumpery things, a mere nothing; nobodies, cads

Berniesque, *adj.* (*Italian liter.*) in the style of Berni, burlesque

Bernique, *int.* not a bit of it, no use, no go

Berniquet, *s.m.* bran-chest; (*pop.*) beggary, last shift [of Berne

Bernois, e, *adj. s.* of Berne, Bernese, native

Béroé, *s.m.* (*zool.*) beroe

Berrichon, ne, *adj. s.* of Berri (*or* Berry); native of Berri; Berri horse *or* mare; Berri sheep

Bertavelle, *s.f.* bow-net; red-legged partridge

Bertellage, *s.m.* (*mas.*) setting (*plastering*)

Berteller, *v.a.n.* (*mas.*) to set (*plaster*)

Bertelo, *s.m.* (*slang*) bob (*coin*)

Berthe, *s.f.* bertha; cape; fur-collarette

Berthelot, *s.m.* (*nav.*) prow

Bertholletia, *s.m.* (*bot.*) bertholletia

Bertrand, *s.m.* confederate, accomplice, pa

Bérule, *s.f.* (*bot.*) *V.* **Berle**

Béryl, *s.m.* (*min.*) beryl

Besace, *s.f.* wallet; beggary. *Être à la* —, to be reduced to beggary, to be beggared, to be ruined, to be a beggar [tramp

Besacier, *s.m.* wallet-bearer, walleteer, beggar,

Besaigre, *adj.* sourish

Besaiguë, *s.f.* twibil

Besant, *s.m.* (*coin, and her.*) bezant, besant

Besanté, e, *adj.* (*her.*) bezanty

Beseau, *s.m.* (*agr.*) trench

Beset, Besas, *s.m.* double ace, ambsace

Besi, *s.m.* species of pear [(*tech.*) face-guard

Besicles, *s.f.pl.* (*obsolete*) spectacles, barnacles;

Besigue, *s.m.* (a game at cards)

Beslère, Beslérie, *s.f.* (*bot.*) besleria

Besoche, *s.f.* mattock

†Besogne, *s.f.* work, task; piece of work; business; job; trouble; (*obsolete*) requisite; fare. *Aimer la — faite*, to hate work

†Besogner, *v.n.a.* to work, to labour; to do

†Besogneu-x, se, Besoigneu-x, se, *adj.* needy, necessitous

Besoin, *s.m.* need; want; necessity; requirement; exigency; emergency; occasion; hunger; necessaries. *Au* —, in case of need, if need be, if necessary; when necessary, when *or* whenever one wants; on the occasion; in need; at a pinch; as the case may be. *Avoir — de*, to want, to need, to require; to be *or* stand in need of; must; to be anxious; to have business. *Être — de, y avoir — de*, (*imp.*, there be need of; to be necessary to; to want, to require. *Faire* —, to be wanted; to be necessary; to be missed. *On connaît les amis au* —, a friend in need is a friend indeed

Besolet, *s.m.* (*Swiss French*) sea-gull

Besson, ne, *s.m.f.* (*local*) twin

Bestiaire, *s.m.* beast-fighter, gladiator, bestiarius; beast-tamer; (*old Fr. liter.*) fable-book, [bestiaire

Bestial, e, *adj.* bestial, beastly

Bestialement, *adv.* bestially

Bestialiser, *v.a.* to bestialize

Se —, *v.r.* to become bestialized

Bestialité, *s.f.* bestiality, beastliness

Bestiasse, *s.f.* stupid ass, foolish creature

Bestiaux, *s.m.pl.* cattle; beasts

Bestiole, *s.f.* little animal; (*pers.*) dunce

Bestion, *s.m.* little animal

Bésy, *s.m. V.* **Besigue**

Béta, sse, *s.m.f.* fool, blockhead, simpleton

†Bétail, *s.m.* cattle; (*fig.*) herd; flock

Bête, *s.f.* animal; beast; brute; vermin; fool; creature, thing; fellow; aversion; animal nature; body, carcass, self, inside; (*game*) beast. — *brute*, brute. — *à cornes*, horned beast *or* animal; horned cattle. — *à laine*, sheep. — *à Dieu*, — *à bon Dieu*, lady-bird. — *du bon Dieu*, good foolish creature. — *noire*, black beetle; (*hunt.*) wild boar; (*fig.*) aversion. — *rousse*, (*hunt.*) fox. *Faire la* —, to play the fool; to be silly *or* foolish; (*at cards*) to beast

Bête, *adj.* stupid, foolish, silly; amiss. — *à manger du foin*, exceedingly stupid

Bétel, *s.m.* (*bot.*) betel
Bêtement, *adv.* foolishly, stupidly
Bétaune, *s.f.* cesspool
Bétille, *s.f.* (Indian) muslin
Bêtise, *s.f.* stupidity, foolishness, silliness; absurdity; folly; piece of folly; blunder; stupid *or* foolish *or* silly thing, nonsense, foolery; oddity, farce, joke; broad talk; trifle
Bétoine, *s.f.* (*bot.*) betony
Bétoire, *s.m.* drain-pit, drain-hole
Béton, *s.m.* (*mas.*) concrete; (*med.*) colostrum
Bétonnage, *s.m.* (*mas.*) concrete-work
Bétonner, *v.a.* (*mas.*) to build with concrete
Bette, *s.f.* (*bot.*) beet; (*fish.*) fishing-boat; (*nav.*) mud-lighter
Betterave, *s.f.* (*bot.*) beet-root; mangold-wurzel
Bétuline, *s.f.* (*chem.*) betuline
Bétuse, *s.f.* oat-bin; (*fish.*) cauf [outcry, roar
Beuglement, *s.m.* bellowing; lowing; loud
Beugler, *v.n.* to bellow; to low; to clamour, to vociferate, to roar
Beurre, *s.m.* butter; pat of butter; (*old chem.*) chloride (*the modern name*), butter (*obsolete*); (*slang*) rhino. *Lait de* —, butter-milk. *Au* —, in *or* with butter; buttered. *Au — noir*, with browned butter sauce; (*jest.*) black and blue, with a black eye. *Faire son* —, (*pop.*) to make nice pickings, to make a good deal of
Beurré, e, *adj.* buttered; buttery [money
Beurré, *s.m.* beurré (*pear*)
Beurrée, *s.f.* slice of bread and butter
Beurrer, *v.a.* to butter
Beurrerie, *s.f.* butter-dairy; butter-room
Beurri-er, ère, *adj.* of butter, butter [terman
Beurrier, *s.m.* butter-dish; butter-cooler; but-
Beurrière, *s.f.* churn; butter-dish; butter-
Beuvante, *s.f.* (*nav.*) bonus [woman
Bévue, *s.f.* blunder, oversight, mistake
Bey, *s.m.* bey
Beylik, *s.m.* beylic
Bezan, *s.m.* (*com.*) bezan [**set; Besi**
Bezant; Bezet; Bezi. *V.* **Besant; Be-**
Bezeau, *s.m.* bevelled timber
Bezigue, Bézy, *s.m. V.* **Besigue**
Bézoard, *s.m.* bezoar
Bezoche, *s.f. V.* **Besoche**
Bi-, (*in compounds, chem. &c.*) bi-...
Biais, *s.m.* bias; slope, slant; way; expedient, shift. *De* —, *en* —, sloping, slanting; obliquely. *Aller en* —, to slope, to slant; to bevel [shift
Biaisement, *s.m.* sloping, slanting; evasion,
Biaiser, *v.n.* to slope, to slant; to shift, to shuffle; to dodge; to evade; — *v.a.* to distort
Biaiseu-r, se, *s.m.f.* shifter, shuffler, dodger
Biangulaire, Biangulé, e, *adj.* biangulated
Biasse, *s.f.* raw silk (*from the Levant*)
Bibace, *adj.* bibacious
Bibacité, *s.f.* bibacity [drunkard
Bibard, Bibacier, *s.m.* (*pop.*) wine-bibber,
Bibelot, *s.m.* nicknack, gewgaw
Biberon, *s.m.* feeding-bottle. *Élever au* —, to bring up by hand [drunkard
Biberon, ne, *s.m.f.* wine-bibber, tippler, toper;
Bibi, *s.m.* (*obsolete*) small (*lady's*) bonnet; (*fam.*)
Bibion, *s.m.* (*zool.*) bibio [darling, ducky, tit
Bible, *s.f.* bible
Bibliographe, *s.m.* bibliographer [*V.* p. 3, § 1
Biblio-graphie, -logie, ique, iquement.
Bibliomane, *s.m.f. adj.* bibliomaniac
Bibliomanie, *s.f.* bibliomania
Bibliophile, *s.m.* bibliophile, bibliophilist
Bibliophilie, *s.f.* bibliophilism
Bibliopole, *s.m.* bibliopolist
Bibliothécaire, *s.m.* librarian
Bibliothèque, *s.f.* library; book-case, book-stand, book-shelves; catalogue
Biblique, *adj.*, **Bibliste,** *s.m. V.* page 3, § 1
Bibus, *s.m.* trifle. *De* —, insignificant, trifling,
Bicarbonate, *s.m.* (*chem.*) bicarbonate [paltry
Bicéphale, *adj.* (*zool.*) bicephalous, having two heads

Biceps, *adj.* (*anat.*) bicipital; — *s.m.* (*anat.*) biceps; (*fam.*) arm, fist; strength, vigour
Bicêtre, *s.m.* Bicêtre (*the French Bedlam*), a mad-house; (*obsolete*) misfortune, disgrace
Bicharrière, *s.f.* trammel (*for shad and salmon*)
Biche, *s.f.* hind, roe; dear, love; gay woman, mot. *Pied de* —, hind's foot; (*tech.*) claw; key; fork; handle (*of a bell-pull*); (*surg.*) elevator. *A pied de* —, claw-footed; claw
Bicherie, *s.f.* class of gay women, gay world
Bichette, *s.f.* little dear, love
Bichon, ne, *s.m.f.* Maltese lapdog, pugdog; dear, love, duck, ducky
Bichonner, *v.a.* to curl; to curl the hair of; to trim up, to dress up, to spruce up, to make
‡**Bichromate,** *s.m.* (*chem.*) bichromate [spruce
Bicipital, e, *adj.* (*anat.*) bicipital
Bicipité, e, *adj.* (*nat. hist.*) bicipitous, bicipital
Bicolore, *adj.* bicoloured, two-coloured
Biconcave, *adj.* biconcave
Biconvexe, *adj.* biconvex
Bicoque, *s.f.* paltry town; hovel, hut, shed, shanty; shabby household
Bicoquet, *s.m.* hood, bonnet
Bicorde, *adj.* (*mus.*) bichord
Bicorne, Bicornu, e, *adj.* bicorn, bicorned, bicornous, two-horned; two-cornered; — *s.m.* two-cornered hat
Bicuspidé, e, *adj.* bicuspid, bicuspidate
Bicycle, *s.m.* bicycle, two-wheeled carriage, two-wheeler
Bident, *s.m.* two-pronged fork *or* spear, bident
Bidenté, e, *adj.* bidental; (*bot., zool.*) biden[illegible]
Bidet, *s.m.* nag; roadster; bidet [*guns*) slug
Bidon, *s.m.* can; camp-kettle; bidon; (*for*
Bief, *s.m.* mill-course, mill-race; pond; (*of canals*) reach, level
Bielle, *s.f.* (*mach.*) connecting rod, rod
Bien, *s.m.* good; benefit; advantage; interest; welfare; comfort; blessing; happiness; pleasure; good thing; gift; boon; favour; kindness; mercy; production, fruit; possession; property, wealth, riches, fortune; treasure; estate; what is good *or* right; probity, honesty; virtue; good character; well. — *au soleil*, landed property. *En* —, well; favourably; in a good sense; for the better; honestly. *En tout — et tout honneur*, with honourable intentions. *Homme* (or *femme*) *de* —, honest *or* good man (*or* woman). *Aller* or *venir* or *arriver à* —, to go on successfully. *Être du dernier — avec*, to be on the very best of terms with. *Faire du* —, to do good; to be pleasant. *Mener à* —, to bring to a good end. *Tourner à* —, to take a good turn. *Le — cherche le* —, money makes money. *Abondance de —s ne nuit pas*, store is no sore. *Grand — vous fasse!* much good may it do you! *Nul — sans peine*, no gains without pains
Bien, *adv.* well; right; proper; rightly; properly; nicely; duly; correctly; all right; carefully; particularly; willingly; easily; clearly; fully, full; quite; enough, sufficiently; abundantly; to the full; o.'s fill; strictly; exactly, just; certainly; surely; really; indeed; in truth; in fact; possibly; perhaps; likely; much; a great deal; many; a great many; very much; very well; very; highly; long; far; fast, hard; steadfastly; soon; comfortable; comfortably; well off; in a fine plight; on good terms; in favour; in good part; good-looking; gentlemanly; ladylike; rather tipsy, mellow, fresh; pray, do, just, now; (*nav.*) ship-shape. — *de, du, de la, des*, much, a great deal, many, a great many. — ! good! yes! — *que*, although, though. *C'est* — ! that will do! that is right! that is all right! that is good! good! all right! very good! *Eh* — ! well! well then! well now! why; how now! yet now; nay. *Très* — ! very well! very good! hear, hear! — *avant*, long before; very far *or* deep; very

late. — *bon*, very good; very kind. — *meilleur*, — *mieux*, much better. — *mal*, very badly, very ill, &c. (*V.* **Mal,** *adv.*). — *du mal*, much trouble, &c. (*V.* **Mal,** *s.m.*) [ling; love
Bien-aimé, e, *adj. s.* beloved; favourite, dar-
Bien-aise, *s.m. V.* **Content,** *s.m.*; — *adj.* very glad, glad
Bien-dire, *s.m.* fine speaking, fine talk, elegance of speech; fine *or* good words; eloquence. *Être* or *se mettre sur son* —, to mind o.'s P's and Q's [spoken, eloquent; fine speaker
Bien-disant, e, *adj. s.* well-spoken, fair-
Bien-être, *s.m.* welfare, well-being; comfort; comforts; comfortableness; sensation of de-
Bien-faire, *s.m.* good actions [light
Bienfaisance, *s.f.* beneficence, benevolence, charity. *Bureau de* —, charitable board, relief-committee. *Institution de* —, charitable institution. *Œuvre de* —, charity. *Société de* —, benevolent society
Bienfaisant, e, *adj.* beneficent, benevolent; charitable; bountiful; kind; kindly; good; generous; beneficial; salutary; grateful
Bienfait, *s.m.* benefit, kindness, good office, service, boon; favour; good action, good act; charity; gift; mercy; blessing; advantage
Bienfai-teur, trice, *s.m.f.* benefactor; benefactress; patron; patroness
Bien-fonds, *s.m.* landed property, land
Bienheureu-x, se, *adj. s.* happy, blessed, blissful; fortunate; happy man *or* woman, happy being *or* creature; saint
Biennal, e, *adj.* biennial
Bienséance, *s.f.* propriety, decorum, decency; good manners; convenience
Bienséant, e, *adj.* proper, becoming, decent, decorous, suitable; convenient
Bientôt, *adv.* soon; very soon; quickly; shortly; before long; presently; nearly, very nearly, very near; easily. *A —!* I hope to see you again soon
†Bienveillance, *s.f.* kindness, kindliness, benevolence, good will; friendliness; affection; good graces; favour; protection
†Bienveillant, e, *adj.* kind, kindly, benevolent, well-wishing, friendly [come!
Bienvenu, e, *adj.* welcome. *Soyez le —!* wel-
Bienvenue, *s.f.* welcome; footing, entrance;
Bien-vivre, *s.m.* comfort [garnish-money
Bienvoulu, e, *adj.* beloved, dear, liked, esteemed, desirable, much sought after, welcome;
Bière, *s.f.* beer; coffin, bier [patronized, favoured
Bièvre, *s.m.* (*obsolete for* "castor") beaver; (*bird*) goosander, merganser, smew
Biez, *s.m. V.* **Bief**
Bifère, *adj.* (*bot.*) biferous
Biffage, Biffement, *s.m.* cancelling; erasure
Biffe, *s.f.* imitation jewel, paste, duffer, sham
Biffer, *v.a.* to cancel; to erase; to cross off; to strike out; to scratch out
Biffure, *s.f.* erasure, stroke of the pen
Bifide, *adj.* (*bot.*) bifid, bifidate [flowered
Biflore, *adj.* (*bot.*) biflorate, biflorous, two-
Bifolié, e, *adj.* (*bot.*) bifoliate, two-leaved
Bifoliolé, e, *adj.* (*bot.*) bifoliolate
Biforé, e, *adj.* (*bot.*) biforate
Biforme, *adj.* biform, biformed [rump-steak
Bifteck, *s.m.* beef-steak. — *chateaubriand*,
Bifurcation, *s.f.* bifurcation, forking; division
Bifurquer (Se), *v.r.* to bifurcate, to be bifurcated, to be forked; to fork
†Bigaille, *s.f.* winged insects, winged parasites
Bigame, *adj.* bigamous, guilty of bigamy; — *s.m.f.* bigamist [plurality
Bigamie, *s.f.* bigamy. — *spirituelle*, (*eccl.*)
Bigamique, *adj.* bigamic
Bigarade, *s.f.* Seville orange
Bigaradier, *s.m.* Seville orange-tree
Bigarré, e, *adj. V.* **Bariolé**
Bigarreau, *s.m.* bigaroon, whiteheart cherry
Bigarreautier, *s.m.* bigaroon-tree, whiteheart-
Bigarrer, *v.a. V.* **Barioler** [cherry tree

Bigarrure, *s.f. V.* **Bariolure**
Bige, *s.m.* (*Rom. antiquity*) biga
Bigéminé, e, *adj.* (*bot.*) bigeminate [squinter
Bigle, *s.m.* beagle; — *adj. s.m.f.* squint-eyed;
Bigler, *v.n.* to squint
†Bignon, *s.m.* (*fish.*) hoop-net [trumpet-flower
†Bignone, Bignonie, *s.f.* (*bot.*) bignonia,
Bigorne, *s.f.* beaked anvil; beak-iron, bickern; beak; (*zool.*) periwinkle, winkle
Bigorneau, *s.m.* small beaked-anvil; small bickern; (*zool.*) periwinkle, winkle; (*pop.*) policeman, peeler, bobby, blue-bottle, slop
Bigot, e, *adj. s.* bigoted; bigot; — *s.m.* two-pronged pickaxe; (*nav.*) rib
Bigoter, *v.n.* to play the bigot
Bigoterie, *s.f.*, **Bigotisme,** *s.m.* bigotry
Bigourneau, *s.m.* (*zool.*) *V.* **Bigorneau**
Bigre, *int.* hang it! confound it! bother! indeed! bless me!
Bigrement, *adv.* confoundedly, deucedly, tremendously, awfully, with a vengeance; an
Bigue, *s.f.* (*nav.*) sheers, shears [awful lot
Biguer, *v.a.n.* to exchange, to barter, to swap
Bihoreau, *s.m.* (*bird*) night-heron
Bijon, *s.m.* liquid resin
Bijou, *s.m.* jewel; trinket; ornament; darling, dear, love. — *d'acier*, polished steel article
Bijouterie, *s.f.* jewellery, jewelry; jeweller's trade *or* business; (*pop.*) advances, outlay. — *d'acier*, polished steel articles, steel jewellery. — *en fin*, gold jewellery
Bijouti-er, ère, *s.m.f.* jeweller
Bijugué, e, *adj.* (*bot.*) bijugate
Bilabié, e, *adj.* (*nat. hist.*) bilabiate
Bilamellé, e, *adj.* bilamellate, bilamellated
Bilan, *s.m.* balance-sheet; balance; return; schedule. *Déposer son* —, to file a schedule, to give in o.'s schedule; to stop payment
Bilatéral, e, *adj.* bilateral; (*of contracts*) binding to the two contracting parties, reciprocal, bipartite
Bilatéralement, *adv.* bilaterally; reciprocally
Bilboquet, *s.m.* cup and ball; tumbler; giddy-head; sport, laughing-stock; (*print.*) jobbing, jobs
Bile, *s.f.* bile; gall; spleen; anger, passion. *Se faire de la* —, to fret. *Ne pas se faire de* —, to take things easy
Biliaire, *adj.* (*anat., med.*) biliary
Bilieu-x, se, *adj.* bilious; choleric; splenetic; irascible, irritable, passionate; — *s.m.f.* bilious
Biline, *s.f.* (*chem.*) biline [person; bilious people
Bilingue, *adj.* (*nat. hist.*) bilinguous, two-tongued; (*philology*) bilingual
Bilitère, *adj.* (*gram.*) biliteral
Bill, *s.m.* (*English parl.*) bill; act
†Billard, *s.m.* billiards; billiard-table *or* room
†Billardier, *s.m.* billiard-maker
†Billardière, *s.f.* (*bot.*) billardiera, appleberry
†Bille, *s.f.* ball; marble; taw; log, baulk; (*agr.*) sucker; slip. *Faire une* —, to pocket (*or* to
†Billebarrer, *v.a. V.* **Barioler** [hole) a ball
†Billebaude, *s.f.* confusion, disorder. *A la* —, in confusion, in disorder, without order, confusedly; irregularly, at random; irregular; independent [wrong
†Billebauder, *v.n.* to hunt irregularly, to go
†Billet, *s.m.* bill; note; ticket; invitation; circular; certificate; notice; billet. — *blanc*, blank. — *doux*, love-letter. — *de banque*, bank-note. — *de complaisance*, accommodation bill. — *de faveur*, free admission ticket, order. — *de logement*, billet. — *d'aller*, (*rail.*) single ticket. — *d'aller et retour*, — *de retour*, return-ticket. *Je vous en donne* (or *fiche*) *mon* —, (*fam.*) I warrant you, I can tell you, I promise you, and no mis-
†Billeté, e, *adj.* (*mil., her.*) billeted [take!
†Billeter, *v.a.* (*obsolete for* "étiqueter"); (*mil.*) to billet [(*of firewood*), billet; (*her., arch.*) billet
†Billette, *s.f.* toll-board, notice; cocket; stick
†Billettement, *s.m.* (*mil.*) billeting
†Billevesée, *s.f.* silly stuff, nonsense, idle story, idle trash; crotchet

Billion, *s.m.* thousand millions
†Billon, *s.m.* coin *or* medal of copper with silver; copper coin, copper; base coin; firspar *or* baulk; (*agr.*) ridge; vine-twig
†Billonnage, Billonnement, *s.m.* dealing in base coin, circulating bad money; sorting; buying up gold or silver coin for exporting or melting; gelding; (*agr.*) ridging
†Billonner, *v.n.a.* to deal in base coin; to circulate (*bad money*); to buy up (*gold or silver for exporting or melting*); to geld; (*agr.*) to ridge
†Billonneur, *s.m.* dealer in base coin, utterer of bad money, smasher
†Billoquer, *v.a.* (*agr.*) to plough deep
†Billot, *s.m.* block; chopping-block; clog; (*vet.*) medicated bit
†Billotée, *s.f.* lot (*of small fish*)
Bilobé, e, *adj.* (*bot.*) bilobate, bilobed, two-lobed
Biloculaire, *adj.* (*bot.*) bilocular
Bimane, *adj.* (*zool.*) bimanous, two-handed; — *s.m.* bimane, biman
Bimbelot, *s.m.* toy, plaything
Bimbeloterie, *s.f.* toy-trade; toys
Bimbeloti-er, ère, *s.m.f.* toyman, toywoman, toy-maker *or* dealer
Bimensuel, le, *adj.* bimonthly
Binage, *s.m.* (*agr.*) second dressing *or* ploughing; (*hort.*) hoeing; (*eccl.*) saying mass twice in one day
Binaire, *adj.* binary
Binard, *s.m.* (stone and timber) waggon, trolly, tug, gill; (*build.*) truck
Biné, e, *adj.* (*bot.*) binate
Binée, *s.f.* (*agr.*) small crib (*for oxen*)
Biner, *v.a.n.* (*agr.*) to dress *or* till a second time; (*hort.*) to hoe; (*eccl.*) to say mass twice in one day; (*fam.*) to begin again, to repeat, to have it again, to have some more, to cut and come again, to have a second game
Binet, *s.m.* save-all; flat candlestick; light plough, binot
Binette, *s.f.* hoe; face, phiz
Bineuse, *s.f.* dresser, hoe
Binochon, *s.m.* weeding-hook
Binocle, *s.m.* double eye-glass, double opera-glass, binocular glass, binocle
Binoculaire, *adj.* binocular
Binoculé, e, *adj.* (*zool.*) binoculate
Binôme, *s.m. adj.* (*alg.*) binomial
Binot, Binoir, *s.m.* binot, light plough
Binotage, *s.m.* light tillage
Binoter, *v.a.n.* to plough lightly
Biographe, *s.m.* biographer
Biograph-ie, -ique. *V.* page 3, § 1
Biographier, *v.a.* to biograph
Bio-logie, -logique, -logiste, -technie, &c. *V.* page 3, § 1
Bipare, *adj.* (*zool.*) biparous
Biparti, e, *adj.* bipartite
Bipartible, *adj.* bipartible
Bipartition, *s.f.* bipartition
Bipédal, e, *adj.* bipedal, two-footed, two-legged
Bipède, *adj.m.f.*, *s.m.* biped; (*rid.*) (two) limbs
Bipenne, *s.f.* two-edged battle-axe
Bipenne, Bipenné, e, *adj.* (*zool.*) bipennate, bipennated
Bipétalé, e, *adj.* (*bot.*) bipetalous
Biphosphate, *s.m.* (*chem.*) biphosphate
Bipinné, e, *adj.* (*bot.*) bipinnate, bipinnated
Bipolaire, *adj.* (*phys.*) bipolar
***Biquadratique,** *adj.* (*alg.*) biquadratic
Bique, *s.f.* she-goat; little horse, pony, nag, tit; sorry horse, jade
Biquet, *s.m.* kid; assay-scales
Biqueter, *v.n.* to kid; — *v.a.* to weigh
Biquette, *s.f.* she-kid
Biqui-er, ère, *s.m.f.* goatherd, goat-keeper
Birambrot, *s.m.* (Dutch) beer-soup
Bire, *s.f.* (*fish.*) bow-net; (*tech.*) wicker bottle
Birème, *s.f.* (*anc. nav.*) bireme
Biribi, *s.m.* biribi (*game*); back-lining (*of a shoe*)
Birloir, *s.m.* window-spring
Birman, e, *adj. s.* Birman
Bis, e, *adj.* brown; (*pers.*) tawny, swarthy. — *blanc*, whity-brown. *A — et à blanc*, anyhow
Bis, *adv.int.s.m.adj.* twice; again, over again; encore! A, ½
Bisage, *s.m.* second dyeing, fresh dyeing
Bisaïeul, e, *s.m.f.* great-grandfather *or* mother
Bisaiguë, *s.f.* *V.* **Besaiguë**
†Bisaille, *s.f.* coarse groats; grey pea, field pea; mixture of peas and vetch
†Bisailler, *v.n.* to get brownish
Bisannuel, le, *adj.* biennial
†Bisbille, *s.f.* bickering, jangling, quarrel; disagreement. *En* —, bickering, jangling; at variance
Biscaïen, *s.m.* small iron ball (*usually put in grape shot*); long-barrelled musket
Biscayen, ne, *adj. s.m.f.* Biscayan
Biscayenne, *s.f.* long boat, Biscayan boat
Bischof, *s.m.* bishop (*liquor*)
Biscornu, e, *adj.* odd; queer; irregular; crooked, out of shape
Biscotin, *s.m.* biscotin
Biscotte, *s.f.* rusk
Biscuit, *s.m.* biscuit; sponge-cake. — *à la cuiller*, finger biscuit, lady's finger. — *de mer*, sea-biscuit; cuttle-fish
Biscuiter, *v.a.* to bake
Biscuiterie, *s.f.* biscuit-baking, biscuit-making *or* trade *or* business; biscuit-bakery *or* manufactory, biscuit-works
Bise, *s.f.* north wind, cold wind, cold blast; (*fig.*) winter time, winter; blast
Biseau, *s.m.* bevelling; bezel; feather-edge; kissing-crust; (*print.*) foot-stick; side-stick
Biseauter, *v.a.* to bevel
Biser, *v.a.* to dye again; — *v.n.* to degenerate, to get brown, to blacken
Biset, *s.m.* wild-rock pigeon, roving pigeon; national guard on duty in plain clothes; coarse brown stuff
Bisette, *s.f.* footing-lace; (*bird*) sea-duck
Bisettière, *s.f.* footing-lace maker
Bisexe, Bisexuel. *V.* **Bissexuel**
Bishop, *s.m.* bishop (*liquor*)
Bismuth, *s.m.* (*min.*) bismuth
Bisoc, *s.m.* *V.* **Bissoc**
Bison, *s.m.* (*zool.*) bison
Bisonne, *s.f.* grey cloth used for lining
Bisontin, e, *adj. s.* of Besançon; native of Besançon
Bisquain, *s.m.* sheep's skin with the wool on, horse-cloth, mat
Bisquant, e, *adj.* (*fam.*) bothering, vexing
Bisque, *s.f.* odds; bisk, soup, broth, sauce, pulp. *Prendre sa* —, to choose o.'s time, to avail oneself of the opportunity, to look out; to leave o.'s work, to give oneself a holiday
Bisquer, *v.n.* to be bothered *or* vexed, to fret. *Faire* —, to bother, to vex, to plague, to rile
Bisquin, *s.m.* *V.* **Bisquain**; (*agr.*) Norman sheep
Bisquine, *s.f.* long boat
Bissac, *s.m.* wallet, bag, knapsack; beggary
Bisse, *s.f.* (*bird*) red-breast; (*her.*) snake
Bissection, *s.f.* (*geom.*) bisection
Bisser, *v.n.* to cry encore; — *v.a.* to encore
Bissêtre, *s.m.* (*obsolete*) misfortune, mishap, disgrace
Bissexe, *adj.* *V.* **Bissexuel**
Bissexte, *s.m.* bissextile day, bissextile
Bissextil, e, *adj.* bissextile. *Année —e*, bissextile, leap-year
Bissexuel, le, Bissexué, e, *adj.* bisexous; (*bot.*) bisexual
Bissoc, *s.m.* two-shared plough, double-furrow plough
Bissus, *s.m.* *V.* **Byssus**
Bistord, *s.m.* *V.* **Bitord**
Bistorte, *s.f.* (*bot.*) bistort, snake-weed
Bistortier, Bistotier, *s.m.* (*pharm.*) pestle
Bistouri, *s.m.* (*surg.*) bistoury, knife
Bistourner, *v.a.* to twist, to crook
Bistre, *s.m.* (*paint.*) bistre
Bistré, e, *adj.* bistre-coloured. imbrowned, tanned
Bistrer, *v.a.* to paint in bistre; to imbrown, to tan
Bistreu-x, se, *adj.* of bistre
Bisulce, Bisulque, *adj.* (*zool.*) cloven-footed
Bisulfate, *s.m.* (*chem.*) bisulphate
Bisulfite, *s.m.* (*chem.*) bisulphite
Bisulfure, *s.m.* (*chem.*) bisulphide, bisulphuret
Bitartrate, *s.m.* (*chem.*) bitartrate
Biterné, e, *adj.* (*bot.*) biternate
Bithynien, ne, *adj. s.* Bithynian
Bitord, Bitors, *s.m.* (*nav.*) spun yarn, twine
Bitte, *s.f.* (*nav.*) bitt
Bitter, *v.a.* (*nav.*) to bitt (*a cable*)
Bitter, *s.m.* bitters (*drink*)

Bitton, *s.m.* (*nav.*) timber-head
Bitture, *s.f.* (*nav.*) range (of the cable)
Bitume, *s.m.* bitumen. *Faire le —,* (*pop.*) to walk the streets
Bitumer, Bituminer, *v.a.* to bituminate; to asphalt; — *v.n.* (*pop.*) to walk the streets
Bitumineu-x, se, *adj.* bituminous
Bituminifère, *adj.* bituminiferous
Bituminisation, *s.f.* bituminization
Bituminiser, *v.a.* to bituminize
Se —, *v.r.* to become bituminized
Bivac, Bivouac, *s.m.* (*mil.*) bivouac
Bivalve, *adj.* (*nat. hist.*) bivalve, bivalved; — *s.m.* bivalve
Bivaquer, Bivouaquer, *v.n.* (*mil.*) to bivouac
Bivoie, *s.f.* junction of two roads
Bizarre, *adj.* odd; strange; queer; uncouth; whimsical; fantastic; singular; eccentric; extravagant; out of the way; — *s.m.* *V.* **Bizarrerie**
Bizarrement, *adv.* oddly; strangely; queerly; whimsically; fantastically; singularly
Bizarrerie, *s.f.* oddness, oddity; strangeness; fantasticalness; singularity; eccentricity; extravagance; whimsicalness; whim, caprice
Bizet, *s.m.* *V.* **Biset**
Blafard, e, *adj.* dim, dull, pale, pallid, wan, sallow, lurid
Blague, *s.f.* tobacco-pouch; gammon, humbug, fudge, bosh, blarney, flam; story, bouncer; hoax; nonsense, stuff; unmeaning *or* flimsy stuff; insignificant *or* trumpery thing; clap-trap; trick; gift of the gab; great conversational powers; wit, fun, humour; gentle raillery, pleasantry; joking, joke; chaffing, chaff; random chit-chat, chat, gossip, talk. *Avoir la — du métier,* to make the most of what one knows; to talk to the best advantage of what one does
Blaguer, *v.a.n.* to humbug; to gammon; to hoax; to make fun of; to chaff; to joke, to jest; to tell stories *or* a story; to have the gift of the gab; to be an agreeable talker; to fascinate *or* captivate by o.'s talk; to talk; to have a random chit-chat, to chat at random, to chat, to gossip
Blagueu-r, se, *s.m.f.* humbug; story-teller; hoaxer; joker; wag; great talker; agreeable talker
Blaireau, *s.m.* badger; shaving-brush; softener, blender
Blâmable, *adj.* blamable, culpable, faulty
Blâme, *s.m.* blame, fault, censure, reprimand; reflection; obloquy; disapprobation
Blâmer, *v.a.* to blame, to censure, to reprimand, to reprove, to find fault with; to disapprove
Blan-c, che, *adj.* white; clean; blank; hoar, hoary; grey; fair; pale; dead (*wall*); sleepless; silver; clear; pure, innocent, spotless; bleached; washed. *Se faire — de son épée,* to boast of a power one has not, to boast of great interest
Blanc, *s.m.* white; whiteness; blank; mark, aim, target; blank cartridge; white man; white cloth; linen; white chalk; paint; white heat; white sauce; breast; small fry, bait; margin; (white) water; (*old French copper coin*) blank (*about a farthing:* "six —s" *made* $1\frac{1}{4}$*d. English coin*). — *d'argent,* best white lead. — *de baleine,* sperm, spermaceti. — *de chaux,* whitewash, limewash. — *d'Espagne,* whiting, Spanish white, ground chalk. — *de fard,* — *de perle,* pearl-powder, pearl-white. — *de plomb,* white lead. — *de zinc,* oxide of zinc. *A —,* blank; white; with blank cartridge; completely, entirely, outright. *Donner* or *mettre dans le —,* to hit the mark. *Tirer à —,* to fire with blank cartridge. *Tirer au —,* to fire at the target
Blancard, *s.m.* (*com.*) blancard (*linen cloth*)
Blanc-aune, *s.m.* (*bot.*) white beam-tree
Blanc-bec, *s.m.* beardless boy, youngster; greenhorn, simpleton, novice, raw recruit
Blanc-bourgeois, *s.m.* best flour, whites, first
†Blanchaille, *s.f.* young fish, small fish, fry, small fry
Blanchard, *s.m.* (*zool.*) white eagle; (*com.*) *V.* **Blancard.** — *velouté,* (*bot.*) soft-grass
Blanchâtre, *adj.* whitish; pale; wan
Blanche, *s.f.* white woman *or* girl; white ball (*at billiards*); sea-gull; (*mus.*) minim
Blanchement, *adv.* cleanly, neatly, clean, in *or* with clean linen
Blancherie, *s.f.* *V.* **Blanchisserie**
Blanchet, *s.m.* felt filtering-bag; corn-salad; (*med.*) thrush; (*print.*) blanket
Blanchet, te, *adj.* of a pretty white colour, cleanly, tidy
Blanchette, *s.f.* (*bot.*) corn-salad, lamb's-lettuce
Blancheur, *s.f.* whiteness; hoariness; paleness; cleanliness; white spot; white colour; white *or* bright tone; light; purity, innocence, virtue
Blanchiment, *s.m.* blanching; bleaching; whitening, washing; whitewashing
Blanchir, *v.a.n.* to whiten; to make white; to blanch; to bleach; to wash; to wash for; to find in washing; to wash white; to whitewash; to boil off, to scald; to plane, to polish; to rough down; to dress, to trim; to blaze (*a tree*); to clear; to purify; to half-cure; to light up; to illuminate; to shine; to appear, to peep; to graze; to glance off; to fail; to foam; to grow *or* get white; to grow *or* turn grey; to grow old; to turn *or* grow pale; to pale. — *à la chaux,* to whitelime, to limewash. — *à neuf,* to clear-starch
Se —, *v.r.* to whiten *or* &c. oneself; to be whitened *or* &c.; to wash; to get o.'s clothes washed, to get o.'s washing done, to find o.'s own washing
Blanchissage, *s.m.* washing; wash; bleaching; whitening; whitewashing. — *de fin* or *à neuf,* clear-starching
Blanchisserie, *s.f.* bleaching-ground; bleach-works; laundry, laundry-works
Blanchisseu-r, se, *s.m.f.* washerman, laundryman, launderer; washerwoman, laundress; washer, cleaner; bleacher; blancher; whitener; (*fam.*) reviser, publisher's literary man; (*pop.*) barrister, counsel. —*se de fin,* clear-starcher. —*se de tuyaux de pipes,* (*pop.*) trollop, trull, drab
Blanchœuvrier, *s.m.* edge-tool maker
Blanchoyer, *v.n.* to whiten, to be hoary
Blanc-manger, *s.m.* (*cook.*) blanc-mange, blanc-manger
Blanc-seing, *s.m.* (**Blanc-seings,** *pl.*) signature on a blank paper, carte blanche, full power
†Blanc-signé, *s.m.* (**Blancs-signés,** *pl.*) *V.* **Blanc-seing**
Blanque, *s.f.* lottery; blank
Blanquet, *s.m.* (*pear*) *V.* **Blanquette;** (*fish*) *V.* **Blanchaille**
Blanquette, *s.f.* (*pear*) blanket, blanquet; kind of grape, and of white wine from Languedoc; corn-salad, lamb's-lettuce; (*cook.*) blanquette, stew *or* fricassee (*of veal or lamb, &c.*) with white sauce, blanquette; (*fish*) *V.* **Blanchaille**
Blaps, *s.m.* (*zool.*) blaps
Blaquet, *s.m.* small fish, small fry, fry; bait
Blaser, *v.a.* to pall, to blunt, to dull, to deaden; to surfeit; to pall *or* blunt the taste of; to deaden all feeling in; to harden; to use up
Se —, *v.r.* to become (*or* be) palled *or* surfeited *or* satiated *or* used up
Blason, *s.m.* heraldry; coat of arms
Blasonnement, *s.m.* blazoning, blazonry
Blasonner, *v.a.* to blazon; to emblazon; to criticize
Blasonneur, *s.m.* blazoner; censurer
Blasphéma-teur, trice, *s.m.f. adj.* blasphemer; blasphemous
Blasphématoire, *adj.* blasphemous
Blasphème, *s.m.* blasphemy
Blasphémer, *v.a.n.* to blaspheme
Blater, Blatrer, *v.a.* to adulterate, to sophisticate (*corn*)
Blatérer, *v.n.* to bleat
Blatier, *s.m.* corn-chandler
Blatte, *s.f.* black beetle; cockroach
Blaude, *s.f.* smockfrock, frock
Blavelle, Blavéole, *s.f.* *V.* **Bluet**

Blé, *s.m.* corn, wheat; cornfield. — *noir*, buck-wheat. — *de Turquie*, Indian corn. *Grands* or *gros —s*, wheat and rye. *Petits —s*, barley and oats. — *de mars*, spring-corn. *Manger son — en herbe*, to anticipate o.'s revenues
Bleime, *s.f.* (*vet.*) bleyme
Blême, *adj.* pale, ghastly, sallow; wan [to fade
Blêmir, *v.n.* to turn *or* grow pale; to grow wan;
Blêmissement, *s.m.* turning pale, paleness
Blende, *s.f.* (*min.*) blende, mock lead, black-
Blenne, Blennie, *s.m.* (*fish*) blenny [jack
Blennorrhagie, *s.f.* (*med.*) blennorrhagia
Blennorrhée, *s.f.* (*med.*) blennorrhœa, gleet
Blépharite, *s.f.* (*med.*) blepharitis
Blésement, *s.m.* speaking thick
Bléser, *v.n.* to speak thick
Blésité, *s.f.* speaking thick
Blessant, e, *adj.* offensive; shocking [wounded
Blessé, *s.m.* wounded man, injured man;
Blesser, *v.a.* to wound; to hurt; to offend against; to injure; to wrong; to offend; to shock; to pinch; to gall; to be repugnant *or* contrary to, to clash with, to militate against
Se —, *v.r.* to hurt *or* wound oneself *or* each other; to be offended, to take offence; to offend *or* shock each other; to be hurt *or* wounded, &c.
Blessir, *v.n.* *V.* **Blettir**
Blessure, *s.f.* wound; hurt; cut; bruise; sore; injury; wrong; offence; pang, torture. *Coups et —s*, (*law*) aggravated assault, cutting and
Blet, te, *adj.* sleepy, overripe; mellow [wounding
Blette, Blète, *s.f.* (*bot.*) blite, strawberry spinach
Blettir, *v.n.* (*of fruit*) to become sleepy; to mellow
Blettissement, *s.m.* (*of fruit*) becoming sleepy; mellowing [ness
Blettissure, *s.f.* (*of fruit*) sleepiness; mellow-
Bleu, e, *adj.* blue; black and blue; wonderful, amazing, too good to be true. *Noir —*, blue-black, bluish black
Bleu, *s.m.* blue; blue colour; blueness; blue mark; blue spot; blue-stone; blue chalk; blue wine, bad wine; (*pop.*) recruit. — *d'azur*, azure blue, smalt. — *de ciel*, sky-blue. — *de Prusse*, Prussian blue. — *de roi*, king's blue, black blue. *Mettre en —* (*dyeing*), *passer au —* (*wash-*
Bleuâtre, *adj.* bluish; dark blue [*ing*), to blue
Bleuet, *s.m.* *V.* **Bluet**
Bleuette, *s.f.* *V.* **Bluette**
Bleuir, *v.a.* to make blue, to blue; — *v.n.* to turn *or* become blue; to appear tinged with blue
Bleuissage, Bleuissement, *s.m.* bluing; [turning blue
Blin, *s.m.* (*nav.*) battering-ram
Blindage, *s.m.* (*mil.*) covering with blinds; blindage; (*nav.*) iron-plating, iron-casing, armour-plating, plating; armour-plates, armour; (*engin.*) sheeting, poling; screen
Blinde, *s.f.* (*fort.*) blind [iron-clad
Blindé, e, *adj.* (*nav.*) iron-plated, iron-cased,
Blinder, *v.a.* (*mil.*) to cover with blinds; (*nav.*) to plate; (*engin.*) to sheet, to screen
Bliner, *v.a.* (*nav.*) to ram
Bloc, *s.m.* block; log; lump; clump; stocks; (*geol.*) boulder; (*pop.*) prison, station-house, quod, lock-up; (*soldiers' slang*) dry-room
Blocage, *s.m.* rubble, rubble-work; (*print.*) turned letter; (*at billiards*) pocketing
†Blocaille, *s.f.* rubble, rubble-stone
Blochet, *s.m.* (*carp.*) *V.* **Entretoise**
Blockaus, *s.m.* (*mil.*) blockhouse
Blocus, *s.m.* blockade
Blond, e, *adj. s.m.f.* fair; light; flaxen; yellow, golden; fair person, blonde; fair friend; fair one; — *s.m.* fairness, fair; lightness, light colour; — *s.f.* blond-lace, blonde. — *ardent*, [sandy colour
Blondasse, *adj.* insipidly fair
Blond-ier, ière, *s.m.f.* blond-lace maker
Blondin, e, *s.m.f.* light-haired person, light-haired man *or* boy *or* woman *or* girl; ladies' man, young fop, spark, beau
Blondir, *v.n.* to assume a golden hue; — *v.a.* to dye in a golden colour

Blondissant, e, Blondoyant, e, *adj.* golden, yellow
Blondoîment, *s.m.* golden hue, yellow tinge
Blondoyer, *v.n.* to assume a golden hue
Bloquer, *v.a.* to blockade; to block up; (*print.*) to turn; (*at billiards*) to pocket, to hole; (*pop.*) to lock up, to cage, to quod
Bloquette, *s.f.* (*game at marbles*) nine-holes
Blottir, (Se), *v.r.* to squat, to cower down, to crouch, to cuddle, to roll oneself up; to lie hid
Blouse, *s.f.* frock; smockfrock, smock; slop; pinafore; blouse; wrapper; working-man; (*genteel slang*) working-men, lower orders, fustian jackets, fustian; (*of billiards*) pocket
Blouser, *v.a.* (*at billiards*) to pocket, to hole; (*fig.*) to deceive, to mislead
Se —, *v.r.* to pocket o.'s own ball; to take oneself in, to make a mistake *or* a blunder, to make a mess of it
Blousier, *s.m.* (*genteel slang*) *V.* **Voyou**
Bluet, *s.m.* (*plant, flower*) blue-bottle, corn-flower; (*bird*) kingfisher; (*fish*) blue dog-fish
Bluette, *s.f.* spark; flash; sparks of wit; smart light production, literary trifle
Blutage, *s.m.* bolting, sifting
Bluteau, *s.m.* *V.* **Blutoir**
Bluter, *v.a.* to bolt, to sift [bolting-mill
Bluterie, *s.f.* bolting-room; bolting-house;
Blutoir, *s.m.* bolter, bolting-mill
Boa, *s.m.* (*serpent, fur*) boa. — *constricteur* or [*devin*, boa-constrictor
Bobe, *s.f.* (*pop.*) *V.* **Moue**
Bobèche, *s.f.* socket; sconce; — *s.m.* block-head, tom-fool [noddle; face, phiz
Bobine, *s.f.* bobbin, spool; reel; (*pop.*) sconce,
Bobiner, *v.a.* to wind on a bobbin
Bobinette, *s.f.* peg, wooden bolt
Bobineuse, *s.f.* (*pers., thing*), **Bobinoir,** *s.m.* (*thing*) winder [hurt, harm, sore
Bobo, *s.m.* (*fam.*) slight hurt, small ailment,
Bocage, *s.m.* grove, boscage [rural
Bocag-er, ère, *adj.* of groves; woody; shady;
Bocal, *s.m.* bottle; jar; glass bowl; globe; mouthpiece; (*pop.*) stomach, inside, bread-basket; lodging
Bocard, *s.m.* (*metal.*) crushing-mill, stamps
Bocardage, *s.m.* (*metal.*) crushing, stamping
Bocarder, *v.a.* (*metal.*) to crush, to stamp
Bocassin, *s.m.* (*com.*) *V.* **Boucassin**
Bock, *s.m.* *V.* **Chope**
Bodruche, *s.f.* *V.* **Baudruche**
Boesse, *s.f.* smoothing-tool
Boesser, *v.a.* to smooth, to even
Bœuf, *s.m.* ox; bullock; neat; beef; piece *or* plate of beef; (*fig.*) fat fellow, heavy fellow, lubber; drudge; victim, dupe; kind of fishing-boat; — *adj.* (*pop.*) enormous, extraordinary, bouncing, tremendous. *Le — gras*, the fat ox, [the prize ox
Bog, *s.m.* (kind of game at cards)
Boghead, *s.m.* (*min.*) Boghead coal, boghead
Boghei, *s.m.* (*carriage*) buggy, gig
Bogue, *s.f.* chestnut-bur; — *s.m.* (*fish*) bogus
Boguey, *s.m.* *V.* **Boghei**
Bohé, Bohéa, *s.m. adj.* bohea (*tea*)
Bohême (La), *s.f.* Bohemia; wild and disorderly people (*or* life), the loafing fraternity; vagrants, tramps; — *s.m.f.* Bohemian, gypsy, gipsy; wild and disorderly fellow, loafer; vagrant, wanderer, tramp. *De —*, Bohemian; gypsy, wandering, irregular, disorderly; low; poor, paltry, shabby, sorry
Bohémien, ne, *s.m.f.* Bohemian; gypsy, gipsy; loose fish; vagrant; hussy, trollop; — *s.f.* Bohemian fashion; gypsy fashion
Boïard, *s.m.* *V.* **Boyard** *and* **Bayard**
Boire, *v.a.n.* to drink; to tipple; to drink in *or* down; to drink up; to sup, to sup up; to suck up; to soak in; to imbibe; to absorb; to swallow; to brook, to pocket, to put up with; to lose; to blot; to be drowning; (*need.*) to be puckered. — *comme un trou, comme une éponge, comme un tonneau, comme un templier, comme un sonneur, comme un chantre, comme un Polonais,*

to drink like a fish. *A* —, to drink; something to drink, some drink, drink; drinking; water, refreshment. *Pour* —, to drink; for oneself; something for oneself. *Qui a bu boira*, use is second nature

Se —, *v.r.* to be drunk

Boire, *s.m.* drink; drinking; — *s.f.* creek, cove, bay; pool, freshet; channel; ditch

Bois, *s.m.* wood; timber; stock; shaft; staff; frame; bedstead; material, stuff; horns, antlers, head; cross; woodland; forest; park; trees; branches, shoots; fuel. — *amaranthe*, purple-wood. — *blanc*, deal. — *dentelle*, (*bot.*) lace-bark tree. — *flotté*, — *de train*, float wood. — *gentil*, (*bot.*) mezereon. — *mort*, dead wood. *Mort* —, brambles, briars. — *neuf*, cord wood. — *puant*, (*bot.*) bird-cherry. — *satiné*, *V.* **Satiné.** — *à brûler*, — *de chauffage*, firewood, fuel. — *de chandelle*, torch-wood, resinous wood. — *de charpente*, — *de construction*, timber. — *de citron*, satinwood, lemon-wood. — *de couleuvre*, snakewood. — *de démolition*, old timber. — *de fer*, iron-wood. — *des îles*, wood from the West India islands, foreign wood. — *de lit*, bedstead. — *de mai*, (*bot.*) hawthorn. — *de rose*, tulipwood. — *de Sainte-Lucie*, mahaleb-wood. — *de Spa*, chestnut-wood. — *de teinture*, dye-wood. — *violet*, purple-wood. — *de violette*, king-wood. *De* or *en* —, wooden. *De* or *des* —, of *or* with wood; of *or* with woods; of the woods; woodland; wooded, woody. *Sous* —, in the brushwood. *Faire du* —, (*nav.*) to make a provision of wood, to get wood. *Être du* — *dont on fait les flûtes*, to be of an easy temper, to be of everybody's opinion. *Vous verrez de quel* — *je me chauffe*, you shall see what metal I am made of

Boisage, *s.m.* wood-work; timbering; wainscoting

Boisé, e, *adj.* woody, wooded; planted with trees; wainscoted

Boisement, *s.m.* stocking with woods *or* trees, planting, plantation; woodiness; timbering

Boiser, *v.a.* to put wood-work to; to do the wood-work in; to timber; to stock with woods *or* trees, to plant; to wainscot

Boiserie, *s.f.* wainscot; wainscoting; floor-boards; wood-work, carpenter's work; screen

Boiseur, *s.m.* timberman

Boiseu-x, se, *adj.* woody; ligneous

Boisseau, *s.m.* bushel

Boisselage, *s.m.* corn-measuring, corn-meter's employment

Boisselée, *s.f.* bushelful

Boisselier, *s.m.* cooper, bushel-maker

Boissellerie, *s.f.* cooperage; cooper's wares

Boisson, *s.f.* drink; drinking; liquor; drunkenness; grape-water, weak wine; weak cider; (*nav.*) vinegar and water

Boissonner, *v.n.* (*pop.*) to tipple, to guzzle, to booze

Boissonnier, *s.m.* (*pop.*) tippler, guzzler, boozer

Boîte, *s.f.* box; case; caddy; canister; chest; casket; can; snuff-box; firework-box; (*of wheels*) chair; (*print.*) hose (*of a press*). — *à* or *de couleurs*, colour-box, paint-box. — *à graisse*, (*rail.*) axle-box. — *à savon*, soap-tray. — *à savonnette*, round box opening in the middle; (*bot.*) pyxidium. — *de quartier*, receiving-house *or* office. — *du crâne*, cranium, skull. — *du genou*, (*pop.*) knee-cap, knee-pan

Boite, *s.f.* maturity, ripeness; grape-water, weak wine; (*of cattle*) foot-sore. *En* —, matured, fit for drinking

Boitement, *s.m.* halting, limping, hobble; lameness; imperfection, weakness

Boiter, *v.n.* to be lame, to walk lame, to halt, to limp, to hobble. *En boitant*, haltingly; lamely

Boiterie, *s.f.* (*vet.*) halting; lameness

Boiteu-x, se, *adj. s.m.f.* lame, limping, halt; unsteady, rickety; (*shawl*) with a single border; (*ribbon*) with two different borders; (*devil*) on two sticks; halter, limper, lame person, cripple; — *s.f.* (kind of dance and tune). *Attendre le* —, to wait for confirmation of intelligence; to bide o.'s time

Boîtier, *s.m.* case of surgical instruments; ointment-box; case; box; watch-case maker

Boitte, Boittée, *s.f.* bait (*for cod*); young fish

Boit-tout, *s.m.* glass with a broken foot

Bol, *s.m.* bowl; basin; finger-glass; (*pharm., vet.*) bolus, ball; (*min.*) bole. — *alimentaire*, (*physiology*) mass of food in the process of deglutition, bolus *or* pellet of food, alimentary pellet

Bolaire, *adj.* (*min.*) bolary

Bolasse, *s.f.* indifferently productive land, poor land

Bolduc, *s.m.* (narrow) tape

Boléro, *s.m.* bolero (*Spanish dance, tune, song*)

Bolet, *s.m.* (*bot.*) boletus

Bolétique, *adj.* (*chem.*) boletic

Boliche, *s.f.* (*fish.*) winged net

Bolide, *s.m.f.* (*meteor*) bolis (*pl.* bolides)

Bolivar, *s.m.* bell-crowned hat; (*pop.*) hat, tile

Bolivien, ne, *adj. s.* Bolivian

Bolonais, e, *adj. s.* Bolognese; Bolognese fashion

Bolus, *s.m.* (*pharm., vet.*) bolus, ball

Bombance, *s.f. V.* **Ripaille**

Bombarde, *s.f.* (*nav.*) bomb-vessel (*mil.*) bombard; (*mus.*) bombardo; full organ

Bombardement, *s.m.* bombardment

Bombarder, *v.a.* to bombard; to shell

Bombardier, *s.m.* (*mil.*) bombardier; (*zool.*) bombardier-beetle

Bombasin, *s.m.*, **Bombasine,** *s.f.* bombazine

Bombe, *s.f.* bomb, shell; glass bowl; round cake; round ice. — *de signaux*, (*nav.*) signal-ball

Bombé, e, *adj.* convex; bulged; swelled out; arched; prominent; round; circular; (*of roads*) barrelled; (*pop.*) round-shouldered, crook-backed

Bombement, *s.m.* convexity; bulging; jutting out; swelling *or* bunching out; curving; curvature; protuberance; (*of roads*) barrelling; (*med.*) noise in the ears

Bomber, *v.a.* to make *or* render convex; to cause to bulge; to swell *or* bunch out; to make jut out; to arch; to curve; to barrel (*roads*); — *v.n.*, **Se** —, *v.r.* to be convex; to bulge; to swell out; to jut out; to become round

Bomberie, *s.f.* shell-foundry, bomb-foundry

Bombeur, *s.m.* convex glass maker

Bombure, *s.f. V.* **Bombement**

Bombyle, *s.m.* (*zool.*) humble-bee fly

Bombyx, *s.m.* (*zool.*) bombyx

Bôme, *s.f.* (*nav.*) spanker

Bomerie, *s.f.* (*nav.*) bottomry

Bon, ne, *adj.* good; nice; excellent; good-natured; good-tempered; kind; kind-hearted; benevolent; simple, foolish, silly; right; fit, proper, due; able; well; fair; comfortable; pleasant; happy; lucky; fine; sound; goodly; large; long; great; full; famous; funny, amusing; useful, of use; convenient; advantageous; profitable; lucrative; beneficial; wholesome; favourable; bountiful; plain; worth; worthy; safe; solvent; not amiss; much, a good deal; dear. — *! int.* good! well! very well! right! be it so! well now! nonsense! pooh! indeed! oh! — *à rien*, good *or* fit for nothing; of no use. —*ne femme*, good *or* kind woman; good *or* kind wife; good soul; simple soul; old woman, biddy. — *homme*, *V.* **Bonhomme.** *A quoi* —*?* what is the use (of)? to what purpose? what is the good of it *or* that? what signifies? what use is it? what avails it? what for? *C'est* — *!* good! very good! very well! that is right! all right! right! that will do! well and good! *Comme* — *me semble*, as I think proper, as I please *or* like. *Pour de* —, *pour tout de* —, *tout de* —, in earnest, in good earnest; really; seriously; real; true, very true; for certain; for good, for good and all; indeed! *Être* — *là*, (*pop.*) to be a fine fellow indeed, to be very cool *or* cheeky. *Faire* —, to be comfortable *or* pleasant; to be safe

Bon, *s.m.* good; good qualities; good fellow, good friend; good one; crack one. clever fellow; best; fun, joke; advantage; gain; profit; cheque; order; bond; bill; ticket; admittance; acceptance; signature; promise, assurance. *Du* —, what is good, something good, good things, good stuff; a good article; some good qualities; some good points; some advantage *or* profit

Bonace, *s.f.* (*nav.*) calm, smooth sea; lull

Bonapartea, *s.m.*, **Bonapartée,** *s.f.* (*bot.*) bonapartea

Bonapart-isme, -iste. *V.* page 3, § 1

Bonasse, *adj.* simple, innocent, silly, foolish; credulous; too good-natured; complying

Bonassement, *adv.* sillily, foolishly, innocently

Bonbanc, *s.m.* white stone

Bonbec, *s.f.* gossip; chatterbox

Bonbon, *s.m.* sweetmeat, sweet, comfit, bonbon

Bonbonne, *s.f.* jar, demijohn, carboy, large bottle; can

Bonbonnière, *s.f.* sweetmeat-box; neat little house, snug little house, small house; kind of carriage

†Bon-chrétien, *s.m.* bon-chrétien (*pear*); [william

Bond, *s.m.* bound; rebound; skip; leap, jump; spring; gambol. *Par sauts et par —s*, by bounds and leaps; by fits and starts. *Tant de — que de volée*, anyhow, as one can, by hook and by crook. *Faire faux* —, to fail; to disappoint; to give the slip

Bonde, *s.f.* sluice; bung-hole; bung; plug. *Lâcher la — à*, (*fig.*) to give vent to

Bondé, e, *adj.* (*of casks*) quite full, full to the [bung

Bonder, *v.a.* (*nav.*) to lade full, to fill

Bondieu, *s.m.* (sawyer's) wedge

Bondir, *v.n.* to bound; to rebound; to skip; to leap, to jump; to spring; to start; to rush; to bounce; to prance; to gambol, to frisk; to rise; to heave; to beat

Bondissement, *s.m.* bounding; rebounding; skipping; bouncing; frisking; rushing; rising; heaving; beating, throbbing, throb; bound; rebound; leap; spring; gambol; friskiness

Bondon, *s.m.* bung; bung-hole; small cheese

Bondonner, *v.a.* to bung

Bondonnière, *s.f.* (*tool*) bung-borer

Bondrée, *s.f.* (*bird*) pernis, pern, honey-buzzard

Bonduc, *s.m.* (*bot.*) bonduc, nickar-tree, yellow [nickar

Bon-frais, *s.m.* (*nav.*) fresh gale

Bongare, *s.m.* (*zool.*) bongar, rock-snake

Bon-henri, *s.m.* (*bot.*) Good-Henry, Good King Henry, all-good (*a plant, species of goose-foot*); bon-henri (*kind of pear*)

Bonheur, *s.m.* happiness; felicity; delight; joy; pleasure; good luck, good fortune, luck, chance; success; welfare, good; blessing, happy thing; happy effect. — *du jour*, davenport. *Au petit* —, happen *or* come what may. *Par* —, happily, fortunately; luckily. *Avoir le — de*, to have the happiness of *or* to. *Avoir du* —, to be lucky *or* fortunate

Bonhomie, *s.f.* good-nature; simplicity; silliness; credulity; humour

Bonhomme, *s.m.* good-natured man; good soul; simple soul; good man; good fellow; old man; codger, old codger; fogy, old fogy; figure; peasant; fellow; (*bot.*) mullein; — *adj.* old; good-natured; simple. *Mon* —, my good fellow, old boy. *Petit* —, little fellow. *Vieux* —, old man; old fellow; old codger, old buffer; [old fogy

Boni, *s.m.* bonus; profit; surplus

Boniface, *adj. s.m.* simple, artless; simpleton

Bonifacement, *adv.* simply, artlessly, frankly; plainly [allowance, bonus

Bonification, *s.f.* improvement, amelioration;

Bonifier, *v.a.* to improve; to better; to make good; to make up; to allow

Se —, *v.r.* to improve

Boniment, *s.m.* quack's show; puff, humbug, clap-trap speech, speech, harangue; clap-trap

Bonisseur, *s.m.* showman's puffer, speaker

Bonite, *s.f.* (*fish*) bonito, stripe-bellied tunny

Bonjour, *s.m.* good morning; good day; good evening; o.'s compliments. *Dire un petit* —, to give a look-in. *Bien le* —, good morning to you [tor

Bonjourier, *s.m.* thief pretending to be a visi-

Bonne, *s.f.* (*and adj. feminine of* **Bon,** *which see*) servant, maid, maid-servant, servant-maid; nurse-maid, nurse; good woman, good friend; dear, honey, sweet, goody; good one; extraordinary *or* wonderful *or* strange thing; fine *or* strange story; bounce, bouncer, whapper; funny thing; fine trick *or* prank; sharp thing. — *d'enfant*, nursery-maid. — *à* (or *pour*) *tout faire*, maid of all work, general servant. — **-dame,** *s.f.* (*bot.*) *V.* **Arroche.** — **-grâce,** *s.f. V.* **Grâce** [(*nav.*) buoy (*of an anchor*)

Bonneau, *s.m.* pander; simple *or* silly fellow;

Bonnement, *adv.* simply; innocently; ingenuously; candidly; sincerely; honestly; truly; really; plainly; foolishly; merely; well. *Tout* —, simply; plainly; merely; literally; foolishly

Bonnet, *s.m.* cap; (*mil.*, *tech.*) cap; (*a Scotchman's, mil., tech.*) bonnet; (*fig.*) doctor's degree; (*of ruminants*) honey-comb bag. — *chinois*, Chinese bells. — *-coiffure, s.m.* dress-cap. — *ducal*, cap of maintenance. — *grec*, Greek cap, smoking-cap. — *jaune*, (*pop.*) yellow-boy. — *vert*, convict's cap. — *de coton*, (man's) night-cap. — *d'évêque*, (*of a fowl*) hinder part, bishop; (*theat.*) small upper-box. — *de linge*, morning-cap. — *de nuit*, (*man's or woman's*) night-cap. — *à poil*, bear-skin cap; busby. — *de police*, forage-cap, undress cap. — *blanc et blanc* —, six of one and half-a-dozen of the other. *Gros* —, don, big-wig, nob. *Mettre* (or *Avoir mis*) *son — de travers*, to be cross. *Prendre sous son* —, to find in o.'s own head; to invent; to take upon oneself. *Y jeter son* —, to give it up. *V.* **Moulin, Opiner,** *and* **Tête**

Bonnetage, *s.m.* (*tech.*) capping

Bonneter, *v.a.* (*tech.*) to cap

Bonneterie, *s.f.* hosiery; hosier's business

Bonneteur, *s.m.* card-sharper

Bonnetier, *s.m.* hosier; (*literary slang*) vulgar fellow, shop-keeper [sail

Bonnette, *s.f.* (*fort.*) bonnet; (*nav.*) studding-

Bonnichon, *s.m.* (*pop.*) little cap

Bonsoir, *s.m.* good night; good evening; not a bit of it; that's enough; gone! go to! good-bye! *Bien le* —, good evening to you. — *et bonne nuit*, a good night's rest to you. *Dire — à la compagnie*, (*fig., jest.*) to kick the bucket, to die

Bonté, *s.f.* goodness; kindness; act of kindness; attention; civility; favour; good-nature; [excellence

Bonze, *s.m.* bonze (*buddhist priest*)

Bonzerie, *s.f.* convent of bonze nuns

Bonzesse, Bonzelle, *s.f.* bonze nun, bonzess

Boquet, *s.m.* (*tech.*) scoop, shovel

Boqueteau, *s.m.* (*obsolete*) small wood [man

†Boquillon, *s.m.* (*obsolete*) wood-cutter, wood-

Boracique, *adj.* (*chem.*) boracic

Boracite, *s.f.* (*min.*) boracite

Borate, *s.m.* (*chem.*) borate

Borax, *s.m.* (*chem.*) borax [in the bowels

Borborygme, *s.m.* (*med.*) borborygm, rumbling

Bord, *s.m.* border; edge; brink; verge; brim, flap; rim; skirt; binding; hem; edging; margin; extremity; side; bank; strand; shore; coast; board; ship, vessel, boat; broadside; tack; way of thinking, party; kind. — *bas*, (*nav.*) port. — *de l'eau*, water's edge, water-side; river-side; bank. — *de la mer*, sea-side. *Franc-* —, clear bank; (*nav.*) planks of the bottom. *Coffre de* —, (*nav.*) sea-chest. *Lit de* —, (*nav.*) cot. *Livre de* —, ship's journal, journal. — *à* —, (*nav.*) alongside. — *à terre*, — *au large*, (*nav.*) off and on. *A* —, *à — de*, on board. *A larges —s*, (*of hats*) broad-brimmed. *De bas* —, (*nav.*) low-built. *De haut* —, (*nav.*) large, of several decks. *Par-dessus le* —, (*nav.*) overboard. *Changer* or *renverser* or *tourner le* —, (*nav.*) to veer. *Courir même — que*, (*nav.*) to stand on the same tack with

Bordage, *s.m.* boarding; poling; planking; planks; weather-boards; hemming, binding, &c. (*V.* **Border**)
Bordé, *s.m.* hem, edging, bordering, border
Bordeaux, *s.m.* Bordeaux wine, claret; Bordeaux cigar, halfpenny cigar
Bordée, *s.f.* broadside; volley; salvo; volley of abuse; round; shower; tack; watch. *Courir des —s,* to tack, to tack about; (*pop.*) to take French leave. *Tirer une —,* to fire a broadside; (*pop.*) to run riot
Bordel, *s.m.* brothel; penny bundle (*of wood*)
Bordelais, e, *adj. s.m.f.* of Bordeaux; native of Bordeaux; — *s.m.* Bordeaux district; — [*s.f.* Bordeaux fashion
Bordement, *s.m.* edge
Borde-plats, *s.m.* (*cook.*) garnish
Border, *v.a.* to border; to hem; to edge; to skirt; to bind; to line; to bound; to lace; to tuck in *or* up; to encircle; to set off; to dispose, to form; to plank (*a ship*); to lay (*a deck*); to unfurl; to haul aft; to ship (*the oars*); to sail *or* run along, to coast. *Borde au vent!* (*nav.*) haul aft the sheets!
Bordereau, *s.m.* memorandum, note, account
Bordeu-r, se, *s.m.f.* binder, shoe *or* hat *or* &c. [binder
Bordeyer, *v.n.* (*nav.*) *V.* **Louvoyer**
Bordier, *s.m.* (*nav.*) lap-sided ship
Bordigue, *s.f.* (*fish.*) crawl
Bordure, *s.f.* border; edge; edging; verge; binding; frame; skirt; rim; kerb-stone, kerb, curb-stone, curb; (*nav.*) flat; foot
Borduré, e, *adj.* bordered
Bore, *s.m.* (*chem.*) boron [north
Boréal, e, *adj.* boreal, northern, northerly,
Borée, *s.m.* (*myth.*) Boreas; (*poet.*) the north wind
†**Borgne,** *adj. s.* blind of one eye, one-eyed; one-eyed man *or* woman; (*zool.*) blind-worm; (*of things*) blind; obscure; dingy; paltry; low; small; lame
†**Borgner,** *v.a.* to look with one eye at
†**Borgnesse,** *s.f.* one-eyed woman *or* girl
Borin, *s.m.* coal-miner, hitcher
Borinage, *s.m.* coal-miners; coal-mining
Borique, *adj.* (*chem.*) boracic
Bornage, *s.m.* setting bounds *or* boundaries, fixing limits, bounding, limiting
Borne, *s.f.* bound; boundary; limit; frontier; land-mark; mile-stone; stone-post, post, stone, pillar; starting-post; spur-post; end; library *or* dining-room clock; centre ottoman. — **-boite,** *s.f.* (*post.*) pillar-box. — **-fontaine,** *s.f.* water-post
Borné, e, *adj.* bounded; limited; confined; stinted; narrow; shallow; mean; small; narrow-minded; ignorant, uninformed; dull; stunted
Borner, *v.a.* to bound; to limit; to confine; to set bounds *or* boundaries to; to end; to put an end to; to stint; to restrain; to restrict; to moderate; to border, to edge; to cut off
 Se —, *v.r.* to keep within bounds; to confine *or* limit oneself; to restrain *or* moderate oneself; to be content *or* satisfied (with); to stop (with); to end (in); to be confined *or* limited [(to)
Bornous, *s.m.* *V.* **Burnous**
Bornoyer, *v.a.* to look with one eye at; to set marks in [aceæ
Borraginées, *s.f.pl.* (*bot.*) boragineæ, boragin-
Borure, *s.m.* (*chem.*) boride
Bosan, *s.m.* bosa (*Eastern drink*)
Bosel, *s.m.* (*arch.*) *V.* **Tore**
Bosniaque, Bosnien, ne, *adj. s.* Bosnian
Bosphore, *s.m.* (*geog.*) Bosphorus; strait
Bosquet, *s.m.* grove; thicket
Bossage, *s.m.* embossing; jut, eminence; relief; (*arch.*) bossage, embossment
Bosse, *s.f.* hump; bump; bunch; swelling; rise; protuberance; roughness, unevenness, ruggedness; bruise, dent, dint; boss; knob; knot; bosset; figure, statue, statuette, bust; model; (*draw.*) round, bust; (*sculp.*) embossment; relief; (*fig.*) turn, aptitude, disposition, inclination, propensity; spree, blow-out; snare; (*nav.*) stopper; (*mil.*) powder-flask *or* horn. *D'après la —,* from the round, from the bust. *En —,* embossed, in relief. *Ouvrage en —,* fret, fretwork, relief. *Relevé en —,* embossed, in relief. *Ronde- —,* round, full relief; statue, statuette, bust; drawing from the round. *Rouler sa —,* (*pop.*) to get along; to knock about. *Travailler* or *relever en —,* to emboss
Bosselage, *s.m.* embossing
Bosseler, *v.a.* to emboss; to bruise, to dent, to dint, to indent, to batter [bruised *or* &c.
 Se —, *v.r.* to be embossed; to get (*or* be)
Bosselure, *s.f.* embossment; denting, indenting, dents, dints, bruises
Bosseman, *s.m.* (*obsolete*) boatswain's mate
Bosser, *v.a.* (*nav.*) to stopper
Bossette, *s.f.* boss, stud; (*of mules*) blinker, [winker
Bossoir, *s.m.* (*nav.*) cat-head; bow
Bossu, e, *adj.* hunchbacked, humpbacked, deformed (in the chest); irregular, uneven, unequal, rugged, tortuous, crooked; — *s.m.f.* hunchback, humpback, deformed person. — *par-devant,* pigeon-breasted. *V.* **Rire**
Bossuer, *v.a.* to bruise, to dent, to dint, to indent, to batter
 Se —, *v.r.* to get (*or* be) bruised *or* dented, &c.
Bostandji, Bostangi, *s.m.* bostandji (*Sultan's gardener; Turkish militiaman*). — **-bachi,** chief of the bostandjis
Boston, *s.m.* boston (*game at cards*)
Bostonien, ne, *adj. s.* Bostonian
Bostrychite, *s.f.* (*min.*) bostrychite
Bot, *adj. Pied —,* *adj. s.* club-footed; club-foot
Bot, *s.m.* Dutch-boat
Botanique, *s.f.* botany [page 3, § 1
Botan-ique (*adj.*), **-iquement, -iste.** *V.*
Botaniser, *v.n.* to botanize
Botargue, *s.f.* botargo (*kind of caviar*)
Bothniaque, *adj. s.* Bothnian
Botte, *s.f.* boot, Wellington boot; bundle; truss; bunch; hank; clod; cask; bucket; rest; case; collar; step; thrust, lunge; (*on a horse's foot*) cutting-boot, boot. *—s fines,* light boots, dress-boots. *—s molles,* hunting-boots. *—s à revers* or *à retroussis,* top-boots. *Grosses —s, —s fortes,* thick boots; jack-boots. *A propos de —s,* *V.* **Propos.** *Porter* or *pousser une —,* (*fenc.*) to make a thrust, to thrust
Botté, e, *adj.* in boots, with o.'s boots on; booted
Bottelage, *s.m.* putting up in bundles; trussing
Botteler, *v.a.* to put up in bundles; to truss
Bottelette, *s.f.* small bundle *or* truss
Botteleur, *s.m.* sheaf-binder, binder, bandster; hay-trusser; (— *mécanique*) *V.* **Botteloir**
Botteloir, *s.m.* binding *or* hay-trussing apparatus
Botter, *v.a.* to put (*a person's*) boots on (*for him*); to help (*one*) on with (*his*) boots; to boot; to supply with boots; to make boots for; to fit; (*fam.*) to suit; to kick
 Se —, *v.r.* to put o.'s boots on; to wear (*good or bad*) boots; to get clods on o.'s feet; (*of horses*) to ball snow *or* mud, to ball
Botterie, *s.f.* boot-shop; boot-room; boot-making; boot-trade; boot-manufactory; boots
Bottier, *s.m.* boot-maker
†**Bottillon,** *s.m.* small bundle *or* bunch
Bottine, *s.f.* half-boot, boot; (*surg.*) stocks; (*on a horse's foot*) cutting-boot, boot. — *à élastiques,* side-spring boot, elastic-side boot
Bou, *s.m. adj. V.* **Bohé**
Boubie, *s.f.* (*bird*) booby, gannet
†**Boubouille,** *s.f.* (*fam.*) boiling, cooking, pot, mess, victuals, grub
Boubouler, *v.n. V.* **Houhouler**
Bouc, *s.m.* goat, he-goat; goat-skin; pulley. — *émissaire,* scapegoat
Boucage, *s.m.* (*bot.*) burnet saxifrage; anise
Boucan, *s.m.* smoking-place; buccan; smoke-dried meat; row, dust, shindy; blowing-up; drubbing, dressing; bawdy house

Boucanage, *s.m.* smoking, buccaning
Boucaner, *v.a.* to smoke-dry, to dry, to buccan; — *v.n.* to hunt wild cattle; to kick up a row; [to grumble
Boucaneur, *s.m.* rioter, rake
Boucanier, *s.m.* buccaneer; buccaneer's gun
Boucanière, *s.f.* trollop, trull, drab, bitch
Boucarde, *s.f. V.* **Bucarde**
Boucardier, *s.m.* (*pop.*) shoplifter
Boucaro, *s.m.* boucaro, red clay
Boucassin, *s.m.*, **Boucassine,** *s.f.* (*com.*) [bocasine
Boucassiné, e, *adj.* bocasine-like
Boucaut, *s.m.* cask; hogshead; goat-skin
Bouchage, *s.m.* stopping; stuffing; corking
Boucharde, *s.f.* chisel
Bouche, *s.f.* mouth; lips, tongue; talk; speaker; palate; eater, feeder, drinker; victuals, food, living, eating; (sovereign's) table, kitchen, cooks; opening, aperture, orifice; entrance. — *à feu*, piece of ordnance, cannon, gun (*also*, mortar, &c.). — *à* —, face to face. — *close!* — *cousue!* not a word (*or* mum) about that! keep it to yourself! mum! — *de chaleur*, hot air-hole. — *d'eau*, plug-hole, water-plug, plug, hydrant; fire-plug. — *d'incendie*, — *de secours*, fire-plug. — *-en-flûte*, (*fish*) flute-mouth, pipe-mouth, aulostoma, fistularia, tobacco-pipe fish. *Bonne* —, tit-bit, last and best bit; end; pleasant taste; hope, fair prospect, expectation. *A — que veux-tu*, freely, liberally, plentifully, in clover. *De* —, by word of mouth. *Avoir la — mauvaise*, to have a disagreeable taste in o.'s mouth. *Être sur sa —, être porté sur* or *sujet à sa* —, to study good living, to be dainty, to make a god of o.'s stomach. *Faire la — en cœur*, to purse up o.'s mouth (*or* lips), to screw up o.'s mouth, to make a mouth. *Faire la petite* —, to eat very little; to be dainty *or* hard to please; to turn up o.'s nose; to mince; to mince matters (*or* the matter), not to speak freely. *Faire venir l'eau à la* —, to make o.'s mouth water (*L'eau me vient à la* —, my mouth waters). *Fermer* (or *clore*) *la — à*, to silence. *Garder pour la bonne* —, to keep the best bit (*or* thing) for the last. *Prendre sur sa* —, to stint oneself
Bouché, e, *part. adj.* covered, stopped, &c. (*V.* **Boucher,** *v.a.*); stupid, dull; (*of sounds, in music*) fainter, deadened [bit
Bouchée, *s.f.* mouthful; morsel; small quantity,
Bouchement, *s.m.* stopping up, walling up
Bouche-nez, *s.m.* (*jest.*) stench-trap, stink-destroyer, deodorizer
Boucher, *v.a.* to stop, to stop up; to shut; to stuff; to choke up; to block up; to obstruct; to prevent; to cork; to bung; to wall up; to dam up; to fill up; to repair
Se —, *v.r.* to become (*or* be) stopped, &c.; (*le, la, les* ...) to stop *or* shut (o.'s ...). *Se — le nez*, to hold o.'s nose
Bouch-er, ère, *s.m.f.* butcher; butcher's wife
Boucherie, *s.f.* slaughter-house; shambles; butchery; slaughter; butcher's trade *or* shop; [butchers
Bouchet, *s.m.* bouchet (*kind of pear*)
Bouche-trou, *s.m.* stop-gap
Boucheture, *s.f.* enclosure, fence
Bouchoir, *s.m.* oven-door, lid, cover, stopper
Bouchon, *s.m.* cork; stopper; nose-cap, muzzle-stopper; wisp; bundle; plug; bush; public-house; pot-house, dram-shop; bobber, float; kind of game; (*pop.*) sort, kind, kidney; (*obsolete*) darling
Bouchonnement, *s.m.* wisping
Bouchonner, *v.a.* to wisp, to rub down; to rumple; (*obsolete*) to caress, to fondle, to pet
Bouchonnier, *s.m.* cork-manufacturer *or* merchant *or* seller *or* cutter
Bouchot, *s.m.* fishing-hurdles, crawl; bed, mussel-bed, mussel-farm
Bouchure, *s.f.* quickset hedge
Boucle, *s.f.* buckle; ring; ear-ring; curl, lock, ringlet; knocker, rapper; loop; irons; (*vet.*) stomatitis. — *d'oreille*, ear-ring
Bouclé, e, *adj.* (*of hair*) curled; curly; (*of carpets*) tapestry
Bouclement, *s.m.* ringing
Boucler, *v.a.n.* to buckle; to ring; to curl; to bulge, to jut out; (*hunt.*) to ferret out, to dislodge; (*pop.*) to shut up, to lock up, to cage, to quod [buckles, rings
Bouclerie, *s.f.* buckle-trade *or* manufactory;
Bouclette, *s.f.* small buckle *or* ring
Bouclier, *s.m.* shield, buckler; defence, protection; defender, protector; (*zool.*) lumpfish; clavicorn beetle. *Levée de —s*, rising in arms; insurrection; opposition, resistance; unsuccessful attack
Boucon, *s.m.* (*obsolete*) poison
Boucquetine, *s.f.* (*bot.*) *V.* **Boucage**
Bouddhique, *adj.* buddhistic
Bouddhisme, *s.m.* buddhism
Bouddhiste, *s.m.f. adj.* buddhist
Bouder, *v.a.n.* to pout (at); to sulk (with), to be sulky *or* cool (with); to be afraid, to funk; to shirk it; not to be forward; (*at dominoes*) not to be able to play (*or* to go), to refuse (*Je boude*, I can't); (*hort.*) not to grow well
Bouderie, *s.f.* pouting; sulking; sulkiness
Boudeu-r, se, *adj. s.* pouting; sulky; sullen; pouter, sulky person, sulker
Boudin, *s.m.* black-pudding; sausage; roll; roller; sand-bag; wire spring; bell-spring; spring; long curl; portmanteau; sausage-finger; excrement; (*rail.*) flange; (*nav.*) pudding-bag; middle rail of the head; (*mil.*) saucisson, saucisse; (*arch.*) torus. *V.* **Eau** *and* **Fer.** — *blanc*, poultry sausage
Boudinade, *s.f.* (*cook.*) lamb with sausages
Boudinage, *s.m.* (*spin.*) roving, slubbing
Boudine, *s.f.* (*of glass*) knot, bull's-eye
Boudinée, *s.f.* dish of black-pudding
Boudiner, *v.a.* (*spin.*) to rove, to slub; (*paint.*) to paint (*fingers, &c.*) sausage-like
Boudineu-r, se, *s.m.f.* (*spin.*) rover, slubber
Boudinier, *s.m.* sausage-maker
Boudinière, *s.f.* sausage-making machine
Boudinoir, *s.m.* (*spin.*) roving-frame
Boudinure, *s.f.* (*nav.*) puddening
Boudjou, *s.m.* boudjou (*Algerian coin, worth* 1*s.* 6*d.*)
Boudoir, *s.m.* withdrawing-room, private room, boudoir
Boudrière, Boudrine, *s.f.* (*agr.*) brown rust
Boue, *s.f.* mud; dirt; mire; filth; clay; sediment; matter; meanness, sordidness; abjection, abject condition; wretched state; misery; corruption. *De* —, of mud, &c.; muddy; dirty; filthy; mean, sordid, base, abject, vile, groveling, corrupt
Bouée, *s.f.* (*nav.*) buoy; (*pop.*) hole
Bouette, *s.f. V.* **Boitte**
Boueu-r, se, Boueu-x, se, *s.m.f.* scavenger, street-orderly, street-sweeper; dustman
Boueu-x, se, *adj.* muddy; miry; dirty; foul; bad; thick
Bouffant, e, *adj.* puffing, puffed
Bouffant, *s.m.* puff (*of a sleeve*)
Bouffante, *s.f.* (*old*) hoop, farthingale; stomacher
Bouffard, *s.m.* smoker, whiffer, whiffler
Bouffarde, *s.f.* bacca-pipe, clay. *Fumer une* or *sa* —, to have a whiff
Bouffarder, *v.n.* to whiff, to have a whiff
Bouffardière, *s.f.* (*jest.*) smoking-room, whiffing-room
Bouffe, *adj.* comic; — *s.m.* buffo, Italian comic actor *or* buffoon; Italian singer; —**s,** *s.m.pl.* Italian opera (*in Paris*) [burst; flight
Bouffée, *s.f.* puff; gust; whiff; fume; fit;
Bouffer, *v.n.* to puff; to swell; to swell out; to rise; to bulge, to jut out; (*fam.*) to eat, to feed, to grub, to guttle; — *v.a.* to blow (*meat*); (*fam.*) to gobble up; (*pop.*) to buffet, to punch
Bouffette, *s.f.* tuft; bow; ear-knot, rosette
Bouffir, *v.a.n.* to puff up, to bloat: to inflate; to swell out; to swell
Bouffissure, *s.f.* puffing up; bloatedness; swelling; bombast; pride, conceit, vanity
Bouffoir, *s.m.* blower, bellows
Bouffon, ne, *adj. s.m.f.* droll, facetious, funny, comical, comic; buffoon; clown; jester, fool; — *s.m.* burlesque, buffoonery; (*old*) *V.* **Bouffo**
Bouffonner, *v.n.* to play the buffoon; to jest

Bouffonnerie, *s.f.* buffoonery, drollery
Bouge, *s.m.* closet; hole, hovel, small room, poor dwelling; den; low pot-house; bawdy house; convexity, rounding, bulge, bilge; cowry
Bougeoir, *s.m.* flat *or* bedroom candlestick; [taper-stand
Bougeon, *s.m.* (*pop.*) fidgety child
Bougeotte, *s.f.* pigeon-hole
Bouger, *v.n.* to move, to stir, to budge; to wag; to fidget; to go out (of) *or* away (from); to change
Bougie, *s.f.* candle, light; wax-candle, wax-light; taper; candle-light; (*surg.*) bougie. — *diaphane,* sperm *or* spermaceti candle. — *filée,* taper. — *de cire,* wax-candle *or* light
Bougier, *v.a.* to wax
†**Bougillon,** *s.m.* (*pop.*) fidgety child
Bougon, ne, *adj. s.* grumbling; grumbler
Bougonner, *v.n.* to grumble, to jaw; — *v.a.* to grumble at, to scold, to jaw
Bougonneu-r, se, *s.m.f.* grumbler, jawer
Bougraine, Bougrane, *s.f. V.* **Bugrane**
Bougran, *s.m.* buckram
Bougraner, *v.a.* to dress buckram-like, to stiffen
Bougre, *s.m.* (*pop.*) blackguard; fellow; buck, brick; famous fellow; determined dog; — *int. V.* **Bigre.** — *de,* confounded. *Bon* —, good sort of fellow. *Mauvais* —, *vilain* —, surly *or* snappish fellow, nasty fellow, ugly customer, downright blackguard
Bougrement, *adv.* (*pop.*) *V.* **Bigrement**
Bougresse, *s.f.* (*pop.*) jade, bitch; creature, thing. *Bonne* —, good sort of creature
Bougue, *s.f.* shifting sand, drift sand
Bouguière, *s.f.* (*fish.*) very thin net
†**Bouillabaisse,** *s.f. V.* **Bouille-abaisse**
†**Bouillaison,** *s.f.* fermentation (*of cider*)
†**Bouillant, e,** *adj.* boiling; burning; ardent, hot, fiery, impetuous; hasty, hot-headed; fierce; eager; — *s.m.* fieriness, impetuosity; hastiness. *Tout* —, boiling hot
†**Bouillard,** *s.m.* (*nav.*) stormy cloud
†**Bouille,** *s.f.* (*fisherman's*) pole
†**Bouille-abaisse,** *s.f.* [Provençal soup made up of fish, &c.]; (*fig.*) mishmash
†**Bouiller,** *v.a.* (*fish.*) to beat (*the water*)
†**Bouillerie,** *s.f.* boilery; brandy-distillery
†**Bouilleur,** *s.m.* (*pers.*) boiler; brandy-distiller; (*fish.*) beater; (*of steam-engines*) boiler-tube
†**Bouilli, e,** *part. adj.* boiled; waxed (*leather*)
†**Bouilli,** *s.m.* (fresh) boiled beef (of which soup has been made); boiled meat
†**Bouillie,** *s.f.* pap; porridge; hasty-pudding; pulp. — *pour les chats,* (*fig.*) vain *or* fruitless labour, useless toil, unprofitable undertaking; failure
†**Bouillir,** *v.n.a.* to boil; to bubble up; to burn; to work, to ferment; to be agitated, to be mad (with). — *à gros bouillons,* to boil fast. — *à petits bouillons,* to boil gently; to simmer. *Faire* —, to boil, to make boil
†**Bouilloire,** *s.f.* boiler; kettle, tea-kettle
†**Bouillon,** *s.m.* broth; soup; basin *or* plate of soup; (*of some kinds of meat, of some herbs*) tea; bubble; ripple; gush; foam, froth; puff; bull's-eye; shoal; farm-yard liquid manure; (*vet.*) bouillon; (*fig.*) burst; fit; impetuosity, ardour; (*fam.*) bad job, bad spec, failure; unsold book *or* newspaper; mouthful of water; poisonous draught, poison; (*pop.*) shower, rain, soaking. — *aveugle,* (*pop.*) poor soup. — *-blanc,* (*bot.*) mullein. — *pointu,* (*fam.*) enema, injection; (*pop.*) bayonet-thrust. — *de canard,* (*pop.*) water. — *d'onze heures,* (*fam.*) drowning; poisonous draught, poison. — *qui chauffe,* (*pop.*) storm brewing. *Boire un* —, to swallow a good deal of water (*after plunging*); to make a bad spec, to lose a good deal of money; to drink poison
†**Bouillonnement,** *s.m.* bubbling; gush; boiling; ebullition; effervescence; agitation; buoyancy
†**Bouillonner,** *v.n.* to bubble; to ripple; to gush out; to boil up *or* over; (*pop.*) to lose money; — *v.a.* to put puffs to, to full, to full in
†**Bouillote, Bouillotte,** *s.f.* boiler; kettle; foot-warmer; bouillote (*game at cards*)
Boujaron, Boujarron, *s.m.* (*nav.*) gill
Boulaie, *s.f.* birch-grove, birch-plantation
Boulang-er, ère, *s.m.f.* baker; baker's wife; — *s.f.* round (*dance, tune*)
Boulanger, *v.n.a.* to make bread, to bake
Boulangerie, *s.f.* bread-making, baking; bake-house, bakery; baker's trade *or* shop *or* business; bakers
Boule, *s.f.* ball; bowl; sconce, pate, noddle, head; face, phiz; wits, senses; assurance, self-possession, presence of mind; vote. — *grasse,* fire-ball (*fuel*). — *d'eau chaude,* hot-water bottle. — *-de-neige, V.* **Neige.** *Jeu de* —, bowl, bowls; bowling-alley *or* ground, bowling-green. *Perdre la* —, (*pop. for* "perdre la tête") *V.* **Tête.** *A — vue,* hastily
Boule, *s.m.* (*of furniture*) buhl, buhl-work, buhl-marquetry. *De* —, buhl
Bouleau, *s.m.* birch, birch-tree
Bouledogue, *s.m.* bull-dog
Boulejon, *s.m.* sardine-net
Bouler, *v.n.* to swell; (*of pigeons*) to pout; (*pop.*) to get on; — *v.a. V.* **Bouiller;** (*pop.*) to thrash, to whack, to lick; to blow up, to bully; to [hustle
Bouleraie, *s.f. V.* **Boulaie**
Boulereau, *s.m.* (*fish*) goby, groundling
Boulet, *s.m.* cannon-ball, ball, round shot, shot; (*punishment*) chain and ball, dragging a cannon-ball; (*of horses*) bullet, fetlock-joint. — *mort,* spent ball. — *ramé,* chain-shot, bar-shot
Bouleté, e, *adj. Cheval* —, *jument* —*e,* boulet horse *or* mare, boulet
Boulette, *s.f.* ball; pellet; cob; forcemeat ball; poison-ball; trip, slip; blunder, bull
Bouleur, *s.m.* (*fish.*) beater
Bouleu-x, se, *s.m.f.* roadster; (*pers.*) drudge
Boulevard, Boulevart, *s.m.* bulwark, rampart; public walk, walk; street; Boulevard
Boulevardier, *s.m.* lounger on the Boulevards (of Paris); Grub-street writer; —**ière,** *s.f.* street-walker
Boulevari, *s.m.* (*pop.*) *V.* **Hourvari**
Bouleversement, *s.m.* overthrow; overturning; destruction; ruin; upsetting; subversion; turning up *or* over; confusion, disorder; convulsion; distraction
Bouleverser, *v.a.* to overthrow; to overturn; to destroy; to ruin; to upset; to subvert; to turn up *or* over, to turn upside down *or* topsy-turvy; to throw into confusion; to derange, to disturb; to agitate; to convulse; to distract
Boulevue. *A la* —, hastily [drag-net
Bouliche, Boulièche, *s.f.* (*fish.*) trawl-net,
Boulier, *s.m.* pipkin; (*arith.*) abacus; (*fish.*) [bag-net
Bouligon, *s.m.* close fishing-net
Boulimie, *s.f.* (*med.*) bulimia, bulimy, voracious [appetite
Boulimique, *adj.* (*med.*) bulimic
Boulin, *s.m.* pigeon-hole; putlog-hole; putlog
Bouline, *s.f.* (*nav.*) bowline. *Vent de* —, tack-wind, scant wind. *Aller à la* —, to sail close to the wind. *Courir la* —, to run the gauntlet
Bouliner, *v.a.* (*nav.*) to haul to windward; — *v.n.* (*nav.*) to sail close to the wind; (*fam.*) to [slouch
Boulineur, *s.m.* camp-follower
Boulingrin, *s.m.* grass-plot, lawn; bowling-[green
Boulingue, *s.f.* (*nav.*) royal sail
Boulinier, *s.m.* (*nav.*) plyer
Boulle, *s.m. V.* **Boule,** *s.m.* [(*mas.*) larry
Bouloir, *s.m.* copper vessel; (*fisherman's*) pole;
Boulon, *s.m.* bolt; pin
Boulonais, e, Boulonnais, e, *adj. s.m.f.* of Boulogne, Boulognese, native of Boulogne; — *s.m.* Boulogne district; — *s.f.* Boulogne fashion
Boulonnement, *s.m.* bolting, pinning
Boulonner, *v.a.* to bolt, to pin
Boulot, te, *adj. s.* squabby, dumpy; fat, plump; squabby (*or* &c.) fellow *or* woman *or* girl *or* thing
Boulotter, *v.n.* to go (*or* get) on so so; to scrape along; — *v.a.* to jog on through, to get easily through

Boulure, *s.f.* (*hort.*) sucker
Boulvari, *s.m.* (*pop.*) *V.* **Hourvari**
Bouque, *s.f.* (*nav.*) mouth (*of a river*)
Bouquer, *v.n.* to yield, to truckle. *Faire —*, (*hunt.*) to dislodge, to ferret out
Bouquet, *s.m.* nosegay, posy, bouquet; bunch; tuft; cluster; clump; wisp; birthday compliment; ode, sonnet; present; end, crowning-piece; prawn, prawns; (*of wine*) odour, perfume, aroma, bouquet; (*of precious stones, fireworks*) bouquet
Bouquetier, *s.m.* flower-man; flower-vase
Bouquetière, *s.f.* flower-girl *or* woman
Bouquetin, *s.m.* ibex, bouquetin, wild goat
Bouquetine, *s.f.* (*bot.*) *V.* **Boucage**
Bouqueton, Bouquetout, *s.m.* shrimp-net
Bouquin, *s.m.* old (he-)goat; buck-hare; buck-rabbit; old hare; worthless *or* stupid *or* musty old book, old book; (*fam.*) book; (*of a pipe*) mouthpiece, tip. *Mauvais —*, worthless book
Bouquinage, *s.m.* hunting after (*or* reading) old books; (*fam.*) hunting after books
Bouquine, *s.f.* (*pop.*) billygoat-beard
Bouquiner, *v.n.* to hunt after old books; to read old books; (*fam.*) to hunt after books; to buck, to couple
Bouquinerie, *s.f.* heap of old books; old books; old book trade; passion for old books
Bouquineur, *s.m.* hunter after (*or* collector *or* lover *or* fancier of) old books; bookworm
Bouquiniste, *s.m.* dealer in old books, second-hand bookseller; collector *or* lover *or* fancier of old books
Bouracan, *s.m.* barracan
Bouracanier, *s.m.* barracan-maker
Bouracher, *s.m.* silk-weaver
†**Bouragne, Bouraque,** *s.f.* (*fish.*) bow-net
Bourbe, *s.f.* mud, mire; (*pop.*) lying-in hospital
Bourbeu-x, se, *adj.* muddy, miry
Bourbier, *s.m.* slough; bog; mire; mud; puddle; mess, scrape; fix; danger; lurch; sink of vice
†**Bourbillon,** *s.m.* mud; clot of ink; (*med.*) core (*of a boil*)
Bourbonien, ne, *adj.* Bourbonic
Bourbon-isme, iste. *V.* page 3, § 1
Bourbonnaise, *s.f.* bourbonnaise (*farcical song*)
Bourbotte, *s.f.* *V.* **Barbote**
Bourcette, *s.f.* (*bot.*) corn-salad, lamb's-lettuce
Bourdaine, *s.f.* (*bot.*) black alder
Bourdalou, *s.m.* hat-band; bed-pan, slipper-pan, slipper
Bourde, *s.f.* fib, sham, flam, bounce, bouncer, whapper, humbug, lie; (*nav.*) shore, prop
Bourder, *v.n.* to fib, to sham, to humbug
Bourdeu-r, se, *s.m.f.* fibber, shammer
Bourdigue, *s.f.* *V.* **Bordigue**
†**Bourdillon,** *s.m.* (*coop.*) *V.* **Merrain**
Bourdon, *s.m.* staff; pilgrim's staff; scaffold-pole; humble-bee; drone-bee, drone; great bell, tom-bell, tom; (*mus.*) drone; bass; (*of organs*) bourdon; (*print.*) out, omission. *Faux —*, (*zool.*) drone-bee, drone; (*mus.*) faux bourdon
Bourdonné, e, *adj.* corrugated, wrinkled; (*her.*) pommee
Bourdonnement, *s.m.* hum, humming; buzz, buzzing; boom, booming; murmur; whisper, whispering; tingling, singing, noise
Bourdonner, *v.n.a.* to hum; to buzz; to drone; to boom; to murmur; to mutter; to whisper; to bore, to bother; to swing
Bourdonnet, *s.m.* (*surg.*) pledget
Bourdonneur, *adj.m.*, *s.m.* humming; humming-bird
Bourg, *s.m.* borough; market-town
Bourgade, *s.f.* small borough; small market-town; long straggling village, village
Bourgène, *s.f.* (*bot.*) *V.* **Bourdaine**
Bourgeois, e, *s.m.f.* citizen; commoner; plebeian; civilian; independent man *or* woman with a small competency; respectable man *or* woman; private person; plain Mr.; plain Mrs.; plain homely man *or* woman; cit; employer; master, governor; mistress; landlord; landlady; gentleman; lady; sir; ma'am; tradesman, shopkeeper; common *or* vulgar person; snob; burgess; burgher; (*nav.*) ship-owner, owner. *A la —e*, (*cook.*) plain, plainly dressed. *Être en —*, to be (dressed) in plain clothes (*not in uniform*)
Bourgeois, e, *adj.* citizenlike; civil; private; homely; plain; family; common, vulgar; snobbish; mean
Bourgeoisade, *s.f.* mean action, shabby thing
Bourgeoisement, *adv.* in a plain *or* homely way (*or* manner), plainly; commonly; vulgarly; snobbishly; meanly
Bourgeoisie, *s.f.* citizenship; citizens; burgesses; burghers; middle class; small gentry; freedom of the city. *Droit de —*, burghership; freedom of the city; (*fig.*) sanction, recognition, admittance, adoption; footing
Bourgeon, *s.m.* bud; gem; tiller; (*of vines*) shoot; (*on the face*) pimple. *—s charnus*, proud flesh
Bourgeonné, e, *adj.* pimpled
Bourgeonnement, *s.m.* budding; budding-time
Bourgeonner, *v.n.* to bud; to tiller; (*of vines*) to shoot; (*fig.*) to break (*or* come) out in pimples, to become pimpled; to blossom
Bourgeonnier, *s.m.* bullfinch
Bourg-épine, Bourgue-épine, *s.m.* *V.* **Alaterne**
Bourgeron, *s.m.* short frock, slop
Bourgeteur, *s.m.* wool-worker
Bourgin, *s.m.* *V.* **Bregin**
Bourgmestre, *s.m.* burgomaster
†**Bourgne,** *s.f.*, **Bourgnon,** *s.m.* (*fish.*) bow-net
†**Bourgogne,** *s.m.* burgundy (wine)
†**Bourguignon, ne,** *adj.* *s.m.f.* Burgundian; — *s.m.* iceberg, floe; kind of grape; — *s.f.* Burgundian fashion
Bourle, *s.f.* (*obsolete*) trick, hoax
Bourlet, *s.m.* (*old spelling*) *V.* **Bourrelet**
Bourlinguer, *v.n.* (*nav.*) to work
Bournous, *s.m.* *V.* **Burnous**
Bourrache, *s.f.* (*bot.*) borage
Bourrade, *s.f.* snapping; cuff; blow; beating; blowing-up, bullying; taunt, hard hit, home-thrust; blow with a musket-butt; recoil, kick
Bourrage, *s.m.* stuffing; wadding; filling; ramming; tamping
Bourrague, *s.m.* (*fish.*) bow-net
Bourras, *s.m.* *V.* **Bure**
Bourrasque, *s.f.* squall; fit of anger; caprice, whim; tiff; fit; burst, explosion; violent attack; commotion; vexation
Bourre, *s.f.* hair; flock; floss; fluff; stuffing; wadding, wad; padding; tamping; down; bud; dried husk; (*fig.*) padding, surplusage, worthless matter, trash. *— de coco*, cocoa-nut fibre, cocoa-fibre, coir. *— de soie*, floss-silk
Bourreau, *s.m.* executioner; hangman; cruel wretch; tormenter; persecutor; tyrant; murderer; enemy; torment; (*obsolete*) sirrah. *— d'argent*, great spendthrift
Bourrée, *s.f.* small fagot, chatwood; blowing-up, bullying; quail-catching; boree (*dance, tune, in Auvergne*)
Bourreler, *v.a.* to torment, to torture, to rack, to sting, to goad
Bourrelet, *s.m.* pad; cushion; sand-bag; tumbling-cap; (*horse's*) collar; round (*cylindrical*) border, border; round swelling, swelling, swell; (*vet.*) coronet; (*nav.*) puddening
Bourrelier, *s.m.* harness-maker
Bourrellement, *s.m.* torment, torture; twinge, twitch; sting
Bourrellerie, *s.f.* harness-making; harness
Bourre-pipe, *s.m.* tobacco-stopper
Bourrer, *v.a.* to stuff; to wad; to pad; to cram; to fill; to choke up; to ram; to tamp (*a mine*); to thrust; to push; to snap; to take to task, to blow up, to bully; to beat; to abuse; — *v.n.* (*of horses*) to bolt, to start. *— de coups*, to beat soundly
Bourriche, *s.f.* frail, basket (*for poultry, game, or fish; also, a basket containing 12 dozen of oysters, that is, about half the quantity of a "cloyère"*)
Bourriers, *s.m.pl.* chaff; leather-parings
Bourrique, *s.f.* she-ass, jenny-ass; donkey; handbarrow

Bourriquet, *s.m.* young *or* little ass; hand-barrow; windlass; horse (*tech.*)
Bourriqui-er, ère, *s.m.f.* donkey-driver
Bourrir, *v.n.* (*of partridges*) to whir [whir
Bourrissement, *s.m.* (*of partridges*) whirring,
Bourroir, *s.m.* tamping-bar
Bourru, e, *adj.* surly, cross, crabbed, peevish; downy; uneven; unfermented; — *s.m.* surly man, churl. — *bienfaisant,* good-hearted
Boursal, *s.m.* (*fish.*) purse-net [grumbler
Bourse, *s.f.* purse; bag; pouch; saddle-bag; purse-net; exhibition, scholarship, bursary; free education; nomination; exchange, change, stock-exchange, money-market; (*anat.*) sac; (*surg.*) suspensory bandage; (*bot.*) wrapper; —**s,** *pl.* (*of colleges*) foundation; (*anat.*) scrotum, cod. — *de filet,* network purse. *Filet en* —, purse-net. *Sans — délier,* without any expense. *Selon ta — gouverne ta bouche,* (*Proverb*) cut your coat according to your cloth
Boursette, *s.f.* little purse; (*bot.*) shepherd's-purse; corn-salad, lamb's-lettuce
Boursicaut, Boursicot, *s.m.* little purse, purse; savings, hoard
Boursicoter, *v.n.* to save a little money; to do a little stock-jobbing, to make small speculations on 'Change; to club together
Boursicoteur, Boursicotier, *s.m.* petty stock-jobber, stock-jobber in a small way, small speculator
Boursi-er, ère, *s.m.f.* foundation scholar, foundationer, exhibitioner, bursar; speculator on 'Change; purse-maker; purser, treasurer
†**Boursiller, Boursillonner,** *v.n.* to club together; to contribute something; to spend money, to pay money, to come down, to fork
†**Boursillon,** *s.m.* little purse [out
Boursouflage, *s.m.* bombast, fustian; pomposity; swelling; bloatedness; puffiness; puffing stuff
Boursouflé, e, *adj.* swollen; puffed up, bloated; puffy; bombastic; — *s.m.f.* puffy man *or* woman *or* girl; — *s.m.* bombast, bombastic style, pomposity [(*chem.*) expansion
Boursouflement, *s.m. V.* **Boursouflage;**
Boursoufler, *v.a.* to swell; to puff up, to bloat; to inflate; to make bombastic *or* turgid
Se —, *v.r.* to swell; to become bloated; (*chem.*) to expand
Boursouflure, *s.f. V.* **Boursouflage**
Bousage, *s.m.* (*manu.*) dunging
Bousard, *s.m.* deer's dung
Bousculade, Bousculée, *s.f.,* **Bousculement,** *s.m.* hustling, jostling, pushing, push; blowing-up, bullying
Bousculer, *v.a.* to turn topsy-turvy; to upset; to hustle, to jostle, to push about; to drive; to hurry; to blow up, to bully
Bouse, *s.f.* dung (*of cows, oxen*)
Bousier, *s.m.* (*zool.*) coprophagan, dung-beetle, tumble-dung, shard-borne beetle
†**Bousillage,** *s.m.* mud; mud-wall, cob-wall; mud-walling, mud-wall building; (*fig.*) bungling piece of work, botch [bungle, to botch
†**Bousiller,** *v.n.* to build with mud; — *v.a.* to
†**Bousilleu-r, se,** *s.m.f.* mud-wall builder; bungler, botcher; slut
Bousin, *s.m.* sandvent (*soft crust of freestone*); inferior turf *or* peat; row, dust, shindy; bawdy house; low pot-house
Bousineur, *s.m.* (*pop.*) roisterer, rioter
Bousingot, *s.m.* sailor's hat; (*pers.*) nondescript
Bousquer, *v.a.* to compel (*a lazy sailor*) to do
Boussard, *s.m.* shotten herring [his work
Bousserade, Bousserole, *s.f. V.* **Busserole**
Boussole, *s.f.* mariner's compass, sea-compass, compass; circumferentor; guide; rule; (*pop.*) headpiece, head, wits, senses [comforts
†**Boustifaille,** *s.f.* stuffing, grub, creature
†**Boustifailler,** *v.n.* (*pop.*) to feed, to grub
Boustrophédon, *s.m.,* **Boustrophédone,** *adj.f.* (*antiquity*) boustrophedon

Bout, *s.m.* end; extremity; tip; top; point; bit; piece; stump; nipple; ferrule; muzzle; (*of foils*) button; (*tech.*) end-piece; (*nav.*) head, bow (*of a ship*); (*fish*) sun-fish. — *coupé,* cheroot. — *ferré,* tag; ferrule. —*s rimés* [words that rhyme given to be formed into verse; pieces of poetry made from given rhymes]; crambo. — *de sein,* nipple, teat. — *de vergue,* (*nav.*) yard-arm. — *de lof,* (*nav.*) bumkin. *A* —, at an end; at a stand; exhausted; hard up; at o.'s wits' end; at the end of o.'s tether; out of temper; out of patience. *A — de ...,* out of ..., at o.'s last ..., having exhausted o.'s ... *A — de forces,* exhausted, spent. *A — portant, V.* **Portant.** *D'un — à l'autre, de — en* —, from one end to the other, from end to end; from beginning to end; all over, all through, throughout. *Tout le — du monde,* the very utmost. *Joindre les deux —s,* to make both ends meet. *Mettre* or *Pousser à* —, to confound, to nonplus, to drive into a corner, to put to a stand, to stop the mouth of, to put *or* reduce to o.'s last shifts; to exhaust; to reduce; to overcome; to drive to extremities; to put out of patience, to provoke *or* excite beyond endurance; to go through with; to press home; to tire out. *Savoir sur le — du doigt,* to have at o.'s finger-ends. *Venir à — de,* to bring about; to succeed in; to accomplish; to be able (to); to manage (to); to manage to do; to get through; to make out; to bring round; to overcome, to master, to get the better of [sally; humouristic verses
Boutade, *s.f.* whim, freak, fit, fancy; start,
Boutant, e, *adj.* (*arch.*) butting
Boutargue, *s.f. V.* **Botargue**
Bout-dehors, *s.m.* (*nav.*) boom
Bout-de-quièvre, *s.m.* (*fish.*) hoop-net
Boute, *s.f.* wine leathern bottle; tobacco cask
Bouté, e, *adj.* (*of horses*) *V.* **Bouleté;** (*of wine*) getting ropy
Bouteau, *s.m.* kind of fishing-net [horses
Boute-charge, *s.m.* (*mil.*) signal to load the
Boutée, *s.f.* (*arch.*) abutment; butment
Boute-en-train, *s.m.* breeding horse; tarin, siskin, piping bird, call-bird; exhilarating companion, leader, life and soul, life of the party [(*in old gunnery*) portfire-stick
Boute-feu, *s.m.* (*pers.*) incendiary, firebrand;
Boute-hors, *s.m.* (*nav.*) *V.* **Bout-dehors**
†**Bouteille,** *s.f.* bottle; flask; jar; bottleful; bubble; (*vet.*) rot; —**s,** *pl.* (*nav.*) quarter gallery; privy. *Fausse* —, (*nav.*) badge. *La — à l'encre, V.* **Encre**
†**Bouteiller,** *s.m.* (*obsolete*) butler; cup-bearer; — *v.n.* to bubble
†**Bouteillerie,** *s.f.* bottle-making; bottle-trade; bottle-warehouse; bottle-room; butlership
Boute-lof, *s.m.* (*nav.*) bumkin
Bouter, *v.a.* to pare; to flesh; (*obsolete*) to put; — *v.n.* (*of wine*) to become ropy, to get thick
Bouterolle, *s.f.* kind of fishing-net; (*mil.*) chape *or* crampit (*of a scabbard*)
Bouteroue, *s.f.m.* tramway; spur-post
Boute-selle, *s.m.* (*mil.*) signal to saddle. *Sonner le* —, to sound to horse
Boute-tout-cuire, *s.m.* spendthrift
Bouteuse, *s.f.* (*pers.*) pin-sticker
Bouteux, *s.m.* (*fish.*) putting-net, shrimp-net
Bouticlar, *s.m.* (*fish.*) well-boat; cauf
†**Boutillier, Boutiller,** *s.m. V.* **Bouteiller**
Boutique, *s.f.* shop; concern; workshop; stall; booth, stand, standing; shop-goods, goods; wares; stock; pedlar's basket, packman's pack; set of tools, tools, implements; workmen, men, people, hands; business; work, doing; set, clan, gang, coterie, clique; well-boat; cauf
Boutiquer, *v.a.* (*pop.*) to bundle up, to botch up
Boutiqui-er, ère, *s.m.f. adj.* shopkeeper; vulgar *or* grovelling fellow; shopkeeping
Boutis, *s.m.* (*hunt.*) rooting-place; holes
Boutisse, *s.f.* (*mas.*) header, bond-stone
Boutoir, *s.m.* snout; tusks; parer; buttress

Bouton, *s.m.* button; bud; gem; pimple; pustule; nipple; stud; knob; handle; bead sight, bead, sight. — *d'or,* (*bot.*) *V.* **Bassinet.** *Serrer le — à,* to keep a tight hand over; to urge, to press hard, to put on the screw
Boutonné, e, *adj.* buttoned; buttoned up; close, reserved; budding; pimpled; (*of surg. instr.*) probe-pointed
Boutonnement, *s.m.* budding; buttoning
Boutonner, *v.a.* to button; to button up; — *v.n.* to bud; to break out in pimples
Se —, *v.r.* to button o.'s clothes; to button; to become pimpled
Boutonnerie, *s.f.* button-trade, button-making *or* manufacture, button-manufactory; buttons, [button-ware
Boutonnier, *s.m.* button-maker
Boutonnière, *s.f.* button-hole; (*fig.*) incision; cut, gash, wound [pagation by slips
Bouturage, *s.m.* (*hort.*) planting of slips, pro-
Bouture, *s.f.* (*hort.*) slip, cutting, piping; sucker
Bouturer, *v.a.* to propagate by slips; — *v.n.* to [shoot suckers
Bouvart, *s.m.* young bull
Bouveau, Bouvelet, *s.m.* young bullock, steer
Bouverie, *s.f.,* **Bouverin,** *s.m.* ox-stall; cow- [stable
Bouvet, *s.m.* grooving-plane
Bouvi-er, ère, *s.m.f.* neat-herd, ox-driver, drover; cow-herd; (*fig.*) churl; — *s.m.* (*astr.*) [Bootes
†Bouvillon, *s.m.* young bullock, steer
Bouvrette, *s.f.* bullfinch-organ
†Bouvreuil, *s.m.* bullfinch [—, cattle plague
Bovine, *adj.f.* bovine. *Bêtes —s,* oxen. *Peste*
Bovista, Boviste, *s.m.* (*bot.*) giant puff-ball
Box, *s.m.* box (*in a stable*)
Boxe, *s.f.* boxing
Boxer, *v.n.a.,* **Se —,** *v.r.* to box; to fight
Boxeu-r, se, *s.m.f.* boxer
Boxon, *s.m.* (*pop.*) bawdy house [*man*)
Boyard, *s.m. adj.* boyar, boyard (*Russian noble-*
Boyart, *s.m.* handbarrow
Boyau, *s.m.* gut; bowel; cat-gut; chitterlings; long and narrow place; small gallery; passage; slip, strip; fiddle-string, string; belly; hose-pipe, hose (*to carry water*); (*fort.*) boyau, small trench, branch (of a trench). *Corde à* (or *de*) —, cat-gut; fiddle-string, string. *Descente de —x,* rupture
Boyauderie, *s.f.* gut-works, cat-gut factory; gut-work; gut-working; fiddle-string making
Boyaudier, *s.m.* gut-worker, cat-gut maker; fiddle-string maker
Boyer, *s.m.* (*nav.*) Flemish sloop
Brabançon, ne, *adj.* Brabantine; — *s.m.f.* Brabanter; — *s.f.* brabançonne (*Belgian national* [*anthem*)
Brabant, *s.m.* Belgian plough
Bracelet, *s.m.* bracelet, armlet
‡Brachial, e, *adj.* (*anat.*) brachial
‡Brachmane, *s.m. V.* **Brahmane**
‡Brachy-graphie, -logie. *V.* page 3, § 1
Bracon, *s.m.* post, beam (*of a sluice*)
Braconnage, *s.m.* poaching
Braconner, *v.n.* to poach
Braconnier, *s.m.* poacher; game-slaughterer
Bractéaire, Bractéal, e, *adj.* (*bot.*) bracteal
Bractée, *s.f.* (*bot.*) bract, bractea
Bractéifère, *adj.* (*bot.*) bracteate
Bractéiforme, *adj.* (*bot.*) bracteiform
Bractéolaire, *adj.* (*bot.*) bracteolar [bracteole
Bractéole, *s.f.* gold leaf; gold clippings; (*bot.*)
Bractéolé, e, *adj.* (*bot.*) bracteolate
Bradype, *s.m.* (*zool.*) bradypus, sloth
Bradypepsie, *s.f.* (*med.*) *V.* page 3, § 1
Brague, *s.f.* (*nav.*) breeching; stoppers; span; —**s,** *pl.* (*in Brittany*) breeches, knickerbockers
Brahmane, Brahme, *s.m.* Brahmin
Brahmanique, *adj.* Brahminical
Brahmanisme, *s.m.* Brahminism
Brahmine, *s.m. V.* **Brahmane** [crushed malt
Brai, *s.m.* resin, rosin; pitch; tar; bird-trap;
Braie, *s.f.* napkin, clout; breeches, pair of breeches; drawers, pair of drawers; fishing-weir, bow-net; (*nav.*) coat; (*fort.*) trench
†Braillard, e, *adj. s.* bawling, brawling, squalling, noisy, obstreperous; bawler, brawler, squaller; scold
†Braille, *s.f.* herring salting-shovel; (*agr.*) husk
†Braillement, *s.m.* bawling, brawling, squalling
†Brailler, *v.n.* to bawl, to brawl, to squall; — *v.a.* to salt (*herrings*) in a shovel
†Brailleu-r, se, *adj. s. V.* **Braillard**
Braiment, Braire, *s.m.* braying
Braire, *v.n.* to bray; (*pop.*) to cry, to whine
Braise, *s.f.* embers, burning embers; wood-cinders; quenched charcoal; (*pop.*) cash, tin, rhino, dust. *A la —,* (*cook.*) braised
Braiser, *v.a.n.* (*cook.*) to braise; (*pop.*) to spend [*or* pay some tin
Braisier, *s.m.* charcoal-bin
Braisière, *s.f.* braising-pan, stewpan; cinder- [pail
Brak, *adj.m.* half-salted (*herring*)
Brame, *s.m. V.* **Brahmane;** — *s.f. V.* **Brème**
Bramement, *s.m.* (*of deer*) belling
Bramer, *v.n.* (*of deer*) to bell
Bramin, Bramine, *s.m. V.* **Brahmane**
Bran, *s.m.* coarse bran; (*pop.*) excrement, dirt; (*old*) brand, sword. — *de Judas,* freckles. — *de scie,* sawdust. — *de son,* coarse bran
Brancard, *s.m.* stretcher; handbarrow; litter; shaft (*of a carriage*); rocker (*in the body of a carriage*). *Cheval de —, V.* **Cheval**
Brancardier, *s.m.* handbarrowman; shaft-horse, wheeler
Branchage, *s.m.* branches, boughs
Branche, *s.f.* branch; bough; pin-wire; side (*of a ladder*); rib (*of an umbrella*); bow (*of a sword*); shank (*of a key*); (*pop.*) friend. — *gourmande,* proud branch, sucker. — *-ursine,* (*bot.*) brankursine, acanthus. *Comme l'oiseau sur la —,* unsettled
Branchement, *s.m.* branching
Brancher, *v.n.,* **Se —,** *v.r.* to perch (*on a tree, on trees*); to tree; (*fig.*) to perch (*anywhere*), to be perched; to branch; — *v.a.* to hang (*on a tree*); to branch; (*pop.*) to hang
Branchette, *s.f.* small branch, twig, wattle
Branchial, e, *adj.* (*anat.*) branchial
Branchier, *adj.m. Oiseau —,* brancher, percher
Branchies, *s.f.pl.* (*anat.*) branchiæ, gills
Branchiopode, *s.m.* (*zool.*) branchiopod
Branchu, e, *adj.* branchy; forked, bifurcated; two-horned
Branc-ursine, *s.f.* (*bot.*) brankursine, acanthus
Brandade, *s.f.* (*cook.*) brandade (*ragout of cod*)
Brande, *s.f.* heath; boughs
Brandebourg, *s.m.* gimp, braid, frog, loop *or* stripe of lace; — *s.f.* (*obsolete*) summer-house; huke, cassock [Brandenburger
Brandebourgeois, e, *adj. s.* of Brandenburg;
Branderie, *s.f.* brandy-distillery
Brandevin, *s.m.* brandy [sutler
Brandevini-er, ère, *s.m.f.* brandy-distiller;
†Brandillement, *s.m.* swinging, tossing, shaking about [toss, to shake about
†Brandiller, *v.a.n.,* **Se —,** *v.r.* to swing, to
†Brandilloire, *s.f.* (*obsolete*) swing-plough; swing [to pin
Brandir, *v.a.* to brandish, to flourish; (*carp.*)
Brandissoire, *s.f.* (*obsolete*) swing-plough
Brandon, *s.m.* wisp of straw (*to indicate seizure of crops*); lighted wisp of straw, link; brand, firebrand. *Saisie- —, V.* **Saisie** [legally seized
Brandonner, *v.a.* to mark (*a piece of land*) as
Branée, *s.f.* bran-and-water, hog-wash
Branlant, e, *adj.* swinging; shaking, shaky; wagging; loose; tottering
Branle, *s.m.* swinging, shaking; swing, full swing; peal; impetus, first impulse, impulse; motion; agitation; brawl (*dance, tune, in Poitou*); (*nav.*) hammock. *Donner le — à,* to set going, to give an impulse (*or* the first impulse) to. *Mener le —,* to lead the dance, to take the lead, to set the example
Branle-bas, *s.m.* (*nav.*) clearing; (*fam.*) turning upside down, confusion, disorder, disturbance; hubbub, uproar; moving, removal, flitting; rush. — ! (*nav.*) down *or* up all hammocks!

Faire —, (*nav.*) to clear the decks. *Faire — de combat*, (*nav.*) to clear for action. *Faire du* —, (*fam.*) to kick up a row

Branlement, *s.m.* swinging, shaking, shake; wagging; agitation; tottering; wavering

Branle-queue, *s.m.* (*bird*) wagtail; (*worm*) brandling

Branler, *v.a.n.* to swing; to shake; to wag; to move; to totter; to stir; to be loose *or* unsteady; (*mil.*) to give way, to waver. — *dans le manche*, to be shaky; to totter; to decline; to lose popularity; to be in an unsafe position; to be in a dangerous state; to hesitate, to waver, to be irresolute [staff

Branloire, *s.f.* see-saw; swing; (*tech.*) rock-

Braque, *s.m.f.* brack-hound, brack, brach; (*fig.*) hare-brained *or* eccentric fellow, mad-cap; — *adj.* hare-brained, eccentric, touched, cracked; —**s,** *s.f.pl.* claws (*of a crab*, &c.)

Braquemart, *s.m.* (*old*) broadsword, hanger

Braquement, *s.m.* pointing; turning [fix

Braquer, *v.a.* to point; to turn, to direct; to

Bras, *s.m.* arm; (*person, and fig.*) hand; handle; bracket, sconce; shaft; (*of a crab*, &c.) claw; (*of a whale*) fin; (*fig.*) power; might; influence, credit; strength; courage, valour; assistance, aid; labour, labour of o.'s hands; jaws (*of death*); agent, instrument; inlet, canal, strait; (*nav.*) brace (*of a yard*). — *de fer*, (*hist.*) iron-side. — *dessus — dessous*, arm in arm. *A* —, with arms; by strength of arms; by hand; (*in compounds: of utensils*) hand [*Ex.*: = *Moulin à* —, *Râteau à* —, *&c.*, hand-mill, hand-rake, &c.]. *A — raccourci*, with all o.'s might. *A — -le-corps*, round the waist. *A tour de* —, with all o.'s might. *Gros comme le* —, (*fig.*) plenty; with a vengeance; at every word. *Sur les* —, on (*or* in) o.'s arms; on o.'s hands; against one, to contend with; to maintain; about one, on o.'s heels. *Couper* or *casser — et jambes à*, (*fig.*) to disable completely, to render powerless, to put a spoke in ...'s wheel, to take the wind out of ...'s sails; to astound, to dumbfound; to discourage. *Se donner le* —, to go arm in arm, to take hold of each other's arm. *Faire les beaux* —, to be full of affectation. *Tendre les — à*, to hold out o.'s arms to; to offer assistance to; to succour; to implore the aid of. *Les — m'en sont tombés*, I was astounded

Brase, *s.f.* (*chem.*) charcoal, coal

Brasement, *s.m.* soldering; brazing; crackling

Braser, *v.a.* to solder; to braze; — *v.n.* to crackle

Brasero, *s.m.* (*Spanish*) coal-pan, brasier

Brasier, *s.m.* coal-fire, red-hot fire; furnace; coal-pan, brasier [sparkling

†**Brasillement,** *s.m.* broiling, roasting; (*nav.*)

†**Brasiller,** *v.a.* to broil, to grill, to roast; — *v.n.* (*nav.*) to sparkle [dust

Brasque, *s.f.* mixture of loam and charcoal-

Brassadelle, *s.f.* (*of muskets, obsolete*) upper band

Brassage, *s.m.*, **Brassaison,** *s.f.* mashing; brewing; stirring up; raking; (*nav.*) bracing; (*coin.*) mixing; (*obsolete*) mintage

Brassard, *s.m.* bracer, brace, armlet, arm-guard, vambrace, vantbrace, brassart

Brasse, *s.f.* six feet, two yards; (*of depth, nav.*) fathom; (*foreign measure*) brace; (*in swimming*) stroke; (*of targets*) bull's-eye

Brassée, *s.f.* armful; (*in swimming*) stroke

Brasseïer, *v.a.* *V.* **Brasseyer**

Brasser, *v.a.* to mash; to brew; to stir up; to rake and stir; to mix; (*fish.*) to beat (*the water*); (*fig.*) to devise, to plot, to concoct, to contrive, to hatch; to despatch, to knock off; (*nav.*) to brace

Se —, *v.r.* to be mashed *or* brewed *or* &c.

Brasserie, *s.f.* brewery; brew-house; beer-shop, beer-house, ale-house, public-house

Brasseu-r, se, *s.m.f.* brewer [bracing

Brasseyage, *s.m.* (*nav.*) quarter (*of a yard*);

Brasseyer, *v.a.* (*nav.*) to brace [water, depth

Brassiage, *s.m.* (*nav.*) fathoming; depth of

Brassicourt, *adj. s.m.* bandy-legged (horse)

Brassière, *s.f.* stays (*for children*); brace, strap; (*fig.*) leading-strings

Brassin, *s.m.* mash-tub, mash-tun; mash-tub-ful, mash-tunful; (*of soap*) boiling (*quantity*

Brasure, *s.f.* soldering; brazing [*boiled*)

Brava, *int.* bravo! (*to a female singer*)

Bravache, *s.m.* blusterer, swaggerer, bully

Bravade, *s.f.* bravado, boast, bluster

Brave, *adj.* brave, courageous; gallant, valiant; bold; honest; good, excellent, worthy, nice; smart, fine. *Un homme* —, a brave *or* courageous man. *Un — homme*, an honest man; a good *or* worthy *or* nice man (*or* fellow). *Un — garçon*, a good boy; an honest lad *or* fellow; a good fellow; a nice *or* fine fellow, a brick

Brave, *s.m.* brave *or* courageous *or* valiant man, gallant fellow, hero; brave soldier; good *or* worthy man; nice *or* fine fellow; good friend; (*obsolete*) bravo, ruffian. — *à trois poils*, hard-fighter; man of courage, true blue, regular game. *Faux* —, braggart. *Vieux* —, brave veteran. *En* —, bravely, gallantly. *Faire le* —, to look big

Brave, *int.* bravo! (*to two or more female singers*)

Bravement, *adv.* bravely, courageously, gallantly, valiantly, stoutly; ably, skilfully, cleverly, adroitly, well; gloriously, capitally; boldly, unhesitatingly, without ceremony

Braver, *v.a.* to brave; to affront, to face; to dare, to defy, to set at defiance; to beard; not to fear; to despise; to taunt

Braverie, *s.f.* (*old*) bravery; finery, fine clothes

Bravi, *int.* bravo! (*to two or more male singers*)

Bravissimo, *int.* bravissimo!

Bravo, *s.m.* cheer, applause, approbation; bravo; — *int.* hurrah! hurrah for ...! well done! excellent! capital! bravo!

Bravoure, *s.f.* bravery, valour, gallantry, courage; —**s,** *pl.* exploits. *Air de* —, (*mus.*)

Braye, *s.f.* clay, mud, slime [bravura, bravoura

Brayer, *s.m.* (*surg.*) truss; (*tech.*) belt, strap

Brayer, *v.a.* (*nav.*) to pitch; to pay

Brayère, *s.f.* *V.* **Kousso**

Brayette, *s.f.* fly, slit (*of trousers*); (*bot.*) cowslip

Brayon, *s.m.* fox-trap, trap (*for vermin*)

Breack, Break, *s.m.* break (*carriage*)

Bréant, *s.m.* *V.* **Bruant**

Brebis, *s.f.* sheep, ewe; —**s,** *pl.* sheep; flock. — *galeuse*, scabby sheep; (*pers.*) black sheep. *Repas de* —, dry meal. *A — tondue Dieu mesure le vent*, God tempers the wind to the shorn lamb. *C'est bien la — du bon Dieu*, he is as gentle as a lamb. — *comptées le loup les mange*, we must watch as well as count

Brèche, *s.f.* breach; gap; opening; hole; notch; break; flaw; deficiency; infraction; injury, wrong, damage; (*min.*) breccia, brockram

Brèche-dents, *adj. s.m.f.* broken-mouthed; broken-mouthed person

Brechet, *s.m.* (*anat.*) breast-bone; (*fam.*) stomach

Brèchetelle, *s.f.* beer-biscuit, lunch-biscuit

Bredi-breda, *adv.* hurriedly, hastily, desultori-

Bredindin, *s.m.* (*nav.*) garnet [ly, harum-scarum

†**Bredouillage,** *s.m.* sputtering, jabbering, jabber, broken words *or* sentences

†**Bredouille,** *s.f.* (*at backgammon*) lurch; (*of sportsmen*) ill-luck, failure, empty bag, blank; — *adj.* (*of sportsmen, and fig.*) with an empty bag (*or* game-bag), without having killed *or* taken any game *or* caught any fish, without having found *or* done anything, with a blank, empty-handed, disappointed. *Sortir* —, to go away as one came. *Se coucher* —, to go to bed supperless [jabbering

†**Bredouillement,** *s.m.* sputtering, sputter,

†**Bredouiller,** *v.a.n.* to sputter, to jabber

†**Bredouilleu-r, se,** *s.m.f.* sputterer, jabberer

Bref, *m.*, **Brève,** *f.*, *adj.* short; brief, curt, concise; laconic; quick

Bref, *s.m.* brief; church-calendar; (*nav.*) pass, passport, warrant
Bref, *adv.* in short, finally, in a few words, in one word, to cut the matter short; briefly, concisely, curtly; sharply
Bregin, *s.m.*, **Brége,** *s.f.* (*fish.*) close net
†**Bréhaigne,** *adj.f.* (*of animals, and pop. of women*) barren, sterile
Brelan, *s.m.* brelan (*game at cards*); gambling-house; (*of cards*) pair-royal, prial
Brelander, *v.n.* to play cards; to gamble; (*pop.*) to loiter, to trifle, to dawdle
Brelandi-er, ère, *s.m.f.* card-player; gambler
Brelée, *s.f.* sheep-fodder [piggledy, slapdash
Brelique-breloque, *adv.* at random, higgledy-
Brelle, *s.f.* raft [*V.* **Berloque**; (*pop.*) clock
Breloque, *s.f.* trinket; charm; (*mil., and fig.*)
Breluche, *s.f.* (*obsolete*) drugget; linsey-woolsey
Brème, *s.f.* bream (*fish*)
Brémois, e, *adj. s.* of Bremen; native of Bremen
Brenade, Brenée, *s.f. V.* **Branée**
Breneu-x, se, *adj.* (*pop.*) dirty, soiled
Brequin, *s.m.* wimble, drill; centre-bit, bit
Brésil, *s.m.* Brazil wood
Brésilien, ne, *adj. s.* Brazilian; Brazilian fashion. *Chapeau* —, chip-hat
†**Brésiller,** *v.a.* to break small, to smash; to dye with Brazil wood; — *v.n.* to crumble into
†**Brésillet,** *s.m.* Brazil wood [dust
Bresolles, *s.f.pl.* (*cook.*) veal-collops
Bressan, e, *adj. s.* of Bresse; native of Bresse
Breste, *s.f.* catching birds with lime-twigs
†**Bretagne,** *s.f.* Brittany linen-cloth; kind of dance [bully
†**Bretailler,** *v.n.* to fight, to fence, to tilt; to
†**Bretailleur,** *s.m.* fighter, bully
Bretaudé, e, *adj.* crop-eared
Bretauder, *v.a.* to crop
Bretèche, *s.f.* (*old*) fortress, castle
Bretelle, *s.f.* brace; strap; (*mil.*) suspender
Breton, ne, *adj. s.m.f.* Breton (*of Brittany*); Breton horse *or* mare; — *s.f.* Breton fashion
Bretonnant, e, *adj.* speaking the low Breton;
Brette, *s.f.* rapier, sword [of Lower Brittany
Bretteler, Bretter, *v.a.* to indent, to tooth;
Bretteur, *s.m.* fighter, bully [to boast; to point
Bretture, *s.f.* teeth, notches; boasting; pointing
†**Breuil,** *s.m.* thicket; (*nav.*) *V.* **Cargue**
†**Breuilles,** *s.f.pl.* (*fish.*) guts (*of fish*)
Breuvage, *s.m.* beverage, drink; draught; potion; liquor; (*vet.*) drench
Brève, *adj., feminine of* **Bref;** — *s.f.* (*gram.*) short, short syllable; (*mus.*) breve
Brevet, *s.m.* patent; letters patent; brevet; certificate, diploma; (*of printers and booksellers*) licence; (*mil.*) commission; (*admin.*) warrant; indentures, indenture (*of apprenticeship*)
Brevetable, *adj.* patentable
Breveté, e, *part. adj.* patented, &c. (*V.* **Breveter**); patent; by appointment; warrant; — *s.m.f.* patentee
Breveter, *v.a.* to grant a patent to; to patent; to license; to brevet; to certificate; to com-
Breveux, *s.m.* (*fish.*) gaff [mission
Bréviaire, *s.m.* breviary
Bribe, *s.f.* hunch; scrap, bit; leavings
Bric. *De — et de broc, V.* **Broc**
Bric-à-brac, *s.m.* marine stores, old stores, old curiosities; marine store dealer, curiosity-
Brick, *s.m.* (*nav.*) brig [dealer
Bricole, *s.f.* breast-strap, breast-plate; breast-collar; strap; (*of carriage-windows*) glass-holder, glass-string; (*billiards, tennis*) back-stroke; (*fam.*) flam; small job, poor business; —**s,** *pl.* (*hunt.*) toils. *De* or *par* —, indirectly; by a fluke
Bricoler, *v.n.* to hit a back-stroke; to shuffle; to shift; to dodge; to do small jobs; to strive, to work; — *v.a.* to botch up
Bricoleur, *s.m.* shuffler; jobber, loafer
Bricolier, *s.m.* outrigger, off-horse; (*pers.*) shuffler; jobber, loafer

Bride, *s.f.* bridle, rein; string; loop; strap; band; stitches; stay; flange; (*fig.*) restraint, curb, check. *A — abattue, à toute* —, at full speed; at full gallop; headlong; eagerly; unreservedly. *Lâcher la* —, to give the reins, to give head; to give rope; to let loose. *Laisser* or *mettre la — sur le cou,* to give head entirely; to give full liberty, to let (*one*) go on his own way. *Tenir en* —, to keep within bounds. *Tenir la — haute* (or *courte* or *serrée*) *à,* to keep a tight hand over. —*s à veaux,* (*pop.*) specious reasons, humbug. *Tourner* —, to turn back
Bridé, e, *adj.* bridled; silly; ignorant; regular
Brider, *v.a.* to bridle; to curb, to check, to restrain; to tie; to bind; to confine; to pinch; to lash, to cut; to truss (*a fowl*); (*nav.*) to span; to shoe *or* stow (*an anchor*)
Bridoir, *s.m.* chin-band, chin-piece; strap
Bridoison, *s.m.* booby, nincompoop, (a) silly Billy *or* simple Simon
Bridon, *s.m.* snaffle-bridle, snaffle, bridoon
Brie, *s.f.* break-staff, break-handle; — *s.m.* Brie cheese [quick
Bri-ef, ève, *adj.* brief, curt, short; prompt,
Brier, *v.a.* to break (*dough, paste*)
Brièvement, *adv.* briefly, curtly, shortly; promptly, quickly
Brièveté, *s.f.* brevity, curtness, shortness
Brifaud, Brifaut, *s.m.* (*pop.*) glutton, greedy gut; ill bred cub, urchin
Brife, *s.f.* (*pop.*) hunch (of bread)
Brifer, *v.a.n.* (*pop.*) *V.* **Bouffer** [guttler
Brifeu-r, se, *s.m.f.* trencher-man, greedy eater,
Brig, *s.m.* (*nav.*) *V.* **Brick**
Brigade, *s.f.* brigade; troop; body; company; gang (*of workmen*); station; boat-hook. — *de sûreté,* company of policemen; body *or* company of detectives, detective police, detectives. *Chef de* —, *V.* **Chef.** *Général de* —, (*mil.*) brigadier-general, brigadier
Brigadier, *s.m.* corporal (*of cavalry*); sergeant (*of police*); ganger (*of workmen*); (*nav.*) bowman, strokesman
Brigand, *s.m.* brigand, highwayman, robber, bandit, ruffian, plunderer, thief; extortioner
Brigandage, *s.m.* brigandage; highway robbery, robbery; plunder, rapine, pillage, depredation; extortion
Brigandeau, *s.m.* cheat, rogue, knave, shark, shaver, thief, petty extortioner; sharp attorney
Brigander, *v.n.* to rob, to plunder; to extort
Brigandine, *s.f.* brigandine (*coat of mail*) [bed
Brigantin, *s.m.* (*nav.*) brigantine; (*mil.*) field-
Brigantine, *s.f.* (*nav.*) small brigantine; brigantine-sail, spanker
†**Brignole,** *s.f.* Brignoles prune (*French plum*)
Brigot, Brigaut, *s.m.* birch-billets and oak-toppings (*for firewood*)
Brigue, *s.f.* intrigue; canvassing; indirect means; bribery; cabal; faction; party
Briguer, *v.a.* to solicit, to court, to sue for; to canvass for; to seek, to aspire to
Brigueu-r, se, *s.m.f.* solicitor, canvasser
†**Brillamment,** *adv.* brilliantly, brightly, splendidly
†**Brillant, e,** *adj.* brilliant, bright, glittering, shining, sparkling, glistening; splendid; gorgeous; glorious; beaming; radiant; gay; blooming; flourishing; robust
†**Brillant,** *s.m.* brilliancy; brightness; splendour, lustre; brilliant (*diamond*). *Faux* —, false *or* imitation brilliant; (*fig.*) tinsel, false ornament [tinselled, showy, gaudy, florid
†**Brillanté, e,** *part. adj.* cut into a brilliant;
†**Brillanté,** *s.m.* damask, diaper; imitation lace
†**Brillanter,** *v.a.* to cut into a brilliant; to tinsel
†**Briller,** *v.n.* to shine; to be bright *or* brilliant; to brighten; to glitter; to sparkle; to glisten; to gleam; to glare; to blaze; to flash; to glance; to be eminent *or* remarkable *or* conspicuous; to be splendid; to bloom; to appear; to be seen; to be displayed; to make a show, to

show off; to make a figure; to distinguish oneself; to excel; (*hunt.*) to range, to quest. *Faire* —, to brighten; to blazon; to show, to display

†**Brilloter,** *v.n.* to shine a little; to shine but little; to shine faintly, to glimmer; to make some little show; to make a certain figure

Brimade, *s.f.* (*mil. slang, pop.*) practical joke; fagging

Brimbale, *s.f.* (*of a pump*) handle, brake [away

Brimbaler, *v.a.n.* to swing; to toss; to ring

Brimborion, *s.m.* nicknack, bauble, gewgaw

Brimé, e, *adj.* (*of grapes*) spotted

Brimer, *v.a.* (*mil. school slang*) to fag (*a new boy*)

Brin, *s.m.* blade (*of grass*); slip, sprig; shoot; slender stalk; straight piece (*of timber*); bit, morsel; jot, iota, whit, bit, little; (*of stuffs*) staple. *Beau — de fille,* (*fam.*) tall well-made girl, fine-grown girl. *De* or *en* —, (*of wood*) unhewn. *Arbre de* —, seedling, straight tree. — *-d'estoc,* quarter-staff; leaping-pole, long pole shod at both ends [tipsy, tight

Brinde, *s.f.* (*old*) health, toast. *Dans les —s,*

Brindezingues. *Dans les* —, (*pop.*) dead

†**Brindille,** *s.f.* branchlet, sprig, twig [drunk

Bringue, *s.f.* ill-shaped horse; (*pop.*) lanky dowdy. *En —s,* (*pop.*) in *or* to pieces; at sixes and sevens, in disorder, in confusion

Bringuebale, *s.f. V.* **Brimbale**

Brio, *s.m.* dash, spirit, vigour, pluck, mettle, raciness, vivacity, animation, brilliancy, go

Brioche, *s.f.* cake, bun; blunder, bull

Briolet, *s.m.* (*pop.*) sourish wine

Brion, Brione. *V.* **Bryon, Bryone**

†**Briquaillons,** *s.m.pl.* old brickbats

Brique, *s.f.* brick; (*of soap, &c.*) wedge. *De* —, of brick, brick; brick-red

Briquet, *s.m.* matches, fusees; steel; steel and flint; tinder-box; short broadsword, dirk; fox-beagle; harrier, harier. *Battre le* —, to strike a light [tion brick-work

Briquetage, *s.m.* brick-work; bricks; imita-

Briqueté, e, *adj.* brick-coloured, tile-coloured, brick-red; in imitation of brick-work

Briqueter, *v.a.* to brick

Briqueterie, *s.f.* brick-field *or* yard, brick-kiln; brick-making; lucifer match-manufactory

Briqueteur, *s.m.* bricklayer

Briquetier, *s.m.* brick-maker

Briquette, *s.f.* fire-ball, patent fuel; cake

Bris, *s.m.* breaking open; breaking; breaking loose, escape; breach; wrecking, wreckage, wreck; fragment; rigging (*the market*)

Brisable, *adj.* breakable, brittle, fragile

Brisant, e, *adj.* (*of gunpowder*) violently explosive; too explosive

Brisant, *s.m.* (*nav.*) breaker; breakwater

†**Briscambille,** *s.f. V.* **Brusquembille**

Brise, *s.f.* breeze; (*bot.*) *V.* **Brize;** — *s.m.f.* (*in compounds, from* **Briser,** "to break") thing (*m.*) *or* person (*m.f.*) that breaks, breaker. — **-cou,** *s.m. V.* **Casse-cou.** — **-eau,** *s.m.* breakwater. — **-glace,** *s.m.* ice-breaker; (*of bridges*) starling. — **-lames,** *s.m.* breakwater; groyne. — **-mottes,** *s.m.* (*agr.*) clod-crusher. — **-pierre,** *s.m.* (*surg.*) lithotrite. — **-raison,** *s.m.f.* wrong-headed fellow *or* woman *or* girl. — **-tourteaux,** *s.m.* (*agr.*) oil-cake breaker. — **-tout,** *s.m.f.* clumsy break-all. — **-vent,** *s.m.* (*agr., hort.*) screen

Brisé, e, *part. adj.* broken, &c. (*V.* **Briser**); short, crisp; jagged, indented; (*of doors, ladders,* &c.) folding; (*of parasols,* &c.) jointed-handle; (*of rings*) split; (*of roofs*) with attics *or* lofts; (*pers.*) harassed, jaded, knocked up, exhausted, spent; bowed down; (*her.*) brisé, rompu

Brisée, *s.f.* (*of parasols,* &c.) fan-joint; (*mus.*) turn; —**s,** *pl.* boughs cut off, blinks; (*fig.*) footsteps, steps, shoes, heels, ground [fracture; contrition

Brisement, *s.m.* dashing; breaking; break;

Briser, *v.a.n.* to break; to break *or* dash to pieces; to shatter; to shiver; to smash; to crush; to split; to break open; to break off; to break down; to bow down; to overwhelm; to harass, to exhaust, to knock up; to destroy; to ruin; to blight; to refract; to dash. *Brisons là* or *là-dessus!* let us say no more about it! no more of that! that is enough!

Se —, *v.r.* to break; to break to pieces; to split; to dash; to break o.'s bones; to break down; to fail; to prove useless, to be powerless; to fold, to fold up; to be broken *or* shattered *or* smashed; to be lost *or* destroyed; to be curved; to be refracted. *Se la* —, (*pop.*) to [be off, to bolt

Briseu-r, se, *s.m.f.* breaker

Brisis, *s.m.* (*arch.*) hip; attic

Briska, *s.m.* britzska, britska (*carriage*)

Brisoir, *s.m.* brake, scutcher (*for hemp and flax*); breaker [ditto

Brisque, *s.f.* brisque (*game at cards*); trump (*at*

Brisure, *s.f.* broken place, break; fold; hook, catch, fastening; (*fort.*) brisure; (*her.*) rebatement

Britannique, *adj.* British, English, Britannic

Brize, *s.f.* (*bot.*) St. Peter's corn, spelt wheat, quaking-grass

Broc, *s.m.* jug; jugful; can: pitcher; (*obsolete*) spit. *De bric et de* —, anyhow, by hook and by crook. *De — en bouche,* burning hot from the spit; hurriedly; summarily

†**Brocaille,** *s.f. V.* **Blocaille**

Brocantage, *s.m.* buying *or* selling (*or* buying and selling) second-hand goods, bartering, swapping, chopping and changing; broker's trade

Brocante, *s.f.* (*fam.*) exchange, barter, swap; (*pop.*) trumpery thing, trash, duffer; overtime job, small job

Brocanter, *v.a.n.* to buy; to sell; to buy and sell; to exchange, to barter, to swap, to chop and change; to buy *or* to buy and sell second-hand goods, to deal in second-hand goods, to be a broker

Brocanteu-r, se, *s.m.f.* broker, furniture-broker, dealer in second-hand goods; barterer, swapper [poon, satire; (*hunt.*) *V.* **Broquart**

Brocard, *s.m.* taunt, scoff, jeer, raillery; lam-

Brocarder, *v.a.* to taunt, to scoff at, to jeer; to lampoon [lampooner

Brocardeu-r, se, *s.m.f.* taunter, scoffer, jeerer;

Brocart, *s.m.* brocade; (*hunt.*) *V.* **Broquart**

Brocatelle, *s.f.* (*stuff*) brocatelle; (*min.*) broca-

Brochage, *s.m.* stitching (*of books*) [telli marble

Brochant, *part. of* **Brocher.** — *sur le tout,* (*her.*) over all; (*fig.*) out-topping all, conspicuous, though last not least; besides, to boot, into the bargain

Brochantite, *s.f.* (*min.*) brochantite

Broche, *s.f.* spit; brooch; knitting-needle; pin; peg; spike; nail; rod, stick; herring-stick; broach, broche; (*spinning*) spindle; (*weaving*) shuttle-pike; (*of wild boars*) tusk; (*of stags*) broach; (*com.*) small bill; (*nav.*) skewer; (*slang*) tooth, snag, tusk

Broché, e, *part. of* **Brocher** [figured shawl

Broché, *s.m.* figured stuff; figured silk ribbon;

Brochée, *s.f.* spitful, roasting, roast meat; stickful; rodful; broachful

Brocher, *v.a.* to figure (*stuffs*); to emboss (*linen*); to stitch, to sew (*books*); to peg; to nail; to drive (*nails*) in; to give a slight dressing to (*vine*), to touch up; (*fig.*) to hurry over, to despatch; — *v.n.* (*hort.*) to shoot, to grow

Brochet, *s.m.* (*fish*) pike; jack

Brocheter, *v.a.* to skewer

Brocheton, *s.m.* (*fish*) jack, pickerel

Brochette, *s.f.* skewer; pin; small stick; (*of orders of knighthood*) file, row; (*dish*) brochette. *A la* —, roasted *or* broiled on skewers. *Élever à la* —, to bring up (*a bird*) by hand; (*fig.*) to bring up tenderly *or* with great care, to coddle, to nurse up [knitter

Brocheu-r, se, *s.m.f.* stitcher (*of books*);

Brochoir, *s.m.* (farrier's) shoeing-hammer
Brochure, *s.f.* pamphlet; chapbook; (*of books*) stitching: (*of stuffs*) figures, ornaments; (*on linen*)
Brocoli, *s.m.* (*bot.*) broccoli; sprout [embossment
Brodequin, *s.m.* lace-boot, half-boot, boot; buskin; sock, comedy; (*instrument of torture*) boot; (*fam.*) red feet (*after a hot foot-bath*)
Broder, *v.a.n.* to embroider, to work; (*fig.*) to embellish, to amplify; (*pop.*) to write
Broderie, *s.f.* embroidery; (*fig.*) embellishment, amplification; (*need.*) work; (*mus.*) grace-note; (*hort.*) border; (*pop.*) writing
Brodeu-r, se, *s.m.f.* embroiderer; embroideress; (*fig.*) embellisher; (*pop.*) writer; — *s.f.* (— *mécanique*) embroidering-machine
Brodoir, *s.m.* bobbin, frame
Brogue, *s.f.* brogue (*shoe*)
Broie, *s.f.* *V.* **Brisoir**
Broiement, Broîment, *s.m.* *V.* **Broyage**
Broma, *s.m.* broma
Bromate, *s.m.* (*chem.*) bromate
Bromatolog-ie, -ique. *V.* page 3, § 1
Brome, *s.m.* (*chem.*) bromine
Brôme, *s.m.* (*bot.*) brome-grass
Bromer, *v.a.* to bromize
Bromhydrate, *s.m.* (*chem.*) hydrobromate
Bromhydrique, *adj.* (*chem.*) hydrobromic
Bromique, *adj.* (*chem.*) bromic
Bromograph-ie, -ique. *V.* page 3, § 1
Bromure, *s.m.* (*chem.*) bromide
Bromurer, *v.a.* to bromidize
Bronchade, *s.f.*, **Bronchement,** *s.m.* stumbling, stumble, tripping, trip
Broncher, *v.n.* to stumble; to trip; to flinch; to falter; to hesitate; to fail; to err; to do wrong; to stir
Bronches, *s.f.pl.* bronchiæ
Bronchial, e, Bronchique, *adj.* (*anat.*) bronchial
Bronchite, *s.f.* (*med.*) bronchitis
‡**Bronchocèle,** *s.f.* (*med.*) bronchocele
‡**Broncho-phonie, -tomie.** *V.* page 3, § 1
Bronzage, *s.m.* bronzing
Bronze, *s.m.* bronze; bronze work; bronze figure; medal; cannon; bell, bells; bronze colour, bronze paint; (*fig.*) flint, iron, steel; impudence, brass
Bronzé, e, *adj.* bronzed; tawny, tanned, sun-browned, sun-burnt; hardened; proof (against); fearless; impudent
Bronzer, *v.a.* to bronze; to tan (*the face*); to steel; to harden
Se —, *v.r.* to be bronzed; to be sun-burnt, to become tawny; to become hard *or* hardened, to be steeled
Bronzeur, *s.m.* bronzer, bronzist
Bronzier, *s.m.* bronzist, maker *or* seller of bronze works of art
Bronzite, *s.f.* (*min.*) bronzite
Broquart, *s.m.* (*hunt.*) brocket, pricket
Broqueteur, *s.m.* (*agr.*) pitcher, loader
Broquette, *s.f.* tack, tin-tack
Brosime, *s.m.* (*bot.*) cow-tree
Brossage, *s.m.* brushing
Brosse, *s.f.* brush; (*forestry*) bush; (*zool.*) hair; tuft of hair; **—s,** *pl.* brushes; brushwood, heath, waste land. — *à barbe*, *V.* **Pinceau.** — *à décrotter*, hard-brush. — *à tête* or *à cheveux*, hair-brush
Brossée, *s.f.* brush, brushing, rub
Brosser, *v.a.* to brush; to rub; to beat; — *v.n.* (*hunt.*) to scour
Se —, *v.r.* to brush oneself; to rub oneself with a flesh-brush; to brush (o.'s . . .); to be brushed; to have a brush together, to fight. *Se — le ventre*, to fast, to starve, to go to bed supperless
Brosserie, *s.f.* brush-making; brush-manufactory; brushes; brush-trade;
Brosseur, *s.m.* brusher; Boots; (*mil.*) officer's servant, batman
Brossier, *s.m.* brush-maker
Brou, *s.m* husk, hull, peel, green shell; (*vet.*) gastro-enteritis. — *de noix*, walnut husk; ratafia of walnut husks, walnut-brandy
†**Brouailles,** *s.f.pl.* *V.* **Breuilles**
Brouée, *s.f* mist, fog, drizzle; passing shower; blight; (*pop.*) sparring, fight, cuffs
Brouet, *s m.* (thin) broth *or* soup; porridge (*for lying-in women in olden times*) caudle, milk-porridge, gruel; (*in contempt*) mess, cagmag. — *noir*, (*of the Spartans*) black broth
Brouette, *s.f.* wheel-barrow, barrow; truck; Bath chair, hand-chair
Brouettée, *s.f.* wheel-barrowful, barrowful
Brouetter, *v.a.* to wheel in a barrow, to wheel, to carry, to convey, to take; to draw in a Bath chair
Brouetteur, Brouettier, *s.m.* wheel-barrow-man, porter; chairman (*of a Bath chair*)
Brouhaha, *s.m.* hubbub, uproar, hurly-burly
†**Brouillage,** *s.m.* mixing, spreading
†**Brouillamini,** *s.m.* confusion, disorder, muddle; misunderstanding, disagreement
†**Brouillard,** *s.m.* fog, mist, haze; spray; obscurity, confusion, intricacy; (*com.*) waste-book; — *adj.m.* blotting. *Faire du —*, to be foggy. *Être dans les —s*, to be muddled, to be tipsy
†**Brouillasse,** *s.f.* (*nav.*) thin fog
†**Brouillasser,** *v.n.* to drizzle, to mizzle
†**Brouille,** *s.f.* misunderstanding, disagreement, falling out, quarrel; broil, disturbance. *Être en — avec*, to be on bad terms with, to be at variance with
†**Brouillement,** *s.m.* confusion; mixing up, mingling, mixture; jumbling; shuffling
†**Brouiller,** *v.a.* to throw into confusion; to put out of order; to mix up; to mingle; to blend; to embroil; to jumble; to confuse; to confound; to muddle; to make a mess of; to trouble; to perplex; to mar; to alter; to turn (*the brain*); to beat up, to beat; to shuffle; to scribble over, to waste; to set at variance; — *v.n.* to blunder, to bungle. *Un teint brouillé*, a mottled complexion. *Être brouillé avec*, to have disagreed *or* quarrelled with, to have fallen out with, to be at variance with, to have cut; to have given up; to be destitute of; to be out of; never to have any, to have violated (*the law*, "la justice")
Se —, *v.r.* to become confused *or* embroiled *or* &c.; to be bewildered; to be altered; to disagree, to fall out, to quarrel, to be on bad terms *or* at variance; to be out (*in speaking*); to get cloudy. *Se — avec la justice*, to bring on oneself a criminal prosecution, to put oneself within the reach of the law, to fall into the clutches of the law
†**Brouillerie,** *s.f.* *V.* **Brouille**
†**Brouillon, ne,** *adj.* *s.* blundering, bungling, meddling; blunderer, bungler, blunderhead, busybody, marplot
†**Brouillon,** *s.m.* rough draught, draught; rough copy; (*com.*) waste-book
†**Brouillonner,** *v.a.* to rough-draw
Brouir, *v.a.* to blight, to blast, to nip, to burn up, to scorch up
Brouissure, *s.f.* blight, blast
†**Broussailles,** *s.f.pl.* brushwood, bushes, brambles, briars, thorns. *Dans les —*, (*pop.*) in o.'s cups
Brousse, *s.f.* (kind of cheese)
Brousser, *v.n.* (*hunt.*) to scour, to range (the woods)
Broussette, *s.f.* (*bot.*) corn-salad, lamb's-lettuce
Broussin, *s.m.* excrescence (*of trees*); melted cheese with vinegar and pepper
Broussonétie, *s.f.* (*bot.*) broussonetia, paper-mulberry
Broussure, *s.f.* (*agr.*) brown rust [(*vet.*) *V.* **Brou**
Brout, *s.m.* browse-wood, browse; browsing;
Broutement, *s.m.* browsing; grazing; (*hort.*) topping
Brouter, *v.n.a.* to browse, to browse on, to crop; to graze; to feed; (*hort.*) to top
†**Broutille,** *s.f.* sprig, sprigs, small wood; axillary bud (*of vine*); (*fig.*) rubbish, trifle, bauble, nicknack
Brouture, *s.f.* browsed branch; browsing
Broyage, *s.m.* pounding; grinding; crushing; breaking; scutching
Broye, Broie, *s.f.* *V.* **Brisoir**
Broyement, Broiement, *s.m.* *V.* **Broyage**
Broyer, *v.a.* to pound; to grind; to crush; to break; to scutch; to pulverize; to shatter; to mangle. — *du noir*, to be in a gloomy mood, to be in a brown study

Broyeu-r, se, *s.m.f.* pounder; grinder; crusher; breaker; scutcher. — *de noir*, hypochondriac. — *d'ocre*, bad painter, dauber
Broyoire, *s.f. V.* **Brisoir**
Broyon, *s.m. V.* **Brayon**
Brrr, *int. V.* **Bah**
Bru, *s.f.* (*obsolete*) daughter-in-law
Bruant, *s.m.* (*bird*) yellow-hammer; bunting
Bruantin, *s.m.* (*bird*) rice-bunting, rice-bird, reed-bird
Brucée, *s.f.* (*bot.*) brucea
Brucelles, *s.f.pl.* spring nippers, tweezers
Bruche, *s.m.* (*insect*) bruchus
Brucine, *s.f.* (*chem.*) brucine
Bruée, *s.f.* steaming *or* reeking *or* roking of hot bread, steam
Brugeois, e, *adj. s.* of Bruges; native of Bruges
†Brugnon, *s.m.* (clingstone) nectarine
Bruine, *s.f.* drizzling rain, drizzle; spray
Bruiné, e, *adj.* (*agr.*) spoilt by drizzle
Bruinement, *s.m.* drizzling; (*agr.*) damage done by drizzle
Bruiner, *v.n.* to drizzle
Bruineu-x, se, *adj.* drizzly
Bruir, *v.a.* (*tech.*) to steam
Bruire, *v.n.* to make a noise; to rustle; to roar; to rattle; to whistle; to whir; to buzz; to tingle; to be heard; — *v.a.n.* to resound
Bruisiner, *v.a.* to crush (*malt*)
Bruissage, *s.m.* (*tech.*) steaming
Bruissant, e, *part. adj.* rustling, roaring, &c. (*V.* **Bruire**); noisy
Bruissement, *s.m.* noise; rustling; roaring; rattling; whistling; whirring; buzzing; tingling
Bruit, *s.m.* noise; sound; disturbance; row; din; bustle; ado, fuss; report; rumour; talk; fame, renown; sensation; clamour; cry; voice; roar, roaring; rattle, rattling; creaking; rustle, rustling; whir, whirring; clatter; boom, booming; peal. *A grand* —, noisily, loudly; (*fig.*) ostentatiously, with pomp, with fuss. *A petit* —, quietly, privately, secretly. *Le — court que ...*, it is reported *or* said that ...
Brûlable, *adj.* burnable, fit for burning, to be burnt; (*obsolete*) deserving to be burnt
Brûlage, *s.m.* burning; (*agr.*) burning of weeds; (*pop.*) break-down, ruin
Brûlant, e, *adj.* burning; scorching; scalding; hot; ardent; glowing; eager; impatient; dangerous; slippery; knotty; delicate; ticklish
Brûlé, e, *part. adj.* burnt, &c. (*V.* **Brûler**); animated; brown; deep, dark
Brûlé, *s.m.* burnt; burning burnt taste *or* smell; something burnt
Brûle-bout, *s.m.* save-all
Brûle-cigare, *s.m.* cigar-tube, cigar-holder
Brûlée, *s.f.* (*pop.*) fight, cuffs; drubbing, whacking, licking
Brûle-gueule, *s.m.* short pipe, cutty-pipe, cutty, (*in Ireland*) dhudeen, dudeen
Brûlement, *s.m.* burning
Brûle-pourpoint (A), *adv.* (at me *or* him *or* her *or* it, *&c.*) close, point-blank; by a point-blank discharge; to o.'s face, in o.'s teeth; home, irrefutable
Brûle-queue, *s.m.* (*vet.*) tail-iron
Brûler, *v.a.n.* to burn; to scorch; to parch; to scald; to sear; to roast; to mull; to brown; to blast; to set on fire; to consume; to blow out; to avoid; to throw out (*cards*); to pass without stopping; not to touch; to outstrip, to nurse; to be on fire; to long (to, for), to be eager *or* impatient; to be animated (with); to be inflamed (*with passion*); to be close to it, not to be far off, to burn; (*pop.*) to find out, to discredit, to ruin, to lose for ever. — *la cervelle à*, to blow out ...'s brains. *Cerveau brûlé, V.* **Cerveau.** — *le jour*, to shut out daylight. — *le papier*, to write in a glowing style. — *le pavé, V.* **Pavé.** — *les planches*, (*theat.*) to act splendidly, to star it; to be quite at home on the stage. — *la politesse à*, to act very unceremoniously with; to leave abruptly. — *les yeux*, to dazzle the eyes; to hurt *or* spoil the eyes; to destroy o.'s sight [(o.'s ...); to be burnt *or* &c. **Se** —, *v.r.* to burn *or* &c. oneself: to burn

Brûlerie, *s.f.* burning; brandy-distillery
Brûle-tout, *s.m.* save-all
Brûleur, *s.m.* burner, incendiary; brandy-distiller
Brûlis, *s.m.* part of a forest burnt down; (*agr.*) burning of weeds
Brûloir, *s.m.* roaster (*for coffee*)
Brûlot, *s.m.* (*nav.*) fire-ship; (*pers.*) incendiary, firebrand, dare-devil, desperado; (*fam.*) devil (*highly-seasoned dish*); burnt brandy, punch; (*tobacco-pipe*) *V.* **Brûle-gueule**
Brûlotier, *s.m.* captain of a fire-ship
Brûlure, *s.f.* burn; burning; scald; (*agr.*) blast; rust
†Brumaille, *s.f.* (*nav.*) *V.* **Brouillasse**
Brumaire, *s.m.* Brumaire (*second month of the calendar of the first French Republic, from October* 23 *to November* 21)
Brumal, e, *adj.* brumal, winterly, wintry
Brumasser, *v.n.* (*nav.*) to be rather foggy
Brume, *s.f.* fog; mist, haze
Brumer, *v.n.* (*nav.*) to be foggy
Brumeu-x, se, *adj.* foggy; misty, hazy
Brun, e, *adj.* brown; dusky, dusk; gloomy; (*of complexion*) dark
Brun, *s.m.* brown (*colour*); (*paint.*) shade; dark man *or* boy
Brunâtre, *adj.* brownish
Brune, *s.f.* dusk of the evening, dusk; dark woman *or* girl; (*fish*) wrasse
Brunelle, *s.f.* (*bot.*) self-heal; (*zool.*) brown snake
Brunet, te, *adj.* brownish; (*pers.*) darkish
Brunet, *s.m.* dark boy *or* fellow; kind of blackbird
Brunette, *s.f.* dark girl *or* woman, brunette; (*obsolete*) love-song; (*bird*) pygmy curlew; (*bot.*) self-heal
Bruni, *s.m.* burnish
Brunir, *v.a.* to burnish; to brown; to paint brown; to darken; — *v.n.,* **Se** —, *v.r.* to get brown *or* dark; to become bright, to brighten, to shine
Brunissage, *s.m.* burnishing; browning
Brunisseu-r, se, *s.m.f.* burnisher (*person*)
Brunissoir, *s.m.* burnisher (*tool*)
Brunissure, *s.f.* burnish; burnishing; browning
Brusc, *s.m.* (*bot.*) knee-holly, butcher's-broom
Brusque, *adj.* blunt; rough, gruff; rude; sudden, abrupt, unexpected; short; overhasty; sharp; quick; strong
†Brusquembille, *s.f.* brusquembille (*game at cards*)
Brusquement, *adv.* bluntly; roughly, gruffly; rudely; abruptly; sharply; suddenly; unexpectedly; all at once; hastily; quickly; strongly
Brusquer, *v.a.* to be sharp *or* blunt *or* rude with; to treat roughly; to do abruptly *or* hastily, to hurry over; to hurry on; to hurry; to attempt *or* try at once; to take at the first onset; to do violence to; to force. — *l'aventure*, to decide at once. — *la fortune*, to take the shortest way to fortune, to tempt fortune
Brusquerie, *s.f.* bluntness; roughness; rough way of speaking; blunt manner, rough thing, hasty expression; gruffness; rudeness; rude behaviour; sharpness; abruptness; suddenness; hastiness
Brusquet, te, *adj.* rather blunt *or* rough *or* &c. (*V.* **Brusque**). *A brusquin* —, tit for tat
Brut, e, *adj.* raw, unwrought, crude; inorganic, unorganized; rough; rude; coarse; unpolished; uncultivated; brute; brutish; — *adj. adv.* gross; gross weight
Brutal, e, *adj.* brutal; brutish; brute; sturdy; coarse, rough, rude; surly; — *s.m.f.* churl, brute; — *s.m.* (*pop.*) cannon
Brutalement, *adv.* brutally; brutishly; sturdily; coarsely, roughly, rudely
Brutaliser, *v.a.* to treat brutally *or* harshly, to use roughly, to abuse
Brutalité, *s.f.* brutality; brutishness; brutal act *or* thing; brutal passion; sturdiness; coarseness, roughness, rudeness; rough usage; coarse abuse
Brute, *s.f.* brute
Brutier, Bruthier, *s.m.* (*bird*) buzzard
Brutification, *s.f. V.* **Abrutissement**
Brutifier, *v.a. V.* **Abrutir**
Brutus, *s.m.* republican

Bruxellois, e, *adj. s.* of Brussels; native of Brussels [perously; clamorously
Bruyamment, *adv.* noisily; loudly; obstre-
Bruyant, e, *adj.* noisy; loud; obstreperous;
Bruyère, *s.f.* (*bot.*) heath [clamorous; blustering
Bryologie, *s.f.* bryology
Bryon, *s.m.* (*bot.*) bryum, tree-moss
Bryone, *s.f.* (*bot.*) bryony
Bryonine, *s.f.* (*chem.*) bryonine
Buanderie, *s.f.* wash-house; laundry
Buandi-er, ère, *s.m.f.* washerman, laundryman, launderer; washerwoman, laundress; bleacher
Bubale, *s.m.* (*zool.*) bubalus *or* bubalis (*antelope*)
Bube, Bubelette, *s f.* pimple, blotch, blain
Bubon, *s.m.* (*med.*) bubo; (*bot.*) bubon
Bubonocèle, *s.f.* (*med.*) bubonocele
Bubuler, *v.n.* *V.* **Houhouler**
†**Bucail,** *s.m.*, **Bucaille,** *s.f.* buck-wheat
Bucarde, *s.f.* (*shell-fish*) cockle; heart-shell
Buccal, e, *adj.* (*anat.*) buccal
Buccin, *s.m.* (*mollusc*) whelk, trumpet-shell, buckie, hen-buckie; (*mus.*) bass-trombone
Buccinateur, *s.m., adj.m.* (*anat.*) buccinator
Bucentaure, *s.m.* Bucentaur
Bucéphale, *s.m* Bucephalus (*Alexander's horse*); (*fig.*) charger, steed, horse; jade
Bûche, *s.f.* log of wood, log, billet; stock; piece, lump; (*pers.*) loggerhead, blockhead; (*nav.*) buss (*fishing-boat*). — *économique,* fire-ball. — *de Noël,* Yule log, Christmas-log
Bûcher, *s.m.* wood-house *or* shed *or* hole; wood-pile; funeral pile, pile, stake, pyre
Bûcher, *v.a.n.* to rough-hew; to destroy; to cut down; to dress, to trim; (*pop.*) to strike, to thump; to fag at; to work hard, to drudge
Se —, *v.r.* (*pop.*) to fight, to have a fight *or* a
Bûcherie, *s.f.* (*pop.*) set-to, tussle [set-to
Bûcheron, *s.m.* wood-cutter, woodman
Bûchette, *s.f.* stick (*small bit of wood*)
Bûcheur, *s.m.* (*pop.*) hard worker
Bûcheux, *s.m.* (*pop.*) *V.* **Bûcheron**
Bucoliaste, *s.m.* bucolic (*poet*)
Bucolique, *adj.* bucolic; —*s.f.* bucolic (*poem*); —**s,** *s.f.pl.* bucolics; (*fam.*) rattle-traps; tackle
Bucrane, *s.m.* (*anc. arch.*) bucrane
Buddlée, *s.f.* (*bot.*) buddlea
Budget, *s.m.* budget
Budgétaire, *adj.* of the budget
Buée, *s.f.* lye; wash; (lye-)washing, bucking; steam; reeking *or* roking of hot bread; vapour, mist; moisture [*bread*) to steam, to reek, to roke
Buer, *v.a.n.* to wash, to do the washing; (*of*
Buffet, *s.m.* cupboard; sideboard, refreshment-table, table, buffet; refreshment-room; set, service (*of plate*); case (*of an organ*). *Vins du —,* choice wines [suck the monkey
Buffeter, *v.n.* to broach and sip (*thievishly*), to
Buffeteur, *s.m.* thievish carrier who sips from the casks he carries; (*jest.*) self-appointed wine-taster [cow
Buffle, *s.m.* buffalo; buff (*skin*); — *s.f.* buffalo-
Bufflesse, *s.f.* *V.* **Bufflonne**
Buffleterie, *s.f.* buff-factory; buff-leather, buff-skin, buff; (*mil.*) belts, buffs
Buffletier, *s.m.* buff-dresser [calf
Buffletin, Bufflon, *s.m.* young buffalo, buffalo-
Bufflonne, *s.f.* buffalo-cow
Bugalet, *s.m.* (*nav.*) Breton bark
Bugle, *s.m.* (*mus.*) bugle; — *s.f.* (*bot.*) bugle
Buglose, Buglosse, *s.f.* (*bot.*) bugloss
†**Bugne,** *s.f.* pancake
Bugrane, *s.f.* (*bot.*) rest-harrow
Buhoriau, *s.m.* *V.* **Bihoreau**
Buhotier, *s.m.* (*fish*) shrimp-net
Buie, *s.f.* pitcher
Buire, *s.f.* (*old*) *V* **Burette**
Buis, *s.m.* (*bot.*) box, box-tree, box-wood [grove
Buissaie, Buissière, *s.f.* box-plantation, box-
Buisson, *s.m.* bush; thicket. — *creux,* the game gone; nothing; nobody. — *d'écrevisses,* dish of piled-up crayfish. — *ardent,* (*bot.*) evergreen thorn; (*in Scripture*) burning bush
Buissonnaie, *s.f.* brake, thicket
Buissonner, *v.n.* (*bot.*) to bush
Buissonnet, *s.m.* little bush, bushet
Buissonneu-x, se, *adj* bushy
Buissonni-er, ère, *adj.* (*of rabbits*) bush. *Écoles —ères,* hedge-schools. *Faire l'école —ère,* to play truant
Buissonnier, *s.m.* shrubbery; bush, shrub
Bulbe, *s.f.m.* (*bot.*) bulb; — *s.m.* (*anat*) bulb
Bulbeu-x, se, *adj.* bulbous
Bulbifère, *adj.* (*bot.*) bulbiferous
Bulbiforme, *adj.* bulbiform
†**Bulbille,** *s.f.* (*bot.*) bulbil
Bulbul, *s.m.* (*bird*) bulbul, Persian nightingale
Bulbule, *s.f.* (*bot.*) bulbule
Bulgare, *s.m.f. adj.* Bulgarian
Bulithe, *s.m.* bulithos, ox bezoar [(*bot.*) fungus
Bullaire, *s.m.* bullary (*collection of papal bulls*);
Bulle, *s f.* bubble; bead; (*med.*) bulla, blister, bleb; (*of the Pope*) bull; — *adj.* (*of paper*) whity-brown; — *s.m.* whity-brown paper
Bullé, e, *adj.* bubbly, bubbling; blistered, blistery; by bull, authentic
Bulletin, *s.m.* paper; circular; (official) account; bulletin; report; note; list; certificate; receipt; notice; ticket; voting-paper, ballot; vote; summary of news; intelligence; collection, rolls, records. — *judiciaire,* law-report. — *des lois,* statute-book
Bulleu-x, se, *adj* *V.* **Bullé** [—, to top
Bulteau, *s.m.* tree forming a bowl. *Mettre en*
Bumélie, *s.f.* (*bot*) bumelia, bastard bully-tree
Bunette, *s.f.* (*bird*) winter warbler
Bunias, *s.m.* (*bot.*) bunias
Bunion, *s m.* (*bot.*) bunium, earth-nut, hawk-nut, kipper-nut, pig-nut
Buphage, *s.m.* (*bird*) *V.* **Pique-bœufs**
Buphthalme, *s.m.* (*bot.*) ox-eye
Buphthalmie, *s.f.* (*med.*) buphthalmus, buph- [thalmia
Buplèvre, *s.m.* (*bot.*) hare's-ear
Bupreste, *s.m.* (*zool.*) buprestis, buprestidan, burn-cow [conist; (*theat.*) money-taker
Buraliste, *s.m.f.* office-keeper; clerk; tobac-
Burat, *s.m.* (*stuff*) bunting; drugget
Buratin, *s.m.*, **Buratine,** *s.f.* poplin
Burbat, *s.m.*, **Burbe,** *s.f.* burbat (*Tunisian coin*)
Burbot, *s.m.* *V.* **Barbote** [shaft; (*fish.*) *V.* **Bire**
Bure, *s.f.* (*stuff*) drugget; fustian; (*mining*)
Bureau, *s m.* writing-table, desk, davenport; table; bureau (*president, vice-president, and secretaries*); office; counting-house; department; government office; post-office; board; bench; court; committee; committee-room; (*obsolete for* "bure") *V.* **Bure** (*stuff*); (*fig.*) door. — *d'affaires,* (general) agency office, agency. — *de tabac,* tobacconist's shop, tobacco-shop, cigar-shop; licence to sell tobacco. *Air* or *vent du —,* aspect of affairs. *Chef de —,* *V.* **Chef.** *Garçon de —,* office-porter, porter, messenger, man. *Petit —,* (*post.*) receiving-house *or* office. *Payer à — ouvert,* (*com.*) to pay on demand. *Prendre l'air du —,* to see how matters stand, to go and hear the news
Bureaucrate, *s.m.* bureaucrat; red-tapist; — *adj* bureaucratic; red-tape
Bureaucratie, *s.f* bureaucracy; over-centralized administration; government by officials, influence of officials; red-tapism; red-tapists; red-tape
Bureaucratique, *adj.* bureaucratic; red-tape
Burelé, e, *adj.* (*her.*) barry, barruly
Burèle, Burelle, *s.f.* (*her.*) barrulet
Burette, *s.f.* cruet; can; oil-can; jug; (*eccl.*) flagon; (*chem.*) burette
Burgalèse, *s.f* Burgos wool
Burgau, *s.m.* burgau (*West Indian mother-of-pearl-shell, marbled turbo*)
Burgaudine, *s.f., adj.f.* burgau mother of pearl,
Burgrave, *s.m.* burgrave [finest mother of pearl
Burgraviat, *s.m.* burgraviate
Burin, *s.m.* graver, burin; manner of engraving; (*fig.*) pen (*of an historian*); engraver

Buriner, *v.a.n.* to engrave; (*fig.*) to write, to trace, to portray, to record, to engrave; to impress deeply; to write forcibly; to write to perfection; (*nav.*) *V.* **Bliner**
Se —, *v.r.* to be engraved *or* &c.
Burlesque, *adj.* burlesque; ludicrous, comical; — *s.m.* burlesque style, burlesque
Burlesquement, *adv.* in a burlesque manner; ludicrously, comically
Burletta, *s.f.* (*mus.*) burletta
Burnous, *s.m.* burnoose, burnous, bournous (*Arabian cloak*), cloak with a hood
Buron, *s.m.* cottage, hut
Bursaire, *adj.* purse-shaped
Bursal, e, *adj.* pecuniary
Bursère, *s.f.* (*bot.*) bursera
Bursiforme, *adj.* purse-shaped
Burtonie, *s.f.* (*bot.*) burtonia
Bus, *s.m.* (*her.*) head
Busaigle, *s.m.* (*bird*) rough-legged buzzard
Busard, *s.m.* (*bird*) buzzard; (*pers.*) blockhead, fool [mitre; (*of a gun-stock*) *V.* **Busque**
Busc, *s.m.* busk, stay-steel; (*of a canal-lock*)
Buse, *s.f.* (*bird*) buzzard; (*pers.*) blockhead; (*of bellows*) nozzle; (*of a copper*) tap; (*in a mine*) air-pipe, ventilator; (*nav.*) *V.* **Bûche**
Buson, *s.m.* (*bird*) buteo (*kind of buzzard*); (*pers.*) blockhead
Busque, *s.m.* hollow cheek (*of a gun-stock*)
Busqué, e, *adj.* busked; curved; arched
Busquer, *v.a.* to put a busk in *or* on; to make (...) wear a busk; to shorten
Se —, *v.r.* to wear a busk
Busquière, *s.f.* busk-case, busk-casing
Bussard, *s.m.*, **Busse,** *s.f.* hogshead
Busserole, *s.f.* (*bot.*) bear's whortleberry
Buste, *s.m.* bust; head and shoulders. *En* —, (*of portraits*) half-length
Bustrophe, *s.f.* *V.* **Boustrophédon**
But, *s.m.* butt, mark; goal; ending-post, winning-post; aim, object, end, end in view, purpose, view, intent; point. — *à* —, without any odds, even; even-handed. *De — en blanc,* point-blank; bluntly; abruptly
Butant, e, *adj.* (*arch.*) *V.* **Boutant**
Bute, *s.f.* (*farrier's*) butteris, parer
Butée, *s.f.* (*arch.*) abutment-pier
Buter, *v.a.* to set (against); (*mas.*) to prop, to buttress; (*fig.*) to press (against); (*nav.*) to place end to end; (*hort., agr.*) *V.* **Butter;** — *v.n.* to hit the mark; to tend, to aim; to end; to stumble; to meet (with); (*nav.*) to butt, to abut [oppose
Se —, *v.r.* to stick (to), to be bent (on); to
Butin, *s.m.* booty, spoil, plunder, prize; discovery; (soldier's) kit; (*pop.*) profit [pilfering
Butinement, *s.m.* plundering; despoiling;
Butiner, *v.a.n.* to pillage, to sack, to plunder, to spoil, to despoil, to carry off by rapine; to seek o.'s booty; to pilfer; to collect, to gather; to make o.'s provisions
Butineu-r, se, *adj.* plundering; pilfering
Butireu-x, se, *adj.* *V.* **Butyreux** [stone
Butoir, *s.m.* parer; buttress; (*of a gate*) stop-
Butome, *s.m.* (*bot.*) flowering-rush
Butor, *s.m.* (*bird*) bittern; (*pers.*) pig-headed churl, booby, clod [booby, dolt
Butorde, *s.f.* pig-headed coarse woman *or* girl,
Buttage, *s.m.* raising, mounding, banking up; (*hort., agr.*) earthing up, moulding, ridging; hoeing
Butte, *s.f.* mound; ridge; bank; butt; knoll, hillock, rising ground, rise, hill. *En — à,* exposed to; the object *or* aim of
Buttée, *s.f.* (*arch.*) *V.* **Butée**
Butter, *v.a.* to raise, to mound, to bank up, to embank; (*hort., agr.*) to earth up, to mould, to ridge; to hoe; (*nav.*) to place end to end; (*mas.*) *V.* **Buter;** — *v.n.* to stumble; to meet (with); (*nav.*) to butt, to abut
Se —, *v.r.* to be raised *or* &c.
Butteur, *s.m.*, **Butteuse,** *s.f.* (*agr.*) *V.* **Buttoir**
Buttoir, *s.m.* (*agr.*) ridging-plough, moulding-plough; (*tech.*) buttress; stop-stone
Butyracé, e, *adj.* butyraceous, buttery
Butyrate, *s.m.* (*chem.*) butyrate
Butyreu-x, se, *adj.* butyrous, buttery
Butyrine, *s.f.* (*chem.*) butyrine
Butyrique, *adj.* (*chem.*) butyric
Butyromètre, *s.m.* butyrometer
Buvable, *adj.* drinkable, fit to drink
†**Buvailler,** *v.n.a.* (*fam.*) to sip
†**Buvailleu-r, se,** *s.m.f.* (*fam.*) sipper
Buvard, *adj.m.* blotting; — *s.m.* blotting-book, blotting-case, blotting-pad. — *de voyage,* despatch-box, writing-desk *or* case
Buvée, *s.f.* (*agr.*) cow-mash
Buverie, *s.f.* drinking, potations, carousal
Buveti-er, ère, *s.m.f.* (*obsolete*) tavern-keeper, keeper of a refreshment-room
Buvette, *s.f.* refreshment-room; tea-room; pump-room, well-room; buttery; tap-room; refreshment-booth *or* marquee *or* stand; sutling-booth; drinking-counter; (*rail.*) third-class refreshment-room; (*obsolete*) tavern, coffee-house; (*fam.*) sip, sipping; tippling; (*obsolete*) jollification, merry bout, feast; (*garment*) pinafore,
Buveu-r, se, *s.m.f.* drinker; toper [tier, tire
Buvoter, *v.n.* to sip; to tipple
Buze, *s.f.* (*tech.*) *V.* **Buse**
By, *s.m.* (*of a pond*) trench
Byronien, ne, *adj. s.* Byronian, Byronic
Byronisme, *s.m.* Byronism
Bysse, Byssus, *s.m.* (*antiq., bot.*) byssus
Byzantin, e, *adj. s.m.f.* Byzantine; — *s.m.* Byzantine style; rose-colour

C

C, *s.m* c
C', *contraction of* **Ce.** *V.* **Ce,** *pron.*
Çà, *adv.* here. — *et là,* here and there; up and down; to and fro; about, all about. *En* —, (*obsolete*) nearly, about, some
Çà, *int.* come! now! *Ah* — ! *V.* **Ah**
Ça, *pron., contraction of* **Cela,** that, &c. (*V.* **Cela**); just the thing, the very thing; one jot, a trifle, a bit, a shade. — *et* —, this and that, this and that and the other, so and so. — *ira,* it shall *or* will go on; that will do! go on! go it! *Pas de* — ! none of that! nay, nay! that won't do!
Cab, *s.m.* hansom cab, hansom
Cabade, *s.m.* (modern Greek military costume)
Cabajoutis, *s.m.* old patchwork house
Cabale, *s.f* cabal; cabala
Cabaler, *v.n.* to cabal, to plot
Cabalette, *s.f.* (*mus.*) cabaletta
Cabaleu-r, se, *s.m.f.* caballer [page 3, § 1
Cabal-iste, -istique, -istiquement. *V.*
Caballin, e, *adj.* caballine [nought-coat, caban
Caban, *s.m.* cloak (*with a hood*); (*nav.*) dread-
Cabanage, *s.m.* hutting; huts, tents; encampment, camp (*of savages*)
Cabane, *s.f.* cottage; cot; cabin; hut; shed; kennel; hutch; awning; flat-bottomed boat
Cabaneau, *s.m.* (*fish.*) hut [(*covered over*)
Cabaner, *v.a.n.* to hut; (*nav.*) to upset, to cap-
Se —, *v.r.* to hut [size; (*nav.*) to gimlet
Cabanon, *s.m.* small hut, cabin; (*in prisons,* &c.) black-hole; cell
Cabaret, *s.m.* wine-shop, public-house, tavern, pot-house, dram-shop; tea-board, tea-service, tea-set, service, set; (*bot.*) *V.* **Asaret;** (*zool.*) *V.* **Sizerin** [publican, tavern-keeper
Cabaret-ier, ière, *s.m.f.* wine-shop keeper,
Cabas, *s.m.* frail, rush basket, bulrush-mat bag, flat straw-basket, hand-basket, shopping *or* marketing-basket, basket; work-bag; basket-carriage; (*jest.*) old-fashioned carriage; old straw-hat *or* bonnet; round bed

Cabasser, *v.n.a.* (*pop.*) to prattle, to gossip; to cheat; to thieve; to swindle; to bag, to prig [thief
Cabasset, *s.m.* (*obsolete*) helmet (*small*)
Cabasseu-r, se, *s.m.f.* (*pop.*) gossip; cheat;
Cabéliau, *s.m. V.* **Cabillaud**
Cabestan, *s.m.* capstan [water-hog
Cabiai, *s.m.* (*zool.*) cabiai, capibara, capybara,
†Cabillaud, *s.m.* (*fish*) keeling, cod [soldier
†Cabillot, *s.m.* (*nav.*) toggel, toggle; (*nav. slang*)
Cabine, *s.f.* (*nav.*) cabin
Cabinet, *s.m.* small room; room; closet; study; private room; consulting-room; office; chambers; practice, business; museum, collection; cabinet; state; private secretary's office; case (*of a clock, of an organ*); summer-house, bower, arbour. — *d'affaires*, (general) agency office, agency. — *d'étude* or *de travail*, study. — *de lecture*, reading-room, news-room; circulating library. — *de toilette*, dressing-room. *Affaires de* —, (*of a lawyer*) chamber-practice
Câble, *s.m.* cable; rope; line; wire; curtain-cord; cable's length. *Grand* or *maitre* —, sheet cable. — *-chaine*, chain-cable. *Filer du* —, to give more cable; (*fig.*) to gain time; to boggle
Câblé, e, *part. adj.* cabled; twisted; cable-laid
Câblé, *s.m.* cord
Câbleau, *s.m.* boat-rope, cablet, mooring-rope
Câblée, *s.f.* cable's length
Câbler, *v.a.* to cable; to make a cable of, to twist into a cable *or* a cord, to twist, to lay
Cabliau, *s.m. V.* **Cabillaud**
Câblot, *s.m. V.* **Câbleau**
Caboche, *s.f.* pate, nob, noddle; headpiece, head, brain-box; (*tech.*) hobnail
Caboché, e, *adj.* (*her.*) caboched, caboshed
Cabochon, *adj.m.* (*jewel.*) polished but uncut; — *s.m.* polished uncut stone; (*mollusc*) pileopsis, foolscap limpet; (*tech.*) hobnail; (*pop.*) knock on the head, thump [bruise
Cabosse, *s.f.* (*bot.*) cacao-pod; (*pop.*) bump,
Cabosser, *v.a.* (*pop.*) to bump, to bruise
Cabot, *s.m.* (*fish*) *V.* **Chabot;** (*pop.*) *V.* **Cabotin**
Cabotage, *s.m.* (*nav.*) coasting; coasting-trade
Caboter, *v.n.* (*nav.*) to coast
Caboteur, Cabotier, *s.m.* (*nav.*) coaster
Cabotin, e, *s.m.f.* strolling player; bad actor *or* actress, low comedian
Cabotinage, *s.m.* bad acting; bad actors; drudgery of the stage; novitiate on the stage; strolling
Cabotiner, *v.n.* to drudge on the stage; to stroll about; to dabble in stage-playing [shop
Caboulot, *s.m.* small tavern, pot-house, dram-
Cabre, *s.f.* (*tech.*) gin; (*nav.*) sheers; — *s.m.f.* (*pers.*) cubra, sambo *or* zambo, samba *or* zamba
Cabrer, *v.a.* to offend, to shock, to provoke, to irritate, to make angry, to put into a passion; to scare, to frighten; — (*Se*), *v.r.* (*of horses*) to rear; — *v.n.* (*Se*), *v.r.* (*fig.*) to rebel, to kick; to take fright *or* offence; to fly into a passion
†Cabretille, *s.m. V.* **Canepin**
Cabri, *s.m.* kid
†Cabrillon, *s.m.* goat-milk cheese
Cabriole, *s.f.* caper; capriole, cabriole
Cabrioler, *v.n.* to caper [hood; outside
Cabriolet, *s.m.* cabriolet; gig; hansom cab;
Cabrioleu-r, se, *s.m.f.* caperer
Cabrion, *s.m.* (*nav.*) wedge; (*pop.*) wag; humbug
Cabrouet, *s.m.* waggon, truck
Cabu, Cabus, *adj.m.* (*of cabbages*) headed
Caca, *s.m.* (*children's word*) cack, ta, nasty dirty thing. *Faire* —, to cack, to go ta
Cacaber, *v.n.* (*of partridges*) to call
Cacade, *s.f.* failure, mess, mull; cowardice, slinking; shameful retreat *or* flight; evacuation, cacking
Cacalie, *s.f.* (*bot.*) cacalia, Alpine colt's-foot
Cacao, *s.m.* (*bot.*) cacao, cacao-nut, chocolate-nut; (*com.*) cocoa
Cacaotier, Cacaoyer, *s.m.* cacao-tree
Cacaotière, Cacaoyère, *s.f.* cacao-plantation
Cacarder, *v.n.* (*of geese*) to cackle, to gabble
Cacatoès, *s.m.* (*bird*) *V.* **Kakatoès**
Cacatois, Cacatoi, *s.m.* (*nav.*) top gallant royal; (*bird*) *V.* **Kakatoès** [sperm-whale
Cachalot, *s.m.* cachalot, spermaceti-whale,
Cache, *s.f.* hiding-place; (*hunt.*) stake-net; (*nav.*) *V.* **Quaiche;** — *s.m.* (*in compounds, from* **Cacher,** "to hide," "to conceal,") thing that conceals. — **-boue,** *s.m.* (*artil.*) bolster-lip. — **-cache,** *s.m.* (*game*) hide and seek. — **-cou,** *s.m.* neckerchief. — **-entrée,** *s.m.* scutcheon (*of a key-hole*). — **-folie,** *s.m.* (*obsolete*) false curls; foretop; scalp; wig; front. — **-lumière,** *s.m.* (*artil.*) apron. — **-marée,** *s.m. V.* **Chasse-marée.** — **-misère,** *s.m.* (*pop.*) coat buttoned up to the chin so as to conceal the absence of a shirt. — **-nez,** *s.m.* muffler, wrapper, comforter. — **-peigne,** *s.m.* curl *or* ornament *or* head-gear to conceal the comb. — **-pot,** *s.m.* flower-pot cover. *A* — *-pot*, (*adv.*) fraudulently, without paying (excise or customs) duty. — **-sottise,** *s.m.* (*fig.*) concealer of fooleries, fools' screen. — **-tampon,** *s.m.* (*game*) hide-stick
Caché, e, *part. adj.* hidden, concealed; disguised; unseen, unperceived; out of the way; retired; in seclusion; in obscurity; latent; secret; close, reserved; dissembling, deceitful, sly [tical
Cachectique, *adj.* (*med.*) cachectic, cachec-
Cachement, *s.m.* hiding, concealment
Cachemire, *s.m.* cashmere
Cachemirette, *s.f.* cashmerette
Cacher, *v.a.* to hide, to conceal; to secrete; to keep close *or* secret; to disguise; to deny
Se —, *v.r.* to hide *or* &c. oneself; to conceal from oneself; to keep out of the way; to keep away; to keep from sight; to be hidden *or* concealed; to lie concealed; to live retired; to lurk; to sculk; to abscond; to make a secret *or* a mystery; to deny; to be close *or* reserved; to dissemble
Cachet, *s.m.* seal; signet; stamp; impression, mark; character; characteristic; style; ticket; lesson. *Courir le* —, to run about giving private lessons, to go out teaching. *Lettre de* —, (sealed official letter, letter under the king's seal, arbitrary warrant of imprisonment)
Cacheté, e, *part. adj.* sealed, sealed up. *Tout* —, unopened
Cacheter, *v.a.* to seal; to seal up [
Cacheteu-r, se, *s.m.f.* sealer
Cachette, *s.f.* hiding-place; lurking-hole. *En* —, secretly, underhand, slily, on the sly; stealthily, by stealth; without the knowledge (of), out of the sight (of)
Cacheu-r, se, *s.m.f.* concealer; sly boots
Cachexie, *s.f.* (*med.*) cachexia, cachexy
Cachiment, Cachiman, *s.m.* (*bot.*) *V.* **Corossol** [**Corossolier**
Cachimentier, Cachiman, *s.m.* (*bot.*) *V.*
Cachiri, *s.m.* cachiri (*liquor*)
Cachot, *s.m.* dungeon, prison; black-hole; cell
Cachotte, *s.f.* tobacco-pipe without a heel at the bowl
Cachotter, *v.n.* to make mysteries about trifles
Cachotterie, *s.f.* mystery about trifles, mystery, mysterious ways, secret practice
Cachotti-er, ère, *adj* mysterious, sly; — *s.m.f.* mysterious fellow *or* thing, close person, [sly boots
Cachou, *s.m.* cashoo, catechu
Cachucha, *s.f.* cachuca (*Spanish dance, tune*)
Cacique, *s.m.* cacique (*American Indian chief*);
Cacis, *s.m. V.* **Cassis** [(*bird*) *V.* **Cassique**
Caco, (*in compounds*) caco (*bad*)
Cacochyme, *adj.* (*med.*) cacochymic; (*fig.*) odd, eccentric, peevish, fretful [*V.* page 3, § 1
Caco-chymie, -graphie, -logie, -phonie.
Cacolet, *s.m.* mule-litter, pannier, cacolet
Cactier, Cactus, *s.m.* (*bot.*) cactus
Cadastral, e, *adj.* cadastral, pertaining to real estate, relative to the government survey of lands

Cadastre, *s.m.* cadastre, official statement of the quantity and value of real property, surveying and valuing, cadastral survey, survey, valuation, assessment, return, register (*of landed property*); plan; surveying department, land registry

Cadastrer, *v.a.n.* to (officially) survey and value

Cadastreur, *s.m.* surveyor [(*land*)

Cadavéreu-x, se, *adj.* cadaverous

Cadavérique, *adj.* cadaveric, of a dead body

Cadavre, *s.m.* corpse, dead body, body; carcass; (*fig.*) ghost; skeleton; ruins [huile de cade

Cade, *s.m.* (*bot.*) Spanish juniper. *Huile de —,*

Cadeau, *s.m.* present, gift; compliment; (*obsolete*) entertainment; flourish [*s.m.* Gascon

Cadédis, *int.* (*old and local*) zounds! faith! —

Cadelle, *s.f.* cadelle (*insect*)

Cadenas, *s.m.* padlock; clasp, snap

Cadenasser, *v.a.* to padlock; to clasp

Cadence, *s.f.* cadence; time; shake

Cadencé, e, *adj.* cadenced; musical, harmonious; (*pers.*) formal, stiff, systematic

Cadencer, *v.a.* to cadence; to regulate; to time; to harmonize; to shake

Cadène, *s.f.* chain; chain-gang; Turkish carpet

Cadenette, *s.f.* tress (*of hair*)

Cadet, te, *adj. s.* younger; junior; youngest; least, smallest; young fellow, boy, sort of a fellow, fellow, chap; (*mil.*) cadet; (*pop.*) bum; (*thieves' slang*) crow-bar, jemmy

Cadette, *s.f.* free paving-stone

Cadetter, *v.a.* to pave in free stone

Cadi, *s.m.* cadi (*Turkish civil judge*) [*judge*)

Cadilesker, *s.m.* cadilesker (*Turkish military*

Cadis, Cadisé, *s.m.* cadis (*serge*)

Cadméen, ne, *adj.* Cadmean

Cadmie, *s.f.* (*chem.*) cadmia

Cadmium, *s.m.* (*chem.*) cadmium

Cadogan, *s.m. V.* **Catogan**

Cadole, *s.f.* latch [dial

Cadran, *s.m.* dial-plate; dial. — *solaire,* sun-

Cadrané, e, *adj.* (*of trees*) split from the centre

Cadranerie, *s.f.* nautical instrument making

Cadranier, *s.m.* dialist [*or* manufactory

Cadranure, *s.f.* (*of trees*) splitting from the

Cadrat, *s.m.* (*print.*) quadrat [centre

Cadratin, *s.m.* (*print.*) m quadrat. *Demi- —,* n quadrat [works

Cadrature, *s.f.* (*horol.*) dial-works; repeating-

Cadraturier, *s.m.* (*horol.*) dial-work maker, repeating-work maker

Cadre, *s.m.* frame; framework; border; compass, limits; outline; plan; (*mil.*) list of officers, list, rolls, staff, skeleton, cadre; (*admin.*) staff, officials, men, servants; (*nav.*) cot, bed-frame. *Sur les —s,* (*nav.*) on the sick-list

Cadrer, *v.n.* to agree, to square, to tally, to answer, to correspond, to suit, to fit, to match

†**Cadrillage,** *s.m.* ruling in squares; checkering, checking; checker-work, checks; squares; checked pavement, square tiles

†**Cadrille,** *s.m.* check, square, lozenge

†**Cadriller,** *v.a.* to rule (*paper*) in squares; to checker, to check (*stuffs,* &c.); to lay *or* dispose in squares *or* checker-work

†**Cadrilleu-r, se,** *s.m.f.* checkerer

Cadu-c, que, *adj.* broken down, infirm, decaying, declining, decayed, decrepit, frail, feeble, weak, rickety, crazy, tumbledown, falling, old; perishable; unclaimed; null, void, null and void, lapsed; barred by limitation; (*bot.*) cadu-

Caducée, *s.m.* caduceus, rod [cous

Caducité, *s.f.* caducity, decay, decline, decrepitude, ruinous state; falling off; nullity,

Cæcal, e, *adj.* (*anat.*) cæcal [lapsing

Cæcum, *s.m.* (*anat.*) cæcum, blind gut

Caennais, e, *adj. s.* of Caen; native of Caen

Cæsium, *s.m.* (*chem.*) cæsium

Cafard, *s.m.* (*insect*) *V.* **Blatte**

Cafard, e, *adj. s.m.f.* (*pers.*) canting, hypocritical, sanctimonious; canter, canting humbug *or* rascal, hypocrite, mawworm; sneak

Cafarder, *v.n.* to cant, to play the hypocrite, to affect sanctity; to sneak [canting; sneaking

Cafarderie, Cafardise, *s.f.* cant, hypocrisy;

Café, *s.m.* coffee; coffee-house, refreshment and oyster-rooms, luncheon-rooms, tavern; coffee-room; coffee-time (*after dinner*). — *chantant,* — *-concert,* concert coffee-house, music-hall, tavern. — *au lait,* coffee with milk (in it); (*adject.*) cream-coloured. *Couleur — au lait,* cream colour; cream-coloured

Caféier, Cafeyer, Cafier, *s.m.* coffee-tree

Caféi-er, ère, *s.m.f.* coffee-planter, coffee-grower

Caféière, Cafeyère, Caféirie, Cafeterie, *s.f.* coffee-plantation; coffee-dressing establish-

Caféine, *s.f.* (*chem.*) caffeine [ment

Caféique, *adj.* (*chem.*) caffeic

Cafetan, *s.m.* caftan (*Persian and Turkish*

Cafeté, e, *adj.* mixed with coffee [*garment*)

Cafetier, *s.m.* coffee-house keeper

Cafetière, *s.f.* coffee-pot; mug

Cafier, *s.m.* coffee-tree

Cafre, *adj. s.m.f.* Caffre, Kafir, Kaffir

Caftan, *s.m. V.* **Cafetan**

Cage, *s.f.* cage; coop; crate; case; frame; shell; carcass; wire-guard; wicker-work; trellis-work; grate; weel, weir, bow-net; glass shade. — *à poulets,* hen-coop; (*fig.*) small dirty room. — *à chapons,* (*pop.*) monastery. — *à jacasses,* (*pop.*) nunnery

Cagée, *s.f.* cageful, all the birds

Cagerotte, *s.f.* cheese-hurdle *or* drainer *or* vat

Cagette, *s.f.* little cage; bird-trap, trap

Cagi-er, ère, *s.m.f.* cage-maker; falconer, hawker, bird-fancier

†**Cagnard, e,** *adj. s.m.f.* lazy, idle, sculking; lazy-bones, sluggard, sculker, loafer; — *s.m.* (*nav.*) tarpaulin [lazy life; to sculk

†**Cagnarder,** *v.n.* to idle time away, to lead a

†**Cagnarderie, Cagnardise,** *s.f.* laziness; sculking

†**Cagne,** *s.f.* lazy-bones, slut; sculker; coward

†**Cagneu-x, se,** *adj.* crook-kneed, knock-kneed; crooked; — *s.m.f.* crook-kneed person

†**Cagnot,** *s.m.* (*fish*) tope

†**Cagnotte,** *s.f.* (*gaming*) money reserved out of stakes; hell-keeper's bonus *or* fee; money-box

Cagot, e, *adj. s.m.f.* bigoted; hypocritical; bigot; cunning saint, hypocrite, mawworm; — *s.m.* (*hist.*) cagot, cretin, idiot [hypocrisy

Cagoterie, *s.f.,* **Cagotisme,** *s.m.* bigotry;

Cagou, *s.m.* misanthrope, solitary; solitary

Cague, *s.f.* (*nav.*) Dutch sloop [thief

Cahier, *s.m.* book; copy-book; writing-book; exercise-book; manuscript; part of a book, part; (folded) sheet; (*of writing-paper, note-paper*) quarter of a quire, six sheets; written lectures; resolutions; report; memorandum; (*in Fr. hist.*) memorial, cahier. — *des charges,* (*admin.*) conditions, specifications. — *des frais,* bill of costs [lamely; slowly; reluctantly

Cahin-caha, *adv.* so so, middling, indifferently,

Cahorsin, e, *adj. s.* of Cahors; native of Cahors

Cahot, *s.m.* jolt; impediment, obstacle, hitch

Cahotage, Cahotement, *s.m.* jolting

Cahoter, *v.a.n.* to jolt; to toss about

Cahute, *s.f.* hut, hovel; (*nav.*) small cabin

Caïc, *s.m. V.* **Caïque**

Caiche, *s.f. V.* **Quaiche**

Caïd, *s.m.* caid (*judge in the Barbary States*)

Caïdji, *s.m.* caidji (*boatman of a caïque*)

Caie, *s.f.* (*geog.*) key (*rock, shoal, rocky islet*)

Caïeu, *s.m.* (*hort.*) clove

†**Caille,** *s.f.* quail. — *coiffée,* (*fam.*) gay woman

†**Caillé, e,** *adj.* curdled, curdy; clotted, clotty

†**Caillé,** *s.m.* curd

†**Caillebot,** *s.m.* guelder rose

†**Caillebotis,** *s.m.* (*nav.*) grating

†**Caillebottage,** *s.m.* curdling

†**Caillebotte,** *s.f.* curds

†**Caillebotter,** *v.a. V.* **Cailler**

†**Caille-lait,** *s.m.* (*bot.*) bedstraw, cheese-rennet
†**Caillement,** *s.m.* curdling; clotting [to clot
†**Cailler,** *v.a.*, **Se** —, *v.r.* to curdle, to curd;
†**Cailler,** *s.m.* quail-net; quail-pipe, quail-call
†**Cailletage,** *s.m.* gossiping, tittle-tattle, twad-
†**Cailleteau,** *s.m.* young quail [dling
†**Cailleter,** *v.n.* to gossip, to chatter, to twaddle
†**Cailletot,** *s.m.* young turbot
†**Caillette,** *s.f.* (*anat.*) rennet, reed; (*pers.*) gossip, chatterer, twaddler [water pear
†**Caillot,** *s.m.* clot, coagulum. — *-rosat,* rose-
†**Caillotis,** *s.m.* kelp
†**Caillou,** *s.m.* flint; pebble; stone
†**Cailloutage,** *s.m.* stoning, gravelling, ballasting; stones, flints, gravel, ballast; pebble-work; rock-work; pipe-clay; (*pottery*) flint-ware
†**Cailloutée,** *s.f.* pebble-work; rock-work; (*pottery*) flint-ware [to metal
†**Caillouter,** *v.a.* to stone, to gravel, to ballast,
†**Caillouteur,** *s.m.* ballaster
†**Caillouteu-x, se,** *adj.* flinty, pebbly, stony
†**Cailloutis,** *s.m.* broken stone, stones, flints, gravel, ballast, metal; stoning, gravelling, ballasting [*tenant*)
Caïmacan, *s.m.* caimacan (*grand-vizier's lieu-*
Caïman, *s.m.* cayman, caiman, alligator
Caïque, *s.m.* (*nav.*) caïque, caïc (*Turkish boat*); galley-boat, skiff
Caire, *s.m.* coir, cocoa-nut fibre, cocoa-fibre
Cairn, *s.m.* cairn
Caisse, *s.f.* case; box; chest; bin; cash-box; till; coffer; cash; cashier's office *or* desk; pay office; counting-house; cash-account; fund; bank; treasury; drum; barrel (*of a drum*); frame, body; (*hort.*) tub; (*rail.*) compartment; (*rail., nav.*) tank (*for water*); (*nav.*) chest; shell (*of a block*); mooring-buoy. — *d'épargne,* savings-bank. — *de secours mutuels,* sick-fund. *Garçon de* —, collecting-clerk. *En* —, (*com., fin.*) in hand. *Faire la* —, to make up the cash-account. *Tenir la* —, to act as cashier, to be cashier, to keep the cash-account
Caissetin, *s.m.* box (*small deal-box for raisins*)
Caissi-er, ère, *s.m.f.* cashier, cash-keeper; treasurer
Caisson, *s.m.* (*mil.*) ammunition waggon *or* cart, waggon, tumbril, chest; caisson; limber; (*nav.*) locker; cartridge-chest, chest; (*of carriages*) box; (*arch.*) coffer, caisson, sunk panel; (*build.*) caisson; (*soldiers' slang*) head, brains
Cajeput, *s.m.* (*bot.*) cajeput; (*pharm.*) cajeput oil
Cajoler, *v.a.* to cajole, to wheedle; to coax; to fawn upon; — *v.a.n.* (*nav.*) (— *le vent*) to tide up; to sail by small tacks [fawning
Cajolerie, *s.f.* cajolery, wheedling, coaxing;
Cajoleu-r, se, *s.m.f.* cajoler, wheedler, coaxer; fawner; — *adj.* cajoling, wheedling, coaxing;
Cajotte, *s.f. V.* **Cachotte** [fawning
Cajute, *s.f.* (*nav.*) small cabin; captain's cabin;
Cal, *s.m.* callosity; (*surg.*) callus [berth, bed
Calabrais, e, *adj. s.* Calabrian; Calabrian
Calade, *s.f.* (*rid.*) descent, slope, calade [fashion
Calage, *s.m.* wedging; lowering; sinking
Calais, *s.m.* (*in markets*) basket; dozen-basket
Calaisien, ne, *adj. s.* of Calais, Calaisian, native of Calais
Calaison, *s.f.* (*nav.*) ship's gage, sea-gage, draught of water, draught, immersion
Calamagrostide, *s.f.* (*bot.*) calamagrostis,
Calambac, *s.m.* calambac (*wood*) [small-reed
Calambour, *s.m.* calambour (*wood*)
Calament, *s.m.* (*bot.*) calamint
Calamine, *s.f.* (*min.*) calamine [toad
Calamite, *s.f.* (*min.*) calamite; (*zool.*) striped
Calamité, *s.f.* calamity; distress
Calamiteusement, *adv.* calamitously
Calamiteu-x, se, *adj.* calamitous; distressing
Calandrage, *s.m.* calendering, mangling
Calandre, *s.f.* calender, mangle; (*a bird, kind of lark*) calandra; (*insect*) calandra, calandre, corn-weevil
Calandrer, *v.a.* to calender, to mangle
Calandreu-r, se, *s.m.f.* calenderer, mangler
Calangue, *s.f.* cove, creek
Calanque, *s.f.* (*nav.*) wedge; *V.* **Calangue**
Calao, *s.m.* (*bird*) hornbill
Calapé, *s.m.* (*cook.*) calipee, calipash
Calappe, *s.m.* (*zool.*) calappa (*kind of crab*)
Calcaire, *adj.m.f.* calcareous, limy, lime; *s.m.* calcareous soil *or* rock, limestone
Calcanéen, ne, *adj.* (*anat.*) calcaneal
Calcanéum, *s.m.* (*anat.*) calcaneum, os calcis,
Calcédoine, *s.f.* (*min.*) chalcedony [heel-bone
Calcédonien, ne, Calcédoineu-x, se, Calcédonieu-x, se, Calcédonique, *adj.* chalcedonian, chalcedonic
Calcéolaire, *s.f.* (*bot.*) calceolaria, slipperw
Calcin, *s.m.* calcined glass
Calcinable, *adj.* calcinable
Calcination, *s.f.* calcination, calcining
Calciner, *v.a.*, **Se** —, *v.r.* to calcine; to burn
Calcium, *s.m.* (*chem.*) calcium
Calcographe, *s.m.* calcographer
Calcograph-ie, -ique. *V.* page 8, § 1
Calcul, *s.m.* calculation, reckoning, computation; forecast; ciphering; arithmetic; sum; account; estimate; design; consideration of personal interest, selfish motive; (*math.*) calculus; (*med.*) calculus, concretion, stone. *De* — *fait,* everything being reckoned
Calculable, *adj.* calculable, computable
Calcula-teur, trice, *adj. s.* calculating; calculator, reckoner; actuary; accountant; schemer; calculating-machine. — *mécanique,* calculating-machine
Calculatoire, *adj.* calculatory; calculating
Calculer, *v.a.n.* to calculate, to reckon, to compute; to estimate; to cipher; to forecast, to foresee, to foretell; to scheme; to adjust; to combine, to contrive, to devise; to judge, to appreciate, to determine; to rely, to depend (on)

Se —, *v.r.* to be calculated *or* reckoned *or* &c.
Calculeu-x, se, *adj. s.* (*med.*) calculous; person affected with calculus
Cale, *s.f.* wedge; block; chock, quoin; slip; slope; stock (*for ship-building*); hold (*of a ship*); ducking, keel-hauling; (*obsolete*) cove, creek; (*obsolete*) skull-cap; (*fish.*) lead, shot. *Eau de la* —, bilge-water. *A fond de* —, (*nav.*) down in the hold; (*pop.*) out of cash, beggared, hard up, done up, done for
Calé, e, *part. adj.* wedged, &c. (*V.* **Caler**); well-to-do, wealthy, warm; strong
Calebasse, *s.f.* calabash, gourd; (*pop.*) pate, nob, noddle, sconce; lanky dowdy
Calebassier, *s.m.* (*bot.*) calabash-tree
Calèche, *s.f.* barouch, barouche; (*old-fashioned*) calash; (*for the head, obsolete*) calash
Caleçon, *s.m.* drawers, pair of drawers. — *rouge,* red (bathing-)drawers; first-rate swimmer
Caleçonnier, *s.m.* drawers-maker
Calédonien, ne, *adj. s.* Caledonian
Calédonite, *s.f.* (*min.*) caledonite
Caléfacteur, *s.m.* cooking-apparatus, steam-kitchen, calefactor; — *adj.m.* (**-trice,** *f.*) cook-
Caléfaction, *s.f.* calefaction [ing; heating
Caléidophone, *s.m.* (*phys.*) kaleidophon, kaleidophone
Caléidoscope, *s.m.* kaleidoscope (*optical toy*)
Calemande, *s.f. V.* **Calmande**
Calembour, *s.m.* pun
Calembourique, *adj.* punning, jocular
Calembouriste, *s.m.f.* punster
Calembredaine, *s.f.* sham; bosh; humbug, gammon; random *or* idle talk, idle story, foolery, nonsense, stuff
Calendaire, *s.m.* church-register
Calende, *s.f.* (*tech.*) crane
Calender, *s.m.* calender, kalender (*dervis*)
Calendes, *s.f.pl.* calends; assembly (*of vicars*). — *grecques,* Greek calends, Tib's eve, latter Lammas, (till) doomsday, never
Calendrier, *s.m.* calendar, almanac

Calenture, *s.f.* (*med.*) calenture
Calepin, *s.m.* note-book, memorandum-book
Caler, *v.a.* to wedge up; to wedge in; to support, to prop, to stay; to steady; to fix; to fasten; to tighten; to strengthen; to secure; to establish firmly; to give a position to; to strike (*a marble*); to keep away from (*school*); (*nav.*) to lower; (*of a vessel*) to draw (*... feet of water*); — *v.n.* (*nav., fish.*) to sink low *or* lower in the water, to sink; (*fig.*) to yield, to submit; (*pop.*) to be idle; (*among printers*) to wait *or* stop for copy; (*at marbles*) to rest o.'s right hand on o.'s left hand, to knuckle down
Se —, *v.r.* to be wedged up, &c.; to get a firm footing
Calessine, *s.f.* (*Spanish*) chaise, fly, van, carriage
Calfait, *s.m.* (*nav.*) calking-iron
Calfat, *s.m.* (*nav.*) calker
Calfatage, *s.m.* (*nav.*) calking
Calfater, *v.a.* (*nav.*) to calk
Calfateur, *s.m.* (*nav.*) calker
Calfatin, *s.m.* (*nav.*) calker's boy
Calfeutrage, *s.m.* stopping of chinks [snug
Calfeutré, e, *adj.* made air-tight; close, warm,
Calfeutrer, *v.a.* to stop the chinks of
Se —, *v.r.* to be made air-tight; (*pers.*) to shut oneself up close *or* snugly, to keep oneself warm and comfortable; (*fig.*) to keep o.'s own counsel [tioning, sizing
Calibrage, *s.m.* giving the calibre to, propor-
Calibre, *s.m.* (*of firearms,* &c.) calibre; size; (*fig.*) calibre; sort, kind, stamp
Calibrer, *v.a.* to give the calibre to, to proportion, to size; to take the calibre of
Calice, *s.m.* chalice, communion-cup, cup; (*bot.*) calyx, cup, flower-cup; (*fig.*) cup; cup of bitterness; grief, affliction, humiliation, sacrifice
Calicé, e, *adj.* (*bot.*) with a calyx
Caliciforme, *adj.* (*bot.*) calyciform
Calicinal, e, *adj.* (*bot.*) calycinal, calycine
Calicot, *s.m.* calico; counter-jumper
Calicote, *s.f.* counter-jumper's sweetheart
Calicotier, *s.m.* calico manufacturer *or* ware-
Caliculaire, *adj.* (*bot.*) calycular [houseman
Calicule, *s.m.* (*bot.*) calycule, calycle
Caliculé, e, *adj.* (*bot.*) calyculate, calycled
Calier, *s.m.* (*nav.*) captain of the hold
Califal, e, *adj.* caliphal
Califat, *s.m.* caliphate
Calife, *s.m.* caliph
Californien, ne, *adj. s.* Californian [straddle
Califourchon, *s.m.* hobby. *A* —, astride, a-
Calige, *s.m.* caligus, fish-louse, sea-louse
Calimande, *s.f.* (*fish*) whiff
Calin, *s.m.* calin (*tea-canister metal*)
Câlin, e, *adj. s.* fawning, caressing, wheedling, coaxing, cajoling, bland; indolent, lazy; fawner, wheedler, coaxer, cajoler; lazy-bones, dullard
Calinage, *s.m.* beech-wood
Câliner, *v.a.* to fawn upon; to fondle, to caress, to indulge, to coddle, to pet; to wheedle, to coax, to cajole [ease; to indulge in idleness
Se —, *v.r.* to coddle oneself; to take o.'s
Câlinerie, *s.f.* fawning, fondling, caressing, caress, caresses, fond ways; wheedling, coaxing, cajolery; indulgence; indolence, laziness
Caliorne, *s.f.* (*nav.*) winding-tackle
Calle, *s.f.* (*bot.*) calla [callose
Calleu-x, se, *adj.* callous, hard, horny; (*bot.*)
‡Callichrome, *s.m.* (*zool.*) callichroma, musk-beetle [penmanship, good penman
Calligraphe, *s.m.* calligrapher, one skilled in
Calligraphie, *s.f.* calligraphy; penmanship
Calligraphique, *adj.* calligraphic; writing
Callionyme, *s.m.* (*fish*) dragonet
Callisthénie, *s.f.* callisthenics, calisthenics
Callisthénique, *adj.* callisthenic, calisthenic
Callosité, *s.f.* callosity; callousness
Callot, *s.m.* block of slate-stone; taw. *Figure à la* —, grotesque figure (*in the style of Callot, a celebrated engraver*)
Calmande, *s.f.* calamanco (*glossy woollen stuff*)
Calmant, *s.m.* (*med.*) soothing remedy, sedative, anodyne, composing draught [squid, sleeve-fish
Calmar, *s.m.* (*mollusc*) calamar, calamary,
Calme, *adj.* calm, quiet, still; undisturbed; unruffled; serene; unimpassioned; dispassionate; composed; collected; cool; sedate; dull, flat
Calme, *s.m.* calm, calmness, quietness, quiet, stillness; tranquillity; repose; serenity; composedness, composure, coolness; dulness, flatness; interruption
Calmée, *s.f.* (*nav.*) *V.* **Embellie**
Calmer, *v.a.* to calm, to quiet, to still, to pacify, to appease, to soothe, to compose, to ease; to mitigate; to soften; — *v.n.* (*nav.*) to fall calm, to be becalmed
Se —, *v.r.* to become calm *or* quiet *or* still *or* easy; to be *or* become appeased *or* soothed *or* &c.; to calm oneself; to compose oneself; to blow over; to subside, to abate, to fall
Calmie, *s.f.* (*nav.*) *V.* **Embellie**
Calmir, *v.n.* (*nav.*) *V.* **Calmer,** *v.n.*
Calmouk, *s.m.* Calmuck-Tartar, Calmuck, Kalmuck; (*stuff*) calmuck, kalmuck
Calomel, *s.m.* (*pharm.*) calomel
Calomnia-teur, trice, *s.m.f.* calumniator, slanderer; — *adj.* calumnious, slanderous
Calomnie, *s.f.* calumny, slander
Calomnier, *v.a.n.* to calumniate, to slander
Calomnieusement, *adv.* calumniously, slanderously
Calomnieu-x, se, *adj.* calumnious, slanderous
Calonière, *s.f.* (*pop. for* **Canonnière**) pop-gun
Calophylle, *s.m.* (*bot.*) calophyllum, calaba-tree
Caloricité, *s.f.* caloricity
Calorie, *s.f.* unit of specific heat
Calorifère, *s.m.* heating *or* warming apparatus; air-stove, hot-air stove, stove; hot-water pipe; calorifere; — *adj.* heating, warming, hot-air, hot-water
Calorification, *s.f.* calorification
Calorifique, *adj.m.f., s.m.* calorific
Calorimètre, *s.m.* calorimeter
Calorimétr-ie, -ique. *V.* page 3, § 1
Calorimoteur, *s.m.* (*phys.*) calorimotor
Calorique, *s.m.* caloric, heat
Calot, *s.m.* wedge; block of slate-stone; taw; (*pop.*) goggle eye; (*mil.*) crown (*of a shako*);
Calotin, *s.m. V.* **Calottin** [(*obsolete*) sturdy beggar
Calotte, *s.f.* skull-cap; smoking-cap; cap; coif; caul; top of the crown, tip (*of a hat*); top (*of a man's cap*); box on the ear; (*of priests, arch.*) calotte; (*fig., fam.*) priesthood; cardinalate; canopy, vault; (*anat.*) pan (*of the skull*). — *grecque*, Greek cap, smoking-cap
Calotter, *v.a.* to box the ears of
Calotti-er, ère, *s.m.f.* calotte *or* cap-maker
Calottin, *s.m.* priest (calotte-wearer; white-
Calotype, *s.m.* calotype [choker *in English*)
Caloy-er, ère, *s.m.f.* caloyer (*Greek monk* or *nun*)
Calque, *s.m.* tracing, calquing; copy
Calquer, *v.a.* to trace, to calque; to copy
Se —, *v.r.* to be traced *or* copied; to take example, to follow, to take as o.'s model
Calquoir, *s.m.* tracing-point, calquing-point
Calumet, *s.m.* calumet, pipe, pipe of peace
Calus, *s.m.* callus, callosity, hard skin; (*fig.*) callousness, obduracy; (*surg.*) callus; (*bot.*)
Calvaire, *s.m.* Calvary [callosity
Calvanier, *s.m.* (*agr.*) stacker
Calville, *s.m.f.* calville (*apple*)
Calvinien, ne, *adj.* Calvinistic
Calvinisme, *s.m.* Calvinism
Calviniste, *s.m.f.* Calvinist; — *adj.* Calvinistic
Calvitie, *s.f.* baldness. — *des paupières*, loss of the eyelashes [allspice, Japan allspice
Calycanthe, *s.m.* (*bot.*) calycanthus, Carolina
Camaïeu, *s.m.* cameo, camaieu; (*paint.*) camaieu, camayeu; (*fig.*) monotonous piece
†Camail, *s.m.* (*garment*) camail; cardinal
Camarade, *s.m.f.* comrade, fellow, mate, chum, companion, associate, partner; friend; lad; play-

fellow; school-fellow; fellow-servant. — *d'école* or *de pension* or *de collège* or *d'étude* or *de classe*, school-fellow, class-fellow, fellow-student
Camaraderie, *s.f.* party association, coalition, coterie, clique, clan, close fraternity, club *or* set of stanch friends; party spirit; favouritism, jobbery; companionship, fellowship; friendship, intimacy
Camard, e, *adj. s.* flat-nosed; flat; flat-nosed person, flat-nose. *La —e,* Death, grim Death
Camarilla, *s.f.* camarilla
Camarine, *s.f.* (*bot.*) crowberry
Camassie, *s.f.* (*bot.*) camassia, quamash, biscuit-root
Cambiste, *s.m.* cambist
Cambium, *s.m.* (*bot.*) cambium
Cambouis, *s.m.* cart-grease, coom, gome
Cambrai, *s.m.* imitation lace of Cambrai
Cambraisien, ne, *adj. s.* of Cambrai; native
Cambre, *s.f.*, **Cambrement,** *s.m.* camber, cambering, curving, arching, bending
Cambré, e, *part. adj.* cambering, cambered, &c. (*V.* **Cambrer**); well set
Cambrer, *v.a.* to camber, to curve, to arch; to bend up
Se —, *v.r.* to camber; to warp; to bend up o.'s back
Cambrésien, ne, *adj. s. V.* **Cambraisien**
Cambreu-r, se, *s.m.f.* camberer, bender
Cambrien, ne, *adj. s.* Cambrian
†**Cambrillon,** *s.m.* (*of shoes*) stiffener
Cambrioleur, *s.m.* housebreaker
Cambrique, *adj.m.f.*, *s.m.* Welsh
Cambrure, *s.f.* camber, bend, arch, curve; cambering, bending; warping
Cambuse, *s.f.* (*nav.*) steward's room, storeroom; (*pop.*) pot-house, dram-shop; hole, hovel
Cambusier, *s.m.* (*nav.*) steward's mate, storekeeper
Came, *s.f.* (*shell*) chama, gaping-cockle; (*tech.*) peg-cam, cog
Camée, *s.m.* cameo
Camélée, *s.f.* (*bot.*) widow-wail
Caméléon, *s.m.* chameleon, cameleon; (*pers.*) weathercock, time-server; — *adj.* fickle
Caméléopard, Camelopard, *s.m.* camelopard, giraffe
Camélia, *s.m.* (*bot.*) camelia, camellia. *Dame aux —s,* gay woman
Caméline, *s.f.* (*bot.*) camelina, gold of pleasure
Camellia, *s.m.* (*bot.*) camellia, camelia. *Dame aux —s,* gay woman
Camelot, *s.m.*(*stuff*) camlet; (*pers.*) cheap Jack, pedlar, packman, hawker; toyman; huckster
Camelote, *s.f.* trash, rubbish, trumpery; bosh
Cameloté, e, *adj.* camleted
Cameloter, *v.a.* to dress camlet-like; — *v.n.* to make trash, to bungle, to deal in trumpery articles; to loaf; to beg
Cameloteur, *s.m.* pedlar, packman, hawker; duffer; loafer
Camelotier, *s.m.* coarse paper; camlet-weaver; bungler; blackguard; cheap Jack, &c. (*V* **Camelot**
Camelotine, *s.f.* (*stuff*) camleteen
Caméra-lucida, *s.f* (*opt.*) camera lucida
Camérier, *s.m.* (*of the Pope*) chamberlain
Camérisier, *s.m.* (*bot.*) fly-honeysuckle
Caméristе, Camérière, *s.f.* waiting-woman; lady's maid; chambermaid
Camerlingat, *s.m* camerlingate (*at Rome*)
Camerlingue, *s.m* (*of the Pope*) camerlingo
Camion, *s.m.* truck; waggon; minikin-pin, small pin
Camionnage, *s.m.* carriage. cartage
Camionner, *v.a.* to convey on a truck, to carry
Camionneur, *s.m.* carrier; porter
Camisade, *s.f.* (*obsolete, mil.*) camisado, camisade, night attack
Camisard, *s.m.* (*Fr. hist.*) camisard (*Calvinistic rebel*)
Camisole, *s.f.* dressing-jacket; strait-waistcoat *or* jacket. — *de force,* strait-waistcoat *or* jacket
Camme, *s.f.* (*tech.*) *V.* **Came**
Camoïard, *s.m. V.* **Mohair**
†**Camomille,** *s.f.* (*bot.*) camomile, chamomile
Çamon, *int.* (*old*) ay! oh,yes! indeed! forsooth!
Camouflet, *s.m.* whiff of smoke (*in the face*); (*mil.*) camouflet, stifler; (*fig.*) affront; rap over the knuckles, snub
Camourlot, *s.m.* mastic cement
Camp, *s.m.* camp; (*fig.*) army; party; (*old*) lists; single combat; field. *Lever le —,* to break up the camp. *Prendre le —, V.* **Ficher**
†**Campagnard, e,** *adj.* country; rustic, rural, countrified; — *s.m.f.* countryman; countrywoman; rustic; farmer
†**Campagne,** *s.f.* country, fields; champaign, champaign country, open *or* flat country; plain, plains; regions; country-place; country-house, seat; (*mil., fig.*) campaign; field; expedition; (*nav.*) voyage, cruise; (*public works*) season. *En —,* in the field; away from home; away; out; at work. *En pleine —, en rase —,* in the open fields *or* country, in the plain. *La — de ...,* the country around ...; the campaign *or* expedition to ..., the ... campaign; the voyage to ... *La — de Rome,* Campagna di Roma. *Battre la —,* to scour the country; to beat about the bush; to ramble, to rove; to speak at random; to talk nonsense; to wander from the subject; to be deranged; to be delirious, to wander, to rave. *Entrer en —,* to take the field. *Être à la —,* to be in the country. *Être en —,* to be in the field; to be from home; to be at work. *Mettre en —,* to bring into the field; to set (...) to work; to send on the search. *Se mettre en —,* to take the field; to set out on an (*or* o.'s) expedition; to set out; to set (oneself) to work; to go out on the search. *Tenir la —,* to keep the field
†**Campagnol,** *s.m.* (*zool.*) vole; field-vole, short-tailed field-mouse, meadow-mouse. — *volant,* bristly bat (*of Senegal*)
Campan, *s.m.* Campan marble
Campane, *s.f.* (*arch.*) bell; (*sculp.*, &c.) ornament with fringe and tassels; fringe, tuft; (*bot.*) campana, pasque-flower
Campanelle, Campanette, *s.f.* (*bot.*) bell-flower, Canterbury-bell
Campaniforme, *adj.* (*bot.*) campaniform, bell-shaped
Campanile, *s.m.* (*arch.*) campanile, bell-tower
Campanule, *s.f.* (*bot.*) campanula, bell-flower
Campanulé, e, *adj.* (*bot.*) campanulate, bell-shaped
Campé, e, *part. adj.* encamped, &c. (*V.* **Camper**); situated; firm; standing bolt upright. *Être bien —,* (*pers.*) to have a firm footing *or* a good standing; to stand well on o.'s stumps, to have a good pair of legs; (*ironically*) to be in a fine plight, to be in a pretty pickle
Campêche (Bois de), *s.m.* logwood, Campeachy wood
Campement, *s.m.* encampment; camping; camp
Camper, *v.n.a.* to encamp; to camp; to seat; to put, to place; to clap; to thrust; to give; to fix; to stick. — *là,* to leave in the lurch, to leave
Se —, *v.r.* to encamp; to place *or* put *or* seat *or* &c. oneself; to give each other; to stand, to squar
Camphène, *s.m.* (*chem.*) camphene
Camphine, *s.f.* (*chem.*) camphine
Camphogène, *s.m.* (*chem.*) camphogen
Camphorate, *s.m.* (*chem.*) camphorate
Camphorique, *adj.* (*chem.*) camphoric
Camphre, *s.m.* camphor; (*pop.*) rough brandy
Camphrée, *s.f.* (*bot.*) camphorosma, stinking ground-pine
Camphrer, *v.a.* to camphorate
Camphrier, *s.m.* (*bot.*) camphor-tree; (*pop.*) publican; dram-shop; brandy-drinker
Campine, *s.f.* fine fat pullet
Campos, *s.m.* holiday; rest, relaxation
Camsin, *s.m. V.* **Kamsin**
Camus, e, *adj.* flat; flat-nosed; balked, disappointed; abashed, looking very small; astonished, dumbfounded. *La —e,* (*pop.*) Death, grim Death
Camuson, *s.f.* flat-nosed girl
Canadien, ne, *adj. s.* Canadian
†**Canaille,** *s.f.* rabble, mob, blackguards, roughs, cads; scoundrel, villain, vile wretch, blackguard; brats; — *adj.* blackguardly, blackguard, coarse, low, vulgar
Canal, *s.m.* canal; channel; strait; water-pipe,

pipe, tube; duct; gutter; drain; flue; (*of mills*) water-course, course; (*fig.*) way, means, medium, channel. *Faire* —, (*nav.*) to cross a channel; to lose sight of the land
Canalicule, *s.m.* small canal *or* channel
Canaliculé, e, *adj.* (*nat. hist.*) canaliculate
Canalisable, *adj.* canalizable
Canalisation, *s.f.* canalization
Canaliser, *v.a.* to canalize
Canamelle, *s.f.* (*bot.*) sugar-cane, reed
Cananéen, ne, *adj. s.* Cananean (*of Cana*)
Canapé, *s.m.* sofa
Canard, *s.m.* duck, drake; hen-pecked husband; printed account of an accident or murder or &c. cried and sold in the streets, broadside; false news, hoax; false note, quack; bit of sugar dipped in brandy or coffee; —, *m.*, **e,** *f.*, *adj.* sinking (*wood*); pitching (*ship*). *Chien* —, water-spaniel. — *privé*, tame duck; (*pers.*) decoy
Canardeau, *s.m.* duckling, young duck
Canarder, *v.a.* to fire at, to shoot (*from under cover*); to hoax, to humbug, to gammon; — *v.n.* to make a quack, to make quacks, to quack (*in music*); (*nav.*) to pitch
Canarderie, *s.f.* duck-yard, duck-house
Canardier, *s.m.* wild-duck shooter; hoaxer; news-writer, penny-a-liner, journalist; news-monger, news-crier
Canardière, *s.f.* place for catching wild ducks, decoy-pond, decoy; duck-pond; duck-gun; (*fort.*) loophole [flat, muff
Canari, *s.m.* canary, canary-bird; simpleton,
Canarien, ne, *adj. s.* Canary, Canarian, Can-
Canarine, *s.f.* (*bot.*) Canary-plant [arese
Canasse, Canastre, *s.m.* tea-canister, canister; canaster (*tobacco*); tobacco-box
Cancan, *s.m.* tittle-tattle; gossip; backbiting, scandal, slander; piece of scandal, scandalous story; tale-bearing; cancan (*vulgar dance*); (*obsolete*) noise, much ado about nothing
Cancaner, *v.n.* to tattle, to gossip; to talk scandal, to spread scandalous stories; to dance the cancan
Cancani-er, ère, Cancaneu-r, se, *adj. s.* gossiping, fond of gossip *or* of scandal, babbling, blabbing; lover of tittle-tattle, gossip, blab, tale-bearer; dancer of the cancan
Cancer, *s.m.* (*med., astr.*) cancer
Cancéreu-x, se, *adj.* (*med.*) cancerous
Cancériforme, *adj.* (*med.*) canceriform
Canche, *s.f.* (*bot.*) hair-grass
Cancre, *s.m.* crab, crab-fish; dunce, lazy fellow, slow boy, backward boy; miser; miserable creature, poor wretch, good-for-nothing fellow
Cancrelas, Cancrelat, *s.m.* kakerlac, American cockroach
Cancriforme, *adj.* (*zool.*) cancriform
Candélabre, *s.m.* candelabrum, candlestick; lamp-post; street-lamp, lamp; (*fig.*) luminary
Candelette, *s.f.* (*nav.*) fore-tackle [ness; purity
Candeur, *s.f.* candour, frankness, ingenuous-
Candi, e, *adj.m.f.*, *s.m.* candied; candy
Candidat, e, *s.m.f.* candidate [putting up, canvass
Candidature, *s.f.* candidature, candidateship,
Candide, *adj.* candid, frank, ingenuous, fair, open, sincere; pure
Candidement, *adv.* candidly, frankly, ingenuously, fairly, openly, sincerely; purely
Candiote, *s.m.f. adj.* Candian, Candiot, Candiote; — *s.f.* candiote (*dance, tune*) [to candy
Candir, *v.a.n.*, **Se** —, *v.r.* to candy. *Faire* —,
Candisation, *s.f.* candying [pan
Candissoire, *s.f.* candying-pan, preserving-
Candite, *s.f.* (*min.*) candite
Candjiar, *s.m.* *V.* **Kandjiar** [*v.n.*
Cane, *s.f.* duck (*female*). *Faire la* —, *V.* **Caner,**
Canéficier, *s.m.* (*bot.*) cassia-tree
Canelle, *s.f.* (*bad spelling for* **Cannelle**)
Canepetière, *s.f.* (*bird*) little bustard
Canéphore, *s.f.* (*Gr. antiquity, arch.*) canephore (*basket-bearer*)
Canepin, *s.m.* outer lamb-skin, kid-skin
Caner, *v.n.* (*pop.*) to shirk danger, to shirk it, to funk, to show the white feather, to run away; to cack; — *v.a.* to shirk; to leave undone
Canescent, e, *adj.* canescent
Canesou, *s.m.* *V.* **Canezou**
Caneter, *v.n.* (*old*) to waddle; to chatter
Caneton, *s.m.* duckling (*male*); (*cook.*) young duck, half-grown duck, duckling
Canette, *s.f.* duckling (*female*); pint-bottle, pint-jug, jug, pint (*of beer*); tap; (*tech.*) spindle, bobbin; (*her.*) bird without feathers; duck without legs or beak [plan, outlines; subject
Canevas, *s.m.* canvas; sketch, groundwork,
Caneveau, *s.m.* sail-cloth
Canevette, *s.f.* (*nav.*) liquor-case, cellaret
Canezou, *s.m.* (*woman's*) jacket, canezou
Cange, *s.f.* (kind of light boat, on the Nile)
Cangette, *s.f.* (*com.*) coarse serge
Cangue, *s.f.* (*in China*) cang, canque, kea (*kind*
Caniche, *s.m.* poodle; water-spaniel [*of pillory*)
Canicide, *s.m.* (*jest.*) canicide
Caniculaire, *adj.* canicular; excessive (*heat*). *Jours* —*s*, dog-days [cula, dog-star
Canicule, *s.f.* dog-days; (*astr.*) canicule, cani-
Canif, *s.m.* penknife. *Donner un coup de* — *dans un* (or *le*) *contrat*, to break a (*or* the) contract, to commit an infidelity, to be unfaithful; to break o.'s marriage vow
†**Canillée,** *s.f.* (*bot.*) duck-weed
Canin, e, *adj.m.f.* canine; ravenous; — *s.f.* canine tooth; (*of animals*) fang, tusk. *Lettre* —*e*, canine letter (*the letter* r). *Rire* or *ris* —, grin, sneer [turning white or grey
Canitie, *s.f.* whiteness *or* hoariness (*of the hair*),
Caniveau, *s.m.* kennel-stone; largest kind of paving-stone; drain, sewer; gutter
Canivet (Madame), *s.f.* (*counter-jumpers'*
Canjare, *s.m.* *V.* **Kangiar** [*slang*) lady Quiz
Canna, *s.f.* (*bot.*) canna, Indian shot, shot
Cannage, *s.m.* measuring by the cane
Cannaie, *s.f.* cane-brake *or* field
Cannamelle, *s.f.* *V.* **Canamelle**
Canne, *s.f.* cane; stick; walking-stick; single-stick; rod; tube (*for blowing glass, &c.*); pipe; (*literary slang*) dismissal, sack, thanks for o.'s services. — *à épée*, sword-stick. — *à pêche*, fishing-rod. — *à vent*, air-cane. — *à sucre*, sugar-cane. *Sucre de* —, cane-sugar. *La* — *à la main*, (*fig.*) idly; quietly, coolly, in an off-
Canneberge, *s.f.* cranberry [hand manner
Cannel (Charbon-), *s.m.* cannel-coal
Cannelas, *s.m.* cinnamon sugar-plum
Cannelé, *s.m.* stout silk, gros grain
Canneler, *v.a.* to channel; to flute; to reed; to groove; to rifle
Cannelle, *s.f.* cinnamon; tap; eye-groove (*of a needle*). — *blanche*, (*bot., pharm.*) canella. *En* —, (*fig., fam.*) in *or* to pieces
Cannellier, *s.m.* (*bot.*) cinnamon-tree
Cannelon, *s.m.* ice-mould, jelly-mould, cheese-mould, &c. (*fluted*); (*cook.*) cannelon, fried puff; roll [groove
Cannelure, *s.f.* channelling; fluting; reeding;
Cannequin, *s.m.* cannequin (*cotton cloth*)
Canner, *v.a.* to measure by *or* with the cane
†**Cannetille,** *s.f.* gold *or* silver twist, bullion, purl; silver thread; brass wire; ribbon-wire, cap-wire; silk-wire; satin-wire
†**Cannetiller,** *v.a.* to adorn with gold *or* silver twist, to surround with metallic threads, to purl; to tie; to wire
Cannette, *s.f.* tap; fuze, tube; (*of needles*) eye-groove; (*of beer, and tech.*) *V.* **Canette**
Cannibale, *s.m.* cannibal, man-eater; savage, cruel man
Cannibalisme, *s.m.* cannibalism; ferocity
Cannier, *s.m.* cane-worker; walking-stick
Canole, *s.f.* (kind of pastry) [maker
Canon, *s.m.* cannon; gun; barrel; cylinder; tube; pipe; shank; key-hole; gutter; (*of bellows*) nose, nozzle; (*of horses*) canon, cannon,

cannon-bone, instep, shank-bone, shank; (*rid.*) mouthpiece; (*obsolete*) breeches lower trimming; (*obsolete*) leg (*of breeches, drawers,* &c.); (*print., mus., chron., math., a law or rule or decision, eccl., of the Mass, adject.*) canon; (*pop.*) quarter of a pint, quartern, gill. — *rayé*, rifled cannon *or* gun; rifled barrel. *A — rayé*, rifle-barrelled, rifled. — *de retraite*, (*nav.*) stern-chaser; (*mil.*) evening-gun. *Gros* —, (*print.*) canon. *Petit* —, (*print.*) two-line English
Canonial, e, *adj.* canonical; prebendal
Canonialement, *adv.* canonically
Canonicat, *s.m.* canonry; (*fig.*) sinecure
Canonicité, *s.f.* canonicity, canonicalness
Canon-ique, -iquement. *V.* page 3, § 1
Canonisation, *s.f.* canonization
Canoniser, *v.a.* to canonize; (*fig.*) to glorify
Canoniste, *s.m.* canonist
Canonnade, *s.f.* cannonade, cannonading
Canonnage, *s.m.* gunnery [tipple
Canonner, *v.a.* to cannonade; — *v.n.* (*pop.*) to
Canonnerie, *s.f.* gun-foundry
Canonneu-r, se, *s.m.f.* tippler
Canonnier, *s.m.* gunner; barrel-maker
Canonnière, *s.f.* gun-boat, gun-vessel; pop-gun; tent; tilt; drain-hole; (*obsolete*) loop-
Canot, *s.m.* boat; barge; canoe [hole (*in a wall*)
Canotage, *s.m.* boating, aquatics
Canoti-er, ère, *s.m.f.* rower; oarsman; barge-man; boat-keeper, boatman, boatwoman
Cantabile, *s.m.* (*mus.*) cantabile, graceful air,
Cantabre, *adj. s.* Cantabrian [melody
Cantal, *s.m.* Cantal cheese
Cantalabre, *s.m.* door-case, casing
Cantalite, *s.f.* (*min.*) cantalite
Cantaloup, *s.m.* cantaloup, musk-melon; (*pop.*)
Cantate, *s.f.* (*mus.*) cantata [simpleton, flat, muff
†**Cantatille,** *s.f.* (*mus.*) cantatilla
Cantatrice, *s.f.* professional singer, singer, vocalist, cantatrice [fly
Cantharide, *s.f.* cantharis, cantharide, Spanish
Cantharider, *v.a.* (*pharm.*) to sprinkle with cantharides
Cantharidine, *s.f.* (*chem.*) cantharidine
Canthère, *s.m.* (*fish*) sea-bream
Canthus, *s.m.* (*anat.*) canthus, corner of the eye
Cantilène, *s.f.* (*mus.*) cantilena, melody
Cantine, *s.f.* bottle-case; (*mil.*) canteen
Cantini-er, ère, *s.m.f.* sutler, canteen-woman
Cantique, *s.m.* canticle, song, hymn
Canton, *s.m.* canton, district, division, part; (*admin.*) sub-district; (*her.*) canton
Cantonade, *s.f.* side-scenes (*behind the scenes*). *Parler à la* —, to speak to an actor off the stage; (*fig.*) to get no audience *or* hearers, to speak to empty benches; to talk to a post; to get no readers for o.'s books [*China*)
Cantonais, e, *adj. s.* Cantonese (*of Canton, in*
Cantonal, e, *adj.* cantonal
Cantonné, e, *adj.* (*arch., her., mil.*) cantoned
Cantonnement, *s.m.* cantonment; cantoning; district
Cantonner, *v.a.* to canton; (*obsolete*) to flank, to accompany, to surround; — *v.n.* to be cantoned, to be in cantonments. *Faire* —, to canton
Se —, *v.r.* to take up a position; to take up o.'s quarters, to fix o.'s abode; to fortify oneself
Cantonni-er, ère, *s.m.f.* road-labourer, roads-man; (*rail.*) plate-layer; signal-man *or* woman; gate-keeper; — *s.f.* valance; iron binding, corner-iron, angle-iron; (*nav.*) tackle-hook
Canule, *s.f.* injection-pipe; tap; pipe, tube; (*surg.*) canula, pipe; (*pers., fam.*) bore, plague
Canulé, e, *adj.* pipe-shaped, pipe-like, tubular
Canuler, *v.a.* (*fam.*) to bore, to plague
Canut, *s.m.* silk-weaver (*at Lyons*)
Canzone, *s.f.* (*poet., mus.*) canzone
Canzonette, *s.f.* (*poet., mus.*) canzonet
Caolin, *s.m.* *V.* **Kaolin**
Caouane, *s.f.* (*zool.*) loggerhead turtle [oucine
Caoutchine, *s.f.* (*chem.*) caoutchine, caoutch-
Caoutchouc, *s.m.* caoutchouc, indiarubber; indiarubber band *or* &c., elastic band *or* &c., hat-guard, overshoe [caoutchouc
Caoutchouter, *v.a.* to work in *or* cover with
Cap, *s.m.* cape, headland, foreland; head (*of a ship*); (*obsolete*) head *or* face (*of a person*). *De pied en* —, cap-a-pie, from head to foot. *Mettre* or *porter le* — *à* (or *sur*), (*nav.*) to steer *or* bear towards. — **-de-more,** *adj.* black-headed
Capable, *adj.* capable; able; skilful; clever; qualified; fit, competent, efficient; sufficient, enough; calculated; apt; likely, likely enough; just the man (to); assuming; knowing. *Prendre un air* —, to put on a wise look, to take *or* have a knowing
Capablement, *adv.* ably, with ability [look
Capacité, *s.f.* capacity; capaciousness; size; extent; reach; capability; ability; skill, talent; competency; qualification; able man, competent *or* qualified person; (*nav.*) bulk; (*nav.*) burden, tonnage [eunuch
Capade, *s.f.* (*in hat-making*) bat; — *s.m.* black
Caparaçon, *s.m.* caparison, trappings
Caparaçonner, *v.a.* to caparison
Caparasse, *s.f.* (*nav.*) overcoat, overall
Cape, *s.f.* cloak with a hood; riding-hood; hood; cloak; (*nav.*) try-sail; (*of anchors*) stock. *Sous* —, clandestinely; by stealth; on the sly, slily; in o.'s sleeve. *N'avoir que la — et l'épée*, to have nothing but o.'s title; to be worth nothing. *Être à la* —, (*nav.*) to try, to be lying to. *Mettre à la* —, (*nav.*) to bring to
Capéer, Capeyer, *v.n.* (*nav.*) to try, to lie to
Capel, *s.m.* (*fish*) capelin, caplin, capelan
Capelan, *s.m.* scrubby parson; male glow-worm; (*fish*) capelin, caplin, capelan
Capelet, *s.m.* (*vet.*) capellet
Capeline, *s.f.* hood; (*of armour*) cappeline
Capendu, *s.m.* capendu (*kind of apple*)
Caperon, *s.m.* *V.* **Capron**
Capétien, ne, *adj.*, **Capétien,** *s.m.* Capetian
Capharnaüm, *s.m.* place of confusion, place of disorder and debauchery, Noah's ark, Babel, bear-garden, chaos, jumble, litter, huddle, omnium gatherum [agassi (*keeper of the seraglio*)
Capi-aga, Capi-agassi, *s.m.* capi-aga, capi-
Capidgi, Capigi, *s.m.* capigi, porter (*of the seraglio*). — *-bachi*, head porter (*of ditto*); executioner
Capillaire, *adj.* capillary, hair-shaped; — *s.m.* (*anat.*) capillary; (*bot.*) maiden-hair. *Sirop de* —, capillaire [attraction
Capillarité, *s.f.* (*phys.*) capillarity; capillary
Capilotade, *s.f.* hash, mince-meat
Capitaine, *s.m.* captain; master; chief; chieftain. — *des chasses*, ranger. — *de pavillon*, flag-captain, captain of a flag-ship. — *de vaisseau*, captain of a man-of-war, captain R.N. — *de navire*, captain *or* master of a merchant-ship. — *de port*, harbour-master. — *au long cours*, captain of a trading vessel going to foreign parts. *Grade de* —, captaincy [gership
Capitainerie, *s.f.* captaincy; captainry; ran-
Capitainesse, *s.f.* (*anc. nav.*) commodore-ship, commodore (*galley*)
Capital, e, *adj.* capital; principal, chief, main, leading, great, considerable, important; deadly, mortal [fund; cash
Capital, *s.m.* main point; (*com.*) capital; stock;
Capitale, *s.f.* capital (*city, letter*)
Capitalement, *adv.* capitally
Capitalisable, *adj.* capitalizable
Capitalisation, *s.f.* capitalization [capitalized
Capitaliser, *v.a.* to capitalize. *Se* —, to be
Capitaliste, *s.m.f.* capitalist; fund-holder
Capitan, *s.m.* bully, hector; swaggerer, boaster; capitan (*Turkish flag-ship*). — *-pacha*, capitan-pasha, capudan-pasha, captain-pasha (*Turkish high-admiral, Turkish flag-ship*) [galley
Capitane, *s.f.*, *adj.f.* *Galère* —, —, admiral's
Capitation, *s.f.* poll-tax, capitation
Capité, e, *adj.* (*nat. hist.*) capitate
Capitellé, e, *adj.* (*nat. hist.*) capitellate
Capiteu-x, se, *adj.* (*of wines,* &c.) heady, strong

Capitiluve, *s.m.* (*med.*) head-bath
Capitole, *s.m.* capitol; town-hall
Capitolin, e, *adj.* capitoline [strawberry
Capiton, *s.m.* (*com.*) cappadine; (*hort.*) large
Capitonner, *v.a.* to stuff, to pad (with cappadine)
Capitoul, *s.m.* (*old*) capitoul (*mayor, alderman, of Toulouse*)
Capitoulat, *s.m.* (*old*) mayoralty, aldermanship (*of Toulouse*); ward (*of Toulouse*)
Capitulaire, *adj.m.f., s.m.* capitular, capitulary
Capitulairement, *adv.* capitularly
Capitulant, *adj.m.* having a vote in a chapter; (*of Swiss cantons, formerly*) furnishing mercenary troops; — *s.m.* (*pers.*) capitulary
Capitulation, *s.f.* capitulation; convention, treaty; compromise
Capitule, *s.m.* (*bot.*) capitulum; (*lit.*) capitule
Capitulé, e, *adj.* (*bot.*) in a capitulum; (*of Swiss troops, formerly*) subsidized, hired, mercenary
Capituler, *v.n.* to capitulate; to compound
Capivard, Capiverd, Capivert, *s.m. V.*
Caplan, *s.m. V.* **Capelan** [**Cabiai**
Capoc, *s.m.* capoc (*Indian cotton-wool*)
Capon, ne, *s.m.f.* coward; sculker; sneak; hypocrite; fawner; cunning fellow; money-lender; — *s.m.* (*nav.*) cat; — *adj.m.f.* cowardly; sculking; sneaking; hypocritical; fawning; cunning, clever
Caponner, *v.n.* to show oneself a coward, to show the white feather, to funk; to shirk it; to sculk away; to sneak; to deal cunningly; — *v.a.* to cajole, to fawn upon; (*nav.*) to cat (*the anchor*) [covered lodgment; rifle-pit
Caponnière, *s.f.* (*fort.*) caponier, caponniere,
Caporal, *s.m.* corporal; shag (*tobacco*). — *de consigne*, senior corporal (*of a guard*). — *de pose*, junior corporal (*of a guard*). *Le petit* —, (*Fr. hist.*) Napoleon I. (*he was so nicknamed familiarly by his soldiers*) [bed; (*nav.*) hood
Capot, *s.m.* (*at play*) capot; (*hort.*) small hot-
Capot, *adj.* (*at play*) capot, having lost all the tricks; beaten hollow; (*fig.*) abashed, confused, foolish, sheepish. *Être* —, to have lost all the tricks. *Demeurer* or *être* —, (*fig.*) to be balked; to look foolish; to stand confounded. *Faire* —, (*at play*) to capot, to win all the tricks from; to beat hollow, to beat out and out; (*nav.*) to upset, to capsize, to cant
Capote, *s.f.* cloak with a hood; cloak; capote (*obsolete*); long coat, great-coat, coat; hood; drawn bonnet, close bonnet, bonnet; (*of carriages*) head, hood; (*of chimneys*) top-pipe; (*at play*) capot
Capoter, *v.n.* (*nav.*) to upset, to capsize, to cant
Capouan, e, *adj. s.* Capuan (*of Capua*) [weed
Capraire, *s.f.* (*bot.*) capraria, goat-weed, sweet-
Câpre, *s.f.* (*bot.*) caper
Capricant, e, *adj. V.* **Caprisant**
Caprice, *s.m.* caprice, whim, freak; fit, start; oddness, oddity; irregularity; peculiarity; fancy, liking; person one has taken a fancy to. *Faire un* —, to win a heart, to take someone's fancy [sically
Capricieusement, *adv.* capriciously, whim-
Capricieu-x, se, *adj.* capricious, whimsical, freakish; skittish
Capricorne, *s.m.* (*astr.*) capricorn; (*zool.*) capricorn, capricorn-beetle, goat-chafer
Câprier, *s.m.* (*bot.*) caper-bush, caper-tree
Câprière, *s.f.* caper-plantation; caper-box
Caprification, *s.f.* caprification
Caprifiguier, *s.m.* wild fig-tree, goat-fig
Caprin, e, *adj.* caprine
Capripède, *adj.m.f., s.m.* capriped
Caprique, *adj.* (*chem.*) capric [(*med.*) caprizant
Caprisant, e, *adj.* leaping; uneven; freakish;
Capromys, *s.m.* (*zool.*) capromys, hog-rat
Capron, *s.m.* hautboy (*large strawberry*)
Capronier, *s.m.* hautboy strawberry-plant
Capselle, *s.f.* (*bot.*) cassweed
Capsulaire, *adj.* capsular, capsulary
Capsule, *s.f.* capsule; percussion-cap, cap
Capsulifère, *adj.* (*nat. hist.*) capsuliferous
Captal, *s.m.* (*Fr. hist.*) lord, chief
Captale, *s.f.* (*feud.*) lady
Capta-teur, trice, *s.m.f.* (*law*) inveigler
Captation, *s.f.* (*law*) undue influence, inveigling, gaining insidiously; (*fig.*) captation
Captatoire, *adj.* (*law*) inveigling; legacy-hunting; inveigled, obtained by the exercise of undue influence
Capter, *v.a.* to inveigle; to exercise undue influence over; to gain *or* win insidiously; to get by bribery; to gain over unfairly; to seduce; to attract; to captivate; to win, to gain; to court; to curry; to coax; to bribe; to take by surprise
Capteur, *s.m.* captor; — *adj.m.* capturing
Captieusement, *adv.* captiously
Captieu-x, se, *adj.* captious [prisoner
Capti-f, ve, *adj. s.* captive; under restraint;
Captiver, *v.a.* to captivate; to charm; to enslave; to keep a prisoner; to confine; to subdue, to bring under subjection [win
Se —, *v.r.* to lay a restraint upon oneself; to
Captiverie, *s.f.* barracoon
Captivité, *s.f.* captivity, bondage [catch, take
Capture, *s.f.* capture; seizure; prize; booty;
Capturer, *v.a.* to capture; to seize; to apprehend, to arrest; to catch
Captureur, *s.m.* captor; — *adj.m.* capturing
Capuce, *s.m.*, **Capuche,** *s.f.*, **Capuchon,** *s.m.* cowl; hood; bonnet; veranda, verandah; (*nav.*) whipping; hood
Capuchonné, e, *adj.* cowled; hooded
Capuchonner, *v.n.* (*rid.*) to arch the neck
Capucin, *s.m.* capuchin friar, capuchin; (*fig.*) bigot; (*zool.*) capuchin (*pigeon*); capuchin-monkey, capuchin. —*s de cartes*, monks made in bent cards. *Tomber comme des —s de cartes*, to tumble over one another [discourse, cant
Capucinade, *s.f.* wretched sermon; canting
Capucine, *s.f.* capuchin nun; (*bot.*) nasturtium, Indian cress; (*of guns, muskets*) band; (*nav.*) standard; — *adj.* capucine (*colour*). *Câpre* —, pickled nasturtium. *Première* —, (*mil.*) upper band. *Jusqu'à la troisième* —, (*soldiers' slang*) completely, outright, dead; over head and ears
Capucinière, *s.f.* (*jest.*) capuchin-friary,
Capulet, *s.m.* cap [monks' house; bigoted house
Caput-mortuum, *s.m.* caput-mortuum
Capvirade, *s.f.* (*agr.*) headland, head ridge, fur-
Capybara, *s.m. V.* **Cabiai** [row-ends
Caquage, *s.m.* barrelling; curing
Caque, *s.f.* keg, barrel, cran; octave-cask (*of Champagne wine*). *La — sent toujours le hareng*, (*Proverb*) what is bred in the bone will never out of the flesh [to cack
Caquer, *v.a.* to barrel; to cure; — *v.n.* (*pop.*)
Caquet, *s.m.* cackle; prattle, talk; tongue; tone; **—s,** *pl.* tittle-tattle, gossip, scandal. **—-bon-bec,** *s.f.* magpie, mag; gossip; chatterbox. *Rabaisser* (or *Rabattre*) *le* —, to make (*one*) lower his tone, to silence, to humble the pride (of)
Caquetage, *s.m.*, **Caqueterie,** *s.f* cackling; prattling, chattering, talk; tittle-tattle, gossip-
Caquète, *s.f V.* **Caquette** [ing, scandal
Caqueter, *v.n.* to cackle; to prattle, to chatter, to talk; to gossip [gossip
Caqueteu-r, se, *s.m.f.* prattler, chatterer,
Caquetoire, *s.f.* (*obsolete*) *V.* **Chauffeuse**
Caquette, *s.f.* fish-tub
Caqueu-r, se, *s.m.f.* fish-curer
Caqueu-x, se, *s.m.f.* Breton pariah
Car, *conj. s.m.* for, because, as
Caraba, *s.m.* cashew-nut oil
Carabas, *s.m.* (*pop.*) old lumber-tub (*heavy old*
Carabe, *s.m.* beetle [*carriage*); nabob, warm man
Carabé, *s.m.* amber
Carabin, *s.m.* saw-bones, medical student; (*of gloves*) quirk; (*old*) skirmisher
Carabinade, *s.f.* discharge of carbines
Carabinage, *s.m.* rifling (*of gun-barrels*)

Carabine, *s.f.* rifle; (*obsolete for* "mousqueton") carbine, carabine; (*pers.*) young sawbones' sweetheart (*pop.*)

Carabiné, e, *adj.* rifled; (*of wind*) stiff; (*pop.*) strong, vigorous, sound; hard to swallow; capital, first-rate, crack [to play low

Carabiner, *v.a.* to rifle; — *v.n.* to skirmish;

Carabineur, *s.m.* rifler (*of gun-barrels*)

Carabinier, *s.m.* carabinier; rifleman

Caracal, *s.m.* (*zool.*) caracal

Caracara, *s.m.* (*zool.*) caracara, caracara eagle

Caraco, *s.m.* (*woman's*) jacket

Caracol, *s.m.* (*arch.*) *En* —, winding

Caracole, *s.f.* (*rid.*) circling, caracole; (*fam.*) gambol. *Escalier en* —, (*arch.*) caracole, caracol, winding *or* spiral staircase [to caracole

Caracoler, *v.n.* (*rid.*) to wheel about, to circle,

Caracoli, *s.m.* caracoli (*alloy*); caracoli jewel

Caracouler, *v.n.* to coo (*as pigeons*)

Caractère, *s.m.* character; handwriting; mark; sign; figure; letter; stamp; temper, disposition, humour, nature; manners; firmness; constancy; decision, resolution; spirit; expression; style; capacity; dignity; quality; authority; characteristic; symptom; spell, charm; effect; type, print; (*arith.*) digit. *Avoir le — bien* (or *mal*) *fait*, to be good (*or* ill) tempered

Caractériser, *v.a.* to characterize; to describe; to define; to mark out, to mark; to distinguish; to be the distinguishing feature *or* the mark *or* the sign of, to be peculiar to

Se —, *v.r.* to assume a character; to show o.'s character; to appear such as one is; to be defined *or* distinguished

Caractéristique, *adj.m.f.*, *s.f.* characteristic

Carafe, *s.f.* water-bottle, bottle; decanter

Carafon, *s.m.* liquor-bottle, small bottle *or* decanter, small flagon; half-pint bottle; cooler,

Caragan, *s.m.* (*bot.*) caragana [ice-pail

†Caragne, *s.f. adj.* (*com.*) caranna (*aromatic resin*) [Brazil cabbage

Caraïbe, *s.m.f.adj.* Carib, Caribbee. *Chou* —,

Caraïpé, *s.m.* (*bot.*) carapa

Caraïsme, *s.m.* Caraism (*Jewish doctrine*)

Caraïte, *s.m.f.* Caraite (*Jewish sectarian*)

Carambolage, *s.m.* (*at billiards*) cannon; cannoning; (*fig.*) rebound, double stroke *or* hit, killing two birds with one stone; (*pop.*) general affray *or* tumble

Carambole, *s.f.* (*at billiards*) red ball; (*game*) carambole; (*bot.*) carambola (*fruit*)

Caramboler, *v.n.* (*at billiards*) to cannon, to make *or* strike a cannon; (*fig.*) to rebound; to make a double hit, to kill two birds with one stone; — *v.a.n.* (*pop.*) to knock about, to knock right and left, to lay about; to tumble down; to rebound against; to topple over

Caramboleur, *s.m.* (*pers.*) good cannon-striker (*billiard-player*) [wood-sorrel

Carambolier, *s.m.* (*bot.*) averrhoa, East India

Caramel, *s.m.* caramel, burnt sugar, colouring, browning; burnt-sugar sweet, hard-bake. — *au beurre*, butter-scotch; toffee

Caramélisation, *s.f.* turning into caramel; mixing *or* colouring *or* sweetening with caramel

Caraméliser, *v.a.* to turn into caramel; to put caramel in, to colour *or* sweeten with

Se —, *v.r.* to turn into caramel [caramel

Caramoussal, *s.m.* (*nav.*) caramoussal (*Turkish merchantman*)

Caranate, *s.f.* small shrimp

Carangue, *s.f. V.* **Calangue;** (*fish*) *V.* **Caranx**

Caranguer, *v.n.* (*nav.*) to tack about without making way [erel, bastard mackerel

Caranx, *s.m.* (*fish*) caranx, scad, horse-mack-

Carapa, *s.m. Huile de* —, oil of carapa

Carapace, *s.f.* carapace, calipash, (upper) shell (*of a tortoise, turtle, crab,* &c.)

Caraque, *s.m.* cacao (cocoa) of Caracas (*or* Caraccas), Caracas cocoa, best cocoa; — *s.f.* (*nav.*) carack (*ship*)

Carat, *s.m.* carat; small diamond (*or* diamonds) [sold by weight], bort; (*fig.*) tinsel

Carature, *s.f.* mixture of gold with silver and copper

Caravane, *s.f.* caravan; party, body, troop, band; host; expedition; prank; love adventure. *Faire ses* —, to lead a wild life

Caravaneur, *s.m.* (*nav.*) Levant coaster

Caravanier, *s.m.* caravaneer

Caravaniste, *s.m.f.* caravanist [vansary

†Caravansérail, Caravansérai, *s.m.* cara-

Caravanséraskier, *s.m.* caravanseraskier (*overseer of a caravansary*)

Caravelle, *s.f.* (*nav.*) caravel, carvel (*ship, boat*)

Carbatine, *s.f.* green skin; green hide

Carbazotate, *s.m.* (*chem.*) carbazotate

Carbazotique, *adj.* (*chem.*) carbazotic

Carbet, *s.m.* large common cabin; (*nav.*) shed

Carbolique, *adj.* (*chem.*) carbolic

Carboliser, *v.a.* (*chem.*) to carbolize [broil

Carbonade, *s.f.* (*cook.*) carbonade, carbonado,

Carbonarisme, *s.m.* carbonarism

Carbonaro (*pl.* **Carbonari**), *s.m.* carbonaro, (*pl.* carbonari)

Carbonate, *s.m.* (*chem.*) carbonate

Carbonaté, e, *adj.* (*chem.*) carbonated

Carboncle, *s.m.* carbuncle

Carbone, *s.m.* (*chem.*) carbon

Carboné, e, *adj.* carbonated; carburetted

Carboneu-x, se, *adj.* (*chem.*) carbonous [coal

Carbonifère, *adj.* carboniferous; conveying

Carbonique, *adj.* (*chem.*) carbonic

Carbonisation, *s.f.* carbonization

Carboniser, *v.a.* to carbonize; to char

Se —, *v.r.* to be carbonized; to become charred

Carbonnade, *s.f. V.* **Carbonade**

†Carbouille, *s.f.* (*agr.*) brown rust, bunt

Carburation, *s.f.* (*metal.*) carbonization

Carbure, *s.m.* (*chem.*) carbide, carburet

Carburé, e, *adj.* (*chem.*) carburetted

†Carcagno, *s.m.* (*pop.*) usurer

†Carcailler, *v.n. V.* **Courcailler**

Carcajou, *s.m.* (*zool.*) carcajou (*American badger*)

Carcan, *s.m.* iron collar, pillory; (*for swine*) yoke; (*of jewels*) carcanet; (*fam.*) jade

Carcasse, *s.f.* carcass, carcase; body; skeleton; bones; shell; framework, frame; shape; fish-basket; (*artil.*) carcass, fire-ball

Carcassonnais, e, *adj. s.* of Carcassonne; [native of ditto

Carcel, *s.f.* Carcel lamp

Carcere-duro, *s.m.* (*Italian*) duress, close imprisonment

Carcinolog-ie, -ique, -iste. *V.* page 3, § 1

Carcinomateu-x, se, *adj.* (*med.*) carcinomatous

Carcinome, *s.m.* (*med*) carcinoma

Cardage, *s.m.* carding

Cardamine, *s.f.* (*bot*) cardamine

Cardamome, *s.m.* (*bot.*) cardamom

Carde, *s.f.* card; carding-machine; teasel-frame; (*bot.*) chard (*foot-stalk, midrib*). — **-poirée,** *s.f.* (*bot.*) chard, white beet, Sicilian beet [carded) at a time

Cardée, *s.f.* quantity carded (*or* that can be

Carder, *v.a.* to card. *Se* —, to be carded

Cardère, *s.f.* (*bot.*) teasel, teazel, teazle

Carderie, *s.f.* carding-house; card-manufactory

Cardeu-r, se, *s.m.f.* carder

Cardia, *s.m.* (*anat.*) cardia

Cardiacé, e, *adj.* heart-shaped; **— es,** *s.f.pl.* (*zool.*) cardiaceæ, heart-shells

Cardiaire, *adj.* relating to the heart; in the heart; bred in the heart

Cardiaire, *s.f.* (*bot*) *V.* **Cardère**

Cardialgie, *s.f.* (*med.*) cardialgia, cardialgy, cardiac passion, heartburn

Cardialgique, *adj.* (*med.*) cardialgic

Cardiaque, *adj.m.f.*, *s.m* (*anat., med.*) cardiac

Cardier, *s.m.* wool-card maker

Cardinal, e, *adj.* cardinal; chief, principal, first; — *s.m.* cardinal; cardinal-bird, cardinal-finch, red bird; — *s.f.* (*bot.*) cardinal-flower

Cardinalat, *s.m.* cardinalate, cardinalship

Cardinaliser, *v.a.* to paint red, to redden

Se —, *v.r.* to turn red, to redden, to blush, to flush

Cardinaliste, *s.m.f.* (*Fr. hist.*) cardinalist
Cardine, *s.f.* (*fish*) whiff [*V.* page 3, § 1
Cardio-graphie, -logie, -pathie, -tomie.
Cardite, *s.f.* (*med.*) carditis; (*shell*) cardite,
Carditique, *adj.* (*med.*) carditic [heart-shell
Cardon, *s.m.* (*bot.*) cardoon; (*fish.*) shrimp
Cardonnette, *s.f.* *V.* **Chardonnette**
Care, *s.f.* (*pop.*) hiding-place. *Vol à la* —, shoplifting. *Voleur* (m., *-euse*, f.) *à la* —, shoplifter
Carême, *s.m.* Lent; Lent-sermons; (*proper name*) Carême (*a famous cook*). — *-prenant*, Shrovetide; Shrove-Tuesday; carnival; Shrovetide revellers, mask; masker; guy. *Face de* —, pale face, wan face. *Faire* —, to keep Lent
Carénage, *s.m.* (*nav.*) careening; careenage
Carence, *s.f.* absence of assets, insolvency
Carène, *s.f.* (*nav.*) keel, bottom; careening; (*bot.*) carina, keel. *Demi* —, (*nav.*) boot-topping, parliament-heel. *En* —, keel-shaped; being careened, careening, undergoing careening. *Mettre en* —, to careen
Caréné, e, *part. adj.* (*nav.*) careened; — *adj.* (*bot.* carinate, carinated, keel-shaped
Caréner, *v.a.* (*nav.*) to careen
Caressant, e, *part. adj.* caressing; endearing; fond, affectionate, tender, kind; fawning; wanton
Caresse, *s.f.* caress; endearment; fondness; kindness; kind words; fawning; smile (*of Fortune*); stroking, pat, chuck
Caresser, *v.a.n.* to caress; to fondle; to pamper; to make much of; to fawn upon; to fawn; to flatter; to cajole, to coax, to wheedle; to stroke; to pat; to chuck; to humour; to indulge, to foster, to cherish; to polish, to finish off, to labour; to indicate, to mark, to show; to sweeten [*Fil de* —, rope-yarn
Caret, *s.m.* hawkbill turtle; rope-maker's reel.
Careu-r, se, *s.m.f.* shoplifter
Carex, *s.m.* (*bot.*) carex, sedge
Cargaison, *s.f.* cargo, freight; ship-load;
Cargue, *s.f.* (*nav.*) brail [lading; bill of lading
Carguer, *v.a.* (*nav.*) to brail up, to clue up, to haul up, to reef; — *v.n.* (*nav.*) to heel
Cargueur, *s.m.* (*nav.*) reefer; top-block
Cari, *s.m.* (*cook.*) curry, currie
Caria, *s.m.* (*insect*) wood-fretter
Cariacou, *s.m.* (*zool.*) cariacou, Virginian deer
Cariama, *s.m.* (*bird*) cariama
Cariatide, *s.f.* caryatid, caryatis
Cariatidique, *adj.* caryatidic
Caribou, *s.m.* (*zool.*) caribou, American reindeer
Caricatural, e, *adj.* caricatural, ludicrous
Caricature, *s.f.* caricature; guy, sight
Caricaturer, *v.a.* to caricature, to ridicule
Caricaturiste, *s.m.f.* caricaturist
Carick, *s.m.* *V.* **Cari**
Carie, *s.f.* (*of bones, teeth*) caries, cariosity, rottenness, decay; (*agr., bot.*) brown rust, bunt; fire-blast [smutty
Carié, e, *adj.* carious, rotten, decayed; (*agr.*)
Carien, ne, *adj. s.* Carian [carious; (*agr.*) to smut
Carier, *v.a.* to rot, to cause to decay; to make **Se** —, *v.r.* to rot, to decay; to become carious; to be smutted *or* blighted
†**Carillon,** *s.m.* chime, peal; chimes, musical bells; ding-dong; music; jingling; noise, racket, row. *A* —, musical. *A double* (or *triple*) —, double (*or* treble) peal; (*fig.*) loudly, soundly, lustily, vigorously, violently, tremendously, with a vengeance
†**Carillonnement,** *s.m.* chiming; jingling
†**Carillonner,** *v.n.a.* to chime; to ring away; to ring; to ring a peal; to jingle; to clatter. *Fête carillonnée*, high festival, great holiday
†**Carillonneur,** *s.m.* chimer, bell-ringer, ringer;
Carinaire, *s.f.* (*mollusc*) carinaria [noisy fellow
Carine, *s.f.* (*Gr. antiquity*) weeper, mourner
Cariné, e, *adj.* *V.* **Caréné**
Carique, *s.f.* (*bot.*) carica (*wild fig*)
Carisel, *s.m.* canvas (*for wool-work or tapestry*)
Carive, *s.m.* Guinea pepper

Carlette, *s.f.* square slate [pug
Carlin, *s.m.* pug-dog; (*coin*) carline; — *adj.m.*
Carline, *s.f.* (*bot.*) carline-thistle [step
Carlingue, *s.f.* (*nav.*) carline, carling; (*of masts*)
Carl-isme, -iste. *V.* page 3, § 1
Carlock, *s.m.* (*com.*) carlock (*isinglass*)
Carlovingien, ne, *adj. s.* Carlovingian
†**Carmagnole,** *s.f.* (*obsolete*) carmagnole (*jacket; revolutionary dance and song*)
Carmantine, *s.f.* (*bot.*) justicia
Carme, *s.m.* Carmelite, white-friar; two fours
Carmeline, *s.f.* vicuna wool [(*at backgammon*)
Carmélite, *s.f.* Carmelite (nun); — *adj.* light
Carmentine, *s.f.* (*bot.*) justicia [brown
Carmin, *s.m. adj.* carmine, crimson
Carminati-f, ve, *adj.*, **Carminatif,** *s.m.* (*med.*) carminative
Carmine, *s.f.* (*chem.*) carminic acid [crimson
Carminé, e, *part. adj.* carminated; carmine,
Carminer, *v.a.* to carminate, to paint in carmine; to redden, to flush
Carnage, *s.m.* carnage, slaughter, butchery; destruction; havoc; feeding on flesh; carrion
Carnaire, *adj.* (*nat. hist.*) living on flesh. *Mouche* —, flesh-fly
Carnassi-er, ère, *adj.* carnivorous, flesh-eating; ravenous, (*pers.*) fond of meat; — *s.m.* carnivorous animal, carnivore (*pl.* carnivores *or* carnivora); — *s.f.* game-bag
Carnation, *s.f.* carnation, flesh-tint, flesh-colour; complexion; (*her.*) purple [tube, flue
Carnau, *s.m.* vent-hole, air-hole, pipe; hot-air
Carnaval, *s.m.* carnival, Shrovetide; queer-looking fellow, odd figure, guy
Carnavalesque, *adj.* of carnival
Carne, *s.f.* corner, edge; (*bad meat, fam.*) cagmag; (*pop.*) blackguard woman, bitch, hag;
Carné, e, *adj.* carnationed, flesh-coloured [jade
Carneau, *s.m.* *V.* **Carnau**
Carnèle, *s.f.* border, ring-edge (*of a coin*)
Carneler, *v.a.* (*of coins, her.*) to border
Carner, *v.n.* (*hort.*) to become flesh-coloured
Carnet, *s.m.* note-book, memorandum-book; (*com.*) book. — *d'échéances*, bill-book
Carnier, *s.m.* game-bag
Carnification, *s.f.* (*med.*) carnification
Carnifier (Se), *v.r.* (*med.*) to carnify
†**Carnillet,** *s.m.* (*bot.*) bladder-campion
Carnique, *adj.* (*geog.*) Carnic, Carnian
Carnivore, *adj.* carnivorous; — *s.m.* carnivorous animal, carnivore (*pl.* carnivores *or* car-
Carnosité, *s.f.* (*surg.*) carnosity [nivora)
†**Carogne,** *s.f.* (*pop.*) blackguard woman, bitch, jade, hag, impudent slut
Carolin, *s.m.* (*coin*) carolin
Carolin, e, *adj.* (*hist.*) of Charlemagne
Caron, *s.m.* fat rasher (*of bacon*); mixture of bar-
Caronade, *s.f.* (*artil.*) carronade [ley and wheat
Caronculaire, *adj.* caruncular
Caroncule, *s.f.* (*anat., zool., bot.*) caruncle
Caronculé, e, *adj.* carunculated
Caronculeu-x, se, *adj.* carunculous
Carotide, *adj. s.f.* (*anat.*) carotid
Carotidien, ne, *adj.* (*anat.*) carotidal
Carotique, *adj.* (*med.*) carotic
Carotte, *s.f.* carrot; (*of tobacco*) roll, twist, pig-tail; (*pop.*) chouse, trick; (*at play*) low stakes. *Tirer une* — *à* ..., to get (something) out of ..., to chouse .. out of (a thing), to screw *or* squeeze money out of ...
Carotter, *v.a.n.* to chouse, to diddle; to play low; to speculate on a small scale; to live on little, to spend little, to live low
Carotteu-r, se, Carotti-er, ère, *s.m.f.* timid player; petty jobber; (*pop.*) trickster
Caroube, *s.f.* (*bot.*) carob-bean, locust-bean, St. John's Bread
Caroubier, *s.m.* (*bot.*) carob-tree, locust-tree
Carouble, *s.f.* skeleton-key
Caroubleur, *s.m.* house-breaker
Carouge, *s.f.* (*bot.*) carob-bean; — *s.m.* carob-wood; (*bird*) crested oriole

Carousse, *s.f.* (*obsolete*) *V.* **Ripaille**
Carpe, *s.f.* (*fish*) carp; — *s.m.* (*anat.*) carpus, wrist. *Faire la — pâmée*, to pretend to faint
Carpeau, *s.m.* young carp
Carpellaire, *adj.* (*bot.*) carpellary
Carpelle, *s.m.* (*bot.*) carpel, carpellum
Carpette, *s.f.* young carp; centre-carpet, rug
Carphologie, *s.f.* (*med.*) carphology, floccillation
Carpie, *s.f.* (*cook.*) carp hash
Carpien, ne, *adj.* (*anat.*) carpal
Carpier, *s.m.*, **Carpière,** *s.f.* carp-pond
†**Carpillon,** *s.m.* young carp
Carpion, *s.m.*, **Carpione,** *s.f.* Alpine trout
Carpolithe, *s.m.* carpolite; hard concretion [(*in pears*, &c.)
Carpolog-ie, -ique. *V.* p. 3, § 1
Carquois, *s.m.* quiver
Carrare, *s.m.* Carrara marble
Carre, *s.f.* (*of a hat*) top of the crown, tip; (*of a coat*) back; (*of a boot*) toes; (*of a sword*) side; (*pers.*) back and shoulders; (*at play*) stake; (*obsolete*) square-headed arrow, quarrel, carrel, quarry. *Vol, Voleur à la —*, *V.* **Care**
Carré, e, *adj.* square; quadratic; cornered; strong; well set; full, flowing; bold; resolute; firm; vigorous; straightforward, plain, categorical; peremptory; flat; of four; of two men and two women; (*of paper*) demy
Carré, *s.m.* square; quadrate; quadrangle; square piece; (*of houses*) landing, landing-place, stair-head; flat, floor, story; (*hort.*) bed; (*of mutton*) best end of the neck; (*of paper*) demy; (*arch.*) fillet; (*coin.*) die; (*tech.*) base. — *long*, oblong square, rectangle. — *des officiers*, (*nav.*) ward-room
Carreau, *s.m.* square; lozenge; paving-tile, flooring-tile, floor-tile; paving-brick; tile-flooring, tile-floor, brick-floor, pavement; ground, floor; spot; cushion, hassock; pane of glass, pane; window; (*design*) check; (*at cards*) diamonds; (*of tailors*) goose; (*file*) rubber; (*arch.*) stretcher; (*fish.*) square-net; (*nav.*) gunnel; (*med.*) tabes mesenterica; (*pop.*) eye-glass; (*obsolete*) square-headed arrow, quarrel, carrel, quarry; thunderbolt, bolt. *A —x*, with checks, checked. *Valet de —*, knave of diamonds; (*fig.*) contemptible fellow, pitiful wretch; snob; low swell. *Brochet —*, very large pike
Carrec, *s.m.* (*zool.*) hawkbill turtle
Carrefour, *s.m.* point of junction of cross-roads *or* streets, cross; public place, crowded thoroughfare; low neighbourhood, backslums. *De —*, (*of language*) coarse, low, vulgar, Billingsgate; (*of authors and writings*) Grub-street; (*of orators and oratory*) stump
Carréger, *v.n.* (*local*) *V.* **Louvoyer**
Carrelage, *s.m.* tile-flooring, brick-paving; tile-floor, brick-pavement; cobbling [to cobble
Carreler, *v.a.* to pave (*or* floor) with brick *or* tile;
Carrelet, *s.m.* flounder, plaice; square fishing-net; clap-net; (*shoemaker's*) awl; square file; triangular sword; square ruler
Carrelette, *s.f.* polishing-file [itinerant cobbler
Carreleur, *s.m.* brick *or* tile-pavier, floor-tiler;
Carrelier, *s.m.* paving-tile maker, paving-brick maker [mending, repairing
Carrelure, *s.f.* new soles; new-soling, cobbling,
Carrément, *adv.* square, in a square, at right angles; boldly; straightforwardly, plainly; categorically; peremptorily; outright; flatly; vigorously; firmly
Carrer, *v.a.* to square, to form into a square
Se —, *v.r.* to strut, to stalk; to look big *or* grand; to attitudinize; to sit in state; (*at play*) to double o.'s stake
Carreu-r, se, *s.m.f.* *V.* **Careur**
Carrick, Carrik, *s.m.* box-coat; cape; gig
Carrier, *s.m.* quarrier, quarry-man
Carrière, *s.f.* career; race-course, race-ground; race; course; scope, play; vent; life; field; prospects; quarry; hard concretion (*in pears*, &c.). *Se donner —*, to take free scope
Carriole, *s.f.* light van; pleasure-van, van; chaise; trap; (*bad carriage*) basket, tub

Carrossable, *adj.* passable for carriages, carriageable, for carriages, carriage. *Route* or *chemin —*, carriage-road
Carrosse, *s.m.* (*obsolescent, now* **Voiture** *or* **Équipage**) coach, carriage; (*nav.*) canopy. *Rouler —*, (*obsolete*) *V.* **Équipage**
Carrossée, *s.f.* coachful, carriageful
Carrosser, *v.a.* to convey in a coach *or* carriage; — *v.n.* (*nav.*) to crowd sail
Carrosserie, *s.f.* carriage-making, coach-making, coach-building trade; carriages
Carrossier, *s.m.* carriage-maker, carriage-builder, coach-maker, coach-builder; carriage-horse, coach-horse
Carrossi-er, ère, *adj.* *V.* **Carrossable**
Carrousel, *s.m.* carrousel, tournament, tilt; [tilt-yard
Carrousse, *s.f.* (*obsolete*) *V.* **Ripaille**
Carrure, *s.f.* breadth of shoulders, back and [shoulders, shoulders, back
Carry, *s.m.* *V.* **Cari**
Cartable, *s.m.* satchel
Cartahu, *s.m.* (*nav.*) girt-line
Cartayer, *v.n.* to quarter, to avoid the ruts
Carte, *s.f.* card; cardboard; pasteboard; map; chart; ticket; label; list; bill of fare; bill; carte. — *blanche*, blank card; plain card; (*fig.*) carte blanche, full power. — *écrite*, map with names. — *muette*, outline map. — *payante*, — *à payer*, bill, reckoning. —*s peintes*, (*at cards*) court-cards, figure-cards. *A la —*, from the bill of fare. *Le dessous des —s*, the face of the cards; (*fig.*) the secret (of an affair), the ins and outs (of a thing). *Brouiller les —s*, (*fig.*) to embroil matters; to sow discord. *Connaître* (or *Voir*) *le dessous des —s*, to be in the secret. *Perdre la —*, to get confused, to be put out, to lose o.'s wits. *Ne pas perdre la —*, to know what one is about
Cartel, *s.m.* challenge, cartel; dial-case; antique hanging-clock, cartel, timepiece; frame-ornament, fancy border; ornamented frieze-panel, ornamented panel, frame, cartouche; (*mil., nav.*) cartel. — *d'armoiries*, (*her.*) shield
Cartelle, *s.f.* ass's-skin (*to write on*); board; plank; shelf
Carterie, *s.f.* card-making; card-factory
Cartero, *s.m.* little pocket-book
Carteron, *s.m.* *V.* **Quarteron**
Cartésianisme, *s.m.* (*philos.*) Cartesianism
Cartésien, ne, *adj. s.* (*philos.*) of Descartes, Cartesian
Carthaginois, e, *adj. s.* Carthaginian
Carthame, *s.m.* (*bot.*) carthamus, safflower
Carthamine, *s.f.* (*chem.*) carthamine, carthamic [acid
Cartier, *s.m.* card-maker; card-paper
Cartilage, *s.m.* gristle; (*anat.*) cartilage
Cartilagineu-x, se, *adj.* gristly; cartilaginous
Cartisane, *s.f.* cartisane. *Dentelle à —*, vellum-lace [chartographer, chart-maker
Cartographe, *s.m.* cartographer, map-maker,
Cartographie, *s.f.* cartography, mapping, chartography, chart-making; maps, charts
Cartograph-ique, -iquement. *V.* page 3, § 1
Cartoman-cie, -tique. *V.* page 3, § 1
Cartomancien, ne, *s.m.f.* cartomancer
Carton, *s.m.* pasteboard; cardboard; board; card; ticket; bandbox; pasteboard box, box; case; hat-box; bonnet-box; pasteboard drawer; pasteboard portfolio, portfolio; cartoon; (*print.*) cancel; half-sheet proof. — *de pâte*, millboard. — *-pierre*, statuary pasteboard, carton-pierre [board covering *or* work *or* article
Cartonnage, *s.m.* boarding; boards; paste-
Cartonné, e, *adj.* in boards, boards
Cartonner, *v.a.* to put *or* bind in boards, to board, to put a pasteboard cover on; (*print.*) to cancel
Cartonnerie, *s.f.* pasteboard-manufactory
Cartonneu-r, se, *s.m.f.* boarder (*of books*)
Cartonnier, *s.m.* pasteboard-maker; bandbox-maker; chest of pasteboard drawers, boxes
Cartonnière, *s.f.* bandbox-maker, paper-box maker

Cartouche, *s.f.* cartridge; round; cartouch; case-shot, canister-shot; (*of squibs, &c.*) case; (*of coin*) pile

Cartouche, *s.m.* escutcheon, shield, ring, ornament; (*arch.*) cartouche, modillion; (*for fireworks*) case; (*pers.*) robber, ruffian, Jonathan Wild, Jack Sheppard [ridge-box *or* pouch

Cartouchier, *s.m.*, **Cartouchière,** *s.f.* cart-

Cartulaire, *s.m.* chartulary, cartulary

Carus, *s.m.* (*med.*) carus

Carvi, *s.m.* (*bot.*) caraway, carraway

Carya, *s.m.* (*bot.*) carya, hickory

Caryatide, *s.f.* caryatid, caryatis

Caryatidique, *adj.* caryatidic

Caryer, *s.m. V.* **Carya**

Caryophyllé, e, *adj.* (*bot.*) caryophyllaceous; **—s,** *s.f.pl.* (*bot.*) caryophyllaceæ; chickweed tribe

Caryopse, *s.m.* (*bot.*) caryopsis

Caryote, *s.m.* (*bot.*) caryota

Cas, *s.m.* case; accident; adventure; event; conjuncture; occasion; circumstance; fact; matter; question; point; position; situation; moment, time; supposition; esteem, value; (*pop.*) needs, cack; concern. *Dans le — de,* in case of; able to; in a position to; so situated as to; likely to, likely enough to, capable of, just the man to. *Dans le — où,* in case. *Dans tous les —,* in any case; at all events. *En —,* in case; *s.m. V.* **En-cas** (*at Letter* **E**). *En tout —,* at all events, at any rate, however; *s.m.* sunshade (*parasol*). *Hors le — où,* unless, except. *Faire — de,* to value, to set a value on, to esteem, to think (*a great deal, or little, or nothing*) of; to consider, to care for, to take into account, to mind. *C'est bien le — de le dire,* it may be truly said here, one may indeed say so

Casani-er, ère, *adj.s.* home-keeping, domestic, domesticated, sedentary; stay-at-home; recluse

Casaque, *s.f.* cassock, cloak, great-coat; jacket; coat; stable-coat. — *rouge,* red jacket, convict's jacket. *Tourner —,* to be a turncoat, to change sides, to rat

Casaquin, *s.m.* jacket; (*pop.*) carcass [*and palace*)

Casauba, Casbah, *s.f.* casbah (*Arabian castle*

Cascade, *s.f.* cascade, waterfall; fall; tumble; leap, bound; slip; fit, start, jerk, tossing; irregularity; freak

Cascadeu-r, se, *s.m.f.* (*pop.*) trifler, humbug, loose fish; actor who tampers with his part;

Cascalho, *s.m.* (*min.*) cascalho [loose woman

Cascaret, *s.m.* scrubby fellow, shrimp, runt, monkey

†Cascarille, *s.f.* (*pharm.*) cascarilla bark

Cascatelle, *s.f.* small cascade

Case, *s.f.* (*negro's*) cabin; hut; house, dwelling, place; compartment, division; pigeon-hole; box; (*of a horse-box, rail.*) stall; (*of chess, draughts, registers*) square; (*of backgammon*) point; (*nav.*) berth [checked, checkered

Casé, e, *part. adj.* placed, &c. (*V.* **Caser**);

Caséation, *s.f.* caseation, turning into cheese

Caséeu-x, se, *adj.* caseous, cheesy

Caséine, *s.f.* (*chem.*) caseine

Caséique, *adj.* caseic

Casemate, *s.f.* (*fort.*) casemate; (*fig.*) prison, dungeon, cell; privy; (*hunt.*) blind hole

Casemater, *v.a.* (*fort.*) to casemate

Caser, *v.a.* to place; to find a place for; to provide for; to settle; to fix; to arrange, to put in order; — *v.n.* (*backgammon*) to make a point [settle; to find a place; to find room

Se —, *v.r.* to get settled, to settle oneself, to

Caser·l, *s.m.*, **Caserette,** *s.f.* cheese-mould

Caserne, *s.f.* barrack, barracks. — *de pompiers* (or *de sapeurs-pompiers*), fire-brigade station, fire-station

Casernement, *s.m.* quartering in barracks

Caserner, *v.n.* to be in barracks; — *v.a.* to quarter in barracks; (*fig.*) to pen up, to confine. *Faire —,* to quarter in barracks

Casernet, *s.m.* (*nav.*) register, log-book

Casernier, *s.m.* barrack-porter

Caset, *s.m.* (*fish.*) cad-bait [*pottery*) sagger, seggar

Casette, *s.f.* (*obsolete*) little house, cottage; (*of*

Caséum, *s.m.* (*chem.*) caseum [*justice*)

Casiasquier, *s.m.* casiaskier (*Turkish chief*

Casier, *s.m.* open case with divisions; set of pigeon-holes; nest of drawers; rack; ledger-rack; (*fish.*) weel. — *à musique,* canterbury

†Casilleu-x, se, *adj.* brittle

Casimir, *s.m.* kerseymere

Casino, *s.m.* casino

Casoar, *s.m.* (*bird*) cassowary

Caspien, ne, *adj.* (*geog.*) Caspian

Casque, *s.m.* helmet, headpiece; strong leather; helmet-shell; (*pop.*) head, noddle; brass, impudence; gabble; drop too much. — *à mèche,*

Casqué, e, *adj.* helmeted [(man's) night-cap

Casquet, *s.m.* (*head-gear*) *V.* **Gasquet;** (*obsolete*) light open helmet; (*hort.*) wooden rake

Casquette, *s.f.* cap (*of a man or boy*); — *adject.*

Cassable, *adj.* breakable [(*pop.*) tipsy, tight

Cassade, *s.f.* fib, sham, flam, bouncer, humbug,

Cassage, *s.m.* breaking, breakage [lie

†Cassaille, *s.f.* (*of a field*) breaking up

Cassandre, *s.m.* Cassander; Pantaloon; simple old man, old booby, old fogy, old codger, dotard; — *s.f.* Cassandra, prophetess

Cassant, e, *adj.* brittle; crisp, short; breaking; blunt, abrupt, bluff, gruff, unsociable

Cassation, *s.f.* breaking; (*law*) annulment; reversal; quashing; appeal. *Se pourvoir en*

Cassave, *s.f.* cassava [—, to appeal

Casse, *s.f.* breaking, breakage; ladle, scoop; (*obsolete*) reducing to the ranks; cashiering; dismissal, sack; (*bot.*) cassia; (*print.*) case; — *s.m.f.* (*in compounds, from* **Casser,** "to break") thing (*m.*) *or* person (*m.f.*) that breaks, breaker. — **-bras,** *s.m.* sad misfortune, hard blow; great pressure; sudden pinch *or* difficulty. — **-cœur,** *s.m.* heart-breaker. — **-cou,** *s.m.* break-neck; stumbling-block; dangerous place; danger; break-neck ladder; (*pers.*) rough-rider; reckless fellow, dare-devil, desperado; — *int.* look out! mind! danger! — **-croûte,** *s.m.* crust-breaker. — **-gueule,** *s.m.* (*pop.*) fighter, bully. — **-lunettes,** *s.m.* (*bot.*) blue-bottle; eyebright. — **-mottes,** *s.m.* (*hort.*) clod-breaker; (*bird*) fallow-finch. — **-museau,** *s.m.* (*pop.*) blow on the face, punch on the head; kind of cake. — **-noisettes,** *s.m.* nutcracker, nutcrackers, nutcracks; (*bird*) nuthatch. — **-noix,** *s.m.* nutcracker, nutcrackers, nutcracks; (*bird*) nutcracker. — **-os,** *s.m.* (*agr.*) bone-breaker. — **-pierre,** *s.m.* (*bot.*) parietary, wall-pellitory, saxifrage, break-stone. — **-poitrine,** *s.m.* strong brandy, strong *or* hot stuff, cut-throat stuff. — **-sucre,** *s.m.* sugar-nippers. — **-tête,** *s.m.* tomahawk; life-preserver, bludgeon; shillelagh; heady wine; deafening noise; head-splitting work, bewildering labour; anxiety; worry; puzzle; (*nav.*) overhead netting, net

Cassé, e, *part. adj.* broken, broken down, &c. (*V.* **Casser**); old, infirm, weak, trembling; (*of a ship*) hogged

Casseau, *s.m.* (*print.*) half-case, drawer

Cassement, *s.m.* breaking. — *de tête,* head-splitting; weariness of the brain; anxiety; worry

Casser, *v.a.n.* to break; to crack; to snap; to split; to puzzle, to rack; to wear out, to break down, to weaken; to annul; to reverse; to quash; to suppress; to dissolve; to disband; to reduce to the ranks; (*obsolete*) to cashier; to dismiss; (*of wine*) to get into (*the head*. — *aux gages,* to dismiss, to discharge; to withdraw o.'s confidence from. *A tout —,* (*pop.*) extremely, dreadfully, awfully, with a vengeance

Se —, *v.r.* to break, to get *or* be broken; to break (o.'s ...); to puzzle *or* rack (o.'s brains); to grow old and weak; (*of a ship*) to hog. *Se la —,* (*pop.*) to be off, to bolt [dish; pie

Casserole, *s.f.* saucepan, stewpan; vegetable-

Casserolée, *s.f.* saucepanful

Cassetée, *s.f.* casketful; (*print.*) caseful
Cassetin, *s.m.* (*print.*) box
Cassette, *s.f.* small case *or* box; casket; cash-box; privy purse; pocket-money, pin-money
Casseu-r, se, *s.m.f.* breaker; breaker of things; blusterer, braggart, bully; — *adj.* in the habit of breaking things; blustering, bragging, bullying. — *d'assiettes*, blusterer, braggart, bully, quarrelsome fellow. — *de raquettes*, vigorous fellow
Cassican, *s.m.* (*bird*) baritah, piping crow
Casside, *s.f.* (*insect*) cassida, tortoise-beetle
Cassidoine, *s.f.* (*min.*) cassidony
Cassie, *s.f.* (*bot.*) cassie
Cassier, *s.m.* (*bot.*) cassia-tree
Cassine, *s.f.* country-villa; hut, hovel, hole; stall; booth; (*mil.*) cassine; (*bot.*) cassine, cassioberry, South Sea tea
Cassinoïde, *s.f.* (*rail.*) elliptical curve
Cassiopée, *s.f.* (*astr.*) Cassiopeia
Cassique, *s.m.* (*bird*) cassican
Cassis, *s.m.* black-currant, black-currants; black-currant bush; black-currant wine
Cassolette, *s.f.* perfuming-pan; scent-box; cresset; smell; (*bot.*) dame's violet; (*pop.*) jorden; night-cart, mud-cart [cullet; cocoa-nib
Casson, *s.m.* broken piece, fragment; lump;
Cassonade, *s.f.* moist sugar, brown sugar
Cassure, *s.f.* broken place, break, crack, snap, breaking, fracture; (*of a ship*) hogging
Castagneau, *s.m.* (*fish*) chromis
†Castagnette, *s.f.* castanet; (*stuff*) cassinette
†Castagneux, *s.m.* (*bird*) didapper, black-chin grebe, dab-chick
†Castagnon, *s.m.* dried chestnut
Castalides, *s.f.pl.* (*myth.*) Muses
Castalie, *s.f.* (*myth.*) Castalia. *Les eaux de* —, Castalian spring, poetry
Caste, *s.f.* caste; tribe; set, crew, lot
Castel, *s.m.* (*obsolete*) castle
†Castillan, e, *adj. s.* Castilian [tilt
†Castille, *s.f.* bickering, squabbling, quarrel;
Castine, *s.f.* (*metal.*) flux [hat, tile; bonnet
Castor, *s.m.* beaver, castor; beaver-hat; (*pop.*)
Castoréum, *s.m.* castoreum, castor
Castorin, *s.m.* nutria, newter
Castorine, *s.f.* (*chem.*) castorine; (*cloth*) castor
Castramétation, *s.f.* castrametation
Castrat, *s.m.* castrato, eunuch
Castration, *s.f.* castration
Castrer, *v.a.* to castrate
Casualité, *s.f.* casualty, fortuitousness
Casuarine, *s.f.* (*bot.*) casuarina, cassowary-tree, beef-wood, forest oak
Casuel, le, *adj.* casual, accidental, contingent, fortuitous; precarious, uncertain; (*pop.*) brittle
Casuel, *s.m.* perquisites, profits; fees; surplice-fees; class-fees, course-fees; chance customers *or* custom [fortuitously, by chance
Casuellement, *adv.* casually, accidentally,
Casuiste, *s.m.* casuist
Casuistique, *s.f.* casuistry
Casuistiquer, *v.n.* to play the casuist
‡Catachrèse, *s.f.* (*rhet.*) catachresis
Cataclysme, *s.m.* cataclysm, deluge, flood; desolation, disaster, overthrow, revolution, crash, smash; shower-bath
Catacoi, Catacoua, *s.f.* (*pop.*) *V.* **Catogan**
Catacois, *s.m.* *V.* **Cacatois**
Catacombes, *s.f.pl.* catacombs [coustic
Catacoustique, *s.f.* catacoustics; —*adj.* cata-
Catadioptrique, *s.f.* catadioptrics; — *adj.* catadioptric [ract, fall
Catadoupe, Catadupe, *s.f.* catadupe, cata-
Catafalque, *s.m.* bed of state, canopy, burial scaffolding; imitation tomb, catafalque
Catagmatique, *adj.m.f.*, *s.m.* (*surg.*) catagmatic
Cataire, *s.f.* (*bot.*) cat-mint; — *adj.* (*med.*) of a cat (*V.* **Frémissement**)
Catalan, e, *adj. s.m.f.* Catalonian, Catalan; — *s.m.* Catalan knife; — *s.f.* Catalonian fashion; Catalan forge
Catalaunien, ne, Catalaunique, *adj.* (*geog.*) Catalaunian, of Châlons-sur-Marne
Catalectes, *s.m.pl.* (*of the ancients*) unfinished poems, fragments; imperfect pieces
Catalectique, *adj.* (*anc. vers.*) catalectic
Catalep-sie (*s.f.*), **-tique** (*adj. s.m.f.*), (*med.*) *V.* page 3, § 1
Catalogue, *s.m.* catalogue, roll, list; series
Cataloguement, *s.m.* cataloguing
Cataloguer, *v.a.* to catalogue
Catalogueur, *s.m.* cataloguer
Catalpa, *s.m.* (*bot.*) catalpa
Catalyse, *s.f.* (*chem.*) catalysis
Catalyt-ique, -iquement. *V.* page 3, § 1
Cataménial, e, *adj.* (*physiol.*) catamenial
Cataphonique, *s.f.* (*phys.*) cataphonics
Cataplasme, *s.m.* poultice
Catapuce, *s.f.* (*bot.*) caper-spurge
Catapulte, *s.f.* catapult, catapulta
Cataracte, *s.f.* cataract, waterfall, fall; (*med., mech.*) cataract; —**s,** *pl.* (*fig.*) anger, passion, indignation; windows, flood-gates (*of heaven*)
Cataracté, e, *adj.* (*med.*) affected with a cataract
Cataracter (Se), *v.r.* (*med.*) to become affected with a cataract
Catarrhal, e, *adj.* (*med.*) catarrhal
Catarrhe, *s.m.* (*med.*) catarrh; bad cold. — *d'été*, summer catarrh, hay-asthma, hay-fever. — *pulmonaire*, bronchitis [catarrhal
Catarrheu-x, se, *adj.* (*med.*) catarrhous;
Catastrophe, *s.f.* catastrophe; calamity [bitch
Catau, *s.f.* country-servant; slut; harlot, mot,
Catéchét-ique, -iquement. *V.* page 3, § 1
Catéchine, *s.f.* (*chem.*) catechine
Catéchisation, *s.f.* catechization
Catéchiser, *v.a.* to catechize; to reason with, to try to persuade; to instruct beforehand, to give the cue, to coach up; to train; to lecture
Catéchisme, *s.m.* catechism; (*fig.*) cue, part, instructions [page 3, § 1
Catéch-iste, -istique, -istiquement. *V.*
‡Catéchuménat, *s.m.* catechumenate
‡Catéchumène, *s.m.f.* catechumen
Catégor-ie, -ique, -iquement. *V.* page 3, § 1
Catégoriser, *v.a.* to categorize, to class [senna
Cathartine, *s.f.* (*chem.*) cathartine, bitter of
Cathartique, *adj.m.f.*, *s.m.* (*med.*) cathartic
Cathedrâ (Ex), *adv.* ex cathedrâ; from the chair *or* pulpit; from *or* with high authority;
Cathédrale, *s.f.*, *adj.f.* cathedral [professionally
Cathérétique, *adj.m.f.*, *s.m.* (*med.*) catheretic
Cathéter, *s.m.* (*surg.*) catheter
Cathétomètre, *s.m.* (*phys.*) cathetometer
Catholicisme, *s.m.* catholicism
Catholicité, *s.f.* catholicity; catholicism; catholic countries
Catholicon, *s.m.* (*pharm.*) catholicon
Catholique, *s.m.f.* catholic, Roman catholic; — *adj.* catholic, Roman catholic; (*fam.*) moral; orthodox; right; genuine
Catholiquement, *adv.* like a catholic, in a catholic manner, catholicly
Cati, e, *part. of* **Catir**
Cati, *s.m.* pressing, gloss, lustre
Catiche, *s.f.* (*hunt.*) hole
Catilina, *s.m.* conspirator, agitator
Catilinaire, *s.f.* Catiline oration, Catiline
†Catillac, Catillard, *s.m.* catillac (*pear*)
Catimaron, *s.m.* (*nav.*) catamaran
Catimini (En), *adv.* *V.* **Cachette (En)**
Catin, *s.f.* harlot, strumpet, bitch, mot
Catinerie, *s.f.* harlotry [strumpet
Catiniser (Se), *v.r.* to become a harlot *or* a
Catir, *v.a.* to press, to gloss
Catissage, *s.m.* pressing, glossing (*of cloth*)
Catisseur, *s.m.* cloth-presser, presser
Cat-marin, *s.m.* (*bird*) red-throated diver
Catogan, *s.m.* (*of hair*) club
Catonien, ne, *adj.* Catonian
Catonisme, *s.m.* Catonism [§ 1
Catoptrique, *s.f.* catoptrics; — *adj.* *V.* page 3,
Catoptromancie, *s.f.* catoptromancy

Caucalide, *s.f.* (*bot.*) bur-parsley
Caucasien,ne,Caucasique, *adj.* Caucasian
Cauchemar, *s.m.* nightmare, incubus; bore; nuisance; bugbear [plague
Cauchemarder, *v.a.* to beset, to bore, to
Cauchois, e, *adj. s.* of Caux (*in Normandy*); native of Caux
Caudal, e, *adj.* caudal; — *s.f.* caudal fin
Caudataire, *s.m.* train-bearer; — *adj.* train-
Caudé,e,*adj.* caudate, caudated, tailed [bearing
Caudebec, *s.m.* (*obsolete*) Caudebec hat
Caudex, *s.m.* (*bot.*) caudex
Caudicule, *s.f.* (*bot.*) caudicle, caudicula
Caudimane, *adj.* (*of monkeys*) caudimanous, with a prehensile tail; — *s.m.* caudimane
Caudines, *adj.f.pl.* Caudine
Caulicole, *s.f.* (*arch.*) caulicole
Caulinaire, *adj.* (*bot.*) cauline
Cauris, *s.m.* cowry (*African and Indian money*)
Causal, e, *adj.* causal
Causalité, *s.f.* causality
Causant, e, *adj.* chatty, conversable
Causati-f, ve, *adj.* causative, causal
Causation, *s.f.* causation
Causativement, *adv.* causatively
Cause, *s.f.* cause; motive, reason, grounds; subject; matter; case; trial; brief. —*s célèbres*, sensation trials. —*finale*, final cause. *Gain de* —, success, gaining of o.'s cause. *A* — *de*, on account of; for the sake of, for; through. *A* — *que*, because. *A ces* —*s*, (*law*) accordingly. *En* —, concerned in a suit; concerned; implicated; at stake. *En tout état de* —, in any case. *Et pour* —, not without cause, for a very good reason. *Pour* — *de*, in consequence of, on account of. *Avoir* — *gagnée*, *Avoir* or *obtenir gain de* —, to gain o.'s cause *or* point; to carry the day; to prevail. *Donner gain de* — *à*, to decide *or* be in favour of; to yield the advantage to, to give it up to. *Être hors de* —, not to be concerned in a suit; not to be concerned *or* implicated; to have nothing to do with it; not to be at stake; to be out of the question. *Mettre en* —, to call to appear, to summon; to put (*one*) on his trial; to sue; to implicate in a lawsuit; to implicate. *Mettre hors de* —, to dismiss from a suit; to free from all imputation; to put out of the question. *Prendre fait et* — *pour* ..., to take ...'s part
Causer, *v.a.* to cause, to be the cause of, to occasion; to induce; to produce; to make; to create; to excite; to give; — *v.n.* to talk, to converse, to chat; to tattle. *Assez causé!* enough of that! that's enough! that'll do! hold your jaw! shut up!
Causerie, *s.f.* talk, chat, chit-chat, gossip, tattle
Causette, *s.f.* chat. *Faire la* —, to have a chat
Causeu-r, se, *adj.* talkative, chatty, conversable; — *s.m.f.* talker; tattler; conversationalist, conversationist; — *s.f.* settee
Causoter, *v.n.* to chat, to have a chat
Causticité, *s.f.* causticity
Caustique, *adj.* caustic; biting, cutting; — *s.m.* (*chem., pharm., surg.*) caustic; — *s.f.* (*opt.*) caustic
Caustiquement, *adv.* caustically; cuttingly
Cauteleusement, *adv.* cunningly, craftily
Cauteleu-x, se, *adj.* cunning, crafty
Cautère, *s.m.* cautery; issue; (*vet.*) firing-iron
Cautérisation, *s.f.* cauterization
Cautériser, *v.a.* to cauterize, to sear, to burn
Caution, *s.f.* bail, surety; security. — *bourgeoise*, (*obsolete*) good bail *or* security. *Sujet à* —, not to be trusted, suspicious, doubtful
Cautionnement, *s.m.* security; bail; bailing; bail-bond; caution money
Cautionner, *v.a.* to be surety for; to bail; to answer for; to warrant
Caux, *s.m.* (*agr.*) cow-mash
Cavage, *s.m.* hollowing, digging; cellarage
Ça-va-là-haut, *int.* (*hunt.*) tally-ho! [intrigue
Cavalcade, *s.f.* cavalcade; ride; (*pop.*) love
Cavalcader, *v.n.* to ride [horse
Cavalcadour, *s.m.* equerry; master of the
Cavale, *s.f.* mare; (*pop.*) lanky awkward woman
Cavaler (Se), *v.r.* (*pop.*) to bolt, to skedaddle
Cavalerie, *s.f.* cavalry, horse
Cavalier, *s.m.* horseman, rider; cavalry-man, horse-soldier, trooper; gentleman; man; cavalier; (*dancing*) partner; dancer; (*chess*) knight; (*paper*) royal. — *servant*, lover, gallant, dangler. *Servir de* — *à*, to escort
Cavali-er, ère, *adj.* free, easy; bold; cavalier, blunt, flippant, too free, unceremonious; horse; (*of paper*) royal
Cavalière, *s.f.* horsewoman, rider
Cavalièrement, *adv.* freely; cavalierly, bluntly, flippantly, too freely, unceremoniously
Cavalot, *s.m.* (*pop.*) small change *or* coin, copper
Cavatine, *s.f.* (*mus.*) cavatina
Cave, *s.f.* cellar; vault; cellarage; bottle-case; liquor-case; sarcophagus, cellaret; bin; case; scent-case; freezing-pot, ice-cream mould; cavity, hollow; (*at play*) pool; (*of carriages*) boot
Cave, *adj.* hollow, sunk, sunken. *Année* —, lunar year of 353 days; uncompleted year, in round numbers. *Lune* —, *mois* —, lunar month of 29 days. *Veine* —, (*anat.*) vena cava; vena cava inferior
Cavé, e, *part. adj.* hollowed; sunken; staked
Cavé, *s.m.* (*pop.*) dupe, gull, gudgeon, pigeon
Caveau, *s.m.* cellar, wine-store, shades; vault; literary club; (*nav.*) captain's store-room
Cavecé, e, *adj.* (*of horses*) with a ... head, ... -headed; with a black head [curb
Caveçon, *s.m.* (*rid.*) caveson, cavesson; (*fig.*)
Cavée, *s.f.* (*hunt.*) hollow way
Caver, *v.a.n.* to hollow; to scoop; to undermine; to make a hole; to furrow; to stake (*at play*); to lunge (*in fencing*). — *au plus bas*, to play the lowest stake; to put it at the lowest; to suppose the worst. — *au plus fort*, to cover the highest stake; to carry things to extremes; to suppose an extreme case; to put it at the highest [stake
Se —, *v.r.* to become hollow *or* sunken; to
Caverne, *s.f.* cavern, cave; hollow; den
Caverneu-x, se, *adj.* cavernous; hollow;
Cavernosité,*s.f.* hollowness; hollow [sepulchral
Cavesson, *s.m.* *V.* **Caveçon**
Cavet, *s.m.* (*arch.*) cavetto
Cavi, *s.m.* (*bot.*) tuber of oca
Caviar, *s.m.* (*cook.*) caviar, caviare
Cavillation, *s.f.* cavilling, cavil; sophistry
Cavin, *s.m.* low ground, hollow; bog; (*mil.*) cavin
Caviste, *s.m.* cellarman
Cavité, *s.f.* cavity, hollow
Caye, *s.f.* *V.* **Caie** [ing-house
Cayenne, *s.f.* (*nav.*) old hulk; barrack; cook-
Cayeu, *s.m.* *V.* **Caïeu**
Cazette, *s.f.* (*of pottery*) *V.* **Casette**
Ce, Cet, *m.*, **Cette,** *f.*, *adj.* this, that; such a, such; what a, what. — *livre-ci*, this book. — *-livre-là*, that book
Ce, C', *pron.* this, that, it, they, these, those; he, she; so; the thing; the reason; the fact. — *dont*, that of which; what ... of *or* about; of which; which ... of; which; what. — *qui*, — *que*, what, that which; which. — *sont*, these *or* those are; they are; it is. *A* — *que*, accord- to what; from what; that; as. *De* — *que* from the fact that; because; that. *Sur* —, thereupon; now. *Sur* — *que*, as, when, on
Céans, *adv.* (*old*) within, in here, here, in this house; the house, the place; at home
Ceci, *pron.* this, this thing, these things, these
Cécilie, *s.f.* (*reptile*) cæcilia
Cécité, *s.f.* blindness
Cécropie, *s.f.* (*bot.*) cecropia, trumpet-tree
Cécropien, ne, Cécropique, *adj.* (*Gr. antiquity*) Cecropian
Cécrops, *s.m.* (*zool.*) cecrops
Cécube, *s.m.* (*in antiquity*) Cæcuban wine; (*fig.*) exquisite wine
Cécum, *s.m.* (*anat.*) *V.* **Cæcum**

Cédant, e, *s.m.f.* (*law*) granter; assigner; transferrer; — *part. adj.* granting; &c. (*V.* **Céder**)
Cédat, *s.m.* natural steel
Céder, *v.a.n.* to cede; to yield; to give up; to give in; to give; to let have; to grant; to concede; to assign; to make over; to transfer; to remit; to resign; to part with; to dispose of; to relax; to give way; to submit; to comply; to obey; to listen (to); to be postponed (to). *Le — à,* to be second to, to be inferior to, to be below *or* behind; to stoop to
†**Cédille,** *s.f.* (*gram.*) cedilla
Cédrat, *s.m.* (*bot.*) cedra, cedrat, cedrate, citron [(*fruit, tree*)
Cédratier, *s.m.* (*bot.*) cedra, cedrat, cedrate, citron [(*tree*)
Cèdre, *s.m.* cedar
Cédrie, *s.f.* cedria, cedar resin
Cédrite, *s.m.* cedar-resin wine
Cédule, *s.f.* schedule; scrip; memorandum; notice; bill; note of hand
Ceindre, *v.a.* to surround; to enclose; to fence; to encircle; to bind; to gird, to put on; to wreathe [wreathe o.'s brow; to gird, to put on
Se —, *v.r.* to bind round one; to encircle *or*
Ceinte, *s.f.* (*nav.*) *V.* **Préceinte**
Ceintrage, *s.m.* (*nav.*) frapping
Ceintre, *s.m.* (*nav.*) tender (*for a boat*)
Ceintrer, *v.a.* (*nav.*) to frap
Ceinture, *s.f.* girdle; belt; sash; waistband, band; waist-ribbon; waist; enclosure; zone; circle; (*arch.*) collar, (*of a column*) cincture; (*artil.*) moulding; (*nav.*) swifter. *— funèbre, — de deuil,* band of black cloth with hatchment. *De —,* circular [confined
Ceinturé, e, *adj.* girdled, girt; wearing a sash;
Ceinturer, *v.a.* to girdle, to gird
Ceinturette, *s.f.* (*hunt.*) horn-strap, strap
Ceinturier, *s.m.* girdle-maker, belt-maker
Ceinturon, *s.m.* belt, sword-belt
Ceinturonnerie, *s.f.* belt-making; belts
Ceinturonnier, *s.m.* belt-maker
Cela, *pron.* that; it; so; that thing; the thing; those things, those; that reason; things; then; as to that; (*fam.*) he, him, that boy, that man, that fellow; she, her, that girl, that woman; they, them, those children, those people. *— est,* it is so. *— n'est pas,* it is not so. *C'est —,* that is it; that will do; that is right; just so; to be sure; it is (*or* was) that. *Ce n'est pas —,* that is not it; that will not do; that is not right; not so; it is not (*or* was not) that. *C'est — même,* that is the very thing. *Par — même,* for that very reason; (*que*) for the very reason (that); from the very fact (that). *Pour — même,* for that very thing (*or* purpose); for that very reason. *Pour — non!* no indeed! certainly not! *Pour — oui!* yes indeed! certainly! to be sure! *N'est-ce que —?* is that all? *Pas de —! V.* **Ça**
Céladon, *adj. s.m.* dead sea-green (*colour*); sentimental lover; old beau
Céladonique, *adj.* maudlin [ality, maudlin
Céladonisme, *s.m.* sentimentalism, sentiment-
Célan, *s.m.* (*fish*) pilchard
Célandine, *s.f.* (*bot.*) blood-wort
Célastre, *s.m.* (*bot.*) celastrus, staff-tree
Célation, *s.f.* (*law*) concealing, concealment
Célébrant, *s.m.* celebrant
Célébrateur, *s.m.* celebrator
Célébration, *s.f.* celebration; solemnization
Célèbre, *adj.* celebrated, famous, famed, renowned, illustrious; distinguished, eminent
Célébrer, *v.a.* to celebrate; to praise; to glorify; to extol; to sing; to solemnize; to keep; — *v.n.* to officiate
Se —, *v.r.* to be celebrated *or* solemnized
Célébrité, *s.f.* celebrity; fame; solemnity
Céler, *v.a.* to conceal, to hide. *Se faire —,* (*old*) to deny *or* conceal oneself; to abscond
Célère, *adj.* swift, fast, fleet, rapid, quick
Céleri, *s.m.* celery
Célérifère, *s.m.f. V.* **Accéléré,** *s.*
Célerin, *s.m. V.* **Célan**
Célérité, *s.f.* celerity, speed, swiftness, rapidity, activity, quickness, despatch
Céleste, *adj.* celestial, heavenly, of heaven; divine; excellent, perfect; sky, of the sky
Célestin, e, *s.m.f.* Celestine (*monk, nun*); — *s.f.* (*chem., bot.*) celestine
Céliaque, *adj. V.* **Cœliaque**
Célibat, *s.m.* celibacy, single life, single state
Célibataire, *s.m.* unmarried *or* single man, bachelor; — *adj.* single, of a single man
Celle, *pron. fem. of* **Celui**
Celle, *s.f.* (*obsolete*) cell, hut, hovel
Celleri-er, ère, *s.m.f.* cellarer, cellarist
Cellier, *s.m.* wine-room, wine-store, store-room, cellar (*on the ground floor*)
Cellulaire, *adj.* cellular; solitary. *Régime* or *système —,* solitary system; silent system.
Cellule, *s.f.* cell [*Voiture —,* prison-van
Cellulé, e, *adj.* cellular, cellulose; celled; — *s.m.f.* celled prisoner
Celluleu-x, se, *adj.* cellulose, cellular
Cellulose, *s.f.* (*chem.*) cellulose
Célosie, *s.f.* (*bot.*) cockscomb, amaranth
Celsie, *s.f.* (*bot.*) celsia [*adj.* Celtic
Celte, *s.m.f.* Celt; — *s.m.* (*language*) Celtic; —
Celtibère, Celtibérien, ne, *adj. s.* Celtiberian
Celtique, *adj.* Celtic; — *s.m.* (*language*) Celtic
Celui, *pron.m.* he; him; the one; that; the person. *— -ci,* the latter; this, this one; he; him; who; this man, this fellow. *— -là,* the former; that, that one; he; him; that man, that fellow
Cément, *s.m.* (*chem., metal., anat.*) cement
Cémentation, *s.f.* cementation
Cémentatoire, *adj.* cementatory
Cémenter, *v.a.* to cement
Cémenteu-x, se, *adj.* cementitious
Cémétérial, e, *adj.* cemeterial
Cénacle, *s.m.* cœnaculum; guest-chamber; (*ironically*) club, coterie
Cendre, *s.f.* ashes; cinders, cinder; embers; dust; remains, relics; memory; death. *Jour* or *mercredi des —s,* Ash-Wednesday
Cendré, e, *adj.* ash-coloured, ashy, ash
Cendrée, *s.f.* dust-shot
Cendrer, *v.a.* to paint *or* make ash-grey; to ash
Cendreu-x, se, *adj.* covered with ashes, full of ashes, ashy
Cendrier, *s.m.* ash-hole, ash-pit; ash-pan; ash-tub, cinder-pail; dealer in ashes, ash-man
†**Cendrillon,** *s.f.* Cinderella; little girl who is always sitting near the fire; cinder-wench
Cendrure, *s.f.* (*of steel*) spots, flaws
Cène, *s.f.* Lord's supper, last supper, communion
Cenelle, *s.f.* (*bot.*) haw
Cénobite, *s.m.* cenobite, monk
Cénobit-ique, -isme. *V.* page 3, § 1
Cénotaphe, *s.m.* cenotaph
Cens, *s.m.* (electoral) qualification, (elective) franchise; rating; (*feud.*) quit-rent; (*Rom. hist.*) census; rating
Censable, *adj.* (*feud.*) to whom the quit-rent is due. *Seigneur —,* lord of the manor
Censal, *s.m.* broker (*in the East*)
Cense, *s.f.* (*obsolete*) farm, fee-farm
Censé, e, *adj.* reputed, deemed, accounted, considered, considered as, supposed; supposed to be; pretended, understood, understood to be, put forward as
Censéable, *adj.* (*feud.*) liable to the quit-rent
Censément, *adv.* by supposition, suppositively, as it is *or* was supposed; constructively; vir-
Censerie, *s.f.* (*in the East*) *V.* **Courtage** [tually
Censeur, *s.m.* censor; censurer, critic, fault-finder; reviewer; controller; censor of the press censor, examiner of plays; (*of public schools*) vice-principal; (*univers.*) proctor; (*com.*) auditor
Censi-er, ère, *adj. s.* (*feud.*) of quit-rent; (*pers.*) to whom the quit-rent is due; lord of the manor; farmer, holder of fee-farm lands. *Livre* or *papier —, —, s.m.* rent-roll, rental. *Seigneur —,* lord of the manor

Censitaire, *adj.* (*of electors*) qualified; — *s.m.* (*feud.*) copyholder
Censive, *s.f.* (*feud.*) quit-rent; manor
Censivement, *adv.* (*feud.*) by copyhold
Censorial, e, *adj.* censorial
Censuel, le, *adj.* feudal, of quit-rent
Censurable, *adj.* censurable, blamable
Censure, *s.f.* censorship; censure, blame, reprehension, reproach, reproof, rebuke, disapprobation; criticism; vote of censure; censorship of the press; examinership of plays; censors, board of censors, office of the lord chamberlain
Censurer, *v.a.n.* to censure, to blame, to reprove, to condemn; to criticize; to find fault; to check, to control
Se —, to censure *or* &c. oneself *or* each other; to be censured *or* &c.
Cent, *s.m. adj.* hundred; (*of percentage, kind of coin*) cent. — *pesant*, hundred-weight. ... *pour* —, ... per cent. — **-gardes,** *s.m.* (*one of the Sovereign's hundred guards*) life-guardsman, horse-guard, yeoman (of the guard). — **-gardes,** *s.m.pl.* body-guard, life-guards, horse-guards, yeomen (of the guard), beef-eaters. — **-suisses,** *s.m.* (*old*) Swiss guardsman (*one of the hundred Swiss life-guards*). — **-suisses,** *s.m.pl.* (*old*) Swiss body-guard, Swiss guards (100 *in number*). *Officier des — -gardes*, exon. *Les — Jours*, (*Fr. hist.*) the Hundred Days (*from March* 20 *to end of June*, 1815)
Centaine, *s.f.* hundred, a hundred or so, about a hundred; age of a hundred, a hundred years of age; thread (*that binds a skein*)
Centaure, *s.m.* (*myth., astr.*) centaur
Centaurée, *s.f.* (*bot.*) centaurea
Centenaire, *adj.* centenary, centenarian, centennial; — *s.m.* centenary (100*th anniversary*); — *s.m.f.* (*pers.*) centenarian
Centenier, *s.m.* centurion; hundreder
Centésimal, e, *adj.* centesimal [*dredth part*)
Centi, (*in Fr. weights and meas.*) centi ... (*hun-*
Centiare, *s.m.* (*Fr. meas.*) centiare
Centième, *adj. s.* hundredth
Centigrade, *adj.* centigrade
Centigramme, *s.m.* (*Fr. weight*) centigramme
Centilitre, *s.m.* (*Fr. meas.*) centilitre
Centime, *s.m.* (*Fr. coin, the* 100*th part of a* "franc") centime; (*fig.*) farthing, doit, stiver, rap. *Cinq —s*, a halfpenny [50 *—s*, half-a-franc, *or* 5 pence]. *—s additionnels*, county rate. *Au — le franc*, so much in the pound
Centimètre, *s.m.* (*Fr. meas.*) centimetre
Centinode, *s.f.* (*bot.*) *V.* **Renouée** [centiped
Centipède, *adj.* (*zool.*) centipedal; — *s.m.*
Centistère, *s.m.* (*Fr. meas.*) centistere
Centon, *s.m.* (*liter., mus.*) cento
Central, e, *adj.* central; principal, chief, head
Centralement, *adv.* centrally
Centralisa-teur, trice, *adj.* centralizing; — *s.m.f.* centralizer
Centralisation, *s.f.* centralization
Centraliser, *v.a.* to centralize
Se —, *v.r.* to become *or* be centralized
Centralité, *s.f.* centrality
Centre, *s.m.* centre; middle; element
Centrer, *v.a.* to centre
Centrier, *s.m.* (*fam.*) conservative
Centrifuge, *adj.* (*phys., bot.*) centrifugal
Centripète, *adj.* (*phys., bot.*) centripetal
Centrisque, *s.m.* (*zool.*) trumpet-fish, bellows-fish, snipe-fish, sea-snipe
Centrolophe, *s.m.* (*zool.*) black-fish
Centrope, *s.m.* (*bird*) pheasant-cuckoo
Centumvir, *s.m.* centumvir
Centumviral, e, *adj.* centumviral
Centumvirat, *s.m.* centumvirate
Centuple, *s.m. adj.* centuple, a hundredfold
Centupler, *v.a.n.*, **Se —,** *v.r.* to centuple, to increase a hundredfold
Centuriateur, *s.m.* (*eccl. liter.*) centuriator
Centurie, *s.f.* (*Rom. hist.*, &c.) century; hundred
Centurion, *s.m.* centurion
Cep, *s.m.* vine-plant, vine-stalk *or* stock, plant, stalk, stock, vine; (*hort.*) vine-cane, cane; (*of a plough*) *V.* **Sep; —s,** *pl.* (*obsolete*) stocks, fetters, shackles, irons, chains, bilboes
Cépage, *s.m.* vine-slip, vine-plant, variety of vine; vine-district
Cèpe, *s.m.* (*bot.*) esculent boletus
Cépée, *s.f.* tuft of shoots; young wood
Cependant, *adv. conj.* in the meantime, meanwhile; yet, still, however, nevertheless. — *que*, (*obsolete*) whilst, whereas
Céphalalg-ie, ique. *V.* page 3, § 1
Céphalée, *s.f.* (*med.*) headache
Céphalique, *adj.* (*anat., med.*) cephalic
Céphalite, *s.f.* (*med.*) cephalitis
Céphalo-graphie, -logie. *V.* page 3, § 1
Céphaloïde, *adj.* cephaloid
Céphalonien, ne, *adj. s.* Cephalonian
Céphaloniote, *s.m.f.* Cephaloniot
Céphalopode, *s.m.* (*zool.*) cephalopod
Céphaloptère, *s.m.* (*bird*) dragoon-bird; (*fish*) horned ray
Céphalotribe, *s.m.* (*surg.*) cephalotribe
Céphée, *s.m.* (*astr.*) Cepheus
Cépole, *s.m.* (*zool.*) band-fish, snake-fish. — *rouge*, fire-flame, red ribbon
Ceps, *s.m. V.* **Cèpe; —** *pl. of* **Cep** (*V.* **Cep**)
Céracée, *s.f.* whey
Céraiste, *s.m.* (*bot.*) mouse-ear chickweed
Cérame, *s.f.* Greek vase
Céramique, *adj.* ceramic; — *s.f.* ceramics
Céramograph-ie, ique. *V.* page 3, § 1
Cérasine, *s.f.* (*chem.*) cerasine, cherry-tree gum
Céraste, *s.m.* (*zool.*) cerastes, horned viper
Cérat, *s.m.* ointment, salve, cold cream, cerate
Céraunie, Céraunite, *s.f.* (*min.*) ceraunite, thunderstone
Cerbère, *s.m.* (*myth.*) Cerberus; (*fig.*) Cerberus, savage watch-dog, brutal keeper *or* jailer *or* warder *or* door-porter; (*astr.*) Cerberus; (*serpent*) cerberus; (*bot.*) cerbera, tanghin, ordeal nut-tree
Cerce, *s.f.* hoop, band, binding
Cerceau, *s.m.* hoop; ring; circle; hoop-net;
Cercelle, *s.f. V.* **Sarcelle** [pinion-quill
Cerclage, *s.m.* hooping; hoops
Cercle, *s.m.* circle; round; ring; hoop; orb; sphere; succession, series; club; society; assembly; party; company; (*formerly*) the Queen's drawing-room *or* court. — *vicieux*, circle, begging the question. *Vin en —s*, wine in casks *or* (the) cask *or* in (the) wood
Cercler, *v.a.* to hoop; to encircle
Cercleur, *s.m.* hooper
Cerclier, *s.m.* hoop-maker [hopper
Cercope, *s.m.* (*insect*) froth-fly, frog-fly, frog-
†Cercueil, *s.m.* coffin; grave, tomb; death
Céréale, *adj.f., s.f.* cereal; **—s,** *s.f.pl.* cereal grasses, cereals, corn, corn-plants, corn-crops, bread-plants, bread-stuffs
Céréaline, *s.f* (*chem.*) cerealine
Cérébelleu-x, se, *adj.* (*anat.*) cerebellous
Cérébellite, *s.f.* (*med.*) cerebellitis, inflammation of the cerebellum [*Fievre —*, brain-fever
Cérébral, e, *adj.* cerebral, of the brain, brain.
Cérébrine, *s.f.* (*chem.*) cerebrine
Cérébrique, *adj.* (*chem.*) cerebric
Cérébrite, *s.f.* (*med.*) cerebritis, inflammation of the cerebrum (*or* brain)
Cérébro-spinal, e, *adj.* (*anat.*) cerebro-spinal
Cérémoniaire, *s.m.* (*eccl.*) master of the ceremonies [ceremonial
Cérémonial, e, Cérémoniel, le, *adj.*
Cérémonial, *s.m.* ceremonial; ceremony, ceremonies; formalities; etiquette; state;
Cérémonialisme, *s.m.* ceremonialism [ritual
Cérémonie, *s.f.* ceremony; ceremoniousness; fuss, ado; state. *De —, adj.* state; full-dress; evening. *En —, en grande —*, in state, ceremoniously
Cérémonieu-x, se, *adj.* ceremonious, formal
Céréopse, *s.m.* cereopsis (*Australian bird*)
Cérès, *s.f.* (*myth., astr.*) Ceres; (*fig.*) corn, harvest;

bread. *Les dons, les trésors de* —, (*poet.*) the gifts, the treasures of Ceres; the harvest, the corn
Cerf, *s.m.* stag, deer; hart. — **-volant,** *s.m.* stag-beetle, horn-beetle; (*toy*) kite, paper-kite
†Cerfeuil, *s.m.* (*bot.*) chervil. — *musqué* or *odorant*, sweet cicely [**Serfouir**
Cerfouette; Cerfouir. *V.* **Serfouette;**
Cérine, *s.f.* (*chem.*) cerine
Cerisaie, *s.f.* cherry-orchard, cherry-garden
Cerise, *s.f.* (*fruit*) cherry; berry (*of coffee*); — *s.m.* cherry colour, cherry, cerise; — *adj.* cherry-coloured, cherry, cerise. *Rouge-* —, cherry-red
Cerisette, *s.f.* dried cherry; cerisette (*kind of red plum*)
Cerisier, *s.m.* cherry-tree; cherry-wood, cherry
Cérite, *s.f.* (*min.*) cerite
Cérium, *s.m.* (*chem.*) cerium
Cermoise, *s.f.* (variety of tulip)
Cerne, *s.m.* circle; ring
Cerné, e, *adj.* surrounded; encircled; (*of the eyes*) surrounded with a dark circle, black and blue [unripe walnut; (*slang*) young girl, lass
Cerneau, *s.m.* kernel of an unripe walnut;
Cernement, *s.m.* surrounding; encircling, &c. (*V.* **Cerner**)
Cerner, *v.a.* to surround; to encircle; to gird; to hem in; to encompass; to invest; to circumvent; to cut round; to surround (*eyes*) with a dark circle; to peel (*walnuts*); to dig round (*a tree*); to ring (*a tree, cut out a ring of bark*); (*surg.*) to cut around (*a tumour*)
  Se —, *v.r.* (*of the eyes*) to become *or* be surrounded with a dark circle [ing-shears
Cernoir, *s.m.* pruning-knife, garden-knife, ring-
Cérocome, *s.m.* (*insect*) cerocoma [cierge-bearer
Céroféraire, *s.m.* (*eccl.*) wax-taper bearer,
Cérographe, *s.m.* cerographer
Cérograph-ie, -ique. *V.* page 3, § 1
Céroléine, *s.f.* (*chem.*) ceroleine
Céron, *s.m.* ceroon (*bale*)
Céroplastique, *s.f. adj.* ceroplastic
Cérotique, *adj.* (*chem.*) cerotic
Céroxyle, *s.m.* (*bot.*) wax-palm, wax-tree
Cerre, *s.m.* (*bot.*) cerrus, bitter oak
Certain, e, *adj.* certain, sure, positive; (*when placed* BEFORE *a noun*) some, certain; settled, fixed, appointed, stated; —**s,** *pron.pl.* (*before a verb*) some people, some
Certain, *s.m.* certainty, certain, that which is certain; positive fact; (*in Exchange language*) certain price
Certainement, *adv.* certainly; to be sure; surely; assuredly; to a certainty; by all means; of course
Certes, *adv.* most assuredly, indeed [racter
Certificat, *s.m.* certificate; testimonial, cha-
Certificateur, *s.m.* certifier; guarantee
Certification, *s.f.* certification, certifying; witnessing [to assure; to witness; to guarantee
Certifier, *v.a.* to certify; to testify; to attest;
Certitude, *s.f.* certainty; assurance; steadiness. *Avoir la* —, to be certain
Cérulé, e, *adj.* cerulean
Cérumen, *s.m.* cerumen, ear-wax
Cérumineu-x, se, *adj.* ceruminous, waxy
Céruse, *s.f.* white lead, ceruse. *Blanc de* —, white lead, ceruse
Cervaison, *s.f.* stag-hunting season
Cerveau, *s.m.* brain; intelligence, mind; head; (*of a bell*) shoulder. — *brûlé*, wild *or* crazy fellow. — *creux*, visionary, dreamer
Cervelas, *s.m.* saveloy (*sausage*)
Cervelet, *s.m.* (*anat.*) cerebellum
Cervelle, *s.f.* brains; brain; intelligence
Cervical, e, *adj.* (*anat.*) cervical
Cervier, *adj.m.* *Loup-* —, *chat-* —, lynx
Cervin, e, *adj.* cervine
Cervoise, *s.f.* (*old*) cerevisia, ale, beer
Ces, (*pl. of* **Ce**) *adj.* these, those; such; what. — *livres-ci*, these books. — *livres-là*, those books
César, *s.m.* Cæsar; emperor, prince; warrior, conqueror; great general; brave man
Césarien, ne, *adj. s.* Cæsarean, Cesarean,
Césarisme, *s.m.* Cæsarism [Cæsarian, Cesarian
Cessation, *s.f.* cessation; end; intermission; discontinuance; interruption; suspension; suspense; stoppage
Cesse, *s.f.* ceasing; rest; respite. *Sans* —, without ceasing, unceasingly, incessantly, unremittingly, constantly, continually, ever, for ever
Cesser, *v.a.n.* to cease; to discontinue; to leave off; to break off; to have done; to stop; to forbear; to end; to finish; to expire; to be at an end. *Faire* —, to stop, to put a stop *or* an end to; to do away with; to abate
Cessibilité, *s.f.* transferability
Cessible, *adj.* transferable [cession
Cession, *s.f.* transfer; assignment; surrender;
Cessionnaire, *s.m.f.* transferee; assignee;
C'est-à-dire, *conj. V.* **Dire** [grantee
Ceste, *s.m.* cestus; gauntlet
Cestoïde, *adj.* cestoid
Cestreau, *s.m.* (*bot.*) cestrum, bastard jasmine
Césure, *s.f.* (*vers.*) cæsura, pause, rest
Cet, te, *adj. V.* **Ce,** *adj.*
Cétacé, *s.m.* (*zool.*) cetacean [ous
Cétacé, e, Cétacéen, ne, *adj.* (*zool*) cetace-
Cétérac, *s.m.* (*bot.*) ceterach, spleenwort, scale
Cétine, *s.f.* (*chem.*) cetine [fern
Cétiosaure, *s.m.* (*fossil*) cetiosaurus, cetiosaur
Céto-graphie, -logie. *V.* page 3, § 1
Cétoine, *s.f.* (*zool.*) floral beetle. — *dorée*, green rose-chafer, rose-beetle, rose-bug
Cétraire, *s.f.* (*bot.*) Iceland-moss
Cétrarine, *s.f.* (*chem.*) cetrarine
Cétylique, *adj.* (*chem.*) cetylic
Ceux, *m.pl. of* **Celui**
†Cévadille, *s.f.* (*pharm.*) cevadilla [the Cévennes
Cévenol, e, *adj. s.* of the Cévennes; native of
Ceylanais, e, *adj. s.* Ceylonese
Ceylanite, *s.m.* (*min.*) ceylonite, ceylanite
Chabec, *s.m. V.* **Chebec**
Chablage, *s.m.* fastening; towing
Chable, *s.m.* (*navig.*) rope, tackle
Chableau, *s.m.* (*navig.*) tow-line, warp
Chabler, *v.a.* to fasten; to tow; to beat down (*walnuts*, &c.) [dead twigs, cablis
Chablis, *s.m.* chablis (wine); wind-fallen wood,
Chablot, *s.m.* (*mas.*) rope
Chaboisseau, *s.m.* (*fish*) sea-scorpion
Chabot, *s.m.* (*fish*) chub, miller's thumb, bull, head; (*mas.*) *V.* **Chablot**
Chabraque, *s.f. V.* **Schabraque**
†Chabrillou, *s.m. V.* **Cabrillon**
Chacal, *s.m.* jackal
Chaconne, *s.f.* chacone (*dance, tune*)
Chacun, e, *pron.m.f.* each; every one; — *m.* everybody; —**e,** *s.f.* partner
Chacunière, *s.f.* (*old*) o.'s own house
Chaff, *s.m.* (*agr.*) chaff, provender
Chafouin, e, *s.m.f.* ugly monkey, scrubby sly-looking fellow *or* thing, mean-looking person, runt; — *adj.* ugly, disagreeable, monkey, mean-looking, sly, with an expression of low cunning
Chafrioler (Se), *v.r.* to delight (in), to indulge
Chagrin, *s.m.* grief, sorrow, trouble, vexation, concern, regret, disappointment; fretfulness, peevishness, surliness, anger, chagrin; (*leather*) shagreen. *Faire* or *donner du* — *à*, to give pain to, to pain, to grieve, to vex. *Mourir de* —, to die of a broken heart
Chagrin, e, *adj.* sorrowful, sad, dull; gloomy; grieved, vexed; morose, fretful, peevish, surly, angry, chagrined
Chagrinant, e, *adj.* grievous, sad, distressing; vexatious, vexing, provoking, troublesome
Chagrinement, *adv.* sorrowfully, sadly; fretfully, peevishly
Chagriner, *v.a.* to grieve, to afflict; to trouble; to vex; to fret; to chagrin; to shagreen (*leather*)
  Se —, *v.r.* to grieve, to fret; to grieve *or* &c. each other; to be shagreened
Chagrinier, *s.m.* shagreen-maker
Chah, *s.m. V.* **Schah**

Chahut, *s.m.* chahut (*a vulgar dance*); row, dust, shindy; squabble
Chahuter, *v.n.* to dance the chahut; to make a row, to squabble; — *v.a.* to shake; to upset
Chahuteu-r, se, *s.m.f.* disorderly person, rioter [storehouse; shed; work-yard
Chai, *s.m.* wine-store (*above ground*), spirit-store,
†**Chaillot,** *s.m.* Chaillot (*a district of Paris*). *A —!* (*pop.*) to Bath! to Jericho! to the devil!
Chaînage, *s.m.* measuring (*land*) with a chain; (*build.*) chain-timbers, bond-timbers, chain-bond, bonds
Chaîne, *s.f.* chain; ridge; range; ledge; chain-gang; warp; boom; series; bond; tie; link; continuity; line; (*build.*) *V.* **Chainage.** — *anglaise,* (*dancing*) right and left. — *longue,* watch-guard, guard. — *de cou,* neck-chain, necklet. — *de sûreté,* (*rail.*) coupling-chain. *A la —,* chained, chained up. *Faire la —,* to form in line; to pass from hand to hand buckets of water, &c. (*in a fire,* &c.). *Mettre à la —,* to chain, to chain up
Chaîné, e, *adj.* chained, forming a chain
Chaîner, *v.a.* to measure (*land*) with a chain
Chaînetier, *s.m.* chain-maker
Chaînette, *s.f.* little *or* small chain; chain; chain-stitch, chain-work; pole-chain (*of a carriage*); chainette (wine); (*math.*) catenary *or* funicular curve, catenary
Chaîniste, *s.m.* chain-maker
Chaînon, *s.m.* link of a chain, link
Chaintre, *s.m.* (*agr.*) trench; paddock
Chair, *s.f.* flesh; meat; skin; body, man, human nature; lust. — *vive,* quick. — *de poule,* (*pers.*) goose-flesh, goose-skin. *Avoir la — de poule,* to feel o.'s flesh creep *or* crawl, to shudder. *Donner* (or *Faire venir*) *la — de poule,* to make o.'s flesh creep *or* crawl, to make o.'s blood run cold, to make one shudder. *N'être ni — ni poisson,* to be neither fish, flesh, nor fowl. *En — et en os,* in flesh and blood
Chair, *s.m.* (*rail.*) chair
Chaire, *s.f.* pulpit; desk; throne; see; chair; professorship; preaching. *En pleine —,* before the whole congregation; before the whole class
Chais, *pl. of* **Chai;** (*abusively for the sing.*) *V.* **Chai**
Chaise, *s.f.* chair; chaise; (*build.*) curb, frame-work. — *longue,* couch, lounge, lounging-chair. — *à porteurs,* sedan-chair. — *percée,* commode
Chaisier, *s.m.* chair-maker
Chaisière, *s.f.* chair-letter
Chako, *s.m. V.* **Shako**
Chalade, *s.f. V.* **Calade** [*s.m.* barge, flat, lighter
Chaland, e, *s.m.f.* customer; purchaser; —
Chalandeau, Chalandou, *s.m.* bargeman
Chalandise, *s.f.* (*obsolete*) custom, customers; goodwill
‡**Chalastique,** *adj.m.f., s.m.* (*med.*) chalastic
‡**Chalaze,** *s.f.* (*med.*) sty (*on the eye*), stye; (*bot.*) chalaza, chalaze; (*of eggs*) chalaza; germ,
‡**Chalazion,** *s.m.* (*med.*) *V.* **Chalaze** [treadle
‡**Chalcédoine,** *s.f. V.* **Calcédoine**
‡**Chalcide,** *s.m.* chalcis (*large lizard*)
‡**Chalcidique,** *s.m.* chalcidicum (*porch*)
‡**Chalcographe,** *s.m.* chalcographer
‡**Chalcographie,** *s.f.* chalcography; engraving-establishment; collection of engravings, catalogue of ditto; printing-office (*of the Pope*)
‡**Chalcographique,** *adj.* chalcographic
‡**Chalda-ïque, -ïsme.** *V.* page 3, § 1
‡**Chaldéen, ne,** *adj.* Chaldean, Chaldee; — *s.m.f.* Chaldean; — *s.m.* Chaldaic *or* Chaldee
Châle, *s.m.* shawl [(*language*)
Chalet, *s.m.* Swiss cottage; cheese-house
Chaleur, *s.f.* heat; warmth; glow; ardour, vivacity, animation, fire, zeal; **—s,** *pl.* hot days, hot weather *or* season, heat, summer. *Les grandes —s,* the very hot weather, the height of summer
Chaleureusement, *adv.* hotly, warmly, ardently; with animation; vehemently; zealously
Chaleureu-x, se, *adj.* warm, ardent, glowing, animated, spirited, vehement, zealous
Châli-er, ère, *adj.* of shawls, shawl
Châlier, *s.m.* shawl-manufacturer; clerk of the shawl department
Chalingue, *s.f.* (small Indian vessel)
Châlit, *s.m.* bedstead
Chaloir, *v.n. imp.* (*old*) to matter, to be important. *Il ne m'en chaut,* it matters not to me, I don't care. *Peu m'en chaut,* it signifies little to me, I care little *or* nothing about it
Chalon, *s.m.* (*fish.*) drag-net, trawl-net
Châlonnais, e, *adj. s.m.f.* of Châlons; native of Châlons; — *s.m.* Châlons district
Chaloupe, *s.f.* launch, long-boat, boat; shallop; sloop; (*pop.*) gaudily dressed woman, swell. — *canonnière,* gun-boat, gun-vessel
Chalumeau, *s.m.* pipe; reed; straw; blow-pipe; lime-twig; (*bot.*) flute
Chalumet, *s.m.* tip (*of a tobacco-pipe*)
Chalut, *s.m.* (*fish.*) drag-net, trawl-net
Chaly, *s.m.* (*stuff*) challis [nous, iron, steel
‡**Chalybé, e,** *adj.* (*pharm.*) chalybeate, ferrugi-
Chamade, *s.f.* parley, chamade; drum-beating. *Battre la —,* to sound a parley; to beat a call; to surrender, to yield; to be disconcerted
‡**Chamærops,** *s.m.* (*bot.*) chamærops, fan-palm
†**Chamailler,** *v.n.,* **Se —,** *v.r.* to scuffle, to wrangle, to squabble. — *des dents,* (*pop.*) to feed, to grub, to fall to, to stuff [scuffle, squabble
†**Chamaillerie,** *s.f.,* **Chamaillis,** *s.m.* fray,
Chaman, *s.m.* shaman (*Asiatic priest*)
Chamanisme, *s.m.* shamanism [ornament
Chamarre, *s.f.* smockfrock; lace, embroidery,
Chamarrer, *v.a.* to lace, to embroider; to bedizen; to cover, to load
Chamarrure, *s.f.* lacing, embroidery, trimming, trimmings; bedizening; gaudy orna-
Chambellan, *s.m.* chamberlain [ments; medley
Chambertin, *s.m.* chambertin (wine)
Chambourin, *s.m.* strass; common green glass
Chambrage, *s.m.,* **Chambraie,** *s.f.* (*nav.*) bowsprit-bitts [frame; (chimney-)piece
Chambranle, *s.m.* (door-)case; (window-)
Chambre, *s.f.* chamber; room; bedroom; apartment; lodging; house (*of parliament*); parliament; court (*of justice,* &c.); office; (*nav.*) cabin, room; (*of firearms, of mines, of the eye, opt.*) chamber; covert (*of a stag*); wolf-trap, fox-trap. — *ardente,* lights round a coffin; (*Fr. hist.*) ardent *or* fiery chamber. — *claire,* (*opt.*) camera lucida. — *étoilée,* (*Engl. hist.*) star-chamber. — *garnie,* furnished lodgings. — *introuvable,* (*Fr. hist.*) "matchless chamber" (*Chamber of Deputies in* 1815, *on the second return of Louis XVIII.*). — *noire,* — *obscure,* (*opt.*) camera obscura. — *à coucher,* bedroom
Chambré, e, *adj.* (*of cast metals*) chambered, honeycombed; (*of shells*) chambered
Chambrée, *s.f.* sleeping room, roomful, number in a room; room; barrack-room; mess; (*theat.*) number of spectators, house, receipts
Chambrelan, *s.m.* jobbing workman; single-room lodger
Chambrer, *v.n.* to chum together; (*of a stag*) to lie in a covert, to be lodged; — *v.a.* to chamber; to hollow; to confine, to keep confined; to take aside
Se —, *v.r.* (*artil.*) to become honeycombed
Chambrette, *s.f.* little room, small room [ard
Chambrier, *s.m.* chamberlain; treasurer, stew-
Chambrière, *s.f.* chamber-maid, house-maid, maid; longe-whip; cart-prop, prop, set-stick; (*nav.*) plait of rope; (*nav.*) staple
†**Chambrillon,** *s.f.* (*pop.*) servant-girl
Chambrule, *s.m.* (*agr.*) black rust, smut, bunt
‡**Chame,** *s.f.* (*shell*) chama, gaping-cockle
Chameau, *s.m.* camel; camel-hair; (*nav.*) camel; (*fam.*) mot; cunning fellow
‡**Chamécisse,** *s.m.* (*bot.*) ground-ivy, gill, ale-
Chamelée, *s.f.* camel-load [hoof
Chamelier, *s.m.* camel-driver

Chamelle, *s.f.* she-camel

Chamélon, *s.m.* young camel, camel-calf

‡**Chamérope,** *s.m. V.* **Chamærops**

Chamois, *s.m.* chamois, wild goat of the Alps; chamois leather, shamoy, shammy; wash-leather; — *adj.* buff; drab

Chamoiser, *v.a.* to shamoy-dress

Se —, *v.r.* to be shamoy-dressed

Chamoiserie, *s.f.* shamoy-dressing; shamoy-factory; shamoy *or* shammy (*leather*)

Chamoiseur, *s.m.* shamoy-dresser

Champ, *s.m.* field; career; ground; scope; space, room; region; start; spring; subject; matter; opportunity; (*her., opt.*) field; (*tech.*) edge, side; **—s,** *pl.* fields; country. — *clos*, lists; tilt-yard. —*s-Élysées*, (*myth.*) Elysian fields; (*part of Paris*) Champs-Élysées. — *de courses*, race-course, race-ground. — *de Mars*, parade-ground, Champ de Mars. *A bout de —*, without resources. *A tout bout de —*, at every moment; at every turn; incessantly, ever, constantly, continually. *De —*, edgewise, sideways (*lying on the ground lengthwise but not flat*). *Sur-le- —*, on the spot; immediately, directly, at once, forthwith; at call; off hand. *Avoir la clé* (or *clef*) *des —s*, to be at liberty. *Battre aux —s*, (*mil.*) to beat a salute *or* the march. *Être aux —s*, (*fig.*) to be uneasy; to be angry. *Mettre aux —s*, to make uneasy, to put out; to make angry. *Prendre la clé* (or *clef*) *des —*, to run away, to escape, to bolt

Champagne, *s.m.* champagne (wine, *from* "*la Champagne*," *one of the old provinces of France*); (*her.*) champain; — *s.f. Fine —*, Champagne brandy (*from* "*Champagne*," *a village near Cognac, in the French department of Charente-Inférieure*) [of

Champaniser, *v.a.* to make sham champagne

Champart, *s.m.* (*feud.*) field-rent

Champé, e, *adj.* (*her.*) with a field

Champeau, *s.m.* (*obsolete*) meadow, field

Champelure, *s.f. V.* **Champlure** [of ditto

Champenois, e, *adj. s.* of Champagne; native

Champêtre, *adj.* rural; country; rustic; country-like; countrified; field; sylvan. *Garde —*, *V.* **Garde,** *s.m.* [the fields; foundling; bastard

Champi, sse, *adj. s.* abandoned *or* found in

†**Champignon,** *s.m.* mushroom; toad-stool; fungus; mushroom-jet (*of water*); letter, thief (*in a candle*); (*of liquids*) mother, fur; (*surg.*) proud flesh; bonnet-stand, stand; peg; cap; knob

†**Champignoniste,** *s.m.f.* mushroom-grower

†**Champignonnière,** *s.f.* mushroom-bed *or* ground *or* pit *or* house

Champion, ne, *s.m.f.* champion; championess

Championnat, *s.m.* championship

Champlé, e, *adj.* (*of trees*) frost-bitten

Champlever, *v.a.* to groove; to engrave, to cut

Champlure, *s.f.* frost-bite (*of trees*); hole (*in*

‡**Chamsin,** *s.m. V.* **Khamsin** [*a cask*)

‡**Chananéen, ne,** *s.m.f.* Canaanite; — *adj.*

Chance, *s.f.* chance, luck; hazard [Canaanitish

Chanceau, *s.m.* (*arch.*) rail, railing

Chancelant, e, *part. adj.* tottering, &c. (*V.* **Chanceler**); unsteady; unsettled; irresolute; uncertain, precarious; weak

Chanceler, *v.n.* to totter; to reel; to stagger; to waver; to falter; to be unsteady *or* unsettled

Chancelier, *s.m.* chancellor [*or* precarious

Chancelière, *s.f.* chancellor's wife; foot-muff

Chancellement, *s.m.* tottering; reeling; staggering; unsteadiness; irresolution

Chancellerie, *s.f.* chancery; chancellor's office *or* residence; chancellorship; seal-office

Chanceu-x, se, *adj.* (*pers.*) lucky, fortunate; (*things*) uncertain, doubtful, ticklish

Chanci, e, *adj.* mouldy

Chancir, *v.n.*, **Se —,** *v.r.* to get mouldy

Chancissure, *s.f.* mould, mouldiness

Chancre, *s.m.* (*med.*) chancre; (*agr., hort., vet., fig.*) canker [crous

Chancreu-x, se, *adj.* cankerous; (*med.*) chan-

Chancroïde, *s.m.* (*med.*) chancre-like eruption

Chandeleur, *s.f.* Candlemas

Chandelier, *s.m.* candlestick; bar; stake; (*nav.*) crutch, stanchion; (*pers.*) screen, scape-goat; (*at play*) expenses of the game. — *d'eau*, vertical jet (of water). — *de mineur*, — *de fer*, miner's borer, crowbar. *Sur le —*, (*fig.*) in a conspicuous situation

Chandeli-er, ère, *s.m.f.* chandler, tallow-chandler, candle-manufacturer

Chandelle, *s.f.* candle, tallow-candle; light; candle-light; (*tech.*) stay, support. — *moulée*, mould candle, mould. — *plongée*, — *à la baguette*, dipped candle, dip. — *de glace*, icicle. — *de veille*, rush-light. *Voir des —s*, *voir mille* or *trente-six —s*, to be stunned, to see the stars by daylight [chandlery; candle-trade; candle-shop

Chandellerie, *s.f.* candle-factory; tallow-

Chanfrein, *s.m.* (*of horses*) chanfrin; bunch *or* plume of feathers; (*ancient armour*) chamfrain, chamfron, chanfron; (*tech.*) chamfer, cant

Chanfreiner, *v.a.* to chamfer, to cant

Change, *s.m.* change; changing; exchange; agio. *Agent de —*, stock-broker. *Donner le — à*, *faire prendre le — à*, to put on the wrong scent; to mislead; to impose upon, to deceive. *Gagner* or *perdre au —*, to be a gainer *or* a loser by the change. *Prendre le —*, to allow oneself to be deceived; to be mistaken. *Rendre le — à*, (*fig.*) to pay (*one*) back in his own coin, to give tit for tat, to retaliate upon; to give a clincher [of change

Changeable, *adj.* to be changed, susceptible

Changeant, e, *adj.* changing, changeable; variable; unsettled; fickle; shifting; moving; (*of colours*) shot

Changement, *s.m.* change; alteration; mutation; turn; variation; variety; shifting. — *à vue*, scene-shifting. — *de voie*, (*rail.*) shunting, shifting; shunt

Changeoter, *v.n.* to change often

Changer, *v.a.n.* to change; to alter; to convert; to transform; to exchange; to have a change (of); to turn; to shift. — *de* ..., to change o.'s ..., to change ..., to have a change of ..., to shift o.'s ..., to shift ..., to take another ..., to go to another ...; to alter o.'s ...; to cast its ... — *de voie*, (*rail.*) to shunt, to shift

Se —, *v.r.* to be changed *or* converted *or* turned, &c., to change, to alter, to turn; to change o.'s linen *or* clothes

Changeu-r, se, *s.m.f.* exchange-broker, money-changer; bullion-dealer; bill-broker

Chanlate, Chanlatte, *s.f.* chantlate, eaves-board, eaves-catch, eaves-lath

Chanoine, *s.m.* canon (*pers.*)

Chanoinesse, *s.f.* canoness

Chanoinie, *s.f.* (*old*) *V.* **Canonicat**

Chanson, *s.f.* song; ballad; carol; ditty; sing-song; (*fig.*) story; nonsense; idle story; affair;

Chansonner, *v.a.* to lampoon [rub, hitch

Chansonnette, *s.f.* little song, ditty; comic

Chansonneu-r, se, *s.m.f.* lampooner [song

Chansonni-er, ère, *s.m.f. adj.* song-writer; ballad-writer; ballad-singer; singer of songs;

Chansonnier, *s.m.* song-book [merry, lively

Chant, *s.m.* singing; song; ditty; carol; anthem; hymn; lay; air, tune, strain, melody; music, vocal music; voice; accent; lullaby; chant; canto; warbling; crow, crowing; chirp, chirping, chirrup; dirge. — *funèbre*, dirge

Chantable, *adj.* fit to be sung; worthy of being sung, worth singing

Chantage, *s.m.* extortion of money (*by threats of exposure or promises of eulogy*), extortion of hush-money; extortion

Chantant, e, *adj.* singing; fit to be sung, fit for singing, fitted for song; easily sung; easy to be set to music; tunable, musical, harmonious. *Café —*, *V.* **Café** [(*cut from the piece*)

Chanteau, *s.m.* hunch (*of bread*); bit of stuff

Chantepleure, *s.f.* funnel with a rose; outlet,

gully-hole; tap; water-pot; trench; tub (*for treading grapes*)
Chantepleurer, *v.a.* to tread (*grapes*)
Chanter, *v.a.n.* to sing; to chant; to sing out; to celebrate, to praise; to say, to tell, to talk about; to talk, to speak; to split (upon), to denounce; to confess; to warble; to crow; to chirp; to carol; to fizz; to whiz; to sound; to resound; to be heard; to yield; to fork out money. — *victoire*, to cry victory, to crow over o.'s victory. — *sur tous les tons*, to ring the changes *or* all the changes on. — *toujours la même antienne* or *la même chanson*, to be ever harping on the same string, to harp upon one string. *C'est comme si je chantais* or *vous chantiez*, &c., it is like talking to the wind, it is of no use, it is no go
Se —, *v.r.* to be sung
Chanterelle, *s.f.* treble-string; musical bottle; call-bird; cantharellus mushroom. *Appuyer sur la* —, (*fig.*) to lay stress on the most important part; to touch the sore point; to recommend strongly
Chanteronner, *v.a.n. V.* **Chantonner**
Chanteur, *s.m.* singer; vocalist; songster; singing bird; extorter of hush-money, extortioner; — *adj.m.* singing
Chanteuse, *s.f.* singer, common singer; singing-woman; songstress; — *adj.f.* singing
Chantier, *s.m.* yard; wood *or* timber-yard; coal-yard; stonecutter's yard; work-yard, building-yard, dock-yard; stock; board; cask-stand, gauntree, stillion, scantling, stollage
†**Chantignole,** *s.f.* (*carp.*) wooden block; (*mas.*) paving-brick
Chantonné, e, *adj.* (*of paper*) defective
Chantonner, *v.a.n.* to hum (*a tune*)
Chantonnerie, *s.f.* humming
Chantournage, *s.m.* cutting in profile, sawing round; carving; indentation; setting off
Chantourné, *s.m.* (*of a bedstead*) headpiece
Chantournement, *s.m.* (*tech.*) profile, rounding
Chantourner, *v.a.* to cut in profile, to saw round; to carve; to indent; to set off
Chantre, *s.m.* chorister; precentor, chanter, lay clerk; singer; poet, bard; songster. *Le — de la Thrace*, Orpheus. *Le — thébain*, Pindar. *Le — d'Ionie* or *d'Ilion* or *d'Ulysse*, Homer. *Le — de Téos*, Anacreon. *Le — d'Énée* or *d'Ausonie*, Virgil. *Le — de Roland*, Ariosto. *Le — des jardins*, Delille. *Le — de Henri*, Voltaire
Chantrerie, *s.f.* precentorship
Chanvre, *s.m.* hemp; (*poet.*) rope
Chanvreu-x, se, *adj.* hempen
Chanvri-er, ère, *s.m.f.* hemp-dresser; dealer in hemp
Chanvrière, *s.f.* (*obsolete*) hemp-field
‡**Chao-logie, -logique, -tique.** *V.* page 3, [§ 1
‡**Chaos,** *s.m.* chaos; disorder, confusion
Chape, *s.f.* (*eccl., arch.*) cope; (*of a buckle or hook or scabbard*) chape, catch; (*of a pulley*) block; (*of a dish*) cover; (*of birds*) colour of the back; (*tech.*) cap; cover; head; back; spindle. **—-chute,** *s.f.* godsend, windfall, good job, job. **—-chuter,** *v.n.* to rustle, to rattle, to murmur, to make a slight noise
Chapé, e, *adj.* coped, clad in a (*or* o.'s) cope
Chapeau, *s.m.* hat; bonnet; felt; wreath *or* crown of flowers, wreath, crown; cardinalate, cardinalship, red hat; (*fam.*) man; name, character; (*fish.*) shrimp-net; (*tech.*) cap; bonnet; hood; head; (*bot., nav.*) cap; (*com. nav.*) primage, hat-money. — *chinois*, Chinese bells. *Frère* —, (*monk*) assistant brother
Chapelain, *s.m.* chaplain; incumbent
Chapeler, *v.a.* to rasp *or* grate (*bread*); (*fig.*) to chip, to hack
Chapelet, *s.m.* chaplet, beads, string of beads; bead-roll; string; story; (*dist.*) bead; (*com.*) beads; (*arch., rid.*) chaplet; (*nav.*) chaplet, casters. — *hydraulique*, chain-pump. *Défiler son* —, to tell o.'s beads; (*fig.*) to tell o.'s story, to empty o.'s budget
Chapeli-er, ère, *s.m.f.* hatter, hat-manufacturer
Chapeline, *s.f.* (*of armour*) cappeline
Chapelle, *s.f.* chapel; altar; choir; church-plate; living; vault of an oven; reservoir of a pump; (*print., nav.*) chapel; (*pop.*) dram-shop. — *ardente*, lights round a coffin. — *blanche*, (*fam.*) bed. *Faire* —, (*nav.*) to chapel, to broach to. *Tenir* —, to attend divine service in state. *Pour la petite —, s'il vous plait!* please remember the grotto!
Chapellenie, *s.f.* chaplaincy, chaplainship
Chapellerie, *s.f.* hat-trade; hat-making; hat-manufactory; hats, caps
Chapelure, *s.f.* bread raspings; grated bread; chippings, chips, fragments
Chaperon, *s.m.* hood; riding-hood; (*pers.*) chaperon, chaperone; (*of a robe*) shoulder-knot; (*tech.*) cap, covering; holster-cap; (*arch.*) coping; (*artil.*) apron
Chaperonner, *v.a.* to chaperon *or* chaperone (*a lady*); (*arch.*) to cope; (*falc.*) to hood
Chapier, *s.m.* cope-bearer; cope-maker; cope-closet
Chapiteau, *s.m.* top; head; (*arch.*) capital; (*mach.*) cap; (*artil.*) vent-cover
Chapitral, e, *adj.* chapteral
Chapitre, *s.m.* chapter; chapter-house; subject, matter, head, point, score; account
Chapitrer, *v.a.* to reprimand, to rebuke, to lecture
Chapon, *s.m.* capon; vine-slip; young vine-plant; clove of garlic; piece of bread rubbed with garlic (*for salad*); sop in broth
Chaponneau, *s.m.* young capon
Chaponner, *v.a.* to caponize [*V.* **Caponnière**
Chaponnière, *s.f.* stewpan for capons; (*mil.*)
Chappin, *s.m.* (*Spanish*) overshoe
Chapska, *s.m. V.* **Schapzka**
Chaque, *adj.* each, every
Char, *s.m.* car; chariot; hearse. — *à bancs*, pleasure-van, van; jaunting-car, car; waggonette. — *numéroté*, (*jest.*) hackney-coach [tail
‡**Chara,** *s.m.* (*bot.*) chara, stonewort, water-horse-
Charabia, *s.m.* Auvergne dialect; bad French, broken French, gibberish; native of Auvergne, Auvergnat
Charade, *s.f.* charade
Charadiste, *s.m.f.* charade-maker
†**Charagne,** *s.f. V.* **Chara**
Charançon, *s.m.* weevil, grub, snout-beetle
Charançonné, e, *adj.* attacked by the weevils
Charasse, *s.f.* crate
Charbon, *s.m.* coal; coals; charcoal; embers; cinder; carbon; (*med.*) anthrax, carbuncle; (*agr.*) black rust, smut, bunt. — *de bois*, charcoal. — *de terre*, pit-coal, coals, coal. *Être sur les —s*, to be on thorns
Charbonnage, *s.m.* coal-mining; coal-mine, coal-pit
†**Charbonnaille,** *s.f.* (*metal.*) bed of fireclay, sand, and charcoal-dust
Charbonné, e, *adj.* charred; blackened, daubed; black; black-spotted; (*agr.*) rusty, smutty; (*med.*) carbuncled, carbuncular
Charbonnée, *s.f.* broiled pork *or* beef, broil; sketch made with charcoal; (*of brick-kilns*) breeze; (*coal-mining*) stratum, coal-seam
Charbonner, *v.a.* to coal; to char, to carbonize; to blacken, to black; to daub; to draw *or* sketch *or* scribble over with charcoal; — *v.n.*,
Se —, *v.r.* to char, to be charred, to carbonize, to burn black, to smoulder
Charbonnerie, *s.f.* coal-store; (*polit.*) *V.* **Carbonarisme**
Charbonneu-x, se, *adj.* coaly; (*med.*) carbuncular
Charbonnier, *s.m.* charcoal-burner; charcoal-dealer, coal-man, coal-merchant; coal-heaver; carbonaro; coal-cellar, coal-hole, coal-closet, coal-shed; (*zool.*) coal-fish; (*vessel*) collier; — *adj.m.* carrying coal. — *est maître chez soi*, a man's house is his castle
Charbonnière, *s.f.* coal-woman; place (*in a wood*) where charcoal is made, charcoal-pit, charcoal-kiln; (*bird*) great tit; cole-tit; — *adj.f.* carrying coal
†**Charbouiller,** *v.a.* (*agr.*) to blight
Charbucle, Charbulle, *s.f.* (*agr.*) *V.* **Nielle**
Charcuter, *v.a.* to cut up, to chop up (*meat*); (*fig.*) to hack, to mangle

Charcuterie, *s.f.* pork-butchery, pork-butcher's trade *or* business; dressed pork, pork; dressing of pork; pork butchers
Charcuti-er, ère, *s.m.f.* pork-butcher
Chardon, *s.m.* thistle; (*on a wall*, &c.) spike; (*fish*) white-horse (*kind of skate*). — *du Parnasse*, Grub-street writer [to nap, to teasel
Chardonner, *v.a.* to raise the nap of (*cloth*),
Chardonneret, *s.m.* goldfinch
Chardonnette, *s.f.* (*bot.*) prickly artichoke
Chardonnière, *s.f.* thistle-plantation
Charenton, *s.m.* Charenton (*the French Bedlam or Colney Hatch*), a mad-house
Charge, *s.f.* load; burden; quantity, number; charge; encumbrance; expense; tax; obligation; duty; trust, care, custody; office, place, situation, post, employment, function; public office; practice; orders, directions; cure (*of souls*); caricature; parody; exaggeration; farce, joke, trick; lading; loading; cargo; freight; shot; (*vet.*) horse-poulticing, poulticing, appliance. *A* —, burdensome; a burden; chargeable; (*law*) for the prosecution. *A — de, A la — de* or *que*, on condition of *or* that; provided that. *A la — d'autant*, on condition of a return. *En* —, (*nav.*) lading. *Être à la — de*, to be dependent upon; to fall upon. *Rompre la* —, to break bulk
Chargé, e, *part. adj.* loaded, laden, charged, &c. (*V.* **Charger**); cloudy; heavy; thick; muddy; too deep, dull; foul; furred; swollen; weighed down; tipsy; (*of a letter*) registered; (*of a cab*) taken, with a fare, with people in; (*her.*) charged; (*nav.*) laden; bound (to *or* for); laid upon her side (*by a gust of wind*). — *en côte*, (*nav.*) embayed on a lee-shore with the hard wind
Chargé, *s.m.* person intrusted. — *d'affaires*, ambassador's substitute, envoy, chargé d'affaires; agent. — *de cours*, assistant lecturer *or* professor, substitute
Chargeant, e, *adj.* heavy, clogging, cloggy
Chargement, *s.m.* loading; load; lading, cargo, freight; shipment; bill of lading; filling; (*post.*)
Chargeoir, *s.m.* basket-prop [registration
Charger, *v.a.n.* to load; to lade; to charge; to burden; to encumber; to clog; to saddle; to place; to put on; to lay on; to fill; to cover; to attack; to beat; to commission, to instruct, to order, to intrust, to appoint; to desire; to inscribe, to enter, to carry to; to exaggerate, to overdo, to overcharge; to amplify, to embellish; to make muddy *or* foul; (*of writings*) to write over; (*of cabmen*) to take *or* take up a (*or* the) fare; to engage (*a cabman*), to take (*a cab*); to fetch (*a pump*); (*post.*) to register
Se —, *v.r.* to load; to burden *or* load *or* cover oneself; to load (o.'s ...); to take charge (of); to take upon oneself; to undertake; to undertake *or* promise to see (to); to make it o.'s business; to charge oneself (with); to assume the responsibility (of); to charge each other; to fall upon each other; to be loaded; to get muddy *or* foul; to get fat; to get cloudy
Chargeur, *s.m.* loader; porter; owner of a ship's cargo; skipper; canal-carrier; smelter;
Chargeure, *s.f.* (*her.*) charge [gunner
Charier, *v.a.n.* *V.* **Charrier**
Chariot, *s.m.* chariot; waggon; truck, drag, trolly, tug, gill; carriage; go-cart; (*for ropes*) cart; (*engin.*) cradle; (*tech.*) slide; (*astr.*) Charles's Wain, Waggoner. *Grand* —, (*astr.*) Charles's Wain, Waggoner, Great Bear. *Petit* —, (*astr.*) Lesser Bear
Charitable, *adj.* charitable; benevolent
Charitablement, *adv.* charitably
Charité, *s.f.* charity; charitableness; benevolence; act of charity; almsgiving; alms; charitable board; Charity hospital (*in Paris*). *De* —, of charity; charitable; benevolent; gratuitous; eleemosynary. *Dame de* —, visitor of the poor, lady of the charitable board. *Sœur de* —, sister of charity, sister of mercy. *Demander la* —, to beg. *Faire la* —, to give alms, to bestow charity; to give for nothing, to give, to make a present (of); to dole out. *Prêter une — à*, to make a gratuitous imputation against. *La* —, *s'il vous plait!* (*a beggar's phrase*) a little for charity! please give something to a poor ...! — *bien ordonnée commence par soi-même*, charity begins at home
Charivari, *s.m.* mock serenade, charivari; rough music; discordant music; concert of marrow-bones and cleavers (*to butchers*), concert of lap-stone and hammer (*to shoemakers*); clatter, rattle, row, shindy; (*cavalryman's*) overalls; (*at play*) four queens in the same hand; (*newspaper*) Charivari, Punch
Charivarieu-r, se, *s.m.f.* *V.* **Charivariseur**
Charivarique, *adj.* of a mock serenade; rough; discordant; noisy
Charivariser, *v.a.n.* to give a mock serenade to; to give rough music; to kick up a row
Charivariseu-r, se, Charivariste, *s.m.f.* mock serenader; noisy musician; rioter
Charlatan, e, *s.m.f.* quack, mountebank, charlatan; impostor; — *adj.* quackish
Charlataner, *v.a.n.* to gull, to wheedle, to cajole; to cheat
Charlatanerie, *s.f.*, **Charlatanisme,** *s.m.* quackery, charlatanry, charlatanism; imposition, cheat
Charlatanesque, *adj.* quackish, charlatanical
†**Charlemagne,** *s.m.* Charlemagne; (*pop.*) dirk, short broadsword. *Faire* —, (*at play*) to quit the game (*after winning*)
Charlot, *s.m.* (*bird*) curlew. — *de plage*, sea-lark
Charlotte, *s.f.* (*cook.*) charlotte. — *russe*, charlotte-russe
Charmant, e, *adj.* charming; pleasing, pleasant, sweet, delightful, lovely; (*ironically*) very nice, very fine; — *s.f.* dear, love, sweet love; (*pop.*) (the) itch
Charme, *s.m.* charm; spell; enchantment; fascination; pleasingness; pleasure; beauty; attraction, allurement; (*bot.*) hornbeam. *Comme un* —, (*fig.*) perfectly, in perfection, admirably. *Sous le* —, spell-bound. *Se porter comme un* —, to be in robust health
Charmer, *v.a.* to charm; to delight; to please; to spell; to enchant; to fascinate; to bewitch; to soothe; to beguile; to while away
Charmeu-r, se, *s.m.f.* charmer
†**Charmille,** *s.f.* young hornbeam plantation; young hornbeam trees; row *or* hedge *or* arbour of hornbeam trees; grove, bower, arbour
Charmoie, *s.f.* hornbeam grove *or* plantation
Charnaigre, *s.m.* (kind of greyhound)
Charnalité, *s.f.* carnality
Charnel, le, *adj.* carnal, sensual
Charnellement, *adv.* carnally
Charnier, *s.m.* charnel-house; larder; game-bag; bundle of sticks *or* poles (*for vines*, &c.); (*nav.*)
Charnière, *s.f.* hinge; knuckle [scuttled butt
Charnon, *s.m.* female-joint (*of a hinge*)
Charnu, e, *adj.* fleshy; brawny; plump
Charnure, *s.f.* flesh, skin [blackguard
†**Charogne,** *s.f.* carrion; carcass; cagmag;
Charoi, *s.m.* cod-fishing boat
Charpente, *s.f.* timber-work; wood-work; carpenter's work; framework, frame; framing; skeleton [structed; framed; rough-hewn
Charpenté, e, *adj.* hewn; built, made, con-
Charpenter, *v.a.* to hew, to square; to hack, to mangle; to construct, to plan, to frame
Charpenterie, *s.f.* carpentry; carpenter's trade *or* work; timber-work, framework; timber-yard
Charpentier, *s.m.* carpenter; (*fish.*) whale-cutter; (*zool.*) St. Domingo woodpecker; (*fig.*) framer. — *de navires*, ship-carpenter; shipwright [woodpecker
Charpentière, *s.f.* (*insect*) wood-fretter; (*bird*)
Charpi, *s.m.* cooper's block [to rags
Charpie, *s.f.* lint. *En* —, (*fig.*) boiled *or* done

Charrée, *s.f.* buck-ashes; (*fish.*) gentle, bait
Charretée, *s.f.* cartload
Charreti-er, ère, *s.m.f.* carter, carman, car-woman, waggoner; ploughman, ploughboy; (*astr.*) charioteer; — *adj.* passable for carts, &c., cart. *Chemin* —, cart-way. *Porte —ère*, cart-gate. *Voie —ère*, cart-way, cart-road; width of a cart (*space between the wheels*). *Il n'y a si bon — qui ne verse*, it is a good horse [that never stumbles
Charretin, *s.m.* truck
Charreton, *s.m.* truck; carman, carter
Charrette, *s.f.* cart
Charriable, *adj.* carriageable, transportable
Charriage, *s.m.* carting, cartage, waggoning, waggonage, carriage; conspiracy to defraud, mystification, swindle
Charrier, *v.a.* to draw in a cart *or* waggon, to cart, to waggon; to draw; to carry, to convey; to carry along; to drag; (*of streams*) to drift; (*med.*) to be loaded with; — *v.n.* (*of streams*) to drift ice. — *droit*, (*fam.*) to behave properly, to do what is right, to act right *or* straightforwardly. — *de la voile*, (*nav.*) to crowd sail, to stretch. *La rivière charrie*, ice is (*or* pieces of ice are) floating down the stream
Se —, *v.r.* to be carted *or* &c.
Charrier, *s.m.* bucking-cloth
Charrière, *s.f.* cart-way, cart-road
Charrieur, *s.m.* swindler
Charroi, *s.m.* carting, cartage, waggoning, waggonage, carriage, transport; cart, carts; —**s,** *pl.* (*formerly*) military train. *Chemin de* —, cart-way, cart-road
Charron, *s.m.* wheelwright
Charronnage, *s.m.* wheelwright's trade *or* work. *Atelier de* —, wheelwright's workshop
Charroyer, *v.a.* to cart, to waggon, to carry
Charroyeur, *s.m.* carter, waggoner, carrier
Charruage, *s.m.* (*extent of land*) plough-gang, plough-gate, plough-land (*in its old sense*), ox-gang, carucate; (*old tax*) carucage
Charrue, *s.f.* plough; (*extent of land*) *V.* **Charruage;** (*fig.*) agriculture. *Mettre la — devant les bœufs*, to put the cart before the horse
Charte, *s.f.* charter; policy; muniment; old title-deeds; old rights. *La grande* — (*d'Angleterre*), Magna Charta. — **-partie,** *s.f.* charter-party
Chartier, *s.m. modern spelling for* **Chartrier;** *obsolete spelling for* **Charretier**
Chartil, *s.m.* body of a cart; harvest-waggon; farm-shed, cart-shed, cart-house
Chart-isme, -iste. *V.* page 3, § 1
Chartographe, *s.m.* writer on charters; collector of charters; (*obsolete spelling of* "Cartographe") *V.* **Cartographe**
Chartographie, *s.f.* writing *or* treatise on charters; (*obsolete spelling of* "Cartographie") *V.* **Cartographie**
Charton, *s.m.* (*obsolete*) carter, waggoner, coach-[man, driver
Chartrain, e, *adj. s.* of Chartres; native of Chartres
Chartre, *s.f.* (*obsolete word*) prison, jail; (*obsolete spelling of* "Charte") charter; (*pop.*) consumption, decline. — *privée*, arbitrary imprisonment, illegal confinement
Chartreuse, *s.f.* Carthusian nun; Charterhouse, Chartreuse, Carthusian monastery *or* convent; (*fig.*) solitary country-house; (*cook.*) chartreuse (*dish of mixed vegetables*); (*liquor*) chartreuse (*cordial made by the monks of the "Grande-Chartreuse," near Grenoble, in France*)
Chartreux, *s.m.* Chartreux, Carthusian friar; bluish grey cat; — *adj.m.* Carthusian; bluish grey
Chartrier, *s.m.* muniment-house, muniment-room; collection of charters; keeper of the charters
Chartron, *s.m.* position of the actors at the end of a play. *Faire* or *former le* —, to stand in a row near the foot-lights, to range themselves in front of the stage
‡**Chartulaire,** *s.m. V.* **Cartulaire**

Chas, *s.m.* eye (*of a needle*); (*pop.*) peeper (*a person's eye*); starch; paste; (*tech.*) plumb-rule
Chaseret, *s.m.* cheese-frame, drainer
Châsse, *s.f.* shrine, reliquary; frame; sash handle; (*of a balance*) cheeks; (*pop.*) peeper (*eye*)
Chasse, *s.f.* hunting, sporting; coursing; shooting; shooting-season; hunting-ground, chase, preserve; hunt, chase, chasing, pursuit; sport; huntsmen; game; hunting-air *or* tune, chasse; (*of machines*) play; (*fam.*) blowing-up. — *à courre*, hunting, hunt; coursing. — *à l'oiseau*, hawking. — *aux oiseaux*, fowling. — *à tir* or *au tir* or *au fusil*, shooting; shooting-party. *Canon* or *pièce de* —, (*nav.*) chaser, bow-chaser. *Plaisirs de la* —, field-sports. *Donner* or *faire la — à*, to hunt, to chase, to pursue, to drive away. *Donner une — à*, to give a blowing-up, to blow up. *Prendre* —, (*nav.*) to sheer off. *Soutenir* —, (*nav.*) to keep up a running fight
Chasse, *s.m.f.* (*in compounds, from* **Chasser,** "to drive away," &c.) thing *or* person that drives away *or* drives, &c., driver. — **-avant,** *s.m.* foreman, overseer, task-master, time-keeper; (*fig.*) leader, instigator; driver. — **-bosses,** *s.f.* (*bot.*) loosestrife. — **-chiens,** *s.m.* (*pop.*) porter; keeper; beadle. — **-coquins,** *s.m.* (*pop.*) beggar-driver; beadle. — **-cousins,** *s.m.* stiff fencing-foil; (*fam.*) bad wine, paltry dinner, cold reception, cold shoulder (*anything fitted to drive away poor relations, spongers, &c.*). — **-ennui,** *s.m.* exhilarant. — **-marée,** *s.m.* fish-cart; fish-cart driver; fish-cart horse; (*nav.*) fishing-lugger, lugger. — **-mouches,** *s.m.* fly-fan; fly-flap; fly-net, horse-net. — **-mulet,** *s.m.* miller's man; mule-driver. — **-neige,** *s.m.* snow-plough. — **-pierres,** *s.m.* catapulta, catapult (*toy*); (*rail.*) guard-iron, life-guard, engine guard. — **-punaises,** *s.f.* (*bot.*) stinking bug-wort. — **-rage,** *s.f.* (*bot.*) pepper-grass, pepper-wort. — **-rivets,** *s.m.* riveting-hammer. — **-roues,** *s.m.* spur-post; guard-iron
Chassé, *s.m.* chassé (*a step in dancing*); (*nav.*) chased ship. — **-croisé,** *s.m.* (*dancing*) chassé-croisé; (*fig.*) exchange of places
Chassé, e, *part. of* **Chasser**
Chasselas, *s.m.* chasselas (*kind of grape*)
Chasser, *v.a.n.* to drive away; to drive *or* turn out; to drive forward; to drive; to drift; to propel; to chase; to pursue; to expel; to discharge; to dismiss; to banish; to dispel; to discard; to throw off; to hunt; to course; to shoot; to catch; to carry; to space; (*of carriages*) to swing; (*dancing*) to make a chassé, to slide to the right; (*nav.*) to chase *or* pursue (*a ship*); (*nav.*) to drive (*at anchor*); (*nav.*) to drag the anchor, to drag; (*nav.*) to fall *or* drive aboard (*of another ship, by dragging the anchor*); (*pop.*) to run away, to bolt. — *à courre*, to hunt; to course. — *au fusil* or *à tir* or *au tir*, to shoot. — *au chien d'arrêt*, to set. — *à l'oiseau*, to hawk. — *de race*, to show blood, to take after o.'s parent, to be a chip of the old block. — *la terre*, (*nav.*) to look out for land. — *sur ses ancres*, (*nav.*) to drag the anchors
Se —, *v.r.* to drive away *or* &c. each other; to be hunted *or* shot *or* caught
Chasseresse, *s.f.* huntress
Chasseur, *s.m.* hunter, huntsman; sportsman; courser; shooter; shot (*marksman*); fowler; (*servant*) chasseur, footman; (*mil.*) rifleman; (— *à pied*) light infantryman, rifleman; (— *à cheval*) light cavalry soldier, light horseman; (*nav.*) chasing ship, chaser; herring-smack; —**s,** *pl.* (*mil.*) riflemen, rifles, rifle-corps. —*s à pied*, light infantry troops, light infantry, riflemen, rifles, rifle-corps. — *à cheval*, light cavalry troops, light cavalry, light horse
Chasseu-r, se, *adj.* (*nav.*) chasing
Chasseuse, *s.f.* huntress; roving spider [left
Chassez-déchassez, *s.m.* (*dancing*) right and
Chassie, *s.f.* gum of the eye
Chassieu-x, se, *adj.* blear, bleared, blear-eyed

Châssis, *s.m.* sash; frame; housing; guard (*of wire or wicker-work*); (*hort.*) glass frame; (*print.*) chase; (*theat.*) scene; (*artil.*) chassis; (*pop.*) peeper (*eye*). — *de couches*, garden-frame, glass frame. — *de papier*, paper window

Chassoir, *s.m.* (*coop.*) driver (*tool*); (*tech.*) drift

Chaste, *adj.* chaste; pure; correct

Chastement, *adv.* chastely; purely

Chasteté, *s.f.* chastity; purity

Chasuble, *s.f.* chasuble (*priest's garment*)

Chasublerie, *s.f.* church-vestments, church-furniture; making of ditto [church-furnisher

Chasublier, *s.m.* church-ornament maker,

Chat, Chatte, *s.m.f.* cat; tom-cat, tom; she-cat; puss, pussy; darling; dainty woman *or* girl; hoarseness; (*bot.*) catkin; (*tech.*) cat; plumb-rule; (*artil.*) searcher; (*nav.*) cat; — *adj.m.f.* fawning, caressing, playful, pretty; gentle; dainty. — *coupé*, (*fig.*) a children's game at running. — **-huant,** *s.m.* brown owl, owl. — **-pard,** *s.m. V.* **Pard.** — **-tigre,** *s.m.* tiger-cat. — *en poche*, a pig in a poke. *A bon — bon rat*, tit for tat; diamond cut diamond; well matched; set a thief to catch a thief. *C'est le —!* oh yes, of course! oh yes, indeed! all very well! who is it then? I don't believe it! *Pas un —*, (*fig., fam.*) not a soul, not a living soul. *Un — dans la gorge*, something in o.'s throat, (to be) hoarse. *Appeler un — un —*, to call a spade a spade, not to mince matters. *Emporter le —*, (*fig.*) to steal away, to take French leave; to remove entirely; (*pop.*) to get a rap over the knuckles *or* a punch on the head. *Éveiller le — qui dort*, to rouse the sleeping lion; to wake sleeping sorrow; to rake up the past — *échaudé craint l'eau froide*, a burnt child dreads the fire. *La nuit tous les —s sont gris*, all cats are grey in the dark. *Quand les —s n'y sont pas, les souris dansent*, when the cat is away the mice will play

†Châtaigne, *s.f.* (*bot.*) chestnut; (*vet.*) ergot. — *d'eau*, *V.* **Macre** [grove

†Châtaigneraie, *s.f.* chestnut-plantation *or*

†Châtaignier, *s.m.* chestnut-tree; chestnut-wood, chestnut; chataignier (*kind of red apple*)

Châtain,e, *adj.*, **Châtain,** *s.m.* chestnut colour, chestnut, nut-brown, brown. — *clair*, light

Chataire, *s.f. V.* **Cataire** [brown, auburn

Château, *s.m.* castle; manor; hall; homestead; country-seat, seat, mansion, house; palace; court. — *fort*, stronghold. — *seigneurial*, manorial house, manor-house, manor. — *de cartes*, house of cards, castle of cards. — *d'eau*, (artificial) fountain; water-works; (*rail.*) water-crane. *Faire des —x en Espagne*, — to build castles in the air. — *-Coutet*, — *-Duplessis*, — *-Labranche*, — *-Lafitte*, — *-Larose*, — *-Latour*, — *-Léoville*, — *-Margaux*, — *-Yquem*, (names of vine-estates in the Bordeaux district; kinds of claret wine from ditto) [(*cook.*) rump-steak

Chateaubriand, Chateaubriant, *s.m.*

Chatée, *s.f. V.* **Chattée**

Châtelain, *s.m.* castellan, lord of a manor

Châtelaine, *s.f.* lady of a manor; key-chain; charm (*trinket*); scarf

Châtelé, e, *adj.* (*her.*) turreted

Châtelet, *s.m.* castlet, small castle; Châtelet (*formerly, law-courts and prison in Paris*)

Châtellenie, *s.f.* castellany, castle-ward

Chatepeleuse, *s.f.* (*insect*) corn-weevil

Châtiable, *adj.* chastisable, punishable

Châtier, *v.a.* to chastise, to punish, to correct; to whip; to chasten; to polish; to condemn. *Qui aime bien châtie bien*, spare the rod and spoil the child [ter, water-pipe

Chatière, *s.f.* cat's hole; cat-trap; drain, gut-

Châtieur, *s.m.* chastiser, punisher

Châtiment, *s.m.* chastisement, punishment, correction, castigation [ment; glistening

Chatoiement, *s.m.* play of colours, chatoy-

Chaton, *s.m.* kit, kitten; (*of rings*) bezel; gem, stone; (*bot.*) catkin

Chatonnement, *s.m.* setting (*in a bezel*) [kitten

Chatonner, *v.a.* to set (*in a bezel*); — *v.n.* to

†Chatouille, *s.f.* young lamprey [pleasure

†Chatouillement, *s.m.* tickling, titillation;

†Chatouiller, *v.a.* to tickle, to titillate; to excite; to please, to gratify; to flatter

†Chatouilleu-x, se, *adj.* ticklish; touchy; excitable; delicate, tender; nice

Chatoyant, e, *adj.* changing colour, shot, chatoyant; glistening; (*of style*) florid

Chatoyante, *s.f.* (*min.*) chatoyant (*stone*)

Chatoyer, *v.n.* to change colour, to be chatoyant; to glisten; (*of style*) to be florid

Châtré, *s.m.* eunuch. *Voix de —*, shrill voice

Châtrer, *v.a.* to castrate; to emasculate; to geld; to spay; (*fig.*) to mutilate; to lop, to prune; to top; to curtail, to retrench; to expurgate; to take out of; to take a few sticks out of (*a bundle of wood*) [castrated, &c.

Se —, *v.r.* to castrate *or* &c. oneself; to be

Châtreu-r, se, *s.m.f.* gelder

Châtrure, *s.f.* gelding

Chatte, *s. adj. feminine of* **Chat**

Chattée, *s.f.* cat's litter, litter

Chattement, *adv.* (*fam.*) fawningly, caressingly, playfully, prettily; gently; daintily; deceitfully, hypocritically

Chattemite, *s.f.* demure-looking person, bland hypocrite, hypocrite, dissembler. *Faire la —*, to put on a gentle look, to look demure, to dissemble, to look so gentle

Chattemiterie, *s.f.* demureness, hypocrisy

Chatter, *v.n.* to kitten; — *v.a.* (*artil.*) to search

Chatterie, *s.f.* playfulness; pretty trick *or* way; coaxing way, interested *or* hypocritical caress; daintiness; act of daintiness; dainty,

Chaty, *s.m.* (*stuff*) angola [delicacy, sweets

Chauboulure, *s.f.* scald, blister

Chauche-branche, *s.f.* (*tech.*) crowbar

Chauche-poule, *s.m.* (*pop.*) kite (*bird*)

Chaud, e, *adj.* hot; warm; heated; burning, glowing; ardent; fiery; eager; violent; passionate, hasty; hot-headed; zealous; fervent; vivid; pressing; sudden; fresh, new, recent; mulled; red-hot. —, —! (*pop.*) quick, quick! sharp, sharp! *Avoir —*, (*pers.*) to be warm *or* hot. *Avoir la tête —e*, to be hot-headed. *Faire —*, (*weather*) to be warm *or* hot; (*things*) to be warm *or* hot work. *Cela ne fait ni — ni froid*, that is neither here nor there; that does not alter the matter; it is of no consequence, it does not matter, it is no matter, it is quite indifferent, it is all one; it is of no use; it does neither good nor harm. *Si jamais* (or *Quand*) *je ..., il fera —*, if ever I ..., tell me of it; catch me ..., not I! [hot, while hot

Chaud, *s.m.* heat; warmth; hot; warm. *A —*,

Chaude, *s.f.* brisk fire; fire; heat; heating. *A la —*, (*tech.*) while the metal is hot, while hot; all hot; in the heat of passion *or* of the moment, on the spur of the moment; suddenly. — *adj.f. V.* **Chaud.** — *-pisse*, clap

Chaudeau, *s.m.* caudle; mulled egg, egg-flip; warm beverage

Chaudelait, *s.m.* batter-pudding

Chaudement, *adv* hotly; warmly; briskly; quickly; sharply; hot; warm; quick; sharp

Chauder, *v.a. V.* **Chauler**

Chauderie, *s.f.* chawati, chauti, choltry, choultry (*inn, public lodging-place in India*)

Chaud-froid, *s.m.* (*cook.*) chaud-froid (*peculiar dressing of fowl*); (*local for* "rhume") cold

Chaudier, *v.n.* (*hunt.*) to be proud, to couple

Chaudière, *s.f.* copper; (large) kettle; boiler;

Chaudrerie, *s.f. V.* **Chauderie** [pan; pot

Chaudron, *s.m.* kettle, boiler, caldron; pot; (*fam.*) tin-kettle (*bad piano*) [ronful; potful

Chaudronnée, *s.f.* kettleful, boilerful, cald-

Chaudronner, *v.a.n.* (*fam.*) *V.* **Brocanter**

Chaudronnerie, *s.f.* coppersmith's *or* brazier's trade *or* wares *or* work *or* workshop; copper-wares; boiler-manufactory

Chaudronni-er, ère, *s.m.f.* copper-smith; brazier; tinker; dealer in copper-wares; boiler-maker; (*fam.*) *V.* **Brocanteur.** — *au sifflet,* tinker

Chauffage, *s.m.* heating; warming; fuel; firing; right of cutting wood for fuel; (*nav.*) breaming (*of a ship*); breaming-fuel

Chauffe, *s.f.* heating; heat; furnace; fire-box

Chauffe, *s.m.f.* (*in compounds, from* **Chauffer,** "to warm," "to heat") thing (*m.*) *or* person (*m.f.*) that warms *or* heats, warmer, heater. — **-assiettes,** *s.m.* plate-warmer. — **-cire,** *s.m.* (*pers.*) chafe-wax. — **-la-couche,** *s.m.f.* late riser; *s.m.* useless husband; henpecked husband. — **-linge,** *s.m.* linen-warmer, clothes-horse. — **-lit,** *s.m.* bed-warmer. — **-pieds,** *s.m.* foot-warmer

Chauffer, *v.a.* to heat; to warm; to chafe; to keep in fuel; to air; to bask; to urge; to push briskly; to attack; to smoke; to make love to; to have *or* keep an eye upon; to look out for; to canvass for; to puff; to applaud; (*mil.*) to open *or* keep up a brisk fire upon; (*nav.*) to bream (*a ship*); — *v.n.* to get (*or* grow) hot *or* warm; to give heat; to be preparing *or* brewing; to be urgent *or* pressing; to get up the steam. *Faire* —, to warm. — *le four,* (*pop.*) to get tipsy. *V.* **Éclairé**

Se —, *v.r.* to warm oneself; to bask; to find o.'s own fuel; (*of things*) to heat, to be heating; to warm, to be warming; to be heated *or* warmed

Chaufferette, *s.f.* foot-warmer, foot-stove; [chafing-pan

Chaufferie, *s.f.* chafery (*forge*)

Chauffeur, *s.m.* fireman, stoker; (*hist.*) chauffeur (*robber who used to burn the feet of his victims to make them surrender their money*); (*slang*) courter, sweetheart, lover; exhilarating companion, leader, life and soul; puffer, boaster, braggart, humbug [chair

Chauffeuse, *s.f.* low-seat chair, Elizabethan

Chauffoir, *s.m.* warming-place, warm room, hall; warm cloth; heater, stove, chauffer [*scales*)

Chauffure, *s.f.* burning (*of iron or steel till it*

Chaufour, *s.m.* lime-kiln [chant

Chaufournier, *s.m.* lime-burner; lime-mer-

Chaufourni-er, ère, *adj.* lime-burning, lime

Chaulage, *s.m.* (*agr.*) liming

Chauler, *v.a.* (*agr.*) to lime. *Se* —, to be limed

Chaulier, *s.m.* lime-burner [for ditto

Chaumage, *s.m.* (*agr.*) stubble-cutting; time

Chaume, *s.m.* stubble; haulm, stalk; stubble-ground, stubble-field; thatch; mountain-pasture

Chaumer, *v.a.n.* to clear (*a field*) of stubble, to cut stubble off; to burn (*a tree*) at the foot

Chaumet, *s.m.* stubble-scythe

Chaumier, *s.m.* stubble-cutter; thatcher; stubble-rick [*or* house

Chaumière, *s.f.* cottage, cot, thatched cottage

Chaumine, *s.f.* small cottage, hut

Chaumontel, *s.m.* chaumontel (*pear*)

Chaussant, e, *adj.* easy to put on, fitting the leg *or* foot; suitable, convenient

Chausse, *s.f.* shoulder-knot; pipe; (— *d'Hippocrate*) felt filtering-bag; (*mil.*) bag *or* fly (*of a busby*); (*obsolete*) stocking, hose; (*her.*) chausse; —**s,** *pl.* (*obsolete*) breeches; stockings, hose. *Tirer ses —s,* to run away

Chaussé, e, *part. adj.* with a shoe *or* boot on, with shoes *or* boots on, with o.'s shoes *or* boots on, booted, shod, wearing shoes *or* stockings. — *de,* having on o.'s feet, wearing, dressed in; covered with, in; taken with, wedded to. *Être bien* —, to have nice *or* good shoes, &c. on, to wear shoes that fit well. *Les cordonniers sont les plus mal —s,* the shoemaker's wife is the worst shod. *Elle est des mieux —es,* she is a tiptop lady [road, roadway; highway

Chaussée, *s.f.* bank; causeway; carriage-way,

Chausse-pied, *s.m.* shoe-horn

Chausser, *v.a.* to put (*a person's*) shoes *or* boots *or* slippers *or* stockings on (*for him or her*): to help (*one*) on with (*his or her*) shoes, &c.; to shoe, to boot; to supply with shoes *or* boots; to make shoes *or* boots for, to make the shoes *or* boots of, to be the shoemaker *or* bootmaker of; to fit; to suit; to put on, to wear; to get (*o.'s foot*) in; to cover; (*fig.*) to get into o.'s head; to adopt, to embrace; (*agr., hort.*) to earth up, to mould; to mulch; — *v.n.* to wear shoes *or* &c. (*of a certain size*), o.'s foot to measure (*so much*). — *les étriers,* (*rid.*) to put o.'s feet too far forward in the stirrups. — *au même point,* to wear shoes of the same size; (*fig.*) to suit each other exactly

Se —, *v.r.* to put on o.'s shoes, &c.; to wear (*good or bad*) shoes, &c.; to buy o.'s shoes (of); to be put on. *Se — de,* to put on; (*fig.*) to be taken with, to become wedded to

Chaussetier, *s.m.* hosier [(*bot.*) star-thistle

Chausse-trappe, *s.f.* trap; (*mil.*) caltrop;

Chaussette, *s.f.* sock

Chausson, *s.m.* sock; list-shoe; pump; shoe (*for fencing,* &c.); felt filtering-bag; dumpling; fighting with the feet; (*pop.*) worn-out loose woman. *Comme* —, (*pop.*) downright, regular

Chaussonner, *v.a.* (*pop.*) to kick

Chaussure, *s.f.* foot-gear, covering for o.'s feet, shoes, boots, &c. *Trouver — à son pied* or *à son point,* (*fig.*) to find what suits one; to meet [with o.'s match

Chaut. *V.* **Chaloir**

Chauve, *adj.* bald, bald-headed; — *s.m.* bald man

Chauve-souris, *s.f.* bat; (*arch.*) sun-blind

Chauveté, *s.f.* (*obsolete*) baldness, calvity

Chauvin, *s.m.* fanatical partisan *or* patriot, ultrapatriot, exclusionist, exclusive; chauvinist

Chauvinique, *adj.* fanatical; ultrapatriotic; exclusionary; chauvinistic

Chauvinisme, *s.m.* party fanaticism; fanatical patriotism, ultrapatriotism; exclusionism, exclusivism; exclusiveness; chauvinism

Chauviniste, *s.m.* *V.* **Chauvin**

Chauvir, *v.n.* (*of horses,* &c.) to lay the ears back

Chaux, *s.f.* lime; limestone. *Pierre à* (or *de*) —, limestone. *A — et à sable, A — et à ciment, A — et à mortier,* with mortar, substantially, solidly, strongly

Chavaria, *s.m.* (*bird*) chauna, crested screamer

Chaveri, Chavery, *s.m.* *V.* **Chauderie**

Chavirement, *s.m.* (*nav.*) upsetting, capsizing

Chavirer, *v.a.n.* (*nav.*) to upset, to capsize

Chebec, Chebek, *s.m.* (*ship*) xebec

Chef, *s.m.* head; chief; chieftain; commander; general; leading man, leader; ringleader; principal; master; superior; manager; director; first partner; foreman; guard; head cook; fag-end; principal *or* leading point; chief clause; count; degree; own head; own accord; own right; right; (*her.*) chief. — *d'accusation,* charge, count of indictment. — *d'atelier,* foreman. — *d'attaque* (*mus.*) leader off. — *de bataillon,* major (*of infantry*). — *de brigade* (*of workmen*) ganger; (*post.*) mail-guard. — *de bureau,* (*admin.*) head of an office, first-class clerk, senior clerk (*clerk next below the* "chef de division"). — *du cabinet,* private secretary. — *du contentieux,* (*admin.*) solicitor. — *de corps,* (*mil.*) colonel (*of infantry*); major (*of riflemen*). — *de cuisine,* head cook. — *de dépôt,* station-master. — *de division,* (*admin.*) head of a department, chief clerk; (*nav.*) commodore; (*mil.*) fugleman. — *d'école,* head of a sect. — *d'émeute,* ringleader. — *d'emploi,* (*theat.*) chief actor in his line of character. — *d'équipe,* (*of workmen*) foreman, ganger. — *d'escadre,* (*nav., obsolete*) flag-officer; commodore. — *d'escadron,* major (*of cavalry*). — *d'état-major,* (*mil.*) brigade-major. — *d'état-major général,* (*mil.*) quartermaster general. — *d'exploitation,* manager, general manager. — *de fabrique,* manufacturer; mill-owner. — *de file,* (*mil.*) file-leader; (*nav.*) leading ship, foremost ship, file-leader; (*fig.*) leader, whipper-in. — *de gare* or *de station,* (*rail.*) station-master, station-clerk; superintendent. — *d'industrie,* — *industriel,* great manufacturer. — *d'institution,* head of a school, schoolmaster (*with a first-class certificate*). — *des jurés* or *du jury,* foreman of the jury. — *-lieu, s.m.* chief town; county town; (*fig.*) principal place, seat. — *de maison,* householder, housekeeper. — *du matériel,* (*admin.*) store-keeper. — *de meute,* whipper-in; leader of the band. — *du mouvement,* (*rail.*) traffic-manager. — *de musique,* (*mil.*) band-master. — *-d'œuvre, s.m.* masterpiece, capital performance; chief work; standard work; master-stroke; (*ironically*) piece of work; (*obsolete*) trial-piece. — *d'orchestre,* musical conductor, conductor. — *de parti,* party leader; ringleader. — *de peloton,* (*mil.*) fugleman. — *de pièce,* (*artil.*) captain of a gun. — *de section,* (*mil.*) fugleman. — *du service commercial,* — *du trafic,* (*rail.*) goods-manager. — *de train,* railway-guard, guard

Chèfecier, *s.m. V.* **Chèvecier** [*officer*)

Chefferie, *s.f.* (*mil.*) district (*of an engineer-*

Chégros, *s.m.* (*shoemaker's*) wax-end

Cheik, Cheick, *s.m.* sheik, sheikh (*of the Arabs*)

‡**Chéiroptère,** *s.m. V.* **Chiroptère**

Chelem, *s.m.* (*at whist*) slam. *Faire* —, to slam

‡**Chélidoine,** *s.f.* (*bot.*) celandine

‡**Chélidonine,** *s.f.* (*chem.*) chelidonine

Chelin, *s.m. V.* **Shilling** [masula-boat

Chelingue, *s.f.* (*nav.*) chelingue, masulamanche,

Chelinguer, *v.n.* (*pop.*) to stink

‡**Chélone,** *s.f.* (*bot.*) chelone, tortoise-flower, shell-flower, snake-head

‡**Chélonée,** *s.f.* sea-tortoise, turtle

‡**Chélonien,** *s.m.* (*zool.*) chelonian, tortoise

Cheloup, *s.m.* (*nav.*) sloop

Chêmer, *v.n.,* **Se** —, *v.r.* to get thin, to waste

Chemin, *s.m.* way, road, path; line; track; distance; journey; progress; walk; ride; drive; stair-carpet; floor-cloth. *Beau* —, fair way; clean part of the road. *Grand* —, main road, highroad, highway. *Grand — des vaches,* (*fig.*) plain road, beaten track. — *communal* or *vicinal,* parish road, parochial road, connecting road, by-way. — *de l'école* or *des écoliers,* (*fig.*) roundabout way, longest way round. — *de fer,* railway, railroad. — *ferré, V.* **Ferré.** *En* —, — *faisant,* by *or* on the way. *Son petit bonhomme de* —, jog-trot. *Aller par quatre —s,* to go a roundabout way to work, to mince the matter, to mince matters. *Faire voir du* —,

Chemineau, *s.m.* portable stove [to give trouble

Cheminée, *s.f.* chimney fireplace; hearth; stove; chimney-piece; mantelpiece, mantelshelf; chimney-top; funnel; shaft; (*of firearms*) nipple. *Sous la* —, *sous le manteau de la* —, secretly, privately, under the rose. *Il faut faire une croix à la* —, we must chalk that up

Cheminement, *s.m.* onward march, progressing, progress, approach

Cheminer, *v.n.* to walk, to go along *or* on, to go, to proceed, to get on; to advance; to move on *or* about, to move; to run on, to run; to make o.'s way; to progress, to approach; to be connected

Chemise, *s.f.* shirt; chemise; wrapper; case, casing; envelope; covering; (*mas., fort.*) chemise. — *de nuit,* night-shirt; night-dress,

Chemiser, *v.a.* to cover over [night-gown

Chemiserie, *s.f.* shirt-making; shirt warehouse; shirts [under-waistcoat

Chemisette, *s.f.* front, dicky; chemisette;

Chemisi-er, ère, *s.m.f.* shirt-maker

‡**Chémosis,** *s.m.* (*med.*) chemosis

Chênaie, *s.f.* oak-grove, oak-plantation

Chenal, *s.m.* channel; watercourse; track

Chenaler, *v.n.* (*nav.*) to sail through a channel

Chenapan, *s.m.* scamp, blackguard, ruffian

Chêne, *s.m.* oak. — *-liège,* cork-tree

Chêneau, *s.m.* (*bot.*) oakling; wall-germander

Chéneau, *s.m.* leaden pipe, gutter; —**x**, *pl.* eaves

Chenet, *s.m.* andiron, firedog, dog

Chêneteau, *s.m.* oakling

Chenette, *s.f.* (*bot.*) germander

Chènevière, *s.f.* hemp-field

Chènevis, *s.m.* hemp-seed

Chènevotte, *s.f.* hemp-stalk; boon

Chènevotter, *v.n.* to make weak shoots

Chênier, *s.m.* oak-fungus

Chenil, *s.m.* kennel, dog-kennel; hovel, hole

†**Chenille,** *s.f.* caterpillar; worm; ugly brute; mischievous brute; bore; silk-velvet twist, chenille; (*of a helmet*) crest, comb; (*obsolete*)

†**Chenillère,** *s.f.* nest of caterpillars [undress

†**Chenillette,** *s.f.* (*bot.*) caterpillar

†**Chenillon,** *s.m.* dowdy, slut, mopsey

Chênon, *s.m.* chain-work glass window

‡**Chénopode,** *s.m.* (*bot.*) goose-foot

Chenu, e, *adj.* hoary, white, snowy; grey-headed; denuded, bald; (*pop.*) capital, famous, stunning; — *s.m.* capital thing, famous stuff

Chenument, *adv.* (*pop.*) capitally, famously

Cheptel, *s.m.* lease of cattle; leased-out cattle

Chepteli-er, ère, *s.m.f.* lessee (*of cattle*)

Chèque, *s.m.* cheque. — *barré,* crossed cheque. *Carnet de —s,* cheque-book

Ch-er, ere, *adj.* dear; beloved; fond; high-priced, expensive, costly; precious, valuable; — *s.m.f* dear fellow *or* boy *or* man; dear girl *or* woman; dear friend. *Rendre* —, to endear

Cher, *adv.* dearly, dear; much. *Vous me les faites trop* —, you ask me too much for them. *Il fait — vivre à ...,* living is dear in...

Cherche, *s.f.* search

Cherché, e, *part. adj.* sought, sought for, &c. (*V.* **Chercher**); affected, far-fetched

Chercher, *v.a.n.* to try to find, to try to find out; to search; to search for; to seek; to seek for *or* after; to seek out; to go *or* be in quest of; to look for; to feel for; to look out for; to fetch out; to endeavour to obtain; to cast about for; to try to remember; to endeavour, to try, to attempt; to think; (*fam.*) to fish, to hook for it. — *des yeux,* to look for. *Aller* —, to fetch; to go to *or* for; to go to fetch; to go and fetch; to go and look for; to go in quest of; to go to seek; to invite; to present itself to. *Envoyer* —, *faire* —, to send for; to send out to look for. *Venir* —, to come for; to come to fetch; to come and fetch; to come and look for; to come to seek. — *querelle* or *noise à,* to quarrel with, to pick a quarrel with

Se —, *v.r.* to look for *or* seek each other; to seek oneself; to try o.'s strength *or* skill, to grope o.'s way; to collect oneself; to search o.'s conscience; to seek o.'s own interest

Chercheu-r, se, *s.m.f.* seeker; searcher; explorer; inquirer; hunter; — *s.m.* (*astr.*) finder (*glass*); — *adj.m.f.* seeking; searching; exploring; inquiring

Chère, *s.f.* living, fare, cheer; entertainment, feast. *Faire bonne* or *mauvaise* —, to live well *or* badly, to have good *or* bad fare. *Il n'est — que d'appétit,* hunger is the best sauce. *Il n'est — que de vilain,* there is nothing like a miser's feast [price; preciously

Chèrement, *adv.* dearly; dear; at a high

Chéri, e, *adj. s.* beloved; cherished; dearest; darling; favourite

Chérif, *s.m.* cheriff, scherif, sherif

Chérifat, *s.m.* cheriffship, cheriffate

Chérimolier, *s.m.* (*bot.*) cherimoyer, chirimoya

Chérir, *v.a.* to love, to cherish [precious

Chérissable, *adj.* worthy of our love; lovely;

‡**Chersonèse,** *s.f.* chersonese, peninsula

Cherté, *s.f.* dearness, high price; dearth

Chérubin, *s.m.* cherub

Chérubique, *adj.* cherubic

Chervi, Chervis, *s.m.* (*bot.*) skirret

Chester, *s.m.* Cheshire cheese

Chéti-f, ve, *adj.* mean, sorry, poor, paltry, miserable; thin, puny; slender; stunted; sickly, feeble, weak, delicate

Chétivement, *adv.* meanly, poorly, paltrily, miserably; slenderly; feebly, weakly, delicately

Chétiveté, *s.f.* meanness, poorness, paltriness, miserableness; thinness; slenderness; stuntedness; feebleness

Chevaine, *s.f. V.* **Chevanne**

Cheval, *s.m.* horse; horse-flesh; horse-power. *A* —, on horseback; riding; mounted; astride; on both sides (of a river *or* road, *said of an army or &c.*); firmly fixed, strong; thoroughly acquainted (with), master (of); harping; haughtily; off; horse; *int.* to horse! *De* —, (*adject.*) horse; violent; very strong *or* hard; riding. — *entier*, entire horse, stone-horse. — *fondu*, (*game*) saddle-my-nag. — *-vapeur*, horse-power. — *à une main*, horse for riding or driving only. — *à deux fins* or *à deux mains* or *à toute fin* or *à toutes mains*, horse for driving and riding. — *d'abri*, stalking-horse. — *d'attelage*, harness-horse, carriage-horse. — *de bât*, pack-horse; drudge; stupid fellow, blockhead. — *de bataille*, war-horse, charger; strong point. — *de bois*, wooden horse; hobby horse. — *de brancard*, shaft-horse, wheel-horse, wheeler, thill-horse, thiller. — *de chasse*, hunter. — *de cheville*, horse before the shaft-horse, body-horse. — *de collier*, draught-horse. — *de conduite*, led-horse. — *de course*, racehorse, racer. *Course de chevaux*, horse-race, race; horse-racing. — *de fatigue*, hack. — *de frise*, *s.m.sing.*, *Chevaux de frise*, *s.m.pl.* (*fort.*) cheval-de-frise, chevaux-de-frise, spiked fence or fences. *Chevaux-légers*, *s.m.pl.* (*obsolete*) light cavalry; *s.m.sing.* light horseman. — *de main*, led-horse. — *de race*, blood-horse. — *de renvoi*, return-horse; (*pers.*) old offender. — *de service*, hack. — *de trait*, draught-horse, cart-horse. — *de gros trait*, cart-horse. — *de trompette*, (*pers.*) dreadnought, war-horse, game-cock. — *de trot*, trotter. — *de volée*, leader. *Force de* — or *de chevaux*, (*mach.*) horse-power. *Lettre à* —, sharp letter. *Lune de* — [or, better, *lune de schevas* or *scheval*], month of May (*in Turkey*). *Sur ses grands chevaux*, on the high horse, upon [the high ropes

Chevalée, *s.f.* horseload

Chevalement, *s.m.* (*build.*) prop, stay, shore, bearing up [(*in the arts*) to work on the horse

Chevaler, *v.a.n.* (*build.*) to prop, to bear up;

Chevaleresque, *adj.* chivalrous; knightly

Chevaleresquement, *adv.* chivalrously

Chevalerie, *s.f* knighthood; chivalry; nobility; (*obsolete*) chivalrous feat. — *errante*, knight-errantry

Chevalet, *s.m.* wooden horse (*for torture*); horse (*wooden frame*); rest; stand; trestle; easel; (*build.*) buttress; bridge (*of a stringed instr.*); (*nav.*) trussel; stake-head

Chevalier, *s.m.* knight; Sir Knight (*old style of address*); chevalier; nobleman; cavalier; defender, protector; suitor; (*bird*) totanus, gambet; sandpiper; (*fish*) eques; grayling, char *or* charr. — *de l'aune*, counter-jumper. — *du crochet*, rag-picker. — *d'honneur*, gentleman in waiting. — *d'industrie*, swindler, sharper, knight of the post. — *du lustre*, (*theat.*) (hired) clapper. — *du mètre*, counter-jumper. *Etre le* — *de*, to be the cavalier of; to be very attentive to

Chevalière, *s.f.* (female) knight, chevaliere; knight's wife; signet-ring. — *d'industrie*, adventuress, swindler

Chevaline, *adj.f.* equine, horse, of horses, of the horse. *Bête* —, horse; mare. *Espèce* or *race* —, equine species *or* race, horse species

Chevalis, *s.m.* canal (*cut in the bed of a shallow river*)

Chevance, *s.f.* (*old*) property, fortune, treasure

Chevanne, *s.f.* (*fish*) chavender, cheven, chub

Chevauchable, *adj.* fit for riding

Chevauchage, *s.m.* (*print.*) riding

Chevauchant, e, *adj.* riding; overlapping; (*bot.*) equitant [course; cavalcade

Chevauchée, *s.f.* riding; circuit; journey;

Chevauchement, *s.m.* riding; overlapping; crossing

Chevaucher, *v.n.a.* to ride; to be astride; to overlap; (*nav.*) to cross

Chevaucheur, *s.m.* rider, horseman

Chevauchons (A), *adv.* astride, astraddle

Chevauchure, *s.f.* overlapping

Chevau-léger, *s.m.sing.*, —**s**, *pl.* (*improper spelling of* "chevaux-légers." *V.* **Cheval**)

Chevaux de frise, *s.m.pl. V.* **Cheval**

Chèvecerie, *s.f.* deanery

Chevêche, *s.f.* sparrow-owl

Chèvecier, *s.m.* dean (*of certain chapters*)

Chevelé, e, *adj.* (*her.*) crined

Chevelée, *s.f.* layer (*of vine*)

Cheveline, *s.f.* (*bot.*) coral club-top

Chevelu, e, *adj.* hairy, with a thick head of hair; long-haired; haired; comate; (*of literature*) romantic; (*of roots, seeds*) fibrous, bearded, comose; (*of plants*) branchy, twiggy; leafy; thick, bushy; —*s.m.* romanticist; romanticism; (*bot.*) tuft of hairs, fibres

Chevelure, *s.f.* hair, head of hair; scalp (*cut off by savages*); (*astr.*) coma; hair; (*bot.*) coma; (*poet.*) foliage

Chever, *v.a.* to hollow out (*a gem, a piece of metal*); to mould (*glass, for watches or clocks*)

Chevet, *s.m.* bolster; pillow; bedhead, head (*of a bed*); bedside; (*arch.*) apsis

Chevêtre, *s.m.* halter; (*surg.*) chevaster, chevestre (*bandage for the head and jaw*); (*tech.*) binding-joist, bracer, transom, beam

Cheveu, *s.m.* hair; (*slang*) bother; hitch; rub, difficulty. —*x blancs*, white hair; grey hair. —*x de Vénus*, (*bot.*) maiden-hair. *En* —*x*, wearing nothing on o.'s head, bare-headed. *Être coiffée en* —*x*, *être* or *rester en* —*x*, to wear or have nothing on o.'s head. *Tiré par les* —*x*, (*fig.*) far-fetched. *Il faut prendre l'occasion aux* —*x*, take time by the forelock

†Chevillage, *s.m.* pegging, bolting

†Chevillard, *s.m.* butcher who buys by the quarter *or* joint (*instead of by the carcass* , small butcher

†Cheville, *s.f.* peg, pin; bolt; sprig; plug; spike; spill; tree-nail; nut; ankle; mere peg to fill a gap, stop-gap; expletive; antler, branch; (*her.*) attire. — *ouvrière*, pole-bolt, pole-pin, pivot-bolt; main spring, prime mover. — *du pied*, ankle. *A la* —, (*butch.*) by the quarter *or* joint (*instead of by the carcass*). *Être en* —, (*of horses*) to be before the shaft-horse; (*at play*) to be the middle hand

†Chevillé, e, *part. adj.* pegged, &c. (*V.* **Cheviller**); strong, robust; close-set; antlered, branched; (*her.*) attired

†Cheviller, *v.a.* to peg, to pin, to bolt, to fasten; to rivet; to wring (*silk*); (*liter.*) to fill with expletives

†Chevillette, *s.f.* small peg *or* pin; key

†Chevillier, *s.m.* horse before the shaft-horse,

†Chevillière, *s.f.* red tape; anklet [body-horse

†Chevillon, *s.m.* peg

†Chevillot, *s.m.* (*nav.*) toggle

†Chevillure, *s.f.* bes-antler

Chevin, *s.m. V.* **Chevanne** [master; to enjoy

Chevir, *v.n.* (*obsolete*) to get over, to manage, to

Chèvre, *s.f.* goat, she-goat; (*astr.*) capella; (*tech.*) gin, crab, crane; wheel-setter, carriage-setter, setter, lifting-jack; (*pop.*) ill humour, tiff, pet. *Avoir la* —, to be in an angry mood. *Ménager la* — *et le chou*, to keep on good terms with both sides, to run with the hare and hold with the hounds. *Prendre la* —, to take offence, to fly out. — **-pieds,** *adj.m.* goat-footed; *s.m.* [satyr

Chevreau, *s.m.* kid

†Chèvrefeuille, *s.m.* honeysuckle; woodbine

Chevrer, *v.n.* (*pop.*) to fret; to fidget

Chèvreter, *v.n* to kid

Chevrette, *s.f.* roe; doe; brand-dog, brand-iron, trivet; setter; stand; (*artil.*) chevrette; (*pharm.*) syrup-pot; (*obsolete*) bagpipe; (*obsolete form of* "crevette") shrimp, prawn

†Chevreuil, *s.m.* roebuck, buck; venison

Chevri-er, ère, *s.m.f.* goatherd, goat-keeper
†**Chevrillard,** *s.m.* young roebuck
Chevron, *s.m.* rafter; coping; slip of turf (*across a walk*); spawn (*of fish*); (*arch., her.*) chevron; (*mil.*) stripe, chevron; (*nav.*) scantling, wedge [ron-work
Chevronnage, *s.m.* raftering; rafters; chev-
Chevronner, *v.a.* to rafter; to chevron
Chevrotain, *s.m.* (*zool.*) chevrotain
Chevrotant, e, *adj.* (*of the voice*) tremulous, trembling, quivering, faltering
Chevrotement, *s.m.* tremulousness, quivering, faltering, shake
Chevroter, *v.n.a.* to kid; to speak in a faltering voice; to sing in a tremulous voice; to be tremulous, to tremble, to falter, to shake; to skip, to caper; to fret, to be peevish; to fidget
Chevrotin, *s.m.* curried kid, cheveril; young roebuck; chevrotain; — *adj.* (*pop.*) fretful, peevish; fidgety. *Tirer au* —, to quaff together
Chevrotine, *s.f.* buck-shot
Chevrotiner, *v.n.* to skip, to caper
Chez, *prep.* at *or* in *or* to *or* into the dwelling *or* abode *or* residence (*house, lodgings,* &c.) of; at *or* to ...'s; in *or* into *or* to the house *or* the room *or* the apartment *or* the place *or* the country *or* the dominions of; among, with; in; on, upon. — *moi, toi, lui, elle, soi, nous, &c.,* at *or* to *or* in *or* into my, thy, his, her, o.'s, our, *or* &c. house (*or* room, &c.); home, at home. *De* — ..., from (*or* of) the house of ..., from ...'s. *Un* — *soi,* a house of o.'s own, o.'s home, a home. *Il n'est* (or *Il n'y a*) *pas de petit* — *-soi,* home is home be it ever so homely
Chiaoux, *s.m.* chiaoux (*Turkish messenger, gentleman usher, and deputy-judge*) [*proval*)
‡**Chiasme,** *s.m.* cross (*mark* ✕ *indicating disap-*
Chiasse, *s.f.* dirt (*of insects*); fly-speck; scum, dross; trash; damaged goods; blackguard
‡**Chiastolite,** *s.f.* (*min.*) *V.* **Macle**
Chibouck, Chibouk, *s.m.*, **Chibouque,** *s.m.f.* chibouk, chibouque (*Turkish pipe*)
Chic, *s.m.* knack; style; — *adj.* stylish; swellish, swell; capital, spicy [(*African dance*)
Chica, *s.m.* chica (*American drink*); — *s.f.* chica
Chicandard, e, *adj.* (*pop.*) most stylish *or* swellish; first-rate, famous, crack
Chicane, *s.f.* chicane, chicanery, pettifoggery, pettifogging, law; cavilling; cavil; quibble; shuffle; trumpery *or* groundless quarrel *or* dispute; (*mil.*) skirmish. *Gens de* —, pettifoggers. *Chercher* — *à,* to pick a trumpery quarrel with
Chicaner, *v.a.n.* to quarrel with; to dispute; to defend; to find fault with; to chicane; to cavil; to quibble; to shuffle; to go to law, to sue; to grudge; to puzzle; to annoy, to bother, to tease; (*nav.*) to lie too near (*the wind*), to hug (*the wind*)
Se —, *v.r.* to bicker, to wrangle
Chicanerie, *s.f.* chicanery; cavil
Chicaneu-r, se, Chicani-er, ère, *s.m.f.* chicaner; shuffler; caviller; wrangler; pettifogger; — *adj.* chicaning; disputatious; fault-finding; shuffling; cavilling; wrangling; litigious; pettifogging
Chicard, e, *adj.* (*pop.*) *V.* **Chic,** *adj.*
Chiche, *adj.* stingy, niggardly; sparing; sorry, miserable, poor; — *s.m.* miser; chick-pea
Chichement, *adv.* stingily, niggardly, meanly; sparingly [ingness
Chicherie, *s.f.* stinginess, niggardliness; spar-
Chicocandard, e, *adj.* (*pop.*) *V.* **Chicandard**
Chicon, *s.m.* cos lettuce; salad
Chicoracé, e, *adj.* endive-like, chicoraceous
Chicorée, *s.f.* chicory; endive; (*pop.*) sharp taunt, sound blowing-up, jaw; mincing prude, fastidious humbug; — *s.m.* chicory-colour; — *adj.* chicory-coloured [**Bonduc**
Chicot, *s.m.* stump. — *du Canada,* (*bot.*) *V.*
Chicoter, *v.n.* (*pop.*) to split hairs; to dispute about trifles; to pick, to nibble
Se —, *v.r.* to bicker, to wrangle, to spar

Chicotin, *s.m.* Socotrine aloes, bitter aloes; powder *or* juice of the bitter apple
Chie-en-lit, *s.m.* (*pop.*) masker (*specially one ill-dressed and dirty*): Jack-pudding; queer-looking fellow, odd figure, guy. *A la* —*!* there goes (*or* here comes) another Guy! here's a guy!
Chien, *s.m.* dog; doggy; hound; cur; rubbish; trash; cagmag; spirit, humour; (*of firearms*) cock, hammer; (*pers.*) cur, hound, dog; (*pers., after* "mon") dear, darling. — *couchant,* setting-dog, setter; toad-eater, toady, lick-spittle. — *courant,* hound. — *-loup,* wolf-dog. — *d'agrément,* fancy dog. — *d'appartement,* lapdog. — *d'arrêt,* pointer. — *d'attache,* — *de basse-cour,* house-dog. — *de chasse,* sporting-dog; hound. — *de cour,* — *de ferme,* — *de garde,* watch-dog. — *de luxe,* fancy dog. — *de manchon,* lapdog. — *de mer,* dogfish. — *de Saint-Bernard,* Mount Saint-Bernard dog, Alpine dog. — *de salon,* lapdog. *Entre* — *et loup,* in the dusk of the evening, between hawk and buzzard; half one thing half another; dubious, suspicious. *Faire le* — *couchant,* to cringe, to truckle. *Nos* —*s ne chassent pas ensemble,* we are not friends. *Quand on veut noyer son* — *on dit qu'il est enragé,* give a dog a bad name and hang him. *Le* — *du jardinier* (*qui ne mange point de choux et n'en laisse pas manger aux autres*), the dog in the manger
Chien, ne. *adj.* doggish; currish; canine; dogged; harsh, hard, close; severe, strict; troublesome; bad, villanous. — *de, de* —, doggish; currish; canine; wretched, beastly, dreadful; deuce of (a), devil of (a); troublesome; rascally; ravenous
Chiendent, *s.m.* (*bot.*) dog-grass, couch-grass, twitch-grass, twitch; (*pop.*) rub, difficulty, hitch. *Brosse de* —, carpet-brush, dusting-brush
Chienlit. *V.* **Chie-en-lit**
Chienne, *s.f.* (*feminine of* **Chien**) she-dog, bitch. *Donner* (*à quelqu'un*) *des cochons de sa* —, (*pop.*) to deceive (one) grossly
Chiennée, *s.f.* litter of pups
Chienner, *v.n.* to pup
Chiennerie, *s.f.* filthy thing, nasty thing; stinginess, meanness; beastly *or* scurvy trick
Chier, *v.n.a.* (*fam.*) to shit; (*pop.*) to give up, to yield, to fork out
Chiffarde, *s.f.* (*pop.*) *V.* **Bouffarde**
Chiffe, *s.f.* rag; flimsy stuff, common stuff; weak man, man of no character
Chiffon, *s.m.* bit of stuff; rag; scrap; bit; hunch; (*pers.*) doll, darling; —**s,** *pl.* rags; dress, rigging, trappings, togs, toggery, finery
Chiffonnage, *s.m.* tumbling, rumpling, crumpling; rumpled drapery
Chiffonné, e, *adj.* tumbled, rumpled, crumpled; (*bot.*) wrinkled; (*of the face*) delicate and irregular, pleasant but irregular-featured
Chiffonner, *v.a.* to tumble, to rumple, to crumple, to ruffle; to feel about; to puzzle; to tease, to vex, to annoy, to bother; — *v.n.* to trim up finery, to do odds and ends of needle-
Se —, *v.r.* to become *or* be tumbled, &c. [work
Chiffonnerie, *s.f.* rag-trade, rag-business; nicknack, gewgaw; petty care, slight trouble
Chiffonni-er, ère, *s.m.f.* rag-gatherer, rag-picker; rag-dealer, rag-merchant; (*fig.*) retailer of stories; disorderly fellow; (*piece of furniture*) cheffonier, chiffonier [total, sum, amount; digit
Chiffre, *s.m.* figure, number; cipher; sum
Chiffrer, *v.a.n.* to represent *or* calculate in figures; to cipher; to number; to mark; (*mus.*) to figure
Chiffreu-r, se, *s.m.f.* calculator, reckoner
†**Chigner,** *v.n.* (*pop.*) to weep, to cry, to blubber, to snivel
†**Chignon,** *s.m.* nape; (*of back-hair*) chignon
‡**Chiliade,** *s.f.* chiliad [*modern Greece*)
‡**Chiliarque,** *s.m.* (*mil.*) chiliarch (*colonel in*
‡**Chiliaste,** *s.m.* chiliast
Chilien, ne, *adj. s.* Chilian

Chimère, *s.f.* chimera; idle fancy, fancy; crotchet; hobby
Chimér-ique, -iquement. *V.* page 3, § 1
Chimie, *s.f.* chemistry
Chimique, *adj.* chemical
Chimiquement, *adv.* chemically
Chimiste, *s.m.* (scientific) chemist
Chimoine, *s.m.* artificial marble, stucco
Chimpansé, Chimpanzé, Chimpanzée, *s.m.* chimpanzee (*monkey*)
China, *s.m.* (*bot.*) China-root; (‡) Peruvian bark
Chinage, *s.m.* variegating [chestnut-tree
Chincapin, *s.m.* chincapin, chinquapin, dwarf
Chinche, *s.m.* (*zool.*) skunk
Chinchilla, *s.m.* chinchilla; chinchilla-fur; chinchilla-colour (*pearly grey*)
Chiné, e, *adj.* variegated, chiné [**Brocanter**
Chiner, *v.a.* to variegate, to cloud; — *v.n. V.*
Chineur, *s.m.* dealer in rabbit-skins; old clothes-man; small broker, huckster [on the head
Chinfreniau, *s.m.* (*pop.*) trinket; thump, rap
Chinois, e, *adj.* Chinese; — *s.m.f.* Chinese (*person*); — *s.m.* Chinese (*language*); rum fellow, rum one; brandied orange; — *s.f.* Chinese fashion
Chinoiserie, *s.f.* Chinese ornament *or* curiosity *or* figure; nicknack; folly, oddity; farce, joke; queer story
Chinure, *s.f.* variegation, clouded warp
‡Chionanthe, *s.m.* (*bot.*) fringe-tree, snowflower
Chiote, *adj. s.m.f.* Chian (*of Chios*)
Chiourme, *s.f.* convicts, set of men (*in the hulks*); (*formerly*) gang *or* crew (*of a galley*)
Chipeau, *s.m.* (*duck*) gadwall
Chiper, *v.a.* to pilfer, to filch, to crib, to prig, to bag, to bone [nothing; nothing at all
Chipette, *s.f.* (*pop.*) jot, bit, shade, trifle, mere
Chipeu-r, se, *s.m.f.* pilferer [fastidious humbug
Chipie, *s.f.* finical creature, mincing prude,
Chipoter, *v.n.* to dally; to trifle; to peddle; to potter; to argue *or* contend about trifles; to dawdle; to higgle; to haggle; to pick a bit here and a bit there, to hardly eat anything, to pick, to nibble
Chipoteuse, *s.f.* (*pop.*) *V.* **Chipie**
Chipoti-er, ère, *s.m.f.* dallier; trifler; dawdler; higgler; haggler; fastidious eater, nibbler; — *adj.* dallying; trifling; &c.
Chippes, *s.f.pl.* cuttings, shreds, pieces, cabbage
Chique, *s.f.* quid (*of tobacco*); chigoe, chigre, jigger (*insect*); poor silk; (*provincialism for* "bille") marble (*toy*); (*pop.*) hunch, piece; drinking-bout; drop too much; ill-humour
Chiqué, e, *adj.* chewed; eaten, swallowed; done in style, capital
Chiquement, *adv.* (*fam.*) in style, capitally
Chiquenaude, *s.f.* fillip
Chiquenauder, *v.a.* to fillip
Chiquer, *v.a.n.* to chew (tobacco); to eat and drink, to eat, to drink, to feed, to grub, to guttle, to guzzle, to swallow down, to swill; to do *or* execute in style; to dash off
Se —, *v.r.* to be chewed (*as tobacco*); (*fig. and pop.*) to be eaten
Chiquet, *s.m.* driblet; bit; shred; drop [ments
Chiquetage, *s.m.* tearing up; marking; orna-
Chiqueter, *v.a.* to tear up; to mark, to orna-
Chiquette, *s.f. V.* **Chiquet** [ment
Chiqueur, *s.m.* tobacco-chewer; great feeder, guttler, guzzler; dasher-off
‡Chiragre, *s.f.* (*med.*) chiragra; — *adj.* chiragrical; — *s.m.f.* chiragrical person
‡Chiragrique, *adj.* (*med.*) chiragrical
‡Chirographaire, *adj.* (*law*) on note of hand
‡Chirographe, *s.m.* chirograph; chirographer
‡Chirogymnaste, *s.m.* (*mus.*) chirogymnast
‡Chirolog-ie, -ique. *V.* page 3, § 1
‡Chiromancie, *s.f.* chiromancy, palmistry
‡Chiromancien, ne, *s.m.f.* chiromancer
‡Chiromantique, *adj.* chiromantic
Chirone, Chironie, *s.f.* (*bot.*) centaury
‡Chironomie, *s.f.* chironomy; (*mus.*) time-beating
‡Chiroplaste, *s.m.* (*mus.*) *V.* **Guide-main**
‡Chiroptère, *s.m.* (*zool.*) cheiropter, bat
‡Chirotonie, *s.f.* (*theol.*) imposition of hands; (*Gr. ant.*) voting by a show of hands
Chirouis, *s.m. V.* **Chervis**
Chirurgical, e, *adj.* surgical
Chirurgico-, (*in compounds*) surgico-...
Chirurgie, *s.f.* surgery
Chirurgien, *s.m.* surgeon
Chirurgique, *adj.* surgical
Chiure, *s.f.* dirt (*of insects*); fly-speck
‡Chlamyde, *s.f.* chlamys
‡Chlamyphore, *s.m.* (*zool.*) chlamyphorus
‡Chloral, *s.m.* (*chem.*) chloral
‡Chlorate, *s.m.* (*chem.*) chlorate [yellow-wort
‡Chlore, *s.m.* chlorine; — *s.f.* (*bot.*) chlora,
‡Chlorer, *v.a.* (*chem.*) to chlorinate
‡Chloreu-x, se, *adj.* (*chem.*) chlorous [muriate
‡Chlorhydrate, *s.m.* (*chem.*) hydrochlorate,
‡Chlorhydrique, *adj.* (*chem.*) hydrochloric, chlorhydric, muriatic
‡Chlorhydrure, *s.m.* (*chem.*) hydrochloride
‡Chlorique, *adj.* (*chem.*) chloric
‡Chlorite, (*chem.*) *s.m.*, (*min.*) *s.f.* chlorite
‡Chlorodine, *s.f.* (*pharm.*) chlorodyne
‡Chloroforme, *s.m.* (*chem., surg.*) chloroform
‡Chloroformé, e, Chloroformisé, e, *adj.* (*med.*) chloroformed, under the influence of chloroform
‡Chloroformer, Chloroformiser, *v.a.* to chloroform, to administer chloroform to
‡Chloroformique, *adj.* (*med.*) chloroformic
‡Chloroformisation, *s.f.* (*med.*) administering
‡Chloromètre, *s.m.* chlorometer [chloroform
‡Chlorométr-ie, -ique. *V.* page 3, § 1
‡Chlorophane, *s.f.* (*min.*) chlorophane
‡Chlorophylle, *s.f.* (*chem., bot.*) chlorophyl
‡Chlorose, *s.f.* (*med.*) chlorosis, green-sickness; (*bot.*) chlorosis, etiolation [chlorotic person
‡Chlorotique, *adj.* (*med.*) chlorotic; — *s.m.f.*
‡Chlorure, *s.m.* (*chem.*) chloride
‡Chlorurer, *v.a.* to chloridize, to chloridate
Choc, *s.m.* shock; collision; conflict; clashing; dashing, dash; onset, attack, encounter; brunt; bump; blow; disaster; touch; (*mech.*) impact; (*nav.*) half-hitch; (*of the sea*) rut. — *en retour,* (*phys.*) return shock
Choca, *s.m.* choca (*mixture of chocolate and coffee*)
†Chocaillon, *s.f.* drunkard, slut
Chocard, *s.m. V.* **Choquard** [**Chicard**
Chocnosoff, Chocnosophe, *adj.* (*pop.*) *V.*
Chocolat, *s.m.* chocolate; chocolate-colour
Chocolaterie, *s.f.* chocolate-making *or* trade
Chocolati-er, ère, *s.m.f.* chocolate-maker *or* dealer; — *s.f.* chocolate-pot [band; chancel
‡Chœur, *s.m.* choir; chorus; choristers; chorists;
Choin, *s.m.* (*bot.*) *V.* **Schœnus**
Choir, *v.n. def.* (*obsolete*) to fall
Choisi, e, *adj.* chosen; selected; picked; elected; choice, select; — *s.m.* choice thing *or* article, best; choice things *or* articles, best of everything [pick out; to single out; to elect
Choisir, *v.a.* to choose; to select; to cull; to
Se —, *v.r.* to choose oneself *or* for oneself; to choose each other; to be chosen
Choisissable, *adj.* eligible
Choix, *s.m.* choice; choosing; selection; option; election; distinction; discernment, discrimination; thing chosen; best part. *Au —,* as people choose; as one likes; with right of choice, with choice; all at one price. *Au — 2 francs,* all at 2
‡Cholagogue, *adj.* (*obsolete*) antibilious [francs
‡Cholate, *s.m.* (*chem.*) cholate
‡Cholédoque, *adj.* (*anat.*) biliary
‡Cholélithe, *s.m.* (*med.*) biliary calculus
‡Choléra, *s.m.* (*med.*) cholera; (*pop.*) cagmag
‡Cholériforme, *adj.* (*med.*) of a choleraic
‡Cholérine, *s.f.* (*med.*) cholerine [nature
‡Cholérique, *adj.* (*in physiology*) choleric; (*med.*) choleraic; cholera; affected with cholera; — *s.m.f.* person affected with cholera, cholera patient

‡**Cholestérine,** *s.f.* (*chem.*) cholesterine
‡**Cholique,** *adj.* (*chem.*) choleic, cholic
Chômable, *adj.* to be kept as a holiday
Chômage, *s.m.* want of work, cessation from work, stoppage of work, stoppage; rest; holiday; time spent without work
Chômer, *v.n.* to be out of work; to cease from work, to leave off work; not to work; to stop; to rest; to do nothing; to be at a stand, to stand still, to be idle *or* inactive *or* stopped; to make a holiday; to want; — *v.a.* to keep as a holiday, to keep [carrageen
‡**Chondre,** *s.m.* (*bot.*) chondrus, Irish moss,
‡†**Chondrille,** *s.f.* (*bot.*) gum-chicory, wall-
‡**Chondrine,** *s.f.* (*chem.*) chondrine [lettuce
‡**Chondro-graphie, -logie,** &c. *V.* page 3, § 1
Chope, *s.f.* half-pint (of beer), glass (of beer)
Chopine, *s.f.* pint (*English pint in quantity, being half of the obsolete French* "pinte." *V.* **Pinte**); pint of wine; (*nav.*) lower pump-box.
Chopiner, *v.n.* to tipple [*Payer* —, to treat
Choppe, *s.f. V.* **Chope**
Choppement, *s.m.* (*old*) stumbling; blundering
Chopper, *v.n.* (*old*) to stumble; to blunder
Choquant, e, *adj.* shocking; offensive; unpleasant, disagreeable; improper
Choquard, Choquart, *s.m.* (*bird*) choquard, chocard, Alpine chough, Alpine crow
Choquer, *v.a.* to shock; to strike against; to clash with; to be contrary to; to offend; to displease; to touch (*glasses*); (*nav.*) to check (*the bowline, the braces*), to surge (*the capstan*); — *v.n.* to touch glasses, to hobnob
Se —, *v.r.* to strike against one another; to come into collision; to clash; to encounter; to take offence
‡**Choral, e,** *adj.* choral; — *s.m.* choral, chorale
‡**Chorde,** *s.f.* (*bot.*) chorda, sea-laces
‡**Chorée,** *s.f.* (*med.*) chorea, St. Vitus's dance
‡**Chorége,** *s.m.* (*in antiquity*) choragus
‡**Chorégraphe,** *s.m.* choregrapher [page 3, § 1
‡**Chorégraph-ie, -ique, -iquement.** *V.*
‡**Choréique,** *adj.* (*med.*) choreic; — *s.m.f.* (*med.*) person affected with chorea [**Chorée**
‡**Chorémanie, Choréomanie,** *s.f. V.*
‡**Chorévêque,** *s.m.* chorepiscopus [choriambic
‡**Choriambe,** *s.m.*, **Choriambique,** *adj.*
‡**Choriste,** *s.m.f.* chorist, choralist, chorister
‡**Chorographe,** *s.m.* chorographer [p. 3, § 1
‡**Chorograph-ie, -ique, -iquement.** *V.*
‡**Choroïde,** *adj.m.f.*, *s.f.* (*anat.*) choroid
‡**Choroïdien, ne,** *adj.* (*anat.*) choroidian
‡**Choroïdite,** *s.f.* (*med.*) choroiditis
‡**Chortasthme,** *s.m.* (*med.*) chortasthma, hay-asthma, hay-fever
‡**Chorus,** *s.m.* chorus. *Faire* —, to join *or* sing in chorus; (*fig.*) to join in, to chime in; to agree
Chose, *s.f.* thing; object; subject; matter; affair; business; deed; reality; fact; case; question; stuff; property; chattels; compliment; something; anything; what do you call him *or* her *or* it? what's his *or* her *or* its name? thingumbob; queer, out of sorts, I don't know what. — *publique*, commonwealth. — *qui va sans dire*, matter of course. —*s et d'autres*, one thing and another. —*s de la mer*, —*s de flot*, sea-ware. *Autre* —, different thing, other thing; another thing; else, other; better *or* superior thing; something else; anything else; any other reason; &c. (*V.* **Autre**). *Autre* — *est de ..., et autre — de ...*, it is one thing to ..., another to ... *Bien des —s à, mille —s à*, my best regards to, o.'s best regards to, many compliments to. *Peu de* —, *pas grand'* —, not much, nothing much, little, no great matter, a trifling *or* slight matter, a mere trifle; low birth; of little consequence, insignificant, inconsiderable, trifling. *Quelque* —, *V.* **Quelque,** *adj.*
Chou, *s.m.* cabbage; cole; kale; sprout; (*pastry*) puff; (*of ribbons*, &c.) bow; rosette; (*fam.*) ducky, darling. — *!* — *-là!* — *-pille!* (*hunt.*) tally-ho! seize him! — *de Milan*, savoy. — *pour* —, taken all in all, it is all one. *Bête comme* —, exceedingly stupid. *Des —x et des raves*, what one pleases, ducks and drakes. *Faire — blanc*, to get a blank; to miss the mark; to fail. — **-blanc,** *s.m.* blank; miss; failure. — **-chou,** *s.m.* ducky, darling. — **-fleur,** *s.m.* cauliflower. — **frisé,** *s.m.* savoy. —**x gras,** *s.m.pl.* delight; profit. — **marin,** — **de mer,** sea-kale. — **-navet,** — **-rave,** *s.m.* kohl-rabi. — **palmiste,** *s.m.* palm-cabbage (*fruit of the palmetto or cabbage-tree*). — **vert,** *s.m.* borecole, colewort
Chouan, *s.m.* long-eared owl; (*Fr. hist.*) chouan (*royalist insurgent during the great French Revolution*); royalist, Bourbonist, legitimist
Chouanner, *v.n.* to fight against the French Republic; to join the chouans; to carry on a guerilla warfare
Chouannerie, *s.f.* insurrection of the chouans; party of the chouans, chouans, Vendean royalists and ruffians; guerilla warfare; legitimist opinions
Choucas, *s.m.* (*bird*) jackdaw, daw; chough
Chouchement, *s.m. V.* **Houhoulement**
Chouchouter, *v.a.* to pet, to cocker, to coddle,
Choucroute, *s.f.* sourkrout, sourcrout [to fondle
Chouette, *s.f.* owl, brown owl; (*fig.*) laughing-stock; — *adj.* (*pop.*) capital, excellent, famous, spicy, stunning. *Faire la* —, to be *or* play alone against two (or more)
Chouettement, *adv.* (*pop.*) capitally, famously
Choultry, *s.m. V.* **Chauderie**
Choumac, Choumaque, *s.m.* (*fam.*) cobbler
†**Choupille,** *s.m.* sporting-dog
Chouquet, *s.m.* (*nav.*) cap, saddle [for
Chouriner, *v.a.n.* (*pop.*) to kill, to settle, to do
Chourineur, *s.m.* (*pop.*) killer, murderer
Choyer, *v.a.* to pamper; to pet; to cocker; to coddle; to nurse up; to fondle; to make much of; to cherish; to hug; to take great care of; to treat, to feast
‡**Chrématistique,** *s.f.* chrematistics; — *adj.* chrematistic [**-nomique.** *V.* page 3, § 1
‡**Chrémato - logie, -logique, -nomie,**
‡**Chrême,** *s.m.* chrism, holy oil
‡**Chrémeau,** *s.m.* chrism-cloth [extracts
‡**Chrestomathie,** *s.f.* chrestomathy, select
‡**Chrétien, ne,** *adj. s.* christian; (*of milk*, &c., *pop.*) watered, diluted
‡**Chrétiennement,** *adv.* christianly
‡**Chrétienner,** *v.a.* (*obsolete*) to christen
‡**Chrétienté,** *s.f.* christendom. *Marcher sur la* —, (*fam.*) to walk barefooted *or* in worn-out
‡**Chrismal,** *s.m.* chrismatory [boots
‡**Chrismation,** *s.f.* chrismation
‡**Christ,** *s.m.* Christ; crucifix
‡**Christe,** *s.f.* — *-marine*, (*bot.*) samphire
‡**Christianisation,** *s.f.* christianization
‡**Christianiser,** *v.a.* to christianize
‡**Christianisme,** *s.m.* christianity
‡**Christologie.** *V.* page 3, § 1
‡**Chromate,** *s.m.* (*chem.*) chromate
‡**Chromat-ique** (*adj.*), **-iquement,** (*mus.*, *opt.*) *V.* page 3, § 1 [(*opt.*) chromatics
‡**Chromatique,** *s.m.f.* (*mus.*) chromatic; — *s.f.*
‡**Chromatisme,** *s.m.* coloration, colouring
‡**Chrôme,** *s.m.* (*chem.*) chromium, chrome
‡**Chromé, e,** *adj.* (*chem.*) combined with chro-
‡**Chromique,** *adj.* (*chem.*) chromic [mium
‡**Chromo-,** (*in compounds*) chromo- ...
‡**Chromolithographe,** *s.m.* chromolithographer; — *adj.* chromolithographic
‡**Chromolithographie,** *s.f.* chromolithography; chromolithograph [thograph
‡**Chromolithographier,** *v.a.* to chromoli-
‡**Chromolithographique,** *adj.* chromolitho-
‡**Chromule,** *s.f.* (*chem.*, *bot.*) chromule [graphic
‡**Chronicité,** *s.f.* (*med.*) chronicity, chronic state
‡**Chronique,** *adj.* (*med.*) chronic, chronical; — *s.f.* chronicle, history; report; news; summary. *La* — *scandaleuse*, scandalous reports, the tittle-tattle of the day
‡**Chroniquement,** *adv.* chronically

‡**Chroniqueur,** *s. m.* chronicler; reporter, reviewer, critic
‡**Chronogrammat-ique,-iste.** *V.* page 3, § 1
‡**Chronogramme,** *s.m.* chronogram
‡**Chronographe,** *s.m.* chronograph; chronographer; chronicler
‡**Chronograph-ie, -ique.** *V.* page 3, § 1
‡**Chronolog-ie, -ique, -iquement, -iste.**
‡**Chronomètre,** *s.m.* chronometer [*V.* p. 3, § 1
‡**Chronométr-ie, -ique.** *V.* page 3, § 1
‡**Chrysalide,** *s.f.* chrysalis, chrysalid; (*pers., pop.*) old belle
‡**Chrysalider (Se),** *v.r.* to become a chrysalis
‡**Chrysanthème,** *s.m.* chrysanthemum
‡**Chryséléphantin,e,** *adj.* (*anc. sculp.*) chryselephantine [golden-tailed fly
‡**Chryside, Chrysis,** *s.f.* (*zool.*) golden-wasp,
‡**Chrysobéril,** *s.m.* (*min.*) chrysoberyl
‡**Chrysocale, Chrysocalque, Chryso-(‡)chalque,** *s.m.* pinchbeck
‡**Chrysoclore,** *s.m.* (*zool.*) chrysochlore
‡**Chrysocolle,** *s.f.* (*min.*) chrysocolla [locks
‡**Chrysocome,** *s.f.* (*bot.*) chrysocome, golden-
‡**Chrysographe,** *s.m.* chrysographer
‡**Chrysographie,** *s.f.* chrysography
‡**Chrysolithe,** *s.m.* (*min.*) chrysolite
‡**Chrysolog-ie, -ique.** *V.* page 3, § 1
‡**Chrysomèle,** *s.f.* (*insect*) chrysomela
‡**Chrysoprase,** *s.f.* (*min.*) chrysoprase
‡**Chrysops,** *s.m.* (*insect*) chrysops
‡**Chrysotype,** *s.m.* chrysotype
Chu, e, (*part. of* **Choir**) fallen
Chucheter, *v.n.* (*of sparrows*) to chirp, to twitter
Chuchotement, *s.m.* whispering, whisper
Chuchoter, *v.n.a.* to whisper
Chuchoterie, *s.f.* whispering, whisper
Chuchoteu-r, se, *s.m.f.* whisperer
Chut, *int.* hush! silence!
Chute, *s.f.* fall; downfall; falling; falling off; failure; failing; decay; close; conclusion; end; cadence; (*med.*) prolapsus; (*nav.*) depth (*of the keel, of a sail*); setting (*of a tide or current*). — *d'eau,* waterfall; watercourse
Chuter, *v.n.* (*from* **Chute,** a "fall") to fall, to fail, to be damned; — *v.a.n.* (*from* **Chut,** "hush") to cry "hush" to, to hiss, to damn; [to cry "hush!"
Chyle, *s.m.* chyle
Chyleu-x, se, *adj.* chylous [chylous vessel
Chylifère, *adj.* chyliferous, chylous; — *s.m.*
Chylification, Chylose, *s.f.* chylifaction, chylification
Chylifier, *v.a.,* **Se** —, *v.r.* to chylify, to turn
Chyme, *s.m.* chyme [into chyle
Chymeu-x, se, *adj.* chymous [chymous vessel
Chymifère, *adj.* chymiferous, chymous; — *s.m.*
Chymification, Chymose, *s.f.* chymifaction, chymification [into chyme
Chymifier, *v.a.,* **Se** —, *v.r.* to chymify, to turn
Chypriote, *s.m.f. adj.* Cypriot; Cyprian
Ci, *adv. pron.* here; this; viz. *De- — de-là,* *V.* **Là.** *Par- — par-là,* here and there; about; now and then; at intervals. — *-après,* hereafter, afterwards, further on, by and by; following. — *-contre,* opposite; in the margin. — *-dessous,* below; hereafter; undermentioned. — *-dessus,* above; abovementioned. — *-devant,* (*adv.*) above; before; formerly; previously; ex; former, late; (*s.m.*) ex-noble, noble, nobleman, royalist, man of the past; old buck (*pers.*). — *et ça,* this and that. — *-git,* — *-inclus,* &c., *V.* **Git, Inclus,** &c.
Cibagé, *s.m.* (*bot.*) cibage, Indian pine
Cibaire, *adj.* cibarious
Cibaudière, *s.f.* kind of fishing-net
Cible, *s.f.* target
Ciboire, *s.m.* ciborium, pyx, pix
Ciboule, *s.f.* (*bot.*) scallion
Ciboulette, *s.f.* (*bot.*) chives
Cicatrice, *s.f.* cicatrice, scar, seam, mark
Cicatricule, *s.f.* cicatricle, germ-mass
Cicatrisable, *adj.* cicatrizable [trizant
Cicatrisant, e, *adj.* cicatrizing; — *s.m.* cica-
Cicatrisati-f, ve, *adj.* cicatrisive [closing
Cicatrisation, *s.f.* cicatrization, healing,
Cicatriser, *v.a.,* **Se** —, *v.r.* to cicatrize, to heal, to close; to scar; to seam; to mark
Cicéro, *s.m.* pica (*printing type*)
Cicérole, *s.f.* (*bot.*) chick-pea, dwarf pea
Cicéron, *s.m.* Cicero; great orator
Cicérone (*pl.* **Ciceroni**), *s.m.* cicerone (*guide*)
Cicéronianisme, *s.m.* Ciceronianism
Cicéronien, ne, *adj. s.m.* Ciceronian
Cicindèle, *s.f.* (*zool.*) cicindela, tiger-beetle,
Cicisbée, *s.m.* *V.* **Sigisbée** [sparkler
Ciclamor, *s.m.* (*her.*) *V.* **Orle**
Cicutaire, *s.f.* (*bot.*) cicuta, water-hemlock,
Cicutine, *s.f.* (*chem.*) *V.* **Conicine** [cowbane
Cid, *s.m.* cid (*Arabian chief*)
Cidre, *s.m.* cider, cyder
Cidrerie, *s.f.* cider-mill; cider-making
Cie, Ce, [*abbreviations of Compagnie*] Co.
Ciel, *s.m.* (*pl.* **Cieux, Ciels**) heaven; heavens; sky; climate, clime; weather; air, atmosphere; tester; top; roof, ceiling; canopy. *Juste —!* good Heavens! *A — ouvert,* with open top, open at the top, open, uncovered; in the open air
Cierge, *s.m.* taper, wax-taper *or* candle, church-candle, candle, cierge; (*bot.*) cereus. — *d'eau,* water-jet. — *du Pérou,* (*bot.*) torch-thistle
Ciergé, e, *adj.* (*nav.*) stiff and upright
Ciergier, *s.m.* wax-chandler
Cigale, *s.f.* (*zool.*) cicada; grasshopper
Cigare, *s.m.* cigar
Cigarette, *s.f.* cigarette [maker
Cigareu-r, se, Cigari-er, ère, *s.m.f.* cigar-
†**Cigogne,** *s.f.* (*bird*) stork
†**Cigogneau,** *s.m.* young stork [poison
Ciguë, *s.f.* (*bot.*) hemlock; potion of hemlock,
Cil, *s.m.* eyelash, lash; (*bot.*) hair (*pl.* cilia)
Ciliaire, *adj.* ciliary
Cilice, *s.m.* hair-cloth
Cilicien, ne, *adj. s.* Cilician
Cilié, e, *adj.* ciliated, ciliate
†**Cillement,** *s.m.* winking, twinkling
†**Ciller,** *v.a.n.* to wink, to twinkle; to seel; to
†**Cillo,** *s.m.* winker [blink; to flinch; to stir
†**Cillose,** *s.f.* (*med.*) cillo, cillosis
Cimaise, *s.f.* *V.* **Cymaise**
Cimbalaire, *s.f.* *V.* **Cymbalaire** [fly
Cimbex, Cimbèce, *s.m.* (*zool.*) cimbex, saw-
Cimbre, *s.m.* Cimbric (*language*); —**s,** *pl.* (*hist.*)
Cimbrique, *adj.* (*hist.*) Cimbric [Cimbri
Cime, *s.f.* top, summit; height; (*bot.*) cyme. *La double —, le mont à double —,* (*poet.*) the two-
Ciment, *s.m.* cement [crowned hill, Parnassus
Cimenter, *v.a.* to cement; to consolidate, to strengthen
Se —, *v.r.* to be cemented *or* strengthened
Cimentier, *s.m.* cement-maker
Cimeterre, *s.m.* scimitar, sword
Cimetière, *s.m.* cemetery, burying-ground, burial-ground; graveyard; churchyard; (*fig.*)
Cimeu-x, se, *adj.* (*bot.*) cymose, cymous [grave
Cimicaire, *s.f.* (*bot.*) bugwort
Cimicide, Cimicicide, *adj.* bug-destroying
Cimicifuge, *adj.* that drives away the bugs; — *s.f.* (*bot.*) cimicifuga, bugwort
Cimier, *s.m.* (*of helmets, and her.*) crest; (*of beef*) buttock, round; (*of venison*) haunch
Cimifuge, *adj.* *V.* **Cimicifuge**
Cimmérien, ne, *adj.* (*geog.*) Cimmerian
Cimolé, e, Cimoli, e, *adj.* Cimolian [dust
Cimolée, *s.f.* cimolite, Cimolian earth; cutlers'
Cimolithe, *s.m.* cimolite
Cinabre, *s.m.* cinnabar
Cincenelle, *s.f.* (*navig.*) tow-line
‡**Cinchonine,** *s.f.* (*chem.*) cinchonine
‡**Cinchonique,** *adj.* (*chem.*) cinchonic
Cincle, *s.m.* (*bird*) cinclus, water-ousel, dipper
Cinématique, *adj.* cinematic; — *s.f.* cinematics
Cinéraire, *adj.* cinerary; — *s.f.* (*bot.*) cineraria
Cinération, *s.f.* cineration

Cinériforme, *adj.* cineraceous, cinereous, cineritious
Cingalais, e, *adj. s.* Cingalese
Cinglage, *s.m.* (*nav.*) ship's course, sailing; run in 24 hours; seaman's pay; (*metal.*) shingling
Cinglement, *s.m.* lashing, cutting; lash, cut; (*nav.*) sailing; (*metal.*) shingling
Cingler, *v.n.* (*nav.*) to sail before the wind, to sail, to make sail, to scud along; — *v.a.* to lash, to cut, to whip, to switch; (*metal.*) to shingle
Cinglerie, *s.f.* (*metal.*) shingling-house
Cingleur, *s.m.* (*metal.*) shingler; — *adj.m.* shingling
Cinips, *s.m. V.* **Cynips**
Cinnabre, *s.m. V.* **Cinabre**
Cinname, *s.m. V.* **Cinnamome**
Cinnamique, *adj.* (*chem.*) cinnamic
Cinnamome, *s.m.* (*bot.*) cinnamomum, cinnamon
Cinnor, *s.m.* kinnor (*mus. instr. of the ancient Hebrews*)
Cinq, *adj.m.f., s.m.* five; fifth; cinque. *Donner — et quatre,* (*pop.*) to give a slap and a back-hander
Cinquain, *s.m.* piece of poetry *or* stanza of five lines
Cinquantaine, *s.f.* fifty or so, about fifty, some fifty, fifty, half-hundred; age of fifty; fiftieth year
Cinquante, *adj.m.f., s.m.* fifty; fiftieth
Cinquantenier, *s.m.* (*obsolete*) captain of 50 men; police-officer
Cinquantième, *adj. s.* fiftieth
Cinquième, *adj.* fifth; — *s.m.* fifth; fifth floor; pupil of the fifth form *or* class; (*pop.*) half-pint, half-pint glass, glass (*fifth of a* "litre"); — *s.f.* fifth; fifth form *or* class
Cinquièmement, *adv.* fifthly
Cintrage, *s.m.* arching, curving; centering; arch, arches, curvature; (*nav.*) *V.* **Ceintrage**
Cintre, *s.m.* arch, semicircle; curve; (*build.*) centering, center, centre, cinter; (*of chairs*) top rail, top splat; (*theat.*) barrel-loft, roof, ceiling. *Loges du* (or *de*) —, —*s*, (*theat.*) upper boxes. *En* —, arched. *Plein* —, semicircle. *A* or *en plein* —, semicircular
Cintré, e, *adj.* arched, curved; (*of windows,* &c.) circular-head. *V.* **Fenêtre**
Cintrer, *v.a.* to arch, to curve; (*nav.*) *V.* **Ceintrer**
Cintreur, *s.m.* arch-builder; curver, bender
Cionite, *s.f.* (*med.*) cionitis, inflammation *or* angina of the uvula
Ciotat, Cioutat, *s.m.* kind of grape
Cipaye, *s.m.* Sepoy
Cipolin, *s.m. adj.* cipolin (marble)
Cippe, *s.m.* (*arch.*) cippus (*column*)
Cirage, *s.m.* waxing; blacking
Circassien, ne, *adj. s.* Circassian
Circée, *s.f.* (*bot.*) circæa, enchanter's nightshade
Circinal, e, Circiné, e, *adj.* (*bot.*) circinal, circinate
Circomméridien, ne, *adj.* (*astr.*) circummeridian
Circompolaire, *adj. V.* **Circumpolaire**
Circoncire, *v.a.* to circumcise
Circoncis, *s.m.* one who is circumcised
Circonciseur, *s.m.* circumciser
Circoncision, *s.f.* circumcision
Circonférence, *s.f.* circumference
Circonflexe, *adj. s.m.* (*gram.*) circumflex; (*fam.*) crooked
Circonjacent, e, *adj.* circumjacent
Circonlocution, *s.f.* circumlocution
Circonscription, *s.f.* circumscription; circumscribing; limitation, bound; division; district; constituency; province, department
Circonscrire, *v.a.* to circumscribe; to encircle; to enclose; to bound, to limit; to confine; to stint; to keep down
Se —, *v.r.* to be circumscribed, &c.; to limit *or* &c. oneself
Circonspect, e, *adj.* circumspect; cautious; wary; guarded
Circonspection, *s.f.* circumspection, cautiousness, caution
Circonstance, *s.f.* circumstance; occasion; conjuncture; occurrence; incident; accident; event; state of affairs; particularity; particular, detail; case. *De* —, necessitated by *or* made for *or* composed on the occasion; required by circumstances; adapted to the question of the hour; accidental; transient
Circonstancié, e, Circonstanciel, le, *adj.* circumstantial
Circonstancier, *v.a.* to detail, to particularize, to state the particulars of, to describe minutely, to circumstantiate
Circonvallation, *s.f.* (*fort.*) circumvallation
Circonvenir, *v.a.* to circumvent, to deceive, to impose upon, to overreach; to surround
Circonvention, *s.f.* circumvention
Circonvoisin, e, *adj.* circumjacent, surrounding, neighbouring, adjoining, adjacent
Circonvolution, *s.f.* circumvolution
Circuit, *s.m.* circuit; circumference; compass; circuitous way, way round, roundabout way; circumlocution
Circulaire, *adj.m.f., s.f.* circular
Circulairement, *adv.* circularly
Circulant, e, *adj.* circulating, in circulation
Circularité, *s.f.* circularity
Circulation, *s.f.* circulation; currency; motion, movement, passing, passage, way; communication; traffic
Circulatoire, *adj.* circulatory, circulating
Circuler, *v.n.* to circulate; to go round; to move on, to pass, to go *or* move about; to spread. *Faire* —, to make (people) go *or* move on; to circulate; to spread; to hand *or* pass round
Circumnavigateur, *s.m.* circumnavigator
Circumnavigation, *s.f.* circumnavigation
Circumpolaire, *adj.* circumpolar
Cire, *s.f.* wax; cerumen; (*of the bill of some birds*) cere. — *d'Espagne,* — *à cacheter,* sealing-wax
Ciré, e, *adj.* waxed; oil (*cloth*); clean (*boots*)
Cirer, *v.a.* to wax; to clean, to black, to polish
Se —, *v.r.* to be waxed; to be cleaned, &c.; to clean *or* &c. o.'s boots
Cireu-x, se, *adj.* waxy
Cirier, *s.m.* wax-chandler; wax-shrub *or* tree
Cirière, *adj.f., s.f.* wax-making (bee)
Ciron, *s.m.* (*insect*) flesh-worm; mite
Cirque, *s.m.* circus
Cirre, *s.m.* (*bot., zool.*) cirrus, cirrhus
Cirré, e, Cirreu-x, se, *adj.* (*bot.*) cirrous, cirrhous
Cirrhe, *s.m. V.* **Cirre**
Cirrhée, *s.f.* (*plant*) cirrhæa
Cirrhopode, *s.m. V.* **Cirripède**
Cirrhose, *s.f.* (*med.*) cirrhosis
Cirrifère, *adj.* (*bot.*) cirriferous
Cirriforme, *adj.* cirriform
Cirripède, *s.m.* (*zool.*) cirriped, cirrhopod
Cirrus, Cirrhus, *s.m.* (*meteorology*) cirrus, curl-cloud, mare's-tail
Cirse, *s.m.* (*bot.*) horse-thistle
Cirsocèle, *s.f.* (*med.*) cirsocele
Cirure, *s.f.* wax preparation, waxing
Cis, *s.m.* (*insect*) cis
†Cisaille, *s.f.* shears; (*of coin*) clippings
†Cisailler, *v.a.* to clip (*metals*); to gauffer (*frills,* &c.)
Cisalpin, e, *adj.* cisalpine
Cisatlantique, *adj.* cisatlantic
Cisdanubien, ne, *adj.* cisdanubian
Ciseau, *s.m.* chisel; scissors; **—x,** *pl.* scissors; shears; chisels
Ciseler, *v.a.* to carve; to cut; to sculpture; to chisel; to chase (*metals*)
Se —, *v.r.* to be carved *or* cut *or* &c.
Ciselet, *s.m.* small chisel; graver; (*coin.*) shears
Ciseleur, *s.m.* carver, sculptor; chaser; vigorous writer
Ciselure, *s.f.* carving; carved work; sculpture; chasing; chased work
Cisgangétique, *adj.* cisgangetic
Cisjuran, e, *adj.* cisjurane (*on the Paris side of the Jura mountains*)
Cisleithan, e, *adj.* cisleithan (*on this side of the Leitha river*)
Cismontain, e, *adj.* cismontane
Cisoir, *s. m.,* **Cisoire,** *s.f.* graver; **—s,** *pl.* bench-shears
Cispadan, e, *adj.* cispadan
Cispyrénéen, ne, *adj.* cispyrenean
Cisrhénan, e, *adj.* cisrhenane
Cisse, *s.m.* (*bot.*) cissus, wild grape, Virginian creeper
Cissoïdal, e, *adj.* (*geom.*) cissoidal
Cissoïde, *s.f.* (*geom.*) cissoid; — *adj.* cissoidal
Ciste, *s.m.* (*in antiquity, arch., sculp.*) cist (*basket*); (*bot.*) cistus, rock-rose
Cistèle, *s.f.* (*insect*) cistela

Cistercien, ne, *adj. s.m.* Cistercian
Cistophore, *s.f.* (*in antiquity*) cistophora (*basket-bearer*); — *s.m.* cistophorus (*coin, medal*)
Cistre, *s.m.* cittern (*mus. instr.*)
Citable, *adj.* citable, quotable
Citadelle, *s.f.* citadel, fortress, castle, tower
Citadin, e, *s.m.f.* townsman; townswoman; citizen; cit; cockney; — *s.f.* hackney-coach, cab, fly; — *adj.* of the town, of towns
Cita-teur, trice, *s.m.f.* citer, quoter
Citation, *s.f.* citation, quotation; (*law*) summons; (*of witnesses*) subpœna; (*can. law, divorce* [*court*) citation
Citatoire, *adj.* citatory
Cité, *s.f.* city; old town; district; buildings, close, rents, inn. — *ouvrière*, working-men's lodging-house, model lodging-house. *Droit de* —, *V.* **Bourgeoisie** (*Droit de*)
Cité, e, (*part. of* **Citer**) cited, &c.
Citer, *v.a.* to cite; to summon; to subpœna; to quote; to mention, to name; to speak of; to relate
Citérieur, e, *adj.* (*geog.*) hither, hithermost
Citerne, *s.f.* cistern, reservoir, tank; pit
Citerneau, *s.m.* small cistern *or* tank
Citeur, *s.m. V.* **Citateur**
Cithare, *s.f.* (*anc. mus. instr.*) cithara, (*modern*) zither, zithern, zittar
Citharède, Cithariste, *s.m.f.* citharist
Citharexyle, *s.m.* (*bot.*) fiddle-wood
Citigrade, *adj.* (*zool.*) citigrade; —**s,** *s.f.pl.* [citigrade spiders
Citise, *s.m. V.* **Cytise**
Citole, *s.f.* (*mus. instr.*) citole, dulcimer
Citoyen, ne, *s.m.f.* citizen; freeman (*of a city*); inhabitant; patriot; (*fam.*) fellow; (*obsolete*) Sir; Mr.; Madam; Mrs.; — *adj.* citizen; patriotic; national
Citoyenneté, *s.f.* citizenship
Citragon, *s.m.* (*bot.*) balm-mint, balm
Citramontain, e, *adj.* cismontane
Citrate, *s.m.* (*chem.*) citrate
Citre, *s.m.* thuja-wood
Citré, e, *adj.* lemon-flavoured
Citrin, e, *adj.* citrine; — *s.m.* citrine colour; — *s.f.* (*pharm.*) citrene, essence *or* oil of lemon, [oil of citron
Citrique, *adj.* (*chem.*) citric
Citron, *s.m.* lemon; citron; lemon colour; — *adj.* lemon-coloured [citron
Citronnat, *s.m.* candied lemon-peel, preserved
Citronné, e, *adj.* lemon-flavoured
Citronnelle, *s.f.* citron-water; (*bot.*) southern-wood, old-man; balm-mint, balm
Citronner, *v.a.* to flavour with lemon
Citronnier, *s.m.* lemon-tree; citron-tree; satin-wood, lemon-wood, lemon
Citronyle, *s.f.* (*chem.*) citronyl, citrene
†Citrouille, *s.f.* pumpkin; (*pop.*) booby, lubber
Civade, *s.f.* (*pop.*) oats
Civadière, *s.f.* (*nav.*) sprit-sail
Cive, *s.f.* (*bot.*) *V.* **Civette** [hare
Civet, *s.m.* stew, ragout. — *de lièvre*, jugged
Civette, *s.f.* civet-cat; civet; (*bot.*) chives
Civière, *s.f.* handbarrow; litter; stretcher
Civil, e, *adj.* civil; private, plain; — *s.m.* civil; civil service; civil proceedings *or* matters; [civilian (*not a soldier*)
Civilement, *adv.* civilly
Civilisable, *adj.* civilizable [civilizer
Civilisa-teur, trice, *adj.* civilizing; — *s.m.f.*
Civilisation, *s.f.* civilization [civilized
Civiliser, *v.a.* to civilize. *Se* —, to become
Civiliste, *s.m.* civilian (*lawyer*)
Civilité, *s.f.* civility; attention; compliment
Civ-ique, -isme. *V.* page 3, § 1
Clabaud, *s.m.* (*hunt.*) liar; (*pers.*) brawler; ranter; babbler; (*obsolete*) flop-hat, slouched hat [scolding; ranting
Clabaudage, *s.m.* barking; brawling, clamour;
Clabauder, *v.n.* (*hunt.*) to give tongue falsely, to open false; to yelp, to bark; (*pers.*) to brawl, to clamour; to scold; to rant, to abuse; — *v.a.* to repeat, to tell
Clabauderie, *s.f.* brawling, clamour; scolding; ranting, abuse, scandal, aspersion
Clabaudeu-r, se, *s.m.f.* brawler, clamourer scold; ranter; slanderer; — *s.m.* (*hunt.*) *V* [**Clabaud**
Cladion, *s.m.* (*bot.*) cladium, twig-rush
Claie, *s.f.* hurdle; wattle; screen; (*fish.*) weel
Clair, e, *adj.* clear; bright; light; thin; limpid; plain; evident; obvious; distinct; sure; available; (*of eggs*) ungerminated, barren. *Faire* —, to be light
Clair, *s.m.* light; light part; thin part; clear *or* evident *or* obvious part; sure part; (*pop.*) peeper (*eye*). — *de lune*, moonlight, moonshine. *Tirer au* —, to strain *or* draw *or* bottle off, to filter, to clarify, to fine; to clear up
Clair, *adv.* clearly; thinly; plainly; well. *Je n'y vois pas* —, I can't see [liquoring
Clairçage, *s.m.* (*manuf. of sugar*) decolouring,
Clairce, *s.f.* (*manuf. of sugar*) clarified syrup, fine liquor [liquor
Claircer, *v.a.* (*manuf. of sugar*) to decolour, to
Claire, *s.f.* burnt bones; sugar-boiler; (*of oyster-beds*, &c.) fattening-pit [**Clairce**
Clairée, *s.f.* reservoir; (*manuf. of sugar*) *V.*
Clairement, *adv.* clearly; distinctly; plainly
Clairet, te, *adj.* lightish, palish; (*of wines*) light red, pale, light, weak; — *s.m.* pale *or* light wine, weak wine; (*pharm.*) aromatized wine; (*jewel.*) pale stone [*from the South of France*)
Clairette, *s.f.* clairette (*white sparkling wine*
Claire-voie, *s.f.* opening; railing; open-work gate, gate; skylight. *A* —, in open work, open-worked; open; (*of sowing*) thin [place
Clairière, *s.f.* glade; clear spot; (*tech.*) thin
Clair-obscur, *s.m.* contrast of light and shade, light and shade, clare-obscure, chiaro-oscuro, chiaroscuro; mezzotint
Clairon, *s.m.* clarion, trumpet; bugle; bugler; clear spot; lighted wisp of straw; (*insect*) bee-moth
Clair-semé, e, *adj.* thin-sown; thinly scattered; few and far between; thin; sparse; [scarce; rare
Clairure, *s.f.* (*of stuffs*) thin place
Clairvoyance, *s.f.* perspicacity, sagacity, acuteness, clear-sightedness, clear-seeing; (*in mesmerism*) clairvoyance
Clairvoyant, e, *adj.* clear-sighted, clear-seeing, clear-headed, acute, sharp; (*in mesmerism*) [clairvoyant
Clameur, *s.f.* clamour, outcry
Clameu-x, se, *adj.* noisy
Clamp, *s.m.,* **Clampe,** *s.f.* (*tech.*) clamp
Clampin, e, *adj.* lame; (*pop.*) slow; — *s.m.f.* (*pop.*) slow-coach, laggard; lazy dog
Clampiner, *v.n.* (*fam.*) to lag; to linger; to loiter; to trifle
Clamponnier, *s.m.* long-pasterned horse
Clan, *s.m.* clan; (*nav.*) mortise
Clandestin, e, *adj.* clandestine, secret; — *s.f.* (*bot.*) broom-rape, coral-wort, tooth-wort [ly
Clandestinement, *adv.* clandestinely, secret-
Clandestinité, *s.f.* clandestineness, secrecy
Clangueur, *s.f.* clangor
Clape, *s.f.* (*engin.*) sluice
Claper, *v.n. V.* **Clapper** [flap, flapper
Clapet, *s.m.* clapper, clack, valve, clack-valve,
Clapier, *s.m.* rabbit-burrow, burrow; rabbit-hutch, hutch; hutch-rabbit, tame rabbit; (*surg.*) sinus; (*obsolete*) house of ill fame
Clapir, *v.n.* (*of rabbits*) to squeak
Se —, *v.r.* to earth, to squat, to cower down; to hide oneself
Clapot, *s.m.* (*nav.*) chop, short wave; chopping
Clapotage, *s.m.* plashing, plash, splashing, splash, swashing, swash, rippling, (*nav.*) chopping
Clapoter, *v.n.* to plash, to splash, to swash, to ripple, (*nav.*) to chop; (*fig.*) to move, to stir, to come in contact
Clapoteu-x, se, *adj.* plashing, splashing, swashing, rippling, (*nav.*) chopping, swelling, rolling, short, running in heaps, rough and [turbulent
Clapotis, *s.m. V.* **Clapotage**
Clappement, *s.m.* smacking *or* smack (*of the* [*tongue*, &c.)
Clapper, *v.n.* to smack

Claquade, *s.f.* buffeting, beating, slaps, smacks
Claque, *s.f.* slap, smack, smacker; overshoe, clog, golosh; clap; (hired) clappers (*in theatres*); (*childish slang*) snapper; bladder-senna pod; — *s.m.* opera-hat; cocked hat; little bird. *Figure à —s*, make-game *or* sneering face (*such as one would like to slap*)
Claquebois, *s.m.* American pine-sticks, musical sticks (*wooden harmonica*)
Claquedents, *s.m.* chattering of the teeth; starving beggar, naked wretch; boaster
Claque-faim, Claque-soif, *s.m.* (*pop.*) starving wretch
Claquement, *s.m.* clapping; snapping, snap; chattering (*of the teeth*); smacking, cracking, smack, crack [confine, to closet
Claquemurer, *v.a.* to shut up, to immure, to
†Claque-oreilles, *s.m.* flop-hat, slouched hat
Claquer, *v.a.n.* to clap; to slap; to snap; (*of the teeth*) to chatter; to smack; to crack; to slap *or* smack the face of; to applaud; to golosh (*shoes, boots*); (*fam., pop.*) to die, to kick the bucket, to hop the twig, to pop off; (*pop.*) to eat, to feed; to sell. *Faire —*, to snap; to slap; to smack, to crack
Claquet, *s.m.* (*of mills*) clapper, clack
Claqueter, *v.n.* to chirp; to click, to clack. *Faire —*, to snap [terbox; card-case
Claquette, *s.f.* clapper; rattle; gossip, chat-
Claqueu-r, se, *s.m.f.* (*pers.*) clapper; — *s.m.*
Claquoir, *s.m.* clapper [(*theat.*) (hired) clapper
Clarence, *s.m.* clarence (*carriage*)
Clarequet, *s.m.* jelly (*of fruit*)
Clarette, *s.f. V.* **Clairette**
Claricorde, *s.m.* (*mus. instr.*) clarichord
Clarière, *s.f. V.* **Clairière;** (*nav.*) opening, way, passage (*between floes or icebergs*)
Clarification, *s.f.* clarification; fining
Clarificatoire, *adj.* clarifying [purify
Clarifier, *v.a.* to clarify, to clear; to fine; to
Se —, *v.r.* to clarify, to become clear, to settle; to be clarified *or* fined
Clarine, *s.f.* (*of cattle*) bell
Clariné, e, *adj.* (*her.*) belled [tist, clarionettist
Clarinette, *s.f.* clarinet, clarionet; clarinet-
Clarinettiste, *s.m.* clarinettist, clarionettist
Clarté, *s.f.* clearness; brightness; light; brilliancy; splendour; transparency; limpidity; perspicacity; perspicuity; obviousness
Classe, *s.f.* class; rank; order; rate; sort; form; class-room, school-room; school-time; lesson; school; college; school-day; list of registered seamen. *En —*, at *or* in school; all in! *Faire une —*, to take *or* teach a class; (*of students*) to go through a form. *Faire ses —s*, to be educated, to go through o.'s course of studies [(*nav.*) engagement, enrolment
Classement, *s.m.* classing, classification;
Classer, *v.a.* to class; to sort; (*nav.*) to engage, to enrol, to register [take rank
Se —, *v.r.* to be classed *or* sorted *or* &c.; to
Classeur, *s.m.* portfolio; sorter
Classicisme, *s.m.* (*liter.*) classicism
Classificateur, *s.m.* classifier
Classification, *s.f.* classification
Classifier, *v.a.* to classify
Classique, *adj.* classic, classical; academical; educational; school, class; standard; — *s.m.* classic; classicism; (*pers.*) classicist [ish, silly
Claude, *s.m.* fool, simpleton, noodle; — *adj.* fool-
Claudicant, e, *adj.* halting, limping, lame
Claudication, *s.f.* halting, limping; lameness
Claudien, ne, *adj.* Claudian
Clause, *s.f.* clause, stipulation, condition
Clausoir, *s.m.* (*arch.*) key-stone [tered
Claustral, e, *adj.* claustral, monastic; clois-
Claustration, *s.f.* confinement [brick
Claustre, *s.m.* (*arch.*) tile-baluster, ornamental
Clavaire, *s.f.* (*bot.*) club-top (*club-shaped fungus*)
Clavé, e, *adj.* clavated, clavate, club-shaped; (*nav.*) icebound [(*vet.*) rot
Claveau, *s.m.* (*arch.*) arch-stone, key-stone;
Clavecin, *s.m.* (*mus. instr.*) harpsichord; (*nav.*) officers' cabins, quarter gallery
Claveciniste, *s.m.f.* harpsichordist
Clavelé, e, *adj.* (*vet.*) affected with the rot
Clavelée, *s.f.* (*vet.*) rot
Clavelisation, *s.f.* (*vet.*) inoculation of the rot
Claveliser, *v.a.* (*vet.*) to inoculate with the rot
Clavesin, *s.m.* (*nav.*) *V.* **Clavecin**
Clavet, *s.m.* (*nav.*) malking-iron
Clavette, *s.f.* peg; pin; key; collar
Clavicorde, *s.m.* (*mus. instr.*) clavichord
Clavicorne, *adj.m.f., s.m.* (*zool.*) clavicorn
Claviculaire, *adj.* (*anat.*) clavicular
Clavicule, *s.f.* (*anat.*) clavicle, collar-bone
Clavier, *s.m.* key-ring; key-chain; (*mus.*) keyboard, clavier; compass, full compass; claviary
Claviforme, *adj.* claviform, club-shaped
Clavigère, *s.m.* (*insect*) claviger
Clavin, *s.m. V.* **Clavelée**
Clayer, *s.m.* large hurdle
Clayère, *s.f.* oyster-bed
Clayette, *s.f.* twenty-four punnets of mushrooms (*from* 5 *to* 8 *mushrooms each punnet*); wicker cheese-drainer, stand
Claymore, *s.f.* claymore (*Scottish sword*)
Clayon, *s.m.* small hurdle, hurdle; wattle, plashoot; wicker cheese-drainer, stand
Clayonnage, *s.m.* hurdle-fence, wattle-fence, wattling; basket-work; wicker
Clayonner, *v.a.* to wattle, to fence
Clé, *s.f.* key; plug; tuning-hammer; (*tech.*) wrench; (*of a cart*) trap-stick; (*of a breech-loader*) lever; (*of a stove*) valve; (*arch.*) crown; (*mus.*) key, clef; (*hunt.*) leading dog, leader (*of a pack*); (*nav.*) chock, hitch, fid; (*of a rudder*) woodlock. — *anglaise*, screw-wrench. — *de voûte*, key; key-stone. *Sous —*, locked up, under lock and key. *Enfermer à —*, to lock in. *Fermer à —*, to lock. *Mettre* or *tenir sous —*, to lock up. *Mettre la — sous la porte*, (*fig.*) to move off, to bolt, to abscond
Cleavelandite, *s.f.* (*min.*) cleavelandite
Cléché, e, *adj.* (*her.*) cleche
Clef, *s.f. V.* **Clé** [virgin's-bower
Clématite, *s.f.* (*bot.*) clematis, traveller's-joy,
Clémence, *s.f.* clemency; mercy; indulgence; leniency; pardon, forgiveness
Clément, e, *adj.* clement; merciful; indulgent; lenient; forgiving; mild; gentle
Clémentin, e, *adj. s.* (*hist.*) Clementine
Clenche, Clenchette, *s.f.* latch (*of a door*); (*abusively*) *V.* **Poucier.** — *de loquet*, latch
Clephte, *s.m.* klepht (*modern Greek mountaineer*)
Clephtique, *adj.* klephtic [*glass*)
Clepsydre, *s.f.* clepsydra (*water-clock, hour-*
Cleptomane, *adj. s.m.f.* cleptomaniac, kleptomaniac
Cleptomanie, *s.f.* cleptomania, kleptomania
Clerc, *s.m.* clerk; articled clerk; (*obsolete*) clergyman, clerk in holy orders; scholar; learned
Clergé, *s.m.* clergy [man; member; amanuensis
Clérical, e, *adj.*, **Clérical,** *s.m.* clerical
Cléricalement, *adv.* clerically
Clériċat, *s.m.* clerkship
Cléricature, *s.f.* clerkship; apprenticeship (*as an articled clerk*), articles; lawyers' clerks; holy orders, ecclesiastical state, ministry; priesthood; priests
Cléristère, *s.m.* (*arch.*) clerestory, clearstory
Clermontois, e, *adj. s.* of Clermont; native
Clèvelandite, *s.f. V.* **Cleavelandite** [of ditto
Clic-clac, *s.m.* cracking (*of a whip*) [casting
Clichage, *s.m.* stereotyping; stereotype; (*sculp.*)
Cliché, *s.m.* stereotype plate, plate, stereotype; (*in photography*) negative; (*sculp.*) cast
Clicher, *v.a.* to stereotype; (*sculp.*) to cast
Clicherie, *s.f.* stereotyping
Clicheur, *s.m.* stereotyper
Client, e, *s.m.f.* client; customer; patient
Clientèle, *s.f.* clients; patronage, protection; practice; connection; custom, business; goodwill; (*milkman's*) walk

Clifoire, *s.f.* squirt
†Clignement, *s.m.* winking, blinking, twinkling of the eyes; wink
†Cligne-musette, *s.f.* (*obsolete*) *V.* **Cache-cache**
†Cligner, *v.a.n.* to wink, to blink, to twinkle
†Clignotement, Clignoter. *V.* **Clignement, Cligner**
Climat, *s.m.* climate, clime; (*in Burgundy*) vine-growing district
Climatérique, *adj.* climacteric; climatic
Climato-graphie, -logie, &c. *V.* page 3, § 1
Climature, *s.f.* climate, temperature
Climax, *s.m.* (*rhet.*) climax
Clin, *s.m.* (*arch.*) louvre-boarding, louvre, lufferboarding, lufferboard; (*nav.*) clincher-work. — *d'œil,* twinkling of an eye; trice, instant; wink. *A* —, (*nav.*) with clincher-work, clincher-built
†Clincaille, *s.f.* *V.* **Quincaille**
Clinche, *s.f.* *V.* **Clenche**
Clinfoc, *s.m.* (*nav.*) flying-jib. *Bâton de* —, flying-jib-boom
Clinicien, *adj.m.* clinical; — *s.m.* clinical physician *or* surgeon
Clinique, *adj.m.f.* clinical; — *s.f.* clinical medicine *or* surgery *or* hospital *or* lectures; — *s.m.* [(*eccl. hist.*) clinic
Clinomètre, *s.m.* clinometer
Clinométr-ie, -ique. *V.* page 3, § 1
Clinopode, *s.m.* (*bot.*) field-basil
†Clinquaille, *s.f.* *V.* **Quincaille**
Clinquant, *s.m.* tinsel; foil; glitter; affectation
Clinquanté, e, *adj.* tinselled, showy, gaudy, florid
Clinquanter, *v.a.* to tinsel
Clipper, *s.m.* (*nav.*) clipper
Cliquart, *s.m.* building-stone
Clique, *s.f.* set, clan, gang, clique; party, club, league. *Prendre* (or *emporter*) *ses* —*s et ses claques,* (*fam.*) to pack up bag and baggage, to be off; to die, to kick the bucket
Cliquet, *s.m.* click; catch
Cliqueter, *v.n.* to clack, to click; to clang, to clank; to clash; to jingle
Cliquetis, *s.m.* clacking, clicking; clashing, clash, clang, clanking, clank; din; jingling, jingle [peepers (*eyes*)
Cliquettes, *s.f.pl.* snaps, snappers, bones; (*pop.*)
Cliquot, *s.m.* Cliquot champagne (wine)
Clisse, *s.f.* wicker-work, wicker; wattle; cheese-hurdle, cheese-drainer, cheese-vat; stand; (*surg., obsolete for* "éclisse") splint
Clissé, e, *adj.* cased in wicker-work, wickered, wicker
Clisser, *v.a.* to case in wicker-work, to wicker; [(*surg.*) *V.* **Éclisser**
Clitore, *s.f.* (*bot.*) clitoria
Clitoris, *s.m.* (*anat.*) clitoris
Clivage, *s.m.* (*min.*) cleavage
Cliver, *v.a.* (*jewel., min.*) to cleave. **Se** —, *v.r.* to be cleft
Cloacal, e, *adj.* (*anat.*) cloacal
Cloaque, *s.m.* sink, cesspool, sewer; filthy hole *or* place; (*anat.*) cloaca
Cloche, *s.f.* bell; glass bell, bell-glass; hand-glass; glass shade; dish-cover, meat-cover, cover; bell-shaped stewpan *or* preserving-pan; (*med.*) blister; (*chem., phys.*) receiver; (*nav.*) barrel (*of a capstan*)
Clochement, *s.m.* limping, hobbling; lameness
Cloche-pied, *s.m.* hopping on one leg, hop-race. *A* —, hopping on one leg, hopping. *Sauter à* —, to hop
Clocher, *s.m.* steeple, bell-tower, belfry; parish; village; native village *or* place. *De* —, (*adject., fig.*) village, petty town, local
Clocher, *v.n.* to limp, to halt, to hobble; to trudge; to be lame, to hitch; — *v.a.* (*hort.*) to cover with a hand-glass. *Quelque chose qui cloche,* a hitch
Clocheton, *s.m.* bell-turret
Clochette, *s.f.* hand-bell, little bell, small bell, bell; (*bot.*) bell-flower
Cloison, *s.f.* partition; separation; division; compartment; (*of a lock*) case; (*anat.*) septum; (*nav.*) bulkhead
Cloisonnage, *s.m.* partition-work; wainscoting
Cloisonner, *v.a.* to partition
Cloître, *s.m.* cloister; close; monastery, convent
Cloîtrer, *v.a.* to cloister; (*fig.*) to immure, to confine, to closet, to shut up
Se —, *v.r.* to enter a monastery *or* a convent; to shut oneself up at home
Cloîtri-er, ère, *s.m.f.* cloisterer
Clonique, *adj.* (*med.*) clonic
Clopémanie, *s.f.* *V.* **Cleptomanie**
Clopin-clopant, *adv.* haltingly, limpingly, hobblingly, hobbling along
Clopiner, *v.n.* to hobble, to halt
Cloporte, *s.m.* wood-louse; (*fam.*) door-keeper, house-porter
Cloque, *s.f.* (*agr.*) brown rust, bunt, smut-ball
Cloqué, e, *adj.* (*agr.*) blighted
Clore, *v.a.n.* to close; to shut; to shut up; to close in, to enclose; to end, to conclude; to seal up
Clos, e, *part. adj.* closed; shut; shut up; enclosed; close; ended, at an end, concluded; sealed
Clos, *s.m.* close, enclosure; (enclosed) field *or* garden; vineyard; orchard; paddock; yard. — *de vignes,* vineyard. —*-Vougeot,* clos-Vougeot (*vine-estate, wine*)
Closeau, *s.m.,* **Closerie,** *s.f.* small close *or* enclosure, small garden *or* &c. (*V.* **Clos,** *s.m.*)
Closet, *s.m.* fish-weir
Closier, *s.m.* small farmer; field-keeper
Closser. *V.* **Glousser**
Clostre, *s.m.* *V.* **Claustre**
Clotho, *s.f.* clotho (*spider*)
Clôture, *s.f.* enclosure; fence; close; closing; seclusion
Clôturer, *v.a* to close
Clou, *s.m.* nail (*of metal*); hobnail; spike; stud; (*med.*) boil; (*bot.*) clove; (*slang*) pawnbroker, uncle, spout; (*soldiers' slang*) dry-room; (*thieves' slang*) prison, quod. — *de girofle,* clove. — *à crochet,* tenter-hook. — *à glace,* frost-nail. *A* —*s,* with nails, nailed; with hobnails, hobnailed; &c. *Mettre* or *coller au* —, to pawn, to put up the spout; to clap into the dry-room
Clouage, *s.m.* nailing; nailwork
Cloucourde, *s.f.* *V.* **Coquelourde**
Clouement, *s.m.* nailing
Clouer, *v.a.* to nail; to spike; to rivet, to pin; to tack; to confine; to detain; to fix; to shut, to close; (*pop.*) to pawn
Se —, *v.r.* to be nailed; to buckle to; to shut oneself up; to settle
Clouter, *v.a.* to stud
Clouterie, *s.f.* nail-manufactory; nail-trade; nails, spikes
Clouti-er, ère, *s.m.f.* nailer, nail-maker; nail-seller, ironmonger; — *s.f.* nail-box
Clovis, Clovisse, *s.m.* (*zool.*) clam
Clown, *s.m.* clown
Cloyère, *s.f.* basket (*of oysters, of* 25 *dozen, and* 1 *dozen over to the retailer*); fish-basket
Club, *s.m.* club, political club
Clubiste, *s.m.f.* member of a club, clubbist
Cluniste, *s.m. adj.* (*eccl. hist.*) Cluniac
Cluser, *v.a.* to set the dogs at (*a partridge*)
Clusie, *s.f.,* **Clusier,** *s.m.* (*bot.*) clusia, balsam-tree
Clysoir, *s.m.* injection-tube
Clysopompe, *s.m.* injecting-apparatus, enema; (*vet.*) clyster-pump
Clystère, *s.m.* (*obsolete, jest.*) clyster, injection
Clystériser, *v.a.* (*jest.*) to clysterize
Cnique, *s.m.* (*bot.*) horse-thistle, blessed thistle
Co-, (*in compounds*) co- . . ., joint . . .
Coaccusé, e, *s.m.f.* (*law*) person accused with another *or* several others; fellow-prisoner
Coacquéreu-r, se, *s.m.f.* joint purchaser
Coacquisition, *s.f.* joint purchase
Coacti-f, ve, *adj.* coactive
Coactivement, *adv.* coactively
Coaction, *s.f.* coaction
Coactivité, *s.f.* coactive power
Coadju-teur, trice, *s.m.f.* coadjutor; coadjutress, coadjutrix
Coadjutorerie, *s.f.* coadjutorship
Coadné, e, *adj.* (*bot.*) coadunate
Coagulable, *adj.* coagulable
Coagulant, e, *adj.* coagulative; — *s.m.* coagulant
Coagula-teur, trice, *adj.* coagulative, coagulatory
Coagulation, *s.f.* coagulation
Coaguler, *v.a.,* **Se** —, *v.r.* to coagulate
Coagulum, *s.m.* (*chem.*) coagulum; coagulant

†**Coaille,** *s.f.* (*com.*) tail-wool
Coalescence, *s.f.* coalescence
Coalescent, e, *adj.* coalescent
Coalisé, e, *part. adj.* leagued, combined, allied, united, together; —**s,** *s.m.pl.* allied powers, allies; coalitionists; unionists
Coaliser, *v.a.,* **Se —,** *v.r.* to league, to confederate, to unite in a coalition *or* combination, to unite, to combine, to form a coalition *or* combination
Coalition, *s.f.* coalition; combination
Coaltar, *s.m.* coal-tar
Coaptation, *s.f.* (*surg.*) setting
Coassement, *s.m.* (*of frogs*) croaking
Coasser, *v.n.* (*of frogs*) to croak [partner
Coassocié, e, *s.m.f.* (*com.*) fellow-partner, co-
Coati, *s.m.* (*zool.*) coati
Cobalt, *s.m.* (*min.*) cobalt
Cobaltifère, *adj.* cobaltiferous
Cobaltique, *adj.* cobaltic
Cobaltisage, *s.m.* cobaltizing
Cobaltiser, *v.a.* to cobaltize
Cobaye, *s.m.* cavy, Guinea-pig
Cobéa, *s.m.,* **Cobée,** *s.f.* (*bot.*) cobæa
Cobelligérant, e, *adj. s.* cobelligerent
Cobite, *s.m.* (*fish*) cobitis, loach
Cobolt, *s.m.* fly-powder
Cobourg, *s.m.* coburg (*stuff*)
Co-bourgeois, *s.m.* copartner in a ship
Cobra-de-capello, *s.m.* (*zool.*) cobra de (*or* da) capello, hooded snake, spectacle-snake *or*
Coca, *s.m.* (*bot.*) coca [viper
†**Cocagne,** *s.f.* feast, treat; festivity, rejoicing; Cocagne, Cockaigne, Utopia. *Pays de —,* land flowing with milk and honey, land of plenty, Cocagne, Cockaigne, Utopia. *Mât de —,* greasy
Cocaïne, *s.f.* (*chem.*) cocaine [pole
Cocard, Cocardeau. *V.* **Coquard,** &c.
Cocarde, *s.f.* cockade; (*pop.*) drinking bout; drop too much [rum
Cocasse, *adj.* funny, comical, droll, odd, queer,
Cocasserie, *s.f.* drollery, oddity, caricature
Cocâtre, *s.m. V.* **Coquâtre**
Cocatris, *s.m.* cock's egg
Cocatrix, *s.m.* cockatrice
Coccifère, *adj.* (*bot.*) cocciferous
Coccigrue, *s.f. V.* **Coquecigrue**
Coccine, *s.f.* (*chem.*) cochinilline
Coccinelle, *s.f.* (*insect*) lady-bird
Coccoloba, *s.m. V.* **Raisinier**
Coccule, *s.m.* (*bot.*) cocculus
Coccyx, *s.m.* (*anat.*) coccyx
Coche, *s.f.* notch; tally; sow; tread; — *s.m.* (*obsolete*) tow-barge; (*obsolete*) coach. — *d'eau,* tow-barge, passage-boat. *En —,* (*nav.*) a-trip. *La mouche du —,* the fly on the coach-wheel, a busybody [sunk, deep; (*of pills*) drastic
Coché, e, *part. V.* **Cocher,** *v.a.*; — *adj.* hollow,
Cochelivier, *s.m.* wood-lark
†**Cochenillage,** *s.m.* cochineal dyeing *or* dye
†**Cochenille,** *s.f.* cochineal
†**Cocheniller,** *v.a.* to dye with cochineal
†**Cochenillier,** *s.m.* (*bot.*) cochineal-tree, nopal
†**Cochenilline,** *s.f.* (*chem.*) cochinilline
Cocher, *s.m.* coachman; cabman; driver; (*astr.*) charioteer. — *de voiture de place,* — *de place,* — *de fiacre,* cab-driver, cabman; fly-driver, flyman
Cocher, *v.a.* to notch; (*of birds*) to tread
Cochère, *adj.f.* for carriages. *Porte —,* carriage-entrance; gateway; courtyard gate
Cochet, *s.m.* young cock, cockerel
Cochevis, *s.m.* (*bird*) crested lark
Cochinchinois, e, *adj. s.* Cochin-Chinese
‡**Cochléaire,** *adj.* (*nat. hist.*) cochleary, cochleate [grass
‡**Cochléaria,** *s.m.* (*bot.*) cochlearia, scurvy-
‡**Cochlée,** *s.f.* (*anat.*) cochlea
Cochon, *s.m.* hog; pig; swine; boar; pork. — *de lait,* sucking pig. — *d'Inde,* Guinea-pig
Cochon, ne, *adj. s.* dirty, nasty, filthy, beastly; lewd; naughty; beast; dirty blackguard

†**Cochonnaille,** *s.f.* (*pop.*) dressed pork, sau-
Cochonnée, *s.f.* farrow, litter [sage meat
Cochonner, *v.n.* to farrow, to pig; — *v.a.* to bungle, to botch, to cobble
Cochonnerie, *s.f.* filthiness; nastiness; nasty *or* beastly thing *or* stuff, trash; wretched work; nasty dealing, blackguard trick [(*at bowls*) jack
Cochonnet, *s.m.* little pig; twelve-faced die;
Coco, *s.m.* coco, cocoa, coco-nut, cocoa-nut; liquorice-root water; (*fam.*) chap, fellow; ducky, darling; horse, nag; (*childish slang*) egg; shoe; (*pop. slang*) head, pate, noddle. *Noix de —,* coco-nut, cocoa-nut
Cocodès, *s.m.* swell, fop; fast man
Cocodette, *s.f.* gay woman
Cocon, *s.m.* cocoon
†**Coconille,** *s.f.* (*silk*) knubs, husks
Coconnage, *s.m.* formation of the cocoons
Coconner, *v.n.* to make its cocoon
Coconnière, *s.f.* cocoonery
Cocorli, *s.m.* (*bird*) dunlin, purr, purre, sea-lark
Cocote, Cocotte, *s.f.* chickabiddy, biddy; ducky, darling, dear; lass, wench; gay woman; egg-boiler; sore eyes; (*mus. slang*) grace
Cocoterie, *s.f.* gay world, courtesans
Cocotier, *s.m.* coco-nut-tree, cocoa-nut-tree, coco-tree, cocoa-tree, coco, cocoa
Cocréanci-er, ère, *s.m.f.* joint creditor
Cocrète, *s.f.* (*bot.*) *V.* **Rhinanthe**
Cocsigrue, *s.f. V.* **Coquecigrue**
Coction, *s.f.* coction, boiling
Cocu, *s.m.* cuckold
Cocuage, *s.m.* cuckoldom
Cocufier, *v.a.* to cuckold
Coda, *s.f.* (*mus.*) coda
Code, *s.m.* code, law, laws, digest, collection of laws; (*pharm.*) pharmacopœia
Codébi-teur, trice, *s.m.f.* joint debtor
Codéine, *s.f.* (*chem.*) codeia, codeine
Codemand - eur, eresse, *s.m.f.* (*law*) co-plaintiff; coapplicant; copetitioner
Codéten-teur, trice, *s.m.f.* joint holder
Codétenu, e, *s.m.f.* (*law*) fellow-prisoner
Codetta, *s.f.* (*mus.*) codetta
Codex, *s.m.* pharmacopœia
Codicillaire, *adj.* (*law*) codicillary
Codicille, *s.m.* (*law*) codicil
Codificateur, *s.m.* codifier, codist
Codification, *s.f.* codification
Codifier, *v.a.* to codify
†**Codille,** *s.f.* (*of hemp or flax*) codilla, scutching-tow; — *s.m.* (*at the game of ombre*) codille
Codirec-teur, trice, *s.m.f.* codirector; co-
Codonataire, *s.m.f.* (*law*) joint donee [directress
Cœcal, Cœcum. *V.* **Cæcal, Cæcum**
Coefficient, e, *adj.,* **Coefficient,** *s.m.* (*alg.*)
Coégal, e, *adj.* coequal [coefficient
Coégalité, *s.f.* coequality
Coélecteur, *s.m.* coelector
Cœliaque, *adj.* (*anat., med.*) cœliac
Coemption, *s.f.* (*civ. law*) coemption
Coercer, *v.a.* (*old*) to coerce
Coercible, *adj.* coercible
Coerciti-f, ve, *adj.* coercive
Coercition, *s.f.* coercion
Coéternel, le, *adj.* coeternal
Coéternité, *s.f.* coeternity
Cœur, *s.m.* heart; stomach; soul; mind; feeling; love; affections; liking, inclination, desire; spirit; mettle; courage; resolution; vigour, strength; middle; midst; core; depth; height; (*at cards*) hearts; (*her.*) heart-point. — *au ventre,* courage, energy. — *d'artichaut,* (*fig.*) everybody's friend; everybody's lover. — *-de-lion,* (*Engl. hist.*) the Lion-hearted. *Joli —,* dangler, spark, beau, ladies' man. *A — joie,* to o.'s heart's content. *A contre- —,* reluctantly, against the grain; grudgingly. *De bon —, de grand —,* with all o.'s heart, heartily, sincerely, cheerfully, gladly, willingly, readily. *D'un bon —,* good-hearted. *De gaieté de —,* on purpose, purposely, deliberately; wantonly;

sportively; gratuitously. *De tout* —, sincerely; devotedly; most willingly. *De tout son* —, *de plein* —, with all o.'s heart. *Mal de* or *au* —, sickness, feeling of sickness. *Maladie de* —, disease of the heart. *Avoir mal au* —, to feel *or* be sick. *Avoir le — gros*, to have o.'s heart full, o.'s heart to be full. *Avoir le — net de*, to have o.'s mind clear about; to disburden o.'s mind (*or* conscience *or* heart) of, to make a clean breast of. *Avoir le — sur les lèvres* (or *sur le bord des lèvres*), to be very nearly sick; (*fig.*) to be open-hearted. *Faire mal au* —, to make sick, to sicken; to disgust, to shock, to displease, to vex. *Faire le joli* —, to play the agreeable. *Faire contre fortune bon* —, to bear up against bad fortune, to keep up o.'s spirits; to put a good face on a bad matter. *Jeter du — sur le carreau, jouer du* —, (*jest.*) to vomit, to spew. *Se ronger le* —, to fret oneself to death. *Si le — vous en dit*, if you wish for any; if you have a mind to it. *Il a le — gros*, his heart is full

Coévêque, *s.m.* cobishop, coadjutor

Coexécu-teur, trice, *s.m.f.* (*law*) coexecutor; coexecutrix

Coexistant, e, *adj.* coexistent

Coexistence, *s.f.* coexistence

Coexister, *v.n.* to coexist

Coffiner (Se), *v.r.* to curl, to turn up; to bend, to camber

Coffre, *s.m.* chest; trunk; box; bin; coffer; locker; case; frame; carcass; body; (*of carriages*) boot; (*print.*) coffin; (*arch., fort.*) coffer; (*zool.*) coffer-fish, trunk-fish. *— -fort*, strong-box, safe. *—s de l'état*, treasury

Coffrer, *v.a.* (*fam.*) to lock up, to clap up, to cage, to quod

Coffret, *s.m.* small chest, box, casket

Coffretier, *s.m.* trunk-maker

Cofidéjusseur, *s.m.* (*law*) cosurety

Cogérant, e, *s m.f.* comanager; comanageress

†Cognac, *s.m.* Cognac brandy, cognac

†Cognasse, *s.f.* wild quince

†Cognassier, *s.m.* quince-tree

Cognat, *s.m.* (*law*) cognate

Cognation, *s.f.* (*law*) cognation

†Cogne, *s.m.* (*pop.*) policeman, constable; — *s.f.* (*pop.*) police, constabulary

†Cognée, *s.f.* axe, hatchet

†Cogne-fétu, *s.m.* great worker and little doer

†Cogner, *v.a.n.* to knock; to strike; to bump; to beat; to thump, to rap, to hit, to maul; to hammer

Se —, *v.r.* to knock, to strike; to knock *or* run (o.'s ...); to beat each other; to fight, to have a fight

†Cognet, *s.m.* roll of tobacco

Cogniti-f, ve, *adj.* cognitive

Cognition, *s.f.* cognition

†Cognoir, *s.m. V* **Décognoir**

Coguenosco, *s.m.* (*nav.*) mastic

Cohabitation, *s.f.* cohabitation

Cohabiter, *v.n.* to cohabit

Cohéremment, *adv.* coherently

Cohérence, *s.f.* coherence, coherency

Cohérent, e, *adj.* coherent

Cohériter, *v.n.* to inherit conjointly with another *or* several others

Cohériti-er, ère, *s.m.f.* coheir, joint heir; coheiress, joint heiress

Cohésion, *s.f.* cohesion; cohesiveness

Cohésionner, *v.a.* to make coherent

Cohibant, e, *adj.* (*phys.*) insulating

Cohibition, *s.f.* hindrance, cohibition

Cohobation, *s.f.* (*pharm.*) cohobation

Cohober, *v.a.* (*pharm.*) to cohobate

Cohortal, e, *adj.* cohortal

Cohorte, *s.f.* cohort; troop, band, horde, company, party, crew, gang; multitude

Cohue, *s.f.* crowd, mob, rout; crush

Coi, te, *adj.* still, quiet; snug

Coiffe, *s.f.* head-dress, cap, hood; coif; network, net; (*of hats*) lining; (*anat., butch.*) caul; (*bot.*) galea, calyptra; (*tech.*) cap

Coiffé, e, *part. adj.* (*V.* **Coiffer**) with o.'s hair dressed, having o.'s hair dressed; (*fig.*) smitten; tipsy, tight, fuddled, muddled; (*nav.*) with her sails laid aback. *— de*, having on o.'s head, wearing, dressed in (...), having on (...), with (...) on; having (*or* with ...) in o.'s hair; (*fig.*) infatuated *or* taken with, wedded to; surmounted *or* capped with. *Être bien* —, to have o.'s hair well dressed; to have a nice bonnet *or* cap *or* hat on; (*of dogs, horses*) to have handsome ears. *Être né* —, (to have been born with a *coiffe* or 'caul') to be born to good luck, to be born with a silver spoon in o.'s mouth. *Être —e en cheveux*, *V.* **Cheveu**

Coiffer, *v.a.n.* to put on *or* cover the head of; to place (...) in the hair of; to fit *or* suit (the head of), to become; to dress the hair of; to dress hair; (*fig.*) to infatuate; to cap; to surmount; (*vulgar*) to throw (...) at the head of; to box the ears of; to make tipsy, to fuddle, to muddle; to deceive (*o.'s husband*); (*hunt.*) to take by the ears; (*v.a., nav.*) to back, to lay aback; (*v.n., nav.*) to be laid aback. *— sainte Catherine*, to remain an old maid

Se —, *v.r.* to put on o.'s head, to put on; to wear; to dress o.'s hair; to be taken (with), to become infatuated (with) *or* wedded (to); to get tipsy; (*nav.*) to be laid aback. *Se — en cheveux*, (*of a woman*) to put *or* wear nothing on o.'s head

Coiffeu-r, se, *s.m.f.* hair-dresser, hair-cutter; tire-woman

Coiffure, *s.f.* head-dress; manner of dressing the hair, style of arranging the hair; hair-dressing; hair (*dressed*). *— en cheveux*, head-dress without a cap

†Coignassier, *s.m. V.* **Cognassier**

Coin, *s.m.* corner; angle; nook; side; patch (*of land*); wedge; stamp; die; mark; corner-piece (of furniture); (*of stockings*) clock; (*vet.*) corner-tooth; (*print.*) coin, quoin; (*rail.*) key. *— de mire*, (*artil.*) coin. *Marqué* or *frappé au bon* —, excellent, very good, of the right sort. *A fleur de* —, looking as fresh from the Mint, quite new *or* fresh. *Les quatre —s*, (*game*) Puss in the corner

Coinçage, *s.m.* wedging; (*rail.*) keying

Coincer, *v.a.* to wedge; (*rail.*) to key

Coïncidence, *s.f.* coincidence

Coïncident, e, *adj.* coincident

Coïncider, *v.n.* to coincide

Coïndicant, e, *adj.* (*med.*) coindicant

Coïndication, *s.f.* (*med.*) coindication

Coïndiquer, *v.n.* (*med.*) to coindicate

Coing, *s.m.* quince

Coïntéressé, e, *s.m.f.* party having a joint interest, associate, partner

Coïon, (*old spelling*) *V.* **Couillon**

Coït, *s.m.* coition, copulation

Coites, Coittes, *s.f.pl.* (*nav.*) bilge-ways, ways

Coïx, *s.m.* (*bot.*) coix, Job's-tears

Cojouissance, *s.f.* (*law*) joint use

Coke, *s.m.* coke

Col, *s.m.* collar; stock, cravat; tie; stiffener, pad; neck; pass, defile, strait; mouth; canal. *— -cravate*, (*s.m.*) stock. *— de cravate*, stiffener, pad. *Faux-* —, shirt-collar

Cola, *s.m. V.* **Kola**

Colachon, *s.m.* Italian lute

Colao, *s.m. V.* **Kolao**

Colaphiser, *v.a.* (*old*) to colaphize, to buffet

Colarin, *s.m.* (*arch.*) colarin

Colas, *s.m.* booby, spoony, simpleton, fool; sheepish fellow

Colatitude, *s.f.* (*astr.*) colatitude

Colature, *s.f.* (*pharm.*) straining, colature. — *de* ..., strained ...

Colback, *s.m.* (*mil.*) busby; (*pop.*) hat, tile

Colchicine, *s.f.* (*chem.*) colchicine

Colchique, *s.m.* (*bot.*) colchicum, meadow saffron; — *adj.* (*anc. geogr., myth.*) Colchian

Colcotar, Colcothar, *s.m.* (*chem.*) colcothar

Cold-cream, *s.m.* cold cream

Colégataire, *s.m.f.* (*law*) colegatee

Coléoptère, *s.m.* (*zool.*) coleopteran, beetle; — *adj.* coleopteral, coleopterous

Colère, *s.f.* anger, passion, wrath; fury, rage; fit of passion. *En* —, angry, in *or* into a passion; raging

Colère, *adj.* passionate, irascible, hasty

Colérer (Se), *v.r.* (*old*) to get angry; to be hasty
Coleret, *s.m.* (*fish.*) drag-net
Colérique, *adj.* passionate, irascible, hasty
Colériquement, *adv.* angrily; hastily
Coliart, *s.m.* (*fish*) skate
Colibri, *s.m.* humming-bird
Colicitant, e, *s.m.f.* (*law*) joint tenant (*of an estate put up to auction*)
Colifichet, *s.m.* gewgaw, bauble, nicknack, trinket, trifle, toy; trumpery; tinsel; finery; [bird-cake
Colimaçon, *s.m. V.* **Limaçon**
Colin, *s.m.* (*zool.*) colin, ortyx, American partridge *or* quail; coal-fish; (*theat.*) shepherd, swain
Colinette, *s.f.* (*obsolete*) (woman's) morning-cap
†**Colin-maillard,** *s.m.* blindman's buff
Colin-tampon, *s.m.* Swiss march. *S'en moquer* (or *S'en soucier* or *S'en ficher*) *comme de* —, not to care a fig *or* a straw about it
Coliou, *s.m.* (*bird*) colius, mouse-bird
Colique, *s.f. adj.* colic
Colis, *s.m.* package, parcel, case, bale, article
Colisée, *s.m.* colosseum, coliseum
Colite, *s.f.* (*med.*) colitis, colonitis
Colitigant, e, *adj. s.* colitigant
Collabora-teur, trice, *s.m.f.* collaborator; associate; assistant; fellow-labourer; contributor; contributress
Collaboration, *s.f.* collaboration; assistance; cooperation; contribution; common industry
Collaborer, *v.n.* to work together; to assist; to cooperate; to contribute [hanging; fining
Collage, *s.m.* pasting; gluing; sizing; sticking;
Collaire, *adj.* (*zool.*) of the neck
Collant, e, *adj.* sticky; tight, close-fitting
Collants, *s.m.pl.* tights
Collapsus, *s.m.* (*med.*) collapse
Collataire, *s.m.* (*eccl.*) presentee
Collatéral, e, *adj.* collateral; side; — *s.m.* (*law*) collateral; (*of churches*) aisle
Collatéralement, *adv.* collaterally [vowee
Collateur, *s.m.* (*eccl.*) collator, presenter, ad-
Collati-f, ve, *adj.* (*eccl.*) collative
Collation, *s.f.* collation; refreshment, meal; presentation; advowson, gift; conferring
Collationnage, *s.m.* collating, collation, comparing [*v.n.* to take a collation
Collationner, *v.a.* to collate, to compare; —
Colle, *s.f.* paste; glue; size; finings; sham, story, bouncer; (*univers.*) little-go. — *forte*, glue. — *à bouche*, mouth-glue. — *de pâte*, paste. — *de poisson*, isinglass. *Professeur* or *maître de —s*, examiner (for the little-go), coach, crammer, grinder
Collectaire, *s.m.* (*eccl.*) collect-book [(*prayer*)
Collecte, *s.f.* collection (*of money*); collect
Collecter, *v.n.* to make collections *or* a collection (*of money*)
Collec-teur, trice, *s.m.f.* collector; collectress; — *s.m.* main sewer; — *adj.* collecting
Collecti-f, ve, *adj.*, **Collectif,** *s.m.* collective
Collection, *s.f.* collection; set
Collectionner, *v.n.* to make collections *or* a collection (*of works of art*, &c.); — *v.a.* to collect (*works of art*, &c.)
Collectionneu-r, se, *s.m.f.* (*of works of art*, &c.) collector; collectress; — *adj.* collecting
Collectivement, *adv.* collectively
Collége, *s.m.* college; grammar-school, school; assembly; district; constituency. — *communal*, grammar-school. — *de plein exercice*, college with a full staff of professors [collegiate church
Collégial, e, *adj.* collegial; collegiate; — *s.f.*
Collégialement, *adv.* scholastically
Collégien, *s.m.* collegian; school-boy, boy at [school
Collègue, *s.m.* colleague
Collement, *s.m.* adhesion, cohesion
Coller, *v.a.* to paste; to glue; to size; to stick; to hang; to fine; to mat; to fix; to apply; to fasten (on); to rivet; to put, to place, to clap; to put close (to); to press; to give; to pass on (to); to send; to catch at fault; to catch; to puzzle, to pose, to stump; to silence, to shut up; (*at billiards*) to put close to the cushion; — *v.n.* to stick, to adhere; to fit tight
Se —, *v.r.* to stick, to stick on; to adhere; to cling; to cleave; to lie *or* stand close; to rest *or* lean (against); to cake; to be pasted *or* glued *or* &c.; to give oneself; (*billiards*) to put o.'s own ball close to the cushion
Colleret, *s.m. V.* **Coleret**
Collerette, *s.f.* tucker, collarette, collar; (*bot.*) involucre; (*tech.*) flange
Collet, *s.m.* collar (*of a coat*); cape; (*butch.*) neck; snare; crown (*of an anchor*); neck (*of a tooth*); (*bot., tech.*) collar, collet. — *montant*, stand-up collar. — *monté*, (*obsolete*) stiff stand-up collar; (*fig.*) stuck-up, stiff, formal, strait-laced, prudish, pedantic; stiff *or* &c. person. *Prêter le — à*, to try o.'s strength with, to cope with
Colleter, *v.a.* to collar; to take *or* seize by the collar *or* by the neck; — *v.n.* to lay *or* set snares
Se —, *v.r.* to collar each other, to seize each other by the collar; to grapple; to wrestle, to fight, to come to blows; to contend, to wrangle; to commit oneself (with) [wrangler, fighter
Colleteur, *s.m.* snarer, gin-setter; (*pop.*)
Collétique, *adj.m.f., s.m.* (*med.*) colletic
Colleur, *s.m.* paper-hanger; bill-sticker, bill-poster; paster; gluer; sizer; (*fam.*) story-teller, boaster, humbug; troublesome twaddler; examiner (for the little-go), coach, crammer, grinder; stumper
Collier, *s.m.* necklace; necklet; collar; (*mark*) ring; (*of spurs*) bow; (*butch.*) neck, clod (*of beef*). — *de force*, training-collar. — *de misère*, toil, drudgery [wood
Collières, *s.f.pl.* framework of a raft of fire-
Colliger, *v.a.* to collect, to cull [tion
Collimation, *s.f.* (*obsolete spelling*) *V.* **Collinéa-**
Collinaire, *adj.* (*bot.*) growing on hills, mountain [the two-crowned hill, Parnassus
Colline, *s.f.* hill; hillock. *La double* —, (*poet.*)
Collinéation, *s.f.* (*astr.*) collineation, collima-
***Colliquati-f, ve,** *adj.* (*med.*) colliquative [tion
***Colliquation,** *s.f.* (*med.*) colliquation
Collision, *s.f.* collision [share; investment
Collocation, *s.f.* collocation, classing; order;
Collodier, *v.a. V.* **Collodionner**
Collodion, *s.m.* (*chem.*) collodion
Collodionner, *v.a.* to collodionize
Colloïde, *adj.* (*surg.*) colloid
Colloque, *s.m.* colloquy; conference; conversation; dialogue [give; to class; to invest
Colloquer, *v.a.* to place, to clap; to seat; to
Colluder, *v.n.* to collude
Collure, *s.f. V.* **Collage**
Collusion, *s.f.* collusion
Collusoire, *adj.* collusive, collusory
Collusoirement, *adv.* collusively
Collutoire, *s.m.* (*med.*) collutorium [eye-water
Collyre, *s.m.* collyrium, eye-salve, eye-wash,
Colmar, *s.m.* colmar (*pear*)
Colmatage, *s.m.* (*agr.*) raising of low marshy lands by artificial alluvia, warping, raising, fertilizing [*marshy lands*), warped land
Colmate, *s.m.* (*agr.*) artificial alluvium (*on low*
Colmater, *v.a.* (*agr.*) to raise low marshy lands by artificial alluvia, to warp, to raise, to fertilize
Colobe, *s.m.* (*zool.*) colobus
Colobome, *s.m.* (*med.*) coloboma
Colocase, Colocasie, *s.f.* (*bot.*) colocasia, cocco, cocoa root, eddoes [colessee
Colocataire, *s.m.f.* cotenant; joint tenant;
Colocation, *s.f.* joint tenancy; joint lease
Colocynthine, *s.f.* (*chem.*) colocynthine
Colombage, *s.m.* (*build.*) stud-work
Colombaire, *adj.* (*zool.*) columbine; — *s.m.* (*in antiquity*) columbarium
Colombe, *s.m.* dove; (*carp.*) joist
Colombelle, *s.f.* (*print.*) column-rule
Colombien, ne, *adj. s.m.f.* Columbian, Colombian; — *s.f.* printing-press

Colombier, *s.m.* pigeon-house, dove-cot, dove-cote; (*print.*) wide spacing, pigeon-hole; (*theat.*) upper gallery; (*paper*) columbier; (*nav.*) blocking-up. *Grand* —, (*paper*) atlas
Colombi-galline, *s.f. V.* **Goura**
Colombin, e, *adj.* (*of colour*) columbine; — *s.m.* stock-dove; lead ore; innocent-looking fellow; — *s.f.* columbine; pigeon-dung, poultry-yard manure
Colombium, *s.m.* (*chem.*) columbium
Colombo, *s.m.* (*bot.*) calumba, columbo
Colomnaire, *adj.* columnar
Colon, *s.m.* colonist; settler; planter; cultivator, husbandman, farmer; convict; West Indian;
Côlon, *s.m.* (*anat.*) *V.* **Colon** [(*anat.*) colon
Colonel, *s.m.* colonel
Colonelle, *s.f.* colonel's wife; — *s.f., adj.f.* (*obsolete*) colonel's company (*first company of a*
Colonial, e, *adj.* colonial [*regiment*)
Colonie, *s.f.* colony; settlement; agricultural school; agricultural penitentiary. — *pénale* or *pénitentiaire*, penal settlement; agricultural penitentiary, convict establishment
Colonisable, *adj.* colonizable [*s.m.f.* colonizer
Colonisa-teur, trice, *adj.* colonizing; —
Colonisation, *s.f.* colonization; settlement
Coloniser, *v.a.* to colonize; to settle
Se —, *v.r.* to become colonized
Coloniste, *s.m. adj.* colonizationist
Colonnade, *s.f.* colonnade
Colonnaison, *s.f.* front columns
Colonnation, *s.f.* columniation
Colonne, *s.f.* column; pillar; monument; post; (*arith.*) row. *A* —*s*, with columns, columned; (*of bedsteads*) four-post. — *d'attaque*, (*mil.*) attacking-party. *Les* —*s d'Hercule*, Hercules' Pillars
Colonnette, *s.f.* small column, little column
Colophane, *s.f.* colophony, black *or* brown rosin
Colophonite, *s.f.* (*min.*) colophonite
Coloquinte, *s.f.* (*bot.*) colocynth, bitter apple, bitter cucumber; (*pop.*) sconce, pate, noddle, head
Coloration, *s.f.* coloration; colouring; colour
Coloré, e, *adj.* coloured; varnished; deep-coloured; ruddy; lively, glowing; plausible, specious, sham
Colorer, *v.a.* to colour; to dye; to tinge; to suffuse; to embellish; to varnish, to gild over, to disguise, to palliate, to excuse, to cloak
Se —, *v.r.* to colour; to be tinged; to assume a colour; to take its colour
Coloriage, *s.m. V.* **Enluminure**
Colorier, *v.a.n.* to colour, to illuminate; to understand colouring, to paint
Coloris, *s.f.* colouring; colour; hue
Coloriste, *s.m.f.* colourist; colourer; illuminator
Colossal, e, *adj.* colossal [nator
Colosse, *s.m.* colossus
Colossien, ne, *adj. s.* Colossian
Colostration, *s.f.* (*med.*) colostration [(*milk*)
Colostre, Colostrum, *s.m.* (*med.*) colostrum
Colportage, *s.m.* hawking; hawker's trade; pedlary; book-hawking; book-stall trade; news-vending; sale (*of books by hawkers and at railway stalls*)
Colporter, *v.a.* to hawk, to hawk about; (*fig.*) to spread [circulate
Se —, *v.r.* to be hawked about; to spread; to
Colporteu-r, se, *s.m.f.* hawker; pedlar; book-hawker; news-vendor; spreader
Coltis, *s.m.* (*nav.*) beak-head
Colubrin, e, *adj.* (*zool.*) colubrine [**lombaire**
Columbaire, Columbarium, *s.m. V.* **Co-**
Columelle, *s.f.* (*nat. hist.*) columella; (*arch.*)
Colure, *s.m.* (*astr., geog.*) colure [cippus
Colza, *s.m.* (*bot.*) colza, rape; rape-seed
Coma, *s.m.* (*med., bot.*) coma
Comaret, *s.m.* (*bot.*) marsh-cinquefoil
Comateu-x, se, *adj.* (*med.*) comatose
Combat, *s.m.* fight, battle, action, engagement, encounter; combat; contest; struggle; strife; conflict; contention; opposition; attack; assault; match. — *en chasse*, (*nav.*) running fight. *Hors de* —, disabled. *Mettre hors de* —,
Combativité, *s.f.* combativeness [to disable
Combattable, *adj.* combatable
Combattant, e, *s.m.f.* combatant; fighting-man *or* woman; fighter; champion, championess; soldier, warrior; supporter; — *s.m.* (*bird*) ruff (*female*, reeve)
Combattre, *v.a.n.* to fight; to fight against; to combat; to encounter; to contend with; to contend; to strive against; to strive; to struggle with; to struggle; to oppose; to resist; to vie; to contest; to impugn
Combe, *s.f.* (*in the Alps*) valley, combe, comb, coombe, coomb, (*in Wales*) cwm; (*mil.*) esplanade
Combien, *adv.* how much; how many; how long; how far, what distance; how; what. — *de temps?* how much time? how long?
Combinable, *adj.* combinable
Combinaison, *s.f.* combination; contrivance; ingenuity; management; calculation [triver
Combina-teur, trice, *s.m.f.* combiner; con-
Combiné, *s.m.* (*chem.*) combination, compound
Combiner, *v.a.* to combine; to contrive
Se —, *v.r.* to combine; to be combined *or* contrived
Comble, *s.m.* heaping; completion, consummation; top; height, summit, utmost, acme, zenith; perfection; roof; roof-timbers; shed. *Au* —, at the height; complete, to the full, full. *Pour* — *de*, to complete, to crown. *Mettre le* — *à*, to complete, to crown
Comble, *adj.* heaped; full, quite full, full to overflowing, overfull, crowded, crammed; ex-
Combleau, *s.m.* (*artil.*) gun-tackle [cessive
Comblement, *s.m.* heaping up; filling up
Combler, *v.a.* to heap; to heap up; to pile up; to fill; to fill up; to fulfil; to gratify; to make up; to supply; to complete; to crown; to load; to overwhelm; (*obsolete*) to delight, to overjoy;
Se —, *v.r.* to be filled [(*fin.*) to cover (*a deficit*)
Comblète, Comblette, *s.f.* cleft (*in a stag's*
Combrière, *s.f.* (*fish.*) tunny-net [*foot*)
Combuger, *v.a.* to season (*with water*)
Comburant, e, *adj.* (*chem.*) comburent, burning, combining with evolution of light and heat; — *s.m.* supporter of combustion
Combustibilité, *s.f.* combustibility
Combustible, *adj.* combustible; — *s.m.* fuel, firing; article of fuel; (*chem.*) combustible
Combustion, *s.f.* combustion; (*fig.*) conflagration, flame, tumult, uproar
Come, *s.m.* warder (*of convicts*) [comediatress
Comédia-teur, trice, *s.m.f.* comediator;
Comédie, *s.f.* comedy; play; theatre; theatricals; sport; fun; farce; dissembling, sham; play-book; book of the play; players, company. *Donner la* —, to make one *or* people laugh; to make oneself an object of laughter; to expose oneself
Comédien, ne, *s.m.f.* comedian; actor, actress, player, performer; dissembler, hypocrite; — *adj.* theatrical; affected, artificial; sham;
Comestibilité, *s.f.* edibleness [quackish
Comestible, *adj.m.f., s.m.* eatable, esculent, edible; —**s,** *s.m.pl.* eatables, esculents, victuals,
Cométaire, *adj.* (*astr.*) cometary [provisions
Comète, *s.f.* (*astr., fireworks, her., game at cards*) comet; (*com.*) satin ribbon
Cométographe, *s.m.* cometographer
Cométo-graphie, -graphique, -logie, -logique. *V.* page 3, § 1 [&c.
Comfort, Comfortable, &c. *V.* **Confort,**
Comice, *s.m.* meeting; society; agricultural meeting *or* society; electoral meeting; —**s,** *pl.* meetings, &c.; (*Rom. hist.*) comitia
Comicial, e, *adj. V.* **Comitial**
Comifère, *adj.* (*bot.*) comose
Comique, *adj.* comic; comical; — *s.m.* comedy, comic art *or* style *or* actor *or* character *or* author *or* subjects; comic singer; comical part *or* side; something comical; humour

Comiquement, *adv.* comically
Comitat, *s.m.* comitat (*district of Hungary*)
Comite, *s.m. V.* **Come**
Comité, *s.m.* committee; board; (*fam.*) meeting, club. *En petit* —, a small party; with a few intimate friends, with a select few; among ourselves *or* yourselves *or* themselves. — *de lecture*, committee (*for deciding upon new plays offered for performance*)
Comitial, e, *adj.* of agricultural *or* electoral meetings; of agricultural societies; agricultural; electoral; (*Rom. hist.*) comitial
Comma, *s.m.* (*print.*) colon; (*mus.*) comma
Command, *s.m.* (*law*) purchaser, principal
Commandant, e, *part. adj.* commanding
Commandant, *s.m.* commander; commandant; commanding officer; major; governor; —**e,** *s.f.* ditto's wife
Commande, *s.f.* order; —*!* *int.* (*nav.*) halloo! *De* —, to order; made to order; ordered; bespoken; prescribed; feigned, forced; at command. *Sur* —, to order
Commandement, *s.m.* command; commandment; order; bidding; mandate, precept; word of command; manner of commanding; (*law*) writ; (*fort.*) command. *Secrétaire des* —*s*, private secretary. *Être de* —, to be prescribed *or* ordered
Commander, *v.a.n.* to command; to order; to bid; to direct; to prescribe; to require; to bespeak; to govern; to rule; to dictate; to lead, to conduct; to give the word of command; to command a view of, to overlook; to shape (*a ship's course*) [come at command *or* at call
Se —, *v.r.* to command oneself; (*of things*) to
Commanderie, *s.f.* commandery [**Troupiale**
Commandeur, *s.m.* commander; (*bird*) *V.*
Commanditaire, *s.m.f. adj.* (*com.*) sleeping partner
Commandite, *s.f.* (*com.*) limited liability; funds advanced, share of capital, interest
Commanditer, *v.a.* (*com.*) to advance funds to, to take an interest in (as a sleeping partner)
Se —, *v.r.* to be assisted with an advance of funds, to find sleeping partners *or* a sleeping partner
Comme, *adv.* as; like; such as; as much as; so much as; as well as; as good as; almost, nearly; as if; as it were; in a manner; how; how much; how many; when. — *cela*, — *ça*, like that; in this way, in that way; thus; so; this way; as it is; middling, indifferently, so so. — *quoi*, how; in what. — *il faut*, *V.* **Falloir**
Commeline, *s.f.* (*bot.*) commelin
Commémoraison, *s.f.* commemoration
Commémorati-f, ve, *adj.* commemorative, memorial [tion
Commémoration, *s.f.* commemoration; men-
Commémorer, *v.a.* to commemorate
Commençant, e, *adj.* beginning; incipient; — *s.m.f.* beginner; tyro
Commencement, *s.m.* beginning, commencement; rise; origin; setting in; setting out. *Au* —, in the beginning, at first
Commencer, *v.a.n.* to begin, to commence
Se —, *v.r.* to be begun; to begin
Commendataire, *adj.* (*can. law*) commendatory; — *s.m.* commendator
Commende, *s.f.* (*can. law*) commendam
Commender, *v.a.* (*can. law*) to give in commendam [habitual guest, guest; boarder
Commensal, e, *s.m.f.* commensal; messmate;
Commensalité, *s.f.* commensality
Commensurabilité, *s.f.* commensurability
Commensurable, *adj.* commensurable
Commensuration, *s.f.* commensuration
Comment, *adv.* how; why; what; how now? what do you mean (by)? — *cela?* how is that? how so? — *donc!* oh dear yes, to be sure, certainly; oh dear no, certainly not. ... — *faire*, ... what to do, ... how to manage it, ... how to help it. — *faire?* what is (*or* was) to be done? what can (*or* could) be done? what are (*or* were) we to do? how can (*or* could) it be helped? — *s.m. Le pourquoi et le* —, the why and the wherefore, the reason [remark; observation
Commentaire, *s.m.* comment; commentary;
Commenta-teur, trice, *s.m.f.* commentator, commenter; expositor
Commenter, *v.a.n.* to comment on, to comment, to make comments; to gloss, to give a gloss; to criticize; to put an ill construction
Se —, *v.r.* to be commented on [upon
Commérage, *s.m.* gossiping, gossip, tittle-tattle
Commerçable, *adj.* (*old*) negotiable
Commerçant, e, *adj. s.m.f.* commercial, mercantile, trading; commercial man, merchant, trader, dealer, tradesman
Commerce, *s.m.* commerce, trade; business; commercial people, tradespeople; intercourse, connection, dealing; correspondence; communication; interchange; cultivation; acquaintance; society; intimacy; communion; conversation. — *actif*, brisk trade; exports; excess of exports over imports. — *passif*, imports; excess of imports over exports. — *de vins*, wine-trade; wine-stores. *De* or *du* —, of commerce, of trade; commercial, mercantile, trading, merchant. *Le haut* —, the higher branches of commerce, the great merchants, merchants. *Le petit* —, the small trade, the shopkeepers, the tradespeople. *Faire le* — *de*, to deal in, to carry on the business of. *Dans le* — *de la vie*, in our dealings with the world
Commercer, *v.n.* to trade, to traffic; to deal; to hold intercourse
Commercial, e, *adj.* commercial, trading
Commercialement, *adv.* commercially
Commère, *s.f.* fellow-godmother; gossip; mother, gammer, friend, good woman; body, thing; artful and clever woman, shrewd woman
Commérer, *v.n.* to gossip, to tittle-tattle
Commettage, *s.m.* (*nav.*) laying (of ropes and cables) [principal; warrantor
Commettant, *s.m.* constituent; employer;
Commetteur, *s.m.* (*pers., nav.*) layer (of ropes and cables)
Commettre, *v.a.* to commit; to do; to intrust; to confide; to appoint; to commission; to employ; to compromise, to expose; to set at variance; (*nav.*) to lay (*a rope*)
Se —, *v.r.* to commit *or* expose oneself; to trust oneself; to measure o.'s strength, to contend, to fight; to be committed
Commination, *s.f.* commination
Comminatoire, *adj.* comminatory
Comminuer, *v.a.* to comminute [comminuted
Comminuti-f, ve, *adj.* comminuting; (*surg.*)
Comminution, *s.f.* comminution
Commis, *s.m.* clerk; book-keeper; shopman; officer; assistant; deputy. — *voyageur*, (commercial) traveller, bagman. — *aux écritures*, clerk. — *aux vivres*, (*nav.*) steward. — *d'administration*, accountant; (*nav.*) purser. — *de barrière*, — *aux barrières*, toll-clerk, exciseman. — *de boutique* or *de magasin*, shopman
Commise, *s.f.* (*feud. law*) forfeiture
Commisération, *s.f.* commiseration
Commissaire, *s. m.* commissary; commissioner; trustee; steward; peace-officer; superintendent of police; chief constable. — -*priseur*, appraiser; auctioneer. — *des pauvres*, relieving-officer. — *de police*, superintendent of police; chief constable
Commissariat, *s.m.* commission; commissioners' office; police-station, police-office; commissaryship; commissionership; trusteeship; stewardship; (*nav.*) commissioners (of the admiralty), naval commissioners. — *de police*, police-station, police-office
Commission, *s.f.* commission; charge; trust; warrant; mandate; mission; message; errand; committee; commission-agency
Commissionnaire, *s.m.f.* street-messenger,

errand-porter, ticket-porter, commissionaire; messenger; porter; carrier; agent; commission-agent. — *-chargeur*, canal-carrier. — *expéditeur*, shipping-agent

Commissionner, *v.a.* to commission

Commissoire, *adj.* (*law*) binding

Commissural, e, *adj.* commissural

Commissure, *s.f.* (*anat., bot., arch.*) commissure

Commixtion, *s.f.* commixtion

Commodant, e, *s.m.f.* lender by commodate

Commodat, *s.m.* (*law*) commodate

Commodataire, *s.m.f.* borrower by commodate

Commode, *adj.* convenient; commodious; suitable; serviceable; handy; comfortable; agreeable; easy; easy to deal with, accommodating; lax, loose

Commode, *s.f.* chest of drawers, drawers; (*ancient head-dress*) commode. — *-toilette, toilette-* —, pedestal dressing-table *or* toilet-table *or* washstand

Commodément, *adv.* conveniently; commodiously; suitably; comfortably; easily

Commodité, *s.f.* convenience; commodiousness; comfort; ease; accommodation; (*obsolete*) conveyance; means, way; opportunity; —**s,** *pl.* water-closet

Commodore, *s.m.* (*Engl. and Amer. nav.*) commodore

Commotion, *s.f.* commotion; shock

Commuabilité, *s.f.* commutability

Commuable, *adj.* commutable

Commuer, *v.a.* to commute

Commun, e, *adj.* common; public, general; universal; unanimous; joint; mutual; usual, ordinary, every-day; familiar; commonplace; trite; trivial; coarse; vulgar; low; mean; average, one with another; conventual. *Peu* —, uncommon, rare, unusual, extraordinary

Commun, *s.m.* common; generality; generality of men, most people, general public, everybody; common stock; common way; ordinary class; lower servants, servants; common people, lower class; —**s,** *pl.* servants' offices, domestic offices, outbuildings; privy. *Le — des hommes* or *des mortels*, the generality of men, most people; the vulgar. *Le — des martyrs*, the common herd

Communal, e, *adj.* communal, parish, parochial, town; —*s.m.*(*pl.* **Communaux**) common, common land, common pasture, public ground, parish property

Communauté, *s.f.* community; convent; corporation; company; body; society; communion; property in common. *Biens de* —, (*law*) common property, common estate

Commune, *s.f.* parish; town; township; town-hall; parishioners; townspeople, inhabitants; common council; commonalty; —**s,** *pl.* parishes, &c.; (*Engl. parl.*) commons. *La* —, (*Fr. hist.*) the Commune (*a revolutionary committee*)

Communément, *adv.* commonly, generally, usually

Communéro, *s.m.* communero (*Spanish democrat*)

Communiant, e, *s.m.f.* communicant

Communicabilité, *s.f.* communicability

Communicable, *adj.* communicable

Communicant, e, *adj.* communicating

Communicateur, *s.m.* communicator

Communicati-f, ve, *adj.* communicative

Communication, *s.f.* communication; correspondence; intercourse; communion; connection; cognizance; message; producing *or* production (*of documents*). *De* —, (*adject.*) communicating, connecting

Communicativement, *adv.* communicatively

Communier, *v.n.* to receive the sacrament, to communicate; — *v.a.* to administer the sacrament to

Communion, *s.f.* communion; sacrament; communion-prayer; union, fellowship

Communiquant, *part.* communicating, &c. (*V.* **Communiquer**)

Communiqué, *s.m.* official communication

Communiquer, *v.a.n.* to communicate; to convey; to impart; to infuse; to produce, to show; to inform, to acquaint, to tell; to correspond, to hold a correspondence; to have communication; to be in communication; to confer; to consult; to lead

Se —, *v.r.* to communicate; to be communicable *or* communicated; to be communicative *or* accessible; to open o.'s heart; to be catching *or* infectious; to spread; to communicate *or* impart to each other

Communisme, *s.m.* communism

Communiste, *s.m.f.* communist; (*law*) tenant in common; — *adj.* communistic

Commutati-f, ve, *adj.* commutative

Commutation, *s.f.* commutation

Comocladie, *s.f.* (*bot.*) comocladia, maiden-plum

Compacité, *s.f.* compactness, density, closeness, firmness

Compact, *s.m.* compact, agreement, contract, convention

Compacte, *adj.* compact, dense, close, solid, firm; serried; concise

†**Compagne,** *s.f.* female companion, companion; consort, partner; wife; friend; equal; helpmate; playmate; mate; attendant, concomitant; (*in compounds*) mate, fellow, companion

†**Compagnie,** *s.f.* company; society; companionship; association; fellowship; partnership; covey, bevy; troop. *Dame* or *demoiselle de* —, lady's companion, companion (*to a lady*). *De bonne* —, of good breeding *or* manners; well-bred; proper; gentlemanly; ladylike. *De mauvaise* —, of bad breeding *or* manners; ill-bred; improper; ungentlemanly; unladylike. *Fausser* —, to give the slip, to steal away; to disappoint. *Il n'est* (or *Il n'y a*) *si bonne — qui ne se sépare*, the best of friends must part

†**Compagnon,** *s. m.* companion; partner; friend; equal; fellow; mate; playfellow, playmate; droll fellow; journeyman, workman; associate, member of a (trade) society *or* union, trade-unionist, trades-unionist, unionist; attendant, concomitant; (*in compounds*) fellow, mate, companion

†**Compagnonnage,** *s.m.* trade-union, trades-union, union; trade-unions, trades-unions, unions; time of service as journeyman; condition of a journeyman, journeymanship

Comparabilité, *s.f.* comparableness

Comparable, *adj.* comparable, to be compared

Comparablement, *adv.* comparably; in comparison (with)

Comparaison, *s.f.* comparison; simile

Comparaître, *v.n.* to appear

Comparant, e, *adj.* (*law*) appearing; — *s.m.f.* appearer

Compara-teur, trice, *s.m.f.* comparer; — *adj.* comparing

Comparati-f, ve, *adj. s.m.* comparative

Comparativement, *adv.* comparatively

Comparé, e, *part. adj.* compared; comparative

Comparer, *v.a.* to compare

Se —, *v.r.* to compare oneself; to be compared; can be compared

Comparoir, *v.n.* (*law, obsolete*) to appear

Comparse, *s.m.f.* (*theat.*) figurant, figurante

Compartiment, *s.m.* compartment; cell; division; (*hort.*) knot; (*mining*) rib-wall, panel

Compartimenté, e, *adj.* with compartments

Comparution, *s.f.* (*law*) appearance, forthcoming

Compas, *s.m.* compass; compasses; pair of compasses; (*of shoemakers*) size; (*pop.*) shanks, stumps. — *de proportion*, sector. — *de réduction*, proportional compass. *Avoir le — dans l'œil*, to have a sure eye

Compassage, *s.m.* compassing

Compassé, e, *adj.* measured, &c. (*V.* **Compasser**); formal, stiff, starched, affected; systematic; precise

Compassement, *s.m.* compassing; (*fig.*) formality, starchedness, punctiliousness, studied regularity

Compasser, *v.a.* to measure with compasses, to compass; to measure; to arrange, to dispose, to lay out; to regulate; to proportion; to weigh, to consider; (*nav.*) to point, to prick (*a chart*) [poser, regulator
Compasseur, *s.m.* measurer, arranger, dis-
Compassion, *s.f.* compassion, pity, mercy
Compaternité, *s.f.* (*theol.*) compaternity
Compatibilité, *s.f.* compatibility
Compatible, *adj.* compatible, consistent
Compatir, *v.n.* to sympathize (with), to compassionate, to commiserate, to pity; to bear (with); to be compatible, to agree
Compatissance, *s.f.* pity, sympathy
Compatissant, e. *adj.* compassionate, sympathizing, feeling, tender
Compatriote, *s.m.f.* (fellow-)countryman *or* countrywoman, compatriot
Compatriotisme, *s.m.* compatriotism
Compellati-f, ve, *adj.*, **Compellatif,** *s.m.* (*gram.*) compellative
Compendiaire, *s.m.* abridger
Compendieusement, *adv.* compendiously
Compendieu-x, se, *adj.* compendious, summary [summary, epitome
Compendium, *s.m.* compendium, abridgment,
Compensable, *adj.* compensable
Compensa-teur, trice, *adj.* compensating, compensative, compensation. *Balancier* or *pendule* —, compensation-balance *or* pendulum
Compensateur, *s. m.* (*phys.*) compensator; (*horol.*) compensation-balance *or* pendulum. — *magnétique*, magnetic compensator
Compensation, *s.f.* compensation; set-off
Compensatoire, *adj.* compensatory
Compenser, *v.a.* to compensate; to set off; to make up for; to make amends for; to balance; to counteract [balanced
Se —, *v.r.* to compensate each other; to be
Compérage, *s.m.* relation between godfather and godmother, compaternity; being a godfather; confederacy; collusion; deception, trickery
Compère, *s.m.* fellow-godfather; daddy, gaffer, fellow, comrade, crony, friend, body, blade; cunning fellow, sly blade; confederate, pal; partner; compeer; squire. *Par — et par commère*, by favour and interest. — **-cochon,** *s.m.* a fellow more free than welcome. — **-loriot,** *s.m.* sty (*on the eye*), stye; (*bird*) oriole, loriot
Compétemment, *adv.* competently
Compétence, *s.f.* competency, competence; sphere, province, department; cognizance
Compétent, e, *adj.* competent; fit; requisite; due; cognizant [the competency (of); to be due
Compéter, *v.n.* (*law*) to be cognizable, to be in
Compéti-teur, trice, *s.m.f.* competitor, competitress; candidate
Compétition, *s.f.* competition, rivalry
Compila-teur, trice, *s.m.f.* compiler
Compilation, *s.f.* compilation
Compiler, *v.a.n.* to compile
Complaindre, *v.a.* (*obsolete*) *V.* **Plaindre**
Complainte, *s.f.* lamentation, wailing; lament, ballad, narrative; (*law*) complaint; (*mus.*) tragedy
Complaire, *v.n.* to please, to gratify; to humour; to comply with the wishes (of); to comply (with); to condescend (to)
Se —, *v.r.* to delight, to take delight *or* pleasure (in); to please oneself; to be satisfied with oneself; to admire oneself
Complaisamment, *adv.* complaisantly, obligingly, with kindness; complacently
Complaisance, *s.f.* complaisance, obligingness, readiness to oblige, goodness, kindness; compliance; condescension; courtesy; attention; accommodation; complacency; pleasure, delight; —**s,** *pl.* (*obsolete*) love, affection
Complaisant, e, *adj.* complaisant, obliging, kind; compliant; yielding; tractable, manageable; condescending; courteous; considerate; accommodating; fawning; complacent; — *s.m.f.* fawner, flatterer, toad-eater; complier; pander

Complant, *s.m.* plantation; vine-estate, vineyard [*trees*)
Complanter, *v.a.* to plant together (*vines and*
Complément, *s.m.* complement; completion; supplement; (*gram.*) object; (*gram.*, *astr.*, *math.*, *mus.*, *fort.*) complement
Complémentaire, *adj.* complementary, completory, completing
Compl-et, ète, *adj.* complete; entire, total, whole; full; well-filled; finished; perfect; utter; strict; (*fam.*) drunk, finished up
Complet, *s.m.* full number, complement; completeness, completion. *Au* —, complete, full; all present; whole, entire; all right. *Au grand* —, quite complete, quite full; present each and all
Complètement, *adv.* completely; entirely, totally, wholly; fully; perfectly; thoroughly; utterly; — *s.m.* completion
Compléter, *v.a.* to complete; to finish; to perfect; to make up; to fill up
Se —, *v.r.* to become *or* be complete; to perfect itself; to complete o.'s set *or* collection; to realize; (*fam.*) to get quite drunk, to finish oneself up
Compléti-f, ve, *adj.* (*gram.*) completive
Complexe, *adj.* complex; compound
Complexion, *s.f.* constitution, habit of body; disposition, temper, humour, inclination
Complexionné, e, *adj.* constituted; inclined
Complexité, *s.f.* complexity
Complexus, *s.m.* (*anat.*) complexus
Complication, *s.f.* complication; intricacy
Complice, *s.m.f.* accomplice; confederate; — *adj.* accessory, privy, instrumental, a party (to)
Complicité, *s.f.* complicity, participation
Complies, *s.f.pl.* (*Cath. lit.*) compline
Compliment, *s.m.* compliment; congratulation. *Faire* — or *son* —, to compliment; to congratulate; to wish joy *Faire ses —s*, to give o.'s compliments
Complimenter, *v.a.n.* to compliment; to congratulate; to make *or* pay compliments
Complimenteu-r, se, *adj. s.* complimentary; complimenter [(*surg.*) compound (*fracture*)
Compliqué, e, *adj.* complicated; intricate;
Compliquer, *v.a.* to complicate
Se —, *v.r.* to become (*or* get) complicated *or*
Complot, *s.m.* plot, conspiracy [intricate
Comploter, *v.a.n.* to plot
Comploteu-r, se, *s.m.f.* plotter
Compon, *s.m.* (*her.*) compon
Componction, *s.f.* compunction, contrition
Componé, e, *adj.* (*her.*) compony
Componium, *s.m.* (*mus. instr.*) componium
Componure, *s.f.* (*her.*) componure
Comportement, *s.m.* (*obsolete*) deportment, behaviour, demeanour, conduct, course of life
Comporter, *v.a.* to admit of, to allow; to require [act; to manage; to be
Se —, *v.r.* to behave, to behave oneself; to
Composant, e, *adj. s.* component
Composé, e, *adj.* composed; compound; composite; component; complicated; complex; (*fig.*) affected, stiff. *Bien* —, select, respectable. *Mal* —, low
Composé, *s.m.* compound; component; mixture
Composée, *s.f.* (*bot.*) compound *or* composite flower, composite; (*min.*) compound mineral
Composer, *v.a.n.* to compose; to compound; to form; to make; to adjust, to fashion, to make up; to set; to settle; to write an examination paper; to come to terms; to capitulate. *A* —, (*print.*) composing
Se —, *v.r.* to be composed, to consist; to be compounded; to compose o.'s looks; to assume; to make for oneself, to form [botcher
Composeur, *s.m.* paltry writer, scribbler,
Composite, *adj.m.f.*, *s.m.* (*arch.*) composite; composite order
Compositeur, *s.m.* (*mus.*) composer; (*print.*) compositor; (*law*) compounder, arbitrator

Composition, *s.f.* composition; composing; compounding; compound; mixture; setting; arrangement, settlement, agreement; terms; capitulation, surrender; disposition to come to terms; temper, disposition, nature; theme, examination paper, (written) examination

Compost, *s.m.* (*agr.*) compost

Composter, *v.a.* (*agr.*) to compost

Composteur, *s.m.* (*print.*) composing-stick

Compote, *s.f.* stewed fruit; stew; sauce. — *de* ..., stew of ..., stewed ...; sauce of ..., ... -sauce. *En* —, stewed; smashed; bruised; black (*eyes*); boiled *or* done to rags. *Avoir l'œil en* —, to have a black eye. *Avoir les yeux en* —, to have a pair of black eyes. *Mettre en* —, to stew; to smash; to bruise; to boil to rags

Compotier, *s.m.* dish for stewed fruit

Compréhensibilité, *s.f.* comprehensibility

Compréhensible, *adj.* comprehensible, conceivable, intelligible

Compréhensi-f, ve, *adj.* comprehensive

Compréhension, *s.f.* comprehension

Comprendre, *v.a.* to comprehend; to comprise; to include; to contain; to understand; to make out. *Faire* —, *V.* **Faire**

Se —, *v.r.* to understand oneself *or* each other; to know o.'s own meaning, to know what one means; to be understood *or* intelligible; to be comprised *or* included

Compresse, *s.f.* (*surg.*) compress

Compresseur, *s.m.* compressor

Compressibilité, *s.f.* compressibility

Compressible, *adj.* compressible; repressible

Compressi-f, ve, *adj.* compressive; repressive

Compression, *s.f.* compression; squeezing; pressure; repression

Comprimable, *adj.* compressible; repressible

Comprimer, *v.a.* to compress; to squeeze; to press; to repress, to keep down, to restrain, to check, to curb; to suppress; to put down; to prevent; to flatten. *Se* —, to be compressed, &c.

Compris, e, *part. adj.* understood, included, &c. (*V.* **Comprendre**). **Y** —, *adj. prep. part.* including, inclusive of, with; included. **Non** —, not including, exclusive of, without; not included

Compromettant, e, *adj.* unsafe, dangerous; disreputable; inculpatory, incriminating

Compromettre, *v.a.* to compromise; to expose; to commit; to put in jeopardy, to endanger, to imperil; to discredit; to implicate; to inculpate, to incriminate; to injure; to bring *or* call into question; to forfeit; — *v.n.* to make a compromise, to agree, to compound

Compromis, *s.m.* compromise; deed stipulating forfeiture; jeopardy, hazard, danger, peril; dissent, disagreement; doubt, question, dispute; — *part. adj.m.*, —**e,** *f.* compromised, &c. (*V.* **Compromettre**)

Compromissaire, *s.m.* arbitrator, referee

Compromission, *s.f.* committing word or action, commitment

Compromissionnaire, *adj.* by compromise

Compromissoire, *adj.* compromissorial

Comprovincial, e, *adj.*, **Comprovincial,** *s.m.* comprovincial

Comptabilité, *s.f.* book-keeping, accounts; account-office, accountant's office; responsibility

Comptable, *adj.* accountable; responsible; valid; — *s.m.*, *Agent* —, accountant; responsible agent; (*nav.*) purser

Comptant, *adj.m.* (*of money*) ready; cash *or* prompt (*payment*); — *s.m.* ready money, cash; — *adv.* in cash, for cash, cash, in ready money, ready money. *Au* —, for cash; (*on Change*) for delivery

Compte, *s.m.* account; reckoning; computation; calculation; score; rate; statement; reason, motive; number; quantity; amount, sum; right sum, due; discharge; part, share; right quantity, everything all right; expense; advantage, benefit, interest; profit; quietus; esteem, regard; audit. — *borgne*, odd number *or* money; obscure *or* suspicious account. — *-rendu*, report; statement; return; review, notice. — *rond*, round number; even money. *A* —, on account; in part payment; instalment. *A bon* —, cheap; easily; freely. *A ce* —, at this *or* that rate; according to that; in that case; in that way. *Au bout du* —, after all, finally, at last; everything considered; upon the whole; happen what may. *De* — *à demi*, on joint account; on half profits. *De bon* —, candid, sincere, honest. *De* — *fait*, on computation. *En fin de* —, in the end, at last, after all, finally; in short. *Pour mon* —, on my own account; for myself; for my part, as for me, as far as I am concerned. *Son* — *est bon*, he will catch it, he is done for. *Sur le* — *de*, on *or* to the score (*or* account) of; about, concerning (*sur mon*, &c. —, about *or* concerning me, &c.). *Avoir son* —, to have o.'s number *or* all o.'s things; to have the right sum; to have what one wants; to have o.'s due; to be dismissed *or* turned out; to have received o.'s quietus, to be sure to die, to be a dead man; to be drunk. *Devoir* —, to be accountable. *Donner son* — *à*, to give (...) his due; to dismiss, to discharge, to pay off; to serve out; to give it to; to give (...) his quietus, to settle, to do for, to kill. *Entrer en ligne de* —, to enter into the computation, to be reckoned, to be taken into account. *Être* or *Faire le* — *de*, to do for, to suit. *Faire* — *de*, to set a value on, to value, to esteem; to pay attention to, to take notice of, to notice. *Faire bon, meilleur* —, to sell cheap, cheaper; to give good, better measure (*or* weight) *Faire son* — *pour*, to contrive *or* manage to. *Laisser pour* —, to leave and not pay for. *Mettre en ligne de* —, to take into account, to set *or* carry to account, to charge. *Mettre sur le* — *de*, to impute to, to ascribe to, to charge with, to lay to ...'s charge, to lay at ...'s door, to lay to the account *or* score of. *Prendre sur son* —, to take upon oneself. *Rendre* — *de*, to render *or* give an account of; to account for; to review, to notice, to give a notice of. *Rester pour* —, to be left and not to be paid for. *Se rendre* — *de*, to account for; to make out, to understand; to see to; to think of. *Tenir* — *de*, to carry to account; to take into consideration; to account; to give back; to be grateful *or* thankful for; to give credit for; to pay attention to, to mind. *Tenir un* —, to keep an account. *Les bons* —*s font les bons amis*, short reckonings make long friends

Compte, *s.m.* (*in compounds, from* **Compter,** "to count," "to tell," &c.) thing which tells *or* &c., teller. — **-fils,** *s.m.* (*opt. instr.*) waling-glass; linen-prover. — **-pas,** *s.m. V.* **Hodomètre**

Compté, e, *part. adj.* (*V.* **Compter**). *Bien* —, complete, full. *Tout bien* —, everything reckoned; everything considered. *Tout bien* —, *tout rabattu*, everything considered *or* taken into consideration

Compter, *v.a.n.* to count; to reckon; to tell; to number; to compute; to calculate; to sum up, to add up; to measure; to grudge; to take into account; to account; to pay; to charge; to include; to value; to consider (as), to esteem (as); to pay regard (to); to date; to settle; to expect, to think; to intend, to purpose; to rely, to depend (upon); to speculate (upon). *A* — *de*, reckoning from, from, from ... forward. *Comptez que*, depend upon it

Se — *v.r.* to count *or* reckon *or* include *or* consider oneself *or* each other; to be counted *or* reckoned *or* &c.; to be taken into account

Compteur, *s.m.* reckoner; counter; teller, tell-tale, indicator; meter; gas-meter; (*nav.*) chronometer; (*mil.*) *V.* **Hodomètre**; — *adj.m.* reckoning

Compteuse, *s.f.* reckoner; — *adj.f.* reckoning

Comptoir, *s.m.* counter; bar; tap; counting-house; office; cashier's desk, desk; branch-bank, branch-establishment; bank; factory
Compulsation, *s.f.* inspection; examination, looking over, perusal [look over, to peruse
Compulser, *v.a.* to inspect; to examine, to
Compulseur, *s.m.* peruser
Compulsi-f, ve, *adj.* compulsive [tion
Compulsion, *s.f.* compulsion. *V.* **Compulsa-**
Compulsoire, *s.m.* (*law*) order to produce papers; inspection by virtue of a judge's order
Comput, *s.m.* (*chron.*) computation
Computation, *s.f.* computation
Computer, *v.a.* to compute
Computiste, *s.m.* computist, computer
Comtal, e, *adj.* of a count *or* earl, of a countess,
Comtat, *s.m.* county [count's, earl's
Comte, *s.m.* count; earl
Comté, *s.m.* earldom; county, shire
Comtesse, *s.f.* countess
Concassage, *s.m.*, **Concassation,** *s.f.*, **Concassement,** *s.m.* pounding, crushing, bruising; breaking [to break
Concasser, *v.a.* to pound, to crush, to bruise;
Concasseur, *s.m.* (*agr.*) crushing *or* bruising-mill, crusher, bruiser; breaker; (*tech.*) steam-
Concaténation, *s.f.* concatenation [roller
Concave, *adj.m.f., s.m.* concave
Concavité, *s.f.* concavity, concaveness
Concavo-concave, *adj.* concavo-concave
Concavo-convexe, *adj.* concavo-convex
Concédant, e, *s.m.f.* grantor [concede
Concéder, *v.a.* to grant, to allow, to yield, to
Se —, *v.r.* to be granted *or* allowed *or* &c.
Concentrateur, *s.m.* concentrator; — *adj.m.* concentrative
Concentration, *s.f.* concentration
Concentré, e, *part. adj.* concentrated, &c. (*V.* **Concentrer**); close-tongued, close, reserved, silent; thoughtful; uncommunicative; inward; very strong
Concentrer, *v.a.* to concentrate; to concentre; to centre; to wrap up; to dissemble, to conceal; to repress, to suppress, to smother
Se —, *v.r.* to concentrate; to centre; to concentrate oneself; to be concentrated *or* centred *or* &c.; to retire within oneself
Concentr-ique, -iquement. *V.* page 3, § 1
Concept, *s.m.* (*philos., log.*) concept
Conceptacle, *s.m.* (*bot.*) conceptacle
Conceptibilité, *s.f.* conceivableness
Conceptible, *adj.* conceivable
Concepti-f, ve, *adj.* conceptive
Conception, *s.f.* conception; apprehension; idea, notion, thought; understanding; wit;
Conceptuel, le, *adj.* conceptual [conceit
Concernant, *prep.* concerning, touching, about, relating to, in reference to [concerned with
Concerner, *v.a.* to concern; to relate to; to be
Concert, *s.m.* concert; music; song; strain; chorus; harmony; melody; accord; concord; union; concurrence; unanimity; agreement; mutual understanding; performers, musicians. — *spirituel,* oratorio. *De* —, in concert; jointly; hand in hand; agreed; together; unanimously; by mutual consent
Concertant, e, *s.m.f.* performer (*in a concert*), musician; — *s.f.* concertante (*piece of music*); — *adj.* concertante; playing; harmonic
Concerté, e, *adj.* concerted, planned; prudent; affected, formal; — *s.m.* concertante style of music
Concerter, *v.a.* to concert, to contrive, to plan, to devise; to deliberate upon; to settle; to adjust; (*obsolete*) to practise, to rehearse; — *v.n.* to make *or* give *or* have a concert; to play alternately
Se —, *v.r.* to consult together, to deliberate
Concertina, *s.m.* (*mus. instr.*) concertina
Concertino, *s.m.* (*mus.*) concertino [musician
Concertiste, *s.m.f.* performer (*in a concert*),
Concerto, *s.m.* (*mus.*) concerto

Concesseur, *s.m.* grantor; — *adj.m.* granting
Concession, *s.f.* concession; grant; privilege; grant of land [privileged
Concessionnaire, *s.m.f.* grantee; — *adj.*
Concetti, *s.m.pl.* (*an Italian word, pl. of* **Concetto**) concetti, conceits, affected wit, point
Concevable, *adj.* conceivable, imaginable, intelligible, comprehensible
Concevoir, *v.a.* to conceive; to imagine; to invent; to plan; to think; to feel; to understand; to entertain; to express, to couch, to word; to form; to construct
Se —, *v.r.* to be conceived *or* imagined *or* understood; to be conceivable *or* intelligible
Conche, *s.f.* second brine-pit (*of a salt-garden*)
‡**Conchifère,** *s.m.* (*zool.*) conchifer; — *adj.* con-
‡**Conchiforme,** *adj.* conchiform [chiferous
‡**Conchite,** *s.f.* conchite (*shell*)
‡**Conchoïdal, e,** *adj.* conchoidal [choidal
‡**Conchoïde,** *s.f.* (*geom.*) conchoid; — *adj.* con-
‡**Concholog-ie, Conchyliolog-ie, -ique, -iste.** *V.* page 3, § 1
Concierge, *s.m.f.* door-porter, porter, portress, house-porter, hall-porter, hall-keeper, door-keeper; keeper; jailer, turnkey
Conciergerie, *s.f.* place of porter *or* door-keeper; porter's lodge; Conciergerie (*a prison*
Concile, *s.m.* (*eccl. hist.*) council [*in Paris*)
Conciliable, *adj.* reconcilable
Conciliabule, *s.m.* conventicle, conciliabule; cabal; secret meeting
Conciliaire, *adj.* of a council, conciliar
Conciliairement, *adv.* in council
Conciliant, e, *adj.* conciliatory, conciliating
Concilia-teur, trice, *adj. s.* conciliatory, conciliating, reconciling; conciliator, reconciler
Conciliation, *s.f.* conciliation; reconciliation
Conciliatoire, *adj.* conciliatory
Concilier, *v.a.* to conciliate; to reconcile; to gain over, to gain, to win
Se —, *v.r.* to be reconciled; to agree; to conciliate, to gain, to win; to ingratiate oneself
Concis, e, *adj.* concise, brief [with
Concision, *s.f.* conciseness, brevity
Concitoyen, ne, *s.m.f.* fellow-citizen; fellow-townsman *or* townswoman
Concitoyenneté, *s.f.* fellow-citizenship
Conclave, *s.m.* conclave (*of cardinals*)
Conclaviste, *s.m.* conclavist
Concluant, e, *adj.* conclusive, decisive
Conclure, *v.a.n.* to conclude; to close; to end; to wind up; to infer; to prove; to judge, to think; to move, to make a motion; to decide; to determine; to agree (upon); to declare o.'s opinion; to demand; to vote (for); to come to a conclusion; to be conclusive
Se —, *v.r.* to be concluded *or* &c.
Conclusi-f, ve, *adj.* conclusive
Conclusion, *s.f.* conclusion; close; end; issue; inference; consequence; determination, final decision; demand; request; motion; (*adverb.*) in short, briefly, in one word, in conclusion
Conclusum, *s.m.* conclusion
Concoc-teur, trice, *adj.* (*med.*) concoctive
Concoction, *s.f.* (*med.*) concoction
Concombre, *s.m.* cucumber
Concomitance, *s.f.* concomitance
Concomitant, e, *adj.* concomitant [agreement
Concordance, *s.f.* concordance; concord;
Concordant, e, *adj.* concordant
Concordat, *s.m.* concordat; (*com.*) composition; (*com.*) certificate [*s.m.f.* certificated bankrupt
Concordataire, *adj.* (*com.*) certificated; —
Concorde, *s.f.* concord, union, harmony, good understanding [to concur
Concorder, *v.n.* to live in concord; to agree;
Concourant, e, *adj.* concurrent
Concourir, *v.n.* to concur; to contribute; to cooperate; to tend; to conspire; to compete; to unite; to meet; to coincide
Concours, *s.m.* concourse; conjuncture; assembling; meeting; cooperation; assistance;

concurrence; coincidence; competition; competitive examination, examination; contest; match; prize-show, show. *Grand* —, — *général*, university examination, tripos

Concréfier, *v.a.*, **Se** —, *v.r.* to concrete

Concrescible, *adj.* concrescible

Concr-et, ète, *adj.* concrete

Concréter, *v.a.*, **Se** —, *v.r.* to concrete

Concrétion, *s.f.* concretion

Concrétionnaire, *adj.* concretionary

Concrétionner, *v.a.*, **Se** —, *v.r.* to concrete

Concubinage, *s.m.* concubinage

Concubinaire, *s.m.* one who keeps a concubine

Concubine, *s.f.* concubine

Concupiscence, *s.f.* concupiscence, lust

Concupiscent, e, *adj.* concupiscent, libidinous

Concupiscible, *adj.* concupiscible

Concurremment, *adv.* concurrently, in concurrence, jointly, together; in competition

Concurrence, *s.f.* competition; emulation; rivalry; opposition. *Faire — à*, to compete with, to be in competition with; to oppose. *Jusqu'à — de*, to the amount of; to the extent of; till ... is duly discharged

Concurrent, e, *s.m.f.* competitor, rival, opponent; — *adj.* concurrent; — *s.m.* (*chron.*) concurrent. *Jour* —, (*chron.*) concurrent

Concussion, *s.f.* peculation, embezzlement; exaction; bribery

Concussionnaire, *s.m.* peculator, embezzler; exactor; — *adj.* peculating, embezzling; exacting [culpable, guilty, criminal

Condamnable, *adj.* condemnable, blamable,

Condamnation, *s.f.* condemnation; sentence, judgment; conviction; doom; blame, censure, reproof; —**s,** *pl.* fines, damages and costs. *Passer* —, to pass sentence; to condemn, to animadvert (upon); to pass judgment upon oneself, to confess oneself to be in the wrong, to own oneself in fault *or* in the wrong, to plead guilty; to give up o.'s claim; not to wish to press the point; to forgive, to excuse. *Subir* —, to suffer judgment. *Subir sa* —, to undergo o.'s sentence. *Subir plusieurs —s*, to be convicted several times

Condamnatoire, *adj.* condemnatory

Condamné, e, *s.m.f.* condemned; convict; man *or* woman condemned to death

Condamner, *v.a.* to condemn; to find guilty; to convict; to sentence; to doom; to blame, to censure; to tell *or* go against; to explode; to force, to compel; to give over (*a patient*); to stop up (*a door*, &c.)

Condensabilité, *s.f.* condensability

Condensable, *adj.* condensable

Condensateur, *s.m.* condenser

Condensa-teur, trice, *adj.* condensing

Condensati-f, ve, *adj.* condensative

Condensation, *s.f.* condensation, condensing

Condenser, *v.a.* to condense

Se —, *v.r.* to condense, to be condensed

Condenseur, *s.m.* condenser; — *adj.m.* condensing [descension; compliance

Condescendance, *s.f.* condescendence; con-

Condescendre, *v.n.* to condescend; to comply; to bear (with)

†**Condigne,** *adj.* (*theol.*) condign

†**Condignement,** *adv.* (*theol.*) condignly

†**Condignité,** *s.f.* (*theol.*) condignity

Condiment, *s.m.* condiment [class-fellow

Condisciple, *s.m.* condisciple; school-fellow,

Condit, *s.m.* (*pharm.*) confection

Condition, *s.f.* condition; rank; station; state; profession; situation; place; service; terms; offer; stipulation; (*silk manu.*) drying-room; (*silk manu.*) Condition (*assay-office*)

Conditionnalité, *s.f.* conditionality

Conditionné, e, *adj.* conditioned; made; sound; downright, egregious; tight, tipsy. *Bien* —, well-conditioned, in good condition; well-made; in a pretty state; sound; downright, egregious; pretty tight, drunk

Conditionnel, le, *adj.* conditional; (*law*) provisory; — *s.m.* (*Fr. gram.*) conditional mood, conditional

Conditionnellement, *adv.* conditionally

Conditionnement, *s.m.* making up; condition; (*of silk*) drying [(*law*) to article

Conditionner, *v.a.* to make up; (*silk*) to dry;

Se —, *v.r.* to be made up; (*of silk*) to be dried

Condoléance, *s.f.* condolence

Condoma, *s.m.* (*zool.*) condoma (*kind of antelope*)

Condor, *s.m.* (*bird*) condor

Condottiere, *s.m.* (*an Italian word, pl.* **Condottieri**) condottiere

Condouloir (Se), *v.r.* (*old*) to condole

†**Condrille,** *s.f. V.* **Chondrille**

Conduc-teur, trice, *s.m.f.* conductor; conductress; leader; chief; guide; director; directress; manager; manageress; superintendent; driver; guard; steersman, coxswain; assistant-engineer; — *adj.* leading; (*phys.*) conducting, conductive. — *de machine* (*à imprimer*), (*print.*) machine-minder

Conductibilité, *s.f.* (*phys., abusively, and just the reverse of its proper meaning*) conductivity, conduction; (*proper meaning*) conductibility

Conductible, *adj.* (*phys., abusively as with* "Conductibilité") conductive, conducting; (*proper meaning*) conductible

Conduction, *s.f.* (*phys.*) conduction; conductivity; (*civ. law*) hiring

Conduire, *v.a.* to conduct; to lead; to show the way to, to show; to take; to attend, to accompany; to escort; to head; to guide; to manage; to direct; to superintend; to rule; to govern; to sway; to command; to carry on; to carry; to convey; to bring; to conduce; to induce; to drive; to steer

Se —, *v.r.* to behave; to take care of oneself; to find o.'s way; to go; to be conducted *or* led

Conduit, e, *part. of* **Conduire** [*or* &c.

Conduit, *s.m.* pipe, tube, conduit, duct, canal, passage, cut. — *acoustique*, speaking-pipe

Conduite, *s.f.* conduct; behaviour; morals; habits; care; charge; guidance; management; direction; superintendence; government; command; disposition; execution; leading; conducting; taking; attending, accompanying, escorting; conveyance; delivery; driving; conduit, pipes; (*nav.*) conduct-money. *Faire la — à*, to accompany, to escort; (*jest.*) to drive

Condyle, *s.m.* (*anat.*) condyle [away, to expel

Condylome, *s.m.* (*med.*) condyloma

Condylure, *s.m.* (*zool.*) condylura, star-nose

Cône, *s.m.* cone; cone-shell. *En* —, conical;

Conéine, *s.f.* (*chem.*) *V.* **Conicine** [conically

Confabulateur, *s.m.* conversational speaker

Confabulation, *s.f.* confabulation

Confabuler, *v.n.* to confabulate, to chat

Confection, *s.f.* making; preparation; execution; construction; drawing up; completion; making up; ready-made clothes business; outfitting; ready-made clothes, slops; slop-article; slop-work; slop-trade; outfitting department; (*pharm., obsolete for* "opiat") confection

Confectionné, e, *adj.* made; manufactured; made up; ready-made

Confectionner, *v.a.* to make; to execute; to draw up; to make up; to manufacture

Se —, *v.r.* to be made *or* made up *or* &c.

Confectionneu-r, se, *s.m.f.* maker; clothier, ready-made clothier, slop-seller; outfitter

Confédéra-teur, trice, *s.m.f. adj.* confederator; confederating [federate

Confédérati-f, ve, *adj.* confederative, federal,

Confédération, *s.f.* confederation, confederacy; league

Confédéré, e, *adj. s.* confederate; federal

Confédérer, *v.a.*, **Se** —, *v.r.* to confederate

Conférence, *s.f.* conference; lecture; conversazione; recital; sermon; debate; debating-society; meeting; comparison

Conférenci-er, ère, *s.m.f.* lecturer

Conférer, *v.a.n.* to confer; to bestow; to give; to grant; to present to; to collate; to administer; to compare; (*print.*) to revise

Se —, *v.r.* to bestow upon oneself, to take to oneself, to assume; to be bestowed *or* &c.

Conferve, *s.f.* (*bot.*) conferva, hair-weed, frog-spittle [(*to a priest*)

Conf-ès, esse, *adj.* (*pers., obsolete*) confessed

Confesse, *s.f.* confession (*to a priest*)

Confesser, *v.a.* to confess; to own, to avow, to acknowledge, to grant, to admit; to disclose; to hear in confession [be confessed, &c.

Se —, *v.r.* to confess o.'s sins, to confess; to

Confesseur, *s.m.* confessor

Confession, *s.f.* confession; avowal, acknowledgment; disclosure. *Donner le bon Dieu sans* —, to trust with untold gold

Confessioniste, *s.m.* confessionist

Confessionnaire, *adj.* confessionary

Confessionnal, *s.m.* confessional

Confessionnel, le, *adj.* confessionary

Confiance, *s.f.* confidence; trust, reliance; faith; hope; security, safety; courage; assurance; presumption. *De* —, of confidence; of trust; trustworthy, trusty; reliable; confidential; confidentially, upon trust; confident; confidently. *Abus de* —, breach of trust; embezzlement

Confiant, e, *adj.* confident; confiding; unsuspicious, unsuspecting; bold; presumptuous; sanguine [fidence; (*old*) confidently

Confidemment, *adv.* confidentially, in con-

Confidence, *s.f.* confidence; secrecy; secret; disclosure; intimacy. *En* —, in confidence, confidentially, as a secret; (*of eccl. livings*) in trust. *Faire une* —, to tell a secret; to make a disclosure

Confident, e, *s.m.f.* confidant; confidante

Confidentiaire, *s.m.* holder (of a living) in trust; trustee

Confidentialité, *s.f.* confidentiality

Confidentiel, le, *adj.* confidential

Confidentiellement, *adv.* confidentially

Confier, *v.a.* to confide; to intrust; to trust; to commit; to tell in confidence

Se —, *v.r.* to confide (in), to rely (on), to trust (in, to); to trust *or* &c. oneself; to be confiding; to unbosom oneself; to confide *or* &c. to each other; to be trusted *or* &c.

Configuration, *s.f.* configuration, form, shape

Configurer, *v.a.* to configure, to configurate, to form, to shape

Confinement, *s.m.* (*law*) confinement

Confiner, *v.a.n.* to confine; to shut up; to limit; to border (upon, on), to be contiguous *or* adjacent (to), to adjoin

Confinité, *s.f.* confinity, contiguity

Confins, *s.m.pl.* confines, borders, limits, ends

Confire, *v.a.* to preserve; to pickle

Se —, to be preserved; to be pickled

Confirmateur, *s.m.* confirmer [tory

Confirmati-f, ve, *adj.* confirmative, confirma-

Confirmation, *s.f.* confirmation; ratification; sanction; slap on the face

Confirmativement, *adv.* confirmatively

Confirmatoire, *adj.* confirmatory

Confirmer, *v.a.* to confirm; to strengthen; to secure; to ratify; to sanction; to show, to prove; to slap ...'s face

Se —, *v.r.* to become *or* be confirmed

Confiscable, *adj.* confiscable; forfeitable

Confiscant, e, *adj.* confiscating

Confiscation, *s.f.* confiscation; forfeiture; for-

Confiserie, *s.f.* confectionery [feit; impounding

Confiseu-r, se, *s.m.f.* confectioner [**fisquer**)

Confisquant, *part.* confiscating, &c. (*V.* **Con-**

Confisquer, *v.a.* to confiscate; to forfeit; to impound; (*fam.*) to ruin, to swamp

Confit, e, *part. adj.* preserved; pickled; steeped; accomplished, consummate, perfect; ruined, done for; — *s.m.* bran-and-water, hog-mash

Confiteor, *s.m.* (*Cath. rel.*) confiteor

Confiture, *s.f.* jam; preserve

Confiturerie, *s.f.* jam and marmalade manufactory *or* making *or* trade [maker

Confituri-er, ère, *s.m.f.* jam and marmalade

Conflagration, *s.f.* conflagration

Conflit, *s.m.* conflict; collision; clashing; jarring; quarrel; rivalry; contention; contest; strife; combat; struggle; agony

Confluence, *s.f.* (*med.*) confluence [junction

Confluent, *s.m.* (*geog.*) confluence, confluent,

Confluent, e, *adj.* confluent

Confluer, *v.n.* to be confluent, to meet, to join

Confondre, *v.a.* to confound; to make a confusion of; to blend; to mingle; to mix; to unite; to jumble; to huddle; to involve; to confuse; to overpower; to amaze; to abash; to perplex; to baffle; to confute; to spoil; — *v.n.* to make a confusion

Se —, *v.r.* to be confounded; to blend; to mingle; to unite; to huddle; to be but one thing, to be one and the same thing; to become *or* be confused; to be lost (in); to overwhelm ... (with), to make all sorts *or* no end (of)

Conformation, *s.f.* conformation

Conforme, *adj.* conformable; according; suitable; agreeable; apposite; congenial; consistent; alike; (*of copies*) true

Conformément, *adv.* conformably; suitably; agreeably; according [to shape, to make

Conformer, *v.a.* to conform; to suit; to form,

Se —, *v.r.* to conform; to comply; to submit; to follow; to share [forming, conformist

Conformiste, *s.m.f.* conformist; — *adj.* con-

Conformité, *s.f.* conformity; compliance; submission. *En* —, in compliance (with), conformably (to), according (to)

Confort, *s.m.* comfort; (*obsolete*) assistance, help, support, countenance [comfort; easy chair

Confortable, *adj.* comfortable; easy; — *s.m.*

Confortablement, *adv.* comfortably

Confortant, e, Confortati-f, ve, *adj.* (*med.*) strengthening, corroborative; — *s.m.* (*med.*) corroborant, corroborative

Confortation, *s.f.* strengthening

Conforter, *v.a.* to strengthen; to comfort

Confraternel, le, *adj.* mutually fraternal

Confraternité, *s.f.* brotherhood, fellowship, confraternity

Confrère, *s.m.* brother, fellow; fellow-member; colleague; brother magistrate *or* barrister *or* physician *or* &c.; fellow-tradesman; compeer; (*of newspapers*) contemporary [therhood

Confrérie, *s.f.* confraternity, fraternity, bro-

Confrication, *s.f.* (*pharm.*) confrication

Confrontation, *s.f.* confrontation; comparing

Confronté, e, *part. adj.* confronted, &c. (*V.* **Confronter**); (*her.*) confronté

Confronter, *v.a.* to confront; to compare; — *v.n.* to border (upon), to adjoin

Confus, e, *adj.* confused; jumbled; indistinct; uncertain; vague; obscure; dim; faint; embarrassed; nonplussed; bewildered; overpowered; abashed; crestfallen; ashamed; (*law, obsolete*) confounded

Confusément, *adv.* confusedly; indistinctly; vaguely; dimly; faintly; tumultuously

Confusion, *s.f.* confusion; disorder; jumble; medley; disturbance; trouble; embarrassment, shame; blush; mortification; (*obsolete*) profusion, affluence, crowd

Confutation, *s.f.* confutation, refutation

Confuter, *v.a.* to confute, to refute, to disprove

Conge, *s.m.* (*kind of tea*) *V.* **Congo**

Congé, *s.m.* leave; permission; discharge; dismissal; sack; notice, notice to quit; warning; holiday; leave of absence; (*cust.*) permit; (*mil.*) furlough; (*mil.*) (full) discharge; (*mil.*) time of service, time; (*nav.*) pass, clearance; (*law*) nonsuit; (*arch.*) conge. — *absolu* or *définitif*, (*mil.*) discharge. *Jour de* —, holiday

Congéable, *adj.* dischargeable, dismissable; (*law*) held under tenancy at will

Congédiement, *s.m.* discharge, dismissal
Congédier, *v.a.* to discharge; to dismiss; to send *or* turn away; to discard; to pay off; to disband, to break up
Congélabilité, *s.f.* congealableness
Congelable, *adj.* congealable
Congélateur, *s.m.* freezing-machine, refrigerator
Congéla-teur, trice, *adj.* freezing, refrigerating
Congélation, *s.f.* congelation, freezing; imitation icicle
Congeler, *v.a.*, **Se** —, *v.r.* to congeal, to freeze
Congénère, *adj.* congeneric; — *s.m.f.* congener
Congénial, e, *adj.* congenial; (*abusively*) congenital
Congénital, e, *adj.* congenital
Congesti-f, ve, *adj.* (*med.*) congestive
Congestion, *s.f.* (*med.*) congestion
Congestionner, *v.a.* (*med.*) to congest
Se —, *v.r.* to become congested
Conglobation, *s.f.* conglobation
Conglober, *v.a.* to conglobate
Conglomérat, *s.m.* (*geol.*) conglomerate
Conglomération, *s.f.* conglomeration
Congloméré, e, *adj.* conglomerate
Conglomérer, *v.a.*, **Se** —, *v.r.* to conglomerate
Conglutinant, e, *adj.*, **Conglutinant,** *s.m.* conglutinant
Conglutinati-f, ve, *adj.* conglutinative; — *s.m.* conglutinant
Conglutination, *s.f.* conglutination
Conglutiner, *v.a.*, **Se** —, *v.r.* to conglutinate
Congo, *s.m.* (*tea*) congou; (*geog.*) Congo
Congratula-teur, trice, *s.m.f. adj.* congratulator; congratulating
Congratulation, *s.f.* congratulation
Congratulatoire, *adj.* congratulatory
Congratuler, *v.a.* to congratulate
Congre, *s.m.* conger, sea-eel; (*fish.*) stake-net
Congréage, *s.m.* (*nav.*) worming (*of a cable*, &c.)
Congréer, *v.a.* (*nav.*) to worm (*a cable*, &c.)
Congréganisme, *s.m.* jesuitism, monasticism
Congréganiste, *s.m.* member of a religious congregation; — *adj.* congregational, ecclesiastical, clerical
Congrégation, *s.f.* congregation; meeting-house. — *des fidèles*, universal Church
Congrégational-isme, -iste. *V.* page 3, § 1
Congrès, *s.m.* congress
Congrève, *s.f.* (*mil.*) *Fusée à la* —, Congreve rocket
Congrier, *s.m.* (*fish.*) stake-net
Congru, e, *adj.* congruous; proper
Congruence, *s.f.* (*arith.*) congruence
Congruent, e, *adj.* congruent
Congruité, *s.f.* congruity; propriety
Congrûment, *adv.* congruously; properly
Conicine, *s.f.* (*chem.*) coniine
Conicité, *s.f.* conicalness
Conifère, *adj.* (*bot.*) coniferous; — *s.m.* conifer
Coniforme, *adj.* coniform
Coniine, Conine, *s.f.* (*chem.*) coniine
†**Conillier,** *v.n.* (*pop.*) to shirk, to sculk
Conique, *adj.* conical, conic; —**s,** *s.f.pl.* conics, conic sections
Conirostre, *s.m.* (*zool.*) conirostre; — *adj.* conirostral
Conise, *s.f.* *V.* **Conyze**
Conite, *s.m.* (*min.*) conite
Conjectural, e, *adj.* conjectural
Conjecturalement, *adv.* conjecturally, by conjecture, by guess
Conjecture, *s.f.* conjecture, guess, surmise, supposition
Conjecturer, *v.a.n.* to conjecture, to guess, to surmise, to suppose
Conjectureu-r, se, *s.m.f.* conjecturer, guesser
Conjoindre, *v.a.* to conjoin, to join, to connect, to unite [conjoint. *Règle—e*, (*arith.*) chain-rule
Conjoint, e, *part. adj* joined, united; (*mus.*) conjoint
Conjoint, *s.m.* (*law.*) spouse, husband *or* wife; —**s,** *pl.* husband and wife, bride and bride-groom, consorts, married parties [union, together
Conjointement, *adv.* conjointly, jointly, in
Conjoncti-f, ve, *adj.* (*gram.*) conjunctive; — *s.f.* (*anat.*) conjunctiva [(*pers.*) union
Conjonction, *s.f.* (*astr., gram.*) conjunction;
Conjonctivement, *adv.* conjunctively
Conjonctivite, *s.f.* (*med.*) conjunctivitis
Conjoncture, *s.f.* conjuncture, juncture
Conjouir (Se), *v.r.* (*obsolete*) to rejoice (together with ...), to congratulate
Conjouissance, *s.f.* (*old*) congratulation
Conjugable, *adj.* (*gram.*) conjugable
Conjugaison, *s.f.* (*gram., anat.*) conjugation
Conjugal, e, *adj.* conjugal, matrimonial
Conjugalement, *adv.* conjugally
Conjugati-f, ve, *adj.* (*gram.*) conjugational
Conjugué, e, *adj.* (*bot., chem., geom., opt.,* &c.) conjugate; (*gram., of words*) conjugate; (*gram., of verbs*) conjugated; (*of machines*) connected
Conjuguer, *v.a.* (*gram.*) to conjugate
Se —, *v.r.* to be conjugated
Conjungo, *s.m.* (*jest.*) wedding, marriage, union, matrimony; (*dipl.*) writing without stops or space between the words
Conjurateur, *s.m.* conjurer; (*obsolete*) conspirator
Conjuration, *s.f.* conspiracy; league, cabal; conjuration, incantation; exorcism; (*obsolete*) entreaty
Conjuré, e, *part. adj.* conjured, &c. (*V.* **Conjurer**); conspiring; leagued; sworn; — *s.m.* conspirator
Conjurer, *v.a.* to conspire, to plot; to conjure; to deprecate; to exorcise, to charm away; to avert, to turn aside, to ward *or* keep off, to avoid; to calm, to appease; to entreat, to beseech, to implore; — *v.n.* to conspire, to plot; to swear, to resolve
Se —, *v.r.* to league; to conspire
Conjureur, *s.m.* conjurer
Connaissable, *adj.* knowable, recognizable to be known *or* recognized
Connaissance, *s.f.* knowledge; acquaintance; senses; consciousness; notice; cognizance; sight; (*hunt.*) print; (*pop.*) sweetheart, mistress, paramour; —**s,** *pl.* knowledge, information, learning, acquirements. *Avec* or *en — de cause*, with knowledge of the subject *or* of the matter, knowingly; from experience; on good grounds. *De* —, of o.'s acquaintance; known to each other; known; familiar. *Sans* —, senseless, insensible, unconscious. *Avoir — de*, to be aware of *or* acquainted with *or* informed of, to know; to have notice of. *Donner — de*, to acquaint with, to inform of; to give notice of. *Être en âge de* —, to have come to years of discretion. *Être en pays de* —, to be with people one knows; to be among old acquaintances; to be at home. *Faire — avec*, to become *or* get acquainted with. *Faire faire* —, to make (*people*) acquainted with each other, to introduce. *Porter à la — de*, to acquaint with, to inform of, to bring before. *Perdre* —, to faint, to become senseless *or* insensible *or* unconscious. *Prendre — de*, to take notice of; to take cognizance of; to make oneself acquainted with; to look *or* inquire into. *Reprendre* —, to recover consciousness *or* o.'s senses, to become conscious again, to come to o.'s senses, to come to oneself. — *des temps*, nautical almanac
Connaissement, *s.m.* (*nav.*) bill of lading
Connaisseu-r, se, *s.m.f.* judge, good judge, connoisseur; acquaintance-maker; — *adj.* knowing, of a connoisseur
Connaître, *v.a.n.* to know; to understand, to be skilled in; to be *or* become acquainted with; to be aware of; to be informed of; to have connection with; to experience, to feel; to discern, to distinguish; to perceive; to see; to recognize; to acknowledge; to admit; to take cognizance. — *à quelqu'un*, to know that someone has. *Faire* —, *V.* **Faire.** *Je ne connais que cela*, that's all I know; that's all I can say, that's all
Se —, *v.r.* to know oneself; to know each other, to be acquainted; (*of things*) to be known. *Se — à* or *en*, to be a judge *or* a good judge of, to understand, to know. *Ne plus se* —, to be out of o.'s senses; to have become unconscious;

to know no bounds. *Ne point se* —, to forget what one is, to forget oneself. *Je m'y connais*, I understand it; I know all about that
Conné, e, *adj.* (*bot.*) connate [connective
Connecti-f, ve, *adj.*, **Connectif,** *s.m.* (*bot.*)
Connétable, *s.m.* (*hist.*) constable, high constable, commander-in-chief; — *s.f.* constable's wife, constabless
Connétablie, *s.f.* (*hist.*) jurisdiction *or* court of a high constable (*viz.*, *commander-in-chief*)
Connexe, *adj.* connected [connexion
Connexion, Connexité, *s.f.* connection,
†**Conniller,** *v.n. V.* **Coniller**
Connivence, *s.f.* connivance
Connivent, e, *adj.* (*nat. hist.*) connivent
Conniver, *v.n.* to connive, to wink
Connotati-f, ve, *adj.* connotative
Connotation, *s.f.* connotation
Connu, e, *adj.*, **Connu,** *s.m.* known. —*!* we know what that is! we know all about that! that is an old story *or* trick *or* dodge! that won't do for me (*or* for us)! *Ni vu ni* —, neither heard nor seen, perfectly unknown
Conoïdal, e, *adj.* conoidal
Conoïde, *adj.m.f.*, *s.m.* conoid [trating
Conquassant, e, *adj.* (*med.*) exhausting, pros-
Conquassation, *s.f. V.* **Concassation**
Conque, *s.f.* shell; conch; pavilion of the ear
Conquérant, e, *s.m.f.* conqueror; conqueress; (*fam.*) lady-killer; belle; — *adj.* conquering, victorious; fond of conquest; (*fam.*) killing; spruce, smart
Conquérir, *v.a.* to conquer; to subdue; to overcome; to gain, to win, to win over; to obtain *or* acquire forcibly *or* by o.'s efforts; to wrest (from)
Se —, *v.r.* to subdue each other; to acquire, to obtain, to gain, to win, to gain *or* win over; to be conquered *or* subdued *or* &c.
Conquêt, *s.m.* (*law*) acquired property, acquisition; —**s,** *pl.* property acquired by two married people [acquisition; success
Conquête, *s.f.* conquest; victory; subjection;
Consacrant, *adj.m.* (*eccl.*) consecrating; ordaining; officiating; — *s.m.* consecrator; ordainer; celebrant
Consacrer, *v.a.* to consecrate; to dedicate; to ordain; to devote; to appropriate; to sanction; to perpetuate; to establish; to hallow; to employ; to give
Consanguin, e, *adj.* on the father's side; — *s.m.* relation on the father's side. *Les —s et les utérins*, half-blood relations
Consanguinité, *s.f.* (*law*) relationship on the father's side; (*can. law*) consanguinity; (*of animals*) breeding in and in
Conscience, *s.f.* conscience; conscientiousness; consciousness; sense; scruple; (a) shame; private thoughts; secrets of the heart; religious opinion; heart; mind; stomach; (*print.*) time-work; compositors working by time, establishment hands; (*tech.*) breastplate. *Avec* —, conscientiously. *En* —, in conscience, conscientiously; fairly; indeed, in truth, in reason, candidly. *En* —, *à la* —, (*print.*) on time-work, on the establishment. *En sûreté de* —, with a safe conscience. *Avoir la — de*, to be conscious of. *Avoir la — large*, not to be overscrupulous. *Mettre la main sur la* (or *sa*) —, to lay o.'s hand to o.'s heart; to be candid *or* sincere. *La main sur la* —, candidly, sincerely
Consciencieusement, *adv.* conscientiously
Consciencieu-x, se, *adj.* conscientious
Conscient, e, *adj.* (*philos.*) conscious
Conscriptible, *adj.* liable to the conscription, liable to be called (for military service)
Conscription, *s.f.* (*mil.*) conscription, recruiting, enrolling, enrolment, enlistment
Conscriptionnaire, *s.m.* one subject to the (military) conscription
Conscriptionnel, le, *adj.* conscriptional
Conscrit, *s.m.* conscript; recruit; raw soldier; novice; freshman; youngster; greenhorn; — *adj.m.* conscript
Consécrateur, *s.m. V.* **Consacrant,** *s.m.*
Consécration, *s.f.* consecration; dedication; ordination; destination; sanction; perpetuation; hallowing [quent; following; secondary
Consécuti-f, ve, *adj.* consecutive; conse-
Consécution, *s.f.* consecution
Consécutivement, *adv.* consecutively
Conseigle, *s.m.* meslin (*mixture of rye and wheat or oats*)
†**Conseil,** *s.m.* advice; counsel; adviser; counsellor; resolution; course; determination; deliberation; consultation; council; board; court. — *d'état*, council of state; (*formerly*) privy council. — *de famille*, family council; commission of lunacy. — *de guerre*, council of war; court-martial. — *municipal*, town-council, common-council. — *des ministres*, cabinet council. — *de révision*, (military) court of appeal; board to examine claims of exemption from military service. *Homme de bon* —, good adviser. *Tenir* —, to hold a council. *La nuit porte* —, consult your pillow
†**Conseillable,** *adj.* advisable
†**Conseiller,** *v.a.* to advise, to counsel
Se —, *v.r.* to advise *or* counsel each other; to be advised *or* counselled
†**Conseill-er, ère,** *s.m.f.* adviser, counsellor; councillor; puisne justice, judge; bencher; councillor's wife. — *d'état*, councillor of state; (*formerly*) privy councillor. — *municipal*, town-councillor, common-councilman; alderman. — *des grâces*, (*euphuistic style*) looking-glass
†**Conseilleu-r, se,** *s.m.f.* adviser, officious person, intermeddler, busybody
Consensuel, le, *adj.* (*law*) consensual
Consentement, *s.m.* consent; assent
Consentir, *v.n.* to consent; to assent; to agree; to acquiesce; to comply; to yield; to adhere; to be content (to); (*nav.*, *of masts*, &c.) to spring, to give way, to break; — *v.a.* to consent to; to assent to; to agree to; to subscribe to; to approve; to authorize; to sanction; to grant
Conséquemment, *adv.* consequently; accordingly; therefore; conformably; according; consistently
Conséquence, *s.f.* consequence; event, sequel; issue; conclusion; result; deduction; inference; importance, moment, weight; consistency. *En* —, in consequence; consequently, accordingly. *Sans* —, of no consequence, of no importance; immaterial. *Tirer une* —, to draw an inference. *Tirer à* —, to be drawn into a precedent; to be of importance
Conséquent, e, *adj.* consistent; coherent; just; rational; (*gram.*, *phys.*, &c.) consequent; (*pop.*) important, considerable
Conséquent, *s.m.* (*log.*, *gram.*, *math.*) consequent. *Par* —, consequently, therefore
Conserva-teur, trice, *adj. s.* preservative; conservative; preserver; protector, protectress, defender, guardian; conservator; conservatrix; keeper; curator; trustee; commissioner; ranger; bencher; registrar (*of mortgages*)
Conservati-f, ve, *adj. s.m.* preservative; conservative
Conservation, *s.f.* preservation; conservation; conservancy; registration (*of mortgages*)
Conservatisme, *s.m.* conservatism
Conservatoire, *adj.* preservative; conservatory, conservative; protective; — *s.m.* conservatory; academy, school (*for science or art*); academy of music; school of elocution; museum; board of conservators *or* trustees *or* commissioners *or* &c.; (*pop.*) pawn-shop
Conserve, *s.f.* preserve; pickle; (*pharm.*) conserve; (*nav.*) convoy; consort; (*fort.*) counterguard; —**s,** *pl.* preserves, &c.; (*opt.*) preservers (*spectacles*). — *alimentaire*, preserved article of food. — *au vinaigre*, pickle. *De* —, in company

Conservé, e, *part. adj.* preserved, &c. (*V.* **Conserver**); sound, fresh, strong, green, vigorous. *Être bien* —, (*pers.*) to carry o.'s age well, to be still hale and hearty

Conserver, *v.a.* to preserve; to keep; to save; to treasure; to take care of; to protect, to defend, to guard; to watch; to keep in sight; to keep up; to maintain; to retain; to reserve; to have left, to have still; to continue; to secure; to pickle

Se —, *v.r.* to preserve oneself; to be preserved; to keep; to keep up; to keep safe; to subsist; to obtain; to reserve oneself; to take care of oneself; to carry o.'s age well, to wear well, not to grow old

Considence, *s.f.* subsidence, subsiding, sinking

Considérable, *adj.* considerable; eminent

Considérablement, *adv.* considerably; a considerable amount *or* quantity

Considérant, *s.m.* (*law*) preamble, recital

Considération, *s.f.* consideration; attention; reflection; observation; examination; inspection; regard, respect, esteem; respectability; importance, consequence; motive; view. *A la* — (*de* ...), on (...'s) account. *En* — *de*, in consideration of, out of regard for, on account of, for the sake of [**Considérer**); considerate

Considéré, e, *part. adj.* considered, &c. (*V.*

Considérément, *adv.* considerately

Considérer, *v.a.* to consider; to look at, to examine; to inspect; to view; to behold; to study; to value, to esteem, to respect; to pay regard to; to mind; to look up to

Se —, *v.r.* to consider *or* &c. oneself *or* each other; to be considered, &c. [trustee

†**Consignataire,** *s.m.f.* consignee; depositary,

†**Consigna-teur, trice,** *s.m.f.* consigner

†**Consignation,** *s.f.* consignment; depositing; deposit; advance of funds; advance money; record; mention; entry; registering; booking

†**Consigne,** *s.f.* (*mil.*, &c.) orders; instructions; confinement to barracks; confinement; (*rail.*) cloak-room. *Forcer la* —, to force a sentry; to infringe the orders. *Lever la* —, to revoke orders; to release from confinement

†**Consigner,** *v.a.* to consign; to deposit; to record; to mention, to state; to write *or* put *or* take *or* note down; to enter; to register; to book; to confine to barracks; to confine; to keep in; to give orders not to admit; to refuse admittance *or* egress to; to forbid; — *v.n.* to give orders

Consistance, *s.f.* consistence, consistency, thickness, firmness; stability; steadiness; solidity; credit; consideration; confirmation; full growth; extent; nature

Consistant, e, *part.adj.* consisting; consistent; firm, solid, fixed, compact

Consister, *v.n.* to consist

Consistoire, *s.m.* consistory

Consistorial, e, *adj.* consistorial

Consistorialement, *adv.* in a consistory

Consœur, *s.f.* associate, sister

Consolable, *adj.* consolable

Consola-teur, trice, *adj. s.* consoling, comforting; consoler, comforter

Consolation, *s.f.* consolation, comfort; (*at play*) forfeits; (*pop.*) brandy, liquor, comfort. *Débit de* —, dram-shop

Consolatoire, *adj.* consolatory

Console, *s.f.* (*arch.*) console; bracket; corbel; (*furniture*) console-table, pier-table, console

Consoler, *v.a.* to console, to comfort, to solace; to cheer; to soothe, to alleviate; (*pop.*) to brandy (*o.'s coffee*, &c.)

Se —, *v.r.* to console oneself *or* each other, to be comforted, to take comfort; to recover (from), to get (over)

Consolidable, *adj.* consolidable

Consolidant, e, *adj.*, **Consolidant,** *s.m.* (*surg.*, *med.*) consolidant

Consolidati-f, ve, *adj.* consolidative

Consolidation, *s.f.* consolidation; funding

Consolidé, *s.m.*, —**s,** *pl.* consolidated fund *or* stock *or* annuities, consols [to secure; to fund

Consolider, *v.a.* to consolidate; to strengthen;

Se —, *v.r.* to consolidate; to grow firm *or* hard *or* solid *or* stronger; to improve

Consommable, *adj.* consumable

Consomma-teur, trice, *s.m.f.* consumer; eater, drinker; diner; customer; — *s.m.* (*theol.*) perfecter; — *adj.* consuming

Consommation, *s.f.* consummation; consumption; expense; destruction, waste; business done; eating and drinking; refreshments; feast; using; use; consumable commodities; human food; (*nav.*) expenditure of the stores during a sea-voyage; (*mil. admin.*) account of expenditure. *Prêt de* —, loan in kind. — *des siècles* or *des temps*, end of the world

Consomme, *s.f.* (*pop.*) consumpt [broth, stock

Consommé, *s.m.* gravy soup, jelly broth, rich

Consommé, e, *part. adj.* consummated; accomplished; complete, consummate, perfect; finished, ended, at an end; consumed; used up, used; spent. *Bien* —, (*of soup*) rich

Consommer, *v.a.* to consummate; to accomplish; to complete; to perfect; to finish, to end; to consume; to use up; to use; to spend. *Faire* —, to boil down (*meat*) [to boil down

Se —, *v.r.* to be consummated, &c.; (*of meat*)

Consompti-f, ve, *adj.*, **Consomptif,** *s.m.* (*med.*) consumptive

Consomption, *s.f.* consumption

Consonnance, *s.f.* (*mus.*, *gram.*) consonance

Consonnant, e, *adj.* consonant

Consonne, *s.f.* (*gram.*) consonant

Consonner, *v.n.* to be consonant, to harmonize

Consorts, *s.m.pl.* associates, partners, company. ... *et* —, (*law*) ... and others

Consoude, *s.f.* (*bot.*) consound, comfrey

Conspira-teur, trice, *s.m.f.* conspirator

Conspiration, *s.f.* conspiracy, plot

Conspirer, *v.n.a.* to conspire; to plot; to concur

Conspuer, *v.a.* to scorn, to scout, to flout, to spurn [*America*)

Constable, *s.m.* constable (*in England and*

Constamment, *adv.* constantly, always; with constancy

Constance, *s.f.* constancy; perseverance; steadiness; stability; consistency; patience; firmness; (*old*) insensibility, heartlessness

Constant, e, *adj.* constant; persevering; steadfast; steady; stable; unremitting; unvarying, invariable, unchangeable; lasting; firm; resolute; certain, positive, unquestion-

Constante, *s.f.* (*math.*) constant [able, undoubted

Constantinopolitain, e, *adj. s.* Constanti-

Constat, *s.m.* (*law*) constat [nopolitan

Constatation, *s.f.* ascertaining; verifying, proving; establishment; inquiry, inquest, hearing of witnesses; evidence given; statement; declaration; mention; discovery; authentication

Constater, *v.a.* to ascertain; to verify, to prove; to testify to; to establish; to state; to declare; to certify; to mention; to note down; to record; to mark, to remark; to discover, t find; to experience; to authenticate

Se —, *v.r.* to be ascertained *or* &c.

Constellation, *s.f.* constellation

Constellé, e, *part. adj.* constellated, &c. (*V.* **Consteller**); (*nat. hist.*) stellate, stellated; (*astrology*) made under the influence of a certain constellation [strew, to stud, to cover

Consteller, *v.a.* to constellate; to dot, to

Conster, *v.n.imp.* (*old*) to appear; to be clear *or* evident *or* certain

Consternation, *s.f.* consternation, dismay

Consterné, e, *adj.* dismayed; scared; of consternation [consternation

Consterner, *v.a.* to dismay, to strike wi

Constipation, *s.f.* constipation, costiveness

Constipé, e, *adj.* constipated, costive

Constiper, *v.a.n.* to constipate, to bind, to make costive; to be binding

Constituant, e, *adj.* constituent; (*law*) giving a power of attorney, settling an annuity; — *s.m.* constituent; (*Fr. hist.*) member of the Constituent Assembly; — *s.f.* constituent; (*Fr. hist.*) Constituent Assembly

Constituer, *v.a.* to constitute; to establish; to place; to put; to organize; to form; to resolve; to settle; to assign; to appoint; to make; to depute; to raise. — *prisonnier*, to commit to prison. *Se — prisonnier*, to surrender, to give oneself up [constitutress

Constitu-teur, trice, *s.m.f.* constituter;

Constituti-f, ve, *adj.* constitutive

Constitution, *s.f.* constitution; establishment; formation; composition; order, arrangement; organization; appointment; settlement (*of an annuity*, &c.); (*obsolete*) annuity

Constitutionnaliser, *v.a.* to constitutionalize

Constitutionnalisme, *s.m.* constitutionalism

Constitutionnalité, *s.f.* constitutionality

Constitutionnel, le, *adj.* constitutional; — *s.m.* constitutionalist [ally

Constitutionnellement, *adv.* constitution-

Constricteur, *adj.m., s.m.* (*anat., zool.*) con-

Constricti-f, ve, *adj.* constrictive [strictor

Constriction, *s.f.* constriction

Constringent, e, *adj.* constringent

Constructeur, *s.m.* builder, constructor; maker; wright; shipbuilder, shipwright

Constructibilité, *s.f.* constructibility

Constructible, *adj.* constructible

Constructi-f, ve, *adj.* constructive

Construction, *s.f.* construction; build; building; erection; structure; edifice; ship-making; ship-building. *De —*, (*adject.*) building; built. *En —*, in course of construction, building, being built, on the stocks. *Faire la —*, (*gram.*) to construe

Constructivité, *s.f.* constructiveness

Construire, *v.a.* to construct; to build; to erect; to frame; to make; (*gram.*) to construe

Se —, *v.r.* to be building, to be in course of construction; to be constructed *or* built *or* erected; to be construed; to construct *or* build for oneself; to raise

Consubstantialité, *s.f.* consubstantiality

Consubstantiation, *s.f.* consubstantiation

Consubstantiel, le, *adj.* consubstantial

Consubstantiellement, *adv.* consubstan-

Consul, *s.m.* consul [tially

Consulaire, *adj.m.f., s.m.* consular

Consulairement, *adv.* by consuls

Consulat, *s.m.* consulate; consulship

Consultable, *adj* consultable

Consultant, *adj.m.* consulting; — *s.m.* consulting physician, physician; consulting barrister, chamber-counsel; consulting engineer; person consulted, adviser, counsellor

Consultant, e, *s.m.f.* consulter

Consultati-f, ve, *adj.* consultative

Consultation, *s.f.* consultation; conference; opinion; advice; deliberation

Consulte, *s.f.* council, assembly, senate; (*obsolete, boorish*) consultation, opinion, advice

Consulter, *v.a.n.* to consult; to heed; to give consultations; (*obsolete*) to consult about. *Ouvrage à —*, book of reference

Se —, *v.r.* to reflect, to consider; to consult each other, to confer, to hold a consultation; (*things*) to be consulted [viser, examiner

Consulteur, *s.m.* consulter; counsellor, ad-

Consumable, *adj.* consumable

Consumer, *v.a.* to consume; to burn; to devour; to wear out *or* away; to waste away; to waste; to squander; to destroy; to spend

Se —, *v.r.* to be consumed *or* &c.; to burn out; to waste away; to pine away; to waste o.'s time *or* strength; to exhaust oneself; to ruin oneself

Contabescence, *s.f.* (*med.*) consumption

Contabescent, e, *adj.* (*med.*) consumptive

Contact, *s.m.* contact; touch; connection

Contage, Contagium, *s.m.* (*med.*) contagious matter *or* poison, virus [to infect

Contagier, *v.a.* (*med.*) to affect by contagion,

Contagieu-x, se, *adj.* contagious, catching; infectious

Contagion, *s.f.* contagion; infection; plague

Contagioniste, *s.m.* contagionist

Contagiosité, *s.f.* contagiousness

†**Contaille,** *adj.f.* (*of silk*) coarse, waste

Contaminable, *adj.* contaminable

Contamination, *s.f.* contamination

Contaminer, *v.a.* to contaminate

Conte, *s.m.* tale; story; fiction, fable, romance; falsehood, fib; nonsense. — *bleu*, — *borgne*, — *à dormir debout*, tale of a tub, rigmarole story, stupid stuff. *Faire des —s*, to tell stories

Contempla-teur, trice, *s.m.f.* contemplator; — *adj.* contemplative

Contemplati-f, ve, *adj.* contemplative; — *s.m.* contemplator; (*eccl.*) contemplative

Contemplation, *s.f.* contemplation; gazing, gaze; admiration; meditation

Contemplativement, *adv.* contemplatively

Contempler, *v.a.n.* to contemplate; to behold; to view, to look at; to gaze on *or* at; to have o.'s eyes fixed upon; to admire; to meditate

Se —, *v.r.* to contemplate *or* &c. oneself *or* each other; to be contemplated, &c.

Contemporain, e, *adj. s.* contemporary

Contemporanéité, *s.f.* contemporaneity

Contemp-teur, trice, *s.m.f.* contemner, despiser, scorner; — *adj.* contemptuous, scornful

Contemptible, *adj.* (*old*) contemptible

Contenance, *s.f.* countenance, air, look; demeanour, bearing, attitude; extent; capacity, capaciousness; (*nav.*) burden. *Bonne —*, firm attitude; stout resistance; spirit; bold look. *Par —, pour se donner une —*, to keep oneself in countenance. *Être embarrassé de sa —, n'avoir point de —, ne savoir quelle — prendre*, to have an awkward look, not to know which way to look *or* what to do with oneself. *Faire bonne —*, to assume a fair attitude; to show spirit *or* resolution; to resist firmly; to put a good face on a bad matter *or* on the matter; to put on a bold look. *Faire perdre —*, to put out of countenance. *Perdre —*, to be out of countenance. *Servir de —*, to serve to keep (one) in countenance [— *s.m.* container, holder

Contenant, e, *part. adj.* containing, holding;

Contendant, e, *adj. s.* contending; contender

Contenir, *v.a.* to contain, to hold; to comprise; to include; to restrain; to refrain; to repress; to moderate; to check; to curb; to confine; to keep within bounds; to keep down *or* back *or* in; to keep; to dam in [pleased; glad; happy

Content, e, *adj.* content, contented; satisfied;

Content, *s.m.* fill, bellyful; heart's content; (*game at cards*) trente-et-un. *Tout son —*, all one wants, as much as one likes *or* could wish, o.'s fill

Contentement, *s.m.* content; contentment; contentedness; satisfaction; gratification; pleasure; joy; happiness; enough. — *passe richesse*, (*Proverb*) content is beyond riches

Contenter, *v.a.* to content; to satisfy; to gratify; to please; to humour; to quiet, to appease; (*obsolete*) to requite, to pay (for)

Se —, *v.r.* to content *or* satisfy *or* please *or* indulge oneself; to be content *or* contented *or* satisfied *or* pleased; to rest satisfied; to merely ... [*lete*) contentiously

Contentieusement, *adv.* litigiously; (*obso-*

Contentieu-x, se, *adj.* disputed; disputable, contestable; litigious; (*obsolete, except as a term of law*) contentious (*jurisdiction*); — *s.m.* affairs in litigation; disputed claims; law business; solicitor's department. *Agent* or *Chef du —*, *V.* **Chef** [ing, binding

Contenti-f, ve, *adj.* (*surg.*) retentive, retain-

Contention, *s.f.* contention; intenseness, intensity; application; vehemence; warmth; fervour; dispute, debate; (*surg.*) keeping reduced (*a fracture, hernia, &c.*)

Contenu, e, *part. adj.* contained, &c (*V.* **Contenir**); reserved; sober, moderate; — *s.m.* contents; enclosure; tenour, terms

Conter, *v.a.n.* to relate, to tell; to report; to confide; to talk; to relate stories *or* a story. *En — à,* to tell stories to; to hoax, to humbug; to talk soft nonsense to, to make love to. *S'en faire —, S'en laisser —,* to listen to soft nonsense

Se —, *v.r.* to tell each other; to be related *or* [told

Conterie, *s.f.* coarse Venetian glass-ware

Contestabilité, *s.f.* questionableness

Contestable, *adj.* contestable, questionable, disputable

Contestablement, *adv.* questionably

Contestant, e, *adj.* contending, litigant, at law; — *s.m.f.* contending party, suitor, litigant; opponent, opposer; opposing creditor

Contestation, *s.f.* contestation; contest; debate; dispute; difference; strife; wrangling; variance; opposition; question; litigation; suit

Conteste, *s.f.* (*obsolete form of* "Contestation"). *Sans —* (*obsolete for* "sans contredit")

Contester, *v.n.a.* to contest, to contend, to dispute, to debate; to call in question; to deny; to oppose; to defend [each other; to contend for

Se —, *v.r.* to be contested, &c.; to deny to

Conteu-r, se, *s.m.f.* teller; relater; narrator; talker; story-teller; tale-writer; — *adj.* fond of [relating stories

Contexte, *s.m.* context; text

Contexture, *s.f.* contexture; texture

Contignation, *s.f.* contignation

Contigu, ë, *adj.* contiguous, adjoining

Contiguïté, *s.f.* contiguity

Continence, *s.f.* continence

Continent, e, *adj.*, **Continent,** *s.m.* continent. *Fièvre —e,* continued fever

Continental, e, *adj.* continental

Contingence, *s.f.* contingence, contingency

Contingent, e, *adj.* contingent; — *s.m.* contingent, share, quota, proportion, contribution; number

Continu, e, *adj.* continued; continual; continuous; uninterrupted; incessant; consecutive. *A la —e,* by continuance, for a length of time, in time, in the end, in the long run, in process of time, at length [tinuator; successor

Continua-teur, trice, *s.m.f.* continuer, con-

Continuation, *s.f.* continuation; continuance

Continuel, le, *adj.* continual; constant; uninterrupted; perpetual; endless

Continuellement, *adv.* continually; constantly; perpetually

Continuer, *v.a.n.* to continue; to carry on; to prolong; to protract; to persevere in; to pursue; to go on with; to go on; to proceed; to last; to hold out; to extend; to run on; to keep; to keep on; to continue the work of, to be the successor of, to succeed

Se —, *v.r.* to continue; to be continued *or* kept up *or* prolonged *or* protracted; to go on; to go on longer; to last; to extend

Continuité, *s.f.* continuity; continuance

Continûment, *adv.* continuedly [ing

Contondant, e, *adj.* blunt, contusing, bruis-

Contondre, *v.a.* to contuse, to bruise [torniate

Contorniate, *adj.* contourniated; — *s.m.* con-

Contorsion, *s.f.* contortion; distortion; twist; wry face, face, grimace [circuit; winding; fold

Contour, *s.m.* contour, outline; circumference,

Contourné, e, *adj.* outlined; encircled, surrounded; spiral; twisted; distorted; crooked, deformed, ill-shaped; forced; (*bot.*) contorted; (*of medals*) contourniated

Contournement, *s.m.* outlining; twisting; distortion; winding; rounding; convolution

Contourner, *v.a.* to outline; to give a proper contour *or* outline to; to encircle, to surround; to twine *or* twist round; to turn around; to pass round; to go round; to round; to twist; to distort; to deform; to bend

Se —, *v.r.* to become *or* be twisted *or* distorted *or* bent, to get out of shape, to get crooked

Contourneu-r, se, *s.m.f.* rounder

Contourniate, *s.m.* *V.* **Contorniate**

Contractable, *adj.* contractable

Contractant, e, *adj. s.* contracting; contracting party, contractor, stipulator, covenanter

Contractation, *s.f.* contracting

Contracter, *v.a.n.* to contract; to covenant, to stipulate, to bargain; to shrink; to straiten; to shorten; to abridge; to condense; to enter into; to make; to form; to acquire, to get; to catch [to shrink

Se —, *v.r.* to be contracted, &c.; to contract,

Contracti-f, ve, *adj.* contractive

Contractile, *adj.* contractile, contractible

Contractilité, *s.f.* contractility, contractibility

Contraction, *s.f.* contraction

Contractuel, le, *adj.* stipulated *or* done by contract, contractual

Contractuellement, *adv.* by contract

Contracture, *s.f.* (*arch.*) diminution; (*med.*) contraction [minish; (*med.*) to contract

Contracturer, *v.a.*, **Se —,** *v.r.* (*arch.*) to di-

Contradicteur, *s.m.* contradicter, gainsayer; opposer, opponent, adversary

Contradiction, *s.f.* contradiction; denial; opposition; inconsistency; discrepancy; incongruity; contrariety; variance; obstacle

Contradictoire, *adj.* contradictory; inconsistent; conflicting; opposed; (*law*) after hearing both sides, in presence of the adverse parties

Contradictoirement, *adv.* contradictorily; inconsistently; (*law*) after hearing both parties

†**Contraignable,** *adj.* compellable; constrainable. — *par corps,* liable to arrest *or* imprisonment, attachable

†**Contraignant, e,** *adj.* compelling, compulsive; constraining; causing restraint; troublesome

Contraindre, *v.a.* to compel, to force, to make; to constrain; to restrain; to put a constraint upon; to put under restraint; to hinder; to strain; (*law*) to attach. — *par corps,* to arrest (for debt), to attach

Contraint, e, *part. adj.* constrained, forced, stiff, unnatural, affected; cramped; compelled, &c. (*V.* **Contraindre**)

Contrainte, *s.f.* compulsion; force; constraint; restraint; stiffness; tightness; summons; (*law*) attachment; duress; warrant. — *par corps,* arrest *or* imprisonment (for debt); warrant

Contraire, *adj.* contrary; opposite; opposed; adverse; unfavourable; hostile; inconsistent; injurious, prejudicial, hurtful, bad; (*in compounds*) counter

Contraire, *s.m.* contrary; reverse; opposite; opposition; inconsistency; repugnance; (*gram.*) antonym; (*nav.*) foul tide *or* current *or* wind. *Au —,* on the contrary; on the other hand. *Au — de,* contrary to. *Bien au —, tout au —, tout le —,* quite the contrary, quite the reverse

Contrairement, *adv.* contrarily, contrary

Contralte, *s.m.* *V.* **Contralto**

Contraltiste, *s.m.f.* (*mus.*) contralto (*person*)

Contralto, *s.m.* (*mus.*) contralto, counter-tenor

Contrapontiste, Contrapuntiste, *s.m.* (*mus.*) contrapuntist

Contrarier, *v.a.* to contradict; to counteract; to oppose; to thwart; to cross; to interfere with; to inconvenience; to frustrate; to baffle; to disappoint; to provoke, to vex, to annoy, to trouble, to tease

Contrariété, *s.f.* contrariety; contradiction; opposition; obstacle, hindrance; difficulty; cross; disappointment; vexation, annoyance; unpleasantness [foil

Contraste, *s.m.* contrast; contradistinction;

Contraster, *v.a.n.* to contrast

Contrat, *s.m.* contract; deed; agreement; settlement; indentures, indenture, articles; convention; treaty; bargain; compact; covenant; (*at play*) square fish

Contraténor, *s.m.* (*mus.*) counter-tenor

Contravention, *s.f.* contravention; infraction; offence. *Être en* —, to commit an offence; to infringe regulations

Contrayerva, *s.m.* (*bot., pharm.*) contrayerva

Contre, *prep. adv.* against; contrary to; in opposition to; in spite of; near, close to, close by; to; towards; for; in exchange for; at; on, upon; with; versus; counter; cross; against it, against them; to the contrary; — *s.m.* against, con, opposite side; challenger; (*at billiards*) kiss. *Par* —, by way of compensation, to make up, on the other hand. *Tout* —, quite close; ajar. *Faire* —, to challenge. — **-accusation,** *s.f.* counter-charge, cross-charge. — **-à-contre,** *adv.* (*nav.*) alongside. — **-allée,** *s.f.* side-walk, side-alley. — **-amiral,** *s.m.* rear-admiral; rear-admiral's ship. — **-appel,** *s.m.* second calling over, second call, check-roll; (*fenc.*) caveating. — **-applaudissement,** *s.m.* counter-cheer. — **-approche,** *s.f.* (*fort.*) counter-approach. — **-attaque,** *s.f.* (*fort.*) counter-works. — **-balancer,** *v.a.* to counterbalance, to counterpoise; to countervail. *Se* — *-balancer*, to counterbalance *or* &c. each other; to be counterbalanced *or* &c. — **-bandé, e,** *adj.* (*her.*) counter-bended. — **-barré, e,** *adj.* (*her.*) counter-barred. — **-bas (En),** *adv. prep.* downward; below. — **-basse,** *s.f.* (*mus.*) counter-bass, double bass, contrabass, contrabasso (*instr. and player*). — **-bassier,** — **-bassiste,** *s.m.* (*mus.*) contrabasso (*player*). — **-basson,** *s.m.* (*mus.*) double bassoon; double-bassoonist. — **-batterie,** *s.f.* cross-battery, counter-battery; counter-plot. — **-battre,** *v.a.* to counter-batter; to oppose. — **-biais, (A),** *adv.* in a contrary direction, contrariwise; the other way; the wrong way. — **-bittes,** *s.f.pl.* (*nav.*) spurs of the bitts. — **-bord (A),** *adv.* (*nav.*) upon a contrary tack. — **-bordée,** *s.f.* (*nav.*) counter-tack. — **-boutant,** *s.m.* counterfort, buttress. — **-bouter,** *v.a.* to buttress, to prop, to shore up. — **-brasser,** *v.a.* (*nav.*) to counter-brace. — **-bretêché, e,** *adj.* (*her.*) counter-embattled. — **-buter,** *v.a.* (*V.* — **-bouter**). — **-calquer,** *v.a.* to reverse the tracing of. — **-caution,** *s.f.* counter-surety, counter-security, counter-bond. — **-change,** *s.m.* counter-change. — **-changer,** *v.a.* to counter-change. — **-charge,** *s.f.* counterpoise. — **-charme,** *s.m.* counter-charm. — **-châssis,** *s.m.* outer sash, outer window, counter-sash, counter-frame, double casement. — **-chef,** *s.m.* foreman. — **-chevron,** *s.m.* (*her.*) counter-chevron. — **-chevronné, e,** *adj.* (*her.*) counter-chevrony. — **-civadière,** *s.f.* (*nav.*) bowsprit top-sail. — **-clé,** — **-clef,** *s.f.* (*arch.*) counter-keystone. — **-cœur,** *s.m.* back (*of a fireplace*). *A* — *-cœur*, *V.* **Cœur.** — **-componé, e,** *adj.* (*her.*) counter-compony. — **-coup,** *s.m.* counter-blow, counter-stroke, counter-buff; rebound; consequence, result, effect; shock; (*at billiards*) kiss; (*rid.*) start, leap. *Par* — *-coup*, as a consequence, indirectly. — **-courant,** *s.m.* counter-current. — **-critique,** *s.f.* counter-criticism. — **-dater,** *v.a.* to counter-date. — **-déclaration,** *s.f.* counter-declaration. — **-dégagement,** *s.m.* (*fenc.*) counter-disengaging. — **-dégager,** *v.n.a.* (*fenc.*) to counter-disengage. — **-écaille,** *s.f.* under-shell. — **-écart,** *s.m.* (*her.*) counter-quarter. — **-écarteler,** *v.a.* (*her.*) to counter-quarter. — **-échange,** *s.m.* mutual exchange. — **-enquête,** *s.f.* counter-inquiry; counter-inquest. — **-épaulette,** *s.f.* (*mil.*) scale, shoulder-scale. — **-épreuve,** *s.f.* counter-proof; imitation; counter-verification. — **-épreuver,** *v.a.* (*engr.*, &c.) to counter-prove. *Se* — *-épreuver*, to be counter-proved. — **-espalier,** *s.m.* espalier facing another, second espalier. — **-étais,** *s.m.pl.* (*nav.*) back stays. — **-étambot,** *s.m.* (*nav.*) (*intérieur*) inner post, (*extérieur*) back of the stern-post. — **-étrave,** *s.f.* (*nav.*) apron. — **-expertise,** *s.f.* counter-valuation; counter-survey. — **-extension,** *s.f.* (*surg.*) counter-extension. — **-fenêtre,** *s.f.* inside sash. — **-fente,** *s.f.* (*surg.*) contra-fissure. — **-feu,** *s.m.* back (*of a fireplace*). — **-fiche,** *s.f.* (*carp.*) brace, strut, bearer. — **-fil,** *s.m.* contrary direction. *A* — *-fil*, the wrong way, backward, against the grain; against the stream. — **-filet,** *s.m.* (*butch.*) outside of the sirloin, outside-cut. — **-fin (A),** *adv.* against o.'s purpose. — **-finesse,** *s.f.* counter-trick, counter-cunning, trick for trick, diamond cut diamond. — **-fissure,** *s.f.* (*surg.*) contra-fissure. — **-fleuri, e,** — **-fleuronné, e,** *adj.* (*her.*) counter-flory. — **-foc,** *s.m.* (*nav.*) foretop stay-sail. — **-force,** *s.f.* counter-force. — **-fort,** *s.m.* counterfort, buttress, shoulder, pier; counter (*of boots, shoes*); branch of a chain (*of mountains*). — **-fossé,** *s.m.* (*engin.*) counter-drain; (*fort.*) advance-fosse. — **-foulement,** *s.m.* forcing up, rise, rising. — **-fracture,** *s.f.* (*surg.*) contra-fissure. — **-frasage,** *s.m.* completion of the process of mixing the flour with water (*in making bread*). — **-fruit,** *s.m.* (*arch.*) over-span. — **-fugue,** *s.f.* (*mus.*) counter-fugue. — **-gage,** *s.m.* double security, pledge. — **-garde,** *s.f.* (*arch., fort.*) counter-guard. — **-gardé, e,** *adj.* counter-guarded. — **-hacher,** *v.a.* (*draw., engr.*) to cross-hatch. — **-hachure,** *s.f.* (*draw., engr.*) cross-hatching. — **-hâtier,** *s.m.* kitchen fire-dog, spit-rack. — **-haut (En),** *adv. prep.* upward; above. — **-herminé, e,** *adj.* (*her.*) counter-ermined. — **-heurtoir,** *s.m.* knocker-stop. — **-indication,** *s.f.* (*med.*) contra-indication. — **-indiquer,** *v.a.* (*med.*) to contra-indicate. — **-interrogatoire,** *s.m.* (*law*) cross-examination. — **-issant, e,** *adj.* (*her.*) counter-salient. — **-jauger,** *v.a.* (*carp.*) to counter-gauge, to regauge. — **-jour,** *s.m.* false light; counter-light. *A* — *-jour*, against the light, in a false *or* unfavourable light, in a contrary point of view. — **-jumelles,** *s.f.pl.* kennel-stones. — **-latte,** *s.f.* counter-lath. — **-latter,** *v.a.* to counter-lath. — **-lettre,** *s.f.* counter-deed, private agreement, defeasance, deed of defeasance. — **-ligne,** *s.f.* (*fort.*) counter-line. — **-maille,** *s.f.* double-mesh; double-meshed net. — **-mailler,** *v.a.* to double-mesh. — **-maître,** *s.m.* foreman; overseer; (*of mines*) overman; under-captain; (*nav.*) boatswain's mate, master's mate; — *-maître charpentier*, (*nav.*) carpenter's mate. — **-manœuvre,** *s.f.* counter-manœuvre. — **-marche,** *s.f.* counter-march, counter-marching; counter-movement; (*of a stair*) riser, raiser. — **-marcher,** *v.n.* to counter-march. — **-marée,** *s.f.* counter-tide. — **-marque,** *s.f.* (*com., vet., of medals*, &c.) counter-mark; (*of theatres*, &c.) check. — **-marquer,** *v.a.* to counter-mark; (*a horse*) to counter-mark, to bishop. — **-marqueur, se,** *s.m.f.* check-taker. — **-mesure (A),** *adv.* against time (*in music*). — **-mine,** *s.f.* counter-mine. — **-miner,** *v.a.* to countermine. — **-mineur,** *s.m.* counterminer. — **-mont (A),** *adv.* uphill; upward; up stream. — **-mot,** *s.m.* (*mil.*) countersign, counter-parole. — **-mouvement,** *s.m.* counter-movement. — **-mur,** *s.m.* contramure, countermure, outer wall. — **-murer,** *v.a.* to contramure, to countermure, to double-wall. — **-opération,** *s.f.* counter-operation. — **-opposition,** *s.f.* counter-opposition. — **-ordre,** *s.m.* counter-order. — **-ouverture,** *s.f.* (*surg.*) counter-opening. — **-pal,** *s.m.* (*her.*) counter-pale. — **-palé, e,** *adj.* (*her.*) counter-paled. — **-partie,** *s.f.* counterpart; reverse, contrary, opposite; opposite opinion; (*at play*) revenge, return-match another game. — **-pas,** *s.m.* counter-pace, counter-step; (*in drilling*) change-step. — **-passant, e,** *adj.* (*her.*) counter-passant. — **-passation,** *s.f.* (*com.*) reendorsement. — **-passer,** *v.a.* (*com.*) to reendorse. — **-pente,** *s.f.* counter-slope; steep slope; slope; unevenness of ground, stop (*of a drain*). — **-percer,** *v.a.* to counter-pierce. — **-peser,** *v.a.* to counterpoise, to counterbalance. — **-pétition,** *s.f.* counter-petition. — **-petterie,** *s.f.* [a slip of the tongue consisting in an inversion of letters from one word to another, and making a new and often ridiculous sense, as if one said, in French, "Trompez, sonnettes!" for "Sonnez, trompettes!" or, in English, "to boil one's sprats" for "to spoil one's brats," "I told cook" for "I took cold," &c.] — **-pied,** *s.m.* reverse, contrary; (*hunt.*) wrong scent, back scent. *A — -pied de,* contrary to, against. — **-planche,** *s.f.* counter-plate. — **-platine,** *s.f.* side-plate (*of a firelock*). — **-poids,** *s.m.* counterpoise, counterbalance; balance-weight; equipoise; equilibrium, balance; balancing-pole (*of acrobats*), poy. — **-poil,** *s.m.* wrong way of the hair *or* of the nap. *A — -poil,* against the grain; the wrong way. — **-poinçon,** *s.m.* die. — **-poinçonner,** *v.a.* to stamp (with a die). — **-point,** *s.m.* (*mus., nav.*) counterpoint. — **-pointe,** *s.f.* sharp-edged point (*of a sword*); broadsword exercise; cut and thrust. — **-pointé, e,** *adj.* (*her.*) counter-pointe. — **-pointer,** *v.a.* to quilt on both sides; to oppose (*cannon to cannon*); to contradict, to oppose, to thwart. — **-pointiste,** *s.m.* (*mus.*) contrapuntist. — **-poison,** *s.m.* counter-poison, antidote; corrective. — **-police,** *s.f.* police-inspectors. — **-porte,** *s.f.* double door, baize door; double gate. — **-poser,** *v.a.* to misplace; (*com.*) to misenter. — **-poseur,** *s.m.* setter. — **-position,** *s.f.* contraposition; (*com.*) misentry. — **-pression,** *s.f.* counter-pressure. — **-preuve,** *s.f.* counter-evidence. — **-projet,** *s.m.* counter-project. — **-promesse,** *s.f.* waiver. — **-propos,** *s.m.* retort. — **-proposition,** *s.f.* counter-proposition, counter-proposal. — **-quille,** *s.f.* (*nav.*) keelson. — **-rail,** *s.m.* check-rail. — **-retable,** *s.m.* back of the altar-piece. — **-révolution,** *s.f.* counter-revolution. — **-révolutionnaire,** *adj.* counter-revolutionary; *s.m.f.* counter-revolutionist. — **-révolutionner,** *v.n.* to effect a counter-revolution. — **-riposte,** *s.f.* (*fenc.*) counter-thrust. — **-ronde,** *s.f.* (*mil.*) counter-round. — **-ruse,** *s.f.* counter-plot, counter-trick. — **-sabord,** *s.m.* (*nav.*) port-lid. — **-saillant, e,** *adj.* (*her.*) counter-salient. — **-saison,** *s.f.* (*hort.*) growth out of season. *A — -saison,* out of season, unseasonable, unseasonably. — **-salut,** *s.m.* (*nav.*) answer to a salute. — **-sangle,** *s.f.,* — **-sanglon,** *s.m.* girth-strap; strap. — **-scel,** *s.m.* counter-seal. — **-sceller,** *v.a.* to counter-seal. — **-seing,** *s.m.* counter-signature, counter-sign; frank (*privilege*). — **-sens,** *s.m.* opposite *or* contrary meaning, wrong sense; mistake (in the sense), mistranslation; wrong construction, misconstruction; misinterpretation; nonsense, absurdity; wrong way; wrong direction; wrong side. *A — -sens,* in a wrong way *or* direction, wrong; on the wrong side; contrary to sense (*or* to the sense); the other way. — **-signal,** *s.m.* counter-signal. — **-signataire,** *s.m.f.* countersigner; *adj.* countersigning. — **-signer,** *v.a.* to countersign; to sign on the envelope, to frank. — **-sol,** *s.m.* (*hort.*) shade. — **-sortie,** *s.f.* (*mil.*) counter-sortie. — **-stimulant, e,** *adj.,* — **-stimulant,** *s.m.* (*med.*) counter-stimulant. — **-sûreté,** *s.f.* counter-security. — **-table,** *s.f.* back of the altar-piece. — **-taille,** *s.f.* (*com.*) counter-tally; (*engr.*) cross-cut. — **-tailler,** *v.a.* (*com.*) to counter-tally; (*engr.*) to cross-cut. — **-temps,** *s.m.* unseasonableness, improper time; preposterousness; unlucky *or* untoward accident, mischance, mishap; disappointment; (*mus.*) counter-measure; (*dancing*) contretemps; (*rid.*) counter-time. *A — -temps,* unseasonably, out of season; preposterously; (*mus.*) out of time. — **-tenant,** *s.m.* (*of tournaments*) challenger, champion. — **-tenir,** *v.a.* (*tech.*) to back. — **-terrasse,** *s.f.* lower terrace. — **-tirer,** *v.a.* to counter-prove; to counter-draw, to trace. — **-tranchée,** *s.f.* (*fort.*) counter-trench. — **-vair,** *s.m.* (*her.*) counter-vair. — **-vairé, e,** *adj.* (*her.*) counter-vairy. — **-val (A),** *adv.* downhill; downward; down stream. — **-vapeur,** *s.f.* counter-steam. — **-vérité,** *s.f.* irony, antiphrasis, mock praise, satire, criticism. — **-visite,** *s.f.* second visit *or* search *or* survey. — **-voile d'étai,** *s.f.* (*nav.*) middle stay-sail. — **-volte,** *s.f.* (*of cavalry*) counter-volt. — **-volter,** *v.n.* to make a counter-volt. — **-vue,** *s.f.* counter-view

Contrebande, *s.f.* smuggling; contraband; smuggled *or* contraband goods. *De —,* contraband; smuggled; prohibited; intruding; obnoxious; flash, false, would-be. *Faire la — de,* to smuggle. *Passer en —,* to smuggle in

Contrebandi-er, ère, *s.m.f.* smuggler, contrabandist

Contrecarrer, *v.a.* to thwart, to cross, to oppose; to counteract

Contredanse, *s.f.* quadrille

Contredire, *v.a.n.* to contradict; to gainsay; to be inconsistent with; to contest; to disprove; to oppose, to combat; to be opposed *or* in opposition to; to object (to); to find fault (with); to deny

Contredit, *s.m.* reply, rejoinder, answer; contrary assertion, contradiction; discussion; opposition; confutation; — *m.,* **e,** *f.* (*part. of* **Contredire**) contradicted, &c. *Sans —,* unquestionably, most assuredly

Contrée, *s.f.* country; region, land; district

Contrefaçon, *s.f.* counterfeiting; forgery; piracy (*of copyright*); infringement (*of patents*); imitation; counterfeit; spurious edition *or* copy

Contrefacteur, *s.m.* counterfeiter; forger; plagiarist, pirate; infringer (*of a patent*); imitator [forgery

Contrefaction, *s.f.* (*obsolete*) counterfeiting;

Contrefaire, *v.a.* to counterfeit; to forge; to pirate; to infringe; to imitate; to mimic; to ape; to act, to play, to feign *or* pretend to be; to feign; to sham; to disguise; to deform; to disfigure

Se —, *v.r.* to dissemble, to disguise oneself, to sham; to be counterfeited *or* forged *or* &c.

Contrefaiseu-r, se, *s.m.f.* imitator; mimicker

Contremandement, *s.m.* countermand countermanding; counter-order

Contremander, *v.a.* to countermand

Contrer, *v.n.* (*at play*) to challenge

Contrescarpe, *s.f.* (*fort.*) counterscarp

Contrescarper, *v.a.* (*fort.*) to counterscarp

Contrevallation, *s.f.* (*fort.*) contravallation

Contrevaller, *v.a.* (*fort.*) to enclose by a contravallation

Contrevenant, e, *s.m.f.* contravener; infractor; offender; transgressor; — *adj.* contravening; infringing; offending; transgressing

Contrevenir, *v.n.* to contravene, to act contrary (to), to infringe, to offend (against), to violate, to transgress, to disobey

Contrevent, *s.m.* outside shutter, shutter

Contreventer, *v.a.* to provide with shutters, to protect from the wind

Contribuable, *s.m.f.* tax-payer; rate-payer; — *adj.* taxable; ratable [tress

Contribuant, e, *s.m.f.* contributor, contribu-

Contribuer, *v.n.* to contribute; to be laid under contribution

Contributaire, *s.m.f.* contributor; tax-payer; — *adj.* contributary; contributional; tax-paying

Contributeur, *s.m.* contributor

Contributi-f, ve, *adj.* contributive

Contribution, *s.f.* contribution; tax; share, part, portion; dividing among the creditors; so much in the pound; loss; (*nav.*) average. *Mettre à* —, to lay under contribution; to put in requisition; to tax; to ransack [tional

Contributoire, *adj.* contributory; contribu-

Contributoirement, *adv.* contributorily [pain

Contrister, *v.a.* to grieve, to afflict, to sadden, to

Contrit, e, *adj.* contrite; grieved, afflicted;

Contrition, *s.f.* contrition [penitent

Contrôlage, *s.m.* controlling, control; hall-marking, stamping; trying; ringing (*of the vine*)

Contrôle, *s.m.* control; controllership; controller's office; inspection; inspectorship; supervision; surveying; surveyorship; surveyor's office; plate-mark, assay-mark, hall-mark, stamp; stamp office; list; rolls

Contrôlement, *s.m.* controlling, control; stamping; trying; clipping (*of tickets*)

Contrôler, *v.a.n.* to control; to check, to verify, to examine; to superintend; to register, to put upon the rolls; to stamp (*gold, silver, arms*); to try (*weights, measures*); to clip, to nick (*tickets*); to censure, to find fault

Contrôleur, *s.m.* controller, comptroller; checker; inspector; superintendent; supervisor; overseer; surveyor (*of assessed taxes*); time-keeper; check-taker; ticket-collector; stamper (*of gold, silver, arms*); censurer, fault-finder [fault-finder

Contrôleuse, *s.f.* controller, checker, censurer,

Controuver, *v.a.* to forge, to invent, to fabricate

Controuveur, *s.m.* forger, inventor, fabricator

Controversable, *adj.* controvertible; contro-

Controverse, *s.f.* controversy [versial

Controverser, *v.a.n.* to controvert, to moot, to debate, to dispute

Controversiste, *s.m.f.* controversialist

Contumace, *s.f.* (*law*) contumacy, non-appearance, default, contempt (of court); — *adj. s.m.f.* contumacious, defaulting; defaulter

Contumacer, *v.a.* to try *or* condemn by default

Contumacial, e, *adj.* (*law*) in contumacy, in default

Contumax, *adj.s.m.f.* contumacious, defaulting;

Contus, e, *adj.* contused [defaulter

Contusi-f, ve, *adj.* contusing, bruising; dull

Contusion, *s.f.* contusion, bruise [(*pain*)

Contusionner, *v.a.* to contuse, to bruise

Convaincant, e, *adj.* convincing

Convaincre, *v.a.* to convince; to convict

Convaincu, e, *adj.* convicted; convinced; of conviction; sincere, earnest

Convainquant, *part.* convincing; convicting

Convalescence, *s.f.* convalescence

Convalescent, e, *adj. s.* convalescent

Convallaire, *s.f.* (*bot.*) convallary, lily of the valley, Solomon's seal

Convenable, *adj.* proper; fit; fitting; fitted; becoming; seemly; decent; right; due; suitable; suited; agreeable; expedient, advisable; seasonable; convenient; — *s.m.* propriety

Convenablement, *adv.* properly; fittingly; becomingly; decently; duly; suitably; agreeably; expediently, advisably; seasonably; conveniently

Convenance, *s.f.* conformity; concord, harmony, proportion; fitness; suitableness; expediency; seasonableness; convenience; leisure; liking, taste; propriety; seemliness; becomingness; decency; decorum; —**s,** *pl.* propriety, decorum, good manners, common civility; etiquette

Convenant, e, *adj.* (*old*) *V.* **Convenable**

Convenant, *s.m.* *V.* **Covenant**

Convenir, *v.n.* to agree; to admit, to acknowledge, to own, to confess, to allow, to grant; to suit; to be suitable *or* suited (to), to be fit (for); to become; to be right *or* proper; to be expedient *or* advisable; to be convenient; to please

Se —, *v.r.* to suit *or* like each other, to please (*or* be pleased with) each other, to be suited to each other, to agree together, to agree

Conventicule, *s.m.* conventicle

Convention, *s.f.* agreement; convention; condition; covenant; treaty; capitulation; assembly, parliament, Convention. *De* —, conventional

Conventionnel, le, *adj.* conventional; (*hist.*) of the (National) Convention, Conventional; — *s.m.* (*hist.*) Conventionalist [by agreement

Conventionnellement, *adv.* conventionally,

Conventualité, *s.f.* conventual life

Conventuel, le, *adj. s.* conventual

Conventuellement, *adv.* conventually

Convergence, *s.f.* convergence

Convergent, e, *adj.* convergent, converging

Converger, *v.n.* to converge; to tend

Convers, e, *adj.* lay; (*geom., log.*) converse; — *s.m.f.* lay brother *or* sister, convert; — *s.f.* (*geom., log.*) converse proposition, converse

Conversable, *adj.* conversable, sociable

Conversation, *s.f.* conversation, converse, talk. *Faire la* —, to carry on a conversation, to talk

Converser, *v.n.* to converse, to talk; to commune; to hold intercourse; to live (with); (*mil.*) to turn, to wheel about

Conversible, *adj.* conversible, convertible

Conversion, *s.f.* conversion; (*mil.*) wheeling, wheel, change of front, conversion. *Demi-* —, wheeling about. *Quart de* —, wheel of the quarter-circle

Conversioniste, *s.m.f. adj.* conversionist

Converso, *s.m.* (*nav.*) waist, main-deck

Converti, e, *adj. s.* converted; convert

Convertibilité, *s.f.* convertibility

Convertible, *adj.* convertible

Convertiblement, *adv.* convertibly

Convertir, *v.a.* to convert; to change, to turn; to bring over

Se —, *v.r.* to be converted; to change; to turn; to become a convert; to be convertible

Convertissable, *adj.* convertible

Convertissement, *s.m.* conversion

Convertisseu-r, se, *s.m.f.* converter

Convexe, *adj.* convex

Convexité, *s.f.* convexity

Convexo-concave, *adj.* convexo-concave

Convexo-convexe, *adj.* convexo-convex

Conviction, *s.f.* conviction; convincing proof

Convictionnel, le, *adj.* convictive

Convictionnellement, *adv.* convictively

Convié, e, *s.m.f.* guest

Convier, *v.a.* to invite; to request, to desire; to bid; to incite, to urge; to induce

Convive, *s.m.f.* guest; table-companion

Convivial, e, *adj.* convivial

Convivialement, *adv.* convivially

Convivialité, *s.f.* conviviality [guest

Conviviat, *s.m.* being a guest, attendance as a

Convocable, *adj.* convocable

Convoca-teur, trice, *s.m.f.* convoker; requisitionist; summoner [summons

Convocation, *s.f.* convocation; requisition;

Convoi, *s.m.* funeral procession, procession, funeral; (*mil., nav.*) convoy; (*of boats, and rail., obsolete for* "train") train. *V.* **Train** [voy

Convoiement, *s.m.* (*mil., nav.*) convoying, con-

Convoitable, *adj.* covetable, desirable [over

Convoiter, *v.a.* to covet. — *des yeux,* to gloat

Se —, *v.r.* to be coveted

Convoiteu-r, se, *s.m.f. adj.* coveter; covetous

Convoiteusement, *adv.* covetously

Convoiteu-x, se, *adj. s.* covetous; coveter

Convoitise, *s.f.* covetousness, eager desire, lust

Convol, *s.m.* remarriage

Convoler, *v.n.* to marry again. — *en secondes noces,* to marry a second time

Convoluté, e, Convoluti-f, ve, *adj.* (*nat. hist.*) convolute, convoluted [vulus

Convolve, Convolvulus, *s.m.* (*bot.*) convol-

Convoquer, *v.a.* to convoke; to convene; to call together; to summon; to assemble

Se —, *v.r.* to be convoked, &c.

Convoyer, *v.a.* (*mil., nav.*) to convoy
Convoyeur, *s.m.* (*nav.*) convoy-ship, convoy; commodore; (*post.*) mail-cart driver, mail-driver
Convulser, *v.a.* to convulse. *Se* —, to become *or* be convulsed
Convulsibilité, *s.f.* convulsibility
Convulsible, *adj.* convulsible
Convulsi-f, ve, *adj.* convulsive
Convulsion, *s.f.* convulsion
Convulsioniste, *s.m.f.* convulsionist
Convulsionnaire, *adj. s m.f.* convulsionary
Convulsionner, *v.a. V.* **Convulser**
Convulsivement, *adv.* convulsively
Conyze, Conyse, *s.f.* (*bot.*) conyza, fleabane
Coobligation, *s.f.* joint obligation
Coobligé, e, *s.m.f.* (*law*) coobligor, joint bondsman, party in a bond
Cooli, *s.m* coolie
Coopéra-teur, trice, *s.m.f. adj.* cooperator; cooperating
Coopérati-f, ve, *adj.* cooperative
Coopération, *s.f.* cooperation, concurrence
Coopérer, *v.n.* to cooperate, to concur
Cooptation, *s.f.* cooptation
Coopter, *v.a.* to cooptate
Coordination, *s.f.* coordination, arrangement, disposition
Coordonna-teur, trice, *s.m.f. adj.* coordinator, disposer; coordinating, disposing
Coordonnées, *s.f.pl.* (*geom.*) coordinates
Coordonner, *v.a.* to coordinate, to arrange, to dispose
Copahier, *s.m. V.* **Copayer**
Copahine, *s.f.* (*chem.*) copaivine
Copahu, *s.m.* (*bot., pharm.*) copaiva
Copaïer, *s.m. V.* **Copayer**
Copain, *s.m.* joint sharer; chum, crony, companion; confederate. *Être le — de*, to go halves with; to be ...'s chum, &c.
Copal, *s.m.*, **Copale,** *s.f.* copal
Copaline, *s.f.* (*chem.*) copaline
Copartageant, e, *adj. s.* having a joint share; joint sharer
Copayer, *s.m.* (*bot.*) copaiva-tree
Copeau, *s.m.* chip; shaving. *Vin de* —, rape-wine
Copec, Copeck, *s.m.* copec, copeck, kopek (*Russian coin, about* ½*d.*)
Copermutant, *s.m.* joint sharer in an exchange
Copernicien, ne, *adj. s.* Copernican
Copétitionnaire, *s.m.f.* copetitioner
Copette, *s.f.* inside pan
Cophose, *s.f.* (*med.*) cophosis, deafness
Cophte, *s.m.* Copt (*Egyptian christian*); Coptic (*language*); — *adj.* Coptic
Cophtique, *adj.* Coptic
Copie, *s.f.* copy; image; likeness; match; (*in schools*) paper. — *au net*, fair copy. *A la* —, being copied. *Pour — conforme*, a true copy
Copier, *v.a.* to copy; to transcribe; to imitate; to ape; to mimic, to take off

Se —, *v.r.* to copy each other; to copy *or* repeat oneself; to be always the same; (*of things*) to be copied
Copieusement, *adv.* copiously; (*of feeding*) heartily
Copieu-x, se, *adj.* copious; (*of meals*) hearty
Copiste, *s.m.f.* copier, copyist
Copreneur, *s.m.* (*law*) joint tenant, colessee
Coprévenu, e, *s.m.f. V.* **Coaccusé**
Coprolithe, *s.m.* coprolite
Coprophage, *adj.* (*zool.*) coprophagous; — *s.m.* coprophagan
Copropriétaire, *s.m.f.* coproprietor; cotenant, tenant in common; joint owner *or* proprietor *or* tenant
Copropriété, *s.f.* joint property; tenancy in common; joint tenancy
Coprose, *s.f.* (*bot.*) coprose, corn-poppy
Copte, Coptique. *V.* **Cophte, Cophtique**
Coptée, *s.f.* tolling, toll, stroke
Copter, *v.a.n.* to toll
Copulati-f, ve, *adj.*, **Copulative,** *s.f.* (*gram.*) copulative
Copulation, *s.f.* copulation
Copulativement, *adv.* copulatively
Copule, *s.f.* copula; copulation
Copuler, *v.a.* to copulate
Coq, *s.m.* cock; weather-cock; (*of a ship*) cook. — *-à-l'âne*, cock and bull story, nonsense. — *de bruyère*, grouse, moor-cock, heath-cock. — *d'Inde*, turkey-cock, turkey; (*pers.*) ninny, goose. — *Indien*, (*bird*) curassow. — *des jardins*, (*bot.*) costmary. *Être comme un — en pâte*, to be very comfortable, to live in clover. *Rouge comme un* —, red as a turkey-cock
Coquage, *s.m.* (*slang*) spying, denouncing, splitting
Coqualin, *s.m.* striped squirrel
Coquard, *s.m.* old cock; old beau; fool, ninny, simpleton; mongrel pheasant; (*children's slang*) egg
Coquardeau, *s.m.* fool, simpleton; (*bot.*) wall-flower
Coquâtre, *s.m.* half-gelded cock
Coque, *s.f.* shell; hull; husk; pod; bow (*of ribbon*); cocoon; cockle (*shell-fish*); (*her.*) green nut. — *du Levant*, Indian berry. *V.* **Œuf**
Coquecigrue, *s.f.* sea-stork; sea-locust; silly fool; fiddle-faddle. *La venue des —s*, Tib's eve, latter Lammas, never
Coquelicot, *s.m.* corn-poppy, wild poppy, red poppy; (*colour*) coquelicot; — *adj.* coquelicot
Coqueliner, *v.n.* (*pop.*) to crow; to flirt
Coquelourde, *s.f.* (*bot.*) rose-campion; pasque-flower
Coqueluche, *s.f.* hooping-cough, whooping-cough; (*fig.*) darling (of), (a) great favourite (with); reigning fancy, rage; (*obsolete*) hood, cowl
Coqueluchon, *s.m.* (*obsolete*) cowl, hood
Coquemar, *s.m.* pipkin, skillet, kettle, boiler
Coquer, *v.a.* (*thieves' slang*) to split upon (*denounce*)
Coquereau, *s.m.* (*nav.*) hoy, lighter
Coquerelle, *s.f.*, **Coqueret,** *s.m.* winter-cherry
Coquerico, *s.m. int.* crowing, cock-a-doodle-doo
Coquerie, *s.f.* (*nav.*) cook-house; cook-room, cuddy
Coqueriquer, *v.n.* to crow
Coqueron, *s.m.* (*nav.*) cook-room; forecastle
Coquesigrue, *s.f. V.* **Coquecigrue**
Coquet, te, *adj.* coquettish; fond of dress; pretty, stylish, elegant; smart, spruce, natty, quaint; affected; — *s.m.* ladies' man, beau; (*nav.*) cock-boat; — *s.f.* jilt, flirt, coquette. *Faire le — or la —te*, *V.* **Coqueter**
Coqueter, *v.n.* to play the lady-killer *or* the jilt, to flirt, to coquet; — *v.a.n.* (*nav.*) to paddle, to scull; — *v.a.* (*of birds*) *V.* **Cocher,** *v.a.*
Coquetier, *s.m.* egg-cup; egg-merchant; poultry-salesman, poulterer
Coquettement, *adv.* coquettishly; prettily, stylishly, elegantly; smartly, sprucely, nattily, quaintly; affectedly
Coquetterie, *s.f.* coquetry, coquettishness; jilting; flirtation; love of dress; prettiness, stylishness, style, elegance; smartness, spruceness, quaintness; affectation
Coqueur, *s.m.* (*slang*) police-spy, decoy
†Coquillage, *s.m.* shell; shell-fish; shell-work
†Coquillard, *s.m.* (*min.*) shelly bed; (*pop.*) pilgrim
†Coquille, *s.f.* shell; scollop, scallop; stew, ragout, hash, minced ...; pat (*of butter*); roaster (*for meat*); blister (*on a loaf of bread*); spandrel (*of a staircase*); foot-board (*of a carriage-box*); post (*paper*); (*of a thumb-latch*) *V.* **Poucier;** mould (*for shot*, &c.); (*of a sword*) basket-hilt; (*print.*) wrong letter, misprint; (*fig.*) blunder; hoax; —**s**, *pl.* (*fig.*) goods, wares, articles, things. — *de Saint-Jacques*, scollop, scallop. *Rentrer dans sa* —, to draw in o.'s horns
†Coquiller, *v.a.n.* (*of bread*) to blister
†Coquilleu-x, se, *adj.* shelly
†Coquilli-er, ère, *adj.* shelly, conchiferous; — *s.m.* collection *or* case of shells; shelly ground; — *s.f.* shelly quarry
Coquin, *s.m.* rogue, rascal, knave, scamp, dog; coward; big fellow. *De* —, rascally, knavish
Coquin, e, *adj.* roguish, rascally, knavish, mean; good-for-nothing; idle, easy; lewd; debauched
Coquine, *s.f.* hussy, slut, jade, wretch, bitch
Coquiner, *v.a.* to cheat, to swindle
Coquinerie, *s.f.* knavery, roguery; knavish *or* rascally *or* roguish trick, piece of knavery
Cor, *s.m.* corn (*on the foot*); horn (*mus. instr.*); horn-player, cornist; antler (*of a stag*); —**s**, *pl.* corns; horns; antlers, starts, branches;

(*her.*) horns, attire. *Cerf dix —s*, full-grown stag. — *de basset*, basset-horn. — *de chasse*, hunting-horn. — *d'harmonie*, French horn. *A — et à cri*, with horn and voice; with hue and cry; loudly; vehemently

Coracoïde, *s.f. adj.* (*anat.*) coracoid

†**Corail,** *s.m.* coral. — *des jardins*, (*bot.*) capsicum

†**Corraillé, e,** *adj.* coralled

†**Corailler,** *v.n.* (*of crows*) to croak

†**Coraillère,** *s.f.* coral-fishing boat, coralline

†**Corailleur,** *s.m.* coral-fisher; — *adj.* coral-fishing [coralline

Coraline, *s.f.* coral-fishing boat, coralline; (*bot.*)

Corallaire, *adj.* corallaceous

Corallé, e, *adj.* coralled

Corallifère, *adj.* coralliferous

Coralliforme, *adj.* coralliform

Coralligène, *adj.* coralligenous [coralline

Corallin, e, *adj.*, **Coralline,** *s.f.* (*bot., jewel.*)

Coralloïde, *adj.* coralloid, coralloidal

Coran, *s.m.* Koran, Alcoran

Corbeau, *s.m.* crow; raven; (*astr.*) corvus; (*arch.*) corbel; bracket; (*tech.*) crane, lift; (*ancient navy*) corvus, grapnel; (*pop.*) undertaker's man; (*pop.*) priest, parson, brother of charity

†**Corbeille,** *s.f.* basket; wedding-presents; flower-bed; (*of trees*) clump; (*arch.*) corbeil, corbel; (*fort.*) corbeil; (*in the stock-exchange*) reserved enclosure. — *d'or*, (*bot.*) gold-dust

†**Corbeillée,** *s.f.* basketful

Corbejeau, Corbigeau, *s.m. V.* **Courlis**

†**Corbillard,** *s.m.* hearse; young raven

†**Corbillat, Corbillot,** *s.m.* young raven

†**Corbillon,** *s.m.* small basket; crambo (*game*)

Corbin, e, *s.m.f.* (*obsolete*) crow, raven. *V.* **Bec**

Corbleu, *int.* by the Powers! by Jupiter! by Jove! hang it!

Corbusée, *s.f.* (*bird*) black-neb

Corcelet, *s.m. V.* **Corselet**

Corceron, *s.m.* (*fish.*) float

‡**Corchore,** *s.m.* (*bot.*) corchorus, Jews'-mallow

Cordace, *s.f.* cordace (*ancient dance*)

Cordage, *s.m.* rope; cord; cordage; rigging; measuring (*of wood*) by the cord

Cordat, *s.m.* serge; packing-cloth

Corde, *s.f.* string; line; cord; rope; halter; hanging, gallows; thread (*of cloth*); twist; chord; tone, note. — *à boyau*, catgut. — *à feu*, slow match. *A —s*, with ropes; stringed; string. *Friser la —*, to have a narrow escape. *Passer à fleur de —*, to very nearly fail. *Use jusqu'a la —*, threadbare, hackneyed, stale, worn out; done up

Cordé, e, *part. adj.* corded; twisted; stringy; cordate, cordated, heart-shaped; (*med.*) chordee

Cordeau, *s.m.* line; string. *Tirer au —*, to lay out by rule and line

Cordée, *s.f.* eel-fishing line *or* rope, trawl

Cordeler, *v.a.* to twist

Cordelette, *s.f.* string, small cord

Cordelier, *s.m.* cordelier, Franciscan, grey-friar

Cordelière, *s.f.* Franciscan nun; girdle (of cord), twist, torsel; cord and tassels; border of woodcuts; (*arch.*) twisted fillet

Cordelle, *s.f.* line; tow-line, tow-rope

Corder, *v.a.* to cord; to twist; — *v.n.* (*pop.*) to agree; to fraternize [corded

Se —, *v.r.* to twist; to get stringy; to be

Corderie, *s.f.* ropery, rope-walk; rope-house; rope-making; rope-trade

Cordial, e, *adj.*, **Cordial,** *s.m.* cordial

Cordialement, *adv.* cordially, heartily

Cordialité, *s.f.* cordiality, heartiness

Cordier, *s.m.* rope-maker; one who fishes with a rope and hooks, trawler; (*of violins*, &c.) tail-piece, stop

Cordiérite, *s.f.* (*min.*) cordierite

Cordieu, *int. V.* **Corbleu**

Cordiforme, *adj.* cordiform, heart-shaped

Cordon, *s.m.* twist; string; cord; lace; line; girdle; belt; band; rope, pull; check-string; bow-string; ribbon; border; slip; edge; row; (*arch., fort., mil.*) cordon. — *acoustique*, speaking-pipe. — *bleu*, blue ribbon; knight of the Holy Ghost; first-rate cook; proficient, crack man. — *rouge*, knight of St. Louis. *Tirer le —*, to pull the string *or* the check-string; to open the (house-)door *or* gate; to be a house-porter *or* portress; to pull the bell. *Le —, s'il vous plait!* (open the) door, please!

Cordonnage, *s.m.* (*coin.*) milling; edging

Cordonner, *v.a.* to twist; to braid; to plait; to plat; to entwine; to wreathe; to line; (*coin.*) to mill; to edge

Cordonnerie, *s.f.* shoe-shop; shoe-room; shoe-making; shoe-trade; shoe-manufactory; shoes

Cordonnet, *s.m.* twist; lace; string; braid; netting-silk; (*of coin*) milled edge *or* border

Cordonni-er, ère, *s.m.f.* shoemaker, cord-wainer [cordovan (*leather*)

Cordouan, e, *adj. s.m.f.* Cordovan; — *s.m.*

Cordouanier, *s.m.* cordovan-dresser, cord-wainer

Corée, *s.f.* (*med.*) *V.* **Chorée**

Coréen, ne, *adj. s.* Corean

Corégence, *s.f.* coregency

Corégent, e, *s.m.f.* coregent

Coreligionnaire, *s.m.f.* coreligionist

Coréopsis, *s.m.* (*bot.*) coreopsis, tick-seeded sun-flower [petitioner; coplaintiff

Corequérant, e, *s.m.f.* (*law*) coapplicant; co-

Coresse, *s.f.* salting house (*for herrings*)

Corète, Corette, *s.f. V.* **Corchore**

Corfiote, *adj. s.m.f.* of Corfu; Corfiote, Corfuote

Coriace, *adj.* leathery, tough; close-fisted

Coriacé, e, *adj.* coriaceous

Coriaire, *s.f.* (*bot.*) *V.* **Corroyère**

Coriandre, *s.f.* (*bot.*) coriander

Corindon, *s.m.* (*min.*) corundum

Corinthien, ne, *adj. s.* Corinthian

Corion, *s.m.* (*anat.*) corium

Coriope, *s.m. V.* **Coréopsis**

Coris, *s.m. V.* **Cauris**

Corise, Corize, *s.f.* (*zool.*) water-bug

Corlieu, Corlis, *s.m. V.* **Courlieu**

Corme, *s.f.* (*bot.*) sorb-apple, sorb, service-berry

Cormé, *s.m.* sorb-wine

Cormier, *s.m.* (*bot.*) service-tree

Cormoran, *s.m.* cormorant

Cornac, *s.m.* elephant-driver *or* keeper; keeper of wild beasts; (*jest.*) showman, puffer, bear-leader, chaperon, Mentor

Cornage, *s.m.* roaring (*of horses*)

Cornaline, *s.f.* carnelian *or* cornelian (stone)

Cornard, e, *adj. s.* (*vet.*) roaring; roaring horse *or* mare, roarer

Cornard, *s.m., adj.m.* (*jest.*) fooled husband, cornuto; fooled *or* deceived by o.'s wife, cornute, cornuted

Corne, *s.f.* horn; hoof, outside rind; shoe-horn; corner; dog's-ear; (*nav.*) gaff, crutch, throat; (*bot.*) *V.* **Cornouille**; — *s.m.* cap (*of the doge of Venice*). — *d'abondance*, cornucopia, horn of plenty. — *d'Ammon*, ammonite. — *de cerf*, hartshorn. *A —*, horned; cocked. *A trois —s*, three-cornered. *Ouvrage à —*, (*fort.*) hornwork. *Faire les —s à*, to snap o.'s fingers at. *Faire des —s à un livre*, to dog's-ear a book. *Faire une — au feuillet* or *à la page*, to turn down the leaf. *Faire une — à une carte de visite*, to turn down the corner of a visiting card. *Montrer les —s*, to show o.'s teeth

Corné, e, *adj.* horny; — *part. V.* **Corner**

Corneau, *s.m.* cross between a mastiff and a hound

Cornée, *s.f.* (*anat.*) cornea

Cornéenne, *s.f.* (*min.*) horn-stone, chert [rook

†**Corneillard,** *s.m.* young crow *or* jackdaw *or*

†**Corneille,** *s.f.* crow; jackdaw, daw; rook; (*bot.*) *V.* **Lysimachie.** *Comme une — qui abat des noix*, headlong, rashly, blindly, thoughtlessly, at random, slapdash

†**Corneillon,** *s.m. V.* **Corneillard**

Cornéite, *s.f.* (*med.*) corneitis

Cornélien, ne, *adj.* of Corneille (*Pierre Corneille, the French dramatist*), in the style of Corneille; about Corneille [roaring (*of a pipe*)

Cornement, *s.m.* tingling, noise (*in the ears*);

Cornemuse, *s.f.* bagpipe

Cornemuseur, *s.m.* bagpiper
Cornéole, *s.f.* (*bot.*) green-broom, dyer's-weed
Corner, *v.n.* to blow a horn; to speak in an ear-trumpet; to din; (*of the ears*) to tingle; (*of horses*, &c.) to roar; (*pop.*) to stink; — *v.a.* to trumpet about, to trumpet; to call (*with a horn*); to din; to gore (*with its horns*); to dog's-ear, to turn down, to turn down the corner of
Se —, *v.r.* to gore each other; to become horny
Cornet, *s.m.* horn, cornet (*mus. instr.*); ear-trumpet; corneter (*player*); cone, cap, extinguisher, conical vase *or* &c.; paper cone, paper cup *or* cap, screw, paper; rolled wafer; dice-box; ink-horn; (*game*) cup and shuttlecock, coronella cup; (*anat.*) turbinated *or* spongy bone; (*mollusc*) *V.* **Calmar;** (*nav.*) case (*of a mast*); (*pop.*) stomach, inside, bread-basket. — *acoustique*, ear-trumpet, hearing-trumpet, ear-cornet. — *à bouquin*, cowherd's horn. — *à pistons*, cornopean
Cornetier, *s.m.* horn-worker
Cornette, *s.f.* (*nav.*) broad pendant; (*bot.*) cow-wheat; (*mas.*) corner-clamp; (*jest.*) wife deceived by her husband; (*obsolete*) (female's) night *or* morning cap, mob-cap, cornet; (*obsolete*) cornet (*company of cavalry, standard*); (*obsolete*) cornetcy; — *s.m.* (*obsolete*) cornet (*officer*)
Corneu-r, se, *s.m.f. adj.* horn-blower; (*pop.*) blubberer, bawler, squaller; (*of horses*) *V.* **Cornard, e,** *adj.s.*
Corniche, *s.f.* (*arch.*) cornice
Cornichon, *s.m.* cornicle, little horn; horn-tip; gherkin; (*fam.*) greenhorn, simpleton, flat, muff
Cornicule, *s.f.* cornicle, little horn
Corniculé, e, *adj.* corniculate, horned
Corni-er, ère, *adj.* at *or* of the corner, corner; angle; — *s.m.* (*bot.*) *V.* **Cornouiller;** — *s.f.* corner-gutter *or* channel; corner-iron, angle-iron; T iron; (*nav.*) fashion-piece
Cornifle, *s.f.* (*bot.*) horn-wort
Corniforme, *adj.* corniform
Cornigère, *adj.* cornigerous
†**Cornillat, Cornillon,** *s.m. V.* **Corneillard**
Corniste, *s.m.* cornist, horn-player
†**Cornouille,** *s.f.* (*bot.*) cornel, cornelian cherry, dog-berry
†**Cornouiller,** *s.m.* (*bot.*) cornel-tree, cornelian-tree, dog-wood
Cornu, e, *adj.* horned; cornute, cornuted; angular; cornered; absurd, extravagant, wild, mad
Cornue, *s.f.* (*chem.*) retort
Cornuet, *s.m.* three-cornered tart, puff
Cornupède, *adj.* horn-foot, hoofed; — *s.m.* hoofed animal
Corollaire, *s.m.* corollary
Corolle, *s.f.* (*bot.*) corolla
Coronaire, *adj.* (*anat.*) coronary
Coronal, e, *adj.*, **Coronal,** *s.m.* (*anat.*) coronal; coronal bone
Coroner, *s.m.* coroner (*in England and America*)
Coronet, *s.m.* (*English*) coronet
Coroniforme, *adj.* coroniform
†**Coronille,** *s.f.* (*bot.*) coronilla, scorpion-senna
Coronoïde, *adj.* (*anat.*) coronoid
Coronope, *s.m.* (*bot.*) wart-cress; crow's-foot
Corossol, *s.m.* (*bot.*) sour sop (*fruit*)
Corossolier, *s.m.* (*bot.*) sour sop (*tree*)
Corozo, *s.m.* corozo, corrozzo, corosso (*vegetable ivory*)
Corporal, *s.m.* (*Cath. rel.*) corporal
Corporalité, *s.f.* corporality, corporeality
Corporati-f, ve, *adj.* corporate
Corporation, *s.f.* corporation
Corporéité, *s.f.* corporeity
Corporel, le, *adj.* corporal; corporeal; bodily; material
Corporellement, *adv.* corporally; corporeally; bodily; materially
Corporification, Corporisation, *s.f.* corporification, embodiment
Corporifier, Corporiser, *v.a.* to corporify, to embody
Corps, *s.m.* body; matter; substance; thickness, consistence; solidity; strength, vigour; frame; figure, shape; dead body, corpse; person; fellow; creature; corporation; corps; staff; college; society, company; brigade; force; mass, collection; block; shell; case; hull; barrel; stock; shank; main point, main thing; emblem; (*print.*) depth. — *morts*, (*pl.*) dead bodies; (*nav.*) moorings. — *à* —, hand to hand. — *d'armée*, main body of troops, main body; division, corps; force. — *de bataille*, (*mil.*) main body, (*nav.*) centre. — *de bâtiment* or *de logis*, main building; detached building; part of a building, suite of rooms. — *de bâtiments*, block of buildings. — *de cheminée*, chimney stack; chimney. — *de délit*, (*law*) main proof, main evidence, substance of the offence *or* crime, material evidence, "corpus delicti." — *d'état* or *de métier*, corporation, trade; profession. — *de fichu*, &c. *V.* **Fichu,** &c. — *de garde* [*See below*]. — *de santé*, medical staff. — *et biens*, (*nav.*) crew and cargo; (*law*) person and property; (from) bed and board, "(a) mensâ et thoro." *Condamnation par* —, sentence of imprisonment. *Garde-* —, hand-rail. *Garde du* —, life-guard, body-guard. — *de garde*, guard; guard-house, military post; guard-room; station-house. *A* — *perdu*, with might and main; with heart and soul; headlong; desperately. *A son* — *défendant*, against o.'s will, reluctantly; in self-defence. *Par* —, (*law*) in person, personally; of *or* for arrest, of *or* for *or* to imprisonment; (*s.m.*) arrest, imprisonment. *Faire* —, to form one body; to be connected *or* joined, to unite. *Faire* — *neuf*, to take a new (*or* a fresh) lease of life. *Passer sur le* — *à* or *de*, to pass over the body of; to run over; (*fig.*) to trample *or* bear down, to rout; (*fig.*) to pass over the head of. *Prendre du* —, to get fat *or* stout; to set. *Se prendre* — *à* —, to wrestle. — *-Dieu!* *V.* **Corbleu**
Corpulence, *s.f.* corpulence, corpulency, stoutness; size
Corpulent, e, *adj.* corpulent, stout
Corpusculaire, *adj.* corpuscular
Corpuscule, *s.m.* corpuscule, corpuscle
Corpusculiste, *s.m.* corpuscularian
Correct, e, *adj.* correct; accurate; right
Correctement, *adv.* correctly; accurately; rightly, right
Correc-teur, trice, *s.m.f.* corrector; correctress; punisher; (printer's) reader; — *adj.* correcting; punishing
Correcti-f, ve, *adj.*, **Correctif,** *s.m.* corrective
Correction, *s.f.* correction; correctness, accuracy; reading, correcting
Correctionnel, le, *adj.* (*law*) relating to misdemeanours; for the trial of misdemeanours; correctional, reformatory; punishable by fine *or* imprisonment. *Tribunal de police* —*le*, police-court. *La* —*le*, *s.f.* (*pop.*) the police-court *or* courts, the magistrate, the beak
Correctionnellement, *adv.* for misdemeanour *or* misdemeanours; relative to misdemeanours; as a misdemeanour; correctionally; before the magistrate
Correctivement, *adv.* correctively
Corrégidor, *s.m.* corregidor (*Spanish magistrate*)
Corrélati-f, ve, *adj.*, **Corrélatif,** *s.m.* correlative
Corrélation, *s.f.* correlation
Corrélativement, *adv.* correlatively
Correspondance, *s.f.* correspondence; communication; intercourse; connection; relation; conformity; harmony; reciprocity, reciprocation, return; correspondence omnibus; railway omnibus; correspondence (omnibus) ticket. *Service de* —, (*post.*) cross-post
Correspondant, e, *adj. s.* corresponding; correspondent; representative of parents, guardian; reporter; informant
Correspondre, *v.n.*, **Se** —, *v.r.* to correspond; to communicate; to answer; to agree; to suit
Corridor, *s.m.* corridor, passage, gallery, gangway
Corrigé, *s.m.* corrected copy; (*of books*) key
Corriger, *v.a.* to correct; to amend; to improve; to repair; to mend; to redress; to rectify; to set right; to restore; to refresh; to reclaim; to redeem; to reform; to punish, to chastise; to reprehend, to reprimand; to read, to revise; to cure; to rid; to temper; to allay; to soften

Se —, *v.r.* to correct oneself *or* each other; to amend; to mend; to reform; to improve; to get rid (of); to get *or* be cured, to be got rid of; to be corrected *or* &c.
Corrigeur, *s.m.* corrector
Corrigibilité, *s.f.* corrigibility, corrigibleness
Corrigible, *adj.* corrigible
Corrigiole, *s.f.* (*bot.*) strap-wort [corroborant
Corroborant, e, *adj.*, **Corroborant,** *s.m.*
Corroborati-f, ve, *adj.*, **Corroboratif,** *s.m.* corroborative [ening
Corroboration, *s.f.* corroboration; strength-
Corroborer, *v.a.* to corroborate; to strengthen
Corrodant, e, *adj.* corroding; — *s.m.* corrodent
Corroder, *v.a.* to corrode. *Se* —, to be corroded
Corrodible, *adj.* corrodible
Corroi, *s.m.* (*of leather*) currying; (*mas.*) claying, puddling; puddle; (*tech.*) tenter; (*nav.*) *V.* **Courai**
Corroierie, *s.f.* currier's shop; currying
Corrompre, *v.a.* to corrupt; to taint; to vitiate; to deprave; to pervert; to spoil; to mar; to seduce; to debauch; to bribe; (*tech.*) to work [taint; to fester; to spoil
Se —, *v.r.* to become corrupt *or* vitiated; to
Corrompu, e, *part. adj.* corrupted, &c. (*V.* **Corrompre**); corrupt; putrid; rotten; unsound; dissolute
Corrosi-f, ve, *adj.*, **Corrosif,** *s.m.* corrosive
Corrosion, *s.f.* corrosion
Corrosiveté, *s.f.* corrosiveness
Corroyage, *s.m.* currying, &c. (*V.* **Corroyer,** *v.a.*)
Corroyer, *v.a.* to curry; to beat up; to puddle; to hammer, to forge; to weld; to plane; to tenter [**Roudou**
Corroyer, *s.m.*, **Corroyère,** *s.f.* (*bot.*) *V.*
Corroyerie, *s.f.* *V.* **Corroierie**
Corroyeur, *s.m.* currier
Corrude, *s.f.* wild asparagus
Corruga-teur, trice, *adj.* (*anat.*) corrugent; — *s.m.* (*anat.*) corrugator
Corrugation, *s.f.* corrugation, wrinkling
Corruguer, *v.a.*, **Se** —, *v.r.* to corrugate, to wrinkle
Corrup-teur, trice, *s.m.f.* corrupter; corruptress; spoiler; perverter; seducer; briber; — *adj.* corrupting; infectious; perverting
Corruptibilité, *s.f.* corruptibility
Corruptible, *adj.* corruptible
Corruption, *s.f.* corruption; taint; depravation, depravity; defilement; perversion; spoil-
Corrupti-f, ve, *adj.* corruptive [ing; bribery
Corsac, *s.m.* (*zool.*) corsac
Corsage, *s.m.* bust; chest; body — *de dessous*, petticoat-body, bodice
Corsaire, *s.m.* corsair; privateer; privateersman; captain of a privateer; (*fig.*) shark, Jew. *A — — et demi*, diamond cut diamond; tit for tat; the biter bit; set a thief to catch a thief
Corse, *adj. s.m.f.* Corsican; — *s.f.* Corsican woman *or* lady *or* girl, Corsican; — (*La*), *s.f.* Corsica; (the) Corsican fashion
Corsé, e, *adj.* rich, having body *or* good body, full-bodied; succulent; thick; stout; substantial; plentiful, copious
Corselet, *s.m.* corselet, thorax; bodice, spencer
Corser, *v.a.* (*of stays*) to fit; (*fig.*) to thicken; to strengthen; to complicate
Se —, *v.r.* to put o.'s stays on; (*fig.*) to thicken; to acquire strength, to get strong; to become complicated *or* serious
Corseron, *s.m.* (*fish.*) float
Corset, *s.m.* stays, pair of stays, corset; bodice; spencer; bandage for the chest; tree-guard
Corseti-er, ère, *s.m.f.* stay-maker, corset-maker, bodice-maker
Corsin, *s.m.* (*obsolete*) usurer, money-dealer
Cortége, *s.m.* retinue, train; attendants; company; procession; troop, crowd; pomp, pageant. *En grand* —, in state. *Faire — à*, to attend
Cortès, *s.f.pl.* cortes (*Spanish parliament*)
Cortical, e, *adj.* (*bot.*, *anat.*) cortical
Cortiqueu-x, se, *adj.* (*bot.*) corticose
Corton, *s.m.* corton (wine)
Coruscation, *s.f.* (*phys.*) coruscation
Corve, *s.m.* corve (*Dutch fishing-boat*)
Corvéable, *adj.* (*feud.*) liable to forced labour, liable to contribution in forced labour; — *s.m.* one liable to ditto
Corvée, *s.f.* (*feud.*) statute-labour, duty-service, forced labour; (*fig.*) extra duty *or* labour; (*mil.*) fatigue-duty, fatigue; (*mil.*) fatigue-party; (*fam.*) drudgery; toil; unpleasant task, troublesome job, bore
Corvéieur, Corveyeur, *s.m.* (*feud.*) statute-labourer; (*mil.*) man on fatigue-duty
Corvette, *s.f.* (*nav.*) corvette, sloop of war
Corvin, e, *adj.* corvine
Corybante, *s.m.* (*in antiquity*) corybant
Corybantique, *adj.* corybantic
Corybantisme, *s.m.* (*old med.*) corybantiasm
Corymbe, *s.m.* (*bot.*) corymb; (*sculp.*, *and of hair, antiquated*) corymbus
Corymbé, e, *adj.* (*bot.*) corymbiate, corymbiated
Corymbeu-x, se, *adj.* (*bot.*) corymbose
Corymbifère, *adj.* (*bot.*) corymbiferous; — *s.f.* corymbiferous plant [palm
Coryphe, *s.m.* (*bot.*) corypha, talipot-tree, fan-
Coryphée, *s.m.* corypheus, coryphæus; chorus-master; leader, leading man, chief, principal man, hero, don, cock, star
Coryphène, *s.m.* (*fish*) coryphene, dolphin, razor-fish [the head
Coryza, Coryse, *s.m.* (*med.*) coryza, cold in
Cosaque, *s.m.* Cossack; — *s.f.* Cossack dance; Cossack fashion [thing, brutality
Cosaquerie, *s.f.* raid, foray; savage act, brutal
Coscossons, Coscotons, *s.m.pl.* *V.* **Cous-**
Cosécante, *s.f.* (*geom.*) cosecant [**cous**
†**Coseigneur,** *s.m.* joint lord
†**Coseigneurie,** *s.f.* joint lordship
†**Cosignataire,** *s.m.f. adj.* cosigner; cosigna-
Cosinus, *s.m.* (*geom.*) cosine [tary
Cosmétique, *adj.m.f.*, *s.m.* cosmetic; — *s.f.* use of cosmetics
Cosm-ique, -iquement. *V.* page 3, § 1
Cosmo-gonie, -gonique, -goniquement, -graphie, -graphique, -logie, -logique, -logiste, -métrie, &c. *V.* page 3, § 1
Cosmographe, *s.m.* cosmographer [politan
Cosmopolite, *s.m.f. adj.* cosmopolite; cosmo-
Cosmopolitisme, *s.m.* cosmopolitism
Cosmorama, *s.m.* cosmorama
Cosmoramique, *adj.* cosmoramic
Cosmos, *s.m.* Cosmos (*Humboldt's work*)
Coss, *s.m.* coss (*Indian road-measure*)
Cossat, *s.m.* pods, shells, husks, refuse
Cosse, *s.f.* pod, shell, husk, cod; (*nav.*) thimble; — *s.m* (*zool.*) cossus, goat-moth; (*pop.*) weevil; (*Indian measure*) *V.* **Coss**
Cosser, *v.n.* (*of rams*) to butt
Cosson, *s.m.* weevil; wood-worm; vine-shoot
Cossu, e, *adj.* podded, husky; rich, substantial, wealthy, warm; smart; whapping
Costal, e, *adj.* costal
Costières, *s.f.pl.* (*theat.*) grooves (*for the side-lights*). *Tomber dans les* —, to be lost or stolen at the theatre
Costume, *s.m.* costume; dress; garb; uniform; manners, habits. *Grand* —, full dress
Costumer, *v.a.* to dress in a fancy dress, to dress up *or* out, to dress
Se —, *v.r.* to put on a fancy dress, to dress oneself up, to dress (as), to wear the costume *or* dress (of) [keeper
Costumi-er, ère, *s.m.f.* costumier; wardrobe-
Costus, *s.m.* (*bot.*, *pharm.*) costus
Cotangente, *s.f.* (*geom.*) cotangent
Cotarnine, *s.f.* (*chem.*) cotarnine
Cotation, *s.f.* quotation
Cote, *s.f.* letter, number, figure, mark; quota, share; contribution; imposition; assessment; rating; quotation, price; price-list — *mal taillée*, settlement in the lump

Côte, *s.f.* rib; hill; slope; coast; shore, sea-shore; district; stem; (*of fruit*) slice; (*agr.*) edge. —*s découvertes*, (*butch.*) chuck-ribs. — *de fer*, (*hist.*) ironside. — *à* —, side by side. *A* —*s*, ribbed; corded. *A la* —, ashore. *Fausses* —*s*, short ribs. *Faire* —, to run ashore. — **-du-Rhône**, *s.m.* côte-du-Rhône (wine). — **-rôtie**, [*s.m.* côte-rôtie (wine)

Coté, e, *part. of* **Coter**

Côté, *s.m.* side; way; part, quarter; direction; point; flank. — *de l'endroit*, right side. — *de l'envers*, wrong side. *A* —, by, by the side, near, not far off; beside; beside the mark; next; close (to); on one side; on a par (with); close by; close by here; by it, near it, next to it; by them, near them, next to them. *Bas* —, *V.* **Bas-côté.** *D'à-* —, adjoining; next; next to it *or* them; next house; next door; close by. *De* —, side; sideways; aside; by; aslant; askance; on one side; to oneself. *De* — *et d'autre*, on both sides; in every direction; here and there; up and down; about. *De ce* — *-ci*, on this side; this way. *De ce* — *-là*, on that side; that way; from that quarter; in that respect; on that score. *Des deux* —*s*, on both sides. *De l'autre* —, on the other side; over the way; in the other room; on the other hand. *De mon* (*ton*, &c.) —, on my (thy, &c.) side; for *or* on my (thy, &c.) part; my (thy, &c.) way; towards me (thee, &c.); from me (thee, &c.); by myself (thyself, &c.). *De tout* —, *de tous*—*s*, on all sides; in every direction; everywhere; from all quarters. *Du* — *de*, on the side *or* part of; on the score of; about; towards; from. *D'un* —, on one side; on the one hand; one way. *Donner à* —, to miss the mark, to miss it

Coteau, *s.m.* hillock; hill; rising ground, rise; hill-side, slope; —**x,** *pl.* hillocks, &c.; (*obsolete*) epicure, gastronomist, good liver, judge of wines [and good living

Côtelé, e, *adj.* ribbed

Côtelette, *s.f.* chop; cutlet

Cotenanci-er, ère, *s.m.f.* cotenant

Cotentin (Le), *s.m.* Cotentin (*formerly, a part of Lower Normandy*); —, **e,** *s.m.f. adj.* native of Cotentin, of *or* from Cotentin

Cotepalis, *s.m.* (*obsolete*) mohair

Coter, *v.a.* to letter, to number; to mark; to fix; to price; to quote; to assess; to rate; to [tax; to allege

Se —, *v.r.* to be quoted *or* &c.

Cotereau, *s.m.* (*Fr. hist.*) cotereau (*brigand*)

Coterie, *s.f.* coterie, set, clan; circle; society; club; (*pop.*) fellow-workman, mate

Cothurne, *s.m.* buskin, cothurn; tragedy

Cothurné, e, *adj.* buskined, cothurnated

Cotice, *s.f.* (*her.*) cotice, cotise, cottise, cost

Coticé, e, *adj.* (*her.*) coticed, cotised, cottised

Côti-er, ère, *adj.* coasting, coast; (*of rivers*) running along (...); — *s.m.* coast-pilot; coaster; — *s.f.* (*hort.*) shelving bed; (*nav.*) range of coast, coast

†**Cotignac,** *s.m.* quince preserve *or* marmalade

†**Cotignelle,** *s.f.* quince wine

†**Cotillon,** *s.m.* petticoat, under-petticoat; girls, women; cotillon (*dance, tune*)

Cotin, *s.m.* (*bot.*) *V.* **Fustet**

Cotinga, *s.m.* (*bird*) cotinga, chatterer

Cotir, *v.a.* (*pop.*) to bruise *or* damage (*fruit*)

Se —, *v.r.* to become bruised, to be damaged

Cotisation, *s.f.* clubbing; subscription; raising a fund by collection *or* subscription; fund raised by ditto; quota, share, contribution; assessment, rating

Cotiser, *v.a.* to assess, to rate

Se —, *v.r.* to get up a subscription, to club together, to join; to subscribe, to contribute

Cotissure, *s.f.* (*pop.*) (*of fruit*) bruising, bruise, damage

Coton, *s.m.* cotton; (*fig.*) down; softness; delicacy; indulgence; (*pop.*) trouble, bother, row, scuffle. — *plat*, darning-cotton. — *-poudre*, gun-cotton. *Filer* or *jeter un mauvais* (or *un vilain*) —, to be going on in a bad way, to be going to the dogs; to be a bad life; to be a bad sign. *Élever dans du* —, to bring up delicately. *Mettre dans du* —, to coddle, to nurse up; to indulge; to take great care of, to put in lavender

Cotonéastre, *s.m.* (*bot.*) cotoneaster

Cotonnade, *s.f.* cotton cloth, cotton stuff; cotton check; cotton goods

Cotonné, é, *part. adj.* wadded, padded; cottony; downy; (*of hair*) woolly; (*of a sail*) worn out

Cotonner, *v.a.* to stuff with cotton, to wad, to pad; to cover with down; — *v.n.*, **Se** —, *v.r.* to cotton; to be covered with down, to become (*or* get) downy; to become (*or* get) mealy

Cotonnerie, *s.f.* cotton-growing; cotton-plantation; cotton-dressing establishment

Cotonneu-x, se, *adj.* cottony; downy; mealy; (*of style*) spun out, long-spun, loose, lax, diffuse

Cotonni-er, ère, *adj.* cotton; cotton-growing; — *s.m.* cotton-plant *or* tree; manufacturer of cotton stuffs; — *s.f.* (*bot.*) cotton-rose, cotton-[weed, cudweed

Cotonnine, *s.f.* cotton canvas

Côtoyer, *v.a.n.* to coast; to coast along; to go along the bank of; to go along *or* at the side of, to walk by the side of, to go *or* be side by side with; to march on the flank of; to skirt; to border upon; to touch upon; to accompany; to keep close to the shore

Cotre, *s.m.* (*nav.*) cutter

Cotret, *s.m.* small fagot, bundle of wood; stick; (*pop.*) thin shank, shank, stump. *Huile de* —, [stirrup-oil, drubbing

Cottage, *s.m.* cottage

Cottager, *s.m.* cottager

Cotte, *s.f.* petticoat; jacket; coat; (*workman's*) overalls (*trousers*); gut *or* skin (*of a sausage*). — *d'armes*, coat of arms; tabard. — *de mailles*, coat of mail. — *morte*, estate (*of a deceased monk*) [*scorpion*, sea-scorpion

Cotte, *s.m.* (*fish*) bull-head, father-lasher. —

Cottiennes, *adj.f.pl.* (*geogr.*) Cottian (*Alps*)

Cotu-teur, trice, *s.m.f.* joint guardian *or* trustee, coguardian, cotrustee

Cotyle, *s.f.* (*anat.*) cotyla, cotyle

Cotylédon, *s.m.* (*anat., bot.*) cotyledon

Cotylédonaire, *adj.* (*bot.*) cotyledonal

Cotylédoné, e, *adj.* (*bot.*) cotyledonous

Cotylet, Cotylier, *s.m.* (*bot.*) navel-wort

Cotyloïde, *adj.* (*anat.*) cotyloid

Cou, *s.m.* neck. *Couper le* — *à* ..., to cut ...'s head off. — **-de-pied,** *s.m.* instep

Couac, *s.m.* quack (*sound*); (*pop.*) priest, parson

Couagga, *s.m.* (*zool.*) quagga

Couard, e, *s.m.f. adj.* coward; cowardly

Couardement, *adv.* in a cowardly manner, [cowardly

Couardise, *s.f.* cowardice

Coucal, *s.m.* (*bird*) pheasant-cuckoo

Couchage, *s.m.* laying; sleeping; bedding; night's lodging, bed; providing beds

Couchant, e, *adj.* lying; setting; (*her.*) couchant; — *s.m.* west; decline, wane

Couche, *s.f.* couch; bed; bedstead; marriage, confinement; lying-in; child-bed; delivery; birth; child's linen, napkin, wrapper, clout, pilch; hot-bed; coat, coating; layer; stratum; (*at play*) lay, stake; (*of a gun-butt*) bend (*from heel to toe*); (*pop.*) fuddle, drop too much. — *sourde*, (*hort.*) forcing-pit. *Fausse* —, miscarriage; (*vulgar*) exoneirosis. *Plaque de* —, (*of a gun-butt*) heel-plate. *Être en* —*s* or *en* —, *Faire ses* —*s*, to be confined, to lie in

Couché, e, *part. adj.* laid, &c. (*V.* **Coucher,** *v.a.* & *v.n.*); lying down; lying; lolling; recumbent; on the side; in bed; gone to bed; set; (*her.*) couché; — *s.m.* (*obsolete spelling*) *V.* **Coucher,** *s.m.* *Être bien* or *mal* —, to have a good *or* bad bed, to be comfortable *or* uncomfortable (*in a bed*) [lodging, bed

Couchée, *s.f.* resting-place; night's lodging,

Coucher, *v.a.* to lay; to lay down; to lay low, to strike down; to lay flat; to lay on the side; to lodge (*corn*, &c.); to slope, to incline; to bend; to lay on; to place; to put to bed; to undress; to give a bed to; to put down (in writing).

to take down, to write down, to write, to inscribe, to enter, to insert; to stake; — *v.n.* to lie, to lie down; to sleep; to pass the night. *A* —, a resting-place, a bed

Se —, *v.r.* to lie, to lie down; to loll; to lie flat; (*of corn*, &c.) to lodge; to go to bed; to get into bed; to set, to go down. *Aller se* —, to go to bed; to be off, to go along, to go to Bath *or* to Jericho. *Se — comme les poules*, to go to bed with the birds (*very early*)

Coucher, *s.m.* bed-time; going to bed; bedding; bed; resting-place; night's lodging; setting (*of the sun*, &c.); lying down, position; rest, sleep; couchee (*formerly*, the king's company about his bed-time). *Petit* —, (*formerly*, the king's select and familiar circle while he was undressing and getting into bed)

Coucherie, *s.f.* carnal intercourse *or* connection, wenching [bed; crib; berth

Couchette, *s.f.* bedstead; small bed, little bed,

Coucheu-r, se, *s.m.f.* bed-fellow, sleeping partner. *Mauvais* —, (*fig.*) disagreeable fellow, ugly customer, cross-patch. *Bon* —, (*fig., little used*) good easy sort of a fellow

Couchis, *s.m.* layer; stratum; bolster

Couci-couci, *adv.* so so, middling, indifferently

Coucou, *s.m.* cuckoo; cuckoo-clock; wooden clock, Dutch clock; cuckoo-toy; old-fashioned coach *or* omnibus; (*bot.*) cowslip; daffodil; barren strawberry-plant; (*pop.*) ticker. *Faire* —, (*children's slang*) to play at hide and seek

Coucouer, Coucouler, *v.n.* (*of cuckoos*) to cuculate, to call

Coude, *s.m.* elbow; turning, turn; bend; angle; neck (*of a bayonet*); elbow-pipe; (*mach.*) knee. *Lever* or *hausser le* —, to tipple; to drink hard, to fuddle. — **-pied,** *s.m.* *V.* **Cou-de-pied**

Coudé, e, *adj.* bent, kneed, cranked

Coudée, *s.f.* cubit; arm's length. —*s franches*, elbow-room; full play; freedom, liberty

Couder, *v.a.* to bend; to make an elbow to

Se —, *v.r.* to form an elbow

Coudière, *s.f.* elbow-piece [dling

Coudoiement, *s.m.* elbowing; jostling; hud-

Coudoir, *s.m.* *V.* **Accoudoir**

Coudoyer, *v.a.* to elbow; to jostle; to huddle

Coudraie, *s.f.* hazel-copse; grove

Coudran, Coudranner. *V.* **Goudron,**

Coudre, *s.m.* *V.* **Coudrier** [**Goudronner**

Coudre, *v.a.n.* to sew; to sew up; to stitch; to tack, to unite, to join, to add; to connect

Se —, *v.r.* to be sewed *or* &c.

Coudrement, *s.m.* (*of leather*) soaking, washing

Coudrer, *v.a.* to soak, to wash (*leather*)

Coudrette, *s.f.* *V.* **Coudraie**

Coudrier, *s.m.* nut-tree, hazel-tree, hazel;

Coudure, *s.f.* bending, bend [filbert-tree

Couenne, *s.f.* pig's skin; rind *or* sward (*of bacon*); porpoise-skin; (*med.*) birth-mark, mother-spot, mole, nævus; (*med.*) skin, buff, buffy-coat; (*pop.*) flesh; (*pop.*) milksop; spoony, flat, muff; — *adj.* (*pop.*) silly, simple, stupid, spoony; —**s,** *s.f.pl.* (*pop.*) chops (*of a person*), chaps

Couenneu-x, se, *adj.* (*med.*) buffy. *V.* **Angine**

Couette, *s.f.* little tail; tuft; sea-gull; (*obsolete*) feather-bed; —**s,** *pl.* (*nav.*) *V.* **Coites**

Couffe, Couffle, *s.m.* frail, basket [gourd

Cougourde, Cougourdette, *s.f.* (*bot.*) bottle-

Couguar, Couguard, *s.m.* (*zool.*) cougar

†**Couillard,** *s.m.* (*nav.*) spilling-line

†**Couillon, ne,** *s.m.f.* (*pop.*) coward, dastard, poltroon, funky fellow; milksop; lazy-bones; simpleton, fool, spoony; — *adj.* cowardly; spoony

†**Couillonnade,** *s.f.* (*pop.*) gammon, humbug, fudge, nonsense, rubbish, bosh; trick, bad joke; cowardice

†**Couillonner,** *v.a.n.* (*pop.*) to gammon, to humbug, to bamboozle; to bother, to bore; to joke, to jest; to show the white feather; to funk; to shirk it, to back out

†**Couillonnerie,** *s.f.* (*pop.*) *V.* **Couillonnade**

Coulage, *s.m.* leakage; wasting, waste; running; guttering; melting; casting; straining; scalding (*of linen*)

Coulamment, *adv.* fluently, freely, easily

Coulant, e, *adj.* flowing; fluent; running; liquid; soft; smooth; easy; easy to deal with, accommodating; indulgent, lenient, tolerant; insinuating; off-hand; (*of knots*) running, slip

Coulant, *s.m.* slide; (*obsolete*) diamond and cross (*round the neck*); (*of a lamp*) chimney-holder; (*hort.*) creeping stalk; (*of strawberries*) runner

Coule, *s.f.* (*obsolete*) cowl; (*fam.*) waste, servants' profits. *Être à la* —, (*fam.*) to look sharp after the servants *or* waiters; (*pop.*) to be easy to deal with, to be accommodating; (*pop.*) to be up to snuff

Coulé, *s.m.* cast; dead colour; (*dancing*) slide; (*mus.*) slur; (*billiards*) following-stroke

Coulé, e, *part. adj.* strained, &c. (*V.* **Couler**); gone; (*of fruit*, &c.) abortive, stunted, come to nothing; (*of handwriting*) running

Coulée, *s.f.* running, flowing, flow; (*of writing*) running-hand; (*metal.*) casting; tapping; (*hunt.*) track, path; (*hort.*) slip (*of turf*); (*nav.*) fair curve [*d'épée*, (*fenc.*) glissade

Coulement, *s.m.* running, flow; abortion. —

Coulequin, *s.m.* *V.* **Cécropie**

Couler, *v.n.* to flow; to run; to trickle, to trickle down, to stream; to glide; to leak; to slip; to slide; to gutter; to melt; to be shed *or* spilt; to pass away; (*of fruit*, &c.) not to set, to prove *or* be abortive, to drop, to fall off, to fail; (*at billiards*) to make the ball follow; — *v.a.* to strain; to scald (*linen*); to cast; to pour; to slip; to foist; to edge in, to whisper; to insinuate; to spend, to pass (*time*); to settle; to exhaust; to run down; to sink; to ruin, to swamp, to do up, to do for; to do away with; (*dancing*) to glide over; (*mus.*) to tie, to slur; — *bas* or *à fond*, to sink; to run down; to ruin; to wind up; to settle; to exhaust. — *plein*, (*of metals*) to cast solid. *En* — *à*, to put upon, to hoax. *Faire* —, to cause to flow *or* &c.; to shed, to spill

Se —, *v.r.* to slip; to slide; to glide; to creep; to find its way; to swamp oneself; to be cast

Couleur, *s.f.* colour; colouring; hue; tint, tinge; paint; dye; suit (*at cards*); aspect; appearance; pretence; excuse; show; sham; fib, story; favour (*ribbon*); livery; complexion; blush, flush; (*adject.*) coloured. — *locale*, local colour *or* colouring, characteristicalness, peculiarities (*of dress or manners*, &c.); appearance *or* look of reality. — *de rose*, rose-colour; rose-coloured; (*fig.*) bright colours, bright side of things; bright and pleasant; on the bright side, under an aspect of beauty and attractiveness. *De* —, of colour; coloured; stained; (*of lamps*) variegated. *Mettre en* —, to colour, to paint, to stain. *Monter une* — *à*, *faire voir des* —*s à*, to put upon, to impose upon. *Prendre* —, (*things*) to assume a character, to take a turn; (*pers.*) to take a side

Couleuvre, *s.f.* (common) snake; (*fam.*) vexation, mortification, humiliation, bitter pill

Couleuvreau, *s.m.* young snake

Couleuvrée, *s.f.* (*bot.*) wild bryony

Couleuvrin, e, *adj.* colubrine

Couleuvrine, Coulevrine, *s.f.* culverin

Couli, *s.m.* coolie

Coulinage, *s.m.* singeing (*of trees*)

Coulis, *s.m.* (*cook.*) cullis; jelly; gravy soup; (*build.*) grout, solder [(*pop.*) noiseless wind

Coulis, *adj.m.* *Vent* —, draught of air, air;

Coulisse, *s.f.* groove; running-string; string-case; slip-board; slide; sliding tray, tray; (*theat.*) side-scene, wing; (*fig.*) behind the scenes, green-room, stage, theatre; (*on 'Change*) outside; afterhours 'Change; outsiders; (*print.*) galley-slice; (*of presses*) rib; (*of crossbows*) chase;

(*agr.*) pipe; (*her.*) portcullis. *A —*, grooved; sliding. *Faire les yeux en —, regarder en —*, to cast side-looks (upon), to ogle, to leer

Coulissé, e, *adj.* grooved; (*her.*) portcullised

Coulisseau, *s.m.* slide, guide-bar, guide

Coulisser, *v.n.* to speculate on 'Change as an outsider [green-room frequenter

Coulissier, *s.m.* outsider *or* stag (*on 'Change*);

Couloir, *s.m.* strainer, filter; passage; lobby; gangway; conduit; (*for letting timber down a mountain*) slide; (*pop.*) throat, whistle; mouth; mug

Couloire, *s.f.* strainer, filter; tap-tub

Coulpe, *s.f.* (*theol.*) sin, fault, trespasses, guilt. *Dire sa —*, to confess and repent

Coulure, *s.f.* running; running out; (*of fruit, &c.*) abortion, dropping, falling off

Coumarine, *s.f.* (*chem.*) coumarine [dipterix

Coumarou, *s.m.* (*bot.*) coumarou, coumarouna,

Coup, *s.m.* blow; stroke; knock; rap; tap; hit; flick; thump; bump; slap; smack; pat; chuck; cut; stab; thrust; push; shove; kick; stamp; butt; lash; sting; prick; incision; wound; gash; bruise; throw, cast; dash; shake; sweep; rub; touch; pull; ring, toll, call; beat; aim; effort; effect; trick; deed; action; act; piece; feat; affair; job; event; accident; time; bout; go; firing; shot; report; round; charge; barrel; arm; draught; drop; peal, clap; gust; flash; move; sudden action *or* motion. *Fusil à un —, à deux —s*, single-barrelled, double-barrelled gun. *Révolver à six —s*, six-chambered revolver. — *d'***aile,** flap. — *d'***air,** cold. — *de l'***art,** masterpiece of skill, masterly stroke, master-stroke. — *d'***assommoir,** (*fig.*) overwhelming blow, dreadful blow. — *d'***autorité,** act of authority, exercise *or* abuse of power; illegal measure. — *de* **balai,** sweep. —*s de* **bâton,** cudgelling. — *de* **bec,** peck; by-stroke; fling, cut. —*s et* **blessures,** *V.* **Blessure.** — **bleu,** useless effort *or* attempt. — *de* **bonheur,** lucky hit; piece of good-fortune. — *de* **botte,** kick. — *de* **boulet,** cannon-shot. — *de* **bourse,** successful speculation on 'Change. — *de* **boutoir,** (*fig.*) wipe, gibe, fling; rough answer; pet, tiff. — *de* **brosse,** brush, rub. — *de* **canif,** cut; infidelity (*V.* **Canif**). —*s de* **canne,** caning. — *de* **canon,** cannon-shot, gun-shot; cannon, gun. — *de* **caveçon,** (*fig.*) rap over the knuckles. — *de* **chapeau,** salutation (by taking off o.'s hat), bow. — *du* **ciel,** special providence. — *de* **collier,** fresh pull, new effort, pull, effort. — *de* **corne,** butt, blow with the horns. *Donner un —* (or *des —s*) *de corne à*, to butt; to gore. — *de* **coude,** nudge. — *de* **couteau,** cut, stab. —*s de* **cravache,** whipping; horse-whipping. — *de* **crayon,** stroke. — *de* **croc,** bite; (*slang*) drop of brandy. — *de* **dé,** cast of the die; throw. — *de* **dent,** bite; fling, cut. — *de* **désespoir,** act of despair, desperate attempt. — *dans l'***eau,** useless effort *or* attempt. — *d'***éclat,** brilliant exploit *or* action; bold stroke. —*s d'***encensoir,** fulsome flattery; blarney. — *d'***épaule,** lift, help. — *d'***épée,** sword-thrust; sword-wound. — *d'***épingle,** prick, sting; fling; provocation. *A —s d'épingle*, (*fig.*) inch by inch, by inches. — *d'***essai,** first attempt. — *d'***état,** politic stroke, unexpected state-measure, violent measure, revolution, decisive event, state-stroke, coup d'état. — *de l'***étrier,** stirrup-cup, parting-glass. — *d'***étrivières,** lashing, flogging, the lash. — *de* **feu,** shot; shot-wound; great heat; roasting heat; last turn; scorch, burn; overdoing; (*fig.*) busy time; bustle, great pressure, heat of it. — *de* **filet,** haul, pull, cast, sweep, catch, take. — *de* **fleuret,** (*fenc.*) pass. — *de* **fond,** (*fenc.*) home thrust. — *de* **fortune,** lucky and unexpected chance, capital speculation. — *de* **la fortune,** frown of fortune. — *de* **foudre,** stroke of lightning; (*fig.*) thunder-stroke. — *de* **fouet,** stroke of (*or* with) a whip, lash, lashing, cut; smack *or* smacking *or* crack *or* cracking (*of a whip*); stimulus, spurring, fillip; (*mus.*) brilliant finale. — *de* **fourchette,** dig *or* twist of the fork. —*s de* **fusil,** gun *or* musket shots; reports of guns *or* muskets; musketry. — *de* **gosier,** effort of the voice, strain, sound; (*mus.*) breath. — *de* **grâce,** death-blow; finishing-blow. — *de* **griffe,** scratch. — *de* **hache,** (*in o.'s head, fig. V.* — de marteau). — *de* **hasard,** mere chance; fluke. — *de* **Jarnac,** treacherous blow. — *de* **lance,** thrust. — *de* **lancette,** incision with a lancet. *Donner un — de lancette à*, to lance. — *de* **langue,** backbiting, slander; reflection; clapper-clawing, invective. — *de* **main,** bold stroke; sudden attack; surprise; lift, help; (*in English mil. slang*) coup de main. — *de* **maître,** masterly stroke, master-stroke. — *de* **malheur,** unlucky hit; piece of ill-luck. —*s de* **manche,** begging-letter impostor. — *de* **manchette,** (*fenc.*) cut on the wrist. — **manqué,** failure, miss. — *de* **marteau,** knock, rap; (*in o.'s head*) crack in the upper works, bee in o.'s bonnet, tile off. — *de* **massue,** (*fig.*) stunning blow, thunder-stroke. — *de* **mer,** heavy wave, heavy sea, wave, billow, sea. — **monté,** got-up affair. — *de la* **mort,** — **mortel,** death-blow, deadly blow; death-shot. — *d'***œil,** glance, look; peep; ogle; talent of rapid observation; sagacity, penetration; eye; sight; aspect; appearance; prospect, view. — *d'***ongle,** scratch. — *de* **partance,** sailing-gun, farewell-gun; signal of departure. — *de* **partie,** winning throw *or* move *or* stroke; decisive blow; masterly move. — *de* **patte,** claw; cuff; back-stroke, fling, cut, wipe, rub. — *de* **peigne,** hasty combing, flick; (*fig.*) drubbing, rub, brush. — **perdu,** useless effort, miss; random shot. — *de* **pied,** kick, kicking; stamp, stamping; step. — *de* **pinceau,** stroke, touch. — *de* **plume,** dash, stroke (of the pen); literary attack. — *de* **poignard,** stab; stabbing. — *de* **poing,** cuff, punch; fisticuff; pocket-pistol; knuckle-duster; (*tool*) borer, fret. — *de* **pouce,** thrust with the thumb; trick to turn down the scale, weighing o.'s thumb; strangling; screwing, putting on the screw; something more at the end, extra. — *de* **Raguse,** (*pop.*) treacherous act, treachery. — *de* **revers,** back-stroke *or* blow, backhanded blow, backhander. — *de* **sabre,** sword-cut. — *de* **sang,** apoplectic fit, congestion of the brain. — *de* **sec,** (*slang*) drop of brandy. — *de* **sifflet** whistle; hiss, hissing; signal. — *de* **soleil,** sunstroke; (*fam.*) flush; blush. — *de* **sonnette,** ring (*of a small or house-bell*), pull (*at ditto*). — *du* **sort,** chance. — *de* **stylet,** stab. — *de* **talon,** (*nav.*) grounding, bump. — *de* **tampon,** (*pop.*) buffet, bunch of fives. — *de* **temps,** chance, opportunity. — *de* **tête,** inconsiderate act, freak; toss; nod; butt. — *de* **théâtre,** unexpected event *or* incident, striking event *or* effect, sudden change, stage effect; stage trick; clap-trap. — *de* **tonnerre,** peal of thunder, thunder-clap. — *de* **vent,** gust of wind, squall, gale. —*s de* **verges,** (a) birching, (the) birch

A- —, (*s.m.*) *V.* **Acoup.** *A —s de*, with a, with. *A — perdu*, in vain; at random. *A — sûr*, surely, assuredly, to be sure, most certainly, for certain, to *or* with a certainty; on sure ground; without fail, infallibly; unerringly. *A ce —*, (*old*) this time; now; then. *Après —*, after the event, afterwards; too late. *A tous —s*, at every turn, every moment. *— sur —*, in close succession, close upon each other; without intermission, without stopping; repeatedly. *Du —, d'un —, d'un seul —*, at a stroke, at one blow; at one swoop; at once, all at once. *Du premier —*, at the first stroke *or* blow; at once; the first time, from the first. *Encore un —*, (*fig.*) once more. *Pour ce* or *le —*, this time; now; then; as to this, as to that; for once. *Sous le — de* under; threatened with, exposed to. *Sur le —*, instantly, on the spot. *Tout à —, tout d'un —*, all of a sudden, on a sudden, suddenly, all at once; abruptly. *Être aux cent —s*, to be upset *or* bewildered, to be at o.'s wits' end, not to know which way to turn *or* what to do. *Être sûr de son —*, to be certain of o.'s aim; to feel sure of success. *Faire — double*, to kill two heads of game with one shot; to kill two birds with one stone. *Faire le* or *son —*, to do it; to succeed. *Faire un bon —*, to make a good bargain *or* speculation. *Faire un mauvais —*, to do a bad action, to play a bad trick, to commit a crime. *Faire le — de fusil*, to take up the musket, to shoot, to fight. *Faire le — de poing, se battre à —s de poing*, to box. *Faire les cent —s*, to play all sorts of pranks, to run riot; to do every mortal thing, to strain every nerve. *Manquer son —*, to miss o.'s aim *or* shot; to fail. *Monter un —*, to get up an affair *or* a job; to lay a snare; to invent a pretext. *Monter (Se) le —*, *v.r.* to delude oneself. *Porter —*, to take effect, to tell, to strike *or* hit home; to injure. *Porter un —*, to deal *or* give a blow. *Tirer un —*, to fire a shot

Coupable, *adj. s.m.f.* guilty; culpable, blamable; sinful; criminal; guilty party; culprit

Coupablement, *adv.* culpably

Coupage, *s.m.* cutting; mixing; diluting

Coupant, e, *adj.* cutting; sharp; keen; edged

Coupant, *s.m.* edge; sharpness

Coupe, *s.f.* cutting; cut; felling; wood to be cut *or* felled; wood cut *or* felled; division; cup; chalice; basin; dish; cupola; section; plan; power; (*of swimming*) hand-over-hand. *— réglée*, annual cutting; (*fig.*) regular contribution. *— de l'amitié*, loving-cup. *En —*, (*of wood*) for felling *or* cutting. *Faire la —*, to cut; to swim hand-over-hand. *Faire sauter la —*, to turn the king or ace at will. *Mettre en — réglée*, to cut down periodically; (*fig.*) to lay regularly under contribution

Coupe, *s.m.f.* (*in compounds, from* **Couper,** "to cut") thing (*m.*) or person (*m.f.*) that cuts, cutter. — **-asperges,** *s.m.* asparagus-knife. — **-bourgeons,** *s.m.* (*zool.*) vine-fretter, vine-gall, vine-grub. — **-bourses,** *s.m.* (*old*) cut-purse. — **-cercle,** *s. m.* round punch. — **-choux,** *s.m.* cabbage-cutter; (*jest.*) drudge (*in a convent*), petty monk; (*jest.*) short broad-sword, dirk. — **-cigares,** *s.m.* (*instr.*) cigar-cutter. — **-cors,** *s.m.* corn-knife. — **-cul (A),** *adv.* (*pop.*) in one game. — **-faucille,** *s.m.* (*bot.*) snapdragon, calves'-snout. — **-foin,** *s.m.* hay-knife. — **-gazon,** *s.m.* turf-knife, turfing-iron. — **-gorge,** *s.m.* cut-throat place *or* slum, den of thieves; (*at lansquenet*) the dealer turning up his own card first. — **-jarrets,** *s.m.* cut-throat, ruffian. — **-lande,** *s.m.* (*instr.*) weeder. — **-légumes,** *s.m.* (*instr.*) vegetable-cutter. — **-paille,** *s.m.* (*instr.*) straw-cutter, chaff-cutter. — **-papier,** *s.m.* paper-cutting machine, paper-cutter, paper-knife. — **-pâte,** *s.m.* dough-knife. — **-queue,** *s.m.* (*vet.*) docking-knife, docking-machine. — **-racines,** *s.m.* (*instr.*) root-cutter, turnip-cutter. — **-sève,** *s.m.* (*hort.*) ringing-shears. — **-sifflet,** *s.m.* (*pop.*) knife. — **-tête,** *s.m.* head-cutter, executioner; head-cutting; leap-frog

Coupé, *s.m.* brougham (*carriage*); coupé, front-seats (*front part of a French stage-coach; front or back compartment of a railway-carriage*); coupee (*in dancing*); cut-over (*in fencing*). — **-lit,** *s.m.* (*rail.*) invalid-carriage

Coupé, e, *part. adj.* cut, &c. (*V.* **Couper**); broken, desultory, unconnected, short, concise, laconic; abrupt; varied; narrow; half-size; half; (*her.*) impaled; (*her.*) couped. *Lait —*, milk-and-water. *Porte —e*, half-door. *Voiture —e*, brougham [(*pop. for* "copeau") chip, shaving

Coupeau, *s.m.* (*old*) top, summit (*of a hill*), cop;

Coupellation, *s.f.* (*chem.*) cupellation, cupel-assay, refining; (*metal.*) testing

Coupelle, *s.f.* (*chem.*) cupel; (*artil.*) shovel; (*fig.*) test. *Argent de —*, purest silver. *Or de* [—, purest gold

Coupeller, *v.a.* to test (*metals*)

Coupement, *s.m.* (*tech.*) cutting, sawing

Couper, *v.a.n.* to cut; to cut off *or* away *or* out *or* up *or* down; to cut asunder; to cut open; to crop; to clip; to pare; to prune; to nip; to chop; to carve; to amputate; to castrate; to geld; to spay; to divide; to break; to cross; to get before, to get past, to pass; to cut across; to go *or* run across; to intersect; to interrupt; to stop; to intercept; to mix; to dilute. *La — à*, (*pop.*) to take away ...'s breath, to take aback, to do

Se —, *v.r.* to cut oneself; to cut; to cut *or* cut off (o.'s ... *or* each other's ...); to crack; to break; to contradict oneself; to cross *or* intersect each other; to be cut; to be galled *or* chafed; to be mixed *or* diluted, to mix

Couperet, *s.m.* cleaver, chopper, chopping-knife; hatchet; knife; enameller's file

Couperie, *s.f.* cutting-house; cutting

Couperose, *s.f.* copperas, vitriol; (*med.*) acne, grog-blossoms, carbuncled face, blotched and pimpled face [pimpled, red

Couperosé, e, *adj.* full of red pimples, blotched,

Couperoser, *v.a.* to blotch. **Se —,** *v.r.* to be-

Coupetée, *s.f. V.* **Coptée** [come blotchy

Coupeu-r, se, *s.m.f.* cutter; clicker; lumberer, lumberman; gelder; (*at lansquenet*) player. *— de bourses*, cut-purse, pickpocket. *— d'eau*, (*bird*) cutwater [of boats

Couplage, *s.m.* coupling; part of a raft; pair

Couple, *s.m.f.* couple; brace; pair; —*s.m.* (*nav.*) frame, timber. *Maître —*, midship-frame

Coupler, *v.a.* to couple; to tack

Couplet, *s.m.* verse, stanza; song; tirade; hinge

Coupleter, *v.a.* to lampoon, to make a song on

Coupletier, *s.m.* (*obsolete*) song-writer

Couplière, *s.f.* part of a raft [cutter

Coupoir, *s.m.* cutter; knife; blade; (*print.*) lead-

Coupole, *s.f.* (*arch.*) cupola

Coupon, *s.m.* coupon, cheque, part, (dividend) warrant; ticket; (*of stuffs*) remnant, short length; cutting, shred. *— détaché*, (*fin.*) ex-dividend. *— de loge*, (*theat.*) box-ticket

Coupure, *s.f.* cut; gash; separation; division; suppression, erasure; smaller coin; smaller banknote; trench; (*fort.*) coupure

Cour, *s.f.* yard; court; courtyard; playground; bench; board; courtship, addresses. *Basse-—*, *V. Letter* **B.** *— des comptes*, audit-office. *— des miracles*, den of thieves, Alsatia. *— de récréation*, playground. *Hors de —*, nonsuited; *s.m.* nonsuit. *Faire la — à*, to court, to pay o.'s addresses to, to make love to. *Faire sa —*, to pay court *or* o.'s respects (to); to do homage to; to court (the) favour (of); to flatter. *Faire un doigt de — à*, to show some attentions to. *Mettre* or *Renvoyer hors de —* (or *hors de — et de procès*); (*law*) to nonsuit, to dismiss the case

Courable, *adj.* (*hunt.*) that may be hunted

Courage, *s.m.* courage; gallantry; boldness; mettle; spirit; heart; soul; zeal; fortitude; resolution; cheer; passion; temper. *— ! du — ! bon — !* come! take courage! cheer up! *Prendre* or *tenir son — à deux mains*, to summon up all o.'s courage

Courageusement, *adv.* courageously; bravely; gallantly; boldly; spiritedly; resolutely

Courageu-x, se, *adj.* courageous; brave; gallant; bold; spirited; resolute; industrious

Courai, *s.m.* stuff to pay a ship's bottom, white stuff, coat [irregular *or* disorderly life

†Courailler, *v.n.* to run about; to lead an

Couramment, *adv.* fluently, readily, off-hand

Courant, e, (*part., V.* **Courir**) *adj.* running; flowing; current; ordinary; prevalent; present; instant; market; (*of goods*) fair, middling; (*of measures*) lineal; (*her.*) courant. *Chien —, Main —e*, &c., *V.* **Chien, Main,** &c.

Courant, *s.m.* stream; current; tide; course;

regular course, ordinary run, routine; running; instant, present month; present quarter; present price; current debt *or* claim; (*pop.*) what is up; what's what; dodge, trick. — *d'air*, draught, draught of air, current of air, current. *Au* —, right up to the present time, with no arrears; acquainted with the news, acquainted with the whole thing; up to the business. *Au — de*, acquainted *or* conversant with, up to; aware of; at the running of; with the current of, &c. *Fin* —, (*com.*) (at the) end of the present month. *Mettre au* — (*de*), to inform (of), to acquaint (with)

Courante, *s.f.* running hand (*writing*); runner, upper mill-stone; (*fam.*) diarrhœa; (*obsolete*) courant (*dance, tune*)

†**Courantille**, *s.f.* tunny-net

Courantin, e, *s.m.f.* truant; — *s.m.* line-rocket

Courap, *s.m.* (*med.*) courap

Courau, *s.m.* small fishing-boat, lighter

Couray, *s.m. V.* **Courai** [ship, to lay on the stuff

Courayer, *v.a.n.* (*nav.*) to pay the bottom of a

Courbable, *adj.* bendable, flexible

Courbage, *s.m.* bending, curving [zebra-wood

Courbaril, *s.m.* (*bot.*) locust-tree. *Bois de* —,

Courbatu, e, *adj.* foundered; knocked up, bruised *or* stiff all over, cramped

Courbature, *s.f.* stiffness in the joints, pains in the back and limbs, great lassitude, over-fatigue, cramp; (*vet.*) founder, foundering

Courbaturé, e, *adj.* knocked up, bruised *or* stiff all over, cramped

Courbaturer, *v.a.* to knock up, to make (*one*) feel stiff all over, to cramp

Se —, *v.r.* to get knocked up *or* cramped

Courbe, *adj.m.f.*, *s.f.* curved, crooked, bent; curve; turn; knee; couple, team; (*vet.*) curb

Courbement, *s.m.* bending

Courber, *v.a.n.* to bend; to bend down; to bow; to bow down; to curve, to incurvate; to crook; to sag; to give way, to comply, to submit. *Se tenir courbé*, to stoop

Se —, *v.r.* to bend; to bow; to bow down; to bow o.'s head; to stoop; to couch down; to give way, to comply, to submit

Courbet, *s.m.* bill-hook; bow (*of a pack-saddle*)

Courbette, *s.f.* (*rid.*) curvet; (*pers.*) servile bow, cringing, bowing and scraping

Courbetter, *v.n.* (*rid.*) to curvet

Courbotte, *s.f.* rock-staff

Courbure, *s.f.* bend; bending; crookedness; crook; curvature, curve, curvation, incurvation; flexion, flexure; sagging

†**Courcailler**, *v.n.* (*of quails*) to call

†**Courcaillet**, *s.m.* cry *or* call of the quail; quail-pipe, quail-call

Courcelle, *s.f.* (*obsolete*) small court *or* yard

Courcet, *s.m.* pruning-bill, pruning-hook

Courcive, *s.f. V.* **Coursive**

Courçon, *s.m.* short piece (*of wood*); (*mil.*) stake set under water; (*artil.*) bandage

Coureau, *s.m.* (*nav.*) strait, channel; yawl, flat

Courée, *s.f.*, **Couret**, *s.m. V.* **Courai**

Coureur, *s.m.* runner; racer; courser; running horse; hunter; running footman; light porter, messenger; stroller; rover, rambler; vagabond; scout; skirmisher; (*in compounds*) . . . -hunter; . . . -goer, . . . -frequenter; (*fam.*) walker, idler, truant; (*fam.*) inconstant lover, libertine, rake, gay man; — *adj.m.* running. — *de cachets*, (*in contempt*) visiting tutor

Coureuse, *s.f.* runner; racer; rover, rambler; vagabond; walker, stroller, idler; (*in compounds*) . . . -huntress; . . . -goer, . . . -frequenter; (*fam.*) street-walker; gay woman; — *adj.f.* running. — *de cachets*, (*in contempt*) visiting *or* daily

Coure-vite, *s.m. V.* **Court-vite** [governess

Courge, *s.f.* gourd, pumpkin; yoke (*to carry pails*, &c.); (*arch.*) corbel, bracket. — *à la moelle*,

Courgée, *s.f.* yoke-load [vegetable marrow

Courir, *v.n.a.* to run; to run on *or* about; to hurry, to hasten; to go *or* be about; to stroll, to stroll about; to ramble; to rove; to rove about; to lead an irregular *or* disorderly life; to slip, to pass away; to draw near, to get on fast; to be on the way *or* on the road (to); to circulate; to go round; to spread; to be abroad; to be reported; to be current; to be prevalent, to prevail; to be in fashion; to abound; to run along, to extend; to ride; to drive; to rush; to fall; to scour; to sail, to scud; to travel over; to go over; to run after; to seek after; to pursue; to run for; to hunt; to course; to frequent; to follow, to attend; to visit; to encounter; (*post*) to travel, to ride. *En courant*, while running; hastily; cursorily; off-hand. *Tout courant*, as fast as one can, unhesitatingly; readily; fluently. *Faire* —, to run; to course; to drive; to trundle; to spread (*a report*, &c.); to circulate; to pass round; to run horses, to be on the turf. *Par le temps qui* —, as times go, in these days

Couris, *s.m. V.* **Cauris** [lander

Courlandais, e, *adj. s.* Courlandish; Cour-

Courlieu, Courlis, *s.m.* (*bird*) curlew; whim-

Couroi, *s.m. V.* **Courai** [brel

Couronnade, *s.f.* (*mil.*) surrounding

Couronne, *s.f.* crown; corona; coronet; wreath, circlet; halo; ring; rim; chaplet; chimney-holder (*of a lamp*); large foolscap (*paper*); prize; (*fort.*) crown-work; (*vet.*) coronet, cornet. — *impériale*, (*bot.*) crown imperial; (*shell*) crown-imperial shell

Couronné, e, *adj.* crowned; capped; rewarded with a prize, rewarded, prize; surrounded, encompassed; (*of a plain*) surrounded with hills; (*of horses*) broken-kneed; (*of trees*) with the top decayed

Couronnement, *s.m.* coronation; crowning-piece; top-piece; top; crowning; crown; completion; perfection; (*arch.*) crowning, finial; (*nav.*) taffrail; (*of horses*) broken knees *or* knee; (*of trees*) withering at the top

Couronner, *v.a.* to crown; to wreathe; to cap; to complete, to perfect, to terminate, to finish; to adorn, to embellish; to reward with a prize, to reward; to honour; to surround, to encompass

Se —, *v.r.* to crown oneself; (*of things*) to be crowned; to wear a crown; (*of a horse*) to break its knees; (*of a tree*) to wither at the top

Couronnure, *s.f.* crown (*on a stag's head*)

Couroyer, *v.a.n. V.* **Courayer**

Courre, *v.a.n.* (*hunt.*) to hunt; to course; (*rid.*) to ride full gallop; (*old*) to run after; to run. *Laisser* —, to slip, to uncouple, to let go the hounds; *s.m.* starting-place, uncoupling of the hounds [coursing-country

Courre, *s.m.* (*hunt.*) starting-place; hunting *or*

Courrier, *s.m.* courier; post-boy; messenger; outrider; mail; mail-coach; mail-cart driver, mail-driver; post; letters; (*of a paper kite*) messenger. — *de la malle*, mail-guard; mail-coach, mail. — *pour* —, by return of post. *Faire son* —, to write o.'s letters

Courrière, *s.f.* (*poet.*) wanderer; forerunner, harbinger; messenger

Courroi, *s.m.* (*tech.*) roller; tenter; rolling

Courroie, *s.f.* (leather) strap, thong, belt, girth *or* girt, band. *Allonger* or *étendre la* —, (*fig.*) to make the most of a place; to stretch o.'s perquisites *or* privileges; to husband o.'s resources, to make the most of o.'s money, to make a penny go a great way; to stretch, to draw out in length. *Lâcher la* —, (*fig.*) to loosen the tether, to give rope, to let (...) go on, to be easy (with), to accommodate. *Serrer la* — *à*, (*fig.*) to diminish ...'s supplies *or* means, to curtail ...'s allowance [raging, in wrath

Courroucé, e, *adj.* angry, incensed, irritated,

Courroucer, *v.a.* to incense, to irritate, to anger, to provoke, to rouse [censed; to rage

Se —, *v.r.* to become (*or* grow) angry *or* in-

Courroux, *s.m.* anger, wrath, ire, rage, fury

Courroyage, *s.m.* tentering

Courroyer, *v.a.* to tenter

Cours, *s.m.* course; flow; run; stream; voyage; path, track; walk *or* parade (*in some towns*), public walk, row, park, ride, drive; extent; length; direction; turn; current; progress, way; lapse; scope, vent; vogue, credit; market-price, current price, price; rate; circulation; currency; class, classes, lecture, lectures, lecturing, course of lectures, course of study, course. — *d'eau*, stream, watercourse. — *de ventre*, diarrhœa; (*vet.*) scouring, break-share. *Long* —, *Voyage de long* —, Ocean voyage, voyage to foreign parts, distant voyage (*V.* **Capitaine**). *Avoir* —, to be current; to be in vogue; to obtain; to take. *Avoir son* —, to take its course, to have its run. *Faire un* —, to give a course, to conduct a class, to lecture, to teach

Course, *s.f.* running; run; race; match; chase; course; career; tilting; ride; drive; excursion; trip; ramble; journey; journeying; distance; walk on business; round; call; errand; incursion, inroad; flight; (*sporting*) turf; (*of public carriages*) fare; (*nav.*) cruise, privateering. — *à cheval*, ride. — *à la voile*, sail. — *au clocher*, steeple-chase. — *de chevaux*, *V.* **Cheval.** — *de haies*, hurdle-race. *A la* —, by *or* in running; running; by the drive. *En* —, out; out on business *or* on an errand; on a cruise; privateering. *Terrain de —s*, *V.* **Champ.** *Faire la* —, (*nav.*) to cruise; to privateer

Coursi-er, ère, *s.m.f.* courser, charger, steed, racer, horse, mare; — *s.m.* (*nav.*) bow-chaser; (*tech.*) float-board [gangway, waist

Coursière, Coursive, *s.f* (*nav.*) half-deck,

Courson, *s.m.* (*hort.*, *agr.*) shoot with the top lopped off

Court, e, *adj.* short; brief, concise, curt; short-lived; narrow, limited, contracted; defective; scant, scanty. *Prendre le plus* —, to take the shortest way

Court, *adv.* short. *Tout* —, short; and no more, simply, only; curtly; bluntly; immediately. *A — de*, short of. *Couper — à*, to cut short; to curtail; to do away at once with, to put an end to. *Demeurer* or *rester* —, to stop short. *Prendre de* —, to press, to take short; to surprise in an unguarded moment. *Tenir* —, to keep short *or* close *or* under

Courtage, *s.m.* brokerage; business of a broker

Courtain, *s.m.* curtein, curtana (*sword*)

Courtaud, e, *adj.* thickset, dumpy, punchy, podgy, stubby; docked, crop-eared; — *s.m.* docked horse, crop-eared horse *or* dog; (*obsolete*) thickset horse, roadster; (*fam.*, — *de boutique*) shopman, counter-jumper, drudge; (*mus.*) short bassoon; — *s.m.f.* dumpy fellow *or* woman *or* girl, punch

Courtauder, *v.a.* to dock, to crop (*horses, dogs*)

†Court-bouillon, *s.m.* (*cook.*) court-bouillon (*particular way of boiling fish*) [court-bouillon

†Court-bouillonné, e, *adj.* (*cook.*) done in

Courte-botte, *s.m.* short man, shrimp, dwarf,

Courtement, *adv.* shortly, briefly [pygmy

†Courte-paille, *s.f.* *V.* **Paille**

Courte-pointe, *s.f.* quilt (*for a bed*)

Courte-pointier, *s.m.* quilt-maker

Courter, *v.n.a.* to buy and sell on commission; to try to sell

Courtier, *s.m.* broker; agent. — *électoral*, electioneering agent, canvasser (*at elections*). — *maritime* or *de navires*, shipbroker. — *de mariages*, matrimonial agent, match-maker

Courtière, *s.f.* broker, agent, go-between. — *de mariages*, matrimonial agent, match-maker

Courtil, *s.m.* (*obsolete*) croft

Courtilière, *s.f.* (*insect*) mole-cricket

†Courtille, *s.f.* tea-gardens, public balls

Courtine, *s.f.* curtain

Courtisan, *s.m.* courtier; courtling; flatterer, fawner, toady; courter; — *adj.m.* courtly

Courtisane, *s.f.* courtesan; — *adj.f.* courtly

Courtisanerie, *s.f.* court-flattery, courtier's adulation, flattery, fawning, toadyism; courtesanship [like, courtly; of a courtesan

Courtisanesque, *adj.* of a courtier, courtier-

Courtiser, *v.a.* to court, to pay court to; to woo, to make love to; to flatter, to fawn upon; to honour

Court-mancher, *v.a.* (*cook.*) to skewer

Court-monté, e, *adj.* (*of horses*) low-backed

Courtois, e, *adj.* courteous, civil; (*of arms*) of courtesy, of parade, blunt [tesy

Courtoisement, *adv.* courteously, with cour-

Courtoisie, *s.f.* courtesy, courteousness; good office, kind service

Court-vite, *s.m.* (*bird*) courser

Couru, e, *part. adj.* run, run for, run over, overrun, run after, pursued, hunted, hunted down, sought after, &c. (*V.* **Courir**); in demand, in request; in vogue, in fashion, fashionable, popular, favourite; frequented

Couscous, Couscoussou, *s.m.* couscous, [kuskus, pilaw

Couseur, *s.m.* sewer; stitcher

Couseuse, *s.f.* sewer; stitcher; (— *mécanique*) sewing-machine

Cousin, e, *s.m.f.* cousin; relation; friend, crony; parasite, sponger, poor relation; — *s.m.* gnat (*insect*), midge [hood; kindred, relations

Cousinage, *s.m.* relationship of cousins, cousin-

Cousiner, *v.a.n.* to call cousin; to sponge; to agree, to be on good terms, to be friends *or* cronies

Se —, *v.r.* to call each other cousin

Cousinerie, Cousinière, *s.f.* host of cousins *or* of poor relations

Cousinière, *s.f.* mosquito-net

Cousoir, *s.m.* sewing-press (*for book-binding*); glove-sewing apparatus [ster; pillow; pad

Coussin, *s.m.* cushion; hassock; squab; bol-

Coussiner, *v.a.* to cushion; to bolster; to pad

Coussinet, *s.m.* small cushion; pad; squab; (*techn.*, &c.) cushion; pillow; rest; iron wedge; (*surg.*) bolster; (*rail.*) chair; (*arch.*) coussinet; (*bot.*) cranberry

Cousu, e, *part. adj.* sewed, &c. (*V.* **Coudre**); seamed; closed; covered; marked; lean, lanky; hollow; full; made (*of money*). — *de fil blanc*, (*fig.*) transparent, shallow, clumsy

Coût, *s.m.* cost

Coûtant, *adj.m.* *Prix* —, *V.* **Prix**

Coutarde, *s.f.* custard

Couteau, *s.m.* knife; steel. — *à découper*, *grand* —, carving-knife, carver. — *à deux manches*, draw-knife. — *à fromage*, cheese-scoop. — *à mouche*, spring-knife. — *de chaleur*, horse-scraper. — *de chasse*, hunting-knife, hanger. — *pliant*, clasp-knife. — *-poignard*, dagger-knife, jack-knife, bowie-knife. *A —x tirés*, at daggers drawn. *Le — de Jeannot*, the old knife with a new blade and a new handle

Coutelas, *s.m.* cutlass, hanger

Couteli-er, ère, *s.m.f.* cutler

Coutellerie, *s.f.* cutlery; cutlery-works

Coûter, *v.n.a.* to cost; to be expensive; to be painful, to be an effort *or* a trial; to be troublesome *or* disagreeable *or* difficult, to be some trouble; to be an object, to matter. — *cher*, to be dear *or* expensive, to cost much *or* a great deal; to cost dear. — *les yeux de la tête*, to cost enormously, to cost no end of money, to be a fearful pull (upon). *En* —, to cost; to be painful; to be an effort *or* a trial; to be troublesome, to be some trouble. *Coûte que coûte*, cost what it may *or* will, at any cost; at any rate, happen (*or* come) what may. *Rien ne lui coûte*, nothing is too great a sacrifice for him; he sticks *or* scruples at nothing; he spares no pains [cost

Coûteusement, *adv.* expensively, at a great

Coûteu-x, se, *adj.* expensive, costly, dear

Coutier, *s.m.* tick-maker [cloth, drill, duck

Coutil, *s.m.* ticking, canvas-ticking, tick, tent-

†Coutille, *s.f.* fescue (*plant*)

Coutre, *s.m.* (*agr.*) coulter; (*tech.*) cleaver

Coutrier, *s.m.* subsoil-plough

Coutume, *s.f.* custom, habit; practice; common law; common-law book; (*old*) toll, tax. *De* —, usual; usually; generally. *Avoir — de*, to be in the habit of; to ... usually, to use (to)
Coutumi-er, ère, *adj.* (*pers.*) in the habit (of), accustomed (to), in the habit of doing *or* committing (...); (*things*) customary, habitual, usual, ordinary, wonted; (*of laws*) common, customary, unwritten, consuetudinary; (*country*) governed by common law; (*pers.*) having a joint right in common ground. — *du fait*, an old hand at it, inclined that way, an old offender
Coutumier, *s.m.* common-law book, customary; (*pers.*) commoner [ally
Coutumièrement, *adv.* customarily, habitu-
Couture, *s.f.* sewing; plain needlework, plain work, needlework; seam; scar. *A plate* —, hollow, utterly, soundly
Couturer, *v.a.* (*fig.*) to seam, to scar
Couturerie, *s.f.* needlewomen's *or* sempstresses' work-room
Couturier, *s.m.* sempster, seamster, sewer; (*anat.*) sartorius muscle, tailor's muscle
Couturière, *s.f.* dress-maker, mantle-maker; needlewoman, sempstress, seamstress; (*pop.*) warbler (*bird*); (*pop.*) vine-weevil (*insect*); (*children's slang for* "courtilière") mole-cricket (*insect*). *Mouche* —, *V.* **Tipule**
Couvage, *s.m.* brooding, sitting
Couvain, *s.m.* (*of some insects*) nest of eggs; (*of bees*) larvæ, maggots; (*of bees*) breeding-cells
Couvaison, *s.f.* brooding-time *or* season, brooding, sitting [(*abusively*) addled, addle
Couvé, e, *part. adj.* hatched, &c. (*V.* **Couver**);
Couvée, *s.f.* nest of eggs; covey; hatch; brood; progeny, breed, generation
Couvent, *s.m.* convent; monastery; nunnery; convent-school; (*pop.*) house of ill fame. — *de religieuses*, nunnery
Couver, *v.a.n.*, **Se** —, *v.r.* to brood on, to sit on, to brood, to sit; to incubate; to hatch; to breed; to brew; to be pregnant with; to brood over, to meditate; to fondle; to cherish; to shelter; to harbour; to lie hid, to lurk; to smoulder; to ripen. —*des yeux*, to devour with o.'s eyes, to look fondly *or* complacently on, to gloat over [ter; (*pop.*) hat, tile
Couvercle, *s.m.* cover; lid; (*tech.*) cap; shut-
Couvert, *s.m.* things on the table, dinner-things, breakfast-things, &c., cloth; knife and fork; spoon and fork; spoon and fork with knife to match (*in a case*); cover; plate; place (*at table*); shelter, refuge, covert; protection; lodging; roof; house; thicket; shady place; shade; wrapper; envelope. *A* —, under cover, under shelter, sheltered; protected; secured; secure, in safety, safe. *Lever le* —, to clear the table. *Mettre le* —, to lay the cloth, to lay the table. *Mettre à* —, to shelter, to screen, to protect, to secure; to house. *Ôter le* —, to take away, to remove the cloth. *Dîner de* 50 —*s*, dinner of 50 covers. *Table de dix —s*, table laid for ten
Couvert, e, *part. adj.* covered, &c. (*V.* **Couvrir**); sheltered; protected; secured; clad; clothed; wrapped up; with o.'s hat on; full; loaded; hidden; secret; mysterious; ambiguous; dark, obscure; veiled; cloudy; shady; woody; (*of carriages*) close; (*of wine*) deep-coloured; (*of the voice*) husky; (*of the voice, of sounds*) drowned (by); (*fort., fig.*) covert, covered; (*obsolete*) sown over [blanket; (*nav.*) deck
Couverte, *s.f.* glaze, glazing; cover; covering,
Couvertement, *adv.* covertly, secretly, privately, closely
Couverture, *s.f.* cover; covering; wrapper; rug; cloth; clothing; blanket; counterpane; bed-clothes; screen, mat; roof; roofing; pretence, cloak, show; security; payment. — *piquée*, quilt. *Faire la* —, to turn down the bed
Couverturier, *s.m.* blanket-maker *or* seller
Couvet, *s.m.* *V.* **Chaufferette**
Couveuse, *s.f.* brood-hen, sitter; (— *artificielle*) incubator; — *adj.f.* brooding, brood. *Poule* —, [brood-hen
Couvi, *adj.m.* addled, addle
Couvoir, *s.m.* incubator
Couvre, *s.m.* (*in compounds, from* **Couvrir,** "to cover") thing that covers, covering, cover. —**-chef,** *s.m.* (*jest.*) covering for the head, head-gear, head-dress, hat, cap, bonnet, kerchief, &c., (*slang*) tile; (*surg.*) bandage round the head. —**-feu,** *s.m.* fire-cover, fire-plate; curfew, curfew-bell; retreat. —**-fonte,** *s.m.* holster-cap. —**-lit,** *s.m.* bed-cover, coverlet. —**-lumière,** *s.m.* (*artil.*) apron. —**-pieds,** *s.m.* counterpane; quilt; coverlet (— *-pieds piqué*, quilt). —**-plat,** *s.m.* dish-cover; meat-cover
Couvreur, *s.m.* coverer; roofer; (— *en ardoise*) slater; (— *en tuiles*) tiler; (— *en chaume*) thatcher; (— *en zinc*) *V.* **Zingueur**
Couvrir, *v.a.* to cover; to lay over; to wrap up; to envelop; to clothe; to overlay; to overspread; to overflow; to overrun; to fill; to hide, to conceal; to disguise; to shelter; to screen; to protect; to secure; to pay; to defray; to reimburse; to indemnify; to make good; to bar; to obliterate; to overwhelm; to load; to drown (*sounds, the voice*); to stifle; to darken, to cloud; to excuse, to palliate; to roof; to slate; to tile; to thatch; (*at dominoes*) to fit, to match; (*at draughts*) to crown; (*at cards*) to cover, to stake on

Se —, *v.r.* to cover *or* &c. oneself; to cover o.'s head; to put on o.'s head, to wear; to put o.'s hat on; to fill; to darken, to cloud; to be overcast, to get cloudy; to abound, to teem; to be covered, &c.

Covenant, *s.m.* (*Engl. hist.*) covenant
Covenantaire, *s.m.* (*Engl. hist.*) covenanter
Covend-eur, euse (*or* **eresse**), *s.m.f.* co-vendor, joint seller [**Couillon,** &c.
Couyon, Couyonnade, Couyonner. *V.*
Cowpox, *s.m.* (*med.*) cow-pox
Coxal, e, *adj.* (*anat.*) coxal
Coxalg-ie, -ique, (*med.*) *V.* page 3, § 1
Coypou, *s.m.* (*zool.*) coypu, nutria
Crabe, *s.m.* crab, crab-fish
Crabier, *s.m.* (*zool.*) crab-catcher, crab-eater
Crabite, *s.m.* (*fossil*) crabite
Crabosser, *v.a.* (*fam.*) *V.* **Bossuer**
Crabron, *s.m.* (*zool.*) hornet
Crac, *s.m.* crack, cracking; creaking; —*! int.* in a second! suddenly! pop! quick! before you can (*or* could) say Jack Robinson! *Monsieur de Crac*, Baron Munchausen
Crachat, *s.m.* spittle; sputter, spawl; (*med.*) expectoration, sputum (*pl.* sputa); (*fam., of orders*) star; (*of buildings*) slight materials
Craché, e, *part. adj.* (*V.* **Cracher**). *Tout* —, *toute —e*, (*fam.*) the very image of, to a T
Crachement, *s.m.* spitting; expectoration; sputtering
Cracher, *v.n.a.* to spit; to spit out; to expectorate; to sputter, to spawl; to sputter out; to spirt; to utter, to speak, to tell; to spout; to mouth; to be always quoting; to fork out (*money*). — *blanc*, — *du coton*, (*pop.*) to be thirsty *or* dry. — *en l'air*, to be hoisted with o.'s own petard. *C'est à — dessus*, it is a most des-
Cracheu-r, se, *s.m.f.* spitter [picable thing
Crachoir, *s.m.* spittoon; spitting-box; (*pop.*) talk, jaw, gabble, mouthing [spitting
Crachotement, *s.m.* frequent *or* constant
Crachoter, *v.n.* to spit frequently, to keep spitting [Cracovian fashion; cracovienne (*dance, tune*)
Cracovien, ne, *adj. s.m.f.* Cracovian; — *s.f.*
Crag, *s.m.* (*geol.*) crag
Craie, *s.f.* chalk
Craïer, *s.m.* (*nav.*) pole-masted vessel
Craière, *s.f.* *V.* **Crayère** [&c.
†**Craillement, Crailler,** *V.* **Croassement,**
Craindre, *v.a.* to fear, to be afraid of, to apprehend, to dread; to dislike; to be injured by, to be unable to stand (*or* to bear). *A* —, to fear; to be feared; formidable; dreadful; dangerous

Crainte, *s.f.* fear; apprehension; anxiety; dread; awe; terror; faint-heartedness. *De — de, — de*, for fear of. *De — que*, for fear, lest

Crainti-f, ve, *adj.* timid, timorous, fearful; afraid; anxious [fearfully

Craintivement, *adv.* timidly, timorously,

Crambe, Crambé, *s.m.* (*bot.*) crambe, colza, sea-kale; (*zool.*) crambus, veneer, grass-moth

Cramoisi, e, *adj.*, **Cramoisi,** *s.m.* crimson

Crampe, *s.f.* cramp. *Tirer sa —*, (*pop.*) to run away, to bolt

Crampon, *s.m.* cramp-iron, cramp; crampoon; holdfast; crank, catch; staple; brace; calk, calkin, frost-nail; (*mach.*) click; (*bot.*) fulcrum, prop; (*hort.*) climbing-spur; (*her.*) crampoon; (*fam.*) tenacious fellow *or* dog *or* thing, bore

Cramponné, e, *part. adj.* (*V.* **Cramponner**); (*her.*) cramponee [rough-shoe (*a horse*)

Cramponner, *v.a.* to cramp; to fasten; to

Se —, *v.r.* to cling, to hold fast, to fasten

Cramponnet, *s.m.* small cramp; staple

Cran, *s.m.* notch; cog; (*print.*) nick; (*fig.*) peg; (*plant*) *V.* **Cranson.** *Lâcher d'un —*, (*pop. for* "planter là." *V.* **Planter**)

Crâne, *s.m.* skull; (*fam.*) swaggerer, blusterer; (*pop.*) bold *or* brave fellow, gamecock; — *adj.* (*fam.*) swaggering, blustering; (*pop.*) bold, brave; mighty, fine, capital, famous, spicy, stunning, awful, first-rate, crack, A 1

Crânement, *adv.* (*fam.*) swaggeringly; saucily; (*pop.*) boldly, fearlessly; mightily, finely, capitally, in the style, famously, spicily, stunningly, awfully; an awful lot

Crânerie, *s.f.* (*fam.*) swaggering, blustering, bluster; (*pop.*) boldness

Crangon, *s.m.* *V.* **Crevette**

Crânien, ne, *adj.* (*anat.*) cranial

Crâniographe, *s.m.* craniographer

Crânio-graphie, -graphique, -logie, -logique, -logiste, -mancie, -mantique, -métrie, -métrique, -scopie, -scopique, -tomie, &c. *V.* page 3, § 1

Crâniologue, *s.m.* craniologist

Crâniomètre, *s.m.* craniometer

Crâniotome, *s.m.* (*surg.*) craniotomy forceps

Cranson, *s.m.* scurvy-grass, horse-radish

Crapaud, *s.m.* toad; brat, urchin; fellow, chap; low-seat chair; (*obsolete*) hair-bag; (*vet.*) fig; (*artil.*) mortar-bed; (*nav.*) *V.* **Crapeau;** (*slang*) purse. — *volant*, (*bird*) goat-sucker. — *de mer*, toad-fish. — *de timon*, pole-crab (*of a carriage*)

†**Crapaudaille,** *s.f.* *V.* **Crépodaille**

Crapaudière, *s.f.* toad-hole

Crapaudine, *s.f.* toad-stone; (*bot.*) iron-wort; (*zool.*) wolf-fish; (*vet.*) crapaudine; crepance, crepane; (*tech.*) collar, socket; valve; water-plug, plug; grating. *A la —*, (*cook.*) flattened and broiled on the gridiron, spitchcocked

Crapeau, *s.m.* (*nav.*) goose-neck (*of the tiller*)

Crapelet, *s.m.* young toad

†**Crapodaille,** *s.f.* *V.* **Crépodaille**

Crapoussin, e, *s.m.f.* scrubby little fellow *or* thing, runt, bloated little shrimp

Crapule, *s.f.* low vice, low habits, low *or* dissolute life; low people, lowest of the low

Crapuler, *v.n.* to indulge in low vice, to lead a low *or* dissolute life, to frequent low people [ly

Crapuleusement, *adv.* in a low way, dissolute-

Crapuleu-x, se, *adj.* low, grossly vicious, dissolute, corrupt, filthy, beastly [brag, crack

Craque, *s.f.* fib, sham, humbug, fudge, bouncer,

Craquelage, *s.m.* cracking, chinking

Craqueler, *v.a.* to crack, to chink; to crack the glazing of. *Porcelaine craquelée*, cracklin

Craquelin, *s.m.* cracknel, crisp biscuit or cake, cracker, snap; (*fam.*) rickety ship; (*pop.*) weak-

Craquelot, *s.m.* new red-herring [ling, poor stick

Craquelotière, *s.f.* herring-curer

Craquelure, *s.f.* crack, chink

Craquement, *s.m.* cracking; crack; crackling; creaking; craunching; scraunching; snapping, snap; (*of teeth*) grating,

Craquer, *v.n.* to crack; to crackle; to creak; to craunch, to crunch; to scraunch, to scrunch; to burst; to snap; (*of the teeth*) to grate; (*fig.*, *fam.*) to fib, to bounce, to brag, to boast, to crack

Craquerie, *s.f.* fibbing, bragging, boasting, cracking; fib, humbug, fudge, bouncer, brag, crack

Craquètement, *s.m.* crackling, crepitation; snapping; (*of storks and cranes*) gabble, gabbling

Craqueter, *v.n.* to crackle, to crepitate; to snap; (*of storks and cranes*) to gabble

Craqueu-r, se, *s.m.f.* story-teller, bouncer, braggart, boaster, cracker

Crase, *s.f.* (*med.*, *gram.*) crasis

Crasio-graphie, -logie, (*med.*) *V.* page 3, § 1

Crassamentum, *s.m.* (*med.*) crassamentum,

Crassane, *s.f.* *V.* **Cresane** [crassament, clot

Crasse, *s.f.* dirt, filth; scurf; dandriff; foulness, fouling; squalidness; layer of dirt; fur; grease; (*of metals*) scum, dross, scales; (*of coals*) ashes, cinders; (*fig.*) rust, rusticity; abject condition, abjection; sordid avarice, sordidness, stinginess; — *adj.* gross, thick,

Crassement, *s.m.* fouling [coarse; sordid

Crasser, *v.a.* to foul, to dirty

Se —, *v.r.* to become (*or* get) foul *or* dirty

Crasseu-x, se, *adj.* dirty, filthy; foul; squalid; scurfy; greasy; unwashed; sordid, stingy; abject, mean; — *s.m.f.* unwashed, sloven, slut, dirty fellow *or* thing, beast; miser

Crassule, *s.f.* (*bot.*) crassula

Cratère, *s.m.* crater; cup, bowl

Cratériforme, *adj.* crateriform

Craticulaire, Craticulation, Craticuler. *V.* **Graticulaire,** &c.

Cravache, *s.f.* riding-whip, horse-whip

Cravacher, *v.a.* to horse-whip, to whip

Cravan, Cravant, *s.m.* (*shell-fish*) barnacle; (*bird*) brent-goose, brent, brant

Cravate, *s.f.* neck-tie, tie, neck-cloth, cravat, (*jest.*) choker; (*of curtains*) band; (*mil.*) tassel (*of a flag*). — *longue*, scarf

Cravate, *s.m.* Croatian horse; (*obsolete*) croat (*horse-soldier*); — *adj.* (*of horses*) Croatian

Cravaté, e, *adj.* cravatted; with a (*or* one's) neck-tie *or* choker on; having round o.'s neck

Cravater, *v.a.* to put (*a person's*) neck-tie *or* cravat on (*for him*)

Se —, *v.r.* to put o.'s neck-tie *or* cravat on

Crayer, *s.m.* (*nav.*) *V.* **Craïer**

Crayère, *s.f.* chalk-pit

Crayeu-x, se, *adj.* chalky

Crayon, *s.m.* pencil; crayon; chalk; pencil drawing, portrait in crayons; manner, style; rough draught, sketch, outline. *Au —*, in pencil; in crayon

Crayonner, *v.a.* to draw in pencil, to pencil; to crayon; to sketch; to chalk; to write with a pencil [rough-sketcher

Crayonneu-r, se, *s.m.f.* drawer in pencil;

Crayonneu-x, se, *adj.* chalky

Cré, e, *adj.* (*pop. abbreviation of* "sacré") cursed, confounded, damned. — *chien!* — *nom!* by George! by Jove! confound it! hang it!

Créable, *adj.* creatable

Créance, *s.f.* credit, credence; trust; confidence; book-debt, debt; claim; (*dipl.*) credence; (*hunt.*) command. *Lettre de —*, credentials; (*bank.*) letter of credit

Créanci-er, ère, *s.m.f.* creditor

Créat, *s.m.* usher (to a riding-master), creat

Créa-teur, trice, *s.m.f.* creator, creatress, maker; — *adj.* creative

Créatine, *s.f.* (*chem.*) creatine

Créatinine, *s.f.* (*chem.*) creatinine

Création, *s.f.* creation; production; foundation; establishment; &c. (*V.* **Créer**)

Créature, *s.f.* creature; thing; tool; bad woman

Crécelle, *s.f.* rattle; cresselle [row-hawk

Crécerelle, *s.f.* (*bird*) kestrel, windhover, spar-

Crèche, *s.f.* crib, manger; rack; infant-asylum,

day-nursery (*for the infants of working mothers*), crèche; foundling-hospital; (*mas.*) starling
Crécy, *s.f.* crecy (*kind of carrot*). *Potage* or *purée* — (or *à la* —), crecy-carrot soup
Crédence, *s.f.* credence, credence-table; buttery, pantry; safe; sideboard
Crédencier, *s.m.* pantler
Crédibilité, *s.f.* credibility
Crédit, *s.m.* credit; trust; interest, influence, patronage; repute, vogue, name; esteem, consideration; favour; request; (*book-keep.*) credit, creditor, credit-side. *A* —, on credit, on trust; (*fig.*) to no purpose, uselessly; without proof, gratuitously. *Lettre de* —, letter of credit; credentials. *Faire* — (*à*), to sell on credit, to give credit, to trust (...)
Créditer, *v.a.* to credit (with). *Être crédité sur une ville*, to have a credit in *or* letters of credit for a town. **Se** —, *v.r.* to gain credit, to be credited
Créditeur, *s.m.* creditor
Credo, *s.m.* credo, creed, belief
Crédule, *adj.* credulous
Crédulement, *adv.* credulously
Crédulité, *s.f.* credulity
Créé, e, *part. adj. V.* **Créer;** — *s.m.* creature; creatures
Créer, *v.a.* to create; to make; to produce; to cause; to form; to invent; to imagine; to find; to raise; to contract; to issue; to appoint, to establish; to found; to settle (*an annuity*)
Se —, *v.r.* to create *or* make *or* &c. (to *or* for) oneself; to procure to oneself; to find; to raise; to be created, &c.
†**Crémaillère,** *s.f.* pot-hanger, pot-hook; rack, toothed rack; spring; (*fort.*) crémaillère; (*bot.*) dodder. *Pendre la* —, to give *or* have a house-warming
†**Crémaillon,** *s.m.* small pot-hook
Crémant, *adj.m.* (*of Champagne wine*) creaming
Crémation, *s.f.* cremation
Crème, *s.f.* cream; custard; (*fig.*) cream, flower, pink, best, first, worthiest. — *fouettée*, whipped cream; (*fig.*) frothy matter, flimsy stuff. — *à la glace*, ice-cream. — *de Bouzy*, crème de Bouzy (*variety of Champagne wine*). *Fromage à la* —, cream-cheese. *Pot de* —, custard
Crément, *s.m.* increment, increase; accretion, alluvion; (*gram.*) suffix (*of a noun or verb*)
Crémer, *v.n.* to cream
Crèmerie, *s.f.* milk-shop, coffee-shop, coffee-house
Crémeu-x, se, *adj.* creamy
Crémi-er, ère, *s.m.f.* dairyman *or* woman, keeper of a coffee-shop, coffee-house keeper; — *s.f.* cream-ewer, cream-jug
Crémomètre, *s.m.* cremometer, cream-gauge
Crémonais, e, *adj. s.* Cremonese
Crémone, *s.m.* Cremona violin, cremona; — *s.f.* window-fastening, spring
Crénage, *s.m.* (*type-founding*) kerning
Crénate, *s.m.* (*chem.*) crenate
Crénaté, e, *adj.* (*chem.*) crenated
Crénatule, *s.f.* (*shell-fish*) crenatula
Créné, e, *adj.* (*type-founding*) kerned (*letter*); (*bot.*) crenate, crenated
Créneau, *s.m.* (*fort.*) battlement; crenelle; embrasure; loophole; (*mil.*) right of the company; (*nav.*) soil-pipe
Crénelage, *s.m.* (*coin.*) milling; milled edge
Crénelé, e, *part. adj.* embattled, battlemented; crenellated; indented; notched; (*of wheels*) cogged; (*of coin*) milled; (*bot.*) crenelled
Créneler, *v.a.* to embattle; to crenellate; to indent; to notch; to cog (*wheels*); to mill (*coin*)
Crénelure, *s.f.* crenellation, crenelle; indenting, notching, indentation, denticulation; (*bot.*) crenature, crenelle
Créner, *v.a.* (*type-founding*) to kern
Crénerie, *s.f.* (*type-founding*) kerning
Crenet, *s.m.* (*local*) curlew (*bird*)
Crénilabre, *s.m.* (*fish*) goldsinny, goldfinny, gilthead
Crénique, *adj.* (*chem.*) crenic
Crénom, *int.* (*pop.*) by George! by Jove! confound it! hang it!
Crénulé, e, *adj.* (*nat. hist.*) crenulate, crenulated

Créole, *s.m.f.* creole, West Indian; — *adj.* creole creolean
Créolisé, e, *adj.* acclimatized in the West Indies
Créoliser, *v.n.* to lead an indolent life
Créosote, *s.f.* (*chem.*) creosote, creasote
Crépage, *s.m.* dressing of crape; crisping; craping
Crêpe, *s.m.* crape; piece of crape; mourning hat-band, band; weed; (*fig.*) dark veil, pall, veil, gloom; (*of hair*) frizz, frizzle; — *s.f.* pancake
Crépé, *s.m.* frizz, frizzle; frisette, frizzet
Créper, *v.a.* to crisp; (*hair*) to crape, to crimp, to frizzle
Se —, *v.r.* to crisp; to become craped *or* frizzled; to crape *or* &c. o.'s hair. *Se — le toupet* (*of men*) or *le chignon* (*of women*), (*pop.*) to have a set-to, to fight, to pull each other by the hair
Crépi, *s.m.* (*mas.*) rough-cast
Crépide, *s.f.* (*bot.*) bastard hawkweed
Crêpière, *s.f.* pancake-woman
Crépin, *s.m.* *Saint-* —, Saint Crispin (*the patron saint of shoemakers*); shoemaker's kit. *Son Saint-* —, o.'s all. *Être dans la prison de Saint-* —, to be in St. Crispin's vice (*in shoes that pinch*). —, (*fam.*) Crispin, shoemaker, cobbler. —**s,** *pl.* grindery
Crépine, *s.f.* fringe; (*of metal*) rose; (*butch.*) caul
Crépinette, *s.f.* flat sausage wrapped in caul
Crépinière, *s.f.* (*pop.*) barberry (*plant*)
Crépir, *v.a.* to roughcast (*a wall*); to grain (*leather*); to crisp (*horse-hair*)
Crépissage, Crépissement, *s.m.*, **Crépissure,** *s.f.* (*mas.*) roughcasting
Crépitation, *s.f.*, **Crépitement,** *s.m.* crepitation, crackling; pattering
Crépiter, *v.n.* to crepitate, to crackle; to patter
†**Crépodaille,** *s.f.* thin crape
Crépon, *s.m.* crepon (*thick crape*); rouge-spreader
†**Créponaille,** *s.f. V.* **Crépodaille**
Creps, *s.m.* (kind of game at dice)
Crépu, e, *adj.* woolly (*hair*); crisped
Crépure, *s.f. V.* **Crépage**
Crépusculaire, *adj.m.f.*, *s.m.* crepuscular
Crépuscule, *s.m.* twilight, evening twilight, owl's light; (*fig.*) decline; (*abusively*) dawn, morning twilight; (*fig., abusively*) dawn
Crépusculin, e, *adj.* crepuscular
Crèque, *s.f.* (*bot.*) sloe
Créquier, *s.m.* (*bot.*) sloe-tree, blackthorn
Cresane, *s.f.* cresane (*pear*)
Crescendo, *adv. s.m.* (*mus.*) crescendo (*gradual increase from soft to loud*); (*fig.*) increasing, more and more, better and better, worse and worse; increase, rise, swell
Crescentie, *s.f.* (*bot.*) crescentia, calabash-tree
Créseau, *s.m. V.* **Carisel**
Cressane, *s.f. V.* **Cresane**
Cresse, *s.f.* (*bot.*) *V.* **Passerage**
Cresserelle, *s.f. V.* **Crécerelle**
Cresson, *s.m.* cress, cresses, water-cress, water-cresses. — *alénois*, — *à la noix*, dittander, garden-cress (*part of the small salad called "mustard and cress"*). — *de fontaine*, water-cress
Cressonnière, *s.f.* cress-bed; water-cress woman
Crésus, *s.m.* very rich man, man as rich as Crœsus
Crétacé, e, *adj.* cretaceous
Créte, *s.f.* crest; comb; tuft; ridge, top; bank; coping; vandyke border; heap. — *baissée*, crest-fallen. — *-marine*, (*bot.*) crest-marine, samphire. — *de coq*, cock's comb; (*bot.*) cocks-comb, coxcomb. *A* —, crested, tufted. *Baisser la* —, to be crest-fallen, to look humble *or* small, to come down a peg. *Donner sur la* —, (*V. Rabaisser la* —). *Lever la* —, to hold o.'s head up, to bear o.'s head high, to carry it high, to be conceited *or* bumptious. *Rabaisser la* — *à*, to lower ...'s crest, to humble ...'s pride, to bring down a peg
Crêté, e, *adj.* crested, tufted; vandyked; tacked
Crételer, *v.n.* (*of hens*) to cackle
Cretelle, *s.f.* (*bot.*) crested dog's-tail grass
Crêter, *v.a.* to vandyke; to tack

Crétin, *s.m.* cretin; idiot, fool
Crétiniser, *v.a.* to stupefy, to brutalize, to brutify, to make (...) an idiot
Se —, *v.r.* to become stupid, to become an [idiot
Crétinisme, *s.m.* cretinism; idiocy, imbecility
Crétois, e, *adj. s.* Cretan
Creton, *s.m.* —**s,** *pl.* (tallow-)graves *or* greaves; (*pain de* —) cracklings, dog-biscuit
Cretonne, *s.f.* linen cloth; long-cloth; chintz
Cretonnier, *s.m.* fat-gatherer
Creusage, Creusement, *s.m.* digging; hollowing; excavating, excavation; scooping; sinking; deepening
Creuser, *v.a.n.* to dig; to hollow; to excavate; to scoop; to sink; to deepen; to dive into, to fathom, to examine thoroughly, to study carefully. **Se** —, *v.r.* to become hollow; to puzzle *or* rack (*o.'s brains*); to dig (for) oneself, to work; to be dug, &c.
Creuset, *s.m.* crucible; cruset, crevet; melting-[pot; test
Creusiste, *s.m.* crucible-maker
Creusure, *s.f* hollow, cavity
Creutzer, *s.m. V.* **Kreutzer**
Creu-x, se, *adj.* hollow, deep; sunk, sunken; shallow; empty; unsubstantial; frothy; vain; foolish; chimerical; fantastic; incomplete. *Songer* —, to indulge in *or* be full of idle fancies
Creux, *s.m.* hollow; cavity; hole; pit; hollowness; emptiness; depth; hollow *or* bass voice; voice; chest, stomach, bread-basket, inside; cast, mould; die; intaglio
†**Crevaille,** *s.f.* (*pop.*) guttling, blow-out
Crevaison, *s.f.* (*pop.*) death, exit, going off, kicking the bucket
Crevant, e, *part. adj. V.* **Crever;** (*pop.*) provoking, aggravating, bothering, a bother
Crevasse, *s.f.* crevice; chink, cranny; crack; gap; chap; crevasse; (*vet.*) scratches
Crevasser, *v.a.,* **Se** —, *v.r.* to crevice; to chink; to cranny; to crack; to chap; to split; to burst
Crève, *s.m.* (*in compounds, from* **Crever,** "to burst," "to break," &c.) thing that bursts *or* breaks *or* &c., breaker. — **-cœur,** *s.m.* heart-breaking thing, heart-break, heart-sore, vexation; large species of cocks and hens
Crevé, e, *part. adj.* burst, &c. (*V.* **Crever**); slashed; bloated, puffy; dead; (*pop.*) thin, emaciated, used up, done up, on o.'s last legs; — *s.m.f.* (*pop.*) mere skeleton, poor stick. *Gros* —, big fat man, bloated *or* puffy fellow (*looking as if ready to burst*). *Grosse —e,* big fat woman, bloated *or* puffy creature. *Petit* —, scrubby little fellow, poor stick; fast young fellow used up *or* done up (*looking as if ready to die*). *Comme un* —, immoderately, outright, dead, with a vengeance. — *s.m.* (*of old costumes*) slash
Crèvement, *s.m.* bursting
Crever, *v.a.n.* to burst; to pierce; to break; to stave, to stave in; to crack; to split; to cram; to kill; to work to death; to die, to go off, to kick the bucket; to put out (*the eyes*); (*nav.*) to bilge, to stave in, to split. — *de faim,* to starve; to be dying with hunger, to be ravenously hungry. — *de rire,* to split o.'s sides with laughing. — *les yeux à,* to put out the eyes of; (*fig.*) to stare in the face; to be obvious. *Faire* —, to kill [oneself; (*nav.*) to bilge, to split
Se —, *v.r.* to burst; to cram *or* kill *or* &c.
Crevet, *s.m.* stay-lace with tags at both ends
Crevette, *s.f.* shrimp, prawn; (*fam.*) gay woman
Cri, *s.m.* cry; shout; scream, screaming; shriek, shrieking; screech; yell; squall, squalling; squeak; creaking; screaking; gabble; chirp; whoop; noise; call; voice; clamour; crying; outcry; complaint; lamentation; qualm; opinion. — *d'armes,* (*her.*) motto. *Jeter* or *pousser les hauts —s,* to cry out lustily, to scream out; to raise an outcry, to complain loudly
Criage, *s.m.* public crying
†**Criaillement,** *s.m. V.* **Criaillerie**
†**Criailler,** *v.n.* to bawl, to squall, to cry out, to cry; to clamour; to gabble; to grumble; to scold; to wrangle
†**Criaillerie,** *s.f.* bawling; crying; squalling; clamouring, clamour; outcry; gabbling; grumbling; scolding; wrangling; noise, racket, row
†**Criailleu-r, se,** *adj.* bawling, squalling; scolding; — *s.m.f.* bawler; grumbler; scolder, scold; wrangler [ful; noisy
Criant, e, *adj.* crying, glaring, shocking, shame-
Criard, e, *adj.* clamorous, squalling, noisy; scolding; screaming; shrill; squeaking; creaking; discordant, harsh, rough; glaring; (*of debts*) paltry, trifling, dribbling, small; — *s.m.f.* bawler, squaller, noisy person; scolder, scold, vixen; — *s.f.* thick-gummed cloth
Criblage, *s.m.* sifting
Crible, *s.m.* sieve; riddle; cribble
Cribler, *v.a* to sift; to riddle; to scan; to pierce all over, to pepper; to perforate; to cover; to fill; to load; to overwhelm. *Criblé de dettes,* over head and ears in debt
Se —, *v.r.* to riddle *or* &c. each other; to be sifted *or* riddled *or* &c.
Cribleu-r, se, *s.m.f.* sifter [form
Cribleu-x, se, *adj.* cribrate, cribrose; cribri-
Criblier, *s.m.* sieve-maker, riddle-maker
Criblure, *s.f.* siftings
Cribration, *s.f.* (*pharm.*) sifting, cribration
Cribriforme, *adj.* cribriform
Cric, *s.m.* creese *or* kris (*Malay dagger*); (*tech.*) lifting-jack, screw-jack, jack, lift; (*of a carriage*) spring-jack; (*noise*) creaking, crick; (*pop.*) rough brandy. — *à baril,* patent cask-stand, hance, tilting-jack
Cric-crac, *s.m., adv., int.* crick-crack
Cricket, *s.m.* cricket (*game*)
Cricoïde, *adj.* (*anat.*) cricoid
Cri-cri, *s.m.* (*insect*) cricket; (*bird*) bunting
Crid, *s.m.* creese, kris (*Malay dagger*)
Criée, *s.f.* auction; announcement; outcry. *A la* —, by auction
Crier, *v.n.a.* to cry; to cry out; to shout; to scream; to shriek; to screech; to yell; to squeak; to holloa; to call out; to squall; to bawl; to roar; to creak; to screak; to grate; to rustle; to rumble; to gabble; to chirp; to make a noise; to clamour; to talk loudly; to complain; to protest; to exclaim; to inveigh; to rant; to grumble; to scold; to keep telling; to proclaim; to publish; to hawk, to hawk about; to sell by auction, to put up for sale, to put up; to be crying *or* glaring
Se —, *v.r.* to be cried; to be proclaimed *or* [published *or* &c.
Crierie, *s.f. V.* **Criaillerie**
Crieu-r, se, *s.m.f.* bawler, squaller; crier; auctioneer; hawker. — *public,* town-crier, common crier, crier
Crime, *s.m.* crime; guilt; offence; felony
Criméen, ne, *adj. s.* Crimean
Criminalisant, e, *adj.* leading to criminality
Criminaliser, *v.a.* to remove (*an affair, a case*) from a civil to a criminal court
Se —, *v.r.* to be removed ditto
Criminaliste, *s.m.* criminalist
Criminalité, *s.f.* criminality
Criminel, le, *adj.* criminal; guilty; unlawful; — *s.m.f.* criminal; culprit; offender; — *s.m.* criminal proceedings *or* matters. *Au* —, in criminal matters; criminally [wickedly
Criminellement, *adv.* criminally, guiltily,
Crin, *s.m.* (*of some animals*) hair (*of the mane or tail*); horse-hair; hair-cloth; fibre (*of some plants*); (*jest., of pers.*) hair; (*pop., s.m. adj.*) disagreeable fellow *or* creature; disagreeable, cross; —**s,** *pl.* mane; hair. — *marin,* silkworm-gut. — *végétal,* alva marina, vegetable fibre. *A tous —s,* (*of horses*) with flowing mane and tail; (*of a lion,* &c.) with a thick mane; (*pers., jest.*) shock-headed. *Comme un* —, (*pop.*) as cross as two sticks
Crincrin, *s.m.* screeching fiddle; scraper
Crinier, *s.m.* horse-hair worker
Crinière, *s.f.* mane; mane-sheet; (horse-hair) plume (*of a helmet*); (*jest.*) mop, shock (*head of hair*), caxon (*wig*). — *en brosse,* hog-mane

Crinole, *s.f.* (*bot.*) crinum
Crinoline, *s.f.* hair-cloth; crinoline
Crinon, *s.m.* (*zool., med.*) crino
Criocère, *s.m.* (*zool.*) crioceris, asparagus-beetle
Crique, *s.f.* creek, cove; flaw, crack; (*fort.*) ditches; (*pop.*) rough brandy
Criquer, *v.n.* (*of steel*) to crack, to chink
Criquet, *s.m.* cricket (*insect*); grasshopper; tit (*little horse*); tom-tit (*bit of a man*); (*pop.*) weak wine [sleep
Crise, *s.f.* crisis; fit; convulsion; mesmeric
Crisiaque, *adj. s.* mesmeric, mesmerized
Crispation, *s.f.* shrivelling, contraction; twitch, twitching; irritation; (*fam.*) fidget
Crisper, *v.a.* to shrivel, to contract; to irritate; to put in a fidget
Se —, *v.r.* to shrivel up; to contract; to twitch; to become irritated; to be in a fidget
Crispin, *s.m.* jester, joker; short cloak
Criss, *s.m.* creese, kris (*Malay dagger*)
Crissement, *s.m.* (*of the teeth*) grating
Crisser, *v.n.* (*of the teeth*) to grate
Cristal, *s.m.* crystal; glass; limpidity. — *de roche*, rock-crystal
Cristallerie, *s.f.* glass-works; crystal-making
Cristallier, *s.m.* glass-cutter; case of crystals
Cristallière, *s.f.* crystal-mine
Cristallifère, *adj.* crystalliferous [line
Cristallin, e, *adj.*, **Cristallin,** *s.m.* crystal-
Cristallisable, *adj.* crystallizable
Cristallisation, *s.f.* crystallization
Cristalliser, *v.a.n.*, **Se —,** *v.r.* to crystallize
Cristalliseur, Cristallisoir, *s.m.* crystallizing-pan; crystallizer
Cristallographe, *s.m.* crystallographer
Cristallo-graphie, -graphique, &c. *V.*
Cristalloïde, *adj.* crystalloid [page 3, § 1
Cristatelle, *s.f.* spongilla fluviatilis, river-
Criste, *s.f.* *V.* **Christe** [sponge
Cristi, *int.* (*abbreviation of* **Sacristi**) [stone
Critérium, *s.m.* criterion, standard, test, touch-
Crithe, *s.m.* (*med.*) *V.* **Orgelet**
Crithme, *s.m.* (*bot.*) samphire
Criticisme, *s.m.* (*philos.*) criticism, critical philosophy (*Kant's system*) [*follower*)
Criticiste, *s.m. adj.* (*philos.*) criticist (*Kant's*
Critiquable, *adj.* criticizable, censurable
Critique, *adj.* critical; censorious; — *s.f.* criticism; critique; review; critics; stricture, censure, reflection; — *s.m.* critic; censurer, fault-finder
Critiquer, *v.a.n.* to criticize; to censure, to reflect on, to animadvert on, to find fault (with)
Se —, *v.r.* to criticize *or* &c. oneself *or* each other; to be criticized *or* &c.
Critiqueu-r, se, *s.m.f.* criticizer, fault-finder
Croassement, *s.m.* (*of crows*) croaking, croak, cawing, caw
Croasser, *v.n.* (*of crows*) to croak, to caw
Croate, *adj. s.* Croatian; croat
Croc, *s.m.* hook; boat-hook; drag-hook; gaff; fang; tusk; dog-tooth, canine tooth; tooth; curling moustache, curl, twist; crackling, craunching; (*pers.*) sharper, bully; — *adv.* crisp. *En* —, hooked; curled up, twisted up. *Faire* —, to crackle (*under the teeth*), to craunch. *Mettre* or *pendre au* —, to hook; to hang up; to lay by, to lay on the shelf, to suspend. — **-en-jambe,** *s.m.* trip; dirty trick. *Donner un — -en-jambe à*, to trip up; to supplant; to serve a dirty trick
Croche, *adj.m.f.* *V.* **Crochu;** — *s.f.* (*mus.*) quaver. *Double* —, semiquaver. *Triple* —, demi-semiquaver. *Quadruple* —, semi-demi-semiquaver. —**s,** *s.f.pl.* (*tech.*) forge-tongs
Crocher, *v.a.* to hook; to crook. **Se —,** *v.r.* (*pop.*) to come to blows, to have a set-to, to fight
Crochet, *s.m.* hook; gaff; tenter; steelyard; picklock, skeleton-key; clasp; claw; hasp; forked hoe; sudden *or* sharp turning *or* turn, turning, turn, bend; porter's knot, shoulder-strap; curl, twist, heart-breaker; fang; tush; tooth; wire; (*arch.*) crocket; (*print.*) bracket; crotchet; crochet-hook, crochet-needle; crochet. *Être sur les —s de, vivre aux —s de*, to live at the expense *or* charge of
Crochetable, *adj.* (*of locks*) pickable
Crochetage, *s.m.* lock-picking, picking; porterage; (*agr.*) hoeing
Crochetée, *s.f.* porter's load, load
Crocheter, *v.a.* to pick (*a lock*); to pick the lock of; to hoe; (*fig.*) to penetrate
Se —, *v.r.* to fight like blackguards, to fight
Crocheteur, *s.m.* street-porter, porter; (*in genteel slang*) common blackguard; (*of locks*) picklock, house-breaker
Crochetier, *s.m.* hook-maker, clasp-maker
Crocheton, *s.m.* small hook
Crochu, e, *adj.* hooked, crooked; bent; forked. *Avoir les mains —es*, (*fig.*) to be light-fingered
Crocidisme, *s.m.* (*obsolete*) *V.* **Carphologie**
Crocine, *s.f.* (*chem.*) crocine
Crocique, *adj.* (*chem.*) *V.* **Croconique**
Crocodile, *s.m.* crocodile; (*pop.*) cheat; ugly customer, cross-patch; creditor, dun
Crocodiléen, ne, Crocodilien, ne, *adj.*, **Crocodilien,** *s.m.* crocodilean
Croconate, *s.m.* (*chem.*) croconate
Croconique, *adj.* (*chem.*) croconic [wolf-dog
Crocotte, *s.m.* cross between a dog and a wolf,
Crocus, *s.m.* (*bot.*) crocus, saffron-flower
Crocydisme, *s.m.* *V.* **Crocidisme**
Croire, *v.a.n.* to believe; to think; to deem; to be of opinion; to think it; to think so; to believe *or* think to be; to give credit for; to credit; to trust to; to take the advice *or* the word of; to fancy, to imagine; to suppose; to presume; to expect. *A* —, to believe, &c.; to be believed, to be presumed, likely. *En* —, to believe, to trust to; to take ...'s advice *or* ...'s word for it. *A l'en* —, if we are to believe him; according to him. *Je crois bien!* I should think so! I believe you! no wonder! *Je crois bien que* ..., I fully *or* really *or* do believe that ...; I dare say (that) ...; indeed. *Je n'en crois rien*, I do not believe a word of it. *Je crois voir*, I think *or* fancy I see. *Croyez bien, croyez-le bien*, depend upon it
Se —, *v.r.* to believe *or* think oneself; to believe *or* &c. oneself to be, to think one is; to think one has; (*of things*) to be believed. *S'en* —, to consult oneself; to rely upon o.'s own judgment. *S'en — beaucoup*, to think a great deal of oneself. *Il se croit tout permis*, he thinks
Croisade, *s.f.* crusade [he may do anything
Croisé, e, *adj.* crossed; cross; across; folded; twilled; double-milled; (*of waistcoats*, &c.) double-breasted; (*of rhymes*) alternate; (*anat.*) crucial; (*pers.*) crusading. *Les bras —s*, with folded arms; doing nothing, idle
Croisé, *s.m.* intersection; crossing; (*in compounds*) cross- ...; (*stuff*) twill; (*pers.*) crusader
Croisée, *s.f.* cross; (*arch.*) window, &c. (*V.* **Fenêtre**)
Croisement, *s.m.* crossing; cross-breeding
Croiser, *v.a.n.* to cross; to cross off; to thwart; to come across; to pass; to fold; to clasp; to lap over; to alternate (*rhymes*); to twill; (*nav.*) to cruise
Se —, *v.r.* to cross each other; to cross; to pass each other; to thwart each other; to sit cross-legged; to contradict oneself; (*of rhymes*) to alternate; (*hist.*) to take the cross, to engage in a crusade, to crusade. *Se — avec*, (*pers.*) to pass. *Se — les bras*, to fold o.'s arms; to remain
Croiserie, *s.f.* wicker-work [idle
Croisette, *s.f.* (*her.*) crosslet; (*nav.*) cross-tree of the topmast; (*fenc.*) fencing-master's foil; (*bot.*) cross-wort; (*obsolete*) cross-row, alphabet
Croiseur, *s.m.* (*mining*) cross-lode, cross-course; (*nav.*) cruiser; — *adj.m.* cruising
Croisière, *s.f.* (*nav.*) cruise; cruising-party; cruising-latitude; (*of roads*) crossing; (*rail.*)
†Croisille, *s.f.* cross-piece [siding

†**Croisillon,** *s.m.* cross-bar, sash-bar; (*of crosses*) arm

Croissance, *s.f.* growth; growing; increase; vegetation. *Avoir pris toute sa —*, to be full-grown [&c. (*V.* **Croitre**)

Croissant, e, *part. adj.* growing, increasing,

Croissant, *s.m.* increase; crescent; pruning-hook *or* bill; hook, rest, holder; fire-irons holder; curtain-rest; crescent-shaped roll *or* cake *or* puff (*or anything else*)

Croisure, *s.f.* crossing; cross; twilling; (*of rhymes*) alternation; (*of verses of different measure*) intermixture, mingling

Croît, *s.m.* (*of cattle, plants*) increase from breeding, increase, growth, production

Croître, *v.n.a.* to grow; to grow up; to increase; to lengthen; to spring, to spring up; to shoot, to shoot up; to rise; to swell; to improve; to thrive; to multiply; to spread. *Ne faire que — et embellir*, to improve *or* increase every day

Croix, *s.f.* cross; mark (*as o.'s signature*); (*print.*) dagger; (*fig.*) affliction, sorrow, tribulation, trouble; (*of knighthood*) cross, star; (*mil.*) cross, medal. *— de par Dieu, — de Dieu, — de Jésus*, Christ-cross-row, criss-cross-row, cross-row, alphabet, letters; spelling-book, primer, horn-book; A B C, elements. *— de Jérusalem, — de Malte*, (*bot.*) caltrop. *— de Saint-André*, St. Andrew's cross; cross columns; cross roads *or* streets; (*her.*) saltier, St. Andrew's cross. *— du sud*, (*astr.*) Crosier, Southern Cross. *— ou pile*, *V.* **Pile.** *En —*, crossways, as a cross, in the shape *or* form of a cross; crossed; cruciate. *Grand'—*, *s.f.* & *s.m.* (*V.* **Grand'croix,** *at letter* **G**). *La —, la — d'honneur, la — de la Légion d'honneur*, the cross of the Legion of Honour (*a French order*), knighthood (*in England*), a medal *or* a cross (*in England, for soldiers*). *Faire le signe de la —, faire un signe de —*, to make the sign of the cross, to cross oneself. *Faire le signe de la — sur*, to cross. *Jouer à — ou pile; N'avoir ni — ni pile; V.* **Pile**

‡**Cromlech, Cromlek,** *s.m.* cromlech (*druidical remains*)

Cromorne, *s.m.* (*mus.*) cromorna (*of an organ*); [krum-horn (*trumpet*)

Cron, *s.m.* shell-marl, crag

Crône, *s.f.* (*fish.*) weedy spot, holt; *— s.m.* (*nav.*) [crane

Croquade, *s.f.* (*paint.*) rough sketch

Croquant, *s.m.* crackling; gristle; crisp almond-cake; (*obsolete*) peasant; boor; churl; vulgar fellow; ragamuffin; beggar; poor wretch

Croquant, e, *adj.* crisp, short, crackling, craunching [cake

Croquante, *s.f.* crisp tart *or* pie; crisp almond-

Croque, *s.m.f.* (*in compounds, from* **Croquer,** "to craunch," &c.) thing (*m.*) that craunches, animal (*m.*) *or* person (*m.f.*) that craunches *or* eats, craunecher, eater, devourer, swallower, gobbler. — **-abeilles,** *s.m.* (*bird*) bee-eater. — **-au-sel (A la),** *adv.* with salt only; as plainly *or* as easily as possible. — **-en-bouche,** *s.m.* crisp sweetmeat; crisp cake, cracker, snap. — **-lardon,** *s.m.f.* (*obsolete*) dinner-hunter, parasite, sponger. — **-mitaine,** *s.m.* bogie, bogy, bogey, old bogie; bugbear. — **-morts,** (*fam.*) undertaker's man, death-hunter, dismal. — **-noisettes,** — **-noix,** *s.m.* (*zool.*) muscardin dormouse. — **-notes,** — **-sol,** *s.m.f.* (*fam.*) sorry musician, scraper, strummer, thrummer, grinder, squeaker; player [(*under* **Croque**)

Croquembouche. *V.* **Croque-en-bouche**

Croquement, *s.m.* craunching, scraunching

Croquemitaine. *V.* **Croque-mitaine** (*under* **Croque**)

Croquer, *v. a. n.* to craunch, to crunch, to scraunch, to scrunch; to eat up, to devour, to swallow, to gobble up; to steal, to filch, to pilfer, to bone, to bag; to enjoy; to sketch; (*nav.*) to hook. *Être à —, être gentil* or *joli à —*, to be very pretty

Se —, *v.r.* to be craunched *or* devoured *or* &c.

Croquet, *s.m.* crisp biscuit *or* cake, cracker, snap; (*pop.*) cross-patch. *Être comme un —*, (*pop.*) to be as cross as two sticks

Croquette, *s.f.* (*cook.*) croquette; (*game*) croquet

Croqueu-r, se, *s.m.f.* craunecher, eater, devourer, swallower, gobbler, glutton; pilferer; sketcher. *— de femmes*, lady-killer

†**Croquignole,** *s.f.* fillip; cracknel

†**Croquignoler,** *v.a.* to fillip

Croquis, *s.m.* sketch, rough draught

Crore, *s.m.* (*Indian*) crore (£1,000,000)

Crosse, *s.f.* hooked stick; hook (*of a stick*); crutch; (*bishop's*) crosier; butt, butt-end (*of a gun*); hockey-stick; hockey; (*the Canadian game, and battledore for ditto*) crosse; (*agr.*) stick; (*anat.*) arch (*of the aorta*)

Crossé, e, *adj.* crosiered

Crosser, *v.a.* to drive with a hockey-stick; (*fig.*) to rate soundly; to bully; to spurn, to kick; to abuse, to clapper-claw; to beat; *— v.n.* to play at hockey [ear, elbow, ancone

Crossette, *s.f.* (*agr.*) layer; (*arch.*) crossette,

Crosseur, *s.m.* hockey-player

†**Crossillon,** *s.m.* curve *or* crook (*of a crosier*)

Crotalaire, *s.f.* (*bot.*) crotalaria, rattle-wort

Crotale, *s.m.* (*in antiquity*) crotalum, castanet; (*modern mus.*) Chinese bells; (*zool.*) crotalus, [rattle-snake

Croton, *s.m.* (*bot.*) croton

Crotonate, *s.m.* (*chem.*) crotonate

Crotonine, *s.f.* (*chem.*) crotonine

Crotonique, *adj.* (*chem.*) crotonic

Crotte, *s.f.* mud, dirt; filth; poverty, misery; degradation, abjection; low debauchery; (*of some animals*) dung; dung-ball

Crotté, e, *adj.* muddy; dirty; (*fig.*) sorry, paltry. *Il fait —*, it is muddy *or* dirty

Crotter, *v.a.* to draggle, to bedraggle, to drabble, to splash, to spatter, to bespatter, to dirty

Se —, *v.r.* to dirty oneself, to get dirty; to draggle, to drabble [horse-dung

Crottin, *s.m.* dung (*of several quadrupeds*);

Crotton, *s.m.* lump of sugar

Crotu, e, *adj.* (*obsolete*) pock-pitted

Crou, *s.m.* sandy and clayey soil

Crouchaut, *s.m.* (*nav.*) crotch, floor-timber

Croulant, e, *adj.* falling, sinking, crumbling, ruinous, tottering, tumbledown, ramshackle

Croulement, *s.m.* falling in, falling, sinking, fall, downfall, ruin

Crouler, *v.n.* to fall in *or* down, to fall, to sink, to give way, to crumble, to go to ruin, to totter, to tumble down; *— v.a.* to shake; to wag; to launch (*a ship*)

Se —, *v.r.* to ruin oneself, to sink, to fail

Crouli-er, ère, *adj.* (*of land*) moving, shifting, sinking, boggy, swampy; *— s.f.* light shifting soil, boggy land

Croumier, *s.m.* horse-jockey [soil, boggy land

Croup, *s.m.* (*med.*) croup

Croupade, *s.f.* (*rid.*) croupade

Croupal, e, *adj.* (*med.*) croupal, croup

Croupe, *s.f.* crupper, croup, rump; (*of hills*) top, ridge, brow; (*arch.*) hip-roof; half-cylinder (*of a church*); (*fin.*) share, interest. *En —*, behind (*on a horse* or *ass* or *&c.*); double load. *Monter en —*, to ride behind [fine crupper

Croupé, e, *adj.* with a crupper. *Bien —*, with a

Croupeton (A), *adv.* squatting down

Croupeu-x, se, *adj.* (*med.*) croupal, croup

Croupi, e, *adj.* stagnant, putrid, ditch (*water*)

Croupiader, *v.n.* (*nav.*) to moor by a stern-cable

Croupiat, *s.m.* (*nav.*) sternfast, stern-cable

Croupier, *s.m.* partner, shareholder; (*at play*) partner; (*of gambling*) croupier

Croupière, *s.f.* (*of saddles*) crupper; (*nav.*) sternfast. *Mouiller en —*, to cast anchor by the stern. *Tailler des —s à*, to cut out work for; to put to flight, to rout, to pursue close

Croupion, *s.m.* rump [o.'s rump about

Croupionner, *v.n.* to raise the rump, to move

Croupir, *v.n.* to stand still; to stagnate; to become putrid; to lie rotting, to rot; to lie in filth; to wallow; to be sunk, to lie, to remain, to live

Croupissant, e, *part. adj.* stagnating, stagnant, standing still, standing, &c. (*V.* **Croupir**), putrescent [tion, putrefaction
Croupissement, *s.m.* standing still, stagna-
Croupon, *s.m.* square hide, butt
Croustade, *s.f.* pie, patty
†**Croustillant, e,** *adj.* crisp, crusty
†**Croustille,** *s.f.* bit of crust
†**Croustiller,** *v.n.* to pick *or* nibble bits of crust, to munch; to craunch, to crunch; — *v.a.* to pick, to nibble, to munch
†**Croustilleusement,** *adv.* smuttily
†**Croustilleu-x, se,** *adj.* smutty, free
Croûte, *s.f.* crust; toast, bit of toast, sippet; scurf, scab; daub; fogy, old fogy; bungler. — *de lait,* — *laiteuse,* (*med.*) achor
Croûté, e, *adj.* crusted, caked, crusty
Croûtelette, *s.f.* bit of crust
Crouter (Se), *v.r.* to cake, to crust
Croûteu-x, se, *adj.* crusty; scurfy, scabby
Croûtier, *s.m.* bad painter, dauber; picture-dealer *or* broker
Croûton, *s.m.* crust-end; crust, bit of crust; sippet, bit of toast, toast; dauber; bungler; [fogy, old fogy
Croûtonner, *v.n.* to daub
Crown-glass, *s.m.* crown-glass [likely
Croyable, *adj.* credible, believable; reliable;
Croyance, *s.f.* belief; creed; credit; trust; persuasion; faith; opinion; expectation
Croyant, e, *adj.* believing; — *s.m.f.* believer; [faithful
Crû, *m.,* **Crue,** *f., part. of* **Croître**
Cru, *m.,* **Crue,** *f., part. of* **Croire;** — *adj.* raw; uncooked; crude; unwrought, undressed; rough; undigested; harsh; blunt; coarse; bare; free, indecent, smutty, obscene; (*of water*) hard; (*paint., med.*) crude. *A* —, on the bare skin, next the skin; on the bare soil *or* ground; on the bare ...; right on, right in *or* into; bare
Cru, Crû, *s.m.* growth; growing; production; make; fabrication; invention; (o.'s) own; vine-estate, vineyard; variety of wine; wine; soil; country. *Vin du* —, wine of the country; wine of o.'s own growth
Cruauté, *s.f.* cruelty; hardship [mush
Cruchade, *s.f.* maize hasty-pudding, hominy,
Cruche, *s.f.* pitcher, jug, jar; dunce, dolt, fool. *Tant va la* — *à l'eau qu'à la fin elle se casse,* the pitcher goes so often to the well that it comes home broken at last
Cruchée, *s.f.* pitcherful, jugful, jarful
Crucherie, *s.f.* foolery, stupidity
Cruchette, *s.f.* small pitcher, jug
Cruchon, *s.m.* small pitcher, jug; stone bottle
Crucial, e, *adj.* crucial, cross-like
Crucianelle, *s.f.* (*bot.*) cross-wort [(*bot.*) crucifer
Crucifère, *adj.* (*bot.,* &c.) cruciferous; — *s.f.*
Crucifiement, Crucifîment, *s.m.* crucifi- [xion
Crucifier, *v.a.* to crucify
Crucifix, *s.m.* crucifix, cross. *Mangeur de* —, bigot. *Faire le demi-* —, (*pop.*) to beg
Crucifixion, *s.f.* crucifixion
Cruciforme, *adj.* cruciform, cross-shaped
Crucigère, *adj.* crucigerous
Crudité, *s.f.* crudity, rawness, crudeness; crude *or* raw thing; raw fruit *or* vegetable; indecency, coarse expression; blunt words; (*of water*) hardness
Crue, *s.f.* growth; increase, rising, rise, swelling, flood, inundation; freshet; surge. *Avoir pris toute sa* —, to be full-grown
Crue, *adj. part., feminine of* **Cru** *and of* **Crû**
Cruel, le, *adj.* cruel; hard-hearted; unkind; painful; sore; fierce; grievous; sad; hard; tiresome, disagreeable, annoying; unfavourable; — *s.m.f.* cruel *or* unkind man *or* woman, cruel one; — *s.f.* unkind beauty; hot-burning brandy
Cruellement, *adv.* cruelly; unkindly; painfully; sorely; fiercely; grievously; sadly
Crûment, *adv.* bluntly; crudely; harshly; [roughly; coarsely
Cruor, *s.m.* (*anat.*) cruor
Cruorique, *adj.* (*anat.*) cruoric
Crural, e, *adj.* (*anat.*) crural [purism
Cruscantisme, *s.m.* cruscantism (*Italian*
Crustacé, e, *adj.* crustaceous; — *s.m.* crustacean
Crustacéen, ne, *adj.* crustacean
Crustacéolog-ie, -ique. *V.* page 3, § 1
Crustacéologue, *s.m.* crustaceologist
Cruzade, *s.f.* cruzado, cruzade, crusade (*Portuguese and Brazilian coin*)
Cryolithe, *s.m.* (*min.*) cryolite
Cryophore, *s.m.* (*phys. instr.*) cryophorus
Crypte, *s.f.* crypt (*vault,* &c.); — *s.m.* (*anat.*) crypt
Cryptogame, *adj.* (*bot.*) cryptogamous; — *s.m.f.*
Cryptogam-ie, -ique. *V.* p. 3, § 1 [cryptogam
Crypto-graphie, -graphique, &c. *V.* page
Cryptonyme, *adj.* cryptonymous [3, § 1
Cryptoportique, *s.m.* (*arch.*) crypto-porticus
Cu, *s.m. V.* **Cul**
Cubage, *s.m.,* **Cubation, Cubature,** *s.f.*
Cubain, e, *adj. s.* Cuban [cubature
Cube, *s.m.* cube; — *adj.* cubic; cube
Cubèbe, *s.m.* (*bot.*) cubebs
Cubébine, *s.f.* (*chem.*) cubebine
Cuber, *v.a.* to cube. *Se* —, to be cubed
Cubilot, *s.m.* (*metal.*) cupola [root
Cubique, *adj.* cubic, cubical. *Racine* —, cube
Cubital, e, *adj.* (*anat.*) ulnar, cubital
Cubital, *s.m.* elbow-rest
Cubitus, *s.m.* (*anat.*) ulna
Cuboïde, *adj.* cuboid, cuboidal
Cuceron, *s.m.* (*zool.*) grub
Cucifère, *s.m.* (*bot.*) doom palm, dum palm
Cucubale, *s.m.* (*bot.*) campion
Cucurbitacé, e, *adj.* (*bot.*) cucurbitaceous
Cucurbite, *s.f.* (*chem.*) cucurbit
†**Cueillage,** *s.m.,* **Cueillaison,** *s.f.* gathering; picking; gathering *or* picking season
†**Cueille,** *s.f.* gathering; picking; (*nav.*) coil, fake; (*nav.*) breadth of sail-cloth
†**Cueillement,** *s.m.* gathering; picking
†**Cueillette,** *s.f.* crop; gathering; picking; nutting; gathering *or* picking *or* nutting season; collection; harvest; (*nav.*) mixed cargo
†**Cueilleu-r, se,** *s.m.f.* gatherer [gathering
†**Cueillie,** *s.f.* (*mas.*) rendering
†**Cueillir,** *v.a.* to gather; to pick, to pluck; to pull; to snatch; (*mas.*) to render; (*nav.*) to coil
Se —, *v.r.* to be gathered *or* picked *or* &c.
†**Cueilloir,** *s.m.* fruit-basket; (*instr.*) fruit-gatherer; grape-gatherer; flower-gatherer
Cuffat, *s.m.* (*mining*) cage, corf *or* corve, kibble,
Cuider, *s.m.* fruit-basket [skip
Cuider, *v.n.a.* (*old*) to think, to imagine
†**Cuiller, Cuillère,** *s.f.* spoon; table-spoon; ladle; (*bird*) spoonbill. — *à bouche,* table-spoon. — *à café, petite* —, tea-spoon. — *à pot,* cooking-ladle. — *à potage,* — *à soupe, grande* —, soup-ladle; (*abusively*) table-spoon. — *à ragoût,* gravy-spoon. — *à sucre,* sugar-sifter. *Élever à la* —, to bring up by hand
†**Cuillerée,** *s.f.* spoonful; ladleful. *Grande* —, — *à bouche,* table-spoonful. *Petite* —, — *à café,* [tea-spoonful
†**Cuilleriste,** *s.m.* spoon-maker
†**Cuilleron,** *s.m.* bowl of a spoon
Cuir, *s.m.* skin; hide; leather; strop; dreadful slip [*of the tongue, consisting in the pronunciation, at the end of words, of* s *or* t *for each other, or where there is neither*]. — *chevelu,* scalp. — *à repasser,* strop. — *de brouette,* (*pop.*) wood. — *de laine,* double-milled cloth. *Entre* — *et chair,* under the skin; inwardly; to oneself. *Faire des* —*s,* not to mind o.'s H's
Cuirasse, *s.f.* cuirass; breastplate; (*nav.*) armour, armour-plate; (*zool.*) carapace, shell. — *marine* or *flottante,* cork-jacket, float. *Défaut de la* —, break *or* extremity of the cuirass; (*fig.*) vulnerable part *or* point, weak side
Cuirassé, e, *adj.* cuirassed; with a breastplate; protected; ready-armed, fully prepared; hardened; case-hardened; proof; seasoned; close; (*mil.*) armed with a cuirass; (*nav.*) armoured, armour-plated, iron-plated, iron-cased, iron-clad, iron-coated

Cuirasseau, *s.m.* (*pop.*) *V.* **Curaçao**
Cuirasser, *v.a.* to cuirass; to put a breastplate on; to supply with weapons; to arm; to fortify; to protect; to harden; to season; (*mil.*) to arm with a cuirass; (*nav.*) to plate
Se —, *v.r.* to put on a breastplate *or* a (*or* o.'s) cuirass; to arm *or* fortify *or* harden oneself
Cuirassier, *s.m.* cuirassier; (*pop.*) one who habitually makes those slips of the tongue called "cuirs" in French (*V.* **Cuir**)
Cuiratier, *s.m.* leather-dresser
Cuire, *v.a.n.* to cook; to dress, to do; to roast; to boil; to stew; to fry; to broil; to bake; to burn; to dry; to ripen; to mature; to digest; to scorch; (*of pain*) to smart; to be cooking, &c. — *dans sa peau* or *dans son jus*, (*pers.*, *fam.*) to be suffocated with heat, to swelter, to be all in a sweat, to stew. *Faire* —, to cook, to dress, to do; to roast; &c. *La main me cuit*, my hand smarts. *Il vous en cuira*, you will smart for it
Se —, *v.r.* to be cooked, &c.
Cuirer, *v.a.* to cover in leather
Cuisage, *s.m.* burning, charring
Cuisant, e, *adj.* easy to cook; burning, scorching; smarting; smart; acute, sharp, piercing, biting, pinching, keen, severe; poignant, bitter; painful, afflicting; vexing; harassing, worrying, corroding, consuming
Cuiseur, *s.m.* brick-burner
Cuisine, *s.f.* kitchen; cookery; cooking; living; fare, cheer; table; mess; cooks; (*nav.*) cook-room, cuddy, cook-house, caboose, galley. — *bourgeoise*, homely living; plain cookery *or* fare *or* dinner; ordinary, chops and steaks; cook-shop. *Chef de* —, *V.* **Chef.** *Fille de* —, kitchen-maid. *Garçon de* —, under-cook. *Être chargé de* —, to be as fat as a mole, to be swag-bellied. *Faire la* — (*de*), to cook (for)
Cuisiner, *v.n.a.* to cook
Cuisinerie, *s.f.* (*fam.*) cooking, doing
Cuisinier, *s.m.* cook, man-cook; messman; (*slang*) police-spy, decoy; policeman, bobby, slop
Cuisinière, *s.f.* cook, woman-cook, cook-maid; meat-screen; Dutch oven. — *tourne-broche*, veruvolver [(*surg.*) bucket-leg
Cuissard, *s.m.* (*armour*) cuissart, cuish, cuisse;
Cuisse, *s.f.* thigh; (*of beef*) rump; (*of poultry*) leg; (*of walnuts*) quarter. — **-madame,** *s.f.* (kind of pear)
Cuisseau, *s.m.* (*of veal*) chump end of the loin
Cuisson, *s.f.* cooking, doing; roasting; baking; boiling; stewing; frying; broiling; ripening; drying; digestion; (*pain*) smart, smarting
Cuissot, *s.m.* (*of venison*) haunch [snob
Cuistre, *s.m.* college-scout, college-fag; pedant;
Cuit, e, *part.adj.* cooked, done, &c. (*V.* **Cuire**); ripe, mature, matured; (*pop.*) done for, dished. *Des pommes* —*es*, baked apples. *Des poires* —*es*, stewed pears
Cuite, *s.f.* burn; burning; baking; boiling; firing; batch; (*pop.*) fuddle, drop too much, finish
Cuivrage, *s.m.* coppering
Cuivre, *s.m.* copper; brass; copper plate; brass instruments. — *jaune*, brass
Cuivré, e, *adj.* copper-coloured, copper; ring-
Cuivrée, *s.f.* coppering [ing, clear, sonorous
Cuivrer, *v.a.* to copper
Cuivrerie, *s.f.* copper wares; brass wares
Cuivrette, *s.f.* (*mus.*) brass reed
Cuivreu-x, se, *adj.* coppery; copper; brass; ringing, clear, sonorous
Cujelier, *s.m.* (*bird*) wood-lark
Cul, *s.m.* bottom; breech; rump; back; (*of carts*) tail; (*of bottles*) punt; (*nav.*) tuck. — **-de -basse-fosse,** *s.m.* black hole under a dungeon. — **-blanc,** *s.m.* (*bird*) *V.* **Motteux.** — **-de -bouteille,** *s.m.* punt of a bottle; *adj.* dark green. — **-de-four,** *s.m.* (*arch.*) demi-cupola. — **-de-jatte,** *s.m.* cripple (seated in a wooden bowl). — **-de-lampe,** *s.m.* (*print.*) tail-piece; (*arch.*) pendant, bracket. — **-de-plomb,** *s.m.* heavy-sides; drudge, sedentary person; red-tapist. — **de-porc,** — **de-pot,** *s.m.* (*nav.*) wale-knot, wall-knot. — **-de-sac,** *s.m.* *V.* **Impasse;** (*tech.*) hollow; bottom; (*mil.*, *nat. hist.*, &c.) cul-de-sac; (*nav.*) cove, harbour
Culasse, *s.f.* (*of fire-arms*) breech; (*of diamonds*) pavilion. *Fusil* or &c. *se chargeant par la* —, breech-loader. *Se chargeant par la* —, breech-loading [tumbler
Culbutant, e, *adj.* tumbling; — *s.m.* (*bird*)
Culbute, *s.f.* somerset, somersault; tumble, fall; failure, bankruptcy, insolvency, ruin. *Faire la* —, to tumble head over heels; to turn over; to tumble, to fall; to fail, to break. *Au bout du fossé la* —, neck or nothing, happen what may
Culbuter, *v.a.n.* to throw down head over heels; to throw down; to overthrow; to turn over; to overturn; to overset; to upset; to rout; to ruin, to undo, to destroy; to tumble head over heels; to tumble, to fall; to fail, to break, to be ruined
Se —, to throw down *or* &c. each other; to push each other down; to tumble; to be thrown
Culbuteur, *s.m.* automaton tumbler [down, &c.
Culbutis, *s.m.* things thrown down, confused heap of things upset, jumble; somerset; tumble, fall [(*nav.*) sternway
Culée, *s.f.* (*of hides*) tail-piece; (*arch.*) abutment;
Culement, *s.m.* (*nav.*) *V.* **Acculement**
Culer, *v.n.* to go back, to back; (*nav.*) to fall astern, to make sternway; (*of the wind*) to veer
Culeron, *s.m.* (*saddlery*) crupper-loop, crupper-dock, dock
Culière, *s.f.* hind-girth; gutter-stone
Culinaire, *adj.* culinary
Culinairement, *adv.* culinarily
Culmifère, *adj.* (*bot.*) culmiferous
Culminance, *s.f.* summit, top, height
Culminant, e, *adj.* culminating; highest;
Culmination, *s.f.* culmination [prominent
Culminer, *v.n.* to culminate
Culot, *s.m.* bottom; residuum; (*of a tobacco-pipe*) plug, black at the bottom, black bottom, bottom of the bowl; (*of a cartridge*) metal end, base-cup, capsule; (*of animals, and jest. of persons*) youngest, last born; youngest member (*of a society or company*) [blackening
Culottage, *s.m.* (*of tobacco-pipes*) colouring,
Culotte, *s.f.* breeches, pair of breeches, small-clothes, smalls; (*of beef, of pigeons*) rump; (*of a tobacco-pipe*) black bottom; (*of a pistol*) trap; (*at play*) loss, run of losses; (*pop.*) spree, blow-out, fuddle, drop too much. — *courte*, shorts, pair of shorts
Culotter, *v.n.* to make breeches; — *v.a.* (*pers.*) to put breeches on, to put into breeches, to breech; (*a tobacco-pipe*) to colour, to blacken, to season; (*the eyes*) to surround with a dark circle; (*pers.*) to season, to inure, to harden, to steel
Se —, *v.r.* (*pers.*) to put on o.'s breeches; (*of a pipe*) to get (*or* become) coloured *or* black; (*of the eyes*) to become *or* be surrounded with a dark circle; (*of the face*) to get grog-blossoms, to get red; (*pers.*) to get (*or* become) inured *or* hardened; to wear out; (*pop.*) to fuddle, to booze, to get tipsy *or* tight
Culotteu-r, se, *s.m.f.* — *de pipes*, confirmed pipe-smoker, pot-house frequenter
Culotti-er, ère, *s.m.f.* breeches-maker
Culottin, *s.m.* tights; child newly breeched
Culpabilité, *s.f.* culpability; guilt
Culte, *s.m.* worship; adoration; religion, creed, persuasion; veneration, honour, respect; love cultivation
Cultivable, *adj.* cultivable, fit for cultivation
Cultivateur, *s.m.* agriculturist, husbandman, farmer, grower, tiller, ploughman, cultivator; (*machine*) cultivator; — *adj.m.* agricultural
Cultivation, *s.f.* cultivation
Cultivatrice, *s.f.* agriculturist, farmeress, grower; — *adj.f.* agricultural

Cultiver, *v.a.* to cultivate; to till; to improve; to tutor; to exercise; to practise; to cultivate the acquaintance of
Se —, *v.r.* to be cultivated *or* tilled *or* &c.
Cultural, e, *adj.* cultural
Culture, *s.f.* culture, cultivation; tillage; farming; husbandry; land under cultivation; crop; growing, growth; rearing; education; improvement
Cuméen, ne, *adj. s.* Cumæan
Cumin, *s.m.* (*bot.*) cumin. — *des prés,* caraway
Cumine, *s.f.* (*chem.*) cumine
Cuminique, Cuminylique, *adj.* (*chem.*) cuminic
Cumul, *s.m.* accumulation; holding of several offices, pluralism, plurality
Cumulard, *s.m.* pluralist
Cumulati-f, ve, *adj.* cumulative
Cumulation, *s.f.* accumulation, cumulation
Cumulativement, *adv.* by accumulation
Cumuler, *v.a.* to accumulate, to cumulate; to hold at the same time; — *v.n.* to hold several offices held at the same time
Se —, *v.r.* to be accumulated, &c.; to be
Cumulo-stratus, *s.m.* (*meteorology*) cumulo-stratus
Cumulus, *s.m.* (*meteorology*) cumulus
Cunéaire, *adj.* cuneal, cuneate, cuneated
Cunéiforme, *adj.* cuneiform
Cunette, *s.f.* (*fort.*) cunette
Cupide, *adj.* covetous, greedy, grasping
Cupidement, *adv.* covetously, greedily
Cupidité, *s.f.* cupidity; covetousness; concupiscence
Cupidon, *s.m.* Cupid, Love; beau. *Vieux —,* old beau; (*pop.*) rag-picker
Cuprate, *s.m.* (*chem.*) cuprate
Cuprique, *adj.* (*chem.*) cupric
Cupulaire, *adj.* cup-shaped
Cupule, *s.f.* cupule, cup
Cupulé, e, *adj.* (*bot.*) cupulate
Cupulifère, *adj.* (*bot.*) cupuliferous
Cupuliforme, *adj.* cupuliform
Curabilité, *s.f.* curability, curableness
Curable, *adj.* curable
Curaçao, *s.m.* curaçoa
Curage, *s.m.* cleansing, cleaning; (*bot.*) water-pepper
Curare, *s.m.* curare, curari, ourari, arrow-poison
Curarine, *s.f.* (*chem.*) curarine
Curatelle, *s.f.* trusteeship, guardianship; committeeship
Cura-teur, trice, *s.m.f.* trustee, curator, curatrix, guardian; committee
Curati-f, ve, *adj.* curative; — *s.m.* curative agent
Curation, *s.f.* (*med.*) curing, cure
Curcuma, *s.m.* (*bot.*) curcuma, turmeric
Curcumine, *s.f.* (*chem.*) curcumine
Cure, *s.f.* (*med.*) cure; (*eccl.*) living; parsonage; vicarage; rectory; parish; (*obsolete*) care, heed. *N'en avoir —,* (*old*) not to care for it, to take no notice of it
Cure, *s.m.* (*in compounds, from* **Curer,** "to cleanse," "to clean," "to pick") thing that cleanses *or* cleans *or* picks. — **-dents,** *s.m.* tooth-pick. — **-feu,** *s.m.* forge-poker *or* shovel. — **-langue,** *s.m.* tongue-scraper. — **-môle,** *s.m.* dredging-machine. — **-oreilles,** *s.m.* ear-pick. — **-pieds,** *s.m.* horse-picker, shoe-picker, hoof-pick
Curé, *s.m.* parish priest, parson; vicar; rector. *Monsieur le —,* Reverend Sir, Sir; the *or* our vicar *or* rector
Curée, *s.f.* (*hunt.*) quarry; (*fig.*) prey, booty; gain; feast; scramble. *Mettre en —,* to flesh, to blood; to bait, to allure, to entice, to make (...) thirst for more
Curement, *s.m.* cleansing, cleaning
Curemolle, *s.m.* *V.* **Cure-môle**
Curer, *v.a.* to cleanse, to clean, to clean out; to pick; to prune
Se —, *v.r.* to be cleansed, &c.; to pick (o.'s ...)
Curette, *s.f.* scraper; scoop; (*surg.*) lithotomy scoop, bullet-scoop, foreign body scoop, scoop, (*for the eye*) curette
Cureur, *s.m.* cleanser, well-cleanser, sewer-man
Curial, e, *adj.* vicarial; rectorial. *Maison —e,* parsonage; vicarage; rectory
Curie, *s.f.* (*Rom. hist.*) curia, ward
Curieusement, *adv.* curiously; inquisitively; carefully; minutely
Curieu-x, se, *adj.* curious; inquisitive; inquiring; prying; desirous; eager; fond; careful; particular, nice; studious; rare; singular; — *s.m.f.* inquisitive (*or* prying) person, inquisitive (*or* prying) man *or* boy *or* fellow, inquisitive (*or* prying) woman *or* girl, (*pl.*) inquisitive (*or* prying) people *or* folks *or* men *or* females, &c.; spectator, looker-on; sight-seer; antiquary; amateur; connoisseur; virtuoso; — *s.m.* curious part, curious thing *or* fact, most curious thing
Curion, *s.m.* (*Rom. hist.*) curio
Curiosité, *s.f.* curiosity; inquisitiveness; desire; care; taste (for), love (of); rarity; raree-show; sight
Curoir, Curon, *s.m.* plough-staff
Curseur, *s.m.* (*geom., tech.*) cursor; slider, slide; index; (*astr.*) wire, spider-line (*of a micrometer*); (*pers.*) messenger (*of the Pope*)
Cursi-f, ve, *adj.* cursive, running; cursory; — *s.f.* cursive *or* running hand
Cursivement, *adv.* cursorily
Curule, *adj.* (*Rom. hist.*) curule
Curures, *s.f.pl.* cleansings, mud, sewage matter, sewage, drainage
Curva-teur, trice, *adj.* curving, bending
Curvati-f, ve, *adj.* curvative
Curvi-, (*in compounds*) curvi-... crooked
†Curviligne, *adj.* curvilinear, curvilineal;
Curvirostre, *adj.* (*of birds*) curvirostral, hook-billed, hook-beaked; — *s.m.* curvirostre
Cuscute, *s.f.* (*bot.*) cuscuta, dodder
Cusparé, *s.m.* (*bot.*) cusparia
Cuspide, *s.f.* cuspis
Cuspidé, e, *adj.* cuspidate, cuspidated, cuspidal
Cusson, *s.m.* (*insects*) bruchus; pea-beetle, pea-chafer; wood-worm
Cussoné, e, *adj.* worm-eaten, eaten
Custode, *s.m.* custodian, warden, keeper, curator; — *s.f.* holster-cap; (*of a carriage*) squab; (*Cath. rel.*) pyx-cover; curtain, veil
Cutané, e, *adj.* cutaneous
Cuticulaire, *adj.* cuticular
Cuticule, *s.f.* (*anat., bot.*) cuticle
Cutter, *s.m.* (*nav.*) cutter
Cuvage, *s.m.* (*tech.*) fermenting (*of wine*); place where wine is fermented
Cuve, *s.f.* vat; tub; copper; trough; (*mining*) cage, corf *or* corve, kibble, skip. *A fond de —,* thoroughly, outright; (*fort.*) flat-bottomed
Cuveau, *s.m.* bucket, tub; (*mining*) corf *or* corve, cage, kibble, skip
Cuvée, *s.f.* vatful; tubful; (*fig.*) quality, kind
Cuvelage, *s.m.* (*of mines*) lining, casing; tubbing
Cuveler, *v.a.* (*mines*) to line, to case; to tub
Cuvellement, *s.m.* *V.* **Cuvelage**
Cuver, *v.n.a.* to stand in the vat; to ferment, to work; to settle; to calm, to appease, to sleep off the effects of. — *son vin,* to sleep off o.'s wine, to sleep oneself sober; to cool down
Cuvette, *s.f.* basin; wash-hand basin; (*phys.,* &c.) cistern, reservoir; pan; trench; (*arch.*) cistern-head; (*of a watch*) cap, (*abusively for* "boîte") case; (*fort.*) *V.* **Cunette**
Cuvier, *s.m.* wash-tub, bucking-tub; tub
Cyame, *s.m.* (*zool.*) whale-louse
Cyanate, *s.m.* (*chem.*) cyanate
Cyane, *s.m.* (*chem.*) *V.* **Cyanogène**
Cyaneux, *adj.m.* (*chem.*) cyanous
Cyanhydrate, *s.m.* (*chem.*) hydrocyanate, cyanhydrate
Cyanhydrique, *adj.* (*chem.*) hydrocyanic, cyanhydric
Cyani-, (*in compounds*) cyani-... (*blue* ...)
Cyanique, *adj.* (*chem.*) cyanic
Cyanisme, *s.m.* (*phys.*) cyanism, degree of blueness
Cyanite, *s.f.* (*min.*) kyanite, cyanite
Cyano-, (*in compounds*) cyano-...
Cyanoferrate, *s.m.* (*chem.*) ferrocyanate
Cyanoferre, *s.m.* (*chem.*) ferrocyanogen
Cyanoferrique, *adj.* (*chem.*) ferrocyanic
Cyanoferrure, *s.m.* (*chem.*) ferrocyanide
Cyanogène, *s.m.* (*chem.*) cyanogen
Cyanomètre, *s.m.* (*phys.*) cyanometer

Cyanopathie, *s.f.* (*med.*) cyanopathy
Cyanose, *s.f.* (*med.*) cyanosis ; — *s.m.* (*min.*) [cyanosite
Cyanurate, *s.m.* (*chem.*) cyanurate
Cyanure, *s.m.* (*chem.*) cyanide
Cyanurique, *adj.* (*chem.*) cyanuric
Cyathe, *s.m.* (*bot.*) cyathea (*tree-fern*) ; (*in antiquity*) cyathus
Cyathiforme, *adj.* cyathiform, cup-shaped
Cycas, *s.m.* (*bot.*) cycas
Cyclade, *s.f.* (*zool.*) cyclas, cycle [sow-bread
Cyclame, Cyclamen, *s.m.* (*bot.*) cyclamen,
Cyclamine, *s.f.* (*chem.*) cyclamine
Cyclamor, *s.m.* (*her.*) orle
Cycle, *s.m.* (*chron.*) cycle ; (*liter.*) period
Cyclique, *adj.* cyclic, cyclical
Cyclographe, *s.m.* cyclograph
Cycloïdal, e, *adj.* cycloidal
Cycloïde, *s.f. adj.* cycloid
Cyclométr-ie, ique. *V.* page 3, § 1
Cyclonal, e, *adj.* (*meteorology*) cyclonic
Cyclone, *s.m.* cyclone (*storm*)
Cyclope, *s.m.* (*myth., zool.*) Cyclop, Cyclops
Cyclopéen, ne, *adj.* Cyclopean, Cyclopic
Cyclopie, *s.f.* (*anat.*) cyclopia
Cycloptère, *s.m.* (*fish*) lumpsucker, lumpfish
Cyclorama, *s.m.* cyclorama
Cycloramique, *adj.* cycloramic
†Cygne, *s.m.* swan ; (*astr.*) cygnus. *Le chant du —,* (*fig.*) the song of the dying swan, the swan's death-song. *Le — thébain,* Pindar. *Le — de Mantoue,* Virgil. *Le — de Cambrai,* Fénelon. *Le — de Pesaro,* Rossini
Cylindrage, *s.m.* rolling ; mangling
Cylindre, *s.m.* cylinder ; roller ; mangle, calender ; (*of organs,* &c.) barrel ; (*of clocks*) glass shade ; (*for baths*) heater ; (*nat. hist.*) volute
Cylindrer, *v.a.* to roll ; to mangle, to calender ; to make cylindrical
Cylindricité, *s.f.* cylindricity
Cylindr-ique, -iquement. *V.* page 3, § 1
Cylindroïde, *adj.m.f., s.m.* cylindroid
Cymaise, *s.f.* (*arch.*) cyma, ogee
Cymbalaire, *s.f.* (*bot.*) ivy-leaved toad-flax
Cymbale, *s.f.* (*mus.*) cymbal ; (*of an organ*) cymbel [cymbal-player
Cymbalier, Cymbaliste, *s.m.* cymbalist,
Cymbiforme, *adj.* cymbiform, boat-shaped
Cyme, *s.f.* (*bot.*) cyme
Cymette, *s.f.* (*bot.*) sprouts, Brussels sprouts
Cymeu-x, se, *adj.* (*bot.*) cymose, cymous
Cymophane, *s.f.* (*min.*) cymophane [chum
‡Cynanche, Cynanque, *s.m.* (*bot.*) cynan-
Cynanthropie, *s.f.* (*med.*) cynanthropy
Cynégétique, *s.f. adj.* hunting, sporting, sport
Cyngalais, e, *adj. s. V.* **Cingalais**
Cynips, *s.m.* (*zool.*) gall-fly
Cynique, *adj.* cynic, cynical ; impudent, barefaced ; obscene, filthy ; — *s.m.* cynic
Cyniquement, *adv.* cynically ; impudently, barefacedly ; obscenely, filthily
Cynisme, *s.m.* cynicism, cynicalness ; impudence, barefacedness ; obscenity, filthiness
Cynocéphale, *s.m.* (*zool.*) cynocephalus
Cynodon, *s.m.* (*bot.*) cynodon, dog-tooth grass, dog-tooth violet [tongue
Cynoglosse, *s.f.* (*bot.*) cynoglossum, hound's-
Cynorexie, *s.f.* (*med.*) cynorexia
Cynorrhodon, *s.m.* (*bot.*) cynarrhodium, hip
Cynosure, *s.f.* (*astr., obsolete*) cynosure, Lesser Bear ; (*bot.*) cynosurus, dog's-tail grass, gold-
Cyprès, *s.m.* cypress [seed
Cyprien, ne, *adj. s.* Cyprian
Cyprière, *s.f.* cypress-grove
Cyprin, *s.m.* (*fish*) cyprinus. *— doré,* gold-fish
Cypriote. *V.* **Chypriote**
Cypripède, *s.m.* (*bot.*) cypripedium, lady's-slipper
Cyropédie, *s.f.* (*liter.*) Cyropædeia (*of Xenophon*)
Cysticerque, *s.m.* (*zool.*) cysticercus, tailed
Cystique, *adj.* (*anat.*) cystic [bladder-worm
Cystirrhée, *s.f.* (*med.*) cystirrhœa
Cystite, *s.f.* (*med.*) cystitis
Cystocèle, *s.f.* (*med.*) cystocele
Cystotome, *s.m.* (*surg.*) lithotomy knife
Cystotomie, *s.f.* (*surg.*) lithotomy, cystotomy
Cythare, *s.f. V.* **Cithare**
Cytinelle, *s.f.* (*bot.*) cytinus
Cytise, *s.m.* (*bot.*) cytisus, laburnum
Czapska, *s.m. V.* **Schapzka**
Czar, *s.m.* czar
Czarien, ne, *adj.* czarinian, czarish
Czarine, *s.f.* czarina
Czarowitz, *s.m.* czarowitz

D

D, *s.m.* d
D', *contraction of* **De.** *V.* **De** [Nenni
Dà, *adv. int.* indeed, truly, forsooth. *V.* **Oui** *and*
Dab, Dabe, *s.m.* (*pop.*) master, governor
Da-capo, *adv.* (*mus.*) da capo
Dace, *adj. s.m.f.* Dacian
Dache, *s.m.* (*pop.*) Old Nick, the devil
Dactyle, *s.m.* (*vers.*) dactyl, dactyle ; (*bot.*) dactylis, cock's-foot grass, orchard grass, tussac grass [3, § 1
Dactyl-iologie, -ique, -ologie, &c. *V.* page
Dactylion, *s.m.* (*mus.*) dactylion
Dactyloptère, *adj.* finger-finned, dactylopterous ; — *s.m.* flying gurnard, flying fish
Dada, *s.m.* cock-horse ; hobby-horse, hobby
Dadais, *s.m.* booby, ninny, spoony
Dagard, *s.m. V.* **Daguet** [dam, hag
Dagorne, *s.f.* one-horned cow ; beldame, bel-
Dague, *s.f.* dagger, dirk ; (*tech.*) scraping-knife, scraper ; (*obsolete*) cat o' nine tails, lash ; **—s,** *pl.* (*of deer,* &c.) dags
Daguer, *v.a.n.* to stab, to strike ; to cover, to buck ; to butt ; to fly rapidly ; to lash
Daguerréotypage, *s.m.* daguerreotyping
Daguerréotype, *s.m.* daguerreotype
Daguerréotyper, *v.a.* to daguerreotype
Daguerréotypie, *s.f.* daguerreotypy
Daguerrien, ne, *adj.* daguerrean [haddock
Daguet, *s.m.* (*hunt.*) brocket, pricket ; (*fish*)
Daguette, *s.f.* small dagger *or* dirk
Dahlia, *s.m.* (*bot.*) dahlia
Dahline, *s.f.* (*chem.*) dahline
†Daigner, *v.n.* to deign, to condescend, to be pleased, to please, to vouchsafe ; (*in court-slang*) to be graciously pleased
†Daillot, *s.m.* (*nav.*) *V.* **Andaillot**
Daim, *s.m.* deer ; buck ; (*fam.*) swell, fast man ;
Daine, *s.f.* doe, deer [fop ; simpleton, muff
Daintiers, *s.m.pl.* (*hunt.*) dowcets
Dais, *s.m.* canopy ; dais ; platform
Dalberge, *s.m.,* **Dalbergie,** *s.f.* (*bot.*) dalbergia
Dalécarlien, ne, *adj. s.* Dalecarlian
Dalème, *s.f.* smoke-consuming apparatus
Dallage, *s.m.* flagging ; flag-stone pavement
Dalle, *s.f.* flag-stone, flag ; slab ; gutter ; sink-stone ; (*of fish*) slice ; (*pop.*) throat, whistle. *— de pompe,* (*nav.*) pump-dale
Daller, *v.a.* to flag, to pave with flag-stones
Dalmate, *adj. s.m.f.* Dalmatian
Dalmatique, *s.f.* dalmatic, tunic
Dalot, *s.m.* (*nav.*) scupper, scupper-hole
Daltonisme, *s.m.* (*med.*) daltonism
Dam, *int. V.* **Dame,** *int.* ; — *s.m.* (*obsolete*) damnation, destruction, loss, damage, injury, hurt, prejudice, misfortune, peril, cost
Damage, *s.m.* puddling, ramming
Daman, *s.m.* (*zool.*) daman, rock-badger
Damas, *s.m.* (*geog.*) Damascus ; (*stuff*) damask ; damask linen ; Damascus blade, damaskin ; damasked steel ; damson (*plum*) ; dame's-violet (*plant*). *— de laine,* moreen
Damascène, *adj.* Damascene
Damasquette, *s.f.* (*stuff*) damassin [embossing
Damasquinage, *s.m.* damascening ; damascene ;
Damasquine, *s.f.* damascened piece
Damasquiner, *v.a.* to damascene, to damaskeen ; to emboss, to frost

Damasquinerie, Damasquinure, *s.f. V.* **Damasquinage**

Damasquineur, *s.m.* damascener

Damassade, *s.f.* damask (*silk*)

Damassé, *s.m.* damask (*linen*)

Damassé, e, *part. adj.* damasked, damask. *Acier* —, wootz, Indian steel

Damasser, *v.a.* to damask, to work damask-like

Damasserie, *s.f.* damask-linen factory

Damasseur, *s.m.* damask-weaver, damask-

Damassin, *s.m.* damassin (*stuff*) [worker

Damassure, *s.f.* damasking, damask-work

Dame, *int.* why! indeed! to be sure; well! nay!

Dame, *s.f.* lady; married lady *or* woman; mistress; madam; dame; nun; (*in dancing*) partner; (*at cards, chess*) queen; (*at draughts*) king; (*at backgammon*) man; (*tech.*) rammer; dam, sluice; —*s, pl.* ladies, &c.; draughts (*game*). *La* —..., (*law*) Mrs.... *Les* —*s*, the ladies; Mesdames. *Notre* —, our Lady (*the Virgin Mary*); Notre-Dame (*the name of the cathedral of Paris, and of many churches*). *Petite* —, little lady; (*fam.*) gay woman, wench. — *damée*, (*at draughts*) king. *Aller à* —, to make a queen (*at chess*); to make a king (*at draughts*). *De* —, lady's; ladylike. *La* — *de ses pensées*, o.'s lady-love. — *d'onze heures*, (*bot.*) star of Bethlehem. — **-jeanne,** *s.f.* jar, demijohn; carboy

Damer, *v.a.* to crown (*a man, at draughts*); to queen (*a pawn, at chess*); (*tech.*) to puddle, to ram; (*fam.*) to marry; to seduce. — *le pion à*, to outdo, to beat, to be more than a match for

Dameret, *s.m.* (*obsolete*) ladies' man, spark, beau, fop; — *adj.m.* foppish

Damier, *s.m.* draught-board; chess-board

Dammar, *s.m.* dammar (*resin*)

Damnable, *adj.* damnable

Damnablement, *adv.* damnably

Damnation, *s.f.* damnation

Damné, e, *part. adj. s.* damned; devil (of); soul in Hell. *Souffrir comme un* —, to suffer Hell torments [to plague to death, to drive mad

Damner, *v.a.* to damn. *Faire* —, to torment,
Se —, *v.r.* to damn oneself; to curse and swear

Damoiseau, Damoisel, *s.m.* (*obsolete*) fop, spark; page [ladyship

Damoiselle, *s.f.* (*obsolete*) damsel, lady, her

Danaïde, *s.f.* (*machine*) danaide; —**s,** *pl.* (*myth.*)

Danché, e, *adj.* (*her.*) dancette [(the) Danaids

†Dandiller, *v.n.* (*pop.*) to ring

†Dandillon, *s.m.* (*pop.*) bell

Dandin, *s.m.* ninny. *Perrin* —, rapacious lawyer

Dandinement, *s.m.* waddling; swinging; slouching

Dandiner, *v.n.*, **Se** —, *v.r.* to waddle; to swing; to slouch; to traipse; to trifle, to dilly-dally, to dally [drubbing

Dandinette, *s.f.* (*pop.*) dressing, trimming,

Dandy, *s.m.* dandy

Dandysme, *s.m.* dandyism

Danger, *s.m.* danger; peril; risk; hazard; jeopardy; fear; harm; disadvantage; objection

Dangereusement, *adv.* dangerously

Dangereu-x, se, *adj.* dangerous; to be feared, formidable [Danish fashion

Danois, e, *adj. s.* Danish; Dane; Danish dog;

Dans, *prep.* in; into; to; within; through; with; amidst; according to; out of, from

Dansable, *adj.* to be danced, fit to be danced

Dansant, e, *adj.* dancing; lively, inviting to dance

Danse, *s.f.* dance; dancing; (*fam.*) dressing, trimming, drubbing; set-to, fight. — *des morts*, dance of Death. — *de Saint-Guy* or *de Saint-Wit*, (*med.*) Saint Vitus's dance. *Entrer en* —, to join the dance; to join in

Danser, *v.n.a.* to dance; to leap; to skip; to bound. *Ne savoir sur quel pied* —, to be at o.'s
Se—, *v.r.* to be danced [wits' end

Danseu-r, se, *s.m.f.* dancer; gentleman *or* lady *or* partner (*at a ball*). — *de corde*, rope-dancer

Dansomane, *s.m.f.* person passionately fond of

Dansomanie, *s.f.* mania for dancing [dancing

Dansoter, *v.n.* to dance a little, to skip

Dantesque, *adj.* (*liter.*) of Dante

Dantzickois, e, *adj. s.* of Dantzic; Dantzicker

Danubien, ne, *adj.* Danubian

Dapêche, *s.m. V.* **Elatérite**

Daphné, *s.m.* (*bot.*) daphne

Daphnéine, Daphnine, *s.f.* (*chem.*) daphnine

Daphnie, *s.f.* (*insect.*) water-flea

Dapifer, *s.m.* (*hist.*) dapifer

Daraise, *s.f.* sluice (*of a pond*)

Darce, *s.f. V.* **Darse**

Dard, *s.m.* dart; sting; (*of a scabbard*) shoe tip; (*bot.*) pistil; (*a fish*) dace, dare, dart

Dardelle, *s.f.* (*pop.*) penny, copper, brown

Darder, *v.a.n.* to dart; to hurl; to shoot; to harpoon; to spear; to pierce; to beam

†Dardille, *s.f.* (*bot.*) spindle [spindle

†Dardiller, *v.n.* (*bot.*) to shoot spindles, to

†Dardillon, *s.m.* barb (*of a fish-hook*)

Dare, *adv. int.* quick [cuff, punch, thump

Dariole, *s.f.* cream-cake, dariole, dariol; (*pop.*)

Dariolette, *s.f.* (*obsolete*) confidante

Darique, *s.f.* daric (*Persian coin*)

Darne, *s.f.* slice (*of fish*)

Darse, *s.f.* (*nav.*) wet-dock

Dartre, *s.f.* (*med.*) herpes, disease of the skin, skin eruption (*rash, tetter, ringworm, shingles, acne,* &c.). — *farineuse*, pityriasis, scurf

Dartreu-x, se, *adj. s.* herpetic, scurfy, scabby; person affected with skin disease

Dasymètre, *s.m.* (*phys.*) dasymeter

Dasyure, *s.m.* (*zool.*) dasyure [*Rome*)

Dataire, *s.m.* datary (*officer of the chancery in*

Date, *s.f.* date; period. *D'ancienne* or *de vieille* or *de longue* —, of old date; of long standing; long since, long before, long ago. *En* — *de*, under date of, bearing date of. *Prendre* —, to have the priority; to fix a day; to make a note (of); to be recorded

Dater, *v.a.n.* to date; to reckon; to form an era. — *de loin*, to be old; to be of long standing. *A* — *de*, reckoning from, from
Se —, *v.r.* to be dated

Daterie, *s.f.* datary's office, dataria

Datif, *s.m.* (*gram.*) dative, dative case

Dati-f, ve, *adj.* (*law*) dative

Dation, *s.f.* (*law*) giving

Datisme, *s.m.* tautology

Datte, *s.f.* date (*fruit*)

Dattier, *s.m.* (*bot.*) date-tree, date-palm

Datura, *s.m.* (*bot.*) datura, thorn-apple

Daturine, *s.f.* (*chem.*) daturine

Daube, *s.f.* (*cook.*) stew, daube

Dauber, *v.a.n.* to cuff, to beat, to strike, to hit; to jeer, to banter; to backbite, to slander; to stew

Daubeu-r, se, *s.m.f.* jeerer, banterer, sneerer;

Daubière, *s.f.* stew-pan [slanderer

Daudinage, *s.m.* (*of wine*) rummaging

Daudine, *s.f.* rummaging-stick (*for wine*)

Daudiner, *v.a.* to rummage (*wine*)

Daumont, *s.m.* postilion-chaise *or* carriage

Daunien, ne, *adj. s.* Daunian

Dauphin, *s.m.* dauphin, heir apparent; dolphin; Delphin Classic; (*fam.*) bully; (*nav.*) cheek; — *adj.m.* Delphin

Dauphine, *s.f.* dauphiness; — *adj.f.* Delphin

Dauphinelle, *s.f.* (*bot.*) larkspur

Dauphinois, e, *adj. s.* Dauphinese

Daurade, *s.f.* (*fish*) gilthead

Dauw, *s.m.* (*zool.*) dauw (*African wild horse*)

Davantage, *adv.* more; further, farther; longer; upwards; most. *Pas* —, not more, not any more, no more; not any longer, &c.; nothing else, that's all

Davéridion, *s.m.* oil of spike

Davier, *s.m.* tooth-forceps; (*nav.*) davit

Davidique, *adj.* Davidic

Daw, *s.m.* (*zool.*) *V.* **Dauw**

De, D', *prep.* of; from; out of; on account of; in; within; with; by; through; on; upon;

for; at; some; any; some of; any of; a; to; about; than; between; among; since; during; for the whole of; of the length of ..., ... long; of the height of ..., ... in height, ... high; the act of, the dealing of, worthy of; worth; the part of; the lot of; inherent in; that of, those of; as a, as; and. **Maison — campagne,** country-house. **Chevaux — course,** race-horses. **Course — chevaux,** horse-race. — *soi-même,* of o.'s own accord

Dé, *s.m.* thimble; die; (*at dominoes*) domino; (*build.*) block; (*arch.*) dado, die; (*for vases,* &c.) stand; (*nav.*) coak (*of a block*). *A vous le —,* it is your throw, it is your turn. *Tenir le — de la conversation,* to engross all the conversation

Dead-heat, *s.m.* (*in horse-racing*) dead heat

Déalbation, *s.f.* whitening by fire; blanching

Débâchage, *s.m.* untilting, uncovering

Débâcher, *v.a.* to untilt, to uncover

Débâcheur, *s.m.* (*jest.*) untilter

Débâclage, *s.m.* clearing; unbarring, opening

Débâcle, *s.f.* breaking up (of the ice), thaw; breaking out, eruption; confusion; clearing; downfall, collapse, break-down, disaster; (*pop.*) riddance

Débâclement, *s.m.* clearing; unbarring, opening; time of breaking up, breaking up (of the ice)

Débâcler, *v.a.* to clear; to unbar, to open; — *v.n.* (*of ice*) to break up; (*fam.*) to move off, to go away

Débâcleur, *s.m.* water-bailiff

Débagouler, *v.n.* to spew, to puke, to shoot the cat; — *v.a.* to vomit, to vomit forth; to blurt out; to blab; to babble; to jabber

Débagouleu-r, se, *s.m.f.* blab; babbler; abuser; jabberer

†Débâillonner, *v.a.* to ungag

Déballage, *s.m.* unpacking; goods exposed for sale, show

Déballer, *v.a.n.* to unpack; to expose goods for sale

Débandade, *s.f.* breaking the ranks; stampede. *A la —,* helter-skelter, in disorder, in confusion; at random; disorderly; at sixes and sevens

Débandement, *s.m.* disbanding, breaking *or* quitting the ranks

Débander, *v.a.* to unbind; to unbend; to unbrace; to loosen; to uncock (*fire-arms*); to rout, to disperse

Se —, *v.r.* to slacken; to relax; to get loose; to come unbound; to become uncocked; to get milder, to break up, to give; to disband; to break *or* quit the ranks; to run away, to disperse; to unbind (o.'s ...)

Débanquer, *v.a.* (*at play*) to break the bank; — *v.n.* (*nav.*) to leave a fishing-bank; to come away from the cod-fishing on the Newfoundland bank

Débaptiser, *v.a.* to unchristen; to change the name of; to call by a wrong name

Se —, *v.r.* to change o.'s name; to renounce baptism

†Débarbouiller, *v.a.* to wash the face of; to wash, to clean; to clear, to clear up; to extricate

†Débarbouilloir, *s.m.*, **Débarbouilloire,** *s.f.* towel (for the face)

Débarcadère, *s.m.* wharf; landing-stage *or* pier; landing-place; terminus, station

Débardage, *s.m.* unlading; landing; carrying, moving; clearing off; breaking up (*boats*)

Débarder, *v.a.* to unlade; to land; to carry, to move; to clear off; to break up (*boats*)

Débardeur, *s.m.* lumper, lighterman; boat-ripper

Débarqué, e, *part. adj.* landed, &c. (*V.* **Débarquer**); — *s.m.f.* person landed *or* arrived

Débarquement, *s.m.* landing, disembarcation, debarcation, disembarking, disembarkment

Débarquer, *v.a.n.* to land, to disembark; to unship; to arrive; to put up

Débarquer, *s.m.* landing; arriving, arrival. *Au —,* on landing; on arriving

Débarras, *s.m.* riddance, disencumbrance; lumber-place, lumber-room. *Chambre de —,* lumber-room

Débarrassement, *s.m.* disembarrassment; clearance; riddance; disentanglement; extrication

Débarrasser, *v.a.* to disembarrass; to disencumber; to clear; to clear away *or* up; to rid; to free; to disentangle; to extricate; to unload; to disburden

Se —, *v.r.* to get rid; to shake off; to extricate *or* &c. oneself; to get clear (of); to get clearer; to be cleared *or* &c.; to be relieved

Débarrer, *v.a.* to unbar

Débarricader, *v.a.* to unbarricade

Débat, *s.m.* debate; discussion; strife; contest; contention; difference; dispute, quarrel; resistance, struggle; trial, pleadings; **—s,** *pl.* debates, &c.; trial, pleadings, evidence

Débatelage, *s.m.* unlading (of boats)

Débateler, *v.a.* to unlade (*boats*)

Débâter, *v.a.* to unsaddle, to take the pack-saddle off. *Ane débâté,* (*fig.*) regular ram

Débâtir, *v.a.* to unbuild; to unbaste, to untack

Débattre, *v.a.* to debate, to discuss, to argue, to dispute; to examine, to consider

Se —, *v.r.* to struggle, to strive; to flounder; to flutter; to writhe; to dispute; to be debated *or* discussed *or* argued

Débauche, *s.f.* debauch; debauchery; lewdness; dissoluteness; carousal, potations; jollification, feast, revel, revelry; riot; flight; excess; luxuriance, exuberance, profusion

Débauché, e, *adj.* dissolute, lewd; — *s.m.f.* debauchee, rake

Débaucher, *v.a.* to debauch; to entice away, to get away; to lead away; to bribe; (*print.*) to dismiss, to send away

Se —, *v.r.* to follow ill courses; to be led away from (*or* to neglect) o.'s work; to give oneself relaxation *or* a treat

Débaucheu-r, se, *s.m.f.* debaucher

Débauger, *v.n.a* (*hunt., of wild boars*) to start

Débet, *s.m.* balance due, debit. *Être* or *rester en —,* to owe a balance

Débiffer, *v.a.* (*old*) to debilitate, to weaken; to disorder, to put out of order *or* out of sorts; to discompose

Débile, *adj.* weak, weakly, feeble; debilitated

Débilement, *adv.* weakly, feebly, faintly

Débilitant, e, *adj.* (*med.*) debilitating; — *s.m.* debilitant

Débilitation, *s.f.* debilitation, weakening, enfeebling; weakness, feebleness

Débilité, *s.f.* debility, weakness, feebleness

Débiliter, *v.a.* to debilitate, to weaken, to enfeeble

Se —, *v.r.* to become debilitated *or* weak *or* feeble

†Débillardement, *s.m.* rough-hewing; canting

†Débillarder, *v.a.* to rough-hew; to cant

†Débiller, *v.a.* to loosen (*horses*)

Débinage, *s.m.* (*pop.*) disparagement; slander

Débine, *s.f.* straits, straitened circumstances, destitution, distress, need, misery, beggary

Débiner, *v.a.* (*pop.*) to disparage, to cry down, to run down, to slander; to ruin, to beggar, to put into a mess; (*agr.*) *V.* **Biner**

Se —, *v.r.* (*pop.*) to disparage *or* &c. each other; to bolt, to vanish

Débineu-r, se, *s.m.f.* (*pop.*) disparager, slanderer

Débit, *s.m.* sale, market; shop, retail-shop; supply; licence; (*book-keep.*) debit, debtor, debit-side; (*fig.*) delivery, utterance, elocution; cutting up; distribution; flow, discharge; (*mus.*) recitative. *— de tabac, V.* **Bureau**

Débitable, *adj.* that may *or* can be cut up *or* &c. (*V.* **Débiter**)

Débitage, *s.m.* cutting up, &c. (*V.* **Débiter**)

Débitant, e, *s.m.f.* dealer; retailer

Débiter, *v.a.* to sell; to sell by retail; to retail; (*book-keep.*) to debit; (*fig.*) to deliver; to utter; to recite; to sing; to tell; to say; to talk; to relate; to report; to spread; to cut up; to saw; to go through, to knock off (*work*); to distribute; to discharge (*water*). **Se —,** *v.r.* to be sold *or* &c.

Débiteur, *s.m.* debtor; seller; retailer; cutter, sawyer; spreader, teller

Débiteuse, *s.f.* seller; retailer; spreader, teller

Débiti-f, ve, *adj.* (*com.*) debtor's

Débitrice, *s.f.* debtor

Débitter, *v.a.* (*nav.*) to unbitt (*a cable*)

Débituminisation, *s.f.* debituminization

Débituminiser, *v.a.* to debituminize

Déblai, *s.m.* clearing; cutting; digging: excavation; rubbish, earth, gravel; (*fort.*) deblai; (*fig.*) riddance, clearance

Déblaiement, Déblayement, *s.m.* clearing, clearance; clearing away; freeing; cutting; digging [*from the fillets*

Déblanchir, *v.a.* (*coin.*) to punch out (*blanks*

Déblatération, *s.f.* abuse, ranting

Déblatérer, *v.n.* to break out into abuse, to rant

Déblayer, *v.a.* to clear; to clear away; to free; to rid; to cut; to dig

Se —, *v.r.* to be cleared *or* &c.

Déblocage, *s.m.* (*print.*) turning back

Déblocus, Débloquement, *s.m.* (*mil.*) raising the (*or* a) blockade

Débloquer, *v.a.* (*mil.*) to raise the blockade of; (*print.*) to turn back; (*pop.*) to release, to uncage

Déboire, *s.m.* after-taste; drawback; vexation, sorrow, mortification, disappointment

Déboisement, *s.m.* (*of land*) clearing (*or* denudation) of woods *or* trees [trees

Déboiser, *v.a.* to clear *or* denude of woods *or*

Se —, *v.r.* to become denuded of woods *or* trees

Déboîtement, *s.m.* dislocation; disjointing

Déboîter, *v.a.* to dislocate, to put out of joint; to disjoint [jointed; to dislocate (o.'s ...)

Se —, *v.r.* to be dislocated; to become dis-

Débonder, *v.a.* to open the sluice of; to unbung; to relax; — *v.n.*, **Se** —, *v.r.* to burst *or* gush forth; to flow, to run out; to scour, to be purged *or* relaxed; to have o.'s bowels open

Débondonner, *v.a.* to unbung [meek

Débonnaire, *adj.* good-natured, easy, kind,

Débonnairement, *adv.* good-naturedly, kindly, meekly [nature, kindness, meekness

Débonnaireté, *s.f.* good-naturedness, good-

Débord, *s.m.* edge, border, side; overflow

Débordé, e, *part. adj.* overflowed, &c. (*V.* **Déborder**); overflowing; without its border; untucked; loose; dissolute, profligate, lewd

Débordément, *adv.* dissolutely; disorderly, irregularly

Débordement, *s.m.* overflowing, overflow; inundation, flood; shower; rush; invasion, irruption; outbreak, outburst; excess; dissoluteness, profligacy, debauchery; (*mil.*) outflanking

Déborder, *v.n.* to overflow; to run over; to jut out; to sag; to burst forth; to break out; (*nav.*) to sheer off, to get clear; (*pop.*) to spew; — *v.a.* to take the border off, to unborder; to untuck; to project *or* go beyond; to outrun; to leave behind; to outnumber; (*mil.*) to outflank; (*nav.*) to rip off (*the planks*), to unship (*the oars*)

Se —, *v.r.* to overflow; to run over; to lose its border, to come unbordered; to untuck oneself; to come untucked; to pour forth; to burst forth; to break out; (*nav.*) to sheer off, to get clear [out of

Débosseler, *v.a.* to take the dents *or* bruises

Débosser, *v.a.* (*nav.*) to take the stoppers off (*a cable*), to unstopper [**Débotter,** *s.m.*

Débotté, e, *adj.* with boots off; — *s.m. V.*

Débotter, *v.a.* to take off the boots of

Se —, *v.r.* to take o.'s boots off

Débotter, *s.m.* taking the boots off. *Au* —, immediately after arriving

Débouché, *s.m.* issue, outlet; opening, sale, market; expedient; prospect; (*of a bridge*) water-way

Débouchement, *s.m.* unstopping; uncorking; opening; outlet, issue; issuing forth, debouching; falling, fall; disemboguement; sale, market

Déboucher, *v.a.* to open; to clear; to unstop; to uncork; (*fam.*) to open the mind of, to sharpen; (*pop.*) to open the bowels of; — *v.n.* to pass out; to run (into); to fall, to empty itself; (*mil.*) to issue forth, to debouch

Se —, *v.r.* to become *or* be opened, &c.; to become intelligent, to get sharp

Déboucler, *v.a.* to unbuckle; to unring; to uncurl; (*of harbours*) to clear; (*pop.*) to release, to uncage [(*pop.*) to escape, to bolt

Se —, *v.r.* to come unbuckled; to uncurl;

†**Débouilli,** *s.m.* (*dyeing*) boiling

†**Débouillir,** *v.a.* (*dyeing*) to boil

†**Débouillissage,** *s.m.* (*dyeing*) boiling

Débouquement, *s.m.* (*nav.*) disemboguement; narrow channel

Débouquer, *v.n.* (*nav.*) to disembogue

Débourbage, *s.m.* (*metal.*) trunking

Débourber, *v.a.* to cleanse; to extricate from the mud; to draw off; (*metal.*) to trunk. *Faire* —, to purge (*fish*) [gentleman *or* a lady of

Débourgeoiser, *v.a.* to polish, to make a

Se —, *v.r.* to become polished, to become a gentleman *or* a lady

Débourgeonner, *v.a. V.* **Ébourgeonner**

Débourrement, *s.m.* taking off the fleece

Débourrer, *v.a.* to take the fleece off; to worm (*fire-arms*); to empty (*a pipe*, &c.); to polish *or* sharpen (*a person*); to break in (*a horse*)

Se —, *v.r.* to become polished; to get sharp; to empty o.'s pipe

Débours, Déboursé, Déboursement, *s.m.* disbursement; outlay; expense, cost; payment

Débourser, *v.a.* to disburse, to lay out, to expend, to pay; — *v.n.* to pay *or* spend money, to come down, to fork out

†**Débouscailler,** *v.a.* (*pop. for* **Décrotter**)

†**Débouscailleur,** *s.m.* (*pop.*) *V.* **Décrotteur**

Debout, *adv.* upright, on end; standing; up; stirring; on o.'s legs; subsisting; ahead; (*of goods in transit*) unloaded, without examination

Débouté, Déboutement, *s.m.* (*law*) dismission, setting aside, nonsuit

Débouter, *v.a.* (*law*) to dismiss, to reject, to set aside, to refuse; to nonsuit; to overrule

Déboutonné, e, *part. adj.* unbuttoned; buttonless; free, unreserved

Déboutonner, *v.a.* to unbutton

Se —, *v.r.* to unbutton o.'s clothes (*or* o.'s coat, &c.); to come unbuttoned; to unbosom oneself; to disburden o.'s mind; to speak o.'s mind

†**Débraillé, e,** *adj.* with o.'s breast uncovered, with o.'s shirt and waistcoat unbuttoned, loosely dressed, loose, untidy

†**Débraillé, Débraillement,** *s.m.* looseness, untidiness; licence, licentiousness

†**Débrailler,** *v.a.* to uncover the breast of, to disorder the dress of; to disorder

Se —, *v.r.* to uncover o.'s breast, to dress loosely; to become loose *or* untidy [necting

Débrayage, *s.m.* (*mach.*) disengaging, discon-

Débrayer, *v.a.* (*mach.*) to disengage, to disconnect

†**Débredouiller,** *v.a.*, **Se** —, *v.r.* (*at backgammon*) to save the lurch

Débridement, *s.m.* unbridling; despatching, hurrying; (*surg.*) opening, incising, incision

Débrider, *v.a.n.* to unbridle; to despatch, to hurry; to halt; to stop; (*surg.*) to open, to incise; (*pop.*) to open. *Sans* —, without intermission, without stopping, at a stretch

†**Débrillanter,** *v.a.* to deaden, to dull [*or* dull

Se —, *v.r.* to lose its brilliancy, to become dead

Débris, *s.m.* fragment; remains; remnant; ruins; waste; rubbish; wreck; (*obsolete*) breaking, breakage, fracture, damage, havoc

Débrochage, *s.m.* unstitching; unspitting

Débrocher, *v.a.* to unstitch, to unspit

†**Débrouillement,** *s.m.* disentanglement; unravelling; unfolding; clearing up; explanation

†**Débrouiller,** *v.a.* to disentangle; to unravel; to unfold; to set to rights; to extricate; to clear up; to explain; to teach, to enlighten

Se —, *v.r.* to get disentangled; to get over difficulties; to extricate oneself; to get out of it; to clear up, to get clear *or* clearer; to become more intelligent [smooth; to thin

Débrutir, *v.a.* to polish, to rough-polish; to

Débrutissement, *s.m.* polishing, rough-polishing; smoothing; thinning

Débûché, *s.m.* start; — *part. V.* **Débûcher**

Débûcher, *v.a.n.* (*hunt.*) to dislodge, to start; — *s.m.* start [expulsion; ousting
Débusquement, *s.m.* dislodging, driving out,
Débusquer, *v.a.* to dislodge; to drive out, to expel; to oust, to turn out; to start; to take the busk off
Début, *s.m.* (*at play*) lead, first play; (*fig.*) beginning, outset; entering, entrance; first step; first attempt *or* trial; first appearance (before the public), debut; first work; first *or* maiden speech; first engagement
Débutant, e, *s.m.f.* beginner; performer making his *or* her first appearance, debutant, debutante
Débuter, *v.n.* to throw *or* toss *or* string for the lead; to lead, to play first; to begin, to set out, to start; to enter (into, upon); to make o.'s first appearance; — *v.a.* (*at play*) to knock away
Deçà, *prep. adv.* on this side (of). *En —, au —, par —*, on this side. *— et delà*, here and there, to and fro, on all sides, everywhere, about; on both sides [(*tenfold greater*)
Déca..., (*in Fr. weights and meas.*) deca...
Décachetable, *adj.* to be unsealed; to be opened
Décachetage, Décachètement, *s.m.* unsealing; opening [open) the seal of, to open
Décacheter, *v.a.* to unseal, to break (*or* break
  Se —, *v.r.* to come unsealed
Décacorde, *s.m. adj.* decachord
Décadaire, *adj.* decadal
Décade, *s.f.* decade
Décadenasser, *v.a.* to unpadlock
Décadence, *s.f.* decay, decadence; decline; downfall, fall; ruin [to set at liberty
Décadener, *v.a.* (*pop.*) to unchain, to release,
Décadi, *s.m.* decadi (*tenth and last day of the decade in the calendar of the first French Republic*), day of rest, sabbath [decahedral
Décaèdre, *s.m.* (*geom.*) decahedron; — *adj.*
Décagonal, e, *adj.* decagonal, decangular
Décagone, *s.m.* (*geom., fort.*) decagon; — *adj.* decagonal, decangular
Décagramme, *s.m.* (*Fr. weight*) decagramme
Décaissage, Décaissement, *s.m.* uncasing, unpacking; untubbing; withdrawal
Décaisser, *v.a.* to take out of its *or* their case (*or* box), to uncase, to unpack; (*hort.*) to untub;
Décalage, *s.m.* unwedging [*V. Supplement*
Décaler, *v.a.* to unwedge
Décalitre, *s.m.* (*Fr. meas.*) decalitre (2¼ *gallons*);
Décalogue, *s.m.* Decalogue [(*pop.*) hat, tile
Décalotter, *v.a.* to take the top off, to uncover
Décalque, *s.m.* transfer of the tracing [the top of
Décalquer, *v.a.* to transfer the tracing of
Décaméron, *s.m.* Decameron (*Boccaccio's work*)
Décamètre, *s.m.* (*Fr. meas.*) decametre [off
Décampement, *s.m.* decampment; marching
Décamper, *v.n.* to decamp; to march off; to run away, to scamper away, to levant, to bolt; to go away, to be off, to toddle [raise
†Décanailler, *v.a.* to raise from the rabble, to
  Se —, *v.r.* to rise from the rabble, to rise in the world, to rise; to lose o.'s low habits; to
Décanal, e, *adj.* decanal [keep better company
Décanat, *s.m.* deanery [oneself off, to levant
†Décaniller, *v.n.* (*pop.*) to turn tail, to take
Décanoniser, *v.a.* to uncanonize
Décantage, *s.m.* decanting
Décantation, *s.f.* decantation
Décanter, *v.a.* to decant
Décapage, *s.m.* cleaning, scraping (*of metals*)
Décapeler, *v.a.* (*nav.*) to unrig
Décaper, *v.a.* to clean, to scrape (*metals*); — *v.n.* (*nav.*) to clear a cape
Décapitalisation, *s.f.* decapitalization
Décapitaliser, *v.a.* to decapitalize
Décapitation, *s.f.* beheading, decapitation
Décapiter, *v.a.* to behead, to decapitate
Décapode, *s.m. adj.* (*zool.*) decapod [hood
Décapuchonner, *v.a.* to take off ...'s cowl *or*
  Se —, *v.r.* to take off o.'s (own) cowl *or* hood; to throw off o's cowl

Décarbonater, *v.a.* (*chem.*) to decarbonate
  Se —, *v.r.* to become (*or* be) decarbonated
Décarbonisation, *s.f.* (*chem.*) decarbonization
Décarboniser, *v.a.* (*chem.*) to decarbonize
  Se —, *v.r.* to become (*or* be) decarbonized
Décarbur-ation, -er. *V.* **Décarbonis-ation,**
Décardinaliser, *v.a.* to decardinalize [**-er**
Décare, *s.m.* (*Fr. meas.*) decare (*ten "ares," or the tenth part of an "hectare"*)
Décarêmer (Se), *v.r.* to make up for a fast, to
Décarrelage, *s.m.* unpaving [feast after fasting
Décarreler, *v.a.* to unpave, to take up the tile-floor *or* brick-floor of
Décarrer, *v.n.* (*pop.*) to run away, to be off
Décaser, *v.a.* to remove from its proper place; to oust, to dislodge [to change caste
Décaster, *v.a.* to change the caste of. *Se —,*
Décastère, *s.m.* (*Fr. meas.*) decastere
Décastyle, *s.m. adj.* (*arch.*) decastyle [syllabic
Décasyllabe, *s.m.* decasyllable; — *adj.* deca-
Décasyllabique, *adj.* decasyllabic
Décatir, *v.a.* to ungloss, to sponge; (*fig.*) to take the bloom off, to cause to fade, to wither, to wear out
  Se —, *v.r.* to lose its gloss, to be unglossed; (*fig.*) to lose o.'s bloom, to fade, to wear out, to grow old *or* ugly
Décatissage, *s.m.* unglossing, sponging
Décatisseur, *s.m.* unglosser, sponger
Décavé, e, *adj.* having lost o.'s stake; out; ruined, beggared; out of repute
Décaver, *v.a.* (*at play*) to win the stake of, to gain the pool of; (*fig.*) to ruin, to beggar; to bring into disrepute; (*old*) to take out of a cellar
  Se —, *v.r.* to lose o.'s stake *or* pool; to bring oneself into disrepute; to write oneself out
Décéder, *v.n.* to die; to decease
Déceindre, *v.a.* to ungird; to loosen
Décèlement, *s.m.* disclosure; betrayal
Déceler, *v.a.* to disclose; to reveal; to betray
Déceleu-r, se, *s.m.f.* discloser; revealer; be-
Décembre, *s.m.* December [trayer
Décembrisade, *s.f.* (*Fr. hist.*) Decembrisade (*massacre, in Paris, December* 2, 1851)
Décembriseur, *s.m.* (*Fr. hist.*) Decembrist (*agent of the massacre, in Paris, December* 2, 1851)
Décemment, *adv.* decently
Décemvir, *s.m.* decemvir
Décemviral, e, *adj.* decemviral
Décemvirat, *s.m.* decemvirate
Décence, *s.f.* decency, propriety
Décennaire, *adj.* decennary
Décennal, e, *adj.* decennial
Décent, e, *adj.* decent, becoming
Décentralisable, *adj.* decentralizable
Décentralisa-teur, trice, *adj.* decentralizing; — *s.m.f.* decentralizer
Décentralisation, *s.f.* decentralization
Décentraliser, *v.a.* to decentralize
  Se —, *v.r.* to become *or* be decentralized
Décepti-f, ve, *adj.* deceptive
Déception, *s.f.* deception; deceit, fraud
Déceptivement, *adv.* deceptively [hooped
Décercler, *v.a.* to unhoop. *Se —,* to come un-
Décernement, *s.m.* decreeing; enactment; bestowing, awarding, award; (*law*) issuing
Décerner, *v.a.* to decree; to enact; to bestow; to award; (*law*) to issue (*a summons, &c.*)
  Se —, *v.r.* to be decreed *or* &c.
Décerveler, *v.a.* to brain
Décès, *s.m.* death; decease; demise
Décesser, *v.n.* (*pop. for* **Cesser**)
Décevable, *adj.* deceivable
Décevant, e, *adj.* deceptive, deceitful
Décevoir, *v.a.* to deceive; to disappoint [joice
Déchagriner, *v.a.* to comfort, to cheer, to re-
Déchaîné, e, *adj.* unchained, let loose, broken loose, loose; uncontrolled; raging, furious, wild
Déchaînement, *s.m.* unchaining, letting loose, breaking loose; unbridling; fury, rage, wildness, violence, outburst; exasperation; inveighing, invective

Déchaîner, *v.a.* to unchain; to turn loose; to let loose; to exasperate

Se —, *v.r.* to break loose, to get loose; to inveigh; to fly out; to run riot; to vent o.'s *or* its fury, to rage; to blow

Déchalander, *v.a. V.* **Désachalander**

Déchalasser, *v.a.* (*hort., agr.*) to unprop

Déchalement, *s.m.* (*nav.*) leaving dry *or* bare; lying dry; ebbing far out [lie dry; to ebb far out

Déchaler, *v.a.n.* (*nav.*) to leave dry *or* bare; to

Déchanter, *v.n.* to change o.'s note, to alter *or* lower o.'s tone; to come down a peg; to alter o.'s opinion; to be undeceived; to be disappointed [uncope (*a wall*)

Déchaperonner, *v.a.* to unhood (*a hawk*); to

Décharge, *s.f.* unloading; unlading; shooting (*of rubbish,* &c.); lumber-place, lumber-room; rubbish-hole; outlet; reservoir; rubbish, waste; discharge; release; allowance; ease, easement; relief; exoneration; exculpation; stamp; (*fam.*) shower (*of blows*). *Cabinet* or *pièce de —,* lumber-room. *Table de —,* dinner-waggon. *A —,* (*law*) for the defence, for the prisoner. *— générale,* (*mil.*) round [tilting

Déchargement, *s.m.* unloading; unlading;

Déchargeoir, *s.m.* opening; outlet; (*weaving*) roller, breast-roll

Décharger, *v.a.n.* to unload; to unlade; to discharge; to shoot; to unburden, to disburden; to disencumber; to lighten; to ease, to free; to release; to relieve; to exonerate; to exculpate; to clear; to vent, to give vent to; to visit; to strike, to give; to empty; to tilt; (*of ink, colours*) to come off

Se —, *v.r.* to unload *or* &c. oneself; to lay the blame; to give vent to; to go off; (*of colours*) to change, to come off; (*of rivers*) to empty itself, to fall [whipper, lumper; wharfinger

Déchargeur, *s.m.* unloader, porter, heaver,

Décharmer, *v.a.* to decharm, to disencharm, to uncharm, to unspell, to disenchant

Décharné, e, *adj.* emaciated, lean, thin, spare, gaunt, bony, fleshless; stripped; meagre, poor; (*of style*) bald, meagre, poor

Décharnement, *s.m.* emaciation; meagreness, poverty; baldness (*of style*)

Décharner, *v.a.* to strip *or* pick the flesh off; to emaciate; to impoverish

Se —, *v.r.* to become emaciated, &c.

Décharpir, *v.a.* (*old*) to tear into rags; to part *or* separate (*fighters*)

Déchassé, *s.m.* (*dancing*) slide to the left

Déchasser, *v.a.* to drive out (*nails, pegs,* &c.); *— v.n.* (*dancing*) to slide to the left

Déchaumage, *s.m.* (*agr.*) digging up *or* ploughing up the stubble

Déchaumer, *v.a.* to dig up *or* plough up the stubble of; to break up (*fallow land*)

Déchaussage, *s.m. V.* **Déchaussement**

Déchaussé, e, *adj.* with shoes *or* boots *or* stockings off; (*of friars*) barefooted; (*for other senses, V.* **Déchausser**)

Déchaussement, *s.m.* laying bare, baring; clearing; lancing the gums; shrinking away of the gums

Déchausser, *v.a.* to pull off the shoes *or* boots *or* stockings of; to lay bare, to bare; to clear; to break up (*a road*)

Se —, *v.r.* to take off o.'s shoes *or* boots *or* stockings; to become *or* get bare

Déchaussière, *s.f.* wolf's form *or* lair

Déchaussoir, *s.m.* gum-lancet

Déchaussure, *s.f. V.* **Déchaussière**

Déchaux, *adj.m.* (*of friars*) barefooted

Dèche, *s.f.* (*pop.*) pinching need, ruin, misery, beggary. *En —,* out of pocket

Déchéance, *s.f.* forfeiture, loss; deposition, dethronement; downfall, fall; decay

Déchet, *s.m.* waste, loss; allowance for waste; (*fig.*) drawback, disappointment

Décheu-x, se, *adj.* (*pop.*) needy, beggared, beggarly; *— s.m.f.* pauper, beggar

Décheveler, *v.a. V.* **Écheveler**

Déchevêtrer, *v.a.* to take the halter off, to unhalter; to disentangle; to release [its halter

Se —, *v.r.* to get its halter off, to break from

†**Décheviller,** *v.a.* to unpeg, to unpin

Se —, *v.r.* to come unpegged *or* unpinned

Déchiffrable, *adj.* decipherable; legible, intelligible

Déchiffrement, *s.m.* deciphering; interpretation; explanation; reading *or* playing at sight

Déchiffrer, *v.a.n.* to decipher; to make out; to unravel; to see through; to interpret; to explain; to clear up; to read *or* play at sight

Se —, *v.r.* to be deciphered *or* &c.

Déchiffreu-r, se, *s.m.f.* decipherer; reader *or* player at sight [ting up; pinking

Déchiquetage, *s.m.* slashing; mangling; cut-

Déchiqueter, *v.a.* to slash; to mangle; to cut up; to whittle; to jag; to pink

Déchiqueteu-r, se, *s.m.f.* slasher, cutter, ripper

Déchiqueture, *s.f. V.* **Déchiquetage**

Déchirage, *s.m.* breaking up. *Bois de —,* old ship-timber [excruciating

Déchirant, e, *adj.* heartrending, harrowing;

Déchiré, e, *part. adj.* torn, &c. (*V.* **Déchirer**); ragged, tattered, in tatters; cragged, craggy. *N'être pas trop —e,* (*fam.*) to be a pretty *or* desirable woman

Déchirement, *s.m.* tearing, rending; breaking; tear, rent; laceration; twitching, twitch; great pain; anguish; pang; commotion; broil

Déchirer, *v.a.* to tear; to rend; to lacerate; to tear off *or* up; to tear to pieces; to mangle; to mutilate; to rip, to rip up; to break up; to cut up; to divide; to split; to jag; to torture, to harrow; to grate on *or* split (*the ear*); to sting; to defame, to slander; to revile, to abuse; (*mil., obsolete*) to bite (*the cartridge*). *— à belles dents,* to pull *or* tear to pieces, to fall foul of. *— de la toile,* (*mil. slang*) to fire irregularly, to keep up a straggling fire [boat-ripper

Déchireu-r, se, *s.m.f.* tearer, render, ripper;

Déchirure, *s.f.* tear, rent; laceration; breaking

Déchoir, *v.n. def.* to fall, to sink; to decline; to decay; to forfeit, to lose

Déchouer, *v.a. V.* **Déséchouer**

‡**Déchristianiser,** *v.a.* to unchristianize, to

Déchu, e, *part. of* **Déchoir** [dechristianize

Déci, (*in Fr. weights and meas.*) deci... (*tenth part, one tenth*) [*an "are"*)

Déciare, *s.m.* (*Fr. meas.*) deciare (*tenth part of*

Décidé, e, *adj.* decided; determined; settled; fixed; resolute; bold; confident; of decision

Décidément, *adv.* decidedly; on consideration; finally; positively, actually

Décider, *v.a.n.* to decide; to settle; to fix; to determine; to persuade; to induce; to resolve

Se —, *v.r.* to make up o.'s mind; to decide; to determine; to settle; to resolve; to take a resolution; to come to a decision *or* to a conclusion; to choose, to fix o.'s choice (upon); (*of things*) to be decided, &c.

Décidu, e, *adj.* (*bot.*) deciduous [(*See* table, p. 6.)

Décigramme, *s.m.* (*Fr. weight*) decigramme

Décilitre, *s.m.* (*Fr. meas.*) decilitre (*See* table,

†**Déciller,** *v.a. V.* **Dessiller** [p. 6.)

Décimable, *adj.* tithable [decimal

Décimal, e, *adj.,* **Décimale,** *s.f.* (*arith.*)

Décimateur, *s.m.* tithe-owner

Décimation, *s.f.* decimation

Décime, *s.m.* (*Fr. coin, the tenth part of a "franc"*) decime (*penny*); tenth; tithe; ten per cent. *— de guerre,* war-tax [off, to carry off, to destroy

Décimer, *v.a.* to decimate; to thin; to sweep

Décimètre, *s.m.* (*Fr. meas.*) decimetre

Décintrage, Décintrement, *s.m.* removing the centering (*of a vault*)

Décintrer, *v.a.* to remove the centering of

Décintroir, *s.m.* cutting-hammer

Décirer, *v.a.* to take the wax off, to unwax

Se —, *v.r.* to lose its wax, to get unwaxed

Décisi-f, ve, *adj.* decisive; positive; peremptory

Décision, *s.f.* decision, resolution [peremptorily
Décisivement, *adv.* decisively; positively;
Décisoire, *adj.* decisory, deciding, decisive
Décistère, *s.m.* (*Fr. meas.*) decistere (*See* table, [p. 6.)
Déciviliser, *v.a.* to uncivilize
Déclama-teur, trice, *s.m.f.* declaimer; stump-orator; twaddler; — *adj.* declamatory, stilted, bombastic, high-flown
Déclamation, *s.f.* declamation; elocution; stump-oratory; bombast; twaddle; abuse; invective; rant
Déclamatoire, *adj.* declamatory [vective; rant
Déclamer, *v.a.n.* to recite; to read; to declaim; to deliver; to spout; to mouth; to inveigh; to rant [out of joint
Déclancher (Se), *v.r.* (*pop.*) to put o.'s shoulder
Déclarable, *adj.* declarable
Déclara-teur, trice, *s.m.f.* declarer
Déclarati-f, ve, *adj.* declarative, declaratory
Déclaration, *s.f.* declaration; proclamation; statement; report; schedule; disclosure; affidavit; verdict. — *de faillite,* adjudication [in bankruptcy
Déclaratoire, *adj.* declaratory [in bankruptcy
Déclaré, e, *adj.* declared; open; public; acknowledged; recognized
Déclarer, *v.a.* to declare; to make known; to proclaim; to state; to disclose; to reveal; to denounce; to certify; (*of juries*) to find (*guilty or not guilty*). — (*quelqu'un*) *en faillite,* to adjudicate (one) a bankrupt; to gazette
Se —, *v.r.* to declare; to declare oneself; to make a declaration; to break out; to come out; to begin; (*of the weather*) to set in; (*of prisoners*) to plead (*guilty or not guilty*)
Déclassé, e, *adj.* taken out of its class, transferred to another class, unclassed; belonging to no particular class; nondescript; of no defined position, out of his sphere; undervalued, depreciated; struck off the rolls, dismissed from the service
Déclassement, *s.m.* alteration in the classes, unclassing; confusion of classes; undervalue, depreciation; striking off the rolls, dismissal from the service
Déclasser, *v.a.* to change the class of, to transfer to another class, to unclass; to alter the classing of; to throw classes into confusion; to undervalue, to depreciate; to strike off the rolls, to dismiss from the service
Se —, *v.r.* to get out of o.'s (*or* its) class; to go out of o.'s sphere; to alter o.'s position; to become undervalued *or* depreciated [unlatching
Déclenchement, *s.m.* unhooking, loosening;
Déclencher, *v.a.* to unhook, to loosen; to unlatch [to go off
Se —, *v.r.* to come unhooked, to get loose;
Déclic, *s.m.* trigger, catch; click; unhitching
Déclimater, *v.a.* to declimatize
Déclin, *s.m.* decline; decay; ebb; wane; close; (*of fire-arms, obsolete*) main spring
Déclinabilité, *s.f.* (*gram.*) declinability
Déclinable, *adj.* (*gram.*) declinable [sion
Déclinaison, *s.f.* declination; (*gram.*) declen-
Déclinateur, *s.m.* (*instr.*) declinator
Déclination, *s.f.* declining; declination; deflection; sloping, slope, declivity
Déclinatoire, *adj.* declinatory; — *s.m.* (*law*) declinatory plea, exception; (*phys.*) declinometer
Décliné, e, *adj.* declined, &c. (*V.* **Décliner**); (*bot.*) declinate, declinous
Déclinement, *s.m.* declining, declination
Décliner, *v.a.n.* to decline; to decline to entertain (*a proposal,* &c.); to state *or* give (*o.'s name,* &c.); to except to; to disclaim to fall off; to [abate
Se —, *v.r.* to be declined, &c.
Décliquer, *v.a.* to unhitch, to loosen
Déclive, *adj.* declivous, sloping; (*surg.*) depend-
Décliver, *v.n.* to slope [ent
Déclivité, *s.f.* declivity, slope
Décloîtrer, *v.a.* to uncloister, to secularize
Se —, *v.r.* to leave the cloister, to return into the world
Déclore, *v.a.* to unclose, to lay open, to open
Déclos, e, *adj.* unclosed, laid open, open
Déclôture, *s.f.* unclosing, opening
Déclouer, *v.a.* to unnail; (*pop.*) to redeem from pawn, to take out of the spout
Se —, *v.r.* to be unnailed; to come unnailed
Décochement, *s.m.* (*of arrows*) shooting, discharge [fly, to let off; to bring out
Décocher, *v.a.* to shoot, to discharge, to let
Décocté, *s.m.* (*pharm.*) decoction
Décoction, *s.f.* decoction
†**Décognoir,** *s.m.* (*print.*) shooting-stick, shooter
Décoiffer, *v.a.* to take off the head-dress of; to undo *or* disorder the hair of; to uncap; to uncork, to empty; to put out of conceit (with)
Se —, *v.r.* to take off (*or* pull off) o.'s head-dress; to undo *or* disorder o.'s (*or* each other's) hair
Décoinçage, *s.m.* unwedging; (*rail.*) unkeying
Décoincer, *v.a.* to unwedge; (*rail.*) to unkey
Se —, *v.r.* to get (*or* come) unwedged, &c.
Décolérer, *v.n.* (*pop.*) to cease to be angry (*or* in a passion)
Décollation, *s.f.* decollation, beheading
Décollement, *s. m.* ungluing; unpasting; coming off; (*surg.*) detachment
Décoller, *v.a.* to unglue; to unpaste; to behead, to cut off the head of, to decollate; (*at billiards*) to disengage from the cushion; — *v.n.* (*pop.*) to move off, to get away
Se —, *v.r.* to get (*or* come *or* be) unglued *or* unpasted, to come off; to disengage o.'s ball from the cushion
Décolleté, e, *adj.* (*pers.*) in a low dress; (*of dresses*) low; (*fig.*) free, broad, licentious
Décolleter, *v.a.* to uncover the neck and shoulders of; to make (*a dress*) come low down
Se —, *v.r.* to uncover o.'s neck and shoulders; to wear a low dress [— *s.m.* decolorant
Décolorant, e, *adj.* decolouring, discolouring;
Décoloration, *s.f.* discoloration, decoloration, decolouring
Décoloré, e, *adj.* discoloured, colourless, faded, pale; (*of style*) cold, poor, tame, colourless
Décolorer, *v.a.* to discolour, to decolour; (*fig.*) to deprive of life [come discoloured; to fade
Se —, *v.r.* to lose o.'s (*or* its) colour; to be-
Décolorimètre, *s.m.* decolorimeter
Décoloris, *s.m.* discoloration
Décombant, e, *adj.* (*bot.*) decumbent
Décombler, *v.a.* to empty
Décombrer, *v.a.* to clear the rubbish from, to clear from rubbish, to clear [ruins
Décombres, *s.m.pl.* rubbish, building materials;
Décommander, *v.a.* to countermand
Se —, *v.r.* to be countermanded
Décompléter, *v.a.* to render incomplete
Décomposable, *adj.* decomposable, decompoundable
Décomposé, e, *part. adj.* decomposed, &c. (*V.* **Décomposer**); (*bot.*) decompound, decomposite
Décomposer, *v.a.* to decompose; to decompound; to analyze; to discompose; to distort
Se —, *v.r.* to decompose; to be decomposed; to become discomposed *or* distorted
Décomposition, *s.f.* decomposition; analysis; discomposure
Décompte, *s.m.* deduction; allowance; stoppage; deficiency; disappointment, drawback; (*soldiers' slang*) death-shot, death-blow, quietus
Décompter, *v.a.n.* to deduct; to make deductions; to be disappointed; to alter o.'s opinion; (*at play*) to begin a fresh count; (*mus.*) to sing the intermediate notes
Se —, *v.r.* to be deducted *or* &c.
Déconcert, *s.m.* disconcert
Déconcertement, *s.m.* disconcertion
Déconcerter, *v.a.* to disconcert; to put out; to abash; to baffle
Se —, *v.r.* to be disconcerted *or* put out
Déconclure, *v.a.* to annul, to break off
Déconf-ès, esse, *adj.* (*pers., obsolete*) unconfessed (*to a priest*), without confession

Déconfire, *v.a.* to discomfit; to nonplus, to puzzle, to shut up; to abash [**Déconfire**

Déconfit, e, *adj. s.* insolvent; — *part. adj. V.*

Déconfiture, *s.f.* discomfiture; havoc, slaughter; consumption; break-down, smash, ruin; insolvency; dilapidation [tress

Déconfort, *s.m.* (*old*) discomfort, sorrow, dis-

Déconforter, *v.a.* to discomfort, to discourage, to dishearten, to grieve, to distress

Déconsacrer, *v.a.* to desecrate

†**Déconseiller,** *v.a.* to dissuade; to dissuade from; to object to, to oppose, to disapprove of

Déconsidération, *s.f.* discredit, disrepute

Déconsidérer, *v.a.* to discredit, to bring into discredit (*or* into disrepute). *Faire* —, to bring into discredit (*or* into disrepute)

Se —, *v.r.* to bring oneself (*or* to fall) into discredit (*or* into disrepute), to lose o.'s credit

Déconstruire, *v.a.* to take to pieces; to demolish, to pull down; to decompose; (*gram.*) to construct badly; (*liter.*) to turn (*verse*) into prose. *Se* —, to be taken to pieces, &c.

Décontenancer, *v.a.* to put out of countenance, to abash [be abashed

Se —, *v.r.* to be put out of countenance, to

Déconvenue, *s.f.* discomfiture, disaster, mishap, ill-luck, failure, disappointment

Décor, *s.m.* decoration; ornamentation; decorative *or* ornamental painting; graining; (*theat.*) scenery, scene; —**s,** *pl.* (*theat.*) scenes, scenery; (*of freemasons*) regalia. *Peintre en —s,* decorator, house-decorator, ornamental painter, scene-painter; grainer

Décora-teur, trice, *s.m.f.* decorator; trimmer; house-decorator; paper-hanger; ornamental painter; scene-painter. *Peintre* —, decorator, house-decorator, ornamental painter, scene-painter; grainer

Décorati-f, ve, *adj.* decorative

Décoration, *s.f.* decoration; ornamentation; ornament; scene, scenery; order (of knighthood); insignia; badge; star; medal; cross *or* ribbon of the Legion of Honour (*a French*

Décordage, *s.m.* untwisting; picking. [*order*)

Décorder, *v.a.* to untwist (*a rope*), to pick

Se —, *v.r.* to come untwisted [(*oakum*)

Décoré, e, *part. adj.m.f., s.m.* decorated, &c. (*V.* **Décorer**); knighted; wearing the insignia (of); wearing orders; wearing a medal; wearing the cross *or* the ribbon of the Legion of Honour; knight; medallist; knight *or* member of the Legion of Honour

Décorer, *v.a.* to decorate; to adorn; to ornament; to set off; to trim; to paint; to varnish; to dignify; to confer (*titles*); to knight; to confer a medal on; to confer the knighthood of the Legion of Honour on

Décorner, *v.a.* to dishorn, to break the horns of; to undo the dog's-ear of, to turn up again, to turn up again the corner of

Décorporation, *s.f.* (*mil.*) disembodying

Décorticant, e, *adj.* decorticating; pulping, husking, shelling, peeling

Décortication, *s.f.* decortication, barking; pulping, husking, shelling, peeling

Décortiquant, *part.* decorticating, barking; pulping, husking, shelling, peeling

Décortiquer, *v.a.* to decorticate, to bark; to pulp, to husk, to shell, to peel

Se —, *v.r.* to be decorticated, &c.

Décortiqueur, *s.m.,* **Décortiqueuse,** *s.f.* barking-iron; (*agr. machine*) pulper, sheller

Décorum, *s.m.* decorum, propriety

Découcher, *v.n.* to sleep out, to stay out all night; to sleep away (from); — *v.a.* to turn (*one*) out *or* deprive (*one*) of his *or* her bed

Découdre, *v.a.* to unsew; to unstitch; to rip; to rip up, to rip open. *En* —, to come to blows, to fight it out, to have a brush (with); to dispute; to run away [to get on badly

Se —, *v.r.* to come unsewed *or* unstitched;

Découlement, *s.m.* flowing, running

Découler, *v n.* to flow; to run down; to trickle; to drop; to proceed, to spring

Découpage, *s.m.* cutting up *or* out; fret-cutting; carving; punching; pinking; figure cut out

Découpé, e, *part. adj.* cut up *or* out, cut, &c. (*V.* **Découper**); shaped; coming out, standing out, showing off; defined; sharp; clear; — *s.m.* (*hort.*) group of beds

Découper, *v.a.* to cut up *or* out; to cut; to fret; to carve; to punch; to pink; to define; to show off. *Service à* —, carving knife and fork

Se —, *v.r.* to be cut up *or* out; to be carved *or* &c.; to come out, to stand out, to show off

Découpeu-r, se, *s.m.f.* fret-cutter; carver; pinker

Découple, Découpler, *s.m.* (*hunt.*) uncoupling

Découplé, e, *part. adj.* uncoupled, &c. *Bien* —, strapping, well-set, well-made, strong-limbed

Découpler, *v.a.* to uncouple; to unmatch; to unyoke; to separate; to let loose; to set (at

Se —, *v.r.* to get uncoupled *or* &c. [*or* on)

Découpoir, *s.m.* punch; butler's tray

Découpure, *s.f.* cutting out; pinking; figure *or* work cut out; fret-work; open-work; cut paper-work; shred; (*bot.*) notch

Décourageable, *adj.* discourageable [dency

Découragement, *s.m.* discouragement; despon-

Décourager, *v.a.* to discourage, to dishearten, to dispirit, to unnerve; to deter (from)

Se —, *v.r.* to be discouraged *or* disheartened, to lose courage; to despond

Décourant, e, *adj. V.* **Décurrent**

Décourber, *v.a.* to unbend, to straighten

Découronnement, *s.m.* discrowning; laying bare; (*mil.*) clearing, sweeping

Découronner, *v.a.* to discrown; to lay bare; (*mil.*) to clear, to sweep

Se —, *v.r.* to abdicate the crown; to become (*or* be) discrowned *or* &c. [ment

Décours, *s.m.* wane, decrease; decline; abate-

Décousu, e, *adj.* unsewed; unstitched; ripped; unconnected, loose, desultory; irregular; unsteady; incoherent; — *s.m.* looseness, desultoriness, irregularity, incoherence [wound

Décousure, *s.f.* place ripped; seam-rent; gash,

Découvert, *s.m.* deficit; loss; stock sold as a time bargain; open ground

Découvert, e, *adj.* uncovered; discovered; open; bare; unguarded; (*of boats*) undecked. *A* —, uncovered; open; in the open air; unprotected, exposed; unsecured; unveiled, barefaced; unmasked; overdrawn (*account*); openly, plainly; (*on 'Change*) as a time bargain

Découverte, *s.f.* discovery; detection; finding out; exposure; (*mil., nav.*) reconnoitring; (*nav.*) discovery; (*nav.*) look-out [roofing

Découverture, *s.f.* stripping off (*a roof*), un-

Découvreur, *s.m.* discoverer

Découvrir, *v.a.* to uncover; to lay bare, to bare; to lay open; to open; to unwrap; to unmuffle; to unveil; to uncase; to unroof; to untile; to discover; to perceive, to descry, to spy out, to see, to discern; to find; to find out; to detect; to learn; to hunt out; to disclose, to reveal, to let know, to tell; to betray; to show; to unguard; to expose; to unmask

Se —, *v.r.* to uncover *or* &c. oneself; to uncover *or* &c. (o.'s ...); to take off o.'s hat *or* cap; to uncover o.'s head *or* face; to make oneself known; to expose oneself; to betray oneself; to be uncovered; to be discovered *or* perceived *or* &c.; to be found out *or* detected *or* &c.; to become known; to come out; to appear; to open; to be open; (*of the sky*) to clear up [to pull off, to make (*one*) let go his hold

Décramponner, *v.a.* to uncramp, to loosen;

Se —, *v.r.* to let go o.'s hold [brush

†**Décrasse-peignes,** *s.m.* comb-cleaner, comb-

Décrasser, *v.a.* to clean; to wash; to scour; to polish, to brush up, to rub off the rust of ignorance, to teach the rudiments; to make a gentleman *or* a lady of

Se —, *v.r.* to clean oneself; to clean (o.'s ...); (*of things*) to be cleaned *or* washed *or* scoured, to get clean; (*fig.*) to become polished, to learn the rudiments; to become a gentleman *or* a lady; to lose (*or* get rid of) its rust
Décravater, *v.a.* to take off the neck-tie *or* neck-cloth *or* cravat of
Se —, *v.r.* to take off o.'s (own) neck-tie *or* &c.
Décréditement, *s.m.* discrediting; discredit, [disrepute
Décréditer, *v.a. V.* **Déconsidérer**
Décrépit, e, *adj.* decrepit, broken down, worn out
Décrépitation, *s.f.*, **Décrépitement,** *s.m.* decrepitation, crepitation, crackling; pattering
Décrépiter, *v.n.* to decrepitate, to crepitate, to crackle; to patter
Décrépitude, *s.f.* decrepitude
Decrescendo, *adv.* (*mus.*) decrescendo; (*fig.*) decreasing, diminishing, less and less; — *s.m.* (*mus.*) decrescendo (*gradual decrease from loud to soft*); (*fig.*) decrease, diminution
Décret, *s.m.* decree; order; enactment; fiat; [writ; warrant
Décrétale, *s.f.* decretal
Décrétaliste, *s.m.* decretist
Décréter, *v.a.* to decree; to order; to enact; to dictate; to award; to issue a writ against
Décrétiste, *s.m.* decretist
Décrétoire, *adj.* decretory [&c.
Décreus-age, -ement, -er. *V.* **Décrusage,**
Décri, *s.m.* prohibition; decrial, crying down; discredit, disrepute
Décrier, *v.a.* to decry; to cry down; to discredit, to bring into discredit *or* into disrepute; to prohibit [form, to make
Décrire, *v.a.* to describe; to trace, to draw; to
Se —, *v.r.* to be described *or* &c.
Décrochement, *s.m.* unhooking
Décrocher, *v.a.* to unhook; to take down; to free, to disengage; (*pop.*) to redeem from pawn, to take out of the spout; (*pop.*) to bring *or* fetch down, to shoot [down *or* &c.
Se —, *v.r.* to come unhooked; to be taken
Décroire, *v.a.n.* to disbelieve
Décroisement, *s.m.* uncrossing
Décroiser, *v.a.* to uncross
Décroissance, *s.f. V.* **Décroissement**
Décroissant, e, *adj.* decreasing, diminishing; decrescent; (*math.*) descending
Décroissement, *s.m.* decrease; wane; decline
Décroît, *s.m.* decrease; wane
Décroître, *v.n.* to decrease, to diminish; to go down, to fall; to shorten; to wane
Décrottage, *s.m.* cleaning; brushing; polishing
Décrotter, *v.a.* to clean; to scrape; to brush; to polish; to pick; to rub off the rust of ignorance, to brush up, to teach the rudiments; (*pop.*) to eat up
Se —, *v.r.* to clean *or* brush oneself; to be cleaned *or* brushed *or* polished; to be taught *or* to learn the rudiments; (*pop.*) to be eaten up
Décrotteur, *s.m.* boot-cleaner, shoeblack; Boots; (*fam.*) teacher for beginners, junior [master
Décrottoir, *s.m.* scraper, door-scraper
Décrottoire, *s.f.* hard-brush
Décru, e, *part. of* **Décroître**
Décruage, *s.m.* scouring
Décrue, *s.f.* (*of waters*) decrease, fall
Décruer, *v.a.* to scour (*silk*, &c.)
Décrument, *s.m.* scouring
Décrusage, Décrusement, *s.m.* ungumming
Décruser, *v.a.* to ungum
Décubitus, *s.m.* (*med.*) decubitus, decumbency
Décuire, *v.a.* (*of syrups*, &c.) to thin. *Se* —, to give
Déculassement, *s.m.* unbreeching (*of fire-arms*)
Déculasser, *v.a.* to unbreech (*fire-arms*)
Déculotter, *v.a.* to take off *or* down the breeches of, to unbreech [to unbreech oneself
Se —, *v.r.* to take o.'s breeches off *or* down,
Décuple, *s.m. adj.* decuple, tenfold
Décupler, *v.a.n.*, **Se** —, *v.r.* to decuple, to in- [crease tenfold
Décurie, *s.f.* (*Rom. hist.*) decury
Décurion, *s.m.* (*Rom. hist.*) decurion
Décurionat, *s.m.* (*Rom. hist.*) decurionate
Décurrent, e, *adj.* (*bot.*) decurrent
Décursi-f, ve, *adj.* (*bot.*) decursive
Décurtation, *s.f.* (*of trees*) withering at the top
Décussati-f, ve, Décussé, e, *adj.* (*bot.*) decussate, decussated
Décussation, *s.f.* decussation
Décuvage, *s.m.*, **Décuvaison,** *s.f.* tunning
Décuver, *v.a.* to tun
†**Dédaignable,** *adj.* to be disdained
†**Dédaigner,** *v.a.* to disdain; to scorn; to despise; to slight; to disregard; not to care for; to set oneself above; to turn up o.'s nose at
†**Dédaigneusement,** *adv.* disdainfully, scornfully
†**Dédaigneu-x, se,** *adj.* disdainful, scornful; regardless, careless. *Faire le* —, to turn up o.'s nose [*en* —, to disdain
Dédain, *s.m.* disdain, scorn; disregard. *Prendre*
Dédale, *s.m.* labyrinth, maze: (*pers.*) Dædalus
Dédaléen, ne, *adj.* Dædalian
Dédallage, *s.m.* unflagging, unpaving
Dédaller, *v.a.* to take up the flag-stones *or* slabs of, to unflag, to unpave
Se —, *v.r.* to get unflagged *or* unpaved
Dédamer, *v.n.* (*at draughts*) to displace a man; — *v.a.* (*at draughts*) to uncrown (*a king*)
Dedans, *adv.* inside; in; within; in it, into it, within it; in them, into them, within them; in for it; tipsy; — *s.m.* inside; interior; home; country; in; (*rid.*) near side. *Au* —, inside; within; at home; in doors; in the country; in; inward, internal; inwardly, internally. *De* —, from within; inside. *Du* —, of *or* from the inside, of *or* from the interior; from within; inner; (*rid.*) near. *En* —, inside; within; in; inward; included; turned in; bashful, uncommunicative, close. *Donner* —, to be taken in. *Mettre* —, to put in; (*fig.*) to take in; to cage, to lock up; to make tipsy, to fuddle. *Se mettre* —, to put *or* take oneself in; to get into a scrape; to get tipsy, to fuddle
Dédicace, *s.f.* dedication; consecration; in- [scription, address
Dédicatoire, *adj.* dedicatory
Dédier, *v.a.* to dedicate; to consecrate; to devote; to offer; to inscribe, to address
Dédire, *v.a.* to contradict, to gainsay, to disown
Se —, *v.r.* to retract, to recant; to revoke *or* forfeit o.'s word; to desist, to withdraw, to recede, to go back
Dédit, *s.m.* forfeit, forfeiture; deed stipulating forfeiture; retractation, recantation; unsaying; breach of promise. *Avoir son dit et son* —, to say and unsay
Dédommagement, *s.m.* indemnification; indemnity; damages; compensation, consolation, amends
Dédommager, *v.a.* to indemnify; to make good; to compensate; to recoup; to make up (for)
Dédorer, *v.a.* to ungild [gilding
Se —, *v.r.* to come ungilt, to lose its gilt *or*
Dédoreu-r, se, *s.m.f.* ungilder
Dédorure, *s.f.* ungilding
Dédoublage, *s.m.* unlining; unfolding; dividing into two; diluting, mixing; (*nav.*) un- [sheathing
Dédoublé, *s.m.* diluted alcohol
Dédoublement, *s.m. V.* **Dédoublage**
Dédoubler, *v.a.* to take out the lining of, to unline; to unfold; to divide into two; to dilute, to mix; (*nav.*) to unsheathe
Se —, *v.r.* to come unlined; to be unfolded; to be divided into two; to be reduced one half; to be diluted *or* mixed; (*nav.*) to be unsheathed
Déducti-f, ve, *adj.* deductive
Déduction, *s.f.* deduction; set-off; inference; (*obsolete*) enumeration, recital
Déductivement, *adv.* deductively
Déduire, *v.a.* to deduct, to subtract, to take off; to deduce, to infer; (*old*) to enumerate, to relate
Se —, *v.r.* to be deducted *or* &c.
Déduit, *s.m.* (*obsolete*) pleasure, enjoyment, pastime, diversion, entertainment, sport
Déesse, *s.f.* goddess

Défâcher, *v.a.* to pacify; — *v.n.* to cease to be angry

Se —, *v.r.* to be pacified, to get *or* be pleased [again

Défaçonner, *v.a.* to put out of shape; to make (*one*) lose his good manners

Se —, *v.r.* to get out of shape; to lose o.'s [good manners

†**Défaillance,** *s.f.* swoon, fainting, fainting fit; exhaustion; decay; failing; weakness; faltering; (*law*) non-accomplishment, failing, failure, default

†**Défaillant, e,** *adj.* fainting; decaying; faint, weak, feeble; trembling, faltering; failing; (*law*) defaulting; — *s.m.f.* (*law*) defaulter

†**Défaillir,** *v.n.* to faint; to decay; to fall; to sink, to give way; to tremble, to falter; to fail

Défaire, *v.a.* to undo; to unmake; to untie; to take off; to unpin; to unpack; to unbraid; to unstitch; to unravel; to break off, to annul; to emaciate; to distort; to discompose; to spoil; to rid, to free, to deliver; to kill; to defeat, to rout

Se —, *v.r.* to come undone; to get loose; to get out of shape; to break down; to unravel; to rid oneself, to get rid; to part (with); to dispose; to throw off; to take off; to kill, to make away (with); to get thin; to become distorted *or* discomposed; (*of wine*, &c.) to get flat

Défaiseu-r, se, *s.m.f.* undoer; unmaker

Défait, e, *part. adj.* undone, &c. (*V.* **Défaire**); defeated; distorted; discomposed; emaciated, exhausted, fagged, seedy; dejected; pale, wan, ghastly

Défaite, *s.f.* defeat; rout; overthrow; ruin, destruction; check; evasion, shuffle, shift, excuse, pretence, sham; sale; riddance

Défalcation, *s.f.* defalcation; deduction

Défalquer, *v.a.* to defalcate; to deduct

Défatiguer, *v.a.* *V.* **Délasser**

Défaufiler, *v.a.* to untack, to unbaste

Défausser, *v.a.* to straighten. *Se —*, to play a card of another suit

Défaut, *s.m.* defect; blemish; flaw; fault; imperfection; deficiency, want; shortcoming; failure; (*of the ribs*) small; (*of a cuirass*) *V.* **Cuirasse;** (*law*) default. *A* or *au — de*, for want of; on failure of, failing; in the absence of, in the place of, instead of. *En —*, at fault; on the wrong scent, at a loss; defective, wanting. *Faire —*, to fail; to be wanting *or* wanted; to be missed. *Mettre en —*, to put on the wrong scent, to throw off the scent; to baffle, to foil

Défaveur, *s.f.* disfavour, disgrace; displeasure; discredit

Défavorable, *adj.* unfavourable; disparaging

Défavorablement, *adv.* unfavourably; disparagingly

Défécation, *s.f.* defecation

Défecti-f, ve, *adj.* defective

Défection, *s.f.* defection; disloyalty

Défectionnaire, *s.m.f.* defectionist

Défectionner, *v.n.* to abandon, to betray, to fall away *or* off

Défectivité, *s.f.* defectiveness

Défectueusement, *adv.* defectively

Défectueu-x, se, *adj.* defective; imperfect; deficient, wanting; faulty

Défectuosité, *s.f.* defectiveness; defect; flaw

Défendable, *adj.* defensible; tenable

Défend-eur, eresse, *s.m.f.* (*law*) defendant; respondent

Défendre, *v.a.n.* to defend; to oppose; to protect; to preserve; to maintain, to uphold, to support, to vindicate; to shelter, to screen; to prohibit, to forbid, to interdict; to prevent; (*nav.*) to fend off. — or *faire — sa porte*, *V.* **Porte**

Se —, *v.r.* to defend *or* protect *or* shelter *or* justify *or* forbid oneself; to contend; to resist; to beware; to forbear, to help, to refrain; to avoid, to shun; to decline, to refuse, to excuse oneself; to deny; to disclaim; (*of horses*) to jib, to wince, to resist; (*nav.*) to stand (*the sea*)

Défends, *s.m.* (*of woods*) defence

Défendures, *s.f.pl.* fences, hurdles

Défenestration, *s.f.* (*hist.*) defenestration

Défens, *s.m.* *V.* **Défends**

Défense, *s.f.* defence; means of defence; protection; screen; vindication; justification; prohibition, interdiction; warning; notice of danger; countermove; opposition; resistance; tusk; fang; (*bot.*) prickles; (*fort.*) outworks; (*nav.*) fender. — *d'entrer*, no admittance, no admittance except on business. — *de fumer*, no smoking allowed. — *d'uriner*, commit no nuisance. *Hors de —*, *sans —*, defenceless, undefended, unprotected. *Faire —*, to forbid, to prohibit

Défenseur, *s.m.* defender; protector; upholder, supporter, champion, vindicator; counsel for a prisoner, counsel

Défensi-f, ve, *adj.*, **Défensive,** *s.f.* defensive

Défensivement, *adv.* defensively

Déféquer, *v.a.* (*chem.*) to defecate

Déférence, *s.f.* deference, regard, respect

Déférent, e, *adj.* deferent, deferential; — *s.m.* [mark

Déférer, *v.a.* to confer, to bestow; to denounce, to inform against; to give up; to bring (before); to administer, to tender; — *v.n.* to defer; to comply, to yield

Se —, *v.r.* to be conferred *or* &c.

Déferlage, *s.m.* (*nav.*) unfurling (*of sails*)

Déferler, *v.a.* (*nav.*) to unfurl (*sails*); — *v.n.*, **Se —,** *v.r.* to break into foam, to come rolling, to dash

Déferrer, *v.a.* to unshoe (*a horse*); to untag; to take off the irons from; to abash, to confuse, to put out; to deprive

Se —, *v.r.* to get unshod; to come untagged; to lose its irons; to be abashed *or* put out, to get confused

Défet, *s.m.* waste, waste-sheet

†**Défeuillaison,** *s.f.* defoliation

†**Défeuiller,** *v.a.* *V.* **Effeuiller**

Défi, *s.m.* defiance; challenge

Défiance, *s.f.* distrust; mistrust; suspicion; jealousy; caution; diffidence

Défiant, e, *adj.* distrustful; mistrustful; suspicious; jealous; cautious; diffident

Déficeler, *v.a.* to untie, to unstring

Déficient, e, *adj.*, **Déficient,** *s.m.* (*arith.*) deficient

Déficit, *s.m.* deficit; deficiency

Défier, *v.a.* to defy; to challenge; to dare, to brave; to provoke; to set at defiance; to bid defiance to; to beard; to baffle; — *v.n.* (*nav.*) to bear off, to fend

Se —, *v.r.* to defy *or* challenge each other; to distrust; to mistrust; to suspect; to be diffident *or* suspicious *or* cautious; to beware; to be on o.'s guard (against); to doubt, to disbelieve

Défiger, *v.a.* to melt again, to warm up

Se —, *v.r.* to become liquid again

Défigurement, *s.m.* disfigurement; deformation, defacement

Défigurer, *v.a.* to disfigure; to deform, to deface; to distort; to mangle

Se —, *v.r.* to disfigure oneself *or* each other; to become disfigured *or* deformed *or* &c.

Défilade, *s.f.* filing off; going off

Défilage, *s.m.* unstringing; unthreading; tearing up

Défilé, *s.m.* defile, strait, pass; difficulty, fix; filing off, defiling, march *or* marching past

Défilement, *s.m.* (*mil.*) filing off, defiling, marching (*or* going) past; (*fort.*) defilading, defilement

Défiler, *v.a.* to unstring; to unthread; to tear up; (*fort.*) to defilade; — *v.n.* (*mil.*) to file off, to defile, to march (*or* go) past; (*jest.*) to pass away in succession, to die off, to go off, to drop off one by one; — *s.m.* filing off, defiling, march *or* marching past. — *la parade*, to file off after the parade; (*jest.*) to die, to go off, to kick the bucket

Se —, *v.r.* to get unstrung *or* unthreaded

Défini, e, *adj.*, **Défini,** *s.m.* definite, determinate

Définir, *v.a.* to define; to determine; to describe; to make out

Se —, *v.r.* to be defined *or* determined *or* &c.

Définissable, *adj.* definable

Définisseu-r, se, *s.m.f.* definer

Définiteur, *s.m.* (*in convents*) definitor
Définiti-f, ve, *adj.* definitive; final; ultimate; eventual; decided, decisive, positive; absolute. *En —, en —ve,* finally, after all, in the end; decidedly; definitively; in short, in a word, in fact [cision
Définition, *s.f.* definition; determination, de-
Définitivement, *adv* definitively; finally; ultimately; eventually; decidedly, decisively, posi-
Définitoire, *s.m.* chapter-house; chapter [tively
Déflagrateur, *s.m.* (*phys.*) deflagrator
Déflagration, *s.f.* (*chem.*) deflagration
Défléchir, *v.a n.*, **Se —,** *v r.* to deflect
Déflegmation, *s.f.* (*chem.*) dephlegmation
Déflegmer, *v a.* (*chem*) to dephlegmate
Défleuraison, *s.f.* fall of the blossom
Défleuri, e, *adj.* having lost its blossoms; with the bloom off; flowerless
Défleurir, *v a.* to nip *or* blow off the blossoms of; to deflower; to take the bloom off; — *v.n.*, **Se —,** *v.r.* to shed *or* lose its blossoms; to lose
Déflexion, *s.f.* deflection [its bloom
Défloraison, *s.f. V.* **Défleuraison**
Déflorateur, *s.m.* deflowerer
Défloration, *s.f.*, **Déflorement,** *s.m.* deflora-
Déflorer, *v.a.* to deflower [tion
Défoliation, *s.f.* defoliation
Défonçage, Défoncement, *s.m.* staving; staving in; digging up; breaking up; subsoil ploughing
Défoncer, *v.a.* to stave, to stave in; to bilge; to dig up; to break up, to break; to shove (*a sail*)
Se —, *v.r.* to give way at the bottom; (*of roads*) to break up
Défonceu-r, se, *adj. s.* (*agr.*) *V.* **Fouilleur**
Déforma-teur, trice, *s.m.f.* deformer; — *adj.* deforming
Déformation, *s.f.* deformation [to distort
Déformer, *v.a.* to deform, to put out of shape;
Se —, *v.r.* to get out of shape; to get deformed
Défortifier, *v.a.* to dismantle
Défournement, *s.m.* taking out of the oven
Défourner, *v.a.* to take out of the oven
Défournir, *v.a.* to unfurnish, to unstock
Défourrer, *v.a.* to unfur; to unwrap, to uncover
Défrai, *s.m.* defraying; keeping
Défraîchi, e, *adj.* no longer fresh; faded
Défraîchir, *v.a.* to take the freshness off
Se —, *v.r.* to lose its freshness; to fade
Défranciser, *v.a.* to unfrenchify
Défrayement, *s.m.* defraying
Défrayer, *v.a.* to defray; to defray the expenses of; to form *or* be the subject *or* substance of; to be a theme for; to afford matter for; to supply; to entertain, to amuse, to divert
Se —, *v.r.* to pay o.'s own expenses; to be
Défrayeu-r, se, *s.m.f.* defrayer [defrayed *or* &c.
Défrichage, Défrichement, *s.m.* (*agr.*) clearing [*s.m.* clearing (*land cleared*)
Défriché, e, *part. adj.* (*of lands*) cleared; —
Défricher, *v.a.* (*agr.*) to clear; (*fig.*) to polish;
Se —, *v.r.* to be cleared *or* &c. [to clear up
Défricheur, *s.m.* (*agr.*) clearer
Défriper, *v.a.* to unrumple
Défrisement, *s.m.* uncurling; (*pop.*) disappointment, balk, bother
Défriser, *v.a.* to uncurl; to uncurl the hair of; (*pop.*) to disappoint, to balk, to put out, to ruffle, to vex, to fret [to uncurl o.'s hair
Se —, *v.r.* to come *or* get uncurled, to uncurl;
Défroncement, *s.m.* unplaiting, unfolding
Défroncer, *v.a.* to unplait; to unfold; (*fig.*) to smooth (*o.'s brow*), to unknit
Défroque, *s.f.* old clothes, left-off *or* cast-off clothes, clothes; old things; effects, property
Défroquer, *v.a.* to unfrock; (*fig.*) to strip (*one*) of all [the cloth
Se —, *v.r.* to quit the frock; (*jest.*) to quit
Défruiter, *v.a.* to strip of its fruit [clothes
Défrusquer, *v.a.* (*pop.*) to strip (*one*) of his
Défuner, *v.a.* (*nav.*) to strip (*a mast*) [parted
Défunt, e, *adj. s.* deceased; dead; late; de-

Dégagé, e, *part. adj.* redeemed, &c. (*V.* **Dégager**); unconstrained; easy; loose; disengaged; disembarrassed; free; clear; sharp; open; offhand; flippant; slender; graceful; private *or* back (*staircase*); (*of rooms*) with a private entrance
Dégagement, *s.m.* redeeming; clearing; disengagement; extrication; release; liberation; discharge; escape, issue; passage; private entrance; back-door; exit; clearance; (*chem.*) evolution. *De —,* (*adject., of staircases and doors*) back
Dégager, *v.a.* to redeem; to clear; to disengage; to disentangle; to extricate; to loose; to loosen; to release; to relieve; to liberate; to deliver; to rescue; to discharge; to free; to ease; to separate; to withdraw; to set off; to get off; to reveal; to rake (*a fire*); (*chem.*) to evolve; to emit; (*math.*) to find
Se —, *v.r.* to disengage *or* &c. oneself; to get off *or* away; to escape; to break loose, to break; to get rid; to come out, to be seen; to get clear; to be cleared *or* &c.; to become easier; to become free; (*chem.*) to evolve
Dégaîne, *s.f.* odd manner, awkward way, loutish gait, odd *or* awkward figure, figure
Dégaîner, *v.a.* to unsheathe, to draw; to fork out; — *v.n.* to draw o.'s (*or* the) sword; to fork out money; — *s.m.* unsheathing, drawing (the sword); forking out (money). *Être brave jusqu'au —,* to be brave till it comes to the scratch
Dégaîneur, *s.m.* fighter; bully [*or* to the push
Dégalonner, *v.a.* to unlace; to unstripe
Déganter, *v.a.* to take off the gloves of, to un-
Se —, *v.r.* to take off o.'s (own) gloves [glove
Dégarni, e, *part. adj.* unfurnished, &c. (*V.* **Dégarnir**); naked; bare; thin; empty; unprovided
Dégarnir, *v.a.* to unfurnish; to disgarnish; to strip; to deprive; to uncover; to untrim; to thin; to unrig; to dismantle; to disgarrison
Se —, *v.r.* to strip oneself; to get bare *or* bald *or* thin *or* empty; to lose; to part (with); to leave oneself unprovided; to part with o.'s ready money; to wear lighter clothing
Dégarnissement, *s.m.* unfurnishing, &c. (*V.* **Dégarnir**) [Gascon accent
Dégasconner, *v.a.* to make (*one*) lose the
Se —, *v.r.* to lose the Gascon accent
Dégât, *s.m.* damage; havoc; mischief; ravage; devastation; depredation; waste; ruins, rubbish
Dégauchir, *v.a.* to smooth; to polish; to straighten [o.'s awkward manners
Se —, *v.r.* to become polished, to get rid of
Dégauchissage, Dégauchissement, *s.m.* smoothing; polishing; straightening
Dégazer, *v.a.* (*chem.*) to free from gas
Dégazonnement, *s.m.* unturfing
Dégazonner, *v.a.* to unturf
Dégel, *s.m.* thaw [caning
Dégelée, *s.f.* (*pop.*) volley; drubbing, sound
Dégeler, *v.a.n.*, **Se —,** *v.r.* to thaw, to melt
Dégénéra-teur, trice, *adj.* degenerative
Dégénération, *s.f.* degeneracy; deterioration
Dégénéré, e, *part. adj.* degenerated, degenerate
Dégénérer, *v.n.* to degenerate
Dégénérescence, *s.f. V.* **Dégénération**
Dégénérescent, e, *adj.* degenerating
Dégingandé, e, *adj.* awkward, gawky, ungainly, ill-shaped, loose, disjointed; unconnected [ness; desultoriness
Dégingandement, *s.m.* awkwardness, loose-
Dégingander, *v.a.* to put out of shape, to disjoint [jointed; to swing, to move o.'s rump about
Se —, *v.r.* to get out of shape, to get dis-
Dégîter, *v.a.n.*, **Se —,** *v.r.* (*hunt.*) to dislodge, to start [lime from; to clear
Dégluer, *v.a.* to unglue; to take off the bird-
Se —, *v.r.* to get rid of bird-lime; to get un-
Déglutition, *s.f.* deglutition [glued *or* cleared
†**Dégobillade,** *s.f.* (*fam.*) spewing
†**Dégobillage, Dégobillis,** *s.m.* (*fam.*) vomit,
†**Dégobiller,** *v.a.n.* (*fam.*) to spew [spew

Dégoiser, *v.a.n.* to blab, to rattle, to clatter, to chatter, to talk; to chirp
Dégommage, *s.m.* ungumming
Dégommer, *v.a.* to ungum; (*fam.*) to oust, to dislodge from o.'s berth *or* perch; to turn off; to unseat; to reduce; to kill [decay, to fade
Se —, *v.r.* to oust *or* &c. each other; (*pop.*) to
Dégonder, *v.a.* to unhinge [off its hinges
Se —, *v.r.* to come *or* be unhinged, to come
Dégonflement, *s.m.* reduction; reduction of volume; subsiding; going down; falling; collapse
Dégonfler, *v.a.* to reduce; to bring down; to reduce the swelling *or* volume of; to let the air *or* the gas out of (*a balloon*, &c.); to empty; to relieve
Se —, *v.r.* to subside; to go down; to become less swollen; to be no longer swollen; to collapse; to find relief
Dégorgement, *s.m.* disgorgement, disgorging; clearing, unstopping; cleansing; outfall, outflow; overflowing
Dégorgeoir, *s.m.* outlet, issue; spout; (*fish.*) disgorger; (*artil.*) vent-bit
Dégorger, *v.a.n.* to disgorge; to clear, to unstop, to open; to cleanse, to scour; to purge (*fish*); to empty; to empty *or* discharge itself; to get unstopped, to get clear; to overflow. *Faire —*, to make (...) disgorge; to purge (*fish*); to cleanse *or* scour (*wool*, *silk*, &c.)
Se —, *v.r.* to empty *or* discharge itself; to overflow; to discharge, to disgorge; to get unstopped, to get clear; (*of fish*) to be purged; (*of wool*, *silk*, &c.) to be cleansed *or* scoured
Dégoter, Dégotter, *v.a.* (*fam.*) to fetch down, to bring *or* get down, to shoot down; to oust, to displace, to push off, to supplant; to outdo; to astonish (*the natives*, &c.); to find out, to find
Dégouliner, *v.n. pop. for* **Dégoutter**
Dégourdi, e, *part. adj.* revived; restored to warmth; with the chill off; sharp, acute, shrewd, knowing; forward; — *s.m.f.* knowing one
Dégourdir, *v.a.* to remove numbness from; to warm, to revive; to stretch (*o.'s legs*); (*fig.*) to sharpen the wits of, to sharpen; to polish. *Faire —*, to take the chill off (*water*, &c.)
Se —, *v.r.* to lose its numbness; to lose its chill; to get warm; to warm *or* stretch (o.'s ...); to look sharp, to bestir oneself; (*fig.*) to get sharp *or* acute; to polish up; to enjoy oneself
Dégourdissement, *s.m.* removal of numbness, return of circulation, reviving; taking the chill off (*water*, &c.); (*fig.*) sharpening, polishing
Dégout, *s.m.* dripping; (*at ombre*) payment
Dégoût, *s.m.* distaste, dislike; disrelish; disinclination; surfeit; nauseousness; loathing; disgust; aversion; disdain, contempt; mortification, vexation; dissatisfaction, displeasure; weariness; tedium [fully; nauseously, fulsomely
Dégoûtamment, *adv.* disgustingly; distaste-
Dégoûtant, e, *adj.* disgusting; distasteful; nauseous, loathsome, fulsome; sickening; disheartening; beastly
Dégoûté, e, *adj.* disgusted; surfeited; fastidious, squeamish; particular; wearied (of), weary (of), tired (of), sick (of); out of conceit (with); dissatisfied, displeased; disaffected; disdainful, contemptuous. *Faire le —* (or *la —e*), to be fastidious *or* squeamish. *N'être pas —*, (*ironically*) not to be over fastidious, not to have a bad taste
Dégoûter, *v.a.* to disgust (with); to give a dislike (for); to surfeit; to sicken; to weary, to tire; to put out of conceit; to take away (...'s) appetite; to dissatisfy, to displease
Se —, *v.r.* to take a dislike (to); to be disgusted *or* surfeited (with); to get tired (of); to be discouraged *or* disheartened, to lose courage
Dégouttement, *s.m.*, **Dégoutture,** *s.f.* dropping; dripping; drippings
Dégoutter, *v.n.* to drop; to drip; to trickle, to trickle down, to run down; to run; to dribble

Dégradation, *s.f.* degradation; debasement; disgrace; damage; defacement; dilapidation; (*law*) waste; (*mil.*) degradation, cashiering, discharge with ignominy, drumming out
Dégrader, *v.a.* to degrade; to debase; to demean; to lower; to disgrace; to damage; to deface; to dilapidate; (*law*) to waste; (*nav.*) to unrig; (*mil.*) to degrade, to reduce, to cashier, to discharge with ignominy, to drum out; — *v.n.* (*nav.*) to drift, to be adrift
Se —, *v.r.* to degrade *or* debase *or* demean *or* lower *or* disgrace oneself; to become damaged *or* defaced *or* dilapidated; to wear away; (*of colours*) to be degraded; (*law*) to waste
Dégrafer, *v.a.* to unhook; to unclasp; to unbuckle; to unpin [unhooked *or* unclasped
Se —, *v.r.* to unhook *or* unclasp oneself; to come
Dégraissage, Dégraissement, *s.m.* scouring, cleaning
Dégraisser, *v.a.* to scour; to clean; to take the fat out of; to skim; to impoverish; to correct the ropiness of (*wine*); to thin; to make thin, to reduce; (*pop.*) to fleece, to bleed, to drain, to ruin; to make (...) disgorge. *Savon à —*, soft soap [to waste, to get thin
Se —, *v.r.* to be scoured *or* &c.; to fall away,
Dégraisseu-r, se, *s.m.f.* scourer
Dégraissis, *s.m.* scourings
Dégraissoir, *s.m.* scraper [*V.* **Égrappage,** &c.
Dégrappage, Dégrapper, Dégrappoir.
Dégrappiner, *v.n.* (*nav.*) to lift the grapple *or* small anchor; — *v.a.* to clear from the ice
Dégras, *s.m.* dubbin, dubbing (*grease*)
Dégraveler, Dégraver, *v.a.* to remove the gravel from, to clean out [bare, baring, mining
Dégravoiement, *s.m.* washing away, laying
Dégravoyer, *v.a.* to wash away, to lay bare, to bare, to mine
Degré, *s.m.* degree; step; stair; stage; grade; gradation; extent, point, pitch; remove; (*obsolete*) staircase; ladder [ging, dismantling
Dégréage, Dégréement, *s.m.* (*nav.*) unrig-
Dégréer, *v.a.* (*nav.*) to unrig, to dismantle (*a ship*); to strip (*a mast*)
Dégrèvement, *s.m.* reduction; relief; redeeming, redemption; disencumbrance
Dégrever, *v.a.* to reduce, to take off; to relieve, to free, to disburden, to lighten; to redeem; to disencumber [cloister
†**Dégriller,** *v.a.* to unrail; to ungrate; to un-
Dégringolade, *s.f.* going down; tumble, fall; break-down. *Faire une —*, *V.* **Dégringoler**
Dégringoler, *v.n.a.* to run *or* rush down, to go down, to roll down, to topple down *or* over, to tumble down, to fall from top to bottom, to fall; to break down; to go on from bad to worse, to go to the dogs
Dégrisement, *s.m.* dispelling of intoxication, returning to o.'s senses, sobering down, cooling down, cooling
Dégriser, *v.a.* to dispel ...'s intoxication, to bring back to o.'s senses, to sober down, to sober, to cool down, to cool; to awake from a dream
Se —, *v.r.* to return to o.'s senses, to get sober, to sober *or* cool down; to lose o.'s illusions, to awake from o.'s dream; to recover (from), to be cured (of)
Dégrossage, *s.m.* (*of ingots*) reducing, thinning
Dégrosser, *v.a.* to reduce, to thin (*ingots*)
Dégrossi, *s.m.* roughing down; rough-hewing; dressing; drawing; boasting; pointing
Dégrossir, *v.a.* to rough down, to take the rough off; to rough-hew; to dress; to draw; to boast; to point; to make a rough sketch of, to sketch out; to read (*a proof*); to clear up; (*pers.*) to fashion, to polish; to sharpen
Se —, *v.r.* to be roughed down, &c.; to become polished *or* sharp [*V.* **Dégrossi**
Dégrossissage, Dégrossissement, *s.m.*
Dégrossisseur, *s.m.* (*adj.m.*, *Cylindre —*) draw- [ing-cylinder
Dégu, *s.m.* (*zool.*) degu

†Déguenillé, e, *adj.* tattered, ragged, in tatters, in rags; — *s.m.f.* ragged creature, tatterdemalion
†Déguenillement, *s.m.* tattering; raggedness; beggary [to beggar; (*pop.*) to abuse, to jaw
†Déguenîller, *v.a.* to tatter, to tear to rags;
Déguerpir, *v.n.* to pack off, to move off, to be off, to go; — *v.a.* to give up, to leave, to quit
Déguerpissement, *s.m.* giving up, quitting, yielding; departure, removal
Déguerpisseur, *s.m.* outgoer
Dégueulement, *s.m.* (*fam.*) spewing
Dégueuler, *v.n.a.* (*fam.*) to spew, to vomit
Dégueulis, *s.m.* (*fam.*) spew, vomit
†Déguignonné, e, *adj.* having better luck, in a run of better luck
†Déguignonner, *v.a.* to bring better luck to, to put into a run of better luck
Déguisable, *adj.* disguisable, concealable
Déguisement, *s.m.* disguise; concealment
Déguiser, *v.a.* to disguise; to conceal
Se —, *v.r.* to disguise oneself; to conceal from oneself; to deceive oneself; (*of things*) to disguise itself, to assume a disguise, to be disguised *or* concealed
Dégustateur, *s.m.* taster (*of wines*, &c.)
Dégusta-teur, trice, *adj.* tasting
Dégustation, *s.f.* tasting (*of wines*, &c.)
Déguster, *v.a.* to taste (*wines*, &c.); (*fam.*) to sip
Se —, *v.r.* to be tasted; to be sipped
Déhaler, *v.a.* (*nav.*) to tow out *or* back, to raise; (*pop.*) to get out of a hobble *or* scrape
Déhâler, *v.a.* to take off the sun-burn from, to clear the complexion of
Se —, *v.r.* to clear o.'s complexion from sun-burn; to be cleared from sun-burn
Déhanché, e, *adj.* hipshot, hipped; (*fig.*) ungainly; — *s.m.f.* hipshot person; ungainly fellow *or* woman *or* girl [of the rump
Déhanchement, *s.m.* swinging about, motion
Déhancher, *v.a.* to dislocate the hip of, to hip
Se —, *v.r.* to dislocate o.'s hip; to swing about, to move o.'s rump about; to bustle, to make much ado about nothing
Déharder, *v.a.* (*hunt.*) to unleash [unrigging
Déharnachement, *s.m.* unharnessing; (*fig.*)
Déharnacher, *v.a.* to unharness; (*fig.*) to unrig
Déhiscence, *s.f.* (*bot.*) dehiscence
Déhiscent, e, *adj.* (*bot.*) dehiscent [less creature
Déhonté, e, *adj.* shameless; — *s.m.f.* shame-
Dehors, *adv.* outside; out; without; abroad; out of doors; out at sea, out to sea, in the offing; out of it, out of them; without it, without them; — *s.m.* outside; exterior; appearances; show; external *or* personal appearance, person; approaches, grounds, dependencies; foreign countries *or* parts; out; (*fort.*) outworks; (*rid.*) off side. *Au* —, outside; without; abroad; out of doors; out; with the world; outward, external; outwardly, externally. *De* —, from without; outside. *Du* —, of *or* from the outside, of *or* from the exterior; from without; from abroad; outer; (*rid.*) off. *En* —, outside; without; out; outward; not included; turned out; apart (from); besides; beyond; between; unconcerned (for, about); frank, open. *Mettre* —, to put *or* turn out; to discharge,
Déhortatoire, *adj.* dehortatory [to dismiss
Déicide, (*murder*) *s.m.*, (*pers.*) *s.m.f.* deicide; —
Déification, *s.f.* deification [*adj.* deicidal
Déifier, *v.a.* to deify
Déifique, *adj.* deific, deifical
Déisme, *s.m.* deism
Déiste, *s.m.f.* deist; — *adj.* deistic, deistical
Déité, *s.f.* deity, divinity, god, goddess
Déjà, *adv.* already; yet; now; then; before; before this; as long ago as; so far; as it is *or* stands; as they are; to begin with; just; first. *Pas — si ...*, not so very ...; not so very much ...; not such great ... *Pas — tant*, not so very much; not such a great quantity *or* amount
Déjection, *s.f.* (*med.*) dejection, ejection, evacuation
Déjeté, e, *adj.* warped; crooked; perverted
Déjeter (Se), *v.r.* to warp; to grow crooked; (*med.*) to deviate [(*med.*) deviation
Déjettement, *s.m.* warping; crookedness;
Déjeuné, *part. of* **Déjeuner,** *v.n.*; — *s.m.* (*old spelling*) *V.* **Déjeuner,** *s.m.*
Déjeuner, *s.m.* luncheon, lunch; breakfast; breakfast-service. *Premier* —, breakfast. *Second* —, luncheon, lunch. — *à la fourchette*, *V.* **Fourchette**
Déjeuner, *v.n.* to take *or* have *or* partake of luncheon *or* lunch, to lunch; to breakfast; to be at luncheon, to be having o.'s lunch; to be at breakfast; to eat o.'s lunch *or* breakfast. *A* —, to (*or* at) lunch *or* breakfast; some (*or* o.'s *or* a) lunch *or* breakfast [separate; to sunder; to sever
Déjoindre, *v.a.* to disjoin; to disunite; to
Se —, *v.r.* to become disjoined *or* &c., to separate, to part, to come apart *or* asunder
Déjouer, *v.a.* to baffle; to frustrate; to foil; to defeat; to counteract; — *v.n.* to play badly; (*nav.*) to wave, to flutter; to shift, to veer
Déjucher, *v.a.* to unroost; (*fig.*) to bring down from o.'s perch, to bring down; to turn out, to dislodge; — *v.n.* to leave the roost; (*fig.*) to come down from o.'s perch, to come down; to move off, to get away
Déjuger, *v.a.* to judge differently
Se —, *v.r.* to reverse o.'s own judgment; to alter o.'s own resolution; to change o.'s opinion
Delà, *prep. adv.* beyond, on the other side (of). *Au-* —, *par-* —, beyond, on the other side (of); above; upwards; more; farther; further; past. *En* —, beyond, farther, further
Délabre, *s.m. V.* **Délabrement**
Délabré, e, *part. adj.* tattered, &c. (*V.* **Délabrer**); in a ruinous state; in a wretched condition, wretched; ragged, in rags; torn; worn out; shabby, seedy; ramshackle; broken; emaciated, wasted
Délabrement, *s.m.* dilapidation; impairment; decay, ruin; raggedness, ragged *or* wretched state; shabbiness; ruinous condition; disorderly *or* disordered state
Délabrer, *v.a.* to tatter, to tear to pieces *or* to rags; to shatter; to batter; to dilapidate; to impair; to ruin; to disorder
Se —, *v.r.* to fall to pieces; to dilapidate; to become impaired; to go to ruin; to decay
Délacer, *v.a.* to unlace [come unlaced
Se —, *v.r.* to unlace oneself; (*of things*) to
Délai, *s.m.* delay; extension of time; adjournment; reprieve; interval; period of time, period, time; term; notice. *Dans un — de*,
Délaiement, *s.m.* diluting [within
Délaissé, e, *adj.* forsaken, deserted, abandoned, destitute, forlorn, friendless, helpless; —**e,** *s.f.* deserted wife; cast-off mistress
Délaissement, *s.m.* destitution; forlornness; helplessness; desertion; abandonment
Délaisser, *v.a.* to forsake, to desert, to leave, to abandon; to cast off; to relinquish
Délardement, *s.m.* unlarding; (*tech.*) chamfering, bevelling, splaying, splay, slope
Délarder, *v.a.* to unlard; (*tech.*) to chamfer, to bevel, to splay, to slope
Délassement, *s.m.* rest, repose, relaxation, ease, refreshment, recreation, diversion, play, sport
Délasser, *v.a.* to refresh; to rest; to relax
Déla-teur, trice, *s.m.f.* informer, denouncer, accuser; — *adj.* informing, denouncing, accusing, treacherous
Délation, *s.f.* information, denunciation, accusation, delation; administering, tendering
Délatter, *v.a.* to unlath. *Se* —, to come unlathed
Délavage, *s.m.* soaking; diluting
Délavé, e, *adj.* soaked; diluted; washy; pale, dim, weak, faint in colour
Délaver, *v.a.* to soak; to dilute
Se —, *v.r.* to be soaked *or* diluted; to become pale *or* weak; to lose its colour
Délayable, *adj.* dilutable

Délayage, *s.m.* diluting, dilution
Délayant, e, *adj.*, **Délayant,** *s.m.* diluent
Délayement, *s.m. V.* **Délaiement**
Délayer, *v.a.* to dilute; to draw out, to spin [out; to temper (*lime*)
Déléatur, *s.m.* (*print.*) dele
Délébile, *adj.* delible
Délectable, *adj.* delectable delicious, delightful
Délectablement, *adv.* delectably, deliciously, delightfully
Délectation, *s.f.* delectation, delight; gratification
Délecter, *v.a.*, **Se —,** *v.r.* to delight
Délégant, e, Déléga-teur, trice, *s.m.f.* (*law*) delegator
Délégataire, *s.m.f.* (*law*) delegatee
Délégation, *s.f.* delegation; proxy; assignment
Délégatoire, *adj.* (*law*) delegatory
Délégué, e, *adj.* delegated; — *s.m.f.* delegate, deputy; proxy
Déléguer, *v.a.* to delegate; to assign
Se —, *v.r.* to be delegated; to be assigned
Délestage, *s.m.* unballasting
Délester, *v.a.* to unballast
Délesteur, *s.m.* (*nav.*) ballast-boat, ballast-lighter; ballast-heaver. *Bateau —,* ballast-boat, ballast-lighter
Délétère, *adj.* deleterious
Déliaque, *adj.* Deliac, of Delos
Délibérant, e, Délibérati-f, ve, *adj.* deliberative
Délibérant, *s.m.* deliberator
Délibération, *s.f.* deliberation; resolution; decision. *Mettre en —,* to bring under deliberation
Délibérativement, *adv.* deliberatively
Délibératoire, *adj.* of deliberation, deliberatory
Délibéré, e, *adj.* easy; free; deliberate; determined; decided; bold, resolute; — *s.m.* (*law*) deliberation
Délibérément, *adv.* deliberately; boldly, resolutely; easily, with ease; freely
Délibérer, *v.n.a.* to deliberate; to resolve; to determine; to decide
Délicat, e, *adj.* delicate; nice; refined; tender; scrupulous; ticklish; difficult; dainty; fastidious; light; soft; gentle; considerate
Délicatement, *adv.* delicately; nicely; daintily; tenderly; softly; gently; considerately
Délicater, *v.a. V.* **Dorloter**
Délicatesse, *s.f.* delicacy; nicety; refinement; delicate taste; tenderness; ticklishness; scrupulousness; softness; daintiness; considerateness; delicate proceeding. *En —,* slightly at variance
Délice, *s.m.* delight, pleasure; **—s,** *s.m.f.pl.* delight, delights, pleasures; delightfulness; deliciousness; darling
Délicieusement, *adv.* deliciously; delightfully
Délicieu-x, se, *adj.* delicious; delightful; sweet; capital; very fine
Délicoter, *v.a.*, **Se —,** *v.r.* to unhalter
Délictueu-x, se, *adj.* (*law*) of a (*or* the) delict [*or* offence
Délié, e, *adj.* untied, loose; slender, fine, thin; small; light, easy; subtle, acute, shrewd, sharp, clever; crafty, cunning; (*of the tongue*) voluble, glib, nimble; — *s.m.* (*in writing*) thin stroke, up stroke
Déliement, *s.m.* untying, &c. (*V.* **Délier**)
Délier, *v.a.* to untie, to undo, to unfasten; to unbind; to loosen, to loose; to release; to free; to absolve
Se —, *v.r.* to come untied *or* undone; to get [loose
Déligation, *s.f.* (*surg.*) deligation
Délimitation, *s.f.* fixing the limits, limiting, bounding; limits, boundaries
Délimiter, *v.a.* to fix the limits of; to mark the boundaries of; to limit, to bound
Délinéateur, *s.m.* delineator
Délinéation, *s.f.* delineation; delineament
Délinéer, *v.a.* to delineate
Délinquant, e, *s.m.f.* delinquent; offender
Délinquer, *v.n.* (*old*) to offend, to commit an offence
Déliot, *s.m.* finger-stall, thumb-stall
Déliquescence, *s.f.* (*chem.*) deliquescence
Déliquescent, e, *adj.* (*chem.*) deliquescent
§Déliquium, *s.m.* (*chem.*) deliquium

Délirant, e, *adj.* delirious; frenzied, frantic, raving; maddening, enrapturing, rapturous
Délire, *s.m.* delirium; deliriousness; lightheadedness; frenzy; raving; folly. *Dans le —, en —,* delirious, light-headed. *Avoir le —, être dans le —, être en —, V.* **Délirer**
Délirer, *v.n.* to be delirious *or* light-headed, to wander, to rave; to be distracted *or* bewildered *or* disconcerted
Delirium tremens, *s.m.* (*med.*) delirium tremens
Délissage, *s.m.* roughing, roughening; ruffling; sorting (*of rags*)
Délisser, *v.a.* to rough, to roughen; to ruffle; [to sort (*rags*)
Délisseu-r, se, *s.m.f.* sorter (*of rags*)
Délit, *s.m.* delict, offence, delinquency; misdemeanour; (*mas.*) wrong bed (*of stone*). *En flagrant —,* in the very act. *En —,* (*mas.*) against the stratum
Déliter, *v.a.* (*mas.*) to lay (*stones*) in their wrong [bed; to cleave
Se —, *v.r.* (*of stones*) to break in the grain, [to cleave
Délitescence, *s.f.* delitescence
Délivrance, *s.f.* deliverance; delivery; release; rescue; relief
Délivre, *s.m.* (*med.*) after-birth, placenta, secundine; (*of animals*) heam
Délivrer, *v.a.* to deliver; to rescue; to save; to release; to set free; to free, to rid; to hand over; to surrender; to give; to issue; (*nav.*) to rip off (*planks*). *Se faire —,* to ask for; to apply for; to take out; to take
Délivreur, *s.m.* deliverer; rescuer; feeder, [groom, ostler
Délogement, *s.m.* removal; change of quarters; departure; decamping
Déloger, *v.a.* to dislodge; to unhouse; to turn out; to oust; to drive away; — *v.n.* to dislodge; to move, to remove, to leave o.'s house *or* lodging; to move out; to quit; to decamp, to march away *or* off, to run away, to get *or* go away. — *sans tambour ni trompette, — sans trompette,* to march off in silence, to decamp quietly, to steal away, to bolt in the night; to [move out at once
Délot, *s.m. V.* **Déliot**
Délover, *v.a.* (*nav.*) to uncoil
Déloyal, e, *adj.* dishonest; unfair; perfidious, treacherous, unfaithful, faithless, false; (*old*) disloyal
Déloyalement, *adv.* dishonestly; unfairly; perfidiously, treacherously, unfaithfully, faithlessly, falsely; (*old*) disloyally
Déloyauté, *s.f.* dishonesty; unfairness; perfidy, treachery, infidelity; (*old*) disloyalty
Delphien, ne, *adj.* Delphian
Delphinal, e, *adj.* of the dauphin
Delphinaptère, *s.m.* (*zool.*) delphinaptera, whale-porpoise
Delphine, Delphinine, *s.f.* (*chem.*) delphinia
Delphinorhynque, *s.m.* (*fish*) delphinorhynchus
Delphique, *adj.* Delphic
Delta, *s.m.* delta
Deltoïde, *adj.* (*anat., bot.*) deltoid; — *s.m.* deltoid muscle
Déluge, *s.m.* deluge, flood
Déluré, e, *adj.* sharp, knowing; smart; humorous
Délustrer, *v.a.* to take off the gloss from. *Se —,* to lose its gloss
Délutage, *s.m.* unluting
Déluter, *v.a.* to unlute
†Démagnétisation, *s.f.* demagnetization
†Démagnétiser, *v.a.* to demagnetize
Démagog-ie, -ique, -isme. *V.* page 3, § 1
Démagogue, *s.m.f.* demagogue; — *adj.* demagogic
Démaigrir, *v.n.* to recover flesh; — *v.a.* (*carp., mas.*) to thin
Démaigrissement, *s.m.* (*carp., mas.*) thinning
†Démailler, *v.a.* to undo the meshes of, to undo
Se —, *v.r.* to come undone
†Démaillotter, *v.a.* to unswathe
Demain, *adv. s.m.* to-morrow
Démanché, e, *adj.* off the handle; (*fig.*) dislocated; ungainly, awkward, loose, disjointed; — *s.m.* ungainly fellow; (*mus.*) shift
Démanchement, *s.m.* taking off the handle, unhafting, being without a handle; (*fig.*) dislocation; (*mus.*) shifting
Démancher, *v.a.* to take the handle *or* stick

off, to unhaft; (*fig.*) to dislocate; — *v.n.* (*mus.*) to shift; (*nav.*) to get out of the channel

Se —, *v.r.* to get loose at the handle, to lose its handle; (*mus.*) to shift; (*fig.*) to go wrong, to get unhinged *or* out of joint; (*pop.*) to bestir oneself, to strive hard, to take pains, to bustle, to make much ado

Demande, *s.f.* question; query; request; application; inquiry; demand; claim; desire; call; order; suit, prayer, petition; proposal; price

Demander, *v.a.n.* to ask; to request; to beg; to beg leave; to bid; to solicit; to want; to wish; to desire; to require; to demand; to claim; to inquire; to query; to ask for; to apply for; to call for; to call; to order; to send for; to pray for; to pray; to propose to. *Faire* —, to send for; to send to ask; to order, to ask for. *Ne pas — mieux,* to ask for nothing better, to wish for no better; to be most willing, to be quite willing *or* content, to be only too glad, to be delighted; to accept *or* comply with the greatest pleasure; to be most happy to do it. *On demande ...,* wanted ... *Je vous le demande,* I ask you about it, I ask you; I don't know any more than you do

Se —, *v.r.* to ask oneself *or* each other; to wonder; to be asked; to be asked for. *Ces choses-là ne se demandent pas,* these are not things to be asked; these things are plain enough [demander

Demandeu-r, se, *s.m.f.* asker; applicant;

Demand-eur, eresse, *s.m.f.* (*law*) plaintiff; applicant; petitioner; demandant

Démangeaison, *s.f.* itching, itch; longing

Démanger, *v.n.* to itch; to long [to dismantle

Démanteler, *v.a.* *V.* **Démantibuler;** (*mil.*)

Démantellement, *s.m.* dismantling

Démantibuler, *v.a.* to break, to dislocate, to put out of order [get out of order

Se —, *v.r.* to break, to become dislocated, to

Démarcati-f, ve, *adj.* of demarcation

Démarcation, *s.f.* demarcation

Démarche, *s.f.* gait, walk; bearing; step, measure, proceeding, conduct; attempt, application, overture [married

Démarier, *v.a.* to unmarry. *Se* —, to be un-

Démarquer, *v.a.* to take the mark off, to unmark; — *v.n.* (*of horses*) to cease to mark, to

Se —, *v.r.* to become *or* get unmarked [be aged

Démarrage, *s.m.* (*nav.*) unmooring

Démarrer, *v.a.n.* (*nav.*) to unmoor; to unbend (*a rope*); to leave her moorings; to slip from her moorings; to get under sail; (*fig.*) to move, to stir, to get away

Démasquer, *v.a.* to unmask; to show up

Se —, *v.r.* to unmask, to take (*or* pull) off o.'s mask; to let o.'s mask fall

Démastiquer, *v.a.* to take the mastic off

Dématage, Dématement, *s.m.* (*nav.*) dismasting [*v.r.* to lose her masts, to be dismasted

Dématér, *v.a.* (*nav.*) to dismast; — *v.n.*, **Se** —,

Dématérialiser, *v.a.* to dematerialize

Démêlé, *s.m.* quarrel, strife, contest, contention, debate, dispute, difference

Démêler, *v.a.* to unmingle; to disentangle; to comb out; to unravel, to clear up; to make out; to perceive, to discover, to find out; to guess; to fathom; to penetrate; to read; to separate; to distinguish; to discern; to recognize; to contest; to dispute; to contend for; to quarrel about; to settle; to do

Se —, *v.r.* to be unmingled *or* disentangled *or* &c.; to disentangle *or* extricate oneself, to get out, to get clear off

Démêloir, *s.m.* large-tooth comb; (*tech.*) hackle

Démembrement, *s.m.* dismemberment; dismembered part [to disjoint; to divide

Démembrer, *v.a.* to dismember; to quarter;

Se —, *v.r.* to be dismembered *or* &c.

Déménagement, *s.m.* removal, remove, removing, moving; removal of furniture. *Voiture de* —, furniture-van

Déménager, *v.a.n.* to remove, to move; to get away, to be off; to be going off; to die, to kick the bucket; to lose o.'s wits. *Sa raison* (or *sa tête*) *déménage,* he is getting childish

Déménageur, *s.m.* furniture-carrier

Démence, *s.f.* insanity; lunacy; madness. *En* —, insane, mad. *Tomber en* —, to become insane, to run *or* go mad

Démener (Se), *v.r.* to throw oneself about; to jump about; to move about; to bestir *or* exert oneself; to strive *or* work hard; to struggle; to flounder; to toss *or* kick about [dement

Dément, e, *adj. s.* insane, lunatic, demented,

Démenti, *s.m.* lie; flat contradiction *or* denial; balk, disappointment. *Donner un — à,* to give the lie to; to contradict. *En avoir le* —, to fail; to be balked *or* baffled *or* defeated; to be worsted, to get the worst of it; to find oneself wrong *or* mistaken

Démentir, *v.a.* to give the lie to; to contradict; to deny; to disown; to belie; to speak *or* act against (*or* contrary to); to show to be false; to refute, to confute; to baffle, to disappoint

Se —, *v.r.* to contradict oneself *or* each other; to belie oneself; to forfeit o.'s word; to be inconsistent; to degenerate; to change, to relax, to flag, to fall off, to fail; to cease, to discontinue; to give way

Démerger, *v.n.*, **Se** —, *v.r.* to come out of the water again, to emerge, to float

Démérite, *s.m.* demerit, unworthiness

Démériter, *v.n.* to demerit, to incur blame, to do amiss, to forfeit esteem

Déméritoire, *adj.* demeritorious

Déméritoirement, *adv.* demeritoriously

Démesuré, e, *adj.* beyond measure, immoderate, inordinate, unbounded, excessive, enormous, huge

Démesurément, *adv.* beyond measure, immoderately, inordinately, excessively, enormously, hugely

Démettre, *v.a.* to dislocate, to put out of joint; to dismiss, to turn out, to discard, to remove; (*law*) to nonsuit; to overrule

Se —, *v.r.* to be (*or* get) dislocated *or* put out of joint; to dislocate (o.'s ...), to put (o.'s ...) out of joint; to resign, to lay down, to give up, to throw up; to abdicate [nished state

Démeublement, *s.m.* unfurnishing; unfur-

Démeubler, *v.a.* to unfurnish, to strip of furniture [to become unfurnished

Se —, *v.r.* to unfurnish o.'s house *or* lodgings;

Demeurant, e, *part. adj.* residing, &c. (*V.* **Demeurer**); — *s.m.f.* resident

Demeurant, *s.m.* (*obsolete*) remainder, remnant, residue, rest. *Au* —, after all; notwithstanding, however; upon the whole; at bottom

Demeure, *s.f.* residence; abode, dwelling, house, home; stay; delay. *A* —, *à — fixe,* residing, resident; fixed, a fixture, stationary, immovable; immovably; for good. *En* —, in arrears, behindhand; prepared. *Mettre en* —, to summon, to call upon, to compel, to oblige, to force, to lay under the necessity (of), to demand, to put in suit. *Péril en la* —, danger in delay, great urgency

Demeurer, *v.n.* to reside, to live, to dwell; to abide; to remain; to stay; to stop; to last, to continue; to stand; to be; to lie; to sit; to stick; to be left. *En — là,* to stop there; to keep to that; to leave off; to go *or* proceed no farther; to say no more about it

Demi, e, *adj.* half; semi; demi; middle; — *s.m. adv.* half; slightly; —**e,** *s.f.* half; half-hour; half-past. ... *et* —, ... and a half; half-past ... *A* —, half; by halves. *N'en pas faire à* —, not to stop half-way, to go right through the business. *A trompeur* (or *A fourbe, menteur,* &c.), *trompeur* (or *fourbe, menteur,* &c.) *et* —, the biter bit, diamond cut diamond; set a thief to catch a thief. — **-bain,** *s.m.* demi-bath, slipper-bath, hip-bath. — **-bosse,** *s.f.* (*sculp.*)

demi-relief. — **-bouteille,** *s.f.* half-bottle. — **-cercle,** *s.m.* semicircle. *En — -cercle,* semicircular. — **-dieu,** *s.m.* demi-god. — **-fin, e,** *adj.* middling quality *or* size; 12 carat (*gold*); gilt, silvered, plated; (*of handwriting*) double-small; *s.m.* 12 carat gold; fringe *or* lace *or* embroidery in imitation gold *or* silver, plated articles, gilt jewellery; double-small hand (*writing*). — **-fortune,** *s.f.* one-horse (private) carriage. **-gros,** *s.m.* (*writing*) round hand; (*com.*) wholesale in small quantities. — **-heure,** *s.f.* half-hour. — **-jour,** *s.m.* twilight; subdued light, faint light. — **-lune,** *s.f.* crescent; (*fort.*) demi-lune, half-moon. — **-mondaine,** *s.f.* gay woman. — **-monde,** *s.m.* mock high life, flash society, fashionable blackguards, common swells, fast men and courtesans; gay world, gay life. — **-mot,** *s.m.* hint. (*Le sage entend à — -mot, V.* **Entendeur.**) — **-nature,** *s.f.* half life-size. — **-pause,** *s.f.* (*mus.*) minim-rest. — **-pension,** *s.f.* half-board. — **-pensionnaire,** *s.m.f.* half-boarder. — **-sang,** *s.m.* half-blood; *adj.* half-bred. — **-savant,** *s.m.* smatterer, sciolist. — **-savoir,** *s.m.,* — **-science,** *s.f.* imperfect learning, smattering, sciolism. — **-solde,** *s.f.* half-pay. — **-soupir,** *s.m.* (*mus.*) quaver-rest. — **-talent,** *s.m.* imperfect skill; person of imperfect skill. — **-tasse,** *s.f. V.* **Tasse.** — **-teinte,** *s.f.* (*paint.*) demi-tint, half-tint. — **-ton,** *s.m.* (*mus.*) semitone, half-note. — **-tour,** *s.m.* half-turn. — *-tour à droite!* (*mil.*) right about face! — *-tour à gauche!* left about face! — **-vent,** *s.m.* (*nav.*) side-wind. — **-vertu,** *s.f.* demirep, kept mistress. — **-voix (A),** *adv.* in an under-tone

Démieller, *v.a.* to take the honey off

Démis, e, (*part. of* **Démettre**) dislocated, out of joint, &c.

Démission, *s.f.* resignation. *Donner sa —,* to tender *or* give in o.'s resignation, to resign

Démissionnaire, *s.m.f. adj.* resigner; resigned

Démissoire, *s.m. V.* **Dimissoire**

Démitrer, *v.a.* to unmitre

Démobilisation, *s.f.* demobilization

Démobiliser, *v.a.* to demobilize

Démocrate, *adj. s.m.f.* democratic; democrat

Démocratie, *s.f.* democracy [page 3, § 1

Démocrat-ique, -iquement, -isme. *V.*

Démocratiser, *v.a.n.* to democratize

Se —, *v.r.* to become democratic

Démodé, e, *adj.* out of fashion, worn out, antiquated, old-fashioned, superseded

Démoder, *v.a.* to supersede, to put out of fashion [seded

Se —, *v.r.* to get out of fashion, to be super-

Démographe, *s.m.* demographer [page 3, § 1

Démograph-ie, -ique, -iquement. *V.*

Demoiselle, *s.f.* young lady; girl; unmarried *or* single lady, single woman; maid; miss; spinster; damsel; attendant, waitress; (*formerly*) gentlewoman; paving-rammer *or* beetle, commander; foot-warmer; (*insect*) dragon-fly; (*bird*) long-tailed titmouse; (*bird*) Numidian crane, demoiselle. *La — . . .,* (*law*) Miss . . .

Démolir, *v.a.* to demolish; to throw *or* pull down; to break up; to smash; to destroy; to overthrow, to subvert; (*pers.*) to cut to pieces, to cut up; to smash; to floor; to ruin; to kill

Se —, *v.r.* to be demolished *or* &c.

Démolisseur, *s.m.* demolisher; subverter

Démolition, *s.f.* demolition; **—s,** *pl.* (building) materials, rubbish

Démon, *s.m.* demon, devil; fiend; spirit, genius; wild child, imp. *Faire le —,* to play the devil

Démonétisation, *s.f.* demonetization, withdrawing from circulation, calling in

Démonétiser, *v.a.* to demonetize, to withdraw from circulation, to call in; (*fig.*) *V.* **Déconsidérer** [**Déconsidérer (Se)**

Se —, *v.r.* to be demonetized, &c.; (*fig.*) *V.*

Démoniaque, *adj. s.m.f.* demoniac

Démonicole, *s.m.f.* demon-worshipper

Démon-isme, -iste. *V.* page 3, § 1

Démonocratie, *s.f.* demonocracy

Démonographe, *s.m.* demonographer

Démono-graphie,-lâtrie,-logie,-logique, -mancie, &c. *V.* page 3, § 1

Démonomane, *adj. s.m.f.* demonomaniac

Démonomanie, *s.f.* demonomania; (*treatise*) demonology [lecturer

Démonstra-teur, trice, *s.m.f.* demonstrator;

Démonstrati-f, ve, *adj.* demonstrative; manifest; making a show of earnestness

Démonstration, *s.f.* demonstration; manifestation; proof; show; assurance; profession; movement; lecture

Démonstrativement, *adv.* demonstratively

Démontage, *s.m.* taking to pieces

Démonté, e, *part. adj.* dismounted, &c. (*V.* **Démonter**); unmounted, without a horse, without horses; (*of partridges*) with a wing broken; (*of the sea*) furious

Démonter, *v.a.* to dismount; to unhorse; to throw down; to bring down; to disable; to break the wing of (*a partridge*); to take to pieces; to undo; to take down; to disjoint; to unset; to unhinge; to put out; to disconcert; to put out of order, to disorder; to madden; to upset; to derange; to baffle, to foil; to nonplus; to shock; (*nav.*) to unship; to supersede (*in the command of a ship*)

Se —, *v.r.* to become deranged, to get out of order; to be taken to pieces, to take to pieces; to dislocate (*o.'s jaw*); to alter *or* change *or* distort (*o.'s countenance*); to become (*or* be) unhinged *or* &c. [monstrableness

Démontrabilité, *s.f.* demonstrability, de-

Démontrable, *adj.* demonstrable

Démontrer, *v.a.* to demonstrate; to prove, to

Se —, *v.r.* to be demonstrated, &c. [show

Démoralisa-teur, trice, *adj. s.m.f.* demoralizing; demoralizer

Démoralisation, *s.f.* demoralization

Démoraliser, *v.a.* to demoralize

Se —, *v.r.* to demoralize each other; to become *or* be demoralized

Démoraliseur, *s.m.* demoralizer

Démordre, *v.n.* (*of animals*) to let go o.'s hold; (*pers.*) to desist; to give up; to depart; to retract. *En —,* to give it up, to yield. *N'en pas —,* to hold hard *or* fast; to stick to it; not to

Démosthénique, *adj.* Demosthenic [give it up

Démotique, *adj.* demotic

Démoucheter, *v.a.* to uncap (*foils, swords*)

Se —, *v.r.* to come uncapped; to be uncapped

Démoulage, *s.m.* taking from the mould

Démouler, *v.a.* to take from the mould

Démouvoir, *v.a.* (*old*) to make (*one*) give up

Démunir, *v.a.* to deprive of ammunition; to unfurnish; to deprive; to divest; to leave unprovided

Se —, *v.r.* to deprive *or* divest oneself (of), to part (with); to leave oneself unprovided

Démurer, *v.a.* to unwall, to open, to reopen

Démuseler, *v.a.* to unmuzzle

Dénaire, *adj.* denary [stripped; bare

Dénanti, e, *adj.* unsecured; unprovided;

Dénantir, *v.a.* to deprive of security; to deprive, to strip; to leave unprovided

Se —, *v.r.* to deprive oneself of security; to part with a pledge; to deprive *or* strip oneself; to part (with), to give up; to leave oneself unprovided

Dénationalisation, *s.f.* denationalization

Dénationaliser, *v.a.* to denationalize

Se —, *v.r.* to become denationalized

Dénatter, *v.a.* to unmat; to untwist; to unplat; to unplait [plat o.'s hair

Se —, *v.r.* to come unmatted *or* &c.; to un-

Dénaturalisation, *s.f.* denaturalization

Dénaturaliser, *v.a.* to denaturalize

Dénaturation, *s.f.* misrepresentation; misconstruction; perversion; alteration; adulteration, sophistication

Dénaturé, e, *adj.* unnatural; barbarous, cruel; — *part. adj. V.* **Dénaturer**

Dénaturer, *v.a.* to alter *or* change the nature of; to alter; (*fig.*) to disfigure; to misrepresent; to misconstrue; to alter the sense of; to misapply; to pervert; to unnaturalize; to adulterate, to sophisticate

Se —, *v.r.* to change its nature; to be altered *or* &c.; to lose o.'s natural sentiments

Dendrite, *s.f.* (*min.*) dendrite

Dendritique, *adj.* dendritic

Dendro-graphie, -logie, &c. *V.* page 3, § 1

Dendroïde, *adj.* dendroid

Dendroïte, *s.f.* (*nat. hist.*) dendroit

Dendrolithe, *s.m.* (*nat. hist.*) dendrolite

Dendromètre, *s.m.* dendrometer

Dendrophage, *adj.* (*nat. hist.*) that eats wood

Dendrophide, *s.m.* (*zool.*) dendrophis, tree-snake

Dénéga-teur, trice, *s.m.f.* denier; — *adj.* denying

Dénégation, *s.f.* denial; (*law*) traverse

Dénégatoire, *adj.* (*law*) traversing

Dénéral, *s.m.* coiner's standard

Déni, *s.m.* (*law*) denial, refusal

Déniaisé, e, *part. adj.* sharpened, sharp, knowing, cunning

Déniaiser, *v.a.* to sharpen the wits of, to sharpen, to make sharp, to teach wit to; to trick, to dupe, to cheat, to take in

Se —, *v.r.* to get sharp, to grow wiser, to learn wit

Dénicher, *v.a.* to take out of its nest *or* niche; to dislodge, to turn out; to find out; — *v.n.* to fly off *or* away, to forsake its nest; (*pers.*) to be off, to get *or* run away. — *des oiseaux*, to take birds out of their (*or* the) nest, to birds'-nest, to go birds'-nesting

Dénicheu-r, se, *s.m.f.* birds'-nester; (*fig.*) hunter, seeker. — *de merles*, sharper. — *de fauvettes*, fortune-hunter; gay man, lady-killer

Dénier, *v.a.* to deny. *Se —*, to be denied

Denier, *s.m.* (*old French coin*) denier (*twelfth part of a* "sou"); (*coin in Roman antiquity*) denarius; (*fig.*) farthing; mite; pence; money, funds; sum; hard cash, specie; profit; (*fraction*) penny, so much in the pound, quota; (*share*) one twelfth; (*obsolete*) rate of interest. —*s publics*, public money. — *sterling*, (*Engl. coin*) penny. — *à Dieu*, earnest money. — *de fin* or *de loi*, standard of the fineness of silver. —*s d'octroi*, toll. — *de poids*, penny-weight. —*s du roi*, king's revenue. *Le — de la veuve*, the widow's mite. *Le — de Saint-Pierre*, (St.) Peter's pence. *A beaux —s comptants, A —s découverts*, in cash, in ready money. *Le — quatre*, (*obsolete*) twenty-five per cent. *Le — cinq*, (*obsolete*) twenty per cent. *Le — dix*, (*obsolete*) ten per cent. *Le — vingt*, (*obsolete*) five per cent. *Le — vingt-cinq*, (*obsolete*) four per cent

Dénigrement, *s.m.* disparagement, traducing; discredit, contempt

Dénigrer, *v.a.* to disparage, to traduce, to vilify, to revile, to asperse, to run down, to decry, to sneer at, to animadvert upon

Dénigreu-r, se, *s.m.f.* disparager

Déniveler, *v.a.* to make uneven, to put out of level, to unlevel

Dénivellation, *s.f.*, **Dénivellement,** *s.m.* making uneven, putting out of level, unlevelling; unevenness, inequality

Dénization, *s.f.* denization

Dénoircir, *v.a.* to clean, to wash clean, to wash white; to clear, to vindicate, to whitewash

Dénombrement, *s.m.* enumeration; numbering; catalogue, list; census

Dénombrer, *v.a.* to enumerate; to number; to count

Se —, *v.r.* to be enumerated *or* &c.

Dénominateur, *s.m.* denominator

Dénominati-f, ve, *adj.*, **Dénominatif,** *s.m.* denominative

Dénomination, *s.f.* denomination, name

Dénominativement, *adv.* denominatively

Dénommer, *v.a.* to denominate, to name

Se —, *v.r.* to be denominated *or* named

Dénoncer, *v.a.* to denounce; to accuse; to impeach; to inform against; to give notice of; to announce; to proclaim; to declare; to tell; to point out

Dénoncia-teur, trice, *s.m.f.* denouncer, denunciator; informer; accuser; — *adj.* denouncing, denunciatory

Dénonciati-f, ve, *adj.* denunciatory

Dénonciation, *s.f.* denunciation; accusation; impeachment; information; notice; announcement; proclamation; declaration

Dénotation, *s.f.* denotation

Dénoter, *v.a.* to denote, to betoken, to indicate, to show; to designate; to describe; to characterize

Dénouement, *s.m. V.* **Dénoûment**

Dénouer, *v.a.* to untie; to undo; to unknot; to loosen; to break; to make more supple; to help the growth of; to develop; to unravel; to disentangle; to unfold; to clear up; to solve

Se —, *v.r.* to come *or* be untied; to come undone; to grow; to become more supple; to unravel; to unfold; to clear up; to be unknotted *or* developed *or* solved; to be wound up, to wind up

Dénoûment, *s.m.* event, issue, end, conclusion, solution, catastrophe, denouement; untying, undoing, unknotting, loosening; development, growth

Denrée, *s.f.* commodity; ware; food, provisions; produce

Dense, *adj.* dense, close, thick, compact; concise, terse

Densité, *s.f.* density, thickness

Dent, *s.f.* tooth; tusk; notch; cog; prong; tine. *Mal de —s*, toothache. *A belles —s*, unmercifully; heartily. *Avoir les —s longues*, (*fig.*) to be hungry. *Avoir mal aux —s*, to have the toothache. *Avoir* or *garder une —* (*une — de lait*) *contre*, to owe a grudge (an old grudge). *Être sur les —s*, to be tired out *or* knocked up, to be off o.'s legs. *Faire ses —s*, to cut o.'s teeth. *Mettre sur les —s*, to tire out, to knock up. *Parler des grosses —s*, to talk big, to threaten. *Parler du bout des —s*, to lisp. *Rire, manger du bout des —s*, *V.* **Rire** *and* **Manger.** — **-de-chien,** *s.f.* (*bot.*) *V.* **Cynodon.** — **-de-lion,** *s.f.* (*bot.*) dandelion. — **-de-loup,** *s.f.* (*tech.*) transom; dog-nail; burnisher

Dentaire, *adj.* dental; — *s.f.* (*bot.*) dentaria, coral-wort, tooth-wort

Dental, e, *adj.* (*gram.*) dental

Dentale, *s.f.* (*gram.*) dental; — *s.m.* (*zool.*) dentalium, tooth-shell

Denté, e, *adj.* toothed; cogged; dentate, dentated; indented; (— *en scie*) serrate, serrated; — *s.m.* (*fish*) dentex; — *s.f.* (*hunt.*) bite (*of a dog*), blow (*of a boar*)

Dentelaire, *s.f.* (*bot.*) leadwort

Dentelé, e, *adj.* indented, toothed; notched; jagged; dentate, dentated; denticulated; serrated; cogged

Denteler, *v.a.* to indent, to tooth; to notch; to jag

Dentelle, *s.f.* lace; lace-work

Dentellière, *s.f.* lace-woman, lace-maker

Dentelure, *s.f.* indentation; denticulation; (*arch.*) embrasure

Denter, *v.a.* to tooth; to cog

Dentex, *s.m.* (*fish*) dentex

Denticule, *s.f.* denticle; (*arch.*) denticule, dentil

Denticulé, e, *adj.* denticulate

Dentier, *s.m.* set of (artificial) teeth

Dentiforme, *adj.* dentiform

Dentifrice, *s.m.* dentifrice; — *adj.* tooth, for the teeth

Dentine, *s.f.* dentine

Dentirostre, *adj.* (*zool.*) dentirostral; — *s.m.* dentirostre

Dentiste, *s.m.* dentist

Dentition, *s.f.* dentition, teething, cutting of the teeth

Dentu, e, *adj.* toothed, with teeth in o.'s mouth *or* in o.'s head

Denture, *s.f.* set of teeth; (*of wheels*, &c.) teeth-range

Dénudation, *s.f.* denudation

Dénuder, *v.a.* to denude, to lay bare, to bare; to strip; to bark (*a tree*)

Se —, *v.r.* to become *or* be denuded, &c.

Dénué, e, *part. adj.* deprived, stripped; destitute; void, devoid

Dénuement, *s.m.* *V.* **Dénûment** [titute
Dénuer, *v.a.* to deprive, to strip, to leave destitute
Dénûment, *s.m.* destitution, want, poverty, penury; deprivation
Déontolog-ie, -ique, -iste. *V.* page 3, § 1
†**Dépaillage,** *s.m.* unbottoming (*of chairs*)
†**Dépailler,** *v.a.* to unbottom (*chairs*)
Se —, *v.r.* to lose its straw bottom
Dépaissance, *s.f.* pasture
Dépaler, *v.n.* (*nav.*) to drift
Dépalissage, *s.m.* (*hort.*) unpaling
Dépalisser, *v.a.* (*hort.*) to unpale [unpacked
Dépaqueter, *v.a.* to unpack. *Se —,* to come unpacked
†**Dépareil, le,** *adj.* (*old*) dissimilar, unlike
†**Dépareillé, e,** *adj.* unmatched, incomplete, imperfect, odd
†**Dépareiller,** *v.a.* to unmatch; to render incomplete; to mix; to spoil a set *or* a pair of
Déparer, *v.a.* to spoil; to injure; to disfigure; to spoil the look of; to disparage; to disgrace; to undress; to strip
Déparier, *v.a.* to unmatch; to separate, to part
Déparler, *v.n.* to leave off talking, to cease speaking; (*pop.*) not to know what one (*oneself*) is talking about
Déparquer, *v.a.* to unpen; to unfold; to disempark; to unbed (*oysters*); — *v.n.* to leave the fold
Départ, *s.m.* departure, leaving, setting out, starting, start; parting, separation, sorting; distinction [to make a majority (*of votes*) in
Départager, *v.a.* to settle by a casting vote, to make a majority (*of votes*)
Département, *s.m.* department; county; district; division; office; line, business, province; —**s,** *pl.* departments, counties, country
Départemental,e, *adj.* departmental, county, country [in *or* by departments
Départementalement, *adv.* departmentally, in *or* by departments
Départir, *v.a.* to distribute, to dispense, to allot; to divide; to assign; to bestow, to grant, to endow, to gift
Se —, *v.r.* to desist; to give up; to abandon; to quit; to depart, to swerve; to be distributed
Dépassement, *s.m.* overextension; excess [*or* &c.
Dépasser, *v.a.n.* to pass, to go beyond; to extend *or* reach beyond; to sail beyond; to exceed; to overstep; to outstrip, to outrun, to outsail, to distance, to leave behind; to overreach; to overshoot; to fall below; to rise above; to be higher *or* taller *or* longer than; to draw out (*ribbons,* &c.); to unreeve (*ropes, nav.*); to surpass, to excel, to outdo; to jut out; to sag [from passion
Dépassionner, *v.a.* to disimpassion, to free from passion
Se —, *v.r.* to become disimpassioned *or* free from passion [tion of pie (*or* pi)
Dépâtissage, *s.m.* (*print.*) sorting and distribution of pie (*or* pi)
Dépâtisser, *v.a.* (*print.*) to sort and distribute
Dépavage, *s.m.* unpaving [pie (*or* pi)
Dépaver, *v.a.* to unpave
Se —, *v.r.* to become *or* get *or* be unpaved
Dépaysement, *s.m.* sending to another country *or* &c. (*V.* **Dépayser**); change of habits *or* occupations
Dépayser, *v.a.* to place on strange ground; to send to a strange place; to put into another country; to send abroad *or* away from home; to take out of o.'s habits *or* element; to carry out of o.'s depth; to bewilder; to put on the wrong scent, to put out
Se —, *v.r.* to leave o.'s country *or* home; to go to a strange place *or* on strange ground; to go abroad; to get out of o.'s habits *or* element
Dépeçage, Dépècement, *s.m.* cutting up; carving; breaking up; tearing up; dismemberment
Dépecer, *v.a.* to cut up; to carve; to take to pieces; to break up; to tear up; to dismember
Se —, *v.r.* to be cut up *or* carved *or* &c.; to cut up [ripper; meat-dresser
Dépeceur, *s.m.* cutter; carver; breaker; boat-ripper; meat-dresser
Dépêche, *s.f.* despatch; message; telegram; mail; —**s,** *pl.* despatches; messages; correspondence; bag; mail; mails
†**Dépêche-compagnon (A),** *adv.* hurriedly, negligently, carelessly; to the death, without quarter
Dépêcher, *v.a.* to despatch; to hurry over; — *v.n.* to send off despatches *or* a despatch; (*fam.*) to be quick, to look sharp
Se —, *v.r.* to make haste, to be quick, to hasten
Dépeçoir, *s.m.* chopping-knife, carver, ripper
Dépeindre, *v.a.* to depict, to describe, to paint, to portray, to picture, to represent
Se —, *v.r.* to depict *or* &c. oneself; (*of things*) to be depicted, &c.
Dépelotonner, *v.a.* to unwind (*thread,* &c.)
Se —, *v.r.* to come unwound
†**Dépenaillé, e,** *adj.* ragged, in rags; loosely dressed, ill-dressed, ill-clad, slovenly, slatternly; emaciated; ruined [emaciation; ruin
†**Dépenaillement,** *s.m.* raggedness; disorder; emaciation; ruin
Dépendamment, *adv.* dependently
Dépendance, *s.f.* dependence, dependency; appendage; outbuilding, outhouse; offices
Dépendant, e, *adj. s.* dependent. *En —,* (*nav.*) edging away [(*pop.*) tall lanky fellow
Dépendeur, *s.m.* unhanger. — *d'andouilles,* (*pop.*) tall lanky fellow
Dépendre, *v.n.* to depend; to be dependent; to be subject; to be a dependency; to lie (*or* be) in ...'s power; to rest (with); to result, to proceed; — *v.a.* to unhang, to take down; (*old*) to expend, to spend. *A pendre* (or *à vendre*) *et à —,* fast, stanch; through thick and thin; entirely
Dépens, *s.m.pl.* expense, cost; (*law*) costs [entirely
Dépense, *s.f.* expense; expenditure; outlay waste; flow, discharge; pantry, larder; steward's room. *Faire de la —,* to spend (much) money. *Faire la —,* to attend to the housekeeping. *Porter en —,* (*of accounts*) to set down
Dépenser, *v.a.* to spend; to expend; to lay out; to consume, to waste
Se —, *v.r.* to be spent *or* &c.
Dépensi-er, ère, *adj. s.* extravagant, lavish prodigal; spendthrift, extravagant person steward; bursar
Dépensionné, e, *adj.* who has lost his *or* her pension, deprived of ditto [(*med.*) discharges
Déperdition, *s.f.* loss, waste; destruction; (*med.*) discharges
Dépérir, *v.n.* to decay; to fall off *or* away; to die away; to decline; to waste away; to dwindle away; to wither
Dépérissement, *s.m.* decaying, decay, ruin; decline; dwindling away; pining away; withering
Dépersuader, *v.a.* to persuade to the contrary, to convert; to get (...) out of the head of
Dépêtrer, *v.a.* to disentangle, to extricate, to disengage, to clear, to free, to rid
Se —, *v.r.* to disentangle *or* &c. oneself; to get out (of) *or* away (from), to get clear, to get rid
Dépeuplement, *s.m.* depopulation; unstocking; thinning (*of forests*); drawing (*of ponds*); destruction of game
Dépeupler, *v.a.* to depopulate, to unpeople; to unstock; to thin (*a forest*); to draw (*a pond*); to destroy the game of
Se —, *v.r.* to become depopulated, &c.; to get unstocked, &c.; to get thin
Déphlegm-ation, -er. *V.* **Déflegmation,** &c.
Dépiauter, *v.a.* (*pop.*) to skin, to peel off; to undress
Dépicage, *s.m.* *V.* **Dépiquage** [undress
Dépicatoire, *adj.* (*agr.*) of *or* for treading out (*corn*)
Dépiècement, *s.m.* *V.* **Dépècement** [(*corn*)
Dépiécer, *v.a.* *V.* **Dépecer** [fleece
Dépilage, *s.m.* (*tech.*) taking off the hair *or* the fleece
Dépilateur, Dépilatif, Dépilatoire, &c. *V.* **Épilateur,** &c. [taking off the fleece
Dépilation, *s.f.* depilation; falling of the hair; taking off the fleece
Dépiler, *v.a.* *V.* **Épiler.** *Se —,* to lose its hair
Dépinglage, *s.m.* (*tech.*) unpinning
Dépingler, *v.a.* (*tech.*) to unpin
Dépioter, *v.a.* *V.* **Dépiauter**
Dépiquage, *s.m.* (*old agr.*) treading out (*corn*)

Dépiquer, *v.a.* to unquilt, to unstitch; (*hort.*) to transplant; (*pers.*) to put in good humour again, to put into better humour, to restore to good humour; (*agr., obsolete*) to tread out (*corn*)
Se —, *v.r.* to come unquilted *or* unstitched; to be unquilted *or* unstitched *or* &c.; (*pers.*) to recover o.'s good humour; to compensate *or* recoup *or* console *or* revenge oneself
Dépiqueuse, *s.f.* (*agr. instr.*) sheller
Dépister, *v.a.* to track; to slot; to hunt out; to find out, to discover; to throw off the scent; to put out
Dépit, *s.m.* vexation; spite. *En — de*, in spite of; in contempt of, in defiance of, contrary to, against. *En — qu'on en ait* (obsolete for *Malgré qu'on en ait*, which See under **Avoir**) [humour
Dépiter, *v.a.* to vex, to spite, to put out of
Se —, *v.r.* to be vexed, to get out of humour, to fret, to be in a pet
Déplacé, e, *part. adj.* displaced, &c. (*V.* **Déplacer**); in the wrong place; out of place; out of o.'s *or* its place; ill-timed, out of season; inappropriate; irrelevant; uncalled for, improper, unbecoming
Déplacement, *s.m.* displacement, displacing, removal, change of place; travelling, journey, call, attendance
Déplacer, *v.a.* to displace; to misplace; to put out of its place; to take ...'s place; to remove; to change
Se —, *v.r.* to change *or* leave o.'s place; to change *or* leave o.'s residence *or* home; to remove; to move; to leave o.'s seat; (*of things*) to have its place changed; to be displaced *or* &c.
Déplaire, *v.n.* to displease; to be displeasing *or* unpleasant *or* disagreeable *or* obnoxious; to give dissatisfaction *or* offence, to offend; to incur (...'s) displeasure; (*imp.*) to dislike. *N'en déplaise à*, by *or* with the leave of; with all due deference to; no offence *or* disparagement to
Se —, *v.r.* to dislike; not to like; to be displeased; to find it unpleasant; not to thrive; to displease each other
Déplaisamment, *adv.* unpleasantly
Déplaisance, *s.f.* dislike, aversion
Déplaisant, e, *adj.* unpleasant, unpleasing, displeasing, disagreeable, annoying, obnoxious
Déplaisir, *s.m.* displeasure; dislike; dissatisfaction; vexation; sorrow, grief, trouble
Déplancher, Déplanchéier, *v.a.* to unplank; to unboard; to unfloor [plantation
Déplantage, *s.m.*, **Déplantation,** *s.f.* dis-
Déplanter, *v.a.* to displant; (*nav.*) to start
Déplantoir, *s.m.* (*hort.*) trowel [(*the anchor*)
Déplâtrage, *s.m.* unplastering
Déplâtrer, *v.a.* to unplaster; (*fig.*) to unmask
Dépléti-f, ve, *adj.* (*med.*) depletory
Déplétion, *s.f.* (*med.*) depletion
Dépleurer, *v.n.* to cease weeping *or* crying
Déplier, *v.a.* to unfold; to open; to lay out; to display; to expose; to unfurl
Se —, *v.r.* to come *or* be unfolded
Déplissage, *s.m.* unplaiting [of plait
Déplisser, *v.a.* to unplait. *Se —*, to come out
Déploiement, *s.m.* unfolding; display; deploying, deployment, deploy
Déplombage, *s.m.* unsealing; unstopping
Déplomber, *v.a.* to unlead; to unload (*a stick*); (*cust.*) to unseal; to unstop (*a tooth*) [wretched
Déplorable, *adj.* deplorable, lamentable, sad;
Déplorablement, *adv.* deplorably, lamentably, sadly; wretchedly
Déplorer, *v.a.* to deplore, to lament, to bewail, to mourn; to pity; to regret
Se —, *v.r.* to be deplored *or* &c.
Déployé, e, *part. adj.* unfolded, &c. (*V.* **Déployer**); open; flying (*colours*); (*nav.*) out. *A gorge —e*, with full *or* open throat; at the top of o.'s voice; heartily. *Voguer à voiles —es*, to be under full sail
Déployer, *v.a.* to unfold; to unroll; to unfurl; to expand; to open; to display; to set *or* forth; to exert; to use; to stretch *or* hold out; to lay out; to show; to spread; to array; to deploy; to take (*its flight*)
Déplumé, e, *part. adj.* unplumed, &c. (*V.* **Déplumer**); unfeathered; shabby, shabby-genteel; bald [to fleece
Deplumer, *v.a.* to unplume, to pluck, to pick;
Se —, *v.r.* to pluck its feathers *or* each other's feathers; to shed its feathers; (*jest.*) to lose o.'s hair [fork out
Dépocher, *v.a.n.* to take out of o.'s pocket; to
Dépointage, *s.m.* unstitching
Dépointer, *v.a.* to unstitch
Dépolarisation, *s.f.* (*phys.*) depolarization
Dépolariser, *v.a.* (*phys.*) to depolarize
Dépoli, e, *part. adj.* with its polish off, having lost its polish; roughened, rough; ground; — *s.m.* roughing [to grind
Dépolir, *v.a.* to take the polish off; to rough;
Se —, *v.r.* to lose its polish; to get rough
Dépolissage, Dépolissement, *s.m.* roughing; grinding [*gram.*) deponent
Déponent, e, *adj.*, **Déponent,** *s.m.* (*Lat.*
Dépopularisation, *s.f.* loss of popularity, unpopularity [popular
Dépopulariser, *v.a.* to make *or* render un-
Se —, *v.r.* to make oneself unpopular, to become unpopular, to lose o.'s popularity
Dépopula-teur, trice, *adj.* depopulating; — *s.m.* depopulator
Dépopulation, *s.f.* depopulation
Déport, *s.m.* delay; (*law*) challenging oneself; (*'Change*) backwardation [exile, banishment
Déportation, *s.f.* transportation, deportation;
Déporté, *s.m.* transported convict, transport; exile. *Transport des —s*, convict-ship
Déportements, *s.m.pl.* misconduct; doings
Déporter, *v.a.* to transport; to exile, to banish
Se —, *v.r.* to desist; to refrain [deposited
Déposable, *adj.* deposable; that may be
Déposant, e, *s.m.f.* depositor; witness, deponent; — *adj.* deposing, giving evidence; depositing
Dépose, *s.f.* (*tech.*) taking up *or* off, removal
Déposer, *v.a.* to put *or* lay *or* set down; to lay aside; to lay, to put, to place; to depose; to divest; to deprive; to deposit; to leave; to shoot (*rubbish*); to resign; to divest oneself of; to intrust, to commit; to give; to send *or* give in; to prefer; to lodge; to register; to state; (*tech.*) to take up *or* off, to remove; — *v.n.* to give evidence; to depose; to state; to testify; to bear witness; (*of liquids*) to settle, to leave a sediment *or* deposit; (*by ellipsis*) to shoot rubbish, to commit a nuisance
Se —, *v.r.* to be put *or* laid down *or* deposited *or* &c.; to resign, to abdicate; to deposit itself; to settle, to sink to the bottom
Déposeur, *s.m.* deposer
Dépositaire, *s.m.f.* depositary, trustee; consignee; holder; guardian; treasurer; confidant
Déposi-teur, trice, *s.m.f.* depositor, consigner
Déposition, *s.f.* deposition; divestiture; deprivation; testimony, evidence; statement
Déposséder, *v.a.* to dispossess; (*law*) to oust
Dépossesseur, *s.m.* dispossessor
Dépossession, *s.f.* dispossession; (*law*) ouster
Déposter, *v.a.*, **Se —,** *v.r.* to dislodge
Dépôt, *s.m.* deposit; depositing; trust; charge; sale or return; repository, depository; store-room, store-house, depôt; magazine; warehouse; station; wharf; agency; chest; vault; sediment, settlement, settling, fur; gathering, abscess; (*of designs, &c.*) registration; entry; (*of prisoners*) commitment; (*in a police-office*) cells. — *de mendicité*, workhouse, poor-house. *Lieu de —*, spoil-bank; depôt
Dépotage, Dépotement, *s.m.* unpotting; potting off; decanting, decantation
Dépoter, *v.a.* to unpot, to take out of the pot; to pot off; to decant
Dépotoir, *s.m.* general deposit of night-soil; (*pop.*) jorden; strong-box, safe; confessional

Dépoudrer, *v.a.* to unpowder; to dust [o.'s hair
Se —, *v.r.* to come unpowdered; to unpowder
†Dépouille, *s.f.* spoil; skin; crop; remains, relics; wardrobe; clothes; inheritance; **—s,** *pl.* spoils, booty
†Dépouillement, *s.m.* stripping; spoliation; despoiling; throwing *or* casting off; renunciation; self-denial; privation; denudation; destitution; abstract; summary; counting up (*of votes by ballot*)
†Dépouiller, *v.a.* to strip; to unclothe, to pull off the clothes of; to skin; to lay bare, to bare; to throw *or* cast off, to leave off; to lay aside; to put off; to renounce; to give up; to despoil, to spoil, to plunder; to divest; to deprive; to reap; to give an abstract *or* a summary of; to count up (*votes by ballot*)
Se —, *v.r.* to strip oneself *or* each other; to pull off o.'s clothes; to divest oneself; to cast *or* throw off, to leave off; to lay aside; to put off; to renounce; to dispense; to cast *or* shed its skin, to moult; to shed; to be stripped *or* laid bare *or* &c.; (*of liquids*) to become clear
†Dépouilleu-r, se, *s.m.f.* stripper; despoiler; gatherer, reaper; teller (*of votes by ballot*)
Dépourrissage, Dépourrissement, *s.m.* picking off the rotten part
Dépourvoir, *v.a.* to divest, to deprive, to strip, to leave unprovided *or* destitute
Dépourvu, e, *part. adj.* divested, deprived, stripped; unprovided; destitute; void, devoid. *Au —,* unawares; unprovided; napping; by surprise [depraving
Déprava-teur, trice, *s.m.f.* depraver; — *adj.*
Dépravation, *s.f.* depravation; depravity; deterioration
Dépraver, *v.a.* to deprave; to deteriorate
Se —, *v.r.* to become depraved *or* deteriorated
Déprécati-f, ve, *adj.* deprecative
Déprécation, *s.f.* deprecation
Déprécatoire, *adj.* deprecatory
Déprécia-teur, trice, *s.m.f.* depreciator; — *adj.* depreciating, depreciative, depreciatory
Dépréciati-f, ve, *adj.* depreciative, deprecia-
Dépréciation, *s.f.* depreciation [tory
Déprécier, *v.a.* to depreciate, to run down, to disparage, to undervalue, to underrate
Se —, *v.r.* to depreciate *or* &c. oneself *or* each other; (*of things*) to fall in value, to become depreciated [*adj.* depredatory, predatory
Dépréda-teur, trice, *s.m.f.* depredator; —
Déprédati-f, ve, *adj.* depredatory, predatory
Déprédation, *s.f.* depredation
Dépréder, *v.a.n.* (*old*) to depredate, to plunder
Déprendre, *v.a.* (*old*) *V.* **Détacher**
Se —, *v.r.* to get detached *or* loose, to extricate *or* free oneself, to get off *or* away; to lay aside, to give up, to renounce, to quit, to part (with), to leave off, to desist [take the gloss off
Dépresser, *v.a.* to take out of the press; to
Dépressible, *adj.* depressible; compressible
Dépressi-f, ve, *adj.* depressive
Dépression, *s.f.* depression; depreciation
Déprêtrer, Déprêtriser, *v.a.* (*fam.*) to
Déprévenir, *v.a.* to disprejudice [unpriest
Déprier, *v.a.* to disinvite
Déprimage, *s.m.* (*agr.*) feeding off
Déprimer, *v.a.* to depress; to abase; to humble; to depreciate; to underrate; (*agr.*) to feed off
Se —, *v.r.* to become depressed; to detract from each other's merit
Dépriser, *v.a.* to undervalue, to underrate, to depreciate, to run down, to disparage [release
Déprisonner, *v.a.* to disprison, to set free, to
De profundis, *adv. s.m.* de profundis [ering
Dépucelage, Dépucellement, *s.m.* deflow-
Dépuceler, *v.a.* to deflower [(*fam.*) braggart
Dépuceleur, *s.m.* deflowerer. — *de nourrices,*
Depuis, *prep.* since; from; for; after; for the last; for some; ago; past; — *adv.* since *or* from that time, since, ever since; afterwards, ever after. — *longtemps,* long since, long ago; for a long time. — *peu,* — *peu de temps,* for some little time past, not long since, not long ago; lately, of late; recently. — *quand?* — *combien de temps?* how long? how long is it since? since what time *or* period? since when? — *que,* since, ever since. — *quelque temps,* for some time past, for some time [rative
Dépurati-f, ve, *adj.*, **Dépuratif,** *s.m.* depu-
Dépuration, *s.f.* depuration
Dépuratoire, *adj.* depuratory
Dépurer, *v.a.* to depurate. *Se—,* to be depurated
Députation, *s.f.* deputation; deputyship, representation, (a) seat in Parliament
Député, *s.m.* deputy; delegate; representative, member of Parliament, M.P. [send a deputation
Députer, *v.a.* to depute, to send; — *v.n.* to
Déqualifier, *v.a.* to disqualify [dislodge, to oust
†Déquiller, *v.a.* to bowl away, to knock off, to
Déracinement, *s.m.* uprooting; eradication
Déraciner, *v.a.* to uproot, to root up *or* out; to eradicate; to pluck up; to extirpate; to extract
Se —, *v.r.* to unroot; to be eradicated *or* &c.
Déracineur, *s.m.* rooter
Dérader, *v.a.* to drive out to sea; — *v.n.* to be driven out to sea, to get out to sea
Déraidir, *v.a.* to unstiffen, to remove the stiffness of, to make pliant, to soften
Se —, *v.r.* to lose its *or* o.'s stiffness, to get pliant *or* soft *or* supple
†Déraillement, *s.m.* running off the rails; throwing off the rails, upsetting a railway-train
†Dérailler, *v.n.* to run off the rails; — *v.a.* to throw off the rails, to upset [tuation
Déraison, *s.f.* unreasonableness; folly; infa-
Déraisonnable, *adj.* unreasonable
Déraisonnablement, *adv.* unreasonably
Déraisonnement, *s.m.* irrational talk
Déraisonner, *v.n.* to talk irrationally, to talk nonsense, to wander
Déralinguer, *v.a.* (*nav.*) to detach *or* blow from the bolt-rope; — *v.n.* to be detached *or* &c. ditto; (*slang*) to die, to kick the bucket
Dérangé, e, *part. adj.* out of order; relaxed; irregular, disorderly; deranged; disordered, &c. (*V.* **Déranger**)
Dérangement, *s.m.* derangement; disorder; inconvenience; disturbance; trouble; discomposure; misconduct; embarrassment; confusion; looseness, diarrhœa
Déranger, *v.a.* to derange; to put out of order; to throw into disorder; to put out of its place, to displace; to upset; to disorder; to impair; to inconvenience, to incommode, to put to inconvenience, to put out of o.'s way; to disturb; to trouble; to put out *or* about; to interfere with; to lead astray; to disconcert; to discompose; to unsettle; to embarrass; to relax, to give the diarrhœa
Se —, *v.r.* to be *or* become deranged; to get out of order; to disturb *or* trouble *or* inconvenience oneself; to move *or* put oneself out of the way; to go out of o.'s way; to leave o.'s seat; to stir; to go astray; to get into irregular habits; to become impaired *or* embarrassed; to unsettle
Déraper, *v.n.* (*nav., of the anchor*) to get atrip, to come home. *Faire —,* to trip (*loosen from the ground*)
Dérâper, *v.a.* to pick (*grapes*) from the bunch
Dératé, e, *adj.* spleened, deprived of spleen; (*fig.*) lively; sharp, knowing, forward; hurried; — *s.m.f.* spleened dog; lively *or* sharp *or* knowing fellow *or* creature *or* thing. *Courir comme un —,* to run like a spleened dog, to run like a greyhound, to run at a smart rate
Dérater, *v.a.* to spleen, to extract the spleen of
Derechef, *adv.* (*obsolete*) again, anew, afresh, over again; once more
Déréglé, e, *adj.* irregular; out of order; intemperate; inordinate; immoderate; exorbitant; disorderly; disordered; unruly; lawless; dissolute, licentious, profligate

Dérèglement, *s.m.* irregularity; intemperateness; excess; riot; disorder; unruliness; lawlessness; dissoluteness, licentiousness, debauchery, profligacy, wildness

Déréglément, *adv.* irregularly; intemperately; inordinately; immoderately; exorbitantly; disorderly; dissolutely; loosely

Dérégler, *v.a.* to put out of order, to disorder, to derange, to unsettle

Se —, *v.r.* to get out of order; to become *or* be disordered *or* deranged *or* unsettled; to go astray, to misconduct oneself

Dérêner, *v.a.* to unrein, to unbridle

Dérider, *v.a.* to unwrinkle; to smooth; to cheer up; to make lively *or* cheerful; to amuse

Se —, *v.r.* to become unwrinkled *or* smooth; to unbend; to relax; to unbend *or* smooth o.'s brow; to cheer up; to brighten up; to make merry, to laugh

Dérimer, *v.a.* to turn (*verse*) into prose

Dérision, *s.f.* derision, mockery; ridicule

Dérisoire, *adj.* derisive, derisory, mocking

Dérisoirement, *adv.* derisively

Dérivable, *adj.* derivable [counter-irritant

Dérivati-f, ve, *adj.*, **Dérivatif,** *s.m.* derivative;

Dérivation, *s.f.* derivation; (*nav.*) yawing, deviation from the course

Dérive, *s.f.* (*nav.*) drift, lee-way. *A la —, en —,* drifting, adrift. *Aller en —,* to drift; to part. *Avoir une belle —,* to have good sea-room

Dérivé, e, *adj.*, **Dérivé,** *s.m.* derivative

Dériver, *v.n.* to derive; to be derived; to originate, to spring, to proceed; to leave the shore; to drift; — *v.a.* to derive; to turn off; (*tech.*) to unrivet, to unclinch. *Faire —,* to derive; [to turn off

Dermatite, *s.f.* (*med.*) dermatitis

Dermato-graphie, -graphique, -logie, -logique, -logiste, &c. *V.* page 3, § 1

Dermatose, *s.f.* (*med.*) dermatose

Derme, *s.m.* (*anat.*) dermis, derm [moth

Dermeste, *s.m.* (*zool.*) dermestes, bacon-beetle,

Dermique, *adj.* dermic, dermal [page 3, § 1

Dermo-logie, -logique, -pathie, &c. *V.*

Derni-er, ère, *adj. s.* latter; last; final; finishing; closing; dying; latest; highest, greatest, utmost, extreme; lowest, vilest, meanest, basest, worst; youngest; last person; last man; last word, last reply; (*at tennis*) end of the gallery. *La semaine* (or *année,* &c.) *—e,* last week (*or* year, &c.). *La —e semaine* (or *année,* &c.), the last week (*or* year, &c.). *La —e fois,* last *or* the last time. *Aux —s les bons* [*morceaux*], last come best served. *Du — . . .,* (*before an adj.*) . . . in the highest degree, in the extreme, extremely . . . [recently

Dernièrement, *adv.* lately, of late, latterly,

Dérobé, e, *part. adj.* stolen, &c. (*V.* **Dérober**); private, secret, back; (*of time*) spare, leisure; (*of a horse's hoof*) worn. *A la —e,* by stealth, stealthily; privately; secretly; clandestinely; slily, on the sly; without being seen, unseen

Dérober, *v.a.* to steal, to rob; to pilfer, to purloin; to steal away; to take away; to take; to snatch; to divest; to deprive; to conceal, to hide; to protect, to shelter, to screen, to shield, to preserve; to rescue; to spare; to unrobe, to disrobe; to shell (*beans,* &c.)

Se —, *v.r.* to steal away; to shun, to avoid, to shrink; to decline; to escape; to disappear, to vanish, to fly; to get behind; to fail, to sink; to conceal *or* hide oneself; to be concealed *or* hidden; (*rid.*) to slip from under the rider; to [swerve

Dérochage, *s.m.* scouring (*metals*)

Dérocher, *v.a.* to scour (*metals*)

Dérogation, *s.f.* derogation

Dérogatoire, Dérogeant, e, *adj.* derogatory

Déroger, *v.n.* to derogate; to detract; to act contrary (to); to condescend, to stoop; to [degrade oneself

Déroidir, *v.a. V.* **Déraidir**

Dérougir, *v.a.* to take the redness off; — *v.n.,* **Se —,** *v.r.* to become less red; to lose its redness

†Dérouillement, *s.m.* rubbing off the rust

†Dérouiller, *v.a.* to rub the rust off; to polish, to brighten up

Se —, *v.r.* to lose its *or* o.'s rust, to brighten up, to polish; to get up again, to rub up

Déroulement, *s.m.* unrolling

Dérouler, *v.a.* to unroll; to unfold; to display

Déroute, *s.f.* rout; defeat; overthrow; subversion; disorder; confusion; failure; ruin. *En —,* in flight and disorder, routed; overthrown; ruined. *En pleine —,* completely routed; entirely overthrown; totally ruined. *Mettre en —,* to rout; to overthrow; to ruin; to puzzle, to pose

Dérouter, *v.a.* to lead astray; to confuse, to put out; to puzzle, to perplex; to bewilder; to disconcert; to baffle, to foil

Se —, *v.r.* to go astray, to lose o.'s way; to become *or* be confused, &c.

Derrière, *prep. adv.* behind; after; back; behind it; behind them; — *s.m.* back; backpart; hinder part, hind; rear; backside, bottom, breech; (*of carts,* &c.) tail; (*paint.*) background; (*artil.*) train; **—s,** *s.m.pl.* back; rear. *De —,* hind, hinder; back; after. *Par —,* behind, from behind; aback; behind the back of, in the absence of. *Porte de —,* back-door; evasion. *Montrer le —,* to turn tail, to show the white feather; to fail in o.'s promise; (*pop.*) to be in [rags

Derviche, Dervis, *s.m.* dervis, dervise

Des [*contraction of* **De les,** *art.*] of the, of; from the, from; some; any

Dès, *prep.* even from, as early as, no later than, at the very beginning of, from, since; at; on; even in. *— aujourd'hui,* this very day; at once; from this day. *— l'aube, — le matin,* at daybreak, at dawn. *— ce soir,* this very evening. *— demain,* not later than to-morrow; to-morrow morning at once. *— le lendemain,* the very next day. *— que,* from the time that; as soon as, when; since; as [scription

Désabonnement, *s.m.* discontinuing o.'s sub-

Désabonner, *v.a.* to withdraw the subscription of (. . .), to strike (. . .) off the list of subscribers

Se —, *v.r.* to discontinue *or* withdraw o.'s subscription, to cease to be a subscriber; to cease to contract; to cease to compound; to drop o.'s season *or* annual ticket

Désabusement, *s.m.* disabusing, undeceiving, destruction of illusions, loss of o.'s illusions

Désabuser, *v.a.* to disabuse, to undeceive, to destroy the illusions of

Se —, *v.r.* to disabuse *or* undeceive oneself, to be disabused, to lose o.'s illusions [ance

Désaccointance, *s.f.* (*obsolete*) disacquaint-

Désaccointer, *v.a.* (*old*) to disacquaint

Se —, *v.r.* to become disacquainted

Désaccord, *s.m.* disagreement; discord; opposition; want of harmony. *En —,* not agreed, disagreeing; at variance; on bad terms; in contradiction; inconsistent

Désaccordé, e, *part. adj.* disunited; at variance; incongruous; (*mus.*) untuned, out of tune

Désaccorder, *v.a.* to disunite; to set at variance; to make incongruous; (*mus.*) to untune, to put out of tune

Se —, *v.r.* to come *or* get out of tune

Désaccouplement, *s.m.* uncoupling

Désaccoupler, *v.a.* to uncouple. *Se —,* to get uncoupled

Désaccoutumance, *s.f.* (*obsolete*) disuse

Désaccoutumer, *v.a.* to disaccustom, to disuse, to break of the habit, to break (of), to wean (from)

Se —, *v.r.* to break oneself (of), to lose (*or* get rid of) the habit *or* custom (of), to wean oneself *or* be weaned (from), to leave off [customers

Désachalandage, *s.m.* loss of custom *or*

Désachalander, *v.a.* to take away the custom *or* customers from, to injure the custom of, to drive the customers away from, to make (*a person, a shop*) lose his *or* its customers

Se —, *v.r.* to lose o.'s (*or* its) custom *or* customers [*s.m.* disaffection
Désaffection, *s.f.*, **Désaffectionnement,**
Désaffectionner, *v.a.* to disaffect, to make disaffected [lose the affection of
Se —, *v.r.* to become *or* get disaffected; to
Désaffourcher, *v.a.n.* (*nav.*) to unmoor
Désaffubler, *v.a.* to unmuffle
Désagencement, *s.m.* putting out of order; disarrangement, disorder; throwing out of gear
Désagencer, *v.a.* to put out of order, to disarrange, to disorder; to throw out of gear
Se —, *v.r.* to get out of order; to be thrown
Désagrafer, *v.a. V.* **Dégrafer** [out of gear
Désagreable, *adj.* disagreeable, unpleasant; uncomfortable; ungracious; ungrateful; unwelcome; distasteful; obnoxious
Désagréablement, *adv.* disagreeably, unpleasantly; uncomfortably; ungraciously; ungratefully [*V.* **Dégréer**
Désagréer, *v.n.* (*old*) to displease; — *v.a.* (*nav.*)
Désagrégation, *s.f.* disaggregation
Désagréger, *v.a.* to disaggregate. *Se* —, to become disaggregated
Désagrément, *s.m.* disagreeableness, unpleasantness; uncomfortableness; disagreeable *or* unpleasant thing; discomfort; annoyance, vexation; defect, blemish
Désaguerrir, *v.a.* to disinure
Désaimanter, *v.a.*, **Se** —, *v.r.* to unmagnetize
Désajustement, *s.m.* derangement, disarrangement, putting out of order, disorder
Désajuster, *v.a.* to derange, to disarrange, to disorder, to put out of order
Se —, *v.r.* to come *or* get out of order
†**Désalignement,** *s.m.* breaking the line, coming out of the line [of the line
†**Désaligner,** *v.a.* to break the line, to put out
Se —, *v.r.* to come *or* fall out of the line
Désallier, *v.a.* to disunite [the alliance
Se —, *v.r.* to become disunited, to break off
Désaltérer, *v.a.* to quench the thirst of, to refresh [oneself, to drink
Se —, *v.r.* to quench o.'s thirst, to refresh
Désamarrer, *v.a. V.* **Démarrer**
Désamorcer, *v.a.* to uncap (*fire-arms*)
Désancrer, *v.n.* (*nav.*) to weigh anchor; — *v.a.* (*fig.*) to unfix, to detach, to get away *or* off *or* out [*v.n.* (*nav.*) to lower and fasten the sails
†**Désappareiller,** *v.a. V.* **Dépareiller;** —
Désapparier, *v.a. V.* **Déparier**
Désappointement, *s.m.* disappointment
Désappointer, *v.a.* to disappoint; to unstitch
Désapprendre, *v.a.* to unlearn, to forget
Désapproba-teur, trice, *adj.* disapproving, disapprobatory; of disapprobation; censuring, carping; — *s.m.f.* disapprover; disliker; censurer, fault-finder
Désapprobati-f, ve, *adj.* disapproving, disapprobative; of disapprobation; censuring, carping [with disapprobation
Désapprobativement, *adv.* disapprovingly,
Désapprobation, *s.f.* disapprobation, disap-
Désappropriation, *s.f.* renunciation [proval
Désapproprier (Se), *v.r.* to renounce
Désapprouver, *v.a.* to disapprove of, to blame
Désarborer, *v.a.* (*nav.*) to strike, to haul down
Désarçonner, *v.a.* to throw off the saddle, to dismount, to unhorse; to throw down; to nonplus, to disconcert, to silence, to floor, to shut up; to oust, to supplant
Désargenter, *v.a.* to unsilver; to drain of cash
Se —, *v.r.* to lose its silvering *or* plating, to become *or* get unsilvered; to spend all o.'s money [**Désarmer**); unarmed
Désarmé, e, *part. adj.* disarmed, &c. (*V.*
Désarmement, *s.m.* disarming; disarmament; dismantling; discharging
Désarmer, *v.a.* to disarm; to uncock (*fire-arms*); to dismantle, to lay up; to discharge; to unman; to unship (*the oars*); to appease, to calm; to baffle

Désarrimer, *v.a.* (*nav.*) to shift the stowage of
Désarroi, *s.m.* disarray, disorder, confusion
Désarticulation, *s.f.* disarticulation
Désarticuler, *v.a.* to disarticulate; to disjoint; to dislocate [lated, &c.
Se —, *v.r.* to become *or* get *or* be disarticu-
Désassemblage, Désassemblement, *s.m.* taking *or* coming to pieces, disjoining
Désassembler, *v.a.* to take to pieces, to disjoin; to separate, to part [joined
Se —, *v.r.* to come to pieces, to get *or* be dis-
Désassiéger, *v.a.* to raise the siege of [tion
Désassociation, *s.f.* dissociation, disassocia-
Désassocier, *v.a.* to dissociate, to disassociate
Désassorti, e, *adj.* unmatched; ill-matched, ill-sorted; jarring; unsuitable; unstocked
Désassortiment, *s.m.* unmatching; unstocking; bad assortment
Désassortir, *v.a.* to unmatch; to unstock
Désassurer, *v.a.* to disinsure
Désastre, *s.m.* disaster; break-down, failure
Désastreusement, *adv.* disastrously; very sadly
Désastreu-x, se, *adj.* disastrous; very sad
Désattrister, *v.a.*, **Se** —, *v.r.* to cheer up
Désavantage, *s.m.* disadvantage; disadvantageousness; detriment, prejudice; injury; damage; loss
Désavantager, *v.a.* to deprive of an advantage; to prejudice; to injure; to wrong; to spoil the look of; to reduce the share of (*a joint heir*)
Désavantageusement, *adv.* disadvantageously; unprofitably; unfavourably; disparagingly; unsuitably
Désavantageu-x, se, *adj.* disadvantageous; detrimental, prejudicial, injurious; unprofitable; ineligible; unfavourable; discreditable; disparaging; unsuitable; disagreeable; unprepossessing; ungainly
Désaveu, *s.m.* disavowal, denial; recantation
Désaveugler, *v.a.* to open the eyes of, to undeceive
Désavouer, *v.a.* to disavow; to disown; to deny; to disclaim; to repudiate; to disapprove; to disallow; to retract
Déscellement, *s.m.* unsealing; loosening
Désceller, *v.a.* to unseal; to loosen [loose
Se —, *v.r.* to become *or* be unsealed; to get
Descendance, *s.f.* descent, birth, extraction, lineage, pedigree, offspring, race, posterity
Descendant, e, *part. adj.* descending, going down, sloping, &c. (*V.* **Descendre**); downward, down; (*of tides*) ebb; (*mil.*) coming off duty; — *s.m.f.* descendant, offspring, progeny; — *s.m.* (*nav.*) ebb-tide, ebb. *En* —, on descending *or* going down, &c.; sloping; downward; downhill. *Aller en* —, to go down-hill, to slope
Descendre, *v.n.* to descend; to come *or* go down; to walk down; to run down; to dismount; to alight; to get down *or* out; to put up; to stay, to stop; to slope, to incline; to go down-hill; to fall; to reach; to sink, to sink down; to condescend, to stoop; to proceed, to come, to pass, to go; to enter; to land; to make a descent; to make a search; — *v.a.* to descend, to go *or* come down; to take down; to carry *or* bring down; to reach down; to get down; to fetch *or* knock down, to shoot, to kill; to let down, to lower; to put *or* set down; to take; to land; to come off. *Faire* —, to make (...) go *or* get *or* come down *or* descend; to bring down; to fetch down; to let down; to send down; to call down; to force down; to lower;
Descension, *s.f.* descension [to sink
Descensionnel, le, *adj.* descensional
Descente, *s.f.* descent; coming *or* going down; down journey; way down; taking down; getting down; letting down; alighting; declivity; fall; landing; invasion, irruption; run; search; (*of guard, mil.*) coming off; (*med.*) rupture, prolapsus, hernia; (*tech.*) pipe. — *de lit*, bedside carpet, rug

Descripteur, *s.m.* describer
Descriptible, *adj.* describable
Descripti-f, ve, *adj.* descriptive [specification
Description, *s.f.* description; inventory;
Descriptivement, *adv.* descriptively
Desdites, *adj.f.pl.*, **Desdits,** *adj.m.pl.* of *or* from the said; of *or* from the same; of *or* from
Déséchalasser, *v.a. V.* **Déchalasser** [ditto
Déséchouement, *s.m.*(*nav.*) setting afloat again
Déséchouer, *v.a.* (*nav.*) to get off, to set afloat again
Désemball-age, -er. *V.* **Déballage,** &c.
Désembarque-ment, -r. *V.* **Débarquement,** &c. [—, *v.r.* to lose o.'s *or* its beauty
Désembellir, *v.a.* to disembellish; — *v.n.*, **Se**
Désembellissement, *s.m.* disembellishment, [loss of beauty
Désemboîter, *v.a. V.* **Déboîter**
Désembourber, *v.a.* to extricate from the mire
Désembrayer, *v.a.* (*tech.*) to disengage; to separate; to reverse
Désemmancher, *v.a. V.* **Démancher**
Désemmuseler, *v.a. V.* **Démuseler**
Désemparer, *v.n.a.* to leave, to quit; to clear; to dislodge; to deprive; to disable. *Sans* —, without quitting the place; on the spot, at once; without once leaving off, without interruption *or* intermission
Désempenné, e, *adj.* stripped of feathers
Désempeser, *v.a.* to unstarch
Se —, *v.r.* to become unstarched, to lose its starch, to become limp
Désempli, e, *adj.* emptied in part, less full
Désemplir, *v.a.* to make less full, to empty; — *v.n.*, **Se** —, *v.r.* to become *or* get less full, to become *or* get empty, to be getting empty. *Ne pas* —, to be always full; to fill
Désempoissonner, *v.a.* to unstock (*a pond*)
Désemprisonner, *v.a. V.* **Déprisonner**
Désenchantement, *s.m.* disenchantment
Désenchanter, *v.a.* to disenchant. *Se* —, to be disenchanted
Désenchan-teur, teresse, *adj. s.* disenchanting; disenchanter, disenchantress
Désenchâsser, *v.a.* to unset
Désenclouage, *s.m.* unnailing; unspiking
Désenclouer, *v.a.* to unnail; to unspike
Désencombrement, *s.m.* disencumbrance
Désencombrer, *v.a.* to disencumber, to clear
Se —, *v.r.* to be disencumbered, to get clear
Désencroûter, *v.a.* to sharpen the wits of, to sharpen, to make sharp, to teach wit to, to teach, to instruct, to polish
Se —, *v.r.* to become sharp, to become less stupid *or* ignorant, to learn something
Désendetter (Se), *v.r.* to get out of debt
Désenfiler, *v.a.* to unthread; to unstring
Se —, *v.r.* to come unthreaded *or* unstrung
Désenflement, *s.m. V.* **Dégonflement**
Désenfler, *v.a. V.* **Dégonfler**; — *v.n.*, **Se** —, *v.r. V.* **Se Dégonfler** [swelling
Désenflure, *s.f.* diminution *or* cessation of
Désenfumer, *v.a.* to clear from smoke
Désengagement, *s.m.* disengagement
Désengager, *v.a.* to disengage
Désengrené, e, *adj.* out of gear
Désengrener, *v.a.* to throw out of gear
Se —, *v.r.* to be thrown out of gear
Désenivrement, *s.m. V.* **Dégrisement**
Désenivrer, *v.a.*, **Se** —, *v.r. V.* **Dégriser**; — *v.n. Ne pas* —, to be always drunk, never to [be sober
Désenlacer, *v.a.* to disentangle
Désenlaidir, *v.a.* to make *or* render less ugly; — *v.n.*, **Se** —, *v.r.* to become *or* get less ugly
Désennui, *s.m.* solacement, amusement, recreation, diversion [amuse, to divert
Désennuyer, *v.a.* to dispel the tedium of, to
Se —, *v.r.* to dispel *or* drive away o.'s tedium *or* dulness, to amuse *or* divert oneself, to find amusement, to kill time
Désenrayer, *v.a.* to unskid
Désenrhumer, *v.a.* to cure of a cold; — *v.n. Ne pas* —, to have always a cold
Se —, *v.r.* to cure o.'s cold, to get rid of o.'s (*or* a) cold
Désenrôlement, *s.m.* disenrolment, discharge
Désenrôler, *v.a.* to disenroll, to discharge
Désenrouement, *s.m.* cessation of hoarseness
Désenrouer, *v.a.* to cure of hoarseness; — *v.n. Ne pas* —, to be always hoarse
Se —, *v.r.* to cure (*or* get rid of) o.'s hoarseness
Désensabler, *v.a. V.* **Déséchouer**
†**Désenseigner,** *v.a.* to unteach
Désensevelir, *v.a.* to unwrap, to unshroud; to exhume, to disinter
Désensevelissement, *s.m.* unwrapping, unshrouding; exhumation, disinterment
Désensorceler, *v.a.* to unbewitch
Se —, *v.r.* to be unbewitched
Désensorcellement, *s.m.* unbewitching
Désentêter, *v.a.* to drive out of the head of; to cure of infatuation *or* obstinacy; to dispel the headache of [of obstinacy
Se —, *v.r.* to get out of o.'s head; to be cured
†**Désentortiller,** *v.a. V.* **Détortiller**
Désentraver, *v.a.* to unfetter; to unshackle
Désenverguer, *v.a.* (*nav.*) to unbend (*sails*)
Désert, e, *adj.* desert, deserted, solitary; uninhabited; unfrequented; wild, waste, uncultivated; empty
Désert, *s.m.* desert, wilderness, solitude, waste
Déserter, *v.a.n.* to desert; to leave; to forsake, [to abandon
Déserteur, *s.m.* deserter
Désertion, *s.f.* desertion
Désespérance, *s.f.* despair
Désespérant, e, *part. adj.* despairing, &c. (*V.* **Désespérer**); desperate, hopeless; disheartening, dispiriting, discouraging; grievous, afflicting, distressing, distracting, provoking; unconquerable; unmanageable; inimitable, unapproachable, matchless
Désespéré, e, *adj.* desperate, hopeless; disheartened, despondent, disconsolate, in despair; distressed, grieved; despaired of, past recovery; very sorry; — *s.m.f.* desperate man *or* woman, desperado; madman, mad woman. *En* —, desperately; furiously; madly, like a madman
Désespérément, *adv.* desperately; with a desperate effort; despairingly; hopelessly
Désespérer, *v.n.* to despair, to despond, to give over; — *v.a.* to drive to despair; to dishearten, to dispirit, to discourage; to torment; to give great anxiety to, to distress; to provoke
Se —, *v.r.* to give oneself up to despair, to give way to despair, to be in despair, to despair, to despond
Désespoir, *s.m.* despair; desperation; hopelessness; despondency; grief, affliction; "ne plus ultra." *Au* —, in despair; grieved, distressed; vexed, very sorry. *Mettre au* —, to drive to despair, to grieve, to distress; to vex. *En — de cause*, despairing of success; as a last shift [dishabille
†**Déshabillé,** *s.m.* undress, morning-wrapper,
†**Déshabiller,** *v.a.* to undress; to strip
Déshabité, e, *adj.* uninhabited, no longer inhabited, deserted
Déshabituer, *v.a. V.* **Désaccoutumer**
Désharmonie, *s.f.* disharmony
Désharmonier, Désharmoniser, *v.a.*, **Se** —, *v.r.* to disharmonize
Désharmonieu-x, se, Désharmonique, *adj.* unharmonious, discordant
Désharmonisation, *s.f.* disharmonization
Déshérence, *s.f.* escheat [herison
Déshéritement, *s.m.* disinheritance, disin-
Déshériter, *v.a.* to disinherit
Désheurer, *v.a.* to derange the hours of, to disturb, to disturb (*one*) in his occupations *or* habits; — *v.n.* (*of clocks*) to strike one time and mark another
Se —, *v.r.* to change o.'s hours, to disturb oneself, to disturb oneself *or* be disturbed in o.'s occupations *or* habits

Déshonnête, *adj.* immodest, indecent [cently
Déshonnêtement, *adv.* immodestly, inde-
Déshonnêteté, *s.f.* immodesty, indecency
Déshonneur, *s.m.* dishonour; disgrace; shame; discredit; ruin. *Tenir à —*, to consider as dishonourable
Déshonorable, *adj. V.* **Déshonorant**
Déshonorablement, *adv.* dishonourably
Déshonorant, e, *adj.* dishonourable; disgraceful; shameful; discreditable; disparaging
Déshonorer, *v.a.* to dishonour; to disgrace, to be a disgrace to; to bring shame upon; to discredit; to tarnish; to disparage; to accomplish the ruin of, to ruin; to spoil
Desideratum, *s.m.*, **Desiderata,** *s.m.pl.* desideratum, desiderata [distinctive
†**Désignati-f, ve,** *adj.* designative, indicative,
†**Désignation,** *s.f.* designation; indication; description; election, choice; appointment, nomination
†**Désigner,** *v.a.* to designate; to indicate; to describe; to point out; to point to; to denote, to betoken; to elect, to choose; to appoint; to mention; to name; to call; to nominate; to assign; to fix
Désillusion, *s.f.*, **Désillusionnement,** *s.m.* disillusion, loss of illusions, return to reality; disappointment
Désillusionner, *v.a.* to destroy *or* dispel the illusions of, to bring back *or* to open the eyes (of ...) to reality, to undeceive; to disappoint
Se —, *v.r.* to lose o.'s illusions, to be undeceived *or* disappointed [disembodying
Désincorporation, *s.f.* disincorporation;
Désincorporer, *v.a.* to disincorporate; to dis-
Désinence, *s.f.* termination, ending [embody
Désinfatuer, *v.a.* to cure of infatuation, to disabuse, to undeceive [cease to be infatuated
Se —, *v.r.* to cure oneself of infatuation, to
Désinfectant, e, *part. adj.* disinfecting; deodorizing; — *s.m.* disinfectant; deodorizer
Désinfecter, *v.a.* to disinfect; to deodorize
Se —, *v.r.* to become *or* be disinfected *or* deodorized
Désinfec-teur, trice, *adj.* disinfecting; deodorizing; — *s.m.* disinfectant; deodorizer
Désinfection, *s.f.* disinfection; deodorization, deodorizing
Désintéressé, e, *adj.* disinterested; uninterested; unconcerned; indifferent; unselfish; unbiassed; impartial; indemnified, &c. (*V.* **Désintéresser**)
Désintéressement, *s.m.* disinterestedness; self-denial; indifference; impartiality
Désintéressément, *adv.* disinterestedly
Désintéresser, *v.a.* to indemnify; to buy out the interest of; to reimburse, to refund, to repay; to satisfy
Se —, *v.r.* to indemnify oneself; to lose o.'s interest (in); to be indifferent (to)
†**Désinterligner,** *v.a.* (*print.*) to unlead
Désinvestir, *v.a.* to deprive, to divest; (*law*) to devest; (*mil.*) to raise the siege of
Désinvestissement, *s.m.* deprivation, disinvestiture; (*mil.*) raising the siege
Désinviter, *v.a.* to disinvite
Désinvolte, *adj.* unconstrained, unrestrained; free, easy; open, straightforward
Désinvolture, *s.f.* easy and graceful manners, easy carriage, unconstrained motion, free and easy manner, ease, gracefulness
Désir, *s.m.* desire, wish; longing
Désirable, *adj.* desirable
Désirer, *v.a.* to desire, to wish; to wish for; to long for; to want. *A —*, to desire, &c.; to be desired; desirable; wanting. *Laisser à —*, to be below the mark, to be inferior; to leave (...) to be desired. *Se faire —*, not to make oneself cheap; to keep people waiting
Désireu-x, se, *adj.* desirous; anxious; solicitous; eager
Désistement, *s.m.* desistance; (*law*) nonsuit

Désister (Se), *v.r.* to desist; to give over; to abandon; to renounce; to waive
Desman, *s.m.* (*zool.*) desman, musk-rat
Desmite, *s.f.* (*med.*) desmitis
Desmo-graphie, -logie, -pathie, -tomie, &c. *V.* page 3, § 1 [to be disobedient
Désobéir, *v.n.* to disobey; to refuse to obey;
Désobéissance, *s.f.* disobedience; undutifulness; act of disobedience; (*law*) contempt, contumacy [contumacious
Désobéissant, e, *adj.* disobedient; undutiful;
Désobligeamment, *adv.* disobligingly, unkindly, offensively [ness, offensiveness
Désobligeance, *s.f.* disobligingness, unkind-
Désobligeant, e, *adj.* disobliging, unkind, ungracious, unaccommodating, unfriendly, offensive; — *s.f.* (*sort of carriage*) sulky [offend
Désobliger, *v.a.* to disoblige; to displease; to
Désobstruant, e, *adj.*, **Désobstruant,** *s.m.* (*med.*) deobstruent [ant
Désobstructi-f, ve, *adj.*, *s.m. V.* **Désobstru-**
Désobstruction, *s.f.* deobstruction, clearance
Désobstruer, *v.a.* to deobstruct, to clear from obstruction, to clear, to free, to disencumber
Se —, *v.r.* to become *or* be deobstructed, &c.
Désoccupation, *s.f.* inactivity, want of occupation *or* employment, leisure
Désoccupé, e, *adj.* unoccupied, unemployed; disengaged, at leisure; vacant; idle; without an object
Désoccuper (Se), *v.r.* to cease to be occupied, to leave o.'s occupation; (*de* ...) to give up ..., to dismiss ...
Désœuvré, e, *adj. s.* unoccupied, unemployed, free from business, inactive, idle; idler
Désœuvrement, *s.m.* want of employment *or* occupation, want of something to do, idleness
Désolant, e, *adj.* disheartening, distressing, grievous; sad; tiresome; vexing, provoking
Désola-teur, trice, *s.m.f. adj.* desolator, ravager, destroyer; bore, plague; desolating, ravaging, destructive [vexation
Désolation, *s.f.* desolation; grief, affliction;
Désolé, e, *part. adj.* desolated, &c. (*V.* **Désoler**); desolate; disconsolate, distressed, grieved; vexed, annoyed; extremely sorry
Désoler, *v.a.* to desolate, to waste, to lay waste; to distress, to grieve, to afflict; to vex, to annoy, to trouble, to worry, to plague; to harass
Se —, *v.r.* to lament, to grieve; to be distressed [deobstruent; — *s.m.* (*med.*) deobstruent
Désopilant, e, *adj.* funny, laughable; (*med.*)
Désopilati-f, ve, *adj.*, **Désopilatif,** *s.m.* (*med.*) *V.* **Désobstruant**
Désopilation, *s.f.* (*med.*) deobstruction, clearance [— *la rate*, (*fig.*) *V.* **Rate**
Désopiler, *v.a.* (*med.*) to deobstruct, to clear.
Se —, *v.r.* to be *or* become deobstructed *or* cleared; to be *or* make merry, to cheer up, to brighten up, to be amused
Désordonné, e, *adj.* disorderly; irregular; unruly; inordinate; immoderate; excessive; extravagant
Désordonnément, *adv.* disorderly; irregularly; inordinately; immoderately; excessively
Désordonner, *v.a.* to disorder, to disturb [order
Se —, *v.r.* to become disordered, to get out of
Désordre, *s.m.* disorder; confusion; irregularity; perturbation; disturbance; tumult; riot; licentiousness, debauchery, dissipation; excess; dissension; devastation, havoc, ravage, plunder; agitation [ing; disorganizer
Désorganisa-teur, trice, *adj. s.* disorganiz-
Désorganisation, *s.f.* disorganization; disorder [**Se —,** *v.r.* to become disorganized, &c.
Désorganiser, *v.a.* to disorganize; to disorder.
Désorienter, *v.a.* to turn from the east; to make (*one*) lose his way; to lead astray; to mislead; to put out, to disconcert, to bewilder, to confuse; to put out of o.'s element *or* latitude. *Être désorienté*, to lose o.'s way; to be out of o.'s way, to have lost o.'s way; to be out

of o.'s element *or* latitude; to be put out *or* disconcerted *or* &c.

Se —, *v.r.* to lose o.'s way, not to know where one is; to get confused, to be disconcerted

Désormais, *adv.* henceforth, hereafter, from this time *or* moment, in future

Désorner, *v.a.* to disadorn

Désossement, *s.m.* boning

Désosser, *v.a.* to bone

Se —, *v.r.* to be boned; to disjoint oneself

Désouci, *s.m.* carelessness, heedlessness

Désourdir, *v.a.* to unweave

Désoxydation, *s.f.* (*chem.*) deoxidation, deoxidization, deoxydation, deoxydization, disoxidation, &c.

Désoxyder, *v.a.*, **Se —,** *v.r.* (*chem.*) to deoxidate, to deoxidize, to deoxydate, to deoxydize, to disoxidate, &c. [genation

Désoxygénation, *s.f.* deoxygenation, disoxy-

Désoxygéner, *v.a.*, **Se —,** *v.r.* (*chem.*) to deoxygenate, to disoxygenate

Despote, *s.m.* despot; — *adj.* despotic

Despot-ique, -iquement, -isme. *V.* page 3, [§ 1

Despumation, *s.f.* despumation

Despumer, *v.a.* to despumate

***Desquamation,** *s.f.* desquamation

***Desquamer,** *v.a.*, **Se —,** *v.r.* to desquamate

Desquelles [*contraction of* **De lesquelles;** *has some of the senses of* **Dont**]

Desquels [*contraction of* **De lesquels;** *has some of the senses of* **Dont**] [of sand

Dessabler, *v.a.* to take the sand out of, to clear

Dessaboté, e, *adj.* unhoofed

Dessaisir, *v.a.* to dispossess; (*nav.*) to unfasten

Se —, *v.r.* to part (with), to let go, to give up, to yield, to resign; to divest oneself

Dessaisissement, *s.m.* parting (with), giving up, divesting oneself, cession, relinquishment, renunciation

Dessaisonnement, *s.m.* (*agr.*) alteration in the rotation of crops; (*hort.*) growing out of season

Dessaisonner, *v.a.* (*agr.*) to change the rotation of crops on; (*hort.*) to grow out of season

Dessalaison, *s.f.* *V.* **Dessalement**

Dessalé, e, *part. adj.* freshened, soaked, unsalted; (*pers.*) sharp, cunning; — *s.m.f.* sharp fellow, sharp woman; bad woman, harlot

Dessalement, *s.m* clearing from salt; soaking

Dessaler, *v.a.*, **Se —,** *v.r.* to freshen, to soak; to water

Dessangler, *v.a.* to ungirth, to ungirt, to ungird

Desséché, e, *part. adj.* dried up, dried, &c. (*V.* **Dessécher**); dry

Dessèchement, *s.m.* drying up, drying; dryness; drainage; withering; emaciation

Dessécher, *v.a.* to dry up, to dry; to parch; to drain; to emaciate, to waste; to wither; to heal up; to deprive of feeling, to harden

Se —, *v.r.* to dry up, to dry, to become dry; to be parched; to be drained; to waste away; to wither; to harden

Dessein, *s.m.* design, intention, intent, purpose, aim, end, project, view, scheme, plan, resolution. *A* —, designedly, intentionally, purposely, on purpose. *A — de,* in order to. *Avoir* — or *le — de,* to intend

Desseller, *v.a.* to unsaddle

Dessemelé, e, *adj.* without sole *or* soles

Dessemeler, *v.a.* to take the sole *or* soles off; to wear out the sole *or* soles of

Desserrage, *s.m.* loosening; unlocking

Desserre, *s.f.* loosening; loosening of the purse-strings; opening; breaking up. *Dur à la* —, close-fisted

Desserrer, *v.a.* to loosen, to loose; to slacken; to relax; to open; to undo; to unlock; to give (*a kick, a blow,* &c.). — *les dents,* to open o.'s mouth *or* lips, to speak, to utter one word

Se —, *v.r.* to get loose; to relax; to loosen [o.'s clothes

Dessert, *s.m.* dessert

Desserte, *s.f.* leavings (*of a table*); duty, duties (*of churches*), officiating; serving, service; working; connection; taking away, clearing. *Chemin de* —, connecting road

Dessertir, *v.a.* to unset (*gems,* &c.)

Se —, *v.r.* to come unset [clergyman; curate

Desservant, *s.m.* worker; officiating priest *or*

Desservir, *v.n.a.* to take away, to remove the cloth, to clear (the table); to do an ill office to (*a person*); to perform the service *or* work *or* duty of; to do duty *or* officiate in *or* at, to serve; to serve for; to work; to ply on, to run *or* ply between ... and ..., to run on, to run *or* go to; to meet, to wait on; to connect; to lead to

Dessiccant, e, *adj.* desiccant, drying

Dessiccateur, *s.m.* desiccator, exsiccator

Dessiccati-f, ve, *adj.* desiccative, desiccant, drying; — *s.m.* desiccative, desiccant

Dessiccation, *s.f.* desiccation, drying

†Dessiller, *v.a.*, **Se —,** *v.r.* (*of eyes*) to open

Dessin, *s.m.* drawing; design; pattern; sketch, outline; draught, plan; model; (*mus.*) arrangement

Dessina-teur, trice, *s.m.f.* draughtsman, drawer; pattern-drawer; designer; modeller. — *de jardins,* landscape-gardener

Dessiner, *v.a.* to draw; to design; to sketch; to delineate; to define; to mark; to indicate; to trace; to form; to frame; to make; to lay out; to represent; to set off, to show off, to show; (*mus.*) to arrange

Se —, *v.r.* to appear, to become perceptible, to be visible *or* seen; to assume a form; to be delineated *or* marked; to become evident; to be conspicuous; to come out, to show off, to show, to stand out in relief, to stand out, to be set off; to display o.'s shape to advantage; to show oneself as one is; to declare o.'s intentions [rotation of crops

Dessolement, *s.m.* (*agr.*) alteration in the

Dessoler, *v.a.* to unsole, to take off the sole of (*a horse,* &c.); (*agr.*) to change the rotation of crops on [&c.); (*agr.*) *V.* **Dessolement**

Dessolure, *s.f.* taking off the sole (*of a horse,*

Dessouder, *v.a.* to unsolder

Se —, *v.r.* to get unsoldered

Dessoudure, *s.f.* unsoldering

Dessoufrage, *s.m.* desulphuration

Dessoufrer, *v.a.* to desulphurate, to desulphurize [desulphurated

Se —, *v.r.* to lose its sulphur, to become *or* be

†Dessouiller, *v.a.* to purify, to cleanse

Se —, *v.r.* to become purified, &c.

Dessoûler, *v.a.n.* *V.* **Désenivrer** *&* **Dégriser**

Dessous, *adv. prep.* under, underneath; below; undermost; under it; under them; under him; under her; — *s.m.* under *or* lower part; under side; under-stratum; bottom; basement floor; wrong side; face (*of a card*); stand; mat; inferiority, disadvantage, worst, defeat; secret; (*nav.*) lee. — *de chapeau,* bonnet-cap. — *de lampe,* lamp-mat. *Au-* —, under; below; underneath; beneath; lower down; under it *or* him *or* her *or* them; below it *or* him *or* her *or* them. *De* —, from under; from below; under, lower. *En* —, underneath; downward; artful, sly, hypocritical; artfully, slily. *Par* —, under, underneath. *Avoir le* —, to have *or* get the worst of it, to be worsted, to get *or* be beaten. *Le — des cartes, V.* **Carte.** *Le — du vent,* (*nav.*) leeward. *Jusqu'au troisième* —, very [deep

Dessuintage, *s.m.* scouring (*of wool*)

Dessuinter, *v.a.* to scour (*wool*)

Dessus, *adv. prep.* on, upon; over; above; uppermost; upwards; at; in; on *or* upon it, on *or* upon them; over it, over them; above it, above them; on *or* upon him *or* her; over him *or* her; — *s.m.* upper part; upper side; upper stratum; roof, loft; top; cover; superscription (*of letters,* &c.), address; back; right side; upper hand, superiority, advantage, best, victory; (*mus.*) treble; (*nav.*) weathergage. — *de fauteuil,* antimacassar. — *de marbre,* marble top. — *de porte,* frieze-panel. — *de table,* table-cover; epergne. — *de toilette,* toilet-cover. *Au-* —, on, upon; over; above; higher up; on or upon or &c. it or him or her or them; beyond; upwards; beyond the reach (of). *De* —, off; from; from above; upper, top; outer; (*mus.*) treble. *En* —, on, upon; over; above; at or on the top; on the upper side. *Par* —, on, upon; over; above; besides; over and above; into; uppermost; — *s.m.* overcoat. *Avoir le* —, to have the best of it or the advantage, to get the upper hand; to be uppermost. *Prendre le* —, to gain the ascendant or the ascendency (over), to assume the mastery (over), to get the better (of), to get the upper hand. *Le* — *du vent*, (*nav.*) the weathergage. *Être au-* — *du vent*, (*nav.*) to be to windward [career, course, life

Destin, *s.m.* destiny, fate; fatality; lot; doom;

Destinataire, *s.m.f.* receiver, recipient; (*post.*)

Destina-teur, trice, *s.m.f.* sender [addressee

Destination, *s.f.* destination; intention; destiny. *A* or *en* — *de*, (*post.*) addressed to; (*nav.*) bound to

Destiné, e, *part. adj.* (*V.* **Destiner**) destined; doomed; fated; intended; born; (*post.*) addressed (to); (*nav.*) bound (to)

Destinée, *s.f. V.* **Destin**

Destiner, *v.a.* to destine; to doom; to fate; to intend; to mean (for); to design; to appoint; to assign; to reserve; to have or lay in store (for); to prepare; to devote

Se —, *v.r.* to be destined or intended

Destituable, *adj.* removable (*from office*)

Destitué, e, *part. adj.* dismissed, removed, discharged, cashiered; destitute, devoid, void

Destituer, *v.a.* to dismiss, to remove, to discharge, to cashier, to turn out; to deprive

Destitution, *s.f.* dismissal, removal, discharge

Destrier, *s.m.* (*obsolete*) destrer, war-horse, steed, charger

Destruc-teur, trice, *adj.* destructive, destroying; blasting; subversive; mischievous; — *s.m.f.* destroyer

Destructibilité, *s.f.* destructibility

Destructible, *adj.* destructible

Destructi-f, ve, *adj.* destructive, destroying

Destruction, *s.f.* destruction

Destructioniste, *s.m.f.* destructionist

Destructivité, *s.f.* destructiveness

Désudation, *s.f.* (*med.*) desudation

Désuétude, *s.f.* desuetude, disuse

Désuint-age, -er. *V.* **Dessuintage,** &c.

Désulfuration, *s.f. V.* **Dessoufrage**

Désulfurer, *v.a. V.* **Dessoufrer** [loose

Désuni, e, *part. adj.* disunited, &c. (*V.* **Désunir**);

Désunion, *s.f.* disunion; separation; disjunction

Désunir, *v.a.* to disunite; to separate, to part; to divide; to disjoin; to disjoint; to disconnect

Se —, *v.r.* to disunite; to separate, to part; to divide; to fall out; to be disunited or disjoined or disjointed

Désusité, e, *adj.* out of use, obsolete, exploded

Détachage, *s.m.* removal of spots, scouring, cleaning

Détaché, e, *part. adj.* detached, &c. (*V.* **Détacher**); loose; unconnected; rambling; indifferent; of indifference; disinterested; isolated, alone, separated from the rest. *Morceaux* —*s*, *pièces* —*es*, (*liter.*) extracts, unconnected pieces

Détachement, *s.m.* disengagement; indifference; disinterestedness; (*mil.*) detachment; draught

Détacher, *v.a.n.* to detach; to loose, to loosen; to let loose; to send off, to send; to untie; to unbind; to unfasten; to undo; to unfix; to unrivet; to unchain; to take off or out or away or down; to cut or break off; to pluck; to part; to separate; to remove; to disengage; to wean; to show in relief, to show off; to give or fetch or deal (*a blow, a kick,* &c.); to take out the spots or stains of, to scour, to clean; to remove spots or stains; (*mil.*) to detach; to draught

Se —, *v.r.* to be loosened or &c.; to get loose; to get untied; to come off or out; to come undone; to fall off or away; to detach or disengage or separate or wean oneself; to be detached or disengaged or separated or weaned; to part (with); to give up; to leave off; to break or break off (from); to quit, to leave; to stand (or come) out in relief, to show off, to appear; to be scoured or cleaned

Détacheu-r, se, *s.m.f.* scourer

†**Détail,** *s.m.* detail, particular; circumstance; detailed or circumstantial account; item; (*fam.*) small matter or affair, trifle, minor point, mere nothing; (*com.*) retail; retail trade or business. *En* —, in detail; minutely; bit by bit; by inches; by degrees; in parts; each separately; (*com.*) by retail, retail [retail dealer; publican

†**Détaillant, e,** *adj.* retail; — *s.m.f.* retailer,

†**Détaillé, e,** *part. adj.* cut up, &c. (*V.* **Détailler**); detailed, particular, circumstantial, with every particular, minute, lengthened, lengthy

†**Détailler,** *v.a.n.* to cut up, to cut in pieces; to detail, to relate minutely, to tell the particulars of; to give a full or particular account of; to examine or consider separately; to enter into particulars; to retail, to sell by retail

Se —, *v.r.* to be cut up; to be detailed or related minutely; to be examined or considered separately; to be retailed or sold by retail

†**Détailleu-r, se,** *s.m.f.* detailer; retailer

†**Détailliste,** *s.m.f.* detailer, writer who abounds or excels in details, minute describer

Détalage, *s.m.* (*of goods*) taking in; packing up

Détaler, *v.a.n.* to take in (*goods*); to pack up; to shut up shop; to scamper away, to be off, to move off or on, to go on, to toddle

Détalinguer, *v.a.n.* (*nav.*) to unbend (*a cable*)

Détaper, *v.a.* (*artil.*) to take the tampion out of

Détaxe, *s.f.* taking off a tax or charge [(*a gun*)

Détaxer, *v.a.* to take the tax or charge off

Déteindre, *v.a.* to take out the colour of; — *v.n.*, **Se** —, *v.r.* to lose its dye or colour, to fade; to come off; to wash off; (*fig.*) to be inconsistent. — *sur* ..., the dye (of ...) to come off upon ...; (*fig.*) to leave its mark on ..., to leave a mark or a stain on ...; to have an influence on ..., to make its influence felt on or in ... [unyoking; uncoupling

Dételage, *s.m.* taking out or off, unharnessing;

Dételer, *v.a.n.* to take out or off, to unharness; to unyoke; to detach; to uncouple; to separate; (*fig.*) to stop, to shut up

Détendre, *v.a.* to unbend; to unstring; to slacken; to loosen; to relax; to take down; to unhang; to strike; (*of weather*) to make milder; — *v.n.* to take down the tapestry or hangings; to strike tents

Se —, *v.r.* to unbend; to slacken; to loosen; to become milder, to give; to become easier

Détenir, *v.a.* to detain; to withhold; to keep; to confine

Détente, *s.f.* unbending, relaxing; (*of fire-arms*) trigger; (*of clocks*) detent, stop; (*mach.*) expansion; (*fig.*) relaxation. *A la* —, in pulling the trigger. *Dur à la* —, stiff in the trigger; (*fig.*) close-fisted

Déten-teur, trice, *s.m.f.* holder, detainer

Détention, *s.f.* detention; confinement, imprisonment

Détenu, e, *part. adj.* detained; withheld; kept; confined, in confinement, in prison; — *s.m.f.* prisoner; convict; — *s.f.* (*law*) detinue

Détergent, e, *adj.*, **Détergent,** *s.m.* detergent

Déterger, *v.a.* to deterge, to cleanse

Détérioration, *s.f.* deterioration; impairment; damage; debasement; defacement; wear and tear

Détériorer, *v.a.* to deteriorate; to impair; to damage; to spoil; to make worse; to debase; to deface [impaired or &c., to grow worse

Se —, *v.r.* to deteriorate; to become (or get)

Déterminable, *adj.* determinable

Déterminant, e, *adj.* determinative; decisive; inducing; efficient
Déterminati-f, ve, *adj.*, **Déterminatif,** *s.m.* determinative, definitive
Détermination, *s.f.* determination; tendency
Déterminé, e, *part. adj.* determined, &c. (*V.* **Déterminer**); determinate; bold; resolute; firm; confirmed; — *s.m.f.* determined *or* resolute *or* desperate man *or* woman *or* fellow *or* girl *or* thing [minedly, resolutely; firmly
Déterminément, *adv.* determinately; deter-
Déterminer, *v.a.* to determine; to fix; to appoint; to settle; to limit; to ascertain; to resolve; to decide; to cause, to occasion, to bring on *or* about; to induce; to lead; to persuade, to influence [to be determined *or* &c.
Se —, *v.r.* to come to a decision; to resolve;
Déterré, e, *part. of* **Déterrer**; — *s.m.* exhumed body. *Avoir l'air* or *le visage d'un* —, *avoir une mine de* —, to look like a corpse, to have a ghastly look [exhumation; discovery
Déterrement, *s.m.* digging up, disinterment,
Déterrer, *v.a.* to take out of the ground, to unearth, to dig up; to disinter, to exhume; to discover, to find out, to find, to search out, to hunt out, to ferret out, to bring to light
Déterreur, *s.m.* resurrectionist, resurrection-man; discoverer, hunter, ferreter
Détersi-f, ve, *adj.*, **Détersif,** *s.m.* detergent,
Détersion, *s.f.* detersion [detersive
Détestable, *adj.* detestable, hateful, abominable, odious; wretchedly bad, wretched
Détestablement, *adv.* detestably, hatefully, abominably; wretchedly [rence
Détestation, *s.f.* detestation, hatred, abhor-
Détester, *v.a.* to detest, to hate, to abhor; to dislike; — *v.n.* (*old*) to curse, to swear
†**Détignonner,** *v.a.* (*pop.*) to tear the hair of
Détirer, *v.a.* to draw out, to draw; to stretch, to stretch out; to wire-draw [calm, to quell
Détiser, *v.a.* to rake out (*the fire*); to still, to
Détisser, *v.a.* to unweave. *Se* —, to get un-
Détitrer, *v.a.* to distitle [weaved
Détonation, *s.f.* detonation, report. *A* —, detonating [*or* conspicuous
Détoner, *v.n.* to detonate; (*fig.*) to be too loud
Détonnation, *s.f.* being *or* playing *or* singing out of tune
Détonneler, *v.a.* to draw out of a cask
Détonner, *v.n.a.* to be out of tune, to play *or* sing out of tune; to bawl out; to jar, to clash
Détordage, *s.m.* untwisting; picking
Détordre, *v.a.* to untwist; to pick (*oakum*)
Se —, *v.r.* to come untwisted
Détorquer, *v.a.* to wrest, to distort
Détors, e, *adj.* untwisted
†**Détortiller,** *v.a.* to untwist; to unravel
Se —, *v.r.* to come *or* be untwisted; to be
Détoucher, *v.n.* (*nav.*) to get off [unravelled
Détouper, *v.a.* to unstop, to take the tow out of; to open; (*agr.*) to clear of thorns *or* brambles
†**Détoupillonner,** *v.a.* to prune (*orange-trees*)
Détour, *s.m.* winding; turn, turning; way round, roundabout way, circuit; recess; fold; evasion, subterfuge, shift, dodge. *Sans* —, straightforward, plain; straightforwardly, plainly; sincerely. *Faire* or *prendre un* —, to go a roundabout way, to go round; to wind; to turn
Détourne, *s.f.* *Vol à la* —, (*pop.*) shop-lifting
Détourné, e, *part.* (*V.* **Détourner**); — *adj.* (*of roads*, &c.) retired, by; (*fig.*) indirect. *Chemin* —, by-way, by-road
Détournement, *s.m.* turning aside *or* away; making away (with); misappropriation; embezzlement; defalcation; abstraction. — *de mineur*, (*law*) abduction of a minor
Détourner, *v.a.* to take out of o.'s road *or* way; to lead astray; to turn aside *or* away *or* off; to turn; to avert, to keep off, to ward off, to ward; to divert; to wrest, to strain; to deter, to dissuade; to disturb; to misappropriate; to embezzle; to take away, to steal away, to abstract; to abduct; (*hunt.*) to start; (*old*) to turn up; — *v.n.* to turn off, to turn
Se —, *v.r.* to go out of the (*or* o.'s) road *or* way, to deviate from the road; to turn aside *or* away *or* round; to swerve, to deviate; to be diverted; to leave off
Détourneu-r, se, *s.m.f.* (*pop.*) shop-lifter
Détracter, *v.a.n.* to detract, to traduce, to slander [slanderer; — *adj.* detracting
Détrac-teur, trice, *s.m.f.* detractor, traducer,
Détraction, *s.f.* detraction [*animals*)
Détranger, *v.a.* (*hort.*) to drive away (*noxious*
Détraqué, e, *part. adj.* deranged, &c. (*V.* **Détraquer**); out of order; crazy; having lost its paces
Détraquement, *s.m.* derangement; disorder
Détraquer, *v.a.* to spoil the paces of (*a horse*); to derange, to put out of order, to disorder; to throw into disorder; to unsettle; to lead astray
Se —, *v.r.* to get out of order, to become (*or* get) deranged *or* disordered *or* unsettled; to break up; to go wrong *or* astray; to lose its paces
Détrempe, *s.f.* distemper; painting in distemper. *En* —, *à la* —, in distemper; (*fig.*) sham, mock, pretended; feeble; slight. *Ouvrage en* —, work which is a feeble imitation of another
Détremper, *v.a.* to soak; to dilute; to dissolve; to moisten; to water, to temper (*lime, mortar*); to soften (*steel*); (*fig.*) to weaken, to enervate, to soften [*or* enervated
Se —, *v.r.* to soak; to soften; to be weakened
Détresse, *s.f.* distress; misery; affliction, sorrow, grief, trouble; anguish [plait; to untwist
Détresser, *v.a.* to unweave; to unplat; to un-
Se —, *v.r.* to come unweaved, &c.; to unplat o.'s hair [(*obsolete*) remains
Détriment, *s.m.* detriment, injury, prejudice;
Détritage, *s.m.* (*tech.*) crushing
Détriter, *v.a.* (*tech.*) to crush
Détrition, *s.f.* detrition
Détritique, *adj.* detrital
Détritoir, *s.m.* edge-mill (*for crushing olives*)
Détritus, *s.m.* detritus; remains; residue; refuse; heap of rubbish
Détroit, *s.m.* strait; pass; narrow; sound; frith, firth; (British) Channel; (*obsolete*) district
Détrompement, *s.m.* undeceiving
Détromper, *v.a.* to undeceive [deceived
Se —, *v.r.* to undeceive oneself, to be un-
Détroncation, *s.f.* (*surg.*) detruncation
Détrônement, *s.m.* dethronement
Détrôner, *v.a.* to dethrone
Détrôneur, *s.m.* dethroner
Détrousser, *v.a.* to untuck; to let down; to rifle, to rob, to plunder
Se —, *v.r.* to let down o.'s dress
Détrousseur, *s.m.* robber, highwayman
Détruire, *v.a.* to destroy; to ruin; to pull down; to demolish; to overthrow; to defeat; to do away with; to put to death, to kill; to annul; to neutralize; to tear up; to break up
Se —, *v.r.* to destroy oneself, to make away with oneself; to ruin oneself; to destroy *or* ruin *or* neutralize each other; to be destroyed; to fall to ruin *or* into decay; to wear itself out; to die away
Dette, *s.f.* debt; (*fig.*) debt, obligation, duty, promise, pledge. —*s actives*, debts due from others, book-debts, assets. —*s passives*, debts due to others, debts, liabilities. *La Dette*, (*obsolete*) the debtors' prison, the Fleet
Détumescence, *s.f.* (*med.*) detumescence
†**Deuil,** *s.m.* mourning; sorrow, grief, affliction; mournful aspect; gloom, gloominess; mourners; black. *Demi-* —, *petit* —, half *or* second mourning. *Grand* —, deep mourning. *Conduire* or *mener le* —, to be chief mourner. *Faire son* — *de*, to make up o.'s mind to the loss of, to give up for lost *or* as a bad job; to make up o.'s mind *or* reconcile oneself to. *Porter le* —, to wear *or* put on mourning; to be in mourning (for); to mourn (for). *Prendre le* —, to go into

mourning. *Faire prendre le — à*, to make (*one*) wear mourning, to put (*one*) into mourning. *Suivre le —*, to be a mourner, to be one of the mourners

Deus ex machinâ, *s.m.* (*Latin*) Deus ex machinâ, supernatural agency, machinery; evasion, wonderful means *or* shift

Deutérogame, *s.m.f.* deuterogamist

Deutéro-gamie, -logie. *V.* page 3, § 1

Deutéronome, *s.m.* Deuteronomy

Deuto-, (*in compounds, chem.*) deuto-...

Deutoxyde, *s.m.* (*chem.*) deutoxide

Deux, *adj.m.f.*, *s.m.* two; both; second; deuce; two things, two different things; (*rid.*) both spurs. *— à —*, two by two. *De — en —*, every other, every two. *De — jours l'un*, every other day. *En —*, in *or* into two; asunder. *Nous —*, both of us. *A nous —*, to *or* at *or* &c. both of us; between us; between you and me; I am your man, I'll settle with you, now I am ready for you. *Tous —, tous les —*, both. *Tous les — jours, ans*, &c., every other day, year, &c. *Piquer* (or *donner*) *des —*, to spur o.'s horse, to spur away; to speed, to lose no time. **—-mâts,** *s.m.* (*nav.*) two-master. **—-ponts,** *s.m.* (*nav.*) two-decker [second floor; — *s.f. V.* **Seconde,** *s.f.*

Deuxième, *adj.* second; other; — *s.m.* second;

Deuxièmement, *adv.* secondly

Dévalement, *s.m.* sloping, slope; going down; letting down, lowering

Dévaler, *v.n.* to slope; to descend, to go *or* come down, to slip down; — *v.a.* to descend, to go *or* come down; to let down, to lower

Dévalisement, *s.m.* rifling, robbing, robbery, plundering, plunder, stripping

Dévaliser, *v.a.* to rifle, to rob, to plunder, to

Dévaliseu-r, se, *s.m.f.* robber, plunderer [strip

Devancer, *v.a.* to precede, to go before; to outrun, to outstrip, to distance, to get ahead of, to head; to get the start of, to anticipate, to forestall; to take precedence of; to excel, to surpass, to outdo; to be beyond *or* above

Devanci-er, ère, *s.m.f.* predecessor; forefather, ancestor

Devant, *prep. adv.* before; in front of; opposite to; in advance of; ahead of; in (*or* in the) presence of; from; at; to; with; in front; opposite; in advance; ahead; forward; foremost; before it, before them; in front of it *or* them; ahead of it *or* them; — *s.m.* front; front part; forepart; (*of boots, shoes*) vamp; (*paint.*) foreground. *— d'autel*, frontal. *— de cheminée*, chimney-board. *Au- —*, towards, forward to meet, to meet; before; on before; in front; over against. *De —*, fore; front. *Par —*, before; forward; in front; in (*or* in the) presence of. *Sur le —*, in front. *Aller* or *venir au- — de*, to go *or* come to meet; to anticipate; to meet half-way; to provide for *or* against; to secure; to make sure of; to prevent; to be beforehand; to obviate; to meet; to encounter, to brave, to oppose; to seek. *Aller droit — soi*, to go straight on, to go straight ahead. *Avoir de l'argent — soi*, to have money at hand. *Bâtir sur le —*, (*fig., fam.*) to get stout; to be in the family way. *Marcher — soi*, to walk on; to go forward. *Prendre* or *gagner les —s*, to go *or* start first; to take the first steps; to go before *or* ahead; to get the start (of), to be beforehand (with), to forestall. *Ôtez-vous de — moi*, stand out of my sight; get out of my light. *Les premiers vont —*, first come, first served

Devant, [*part. of* **Devoir**] owing; intending; intended; being on the point of; being certain, being sure; being likely; who *or* which must;

Devantier, *s.m.* (*pop.*) apron [who *or* which is (to)

Devantière, *s.f.* riding-petticoat

Devanture, *s.f.* front (*of buildings*)

Dévasta-teur, trice, *adj. s.* destructive, devastating; destroyer, ravager

Dévastation, *s.f.* devastation; ravage; havoc

Dévaster, *v.a.* to lay waste, to devastate, to ravage, to spoil

Déveine, *s.f.* change of a run of good luck to bad, reverses, run of ill luck, ill luck

Développable, *adj.* developable, that may be developed, capable of development

Développante, *s.f.* (*geom.*) evolvent, involute

Développée, *s.f.* (*geom.*) evolute

Développement, *s.m.* unfolding; unwrapping; opening; development; growth; progress; enlargement; expansion; extent; display; explanation, exposition; elucidation; clearing up; (*geom.*) evolution

Développer, *v.a.* to unfold; to unwrap; to open; to develop; to evolve; to enlarge; to expand; to spread out; to extend; to display; to explain, to expound; to unravel; to elucidate; to clear up; to bring to light; to carry out

Se —, *v.r.* to develop oneself *or* itself; to display *or* &c. itself; to evolve; to expand; to spread out; to extend; to grow; to thrive; to clear up; to become (*or* be) developed, &c.

Devenir, *v.n.* to become, to grow, to get, to turn; to be made; to turn to; to become of; to do; to come (to); to turn out, to end; to prove; to be. *Faire —*, to make; to drive, to turn

Déventer, *v.a.* (*nav.*) to take the wind out of, to spill, to shiver (*sails*)

Dévergondage, *s.m.* open profligacy; shamelessness; intemperance; disorder, irregularity; eccentricity

Dévergondé, e, *adj.* dissolute, licentious, profligate; shameless, lost to shame, barefaced, impudent; intemperate; disorderly, irregular; eccentric; — *s.m.f.* profligate; shameless *or* barefaced person

Dévergonder, *v.a.* to render dissolute *or* shameless; to make intemperate *or* &c. (*V.* **Dévergondé**)

Se —, *v.r.* to become dissolute *or* licentious; to throw off all restraint; to run riot; to lose all shame; to become intemperate *or* &c. (*V.* **Dévergondé**)

Déverguer, *v.a.* (*nav.*) *V.* **Désenverguer**

Dévernir, *v.a.* to unvarnish

Se —, *v.r.* to come unvarnished, to lose its

†Déverrouillement, *s.m.* unbolting [varnish

†Déverrouiller, *v.a.* to unbolt

Devers, *prep.* (*old*) towards; about; to; near. *Par —*, (*law*) before; to. *Par — soi*, in o.'s possession; for *or* to oneself [ing, jutting out

Dévers, e, *adj.* (*tech.*) inclining, leaning, bend-

Dévers, *s.m.* (*tech.*) inclination

Déversement, *s.m.* inclining, leaning, bending, inclination, bent, warping; pouring, flowing, running, falling, fall, discharge, overflow; casting, throwing

Déverser, *v.n.a.* to incline, to lean, to bend, to warp; to pour out *or* down, to pour; to turn off; to discharge; to flow, to run, to fall, to overflow; to cast, to throw

Se —, *v.r.* to incline, to lean, to bend, to warp; to discharge *or* empty itself, to fall, to overflow; to be cast *or* thrown

Déversoir, *s.m.* weir; drain; (*fig.*) outlet

Dévestiture, *s.f.* divestiture

Dévêtement, *s.m.* stripping

Dévêtir, *v.a.* to unclothe, to undress; to strip; to take off, to throw off; to divest

Dévêtissement, *s.m.* divestiture

Déviation, *s.f.* deviation

Dévidage, *s.m.* winding

Dévider, *v.a.* to wind (*thread*)

Dévideu-r, se, *s.m.f.* winder (*pers.*)

Dévidoir, *s.m.* winder, reel [off; to swerve

Dévier, *v.n.a.*, **Se —,** *v.r.* to deviate; to glance

Devin, e, *s.m.f.* diviner, divineress, soothsayer, conjurer; — *s.m.* (*zool.*) buffalo-snake

Devinable, *adj.* guessable, to be guessed

Deviner, *v.a.* to divine; to guess; to guess at; to conjecture; to forecast, to foretell, to predict; to find out; to recognize, to know [other

Se —, *v.r.* to be guessed; to understand each

Devineresse, *s.f.* (*fem. of* **Devineur**) divineress, soothsayer, conjurer

Devineur, *s.m.* diviner, soothsayer, conjurer; guesser, diviner

Devineuse, *s.f.* (*fem. of* **Devineur**) diviner-ess, soothsayer, conjurer; guesser, diviner

Dévirer, *v.a.* (*nav.*) to recoil, to heave back

Devis, *s.m.* estimate; specification; plan; (*obsolete*) conversation, talk, chat

Dévisager, *v.a.* to disfigure; to tear the face of; to stare at, to stare right in the face of, to stare out of countenance, to outface

Devise, *s.f.* device; motto; posy; emblem

Deviser, *v.n.* (*old*) to converse, to talk, to chat

Dévissage, Dévissement, *s.m.* unscrewing

Dévisser, *v.a.* to unscrew

Se —, *v.r.* to unscrew; to come *or* be unscrewed

Dévitrifiable, *adj.* devitrifiable

Dévitrification, *s.f.* devitrification

Dévitrifier, *v.a.* to devitrify

Dévoiement, *s.m.* relaxation, looseness, diarrhœa; (*arch.*) inclination, slope

Dévoilement, *s.m.* unveiling; disclosing; exposition; display

Dévoiler, *v.a.* to unveil; to uncover; to disclose; to discover; to display; to reveal; to expose; to show; to absolve (*a nun*) from her vows

Se —, *v.r.* to unveil; to be unveiled *or* &c.; to open; to display itself; to betray oneself; to be found out

Devoir, *s.m.* duty; (*of schools*) work, task; exercise; paper; (*of workmen*) trade-union; **—s**, *pl.* duties, &c.; work; respects. *En — de*, ready to. *Se faire un — de*, to make it o.'s duty to; to make a point of, to make it a point to. *Se mettre en — de*, to prepare, to set oneself, to set about, to set to work. *Compagnon du —*, *V.* **Dévorant**, *s.m.*

Devoir, *v.a.n.* to owe; to be indebted for; to owe money, to be in debt; must; to be obliged *or* bound *or* compelled, to have (to); to have need (of), to need; to be (to); to intend; to be intended; to be certain *or* likely; cannot but; should, ought; were to; shall; must do, ought to do; to have reason (to); (*obsolete*) to be inferior *or* second (to). **Se —**, *v.r.* to owe oneself; to owe it to oneself; to be a duty; must *or* should be done; to be right; ought to be; to be owing; to owe to each other. *Vous devez être fatigué*, you must be tired. *Comme vous avez dû souffrir!* how you must have suffered! *Il a dû payer le dégât*, he has had to pay for the damage. *J'ai dû en être blessé*, I could not but be (*or* I could not help being) offended at it. *La douleur qu'il dut éprouver*, the pain which he must have felt. *Cela ne se doit pas*, that must (*or* should) not be done, that ought not to be, that is not right. *Je le dois*, I ought to *or* must do it. *Je dois lui répondre demain*, I am to (*or* I intend to) answer him to-morrow. *Il devait quitter Paris hier*, he was to leave Paris yesterday. *Il a dû* (or *il avait dû*) *quitter Paris hier*, he was to have left Paris yesterday. *Dans sa jeunesse il devait être à craindre*, in his youth he must have been formidable. *Je crois — lui répondre*, I think it my duty (I think it right *or* proper) to answer him. *Il semblait — réussir*, he seemed sure *or* likely to succeed (his success seemed certain). *Vous deviez sortir*, you were obliged to go out; you were to (*or* must) go out; you were to have gone out; you must have gone out; you ought to *or* should have gone out. *Vous aviez dû sortir*, you must have gone out. *Vous devrez sortir*, you will have to go out. *Vous aurez dû sortir*, you must have gone out. *Vous devriez sortir*, you ought to *or* should go out. *Vous auriez dû sortir*, you ought to *or* should have gone out. *Il devait être dix heures*, it must have been ten o'clock. *Dussé-je*, though I should, were I to

Dévoirant, *s.m.* *V.* **Dévorant**

Dévole, *s.f.* (*at cards*) having no trick. *Être en —, faire la —*, to lose all the tricks

Dévoler, *v.n.* (*at cards*) to lose all the tricks

Dévolu, e, *adj.* devolved; vested; awarded; fallen; due; belonging; imposed; doomed. *Être —*, to devolve; to be vested *or* awarded *or* &c.

Dévolu, *s.m.* lapse of right. *Jeter son — sur*, to fix o.'s choice upon

Dévolution, *s.f.* devolution; escheat

Dévorant, e, *adj.* devouring; consuming; wasting; burning; sultry; ravenous, voracious; — *s.m.f.* voracious person, great eater; — *s.m.* member of the "Duty" [*Devoir*] society *or* trade-union, trade-unionist

Dévora-teur, trice, *s.m.f. adj.* devourer; devouring; consuming [**Dévorer**); a prey (to)

Dévoré, e, *part. adj.* devoured, &c. (*V.* **Dévorer**)

Dévorer, *v.a.* to devour; to eat up; to swallow up; to consume; to waste; to destroy; to squander; to run through; to plunder; to prey upon; to distract; to inflame; to stifle, to suppress, to check; to master, to surmount, to overcome; to swallow, to brook, to pocket; to covet; to pore over; to read right through; to sweep along, to sweep; (*fam.*) to scratch furiously. — *des yeux*, to devour with o.'s eyes, to gaze at, to pore over, to gloat over. — *l'espace*, to go at full speed, to glide through space. — *la route*, to tear along the road. — *le temps*, to make the most of o.'s time; to burn with impatience

Dévoreu-r, se, *s.m.f.* devourer, — *de livres*, devourer of books, hard reader, bookworm

Dévot, e, *adj.* devout, godly, pious, religious; bigoted; — *s.m.f.* devout *or* pious *or* religious person; devotee, bigot. *Faux —*, devotee, bigot

Dévotement, Dévotieusement, *adv.* devoutly, piously, religiously; bigotedly, like a bigot

Dévotieu-x, se, *adj. s. V.* **Dévot**

Dévotion, *s.f.* devotion, piety, religion; bigotry; devotedness; disposal, service, command, bidding. *Faire ses —s*, to receive the sacrament

Dévoué, e, *adj.* devoted; unselfish; true, sincere; faithful; trusty; zealous; affectionate, loving; at the service (of). *Votre —, votre tout —*, yours truly *or* sincerely *or* faithfully, yours

Dévouement, *s.m.* devotedness, devotion; self-denial, self-devotion, self-sacrifice; attachment; zeal

Dévouer, *v.a.* to devote, to consecrate, to dedicate; to consign; to sacrifice

Dévoûment, *s.m.* *V.* **Dévouement**

Dévoyé, e, *part. adj.* misled, &c. (*V.* **Dévoyer**); sloping; — *s.m.f.* wanderer, stray *or* lost sheep

Dévoyer, *v.a.* to take *or* place the wrong way; to mislead, to misguide, to lead astray; to place obliquely; to put out of order, to relax, to give the diarrhœa; — *v.n.*, **Se —**, *v.r.* to lose o.'s way; to go astray; to swerve; to be placed obliquely; to be relaxed, to have *or* give oneself the diarrhœa

Dextérité, *s.f.* dexterity, skill

Dextre, *adj.* (*her.*) dexter; (*obsolete*) right; dexterous, skilful; — *s.f.* (*obsolete*) right hand; right-hand side, right

Dextrement, *adv.* (*old*) dexterously, skilfully

Dextrine, *s.f.* (*chem.*) dextrine

Dey, *s.m.* dey

Dia, *int.* (*to horses*) hoi! (*to the left!*) *A —*, on *or* to the left

Diabase, *s.m.* (*min.*) diabase, greenstone

Diabète, *s.m.* (*med.*) diabetes; (*phys.*) Tantalus's cup

Diabétique, *adj. s.m.f.* (*med.*) diabetic

Diable, *s.m. int.* devil; deuce; the devil, the deuce; old Nick; hell; wild child; fellow; dog; wretch; truck, drag, trolly, tug, gill; (*machine*) willow, willy, devil; (*toys*) humming-top; devil on two sticks; Jack-in-the-box; (*fig.*) difficulty, rub; (a) dreadful job; — *adj.* bad; mischievous. — *à quatre*, regular devil, arrant imp. — *de, du —, de tous les —s*, devil of, devilish, wretched, terrible, tremendous, dreadful; terribly, dreadfully. *A la —*, devilish bad; wretchedly; in a slipslop way; slovenly; at sixes and sevens; higgledy-piggledy; at random; anyhow; as well as one can *or* could; (*cook.*) devilled. *Au —, à tous les —s*, to *or* at the devil *or* deuce; confound ...! hang ...

out upon ...! the devil take ...! the devil take it! a very long way off. *Au — vert*, a tremendous long way off, a devil of a way. *Bien le — si*, very hard if. *Du — si*, the devil a bit if; the devil take me if. *En —*, like the devil, devilishly, devilish; terribly, tremendously. *Avoir le — au corps*, to have the devil *or* deuce in one, to be mad *or* restless. *Faire le — à quatre*, to play the very devil. *Faire voir le — à*, to play all sorts of tricks to; to be a dreadful plague to. *Tirer le — par la queue*, to struggle hard for a living, to be miserably poor, to be hard up. *Ne valoir pas le —*, not to be worth a rap. *Le — s'en mêle*, the devil is in it. *C'est là le —*, there is the devil of it, there is the rub. *Ce n'est pas le —*, it is no great catch; it is not much. *Il a le — au corps*, the devil is in him, he is mad. *Que —!* what the devil! hang it! come! *Que le — emporte ...! le — soit de ...!* the devil take ...! *Le — bat sa femme et marie sa fille*, it rains and shines at the same time. *La beauté du —*, youth, freshness [ish lot

Diablement, *adv.* devilishly, devilish; a devil-

Diablerie, *s.f.* witchcraft; devilry; jugglery; sly *or* wicked trick; mischievousness, wildness; (*drawing*) devil, devils

Diablesse, *s.f.* vixen, shrew, she-devil, devil; bitch; wretch; creature, thing

Diablotin, *s.m.* imp, little devil; chocolate-cracker, cracker; cream-cake; (*nav.*) mizzen-top stay-sail

Diabolique, *adj.* diabolical, devilish

Diaboliquement, *adv.* diabolically, devilishly

Diabrose, *s.f.* (*med.*) diabrosis

Diabrotique, *adj.m.f., s.m.* (*med.*) diabrotic

Diacaustique, *adj.m.f., s.f.* diacaustic

Diachylon, Diachylum, *s.m.* (*pharm.*) diachylon, diachylum [poppies

Diacode, *s.m.* (*pharm.*) diacodium, syrup of

Diaconal, e, *adj.* diaconal

Diaconat, *s.m.* deacon's orders; deaconry

Diaconesse, *s.f.* deaconess

Diaconie, *s.f.* almonry

Diaconiser, *v.a.* to ordain a deacon

Diacope, *s.f.* (*fish*) diacope [tics

Diacoustique, *adj.* diacoustic; — *s.f.* diacous-

Diacre, *s.m.* deacon

Diacritique, *adj.* diacritic, diacritical

Diadelphe, *adj.* (*bot.*) diadelphous

Diadelphie, *s.f.* (*bot.*) diadelphia

Diadelphique, *adj.* (*bot.*) diadelphian

Diadème, *s.m.* diadem; crown; royalty

Diaggot, *s.m.* birch-oil

Diagnose, *s.f.* (*med., nat. hist.*) diagnosis

Diagnostic, *s.m.* (*med.*) diagnosis

Diagnostique, *adj.* (*med.*) diagnostic; — *s.f.* diagnostics, diagnosis [to diagnose

Diagnostiquer, *v.a.* (*med.*) to diagnosticate,
 Se —, *v.r.* to be diagnosticated *or* diagnosed

Diagomètre, *s.m.* (*phys.*) diagometer

Diagométr-ie, -ique. *V.* page 3, § 1 [diagonal

Diagonal, e, *adj.* (*geom.*), *s.f.* (*geom.*), *s.m.* (*rid.*)

Diagonalement, *adv.* diagonally

Diagramme, *s.m.* diagram; (*fish*) diagramma

Diagraphe, *s.m.* diagraph

Diagraphie, *s.f.* diagraphics

Diagraphique, *adj.* diagraphic

Dialecte, *s.m.* dialect

Dialecticien, ne, *s.m.f.* dialectician

Dialectique, *s.f.* dialectics

Dialect-ique (*adj.*), **-iquement.** *V.* page 3, § 1

Diallage, *s.f.* (*min.*) diallage

Dialogique, *adj.* dialogistic

Dialogiquement, *adv.* dialogistically

Dialog-isme, -iste. *V.* page 3, § 1

Dialogue, *s.m.* dialogue

Dialoguer, *v.n.a.* to converse, to talk; to carry on *or* conduct a dialogue; to put in dialogue
 Se —, *v.r.* to be put in dialogue

Dialogueur, *s.m.* dialogue-writer, dialogist

Dialyse, *s.f.* (*chem., surg., rhet.,* &c.) dialysis

Dialyser, *v.a.* (*chem.*) to dialyze

Dialyseur, *s.m.* (*chem.*) dialyzer

Dialytique, *adj.* dialytic

†**Diamagnét-ique, -isme.** *V.* page 3, § 1

Diamant, *s.m.* diamond; adamant; jewel; gem; diamond-ring; (*nav.*) crown *or* throat (*of an anchor*)

Diamantaire, *adj.* diamond-like, brilliant like diamond; — *s.m.* diamond-cutter *or* worker

Diamanter, *v.a.* to adorn *or* cover with diamonds, to diamondize; to make diamond-like; to render sparkling *or* brilliant; to tinsel; to frost [diamantiferous

Diamantifère, *adj.* productive of diamonds,

Diamantin, e, *adj.* adamantine

Diamétral, e, *adj.* diametrical, diametral

Diamétralement, *adv.* diametrically

Diamètre, *s.m.* diameter

Diandre, *adj.* (*bot.*) diandrous

Diandrie, *s.f.* (*bot.*) diandria

Diandrique, *adj.* (*bot.*) diandrian, diandrous

Diane, *s.f.* (*mil., nav.*) morning drum, morning gun *or* flourish, morning call, reveille

Diantre, *s.m. int.* (the) deuce, (the) dickens. — — *de*, deuced. — *soit de ...!* the deuce take ...!

Diantrement, *adv.* deucedly; a deuced lot

Diapason, *s.m.* diapason, pitch; compass; tuning-fork; (*sifflet-* —) pitch-pipe; (*fig.*) pitch; tune; tone; level; standard, measure. *Mettre au — de*, to tune to, to attune to; to adapt to; to chime *or* join in with

Diapasonner, *v.a.* to tune, to attune

Diapédèse, *s.f.* (*med.*) diapedesis [parent

Diaphane, *adj.* diaphanous, translucent; trans-

Diaphanéité, *s.f.* diaphaneity, transparency

Diaphanomètre, *s.m.* (*phys.*) diaphanometer

Diaphanométr-ie, -ique. *V.* page 3, § 1

Diaphanorama, *s.m.* diaphanorama

Diaphanoscope, *s.m.* diaphanoscope

Diaphorèse, *s.f.* (*med.*) diaphoresis

Diaphorétique, *adj.m.f., s.m.* (*med.*) diaphoretic

Diaphragmatique, *adj.* diaphragmatic

Diaphragmatite, *s.f.* (*med.*) diaphragmatitis

Diaphragme, *s.m.* diaphragm; (*anat.*) diaphragm, midriff [diaphragmitis

Diaphragmite, *s.f.* (*med.*) diaphragmatitis,

Diapré, e, *adj.* diapered, variegated; violet (*plum*); — *s.m.* diapering, diaper work; — *s.f.*

Diaprer, *v.a.* to diaper, to variegate [violet plum
 Se —, *v.r.* to become diapered *or* variegated

Diaprure, *s.f.* diapering, variegation

Diapyétique, *adj.m.f., s.m.* (*med.*) diapyetic

Diarrhée, *s.f.* diarrhœa

Diarrhéique, *adj. s.* (*med.*) diarrhœtic

Diarthrose, *s.f.* (*anat.*) diarthrosis

Diascordium, *s.m.* (*pharm.*) diascordium

Diaspore, *s.m.* (*min.*) diaspore

Diastase, *s.f.* (*surg.*) diastasis; (*chem.*) diastase

Diastole, *s.f.* (*anat.*) diastole

Diastolique, *adj.* (*anat.*) diastolic

Diastyle, *s.m. adj.* (*arch.*) diastyle

Diathèse, *s.f.* (*med.*) diathesis

Diatome, *s.m.* (*bot.*) diatom

Diatomées, *s.f.pl.* (*bot.*) diatomaceæ, diatoms

Diaton-ique, -iquement. *V.* page 3, § 1

Diatribe, *s.f.* diatribe; castigation

Dicacité, *s.f.* (*obsolete*) waggery, causticity

Dicéphale, *adj.* dicephalous

‡**Dichotome,** *adj.* (*nat. hist., astr.*) dichotomous

‡**Dichotom-ie, -ique.** *V.* page 3, § 1

‡**Dichroïsme,** *s.m.* (*phys.*) dichroism

‡**Dichromatique,** *adj.* (*phys.*) dichromatic

Dicline, *adj.* (*bot.*) diclinous [*s.f.* dicotyledon

Dicotylédone, *adj.* (*bot.*) dicotyledonous; —

Dicotylédoné, e, *adj.* (*bot.*) dicotyledonous;

Dicrane, *s.m.* (*bot.*) dicranum [— *s.f.* dicotyledon

Dicrote, *adj.* (*med.*) dicrotic

Dictame, *s.m.* (*bot.*) dittany (of Crete, *kind of marjoram*); (*fig.*) balm, remedy

Dictamen, *s.m.* dictates

Dictamne, *s.m.* (*bot.*) dictamnus, dittany, frax-

Dictateur, *s.m.* dictator [inella

Dictatorial, e, *adj.* dictatorial

Dictature, *s.f.* dictatorship, dictature
Dictée, *s.f.* dictation
Dicter, *v.a.* to dictate; to suggest, to prompt; to inspire with; to prescribe, to impose
Diction, *s.f.* diction; delivery [gazetteer
Dictionnaire, *s.m.* dictionary; vocabulary;
Dictionnariste, *s.m.f.* dictionary-maker
Dicton, *s.m.* saying, common saying, old saw, byword; jeer
Dictum, *s.m.* (*law*) *V.* **Dispositif,** *s.m.*
Didactique, *s.f.* didactics; — *s.m.* didactic language *or* style
Didact-ique (*adj.*), **-iquement.** *V.* page 3, § 1
Didactyle, *adj.m.f.*, *s.m.* (*zool.*) didactyle, di-
Dideau, *s.m.* (*fish.*) crossing-net [dactylous
Didelphe, *s.m.* (*zool.*) didelph, didelphys; —
Didisque, *s.m.* (*bot.*) didiscus [*adj.* didelphic
Didyme, *adj.* (*bot.*) didymous; — *s.m.* (*chem.*)
Didymite, *s.f.* (*med.*) didymitis [didymium
Didyname, *adj.* (*bot.*) didynamous
Didynamie, *s.f.* (*bot.*) didynamia
Didynamique, *adj.* (*bot.*) didynamian
Dièdre, *adj.* (*geom.*) dihedral
Dieppois, e, *adj.s.* of Dieppe; native of Dieppe
Diérèse, *s.f.* (*gram.*, *surg.*) diæresis
Dièse, *s.m. adj.* (*mus.*) sharp
Diéser, *v.a.* (*mus.*) to sharp [*or* nothing, to diet
Diète, *s.f.* diet; low diet. *Faire* —, to eat little
Diététique, *adj.* (*med.*) dietary, dietetic; — *s.f.*
Diététiquement, *adv.* dietetically [dietetics
Diététiste, *s.m.* dietetist
Diétine, *s.f.* dietine
Dieu, *s.m.* God, deity; (*fam.*) Goodness. — *veuille!* God grant! *Grâce à* —, — *merci*, thank God, thank Goodness; I am thankful to say. *Mon* —! —! good God! good Heavens! Lord! my Goodness! dear me! dear! bless me! why, well, indeed. *Bon* —! *Grand* —! good God! *Le bon* —, (*fam.*) God; the host. *Jurer ses grands* —*x*, to swear by all that is sacred. *Pour l'amour de* —, *pour* —, for God's sake, for the love of God, for Goodness' sake. *Comme pour l'— de Dieu*, as if one did not care, carelessly, slovenly; reluctantly
Dieudonné, *s.m.* Heaven-sent, Heaven-born
Diffamant, e, *adj.* defamatory, libellous, slanderous [slanderer
Diffama-teur, trice, *s.m.f.* defamer, libeller,
Diffamation, *s.f.* defamation, libel, libelling,
Diffamatoire, *adj. V.* **Diffamant** [slander
Diffamer, *v.a.* to defame, to libel, to slander,
Différemment, *adv.* differently [to traduce
Différence, *s.f.* difference; distinction; dissimilarity; disagreement; discrepancy; diversity; contrast; disproportion; disparity; odds; test. — *de longitude*, (*geogr.*) meridian distance. — *en longitude*, (*nav.*) departure. — *en moins*, difference against (...); decrease. — *en plus*, difference in favour of (...); increase. *A la* — *de*, contrary to, quite contrary to. *A la* — *que*, except that [tion
Différenciation, *s.f.* distinction; differentia-
Différencier, *v.a.* to distinguish, to make a difference between; (*math.*) to differentiate
Se —, *v.r.* to be distinguished, to differ (from), to be different (from), to be dissimilar (to), to grow different
Différenciomètre, *s.m.* (*nav.*) draught-gauge
Différend, *s.m.* difference, dispute, quarrel, variance; (*of value*) difference. *Partager le* —, to split the difference
Différent, e, *adj.* different; differing; unlike; distinct; various, divers, sundry
Différentiation, *s.f.* (*math.*) differentiation
Différentiel, le, *adj.*, **Différentielle,** *s.f.* differential
Différentier, *v.a.* (*math.*) to differentiate
Différer, *v.a.n.* to defer, to delay, to put off; — *v.n.* to differ; to be different; to disagree
Se —, *v.r.* to be deferred *or* delayed *or* put off
Difficile, *adj.* difficult, hard; trying; painful; troublesome; rough, steep, narrow *or* &c., difficult of access; unaccommodating; exacting; hard to please, fastidious; particular, nice; (*of horses*) shy, skittish, wilful; — *s.m.f.* fastidious person; — *s.m.* difficulty, difficult thing; objection [hardly
Difficilement, *adv.* with difficulty, not easily,
Difficulté, *s.f.* difficulty; impediment, hindrance, obstacle; perplexity, embarrassment; trouble; roughness; objection; scruple; difference, quarrel, tiff; fuss; rub
Difficultueusement, *adv.* fastidiously; scrupulously; with difficulty; with fuss
Difficultueu-x, se, *adj.* unreasonably fastidious, squeamish, fidgety, never satisfied; over particular; over scrupulous; fussy; captious; crotchety; cross-grained; full of diffi-
Difforme, *adj.* deformed [culties, intricate
Difformer, *v.a.* to deform; to deface (*coins*)
Difformité, *s.f.* deformity [diffracted
Diffracter, *v.a.* (*phys.*) to diffract. *Se* —, to be
Diffracti-f, ve, *adj.* (*phys.*) diffractive
Diffraction, *s.f.* (*phys.*) diffraction
Diffrangibilité, *s.f.* (*phys.*) diffrangibility
Diffrangible, *adj.* (*phys.*) diffrangible
Diffringence, *s.f.* (*phys.*) diffringency
Diffringent, e, *adj.* (*phys.*) diffringent [vague
Diffus, e, *adj.* diffuse; prolix; wordy, verbose;
Diffusément, *adv.* diffusely; wordily
Diffusibilité, *s.f.* diffusibility
Diffusible, *adj.* diffusible
Diffusi-f, ve, *adj.* diffusive
Diffusion, *s.f.* diffusion; diffuseness, diffusiveness; prolixity; wordiness, verbosity; vagueness
Diffusivement, *adv.* diffusively [gastric muscle
Digastrique, *adj.* (*anat.*) digastric; — *s.m.* di-
Digérer, *v.n.a.* to digest; to brook, to stomach; to bear, to stand, to tolerate, to put up with; to believe, to swallow
Se —, *v.r.* to be digested *or* &c.
Digeste, *s.m.* digest
Digesteur, *s.m.* digester (*vessel*)
Digestibilité, *s.f.* digestibility
Digestible, *adj.* digestible
Digesti-f, ve, *adj.*, **Digestif,** *s.m.* digestive
Digestion, *s.f.* digestion
Digital, e, *adj.* (*anat.*) digital; — *s.f.* (*bot.*) digitalis, foxglove; (*fish.*) parr, brandling, fingerling (*young salmon*)
Digitaline, *s.f.* (*chem.*) digitaline
Digitalique, *adj.* (*chem.*) digitalic
Digitation, *s.f.* digitation
Digité, e, *adj.* digitate
Digitiforme, *adj.* digitiform
Digitigrade, *adj.m.f.*, *s.m.* (*zool.*) digitigrade
Diglyphe, *s.m.* (*arch.*) diglyph [(*fam.*) just like
†Digne, *adj.* worthy; deserving; dignified;
†Dignement, *adv.* worthily; handsomely, nobly; properly, suitably; with dignity
†Dignifier, *v.a.* to dignify
†Dignitaire, *s.m.f.* officer, dignitary
†Dignité, *s.f.* dignity; title; stateliness; power; dignitary. *Constitué en* —, raised to dignity *or* to power; dignified. *Faire de la* —, to play at dignity, to assume an air of dignity *or* of offended dignity [(*fish.*) hook
Digon, *s.m.* (*nav.*) pole (*of a mast*), flag-yard;
Digresser, *v.n.* to digress
Digresseur, *s.m.* digresser
Digressi-f, ve, *adj.* digressive
Digression, *s.f.* digression
Digressivement, *adv.* digressively
†Diguail, *s.m.* (*fish.*) crossing-net
Digue, *s.f.* dike, dam, embankment, bank, mound, causeway, pier, mole; (*fig.*) barrier, bound, check, obstacle; bulwark, security
Diguement, *s.m.* embankment; dike, dam, causeway [to spur up
Diguer, *v.a.* to dike, to dam, to embank; (*rid.*)
Se —, *v.r.* to be diked *or* &c.
Diguial, *s.m.* (*fish.*) crossing-net
Digyne, *adj.* (*bot.*) digynous
Digynie, *s.f.* (*bot.*) digynia

Digynique, *adj.* (*bot.*) digynian
Dijonais, e, Dijonnais, e, *adj. s.* of Dijon, Dijonese, native of Dijon
Dilacération, *s.f.* dilaceration, tearing
Dilacérer, *v.a.* to dilacerate, to tear
Dilapida-teur, trice, *s.m.f.* dilapidator; embezzler; — *adj.* wasteful, extravagant; embezzling [bezzlement
Dilapidation, *s.f.* dilapidation, waste; em-
Dilapider, *v.a.* to dilapidate, to waste; to em-
Dilatabilité, *s.f.* dilatability [bezzle
Dilatable, *adj.* dilatable, expansible
Dilatant, e, *adj.* dilating; of dilatation; — *s.m.* dilater, dilatator
Dilatateur, *s.m.* (*surg.*) dilatator, dilatatorium; (*anat.*) dilatator; — *m.*, **-trice,** *f.*, *adj.* dilating
Dilatation, *s.f.* dilatation, dilation, expansion, distension; (*med.*) enlargement
Dilatatoire, *s.m.* (*surg.*) *V.* **Dilatateur**
Dilater, *v.a.*, **Se** —, *v.r.* to dilate, to expand, to extend, to distend, to enlarge
Dilateur, *s.m.* dilater
Dilation, *s.f.* delay
Dilatoire, *adj.* dilatory
Dilatoirement, *adv.* dilatorily
Dilection, *s.f.* (*obsolete*) dilection, love, charity
Dilemmatique, *adj.* dilemmatic
Dilemme, *s.m.* dilemma [(*pl.* dilettanti)
Dilettante (*pl.* **Dilettanti**), *s.m.* dilettante
Dilettantisme, *s.m.* dilettantism
Diligemment, *adv.* diligently; speedily, promptly, quickly, expeditiously
Diligence, *s.f.* diligence; speed, promptitude, expedition, despatch, haste; lesson, work, summary of a lecture; stage-coach, coach, "diligence"; (*rail., obsolete*) first-class carriage; (*law*) suit, proceedings. — *d'eau,* (*obsolete*) passage-boat
Diligent, e, *adj.* diligent, industrious, assiduous, careful; speedy, prompt, quick, expeditious; active, watchful
Diligenter, *v.a.* to hasten, to speed, to despatch, to forward, to urge on, to push on; — *v.n.*, **Se** —, *v.r.* to hasten, to make haste, to be
Dillénie, *s.f.* (*bot.*) dillenia [quick
Dilogie, *s.f.* dilogy (*drama in two distinct parts*)
Diluer, *v.a.* to dilute. *Se* —, to be diluted
Dilution, *s.f.* dilution [diluvian
Diluvial, e, Diluvien, ne, *adj.* diluvial,
Diluvion, Diluvium, *s.m.* diluvium
Dîmable, *adj.* tithable [Shrove Sunday
Dimanche, *s.m.* Sunday; sabbath. — *gras,*
Dimanchi-er, ère, *s.m.f.* (*pop.*) sabbatarian
Dîme, *s.f.* tithe; (*American coin*) dime
Dîmée, *s.f.* tithing
Dimension, *s.f.* dimension; measure
Dîmer, *v.n.a.* to tithe
Dîmeur, *s.m.* tithe-collector, tithe-gatherer
Diminué, e, *part. adj.* diminished, &c. (*V.* **Diminuer**); (*of columns*) tapering
Diminuendo, *adv. s.m.* (*mus.*) diminuendo (*gradual decrease from loud to soft*); (*fig.*) *V.* **Decrescendo**
Diminuer, *v.a.n.* to diminish; to decrease; to lessen; to shorten; to abridge; to curtail; to retrench; to take off; to dwindle; to reduce; to lower; to abate; to slacken; to impair; to weaken; to sink; to go down; to fall; to fall away; (*of columns*) to taper [nutive
Diminuti-f, ve, *adj.*, **Diminutif,** *s.m.* dimi-
Diminution, *s.f.* diminution; decrease; abridgment; curtailment; retrenchment; deduction; reduction; abatement; impairment; sinking;
Diminutivement, *adv.* diminutively [tapering
Dimissoire, *s.m.* (*eccl.*) letter dimissory
Dimissorial, e, *adj.* (*eccl.*) dimissory
Dimorphe, *adj.* (*nat. hist.*) dimorphous [phism
Dimorphie, *s.f.*, **Dimorphisme,** *s.m.* dimor-
Dinanais, e, *adj. s.* of Dinan, Dinanese, native
Dinanderie, *s.f.* brass wares [of Dinan
Dinandier, *s.m.* brazier
Dinandois, e, *adj. s.* (*obsolete*) *V.* **Dinanais**

Dinarique, *adj.* (*geog.*) Dinaric
Dînatoire, *adj.* of dinner, dinner. *Déjeuner* —, late lunch, lunch-dinner
Dinde, *s.f.* turkey-hen, turkey; (*pers.*) goose, fool; — *s.m.* (*any*) turkey (*cooked*)
Dindon, *s.m.* turkey, turkey-cock; (*pers.*) goose, fool, dupe; —**s,** *pl.* turkeys (*either cocks only, or cocks and hens*)
Dindonneau, *s.m.* young turkey, turkey-poult
Dindonner, *v.a.* to fool, to dupe, to bamboozle
Dindonni-er, ère, *s.m.f.* turkey-keeper; country dowdy; — *adj.* of turkeys, turkey
Dîné, *part. of* **Dîner,** *v.n.*; — *s.m.* (*old spelling*) *V.* **Dîner,** *s.m.* [place (*on the road*)
Dînée, *s.f.* (*obsolete*) dinner (*at an inn*); dining-
Dîner, *s.m.* dinner; dinner-party
Dîner, *v.n.* to dine; to be at dinner; to eat o.'s dinner. — *par cœur,* to go without o.'s dinner. *A* —, to dine; to dinner; some dinner; o.'s dinner; a dinner; dinners; a dinner-party
Dînette, *s.f.* feast, treat; doll's dinner. *Faire la* —, to have a feast *or* treat; to play dinners
Dîneu-r, se, *s.m.f.* diner; trencherman, eater, feeder
Dinguer, *v.n.* (*pop.*) to saunter, to stroll, to lounge; (*theatrical slang*) to incline; to shake, to totter, to reel. *Envoyer* —, to send away *or* about o.'s business
Dinosaurien, *s.m.* (*fossil*) dinosaurian
Dinothérium, *s.m.* (*fossil*) dinotherium
Diocésain, e, *adj.m.f.* diocesan; — *s.m.f.* inhabitant of a diocese; — *s.m.*, *adj.m.* *Évêque* [—, diocesan
Diocèse, *s.m.* diocese
Dioclée, *s.f.* (*bot.*) dioclea
Diodon, *s.m.* (*zool.*) diodon, globe-fish
Diœcie, *s.f.* (*bot.*) diœcia
Diœcique, *adj.* (*bot.*) diœcious, diœcian, dioicous
Dioggot, *s.m.* *V.* **Diaggot**
Dioïque, *adj.* (*bot.*) *V.* **Diœcique**
Diomédée, *s.f.* (*bird, plant*) diomedea
Dionée, *s.f.* (*bot.*) dionæa, Venus's fly-trap, Carolina fly-trap, fly-trap
Dionysiaques, *s.f.pl.* (*in anc. Greece*) Dionysia
Dioptase, *s.f.* (*min.*) dioptase, emerald copper-ore
Dioptrique, *s.f.* (*opt.*) dioptrics; — *adj.* diop-
Diorama, *s.m.* diorama [tric, dioptrical
Dioramique, *adj.* dioramic
Diorite, *s.m.* (*min.*) diorite, greenstone
Dioscorée, *s.f.* (*bot.*) dioscorea, yam
Diosma, *s.m.* (*bot.*) diosma
Dipétale, Dipétalé, e, *adj.* (*bot.*) dipetalous
Diphthérie, (*formerly*) **Diphthérite,** *s.f.* (*med.*) diphtheria (*formerly,* diphtheritis)
Diphthéritique, *adj.* (*med.*) diphtheric, diph-
Diphthongue, *s.f.* diphthong [theritic
Diphylle, *adj.* (*bot.*) diphyllous
Diploé, *s.m.* (*anat.*) diploe
Diplomate, *s.m.* diplomatist; — *adj.* diplomatic
Diplomatie, *s.f.* diplomacy [matics
Diplomatique, *adj.* diplomatic; — *s.f.* diplo-
Diplomatiquement, *adv.* diplomatically; shrewdly, cautiously, cleverly
Diplomatiste, *s.m.* one versed in diplomatics
Diplôme, *s.m.* diploma
Diplômé, e, *adj.* with a diploma, graduated; certificated; — *s.m.f.* graduate
Diplopie, *s.f.* (*med.*) diplopia
Dipode, *adj.* having two feet *or* two fins
Dipsade, *s.f.* (*serpent*) dipsas
Dipsétique, *adj.m.f.*, *s.m.* (*med.*) dipsetic
Dipsomanie, *s.f.* (*med.*) dipsomania
Diptère, *adj.* (*zool., bot.*) dipterous, dipteral; — *s.m.* (*zool.*) dipterous insect, dipteran; (*arch.*)
Diptérique, *adj.* (*arch.*) dipteral [dipteron
Diptérygien, ne, *adj.m.f.*, *s.m.* (*zool.*) dipterygian (*fish*)
Diptéryx, *s.m.* (*bot.*) dipterix, dipteryx
Diptyque, *s.m.* diptych
Dirca, *s.m.* (*bot.*) dirca
Dire, *v.a.* to say; to tell; to speak; to talk; to state; to mention; to name; to appoint; to assert; to declare; to express; to mean; to signify; to bid;

to order; to relate; to describe; to recite; to sing; to report; to repeat; to whisper; to suggest; to own; to forebode; to show, to indicate, to announce, to bespeak; to think; to fancy; (*pop.*) to please, to take the fancy (of), to tempt, to suit; — *v.n.* (*fam.*) to scold, to grumble. — *du bien* or *du mal de*, to speak well *or* ill of. *A bien* —, properly speaking. *Pour ainsi* —, so to speak, as it were. *Faire* —, *V.* **Faire.** *Se faire* —, *V.* **Faire (Se).** *Trouver à* —, to find fault (with); (*old*) to miss, to find missing. *Cela va sans* —, that is (*or* follows as) a matter of course, that is understood; of course. *C'est-à-* —, that is to say, that is; to wit; namely, viz.; this means; in fact, the fact is. *C'est assez* —, that is as much as to say. *C'est tout* —, it is saying all, that is all, that includes everything. *C'est dit!* all right! *Ce n'est pas à — que ...*, it does not mean *or* follow that ... *Comme qui dirait*, as we should say; some sort of, something like; in a manner. *Comme vous dites*, as you say; just so, ay, to be sure. *Dis* or *dites*, speak; tell me; pray; now then; go on; if you please; will you; you mean. *Dis donc! dites donc!* I say! *Disons 5 francs*, say 5 francs. *Est-ce à — que ...?* does it mean *or* follow that ...? *Il n'y a pas à* —, it is of no use to say; it is of no use talking, there is no saying nay, say *or* do what we *or* you will, it is of no use, there is no helping it; there is no denying it. *Il va sans* —, it is unnecessary to say; of course. *Il était* (or *est*) *dit* (*que*), it was (*or* is) fated (that), it was (*or* is) to be (that). *Je ne dis pas*, I don't say *or* &c.; I don't say no, perhaps. *On dit*, *V.* **On.** *On disait*, it was said. *On le dit habile*, they say that he is skilful, he is said to be skilful. *On dirait un fou*, he looks like a madman, one would think he is mad. *Pour tout* —, in a word, to sum up all in one word. *Quand je vous le disais*, or *Je vous le disais bien*, or *Je vous l'avais bien dit*, did I not say so now? now I told you so. *Qu'est-ce à —?* what does this mean? what then? eh? what? what is that? *Que je lui dis*, (*pop.*) says I. *Tout est dit*, all is said; all is agreed; all is over; that's all; there is an end of it. *Vous l'avez dit*, precisely, just so. *Vous m'en direz tant!* well, if it comes to all this! who could wonder? *A qui le dites-vous?* don't I know it? *Si le cœur vous en dit*, *V.* **Cœur**

Se —, *v.r.* to call *or* style oneself; to say one is; to give oneself out for; to profess to be; to say to oneself; to say to each other, to tell each other; to be said *or* told *or* &c.; to be called; to be used. *Cela ne se dit pas*, people don't say that; that is not used

Dire, *s.m.* what one says, saying, say, statement, assertion, point, words; speaking; talk; account, report; opinion; (*law*) allegation. *Au — de ...*, by what ... says, according to ... *Au — de tout le monde*, by all accounts, according to what everybody says. *Le bien* —, *V.* **Bien-dire,** *s.m.* (*at Letter* **B**)

Direct, e, *adj.* direct; straight; immediate; (*of taxes*) direct, assessed; (*rail.*) express, through [immediately; entirely, quite; exactly

Directement, *adv.* directly; direct; straight;

Directeur, *s.m.* director; manager; conductor; superintendent; governor; warden; editor; principal; master; head; president; guide; (*Cath. rel.*) confessor, spiritual director; — *adj.m.* directing; managing. — *de l'exploitation*, general manager. — *général des postes*, postmaster-general

Direction, *s.f.* direction; side; conduct; management; directorship; superintendence; government; steerage; governorship; mastership; editorship; presidency; manager's office; directors; (*math.*) bearing; (*mining*) stretch, bearing. — *générale des postes*, postmaster-general's office. *Être dans la — de*, to be exactly opposite

Directoire, *s.m.* directory

Directorat, *s.m.* directorate; directorship;

Directorial, e, *adj.* directorial [presidency

Directrice, *s.f.* directress; manageress; conductress; superintendent; governess; editress; principal; mistress; head; president; guide; (*geom.*) directrix, dirigent; — *adj.f.* directing; managing

Dirigeant, e, *adj.* directing; leading; acting

Diriger, *v.a.* to direct; to manage; to conduct; to guide; to regulate; to govern; to rule; to turn; to aim; to level; to point; to send off *or* on; to forward; to march (*troops*); to take (*proceedings*)

Se —, *v.r.* to direct o.'s steps *or* course; to go (towards), to proceed, to make (for); to turn; to cross; to direct *or* guide *or* govern oneself; to take care of oneself; to take example (from), to go (by), to be guided (by); to be directed *or* managed *or* &c.; to extend, to stretch; (*nav.*) to stand in [to solve

Dirimer, *v.a.* to invalidate, to annul; to settle,

Discale, *s.f.* (*com.*) shrinkage, waste, tret

Discaler, *v.n.* (*com.*) to shrink, to waste, to lose

Disceptation, *s.f.* disceptation

Discernable, *adj.* discernible

Discernablement, *adv.* discernibly

Discernement, *s.m.* discernment; discrimination; distinction; discretion; judgment

Discerner, *v.a.* to discern; to discriminate; to distinguish; to judge

Se —, *v.r.* to be discerned *or* &c.

Dischidie, *s.f.* (*bot.*) dischidia

Disciple, *s.m.* disciple; scholar, pupil; follower;

Disciplinable, *adj.* disciplinable [apostle

Disciplinaire, *adj.* disciplinary

Disciplinairement, *adv.* disciplinarily

Discipline, *s.f.* discipline; training; drill; knowledge; castigation; whip, scourge, cat

Disciplinement, *s.m.* disciplining, training

Discipliner, *v.a.* to discipline; to train; to drill; to chastise, to whip, to scourge

Se —, *v.r.* to become disciplined, to be formed to discipline; to scourge oneself

Discobole, *s.m.* discobolus [discoidal, discoid

Discoïdal, e, Discoïde, Discoïdé, e, *adj.*

Discontinu, e, *adj.* discontinuous

Discontinuation, *s.f.* discontinuance, discontinuation

Discontinuer, *v.a.n.* to discontinue, to interrupt, to suspend, to cease, to leave off, to give

Se —, *v.r.* to be discontinued *or* &c. [over

Discontinuité, *s.f.* discontinuity, discontinuance [unbecoming

Disconvenable, *adj.* unsuitable, improper,

Disconvenablement, *adv.* unsuitably, improperly

Disconvenance, *s.f.* incongruity; unsuitableness; dissimilarity; difference; disagreement; discrepancy; disproportion; disparity; incompatibility

Disconvenir, *v.n.* to deny, to disown; to be unsuitable, not to suit, to disagree

Discord, *s.m.* disagreement, misunderstanding, dissension, discord; —*adj.m.* out of tune, discordant; (*fig.*) inconsistent

Discordamment, *adv.* discordantly

Discordance, *s.f.* discordance, discordancy, discord, disagreement, inconsonancy, dissonance [nant, inharmonious; out of tune

Discordant, e, *adj.* discordant, jarring, disso-

Discorde, *s.f.* discord; disagreement; dissension; variance; contention; strife; quarrel

Discorder, *v.n.* to be discordant; to jar; to disagree; to be out of tune [twaddler

Discoureu-r, se, *s.m.f.* discourser; talker;

Discourir, *v.n.* to discourse; to descant; to talk; to twaddle

Discours, *s.m.* discourse; speech; oration; harangue; address; lecture; dissertation; treatise; conversation; talking, speaking; talk; words; subject; matter

Discourtois, e, *adj.* discourteous
Discourtoisement, *adv.* discourteously
Discourtoisie, *s.f.* discourtesy
Discrase, *s.m.* (*min.*) discrase, discrasite
Discrédit, *s.m.* discredit, disrepute; disgrace
Discréditer, *v.a. V.* **Déconsidérer**
Discr-et, ète, *adj.* discreet; prudent; circumspect; cautious; wary; reserved; secret, close; unobtrusive; considerate; reasonable; discrete
Discrètement, *adv.* discreetly; prudently; cautiously; warily; reservedly; unobtrusively; considerately; reasonably; trustfully; closely
Discrétion, *s.f.* discretion; prudence; circumspection; cautiousness, caution; reservedness, reserve; secrecy; considerateness; reasonableness; mercy. *A* —, at discretion, without terms; at will, at pleasure, "ad libitum"; as much as one wants *or* likes, without restriction *or* stint *or* limitation; plentifully; at free quarters; freely. *A la — de*, at the mercy of, at ...'s mercy; at *or* to ...'s discretion
Discrétionnaire, *adj.* discretionary
Discrétoire, *s.m.* council-room; council
Disculpation, *s.f.* exculpation
Disculper, *v.a.* to exculpate, to clear
Discursi-f, ve, *adj.* discursive
Discussi-f, ve, *adj.*, **Discussif,** *s.m.* (*med.*, *obsolete*) discutient
Discussion, *s.f.* discussion; debate; altercation, dispute, words; (*law*) execution, distress
Discutable, *adj.* arguable, debatable, disputable, questionable, contestable
Discuter, *v.a.n.* to discuss, to debate, to dispute, to argue; to examine, to inquire into; to discuss the claims of; (*law*) to distrain, to distress
  Se —, *v.r.* to be discussed *or* &c.
Discuteur, *s.m.* debater
Disépale, *adj.* (*bot.*) disepalous
Disert, e, *adj.* fluent, copious, somewhat eloquent
Disertement, *adv.* fluently, copiously, somewhat eloquently
Disette, *s.f.* dearth; scarcity; want; poverty; penury
Disetteu-x, se, *adj.* needy, necessitous
Diseu-r, se, *s.m.f.* sayer; teller; talker; speaker
Disgrâce, *s.f.* disgrace; disfavour; displeasure; misfortune; reverse; downfall; affliction; awkwardness, ungracefulness
Disgracié, e, *adj.* disgraced; out of favour; (— *de* or *par la nature*) ill-favoured; deformed; disfigured; blunt, stupid
Disgracier, *v.a.* to disgrace, to put out of favour
Disgracieusement, *adv.* ungracefully, ungraciously, unpleasantly, awkwardly
Disgracieu-x, se, *adj.* ungraceful, ungracious, unsightly, uncouth, unpleasant, disagreeable, awkward
Disgrég-ation, -er. *V.* **Désagrégation,** &c.
Disharmonie, *s.f.* disharmony
Disjoindre, *v.a. V.* **Déjoindre**
Disjoint, e, (*part. of* **Disjoindre**) *adj.* disjoined, &c.; (*mus.*) disjunct
Disjoncti-f, ve, *adj. s.* disjunctive
Disjonction, *s.f.* disjunction, separation, severance
Dislocation, *s.f.*, **Disloquement,** *s.m.* dislocation; taking to pieces; derangement; separation; division; dismemberment; (*mil.*) breaking up
Disloquer, *v.a.* to dislocate; to disjoint; to put out of joint; to take to pieces; to put out of order; to derange; to separate; to divide; to dismember; (*mil.*) to break up
  Se —, *v.r.* to be dislocated *or* disjointed *or* put out of joint; to dislocate (o.'s ...), to put (o.'s ...) out of joint; to be taken to pieces; to take to pieces; to fall to pieces; to get out of order, to become deranged
Dispache, *s.f.* (*in ship-insur.*) assessment
Dispacheur, *s.m.* nautical assessor, average-stater
Disparaître, *v.n.* to disappear; to vanish; to pass away, to pass; to go; to flee, to fly, to fly away; to abscond; to elope; to be eclipsed
Disparate, *adj.* disparate; incongruous; unlike, dissimilar; ill-matched; unsymmetrical; — *s.f.* disparate; incongruity
Disparité, *s.f.* disparity, dissimilarity
Disparition, *s.f.* disappearance
Disparu, e, *part. adj.* disappeared, &c. (*V.* **Disparaître**); (*mil.*) missing
Dispendieusement, *adv.* expensively
Dispendieu-x, se, *adj.* expensive, costly
Dispensable, *adj.* exemptible, licensable, privileged
Dispensaire, *s.m.* dispensatory, pharmacopœia; dispensary
Dispensataire, *s.m.f.* recipient, receiver, sharer
Dispensa-teur, trice, *s.m.f.* dispenser; manager; ruler
Dispensation, *s.f.* dispensation, distribution; management
Dispense, *s.f.* dispensation, exemption; licence; permission
Dispenser, *v.a.* to dispense; to exempt; to excuse; to spare; to let off; to distribute; to bestow
  Se —, *v.r.* to dispense (with); to exempt *or* excuse oneself; to spare oneself, to spare; to be dispensed *or* distributed *or* bestowed
Disperser, *v.a.*, **Se** —, *v.r.* to disperse; to scatter; to dispel; to dissipate; to break up
Dispersi-f, ve, *adj.* dispersive
Dispersion, *s.f.* dispersion; scattering; spreading; breaking up
Disponibilité, *s.f.* disposableness; power of disposal; suspension; disposable fund. *En* —, disposable; (*mil.*, *admin.*) unattached; on the unattached list; suspended; (*nav.*) on the reserved list
Disponible, *adj.* disposable; available; disengaged; unengaged; unoccupied; free; vacant; unattached; transferable; (*of goods*) in bond; — *s.m.* goods in bond, bonded goods
Dispos, e, *adj.* active, nimble; cheerful; well. *Frais et —, gaillard et —*, hale and hearty
Disposant, e, *s.m.f.* donor, giver; testator, testatrix; devisor
Disposé, e, *part.adj.* disposed, &c. (*V.* **Disposer**); ready; willing; inclined; apt; liable. *Bien* —, well disposed; well. *Mal* —, ill disposed; unwell
Disposer, *v.a.n.* to dispose; to arrange; to order; to regulate; to lay out; to direct; to provide; to prepare; to fit; to shape; to incline; to induce; to prevail upon; to possess; to have at command; to spare; to draw (*a bill*)
  Se —, *v.r.* to prepare, to get ready; to be about; to dispose *or* &c. oneself; to array oneself; to be disposed *or* arranged *or* &c.
Dispositi-f, ve, *adj.* preparatory; — *s.m.* dictum; recital; purview, terms; sentence, decision; arrangement, plan, disposition
Disposition, *s.f.* disposition; arrangement; order; preparation; disposal; command; service; inclination, taste; aptitude; natural ability; tendency; state, condition; mind, humour; habit; intention; (*law*) provision; (*law*) bequest. —*s testamentaires*, last will, testament, devise
Disproportion, *s.f.* disproportion
Disproportionné, e, *adj.* disproportionate
Disproportionnel, le, *adj.* disproportional
Disproportionnellement, *adv.* disproportionally
Disproportionnément, *adv.* disproportionately
Disproportionner, *v.a.* to disproportion
Disputable, *adj.* disputable, debatable, contestable, controvertible, doubtful
†**Disputailler,** *v.n.*, **Se** —, *v.r.* to cavil, to wrangle, to squabble, to bicker
†**Disputaillerie,** *s.f.* trumpery cavilling, wrangling, squabbling, bickering
†**Disputailleu-r, se,** *s.m.f.* caviller, wrangler, bickerer; — *adj.* cavilling, wrangling, disputatious
Disputant, e, *adj. s.* disputant
Disputation, *s.f.* disputation
Dispute, *s.f.* dispute, contest, wrangle, wrangling, quarrel; discussion, debate; controversy; disputation
Disputer, *v.a.n.* to dispute; to contest; to oppose; to quarrel with; to quarrel; to wrangle; to contend for; to contend; to argue, to debate,

to discuss; to struggle; to attempt to rescue; to snatch; to call in question; to deny; to vie. *Le — à*, to vie *or* contend with; to struggle for the mastery with

Se —, *v.r.* to dispute, to strive *or* contend *or* struggle for; to be disputed; to quarrel, to wrangle; to deny oneself

Disputeu-r, se, *s.m.f.* disputer; disputant; wrangler; — *adj.* disputatious, quarrelsome

Disqualification, *s.f.* disqualification

Disqualifier, *v.a.* to disqualify

Disque, *s.m.* disc; quoit

Disquisition, *s.f.* disquisition

Disruption, *s.f.* disruption

Dissecteur, *s.m.* dissector

Dissection, *s.f.* dissection

Dissemblable, *adj.* dissimilar, unlike, different

Dissemblablement, *adv.* dissimilarly, differently [tude, unlikeness, difference

Dissemblance, *s.f.* dissimilarity, dissimilitude, unlikeness, difference

Dissembler, *v.n.* to be dissimilar *or* unlike, to differ [dissemination, scattering, spreading

Dissémination, *s.f.*, **Disséminement,** *s.m.* dissemination, scattering, spreading

Disséminer, *v.a.* to disseminate, to scatter, to spread [spread; to scatter, to spread

Se —, *v.r.* to be disseminated *or* scattered *or* spread; to scatter, to spread

Dissension, *s.f.* dissension, disagreement, strife, feud

Dissentiment, *s.m.* dissent, disagreement

Dissentir, *v.n.* to dissent

Dissépale, *adj.* (*bot.*) *V.* **Disépale**

Disséquer, *v.a.* to dissect

Disséqueur, *s.m.* dissector

Disserta-teur, trice, *s.m.f.* dissertator

Dissertati-f, ve, *adj.* dissertative, disquisitive

Dissertation, *s.f.* dissertation; (*in schools*) composition

Disserter, *v.n.* to dissert, to discourse

Disserteu-r, se, *s.m.f.* dissertator [dissidence

Dissidence, *s.f.* dissent, division, difference, dissidence

Dissident, e, *adj.* dissenting; — *s.m.f.* dissenter, dissentient, dissident

Dissimilaire, *adj.* dissimilar

Dissimilarité, *s.f.* dissimilarity

Dissimilitude, *s.f.* dissimilitude

Dissimula-teur, trice, *s.m.f.* dissembler, hypocrite; — *adj.* dissembling, hypocritical

Dissimulation, *s.f.* dissimulation, dissembling, hypocrisy, double-dealing; concealment

Dissimulé, e, *part. adj.* dissembled, concealed, suppressed; dissembling, hypocritical, double-faced, artful, deceitful; — *s.m.f.* dissembler, hypocrite

Dissimuler, *v.a.n.* to dissemble, to conceal, to hide; to suppress; to pretend *or* feign not to notice; to pass over; to pretend, to feign

Se —, *v.r.* to conceal *or* hide oneself; to steal away, to slip out; to conceal from oneself; to be concealed *or* hid *or* suppressed

Dissipa-teur, trice, *s.m.f.* spendthrift, squanderer; — *adj.* wasteful, profuse, extravagant

Dissipation, *s.f.* dissipation; squandering; waste; relaxation, recreation, diversion; inattention, idleness

Dissipé, e, *part. adj.* dissipated, &c. (*V.* **Dissiper**); inattentive, not attentive, not studious, trifling; wild; — *s.m.f.* dissipated *or* &c. person (fellow, man, woman, girl)

Dissiper, *v.a.* to dissipate; to disperse; to scatter; to drive away; to dispel; to waste, to squander, to fritter away; to spend; to relax, to recreate, to divert

Se —, *v.r.* to dissipate, to disperse, to scatter; to clear, to clear off; to disappear, to vanish, to pass away; to be dissipated *or* &c.; to relax o.'s mind, to recreate *or* divert oneself; to become dissipated *or* inattentive *or* wild

Dissociable, *adj.* dissociable

Dissocial, e, *adj.* dissocial

Dissoci-ation, -er. *V.* **Désassociation,** &c.

Dissolu, e, *adj. s.* dissolute; profligate

Dissolubilité, *s.f.* dissolubility; dissolvability

Dissoluble, *adj.* dissoluble; dissolvable

Dissolûment, *adv.* dissolutely, loosely

Dissoluti-f, ve, *adj. s.m. V.* **Dissolvant**

Dissolution, *s.f.* dissolution; dissoluteness, looseness, profligacy; solution

Dissolvant, e, *adj.* dissolving, dissolvent; (*chem.*) solutive; — *s.m.* (*med.*, &c.) dissolvent; (*chem.*) solvent, menstruum

Dissonnance, *s.f.* dissonance, discord

Dissonnant, e, *adj.* dissonant, discordant

Dissonner, *v.n.* to be dissonant *or* discordant,

Dissoudre, *v.a.* to dissolve; to break up [to jar

Se —, *v.r.* to be dissolved; to dissolve; to break up

Dissuader, *v.a.* to dissuade

Dissuasi-f, ve, *adj.* dissuasive

Dissuasion, *s.f.* dissuasion

Dissyllabe, *s.m.* dissyllable; — *adj.* dissyllabic

Dissyllabique, *adj.* dissyllabic

Distance, *s.f.* distance [to distance

Distancer, *v.a.* to lay out at equal distances; to distance

Distant, e, *adj.* distant, remote, far

Distendre, *v.a.* to distend [tend

Se —, *v.r.* to become *or* be distended, to distend

Distension, *s.f.* distension

Disthène, *s.m.* (*min.*) disthene, kyanite

‡**Distichiase, Distichiasis,** *s.m.* (*med.*) distichiasis, trichiasis

Distillable, *adj.* distillable

Distilla-teur, trice, *s.m.f.* distiller

Distillation, *s.f.* distillation

Distillatoire, *adj.* distillatory

Distiller, *v.a.n.* to distil; to drop; to trickle; to discharge, to vent; to be discharged *or* vented; (*fam.*) to elaborate, to do in style; (*old*) to puzzle (*o.'s brains*). *Se* —, to be distilled *or* &c.

Distillerie, *s.f.* distillery; distilling

Distinct, e, *adj.* distinct

Distinctement, *adv.* distinctly

Distincti-f, ve, *adj.* distinctive, distinguishing, characteristic

Distinction, *s.f.* distinction; eminence; rank; polish, politeness, refinement, elegance, good manners

Distinctivement, *adv.* distinctively

Distingué, e, *part. adj.* distinguished, &c. (*V.* **Distinguer**); eminent; noble; high; polished; refined; elegant; genteel; gentlemanly; ladylike

Distinguer, *v.a.n.* to distinguish; to discern; to discriminate; to recognize; to perceive; to take notice of; to mark; to single out; to treat with regard; to honour; to distinguish from the rest; not to make a confusion

Se —, *v.r.* to distinguish oneself; to be distinguished *or* conspicuous [distichous

Distique, *s.m.* distich, couplet; — *adj.* (*bot.*) distichous

Distome, *s.m. adj.* (*zool.*) distoma

Distordre, *v.a.* to distort; to sprain

Se —, *v.r.* to become *or* be distorted *or* sprained

Distors, e, *adj.* distorted

Distorsion, *s.f.* distortion; sprain

Distracti-f, ve, *adj.* distractive; distractile

Distractile, *adj.* distractile

Distraction, *s.f.* inattention; listlessness; absence of mind, abstraction; diversion, interruption, relaxation, recreation; amusement; relief; (*law*) separation. *Par* —, by way of amusement; inadvertently

Distraire, *v.a.* to distract; to divert; to entertain, to amuse; to disturb; to abstract; to take away *or* off *or* out; to take (from); to call off; to turn (from); to deprive; (*law*) to separate

Se —, *v.r.* to divert *or* amuse oneself; to take some relaxation, to relax o.'s mind; to forget o.'s troubles; to divert o.'s attention; to be disturbed *or* &c.

Distrait, e, *part. adj.* diverted, &c. (*V.* **Distraire**); absorbed; inattentive, listless, heedless; absent (*in mind*); vacant; wandering; — *s.m.f.* absent person, absent man *or* woman *or* girl

Distribuable, *adj.* distributable

Distribuer, *v.a.* to distribute; to portion *or* serve out; to deal out; to dole out; to dispose;

to arrange; to lay out; to deliver; to issue; to supply; to allot; to bestow; to allow; to give; to share; to divide; (*theat.*) to cast (*the parts*) [perse; to share among themselves

Se —, *v.r.* to be distributed *or* &c.; to dis-

Distributaire, *s.m.f.* sharer, recipient, receiver

Distribu-teur, trice, *s.m.f.* distributer, dispenser, bestower; foot-post, letter-carrier. — *des vivres*, (*nav.*) purser's steward, steward's

Distributi-f, ve, *adj.* distributive [mate

Distribution, *s.f.* distribution; disposition; disposing; arrangement; laying out; delivery; issue; supply; allowance; division; (*theat.*) cast (*of the parts*)

Distributivement, *adv.* distributively; singly

District, *s.m.* district; (*fig.*) department, province; jurisdiction [distylous

Distyle, *s.m. adj.* (*arch.*) distyle; — *adj.* (*bot.*)

Dit, e, *part. adj.* said, told, &c. (*V.* **Dire**); called; surnamed; so-called; alias; agreed, settled, concluded, decided; granted. *Autrement* —, in other words; alias. *Cela* —, thereupon. *Tout est dit*, &c., *V.* **Dire.** *Prendre pour* —, *Tenir pour* —, *Se le tenir pour* —, *V.* **Prendre** *and* **Tenir** [**Dédit**

Dit, *s.m.* saying, maxim; (*old*) story, fable. *V.*

Dithéisme, *s.m.* ditheism

Dithéiste, *s.m.f.* ditheist; — *adj.* ditheistic

Dithyrambe, *s.m.* dithyramb; dithyrambic

Dithyrambique, *adj.* dithyrambic

Dito, Ditto, *adv. s.m.* ditto, do.

Diton, *s.m.* (*mus.*) ditone

Ditriglyphe, *s.m.* (*arch.*) ditriglyph

Diurèse, *s.f.* (*med.*) diuresis

Diurétique, *adj.m.f., s.m.* (*med.*) diuretic

Diurnal, *s.m.* (*Cath. rel.*) diurnal

Diurnal, e, *adj.* (*old*) diurnal, daily [*sect, bird*)

Diurne, *adj.* diurnal, daily; — *s.m.* diurnal (*in-*

Diva, *adj.f.* (*Italian*) diva

Divagant, e, *adj.* rambling, wandering

Divaga-teur, trice, *adj.* rambling, wandering; — *s.m.f.* rambling writer *or* speaker, rambler [wandering, raving; straying

Divagation, *s.f.* divagation, vagary, rambling,

Divaguant, *part.* wandering, &c. (*V.* **Divaguer**)

Divaguer, *v.n.* to ramble, to wander; to stray; to rave; to muse; to digress, to wander from the question; to talk at random; to have a random chit-chat, to gossip

Divagueu-r, se, *s.m.f. adj. V.* **Divagateur**

Divan, *s.m.* divan

Divarication, *s.f.* divarication

Divariqué, e, *adj.* (*bot.*) divaricate

Dive, *adj.f.* (*old*) divine; — *s.f.* (*Eastern myth.*) dive (*goddess*) [ference; difference of opinion

Divergence, *s.f.* divergence, divergency; dif-

Divergent, e, *adj.* divergent; different; (*bot.*) (*of branches*) spreading, (*of the veins of leaves*) diverging [spread; to differ

Diverger, *v.n.* to diverge; to branch off; to

Divers, e, *adj.* different, diverse, divers, varied, various, several, sundry; miscellaneous; — *s.m.pl.* sundries [variously, in various ways

Diversement, *adv.* differently, diversely,

Diversicolore, *adj.* diversicoloured

Diversi-f, ve, *adj.* diversive

Diversifiable, *adj.* diversifiable

Diversification, *s.f.* diversification [vary

Diversifier, *v.a.* to diversify; to variegate; to

Se —, *v.r.* to be diversified, &c.

Diversiflore, *adj.* (*bot.*) diversiflorous

Diversiforme, *adj.* diversiform

Diversion, *s.f.* diversion

Diversité, *s.f.* diversity; variety; difference

Divertir, *v.a.* to divert; to amuse, to entertain; to abstract; to misappropriate; to embezzle

Se —, *v.r.* to divert *or* amuse *or* enjoy oneself, to be merry, to sport, to be amused, to laugh (at), to make merry (with), to make fun (of), to joke, to jest [amused *or* diverted

Divertissable, *adj.* amusable, capable of being

Divertissement, *s.m.* entertainment, amusement, sport; recreation; diversion; abstraction; misappropriation; embezzlement; (*theat.*,

Dividende, *s.m.* dividend [*mus.*) divertisement

Dividivi, *s.m.* dividivi, libidibi

Divin, e, *adj.* divine; heavenly; gracious; admirable, exquisite

Divina-teur, trice, *adj.* divining, prophetic, foreseeing; — *s.m.f.* diviner

Divination, *s.f.* divination

Divinatoire, *adj.* divinatory; divining

Divinement, *adv.* divinely; heavenly; admi-

Divinisation, *s.f.* deification [rably, exquisitely

Diviniser, *v.a.* to deify; to extol to the skies

Se —, *v.r.* to become divine

Divinité, *s.f.* divinity, deity; (*fig.*) angel

Divis, *s.m.* (*law*) division, share

Divise, *s.f.* (*her.*) narrow band

Diviser, *v.a.* to divide; to separate, to part; to parcel out; to disunite [into portions

Se —, *v.r.* to divide; to be divided; to split

Diviseur, *s.m.* divisor; divider; — *adj.m.* di-

Divisibilité, *s.f.* divisibility [visive, dividing

Divisible, *adj.* divisible; separable

Divisiblement, *adv.* divisibly; separably

Divisi-f, ve, *adj.* divisive

Division, *s.f.* division; partition; department; quarrel; (*nav.*) squadron. *Chef de* —, *V.* **Chef.** *Être en* —, to be at variance

Divisionnaire, *adj.* divisional; fractional, fractionary; — *s.m.* (*in schools*) assistant formmaster; (*mil.*) *V.* **Général de division**

Divorce, *s.m.* divorce. *Faire* —, to divorce, to be divorced; (*fig.*) to give up, to renounce

Divorcé, e, *part. adj.* divorced; — *s.m.f.* divorced person, divorcee, divorced husband *or* wife

Divorcer, *v.a.n.* to divorce; to repudiate; to be divorced [divulging

Divulga-teur, trice, *s.m.f.* divulger; — *adj.*

Divulgation, *s.f.* divulgation, publishing

Divulguer, *v.a.* to divulge, to publish, to reveal,

Se —, *v.r.* to be divulged, &c. [to noise abroad

Divulsion, *s.f.* divulsion

Dix, *adj.m.f., s.m.* ten; tenth. — **-cors,** *s.m.* (*hunt.*) full-grown stag. — **-huit,** *adj.m.f., s.m.* eighteen; eighteenth. — **-huitième,** *adj. s.* eighteenth. — **-neuf,** *adj.m.f., s.m.* nineteen; nineteenth. — **-neuvième,** *adj. s.* nineteenth. — **-sept,** *adj.m.f., s.m.* seventeen; seventeenth. — **-septième,** *adj. s.* seventeenth

Dixain, *s.m. V.* **Dizain** [(*mus.*), *s.m.f.* (*pers.*) tenth

Dixième, *adj.m.f., s.m.* tenth; tenth part; — *s.f.*

Dixièmement, *adv.* tenthly

Dizain, *s.m.* piece of poetry *or* stanza of ten lines, decastich; decade (*of a chaplet or rosary*); ten packs (*of cards*); set of ten

Dizaine, *s.f.* ten or so, about ten, some ten, ten, half-score; (*hist.*) decennary, tithing

Dizainier, Dizenier, *s.m.* (*hist.*) tithing-man

Dizeau, *s.m.* (*agr.*) shock of ten sheaves, shock, ten trusses of hay

Djérid, *s.m.* djerrid (*Turkish javelin*)

Djerme, *s.f.* (*nav.*) djerme (*Egyptian vessel*)

Djinn, *s.m.* djinn *or* jinn (*Arabian genius*)

Do, *s.m.* (*mus.*) *V.* **Ut**

Dobrao, *s.m.* dobrao (*Portuguese gold coin*)

Dobule, *s.m.* (*fish*) dobule

Docart, *s.m.* dog-cart [ing, tractable, manageable

Docile, *adj.* docile, submissive, obedient, yield-

Docilement, *adv.* with docility, submissively,

Dociliser, *v.a.* to docilize [obediently

Docilité, *s.f.* docility, submissiveness, obedience, tractableness, manageableness

Docimasie, *s.f.* (*chem., med.*) docimacy

Docimastique, *adj.* (*chem., med.*) docimastic; — *s.f.* docimastic art [warehouse

Dock, *s.m.* (*nav., com.*) dock; bonded store *or*

Docte, *adj.* learned; — *s.m.* learned man, scholar

Doctement, *adv.* learnedly; scientifically; pedantically

Docteur, *s.m.* doctor. — ***-médecin,* — *en médecine*,** doctor of medicine, M.D. — ***en droit*,** doctor of laws

Doctissime, *adj.* (*jest.*) most learned
Doctoral, e, *adj.* doctoral, doctor's, doctors'
Doctoralement, *adv.* doctorally [torship
Doctorat, *s.m.* doctor's degree, doctorate, doc-
Doctorerie, *s.f.* examination for the degree
Doctoresse, *s.f.* doctoress, doctress [of D.D.
Doctorifier, Doctoriser, *v.a.* (*jest.*) to dub *or* style doctor, to doctor
Doctrinaire, *adj.m.f.*, *s.m.* stiff, formal, systematic, pedantic; conservative, tory, doctrinaire; lay brother [tematically, pedantically; illiberally
Doctrinairement, *adv.* stiffly, formally, sys-
Doctrinal, e, *adj.* doctrinal
Doctrinalement, *adv.* doctrinally
Doctrinarisme, *s.m.* doctrinaireism, doctrinarianism, conservatism, toryism
Doctrinariste, *s.m.f. adj.* doctrinarian
Doctrine, *s.f.* doctrine; (*polit.*) conservatism, conservatives; (*obsolete*) learning, erudition, lore
Document, *s.m.* document; instrument; paper; title; title-deed; muniment; charter; certificate; (*obsolete*) precept, instruction, teaching
Dodéca-, (*in compounds*) dodeca-... (*twelve*)
Dodécaèdre, *s.m.* (*geom.*) dodecahedron; — *adj.* dodecahedral
Dodécagonal, e, *adj.* dodecagonal
Dodécagone, *s.m.* (*geom.*) dodecagon; — *adj.* dodecagonal
Dodécastyle, *s.m. adj.* (*arch.*) dodecastyle
Dodelinement, *s.m.* rocking; fondling; wagging; nodding; waddling, swinging
Dodeliner, *v.a.n.* to rock; to fondle; to wag; to nod; to waddle, to swing; to loll about
Dodinage, *s.m.* shaking, stirring; (*of wine*) rummaging
Dodine, *s.f.* rummaging-stick (*for wine*)
Dodiner, *v.a.* to shake, to stir; to rock; to swing; to fondle; (*of wine*) to rummage; — *v.n.* to indulge oneself; to waddle, to swing
Se —, *v.r.* to nurse oneself up, to coddle *or* indulge oneself; to waddle, to swing
Dodinette, *s.f.* (*children's slang*) *V.* **Dodo**
Dodo, *s.m.* (*children's slang*) bed; sleep; (*bird*) dodo. *Aller faire* —, to go to bye-bye. *Faire* —, to sleep
Dodu, e, *adj.* plump
Dogaresse, *s.f.* wife of the doge
Dogat, *s.m.* dogate, dogeate
Dog-cart, *s.m.* dog-cart
Doge, *s.m.* doge
Dogesse, *s.f.* *V.* **Dogaresse**
Dogmatique, *s.f.* dogmatics
Dogmat-ique (*adj.m.f.*, *s.m.*), **-iquement, -isme, -iste.** *V.* page 3, § 1
Dogmatiser, *v.n.* to dogmatize
Dogmatiseur, *s.m.* dogmatizer
Dogme, *s.m.* dogma, tenet, doctrine [boat
Dogre, Dogrebot, *s.m.* (*nav.*) dogger, dogger-
Dogue, *s.m.* mastiff, house-dog
Doguer (Se), *v.r.* to butt each other, to butt
Doguet, *s.m.* codling, young cod
Doguin, e, *s.m.f.* pug-dog, pug
Doigt, *s.m.* finger; toe; (*fig.*) finger, hand; knuckle; finger's breadth; little bit; drop; (*astr.*) digit. — *du pied*, toe. *A deux —s de*, within an inch *or* an ace of, on the brink of. *Au — et à l'œil*, at o.'s beck and call, at a nod; (*of watches*) very badly. *Donner sur les —s à*, to give a rap over the knuckles, to rap ...'s knuckles. *Mettre le — dessus*, to hit the nail (*or* the right nail) on the head, to hit it. *Montrer au* or *du* —, to point at. *Tirer au — mouillé*, to draw lots. *Mon petit — me l'a dit*, a little bird told it me [ing well indicated
Doigté, e, *adj.* (*mus.*) *Bien* —, with the finger-
Doigté, Doigter, *s.m.* (*mus.*) fingering
Doigter, *v.n.a.* (*mus.*) to finger; to mark *or* indicate the fingering on
Doigtier, *s.m.* finger-stall, thumb-stall; thimble
Dois, *s.m.* rill, rivulet, runlet, streamlet
Doit, *s.m.* debit, debtor; rill, rivulet, runlet, streamlet
Doite, *s.f.* thickness *or* size of thread
Doitée, *s.f.* bit of thread

Dol, *s.m.* fraud, deceit; drum [dolabella
Dolabelle, *s.f.* small axe *or* hatchet; (*mollusc*)
Dolabre, *s.f.* (*ancient hatchet*) dolabra, celt
Dolabriforme, *adj.* (*nat. hist.*) dolabriform
Dolage, *s.m.* adzing; chipping; planing; paring
Dolce, *adv.* (*mus.*) dolce (*softly, sweetly*) [ance
Doléance, *s.f.* complaint; lamentation; griev-
Dolemment, *adv.* dolefully, mournfully, whiningly [*s.m.f.* mourner
Dolent, e, *adj.* doleful, mournful, whining; —
Doler, *v.a.* to adze; to chip; to plane; to pare
Dolérine, Dolérite, *s.f.* (*min.*) dolerite
Dolic, Dolique, *s.m.* (*bot.*) dolichos
Doliman, *s.m.* (*Turkish garment*) doliman, dolman; (*mil.*) *V.* **Dolman**
Dollar, *s.m.* dollar (*coin*)
Dolman, *s.m.* (*mil., of hussars and other cavalry corps*) shell-jacket, jacket; (*obsolete*) hussar's pelisse, pelisse, slung-jacket
Dolmen, Dolmin, *s.m.* dolmen, tolmen, cromlech (*druidical remains*)
Doloir, *s.m.* paring-knife, parer [hatchet
Doloire, *s.f.* cooper's adze, adze, chip-axe, axe,
Dolomie, Dolomite, *s.f.* (*min.*) dolomite
Dolorifuge, *adj.m.f.*, *s.m.* soothing; soothing remedy
Dom, *s.m.* dom, don
Domaine, *s.m.* domain; demesne; estate; homestead; land; property; possession; department, province; limits, compass, sphere. *Tomber dans le — public*, to become public property
Domanial, e, *adj.* domanial
Domanialiser, *v.a.* to annex (to a domain)
Dombéye, *s.f.* (*bot.*) dombeya
Dôme, *s.m.* dome; canopy; round top, swelling hill
Domerie, *s.f.* abbey
Domestication, *s.f.* domestication
Domesticité, *s.f.* domesticity, being in service, menial condition; domestic servants, servants, domestics, domestic establishment, household; domesticated state, tameness
Domestique, *adj.* domestic; household; house; homely; home-bred; internal, home; menial; familiar; tame, domesticated; — *s.m.f.* servant, domestic, domestic servant; man-servant; female servant, woman-servant, maid servant; — *s.m.* servants, domestics; household; home. — *à* (or *pour*) *tout faire*, servant of all work, general servant [tically; familiarly
Domestiquement, *adv.* as a servant; domes-
Domestiquer, *v.a.* to domesticate, to tame
Se —, *v.r.* to become domesticated
Domicile, *s.m.* residence, abode, dwelling, home; domicile. *A* —, at *or* to o.'s (own) house, at *or* to people's houses, at home; outdoor. *Élire —, faire élection de* —, *V.* **Élire**
Domiciliaire, *adj.* domiciliary
Domicilié, e, *adj.* resident; residing; settled; domiciled; — *s.m.f.* resident, inhabitant
Domicilier (Se), *v.r.* to settle; to be settled
Dominance, *s.f.* dominance, predominance
Dominant, e, *adj.* dominant; predominant; ruling; commanding; overbearing, domineering; prevailing, prevalent; reigning; presiding; leading; established; — *s.f.* (*mus.*) dominant
Domina-teur, trice, *adj.* ruling, governing, dominant; overbearing, domineering; commanding; — *s.m.f.* ruler, dominator; tyrant
Dominati-f, ve, *adj.* dominative
Domination, *s.f.* dominion, government, power, rule, sway, command; domination
Dominer, *v.a.n.* to rule, to sway, to govern; to get over, to master; to domineer; to lord it over; to drown (*sounds*); to rise above; to overlook, to tower over, to command a view of; to command; to hang over, to overhang; to predominate, to prevail [of ditto
Domingois, e, *adj. s.* of St. Domingo; native
Dominicain, e, *adj. s.* Dominican, Dominican (black) friar *or* nun [sermon
Dominical, e, *adj.* dominical; — *s.f.* Sunday
Domino, *s.m.* domino; coloured paper. *Faire* —, to play out. — ! *int.* out !

Dominoterie, *s.f.* coloured paper
Dominoti-er, ère, *s.m.f.* paper-stainer
Domite, *s.f.* (*min.*) domite
Dommage, *s.m.* damage, injury, harm, loss; prejudice, wrong; pity. —*s-intérêts*, —*s et intérêts*, damages. *C'est* —, it is a pity [judicial
Dommageable, *adj.* injurious, hurtful, pre-
Dommageablement, *adv.* injuriously, hurtfully, prejudicially
Domptable, *adj.* tamable, governable, manageable, conquerable, to be subdued [breaker
Domptaire, *s.m.* (*of oxen*) quiet yoke-mate,
Domptement, *s.m.* taming
Dompter, *v.a.* to subdue; to conquer; to overcome; to master; to quell; to restrain; to keep under; to tame, to break
Se —, *v.r.* to govern *or* subdue o.'s passions; to contain oneself; to be subdued *or* &c.
Dompteur, *s.m.* subduer; tamer, breaker
Dompte-venin, *s.m.* (*bot.*) swallow-wort, tame-poison
Don, *s.m.* gift; present; donation; endowment; allowance; grant; advantage; boon; favour; talent; knack; command; habit; (*title*) don
Dona, *s.f.* (*title*) dona, donna
Donace, *s.f.* (*shell-fish*) donax
Donataire, *s.m.f.* donee
Dona-teur, trice, *s.m.f.* donor, giver
Donation, *s.f.* donation; gift; grant; deed of gift. — *entre-vifs*, donation *or* gift inter vivos
Donat-isme, -iste. *V.* page 3, § 1
Donax, *s.m.* (*bot.*) donax
Donc, *conj. adv. int.* then; therefore, consequently, hence, accordingly, so; pray; do; just; now; now then; come; eh; to be sure
Dondon, *s.f.* plump *or* jolly woman *or* girl, bouncer [belvedere
Donjon, *s.m.* castle-keep, keep, donjon; turret;
Donjonné, e, *adj.* turreted
Donnant, e, *adj.* giving, liberal, generous. — *donnant*, give and take, tit for tat, giff-gaff
Donne, *s.f.* deal (*at cards*)
Donné, e, *part. adj.* given, &c. (*V.* **Donner**). *Marché* —, dead bargain. *Être* — *à*, to be given to. *Être* — *à* ... *de*, (*imp.*) ... to be permitted *or* allowed to; to fall to ...'s lot to, to be ...'s lot *or* fortune to; to be in ...'s power to; to be in ... to; to have the advantage *or* the good luck to
Donnée, *s.f.* giving; gift; dead bargain; distribution; notion, idea, conception; information; indication, clue; datum (*pl.* data); fact; basis; canvas; subject; known *or* given quantity
Donner, *v.a.n.* to give; to give away *or* out; to give in; to bestow, to confer; to present; to grant; to allow; to afford; to furnish, to supply, to provide; to devote, to consecrate; to let have; to leave; to deliver; to consign; to produce, to yield, to bear; to bring in; to bring; to pay; to lay down; to stake; to administer; to impart, to communicate; to cause, to occasion; to inspire; to infuse; to rouse, to arouse; to call (*names*); to pass off (for); to warrant; to ascribe, to attribute; to suppose; to take (...) to be; to give to guess; to afford matter (for); to make; to permit, to allow; to let; to wish *or* bid (*good morning*, &c.); to set (*an example, task*, &c.); to perform, to act, to play; to publish; to show; to appoint, to fix; to strike, to knock, to hit, to beat, to rap; to dash; to attack; to blow *or* wind (*a horn*); to look *or* look out (into), to front, to face; to go, to lead, to communicate, to open (into); to get; to run; to rush; to fall; to shine, to dart its beams; to drive; to blow; to believe; to indulge, to like; to devote oneself, to give oneself up (to); to take up, to embrace; to be abundant *or* plentiful; to act (*on the nerves*); (*of liquors*) to get (*into o.'s head*); (*at cards*) to deal; (*mil.*) to give (*battle*), to fight (*a battle*); to charge, to engage, to attack, to fight; (*nav.*) to shape (*the course*); to run (*ashore*, &c.); (*law*) to issue (*writs*); (*com.*) to sell, to let have; (*slang*) to split upon, to denounce. — *à penser* or *à réfléchir*, to set thinking, to make (one) think; to puzzle. — *à rire*, to provoke a laugh, to make (one) laugh. *La* — *belle* or *bonne à, le* — *beau a, en* — *d'une belle à*, to give a fair opportunity *or* a fine chance; to tell stories *or* fine stories; to make fun of; to make a fool of; to deceive, to impose upon, to put upon; to try to gull; to humbug. *Vous me la donnez belle*, you are telling me fine stories *or* a fine story; a pretty story that! that's all very well. *Le* — *en dix, vingt* or *&c.*, to give ten, twenty *or* &c. times to guess it in. — *a quelqu'un dix, vingt* or *&c. ans*, to take one to be ten, twenty *or* &c. years old. *Quel âge lui donneriez-vous?* how old should you take him (*or* her) to be? — *du monseigneur* or *de l'altesse* or *&c. à*, to call (*or* style, "my Lord" *or* "your Highness" *or* &c. — *à la tête*; — *de la tête contre*; *Ne savoir où* — *de la tête*; *V.* **Tête.** *Il m'a été donné de*, I have been permitted *or* allowed **to**; it has fallen to my lot to; &c. (*V.* **Donné**)
Se —, *v.r.* to give oneself *or* to oneself; to procure, to get; to gain; to acquire; to give oneself up; to devote oneself; to attach oneself; to be addicted; to take (to); to assume; to take; to have; to ascribe *or* attribute *or* appropriate *or* take to oneself; to strike, to knock, to hit (o.'s ...); to give *or* &c. (*V.* **Donner**) each other *or* to each other; to be given *or* bestowed *or* &c. (*V.* **Donner**); to take place; (*of battles*) to be fought, to be given, to take place; (*of diseases*) to be catching. *Se* — *pour*, to give oneself out for, to pass oneself off for (*or* as), to set up for, to pretend *or* profess to be. *S'en* —, to indulge *or* enjoy oneself; to have such fun *or* such a treat; to have a nice *or* fine time of it; to have a bout of it; to keep it up; to take o.'s fill; to have o.'s fling. *Se la* —, (*pop.*) to run away, to bolt. *Se* — *de la peine*; *Se* — *la peine de* ...; *V.* **Peine**
Donneu-r, se, *s.m.f.* giver; — *adj.* fond of giving, of a giving disposition
Don-Quichotte, *s.m.* Don Quixote; madcap; volunteer champion; lanky fellow
Don-Quichottique, *adj.* Quixotic
Don-Quichottisme, *s.m.* Quixotism
Dont, *pron.* (*stands for* **De** *and* **lequel** *or* **laquelle,** &c., *or for* **De qui,** *or for* **De quoi,** *or for* **D'où**) whose, of whom; from whom; out of whom; of which; from which; whereof; wherefrom; with *or* by *or* about *or* to *or* for *or* &c. (*V.* **De**) whom; with *or* by *or* about *or* to *or* for *or* &c. (*V.* **De**) which; wherewith; by means of which; out of which; in which; whom; which; from where, whence, from
Donte, *s.f.* body (*of a lute*, &c.) [whence
Donville, *s.m.f.* donville (*kind of late pear*)
Donzelle, *s.f.* damsel, wench; (*fish*) ophidion
Dorade, *s.f.* (*zool.*) gold-fish; coryphene, dolphin, razor-fish, dorado; (*astr.*) dorado, sword-
†**Doradille,** *s.f.* (*bot.*) spleenwort, miltwort [fish
Dorage, *s.m.* gilding; (*of meat-pies, cakes*) glazing; (*of head-dresses*) doing up
Doré, e, *adj.* gilt; gilded; golden; yellow; gold (*colour*); glazed; rich, fine, brilliant, smooth; — *s.m.* gilding; gilt metal; gilt articles; —**e,** *s.f.* slice of bread and butter (*or* jam); (*fish*) John Dory, dory. *Langue* —*e*, silver tongue
Dorême, *s.m.* (*bot.*) dorema
Dorénavant, *adv.* henceforth, in future
Dorer, *v.a.* to gild; to glaze (*a meat-pie, a cake*); to do up (*a head-dress*)
Se —, *v.r.* to be gilded, to gild; to become yellow, to assume a golden hue
Doreu-r, se, *s.m.f.* gilder
Dorien, ne, *adj. s.* Dorian, Doric
Dorine, *s.f.* (*bot.*) golden saxifrage
Dorique, *adj.m.f., s.m.* Doric
Doris, *s.f.* (*mollusc*) doris

Dorloter, *v.a.* to coddle; to nurse up, to nurse; to pet; to pamper; to cocker; to fondle; to make much of; to indulge

Se —, *v.r.* to nurse oneself up; to indulge oneself; to take great care of oneself; to take o.'s ease [to have a broken sleep

†**Dormailler, Dormasser,** *v.n.* to sleep badly,

Dormant, e, *adj.* sleeping; dormant; standing; still, stagnant; fixed; dead; unemployed; dull; quiet; (*her.*) dormant; — *s.m.* sleeper; dormant; post; fixed frame; epergne

Dormeu-r, se, *s.m.f.* sleeper; sluggard; — *s.f.* lounging chair, easy chair; easy travelling-carriage; ear-ring, ear-wire, sleeper

†**Dormille,** *s.f.* (*fish*) loach

Dormir, *v.n.a.* to sleep; to be asleep; to rest; to lie dormant; to be stagnant *or* still; to be inactive; to be dead; to smoulder. — *sur les deux oreilles*, to sleep soundly; (*fig.*) to feel perfectly safe *or* at ease, to be in security. — *debout* or *tout debout*, to sleep standing; not to be able to keep o.'s eyes open. *A — debout*, to sleep standing; enough to sleep standing; (*of tales*) to send one to sleep, dull, tedious, tiresome, idle, nonsensical; (*of some people's feet*) very large, enormous. *Qui dort dine*, sleeping is as good as eating, he who sleeps wants no

Dormir, *s.m.* rest, sleep; sleeping [dinner

Dormiti-f, ve, *adj.*, **Dormitif,** *s.m.* dormitive,

Doroir, *s.m.* paste-brush, glazing-brush [soporific

Doronic, *s.m.* (*bot.*) leopard's-bane

Dorque, *s.m. V.* **Orque**

Dorsal, e, *adj.* (*anat.*) dorsal; — *s.m.* dorsal

Dorsay, *s.m.* jacket [muscle; — *s.f.* dorsal fin

Dorsch, *s.m.* (*fish*) dorse, variable cod, Baltic

Dorset, *s.m.* Dorset sheep [cod

Dorso-, (*in compounds, anat.*) dorso-...

Dorsténie, *s.f.* (*bot.*) dorstenia, contrayerva

Dortoir, *s.m.* dormitory, sleeping-room, bedroom

Dorure, *s.f.* gilding; gilt object *or* article; (*of meat-pies, cakes*) glazing

Dos, *s.m.* back; rear; top; ridge; (*of the nose*) bridge. — *d'âne*, ass's back; (*tech.*) saddle-back; (*arch.*) shelving-ridge. *A — d'âne, de mulet*, &c., on an ass's back (*or* on asses' backs), on a mule's back (*or* on mules' backs), &c. *En — d'âne*, with a saddle-back, saddle-backed; with a shelving-ridge, sharp-ridged. *Sur le —*, on o.'s back; (*fig.*) on o.'s hands; about o.'s ears; at o.'s elbow; to o.'s account, at o.'s door. *Avoir à —*, to have against one *Avoir bon —*, to have a strong back. *Avoir plein le — de*, (*fam.*) to be heartily sick of. *Faire le gros —*, (*of the cat*) to set up its back; (*fig.*) to scold, to bluster, to talk big; to assume an air of importance, to look big. *Mettre* (or, fam., *Camper*) *sur le — à*, (*fig.*) to load, to saddle (with); to charge (with); to attribute to; to blame (for); to lay to ...'s account *or* at ...'s door. *Se mettre quelqu'un à —*, to make an enemy of a person. *Prendre à —*, (*mil.*) to attack in the rear. *Tourner le —*, to turn o.'s back; to turn tail, to take to flight; to forsake

Dosable, *adj.* measurable

Dosage, *s.m.* (*chem.*) quantitative analysis; (*pharm.*, &c.) dosing; proportion; mixture

Dose, *s.f.* dose; quantity; portion; share; pro-

Doser, *v.a.* to dose; to proportion; to mix [portion

Dosse, *s.f.* plank; wooden pile

Dosseret, *s.m.* pilaster; back-piece

Dossier, *s.m.* back-piece; back (*of a seat, chair*, &c.); chair-screen; head-board (*of a bed*); back-board (*of a boat*); (*of lawyers, admin.*) brief, bag; bundle of papers, papers, documents, papers in the case

Dossière, *s.f.* (*of harness*) back-band, ridge-band; (*of a cuirass*, &c.) backplate, back

Dot, *s.f.* marriage-portion, portion; dowry; independent settlement

Dotal, e, *adj.* of a *or* of the marriage-portion *or* dowry, dotal; of separate property *or* marriage-settlements; separate [entail

Dotation, *s.f.* endowment, dotation; dowry;

Doter, *v.a.* to give a portion to, to portion; to endow; to gift, to favour [ment

Douaire, *s.m.* dower, jointure, marriage-settle-

Douairière, *s.f.*, *adj.f.* dowager; (*fig.*) matron

Douaisien, ne, *adj.s.* of Douai; native of Douai

Douane, *s.f.* customs; custom-house; custom-duty, duty [to pass (*through ditto*); to seal

Douaner, *v.a.* to clear (*goods at the custom-house*);

Douanier, *s.m.* tidewaiter; custom-house officer

Douani-er, ère, *adj.* of customs, relating to the custom-house [*tribe in Algeria*)

Douar, *s.m.* douar (*Arabian village, part of a*

Doublage, *s.m.* doubling; lining; plating; (*of boats and ships*) sheathing; (*print.*) double

Doublant, e, *adj.* (*theat.*) fit to be a substitute

Double, *s.m. adj.* double; twofold; two; twin; twice as much, as much again; twice as many, as many again; twice the quantity *or* number *or* value; duplicate; replica; fold; bight (*of a rope, nav.*); double (*small anc. coin*), doit; substitute, supernumerary (*theat.*); (*of fire-arms*) double-barrelled; (*fig.*) strong (*of superior quality*); deceitful, double-faced; downright, regular, arrant. **—-main,** *s.f.* (*mus.*) *V.* **Main**

Doublé, e, *part. adj. of* **Doubler;** — *s.m. V.* **Plaqué,** *s.m.*; (*at billiards*) doublet

Doubleau, *s.m.* (*carp.*) binding-joist; — *adj. Arc —, V.* **Arc** [(*mil.*) forming two-deep

Doublement, *adv.* doubly; — *s.m.* doubling;

Doubler, *v.a.n.* to double; to double up; to fold; to line; to fur; to plate; to sheathe (*boats and ships*); to duplicate; to reduplicate; to repeat; to go through (...) over again; to superadd; to increase; to complicate; to mend (*o.'s pace*); to outsail, to outrun, to outstrip; to clear; to double *or* round *or* weather (*a cape*); (*mil.*) to form two-deep; (*theat.*) to act as substitute of (*another actor*) *or* in (*a part*), to replace (*another actor*)

Se —, *v.r.* to double, to become double, to be doubled; to be folded *or* lined *or* &c. [doublet

Doublet, *s.m.* (*backgammon, billiards, opt., jewel.*)

Doublette, *s.f.* thick board; (*mus.*) principal (*of an organ*) [(*pers.*) plater; (*phys. instr.*) doubler

Doubleu-r, se, *s.m.f.* (*pers.*) doubler; — *s.m.*

Doublon, *s.m.* (*coin*) doubloon; (*print.*) double; (*tech.*) double; (*local*) two-year old (*colt or calf*)

Doublure, *s.f.* lining; plating, plate (*of gold or silver*); (*theat.*) substitute, supernumerary

Douc, *s.m.* (*monkey*) douc

Douce, *fem. of* **Doux.** *A la —, adv. pop. for* **Doucement;** *int.* sweet cherries!

Douce-amère, *s.f.* (*bot.*) bitter-sweet, woody nightshade, dulcamara

Douceâtre, *adj.* sweetish

Doucement, *adv.* sweetly; softly; smoothly; mildly; gently; quietly; slowly; leisurely; gradually, by degrees; lightly; faintly; weakly; kindly; meekly; easily; comfortably; pleasantly; indifferently, so so; poorly; (*nav.*) ease her! [creature

Douceret, te, *s.m.f.* mild *or* bland-looking

Doucereusement, *adv.* sweetishly; mawkishly; blandly; coaxingly

Doucereu-x, se, *adj.* sweetish; mawkish; bland; mealy-mouthed; honeyed, sugared; coaxing

Doucet, te, *adj.* sweetish; gentle, mild, bland, demure; — *s.m.* gentle (*or* &c.) -looking fellow *or* creature; (*fish*) gemmeous *or* golden dragonet, yellow sculpin; (*bot.*) doucet (*kind of grape; kind of cider-apple*); — *s.f.* gentle (*or* &c.) -looking woman *or* girl *or* creature; thin silk; (*bot.*) corn-salad, lamb's-lettuce; (*bad spelling of* "Roussette") spotted dog fish; cane-juice

Doucettement, *adv.* gently, softly, so so

Douceur, *s.f.* sweetness; softness; smoothness; mildness; gentleness; gentle means, good words; slowness; moderation; kindness; meekness; easiness; indulgence; sweet thing; pleasure, comfort, delight, charm, consolation;

gratuity, present, fee, profit, douceur; dainty; compliment; flattery; **—s,** *pl.* sweet things, &c.; sweets; soft words. *En* —, gently; quietly; gradually, by degrees; (*nav.*) ease her!
Douche, *s.f.* shower-bath, douche; pumping
Doucher, *v.a.* to shower; to pump
Doucheu-r, se, *s.m.f.* shower-bath man *or* woman
Douchi, Douci, *s.m.* polishing; polish
Doucin, *s.m.* wild apple-tree; brackish water
Doucine, *s.f.* (*carp.*) moulding-plane; (*arch.*) doucine
Doucir, *v.a.* to polish (*looking-glasses*)
Doucissage, *s.m.* polishing
Doué, e, *part. adj.* endowed; gifted; possessed
Douelle, *s.f.* side (*of an arch-stone*); (*abusively*) curve (*of an arch*); stave (*of a cask*)
Douer, *v.a.* to endow; to gift, to favour
Douet, *s.m.* rill, rivulet, runlet, streamlet
†**Douil,** *s.m.* bucket
†**Douillage,** *s.m.* bad texture
†**Douille,** *s.f.* socket, hose; pipe; nozzle (*of a bellows*); case *or* shell (*of a cartridge*); cartridge
†**Douillet, te,** *adj.* soft; delicate, tender, effeminate; — *s.m.f.* delicate person, person who cannot bear the slightest pain, great coward; — *s.f.* wadded gown; wadded slipper, furred shoe
†**Douillettement,** *adv.* softly; delicately, tenderly, effeminately; at ease
†**Douilletter,** *v.a. V.* **Dorloter**
†**Douilletterie,** *s.f.* over-sensitiveness; effeminacy; indulgence
†**Douilleu-x, se,** *adj.* badly woven
†**Douillon,** *s.m.* inferior wool
Douleur, *s.f.* pain; ache; suffering; soreness; grief; sorrow; throe, pang
Douloir (Se), *v.r.* (*old*) to feel pain; to wail, to moan; to complain; to grieve
Douloureusement, *adv.* painfully; sorrowfully; grievously; sadly
Douloureu-x, se, *adj.* painful; smarting; tender, sore; sorrowful; grievous; afflicting; sad; mournful
Doum, *s.m. V.* **Cucifère**
Doupion, *s.m.* twin thread (*of the cocoon*), double thread
Doura, Dourah, *s.m.* (Indian) millet, doura, dourra, dura, durra, dhura
Douro, *s.m.* douro (*Spanish coin, about four shillings*)
Doute, *s.m.* doubt; doubtfulness; misgiving; suspicion; scruple; fear, apprehension. *Hors de* —, beyond doubt, out of the question. *Sans* —, without doubt, doubtless, undoubtedly, unquestionably, no doubt, certainly, to be sure; most likely; likely enough. *Mettre* or *révoquer en* —, to question, to call in question; to doubt. *Cela ne fait pas de* (or *Cela ne fait aucun*) —, there is no doubt of it
Douter, *v.n.* to doubt; to question; to distrust, to mistrust; to be diffident; to suspect; to hesitate. *Ne* — *de rien*, to doubt nothing, to be credulous *or* full of illusions; to be full of self-confidence
Se —, *v.r.* to suspect; to distrust, to mistrust; to have some notion (of); to have the least (*or* any) idea *or* notion (that, of); to imagine, to fancy, to think; to conjecture; to expect; to foresee. *Ne se* — *de rien*, to know nothing of what is going on, to suspect *or* &c. nothing
Douteu-r, se, *s.m.f.* doubter; — *adj.* doubting, incredulous
Douteusement, *adv.* doubtfully; questionably; ambiguously; faintly
Douteu-x, se, *adj.* doubtful; questionable; suspicious; ambiguous; obscure; undecided; uncertain; indistinct; vague; faint; (*obsolete*) wavering, irresolute, timorous, timid, fearful; — *s.m.* uncertain, uncertainty
Douvain, *s.m.* stave-wood, clap-boards, clap-board
Douve, *s.f.* stave; clap-board; trench; moat; walled facing; cave; salt-marsh; freshet; (*zool.*) fluke-worm, liver-fluke, gourd-worm; (*bot.*) spearwort
Douvelle, *s.f.* stave; clap-board
Douville, *s.m.f. V.* **Donville**
Dou-x, ce, *adj.* sweet; soft; smooth; mild; gentle; easy; quiet; calm; tranquil; moderate; pleasant, pleasing, agreeable, delightful, delicious, charming; fond; harmonious; bland; meek; kind; tractable; mellow; unfermented; (*of water*) fresh (*not salt*); (*of water*) soft; — *adv.* gently, softly (*V.* **Tout** —); — *s.m.* sweet, &c.; sweetness, softness, &c. (*V.* **Douceur**); sweet *or* mild stuff *or* substance
Douzain, *s.m.* piece of poetry *or* stanza of twelve lines; twelve packs (*of cards*)
Douzaine, *s.f.* dozen. *A la* —, by the dozen; to the dozen; very ordinary, indifferent
Douze, *adj.m.f.*, *s.m.* twelve; twelfth
Douzième, *adj.m.f.*, *s.m.* twelfth; twelfth part; — *s.f.* (*mus.*), *s.m.f.* (*pers.*) twelfth
Douzièmement, *adv.* twelfthly
Douzil, *s.m.* (*local*) spigot, peg
Doxolog-ie, -ique. *V.* page 3, § 1
Doyen, *s.m.* dean; senior *or* oldest member, senior, oldest
Doyenne, *s.f.* senior member, senior; superioress
Doyenné, *s.m.* deanery; (*hort.*) doyenne (*pear*)
Doyenneté, *s.f.* seniority
Draban, *s.m. V.* **Traban**
Dracène, *s.f.* she-dragon
‡**Drachme,** *s.m.f.* (*Gr. coin and weight*) drachm, drachma; (*weight in old pharm.*) dram, drachm
Dracine, *s.f.* (*chem.*) dracine, draconine
Dracocéphale, *s.m.* (*bot.*) dragon's-head
Draconcule, *s.m.* (*fish*) dragonet, sculpin; (*bot.*) dragon's-wort
Draconien, ne, *adj.* Draconian; Draconic; (*zool.*) dracontine
Draconine, *s.f.* (*chem.*) draconine, dracine
Draconte, *s.m.*, **Dracontie,** *s.f.*, **Dracontion,** *s.m.* (*bot.*) dracontium
Drag, *s.m.* drag (*carriage*)
Dragage, *s.m.* dredging
Dragante, *s.f.* dracanth
Drage, *s.f. V.* **Drèche**
Dragée, *s.f.* sugar-plum, comfit, bull's-eye, sugared almond; dust-shot; (*agr.*) meslin; (*jest.*) pill; (*jest.*) bullet. *Tenir la* — *haute à*, to keep long in suspense; to make (*one*) pay a high price (for ...); to keep o.'s terms high with
Drageoir, *s.m.* comfit-dish; comfit-box; groove
Drageon, *s.m.* (*bot.*) sucker, root-shoot
Drageonner, *v.n.* (*bot.*) to shoot suckers
Dragier, *s.m. V.* **Drageoir**
Dragme, *s.m. V.* **Drachme**
Dragoman, *s.m. V.* **Drogman**
Dragon, *s.m.* (*myth., astr., zool., her.*, &c.) dragon; (*mil.*) dragoon; (*fig.*) termagant, virago; imp; (*obsolete*) spot (*in the eye*); (*obsolete*) care, grief, blue devils. — *de vertu*, person affecting an austere virtue, great prude
Dragonnade, *s.f.* dragoonade, dragonnade
Dragonne, *s.f.* termagant, virago; (*mil.*) sword-knot. *A la* —, in dragoon fashion; unceremoniously, cavalierly; with a high hand
Dragonné, e, *adj.* (*her.*) dragonnee
Dragonneau, *s.m.* (*worm*) Guinea-worm, thread-worm; (*fish*) dragonet, sculpin; (*jewel.*) spot (*in a diamond*)
Dragonner, *v.a.* to dragoon; to harass, to torment, to worry
Dragonnier, *s.m.* (*bot.*) dragon-tree
Drague, *s.f.* dredge-net, dredge, drag-net, drag; dredging-machine, dredger, dredge; grains (*of malt*)
Draguer, *v.a.* to dredge; to drag
Draguette, *s.f.* small dredge *or* drag-net
Dragueu-r, se, *s.m.f.* (*pers.*) dredger; — *s.m.* (*adj.m., Bateau* —) dredging-machine, dredger, dredge; fishing-boat; — *adj.m.f.* dredging
Drain, *s.m.* (*agr.*) drain; drain-pipe
Drainage, *s.m.* (*agr., surg., fig.*) drainage, draining
Draine, *s.f.* (*bird*) missel thrush
Drainer, *v.a.* (*agr., surg., fig.*) to drain
Drainette, *s.f.* small fishing-net
Draineur, *s.m.* (*agr.*) drainer; — *adj.m.*, **-euse,** *f.* draining
Draisienne, *s.f.* velocipede
Dramatique, *adj.m.f.*, *s.m.* dramatic; drama, dramatic style *or* form *or* interest *or* situations; dramatist

Dramatiquement, *adv.* dramatically
Dramatiser, *v.a.* to dramatize [matist
Dramatiste, *s.m.f.*, **Dramaturge,** *s.m.* dra-
Dramaturg-ie, -ique. *V.* page 3, § 1
Drame, *s.m.* drama
Drap, *s.m.* cloth; (*of beds*) sheet. — *marin*, — *de mer*, (*of shells*) periostracum. *Dans de beaux —s*, (*fam., jest.*) in a fine mess *or* pickle
Drapé, e, *part. adj.* covered, draped, hung, &c. (*V.* **Draper**); cloth-like; milled; woollen; (*bot.*) dense
Drapeau, *s.m.* flag, standard, banner, ensign, colours; (*obsolete*) rag, clout; (*med.*) pterygium. *Sous les —x*, in the service. *Se ranger sous les —x de*, to serve under; (*fig.*) to espouse the cause of, to side with
Draper, *v.a.* to cover; to cover with black cloth; to hang with drapery, to drape; to arrange, to dispose; to make the drapery of; to mill; to censure, to ridicule, to rail at, to banter, to abuse
Se —, *v.r.* to wrap oneself up; to dress; to make a show, to boast; to attitudinize; to be covered *or* &c.; to censure *or* &c. each other
Draperie, *s.f.* drapery; woollen cloths *or* stuffs, cloth-work, cloth; cloth-trade; cloth-making; cloth-manufactory
Drapi-er, ère, *s.m.f.* woollen-draper, draper; clothier; — *s.f.* skewer (*pin*); — *adj.m.f.* of the cloth-trade, cloth
Drastique, *adj.m.f.*, *s.m.* drastic
Drave, *s.f.* (*bot.*) whitlow-grass
Drawback, *s.m.* (*com.*) drawback
Drayage, *s.m.* fleshing (*of hides*)
Drayer, *v.a.* to flesh (*hides*)
Drayoire, *s.f.* fleshing-knife
Drayure, *s.f.* fleshings (*of hides*)
Drèche, *s.f.* malt; grains
Drège, Dreige, *s.f. V.* **Drague**
Drégeur, Dreigeur, *s.m. V.* **Dragueur**
Drelin, *s.m.* tinkling, tinkle, ding; jingling, jingle
Drenne, *s.f. V.* **Draine**
Dressage, *s.m.* erecting, erection; raising; laying out; preparation; putting *or* setting up; training; &c. (*V.* **Dresser**)
Dresse, *s.f.* (*of shoes*, &c.) filling-up stuff
Dressé, e, *part. adj.* erected, &c. (*V.* **Dresser**); erect; straight; upright; standing; sticking up; — *s.m.* training
Dresser, *v.a.n.* to erect; to raise; to put *or* set up; to lift up; to hold upright; to lay out; to arrange; to prepare; to spread; to lay; to draw up; to make out (*accounts*); to make; to train; to teach; to break; to form; to direct; to point; to prick up; to stand on end; to pitch; to straighten; to smooth; to trim; to dress
Se —, *v.r.* to stand up *or* erect; to stand; to stick up; to start up; to stand on end; to rise; to rear; to form oneself; to erect *or* raise to oneself; to be erected *or* raised *or* &c.; to be trained [mer; dresser
Dresseur, *s.m.* trainer; breaker; raiser; trim-
Dressoir, *s.m.* sideboard; dresser
Drill, *s.m.* (*zool., agr.*) drill
†Drille, *s.m.* fellow, dog, buck; — *s.f.* drill (*borer*); —**s,** *s.f.pl.* (*cust.*) rags (*woollen and others*), old ropes, oakum. *Bon —*, jolly fellow
†Drillé, e, *adj.* drilled, drill-eyed (*needle*)
Drimyde, *s.f.* (*bot.*) drimys
Drisse, *s.f.* (*nav.*) gear; halyard; hoist
Drogman, *s.m.* dragoman, drogman, interpreter
Drogmanat, *s.m.* dragomanship
Drogue, *s.f.* drug; stuff, trash, rubbish, refuse; nasty ill-tempered fellow *or* thing, disagreeable ditto, cross-patch, ugly customer, bitch; drogue (*game at cards among soldiers; forked stick or split peg which the loser at ditto has to keep on his nose*)
Droguer, *v.a.n.* to drug; to physic; to doctor; to adulterate; to wait *or* trudge in vain *or* for nothing, to dance attendance; to drudge; to play the game of "drogue"

Droguerie, *s.f.* drugs; drug-trade; druggist's
Droguet, *s.m.* drugget [business, drysaltery
Droguetier, *s.m.* drugget-maker
Drogueur, *s.m.* drugging doctor; impostor collecting money for some imaginary misfortune
Droguier, *s.m.* medicine-chest; collection of
Droguiste, *s.m.f.* druggist; drysalter [drugs
Droit, e, *adj.* straight; direct; right; right-hand; upright; up, erect; stand-up, stick-up; single-breasted; sound; straightforward; righteous. — *comme un* I, *comme un jonc, comme un cierge*, as straight as an arrow, bolt upright. *Se tenir —*, to stand upright; to sit up; to hold up o.'s head
Droit, *adv.* straight; right, directly; upright; uprightly, fairly, honestly, justly; rightly. *Tout —*, quite straight; straight; straight on, right on; right; upright
Droit, *s.m.* right; power; claim, title; law; justice; due, duty (*tax*); toll; fee; franchise; freedom (*of the city*). — *canon*, canon law. — *écrit*, statute law. —*s réunis*, (*obsolete*) excise. *A bon —*, justly, with justice, with reason. *Au — de*, opposite. *De —*, of course; by right; in reason; in law; of law, law. *Qui de —*, those whom it may concern; the proper person *or* persons; the proper quarter. *Donner — à*, to give a right to; to entitle to; to decide in favour of. *Être en — de*, to have a right to; to be entitled to; to be justified in *or* to; to be authorized *or* allowed to. *Faire — à*, to do justice to; to give (*one*) his due; to accede to, to grant. *Faire son —*, to study the law. *Mettre en — de*, to give a right to; to entitle to; to justify in *or* to. *En avoir le —*, to have a right to do (*or* say) so. *Y avoir —*, to have a right to it
Droite, *s.f.* right, right hand, right-hand side, right side; right wing (*of an army*); (*geom.*) straight line. *A —*, on *or* to the right, right; (*mil.*) right face!
Droitement, *adv.* rightly; uprightly; judiciously; soundly; straightforwardly
Droiti-er, ère, *adj. s.* right-handed
Droiture, *s.f.* uprightness, justice, equity; rectitude, soundness; straightforwardness. *En —*, directly, direct, straight
Drolatique, *adj.* droll, funny, comical, facetious, merry, humorous
Drolatiquement, *adv.* comically, humorously
Drôle, *adj.* droll, funny, comical; humorous; odd, queer, queer sort of; strange; pleasant; — *s.m.* rogue, knave, rascal, scoundrel, blackguard, scamp; fellow. — *de corps*, odd *or* queer fellow, odd fish. *Mauvais —*, thorough blackguard [forsooth
Drôlement, *adv.* comically; queerly; indeed,
Drôlerie, *s.f.* drollery, droll thing; piece of fun; funny trick; trifle; roguish trick
Drôlesse, *s.f.* wench, hussy, jade, bitch
Drôlichon, ne, *adj.* (*pop.*) funny, rum
Dromadaire, *s.m.* dromedary
Drome, *s.f.* (*nav.*) float, raft; spare masts *or* yards; — *s.m.* (*bird*) dromas
Dromie, *s.f.* (*zool.*) dromia, sponge-crab
Dromon, *s.m.* (*ancient boat*) dromond
Drongo, *s.m.* (*bird*) drongo
Dronte, *s.m.* (*bird*) dronte, dodo
Dropax, *s.m.* (*pharm.*) dropax
Droschki, *s.m.* drosky (*Russian carriage*)
Drosère, *s.f.* (*bot.*) drosera, sundew
Drosomètre, *s.m.* drosometer
Drosométr-ie, -ique. *V.* page 3, § 1
Drosophile, *s.f.* (*insect*) drosophila
Drosse, *s.f.* (*nav.*) truss, rope
Drosser, *v.a.n.* to drive *or* drift ashore, to drive,
†Drouillette, *s.f.* mackerel-net [to drift
Drouine, *s.f.* tinker's bag
Drouineur, Drouinier, *s.m.* tinker
Droussage, *s.m.* oiling and carding (*wool*)
Drousser, *v.a.* to card (*wool*)
Droussette, *s.f.* coarse comb (*for wool*)
Drousseur, *s.m.* wool-comber, cloth-dresser

Dru, e, *adj.* fledged; brisk, lively; sturdy, strong; thick, close; — *adv.* thick, close, hard, fast. — *comme mouches,* as thick as hail
Druidal, e, *adj.* druidical
Druide, *s.m.* druid
Druidesse, *s.f.* druidess
Druid-ique, -isme. *V.* page 3, § 1
Drupacé, e, *adj.* (*bot.*) drupaceous
Drupe, *s.m.* (*bot.*) drupe
Druse, *s.f.* (*min.*) druse; — *s.m. adj.* (*geog.*) Druse
Dryade, *s.f.* (*myth.*) dryad, wood-nymph; (*bot.*) dryas
Du, *art.m.* [*contraction of* **De le,** *art.*] of the, of; from the, from; &c. (*V.* **De**); some; any; something; anything; something of; anything of
Dû, *m.*, **Due,** *f.*, *part. adj.* owed; been obliged; &c. (*V.* **Devoir**); due; owing; proceeding, coming (from); the work (of)
Dû, *s.m.* due; (*obsolete*) duty, duties
Dualisme, *s.m.* dualism
Dualiste, *s.m.f.* dualist; — *adj.* dualistic
Dualistique, *adj.* dualistic
Dualité, *s.f.* duality
Duarchie, *s.f.* duarchy
Dubita-teur, trice, *adj. s. V.* **Douteur**
Dubitati-f, ve, *adj.* dubitative, expressing *or* implying doubt
Dubitation, *s.f.* dubitation, doubt
Dubitativement, *adv.* doubtingly
Duc, *s.m.* duke; (*bird*) horn-owl
Ducal, e, *adj.* ducal
Ducat, *s.m.* (*coin*) ducat
Ducaton, *s.m.* (*coin*) ducatoon
Duché, *s.m.* duchy; dukedom. — **-pairie,** *s.m.f.* dukedom with a peerage (attached to it)
Duchesse, *s.f.* duchess; couch. — *d'Angoulême,* —, duchess (*pear*). *Lit à la* —, four-post bedstead
Ducroire, *s.m.* (*com.*) del credere
Ductile, *adj.* ductile
Ductilimètre, *s.m.* ductilimeter
Ductilité, *s.f.* ductility [the same, of *or* from ditto
Dudit, *adj.m.* of *or* from the said; of *or* from
†**Duègne,** *s.f.* duenna, governess (*in Spain and Portugal*); (*jest.*) old woman
Duel, *s.m.* duel; duelling; duello; (*Gr. gram.*)
Duelliste, *s.m.* duellist [dual number
Duettino, *s.m.* (*mus.*) duettino
Dugazon, *s.f.* fond woman, lover
Dugong, *s.m.* (*fish*) dugong
Duire, *v.n.* (*old*) to become; to fit; to suit; to
Duis, *s.m.* canal [be agreeable, to please
Duit, *s.m.* (*fish.*) stake-net, poke-net, weir; (*old*
Duite, *s.f.* weft [(*coin*) doit
Dulcamarine, *s.f.* (*chem.*) dulcamarine
Dulcification, *s.f.* dulcification
Dulcifier, *v.a.* to dulcify, to sweeten
Dulcimer, *s.m.* (*mus. instr.*) dulcimer
Dulcine, *s.f.* (*chem.*) dulcine
Dulcinée, *s.f.* sweetheart, Dulcinea
Dulie, *s.f.* (*worship of saints*) dulia
Dumasine, *s.f.* (*chem.*) dumasine
Dûment, *adv.* duly
Dune, *s.f.* sand-drift, sand-hill, dune; down
Dunette, *s.f.* (*nav.*) poop
Dunkerque, *s.m. Petit* —, curiosity shop, collection of curiosities; whatnot
Dunkerquois, e, *adj. s.* of Dunkirk; Dunkirker
Duo, *s.m.* (*mus., fig.*) duet [kirker
Duodécimal, e, *adj.* duodecimal
Duodécimo, *adv.* twelfthly
Duodénaire, *adj.* duodenary
Duodénal, e, *adj.* (*anat.*) duodenal
Duodénite, *s.f.* (*med.*) duodenitis
Duodénum, *s.m.* (*anat.*) duodenum
Duodi, *s.m.* duodi (*second day of the decade in the calendar of the first French Republic*)
Dupe, *s.f.* dupe; gull [to cheat, to take in, to gull
Duper, *v.a.* to dupe, to deceive, to impose upon,
Duperie, *s.f.* dupery, trickery, trick, fraud, cheat, imposition, take-in, sell; blunder, mull; gullibility
Dupeu-r, se, *s.m.f.* duper, cheat, trickster

Duplicata, *s.m.* duplicate
Duplicati-f, ve, *adj.* duplicative
Duplication, *s.f.* duplication
Duplicature, *s.f.* duplicature [double-dealing
Duplicité, *s.f.* duplicity; doubleness; deceit,
Duplique, *s.f.* (*law*) rebutter; sur-rejoinder
Dupliquer, *v.n.* (*law*) to rebut, to put in a rebutter; to sur-rejoin, to put in a sur-rejoinder
Duquel [*contraction of* **De lequel;** *has some of the senses of* **Dont**]
Dur, e, *adj.* hard; hardened; firm; tough; harsh; severe; hard-hearted; painful; rough; sharp; thick, dull; stiff; miserable; — *adv.* hard; hardly; firmly; — *s.m.* hard, &c.; hardness; firmness; toughness; &c.; (*pop.*) brandy; — *s.f.* bare ground *or* floor; bare board; hard bed. — *à cuire,* (*fig., pop.*) tough, hardy; *s.m.* tough fellow. *A la* —*e,* hardily. — **-bec,** *s.m.* (*bird*) hawfinch. —**e-mère,** *s.f.* (*anat.*) dura-mater
Durabilité, *s.f.* durability, durableness [mater
Durable, *adj.* durable, lasting; strong
Durablement, *adv.* durably, lastingly
Duracine, *s.f.* duracine (*kind of peach*)
Duramen, *s.m.* (*bot.*) duramen, heart-wood
Durandal, *s.f.* falchion, brand [while, whilst
Durant, *prep.* during; for; in. — *que,* (*old*)
Durbar, *s.m.* durbar
Durcir, *v.a.n.*, **Se** —, *v.r.* to harden; to stiffen; to indurate; to make *or* get (*or* become) hard *or* tough *or* stiff [induration
Durcissement, *s.m.* hardening; stiffening;
Dure, *adj.f.*, *s.f. V.* **Dur**
Durée, *s.f.* duration; continuance
Durelin, *s.m.* (*bot.*) *V.* **Rouvre**
Durement, *adv.* hard, hardly; harshly; roughly; strongly; sharply; stiffly; severely; austerely
Durer, *v.n.* to last; to continue; to hold out; to endure, to stand; to subsist; to remain; to live; to seem *or* appear long [toughish
Duret, te, *adj.* rather hard *or* tough, hardish,
Dureté, *s.f.* hardness; toughness; harshness; harsh thing; harsh *or* cutting words; hard-heartedness; severity, rigour; austerity; painfulness; roughness; sharpness; stiffness; dulness; hard swelling
Durham, *adj.m.f.*, *s.m.* Durham (ox)
†**Durillon,** *s.m.* callosity, hard skin; corn; flaw
†**Durillonné, e,** *adj.* callous, hard, horny; flawy
†**Durillonner (Se),** *v.r.* to grow callous *or* hard
Durissime, *adj.* (*jest.*) very hard *or* tough
Duriuscule, *adj.* (*jest.*) *V.* **Duret**
Dusi, Dusil, *s.m. V.* **Douzil**
Dusodyle, *s.m. V.* **Dysodyle**
Dussé-je. *V. end of* **Devoir,** *v.a.n.*
Duumvir, *s.m.* duumvir
Duumviral, e, *adj.* duumviral
Duumvirat, *s.m.* duumvirate
Duvet, *s.m.* down; wool, nap
Duveté, e, Duveteu-x, se, *adj.* downy
Dyade, *s.f.* duad, dyad
Dyarchie, *s.f.* duarchy
Dynactinomètre, *s.m.* dynactinometer
Dyname, *s.m.*, **Dynamie,** *s.f.* (*mech.*) dynam, dynamical unit, efficiency, duty
Dynamètre, *s.m.* (*opt.*) dynameter
Dynamique, *s.f.* dynamics; — *adj.* dynamical
Dynam-isme, -iste. *V.* page 3, § 1
Dynamomètre, *s.m.* dynamometer
Dynamométr-ie, -ique. *V.* page 3, § 1
Dynamoscope, *s.m.* (*med.*) dynamoscope
Dynamoscopie, *s.f.* (*med.*) dynamoscopy
Dynaste, *s.m.* dynast, petty ruler, kinglet
Dynast-ie, -ique. *V.* page 3, § 1
Dyostyle, *s.m. adj. V.* **Distyle**
Dyscinésie, *s.f.* (*med.*) dyscinesia
Dyscole, *adj.* (*obsolete*) unsociable
Dyscrasie, *s.f.* (*med.*) dyscrasia, dyscrasy
Dysécée, *s.f.* (*med.*) dysecoia
Dysesthésie, *s.f.* (*med.*) dysæsthesia
Dyslochie, *s.f.* (*med.*) dyslochia
Dysménie, Dysménorrhée, *s.f.* (*med.*) dysmenia, dysmenorrhœa

Dysodie, *s.f.* (*med.*) dysodia
Dysodyle, *s.m.* (*min.*) dysodile
Dysopie, *s.f.* (*med.*) dysopsia, dysopsy
Dysosmie, *s.f.* (*med.*) dysosmia
Dyspepsie, *s.f.* (*med.*) dyspepsia, dyspepsy
Dyspeptique, *adj. s.m.f.* dyspeptic
Dysphagie, *s.f.* (*med.*) dysphagia
Dysphonie, *s.f.* (*med.*) disphony
Dyspnée, *s.f.* (*med.*) dyspnœa
Dyssenterie, *s.f.* dysentery [dysenteric patient
Dyssentérique, *adj.* dysenteric; — *s.m.f.*
Dyssymétrie, *s.f.* want of symmetry
Dyssymétrique, *adj.* unsymmetrical
Dysurie, *s.f.* (*med.*) dysuria, dysury
Dysurique, *adj.* dysuric
Dytique, *adj.* diving; — *s.m.* (*insect*) dytiscus, water-beetle; (*bird*) diver [*horse*)
Dziggueta, *s.m.* dziggetai, kiang (*Tartarian*

E

E, *s.m.* e
Eau, *s.f.* water; rain; stream; river; sea; pond; lake; waves; liquid; vapour; perspiration, sweat; tears; wash (*cosmetic*, &c.); tea (*of plants, meat*); broth; juice (*of fruit*); serum, serosity; gloss, lustre (*of stuffs*); **—x,** *pl.* waters, &c.; watering-place; mineral waters; waterworks; (*artificial*) fountains; tide; flood; wake, track (*of a ship*); (*fig.*) funds. — **bénite,** holy water; (*elliptically for* "— bénite de cour," *See below*). — **bénite de cour,** fair promises, empty promises, blarney, soft sawder, soft soap. — **blanche,** bran-water, bran and water; (*pharm.*) Goulard water. — *de* **boudin,** thin air, smoke, nothing. — *du* **ciel,** rain; rain-water. — **claire,** (*fig.*) very poor work, no good, lost trouble. — *de* **Cologne,** eau de Cologne. **—x et forêts,** (*admin.*) woods and forests. — **forte,** aquafortis; etching. — **-fortier,** *s.m.* etcher. — *de* **Javel,** — *de* **javelle,** eau de javelle (*solution of hypochlorite of potash, bleaching and disinfecting liquid*). — *de* **Luce,** eau de Luce. — **mère,** (*chem.*) mother water; bittern. **—x mortes,** neap tide. — **panée,** toast-water, toast and water. — *de* **puits,** well-water, pump-water. — **régale,** aqua regia. — **rougie,** (weak) wine and water. — *de* **savon,** soapsuds. — **seconde,** (*chem.*) lye-water. — *de* **Seltz,** Seltzer water; soda water. — *de* **vaisselle,** dish-water. **—x-vannes,** *V.* **Vannes.** — **-de-vie,** brandy. — **vive,** spring water; running water; hard water. **—x vives,** (*nav.*) spring tide. *Grandes —x*, great fountains; (*of rivers*) high flood. *Hautes —x*, high-water. *Pleine —*, *V.* **Plein,** *adj. A grande —*, in plenty of water. *D'—*, of *or* from *or* &c. water; (*adject.*) water. *Entre deux —x*, between wind and water; under water. *Faire —*, (*nav.*) to leak, to be leaky, to spring a leak, to make water. *Faire de l'—*, (*nav.*, &c.) to take in water *or* fresh water, to water. *Faire* or *lâcher de l'—*, (*pers.*) to make water, (*fam.*) to pump ship. *Porter de l'— à la mer* or *à la rivière*, to carry coals to Newcastle. *Prendre l'—*, to let in water. *Prendre les —x*, to drink mineral waters, to drink *or* take the waters. *Il n'est* (or *Il n'y a*) *pire —* (or *point de pire —*) *que celle* (or *que l'—*) *qui dort*, still waters run deep. [*For other phrases, V.* **Bec, Bouche, Chute, Cours, Épée, Fleur, Mettre, Mise, Moulin, Sentir, Vin, Voie,** &c.] [wondering
Ébahi, e, *part. adj.* amazed, dumbfounded,
Ébahir (S'), *v.r.* to be amazed, to wonder
Ébahissement, *s.m.* amazement, wonder
Ébarbage, Ébarbement, *s.m.* paring, clipping, &c. (*V.* **Ébarber**)
Ébarber, *v.a.* to pare, to clip, to trim, to cut down; to strip; to scrape; to edge off
Ébarboir, *s.m.* (*tool*) parer, scraper
Ébarbure, *s.f.* chip, chips, parings, clippings,
Ébarouir, *v.a.* (*nav.*) to dry up [scrapings
Ébarouissage, *s.m.* (*nav.*) drying up; shakes
Ébat, *s.m.* sport, play, diversion; pastime; fun; gambol, frolic; turn-out, exercise. *Prendre ses —s*, *V.* **Ébattre (S')**
Ébattement, *s.m.* (*obsolete*) *V.* **Ébat;** (*of a vehicle*) balancing, swinging
Ébattre (S'), *v.r.* to disport *or* enjoy oneself, to sport, to play, to gambol, to frolic
Ébaubi, e, *adj.* dumbfounded, amazed, astounded, astonished, wondering, wonder-struck
Ébaubir (S'), *v.r.* to marvel, to wonder, to be dumbfounded *or* &c. (*V.* **Ébaubi**)
Ébauchage, *s.m.* sketching, &c. (*V.* **Ébaucher**)
Ébauche, *s.f.* sketch; rough draught; rough model; rough cast; rough attempt; outline; sign, mark, indication
Ébauchement, *s.m.* *V.* **Ébauchage**
Ébaucher, *v.a.* to sketch; to rough-model; to rough-cast; to rough-hew; to rough; to half-finish; to begin; to outline; to trace out; to prepare, to get up; to attempt; (*mas.*) to boast; **S'—,** *v.r.* to be sketched *or* &c. [(*sculp.*) to point
Ébaucheur, *s.m.*, *adj.m.* *V.* **Dégrossisseur**
Ébauchoir, *s.m.* (*mason's*) boaster; (*sculptor's*) point; (*carpenter's*) mortise-chisel [to delight
Ébaudir, *v.a.* to cheer, to exhilarate, to enliven; **S'—,** *v.r.* to cheer, to be *or* make merry, to be in high glee, to be delighted *or* overjoyed, to frisk, to skip about
Ébaudissement, *s.m.* cheering, amusement, sport, merry-making, glee, mirth, delight, frisking, skipping about
Ebbe, Èbe, *s.f.m.* (*local*) ebb, ebb-tide
Ébène, *s.f.m.* (*wood*) ebony; — *s.m.* (*colour, work*) ebony, jet-black; ebony-work. — *rouge*, Grenada cocus, grenadillo
Ébéner, *v.a.* to ebonize [burnum
Ébénier, *s.m.* (*bot.*) ebony-tree. *Faux-* —, laburnum
Ébénin, e, *adj.* ebon
Ébéniste, *s.m.* cabinet-maker; ebonist
Ébénisterie, *s.f.* cabinet-making *or* work
Éberluer, *v.a.* to dazzle, to strike with dizziness, to wonder-strike, to amaze
Éberner, *v.a.* *V.* **Ébrener** [**Abêtir**
Ébêtement, Ébêtir. *V.* **Abêtissement** *and*
Ébloui, e, *part. adj.* dazzled, &c. (*V.* **Éblouir**); dizzy [to fascinate; to deceive
Éblouir, *v.a.* to dazzle; to dim; to make dizzy; **S'—,** *v.r.* to be dazzled *or* confused
Éblouissement, *s.m.* dazzling; flash; dimness; dizziness; fascination, charm; error
†**Éborgnage,** *s.m.* (*hort.*) nipping off buds
†**Éborgner,** *v.a.* to blind of one eye; to almost blind; to shut out the light from (*a house*, &c.); (*hort.*) to nip the buds off
Ébotter, *v.a.* to top; to prune
Ébouage, *s.m.* scavenging
Ébouer, *v.a.* to scavenge
Éboueur, *s.m.* road-scraper, scavenger
Ébouffer (S'), *v.r.* — *de rire*, to burst out laughing, to roar with laughter
†**Ébouillanter,** *v.a.* to apply boiling water to
†**Ébouillir,** *v.n.* to boil down, to boil away
Éboulement, *s.m.* falling, fall, falling in, falling down, sinking; earth-fall, earth-slip; landslip; rubbish
Ébouler, *v.n.*, **S'—,** *v.r.* to fall, to fall in *or* down, to sink; — *v.a.* to cause to fall, to bring
Ébouleu-x, se, *adj.* liable to fall, loose [down
Éboulis, *s.m.* rubbish, heap of fallen rubbish, fallen ground
Ébouqueu-r, se, *s.m.f.* (*manu.*) burler
Ébourgeonnage, Ébourgeonnement, *s.m.* (*hort.*) nipping off buds, disbudding
Ébourgeonner, *v.a.* (*hort.*) to disbud, to nip the buds off [*adj.m.* bud-picking
Ébourgeonneur, *s.m.* (*bird*) bud-picker; —
Ébourgeonnoir, *s.m.* (*hort.*) nipping-knife
Ébouriffé, e, *adj.* disordered, ruffled, rough; with o.'s hair in disorder; dazzled, astounded,

stunned, astonished, amazed, dumbfounded; startled, staggered; scandalized; flurried, in a flurry, in a flutter

Ébouriffer, *v.a.* to disorder, to ruffle; to disorder *or* make rough *or* ruffle the hair of; to dazzle, to astound, to stun, to astonish, to amaze, to dumbfound; to startle, to stagger; to scandalize; to flurry, to flutter

S'—, *v.r.* to disorder *or* ruffle o.'s (own) *or* each other's hair; to be dazzled *or* astounded [*or* &c.

Ébourrer, *v.a.* to peel (*a hide*)

Ébousiner, *v.a.* (*mas.*) to clean off

Ébraisoir, *s.m.* furnace-shovel

Ébranchage, Ébranchement, *s.m.* lopping, trimming, pruning; breaking branches off

Ébranché, e, *part. adj.* lopped, trimmed, pruned; with broken branches; deprived of branches; branchless

Ébrancher, *v.a.* to lop, to trim, to prune; to break branches off; to deprive of branches

Ébranchoir, *s.m.* bill-hook, pruning-hook

Ébranlement, *s.m.* shaking; tottering; concussion; shock; commotion, disturbance, perturbation, trouble; agitation; emotion; decay; motion, movement; (*of a ship*) straining

Ébranler, *v.a.* to shake; to stagger; to shock; to disturb; to unsettle; to loosen; to agitate; to stir; to move; to put in motion

S'—, *v.r.* to shake; to be shaken *or* &c.; to totter; to flinch; to waver; to give way; to begin to move, to move on; to be set in motion

Ébrasement, *s.m.* (*arch.*) splaying, splay

Ébraser, *v.a.* (*arch.*) to splay

Ébrèchement, *s.m.* notching, &c. (*V.* **Ébrécher**)

Ébrécher, *v.a.* to notch; to jag, to indent; to break off a piece of; to break; to make a gap *or* a hole in; to cut into; to diminish; to impair [&c.; to break a piece off (*o.'s tooth*)

S'—, *v.r.* to become (*or* get) *or* be notched *or*

Ébrener, *v.a.* (*fam.*) to clean (*a child*)

Ébriété, *s.f.* ebriety, inebriety

Ébrieu-x, se, *adj.* ebrious [bridle

†Ébrillade, *s.f.* (*rid.*) ebrillade, jerk with the

Ébriosité, *s.f.* ebriosity

Ébrouage, *s.m.* washing in bran-and-water [ing

Ébrouement, *s.m.* (*rid.*) snorting; (*vet.*) sneez-

Ébrouer, *v.a.* to wash in bran-and-water; to shell *or* husk (*walnuts*)

S'—, *v.r.* (*rid.*) to snort; (*vet.*) to sneeze

Ébroueu-r, se, *s.m.f.* walnut-sheller

Ébruitement, *s.m.* divulgation, disclosure, oozing out

Ébruiter, *v.a.* to divulge, to disclose, to make known, to spread, to report, to noise *or* rumour *or* bruit abroad. *S'—*, to be divulged *or* &c., to be talked of, to get wind, to spread about, to [ooze out

Ébrun, *s.m.* horned rye

Ébuard, *s.m.* wooden wedge

Ébullioscope, *s.m.* ebullioscope

Ébullition, *s.f.* ebullition, boiling; effervescence; rash, breaking out, eruption

Éburne, *s.f.* (*mollusc*) eburna, ivory-shell

Éburné, e, Éburnéen, ne Éburnin, e, *adj.* eburnean [ing, break; flattening; flatness

Écachement, *s.m.* squashing, crushing; break-

Écacher, *v.a.* to squash; to crush; to flatten, to beat flat. *Nez écaché*, flat *or* pug nose [**S'—**)

†Écaillage, *s.m.* scaling, &c. (*V.* **Écailler** *&*

†Écaille, *s.f.* scale; shell; tortoise-shell; chip-

†Écaillé, e, *adj.* scaled, scaly [ping

†Écaillement, *s.m.* scaling, &c. (*V.* **Écailler** *&* **S'—**); copper shells

†Écailler, *v.a.* to scale; to open (*oysters*, &c.)

S'—, *v.r.* to scale off; to peel off; to shell; to chip off; to be scaled; to be opened [woman

†Écaill-er, ère, *s.m.f.* oyster-man; oyster-

†Écailleu-x, se, *adj.* scaly, squamous

Écale, *s.f.* (*bot.*) husk, hull; shell; (*mas.*) rubble; (*nav.*) *V.* **Escale** [*écalée*, separate piece of land

Écaler, *v.a.* to husk, to hull; to shell. *Terre*

S'—, *v.r.* to shell, to come out of the shell *or* husk; to be husked *or* shelled; to chip off

Écaleu-r, se, *s.m.f. V.* **Ébroueur**

Écanguer, *v.a.* to clean (*flax or hemp*)

†Écarbouiller, *v.a.* to crush, to squash

Écarlate, *s.f. adj.* scarlet [ing wide

†Écarquillement, *s.m.* spreading out; open-

†Écarquiller, *v.a.* to spread out; to open wide

Écarrir, &c. *V.* **Équarrir,** &c. [shoulders

Écarrure, *s.f.* top of the back, breadth of

Écart, *s.m.* step aside; opening of the legs; strain; digression; flight; error; fault; mistake; deviation; ramble; range; distance; difference; discarding; cards thrown out; (*mas.*) rubble; (*her.*) quarter; (*nav.*) scarf. *A l'—*, aside; away; off; aloof; on one side; apart; out of the way; in a lonely place; in a retired place, in retirement; in reserve; excluded; by oneself; left to oneself. *Faire un —*, to step *or* start aside; to shy; to make a digression. *Se donner un —*, to strain oneself

Écartable, *adj.* discardable

Écarté, e, *part. adj.* discarded, &c. (*V.* **Écarter**); remote, out of the way, retired, secluded, lonely; — *s.m.* écarté (*game at cards*)

Écarteler, *v.a.* (*pers.*) to quarter, to draw and quarter; (*her.*) to quarter

Écartellement, *s.m.* quartering

Écartelure, *s.f.* (*her.*) quartering

Écartement, *s.m.* removal; scattering; spreading; opening; divergence; separation; parting; space between, interval

Écarter, *v.a.* to discard; to throw out *or* away *or* back; to divert; to avert; to turn aside *or* away *or* off; to ward off; to remove; to lay *or* put *or* set aside; to put by; to put out of the way; to put *or* place *or* set apart (*or* wide apart); to keep away *or* off *or* out *or* back; to exclude; to lead (from); to drive away; to disperse; to scatter; to put to flight; to dissipate; to dispel; to dismiss; to reject; to waive; to elude; to separate; to spread out, to spread; to open, to spread open; to widen; to extend; (*jest.*) to sputter, to spawl

S'—, *v.r.* to deviate; to turn aside *or* away; to turn; to go; to step *or* stand aside; to make way; to go out of the way; to go away *or* far; to remove; to separate; to disperse; to take to flight; to ramble; to rove; to wander; to stray; to go astray; to err; to straggle; to depart; to leave; to swerve; to recede; to diverge; to open; to be discarded, &c.; to be scattered wide apart; to scatter; to strain [oneself

Écarteur, *s.m.* bull-baiter, bull-fighter

Écatir, &c. *V.* **Catir,** &c.

Ecbolique, *adj.m.f., s.m.* (*med.*) ecbolic [person

Ecce homo, *s.m.* ecce homo; (*jest.*) pale thin

‡Ecchymose, *s.f.* (*med.*) ecchymosis

‡Ecchymoser, *v.a.* (*med.*) to ecchymose

S'—, *v.r.* (*med.*) to become ecchymosed

‡Ecchymotique, *adj.* (*med.*) ecchymotic

Ecclésiaste, *s.m.* Ecclesiastes

Ecclésiastique, *adj.m.f., s.m.* ecclesiastical; ecclesiastic; clerical; clergyman, priest, churchman; Ecclesiasticus

Ecclésiastiquement, *adv.* ecclesiastically

Ecclésiolog-ie, -ique, -iste. *V.* page 3, § 1

Eccoprotique, *adj.m.f., s.m.,* **Eccrinologie,** &c. *V.* page 3, § 1

Écervelé, e, *adj.* brainless, mad-brained, hare-brained, wild, rash, giddy; — *s.m.f.* lackbrain, mad-cap, giddy-head, giddy goose

Écerveler, *v.a.* to brain

Échafaud, *s.m.* scaffold; stage; stand; gallows; drop; execution. — *de service*, temporary stage

Échafaudage, *s.m.* scaffolding; great preparations, fuss; display; heap

Échafauder, *v.n.a.* to scaffold, to erect scaffolding *or* a stage; to make great preparations; to make a fuss about; to make a great display of; to raise, to erect; to pile up; to rest; to ground; to prepare

Échalas, *s.m.* prop, pole, stick; vine-stick; hop-pole; lath; thin leg *or* shank

Échalassement, *s.m.* (*hort., agr.*) propping
Échalasser, *v.a.* (*hort., agr.*) to prop (*shrubs, vines, &c.*)
Échalier, *s.m.* hurdle, fence; stile
Échalis, *s.m.* stile
Échalote, *s.f.* shallot, eschalot
Échampir, *v.a. V.* **Réchampir**
Échancrer, *v.a.* to slope, to cut sloping; to hollow; to indent
S'—, *v.r.* to hollow inwards, to form a crescent *or* a semicircle *or* a horseshoe; to be indented
Échancrure, *s.f.* sloping; hollowing; scallop; slope; notch; hollow cut; indentation
Échange, *s.m.* exchange, barter; interchange; reciprocation. *Libre —, liberté des —s,* free-trade
Échangeabilité, *s.f.* exchangeability
Échangeable, *adj.* exchangeable
Échangeage, *s.m. V.* **Essangeage**
Échanger, *v.a.* to exchange, to barter; to interchange; to reciprocate; (*linen*) *V.* **Essanger**
S'—, *v.r.* to be exchanged *or* &c.
Échangeu-r, se, *s.m.f.* exchanger
Échangiste (Libre-). *V.* **Libre-** —, *at letter* **L**
Échanson, *s.m.* cup-bearer
Échansonnerie, *s.f.* (*of princes*) wine-cellar; cup-bearers
†**Échantignole,** *s.f.* (*tech.*) lining; bracket; block
†**Échantillon,** *s.m.* sample; pattern; specimen; tally; (*nav.*) scantling; (*tech.*) gauge
†**Échantillonnage,** *s.m.* sampling; cutting out patterns; gauging
†**Échantillonner,** *v.a.n.* to sample; to make a pattern of; to cut out patterns; (*tech.*) to gauge
Échanvrer, *v.a. V.* **Serancer**
Échanvroir, *s.m.* hackle
Échappade, *s.f.* slip. *En —,* by stealth
Échappatoire, *s.f.* evasion, shuffle, shift, subterfuge, loophole, creep-hole
Échappé, e, *part. adj.* escaped, &c. (*V.* **Échapper**); — *adj. s.* runaway; mongrel, cross; imitation, counterfeit
Échappée, *s.f.* escape; oversight; prank, frolic; vista; snatch; sally; short interval; space to turn in, rounding off. *— de lumière,* (*paint.*) accidental light. *— de vue,* vista. *A l'—,* by stealth. *Par —s,* by snatches, by fits and starts
Échappement, *s.m.* (*mech., horol.*) escapement; (*of steam, &c.*) escape; (*arch.*) space to turn in, rounding off. *— à ancre,* anchor *or* lever escapement. *— à repos,* dead-beat escapement
Échapper, *v.n.a.* to escape; to make o.'s escape; to get away *or* off *or* out; to recover, to get over; to slip; to fall, to drop; to happen, to occur; to avoid; to put to the greatest speed. *L'— belle,* to have a narrow escape, to escape narrowly. *Laisser —,* to let escape; to let off *or* out; to utter; to blurt out; to heave; to let slip *or* fall; to drop; to let go; to give vent to; to overlook; to turn off (*gas, &c.*). *Il lui est échappé de …,* he has inadvertently …, it has happened *or* occurred to him to …
S'—, *v.r.* to escape; to make o.'s escape; to run *or* fly away; to break loose; to steal *or* slip away *or* off *or* out; to sneak *or* slink away *or* off *or* out; to vanish, to disappear; to slip; to fall, to drop; to burst; to break out (into); to forget oneself
Écharbot, *s.m.* (*bot.*) *V.* **Macre**
Écharde, *s.f.* splinter; thorn; (*bot.*) prickle (*of a thistle*); (*fish*) stickleback
Échardonnage, *s.m.* clearing of thistles
Échardonner, *v.a.* to clear of thistles
Échardonnet, Échardonnoir, *s.m.* thistle-extirpator
Écharnage, Écharnement, *s.m.* fleshing (*of hides*)
Écharner, *v.a.* to flesh (*hides*), to clear of flesh
Écharnoir, *s.m.* fleshing-knife
Écharnure, *s.f.* (*of hides*) fleshing, fleshings, parings
Écharpe, *s.f.* scarf; sash; arm-sling, sling; tassel (*of a flag*); colours, side, party; (*engin.*) surface-table, water-table; (*tech.*) tie; cross-piece; (*her.*) scarp. *En —,* over the shoulder; in a sling; slantingly, obliquely, sideways; slanting, oblique. *L'— d'Iris,* (*poet.*) the rainbow
Écharpement, *s.m.* (*mil.*) oblique march
Écharper, †Écharpiller, *v.a.* to slash, to cut; to hack; to cut to pieces; to smash; **(Écharper)** *v.n.* to march obliquely; *v.a.* (*tech.*) to sling
Échars, e, *adj.* light; (*nav.*) scant, shifting
Écharser, *v.n.* (*nav.*) to scant, to veer, to shift
Échasse, *s.f.* stilt; (*tech.*) ruler; pole (*of a scaffold*); (*zool.*) stilt-bird. *— à manteau noir,* long-legged plover
Échassier, *s.m.* long-legged water-fowl, wading bird, wader
Échauboulé, e, *adj.* pimpled, full of pimples
Échauboulure, *s.f.* pimple, blotch, rash, pustule; burn, scald
Échaudage, *s.m.* testing (*casks*) with hot water; limewashing; limewash
Échaudé, *s.m.* cracknel
Échaudement, *s.m.* (*agr.*) parching, withering, blighting
Échauder, *v.a.* to scald; to overheat; to burn; to parch, to wither, to blight; to wash in hot water; to test (*a cask*) with hot water; to limewash; (*fig.*) to catch, to bite; to cheat, to fleece, to overcharge, to chouse
S'—, *v.r.* to scald *or* burn oneself (*or* o.'s …); (*fig.*) to smart, to burn o.'s fingers; (*things*) to be scalded *or* &c.
Échaudeu-r, se, *s.m.f.* scalder; limewasher; cheat, fleecer
Échaudoir, *s.m.* scalding-house; scalding-tub
Échaudure, *s.f.* scald
Échauffaison, *s.f.* overheating, eruption, rash
Échauffant, e, *adj.* heating; binding; — *s.m.* heating *or* binding food *or* substance
Échauffé, e, *part. adj.* warmed, heated, &c. (*V.* **Échauffer**); (*of wood*) dry, rotten; — *s.m.* heat (*Sentir l'—,* to have *or* exhale a hot smell)
Échauffement, *s.m.* heating; over-excitement; costiveness, constipation
Échauffer, *v.a.* to warm, to heat, to make warm *or* hot; to overheat; to excite; to over-excite; to inflame; to animate; to chafe; to irritate; to provoke; to work up; to stir up; to constipate, to bind
S'—, *v.r.* to become (*or* get *or* grow) warm *or* hot *or* heated *or* overheated *or* inflamed; to warm; to heat; to heat oneself; to overheat oneself; to become (*or* get *or* grow) *or* be chafed; to become animated; to become (*or* get *or* grow) excited *or* angry, to chafe, to fume; to get stirred up; to ferment; to mowburn; (*of quarrels*) to get *or* run high
Échauffourée, *s.f.* affray, scuffle; skirmish; rash enterprise; unlucky move; blunder; failure, mess
Échauffure, *s.f.* overheating; heat; rash, eruption, pimple
Échauguette, *s.f.* watch-tower
Échauler, *v.a. V.* **Chauler**
Échaumer, *v.a. V.* **Déchaumer**
Échaux, *s.m.* (*agr.*) drain, watercourse
Èche, *s.f.* lob-worm, lug-worm
Échéable, *adj.* falling due, payable
Échéance, *s.f.* expiration; falling due; maturity; term of payment; bill to meet. *A courte —,* at a short date, short-dated; short. *A longue —,* at a long date, long-dated; long
Échéancier, *s.m.* bill-book
Échéant, *part.* falling, &c. (*V.* **Échoir**). *Le cas —,* the case occurring, in that case, if it should so occur *or* happen, if such should be the case; on the (*or* on such an) occasion; occasionally
Échec, *s.m.* check; repulse; defeat; loss; blow; failure, foil; disappointment. *— et mat,* checkmate. **—s,** *pl.* checks, &c.; (*game*) chess; chessmen
Échelette, *s.f.* rack; rathe, rave, shelving; (*bird*) wall-creeper; (*mus.*) regal
Échelier, *s.m. V.* **Rancher**
Échelle, *s.f.* ladder; steps; scale; degree; rack; seaport. *— anglaise,* Gunter's scale. *— double,* trestles; pair of steps. *— de commandement* accommodation-ladder. *— de meunier,* trap-ladder. *— de siége,* scaling-ladder.

Faire —, (*nav.*) to touch. *Faire la courte* —, to climb upon each other's shoulders, to let another get upon o.'s back. *Faire la courte — à*, to let (...) get upon o.'s back; (*fig.*) to help up *or* through; to pave the way for. *Après lui il faut tirer l'*—, no one can do better

Échellier, *s.m. V.* **Rancher**

Échelon, *s.m.* round; step; stepping-stone; degree; rank; (*mil.*) echelon

Échelonner, *v.a.* to arrange *or* draw up in degrees, to graduate; to place apart; to proportion; (*mil.*) to range *or* place *or* draw up in echelons, to echelon

S'—, *v.r.* to be arranged in degrees, to be graduated; (*mil.*) to be ranged *or* &c. in echelons, to be echeloned, to extend in echelons

Échenal, *s.m.* gutter; basin

‡**Échène, Échénéide,** *s.m.* (*zool.*) echeneis, sucking-fish, sucker

Écheneau, Échenet, *s.m. V.* **Échenal**

†**Échenillage,** *s.m.* clearing of caterpillars, destruction of caterpillars

†**Écheniller,** *v.a.* (*hort.*) to clear (*trees*) of caterpillars; (*arch.*) to vermiculate

†**Échenilleur,** *s.m.* caterpillar-destroyer; (*bird*) caterpillar-catcher, caterpillar-eater

†**Échenilloir,** *s.m.* (*hort.*) averruncator

Échet, *s.m. V.* **Écheveau**

Écheveau, *s.m.* skein

Échevelé, e, *adj.* dishevelled, in disorder; with dishevelled hair; (*fig.*) disordered, disorderly, in disorder, extravagant; romantic

Écheveler, *v.a.* to dishevel *or* disorder the hair of [to come dishevelled, to flow in disorder

S'—, *v.r.* to disorder o.'s *or* each other's hair;

Échevette, *s.f.* small skein, lea

Échevin, *s.m.* (*obsolete, except in the Netherlands*) sheriff, alderman; mayor

Échevinage, *s.m.* sheriffship, shrievalty, aldermanship; mayoralty; sheriffs, aldermen, corporation, town *or* common council

Échevinal, e, *adj.* of a sheriff *or* alderman, of sheriffs *or* aldermen; mayor's, mayors' [eater

‡**Échidné,** *s.m.* (*zool.*) echidna, porcupine ant-

‡**Échidnine,** *s.f.* (*chem.*) echidnine, serpent

Échi-f, ve, *adj.* (*hunt.*) voracious, greedy [poison

Échiffe, Échiffre, *s.m.* partition-wall (*of a*

†**Échigner,** *v.a. pop. for* **Échiner** [*staircase*)

†**Échillon,** *s.m.* waterspout

‡**Échimys,** *s.m.* (*zool.*) echimyd, spiny rat

Échin, *s.m.* echin (*physician of the seraglio*)

Échine, *s.f.* chine; spine; backbone; back; (*arch.*) echinus, egg and anchor moulding. *Longue* or *maigre* —, (*pop.*) lanky-bones

Échiné, e, *part. adj.* broken-backed; beaten to death; belaboured; knocked up, tired out; — *s.f.* chine (of pork), chine-piece, griskin

‡**Échiné, e,** *adj.* (*nat. hist.*) echinate, echinated

Échiner, *v.a.* to break the back of; to beat to death; to kill; to murder; to cut up; to belabour; to knock up, to tire out; to use up, to wear right out; to exhaust; to spoil entirely; to crush, to smash

S'—, *v.r.* to break o.'s back; to knock oneself up; to toil hard; to work oneself to death; to break each other's back, to beat each other to death, to kill *or* &c. each other; (*things*) to get *or* be used

‡**Échinide,** *s.m.* (*zool.*) echinidan [up *or* &c.

‡**Échinite,** *s.m.* (*fossil*) echinite

‡**Échinocoque,** *s.m.* (*zool.*) echinococcus

‡**Échinoderme,** *s.m.* (*zool.*) echinoderm; — *adj.* echinodermatous

‡**Échinope,** *s.m.* (*bot.*) echinops, globe-thistle

‡**Échinophore,** *s.f.* (*bot.*) echinophora, prickly samphire [*tinal worm*)

‡**Échinorhynque,** *s.m.* echinorhyncus (*intes-*

Échiqueté, e, *adj.* checkered; (*her.*) checky

Échiquier, *s.m.* chess-board; checker, chequer, checks, squares; exchequer; square net. *En* —, like a chess-board, checkerwise, checker, in squares; (*mil.*) alternately; (*nav.*) in a bow and quarter line. *Table à* —, chess-table

‡**Écho,** *s.m.* echo; town *or* theatrical gossip; — *s.f.* (*myth.*) Echo. *Faire* —, to echo

‡**Échoïque,** *adj.* (*vers.*) echoing

Échoir, *v.n. def.* to fall (to), to come (to), to fall to the lot (of); to occur, to happen; to expire; to become *or* fall due, to mature, to arrive at maturity. *A* —, (*of bills*) running, not due,

Échome, *s.m. V.* **Tolet** [undue

‡**Échomètre,** *s.m.* echometer

‡**Échométr-ie, -ique.** *V.* page 3, § 1

Échoppage, *s.m.* (*tech.*) scorping, edging

Échoppe, *s.f.* stall; (*tool*) scorper, graver

Échopper, *v.a.* (*tech.*) to scorp, to edge

Échoppi-er, ère, *s.m.f.* stall-keeper

‡**Échoter,** *v.n.* (*newspaper slang*) to write the town *or* theatrical gossip

‡**Échotier,** *s.m.* (*newspaper slang*) writer of the town *or* theatrical gossip

Échouage, *s.m.* (*nav.*) beaching; stranding, running aground [aground

Échouement, *s.m.* (*nav.*) stranding, running

Échouer, *v.a.n.* (*nav.*) to strand, to run aground; to strike; to beach; to lie dry; (*fig.*) to fail; to be foiled; to founder; to miscarry; to prove useless, to be powerless. *S'*—, to run aground; to strike [become due, due

Échu, e, (*part. of* **Échoir**) fallen, &c.; fallen *or*

Écimage, *s.m.* topping, polling

Écimer, *v.a.* to top, to poll

Éclaboussement, *s.m.* splashing

Éclabousser, *v.a.* to splash

Éclaboussure, *s.f.* splash; spray, spoondrift

Éclair, *s.m.* lightning; flash of lightning; flash; gleam; light; fire; snatch; kind of cake. *Faire des* —*s*, (*imp.*) to lighten. *Jeter* or *lancer des* —*s*, to flash

Éclairage, *s.m.* lighting; light; illumination, illuminating. — *au gaz*, gas-lighting, gas-illumination, gas-light. *Gaz d'*—, illuminating gas [spot; spacing out; thinning

Éclaircie, *s.f.* glade; vista; opening; clear

Éclaircir, *v.a.* to clear; to clear up; to clarify; to brighten up, to brighten, to polish; to space out; to thin; to illustrate, to elucidate, to throw light upon; to explain; to inquire into; to unravel; to solve; to instruct, to inform, to enlighten, to satisfy

S'—, *v.r.* to become *or* get clear; to clear; to clear up; to get bright, to brighten; to become *or* grow *or* get thin; to be solved; to unravel; to be illustrated *or* elucidated *or* cleared up *or* explained; to inquire (into); to gain information, to satisfy o.'s mind; to come to an

Éclaircissage, *s.m.* polishing [explanation

Éclaircissement, *s.m.* clearing up; solution; explanation; elucidation; illustration; hint; light; discovery; insight; spacing out; thinning

Éclaire, *s.f.* (*bot.*) celandine, tetterwort, pilewort

Éclairé, e, *part. adj.* lighted, &c. (*V.* **Éclairer**); enlightened, judicious, discriminating, intelligent, clear-sighted, well-informed; open, exposed. *Être nourri, logé, chauffé et* —, to have board, lodging, fuel and light

Éclairer, *v.a.* to light; to light up; to illuminate, to illumine; to give light to; to show a light to; to inform, to instruct, to enlighten; to throw a light upon; to watch; (*mil.*) to reconnoitre; — *v.n.* to give light; to light; to hold the light; to shine; to sparkle, to glitter; to glisten; (*imp.*) to lighten; (*pop.*) to show o.'s shiners, to fork out

S'—, *v.r.* to be lighted *or* lighted up; to become *or* grow *or* get enlightened; to get information; to find o.'s own light; to inform *or* instruct *or* enlighten each other

Éclaireur, *s.m.* (*mil., nav.*) scout

Éclamé, e, *adj.* broken-legged, broken-winged

Éclampsie, *s.f.* (*med.*) eclampsia, eclampsy

Éclanche, *s.f.* (*obsolete*) shoulder (of mutton); (*still more obsolete*) leg (of mutton)

Éclancher, *v.a.* to unrumple

Éclat, *s.m.* fragment, piece; splinter; shiver;

explosion; loud sound *or* noise; bursting; burst; peal; clap; shout; flash; fire; flare; glare; brightness, brilliancy, splendour, lustre; resplendence; magnificence; glory; eminence; honour; glitter; vividness; gaudiness; show; pomp; display; expression; shrillness; noise, scandal, exposure, discovery; infamy; violent measure; rupture; open declaration; éclat. — *de rire*, burst *or* roar of laughter. *Action d'*—, splendid achievement, brilliant action, remarkable deed [plosive

Éclatable, *adj.* liable to split *or* to burst, ex-

Éclatant, e, *adj.* bright; brilliant; shining; splendid; resplendent; magnificent; noble; grand; pompous; gorgeous; sparkling; glittering; dazzling; radiant; blooming; vivid; glowing; garish; showy; flashy; gaudy, tawdry; glaring; loud, piercing; shrill; noisy; sonorous; striking; signal; remarkable; eminent; glorious; illustrious; famous; conspicuous; notorious; open, public

Éclaté, e, *part. adj.* shivered, split, &c. (*V.* **Éclater**); (*her.*) rompu [bursting, cracking

Éclatement, *s.m.* breaking up, breaking,

Éclater, *v.n.*, **S'—,** *v.r.* to shiver, to splinter, to fly into shivers *or* splinters *or* pieces *or* fragments; to chip, to chip off; to split; to snap; to break; to explode; to burst; to burst out *or* forth; to break out *or* forth; to fly; to exclaim; to shine; to shine forth; to sparkle; to glitter; to blaze out; to flash; to fall; to show; to come to light, to appear; to display *or* show itself, to be displayed *or* made conspicuous; to be exposed *or* discovered; to make a noise; to resound; to roar. — *sur*, (*of lightning*) to strike. — *de rire*, to burst out laughing. *Faire* —, to shiver, to shatter, to splinter; to chip; to split; to snap; to break off; to burst; to blow up; to give vent to; to blaze forth; to show forth, to show, to display; to discover; to draw, to draw down, to bring, to bring down

Éclecticien, ne, *adj. s.* eclectic

Éclect-ique (*adj. s.*), **-iquement.** *V.* page 3,

Éclectiser, *v.n.* to eclectize [§ 1

Éclectisme, *s.m.* eclecticism

Éclefin, *s.m.* *V.* **Églefin**

Écli, *s.m.* (*nav.*) splinter

Éclié, e, *adj.* (*nav.*) splintered, sprung

Éclingure, *s.f.* (*nav.*) rabbet [sence

Éclipse, *s.f.* eclipse; disappearance, exit; ab-

Éclipsement, *s.m.* obscuration; disappearance

Éclipser, *v.a.* to eclipse

S'—, *v.r.* to be eclipsed; to disappear, to vanish, to go; to steal away

Écliptique, *s.f. adj.* (*astr.*) ecliptic

Éclisse, *s.f.* splinter; split-wood; wicker; wattle; cheese-hurdle, cheese-drainer, cheese-vat; stand; (*of violins*, &c.) side-piece, rib; [(*surg.*) splint

Éclisser, *v.a.* (*surg.*) to splint

Éclogue, *s.f.* *V.* **Églogue**

Écloppé, e, *adj. s.* lame, cripple, halt, badly hurt

Éclopper, *v.a.* to lame, to cripple, to hurt badly

Éclore, *v.n.* to hatch; to blow, to open; to dawn, to break; to come to light; to come out; to be disclosed *or* discovered. *Faire* —, to hatch; to cause to blow; to bring to light; to bring out; to give birth to; to produce; to usher in; to disclose, to discover

Éclosion, *s.f.* hatching; blowing, opening

Écluse, *s.f.* lock, sluice, flood-gate; dam, mill-dam; oyster-bed, mussel-bed; fishing-weir, [crawl

Éclusée, *s.f.* lock of water, lockage

Écluser, *v.a.* to lock (*canals*, &c.); to pass (*a vessel*) through the locks *or* through a lock

Éclusi-er, ère, *s.m.f.* lockman, lock-keeper; — *adj.* of locks, of a lock

Écobuage, *s.m.* paring and burning (*peat-lands*, &c.), burning weeds *or* turf *or* sod; weeds, sod, flag, turf-ashes

Écobue, *s.f.* weeder, turfing-iron, turf-knife, paring-spade; breast-plough, paring-plough; —**s**, *pl.* weeds, sod, flag, turf-ashes

Écobuer, *v.a.* to pare and burn (*peat-lands*, &c.), to burn weeds *or* turf *or* sod on (*land*)

Écobueuse, *s.f.* (*agr. inst.*) *V.* **Écobue**

Écochelage, *s.m.* raking (*of corn*)

Écocheler, *v.a.* to rake (*corn*)

Écœurer, *v.a.* to sicken, to make sick

Écofrai, Écofroi, *s.m.* (*tech.*) cutting-board

Écoinçon, Écoinson, *s.m.* (*mas., carp.*) diagonal *or* angle-tie, angle stuff-bead; jamb (*of a door*); reveal (*of a window*); corner-piece (of [furniture)

Écolage, *s.m.* schooling

Écolâtre, *s.m.* (*obsolete*) master of a cathedral school

École, *s.f.* school; college; sect; scholastic philosophy; training; practice; apprenticeship; discipline; exercise; drill; trial, experiment; blunder. — *centrale*, central school, school of science and art. — *de charité*, — *gratuite*, charity school, ragged school. — *libre*, free school, private school. — *maternelle*, infant-school. — *normale*, normal school. — *normale primaire*, training college. — *d'enseignement mutuel*, — *mutuelle*, school for mutual instruction, national school. — *régionale*, agricultural school. *Basse* —, elements of horsemanship. *Haute* —, high horsemanship. *Pas d'*—, balance *or* goose-step. *Faire* —, to be the head of a school; to be a fundamental doctrine. *Faire une* —, to make *or* commit a blunder; to make a trial *or* experiment; (*at backgammon*) to be pegged

Écoli-er, ère, *s.m.f.* pupil, student, scholar, learner; schoolboy *or* girl; novice, tyro. *Papier* —, exercise-paper

Écolleter, *v.a.* (*tech.*) to cut off, to round

Éconduire, *v.a.* to refuse, to deny; to put off; to bow out; to show out; to dismiss

Économat, *s.m.* stewardship; treasurership; bursarship; steward's *or* treasurer's office, bursary

Économe, *s.m.f.* economist; manager; manageress; steward; stewardess; treasurer; bursar; — *adj.* saving, sparing, economical, thrifty

Économie, *s.f.* economy; thrift, thriftiness; saving; management; arrangement; disposition; order; system; plan; constitution; structure. — *domestique*, domestic economy, household matters. *Faire des* —*s*, to economize, to put by, to save, to save money

Économique, *adj.* economic, economical; cheap; — *s.f.* economics

Économiquement, *adv.* economically

Économiser, *v.a.* to economize, to save, to put by; to spare, to husband, to use sparingly, to be sparing *or* chary of

S'—, *v.r.* to be economized *or* &c.

Économiste, *s.m.* economist

Écope, *s.f.* scoop, skeet, ladle

Écoper, *v.a.* to scoop, to bale, to lade out

Écoperche, *s.f.* lift, derrick; scaffold-pole

Écorçage, *s.m.* barking (*of trees*)

Écorce, *s.f.* bark; rind, peel; shell; skin; crust; outside, surface, exterior, appearance

Écorcement, *s.m.* barking (*of trees*)

Écorcer, *v.a.* to bark, to strip, to peel

S'—, *v.r.* to lose its bark; to be barked *or* &c.

Écorceur, *s.m.* barker, stripper

Écorché, *s.m.* (*paint.*) figure without skin (*for the study of the muscles*), écorché

Écorche-cul (A), *adv.* sliding down *or* dragging on the backside; (*fig.*) against the grain, by force [lots *or* small parts

Écorchée, *s.f.* (*shell*) striated cone. *A l'*—, in

Écorcheler, *v.a.* (*agr.*) to cock [ning

Écorchement, *s.m.* excoriation; flaying, skin-

Écorcher, *v.a.* to rub the bark off; to flay, to skin; to rub *or* graze *or* tear *or* cut the skin off; to tear; to gall; to peel off; to excoriate; to scrape; to fleece (*overcharge*); to grate upon (*the ear*), to grate; to burn *or* be rough to (*the palate*); to murder *or* hack (*a language*, &c.); to thrum (*an air*, &c.). — *vif*, to flay *or* skin alive

— *l'anguille par la queue*, to begin at the wrong end, to go the wrong way to work. *Il crie avant qu'on l'écorche*, he cries before he is hurt

S'—, *v.r.* to rub *or* tear *or* cut o.'s skin off, to rub the skin off *or* tear *or* gall (o.'s ...); to be galled; (*fig.*) to speak ill of oneself

Écorcherie, *s.f.* knacker's yard; inn in which travellers are fleeced, outrageously expensive place; fleecing

Écorcheur, *s.m.* flayer; knacker; fleecer

Écorchure, *s.f.* graze, grazing, gall, sore, excoriation, abrasion

Écore, *s.f. adj.* (*nav.*) *V.* **Accore**

Écorné, e, *part. adj.* broken-horned; broken-cornered; worn out *or* off at the corners; curtailed, begun, cut into, partly spent *or* gone

Écorner, *v.a.* to break the horn *or* horns of; to break the corner *or* corners off; to spoil the corners of, to dog's-ear; to curtail, to impair, to lessen, to diminish; to make a gap *or* a hole in; (*pop.*) to slander [sponging

Écornifler, *v.a.* to sponge upon; to get by

Écorniflerie, *s.f.* sponging [pilferer, prig, thief

Écornifleu-r, se, *s.m.f.* sponger, hanger-on;

Écornure, *s.f.* corner broken off, breaking *or* break at the corner *or* corners, chipping

Écossais, e, *adj. s.* Scotch, Scottish; — *s.m.* Scotchman; Scotch boy; Scotch plaid, plaid-stuff, plaid, tartan; (*Fr. hist.*) Scotch guard; — *s.f.* Scotch woman *or* lady *or* girl; Scotch fashion; écossaise (*Scottish dance, tune*). *Étoffe —e*, Scotch plaid, plaid-stuff, plaid, tartan. *Nouvel-* —, Nova Scotian

Écosse, *s.f. V.* **Cosse**

Écosser, *v.a.*, **S'—**, *v.r.* to shell, to husk

Écosseu-r, se, *s.m.f.* sheller

Écot, *s.m.* share, quota; reckoning, score, shot, scot; expense; company, party; stump (*of a tree*). *De tous —s*, meddling with everything

Écôtage, *s.m.* stemming (*of tobacco*)

Écoté, e, *adj.* (*her.*) lopped [stemmed

Écôter, *v.a.* to stem (*tobacco*). *S'—*, to be

Écôteu-r, se, *s.m.f.* stemmer (*of tobacco*)

†Écouailles, *s.f.pl.* tail-wool, coarse wool

Écouane, Écouenne, *s.f.* (*tech.*) file

Écouaner, Écouenner, *v.a.* to file

Écouer, *v.a.* to cut off the tail of

Écouet, *s.m.* (*nav.*) tack

Écoufle, *s.m.* (*pop.*) kite (*bird, toy*)

Écoulé, e, *part. adj.* elapsed, &c. (*V.* **S'écouler**); expired; gone; gone by; bygone; over; out; sold

Ecoulement, *s.m.* flow, flowing, running; running out, passing out; drainage, draining; discharge; outlet; sale; gleet

Écouler, *v.a.* to sell; to pour away; to drain; — *v.n.* (*elliptically for* "S'écouler," *after* "Faire," "Laisser," "Sentir," "Voir," &c.) *V.* **S'écouler**

S'—, *v.r.* to flow away *or* out, to run off *or* out; to glide *or* slide *or* slip away; to pass away, to elapse, to pass; to be spent; to pass out, to go off; to escape; to disperse; to sell off, to go off. *Faire* —, to drain *or* let off; to disperse; to sell off

Écoupe, *s.f.* (*agr.*) spade; (*nav.*) swab

Écourgée, *s.f. V.* **Escourgée**

Écourgeon, *s.m. V.* **Escourgeon**

Écourté, e, *part. adj.* curtailed, &c. (*V.* **Écourter**); short; narrow; snub (*nose*); shortly dressed; — *s.m.f. Le pauvre* —, poor Master Bobtail [to shorten; to dock; to crop

Écourter, *v.a.* to curtail, to cut short *or* shorter,

Écoutant, e, *part. adj.* listening, &c. (*V.* **Écouter**); (*obsolete*) briefless (*barrister*); — *s.m.f.* hearer, listener

Écoute, *s.f.* listening-place; private box; (*fort.*) listening-gallery, listener, écoute; (*nav.*) sheet. *Être aux —s*, to eavesdrop, to listen, to be listening; to be attentive; to be on the watch *or* on the look-out. *Entre deux —s*, (*nav.*) both sheets aft. *Sœur* —, listening nun

Écouter, *v.a.n.* to listen, to listen to; to hear; to hearken; to attend to, to attend; to pay attention to, to mind. *Écoutez !* hark! listen! listen to me! hear! hear me! look here! come! *Écoutez donc !* do listen! let me tell you! well, you know! well! why! *Se faire* —, to obtain a hearing; to command attention; to excite interest; to get an audience; to enforce obedience

S'—, *v.r.* to listen to oneself; to follow o.'s own inspiration; to like to hear oneself; to indulge oneself, to nurse oneself up

Écoute-s'il-pleut, *s.m.* mill worked by sluices; vain hope; hoper against hope; trifle, fiddle-faddle, trash, rubbish [— *adj. V.* **Écouteux**

Écouteu-r, se, *s.m.f.* listener; eaves-dropper;

Écouteu-x, se, *adj.* (*of horses and mares*) shy, skittish, jibbing

†Écoutille, *s.f.* (*nav.*) hatchway, hatch

†Écoutillon, *s.m.* (*nav.*) scuttle

Écoutoir, *s.m.* ear-trumpet, hearing-trumpet

†Écouvillon, *s.m.* scovel, swab, mop, malkin; (*artil.*) sponge-rod, sponge, rammer

†Écouvillonner, *v.a.* to mop; to sweep; (*artil.*) to sponge

Écran, *s.m.* fire-screen, screen; (*phys.*) white ground. — *à main*, hand-screen. — *à pied*, pole-screen. — *de cheminée*, cheval-screen

Écrancher, *v.a.* to unrumple [mashing

Écrasage, *s.m.* crushing; bruising; squashing;

Écrasant, e, *adj.* crushing; overwhelming; oppressive; humiliating; withering; astounding; exorbitant; excessive; extraordinary

Écrasé, e, *part. adj.* crushed, &c. (*V.* **Écraser**); flat; squat, short; low; (*bot.*) depressed

Écrasement, *s.m.* crushing; crush; bruising; squashing; mashing; squelching; overwhelming, ruin, destruction

Écraser, *v.a.* to crush; to bruise; to squash; to mash; to smash; to shatter; to run over; to squelch; to overwhelm; to smother; to eclipse

S'—, *v.r.* to crush (o.'s ...); to crush; to be crushed, &c.; (*fenc.*) to stoop; (*rid.*) to sink down

Écraseur, *s.m.* crusher; bruiser; (*surg.*) ecraseur

Écrelet, *s.m.* (Swiss) gingerbread

Écrémage, *s.m.* creaming, skimming

Écrémer, *v.a.* to cream, to cream off, to skim; to take the best of

S'—, *v.r.* to be creamed *or* &c.

Écrémière, *s.f.* large freshwater mussel

Écrémoire, *s.f.* cream-skimmer, skimming-dish; (*tech.*) slice, ladle, scraper

Écrén-age, -er. *V.* **Crénage** *and* **Créner**

Écrêter, *v.a.* to cut off *or* remove the comb of (*a cock*); to take *or* remove the top off; to lower (*a slope, a road*); (*mil.*) to batter the top of (*a work*)

Écrevisse, *s.f.* crayfish, crawfish; crab; (*astr.*) Cancer, crab; (*tech.*) smith's tongs. — *de mer*, crab, lobster. *Rouge comme une* —, red as a lobster

Écrier (S'), *v.r.* to cry out, to exclaim, to cry

†Écrille, *s.f.* grate (*of a fish-pond*)

Écrin, *s.m.* jewel-box *or* case, casket; case

Écrire, *v.a.n.* to write; to write down, to set down; to pen; to write word; to state; to spell. — *que*, to write to say that; to state that

S'—, *v.r.* to write to each other; to be written; to be spelt; to sign oneself; to write *or* sign *or* leave o.'s name

Écrit, e, *part. adj.* written, &c. (*V.* **Écrire**); written on; (*of maps*) with names; (*of law*) statute

Écrit, *s.m.* writing; written agreement; work; pamphlet. *Mot d'—*, short writing; short note. *Par* —, in writing

Écriteau, *s.m.* bill; board; sign-board; label;

Écritoire, *s.f.* inkstand [ticket

Écriture, *s.f.* writing; handwriting, hand; Scripture; **—s,** *pl.* accounts, books, papers, letters; Scriptures

Écriturer, *v.n.* to do writing *or* copying work

Écrituri-er, ère, *s.m.f.* copying-clerk, copier, copyist; book-keeper

†Écrivailler, *v.n.a.* to scribble

†**Écrivaillerie,** *s.f.* scribbling, writing silly *or* fashionable novels
†**Écrivailleu-r, se,** *s.m.f.* scribbler, fashionable novel-writer; — *adj.* scribbling
Écrivain, *s.m.* writer; writing-master; (— *public*) copier, letter-writer; (*nav.*) purser, captain's clerk; (*zool.*) vine-fretter
Écrivass-er, -erie. *V.* **Écrivailler, Écrivaillerie**
Écrivassi-er, ère, *s.m.f. adj.* *V.* **Écrivailleur**
Écriveu-r, se, *adj.* fond of writing *or* scribbling, always writing *or* scribbling; — *s.m.f.* person ditto
Écrou, *s.m.* female screw; screw-nut, nut; entry in the jail-book. *Livre* or *registre d'*—, jail-book
Écrouelle, *s.f.* freshwater shrimp; —**s,** *pl.* (*med., obsolete for* "scrofules") king's evil, scrofula
Écrouellé, e, Écrouelleu-x, se, *adj. s. V.* **Scrofuleux**
Écrouer, *v.a.* to enter in the jail-book; to commit to prison, to imprison, to confine
Écrouir, *v.a.* to hammer-harden (*metals*)
Écrouissage, Écrouissement, *s.m.* hammer-hardening
Écroulement, *s.m.* falling in *or* down, falling, tumbling *or* crumbling down, fall, downfall, break-down, collapse, wreck, ruin
Écrouler (S'), *v.r.* to fall in *or* down, to tumble *or* crumble down, to break down, to collapse, to fall, to sink, to give way; to fall into decay, to fall to pieces, to perish. *Faire* —, to shake *or* pull *or* bring down
Écroûter, *v.a.* to cut *or* chip the crust off
S'—, *v.r.* to lose its crust *or* outside; to be deprived of its crust
Écru, e, *adj.* unbleached; raw; brown; — *s.m.* unbleached *or* raw state; unbleached stuff; brown colour
Écrues, *s.f.pl.* wood of recent growth
Ecthyma, *s.m.* (*med.*) ecthyma
Ectozoaire, *s.m.* (*zool.*) ectozoan, ectozoon (*pl.* ectozoa); — *adj.* ectozoal, ectozoic
Ectropion, *s.m.* (*med.*) ectropium, ectropion, eversion of the eyelids
Ectrotique, *adj.m.f., s.m.* (*med.*) ectrotic
Ectype, *s.f.* ectype
Écu, *s.m.* shield; (*old coin*) half-crown; (*old coin*) crown; (*fig.*) shilling; (*stat.*) post-paper; —**s,** *pl.* shields, &c.; money, cash. *Petit* —, (*old coin*) half-crown (3 *francs*). *Père aux —s,* moneyed man, ready-money man, man made of money
Écuage, *s.m.* (*feud.*) escuage, scutage, land-tax
Écubier, *s.m.* (*nav.*) hawse-hole
†**Écueil,** *s.m.* rock, reef, shelf, breaker, sandbank; stumbling-block; obstacle, impediment; difficulty; danger, peril
Écuelle, *s.f.* porringer, bowl, basin, dish, plate, trencher
Écuellée, *s.f.* porringerful, bowlful
Écuire, *v.a.n.,* **S'**—, *v.r.* to seethe
Écuisser, *v.a.* to thin (*a tree*) at the foot
Éculer, *v.a.* to tread down at the heel
S'—, *v.r.* to wear down at the heel
Écumage, *s.m.* skimming, scumming
Écumant, e, *adj.* foaming; frothy
Écume, *s.f.* foam; froth; scum; dross; dregs; lather. — *de mer,* meerschaum; foam of the sea; sea-ware. — *de terre,* (*pop.*) pewter
Écuménique, &c. *V.* **Œcuménique,** &c.
Écumer, *v.n.* to foam; to froth; — *v.a.* to skim; to scum; to pick up, to collect, to gather, to rake; to rid, to clear; (*nav.*) to scour, to infest (*the seas*). — *les marmites,* (*fig.*) to sponge
S'—, *v.r.* to be skimmed *or* &c.
Écumeu-r, se, *s.m.f.* skimmer; collector; pirate; plagiarist; parasite, sponger. — *de marmites,* parasite, sponger. — *de mer,* pirate, sea-rover
Écumeu-x, se, *adj.* foamy, foaming, frothy
Écumoire, *s.f.* skimmer; slice; (*pop.*) pock-pitted face
Écurage, *s.m.* scouring, cleaning, cleansing
Écurement, *s.m.* (*agr.*) trench
Écurer, *v.a.* to scour; to clean; to cleanse
†**Écureuil,** *s.m.* squirrel
Écureu-r, se, *s.m.f.* scourer; cleanser
Écurie, *s.f.* stable; stabling; mews; repository; stud; equipage; (*rail.*) horse-box. *Garçon* or *valet d'*—, stable-boy, groom; ostler
Écusson, *s.m.* escutcheon; scutcheon; shield; coat of arms; hatchment; crest; (*of a keyhole*) scutcheon; (*of grafting*) leaf-bud, gem. *Enter* or *greffer en* —, to bud
Écussonné, e, *adj.* escutcheoned; (*hort.*) budded
Écussonner, *v.a.* (*hort.*) to bud
Écussonnoir, *s.m.* (*hort.*) budding-knife
Écuyer, *s.m.* squire; esquire; equerry; shield-bearer; rider, horseman; equestrian performer; riding-master; horse-breaker; prop, stay; wall hand-rail. *Grand* —, master of the horse. — *tranchant,* carver. — *de bouche* or *de cuisine,* head cook; house-steward
Écuyère, *s.f.* horsewoman, rider; female equestrian performer. *A l'*—, in horse-riding fashion. *Bottes à l'*—, riding-boots, Hessian boots
Eczéma, *s.m.* (*med.*) eczema
Eczémateu-x, se, *adj.* (*med.*) eczematous
Edda, *s.f.* Edda
Éden, *s.m.* Eden
Édénien, ne, *adj.* of Eden
Édenté, e, *adj.* toothless; (*of things*) with broken teeth; — *adj. s.m.* (*zool.*) edental, edentate
Édenter, *v.a.* to deprive of o.'s teeth, to make (...) lose his *or* her teeth; to extract all the teeth of; (*of things*) to break *or* wear out the teeth of
S'—, *v.r.* to lose its *or* o.'s teeth
Édictal, e, *adj.* edictal
Édicter, *v.a.* to decree, to enact; to pass; to impose; to inflict
Édificateur, *s.m.* constructor, builder
Édification, *s.f.* erection, raising, construction, building; edification
Édifice, *s.m.* edifice; building; construction; fabric, structure
Édifier, *v.a.* to erect, to raise, to construct, to build, to build up; to edify; to instruct, to enlighten; to satisfy, to settle
S'—, *v.r.* to be building *or* built; to edify each other, to be edified
Édile, *s.m.* edile, ædile; municipal officer, town-councillor
Édilité, *s.f.* edileship, ædileship; town-council, corporation, municipality; resolutions *or* doings of the town-council; administration, aldermanship, mayoralty; construction of public buildings, building; city improvements
Édimbourgeois, e, *s.m.f.* Edinburgher; — *adj.* of Edinburgh
Édit, *s.m.* edict; decree
Éditer, *v.a.* (*of books,* &c.) to edit; to publish; (*law*) to quote
S'—, *v.r.* to be published; to be o.'s own publisher
Éditeur, *s.m.* editor; publisher
Édition, *s.f.* edition
Édolie, *s.m.* (*bird*) drongo
Édosser, *v.a.* (*hort., agr.*) to pare off
Édredon, *s.m.* eider-down; eider-down quilt *or* cushion *or* pillow; soft bed
Éducabilité, *s.f.* educability
Éducable, *adj.* educable, teachable
Éduca-teur, trice, *s.m.f.* educator, teacher, instructor, instructress; rearer, breeder, grower, producer; — *adj.* educating, educative, instructing. — *de vers à soie, V.* **Magnanier**
Éducati-f, ve, *adj.* educative
Éducation, *s.f.* education; instruction; training; rearing; breeding; manners
Éducationiste, *s.m.f.* educationist
Édulcoration, *s.f.* edulcoration, sweetening
Édulcorer, *v.a.* to edulcorate, to sweeten
S'—, *v.r.* to be edulcorated *or* sweetened
Éduquer, *v.a.* (*fam.*) to educate, to bring up, to rear, to school
Éfaufiler, *v.a.* to reeve out
Effaçable, *adj.* that can be effaced *or* obliterated, effaceable, delible
Effaçage, *s.m.* effacing, &c. (*V.* **Effacer**)
Effacement, *s.m.* effacement, effacing; defacement; erasion, erasure; obliteration; blot-

ting out; removal; eclipsing, obscuration; subordinate position; disappearance; keeping (*or* holding) in *or* sideways; throwing back; yielding, giving way; keeping in the background; humility

Effacer, *v.a.* to efface; to deface; to erase; to expunge; to obliterate; to do away with; to remove; to rub *or* strike *or* scratch out; to blot out; to wash away *or* off *or* out; to wipe away *or* off *or* out; to wear away *or* off *or* out; to fade; to eclipse, to outshine, to throw into the shade; to surpass, to excel, to outdo; to keep (*or* hold) in *or* sideways; to throw back; to keep in the background; to forgive; to forget; (*pop.*) to swallow

S'—, *v.r.* to come out; to become (*or* be) effaced *or* obliterated *or* erased; to wash out; to be blotted out; to wear away *or* off *or* out; to grow dim; to fade; to keep (oneself) in the background, to keep from sight; to yield, to give way; to be eclipsed *or* thrown into the shade; to be subordinate *or* inferior; to disappear, to vanish; to be forgotten; to be forgiven; to draw in, to stand sideways, to show less front, to cover the body, to draw in the shoulders; (*mil.*) to keep the line; (*nav.*) to present the broadside

Effaceu-r, se, *s.m.f.* eraser

Effaçure, *s.f.* erasure; obliteration; blot [ping

Effanage, *s.m.* stripping of leaves *or* tops, top-

Effaner, *v.a.* to strip of leaves *or* tops, to top

Effanure, *s.f.* leaves *or* tops (*cut off*)

Effaré, e, *adj.* scared, frightened; bewildered; wild; of fright; (*her.*) effaré (*rearing*)

Effarement, *s.m.* fright, terror; bewilderment

Effarer, *v.a.* to scare, to frighten; to bewilder

S'—, *v.r.* to be scared *or* &c.; to take fright

Effarouchement, *s.m.* fright; umbrage; alarm

Effaroucher, *v.a.* to scare, to frighten away; to shock, to startle; to give umbrage to

S'—, *v.r.* to be scared *or* frightened away, to take fright; to be shocked *or* startled; to take umbrage *or* alarm

Effauchetter, *v.a.* (*agr.*) to rake up

Effecti-f, ve, *adj.* effective; real; positive; in cash. *Homme —,* man of his word [strength

Effectif, *s.m.* (*mil.*) effective force; effective

Effectivement, *adv.* indeed, in fact, in reality, really, actually, positively, certainly, to be sure; yes; ay; so it is

Effectuer, *v.a.* to effect, to carry into effect, to realize, to make, to perform, to fulfil, to accomplish, to work out, to execute, to put into execution [to take place

S'—, *v.r.* to be effected *or* &c.; to take effect;

Effémination, *s.f.* effeminating; effeminacy

Efféminé, e, *adj.* effeminate; womanish; tame; — *s.m.* effeminate man

Efféminément, *adv.* effeminately

Efféminer, *v.a.* to effeminate, to render effem-

S'—, *v.r.* to become effeminate [inate; to soften

Effendi, *s.m.* effendi (*Turkish title*)

Efférent, e, *adj.* efferent

Effervescence, *s.f.* effervescence; excitement

Effervescent, e, *adj.* effervescent, effervescing; excitable; excited

Effet, *s.m.* effect; consequence, result; end; purpose, intent; show; execution; performance; deed; work; action; sensation; impression; mark; bill; security; (*mach.*) action, power; **—s,** *pl.* effects, goods, property, chattels; things; luggage; traps; stores; equipage; commercial bills, bills; bonds, stocks, shares, funds, securities. *— rétrograde,* (*billiards*) screwing back. *— de côté,* (*billiards*) side. *— de clair de lune,* (*paint.*) moonlight scenery. *— de nuit,* (*paint.*) night-piece. *A —,* intended for effect; show; sensation, sensational; clap-trap; (*mach.*) with ... action *or* power, ...-acting. *A l'— de,* in order to, with a view to. *En —,* in fact; in reality, indeed; it is true; to be sure; really; substantially; certainly; for indeed, for; yes; ay; so it is. *Faire —,* to take effect. *Faire* or *produire de l'—,* to produce an effect; to make an impression; to create a sensation; to be efficient; to operate. *Faire l'— de,* to have the same effect as; to seem *or* look *or* smell *or* taste *or* feel *or* sound like (*or* as if); to represent; to remind of. *Faire un bon* or *mauvais —,* to produce a good *or* bad effect; to look well *or* ill. *Cela me fait cet — -là,* it seems so to me. (*At billiards*) *Faire un — rétrograde,* to screw back; *faire un — de côté,* to put on "side" [ping of the leaves

†**Effeuillage,** *s.m.*, **Effeuillaison,** *s.f.* strip-

†**Effeuillement,** *s.m.* fall *or* loss of the leaves, defoliation; leaflessness

†**Effeuiller,** *v.a.* to strip *or* deprive of leaves, to pick *or* pluck the leaves of; to pick (*a flower*)

S'—, *v.r.* to lose *or* shed its leaves [to pieces

†**Effeuilleu-r, se,** *s.m.f.* leaf-stripper

†**Effeuillure,** *s.f.* leaves (*plucked off*)

Efficace, *adj.* efficacious, efficient, effectual, effective; — *s.f.* (*old*) *V.* **Efficacité** [effectually

Efficacement, *adv.* efficaciously, efficiently,

Efficacité, *s.f.* efficacy, efficiency, effectualness

Efficient, e, *adj.* efficient

Effigial, e, *adj.* effigial

Effigie, *s.f.* effigy [*or* burn in effigy

Effigier, *v.a.* to make an effigy of; (*old*) to hang

Effilage, *s.m.* unravelling; tapering; thinning

Effilé, e, *adj.* slender; slim; thin; fine; sharp; tapering; thin-shouldered (*horse*); — *s.m.* fringe

Effiler, *v.a.* to unravel, to ravel out, to unweave; to fray; to taper; to thin; to string; (*hunt.*) to fatigue, to emaciate

S'—, *v.r.* to come unravelled; to fray out; to taper; to become slender *or* thin

Effilochage, *s.m.* tearing up; (*— de laines*) shoddy; mungo; shoddy-trade [fray

Effiloche, *s.f.* light refuse silk; untwisted silk;

Effiloché, *s.m.* shoddy; mungo

Effilocher, *v.a.* to tear up, to devil

Effilocheu-r, se, *s.m.f.* (*— de laines*) shoddy-manufacturer; — *s.f.* shoddy-mill, devil

Effiloque, *s.f. V.* **Effiloche**

Effiloquer, *v.a.* to ravel out; to fray

Effilure, *s.f.* ravellings, ravelling

Effioler, *v.a.* (*agr.*) to mow off, to feed off

Efflanqué, e, *adj.* emaciated, lean, thin, lank, raw-boned; meagre; — *s.m.f.* longshanks

Efflanquer, *v.a.* to emaciate

Effleurer, *v.a.* to graze; to brush; to skim the surface of, to skim over *or* along, to skim; to touch slightly; to touch upon, to touch; to dip into; to glance at; to take the surface off, to pare, to shave, to scrape; to strip of its flower *or* flowers

S'—, *v.r.* to graze (o.'s ...); to be grazed *or* skimmed *or* &c.; to come very near each other; to lose its flower *or* flowers

Effleurir, *v.n.*, **S'—,** *v.r.* (*chem., min.*) to effloresce

Efflorescence, *s.f.* efflorescence

Efflorescent, e, *adj.* efflorescent

Effluence, *s.f.* effluence

Effluent, e, *adj.*, **Effluent,** *s.m.* effluent

Effluve, *s.m.* effluvium; **—s,** *pl.* effluvia

Effondrement, *s.m.* deep digging, subsoil-digging *or* ploughing; breaking up; breaking open *or* in; falling in, sinking

Effondrer, *v.a.* to dig deep; to break up; to break open *or* in; to stave in; to weigh down, to sink; to draw (*poultry*); to gut (*fish*); — *v.n.*, **S'—,** *v.r.* to fall in, to give way, to sink

†**Effondrilles,** *s.f.pl.* sediment, grounds, grout, grouts, dregs

Efforcer (S'), *v.r.* to strive, to labour, to exert oneself, to endeavour, to attempt, to try

Effort, *s.m.* effort, exertion; endeavour; attempt; strain; force, strength; weight; stress; difficulty; labour. *Faire un — sur soi-même,* to strive to overcome o.'s repugnance, to do oneself violence. *Se donner un —,* to overstrain oneself; to sprain o.'s back

Effraction, *s.f.* breaking open. *Vol avec —,* (robbery with) house-breaking. *Vol de nuit* [*avec —,* burglary
Effraie, *s.f.* barn-owl
Effranger, *v.a.* to fringe; to fray
Effrayant, e, *adj.* frightful, fearful, dreadful, terrific, appalling, tremendous, awful; grim, horrible, hideous
Effrayé, e, *part. adj.* frightened, &c. (*V.* **Effrayer**); afraid; affrighted; of fright, of dismay; (*her.*) effrayé (*rearing*)
Effrayer, *v.a.* to frighten; to frighten away; to scare; to dismay; to alarm; to deter
S'—, *v.r.* to be frightened *or* &c.; to take fright; to become *or* be alarmed, to take alarm; to mind
Effréné, e, *adj.* unbridled; unrestrained; ungovernable; unruly; lawless; immoderate; unbounded; excessive; extravagant; frantic; wild
Effrènement, *s.m.* unruliness; lawlessness; wildness; violence; excess; extravagance; frenzy
Effrénément, *adv.* lawlessly; wildly; immoderately; extravagantly; frantically; excessively [crumbling to dust
Effritement, *s.m.* (*agr.*) exhaustion; (*tech.*)
Effriter, *v.a.* (*agr.*) to exhaust
S'—, *v.r.* to become exhausted; (*tech.*) to crumble to dust, to crumble
Effroi, *s.m.* fright, terror, fear, dread, dismay
Effronté, e, *adj.* shameless, impudent, brazen-faced, brazen, bold-faced, bold; — *s.m.f.* brazen-face, bold-face [shamelessly
Effrontément, *adv.* impudently, boldly,
Effronterie, *s.f.* effrontery, impudence, shamelessness, boldness, assurance
Effroyable, *adj.* frightful, fearful, dreadful, awful; horrid, horrible; shocking
Effroyablement, *adv.* frightfully, fearfully, dreadfully, awfully, horribly, shockingly
Effruiter, *v.a.* to strip of fruit, to gather the
S'—, *v.r.* to drop its fruit [fruit of
Effumer, *v.a.* (*paint.*) to soften the colours of
Effusion, *s.f.* effusion; overflowing; shedding
Éfourceau, *s.m.* pair of wheels, gill, tug,
Égagre, *s.f. V.* **Ægagre** [trolly
Égagropile, *s.m.* (*vet.*) wool-ball
Égal, e, *adj. s.* equal; like, alike; even; level; uniform; regular; indifferent, (all) the same, all one; unmoved; worthy (of). *A l'— de,* equally with, equal to, as much as, like; in comparison with. *D'— à —,* between equals; as between equals; on equal terms. *Sans —,* without an equal, matchless, peerless, unequalled, unrivalled, unparalleled, unprecedented, unexampled, incomparable. *C'est —,* never mind; after all; well; but, yet
Égalable, *adj.* to be equalled *or* compared
Également, *adv.* equally; uniformly; impartially; alike; also, likewise, too; both; — *s.m.* (*obsolete*) equalization
Égaler, *v.a.* to equal; to match, to come up to; to rival, to emulate; to compare; to make even
S'—, *v.r.* to compare oneself (to), to make [oneself equal (to)
Égalisation, *s.f.* equalization
Égaliser, *v.a.* to equalize; to level; to square (*accounts*) [equal; to find its own level
S'—, *v.r.* to become (*or* be) equalized *or*
Égalitaire, *adj.* (*polit.*) of equality; based on equality *or* equal rights; levelling; — *s.m.f.* partisan of equality; leveller
Égalité, *s.f.* equality; parity; evenness; uniformity; regularity; congruity; fairness
Égard, *s.m.* regard; respect; consideration, account; deference; attentions. *A cet —,* in this or that respect. *A l'— de,* regarding, with regard (*or* respect) to, as for; towards, to; in comparison with, compared with. *A mon —,* with regard to me; towards me, to me. *A son —,* with regard to him (*or* her); towards him (*or* her), to him (*or* her). *A quelques —s,* in some respects. *A tous —s,* in all respects, in every respect. *Eu — à,* considering. *Par — pour,* out of regard for (*or* to); for the sake of, on account of. *Avoir — à,* to have regard to; to make allowance for; to consider; to take notice of. *Avoir des —s pour,* to pay consideration *or* respect to, to show deference *or* attentions to
Égaré, e, *part. adj.* lost; stray; wandering; erring; out of the way; that has lost his way; misled, misguided, led astray; mislaid; disordered; deranged; distracted; bewildered; wild; scattered; (*of a horse's mouth*) spoilt; (*of paths*) devious
Égarement, *s.m.* losing o.'s way, straying, wandering; error; mistake; confusion; disorder; misconduct; excess; frenzy; bewilderment; wildness; derangement, alienation
Égarer, *v.a.* to mislead; to misguide; to lead astray; to lead *or* take out of the way; to turn; to lead into error; to let (...) wander; to mislay; to lose; to disorder; to derange; to bewilder; to spoil (*a horse's mouth*)
S'—, *v.r.* to lose o.'s way; to lose oneself; to wander, to ramble, to err, to stray, to go astray, to go wrong; to fall into error; to be mislaid *or* lost
Égarrotté, e, *part. adj.* (*vet.*) wither-wrung
Égarrotter, *v.a.* (*vet.*) to injure *or* hurt in the withers [(*agr.*) trench
Égayement, *s.m.* enlivening, &c. (*V.* **Égayer**);
Égayer, *v.a.* to enliven; to cheer up; to make cheerful; to lighten; to let light into; to make lighter; to go out of (*deep mourning*); to thin (*trees*); to hiss (*in theat. slang*); (*abusively for* "aiguayer") *V.* **Aiguayer**
S'—, *v.r.* to cheer up; to amuse oneself; to make *or* be merry; to sport
Égérie, *s.f.* (*myth., astr., zool.*) Egeria; (*fig.*)
Égide, *s.f.* ægis, shield; protection [inspirer
Égilope, *s.f.* (*bot.*) ægilops, hard-grass
Égilops, *s.m.* (*med.*) ægilops, anchilops
Égipan, *s.m.* (*myth.*) ægipan, satyr
Églantier, *s.m.* (*tree*) dog-rose tree. — *odorant,* sweet-briar, eglantine
Églantine, *s.f.* (*flower*) wild rose, dog-rose; sweet-briar rose, eglantine
Églefin, *s.m.* (*fish*) haddock
Église, *s.f.* church; chimney-cowl, cowl
Églisi-er, ère, *s.m.f.* (*pop.*) inveterate church-
Églogaire, *s.m.* excerptor [goer
Églogue, *s.f.* eclogue; selection, excerpts
Égoger, *v.a.* to square (*hides*)
Égohine, Égoïne, *s.f.* hand-saw
Égoïser, *v.n.* to egotize [(*philos.*) egoism
Égoïsme, *s.m.* selfishness, egoism, egotism;
Égoïste, *adj.* selfish, egoistic, egotistic; (*philos.*) egoistic; — *s.m.f.* selfish person, selfish man *or* fellow *or* woman *or* girl *or* creature, egoist, egotist; (*philos.*) egoist [tistically
Égoïstement, *adv.* selfishly, egoistically, ego-
Égoïst-ique (*adj.*), **-iquement** (*adv.*). *V.* **Égoïst-e, -ement**
Égophonie, *s.f.* (*med.*) egophony
Égopode, *s.m.* (*bot.*) gout-weed, gout-wort
Égorgement, *s.m.* slaughter, butchery; murder
Égorgeoir, *s.m.* slaughter-house, cut-throat place; (*nav.*) spilling-line
Égorger, *v.a.* to cut the throat of; to slaughter, to kill, to slay, to butcher; to murder; to immolate, to sacrifice; to ruin; to cut to pieces; to fleece [assassin, murderer, murderess
Égorgeu-r, se, *s.m.f.* cut-throat, slaughterer,
†**Égosiller (S'),** *v.r.* to make oneself hoarse, to bawl *or* shout oneself hoarse, to make o.'s throat sore, to strain o.'s voice; to sing *or*
Égot-isme, -iste. *V.* page 3, § 1 [chirp loud
Égout, *s.m.* sewer, drain, sink; down pipe, trunk-pipe; drip, fall; projecting roof; eaves. — *collecteur,* main sewer
Égoutier, *s.m.* sewerman [draining, dripping
Égouttage, Égouttement, *s.m.* drainage,
Égoutter, *v.a.n.*, **S'—,** *v.r.* to drain; to drop;
Égouttoir, *s.m.* drainer; plate-rack [to drip

Égoutture, *s.f.* drainings, drippings
†**Égraffigner,** *v.a. pop. for* **Égratigner**
Égrain, *s.m.* seedling pear *or* apple-tree
Égrainage, Égrainer, &c. *V.* **Égrenage,** &c.
Égrappage, *s.m.* picking (*of grapes,* &c.)
Égrapper, *v.a.* to pick (*grapes,* &c.) from the bunch; to dress (*the ore*)
S'—, *v.r.* to be picked; to come off the stalk
Égrappoir, *s.m.* picking utensil (*for grapes,* &c.)
†**Égratigner,** *v.a.n.* to scratch; (*paint.*) to stencil [stenciller; — *adj.* scratching
†**Égratigneu-r, se,** *s.m.f.* scratcher; (*paint.*)
†**Égratignure,** *s.f.* scratch
†**Égravillonner,** *v.a.* (*hort.*) to ablaqueate
Égrefin, *s.m.* (*fish*) haddock
Égrenage, *s.m.* shelling, husking; picking;
Égrène, *s.f.* corner-iron, angle-iron [ginning
Égrener, *v.a.* to shell, to husk; to pick (*grapes,* &c.); (*manu.*) to gin; (*fig.*) to tell (*o.'s beads*); — *v.n.* to grain [fall from the stalk
S'—, *v.r.* to shell; to shed seed, to seed; to
Égreneuse, *s.f.,* **Égrenoir,** *s.m.* sheller, corn-sheller; gin, cotton-gin
†**Égrillard, e,** *adj.* sprightly, lively, brisk, jolly; fast; free; — *s.m.f.* grig, spark, fast fellow *or* woman *or* girl
†**Égrilloir,** *s.m.* weir; grate [ting (*diamonds*)
Égrisage, *s.m.* grinding, roughing down; cut-
Égrisé, *s.m.,* **Égrisée,** *s.f.* diamond dust
Égriser, *v.a.* to grind, to rough down; to cut
Égrisoir, *s.m.* diamond-dust box [(*diamonds*)
Égrugeoir, *s.m.* mortar
Égruger, *v.a.* to pound, to crush, to grate
Égrugeure, *s.f.* poundings, gratings, raspings, powder, dust
Égueulé, e, *part. adj.* (*things*) broken-mouthed, broken-necked; (*pers.*) hoarse; foul-mouthed; — *s.m.f.* foul-mouthed person [mouth *or* spout
Égueulement, *s.m.* breaking *or* break at the
Égueuler, *v.a.* to break the mouth *or* spout *or* neck of
S'—, *v.r.* to break at the mouth; (*pers.*) to bawl *or* shout oneself hoarse, to make oneself hoarse, to strain o.'s voice
†**Éguille,** *s.f. V.* **Équille**
Égyptiac, *adj.m. Onguent* —, (*pharm.*) Ægyptiacum unguentum (*oxymel of verdigris*)
Égyptien, ne, *adj. s.* Egyptian; gypsy; Egyptian fashion
Eh, *int.* eh! ah! oh! well! alas! what! — *bien!*
Éhanché, e, *adj. V.* **Déhanché** [*V.* **Bien,** *adv.*
Éherber, *v.a.* to weed
Éhonté, e, *adj. s. V.* **Déhonté**
Éhoupper, *v.a.* to top (*trees*)
Eider, *s.m.* (*bird*) eider, eider-duck
Éjacula-teur, trice, Éjaculatoire, *adj.* ejaculating, ejaculatory
Éjaculation, *s.f.* ejaculation
Éjaculer, *v.a.* to ejaculate, to throw out
Éjamber, *v.a. V.* **Écôter**
Éjarrage, *s.m.* removal of the coarse hairs
Éjarrer, *v.a.* to remove the coarse hairs of (*a fur*)
Éjec-teur, trice, *adj.* ejecting. *Tuyau* —,
Éjection, *s.f.* ejection [discharge pipe
Éjointer, *v.a.* (*falc.*) to clip one of the wings of
Éjouir, *v.a.* (*old*) *V.* **Réjouir**
Élabora-teur, trice, *adj.* elaborating, ela-
Élaboration, *s.f.* elaboration [borative
Élaboré, e, *part. adj.* elaborated, elaborate, laboured, wrought
Élaborer, *v.a.* to elaborate; to work out
S'—, *v.r.* to become *or* be elaborated, &c.
Élæolithe, *s.m.* (*min.*) elæolite
Élæomètre, *s.m.* elæometer
Élagage, *s.m.* lopping, pruning
Élaguer, *v.a.* to lop, to prune, to cut off; to suppress, to cut out, to curtail, to remove; to shorten; to condense
Élagueu-r, se, *s.m.f.* lopper, pruner
Élan, *s.m.* spring, start; bound; flight, soaring; burst; sally; impulse; rush, dash; impetuosity; spirit; glow, warmth, life; transport, yearning; enthusiasm; (*animal*) elk, moose, moose deer. — *du Cap,* Cape-elk, eland
Élancé, e, *adj.* slender, slim, lank, thin
Élancement, *s.m.* shooting (*pain*), twinge, twitch, twitching; (*nav.*) rake; (*obsolete*) springing, spring, starting, start, bounding, bound, rushing, rush, dashing, dash; transport, yearning
Élancer, *v.a.* to launch, to dart, to shoot; to incite, to urge on, to impel, to drive, to push on; — *v.n.* to shoot (*pain*), to twinge, to twitch
S'—, *v.r.* to spring, to start; to bound, to leap; to throw oneself; to pounce; to rush, to rush on *or* forward; to dash; to dart, to dart forth; to shoot, to shoot forth; to burst; to take o.'s flight; to grow upward; to become
Élane, *s.m.* (*bird*) elanet [slender
Élargi, e, *part. adj.* widened, &c. (*V.* **Élargir**); wider; broader; wide; broad
Élargir, *v.a.,* **S'—,** *v.r.* to widen; to enlarge; to extend; to spread; to stretch; to let out; to release, to set at liberty; to get at a distance; to enlarge o.'s estate; to get loose, to gain o.'s liberty [enlargement; release
Élargissement, *s.m.* widening; enlarging;
Élargissure, *s.f.* piece let in, eking-piece, inlay
Élasticité, *s.f.* elasticity, springiness, spring
Élastique, *adj.m.f., s.m.* elastic; springy; spring; indiarubber
Élater, *s.m.* (*insect*) elater, &c. (*V.* **Taupin**)
Élatérine, *s.f.* (*chem.*) elaterine
Élatérite, *s.f.* (*min.*) elaterite, elastic bitumen, mineral caoutchouc
Élatérium, *s.m.* (*pharm.*) elaterium
Élatéromètre, *s.m.* elaterometer
Élatine, *s.f.* (*bot.*) elatine, water-pepper, water-
Élavé, e, *adj.* soft and discoloured [wort
Elbeuf, *s.m.* Elbeuf cloth; (*pop.*) coat
Elbeuvien, ne, *adj. s.* of Elbeuf; native of
Eldorado, *s.m.* eldorado [Elbeuf
Éléatique, *adj.* Eleatic
Électeur, *s.m.* elector
Électi-f, ve, *adj.* elective
Élection, *s.f.* election; polling; choosing, choice; return; appointment
Électoral, e, *adj.* electoral; elective
Électorat, *s.m.* electorate; vote, right to vote
Électrice, *s.f.* electress
Électricien, *s.m.* electrician
Électricité, *s.f.* electricity
Électr-ique, -iquement. *V.* page 3, § 1
Électrisable, *adj.* electrifiable
Électrisation, *s.f.* electrification; electrization
Électriser, *v.a.* to electrify, to electrize
S'—, *v.r.* to be electrified; to become electric
Électriseur, *s.m.* electrizer
Électro-, (*in compounds*) electro-...
Électro-aimant, *s.m.* electro-magnet
Électrode, *s.f.* electrode
Électrographe, *s.m.* electrician
Électrolog-ie, -ique. *V.* page 3, § 1
Électrolysable, *adj.* electrolyzable
Électrolysation, *s.f.* electrolyzation
Électrolyse, *s.f.* electrolysis, electro-chemical decomposition
Électrolyser, *v.a.* to electrolyze
Électrolyte, *s.m.* electrolyte
Électrolytique, *adj.* electrolytic
Électromètre, *s.m.* electrometer
Électromètr-ie, -ique. *V.* page 3, § 1
Électromo-teur, trice, *adj.* electromotive; — *s.m.* electromotor
Électrophore, *s.m.* electrophorus
Électroscope, *s.m.* electroscope
Électroscop-ie, -ique. *V.* page 3, § 1
Électrotypage, *s.m.* electrotyping
Électrotype, *s.m.* electrotype
Électrotyper, *v.a.* to electrotype
Électrotypeur, *s.m.* electrotyper
Électrotyp-ie, -ique. *V.* page 3, § 1
Électuaire, *s.m.* electuary
Élédone, *s.f.* (*mollusc*) eledone
Élégamment, *adv.* elegantly

Élégance, *s.f.* elegance
Élégant, e, *adj. s.* elegant; fashionable; fashionable man *or* lady, beau, belle, exquisite, swell
Élégiaque, *adj.* elegiac; — *s.m.* elegiast, elegist
Élégie, *s.f.* elegy
Élément, *s.m.* element; component part
Élémentaire, *adj.* elementary; elemental
Élémi, *s.m.* (*pharm.*) elemi
Éléphant, e, *s.m.f.* elephant
Éléphantiaque, *adj. s.* (*med.*) elephantiac
Éléphantiasis, *s.f.* (*med.*) elephantiasis
Éléphantin, e, *adj.* elephantine [phantiac
Éléphantique, *adj.* elephantine; (*med.*) ele-
Élevage, *s.m.* breeding, raising, rearing, growing
Éléva-teur, trice, *adj.m.f.* elevatory, raising, lifting; — *adj.m.* (*anat.*) elevator; — *s.m.* (*anat.*, *mech.*, &c.) elevator
Élévation, *s.f.* elevation; raising; heaving, heave; rising ground, ridge; height; eminence; rise; increase; preferment; dignity; exaltation; nobleness; (*of sound*) acuteness; (*draw.*) view; (*at mass*) elevation of the host
Élévatoire, *s.m.* (*surg.*) elevator; — *adj.* elevatory, raising, lifting, lift
Élève, *s.m.f.* pupil, student, scholar; schoolboy, boy, school-girl, girl; apprentice; cadet; midshipman; animal reared; plant raised, nursling; — *s.f. V.* **Élevage.** — *caporal*, lance corporal. — **-maître** (*m.*), — **-maîtresse** (*f.*), pupil-teacher, governess-pupil, articled pupil. — *en chambre*, parlour boarder. *Faire des —s*, to make *or* educate pupils *or* scholars; to rear cattle *or* horses *or* &c.; to raise *or* grow plants *or* flowers
Élevé, e, *part. adj.* elevated, raised, &c. (*V.* **Élever**); high; lofty; eminent; erect; bred, brought up, &c.; grown up
Élèvement, *s.m.* raising; rise
Élever, *v.a.* to elevate; to raise; to exalt; to extol; to elate; to erect; to build; to set up; to lift up; to heave; to bring up; to train up; to educate; to rear; to breed; to cultivate, to grow; to give rise to, to start; (*of accounts*, &c.) to run up, to increase; (*nav.*) to near
S'—, *v.r.* to rise; to arise; to ascend; to spring up; to grow up; to come *or* go up; to run up *or* high; to increase; to advance; to reach; to amount; to tower; to raise *or* &c. oneself (*or* to oneself); to become elated, to grow proud; to be raised *or* &c.; to be built *or* building; (*of the weather*) to clear up
Éleveur, *s.m.* breeder; grazier; cattle-dealer; (— *de moutons*) sheep-farmer; (*thing*) elevator. — *d'abeilles, V.* **Apiculteur.** — *de vers à soie, V.* **Magnanier**
Élevure, *s.f.* blister; eruption, pimple, pustule,
Elfe, *s.m.* elf [blotch, blain
Élider, *v.a.* (*gram.*) to elide, to cut off
S'—, *v.r.* to be elided, to be cut off
Élier, *v.a.* to draw off, to rack off, to rack
Éligibilité, *s.f.* eligibility
Éligible, *adj. s.* eligible; eligible person
Éligiblement, *adv.* eligibly
Élimer, *v.a.*, **S'—,** *v.r.* to wear out
Élimina-teur, trice, *adj.* eliminating
Élimination, *s.f.* elimination; dismissal, removal, expulsion, extrusion, rejection
Éliminer, *v.a.* to eliminate; to discard; to dismiss, to remove, to expel, to extrude, to exclude; to strike off *or* out
Élingue, *s.f.* (*nav.*) sling
Élinguer, *v.a.* (*nav.*) to sling
Élire, *v.a.* to elect, to choose; to return; to appoint; to designate. — *domicile*, to appoint o.'s domicile; to fix o.'s residence, to take up o.'s abode *or* quarters, to establish oneself, to
Élision, *s.f.* elision [settle
Élite, *s.f.* choice; flower, prime, best. *D'—*, select; choicest; picked; superior; crack
Éliter, *v.a.* (*pop.*) to choose *or* take the best of
Élixation, *s.f.* elixation
Élixir, *s.m.* elixir

Elle, *pron.f.* she; her; it; for her part; herself; itself; **—s,** *pl.* they; them; for their part; themselves; each other, one another. *A —*, to *or* at *or* with her; to *or* at herself; hers, her own; of hers, of her own; peculiar; to spare. *A —s*, to *or* at *or* with them; to *or* at themselves; theirs, their own; of theirs, of their own; peculiar; to spare. *A — or —s à; A — or —s de; V.* **A.** — *-même*, herself; itself; alone; too, also, likewise. *—s-mêmes*, themselves; alone; too, also, likewise
Ellébore, *s.m.* (*bot.*) hellebore
Elléborine, *s.f.* (*bot.*) helleborine
Ellipse, *s.f.* (*geom.*) ellipse; (*gram.*, *rhet.*) ellipsis
Ellipser, *v.a.* (*gram.*, *rhet.*) to ellipsize, to leave out by ellipsis
Ellipsographe, *s.m.* ellipsograph
Ellipsoïdal, e, *adj.* (*geom.*) ellipsoidal
Ellipsoïde, *s.m.* (*geom.*) ellipsoid; — *s.f.* elliptical curve; — *adj.* ellipsoidal
Ellipsologie, *s.f.* ellipsology
Ellipticité, *s.f.* ellipticity
Ellipt-ique, -iquement. *V.* page 3, § 1
Elme (Feu saint-), *V.* **Feu**
Élocher, *v.a.* to shake, to loosen
Élocution, *s.f.* elocution
Éloge, *s.m.* praise; commendation; eulogy, eulogium, encomium, panegyric. — *funèbre*, funeral oration. *Faire l'— de*, to praise, to eulogize, to bestow praise on, to speak in praise of, to speak highly of; to be creditable to, to
Élogier, *v.a.* to eulogize [tell in favour of
Élogieu-x, se, *adj.* eulogistic, flattering
Élogiste, *s.m.f.* eulogist
Élohiste, *s.m.* elohist; — *adj.* elohistic
†**Éloigné, e,** *part. adj.* removed, &c. (*V.* **Éloigner**); remote; distant; far; wide; foreign; absent; away; disinclined, indisposed, reluctant, averse, unwilling
†**Éloignement,** *s.m.* removal, removing; distance; remoteness; absence; separation; departure; retirement; estrangement; dislike, aversion, antipathy; reluctance, unwillingness; neglect, forgetfulness
†**Éloigner,** *v.a.* to remove; to remove further; to put *or* take *or* send *or* drive away *or* off; to send to a distance; to dismiss; to discard; to repudiate; to repulse; to put to flight; to dispel; to banish; to keep away *or* off, to keep at a distance; to avert; to separate; to withhold; to delay, to defer, to put off; to divert; to deter; to waive; to alienate, to estrange; to indispose
S'—, *v.r.* to go *or* move away *or* off, to go to a distance, to get *or* turn away; to go (from); to remove; to withdraw, to leave, to quit; to recede; to ramble, to wander; to straggle; to keep away *or* off, to keep at a distance; to avoid; to depart; to swerve, to deviate; to be more remote; to be wide (of); to be wanting, to fall off, to fail; to forsake; to neglect; to differ, to be different; to be delayed *or* deferred; to be estranged; to dislike, to be averse; to appear in the distance; to disappear; to depress (*the pole*, &c.); (*nav.*) to stand away, to
Élongation, *s.f.* elongation [sheer off
Élonger, *v.a.* (*nav.*) to lay alongside of. — *une manœuvre*, to stretch out a rope, to run out
Élope, *s.m.* (*fish*) elops [a warp
Éloquemment, *adv.* eloquently
Éloquence, *s.f.* eloquence; oratory
Éloquent, e, *adj.* eloquent
Élu, e, *part. adj. s.* elected; chosen; returned; appointed; designate; choice; select; elect; (*obsolete*) county-court judge, wife of ditto
Élucidation, *s.f.* elucidation [dated
Élucider, *v.a.* to elucidate. *S'—*, to be eluci-
Élucubrateur, *s.m.* lucubrator
Élucubrati-f, ve, *adj.* lucubratory
Élucubration, *s.f.* lucubration
Élucubrer, *v.a.n.* to lucubrate
Éludable, *adj.* eludible, evasible, evadible
Éluder, *v.a.n.* to elude, to evade

Éludeu-r, se, *s.m.f.* eluder, evader, shuffler
Éludorique, *adj.* (*paint.*) elydoric
Élutriation, *s.f.* elutriation
Élyme, *s.m.* (*bot.*) lyme grass
Élysée, *s.m.* Elysium; — *adj.m.* Elysian
Élyséen, ne, *adj.m.f.*, **Élysien,** *adj.m.* Elysian
Élytre, *s.m.* (*of insects*) elytrum, wing-case, [wing-shell
Élytrite, *s.f.* (*med.*) elytritis
Élytrocèle, *s.f.* (*med.*) elytrocele
Elzévir, *s.m.* Elzevir edition, Elzevir
Elzévirien, ne, *adj.* Elzevirian, Elzevir
Émaciation, *s.f.* emaciation
Émacié, e, *adj.* emaciate, emaciated
†**Émail,** *s.m.* enamel; (*fig.*) gloss, brilliancy; ornament; flowers; (*her.*) tincture
†**Émaillage,** *s.m.* enamelling
†**Émaillé, e,** *part. adj.* enamelled, &c. (*V.* **Émailler**); glossy, brilliant; (*her.*) tinctured
†**Émailler,** *v.a.* to enamel; (*fig.*) to enamel, to adorn, to embellish, to deck, to cover, to stud, to diversify

S'—, *v.r.* to become (*or* be) enamelled *or* &c.; to become *or* be covered with flowers
†**Émaillerie,** *s.f.* enamelling
†**Émailleu-r, se,** *s.m.f.* enameller
†**Émaillure,** *s.f.* enamelling
Émanation, *s.f.* emanation
Émancipa-teur, trice, *s.m.f.* emancipator; — *adj.* emancipating [livery
Émancipation, *s.f.* emancipation; (*of a minor*)
Émanciper, *v.a.* to emancipate

S'—, *v.r.* to gain o.'s liberty; to free oneself; to make *or* be too free, to take too much liberty, to take liberties, to go beyond bounds, to be fast, to go far, to go so far (as to), to forget oneself; to play pranks
Émané, e, *part.* emanated, emanating
Émaner, *v.n.* to emanate
Émargement, *s.m.* emargination; writing *or* signature in the margin, marginal note *or* notes, signature
Émarger, *v.a.n.* to emarginate; to write *or* sign in the margin of; to sign; to receipt; to sign the receipt; to sign the receipt of o.'s salary
Émarginé, e, *adj.* (*nat. hist.*) emarginate
Émasculation, *s.f.* emasculation
Émasculer, *v.a.* to emasculate [*V.* **Ababouiné**
Embabouiné, e, *adj.* wheedled, coaxed; (*nav.*)
Embabouiner, *v.a.* to wheedle, to coax, to gammon
Embâcle, *s.m.* ice-pack, obstruction, stoppage
Emballage, *s.m.* packing, packing up; wrapping; package
Emballer, *v.a.* to pack, to pack up; to wrap up; to pack off, to bundle off; to clap up, to lock up, to quod; (*old*) to inveigle; — *v.n.* (*slang*) (*of horses*) to run away
Emballeur, *s.m.* packer; (*pop.*) policeman, bobby; (*obsolete*) inveigler
Emballuchonner, *v.a.* (*pop.*) to bundle up
Embander, *v.a.* to bandage up, to bind up, to [swathe
Embanquer, *v.n.* (*nav.*) *V.* **Banquer**
Embarbé, e, *adj.* (*jest.*) bearded
Embarboter, †**Embarbouiller,** *v.a.* (*pop.*) to muddle; to entangle

S'—, *v.r.* to get muddled, to get into a mess, to get into confusion worse confounded
Embarcadère, *s.m.* wharf; pier; steps; terminus, station [gers
Embarcation, *s.f.* boat, craft; crew; passen-
Embardée, *s.f.* (*nav.*) yaw, lurch
Embarder, *v.n.* (*nav.*) to yaw, to lurch, to sheer
Embargo, *s.m.* embargo
†**Embarillage,** *s.m.* barrelling
†**Embariller,** *v.a.* to barrel, to barrel up
Embarlificoter, *v.a.* (*pop.*) *V.* **Emberlificoter**
Embarquement, *s.m.* embarcation, embarking, embarkment; shipping, shipment
Embarquer, *v.a.n.* to embark; to ship; to put *or* take on board; to engage, to involve; to see off

S'—, *v.r.* to embark, to go on board, to take shipping, to put *or* go to sea; to sail; to set out; to engage
Embarras, *s.m.* encumbrance; obstruction; stoppage; impediment; obstacle; hindrance; clog; embarrassment; confusion; derangement; intricacy; difficulty; difficulties; scrape; perplexity; puzzle; trouble; inconvenience; fuss; dash; family way. *Ce n'est pas l'—*, that is easy enough; I see no objection; there is something in that; after all; yet; for all that; for the matter of that; as to that
Embarrassant, e, *adj.* encumbering, cumbrous, cumbersome; awkward; embarrassing; intricate; perplexing, puzzling; troublesome
Embarrassé, e, *part. adj.* encumbered, embarrassed, &c. (*V.* **Embarrasser**); at a loss (to, for); constrained; out of countenance; awkward; intricate; indistinct; in the family way; uncomfortable; pinched *or* pressed (*for money*). *Être — de sa personne*, not to know what to do with oneself
Embarrasser, *v.a.* to encumber; to hamper; to clog; to obstruct; to block up; to hinder; to impede; to be in the way of; to inconvenience, to incommode; to crowd; to entangle; to embroil; to complicate; to embarrass; to straiten; to trouble; to confuse; to confound; to disconcert; to perplex; to puzzle; to come amiss to

S'—, *v.r.* to encumber *or* &c. oneself; to become (*or* be) encumbered *or* &c.; to entangle oneself, to become *or* be entangled; to stick, to clog; to become (*or* get) confused *or* perplexed; to trouble oneself (with, about); to meddle (with); to care (for), to mind; to concern oneself, to be uneasy (about); to be affected; to take notice; to be solicitous (about)
Embarrure, *s.f.* comminuted fracture of the [skull
Embase, *s.f.* (*tech.*) shoulder
Embasement, *s.m.* (*arch.*) continued base
†**Embastillement,** *s.m.* imprisoning, imprisonment; surrounding with forts
†**Embastiller,** *v.a.* to imprison; to surround with forts, to fortify with towers
†**Embataillement,** *s.m.* embattling
†**Embatailler,** *v.a.* to embattle
†**Embataillonner,** *v.a.* to form into battalions
Embâter, *v.a.* to saddle [with a stick *or* cudgel
Embâtonné, e, (*her.*) reeded; (*obsolete*) armed
Embattage, *s.m.* shoeing (*of wheels*), tiring
Embattés, *s.m pl.* periodical winds
Embattoir, *s.m.* shoeing-pit (*for wheels*)
Embattre, *v.a.* to shoe (*wheels*), to tire
Embauchage, Embauchement, *s.m.* engaging, engagement; hiring; decoying, enticing away; enlisting, recruiting; crimping; paying o.'s footing
Embaucher, *v.a.* to engage, to hire; to decoy, to entice away, to tamper with; to enlist, to recruit; to crimp [recruiting officer; crimp
Embaucheur, *s.m.* hirer; enticer, decoy;
Embauchoir, *s.m.* boot-last, boot-tree, boot-crimp
Embaumé, e, *part. adj.* enbalmed; balmy, perfumed, sweet-scented, sweet-smelling, sweet
Embaumement, *s.m.* embalming
Embaumer, *v.a.* to embalm; to perfume, to scent; — *v.n.* to smell very sweet

S'—, *v.r.* to be embalmed; to be *or* become perfumed *or* scented
Embaumeur, *s.m.* embalmer [*fishing-hook*)
Embecquer, *v.a.* to feed (*a bird*); to bait (*a*
Embecqueter, *v.n.a.* (*nav.*) *V.* **Embouquer**
Embéguiné, e, *part. adj.* muffled up; wrapped up; bigoted; infatuated
Embéguiner, *v.a.* to muffle up; to wrap up; to infatuate, to bewitch

S'—, *v.r.* to muffle *or* wrap oneself up; to become (*or* be) infatuated *or* bewitched, to be wrapped up (in), to be wedded (to), to be taken [(with)
Embelle, *s.f.* (*nav.*) gangway, waist

Embellie, *s.f.* (*nav.*) lull, calm, moment of calm *or* of fair weather, momentary fall of the swell, favourable change (of weather), smooth interval

Embellir, *v.a.* to embellish, to beautify, to adorn, to grace, to decorate, to set off; to exaggerate; — *v.n.*, **S'—,** *v.r.* to improve, to grow beautiful *or* handsome *or* handsomer; to look *or* appear more beautiful

Embellissement, *s.m.* embellishing, embellishment, improvement, adornment, ornament, decoration [improver

Embellisseur, *s.m.* embellisher, beautifier,

Embérize, *s.f.* (*bird*) bunting

Emberlificoter, *v.a.* (*pop.*) to entangle; to muddle; to practise upon, to coax, to wheedle, to bring round

S'—, *v.r.* to get entangled *or* muddled, to get into a mess, to get into confusion worse confounded [wheedler

Emberlificoteu-r, se, *s.m.f.* (*pop.*) coaxer,

Emberlucoquer (S'), *v.r.* *V.* **Embéguiner (S'),** *v.r.*

†Embesogné, e, *adj.* busy, busily engaged

Embêtement, *s.m.* (*fam.*) annoyance, bother, botheration, nuisance, bore

Embêter, *v.a.* (*fam.*) to annoy, to bother, to plague, to tease, to rile; to vex; to pester; to worry; to tire, to weary; to dissatisfy; to disappoint; to be obnoxious to, to be in ...'s way

S'—, *v.r.* to bother oneself *or* each other; to find it dreadfully dull *or* slow, not to know what to do with oneself

Emblaison, *s.f.* sowing-time

Emblavage, *s.m.* sowing with corn, sowing

Emblaver, *v.a.* to sow with corn, to sow

Emblavure, *s.f.* land sown with corn, cornfield; sowing with corn, sowing

Emblée (D'), *adv.* at the first onset; at once, all at once; instantly; slapdash; without any opposition

Emblémat-ique, -iquement. *V.* page 3, § 1

Emblème, *s.m.* emblem

Embobeliner, Embobiner, *v.a.* to circumvent, to coax, to wheedle, to cozen; to muffle *or* [wrap up

Embodinure, *s.f.* *V.* **Emboudinure**

Emboire, *v.a.* to coat *or* cover (*a mould*) with wax *or* oil [*sucked up, imbibed*)

S'—, *v.r.* (*paint.*) to become chilled (*absorbed,*

Emboiser, *v.a.* (*old*) *V.* **Enjôler** [insertion; fit

Emboîtement, *s.m.* fitting, fitting in, jointing,

Emboîter, *v.a.* to fit, to fit in, to set, to clamp, to joint, to insert; to box. — *le pas*, (*mil.*) to cover the step; to lock up; (*fig.*) to yield, to submit, to knuckle down

S'—, *v.r.* to fit, to fit in

Emboîture, *s.f.* juncture; joint; socket; lamp; fitting, fit; panel-frame

Embolie, *s.f.* (*med.*) embolism

Embol-isme, -ismique, (*chron.*) *V.* page 3, § 1

Embonpoint, *s.m.* stoutness, plumpness, good condition. *Avoir de l'—*, to be stout. *Prendre de l'—*, to get stout, to get *or* pick up flesh. *Perdre son —*, to lose flesh, to waste, to fall away

Emboquer, *v.a.* to feed, to cram [to bear

Embossage, *s.m.* (*nav.*) bringing the broadside

Embosser, *v.a* (*nav.*) to bring the broadside to

S'—, *v.r.* to get the broadside to bear [bear on

Embossure, *s.f.* (*nav.*) spring

Embouché, e, *part. adj.* blown, &c. (*V.* **Emboucher**); mouthed. *Bien —*, fair-spoken. *Mal —*, foul-mouthed, foul-spoken, coarse, ill-bred, impertinent

Emboucher, *v.a.* (*mus.*) to put to o.'s mouth; to blow, to sound; to bit (*a horse*); to prompt, to instruct, to give (*one*) his cue, to prepare, to coach up; (*of boats*) to enter [itself, to fall

S'—, *v.r.* (*of a river*) to discharge *or* empty

Embouchoir, *s.m.* boot-last, boot-tree, boot-crimp; (*of muskets*, &c.) upper band; (*obsolete*) mouthpiece (*of a wind-instr.*)

Embouchure, *s.f.* (*of rivers*, &c.) mouth; (*of a wind-instr.*) mouthpiece; mouth, tonguing, blowing; (*of a horse's bit*) mouthpiece; (*engin.*) [outfall

Emboudinure, *s.f.* (*nav.*) puddening

Embouer, *v.a.* to cover with mud, to bemire; to vilify [entrance of) a strait *or* narrow passage

Embouquement, *s.m.* (*nav.*) entering (*or*

Embouquer, *v.n.* (*nav.*) to enter a strait *or* narrow passage; — *v.a.* to enter [mess, muddle

Embourbement, *s.m.* getting into the mire;

Embourber, *v.a.*, **S'—,** *v.r.* to get (*or* sink) into the mire *or* mud; to stick fast; to involve; to involve oneself

Embourrer, *v.a.* *V.* **Rembourrer**

Embourseraent, *s.m.* pocketing

Embourser, *v.a.* to put into o.'s purse; to [pocket; to receive, to get

Embout, *s.m.* ferrule

†Embouteillage, *s.m.* bottling

†Embouteiller, *v.a.* to bottle

Embouter, *v.a.* to ferrule, to tip

Emboutir, *v.a.* to beat out, to scoop out, to relieve, to stamp; to plate; to tip

Embranchement, *s.m.* branching, branching off; branch-road, branch-line, branch, junction

Embrancher, *v.a.* to branch, to put together, to join [each other, to abut

S'—; *v.r.* to branch, to branch off; to join

Embraquer, *v.a.* *V.* **Abraquer** [burning

Embrasé, e, *adj.* in flames, inflamed, on fire,

Embrasement, *s.m.* conflagration; combustion; inflammation; burning; fire

Embraser, *v.a.* to set on fire; to fire; to kindle; to burn; to consume by fire; to throw into a conflagration; to inflame

S'—, *v.r.* to take fire; to be kindled, to kindle; to become inflamed, to glow, to be in a glow [hug; kissing, kiss

Embrassade, *s.f.* embrace; clasping, clasp;

Embrasse, *s.f.* curtain-loop, curtain-band

Embrassement, *s.m.* *V.* **Embrassade**

Embrasser, *v.a.* to embrace; to take in o.'s arms; to put o.'s arms round; to clasp; to hug; to kiss; to encompass; to encircle; to comprise, to comprehend, to include, to contain; to take in; to undertake; to avail oneself of; to seize; to take up. *Se tenir embrassés*, to remain locked in each other's arms. *Qui trop embrasse mal étreint*, grasp all lose all

Embrasseu-r, se, *s.m.f.* embracer, kisser

Embrassure, *s.f.* (*tech.*) iron binder

Embrasure, *s.f.* embrasure [cogged wheels

Embrayage, *s.m.* engaging; connection of

Embrayer, *v.a.* (*mach.*) to engage; to connect

Embrelage, *s.m.* fastening, cording, cords

Embreler, *v.a.* to fasten, to cord (*a waggon-load*)

Embrènement, *s.m.* (*fam.*) dirtying, soiling, beshitting

Embrener, *v.a.* (*fam.*) to dirty, to soil, to beshit; (*pop.*) to get into a scrape *or* mess

Embrèvement, *s.m.* (*carp.*) franking [tise

Embrever, *v.a.* (*carp.*) to frank, to join, to mor-

Embrigadement, *s.m.* brigading; enlisting, recruiting [recruit

Embrigader, *v.a.* to brigade; to enlist, to

Embrocation, *s.f.* (*med.*) embrocation

Embrochement, *s.m.* spitting (*of meat*)

Embrocher, *v.a.* to spit, to put on the spit; to pierce; to run through; to run through the [body

Embroncher, *v.a.* (*tech.*) to overlap

†Embrouillamini, *s.m.* confusion, disorder, muddle [fuddled *or* muddled

†Embrouillarder (S'), *v.r.* (*pop.*) to get

†Embrouillé, e, *part. adj.* entangled; intricate; obscure; confused; perplexed

†Embrouillement, *s.m.* entanglement; embroiling; confusion; intricacy; perplexity

†Embrouiller, *v.a.* to entangle; to embroil; to obscure; to confound; to jumble; to confuse; to put out, to perplex; (*nav.*) to brail up (*sails*)

S'—, *v.r.* to become entangled *or* intricate; to get confused; to perplex oneself; (*nav.*) to get cloudy; (*pop.*) to get fuddled *or* muddled

†Embrouilleu-r, se, *s.m.f.* jumbler; blunderer; mar-plot [rain

Embruiné, e, *adj.* (*agr.*) spoilt by drizzling

Embrumé, e, *adj.* foggy, misty, hazy; cloudy; dark; heavy [shroud

Embrumer, *v.a.* to cover with fog *or* mist, to

S'—, *v.r.* to be covered with fog *or* mist, to get foggy

Embrun, *s.m.* (*nav.*) foggy weather; spray

Embrunir, *v.a.* *V.* **Rembrunir**

Embryo-ctonie, -génie, -génique, -graphie, -logie, -logique, -logiste, &c. *V.* page 3, § 1

Embryologue, *s.m.* embryologist [shrimp

Embryon, *s.m.* embryo; little bit of a man, dwarf,

Embryonnaire, *adj.* embryonary, embryonal, embryonic; in the germ, incipient, nascent; very small

Embryonné, e, *adj.* embryonate, embryonated

Embryotomie, *s.f.* embryotomy

Embu, e, *part.* *of* **Emboire,** *adj.* (*paint.*) chilled; — *s.m.* (*paint.*) blooming

Embûche, *s.f.* ambush; snare; danger

Embûcher, *v.a.* to begin cutting (*trees*); (*hunt.*) to drive back to the lair *or* to covert; — *v.n.*, **S'—,** *v.r.* to go back (*or* return) to the lair *or* to covert

Embuscade, *s.f.* ambuscade; ambush; lurking-place. *Être* or *Se mettre* or *Se tenir en —*, to lie in wait [*or* in ambush; lying in wait; posted

Embusqué, e, *part. adj.* placed in ambuscade

Embusquer, *v.a.* to place in ambuscade *or* in ambush, to ambush; to post

S'—, *v.r.* to place oneself in ambuscade *or* in ambush, to lie in wait; to post oneself

Émécher (S'), *v.r.* (*pop.*) to get mellow (*tipsy*)

Émendateur, *s.m.* emendator

Émendati-f, ve, *adj.* emendatory

Émendation, *s.f.* emendation

Émender, *v.a.* to amend, to correct

Émeraude, *s.f.* emerald

Émère, *s.m.* (*bot.*) scorpion-senna

Émergé, e, *part. adj.* emerged; unimmersed

Émergence, *s.f.* emergence, emergency

Émergent, e, *adj.* emergent

Émerger, *v.n.* to emerge, to rise out

Émeri, *s.m.* (*min.*) emery

†Émerillon, *s.m.* large fishing-hook, swivel-hook; (*nav.*) iron swivel; (*tech.*) whirl; (*bird*) stone-falcon, merlin

†Émerillonné, e, *part. adj.* brightened up, &c. (*V.* **Émerillonner**); bright; ruddy; brisk, sprightly, lively, merry, gay, jovial, buxom

†Émerillonner, *v.a.* to brighten up, to brighten; to brisk up, to enliven; to flush; to ogle, to leer upon, to leer

S'—, *v.r.* to brighten up, to sparkle; to flush, to get flushed; to become lively *or* merry; to get *or* be excited with drink

Émeriser, *v.a.* to cover with ground emery. *Papier émerisé*, emery paper. *Toile émerisée*, emery cloth

Éméritat, *s.m.* retiring pension, superannuation

Émérite, *adj.* retired, pensioned, superannuated, emeritus; deserving; accomplished, consummate, experienced, practised, adept;

Émersion, *s.f.* emersion [old, confirmed

Émérus, *s.m.* *V.* **Émère**

†Émerveillement, *s.m.* wonder, astonishment

†Émerveiller, *v.a.* to seize with admiration, to astonish, to amaze

S'—, *v.r.* to wonder, to be astonished *or*

Émétine, *s.f.* (*chem.*) emetine [amazed

Émétique, *adj.m.f.*, *s.m.* (*pharm.*) emetic

Émétiser, *v.a.* to put some emetic in; to give an emetic to, to treat with emetics

Émettre, *v.a.* to emit; to send *or* put forth; to express; to utter; to give out, to give; to issue

Émeu, *s.m.* (*bird*) emu

Émeute, *s.f.* riot, disturbance, commotion, uproar, tumult, stir, rising, insurrection, sedition, mutiny

Émeuter, *v.a.* to rouse, to excite, to stir up

Émeutier, *s.m.* rioter

Émiettement, *s.m.* crumbling

Émietter, Émier, *v.a.*, **S'—,** *v.r.* to crumble

Émigrant, e, *adj. s.* emigrating; emigrant

Émigration, *s.f.* emigration; migration; emi-

Émigré, e, *s.m.f.* emigrant; refugee [grants

Émigrer, *v.n.* to emigrate; to migrate

Émincé, *s.m.* mince-meat

Émincer, *v.a.* to mince

Éminemment, *adv.* eminently, in a high degree

Éminence, *s.f.* eminence; height; elevation; rising ground [lofty; conspicuous

Éminent, e, *adj.* eminent; high; elevated;

Éminentissime, *adj.* most eminent

Émir, *s.m.* emir

Émissaire, *s.m.* emissary; drain, viaduct

Émissi-f, ve, *adj.* emissive, emissory

Émission, *s.f.* emission; issue; uttering; utterance; discharge; taking (*vows*) [smasher

Émissionnaire, *s.m.f.* utterer (*of bad money*),

Emmagasinage, Emmagasinement, *s.m.* warehousing; storage

Emmagasiner, *v.a.* to warehouse; to store

†Emmaillottement, *s.m.* swathing; wrapping up

†Emmaillotter, *v.a.* to swathe; to wrap up

Emmanchement, *s.m.* putting a handle *or* stick, hafting, helving; fitting; joining; beginning, getting up, first move

Emmancher, *v.a.* to put a handle *or* stick to, to haft, to helve; to adjust; to fit; to join; to attach; to arrange; to manage; to make a beginning of, to begin, to get on with, to set about, to get up; — *v.n.* (*nav.*) to enter the channel [done; to be easy

S'—, *v.r.* to fit; to begin; to get on; to be

Emmancheur, *s.m.* handle-setter *or* maker;

Emmanchure, *s.f.* arm-hole [promoter

Emmannequiner, *v.a.* to put in hampers, to basket (*plants*) [*crows*) hooded; (*mil.*) fortified

Emmantelé, e, *adj.* covered with a cloak; (*of*

Emmanteler, *v.a.* (*mil.*) to wall round

†Emmargouiller, *v.a.* to mess, to soil, to be-

Emmariner, *v.a.* *V.* **Amariner** [daub

Emmêlement, *s.m.* entanglement

Emmêler, *v.a.* to entangle, to mix [tangled

S'—, *v.r.* to entangle oneself, to become en-

Emménagement, *s.m.* removal; installation; arrangement; (*nav.*) conveniences, accommodations [settle; to arrange; to buy in furniture

Emménager, *v.n.a.*, **S'—,** *v.r.* to move in; to

Emménagogue, *s.m.* (*med.*) emmenagogue; — *adj.* emmenagogic

Emmener, *v.a.* to take away; to carry away; to bring away; to fetch away; to lead away;

Emménologie, *s.f.* (*med.*) emmenology [to take

Emmenotter, *v.a.* to handcuff, to manacle

Emmerdement, *s.m.* (*fam.*) dirtying, soiling, beshitting; (*pop.*) confounded *or* beastly bother

Emmerder, *v.a.* (*fam.*) to dirty, to soil, to beshit; (*pop.*) to bother, to bore, to plague; not to care a damn for ["s'embêter" *and* "s'ennuyer")

S'—, *v.r.* to dirty *or* &c. oneself; (*pop. for*

Emmeulage, *s.m.* (*agr.*) stacking

Emmeuler, *v.a.* (*agr.*) to stack

Emmiellé, e, *part.adj.* honeyed, sweet; coaxing

Emmieller, *v.a.* to honey, to cover *or* sweeten with honey; to coax; (*jest., and genteel slang for* **Emmerder**) to bother, to bore, to plague

Emmitonner, *v.a.* to wrap up, to cover; to wheedle, to coax, to lull

Emmitoufler, *v.a.* to muffle, to wrap up

Emmitrer, *v.a.* to mitre

Emmortaiser, *v.a.* to mortise

Emmotter, *v.a.* to cover up (*a root*) with soil

Emmouracher, *v.a.* *pop. for* **Amouracher**

Emmoustaché, e, *adj.* moustached

Emmuseler, *v.a.* *V.* **Museler**

Emmusquer, *v.a.* *V.* **Musquer**

Émoeller, *v.a.* to take the marrow out of

Émoi, *s.m.* anxiety; agitation; flutter; flurry; emotion

Émollient,e, *adj.*, **Émollient,** *s.m.* emollient
Émolument, *s.m.* emolument, fee, perquisite
Émolumentaire, *adj.* emolumental
Émolumenter, *v.n.* to profit, to gain, to get fees *or* perquisites
Émonctoire, *s.m.* (*anat.*) emunctory
Émondage, *s.m.* pruning, trimming, lopping; cleaning, picking [clean, to pick, to dress
Émonder, *v.a.* to prune, to trim, to lop; to
S'—, *v.r.* to be pruned *or* &c. [trash
Émondes, *s.f.pl.* prunings, loppings; refuse,
Émondeu-r, se, *s.m.f.* pruner; picker, dresser; — *s.m.* riddle, sieve [the edge of
Émorfiler, *v.a.* to beard off, to blunt *or* dull
Émotion, *s.f.* emotion; commotion, agitation, stir; excitement; disturbance
Émotionner, *v.a.* to impress, to affect, to move, to stir, to agitate, to flurry
S'—, *v.r.* to be impressed *or* &c. [*or* breaking
Émottage,Émottement, *s.m.* clod-crushing
Émotter, *v.a.* to crush *or* break the clods in
Émotteu-r, se, *s.m.f.* (*pers.*), **Émottoir,** *s.m.* (*instr.*), clod-crusher *or* breaker
Émou, *s.m.* *V.* **Émeu**
Émoucher, *v.a.* to drive away the flies from; to clear of flies; (*foils*, &c.) *V.* **Démoucheter**
Émouchet, *s.m.* sparrow-hawk
Émoucheter, *v.a.* *V.* **Épointer**
Émouchette, *s.f.* horse-net, fly-net
Émoucheu-r, se, *s.m.f.* fly-flapper
Émouchoir, *s.m.* fly-flap
Émoudre, *v.a.* to grind, to whet, to sharpen
Émouleur, *s.m.* knife-grinder, grinder
Émoulu, e, *part. adj.* ground, sharpened, sharp. *Frais — de*, fresh from; full of; well up in [moss, emuscation
Émoussage, *s.m.* clearing *or* freeing from
Émoussé, e, *part. adj.* blunted, &c. (*V.* **Émousser**); blunt; dull
Émousser, *v.a.* to blunt; to take off the edge of; to dull; to deaden; to soften down; to weaken; to enervate; to damp; to depress; to daunt; to repress; to take the moss off, to clear *or* free from moss
S'—, *v.r.* to get blunt *or* dull, to lose its edge; to deaden; to be softened down *or* weakened *or* &c.; to be cleared of moss
Émoussoir, *s.m.* moss-scraper
†Émoustillé, e, *part. adj.* brisked up, &c. (*V.* **Émoustiller**); brisk, sprightly, lively
†Émoustiller, *v.a.* to brisk up, to rouse, to stir up, to excite, to stimulate, to provoke, to exhilarate, to cheer up, to raise the spirits of
S'—, *v.r.* to become brisk *or* lively, to cheer up; to stir about; to bestir oneself; to bustle; to look sharp *or* alive
Émouvoir, *v.a.* to move; to agitate; to stir up; to stir; to raise; to rouse; to excite; to provoke; to alarm; to affect, to touch
S'—, *v.r.* to become *or* be moved *or* agitated *or* &c.; to rise; to arise; to move
†Empaillage, Empaillement, *s.m.* covering with straw; packing; stuffing; bottoming
†Empailler, *v.a.* to cover with straw; to pack up in straw; to put a straw bottom to; to stuff
†Empailleu-r, se, *s.m.f.* chair-bottomer; bird-stuffer, naturalist
S'—, *v.r.* to be covered with straw, *or* &c.
Empalement, *s.m.* impalement; paddle, shut-
Empaler, *v.a.* to impale [tle; paddles, shuttles
Empaletoquer (S'), *v.r.* (*pop.*) to wrap one-
Empaleur, *s.m.* impaler [self up
Empan, *s.m.* span [a plume *or* with plumes
Empanacher, *v.a.* to plume, to adorn with
Empanner, *v.a.* (*nav.*) to bring to
Empaquetage, *s.m.* packing, packing up
Empaqueter, *v.a.* to pack, to pack up; to
Emparenter, *v.a.* *V.* **Apparenter** [wrap up
Emparer (S'), *v.r.* to seize, to take possession, to possess oneself (of), to lay *or* get hold (of); to secure; to take up; to take; to engross; to master; to possess; to come over; to pervade

Empasme, *s.m.* empasm
Empâté, e, *part. adj.* crammed, fattened; sticky, clammy; sodden; thick; impasted; worked up
Empâtement, *s.m.* stickiness, clamminess; thickness; cramming, fattening; (*paint.*) impasting; (*surg.*) puffiness
Empâter, *v.a.* to cover with paste; to make sticky *or* clammy *or* thick; to cram, to fatten; (*paint.*) to impaste [thick; to eat thick food
S'—, *v.r.* to become sticky *or* clammy *or*
Empâteu-r, se, *s.m.f.* fattener
Empattement, *s.m.* footing, foot, base, basement; water-table; (*nav.*) splicing
Empatter, *v.a.* to foot, to base; to fix, to tie, to fasten; (*nav.*) to splice
Empaumer, *v.a.* to strike (*a ball*) with the palm of the hand *or* with a bat, to strike; to catch; to grasp; to take in hand; to take up; to engross; to go the right way about, to manage well; to wheedle, to get hold of, to gain over, to fool
Empaumure, *s.f.* palm (*of a glove*); bes-antlers
Empeau, *s.m.* (*hort.*) flute-grafting
Empêchable, *adj.* preventable, preventible
Empêché, e, *part. adj.* prevented, &c. (*V.* **Empêcher**); embarrassed; at a loss (to); busy. *Faire l'—*, to affect to be busy
Empêchement, *s.m.* obstacle; impediment; hindrance; obstruction; opposition; difficulty; objection
Empêcher, *v.a.* to prevent, to hinder; to stop; to impede; to obstruct; to oppose; to forbid; to prohibit; to resist; to preclude; to bar; to keep (from). *Cela* (or *ce qui*) *n'empêche pas que*, (*fam.*) and yet, for all that
S'—, *v.r.* to forbear; to help; to refrain; to abstain; to keep (from); (*obsolete*) to trouble oneself (about)
Empédocléen, ne, *adj.* Empedoclean
†Empeigne, *s.f.* upper-leather, vamp
Empellement, *s.m.* sluice, dam
Empenneler, *v.a.* (*nav.*) to back (*an anchor*)
Empennelle, *s.f.* small anchor, kedge
Empenner, *v.a.* to feather
Empenoir, *s.m.* lock-chisel
Empereur, *s.m.* emperor
Emperler, *v.a.* to adorn *or* set off with pearls;
Empesage, *s.m.* starching [to bead
Empesé, e, *adj.* starched; stiff, formal, affected
Empeser, *v.a.* to starch; to wet (*a sail*). *S'—*,
Empeseu-r, se, *s.m.f.* starcher [to be starched
Empesté, e, *adj.* infected; tainted; stinking
Empester, *v.a.* to infect; to taint; — *v.n.* to stink horridly
Empêtrer, *v.a.* to entangle; to embarrass; to hamper; to encumber; to saddle; to engage; to involve; to fetter
S'—, *v.r.* to entangle *or* &c. oneself; to become (*or* get *or* be) entangled, &c.
Empetrum, *s.m.* (*bot.*) crowberry, crakeberry
Emphase, *s.f.* bombast, pomposity, magniloquence; affectation; emphasis, stress
Emphatique, *adj.* bombastic, pompous, magniloquent; affected; emphatic
Emphatiquement, *adv.* bombastically, pompously, magniloquently; affectedly; emphatically [tic
Emphractique, *adj.m.f.*, *s.m.* (*med.*) emphrac-
Emphraxie, *s.f.* (*med.*) emphraxis, obstruction
Emphysémateu-x, se, *adj.* (*med.*) emphysematous [dropsy
Emphysème, *s.m.* (*med.*) emphysema, wind-
Emphytéose, *s.f.* emphyteusis, feudal holding, long lease [on a long lease
Emphytéote, *s.m.f.* emphyteuticary, tenant
Emphytéotique, *adj.* emphyteutic, for a long term of years, for 99 years. *Redevance —*, ground-rent
Empierrement, *s.m.* stoning, ballasting, metalling; broken stone ballast, metal; metalled road

Empierrer, *v.a.* to stone, to metal (*roads*)
Empiètement, *s.m.* encroachment, encroaching; infringement; trespassing
Empiéter, *v.n.a.* to encroach, to intrench or trench (on), to infringe (on), to trespass (on); to intrude; to usurp; (*falc.*) to pounce
Empiffrer, *v.a.* to cram, to stuff; to bloat
Empiffrerie, *s.f.* cramming, stuffing, guttling, gluttony
Empilage, *s.m.* piling; stacking; binning
Empile, *s.f.* (*fish.*) gut-line
Empilement, *s.m.* *V.* **Empilage**
Empiler, *v.a.* to pile up, to pile; to stack; to bin; to attach (*a fishing-hook*)
Empileu-r, se, *s.m.f.* piler; stacker; binner
Empirance, *s.f.* waste, damage, loss
Empire, *s.m.* empire; dominions, sway, rule, dominion; sovereignty; authority; power; influence; ascendency; control, command; reign
Empirement, *s.m.* getting worse, aggravation
Empirer, *v.a.* to make worse, to aggravate; — *v.n.* to become or grow or get worse; to be aggravated; to become or be damaged
Empir-ique (*adj.s.*),**-iquement.** *V.* page 3, § 1
Empirisme, *s.m.* empiricism
Emplacement, *s.m.* site, situation, place, seat, ground, piece of ground, plot, lot
Emplage, *s.m.* *V.* **Remplage**
Emplanter, *v.a.* to plant
Emplanture, *s.f.* (*nav.*) step (*of a mast*)
Emplastique, *adj.m.f.*, *s.m.* (*med.*) emplastic
Emplastration, *s.f.* (*hort.*) budding
Emplastrer, *v.a.* (*hort.*) to bud
Emplâtre, *s.m.* plaster, salve, ointment; sickly person, helpless creature, poor stick. *Mettre un — à*, to put a plaster on; (*fig.*) to patch up
Emplâtrer, *v.a.* to lay the gold colour on; (*fig.*) [to encumber, to saddle
Emplette, *s.f.* purchase
Emplir, *v.a.*, **S'—,** *v.r.* to fill, to fill up
Emploi, *s.m.* employment; employ; use; occupation; situation, office; service; appropriation; outlay; investment; entry; (*theat.*) department; line of character. *Double —*, useless repetition or duplicate. *Sans —*, unemployed; out of employment
Employable, *adj.* employable
Employé, e, *s.m.f.* person employed or in o.'s employ, employé, clerk, official, officer, servant (*not domestic*), man, boy, woman, girl
Employer, *v.a.* to employ; to use, to make use of; to occupy; to take; to devote, to bestow; to exert; to lay out; to invest; to spend; to pass away; (*book-keep.*) to enter
S'—, *v.r.* to employ or occupy oneself; to apply oneself; to exert oneself; to use o.'s interest or influence; to be employed or used
Employeur, *s.m.* (*polit. economy*) employer
Emplumer, *v.a.* to feather; to fledge; to quill
S'—, *v.r.* to become feathered or fledged; to feather o.'s nest; to pick up flesh
Empocher, *v.a.* to pocket, to put in o.'s pocket
S'—, *v.r.* to be pocketed [apprehension
†Empoignement, *s.m.* taking up, capture,
†Empoigner, *v.a.* to grasp, to gripe, to clutch, to grab, to seize, to lay hold of; to take up, to capture, to apprehend, to nab [grasped, &c.
S'—, *v.r.* to grasp or &c. each other; to be
†Empoigneu-r, se, *s.m.f.* clutcher, grabber
Empointage, *s.m.* (*of needles*, &c.) pointing
Empointer, *v.a.* to stitch; (*needles*, &c.) to point
Empointeu-r, se, *s.m.f.* stitcher; (*of needles*, &c.) pointer
Empointure, *s.f.* (*nav.*) earing
Empois, *s.m.* starch
Empoisonné, e, *part. adj.* poisoned, &c. (*V.* **Empoisonner**); poisonous; stinking
Empoisonnement, *s.m.* poisoning
Empoisonner, *v.a.* to poison; to infect; to corrupt; to mar; to envenom, to embitter; — *v.n.* to be poisonous; to stink horridly
Empoisonneu-r, se, *s.m.f.* poisoner; corrupter; pest; wretched cook; —*adj.* poisonous
Empoisser, *v.a.* *V.* **Poisser**

Empoissonnement, *s.m.* (*of a pond*, &c.) stocking (with fish)
Empoissonner, *v.a.* to stock (with fish)
Emport, *s.m.* (*law*) carrying away
Emporté, e, *adj.* passionate, hasty, violent, fiery, hot, hot-headed; runaway, unmanageable; — *part.* carried away, &c. (*V.* **Emporter**)
Emportement, *s.m.* transport, fit; burst, outburst; passion; fit of anger, anger, rage; hastiness; frenzy; violence; excess; extravagance, wildness; freak [press; bitter satirist
Emporte-pièce, *s.m.* punch, puncher, fly-
Emporter, *v.a.* to carry away; to carry; to bear away or off or along; to take away or off or out; to bring away; to convey away; to run away with; to gain, to obtain; to fetch away or out; to hurry away; to carry beyond bounds; to sweep away or off; to carry off; to carry down, to sink; to blow off; to wash away or off; to bite off; to cut off; to remove; to tear; to peel off; to burn (*the mouth*); to take; to transport; to involve, to entail; to imply; to prevail over; to outweigh; to turn. *— la pièce*, to be very cutting, to strike home. *L'— (sur)*, to have the advantage or get the mastery (over); to get the better (of); to overcome; to outweigh; to excel, to surpass; to prevail; to be superior (to)
S'—, *v.r.* to get out of temper, to lose o.'s temper, to give way to anger, to fly into a passion; to fly out; to inveigh, to declaim, to abuse; to get wild; to become unmanageable, to run away, to bolt; to hurry away; to go beyond bounds; to run riot; to be violent; to rub off; to tear or &c. (o.'s ... or each other's ...); to be carried away or &c.; (*hort.*) to grow upward, [to grow irregularly
Empotage, *s.m.* potting
Empoter, *v.a.* to pot
Empourpré, e, *adj.* purpled, purple
Empourprer, *v.a.* to purple
Empreindre, *v.a.* to imprint, to stamp, to mark; to impress; to tinge, to tincture
S'—, *v.r.* to become (or be) imprinted or marked or &c.
Empreinte, *s.f.* impression; impress; print; stamp; mark; trace; (*paint.*) priming, dead-colouring
Empressé, e, *adj.* eager, earnest; forward; obsequious; attentive, assiduous; ready, prompt; active; ardent; impetuous; zealous; hasty, in haste; busy; sincere, best. *Faire l'—*, to show oneself to be very busy; to put oneself forward
Empressement, *s.m.* eagerness, earnestness; forwardness; obsequiousness; attention, assiduity; readiness, promptitude; bustle; cheerfulness; ardour; zeal; hastiness, haste; hurry; interest
Empresser (S'), *v.r.* to be eager or earnest or forward or assiduous; to hasten; to flock, to crowd; to press forward; to bestir or busy one- [self
Emprise, *s.f.* (*rail.*) breadth of formation
Emprisonnement, *s.m.* imprisonment; confinement; commitment [to commit
Emprisonner, *v.a.* to imprison, to confine;
Emprunt, *s.m.* loan; borrowing; artifice. *D'—*, borrowed; assumed; supposed; fictitious; factitious; false; artificial; affected. *Faire un —*, to contract a loan, to borrow
Emprunté, e, *adj.* borrowed; assumed; supposed; fictitious; factitious; false; artificial; affected; embarrassed, constrained, stiff, awkward, ill at ease
Emprunter, *v.a.* to borrow; to derive, to receive
S'—, *v.r.* to borrow from each other; to be borrowed
Emprunteu-r, se, *s.m.f.* borrower; — *adj.* borrowing, fond of borrowing, of a borrowing disposition; not original
Empuantir, *v.a.* to infect. *S'—*, to stink
Empuantissement, *s.m.* infection; stink, [stench
Empyème, *s.m.* (*med.*) empyema
Empyréal, e, *adj.* empyreal

Empyrée, *s.m. adj.* empyrean
Empyreumatique, *adj.(chem.)* empyreumatic
Empyreume, *s.m.* (*chem.*) empyreuma
Ému, e, *part. adj.* moved, &c. (*V.* **Émouvoir**); of emotion; in earnest; trembling; shaking; moving; uneasy, anxious; angry; fuddled, maudlin [tress; — *adj.* emulative
Émula-teur, trice, *s.m.f.* emulator, emula-
Émulati-f, ve, *adj.* emulative
Émulation, *s.f.* emulation
Émule, *s.m.f.* emulator, emulatress; rival; competitor, competitress
Émulgent, e, *adj.* (*anat.*) emulgent
Émulsi-f, ve, *adj.*, **Émulsif,** *s.m.* emulsive
Émulsine, *s.f.* (*chem.*) emulsine
Émulsion, *s.f.* emulsion
Émulsionner, *v.a.* to mix an emulsion with
Émyde, *s.f.* emys, marsh-tortoise
Émy-saure, *s.f.* alligator tortoise
En, *prep.* in; into; to; within; with; in the shape of; like a, like; as a, as; in course of; by; at; on; for; of; made of; from; out of; through; while; when; dressed in (*or* in a); dressed as (*or* as a)
En, *pron.m.f., adv.* of him, his, of her, her, of it, its, of them, their; of that; of doing so, to do so; of saying so, to say so; of the party; from him, from her, from it, from them; from that, from this; from that *or* this place, from there, from here, away; by him, by her, by it, by them; for that; for it, for them; on that account; with him *or* her *or* it *or* them; about him *or* her *or* it *or* them; at *or* on it, at *or* on them; to it, to them; him, her, it, them; like it, like them; so; some, any; one, ones. — *voici un,* — *voici deux,* here is one, here are two. — *voici un bon,* — *voici deux bons,* here is a good one, here are two good ones. *C'— est* or — *voilà assez, trop,* it *or* that is enough, too much
Énallage, *s.f.* (*gram.*) enallage
Énamourer, *v.a.* (*old*) *V.* **Amouracher**
Énanthème, *s.m.* (*med.*) enanthema
Énantiopath-ie, -ique. *V.* page 3, § 1
Énantiose, *s.f.* enantiosis
Énarrable, *adj.* expressible, describable
Énarrer, *v.a.* to narrate
Énarrher, *v.a.* *V.* **Arrher**
Énarthrose, *s.f.* (*anat.*) enarthrosis
Énaser, *v.a.* to crush ...'s nose
En-belle, *s.f.* (*nav.*) direct fire; — *adj.* direct; — *adv.* directly, fairly, in the middle [wild life
Enbohêmer (S'), *v.r.* to get wild, to lead a
Encâblure, *s.f.* (*nav.*) cable's length
Encadenasser, *v.a.* to padlock; to shut up
Encadrement, *s.m.* framing; frame; (*mil.*) enlistment
Encadrer, *v.a.* to frame; to encircle, to surround, to encompass; to insert, to introduce; (*mil.*) to enlist
S'—, *v.r.* to be framed *or* &c.; to stand out
Encadreur, *s.m.* framer
Encager, *v.a.* to cage
Encaissage, *s.m.* *V.* **Encaissement**
Encaisse, *s.f.* cash in hand. — *métallique,* stock of bullion
Encaissé, e, *part. adj.* incased, &c. (*V.* **Encaisser**); with high and steep banks; sunk; hollow
Encaissement, *s.m.* incasing, casing, packing, packing *or* putting in a case *or* box; payment; encashment; receipt; collecting, collection; embankment; bed; height (*of a bank*); (*hort.*) tubbing. *Sauf —,* when paid, if paid
Encaisser, *v.a.* to incase, to case, to pack, to pack up, to pack *or* put in a case *or* box; to enclose; to sink; to place; to put in a cash-box; to get cashed; to receive; to collect; to lay up; to embank; to lay a bed to; (*hort.*) to tub
Encalminé, e, *adj.* (*nav.*) becalmed
Encampanement, *s.m.* wide opening (*of a*
Encan, *s.m.* auction [*cannon*)

†Encanailler, *v.a.* to degrade, to lower to the level of the rabble, to lower; to mix with low people
S'—, *v.r.* to keep low company; to get into low habits; to lose caste; to degrade *or* lower oneself; to get low
Encanthis, *s.m.* (*med.*) encanthis
Encaper, *v.a.n.* (*nav.*) to embay [muffled up
Encapuchonné, e, *adj.* hooded, cowled;
Encapuchonner, *v.a.* to put a hood *or* a cowl on; to muffle up; to make a monk of
S'—, *v.r.* to put on (*or* wear) a hood *or* a cowl; to muffle oneself up; to turn monk
Encaquement, *s.m.* packing, barrelling
Encaquer, *v.a.* to pack, to pack up, to barrel; to cram up, to stow up
Encaqueu-r, se, *s.m.f.* packer
Encarpe, *s.m.* (*anc. arch.*) encarpus
Encarter, *v.a.* to insert; to enclose
S'—, *v.r.* to be inserted *or* enclosed
En-cas, *s.m.* something prepared in case of need, something to meet an emergency, provision against a contingency; collation kept in readiness; carriage in case of rain; sun-shade (*parasol large enough to serve as an umbrella in case of rain*)
Encastelé, e, *adj.* (*vet.*) hoof-bound [hoof-bound
Encasteler (S'), *v.r.* (*vet.*) to become (*or* get)
Encastelure, *s.f.* (*vet.*) contraction of the hoof
†Encastill-age, é. *V.* **Accastillage,** &c.
Encastrement, *s.m.* fitting, fitting in; rece
Encastrer, *v.a.,* **S'—,** *v.r.* to fit, to fit in, to fit
Encaume, *s.m.* (*med.*) encauma [into a recess
Encaustique, *adj.m.f., s.f.* encaustic; furni-
Encaustiquer, *v.a.* to polish [ture-paste
Encavage, Encavement, *s.m.* putting *or* storing in a cellar; cellarage [cellar
Encaver, *v.a.* to put *or* store in a cellar, to
S'—, to be put in a cellar; (*jest.*) to fall into
Encaveur, *s.m.* cellarman, wine-porter [a cellar
Enceindre, *v.a.* to enclose, to encircle, to encompass, to surround
Enceint, e, *part.m.f. of* **Enceindre;** — *adj.f.* pregnant, in the family way, with child
Enceinte, *s.f.* circumference, circuit; enclosure; compass; precincts; walls; fence; place; spot; premises; building; hall; (*fort.*) body of the place, enceinte
Encellulement, *s.m.* confinement in a cell
Encelluler, *v.a.* to confine in a cell, to cell
Encens, *s.m.* frankincense; incense; fragrance; homage; praise; flattery
Encensement, *s.m.* incensing; perfuming; praising, praise; flattering, flattery
Encenser, *v.a.* to incense; to worship; to pay homage to; to praise; to flatter; to perfume; — *v.n.* to burn incense; (*rid.*) to boar
Encenseur, *s.m.* burner of incense; flatterer
Encensier, *s.m.* (*bot.*) rosemary
Encensoir, *s.m.* censer, thurible; (*fig.*) ecclesiastical power; flattery; (*astr.*) Ara. *Mettre la main à l'—,* to interfere with ecclesiastical affairs. *Donner de l'— par le nez, casser le nez à coups d'—,* to flatter fulsomely
Encéphalalgie, *s.f.* (*med.*) encephalalgia
Encéphalalgique, *adj.* (*med.*) encephalalgic
Encéphale, *s.m.* (*anat.*) encephalon, encephalos,
Encéphalique, *adj.* (*anat.*) encephalic [brain
Encéphalite, *s.f.* (*med.*) encephalitis, inflammation of the brain
Encéphalocèle, *s.f.* (*med.*) encephalocele, hernia of the brain [(*min.*) brainstone coral
Encéphaloïde, *adj.* encephaloid; — *s.m.*
Encéphalologie, &c. *V.* page 3, § 1
Enchaînement, *s.m.* chaining; chain; links; series; connection; concatenation
Enchaîner, *v.a.* to chain; to chain up *or* down; to shackle, to fetter; to tie down, to tie, to bind; to captivate; to enslave; to detain; to restrain; to check; to stop; to link, to connect; to concatenate
S'—, *v.r.* to link, to be linked *or* connected

Enchaînure, *s.f.* chain, chain-work; links; connection; concatenation

Enchanteler, *v.a.* to put (*timber, wood*) in a yard, to put (*casks*) on a stand, to place, to range

Enchantement, *s.m.* enchantment; magic; witchcraft; delusion; charm; delight

Enchanter, *v.a.* to enchant; to bewitch; to fascinate; to charm; to delight

Enchan-teur, teresse, *adj. s.* enchanting, bewitching, charming, delightful; enchanter, enchantress, bewitcher, charmer, witch, fairy

Enchaper, *v.a.* to hook, to fasten; to enclose (*one cask*) in another, to case

Enchaperonner, *v.a.* to hood

Enchapure, *s.f.* fastening [to puzzle

Encharibotter, *v.a.* (*pop.*) to bother, to vex;

Encharner, *v.a.* to hinge

Enchâsser, *v.a.* to enchase; to enshrine; to set; to insert, to introduce [tion

Enchâssure, *s.f.* setting; insertion, introduc-

Enchatonnement, *s.m. V.* **Sertissure**

Enchatonner, *v.a. V.* **Sertir**

Enchausser, *v.a.* (*hort.*) to mulch

Enchère, *s.f.* bidding, bid; auction. *A l'—, aux —s,* to auction; by auction; put up for sale; to the highest bidder. *Folle —,* bidding what one cannot pay. *Couvrir l'—,* to make a higher bid, to outbid. *Payer la folle —,* to pay for o.'s rashness, to pay dear for o.'s folly, to bear the penalty (of ..., of it), to pay (for ..., for it)

Enchérir, *v.a.* to bid for; to outbid; to raise the value *or* price of, to raise, to increase; — *v.n.* to bid; to grow (*or* get *or* become) dear *or* dearer, to rise in value *or* price, to rise. — *sur,* to outbid; to outdo, to surpass, to improve upon, to refine upon, to add to, to go beyond, to go farther in (*a thing*) *or* than (*a person*), to be stronger than [of price

Enchérissement, *s.m.* rise, increase, increase

Enchérisseur, *s.m.* bidder. *Fol —,* bidder who cannot fulfil the conditions. *Moins —,* lowest tenderer

Enchevalement, *s.m.* propping, props

Enchevaucher, *v.a.* to overlap

Enchevauchure, *s.f.* overlapping [sion

Enchevêtrement, *s.m.* entanglement; confu-

Enchevêtrer, *v.a.* to halter; to entangle; to embarrass; to confuse [halter-cast

Enchevêtrure, *s.f.* (*arch.*) binding; (*vet.*)

Enchifrené, e, *adj.* stuffed up; having o.'s nose stuffed up

Enchifrènement, *s.m.* obstruction *or* stuffing up of (*or* stoppage in) the nose, snuffles

Enchifrener, *v.a.* to give a cold in the head, to cause a stoppage in the nose. *S'—,* to get

‡**Enchiridion,** *s.m.* enchiridion, manual [ditto

‡**Enchondrome,** *s.m.* (*med.*) enchondroma

‡**Enchorial, e, Enchorique,** *adj.* enchorial, [enchoric

‡**Enchymose,** *s.f.* (*med.*) enchymosis

Enclave, *s.f.* piece of land enclosed in another land and independent of it; territory lying within the bounds of another state; boundary, limit; (*of a lock on a river*) recess; (*her.*) enclave

Enclavement, *s.m.* enclosing

Enclaver, *v.a.* to enclose (in), to lock (in), to hem in, to shut in, to wedge in; to bind; to [fix; to fit in

S'—, *v.r.* to be enclosed *or* &c.

Enclin, e, *adj.* inclined, prone, apt, given

Encliquetage, *s.m.* (*tech.*) catch [catch

Encliqueter, *v.a.* (*tech.*) to provide with a

Enclitique, *adj.m.f., s.f.* (*gram.*) enclitic

Encloîtrer, *v.a. V.* **Cloitrer** [in; to shut in

Enclore, *v.a.* to enclose; to fence in; to take

S'—, *v.r.* to fence oneself in; to be enclosed *or* &c. [vineyard; orchard; paddock

Enclos, *s.m.* enclosure; close; (enclosed) field;

Enclotir, *v.n.* (*hunt.*) to burrow

Enclouage, *s.m.* (*artil.*) spiking

Enclouer, *v.a.* (*artil.*) to spike; (*of horses,* &c.) to prick (*in shoeing*) [dict *or* betray oneself

S'—, *v.r.* to get a nail in the foot; to contra-

Enclouure, *s.f.* prick (*in the foot of an animal*); (*fig.*) hitch, impediment

Enclume, *s.f.* anvil; (*anat.*) incus

Enclumeau, Enclumot, *s.m.,* **Enclumette,** [*s.f.* hand-anvil

Encoche, *s.f.* notch

Encochement, *s.m.* notching [the bow

Encocher, *v.a.* to notch; to fit (*an arrow*) in

Encoffrer, *v.a.* to coffer, to lay up; to pocket, to bag; to cage, to lock up, to quod

†**Encognure, Encoignure,** *s.f.* corner, angle; corner-piece (of furniture)

Encollage, *s.m.* sizing

Encoller, *v.a.* to size

Encolleur, *s.m.* sizer [look, looks, appearance

Encolure, *s.f.* (*of horses,* &c.) neck; (*pers.*)

Encombre, *s.m.* hindrance, impediment, obstacle, accident

Encombrement, *s.m.* obstruction; stoppage; crowding, crowd; glutting, glut; encumbrance, impediment, hindrance

Encombrer, *v.a.* to obstruct; to stop, to block up; to crowd, to throng, to cram; to glut; to encumber

S'—, *v.r.* to become (*or* be) obstructed *or* &c.

Encontre, *s.f.* (*old*) occurrence, occasion; chance, luck. *A l'—,* against, counter, con- [trary (to)

Encor, *poet. for* **Encore**

Encorbellement, *s.m.* (*arch.*) corbelling, corbel

Encore, *adv. conj.* still; yet; as yet; again; besides, further, also, too; more; still more; moreover; another, one more; longer; left; even; even then; at least; but, only; else; however; and yet; what next? what else? what of that? — *un,* — *un autre,* one more, another. — *une fois,* once more, over again. — *un peu,* a little more; a few more; a little longer. — *longtemps,* much longer. — *que,* (*obsolete*) *V.* **Quoique.** *Ou bien —,* or else, or again

Encorner, *v.a.* to horn; to gore (*with its horns*)

Encornet, *s.m.* (*mollusc*) calamar, calamary, squid, sleeve-fish; poulp, devil-fish, blood-sucker [vernment; henpecked

†**Encotillonné,** *adj.m.* under petticoat-go-

†**Encotillonner (S'),** *v.r.* to fall under (*or* submit to) petticoat government; to become (*or* be) a henpecked husband

Encouragement, *s.m.* encouragement; inspiriting; incitement, incentive; excitement; countenance; support; promotion; abetment

Encourager, *v.a.* to encourage; to inspirit; to cheer; to incite; to excite; to countenance; to support; to promote; to abet; to spur

Encourir, *v.a.* to incur, to bring *or* draw upon

S'—, *v.r.* to be incurred; (*old*) to run [oneself

Encouture, *s.f.* (*nav.*) clincher-work [work

Encouturer, *v.a.* (*nav.*) to build with clincher-

Encrage, *s.m.* (*print.*) inking

Encrasser, *v.a.* to foul, to dirty, to grease, to make greasy *or* dirty

S'—, *v.r.* to get foul *or* greasy *or* dirty; to get rusty *or* thick; to become vulgar; to debase *or* lower oneself

Encre, *s.f.* ink. — *de Chine,* Indian ink, China ink. *A l'—,* with ink. *Écrire de bonne — à quelqu'un,* to write in strong terms to a person. *C'est la bouteille à l'—,* it is an affair that cannot be seen through, it is an obscure *or* confused business

Encrêper, *v.a.* to cover with a crape, to put a crape *or* a weed *or* a band on; to muffle; to dress in mourning [ink

Encrer, *v.a.* (*print.*) to ink; — *v.n.* to take the

Encrier, *s.m.* ink-bottle, inkstand

Encrinite, *s.m.* (*fossil*) encrinite, stone-lily

Encroué, e, *adj.* (*of trees*) entangled

Encroûté, e, *adj.* covered with a crust; (*fig.*) rusty; wedded (to); full of prejudices

Encroûter, *v.a.* to crust, to cover with a crust

S'—, *v.r.* to crust; to cake; to get hard; to get heavy *or* stupid; to get full of prejudices

Encuirasser, *v.a.* to cover with a cuirass
S'—, *v.r.* to put on o.'s cuirass; to get dirty *or* rusty; to become hardened
Enculasser, *v.a.* to breech (*a gun*)
Encuvage, Encuvement, *s.m.* tubbing
Encuver, *v.a.* to tub, to put into a tub *or* vat
Encyclie, *s.f.* concentric circles (*on the surface of the water*)
Encyclique, *adj.m.f.*, *s.f.* encyclical
Encyclopédie, *s.f.* encyclopædia, encyclopedia, cyclopædia, cyclopedia [§ 1
Encyclopéd-ique, -isme, -iste. *V.* page 3,
Endaubage, *s.m.* (*cook.*) daubing; (*nav.*) sea-
Endéans, *prep.* within [provisions
Endécagone, *adj. s. V.* **Hendécagone**
Endécher, *v.a.* (*pop.*) to beggar
Endémie, *s.f.*, **Endémique,** *adj.* endemic
Endenter, *v.a.* to provide *or* supply with teeth; to tooth; to indent; to cog
Endermique, *adj.* (*med.*) endermatic, endermic
Endetté, e, *adj.* in debt, indebted [into debt
Endetter, *v.a.* to cause to run into debt, to get
S'—, *v.r.* to contract debts, to get *or* run into
Endêvé, e, *adj.* mad, irritable, passionate [debt
Endêver, *v.n.* to fume, to be vexed *or* mad. *Faire* —, to tease, to vex, to rile, to drive mad, to aggravate
Endiablé, e, *adj.* possessed, mad; furious; devilish bad; wicked, detestable, abominable
Endiabler, *v.n.* to be furious *or* raving mad. *Faire* —, to torment, to plague to death
Endigage, Endiguement, *s.m.* damming, dam; embankment
Endiguer, *v.a.* to dam; to embank
Endimancher, *v.a.* to dress in o.'s Sunday
Endive, *s.f.* (*bot.*) endive [clothes
Endocarde, *s.m.* (*anat.*) endocardium
Endocardite, *s.f.* (*med.*) endocarditis
Endoctrinement, *s.m.* instruction, teaching; prompting; wheedling
Endoctriner, *v.a.* to indoctrinate, to instruct, to teach; to coach up; to prompt, to give (*one*) his cue; to bring *or* get round, to gain over, to get hold of, to circumvent, to wheedle
Endoctrineur, *s.m.* instructor, teacher; prompter; wheedler [dogen
Endogène, *adj.* (*bot.*) endogenous; — *s.f.* en-
Endolori, e, *part. adj.* made sore, aching, sore
Endolorir, *v.a.* to make sore
S'—, *v.r.* to become sore, to ache [ness
Endolorissement, *s.m.* pain, aching, sore-
Endommageable, *adj.* damageable
Endommagement, *s.m.* damage, injury
Endommager, *v.a.* to damage, to injure
S'—, *v.r.* to become (*or* get) damaged, &c.
Endormant, e, *adj. V.* **Assoupissant**
Endormeu-r, se, *s.m.f.* wheedler, coaxer
Endormi, e, *adj.* asleep; sleeping; sleepy; drowsy; sluggish; benumbed; calm; — *s.m.f.* sleepy-head; person asleep. *Faire l'*—, to sham sleep
Endormir, *v.a.* to send *or* set to sleep, to lull to sleep, to lull asleep; to rock to sleep; to benumb; to wheedle; to lull
S'—, *v.r.* to fall asleep, to go to sleep; to be sleepy; to slumber; to be lulled into security; to be wanting in vigilance; to become careless *or* idle, to grow lazy; to remain buried. *S'— sur le rôti*, to neglect the favourable opportunity,
Endos, *s.m.* (*com.*) endorsement [to stop half-way
Endosmomètre, *s.m.* (*phys.*) endosmometer
Endosmose, *s.f.* (*phys.*) endosmose, endosmosis
Endosmotique, *adj.* (*phys.*) endosmotic
Endosse, *s.f.* trouble, burden
Endossement, *s.m.* (*com.*) endorsement
Endosser, *v.a.* to put on o.'s back, to put on, to don; to buckle on; (*fig.*) to saddle; (*com.*, *fig.*) to endorse; (*fig.*) to take upon oneself, to assume; to own, to acknowledge; (*agr.*) to
S'—, *v.r.* to be put on [ridge
Endosseur, *s.m.* (*com.*) endorser
Endroit, *s.m.* place; spot; part; passage; side; point; (*of a stuff*) right side. *A l'— de*, with regard *or* respect to; towards. *A cet* —, in this *or* that respect. *A mon* (*ton*, &c.) —, with regard to me (thee, &c.), towards me (thee, &c.). *A deux* —*s*, (*of stuffs and clothes*) reversible
Enduire, *v.a.* to do over, to lay over, to coat, to cover, to rub; to plaster; to daub; (*mas.*) to render
Enduit, *s.m.* coat, layer, coating; plastering; daub; paint; varnish; glaze, glazing; polish;
Endurable, *adj.* endurable [(*mas.*) rendering
Endurance, *s.f.* endurance [placid
Endurant, e, *adj.* patient, enduring, tolerant,
Endurci, e, *part. adj.* hardened, &c. (*V.* **Endurcir**); obdurate; hardy; callous; — *s.m.f.* hardened sinner
Endurcir, *v.a.* to harden, to make hard; to toughen; to steel; to make hardy; to inure; to confirm; to render callous; to indurate
S'—, *v.r.* to harden, to become (*or* grow *or* get) hard *or* hardened; to become obdurate; to be steeled; to steel oneself; to inure oneself; to become hardy *or* inured *or* callous; to indurate [obduracy; callousness; induration
Endurcissement, *s.m.* hardening, hardness,
Endurer, *v.a.* to endure; to suffer; to undergo; to go through; to bear; to put up with; to support; to allow, to permit
S'—, *v.r.* to be endured *or* &c.
Énéide, *s.f.* Eneid, Æneid
Énéorème, *s.m.* (*med.*) eneorema
Énergie, *s.f.* energy; strength; force; vigour; power; spirit; pith, pithiness; emphasis
Énergique, *adj.* energetic; strong; vigorous; forcible; powerful; strenuous; spirited; pithy; emphatic
Énergiquement, *adv.* energetically, with energy; strongly; vigorously, with vigour; forcibly; powerfully; strenuously; spiritedly; pithily; emphatically
Énergumène, *s.m.f.* energumen, demoniac; frantic *or* wild person; fanatic; ranter; desperado [tion
Énervation, *s.f.*, **Énervement,** *s.m.* enerva-
Énerver, *v.a.* to enervate. *S'*—, to become
Enfaîteau, *s.m.* ridge-tile, gutter-tile [enervated
Enfaîtement, *s.m.* ridge-lead, ridge
Enfaîter, *v.a.* to cover the ridge of
Enfance, *s.f.* infancy; childhood; babyhood; boyhood; girlhood; boyish *or* girlish days; children; young people, young; childishness, dotage; puerility; childish action *or* thing
Enfant, *s.m.f.* child; infant, baby; offspring; youth; boy, lad; son; girl; daughter; fellow; dear; issue; native; (*adject.*) childish. —*s perdus*, (*mil.*) forlorn hope. — *trouvé*, foundling. — *à la mamelle*, sucking child, baby. — *de chœur*, singing-boy. —*s de France*, royal children of France. — *de troupe*, soldier's boy (*brought up in a regiment*). *Bon* —, *bonne* —, good fellow; jolly fellow; good girl *or* thing; good-natured; simpleton; simple. *Bonne d'*—, *V.* **Bonne,** *s.f.* *Mal d'*—, *travail d'*—, labour, travail, child-birth. *Petits* —*s*, (*without a hyphen*) little children; (*with a hyphen*) grandchildren. *Faire l'*—, to play the child, to behave like a child, to be childish *or* foolish. *Faire un* —, to have a child. *Faire un* — *à* . . ., to get . . . with child [production
Enfantement, *s.m.* childbirth, parturition;
Enfanter, *v.a.* to bring forth; to give birth to; to produce [thing; child's play; trifle
†Enfantillage. *s.m.* childishness; childish
Enfantin, e, *adj.* infantine, childish
Enfariner, *v.a.* to cover with flour, to beflour. *Être enfariné de*, to be tainted with, to be prepossessed in favour of, to be taken with; to have a smattering of. *La gueule enfarinée*, big with expectation
Enfer, *s.m.* hell; eternal punishment; infernal regions, lower regions. *D'*—, infernal; furious, terrible, dreadful, awful

Enfermer, *v.a.* to shut, to shut up *or* in; to lock up; to put in *or* away; to enclose; to surround; to hem in; to confine; to comprehend, to include; to contain; to harbour; to coop up; to conceal

Enferrer, *v.a.* to run through, to pierce

S'—, *v.r.* to run oneself through; to injure oneself; to contradict *or* betray oneself; to play oneself a trick, to take oneself in; to fall into the snare; to get into a mess *or* a fix; to make a mess of it

Enficeler, *v.a. V.* **Ficeler**

Enfiévrer, *v.a.* to fever

Enfilade, *s.f.* suite; series; row; range; long string; length; (*mil.*) enfilade. *D'—,* (*mil.*) raking

Enfiler, *v.a.* to thread; to string; to pierce; to run through; to go through; to engage in, to enter *or* get into; to begin; to run o.'s arms *or* legs through, to slip on; to cozen; to swindle, to cheat; (*mil.*) to enfilade, to rake

S'—, *v.r.* to be run through, &c.; to get engaged *or* involved; (*pop.*) to lose a good deal; to get into debt; to play high

Enfileu-r, se, *s.m.f.* (*tech.*) header; (*fig.*) cozener, cheat

Enfin, *adv.* in fine, finally, lastly, in short; at last, at length; in the end; after all; in fact; upon the whole; yet; come, now then; well

Enflammé, e, *part. adj.* kindled, &c. (*V.* **Enflammer**); on fire, in flames, in a blaze; burning; flaming; fiery; glowing; fervid; flushed, red

Enflammer, *v.a.* to set on fire, to set fire to; to ignite; to fire; to kindle; to set in a blaze; to inflame; to incense; to provoke, to excite; to heat

S'—, *v.r.* to take *or* catch fire; to ignite; to blaze; to kindle; to become *or* be inflamed; to be incensed

Enflaquer, *v.a.* (*pop.*) to bother; to quod

Enflé, e, *part. adj.* swollen, &c. (*V.* **Enfler**); puffy; tumid; turgid; bombastic; — *s.m.f.* (*pop.*) fool, muff

Enfle-bœuf, *s.m.* (*zool.*) golden beetle, buprestis, burn-cow

Enflécher, *v.n.* (*nav.*) to go up the ratlines

Enfléchure, *s.f.* (*nav.*) ratline

Enflement, *s.m. V.* **Gonflement**

Enfler, *v.a.n.*, **S'—,** *v.r.* to swell; to swell out; to blow out; to bloat; to puff up *or* out; to inflate; to distend; to elate; to raise, to excite; to rise; (*pop.*) to drink, to soak

Enfleurage, *s.m.* (*in perfumery*) scenting with flowers, enfleurage

Enfleurer, *v.a.* (*in perfumery*) to scent with flowers

Enflure, *s.f.* swelling; puffiness; inflation; elation, pride; turgidness; bombast

Enfonçage, *s.m.* sinking; plunging; driving *or* forcing in; bottoming, heading

Enfoncé, e, *part. adj.* sunk, sunken, &c. (*V.* **Enfoncer**); deep, hollow; (*of ships*) low, low-built

Enfoncement, *s.m.* sinking, sinking down; breaking in *or* down *or* open *or* through; driving in; forcing in; farthest end *or* part, depth, bottom; recess; hollow; (*paint.*) background

Enfoncer, *v.a.n.* to sink, to sink down, to sink to the bottom; to thrust; to stick; to fix; to plunge; to immerse; to swamp; to bury; to break; to break in *or* into *or* down *or* open *or* through; to stave in; to drive in; to force in; to deepen; to hollow; to pull down; to pull over o.'s eyes; to balk; to beat, to excel, to surpass; to outwit; to outdo, to dish, to diddle; to take in; to ruin, to do for; (*tech.*) to bottom, to head (*a cask*); (*old*) to probe, to examine

S'—, *v.r.* to sink down, to sink; to go deep *or* deeper; to penetrate; to plunge; to dive; to bury oneself; to recede; to break down; to give way; to swamp oneself, to make a mess of it

Enfonceu-r, se, *s.m.f.* person *or* thing that breaks open; diddler, cheat; jobber. — *de portes ouvertes,* braggart, boaster

Enfonçure, *s.f.* cavity, hole, hollow; (*of casks*) bottom-pieces, head-pieces, bottom, head; (*of beds*) boarding, bottom

Enforcir, *v.a.* to strengthen; — *v.n.*, **S'—,** *v.r.* to gather *or* acquire strength, to become (*or* grow *or* get) strong *or* stout; to grow up well; to thrive

Enformer, *v.a.* to put on the block *or* form

Enfouir, *v.a.* to bury, to hide; to bury *or* hide in the ground; to cover with earth; to earth

Enfouissement, *s.m.* burying, hiding in the ground

Enfouisseur, *s.m.* burier; (*zool.*) necrophore, sexton-beetle, burying beetle

Enfourchement, *s m.* (*tech.*) crossing; (*hort.*) saddle-grafting

Enfourcher, *v.a.* to bestride

Enfourchure, *s.f.* fork (*of the legs, of trousers, of boughs,* &c.); forked antlers, forked head (*of a stag*)

Enfournage, *s.m.*, **Enfournée,** *s.f.*, **Enfournement,** *s.m.* putting in the oven

Enfourner, *v.a.* to put in the oven; (*fig.*) to begin; — *s.m.* beginning, outset

S'—, *v.r.* to engage (right in); to get into a fix

Enfranger, *v.a. V.* **Franger**

Enfreindre, *v.a.* to infringe, to break, to violate

S'—, *v.r.* to be infringed *or* &c.

Enfroquer, *v.a.* to make a monk of. *S'—,* to turn monk

Enfuir (S'), *v.r.* to flee, to take flight, to run away *or* off, to get away *or* off, to go *or* be off; to escape, to make o.'s escape; to abscond; to elope; to fly; to go, to disappear, to vanish; to run out; to leak; to run over, to boil over

Enfumé, e, *adj.* besmoked, smoked, smoky

Enfumer, *v.a.* to besmoke, to smoke, to fill *or* smother with smoke; to smoke out; to fume; to intoxicate; to elate

†**Enfutaillement,** *s.m.* casking

†**Enfutailler,** *v.a.* to cask

Engagé, e, *part. adj.* engaged, &c. (*V.* **Engager**); (*nav.*) in action; water-logged; — *s.m.* soldier enlisted

Engageant, e, *adj.* engaging, inviting, pleasing, winning, taking, attractive, prepossessing

Engagement, *s.m.* engagement; pledging; pawning; mortgage; assignment; hiring; enlistment; bounty; liabilities; action

Engager, *v.a.* to engage; to pledge; to pawn; to mortgage; to assign; to hire; to bind; to entangle; to involve; to invite, to advise; to induce; to persuade; to urge; to win over; to oblige, to compel; to begin, to enter upon; to enter; to enlist

S'—, *v.r.* to engage *or* &c. oneself; to engage; to undertake; to promise; to be a security; to begin; to arise; to take place; to enter; to get (into); to penetrate; to be affected; to enlist; (*of a ship*) to incline

Engagiste, *s.m.f.* (*obsolete*) tenant

Engaîner, *v.a.* to case, to sheathe

Engallage, *s.m.* (*dyeing*) galling

Engaller, *v.a.* (*dyeing*) to gall

Engamer, *v.n.* (*fish.*) to swallow the hook

Enganter, *v.a.* (*nav.*) to come up with, to join, to overtake, to catch, to reach; (*fig.*) to infatuate; to wheedle, to get hold of; (*pop.*) to grab, to snatch, to clutch, to steal

S'—, *v.r.* to become infatuated; to become thick *or* intimate (with)

Engarrotté, e, *adj. V.* **Égarrotté**

Engaver, *v.a. V.* **Gaver**

Engazonnement, *s.m.* turfing

Engazonner, *v.a.* to turf

Engeance, *s.f.* breed; race, brood, set, lot

Engeancer, *v.a.* to encumber, to saddle

†**Engeigner,** *v.a.* (*old*) to entrap, to deceive, to cheat, to take in

Engelure, *s.f.* chilblain

Engendrer, *v.a.* to beget, to engender; to generate; to breed, to produce; to spawn; (*old*) to give a son-in-law to; to take for o.'s son-in-law

S'—, *v.r.* to be begot *or* &c.; to breed; (*old*) to choose a son-in-law, to take for o.'s son-in-law

Enger, *v.a.* (*old*) *V.* **Engeancer**

Engerbage, *s.m.* binding in sheaves; piling up, heaping up

Engerber, *v.a.* to bind in sheaves, to sheaf; to pile up, to heap up

Engin, *s.m.* engine, machine; contrivance; utensil, implement, instrument, tool; tackle; gear; appliance; lift; snare, gin, net; *(obsolete)* skill, dexterity
Englober, *v.a.* to annex, to unite; to put together; to merge; to encompass; to include; [to contain
S'—, *v.r.* to be annexed *or* &c.
Engloutir, *v.a.* to swallow up *or* down; to ingulf; to absorb; to squander
S'—, *v.r.* to be swallowed up *or* &c.; to sink
Engloutissement, *s.m.* swallowing up *or* down; sinking
Engloutisseu-r,se, *s.m.f.* swallower, devourer
Engluer, *v.a.* to lime; to catch; to ensnare; to take in
S'—, *v.r.* to stick in birdlime; to be caught (as in birdlime), to be ensnared *or* taken in
Engommage, *s.m.* gumming
Engommer, *v.a.* to gum
Engoncement, *s.m.* awkward appearance
Engoncer, *v.a.* to smother, to cover up, to sink, to bury, to cramp, to confine, to give an awkward look
Engorgement, *s.m.* obstruction, choking, choking up, stoppage; *(med.)* engorgement, congestion
Engorger, *v.a.* to obstruct, to choke, to choke up, to stop up; *(med.)* to engorge, to congest
S'—, *v.r.* to become (*or* be) obstructed *or* &c.
Engoué, e, *part. adj.* infatuated (with); wrapped up (in); overfond (of); obstructed, choked
Engouement, *s.m.* infatuation, extreme fondness; obstruction, choking
Engouer, *v.a.* to infatuate; to obstruct, to choke
S'—, *v.r.* to become *or* be infatuated; to admire extravagantly; to choke oneself; to be obstructed
Engouffrer, *v.a.* to ingulf, to swallow up *or* down
S'—, *v.r.* to be ingulfed, to be swallowed up *or* down; to blow hard; to rush
Engoulé, e, *part. adj.* swallowed up, gobbled up; *(her.)* engoulee
Engouler, *v.a.* to swallow up, to gobble up
Engoulevent, *s.m.* *(bird)* goat-sucker, night-jar, fern-owl
Engourdi, e, *adj.* benumbed; torpid; dull
Engourdir, *v.a.* to benumb; to make torpid; to dull; to blunt; to enervate
S'—, *v.r.* to get benumbed; to grow torpid *or* dull; to become enervated
Engourdissement, *s.m.* benumbing; numbness; torpor; dulness; enervation, weakness
Engrain, *s.m.* corn-sowing; *(bot.)* lesser spelt, one-grained wheat
Engrainer, *v.a.* to feed with grain *or* corn; — *v.n.* to put corn in the mill-hopper; *(fig.)* to begin
Engrais, *s.m.* manure; pasture; fatting. *A l'*—, fatting. — *humain,* night-soil manure, night-[manure
Engraissage, *s.m.* fattening, fatting
Engraissement, *s.m.* fattening, fatting; corpulence, stoutness; manuring; manure
Engraisser, *v.a.* to fatten; to fat; to make fat; to enrich; to manure; to grease; — *v.n.,* **S'—,** *v.r.* to get *or* grow fat *or* stout; to fatten; to thrive; to enrich oneself, to grow rich; *(old)* to thicken, to get ropy
Engraisseu-r, se, *s.m.f.* fattener
Engrangement, *s.m.* getting in, housing *(corn)*, ingathering
Engranger, *v.a.* to get in, to house *(corn)*
S'—, *v.r.* to be housing *or* housed
Engravement, *s.m.* stranding [strand
Engraver, *v.a.n.,* **S'—,** *v.r.* to run aground, to
Engrêler, *v.a.* *(of lace)* to purl; *(her.)* to engrail
Engrêlure, *s.f.* *(of lace)* purl; *(her.)* engrailing
Engrenage, *s.m.* *(mach.)* gear, gearing. *A* —, serrated. *Roue d'*—, brake-wheel
Engrener, *v.a.* to throw into gear, to gear; to tooth; to fit together; to fetch *(a pump)*; to feed with grain *or* corn; — *v.n.* to catch, to work into each other; to put corn in the mill-hopper; *(fig.)* to begin
S'—, *v.r.* to work into each other, to catch; to be put in gear [*machine*)
Engreneur, *s.m.* *(agr.)* feeder (*of a thrashing-*
Engrenure, *s.f.* catching, working into each [other
Engrosser, *v.a.* to get with child
Engrumeler, *v.a.,* **S'—,** *v.r.* to coagulate, to clot
†Enguenillé, e, *adj.* tattered, in rags
†Engueniller, *v.a.* to clothe in tatters, to cover with rags [chaff
Engueulement, *s.m.* *(pop.)* abuse, chaffing,
Engueuler, *v.a.* *(pop.)* to shout at, to abuse, to humbug, to chaff
Engueuleu-r, se, *s.m.f.* *(pop.)* abuser, chaffer
Engueuser, *v.a.* to bamboozle, to gammon, to [humbug
Enguichure, *s.f.* *V.* **Anguichure**
Enguirlander, *v.a.* to wreathe
Enhardir, *v.a.* to embolden; to encourage
S'—, *v.r.* to grow bold; to make bold; to pluck up courage enough (for, to)
Enhardissement, *s.m.* emboldening [3, § 1
Enharmon-ie, -ique, -iquement. *V.* page
Enharnach-er, -ement. *V.* **Harnacher,** &c.
Enherber, *v.a.* to sow with grass
Enhuché, e, *adj.* *(nav.)* moon-sheered
Enhydre, *adj.* enhydrous
Éniellage, *s.m.* clearing of corn-cockles
Énieller, *v.a.* to clear of corn-cockles
Énigmat-ique, -iquement. *V.* page 3, § 1
Énigmatiser, *v.n.a.* to enigmatize
Énigme, *s.f.* enigma, riddle
Enivrement, *s.m.* intoxication
Enivrer, *v.a.* to intoxicate, to inebriate, to make drunk *or* tipsy; to elate
S'—, *v.r.* to get *or* be intoxicated, to get drunk *or* tipsy; to be elated
Enjabler, *v.a.* to bottom *or* head *(a cask)*
Enjaler, *v.a.* *(nav.)* to stock *(an anchor)*
Enjambé, e, *adj* *(pers., animals)* legged. *Haut* —, long-legged
Enjambée, *s.f.* stride [sense into the next line
Enjambement, *s.m.* *(vers.)* running of the
Enjamber, *v.a.n.* to stride over, to bestride; to stride; to stride along; to skip over, to skip; to project; to encroach; *(vers.)* to run into the next line, to complete the sense in [another line
Enjaveler, *v.a.* *V.* **Javeler**
Enjeu, *s.m.* *(at play)* stake
Enjoindre, *v.a.* to enjoin, to order, to bid, to direct, to command, to prescribe, to summon, [to charge
S'—, *v.r.* to be enjoined *or* &c.
Enjointé, e, *adj.* *(of birds)* legged
Enjôlement, *s.m.* wheedling, coaxing, inveigling, inveiglement
Enjôler, *v.a.* to wheedle, to coax, to inveigle
Enjôleu-r,se, *s.m.f.* wheedler, coaxer, inveigler
Enjolivement, *s.m.* ornament, embellishment, decoration, set-off, flourish, scroll
Enjoliver, *v.a.* to adorn, to ornament, to set off, to embellish, to beautify, to decorate
S'—, *v.r.* to become (*or* be) adorned *or* &c.
Enjoliveu-r, se, *s.m.f.* setter-off, adorner, em-[bellisher
Enjolivure, *s.f.* *V.* **Enjolivement**
Enjoué, e, *adj.* playful, sportive, humorous, lively, sprightly
Enjouement, *s.m.* playfulness, sportiveness, humour, liveliness, sprightliness
Enjouer, *v.a.* to bring (*the butt of a gun*) against the cheek [by a petticoat (*by a woman*)
Enjuponner (S'), *v.r.* to have o.'s head turned
Enkysté, e, *adj.* *(med.)* encysted
Enkystement, *s.m.* *(med.)* encysting [cysted
Enkyster (S'), *v.r.* to encyst, to become en-
Enlacement, *s.m.* lacing; entwining; interweaving; entanglement
Enlacer, *v.a.* to lace; to entwine, to twine, to twist; to interweave; to entangle; to immesh; to clasp, to fold
Enlaidir, *v.a.* to make ugly, to disfigure, to spoil; — *v.n.* to grow ugly, to be disfigured
Enlaidissement, *s.m.* growing ugly, ugliness, disfigurement
Enlèvement, *s.m.* removal; carrying off *or*

away; carrying; taking off *or* away; taking; buying up, monopoly; kidnapping; rape; abduction; elopement; (*to heaven*) translation

Enlever, *v.a.* to lift, to raise; to take away; to remove; to take out *or* off; to carry away *or* off; to carry; to take; to rub out *or* off; to wash out; to sweep off; to knock off; to despatch; to buy up; to play off; to flay; to peel off; to burn (*the mouth*); to rescue; to kidnap; to run away with; to abduct; to ravish; to transport; to enrapture; to surprise. *Enlevé!* (*pop.*) done!

S'—, *v.r.* to be lifted *or* raised *or* &c.; to rise; to come out *or* off; to peel off; to wipe off; to rub *or* wash out; to go off; to get into a passion, to fly out. *Se faire — par*, to elope with

Enleveur, *s.m.* kidnapper, abductor, ravisher; dashing actor

Enlevure, *s.f.* blister; raised work; shred, chip, fragment

†Enligner, *v.a. V.* **Aligner**

Enliser, Enlizer, *v.a.* to sink in quicksand

Enluminé, e, *adj.* coloured, illuminated; red

Enluminement, *s.m. V.* **Enluminure**

Enluminer, *v.a.* to colour (*prints*); to illuminate; to redden, to flush, to inflame; (*liter.*) to overload with ornaments, to tinsel

S'—, *v.r.* to be coloured *or* &c.; to become red *or* flushed; to become excited with drink; to redden; to paint, to rouge

Enlumineu-r, se, *s.m.f.* colourer, illuminating artist, illuminator, limner

Enluminure, *s.f.* colouring, illuminating; coloured print, illumination; (*of the face*) redness; (*liter.*) far-fetched ornament, overcolouring, tinsel; (*pop.*) slight intoxication, drop too much

Enmouracher, *v.a. pop. for* **Amouracher**

Ennéade, *s.f.* ennead

Ennéagonal, e, *adj.* (*geom.*) enneagonal

Ennéagone, *s.m.* (*geom.*) enneagon; — *adj.* enneagonal

Ennemi, e, *s.m.f.* enemy; foe; adversary; antagonist; opponent; opposite; prejudicial *or* injurious thing; — *adj.* hostile; inimical; adverse; contrary; opposite, opposed; antagonistic; unfriendly; prejudicial, injurious, hurtful; repugnant; enemy's, of the enemy

Ennoblir, *v.a.* to ennoble, to dignify, to exalt, to raise

S'—, *v.r.* to ennoble *or* &c. oneself; to be ennobled, &c.

Ennui, *s.m.* tediousness, weariness, irksomeness, tiresomeness, tedium; dulness, spleen, ennui; annoyance, vexation; nuisance; care; trouble

Ennuyant, e, *adj.* tiresome, annoying

Ennuyé, e, *part. adj.* tired, &c. (*V.* **Ennuyer**); listless; splenetic; — *s.m.f.* ennuyé, ennuyée, splenetic

Ennuyer, *v.a.* to tire, to weary; to annoy, to worry, to tease, to bother, to bore

S'—, *v.r.* to be wearied *or* tired, to weary oneself; to grow weary, to grow *or* get tired; to feel dull, to find it dull, not to know what to do with oneself; to bother oneself *or* each other

Ennuyeusement, *adv.* tediously, wearisomely, irksomely

Ennuyeu-x, se, *adj.* tiresome, wearisome, irksome, dull, tedious; annoying, provoking, vexing, troublesome; — *s.m.f.* bore, tiresome person

Énode, Énodé, e, *adj.* (*bot.*) enode

Énoncé, *s.m.* statement, assertion, declaration, enunciation; terms

Énoncer, *v.a.* to state; to assert; to declare; to give out; to utter; to express; to word; to enunciate

S'—, *v.r.* to express oneself; to be expressed

Énonciati-f, ve, *adj.* enunciative, expressive

Énonciation, *s.f.* statement; declaration; utterance; delivery; expression; wording; proposition; enunciation

†Enorgueillir, *v.a.* to make *or* render proud, to puff up, to elate

S'—, *v.r.* to be *or* get *or* grow proud; to become elated, to be puffed up; to pride oneself (upon)

Énorme, *adj.* enormous; huge; immense; prodigious; excessive; grievous; heinous, atrocious

Énormément, *adv.* enormously; hugely; immensely; prodigiously; excessively, beyond measure; extremely; heinously, atrociously; an enormous amount *or* quantity

Énormité, *s.f.* enormousness; hugeness; enormity; grievousness; heinousness, atrocity

Énostose, *s.f.* (*med.*) enostosis

Énouage, *s.m.* burling

Énouer, *v.a.* to burl

Énoueu-r, se, *s.m.f.* burler

Enquérant, e, *adj.* (*obsolete*) inquisitive, prying, curious

Enquérir (S'), *v.r.* to inquire; to ask

Enquête, *s.f.* inquiry; inquest; search; information; investigation; commission

Enquêter (S'), *v.r.* (*old*) to inquire; to care (for)

Enquêteur, *adj.m.* inquiring, examining; — *s.m.* inquirer

Enquinauder, *v.a.* to wheedle, to coax, to fool

Enraciné, e, *part. adj.* rooted, inveterate

Enracinement, *s.m.* rooting, rootedness; inveteracy

Enraciner, *v.a.n.,* **S'—,** *v.r.* to root; to take root; to grow inveterate

Enragé, e, *adj.* mad, rabid; enraged; furious; raving; outrageous; raging, terrible, desperate; obstinate; determined; unlucky, evil; (*of music*) rough and noisy; — *s.m.f.* hydrophobiac; madman, mad woman, devil. *Manger de la vache —e*, to undergo great hardships, to live miserably, to swallow many a bitter pill

Enrageant, e, *adj.* provoking, vexatious, vexing, maddening

Enrager, *v.n.* to be *or* go mad; to be enraged, to be in a rage, to rage; to be vexed *or* plagued; to fume. *Faire —*, to enrage, to madden, to drive mad, to worry, to plague, to tease, to vex, to rile, to bother

Enraiement, Enrayement, *s.m.* putting on the drag, skidding, locking; first furrow

Enrayer, *v.a.n.* to put spokes to; to put the drag on, to skid, to lock, to apply the break; (*fig.*) to check; to stop; (*agr.*) to trace the first furrow

Enrayure, *s.f.* drag, skid, lock-chain, break; spokes; first furrow; platform; radiated work

Enrégimenter, *v.a.* to embody, to form into a regiment *or* into regiments; to enlist, to enroll

Enregistrement, *s.m.* registration; registry; entry; enrolment; recording

Enregistrer, *v.a.* to register, to book, to enter; to enroll; to record; (*fam.*) to take note of

S'—, *v.r.* to be registered *or* &c.

Enregistreur, *s.m.* registrar

Enréner, *v.a.* to rein in, to tie by the reins

Enrénoire, *s.f.* peg for reins

Enrhumé, e, *part. adj.* with a cold. *Être —*, to have a cold. *Être — du cerveau*, to have a cold in the head

Enrhumer, *v.a.* to give a cold

S'—, *v.r.* to catch cold, to get *or* take cold

Enrichi, e, *s.m.f.* upstart; — *part. V.* **Enrichir**

Enrichir, *v.a.* to enrich; to adorn, to embellish; to store; to set

S'—, *v.r.* to enrich oneself, to get *or* grow rich; to be enriched; to be stored

Enrichissement, *s.m.* enriching; ornament, embellishment

Enrochement, *s.m.* enrockment

Enrocher, *v.a.* to enrock

Enrôlement, *s.m.* enrolment; enlisting, enlistment; engagement

Enrôler, *v.a.* to enroll; to enlist; to engage

S'—, *v.r.* to enroll oneself; to enlist; to engage

Enrôleur, *s.m. V.* **Racoleur**

Enrosser, *v.a.* (*slang*) to bishop (*a horse*)

Enroué, e, *adj.* hoarse; husky

Enrouement, *s.m.* hoarseness; huskiness

Enrouer, *v.a.* to make hoarse *or* husky

S'—, *v.r.* to make oneself hoarse, to get (*or* become) hoarse *or* husky

†Enrouillement, *s.m.* rusting; rustiness

†Enrouiller, *v.a. V.* **Rouiller**

Enroulement, *s.m.* rolling, rolling up; roll; (*bot.*) twisting; (*arch.*) scroll [coil
Enrouler, *v.a.* to roll, to roll up; to twist; to
Enrubaner, *v.a.* to trim *or* deck out with rib-
Enrue, *s.f.* large furrow [bons, to ribbon
Ensablement, *s.m.* sandbank, heap of sand; ballasting; ballast; gravelling
Ensabler, *v.a.* to fill *or* choke up with sand; to ballast; to gravel; to run on a sandbank
S'—, *v.r.* to sink in sand, to fill with sand, to be covered with sand; to run aground, to run on a sandbank, to remain fixed in the sand; to be ballasted; to be gravelled
Ensaboté, e, *adj.* in wooden shoes
Ensaboter, *v.a.* to put wooden shoes on; to skid; to bottom (*round shot*)
Ensachement, *s.m.* bagging, sacking
Ensacher, *v.a.* to bag, to sack
Ensade, *s.m.* (*bot.*) pippul-tree, peepul-tree
Ensanglanté, e, *part. adj.* stained with blood; bloody [with blood; bloodiness
Ensanglantement, *s.m.* staining *or* covering
Ensanglanter, *v.a.* to stain *or* cover with blood, to imbrue *or* drench in blood, to make bloody, to smear with gore, to ensanguine; to
†Enseignable, *adj.* teachable [kill, to murder
†Enseignant, e, *adj.* teaching. *Corps* —, university; educators of youth
†Enseigne, *s.m.* (*pers.*) ensign (*obsolete*); (*nav.*) passed midshipman. — *de vaisseau,* passed midshipman
†Enseigne, *s.f.* sign, sign-board; show-board; (*fig.*) advertisement; mark; token; (*mil.*) ensign (*flag*); ensigncy (*obsolete*); **—s,** *pl.* colours. —*s déployées,* with flying colours. *A bonnes* —*s,* justly; deservedly; on good security; on sure grounds. *A telles —s que,* so much so that, as proof. *A l'— de la lune,* (*pop.*) in the open air. *A bon vin point d'—,* good wine needs no bush. *Être logé à la même —,* (*fig.*) to be in the same predicament
†Enseignement, *s.m.* instruction; precept; lesson; teaching, tuition; education
†Enseigner, *v.a.* to teach; to teach how; to instruct; to inform, to tell; to show; to direct to; to send to [other; (*things*) to be taught
S'—, *v.r.* (*pers.*) to teach oneself · each
Ensellé, e, *adj.* saddle-backed
Ensemble, *adv.* together; at the same time. *Le tout —,* the whole
Ensemble, *s.m.* whole; mass; (general) appearance *or* effect; entirety; unity; series; harmony, uniformity; part-music; ensemble. *D'—,* simultaneous; comprehensive; combined; (*mus.*) concerted, in parts, part. *Morceau d'—,* (*mus.*) concerted piece, piece of music in parts, part-music. *Mouvement d'—,* combined move-
Ensemencement, *s.m.* sowing [ment
Ensemencer, *v.a.* to sow. *S'—,* to be sown
Enserrer, *v.a.* to encompass; to enclose; to surround; to encircle; to hem in; to confine; to contain; to comprehend; to embrace; to clasp; to shut up *or* in; to lock up to put away *or* by; to hoard up; to bury; to take in, to house; to put in a greenhouse
†Enseuillement, *s.m.* (*arch.*) sill
Ensevelir, *v.a.* to put in a shroud, to shroud; to lay out; to bury, to inter, to entomb; to ingulf, to swallow up; to plunge; to absorb
S'—, *v.r.* to bury oneself; (*of things*) to be buried *or* &c.
Ensevelissement, *s.m.* putting in a shroud, shrouding; laying out; burying, burial, interment, entombment
Ensevelisseu-r, se, *s.m.f.* layer-out
Ensiforme, *adj.* ensiform
†Ensoleillé, e, *adj.* sunned; sunny
†Ensoleiller, *v.a.* to sun
Ensorceler, *v.a.* to bewitch [bewitching
Ensorceleu-r, se, *s.m.f.* bewitcher; — *adj.*
Ensorcellement, *s.m.* bewitching, bewitchment
Ensoufrer, *v.a.* *V.* **Soufrer**
Ensuifer, *v.a.* *V.* **Suifer**
Ensuite, *adv.* after, afterwards; then; in the next place, next; what then? what next? what of that? well? — *de cela,* after that. — *de quoi,* after which
Ensuivre (S'), *v.r.* to follow; to ensue; to result; to proceed; to spring [tablement, table
Entablement, *s.m.* (*arch.*) entablature, en-
Entabler (S'), *v.r.* (*rid.*) to entable [to stain
Entacher, *v.a.* to infect; to taint; to sully,
†Entaillage, *s.m.* notching; grooving
†Entaille, *s.f.* notch; cut, cutting; gash; groove; mortise
†Entailler, *v.a.* to notch; to cut
†Entaillure, *s.f.* *V.* **Entaille**
Entalinguer, *v.a.* (*nav.*) to bend (*a cable*)
Entalingure, *s.f.* (*nav.*) clinch
Entame, *s.f.* first cut, first slice
Entamer, *v.a.* to make an incision in; to cut the first piece of, to cut into, to cut; to break through, to break; to bite into; to make a hole in; to open; to graze; to scratch; to touch; to partly spend; to make a beginning of, to begin, to commence; to enter into *or* upon; to broach; to attack; to make an impression upon; to impair, to injure, to damage; to encroach on; to prevail upon; to get over; to run down; to fathom. — *d'un coup de dent,* to bite into [cut *or* graze *or* scratch (o.'s ...)
S'—, *v.r.* to be begun *or* opened *or* &c.; to
Entamure, *s.f.* cut, incision; grazing; first cut; opening; beginning [**ser**); thickset
Entassé, e, *part. adj.* heaped, &c. (*V.* **Entas-**
Entassement, *s.m.* heap; pile; accumulation; crowding; crowd
Entasser, *v.a.* to heap, to heap up; to pile up; to hoard up; to cram, to crowd, to huddle, to pack together; to lumber; to accumulate; to drift
S'—, *v.r.* to be heaped up *or* &c.; to accumulate; to gather; to cram themselves (*or* ourselves, &c.) [lector, collectress
Entasseu-r, se, *s.m.f.* heaper; hoarder; col-
Ente, *s.f.* (*hort.*) graft; stock; (*paint.*) handle (*of a brush*); (*hunt.*) decoy
Entéléchie, *s.f.* (*anc. philos.*) entelechy
Entelle, *s.f.* (*zool.*) entellus monkey, honuman
Entement, *s.m.* grafting; ingrafting; jointing
Entendement, *s.m.* understanding; sense, judgment
Entendeur, *s.m.* (*obsolete*) hearer. *A bon — salut* or *demi-mot* or *peu de paroles,* a word to the wise is enough
Entendre, *v.a.n.* to hear; to listen to; to understand; to know; to mean; to intend; to require; to expect; to think proper; to attend, to pay attention; to approve; to consent. — *mal,* to hear *or* understand badly; to misunderstand. — *dire,* to hear, to hear say, to hear it said. — *parler de,* to hear of; to mean. — *de corne,* to be hard of hearing; to misunderstand. *Donner à —, faire —,* to give to understand; to intimate; to hint; to utter; to sound; to set up; to give. *Se faire —, V.* **Faire (Se).** *A —,* according to. *Ne pas y — malice,* to see no harm in it, to take it innocently, not to suspect anything; to mean no harm by it; to mean no more than what one says; not to have any secret *or* evil intention. *Ne savoir auquel* (or *à qui*) —, not to know which to hear *or* to attend to first
S'—, *v.r.* to hear oneself *or* each other; to understand each other; to know o.'s own meaning, to know what one means; to understand, to know; to be a judge (of); to be skilful (in); to manage; to arrange; to concert; to come to *or* to have an understanding; to come to terms; to act in concert; to be in collusion; to agree; to be heard; to be understood. *S'entend,* or *cela s'entend,* that is understood, of course, as a matter of course

Entendu, e, *part. adj.* heard; understood; agreed; contrived; conceived; ordered, arranged; managed; performed; intelligent, skilful, skilled, clever; versed; knowing; notable, a good manager. *Bien* —, well understood *or* &c.; very intelligent *or* &c.; of course, to be sure; it being understood (that); on condition (that). *Faire l'*—, to put on a knowing look, to pretend to be a judge *or* a skilful manager [ness, to benight

Enténébrer, *v.a.* to involve *or* wrap in dark-

Entente, *s.f.* understanding; agreement; harmony; meaning; skill; knowledge; judgment. *Double* —, double meaning. *Mot à double* —, word with a double meaning, double entendre (*in vulgar English*)

Enter, *v.a.* to graft; to ingraft; to joint

Entéralgie, *s.f.* (*med.*) enteralgy

Entérinement, *s.m.* ratification, confirmation

Entériner, *v.a.* to ratify, to confirm

Entérique, *adj.* (*med.*) enteric

Entérite, *s.f.* (*med.*) enteritis

Entéro-, (*in compounds*) entero-...

Entérocèle, *s.f.* (*med.*) enterocele

Entérolithe, *s.m.* (*med.*) enterolite

Entérologie, *s.f.* enterology

Entérotome, *s.m.* (*surg.*) enterotomy-knife

Entérotomie, *s.f.* (*surg.*) enterotomy

Enterrement, *s.m.* burial, burying, interment; funeral. *Billet d'*—, invitation to a funeral

Enterrer, *v.a.* to bury; to inter, to inhume; to survive, to outlive; to hide; to eclipse; to end, to terminate; to see the end of; to sink (*money*) [sexton-beetle, burying beetle

Enterreur, *s.m.* burier; (*zool.*) necrophore,

En-tête, *s.m.* heading, head

Entêté, e, *adj.* obstinate, headstrong, stubborn, wilful, wayward; infatuated; vain (of); taken (with); — *s.m.f.* obstinate *or* &c. man *or* fellow *or* woman *or* girl

Entêtement, *s.m.* obstinacy, stubbornness, wilfulness, waywardness; infatuation

Entêter, *v.a.* to affect the head, to make giddy; to make vain *or* conceited; to prepossess, to infatuate; (*tech.*) to head (*pins*, &c.)

S'—, *v.r.* to get obstinate; to be obstinately bent (upon); to become *or* be prepossessed *or* infatuated

Entêteu-r, se, *s.m.f.* header (*of pins*, &c.)

Enthousiasme, *s.m.* enthusiasm; rapture, ecstasy

Enthousiasmer, *v.a.* to transport, to enrapture

S'—, *v.r.* to become enthusiastic; to be in rapture

Enthousiaste, *adj.* enthusiastic; rapturous; — *s.m.f.* enthusiast; enthusiastic admirer

Enthymème, *s.m.* (*log.*) enthymeme

Entiché, e, *adj.* tainted, infected; taken (with); overpartial (to), overfond (of)

Enticher, *v.a.* to taint, to infect; to infatuate

S'—, *v.r.* to become (*or* be) tainted *or* infected; to become infatuated; to be taken (with); to get overpartial (to) *or* overfond (of)

Enti-er, ère, *adj.* entire; whole; total; complete; perfect; full; obstinate, positive, self-willed; (*arith.*) integral. *Nombre* —, (*arith.*) integer. *Tout* —, whole, entire; full; wholly, entirely, in full; all

Entier, *s.m.* entireness; entirety; totality; whole; entire horse; (*arith.*) integer. *En* —, *en son* —, entirely, wholly, totally, bodily, fully, in full, all over, through; entire

Entièrement, *adv.* entirely, wholly; totally; bodily; quite; all over; through

Entime, *s.m.* (*zool.*) entimus, diamond-beetle

Entité, *s.f.* entity [mounting

Entoilage, *s.m.* lining; mounting on canvas,

Entoiler, *v.a.* to line; to mount on canvas, to

Entoir, *s.m.* (*old*) *V.* **Greffoir** [mount

Entomo-logie, -logique, -logiste, &c. *V.* page 3, § 1 [casking

Entonnage, Entonnement, *s.m.* tunning,

Entonner, *v.a.* to tun, to cask; to intonate; to strike up, to begin; to begin to sing; to sing; to celebrate; to quaff [rush, to blow

S'—, *v.r.* to be tunned *or* &c.; (*of wind*) to

Entonnoir, *s.m.* funnel; (*jest.*) gullet, swallow; quaffer, tippler, hard drinker

Entophyte, *s.m.* (*bot.*) entophyte

Entorse, *s.f.* sprain; strain; twist; shock

†Entortillage, *s.m.* entanglement, intricacy, obscurity; circumlocution; equivocation; involved *or* obscure discourse *or* style; rigmarole

†Entortillé, e, *part. adj.* twisted, &c. (*V.* **Entortiller**); (*of style*) involved, obscure; (*bot.*) volubilate

†Entortillement, *s.m.* twisting; winding; entanglement; perplexity, intricacy, obscurity, ambiguity

†Entortiller, *v.a.* to twist; to wind; to wrap; to entangle; to perplex; to involve; to circumvent, to get round; to bring round; to captivate; to practise upon, to coax, to wheedle; to bother

†Entortilleu-r, se, *s.m.f.* coaxer, wheedler

Entour, *s.m.* *V.* **Entourage**; —**s**, *pl.* *V.* **Alentours.** *A l'*—, *V.* **Alentour,** *adv.*

Entourage, *s.m.* surroundings; enclosure; fence; railing; frame; mounting; setting; casing, case; connections, intimates, familiars, associates, company, circle, attendants

Entourer, *v.a.* to surround; to encompass; to hem round; to enclose; to encircle; to wreathe; to clasp; to set; to be about, to associate with [hole; (*fig.*) hitch, rub

Entournure, *s.f.* (*of sleeves*, &c.) sloping; arm-

En-tout-cas, *s.m.* sun-shade (*parasol, as described at* **En-cas**)

Entozoaire, *s.m.* (*zool.*) entozoan, entozoon (*pl.* entozoa); — *adj.* entozoal, entozoic

Entr'... (S'), *v.r.* to . . . each other

Entr'abattre (S'), Entr'aborder (S'), Entr'accoler (S'), &c. to ... (*V.* **Abattre, Aborder, Accoler,** &c.) each other

Entr'accorder (S'), *v.r.* to agree together

Entr'accuser (S'), *v.r.* to accuse each other

Entr'acte, *s.m* (*theat.*) interval between the acts; (*mus.*) entr'act; (*obsolete, and abusively for* **Intermède**) interlude; (*fig.*) interval, suspension, rest; (*name of a French newspaper*) "Entr'acte" (*Theatrical News*)

Entr'admirer (S'), *v.r.* to admire each other

Entr'aider (S'), *v.r.* to help each other

†Entrailles, *s.f.pl.* entrails; bowels; feeling, feelings, tenderness, heart; pity

Entr'aimer (S'), *v.r.* to love each other

Entrain, *s.m.* spirits, high spirits; animation; spirit, life; humour; conviviality

Entraînement, *s.m.* force, sway; impulse; spirit; animation; enthusiasm; fascination, seduction, allurement, temptation; irresistible influence; error, mistake; training (*for races or matches*); carrying away, dragging along, &c. (*V.* **Entraîner**)

Entraîner, *v.a.* to carry away; to carry; to hurry away *or* along; to drag away *or* along; to lead away *or* on; to impel; to draw along; to draw; to bring on *or* over; to gain over; to win; to captivate; to fascinate, to seduce; to overpower; to influence; to induce; to persuade; to allure, to entice; to excite; to animate, to inspirit; to involve, to entail; to cause; to turn (*the scale*); to train (*for races or*

Entraîneur, *s.m.* horse-trainer, trainer [*matches*)

Entrait, *s.f.* (*carp.*) tie-beam

Entrant, e, *adj.* ingoing; incoming; going in; coming in; entering; insinuating; — *s.m.* ingoer; incomer

Entr'appeler (S'), *v.r.* to call each other

Entr'attaquer (S'), *v.r.* to attack each other

Entrave, *s.f.* *V.* **Entraves**

Entraver, *v.a.* to shackle, to clog, to fetter, to trammel; to bind, to tie; to entangle; to hinder, to impede, to oppose, to thwart

Entraverser, *v.a.* (*nav.*) to bring the broad-side of

Entr'avertir (S'), *v.r.* to warn each other; to give one another notice

Entraves, *s.f.pl.* fetters, clog, hobbles, trammels; shackles; chains; bonds, ties; obstacles, impediments, obstacle, impediment, hindrance; restraint

Entravon, *s.m.* (*on a horse's leg*) cutting-boot, boot

Entr'avouer (S'), *v.r.* to confess to each other

Entre, *prep.* between; among; with; of; in; into; to; (*as a prefix to a verb*) each other, one another, mutually, reciprocally; together; partly, half-way, half. — *autres*, among other; among others; among them; in the number; particularly. — *tous*, among all; more than all; above all other; above all others; of all other; of all others; in the extreme

†Entre-bâillé, e, *adj.* ajar, on the jar, half-open

†Entre-bâillement, *s.m.* part-opening

†Entre-bâiller, *v.a.*, **S'—**, *v.r.* to half-open

Entre-baiser (S'), *v.r.* to kiss each other

Entre-battre (S'), *v.r.* to fight together

Entre-blesser (S'), Entre-briser (S'), Entre-caresser (S'), Entre-casser (S'), &c. to ... (*V.* **Blesser, Briser, Caresser, Casser,** &c.) each other

Entrechat, *s.m.* (*dancing*) caper

Entre-chercher (S'), *v.r.* to seek each other, to look for each other

Entre-choquement, *s.m.* clashing, clash; conflict

Entre-choquer (S'), *v.r.* to strike *or* knock against each other; to clash; to jar; to thwart each other; to interfere

Entre-clore, *v.a.*, **S'—**, *v.r.* to half-close

Entre-colonnes, Entre-colonnement, *s.m.* (*arch.*) intercolumniation

Entre-combattre (S'), Entre-connaître (S'), Entre-consoler (S'), &c. to ... (*V.* **Combattre, Connaître, Consoler,** &c.) each other

Entre-côtes, *s.f.* piece off the ribs, rib of beef

Entre-coudoyer (S'), *v.r.* to ... (*V.* **Coudoyer**) each other

Entrecoupe, *s.f.* turning-space

Entrecoupement, *s.m.* intersection; cutting; crossing; interspersion; interruption; faltering

Entrecouper, *v.a.* to intersect; to cut; to cross; to intersperse; to break, to interrupt, to stop

Entre-croisé, e, *adj.* crossing each other, intersecting; — *part.* intersected *or* crossed (by, with)

Entre-croisement, *s.m.* intersection, crossing

Entre-croiser (S'), *v.r.* to cross each other, to intercross, to intersect

Entre-déchirer (S'), *v.r.* to tear each other to pieces

Entre-détruire (S'), *v.r.* to destroy each other

Entre-deux, *s.m.* intermediate space *or* situation; partition; pier-piece (of furniture); pier; (*of stuffs*) insertion; (*of cod*) middle; (*agr.*) balk; (*nav.*) waist (*of a ship*); trough *or* hollow (*of the sea*)

Entre-dévorer (S'), Entre-donner (S'), &c. to ... (*V.* **Dévorer, Donner,** &c.) each other

Entrée, *s.f.* entrance; entry; entering; going in; coming in; appearance; introduction; admission, admittance; reception; access; ingress; way in; passage; opening; inlet; mouth; beginning; rise, birth; importation; duty; entrance-money *or* fee; admission-money; admission-ticket; free admission; seat; first course side-dish *or* corner-dish, dish, entrée. *Droit d'—*, import-duty. *Avoir ses —s à*, to have free admission *or* access to. *D'—*, (*adv., obsolete*) at first, from the beginning

Entrefaite, *s.f.*, **Entrefaites,** *s.f.pl.* *Sur l'—, sur ces —s*, during that time, while this is *or* was going on, in the midst of all this

Entre-filets, *s.m.* (short) paragraph

Entre-fin, e, *adj.* (*com.*) middling quality *or* size

Entre-flatter (S'), Entre-frapper (S'), &c. to ... (*V.* **Flatter, Frapper,** &c.) each other

Entregent, *s.m.* ways of the world, pleasing *or* insinuating address; address, tact

Entr'égorger (S'), *v.r.* to cut each other's throat

†Entr'égratigner (S'), Entre-gronder (S'), Entre-haïr (S'), Entre-heurter (S'), &c. to ... (*V.* **Égratigner, Gronder,** &c., &c.) each other

†Entreillisser, *v.a.* *V.* **Treillisser**

Entre-joindre (S'), &c. to ... (*V.* **Joindre,** &c.) each other

Entrelacement, *s.m.* interlacing, interweaving, intermixing, wreathing, twining, twisting, wattling, blending

Entrelacer, *v.a.* to interlace, to interweave, to intermix, to wreathe, to twine, to twist, to wattle, to blend

S'—, *v.r.* to be interlaced *or* &c.; to twine *or* twist round each other; to entwine; to twist; to wreathe

Entrelacs, *s.m.* twine, interlaced ornaments, ciphers; flourishes

Entrelardé, e, *part. adj.* interlarded; streaked, streaky

Entrelardement, *s.m.* interlarding; streakiness

Entrelarder, *v.a.* to interlard

Entre-large, *adj.* (*com.*) of middling width

Entre-lier (S'), *v.r.* to bind *or* &c. (*V.* **Lier**)

†Entre-lignes, *s.m.* *V.* **Interligne**

Entre-louer (S'), *v.r.* to praise each other

Entreluire, *v.n.* to glimmer

Entre-manger (S'), Entr'embarrasser (S'), Entr'embrasser (S'), &c. to ... (*V.* **Manger,** &c., &c.) each other

Entremêlement, *s.m.* intermixing; intermixture

Entremêler, *v.a.* to intermix, to mix up, to mix together, to intermingle; to intersperse; to interweave; to twist; to blend; to vary

S'—, *v.r.* to intermix, &c. (*as above*); to meddle, to intermeddle

Entremets, *s.m.* second course, last course; second *or* last course side-dish (*or* corner-dish), dish (*coming between roast meat and dessert*), entremets

Entremetteu-r, se, *s.m.f.* go-between

Entremettre (S'), *v.r.* to interpose, to intervene, to interfere; to intercede; to meddle, to intermeddle

Entremise, *s.f.* interposition, intervention, interference, mediation; medium, agency; (*nav.*) carling

†Entre-modillons, *s.m.* (*arch.*) intermodillion

Entre-mordre (S'), &c. to ... (*V.* **Mordre,** &c.) each other

Entre-nœuds, *s.m.* (*bot.*) internode

Entre-nouer, *v.a.* to interknot

Entre-nuire (S'), *v.r.* to injure each other

Entre-pardonner (S'), *v.r.* to pardon *or* forgive each other

Entre-parler (S'), *v.r.* to speak to each other, to talk together

Entrepas, *s.m.* (*rid.*) ambling pace

Entre-percer (S'), Entre-persécuter (S'), †Entre-piller (S'), &c. to ... (*V.* **Percer,** &c., &c.) each other

Entrepont, *s.m.* (*nav.*) between-decks; under deck. *Passager d'—*, steerage passenger

Entreposage, *s.m.* bonding, warehousing

Entreposer, *v.a.* to bond, to warehouse

Entreposeur, *s.m.* warehouse-keeper

Entrepositaire, *s.m.f.* bonder

Entrepôt, *s.m.* warehouse; store; bonding *or* bonded warehouse *or* store; free port; mart, emporium; bond; entrepôt

Entre-poursuivre (S'), Entre-pousser (S'), &c. to ... (*V.* **Poursuivre, Pousser,** &c.) each other

Entreprenable, *adj.* undertakable

Entreprenant, e, *adj.* enterprising; pushing; bold, daring; encroaching

Entreprendre, *v.a.* to undertake; to take in hand; to contract for; to attempt; to attack; to set on; to lay hold of; to affect, to seize,

to take up; — *v.n.* to encroach, to intrench, to trench, to infringe, to trespass, to intrude, to usurp; to make an attempt [*or* &c. each other
S'—, *v.r.* to be undertaken *or* &c.; to attack
Entrepreneu-r, se, *s.m.f.* undertaker; contractor; builder; master (...); proprietor; manufacturer (of), manufacturing (...); maker. — *de pompes funèbres,* undertaker (*of funerals*)
Entre-presser (S'), Entre-prêter (S'), &c. to ... (*V.* **Presser, Prêter,** &c.) each other
Entrepris, e, *part. adj.* undertaken, &c. (*V.* **Entreprendre**); crippled, impotent; stiff; diseased; affected; attacked; taken up; taken; caught; (*obsolete*) disconcerted
Entreprise, *s.f.* undertaking, enterprise; contract; attempt; venture; encroachment; usurpation; violence; establishment, concern, house, office, company. *A l'—,* by contract. *Tenter l'—,* to make the attempt [each other
Entre-quereller (S'), *v.r.* to quarrel with
Entrer, *v.n.* to enter; to go in; to come in; to walk *or* step in; to run in; to drop in; to get in; to go on; to penetrate; to go *or* come *or* get *or* pass *or* march (into); to begin; to fall (*into a passion*); to contribute; to share; to participate; to be concerned (in); to be; — *v.a.* to bring *or* carry in; to take in; to get in; to get on; to let in; (*book-keep.*) to enter. — *en âge,* to be of age. — *en maison,* to go into service, to become a servant. — *en religion,* to enter a convent, to become a monk *or* a nun. — *pour quelque chose dans,* to form part of; to have some share in; to have something to do with. *Faire —,* to make (...) go *or* come in; to let in; to ask *or* show in; to introduce; to admit; to take in; to take; to get in *or* into; to get on; to insert; to drive in; to send in; to call in. *On n'entre pas!* no admittance!
†**Entre-rails,** *s.m.* (*rail.*) space between the rails, gauge, four-foot way, four-foot, four-feet (*seven feet or so, on the broad-gauge lines*)
Entre-regarder (S'), Entre-regretter (S'), Entre-répondre (S'), &c. to ... (*V.* **Regarder, Regretter,** &c., &c.) each other
Entre-sabords, *s.m.* (*nav.*) interval between the ports
Entre-saluer (S'), Entre-secourir (S'), &c. to ... (*V.* **Saluer, Secourir,** &c.) each other
Entresol, *s.m.* (*a suite of low rooms between the ground-floor and the first floor*) entresol, mezzanine floor [brows
Entre-sourcils, *s.m.* space between the eye-
Entre-soutenir (S'), Entre-suivre (S'), &c. to ... (*V.* **Soutenir, Suivre,** &c.) each
†**Entre-taille,** *s.f.* (*engr.*) interline [other
†**Entre-tailler (S'),** *v.r.* (*of horses*) to interfere, to cut [crepane
†**Entre-taillure,** *s.f.* (*vet.*) cutting, crepance,
Entre-temps, *s.m.* interval, meantime, meanwhile
Entretènement, *s.m.* (*old*) *V.* **Entretien**
Entreteneur, *s.m.* keeper (*of a woman*)
Entretenir, *v.a.* to hold, to hold *or* keep together; to keep up; to maintain; to sustain; to support; to keep; to feed; to keep alive; to keep in repair; to keep in; to preserve; to converse with, to have a conversation with, to talk with, to speak to; to cherish; to entertain; to indulge in
S'—, *v.r.* to hold together; to keep up; to keep *or* maintain *or* supply oneself; to be kept up *or* maintained *or* sustained *or* supported *or* preserved; to keep; to feed; to subsist; to keep *or* be kept in repair; to converse, to talk, to speak [—*e,* kept woman
Entretenu, e, *part. of* **Entretenir.** *Femme*
Entretien, *s.m.* keeping in repair; maintenance; support; keeping; living, livelihood; dress; conversation, talk; discourse; communication; conference

Entre-tisser, *v.a.* to interweave
Entre-tissu, e, *adj.* interwoven
Entretoile, *s.f.* cut-work, open-work
Entretoise, *s.f.* (*tech.*) intertie, interduce, tie-piece, cross-piece, cross-bar, transom
Entre-toucher (S'), Entre-tromper (S'), Entre-tuer (S'), &c. to ... (*V.* **Toucher, Tromper, Tuer,** &c.) each other
Entre-voies, *s.f.* (*rail.*) space between the lines, six-foot way, six-foot, six-feet
Entrevoir, *v.a.* to see partly, to see but little, to see imperfectly *or* indistinctly *or* dimly, to only just see, to catch *or* have a glimpse of; to catch sight of; to perceive; to discover imperfectly; to have an imperfect idea *or* notion of; to see through; to foresee
S'—, *v.r.* to see each other, to have an interview, to meet; to visit each other; to be seen partly, &c., &c.; to peep; to be foreseen
Entrevous, *s.m.* (*build.*) interjoist
Entrevue, *s.f.* interview, meeting
Entr'exciter (S'), Entre-exhorter (S'), Entr'honorer (S'), Entre-injurier (S'), &c. to ... (*V.* **Exciter, Exhorter,** &c., &c.)
†**Entripaillé, e,** *adj.* swag-bellied [each other
†**Entripailler (S'),** *v.r.* to guttle, to feed like a hog, to batten
Entr'obliger (S'), Entr'offenser (S'), &c. to ... (*V.* **Obliger, Offenser,** &c.) each other
Entropion, *s.m.* (*med.*) entropium, entropion
Entr'ouvert, e, *adj.* half-open, ajar, on the jar; gaping, yawning; (*of horses*) shoulder-pitched
Entr'ouverture, *s.f.* (*vet.*) shoulder-pitch
Entr'ouvrir, *v.a.* to open a little, to half-open; to rend, to open; to put ajar [open; to be ajar
S'—, *v.r.* to half-open; to gape, to yawn; to
Entrure, *s.f.* (*agr.*) depth of the furrow
Entr'user (S'), *v.r.* to wear each other out
Enturbané, e, *adj.* turbaned
Enture, *s.f.* cut, incision (*for grafting*); pegs; scarf, scarf joint; knot
Énucléation, *s.f.* enucleation
Énucléer, *v.a.* to enucleate [*adj.* enumerating
Énuméra-teur, trice, *s.m.f.* enumerator; —
Énumérati-f, ve, *adj.* enumerative
Énumération, *s.f.* enumeration
Énumérer, *v.a.* to enumerate
Énurésie, *s.f.* (*med.*) enuresis
Envahir, *v.a.* to invade; to overrun; to overspread, to spread over; to overgrow; to break in upon; to usurp; to encroach on; to seize upon, to grasp; to fill; to absorb
Envahissement, *s.m.* invasion; overrunning; encroachment; usurpation
Envahisseur, *s.m.* invader; — *adj.m.* invading; encroaching [with mud *or* silt
Envasement, *s.m.* filling up *or* choking up
Envaser, *v.a.* to fill *or* choke up with mud *or* silt, to imbed in mud, to silt up, to silt; to puddle
S'—, *v.r.* to be filled *or* choked up with mud *or* silt, to silt up; to stick in mud, to become imbedded in mud *or* silt [ing (*of hay or grass*)
†**Enveillotage, Enveillotement,** *s.m.* cock-
†**Enveilloter,** *v.a.* to cock (*hay or grass*)
Enveloppe, *s.f.* envelope; wrapper; cover, covering; case, casing; shell; peel; (*anat.*) coat; (*of the eye*) tunic; (*fig.*) exterior, appearance; skin [ing, wrapping
Enveloppement, *s.m.* envelopment, envelop-
Envelopper, *v.a.* to envelop; to wrap, to wrap up; to fold up; to shroud; to muffle, to muffle up; to cover; to disguise; to hide; to hem in; to surround; to involve; to entangle; to beset; to invest [— *adj.* wrapping; casing
Enveloppeu-r, se, *s.m.f.* wrapper; caser;
Envenimement, *s.m.* envenoming; irritation; exasperation [irritate; to exasperate
Envenimer, *v.a.* to envenom; to inflame; to
S'—, *v.r.* to be envenomed *or* &c.; to fester;
Envenimeu-r, se, *s.m.f.* envenomer [to rankle
Enverger, *v.a.* to wicker [yards
Enverguer, *v.a.* (*nav.*) to bend (*the sails*) to the

Envergure, *s.f.* span (of the wings); (*nav.*) bending (*of sails*); square (*of a sail*); length of the yards. *D'—*, (*of a bird's or insect's wings*) from tip to tip, (*of the bird or insect itself*) from tip to tip of the wings

Envers, *prep.* towards; to. *— et contre tous*, against each and all, against all men, against the whole world, in spite of everybody, through thick and thin

Envers, *s.m.* wrong side; under side; reverse; back. *A l'—*, on the wrong side; the wrong side outwards; inside out; upside down; wrong, all wrong; deranged; upset; beside oneself. *Avoir l'esprit* or *la tête à l'—*, to be wrong-headed; to be crack-brained; to have lost o.'s wits; to be all upset; to be beside oneself. *Mettre l'esprit* or *la tête à l'— à*, to turn the brain of

Envi (A l'), *prep.* in emulation (of); *— adv.* emulously, with emulation, in emulation of each other, vying with each other; eagerly

Envi, *s.m.* (*at play*) *V.* **Renvi**

Enviable, *adj.* enviable, to be envied

Envie, *s.f.* envy; inclination; wish, desire, mind; want; longing; fancy; whim; liversick, flaw, hangnail; birth-mark, mother-spot, mole, nævus. *— de dormir*, sleepiness. *— de vomir*, sickness (*of stomach*), nausea. *Avoir — de*, to be inclined to, to have an inclination *or* a desire *or* a mind to; to want; to feel disposed to; to wish for, to wish to have, to wish. *Avoir — de boire, dormir, manger, vomir*, to feel thirsty, sleepy, hungry, sick. *Avoir — de pleurer*, to feel as if one would cry. *Brûler* or *mourir d'— de*, to long to *or* for, to have a desperate longing for. *Faire —*, to be tempting; to excite envy. *Faire — à*, to take the fancy of. *Passer son —*, to gratify o.'s desire. *Porter — à*, to envy. *Si l'— m'en prend*, if I feel inclined to it

†**Envieillir,** *v.a.n.* (*old*) *V.* **Vieillir**

Envier, *v.a.* to envy, to be envious of; to grudge; to wish for, to desire, to covet, to long for; (*old*) to refuse, to deny

Envieu-x, se, *adj.s.* envious; envious person. *Se faire des —*, to excite envy [smelling of wine

Enviné, e, *adj.* saturated (*or* soaked) with *or*

Environ, *prep. adv.* about; thereabouts

Environnement, *s.m.* environment

Environner, *v.a.* to environ, to surround, to encompass, to encircle, to beset, to enclose, to stand (*or* be) round *or* about

Environs, *s.m.pl.* environs, neighbourhood, vicinity, neighbouring places, adjacent parts, country round

Envisager, *v.a.* to look in the face of, to face, to look at; to consider, to view, to look upon

S'—, *v.r.* to look at each other; to consider *or* view oneself; (*of things*) to be looked at *or* &c.

Envoi, *s.m.* sending; expedition; thing *or* article sent; consignment; remittance; parcel, package, goods; goods forwarded *or* to be forwarded; message; (*liter.*) envoy. *Lettre d'—*, letter of advice

Envoiler (S'), *v.r.* (*of metals*) to warp, to bend

Envoilure, *s.f.* warping, bend, bent

Envoisiné, e, *adj.* *V.* **Avoisiné**

Envoisiner, *v.a.* to surround with neighbours

Envoler (S'), *v.r.* to fly away *or* off *or* up; to fly about; to fly; to fleet; to vanish, to disappear; to escape

Envoûtement, *s.m.* magical charm

Envoûter, *v.a.* to throw a spell on

Envoye, *s.m.* slow-worm, blind-worm

Envoyé, *s.m.* envoy, messenger, delegate, deputy

Envoyer, *v.a.* to send; to forward; to despatch; to transmit; to emit; to commit; to give; to throw, to shy; to address; to convey; (*pop.*) to rail at, to banter, to chaff; to cut; to hit. *— chercher, — paitre, — promener*, &c., *V.* **Chercher, Paître, Promener,** &c. *— dire*, to send word. *Envoyez!* (*nav.*) alee!

S'—, *v.r.* to send oneself; to send to each other; to be sent *or* &c. [despatching

Envoyeu-r, se, *s.m.f.* sender; *— adj.* sending,

Enzoot-ie, -ique, -iquement. *V.* page 3, § 1

Éocène, *adj. m.f.*, *s.m.* (*geol.*) eocene

Éolide, *s.f.* (*mollusc*) eolis, æolis

Éolien, ne, *adj. s.* Æolian, Eolian

Éolien, *s.m.* Æolic *or* Eolic (*dialect*)

Éoli-harpe, *s.f.* Æolian harp

Éolipyle, *s.m.* (*phys.*) æolipile, eolipile; smoke-driving apparatus

Éolique, *adj.* Æolic, Eolic [driving apparatus

Éon, *s.m.* eon

Épacris, *s.f.* (*bot.*) epacris

Épactal, e, *adj.* (*astr.*) epactal

Épacte, *s.f.* (*astr.*) epact

†**Épagneul, e,** *s.m.f. adj.* spaniel

Épais, se, *adj.* thick; large; big; dull; heavy; gross; profound [thick, thickly

Épais, *s.m.* thickness; thick part; *— adv.*

Épaisseur, *s.f.* thickness; density; thick part; breadth; depth; dulness

Épaissir, *v.a.* to thicken; *— v.n.*, **S'—**, *v.r.* to thicken, to become *or* grow *or* get thick; to get large; to grow *or* get stout; to get dull *or* heavy

Épaississement, *s.m.* thickening; thickness

Épamprage, Épamprement, *s.m.* pruning (*a vine*); mowing off *or* feeding off (*a corn-field*)

Épamprer, *v.a.* to prune (*a vine*); to mow off *or* to feed off (*a corn-field*)

Épanchement, *s.m.* outpouring; overflowing, overflow; outburst; effusion; opening; discharge; extravasation

Epancher, *v.a.* to pour out; to spill; to shed; to spread; to open; to disclose; to vent; to discharge; to extravasate

S'—, *v.r.* to pour itself out, to overflow; to open o.'s heart, to unbosom oneself; to be spilt *or* &c.; to spread itself, to spread; to open; to be extravasated

Épanchoir, *s.m.* outlet, drain

Épandage, *s.m.* spreading (*of manure*)

Épandre, *v.a.* *V.* **Répandre**

Épanneler, *v.a.* (*tech.*) to cant

Épanorthose, *s.f.* (*rhet.*) epanorthosis

Epanoui, e, *part. adj.* expanded; expansive; full-blown, blown; wide open; cheerful, jolly, beaming with joy

Épanouir, *v.a.*, **S'—**, *v.r.* to expand; to blow, to open; to brighten; to cheer, to gladden

Épanouissement, *s.m.* blowing, opening; expansion; brightening. *— de rate*, cheerfulness, joy, mirth, merriment, hearty laugh

Éparcet, Éparcette, *V.* **Esparcet**

Éparchie, *s.f.* eparchy

Éparer (S'), *v.r.* (*old*) *V.* **Ruer**

†**Épargne,** *s.f.* economy; saving; (*old*) treasury

†**Épargner,** *v.a.n.* to save; to economize; to husband; to lay by; to spare; to be sparing of; to grudge

†**Éparpillement,** *s.m.* scattering, dispersion

†**Éparpiller,** *v.a.* to scatter, to disperse; to fritter away, to squander

S'—, *v.r.* to get (*or* be) scattered about, to disperse; to divide o.'s attention; to be divided

Éparque, *s.m.* eparch

Épars, e, *adj.* scattered, dispersed; straggling; sparse, thin; dishevelled, loose

Éparvin, *s.m.* (*vet.*) spavin [amazement

Épatage, *s.m.*, **Épate,** *s.f.* (*pop.*) dash, fuss;

Épaté, e, *adj.* broad-footed; broad, wide; flat; (*of noses*) flat, pug; (*of glasses*) with a broken foot; (*pop.*) struck all of a heap, dumbfounded

Épatement, *s.m.* flatness; (*pop.*) amazement, dumbfounding

Épater, *v.a.* to break the foot of (*a glass*); to flatten; to widen; (*pop.*) to strike all of a heap, to stun, to astonish, to amaze, to dumbfound, to dazzle; to cow; to take up short, to give a clincher

S'—, *v.r.* to sprawl; to fall plump; to weigh (upon); to get broken at the foot; to be flattened; to get wider

Épaufrure, *s.f.* chipping [tened; to get wider

Épaulard, *s.m.* (*fish*) grampus, orc, ork
Épaule, *s.f.* shoulder; (*fort.*) epaule. *Par dessus l'*—, (*fig.*) over the left shoulder; contemptuously. *Marcher des —s*, to slouch. *Porter sur les —s*, (*fig.*) to be tired of
Épaulé, e, *part. of* **Épauler.** *Bête —e*, animal with a sprain in the shoulder; worn-out animal; (*pers.*) regular fool, stupid ass; bitch of a woman
Epaulée, *s.f.* push *or* shove with the shoulder, shouldering; (*butch.*) fore-quarter (of mutton) without the shoulder. *Par —s*, by fits and starts, by snatches
Épaulement, *s.m.* (*carp.*, *mach.*) shoulder; (*fort.*) epaulment, epaulement, side-work, earthwork, breast-work; rampart; breast-wall
Épauler, *v.a.* to break *or* dislocate *or* sprain the shoulder of, to splay; to bring (*o.'s gun*) to the shoulder; to press (*the butt-end*) against the shoulder; (*fig.*) to support, to back, to assist, to help; (*mil.*) to protect *or* cover by an epaulment
S'—, *v.r.* to break *or* dislocate *or* sprain its shoulder; to be splayed *or* &c.; to support *or* &c. each other; (*mil.*) to protect oneself by an epaulment; to rest
Épaulette, *s.f.* shoulder-piece; shoulder-strap; (*mil.*) epaulet, epaulette [plate, epauliere
Épaulière, *s.f.* brace; (*of anc. armour*) shoulder-
Épaulu, e, *adj.* (*jest.*) broad-shouldered
Épave, *adj.* stray, strayed; — *s.f.*, **—s,** *s.f.pl.* stray; waif, waifs; wreck, wrecks, wreckage,
Épeautre, *s.m.f.* spelt, German wheat [sea-ware
Épée, *s.f.* sword; steel; swordsman; military profession. — *d'assaut*, fencing-sword. — *de chevet*, (*fig.*) advice-friend, adviser; pillow-companion, constant companion; favourite theme, hobby. — *de combat*, duelling-sword. *Combat à l'*—, sword-fight. *Coup d'*—, *V.* **Coup.** *C'est un coup d'— dans l'eau*, it is beating the air, it is an unsuccessful attempt. *L'— à la main*, sword in hand. *L'— dans les reins*, hard, close. *Mettre l'— à la main*, to draw the sword. *Passer au fil de l'*—, to put to the sword. *Se battre à l'*—, to fight with swords. — *de mer*, sword-fish [witwall
Épeiche, *s.f.* (*bird*) great spotted woodpecker,
Épeichette, *s.f.* (*bird*) lesser spotted woodpecker, crank-bird, hickwall
Épeire, *s.f.* epeira (*kind of spider*)
Épeler, *v.a.* to spell
Épellation, *s.f.* spelling
Épenthèse, *s.f.* (*gram.*) epenthesis
Épenthétique, *adj.* (*gram.*) epenthetic
Épépiner, *v.a.* to take the pips out of (*a fruit*)
Éperdu, e, *adj.* distracted; bewildered; dismayed; desperate
Éperdument, *adv.* distractedly; desperately
Éperlan, *s.m.* (*fish*) smelt
Épernay, *s.m.* Epernay champagne (wine)
Éperon, *s.m.* (*for riding, of birds or &c., of mountains, bot., anat., fort.*, &c.) spur; (*of game-cocks*) gaffle; (*of the eyes*) crow's foot, wrinkles; (*arch.*) buttress; pier; breakwater; starling; (*nav.*) cut-water, head, beak-head, prow, stem; (*of an ironclad ship*) spur; (*anc. nav.*) rostrum; (*rock*) breaker
Éperonner, *v.a.* to spur; to spur on; to excite, to stimulate; to gaffle; (*the eyes*) to wrinkle [spurs
Éperonnerie, *s.f.* spur-making, spur-trade;
Éperonnier, *s.m.* spurrier, spur-maker; (*bird*) polyplectron, Indian peacock
Éperonnière, *s.f.* spur-leather; (*bot.*) lark-spur; columbine; toad-flax
Éperverie, *s.f.* art of training sparrow-hawks, hawking, falconry [sweep-net
Épervier, *s.m.* sparrow-hawk, hawk; (*fish.*)
Épervière, *s.f.* (*bot.*) hawkweed
Épervin, *s.m.* *V.* **Éparvin**
Éphèbe, *s.m.* (*Gr. antiq.*) ephebus [tail, sea-grape
Éphèdre, *s.f.* (*bot.*) ephedra, shrubby horse-
Éphélide, *s.f.* (*med.*) ephelis, spot, freckel; scorch; colouration of the skin
Éphémère, *adj.* ephemeral; — *s.m.f.* (*insect*) ephemera, ephemeran, day-fly; — *s.f.* (*bot.*) spider-wort
Éphéméride, *s.f.* ephemeris (*pl.* ephemerides)
Éphémérine, *s.f.* (*insect, and bot.*) *V.* **Éphémère**
Éphésien, ne, *adj. s.* Ephesian
Éphialte, *s.m.* (*med.*) ephialtes, nightmare
Éphidrose, *s.f.* (*med.*) ephidrosis
Éphod, *s.m.* (*Jewish antiquity*) ephod
Éphorat, *s.m.* ephoralty
Éphore, *s.m.* ephor
Éphorie, *s.f.* ephoralty
Éphorique, *adj.* ephoral
Épi, *s.m.* ear (*of corn*, &c.); spike; cluster; top; rough tuft of hair, topknot; (*of horses*) feather; (*surg.*) spica. — *d'eau*, (*bot.*) pondweed
Épiage, *s.m.* (*agr.*), **Épiation,** *s.f.* (*bot.*) earing
Épicarpe, *s.m.* (*bot.*) epicarp
Épice, *s.f.* spice; (*obsolete*) court-fees. *Chère* —, (*fig.*) dear article. *Fine* —, (*fig.*) sharp blade. *Pain d'*—, gingerbread
Épicé, e, *adj.* spiced, spicy, seasoned, hot; biting; dear, high-priced
Épicéa, *s.m.* *V.* **Picéa**
Épicemar, *s.m. pop. for* **Épicier**
Épicène, *adj.m.f.*, *s.m.* (*gram.*) epicene
Épicer, *v.a.* to spice, to season; to charge high, to lay it on; (*pop.*) to rail at, to banter, to chaff; to slander
Épicerie, *s.f.* grocery; spices, spicery; grocery-business *or* trade; grocer's shop; grocers; vulgar fellows
‡Épichérème, *s.m.* (*log.*) epichirema
Épici-er, ère, *s.m.f.* grocer; petty tradesman; vulgar fellow; — *adj.* vulgar
Épicrâne, *s.m.* (*anat.*) epicranium
Épicrise, *s.f.* (*med.*) epicrisis
Épicure, *s.m.* Epicurus
Épicuréisme, *s.m.* (*old*) *V.* **Épicurisme**
Épicurien, ne, *adj.* Epicurean; — *s.m.f.* Epicurean; epicure [(*sensuality*) epicurism
Épicurisme, *s.m.* Epicureanism, Epicurism;
Épicycle, *s.m.* (*astr.*) epicycle
Épicycloïdal, e, *adj.* epicycloidal
Épicycloïde, *s.f.* (*geom.*) epicycloid
Épidaurien, ne, *adj. s.* Epidaurian
Épidémie, *s.f.* epidemic
Épidémio-graphie, -graphique, -logie, -logique. *V.* page 3, § 1
Épidémique, *adj.* epidemic, zymotic
Épidémiquement, *adv.* epidemically
Épiderme, *s.m.* (*anat.*, &c.) epidermis, epiderm, cuticle, scarf-skin
Épidermique, *adj.* epidermic
Épidote, *s.m.* (*min.*) epidote
Épié, e, *part. adj.* eared, &c. (*V.* **Épier,** *v.n.*, *v.a.*); in ear, awny, awned; spicate, spicated, (*of a dog*) with long hair hanging over his eyes; (*of a dog's tail*) ending in a feather
Épier, *v.n.* to ear; — *v.a.* to spy, to watch; to listen to; to pry into
Épierrage, Épierrement, *s.m.* clearing of stones
Épierrer, *v.a.* to clear of stones
Épieu, *s.m.* boar-spear, hunting-spear; heavy weapon, weapon [eavesdropper, Paul Pry
Épieu-r, se, *s.m.f.* spier, watcher, listener,
Épigastralgie, *s.f.* (*med.*) epigastralgia
Épigastralgique, *adj.* (*med.*) epigastralgic
Épigastre, *s.m.* (*anat.*) epigastrium
Épigastrique, *adj.* (*anat.*) epigastric
Épigastrocèle, *s.f.* (*med.*) epigastrocele
Épigenèse, *s.f.* (*physiol.*) epigenesis
Épiglotte, *s.f.* (*anat.*) epiglottis
Épiglottique, *adj.* (*anat.*) epiglottic
Épiglottite, *s.f.* (*med.*) epiglottitis
Épigrammat-ique, -iquement. *V.* page 3, § 1
Épigrammatiser, *v.n.a.* to epigrammatize
Épigrammatiste, *s.m.f.* epigrammatist
Épigramme, *s.f.* epigram
Épigraphe, *s.f.* epigraph
Épigraph-ie, -ique. *V.* page 3, § 1

Épigyne, Épigynique, *adj.* (*bot.*) epigynous
Épilateur, *s.m. V.* **Épilatoire**
Épilati-f, ve, *adj.* depilatory, epilatory
Épilation, *s.f.* depilation
Épilatoire, *s.m.* (*thing*) hair-destroyer, depilatory, epilatory; — *adj.* depilatory, epilatory
Épilep-sie (*s.f.*), **-tique** (*adj. s.m.f.*), *V.* page 3, § 1
Épiler, *v.a.* to depilate, to strip of hair, to pull the hair *or* hairs off; to take out o.'s grey hair
Épileu-r, se, *s.m.f.* (*pers.*) depilator
†**Épillet,** *s.m.* (*bot.*) spikelet
Épilobe, *s.m.* (*bot.*) willow-herb
Épilogage, *s.m.*, **Épilogation,** *s.f.* hair-splitting, fault-finding, nibbling, carping, criticizing
Épilogisme, *s.m.* epilogism
Épilogue, *s.m.* epilogue
Épiloguer, *v.n.a.* to split hairs; to find fault (with), to nibble (at), to carp (at), to criticize, to censure
Épilogueu-r, se, *s.m.f.* hair-splitter, fault-finder, nibbler, carper, criticizer; — *adj.* hair-splitting; fault-finding, nibbling, carping
Épiloir, *s.m.* tweezers
Épimaque, *s.m.* plume-bird
Épimède, *s.m.* (*bot.*) barrenwort
Épinaie, *s.f.* brake, thorn-bush, spinny
Épinard, *s.m.* (*bot.*), **—s,** *s.m.pl.* (*cook.*) spinach, spinage; spinach-green (*colour*). *A graine d'—s,* (*of epaulets,* &c.) with large bullion. *Graine d'—s,* (*slang*) epaulets of a superior officer;
Épinarde, *s.f. V.* **Épinoche**
Épinçage, Épincetage, *s.m.* burling
Épincer, Épinceler, Épinceter, *v.a.* to burl
Épincette, *s.f.* burling-tweezers
Épinceu-r, se, Épinceteu-r, se, *s.m.f.* burler
Épinçoir, *s.m.* pavier's hammer
Épine, *s.f.* thorn; spine. — *blanche,* hawthorn, May, white thorn. — *dorsale* or *du dos,* spine, backbone. — *rouge,* red American larch, hackmatack, tamarac. — *-vinette,* barberry. *Tirer une — du pied à,* to take a thorn out of ...'s side
Épiner, *v.a.* to set with thorns
Épinette, *s.f.* (*old mus. instr.*) spinet; (*for fowls*) coop; (*bot.*) (— *blanche*) hemlock spruce, (— *rouge*) red American larch, hackmatack, tamarac; (*fish.*) thorn hook
Épineu-x, se, *adj.* thorny; spiny; (*fig.*) knotty, intricate, difficult, captious, ticklish; (*nav.*) dangerous. *Pomme —se,* (*bot.*) stramony, thorn-apple
Épingard, Épingare, *s.m.* (*old artil.*) one-pounder
Épingle, *s.f.* pin; scarf-pin, breast-pin; peg; **—s,** *pl.* pins, &c.; present, gratuity, douceur, premium, bonus; pin-money; (*game*) push-pin. — *de cravate,* scarf-pin, breast-pin. *Être tiré à quatre —s,* to look as if one came out of a bandbox; to be precise *or* fine-spun. *Tirer son — du jeu,* to get out of a bad job *or* out of it (skilfully *or* in time), to back out
Épinglé, e, *part. adj.* pinned; (*of fabrics*) Terry
Épingler, *v.a.* to pin; to prick; to clean
Épinglerie, *s.f.* pin-manufactory
Épinglette, *s.f.* (*mil.*) pricker; (*artil.*) priming-wire
Épingli-er, ère, *s.m.f.* pin-maker
Épinier, *s.m.* thorn-bush, spinny; (*bird*) siskin
Épinière, *adj.f.* (*anat.*) spinal; — *s.f.* (*pop.*) hawthorn, May
Épinoche, *s.m.* best coffee; (*fish*) stickleback
Épipactide, *s.f.* (*bot.*) helleborine
Épiphanie, *s.f.* Epiphany
Épiphénomène, *s.m.* (*med.*) accidental symptom
Épiphonème, *s.m.* (*rhet.*) epiphonema
Épiphora, *s.m.* (*med.*) epiphora, watery eye
Épiphore, *s.f.* (*gram.*) epiphora
Épiphyse, *s.f.* (*anat.*) epiphysis
Épiphyte, *s.m.* (*bot.*) epiphyte; — *adj.* epiphytic
Épiphyt-ie, -ique. *V.* page 3, § 1
Épiplocèle, *s.f.* (*med.*) epiplocele
Épiploïque, *adj.* (*anat.*) epiploic
Épiploïte, *s.f.* (*med.*) epiploitis
Épiploon, *s.m.* (*anat.*) epiploon, omentum
Épique, *adj.* epic; heroic

Épirote, *adj. s.* Epirote
‡**Épischèse,** *s.f.* (*med.*) epischesis
Épiscopal, e, *adj.* episcopal; Episcopalian
Épiscopal, *s.m.* Episcopalian
Épiscopalement, *adv.* episcopally
Épiscopat, *s.m.* episcopate; episcopacy; bishopric; bishops
Épiscopiser, *v.n.* to aspire to a bishopric; to play the bishop
Épisode, *s.m.* episode
Épisod-ique, -iquement. *V.* page 3, § 1
Épispastique, *adj.m.f., s.m.* (*med.*) epispastic
Épisperme, *s.m.* (*bot.*) episperm, seed-coat
Épisser, *v.a.* (*nav.*) to splice
Épissoir, *s.m.* (*nav.*) marling-spike, fid
Épissure, *s.f.* (*nav.*) splice
Épistaxis, *s.f.* (*med.*) epistaxis
Épistolaire, *adj.m.f., s.m.* epistolary; letter-writer
Épistoli-er, ère, *s.m.f.* epistolizer, letter-writer; — *s.m.* (*Cath. lit.*) lectionary
Épistolographe, *s.m.* epistolographer
Épistolograph-ie, -ique. *V.* page 3, § 1
Épistrophe, *s.f.* (*rhet.*) epistrophe
Épistyle, *s.m.* (*arch.*) epistyle
Épitaphe, *s.f.* epitaph
Épitase, *s.f.* (*liter., med.*) epitasis
Épithalame, *s.m.* epithalamium, epithalamy, wedding *or* nuptial song
Épithélial, e, *adj.* (*anat.*) epithelial
Épithélium, *s.m.* (*anat.*) epithelium
Épithème, *s.m.* (*pharm.*) epithem
Épithète, *s.f.* epithet
Épithétique, *adj.* epithetic
Épitoge, *s.f.* shoulder-knot; (*obsolete*) cap, coif; (*Rom. antiquity*) epitogium, epitoge (*cassock*)
Épitomé, *s.m.* epitome
Épître, *s.f.* epistle; letter, missive
Épitrope, *s.f.* (*rhet.*) epitrope
Épizoaire, *s.m.* (*zool.*) epizoan, epizoon (*pl.* epizoa); — *adj.* epizoal, epizoic
Épizootie, *s.f.* epizooty, epizootic, murrain
Épizoot-ique, -iquement. *V.* page 3, § 1
†**Éplaigner,** *v.a.* to raise the nap of, to tease *or* dress (*cloth*)
†**Éplaigneu-r, se,** *s.m.f.* cloth-dresser, teaseler
Éploration, *s.f.* lamentation, lament, wailing, tearfulness
Éploré, e, *adj.* in tears, tearful, weeping, distressed
Éployé, e, *adj.* displayed, expanded, spread
Épluchage, *s.m.* picking; scrutinizing, sifting
Épluchement, *s.m.* picking, cleaning
Éplucher, *v.a.* to pick, to clean; to pick out; to pare; to scrutinize, to scan, to sift
S'—, *v.r.* to clean itself; to examine oneself; (*of things*) to be picked *or* cleaned *or* &c.
Éplucheu-r, se, *s.m.f.* picker; cleaner; fault-finder, hair-splitter
Épluchoir, *s.m.* paring-knife
Épluchures, *s.f.pl.* pickings, parings; orts; refuse
Épode, *s.f.* epode
Épointage, *s.m.* blunting
Épointé, e, *adj.* without a point, with broken point, blunt-topped; (*of a horse*) hipshot; (*of a dog*) with a broken thigh
Épointement, *s.m.* bluntness
Épointer, *v.a.* to break the point of, to blunt
S'—, *v.r.* to break at the point, to get blunt-topped
†**Épointiller,** *v.a. V.* **Épincer**
Épointure, *s.f.* hip-shot
Épois, *s.m.pl.* (*hunt.*) trochings
Éponge, *s.f.* sponge; (*bot.*) rose-gall; (*pop.*) drunkard. *Passer l'— sur,* to sponge; to blot out, to obliterate; to forgive, to forget, to overlook, to say no more about
Éponger, *v.a.* to sponge; to sponge up; to dab, to mop; to glaze (*gingerbread*)
Épongeur, *s.m.* (*of public carriages*) waterman
Épongier, *s.m.* spongeman
†**Épontille,** *s.f.* (*nav.*) stanchion, prop
†**Épontiller,** *v.a.* (*nav.*) to prop, to shore
Éponyme, *adj. s.* eponymous; eponym
Épopée, *s.f.* epopee, epic poem *or* poetry; series of brilliant exploits

Époque, *s.f.* epoch; era; time; period; date; (*med.*) course, term. *Faire* —, to form *or* mark [an era

Époucé, e, *adj.* thumbless

Époudrer, *v.a.* (*old*) *V.* **Épousseter**

Époufé, e, *adj.* out of breath, breathless

Épouffer (S'), *v.r.* (*old*) to get out of breath; to steal away. — *de rire, V.* **Pouffer**

†**Épouiller,** *v.a.* to louse, to free from lice

Époularder, *v.a.* to pick, to clean (*tobacco leaves*)

Époumoner, *v.a.* to tire the lungs of, to exhaust

S'—, *v.r.* to tire *or* fatigue o.'s lungs, to exhaust oneself; to vociferate

†**Épousailles,** *s.f.pl.* espousals, wedding

Épouse, *s.f.* spouse, wife, consort, (*jest.*) rib

Épousée, *s.f.* bride

Épouser, *v.a.* to marry; to wed; to espouse, to embrace, to take up; to take to; to adopt

S'—, *v.r.* to marry each other

Épouseur, *s.m.* intended; man to marry, husband; marrying man; marrier

Épouseuse, *s.f.* intended; girl *or* woman to marry, wife; marrying woman; marrier

Époussetage, *s.m.* dusting, whisking

Épousseter, *v.a.* to dust, to whisk, to beat the dust out of; (*fig.*) to whack, to thwack, to [bang

Époussette, *s.f.* duster, whisk

Épouti, *s.m.* filth (*in cloth*) [burl

Époutier, Époutir, *v.a.* to pick, to clean, to

Époutieu-r, se, *s.m.f.* picker, cleaner, burler

Époutissage, *s.m.* picking, cleaning, burling

Épouvantable, *adj.* frightful, dreadful, terrific, terrible, tremendous, appalling, shocking, horrible, abominable

Épouvantablement, *adv.* frightfully, dreadfully, terribly, tremendously, shockingly, horribly, abominably [(*bird*) black tern, scarecrow

†**Épouvantail,** *s.m.* scarecrow; bugbear;

Épouvante, *s.f.* fright, terror

Épouvantement, *s.m.* (*old*) terror, affright

Épouvanter, *v.a.* to frighten, to scare, to terrify, to horrify

S'—, *v.r.* to take fright, to be frightened *or* &c.

Époux, *s.m.* husband, spouse, consort; —, *pl.* husband and wife, married couple, couple, pair

Épreindre, *v.a.* to express, to press, to press out,

S'—, *v.r.* to be expressed *or* &c. [to squeeze out

Épreinte, *s.f.* (*med.*) tenesmus, straining; gripes; (*fig.*) pressure

Éprendre, *v.a.* to make (...) fall in love, to smite, to charm, to captivate, to fascinate, to enamour [ten, to become enamoured

S'—, *v.r.* to fall in love, to be taken *or* smit-

Épreuve, *s.f.* trial; proof; test; experiment; ordeal; probation; examination; vote; (*in races*) heat; (*engr., photography*) proof; print; (*print.*) proof, proof-sheet; revise. *A l'— de* ..., proof to *or* against ..., ...-proof; above ... *A toute —, à l'—,* well-tried, true, trusty, faithful, devoted; unshaken; unwearied, untiring; unchangeable; proof against anything. *Seconde —,* (*print.*) revise. *Troisième —,* second revise. *Faire l'— de, mettre à l'—,* to make a trial of, to try, to test, to put to the test. *A l'—,* (*misused for* "à l'essai") *V.* **Essai**

Épris, e, *adj.* in love, taken (with), smitten, charmed, captivated, fascinated, enamoured

Éprouver, *v.a.* to try; to put to the test; to assay; to experience; to feel; to meet with; to go through, to undergo [to be tried, &c.

S'—, *v.r.* to try *or* &c. oneself *or* each other;

Éprouvette, *s.f.* prover; measurer; gauge; steam-gauge; eprouvette; (*surg.*) probe

Épucer, *v.a.* to flea, to clean from fleas

Épuisable, *adj.* exhaustible

Épuisé, e, *part. adj.* exhausted; drained; wasted; spent; used up; worn out; threadbare; out of print

Épuisement, *s.m.* exhaustion; drainage

Épuiser, *v.a.* to exhaust; to draw; to drain; to waste; to spend; to use up; to work up; to wear out; to eat up, to consume; to dry up; to empty

S'—, *v.r.* to exhaust *or* &c. oneself; to become *or* be exhausted, &c.; to waste; to wear out; to be lost; to sell off, to get out of print

Épuisette, *s.f.* scoop; hand-net; (*fish.*) hoop-net, landing-net

Épulide, Épulie, *s.f.* (*med.*) epulis, gum-boil

Épulons, *s.m.pl.* (*Rom. hist.*) epulones

Épulotique, *adj.m.f., s.m.* (*pharm.*) epulotic

Épura-teur, trice, *s.m.f.* purifier; refiner

Épurati-f, ve, *adj.* purifying; refining

Épuration, *s.f.* purifying; refining; purging, [weeding

Épuratoire, *adj. V.* **Épuratif**

Épure, *s.f.* diagram; working-plan; draught

Épuré, e, *part. adj.* purified, &c. (*V.* **Épurer**);

Épurement, *s.m. V.* **Épuration** [pure

Épurer, *v.a.* to purify; to refine; to clear; to expurgate; to purge, to weed

S'—, *v.r.* to be purified *or* refined; to become more refined; to become pure *or* purer; to [grow finer

Épurge, *s.f.* (*bot.*) caper-spurge

***Équanime,** *adj.* (*obsolete*) equanimous

***Équanimité,** *s.f.* (*obsolete*) equanimity

Équarrir, *v.a.* to square; to kill and skin, to cut up (*horses,* &c.)

Équarrissage, *s.m.* squareness; squaring; killing and skinning, cutting up (*horses,* &c.), knacker's trade. *Bois d'—,* squared timber. *Chantier d'—, clos d'—,* knacker's yard

Équarrissement, *s.m.* squaring

Équarrisseur, *s.m.* horse-slaughterer, knacker

Équarrissoir, *s.m.* squarer; rimer; broach; knacker's knife [Equator

***Équateur,** *s.m.* equator; (*country*) Ecuador,

***Équation,** *s.f.* equation

***Équatorial, e,** *adj.* equatorial; — *s.m.* equatorial, equatorial telescope

***Équatorien, ne,** *adj. s.* Ecuadorean

Équerrage, *s.m.* bevelling, bevel

Équerre, *s.f.* square rule, square; (*of a pipe*) knee. *D'—, en —,* square. *Fausse —,* bevel. *A*

Équerrer, *v.a.* to bevel [*fausse —,* out of square

§**Équestre,** *adj.* equestrian

§**Équiangle,** *adj.* (*geom.*) equiangular

§**Équidifférence,** *s.f.* equidifference

§**Équidifférent, e,** *adj.* equidifferent

§**Équidistance,** *s.f.* equidistance

§**Équidistant, e,** *adj.* equidistant

Équiffle, *s.f.* (*obsolete*) squirt

†**Équignon,** *s.m.* axletree-bar

§**Équilatéral, e, Équilatère,** *adj.* (*geom.*)

Équilboquet, *s.m.* mortise-gauge [equilateral

Équilibre, *s.m.* equilibrium; equipoise, poise; balance [balance

Équilibrer, *v.a.* to equilibrate, to poise, to

Équilibrisme, *s.m.* equilibrism, balancing-

Équilibriste, *s.m.f.* equilibrist, acrobat [tricks

†**Équille,** *s.f.* (*fish*) sand-eel, launce

§**Équimultiple,** *adj.m.f., s.m.* equimultiple

Équin, e, *adj.* equine

Équinoxe, *s.m.* equinox

Équinoxial, e, *adj.* equinoctial

Équipage, *s.m.* equipage; turn-out; carriage; train; equipment, dress; paraphernalia; gear; tackle; implements, machinery, plant, working-stock; (*of horses*) furniture; (*fig.*) situation, plight; (*of a ship*) crew. *Rouler —,* to ride in o.'s carriage, to keep o.'s (*or* a) carriage. *L'— de Jean de Paris,* a brilliant equipage, a Lord Mayor's show

Équipe, *s.f.* train of boats; (*of a boat*) crew; (*of workmen*) gang. *Chef d'—,* foreman, ganger. *Homme d'—,* boatman, rower, oarsman; workman

Équipée, *s.f.* prank, freak, frolic

Équipement, *s.m.* fitting out, outfit; equipment; accoutrement; paraphernalia; equipage; manning; (*of horses*) furniture. *Petit —,* (*mil.*) kit

Équiper, *v.a.* to fit out; to equip; to stock, to furnish, to supply; to man, to appoint; to accoutre; to dress *or* rig out; to ill-treat, to pay [out, to serve out

Équipet, *s.m.* (*nav.*) locker

Équipeur, *s.m.* (*of firelocks*) finisher

Équipollence, *s.f.* (*old*) equipollence

Équipollent, e, *adj.* (*old*) equipollent, equivalent [to be equivalent
Équipoller, *v.a.* (*old*) to balance; — *v.n.* (*old*)
§Équipondérance, *s.f.* equiponderance
§Équipondérant, e, *adj.* equiponderant
§Équisétique, *adj.* (*chem.*) equisetic
Équitable, *adj.* equitable, fair, just
Équitablement, *adv.* equitably, fairly, justly
§Équitant, e, *adj.* (*bot.*) equitant
§Équitation, *s.f.* equitation, riding, horsemanship, equestrianism
Équité, *s.f.* equity, justice
Équivalemment, *adv.* equivalently
Équivalence, *s.f.* equivalence
Équivalent, e, *adj.*, **Équivalent,** *s.m.* equivalent
Équivaloir, *v.n.* to be equivalent
§Équivalve, *adj.* (*of shells*) equivalve
Équivocation, *s.f.* equivocation
Équivoque, *adj.* equivocal, ambiguous; suspicious; doubtful, uncertain, questionable; of doubtful character; — *s.f.* equivocation; ambiguity; play on words, pun; coarse joke; (*paint.*) defect, fault
Équivoquer, *v.n.* to equivocate [make a slip
S'—, *v.r.* to use one word for another, to
Érable, *s.m.* maple, maple-tree. — *à sucre*, sugar-maple. *Sucre d'—*, maple sugar
Éradicati-f, ve, *adj.* eradicative
Éradication, *s.f.* eradication
Éraflement, *s.m.* scratch, graze, grazing
Érafler, *v.a.* to scratch, to graze
Éraflure, *s.f.* scratch, graze
Éragrostide, *s.f.* (*bot.*) eragrostis, love-grass
†Éraillé, e, *part. adj.* frayed; chafed, galled; (*of the eyes*) bloodshot, red; (*of the voice*) rough, husky, hoarse
†Éraillement, *s.m.* fraying, fretting; chafing, galling; roughness, huskiness, hoarseness; (*med.*) eversion; redness
†Érailler, *v.a.*, **S'—,** *v.r.* to fray, to fret; to chafe, to gall; to make *or* become red *or* rough *or* husky *or* hoarse
†Éraillure, *s.f.* fraying, fret; chafing, gall
Érater, *v.a. V.* **Dérater.** *S'—*, to run oneself out of breath
Erbue, *s.f. V.* **Castine**
Ère, *s.f.* era, epoch
Érecteur, *adj.m.*, *s.m.* (*anat.*) erector
Érectile, *adj.* (*anat.*) erectile
Érectilité, *s.f.* (*anat.*) erectility
Érection, *s.f.* erection; raising
Éreintement, *s.m.* cutting up, smashing
Éreinter, *v.a.* to break *or* strain the back of; to tire out, to knock up; to overwork; to overload; to use up; to do up; to wear right out; to exhaust; to spoil entirely; to crush, to smash; to beat unmercifully; to beat all to nothing; to cut to pieces, to cut up; to hiss
S'—, *v.r.* to break *or* strain o.'s back; to tire oneself out, to be knocked up; to overwork oneself, to toil, to drudge; to get *or* be used up *or* &c.; to cut each other up
Éreinteur, *s.m.* slasher, smasher
Érémacausie, *s.f.* (*chem.*) eremacausis
Érémitique, *adj.* hermitical
Érémont, *s.m. V.* **Armon**
Éréné, e, *adj.* (*pop.*) broken-backed; foundered; tired out, knocked up
Érésipèle, *s.m.* (*vulgar*) *V.* **Érysipèle**
Éréth-isme, -istique. *V.* page 3, § 1
Éréthizon, *s.m. V.* **Urson**
Ergo, *adv. s.m.* (*Latin*) "ergo," therefore. —*-glu*, and what then?
Ergot, *s.m.* (*of some birds*) spur; (*of dogs*) dew-claw; (*pharm., vet.*) ergot; (*agr.*) ergot, spur; (*hort.*) dead wood; (*med.*) ergotism; (*pop.*) foot, trotter. *Être sur ses —s*, to assume an air of reserve, to keep o.'s distance; to look big. *Monter* or *se lever sur ses —s*, to ride o.'s high horse
Ergotage, *s.m. V.* **Ergoterie**
Ergoté, e, *adj.* (*of birds*) spurred; (*of dogs*) with dew-claws; (*agr.*) spurred, horned; (*pers.*) shrewd
Ergoter, *v.n.* to cavil, to quibble, to split hairs, to find fault; — *v.a.n.* to cut the dead wood off
Ergoterie, *s.f.* cavilling, quibbling, hair-splitting, fault-finding; cavil, quibble
Ergoteu-r, se, *s.m.f.* caviller, quibbler, hair-splitter, fault-finder; — *adj.* cavilling, quibbling, hair-splitting, fault-finding
Ergotine, *s.f.* (*chem.*) ergotine
Ergotisme, *s.m. V.* **Ergoterie;** (*med.*) ergotism
Éridan, *s.m.* (*astr.*) Eridanus
Ériger, *v.a.* to erect; to raise; to set up; to establish; to institute; to convert
S'—, *v.r.* to set up (for), to set oneself up (for); (*of things*) to be erected *or* &c.
Érigeron, *s.m.* (*bot.*) erigeron, fleabane, fleawort
†Érigne, Érine, *s.f.* (*surg.*) hook
Ériodendron, *s.m.* (*bot.*) eriodendron, wool-tree
Ériomètre, *s.m.* (*phys.*) eriometer
Ermin, *s.m.* customs-duty (*in the Levant*)
Ermine, Erminette. *V.* **Hermine, Herminette**
Ermitage, *s.m.* hermitage; ermitage (wine)
Ermite, *s.m.* hermit; (*zool.*) *V.* **Bernard-l'ermite.** *Pâtés d'—*, dry walnuts
Éroder, *v.a.* to erode, to gnaw, to eat into *or* away
Érodium, *s.m.* (*bot.*) erodium, heron's-bill
Érophile, *s.m. V.* **Drave**
Érosi-f, ve, *adj.* erosive; — *s.m.* erodent
Érosion, *s.f.* erosion
Érot-ique (*adj.m.f.*, *s.m.*), **-iquement.** *V.* page 3, § 1
Érotomanie, *s.f.* (*med.*) erotomania
Erpéto-graphie, -graphique, -logie, -logique, -logiste. *V.* page 3, § 1
Errant, e, *adj.* wandering; roving; rambling; stray, lost; fugitive; erring; erratic; (*of knights*) errant; — *s.m.* (*fig.*) stray *or* lost sheep
Errata, *s.m.* errata; erratum
Erratique, *adj.* erratic
Erre, *s.f.*, **—s,** *pl.* rate; pace; course; way, track; footsteps; fore-quarters. *Aller grand'—*, (*obsolete*) to go very fast
Errements, *s.m.pl.* track, course, way; manner; footsteps; proceedings; vagaries
Errer, *v.n.* to wander; to rove, to ramble, to roam, to stroll; to stray; to err, to be mistaken
Erreur, *s.f.* error; mistake; misreckoning; illusion. —*!* nay! — *n'est pas compte*, misreckoning is no payment. *Être dans l'—*, to be in error, to be mistaken. *Induire en —*, to lead into error, to mislead
Errhin, e, *adj.*, **Errhin,** *s.m.* (*med.*) errhine
Erroné, e, *adj.* erroneous
Erronément, *adv.* erroneously
Ers, *s.m.* (*bot.*) ervum, tare
Erse, *adj.m.f.*, *s.m.* Erse; — *s.f.* (*nav.*) strop
Erseau, *s.m.* (*nav.*) small strop; grommet
Érubescence, *s.f.* erubescence
Érubescent, e, *adj.* erubescent, reddening
Érucage, Érucago, Érucague, *s.f.* (*bot.*) rocket
Érucine, *s.f.* (*chem.*) erucine
Érucique, *adj.* (*chem.*) erucic
Éructation, *s.f.* eructation, belching
Éructer, *v.n.a.* to eructate, to belch
Érudit, e, *adj. s.* learned; erudite; scholar, learned man, learned person
Érudition, *s.f.* erudition, learning, knowledge, scholarship
Érugineu-x, se, *adj.* eruginous
Érupti-f, ve, *adj.* eruptive
Éruption, *s.f.* eruption; breaking out; cutting (*of teeth*)
Érynge, *s.f.*, **Éryngion,** *s.m.* (*bot.*) eryngo
Érysimon, *s.m. V.* **Vélar**
Érysipélateu-x, se, *adj.* erysipelatous
Érysipèle, *s.m.* (*med.*) erysipelas
Érythémateu-x, se, Érythématique, *adj.* (*med.*) erythematous, erythematic
Érythème, *s.m.* (*med.*) erythema
Érythrée, *s.f.* (*bot.*) centaury
Érythrin, *s.m.* (*fish*) erythrinus
Érythrine, *s.f.* (*bot.*) coral-flower, coral-tree; (*chem.*) erythrine
Érythrone, *s.f.* (*bot.*) erythronium, dog-tooth violet
Ès [*contraction of* **En les,** *obsolete except in university degrees*) in the, into the, in, into; at *or* of *or* &c. the, at, of, &c. *Baccalauréat ès-*

lettres, degree of bachelor of arts, B.A. degree. *Bachelier ès-lettres*, bachelor of arts [bolt
†Esbigner (S'), *v.r.* (*pop.*) to be off, to cut, to
Esbrouffe, *s.f.* (*pop.*) fuss, show; bragging, boasting
Esbrouffer, *v.a.* (*pop.*) to dazzle, to astound, to stun, to astonish, to amaze, to dumbfound; to startle, to stagger; to scandalize; to flurry, to flutter; to crush, to kill; to lord it over; to impose upon; to cow, to intimidate; to blow up
S'—, *v.r.* to be dazzled *or* &c.
Esbrouffeu-r, se, *s.m.f.* (*pop.*) fussy *or* showy fellow *or* woman *or* thing, humbug, boaster, braggart, swaggerer, bouncer, flash man *or* woman, low swell; — *adj.* fussy, showy, humbugging, boasting, bragging, swaggering, bouncing, flash
Escabeau, *s.m.*, **Escabelle,** *s.f.* stool; steps. *Déranger les escabelles à*, to put out, to disconcert, to foil, to baffle. *Remuer ses escabelles*, to remove, to change situation
Escabelon, Escablon, *s.m.* pedestal, stand
Escache, *s.f.* (*rid.*) scatch, scatch-mouth [**Chef**
Escadre, *s.f.* (*nav.*) squadron. *Chef d'—*, *V.*
†Escadrille, *s.f.* (*nav.*) small squadron, flotilla
Escadron, *s.m.* (*mil.*) squadron; (*fig.*) troop, set, lot. *Chef d'—*, *V.* **Chef**
Escadronner, *v.n.a.* (*mil.*) to manœuvre; to
Escafe, *s.f.* (*old*) kick [form into squadrons
Escafer, *v.a.n.* (*old*) to kick
†Escafignon, *s.m.* (*pop.*) foot, trotter. *Sentir l'—*, to stink from the feet [escalade
Escalade, *s.f.* climbing over, scaling; (*mil.*)
Escalader, *v.a.* to climb over *or* up, to scale; to ascend, to go up; (*mil.*) to escalade
S'—, *v.r.* to be scaled *or* &c.
Escaladou, Escaladon, *s.m.* winder
Escale, *s.f.* (*nav.*) putting in, stay; harbour, port. *Faire —*, to put in, to touch (at) [in, to touch
Escaler, *v.n.* (*nav.*) to put into harbour, to put
Escalier, *s.m.* staircase; flight of stairs; stairs. — *mécanique*, lift. — *de commandement*, (*nav.*) accommodation-ladder. — *de meunier*, narrow and steep staircase, trap-ladder
Escalin, *s.m.* escalin (*Dutch six-penny piece*)
Escalope, *s.f.* (*cook.*) collop
Escalpe, *s.f.* scalping
Escamotage, *s.m.* juggling, jugglery, juggle, legerdemain, sleight of hand, hocus-pocus, conjuring; trick; filching, prigging
Escamote, *s.f.* juggler's ball
Escamoter, *v.a.* to juggle; to juggle away; to conjure; to filch, to prig, to pilfer, to abstract; to cozen out of; to elude; to get by a trick; (*mil.*) to use lightly
S'—, *v.r.* to be juggled *or* &c.
Escamoteu-r, se, *s.m.f.* juggler, conjurer; light-fingered gentleman *or* lady, filcher, pilferer, pickpocket
Escampative, *s.f.* flight, scampering, running away, bolting, escape, elopement; prank, spree,
Escamper, *v.n.* to scamper away [lark
Escampette, *s.f.* scampering, flight. *Prendre de la poudre d'—*, to scamper away, to cut
Escapade, *s.f.* escapade; prank, freak, trick, frolic, spree, lark; slip; (*of horses*) escapade
Escape, *s.f.* (*arch.*) scape
†Escarbille, *s.f.* coal-cinder; clinker
Escarbot, *s.m.* beetle (*insect*)
Escarboucle, *s.f.* (*min.*) carbuncle; (*her.*) escarbuncle; (*zool.*) ruby-throated humming-bird
†Escarbouiller, *v.a.* *V.* **Écarbouiller**
Escarcelle, *s.f.* (*obsolete*) purse; money-bag; bag, budget, pouch
Escare, *s.f.* (*bad spelling*) *V.* **Eschare**
Escargot, *s.m.* snail; edible snail; Archimedean screw, water-snail, screw-propeller; winding *or* corkscrew staircase; (*pop.*) slovenly fellow, slattern, slut; tramp [escargatoire
Escargotière, *s.f.* snail-nursery, (*in old English*)
Escarmouche, *s.f.* skirmish; skirmishing; brush; cavilling, bickering
Escarmoucher, *v.n.* to skirmish; to cavil, to fence, to bicker
Escarmoucheur, *s.m.* skirmisher; caviller
Escarole, *s.f.* (*bot.*) endive [**rotique**
Escarotique, *adj. s.* (*bad spelling*) *V.* **Escha-**
Escarpe, *s.f.* (*fort.*) scarp, escarp; — *s.m.* (*pop.*) robber, ruffian, murderer
Escarpé, e, *adj.* steep; (*nav.*) bluff
Escarpement, *s.m.* steep; steepness; (*fort.*, &c.) escarpment
Escarper, *v.a.* to cut steep, to scarp; (*pop.*) to kill, to murder, to settle, to do for
S'—, *v.r.* to become steep; to show its steepness; (*pop.*) to kill each other
Escarpin, *s.m.* pump (*shoe*); (*obsolete*) stocks (*torture for the feet*). — *de Limousin*, (*pop.*) wooden shoe. *Jouer de l'—*, (*pop.*) to run away, to bolt, to cut [bolt, to cut
Escarpiner (S'), *v.r.* (*pop.*) to run away, to
Escarpolette, *s.f.* swing, seesaw. *Tête à l'—*, giddy-head
Escarre, *s.f.* (*bad spelling*) *V.* **Eschare** [caveson
Escaveçade, *s.f.* (*rid.*) check *or* jerk with the
‡Eschare, *s.f.* (*med.*) eschar, slough
‡Escharification, *s.f.* (*med.*) escharification
‡Escharifier, *v.a.* (*med.*) to escharify
‡Escharotique, *adj.m.f.*, *s.m.* (*med.*) escharotic
‡Eschatolog-ie, -ique. *V.* page 3, § 1
‡†Eschillon, *s.m.* *V.* **Échillon**
Escient, *s.m.* (*obsolete*) knowledge. *A bon —*, knowingly, wittingly; in good earnest, in earnest; in reality, indeed. *A son —*, to o.'s knowledge, knowingly, wittingly
Esclame, *adj.* (*hunt.*) thin, lank
Esclandre, *s.m.* noise, uproar, scandal, exposure, scandalous scene, scene, quarrel in public, fracas [captivity; (*old*) necklace
Esclavage, *s.m.* slavery; bondage; thraldom;
Esclavagiste, *s.m.f.* *adj.* antiabolitionist
Esclave, *s.m.f.* slave; bondman, bondwoman; captive; — *adj.* slavish
Esclavon, ne, *adj. s.* Sclavonian
Escobar, *s.m.* shuffler
Escobarder, *v.n.* to shuffle; — *v.a.* to chouse, to fob off, to get *or* obtain by fraud
Escobarderie, *s.f.* shuffling
Escobardeu-r, se, *s.m.f.* shuffler [for, to settle
Escoffier, *v.a.* (*pop.*) to kill, to murder, to do
Escoffion, *s.m.* (*obsolete*) hair-net (*woman's*)
Escogriffe, *s.m.* sharper, shark; sponger; lanky lout, lanky *or* ungainly fellow
Escompte, *s.m.* discount. *Règle d'—*, (*arith.*) discount. *Faire l'—*, to discount
Escompter, *v.a.* to discount; to cash; to anticipate; to forestall
S'—, *v.r.* to be discounted *or* &c.
Escompteur, *s.m.* discounter
Escope, *s.f.* (*obsolete spelling*) *V.* **Écope**
Escoperche, *s.f.* *V.* **Écoperche**
Escopette, *s.f.* (*old*) rifle, carbine
Escopettier, *s.m.* (*old*) rifleman
Escors, *s.m.* (*at play, pop.*) distance, start
Escorte, *s.f.* escort; convoy; retinue, train, attendants. *Faire —*, to escort, to accompany
Escorter, *v.a.* to escort; to accompany; to
Escot, *s.m.* serge [attend
Escouade, *s.f.* squad; (*of workmen*) gang
Escouladou, *s.m.* *V.* **Escaladou**
Escourgée, *s.f.* cat o' nine tails, scourge, whip, lash; lashing
Escourgeon, *s.m.* (*bot.*) six-rowed barley, bear, big, bigg; (*agr.*) winter barley
Escousse, *s.f.* run, spring
Escrime, *s.f.* fencing [trial of skill
Escrimer, *v.n.* to fence; to spar; to have a
S'—, *v.r.* to endeavour, to strive, to try, to apply oneself; to work; to fight; to dispute; to dabble (in), to have some knowledge (of)
Escrimeur, *s.m.* fencer
Escroc, *s.m.* sharper, swindler, cheat, blackleg
Escroquer, *v.a.* to swindle, to cheat; to steal
Escroquerie, *s.f.* swindling, swindle

Escroqueu-r, se, *s.m.f.* swindler, cheat, stealer
Escubac, *s.m. V.* **Scubac**
Esculape, *s.m.* Æsculapius; (*jest.*) medical man, physician, doctor
Esculent, e, *adj.* esculent, eatable, edible
Esculine, *s.f.* (*chem.*) esculine, æsculine
Esculique, *adj.* (*chem.*) esculic, æsculic
Escurial, *s.m.* Escurial (*palace of the kings of Spain*)
Esherber, *v.a. V.* **Éherber**
†**Esmiller,** *v.a. V.* **Smiller**
Ésope, *s.m.* Æsop; ugly hunchback
Ésophage, *s.m. V.* **Œsophage**
Ésopique, *adj.* Æsopian
Ésotér-ique, -iquement. *V.* page 3, § 1
Ésotérisme, *s.m.* esotericism, esoterics
Espace, *s.m.* space; place; region, realm; room; distance; extent; duration; interval; — *s.f.* (*print.*) space
Espacement, *s.m.* interval; spread; spacing
Espacer, *v.a.* to place apart; to separate; to put *or* plant *or* set at convenient *or* regular distances; to leave a space between; to space, to space out
S'—, *v.r.* to be placed apart *or* &c.; to extend
Espadon, *s.m.* espadon, two-handed sword; (*fenc.*) broadsword; (*zool.*) sword-fish
Espadonner, *v.n.* to fight with the broad-sword
Espadonneur, *s.m.* swordsman
Espadot, *s.m.* boat-hook
†**Espadrille,** *s.f.* (Spanish) sandal
†**Espagnol, e,** *adj.* Spanish; — *s.m.* Spaniard; Spanish (language); — *s.f.* Spanish woman *or* lady *or* girl, Spaniard; Spanish fashion; Spanish sauce
†**Espagnolette,** *s.f.* baize; window-fastening, fastening
Espalier, *s.m.* espalier; fruit-wall; (*theat. slang*) figurante, wall-flower; (*nav.*) stroke oarsman. *Fruit d'—*, wall-fruit. *Mur en —*, fruit-wall
Espalme, *s.m. V.* **Courai**
Espalmer, *v.a.* (*nav.*) to grave
Espar, *s.m.* lever; pole; (*nav.*) spar
Esparcet, *s.m.*, **Esparcette,** *s.f.* (*pop.*) *V.* **Sainfoin**
Espargoute, *s.f.* (*bot.*) spurrey, spurry
Espèce, *s.f.* species; kind, sort; nature, description; breed; case; present case; case at issue, case in point; (*arith.*) denomination; (*philos.*) form, image; (*theol.*) element; (*fam.*) creature; wretch; (*pharm.*) species; **—s,** *pl.* specie, cash; coin; money; kinds, sorts, &c.; elements. *L'— humaine*, mankind, humankind. *—s sonnantes*, hard cash, ready money
Espérable, *adj.* to be hoped for
Espérance, *s.f.* hope; expectation; confidence; trust
Espérer, *v.a.n.* to hope; to hope for; to expect; to trust. *J'espère bien*, I do hope. *J'espère!* (*very fam.*) indeed! oh, my ...! isn't it fine! isn't it?
Espiègle, *adj. s.m.f.* frolicsome, waggish, roguish; frolicsome child, wag, rogue, roguish fellow *or* thing
Espièglerie, *s.f.* frolic, trick, waggish *or* roguish trick, waggishness, roguishness, waggery, roguery
Espingard, *s.m. V.* **Épingard**
Espingole, *s.f.* blunderbuss
Espion, ne, *s.m.f.* spy; scout; (*at horse-races*) touter
Espionnage, *s.m.* spying; spy-system; espionage
Espionner, *v.a.* to spy; to pry into; to watch
Esplanade, *s.f.* esplanade, parade
Espoir, *s.m. V.* **Espérance**
Espolette, Espoulette, *s.f.* (*artil.*) fuze, fuse
Esponton, *s.m.* spontoon (*half-pike*)
Espringale, *s.f.* espringal, springal
Esprit, *s.m.* spirit; soul; ghost; mind, intellect; brains; brain; head; intelligence; abilities; wit; wits; ingenuity; skill; cleverness; talent; genius; turn; sense; senses; imagination; humour; temper, disposition; feeling; notions; habits; meaning; character; opinion; tendency; spiritedness; emanation, scent; person; fellow; people; (*gram.*) breathing; (*obsolete*) tuft of feathers. *— fort*, freethinker; sceptic; clever fellow. *— de corps*, spirit of association, fellow-feeling, brotherhood, party spirit, partisanship, esprit de corps. *— d'ordre*, orderliness; management. *— de parti*, party spirit, partisanship. *— de suite*, consistency; notions *or* habits of regularity. *Bel —*, (*Beaux —s, pl.*) man of wit; wit; witling. *Homme, femme, gens d'—*, witty *or* clever *or* sensible man, woman, people. *Avoir de l'—*, to be intelligent *or* sensible *or* clever; to be witty, to have wit. *Avoir l'— bien fait*, to be sensible; to be good-tempered. *Être bien dans l'— de*, to be in ...'s favour. *Faire de l'—*, to play the wit, to affect *or* strive to be witty, to be witty *or* facetious, to make jokes. *Se mettre bien dans l'— de*, to gain ...'s favour, to ingratiate oneself with. *Rappeler* or *reprendre ses —s*, to recover o.'s senses *or* wits. *Recueillir ses —s*, to collect o.'s thoughts. *Remettre les —s*, to quiet people's minds. *Rendre l'—*, *V.* **Âme**
Esprité, e, *adj.* intelligent, sensible, clever, witty
Esprot, *s.m.* sprat
Esquicher, *v.n.*, **S'—,** *v.r.* (*at cards*) to forbear taking a trick by playing an inferior card; (*fig.*) to forbear giving an opinion, to forbear taking part in a broil, to shirk it, to decline, to back out
Esquif, *s.m.* skiff
†**Esquille,** *s.f.* splinter (*of a bone*, &c.)
†**Esquilleu-x, se,** *adj.* splintery
Esquiman, *s.m.* (*nav.*) quartermaster
Esquimau (*pl.* **Esquimaux**), *s.m.* Esquimau (*pl.* Esquimaux)
Esquinancie, *s.f.* quinsy
Esquine, *s.f.* (*of horses*) loins; (*bot.*) *V.* **Squine**
Esquintement, *s.m.* (*pop.*) exhaustion; cutting up, smashing
Esquinter, *v.a.* (*pop.*) *V.* **Éreinter**
Esquipot, *s.m.* money-box
Esquisse, *s.f.* sketch; outline; rough drawing, rough draught; rough cast; plan
Esquisser, *v.a.* to sketch; to outline
Esquiver, *v.a.* to avoid, to shun, to evade; — *v.n.* to slip aside *or* away, to get out of the way, to make off, to escape
S'—, *v.r.* to steal away, to slip *or* slink away, to creep out, to escape; to avoid each other
Essai, *s.m.* trial; attempt; endeavour; effort; essay; experiment; assay, assaying, testing; sample; sample-bottle. *A l'—*, on trial
Essaim, *s.m.* swarm; host; bevy
Essaimage, Essaimement, *s.m.* swarming
Essaimer, *v.n.* to swarm
Essange, *s.f.*, **Essangeage,** *s.m.* soaking, scouring (*dirty linen*)
Essanger, *v.a.* to soak, to scour (*dirty linen*)
Essarder, *v.a.* (*nav.*) to swab, to mop
Essarmenter, *v.a. V.* **Épamprer**
Essart, *s.m.* cleared land, assart
Essartage, Essartement, *s.m.* grubbing, clearing, assarting, assart
Essarter, *v.a.* to grub, to clear, to assart
Essarteu-r, se, *s.m.f.* grubber
Essaver, *v.a.* to drain
Essayer, *v.a.n.* to try; to try on; to attempt, to endeavour, to essay; to assay
S'—, *v.r.* to try oneself; to try o.'s hand *or* skill *or* strength; to attempt, to endeavour; to try each other; to spar; to be tried *or* &c.
Essayerie, *s.f.* assay-office
Essayeur, *s.m.* assayer
Essayiste, *s.m.f.* essayist
Esse, *s.f.* S (*anything in the shape of an S*); S-cramp; S-hook; hammer-axe; linch-pin; (*artil.*) fore-lock; (*of violins*, &c.) S-hole, sound-hole
Esseau, *s.m.* (*carp.*) *V.* **Aisseau;** (*tech.*) hammer-axe
Esseiglage, *s.m.* clearing from rye
Esseigler, *v.a.* to clear from rye
Esselier, *s.m.* (*carp.*) brace
Esséminer, *v.a.* (*old*) to scatter, to disperse
Essence, *s.f.* essence; substance; (*of roses*) otto, attar; (*of turpentine*, &c.) spirit, spirits, oil, essence; (*in forestry*) species (*of tree*). *— de la vie*, heart's blood. *— d'Orient*, essence d'Orient (*powdered scales of the bleak*)
Essénien, *s.m.* Essene (*Jewish philosopher*)

Essential-isme, -iste. *V.* page 3, § 1
Essentialité, *s.f.* essentiality [main point
Essentiel, le, *adj. s.m.* essential; material;
Essentiellement, *adv.* essentially; materially
Essère, *s.f.* (*med.*) essera, nettle-rash
Essette, *s.f.* hammer-axe
Esseulé, e, *adj.* solitary, abandoned
Esseuler, *v.a.* to leave alone, to abandon, to forsake, to desert
Essieu, *s.m.* axle, axle-tree; pin (*of a block*)
Essonite, *s.f.* (*min.*) essonite
Essonte, *s.f.* (*carp.*) shingle
Essor, *s.m.* flight; soaring; strain; play, scope, swing; impulsion, impulse; motion; progress; enterprise. *Prendre l'—* or *son —*, to soar; to take its flight, to fly
Essorage, *s.m.* drying; soaring
Essorant, e, (*her.*) essorant
Essorer, *v.a.* to dry, to dry up
S'—, *v.r.* to be dried, to dry; to soar aloft
Essoreu-r, se, *s.m.f.* dryer; — *s.f.* drying-machine, dryer
†**Essorillé, e,** *adj.* crop-eared, cropped
†**Essorillement,** *s.m.* cutting off the ears; cropping
†**Essoriller,** *v.a.* to cut the ears of; to crop
Essouchement, *s.m.* stubbing
Essoucher, *v.a.* to stub
Essoufflé, e, *part. adj.* breathless, out of breath
Essoufflement, *s.m.* breathlessness, panting
Essouffler, *v.a.* to put out of breath; to wind
S'—, *v.r.* to put oneself out of breath, to get *or* be out of breath
Essui, *s.m.* drying-place; drying-room *or* closet
Essuie, *s.m.* (*in compounds, from* **Essuyer,** "to wipe") thing that wipes, wiper. — **-mains,** *s.m.* towel. — **-pieds,** *s.m.* mat, door-mat. — **-plume,** *s.m.* pen-wiper
Essuyage, *s.m.* wiping
Essuyer, *v.a.* to wipe, to wipe off *or* away; to clean; to dry, to dry up; to support; to sustain; to undergo, to go through, to endure; to suffer; to experience, to meet with, to encounter, to receive; to put up with; to bear; to stand; to be exposed to
S'—, *v.r.* to wipe oneself; to wipe (o.'s ...); [to be wiped *or* &c.
Essuyeu-r, se, *s.m.f.* wiper
Est, *s.m.* east; east wind; Great Eastern railway; — *adj.* east, eastern, easterly. *A l'—*, to *or* in *or* on *or* &c. the east; east, eastward, easterly. *D'—, de l'—*, east, eastern, easterly. *Vers l'—*, eastward
Estacade, *s.f.* stockade; (*of harbours*) boom
Estafette, *s.f.* estafette, express messenger, express
Estafier, *s.m.* big strong footman *or* livery servant, flunkey, flunky; bully; (*pop.*) policeman, bobby, slop
Estafion, *s.m.* (*pop.*) cuff, punch, slap
Estafilade, *s.f.* gash, slash, cut; rent
Estafilader, *v.a.* to gash, to slash, to cut
†**Estagnon,** *s.m.* (*local*) can
Estaim, *s.m.* *V.* **Étaim**
Estain, *s.m.* (*nav.*) fashion-piece
Estame, *s.f.* worsted, knitted worsted
Estamet, *s.m.*, **Estamette,** *s.f.* coarse woollen stuff
Estaminet, *s.m.* tavern; smoking-room *or* divan; tap-room; shades
Estampage, *s.m.* stamping; impression
Estampe, *s.f.* print, cut, engraving; stamp; punch
Estamper, *v.a.* to stamp; to mark; to brand;
S'—, *v.r.* to be stamped *or* &c. [to punch
Estampeur, *s.m.* stamper (*pers.*); — *adj.m.* stamping
†**Estampillage,** *s.m.* stamping; marking
†**Estampille,** *s.f.* stamp; mark; trade-mark
†**Estampiller,** *v.a.* to stamp; to mark
S'—, *v.r.* to be stamped *or* marked
Estampoir, *s.m.* stamper (*tool*)
Estance, *s.f.* *V.* **Étance**
Estant (En). *V.* **Étant**
Estelaire, *adj.* (*of stags*) tame, decoy
Ester, *v.n.* (*law*) to appear in court
Estère, *s.f.* rush mat; creek, cove
Esterre, *s.f.* creek, cove
Esteuble, *s.f.* stubble
Esteuf, *s.m.* *V.* **Éteuf**
Esthétique, *adj.* æsthetic; — *s.f.* æsthetics
Esthétiquement, *adv.* æsthetically
Esthonien, ne, *adj. s.* Esthonian
Estimable, *adj.* estimable
Estima-teur, trice, *s.m.f.* appraiser; valuer; appreciator; assessor; — *adj.* valuing, appreciating
Estimati-f, ve, *adj.* *V.* **Appréciatif**
Estimation, *s.f.* estimation; appraising; valuation; estimate
Estime, *s.f.* esteem; estimation; (*nav.*) reckoning
Estimer, *v.a.n.* to estimate, to appraise; to rate; to assess; to value; to esteem, to prize; to deem, to consider, to account; to reckon; to conjecture; to be of opinion
Estivage, *s.m.* summer season, estivation; lading, ship-load
Estival, e, *adj.* estival, summer
Estivation, *s.f.* (*bot., nat. hist.*) estivation
Estive, *s.f.* (*nav.*) tension. *Charger en —*, to compress
Estiver, *v.a.* to turn out to grass during summer; (*nav.*) to compress; — *v.n.* to stay during the summer
Estoc, *s.m.* tuck (*sword*); point of a sword; (*of trees*) trunk, stock; stump; (*nav.*) rock, shelf, ledge. *A blanc —*, down to the root; general, complete; to nothing. *Frapper d'— et de taille*, to cut and thrust, to lay about at random. *Faire l'—*, to shift (*a card*) under
Estocade, *s.f.* thrust, lunge; unexpected attack
Estocader, *v.n.* to thrust, to lunge
Estomac, *s.m.* stomach; breast; chest; (*old, fig.*) belly. *Ardeur d'—*, heartburn
Estomaquer, *v.a.* to offend; to astound, to dumbfound; to exhaust
S'—, *v.r.* to take offence; to be astounded *or* dumbfounded; to exhaust oneself
Estompe, *s.f.* stump; stump-drawing
Estomper, *v.a.* (*draw.*) to stump
Estouffade, *s.f.* *obsolete spelling of* **Étouffade**
Estourbir, *v.a.* (*pop.*) *V.* **Escoffier;** — *v.n.* to die
S'—, *v.r.* (*pop.*) to kill oneself; to die, to kick the bucket; to go off, to be off, to vanish
Estrade, *s.f.* platform, stage, stand, estrade; hustings; (*obsolete*) road. *Battre l'—*, to scout; to wander, to rove; to be on the tramp
Estragon, *s.m.* (*bot.*) tarragon
Estramaçon, *s.m.* two-edged sword
Estramaçonner, *v.a.n.* (*old*) to slash, to cut
Estrapade, *s.f.* strappado; (*rid.*) estrapade
Estrapader, *v.a.* to give the strappado
Estrapasser, *v.a.* to override, to overwork
Estraper, *v.a.* *V.* **Étraper**
Estrope, *s.f.* (*nav.*) strop
Estroper, *v.a.* (*nav.*) to strop
Estropiat, *s.m.* cripple, beggar
Estropié, e, *adj.* crippled; lame; disabled; (*fig.*) mutilated; — *s.m.f.* cripple
Estropiement, *s.m.* crippling, disablement
Estropier, *v.a.* to cripple, to lame, to maim; to disable; (*fig.*) to mutilate; to mangle; to murder; to bungle; to spoil
Estuaire, *s.m.* estuary
Esturgeon, *s.m.* sturgeon
Ésule, *s.f.* (*bot.*) esula
Et, *conj.* and; then, thereupon, immediately, at once. — ... *et*, both ... and
Établage, *s.m.* stabling
Étable, *s.f.* stable, stall, shed, cattle-shed, cattle-house; pig-sty, sty. *Franc- —*, *V.* **Franc,** [*adj.*
Établer, *v.a.* to stable
Établi, *s.m.* work-bench, bench; board; shop-board, counter
Établir, *v.a.* to establish; to institute; to found; to appoint; to lay down; to lay; to set; to fix; to put, to place; to seat; to rest; to impose; to settle; to marry; to provide for; to set up; to take up; to assert, to state; to

prove; to show; to ascertain; to make; to draw up, to make up; to strike (*a balance*)
Établissement, *s.m.* establishment; institution; concern; house; foundation; appointment; settlement; settling; marriage; setting up; setting up in business; situation; fixing; putting, placing; stating; proving, showing; enactment; (*of taxes*) imposition; (*nav.*) establishment (*of a port*), tide-table
Étage, *s.m.* story, floor, flat; flight; row; tier; step; stratum, layer; degree, quality, grade, rank, class. *De bas* —, low
Étagé, e, *part. adj.* rising above one another, rising; in tiers; in lines behind each other; tapered, tapering
Étager, *v.a.* to place *or* arrange *or* dispose in tiers, to place in rows one above the other, to raise; to place in lines behind each other; to taper
S'—, *v.r.* to be placed *or* &c. in tiers *or* in rows one above another, to rise above one another, to rise; to be placed in lines behind each other; to taper [pen-rack
Étagère, *s.f.* whatnot; set of shelves; shelf;
Étai, *s.m.* stay, shore, prop, support; (*nav.*) stay
Étaie, *s.f.* (*her.*) chevronel
Étaiement, *s.m. V.* **Étayement**
†Étaillir, *v.a.* to copse
†Étaillissage, *s.m.* copsing
Étaim, *s.m.* carded wool
Étain, *s.m.* tin; pewter
Étal, *s.m.* stall, butcher's stall *or* shop
Étalage, *s.m.* exposing for sale; laying out, hanging out; goods exposed for sale; shop-window, window; stall; stallage; display, show; finery [window-dresser
Étalagiste, *s.m.f.* stall-holder, stall-keeper;
Étale, *adj.* (*nav.*) slack, still; (*of the wind*) settled, steady; — *s.m.* slackness, stillness
Étaler, *v.a.* to expose for sale; to put in the window; to lay out; to hang out; to spread, to spread out; to display, to show, to make a show *or* a display of; (*fam.*) to upset, to knock down, to floor; (*nav.*) to resist; to pursue
S'—, *v.r.* to sprawl; to loll; to fall down at full length; to stretch *or* spread oneself out; to show oneself off, to show off; to be exposed for sale, &c.
Étaleu-r, se, *s.m.f.* stall-holder *or* keeper
Étalier, *s.m.* butcher's foreman; (*fish.*) stakes
Étalinguer, &c. *V.* **Entalinguer,** &c.
Étalon, *s.m.* stallion; standard (*of weights*, &c.); (*in forestry*) youngest staddle; (*tech.*) full-size draught [ing; gauging
Étalonnage, Étalonnement, *s.m.* stamp-
Étalonner, *v.a.* to stamp; to gauge; to serve, to cover, to horse [measures
Étalonneur, *s.m.* inspector of weights and
Étalonni-er, ère, *adj.* of stallions, stallion
Étamage, *s.m.* tinning; plating, silvering (*of glass*); tinned work
Étambot, *s.m.* (*nav.*) stern-post
Étambrai, *s.m.* (*nav.*) partner (*of a mast*, &c.)
Étamer, *v.a.* to tin; to plate, to silver (*glass*)
Étameur, *s.m.* tinker; tinner; glass-tinner, looking-glass silverer, silverer
Étamine, *s.f.* stamin; bunting; bolting-cloth, sieve, tammy; strainer, colander; (*fig.*) examination; ordeal, trial; hard trial; (*bot.*) stamen. *Passer par l'—*, to sift; to be sifted, to be strictly examined; to be tried, to pass through the ordeal
Étaminé, e, *adj.* (*bot.*) stamened [tammy-maker
Étaminier, *s.m.* stamin *or* bunting-maker;
Étampage, *s.m.* stamping; punching
Étampe, *s.f.* stamp; punch
Étamper, *v.a.* to stamp; to punch
Étampeur, *s.m.* stamper (*pers.*)
Étampoir, *s.m.* stamper (*tool*)
Étamure, *s.f.* tinning
Étance, *s.f.* (*nav.*) stanchion
Étancer, *v.a.* (*nav.*) to prop, to shore
Étanche, *adj.* water-tight, air-tight, wind-tight, steam-tight, tight, stanch; dry
Étanchement, *s.m.* stanching; stopping; drying; quenching *or* slaking (*o.'s thirst*)
Étancher, *v.a.* to stanch; to stop; to free from water; to dry, to dry up; to quench *or* slake (*o.'s thirst*)
S'—, *v.r.* to become *or* be stanched, &c.
Étançon, *s.m.* stay; prop; shore; (*nav.*) stanchion [shoring
Étançonnement, *s.m.* propping, staying;
Étançonner, *v.a.* to prop, to stay; to shore
Étanfiche, *s.f.* quarry-stratum
Étang, *s.m.* fish-pond, pond, pool
Étant (En), (*of forest-trees*) standing
Étape, *s.f.* (*mil., fig.*) rations, allowance; forage; halting-place, stopping-place, station; stage; storehouse; mart. *Brûler l'—*, to pass on *or* through without stopping. *Tout d'une —*, *V.* **Traite**
Étapier, *s.m.* (*mil.*) distributer of rations
État, *s.m.* state; status; position; condition; plight, predicament; case; circumstances; way; calling; trade; profession; business; occupation; station; office; establishment; list; account; bill; inventory; estimate; return; statistics; muster-roll; register; certificate; commonwealth; government; cabinet; estate; **—s,** *pl.* states, &c.; way; dominions; (*Fr. hist.*) States, States-general, Parliament. — *civil*, social state; o.'s state as a citizen, social position, position, condition. *Acte de l'— civil*, certificate of birth, death, or marriage. *Actes* or *registres de l'— civil*, certificates *or* registers *or* registration of births, deaths, and marriages, registers of the parish *or* of the municipality. *Officier de l'— civil*, registrar of births, deaths, and marriages. *Les—s généraux*, (*Fr. hist.*) the States-general, Parliament. *Tiers-* —, (*Fr. hist.*) third estate, Commons; common people. *Dans tous ses —s*, (*pop.*) in a dreadful way; all in a bustle. *De son* —, by trade *or* profession. *En* —, in a proper state, in good condition; in repair; in gear; ready; as it is, in statu quo. *En — de*, in a state of; in a condition *or* position to, able to; ready to. *Hors d'—*, not in a state; not in a condition, unable; out of gear. *Faire — de*, to value, to consider, to care for; to intend to; to rely on. *Mettre en — de*, to put in a state of; to put in a position to, to enable to; to prepare for. *Mettre hors d'—*, to disable, to prevent, to put it out of (o.'s) power (to). *Remettre en* —, to set right again, to repair
État-major, *s.m.* (*mil., nav., fig.*) staff; staff-office; head-quarters; principal station. *Chef d'—*, *Chef d'— général*, *V.* **Chef**
Étau, *s.m.* (*tech.*) vice [moling
Étaupinage, *s. m.* clearing of mole-hills,
Étaupiner, *v.a.* to clear of mole-hills, to mole
Étaux, *s.m.pl.* (*pl. of* **Étau** *and of* **Étal**)
Étayage, Étayement, *s.m.* staying, propping, shoring; support
Étayer, *v.a.* to stay; to shore; to prop; to support; to rest; to back [to be stayed *or* &c.
S'—, *v.r.* to stay *or* &c. oneself *or* each other;
Et cætera, *conj. s.m.* et cætera
Été, *s.m.* summer; summer clothes; prime; (*figure in dancing*) été
Été, *part.* (*of* **Être**). *J'ai* —, I have been, I was; I have gone, I did go, I went
†Éteigneu-r, se, *s.m.f.* (*pers.*) extinguisher
†Éteignoir, *s.m.* extinguisher; damper
Éteindre, *v.a.* to extinguish; to put out; to blow out; to snuff out; to stamp out; to destroy; to put an end to; to abolish; to do away with; to exterminate; to reduce; to dim; to dull; to blunt; to soften; to allay; to still; to calm; to appease; to quench; to slake; to cool; to damp; to stifle; to quell, to squelch, to put down; to obliterate; to cancel, to annul; to strike out; to redeem (*an annuity*);

to pay off *or* liquidate (*a debt*); to silence (*the enemy's batteries*)

S'—, *v.r.* to become *or* be extinguished, &c.; to go out; to die away *or* off *or* out; to die; to disappear; to end; to cease; to decrease; to abate; to cool; to become extinct; to become dim *or* dull *or* blunt *or* faint

Éteint,e, *part. adj.* (*V.* **Éteindre**) extinguished, out; slaked; extinct; dead; lifeless; dim; dull; blunt; faint, inaudible [stick

Étèle, Ételle, *s.f.* (*nav.*) ripple; (*local*) splinter,

Ételon, *s.m.* full-size draught

Étendage, *s.m.* drying-lines; drying-room *or* place; tentering; drying

Étendard, *s.m.* standard; flag, colours, banner

Étendelle, *s.f.* horse-hair bag

Étenderie, *s.f.* drying-room *or* place

Étendeu-r, se, *s.m.f.* stretcher

Étendoir, *s.m.* clothes-posts, clothes-props, drying-poles; tenter; (*print.*) peel; drying-room *or* place

Étendre, *v.a.* to extend; to spread; to spread out; to stretch; to stretch out; to expand; to distend; to lay out *or* on; to lay down; to lay; to hang up; to tenter; to enlarge; to lengthen; to draw out; to wire-draw; to dilute, to mix (with water); to lay dead

S'—, *v.r.* to extend; to stretch oneself out; to lay oneself, to lie down; to loll; to sprawl; to fall down at full length; to spread; to stretch; to reach, to go; to expand; to enlarge; to dilate, to expatiate, to dwell; to lengthen; to draw out; to last; to enlarge o.'s estate

Étendu, e, *part. adj.* extended, spread, &c. (*V.* **Étendre**); extensive; wide; large; of great compass; long; lying down; lolling; sprawling; dilute, diluted, mixed with water

Étendue, *s.f.* extent; extensiveness; extension; expanse; space; tract; compass; volume; capacity; comprehension; greatness; length; duration

Éternel, le, *adj.* eternal; everlasting; endless; perpetual; repeated, continual, constant; tedious; — *s.m.* Eternal, Almighty; — *s.f.* (*obsolete*) *V.* **Immortelle**

Éternellement, *adv.* eternally; everlastingly; for ever; ever, endlessly, perpetually, incessantly, continually, constantly

Éterniser, *v.a.* to eternize; to immortalize; to prolong *or* continue for ever, to make endless, to perpetuate

S'—, *v.r.* to be eternized *or* &c., to become eternal *or* immortal *or* immortalized, to be perpetuated, to last *or* remain *or* be for ever; (*jest.*) to become a fixture [mortality

Éternité, *s.f.* eternity; everlastingness; im-

Éternue, *s.f.* (*bot.*) sneezewort

Éternuement, *s.m.* sneezing; sneeze

Éternuer, *v.n.* to sneeze

Éternueu-r, se, *s.m.f.* sneezer

Éternûment, *s.m.* *V.* **Éternuement**

Étésien, *adj.m.* Etesian

Étêté, e, *adj.* headless

Étêtement, *s.m.* heading down, polling, topping

Étêter, *v.a.* (*of nails*, &c.) to take the head off; (*of trees*) to head down, to poll, to top

Éteuf, *s.m.* (*old*) tennis-ball, ball

Éteule, *s.f.* stubble; (*nav.*) ripple

Éthal, *s.m.* (*chem.*) ethal

Éther, *s.m.* ether

Éthérate, *s.m.* (*chem.*) etherate [canopy of heaven

Éthéré, e, *adj.* ethereal; subtle; pure. *Voûte —e*,

Éthérène, *s.m.* (*chem.*) ethylene

Éthérification, *s.f.* (*chem.*) etherification

Éthérifier, *v.a.* (*chem.*) to etherify, to ether-

Éthérique, *adj.* (*chem.*) etheric [ealize

Éthérisation, *s.f.* (*chem.*, *med.*) etherization

Éthériser, *v.a.* (*chem.*, *med.*) to etherize

Éthérol, *s.m.* (*chem.*) etherol, etherine

Éthiopien, ne, Éthiopique, *adj. s.* Ethiopian, Ethiopic

Éthique, *adj.* ethic, ethical; — *s.f.* ethics, [morals

Ethmoïdal, e, *adj.* (*anat.*) ethmoidal

Ethmoïde, *adj. s.m.* (*anat.*) ethmoid; ethmoid [bone

Ethnarch-ie, -ique. *V.* page 3, § 1

Ethnarque, *s.m.* ethnarch

Ethnique, *adj.* ethnic, ethnical

Ethnographe, *s.m.* ethnographer

Ethnograph-ie, -ique. *V.* page 3, § 1

Ethnolog-ie, -ique, -iste. *V.* page 3, § 1

Étho-graphie, -graphique, -logie, -logique. *V.* page 3, § 1

Éthologue, *s.m.* ethologist

Éthopée, *s.f.* (*rhet.*) ethopœia

Éthrioscope, *s.m.* (*phys.*) æthrioscope

Éthuse, *s.f.* *V.* **Æthuse**

Éthyle, *s.m.* (*chem.*) ethyl

Étiage, *s.m.* (*navig.*) low water, low-water mark

Étier, *s.m.* canal from the sea to a salt-marsh

Étinceler, *v.n.* to sparkle; to glitter; to glisten; to twinkle; to flash; to flare

Étincelette, *s.f.* sparkle

Étincelle, *s.f.* spark; flash

Étincellement, *s.m.* sparkling; glittering; glistening; twinkling; flashing; flaring

Étiolé, e, *part. adj.* etiolated; blanched; pale, wan; emaciated; enfeebled, feeble, weakly, sickly

Étiolement, *s.m.* etiolation; blanching; paleness; emaciation; weakening, feebleness, weakness, sickliness

Étioler, *v.a.* (*of plants*) to etiolate, to blanch; (*pers.*) to etiolate, to make pale *or* wan, to emaciate, to enfeeble, to debilitate, to weaken, to make weak and sickly

S'—, *v.r.* to etiolate; to be blanched; to grow pale *or* wan; to become *or* grow etiolated, to become weak and sickly, to become emaciated, to waste away, to waste; to wither

Étiolog-ie, -ique. *V.* page 3, § 1 [emaciated

Étique, *adj.* hectic; consumptive; lean, lank,

Étiqueter, *v.a.* to label; to docket; to ticket

Étiquette, *s.f.* label; docket; ticket; ceremony; ceremonial; formality, forms, usages; etiquette [drawing

Étirage, *s.m.* drawing out, stretching; wire-

Étirer, *v.a.* *V.* **Détirer** [drawer

Étireu-r, se, *s.m.f.* drawer, stretcher; wire-

Étisie, *s.f.* consumption, decline, emaciation

Étoc, *s.m.* *V.* **Estoc**

Étoffe, *s.f.* stuff; cloth; fabric; material; sort, condition, worth, quality; matter, subject; **—s,** *pl.* stuffs, &c.; (*print.*) plant; wear and tear

Étoffé, e, *part. adj.* stuffed; lined; furnished; appointed; clothed, clad; comfortably off; comfortable; stout, plump, substantial, strong; full-bodied; rich; full; sonorous

Étoffer, *v.a.* to put stuff in, to stuff; to line

Étoile, *s.f.* star; blaze; asterisk; star-wheel; centre (*junction of converging ways*); fate, destiny. — *de mer*, star-fish. *A la belle* —, (*literally*, at the sign of the "Beautiful Star," *that is, jocularly :*) in the star-light, in the open air [light; star

Étoilé, e, *adj.* starry; starred; studded; star-

Étoilement, *s.m.* starring, cracking; star, crack

Étoiler, *v.a.* to star; to stud; to blaze; to light

S'—, *v.r.* to become *or* be covered *or* studded with stars; to star, to crack

Étole, *s.f.* stole (*priest's garment*)

Étolien, ne, *adj. s.* Ætolian, Etolian

Étonnamment, *adv.* astonishingly, wonderfully, surprisingly, amazingly; astoundingly; an astonishing *or* wonderful amount *or* quantity

Étonnant, e, *adj.* astonishing, wonderful, surprising, amazing; astounding; strange

Étonné, e, *part. adj.* astonished, &c. (*V.* **Étonner**); of astonishment; wondering; wavering. *Faire* or *jouer l'—*, to feign astonishment

Étonnement, *s.m.* astonishment, wonder, surprise, amazement; fright, terror; commotion, shock

Étonner, *v.a.* to astonish, to surprise, to amaze; to astound, to stun, to startle, to stagger, to shake; to daunt, to confuse, to frighten

S'—, *v.r.* to be astonished *or* &c.; to wonder; [to waver

Étouffade, *s.f.* (*old*) *V.* **Étouffée**

Étouffage, *s.m.* suffocation, stifling

Étouffant, e, *part. adj.* suffocating, &c. (*V.* **Étouffer**), sweltering, sultry

Étouffée, *s.f.* (*cook.*) *V.* **Étuvée**

Étouffement, *s.m.* suffocation, stifling

Étouffer, *v.a.* to suffocate; to stifle; to smother; to choke; to burke; to extinguish; to destroy; to conceal; to obliterate; to suppress; to quell, to squelch, to put down; to stamp out; to hush up; to deaden *or* drown (*sounds*); (*pop.*) to crack *or* drink (*a bottle*); — *v.n.* to be suffocated *or* stifled *or* smothered; to be suffocating; to choke; to swelter

Étouffeu-r, se, *s.m.f.* stifler, smotherer, choker, burker; — *s.m.* (*zool.*) boa

Étouffoir, *s.m.* cinder-pail; (*of pianos*) damper; (*fig.*) stew, stove; extinguisher

Étoupe, *s.f.* tow; oakum; stuffing. *Mettre le feu aux —s,* (*fig.*) to fan the flame, to blow the coals [calking

Étoupement, *s.m.* stopping; stuffing; (*nav.*)

Étouper, *v.a.* to stop with tow *or* oakum, to stop; to stuff; to stop (*o.'s ears*) with cotton-wool; (*nav.*) to calk

Étouperie, *s.f.* coarse cloth made of tow

Étoupeu-x, se, *adj.* towy

Étoupi-er, ère, *s.m.f.* oakum-picker

†Étoupille, *s.f.* (*artil.*) quick-match; tube. — *fulminante,* friction-tube

†Étoupiller, *v.a.* (*artil.*) to prime

†Étoupillon, *s.m.* (*artil.*) toppin

Étoupin, *s.m.* (*nav. artil.*) wadding, wad; match

Étourdeau, *s.m.* young capon

Étourderie, *s.f.* giddiness, thoughtlessness, heedlessness; giddy trick, thoughtless act; blunder

Étourdi, e, *part. adj.* stunned, &c. (*V.* **Étourdir**); dizzy; giddy, thoughtless, heedless; — *s.m.f.* giddy fellow *or* woman *or* girl *or* creature, giddy-head, giddy goose, madcap, wild spark, blunderer. *A l'—e,* giddily, thoughtlessly, heedlessly; rashly; at random [heedlessly; rashly

Étourdiment, *adv.* giddily, thoughtlessly,

Étourdir, *v.a.* to stun; to din; to deafen; to make giddy *or* dizzy; to astound; to bewilder; to benumb; to allay, to assuage; to divert; to forget; to appease; to parboil; to take the chill off

S'—, *v.r.* to get rid of the thought (of), to shake off the thoughts (of), to forget; to lull *or* forget o.'s sorrow, to forget o.'s troubles; to drive away fear; to get away from o.'s thoughts, to divert o.'s mind

Étourdissant, e, *part. adj.* stunning, &c. (*V.* **Étourdir**); giddy, dizzy; obstreperous; dazzling

Étourdissement, *s.m.* stunning; giddiness; dizziness; amazement, stupefaction; forgetfulness; infatuation

Étourneau, *s.m.* starling; giddy fellow; flea-bitten horse; — *adject.* flea-bitten

Étrange, *adj.* strange; odd, queer; novel. *Chose —!* strange thing! strange! strange to say! [a little

Étrangement, *adv.* strangely; terribly; not

Étrang-er, ère, *adj.* strange; stranger; foreign; outlandish; extraneous; irrelevant; unconcerned; unconnected; unacquainted (with); unknown (to)

Étrang-er, ère, *s.m.f.* stranger; outsider; foreigner; alien; — *s.m.* foreign country; foreign countries *or* parts; exportation. *A l'—,* abroad, in *or* to a foreign country *or* &c. *Passer à l'—,* to go abroad [to alienate

Étranger, *v.a.* (*old*) to drive away; to estrange,

S'—, *v.r.* to desert, to forsake; to be driven away *or* &c. [ness; novelty

Étrangeté, *s.f.* strangeness; oddness, queer-

Étranglant, e, *adj.* overwhelming, amazing; decisive

Étranglé, e, *part. adj.* strangled, &c. (*V.* **Étrangler**); scanty; too narrow *or* tight; too much compressed; strangulated

Étrangle-chien, *s.m.* (*bot.*) cynanchum

Étrangle-loup, *s.m.* (*bot.*) true-love

Étranglement, *s.m.* strangling; strangulation; garotting; contraction; stricture

Étrangler, *v.a.* to strangle; to throttle; to garotte; to choke; to stifle; to make too narrow *or* too tight; to contract; to compress; to confine; to slur over; — *v.n.* to choke, to be choking *or* strangling

S'—, *v.r.* to strangle *or* &c. oneself *or* each other; (*surg.*) to become strangulated; (*fam.*) to hurt o.'s throat (*by straining o.'s voice*)

Étrangleu-r, se, *s.m.f.* strangler; choker; [garotter

Étranglure, *s.f.* crease

†Étranguillon, *s.m.* (*vet.*) strangles. *Poire d'—,* choke-pear

Étrape, *s.f.* sickle (*for stubble*)

Étraper, *v.a.* to cut (*stubble*)

Étraquer, *v.a.* (*hunt.*) to track (*on the snow*)

Étrave, *s.f.* (*nav.*) stem

Être, *v.n.* to be; to exist; to live; to lie; to stand; to subsist; to remain; to dwell; to belong; to be a native (of); to consist (of); to take part (in); to come in (for); to attend (to), to pay attention, to mind; to have come (to); to be reduced (to); to come; to prove, to prove to be, to turn out to be; to happen, to take place; to be true; to be so; to be the case; to embody; to represent; to have. *Ça y est!* it is done! done! now I *or* you *or* &c. have done it! all right! and no mistake! *Ce qui en est,* how *or* what it is, how the case stands, all about it. *C'est,* it *or* that is; it *or* that was; he is; she is; there is. *C'est que,* it is *or* was because, because; the reason is; the fact is, the truth is; for; but; why; suppose that. *Ce n'est pas que,* not that. *Ce n'est pas que ... ne,* not but that. *Ce sont,* it *or* that is; it *or* that was; they are; there are. *Comme si de rien n'était,* as if nothing at all was the matter, as if nothing had happened. *En —,* to be; to be concerned in it; to be one of the party; to be *or* make one; to belong to it; to join it, to join the party *or* the game; to stand; to turn out, to happen; to be the consequence, to come out of it. *En — à,* to be at, to hold at; to leave off at; to have come to; to come to; to be reduced to; to have (to). *En — de ... comme de,* to be with ... as with. *En — là,* to have come to that; to be in that case; to have gone *or* done so far; to know just so much about it. *En — pour,* to be in for, to lose; to get nothing by. *Est-ce que,* is it (true *or* a fact) that: *Est-ce que vous êtes malade?* or, *Êtes-vous malade?* are you ill? *Est-ce qu'il le savait?* or, *Le savait-il?* did he know it? *Être de,* to be of *or* from *or* by *or* &c. (*V.* **De**); to come from; to be concerned in; to be *or* make one of; to form part of; to belong to; to enter into; to be present at; to be a native *or* an inhabitant of; to be (*Si j'étais de vous, Si j'étais que de vous,* if I were you). *Fussé-je,* were I. *Il est,* he *or* it is; it belongs, &c.; there is; there are. *Il n'en est rien,* it is not so, that is not the case, it is nothing of the sort, no such thing; there is no truth in it; nothing comes out of it. *Il n'est pas que vous ne sachiez,* you are not without knowing, you cannot but know, you must know, no doubt you know. *Je n'en suis plus,* I am no longer one of the party, I no longer belong to it, &c. (*V. En —*); I cry off. *N'est-ce pas?* is it not (so)? is it not true *or* a fact? don't you think so? eh? does it not? are you not? do you not? did they not? shall we not? &c. &c. *N'était, N'étaient,* or *Si ce n'était* (or *n'étaient*), were it not (for *or* that), except. *N'eût été* or *Si ce n'eût été,* had it not been (for *or* that), except. *Ne fût-ce que, Ne serait-ce que,* were it only. *Qu'est-ce? Qu'est-ce que c'est?* *V.* **Que,** *pron.* *Si ce n'est,* if it is *or* was not; if not; unless it be, except, but. *S'il en fut, S'il en fut jamais,* if there ever was one. *Voilà ce que c'est,* that is *or* there's the thing; this is what has happened; I'll tell you what; that's the consequence. *Voilà ce que c'est de* (or *que de*), this is what one gets by, this comes of. *Voilà ce que c'est qu'un ...,* that is what a ... is. *Y —,* to have hit it, to have it; to see it, to understand (it); to have come to the point; to have come to it; to be up to the mark; to be ready; to be at home. *Y — pour,* to come in for (*some share*). *Y — pour quelque chose,* to have something to do with it, to have a hand in it. *N'y — pour rien,* to have nothing to do with it, to have no hand in it. *N'y — pas* (or *plus*) *du tout,* to be quite out, to be a long way from it; to be no longer attending. *Vous n'y êtes pas,* you do not see it, you are out, that is not it; &c. (*V. Y —*). *Ne plus savoir où on en est,* to be put out, to be bewildered; not to know how one stands *or* what one is about *or* what to do

Être, *s.m.* being; existence; life; birth; creature; reality; (*in forestry*) *V.* **Estoc;** **—s,** *pl.* (*of a house*) disposition, parts, ins and outs

Étrécir, *v.a.* *V.* **Rétrécir**

Étrécissement, &c. *V.* **Rétrécissement,**&c.

Étreindre, *v.a.* to bind; to tie up; to clasp, to press; to hug; to embrace; to twine; to grasp; to gripe; to draw close

Étreinte, *s.f.* knot; tie; hold; clasping, clasp; embrace; grasp; gripe, grip; (*tech.*) horse-hair bag

Étrenne, *s.f.* handsel; New Year's gift *or* present; Christmas-box, Christmas gift *or* present

Étrenner, *v.a.* to handsel; to use *or* try *or* put on for the first time; to buy the first lot of, to give good luck; to give a New Year's present *or* Christmas-box to; — *v.n.* to sell o.'s first lot, to sell anything; (*pop.*) to get buffeted

Étréper, *v.a.* *V.* **Écobuer**

†Étrésillon, *s.m.* prop, stay, support [port

†Étrésillonner, *v.a.* to prop, to stay, to support

Étrier, *s.m.* stirrup; strap; stirrup-bandage. *Vin* or *coup de l'—,* *V.* **Coup.** *A franc —,* at full speed. *Tenir l'— à,* (*fig.*) to give a lift to

Étrière, *s.f.* *V.* **Étrivière**

†Étrille, *s.f.* curry-comb [fleece

†Étriller, *v.a.* to curry, to comb; to drub; to

Étriper, *v.a.* to gut. *A étripe-cheval,* tantivy, furiously [poor

Étriqué, e, *adj.* scanty; narrow; curtailed,

Étriquer, *v.a.* to scant, to curtail; (*carp.*) to scribe

Étrivière, *s.f.* stirrup-leather. *Les —s,* (*fig.*) a lashing, a horsewhipping, a hiding; a base treatment; a loss. *Allonger l'—,* (*fig.*) to raise a fresh difficulty, to cause further delay

Étroit, e, *adj.* narrow; strait; tight; close; intimate; strict; limited; confined; scanty; small. *A l'—,* confined; straitened; cramped; narrowly, closely, close; sparingly; scantily; in a narrow compass; badly off for room; in too small a house *or* room *or* &c.

Étroitement, *adv.* narrowly; straitly; tightly; closely; intimately; strictly; sparingly; scantily

Étroitesse, *s.f.* narrowness; straitness; tightness; closeness; intimacy; strictness; scantiness; smallness [*Suisse,* lump of gunpowder

Étron, *s.m.* (*pop.*) excrement, turd. — *de*

Étronçonner, *v.a.* (*of trees*) *V.* **Étêter**

Étronner, *v.n.* (*pop.*) to shit

Étrope, *s.f.* *V.* **Estrope**

Étruffé, e, *adj.* (*of dogs*) lame

Étruffure, *s.f.* (*of dogs*) lameness [Etruscan

Étrurien, ne, Étrusque, *adj. s.* Etrurian,

Ette, (*in mil. commands*) *abbrev. of* **Baïonnette**

Étude, *s.f.* study; learning; labour; meditation; examination, consideration; survey; rehearsal; preparing the school-work *or* the lessons, time of ditto, study-time, hours of study; school; school-room; office; chambers; practice; academy figure; sketch; art; disguise; affectation; **—s,** *pl.* studies, &c.; (classical) education; school-days. *A l'—,* (*of schemes,* &c.) being studied, under examination *or* consideration; (*of plays*) being rehearsed, in *or* into rehearsal. *Avoir fait des* or *ses —s,* to have received a classical education, to have been educated, to have had education. *Faire ses —s,* to go through a course of studies; to study; to receive o.'s education. *Faire de bonnes —s,* to be well educated; to learn much. *Se faire une — de,* to make it a study to. *Il a fait ses —s à Rouen,* he was educated at Rouen. *Il a fait toutes ses —s,* he has been thoroughly educated

Étudiant, e, *s.m.f.* student; — *s.m.* undergraduate; — *s.f.* (*fam.*) student's sweetheart. — *en droit,* law student. — *en médecine,* medical student [elaborate; far-fetched; affected

Étudié, e, *part. adj.* studied, &c. (*V.* **Étudier**);

Étudier, *v.a.n.* to study; to learn; to practise; to examine, to consider; to observe; to survey; to prepare; to meditate; to feel (*the ground*); to be a student; to be brought up

S'—, *v.r.* to study oneself *or* each other; to be studied *or* &c.; to endeavour, to make it o.'s study

Étudiole, *s.f.* paper-case [well (*of a boat*)

Étui, *s.m.* case; box; sheath; needle-case; (*fish.*)

Étuve, *s.f.* stove; drying-stove; sweating-house *or* room, stew. — *humide,* vapour bath. — *sèche,* hot-air bath [*Cuire* or *faire cuire à l'—,* to stew

Étuvée, *s.f.* stewing; stew. *A l'—,* stewed.

Étuvement, *s.m.* warming, drying; (*cook.*) stewing; (*of wounds,* &c.) fomentation

Étuver, *v.a.* to warm, to dry; (*cook.*) to stew; (*wounds,* &c.) to foment, to dab

S'—, *v.r.* to be warmed *or* dried; to be stewed; to foment oneself

Étuviste, *s.m.f.* (*old*) *V.* **Baigneur** [*V.* p. 3, § 1

Étymolog-ie, -ique, -iquement, -iste.

Étymologiser, *v.a.n.* to etymologize

Eubage, *s.m.* druid

Eubéen, ne, *adj. s.* Eubœan

Eucalypte, *s.m.* (*bot.*) eucalyptus, gum-tree

‡Eucharistie, *s.f.* eucharist

‡Eucharistique, *adj.* eucharistic

Euclase, *s.f.* (*min.*) euclase

Eucologe, *s.m.* euchology

Eucras-ie, -ique. *V.* page 3, § 1

Eudiomètre, *s.m.* (*chem.*) eudiometer

Eudiométr-ie, -ique. *V.* page 3, § 1

Eufraise, *s.f.* (*bot.*) euphrasia, eyebright

Eugénie, *s.f.* (*bot.*) eugenia

Eugénine, *s.f.* (*chem.*) eugenine

Eugénique, *adj.* (*chem.*) eugenic

Euh, *int.* hem! well! oh! ah! what the deuce!

Eulogie, *s.f.* (*eccl. hist.*) eulogy [what the plague!

Eulophe, *s.m.* (*bird, insect*) eulophus

Euménides, *s.f.pl.* (*myth.*) Eumenides

Eumolpe, *s.m.* (*zool.*) eumolpus, vine-fretter

Eunomia, Eunomie, *s.f.* (*astr.*) Eunomia

‡Eunuchisme, *s.m.* eunuchism

Eunuque, *s.m.* eunuch; (*mus.*) singing-pipe

Eupatoire, *s.f.* (*bot.*) eupatorium

Eupatorine, *s.f.* (*chem.*) eupatorine

Eupepsie, *s.f.* (*med.*) eupepsia, eupepsy

Euphémique, *adj.* euphemistic, euphemistical

Euphémiquement, *adv.* euphemistically

Euphémisme, *s.m.* euphemism

Euphone, *adj.* euphonious; (*zool.*) sweet-voiced; — *s.m.* (*mus.*) euphon, euphonon, euphonium; (*bird*) euphonia, blue-quit, blue-sparrow [of sound

Euphonie, *s.f.* euphony. *Par —,* for the sake

Euphon-ique, -iquement. *V.* page 3, § 1

Euphorbe, *s.f.* (*bot.*) euphorbia, spurge; (*pharm.*) euphorbium

Euphorbine, *s.f.* (*chem.*) euphorbine

Euphorbique, *adj.* (*chem.*) euphorbic

Euphraise, *s.f.* *V.* **Eufraise**
Euphu-ïsme, -ïste, -ïstique. *V.* page 3, § 1
Eupione, *s.f.* (*chem.*) eupione
Euplastique, *adj.* (*med.*) euplastic
Eurasien, ne, *s.m.f.* *adj.* Eurasian
Eurhythm-ie, -ique. *V.* page 3, § 1
Eurite, *s.f.* (*min.*) eurite, white-stone
Européaniser, *v.a.* to europeanize
Européen, ne, *adj.* *s.m.f.* European; — *s.f.* European fashion
Eurus, *s.m.* (*poet.*) eurus, east wind
Euryale, *s.f.* (*bot., zool.*) euryale
Eurythmie, &c. *V.* **Eurhythmie, &c.**
Eustache, *s.m.* clasp-knife, whittle
Eustyle, *s.m.* (*arch.*) eustyle
Euthanasie, *s.f.* euthanasy, easy death
Eutrophie, *s.f.* (*med.*) eutrophy
Eux, *pron.m.pl.* they; them; for their part; themselves; each other, one another. *A* —, to *or* at *or* with them; to *or* at themselves; theirs, their own; of theirs, of their own; peculiar; to spare. *A — à, A — de, V.* **A.** — *-mêmes,* themselves; alone; too, also, likewise
Évacuant, e, *adj.*, **Évacuant,** *s.m.*, **Évacuati-f, ve,** *adj.*, **Évacuatif,** *s.m.* (*med.*) evacuant, aperient [*adj.* evacuating
Évacuateur, *s.m.* evacuator; — *m.*, **-trice,** *f.*,
Évacuation, *s.f.* evacuation; clearing, clearance
Évacuer, *v.a.n.* to evacuate; to clear; to void; to remove; to be purged, to scour. *Faire* —, to clear; to remove
  S'—, *v.r.* to be evacuated *or* &c.
Évadé, e, *part. adj. s.* escaped; runaway
Évader (S'), *v.r.* to make o.'s escape, to escape, to get off. *Faire* —, to favour ...'s escape
Évagation, *s.f.* evagation [assessable
Évaluable, *adj.* appraisable, estimable, ratable,
Évaluation, *s.f.* valuation; estimate; appraisement [praise; to rate; to assess
Évaluer, *v.a.* to value; to estimate; to ap-
  S'—, *v.r.* to be valued, &c.; to rate oneself
Évanescent, e, *adj.* evanescent
Évangéliaire, *s.m.* evangelistary
Évangélique, *adj.* evangelical; protestant
Évangél-iquement, -isme, -iste. *V.* page
Évangélisation, *s.f.* evangelization [3, § 1
Évangéliser, *v.a.n.* to evangelize
Évangélistaire, *s.m.* *V.* **Évangéliaire**
Évangile, *s.m.* Gospel. *Prendre pour parole d'—*, to accept as gospel
Évanoui, e, *adj.* in a swoon, in a fainting fit, insensible, senseless, unconscious; vanished away, dispelled, gone
Évanouir (S'), *v.r.* to faint, to swoon; to vanish, to disappear; to fade away
Évanouissement, *s.m.* fainting; fainting fit, swoon; insensibility, unconsciousness; vanishing, evanishment, disappearance
Évaporable, *adj.* evaporable
Évaporati-f, ve, *adj.* evaporative
Évaporation, *s.f.* evaporation; thoughtlessness
Évaporatoire, *adj.* evaporating; — *s.m.* evaporating-apparatus
Évaporé, e, *adj.* evaporated; thoughtless, giddy; — *s.m.f.* thoughtless fellow *or* thing, giddy-head [to abstract, to filch, to prig
Évaporer, *v.a.* to evaporate; to vent; (*pop.*)
  S'—, *v.r.* to evaporate; to be vented; to get thoughtless *or* giddy
Évasé, e, *part. adj.* widened, &c. (*V.* **Évaser**); wide (at the opening); bell-mouthed; (*of hats*) bell-crowned; (*of noses*) with wide nostrils
Évasement, *s.m.* widening, width (*of the opening*), wide-opening, bell-mouth; bell-crown; (*of doors*, &c.) splay [to extend; (*arch.*) to splay
Évaser, *v.a.* to widen (*an opening*); to spread,
  S'—, *v.r.* to be widened, to widen; to extend,
Évasi-f, ve, *adj.* evasive [to spread itself
Évasion, *s.f.* escape; flight; elopement; (*obso-*
Évasivement, *adv.* evasively [*lete*) evasion
Évasure, *s.f.* opening

Évêché, *s.m.* bishopric; episcopate; episcopal see, cathedral city; episcopal palace, bishop's palace *or* house *or* residence
Évection, *s.f.* (*astr.*) evection
†**Éveil,** *s.m.* hint, warning, alarm, alert; suspicion; awaking, rousing. *En* —, on the alert; on the watch; ready
†**Éveillable,** *adj.* awakable
†**Éveillé, e,** *part. adj.* awakened, &c. (*V.* **Éveiller**); awake; wide awake, watchful, vigilant, alert, attentive; lively, sprightly, brisk, quick, sharp, smart, intelligent; waggish; free, broad; — *s.m.f.* sharp fellow, sprightly lass
†**Éveiller,** *v.a.*, **S'—,** *v.r.* to awake, to wake, to wake up, to awaken; to call; to rouse; to excite; to enliven [waker
†**Éveilleu-r, se,** *s.m.f.* awakener, wakener,
Événement, *s.m.* event; occurrence; incident; issue, end, result, consequence; emergency
Évent, *s.m.* flatness, vapidness; open air, air; vent; air-hole; vent-hole; (*nat. hist.*) blow-hole, spout-hole; (*artil.*) windage. *Sentir l'—*, to smell vapid, to be touched. *Tête à l'—*, giddy-head
Éventable, *adj.* to be aired; liable to get flat
Éventage, *s.m.* airing; (*agr.*) spreading
†**Éventail,** *s.m.* fan. *Bec à* —, (*gas-lighting*) batwing-burner. *Fenêtre en* —, fan-light
†**Éventailliste,** *s.m.f.* fan-maker *or* seller;
Éventaire, *s.m.* flat basket [fan-painter
Éventé, e, *part. adj.* fanned; aired; let out, &c. (*V.* **Éventer**); vapid, flat; thoughtless, giddy; — *s.m.f.* thoughtless fellow *or* thing, giddy-head [**Éventer**)
Éventement, *s.m.* fanning, airing, &c. (*V.*
Éventer, *v.a.* to fan; to air; to vent; to ventilate; to turn over (*corn*, &c.); to spread (*weeds*); (*nav.*) to fill (*sails*); (*of liquors*) to deaden, to let (...) get flat; to injure by exposure to the air; (*fig.*) to let out, to divulge; to get wind of, to discover; to wind, to scent; — *v.n.* (*of horses*) to boar
  S'—, *v.r.* to fan oneself; to get flat; to evaporate; to be injured by exposure to the air; to get wind, to get abroad
Éventi-f, ve, *adj.* contingent
†**Éventiller,** *v.n.* to flap its wings
Éventoir, *s.m.* fire-fan
Éventration, *s.f.* (*med.*) eventration
Éventrer, *v.a.* to disembowel, to embowel; to rip up *or* open; to cut open; to draw (*poultry*); to gut (*fish*); (*nav.*) to split (*a sail*)
Éventualité, *s.f.* contingency, uncertainty
Éventuel, le, *adj.* eventual; contingent, uncertain; — *s.m.* contingency; perquisites; class-fees, course-fees; (*print.*) jobbing, jobs
Éventuellement, *adv.* eventually; contin-
Éventure, *s.f.* crack, flaw [gently
Évêque, *s.m.* bishop. *Un chien regarde bien un* —, a cat may look at a king
Éverrer, *v.a.* to worm (*a dog*)
Éversi-f, ve, *adj.* eversive, subversive
Éversion, *s.f.* eversion, subversion
Évertuer (S'), *v.r.* to strive, to exert *or* bestir
Éviction, *s.f.* (*law*) eviction [oneself
Évidage, Évidement, *s.m.* hollowing; grooving, &c. (*V.* **Évider**); scooping out; unstarching; hollow; groove; scallop
Évidemment, *adv.* evidently, obviously, plainly, clearly; certainly, to be sure
Évidence, *s.f.* evidence; obviousness, plainness, clearness. *En* —, evident, obvious, forward, conspicuous; conspicuously, in a conspicuous situation *or* position; in a clear *or* plain light
Évident, e, *adj.* evident, obvious, plain, clear
Évider, *v.a.* to hollow out; to hollow; to groove; to scoop out; to round; to scallop; to stamp, to pink; to carve; to cut the inner branches off; to unstarch
Évideur, *s.m.* groover (*of needles*)
Évidoir, *s.m.* hollowing-bit

Évidure, *s.f. V.* **Évidage**
Évier, *s.m.* sink; sink-stone; gutter, drain. *Pierre d'—*, sink-stone; gutter-stone
Évilasse, *s.m.* Madagascar ebony
Évincer, *v.a.* to evict; to oust; to turn out
Éviration, *s.f.* eviration
Éviscération, *s.f.* evisceration; (*med.*) even- [tration
Éviscérer, *v.a.* to eviscerate
Évitable, *adj.* avoidable, evitable; preventable
Évitage, *s.m.*, **Évitée,** *s.f.* (*nav.*) swinging; swinging-room, berth; (*navig.*) ship-width (*of a canal or river*) [siding, shunt, turn-out
Évitement, *s.m.* avoiding. *Gare d'—*, (*rail.*)
Éviter, *v.a.* to avoid; to shun; to eschew; to decline; to evade; to elude; to escape; to save, to spare; — *v.n.* (*nav.*) to swing, to tend, to stem
S'—, *v.r.* to avoid *or* &c. each other; to save *or* spare oneself; (*of things*) to be avoided, &c.
Évocable, *adj.* (*law*) removable (*from one court to another*), evokable
Évocation, *s.f.* evocation; raising up; (*law*) removal (*from one court to another*), evocation
Évocatoire, *adj.* (*law*) of *or* for removal (*from one court to another*); that may cause an evocation
Évoluer, *v.n.* to evolve; to revolve; (*mil., nav.*) to make *or* perform *or* go through evolutions
Évoluté, e, *adj.* (*nat. hist.*) convoluted
Évoluti-f, ve, *adj.* evolving [field-practice
Évolution, *s.f.* evolution. *—s de ligne*, (*mil.*)
Évolutionnaire, *adj.* evolutionary
Évoquer, *v.a.* to evoke; to conjure; to raise; to call up; (*law*) to remove (*from one court to another*), to evoke
Évulsi-f, ve, *adj.* evulsive
Évulsion, *s.f.* evulsion
Ex, (*Latin prep., prefix*) ex
Exacerbation, *s.f.* exacerbation
Exact, e, *adj.* exact; accurate; correct; precise; punctual; strict; close
Exactement, *adv.* exactly; accurately; correctly; precisely; punctually; strictly; closely; quite
Exacteur, *s.m.* exactor, extortioner
Exaction, *s.f.* exaction, extortion
Exactitude, *s.f.* exactness; accuracy; correctness; preciseness, precision; punctuality; strictness; closeness
Exagéra-teur, trice, *s.m.f.* exaggerator; — *adj.* exaggeratory, exaggerating, apt to exaggerate [rating
Exagérati-f, ve, *adj.* exaggeratory, exagge-
Exagération, *s.f.* exaggeration; amplification; magnifying; overrating; excess; aggravation; wild fancy
Exagéré, e, *part.* exaggerated, &c. (*V.* **Exagérer**); — *adj.* given to exaggeration, &c. *V.* **Outré;** — *s.m.f.* exaggerator; enthusiast; fanatic; ultra; wild schemer
Exagérément, *adv.* with exaggeration, excessively, unreasonably
Exagérer, *v.a.* to exaggerate; to carry to excess; to amplify; to magnify; to overrate; to aggravate
S'—, *v.r.* to be exaggerated, &c.; to exaggerate *or* &c. to oneself, to exaggerate, to overrate
Exaltable, *adj.* excitable
Exaltation, *s.f.* exaltation; elevation; exaggeration; excitement; over-excitement; ardour; enthusiasm; fanaticism
Exalté, e, *part. adj.* exalted, &c. (*V.* **Exalter**); over-excited; heated; feverish; ardent, enthusiastic; extreme; fanatic; — *s.m.f.* enthusiast; fanatic; hot-headed fellow
Exalter, *v.a.* to exalt; to elate; to extol; to magnify; to glorify; to exaggerate; to excite; to work up; to over-excite; to heat; to inflame
S'—, *v.r.* to exalt *or* &c. each other; to work itself up; to become excited, &c.; to be over-excited; to become enthusiastic; to rise; to be exalted, &c.
Examen, *s.m.* examination; inspection; survey; inquiry; scrutiny; consideration. *Libre —*, freethinking

Examina-teur, trice, *s.m.f.* examiner
Examiner, *v.a.* to examine; to inspect; to look at; to look over *or* into; to survey; to inquire into; to scrutinize; to consider, to weigh; to try, to assay [other; to be examined, &c.
S'—, *v.r.* to examine *or* &c. oneself *or* each
Exanie, *s.f.* (*surg.*) exania
Exanthémateu-x, se, Exanthématique, *adj.* (*med.*) exanthematous, exanthematic
Exanthème, *s.m.* (*med.*) exanthema
‡**Exarchat,** *s.m.* exarchate
Exarque, *s.m.* exarch
Exaspération, *s.f.* exasperation; aggravation; exaggeration; excessive increase; excess; acme
Exaspérer, *v.a.* to exasperate; to inflame; to aggravate; to exaggerate; to increase to excess, to raise excessively
S'—, *v.r.* to become (*or* get) exasperated *or* &c.
Exaucement, *s.m.* hearing; granting
Exaucer, *v.a.* to hear the prayer of, to hear favourably, to hear; to grant
Excarnation, *s.f.* excarnation
Excarner, *v.a.* to excarnate
Excavateur, *s.m.* excavator
Excavation, *s.f.* excavation; hollowing; digging; cavity, hollow
Excaver, *v.a.* to excavate; to hollow; to dig
S'—, *v.r.* to be excavated *or* &c. [**Excéder**)
Excédant, e, *part. adj.* exceeding, &c. (*V.*
Excédant, *s.m.* surplus; overweight; excess
Excéder, *v.a.* to exceed; to weary, to tire out, to tire, to fatigue, to harass, to knock up; to overwhelm; to exhaust, to wear out
Excellemment, *adv.* excellently, surpassingly
Excellence, *s.f.* excellence, excellency. *Par —*, preeminently, above all, of all others; in the highest degree, in the extreme; perfect; unrivalled; excellently, surpassingly; by way of eminence *or* distinction; *the* (*l'endroit par —*, *the* place). *Donner de l'— à*, (*fam.*) to style (*a person*) "Excellency" [ful; capital; very fine
Excellent, e, *adj.* excellent; perfect; delight-
Excellentissime, *adj.* most excellent
Exceller, *v.n.* to excel; to surpass
Excentricité, *s.f.* eccentricity
Excentrique, *adj.m.f., s.m.* eccentric
Excentriquement, *adv.* eccentrically
Excepté, *prep.* except, save, but
Excepter, *v.a.* to except [be excepted
S'—, *v.r.* to except oneself *or* each other; to
Exception, *s.f.* exception; plea; bar. *— péremptoire*, demurrer. *A l'— de*, with the exception of, except. *D'—*, exceptional
Exceptionnel, le, *adj.* exceptional
Exceptionnellement, *adv.* exceptionally
Excès, *s.m.* excess; abuse; violence; intemperance; riot; jollification
Excessi-f, ve, *adj.* excessive; extreme; unreasonable; immoderate; intemperate; extravagant; exorbitant
Excessivement, *adv.* excessively, to excess; exceedingly; extremely; unreasonably; immoderately; intemperately; extravagantly; exorbitantly; enormously, immensely; an immense amount *or* quantity
Excessiveté, *s.f.* excessiveness
Exciper, *v.n.* to plead an exception, to allege, [to plead
Excipient, *s.m.* (*pharm.*) excipient
Excise, *s.f.* (English) excise; excisemen; excise department; excise office [excised *or* cut off
Exciser, *v.a.* to excise, to cut off. *S'—*, to be
Excision, *s.f.* excision, cutting off
Excitabilité, *s.f.* excitability
Excitable, *adj.* excitable
Excitant, e, *part. adj.* exciting, &c. (*V.* **Exciter**); (*med.*) stimulant; — *s.m.* excitant; (*med.*) stimulant [(*phys.*) excitator
Excita-teur, trice, *s.m.f.* exciter; — *s.m.*
Excitati-f, ve, *adj.*, **Excitatif,** *s.m.* excitative; (*med., obsolete*) *V.* **Excitant**
Excitation, *s.f.* excitement; exciting, excitation; inciting; stimulation

Excitement, *s.m.* excitement
Exciter, *v.a.* to excite; to incite; to urge; to animate; to inspirit; to rouse; to stir up, to stir; to stimulate; to inflame; to provoke; to instigate; to set on; to set
S'—, *v.r.* to excite *or* &c. oneself *or* each other; to be excited, &c.
Exciteu-r, se, *s.m.f.* exciter
Excitomo-teur, trice, *adj.* (*in physiology*) excitomotory
Exclamati-f, ve, *adj.* exclamative, exclamatory, of exclamation
Exclamation, *s.f.* exclamation; shout
Exclamativement, *adv.* exclamatively
Exclamer, *v.n.a.,* **S'—,** *v.r.* to exclaim, to cry out, to clamour, to shout; to protest
Exclure, *v.a.* to exclude; to preclude; to debar; to shut out
Exclusi-f, ve, *adj.s.* exclusive
Exclusion, *s.f.* exclusion
Exclusivement, *adv.* exclusively
Exclusivisme, *s.m.* exclusionism, exclusivism; exclusiveness
Exclusiviste, *s.m.f.* exclusionist, exclusive; — *adj.* exclusionary
Excommunicateur, *s.m.* excommunicator
Excommunication, *s.f.* excommunication
Excommunicatoire, *adj.* excommunicatory
Excommunié, e, *part. adj.* excommunicated; — *s.m.f.* excommunicated person, excommunicate
Excommunier, *v.a.* to excommunicate
Excoriation, *s.f.* (*surg.*) excoriation
Excorier, *v.a.* (*surg.*) to excoriate
Excortication, &c. *V.* **Décortication**
Excrément, *s.m.* excrement. *— de la terre,* scum of the earth
Excrémenteu-x, se, Excrémentiel, le, Excrémentitiel, le, *adj.* excrementitious, excremental, excrementitial
Excreta, *s.m.pl.* (*Latin*) excreta, excretions
Excréter, *v.a.* to excrete
Excré-teur, trice, Excrétoire, *adj.* excretory
Excrétion, *s.f.* excretion
Excroissance, *s.f.* excrescence; fungus
Excursion, *s.f.* excursion; ramble; trip
Excursioniste, *s.m.f.* excursionist
Excurvé, e, *adj.* excurvate, curved outward
Excusable, *adj.* excusable
Excusablement, *adv.* excusably
Excuse, *s.f.* excuse; apology; exculpation. *Faire —, faire des* (or *ses*) *—s,* to beg pardon, to apologize, to make an apology. *Faites —!* (*pop.*) excuse me! I beg your pardon!
Excuser, *v.a.* to excuse; to exculpate; to apologize for. *Excusez-moi!* excuse me! pardon me! *Excusez!* (*pop.*) excuse me! I beg your pardon! indeed! upon my word! bless me! *Excusez du peu!* (*fam., ironically*) only that! how modest!
S'—, *v.r.* to excuse *or* exculpate oneself; to plead as an excuse, to plead, to allege; to throw the blame; to apologize; to beg to be excused; to decline; (*of things*) to be excused
Exeat, *s.m.* exeat; pass; leave
Exécrabilité, *s.f.* execrability, execrableness
Exécrable, *adj.* execrable
Exécrablement, *adv.* execrably
Exécration, *s.f.* execration
Exécratoire, *adj.* execratory
Exécrer, *v.a.* to execrate
Exécutable, *adj.* executable, practicable, feasible
Exécutant, e, *s.m.f.* performer, player, musician
Exécuter, *v.a.* to execute; to carry out; to perform; to fulfil; to achieve; to accomplish; to do; to make; to enforce; to distrain; to expel *or* dismiss from the stock-exchange
S'—, *v.r.* to be executed *or* &c.; to sell off o.'s property; to sacrifice oneself; to make a sacrifice; to make an effort, to comply, to yield, to submit; to do it
Exécu-teur, trice, *s.m.f.* executor, executrix; executioner, hangman
Exécuti-f, ve, *adj.,* **Exécutif,** *s.m.* executive
Exécution, *s.f.* execution; working; performance; fulfilment; achievement; accomplishment. *Homme d'—,* bold and enterprising man; practical man [of execution, execution
Exécutoire, *adj.* (*law*) executory; — *s.m.* writ of execution, execution
Exécutoirement, *adv.* (*law*) by execution
Exèdre, *s.m.* (*arch.*) exedra, exhedra
Exégèse, *s.f.* exegesis
Exégète, *s.m.* exegete, exegetist
Exégétique, *adj.* exegetical
Exemplaire, *adj.* exemplary; — *s.m.* (*of a book,* &c.) copy, specimen; (*obsolete*) model, pattern, exemplar
Exemplairement, *adv.* exemplarily
Exemple, *s.m.* example; parallel; precedent; instance; case; pattern; model; copy; slip, copy-slip. *A l'— de,* after the example of, in imitation of. *Par —,* for instance; as to that; but then; but yet, yet; indeed! to be sure! I dare say! only fancy! the idea! well now! bless me! bless my heart! *Pour —,* as an instance. *Sans —,* unexampled, unparalleled, unprecedented. *Prêcher d'—,* to practise what one preaches
Exempt, e, *adj.* exempt, free; exempted; — *s.m.* (*old*) police-officer, officer, constable
Exemptable, *adj.* exemptible
Exempter, *v.a.* to exempt, to free; to exonerate; to dispense
Exemption, *s.f.* exemption; exoneration; dispensation
***Exequatur,** *s.m.* (*dipl.*) exequatur; (*law*) attachment
Exercer, *v.a.n.* to exercise; to instruct; to train up; to drill; to practise; to exert; to use; to employ; to make; to try; to administer; to follow, to carry on; to fill (*an office*); to commit; to act; to visit, to inspect and rate excisable commodities
S'—, *v.r.* to exercise *or* &c. oneself; to practise, to exercise; to be exercised *or* &c.
Exercice, *s.m.* exercise; exertion; use; action; working, work; practice; execution; performance; service, functions; office; receipts and expenditure; financial year, dividend year, year; inspection (*of an exciseman*); drill, drilling; (*obsolete*) trouble, fatigue. *Faire l'—,* to drill. *Faire faire l'— à ...,* to drill ... *Prendre* (or, obsolete, *faire*) *de l'—,* to take exercise
Exérèse, *s.f.* (*surg.*) exeresis
Exergue, *s.m.* exergue
Exert, e, *adj.* (*bad spelling*) *V.* **Exsert**
Exfœtation, *s.f.* (*med.*) exfœtation
Exfoliati-f, ve, *adj.* exfoliative
Exfoliation, *s.f.* exfoliation
Exfolier, *v.a.,* **S'—,** *v.r.* to exfoliate
Exfumer, *v.a.* (*paint.*) to soften
Exhalaison, *s.f.* exhalation, effluvium
Exhalation, *s.f.* exhalation, exhaling
Exhalatoire, *adj.* exhaling, evaporating; — *s.f.* evaporating-apparatus
Exhaler, *v.a.* to exhale; to emit, to send *or* give forth; to evaporate; to breathe out *or* forth; to vent, to give vent to
S'—, *v.r.* to exhale; to evaporate; to find vent; to come out; to break out; to be exhaled *or* &c.
Exhaussement, *s.m.* raising; height; mound; drift
Exhausser, *v.a.* to raise. *S'—,* to raise oneself; to be raised
Exhaustion, *s.f.* (*math., phys.,* &c.) exhaustion
Exhèdre, *s.m.* *V.* **Exèdre**
Exhérédation, *s.f.* (*law*) exheredation, disinherison, disinheritance
Exhéréder, *v.a.* (*law*) to exheredate, to disinherit
Exhiber, *v.a.* (*law, admin., jest.*) to exhibit, to produce, to show
Exhibition, *s.f.* (*law, admin., fam. & jest.*) exhibition, producing, showing, show
Exhibitoire, *adj.* exhibitory
Exhilarant, e, *adj.* exhilarating, exhilarant
Exhorta-teur, trice, *s.m.f.* exhortator, exhorter
Exhortati-f, ve, *adj.* exhortative, hortative
Exhortation, *s.f.* exhortation
Exhortatoire, *adj.* exhortatory, hortatory

Exhorter, *v.a.* to exhort; to admonish
Exhumation, *s.f.* exhumation, disinterment
Exhumer, *v.a.* to exhume; to disinter; to bring to light, to revive, to rake up
Exigeant, e, *adj.* too difficult to please; too particular; over nice; requiring *or* expecting too much; unreasonable; troublesome; exacting, exigent; — *s.m.f.* ditto person
Exigence, *s.f.* exigency; requirement; unreasonableness; fastidiousness; unreasonable wish *or* request *or* demand; troublesome call *or* demand; authoritative demand; authoritativeness
Exiger, *v.a.* to require; to demand; to exact
S'—, *v.r.* to be required *or* &c.
Exigibilité, *s.f.* exigibility [due, payable
Exigible, *adj.* exigible, demandable, requirable,
Exigu, ë, *adj.* scanty, slender; small
Exiguïté, *s.f.* scantiness, slenderness; small-
Exil, *s.m.* exile, banishment [ness
Exilé, e, *s.m.f.* exile, refugee
Exiler, *v.a.* to exile, to banish
Exilité, *s.f.* (*old*) slenderness, smallness
Exinanition, *s.f.* exinanition
Existant, e, *part. adj.* existing, existent, extant, being, living
Existence, *s.f.* existence; being; life; subsistence; living; (social) position
Exister, *v.n.* to exist; to be; to live; to be
Exocet, *s.m.* flying fish [extant; to subsist
Exocyste, *s.f.* (*surg.*) exocystis [ode, exodium
Exode, *s.m.* Exodus; (*Gr. & Rom. antiquity*) ex-
Exodique, *adj.* (*in physiology*) exodic
Exogène, *adj.* (*bot.*) exogenous; — *s.f.* exogen
Exoine, *s.f.* certificate from a medical man; (*old Fr. law*) essoin
Exomètre, *s.f.* (*surg.*) exometra [exomphalos
Exomphale, Exomphalocèle, *s.f.* (*surg.*)
Exonération, *s.f.* exoneration, discharge; exemption [to exempt
Exonérer, *v.a.* to exonerate, to discharge;
Exonirose, *s.f.* (*med.*) exoneirosis, nocturnal pollution
Exophthalmie, *s.f.* (*med.*) exophthalmia
Exorable, *adj.* exorable
Exorbitamment, *adv.* exorbitantly; excessively; extravagantly; outrageously
Exorbitance, *s.f.* exorbitance, exorbitancy; excessiveness; extravagance; outrageousness
Exorbitant, e, *adj.* exorbitant; excessive; extravagant; outrageous
Exorbitisme, *s.m.* (*med.*) *V.* **Exophthalmie**
Exorciser, *v.a.* to exorcise
Exorciseu-r, se, *s.m.f.* exorciser
Exorc-isme, -iste. *V.* page 3, § 1
Exorde, *s.m.* exordium; beginning
Exosmose, *s.f.* (*phys.*) exosmose, exosmosis
Exosmotique, *adj.* (*phys.*) exosmotic
Exostose, *s.f.* (*surg., bot.*) exostosis
Exostoser (S'), *v.r.* to form in exostosis
Exotér-ique, -iquement. *V.* page 3, § 1
Exotérisme, *s.m.* exotericism, exoterics
Exotique, *adj.* exotic, foreign, outlandish
Expansibilité, *s.f.* expansibility
Expansible, *adj.* expansible
Expansi-f, ve, *adj.* expansive; unreserved, open-minded, open-hearted [unreserved joy
Expansion, *s.f.* expansion; unreservedness;
Expatriation, *s.f.* expatriation
Expatrier, *v.a.* to expatriate
S'—, *v.r.* to expatriate oneself, to leave o.'s
Expectance, *s.f.* expectancy [native country
Expectant, e, *adj. s.,* **Expectati-f, ve,** *adj.* expectant [expectant medicine
Expectantisme, *s.m.* (*jest.*) expectantism,
Expectation, *s.f.* (*med.*) expectation
Expectative, *s.f.* expectation; expectancy; hope, hopes; prospects; abeyance; reversion
Expectorant, e, *adj.,* **Expectorant,** *s.m.* (*med.*) expectorant
Expectoration, *s.f.* expectoration
Expectorer, *v.a.n.* to expectorate

Expédiée, *s.f.* (*writ.*) running hand
Expédience, *s.f.* (*old*) expediency
Expédient, e, *adj.* expedient, proper, fit; — *s.m.* expedient, shift
Expédier, *v.a.* to despatch; to expedite, to hasten; to send, to forward; to get *or* go through, to knock off; to clear out *or* off; to draw up; to copy; (*cust.*) to clear
S'—, *v.r.* to be despatched *or* &c.
Expédi-teur, trice, *s.m.f.* sender; commission-agent; shipper
Expéditi-f, ve, *adj.* expeditious, quick
Expédition, *s.f.* expedition; expeditiousness; despatch; forwarding, sending; shipment; copy; (*cust.*) clearance
Expéditionnaire, *adj.* expeditionary; that forwards goods; copying; — *s.m.* commission-agent; sender; copying-clerk, copier; law-stationer, law-writer [— *v.a.* to copy
Expéditionner, *v.n.* to go on an expedition;
Expéditivement, *adv.* expeditiously
Expérience, *s.f.* experience; experiment;
Expérimental, e, *adj.* experimental [trial
Expérimentalement, *adv.* experimentally
Expérimenta-teur, trice, *s.m.f.* experimentalist, experimenter; — *adj.* experimenting
Expérimentation, *s.f.* experimentation
Expérimenter, *v.a.n.* to experience; to experiment; to try; to test [experience
S'—, *v.r.* to be experienced *or* &c.; to acquire
Expert, *s.m.* expert; appraiser, valuer; surveyor; inspector; assessor; arbitrator; medical witness *or* authority. — *-chimiste,* analytical chemist. — *-comptable,* actuary. — *-priseur,* appraiser. *A dire d'—s,* on *or* by official estimation; (*fig.*) outright, unreservedly
Expert, e, *adj.* expert, skilful, skilled, versed
Expertement, *adv.* expertly, skilfully
Expertise, *s.f.* function *or* report of an expert (*or* of experts), report; appraisement, valuation; survey; (official) inspection; assessment; arbitration
Expertiser, *v.a.n.* to appraise, to value, to make valuations; to survey, to examine, to inspect; to assess
S'—, *v.r.* to be appraised *or* &c.
Expiable, *adj.* expiable
Expia-teur, trice, *s.m.f.* expiator, expiatist, atoner; — *adj.* expiatory
Expiation, *s.f.* expiation; atonement
Expiatoire, *adj.* expiatory
Expier, *v.a.* to expiate, to atone for; to pay for
S'—, *v.r.* to be expiated *or* &c. [inaudible
Expirant, e, *part. adj.* expiring; dying; faint;
Expira-teur, trice, *adj.* (*anat.*) expiratory
Expiration, *s.f.* expiration
Expirer, *v.n.* to expire; to die; to die away; to run out; — *v.a.* to expire, to breathe out
Expléti-f, ve, *adj.,* **Explétif,** *s.m.* (*gram.*)
Explétivement, *adv.* expletively [expletive
Explicable, *adj.* explicable, explainable
Explica-teur, trice, *s.m.f.* explainer; show-
Explicati-f, ve, *adj.* explanatory [man; guide
Explication, *s.f.* explanation; translation, reading, construing
Explicit, *s.m.* (*old*) explicit, the end
Explicite, *adj.* explicit; express
Explicité, *s.f.* explicitness
Explicitement, *adv.* explicitly; expressly
Expliquer, *v.a.* to explain; to expound; to illustrate; to express; to declare; to read, to construe, to translate; to account for; to make out; to solve
S'—, *v.r.* to explain oneself *or* o.'s meaning; to speak out; to speak plainly; to be clear; to enter into an explanation, to give explanation, to explain; to make o.'s statements; to account for, to make out, to understand; to have an explanation; to explain itself *or* each other; to be explained *or* &c.; to manifest itself; (*obsolete*) to explicate *or* unfold *or* develop itself
Expliqueu-r, se, *s.m.f.* explainer

Exploit, *s.m.* exploit, deed, achievement, feat; (*law*) writ, process

Exploitabilité, *s.f.* workableness; cultivableness; improvableness; distrainableness; gullibility

Exploitable, *adj.* that may be worked *or* cultivated *or* felled, workable, cultivable; that may be turned to account; improvable; distrainable; gullible

Exploitant, *s.m.* worker; cultivator, farmer; grower; manager, director; — *adj.m.* (*law*) process-serving, writ-serving (*Huissier* —, process-server, summoning officer)

Exploita-teur, trice, *s.m.f.* *V.* **Exploiteur**

Exploitation, *s.f.* working; cultivation, farming, improving; growing; administering, managing, management, direction; enterprise, concern, establishment, farm, forest, works, line (of railway), &c.; speculation; operation; employing, using; turning to account, making capital (out of); taking advantage (of); trading (on, on the merits of); cheating, imposition. — *rurale*, cultivation of the soil, agriculture, farming; farm. — *de l'homme par l'homme*, speculating on the labour of others

Exploiter, *v.a.* to work; to cultivate for sale, to cultivate; to farm; to improve; to grow; to administer, to manage; to employ, to use; to make the most of; to speculate upon; to turn to account, to make capital out of; to take advantage of; to trade on *or* on the merits of; to cheat, to impose *or* put upon; — *v.n.* (*law*) to serve writs *or* processes

S'—, *v.r.* to be worked *or* &c.; to take advantage of *or* &c. each other

Exploiteu-r, se, *s.m.f.* jobber, speculator, trafficker (on), sweater; cheat, knave

Explorable, *adj.* explorable

Explora-teur, trice, *s.m.f.* explorer; — *adj.* exploring

Explorati-f, ve, *adj.* explorative, exploratory

Exploration, *s.f.* exploration

Explorativement, *adv.* exploratively

Explorer, *v.a.* to explore. *S'—*, to be explored

Explosibilité, *s.f.* explosiveness

Explosible, Explosi-f, ve, *adj.* explosive

Explosion, *s.f.* explosion; blowing up; bursting; burst, outburst; breaking out, outbreak; discharge; report. *Faire* —, to explode; to blow up; to burst; to burst out; to break out; to detonate

Exponction, *s.f.* expunction

Exponentiel, le, *adj.* (*alg.*) exponential; — *s.f.* exponential quantity

Exportable, *adj.* exportable

Exporta-teur, trice, *s.m.f.* exporter; — *adj.* exporting

Exportation, *s.f.* exportation; export

Exporter, *v.a.* to export. *S'—*, to be exported

Exporteu-r, se, *s.m.f.* (*old*) *V.* **Exportateur**

Exposant, e, *s.m.f.* exhibitor; (*law*) petitioner; — *s.m.* (*math.*) exponent

Exposé, *s.m.* statement; account; (*law*) recital

Exposé, e, *part. adj.* exposed, &c. (*V.* **Exposer**); in *or* on view; conspicuous; situated; looking (*to the north or south or &c.*); lying open, open; lying; lying in state; uncovered; liable; exposed to danger; abandoned

Exposer, *v.a.* to expose; to exhibit; to show; to disclose; to make known; to lay (before); to state; to explain; to expound; to turn (to); to desert; to venture, to endanger; to lay open; (*of dead bodies*) to lay in state, to expose; (*obsolete*) to utter (*coin*). *Être exposé au nord, au midi*, to have (*or* to be of) a northern, a southern aspect

S'—, *v.r.* to expose oneself; to run the risk (of); to commit oneself; to be exposed *or* exhibited *or* &c.

Exposeur, *s.m.* exposer; expositor, exponent, explainer, expounder

Expositi-f, ve, *adj.* expositive, expository

Exposition, *s.f.* exposition; exposure; exposing; exhibition; show; aspect, situation; statement; account; narration; explanation; (*of dead bodies*) lying in state, exposition

Expr-ès, esse, *adj.* express, positive, plain clear, distinct; strict

Exprès, *adv.* purposely, on purpose. *Tout* —, expressly, for the very purpose (of). *Tout* — *pour cela*, for that very purpose. *C'est un fait* —, it is done on purpose. *C'est comme un fait* —, one would think it was done on purpose

Exprès, *s.m.* express messenger, express

Express, *adj. s.m.* (*rail.*) express

Expressément, *adv.* expressly, positively, plainly, clearly, distinctly; strictly

Expressi-f, ve, *adj.* expressive

Expression, *s.f.* expression; utterance. *La plus simple* —, (*math.*) the lowest terms

Expressivement, *adv.* expressively

Exprimable, *adj.* expressible

Exprimer, *v.a.* to express; to press out, to squeeze out; to be expressive of; to utter; to declare; to tell; to word; to represent

S'—, *v.r.* to express oneself; to be expressed

Expropriation, *s.f.* expropriation; dispossession

Exproprier, *v.a.* to expropriate; to dispossess

Expugnable, *adj.* expugnable

Expuition, *s.f.* *V.* **Exspuition**

Expulser, *v.a.* to expel; to turn out *or* off; to drive; to drive out; to put *or* throw out; to eject; to exclude; to extrude

S'—, *v.r.* to be expelled *or* &c.

Expul-seur, trice, *adj.* expelling

Expulsi-f, ve, *adj.* expulsive

Expulsion, *s.f.* expulsion; ejection, ejectment; exclusion; extrusion

Expurgation, *s.f.* expurgation

Expurgatoire, *adj.* expurgatory

Expurger, *v.a.* to expurgate. *S'—*, to be expurgated

Exquis, e, *adj.* exquisite; — *s.m.* exquisiteness, exquisite

Exquisement, *adv.* exquisitely

Exsangue, Exsanguin, e, *adj.* (*med.*) exsanguious, exsanguineous, bloodless; (*fig.*) weak, feeble, spiritless; colourless

Exsert, e, *adj.* (*nat. hist.*) exsert, exserted

Exsertion, *s.f.* (*nat. hist.*) exsertion

Exsiccation, *s.f.* exsiccation

Exspuition, *s.f.* (*med.*) exspuition, spitting out

Exstrophie, *s.f.* (*surg.*) extroversion

Exsuccion, *s.f.* exsuction

Exsudation, *s.f.* exsudation, exudation, sweating, sweat, perspiration, oozing out

Exsuder, *v.n.* to exsude, to exude, to sweat, to perspire, to ooze out

Exsufflation, *s.f.* exsufflation

Extase, *s.f.* ecstasy, rapture; trance

Extasié, e, *adj.* in ecstasy, in raptures, enraptured, transported; wondering

Extasier, *v.a.* to enrapture, to charm; — *v.n.*, **S'—,** *v.r.* to be in ecstasy *or* in raptures, to be enraptured *or* transported; to be struck with admiration *or* amazement, to wonder

Extatique, *adj. s.* ecstatic

Extemporané, e, *adj.* extemporaneous; unpremeditated

Extemporanéité, *s.f.* extemporaneousness

Extemporanément, *adv.* extemporaneously

Extenseur, *adj.m.*, *s.m.* (*anat.*) extensor

Extensibilité, *s.f.* extensibility, extensibleness

Extensible, *adj.* extensible, extendible

Extensi-f, ve, *adj.* extending, of extension, expanding, of expansion; (*gram.*, *agr.*) extended, extensive

Extension, *s.f.* extension; tension; expansion; span; extent; strain

Extenso (In), *adv.* in extenso, at full length

Exténuation, *s.f.* extenuation; weakening; weakness; exhaustion

Exténuer, *v.a.* to extenuate; to weaken; to exhaust

Extérieur, e, *adj.* exterior, external, outward, outer, outside; extrinsic; foreign; — *s.m.* exterior; outside; appearance; foreign countries, abroad; foreign department. *A l'—*, without, on the outside, outside; externally; out of doors; abroad; outwards, without, outside

Extérieurement, *adv.* externally, outwardly,

Extérioriste, *s.m.* (*philos.*) exteriorist

Extériorité, *s.f.* exteriority
Extermina-teur, trice, *adj.* exterminating, destroying; — *s.m.f.* exterminator, exterminatress, destroyer
Extermination, *s.f.* extermination
Exterminer, *v.a.* to exterminate, to destroy; (*fam.*) to tire out, to knock up, to exhaust
S'—, *v.r.* to exterminate *or* &c. each other; to knock oneself up, &c.; to be exterminated, &c.
Externat, *s.m.* day-school; (*of hospitals*) dressership
Externe, *adj.* external; exterior; outward; outer; out-door, out; non-resident; — *s.m.f.* extern; non-resident; day-pupil; —*s.m.* junior clerk; (*of hospitals*) dresser, physician's clerk
Exterritorialité, *s.f.* exterritoriality
Extinc-teur, trice, *adj.* extinguishing; destroying; fire-extinguishing, fire-annihilating; — *s.m.f.* destroyer; — *s.m.* fire-extinguisher, fire-annihilator
Extinction, *s.f.* extinction; extinguishment; putting out; going out; destruction; abolition; extermination; exhaustion; cessation; reduction, diminution; appeasement; quenching; slaking; quelling, suppression; obliteration; cancelling, annulment; redemption (*of annuities*); liquidation (*of debts*); loss (*of voice*). *A l'— des feux* or *des bougies,* (*at auctions*) by inch [of candle
Extinguible, *adj.* extinguishable
Extirpateur, *s.m.* extirpator; weed-extirpator, grubber [grubbing up; eradication; destruction
Extirpation, *s.f.* extirpation; rooting out;
Extirper, *v.a.* to extirpate; to root out *or* up; to grub up; to eradicate; to destroy utterly
S'—, *v.r.* to be extirpated, &c.
Extorquer, *v.a.* to extort, to wrest
S'—, *v.r.* to be extorted, &c.; to extort *or* &c. from each other
Extorqueu-r, se, *s.m.f.* extortioner
Extorsion, *s.f.* extortion [tionary
Extorsionnaire, *adj.* extortionate, extor-
Extra, *s.m.* extra, something extra; supplement; — *prep.* (*in compounds*) extra-... *D'—, adj.* extra; choice [tress; — *adj.* extracting
Extrac-teur, trice, *s.m.f.* extractor, extrac-
Extracti-f, ve, *adj.*, **Extractif,** *s.m.* extrac-
Extractiforme, *adj.* extractiform [tive
Extraction, *s.f.* extraction; drawing; origin, descent, lineage, birth
Extrader, *v.a.* to surrender *or* deliver *or* give up (*to a foreign state or nation*), to send back
Extradition, *s.f.* extradition
Extrados, *s.m.* (*arch.*) extrados
Extradosser, *v.a.* (*arch.*) to extrados
Extrafin, e, *adj.* extrafine, extra-superfine, extra-refined
Extraire, *v.a.* to extract; to draw out; to draw; to take out; to take; to select; to abstract, to make extracts from, to abridge
S'—, *v.r.* to be extracted *or* &c.
Extrait, *s.m.* extract; abstract, epitome; selection; single number; office copy, copy of certificate, certificate of registry, certificate; [docket
Extrajudiciaire, *adj.* extrajudicial
Extrajudiciairement, *adv.* extrajudicially
Extralégal, e, *adj.* extralegal
Extra-muros. *V.* **Muros**
Extraordinaire, *adj.* extraordinary; uncommon, unusual, out of the way; express; singular, odd, queer; enormous; (*old law*) criminal; — *s.m.* extraordinary *or* unusual thing, what is extraordinary, extraordinary, extraordinaries; extraordinariness; something extra, extra; express messenger, express. *Par —,* extraordinarily; out of the way
Extraordinairement, *adv.* extraordinarily; uncommonly, unusually; singularly, oddly, queerly; enormously; (*old law*) criminally
Extravagamment, *adv.* extravagantly
Extravagance, *s.f.* extravagance, extravagancy; folly; wildness; extravagant thing; extravaganza
Extravagant, e, *adj. s.* extravagant, wild, extravagant person [vaguer
Extravaguant, *part.* raving, &c. (*V.* **Extra-**
Extravaguer, *v.n.* to rave, to talk wildly, to talk like a madman [vasation
Extravasation, Extravasion, *s.f.* extra-
Extravaser, *v.a.* to extravasate; — *v.n.*, **S'—,** *v.r.* to be extravasated *Faire —,* to extravasate
Extrême, *adj.m.f.*, *s.m.* extreme, utmost, excessive. *Les —s se touchent,* extremes meet
Extrêmement, *adv.* extremely, exceedingly; enormously, immensely; an immense amount *or* quantity [the point of death
Extremis (In), *adv.* in extremis, on (*or* at)
Extrémité, *s.f.* extremity; extreme; end; tip; verge, border, brink; excessive want, destitution, misery; last moment; excess. *A l'—,* at *or* to the extremity (of); to extremity; to an extreme; to the last moment; at a push; without resource; dying, on (*or* at) the point of death. *A toute —,* at *or* for the worst
Extrinsèque, *adj.* extrinsic
Extrinsèquement, *adv.* extrinsically
Extrorse, *adj.* (*bot.*) extrorsal, extrorse
Extroversion, *s.f.* (*surg.*) extroversion [antly
Exubéramment, *adv.* exuberantly; luxuri
Exubérance, *s.f.* exuberance; luxuriance
Exubérant, e, *adj.* exuberant; luxuriant
Exubérer, *v.n.* to exuberate, to abound; to luxuriate
Exulcérati-f, ve, *adj.* (*med.*) exulcerative
Exulcération, *s.f.* (*med.*) exulceration
Exulcérer, *v.a.*, **S'—,** *v.r.* (*med.*) to exulcerate
Exultation, *s.f.* (*old*) exultation
Exulter, *v.n.* (*old*) to exult [issue, vent, outlet
Exutoire, *s.m.* (*med.*) exutory, issue; (*fig.*)
Exuviabilité, *s.f.* (*zool.*) exuviability
Exuviable, *adj.* (*zool.*) exuviable
Ex-voto, *s.m. V.* **Voto**

F

F, *s.f.* f. *Les — et les B,* oaths, swearing. *Ne parler que par — et par B,* to be always cursing and swearing, never to speak without swearing
Fa, *s.m.* (*mus.*) fa, F [caper
Fabagelle, *s.f.*, **Fabago,** *s.m.* (*bot.*) bean-
Fable, *s.f.* fable; fiction; story, tale, untruth; mythology; byword, laughing-stock
Fabliau, *s.m.* (*Fr. liter.*) fabliau, tale (*in verse*), little fable, ballad
Fablier, *s.m.* fabulist, fabler; fable-book [tree
Fabrecoulier, Fabreguier, *s.m.* (*bot.*) nettle-
Fabricant, e, *s.m.f.* manufacturer, maker; mill-owner; — *adj.* manufacturing
Fabrica-teur, trice, *s.m.f.* fabricator, fabricatress, maker; coiner, forger
Fabrication, *s.f.* manufacture; fabrication; making; make; coining; forgery [**Marguillier**
Fabricien, Fabricier, *s.m.* (*obsolete*) *V.*
Fabriquant, *part. pres. of* **Fabriquer**
Fabrique, *s.f.* manufacture; making; make; manufactory; factory, works, mill; fabric; building; revenue *or* property (*of a parish church*), church; vestry-board, churchwardens; churchwardens' pew; fabrication, coining, forging. *Marque de —,* trade-mark. *V.* **Prix**
Fabriquer, *v.a.* to manufacture, to make; to make up; to coin; to fabricate, to forge; to
Se —, *v.r.* to be manufactured, &c. [invent
Fabuleusement, *adv.* fabulously; extraordinarily, incredibly; an extraordinary *or* incredible amount *or* quantity
Fabuleu-x, se, *adj.* fabulous; extraordinary, incredible; — *s.m.* fabulous, fable, fiction
Fabuliste, *s.m.* fabulist
Fabulosité, *s.f.* fabulousness
Façade, *s.f.* front, face, frontage, façade

Face, *s.f.* face; front; aspect, appearance; phase; turn; aspect of affairs; state; surface; (*pop.*) halfpenny, copper, brown, mag. — *à main*, folding eye-glass, folder. *A la — de*, in the face *or* presence of, before. *De* —, in front; from the front; with a full front; front; (*of walls*) external. *En* —, in the face *or* presence; to o.'s face; before; in front; opposite; opposite to it *or* to them; over the way. *Faire — à*, to face; to face about; to front; to meet; to fulfil; to go through; to oppose; to make head against

Facé, e, *adj.* (*in compounds, fam.*) ...-faced

Facétie, *s.f.* facetiousness; joke, jest

Facétieusement, *adv.* facetiously, jocosely

Facétieu-x, se, *adj.* facetious, jocose, jocular, droll, merry

Facettage, *s.m.* facetting

Facette, *s.f.* facet, face

Facetter, *v.a.* to cut with facets

Fâché, e, *adj.* (— *contre*) angry *or* displeased (with); (— *de, en, que*) sorry (for *or* to, for it, that), grieved (at, at it, that); (— *avec*) at variance (with), on bad terms (with)

Fâcher, *v.a.* to make angry; to offend; to vex; to grieve, to afflict

Se —, *v.r.* to get *or* be angry; to take offence; to fall out, to quarrel

Fâcherie, *s.f.* angry feeling, disagreement, quarrel; (*obsolete*) grief, vexation, annoyance

Fâcheusement, *adv.* grievously, sadly; unpleasantly, disagreeably, vexatiously; unfortunately, unluckily, awkwardly; unfavourably; peevishly, crossly

Fâcheu-x, se, *adj.* grievous, sad; troublesome, unpleasant, disagreeable, vexatious; unfortunate, unlucky, awkward; unfavourable; a pity, to be regretted; hard; difficult; peevish, cross; — *s.m.f.* tiresome *or* troublesome person (*or* guest), bore, intruder; — *s.m.* unpleasantness, worst part

Facial, e, *adj.* (*anat.*) facial

Facies, *s.m.* (*nat. hist.*) facies; (*pop.*) phiz

Facile, *adj.* easy; compliant; docile; sociable; yielding; condescending; indulgent; weak; facile; off-hand, flowing, fluent, ready, voluble; free; natural

Facilement, *adv.* easily; fluently; readily

Facilité, *s.f.* easiness; ease; facility; readiness; quickness; fluency; aptitude; accommodation

Faciliter, *v.a.* to facilitate, to make easy

Façon, *s.f.* making; make; workmanship; fashion; shape; form; dressing; manner, way; style; sort, kind; imitation; look; appearance, mien; ornament; affectation; ceremony; fuss; ado; compliment. — *de parler*, form of speech, way of speaking. — *de penser*, way of thinking, opinion, mind. — *d'être*, — *de voir*, *V.* **Manière.** *A la — de*, after the manner of. *A sa* —, in o.'s own way; from o.'s manner. *De cette* —, in this (*or* that) manner *or* way, so; at this (*or* that) rate. *De — à*, so as, in such a way as. *De — ou d'autre*, somehow or other, somehow, some way or other, by some means or other. *De — que*, so that; in such a way that. *De sa* —, of o.'s making; of o.'s own. *De toute* —, every way; anyhow; at any rate; at all events. *En — de*, by way of. *En aucune* —, *d'aucune* —, in any way; in no wise; by no means, not at all. *Sans* —, *V.* **Gêne** (*Sans*). *Avoir bonne* —, to look genteel; to look nice. *Donner à* —, to put out to make. *Prendre* or *travailler à* —, (*of tailors*, &c.) to make up people's own materials. *Dernière* —, last touch, finish, completion; perfect workmanship

Faconde, *s.f.* loquacity, talkativeness, fluency of speech, flow of words, gift of the gab; (*obsolete*) eloquence

Façonnage, Façonnement, *s.m.* fashioning, shaping, &c. (*V.* **Façonner**)

Façonné, e, *part. adj.* fashioned, &c. (*V.* **Façonner**); fancy; — *s.m.* fancy *or* figured articles

Façonner, *v.a.* to fashion, to shape, to form; to make; to make up; to work; to work up; to get up; to finish, to finish off; to polish; to improve; to accustom, to use, to inure; to dress; to adorn, to embellish; to figure; — *v.n.* (*old*) to be ceremonious, to make *or* use ceremony, to stand on ceremony

Se —, *v.r.* to be fashioned *or* &c.; to become polished; to improve; to use *or* accustom oneself, to become used *or* accustomed

Façonnerie, *s.f.* figuring (*of stuffs*)

Façonni-er, ère, *adj.* ceremonious; formal, precise, affected; hypocritical; (*manu.*) finishing; figuring; — *s.m.f.* ceremonious *or* &c. person; hypocrite; (*manu.*) finisher; figurer

Fac-similaire, *adj.* fac-similar

Fac-simile, *s.m.* fac-simile

Fac-similer, *v.a.* to fac-simile, to take the fac-simile of, to copy exactly

Factage, *s.m.* carriage; goods *or* parcels delivery, delivery; porterage; (*abusively for* "Factorage") *V.* **Factorage.** — *parisien*, Paris Parcels Delivery Company

Fac-teur, trice, *s.m.f.* factor, factoress; agent; shop-woman *or* girl; maker, manufacturer; builder (*of organs*); postman, letter-carrier; carrier; (*rail.*) porter; (— *de ville*) van-guard; (*math.*) factor. — **-couvoir,** *s.m.* incubator

Factice, *adj.* factitious; artificial; imitation; sham; mock; unnatural; feigned, pretended; forced; got up; (*of words*) made up, unrecognized, unauthorized

Facticement, *adv.* factitiously

Factieusement, *adv.* factiously

Factieu-x, se, *adj.* factious; — *s.m.f.* factious person, factionist

Faction, *s.f.* faction; sentry, watch, duty. *De* or *en* —, factious; on sentry, on guard, on duty; on the watch. *Être de* or *en* —, *faire* —, *V.* **Sentinelle**

Factionnaire, *s.m.* sentry, sentinel; (*pop.*) excrement

Factorage, *s.m.* factorage

Factorat, *s.m.* factorship

Factorerie, Factorie, *s.f.* factory; indigo-factory

Factoriel, le, *adj.*, **Factorielle,** *s.f.* (*alg.*) factorial

Factorin, *s.m.* (*Italian*) broker *or* factor

Factotum, Factoton, *s.m.* factotum, Jack of all work

Factum, *s.m.* factum, memoir, statement, case

Facture, *s.f.* invoice, bill, bill of parcels; fabrication, making; composition; execution; workmanship; (*of organ-pipes*) size. *Couplet de* —, (*theat.*) sensation song. *Morceau de* —, (*mus.*) long and difficult piece. *Faire suivre les frais d'une* —, to require payment on delivery, to charge forward

Facturer, *v.a.* to invoice

Facturier, *s.m.* (*com.*) invoice-book; invoice-clerk; (*theat.*) sensation-song writer

Facule, *s.f.* (*astr.*) facula

Facultati-f, ve, *adj.* optional; discretionary; (*com., of credit*) blank. *Bref* —, pope's licence, dispensation

Facultativement, *adv.* optionally; discretionarily

Faculté, *s.f.* faculty; option; right; ability, talent; power; means; quality; virtue, property; study, branch, subject; **—s,** *pl.* faculties, &c.; mind; means

Fadaise, *s.f.* trifle, fiddle-faddle, twaddle, foolery, trash, rubbish, nonsense, stuff, bosh

Fadasse, *adj.* very mawkish, nauseous, sickening, insipid, dull, insignificant, unmeaning, pale; — *s.f.* very light-complexioned woman *or* girl, insignificant creature (*without expression*)

Fade, *adj.* insipid, unsavoury, tasteless, flat, stale, mawkish; nauseous; loathsome; dull, heavy, pointless; tame; foolish, silly; unmeaning, insignificant; pale; — *s.m.* fop, dundreary; (*pop.*) share, contribution. *Se sentir le cœur* —, to feel o.'s stomach rise

Fadement, *adv.* insipidly, tastelessly, mawkishly, &c. (*V.* **Fade**)

Fadeur, *s.f.* insipidity, unsavouriness, tastelessness, flatness, mawkishness; nauseousness; dulness, heaviness, pointlessness; tameness;

foolishness, silliness; want of expression; paleness; empty talk, nonsense; insipid compliment

Fagine, *s.f.* (*chem.*) fagine

Fagot, *s.m.* fagot; bundle; idle story; (*pop.*) convict; ticket-of-leave man. *Sentir le* —, to be somewhat unprincipled, to be hardly fit to be trusted; (*old*) to be heretical, to be tainted with heresy. *Il y a —s et —s*, all men are not alike, things of the same name differ in quality, there is cheese and cheese

Fagotage, Fagotement, *s.m.* fagot-making; fagot-wood, brushwood, chatwood, fagots; bundling up, botching up; jumble

†**Fagotaille,** *s.f.* fagot fence

Fagoter, *v.a.* to make into fagots; to bundle up, to botch up; to jumble; to make up, to get up; to dress out, to rig out, to dress slovenly *or* frightfully

Se —, *v.r.* to be made into fagots; to be bundled up *or* &c.; to dress oneself out *or* &c.

Fagoteur, *s.m.* fagot-maker; bungler, botcher; scribbler

Fagotin, *s.m.* small fagot, bundle of wood; monkey dressed up; Pug; merry-andrew, Jack-pudding, clown, fool; sorry jester, wag

Fagoue, *s.f.* sweetbread

Faguenas, *s.m.* (*old*) body-smell, stink

Faguette, *s.f.* (*mil.*) small fagot

Faham, *s.m.* (*bot.*) faham, faam, Isle of Bourbon tea

Fahlertz, *s.m.* (*min.*) fahlerz

Fahlunite, *s.f.* (*min.*) fahlunite

Faiblage, *s.m.* shrinkage, waste, damage; thin part

Faible, *adj.* weak; feeble; faint; slight; slender; thin; helpless; deficient; backward; light; short; small; little; low; poor; meagre; slack; — *s.m.* weak person, weak (*people*); backward boy; weak side; weak part *or* point; weakness; failing; foible; partiality; deficiency; small (*of a sword*)

Faiblement, *adv.* weakly; feebly; faintly; slightly; slenderly; thinly; helplessly; poorly

Faiblesse, *s.f.* weakness; feebleness; faintness; slightness; slenderness; thinness; helplessness; deficiency; defect; backwardness; lightness; shortness; smallness; poorness; meagreness; slackness; foible; partiality; frailty; failing; fainting fit, swoon

Faiblir, *v.n.* to become (*or* grow *or* get) weak; to faint; to fail; to slacken, to relax, to flag; to abate; to fall; to give way, to yield

Faïence, *s.f.* earthenware, crockery, crockery-ware. — *de Delft*, Delft-ware

Faïencé, e, *adj.* cracked

Faïencerie, *s.f.* earthenware, crockery, crockery-ware, pottery, crockery-ware factory *or* trade

Faïenci-er, ère, *s.m.f.* manufacturer of *or* dealer in crockery, crockery-ware man *or* woman, potter; — *adj.* of earthenware, of crockery, of pottery

†**Faignant, e,** *adj. s.* (*pop.*) *V.* **Fainéant**

†**Faille,** *s.f.* stout black Flemish silk; Flemish head-dress of ditto; (*geol., mining,* &c.) outthrow; excavation; (*obsolete*) fault

†**Failli, e,** *s.m.f. adj.* bankrupt; insolvent

†**Faillibilité,** *s.f.* fallibility

†**Faillible,** *adj.* fallible, liable to err

†**Faillir,** *v.n.* to err; to be mistaken; to miss, to come short; to transgress; to fail; to break, to be a bankrupt; to end; to be near *or* on the point of, to nearly ... *J'ai failli tomber, attendre,* &c., I was near falling down, I nearly fell, I nearly had to wait, &c. *Il s'en faut; Peu s'en faut; Tant s'en faut: V.* **Falloir** (*S'en*)

†**Faillite,** *s.f.* failure, bankruptcy; insolvency. *Être en* —, to be a bankrupt *or* an insolvent. *Faire* —, to fail; to become bankrupt *or* insolvent

†**Failloise,** *s.f.* (*nav.*) point where the sun sets, sunset

†**Faillouse,** *s.f. V.* **Bloquette**

Faim, *s.f.* hunger; appetite; (*fig.*) thirst. *Grosse* —, most pressing hunger. *Avoir* —, to be hungry. *Apaiser* or *étourdir la grosse* —, to stay o.'s stomach, to take the edge off the appetite. *Réduire par la* —, to starve out. **-valle,** *s.f.* (*vet.*) hungry-evil

Faîne, *s.f.* (*bot.*) beech-nut *or* mast; (*pop.*) half-penny, copper, brown, mag

Fainéant, e, *adj. s.* idle, lazy, sluggish, slothful; sculking; idler, drone, sluggard, loafer, lazy *or* idle person *or* fellow *or* dog *or* creature *or* thing; sculker

Fainéanter, *v.n.* to idle, to laze, to loaf

Fainéantise, *s.f.* idleness, laziness, sluggishness, slothfulness, sloth, loafing

Faînée, *s.f.* crop of beech-nuts

Fainin, *s.m.* (*pop.*) farthing

Faire, *v.a.n.* to make; to do; to make up; to create; to beget; to make out; to perform; to transact; to carry out *or* on; to practise; to effect; to carry into effect; to execute; to accomplish; to work; to commit; to indulge in; to go on; to go on with; to settle, to conclude; to finish; to frame; to form; to constitute; to be; to ask; to ask for; to charge for; to sell; to give; to furnish, to supply; to pass; to accustom, to use; to inure; to improve; to have; to bear; to sustain; to set up for; to pretend *or* feign to be, to pretend; to sham; to counterfeit; to imitate; to play; to act; to personate; to represent; to paint; to draw; to show; to make a show *or* a display of; to affect; to produce; to excite; to bring; to inspire with; to cause, to get, to have, to order, to give orders for; to let; to enable, to allow; to compel, to oblige, to force; to lead, to induce; to celebrate; to keep; to hold; to serve; to pay; to discharge (*a duty*); to compose, to write; to indite; to draw up; to coin; to build; to raise; to lay; to inflict; to exercise; to follow; to carry on; to wage; to travel, to go; to go through; to canvass; to walk; to ride; to drive; to move, to advance; to take; to eat; to receive *or* take in (*a supply*); to lay in; to get; to gain; to reap, to get in; to set (*sail*); to cut; to cast; to set up; to utter; to deliver; to tell; to say; to talk; to report, to give out; to offer up (*prayers*); to clean; to dress; to trim; to clip; to pare; to shave; to deal in; to deal; to look; to suit, to fit; to last; to mean; to signify, to matter; to have ... to do (with); to concern, to be; to manage, to arrange, to contrive; to take care, to see (that); to be the cause of; to be the cause *or* the reason; to be of any use; to satisfy o.'s natural wants, to do o.'s needs, to evacuate. *A* —, to do, &c.; to be done, &c.; undone; something to do; trouble. *A tout* —, to do everything; fit for *or* capable of everything; of all work. *Avoir à — de*, to want, to have occasion for. *Faire* — ..., to make (*one*) do *or* &c. ...; to have *or* get ... made *or* done, to cause *or* order ... to be made *or* done, to order ... — *aller*, — *avertir*, &c., *V.* **Aller, Avertir,** &c. — *avoir*, — *obtenir*, to procure *or* get (for). — *bâtir*, to have *or* get built, to build; to get a house built; to build houses. — *comprendre*, to make (...) understand; to make (...) understood; to let (...) understand; to let (...) be understood; to give to understand; to give it to be understood. — *connaître*, to make (...) known (to); to make (...) acquainted with; to inform; to notify; to let (...) know; to set forth; to declare; to introduce (to); to discover; to reveal; to show; to make it appear; to unmask, to expose. — *courir*, *V.* **Courir.** — *dire*, to make (*one*) say; to have (...) said; to have it said; to send to tell; to send word; to give orders to say; to give notice; to suggest; to suggest the reflection. — *entendre*, — *entrer*, — *jouer*, — *marcher*, &c., *V.* **Entendre, Entrer, Jouer, Marcher,** &c. — *parler*, to make (...) speak; to apply, to enforce; &c. (*V.* **Parler**). — *parler de soi*, to get *or* be talked of. — *penser*, — *savoir*, — *suivre*, — *tomber*. — *venir*, — *voir*, &c., *V.*

Penser, Savoir, Suivre, Tomber, Venir, Voir, &c. *Laisser* —, &c., *V.* **Laisser,** &c. — *le malade*, to pretend to be ill. — *les cartes*, to deal the cards, to deal. *Fasse le ciel*, may Heaven grant, pray to Heaven. *Faites*, do; go on; don't disturb yourself; don't mention it. *Il fait*, (*imp.*, *of the weather, temperature*, &c.) it is; there is; there falls; there blows. *Il fait chaud, doux, froid, sec, jour, noir*, &c., it is warm *or* hot, mild, cold, dry, daylight, dark, &c. *Il fait un brouillard épais*, there is a thick fog. *Le temps qu'il fait; Le vent qu'il fait: V.* **Temps** & **Vent.** *Ça* or *cela fait que*, so that. *Cela fait bien*, that looks well, that produces a good effect. *Cela fait du bien*, that does (*one*) good; that is pleasant. *Vous faites bien*, you do well, you do (*or* act) right *or* &c. (*V.* **Bien,** *adv.*). *Cela fait beaucoup*, that makes a great difference, that matters much, that is important. *Cela ne fait rien*, that makes no difference, that is nothing, that does not matter *or* signify; that is of no consequence; never mind. *Cela ne fait rien à l'affaire* or *à la chose*, that does not alter the case; that is nothing to the purpose; that signifies nothing. *Cela vous fait-il quelque chose?* does it matter to you? does it inconvenience *or* affect you? *C'est bien fait; C'en est fait*, &c.: *V.* **Fait,** *part. adj. C'est* (or *Voilà*) *ce qui fait que*, this is how it happens that, this is why. *Qu'est-ce que cela fait?* what does that signify? what matters it? what has that to do (with ...)? what is that (*to the purpose*)? *Qu'est-ce que cela me fait?* what is that to me? what do I care for (*or* about) that? *Qu'est-ce que cela fait là?* what is that doing there? what does that do there? *N'avoir que* —, to have no business, to have nothing to do, to be useless, not to be wanted. *N'avoir que — de*, not to want, to need not, to have no need of *or* no occasion for; to have no business with; to have nothing to do with; not to care for. *Ne — que* ..., to do nothing but ...; to do only ..., to do but ...; to only ... *Ne — que de* (*sortir*, &c.), to have *or* be but just (gone out, &c.). *Ne rien* —, to do nothing; to make no difference; to be nothing, to go for nothing (in); to be nothing to the purpose; to have nothing to do (with). *N'en rien* —, to do nothing of the sort *or* of the kind, to do no such thing, to let it alone, not to mind it. *Je n'y puis que* —, I cannot help it. *On ne saurait qu'y* —, it cannot be helped. *Que voulez-vous que j'y fasse?* what can I do? how can I help it? *Rien n'y faisait*, nothing would do, everything was in vain. *Rien ne lui fait*, nothing has any effect on him (*or* her); he (*or* she) does not care for anything. *Pour bien* —, properly, by rights. *Pour quoi —?* what for? *Que* or *Qu'y* or *Comment* —, *V.* **Comment**

Se —, *v.r.* to be done *or* made; to happen, to take place, to be; to become, to turn; to get, to grow; to begin; to set in; to come on; to make oneself; to give oneself out as; to pretend to be, to pretend, to set up for; to make for oneself, to make; to make it; to procure, to get, to gain, to earn, to acquire; to do oneself; to accustom *or* use *or* inure oneself, to become (*or* get *or* be) accustomed *or* used *or* inured; to reconcile oneself; to get into; to ripen, to mature; to improve; to form oneself; to form; to realize; to draw; to make *or* &c. each other. *Se — amener* ..., to have ... brought to him (*or* her *or* oneself, &c.). *Se — comprendre*, to make oneself understood. *Se — connaitre*, to make oneself known, to become known. *Se — dire*, to have (...) told; to require *or* have *or* wait to be told. *Se — entendre*, to make oneself heard *or* understood; to be heard; to perform; to sing. *Se — écouter, voir*, &c., *V.* **Écouter, Voir,** &c. *Se — pendre, raser, tuer*, &c., to get hanged, shaved, killed, &c. *Se — couper les cheveux*, to have *or* get o.'s hair cut. *Comment se fait-il?* how is it? *Comment cela se fait-il?* how is that? *Cela ne se fait pas*, that is not done, people don't do that, that is not the custom. *Se peut-il — que*, can it be that, is it possible that. *Il pourrait se — que*, it might happen that. *Si — se peut*, if it can be done, if possible. *Autant que — se peut*, as much *or* as far as one can, as much as possible. *Paris ne s'est pas fait en un jour*, Rome was not built in a day

Faire, *s.m.* doing, making, deed, execution; (*in fine arts*) manner, style; (*com.*) goods, articles, business

Faisable, *adj.* feasible, to be done, practicable; possible; allowable

Faisan, *s.m.* pheasant

Faisance, *s.f.* dues over and above the rent. — *-valoir*, cultivation, farming; land under cultivation

Faisande, *s.f. V.* **Faisane**

Faisandé, e, *adj.* gamy, high; tainted

Faisandeau, *s.m.* young pheasant

Faisander, *v.a.* to give a flavour of game to, to keep (...) till it gets high *or* gamy; — *v.n.*, **Se** —, *v.r.* to get gamy *or* high; to begin to be tainted. *Laisser trop* —, to keep too long

Faisanderie, *s.f.* pheasantry

Faisandi-er, ère, *s.m.f.* pheasant-breeder

Faisane, *s.f.* (*Poule* —) hen-pheasant

Faisant, *s.m.* doer; chum, crony

Faisceau, *s.m.* bundle; parcel; cluster; group; heap; pile; (*mil.*) pile, stack; (*anat.*) fascia; (*opt.*) pencil; (*fig.*) number; union; alliance; —**x,** *pl.* bundles, &c.; (*Rom. hist.*) fasces, (*fig.*) consular dignity *or* authority. *En* —, in a bundle, &c., in bundles, &c.; (*arch.*) clustered. *Former les —x, Mettre* (or *ranger*) *en* — or *en —x*, (*mil.*) to pile

Faiseu-r, se, *s.m.f.* maker; doer; worker, hand; monger; builder; scribbler; hack; jobber; innovator. — *d'affaires*, promoter, speculator, jobber, (general) agent

Faisse, *s.f.* withe

Faisselle, *s.f.* drainer; basket; stand; cheese-drainer, cheese-vat

Faisser, *v.a.* to withe

Faisserie, *s.f.* open wicker-work

Fait, e, *part. adj.* made, done, &c. (*V.* **Faire**); shaped; organized; qualified, fitted, fit; suited; good enough; calculated; intended; destined; full-grown, grown up, grown; ripe, mature, matured; fit for eating *or* drinking; regular; settled; established; ended; over; accustomed *or* used *or* inured (to); clad, dressed, dressed up, rigged out; (*of horses*) trained; (*of phrases*) made up; (*of words*) authorized by custom. *C'est bien* —, it is well done; it serves him *or* her *or* you, &c. right. *C'est* (or *C'en est*) — *de lui*, it is all up *or* all over with him, he is undone, he is done for. *C'en est* —, the thing is done, it is all up, it is all over; it is decided. *C'en est — de*, it is all over with. *Ce qui est — est* —, what is done cannot be undone. *Cela* —, this done, this being done, thereupon. *Cela est* (or *semble*) — *pour moi*, such things happen to me alone, that is just my luck. *Est-ce —?* is it done? have you done? *Tout* —, *V.* **Tout,** *adv.*

Fait, *s.m.* fact; deed, act; doing; making; feat; event; occurrence; matter of fact; reality; case; matter; point; business; share; (o.'s) own; truth told (*to someone about himself*), unpleasant truth, truth; thing *or* man *or* person (*for one*), what suits (*one*), what one wants *or* wanted. —*s et gestes*, doings; sayings and doings. — *d'armes, haut* —, *beau* —, deed, achievement, (military) exploit. —*s divers*, miscellaneous news (accidents, &c.), newspaper gossip *or* tittle-tattle. — *à part*, particular *or* exceptional case; different affair, other matter. *Mon* (or *votre*, &c.) —, my (*or* your, &c.) case *or* business *or* doing *or* making *or* &c.; my (*or* your, &c.) own; the truth about myself (*or* yourself, &c.); the thing *or* man *or* person for me (*or* you, &c.), what suits me (*or* you, &c.),

what I want or wanted (or what you, &c. want or wanted). *Au* —, in fact, indeed, in reality; after all; well; to the fact, to the point or question; acquainted with the whole matter, knowing all about it; up to the business, up to the work, up to it; well instructed; expert, skilful, skilled, proficient. *Au — de*, knowing, understanding, acquainted with, aware of, up to; master of; skilled or proficient in. *Au — et au prendre*, at or to the rub or scratch, at the pinch. *Dans le* —, in fact, indeed, in reality. *De* —, in fact, "de facto," indeed, in reality; actual; certain; a fact. *En* —, in fact. *En — de*, in point of; in matters of; with regard to, as to; as; in the way of; in. *Par le* —, in fact, indeed, in reality. *Si* —, *V.* **Si,** *adv.* *Tout à* —, *V.* **Tout,** *adv.* *Aller* or *venir au* —, to come to the point. *Être au* —, to understand it, to know all about it; to be up to the business or &c. (*V. Au* —). *Être au — de*, to know, to understand, to be acquainted with or aware of or up to or &c. (*V. Au — de*). *Être sûr de son* —, to be sure of what one says, to know well what one is about, to go upon sure grounds, to make sure of success; to be sure of the fact, to be convinced. *Mettre au — de*, to acquaint with, to make acquainted with, to tell all about, to put up to. *Mettre* or *poser en* —, to lay down as a fact, to assert. *Prendre — et cause*, *V.* **Cause.** *Prendre sur le* —, to catch in the act; (*fig.*) to get an insight into; to see (...) as it is or as they are; to represent or take or draw or paint from the life

Faîtage, *s.m.* (*build.*) ridge-piece; ridge-lead, ridge-tiles; (*abusively*) ridge, roofing; finial

Faîte, *s.m.* ridge; top, summit; height, pinnacle, zenith

Fait-exprès, *s.m.* thing done intentionally or on purpose. *C'est un* —, *V.* **Exprès,** *adv.*

Faîtière, *adj.f.* of the ridge; — *s.f.* ridge-tile, gutter-tile, pantile; ridge-lead; skylight; (*of tents*) roof-piece; (*shell*) giant tridacna, hippopus

Faix, *s.m.* burden, load, weight

Fakir, *s.m.* fakir, faquir

Falaise, *s.f.* cliff

Falaiser, *v.n.* to dash against the cliffs

Falbala, *s.m.* furbelow, flounce

Falbalasser, *v.a.* to furbelow, to flounce

Falcade, *s.f.* (*rid.*) falcade

Falciforme, *adj.* falciform, falcate, falcated

Fale, *s.f.* (*pop.*) crop (*of a bird*)

Falerne, *s.m.* Falernian wine, falernian, falernum

Fallacieusement, *adv.* fallaciously

Fallacieu-x, se, *adj.* fallacious

Falle, *s.f.* *V.* **Fale**

Falloir, *v.n. imp.* to be necessary or requisite or wanted or wanting or needed or needful; to become necessary; must; to be obliged or bound, to have (to); should, ought; shall; shall have (to), will have (to); must be; should be; should have been; to require, to want, to need, must have. *Ce qu'il faut*, what is necessary or &c. *Ce qu'il faut faire*, what must be done, what one or I or you or &c. must (or should) do. *Il faut que je sorte*, I must go out. *Il faut sortir*, one, or I, thou, he, &c. must (or should) go out. *Il faut faire cela*, that must be done, it is necessary to do that; one, or I, thou, he, &c. must do that. *Il faut le faire*, it must be done, it is necessary to do it; one, or I, thou, he, &c. must do it. *Il le faut*, *Il faut cela*, it or that must be so; it or that must be done; it or that is necessary; it or that is wanted. *Il me le faut*, I want it, I must have it. *Il me fallut* (or *Il m'a fallu*) *y aller*, I was obliged to go there. *Il le fallait*, *Il fallait cela*, it or that was necessary; it or that was to be done; it or that was to be so; it or that was wanted. *Il fallait le passer*, it was to be crossed, it must (*then*) be crossed; it should have been crossed, I or he or you or &c. should (or ought to) have crossed it. *Il fallait voir*, you should have seen. *Il faudrait voir*, you should see. *Il aurait fallu voir*, you should have seen. *Il faudra* or *il va falloir vous habiller*, you will have to dress yourself. *Il faut de l'argent pour voyager*, money is necessary for travelling. *Il lui faut de l'argent*, he requires or wants or must have some money. *Combien vous faut-il?* how much do you want? *Comme il faut*, as it should be; as one or you or &c. ought to do; properly, well, in proper style, nicely, finely; soundly; hard; with a vengeance; respectably; respectable; genteel; proper; decent; nice; well-bred; gentlemanly; ladylike; (*s.m.*) good manners, gentlemanly or ladylike appearance; respectability. *Comme il en faut*, such as there should be, such as one should have. *Plus qu'il ne* (or *n'en*) *faut*, more than necessary, more than enough. *Pourquoi faut-il que ... ?* why is it that ...? *Le* or *la* or *les ... qu'il faut* or *fallait* or *faudra* or *&c.*, the right or proper or necessary ...

S'en —, *v.r.* to be far; to be wanting; to fall short; (*with* **ne**) to be near, to be on the point. *Il s'en faut* (*de beaucoup*), (very) far from it; there wants (much); it is (very) far from being the fact. *Peu s'en faut*, little short of it, not far from it, nearly so. very near, very nearly. *Tant s'en faut*, far from it; so far from ... *Il s'en faut* (*de beaucoup*) *que le nombre soit complet*, the number is (very) far from being complete. *Il s'en est peu fallu qu'il n'ait été tué*, he was near being killed

Falot, *s.m.* lantern; cresset; light

Falot, e, *adj.* ludicrous; grotesque; funny, droll, laughable; — *s.m.f.* ditto person (fellow, creature, &c.)

Falotement, *adv.* ludicrously; grotesquely; funnily, comically

Faloterie, *s.f.* ludicrous or droll thing, drollery, fun; grotesqueness

Falourde, *s.f.* bundle of logs; sea-swallow

Falque, *s.f.* (*rid.*) falcade; (*of boats*) weather-board, wash-board

Falqué, e, *adj.* (*bot.*) falcate, falcated

Falquer, *v.n.* (*rid.*) to make falcades

Falsifiable, *adj.* falsifiable

Falsifica-teur, trice, *s.m.f.* falsifier, adulterator, adulteratress, debaser; — *adj.* falsifying, adulterating, debasing

Falsification, *s.f.* falsification; adulteration; debasement; forgery

Falsifier, *v.a.* to falsify; to adulterate; to debase; to forge

Se —, *v.r.* to be falsified or &c.

Faltranck, *s.m.* (*pharm.*) faltranck

Falun, *s.m.* shell-marl, crag, falun

Falunage, *s.m.* shell-marl manuring

Faluner, *v.a.* to manure with shell-marl

Faluneur, *s.m.* shell-marl manurer

Falunière, *s.f.* shell-marl pit, falun-bed

Famé, e, *adj.* famed, of (*good, or bad*) character or repute, of (*good, or ill*) fame

Famélique, *adj.* *s.m.f.* famished, hungry, starved, starving, starveling

Fameusement, *adv.* famously; capitally; preciously, uncommonly, prodigiously

Fameu-x, se, *adj.* famous, famed, celebrated, renowned; notorious; first-rate, very good, capital; precious, rare; terrible, awful

Familial, e, *adj.* family

Familiariser, *v.a.* to familiarize, to accustom; to acquaint

Se —, *v.r.* to become or grow or get familiar; to make oneself familiar; to familiarize or accustom oneself, to become accustomed; to become acquainted; to become tame

Familiarité, *s.f.* familiarity; liberty

Famili-er, ère, *adj.* familiar; intimate; free, unconstrained; homely; tame; — *s.m.f.* familiar

Familièrement, *adv.* familiarly; freely

†Famille, *s.f.* family; household; kin, kindred; relatives; race; tribe; parentage. *Enfant de* —, child of good family (*V.* **Fils**). *Père de* —, *chef de* —, father or head of a family, family man, man of family, paterfamilias. *De* —,

family; domestic. *En* —, with *or* in o.'s family; at home; among (*or* by) ourselves *or* yourselves [*or* themselves
Famine, *s.f.* famine
Famosité, *s.f.* famousness; notoriety
Fanage, *s.m.* turning of grass; haymaker's wages; leafage, leaves, tops; drying (*of fodder-plants*)
Fanaison, *s.f.* hay-time
Fanal, *s.m.* ship's lantern, lantern; light-house; beacon; signal-light, watch-light, light; (*of carriages, trains,* &c.) bull's-eye lamp, lamp; (*pop.*) gullet, swallow
Fanariote, *s.m.* Fanariot
Fanatique, *adj. s.m.f.* fanatic
Fanatiser, *v.a.* to fanaticize
Se —, *v.r.* to become fanatic
Fanatiseur, *s.m.* fanaticizer; — *adj.m.* fanaticizing
Fanatisme, *s.m.* fanaticism
Fanchon, *s.f.* handkerchief (*over the head*), kerchief, head-wrapper, wrapper
Fanchonnette, *s.f.* (kind of cake)
Fandango, *s.m.* fandango (*Spanish dance, tune*)
Fane, *s.f.* fallen leaves; dead *or* dry leaves; leaves, tops; envelope of the flower (*of anemones and ranunculuses*)
Faner, *v.a.* to turn (*hay,* &c.); to cause to fade, to fade, to wither; to tarnish
Se —, *v.r.* to fade away, to fade; to wither; to tarnish
Faneu-r, se, *s.m.f.* haymaker; — *s.f.* hay-making machine, haymaker
Fanfan, *s.m.f.* (*fam.*) baby; darling, duck, ducky
Fanfare, *s.f.* flourish, flourish of trumpets, fanfare; military music; brass band. *Musique de* —, brass instruments, brass band
Fanfarer, *v.a.n.* to trumpet; to puff
Fanfaron, ne, *adj.* blustering, swaggering; vain, presumptuous; boasting, bragging; — *s.m.f.* blusterer, swaggerer; boaster, braggart
Fanfaronnade, Fanfaronnerie, *s.f.* fanfaronade, blustering, bluster, swaggering, swagger, boasting, boast, bragging, brag
Fanfinot, *s.m.* baby, ducky
Fanfre, *s.m.* (*zool.*) pilot-fish
Fanfreluche, *s.f.* gewgaw, bauble; tinsel, trumpery
Fanfrelucher, *v.a.* to set out with gewgaws *or* baubles, to tinsel, to rig out in trumpery
Fange, *s.f.* mire, mud, dirt; (*fig.*) vileness, degradation, filth; low condition, low extraction, dunghill
Fangeu-x,se, *adj.* miry, muddy, dirty
Fanion, *s.m.* (*mil.*) small flag
Fanoir, *s.m* hay-drying apparatus
Fanon, *s.m.* dewlap, shaking piece (*of oxen*); wattle (*of cocks, turkeys,* &c.); fetlock (*of horses*); fin *or* bone (*of whales*); pendant (*of a bishop's mitre, of a banner*); fanon (*priest's garment*); (*mil.*) little flag
Fantaisie, *s.f.* fancy; humour; whim, crotchet, freak; caprice; liking, mind, taste; fantasticalness; fancy article *or* thing *or* work *or* production; (*mus.*) fantasia
Fantaisisme, *s.m.* whimsical style of painting *or* writing, fanciful art, humourism
Fantaisiste, *s.m.f.* whimsical painter *or* artist *or* writer, humourist; — *adj.* fanciful, fancy; whimsical; imaginary [*and jest. for* **Fantaisie**
Fantasia, *s.f.* fantasia (*Arabian sport*); *pop.*
Fantasmagorie, *s.f.* phantasmagoria; dissolving views
Fantasmagorique, *adj.* phantasmagoric
Fantasmagoriquement, *adv.* phantasmagorically
Fantasmascope, Fantasmatoscope, *s.m.* phantascope, phantasmascope
Fantasmatique, *adj.* phantasmatical, phantasmal
Fantasme, *s.m.* (*med.*) phantasma, phantasm
Fantasque, *adj.* fantastic, whimsical, fanciful, wayward, odd, freakish
Fantasquement, *adv.* fantastically, whimsically, fancifully, waywardly, oddly
Fantassin, *s.m.* foot-soldier
Fantast-ique, -iquement. *V.* page 3, § 1
Fantoccini, *s.m.pl.* fantoccini
Fantoche, *s.m.* puppet; puppet-show; fantastic *or* fanciful character; — *adj.* fantastic; odd, strange, whimsical

Fantôme, *s.m.* phantom; ghost; spectre; shadow; chimera; vision
Fanton, *s.m. V.* **Fenton**
Fanu, e, *adj.* (*agr.*) leafy
Fanum, *s.m.* (*Rom. antiquity*) fane
Faon, *s.m.* fawn; (*abusively*) whelp
Faonner, *v.n.* to fawn; (*abusively*) to whelp
Faourche, *s.m. V.* **Farouch**
Faquin, *s.m.* jackanapes, fop, puppy, snob; rascallion, rascal, scamp, scoundrel; (*obsolete*) tilting-dummy
Faquinerie, *s.f.*, **Faquinisme,** *s.m.* foppery, puppyism, snobbery, snobbishness; scoundrelism, knavery, rascaldom; rascally action, piece of rascality
Faquir, *s.m.* faquir, fakir
Far, *s.m.* (*local*) custard
Faradisation, *s.f.* (*med.*) faradization
Farandole, *s.f.* farandole (*dance, tune, in Provence*)
Faraud, e, *s.m.f.* low fop, snob, swell; — *adj.* foppish, swellish
Farce, *s.f.* stuffing, forcemeat; (*of vegetables*) — *de* ..., minced ...; farce; broad comedy; drollery; foolery; antic; humbug; practical joke, joke; hoax; trick; prank; infidelity; — *adj.* (*pop.*) farcical, comical, droll, funny, amusing
Farceu-r, se, *s.m.f.* farce-player; buffoon; droll *or* funny fellow *or* thing; joker, jester; trickster; humbug; story-teller; sly blade; wild fellow *or* thing, wild dog, rascal, rogue, rake; gay woman; fellow, thing, blade
Farcin, *s.m.* (*vet.*) farcy, glanders
Farcineu-x, se, *adj.* (*vet.*) farcied, glandered; of farcy, of glanders
Farcinière, *s.f.* (*bot.*) cinquefoil
Farcir, *v.a.* to stuff; to cram; to fill
Se —, *v.r.* to stuff *or* &c. oneself (*or* o.'s ...); to be stuffed *or* &c.
Farcissure, *s.f.* (*cook.*) stuffing
Fard, *s.m.* paint; rouge; (*fig.*) varnish, tinsel; disguise; affectation
Fardage, *s.m.* (*nav.*) dunnage
Farde, *s.f.* bale of mocha; (*of boats*) *V.* **Falque**
Fardeau, *s.m.* burden, load, charge, weight; encumbrance; (*brewing*) mash; (*mining*) mass
Farder, *v.a.* to paint, to rouge; (*fig.*) to gloss; to varnish; to tinsel; to disguise; — *v.n.* to sink, to give way
Fardier, *s.m.* (stone and timber) waggon, trolly, tug, gill
Farfadet, *s.m.* elf, goblin; (*obsolete*) trifler
†**Farfouiller,** *v.a.n.* to feel *or* handle *or* fumble about, to rummage, to fumble, to poke
†**Farfouilleu-r, se,** *s.m.f.* rummager, fumbler
Fargue, *s.f.* (*of boats*) *V.* **Falque**
Faribole, *s.f.* idle story; trifle; foolery, nonsense
Faridondaine, *s.f.* tol-de-rol-lol
†**Farillon,** *s.m.* (*bad spelling*) *V.* **Pharillon**
Farinacé, e, *adj.* farinaceous
Farine, *s.f.* flour, meal; farina; sort, stamp, stuff. *Folle* —, mill-dust
Fariner, *v.a.* to flour; to meal; (*cook.*) to dredge, to flour; — *v.n.* to get floury *or* mealy; to get scurfy
Farinet, *s.m.* one-faced die
Farineu-x, se, *adj.* floury; mealy; farinose; farinaceous; white with flour; scurfy; (*pop.*) capital, famous; — *s.m.pl.* mealy substances, farinaceous food
Farinier, *s.m.* mealman
Farinière, *s.f.* flour-bin, flour-tub, meal-tub; mealman's wife
Farlouse, *s.f.* titlark
Far-niente, *s.m.* (*Italian*) far-niente, doing nothing. *Dolce* —, ease with nothing to do, pleasant laziness
Faro, *s.m.* faro, Brussels beer
Farouch, Farouche, *s.m.* (*bot.*) crimson clover, Italian clover
Farouche, *adj.* wild; fierce; savage; stern; austere; severe; rigid; intractable, unmanageable; unsociable; shy
Farrago, *s.m.* farrago
Farre, *s.m.* freshwater herring
Farthing, *s.m.* (*English coin*) farthing
Fasce, *s.f.* (*arch.*) fascia; (*her.*) fesse, fess
Fascé, e, *adj.* (*her.*) fessed, fessy
Fascer, *v.a.* (*her.*) to fess
Fascia, *s.m.* (*anat.*) fascia

Fascial, e, *adj.* (*anat.*) fascial
Fasciation, *s.f.* fasciation
Fasciculaire, *adj.* fascicular
Fasciculation, *s.f.* fasciculation
Fascicule, *s.m.* fascicle, fasciculus; small bundle; nosegay; number (*of a work published in parts*), part [culated, fascicular
Fasciculé, e, *adj.* fascicled, fasciculate, fasci-
Fascie, *s.f.* fascia, stripe, streak, band; (*of violins*, &c.) side-piece, rib [streaked
Fascié, e, *adj.* fasciate, fasciated, striped,
Fascinage, *s.m.* fascining, fascine-work, fascines, hurdling, bavins, hurdles
Fascina-teur, trice, *adj.* fascinating; —
Fascination, *s.f.* fascination [*s.m.f.* fascinater
Fascine, *s.f.* fascine, fagot, bavin, hurdle, bush,
Fasciner, *v.a.* to fascinate [bundle of twigs
Fasciolaire, *s.f.* (*shell*) fasciolaria
Fasciole, *s.f.* (*zool.*) fluke-worm, liver-fluke
Faséiement, *s.m.* (*nav.*, *of sails*) shivering
Faséier, *v.n.* (*nav.*) *V.* **Fasier**
Faséole, *s.f.* phasel (*bean*)
Fashion, *s.f.* fashion; fashionable world
Fashionable, *adj.s.m.f.* fashionable; fashionable man *or* woman, beau, belle, exquisite, swell
Fashionablement, *adv.* fashionably
Fasier, *v.n.* (*nav.*, *of sails*) to shiver
Faste, *s.m.* pomp, magnificence; pageantry; display, show, ostentation; pride; affectation; — *adj.m.* auspicious; **—s,** *s.m.pl.* records, annals, history, (*Latin*) "fasti"; (*Ovid's*) "Fasti"
Fastidieusement, *adv.* tediously, irksomely
Fastidieu-x, se, *adj.* tedious, tiresome, irksome, wearisome, dull
Fastigié, e, *adj.* (*bot.*) fastigiate, fastigiated
Fastigium, *s.m.* (*anc. arch.*) fastigium
Fastueusement, *adv.* pompously, gorgeously, sumptuously, magnificently, splendidly; ostentatiously; luxuriously
Fastueu-x, se, *adj.* pompous, gorgeous, sumptuous, magnificent, stately; pageant; ostentatious; showy, gaudy; luxurious; proud
Fat, *s.m.* fop, coxcomb; — *adj.m.* foppish
Fatal, e, *adj.* fatal; inevitable; irrevocable; unlucky; unfortunate. *Terme* —, (*admin.*, *com.*) term of grace, latest time
Fatalement, *adv.* fatally; inevitably; irrevocably; unluckily; unfortunately
Fatalisme, *s.m.* fatalism
Fataliste, *s.m.f.* fatalist; — *adj.* fatalistic
Fatalité, *s.f.* fatality
Fata Morgana, *s.f.* Fata Morgana, looming,
Fatidique, *adj.* fatidical, prophetic [mirage
Fatidiquement, *adv.* fatidically, prophetically
Fatigable, *adj.* fatigable [tedious
Fatigant, e, *adj.* fatiguing; tiresome, irksome,
Fatiguant, *part.* fatiguing, tiring, &c. (*V.* **Fatiguer**)
Fatigue, *s.f.* fatigue; weariness; hard work, work, labour, pains, toil, hardship; strain; stress. *De* —, of *or* from *or* with *or* &c. fatigue, &c.; for (*or* fit for) hard work, for (*or* fit for) rough wear, strong; working
Fatiguer, *v.a.* to fatigue, to tire, to weary; to fag; to wear out, to jade; to overwork; to strain; to harass; to tease, to vex, to worry; to impoverish (*land*); to mix well (*a salad*); to thumb (*a book*); to fade (*colours*); — *v.n* to fatigue *or* tire oneself; to work hard, to work, to toil, to labour; to drudge; to sweat; to fag; to bear a weight; to be fatiguing. — *à l'ancre*, (*nav.*) to ride hard

Se —, *v.r.* to fatigue *or* tire oneself; to become *or* grow *or* get tired, to tire; to be jaded
Fatimite, *s.m.* (*hist.*) Fatimite
Fatras, *s.m.* heap, medley, jumble, lumber, litter, farrago, confusion, confused mass; trash, rubbish; balderdash
Fatuité, *s.f.* self-conceitedness, conceitedness, conceit, puppyism, foppishness, foppery; piece
Faubert, *s.m.* (*nav.*) swab, mop [of impertinence
Fauberter, *v.a.* (*nav.*) to swab, to mop
Fauberteur, *s.m.* (*nav.*) swabber
Faubourg, *s.m.* suburb, outskirt; poor *or* low neighbourhood, slums, backslums; (*specifically*) faubourg. *Le — Saint-Germain, Le* —, the faubourg St. Germain, the 'Belgravia' of Paris, the old (French) aristocracy
Faubourien, ne, *adj.* suburban; low; — *s.m.f.* suburban; working man *or* woman; low fellow, low creature
Faucard, *s.m.* weeding-tool (*for canals*)
Faucardement, *s.m.* weeding (*of canals*)
Faucarder, *v.a.* to weed (*canals*)
Faucet, *s.m.* (*mus.*) *V.* **Fausset**
Fauchable, *adj.* mowable
Fauchage, *s.m.* mowing
Fauchaison, *s.f.* mowing-time; mowing
Fauchard, *s.m.* sickle
Fauche, *s.f.* mowing; mowing-time
Fauchée, *s.f.* day's mowing, mow
Faucher, *v.a.* to mow, to mow *or* cut down; to cut off; — *v.n.* (*of horses*) to dish. *Être fauché*, (*pers.*, *pop.*) to have o.'s head cut off. — *le grand pré, aller — au pré, aller au pré*, (*thieves' slang*, *old*) to mow the sea, to be a galley-slave, to be condemned to penal servitude, to be lagged
Fauchet, *s.m.* hay-rake; rake; hedging-bill, bill-hook; (*bird*) scissor-bill
Fauchette, *s.f.* (*hort.*) border-shears
Faucheur, *s.m.* mower, haymaker; (*insect*) *V.* **Faucheux.** *Le* —, (*pop.*) the executioner, Jack Ketch
Faucheuse, *s.f.* mowing-machine, mower
Faucheux, *s.m.* field-spider, shepherd-spider, harvest-man, daddy-longlegs
Fauchon, *s.m.* small scythe
Fauchure, *s.f.* mowing, mow
†**Faucille,** *s.f.* sickle, reaping-hook
†**Faucillon,** *s.m.* hedging-bill, bill-hook
Faucon, *s.m.* falcon, hawk; (*anc. artil.*) falcon
Fauconneau, *s.m.* jashawk; (*anc. artil.*) falconet
Fauconnerie, *s.f.* falconry; hawking
Fauconnier, *s.m.* falconer. *Monter à cheval en* —, to get up on the off-side
Fauconnière, *s.f.* hawking-bag; saddle-bag
Faudr-ai, -as, -a, &c. (*obsolete future tense of* **Faillir**)
Faudra (*future tense of the imp. verb* **Falloir**)
Faufil, *s.m.* tacking-thread, basting-thread
Faufiler, *v.a.n.* (*need.*) to tack, to baste; (*fig.*) to introduce

Se —, *v.r.* to slip (through, in, into), to creep (in, into), to insinuate *or* introduce oneself, to worm *or* edge oneself (in, into), to make o.'s way; to intrude oneself, to intrude, to thrust oneself forward, to pick up acquaintance, to ingratiate oneself, to curry favour
Faufilure, *s.f.* (*need.*) tacking, basting
Faulde, *s.f.* charcoal-burning pit
Faulx, *s.f.* (*old spelling*) *V.* **Faux,** *s.f.*
Faune, *s.m.* (*myth.*) faun; — *s.f.* (*myth.*, *zool.*)
Fauque, *s.f.* (*of boats*) *V.* **Falque** [fauna
Faussaire, *s.m.f.* forger
Fausse, *adj.f.* (*fem. of* **Faux**). **—-braie,** *s.f.* (*fort.*) fausse-braye. **—-côte,** &c., &c. *V.* **Côte,** &c., &c. [fully, wrongly, untruly
Faussement, *adv.* falsely, erroneously, wrong-
Fausser, *v.a.* to bend; to twist; to dent, to dint, to indent; to force; to strain; to warp; to pervert; to violate, to break; to falsify; to put out of tune; — *v.n.* to sing *or* be out of tune

Se —, *v.r.* to bend, to be bent; to become (*or* be) warped *or* strained *or* &c.; to get out of tune
Fausset, *s.m.* spigot, peg, vent-peg; falsetto, falset, shrill treble, shrill voice *or* tone, piping voice, squeaking, squeak
Fausseté, *s.f.* falsity; falseness; falsehood; untruth; duplicity; insincerity; treachery; deceitfulness, deceit; spuriousness; fallacy
Faussure, *s.f.* (*of bells*) sound-bow
Faut, *v.n.* (*3rd pers. sing. pres. Ind. of* **Falloir;** *obsolete ditto of* **Faillir**)

Faute, *s.f.* fault; error; mistake; want; fail. — *de*, for want of; in default of. *A qui la —?* whose fault is it? *Faire —*, *V.* **Défaut** (*Faire*). *Ne pas se faire — de ...*, not to spare ..., to use ... freely; to ... freely; not to refrain from ...

†**Fauteuil,** *s.m.* easy chair, arm-chair, elbow-chair; chair; seat *or* place (*in the French Academy*), academic chair. — *à la Voltaire*, reclining chair [porter

Faut-eur, rice, *s.m.f.* abetter, favourer, sup-

Fauti-f, ve, *adj.* faulty, at fault, incorrect, defective [fectively

Fautivement, *adv.* faultily, incorrectly, de-

Fauve, *adj.* fallow, fawn-coloured, fawn; tawny; reddish; lurid; gloomy, dismal, evil; wild, savage; — *s.m.* fallow, fawn (colour); deer; wild beast *or* beasts. *Bête —*, fallow deer, deer; [wild beast

Fauveau, *s.m.* fawn-coloured ox

Fauvette, *s.f.* (*bird*) warbler, fauvette. — *à tête* [*noire*, blackcap

Faux, *s.f.* scythe; (*anat.*) falx

Fau-x, sse, *adj.* false; untrue; wrong; deceitful; treacherous; insincere; hypocritical; faithless; erroneous; unsound; spurious; bastard; artificial; sham; pretended, feigned; fictitious; mock; imitation; something like; slight; base, bad, counterfeit; forged; irregular; defective; (*of weights and measures*) false, light, short; (*of doors, windows*) sham, blank; (*of doors, gates*) private, back; (*mus.*) false, untuned, untunable, discordant, out of tune. *Acte —*, forgery. *Chose —sse*, untruth, falsehood, sham

Faux, *s.m.* falsehood; false; falsification; forgery; imitation articles, imitation; tinsel; foil; error; discordance

Faux, *adv.* falsely; out of tune; wrong; wrongly; wrongfully; erroneously. *A —*, falsely; false; erroneously; unjustly; wrongfully; wrongly; wrong; amiss; unsuccessfully. *Porter à —*, to bear false; to be out of perpendicular; to be destitute of foundation; to be inconclusive [**don, Col,** &c.

Faux-bourdon, Faux-col, &c. *V.* **Bour-**

Faux-fuyant, *s.m.* by-place, by-way, by-path; (*fig.*) subterfuge, evasion, shift

Faux-pont, &c., &c. *V.* **Pont,** &c., &c.

Favéolé, e, *adj.* (*nat. hist.*) faveolate

Faveur, *s.f.* favour; boon; interest; vogue; grace; ribbon. *A la — de*, under favour *or* cover of; under the protection of; favoured *or* protected by; by the help of; by means of. *De —*, of (*or* from *or* by *or* &c.) favour *or* &c.; of grace; obtained by favour; (*of admission*) free. *En — de*, in behalf of; for the sake of; on account of. *Prendre —*, to get (*or* come) [into favour *or* vogue

Faveu-x, se, *adj.* favose

Faviforme, *adj.* faviform

Favonette, *s.f.* (*bot.*) everlasting pea

Favorable, *adj.* favourable; propitious

Favorablement, *adv.* favourably; propitiously

Favori, te, *adj. s.* favourite

Favori, *s.m.* (*hair*) whisker

Favoriser, *v.a.* to favour; to encourage; to countenance; to befriend; to endow; to support; to defend; to assist, to aid; to protect; to patronize; to be favourable *or* propitious to; to promote; to further; to facilitate; to [grant

Favoritisme, *s.m.* favouritism

Favouette, *s.f.* *V.* **Favonette**

Favus, *s.m.* (*med.*) favus

Fayard, *s.m.* (*vulgar*) beech-tree, beech

Fayence, &c. *V.* **Faïence,** &c.

Fayol, Fayot, *s.m.* (*nav.*) bean

Féage, *s.m.* (*obsolete*) feoffment [ditto friend

Féal, e, *adj.* (*obsolete*) trusty, faithful; — *s.m.*

Féalté, Féauté, *s.f.* (*old*) fealty, fidelity

Fébricitant, e, *adj. s.* feverish; fever patient

Fébricule, *s.f.* (*med.*) febricula

Fébrifuge, *adj.m.f.*, *s.m.* febrifuge, antifebrile. *Gouttes —s, Poudre —*, ague-drops, ague-powder

Fébrile, *adj.* febrile [fæces, excrement

Fécal, e, *adj.* fecal, fæcal. *Matière —e*, feces,

Fécalités, *s.f.pl.* moral filth, corruption, vices

Fèces, *s.m.pl.* (*chem., pharm., med.*) feces, fæces

Féchelle, *s.f.* hurdle, wattle, strainer

Fécial, e, *adj. s.m.* (*Rom. hist.*) fecial

Fécond, e, *adj.* fecund; fruitful; prolific; fertile; productive; pregnant; teeming; rich; voluminous; copious, abundant; genial

Fécondant, e, Féconda-teur, trice, *adj.* fecundating, fertilizing, genial

Fécondation, *s.f.* fecundation, impregnation

Féconder, *v.a.* to fecundate; to fertilize

Se —, *v.r.* to be fecundated *or* &c.

Fécondité, *s.f.* fecundity, fruitfulness, fertility

Fécule, *s.f.* fecula; flour

Féculence, *s.f.* feculence, feculency

Féculent, e, *adj.*, **Féculent,** *s.m.* feculent

Féculer, *v.a.* to reduce to fecula

Féculerie, *s.f.* fecula-making; fecula-works

Féculeu-x, se, *adj.* feculous, feculent

Féculi-er, ère, Féculiste, *s.m.f.* fecula-maker

Fédéral, e, *adj.*, **Fédéral,** *s.m.* federal

Fédéraliser, *v.a.*, **Se —,** *v.r.* to federalize

Fédéral-isme, -iste. *V.* page 3, § 1

Fédérati-f, ve, *adj.* federative

Fédération, *s.f.* federation

Fédéré, e, *adj.*, **Fédéré,** *s.m.* federate

Fédérer, *v.a.*, **Se —,** *v.r.* to federate

Fée, *s.f.* fairy; — *adj.* enchanted, magic. — *-bosse*, — *Carabosse*, old hag

Féer, *v.a.* (*old*) to enchant, to charm

Féerie, *s.f.* enchantment; fairy-land; fairy-scene; power of fairies [vellous, wonderful

Féerique, *adj.* fairy; enchanting, magic, mar-

†**Feignant, e,** *part. adj.* feigning, &c. (*V.* **Feindre**); — *adj. s.m.f.* (*pop.*) *V.* **Fainéant**

Feindre, *v.a.n.* to feign; to sham, to pretend; to dissemble; to disguise; to imagine, to suppose; to limp; (*old*) to hesitate, to scruple; to deceive by telling

Se —, *v.r.* to be feigned *or* &c.; to feign *or* pretend to be; to imagine to oneself

Feint, e, *part. adj.* feigned, &c. (*V.* **Feindre**); sham, mock, imitation, counterfeit

Feinte, *s.f.* feint, pretence, sham; dissimulation; disguise; artifice; invention; (*obsolete*) fiction; (*print.*) friar; (*fenc., mil.*) feint; (*mus.*) accidental; (*vet.*) slight limp; (*fish*) twaite shad

Feintier, *s.m.* shad-net

Feintise, *s.f.* (*old*) feint, pretence, sham

Feld-maréchal, *s.m.* (*in some northern countries*) field-marshal

Feldspath, *s.m.* (*min.*) felspar, feldspar

Feldspathique, *adj.* (*min.*) felspathic [cracked

Fêler, *v.a.* to crack. *Se —*, to crack, to get *or* be

Félicitation, *s.f.* felicitation, congratulation

Félicité, *s.f.* felicity, happiness, bliss, blessing, joy [to wish joy

Féliciter, *v.a.* to congratulate, to felicitate,

Se —, *v.r.* to congratulate oneself *or* each other; to rejoice (at); to be satisfied *or* pleased (with); to speak highly (of)

Félide, *s.m.* felis, cat-tribe

Félin, e, *adj.* feline

Félins, *s.m.pl.* felines, cat-tribe

Félir, *v.n.* (*of cats*) to spit

Fellah, *s.m.* fellah (*Egyptian peasant*)

Félon, ne, *adj.* (*old*) felonious, felon, disloyal, traitorous, treacherous; — *s.m.f.* felon, traitor, traitoress, traitress

Félonie, *s.f.* (*old*) felony, disloyalty, treason, [treachery

Felouque, *s.f.* (*nav.*) felucca

Fêlure, *s.f.* crack, chink, fissure

Femelle, *adj.m.f.*, *s.f.* (*zool., bot.*) female; she; hen; doe; ewe; (*pers., in contempt or jest only*) female, woman, girl; wife, rib; creature, bitch; she

Femelots, *s.m.pl.* (*nav.*) googings (*of the rudder*)

Féminiflore, *adj.* (*bot.*) female-flowered

Féminiforme, *adj.* feminiform

Féminin, e, *adj.* feminine; female; womanly; womanish, effeminate; — *s.m.* (*gram.*) feminine gender, feminine

Fémininement, *adv.* femininely
Fémininité, *s.f.* feminineness, femininity
Féminiser, *v.a.* to make feminine; to render effeminate, to effeminate [effeminate
Se —, *v.r.* to be made feminine; to become
Femme, *s.f.* woman; female; wife; female attendant; lady. — *de chambre*, lady's maid; waiting woman; chambermaid. — *de charge*, housekeeper. — *de journée*, charwoman; laundress. — *de ménage*, charwoman; laundress; manager, housewife. — *publique*, prostitute, woman of the town. *De* —, (*adject.*) of a woman, female, feminine, womanly, womanish
Femmelette, *s.f.* silly woman; (*fig.*) woman, effeminate man
Fémoral, e, *adj.* (*anat.*) femoral
Fémoro-tibial, e, *adj.* (*anat.*) femoro-tibial
Fémur, *s.m.* (*anat.*) femur, thigh-bone
Fenaison, *s.f.* haymaking; hay-harvest; dry-
Fenasse, *s.f.* (*pop.*) *V.* **Sainfoin** [ing up
Fendage, *s.m.* slitting; splitting; cleaving; cutting [hector; — *s.m.* (*obsolete*) slash
Fendant, e, *s.m.f.* swaggerer, blusterer, bully,
Fenderie, *s.f.* slitting; slitting-mill [cutter
Fendeu-r, se, *s.m.f.* slitter; splitter; cleaver;
†Fendillement, *s.m.* splitting, slitting; chinking, cracking, chipping [chink, to crack, to chip
†Fendiller, *v.a.*, **Se —,** *v.r.* to split, to slit; to
Fendoir, *s.m.* cleaver, cleaving-tool
Fendre, *v.a.n.* to cleave, to split; to slit; to cut; to crack; to chink; to chap; to divide; to rend; to burst; to break; to rip up; to break through; to plough (*the sea*)
Se —, *v.r.* to cleave, to split, to slit; to crack, to chink; to chap; to divide, to separate; to break asunder; to gape; (*fenc.*) to open o.'s legs, to make a lunge, to lunge; (*pop.*) to make a great effort, to make a sacrifice, to spend money, to bleed; to come out; (*de* ...) to spend, to fork out; to pay, to stand
Fendu, e, *part. adj.* cleft, split, &c. (*V.* **Fendre**); cloven; extending, reaching. *Bien* —, large, wide, full, full and finely cut; long-legged
Fendue, *s.f.* uncovered trench *or* gallery
Fène, *s.f.* *V.* **Faine**
Fenestral, e, *adj.* (*old*) fenestral
Fenestré, e, *adj.* (*old*) *V.* **Fenêtré**
Fenêtrage, *s.m.* fenestration; windows, lights
Fenêtre, *s.f.* window; casement; (*anat.*) fenestra, opening, aperture. — *cintrée*, — *à plein cintre*, circular-head window. — *cintrée en plan*, bow-window. — *à coulisse* or *à guillotine*, sash-window. — *à pans coupés*, cant-window. — *à plate-bande*, square window. — *en rotonde*, bow-window. — *en saillie*, bay-window. — *en tour creuse*, inside-circular window. — *en tour ronde*, outside-circular window, bow-window. *Jeter par la* —, to throw out of the window; to throw *or* squander away, to play at ducks and drakes with [*hist.*, *surg.*) fenestrate, fenestrated
Fenêtré, e, *adj.* fenestrated, windowed; (*nat.*
Fenêtrer, *v.a.* to window; to fenestrate, to
Fénian, e, *adj. s.* fenian [perforate, to open
Fénianisme, *s.m.* fenianism
Féníaniste, *s.m.f.* fenianist; — *adj.* fenianistic
Fenier, *s.m.* (*local*) hay-stack
Fenière, *s.f.* hay-loft
Fenil, *s.m.* hay-loft
Fennec, *s.m.* (*zool.*) fennec, zerda
†Fenouil, *s.m.* (*bot.*) fennel; fennel-seed
†Fenouillet, *s.m.* fennel-apple
†Fenouillette, *s.f.* fennel-water; fennel-apple
Fente, *s.f.* cleft, split; slit; cut; crack, chink, crevice, cranny; chap; rent; (*min.*) rent, cleavage; (*nav.*) spring
Fentoir, *s.m.* cleaver, chopper
Fenton, *s.m.* iron-cramp, tie; slit iron, iron square rods; peg-wood
Fenugrec, *s.m.* (*bot.*) fenugreek
Féodal, e, *adj.* feudal
Féodalement, *adv.* feudally
Féodaliser, *v.a.* to feudalize
Féodalisme, *s.m.* feudalism
Féodaliste, *s.m.f.* feudalist; — *adj.* feudalistic
Féodalité, *s.f.* feudality; feudalism
Fer, *s.m.* iron; head, point; tag; ferrule; tip; tool; instrument; forceps; sword, brand, steel, weapon, weapons; rail; (*of animals*) shoe; (*jest.*) foot; —**s,** *pl.* iron; iron-work; irons; chains, fetters; bondage, slavery, captivity; shoes. — *-blanc*, tin-plate, sheet-tin, tin, latten. — *chaud*, hot iron; brand-iron; (*med.*) heartburn. — *à boudin*, Italian iron. — *à cheval*, horse-shoe; (*zool.*) horse-shoe bat. — *à friser*, curling-irons, crimping-iron. — *à glace*, frost-shoe. — *à gratiner*, salamander. — *à repasser*, iron, smoothing-iron, flat iron. — *de cheval*, horse-shoe. — *de moulin*, millrind. — *en meubles* (or, better, *Faire en meubles*, *V.* **Faire,** *s.m.*) articles for furniture. *De* —, of iron; iron; made of iron; of rail, rail. *Fil de* —, wire, iron wire. *Ne pas valoir les quatre —s d'un chien*, not to be worth a straw *or* a rap. *Tomber les quatre —s en l'air*, to fall on o.'s back; to be struck all of a heap
Féramine, *s.f.* iron pyrite
Fer-blanc, Ferblanc, *s.m.* *V.* **Fer**
Ferblanterie, *s.f.* tin-plate working; tin-trade; tin-wares [whitesmith, tinman
Ferblantier, *s.m.* tin-plate worker, tinsmith,
Féret, *s.m.* iron-ore, hematite
Fériable, *adj.* to be kept as a holiday
Férial, e, *adj.* ferial
Férie, *s.f.* day of rest, holiday; (*Cath. lit.*) feria (*week-day*); —**s,** *pl.* (*Roman antiquity*) feriæ
Férié, e, *adj.* of holidays, ferial. *Jour* —, holiday
Férin, e, *adj.* ferine, savage, cruel; (*med.*) malignant
Férir, *v.a.* (*old*) to strike. *Sans coup* —, without striking a blow, without meeting resistance,
Ferlage, *s.m.* (*nav.*) furling [easily
Ferlampier, *s.m.* (*pop.*) poor devil, poor wretch,
Ferler, *v.a.* (*nav.*) to furl [beggar
Fermage, *s.m.* farming; leasing; rent, rental;
†Fermail, *s.m.* clasp [rent-charge
Fermant, e, *adj.* closing; with lock and key;
Fermata, *s.f.* (*mus.*) fermata [— *s.m.* cover
Ferme, *s.f.* farm; farmhouse, farmery, farmstead, homestead; farming; (*carp.*) truss, rib, framing, framework, timbers, roof-timbers; (*theat.*) set piece. — *-école*, — *modèle*, practical school of agriculture, agricultural school. *A* —, on lease; on farm (contract). *Bail à* —, lease of ground
Ferme, *adj.* firm; solid; hard; stiff; steady, fast; fixed; resolute; bold; strong; stout; sound; stable; steadfast; unshaken; constant; stanch; (*com.*, *exchange*) "bonâ fide" (*sale, purchase, bargain*); (*admin.*) contract (*price*)
Ferme, *adv. int.* fast, hard, firmly; stoutly; steady! cheer up! courage! go on! go it! *Faire* —, to keep o.'s ground, to resist. *Tenir* —, *V.* **Tenir**
Ferme, *s.m.* (*in compounds, from* **Fermer,** "to shut," "to close") thing that shuts *or* closes, shutter, closer. — **-bourse,** *s.m.* purse-string *or* ring *or* clasp *or* band. — **-porte,** *s.m.* door-spring [**Fermer**); (*of carriages*) close
Fermé, e, *part. adj.* shut, closed, &c. (*V.*
Fermement, *adv.* firmly; steadily; fixedly; resolutely; boldly; strongly; stoutly; steadfastly
Ferment, *s.m.* ferment, leaven, yeast, barm
Fermentabilité, *s.f.* fermentability
Fermentable, *adj.* fermentable
Fermentaire, *s.m.* Leavenite
Fermentati-f, ve, *adj.* fermentative
Fermentation, *s.f.* fermentation; fermenting; working; (*fig.*) ferment
Fermenter, *v.n.* to ferment; to work; to rise
Fermentescibilité, *s.f.* fermentescibility
Fermentescible, *adj.* fermentescible
Fermer, *v.a.n.*, **Se —,** *v.r.* to shut; to shut up *or* down: to close; to close up; to enclose; to

encompass; to fasten; to lock; to obstruct; to stop; to stop up; to turn off; to draw; to clench *or* double (*the fist*); to break up; to be *or* come last in, to be in the rear of. — *au loquet*, to latch; to hasp. — *au verrou*, to bolt

Fermeté, *s.f.* firmness; solidity; hardness; steadiness; fixedness; resolution; boldness; strength; vigour; soundness; stability; steadfastness; constancy

Fermette, *s.f.* (*carp.*) small truss *or* rib

Fermeture, *s.f.* shutting, shutting up, closing; fastening, fastenings, shutter, shutters; chimney-top

Fermi-er, ère, *s.m.f.* farmer; farmeress; farmer's wife; tenant; contractor; — *adj.* farm. — *à bail*, tenant farmer. — *général*, (*Fr. hist.*) farmer-general (*of the public revenues*)

Fermoir, *s.m.* clasp; (*tech.*) chisel

Féro, *s.m.* (*local*) dolphin

Féroce, *adj.* ferocious, fierce, savage; wild; (*fam.*) ravenous; furious; very strict *or* severe; rough; proficient

Férocité, *s.f.* ferocity, ferociousness, fierceness, savageness; (*fam.*) ravenousness; fury; strictness, severity; roughness

Féronie, *s.f.* (*plant, insect*) feronia

Ferrage, *s.m.* ironing; shoeing; pelting; tagging; tipping; stoning; railing; iron tools; putting the irons (on); (*cust.*) sealing and stamping [*or* utensils *or* &c., iron

†Ferraille, *s.f.* old iron, scrap-iron; iron bars

†Ferrailler, *v.n.* to forge, to hammer; to fence; to dabble in fencing, to fence badly; to fight; to dispute, to wrangle

†Ferrailleur, *s.m.* dealer in old iron, metal-dealer; fencer, fighter, bully; wrangler

Ferrandine, *s.f.* (*obsolete*) ferrandine (*stuff*)

Ferrarois, e, *adj. s.* Ferrarese

Ferrate, *s.m.* (*chem.*) ferrate

Ferratier, *s.m.* (*farrier's*) shoe-turning hammer

Ferré, e, *part. adj.* bound *or* mounted *or* &c. (*V.* **Ferrer**) with iron, ironed; iron-shod; shod; pelted; tagged; tipped; with a ferrule, ferruled; metalled, stoned; of rail; ferruginous, chalybeate; (*fig.*) hard, strong; (*pers.*) versed, skilled, well up, strong, at home. — *à glace*, rough-shod; (*pers.*) well versed, much skilled, thoroughly up *or* acquainted, very strong, perfectly at home, armed at all points. *Chemin —, route —e*, metalled *or* stoned road. *Voie —e, ligne —e*, line of rail, railroad

Ferrement, *s.m.* iron tool; forceps; ironing; iron-work, iron fittings; putting the irons (on)

Ferre-mule. *s.m.f.* extortioner; — *adj.* extortionate

Ferrer, *v.a.* to bind *or* mount *or* furnish *or* arm with iron, to iron; to fasten; to shoe (*animals, wheels*, &c.); to pelt (*boots, shoes*); to tag; to tip; to put a ferrule to; (*of roads*) to metal, to stone; (*of railway-lines*) to lay the rails on, to rail, to plate; (*cust.*) to seal and stamp. — *à glace*, to rough-shoe. — *la mule*, to charge more than one gave, to extort money,

Se —, *v.r.* to be ironed *or* &c. [to extort

Ferrerie, *s.f.* *V.* **Ferronnerie**

Ferret, *s.m.* tag; iron-ore, hematite; tin pipe

Ferretier, *s.m.* (*farrier's*) shoe-turning hammer; dealer in old metal, metal-dealer

Ferreur, *s.m.* ironer; locksmith; tagger; (*cust.*) sealer, stamper. — *en voitures*, coach-smith

Ferreu-x, se, *adj.* ferrous; ferreous

Ferrico-, (*in compounds, chem.*) ferrico-...

Ferrière, *s.f.* tool-bag

Ferrifère, *adj.* ferriferous

Ferrique, *adj.* (*chem.*) ferric

Ferro, (*in compounds, chem.*) ferro...

Ferrocyanate, *s.m.* (*chem.*) ferrocyanate

Ferrocyane, *s.m.* (*chem.*) ferrocyanogen

Ferrocyanique, *adj.* (*chem.*) ferrocyanic

Ferrocyanure, *s.m.* (*chem.*) ferrocyanide

Ferron, *s.m.* dealer in iron, iron-dealer, ironmonger

Ferronnerie, *s.f.* iron-foundry; iron-store; iron-trade; ironmongery; iron-ware *or* wares; iron-work, iron fittings

Ferronni-er, ère, *s.m.f.* iron-dealer, ironmonger; — *s.f.* coronet (*lady's head-dress*)

Ferrugineu-x, se, *adj.* ferruginous, chalybeate, iron, steel; — *s.m.* chalybeate

Ferruginosité, *s.f.* ferruginosity

Ferrure, *s.f.* iron-work, iron binding, iron; (*of boots*, &c.) pelting; pelt; (*nav.*) hinges; (*of animals*) shoeing, shoes

Fertile, *adj.* fertile; fruitful

Fertilement, *adv.* fertilely; fruitfully

Fertilisable, *adj.* fertilizable

Fertilisation, *s.f.* fertilization

Fertiliser, *v.a.* to fertilize

Se —, *v.r.* to become fertile, to be fertilized

Fertilité, *s.f.* fertility; fruitfulness

Féru, e, *part.* (*of* **Férir,** *obsolete*) struck; stung; wounded; hurt; smitten, in love, taken (with), overfond (of); (— *contre*) angry, incensed (against). — *d'amour*, enamoured, in love

Férulacé, e, *adj.* (*bot.*) ferulaceous

Férule, *s.f.* ferule; rod; stroke, cut; (*bot.*) ferula, giant fennel

Fervemment, *adv.* fervently

Fervent, e, *adj.* fervent

Ferveur, *s.f.* fervour, fervency

Fescennin, e, *adj.* Fescennine

Fessade, *s.f.* (*obsolete*) *V.* **Fessée**

Fesse, *s.f.* buttock; (*pop.*) wife, better half, rib; **—s,** *pl.* buttocks, rump, bottom, breech; (*nav.*) tuck. — **-cahier,** *s.m.* quill-driver, scribbler, literary hack. — **-mathieu,** *s.m.* miser, usurer, old hunks, skin-flint

Fessée, *s.f.* whipping, flogging, breeching

Fesser, *v.a.* to whip, to flog, to breech; (*fig.*) to despatch; to swell. — *le cahier*, to drive the quill, to scribble, to be a literary hack

Fesseu-r, se, *s.m.f.* flogger

Fessier, *s.m.* breech, bottom; (*anat.*) glutæus, gluteal muscle. *Grand —,* (*anat.*) glutæus maximus. *Moyen —,* (*anat.*) glutæus medius. *Petit —,* (*anat.*) glutæus minimus

Fessi-er, ère, *adj.* (*anat.*) gluteal

Fessu, e, *adj.* full-bottomed, large-breeched

Festin, *s.m.* feast, banquet, entertainment, feasting, banqueting. *Faire —,* to feast, to banquet. *Pour tout —,* as the only fare, to eat

Festiner, *v.n.a.* to feast, to entertain

Festival, *s.m.* (*mus.*) festival

Festoiement, *s.m.* feasting, feast, entertaining, entertainment, treating, treat

Feston, *s.m.* festoon, scallop; (*fam.*) zigzag

Festonner, *v.a.* to festoon, to scallop; — *v.n.* (*fam.*) to reel about, to walk zigzag

Se —, *v.r.* to be festooned *or* scalloped

Festoyant, e, *s.m.f.* feaster

Festoyer, *v.n.a.* to feast; to entertain, to treat

Fête, *s.f.* feast; festivity; festival; holiday; birthday; saint's day; entertainment; treat; pleasure; amusement; sport; merry-making; anniversary feast; fair; fête. — *-Dieu*, — *du saint sacrement*, Corpus Christi day. *Jour de —,* holiday. *Jour de sa —,* o.'s saint's day; o.'s birthday. *Faire — à*, to welcome, to entertain, to give a warm reception *or* a hearty welcome; to hold out to ... the hope (of). *Se faire de —,* to make oneself useful; to intermeddle. *Se faire une — de*, to anticipate *or* promise oneself much pleasure from, to look forward with pleasure to, to rejoice at the idea of. *Souhaiter la — à* ..., to wish ... many happy returns of the day. *Ce n'est pas tous les jours —,* Christmas comes but once a year

Fêter, *v.a.* to keep as a holiday, to observe; to celebrate; to welcome; to entertain, to treat, to feast [*a mufti*)

Fetfa, *s.m.* (*Turkish*) fetwah (*written decision of*

Fétiche, *s.m. adj.* fetish, fetich

Fétichisme, *s.m.* fetishism, fetichism

Fétichiste, *s.m.f. adj.* fetishist, fetichist

Fétide, *adj.* fetid, fœtid
Fétidier, *s.m.* (*bot.*) fœtidia (*tree*)
Fétidité, *s.f.* fetidness, fœtidness
Fétoyer, *v.n.a.* (*old spelling*) *V.* **Festoyer**
Fétu, *s.m.* straw, bit of straw; (*fig.*) rush, fig, pin, rap. — *-en-cul, V.* **Paille-en-queue**
Fétuque, *s.f.* (*bot.*) fescue-grass, fescue
Fétus, *s.m. V.* **Fœtus**
Feu, *s.m.* fire; firing; flame; light; signal-light; beacon; light-house; burning; conflagration; heat; fireplace, chimney; set of fire-irons, fire-irons; hearth, family, house, household; inflammation; ardour; zeal; passion; spirit, mettle; animation; life; inspiration; spur; vivacity; liveliness, sprightliness; flash; lustre, brilliancy; dash; brunt; tan-spot; (*of actors*) extra fee; **—x,** *pl.* fires, &c.; (*poet.*) love. — *sacré,* sacred fire; inspiration; genius; (*obsolete*) glowing zeal. — *d'artifice,* fireworks. — *de cheminée,* chimney on fire. — *de joie,* bonfire; rejoicing. — *de paille,* straw fire, sudden blaze, mere flash. — *du ciel,* lightning. — *saint-Elme,* Elmo's fire, Castor and Pollux, Hellene, corposant. *A* —, (*adject., in compounds*) fire. *A petit* —, on a slow fire; by inches. *Au* —*!* fire! *Coin du* —, fireside, chimney-corner. *Couleur de* —, flame-colour; flame-coloured. *Ni* — *ni lieu,* neither house nor home. *Donner le* — *à,* (*vet.*) to sear; (*nav.*) to bream. *Faire* —, to fire. *Faire du* —, to make a fire. *Faire long* —, to hang fire; to be protracted; to miscarry. *Faire* — *des quatre pieds,* to use every effort, to strain every nerve. *Faire* — (or *Faire vie*) *qui dure, V.* **Vie.** *Jeter* — *et flamme,* to rage, to fume. *Jeter ses premiers* —*x,* to sow o.'s wild oats. *Mettre le* — *à, Mettre en* —, to set fire to, to set on fire, to fire. *Mettre à* — *et à sang,* to put to fire and sword, to lay waste (or to waste) with fire and sword. *N'y voir que du* —, not to see anything (of it); not to make it out; to be dazzled (by it)
Feu, e, *adj.* late, the late, deceased
Feudataire, *s.m.f.* feudatory
Feudiste, *s.m. adj.* feudist
†**Feuillade,** *s.f.* (*of ferns*) frond, leaf
†**Feuillage,** *s.m.* foliage, leafage, leaves
†**Feuillagiste,** *s.m.f.* foliage-maker
†**Feuillaison,** *s.f.* foliation [(*monk; royalist*)
†**Feuillant,** *s.m.* (*eccl. & polit. Fr. hist.*) feuillant
†**Feuillantine,** *s.f.* feuillantine (*nun; kind of light pastry*) [— *de fer,* hoop-iron, plate-iron
†**Feuillard,** *s.m.* browsing cut off; hoop-wood.
†**Feuille,** *s.f.* leaf; blade; sheet (*of paper, metal*); newspaper, paper, journal; way-bill; list; folio; foil; veneer; flake; scale; fold. — *volante,* loose sheet (of paper), flying sheet, slip *or* scrap (of paper). — *à plaquer,* veneer, veneering. — *de route,* way-bill; (*mil.*) march-route, route. *A* —*s,* with leaves; folding. *Vin de deux, trois* —*s,* wine two, three years old. — **-morte,** *s.m., adj.m.f.* feuillemort, (of a) faded-leaf *or* yellow-brown colour
†**Feuillé, e,** *adj.* foliate, leaved, leafy; — *s.m.* (*paint.*) foliage, leaves; — *s.f.* bower, green arbour, foliage; (*bot.*) feuillea (*a plant*)
†**Feuiller,** *v.a.n.,* **Se** —, *v.r.* to leaf; to paint *or* draw *or* represent foliage; — *s.m. V.* **Feuillé,**
†**Feuilleret,** *s.m.* (*old*) *V.* **Guillaume** [*s.m.*
†**Feuillet,** *s.m.* leaf (*of a book*); folio; thin plate *or* board; circular saw; (*bot.*) gill, gills; (*anat., of the pleura,* &c.) fold, layer; (*of ruminants*) manyplies [making of ditto, rolling out
†**Feuilletage,** *s.m.* flaky paste, puff-paste;
†**Feuilleté, e,** *part. adj.* foliated, &c. (*V.* **Feuilleter**); in layers; flaky; — *s.m.* flaky paste, puff-paste
†**Feuilleter,** *v.a.* to turn over the leaves of, to thumb; to read over, to peruse; to run through; to consult; to study; to consider; to examine; to roll out (*paste*), to make flaky; to make of flaky *or* puff paste [thumbed *or* read over *or* &c.
Se —, *v.r.* to split into thin plates; to be
†**Feuilleton,** *s.m.* feuilleton (*bottom part of a French newspaper, reserved for literature, science, art, criticism, and frequently for novels also; article of the kind in ditto*); (*parliam.*) list (*of petitions*); (*obsolete*) small leaf
†**Feuilletoniste,** *s.m.f.* writer of "feuilletons," feuilletonist, feuilletoniste
†**Feuillette,** *s.f.* (*of wine*) quarter-cask
†**Feuillettement,** *s.m.* thumbing, &c. (*V.* **Feuilleter**)
†**Feuilliste,** *s.m.* (*obsolete*) pamphleteer
†**Feuillu, e,** *adj.* leafy [flakes, sheets
†**Feuillure,** *s.f.* cheek (*of a door,* &c.), rabbet,
Feurre, *s.m.* (*obsolete*) straw, thatch
Feutier, *s.m.* fireman (*to keep up fires*)
Feutrabilité, *s.f.* felting quality
Feutrable, *adj.* capable of being felted
Feutrage, *s.m.* felting; padding, packing
Feutre, *s.m.* felt; felt hat; (*jest.*) hat, old hat, tile; felt-slipper; padding, packing
Feutrer, *v.a.* to felt; to pad, to pack. *Se* —,
Feutrier, *s.m.* felt-maker [to be felted *or* &c.
Feutrière, *s.f.* felt-cloth
Fève, *s.f.* bean; broad bean; berry; chrysalis; (*vet.*) lampas, lampass. — *de haricot,* kidney-bean, haricot-bean, haricot. — *de marais,* garden *or* common bean; broad bean. — *de Saint-Ignace,* Ignatius' bean. — *de Tonka,* — *tonka,* Tonka-bean. *Gâteau de la* —, Twelfth-cake. *Roi* or *reine de la* —, Twelfth-night king *or* queen. *Rendre* — *pour pois,* to give tit for tat
Féverole, *s.f.* horse-bean; (*obsolete or local*) dried kidney-bean, bean
Févier, *s.m.* (*bot.*) *V.* **Gléditschia**
Février, *s.m.* February
Fez, *s.m.* fez (*cap worn by Turks,* &c.)
Fi, *int.* fie! — *donc!* fie! fie, fie! for shame! — *de,* fie upon, out upon, away with, hang, confound, cursed be. *Faire* — *de,* to turn up o.'s nose at, to despise, to slight, to disdain
Fiacre, *s.m.* (*old*) hackney-coach, four-wheeled cab, four-wheeler, cab (*not a hansom*), common cab; fly; cab-driver, cabman; fly-driver, flyman. *Place de* —*s,* hackney-coach stand, coach-stand, cab-stand, cab-rank
Fiacrée, *s.f.* (*obsolete, jest.*) cabful
†**Fiançailles,** *s.f.pl.* betrothal, affiancing
Fiancé, e, *s.m.f.* betrothed; bridegroom; bride
Fiancer, *v.a.* to betroth, to affiance
Se —, *v.r.* to be betrothed *or* affianced
Fiasco, *s.m.* failure, fiasco. *Faire* —, to fail, to come to grief, to go to pot
Fiat, *int.* let it be done, be it so; — *s.m.* fiat; (*obsolete*) dependence, trust, reliance, relying
Fibre, *s.f.* fibre; string; thread; filament; feeling; constitution
Fibreu-x, se, *adj.* fibrous; stringy
Fibrillaire, *adj.* fibrillary
Fibrille, *s.f.* fibril
Fibrilleu-x, se, *adj.* fibrillous
Fibrine, *s.f.* (*chem.*) fibrine
Fibrineu-x, se, *adj.* fibrinous
Fibro-, (*in compounds*) fibro-...
Fibule, *s.f.* (*old*) fibula, clasp, buckle
Fic, *s.m.* (*med.*) ficus; (*vet.*) fig
Ficaire, *s.f.* (*bot.*) pilewort, lesser celandine
Ficeler, *v.a.* to tie with string, to tie up; (*fam.*) to do up; to dress up *or* out, to dress
Se —, *v.r.* to be tied up; to be done up; to dress oneself up *or* out, to dress
Ficeleu-r, se, *s.m.f.* packer
Ficelle, *s.f.* string, twine, packthread; dodge, trick, stage-trick; (*pop.*) dodger, trickster; jade; vicious horse *or* mare; — *adj.* (*pop.*) tricky; jadish; vicious [(*pop.*) dodger, trickster
Ficellier, *s.m.* packthread-reel, reel, roller;
Fichaise, *s.f.* (*fam.*) trifle, nonsense, humbug, bosh, rigmarole
Fichant, e, *adj.* (*fam.*) confoundedly annoying *or* troublesome, bothering, a bother, sad, a sad thing; (*obsolete*) darting *or* plunging (*fire*)
Fiche, *s.f.* hook, peg, pin; picket, stake; ground-

depth; mark, ticket, label; *(at play)* fish; — *v.a.n.* *(pop.)* *V.* **Ficher.** — *de consolation,* extra fish given to the winner, forfeit; *(fig.)* compensation, little bit of consolation *or* of comfort, consolatory sop. *Aller se faire* —, to go to the deuce, to go and be hanged, to go to. *Envoyer faire* —, to send to the deuce

Fiché, e, *part. adj.* driven in, &c. (*V.* **Ficher**); dressed; *(her.)* fitchy, fitched, fitché, fiched

Ficher, *v.a.* to drive in; to stick in; to fix; *(fam.)* to give; to throw; to send; to shove; to put; to set; to clap; to get; to lodge; to do; — *v.n.* *(fam.)* to matter, to signify, to be; to strike, to hit, to knock, to rap. — *malheur,* to bother, to vex, to worry. — *le* or *son camp,* to decamp, to run away, to be off, to cut it, to bolt, to toddle; to disappear, to vanish, to go. *Je t'en* (or *vous en*) *fiche!* *(fam.)* nonsense! not a bit of it! indeed? is it though? does it though? will *or* would you though? I wish you may get it

Se —, *v.r.* to stick *or* fix *or* &c. oneself *or* itself; to be driven in *or* stuck *or* &c.; to get *or* enter (into); *(pop.)* to dress oneself. *Se* — *de,* *(fam.)* to laugh (at), to make game (of), to trifle (with), to play the fool (with), to make a fool (of); not to care (for), to snap o.'s fingers [(at)

Ficheron, *s.m.* iron pin

Fichet, *s.m.* peg; hooked point; mark, ticket

Ficheur, *s.m.* *(mas.)* pointer [*a line*)

Fichoir, *s.m.* peg (*for hanging clothes or &c. on*

Fichtre, *int.* *(fam.)* hang it! damn it! confound it! bless me! indeed; certainly

Fichtrement, *adv.* *V.* **Fichument**

Fichu, *s.m.* neckerchief, neck-handkerchief, handkerchief. *Corps de* —, habit-shirt

Fichu,e, *part. adj.* *(fam.)* given, &c. (*V.* **Ficher**); — *adj.* sorry, wretched, confoundedly bad; deuced, infernal, confounded, blasted, damned, *(ironically)* blessed; done, arranged, conditioned; made; shaped; dressed, clad; capable; fit; lost; done for; queer; out of sorts

Fichument, *adv.* *(fam.)* sorrily, wretchedly, confoundedly, deucedly, infernally, damnably, damned; queerly; ridiculously

Fichûre, *s.f.* fish-gig, gig

Ficiforme, *adj.* ficiform, fig-shaped

Ficoïde, *s.f.* *(bot.)* mesembryanthemum (fig-marigold, ice-plant, &c.: *about* 400 *species*)

Fictice, *adj.* *(old)* *V.* **Fictif**

Ficti-f, ve, *adj.* fictitious

Fiction, *s.f.* fiction; fable, figment

Fictionnaire, *adj.* *(old)* founded on fiction

Fictivement, *adv.* fictitiously

Fidéicommis, *s.m.* *(law)* trust, fideicommissum

Fidéicommissaire, *s.m.* transferee (*of property left in trust*)

Fidéiste, *s.m.* *(Cath. rel.)* fideist, traditionalist

Fidéjusseur, *s.m.* *(law)* surety, guarantor

Fidéjussion, *s.f.* *(law)* suretyship; security

Fidèle, *adj.* faithful; true; trusty; loyal; exact; accurate; real; safe; sure; good; — *s.m.f.* faithful friend; (one) of a *or* of the congregation; worshipper; believer; —**s,** *s.m.f.pl.* faithful; church-goers; congregation; worshippers; believers; faithful friends

Fidèlement, *adv.* faithfully; truly; trustily; loyally; exactly; accurately; really; safely; surely; right

Fidélité, *s.f.* fidelity; faithfulness; truthfulness; trustiness; loyalty; allegiance; exactness; accuracy; honesty, probity

Fidibus, *s.m.* *(jest.)* pipe-light, spill

Fiduciaire, *adj.m.f.*, *s.m.* fiduciary. *Circulation* —, paper currency. *Héritier* —, heir in trust. *Monnaie* —, paper-money

Fiduciairement, *adv.* fiduciarily [freehold

Fief, *s.m.* fief, fee, feud. *Franc-* —, frank-fee,

Fieffé, e, *adj.* downright, regular, arrant

Fieffer, *v.a.* to enfeoff

Fiel, *s.m.* gall; hatred, malice, rancour, spleen;

Fiente, *s.f.* dung [bitterness. — *de verre,* sandiver

Fienter, *v.n.a.* to dung

Fienteu-x, se, *adj.* dungy

Fier (Se), *v.r.* to trust; to rely, to depend

Fi-er, ère, *adj.* proud; haughty; high-spirited, spirited; bold; determined; intrepid; boastful; *(her.)* fierce; *(fam., pop.)* extreme, very great, remarkable, precious, rare, famous, stunning, fine, capital; tipsy, tight. — *comme un paon,* — *comme Artaban,* — *comme un Écossais,* as vain *or* as proud as a peacock, as proud as Lucifer

Fier à-bras, *s.m.* bully, hector, braggart

Fièrement, *adv.* proudly; haughtily; spiritedly, with spirit; boldly; *(fam., pop.)* extremely, very greatly, very much, very, remarkably, preciously, famously, finely, capitally; a precious deal, a rare lot

Fiérot, te, *adj. s.* proudish; ditto person

Fiert, *v.* (*from* **Férir,** *obsolete*) strikes

Fierté, *s.f.* pride; haughtiness; high spirit; dignity; boldness [son, lad, boy, child

Fieu, Fieux, *s.m.* (*pop. for* **Fils** *or* **Enfant**)

Fièvre, *s.f.* fever; ague; uneasiness, restlessness; agitation; excitement; heat. — *lente,* hectic fever. — *d'hôpital,* typhus fever. *Tomber de* — *en chaud mal,* to fall out of the frying-pan into the fire. *Que la* — *le serre!* *(obsolete)* a plague on him!

Fiévreu-x, se, *adj. s.* feverish; restless; fever

Fiévrotte, *s.f.* *(fam.)* slight fever [patient

Fifi, *s.m.* *(fam.)* ducky; sweet; *(pop.)* nightman

†Fifille, *s.f.* *(fam.)* little girl

Fifre, *s.m.* fife; fifer

Fifrer, *v.n.a.* to fife [knavish valet; go-between

Figaro, *s.m.* cunning barber, barber, hairdresser;

Figement, *s.m.* congelation; coagulation; curdling [to curdle; to set

Figer, *v.a.*, **Se** —, *v.r.* to congeal; to coagulate;

†Fignoler, *v.n.* *(pop.)* to affect refinement, to mince, to humbug; to dress smartly, to rig oneself out; — *v.a.* *(fam., pop.)* to polish, to finish off; to labour; to do *or* perform in style

Figue, *s.f.* fig. *Moitié* — *moitié raisin,* half one way half the other, so so, not quite the thing, not altogether; reluctantly. *Faire la* — *à,* *(obsolete)* *V. Se* **Moquer** *de*

Figuerie, *s.f.* fig-orchard

Figuier, *s.m.* fig-tree; *(bird)* fig-eater

Figuline, *s.f.* *adj.* figuline, potter's clay; earth-

Figurabilité, *s.f.* figurability [enware, pottery

Figurable, *adj.* figurable

Figurant, e, *s.m.f.* *(theat.)* figurant, figurante

Figurati-f, ve, *adj.* figurative; *(Gr. gram.)* characteristic

Figuration, *s.f.* figuration; *(theat.)* figurants

Figurativement, *adv.* figuratively

Figure, *s.f.* figure; form; shape; face, countenance; look; appearance; image; portrait; diagram; representation; symbol, type; *(at cards)* court-card, figure-card; *(nav.)* figure-head; *(butch., pop.)* sheep's head. *Être bien de* —, to have a handsome face, to be good-looking

Figuré, e, *adj.* figured; figurate; figurative; *(obsolete)* accoutred, equipped; — *s.m.* figures; objects; *(gram.)* figurative sense. *Au* —, in a

Figurément, *adv.* figuratively [figurative sense

Figurer, *v.a.* to figure; to represent; to typify; — *v.n.* to harmonize, to match; to look; to appear; to figure; to make a figure; to dance in figures; *(theat.)* to be a figurant *or* figurante

Se —, *v.r.* to figure *or* picture to oneself; to imagine; to fancy; to suppose; to think; to be figured *or* &c. *Figurez-vous que* ..., suppose that ...; would you believe that ...?

Figurine, *s.f.* little figure; miniature figure; image; postage-stamp, head

Figur-isme, -iste. *V.* page 3, § 1

Fil, *s.m.* thread; yarn; wire; edge (*of razors, swords,* &c.); stream, current; grain; string; chain, series, course; order; clue; (*in marble, stone, glass*) flaw; *(pop.)* dodge, trick; knack. — *retors,* twine. — *d'Écosse,* cotton. — *de la*

Vierge, gossamer, gossamer thread, air-thread. *De — en aiguille*, from one thing to another; insensibly; minutely. *Avoir le —*, to be sharp; to be up to it; to have the knack. *De droit —*, straight, right, straightforward. *Donner du — à retordre à*, to cut out work for, to give a deal of trouble, to plague, to annoy

Filable, *adj.* spinnable

Filadière, *s.f.* flat-bottomed boat, flat [weed

Filage, *s.m.* spinning; (*bot.*) cotton-rose, cud-

Filago, *s.m.* (*bot.*) cotton-rose, cudweed

Filagramme, *s.m. V.* **Filigrane**

Filaire, *s.m.f.* (*zool.*) thread-worm, Guinea-worm

Filament, *s.m.* filament; thread; string; fibre

Filamenteu-x, se, *adj.* filamentous; thready;

Filanderie, *s.f.* (*local*) spinnery [stringy

Filandière, *s.f.* spinster, spinner. *Les sœurs —s*, (*myth.*) the fatal sisters, the fates

Filandres, *s.f.pl.* gossamer, gossamer threads, air-threads; strings; sea-weeds; filanders

Filandreu-x, se, *adj.* stringy, thready; diffuse, loose, involved, cumbrous [shooting, falling

Filant, e, *adj.* ropy, viscous, viscid; (*of stars*)

Filao, *s.m.* (*bot.*) *V.* **Casuarine**

Filardeau, *s.m.* straight sapling; (*fish*) jack,

Filardeu-x, se, *adj.* (*of stones*) flawy [pickerel

Filarets, *s.m.pl.* (*nav.*) rail-netting [*V.* **Filaire**

Filaria, *s.m.* (*bot.*) phyllirea, mock-privet; (*zool.*)

Filasse, *s.f.* tow; harl; bast; (*jest.*) flaxen hair; (*pop.*) mattress; bed

Filassi-er, ère, *s.m.f.* hemp and flax dresser

Filateur, *s.m.* spinner, mill-owner

Filatier, *s.m.* thread-merchant

Filatrice, *s.f.* silk-winder (*woman*)

Filature, *s.f* spinning; spinning-mill, mill, factory; rope-walk

File, *s.f.* file; row; line. *A la —*, in (a) file *or* &c., one after another; in the file. *Chef de —*, *V.* **Chef.** *Par — à droite!* (*mil.*) right file! [*Par — à gauche!* left file!

Filé, *s.m.* thread

Filer, *v.a.* to spin; to conduct, to manage, to carry on; to make; to spend; to spin out; to wire-draw; to net; to slip; to let down; (*nav.*) to veer, to veer away; to pay away *or* out; to run (*knots*); (*mus.*) to hold (*a note*); — *v.n.* to spin; to rope, to be ropy; to run along; to run; to slip away; to take oneself off, to be off, to bolt, to cut away *or* along, to toddle, to make oneself scarce; to vanish; to pur; to flare; to shoot; to file off. *— doux*, to give way, to submit, to be submissive, to be all submission; to draw in o.'s horns; to sing small; to eat humble pie. *— le parfait amour*, to be a sentimental lover, to be all love and sentiment. *Du temps que Berthe filait*, in the time of queen Bess, in old times, in times of old, of yore

Se —, *v r.* to be spun, &c.

Filerie, *s.f.* rope-walk; wire-mill; wire-drawing

Filet, *s m.* thread; string; fillet; net; netting; network; snare; toil; small stream, streamlet, brook; dash, drop; bead; streak; filament; film; ligament; fibre; current, draught; (*butch.*, *cook.*) under-cut, fillet, inside of the sirloin (*of beef*); (*cook.*) fillet (*of fish*, &c.); (*anat.*) frænum, frenum, fillet, string; (*arch.*) fillet, bed-moulding; (*her.*) fillet; (*bot.*) fillet, filament; (*of strawberries*) runner; (*print.*) rule; (*rid.*) snaffle-bridle, snaffle, bridoon. *— de vinaigre*, dash of vinegar; (*fig.*) thin sharp voice. *— de voix*, thin voice. *Faux —*, (*butch.*) *V.* **Contre-filet.** *Couvert à —s*, thread-pattern spoon and fork. *Avoir le —*, to be tongue-tied. *Avoir le — coupé*, to have a glib tongue, not to be tongue-tied

Filetage, *s.m.* filleting; threading; worming; wire-drawing; net-poaching

Fileter, *v.a.n.* to fillet; to thread; to worm; to wire-draw; to poach with nets

Fileu-r, se, *s.m.f.* spinner, spinster; — *s.m.* wire-drawer; — *s.f.* (*spider*) weaver, retiary; — *adj.* spinning; weaving, retiary. *— de cartes*, [card-sharper

Filial, e, *adj.* filial

Filialement, *adv.* filially

Filiation, *s.f.* filiation

Filicifère, *adj.* (*min.*) filiciferous

Filière, *s.f.* draw-plate; screw-plate; vermicelli-gauge; (*of spiders*, &c.) spinneret; (*arch.*) purlin; (*fig.*) string, series; regular course; hierarchy; medium; ordeal, trial

Filiforme, *adj.* filiform, thread-shaped, thread-like; (*med.*, *of the pulse*) thread-like

Filigrane, *s.m.* filigree, filigree-work; (*of paper*) watermark [(*of paper*) to watermark

Filigraner, *v.a.* to work in filigree, to filigree;

Filigraniste, *s.m.* filigree-worker

Filin, *s.m.* (*nav.*) cordage [*s.f.* (*bot.*) dropwort

Filipendule, *adj.* (*nat. hist.*) filipendulous; —

†**Fillasse,** *s.f.* low girl, wench

†**Fille,** *s.f.* girl; maid; maiden; lass; daughter; offspring; servant-maid, servant-girl, servant; waitress; spinster; nun; creature, thing, woman; bad woman, woman of the town. *Petite- —*, (*with a hyphen*) granddaughter; (*without a hyphen*) little girl, little daughter, &c. *— de chambre*, chambermaid; (*obsolete*) lady's-maid. *— de joie*, *— publique*, prostitute, harlot, girl *or* woman of the town. *— de marbre*, gay woman incapable of love, cold *or* hard-hearted wretch, heartless bitch, kept woman, courtesan. *— de salle*, waitress. *— de service*, housemaid; chambermaid. *Rester —*, to remain an old maid, to live single [wench

†**Fillette,** *s.f.* young *or* little girl, lass, maiden;

†**Filleul,** *s.m.* godson; (also, in a duel, either of the fighters is called his own second's *filleul*)

†**Filleule,** *s.f.* goddaughter

†**Fillot,** *s.m. V.* **Fiston**

†**Fillotte,** *s.f.* little girl

Filoche, *s.f.* network; net; rope; thread (*come out of a tissue*), ravelling; (*pop.*) purse

Filoir, *s.m.* spinning-machine

Filon, *s.m.* lode; vein

Filoselle, *s.f.* floss-silk

Filoti-er, ère, *s.m.f.* thread-dealer

Filou, *s.m.* pickpocket, thief; sharper, cheat

Filoutage, *s.m. V.* **Filouterie**

Filouter, *v.a.n.* to steal; to swindle, to cheat, to chisel; to pick pockets

Filouterie, *s.f.* picking pockets, pocket-picking, stealing, stealth; swindling, cheating, cheat

Fils, *s.m.* son; child; offspring; lad, boy; fellow, young fellow; creature; junior. *Petit- —*, grandson. *— de famille*, young gentleman *or* nobleman under age; young gentleman *or* nobleman, young man of good family, gentleman's son. *— de ses œuvres*, a self-made man

Filterie, *s.f.* twine-factory

Filti-er, ère, *s.m.f.* twiner

Filtrage, *s.m.*, **Filtration,** *s.f.* filtering, filtration, straining, percolation [ing

Filtra-teur, trice, *s.m.f.* filterer; — *adj.* filter-

Filtre, *s.m.* filter, filtering-machine; strainer; tammy

Filtrer, *v.a.n.*, **Se —**, *v.r.* to filter, to strain, to [percolate

Filure, *s.f.* spinning

Fin, *s.f.* end; close, conclusion, termination; term; issue; expiration; death; aim, object, design, purpose, intention, view. *A ces —s*, to this *or* that end; consequently. *A deux —s*, *à toute —*, (*of horses*) *V.* **Cheval.** *A la —*, at last, at length; in the end; after all; in fact, now. *A telle — que de raison*, at all events, at any rate. *Sans —*, without end, endless, unending; perpetually. *— de non-recevoir*, (*law*) plea in bar, exception; (*fig.*) objection; put-off. *Faire une —*, to come to an end; to settle, to get married. *Qui veut la — veut les moyens*, where there is a will there is a way. *La — couronne l'œuvre*, "finis coronat opus," the end crowns the work; all is well that ends well

Fin, e, *adj.* fine; thin; slender; small; delicate; nice; dainty; refined; elegant; pure; real; good; choice; exquisite, excellent; skilful, brilliant; ingenious; witty; acute; sharp; keen, shrewd; subtle; quick; cunning, sly;

arch; swift; very, utmost; (*of writing*) small-hand, small; — *s.f.* small hand (writing). —*es herbes*, sweet *or* savoury herbs. *Pierres —es*, precious stones, gems. *Avoir le nez* —, to have a good nose; (*fig.*) to be far-sighted *or* sagacious. *Avoir l'oreille —e*, to have a quick ear

Fin, *s.m.* sly *or* cunning fellow; main point; gist; secret; essence, quintessence; best; cream; perfection; fine materials *or* article; fine linen; pure metal, gold, silver; small hand (writing). — *contre* —, *à* — — *et demi*, diamond cut diamond. *Jouer au* — or *au plus* [—, to vie in cunning

Finage, *s.m.* affinage

Final, e, *adj.* final, last

Finale, *s.f.* (*gram.*) final syllable; (*mus.*) finale (*note*, &c.); (*dancing, and fig.*) finale; — *s.m.* (*mus.*) finale (*piece of music*)

Finalement, *adv.* finally, lastly

Finaliste, *s.m.* (*philos.*) finalist

Finalité, *s.f.* finality

Finance, *s.f.* cash, ready money; finance; financiers; exchequer; treasury [to fork out

Financer, *v.n.* to pay money, to come down,

Financi-er, ère, *adj.* financial; — *s.m.* financier; financialist; — *s.f.* (*cook.*) financière (*an expensive, highly-flavoured, mixed ragout*)

Financièrement, *adv.* financially

Finasser, *v.n.* to use petty tricks, to shirk, to shuffle, to finesse [fice, cunning, finesse

Finasserie, *s.f.* petty trickery, shirking, arti-

Finasseu-r, se, Finassi-er, ère, *s.m.f. adj.* petty trickster, artful *or* sly person; tricky, [artful, sly

Finâtre, *s.f.* inferior silk

Finaud, e, *adj. s.* cunning, sly; cunning one, sly boots, dodger

Finement, *adv.* finely; delicately; skilfully; ingeniously; acutely, shrewdly, keenly, cunningly, slily

Fine-métal, *s.m.* refined white cast-iron

Finerie, *s.f.* finery, refinery

Finesse, *s.f.* fineness; thinness; slenderness; smallness; delicacy; nicety; refinement; purity; clearness; ingenuity; wit; acuteness; sharpness; keenness, shrewdness; subtleness, subtility; quickness; cunning, sliness; archness; artifice, device, trick, finesse. *Entendre* — *à*, to give a malicious construction to; to see something in. *Faire* — *de*, to make a mystery of [stuff *or* tissue

Finet, te, *adj. s.m.f. V.* **Finaud;** — *s.f.* thin

Fini, e, *part. adj.* finished; ended; at an end; concluded; completed; done; done with; settled; over; being over; up; complete; perfect; consummate; accomplished; expert; downright, regular, arrant, thorough; done for, broken down, ruined, finished up; finite, limited; — *s.m.* finish, finishing; completion; perfection; finite

Finir, *v.a.n.* to finish; to end; to terminate; to conclude; to put an end to; to complete; to perfect; to settle; to do; to have done; to have done with; to make an end; to cease; to leave off; to come to an end; to draw to a close; to expire; to die. — *par*, to end by *or* with *or* in; to ... in the end, to ... at last, to ... finally. *En* —, to finish, to end, to leave off, to have done (with), to put an end *or* a stop (to), to make an end (of), to settle (with), to have done with it, to put an end *or* a stop to it, to make an end of it, to cut it (*or* the matter) short; to conclude; to be conclusive *or* decisive. *A n'en plus* —, without end, endless. *Cela n'en finit pas*, there is no end of it, it is endless. *As-tu fini!* (*pop.*) nonsense! fudge! all humbug! hold your jaw! shut up!

Finissage, *s.m.* finishing off, finishing, closing

Finisseu-r, se, *s.m.f.* finisher, closer

Finito, *s.m.* settlement (*of an account*)

Finlandais, e, *adj. s.* Finnish, of Finland; Finlander, Fin, Finn

Finnois, e, *adj. s. V.* **Finlandais**

Fin-or, *s.m.* (kind of pear)

Finot, te, *adj. s. V.* **Finaud**

Finoterie, *s.f.* (*old*) *V.* **Finasserie**

Finte, *s.f.* (*alias* **Feinte**) twaite shad

Fintier, *s.m.* shad-net [corn)

Fiole, *s.f.* phial, vial; bottle; blade *or* flag (*of*

Fioler, *v.a.n.* (*pop.*) to quaff, to tipple, to tope

Fioleu-r, se, *s.m.f.* (*pop.*) tippler, toper

Fion, *s.m.* (*pop.*) finish, finishing touch, last touch, touching up; style; knack

Fionner, *v.a.* (*pop.*) to give the last touch, to give a style; — *v.n.* (*pop.*) to be stylish, to look smart, to be a swell; to parade [beau, belle

Fionneu-r, se, *s.m.f.* (*pop.*) swell, exquisite,

Fiorin, *s.m.* (*bot.*) fiorin, black couch-grass

Fiorite, *s.f.* (*min.*) fiorite

Fioriture, *s.f.* embellishment; (*mus.*) grace, [grace-note

Fiotte, *s.f.* (*pop.*) *V.* **Fillotte**

Firmament, *s.m.* firmament

Firman, *s.m.* firman

Firole, *s.f.* (*mollusc*) firola

Fisc, *s.m.* public treasury, treasury, exchequer, fisc; revenue-officers [— *s.m.* fiscal

Fiscal, e, *adj.* fiscal; financial; extortionate;

Fiscalement, *adv.* fiscally; financially

Fiscalité, *s.f.* fiscality; fiscal matters; fiscal [zeal, exaction

Fissiflore, *adj.* (*bot.*) fissiflorous

Fissile, *adj.* fissile

Fissilité, *s.f.* fissility

Fissipare, *adj.* (*zool.*) fissiparous

Fissiparie, Fissiparité, *s.f.* (*zool.*) fissiparism, fissiparity

Fissipède, *adj.m.f., s.m.* (*zool.*) fissiped

Fissipenne, *s.m.* (*zool.*) plumed moth

Fissirostre, *adj.* (*zool.*) fissirostral; — *s.m.* [fissirostre

Fissuration, *s.f.* fissuration

Fissure, *s.f.* fissure; cleft; crack; rent

Fissurelle, *s.f.* (*mollusc*) fissurella (*shell*), key-hole-limpet

Fissurellier, *s.m.* (*mollusc*) fissurella (*animal*)

Fissurer, *v.a.* to fissure. *Se* —, to become fissured [young one, child; friend

Fiston, Fistot, *s.m.* (*fam.*) son, lad, boy,

Fistulaire, *adj.* fistular, fistuliform; — *s.m.* (*zool.*) fistularia, tobacco-pipe fish; — *s.f.* (*zool.*) fistularia (*mollusc*); (*bot.*) kind of sea-weed

Fistulane, *s.f.* (*zool.*) fistulana

Fistule, *s.f.* (*surg.*) fistula

Fistuleu-x, se, *adj.* fistulous, fistulose

Fistuline, *s.f.* (*bot.*) fistulina (*fungus*)

Fixage, *s.m.* fixing, fixation

Fixateur, *s.m.* fixator, fixative; — *m.*, **-trice,** [*f.*, *adj.* fixative, fixing

Fixati-f, ve, *adj.* fixative

Fixation, *s.f.* fixation; fixing; setting; settling; appointing; assessment

Fixe, *adj.* fixed; firm, steady; steadfast; fast; stable; immovable; set; established; settled; appointed; regular; certain; stationary; — *s.m.* regular salary; regular income; settled weather; (*chem.*) fixed body; — *s.f.* fixed star; — ! (*mil.*) eyes front! steady!

Fixé, e, *part. adj.* fixed, &c. (*V.* **Fixer**); — *s.m.* oil-painting protected by a glass

Fixement, *adv.* fixedly; wistfully; hard; in the face; firmly; steadily; steadfastly; immovably

Fixer, *v.a.*, **Se** —, *v.r.* to fix; to fasten; to stick; to set; to establish; to settle; to appoint; to satisfy; to determine; to attract; to stop; to stare at, to gaze on

Fixité, *s.f.* fixity, fixedness; stability

Fla, *s.m.* double beat of the drum. — **-fla,** *s.m.* [*V.* **Flafla**

Flabellation, *s.f.* flabellation

Flabellé, e, *adj.* flabellate

Flabellifolié, e, *adj.* (*bot.*) flabellifoliate

Flabelliforme, *adj.* flabelliform, fan-shaped

Flac, *int.* plash! smack! slap! bang!

Flaccidité, *s.f.* flaccidity, flabbiness

Flache, *s.f.* hole (*in a paved road*); plash, puddle, pool; (*tech.*) hollow, blister, flaw [fective

Flacheu-x, se, *adj.* full of holes; flawy, de-

Flacon, *s.m.* flagon; flask; phial, vial; bottle; smelling-bottle, scent-bottle; decanter; (*pop.*) shoe. — *d'odeur*, smelling-bottle, scent-bottle

Flaconnerie, *s.f.* flagon-making *or* trade;
Flaconni-er, ère, *s.m.f.* flagon-maker [flagons
Flafla, *s.m.* (*fam.*) clap-trap, effect, show, dash,
Flagellant, *s.m.* flagellant (*fanatic*) [fuss
Flagella-teur, trice, *s.m.f.* whipper, flogger, scourger; lasher; — *adj.* whipping, flogging, scourging; lashing [ging, scourging; lashing
Flagellation, *s.f.* flagellation, whipping, flog-
Flageller, *v.a.* to flagellate, to whip, to flog, to scourge; to lash
Flagelliforme, *adj.* flagelliform, whip-shaped
Flageoler, *v.n.* to totter, to tremble, to shake; (*old*) to play on the flageolet
Flageolet, *s.m.* flageolet; flageolettist; (*haricot* —) dwarf kidney-bean; (*pop.*) thin shank, shaky *or* trembling leg
Flageolettiste, *s.m.* flageolettist
Flagorner, *v.a.* to fawn upon, to toady
Flagornerie, *s.f.* base flattery, toadyism, sycophancy [sycophant, wheedler
Flagorneu-r, se, *s.m.f.* toad-eater, toady,
Flagrance, *s.f.* flagrance, flagrancy
Flagrant, e, *adj.* flagrant
Flair, *s.m.* smelling, scent
Flairer, *v.a.n.* to scent, to smell; to snuff; to smell out; to detect; to suspect; to foresee; — *s.m.* smelling, scent [scented *or* smelt *or* &c.
Se —, *v.r.* to scent *or* &c. each other; to be
Flaireu-r, se, *s.m.f.* smeller; detecter. — *de cuisine* or *de table*, smell-feast, parasite, sponger
Flamand, e, *adj.* Flemish; — *s.m.f.* (*pers.*) Fleming; — *s.m.* Flemish (language); — *s.f.* Flemish fashion; (*dance, tune*) flamande
Flamant, *s.m.* (*bird*) flamingo
Flambage, *s.m.* singeing
Flambant, e, *adj.* flaming; blazing; flaring; bright; natty, neat; flashy; flash; swaggering. — *neuf*, flam-new, brand-new, bran-new
Flambard, e, *adj.* (*pop.*) splendid, bright, flashy
Flambard, Flambart, *s.m.* fishing-smack; brand; half-burnt coal; (*local*) Elmo's fire, corposant; (*pop.*) sailor, jack; (*pop.*) boatman; (*pop.*) jolly fellow, buck; (*old*) sword with a waving blade [flag; (*old*) flaming sword
Flambe, *s.f.* (*bot.*) common iris; yellow water-
Flambé, e, *part. adj.* singed, &c. (*V.* **Flamber**); flamy; (*fam.*) ruined, done, done for, undone; lost, gone
Flambeau, *s.m.* flambeau, torch, link; candle; taper; light; luminary; candlestick; fire-brand, brand. *Clarté* or *lumière de* — (or *des* —*x*), torchlight; candle-light. *Aux* —*x*, by
Flambée, *s.f.* blaze [torchlight; by candle-light
Flamber, *v.n.* to flame; to blaze; to flare; to flash; — *v.a.* to pass before a fire; to fire; to singe; to air; to purify (by fire), to disinfect; to scale *or* prove (*a cannon*); to fire a cap on the nipple of (*a firelock*); (*fig.*) to inflame; to squander; to do, to ruin; to rifle; to lose; to reprimand (*a ship*) by signal; — *s.m.* flaming; blazing
Flamberge, *s.f.* (*obsolete*) sword, brand, falchion. — *au vent*, (*jest.*) with drawn sword. *Mettre — au vent*, (*jest.*) to draw the sword
Flambergeant, *s.m.* (*bird*) oyster-catcher; curlew [flash
Flamboiement, *s.m.* flaming; blazing; flare;
Flamboyant, e, *adj.* flaming; blazing; flaring; bright; gleaming; glistening; shining; flashy; (*paint.*) airy, light; (*arch.*) flamboyant; — *s.f.* flaming rocket; kind of tulip
Flamboyer, *v.n.* to flame; to blaze; to flare; to flash; to gleam; to glisten, to glitter, to shine,
Flambure, *s.f.* flaw (*in a dyed stuff*) [to sparkle
Flamine, *s.m.* (*hist.*) flamen (*Roman priest*)
Flamingant, e, *adj.* speaking Flemish
Flaminien, ne, *adj.* Flaminian; flamineous
Flammant, *s.m.* *V.* **Flamant**
Flamme, *s.f.* flame; blaze; fire; light; brightness, lustre; glow; ardour, passion, love; (*mil.*) bag *or* fly (*of a busby*); (*nav.*) pendant, pennant; (*vet.*) fleam; (*bot.*) spearwort
Flammèche, *s.f.* flake (of fire), spark
Flammerole, *s.f.* fire-drake, wild-fire, will o' the wisp, ignis fatuus, meteor; (*nav.*) corposant
Flammette, *s.f.* small flame, flake (of fire), spark; (*nav.*) small pendant *or* pennant; (*vet.*) fleam; (*bot.*) spearwort
Flammifère, *adj.* flammiferous
Flammigère, *adj.* flammigerous; — *s.f.* flaming fusee (*for smokers*), flamer
Flammivome, *adj.* flammivomous
Flan, *s.m.* custard; (*coin.*) blank
Flanc, *s.m.* flank; side; womb, bosom; entrails, bowels. *Être sur le* —, (*fam.*) to be laid up. *Prêter le — à*, (*fig.*) to give a hold to, to expose oneself to, to lay oneself open to. *Se battre les —s*, (*fig.*) to make great efforts. *Par le — droit!* (*mil.*) to the right about! *Par le — gauche!* to the left about!
Flanche, *s.m.* (*pop.*) dodge, trick, knack
Flanchet, *s.m.* (*of beef*) flank, veiny piece; (*of*
Flanconade, *s.f.* (*fenc.*) flanconade [*cod*) flank
Flandrin, e, *adj.* Flemish; — *s.m.* lanky fellow
Flanelle, *s.f.* flannel
Flâner, *v.n.* to lounge, to saunter; to stroll; to loiter; to idle; to moon; to loaf
Flânerie, *s.f.* lounging, lounge, sauntering, saunter; strolling, stroll; loitering; idling; mooning; loafing
Flâneu-r, se, *s.m.f.* lounger, saunterer; stroller; loiterer; idler; mooner; loafer; — *adj.* lounging; sauntering; &c.
Flânocher, Flânoter, (*pop.*) *V.* **Flâner**
Flanqué, e, *part. adj.* flanked, &c. (*V.* **Flanquer**); accompanied; having at o.'s side
Flanquement, *s.m.* flanking
Flanquer, *v.a.* to flank; to go *or* be alongside of; to cover; (*fam.*) to give, to hit; to throw, to shy, to fling, to pitch; to thrust; to put, to clap. — *à la porte*, to bundle out
Se —, *v.r.* to give *or* &c. oneself *or* each other; to fall; to intrude; to be given, &c.
Flanquette, *s.f.* (*a vulgar corruption of* **Fran-**
Flanqueur, *s.m.* (*mil.*) flanker [**quette**)
Flaque, *s.f.* plash, puddle, pool
Flaquée, *s.f.* dab, dash (*of liquid*)
Flaquer, *v.a.* to dash, to throw (*liquid*)
Flasque, *adj.* lax, slack, lank, loose, soft, flabby, limp, flaccid; effeminate, weak, feeble; indolent; languid; — *s.m.* (*artil.*) cheek; — *s.f.* powder-flask; (*of bellows*) board; (*nav.*) whelp
Flasquement, *adv.* slackly, loosely, flabbily;
Flatir, *v.a.* (*tech.*) to flatten [feebly
Flatoir, *s.m.* flattening-hammer
Flâtrer, *v.a.* (*vet.*) to fire, to cauterize
Se —, *v.r.* (*hunt.*) to crouch [flattering
Flatté, e, *part. adj.* flattered, &c. (*V.* **Flatter**);
Flatter, *v.a.* to flatter; to caress, to stroke, to pat; to humour; to tamper with; to fawn upon; to coax, to wheedle; to delude, to deceive; to gratify; to tickle; to please; to delight; to soothe; to favour; to hold out hopes (of ...) to (*a person*); to touch gently (*strings of mus. instr.*), to run o.'s fingers over; (— *le dé*) to throw (*the dice*) gently, to slide (*the dice*), (*fig.*) to soften (*things*) down, to mince (*the matter*)
Se —, *v.r.* to flatter oneself *or* each other; to hope, to trust; to expect; to delude oneself
Flatterie, *s.f.* flattery; caress; fawning
Flatteu-r, se, *s.m.f.* flatterer; — *adj.* flattering; eulogistic; complimentary; caressing; fawning; gratifying, pleasing
Flatteusement, *adv.* flatteringly; fawningly
Flatueu-x, se, *adj.* (*med.*) flatulent, windy
Flatulence, *s.f.* (*med.*) flatulence, flatulency, windiness
Flatulent, e, *adj.* (*med.*) flatulent, windy
Flatuosité, *s.f.* (*med.*) flatulence, flatulency,
Flavescent, e, *adj.* flavescent, yellowish [wind
Flavine, *s.f.* (*chem.*) flavine
Fléau, *s.m.* flail; scourge, plague; beam (*of a pair of scales*); bar, lever, fastening; hook; (*of forges*) rock-staff; (*bot.*) *V.* **Fléole**

Flèche, *s.f.* arrow; (*of spears*) head; (*of carriages*) crane, perch; (*of artil. waggons*) pole; (*of ploughs*) beam; (*of masts*) pole, flag-yard; (*of plants*) stem, stalk, cane, trunk; (*of steeples*) spire; (*of bacon*) flitch; (*of backgammon*) point; (*arch.*) rise; (*fort.*) fleche; (*of driving*) tandem; (*tech.*) tree, beam, pole, rod, stick, stake, jib. *Faire — de tout bois,* to use every means, to leave no stone unturned. *Ne savoir plus de quel bois faire —,* not to know which way to turn, to be put to o.'s last shift, to be at o.'s wits' end

Flécher, *v.n.* (*of sugar-canes*) to shoot, to grow; — *v.a.* (*of rams*) to tup, to cover

Flécnier, *s.m.* arrow-maker

Fléchière, *s.f.* (*bot.*) arrow-head

Fléchir, *v.a.n.* to bend; to bow; to subdue; to move; to soften; to make (...) yield, to induce to yield, to make (...) relent; to prevail on; to appease; to give way; to submit, to yield; to relent; to waver; (*com.*) to decline

Fléchissable, *adj.* flexible; pliant; to be moved *or* softened *or* prevailed upon

Fléchissement, *s.m.* bending; giving way

Fléchisseur, *adj.m., s.m.* (*anat.*) flexor

Fléchissure, *s.f.* flexure, flexion

Flegmagogue, *s.m.* (*med.*) phlegmagogue; — *adj.* phlegmagogic

Flegmasie, *s.f.* (*med.*) phlegmasia, phlegmasy

Flegmatique, *adj.* phlegmatic

Flegmatiquement, *adv.* phlegmatically

Flegme, *s.m.* phlegm; — *adj.* phlegmatic

Flegmon, *s.m.* (*med.*) phlegmon

Flegmoneu-x, se, *adj.* (*med.*) phlegmonous

Flême, *s.f.* (*pop.*) weariness; idleness, rest

Fléole, *s.f.* (*bot.*) timothy grass, cat's-tail grass

Flet, *s.m.* (*fish*) fluke (*kind of flounder*)

Flétan, *s.m.* (*fish*) halibut

Flétrir, *v.a.* to cause to fade, to fade; to wither; to dry up; to blight, to blast; to tarnish; to sully; to blemish; to brand; to stigmatize; to stain, to dishonour, to disgrace

Se —, *v r.* to fade; to wither; to tarnish; to be blighted *or* &c.; to dishonour oneself

Flétrissure, *s.f.* fading; withering; blight; blemish; stain, disgrace; brand, stigma

Flette, *s.f.* flat-bottomed boat, flat

Fleur, *s.f.* flower; blossom; bloom; choice, best; prime; flourish; first use, first, handsel; **—s,** *pl.* flowers, &c.; (*med.*) monthly courses, courses, terms. *—s blanches,* (*med.*) whites, fluor albus, leucorrhœa. *— de farine,* best flour, flour, first, whites. *— de lis,* lily flower; (*her.*) fleur-de-lis, flower-de-luce. *— des pois,* pink of fashion; pink. *Fine —,* finest *or* choicest flower, very flower, pink, best. *A —s,* with flowers, flowery, flowered. *A — de,* on a level with, level with, even with, close to. *A — d'eau,* level with the surface of the water, on the surface of the water, between wind and water. *Yeux à — de tête,* goggle-eyes. *Entrer en —,* to flower, to blossom, to bloom, to blow

Fleurage, *s.m.* pollard (*flour and bran*)

Fleuraison, *s.f.* flowering, blossoming, blooming, efflorescence; flowering-season

Fleurdeliser, *v.a.* to brand *or* mark *or* adorn with fleur-de-lis *or* flower-de-luce

Fleuré, e, *adj.* (*her.*, &c.) ornamented with flowers, flowery, flowered, fleury, flory; ornamented, adorned; — *s.f.* (*in dyeing*) floree

Fleurer, *v.n.* (*obsolete*) to smell; to smell of; — *v.a.n. old and pop. for* **Flairer**

Fleuret, *s.m.* floss-silk; silk-ferret; (*of cotton, wool, or thread*) best quality, best, choice; (*fenc.*) foil; (*mining*) punch

Fleureté, e, *adj. V.* **Fleuré**

Fleuretis, *s.m.* (*mus.*) grace, grace-note

Fleurette, *s.f.* little flower, floweret; (*bot.*) floret; (*fam.*) soft nonsense; compliment. *Conter —,* to talk soft nonsense, to make love

Fleureu-r, se, *s.m.f.* (*old and pop.*) *V.* **Flaireur**

Fleuri, e, *adj.* flowering, flowery, blooming, bloomy, blossoming, in flower, in bloom, in blossom; flowered; florid; gaudy; richly adorned

Fleurir, *v.n.* to flower, to blossom, to bloom, to blow; to become florid; (*old, more correctly* **Florir**) to flourish, &c., *V.* **Florir**; — *v.a.* to flower, to adorn *or* ornament *or* embellish *or* deck with flowers; to render florid. *Faire —,* (*fig.*) *V.* **Florir** [florist; — *adj.* flower

Fleuriste, *s.m.f.* florist; flower-maker, artificial

Fleuron, *s.m.* flower-work, flower, gem, jewel, ornament; floroon; (*bot.*) floret (of the disc); (*arch.*) flower, finial; (*print.*) tail-piece [lous

Fleuronné, e, *adj. V.* **Fleuré**; (*bot.*) floscu-

Fleuronner, *v.a.* to ornament with flower-work *or* &c. (*V.* **Fleuron**)

Fleurtis, *s.m. V.* **Fleuretis** [god

Fleuve, *s.m.* (*great*) river; stream; (*myth.*) river-

Flexibilité, *s.f.* flexibility, flexibleness, suppleness, pliableness, pliability, pliantness, pliancy

Flexible, *adj.* flexible, supple, pliable, pliant

Flexion, *s.f.* flexion; flexure; bending; inflection; deflection

Flexueu-x, se, *adj.* flexuous, flexuose

Flexuosité, *s.f.* flexuousness, flexuosity

Flibot, *s.m.* fly-boat

Flibuste, *s.f.* corsair; filibustering

Flibuster, *v.n.* to filibuster; — *v.a.* (*fam.*) to rob, to steal, to swindle, to cheat, to chisel

Flibusterie, *s.f.* filibustering, filibusterism; (*fam.*) swindling, swindle, cheating, cheat

Flibustier, *s.m.* filibuster, freebooter, buccaneer; robber; (*fam.*) swindler, cheat

Flic-flac, *int. s.m.* flick-flack, thwick-thwack

Flin, *s.m.* (*min.*) marcasite

Flint-glass, *s.m.* flint-glass

Flion, *s.m.* (*local*) *V.* **Donace**

Floc, *s.m.* flock; tuft; tassel

Floche, *s.f.* rag; flock; tuft; tassel; — *adj.* shaggy. *Soie —,* floss-silk

Flocon, *s.m.* flake; (*of wool,* &c.) flock, lock; tuft; **—s,** *pl.* (*med.*) "muscæ volitantes" [tufts

Floconner, *v.n.,* **Se —,** *v.r.* to form flakes *or*

Floconneu-x, se, *adj.* flaky; tufty

Flonflon, *s.m. int.* tol-de-rol-lol

Floraison, *s.f. V.* **Fleuraison**

Floral, e, *adj.* floral

Florales, *s.f.pl.* (*in antiquity*) floral games

Flore, *s.f.* (*bot.*) flora; anthology; (*myth., astr.*) Flora; — *s.m.* (*nav.*) *V.* **Courai.** *Les dons* or *les présents de —,* (*poet.*) flowers

Floréal, *s.m.* Floreal (*eighth month of the calendar of the first French Republic, from April* 20

Florence, *s.m.* sarcenet [*to May* 20)

Florencé, e, *adj. V.* **Fleuré**

Florentin, e, *adj. s.m.f.* Florentine; — *s.f.* florentine (*figured satin*)

Florer, *v.a.n.* (*nav.*) *V.* **Courayer**

Florès. *Faire —,* to flourish, to thrive, to be flourishing *or* thriving, to be highly successful, to be in vogue; to make a figure, to cut a dash

Floricole, *adj.* floricultural

Floriculteur, *s.m.* floriculturist

Floricultural, e, *adj.* floricultural

Floriculture, *s.f.* floriculture

Florifère, *adj.* (*bot.*) floriferous; flower

Floriforme, *adj.* floriform

Florilége, *s.m.* florilege; anthology

Florin, *s.m.* florin; guilder

Floripare, *adj.* (*bot.*) floriparous

Florir, *v.n.* (*frequently corrupted into* **Fleurir**) to flourish, to prosper, to thrive, to be flourishing *or* prosperous *or* thriving, to be in vogue. *Faire —,* to promote, to encourage, to render

Floriste, *s.m.* florist [flourishing

Florule, *s.f.* floweret, floret, floscule

Floscule, *s.f.* (*bot.*) floscule [lar

Flosculeu-x, se, *adj.* (*bot.*) flosculous, floscu-

Floss, *s.m.* (*metal.*) floss

Flot, *s.m.* wave, billow, surge; tide, flood-tide; flood; water; torrent, stream; crowd; waving, undulation; floating wood; tuft. *A —,* afloat;

floating. *A —s*, in torrents, in streams; in crowds; in abundance. *A — perdu*, loose. *Demi- —*, half-tide

Flottabilité, *s.f.* floatability; flotation

Flottable, *adj.* floatable; navigable (for rafts)

Flottage, *s.m.* flotage, floating; rafting; floating wood [line, water-line

Flottaison, *s.f.* flotation; (*nav.*) load water-

Flottant, e, *part. adj.* floating, &c. (*V.* **Flotter**); buoyant; irresolute, uncertain, unsettled; unfunded *or* floating (*debt*); (*her.*) floating, flotant; — *s.m.* (*of hydraulic wheels*) float

Flotte, *s.f.* fleet; navy; shipping; float; cable-buoy; skein (*of silk*); washer (*of a carriage-wheel*); (*pop.*) crowd, swarm, lot; (*slang*) allowance, pension

Flottement, *s.m.* undulation, waving; floating; irresolution, hesitation, wavering

Flotter, *v.n.a.* to float; to swim; to buoy; to waft; to hull; to undulate, to wave, to stream, to flow, to flaunt, to swing, to flutter; to hover; to wander, to ramble, to rove; to flow *or* hang loosely; to fluctuate, to waver, to vacillate, to

Flotteron, *s.m.* (*fish.*) small float [hesitate

Flotteur, *s.m.* raftsman, wood-floater; (*fish.*, &c.) float; (*nav.*) cable-buoy; (*tech.*) floater, float, water-

†**Flottille**, *s.f.* flotilla [gauge; (*pop.*) swimmer

Flou, *s.m.* (*paint.*) softness, delicacy; — *adj.m.* (**—e**, *f.*) light and soft, soft, delicate; — *adv.* lightly, softly

Flouer, *v.a.* to cheat, to diddle, to chisel

Flouerie, *s.f.* cheating, cheat

Flouette, *s.f.* (*nav.*) vane

Floueu-r, se, *s.m.f.* cheat, sharper, thief

Flouflou, *s.m.* rustling, rustle

Flouve, *s.f.* (*bot.*) vernal grass

Fluant, e, *adj.* flowing; liquid; fleeting; unresisting; (*tech.*) unsized, badly sized, blotting

Fluate, *s.m.* (*old chem.*) fluate, fluoride

Fluaté, e, *adj.* (*chem.*) fluoride of ... *Chaux —e*, fluoride of calcium, fluor spar

Fluctuant, e, *adj.* fluctuant, fluctuating

Fluctuation, *s.f.* fluctuation [terous

Fluctueu-x, se, *adj.* fluctuous, agitated, bois-

Flue, *s.f.* kind of fishing-net

Fluence, *s.f.* fluency [fluent

Fluent, e, *adj.* fluent, flowing; — *s.f.* (*old math.*)

Fluer, *v.n.* to flow, to run [delicate

Fluet, te, *adj.* thin, slender, spare, lean, lank,

Flueurs, *s.f.pl.* — *blanches*, (*obsolete for* "fleurs blanches," *med.*) *V.* **Fleur** [*s.m.* fluid

Fluide, *adj.* fluid, flowing, liquid; fluent; —

Fluidification, *s.f.* fluidizing

Fluidifier, *v.a.* to fluidize

Fluidité, *s.f.* fluidity, fluidness

Fluoborate, *s.m.* (*chem.*) fluoborate

Fluoborique, *adj.* (*chem.*) fluoboric

Fluor, *s.m.* (*chem.*) fluorine; (*old min.*) fluor, fluor spar, fluoride of calcium

Fluoré, e, *adj.* (*chem.*) fluorated

Fluorescence, *s.f.* (*opt.*) fluorescence

Fluorescent, e, *adj.* (*opt.*) fluorescent

Fluorhydrate, *s.m.* (*chem.*) hydrofluate

Fluorhydrique, *adj.* (*chem.*) hydrofluoric

Fluorine, *s.f.* (*min.*, *chem.*) *V.* **Fluor**

Fluorique, *adj.* (*chem.*, *obsolete*) fluoric

Fluorure, *s.m.* (*chem.*) fluoride

Fluosilicate, *s.m.* (*chem.*) fluosilicate

Fluosilicique, *adj.* (*chem.*) fluosilicic [sea-weed

Flustre, *s.f.* (*nat. hist.*) flustra, sea-mat, white

Flûte, *s.f.* flute; flutist; pipe; piper; long roll (*of bread*); butter-prover; (*nav.*) store-ship; (*fish*) sea-eel, murry; (*fam.*, *jest.*) thin shank; clyster-pipe, syringe, squirt, enema; (*pop.*) bottle of wine; (*obsolete*) long drinking-glass. — *à l'ognon*, reed-pipe. — *de Pan*, Pan's-pipes, Pandean pipes, mouth-organ. *Ce qui vient de la — s'en retourne au tambour*, lightly come lightly go [— *part. V.* **Flûter**

Flûté, e, *adj.* fluted, fluty, soft, sweet; piping;

Flûteau, *s.m.* child's whistle-pipe; (*bot.*) water-plantain

Flûter, *v.n.* (*jest.*) to flute, to pipe; (*pop.*) to talk to the wind; — *v.n.a.* (*fam.*) to quaff; to

Flûtet, *s.m. V.* **Galoubet** [tipple

Flûteu-r, se, *s.m.f.* (*jest.*) flute-player, fluter, piper; (*fam.*) tippler, toper

Flûtiste, *s.m.* flutist, flute-player

Fluvial, e, *adj.* fluvial, fluviatic, river

Fluviatile, *adj.* fluviatile, fluviatic, river

Fluvio-marin, e, *adj.* (*geol.*) fluvio-marine

Fluviomètre, *s.m.* fluviometer

Fluviométr-ie, -ique. *V.* page 3, § 1

Flux, *s.m.* flux; flow; stream; flood; tide; rising; (*med.*) flux, profluvium, flow, running, discharge, evacuation; diarrhœa; dysentery; (*chem.*) flux; (*at cards*) flush. — *de bouche*, — *labial*, flow of saliva, salivation; (*fig.*) flow of words, talkativeness, loquacity, garrulity, palaver, twaddle, gabble, talk. — *de sang*, dysentery, bloody flux. — *de ventre*, diarrhœa

Fluxion, *s.f.* inflammation; swelling in the face, swollen face, swelling, cold; (*old math.*) fluxion [inflammatory

Fluxionnaire, *adj.* liable to inflammation;

Foc, *s.m.* (*nav.*) jib, stay-sail. *Grand —*, standing jib. *Petit —*, fore stay-sail. *Bâton de —*,

Focal, e, *adj.* focal [jib-boom

Focimètre, *s.m.* focimeter

Foène, *s.f.* fish-gig, gig

Foéner, *v.a.n.* (*fish.*) to gig

Fœtal, e, *adj.* fœtal

Fœticide, *s.m.* fœticide

Fœtus, *s.m.* fœtus

Foi, *s.f.* faith; belief; fidelity; honour; conscience; word; parole; trust; confidence; reliance; credit; proof, testimony, evidence. *Bonne —*, good faith, sincerity, honesty, uprightness, fairness, plain dealing, fair play. *Mauvaise —*, bad faith, insincerity, dishonesty, unfairness, foul *or* false play. *Profession de —*, profession of faith; creed, belief; address (*to electors*). — *du charbonnier*, implicit *or* blind faith, strong belief. *De bonne —*, sincere, trustworthy, candid, honest, fair, in earnest; sincerely, candidly, honestly, fairly, with good faith, "bonâ fide." *De mauvaise —*, false, dishonest, insincere, not candid, unfair; falsely, dishonestly, insincerely, unfairly, with bad faith. *En bonne —*, indeed, in truth, really, candidly. *En — de quoi*, in witness *or* in testimony whereof. *Ma — !* upon my word! indeed! in truth! really! I declare! to be sure! I am sure! sure! faith! forsooth! *Ajouter — à*, to give credit *or* credence to, to credit, to trust, to believe. *Faire —*, to be a proof, to be evidence, to testify, to prove. *N'avoir ni — ni loi*, to regard neither law nor gospel

Foible, *adj. s.* (*obsolete spelling*) *V.* **Faible**

Foie, *s.m.* liver. *Pâté de — gras*, goose-liver pie

Foin, *s.m.* hay; herd's-grass, grass; (*of artichokes*) choke; — *int.* (*obsolete*) hang it! — *de !* hang! a fig for! a plague on! out upon! away with! *Asthme* or *maladie de —*, hay-asthma, hay-fever. *Avoir du — dans ses bottes*, to be well off, to be rich *or* warm. *Faire les —s*, to make hay. *Mettre du — dans ses bottes*, to feather o.'s nest

Foire, *s.f.* fair; fairing; (*fam.*) diarrhœa, back-door trot; funk. — *de respect*, (*com.*) facility, accommodation, easy terms. *S'entendre comme larrons en —*, to be hand and glove together

Foirer, *v.n.* (*fam.*) to be relaxed in the bowels, to have a back-door trot, to scour; to make a mess; to show the white feather; to funk, to be in a funk, to be funky; (*nav.*) to become slack, to slip

Foireu-x, se, *adj. s.* (*fam.*) relaxed, having the diarrhœa; pale; funky; cowardly; coward

Fois, *s.f.* time. *Une —*, once; once upon a time; when once; for once. *Deux —*, twice. *Trois —*, three times, thrice. *Une bonne —*, *une — pour toutes*, once for all; seriously, in *Une — que*, one time that; when once; if once; as soon as. *A la —, tout à la —*, at a time; at the same time; at once; all at once; alike; together; both. *De — à autre, par —*, from time to time, now and then. *Pour cette —*, for this *or* that time; for the nonce; for once. *N'en pas faire à deux —, N'en faire ni une ni deux*, V. **Un**

Foïsme, *s.m.* foism (*worship of Fo, in China*)

Foison, *s.f.* plenty, abundance. *A —*, plentifully, abundantly, in plenty, in abundance, in crowds

Foisonnement, *s.m.* increase; heaping up

Foisonner, *v.n.* to abound; to be plentiful; to increase; to multiply; to swell; to plump up; to yield; to produce plenty

Fol, le, *adj.* V. **Fou**

Folâtre, *adj.* playful, sportive, frolicsome, wanton

Folâtrement, *adv.* playfully, sportively, frolicsomely, wantonly

Folâtrer, *v.n.* to play, to sport, to frolic, to romp, to gambol, to wanton

Folâtrerie, *s.f.* frolic, frolics, prank, pranks, gambols, game, playful thing, playful trick, play, sport

Folette, *s.f.* tilted boat

Foliacé, e, *adj.* foliaceous

Foliaire, *adj.* (*bot.*) foliar

Foliation, *s.f.* (*bot., arch.,* &c.) foliation

Folichon, ne, *adj. s.* (*fam.*) V. **Folâtre**; (*pop.*) fresh (*tipsy*)

Folichonner, *v.n.* (*fam.*) V. **Folâtrer**

Folichonnerie, *s.f.* (*fam.*) V. **Folâtrerie**

Folie, *s.f.* madness, insanity; folly; distraction; extravagance; excess; foolishness; foolish thing; foolery; nonsense; mania; hobby, passion; frolic, prank; country-seat, seat, villa, cottage

Folié, e, *adj.* leafy; foliated

Foliette, *s.f.* small bottle

Foliifère, *adj.* (*bot.*) foliferous; leaf

Foliiforme, *adj.* (*bot.*) foliform, leaf-like

Foliipare, *adj.* (*bot.*) foliparous

Folio, *s.m.* folio

Foliolaire, *adj.* (*bot.*) foliolar

Foliole, *s.f.* (*bot.*) foliole, leaflet

Foliolé, e, *adj.* (*bot.*) foliolate

Foliotage, *s.m.* folioing

Folioter, *v.a.* to folio

Folle, *adj.f., s.f.* (*fem. of* **Fou,** *which see*); — *s.f.* flat-fish net; turtle-net

Follement, *adv.* madly; foolishly; dotingly; extravagantly; rashly

Follet, te, *adj.* playful, wanton, frolicsome, waggish; downy; — *s.m.* sprite, goblin, elf; — *s.f.* playful *or* &c. creature; (*bot.*) orach, French spinach; (*obsolete*) neckerchief. *Esprit —*, sprite, goblin, hobgoblin, elf, ghost, spectre. *Feu —*, ignis fatuus, Jack o' lantern, will o' the wisp, night-fire; flash. *Poil —*, down, downy *or* soft hair, downy beard

Folliculaire, *s.m.* newspaper scribbler, pamphleteer; — *adj.* journalistic; (*anat., bot.*) follicular

Follicule, *s.m.* (*anat., bot.*) follicle; (*pharm.*) pod

Folliculeu-x, se, *adj.* folliculous

Fomenta-teur, trice, *s.m.f.* fomenter

Fomentation, *s.f.* fomentation

Fomenter, *v.a.* to foment; to feed

Fonçage, *s.m.* bottoming; sinking; driving

†**Fonçailles,** *s.f.pl.* (*of beds*) boarding, bottom; (*of casks*) bottom-pieces, head-pieces, bottom, head

Fonce, *s.m.* V. **Foncet**

Foncé, e, *adj.* dark, deep; substantial; rich, wealthy, moneyed; skilled, skilful, clever, expert, versed, proficient; — *part.* V. **Foncer**

Foncement, *s.m.* sinking

Foncer, *v.a.* to bottom, to put a bottom to; to sink (*wells*); to deepen (*colours*); — *v.n.* to pitch, to dash, to dart, to rush, to run, to fall; to furnish funds

Se —, *v.r.* to deepen, to get deep; (*pop.*) to be getting tipsy

Foncet, *s.m.* barge, boat

Fonceur, *s.m.* sinker (*of wells*)

Fonci-er, ère, *adj.* landed; of *or* on land; land; of *or* on landed property; of *or* on real estate; ground; (*obsolete*) deep-seated, thorough

Foncièrement, *adv.* thoroughly; at the bottom; fully

Fonction, *s.f.* function; functions; office; duty, duties; work, working, action. *En —s*, upon *or* on o.'s duties; in *or* into office: acting; in action; at work

Fonctionnaire, *s.m.f.* functionary, officer

Fonctionnel, le, *adj.* functional

Fonctionnellement, *adv.* functionally

Fonctionnement, *s.m.* working; action; operation

Fonctionner, *v.n.* to perform its functions; to work; to act; to operate

Fond, *s.m.* bottom; depth; ground, foundation; basis, base; groundwork; bottom *or* head (*of a cask*); further end; farthest end *or* part; lower end; end; backpart, back; seat; top *or* crown (*of a man's cap*); caul (*of a woman's cap*); recess; middle, centre, heart, core; ground, background; backscene; inner margin; substance; matter; amount; stock; chief quality; staple; main *or* essential part; essence; gist; inward *or* solid qualities; solidity; strength, power, stamina; stability; stuff; sound judgment, real knowledge. *Fin —*, lowest depth; very bottom; inmost recesses; farthest end *or* extremity, furthest borders; (*nav.*) sharp bottom. *A —*, thoroughly; thorough; to the bottom. *Au —, dans le —*, at *or* to the bottom, &c.; at bottom; in the main, on the whole; in o.'s heart; after all; in reality, in fact. *De — en comble*, from top to bottom; to the ground; entirely; completely; utterly. *Sans —*, without bottom *or* ground *or* &c., bottomless, groundless, &c. *La forme et le —*, the manner and the matter, the form and the substance, the letter and the spirit. *Donner —*, (*nav.*) to cast anchor. *Faire — sur*, to rely *or* depend on. *Perdre —*, to get out of o.'s depth. *Prendre —*, to go in o.'s depth; to cast anchor

Fondage, *s.m.* melting; casting; smelting

Fondamental, e, *adj.* fundamental; foundation, of the foundation; essential; radical

Fondamentalement, *adv.* fundamentally; essentially; radically

Fondant, e, *adj.* melting; dissolvent; discutient; — *s.m.* melting sweetmeat, melting sweet; (*old med.*) dissolvent, discutient; (*chem., tech.*) flux; — *s.f.* fondante (*melting pear*)

Fonda-teur, trice, *s.m.f.* founder; foundress; — *adj.* founding

Fondation, *s.f.* foundation; founding; groundwork; basis; bed; endowment, establishment

Fondé, e, *part. adj. s.* founded, &c. (*V.* **Fonder**); resting; well-founded, authentic; strong; proxy, attorney, agent. *— de pouvoir* or *de pouvoirs, — de procuration*, proxy, attorney, agent. *Être — à*, to have authority to; to be justified in *or* to; to have a right to. *Être — de pouvoir* (or *de pouvoirs*), to have power of attorney, to be (...'s) agent. *Être — en droit*, to have a just cause

Fondement, *s.m.* foundation; groundwork; basis; ground, cause; reliance, trust; (*anat.*) fundament, seat, anus. *Sans —, dénué de —*, without foundation, groundless

Fonder, *v.a.* to lay the foundation of; to found; to establish; to institute; to create; to build; to erect; to raise; to ground; to base; to rest; to endow; to justify; to authorize; to fund. *— de pouvoir* or *de procuration*, to give power of attorney

Se —, *v.r.* to be grounded *or* founded *or* &c.; to rest; to rely, to build, to go

Fonderie, *s.f.* founding; foundry; melting-house; smelting-house, smeltery; type-founding; type-foundry. *— de caractères*, type-founding; type-foundry

Fondeur, *s.m.* founder; caster; melter; smelter. *— en caractères*, type-founder

Fondis, *s.m.* giving way, sinking, settling

Fondoir, *s.m.* melting-house

Fondre, *v.a.* to melt; to melt down *or* away; to cast, to found; to dissolve; to smelt; to blend; to soften; to merge; to fuse; to waste, to squander; to convert; to sell out; — *v.n.* to melt; to dissolve; to sink; to fall away; to wither, to die; to disappear suddenly, to vanish; to fall, to rush, to pounce; to burst

Se —, *v.r.* to melt, to melt down *or* away; to be cast *or* founded; to dissolve; to be blended *or* merged *or* fused, to blend, to merge, to fuse; to coalesce; to diminish; to dwindle away; to come to nothing; to become *or* be extinct; to disappear suddenly, to vanish

Fondrier, *adj.m., s.m. Bois* —, sinking wood

Fondrière, *s.f.* quagmire, bog, slough; pit, gully

†**Fondrilles,** *s.f.pl. V.* **Effondrilles**

Fonds, *s.m.* ground, soil; land; landed property, property, estate; fund; funds; cash; money; capital, principal; outlay, expenses; stock; stock-in-trade; business; mine; subject; matter; solidity, &c. (*V.* **Fond**). — *secrets,* (*pl.*) Secret Service Fund *or* money. — *de boutique,* — *de commerce,* business; stock-in-trade. *Bien* —, *V. Letter* **B.** *Être en* —, to be in cash, to have some cash, to be flush of cash *or* of money; (*fig.*) to be in a position (to). *Faire* — *sur, V.* **Fond.** *Placer* or *prêter à* — *perdu,* to sink (*money*) in an annuity, to sink (*money, a capital*). *Placement à* — *perdu,* sinking ditto

Fondue, *s.f.* (*cook.*) fondue (*cheese and beaten eggs*)

Fongate, *s.m.* (*chem.*) fungate

Fonger, *v.n.* (*of paper*) to blot

Fongible, *adj.* (*law*) fungible

Fongiforme, *adj.* fungiform

Fongine, *s.f.* (*chem.*) fungine

Fongique, *adj.* (*chem.*) fungic

Fongite, *s.f.* (*fossil, min.*) fungite

Fongivore, *adj.* (*zool.*) fungivorous

Fongoïde, *adj.* fungoid

Fongosité, *s.f.* fungosity

Fongueu-x, se, *adj.* fungous

Fongus, *s.m.* (*med., bot.*) fungus

Fontaine, *s.f.* fountain; spring; cistern; cock, tap; plug; (*for tea,* &c.) urn; (*anat.*) fontanel; (*obsolete*) issue. — *-crapaudine,* water-plug

Fontainebleau, *s.m.* Fontainebleau grape

Fontainier, *s.m.* fountain-maker; cistern-maker; turncock

Fontanelle, *s.f.* (*anat., med.*) fontanel

Fontange, *s.f.* (*obsolete*) fontange (*top-knot*)

Fonte, *s.f.* melting; casting; cast; cast iron; pig-iron; gun-metal, brass; smelting; fount *or* font (*of type*); holster. — *de fer, fer de* —, cast iron. *Métal de* —, gun-metal, brass

Fontenier, *s.m.* (*bad spelling*) *V.* **Fontainier**

Fonticule, *s.m.* (*surg., obsolete*) issue

Fontinal, e, *adj.* fountain; spring; — *s.f.* (*bot.*) water-moss

Fontis, *s.m. V.* **Fondis**

Fonts, *s.m.pl.* font. *Tenir sur les* —, to stand godfather *or* godmother to

For, *s.m.* (*obsolete*) tribunal. — *intérieur,* conscience

Forage, *s.m.* boring; drilling; (*feud.*) wine-duty

Forain, e, *adj.* foreign; strange; non-resident; travelling, itinerant; fair, market; — *s.m.* hawker, pedlar. *Chemin* —, carriage-way. *Marchand* —, hawker, pedlar. *Rade* —*e,* (*nav.*) open road. *Spectacle* or *théâtre* —, fair-show. *Traite* —*e,* (*old*) customs-duty

Foraminé, e, *adj.* foraminated

Foraminifère, *adj.* foraminated; — *s.m.* (*zool.*) foraminifer

Forant, *s.m.* (*nav.*) upher, balk, yuffer, spar

Forban, *s.m.* pirate, corsair; plunderer

Forçage, *s.m.* (*coin.*) overweight

Forçat, *s.m.* convict; transport; galley-slave

Force, *s.f.* strength; might; power; authority; force; violence; intensity; vigour; energy; emphasis; full sense, full acceptation; fortitude; command; constraint, compulsion; necessity; virtue, efficacy; validity; proficiency, forwardness; skill; cleverness; plenty, abundance; (*adverb.*) much, a great deal of, many, a great many, no end of; (*nav.*) press (*of sails*); —**s,** *pl.* strength; might; power; forces; troops; shears. — *armée,* — *publique,* armed force, military, soldiery, police. — *vive,* living *or* active force, "vis viva," main strength, available strength. — *majeure, maison de* —, &c., *V.* **Majeur, Maison,** &c. *A* —, extremely; hard. *A* — *de,* by strength of; by much, by many, by repeated, by great, by dint of; from continually. *A toute* —, by all means; at all hazards; absolutely; after all; on the whole; strictly speaking. *De* —, a match for each other. *De* —, *de vive* —, *par* —, by force; forcibly. *De* — *à,* strong enough to; equal to. *De toute sa* —, *de toutes ses* —*s,* with all o.'s might, as hard *or* as fast *or* as loud *or* &c. as one can *or* could. *Être de première* —, to be very proficient *or* skilful. *Faire* — *de,* to use all o.'s ..., to bring all o.'s ... to bear; to ply (*the oars*); to crowd (*sail*). *N'être pas de* —, to be no match. — *m'est,* I am obliged *or* compelled

Forcé, e, *part. adj.* forced, &c. (*V.* **Forcer**); compulsory; involuntary; unnatural; affected; far-fetched; necessary; unavoidable, inevitable; (*of wind, nav.*) violent, boisterous

Forcement, *s.m.* forcing; compulsion; rape

Forcément, *adv.* forcibly; by force; compulsorily; necessarily; unavoidably, inevitably

Forcené, e, *adj. s.* mad, furious, enraged; frantic; passionate; madman, mad woman

Forceps, *s.m.* (*surg.*) forceps

Forcer, *v.a.* to force; to compel, to oblige, to make; to constrain; to do violence to; to extort; to storm; to impel, to drive, to draw; to carry away; to carry; to sway; to subdue; to force open; to break open *or* through; to break; to stretch; to strain; to twist; to bend; to wrench; to wring; to wrest; to swell; to hunt *or* run down; to overwork; (*v.n.*) to blow hard; to crowd (*sail*); to ply (*the oars*). — *le pas,* to hurry o.'s pace

Forcerie, *s.f.* forcing-house, orchard-house

Forcet, *s.m.* whip-cord

Forcettes, *s.f.pl.* small shears

Forceur, *s.m.* forcer

Forcière, *s.f.* small fish-pond, nurse-pond

Forcir, *v.n. V.* **Enforcir**

Forclore, *v.a.* (*law*) to foreclose, to estop, to debar, to preclude, to exclude

Forclusion, *s.f.* (*law*) foreclosure, estoppel, debarring, exclusion

Forer, *v.a.* to perforate; to bore; to drill; to pierce. *Clé* or *clef forée,* piped key

Forerie, *s.f.* boring-house *or* shop; boring

Foresti-er, ère, *adj.* forest, of a forest, of forests. *Garde* —, forester, forest-ranger

Forestier, *s.m.* forester, ranger

Forêt, *s.f.* forest; wood; woodland; roof-timbers; den of thieves, haunt of robbers. *La* — *de Bondy,* (*fig.*) a den of thieves, a haunt of robbers, Hounslow Heath

Foret, *s.m.* (*tool*) drill, borer, fret

Foreur, *s.m.* borer

Forfaire, *v.n.a.def.* to forfeit; to prevaricate; to fail

Forfait, *s.m.* forfeit; crime; contract; job. *A* —, by contract; by the job; by the lump; on speculation

Forfaiture, *s.f.* forfeiture; prevarication

Forfanterie, *s.f.* boasting, bragging; boast, brag

Forficule, *s.f.* (*zool.*) forficula, earwig

Forge, *s.f.* forge; iron-works; smithery, smithy, blacksmith's shop; farrier's shop. *Maître de* —*s, V.* **Maître**

Forgeable, *adj.* forgeable

Forgeage, Forgement, *s.m.* forging; hammering; fabrication; coining (*of words*)

Forger, *v.a.* to forge; to hammer; to fabricate; to make; to invent; to imagine; to coin (*words*); — *v.n.* (*of horses*) to overreach. *Fer forgé,* wrought iron

Se —, *v.r.* to be forged *or* &c.; to frame to oneself, to portray *or* picture to oneself, to make, to create, to imagine, to fancy

Forgerie, *s.f.* forges, iron-works
Forgeron, *s.m.* smith, blacksmith (*V.* **Zée**). *En forgeant on devient* —, practice makes perfect
Forgeur, *s.m.* forger; forgeman; hammerman, hammerer; smith; coiner (*of words*); — *adj.m.* [forging
Forhu, *s.m.* (*hunt.*) recheat
Forhuer, Forhuir, *v.n.* to blow, to wind (*the horn*), to blow the horn, to recall the hounds, to recheat
Forjet, *s.m.* (*arch.*) jutting, projection
Forjeter, *v.n.a.*, **Se** —, *v.r.* to jut out, to project
Forjeture, *s.f.* *V.* **Forjet** [unharbour
Forlancer, *v.a.* (*hunt.*) to start, to dislodge, to
†**Forligner,** *v.n.* (*old*) to degenerate, to derogate, to commit *or* degrade *or* debase *or* disgrace oneself [length, to get ahead
Forlonger, *v.n.*, **Se** —, *v.r.* (*hunt.*) to run a
Formaliser, *v.a.* to offend, to shock
Se —, *v.r.* to take offence, to be offended *or* shocked, to take exception
Formalisme, *s.m.* formalism [— *s.m.f.* formalist
Formaliste, *adj.* formal, precise, ceremonious;
Formalité, *s.f.* formality, form, ceremony
Format, *s.m.* (*of books*, &c.) size, form, shape
Forma-teur, trice, *adj.* forming, formative, creative; — *s.m.f.* former, maker, author, creator
Formati-f, ve, *adj.*, **Formative,** *s.f.* forma-
Formation, *s.f.* formation [tive
Forme, *s.f.* form; shape; figure; make; mould; frame; (*boot-maker's*) last; (*hatter's*) block; (*part of a hat*) crown; (*of a bonnet*) crown; shape; (*of a stocking*) leg; (*of a choir*) stall; (*tech.*) seat *or* bench (*stuffed*); (*with paviers*) bed; (*for cheese*) drainer; (*of a hare*) form; (*vet.*) ring-bone; (*print.*) form, forme; (*nav.*) dock; (*fig.*) form; formality; established rule; manner; way; method; practice; custom; ceremony; civil way, civility. — *brisée*, stretchers. *Dans les* —*s*, *en* —, *en bonne* —, in due form, regularly, regular, in order, all right; formally, formal. *Pour la* —, for form's sake
Formé, e, *part. adj.* formed, &c. (*V.* **Former**); full-grown; mature, matured, ripe; (*of fruit*) set
Formel, le, *adj.* formal; express; explicit; plain; precise; distinct; absolute; positive; strict
Formellement, *adv.* formally; expressly; explicitly; plainly; precisely; distinctly; absolutely; positively; strictly
Former, *v.a.* to form; to shape; to fashion; to frame; to mould; to make; to make up; to compose; to constitute; to establish; to plan, to contrive; to collect; to train, to bring up; to polish; to improve; to raise; to utter; to prefer, to lodge (*a charge, a complaint*)
Se —, *v.r.* to be formed *or* &c.; to take *or* assume a form; to form; to appear; to improve; to grow; to ripen; to set; to be bred; to resolve itself (into)
Formiate, *s.m.* (*chem.*) formiate
Formica-leo, *s.m.* *V.* **Fourmi-lion**
Formicant, e, *adj.* (*med., of the pulse*) formicant
Formication, *s.f.* (*med.*) formication
Formicivore, *adj.* (*zool.*) formicivorous
Formidable, *adj.* formidable, terrible, tremendous, fearful, dreadful
Formidablement, *adv.* formidably, terribly, tremendously, fearfully, dreadfully
Formier, *s.m.* last-maker
Formique, *adj.* (*chem.*) formic
Formulaire, *s.m.* formulary
Formulation, *s.f.* expression, statement
Formule, *s.f.* formula; form; prescription
Formuler, *v.a.* to formulate; to draw up; to express, to state; (*math.*) to reduce to a formula
Se —, *v.r.* to be drawn up *or* &c.
Formyle, *s.m.* (*chem.*) formyle
Fornica-teur, trice, *s.m.f.* fornicator, forni-
Fornication, *s.f.* fornication [catress
Forniquer, *v.n.* to fornicate
Forpaiser, Forpaître, *v.n.* (*hunt.*) to feed far away from the covert
Forquine, *s.f.* (*of arquebuses and old muskets*) rest

Fors, *prep.* (*old*) save, except, but
Forsenant, e, *adj.* (*hunt.*) eager after the game
Fort, e, *adj.* strong; vigorous; firm; stout; lusty; large; copious, plentiful; full; great; violent; intense; deep; severe; bad; stiff; exorbitant; strange; powerful; of great powers; able; skilful; skilled; clever; forward; proficient; well up (in); good (at); ready (to); fond (of); thick; hot; hard; difficult; laborious; heavy; high; loud; emphatic; impressive; cogent; forcible; fortified. *V.* **Eau.** *Au plus* —, at *or* to *or* &c. the strongest *or* &c.; at *or* in the height; in *or* into the midst *or* depth; in the thick; at the worst; at *or* to the hardest part. *Se faire* — (*de*), to undertake; to pledge oneself; to boast; to rely. *Se porter* — *pour*, to answer for. *C'est* —, *voila qui est* —, that is strange, that is hard to swallow. *C'est plus* — *que moi*, I cannot help it. *C'est trop* —, *c'est par trop* —, that (*or* it) is too bad, I cannot stand it. *Cela n'est pas* —, there is not much in that, that is very tame; that is not very nice
Fort, *s.m.* strong man, strong person, strong; market-porter; clever man *or* boy; strong *or* strongest part (*or* side); main point; gist; centre; middle; midst; height; heart; depth; thick *or* thickest part, thick; heat; best part, best; worst part, worst; strength, skill, forte; lair, covert; stronghold, hold; fort, fortress. *Le* — *portant le faible, du* — *au faible*, one thing with another, one with another, on an average. *Connaître* or *savoir le* — *et le faible* (or *le* — *et le fin*) *de*, to be well acquainted with, to know the ins and outs of
Fort, *adv.* very, very much, much, a great deal; extremely, exceedingly; highly; vastly; greatly; strongly; resolutely; vigorously; forcibly; deeply; hard; fast; tightly, tight; loud; earnestly; particularly; widely. *Bien* —, very much, very strongly *or* hard or loud. — *bien*, very well, very good, very properly, &c. (*V.* **Bien,** *adv.*). — *et ferme*, strongly, stoutly, resolutely, strenuously, right well; closely
Forte, *s.f.* strong woman; strange thing, thing hard to believe *or* to swallow, bounce, bouncer, whapper; bad *or* dangerous trick
Forté, *adv. s.m.* (*mus.*) forte. — **-piano,** *s.m.* (*obsolete*) *V.* **Piano**
Fortement, *adv.* strongly; forcibly; stoutly; vigorously; firmly; deeply; hard; fast; tight; very much; much; very; extremely
Forteresse, *s.f.* fortress, stronghold
Fortifiable, *adj.* fortifiable
Fortifiant, e, *adj.* strengthening, invigorating, bracing, fortifying, corroborant; — *s.m.* (*med.*)
Fortificateur, *s.m.* fortifier [corroborant
Fortification, *s.f.* fortification; redoubt, redout
Fortifier, *v.a.* to strengthen; to invigorate; to brace; to corroborate; to confirm; to fortify; — *v.n.* to be strengthening *or* &c.
Se —, *v.r.* to become *or* grow *or* get strong, to gain strength, to strengthen; to be strengthened *or* &c.; to gain proficiency, to make oneself a proficient; to fortify oneself; to strengthen *or* &c. each other
Fortin, *s.m.* fortlet, little fort
Fortiori (A), *adv.* à fortiori, with stronger *or* greater reason, with so much the more reason much more, still more so
Fortissimo, *adv. s.m.* (*mus.*) fortissimo
Fortitrer, *v.n.* (*hunt.*) to avoid the dogs
Fortitude, *s.f.* (*obsolete*) fortitude [spent
Fortrait, e, *adj.* (*of horses*) overworked, over-
Fortraiture, *s.f.* (*of horses*) overworking, overfatigue [*Cas* —, mere accident, mere chance
Fortuit, e, *adj.* fortuitous, accidental, casual.
Fortuité, *s.f.* fortuitousness, fortuity
Fortuitement, *adv.* fortuitously, casually, accidentally, by accident, by chance
Fortune, *s.f.* fortune; chance; accident: hazard; risk; fate; lot; luck; success; pros-

perity; wealth, property; (*nav.*) accident, misfortune. *La — du pot*, pot-luck. *Bonne —*, good fortune *or* luck, piece of ditto, unexpected luck, good windfall, prosperous adventure; a woman's favours, success with the fair, intrigue. *De —*, enriched, self-made; risen from the ranks; (*nav.*) spare, temporary, &c. (*V.* **Hauban, Mât,** *and* **Voile,** *s.f.*); (*obsolete*) by chance. *Homme à bonnes —s*, lady-killer, man of intrigue. *Faire —*, to make a fortune; (*fig.*) to have great success. *Dîner à la — du pot, courir la — du pot*, to take o.'s chance of a dinner, to take pot-luck

Fortuné, e, *adj.* fortunate, happy, lucky, successful, prosperous; (*pop.*) rich, well-to-do

Forum, *s.m.* (*Rom. hist.*) forum

Forure, *s.f.* hole, bore

Forvêtu, *s.m.* (*obsolete*) vulgar swell

Fossane, *s.f.* (*zool.*) fossane (*kind of genet*)

Fosse, *s.f.* pit; hole; grave; den; trench; cesspool; pipe; (*anat.*) fossa, fosse, pit; (*of the nose*) chamber. — *aux câbles*, cable-stage. — *aux lions*, lions' den; (*nav.*) boatswain's store-room; (*jest., obsolete*) swell's stage-box. — *aux mâts*, mast-pond. — *aux ours*, bear-pit. *Mettre la clé sur la —*, to waive o.'s right of inheritance

Fossé, *s.m.* ditch; trench; drain; moat, fosse. *Sauter le —*, (*fig.*) to pass the Rubicon, to cast the die. *Ce qui tombe dans le — est pour le soldat*, "findings, keepings" [peg

Fosset, *s.m.* (*bad spelling for* "fausset") spigot,

Fossette, *s.f.* dimple; pit; (*game*) chuck-farthing, pitch-farthing, cherry-pit

Fossile, *adj.m.f.*, *s.m.* fossil

Fossilifère, *adj.* fossiliferous

Fossilisation, *s.f.* fossilization, fossilification

Fossiliser, *v.a.*, **Se —,** *v.r.* to fossilize

Fossil-isme, -iste. *V.* page 3, § 1

Fossilité, *s.f.* fossility

Fossoiement, *s.m.* *V.* **Fossoyage**

Fossoir, *s.m.* (*agr.*) hoe

Fossoyage, *s.m.* ditching; grave-digging

Fossoyer, *v.a.* to ditch, to surround with a ditch, to dig

Fossoyeur, *s.m.* ditcher; grave-digger, sexton; (*zool.*) necrophore, sexton-beetle, burying beetle

Fossoyeuse, *s.f.* *La —*, Death, grim Death

Fou, Fol, *m.*, **Folle,** *f.*, *adj.* mad; insane; lunatic; crazy; frantic; infuriated, furious; maddened; distracted; wild; madly fond, exceedingly fond; foolish, senseless, silly; thoughtless; frolicsome, sportive, playful, wanton; wandering; erratic; enormous, immense, prodigious; excessive, exorbitant, extravagant; immoderate; uncontrollable; dreadful; (*tech.*) irregular; defective; light; untwisted. — *à lier*, raving *or* stark mad

Fou, *s.m.*, **Folle,** *s.f.* madman; mad woman *or* girl; lunatic; mad boy; foolish *or* silly *or* thoughtless *or* wild fellow, fool; (*formerly, to kings*, &c.) jester, fool; (*at chess*) bishop; (*bird*) booby, gannet. *Plus on est de —s plus on rit*, the more the merrier

Fouace, *s.f.* hearth-cake, griddle-cake [woman

Fouaci-er, ère, *s.m.f.* hearth-cake man *or*

Fouage, *s.m.* (*feud.*) fuage, fumage, hearth-money, hearth-penny, smoke-farthings

†**Fouaille,** *s.f.* (*hunt.*) quarry

†**Fouailler,** *v.a.* to whip, to flog, to lash; — *v.n.* (*pop.*) to show the white feather, to funk, to shirk, to sculk; (*of things*) to fail, to break, to slip *or* run out, to escape

†**Fouailleur,** *s.m.* (*pop.*) funky fellow; milksop

Fouane, Fouanne, *s.f.* *V.* **Foène**

Fouarre, *s.m.* (*obsolete*) *V.* **Feurre**

Foucade, *s.f.* (*pop.*) whim, freak, fit; tiff, pet

Foucault, *s.m.* *pop. for* **Bécassine**

Foudre, *s.f.* lightning; thunder; thunderbolt, bolt; — *s.m.* (*fig.*) thunderbolt; hero; (*for liquids*) tun [thunder-striking

Foudroiement, *s.m.* stroke of lightning;

Foudroyant, e, *adj.* thundering; fulminating; crushing, withering, dreadful; terrible; tremendous; startling; causing sudden death

Foudroyer, *v.a.n.* to strike with lightning; to thunder-strike; to kill as by lightning; to batter down, to destroy; to crush; to ruin; to confound; to fulminate against; to fulminate; to anathematize; to strike; to shoot

Fouée, *s.f.* bat-fowling; oven-fire; fagot

Fouenne, *s.f.* *V.* **Faîne** *and* **Foène**

Fouet, *s.m.* whip; driving-whip; whisk; whipcord; whipping, flogging; cat o' nine tails, cat; (*nat. hist.*: *of the wing*) tip, (*of the tail*) tuft. — *à blancs d'œufs*, egg-whisk, whisk. *De plein —*, (*artil.*) horizontal; horizontally. *Donner le — à*, to whip, to flog, to give a whipping *or* a flogging. *Faire claquer son —*, to crack o.'s whip; (*fig.*) to boast, to make a great noise, to sound o.'s own trumpet. *Se faire donner le —*, to get a whipping, &c., to get *or* be whipped, &c.

Fouetté, e, *part. adj.* whipped, &c. (*V.* **Fouetter**); streaked

Fouette-merle, *s.m.* (*pop.*) *V.* **Émerillon**

Fouette-queue, *s.m.* (*zool.*) star-lizard

Fouetter, *v.a.n.* to whip; to horsewhip; to flog; to scourge; to lash; to cut; to whisk, to flick; to beat; to drive; to patter; to flap; to sweep; to whip away; to spur on, to stimulate; to quicken, to hasten; to toss off, to quaff. *Avoir bien d'autres chiens* (or *chats*) *à —*, to have other fish to fry. *Il n'y a pas là de quoi — un chat*, it is a mere trifle. *Fouette cocher!* whip away, coachman (*or* driver)! onward! forward! all right! let us go ahead! fire away! off we go! off we went! [whipping, flogging

Fouetteu-r, se, *s.m.f.* whipper, flogger; — *adj.*

Fouetteux, *s.m.* (*pop.*) *V.* **Émerillon**

Fougade, *s.f.* (*pop.*) *V.* **Foucade**

Fougasse, *s.f.* (*mil.*) fougasse; (*cake*) *V.* **Fouace**

Fouger, *v.n.* (*of boars*) to grub, to root

Fougeraie, *s.f.* fern-bed *or* brake *or* plot, fernery

Fougère, *s.f.* fern; brake; (*old, poet.*) glass,

Fougon, *s.m.* (*nav.*) cook-room, cuddy [bottle

Fougue, *s.f.* fury, rage, transport, passion; fire; heat; ardour; impetuosity; spirit; mettle; spiritedness; (*nav.*) mizzen-top

Fougueu-x, se, *adj.* furious, fierce; passionate; fiery; hot; ardent; impetuous; impulsive; spirited; mettlesome [searching, search

†**Fouille,** *s.f.* excavation, digging; trench;

†**Fouillement,** *s.m.* excavating, digging; searching [molly-coddle

†**Fouille-au-pot,** *s.m.* (*fam.*) scullion, cook;

†**Fouille-merde,** *s.m.* (*fam.*) *V.* **Bousier**; (*pop.*) nightman

†**Fouiller,** *v.a.n.* to excavate, to dig; to sink; to work; to labour; to search; to rummage; to ransack; to feel; to fumble

Se —, *v.r.* to search o.'s pockets; to search each other; to be excavated *or* &c.

†**Fouilleu-r, se,** *adj.* excavating, digging; searching; (*agr.*) digging, subsoil; — *s.m.f.* excavator, digger; searcher; (*agr.*) digger, digging-plough, subsoiler, subsoil-plough. *Charrue —euse*, digging-plough, digger, subsoil-plough, subsoiler [ley, jumble, litter, mess

†**Fouillis,** *s.m.* confusion, confused mass, med-

†**Fouillure,** *s.f.* (*of boars*) digging, rooting

Fouine, *s.f.* (*zool.*) common marten, beech-marten, stone-marten, marten; (*agr.*) pitch-fork, fork; (*fish.*) *V.* **Foène**

Fouiner, *v.n.* (*pop.*) to intermeddle; to sneak; to sculk; to sneak *or* slink away *or* off, to steal away *or* off, to bolt

Fouineur, Fouinard, *s.m.* (*pop.*) sneak;

Fouir, *v.a.n.* (*old*) to dig [sculker; funky fellow

Fouissement, *s.m.* (*old*) digging

Fouisseur, *s.m.*, *adj.m.* (*zool.*) fossorial

Foulage, *s.m.* fulling, pressing, milling; (*pop.*) pressure, crowding, hurry-work

Foulant, e, *part. adj.* pressing down, pressing &c. (*V.* **Fouler**); (*of pumps*) forcing, force

Foulard, *s.m.* silk handkerchief, handkerchief

scarf; (*material*) foulard, (*Indian*) bandanna, bandanno, corah

Foule, *s.f.* crowd; throng; multitude; great number; host; quantity; mob; herd, common herd; (*tech.*) fulling, pressing; fullery. *Faire* —, to crowd

Foulée, *s.f.* pile (*of skins*); tread (*of steps*); (*rid.*) appui; —**s**, *pl.* (*hunt.*) track, foiling, foil, fusee, slot [ling; oppression; spraining; fulling

Foulement, *s.m.* pressing; treading; tramp-

Fouler, *v.a.* to crowd; to press; to tread *or* trample on, to tread, to trample; to oppress; to sprain; to strain; to hurt; to mill; to full; to plug; (*hunt.*) to bite; to beat (*a wood*); — *v.n.* (*print.*) to press

Se —, *v.r.* to crowd, to throng, to press; to work hard, to overwork oneself, to strain, to fag, to sweat, to hurry; to sprain *or* strain (o.'s ...); to become *or* be sprained *or* strained; to be pressed *or* &c. *Ne pas se* —, (*fam.*) to take it (*or* things) easy, not to overwork oneself

Foulerie, *s.f.* fullery, fulling-mill

Fouleur, *s.m.* fuller; wine-presser

Fouloir, *s.m.* beater; fulling-stock; fullery; pressing-house *or* room; pressing *or* treading-vat; tobacco-stopper; (*dentist's*) plugger (*for stopping teeth*); (*artil.*) rammer, sponge-rod

Fouloire, *s.f.* fulling-board; fulling-tub

Foulon, *s.m.* fuller. *Chardon à* —, teasel, teazel, teazle, thistle-head. *Moulin à* —, fulling-mill.

Foulonnier, *s.m.* fuller [*Terre à* —, fuller's earth

Foulque, *s.f.* (*bird*) coot

Foulure, *s.f.* sprain; strain; fulling, pressing, milling; (*vet.*) warbles; —**s**, *pl.* (*hunt.*) *V.* **Foulées**

Four, *s.m.* oven; kiln, furnace; scorifier; bake-house, bakery; oven-cake, light cake, cake, biscuit; dark room; (*arch.*) demi-cupola; (*fam.*) failure, bungle, mess, mull. — *d'incubation*, — *à poulets*, incubator. *Faire* —, to make a failure *or* &c., to fail; (*old*) to give back the money

Fourbe, *adj.* cheating, deceitful, crafty, knavish; — *s.m.f.* cheat, impostor, knave; — *s.f.* cheating, cheat, imposition, imposture, fraud, trick, knavery [upon

Fourber, *v.a.* to cheat, to deceive, to impose

Fourberie, *s.f.* cheating, cheat, imposition, imposture, fraud, trick, trickery, knavery

Fourbi, *s.m.* (*pop.*) dodge, trick, snare

Fourbir, *v.a.* to furbish

Se —, *v.r.* to be furbished; to furbish o.'s arms

Fourbissage, *s.m.* furbishing

Fourbisserie, *s.f.* sword-cutlery

Fourbisseur, *s.m.* furbisher; sword-cutler

Fourbissime, *adj.* most knavish

Fourbissure, *s.f.* furbishing [up

Fourbu, e, *adj.* (*vet.*) foundered; (*fig.*) knocked

Fourbure, *s.f.* (*vet.*) foot-founder, founder, [foundering

Fourcat, *s.m.* (*nav.*) crotch

Fourche, *s.f.* fork; pitchfork; branch; rest. — *-fière*, pitchfork. —*s patibulaires*, forked gibbet. *A la* —, (*fig.*) carelessly; coarsely, roughly. *Faire la* —, to fork, to branch off

Fourché, e, *adj.* forked; split; (*of feet*) cloven; (*her.*) fourchee; — *part.* *V.* **Fourcher**

Fourchée, *s.f.* forkful, pitchforkful

Fourcher, *v.n.a.*, **Se** —, *v.r.* to fork; to branch off; to split; (*of the tongue*) to trip, to slip

Fourchet, *s.m.* (*hort.*) forking; (*vet.*) foot-rot

Fourcheté, e, *adj.* forked; (*her.*) fourchee

Fourchetée, *s.f.* *V.* **Fourchettée**

Fourchette, *s.f.* fork; trencherman, eater; (*of a vehicle*) prop; (*mil.*) rest; (*of umbrellas*) stretcher; (*of shirts*) sleeve-bit; (*of gloves*) forgett; (*anat.*) fourchette; (*of birds*) fourchette, wish-bone, merry-thought; (*vet.*) frog, frush; (*surg.*) fourchette; (*soldiers' slang*) bayonet. — *à découper*, *grande* —, carving-fork. — *de l'estomac*, (*pop.*) breast-bone. *La* — *d'Adam*, the fingers. *Déjeuner à la* —, (*s.m.*) meat-breakfast; (substantial) lunch; (*v.n.*) to [take ditto

Fourchettée, *s.f.* forkful

Fourchon, *s.m.* prong, tine; (*of a tree*) fork

Fourchu, e, *adj.* forked; (*of feet*) cloven. *N'avoir pas la langue* —*e*, to be plain-spoken. *V.* **Arbre** [branching, splitting

Fourchure, *s.f.* forking, fork, furcation,

Fourgat, *s.m.* (*slang*) *V.* **Attriqueur**

Fourgon, *s.m.* baggage-cart *or* waggon, store-waggon, cart, waggon, tumbril; van, carriage; fruggin, oven-fork, coal-rake, rake, poker

Fourgonner, *v.a.n.* to poke; to stir; to poke *or* stir the fire; to rummage, to rake, to fumble

Fourguer, *v.a.* (*thieves' slang*) to sell (*stolen goods*) to a fence

Fouriérisme, *s.m.* Fourierism

Fouriériste, *adj. s.m.f.* Fourierist, Fourierite

Fourmi, *s.f.* ant; emmet, pismire; —**s**, *pl.* ants, &c.; (*fig.*) tingling. — **-lion,** *s.m.* (*insect*) ant-lion [bear; (*bird*) ant-catcher, ant-thrush

Fourmilier, *s.m.* (*quadruped*) ant-eater, ant-

Fourmilière, *s.f.* ant-hill, ant-nest, swarm of ants; (*fig.*) swarm, crowd, lot; (*vet.*) pumiced feet

†Fourmillement, *s.m.* swarming, teeming; tingling, pricking, creeping sensation, formication [bound, to be full; to tingle

†Fourmiller, *v.n.* to swarm, to teem, to a-

Fournage, *s.m.* charge for baking, baking

Fournaise, *s.f.* furnace

Fournaliste, *s.m.f.* stove *or* furnace-maker

Fourneau, *s.m.* cooking-stove, stove, fire-range, range, kitchen-range, kitchener; kitchen; furnace; hearth; fire-hole; (*of a tobacco-pipe*) bowl; (*of a mine*) chamber, fourneau. *Haut* —, [*V.* **Haut**

Fournée, *s.f.* baking; batch

Fournerie, *s.f.* bakery, bake-house

Fourni, e, *part.adj.* furnished, &c. (*V.* **Fournir**); thick, close, full

Fourni-er, ère, *s.m.f.* oven-man, oven-woman; baker, public baker; waiter who serves the coffee; — *s.m.* (*zool.*) oven-bird [bed

Fournil, *s.m.* bake-house; wash-house; (*pop.*)

†Fournilles, *s.f.pl.* fagot-wood, chatwood

Fourniment, *s.m.* (*mil.*) equipment, suit; belts, buffs; (*obsolete*) powder-flask, powder-horn

Fournir, *v.a.* to furnish, to supply, to provide; to stock; to store; to afford; to give; to find; to procure; to produce; to make up, to complete; to make; to do; (*com.*) to draw (*bills*); (*fig.*) to go *or* run over (*a course*, &c.); to run (*a race*); — *v.n.* to supply; to pay (for); to contribute; to suffice, to be sufficient; to meet; (*com.*) to value (on)

Se —, *v.r.* to furnish *or* supply *or* &c. oneself; to deal (with); to find (o.'s own ...) [share

Fournissement, *s.m.* share of capital, capital,

Fournisseur, *s.m.* contractor; purveyor, supplier; tradesman; (*theat.*) property-man. — *breveté de* ..., by appointment (...) to ...

Fourniture, *s.f.* furnishing; supplying; provision, supply; equipment; furniture; articles, goods; (*of tailors*, &c.) trimmings; (*of salad*) dressing; (*mil.*) supplies, stores, provisions, bedding. —*s de bureau*, stationers' sundries, stationery

Fourrage, *s.m.* forage, fodder, provender; foraging; foraging-party; (*nav.*) *V.* **Fourrure**

Fourragement, *s.m.* foraging

Fourrager, *v.a.n.* to forage; to plunder; to rummage, to tumble, to fumble

Fourrag-er, ère, *adj.* fit for fodder, fodder; — *s.f.* fodder-plant, forage-plant, fodder-grass; meadow; (*mil.*) cap-line

Fourrageur, *s.m.* forager; rummager, fumbler

Fourrageu-x, se, *adj.* fit *or* used for fodder; abounding in fodder

Fourré, *s.m.* thicket; brake; jungle

Fourré, e, *part. adj.* thrust, &c. (*V.* **Fourrer**); furred; furry; feathered; woody; full of thickets; thick; to be found; (*of peace*) patched up; (*of thrusts, blows*) interchanged; counter: underhand, secret; (*of hay, straw*) mixed; (*obsolete for* "plaqué," *of coins, medals*) plated. *Langue* —*e*, savoury tongue. *Toile* —*e*, diaper

Fourreau, *s.m.* scabbard, sheath; cover; case; holster; (*of harness*) tug-safe; (*bird*) long-tailed titmouse; (*obsolete*) straight dress *or* frock; (*child's*) frock. *Coucher dans son —*, (*jest.*) to sleep in o.'s clothes. *L'épée* or *la lame use le —*, the blade wears out the scabbard, the mind is too active for the body

Fourrelier, *s.m.* (*obsolete*) scabbard-maker

Fourrer, *v.a.* to thrust; to put; to poke; to shove; to run; to introduce; to insert; to foist; to give privately; to stuff, to cram; to force; to beat, to knock (into); to mix up, to mix; to line with fur, to fur; (*nav.*) to serve, to keckle

Se —, *v.r.* to thrust *or* &c. oneself; to get (into *or* &c.); to creep (into *or* &c.); to introduce oneself; to put *or* intrude oneself, to intrude; to meddle; to hide oneself; to wear warm clothing, to dress warm, to put on furs

Fourreur, *s.m.* furrier

Fourrier, *s.m.* (*mil.*) quartermaster; (*nav.*) clerk; (*obsolete*) harbinger. *Faire le bon —*, (*fam.*) to help oneself to the best pieces. *Faire le mauvais —*, (*fam.*) to neglect oneself while helping others (*at table*)

Fourrière, *s.f.* pound, greenyard; (*obsolete*) wood-house, coal-hole. *Mettre en —*, to impound, to take to the greenyard

Fourrure, *s.f.* fur; furred gown *or* garment; (*nav.*) service. *— de gouttière*, water-way

Fourvoiement, *s.m.* going astray, straying, wandering; error, mistake, blunder

Fourvoyé, e, *part. adj.* misled, misguided led astray; that has lost his way, out of the way; stray; wandering; erring; in error; mistaken

Fourvoyer, *v.a.* to mislead, to misguide, to lead astray; to lead into error; to put on the wrong scent; to baffle, to foil

Se —, *v.r.* to lose o.'s way, to go out of o.'s way, to go astray, to stray; to be lost; to be mistaken, to blunder, to err, to fall into error (*or* errors *or* an error), to make mistakes (*or* a mistake); to go on the wrong scent

Foustanelle, *s.f.* foustanelle, fustianello (*modern Greek military tunic, kind of kilt*)

Foutaise, *s.f.* (*pop.*) *V.* **Fichaise**

Foutant, e, *adj.* (*pop.*) *V.* **Fichant** (*fam.*)

Fouteau, *s.m.* (*local, vulgar*) beech-tree, beech

Foutelaie, *s.f.* beech-grove, beech-plantation

Foutimasser, *v.n.* (*pop.*) to do no good

Foutimasseur, *s.m.* (*pop.*) idler, do-nothing

Foutre, *int.* (*pop.*) *V.* **Fichtre;** *— v.a.n.* (*pop. for* **Ficher, Donner, Mettre, Faire,** *and* **Dire**). *— le camp*, *V.* **Ficher.** *Aller se faire —*, to go to the devil *or* to Old Nick, to go to blazes, to go and be damned; *envoyer faire —*, to send to ditto

Se —, *v.r.* (*pop. for* **Se Ficher, Se Donner,** &c.). *Se — de*, *V.* **Se Moquer de, Se Ficher de**

Foutrement, *adv.* (*pop.*) *V.* **Fichtrement**

Foutriquet, Foutriot, *s.m.* (*pop.*) bit of a man, scrubby fellow, dwarf, shrimp, runt; (*obsolete*) prig, puppy, fribble [**Fichu,** *part. adj.*

Foutu, e, *part. of* **Foutre** *and adj.* (*pop.*) *V.*

Foutument, *adv.* (*pop.*) *V.* **Fichument**

Fovéolaire, Fovéolé, e, *adj.* (*nat. hist.*) foveolate, foveolated

Foyer, *s.m.* hearth; furnace; fire-hole; fire-box (*of a steam-engine*); bowl (*of a tobacco-pipe*); fire; fireside; home; native land; focus; centre, seat, hotbed; source; (*theat.*) saloon, crush-room; (*theat.*) greenroom; (*com.*) hearth-rug. *— des acteurs*, greenroom. *— du public*, saloon, [crush-room

Frac, *s.m.* dress-coat; full dress

Fracas, *s.m.* crash; roar; uproar, fracas; din; tumult; bustle; noise; fuss; show, display

Fracasser, *v.a.* to break to pieces, to shatter, to shiver; to break in several places, to break

Fraction, *s.f.* fraction; portion; breaking

Fractionnaire, *adj.* fractional, fractionary

Fractionnement, *s.m.* dividing into fractions, dividing, division, splitting, split

Fractionner, *v.a.,* **Se —,** *v.r.* to divide into fractions, to divide, to split; to be divided

Fracture, *s.f.* fracture; breaking; rupture

Fracturer, *v.a.* to fracture; to break

Fragiforme, *adj.* fragiform, strawberry-shaped

Fragile, *adj.* fragile; brittle; frail; weak; fleeting. *— !* with care! glass! [weakness

Fragilité, *s.f.* fragility; brittleness; frailty;

Fragment, *s.m.* fragment, piece, scrap, particle

Fragmentaire, *adj.* fragmentary, fragmental

Fragmentation, *s.f.* fragmentation

Fragmenter, *v.a.,* **Se —,** *v.r.* to fragment, to divide; to be fragmented *or* divided

Fragmenteu-x, se, *adj.* fragmentous

Fragmentiste, *s.m.f.* fragmentist, essayist

Fragon, *s.m.* (*bot.*) *V.* **Brusc**

Fragrance, *s.f.* fragrance, fragrancy

Fragrant, e, *adj.* fragrant [fish; (*of coin*) wear

Frai, *s.m.* spawn; spat; spawning; fry, young

Fraîche, *s.f.* fresh meadow; fresh *or* cool air; breeze; *— adj.f. V.* **Frais,** *adj. A la —*, out in the cool air; on a cool morning *or* evening; refresh yourselves!

Fraîchement, *adv.* freshly; coolly; lately recently, newly, of late; just

Fraîcheur, *s.f.* freshness; coolness; coldness; cold; chill; dampness; ruddiness, floridness; bloom; (*nav.*) breeze, flaw of wind

Fraîchir, *v.n.* to freshen, to begin to blow high; to get cool

Fraie, Fraieson, *s.f.* spawning-time

Frairie, *s.f.* (*old*) entertainment, feast, merry-making, merriment; fair

Frais, *m.,* **Fraîche,** *f., adj.* fresh; cool; cold-ish; cold; ruddy, florid, fresh-coloured; blooming; hale; recent, late; new-laid; new; (*pop.*) in a pretty condition *or* plight; (*adv.*) freshly, recently, lately, newly, new. *Frais-cueilli* (*m.*), *Fraîche-cueillie* (*f.*), fresh-gathered. *Faire —*, to be cool

Frais, *s.m.* freshness, coolness, cool; fresh *or* cool air; cool place *or* spot; cold; (*nav.*) fresh wind, gale; (*jest.*) prison

Frais, *s.m.pl.* expenses, expense, cost; costs; outlay; charges; charge; contribution; efforts; pains, trouble, difficulty; inconvenience; advances; (*pop.*) damage. *Faux —*, incidental *or* casual *or* extra *or* idle *or* unforeseen expenses; (*law*) untaxable costs. *A — communs*, at joint expense, jointly, at the general cost. *A peu de —*, at little cost, cheaply, easily. *Sur nouveaux —*, on a new score; anew, over again. *Tous — faits*, clear of all charges *or* expenses, when all is paid. *En être pour ses —*, to lose (*or* to have lost) o.'s time and money (*or*, *fig.*, o.'s time and trouble). *Faire les — de*, to pay *or* bear the expenses (*or* expense) of, to pay for; to furnish, to supply, to find; to be the chief contributor to; to keep up. *Faire des —*, to go to expense; to make efforts; to take trouble; to make advances; to make efforts to please. *Faire ses —*, to cover o.'s expenses

Fraise, *s.f.* strawberry; strawberry-mark; ruff (*collar*); (*butch.*) crow; (*of bridges*) starling; (*fort.*) fraise; (*hunt.*) start. *— des bois*, wood strawberry, wild strawberry [starlings

Fraisement, *s.m.* (*fort.*) fraising; (*of bridges*)

Fraiser, *v.a.* to ruffle, to plait; (*fort.*) to fraise; (*tech.*) to countersink; (*in baking*) *V.* **Fraser**

Fraiserat, *s.m.* (*bot.*) potentilla

Fraisette, *s.f.* small ruff

Fraisier, *s.m.* strawberry-plant

Fraisière, *s.f.* strawberry-bed [dust; coke-dust

Fraisil, *s.m.* coal-cinders, breeze; charcoal-

Fraisoir, *s.m.* wimble, drill

Frambœsia, *s.m.* (*med.*) frambœsia

Framboise, *s.f.* raspberry [berries

Framboiser, *v.a.* to flavour *or* mix with rasp-

Framboisier, *s.m.* raspberry-bush

Framée, *s.f.* framea, javelin

Franc, *s.m.* franc (*French or &c. silver coin worth about* 20*c.*); (*hort.*) seedling; (*thieves' slang*) pal

Franc, *m.*, **Franche,** *f.*, *adj.* free; independent; scot-free; exempt; frank; candid, sincere, open, open-hearted; fair; uninjured, unscathed, harmless; whole, entire, complete, full, clear; pure; unmixed; genuine; true, real; downright, regular, arrant; bold; mere; very; (*hort.*) natural, ungrafted. — **-alleu,** — **-bord,** &c., *V.* **Alleu, Bord,** &c. — **bourgeois,** *s.m.* (*pop.*) swell-mobsman. — *du* **collier,** free; earnest, obliging, honest. — **-Comtois, e,** *s.m.f. adj.* native of Franche-Comté; of Franche-Comté. — **-étable,** *s.m.* (*nav.*) collision. *De* — *-étable,* (*nav.*) foul. — **-funin,** — **-filin,** *V.* **Funin.** — **-maçon,** *s.m.* freemason, mason. — **-maçonnerie,** *s.f.* freemasonry. — *de* **maison,** *s.m.* (*pop.*) receiver of stolen goods, fence. — **-parler,** *s.m. V.* **Parler,** *s.m.* — **-pineau,** *s.m.* franc-pineau (*Burgundy grape*). — **-réal,** *s.m.* franc-real (*kind of pear*). — **-tenancier,** *V.* **Tenancier.** — **-tillac,** *s.m.* (*nav.*) gun-deck, lower deck. — **-tireur,** *s.m.* independent sharpshooter *or* rifleman, volunteer

Franc, *adv.* frankly, freely, candidly, openly, plainly; wholly, entirely; clear, clean; free

Fran-c, que, *s.m.f. adj.* Frank; Frankish, Francic

Français, e, *adj. s.* French; Frenchman, French boy; (the) French language, French; French woman *or* lady *or* girl; French fashion. *En bon* —, in good *or* plain French; in plain language *or* terms, plainly; like a true Frenchman. *Parler* —, to speak French; (*fig.*) to speak plainly, to speak out. *A la* —*e*, *V.* **A** *and* **Habit.** *Le* —, the French language, French; plain language; the *or* a Frenchman. *Les* —, the French people, the French; (*also used as an abbreviation of* "le Théatre-Français" *in* [*Paris*)

Francatu, *s.m.* francatu (*kind of apple*)

Francfortois, e, *adj. s.* of Frankfort; Frankforter

Franchement, *adv.* freely, candidly, sincerely, frankly, openly; fairly; boldly; arrantly; outright; at once; with a vengeance; and no mistake; really

Franchipanier, *s.m. V.* **Frangipanier**

Franchir, *v.a.* to leap *or* jump (clean) over, to clear; to rush *or* go (right) through *or* across *or* up *or* down, &c.; to pass *or* go over; to cross; to go beyond; to overstep; to break through; to overcome, to surmount; to free (*a ship*)

Se —, *v.r.* to be cleared *or* &c.

Franchise, *s.f.* franchise, immunity, exemption; privilege; asylum, refuge; freedom; frankness, candour, sincerity, plain dealing; fairness; boldness; (*post.*) frank, franking. *En* —, duty free [be crossed *or* gone over

Franchissable, *adj.* passable, superable, to

Franchissement, *s.m.* leaping *or* leap over, &c. (*V.* **Franchir**), passage

Franciade, *s.f.* Franciad

Francique, *adj.* Francic

Francisation, *s.f.* frenchification, frenchifying, gallicizing; (*com. law*) registry as a French vessel [friar

Franciscain, *s.m., adj.m.* Franciscan, grey-

Franciser, *v.a.* to frenchify, to gallicize

Se —, *v.r.* to become *or* be frenchified (*or* gallicized), to become French

Francisque, *s.f.* battle-axe, Francic battle-axe

Franco, *adv.* free of charge *or* expense; free from postage, post-free; prepaid

Francolin, *s.m.* (*bird*) francolin

Frange, *s.f.* fringe; valance [ate

Franger, *v.a.* to fringe; to valance; to fimbri-

Frangibilité, *s.f.* frangibility

Frangible, *adj.* frangible

Frang-ier, ière, (*modern*) **Frang-er, ère,** (*old*) *s.m.f.* fringe-maker

Frangipane, *s.f.* (*pastry*) frangipane, cream and almond cake; (*perfume*) frangipanni, fran-

Frangipanier, *s.m.* (*bot.*) red jasmine [gipane

Franque, *adj.f.* Frank, Frankish, Francic

Franquette, *s.f.* *A la bonne* —, *à la* —, (*fam.*) frankly, freely, sincerely, candidly; simply, plainly, without ceremony [**Frapper**)

Frappage, *s.m.* striking, stamping, &c. (*V.*

Frappant, e, *adj.* striking, impressive

Frappe, *s.f.* (*coin.*) stamp; (*type-founding*) set of matrices [thesis

Frappé, *s.m.* (*mus.*) fall (*of the hand or foot*),

Frappé, e, *part. adj.* struck, &c. (*V.* **Frapper**); made; done; powerful, forcible; spirited; (*of cloth*) strong and close; (*mus.*) of the fall (*of the hand or foot*)

Frappe-main, *s.m.* (*obsolete*) *V.* **Main chaude**

Frappement, *s.m.* striking, clapping, &c. (*V.* **Frapper**)

Frapper, *v.a.n.* to strike; to hit; to smite; to beat; to knock; to rap; to tap; to slap; to dash; to give; to blast; to blemish; to attaint; to afflict; to impress; to make an impression on; to affect, to move; to seize; to startle; to astonish, to surprise; to frighten; to fill with gloom, to gloom; to stamp; to coin; to clap; to patter; to ice (*liquids*); to lay; to be impressive; (*nav.*) to fix. — *juste*, to strike home, to make a home-thrust. *Entendre* —, to hear a knock

Se —, *v.r.* to strike *or* &c. oneself *or* each other; to strike *or* beat (o.'s ...); to impress o.'s imagination, to be impressed *or* affected; to be frightened; to be filled with gloom; (*of things*) to be struck *or* &c.

Frappeu-r, se, *s.m.f.* striker, hitter, beater, knocker, rapper; smith; — *adj.* striking, beating, knocking, rapping. *Esprit* —, rapping spirit, spirit-rapper [water)

Frasage, *s.m.* (*in baking*) mixing (the flour with

Fraser, *v.a.* (*in baking*) to mix (the flour with

Frasque, *s.f.* freak, prank, trick [water)

Frater, *s.m.* (*mil., nav., jest.*) barber; (*obsolete*) barber-surgeon's assistant; (*jest.*) saw-bones

Fraternel, le, *adj.* fraternal, brotherly

Fraternellement, *adv.* fraternally, brotherly

Fraternisation, *s.f.* fraternization, fraterniz-

Fraterniser, *v.n.* to fraternize [ing

Fraternité, *s.f.* fraternity, brotherhood

Fratricide, (*murder*) *s.m.*, (*pers.*) *s.m.f.* fratricide; — *adj.* fratricidal

Fraude, *s.f.* fraudulency, deceit, guile, cheat, imposition, imposture, artifice, trick; smuggling; smuggled *or* contraband goods. *En* —, fraudulently; in the act of defrauding *or* smuggling; (*jest.*) insolvent

Frauder, *v.a.n.* to defraud; to deceive; to cheat; to frustrate; to balk, to baffle, to foil; to avoid; to smuggle

Fraudeu-r, se, *s.m.f.* defrauder; smuggler

Frauduleusement, *adv.* fraudulently

Frauduleu-x, se, *adj.* fraudulent; deceitful; smuggling, contraband

Frauler, *v.a.* to rub (*seeds*) in o.'s hands

Fraxinelle, *s.f.* (*bot.*) fraxinella, bastard dittany

Fraxinine, *s.f.* (*chem.*) fraxinine

Frayant, e, *adj.* (*obsolete*) expensive

Frayer, *v.a.* to trace, to mark out; to open, to cut, to beat; to make; to prepare; to show; to wear away; to fray, to rub; to gall; (*old*) to graze, to rub against; — *v.n.* to wear away; to agree, to be on good terms; to associate; to spawn

Frayère, *s.f.* spawning-place; spawning-time

Frayeur, *s.f.* fright, dread, fear, terror [place

Frayoir, *s.m.* (*hunt.*) fray, rub; (*fish.*) spawning-

Frayone, Frayonne, *s.f.* (*pop.*) rook (*bird*)

Frayure, *s.f.* (*hunt.*) fraying, rubbing

Fredaine, *s.f.* frolic, prank; freak [16*s.* 10*d.*)

Fréderic, *s.m.* frederic (*Prussian gold coin worth*

Fredon, *s.m.* (*obsolete*) (*mus.*) shake, trill, grace; hum; (*at cards*) pair-royal; (*fig.*) trio

Fredonnement, *s.m.* humming

Fredonner, *v.a.n.* to hum (*a tune*); (*old*) to shake, to trill [humming

Fredonneu-r, se, *s.m.f.* hummer; — *adj.*

Frégate, *s.f.* frigate; (*zool.*) frigate-bird

Frégaté, e, *adj.* frigate-built
Frégater, *v.a.* to build as a frigate
Frégaton, *s.m.* frigatoon
Frein, *s.m.* bit; bridle, curb, check, restraint; drag, skid; break, brake; (*anat.*) frænum, frenum, fillet. *Ronger son* —, to champ the bit; (*fig.*) to fret oneself. *Serrer le* —, (*rail.*, &c.) to put on *or* apply the break
Frelatage, Frelatement, *s.m.*, **Frelaterie,** *s.f.* adulteration, sophistication
Frelater, *v.a.* to adulterate, to sophisticate, to doctor
Se —, *v.r.* to be adulterated *or* &c.
Frelateu-r, se, *s.m.f.* adulterater, adulteratress
Frêle, *adj.* frail; brittle; weak, feeble; faint
Frêler, *v.n.a.* (*local*) to crackle; to rub
Freloche, *s.f.* butterfly-net, insect-net
Frelon, *s.m.* hornet; (*old, abusively, fig.*) drone; (*bot.*) *V.* **Fragon**
Freluche, *s.f.* tuft; air-thread; trifle
Freluquet, *s.m.* coxcomb, prig, puppy, fribble, fopling
Frémir, *v.n.* to shudder; to thrill; to shake, to quiver, to tremble; to flutter; to vibrate; to rustle; to murmur; to simmer; (*of the sea*) to boil, to be agitated
Frémissement, *s.m.* shuddering, shudder; thrilling, thrill; shaking, shake; shock; quivering, quiver; trembling; tremor; fluttering, flutter; vibration; rustling, rustle; murmuring, murmur; din; simmering; agitation; motion. — *cataire*, (*med.*) purring tremor, thrill
Frémont, *s.m.* fremont (*kind of pear*)
Frênaie, *s.f.* ash-grove, ash-plantation
Frêne, *s.m.* ash-tree, ash
Frénésie, *s.f.* frenzy, madness, fury, raving
Frénétique, *adj.* frantic, mad, furious, raving; — *s.m.f.* ditto man *or* woman
Fréquemment, *adv.* frequently, often
Fréquence, *s.f.* frequency; (*of the pulse and breathing*) quickness
Fréquent, e, *adj.* frequent; (*of the pulse and breathing*) quick
Fréquentable, *adj.* frequentable
Fréquentati-f, ve, *adj.*, **Fréquentatif,** *s.m.* (*gram.*) frequentative
Fréquentation, *s.f.* frequenting, frequentation; company; frequent use, frequent receiving
Fréquenter, *v.a.n.* to frequent, to go often to, to resort to, to haunt; to associate with; to visit often; to receive frequently
Frequin, *s.m.* barrel, cask (*for sugar*, &c.)
Frère, *s.m.* brother; fellow-christian; friar, monk; brother of charity. — *de mère, de père*, brother on the mother's *or* father's side. *École des* —*s*, ragged school
Frérie, *s.f.* (*old*) *V.* **Frairie**
Frérot, *s.m.* (*fam.*) little brother, dear little brother
Fresaie, *s.f.* *V.* **Effraie**
†**Frésillon,** *s.m.* (*pop.*) privet (*shrub*)
Fresque, *s.f.* (*paint.*) fresco. *A* —, in fresco
Fresquiste, *s.m.* fresco-painter
Fressure, *s.f.* (*butch., cook.*) pluck; fry; haslet; [(*pers., jest.*) gizzard
Fret, *s.m.* freight
Frètement, *s.m.* chartering, letting to charter; (*old*) freighting
Fréter, *v.a.* to charter, to let to charter; (*old*) to freight
Fréteur, *s.m.* charterer; (*old*) freighter
†**Frétillant, e,** *adj.* frisky, wriggling; brisk; fidgety, impatient
†**Frétillement,** *s.m.* frisking, wriggling; briskness; itching, longing, fidget, impatience
†**Frétiller,** *v.n.* to frisk, to frisk about, to wriggle; to itch, to long, to fidget, to be impatient
†**Frétillon,** *s.m.f.* frisky body
Fretin, *s.m.* small fish; young fish; fry, small fry; trash, rubbish
Frettage, *s.m.* hooping, binding
Frette, *s.f.* iron hoop, hoop, band, ring, ferrule, cramp, curbing; (*her.*) fret
Fretté, e, *part. adj.* hooped, iron-bound, secured by an iron hoop *or* band; (*her.*) fretted, fretty
Fretter, *v.a.* to hoop, to bind
Freux, *s.m.* (*bird*) rook
Friabilité, *s.f.* friability, friableness
Friable, *adj.* friable, crisp, short
Friand, e, *adj. s.* dainty, nice, delicate; fond (of), partial (to); greedy (of), eager (for); dainty person, epicure, sweet-tooth
Friandement, *adv.* daintily, nicely; greedily
Friandise, *s.f.* daintiness, epicurism; nicety dainty, dainty bit, titbit, delicacy
Fricandeau, *s.m.* fricandeau, larded veal
Fricassée, *s.f.* (*cook.*) fricassee; (*pop.*) tussle, brush, drubbing; regular smash, smash
Fricasser, *v.a.n.* to fricassee; to squander away, to dissipate, to waste, to spend; to lose, to sell off; to ruin, to do up, to do for, to dish; (*pop.*) to cook the grub. *On t'en fricasse*, don't you wish you may get it?
Se —, *v.r.* to be fricasseed *or* &c.
Fricasseu-r, se, *s.m.f* bad cook; spendthrift drunkard, rake
Friche, *s.f.* waste land; fallow; — *s.m.* (*agr.*) twitch-grass, twitch. *En* —, uncultivated, waste; fallow, lying fallow
Frichti, *s.m.* (*pop.*) stew with potatoes, stew
Fricot, *s.m.* (*fam.*) ragout, stew; meat, dish mess, eating, food, victuals, grub, stuffing
Fricoter, *v.n.* (*fam.*) to make a stew; to cook some grub, to cook; to mess, to grub, to feast, to revel, to live well; to job, to be a jobber; — *v.a.* to squander in feasts, to eat away; to job, to concoct, to plot
Fricoteu-r, se, *s.m.f.* feaster, reveller, good liver; bad cook; jobber; marauder
Friction, *s.f.* friction, rubbing. *A* —*s*, (*adject., of brushes, gloves*, &c.) flesh
Frictionner, *v.a.n.* to rub
Frictionneu-r, se, *s.m.f.* (professional) rubber
Frigard, *s.m.* pickled herring
Frigidité, *s.f.* frigidity
Frigorifique, *adj.* frigorific
Frigoter, *v.n.* (*of the chaffinch*) to chirp
Frigousse, *s.m.* (*pop.*) cooking; grub; stew
Frigousser, *v.a.n.* (*pop.*) to cook
Frileusement, *adv.* chillily, like one who is chilly
Frileu-x, se, *adj.* chilly; (*pop.*) cowardly, funky; — *s.m.f.* chilly person; (*pop.*) coward, funky fellow; — *s.f.* (lady's) warm cap
†**Frilleuse,** *s.f.* *pop. for* **Rouge-gorge**
Frilosité, *s.f.* chilliness
Frimaire, *s.m.* Frimaire (*third month of the calendar of the first French Republic, from Nov.* 21 *to Dec.* 20)
Frimas, *s.m.* white frost, rime; (*nav.*) spray; — *pl.* frost, snow, frost and snow, cold weather, cold, winter; cold climates
Frime, *s.f.* (*fam.*) sham, pretence, show, make-believe; fun of the thing, joke
Frimousse, *s.f.* (*fam.*) face, phiz; own self
Fringale, *s.f.* fit of hunger
Fringant, e, *adj.* frisky; brisk, nimble, smart, dapper; dashing; lively; flippant
Fringille, *s.f.* (*zool.*) fringilla
Fringuer, *v.n.* to frisk, to frisk *or* skip about
Friolerie, *s.f.* (*old*) *V.* **Friandise**
Friolet, *s.m.* friolet (*kind of pear*)
Fripe, *s.f.* (*pop.*) eatable, grub, victuals; eating; cooking; share; (*obsolete*) rag, scrap
Fripé, e, *part. adj.* tumbled, &c. (*V.* **Friper**); no longer fresh; old; shabby; tattered; threadbare
Friper, *v.a.* to tumble, to rumple, to crumple; to take the freshness off; to spoil, to wear out; to waste; to squander; to spend; to gobble down; to pilfer, to crib, to bone, to fork, to bag
Se —, *v.r.* to get *or* be rumpled; to lose its freshness; to wear out; to be spoilt *or* &c.
Friperie, *s.f.* frippery, old clothes, second-hand clothes *or* furniture, marine stores; ditto trade *or* shop, broker's shop, marine store-shop; rag-fair, Petticoat-lane
Fripe-sauce, *s.m.* (*pop.*) glutton, greedy gut; bad cook, cook, scullion
Fripi-er, ère, *s.m.f.* old clothesman, old clothes-woman, second-hand clothier; marine store dealer, marine clothier; furniture-broker; (*obsolete*) compiler, plagiarist

Fripon, ne, *s.m.f. adj.* knave, rogue, rascal, cheat; hussy; knavish, roguish, rascally
Friponneau, *s.m.* little knave *or* &c. (*V.* **Fripon**)
Friponner, *v.a.n.* to cheat; to pilfer
Friponnerie, *s.f.* knavery, roguery, knavish *or* roguish trick, piece of knavery *or* of roguery, cheating, cheat, dishonesty
Friquet, *s.m.* (*bird*) tree-sparrow; (*vers.*) spark; (*local*) slice (*kitchen utensil*)
Frire, *v.a.n.*, **Se** —, *v.r.* to fry; (*pop.*) to eat; to ruin; to squander. *Faire* —, to fry
Frisage, *s.m.* curling, rolling; frizzing; lattice-work, lattice, trellis [border (*sky-border*, &c.)
Frise, *s.f.* (*cloth, arch., nav., tech.*) frieze; (*theat.*)
Frisé, e, *part. adj.* curled, &c. (*V.* **Friser**); curly; crispy, crisp; — *s.m.f.* frizzly-pated fellow *or* woman *or* girl; — *s.m.* curl, curls, curling, curliness, crispness; — *s.f.* curl (*potato disease*)
Friser, *v.a.n.* to curl; to frizzle, to frizz, to frieze; to crimp; to crisp; to curl the hair of; to graze, to touch lightly; to ruffle; to border *or* be close upon, to approach, to come *or* pass very near; to be very near having *or* getting, to narrowly escape; (*print.*) to slur; (*nav.*) to shiver
Se —, *v.r.* to curl o.'s hair; to curl; to crisp; to pass close to each other; (*of horses*) to over-
Frisette, *s.f.* small *or* little curl; frisette [reach
Friseu-r, se, *s.m.f.* curler, crisper, hair-dresser
Frisoir, *s.m.* curling-irons, crimping-iron; chasing-tool
Frison, ne, *adj.* Friesic; (*ancient*) Frisian; — *s.m.f.* Frieslander; (*ancient*) Frisian; — *s.m.* (the) Frisian (language); curl; side-curl (*on the temples*); floss (*of silk*); knubs *or* husks (*of silk*); (*nav.*) can
Frisoter, *v.a.n.* to frizzle, to frizz, to curl
Frisquet, te, *adj.* (*pop.*) smart, dashy, natty; (*of weather*) sharp cold; — *s.f.* (*pop.*) smart young girl; (*print.*) frisket
Frisson, *s.m.* shiver, shivering; chill; cold fit; shudder; quiver; thrill; emotion; agitation; motion; rustle
Frissonnement, *s.m.* shivering, shiver; chilliness; shuddering, shudder; thrilling, thrill; quivering, quiver; emotion; agitation; motion; vibration; rustling
Frissonner, *v.n.* to shiver; to shudder; to thrill; to quiver; to shake; to tremble; to vibrate; to rustle; to flutter
Frisure, *s.f.* curling, crisping, curliness, crispness, crispature, curls, curl; little knot; gold *or* silver thread [squandered, spent, gone
Frit, e, *adj.* fried; ruined; undone; done for;
Friteau, *s.m.* (*cook.*) fry, fried dish
Friteu-r, se, *s.m.f.* special cook for fried dishes, frying-cook; (*dealer*) fried-fish man *or* woman
Fritillaire, *s.f.* (*plant, butterfly*) fritillary. — *impériale*, (*plant*) crown imperial
Frittage, *s.m.* (*in glass-making*) fritting
Fritte, *s.f.* (*in glass-making*) frit, fritt; fritting
Fritter, *v.a.* (*in glass-making*) to frit
Fritteu-x, se, *adj.* fritty
Frittier, *s.m.* (*in glass-making*) fritter
Friture, *s.f.* frying; fry, fried dish *or* dishes; fried fish, dish of fried fish; frying butter *or* oil, dripping [to feed, to grub
Friturer, *v.a.n.* (*pop.*) to fry, to cook; to eat,
Frituri-er, ère, *s.m.f. V.* **Friteur**
Frivole, *adj.* frivolous, trifling, futile, flimsy, shallow, vain, empty; — *s.m.* trifles
Frivolement, *adv.* frivolously
Frivoliste, *s.m.f.* trifler; flimsy writer
Frivolité, *s.f.* frivolity, frivolousness, triflingness, futility; trifle; (*need.*) tatting
Froc, *s.m.* frock, monk's habit; monkery, monkhood, monks. *Jeter le — aux orties*, to throw off the cowl; (*fig.*) to quit the business
†**Frocaille,** *s.f.* (*in contempt*) monks
Frocard, *s.m.* (*in contempt*) monk
Froid, e, *adj.* cold; frigid, lukewarm, indifferent; cool; cold-blooded; inanimate, lifeless; dull; grave, calm, dispassionate; reserved, distant; (*of gout*) atonic. — *aux yeux*, (*pop.*) want of pluck, funk. *Avoir* —, (*pers.*) to be cold. *Faire* —, (*weather*) to be cold. *Avoir — aux yeux*, (*pop.*) to want pluck, to be a coward, to be funky, to funk. *N'avoir pas — aux yeux*, (*pop.*) to be plucky *or* game, to be a plucky fellow *or* a man of pluck, to be a bold *or* a determined fellow
Froid, *s.m.* cold; cold weather; coldness; frigidity; indifference, unconcern; coolness; dulness; gravity; reserve; —**s**, *pl.* cold days, cold weather *or* season, cold, winter. *Les grands —s*, the very cold weather, the depth of winter. *A* —, cold; coldly; coolly; in cold blood
Froidement, *adv.* coldly; frigidly, lukewarmly, with indifference, weakly, faintly; coolly; in cold blood; lifelessly; gravely, calmly, dispassionately; reservedly
Froideur, *s.f.* coldness; chilliness, chill; lukewarmness, indifference, unconcern; coolness; dulness; gravity; reserve
Froidir, *v.a.n.*, **Se** —, *v.r.* (*old*) *V.* **Refroidir**
Froidure, *s.f.* cold temperature, cold air, cold weather, cold, coldness, cold season, winter
Froidureu-x, se, *adj.* (*old*) cold, bleak, chilly
Froissage, *s.m.* (*tech.*) bruising
Froissement, *s.m.* bruising; rumpling; collision; clashing; dashing; crush; crash; pressure; ruffling; rustling; offending; offence; annoyance, vexation
Froisser, *v.a.* to bruise; to rumple; to tumble, to crease, to crumple; to clash with *or* against; to dash; to strike; to push against; to rub; to crush; to wound, to hurt, to ruffle, to gall, to offend; to wound *or* hurt *or* ruffle the feelings of
Se —, *v.r.* to be bruised *or* &c.; to bruise (o.'s ...); to take offence [bruising
Froisseur, *s.m.* bruiser; hurter; — *adj.m.*
Froissis, *s.m.* (*old*) *V.* **Froissement**
Froissure, *s.f.* bruise; rumple; crease
Frôle, *s.f.* Alpine honeysuckle [rustle
Frôlement, *s.m.* grazing; contact; rustling,
Frôler, *v.a.* to graze, to brush; to touch; to rustle against; (*agr.*) to rub (*seeds*) in o.'s hands
Fromage, *s.m.* cheese. — *de cochon*, brawn. — *d'Italie*, Italian brawn [mallow (*plant*)
Fromageon, *s.m.* ewe-milk cheese; (*pop.*)
Fromag-er, ère, *s.m.f.* cheese-maker; cheesemonger; — *s.m.* cheese-mould; (*bot.*) silk-cotton tree [cheese-market *or* shop; cheeses
Fromagerie, *s.f.* cheese-dairy; cheese-trade;
Fromageu-x, se, *adj.* cheesy [monger
Fromagi-er, ère, *s.m.f.* cheese-maker; cheese-
Froment, *s.m.* wheat. *De* —, of wheat; wheaten
Fromentacé, e, *adj.* frumentaceous
Fromental, e, *adj.* fit for wheat-sowing, wheat; — *s.m.* rye-grass [*grape*)
Fromenteau, *s.m.* fromenteau (*Champagne*
Fromentée, *s.f.* (*cook.*) frumenty
Fromenteu-x, se, *adj.* abounding in wheat
Fromenti-er, ère, *adj. V.* **Fromental**
Fronce, *s.f.* (*need.*) gather; (*in paper*) crease
Froncement, *s.m.* wrinkling, knitting, pursing, frowning, frown, contraction, corrugation; (*need.*) gathering, puckering. — *des* or *de sourcils*, knitting of the brows, frowning, frown
Froncer, *v.a.* to wrinkle, to knit, to purse, to contract, to corrugate; (*need.*) to gather, to pucker. — *le sourcil* or *les sourcils*, to knit the brows, to frown [gathers, puckers, folds
Froncis, *s.m.* (*need.*) gathering, puckering,
Fronçure, *s.f.* wrinkling, contraction, corrugation; wrinkle, fold
Frondaison, *s.f.* foliation; foliage
Fronde, *s.f.* sling; (*bot.*) frond; (*surg.*) four-tailed bandage; (*Fr. hist.*) Fronde
Frondée, *s.f.* sling-shot
Fronder, *v.a.* to sling; to hurl, to fling, to throw; to censure, to blame, to animadvert on, to find fault with, to criticize, to rail, to jeer, to carp at, to exclaim against, to oppose

Fronderie, *s.f.* (*Fr. hist.*) riot of the Fronde; (*obsolete*) riot, disturbance
Frondescence, *s.f.* (*nat. hist.*) frondescence
Frondescent, e, *adj.* (*nat. hist.*) frondescent
Frondeu-r, se, *s.m.f.* slinger; censurer, fault-finder; railer, jeerer, carper; grumbler, croaker; (*Fr. hist.*) frondeur, frondeuse; — *adj.* censuring, fault-finding; railing, jeering
Frondifère, *adj.* (*bot.*) frondiferous
Front, *s.m.* forehead; brow; face, countenance; head; front; impudence, boldness, brass, cheek; (*poet.*) bearing, attitude, demeanour; air, look; (*mil.*) front. — *d'airain*, brazen face. *De* —, in front; abreast; simultaneously, at the same time, together. *Faire* —, to face
Frontal, e, *adj.*, **Frontal,** *s.m.* frontal; frontal bone; (*of a horse's head-stall*) front-piece, front
Fronteau, *s.m.* frontlet; (*of a horse's head-stall*) front-piece, front; (*arch.*) frontal; (*nav.*) breast-work
Frontière, *s.f. adj.* frontier; border; confine
†**Frontignan,** *s.m.* frontiniac *or* frontignac (wine)
Frontin, *s.m.* knavish clever valet, confidant
Frontispice, *s.f.* frontispiece
Fronton, *s.m.* (*arch.*) pediment, fronton; (*nav.*) poop-rail, poop-ornaments
Froquer, *v.a.* to frock [of billiards
Frotin, *s.m.* (*pop.*) billiards. *Coup de* —, game
Frottage, *s.m.* rubbing, polishing, waxing and
Frotte, *s.f.* (*pop.*) itch [polishing, scrubbing
Frottée, *s.f.* rubbing; scrubbing; drubbing. — *d'ail*, crust of bread rubbed with garlic
Frottement, *s.m.* rubbing, friction; contact; frequentation; collision, clash
Frotter, *v.a.n.* to rub; to polish; to wax and polish; to scrub; to drub, to pommel; to warm (*the ears*)
Se —, *v.r.* to rub oneself *or* each other; to rub (o.'s ...); to be rubbed *or* &c.; to be in (*or* come into) contact with; to frequent; to fight, to have a set-to; to provoke; to meddle (with), to interfere (with), to have something *or* anything to do (with), to venture, to try; to get a smattering (of). *Qui s'y frotte s'y pique*, meddle and smart for it
Frotteu-r, se, *s.m.f.* rubber; dry-rubber; scrubber; polisher; floor-polisher
Frottis, *s.m.* (*paint.*) light touch
Frottoir, *s.m.* rubber; rubbing-cloth; rough towel; flesh-glove; shaving-cloth; scrubbing-brush, polishing-brush
Frouement, *s.m.* piping, calling (birds)
Frouer, *v.n.* to pipe, to call (birds)
Froufrou, *s.m.* rustling, rustle; (*pop.*) humming-bird; (*slang*) skeleton-key. *Faire* —, to rustle; to cut a dash; to make a fuss
Frousse, *s.f.* (*pop.*) fright, start, shake, shock
Fructidor, *s.m.* Fructidor (*twelfth month of the calendar of the first French Republic, from August* 18 *to September* 16) [*legislative assembly*)
Fructidoriser, *v.a.* to dissolve by force (*a*
Fructifère, *adj.* (*bot.*) fructiferous; fruit
Fructifica-teur, trice, *adj.* fructifying, fer-
Fructification, *s.f.* fructification [tilizing
Fructifier, *v.n.* to fructify; to bear fruit; to be fruitful; to thrive, to prosper
Fructueusement, *adv.* fruitfully, profitably
Fructueu-x, se, *adj.* fruitful; profitable
Fructuosité, *s.f.* fruitfulness
Frugal, e, *adj.* frugal
Frugalement, *adv.* frugally
Frugalité, *s.f.* frugality
Frugardite, *s.f.* (*min.*) frugardite
Fruges, *s.f.pl.* (*slang*) profits, pickings
Frugifère, *adj.* (*bot.*) frugiferous [animal
Frugivore, *adj.* frugivorous; — *s.m.* ditto
Fruit, *s.m.* fruit; dessert; produce, product, production; offspring, child; profit, advantage, benefit, utility; effect, result; (*mas.*) batter. — *sec*, dried fruit; (*fig.*) plucked candidate; indifferent genius, mere nobody
Fruitage, *s.m.* fruitage, fruit
Fruité, e, *adj.* (*her.*) fructed
Fruiterie, *s.f.* fruitery; fruit-room *or* loft; fruit-trade, greengrocery; fruit-shop, greengrocer's shop
Fruiti-er, ère, *adj.* fruit-bearing, fruit; — *s.m.f.* fruiterer, fruiteress, greengrocer, — *s.m.* fruit-room *or* loft; treatise on fruits; (*obsolete*)
Frumentacé, e, *adj.* frumentaceous [orchard
Frusque, *s.f.* (*pop.*) coat; —**s,** *pl.* clothes, effects, things, traps, duds, togs, toggery
Frusquin, *s.m.* (*son saint-* —) o.'s all
Frusquiner (Se), *v.r.* (*pop.*) to put on o.'s
Frusquineur, *s.m.* (*pop.*) tailor [duds, to dress
Fruste, *adj.* worn away, corroded, defaced; *s.m.* defaced inscription *or* effigy, defacement, wear [*adj.* frustrating
Frustra-teur, trice, *s.m.f.* frustrater; —
Frustration, *s.f.* frustration
Frustratoire, *adj.* frustratory; (*of costs*) unnecessary; — *s.m.* digester, negus
Frustratoirement, *adv.* frustratorily
Frustrer, *v.a.* to frustrate; to balk; to baffle; to foil; to defeat; to disappoint; to deprive; to
Frutescent, e, *adj.* (*bot.*) frutescent [defraud
Fruticuleu-x, se, *adj.* (*bot.*) fruticulose
†**Frutille,** *s.f.* Chili strawberry (*fruit*) [(*plant*)
†**Frutiller, Frutillier,** *s.m.* Chili strawberry
Frutiqueu-x, se, *adj.* (*bot.*) fruticose, fruticous
‡**Fuchsia,** *s.m.* (*bot.*) fuchsia
‡**Fuchsine,** *s.f.* (*chem.*) fuchsine
Fucus, *s.m.* (*bot.*) fucus, wrack, sea-wrack
Fuero, *s.m.* (*Spanish*) fuero
Fugace, *adj.* fugacious, fugitive, fleeting, volatile, transient, variable
Fugacité, *s.f.* fugacity, fugaciousness
Fugato, *s.m.* (*mus.*) fugato
Fugiti-f, ve, *adj. s.* fugitive; fleeting; transient; transitory; passing; short-lived; wandering; runaway; wanderer [transiently
Fugitivement, *adv.* fugitively, fleetingly,
Fugue, *s.f.* (*mus.*) fugue; (*fam.*) running away, bolting, flight; wild prank, lark, spree. *Faire une* —, (*fam.*) to run away, to bolt, to take flight; to have a lark *or* a spree
Fugué, e, *adj.* (*mus.*) fugue-like
Fuie, *s.f.* small pigeon-house, coop
Fuir, *v.n.a.* to flee, to fly; to run away; to escape; to vanish; to evade; to shift; to shun; to avoid; to eschew; to desert; to run; to leak; to sink; (*paint.*) to appear at a distance; to recede
Fuite, *s.f.* flight; escape; running away; absconding; elopement; shunning; avoiding; evasion, shift; running out; leakage; crack; vanishing, receding, recession, retreat; per-
Fulcrum, *s.m.* (*bot.*) fulcra [spective
Fulgore, *s.m.* (*zool.*) lantern-fly, fulgora
Fulgural, e, *adj.* fulgural
Fulgurant, e, *adj.* fulgurant, fulgurating, flashing, lightning, vivid
Fulgurateur, *s.m.* fulgurator [ing, flash
Fulguration, *s.f.* fulguration, lightning, flash-
Fulgurite, *s.m.* fulgurite, fossil lightning
Fulguromètre, *s.m.* (*phys.*) fulgurometer
Fuligineu-x, se, *adj.* fuliginous, sooty, sootish, smoky, dusky
Fuliginosité, *s.f.* fuliginosity, sootiness
Fulmar, *s.m.* (*bird*) fulmar
Fulmicoton, *s.m.* gun-cotton
Fulminaire, Fulminal, e, *adj.* fulmineous
Fulminant, e, *adj.* fulminant; fulminating; detonating; thundering; storming; (*of light-*
Fulminate, *s.m.* (*chem.*) fulminate [*ning*) forked
Fulmination, *s.f.* fulmination; detonation;
Fulminatoire, *adj.* fulminatory [explosion
Fulminé, e, *adj.* fulminated; (*nat. hist.*) streaked in zigzags
Fulminer, *v.a.n.* to fulminate; to detonate; to explode; to thunder; to storm
Fulminique, *adj.* (*chem.*) fulminic
Fumable, *adj.* smokable

Fumade, *s.f.* (*agr.*) dunging
Fumage, *s.m.* colouring, lacquering (*of silver*, &c.); smoking (*of meat, fish*, &c.); manuring; (*old tax*) *V.* **Fouage** [dust
Fumagine, *s.f.*, **Fumago,** *s.m.* (*hort.*) black
†Fumailler, *v.n.* to keep smoking, to smoke
†Fumaillerie, *s.f.* constant smoking [away
Fumaison, *s.f.* manuring
Fumarate, *s.m.* (*chem.*) fumarate
Fumarine, *s.f.* (*chem.*) fumarine
Fumarique, *adj.* (*chem.*) fumaric
Fumarolle, *s.f.* *V.* **Fumerolle**
Fumé, e, *part. adj.* smoked; manured; (*pop.*) done for, done, lost, gone
Fumé, *s.m.* (*engr.*) smoke-proof
Fumée, *s.f.* smoke; reek; fume; vapour; steam; vanity, phantom, bubble; dream; vain hope; **—s,** *pl.* fumes, &c.; (*hunt.*) fumet, dung
Fumer, *v.a.n.* to smoke; to smoke-dry; to manure; to reek; to steam; to fume, to fret, to be in a rage, to rage. *Se* —, to become *or* be smoked
Fumerie, *s.f.* opium-smoking room; (*fam.*) smoking (*of tobacco*, &c.) [hole
Fumerolle, *s.f.* (*of volcanoes*) fumarole, smoke-
Fumeron, *s.m.* smoky bit of charcoal, smoking charcoal; (*jest.*) inveterate smoker; (*pop.*) hypocrite, sneak
Fumet, *s.m.* flavour; (*hunt.*) scent
Fumetereau, Fumeteron, *s.m.* lump of
Fumeterre, *s.f.* (*bot.*) fumitory [manure
Fumeu-r, se, *s.m.f.* smoker
Fumeuse, *s.f.* smoking-chair; (female) smoker; — *adj.f.* *V.* **Fumeux** [heady
Fumeu-x, se, *adj.* smoky; fumous, fumy;
Fumier, *s.m.* muck; dung; mulch; manure; dunghill; litter; trash, rubbish
Fumifuge, *adj.* smoke-preventing; — *s.m.* smoke-preventer
Fumigateur, *s.m.* fumigator (*pers., instr.*)
Fumigation, *s.f.* fumigation, fumigating; smoking [*boîte* —, fumigator
Fumigatoire, *adj.* fumigating. *Appareil* or
Fumiger, *v.a.* to fumigate
Fumiste, *s.m.* chimney-builder *or* mender, bricklayer, chimney-doctor
Fumisterie, *s.f.* chimney-building *or* mending
Fumivore, *adj.* smoke-consuming; — *s.m.* smoke-consumer
Fumivorité, *s.f.* smoke-consuming contrivance
Fumoir, *s.m.* smoking-room; smoking-divan;
Fumosité, *s.f.* fumosity [smoking-place
Fumure, *s.f.* dung, manure; manuring
Funaire, *s.f.* (*bot.*) funaria
Funambule, *s.m.f.* funambulist, rope-walker *or* dancer, acrobat; — *adj.* funambulatory,
Funambulie, *s.f.* funambulation [acrobatic
Fune, *s.f.* (*nav.*) cordage, rope, line
Funèbre, *adj.* funeral, funereal; of the dead, dead; mournful; melancholy; dismal; ominous
Funèbrement, *adv.* funerally, funereally, mournfully, dismally, ominously
Funer, *v.a.* (*nav.*) to rig (*a mast*)
†Funérailles, *s.f.pl.* funeral, obsequies, interment, funeral rites [rative, memorial
Funéraire, *adj.* funeral, funereal; commemo-
Funeste, *adj.* fatal, baneful, baleful; disastrous; unlucky; sad, sorrowful, melancholy, distressing
Funestement, *adv.* fatally; unluckily; sadly
Fungate, Fungine, Fungique, Fungus, &c. *V.* **Fongate,** &c. (*with* **o**)
Funiculaire, *adj.* (*mech., math.*) funicular; — *s.f.* (*math.*) funicular curve, catenary curve, catenary
Funicule, *s.m.* (*bot.*) funiculus, funicle
Funin, *s.m.* (*nav.*) running rigging, rope, hawser. *Franc-* —, cable, hawser; white hawser
Fur. *Au — et à mesure*, in proportion, proportionally; in succession, successively, one after another; as soon (as); as fast (as)
Furet, *s.m.* (*zool.*) ferret; (*pers.*) ferreter, Paul Pry; (*also, a game similar to hunt the-slipper*)
Furetage, *s.m.* hunting with a ferret; ferreting
Fureter, *v.n.a.* to hunt with a ferret; to ferret, to ferret out, to search, to search out, to rummage, to ransack, to pry about, to pry into, to hunt after [prier; hunter
Fureteu-r, se, *s.m.f.* ferreter; rummager;
Fureur, *s.f.* fury; rage; madness; frenzy; mania, passion; transport, rapture; enthusiasm; furore. *Faire* —, to be the rage, to be quite the rage, to be all the rage, to be in great vogue or fashion; to rage
Furfuracé, e, *adj.* furfuraceous, scurfy
Furfures, *s.f.pl.* dandriff, scurf
Furfurol, Furfurole, *s.m.* (*chem.*) furfurol
Furibond, e, *adj.* furious, raging, wild, mad; — *s.m.f.* ditto person [fume
Furibonder, *v.n.* to be in a rage, to rage, to
Furie, *s.f.* fury, rage; heat; height; (*myth.*) Fury
Furieusement, *adv.* furiously, tremendously, terribly, awfully, excessively, extraordinarily, prodigiously; with a vengeance; a rare lot
Furieu-x, se, *adj.* furious, mad; enraged; in a rage; raging; raving; impetuous; tremendous, terrible, awful, excessive, extraordinary, prodigious, rare, confounded; — *s.m.f.* madman,
Furin, *s.m.* open sea, deep water [mad woman
Furioso, *adj.m. adv.* (*mus.*) furioso
Furmint, *s.m.* Tokay vine
Furolles, *s.f.pl.* fiery exhalations
Furon, *s.m.* young ferret
Furoncle, *s.m.* furuncle, boil
Furonculeu-x, se, *adj.* (*med.*) furuncular
Furti-f, ve, *adj.* furtive, stealthy, secret; sly
Furtivement, *adv.* furtively, stealthily, by stealth, secretly; slily [away, I went
Fus, *pret. of* **Être.** *Je m'en* —, (*old*) I went
Fusain, *s.m.* (*bot.*) spindle-tree, prick-wood; (*draw.*) prick-wood charcoal, crayon
Fusarolle, *s.f.* (*arch.*) fusarole
Fuscine, *s.f.* (*chem.*) fuscine
Fuscite, *s.m* (*min.*) fuscite [lime
Fusé, e, *part. of* **Fuser.** *Chaux —e*, air-slaked
Fuseau, *s.m.* spindle; bobbin; (*of lace*) bobbin, bone; (*mollusc*) fusus, red whelk, roaring buckie; (*her.*) fusil. *Jambes de* —, spindle-shanks
Fusée, *s.f.* spindleful; bobbinful; (*fireworks, mil.*) rocket; (*artil.*) fuze, fuse; (*horol.*) fusee; (*of kitchen-jacks, of capstans*) barrel; (*mach.*) gudgeon; (*of oars*) dolphin; (*vet.*) splint, splent; (*her.*) fusil; (*fig.*) intricate business, tangle, intrigue; flash, dash, burst, freak, squib; (*mus.*) rapid passage; (*pop.*) spew. — *d'amorce*, (*artil.*) tube. — *porte-amarre*, (*nav.*) life-saving rocket, life-rocket, line-rocket, life-saving *or* ship-saving apparatus. — *volante*, sky-rocket. *Lâcher une* —, (*pop.*) to shoot the cat, to spew
Fuséen, *s.m.* (*mil.*) rocketer, rocket-gunner
Fuselé, e, *adj.* spindle-shaped, taper, tapering, [slender; (*her.*) fusile
Fuseler, *v.a.* to taper
Fuselier, *s.m.* spindle-maker; bobbin-maker
Fusement, *s.m.* expansion; fusion; deflagration
Fuser, *v.n.* to expand, to spread; to fuse, to melt, to dissolve; to deflagrate
Fusibilité, *s.f.* fusibility
Fusible, *adj.* fusible
Fusiforme, *adj.* fusiform, spindle-shaped
Fusil, *s.m.* hand-gun, gun, musket, firelock; steel (*to sharpen knives or to strike a light*); sharpener, whetstone; tinder-box. — *de chasse*, sporting-gun, gun, fowling-piece. — *de munition*, musket. — *de rempart*, wall-piece. — *à aiguille*, needle-gun. — *à piston*, percussion-gun *or* musket. — *à pierre*, flint-gun, flint-lock musket. *Pierre à* —, flint, gun-flint. — *à vent*, air-gun. *Canon de* —, gun-barrel
Fusilier, *s.m.* (*mil.*) fusilier, fusileer
Fusilière, *adj.f.* *Pierre* —, ragstone
†Fusillade, *s.f.* fusillade, discharge *or* volley of musketry; firing, shooting
†Fusiller, *v.a.* to fusillade; to shoot; to fire at; to sharpen, to steel
Fusion, *s.f.* fusion, melting; blending; coali-
Fusioniste, *s.m.f. adj.* fusionist [tion

Fusionnement, *s.m.* fusion, blending, amalgamation, coalescence, union
Fusionner, *v.a.n.*, **Se** —, *v.r.* to fuse, to blend, to amalgamate, to unite, to coalesce (*v.n.*)
Fustanelle, *s.f. V.* **Foustanelle**
Fuste, *s.f.* (*obsolete*) foist (*galley*)
Fustereau, *s.m.* small light boat
Fustet, *s.m.* (*bot.*) Venetian sumach, smoke-tree; (*dye-wood*) fustet, young fustic
Fustigation, *s.f.* fustigation, whipping, flogging, scourging
Fustiger, *v.a.* to whip, to flog, to scourge
Fustine, *s.f.* (*chem.*) fustine [fustic
Fustoc, Fustok, *s.m.* (*dye-wood*) old fustic,
Fût, *s.m.* cask, wood; stock (*of a gun*, &c.); barrel (*of a drum*); shaft (*of a column, of a candelabrum*); trunk; stem; staff (*of a halberd*); case (*of an organ*); horn (*of a deer*); (*nav.*) stock (*of a vane*)
Futaie, *s.f.* wood *or* forest of high *or* lofty trees, forest-trees, timber-trees. *Demi-* —, forest of half-grown trees. *Haute* —, forest of full-grown trees. *Arbre de haute* —, full-grown forest-tree, timber-tree. *Bois de haute* —, wood of full-grown trees, high *or* lofty trees, timber-trees, timber [staves of a cask
†**Futaille,** *s.f.* cask, barrel; casks. — *en bottes*,
†**Futaillerie,** *s.f.* stave-wood
Futaine, *s.f.* fustian
Futainier, *s.m.* fustian-maker
Futé, e, *adj.* crafty, cunning, sly, sharp, shrewd, deep, knowing, clever; (*her.*) fute; — *s.f.* joiner's
Futile, *adj.* futile, trifling, frivolous [putty
Futilité, *s.f.* futility, frivolity; trifle
Futur, e, *adj.* future, to come; intended; — *s.m.* futurity, future, prospects; (*gram.*) future tense, future; — *s.m.f.* intended, future husband *or* wife, bridegroom, bride
Futurition, *s.f.* futurition
Fuyant, e, *part. adj.* flying, fleeing, &c. (*V.* **Fuir**); fleeting; fading; tapering; receding, retreating; — *s.m.* tapering *or* receding part, perspective
Fuyard, e, *adj. s.* fugitive; runaway

G

G, *s.m.* g
Gabarage, *s.m.* lighterage
Gabare, *s.f.* lighter; transport, transport-ship, store ship; barge; fishing-boat; trawl-net,
Gabarer, *v.n.* (*old*) *V.* **Godiller** [drag-net
Gabari, *s.m.* (*nav. arch.*) mould, model, draught, gauge, frame-timber; (*mil.*) capacity, size, model, draught, gauge
Gabariage, *s.m.* (*nav. arch.*) moulding
Gabarier, *s.m.* lighterman; master of a store-ship; lumper; — *v.a.* (*nav. arch.*) to mould, to
Gabarieur, *s.m.* (*nav. arch.*) moulder [model
Gabarit, *s.m. V.* **Gabari** [little boat
Gabarot, *s.m.*, **Gabarote,** *s.f.* small lighter,
Gabatine, *s.f.* (*pop.*) flam, humbug, hoax, trick, practical joke. *Donner de la* —, to bamboozle,
Gabegie, *s.f.* (*pop.*) trickery, cheat [to humbug
Gabelage, *s.m.* time for drying salt; excise
Gabeler, *v.a.* to dry (*salt*) [mark on the salt
Gabeleur, *s.m.* salt-dryer; (*old*) gabeller, gabelman [tax; salt-store; excise; excise-office
Gabelle, *s.f.* (*obsolete*) gabel, duty on salt, salt-
Gabelou, *s.m.* (*pop., in contempt*) custom-house officer; toll-collector; exciseman
Gaber, *v.a., v.n., v.r.* (*old*) *V.* **Gausser**
Gabet, *s.m.* (*nav.*) vane
Gabian, *s.m. Huile de* —, Gabian oil, French
Gabie, *s.f.* (*nav., local*) top [petroleum
Gabier, *s.m.* (*nav.*) top-man
Gabion, *s.m.* (*fort.*) gabion; (*agr.*) basket
Gabionnade, *s.f.* (*fort.*) gabionade
Gabionnage, *s.m.* (*fort.*) gabionage
Gabionner, *v.a.* (*fort.*) to gabion, to cover with
Gabionneur, *s.m.* (*fort.*) gabion-man [gabions
Gabord, *s.m.* (*nav.*) garboard
Gabronite, *s.f.* (*min.*) gabronite
Gaburon, *s.m.* (*nav.*) fish, clamp
Gâche, *s.f.* staple; wall-hook; (*bricklayer's labourer's*) shovel; (*pastrycook's*) spatula *or* pestle
Gâcher, *v.a.* to temper (*mortar*); to rinse (*linen*); (*fig.*) to bungle, to botch, to make a mess of, to spoil; to waste; to fritter away; (*agr.*) to harrow; (*com.*) to sell under price
Gâchette, *s.f.* spring; (*of a firelock*) sear; (*of ditto, abusively for* "détente") trigger
Gâcheu-r, se, *s.m.f.* bricklayer's *or* mason's labourer; bungler, botcher; waster; underseller; — *adj.* bungling, botching; wasteful, extravagant
Gâcheu-x, se, *adj.* miry, muddy, dirty, splashy, sloppy, swampy; — *s.m.* (*jest.*) usher (*in a school*), paltry schoolmaster [waste; row, riot, kick-up
Gâchis, *s.m.* mortar; mess, slush, splash, slop;
Gade, *s.m.* (*zool.*) gadus, cod-fish; — *s.f.* (*local*)
Gadelle, *s.f.* (*local*) currant [currant
Gadellier, *s.m.* (*local*) currant-tree
Gadin, *s.m.* (*pop.*) cork; old ramshackle hat
Gadoïde, *s.m.* (*zool.*) gadoid, cod-fish
Gadolinite, *s.f.* (*min.*) gadolinite [ger
Gadouard, *s.m.* nightman; sewerman; scaven-
Gadoue, *s.f.* night-soil, night-manure, dirt, filth, sewage matter, sewage, drainage; (*pop.*)
Gaduine, *s.f.* (*chem.*) gaduine [trollop, trull
Gaélique, *adj.m.f.*, *s.m.* Gaelic
Gaffe, *s.f.* boat-hook; (*fish.*) gaff; (*pop.*) tongue
Gaffeau, *s.m.* small boat-hook *or* gaff
Gaffer, *v.a.* to hook
Gage, *s.m.* pledge; pawn; deposit; stake, stake security; token; testimony; mark; proof; promise, assurance; gage; (*at play*) forfeit; (*law*) pledge, lien; —**s**, *pl.* pledges, &c.; wages, pay, hire. *A* —*s*, hired, paid. *Prendre à* —*s*, to hire
Gager, *v.a.n.* to bet, to lay, to wager; to lay a wager; to undertake to say, to dare say, to undertake to predict, to be almost certain; to hire; to pay; (*old*) to undertake, to pledge one-
Gagerie, *s.f. V.* **Saisie** [self
Gageu-r, se, *s.m.f. V.* **Parieur**
Gageure, *s.f.* wager, bet, betting; stake, stakes
Gagiste, *s.m.* person hired, hireling, hired assistant, under-clerk, servant (*not domestic*), man, supernumerary; bandsman
†**Gagnable,** *adj.* gainable; to be earned *or* won; obtainable, procurable
†**Gagnage,** *s.m.* pasture-ground, pasture
†**Gagnant, e,** *s.m.f.* winner; — *adj.* winning
†**Gagne,** *s.m.f.* (*in compounds, from* **Gagner,** "to gain," "to earn," "to win," &c.) thing (*m.*) *or* person (*m.f.*) that gains *or* procures *or* wins *or* earns *or* &c., gainer, winner, &c. — **-deniers,** *s.m.* (*obsolete*) labourer, day-labourer. — **-pain,** *s.m.* bread-winner, means of living *or* of subsistence, support, tool, livelihood, daily bread, bread and cheese. — **-petit,** *s.m.* knife-grinder, grinder
†**Gagné, e,** *part. adj.* gained, &c. (*V.* **Gagner**). *Donner* —, to own oneself beaten, to give it up. *Avoir ville* —*e*, to carry the day, to gain o.'s point, to succeed. *Croire* or *crier ville* —*e*, to make sure of success, to cry out victory
†**Gagner,** *v.a.n.* to gain; to be a gainer; to earn; to win; to obtain; to get; to acquire; to procure; to receive; to carry, to take; to save; to prepossess; to persuade; to prevail on; to conciliate; to bring over; to win over; to gain over; to bribe, to corrupt; to entice, to allure, to attract, to captivate, to charm; to catch; to reach; to attain to, to arrive at, to get to; to pervade; to come over, to seize; to overtake; to get the better of; to beat; to deserve; to gain ground; to extend; to spread; to improve; to rise; to be the better (for). — *à être connu*, to improve upon acquaintance

Se —, *v.r.* to be catching *or* contagious; to be caught; to be gained *or* earned *or* &c.; to gain, to acquire, to get, to make
†Gagneu-r, se, *s.m.f.* gainer, winner
Gaguie, *s.f.* (*pop.*) buxom woman
Gai, e, *adj.* gay, lively, cheerful, merry; exhilarating; amusing, entertaining; pleasant; free; loose; (*of herrings*) shotten; (*of horses in heraldry*) without saddle or bridle; — *adv. int.* gaily, merrily; cheer! tol-de-rol-lol!
Gaïac, *s.m.* (*bot.*) guaiacum, guaiac, lignum-vitæ
Gaïacène, *s.f.* (*chem.*) guaiacyl
Gaïacine, *s.f.* (*chem.*) guaiacine
Gaïacique, *adj.* (*chem.*) guaiacic [**Gaîment**
Gaiement, *adv.* (*old and absurd spelling*) *V.*
Gaieté, *s.f.* gaiety, liveliness, cheerfulness, mirth, merriment; humour; fun. *En* —, merry, mellow, fresh (*tipsy*)
†Gaillard, e, *adj.* merry, sprightly, lively, jolly; free, wanton; bold; spirited; brisk; hearty; healthy, fresh; cool, fresh; tipsy, fresh
†Gaillard, *s.m.* merry *or* jolly fellow; determined fellow; fellow, chap, buck, body; (*in fables*) squire, master; (*nav.*) castle. — *d'arrière*, quarter-deck. — *d'avant*, forecastle
†Gaillarde, *s.f.* merry *or* somewhat gay woman; bold *or* determined woman; body; (*obsolete sprightly dance and tune*) gaillarde, galliard; (*print.*) bourgeois
†Gaillardement, *adv.* merrily; freely; briskly; heartily; boldly; rashly; bluntly
†Gaillardise, *s.f.* gaiety, sprightliness, jollity, mirth; frolic, sport, fun; rather free talk
†Gaillet, *s.m.* (*bot.*) *V.* **Caille-lait**
Gaiment, *adv.* gaily, cheerfully, merrily; heartily; willingly, readily; briskly; freely, at o.'s ease [ing; winning; success
Gain, *s.m.* gain, profit; advantage; lucre; gain-
Gaîne, *s.f.* case; sheath; (*arch.*) terminal
Gaînerie, *s.f.* case and sheath-making; case and sheath-trade; cases, sheathes [Judas-tree
Gaînier, *s.m.* case and sheath-maker; (*bot.*)
Gaîté, *s.f.* *V.* **Gaieté**
Gal, *s.m.* (*fish*) zeus gallus (*kind of dory*)
Gala, *s.m.* gala, feast, banquet, entertainment. *De* —, (*adject.*) gala-day, gala, festive; birthday; state [*adj.* galactagogic
Galactagogue, *s.m.* (*med.*) galactagogue; —
Galactite, *s.f.* (*min.*, *bot.*) galactite
Galactodendron, *s.m.* (*bot.*) galactodendron, milk-tree, cow-tree
Galacto-graphie, -logie. *V.* page 3, § 1
Galactomètre, *s.m.* galactometer, lactometer
Galactophage, *s.m.f.* galactophagist; — *adj.* galactophagous [*s.m.* (*instr.*) nipple
Galactophore, *adj.* (*anat.*) galactophorous; —
Galactophorite, *s.f.* (*med.*) galactophoritis
Galactoposie, *s.f.* (*med.*) galactoposia
Galactorrhée, *s.f.* (*med.*) galactorrhœa
Galactose, *s.f.* (*physiology*) galactosis
Galacturie, *s.f.* (*med.*) galacturia
Galago, *s.m.* (*zool.*) galago, gum animal
Galamment, *adv.* politely, courteously, gallantly; flatteringly; handsomely; in fine style; nobly; readily; skilfully, cleverly; tastefully,
Galane, *s.f.* (*bot.*) *V.* **Chélone** [elegantly
Galanga, *s.m.* (*bot.*) galanga
Galant, e, *adj.* polite, courteous (*to ladies*), gallant; complimentary, flattering, civil, kind; worthy, honest; handsome, in good taste, tasteful, genteel, elegant, stylish, pretty; gay; of gallantry, of love. — *homme*, gentleman, man of honour, honest man; fine fellow. *Homme* —, courteous man; ladies' man. *Femme* or *dame* —*e*, gay woman
Galant, *s.m.* spark; gallant, wooer, suitor, lover; (*obsolete*) fellow, brisk *or* sharp *or* shrewd fellow; (*obsolete*) bow (*of ribbons*). *Vert* —, dashing ladies' man, brisk spark, great admirer of the sex
Galanterie, *s.f.* politeness, courtesy, gallantry; compliment; present; attention; love-affair *or* intrigue, love-making, gallantry; the smart consequences of ditto; elegance; (*obsolete*)
Galanthe, *s.m.* (*bot.*) snowdrop [trick; hobble
Galantin, *s.m.* dangler, beau [drop
Galantine, *s.f.* (*cook.*) galantine; (*bot.*) snow-
Galantiser, *v.a.n.* (*old*) to court, to dangle about, to flirt with the ladies
Galapian, Galapiat, *s.m.* (*pop.*) vagabond, dirty fellow, blackguard
Galate, *s.m.f. adj.* Galatian
Galatée, *s.f.* (*shell-fish*) galathæa
Galauban, *s.m.* *V.* **Galhauban**
Galaxie, *s.f.* (*astr.*) galaxy, milky-way
Galbanon, *s.m.* (*pop.*) *V.* **Cabanon** [whiting
Galbanoner, *v.a.* to clean (*windows*) with
Galbanum, *s.m.* (*bot.*, *pharm.*) galbanum; (*fig.*) empty promises, false hopes, humbug, gammon, soft-sawder, blarney
Galbe, *s.m.* graceful outline, outline, swelling, rounding, sweep, curve, contour, entasis; (*fam.*) countenance, look, tidy *or* swellish look, style, elegance [graceful
Galbé, e, *adj.* (*arch.*) outlined, in outline;
Galber, *v.a.* (*arch.*) to outline, to give a graceful contour to
Galbeu-x, se, *adj.* (*fam.*) stylish, swellish
Galbule, *s.m.* (*bot.*) galbulus, galbule, berry; (*bird*) galbula, jacamar
Gale, *s.f.* itch; mange; scab; (*bot.*) scurf; (*pers.*, *fam.*) spiteful *or* peevish *or* mischievous brute. *Mauvais* or *méchant comme la* —, very spiteful,
Galé, *s.m.* (*bot.*) gale [a very demon
Galéace, Galéasse, *s.f.* (*nav.*) galeas, galley
Galée, *s.f.* (*print.*) galley
Galéga, *s.m.* (*bot.*) galega, goat's rue
Galéiforme, *adj.* (*bot.*) galeate, galeated
Galène, *s.f.* (*min.*) galena, lead-glance
Galén-ique, -isme, -iste. *V.* page 3, § 1
Galéopithèque, *s.m.* (*zool.*) galeopithecus, flying lemur, colugo
Galéopsis, *s.m.* (*bot.*) galeopsis, hemp-nettle
Galer, *v.a.* (*pop.*) to scratch, to rub
Galère, *s.f.* galley; hand-truck; Spanish waggon; drudgery; wretched place; —**s**, *pl.* galleys, penal servitude. *Mal de* —, world of trouble; dreadful pain. *Vie de* —, life of a galley-slave, wretched life. *Vogue la* —*!* happen *or* come what may! *Qu'allait-il faire dans cette* —*?* what business has he there?
Galerie, *s.f.* gallery; passage; (*mach.*) footboard; (*mining*) adit, drift, level, gallery; (*of furniture*) gallery, rim, beading; (*for curtains*) cornice; (*fig.*) spectators, lookers-on, company, public; customary walk. — *de l'entrepont* or *du faux pont*, (*nav.*) gangway. *Faire* —, to look on, to make only a show, to be a wall-flower
Galérien, *s.m.* galley-slave, convict
Galérite, *s.f.* (*fossil*) galerite, sugar-loaf
Galerne, *s.f.* (*local*) north-west wind
Galéruque, *s.f.* (*insect*) galeruca
Galet, *s.m.* pebble; shingle; (*tech.*) friction-roller; (*fish.*) buoy; (*old game*) shove-board, shovel-board, shuffle-board
Galetas, *s.m.* garret, attic; (*fig.*) hole
Galette, *s.f.* (flat) cake; buttered roll; (*nav.*) biscuit; (*jest.*) flat mattress, (*soldier's*) shoulder-scale; (*of a hat*) body; (*of silk*) knubs; (*pop.*) blockhead; fogy, old fogy
Galettoire, *s.f.* (*local*) frying-pan
Galeu-x, se, *adj.* itchy; scabby, mangy; scurfy; — *s.m.f.* one infected with the itch; scabby fellow *or* thing
Galgal, *s.m.* barrow, cairn, sepulchral mound
Galgale, *s.f.* (*nav.*) mastic
Galhauban, *s.m.* (*nav.*) back-stay
Galicien, ne, *adj. s.* Galician
Galiléen, ne, *adj. s.* Galilean
Galimafré, *s.m.* clown [mishmash
Galimafrée, *s.f.* gallimaufry, hotch-potch,
Galimatias, *s.m.* nonsense, balderdash, rigmarole, gibberish, stuff, bosh; medley, confusion, bother. — *double*, sheer nonsense

Galion, *s.m.* (*nav.*) galleon
Galiote, *s.f.* (*nav.*) galiot, galliot; (*obsolete*) boat, bark; (*bot.*) bennet; (*slang*) conspiracy of card-sharpers. — *à bombes,* (*old*) bomb-ketch, bomb-vessel
Galipée, *s.f.* (*bot.*) galipea
Galipot, *s.m.* galipot, Burgundy pitch
Galipoter, *v.a.* (*nav.*) to pitch
Gallate, *s.m.* (*chem.*) gallate
Galle, *s.f.* gall; gall-nut; oak-apple, oak-gall
Gallérie, *s.f.* (*zool.*) bee-moth, honeycomb-moth, wax-moth
Galliambe, *s.m.*, **Galliambique,** *adj.* (*ancient vers.*) galliambic
Gallican, e, *adj. s.* Gallican, French
Gallicanisme, Gallicisme. *V.* page 3, § 1
Gallicien, ne, *adj. s.* Galician (*of Austria*)
Gallifère, *adj.* (*bot.*) galliferous
Gallinace, *s.f.* (*min.*) obsidian
Gallinacé, e, *adj.* (*zool.*) gallinaceous; — *s.m.* gallinacean, gallinaceous bird
Galline, *adj.f.* galline, cock, of cocks, of the cock
Gallinsectes, *s.m.pl.* gall-insects, scale-insects, scales
Gallinule, *s.f.* (*zool.*) gallinule, water-hen, moor-hen
Gallique, *adj.* (*chem.*) gallic; (*geog.*) Gallic
Gallisme, *s.m.* Gallism (*system of Dr. Gall*)
Galliste, *s.m.f.* Gallist (*partisan of Dr. Gall's system*); — *adj.* Gallistic
Gallo-, (*in compounds*) gallo-...
Gallois, e, *adj. s.* Welsh; Welshman, Welsh boy; Welsh woman *or* lady *or* girl
Gallomane, *adj. s.m.f.* gallomaniac
Gallomanie, *s.f.* gallomania
Gallomaniser, *v.a.* to make (*one*) a gallomaniac
Se —, *v.r.* to become a gallomaniac
Gallon, *s.m.* (*Engl. meas.*) gallon; (*bot.*) gall acorn
Gallophobe, *adj. s.m.f.* gallophobic; person affected with gallophobia, gallophobist, gallophobiac
Gallophobie, *s.f.* gallophobia
Gallo-romain, e, *adj. s.* Gallo-Roman
Galoche, *s.f.* golosh, clog; (*nav.*) clamp, hollow cleat. *Menton de —,* long peaked chin, turned-up chin
Galochier, *s.m.* golosh-maker
Galon, *s.m.* lace, galloon; tape; binding; band; stripe; (*pop.*) crust, scurf. *Vieux habits, vieux —s! habits, —s!* clo', clo'!
Galonner, *v.a.* to lace; to stripe
Galonnier, *s.m.* lace-maker, galloon-maker
Galop, *s.m.* gallop; galloping; (*dance, tune*) galop; (*fig., fam.*) great haste; blowing-up. *Grand —, — de charge,* full gallop. *Petit —,* hand gallop, canter
Galopade, *s.f.* galloping; gallop; (*old dance*) gallopade; (*fam.*) blowing-up
Galopante, *adj.f.* (*med., of consumption*) galloping, rapid
Galoper, *v.n.* to gallop; to run, to run on *or* about, to hasten, to make haste; to dance the galop; — *v.a.* to gallop; to run *or* hunt after, to pursue; to press; (*of fear, fever, &c.*) to seize, to have got hold of; (*pop.*) to hurry over, to despatch, to knock off, to botch up, to bungle
Galopin, *s.m.* errand-boy; scullion; apprentice; urchin, rogue, imp; vagabond, low *or* dirty fellow, blackguard
Galoubet, *s.m.* galoubet, tabour-pipe, three-hole flute
Galuchat, *s.m.* dog-fish skin, fish-skin
Galvan-ique, -iquement. *V.* page 3, § 1
Galvanisation, *s.f.* galvanization, galvanizing
Galvaniser, *v.a.* to galvanize
Galvaniseur, *s.m.* galvanizer
Galvan-isme, -iste. *V.* page 3, § 1
Galvano-, (*in compounds*) galvano-...
Galvanomètre, *s.m.* galvanometer
Galvanoplaste, *s.m.* electro-plater
Galvanoplastie, *s.f.* electro-plating; electro-plate
Galvanoplastique, *adj.* electro-plating, galvanoplastic
Galvanoscope, *s.m.* galvanoscope
Galvanotypie, &c. *V.* **Électrotypie,** &c.
Galvaudage, *s.m.* (*fam.*) disorder, confusion, jumble; botching, bungling; waste; squandering; ruination; jobbing, jobbery; disgrace
Galvauder, *v.a.n.* (*fam.*) to disorder, to disturb, to confuse, to jumble, to rummage; to spoil, to botch, to bungle; to make a mess of; to waste; to squander; to job; to disgrace, to degrade; (*obsolete*) to taunt, to rate, to blow up
Galvaudeu-x, se, *s.m.f.* (*pop.*) loose fish, rake
Gamache, *s.f.* (*obsolete*) gamash, gambado, spatterdash, legging; (*bird*) blackcap; (*bot.*) kind of apple. *Noces de Gamache,* splendid feast
Gamande, *s.f.* (kind of chestnut)
Gamandier, *s.m.* (kind of chestnut-tree)
Gamay, *s.m.* (inferior kind of Burgundy vine)
Gambade, *s.f.* gambol, caper; soft-sawder, blarney
Gambader, *v.n.* to gambol, to frisk about, to caper, to skip; to play tricks
Gambadeu-r, se, *s.m.f.* gamboller, caperer
Gambe, *s.f.* (*nav.*) foot-hook shroud
Gambette, *s.f.* (*bird*) gambet, redshank
†Gambillard, e, *s.m.f.* (*pop.*) restless person, fidget; great walker
†Gambille, *s.f.* (*pop.*) shank, stump, leg
†Gambiller, *v.n.* (*pop.*) to kick about, to fidget; to caper, to dance
Gambir, *s.m.* gambir, gambeer, gambier
Gambit, *s.m.* (*at chess*) gambit
Gambodique, *adj.* (*chem.*) gambogic, gambodic
Gamelle, *s.f.* (*mil., nav.*) bowl, basin, dish; mess
Gamet, *s.m. V.* **Gamay;** (*pop.*) Paris sour wine grape
Gamin, *s.m.* blackguard-boy, little blackguard, young vagabond, rogue, street-boy, street Arab, cad; urchin, brat, cub, chit, young one; little boy, boy, mere boy
Gamine, *s.f.* romp, hoiden, saucy little baggage; little girl, girl, mere girl
Gaminer, *v.n.* to play the blackguard; to be boyish *or* girlish; to romp, to hoiden
Gaminerie, *s.f.* low trick; boyish trick *or* prank
Gammare, *s.m.* gammarus, freshwater shrimp
Gamme, *s.f.* (*mus.*) gamut, scale; (*fig.*) scale; comprehension; tone; lecture, blowing-up; correction, trimming, dressing. *Hors de —,* put out, out, puzzled, in a fix; unprepared. *Changer de —,* to alter o.'s tone; to turn over a new leaf. *Chanter la* or *sa —,* to give a lecture *or* a blowing-up, to lecture, to blow up; to sing out. *Faire chanter une —,* to give a trimming, to make (*one*) sing out. *Monter une —,* to lecture, to blow up, to give a lecture *or* a blowing-up
Ganache, *s.f.* lower jaw (*of a horse*); easy chair, hall-porter's chair; (*pers.*) blockhead, dolt; fogy, old fogy. *Chargé de —,* heavy-headed
Gandin, *s.m.* swell, dandy, fop, dundreary
Gandine, *s.f.* fast girl, gay woman
Gandinerie, *s.f.*, **Gandinisme,** *s.m.* dandyism, foppery; fops, dundrearies and fast girls
Ganelonnerie, *s.f.* (*obsolete*) treachery, treacherousness
Ganga, *s.m.* (*bird*) ganga, sand-grouse
Gangétique, *adj.* Gangetic
Gangliforme, *adj.* (*anat.*) gangliform
Ganglion, *s.m.* (*anat.*) ganglion; (*med.*) gland
Ganglionite, *s.f.* (*med.*) ganglionitis
Ganglionnaire, *adj.* ganglionary
Ganglionné, e, *adj.* ganglionic, ganglial
Gangrène, *s.f.* gangrene, mortification; (*bot., fig.*) canker
Gangrener, *v.a.*, **Se —,** *v.r.* to gangrene, to mortify; (*bot., fig.*) to canker
Gangrenescence, *s.f.* gangrenescence
Gangrenescent, e, *adj.* gangrenescent
Gangreneu-x, se, *adj.* gangrenous
Gangue, *s.f.* (*min.*) gangue, mineral matrice, stony matrix, vein-stone
Gangui, *s.m.* (kind of fishing-net)
Ganil, *s.m.* (*min.*) ganil
Gannaliser, *v.a.* to embalm
Gannet, *s.m.* (*bird*) wagel
Gano, *s.m.* (*at ombre*) "let the lead come to me, I have the king"
Ganse, *s.f.* cord, string, twist, gimp, edging; loop
Ganser, *v.a.* (*need.*) to cord, to gimp
Gansette, *s.f.* little cord *or* &c. (*V.* **Ganse**)
Gant, *s.m.* glove; gauntlet, gantlet; **—s,** *pl.* gloves; (*fig.*) priority; merit; credit, honour; success; present; precautions. — *bourré,* fencing-glove, boxing-glove

Ganté, e, *part. adj.* gloved, in gloves, with gloves (*or* o.'s gloves) on, &c. (*V.* **Ganter**)
Gantelée, *s.f.* (*bot.*) foxglove; throatwort
Gantelet, *s.m.* gauntlet, gantlet; (*surg.*) glove-bandage; (*tech.*) hand-leather; (*bot.*) *V.* **Gantelée**
Ganteline, *s.f. V.* **Gantelée**
Ganter, *v.a.* to glove; to put gloves on; to supply with gloves; to fit with gloves; to fit; to suit. *Être ganté*, to have (o.'s) gloves on. *Être bien ganté*, to have nice *or* good gloves on, to have on gloves that fit well
Se —, *v.r.* to put on o.'s gloves; to wear gloves that fit (well *or* badly); to supply oneself with gloves; to get o.'s gloves (at); to buy gloves (of); to be gloved *or* &c.
Ganterie, *s.f.* glove-making; glove-trade; glove-shop; gloves
Ganti-er, ère, *s.m.f.* glover, glove-maker
Gantilier, *s.m. V.* **Gantelée**
Gantois, e, *adj. s.* of Ghent, native of Ghent, Ghenter, Gantois
Ganymède, *s.m.* minion
Garage, *s.m.* putting into dock; (*rail.*) shunting. *Voie de —*, (*rail.*) shunt, siding, turn-out
Garançage, *s.m.* maddering, madder-dyeing
Garance, *s.f.* (*bot., dyeing*) madder; — *s.m.* madder colour, madder red, madder, garance; — *adj.* madder-coloured, madder-dyed, red, garance. *Pantalon —*, (*fig.*) (French) soldier
Garancer, *v.a.* to madder, to dye red (with madder)
Garanceur, *s.m.* madder-dyer
Garancière, *s.f.* madder-field; madder-works
Garancine, *s.f.* (*chem.*) garancine
Garant, e, *s.m.f.* guarantee; voucher; warrantor; surety; security; warranty; pledge; authority; informant; proof. *Être — de*, to be guarantee *or* &c. for; to guarantee; to warrant; to pledge oneself for; to be answerable for; to answer for; to attest
Garant, *s.m.* (*nav.*) fall, tackle-fall; laniard
Garanti, e, *s.m.f.* warrantee
Garantie, *s.f.* guarantee; warranty; warranting; voucher; security; pledge; assurance; protection. *Bureau de —*, assay-office
Garantir, *v.a.* to guarantee; to warrant; to answer for; to pledge; to attest; to certify; to declare, to pronounce; to assure; to insure; to secure; to keep, to preserve, to protect, to guard, to shelter, to screen, to shield
Garantisseur, *s.m.* warranter, warrantor
Garbin, *s.m.* (*local*) south-west wind
Garbon, *s.m.* cock-partridge
Garbure, *s.f.* soup of cabbage and bacon
Garce, *s.f.* wretch, beast, bitch, strumpet, wench, drab; (*obsolete, boorish*) girl, lass, wench, woman. *— de ...*, bitch of a ...; wretched ..., beastly ...
Garcette, *s.f.* (*nav.*) gasket, point, line, nipper; cat o' nine tails, cat; (*manu.*) burling-tweezers
Garçon, *s.m.* boy; lad; fellow, chap; bachelor, single man; journeyman; servant, man; assistant; shopboy, shopman; porter; messenger; waiter. *— de collége*, college-servant *or* scout. *— de ferme*, farm-servant, hind. *— de peine*, &c. *V.* **Peine,** &c. *Premier —*, foreman. *V.* **Brave,** *adj.*
Garçonner, *v.n.* to romp, to hoiden
Garçonnet, *s.m.* little boy
Garçonnière, *s.f.* romp, tomboy, hoiden
Gardable, *adj.* to be kept; that keeps; easy to keep; guardable
Garde, *s.f.* guard; keeping; watch; police; defence; protection; custody, charge; care, heed; duty; sick-nurse, nurse; (*of locks*) ward; (*book-bind.*) fly-leaf; (*of certain swords, cross-piece*) guard: (*of certain swords, part protecting the hand*) hilt; (*of certain swords, part protecting the hand, of a peculiar shape*) bow; (*mil.*) guard; guards. *— bourgeoise*, militia. *— à vous!* (*mil.*) attention! *A la —!* police! *A la — de Dieu*, under God's protection, in God's keeping; (*fam.*) happen what may. *En —*, on o.'s guard; (*fenc.*) on guard. *Avoir — de* (*obsolete for* "N'avoir — de"). *Descendre la —*, to come off guard; (*pop.*) to tumble down; to die, to kick the bucket. *Être de —*, (*of things*) to keep; (*pers.*) to be on guard *or* on duty *or* in waiting. *Être* (*or Se tenir*) *sur ses —s*, to be on o.'s guard; to be on the watch. *Faire bonne —*, to keep good watch. *Monter la —*, to mount guard. *Monter une — à*, to rate soundly, to blow up. *N'avoir — de*, to be far from; to be careful not to, to take good care not to; to be too wise to, to know better than to; to have no wish to, to be by no means willing *or* disposed *or* inclined to; not to be likely to; not to be able to, cannot. *Prendre —*, to take care; to be careful; to mind; to beware; to take notice, to notice; to pay attention; to observe; to consider. *Prenez — de tomber*, take care not to fall, mind you don't fall, beware of falling. *Se donner de —*, to beware, to mistrust; to take care not to; to avoid. *Se mettre en —*, to guard (against); (*fenc.*) to put *or* place oneself on guard
Garde, *s.m.* guardsman, guard; keeper; warden; warder; watchman, watcher; attendant; (*in compounds, m.f., but never taking the mark of the plural when followed immediately by a substantive, from* **Garder,** "to keep," "to guard," &c.) person *or* thing that keeps, guards, &c., thing in which one keeps. — **champêtre,** *s.m.* rural guard *or* constable, field-keeper, game-keeper, keeper. — *du* **commerce,** *s.m.* sheriff's officer, bailiff. —**s** *de la* **marine,** —**s-marine,** *s.m.pl.* (*obsolete*) midshipmen, naval cadets. — **-barrière,** *s.m.f.* gate-keeper. — **-bois,** *s.m.* wood-steward, wood-reeve. — **-boutique,** *s.m.* old shopkeeper, unsalable goods. — **-bras,** *s.m.* arm-guard, vambrace. — **-cendres,** *s.m.* fender. — **-chaîne,** *s.m.* chain-guard. — **-charrue,** *s.m.* (*bird*) *V.* **Motteux.** — **-chasse,** *s.m.* game-keeper. — **-chevron,** *s.m.* (*build.*) barge-board, verge-board. — **-chiourme,** *s.m.* convict-keeper, warder. — **-corps,** *s.m.* rail, hand-rail, rails, railing, netting, man-rope; (*of capstans*) swifter. — **-côtes,** *s.m.* coast-guard; guardship, block-ship, cruiser. — **-crotte,** *s.m.* splasher, splash-board, dash-board. — **-éclusier, ière,** *s.m.f.* lock-keeper. — **-essieu,** *s.m.* axle-guard. — **-étalon,** *s.m.* stallion-keeper. — **-feu,** *s.m.* fire-guard; fender; (*nav.*) match-tub; cartridge-box. — **-fous,** *s.m.* parapet, rail, hand-rail, rails, railing; (*of capstans*) swifter. — **-frein,** *s.m.* breaksman, brakesman. — **-ligne,** *s.m.* (*rail.*) watchman. — **-magasin,** *s.m.* store-keeper; barrack-sergeant; warehouse-keeper, warehouseman; unsalable goods. — **-main,** *s.m.* hand-guard; guard-paper, guard-sheet, guard-leaf; writing-pad, blotting-pad, pad. — **-malade,** *s.f.m.* sick-nurse, nurse, attendant, watcher. — **-manche,** *s.m.* sleeve-guard, linen sleeve, half-sleeve. — **-manger,** *s.m.* larder, pantry; meat-safe, safe. — **-meubles,** *s.m.* furniture repository *or* storehouse; ditto of the crown; keeper of ditto; furniture store-warehouse, pantechnicon; store-room, lumber-room. — **-moulin,** *s.m.* mill-watchman. — **-nappe,** *s.m.* table-mat, mat. — **national,** *s.m.* national guard, militiaman. — **nationale,** *s.f.* national guard, militia. — **-notes,** *s.m.* (*obsolete, jest.*) *V.* **Notaire.** — **-pêche,** *s.m.* river-keeper. — **-port,** *s.m.* water-bailiff. — **-robe,** *s.f.* closet; wardrobe; stole; robes; water-closet; dejection, ejection, evacuation, motion, stool; (*bot.*) southernwood, lavender; *s.m.* apron. — **-rôles,** *s.m.* (*obsolete*) master of the rolls. — **-roues,** *s.m.* paddle-box. — **-salle,** *s.m.* (fencing-master's) assistant. — **-scellés,** *s.m.* seal-keeper. — **-sein,** *s.m.* milk-receiver. — **-temps,** *s.m.* time-keeper, chronometer. — **-tranchée,** *s.m.* trench-guard. — **-vaisselle,** *s.m.* yeoman of the ewry. — **-vente,** woodmerchant's agent. — **-vue,** *s.m.* shade (*eye-shade; lamp-shade*)
Gardénie, *s.f.* (*bot.*) gardenia, Cape jasmine

Garder, *v.a.* to keep; to keep on (*clothes*); to preserve; to guard; to protect; to defend; to watch; to look after; to tend; to attend to; to take care of; to nurse; to maintain, to uphold, to keep up; to observe; to let stay; to confine; to have; to save; to lay by; to lay in store; to reserve; to bear (*malice*); to owe (*a grudge*); to entertain; to forbid; to keep down *or* in; — *v.n.* (*poet.*) to beware. *En donner à — à*, to impose upon. *La — bonne à*, to have a rod in pickle for

Se —, *v.r.* to keep; to be kept *or* kept on; to keep down *or* in; to protect *or* shelter oneself; to guard (against); to beware; to take care not to, to be careful not to; to be sure not to; to refrain, to abstain, to forbear; to be far (from). *Je m'en garderai bien*, I will take good care not to do it *or* so. *Garde-t'en bien, gardez-vous-en bien*, don't you do it (*or* that), mind you don't do it (*or* that), do nothing of the kind

Garderie, *s.f.* (*of foresters*) beat, district

Gardeu-r, se, *s.m.f.* keeper, herd

Gardien, ne, *s.m.f. adj.* guardian; guard; custodian; keeper; trustee; protector, protectress; warden; warder; watchman; policeman; door-keeper, porter; bailiff's man, broker's man, possession-man; (*of convents*) superior

Gardiennage, *s.m.* keeping in repair, conservancy; keepership; trusteeship; wardenship; [custody

Gardiennat, *s.m.* superiorship

Gardon, *s.m.* (*fish*) ide, roach [ruff

Gardonnée, *adj.f. Perche —*, (*fish*) pope, ruffe,

Gare, *s.f.* terminus, station, railway-depôt; (*of rivers*) basin, dock; (*of canals*) siding; — *int.* out of the way! look out! take care! beware of; mind. *Crier* or *dire —*, to give warning *or* notice [ren

Garenne, *s.f.* warren. *— forcée*, enclosed war-

Garennier, *s.m.* warrener, warren-keeper

Garer, *v.a.* to shunt, to turn off; (*on rivers*) to put into dock, to dock, to moor, to secure

Se —, *v.r.* to shunt, to turn off; to keep in shore; to get *or* keep out of the way (of), to avoid, to beware, to take care [rant

Gargantua, *s.m.* Gargantua, glutton, cormo-

Gargantuesque, *adj.* of Gargantua; &c. *V.*

Gargariser, *v.a.* to gargle [**Pantagruélique**

Se —, *v.r.* to gargle; (*pop.*) to wet o.'s whistle; to rejoice, to chuckle [drop of something

Gargarisme, *s.m.* gargle; gargling; (*pop.*)

Gargoine, *s.f.* (*pop.*) throat, whistle [**Gargote**

Gargot, *s.m.* pig-salesman, porkman; (*thing*) *V.*

Gargotage, *s.m.* wretched cooking, dirty mess; wretched work

Gargote, *s.f.* low cook-shop, pot-house

Gargoter, *v.n.a.* to frequent low cook-shops and pot-houses; to eat and drink in a slovenly manner; to cook wretchedly; to bungle, to [botch

Gargoterie, *s.f. V.* **Gargotage**

Gargoti-er, ère, *s.m.f.* low *or* small eating-house keeper, low publican; wretched cook; bungler, botcher

†**Gargouillade,** *s.f. V.* **Gargouillement**

†**Gargouille,** *s.f.* gargoyle, gurgoyle, gutter-spout, water-spout, spout; small drain; drain-pipe; (*her.*) snake-head

†**Gargouillée,** *s.f.* spout, splash

†**Gargouillement,** *s.m.* rattling, rumbling, grumbling, gurgling; (*med.*) borborygm

†**Gargouiller,** *v.n.* to rattle, to rumble, to grumble, to gurgle; to dabble, to paddle, to [muddle

†**Gargouillette,** *s.f.* jug, cooler

†**Gargouillis,** *s.m.* gurgling

Gargoulette, *s.f. V.* **Gargouillette**

Gargousse, *s.f.* (*artil.*) cartridge

Gargoussier, *s.m.* (*artil., nav.*) cartridge-box; match-tub; powder-monkey

Gargoussière, *s.f.* (*artil., nav.*) cartridge-box; match-tub [*shirt*, &c.; *felt hat*)

Garibaldi, *s.m.* (*obsolete slang*) garibaldi (*coloured*

Garigue, *s.f.* waste-land, waste

Garite, *s.f.* (*nav.*) top-brims, top-rims

Garnement, *s.m.* worthless fellow, scamp, scapegrace

Garni, *s.m.* furnished lodgings, lodgings; lodging-house; — *m.*, —**e,** *f. part. adj.* furnished &c. (*V.* **Garnir**); thick, bushy; full

Garniment, *s.m. V.* **Garniture**

Garnir, *v.a.* to furnish, to provide, to supply, to stock, to store; to fit up; to adorn, to decorate, to set off *or* out; to trim; to line; to bind; to inlay; to mount; to set; to stuff; to fill; to cover; to fortify, to strengthen; (*cook.*) to garnish; to dress; (*fish.*) to bait (*a hook*); (*nav.*) to rig; to serve

Se —, *v.r.* to furnish *or* &c. oneself; to preserve *or* protect oneself; (*of things*) to be furnished *or* &c.; to fill [bumbailiff

Garnisaire, *s.m.* bailiff's man, under-bailiff,

Garnison, *s.f.* garrison; bailiff's man *or* men; (*pop.*) vermin, varmint

Garnissage, *s.m.* trimming; fitting

Garnisseu-r, se, *s.m.f.* trimmer; fitter

Garniture, *s.f.* fittings, requisites, appointments; furniture; ornaments; set; trimming; lining; binding; mounting; setting; gear; (*cook.*) garnishing, garnish; dressing; (*nav.*) rigging. *— de cheminée*, set of chimney-ornaments. *— de foyer* or *de feu*, set of fire-irons,

Garo, *s.m.* aloes-wood, eagle-wood [fire-irons

Garou, *s.m.* (*bot.*) garou-bush, spurge-laurel; (*pharm.*) garou-bark, garou. *— des bois*, mezereon. *Loup- —*, *V.* **Loup**

Garrot, *s.m.* withers; bending lever; packing-stick; (*killing instr. in Spain*) garotte; (*surg.*) garrot; (*bird*) garrot, golden-eye

Garrotte, *s.f.* garotte, strangulation (*legal killing in Spain, slightly different from the lawless* "garotte" *peculiar to London*)

Garrotter, *v.a.* to tie down, to bind; to pinion, to handcuff; to garotte *or* strangle (*execute in*

Garrulité, *s.f.* garrulity, loquacity [*Spain*)

Gars, *s.m.* lad, boy, fellow, chap

Garus, *s.m. Élixir de —*, elixir of Garus

Gas, *s.m. V.* **Gars**

Gascon, ne, *s.m.f. adj.* Gascon; Gascon fashion; boaster, braggart; gasconading, boastful,

Gasconisme, *s.m.* Gasconism [bragging

Gasconnade, *s.f.* gasconade, boast, brag, vaunt

Gasconner, *v.n.* to speak Gascon; to speak with a Gascon accent; to gasconade, to boast, to brag

Gaspard, *s.m.* (*pop.*) clever fellow, knowing one

Gasparot, Gasperau, *s.m.* (*fish*) alewife, spring herring (*kind of shad*)

†**Gaspillage,** *s.m.* waste, wasting, squandering

†**Gaspiller,** *v.a.* to waste, to squander; to spoil; to fritter away; to trifle away; (*old*) to throw into disorder

†**Gaspilleu-r, se,** *s.m.f. adj.* waster, squanderer, spendthrift; wasteful, extravagant, squan- [dering

Gasquet, *s.m.* red cloth smoking-cap

Gaster, *s.m.* gaster, stomach, belly

Gastéropode, *s.m.* (*zool.*) gasteropod; — *adj.* gasteropodous

Gastralgie, *s.f.* (*med.*) gastralgia, stomach-ache

Gastralgique, *adj.* (*med.*) gastralgic

Gastricisme, *s.m.* (*med.*) gastricism

Gastriloque, *s. adj.* (*obsolete*) *V.* **Ventriloque**

Gastrique, *adj.* (*anat.*) gastric, of the stomach

Gastrite, *s.f.* (*med.*) gastritis

Gastro-, (*anat., med., in compounds*) gastro-...

Gastrobranche, *s.m.* (*fish*) hag-fish, hag

Gastrocèle, *s.f.* (*med.*) gastrocele

Gastrocnémien, *adj.m., s.m.* (*anat.*) gastrocnemius (muscle)

Gastrodynie, *s.f.* (*med.*) gastrodynia

Gastro-entérite, *s.f.* (*med.*) gastro-enteritis

Gastromalacie, *s.f.* (*med.*) gastromalacia

Gastronome, *s.m.f.* gastronomist, gastronomer

Gastronom-ie, -ique, -iquement. *V.* page 3, § 1 [§ 1

Gastro-rraphie, -tomie, (*surg.*) *V.* page 3,

Gastrorrhée, *s.f.* (*med.*) gastrorrhœa

Gât, *s.m.* (*nav.*) steps, stairs, landing

Gatan, *s.m.* (*zool.*) razor-shell, razor-fish

Gatangier, *s.m.* (*zool.*) spotted dog-fish

Gâte, *s.m.f.* (*in compounds, from* **Gâter,** "to spoil," &c.) thing (*m.*) *or* person (*m.f.*) that spoils, &c., spoiler. — **-bois,** *s.m.* bungling joiner *or* carpenter; (*insect*) cossus, goat-moth. — **-cuir,** *s.m.* bungling shoemaker, mere cobbler. — **-enfants,** *s.m.f.* spoiler of children. — **-maison,** *s. m.f.* too good a servant. — **-ménage,** *s.m.f.* too great a household-reformer. — **-métier,** *s.m.f.* spoiler of trade, spoil-trade, underseller, underworker, rat, too reasonable *or* too active *or* too conscientious a workman. — **-papier,** *s.m.f.* scribbler, paltry writer. — **-pâte,** *s.m.f.* bad baker; bad pastrycook; bungler. — **-sauce,** *s.m.* scullion; pastrycook's man *or* boy; bad cook. — **-tout,** *s.m.f.* spoil-all, mar-all

Gâté, e, *part. adj.* spoilt; damaged; tainted; decayed; &c. (*V.* **Gâter**); unwholesome; unhealthy; — *s.m.* tainted *or* decayed part

Gâteau, *s.m.* cake; pudding; tart; comb, honey-comb; profit, booty, spoil; business, job; (*surg.*) pledget. *Papa* or *père* —, Daddy Cake, old coddle

Gâter, *v.a.* to spoil; to mar; to soil; to taint; to contaminate; to vitiate; to injure; to damage; to waste; to make worse; to corrupt, to deprave

Se —, *v.r.* to taint; to soil; to spoil; to get spoilt *or* &c.; to decay; to become corrupt *or* depraved; to be getting bad; to get wrong; to go on badly; to break up

Gâterie, *s.f.* petting, fond indulgence

Gâteu-r, se, *s.m.f.* spoiler; waster; corrupter

Gâteu-x, se, *s.m.f. adj.* (*med.*) one (*patient or idiot*) who has lost control over his evacuations and soils (*gâter,* "to soil") his clothes; (*fig.*) one who has lost self-control, downright idiot

Gatte, *s.f.* (*nav.*) manger

Gattilier, *s.m.* (*bot.*) chaste-tree

Gattine, *s.f.* (a disease of silk-worms)

Gauche, *adj.* left; left-hand; crooked; awkward, clumsy, gawky; (*her.*) sinister; —*s.f.* left, left hand, left-hand side, left side; left wing (*of an army*). *A* —, on *or* to the left, left; wrong; (*mil.*) left face! *Donner à* —, to get into the wrong box, to go wrong, to be mistaken

Gauchement, *adv.* awkwardly, clumsily

Gauch-er, ère, *adj. s.* left-handed; ditto person

Gaucher, *v.a.* (*carp.*) to warp [der

Gaucherie, *s.f.* awkwardness; bungling; blun-

Gauchir, *v.n.* to turn aside; to flinch; to shuffle, to shift; to warp; to get out of shape; — *v.a.* to warp; to put out of shape

Se —, *v.r.* to warp; to get out of shape

Gauchissement, *s.m.* warping

Gaudage, *s.m.* dyeing with weld

Gaude, *s.f.* maize hasty-pudding, hominy, mush; (*bot.*) weld, yellow-weed, dyer's weed

Gaudéamus, *s.m.* rejoicing, jubilee, merry-making, jollification

Gauder, *v.a.* to dye with weld, to dye yellow

Gaudir (Se), *v.r.* (*old*) to rejoice, to make *or* be merry; to laugh (at), to make fun *or* game (of)

Gaudissard, Gaudissart, *s.m.* (*jest.*) commercial traveller, bagman; wag

Gaudisserie, *s.f.* broad humour; waggishness, waggery; joke, jest, fun, drollery

Gaudisseu-r, se, *s.m.f.* jester, banterer, wag

Gaudriole, *s.f.* broad joking; broad joke, funny thing

Gaudrioler, *v.n.* to indulge in broad jokes

Gaudrioleu-r, se, *s.m.f.* broad-joker

Gaudron, &c. *V.* **Godron,** &c. [ing, figuring

Gaufrage, *s.m.* gauffering, crimping; emboss-

Gaufre, *s.f.* honey-comb; waffle; figuring; sufferer, victim, dupe

Gaufrer, *v.a.* to gauffer, to crimp; to emboss,

Se —, *v.r.* to be gauffered *or* &c. [to figure

Gaufreu-r, se, *s.m.f.* gaufferer, crimper; embosser, figurer

Gaufrier, *s.m.* waffle-iron

Gaufroir, *s.m.* gauffering-iron, gauffering-machine, crimping-machine

Gaufrure, *s.f.* *V.* **Gaufrage**

Gaulade, *s.f.* blow with a pole *or* switch *or* rod

Gaulage, *s.m.* beating with a pole, beating *or* knocking down

Gaule, *s.f.* pole; switch; rod; cudgel; staff

Gauler, *v.a.* to beat with a pole, to beat *or* knock down; to cudgel, to thwack

Se —, *v.r.* to be beaten *or* &c.

Gaulette, *s.f.* small pole, rod, stick

Gaulis, *s.m., adj.m.* long sprig; small wood; chip-wood; copse, coppice

Gaulois, e, *adj.* Gallic; old, old French; of the olden time; old-fashioned; rough, untutored; honest, frank, sincere; free; — *s.m.f.* Gaul; frank person; — *s.m.* Gallic language; old French; plain French; — *s.f.* Gallic *or* old

Gault, *s.m.* (*geol.*) gault [French fashion

Gaulthérie, *s.f.* (*bot.*) gaultheria, winter-green, Canada tea

Gaulthérine, *s.f.* (*chem.*) gaultherine

Gaupe, *s.f.* slut, trollop, bitch

Gauperie, *s.f.* beastly manners *or* behaviour

Gaure, *s.m.f.* *V.* **Guèbre**

Gausse, Gausser, &c., (*obsolete spelling*) *V.*

Gautier, *s.m.* sluice [**Gosse, Gosser,** &c.

Gavache, *s.m.* (*obsolete*) ragamuffin

Gavauche, *s.m.* (*old nav.*) disorder, confusion

Gave, *s.m.* (*local*) torrent; — *s.f.* (*pop.*) crop *or*

Gaveau, *s.m.* *V.* **Gavot** [maw (*of a bird*)

Gaver, *v.a.* (*pop.*) to feed; to cram; to fatten; to glut, to fill, to satiate

Gavial, *s.m.* (*zool.*) gavial [gullet, wizen, whistle

Gaviot (*formerly,* **Gavion**), *s.m.* (*pop.*) throat,

Gaviteau, *s.m.* (*nav., local*) buoy

Gavot, *s.m.* (*pop.*) trade-unionist

Gavotte, *s.f.* gavotte (*dance, tune*)

Gayac, *s.m.* *V.* **Gaïac**

Gaylussite, *s.f.* (*min.*) gaylussite

Gaz, *s.m.* gas; gas-light; gas-lighting; gas-company; (*med.*) flatus, wind; (*pop.*) peepers, eyes. *A* —, *De* —, (*adject.*) gas. *Au* —, by gas-light; (*adject.*) gas. *Bec de* —, gas-light, gas-burner, burner, street-lamp. *Fermer le robinet de* —, to turn off the gas. *Ouvrir le robinet de* —, to turn on the gas

Gaze, *s.f.* gauze; (*fig.*) veil, softening

Gazé, *s.m.* (*zool.*) hawthorn-butterfly, black-veined white butterfly; — *m.*, —**e,** *f. part. of* **Gazer**

Gazéifiable, *adj.* gasifiable, convertible into gas

Gazéification, *s.f.* gasification

Gazéifier, *v.a.*, **Se** —, *v.r.* to gasify, to turn *or*

Gazéiforme, *adj.* gasiform [convert into gas

Gazéité, *s.f.* (*chem.*) gaseity

Gazelle, *s.f.* (*zool.*) gazelle

Gazer, *v.a.* to cover with gauze; (*fig.*) to veil, to disguise, to gloss over, to soften down

Gazeti-er, ère, *s.m.f.* (*obsolete*) gazetteer; journalist; newsmonger; (*arch-obsolete*) newsman, newsvendor; — *adj.* journalistic

Gazetin, *s.m.* (*obsolete*) little gazette

Gazette, *s.f.* gazette; newspaper, paper, journal; newsmonger; quidnunc; blab; (*manu. of pottery*) *V.* **Casette** [observer of decency

Gazeu-r, se, *s.m.f.* softener of offensive things,

Gazeu-x, se, *adj.* gaseous; aerated; effervescing; — *s.f.* (*fam.*) effervescing lemonade

Gazi-er, ère, *s.m.f.* gauze-maker; — *s.m.* gas-fitter [apparatus

Gazifère, *adj.* gas-making; — *s.m.* gas-making

Gazofacteur, *s.m.* gas-works

Gazogène, *s.m.* gazogène, gasogene

Gazolitre, *s.m.* (*instr.*) gas-measurer

Gazomètre, *s.m.* gasometer; gas-holder; gas-

Gazométrie, *s.f.* gasometry [meter

Gazométrique, *adj.* gasometric

Gazon, *s.m.* grass; turf; sod; grass-plot, lawn; (*fort.*) gazon; (*jest.*) wig, caxon

Gazonnage, Gazonnement, *s.m.* turfing

Gazonner, *v.a.* to turf. *Se* —, to be turfed

Gazonneu-x, se, Gazonnant, e, *adj.* turfy

Gazoscope, *s.m.* gasoscope

†**Gazouillement,** *s.m.* warbling, chirping, singing; purling; prattle

†**Gazouiller,** *v.n.a.* to warble, to chirp, to sing; to purl; to prattle, to lisp

†**Gazouillis,** *s.m.* (*old*) *V.* **Gazouillement**

Geai, *s.m.* jay; jackdaw [tic, giant

Géant, e, *s.m.f.* giant, giantess; — *adj.* gigan-

Géantisme, *s.m.* giantism, gigantic size

Gecko, *s.m.* (*zool.*) gecko

Géhenne, *s.f.* Gehenna, Hell [— *adj.* whining

†**Geigneu-r, Geigneu-x, se,** *s.m.f.* whiner;

Geindre, *v.n.* to moan; to groan; to whine; to complain; — *s.m.* baker's man (who kneads the dough), baker's second hand, bread-maker

Géine, *s.f.* (*chem.*) geine

Géinique, *adj.* (*chem.*) geinic

Gel, *s.m.* frost [frozen, liable to freeze

Gelable, *adj.* gelable, congealable, that may be

Gélatine, *s.f.* gelatine

Gélatineu-x, se, *adj.* gelatinous

Gélatiniforme, *adj.* gelatiniform

Gélatinisation, *s.f.* gelatinization

Gélatiniser, *v.a.*, **Se** —, *v.r.* to gelatinize

Gelé, e, *part. adj.* frozen; frost-bitten; cold;

Gelée, *s.f.* frost; jelly [jellied

Geler, *v.a.n.*, **Se** —, *v.r.* to freeze; to be frozen

Géli-f, ve, *adj.* cracked by frost

Geline, *s.f.* (*obsolete*) hen

Gelinier, *s.m.* (*obsolete*) hen-house

Gelinotte, *s.f.* bonasia, hazel-grouse; pullet

Gélivure, *s.f.* crack caused by frost, frost-crack

Gémeau, *s.m.* (*obsolete for* **Jumeau**) twin; —**x,** *pl.* (*astr.*) Gemini, twins

Géminé, e, *adj.* duplicate, double, twin, geminate; (*law*) iterated, repeated

Gémir, *v.n.* to groan; to moan; to lament; to bewail; to complain; to grieve; to repine. *Faire — la presse,* to make the press groan, to keep the press going, to print away

Gémissement, *s.m.* groan; moan; groaning; moaning; lamentation; murmur; cooing

Gemmation, *s.f.* (*bot.*) gemmation, budding

Gemme, *s.f.* (*min.*) gem; (*bot.*) gem, leaf-bud; (*zool.*) bud; — *adj. Pierre* —, precious stone, gem. *Sel* —, rock-salt

Gemmé, e, *adj.* gemmated; (*of trees*) tapped

Gemmer, *v.a.* to tap (*a tree*)

Gemmifère, *adj.* gemmiferous [shaped

Gemmiforme, *adj.* (*bot.*) gemmiform, bud-

Gemmipare, *adj.* (*bot., zool.*) gemmiparous

Gemmiparie, *s.f.* (*bot., zool.*) gemmiparity

Gemmule, *s.f.* (*bot.*) gemmule

Gémonies, *s.f.pl.* (*Roman antiquity*) gemoniæ, place of execution, gibbet

Génal, e, *adj.* (*anat.*) of the cheeks, genal

Gênant, e, *adj.* inconvenient; uncomfortable; uneasy; troublesome; in the way; embarrassing; cumbersome; awkward; annoying

Gencive, *s.f.* (*anat.*) gum

Gendarme, *s.m.* (armed) policeman, gendarme; (*obsolete*) man-at-arms; life-guardsman; (*fig.*) virago, termagant, Turk; surly fellow, bear; flaw, spot, speck; lees, sediment, fur; spark (*of fire*); smoothing-iron, flat iron; red herring

Gendarmé, e, *part. adj.* dragooned; out of temper, angry (with), kicking (against)

Gendarmer, *v.a.* to dragoon

Se —, *v.r.* to get angry or out of temper, to fire up, to fly out, to fly into a passion; to bluster; to resist, to struggle, to kick (against)

Gendarmerie, *s.f.* (armed) police, constabulary, gendarmerie, gendarmes; station *or* barracks of ditto; (*obsolete*) men-at-arms; life-guard, body-guard

Gendarmeu-x, se, *adj.* (*min.*) flawy, spotty

Gendelettre, *s.m.* (*a silly slang word, used in contempt by men in trade, out of spite to their betters*) literary man

Gendre, *s.m.* son-in-law

Gêne, *s.f.* inconvenience; uncomfortableness; discomfort; uneasiness; pain; constraint; restraint; restriction; annoyance; trouble; difficulty; embarrassment; narrow circumstances strait, straits, want, need, penury; scarcity; torture, rack; torment. *Sans* —, unconstrained; unrestrained; unceremonious, free, familiar; easy; plain; off-handed; off-hand; unceremoniously, without (any) ceremony, freely, familiarly; plainly; at home; (*s.m.*) *V.* **Sans-gêne,** *s.m.* *Mettre à la* —, to put to trouble; to make uncomfortable; to straiten; to stint; to pinch; to torture, to rack

Gêné, e, *part. adj.* inconvenienced, &c. (*V.* **Gêner**); uncomfortable; uneasy; constrained; under restraint; awkward; stiff; embarrassed; short of cash. *N'être pas* —, not to be ... (*as above*); to be free; to be too free *or* familiar; to be cool *or* impudent

Généalogie, *s.f.* genealogy, pedigree [3, § 1

Généalog-ique, -iquement, -iste. *V.* page

Génépi, *s.m.* (*bot.*) genipi, genipp, Alpine wormwood, Swiss tea

Gêner, *v.a.* to inconvenience; to make uncomfortable *or* uneasy; to trouble; to disturb; to constrain; to restrain; to cramp; to straiten; to clog; to obstruct; to hinder; to impede; to thwart; to be in the way of; to embarrass; to interfere with; to annoy; to put about; to pinch; to hurt; to squeeze

Se —, *v.r.* to inconvenience *or* &c. oneself *or* each other; to put oneself to inconvenience; to put oneself out of the way; to restrain *or* trouble *or* straiten *or* &c. oneself; to stand on ceremony, to make *or* use ceremony. *Ne pas se* —, not to ... (*as above*); to be at o.'s ease; to make *or* use no ceremony; to make oneself at home; to act freely, to make free; not to hesitate *or* mince matters; to ... freely

Général, e, *adj.* general; — *s.m.* general; head, chief, commander; (*obsolete*) generality; — *s.f.* general's wife; head, superioress; (*drum-beating*) fire-drum; (*mil.*) general. — *de brigade, V.* **Brigade.** — *de division,* major-general; lieutenant-general. *En* —, in general, generally. *Battre la* —*e,* (*mil.*) to beat the general, to beat to arms

Généralat, *s.m.* generalship

Généralement, *adv.* generally, in general

Généralisable, *adj.* generalizable

Généralisa-teur, trice, *s.m.f.* generalizer; — *adj.* generalizing [izing

Généralisation, *s.f.* generalization, general-

Généraliser, *v.a.* to generalize; to make general [general

Se —, *v.r.* to be generalized; to become

Généralissime, *s.m.* generalissimo, commander-in-chief

Généralité, *s.f.* generality; general remark

Généra-teur, trice, *adj.* generating; — *s.m.*

Générati-f, ve, *adj.* generative [generator

Génération, *s.f.* generation; descent

Généreusement, *adv.* generously; liberally; bounteously, bountifully; nobly, handsomely; valiantly, bravely, courageously

Généreu-x, se, *adj.* generous; liberal; bounteous, bountiful; grateful; noble, handsome; valiant, brave, courageous

Génér-ique, -iquement. *V.* page 3, § 1

Générosité, *s.f.* generosity; liberality; bounty, bountifulness; nobleness; bravery

Genèse, *s.f.* Genesis

Génésique, *adj.* genetic, genetical

Genestrolle, *s.f.* (*bot.*) dyers' green-weed

Genêt, *s.m.* (*bot.*) broom. — *épineux, V.* **Ajonc.** — *d'Espagne,* rush-broom

Genet, *s.m.* jennet (*Spanish horse*)

Genétaire, *s.m.* (ancient Spanish trooper)

Généthliaque, *s.m. adj.* genethliac (*birthday poem*)

Genétière, *s.f.* broom-land

Genétin, *s.m.* (Orleans grape; ditto wine; kind of apple)

Génétique, *adj.* genetic, genetical

Genette, *s.f.* (*zool.*) genet; (*rid.*) Turkish bit. *A la* —, (*rid.*) with short stirrups

Génevois, e, *adj. s.* Genevese
Genévrette, *s.f.* juniper-wine
Genévrier, *s.m.* juniper-tree, juniper
Genévrière, *s.f.* juniper-ground
Géni, *adj.* (*anat.*) genian
Géniculation, *s.f.* geniculation
Géniculé, e, *adj.* geniculate, geniculated
Génie, *s.m.* genius; spirit; nature; disposition; talent; wit; engineering; engineers. *Officier du* —, engineer-officer. *Soldat du* —, sapper and miner, engineer
Génien, ne, *adj.* (*anat.*) genian
Génieux, *s.m.* (*pop.*) bowl, basin, cup
Genièvre, *s.m.* juniper-berry, juniper-tree, juniper; gin. — *de Hollande*, hollands, schiedam
Genièvrerie, *s.f.* gin-distillery
Génipa, Génipayer, *s.m.* (*bot.*) genipa, marmalade box (*tree*)
Génipat, *s.m.* genipap (*fruit of the genipa*)
Génipi, *s.m.* (*bot.*) *V.* **Génépi**
Génisse, *s.f.* heifer; fast woman
Genistelle, *s.f.* *V.* **Genestrolle**
Génital, e, *adj.* genital [male kept for breeding
Géniteur, *s.m.* genitor, generator; (*agr.*, &c.)
Génitif, *s.m.* (*gram.*) genitive, genitive case
Géniture, *s.f.* (*old*) offspring, progeny
Génois, e, *adj. s.* Genoese [lashing
Genope, *s.f.* (*nav.*) belay, belaying, seizing,
Genoper, *v.a.* (*nav.*) to belay, to seize, to lash
Genou, *s.m.* knee; (*jest.*) hairless scalp, bald head; (*mech.*) ball and socket; crank; (*rail.*) break-wheel, brake-wheel; (*nav.*) futtock; —**x,** *pl.* knees, &c.; lap. *A —x*, on o.'s knees; kneeling. *A ses —x*, at his *or* her knees. *Se mettre à —x*, to kneel down
†**Genouillé, e,** *adj.* *V.* **Géniculé**
†**Genouillère,** *s.f.* knee-piece; knee-guard; knee-pad *or* cap; (*of boots*) top; (*tech.*) hinge; bracket; (*fort.*) genouillère. *Bottes à* —, jack-boots, knee-boots
†**Genouillet,** *s.m.* (*bot.*) Solomon's seal [roots
†**Genouilleu-x, se,** *adj.* (*bot.*) with jointed
Génovéfain, *s.m.* canon of St. Genevieve
Génovine, *s.f.* genovine (*gold coin of Genoa*)
Genre, *s.m.* kind, species, sort; manner; style; fashion; taste; mode; way; course; line; study; system; breeding, manners; (*fam.*) mannerism, affectation, attitudinizing, airs, fuss, dash; (*nat. hist.*, &c.) genus; (*gram.*) gender; (*paint.*, &c.) manner, style; kind of composition; (*paint., said of subjects being neither historical nor landscapes*) genre-painting, genre. *Peintre de* —, genre-painter. *Tableau de* —, genre-picture. *Le — humain*, mankind, humankind. *Le — comique*, comedy. *Le — tragique*, tragedy
Gens, *s.m.f.pl.* people; folks; persons; men; fellows; domestics, servants; attendants. *Droit des* —, law of nations. *Jeunes* —, young men; young people; youths; boys. (*In compound words and in phrases where* **Gens** *is the plural of* **Homme** *or of* **Personne**, *See under each of these words.*) — *d'armes*, — *de chicane*, &c., *V.* **Arme, Chicane,** &c. — *de justice*, law-officers. — *de maison*, servants
Gent, *s.f.* (*jest.*) race, nation, people, tribe
Gent, e, *adj.* (*old*) fair, comely, pretty, gentle,
Gentiane, *s.f.* (*bot.*) gentian [sweet
Gentianelle, *s.f.* (*bot.*) gentianella, small-flowered *or* autumnal gentian [gentianine
Gentianin, *s.m.*, **Gentianine,** *s.f.* (*chem.*)
Gentianique, *adj.* (*chem.*) gentianic
Gentil, e, *s.m.f. adj.* Gentile
Gentil, le, *adj.* nice, pretty; amiable, good, kind, obliging; pleasant, agreeable; sweet; (*obsolete*) noble, gentle. *Faire le* —, to play the agreeable
Gentilé, *s.m.* (*gram.*) gentile noun *or* adjective
†**Gentilhomme,** *s.m.* nobleman; gentleman; esquire; squire [squire
†**Gentilhommeau,** *s.m.* lordling, country
†**Gentilhommerie,** *s.f.* (*disparagingly*) nobility, nobs; gentility, gentry, genteel people *or* folks
†**Gentilhommière,** *s.f.* country squire's house, small country-seat; — *adj.f.* of a nobleman; of a gentleman [dom, Gentile nations
Gentilité, *s.f.* paganism, heathenism, heathen-
†**Gentillâtre,** *s.m.* lordling, poor lord, country
†**Gentille,** *adj.f.* *V.* **Gentil** [squire
†**Gentillesse,** *s.f.* prettiness; gracefulness, elegance, loveliness; pretty thing; pretty saying; pretty trick *or* way; liveliness, playfulness
†**Gentillet, te,** *adj.* prettyish, somewhat nice
Gentiment, *adv.* nicely, prettily; gently; like a good boy *or* girl
Gentisin, *s.m.* (*chem.*) gentisine, gentisic acid
Gentleman, *s.m.* (English) gentleman
Génuflexion, *s.f.* genuflexion, genuflection, kneeling
Géocentr-ique, -iquement. *V.* page 3, § 1
Géode, *s.f.* (*min.*) geode, potato-stone
Géodésie, *s.f.* geodesy
Géodésien, *s.m.* geodesian
Géodésique, *adj.* geodetic, geodetical
Géodésiquement, *adv.* geodetically
Géodique, *adj.* (*min.*) geodic, geode-shaped
Géo-génie, -gnosie. *V.* page 3, § 1
Géognoste, *s.m.* geognost
Géognost-ique, -iquement. *V.* page 3, § 1
Géogon-ie, -ique. *V.* page 3, § 1
Géographe, *s.m. adj.* geographer; geographical
Géograph-ie, -ique, -iquement. *V* p. 3, § 1
Géohydrographe, *s.m.* geohydrographer
Géohydrograph-ie, -ique. *V.* page 3, § 1
Geôlage, *s.m.* prison-fee
Geôle, *s.f.* jail, gaol, prison; jailer's lodge
Geôlier, *s.m.* jailer, gaoler
Geôlière, *s.f.* jailer's wife; jailer
Géolog-ie, -ique, -iquement, -iste. *V.* page
Géologue, *s.m.* geologist [3, § 1
Géoman-cie, -tique. *V.* page 3, § 1
Géomancien, ne, *s.m.f.* geomancer
Géométral, e, *adj.* geometrical. *Chenille —e*, *V.* **Arpenteuse**
Géométralement, *adv.* geometrically
Géomètre, *s.m.* geometrician, geometer; mathematician; surveyor; (*zool.*) *V.* **Arpenteuse;** — *adj.* geometrical, mathematical
Géométrie, *s.f.* geometry
Géométrique, *adj.* geometrical; mathematical; exact, methodical [mathematically
Géométriquement, *adv.* geometrically;
Géométriser, *v.n.* to geometrize
Géonom-ie, -ique. *V.* page 3, § 1 [gist
Géophage, *adj.* geophagous; — *s.m.f.* geopha-
Géophagie, *s.f.* geophagy, geophagism, dirt-
Géoponie, *s.f.* (*old*) geopony, agriculture [eating
Géoponique, *adj.* geoponic; — *s.f.* geoponics; —**s,** *s m.pl.* (*ancient liter.*) Geoponica
Géorama, *s.m.* georama, globe
Géoramique, *adj.* georamic
Géorgien, ne, *adj. s.* Georgian
Géorgique, *adj.* georgic; —**s,** *s.f.pl.* Georgics
Géosphérique, *adj.* geospherical
Géostatique, *s.f.* geostatics
Géotherm-ie, -ique. *V.* page 3, § 1
Géothermomètre, *s.m.* geothermometer
Gérance, *s.f.* management; editorship; sub-editorship
Géraniine, Géranine, *s.f.* (*chem.*) geraniine
Géranium, *s.m.* (*bot.*) geranium
Gérant, e, *s.m.f.* manager, manageress; principal; editor, editress; sub-editor, sub-editress; — *adj.* managing, acting. — *d'un bureau de* *tabac*, tobacconist
Gerbage, *s.m.* sheafing
Gerbe, *s.f.* sheaf; bundle; wheat-sheaf jet, jet, spout; (*of fireworks*) gerbe; (*her.*) garb [fodder
Gerbée, *s.f.* bundle of straw not well thrashed;
Gerber, *v.a.n.* to bind in sheaves; to sheaf; to
Gerbier, *s.m.* (*obsolete*) rick, stack; barn [pile up
Gerbière, *s.f.* harvest-waggon; pile of sheaves,
Gerbiforme, *adj.* sheaf-shaped [fiving
†**Gerbille,** *s.f.* (*zool.*) gerbil
†**Gerbillon,** *s.m.* small sheaf [jumping hare
Gerbo, *s.m.*, **Gerboise,** *s.f.* (*zool.*) jerboa,

Gerçable, *adj.* liable to crack

Gerce, *s.f.* moth; chap, crack; cleft, chink

Gercement, *s.m.* cracking, crack, chapping

Gercer, *v.a.n.,* **Se —,** *v.r.* to chap; to crack

Gerçure, *s.f.* chap; crack; cleft, chink

Gérer, *v.a.* to manage, to conduct, to administer **Se —,** *v.r.* to be managed *or* &c.

Géreur, *s.m.* (*local*) manager

Gerfaut, *s.m.* (*bird*) gyrfalcon, gerfalcon

Germain, e, *s.m.f.* (*law*) own brother *or* sister, brother *or* sister of the whole blood; (*obsolete*) brother, sister; German (*of ancient Germany*); — *adj.* own, of the whole blood; german, first; German (*of ancient Germany*). *Frère —, sœur —e,* own brother *or* sister, brother *or* sister of the whole blood. *Cousin* (*m.*) —, *cousine* (*f.*) —*e,* cousin german, first cousin. *Issu de —, cousin issu de —,* second cousin, cousin once

Germandrée, *s.f.* (*bot.*) germander [removed

German-ique, -isme, -iste. *V.* page 3, § 1

Germaniser, *v.a.* to germanize; — *v.n.* to make germanisms

Germe, *s.m.* germ; bud, seed; sprout, shoot; acrospire; treadle; origin, source, cause, principle, beginning, dawn. — *de fève,* (*vet.*) mark (*in a horse's mouth*)

Germer, *v.n.* to germinate, to shoot, to sprout; (*agr.*) to spire; (*fig.*) to bud, to spring up, to fructify; — *v.a.* (*poet.*) to cause to grow, to produce

Germinal, e, *adj.* germinal; — *s.m.* Germinal (*seventh month of the calendar of the first French Republic, from March* 21 *to April* 19)

Germina-teur, trice, *adj.* germinating

Germinati-f, ve, *adj.* germinative, germinating

Germination, *s.f.* germination

Germinipare, *adj.* germiniparous

Germoir, *s.m.* malt-house; (*hort.*) breeding-

Germon, *s.m.* (*fish*) dolphin [bed *or* pot

Gérocomie, *s.f.* (*old spelling*) *V.* **Gérontocomie**

Gérofle, Gérofiier, *V.* **Girofle, Giroflier**

Géromé, *s.m.* Géromé cheese

Gérondif, *s.m.* (*gram.*) gerund [old codger

Géronte, *s.m.* silly old man, dotard, old fogy,

Gérontisme, *s.m.* dotage, dotingness, senile imbecility, fogyism [comy

Gérontocomie, *s.f.* (*med.*) gerontocomy, gero-

Gérontocratie, *s.f.* gerontocracy; fogyism

Gérontocratique, *adj.* gerontocratic; of old

Gérousse, *s.f.* *V.* **Jarosse** [fogies

Gerzeau, *s.m.* (*bot.*) corn-cockle

Gésier, *s.m.* gizzard

Gésine, *s.f.* (*obsolete*) confinement, lying-in, childbed; (*in some country-hospitals*) lying-in ward. *En —,* (*old, jest.*) confined, lying-in; in

Gésir, *v.n.* (*obsolete*) to lie down, to lie [the straw

Gesse, *s.f.* (*bot.*) vetch, chickling-vetch

Gessette, *s.f.* (*bot.*) vetchling [ture

Gesseu-r, se, *s.m.f.* (*pop.*) fussy fellow *or* crea-

Gestation, *s.f.* gestation [Pope's) sedan-chair

Gestatoire, *adj.* gestatory. *Chaise —,* (the

Geste, *s.m.* gesture; movement, motion; manner; sign; beck; nod; action; gesticulation; —**s,** *pl.* gestures, &c.; doings, deeds, exploits, feats, tricks [*adj.* gesticulating

Gesticula-teur, trice, *s.m.f.* gesticulator; —

Gesticulation, *s.f.* gesticulation

Gesticuler, *v.n.* to gesticulate, to make gestures

Gestion, *s.f.* management, conduct, adminis-

Géum, *s.m.* (*bot.*) geum, avens [tration

Geyser, *s.m.* (*geol.*) geyser

Giaour, *s.m.* (*Turkish*) giaour

Gibbar, *s.m.* rorqual (*kind of whale*)

Gibbeu-x, se, *adj.* gibbous, gibbose, convex

Gibbon, *s.m.* gibbon, long-armed ape [hump

Gibbosité, *s.f.* gibbosity, gibbousness; hunch,

Gibecier, *s.m.* shooting-pouch maker, pouch *or* bag-maker

Gibecière, *s.f.* shooting-pouch; courier-bag; pouch, bag; satchel; scrip. *Tour de —,* sleight of hand trick, juggling, juggle

Gibèle, *s.f.* (*fish*) gibel, Prussian carp

Gibelet, *s.m.* borer, gimlet [Ghibelline

Gibelin, *s.m.,* **Gibelin, e,** *adj.* (*Italian hist.*)

Gibelotte, *s.f.* rabbit-stew, stewed rabbit, stew. — *de gouttière,* (*jest.*) cat-stew, stewed cat (*passed off as rabbit*), cat

Giberne, *s.f.* cartridge-pouch *or* box. *Enfant de —* or *de troupe, V.* **Enfant**

Gibernerie, *s.f.* cartridge-pouch making *or* manufactory *or* trade; cartridge-pouches

Gibet, *s.m.* gibbet, gallows

Gibier, *s.m.* game; venison. — *à commissaire,* prostitute, thief, pickpocket. — *à plumes,* game-birds, winged game. — *de Cayenne,* — *de potence,* gallows-bird, jail-bird, robber, murderer

Gible, *s.f.* clamp (*of bricks*)

Giboudot, *s.m.* (kind of grape)

Giboulée, *s.f.* shower, hail-shower; (*pop.*) drubbing, hiding. — *de mars,* April shower

Giboya, *s.m.* giboya (*serpent*)

Giboyer, *v.n.* (*obsolete*) to go a-hunting *or* shooting, to hunt, to shoot; to poach

Giboyeur, *s.m.* (*obsolete*) huntsman, hunter, sportsman; dealer in game [of game

Giboyeu-x, se, *adj.* abounding in game, full

Giclet, *s.m.* (*bot.*) squirting *or* spirting *or* wild cucumber [smacker, stinger

Gifle, *s.f.* slap on the face, box on the ear,

Gifler, *v.a.* to slap *or* smack the face of, to box

Gifole, *s.f.* (*bot.*) *V.* **Cotonnière** [the ears of

Gigantesque, *adj.m.f., s.m.* gigantic

Gigantesquement, *adv.* gigantically

Gigantisme, *s.m.* giantism [3, § 1

Giganto-graphie, -logie, -machie. *V.* p.

Gigartine, *s.f.* (*bot.*) gigartina, Corsican moss

†**Gigogne,** *s.f.* *Madame —, la mère —,* "the old woman who lived in a shoe." *Une mère —,* (*jest.*) a great breeder [mutton sleeve

Gigot, *s.m.* leg of mutton, leg; hind leg; leg of

Gigotté, e, *adj.* (*of animals*) strong-limbed

Gigotter, *v.n.* to kick, to kick about, to move o.'s legs; to fidget; to dance, to cut capers

Gigue, *s.f.* shank, stump, leg; lanky woman *or* girl; (*dance, tune*) jig, gigg, gigue

Giguer, *v.n.* (*pop.*) to skip, to dance

Gilet, *s.m.* waistcoat, vest; (*fenc.*) jacket; (*fenc.*) complete beating; (*pop.*) stomach, chest, bread-basket. — *à châle,* roll-collar waistcoat. — *d'armes,* fencing-jacket. — *de force,* strait-waistcoat *or* jacket. *Donner un — à,* (*fenc.*) to beat outright

Gileter, *v.a.* to put a waistcoat *or* a vest on. *Se —,* to put o.'s waistcoat *or* vest on. *Être bien gileté,* to have a good *or* a nice-looking waistcoat *or* vest on

Gileti-er, ère, *s.m.f.* waistcoat *or* vest-maker

Gille, *s.m.* clown; ninny, booby, fool. *Faire —,* to run off, to scamper away; to break, to fail, to become bankrupt *or* insolvent

Giller, *v.n.* *V.* **Gille** (*Faire —*)

Gillerie, *s.f.* silly clownish trick, silly thing, silliness, nonsense

Gilquin, *s.m.* (*slang*) bunch of fives

Gimblette, *s.f.* ring-biscuit; jam tart

Gin, *s.m.* (English) gin

Gindre, *s.m.* *V.* **Geindre,** *s.m.*

Gingas, *s.m.* (*stuff*) tick, ticking

Gingembre, *s.m.* ginger

Gingival, e, *adj.* (*anat.*) gingival, of the gums

Gingivite, *s.f.* (*med.*) gingivitis

Gingko, *s.m.* (*bot.*) gingko, ginko

Ginglyme, *s.m.* (*anat.*) ginglymus

Ginglymoïdal, e, Ginglymoïde, *adj.* (*anat.*) ginglymoidal, ginglymoid

Ginguer, *v.n.* (*pop., of animals*) to kick

Ginguet, te, *adj.* weak; poor, sorry; curtailed, scanty, short; small; — *s.m.* (*obsolete*) weak *or*

Ginseng, *s.m.* (*bot.*) ginseng [tart wine

Giocoso, *adj.* (*mus.*) giocoso

Giorno (A), *adv.* (*Italian*) like daylight, bril-

Gir, *v.n.* (*obsolete*) *V.* **Gésir** [liantly, splendidly

Girafe, *s.f.* giraffe, camelopard [*rockets*)

Girande, *s.f.* girande (*cluster of water-jets or of*

Girandole, *s.f.* girandole; (*of gems*) sprig; (*bot.*) chara; whorl [*V.* **Tournesol**
Girasol, *s.m.* (*min.*) girasol, fire opal; (*bot.*)
Giration, *s.f.* gyration
Giratoire, *adj.* gyratory, gyral. *Mouvement* or *évolution* —, gyration. *Point* —, axis of gyration
Giratrice, *adj.f. V.* **Gyratrice**
Giraumon, Giraumont, *s.m.* pumpkin
Girel, *s.m.* (*nav., local*) capstan
Girie, *s.f.* lamentation, whining, whimpering, complaint; fuss, grimace, smirk
Girofle, *s.m.* (*bot.*) clove
Giroflée, *s.f.* (*bot.*) gillyflower, stock. — *jaune*, wall-flower. — *à cinq feuilles*, (*pop.*) bunch of fives, good slap on the face
Giroflée, *adj.* of clove. *Cannelle* —, clove-bark
Giroflier, *s.m.* (*bot.*) clove-tree
Girole, *s.f. V.* **Chervi** [*a step*); (*her.*) gyron
Giron, *s.m.* lap; pale; bosom; (*arch.*) tread (*of*
Gironde, *s.f.* (*Fr. hist.*) Gironde, Girondist party
Girondin, *s.m.*, **Girondin, e,** *adj.* (*Fr. hist.*) Girondist
Gironné,e, *adj.* rounded; winding; (*her.*) gyrony
Gironner, *v.a.* to round, to turn
Girouette, *s.f.* weather-cock; vane; time-server
Girouetterie, *s.f.* fickleness, changing, time-
Gisait, *v.* was lying [serving
Gisaient, *v.* were lying
Gisant, e, *adj.* lying, lying down, stretched; (*nav.*) wrecked, aground; — *s.m.f.* (*obsolete*) patient. *Meule* —*e*, lower stone (*of a mill*) [bed
Gisement, *s.m.* (*nav.*) bearing; (*geol.*) bearing;
Gisent, *v.* lie, are lying [memory of
Gît, *v.* lies. *Ci-* —, here lies, sacred to the
Gitano, *s.m.*, **Gitana,** *s.f.* (*Spanish*) gypsy
Gîte, *s.m.* home; lodging; quarters; resting-place; halting-place; bed; shelter; lair; (*of hares*) form, seat; (*build.*) floor-timbers; (*of a mill, obsolete*) lower stone, nether millstone; (*tech.*) rest, bed; under side; (*min.*) deposit, stratum, layer, bed, locality, field; (*of beef*) mouse buttock, mouse-piece, buttock, round. — *à la noix*, silver (*or* under) side of the round. — *s.f.* (*nav.*) bed
Gîter, *v.a.* to lodge, to house, to accommodate; — *v.n.*, **Se** —, *v.r.* to lodge, to sleep; to live;
Githagine, *s.f.* (*chem.*) githagine [to lie
Giton, *s.m.* minion
Givre, *s.m.* rime, white frost; — *s.f. V.* **Guivre**
Givré,e, *adj.* rimy, white with frost; (*her.*) with
Givreu-x, se, *adj.* chapped, cracked [snakes
Glabre, *adj.* (*bot.*) glabrous, smooth, soft, hairless
Glaçage, *s.m.* icing; frosting; glazing
Glace, *s.f.* ice; looking-glass, mirror; plate-glass; glass window, window; plate-glass door; glass-plate, plate; ice-work; frost-work; icing; glazing; jelly; flaw; coldness; freezing-point. *A la* —, with ice; iced, icy, ice; very cold. *Frapper de* —, to ice
Glacé, e, *part. adj.* frozen; freezing; frosted; frosty; iced; icy; icy cold, cold as ice, cold; chilled; chilling, frigid; preserved; glazed; shot-coloured, shot; damped; overpowered, paralyzed, struck; — *s m.* glazing, glaze; glazed articles; glazed gloves; — *s.f.* (*bot.*) ice-plant
Glacer, *v.a.n.* to freeze; to chill; to damp; to ice; to overpower, to paralyze, to strike; to frost; to glaze; to serge (*stitch*); — *v n.* to freeze; to chill [to become as paralyzed
Se—, *v.r.* to freeze; to chill; to grow weak;
Glacerie, *s.f.* ice-making, ice trade; ices; looking-glass trade *or* manufactory, plate-glass
Glaceu-r, se, *s.m.f.* glazer [manufactory
Glaceu-x, se, *adj.* icy, frosty; flawy
Glaciaire, *adj.* of glaciers [glacialist
Glaciairiste, *s.m.* one who studies glaciers,
Glacial, e, *adj.* freezing, frozen, icy, glacial, frigid, cold; — *s.f.* (*bot.*) ice-plant
Glaciation, *s.f.* glaciation
Glacier, *s.m.* ice-maker, dealer in ice *or* ices, confectioner; looking-glass *or* plate-glass maker; (*field of ice*) glacier

Glacière, *s.f.* ice-house; freezing-machine, refrigerator, ice-safe *or* box; mass of ice; (*geol.*) ice-cave, glacière
Glacis, *s.m.* glacis, slope, sloping bank; glazing, varnish; serging (*stitching*)
Glaçon, *s.m.* piece of ice; icicle; floe
Glaçure, *s.f.* glazing
Gladiateur, *s.m.* gladiator, prize-fighter, fighter
Gladiatoire, *adj.* gladiatorial, gladiatorian,
Gladié, e, *adj.* (*bot.*) gladiate [gladiatory
Glai, *s.m.* cluster of gladioles
Glaïeul, *s.m.* (*bot.*) gladiole, gladiolus, corn-flag
Glairage, *s.m.* glairing
Glaire, *s.m.* mucus, phlegm; (*chem.*) glair, glaire, ovalbumen, albumen, white of an egg (*raw*);
Glairer, *v.a.* to glair [slime, slimy matter
Glaireu-x, se, *adj.* glaireous, glairy; slimy;
Glairine, *s.f.* (*chem.*) glairine [mucous
Glairure, *s.f.* glairings
Glaise, *s.f. adj.* clay, loam. *Terre* —, clay, loam
Glaiser, *v.a.* to clay over, to clay, to loam
Glaiseu-x, se, *adj.* clayey, loamy
Glaisière, *s.f.* clay-pit, loam-pit
Glaive, *s.m.* sword, brand, blade, steel; knife
Glanage, *s.m.* gleaning
Gland, *s.m.* acorn; mast; tassel; (*anat.*) glans. — *de mer*, acorn-shell, acorn-barnacle. — *de terre*, earth-nut
Glandage, *s.m.* pannage (*duty*); (*vet.*) enlargement and induration of the glands (*in glanders*)
Glandaire, *adj.* feeding on acorns
Glande, *s.f.* gland; tumour, glans
Glandé, e, *adj.* (*vet.*) glandered; (*her.*) acorned
Glandée, *s.f.* crop of acorns *or* of masts; acorning; pannage
Glandifère, *adj.* (*bot.*) glandiferous
Glandiforme, *adj.* glandiform, acorn-shaped; (*anat.*) glandiform, gland-shaped [acorns
Glandivore, *adj.* glandivorous, feeding on
Glandulaire, *adj.* glandular, glandulous
Glandule, *s.f.* (*anat., bot.*) glandule
Glanduleu-x, se, *adj.* glandulous, glandular
Glandulifère, *adj.* glanduliferous
Glanduliforme, *adj.* glanduliform
Glane, *s.f.* glean, gleaning; (*of pears, onions*) cluster, rope; (*of straw*) wisp
Glaner, *v.a.n.* to glean
Glaneu-r, se, *s.m.f.* gleaner
Glanis, *s.m.* (*fish*) sly silurus, sheat-fish, shaden
Glanure, *s.f.* gleaning, gleanings
Glapir, *v.n.* to yelp; to squeak, to scream
Glapissement, *s.m.* yelping; squeaking, scream
Glaréole, *s.f.* (*bird*) sea-partridge
Glas, *s.m.* knell, passing-bell; tolling; (*mil.*) salute with guns (*funeral honours*); (*pop.*) grumbler, croaker
Glauber (Sel de), *s.m.* Glauber's salt
Glaubérite, *s.f.* (*min.*) glauberite
Glaucescence, *s.f.* glaucescence
Glaucescent, e, *adj.* glaucescent
Glaucier, *s.m.* (*bot.*) glaucium, horn-poppy
Glaucine, *s.f.* (*chem.*) glaucine
Glaucique, *adj.* (*chem.*) glaucic
Glaucomateu-x, se, *adj.* (*med.*) glaucomatous
Glaucome, *s.m.* (*med.*) glaucoma
Glauconie, Glauconite, *s.f.* (*min.*) glauconite
Glaucope, *s.m.* (*zool.*) glaucopis, wattle-bird
Glaucus, *s.m.* (*mollusc*) glaucus
Glaude, *s.m. adj. V.* **Claude**
Glauque, *adj.* glaucous, sea-green, green; — *s.m.* (*mollusc*) glaucus
Glaviau, *s.m.* (*rustic*) *V.* **Clavelée**
Glaviot, *s.m.* (*pop.*) gob (*spittle*)
Glaviotter, *v.n.* (*pop.*) to gob (*spit*)
Glaviotteu-r, se, *s.m.f.* (*pop.*) gobber (*spitter*)
Glayeul, *s.m. V.* **Glaïeul** [clod
Glèbe, *s.f.* glebe; earth; land; soil; ground;
‡**Glèchome, Glécome,** *s.m.* (*bot.*) ground-ivy
‡**Glèditschia,** *s.m.* (*bot.*) gleditschia, honey locust-tree, three-thorned acacia
Glène, *s.f.* (*anat.*) glene; (*nav.*) coil; (*fish.*) fish-
Gléner, *v.a.* (*nav.*) to coil [basket

Glénoïde, Glénoïdal, e, *adj.* (*anat.*) glenoid, glenoidal; — *s.f.* glenoid cavity
Glénoïdien, ne, *adj.* (*anat.*) of a glenoid cavity, cavity
Glette, *s.f.* (*metal.*) litharge
Gleucomètre, *s.m.* gleucometer, must-gauge
Gleucométr-ie, -ique. *V.* page 3, § 1
Gliadine, *s.f.* (*chem.*) gliadine
Gline, *s.f.* covered fish-basket
Glissade, *s.f.* slide, sliding; slip, slipping; (*dancing*) glissade. *Faire une* —, to have a slide; to make a slip
Glissage, *s.m.* sliding down
Glissant, e, *part. adj.* slipping, sliding, &c. (*V.* **Glisser**); slippery; dangerous; ticklish, delicate, tender; uncertain
Glissé, *s.m.* (*in dancing*) glisse
Glissement, *s.m.* slipping, sliding
Glisser, *v.n.a.* to slip; to slide; to glide; to glance off; to make little impression; to slur, to touch, to glance; to pass (over); to slip in; to slide in; to foist; to insinuate; to edge in; to introduce; to whisper
Se —, *v.r.* to slip; to glide; to insinuate *or* introduce oneself; to creep (in, into), to steal, to find its way
Glisseu-r, se, *s.m.f.* (*pers.*) slider
Glissière, *s.f.* (*tech.*) slide, groove
Glissoir, *s.m.* slider; slide
Glissoire, *s.f.* slide
Globe, *s.m.* globe; orb; ball; glass shade, shade; tut. — *de feu*, fire-ball
Globeu-x, se, *adj.* globous, round
Globo (In), *adv.* (*Latin*) in a mass, in the lump, bodily
Globulaire, *adj.* globular; — *s.f.* (*bot.*) globularia, madwort
Globule, *s.m.* globule; air-hole
Globuleu-x, se, *adj.* globulous, globular
Globuline, *s.f.* globuline
Gloire, *s.f.* glory; fame; homage; vanity; pride; boast, boasting; halo of glory; (*in fireworks*) sun. *Mettre sa* — *à*, to glory in. *Se faire* — *de*, to glory in, to boast of, to make it o.'s boast
Gloria, *s.m.* (*fam.*) coffee with brandy, burnt coffee
Gloriette, *s.f.* pavilion; summer-house, alcove
Glorieusement, *adv.* gloriously; honourably
Glorieu-x, se, *adj. s.* glorious; honourable; glorified, blessed; proud; boastful, vain, vainglorious, conceited; vain *or* conceited person, boaster, braggart
Glorifiable, *adj.* glorifiable
Glorifiant, e, *part. adj.* glorifying; (*pop.*) honourable
Glorification, *s.f.* glorification; glory
Glorifier, *v.a.* to glorify; to honour
Se —, *v.r.* to glory (in); to boast (of), to be proud (of), to pride *or* plume oneself (upon)
Gloriole, *s.f.* vainglory, vanity
Glose, *s.f.* gloss, comment; carping, reflection; criticism; parody
Gloser, *v.a.n.* to gloss, to comment; to carp at, to criticize, to censure, to find fault with
Gloseu-r, se, *s.m.f.* carper, criticizer, censurer, fault-finder
Glossaire, *s.m.* glossary; vocabulary
Glossalgie, *s.f.* (*med.*) glossalgia, glossalgy
Glossanthrax, *s.m.* (*med., vet.*) glossanthrax, carbuncle of the tongue
Glossateur, *s.m.* glossator, glosser, glossarist
Glossien, ne, Glossique, *adj.* of the tongue
Glossite, *s.f.* (*med.*) glossitis
Glosso, (*in compounds*) glosso-...
Glossocèle, *s.f.* (*med.*) glossocele
Glossographe, *s.m.* glossographer
Glossograph-ie, -ique. *V.* page 3, § 1
Glossolog-ie, -ique. *V.* page 3, § 1
Glossologue, *s.m.* glossologist
Glossopètre, *s.m.* (*fossil*) glossopetra
Glossotomie, *s.f.* (*surg.*) glossotomy
Glotte, *s.f.* (*anat.*) glottis
Glottique, *adj.* (*anat.*) glottic, glottal
Glottite, *s.f.* (*med.*) glottitis
Glougloter, *v.n.* (*of turkeys*) *V.* **Glouglouter**
Glouglou, *s.m.* gurgling, gurgle; (*of turkeys*) gobble
Glouglouter, *v.n.* to gurgle; (*of turkeys*) to gobble; (*pop.*) to drink, to swig
Gloume, *s.f.* *V.* **Glume**
Gloussement, *s.m.* clucking, chucking, chuckling, cluck, chuck, chuckle
Glousser, *v.n.* to cluck, to chuck, to chuckle
Glouteron, *s.m.* (*bot.*) burdock, bur
Glouton, ne, *adj. s.m.f.* gluttonous, ravenous, greedy; glutton; — *s.m.* (*zool.*) wolverine, wolverene, glutton
Gloutonnement, *adv.* gluttonously, ravenously, greedily
Gloutonnerie, *s.f.* gluttony, greediness
Glu, *s.f.* birdlime, lime; (*bot., nav.*) glue
Gluant, e, *adj.* limy; slimy, clammy, sticky; tenacious; (*bot.*) glutinous
Gluau, *s.m.* lime-twig
Glucose, *s.f.* (*chem.*) glucose, glycose
Gluer, *v.a.* to lime; to make sticky
Glui, *s.m.* rye-straw
Glumacé, e, *adj.* (*bot.*) glumaceous
Glume, *s.f.* (*bot.*) glume, boll, husk, chaff
Gluten, *s.m.* gluten
Glutinant, e, Glutinati-f, ve, *adj.* glutinative
Glutination, *s.f.* glutination
Glutine, *s.f.* (*chem.*) glutine
Glutineu-x, se, *adj.* glutinous, viscous, viscid, sticky, adhesive
Glutinosité, *s.f.* glutinosity, glutinousness
Glycérie, *s.f.* (*bot.*) glyceria, manna-grass
Glycérine, *s.f.* (*chem.*) glycerine
Glycérinien, ne, Glycérique, *adj.* (*chem.*) glyceric
Glycine, *s.f.* (*chem., bot.*) glycine
Glycol, *s.m.* (*chem.*) glycol
Glyconien, ne, Glyconique, *adj.* (*ancient vers.*) glyconian, glyconic
Glycose, *s.f.* (*chem.*) glycose, glucose
Glycosurie, *s.f.* (*med.*) glycosuria, diabetes
Glyphe, *s.m.* (*arch.*) glyph
Glyptique, *s.f.* glyptics
Glypto-graphie, -logie, &c. *V.* page 3, § 1
Gmelin, *s.m.*, **Gmelinie,** *s.f.* (*bot.*) gmelina, goombar, koombar
†**Gnangnan,** *adj.* (*fam.*) effeminate, indolent, sluggish, lazy, spiritless, fainthearted; — *s.m.f.* ditto person
Gneiss, *s.m.* (*min.*) gneiss
Gnet, *s.m.* (*bot.*) joint-fir
†**Gniaf,** *s.m.* (*pop.*) *V.* **Savetier**
†**Gniaffer,** *v.a.* (*pop.*) *V.* **Saveter**
†**Gniangnian,** *adj. s.* *V.* **Gnangnan**
†**Gniff,** *adj.* (*pop., of wine*) clear, bright
†**Gniole, Gnole,** *s.f.* (*pop., old*) *V.* **Torgnole**
†**Gnognote,** *s.f.* (*pop.*) trash, rubbish, small beer, duffers
Gnome, *s.m.* gnome
Gnomide, *s.f.* gnome
Gnomique, *adj.* gnomic, gnomical
Gnomon, *s.m.* gnomon
Gnomonique, *adj.* gnomonic, gnomonical; — *s.f.* gnomonics, dialling
Gnomoniste, *s.m.* gnomonist
†**Gnon,** *s.m.* (*pop.*) *V.* **Torgnole**
Gnost-icisme, -ique. *V.* page 3, § 1
Gnou, *s.m.* (*zool.*) gnu, antelope gnu, horned horse
Go (Tout de), *adv.* freely, easily, of itself, without difficulty, without ceremony
†**Goailler,** &c. (*old spelling*) *V.* **Gouailler**
Gobe, *s.f.* poison-ball (*for noxious animals, dogs*); fattening-ball, cob (*for poultry*); (*vet.*) wool-ball (*in sheep*); — *s.m.f.* (*in compounds, from* **Gober,** "to swallow," &c.) person *or* animal that swallows, swallower (*V.* **Gobe-mouches,** &c.)
Gobelet, *s.m.* goblet; cup, juggler's cup *or* thimble; (*of palaces, obsolete*) ewry. *Jouer des* —*s*, to thimble-rig. *Joueur de* —*s*, thimble-rigger. *Tours de* —*s*, thimble-rigs, thimble-rigging
Gobelèterie, Gobeletterie, *s.f.* goblet and drinking-glass manufactory *or* trade; goblets, cups, table-glass
Gobeletier, *s.m.* goblet and drinking-glass maker
Gobelin, *s.m.* goblin; —**s,** *pl.* goblins; Gobelins (*manufactory of tapestry in Paris*)
Gobeloter, *v.n.* to tipple
Gobeloterie, *s.f.* tippling
Gobeloteu-r, se, *s.m.f.* tippler
Gobe-moucherie, *s.f.* gullibility, stupidity, spooniness; trifling

Gobe-moucherons, *s.m.* (*bird*) gnat-snapper
Gobe-mouches, *s.m.* (*bird*) fly-catcher; (*plant*) catchfly, fly-trap; (*pers.*) gull, ninny, spoony; trifler
Gober, *v.a.* to gobble up, to gorge, to gulp down, to swallow down, to swallow; to believe easily *or* foolishly; to snap; to catch; to nab; to endure, to put up with, to pocket. — *le morceau*, to swallow the bait, to be caught *or* taken in. — *des mouches* or *du vent*, to trifle o.'s time away, to waste o.'s time [admire oneself
Se —, *v.r.* to be gobbled *or* &c.; (*pop.*) to
Goberge, *s.f.* cross-bar (*of a bedstead*), lath; veneering-stick; large species of cod-fish
Goberger, *v.a.* to entertain, to treat; to indulge, to coddle
Se —, *v.r.* to take o.'s ease, to indulge oneself, to coddle oneself; to feast, to live well; to amuse *or* enjoy oneself; (*obsolete*) to make fun *or* game (of)
Gobet, *s.m.* gobbet, mouthful; joint of meat, joint, piece; credulous person, gull; (*pop.*) scamp; gobet (*kind of cherry*). *Prendre au* —,
Gobetage, *s.m.* (*mas.*) pointing, stopping [to nab
Gobeter, *v.a.* (*mas.*) to point, to stop
Gobetis, *s.m.* (*mas.*) pointing, rough-cast
Gobeu-r, se, *s.m.f.* swallower, gobbler, gulper, eater; simpleton, gull; (*local*) porter. — *de mouches*, (*bird*) fly-catcher
Gobichonnade, *s.f.* (*pop.*) *V.* **Ripaille**
Gobichonner, *v.n.* (*pop.*) *V.* **Riboter**
Gobichonneur, *s.m.* (*pop.*) *V.* **Riboteur**
Gobie, *s.m.* (*fish*) goby
†Gobillard, *s.m.* stave-wood
†Gobille, *s.f.* (*mach.*) ball
Gobin, *s.m.* (*pop.*) hunchback; odd fellow
Godage, *s.m.* puckering, pucker, puckers, creasing, crease, creases
†Godaille, *s.f.* feasting, feast, guttling, guzzling, carousal, blow-out; good cheer, extravagant living; toping; bad wine [feast
†Godailler, *v.n.* to tope, to carouse, to riot, to
†Godailleu-r, se, *s.m.f.* toper, carouser, boozer
Godan, *s.m.* (*pop.*) dodge, trick, snare, fib, flam, sham, shift
Godancer, *v.n.* (*pop.*) to be caught *or* taken in
Goddam, Goddem, *s.m.* (*pop.*) Englishman
Godelureau, *s.m.* fop, coxcomb, spark
Godenot, *s.m.* puppet, juggler's puppet, Jack in the box; (*pers.*) scrubby fellow, runt, ill-shaped
Goder, *v.n.* to crease, to pucker [dwarf, Punch
Godet, *s.m.* cup; bucket; bowl (*of a tobacco-pipe*); crease, pucker
Godiche, Godichon, ne, *adj. s.m.f.* awkward, clumsy, gawky; spoony; silly, foolish, simple; timid, nervous; ditto person, spoony, silly, stupid, simpleton, ninny, booby
†Godille, *s.f.* (*nav.*) scull [merry, to be pleased
†Godiller, *v.n.* (*nav.*) to scull; (*pop.*) to make
†Godilleur, *s.m.* (*nav.*) sculler [pie
Godiveau, *s.m.* (*old*) veal-forcemeat, forcemeat-
Godron, *s.m.* godroon; (*obsolete*) gauffer, round plait [fering, round plaiting
Godronnage, *s.m.* godrooning; (*obsolete*) gauf-
Godronner, *v.a.* to godroon; (*old*) to gauffer, to plait round
Godronneu-r, se, *s.m.f.* godrooner
Godronnoir, *s.m.* hollow punch
Godure, *s.f.* *V.* **Godage** [gomaster, &c.)
Goèland, *s.m.* (large) gull, sea-gull (wagel, bur-
Goèlette, *s.f.* (*nav.*) schooner; (*bird*) sea-swallow
Goèmon, *s.m.* (*local*) sea-weed, sea-ware, sea-grass, sea-wrack, wrack
Goét-ie, -ique. *V.* page 3, § 1
Goffe, *adj.* (*old*) ill-shaped, awkward, churlish
†Gogaille, *s.f.* merry-making, feast, good living; over-eating, over-drinking
Gogo, *s.m.* simpleton, gull, gudgeon. *A* —, in clover, in abundance, in plenty, plentifully, as much as one likes, freely
Goguenard, e, *adj.* jeering, bantering, chaffing; — *s.m.f.* jeerer, banterer, chaffer
Goguenarder, *v.n.* to jeer, to banter, to chaff; to joke, to crack jokes
Goguenarderie, *s.f.* jeering, jeer, bantering, banter, chaffing, chaff; joking, joke, jokes
Goguenot, *s.m.* (*mil.*) can; urinal, privy
Goguette, *s.f.* singing-society (*meeting in a public-house*), free and easy party; merry song; merry talk *or* saying *or* story *or* thing; mirth, merry mood [member of a singing-society
Goguettier, *s.m.* singer of merry songs;
Goinfrade, *s.f.* guttling, blow-out [greedy-gut
Goinfre, *s.m.* gormandizer, guttler, glutton,
Goinfrer, *v.n.* to gormandize, to guttle; to stuff, to cram [tling, stuffing, blow-out
Goinfrerie, *s.f.* gormandizing, gluttony; gut-
Goiran, *s.m.* *V.* **Bondrée**
Goître, *s.m.* (*med.*) goitre, bronchocele, Derbyshire neck, wen (on the neck); (*bot.*) struma
Goîtreu-x, se, *adj. s.* goitrous, goitrous person
Golfe, *s.m.* gulf; bay; frith, firth [beetle
Goliath, *s.m.* Goliath, giant; (*zool.*) Goliath-
Gomariste, *s.m.* (*eccl. hist.*) Gomarite, Gomarist
Gomart, *s.m.* *V.* **Gommart**
Gombaut, Gombo, *s.m.* gombo (*plant, fruit*)
Gommage, *s.m.* gumming
Gommart, *s.m.* (*bot.*) bursera
Gommate, *s.m.* (*chem.*) gummate
Gomme, *s.f.* gum; indiarubber; (*hort.*) gumming (*disease*). — *élastique*, indiarubber. — *gutte*, gamboge
Gommé, e, *part. adj.* gummed, gummy
Gommement, *s.m.* gumming
Gommer, *v.a.* to gum; to mix with gum
Se —, *v.r.* to be gummed *or* &c.
Gommeu-x, se, *adj.* gummous, gummy
Gommier, *s.m.* (*bot.*) gum-tree
Gommifère, *adj.* gummiferous
Gommique, *adj.* (*chem.*) gummic [resinous
Gommo-résineu-x, se, *adj.* (*chem.*) gummo-
Gomorrhéen, ne, *adj. s.* Gomorrhean
Gomphose, *s.f.* (*anat.*) gomphosis
Gomphrène, *s.f.* (*bot.*) *V.* **Amarantine**
Gonagre, *s.f.* (*med.*) gonagra, gout in the knee; — *adj.* affected with ditto
Gonalgie, *s.f.* (*med.*) gonalgia, pain in the knee
Gond, *s.m.* hinge. *Hors des —s*, off the hinges, unhinged; exasperated, beside oneself, out of o.'s senses; out of sorts. *Faire sortir* (or *Mettre*) *hors des —s*, to unhinge; to exasperate;
Gonder, *v.a.* to hinge [to put out of sorts
Gondolage, *s.m.* (*tech.*) warping, swelling, bulging; (*nav.*) sheering round
Gondole, *s.f.* gondola; car (*of a balloon*); drinking-cup; (*med.*) eye-bath, eye-glass; stage-carriage; gondola-chair; gutter, trench
Gondolé, e, *part. adj.* warped, &c. (*V.* **Gondoler**); (*nav.*) round-sheered
Gondoler, *v.n.* (*tech.*) to warp, to swell, to bulge; (*nav.*) to sheer round
Gondolier, *s.m.* gondolier
Gonfalon, Gonfanon, *s.m.* gonfalon
Gonfalonier, *s.m.* gonfalonier
Gonflement, *s.m.* swelling; swelling out; inflation; distension; increase; tumidness; wind
Gonfler, *v.a.n.*, **Se** —, *v.r.* to swell; to swell out; to make ... swell; to puff; to puff up; to inflate; to distend; to increase
Gong, *s.m.* (*mus. instr.*) gong
Gongonner, *v.n.* (*fam.*) to crease, to pucker
Gonin, *s.m.* *Maître* —, (*pop.*) artful dodger, knave, rogue, rascal
Goniomètre, *s.m.* goniometer
Goniométr-ie, -ique. *V.* page 3, § 1
Gonne, *s.f.* barrel, cask, last; tar-barrel
Gonnelle, *s.f.* *V.* **Gunnel**
Gonocèle, *s.f.* (*med.*) gonocele
Gonorrhée, *s.f.* (*med.*) gonorrhœa
Gonorrhéique, *adj.* (*med.*) gonorrhœal
Gord, *s.m.* fishing-weir, bow-net
Gordie, *s.f.* (*zool.*) hair-worm, hair-eel
Gordien, ne, *adj.* Gordian
Gore, *s.f.* (*obsolete*) sow

Goret, *s.m.* little pig, pig; dirty fellow; (*shoemaker's, hatter's*) foreman; (*nav.*) hog
Goreter, *v.a.* (*nav.*) to hog
Gorge, *s.f.* throat; breast, bosom; neck; gullet; orifice, aperture, mouth; pass, strait, defile; (*fort., arch.*) gorge; (*of a chimney*) throat; (*of a pulley, of a wheel*) groove; (*of a wall-map,* &c.) ledge; (*obsolete form of* "courge") yoke. — *chaude,* (*falc.*) hawk's fee; (*fig.*) mouthful, good meal; fun, good laugh. — **-de-pigeon,** *adj.* shot-coloured, shot, columbine; *s.m.* shot-colour, dove-colour. *A — déployée, V.* **Déployé.** *Mal de* —, sore throat. *Avoir mal à la* —, to have a sore throat. *Faire des —s chaudes de, faire — chaude de,* to laugh *or* chuckle at, to make fun of, to have a good laugh over, to be much amused with *or* overjoyed at. *Rendre* —, to disgorge, to vomit
Gorgée, *s.f.* draught, mouthful, gulp, sip
Gorger, *v.a.* to gorge, to glut, to cram, to fill; [to swell
Gorgeret, *s.m.* (*surg.*) gorget
Gorgerette, *s.f.* gorget (*lady's ruff*); (*child's*) cap-string; (*bird*) blackcap
Gorgerin, *s.m.* gorget (*of armour*), neck-piece; (*dog's*) strong collar, collar with spikes; (*arch.*) [gorgerin
Gorget, *s.m.* (*carp.*) moulding-plane
†Gorgniat, *s.m.* (*pop.*) pig, dirty fellow
Gorgone, *s.f.* (*myth.*) Gorgon; (*zool.*) gorgonia
†Gorille, *s.m.* (*zool.*) gorilla
Gosier, *s.m.* throat; gullet; voice
Gossampin, *s.m.* (*bot.*) silk-cotton tree
Gosse, *s.f.* (*fam.*) bad joke; fib, sham, flam, story, bouncer, humbug, hoax
Gosser, *v.a.n.,* **Se** —, *v.r.* to jeer, to banter, to chaff, to joke, to jest, to make game *or* fun (of); to tell stories, to fib, to humbug, to hoax
Gosserie, *s.f.* jeering, banter, chaff; story, fib, flam, humbugging, humbug, hoax
Gosseu-r, se, *s.m.f.* jeerer, banterer, chaffer; story-teller, bouncer, humbug; — *adj.* jeering, bantering, chaffing; fibbing, bouncing, hum- [bugging
Gossypine, *s.f.* (*chem.*) gossypine
Goth, *s.m.* Goth; barbarian
Gothicité, *s.f.* gothicism
Gothique, *adj. s.* Gothic; old-fashioned, antiquated, old; barbarian, savage; black (*letter*); old English, black letter; Elizabethan type
Gothon, Goton, *s.f.* slattern, slut; wench
Gouache, *s.f.* body-colour, body-colours; body-colour painting *or* drawing
Gouacher, *v.a.n.* to paint in body-colour
Gouachiste, *s.m.f.* body-colour painter
†Gouailler, *v.a.n.* (*fam.*) to jeer, to chaff, to humbug
†Gouaillerie, *s.f.* (*fam.*) jeering, chaffing, chaff
†Gouailleu-r, se, *s.m.f.* (*fam.*) jeerer, chaffer; — *adj.* jeering, chaffing [ballad-singer, singer
Gouaieu-r, se, *s. m.f.* (*pop.*) street-singer,
Gouape, &c. *V.* **Gouêpe,** &c.
†Goudille, &c. *V.* **Godille,** &c.
Goudran, *s.m.* (*mil.*) dipped bavin [tar, gas-tar
Goudron, *s.m.* tar. — *minéral,* mineral tar; coal-
Goudronnage, *s.m.* tarring; dipping (*of bot-* [*tles*)
Goudronnaire, *adj.* tarry
Goudronné, e, *part. adj.* tarred. *Eau —e,* tar-water. *Toile —e,* tarpaulin
Goudronner, *v.a.* to tar; to dip (*bottles*)
Goudronnerie, *s.f* tar-works
Goudronneur, *s.m.* tarrer
Goudronneu-x, se, *adj.* tarry
Gouêpe, Goueppe, *s.f.* (*pop.*) idling, loafing, hulking; idler, lazy brute, loafer, hulker
Gouêper, Gouepper, *v.n.* (*pop.*) to idle, to loaf, to hulk
Gouêpeu-r, Goueppeu-r, se, *s.m.f.* idler, lazy brute, loafer, hulker; — *adj.* idling, lazy, loafing, hulking [pint, wake-robin
Gouet, *s.m.* hedging-bill; (*bot.*) arum, cuckoo-
Gouffre, *s.m.* gulf, abyss, pit; whirlpool
Gouge, *s.f.* gouge; (*pop.*) bad woman
Gouger, *v.a.* to gouge
Gougette, *s.f.* small gouge

†Gouille, *s.f.* throwing for a scramble; scram- [ble
Gouin, *s.m.* slovenly sailor
Gouine, *s.f.* trull, wench
Goujat, *s.m.* hodman; (*mil.*) servant, scrub; (*nav.,* — *de vaisseau*) powder-monkey; (*fig.*) dirty *or* vulgar fellow; snob; blackguard; bungler, botcher
Goujon, *s.m.* gudgeon; iron pin. *Avaler le* —, to swallow the bait, to fall into the snare; to make a bad spec; to kick the bucket
Goujonner, *v.a.* to gudgeon; to pin
Goujonnier, *s.m.* gudgeon-net [ruffe, ruff
Goujonnière, *s.f. adj. Perche* —, (*fish*) pope,
Goulard (Eau de), *s.f.* Goulard lotion *or* water
Goule, *s.f.* (*pop.*) mouth; gullet, stomach, guts, eating and drinking, stuffing; (*elf*) ghoul
Goulée, *s.f.* (*pop.*) mouthful, gulp; feed, grub
Goulet, *s.m.* narrow entrance, inlet, mouth, [pass, neck
Goulette, *s.f. V.* **Goulotte**
Gouliafre, *s.m.f.* (*pop.*) *V.* **Goinfre;** — *adj.* [gluttonous, greedy
Goulique, *adj.* ghoulish
Goulot, *s.m.* (*of a bottle,* &c.) neck; (*pop.*) mouth, mug. *Arroser au* —, (*hort.*) to use the water-pot without the rose [canal
Goulotte, *s.f.* water-channel, gullet, gutter;
Goulu, e, *adj. s.* gluttonous, greedy; glutton, gobbler, cormorant
Goulument, *adv.* gluttonously, greedily
Goum, *s.m.* (*Arabian mil. term*) contingent (*in* [*Algeria*)
†Goupille, *s.f.* (*tech.*) pin
†Goupiller, *v.a.* to pin
†Goupillon, *s.m.* holy-water sprinkler; sprinkling-brush; bottle-brush
†Goupillonner, *v.a.* to sprinkle with holy water; to sprinkle; to clean with a brush
Gour, *s.m.* pool, puddle; (*zool.*) gaur, gour
Goura, *s.m.* (*zool.*) goura, crested pigeon, Victoria pigeon [gourami
Gourami, Gouramy, *s.m.* (*fish*) goramy,
Gourbet, *s.m.* (*local*) sand-reed
Gourbi, Gourbil, *s.m.* (*Arabian*) hut *or* village
Gourd, e, *adj.* benumbed; (*of corn*) growy
Gourde, *s.f.* pilgrim's bottle, gourd; wicker bottle, flask; (*bot.*) gourd; (*coin*) gourde, gourd; (*obsolete*) bump; swelling
Gourdin, *s.m.* cudgel, club
Gourdiner, *v.a.* to cudgel
Goure, *s.f.* adulterated drug; (*pop.*) take-in, flam, sham, hoax, duffer, cheat
Gourer, *v.a.* to adulterate (*drugs*); (*pop.*) to take in, to hoax, to cheat
Goureu-r, se, *s.m.f.* adulterator of drugs; (*pop.*) trickster, duffer, cheat
Gourgalle, *s.m. V.* **Poupart**
Gourgandine, *s.f.* woman *or* girl of the town, street-walker, wench [knock about in bad places
Gourgandiner, *v.n.* to lead a dissolute life, to
Gourgane, *s.f.* (*bot.*) Mazagan bean; **—s,** *pl.* (*pop.*) beans, lentils, &c., pulse
Gourgouran, *s.m.* Indian silk
Gourmade, *s.f.* cuff, fisticuff, punch, blow
Gourmand, e, *adj.* gluttonous, greedy; fond of good living, epicurean; dainty; (*hort., agr.*) parasitic, useless, troublesome, exhaustive; — *s.m.f.* gormand, gourmand, gormandizer, glutton, greedy fellow *or* thing; epicure, gastronomist, good liver
Gourmander, *v.a.* to scold, to chide, to reprove, to rebuke, to snub, to taunt; to blame, to accuse; to check, to curb; (*obsolete*) to challenge; to command; (*hort.*) to prune (*trees*); (*of trees themselves*) to injure (*other trees*); (*cook., obsolete*) to lard, to stuff, to season, to garnish; — *v.n.* to gormandize
Gourmandise, *s.f.* gormandizing, gluttony, greediness; daintiness; (*hort.*) parasiticalness, parasitism
Gourme, *s.f.* (*vet.*) strangles; (*of children*) teething eruptions, ill humours; (*obsolete*) stiffness, affected gravity, solemnity. *Jeter sa* —, to have ditto (*as above*), to throw off o.'s ill humours; (*fig.*) to sow o.'s wild oats

Gourmé,e, *part. adj.* curbed, &c. (*V.* **Gourmer**); stiff, formal, affectedly grave, solemn

Gourmer, *v.a.* to curb (*horses*); to cuff, to punch, to box, to pommel, to beat; (*obsolete*) to stiffen

Gourmet, *s.m.* judge of wines and good living; good liver, epicure; (*obsolete*) wine-taster; — *adj.* fond of good living, epicurean

Gourmette, *s.f.* (*rid.*) curb, curb-chain

Gournable, *s.m.* (*nav.*) trenail, treenail

Gournabler, *v.a.* (*nav.*) to trenail [young thief

Gouspin, *s.m.* (*pop.*) cad, rough, tramp, cadger,

Gouspiner, *v.n.* (*pop.*) to be on the tramp, to loaf, to hulk

Goussant, Goussaud, Goussaut, e, *adj. s.* thickset, stubby; ditto horse *or* mare *or* dog, &c.

Gousse, *s.f.* pod, husk, shell, cod; (*of garlic*) clove; **—s,** *pl.* pods, &c.; (*arch.*) honeysuckle

Gousset, *s.m.* fob; pocket; gusset; arm-pit; smell from ditto; (*obsolete, fig.*) purse; (*carp.*) bracket, brace; (*nav.*) helm-port. *Vider un —,* (*obsolete*) to pick a pocket

Goût, *s.m.* taste; palate; relish; savour; flavour; smell; inclination, fancy, liking; style; manner. *De haut —,* rich, high-seasoned, high-flavoured, high-tasted. *Trouver à son —,* to like, to approve of, to be pleased with, to relish, to be partial to [*ing*) *V.* **Goûter,** *s.m.*

Goûté, *part. of* **Goûter,** *v.a.n.*; — *s.m.* (*old spell-*

Goûter, *s.m.* (a light meal that used to be taken, like 'tea' in England, between dinner and supper); (*obsolete or local*) luncheon, lunch; collation

Goûter, *v.a.n.* to taste; to smell; to relish; to enjoy; to like; to approve of, to approve; to appreciate; to delight in; to try; to have a taste (of); to eat something; (*obsolete or local*) to lunch, to take a luncheon [each other

Se —, *v.r.* to be tasted *or* &c.; to like *or* &c.

Gouttant, e, *adj.* dripping; dropping; draining

Goutte, *s.f.* drop; drip; dram, drink, tipple, liquor, creature; small quantity, jot; gout; — *adv.* in the least, at all, anything. — *militaire,* gleet. — *sciatique,* sciatica, hip-gout. — *sereine,* gutta serena, drop serene. — *de sang,* drop of blood; (*bot.*) corn adonis, bird's-eye, pheasant's-eye. *Petite —,* little drop; liquor, creature. *Boire la —,* to take a dram *or* a drop. *Payer la —,* to stand something to drink. *Ne voir —, n'y voir —,* not to see (*or* can't see) at all *or* anything *or* one jot *or* bit; not to see (*or* can't see) through it

Goutté, e, *adj.* (*her.*) gutté, gutty

Gouttelette, *s.f.* little drop

Goutteu-x, se, *adj. s.* gouty; gouty person

Gouttière, *s.f.* gutter; spout; roof, house-top; groove; channel; (*of carriages*) cornice; (*of books*) fore-edge; (*anat.*) groove; (*surg.*) wire splint

Gouvernable, *adj.* governable, manageable

†Gouvernail, *s.m.* rudder, helm; (*of a wind-mill*) flier, fan, fan-tail [governorship; tutorship

Gouvernance, *s.f.* governance, government,

Gouvernant, *s.m.* governor, ruler [housekeeper

Gouvernante, *s.f.* governor's wife; governess;

Gouverne, *s.f.* guidance, direction, rule, government; (*nav.*) steering; sculling

Gouvernement, *s.m.* government; rule, sway; management; direction; care; keeping; command; steering, steerage; governorship; governor's house, government-house

Gouvernemental, e, *adj.* governmental

Gouverner, *v.a.n.* to govern; to rule; to sway; to have great influence over; to manage; to direct; to guide; to conduct; to regulate; to control; to command; to husband; to take care of; to bring up, to educate, to rear, to breed; to rein up; (*nav.*) to steer; to answer the helm

Se —, *v.r.* to govern oneself; to manage o.'s own affairs; to take care of oneself; to behave, to conduct oneself; to be governed *or* &c.

Gouverneur, *s.m.* governor; ruler; manager;

Gouvion, *s.m.* (*tech.*) pin, bolt [steersman; tutor

Goyave, Gouyave, *s.f.* (*bot.*) guava

Goyavier, Gouyavier, *s.m.* (*bot.*) guava-tree

Graal, *s.m.* Grail, Graal, Gral, Greal (*miraculous chalice*)

Grabat, *s.m.* pallet. *Sur le —,* very ill, laid up, bedridden, on a sick-bed; in great poverty, miserably poor

Grabataire, *adj. s.m.f.* ill in bed, bedridden; ditto person, sick man *or* woman

Grabeau, *s.m.* (*com.*) garbles, fragments, crumblings, siftings, dust, waste, refuse

Grabelage, *s.m.* cleaning, sifting

Grabeler, *v.a.* to clean, to sift

Grabeleu-r, se, *s.m.f.* cleaner, sifter

Grabuge, *s.m.* (*pop.*) squabble, squabbling, row, riot, kick-up, set-to

Grâce, *s.f.* grace; favour; pardon; forgiveness; mercy; indulgence; gracefulness; charm; thanks (to), owing (to); **—s,** *pl.* graces; Graces (*in myth.*); grace; favours; charms; thanks; (*game*) graces, sticks and hoops; (*after meals*) grace. *Bonne —,* good grace; good air; genteel way; readiness; (*tailor's*) wrapper; (*of a bed*) head-curtain. *Action de —s,* thanksgiving. *L'an de —,* the year of grace, in the year of our Lord. — *à Dieu, V.* **Dieu.** *A la — de Dieu,* to the mercy of God; (*fam.*) at random, at sixes and sevens, higgledy-piggledy; happen what may! *De — !* pray! I pray! I beg of you! I entreat you! for mercy's sake, for goodness sake. *De bonne —,* with a good grace; gracefully; readily. *De mauvaise —,* with a bad grace; ungracefully; reluctantly, grudgingly. *Par —,* for mercy's sake. *Par — pour,* out of favour to, for the sake of. *Avoir* or *recevoir en —,* to look upon ... mercifully *or* with an eye of favour. *Demander —,* to ask pardon; to cry mercy; to crave quarter. *Demander* or *prier en —,* to beg *or* ask as a favour, to entreat. *Faire — à,* to forgive, to pardon; to be indulgent to. *Faire une* or *la —,* to do a *or* the favour. *Faire — de,* to forgive; to pardon; to excuse, to grant, to spare, to let off for, to dispense with. *Rendre —s à,* to thank, to give *or* return thanks. *Rentrer en —,* to be restored to favour. *Rentrer dans les bonnes —s de,* to regain the favour of

Graciable, *adj.* (*law*) pardonable

Gracier, *v.a.* (*law*) to pardon

Gracieusement, *adv.* graciously, kindly; gracefully; courteously

Gracieuser, *v.a.* to give marks of kindness to, to show kindness to, to treat kindly, to welcome; — *v.n.* to display o.'s graces

Gracieuseté, *s.f.* graciousness, kindness; courtesy, civility; kind attention; gratuity, acknowledgment

Gracieu-x, se, *adj.* gracious, kind; obliging; graceful; pleasant, pleasing, agreeable; courteous, civil; voluntary; — *s.m.* gracefulness; graceful style; (*pers.*) gracioso (*buffoon*). *A titre —,* by mere favour, through mere kindness, merely to oblige [shrillness

Gracilité, *s.f.* gracility, slenderness, slimness;

Graciole, *s.f.* graciole (*kind of pear*)

Gracioso, *s.m.* (*Spanish*) gracioso (*buffoon*)

Gradati-f, ve, *adj.* gradatory

Gradation, *s.f.* gradation; degrees; climax. — *descendante* or *inverse,* anticlimax

Grade, *s.m.* grade; rank; degree; step; dignity; title; post, situation; position

Gradé, *adj.m.* (*mil.*) having an inferior rank; — *s.m.* non-commissioned officer

Grader, *v.a.* to confer rank on

Gradin, *s.m.* bench *or* form *or* seat (*in tiers*), gradin; step; shelf. *Sur les —s,* (*fig.*) at col-

Gradine, *s.f.* gradine (*chisel*) [lege, at school

Gradualité, *s.f.* graduality

Graduateur, *s.m.* graduator

Graduation, *s.f.* graduation; drying-house

Gradué, e, *part. adj.* graduated; progressive; gradual; — *s.m.f.* graduate

Graduel, le, *adj.* gradual; — *s.m.* (*Cath. rel.*) gradual, graduale; choir-book

Graduellement, *adv.* gradually

Graduer, *v.a.* to graduate; to raise, to increase

Gradus, *s.m.* gradus (*dictionary*)

†Graffigner, *v.a.n.* (*pop.*) to grab; to scratch

Graffin, *s.m.* (*pop.*) rag-picker

Grafitto (*pl.* **Grafitti**), *s.m.* grafitto, graffito [(*pl.* —i)

†Graille, *s.f.* (*pop.*) crow

†Graillement, *s.m.* hoarseness, huskiness, hoarse *or* husky voice, hoarse sound

†Grailler, *v.n. V.* **Forhuer**

†Graillon, *s.m.* burnt fat *or* grease, burnt meat; broken meat, broken victuals, scraps, remnants; marble-chippings; gob (*spittle*); — *s.f.*, *Marie* —, slattern, slut, drab, mopsey

†Graillonner, *v.n.* to burn; (*pers.*) to hawk up phlegm, to hawk, to gob

†Graillonneu-r, se, *s.m.f.* gobber; dealer in broken victuals; bad cook

Grain, *s.m.* grain; seed; corn; berry; bead; bullion (*of epaulets*); jot, bit, particle, spark; drop; touch; squall, gust of wind; black cloud; shower; (*slang*) half-franc piece (5*d.*), tanner. — *de beauté*, mole. — *de grêle*, hailstone. — *d'orge*, barley-corn. — *de raisin*, grape. — *de petite vérole*, pock-mark. *Gros —s*, *gros* —, coarse grain, large berries, large beads, large bullion, &c.; (*silk*) gros grain; (*agr.*) wheat and rye. *Menus —s*, barley, oats, and peas, spring-corn. *Petit* —, orange berries; oil of ditto. *A gros —s*, with coarse grain, coarse-grained; &c. (*V. Gros —s*); (*of Catholics*) lax. *A* or *De — d'orge*, *— d'orge*, nappy. *Avoir un — (de folie)*, to be a little crack-brained. *Être dans le* —, (*fig.*, *pop.*) to be on the road to fortune

Grainage, *s.m.* granulating, &c. (*V.* **Grenage**); production of silk-worms' eggs. — *domestique*, ditto on a small scale. — *industriel*, ditto on [a large scale

†Grainaille, *s.f. V.* **Grenaille**

Grainaison, *s.f. V.* **Grenaison**

Grainasse, *s.f.* (*nav.*) light squall

Graine, *s.f.* seed; grain; berry; (*of silk-worms*) eggs, seed; (*pers.*) set, lot. — *de niais*, bait for fools, fool-trap. *Monter en* —, to run to seed; to be growing an old maid

Grainer, *v.a.n. V.* **Grener**

Graineterie, *s.f.* seed-trade; corn-chandlery

Graineti-er, ère, *s.m.f.* seed-merchant, seedsman, seedswoman; corn-chandler

Grainetis, Graineur, &c. *V.* **Grènetis, Greneur,** &c. [collection of seeds

Graini-er, ère, *s.m.f. V.* **Grainetier;** — *s.m.*

Grainoir, *s.m. V.* **Grenoir**

Graissage, *s.m.* greasing; grease

Graisse, *s.f.* fat; fatness; grease; dripping; tallow; (*of wine*, &c.) ropiness; (*slang*) rhino; —**s**, *pl.* kitchen-stuff, kitchen-fat. — *de boucherie*, rough fat. — *de cuisine*, kitchen stuff, kitchen-fat. — *de rôti*, dripping. *Tourner à la* —, (*of wine*, &c.) to become (*or* get) ropy, to get thick

Graisser, *v.a.* to grease; to make greasy; to oil; to dirty; — *v.n.* (*of wine*, &c.) to become (*or* get) ropy, to get thick. — *les bottes à*, to drub; to flatter, to coax, to wheedle. — *ses bottes*, to prepare for a journey *or* for departure, to pack up; to be (*or* get) ready to go to o.'s long home. — *la patte à*, to fee, to bribe, to tip. — *la marmite*, to keep the pot boiling. — *le marteau*, to fee *or* bribe *or* tip the door-keeper *or* porter

Graisserie, *s.f.* grease-trade *or* shop; grease

Graisset, *s.m.* (*zool.*) *V.* **Rainette**

Graisseu-r, se, *s.m.f.* greaser; — *adj.* greasing

Graisseu-x, se, *adj.* greasy; fatty

Graissi-er, ère, *s.m.f.* grease-merchant *or* [dealer

Graissoir, *s.m.* greasing-cloth

Gralle, *s.m. V.* **Échassier**

Gramen, *s.m.* grass

Graminé, e, *adj.* gramineous; — *s.f.* grass, gramineous plant; —**s,** *s.f.pl.* grasses, grass- [tribe

Graminivore, *adj.* graminivorous

Grammaire, *s.f.* grammar

Grammairien, ne, *s.m.f.* grammarian

Grammatical, e, *adj.* grammatical

Grammaticalement, *adv.* grammatically

Grammat-iste, -ologie, -ologique. *V.* page 3, § 1

Gramme, *s.m.* gramme (*French measure of weight; weighing over* 15 *grains troy English:* 500 *grammes make a modern French pound;* 5 *grammes is the legal weight of a franc-piece*)

Granaire, *adj.* (*zool.*) grain-eating, corn-eating

Grand, e, *adj.* great; large; big; tall; grown-up; old; long; extensive; vast; high; broad; wide; open; deep; full; hard; strong; loud; heavy; grand; noble; stately, majestic; greater; major; superior; chief, principal, main, head; capital; general; important; heroic (*verses*); much; many; very; — *s.m.* greatness, nobleness, grandeur, sublime, sublimity; great things, great; great *or* high personage, great lord, great man (*in mere title*), nobleman; grandee; (*at school*) big boy, pupil of the upper forms; —**s,** *s.m.pl.* great *or* high people, great folks, great, high; grandees, grandesse; grown-up people; (*at school*) big boys. *Un — homme*, a great man. *Un homme* —, a tall man. *Un — homme pâle*, *un homme — et pâle*, a tall pale man. *De —s jeunes gens*, grown-up young men. *En* —, on a large scale; largely; at full length, of full size, full-sized; in great style; nobly, grandly. **Grand-amiral,** &c., *V.* **Amiral,** &c. **Grand-aumônier,** *s.m.* grand-almoner. **Grand'chose (Pas),** *V.* **Chose. Grand-cordon,** *s.m.* Grand-Cordon; broad ribbon. **Grand'croix,** *s.f.* Grand-Cross; *s.m.* Knight Grand-Cross, Grand-Cross. **Grand-duc,** *s.m.* grand-duke; (*bird*) great horn-owl, eagle owl. **Grand-ducal, e,** *adj.* grand-ducal. **Grand-duché,** *s.m.* grand-duchy. **Grande-duchesse,** *s. f.* grand-duchess. **Grand'garde,** *s.f.* (*mil.*) grand-guard, main guard, outpost; (*of fire-brigade*) watchmen. **Grand'maman,** *s.f.* grandmamma. **Grand'mère,** *s.f.* grandmother; (*of animals*) grandam. **Grand-oncle,** *s. m.* great-uncle. **Grand ouvert (Tout),** wide open. **Grand'peine (A),** *adv. V.* **Peine. Grand-père,** *s.m.* grandfather, grandsire. **Grand'tante,** *s.f.* great-aunt. **Grand-vizir,** *s.m.* grand-vizier. **Grand-vizirat,** *s.m.* grand-viziership. [*Grand-chemin*, *-livre*, *-maître*, &c., &c., *V.* **Chemin, Livre, Maître,** &c., &c.]

Grande, *s.f.* (*at school*) big girl; (*in Spain*) titled lady; (*obsolete*) great style, grand fashion. *A la* —, (*obsolete*) in great style, grandly, like a [prince

Grandelet, te, *adj.* pretty tall, tallish

Grandement, *adv.* greatly, much, very much; extremely; largely, vastly; highly; high; grandly, nobly, handsomely [dees

Grandesse, *s.f.* grandeeship; grandesse, gran-

Grandeur, *s.f.* greatness; largeness; size; bulk; magnitude; extent; length; tallness; height; dignity; grandeur; great person, high personage; (*titles*) grace, lordship, highness. — *naturelle*, *de — naturelle*, life-size

Grandiose, *adj.* grand; — *s.m.* grandeur

Grandir, *v.n.* to grow tall, to get high, to grow in height, to grow up, to grow; to increase; to spring up; to rise; to become great *or* greater; to flourish; — *v.a.* to make taller; to lengthen; to make great *or* greater; to raise; to magnify; to increase; to give importance to; to make (*one*) appear taller *or* greater

Se —, *v.r.* to make oneself taller *or* appear taller, to become *or* grow taller; to become greater, to make itself greater, to raise oneself, to rise, to grow; to make oneself appear greater

Grandissement, *s.m.* growth, increase, rise, [magnifying

Grandissime, *adj.* very great

Grandoul, *s.m.* (*local*) sand-grouse

Grange, *s.f.* barn [of half the produce

Grangeage, *s.m.* farming where rent consists

Grangée, *s.f.* barnful
Grang-er, ère, *s.m.f.* farmer who gives half the produce as his rent
Grangerie, *s.f.* tenancy *or* farm the rent of which consists of half the produce
Granifère, *adj.* (*bot.*) graniferous
Graniforme, *adj.* graniform
Granilite, *s.f.* fine-grained granite
Granit, *s.m.* granite; (*conf.*) kind of ice
Granitelle, *adj.* granitoid; — *s.m.* granitel
Granitellé, e, *adj.* granit-like
Graniter, *v.a.* to grain (*paint*) granit-like
Graniteu-x, se, *adj.* granitous
Granitin, *s.m.*, **Granitine,** *s.f.* granitine
Granitique, *adj.* granitic
Granitoïde, *adj.* granitoid
Granivore, *adj.* granivorous; **—s,** *s.m.pl.* granivoræ
Granulage, *s.m.* granulation
Granulaire, *adj.* granular
Granulation, *s.f.* granulation
Granule, *s.m.* granule
Granuler, *v.a.*, **Se —,** *v.r.* to granulate
Granuleu-x, se, *adj.* granulous, granular
Granuliforme, *adj.* granuliform
Granulosité, *s.f.* granulosity
Granvillais, e, *adj. s.* of Granville, native of Granville
Graph-ique, -iquement. *V.* page 3, § 1
Graphite, *s.m.* (*min.*) graphite
Graphiteu-x, se, Graphitique, *adj.* graphitic
Grapholithe, *s.m.* (*min.*) grapholite
Graphomètre, *s.m.* graphometer
Graphométrique, *adj.* graphometric
Graphoscope, *s.m.* graphoscope
Graphotype, *s.m.* graphotype
†Grapignan, *s.m.* (*disparagingly*) attorney
Grapin, *s.m. V.* **Grappin**
Grappe, *s.f.* bunch; cluster; (*artil.*) grape-shot; (*vet., tumour*) grape; (*of horse-shoes*) calkin. — *de raisin,* bunch of grapes; (*artil.*) grape-shot
Grappeler, *v.a.* to bunch, to cluster
†Grappillage, *s.m.* gleaning; small picking, pickings, pilfering, plunder
†Grappiller, *v.a.n.* to glean; to pick, to pick up, to scrape up; to pilfer
†Grappilleu-r, se, *s.m.f.* grape-gleaner; pilferer
†Grappillon, *s.m.* cluster *or* small bunch of grapes
Grappin, *s.m.* grapnel, grappling, grapple, grappling-iron, hook; toasting-fork; (*pop.*) clutches, clutch. — *d'abordage,* fire-grappling. — *à rôtir,* toasting-fork. *Mettre* or *poser le — sur,* (*fig.*) to hook, to clutch, to grab, to nab, to catch *or* lay hold of, to lay o.'s hand upon
Grappiner, *v.a.* (*nav.*) to grapple; (*pop.*) to hook, to nab; to gather
Grappu, e, *adj.* loaded with bunches *or* with grapes
Graptolithe, *s.m.* (*fossil*) graptolite
Gras, se, *adj.* fat; plump; fatted; greasy; waxy; rich; fertile; thick; slippery; heavy; made with meat; dressed in meat-gravy; meat; shrove; obscene, broad, smutty; (*of wine, brandy, beer*) ropy; (*print.*) thick-faced; (*of weather*) hazy; (*of coughs*) mucous, humid; — *adverb.* thick; much. *Jour —,* flesh-day. *Les jours —,* Shrovetide; flesh-days. *Potage —, soupe —se,* meat-soup
Gras, *s.m.* fat; fat part, fleshy part; meat, flesh; (*of the leg*) calf; (*of wine,* &c.) ropiness; (*pop.*) profit. *Au —,* dressed in meat-gravy *or* broth; meat; (*of vegetables*) done in butter *or* dripping. *Faire —, manger —,* to eat flesh *or* meat. *Tourner au —,* (*pers.*) to get fat, to get a corporation; (*of wine,* &c.) to become (*or* get) ropy, to get thick. — **-cuit,** *adj.m.* (*of bread*) sodden. — **-double,** *s.m.* tripe. — **-fondu,** *s.m.* melted grease *or* fat; (*vet.*) mucous irritation in the intestines; *adj.* ill of ditto. — **-fondure,** *s.f.* (*vet.*) mucous irritation in the intestines
Grassement, *adv.* liberally, generously, handsomely; comfortably, in plenty
Grasserie, *s.f.* (a disease of silk-worms)
Grasset, te, *adj.* rather fat *or* stout, fatty; — *s.m.* (*of horses*) stifle, stifle-joint; (*butch.*) thin flank; (*zool.*) *V.* **Rainette;** — *s.f.* (*bot.*) butterwort; (*bird*) garganey
Grasseyement, *s.m.* burring, bur, burr, rotacism
Grasseyer, *v.n.* to speak thick, to bur, to burr
Grasseyeu-r, se, *s.m.f.* burrer
†Grassouillet, te, *adj.* plump, fatty
Grat, *s.m.* place scratched by fowls
Grateron, *s.m.* (*bot.*) goose-grass, scratch-weed, cleavers
Gratgal, *s.m.* (*bot.*) gratgal
Graticulaire, *adj.* in *or* by squares
Graticulation, *s.f.* (*draw., engr., paint.*) graticulation, squaring
Graticule, *s.f.* (*draw., engr., paint.*) graticule
Graticuler, *v.a.n.* (*draw., engr., paint.*) to graticulate, to square
Gratification, *s.f.* gratuity, present
Gratifier, *v.a.* to favour, to oblige, to confer, to bestow; to attribute, to ascribe
Gratin, *s.m.* burnt part, scraping, crackling; (*dish*) gratin. *Au —,* dressed with bread raspings *or* grated bread *or* (fried) bread-crumbs
Gratiné, e, *adj.* burnt, done brown, browned
Gratiner, *v.n.*, **Se —,** *v.r.* to begin to burn, to stick at the bottom of the pan; to get brown; — *v.a.* to brown. *Fer à —, V.* **Fer.** *Faire —,* to brown
Gratiole, *s.f.* (*bot.*) gratiola, hedge-hyssop
Gratioline, *s.f.* (*chem.*) gratioline
Gratis, *adv.* gratis, gratuitously, free of cost, free, for nothing, without profit; — *s.m.* gratuitousness; free gift; free admission, order; free list
Gratitude, *s.f.* gratitude
Grattage, *s.m.* scratching, scraping, friction
Gratte, *s.f.* (*nav.*) scraper; (*with dressmakers and tailors*) cabbage; (*with servants*) pickings, profits; (*pop.*) itch; — *s.m.f.* (*in compounds, from* **Gratter,** "to scratch," "to scrape") he *or* she who (*or* that which) scratches *or* scrapes, scratcher, scraper. — **-bosse,** *s.m.* scratch-brush. — **-bosser,** *v.a.* to rub with a scratch-brush. — **-cul,** *s.m.* (*bot.*) hip. — **-langue,** *s.m.* tongue-scraper. — **-menton,** *s.m.* (*jest.*) common barber. — **-papier,** *s.m.* quill-driver, scribbler
Grattée, *s.f.* (*pop.*) rub, brush, set-to, fight
Gratteler, *v.a.* to scratch *or* scrape lightly
Gratteleu-x, se, *adj.* itchy
Grattelle, *s.f.* itching, rash
Gratter, *v.a.n.* to scratch; to scrape; to scrape off; to rub; to claw, to flatter; to dig; to paw; to pick, to pilfer; to cabbage. — *le papier* or *le parchemin,* to drive the quill, to scribble. *Trop — cuit, trop parler nuit,* (*Proverb*) you may hurt yourself by scratching too much or talking too much; one must not rub an old sore; the least said the soonest mended
Gratteu-r, se, *s.m.f.* scratcher; scraper; pilferer. — *de papier,* quill-driver, scribbler
Grattoir, *s.m.* scratching-knife, scratcher; scraper; eraser; (*pop.*) razor
Gratture, *s.f.* scratchings, scrapings
Gratuit, e, *adj.* gratuitous; free; charity; wanton
Gratuité, *s.f.* gratuitousness; wantonness; (*theol.*) grace, gift
Gratuitement, *adv.* gratuitously; gratis, free, for nothing, without profit; wantonly
Graule, *s.f.* (*bad spelling for* **Grolle**)
Grauwacke, *s.f.* (*geol.*) greywacke, grauwacke
Gravan, *s.m.*, **Gravanche,** *s.f.* freshwater herring
Gravatier, *s.m.* rubbish-carter
Gravati-f, ve, *adj.* (*med.*) dull, heavy
Gravats, *s.m.pl.* coarse plaster, rubbish. *Battre les —,* (*fig. and pop.*) to eat up the scraps
Grave, *adj.* grave; serious; solemn; sedate; stern; severe; grievous; weighty, of weight, important; deep, low, hollow, flat; heavy; — *s.m.* grave; gravity; seriousness; weight; heavy body; Grave (wine); (*mus.*) flat; — *s.f.* beach, strand; **—s,** *s.f.pl.* strands; gravelly soil
Gravé, e, *part. adj.* engraved, &c. (*V.* **Graver**); pitted with the small pox, pock-pitted, pock-marked, pitted
Gravelage, *s.m.* gravelling

Gravelée, *adj.f. Cendre* —, pearlash
Graveler, *v.a.* to gravel
Graveleu-x, se, *adj.* gravelly; gritty; smutty, ribald, free, broad; (*med.*) of gravel; containing gravel; affected with gravel; — *s.m.f.* person affected with gravel
Gravelle, *s.f.* (*med.*) gravel
Gravelure, *s.f.* smuttiness, ribaldry
Gravement, *adv.* gravely; seriously; solemnly; sedately; sternly; severely; grievously; slowly, deeply
Graver, *v.a.* to engrave, to grave; to trace; to cut out, to cut, to carve; to impress, to imprint. — *au burin,* to engrave. — *à l'eau forte,* to etch. — *en creux,* to sink. — *en relief,* to carve in relief, to emboss
Se —, *v.r.* to be engraved; to be *or* become impressed, &c.; to impress (on o.'s own mind)
Graves, *s.m.* Graves (wine)
Graveur, *s.m.* engraver, graver. — *à l'eau forte,* etcher. — *sur bois,* wood-engraver, wood-cut engraver, wood-cutter
Gravide, *adj.* (*med.*) gravid
Gravier, *s.m.* gravel; grit
Gravière, *s.f.* (*agr.*) vetch and lentils
Gravigrade, *adj.m.f., s.m.* (*zool.*) gravigrade
Gravimètre, *s.m.* (*phys.*) gravimeter
Gravir, *v.n.a.* to climb, to climb up, to clamber, to ascend, to scale
Gravitation, *s.f.* gravitation
Gravité, *s.f.* gravity; seriousness; solemnity; sedateness; sternness; severity; grievousness; weight, importance; depth, lowness, flatness; heaviness
Graviter, *v.n.* to gravitate
Gravois, *s.m.pl. V.* **Gravats**
Gravure, *s.f.* engraving; print, cut, picture. — *au burin,* stroke-engraving. — *à l'eau forte,* etching. — *au trait,* line-engraving. — *en creux,* intaglio; die-sinking; seal-engraving. — *en relief,* carving in relief, embossing. — *sur bois,* wood-engraving, wood-cutting; wood-cut
Grazioso, *adj. adv.* (*mus.*) grazioso
Gré, *s.m.* will; good will; wish; inclination; liking; taste; mind; accord; consent; gratitude, thankfulness, thanks. *A son* —, to o.'s taste; to o.'s mind; to o.'s satisfaction; at o.'s pleasure; as one pleases *or* wishes; according to one; in o.'s opinion *or* thinking. *Au — de,* according to, agreeable to, agreeably to; with. *Au — du vent,* in the wind; at the mercy of the wind. *Bon — mal* —, whether one will or not, willing or not, willing or unwilling, willingly or unwillingly, will or nill. *Contre son* —, unwillingly, against o.'s will, against the grain. *De* —, from good will; by gentle means. *De bon* —, *de plein* —, *de son* —, willingly, voluntarily, of o.'s own accord *or* consent. *De mauvais* —, unwillingly, with reluctance. *De — à* —, by mutual agreement *or* private contract, with mutual consent, amicably, privately. *De — ou de force,* willing or not, willingly or from compulsion. *Plein* —, free will, own free will. *Prendre* or *recevoir* or *avoir en* —, to take in good part, to approve of, not to take amiss; to be pleased to accept, to be pleased with, to like; to take a liking to; to receive with resignation. *Savoir* — or *bon — de,* to be pleased *or* obliged *or* thankful *or* grateful for, to take kindly; to applaud for. *Savoir mauvais — de,* to take ill *or* unkindly, to be displeased *or* unthankful for. *Se savoir bon — de,* to be pleased with oneself for, to be pleased *or* glad with *or* of *or* to *or* that
Gréage, *s.m.* (*nav.*) rigging
Gréal, *s.m. V.* **Graal**
Grèbe, *s.m.* (*a bird, its plumage*) grebe. — *huppé,* crested grebe, cargoose
Grébiche, *s.f.* reading-portfolio, reading-cover
Grec, que, *adj.* Greek, Grecian; Graian (*Alps*); skilful; — *s.m.f.* Greek (*person*); Greek woman *or* lady *or* girl; — *s.m.* Greek, (the) Greek language; card-sharper, blackleg, cheat; miser; — *s.f.* Greek fashion; Greek head-dress; (*arch.*) fret-work; (*book-bind.*) saw; indentation in the back (*of a book*); (*nav.*) sky-scraper. *Vent* —, (*nav.*) north-east wind
Gréciser, *v.a.n.* to grecize, to grecianize
Gréc-isme, -iste. *V.* **Hellén-isme, -iste**
Grécité, *s.f.* grecity
Grécoliser, *v.n.* (*nav.*) to sail in a north-easterly direction
Gréco-romain, e, *adj.* Greco-Roman
Grecque, *adj.f., s.f. V.* **Grec**
Grecquer, *v.a.* to saw-bind (*books*)
Grecquerie, *s.f.* sharping, cheating; blackleg fraternity, blacklegs
Gredin, e, *s.m.f.* villain, scoundrel, rascal, knave, scamp, blackguard, wretch; (*obsolete*) vagabond, beggar; (*dog*) cocker, lap-dog
Arrediner, *v.n.* to behave like a blackguard, to play knavish tricks
Gredinerie, *s.f.* villany, rascality, knavery, blackguardism; (*obsolete*) beggary
Gréement, *s.m.* (*nav.*) rigging
Gréer, *v.a.* (*nav.*) to rig
Grées, *s.f.pl.* (*nav.*) rigging
Gréeur, *s.m.* (*nav.*) rigger
Greffe, *s.m.* record-office, registrar's *or* clerk's office, registry; — *s.f.* (*agr., hort.*) graft; grafting
Greffer, *v.a.* (*agr., hort.*) to graft
Se —, *v.r.* to be grafted
Greffeur, *s.m.* grafter
Greffier, *s.m.* clerk; registrar; keeper of the records; recorder; (*pop.*) cat, puss, tom
Greffoir, *s.m.* grafting-knife
Grégaire, *adj.* gregarious
Grégalade, *s.f.* (*nav.*) north-easterly gale
Grége, *adj.* (*of silk, thread*) raw
Grégeois, *adj.m. Feu* —, Greek fire, wild-fire
Grégorien, ne, *adj.* Gregorian
Grégou, *s.m.* (*nav.*) north-east wind
Grègues, *s.f.pl.* (*obsolete*) breeches. *Tirer ses* —, (*old*) to take to o.'s heels
Grêle, *adj.* slender, slim, thin, lank, delicate; small; lesser; (*of the voice*) shrill, thin; — *s.f.* hail; hailstorm; (*fig.*) shower; (*med.*) sty (*on the eye*), stye; (*pop.*) small pox; — *s.m.* highest note (*of a horn or trumpet*); cobbles, knubbly coals; (*pop.*) governor
Grêlé, e, *adj.* ravaged by hail; (*pers.*) pitted with the small pox, pock-pitted, pock-marked, pitted; shabby, seedy; not very popular; (*her., of coronets*) adorned with pearls; — *s.m.f.* person pitted with the small pox
Grêleau, *s.m.* small staddle
Grêlée, *s.f.* hailstorm
Grêler, *v.n.* to hail; (*fig.*) to shower down, to fall thick *or* hard; — *v.a.* to ravage *or* destroy by hail, to ruin, to spoil. — *sur le persil,* (*fig.*) to break a butterfly on the wheel. *Il a grêlé sur lui,* (*pop.*) he is pitted with the small pox
Grelet, *s.m.* granite-hammer
Grêlet, te, *adj.* rather slender, somewhat thin, thinnish
Grêleu-x, se, *adj.* haily, hail-like
Grelin, *s.m.* coal-fish; (*nav.*) stream-cable
Grêlon, *s.m.* hailstone
Grelot, *s.m.* rattle, little round bell, hawk's bell, bell. *Attacher le* —, to bell the cat. *Trembler le* —, to shake till o.'s teeth chatter
Grelotter, *v.n.* to shiver with cold, to shiver
Greluchon, *s.m.* favourite *or* favoured lover
Grément, *s.m. V.* **Gréement**
Grémial, *s.m.* gremial (*bishop's apron*)
Grémil, *s.m.* (*bot.*) gromwell
†**Gremille,** *s.f.* (*fish*) pope, ruffe, ruff
†**Grémillet,** *s.m.* (*local*) *V.* **Myosotis**
Grenache, *s.m.* grenache (*vine, grape, wine*)
Grenade, *s.f.* (*bot.*) pomegranate; (*mil.*) grenade; (*local*) shrimp; (*geog.*) Granada; Grenada
Grenadier, *s.m.* pomegranate-tree; grenadier; large shrimp-net; (*pop.*) louse
Grenadière, *s.f.* pomegranate-grove; grenade-pouch; (*of guns, muskets*) middle band, sling-ring; (*fish.*) small shrimp-net. *Mettre à la* —, to sling
†**Grenadille,** *s.f.* (*bot.*) granadilla, passion-flower; (*cabinet-wood*) grenadillo, Grenada cocus
Grenadin, e, *adj.* Granadan, Grenadan; of pomegranate; — *s.m.f.* Granadan, Grenadan;

— *s.m.* (*cook.*) stuffed fowl; — *s.f.* (*chem.*, *and kind of silk*) grenadine [tion; graining
Grenage, *s.m.* granulating, corning; granula-
†Grenaille, *s.f.* minute grains; granulated metal, small shot; (*agr.*) refuse grain *or* seeds, small *or* bad seed, tailings
†Grenaillement, *s.m.* granulating
†Grenailler, *v.a.*, **Se** —, *v.r.* to granulate
Grenaison, *s.f.* seeding, running to seed, pro-
Grenasse, *s.f.* *V.* **Grainasse** [duction of seed
Grenat, *s.m.* (*min.*) garnet; — *s.m. adj.* garnet-
Grenatique, *adj.* (*min.*) of garnet [red, garnet
Grené, *s.m.* grain, grains; (*draw.*, *engr.*) blending; —, *m.*, **e,** *f.*, *part. of* **Grener**
Greneler, *v.a.* to grain
Grener, *v.a.n.* to granulate; to corn; to powder; to grain; (*draw.*, *engr.*) to blend; — *v.n.*
Greneter, *v.a.* to grain [to seed, to produce seed
Grèneterie, Grènetier, (*old spellings*) *V.* **Graineterie, Grainetier**
Grenétine, *s.f.* pure gelatine *or* isinglass
Grènetis, *s.m.* graining; (*of coin*) milling, milled edge; puncheon, punch, stamp
Grenetoir, *s.m.* graining-tool
Grenette, *s.f.* coarse gunpowder; French berry, Avignon berry, yellow berry
Greneur, *s.m.* silk-worm hatcher
Grenier, *s.m.* granary; storehouse; magazine; mow; loft; attic; garret; lumber-room, store-room. — *d'abondance*, public granary *or* store-house. — *à coups de poing*, (*pop.*) drunkard's wife. *En* —, in the granary, in store; (*nav.*) in bulk, unpacked. *Aller du — à la cave* (or *de la cave au* —), to be eccentric *or* full of whims; to talk rigmarole; to write up and down hill
Grenoir, *s.m.* gunpowder-sieve; corning-house
†Grenouillard, *s.m.* (*zool.*) rough-legged buzzard; (*pop.*) teetotaller
†Grenouille, *s.f.* frog; (*pop.*) society's *or* company's fund, common fund, capital stock, capital
†Grenouiller, *v.n.* (*pop.*) to drink Adam's ale
†Grenouillère, *s.f.* place full of frogs; swamp, fen; damp hole; (*pop.*) swimming-baths
†Grenouillet, *s.m.* (*bot.*) Solomon's seal
†Grenouillette, *s.f.* (*bot.*) water crowfoot; buttercup; (*med.*) ranula
Grenu, e, *adj.* grainy, seedy; corned, full of corn; grained; (*of oil*) clotted [blending
Grenure, *s.f.* graining, grain; (*draw.*, *engr.*)
Grès, *s.m.* sandstone; gritstone, grit; paving-stone; stoneware, stone; sand
Gréseu-x, se, *adj.* sandy, gritty
Grésier, *s.m.* sandstone-quarrier
Grésière, *s.f.* sandstone-quarry
Grésiforme, *adj.* like sandstone [cullet
Grésil, *s.m.* sleet; broken *or* pounded glass,
†Grésillement, *s.m.* shrivelling, shrivelling up, shrinking; pattering; crackling; chirping
†Grésiller, *v.n.* to sleet; to patter; to crackle; (*of crickets*) to chirp; — *v.a.* to shrivel, to shrivel up [work; stoneware
Gresserie, *s.f.* sandstone-quarry; sandstone-
Gresset, *s.m.* green frog
Gressoripède, *adj.* (*zool.*) gressorial
Grève, *s.f.* sand, beach, strand; sand-bank, bank; (*of workmen*) strike, turn-out; (*of armour*) greave; (*Fr. hist.*) Grève (*square, in Paris, where public executions used to take place, as at the Old Bailey in London*). *En* —, on strike. *En* —, *en place de* —, on the Grève. *Faire* —, *se mettre en* —, to strike work, to strike, to turn out
Grevé, e, *part. adj.* burdened, &c. (*V.* **Grever**); — *s.m.f.* (*law*) heir of entail
Grever, *v.a.* to burden; to encumber; (*old*) to grieve, to aggrieve, to injure, to wrong
Grianeau, Grianneau, *s m.* young grouse
Grias, *s.m.* (*bot.*) grias, anchovy-pear (*tree*)
Gribane, *s.f.* flat-bottomed boat, flat
Griblette, *s.f.* (*cook.*) broil [scribbling; daub
†Gribouillage, *s.m.* scrawl, scribble, scrawling,
†Gribouille, *s.m.* simpleton, booby [daub
†Gribouiller, *v.a.n.* to scrawl, to scribble; to
†Gribouillette, *s.f.* scramble, scrambling. *A la* —, for a scramble; at random, negligently, higgledy-piggledy
†Gribouilleu-r, se, *s.m.f.* scrawler, scribbler; dauber; — *adj.* scrawling, scribbling; daubing
†Gribouillis, *s.m.* *V.* **Gribouillage**
Gribouri, *s.m.* (*zool.*) vine-fretter
Grièche, *adj.* (*old*) sharp, smart, hurtful, injurious, mischievous. *V.* **Pie,** *s.f.*
Gri-ef, ève, *adj.* (*old*) grave, serious, sad, bad, grievous, severe
Grief, *s.m.* injury, wrong; offence; grievance; cause of complaint; complaint; charge
Grièvement, *adv.* gravely, seriously, sadly, badly, grievously, severely
Grièveté, *s.f.* (*old*) gravity, enormity, heinousness; grievousness, severity
Griffade, *s.f.* clawing, scratch
Griffe, *s.f.* claw; talon; clutch; music-pen; stamped signature, signature, stamp; (*hort.*) offset; (*bot.*, *of climbing plants*) cirrus, tendril, rootlet, adhering disc; (*of cloves*) stalk; (*tech.*) catch; — *s.m.f.* (*pers.*) sambo *or* zambo, samba *or* zamba
Griffer, *v.a.n.* to claw, to scratch; (*pop.*) to clutch, to grab, to hook, to fork, to bone, to crib, to bag
Griffon, *s.m.* (*myth.*, *her.*) griffin; (*bird*) griffin, griffon, tawny vulture; lämmergeier; (*dog*) griffon; (*angling*) pike-spinner
Griffon, ne, *s.m.f.* scrawler, scribbler
Griffonnage, *s.m.* scrawl, scrawling, scribble, scribbling [sketch, scrawling
Griffonnement, *s.m.* rough-drawing, rough
Griffonner, *v.a.n.* to scrawl, to scribble; to rough-draw [— *adj.* scrawling, scribbling
Griffonneu-r, se, *s.m.f.* scrawler, scribbler;
Griffonnis, *s.m.* pen-and-ink sketch; etching in imitation of ditto
†Grignon, *s.m.* hard crust; residuum (*of olives*)
†Grignoter, *v.a.n.* to nibble; to pick, to pick up, to get some pickings, to make a small profit, to get something
†Grignotis, *s.m.* (*engr.*) crispness [ed fellow
Grigou, *s.m.* curmudgeon, miser, hunks, wretch-
Gril, *s.m.* gridiron; toaster; grate; (*frame for ships*) gridiron; (*theat.*) border-batten; barrel-loft, roof, ceiling. *Être sur le* —, (*fig.*) to be on tenter-hooks, to be in a stew
†Grillade, *s.f.* grillade, grilling, broiling; grillade, broil, steak, slice of grilled *or* broiled meat; toast; roast
†Grillage, *s.m.* grilling, broiling; toasting; roasting; burning; singeing; wire-work; wire-lattice; wire-guard; wire-guard work; grating; grate; railing; frame, timber-frame
†Grillager, *v.a.* to wire; to protect by a wire-guard *or* by wire; to grate; to rail
†Grillageur, *s.m.* wire-worker
†Grille, *s.f.* grate; grating; railing; gate
†Grille-pain, *s.m.* gridiron, toaster
†Griller, *v.a.n.* to grill, to broil; to toast; to roast; to scorch, to parch; to burn; to singe; (*slang*) to smoke (*tobacco*); to grate; to wire; to rail, to rail in; to cloister; to burn (with), to long (to), to be very anxious (to); to be on tenter-hooks, to be in a stew. *Faire* —, to grill, to broil, &c. (*as above*). *Loge grillée*, (*theat.*) close box [self; to scorch *or* burn (o.'s ...)
Se —, *v.r.* to be grilled *or* &c.; to roast one-
†Grillet, *s.m.*, **Grillette,** *s.f.* (*her.*) hawk's bell
†Grilleté, e, *adj.* (*her.*) belled
†Grilletier, *s.m.* grate-maker
†Grillon, *s.m.* cricket (*insect*)
†Grilloter, *v.n.* (*of crickets*) to chirp
Grimace, *s.f.* grimace; wry face, face; grin; sham, cant, humbug, show, hypocrisy; pucker, crease; pincushion wafer-box. *Faire la* —, to make faces *or* mouths, to grin (at); to look sour *or* displeased *or* disgusted, not to like it; to pucker, to crease
Grimacer, *v.n.* to grimace, to grin, to make

grimaces *or* wry faces; to be grimacing *or* grimaced *or* distorted; to be forced; to simper, to mince, to sham; to pucker, to crease; — *v.a.* to mimic; to travesty

Grimacerie, *s.f.* (*old*) *V.* **Grimace**

Grimaci-er, ère, *adj.* grimacing; grinning; simpering, mincing, finical, affected, dissembled, hypocritical, shamming, canting, humbugging; — *s.m.f.* grimacer; grinner; simperer, dissembler, hypocrite, canter, humbug

Grimage, *s.m.* (*theat.*) wrinkling o.'s face, painting, making-up, make-up, ruddling

Grimaud, *s.m.* (*old*) backward boy, ignorant fellow, urchin, brat; scribbler; dauber; duffer; pedant; peevish fellow

Grimaud, e, *adj.* cross, peevish, ill-tempered

Grime, *s.m.* (*theat.*) dotard, old fogy; (*obsolete*) urchin, brat

Grimer (Se), *v.r.* (*theat.*) to wrinkle o.'s face, to paint, to make up, to ruddle; (*pop.*) to get drunk

Grimm, *s.m.* grimm (*antelope*)

Grimoire, *s.m.* conjuring-book, black-book; unintelligible thing, double Dutch, jargon, scrawl; obscurity, intricacy, wheels within wheels, confusion worse confounded; black art of the law. *Entendre* or *savoir le* —, to know what one is about, to know what is what, to be up to snuff; to understand the ins and outs of the law

Grimper, *v.n.a.* to climb, to climb up, to clamber, to clamber up, to get up, to get up high, to creep up, to creep. *Plante grimpante,* climbing plant, climber, creeper

Grimpereau, *s.m.* (*bird*) creeper

Grimpeu-r, se, *s.m.f.* climber; — *s.m.* (*zool.*) climbing bird, climber

Grincement, *s.m.* gnashing, grinding; grating

Grincer, *v.a.n.* to gnash, to grind; to grate; to rattle. *Faire* —, to make (...) grate *or* rattle, [to set on edge

Grinche, *s.m.* (*slang*) thief

Grincher, *v.n.* (*of bread*) to blister; — *v.a.n.* (*slang*) to steal

Grincheu-x, se, *adj.* (*pop.*) cross, peevish, surly

Grinchir, *v.a.n.* (*slang*) to steal

Grinchisseu-r, se, *s.m.f.* (*slang*) thief, stealer

Gringalet, *s.m.* thin fellow, small fellow, bit of a man; insignificant fellow, nobody, mere nobody

Gringole, *s.f.* (*her.*) snake-head

Gringolé, e, *adj.* (*her.*) snake-headed [to hum

Gringoter, *v.n.a.* to warble, to chirp, to twitter;

Gringuenaude, *s.f.* dirt, filth; scrap

Griot, *s.m.* (*of meal*) seconds

Griotte, *s.f.* egriot, morella cherry, morella; (*kind of marble*) griotte. *Petites —s à ratafia,* brandy-blacks

Griottier, *s.m.* egriot-tree, morella-tree

Grippe, *s.f.* whim, hobby, crotchet; dislike, aversion; (*med.*) influenza; — *s.m.f.* (*in compounds, from* **Gripper,** "to seize," "to clutch," &c.) person who seizes *or* clutches *or* &c. — **-argent,** *s.m.f.* money-grubber; thief. — **-coquins,** *s.m.* (*jest.*) policeman, constable. — **-fromage,** *s.m.* (*jest., obsolete*) cheese-stealer, cat, pussy. — **-sou,** *s.m.* money-grubber, screw

Grippé, e, *part. adj.* seized, &c. (*V.* **Gripper**); shrunk, shrivelled; ill of the influenza [crisp

Grippeler (Se), *v.r.* to shrink, to shrivel, to

Grippement, *s.m.* shrinking, shrivelling; rubbing, friction

Grippeminaud, *s.m.* Grimalkin

Gripper, *v.a.* to seize, to seize upon, to catch *or* lay hold of, to gripe, to grip, to clutch, to snatch, to grab; to nab; to scrape up, to scrape, to grub; to hook, to fork, to bone, to crib, to bag; to prepossess, to prejudice. — *v.n.* to shrink, to shrivel, to shrivel up

Se —, *v.r.* to shrink, to shrivel, to shrivel up; to be prepossessed *or* prejudiced; to take a dislike (to); to seize *or* &c. each other; to be seized *or* &c.

Grippeu-r, se, *s.m.f.* griper, clutcher, thief

Gris, e, *adj.* grey, gray; grizzled, grizzly; grey-headed; tipsy, drunk; dull, cloudy, foggy; darkish, dark, dusky; unpleasant; gruff; (*print., of letters*) flourished; (*of wine*) pale. *V.* **Papier** *and* **Patrouille.** — *de lin,* gridelin. *Faire —e mine a,* to give a black look to, to look sour upon. *En voir de —es,* to have a hard *or* an unpleasant time of it; to have hot work. *En faire voir de —es à,* to plague terribly; to play all kinds of tricks to, to play pretty tricks to

Gris, *s.m.* grey, gray; grey clothes. — *blanc,* whitish grey, greyish. — *bleu,* bluish grey. — *de lin,* gridelin. — *de more,* dark grey. — *-perle,* pearl-grey; gris-perle (*dye*). *V.* **Petit-gris** *and* **Vert-de-gris**

†**Grisaille,** *s.f.* grey painting *or* camaieu, grisaille; grey colour; grey materials, grey stuff; (*of wigs*) white and brown hair, grizzly hair

†**Grisailler,** *v.a.* to paint grey; — *v.n.* to turn [grey

Grisard, *s.m.* badger; grey gull; grit

Grisâtre, *adj.* greyish, grayish, grizzled, grizzly; gloomy, dull

Grise-bonne, *s.f.* grise-bonne (*kind of pear*)

Griser, *v.a.* to give a grey tint; to make tipsy *or* drunk, to fuddle, to intoxicate, to get into ...'s head; — *v.n.* to turn grey

Se —, *v.r.* to get tipsy *or* drunk *or* fuddled *or* [intoxicated

Griserie, *s.f.* fuddling

Griset, *s.m.* young goldfinch

Grisette, *s.f.* coarse grey stuff; grey gown *or* dress; (*pers.*) grisette, gay work-girl; (*bird*) whitethroat [warble

Grisoller, *v.n.* (*of larks*) to carol, to chirp, to

Grison, ne, *adj.* grey-headed, grey-haired; grey; old; (*geogr.*) Grison; — *s.m.* grey; grey-beard; grey horse; ass, donkey, moke; (*zool.*) grison; (*obsolete*) footman in grey livery; private agent; policeman in plain clothes, detective; (*tech.*) gritstone, grit; —**s,** *s.m.pl.* (*geog.*) Grisons [grizzled, grizzly

Grisonnant, e, *part. adj.* growing grey,

Grisonner, *v.n.* to grow *or* get grey, to turn *or* become grey; to be greyish *or* grizzly

Grisoter (Se), *v.r.* (*fam.*) to get rather tipsy, to get fresh

Grisou, *s.m.* (*adject., Feu* —,) fire-damp

Grisse, *s.f.,* **Grissin,** *s.m.* (*local*) crisp roll *or* [loaf

Grive, *s.f.* thrush

Grivelé, e, *adj.* speckled (*like a thrush*)

Griveler, *v.a.n.* (*old*) to embezzle, to pilfer

Grivelure, *s.f.* speckle, speckles, speckledness

Grivois, e, *adj. s.* jolly; broad, free; jolly fellow, jolly companion; rake

Groenlandais, e, *adj. s.* of Greenland; Greenlander

Grog, *s.m.* grog

†**Grognard, e,** *adj. s.* grumbling, growling, peevish; grumbler, growler; old guardsman (*of Napoleon I.*), old soldier, veteran

†**Grognasserie,** *s.f.* *V.* **Grognerie**

†**Grogne,** *s.f.* grumbling, peevishness, sulks

†**Grognement,** *s.m.* grunt; growl; snarl; grumbling, growling; groan; complaint

†**Grogner,** *v.n.* to grunt; to growl; to snarl; (*pers.*) to grumble, to growl, to croak; to groan; to whine; — *v.a.* to grumble at, to scold, to jaw

†**Grognerie,** *s.f.* grumbling, scolding; complaint; (*of babies*) whining

†**Grogneu-r, se, Grognon,** *adj. s.m.f.* grumbling, growling, croaking, peevish; grumbler, growler, croaker

†**Grognonner.** *V.* **Grogner**

†**Grognonnerie,** *s.f.* grumbling, scolding, [jawing

Groin, *s.m.* snout

Groisil, *s.m.* broken glass, cullet

Grolle, *s.f.* *V.* **Freux** [rummage, to fumble

Groller, *v.n.* to croak, to grumble; — *v.a.* to

Gromatique, *adj.* gromatic; — *s.f.* gromatics

Gromiau, *s.m.* (*pop.*) urchin, brat [mutter

Grommeler, *v.n.a.* to grumble; to growl; to

Grondement, *s.m.* growl; rumbling sound, rumbling, roaring, roar, booming, boom, pealing, peal

Gronder, *v.a.n.* to grumble, to scold, to chide; to mutter; to growl; to roar; to rumble; to boom; to peal

Gronderie, *s.f.* scolding, chiding
Grondeu-r, se, *adj. s.m.f.* grumbling, scolding; grumbler, scolder, scold; — *s.m.* (*fish*) grey
Grondin, *s.m.* (*fish*) gurnard, gurnet [gurnard
Groom, *s.m.* page, buttons, tiger; groom
Gros, se, *adj.* big, large, bulky; broad; great; main; stout; corpulent; plump; fat; strong; pregnant; swollen; swelling; full; coarse; thick; rich, wealthy; substantial; considerable; deep; high; loud; rough; heavy; bad. — *papa*, — *père*, fat jolly fellow, fatty
Gros, *s.m.* main part; body; bulk; generality, mass; main body; (*writing*) large hand; (*com.*) wholesale; wholesale trade *or* business; stout fabric; stout silk, gros grain, gros; common linen; (*old weight*) dram. — *de l'eau*, (*nav.*) spring tide. — *de Naples*, — *de Tours*, (*silks*) gros de Naples, gros de Tours. *En* —, wholesale, by wholesale; in the lump; bodily; taken together, together; on the whole; summarily. *Tout en* —, in all, only [*Plus* —, more; higher
Gros, *adv.* much, a great *or* good deal; high.
Gros-bec, *s.m.* (*bird*) grossbeak, grosbeak
†Groseille, *s.f.* currant; gooseberry; currant syrup; currant jam; — *adj.* currant-coloured (*red*). — *à maquereau*, — *verte*, gooseberry, green gooseberry
†Groseillier, *s.m.* currant-tree; gooseberry-bush. — *à maquereau*, gooseberry-bush
Grosil, *s.m. V.* **Groisil**
Gros-Jean, *s.m.* Thingumbob, a mere nobody, a common fellow. *V.* **Remontrer**
Grosse, *s.f.* (12 *dozen*) gross; (*writing*) large text *or* hand; (*law*) engrossed copy, engrossment, copy; (*com. nav.*) bottomry. *A la* —, by the gross; in a rough way, coarsely; slowly, jog-trot; (*com. nav.*) bottomry (*adject.*). —**-de-fonte,** *s.f.* (*print.*) broadside founts, broadside letter, jobbing-founts
Grossement, *adv.* coarsely, roughly
Grosserie, *s.f.* iron-ware, ironmongery; wholesale trade *or* business, wholesale
Grossesse, *s.f.* pregnancy
Grosseur, *s.f.* bigness, largeness, thickness, stoutness, size, bulk; swelling
Grossi-er, ère, *adj.* coarse; thick; gross; rough; unpolished; rude; blunt; unmannerly; uncouth; boorish; barbarous; scurrilous; homely, plain, common
Grossièrement, *adv.* coarsely; grossly; roughly; rudely; bluntly; unmannerly; uncouthly; boorishly; scurrilously; plainly; summarily
Grossièreté, *s.f.* coarseness; grossness; roughness; rudeness; rude thing *or* action; bluntness; unmannerliness; uncouthness; boorishness; scurrility, bad language; homeliness, plainness
Grossir, *v.a.n.* to make bigger *or* larger *or* greater; to enlarge, to increase; to magnify; to exaggerate; to swell out, to swell; to heighten; to render coarse; to get big *or* large; to grow stout; to thicken
Se —, *v.r.* to grow bigger *or* larger, to grow; to increase; to gather; to magnify; to swell, to rise
Grossissement, *s.m.* enlargement, increasing, increase; magnifying; exaggeration; swelling; thickening; gathering; rise
Grossisseur, *s.m.* magnifier
Grosso-modo, *adv.* roughly, summarily, gene-
Grossoyer, *v.a.n.* to engross [rally
Grossulaire, *s.f.* (*min.*) grossularia
Grossuline, *s.f.* (*chem.*) grossuline
Grotesque, *adj.m.f.*, *s.m.* (*style*), *s.f.* (*ornament*) grotesque; *s.m.* grotesqueness; (*pers.*) clown, fool, antic; grotesque dancer; guy
Grotesquement, *adv.* grotesquely
Grotesquerie, *s.f.* grotesqueness
Grotte, *s.f.* grotto, grot
†Grouillement, *s.m.* stirring; rattling, rumbling, grumbling; swarming, crawling
†Grouiller, *v.n.* to stir, to move; to rattle, to rumble, to grumble; to swarm, to crawl; (*old*) to shake

Group, *s.m.* bag of money
Groupage, *s.m.* (*rail.*) collecting parcels, receiving parcels *or* goods
Groupe, *s.m.* group; cluster; clump; flock; crowd; (*print.*) heading [*part. of* **Grouper**
Groupé, *s.m.* grouping; groups; — *m.*, **e,** *f.*
Groupement, *s.m.* grouping
Grouper, *v.a.n.*, **Se** —, *v.r.* to group, to group together, to cluster, to gather, to crowd
Groupet, *s.m.* (*mus.*) gruppetto
Groux, *s.m.* buckwheat hasty-pudding
Gru, *s.m.* (*local*) gruel
Gruau, *s.m.* meal, grits, groats; oatmeal; first *or* best flour; gruel; (*bird*) young crane; (*mach.*) small crane. — *à l'eau*, water-gruel. *Pain de* —, fine wheaten bread
Grue, *s.f.* crane; ninny, simpleton, fool, goose. *Faire le pied de* —, to stand kicking o.'s heels,
Gruer, *v.a.* to grind (*corn*) [to dance attendance
Gruerie, *s.f.* (*old*) woodmote, forest-court; (*fam.*) stupidity, tomfoolery
Grugeon, *s.m.* lump (*of sugar*) [*or* up
Gruger, *v.a.* to craunch; to devour; to eat out
Grugerie, *s.f.* craunching; devouring; squandering [squanderer; sponger, parasite
Grugeu-r, se, *s.m.f.* cruncher; devourer, eater;
Grume, *s.m.* bark. *En* —, with the bark on, unbarked, undressed, in the rough
Grumeau, *s.m.* clot, lump
Grumeler, *v.a.*, **Se** —, *v.r.* to coagulate, to clot; — *v.n.* (*of wildboars*) to squeak
Grumeleu-x, se, *adj.* clotted, clotty; rugged,
Gruppetto, *s.m.* (*mus.*) gruppetto [rough
Gruyère, *s.m.* Gruyere cheese
Grypose, *s.f.* (*med.*) gryposis
Guacharo, *s.m.* (*bird*) guacharo
Guacine, *s.f.* (*chem.*) guacine
Guaco, *s.m.* (*bot.*) guaco
Guais, *adj.m.* (*of herrings*) shotten
Guan, *s.m.* (*bird*) guan, yacou
Guanaco, *s.m.* (*zool.*) huanaca, guanaco
Guanine, *s.f.* (*chem.*) guanine
Guano, *s.m.* guano
Guarana, *s.f.* Guarana bread, guarana
Guaranine, *s.f.* (*chem.*) guaranine
Guazuma, *s.m.* (*bot.*) guazuma
Gué, *s.m.* ford; — *adv. int. V.* **Gai,** *adv. int.* *Passer* or *traverser à* —, to ford
Guéable, *adj.* fordable
Guèbre, *s.m.f.* guebre (*fire-worshipper*)
Guède, *s.f.* (*bot.*) woad, dyer's woad, pastel
Guéder, *v.a.* to woad, to dye blue; (*old*) to cram, to stuff, to surfeit
Guéderon, Guédron, *s.m.* woad-dyer
Guéer, *v.a.* to ford; to water; to rinse
Se —, *v.r.* to be forded *or* &c.
Guelfe, *s.m. adj.* (*Italian hist.*) Guelph, Guelf
†Guenille, *s.f.* rag, tatter; scrap; piece of rubbish, trumpery, worthless thing; (*jest.*) seedy *or* shabby clothes, old toggery
†Guenilleu-x, se, *adj.* tattered, ragged, in rags; rubbishy, trumpery, worthless [dowdy
†Guenillon, *s.m.* little rag, scrap, rubbish;
Guenipe, *s.f.* slut, slattern; drab
Guenon, *s.f.* pouched monkey, monkey, cercopithecus; she-monkey; fright, ugly woman; drab, trull [ape in petticoats
Guenuche, *s.f.* young she-monkey. — *coiffée*,
Guépard, *s.m.* (*zool.*) cheetah, chittah, hunting leopard
Guêpe, *s.f.* wasp. *Taille de* —, very slender waist
Guêpier, *s.m.* wasps' nest; (*fig.*) nest of hornets, scrape, difficulty, hobble; (*bird*) bee-eater
Guerdon, *s.m.* (*old*) guerdon, reward; salary
Guère, (*poet.*, **Guères,**) *adv.* (*Ne* ... —) not much, not very; little; but little; not many, few, but few; not long; not often, seldom, but seldom; not easily; hardly, scarcely; hardly more, little more; hardly any; hardly anything but; hardly ever
Guéret, *s.m.* ploughed land; fallow land; waste land; headland; (*poet. and old*) field, corn-field, harvest

Guéri, e, *part. adj.* cured; healed; recovered, well again
Guéridon, *s.m.* stand; centre-table, loo-table
Guérilla, *s.f.* (*abusively, pers., s.m.*) guerilla,
Guérillero, *s.m.* guerillero, guerrillero [guerrilla
Guérir, *v.a.n.*, **Se** —, *v.r.* to cure; to heal; to remedy; to undeceive; to comfort, to solace, to console; to recover, to get well again; to be cured; to get rid; to cure oneself; (*fam.*) to be of use, to help, to do good
Guérison, *s.f.* cure; healing; recovery
Guérissable, *adj.* curable
Guérisseu-r, se, *s.m.f.* curer
Guérite, *s.f.* watch-box; (*mil.*) sentry-box; (*fort.*) guerite; (*arch.*) turret, watch-tower, belvedere; (*nav.*) rim
Guerre, *s.f.* war; warfare; dissension, strife, contest, conflict; war-department, war-office. *Petite* —, war on a small scale; sham-fight; skirmishing; desultory warfare, guerilla warfare; bickering. *De* —, of war, war; warlike. *De bonne* —, according to the laws of war; fairly, by fair means; fair play, fair. *De — lasse*, from pure weariness, weary of resistance, quite tired out, after long resistance, against o.'s will. *En* —, at war; at variance. *Faire la* —, to make *or* wage war, to carry on (the) war; to be at war; to war; to fight *or* struggle *or* contend *or* quarrel (with); to be (at); to attack; to tease, to plague, to worry; to censure, to criticize. *A la — comme à la* —, one must take things as they come
Guerri-er, ère, *adj. s.* warlike, martial, of war; warrior, soldier; female warrior [nacious
Guerroyant, e, *adj.* fighting, combative, pug-
Guerroyer, *v.n.* to war, to make *or* wage war
Guerroyeur, *s.m.* warrior
Guet, *s.m.* watch. *Au* —, on the watch. *Avoir l'œil au* —, *faire le* —, to be on the watch *or* look-out, to watch, to keep watch
Guet-apens, *s.m.* lying in wait; ambush, ambuscade; snare, trap; foul play; premeditated design to injure, premeditation; wilful injury; wilful crime; wilful murder; (*fam.*) catch, take-in, surprise
Guêtre, *s.f.* gaiter; legging. *Grande* or *longue* —, — *de chasse*, legging. *Tirer ses* —*s*, (*pop.*) to run away, to hook it
Guêtré, e, *adj.* gaitered, with (o.'s) gaiters on
Guêtrer, *v.a.* to gaiter. *Se* —, to gaiter oneself, to put on o.'s gaiters
Guêtri-er, ère, *s.m.f.* gaiter-maker
Guêtron, *s.m.* short gaiter
Guette, *s.f.* watching, watch; watch-box
Guetter, *v.a.* to watch, to be on the watch for; to wait for, to lie in wait for
Guetteu-r, se, *s.m.f.* watcher, watchman, signal-man, look-out man
Gueulard, e, *s.m.f.* bawler, brawler; greedy gut; — *s.m.* furnace-mouth; wide-mouthed pistol; — *adj.* (*of horses*) hard-mouthed
Gueulardise, *s.f.* gormandizing, gluttony
Gueule, *s.f.* mouth; jaws; hole; muzzle; (*of pers., in contempt or jest*) mug, chops, mouth; greediness, guts; palate; gabble, jaw. — *-de-loup*, chimney-cowl, cowl; (*bot.*) snapdragon, calves'-snout. *Fine* —, (*fam.*) epicure, good liver, judge of good living. *Fort en* —, (*pop.*) full of gabble, a great gabbler *or* talker; very abusive, violent *or* bold in o.'s language, foul-mouthed. *Fort sur la* —, (*pop.*) greedy, a great eater, thinking of nothing but his guts. *Avoir la — morte*, to be down in the mouth. *Être sur sa* —, *être porté sur sa* —, *être sujet à sa* —, (*fam.*) *V.* **Bouche**
Gueulée, *s.f.* (*pop.*) grub, feeding, stuffing; large mouthful; —**s**, *pl.* bawdy things, bawdy stuff
Gueuler, *v.n.* to bark; to bawl, to squall; to mouth, to spout; — *v.a.* (*hunt.*) to take up, to seize
Gueules, *s.m.* (*her.*) gules [blow-out; meal
Gueuleton, *s.m.* (*pop.*) feast, stuffing, guttling,
Gueuletonner, *v.n.* (*pop.*) to feast, to stuff, to guttle, to revel [muffins, riffraff, rabble
†Gueusaille, *s.f.* set of beggars, low set, raga-
†Gueusailler, *v.n.* to go begging, to beg, to be a lazy beggar, to loaf [blackguard, ragamuffin
Gueusard, e, *s.m.f.* beggar; rascal, rogue,
Gueuse, *s.f.* beggar; bad woman, wench, hussy, bitch; wretch; pig iron, sow
Gueuser, *v.a.n.* to beg
Gueuserie, *s.f.* beggary, beggarliness, poverty, misery; mendicity; beggars; knavery, blackguardism, villany, piece of knavery, blackguard trick [wretched
Gueu-x, se, *adj.* beggarly, poor, destitute,
Gueux, *s.m.* beggar; ragamuffin; loafer; rascal, scoundrel, knave, blackguard, villain; wretch; foot-warmer, foot-stove. — *revêtu*, mean upstart, beggar on horseback
Guévoir, *s.m.* (*local*) *V.* **Abreuvoir**
Gui, *s.m.* mistletoe; (*nav.*) main boom
Guibes, Guibolles, *s.f.pl.* (*pop.*) legs, shanks,
Guibre, *s.f.* (*nav.*) cut-water [stumps
Guiche, *s.f.* (*local*) cat, tipcat (*game*)
Guichemar, *s.m. pop. for* **Guichetier**
Guichet, *s.m.* wicket; slip-door; gateway, archway; entrance; grating; opening; little window; shutter; (*obsolete*) door (*of a piece of furniture, as of a wardrobe*, &c.)
Guichetier, *s.m.* turnkey
Guide, *s.m.* person *or* thing that guides, guide; leader; director; guide-book; text-book; (*mach., mus.*) guide; (*mil.*) guide, (*drill*) fugleman; — *s.f.* rein; stage-fee (*to postilions*). *A grandes* —*s*, four-in-hand. — **-âne,** *s.m.* guide-book, guide, directory; (*for writing*) black lines, lines. — **-chaîne,** *s.m.* (*horol.*) ratchet. — **-main,** *s.m.* (*of the piano*) hand-rail, hand-guide, hand-director, chiroplast
Guideau, *s.m.* groyne; (*fish.*) poke-net, stake-net
Guider, *v.a.* to guide; to lead, to conduct; to direct; to steer; to actuate
Se —, *v.r.* to guide oneself; to go (by); to take care of oneself; to direct o.'s steps, to proceed; to be guided *or* &c.
Guidon, *s.m.* (*mil.*) guidon; field-colours; (*formerly*) flag, standard; standard-bearer, cornet; cornetcy; (*nav.*) broad-pendant; (*of a guild or fraternity*) banner, flag, guidon; (*of fire-arms*) sight, fore-sight, bead; (*of writings*) reference, mark; (*on cards, for cheating*) mark; (*mus.*) direct; (*obsolete*) guide-book, guide. — *de renvoi*, reference
Guidonner, *v.a.* to mark (*cards*)
Guifette, *s.f.* sea-swallow
†Guignard, *s.m.* (*bird*) dotterel
†Guignau, *s.m.* *V.* **Guigneau**
†Guigne, *s.f.* black-heart cherry
†Guigne-à-gauche, *s.m.f.* (*pop.*) squinter
†Guigneau, *s.m.* (*build.*) trimmer
†Guigner, *v.n.a.* to cast a sidelong glance; to leer; to peer; to ogle; to look wistfully at; to wink at; to peep at; to have an eye *or* a design upon, to covet, to look after, to watch, to aim at, to expect
†Guignette, *s.f.* (*bird*) common sandpiper, summer snipe; (*shell-fish, local*) periwinkle,
†Guignier, *s.m.* black-heart cherry tree [winkle
†Guignol, *s.m.* puppet; Punch [**nant**)
†Guignolant, e, *adj.* (*abusively for* **Guignon-**
†Guignolet, *s.m.* black-heart cherry wine
†Guignon, *s.m.* ill luck, bad luck
†Guignonnant, e, *adj.* vexing, provoking, bothering, most unfortunate
†Guignonné, e, *adj.* unlucky. *Être* —, to be unlucky, to have the luck of it, to have a run
Guigue, *s.f.* (*nav.*) gig [of ill luck
Guilandine, *s.f.* (*bot.*) guilandina, nickar-tree
Guildive, *s.f.* tafia
Guildiverie, *s.f.* tafia-distillery
Guildivier, *s.m.* tafia-distiller
†Guillage, *s.m.* (*of beer*) working, fermenting
†Guillaume, *s.m.* (*tech.*) fillister-plane, rabbet-
†Guille, *s.f.* (*local*) tap [plane

†Guilledou, *s.m.* places of ill fame
†Guillemet, *s.m.* inverted comma
†Guillemeter, *v.a.* to put between inverted [commas
†Guillemot, *s.m.* (*bird*) guillemot
†Guiller, *v.n.* (*of beer*) to work, to ferment
†Guilleret, te, *adj.* lively, sprightly, brisk, active, dapper; slight; light; flimsy; free
†Guilleri, *s.m.* (*of sparrows*) chirping
†Guillet, *s.m.* (*local*) cat, tipcat (*game*)
†Guillochage, *s.m.* rose-engine turning, engine-[turning
†Guilloche, *s.f.* rose-engine
†Guilloché, *s.m.* *V.* **Guillochis**; —, *m.*, **e,** *f.*, *part. V.* **Guillocher**
†Guillocher, *v.a.* to engine-turn, to guillochee
†Guillocheur, *s.m.* engine-turner
†Guillochis, *s.m.* rose-engine turning, engine-turning, engine-turned work, guilloche
†Guilloire, *s.f.* fermenting-vat (*for beer*)
†Guillotine, *s.f.* guillotine; scaffold; beheading. *V.* **Fenêtre**
†Guillotiné, *s.m.* person guillotined
†Guillotinement, *s.m.* guillotining, beheading
†Guillotiner, *v.a.* to guillotine, to behead
†Guillotineur, *s.m.* guillotiner, guillotinist, partisan of the guillotine
Guimauve, *s.f.* marsh-mallow
Guimbarde, *s.f.* waggon, van; Jew's harp; (*tool*) old woman's tooth
Guimoisseron, Guimoisson, *s.m.* parr, brandling (*young salmon*) [tucker
Guimpe, *s.f.* wimple, stomacher; neckerchief;
Guindage, *s.m.* hoisting
Guindal, *s.m.* derrick, crane, lift, hoist
Guindant, *s.m.* (*nav.*) hoist (*of a flag*)
Guinde, *s.f.* lift, hoist
Guindé, e, *part. adj.* hoisted, &c. (*V.* **Guinder**); strained, forced, unnatural, stiff, stilted, formal; (*nav.*) an-end, a-trip
Guindeau, *s.m.* windlass, lift, hoist
Guinder, *v.a.* to hoist; to wind; to lift, to raise; to hang up; (*fig.*) to strain, to force
Se —, *v.r.* to hoist *or* &c. oneself up; to be hoisted *or* &c.; to fall into bombast; to bridle up
Guinderesse, *s.f.* (*nav.*) top-rope
Guinderie, *s.f.* constraint, stiffness
Guinée, *s.f.* guinea; blue cotton-cloth
Guingamp, Guingan, *s.m.* gingham
Guingois, *s.m.* crookedness. *De —*, crookedly, crooked, awry; cross-grained
Guinguette, *s.f.* tea-garden, public-house (*out of town*), suburban public-house *or* tea-garden; (*jest. and obsolete*) country-box, box
Guiorer, *v.n.* (*of mice*) to squeak
Guipé, *s.m.* imitation vellum-lace; — *m.*, **e,** *f. part. adj.* twisted, &c. (*V.* **Guiper**)
Guiper, *v.a.* to twist; to do in imitation of vel-[lum-lace
Guipon, *s.m.* (*nav.*) mop
Guipure, *s.f.* vellum-lace, guipure; slight lace edging, gimp, guipure [hook, fore-hook, hook
Guirlande, *s.f.* garland, wreath; (*nav.*) breast-
Guirlander, *v.a.* to wreathe
Guisarme, *s.f.* two-edged axe
Guise, *s.f.* wise, manner, way; humour, fancy. *En — de*, by way of; instead of; like, as. *Faire à sa —*, to have o.'s own way, to do as one likes
Guitardin, *s.m.* (*bot.*) fiddle-wood
Guitare, *s.f.* guitar
Guitariste, *s.m.f.* guitarist
Guivre, *s.f.* (*her.*) snake, serpent
Guivré, e, *adj.* (*her.*) with snakes
Gulf-stream, *s.m.* (*geog.*) Gulf Stream
Gumène, *s.f.* (*her.*) cable
Gunnel, *s.m.* (*zool.*) gunnel, butterfish
Gurnard, Gurneau, *s.m.* (*fish*) grey gurnard,
Gustati-f, ve, *adj.* gustatory [grey gurnet
Gustation, *s.f.* gustation, taste
‡Gutta-percha, *s.f.* gutta-percha
Gutte, *adj. V.* **Gomme**
Guttier, *s.m.* (*bot.*) gamboge-tree
Guttifère, *adj.* guttiferous; — *s.f.* guttifer
Guttiforme, *adj.* guttiform, drop-shaped
Guttural, e, *adj.*, **Gutturale,** *s.f.* guttural
Gutturalement, *adv.* gutturally
Gymnase, *s.m.* gymnasium
Gymnasiarque, *s.m.* gymnasiarch; gymnas[t]
Gymnaste, *s.m.f.* gymnast
Gymnastique, *adj.* gymnastic; — *s.f.* gymnastics; gymnasium
Gymnètre, *s.m.* (*fish*) gymnetrus
Gymnique, *adj.* gymnic, gymnical, athletic — *s.f.* gymnics, athletics
Gymnoclade, *s.m.* (*bot.*) gymnocladus
Gymnosoph-ie, -isme, -iste. *V.* page 3, § 1
Gymnosperme, *adj.* (*bot.*) gymnospermous — *s.f.* gymnosperm
Gymnospermie, *s.f.* (*bot.*) gymnospermia
Gymnospermique, *adj.* (*bot.*) gymnospermic
Gymnote, *s.m.* (*zool.*) gymnotus, electric eel
Gynandre, *adj.* (*bot.*) gynandrous
Gynandrie, *s.f.* (*bot.*) gynandria [drous
Gynandrique, *adj.* (*bot.*) gynandrian, gynan-
Gynécée, *s.m.* gynæceum, women's apartment; women's workshop [government, female power
Gynécocratie, *s.f.* gynecocracy, petticoat
Gynéco-cratique, -graphie, -graphique, -logie, -logique, -logiste, &c. *V.* p. 3, § 1
Gypaète, *s.m.* (*zool.*) lämmergeier, bearded vul-
Gypse, *s.m.* gypsum, plaster of Paris [ture
Gypseu-x, se, *adj.* gypseous
Gypsifère, *adj.* gypsiferous [**Girasol,** &c.
Gyrasol, Gyration, Gyratoire, &c. *V.*
Gyratrice, *adj.f. Colombe —*, tumbler (*pigeon*)
Gyrin, *s.m.* (*insect*) whirligig, weaver
Gyrocarpe, *s.m.* (*bot.*) gyrocarpus
Gyroman-cie, -tique. *V.* page 3, § 1
Gyromancien, ne, *s.m.f.* gyromancer
Gyromètre, *s.m.* gyrometer
Gyroscope, *s.m.* gyroscope
Gyrovague, *s.m.* monk-errant

H

H, *s.f.* h
'Ha, *int. s.m.* ha! ah! oh! he! hey!
Habeas corpus, *s.m.* (*English law*) habeas [corpus
Habenaire, *s.f.* (*bot.*) habenaria
Habile, *adj.* able; clever, skilful, skilled; proficient; quick, active, expeditious; competent, qualified, fit, capable; learned; sharp, cunning; — *s.m.f.* clever fellow, clever person, clever one; proficient; sharp practitioner
Habilement, *adv.* ably; cleverly, skilfully
Habileté, *s.f.* ability; cleverness, skill, skilfulness; talent; proficiency; experience; capacity; knowledge; quickness; sharpness [*or* learned
Habilissime, *adj.* (*fam.*) very able *or* skilful
Habilitation, *s.f.* aptitude; qualifying, qualification, capacitation
Habilité, *s.f.* competency, qualification, capacity
Habiliter, *v.a.* to qualify, to capacitate, to en-[able, to entitle
†Habillable, *adj.* dressable
†Habillage, *s.m.* (*tech.*) dressing; trussing; curing [rich
†Habillant, e, *adj.* fit *or* good for dress, nice,
†Habillé, e, *part. adj.* dressed, clad, &c. (*V.* **Habiller**); good for dress, for dress, dress, dressy. *Robe —e*, full dress. *Tout —*, in o.'s clothes, with o.'s clothes on
†Habillement, *s.m.* clothing; clothes, dress, habit, garments, attire, wearing-apparel; suit. — *complet*, suit of clothes, complete suit
†Habiller, *v.a.* to dress; to clothe; to dress out; to trim; to cover; to wrap up; to disguise; to fit, to become; to make clothes for, to work for; to provide *or* supply with clothes, to find in clothes; (*fam.*) to abuse *or* ridicule, to fall foul of; (*tech.*) to dress, to prepare, to skin, to truss, to cure, to gut, to draw; (*of cards*) to illuminate
S'—, *v.r.* to dress *or* &c. oneself, to dress; to have o.'s clothes made, to get *or* buy o.'s

clothes; to find o.'s own clothes; to abuse each other; to be dressed *or* &c. [slop-seller
†**Habilleu-r, se,** *s.m.f.* dresser; skin-dresser;
Habit, *s.m.* coat; dress-coat; full dress; habit, garment, garb, raiment, attire, dress, clothes; (*eccl.*) cloth; (*obsolete*) suit (of clothes); **—s,** *pl.* clothes; vestments; robes; wearing-apparel. — *habillé,* dress-coat; dressy coat; full dress, evening-dress. — *rouge,* red coat; English soldier; Englishman. — *à la française,* cutaway-coat. — *de bord,* (*nav.*) sea-clothes. *Prendre l'—,* to take the veil, to put on the cowl, to become a nun *or* a monk
Habitabilité, *s.f.* habitability, habitableness
Habitable, *adj.* habitable, inhabitable, fit to live in [tation, abode, dwelling
Habitacle, *s.m.* (*nav.*) binnacle; (*obsolete*) habi-
Habitant, e, *s.m.f.* inhabitant; occupant, occupier; resident; inmate; planter, habitant
Habitat, *s.m.* (*nat. hist.*) habitat
Habitation, *s.f.* habitation; abode, dwelling, residence; house; tenement; settlement; plantation [inhabitativeness
Habitativité, *s.f.* (*in phrenology*) inhabitiveness,
Habiter, *v.a.n.* to inhabit, to occupy, to live in, to reside in, to dwell, to live
Habitude, *s.f.* habit, use, custom; practice; trick; (*obsolete*) acquaintance; intercourse. *D'—,* habitual; usual; usually; generally
Habitué, e, *part. adj.* accustomed, used; — *s.m.f.* frequenter; customer
Habituel, le, *adj.* habitual, usual
Habituellement, *adv.* habitually, usually
Habituer, *v.a.* to habituate, &c. (*V.* **Accoutu-**
Habitus, *s.m.* (*nat. hist.*) habitus [**mer**)
'**Hâbler,** *v.n.* to boast, to brag
'**Hâblerie,** *s.f.* boasting, bragging
'**Hâbleu-r, se,** *s.m.f.* boaster, braggart
'**Hachage,** *s.m.* chopping, &c. (*V.* **Hacher**)
'**Hache,** *s.f.* axe; hatchet. — *d'armes,* battle-axe, pole-axe. — *d'abordage,* — *d'armes,* (*nav.*) boarding-hatchet *or* axe, pole-axe. *Coup de —, V.* **Coup.** *Fait à coups de —,* clumsily made, roughly done
'**Hache,** *s.m.* (*in compounds, from* **Hacher,** "to chop," "to cut up," &c.) thing that chops *or* cuts up, chopper, cutter. — **-légumes,** *s.m.* vegetable-cutter. — **-paille,** *s.m.* straw-cutter, chaff-cutter [abrupt, irregular, desultory
'**Haché, e,** *part. adj.* chopped, &c. (*V.* **Hacher**);
'**Hacher,** *v.a.* to chop; to hew; to hack; to cut to pieces, to cut up, to cut; to hash; to mince; (*draw., engr.*) to hatch
'**Hachereau,** *s.m.* small axe, hatchet
'**Hachette,** *s.f.* hatchet; hacking-knife
'**Hachich, Hachisch,** *s.m.* hashish, hasheesh, haschish
'**Hachis,** *s.m.* hash; minced meat, mince-meat, forcemeat; jumble. *En —,* in *or* into a hash, hashed, minced [mincing-machine
'**Hachoir,** *s.m.* chopping-board; mincing-knife;
'**Hachotte,** *s.f. V.* **Hachette**
'**Hachure,** *s.f.* (*draw., engr.*) hatching
'**Hadji,** *s.m.* hadji (*Mahometan pilgrim*)
Hæma..., Hæmo..., *V.* **Héma..., Hémo...**
'**Hagard, e,** *adj.* haggard, wild
'**Hagardement,** *adv.* haggardly, wildly
Hagiographe, *adj.* hagiographal, hagiographic; — *s.m.* hagiographer
Hagio - graphie, -graphique, -logie, -logique, &c. *V.* page 3, § 1
'**Haha,** *s.m.* ha-ha, sunk fence, ditch
'**Hahé,** *int. s.m.* (*hunt.*) ware there!
'**Hai,** *int. V.* **Hé**
'**Haï, e,** *part. of* **Haïr;** — *s.m.* eddy
'**Haie,** *s.f.* hedge; hedgerow; hurdle, fence; line, row; (*of a plough*) beam; — *int. V.* **Aïe.** — *vive,* quickset hedge. — *morte,* fence of branches. *Border la —,* to line the road *or* street, to stand on a line on both sides
'**Haïe,** *int. V.* **Aïe**
'**Haïk,** *s.m.* haik (*Arabian cloak*)
†'**Haillon,** *s.m.* rag, tatter
Haim, Hain, *s.m.* (*local*) fish-hook, hook
'**Haine,** *s.f.* hatred, hate; odium; spite; grudge; abhorrence, aversion, dislike
'**Haineusement,** *adv.* hatefully, spitefully
'**Haineu-x, se,** *adj.* hateful, spiteful
'**Haïr,** *v.a.* to hate, to detest, to abhor; to dislike
'**Haire,** *s.f.* hair-shirt
'**Haïssable,** *adj.* hateful, odious
'**Haïsseu-r, se,** *s.m.f.* hater
Haïtien, ne, *adj. s.* Haytian
'**Halage,** *s.m.* towage; towing; tracking. *Chemin de —,* towing-path, tow-path
'**Halbourg,** *s.m.* shotten herring
'**Halbran,** *s.m.* young wild duck
'**Halbrené, e,** *adj.* broken-feathered; seedy
'**Halbrener,** *v.n.* to shoot young wild duck
Halcyon, *s.m. V.* **Alcyon**
'**Halde,** *s.f.* dross, scum
'**Hâle,** *s.m.* hot *or* sultry air, heat, sun-burn; tawny complexion; (*agr.*) drying wind
'**Halé, e,** *part. adj.* towed, &c. (*V.* **Haler**)
'**Hâlé, e,** *part. of* **Hâler,** *and adj.* sun-burnt, sun-browned, burnt, swarthy, tanned, tawny
Haleine, *s.f.* breath, wind. *Ouvrage de longue —,* work of time, long work. *A perte d'—,* till out of breath; long-winded, without end. *Tenir en —,* to keep in exercise *or* in practice *or* in play *or* in working order; to keep up; to keep at bay; to keep on the alert
Haleiner, *v.n.a. V.* **Halener**
Halenée, *s.f.* breath, whiff, smell
Halener, *v.n.* to breathe; — *v.a.* (*hunt.*) to wind, to get scent of [to excite, to set (on, upon, at)
'**Haler,** *v.a.* to tow; to track; to haul; to heave;
'**Hâler,** *v.a.* to burn, to tan, to brown
Se —, *v.r.* to become *or* get sun-burnt, to become tawny
Halésie, *s.f.* (*bot.*) halesia, snowdrop-tree
'**Haletant, e,** *adj.* panting, breathless, out of breath [breath, to puff, to be out of breath
'**Haleter,** *v.n.* to pant, to pant *or* gasp for
'**Haleu-r, se,** *s.m.f.* hauler, tracker
Halicore, *s.m.* (*fish*) halicore, dugong
Haliète, *s.m.* (*bird*) erne
Halieutique, *adj.* halieutic; **—s,** *s.f.pl.* halieutics (*art*); *s.m.pl.* Halieutics (*treatise*) [sea-ear
Haliotide, *s.f.* (*shell-fish*) haliotis, sea-ear shell,
Halitueu-x, se, *adj.* (*med.*) halituous, moist
'**Hallage,** *s.m.* market-fee, market-dues
Hallali, *s.m.* (*hunt.*) whohoop. *A l'—,* at bay
'**Halle,** *s.f.* market. *Dames de la —,* market-women. *Fort de la —,* market-porter. *Langage des —s,* Billingsgate language
'**Hallebarde,** *s.f.* halberd. *Pleuvoir* or *tomber des —s,* to rain cats and dogs
'**Hallebardier,** *s.m.* halberdier
'**Hallier,** *s.m.* thicket; trammel (*net*); market-keeper, market-officer; market-man
'**Hallope,** *s.m.* (*fish.*) trawl-net
Hallucination, *s.f.* hallucination, delusion
Halluciné, e, *part. adj.* hallucinated, deluded; — *s.m.f.* person given to hallucinations *or* delu-
Halluciner, *v.a.* to hallucinate, to delude [sions
S'—, *v.r.* to become hallucinated, to delude oneself
'**Halo,** *s.m.* (*astr.*) halo; (*anat.*) areola, halo
'**Halochimie,** *s.f.* halochemistry
'**Halogène,** *s.m.* halogen; — *adj.* halogenous
'**Halograph-ie, -ique.** *V.* page 3, § 1
'**Haloïde,** *adj.* (*chem.*) haloid
'**Haloir,** *s.m.* drying-room (*for hemp*)
'**Halolog-ie, -ique.** *V.* page 3, § 1
'**Halo-mancie, -métrie,** &c. *V.* page 3, § 1
'**Haloscope,** *s.m.* (*astr.*) haloscope
'**Halot,** *s.m.* rabbit-hole
Haloxyline, *s.f.* haloxyline
'**Halte,** *s.f.* halt; stop; stand; halting-place, resting-place. —! — *là!* halt! stop! stand! hold! not so fast! that won't do! *Faire —,* to halt; to stop, to make a stop *or* a stand
'**Halter,** *v.n.a.,* **Se —,** *v.r.* to halt

'Haltère, *s.m.* dumb-bell; (*of dipterous insects*) poiser, balancer, halteres
'Halurg-ie, -ique. *V.* page 3, § 1 [cot
'Hamac, *s.m.* hammock. — *à l'anglaise*, (*nav.*)
Hamadryade, *s.f.* hamadryad, wood-nymph
'Hambourg, *s.m.* keg; (*geog.*) Hamburg, Hambro
'Hambourgeois, e, *adj. s.* of Hamburg; Hamburger
'Hambouvreux, *s.m.* tree-sparrow
'Hameau, *s.m.* hamlet
Hameçon, *s.m.* fish-hook, hook; (*fig.*) bait
Hameçonner, *v.a.* to hook
'Hamée, *s.f.* (*artil.*) handle (*of the sponge*)
Hamiltonie, *s.f.* (*bot.*) hamiltonia, elk-nut
'Hampe, *s.f.* staff; handle; (*bot.*) scape; (*butch.*) thin flank; (*hunt.*) breast (*of a stag*)
'Hamster, *s.m.* hamster (*kind of rat*)
'Han, *s.m.* (*in the East*) khan, inn, caravansary; — *int. s.m.* hugh! heave (*of a workman striking a heavy blow*)
'Hanap, *s.m.* (*old*) goblet, tankard
'Hanche, *s.f.* hip, haunch; (*nav.*) quarter
'Handicap, *s.m.* handicap
'Handicaper, *v.n.* to handicap
'Handicapeur, *s.m.* handicapper
'Hanebane, *s.f.* *V.* **Jusquiame**
'Hangar, *s.m.* shed; cart-house; house; out-house; shanty; lean-to
'Hanneton, *s.m.* cockchafer; (*pers.*) giddy goose; (*pop.*) crotchet, hobby. *Étourdi comme un* —, giddy as a goose. *Avoir un — dans le plafond*, (*pop.*) to have a bee in o.'s bonnet
'Hannetonner, *v.a.* to clear of cockchafers; — *v.n.* to act thoughtlessly
'Hanovrien, ne, *adj. s.* Hanoverian
'Hansar, Hansard, *s.m.* crosscut-saw
'Hanse, *s.f.* pin-wire; (*obsolete*) guild, company; (*geog.*, — *teutonique*) Hanseatic towns *or* cities, Hanse Towns
Hanséatique, *adj.* Hanseatic
'Hanter, *v.a.n.* to frequent; to resort to; to associate with, to keep company with; to visit; to haunt
'Hanteu-r, se, *s.m.f.* frequenter; haunter
'Hantise, *s.f.* frequenting, frequentation, intercourse, intimacy, company, associates, connection; haunting
'Happe, *s.f.* cramp-iron; axle-tree-bed
'Happe-chair, *s.m.* torment, plague, teaser; dun; grasping *or* insatiable fellow; bailiff, catchpoll
'Happelourde, *s.f.* false gem, imitation stone, paste; duffer
'Happement, *s.m.* snapping, &c. (*V.* **Happer**)
'Happer, *v.a.* to snap, to snap up; to seize; to apprehend; to catch; to lay hold of; to nab; — *v.n.* to adhere to the tongue; to adhere
'Haquebute, *s.f.* haquebut, hackbut, arquebuse
'Haquenée, *s.f.* (*obsolete*) ambling nag, pad;
'Haquet, *s.m.* dray; truck [gawky woman
'Haquetier, *s.m.* drayman; carman
'Harangue, *s.f.* harangue, speech, oration, address; lecture
'Haranguer, *v.a.n.* to harangue, to address; to lecture; to speechify, to hold forth, to make speeches *or* a speech
'Harangueu-r, se, *s.m.f.* haranguer, orator, speaker; speech-maker, speechifier; twaddler, preacher, lecturer
'Haras, *s.m.* breeding-stud, stud
'Harasse, *s.f.* crate [weariness, fatigue
'Harassement, *s.m.* harassing, wearing out,
'Harasser, *v.a.* to harass, to weary out, to weary, to tire out, to tire, to fatigue, to overwork, to jade
'Harassier, *s.m.* stud-keeper
'Harauder, *v.a.* *V.* **Haroder**
'Harceler, *v.a.* to harass; to torment, to plague, to tease, to annoy
'Harcellement, *s.m.* harassing; teasing
'Harde, *s.f.* (*hunt.*) herd; (*of dogs*) leash; —**s,** *pl.* herds, &c.; clothes, wearing-apparel; traps, luggage
'Hardées, *s.f.pl.* branches broken by fallow deer
'Harder, *v.a.* (*hunt.*) to leash
'Hardi, e, *adj.* bold; daring, courageous, fearless; forward, impudent; elegant, grand; —! *int.* courage! go it!
'Hardiesse, *s.f.* boldness; daring, courage; confidence; forwardness, impudence; licence; liberty; nobleness, grandeur
'Hardiment, *adv.* boldly; daringly, fearlessly; freely; unhesitatingly; flatly; safely; impudently
'Hare, *int. s.m.* (*hunt.*) halloo, holloa
'Harem, *s.m.* harem [bloater
'Hareng, *s.m.* herring. — *saur*, red herring,
'Harengade, *s.f.* herring-net, drift; —**s,** *pl.* packed sardines
'Harengaison, *s.f.* herring-season; herring-fishery, catch *or* take of herrings
'Harengère, *s.f.* herring-woman, fish-woman, fish-fag
'Harengerie, *s.f.* herring-market
'Harenguet, *s.m.* sprat; sill
'Harenguière, *s.f.* herring-net, drift
'Haret, *adj.m.* (*hunt.*, *of cats*) wild; poaching
'Harfang, *s.m.* (*bird*) harfang, snowy owl, hawk-owl [wrangling, bickering
†**'Hargnerie,** *s.f.* surly *or* snappish disposition;
†**'Hargneu-x, se,** *adj.* surly, peevish, cross, quarrelsome, currish; snarling, snappish, vicious
Haria, *s.m.* *V.* **Aria**
'Haricot, *s.m.* kidney-bean, bean, haricot; (— *de mouton*) haricot of mutton, haricot, Irish stew. —*s blancs*, kidney-beans, haricot-beans. — *verts*, French beans. — *d'Espagne*, scarlet runner. —*s*, *Hôtel des —s*, (*jest.*) prison, defaulters' room, dry-room (*for national guards or militiamen*)
'Haricoter, *v.n.* (*pop.*) to play low; to speculate on a small scale; to do small jobs; to do a small business only, to get on so so, to scrape along, to do very little
'Haricoteu-r, se, Haricoti-er, ère, *s.m.f.* timid player; petty jobber [woman
'Haridelle, *s.f.* jade; hack; lanky gawky
'Harle, *s.m.* (*bird*) goosander, merganser, smew
'Harline, *s.f.* (*chem.*) harline
Harmale, *s.f.* (*bot.*) harmala, Syrian rue
Harmaline, *s.f.* (*chem.*) harmaline
Harmattan, *s.m.* harmattan (*hot wind of Africa*)
Harmine, *s.f.* (*chem.*) harmine
Harmonia, *s.f.* (*astr.*) Harmonia
Harmonica, *s.m.* harmonica, musical glasses
Harmonicon, *s.m.* (*mus. instr.*) harmonicon
Harmonicorde, *s.m.* (*mus. instr.*) harmonichord
Harmonie, *s.f.* harmony; harmonics; concert; union, concord; tune; keeping; wind-instruments; (*rhet.*) number; (*anat.*) harmonia
Harmonier, (*old spelling*) *V.* **Harmoniser**
Harmonieusement, *adv.* harmoniously; musically
Harmonieu-x, se, *adj.* harmonious; musical; melodious; sweet, agreeable; (*of colours*) friendly
Harmoniflûte, *s.m.* (*mus. instr.*) harmoniflute
Harmoniphon, *s.m.* (*mus. instr.*) harmoniphon
Harmon-ique, -iquement. *V.* page 3, § 1
Harmonisa-teur, trice, *s.m.f.* harmonizer; — *adj.* harmonizing
Harmonisation, *s.f.* harmonization
Harmoniser, *v.a.n.*, **S'**—, *v.r.* to harmonize
Harmoniste, *s.m.f.* harmonist
Harmonium, *s.m.* harmonium
Harmonomètre, *s.m.* harmonometer
'Harnachement, *s.m.* harnessing; harness; trappings; rig [out, to trap out
'Harnacher, *v.a.* to harness; to trick *or* rig
'Harnacheur, *s.m.* harness-maker; harnessing-groom, harnesser
'Harnais, *s.m.* harness; trappings; armour; equipment; uniform; tackle; gear
'Harnois, *s.m.* (*poet. and old*) *V.* **Harnais**
'Haro, *s.m.* hue and cry, outcry. —! shame! out (upon ...)! *Crier — sur*, to raise an outcry against
'Haroder, *v.a.* (*pop.*) to hoot, to chaff
Harpagon, *s.m.* Harpagon, miser
†**'Harpailler (Se),** *v.r.* to wrangle, to squabble
'Harpaye, *s.m.* (*bird*) harpy, moor-buzzard, marsh-harrier, duck-hawk

'Harpe, *s.f.* harp; harp-shell; toothing-stone, rustic coin; **—s,** *pl.* harps, &c.; toothing

'Harpé, e, *adj.* harp-shaped, well-shaped, [graceful

'Harpeau, *s.m.* (*nav.*) *V.* **Grappin**

Harpége, &c. *V.* **Arpége,** &c.

'Harper, *v.n.* to harp, to play on the harp; (*of horses*) to have the string-halt, to halt; — *v.a.* to catch hold of, to clutch, to gripe, to grasp, to grapple

'Harpeur, *s.m.* (*of the ancients*) harper

'Harpie, *s.f.* harpy; shrew, vixen, scold, hell-cat; (*zool.*) harpy-eagle, harpy

†'Harpigner, Harpiller (Se), *v.r.* (*pop.*) to wrangle, to bicker, to squabble, to scuffle

'Harpin, *s.m.* boat-hook; (*vet.*) carbuncle

'Harpiste, *s.m.f.* harpist [crosscut-saw

'Harpon, *s.m.* harpoon; (*tech.*) cramp-iron;

'Harponnage, Harponnement, *s.m.* harpooning

'Harponner, *v.a.* to harpoon

'Harponneur, *s.m.* harpooner [bramble

'Harponnier, *s.m.* crab-catcher (*bittern*);

'Harpyie, *s.f.* (*zool.*) *V.* **Harpie**

'Hart, *s.f.* withe, band, fagot-band; rope, halter; hanging, gallows

'Hartite, *s.f.* (*chem.*) hartite

Haruspice, *s.m. V.* **Aruspice**

'Hasard, *s.m.* hazard; chance; accident; casualty; risk, danger, peril; good fortune; good bargain, bargain. *Au* —, at a venture; at random; by chance. *A tout* —, at all hazards, at all events. *De* —, second-hand. *Par* —, by chance, by accident, accidentally; I wonder, I should like to know, surely, I suppose; what (if) . . . ? *Corriger le* —, to assist fortune. *Est-ce que par — il nous manquerait de parole?* surely he does not mean to disappoint us?

'Hasardé, e, *adj.* ventured; hazardous; rash; bold; free; strong; deep; going *or* gone far, far gone; stale, tainted. *Blond* —, gingery, ginger [risk; to expose; to try

'Hasarder, *v.a.n.* to hazard; to venture; to

'Hasardeusement, *adv.* hazardously

'Hasardeu-x, se, *adj.* hazardous, venturous, venturesome, bold; dangerous, perilous, unsafe

'Hasardise, *s.f.* venture, trial, attempt

'Haschich, Haschisch, *s.m. V.* **Hachich**

'Hase, *s.f.* doe-hare, doe-rabbit

Hast, *s.m.* staff, haft, spear. *Arme d'*—, long-hafted weapon (*lance, pike,* &c.) [man, pikeman

'Hastaire, Hastat, *s.m.* (*Rom. hist.*) spear-

'Haste, *s.f.* (*old*) spear, pike; (*obsolete*) spit; spitful; (*of a letter*) upright

'Hasté, e, *adj.* (*bot.*) hastate, hastated [liated

'Hastifolié, e, *adj.* (*bot.*) hastifoliate, hastifo-

'Hastiforme, *adj.* hastiform [tine

'Hatchetine, *s.f.* (*chem.*) hatchetine, hatchet-

'Hâte, *s.f.* haste, hurry, speed; (*obsolete*) spit; spitful. *A la* —, in haste, hastily, in a hurry, quickly. *En* —, in haste; forthwith. *En toute* —, with all possible speed. *Avoir — de,* to be in haste, to be in a hurry; to long; to be anxious

'Hâté, e, *part. adj.* hastened, &c. (*V.* **Hâter**); in haste, in a hurry; early, forward; pressing, urgent

'Hâtelet, *s.m.* (*cook.*) skewer

'Hâtelettes, *s.f.pl.* (*cook.*) broil

'Hâter, *v.a.* to hasten; to urge; to quicken; to forward; to hurry; to force; to mend

Se —, *v.r.* to hasten; to make haste; to hurry; to be in a hurry

'Hâtier, *s.m.* spit-rack

'Hâti-f, ve, *adj.* forward; precocious; premature; early; hasty [hastings, early peas

'Hâtiveau, *s.m.* hasting-pear, green chissel;

'Hâtivement, *adv.* prematurely; early; hastily

'Hâtiveté, *s.f.* earliness, forwardness, precocity

'Hatti-chérif, *s.m.* hatti-sherif (*Turkish decree*)

'Hauban, *s.m.* (*nav.*) shroud; (*tech.*) rope. — *de fortune,* swifter, preventer shroud

'Haubergeon, *s.m.* habergeon, small hauberk

'Haubert, *s.m.* hauberk, coat of mail

'Haüs, *s.m.* (*counter-jumpers' slang*) quiz

'Hausse, *s.f.* rise; (*tech.*) lift, block; (*of shoes*) piece; (*artil.*) bridge; (*print.*) overlay. *Être en* —, to be rising

'Hausse-col, *s.m.* (*mil.*) gorget

'Haussement, *s.m.* raising, lifting, rising, rise; shrugging, shrug

'Hausse-pied, *s.m.* wolf-snare, toil

'Hausse-queue, *s.m.* (*bird*) wagtail

'Hausser, *v.a.* to raise; to lift, to lift up; to increase; to shrug; (*nav.*) to near (*another vessel, a coast,* &c.); — *v.n.* to rise; to go *or* come up; to increase

Se —, *v.r.* to be raised *or* lifted up; to rise *or* get higher, to rise; to go *or* come up; to raise oneself; to stand on tiptoe; to increase; (*of the weather*) to clear up

'Haussier, *s.m.* bull, operator for a rise

'Haussière, *s.f. V.* **Aussière**

'Haussoir, *s.m.*, **Haussoire,** *s.f.* sluice-gate

'Haustellé, e, *adj.*, **Haustellé,** *s.m.* (*zool.*) haustellate

'Haut, e, *adj.* high; higher; upper; superior; top; up; erect; aloft; uplifted; raised; lofty; tall; elevated; principal, chief; great; grand; important; eminent; proud, haughty; loud; strong; (*in the almanac*) late; (*of antiquity*) remote; (*of the weather*) clear; — *s.m.* height; top, upper part; summit; eminence; head; upper end; higher notes; up; **—e,** *s.f.* (*pop.*) higher class, crack people, crack *or* swell places *or* place; (*thieves*) swell-mob; — *adv.* high; high up; up; aloft; far back; proudly, haughtily; loudly, loud, aloud, out; boldly. — *en bas!* sweep! — *en couleur,* high-coloured, florid-complexioned, ruddy. — *sur jambes,* — *-monté,* long-legged. *En* —, at the top; on high; aloft; up; over; above; overhead; in Heaven; upward; upstairs; up there. *D'en* —, *du* —, from *or* of the top; from *or* of above; from *or* of Heaven; from *or* of the Court, from *or* of the authorities; upper, top. *De — en bas,* downward; with contempt (*V.* **Regarder**); proudly, haughtily; roughly; from head to foot. *Du — en bas,* from top to bottom; from head to foot; overhead; with contempt; proudly, haughtily; roughly. *Là-* —, *par là-* —, up there, above; in Heaven; upstairs. *Par en* —, at top, at the top; in the upper part; through the top; upward. *Par — et par bas,* upward and downward. *Plus* —, higher; higher up; above; before; louder. *De plus* —, from higher; higher, further up, farther back. *Tout* —, aloud. *Avoir deux mètres de* —, to be six feet high. *Gagner le* or *au* —, (*old*) to take flight, to scamper away. *Le prendre* — or *bien* —, to take it high *or* very high; to assume a high tone, to speak haughtily *or* with arrogance, to carry it high. *Tomber de son* —, to fall flat down; to be astounded *or* amazed *or* thunderstruck. — **-à-bas,** *s.m.* (*obsolete*) pedlar, hawker. — **-à-haut,** *s.m.* (*hunt.*) halloo, hoo-up. — **-Brion,** *s.m.* Haut-Brion (*claret wine*). — **-de-casse,** *s.m.* (*print.*) upper case. — **-de-chausses,** *s.m.* (*obsolete*) breeches, pair of breeches, small clothes, smalls, upper hose. —**e-bonté,** *s.f.* haute-bonté (*kind of pear*). —**e-contre,** *s.f.* counter-tenor, contralto. —**e-licier,** —**e-lissier,** *s.m.* high-warper. — **-fond,** *s.m.* (*nav.*) shoal. — **-fourneau,** *s.m.* blast-furnace, high-furnace. *Propriétaire de —s-fourneaux,* iron-manufacturer, iron-master. — **-le-corps,** *s.m.* skip, bound, start; retching. — **-le-pied** (*adv. int., V.* **Pied**), *s.m.* vagrant, tramp, loafer, scamp. — **-mal,** *s.m.* (*pop.*) falling sickness, epilepsy. — **-pas,** *s.m.* (*arch.*) foot-pace. — **-pendu,** *s.m.* (*nav.*) scud, flying cloud. — **-relief,** *s.m.* high relief [(*agr.*) pole

'Hautain, e, *adj.* haughty, lofty, proud; — *s.m.*

'Hautainement, *adv.* haughtily, proudly

'Hautbois, *s.m.* hautboy, oboe; hautboyist

'Hautboïste, *s.m.f.* hautboyist

'Hautement, *adv.* highly; boldly, resolutely; stoutly; openly; loudly; haughtily, proudly

'Hautesse, *s.f.* Highness
'Hauteur, *s.f.* height, elevation, loftiness; altitude; eminence, hill, down, rising ground; ascent; pride; haughtiness; haughty manner *or* behaviour, arrogance; greatness; superiority; depth. *A la — de*, at *or* to the height of; as high as; equal to; up to; competent for; able to understand, capable of appreciating; on a level with; on a par with; opposite; off. *Tomber de sa —* or *de son haut*, *V.* **Haut**
'Hauturi-er, ère, *adj.* of the high seas, ocean, sea; — *s.m.* sea-pilot
'Havanais, e, *adj. s.* Havanese
'Havane, *s.m.* Havana (cigar), foreign cigar
'Hâve, *adj.* emaciated; wan
'Haveneau, Havenet, *s.m. V.* **Avano**
'Haveron, *s.m.* wild oats [fork
'Havet, *s.m.* slater's hook; tenter-hook; flesh-
'Havi, e, *part. adj.* scorched, burnt; — *s.m. V.*
'Havir, *v.a.n.*, **Se —,** *v.r.* to scorch, to burn [**Avi**
'Havrais, e, *adj. s.* of Havre, Havrese, native of Havre
'Havre, *s.m.* tidal harbour, harbour, haven
'Havrer, *v.n.* to put into harbour [basket, wallet
'Havresac, *s.m.* haversack, knapsack; tool-
'Haye, *s.f.* (*of ploughs*) beam; — *int.* (*hunt.*)
'Hayer, *v.a.n.* to hedge [ware there! soho!
'Hé, *int.* hey! hi! hoy! ho! halloo! I say! ha! there! (*obsolete spelling for* "eh") *V.* **Eh**
'Heaume, *s.m.* (*old*) helmet, helm
'Heaumier, *s.m.* (*pop.*) *V.* **Guignier**
Hebdomadaire, *adj.* weekly, hebdomadal
Hebdomadairement, *adv.* weekly, hebdomadally [hebdomadary
Hebdomadi-er, ère, *s.m.f. adj.* (*Cath. rel.*)
Hébé, *s.f.* (*myth., astr.*, &c.) Hebe
Héberge, *s.f.* point of disjunction, break
Hébergement, *s.m.* harbouring, entertaining, lodging [lodge
Héberger, *v.a.* to harbour, to entertain, to
  S'—, *v.r.* (*arch.*) to rest (against a party wall)
Hébertiste, *s.m.* (*Fr. hist.*) hebertist
Hébété, e, *part. adj.* dulled, stupefied, besotted, dull, stupid; — *s.m.f.* dullard, dolt, dunce, blockhead [ting, imbecility, stupefaction
Hébétement, *s.m.* dulness, stupidity, besot-
Hébéter, *v.a.* to dull, to stupefy, to make dull *or* stupid, to besot, to hebetate
  S'—, *v.r.* to become dull *or* stupid
Hébétude, *s.f.* hebetude
Hébraïque, *adj.* Hebraic, Hebrew
Hébraïquement, *adv.* hebraically
Hébraïsant, *s.m.* hebraist
Hébraïser, *v.n.a.* to hebraize
Hébraïsme, *s.m.* hebraism
Hébraïste, *s.m.* hebraist
Hébreu, *adj. s.* Hebrew
Hécatombe, *s.f.* hecatomb
Hécatonstyle, *s.m.* (*Gr. arch.*) hecatonstylon
'Hèche, *s.f.* heck, rack
Hectare, *s.m.* (*Fr. meas.*) hectare (100 *ares or* 10,000 *square mètres, or about* 2½ *acres English*)
Hectarer, *v.a.* to measure by the hectare, to
Hectique, *adj.* (*med.*) hectic [measure
Hectisie, *s.f.* (*med.*) consumption
Hecto, *s.m.* (*Fr. weight*) hecto, hectogramme (100 *grammes*); — (*in compounds*) hecto... (*one hundredfold greater*) [(100 *grammes*)
Hectogramme, *s.m.* (*Fr. weight*) hectogramme
Hectolitre, *s.m.* (*Fr. meas.*) hectolitre (100 *litres, or somewhat more than* 22 *gallons or than* 2 *bushels English*) [*metres, or* 109 *yards English*)
Hectomètre, *s.m.* (*Fr. meas.*) hectometre (100
Hectométrique, *adj.* (*Fr. meas.*) hectometric
Hectostère, *s.m.* (*Fr. meas.*) hectostere (100
Hédéracé, e, *adj.* (*bot.*) hederaceous [*steres*)
Hédériforme, *adj.* hederiform
Hédérine, *s.f.* (*chem.*) hederine
Hédérique, *adj.* (*chem.*) hederic
Hégélien, ne, *adj. s.* (*philos.*) Hegelian
Hégémonie, *s.f.* hegemony
Hégire, *s.f.* Hegira

Heiduque, *s.m.* Hungarian militiaman; livery
'Hein, *int.* eh! hey! what? [footman
Hélamys, *s.m.* (*zool.*) jumping hare [complaint
Hélas, *int.* alas! ah! — *s.m.* alas, sigh, moan,
'Helbut, *s.m. V.* **Hellebut**
'Héler, *v.a.* to hail, to call; (*nav.*) to hail, to speak, to speak with
Hélianthe, *s.m.* (*bot.*) helianthus, sun-flower
Hélianthème, *s.m.* (*bot.*) helianthemum,
Héliaque, *adj.* (*astr.*) heliacal [rock-rose
Héliaquement, *adv.* (*astr.*) heliacally
Hélice, *s.f.* helix; screw. *A —*, with a screw, screw; spiral, winding. *En —*, in the shape of a screw, spiral, winding. *— propulsive*, *propulseur à —*, screw-propeller
Hélicé, e, *adj.* helical, spiral
Hélicier, *s.m.* snail
Héliciforme, *adj.* heliciform [helicina
Hélicine, *s.f.* helicine, snail mucilage; (*zool.*)
Hélicite, *s.f.* helicite, fossil spiral shell
Hélicoïdal, e, *adj.* helicoidal, helicoid
Hélicoïde, *adj.* helicoid, helicoidal; — *s.m.*
Héliconien, ne, *adj.* Heliconian [helicoid
Hélingue, *s.f. V.* **Élingue**
Héliocentr-ique, -iquement. *V.* p. 3, § 1
‡Héliochrome, *s.m.* heliochrome
‡Héliochrom-ie, -ique. *V.* page 3, § 1
Héliocomète, *s.f.* light from the setting sun like the tail of a comet
Héliographe, *s.m.* heliograph (*instr.*) [(*picture*)
Héliographie, *s.f.* heliography; heliograph
Héliographique, &c. *V.* page 3, § 1
Héliomètre, *s.m.* heliometer
Héliométrique, *adj.* heliometric
Hélioscope, *s.m.* helioscope
Hélioscop-ie, -ique. *V.* page 3, § 1 [stroke
Héliose, *s.f.* (*med.*) heliosis, insolation, sun-
Héliostat, *s.m.* heliostat [statics
Héliostatique, *adj.* heliostatic; — *s.f.* helio-
Héliotrope, *s.m.* (*bot., min., phys.*, &c.) heliotrope
Héliotrop-ie, -ique, -isme. *V.* page 3, § 1
Héliotypograph-ie, -ique, &c. *V.* p. 3, § 1
Hélix, *s.m.* (*anat.*) helix
Hellébore, &c. *V.* **Ellébore,** &c.
'Hellebut, *s.m.* (*fish*) halibut
Hellène, *s.m.* Hellene, Greek
Hellénique, *adj.m.f., s.m.* Hellenic, Greek; —
—**s,** *s.f.pl.* Hellenics (*treatise*) [come hellenized
Helléniser, *v.n.a.* to hellenize. *S'—*, to be-
Hellénisme, *s.m.* hellenism, grecism [scholar
Helléniste, *s.m. adj.* hellenist, Grecian, Greek
Hellénistique, *adj.* Hellenistic
Hellespontiaque, *adj.* Hellespontine
Helminthagogue, *s.m.* (*med.*) helminthagogue; — *adj.* helminthagogic [worm
Helminthe, *s.m.* (*zool.*) helminth, intestinal
Helminthiase, *s.f.* (*med.*) helminthiasis
Helminthique, *adj.* helminthic
Helminthoïde, *adj.* helminthoid
Helmintholog-ie, -ique, -iste. *V.* p. 3, § 1
Helminthologue, *s.m.* helminthologist
Hélode, *adj.* of marshes, marsh. *Fièvres —s*,
Helvètes (Les), *s.m.pl.* Helvetii [helodes
Helvétien, ne, *adj. s.* Helvetian; —**s,** *s.m.pl.* Helvetians; Helvetii [(*geog.*) Helvetian (*Alps*)
Helvétique, *adj.* Helvetic, Swiss; Swiss-like;
Helvétisme, *s.m.* helvetism, Swiss French,
'Hem, *int. s.m.* hem [bad French
Hémadromomètre, *s.m.* hemadromometer, hemadrometer
Hémadynamique, *s.f.* hemadynamics [ter
Hémadynamomètre, *s.m.* hemadynamome-
Hémagogue, *s.m.* (*med.*) hemagogue; — *adj.* hemagogic [hæmalops, bloodshot eye
Hémalopie, *s.f.* (*med.*) hæmalopia, hemalopy,
Hémanthe, *s.m.* (*bot.*) blood-flower [mastatics
Hémastatique, *adj.* hemastatic; — *s.f.* he-
Hématéine, *s.f.* (*chem.*) hemateine
Hématémèse, *s.f.* (*med.*) hematemesis, vomit-
Hématine, *s.f.* (*chem.*) hematine [ing of blood
Hématique, *adj.m.f., s.m.* hematic

Hématite, *s.f.* (*min.*) hematite; —*adj.* hematitic
Hématocèle, *s.f.* (*med.*) hematocele
Hématographe, *s.m.* hematographer
Hémato-graphie, -graphique, -logie, &c. *V.* page 3, § 1
Hématome, *s.m.* (*surg.*) hematome, hæmatoma
Hématomètre, *s.m.* hematometer
Hématose, *s.f.* hematosis
Hématoser (S'), *v.r.* to be converted into arterial blood, to be arterialized
Hématosine, *s.f.* (*chem.*) hematosine, hæmatosine
Hématoxyline, *s.f.* (*chem.*) hematoxyline
Hématozoaire, *s.m.* (*zool.*) hematozoan; — *adj.* hematozoal
Hématurie, *s.f.* (*med.*) hæmaturia, hematuria
Héméralope, *s.m.f.* person affected with hemeralopia, hemeralops
Héméralopie, *s.f.* (*med.*) hemeralopia, night-blindness
Hémérobe, *s.m.* golden-eye fly
Hémérocalle, *s.f.* (*bot.*) hemerocallis, day-lily
Hémi, (*in compounds*) hemi..., demi..., semi..., half-...
Hémicrânie, *s.f.* (*med.*) *V.* **Migraine**
Hémicycle, *s.m.* hemicycle, semicircle
Hémione, *s.m.* hemionus, dziggetai, kiang (*Tartarian horse*)
Hémiopie, *s.f.* (*med.*) hemiopia, hemiopsia
Hémipinique, *adj.* (*chem.*) hemipinic
Hémiplégie, Hémiplexie, *s.f.* (*med.*) hemiplegia, hemiplegy
Hémiplégique, *adj. s.* (*med.*) hemiplegic
Hémiptère, *adj.* (*zool.*) hemipterous, hemipteral; — *s.m.* hemipterous insect, hemipteran, hemipter
Hémisphère, *s.m.* hemisphere
Hémisphérique, *adj. V.* page 3, § 1
Hémisphéroïdal, e, *adj.* hemispheroidal
Hémisphéroïde, *s.m. adj.* hemispheroid
Hémistiche, *s.m.* hemistich
'Hemmer, *v.n.* to hem, to hawk
Hémodynamomètre. *V.* **Hémadynamomètre**
Hémophthalmie, *s.f.* (*med.*) hemophthalmia, hematophthalmia, sanguineous ophthalmia
Hémoplastique, *adj.* (*med.*) hemoplastic, hematoplastic
Hémoptoïque, *adj. s.* (*bad spelling*) *V.* **Hémoptyique**
Hémoptyique, *adj. s.* (*med.*) hemoptic
Hémoptysie, *s.f.* (*med.*) hemoptysis, hæmoptysis, spitting of blood
Hémorragie, Hémorrhagie, *s.f.* (*med.*) hemorrhage. — *cérébrale*, cerebral hemorrhage, effusion of blood on the brain
Hémorragique, Hémorrhagique, *adj.* (*med.*) hemorrhagic
Hémorrhinie, *s.f.* (*med.*) hemorrhinia, bleeding at the nose
Hémorroïdaire, Hémorrhoïdaire, *s.m.f.* (*med.*) person subject to piles
Hémorroïdal, e, Hémorrhoïdal, e, *adj.* (*med.*) hemorrhoidal, of piles; — *s.f.* (*anat.*) hemorrhoidal artery; (*bot.*) *V.* **Ficaire**
Hémorroïdes, Hémorrhoïdes, *s.f.pl.* (*med.*) hemorrhoids, piles
Hémorroïsse, *s.f.* (*obsolete*) woman with a bloody flux
Hémospas-ie, -ique, (*surg.*) *V.* page 3, § 1
Hémostase, *s.f.* (*med., surg.*) hemostasis
Hémostatique, *adj.m.f., s.m.* (*med.*) hemostatic, styptic
Hémotexie, *s.f.* (*med.*) hæmotexia, hæmotexis
Hémothorax, *s.m.* (*med.*) hemothorax
Hendécagonal, e, *adj.* (*geom.*) hendecagonal
Hendécagone, *adj.* (*geom.*) hendecagonal; — *s.m.* hendecagon
Hendécasyllabe, *s.m.* hendecasyllable; — *adj.* hendecasyllabic
Hendécasyllabique, *adj.* hendecasyllabic
'Henné, Henneh, *s.m.* (*bot.*) henna, hinna
'Hennebanne, *s.f. V.* **Jusquiame**
'Hennir, *v.n.* to neigh
'Hennissement, *s.m.* neighing, neigh [*poem*)
'Henriade (La), *s.f.* the Henriade (*Voltaire's*
Hépatalgie, *s.f.* (*med.*) hepatalgia, hepatalgy
Hépatalgique, *adj.* (*med.*) hepatalgic
Hépatique, *adj.* hepatic; — *s.f.* (*bot.*) hepatica, liverwort
Hépatisation, *s.f.* (*med.*) hepatization
Hépatiser, *v.a.* (*med.*) to hepatize
S'—, *v.r.* to become hepatized
Hépatite, *s.f.* (*med.*) hepatitis, inflammation of the liver; (*min.*) hepatite, liver-stone
Hépatocèle, *s.f.* (*med.*) hepatocele
Hépato, (*in compounds*) hepato-...
Hépato-graphie, -graphique, -logie, -scopie, -tomie, &c. *V.* page 3, § 1
Hépatorrhée, *s.f.* (*med.*) hepatorrhœa
Hépiale, *s.f.* (*zool.*) hepialus, swift. — *du houblon*, — *lupuline*, ghost-moth
Heptacorde, *s.m. adj.* heptachord
Heptade, *s.f.* heptade
Heptaèdre, *s.m.* (*geom.*) heptahedron; — *adj.* heptahedral
Heptagonal, e, *adj.* (*geom.*) heptagonal
Heptagone, *adj.* (*geom.*) heptagonal; — *s.m.* (*geom., fort.*) heptagon
Heptaméron, *s.m.* heptameron
Heptamètre, *s.m. adj.* (*vers.*) heptameter
Heptandrie, *s.f.* (*bot.*) heptandria
Heptarch-ie, -ique. *V.* page 3, § 1
Heptarque, *s.m.* heptarch, heptarchist
Heptasyllabe, *s.m.* heptasyllable; — *adj.* heptasyllabic
Heptateuque, *s.m.* Heptateuch
Héraclées, *s.f.pl.* feasts in honour of Hercules
Héraclides, *s.m.pl.* Heraclidæ, descendants of Hercules
Héraldique, *adj.* heraldic
'Héraut, *s.m.* herald
Herbacé, e, *adj.* herbaceous
Herbage, *s.m.* herbage, herbs, herb; grass; green food, pasture; pasture-ground *or* land, grazing-ground *or* land, meadow, paddock; common pasture
Herbager, *s.m.* grazier
Herbageu-x, se, *adj. V.* **Herbeux**
Herbe, *s.f.* herb; grass; wort; weed; blade; plant; root. *Aux —s*, (*cook.*) with herbs, herb; vegetable. *Aux fines —s*, *V.* **Fin,** *adj. Brin d'—*, blade of grass. *En —*, grass; in the blade; in embryo, in expectation, in prospect, future; young, youthful, green, rising; beforehand. *Mauvaise —*, weed; bad grass; bad lot. *Mauvaise — croît toujours* (or *croît trop vite*), ill weeds grow apace. *Faire de l'—*, to cut grass, to mow. — *aux abeilles*, meadow-sweet. — *au chantre*, hedge-mustard. — *aux charpentiers* or *à la coupure*, — *militaire*, yarrow, milfoil. — *aux chats*, catmint. — *au coq*, costmary. — *aux cors*, house-leek. — *à cousin*, fleabane. — *aux cuillers*, scurvy-grass, lemon-grass. — *aux écrouelles*, figwort. — *à éternuer*, sneezewort. — *aux gueux*, traveller's-joy, virgin's-bower. — *au lait*, milkwort. — *à pauvre homme*, *V.* **Gratiole.** — *aux perles*, *V.* **Grémil.** — *de la Saint-Jean*, ground-ivy; (*pop.*) great exertions, great care, o.'s utmost, o.'s best. — *de Saint-Jean*, mugwort. — *aux verrues*, turnsole. — *aux vers*, tansy
†Herbeiller, *v.n.* (*hunt.*) to graze
Herbeline, *s.f.* sickly sheep turned out to grass
Herber, *v.a.* to grass-bleach
Herberie, *s.f.* herb *or* green market; bleach-field
Herbette, *s.f.* grass, tender grass, turf, green-sward
Herbeu-x, se, *adj.* herbous, herby; grassy
Herbier, *s.m.* herbarium, herbal; grass-shed; weedery; (*of ruminants*) paunch
Herbière, *s.f.* herb-woman; grass-cutter
Herbifère, *adj.* herbiferous
Herbiforme, *adj.* herbiform, grass-shaped
Herbivore, *adj.* herbivorous; — *s.m.* herbivorous animal, herbivore (*pl.* herbivores *or* herbivora)
Herborisa-teur, trice, *s.m.f.* herborizer; — *adj.* herborizing
Herborisation, *s.f.* herborization
Herboriser, *v.n.* to herborize
Herboriseur, *s.m.* (*fam.*) herborizer
Herboriste, *s.m.f.* herbalist, herborist
Herboristerie, *s.f.* herb-trade *or* shop *or* room; herbs
Herbu, e, *adj.* grass-grown, grassy; — *s.f. V.* **Castine;** (*agr.*) sod, light mould
'Herclan, *s.m. V.* **Tadorne**
Hercotectonique, *s.f.* fortification (*art*)

Hercule, *s.m.* (*myth.*, *astr.*) Hercules; (*fig.*, Hercules, man of Herculean strength
Herculéen, ne, *adj.* Herculean
'Hère, *s.m.* wretch, wight; (*hunt.*) yearling fawn; (*game at cards*) here
Héréditaire, *adj.* hereditary [heritance
Héréditairement, *adv.* hereditarily, by in-
Hérédité, *s.f.* heirship, right of inheriting, hereditary right, hereditament, succession, in-
Hérésiarque, *s.m.* heresiarch [heritance
Hérésie, *s.f.* heresy
Hérésiographe, *s.m.* heresiographer
Hérésiograph-ie, -ique, &c. *V.* page 3, § 1
Héréticité, *s.f.* heretical nature *or* tendency, hereticalness, heresy
Hérétique, *adj.* heretical; — *s.m.f.* heretic
Hérétiquement, *adv.* heretically
'Héridelle, *s.f.* narrow roofing-slate
'Hérigoté, e, *adj.* (*hunt.*, *of dogs*) spotted *or* having marks on the hind legs [hind legs
'Hérigoture, *s.f.* (*hunt.*, *of dogs*) mark on the
'Hérissé, e, *adj.* standing erect *or* on end, erect; raised upright; bristling; staring; shaggy; rough; repulsive; armed; covered; full; thickset; beset; rough-coated; cross, peevish; (*bot.*) prickly; — *s.m.* bristling, staring, shagginess, roughness; — *s.f.* caterpillar of the cabbage-moth [ness, roughness
'Hérissement, *s.m.* bristling, staring, shaggi-
'Hérisser, *v.a.* to bristle, to bristle up, to erect, to set up; to arm; to cover; to fill; to lard, to mix; (*mas.*) to roughcast
Se —, *v.r.* to stand erect *or* on end; to stand up; to bristle, to bristle up; to be armed; to be *or* become covered; (*old*) to get angry
'Hérisson, *s.m.* hedgehog; crabbed person, waspish fellow; sweep's machine; plate-rack, drainer; spikes; (*fort.*) herisson; (*agr.*) clod-crusher; (*tech.*) spur-wheel, canting-wheel, sprocket-wheel, rag-wheel; (*bot.*) sour sop (*fruit*); chestnut-bur. — *de mer*, sea-urchin
'Hérisson, ne, *adj.* prickly, bristly, hairy; rough; crabbed, cross, peevish, waspish
'Hérissonné, e, *adj.* prickly, bristly, hairy; rough; (*mas.*) roughcast; (*her.*) crouching
'Hérissonnement, *s.m.* prickliness, bristliness, hairiness; roughness; (*mas.*) roughcasting
'Hérissonner, *v.a.* to ruffle up; (*mas.*) to
Héritable, *adj.* heritable [roughcast
Héritage, *s.m.* inheritance, heritage; succession; legacy; estate; patrimony; portion. *Faire un* —, to inherit some property
Hériter, *v.a.n.* to inherit; to be heir; to succeed
Hériti-er, ère, *s.m.f.* heir, heiress; inheritor, inheritress; — *s.f.* (*bot.*) Venus's looking-glass
Hermandad (Sainte), *s.f.* (*Spanish*) Hermandad, Inquisition
Hermaphrodie, *s.f.*, **Hermaphrodisme,** *s.m.* hermaphrodism, hermaphroditism
Hermaphrodite, *s.m. adj.* hermaphrodite
Hermeline, *s.f.* sable [hermeneutics
Herméneutique, *adj.* hermeneutic; — *s.f.*
Hermès, *s.m.* Hermes, bust of Mercury
Herméticité, *s.f.* hermeticalness, closeness
Hermétique, *adj.* hermetic, hermetical, close, air-tight. *Colonne* —, Hermes; column with a bust
Hermétiquement, *adv.* hermetically, closely
Hermine, *s.f.* ermine
Herminé, e, *adj.* ermined, ermine
Herminette, *s.f.* adze
Hermitage, Hermite. *V.* **Ermitage, Ermite**
Hermodacte, Hermodatte, *s.f.*, **Hermodactyle,** *s.m.* (*pharm.*) hermodactyl
Hernandie, *s.f.* (*bot.*) hernandia
'Herniaire, *adj.* hernial; for hernia; — *s.f.* *V.* **Herniole.** *Bandage* —, truss. *Bandagiste* or *chirurgien* —, truss-maker
'Hernie, *s.f.* (*med.*) hernia, rupture; prolapsus
'Hernié, e, *adj.* (*med.*) ruptured; prolapsed
'Hernier, *s.m.* (*nav.*) crowfoot stick
'Hernieu-x, se, *adj.* (*med.*) hernious
'Herniole, *s.f.* (*bot.*) rupture-wort
'Herniotome, *s.m.* (*surg.*) hernia-knife
'Herniotomie, *s.f.* (*surg.*) herniotomy
'Hernute, *s.m.* herrnhuter, Moravian Brother
'Hernutisme, *s.m.* herrnhutism, doctrine and practice of the Moravian Brethren
Hérodien, *s.m.* (*hist.*) Herodian
Héroïcité, *s.f.* heroicalness
Héroï-comique, *adj.* heroi-comic, mock-
Héroïde, *s.f.* heroic epistle [heroic, serio-comic
Héroïne, *s.f.* heroine
Héroïque, *adj.* heroic; (*med.*) powerful
Héro-ïquement, -ïsme. *V.* page 3, § 1
'Héron, *s.m.* heron. *Masse de* —, heron-plume
'Héronneau, *s.m.* young heron
'Héronner, *v.n.* to fly the heron
'Héronni-er, ère, *adj.* heron-like; thin, lean; (*falc.*) trained for flying the heron
'Héronnière, *s.f.* heronry
'Héros, *s.m.* hero
'Herpe, *s.f.* (*hunt.*) claws; (*nav.*) rail; **—s,** *pl.* (*nav.*) rails; (*obsolete*) sea-ware
Herpès, *s.m.* (*med.*) herpes, tetters, shingles
Herpeste, *s.m.* (*zool.*) herpestes, ichneumon
Herpét-ique, -isme, (*med.*) *V.* page 3, § 1
Herpéto-graphie, -graphique, -logie, -logique, -logiste, &c. *V.* page 3, § 1
'Herque, *s.f.* iron rake
'Hersage, *s.m.* (*agr.*) harrowing
'Herse, *s.f.* (*agr.*) harrow; (*fort.*) portcullis, herse; (*of houses*) palisading-gate; (*theat.*) gas-battens; (*in churches*) triangular candlestick, herse; (*bot.*) caltrop
'Hersé, e, *adj.* portcullised, with a herse; (*agr.*)
'Hersement, *s.m.* (*agr.*) harrowing [harrowed
'Herser, *v.a.* (*agr.*) to harrow. *Se* —, to be
'Herseur, *s.m.* harrower [harrowed
†**'Hersillon,** *s.m.* (*mil.*) hersillon
Hésitation, *s.f.* hesitation; faltering
Hésiter, *v.n.* to hesitate; to waver; to demur; to stop, to pause; to falter [evening star
Hesper, *s.m.* Hesper, Hesperus, Venus, the
Hespéridées, *s.f.pl.* (*bot.*) hesperideæ
Hespérides, *s.f.pl.* (*myth.*) Hesperides
Hespéridine, *s.f.* (*chem.*) hesperidine
Hespérie, *s.f.* (*butterfly*) hesperia, skipper
Hespérien, ne, *adj. s.* Hesperian
Hespérique, *adj.* Hesperic
Hespéris, *s.m.* (*bot.*) hesperis, rocket
'Hessois, e, *adj. s.* Hessian
Hétéroclite, *adj.* heteroclite; irregular, anomalous; fantastic, whimsical, odd
Hétérodoxe, *adj.* heterodox
Hétérodoxie, *s.f.* heterodoxy
Hétérogène, *adj.* heterogeneous [neousness
Hétérogénéité, *s.f.* heterogeneity, heteroge-
Hétérogén-ie, -iste. *V.* page 3, § 1
Hétérologue, *adj.* heterologous
Hétéromorphe, *adj.* heteromorphous
Hétéromorphisme, *s.m.* heteromorphism
Hétéronyme, *adj.* heteronymous
Hétérosciens, *s.m.pl.* (*geog.*) heteroscians
Hetman, *s.m.* hetman (*general of the Cossacks*)
'Hêtraie, *s.f.* beech-grove, beech-plantation
'Hêtre, *s.m.* beech, beech-tree
'Heu, *s.m.* (*nav.*) hoy (*vessel*); — *int.* *V.* **Euh**
Heur, *s.m.* (*obsolete*) luck, chance, good luck, good fortune, happiness
Heure, *s.f.* hour; time; moment, moments; present; o'clock; clock; appointment; **—s,** *pl.* hours, &c.; primer, prayer-book. *A cette* —, at this *or* that time; now. *A la bonne* —, well and good; let it be so, be it so; that is right; all right; very good; very well; I am glad of that *or* of it; well done! with all my heart; (*nav.*) very well! (*obsolete*) at the right time, in good time. *A l'*—, by the hour; at the (appointed) time, at *or* to the right time, in good time, in time; right. *A l'— qu'il est*, at present, at the present time *or* moment, now; by this time; nowadays. *De bonne* —, in good time; early. *D'— en* —, hourly, every hour, every

moment. *De meilleure* —, earlier sooner. *Sur l'*—, instantly, forthwith, on the spot. *Sur les deux* or *&c.* —*s*, about two *or* &c. o'clock. *Tout à l'*—, presently, by and by; just now; not long ago, a little while ago; (*obsolete*) immediately, even now, this instant

Heureusement, *adv.* happily; fortunately, luckily; successfully; prosperously; favourably; advantageously; safely

Heureu-x, se, *adj.* happy; pleased, glad, delighted; blessed; fortunate, lucky; felicitous; successful; prosperous; favourable; advantageous; beneficial; safe; good; pleasing, agreeable, prepossessing; in good circumstances, well off; — *s.m.pl.* happy people. *Faire des* —, to make people (*or* some people) happy

Heuristique, Hévristique, *adj.* heuristic, hevristic; — *s.f.* heuristics, hevristics

'Heurt, *s.m.* (*old*) collision, shock; dash; jostle; bumping; knock; blow, hit; mark of a blow, bruise; clash; jar; mishap; crown of a bridge *or* of a pavement; dust-heap

'Heurté, e, *part. adj.* hit, struck, knocked, &c. (*V.* **Heurter**); harsh; roughly done; free, bold

'Heurtement, *s.m.* collision, shock, dashing, dash; jostling, jostle; knock; clashing, clash; jarring, jar; jingling, jingle; hiatus

'Heurter, *v.a.n.* to hit, to strike *or* dash *or* run against, to stumble upon; to come across, to meet; to jostle; to strike, to knock, to touch; to attack; to shock, to offend, to hurt, to injure, to run counter to, to interfere with, to irritate, to clash with, to jar with; to rough-draw; (*old*) to knock at the door, to knock, to rap

Se —, *v.r.* to dash, to strike, to hit; to knock (o.'s ...); to come into collision, to collide; to strike *or* knock *or* dash *or* run against each other; to jostle *or* &c. each other; to clash together, to clash; to jar; to prove useless, to be powerless, to fail

'Heurtoir, *s.m.* stop-stone, stop-iron, stopper; flapper; lock-sill; (*artil.*) hurter; (*obsolete*) knocker

'Heuse, *s.f.* (*nav.*) box (*of a pump*)

Hévée, *s.m.* (*bot.*) hevea, indiarubber-tree

Hexacorde, *s.m. adj.* hexachord

Hexaèdre, *s.m.* (*geom.*) hexahedron; — *adj.* hexahedral

Hexaédrique, *adj.* hexahedral

Hexagonal, e, *adj.* hexagonal

Hexagone, *s.m.* (*geom., fort.*) hexagon; — *adj.* hexagonal

Hexamètre, *s.m. adj.* (*vers.*) hexameter

Hexaples, *s.m.pl.* hexapla

Hexastique, *s.m.* hexastich

Hexastyle *s.m. adj.* (*arch.*) hexastyle

Hexasyllabe, *s.m.* hexasyllable; — *adj.* hexasyllabic

'Hi, *int.* he! hi!

Hiatus, *s.m.* hiatus

Hibernacle, *s.m.* hibernacle, hibernaculum

Hibernal, e, *adj.* hibernal, wintry, winter

Hibernation, *s.f.* hibernation

Hiberner, *v.n.* to hibernate

Hibernien, ne, *adj. s.* Hibernian, Irish

Hiberniser, *v.a.n.* to hibernicize

Hibernisme, *s.m.* hibernianism, hibernicism

Hibernois, e, *adj. s.* Hibernian, Irish; Paddy

Hibiscus, *s.m.* (*bot.*) hibiscus

'Hibou, *s.m.* owl; (*local*) periwinkle; (*pers.*) moper, owl

'Hic, *s.m.* rub, knot, difficulty

'Hic et nunc, *adv.* (*Latin*) forthwith

Hickory, *s.m.* (*bot.*) hickory

Hidalgo, *s.m.* (*Spanish*) hidalgo

'Hideur, *s.f.* hideousness

'Hideusement, *adv.* hideously, frightfully, horribly, horridly, dreadfully, shockingly

'Hideu-x, se, *adj.* hideous, frightful, horrible, horrid, dreadful, shocking

Hidrotique, *adj.m.f., s.m.* (*med.*) hidrotic

'Hie, *s.f.* (*tech.*) fistuca, ram, rammer, beetle, monkey; paving-rammer *or* beetle, commander

Hièble, *s.f.* (*bot.*) dwarf elder, danewort

Hiémal, e, *adj.* hyemal, wintry

Hiémation, *s.f.* hyemation

'Hiement, *s.m.* ramming; rocking; (*of machines*) grating, creaking

Hier, *adv. s.m.* yesterday. — *soir,* — *au soir,* yesterday evening, last evening, last night

'Hier, *v.a.* to ram, to beat *or* drive in; — *v.n.* to rock; to grate, to creak

'Hiérarch-ie, -ique, -iquement. *V.* page 3, § 1

'Hiérarchisation, *s.f.* hierarchization

'Hiérarchiser, *v.a.* to hierarchize

Hiératique, *adj.* hieratic

Hiéroglyphe, *s.m.* hieroglyphic, hieroglyph

Hiéroglyphique, *adj.* hieroglyphic

Hiéro-graphie, -graphique, -logie, -logique, &c. *V.* page 3, § 1

Hiérophante, *s.m.* hierophant

Hilarant, e, Hilariant, e, *adj.* exhilarating, laughing

Hilarité, *s.f.* hilarity, laughter, merriment, mirth, cheerfulness

'Hile, *s.m.* (*bot., anat.*) hilum, hile

'Hiloire, *s.f.* (*nav.*) binding streak, roof-tree

'Hilon, *s.m.* black speck on the eye

Hindi, *s.m. V.* **Hindoustani**

Hindou, e, *adj. s. V.* **Indou**

Hindoustani, Hindouvi, *s.m. adj.* Hindustani

'Hinné, *s.m. V.* **Henné**

Hipparque, *s.m.* (*Gr. antiquity*) hipparch

Hippiatre, *s.m.* horse-doctor, veterinarian

Hippiatrie, *s.f.* veterinary medicine

Hippiatrique, *s.f.* veterinary medicine; — *adj.* veterinary

Hippien, ne, *adj.* hippian

Hippique, *adj.* hippic, of horses, of the horse, horse, equine; racing

Hippobdelle, *s.f.* horse-leech

Hippobosque, *s.f.* horse-fly, forest-fly

Hippocampe, *s.m.* (*myth., anat.*) hippocampus; (*zool.*) hippocampus, hippocamp, sea-horse

Hippocentaure, *s.m.* (*myth.*) hippocentaur

Hippocolle, *s.f.* (*chem.*) hippocolla

Hippocras, *s.m.* (*med.*) hippocras, negus

Hippocrat-ique, -isme, -iste. *V.* page 3, § 1

Hippocrène (L'), *s.f.* Hippocrene

Hippodrome, *s.m.* hippodrome; circus, amphitheatre; race-ground, ground; race-course

Hippodromie, *s.f.* horse-racing; horsemanship

Hippoglosse, *s.m.* (*fish*) halibut

Hippogriffe, *s.m.* hippogriff, hippogryph, winged horse

Hippolithe, *s.m.* (*vet.*) hippolith

Hippolog-ie, -ique. *V.* page 3, § 1

Hippologue, *s.m.* hippologist

Hippomane, *s.f.* (*vet., bot.*) hippomane; — *s.m.f.* (*pers.*) hippomaniac

Hippomanie, *s.f.* hippomania

Hippopatholog-ie, -ique, -iste. *V.* page 3, § 1

Hippope, *s.m.* (*shell*) hippopus, bear's-paw clam

Hippophaé, *s.f. V.* **Argousier**

Hippophage, *adj.* hippophagian, hippophagous, hippophagic, horse-eating; — *s.m.f.* hippophagist, hippophagus, horse-eater

Hippophagie, *s.f.* hippophagy, horse-eating

Hippophagique, *adj.* hippophagic

Hippopotame, *s.m.* hippopotamus

Hippopotamien, ne, *adj.* of the hippopotamus, hippopotamus-like

Hippotomie, *s.f.* hippotomy, anatomy of the horse

Hippurate, *s.m.* (*chem.*) hippurate

Hippuride, *s.f.* (*bot.*) hippuris, mare's-tail

Hippurie, *s.f.* (*med.*) hippuria

Hippurique, *adj.* (*chem.*) hippuric

Hippurite, *s.f.* (*fossil shell*) hippurite

Hircin, e, *adj.*, **Hircine,** *s.f.* hircine

Hircique, *adj.* (*chem.*) hircic

Hircisme, *s.m.* (*med.*) hircismus, hircine smell (*of the arm-pit*)

Hironde, *s.f. V.* **Aronde**

Hirondeau, *s.m.* young swallow

Hirondelle, *s.f.* (*bird*) swallow; (*tech.*) washer; (*pop.*) commercial traveller, bagman; driver of a job-carriage, flyman; cabman plying for hire, crawler

Hirsute, Hirsuté, e, Hirsuteu-x, se, *adj.* hirsute, hairy, bristly, shaggy, rugged, rough

Hirudiné, e, Hirudiniforme, *adj.* hirudinate, hirudiniform, leech-like, leech-shaped

Hirudiniculteur, Hirudiculteur, *s.m.* leech-grower

Hirudiniculture, Hirudiculture, *s.f.* leech-culture
Hispanique, *adj.* Hispanian, Spanish
Hispanisme, *s.m.* hispanicism, Spanish idiom
Hispe, *s.f.* (*zool.*) hispa, little leaf-beetle
Hispide, *adj.* (*nat. hist.*) hispid
Hispidité, *s.f.* (*nat. hist.*) hispidity
'Hisser, *v.a.* to hoist, to raise, to lift
Hister, *s.m.* (*zool.*) hister, mimic-beetle
Histograph-ie, -ique, &c. *V.* page 3, § 1
Histoire, *s.f.* history; tale; account; story; untruth; joke; nonsense; long rigmarole; matter; affair; thing; concern; small matter, trifle; great matter; long affair; difficulty; ceremony; ado; fuss; quarrel, row, blowing-up, scene; noise; disturbance; troublesome affair, trouble, annoyance, bother; lot of things. — *de* ..., merely for the sake of ..., only to ... — *de rire*, for the laugh *or* fun of the thing; it is *or* was only a joke, a mere joke that's all. — *sacrée* or *sainte*, sacred *or* Scripture history. *D'*—, of *or* on *or* &c. history, &c.; historical
Histolog-ie, -ique, &c. *V.* page 3, § 1
Historial, e, *adj.* (*obsolete*) historical
Historié, e, *part. adj.* embellished, &c. (*V.* **Historier**); storied
Historien, ne, *s.m.f.* historian, recorder
Historier, *v.a.* to embellish, to adorn, to ornament, to flourish
Historiette, *s.f.* short tale *or* story, little *or* pretty story, historiette
Historiographe, *s.m.* historiographer
Historiograph-ie, -ique. *V.* page 3, § 1
Histor-ique (*adj.*), **-iquement.** *V.* page 3, § 1
Historique, *s.m.* historical account, history, account
Histrion, *s.m.* stage-player, player, comedian, histrion
Histrionage, *s.m.*, **Histrionie,** *s.f.* (*jest.*) histrionism, stage-playing
Histrionique, *adj.* histrionic
Histrionner, *v.n.* (*jest.*) to histrionize
Hiver, *s.m.* winter; winter clothes. *D'*—, of winter, winter, wintry, winterly
Hivernache, *s.m.* (*agr.*) winter-crop
Hivernage, *s.m.* winter-season *or* time; wintering; wintering-place, winter-harbour; (*agr.*) winter-fallowing; winter-crop
Hivernal, e, *adj.* wintry, winterly, winter, hibernal
Hivernation, *s.f.* hibernation; cold weather in summer
Hiverner, *v.n.* to winter; (*zool.*) to hibernate; — *v.a.* (*agr.*) to winter-fallow; **S'**—, *v.r.* to inure oneself to cold
'Ho, *int.* ho! oh! hoy! (*nav.*) ahoy!
Hoazin, *s.m.* (*bird*) hoazin
'Hobb-isme, -iste. *V.* page 3, § 1
'Hobereau, *s.m.* poor country-squire; (*bird*) hobby
'Hobin, *s.m.* Scotch pad (*horse*)
'Hoc, *s.m.* (*game at cards*) hoc. *Être* —, to be taken. *Cela lui est* —, he is sure of that, he will get that, that will be his. *Ad* —, *Ab* — *et ab hac*, (*Latin*) *V. Letter* **A**
'Hoca, *s.m.* hoca (*game of chance*)
'Hocco, *s.m.* (*bird*) hocco, curassow
'Hoche, *s.f.* notch
'Hochement, *s.m.* jerking, jogging, tossing, toss, shaking, shake, wagging
'Hochepied, *s.m.* (*falc.*) heron-hawk
'Hochepot, *s.m.* hotch-potch, hodge-podge
'Hochequeue, *s.m.* (*bird*) wagtail
'Hocher, *v.a.* to jerk, to jog, to toss, to shake, to wag; to notch, to jag, to indent; — *v.n.* (*of horses*) to jerk the bit
'Hochet, *s.m.* coral, rattle; toy, plaything, bauble
Hodographe, *s.m.* hodograph
Hodograph-ie, -ique. *V.* page 3, § 1
Hodomètre, *s.m.* hodometer, pedometer, perambulator; teller
Hodométr-ie, -ique. *V.* page 3, § 1
†'Hogner, *v.n.* (*pop.*) to growl, to grumble, to mumble, to whine
Hoir, *s.m.* (*law, obsolete*) heir
Hoirie, *s.f.* (*law, old*) inheritance
'Holà, *int. adv.* halloo! hi! hoy! ho! ho, there! stop! enough! gently! hold on! stop him! — *s.m.* interference, hindrance, end, stop. *Mettre le* or *les* —, to interfere, to put a stop (*to a quarrel*, &c.)
'Hôlement, Hôler. *V.* **Houhoulement,** &c.
'Hollandais, e, *adj. s.* Dutch; Dutchman, Dutch boy, Dutchwoman, Dutch lady *or* girl, Hollander; Dutch fashion
'Hollande, *s.f.* Holland; holland (*cloth*); large potato; — *s.m.* Dutch cheese. *De* —, of *or* from Holland, Holland, Dutch
'Hollander, *v.a.* to dress (*quills*). *Batiste hollandée*, stout cambric
Holocauste, *s.m.* holocaust; burnt-offering; sacrifice
Holographe, *adj.* holographic; — *s.m.* holograph
Holographier, *v.a.* to write entirely in o.'s own hand
Holomètre, *s.m.* (*astr.*) holometer
Holothurie, *s.f.* (*zool.*) holothuria, sea-slug, sea-cucumber
Hom, *int.* hum! hem!
'Homard, *s.m.* lobster
Hombre, *s.m.* ombre (*game at cards*)
Homélie, *s.f.* homily, sermon
Homéo..., *V.* **Homœo...**
Homérique, *adj.* Homeric; — *s.m.* Homerian
Homicide, *s.m.* homicide; murder; — *s.m.f.* homicide, manslayer; murderer, murderess; — *adj.* homicidal, murderous, murdering, killing. — *involontaire*, manslaughter. — *de soi-même*, self-destruction, suicide; self-destroyer, suicide; self-destroying, suicidal
Homilétique, *adj.* homiletic; — *s.f.* homiletics
Homiliaire, *s.m.* homiliarium
Homiliaste, *s.m.* homilist
Hominem (Ad), *adv. See Letter* **A**
Hommage, *s.m.* homage; respect; present, gift; presentation; testimony; tribute; justice. — *de l'auteur*, presented by the Author, with the Author's compliments. *Faire* — *de*, to present with
Hommagé, e, *adj.* (*feud.*) held by homage
Hommager, *s.m.* (*feud.*) homager; — *adj.m.* holding by homage
Hommasse, *adj.* (*of women*) masculine
Hommasser (S'), *v.r.* to become masculine
Homme, *s.m.* man; gentleman; fellow; (*pop.*) husband, old man, goodman. *Jeune* —, young man, young gentleman, youth; lad, boy; youngster, young fellow, young one. — *d'***affaires,** man of business; agent; middleman; steward. — **-affiche,** *V.* **Affiche.** — *d'***affût,** *V.* **Affût.** — *d'***armes,** *V.* **Arme.** — *de l'***art,** *V.* **Art.** — *de* **bien,** *V.* **Bien,** *s.m.* — *de* **bois,** wooden man; (*obsolete*) dumb-jockey. — *des* **bois,** man of the woods, wild man, orang-outang. — *de* **cabinet,** studious man. — *de* **cheval,** horseman, rider; cavalry-man, horse-soldier. — *de* **cœur,** man of feeling; man of spirit; courageous man. — *de* **cour,** courtier. — **-Dieu,** God-man. — *d'***église,** churchman, ecclesiastic, clergyman. — *d'***épée,** swordsman; man of the sword, military man, soldier. — *d'***équipe,** *V.* **Équipe.** — *d'***esprit,** *V.* **Esprit.** — *d'***état,** statesman. — *d'***étude,** studious man. — *d'***exécution,** *V.* **Exécution.** — *de* **guerre,** warrior, military man, soldier. — *d'* **hier,** upstart; novice. — *d'* **honneur,** *V.* **Honneur.** — *de* **journée,** day-labourer. — *de* **lettres,** man of letters, literary man. — *de* **loi,** lawyer. — *de* **main,** bold and enterprising man. — *de* **mer,** seaman. — *du* **monde,** man of the world, gentleman. — *de* **paille,** man of straw, dummy. — *de* **palais,** lawyer. — *de* **parti,** party man, partisan. — *de* **peine,** *V.* **Peine.** — *de* **pied,** foot-soldier; pedestrian. — *en* **place,** man *or* person in office, public officer; placeman, place-holder. — *de* **plume,** writer, literary man. — *de* **robe,** gownsman, lawyer. — *de* **tête,** strong-minded man
Hommée, *s.f.* day's work of a man
Hommelette, *s.f.* (*pop.*) milksop, poor stick
Homocentr-ique, -iquement. *V.* page 3, § 1
Homœomorphe, *adj.* homœomorphous
Homœomorphisme, *s.m.* homœomorphism

Homœopathe, *s.m.* homœopathist homœopath; — *adj.* homœopathic [*V.* page 3, § 1
Homœopath-ie, -ique, -iquement, -iste.
Homœopathiser, *v.a.n.* to homœopathize
Homogène, *adj.* homogeneous [ousness
Homogénéité, *s.f.* homogeneity, homogene-
Homogènement, *adv.* homogeneously
Homograph-ie, -ique, (*geom.*) *V.* page 3, § 1
Homologable, *adj.* (*law*) confirmable
Homologati-f, ve, *adj.* (*law*) confirmative
Homologation, *s.f.* (*law*) confirmation, homologation [§ 1
Homolog-ie, -ique, -iquement. *V.* page 3,
Homologue, *adj.* homologous, similar; — *s.m.* homologue [logate
Homologuer, *v.a.* (*law*) to confirm, to homo-
Homomorphe, *adj.* homomorphous
Homoncule, *s.m.* *V.* **Homuncule**
Homonyme, *adj.* homonymous; — *s.m.* homonym; — *s.m.f.* (*pers.*) namesake
Homonym-ie, -ique. *V.* page 3, § 1
Homopétale, *adj.* (*bot.*) homopetalous
Homophone, *adj.* homophonous; — *s.m.*
Homophonie, *s.f.* homophony [homophone
Homotype, *s.m.* homotype [§ 1
Homotyp-ie, -ique, -iquement. *V.* page 3,
Homuncule, *s.m.* manikin, dwarf, little man
'Hon, *int.* hum! what!
'Honchet, *s.m.* (*bad spelling*) *V.* **Onchet**
'Hong, *s.m.* (*Chinese*) hong
'Hongre, *adj. m.* gelded; — *s.m.* gelding
'Hongreline, *s.f.* (*obsolete*) jacket
'Hongrer, *v.a.* to geld
'Hongreur, *s.m.* gelder
'Hongrieur, *s.m.* *V.* **Hongroyeur**
'Hongroierie, *s.f.* tanning *or* tannery of Hungary leather [fashion
'Hongrois, e, *adj. s.* Hungarian; Hungarian
'Hongroyeur, *s.m.* tanner of Hungary leather
'Honguette, *s.f.* (*sculptor's*) point
'Honi (*English corruption of* **Honni**). *V.* **Honnir**
Honnête, *adj.* honest; upright; virtuous, chaste, modest; proper, fit, becoming, decent; genteel; well-bred; respectable; creditable; reasonable, moderate; fair; handsome; satisfactory; (*old, boorish*) civil, polite, obliging, kind; — *s.m.* honesty, (what is) honest, probity
Honnêtement, *adv.* honestly; uprightly; virtuously, chastely, modestly; properly, decently; genteelly; respectably; creditably; reasonably, moderately; sufficiently; fairly; handsomely; (*old*) civilly, politely, kindly
Honnêteté, *s.f.* honesty; probity; integrity; uprightness; virtue, chastity, modesty; propriety, decency; good breeding; respectability; fairness; handsomeness; (*old*) civility, politeness, kindness, attention; present
Honneur, *s.m.* honour; credit; respect; love; —**s,** *pl.* honours; regalia. *D'*—, of (*or* from, &c.) honour, &c.; honourable; respectable; honorary; upon my honour, upon my word; (*of courts*) principal; state; (*of staircases*) grand. *Dame d'*—, lady in waiting. *Demoiselle d'*—, maid of honour; bridesmaid. *Fille d'*—, bridesmaid; (*obsolete*) maid of honour. *Garçon d'*—, bridesman; honest fellow. *Homme d'*—, man of honour, honourable *or* respectable man, gentleman. *En* —, in honour, in favour; indeed. *En tout* —, honourably, uprightly. *Avoir l'*—, to have the honour; to beg leave, to beg. *Faire* — *à*, to do honour to, to honour; to be an honour to, to do credit to, to be creditable to; to give credit to; (*com.*) to honour, to meet. *Faire les* —*s*, to do the honours. *Se faire* — *de*, to glory in, to consider *or* esteem *or* deem it an honour to; to take credit for. *Tenir à* —, to esteem it an honour; to make it a point of honour
'Honnir, *v.a.* to disgrace, to dishonour; to brand; to cover with shame; to scoff at, to revile, to treat with scorn, to scorn, to spurn. *Honni soit qui mal y pense*, evil be to him that evil thinks
'Honnissement, *s.m.* reviling; disgrace, ignominy [ability
Honorabilité, *s.f.* honourableness; respect-
Honorable, *adj.m.f., s.m.* honourable; respectable; reputable; creditable; deserving; proper
Honorablement, *adv.* honourably; respectably; reputably; creditably; properly; nobly, splendidly
Honoraire, *adj.* honorary, titular; —**s,** *s.m.pl.* honorarium, honorary; fee, fees; salary; stipend; retainer [fees, regular fees, fees
Honorariat, *s.m.* honorary membership; legal
Honorée, *s.f.* (*com.*) letter, favour
Honorer, *v.a.* to honour; to do honour to; to do credit to, to be creditable to, to be an honour to; to respect; to favour; to fee
S'—, *v.r.* to honour oneself, to do oneself honour; to acquire honour; to esteem *or* deem *or* consider it an honour; to glory *or* pride oneself (in); to honour each other; to be honoured
Honores (Ad), (*Latin*) honorary, unremune-
Honorifique, *adj.* honorary, titular [rated
'Honte, *s.f.* shame; disgrace; infamy; discredit; reproach, scandal; confusion; bashfulness. *Courte* —, refusal; affront; balk; failure, unsuccessfulness. *Fausse* —, *mauvaise* —, bashfulness, sheepishness. *Avoir* —, to be ashamed. *Avoir perdu* or *mis bas toute* —, *avoir bu toute* —, *avoir toute* — *bue*, to be lost to all shame, to have lost all sense of shame. *Faire* — *à*, to shame, to make ashamed, to put to shame; to disgrace; to outshine, to eclipse. *Faire la* — *de*, to be the shame of; to be a disgrace to. *Vous me faites* —, I am ashamed of you
'Honteusement, *adv.* shamefully, disgracefully, ignominiously; bashfully, sheepishly
'Honteu-x, se, *adj.* shameful, disgraceful, ignominious; ashamed; shamefaced, abashed; bashful, shy, sheepish, looking foolish; — *s.m.* bashful person. *Morceau* —, manners-piece *or* bit (*at table*). *Parties* —*ses*, secret parts, pudenda. *Pauvres* —, poor people who are ashamed to beg. *Il n'y a que les* — *qui perdent*, nothing ask nothing have. *Jamais* — *n'eut belle amie*, faint heart never won fair lady
'Hop, *int.* hoy! gee-up!
Hôpital, *s.m.* hospital; (*obsolete for* "hospice") *V.* **Hospice;** (*fig.*) infirmary; ruin, wreck and ruin, dogs, misery, beggary, workhouse. — *ambulant*, field-hospital. *Vaisseau-*—, hospital-ship. *Mettre à l'*—, (*fig.*) to beggar, to send to the workhouse
'Hoquet, *s.m.* hiccup, hiccough; sob; (*obsolete*) shock, jolt, stumble, stumbling-stone
'Hoqueter, *v.n.* to hiccup, to hiccough
'Hoqueton, *s.m.* (*obsolete*) jacket; smockfrock; archer, yeoman
'Hoquette, *s.f.* *V.* **Honguette**
Horaire, *adj.* horary, horal
Horatien, ne, *adj.* Horatian
'Horde, *s.f.* horde
Hordéiforme, *adj.* hordeiform, barley-shaped
Hordéine, *s.f.* (*med.*) hordeine
'Horion, *s.m.* thump, blow
Horizon, *s.m.* horizon
Horizontal, e, *adj.* horizontal
Horizontalement, *adv.* horizontally [tality
Horizontalité, *s.f.* horizontalness, horizon-
Horloge, *s.f.* clock, turret-clock; (*nav.*) watch-glass, glass. — *marine*, chronometer, timekeeper. — *solaire*, sun-dial. — *d'eau*, water-clock. — *de sable*, sand-glass. — *de la mort*, (*insect*) death-watch. — *de Flore*, table of the time at which certain flowers open, time-paper of flowers, horologium Floræ
Horloger, *s.m.* clock-maker, watch-maker
Horlogère, *s.f.* clock and watch-maker's wife
Horlogerie, *s.f.* clock and watch-making, horology; clock-work; clock and watch trade *or* manufactory; clocks and watches
Hormis, *prep.* except, but, save
'Hornblende, *s.f.m.* (*min.*) hornblende

Horo-graphie, -graphique, &c. *V.* page 3, [§ 1
Horoptère, *s.m.* (*opt.*) horopter
Horoptérique, *adj.* (*opt.*) horopteric
Horoscope, *s.m.* horoscope, casting nativity, fortune-telling; probable fate *or* event *or* issue. *Faire* or *tirer l'— de*, to cast ...'s nativity; to predict the fate of, to prophesy the event of, to foretell the issue of. *Faire tirer son —*, to have o.'s fortune told
Horoscop-ie, -ique. *V.* page 3, § 1
Horoscopiser, *v.n.* to horoscopize
Horreur, *s.f.* horror; horrid *or* frightful *or* shocking thing; fright; dread; awe; shuddering; abhorrence, abomination, hatred, disgust. *Belle —*, scene of terrible grandeur, awful sight. *Avoir — de, avoir en —*, to have a horror of, to abhor, to hold in abomination, to hate. *Faire —*, to be frightful *or* a fright; to be horrifying *or* disgusting, to make one shudder. *Faire — à*, to horrify, to make (...) shudder; to disgust. *Se faire — à soi-même*, to be horrified at *or* disgusted with oneself
Horrible, *adj.* horrible, horrid, frightful, dreadful, awful, shocking; loathsome
Horriblement, *adv.* horribly, horridly, frightfully, dreadfully, awfully, shockingly
Horrifique, *adj.* horrific
Horripilant, e, *adj.* horrifying, thrilling, scandalizing, shocking, offensive
Horripilation, *s.f.* horripilation
Horripiler, *v.a.* to horrify, to thrill, to scandalize, to shock, to offend
S'—, *v.r.* to be *or* become horrified *or* &c.; to [shudder
'Hors, *prep.* out; beyond; past; free (from); away; off; beside; except, save. *— de là*, beyond that, &c.; in other respects *or* cases, otherwise. *— de soi*, beside oneself, out of o.'s senses *or* temper, exasperated. *— que*, (*obsolete*) except that, except, unless
'Hors-d'œuvre, *s.m.* outbuilding; (small) first course side-dish, appetizer; extra; episode, digression; surplusage; accessory; *— adj. adv.* extra, accessory; foreign to the purpose; (*of buildings*) detached, from out to out, outside; (*of gems*) unset
Hortensia, *s.m.* (*bot.*) hortensia, hydrangea
Horticole, *adj.* horticultural
Horticulteur, *s.m.* horticulturist
Horticultural, e, *adj.* horticultural
Horticulture, *s.f.* horticulture. *Exposition d'—*, flower-show
Hosanna, *s.m.* hosanna
Hospice, *s.m.* asylum, refuge, home, hospital (*specially for incurables, children, infirm or old people, whereas* "hôpital" *is for the sick and wounded generally*); alms-house, poor-house; convent, monastery (*in the Alps*, &c.), hospice; *—s*, *pl.* asylums, &c.; (*in lawyers' bad French*) hospitals and asylums. *Hôpitaux et —s*, (*in good modern French*) hospitals and asylums. *— des enfants assistés* (or *des enfants trouvés*), foundling-hospital, Foundlings' Home
Hospitali-er, ère, *adj.* hospitable; of hospitals, of the sick; of charity, charitable; *— s.m.* hospitaller; *— s.f.* sister of charity
Hospitalièrement, *adv.* hospitably
Hospitalisation, *s.f.* admission and stay in [the hospital
Hospitalité, *s.f.* hospitality
Hospodar, *s.m.* hospodar
Hospodarat, *s.m.* hospodarship; hospodar's [palace
Host, *s.m.* (*old*) army, host; flock; enemy
Hostie, *s.f.* host, consecrated wafer, wafer; victim; offering, sacrifice
Hostile, *adj.* hostile, inimical, adverse, unfriendly; of the enemy
Hostilement, *adv.* hostilely, adversely
Hostilité, *s.f.* hostility, enmity, unfriendliness
Hôte, *s.m.* landlord; host; guest; lodger; visitor; inhabitant; denizen; occupant, occupier; tenant. *Table d'—*, ordinary, table d'hôte. *Compter sans son —*, to reckon without o.'s host
Hôtel, *s.m.* hotel, inn; town-mansion, mansion, house; hall; building; hospital. *— des postes*, General Post-Office. *— des ventes*, auction-mart. *— de ville*, town-hall, town-house, guildhall; parochial offices, registrar's office, &c.; mayor's house, mansion-house. *—-Dieu*, Hôtel-Dieu, hospital. *— meublé* or *garni*, lodging-house. *Maître d'—*, *V.* **Maître**
Hôteli-er, ère, *s.m.f.* inn-keeper, hotel-keeper; landlord, host; landlady, hostess
Hôtellerie, *s.f.* inn, hotel
Hôtesse, *s.f.* landlady; hostess; guest; lodger; visitor; inhabitant; occupant, occupier; tenant
'Hotte, *s.f.* basket (*carried on the back*), dosser; [funnel; drain
'Hottée, *s.f.* basketful
'Hottentot, e, *s.m.f. adj.* Hottentot
'Hotter, *v.a.* to carry *or* remove in a basket (*on o.'s back*)
'Hottereau, Hotteret, *s.m.* basket, hamper
'Hotteriau, *s.m.* (*pop.*) rag-picker
'Hotteu-r, se, *s.m.f.* basket-carrier
Hottone, Hottonie, *s.f.* (*bot.*) hottonia, water-violet, featherfoil
'Hou, *int.* hoo! whoop! ho! bo! hi! go along [with ye!
Houache, Houaiche, *s.f.* (*nav.*) wake, track
'Houage, *s.m.* hoeing
Houari, Houary, *s.m.* (*nav.*) wherry
'Houblon, *s.m.* hop, hops
'Houblonner, *v.a.* to hop
'Houblonnière, *s.f.* hop-plantation, hop-[ground, hop-garden
'Houcre, *s.f.* *V.* **Hourque**
'Houe, *s.f.* hoe
'Houement, *s.m.* hoeing
'Houer, *v.a.n.* to hoe
'Houerie, *s.f.* hoeing
'Houette, *s.f.* small hoe
'Houeur, *s.m.* hoer
'Houhou, *s.f.* hag; *— s.m.* (*bird*) pheasant-cuckoo
'Houhoulement, *s.m.* hooting, whooping
'Houhouler, *v.n.* (*of owls*) to hoot, to whoop
†**'Houille,** *s.f.* coal, pit-coal
†**'Houill-er, ère,** *adj.* coal
†**'Houillère,** *s.f.* coal-mine, coal-pit, colliery
†**'Houilleur,** *s.m.* collier, coal-miner
†**'Houilleu-x, se,** *adj.* coaly
'Houin, *s.m.* *V.* **Matteau**
'Houka, *s.m.* hookah (*pipe*)
'Houlan, *s.m.* *V.* **Uhlan**
'Houle, *s.f.* swell, surge, billow
'Houlette, *s.f.* crook, sheep-hook; (*hort.*) trowel; (*tech.*) scoop, spatula, ladle, spoon; (*fig.*) shepherd, peasant
'Houleu-x, se, *adj.* swelling, rough, rolling
'Houlque, *s.f.* *V.* **Houque**
'Houp, *int.* hoy! gee! gee-up! move on! get on! get out! be off! away with you!
'Houpement, *s.m.* hallooing, halloo, hoop, whoop, shout
'Houper, *v.a.n.* to halloo, to hoop, to whoop, [to shout, to call out
'Houpette, *s.f.* (*bird*) black tanager
'Houppe, *s.f.* tuft; tassel; powder-puff, puff. *— à poudrer*, powder-puff. *—s nerveuses*, (*anat.*) nervous expansion
'Houppée, *s.f.* (*nav.*) crest (*of a wave*), crest of [foam
'Houppelande, *s.f.* (*old*) overcoat, pilch
'Houpper, *v.a.* to tuft; to comb (*wool*)
'Houppette, *s.f.* little tuft
'Houppier, *s.m.* wool-comber; lopped tree; tuft; withering at the top
'Houppifère, *adj.* tufted
'Houque, *s.f.* (*bot.*) holcus, soft-grass
'Houra, Hourah. *V.* **Hourra**
†**'Hourailler,** *v.n.* to hunt with bad hounds
†**'Houraillerie,** *s.f.* hunting with bad hounds
†**'Houraillis,** *s.m.* pack of bad hounds
'Hourdage, *s.m.* rough-walling; pugging
'Hourder, *v.a.* to rough-wall; to pug
'Hourdi, Hourdy, *s.m.* (*nav.*) wing-transom
'Hourdis, *s.m.* *V.* **Hourdage**
'Houret, *s.m.* bad hound
'Houri, *s.f.* (*Mahom. rel.*) houri
'Hourque, *s.f.* (*nav.*) hooker, howker, hulk
'Hourra, Hourrah, *s.m. int.* hurrah, hurray
'Hourvari, *s.m.* (*fam.*) uproar, hubbub, row, shindy; (*hunt.*) cry to call back the hounds;

dodging, dodge; (*local*) tornado; (*obsolete*) accident, disappointment
'Housard, *s.m.* (*old*) *V.* **Hussard**
'Housche, *s.f.* (*obsolete*) croft
'Houseaux, *s.m.pl.* (*obsolete*) spatterdashes. *Laisser ses* —, to leave o.'s bones, to die
†'Houspillement, *s.m.* pulling about, tugging, &c. (*V.* **Houspiller**)
†'Houspiller, *v.a.* to pull about, to tug, to mob, to maul, to worry, to handle roughly; to abuse, to cut up, to lash, to give it to
'Houssage, *s.m.* dusting; enclosure (*of a wind-mill*)
'Houssaie, *s.f.* holly-grove
'Houssard, *s.m.* (*old*) *V.* **Hussard**
'Housse, *s.f.* housing, horse-cloth, body-cloth; saddle-cloth; hammer-cloth; cover; case. — *trainante*, — *de pied*, — *en soulier*, foot-cloth
'Houssé, e, *part. adj.* dusted; (*of horses*) housed, clothed; (*formerly, of coaches*) covered
'Housseau, *s.m.* blanket-pin
'Housser, *v.a.* to dust
'Houssette, *s.f.* spring-lock, clasp-lock
'Houssine, *s.f.* switch
'Houssiner, *v.a.* to switch; to cane, to beat
'Houssoir, *s.m.* dusting-brush, whisk, feather-broom
'Housson, *s.m. V.* **Brusc**
'Houtias, *s.m.* (*zool.*) hutia, hog-rat
'Houx, *s.m.* holly; holly-stick. *Petit* —, *V.* **Brusc**
'Hoyau, *s.m.* mattock
'Hoyé, e, *adj.* (*fish.*) bruised
'Hu, *int. V.* **Hue**
'Huaco, *s.m. V.* **Guaco**
'Huage, *s.m.* hooting; shouting
†'Huaille, *s.f.* (*old*) rabble, mob
'Huard, *s.m.* (*bird*) black-throated diver
'Huau, *s.m.* scarecrow
'Hubert, *s.m.* (*insect*) vine-fretter
'Hublot, *s.m.* (*nav.*) light-port
'Huche, *s.f.* bread-pan, pan; kneading-trough, trough; hutch, bin, chest, tub
'Hucher, *v.n.*, **Se** —, *v.r. V.* **Jucher**; — *v.a.* (*old*) to call, to whistle (*Se* —, ditto each other)
'Huchet, *s.m.* call-horn; (*her.*) hunting-horn
'Huchier, *s.m.* (*obsolete*) cabinet-maker *or* turner, wood-carver
'Hue, *int.* (*to horses*) go on! (*to the right, obsolete*) [*V.* **Huhau**
'Huée, *s.f.* hooting; shouting
'Huer, *v.n.a.* to hoot; to holloa; to shout after *or* at
'Huette, *s.f. V.* **Hulotte**
'Huguenot, e, *s.m.f. adj.* Huguenot; — *s.f.* earthen kitchen-stove; pipkin. *Œufs à la* —*e*, eggs cooked in mutton-gravy
'Huguenotisme, *s.m.* huguenotism
'Huhau, Huhaut, *int.* (*to horses*) gee! geeho! (*to the right!*) *A* —, on *or* to the right
Huilage, *s.m.* oiling
Huile, *s.f.* oil; (*slang*) wine; rhino; suspicion. — *blonde*, (*slang*) beer. — *à brûler*, lamp-oil. — *à manger*, salad-oil, table-oil. — *d'aspic* or *de spic*, oil of spike, foreign oil of lavender. — *de bras*, — *de poignet*, (*pop.*) elbow-grease; vigour, stamina. — *de mains*, (*slang*) oil of palms, rhino. — *de pied de bœuf*, neat's foot oil. — *de poisson* or *de baleine*, train-oil. — *de pomme de terre*, potato-spirit, fusel-oil, fusel. *Sentir l'*—, (*of intellectual productions*) to smell of the lamp
Huilé, e, *part. adj.* oiled, &c. (*V.* **Huiler**)
Huilement, *s.m.* oiling
Huiler, *v.a.* to oil; to anoint with oil; to grease
Huilerie, *s.f.* oil-works, oil-mill; oil-shop; oilery
Huileu-x, se, *adj.* oily; greasy; fat; unctuous
Huilier, *s.m.* cruet-frame, cruet-stand; (*old*) oil-cruet; oil-maker; oilman
Huilière, *s.f.* oil-can
Huilure, *s.f.* oiliness
Huis, *s.m.* (*obsolete*) door. — *clos*, (*law*) closed doors, trial with closed doors, secret trial; (*fig.*) secrecy, privacy. *A* — *clos*, (*law, fig.*) with closed doors, privately, in private, secretly
Huisserie, *s.f.* door-frame
Huissier, *s.m.* usher; door-keeper; tipstaff; serjeant; sheriff's officer; bailiff; summoning officer; process-server; (— *-priseur*) appraiser, auctioneer (*obsolete for* "commissaire-priseur")
'Huit, *adj.m.f.*, *s.m.* eight; eighth. — *jours*, (a) week. *En* —, week. *D'aujourd'hui* (or *de demain*, &c.) *en* —, this day (*or* to-morrow, &c.) week. *Il y a aujourd'hui* — *jours*, this day last week. *Il y a eu hier* — *jours*, yesterday week. *Il y a eu lundi* — *jours*, last Monday week
'Huitain, *s.m.* piece of poetry *or* stanza of eight lines
'Huitaine, *s.f.* eight, about eight, some eight; week, eight days; eight-day clock. *A* —, till *or* to this *or* that day week, for a week. *Dans la* —, in the course of the week
'Huitième, *adj.m.f.*, *s.m.* eighth; pupil of the eighth form *or* class; — *s.f.* eighth form *or* class
'Huitièmement, *adv.* eighthly
Huître, *s.f.* oyster; (*pop.*) gob (*spittle*); (*pers.*) booby, fool. *Comme une* —, (*fam.*) like a fool; very badly
Huîtrier, *s.m.* (*bird*) oyster-catcher; — *adj.m.* of oysters, oyster
Huîtrière, *s.f.* oyster-bed, oyster-fishery; — *adj.f.* of oysters, oyster
Huîtrifier (S'), *v.r.* (*fam.*) to get stupid, to become a mope
'Hulan, *s.m. V.* **Uhlan**
'Hulla, *s.m.* (*Turkish*) hulla
'Hulot, *s.m.* (*nav.*) *V.* **Hublot**
'Hulotte, *s.f.* brown owl, wood-owl, owlet
'Hululer, *v.n.* (*old*) *V.* **Houhouler**
'Hum, *int.* hum!
Humain, e, *adj.* human; humane; — *s.m.* human being, man; human nature, human; —**s**, *s.m.pl.* mankind, men
Humainement, *adv.* humanely; humanly
Humanisation, *s.f.* humanization
Humaniser, *v.a.* to humanize; to soften down
S'—, *v.r.* to become humanized, &c.; to adapt oneself to the capacity of others
Humaniste, *s.m.* humanist, classical scholar
Humanitaire, *adj.m.f.*, *s.m.* humanitarian
Humanitarisme, *s.m.* humanitarianism
Humanité, *s.f.* humanity; mankind; human nature; —**s**, *pl.* humanities, classical studies *or* learning
Humantin, *s.m.* (*fish*) centrine
Humble, *adj.* humble, lowly, low, meek, modest, quiet, small
Humblement, *adv.* humbly, lowly, meekly, modestly, quietly
Humectant, e, *adj.*, **Humectant,** *s.m.* humectant [moistening, damping; refreshing
Humectation, *s.f.* humectation, wetting,
Humecter, *v.a.* to wet, to moisten, to damp; to water; to refresh
S'—, *v.r.* to refresh oneself; to wet *or* &c. (o.'s ...); to be moistened *or* &c.
Humec-teur, trice, *adj.* moistening, wetting; — *s.m.* moistener
Humer, *v.a.* to suck in *or* up, to sup up, to sip up, to gulp, to swallow, to swig, to inhale, to sniff up, to snuff up
Huméral, e, *adj.* (*anat.*) brachial, humeral
Humérus, *s.m.* (*anat.*) humerus
Humeur, *s.f.* humour; temper, disposition, mood, turn of mind; caprice, fancy, whim; ill-humour, peevishness, temper. —*s froides*, scrofula. — *noire*, melancholy spleen, brown study, blue devils, dismals. *Belle* —, cheerfulness, merry mood. *Avec* —, peevishly, crossly. *De bonne* —, in *or* into good humour, good-humoured, good-humouredly. *De mauvaise* —, in *or* into ill *or* bad humour, ill-humoured, cross, out of temper, ill-humouredly. *Avoir de l'*—, to be out of temper, to be cross *or* angry. *Être en* — *de*, *être d'*— *à*, to be in the (*or* in a) humour to, to be inclined *or* disposed to. *Prendre de l'*—, to get out of temper
Humeu-r, se, *s.m.f.* sucker, sipper, gulper, swallower, sniffer; — *adj.f.* *Pierre* —*se*, light concretion of humus
Humide, *adj.* humid; damp; moist; wet; watery; liquid; dewy; — *s.m.* humidity, dampness, moisture, wet, damp, moist

Humidement, *adv.* in a damp place
Humider, *v.a.* (*tech.*) to wet
Humidifuge, *adj.* waterproof
Humidité, *s.m.* humidity; dampness, damp; moisture; wetness, wet; wateriness
Humifuse, *adj.* (*bot.*) humifuse
Humiliation, *s.f.* humiliation, abasement
Humilier, *v.a.* to humiliate, to humble, to abase
Humilité, *s.f.* humility; humbleness, lowliness; meekness
Humine, *s.f.* (*chem.*) humine
Humique, *adj.* (*chem.*) humic
Humopinique, *adj.* (*chem.*) humopinic
Humoral, e, *adj.* (*med.*) humoral
Humorique, *adj.* (*med.*) humoric
Humorisme, *s.m.* humourism
Humoriste, *s.m.f. adj.* humourist
Humoristique, *adj.* humouristic, humourist
Humour, *s.m.* (*liter.*) humour
Humuline, *s.f.* (*chem.*) humuline, lupuline
Humus, *s.m.* humus, mould, vegetable mould
'Hun, *s.m.* (*hist.*) Hun
'Hune, *s.f.* (*nav.*) top; (*tech.*) bell-beam
'Hunier, *s.m.* (*nav.*) top-sail; top-mast. *Grand* —, main top-sail. *Petit* —, fore top-sail
'Huppard, *s.m.* crested eagle-hawk
'Huppe, *s.f.* tuft, crest; (*bird*) hoopoe
'Huppé, e, *adj.* tufted, crested; high, tiptop, great, leading; clever, crack, best; smartly dressed
'Huque, *s.f.* (*obsolete*) cap
'Hure, *s.f.* (*of boars,* &c.) head; jowl; (*pers.*) mop, shock (*head of hair*)
'Hurhau, Hurhaut, *int. V.* **Huhau**
'Hurlade, *s.f.* (*old*) howl, yell
'Hurlement, *s.m.* howling, howl; yelling, yell; roaring, roar; shrieking, shriek
'Hurler, *v.n.a.* to howl; to yell; to roar. — *avec les loups,* to howl with the wolves; to do as others do
'Hurleu-r, se, *s.m.f.* howler; — *s.m.* (*zool.*) *V.* **Alouate**
Hurluberlu, *adj.m., s.m.* harebrained, giddy, thoughtless; harebrained person, giddy goose. *En* —, giddily, thoughtlessly, inconsiderately
'Hurlupé, e, *adj.* (*old*) bristly, shaggy, rough, ruffled, in disorder
'Huron, ne, *s.m.f.* Lake Huron Indian, Huron; [(*fig.*) churl, brute, savage
'Hurra, Hurrah. *V.* **Hourra**
†Hurtebiller, *v.a.* (*old*) to cover, to tup
'Hussard, *s.m.* hussar
'Hussarde, *s.f.* hussar style *or* fashion; (*dance, tune*) hussarde. *A la* —, like hussars, in hussar style, after the hussar fashion; by plunder. *Bottes à la* —, riding-boots
'Hussite, *s.m.* (*eccl. hist.*) Hussite
'Hustings, *s.m.pl.* (*English*) hustings
'Hutin, *adj.m.* (*old*) headstrong, stubborn; obstreperous
'Hutinet, *s.m.* mallet, bat
'Hutte, *s.f.* hut, shed, shanty
'Hutter, *v.a.*, **Se** —, *v.r.* to hut, to make a hut or shed, to live in ditto
'Huzza, *s.m. int.* huzza
Hyacinthe, *s.f.* hyacinth (*plant, gem, stuff*); — *adj.* hyacinth-coloured (*blue*)
Hyacinthine, *s.f.* (*min.*) hyacinthine
Hyades, *s.f.pl.* (*myth., astr.*) Hyades
Hyalin, e, *adj.* hyaline
Hyalite, *s.f.* (*min.*) hyalite
Hyalographe, *s.m.* hyalograph
Hyalographie, *s.f.* hyalography
Hyaloïde, *adj.* hyaloid
Hyalurgie, *s.f.* hyalurgy, glass-making
Hybridation, *s.f.* hybridization
Hybride, *adj.m.f., s.m.* hybrid, mongrel
Hybridisme, *s.m.* hybridism
Hybridité, *s.f.* hybridity
Hydarthre, *s.m.*, **Hydarthrose,** *s.f.* (*surg.*) hydarthrus, hydarthrosis, white-swelling
Hydatide, *s.f.* (*med., zool.*) hydatid
Hydat-ique, -isme, (*med.*) *V.* page 3, § 1
Hydne, *s.m.* (*bot.*) hydnum
Hydnore, *s.m.* (*bot.*) hydnora, jackal's kost
Hydracide, *s.m.* (*chem.*) hydracid
Hydragogue, *adj.* (*med.*) hydragogic; — *s.m.* hydragogue
Hydrangée, *s.f.* (*bot.*) hydrangea
Hydrargyrie, *s.f.* (*med.*) hydrargyria
Hydrargyrique, *adj.* hydrargyric
Hydrargyrose, *s.f.* (*med.*) hydrargyrosis, mercurial friction
Hydrarthre, *s.m.* (*bad spelling*) *V.* **Hydarthre**
Hydraste, *s.m.* (*bot.*) hydrastis, warneria, yellow root, orange root
Hydratation, *s.f.* (*chem.*) hydration
Hydrate, *s.m.* (*chem.*) hydrate
Hydraté, e, *adj.* (*chem.*) hydrated
Hydraulicien, *s.m.* hydraulist, hydraulic engineer
Hydraulique, *adj.* hydraulic; water; — *s.f.* hydraulics
Hydre, *s.f.* hydra
Hydriote, *adj. s.m.f.* Hydriot
Hydro, (*in compounds*) hydro... [&c.
Hydrobromate, &c., (*old*) *V.* **Bromhydrate,** &c.
Hydrocarbonate, *s.m.* (*chem.*) hydrocarbonate
Hydrocarbure, *s.m.* (*chem.*) hydrocarbide, hydrocarburet, carburetted hydrogen
Hydrocèle, *s.f.* (*med.*) hydrocele
Hydrocéphale, Hydrocéphalie, *s.f.* (*med.*) hydrocephalus, dropsy of the brain, water in the head *or* on the brain
Hydrocéphale, *s.m.* hydrocephalic person; — *adj.* hydrocephalic
Hydrocérame, *s.m.* porous vase, cooler
Hydrocéramique, *adj.* hydroceramic
‡Hydrochlorate, &c., (*old*) *V.* **Chlorhydrate,** &c.
Hydrocoride, Hydrocorise, *s.f.* water-bug
Hydrocotyle, *s.f.* (*bot.*) hydrocotyle, pennywort
Hydrocyanate, &c., (*old*) *V.* **Cyanhydrate,** &c.
Hydrocyste, *s.f.* (*med.*) hydrocystis
Hydrodynamique, *adj.* hydrodynamic; — *s.f.* hydrodynamics
Hydroélectrique, *adj.* hydroelectric
Hydrofluate, Hydrofluorique, (*old*) *V.* **Fluorhydrate, Fluorhydrique**
Hydrofuge, *adj.m.f., s.m.* hydrofuge
Hydrogénation, *s.f.* (*chem.*) hydrogenation, hydrogenization
Hydrogène, *s.m.* (*chem.*) hydrogen
Hydrogéner, *v.a.*, **S'**—, *v.r.* (*chem.*) to hydrogenate, to hydrogenize
Hydrographe, *s.m.* hydrographer; — *adj.* hydrographic
Hydrograph-ie, -ique. *V.* page 3, § 1
Hydrohém-ie, -ique, (*med.*) *V.* page 3, § 1
Hydrolé, *s.m.* (*pharm.*) wash
Hydrolog-ie, -ique. *V.* page 3, § 1
Hydrologue, *s.m.* hydrologist
Hydroman-cie, -tique. *V.* page 3, § 1
Hydromancien, ne, *s.m.f.* hydromancer
Hydromanie, *s.f.* (*med.*) hydromania
Hydromécanique, *adj.* hydromechanical; — *s.f.* hydromechanics
Hydromel, *s.m.* hydromel, mead. — *vineux,* vinous hydromel
Hydrométéore, *s.m.* hydrometeor
Hydromètre, *s.m.* (*phys.*) hydrometer
Hydrométr-ie, -ique. *V.* page 3, § 1
Hydrominéral, e, *adj.* hydromineral
Hydromphale, *s.f.* (*med.*) hydromphalus
Hydromys, *s.m.* (*zool.*) hydromys, beaver-rat
Hydronéphrose, *s.f.* (*med.*) hydronephrosis
Hydropathe, *s.m.* hydropathist, hydropath, water-cure doctor; — *adj.* hydropathic
Hydropathie, *s.f.* hydropathy, water-cure
Hydropath-ique, -iquement, -iste. *V.* page 3, § 1
Hydropathiser, *v.a.n.* to hydropathize
Hydrophane, *s.f.* (*min.*) hydrophane; — *adj.* hydrophanous
Hydrophide, *s.m.* (*zool.*) hydrophid, water-snake
Hydrophobe, *s.m.f. adj.* hydrophobiac
Hydrophobie, *s.f.* hydrophobia
Hydrophobique, *adj.* hydrophobic
Hydrophosphate, *s.m.* (*chem.*) hydrophosphate
Hydrophthalmie, *s.f.* (*med.*) hydrophthalmia
Hydrophyte, *s.f.* (*bot.*) hydrophyte
Hydrophyto-graphie, -logie, &c. *V.* page 3, § 1
Hydropique, *adj. s.m.f.* (*med.*) dropsical; dropsical person
Hydropisie, *s.f.* (*med.*) dropsy
Hydroplast-ie, -ique. *V.* page 3, § 1
Hydropneumatique, *adj.* hydropneumatic
Hydropote, *s.m.f.* water-drinker

Hydropulte, *s.f.* hydropult
Hydrorachis, *s.m.* (*med.*) hydrorachitis
Hydroscope, *s.m.* hydroscope; bletonist
Hydroscopie, *s.f.* hydroscopy; bletonism
Hydrostatique, *adj.* hydrostatic; — *s.f.* hydrostatics
Hydrostatiquement, *adv.* hydrostatically
Hydrosulfate, &c., (*old*) *V.* **Sulfhydrate,** &c.
Hydrothérapeutique, Hydrothérapie, *s.f.* hydropathy, hydrotherapia, water-cure
Hydrothérapique, *adj.* hydropathic
Hydrothermique, *adj.* hydrothermic
Hydrothorax, *s.m.* (*med.*) hydrothorax, dropsy of the chest
Hydroxyde, *s.m.* (*chem.*) hydroxide
Hydrure, *s.m.* (*chem.*) hydride
Hyèble, *s.f.* *V.* **Hièble**
Hyémal, Hyémation. *V.* **Hiémal,** &c.
Hyène, *s.f.* hyena, hyæna
Hygie, *s.f.* (*myth.*, *astr.*) Hygeia, Hygieia
Hygiène, *s.f.* hygiene, hygienics, preservation of health, health
Hygiénique, *adj.* hygienic, sanitary, health-preserving, of *or* for the preservation of health, of health; — *s.f.* hygienics
Hygiéniquement, *adv.* hygienically
Hygiéniste, *s.m.* hygeist
Hygiocérame, *s.m.* pottery free from noxious substances
Hygiolog-ie, -ique. *V.* page 3, § 1
Hygrolog-ie, -ique. *V.* page 3, § 1
Hygroma, Hygrome, *s.m.* (*surg.*) hygroma
Hygromètre, *s.m.* (*phys.*) hygrometer
Hygrométricité, *s.f.* hygrometricity
Hygrométr-ie, -ique, &c. *V.* page 3, § 1
Hygroscope, *s.m.* (*phys.*) hygroscope
Hygroscopicité, *s.f.* hygroscopicity
Hygroscop-ie, -ique, &c. *V.* page 3, § 1
Hymen, Hyménée, *s.m.* hymen; marriage, matrimony, wedlock, nuptials, union
Hyménoptère, *adj.* (*zool.*) hymenopterous, hymenopteral; — *s.m.* hymenopterous insect, hymenopteran, hymenopter
Hymnaire, *s.m.* hymn-book
Hymne, *s.m.* hymn; anthem
Hymnique, *adj.* hymnic
Hymnographe, *s.m.* hymnographer
Hymno-graphie, -logie, &c. *V.* page 3, § 1
Hymnologue, *s.m.* hymnologist
Hyoïde, *adj.* (*anat.*) hyoid; — *s.m.* hyoid bone, lingual bone, tongue-bone, hyoid
Hyoscyamine, *s.f.* (*chem.*) hyoscyamine
Hypallage, *s.f.* (*rhet.*) hypallage
Hyper, (*in compounds, chem.*, &c.) hyper...
Hyperbate, *s.f.* (*gram.*) hyperbaton, inversion
Hyperbole, *s.f.* (*rhet.*) hyperbole, exaggeration; (*geom.*) hyperbola
Hyperboliforme, *adj.* hyperboliform
Hyperbol-ique, -iquement. *V.* page 3, § 1
Hyperboliser, *v.n.* to hyperbolize
Hyperbolisme, *s.m.* hyperbolism
Hyperboloïde, *s.m.* (*geom.*) hyperboloid; — *adj.* hyperboloidal
Hyperborée, Hyperboréen, ne, *adj.*, **Hyperboréen,** *s.m.* hyperborean
‡**Hyperchlorate,** *s.m.* (*chem.*) hyperchlorate
‡**Hyperchlorique,** *adj.* (*chem.*) hyperchloric
Hypercrise, *s.f.* (*med.*) hypercrisis
Hypercritique, *s.m.* hypercritic; — *s.f.* hypercriticism; — *adj.* hypercritical
Hyperdramatique, *adj.m.f.*, *s.m.* hyperdramatic
Hyperdulie, *s.f.* hyperdulia (*worship of the Virgin Mary*)
Hyperelliptique, *adj.* (*math.*) hyperelliptic
Hyperémie, *s.f.* (*med.*) hyperæmia, superabundance of blood
Hyperesthésie, *s.f.* (*med.*) hyperæsthesia
Hyperostose, *s.f.* (*med.*) hyperostosis
Hyperoxyde, *s.m.* (*chem.*) hyperoxide
Hyperphysique, *adj.* hyperphysical
Hyperstène, *s.m.* (*min.*) hyperstene, hypersthene
Hypersulfure, *s.m.* (*chem.*) hypersulphide, hypersulphuret

Hyperthyron, *s.m.* (*arch.*) hyperthyrum, hyperthyrion
Hypertonie, *s.f.* (*med.*) hypertonia, hypertone
Hypertrophie, *s.f.* (*med.*) hypertrophy, enlargement
Hypertrophié, e, *adj.* (*med.*) hypertrophied, enlarged
Hypertrophier, *v.a.* (*med.*) to enlarge
  S'—, *v.r.* to become hypertrophied *or* enlarged, to enlarge
Hypertrophique, *adj.* (*med.*) hypertrophic
Hypèthre, *s.m.* (*arch.*) hypætron; — *adj.* hypætral
Hypnobate, *s.m.* somnambulist
Hypno-graphie, -graphique, -logie, &c. *V.* page 3, § 1
Hypnot-ique (*adj.m.f.*, *s.m.*), **-isme.** *V.* page 3, § 1
Hypnotiser, *v.a.* to hypnotize
Hypo, (*in compounds, chem.*, &c.) hypo...
Hypocauste, *s.m.* hypocaust
Hypochéride, *s.f.* (*bot.*) hypochæris
‡**Hypochlorate,** *s.m.* (*chem.*) hypochlorate
‡**Hypochloreux,** *adj.m.* (*chem.*) hypochlorous
‡**Hypochlorique,** *adj.* (*chem.*) hypochloric
‡**Hypochlorite,** *s.m.* (*chem.*) hypochlorite
Hypociste, *s.f.* (*bot.*) hypocistis. *Suc d'—,* (*pharm.*) hypocist
Hypocondre, *s.m.* (*anat.*) hypochondrium, hypochonder; — *s.m.f.* *adj.* (*pers.*) hypochondriac, hypochondriacal, splenetic
Hypocondriaque, *adj.* *s.m.f.* hypochondriac, hypochondriacal, splenetic
Hypocondrie, *s.f.* (*med.*) hypochondria, hypochondriasis, spleen
Hypocras, *s.m.* (*bad spelling*) *V.* **Hippocras**
Hypocratériforme, Hypocratérimorphe, *adj.* hypocrateriform, salver-shaped
Hypocrisie, *s.f.* hypocrisy
Hypocrite, *s.m.f.* hypocrite; — *adj.* hypocritical
Hypocritement, *adv.* hypocritically
Hypocycloïdal, e, *adj.* hypocycloidal
Hypocycloïde, *s.f.* (*geom.*) hypocycloid
Hypogastre, *s.m.* (*anat.*) hypogastrium
Hypogastrique, *adj.* (*anat.*) hypogastric
Hypogastrocèle, *s.f.* (*med.*) hypogastrocele
Hypogée, *s.m.* (*ancient arch.*) hypogeum, vault, catacomb; — *adj.* hypogean
Hypoglosse, *adj.* (*anat.*) hypoglossal; — *s.m.* hypoglossal nerve; (*bot.*) butcher's-broom
Hypogyne, *adj.* (*bot.*) hypogynous
Hyponitreux, *adj.m.* (*chem.*) hyponitrous
Hyponitrique, *adj.* (*chem.*) hyponitric
Hypophosphate, *s.m.* (*chem.*) hypophosphate
Hypophosphite, *s.m.* (*chem.*) hypophosphite
Hypophosphoreux, *adj.m.* (*chem.*) hypophosphorous
Hypophosphorique, *adj.* (*chem.*) hypophosphoric
Hypostase, *s.f.* (*med.*, *theol.*) hypostasis
Hypostat-ique, -iquement. *V.* page 3, § 1
Hypostyle, *adj.m.f.*, *s.m.* (*arch.*) hypostyle
Hyposulfate, *s.m.* (*chem.*) hyposulphate
Hyposulfite, *s.m.* (*chem.*) hyposulphite
Hyposulfureux, *adj.m.* (*chem.*) hyposulphurous
Hyposulfurique, *adj.* (*chem.*) hyposulphuric
Hypoténuse, *s.f.* (*geom.*) hypotenuse, hypothenuse
Hypothécable, *adj.* mortgageable
Hypothécaire, *adj.* on mortgage; of mortgage. *Créancier —,* mortgagee
Hypothécairement, *adv.* by *or* with mortgage; relatively to mortgage
Hypothèque, *s.f.* mortgage; (*pop.*) chronic disease
Hypothéqué, e, *part. adj.* mortgaged; (*pers.*) infirm, sickly; cripple; paralytic; done up; embarrassed, in need, hard up
Hypothéquer, *v.a.* to mortgage; (*pers.*, *fam.*) to do up
Hypothèse, *s.f.* hypothesis, supposition
Hypothét-ique, -iquement. *V.* page 3, § 1
Hypotypose, *s.f.* (*rhet.*) hypotyposis
Hypoxanthine, *s.f.* (*chem.*) hypoxanthine
Hypozoïque, *adj.* (*geol.*) hypozoic
Hypsographie, *s.f.* hypsography
Hypsomètre, *s.m.* (*phys.*) hypsometer
Hypsométr-ie, -ique, &c. *V.* page 3, § 1
Hyracéum, *s.m.* hyraceum
Hyrax, *s.m.* (*zool.*) hyrax, daman

Hyrcanien, ne, *adj. s.* Hyrcanian
Hysope, Hyssope, *s.f.* (*bot.*) hyssop
Hysopine, *s.f.* (*chem.*) hyssopine
'Hysson, *s.m.* hyson (*green tea*)
Hystéralgie, *s.f.* (*med.*) hysteralgia
Hystéricisme, *s.m.* (*med.*) hystericism
Hystérie, *s.f.* (*med.*) hysteria, hysterics
Hystérique, *adj.m.f., s.f.* hysteric, hysterical;
Hystérite, *s.f.* (*med.*) hysteritis [ditto person
Hysterocèle, *s.f.* (*med.*) hysterocele
Hystéro-graphie, -logie, &c. *V.* page 3, § 1
Hystérolithe, *s.m.* hysterolite
Hystéromanie, *s.f.* (*med.*) hysteromania
Hystéromètre, *s.m.* (*surg.*) hysterometer
Hystéroptose, *s.f.* (*surg.*) hysteroptosis
Hystérotome, *s.m.* (*surg.*) hysterotomy-knife, hysterotome
Hystérotomie, *s.f.* (*surg.*) hysterotomy

I

I, *s.m.* i [*adj.* iambic
Iambe, Iambique, *s.m.* iambus, iambic; —
Ibère, *s.m. adj.* (*old, poet.*) Spaniard; Spanish
Ibéride, *s.f.* (*bot.*) candytuft
Ibérien, ne, *adj. s.,* **Ibérique,** *adj.* (*old*) Iberian, Iberic, Spaniard, Spanish
Ibidem, *adv. s.m.* (*Latin*) ibidem
Ibis, *s.m.* (*bird*) ibis
Icaque, *s.f.* (*bot.*) cocoa-plum
Icaquier, *s.m.* (*bot.*) cocoa-plum tree
Icarien, ne, *adj.* Icarian
Icelui, *m.,* **Icelle,** *f., pron.* (*obsolete*) he, him, she, her, it, this, that, the said, the aforesaid,
‡**Ichneumon,** *s.m.* (*zool.*) ichneumon [the same
‡**Ichnographe,** *s.m.* ichnographer
‡**Ichnograph-ie, -ique, -iquement.** *V.* page 3, § 1 [3, § 1
‡**Ichnolog-ie, -ique, -iquement.** *V.* page
‡**Ichor,** *s.m.* (*myth., med.*) ichor
‡**Ichoreu-x, se,** *adj.* (*med.*) ichorous
‡**Ichthyique,** *adj.* ichthyic
‡**Ichthyo,** (*in compounds*) ichthyo...
‡**Ichthyocolle,** *s.f.* ichthyocol, ichthyocolla, fish-glue, isinglass
‡**Ichthyographe,** *s.m.* ichthyographer [§ 1
‡**Ichthyograph-ie, -ique,** &c. *V.* page 3,
‡**Ichthyolithe,** *s.m.* ichthyolite [§ 1
‡**Ichthyolog-ie, -ique, -iste,** &c. *V.* page 3,
‡**Ichthyophage,** *s.m.f.* ichthyophagist; — *adj.* ichthyophagous
‡**Ichthyophag-ie, -ique.** *V.* page 3, § 1
‡**Ichthyosaure, Ichthyosaurus,** *s.m.* (*zool.*) ichthyosaur, ichthyosaurus
‡**Ichthyosaurien, ne,** *adj.* ichthyosaurian
‡**Ichthyose,** *s.f.* (*med.*) ichthyosis, fish-skin disease
Ici, *adv.* here; hither; in this place; this place; this; this time, now. — *-bas, V.* **Bas.** — *même,* in this very place. — *près,* near here, close by, hard by. *D'*—, of *or* from here, &c.; hence, from hence; already. *D'— à,* between this and; until; by; for; ... hence. *D'— à ce que,* until. *D'— à deux jours,* within two days; two days hence. *D'— en avant,* henceforward. *D'— là,* from here to there, between this and there; between this and then; until then; in the meantime; by that time. *C'est* —, it is
Iciquier, *s.m.* (*bot.*) icica [*or* was here; this is
Icoglan, *s.m.* icoglan (*Sultan's page*)
Iconoclasme, *s.m.* iconoclasm [clastic
Iconoclaste, *s.m.* iconoclast; — *adj.* icono-
Iconographe, *s.m.* iconographer
Icono-graphie, -graphique, -graphiquement, -lâtrie, -lâtrique, -logie, &c. *V.* page 3, § 1 [image-worshipper
Iconolâtre, *s.m.f.* iconolater, iconolatress,
Iconostase, *s.f.* iconostasis
Iconostrophe, *s.m.* iconostrophe
Icosaèdre, *s.m.* (*geom.*) icosahedron; — *adj.*
Icosandre, *adj.* (*bot.*) icosandrous [icosahedral
Icosandrie, *s.f.* (*bot.*) icosandria [drous
Icosandrique, *adj.* (*bot.*) icosandrian, icosan-
Ictère, *s.m.* (*med.*) icterus, jaundice
Ictère, *s.m.,* **Ictérie,** *s.f.* (*bird*) icterus, oriole;
Ictérique, *adj. s.* (*med.*) icteric [troopial
Ictis, *s.m.* (*zool.*) benturong
Idalien, ne, *adj.* Idalian
Ide, *s.m.* (*fish*) ide; —**s,** *s.f.pl.* (*Rom. ant.*) ides
Idéal, e, *adj.* ideal; vain; imaginary; fictitious; visionary; perfect; — *s.m.* ideal, ideality. *Le beau* —, ideal beauty, the ideal of perfec-
Idéalement, *adv.* ideally [tion, the beau ideal
Idéalisation, *s.f.* idealization [be idealized
Idéaliser, *v.a.* to idealize. *S'*—, to become *or*
Idéalisme, *s.m.* idealism
Idéaliste, *s.m.f.* idealist; — *adj.* idealistic
Idéalistique, *adj.* idealistic
Idéalité, *s.f.* ideality
Idée, *s.f.* idea; notion; conception; conceit; plan; hint; outline, sketch; imagination; fancy; thought; meaning, sense; reason; opinion; image; invention; recollection; mind, head; taste, (the) mere name (of it); jot, bit, shade, trifle. *Avoir dans l'— que,* to have an idea *or* a notion that, to fancy that. *Changer d'*—, to change o.'s mind. *Se mettre dans l'*—, to take it into o.'s head. *Venir à l'*—, to occur to, to strike. *J'ai* —, I rather think; it strikes me. *On n'a pas d'— de ...!* one never heard of ...! *On n'a pas d'— de cela!* one never heard of such a thing! only fancy now! *A-t-on —!* what an idea!
Idem, *adv.* idem, ditto; also, too
Identifiable, *adj.* identifiable
Identification, *s.f.* identification
Identifier, *v.a.* to identify [tified, to identify
S'—, *v.r.* to identify oneself, to become iden-
Ident-ique, -iquement. *V.* page 3, § 1
Identité, *s.f.* identity; sameness
Idéograph-ie, -ique, &c. *V.* page 3, § 1
Idéolog-ie, -ique, &c. *V.* page 3, § 1
Idéologue, *s.m.* ideologist
Idio-électricité, *s.f.* idio-electricity
Idio-électrique, *adj.* idio-electric
Idiomat-ique, -iquement. *V.* page 3, § 1
Idiome, *s.m.* language; dialect
Idiomograph-ie, -ique. *V.* page 3, § 1
Idiopath-ie, -ique. *V.* page 3, § 1
Idiosyncrasie, *s.f.* idiosyncrasy
Idiosyncrasique, *adj.* idiosyncratic
Idiot, e, *s.m.f. adj.* idiot; idiotic
Idiotie, *s.f.* idiocy, idiotcy
Idiotique, *adj.* idiotic; idiomatic
Idiotiquement, *adv.* idiotically; idiomatically
Idiotisme, *s.m.* idiom; idiocy, idiotcy
Idocrase, *s.f.* (*min.*) idocrase, vesuvian
Idolâtre, *adj.* idolatrous; idolizing; excessively fond; — *s.m.f.* idolater, idolatress; idol-
Idolâtrement, *adv.* idolatrously [izer
Idolâtrer, *v.a.n.* to idolize
Idolâtrie, *s.f.* idolatry
Idolâtrique, *adj.* idolatrous
Idole, *s.f.* idol; (*jest.*) doll, statue
Iduméen, ne, *adj. s.* Idumean
Idylle, *s.f.* idyl, idyll
Idyllique, *adj.* idyllic
Ièble, *s.f. V.* **Hièble** [(*for illuminations*)
If, *s.m.* yew, yew-tree; (pyramidal) lamp-stand
Igasurate, *s.m.* (*chem.*) igasurate
Igasurine, *s.f.* (*chem.*) igasurine
Igasurique, *adj.* (*chem.*) igasuric
†**Igname,** *s.f.* (*bot.*) yam [nothing
†**Ignare,** *adj. s.m.f.* ignorant; ignoramus, know-
†**Ignatie,** *s.f.,* **Ignatier,** *s.m.* (*bot.*) ignatia amara, Ignatius' bean tree
Igné, e, *adj.* igneous, fiery
Ignescence, *s.f.* ignescence
Ignescent, e, *adj.* ignescent
Ignicole, *adj.* fire-worshipping; — *s.m.f.* fire-worshipper, ignicolist

Ignition, *s.f.* ignition. *En* —, ignited, in a state of ignition
Ignivome, *adj.* ignivomous, vomiting fire
Ignivore, *adj.* fire-eating, ignivorous; — *s.m.f.* fire-eater
†**Ignobilité,** *s.f.* ignobleness, baseness, vileness
†**Ignoble,** *adj.* ignoble, base, vile, mean, low; horrid; beastly; filthy
†**Ignoblement,** *adv.* ignobly, basely, vilely
†**Ignominie,** *s.f.* ignominy
†**Ignominieusement,** *adv.* ignominiously
†**Ignominieu-x, se,** *adj.* ignominious
†**Ignorable,** *adj.* that one need not know, which it is pardonable not to know [ingly
†**Ignoramment,** *adv.* ignorantly, unknow-
†**Ignorance,** *s.f.* ignorance; error, blunder
†**Ignorant, e,** *adj. s.* ignorant; ignoramus. *Faire l'*—, to pretend ignorance, to pretend to know nothing about it
†**Ignorantin,** *s.m., adj.m. Frère* —, Ignorantine, brother of charity, ragged-school teacher
†**Ignorant-isme, -iste.** *V.* page 3, § 1
†**Ignorantissime,** *adj.* most ignorant
†**Ignoré, e,** *part. adj.* unknown; concealed
†**Ignorer,** *v.a.* to be ignorant of, not to know, not to be aware of; to be unacquainted with. *Ne pas* —, to know, to be acquainted with, to be
Iguane, *s.m.* (*zool.*) iguana [aware of (*or* that)
Il, *pron. m.* he; it; there; —**s,** *pl.* they
Île, *s.f.* island, isle; (*of houses*) block; district. *L'Île de France*, Mauritius; (*formerly, a province of France*) Isle of France. *Les —s*, (*when thus used alone*) the Antilles, the West India islands, the West Indies. *Les —s du vent*, the Windward Islands. *Les —s sous le vent*, the Leeward Islands. *Les —s des Amis*, the Friendly Islands
Iléite, *s.f.* (*med.*) ileitis
Iléo-, (*in compounds, anat., med.*) ileo-...
Iléon, *s.m.* (*anat.*) ileum
Iles, *s.m.pl.* (*anat.*) ilia, flanks
Îlet, *s.m.,* **Îlette,** *s.f.* (*old*) *V.* **Îlot**
Iléum, *s.m.* (*anat.*) ileum
Iléus, *s.m.* (*med.*) iliac passion, ileus
Iliade, *s.f.* Iliad; (*fig.*) long story; long series; string, strain, tirade; world, ocean
Iliaque, *adj.* (*anat., med.*) iliac; (*hist.*) of Ilium,
Ilicine, *s.f.* (*chem.*) ilicine [of Troy, Trojan
Ilio-, (*in compounds, anat.*) ilio-...
Ilion, *s.m.* (*anat.*) ilium, flank-bone, haunch-bone; (*hist.*) Ilium, Troy
Ilium, *s.m.* (*anat.*) *V.* **Ilion**
Illabourable, *adj.* unploughable
Illabouré, e, *adj.* unploughed
Illacérable, *adj.* untearable
Illacéré, e, *adj.* untorn
Illégal, e, *adj.* illegal; unlawful; false
Illégalement, *adv.* illegally; unlawfully
Illégalité, *s.f.* illegality; unlawfulness
Illégitime, *adj.* illegitimate; unlawful, unjust; spurious [fully, unjustly
Illégitimement, *adv.* illegitimately; unlaw-
Illégitimité, *s.f.* illegitimacy; unlawfulness;
Illésé, e, *adj.* uninjured [spuriousness
Illettré, e, *adj.* illiterate, unlettered
Illibéral, e, *adj.* illiberal; mean; mechanical
Illibéralement, *adv.* illiberally; meanly
Illibéralisme, *s.m.* illiberalism
Illibéralité, *s.f.* illiberality; meanness
Illicite, *adj.* illicit, unlawful; illegal
Illicitement, *adv.* illicitly, unlawfully
Illico, *adv.* (*fam.*) directly, at once; — *s.m.*
Illimitable, *adj.* illimitable [(*fam.*) grog
Illimitablement, *adv.* illimitably
Illimitation, *s.f.* illimitation [less, indefinite
Illimité, e, *adj.* unlimited, unbounded, bound-
Illisible, *adj.* illegible; unreadable
Illisiblement, *adv.* illegibly
Illition, *s.f.* (*med.*) anointing
Illittérature, *s.f.* illiterateness
Illogicité, *s.f.* illogicalness [§ 1
Illog-ique, -iquement, -isme. *V.* page 3,
Illuminable, *adj.* illuminable

Illumina-teur, trice, *s.m.f.* illuminator illuminer, enlightener; — *adj.* illuminating, enlightening
Illuminati-f, ve, *adj.* illuminative
Illumination, *s.f.* illumination; lighting; lights; divine light; inspiration
Illuminé, e, *part. adj.* illuminated, &c. (*V.* **Illuminer**); — *s.m.f.* illuminate, illuminee (*pl.* illuminati); visionary; fanatic
Illuminer, *v.a.* to illuminate; to illumine; to light up, to light; to enlighten; to brighten up
S'—, *v.r.* to become *or* be illuminated, &c.; to be illuminating *or* &c.; to brighten up, to
Illuminisme, *s.m.* illuminism [beam
Illuministe, *adj.* illuministic; — *s.m.f.* illuminist
Illusion, *s.f.* illusion; delusion; dece fallacy; chimera; vision; phantom; prestige; error. *Se faire* — (*à soi-même*), to delude *or* de-
Illusioniste, *s.m.f.* illusionist [ceive oneself
Illusionner, *v.a.* to delude, to deceive
Illusoire, *adj.* illusory, illusive; delusive; deceitful; fallacious [fallaciously; deceitfully
Illusoirement, *adv.* illusively; delusively;
Illustrable, *adj.* illustrable
Illustrateur, *s.m.* illustrator
Illustration, *s.f.* illustration; illustriousness; lustre; celebrity; glory; (*obsolete*) illumination
Illustre, *adj.* illustrious; celebrated; notorious; — *s.m.* illustrious man, celebrity
Illustrement, *adv* illustriously
Illustrer, *v.a.* to illustrate; to make *or* render illustrious; (*old*) to illuminate
S'—, *v.r.* to make *or* render oneself illustrious; to be illustrated [reverend
Illustrissime, *adj.* most illustrious; right
Illutation, *s.f.* (*med.*) illutation
Illyrien, ne, *adj. s.,* **Illyrique,** *adj.* Illyrian
Îlot, *s.m.* small island, islet, ait *or* eyot, holm; plot; lot; block; district; (*policeman's*) beat
Ilote, *s.m.* helot
Ilotisme, *s.m.* helotism
Ils, *pron.* (*pl. of* **Il**) they
Image, *s.f.* image; imagery; print; cut; picture; likeness; statue; idea; imagination. *Sage comme une* —, a very good boy (*or* girl)
Imagé, e, *part. adj.* imaged, full of images, figurative, adorned, ornate
Imager, *v.a.* to image, to adorn with images *or* rhetorical figures, to adorn [print-seller
Imag-er, ère, *s.m.f.* (*obsolete*) image-vendor,
Imagerie, *s.f.* image-trade, picture-trade;
Imaginable, *adj.* imaginable [images, pictures
Imaginaire, *adj.* imaginary; visionary; chimerical; fantastic; of fancy, fancy, of *or* in imagination; — *s.f.* (*alg.*) imaginary quantity
Imaginati-f, ve, *adj.* imaginative; — *s.f.* imagination, fancy, imaginative faculty
Imagination, *s.f.* imagination; fancy; whim; thought; idea; invention; conception; conceit; —**s,** *pl.* fancies, &c.; (*med.*) muscæ volitantes
Imaginé, e, *part. adj.* imagined, &c. (*V.* **Imaginer**); fictitious, unreal, false
Imaginer, *v.a.n.,* **S'**—, *v.r.* to imagine; to fancy; to conceive; to contrive; to plan; to invent; to find; to suppose; to surmise; to be imagined
Iman, Imam, *s.m.* iman, imam, imaum
Imanat, Imamat, *s.m.* imanate, imamate
Imaret, *s.m.* imaret (*Turkish inn*)
Imbécile, *adj. s.m.f.* imbecile, silly, foolish, stupid, crazy, idiotic; idiot, fool, oaf
Imbécilement, *adv.* foolishly, stupidly
Imbécillité, *s.f.* imbecility; silliness, foolish-
Imbéni, e, *adj.* unblessed [ness, folly, stupidity
Imberbe, *adj.* beardless; raw
Imbiber, *v.a.,* **S'**—, *v.r.* to imbibe, to soak; to
Imbibition, *s.f.* imbibition [imbue
Imboire, *v.a.* (*old*) to imbue; to become imbued
S'—, *v.r.* to be *or* become imbued [with
Imbricaire, *s.f.* (*bot.*) imbricaria
Imbricati-f, ve, *adj.* (*bot.*) imbricative
Imbrication, *s.f.* imbrication, overlapping

Imbricé, e, *adj.* imbricated [waterproof
Imbrifuge, *adj.* sheltering from the rain,
Imbrim, *s.m.* (*bird*) loon, great northern diver, immer *or* ember goose
Imbriquant, e, *adj.* imbricant, overlapping
Imbriqué, e, *adj.* imbricated
Imbroglio, *s.m.* imbroglio; intricacy, entanglement, complication, wheels within wheels, perplexity, confusion
Imbrûlable, *adj.* unburnable, unfit for burning,
Imbrûlé, e, *adj.* unburnt [not to be burnt
Imbu, e, *adj.* imbued, impressed
Imbuvable, *adj.* undrinkable
Imitable, *adj.* imitable, to be imitated
Imita-teur, trice, *adj. s.* imitative; imitator
Imitati-f, ve, *adj.* imitative
Imitation, *s.f.* imitation; mimicry [to be like
Imiter, *v.a.* to imitate; to mimic; to resemble,
S'—, *v.r.* to imitate *or* &c. oneself *or* each other; to be imitated *or* &c.
Immaculé, e, *adj.* immaculate; spotless
Immanent, e, *adj.* immanent; inherent; con-
Immangeable, *adj.* uneatable [stant
Immanquable, *adj.* infallible, certain, sure
Immanquablement, *adv.* infallibly, certainly
Immarcescible, *adj.* unfading; incorruptible
Immariable, *adj.* unmarriageable
Immatérialiser, *v.a.* to immaterialize
Immatérial-isme, -iste. *V.* page 3, § 1
Immatérialité, *s.f.* immateriality
Immatériel, le, *adj.* immaterial
Immatériellement, *adv.* immaterially
Immatriculation, *s.f.* matriculation; registering [registering
Immatricule, *s.f.* matriculation; enrolment;
Immatriculer, *v.a.* to matriculate; to enroll; to register
Immaturité, *s.f.* immaturity, unripeness
Immédiat, e, *adj.* immediate; direct; next
Immédiatement, *adv.* immediately
Immédiateté, *s.f.* immediateness
Immédité, e, *adj.* unmeditated
Immémorable, *adj.* immemorable
Immémoré, e, *adj.* unremembered
Immémorial, e, *adj.* immemorial
Immémorialement, *adv.* immemorially
Immense, *adj.* immense; unbounded; infinite; enormous; huge; vast; prodigious
Immensément, *adv.* immensely; an immense amount *or* quantity
Immensité, *s.f.* immensity; immense amount *or* quantity; boundlessness; boundless space
Immensurable, *adj.* immeasurable
Immerger, *v.a.* to immerge, to immerse, to plunge, to dip
S'—, *v.r.* to be immerged, to plunge, to sink
Immérité, e, *adj.* unmerited, undeserved; un-
Imméritoire, *adj.* unmeritorious [called for
Immersi-f, ve, *adj.* immersive
Immersion, *s.f.* immersion
Immesurable, *adj.* immeasurable
Immesuré, e, *adj.* unmeasured
Imméthodique, *adj.* unmethodical
Imméthodiquement, *adv.* unmethodically
Immeuble, *adj.* (*law*) immovable, real; — *s.m.* real estate, landed estate *or* property, estate, realty; house; fixture
Immigrant, e, *adj. s.* immigrant
Immigration, *s.f.* immigration
Immigrer, *v.n.* to immigrate
Imminemment, *adv.* imminently
Imminence, *s.f.* imminence
Imminent, e, *adj.* imminent, impending
Immiscer, *v.a.* to mix up; to blend. *S'—,* to meddle, to intermeddle, to interfere; to enter
Immiscibilité, *s.f.* immiscibility [(upon)
Immiscible, *adj.* immiscible
Immiséricorde, *s.f.* unmercifulness [fully
Immiséricordieusement, *adv.* unmerci-
Immiséricordieu-x, se, *adj.* unmerciful
Immission, *s.f.* immission
Immixtion, *s.f.* mixing up; blending; meddling, intermeddling, interference; entering (upon an inheritance)
Immobile, *adj.* immovable, motionless, still; unmoved; unshaken; stable; firm
Immobilement, *adv.* immovably
Immobili-er, ère, *adj.* (*law*) immovable, real, in *or* of real (*or* landed) estate (*or* property), of lands, landed; — *s.m.* (*obsolete*) landed property, land
Immobilièrement, *adv.* as (*or* in) real pro-
Immobilisation, *s.f.* realization [perty
Immobiliser, *v.a.* to realize
Immobilisme, *s.m.* fogyism
Immobiliste, *s.m.* fogy, old fogy; — *adj.* of fogyism, over-conservative
Immobilité, *s.f.* immobility, immovability, immovableness; stillness; stability; firmness; permanency; impassiveness, inertness, indolence, apathy [rateness
Immodération, *s.f.* immoderation, immode-
Immodéré, e, *adj.* immoderate, intemperate, excessive, unreasonable, violent
Immodérément, *adv.* immoderately, intemperately, excessively
Immodeste, *adj.* immodest, indecent
Immodestement, *adv.* immodestly, indecently
Immodestie, *s.f.* immodesty, indecency
Immolateur, *s.m.* immolator, sacrificer
Immolation, *s.f.* immolation, sacrifice
Immoler, *v.a.* to immolate, to sacrifice; to slay; (*fig.*) to ridicule
Immonde, *adj.* unclean, impure, foul
Immondices, *s.f.pl.* dirt, filth, dirty rubbish; (*theol.*) uncleanness, impurity
Immondicité, *s.f.* uncleanness, impurity
Immoral, e, *adj.* immoral
Immoralement, *adv.* immorally
Immoralité, *s.f.* immorality
Immortalisation, *s.f.* immortalization
Immortaliser, *v.a.* to immortalize
Immortalité, *s.f.* immortality
Immortel, le, *adj. s.m.f.* immortal; — *s.f.* (*bot.*) everlasting-flower, immortelle
Immortellement, *adv.* immortally
Immortification, *s.f.* immortification
Immortifié, e, *adj.* unmortified
Immuabilité, *s.f.* (*old*) *V.* **Immutabilité**
Immuable, *adj.* immutable, unchangeable
Immuablement, *adv* immutably, unchangeably
Immunité, *s.f.* immunity [ably
Immuration, *s.f.* immuring, immurement
Immusical, e, *adj.* unmusical
Immutabilité, *s.f.* immutability, unchangeableness
Impact, *s.m.* (*mech.*) impact [ableness
Impaction, *s.f.* (*surg.*) impacted fracture [gous
Impair, e, *adj.* odd, uneven; (*anat.*) single, azy-
Impairement, *adv.* oddly, unevenly; (*anat.*) singly
Impalpabilité. *V.* page 3, § 1 [singly
Impalpable, *adj.* impalpable
Impanateur, *s.m.* (*theol.*) impanator
Impanation, *s.f.* (*theol.*) impanation
Impané, e, *part. adj.* (*theol.*) impanated, impanate
Impaner, *v.a.* (*theol.*) to impanate [nate
Impardonnable, *adj.* unpardonable
Impardonnablement, *adv.* unpardonably
Impardonné, e, *adj.* unpardoned, unforgiven
Imparfait, e, *adj.* imperfect; incomplete; unfinished; defective; — *s.m.* imperfection; (*gram.*) imperfect tense, imperfect
Imparfaitement, *adv.* imperfectly
Imparipenné, e, Imparipinné, e, *adj.* (*bot.*) imparipinnate [imparisyllabic
Imparisyllabe, Imparisyllabique, *adj.*
Imparité, *s.f.* imparity, oddness, unevenness
Impartagé, e, *adj.* undivided; unshared
Impartageable, *adj.* indivisible
Impartial, e, *adj.* impartial
Impartialement, *adv.* impartially
Impartialité, *s.f.* impartiality
Impasse, *s.f.* blind alley; lane without egress, street without a thoroughfare; court; post *or* office *or* charge from which there is no chance

of promotion; difficult position without issue, inextricable difficulty, entanglement, fix; (*at whist*) finesse [ness, impassiveness; calmness
Impassibilité, *s.f.* impassibility, impassible-
Impassible, *adj.* impassible, impassive, unmoved; calm, tranquil
Impassiblement, *adv.* impassively; calmly
Impastation, *s.f.* impastation
Impatiemment, *adv.* impatiently; eagerly
Impatience, *s.f.* impatience; eagerness, longing; anxiety; restlessness; fidget; hastiness
Impatient, e, *adj.* impatient; eager; anxious; restless, fidgety; hasty, passionate; — *s.f.* (*bot.*) touch-me-not [some, irksome, wearisome
Impatientant, e, *part. adj.* provoking, tire-
Impatienté, e, *part. adj.* provoked, out of patience
Impatienter, *v.a.* to put out of patience, to make impatient, to provoke, to tease, to tire
S'—, *v.r* to fret, to get impatient, to lose patience; to grow angry [coming master
Impatronisation, *s.f.* impatronization; be-
Impatroniser, *v.a.* to impatronize
S'—, *v.r.* to gain *or* get authority, to usurp *or* exercise authority, to become master; to get a footing; to make oneself at home
Impayable, *adj.* invaluable; worth any money; exceedingly funny; capital, excellent, admirable; inimitable; precious; extraordinary; passing strange; very fine indeed
Impayé, e, *adj.* unpaid
Impeccabilité, *s.f.* impeccability
Impeccable, *adj.* impeccable; infallible
Impeccance, *s.f.* impeccancy
Impécunieu-x, se, *adj.* (*old*) impecunious
Impécuniosité, *s.f.* (*old*) impecuniosity
Impédiments, *s.m.pl.* (*mil.*) impediments
Impénétrabilité, *s.f.* impenetrability; imperviousness; inscrutableness; closeness
Impénétrable, *adj.* impenetrable; impervious; unfathomable, inscrutable; close; secret
Impénétrablement, *adv.* impenetrably
Impénétré, e, *adj.* unpenetrated; unfathomed
Impénitence, *s.f.* impenitence
Impénitent, e, *adj. s.* impenitent [ments
Impense, *s.f.* expense for repairs *or* improve-
Impenné, e, *adj. s.m.* (*zool.*) impennate
Impérati-f, ve, *adj.* imperative; — *s.m.* (*gram.*) imperative mood, imperative
Impérativement, *adv.* imperatively
Impératoire, *s.f.* (*bot.*) masterwort
Impérator, *s.m.* (*Rom. ant.*) imperator
Impératrice, *s.f.* empress
Imperceptibilité. *V.* page 3, § 1
Imperceptible, *adj.* imperceptible
Imperceptiblement, *adv.* imperceptibly
Imperdable, *adj.* that cannot be lost, not to be
Imperfectibilité, *s.f.* imperfectibility [lost
Imperfectible, *adj.* imperfectible
Imperfectiblement, *adv.* imperfectibly
Imperfection, *s.f.* imperfection [proved
Imperfectionné, e, *adj.* unperfected; unim-
Imperforation, *s.f.* imperforation
Imperforé, e, *adj.* imperforate, imperforated
Impérial, e, *adj.m.f.* imperial; — *s.m.* imperialist; — *s.f.* imperial; (*of omnibuses*, &c.) outside, top, roof; (*of beds*) tester, canopy; (*com.*) imperial serge; (*bot.*) crown imperial; imperial plum; (*game at cards*) all-fours
Impérialement, *adv.* imperially
Impérialiser, *v.a.* to imperialize
Impérialisme, *s.m.* imperialism [perialistic
Impérialiste, *s.m.f.* imperialist; — *adj.* im-
Impérieusement, *adv.* imperiously: urgently
Impérieu-x, se, *adj.* imperious; urgent, [pressing
Impériosité, *s.f.* imperiousness
Impérissabilité, *s.f.* imperishableness
Impérissable, *adj.* imperishable, undying
Impérissablement, *adv.* imperishably [rance
Impéritie, *s.f.* unskilfulness, incapacity, igno-
Imperméabilisation, *s.f.* rendering impermeable
Imperméabiliser, *v.a.* to render impermeable
Imperméabilité. *V* page 3, § 1
Imperméable, *adj.m.f.*, *s.m.* impermeable, impenetrable, impervious; waterproof; proof, tight. — *à l'eau*, waterproof; watertight. — *à l'air*, airtight [perviously
Imperméablement, *adv.* impermeably, im-
Impermutabilité, *s.f.* inexchangeability
Impermutable, *adj.* unexchangeable
Impersonnalité, *s.f.* impersonality
Impersonnel, le, *adj.* impersonal; — *s.m.* impersonal verb
Impersonnellement, *adv.* impersonally
Impersuadé, e, *adj.* unpersuaded
Impersuasible, *adj.* impersuasible
Impertinemment, *adv.* impertinently; improperly; rudely, uncivilly, pertly
Impertinence, *s.f.* impertinence; impropriety; rudeness, incivility, pertness; impertinent thing
Impertinent, e, *adj. s.* impertinent; improper; rude, uncivil, saucy, pert; conceited; impertinent fellow *or* thing, saucy baggage
Imperturbabilité, *s.f* imperturbability
Imperturbable, *adj* imperturbable
Imperturbablement, *adv.* imperturbably
Impesé, e, *adj.* unweighed
Impétigineu-x, se, *adj.* (*med.*) impetiginous
Impétigo, *s.m.* (*med.*) impetigo
Impétrabilité, *s.f.* impetrability
Impétrable, *adj.* (*law*) impetrable, obtainable
Impétrant, e, *s.m.f.* grantee; patentee; (successful) candidate, graduate, recipient
Impétration, *s.f.* (*law*) impetration, obtainment
Impétrer, *v.a.* (*law*) to impetrate, to obtain
Impétueusement, *adv.* impetuously [fiery
Impétueu-x, se, *adj.* impetuous; violent;
Impétuosité, *s.f.* impetuosity; violence; force, impetus; fire [habited
Impeuplé, e, *adj.* without population, unin-
Impey, *s.m.* *V.* **Lophophore**
Impie, *adj.* impious, ungodly; infidel; — *s.m.f.* impious man *or* woman, ungodly person; infidel [profanation
Impiété, *s.f.* impiety; ungodliness, irreligion;
Impitié, *s.f.* (*old*) pitilessness
Impitoyable, *adj.* pitiless, unmerciful, unsparing; inexorable; unrelenting, relentless
Impitoyablement, *adv.* pitilessly, unmercifully, unsparingly; inexorably; unrelentingly
Implacabilité, *s.f.* implacability
Implacable, *adj.* implacable
Implacablement, *adv.* implacably
Implantation, *s.f.* implantation; planting
Implanter, *v.a.* to implant; to plant; to sow; to fix; to lodge; to insert, to place; to ingraft
S'—, *v.r.* to take root; to grow; to be im-
Implexe, *adj.* implex, intricate [planted, &c.
Impliable, *adj.* unbendable, inflexible; unfoldable
Implication, *s.f.* implication; contradiction
Implicite, *adj.* implicit; implied
Implicitement, *adv.* implicitly
Impliquer, *v.a.* to implicate; to involve; to imply; to infer; — *v.n.* to imply *or* involve contradiction, to be contradictory
Implorable, *adj.* implorable
Implora-teur, trice, *s.m.f.* implorer
Imploration, *s.f.* imploration, supplication
Implorer, *v.a.* to implore; to beseech; to crave; to call for
Imploreu-r, se, *s.m.f.* implorer
Imployable, *adj.* *V.* **Impliable**
Impoli, e, *adj.* unpolished, impolite, uncourteous, uncivil, rude, coarse [refined
Impolicé, e, *adj.* uncivilized, unpolished, un-
Impoliment, *adv.* impolitely, uncivilly, rudely
Impolitesse, *s.f.* impoliteness, incivility, rudeness; impolite thing. *Faire une —*, to behave uncivilly
Impolitique, *adj.* impolitic; — *s.f.* impolicy
Impolitiquement, *adv.* impoliticly

Impollué, e, *adj.* unpolluted
Impondérabilité, *s.f.* imponderability
Impondérable, *adj.* imponderable
Impondéré, e, *adj.* unweighed
Impopulaire, *adj.* unpopular
Impopulairement, *adv.* unpopularly
Impopularité, *s.f.* unpopularity
Imporeu-x, se, *adj.* imporous
Imporosité, *s.f.* imporosity
Importable, *adj.* importable
Importance, *s.f.* importance, consequence, moment; worth, note; weight; consequentialness. *D'—*, of importance *or* &c., important, weighty, eminent; consequential; famously, soundly, sharply, heartily, at a high rate. *Avoir de l'—*, to be of importance *or* of consequence. *Faire l'homme d'—*, to set up for a man of importance, to play the man of consequence, to be consequential
Important, e, *adj.* important, of consequence, of moment; main, chief, essential; consequential; overbearing. *Peu —*, of little consequence, immaterial
Important, *s.m.* important *or* main *or* chief point, essential part; important *or* consequential man. *Faire l'—, faire l'homme d'importance, V.* **Importance**
Importa-teur, trice, *s.m.f.* importer; — *adj.* [importing
Importation, *s.f.* importation; import
Importer, *v.a.* to import; — *v.n.* to concern, to be important, to be of importance *or* consequence; to signify, to matter. *N'importe*, no matter, it is *or* makes no matter, it matters not, it does not matter, it does not signify, never mind; any ... (*N'importe comment*, anyhow; *N'importe où*, anywhere; *N'importe quand*, anywhen, at any time; *N'importe quel* ..., any ...; *N'importe qui*, anybody, anyone; *N'importe quoi*, anything, no matter what.) *Peu —*, it matters little, it is immaterial, no matter. *Qu'importe?* what does it signify *or* matter? what of that? *Que m'importe?* what is it (*or* [that) to me?
S'—, *v.r.* to be imported
Importeu-r, se, *s.m.f.* (*old*) *V.* **Importateur**
Importun, e, *adj.* importunate; obtrusive; troublesome; inconvenient; — *s.m.f.* importunate *or* troublesome person, bore; intruder; hanger-on; dun
Importunément, *adv.* importunately
Importuner, *v.a.* to importune; to trouble; to annoy; to pester; to bore; to weary; to intrude upon; to dun
Importunité, *s.f.* importunity
Imposable, *adj.* taxable; ratable, assessable
Imposé, e, *part. adj.* imposed, &c. (*V.* **Imposer**); chargeable; — *s.m.f.* tax-payer; rate-payer
Imposer, *v.a.n.* to impose; to force (upon); to lay on; to inflict; to give; to confer; to obtrude; to command; to tax; to rate, to assess; to charge; to awe; to overpower. *En —*, to overawe; to impose upon, to deceive
S'—, *v.r.* to force oneself (upon); to obtrude, to be obtrusive; to impose oneself *or* on oneself; to impose a tax on oneself; to assess oneself; to be imposed *or* &c. *S'en —*, to de- [ceive oneself
Imposeur, *s.m.* imposer
Imposition, *s.f.* imposition; imposing; infliction; giving; tax, impost; assessment
Impossibilité, *s.f.* impossibility. *De toute —*, quite *or* utterly impossible
Impossible, *adj.* impossible; fabulous, extravagant, beyond all reason; outrageous; entirely out of the way; ineligible, altogether out of the question; inadmissible; unacceptable; most absurd; — *s.m.* (*L'—*) (an) impossibility, impossibilities, impossible things; o.'s utmost; a great deal, an enormous amount *or* quantity, lots, no end (of); enormously. *Par —*, supposing an impossibility, contrary to all probability. *A l'— nul n'est tenu*, there is no doing impossibilities

Impossiblement, *adv.* impossibly
Imposte, *s.f.* (*arch.*) impost; moulding [false
Imposteur, *s.m., adj.m.* impostor; deceitful;
Imposture, *s.f.* imposture; imposition; deception; falsehood; fallacy; illusion
Impôt, *s.m.* tax, impost; taxation, taxes. — *personnel et mobilier*, house-tax
Impotable, *adj.* impotable
Impotence, *s.f.* impotence, infirmity
Impotent, e, *adj. s.* impotent, infirm
Impraticabilité, *s.f.* impracticability
Impraticable, *adj.* impracticable; unmanageable; impassable; uninhabitable; unbearable [untrodden, unfrequented
Impratiqué, e, *adj.* unpractised; unbeaten,
Impréca-teur, trice, *s.m.f.* imprecator; — *adj.* imprecating
Imprécation, *s.f.* imprecation, curse
Imprécatoire, *adj.* imprecatory [tion
†**Imprégnable,** *adj.* susceptible of impregna-
†**Imprégnation,** *s.f.* impregnation
†**Imprégner,** *v.a.* to impregnate. *S'—*, to become impregnated
Imprémeditation, *s.f.* unpremeditatedness
Imprémédité, e, *adj.* unpremeditated
Imprenable, *adj.* impregnable; untakable, not to be taken [ness
Impréparation, *s.f.* unpreparedness, unreadi-
Impréparé, e, *adj.* unprepared, unready
Impresario, *s.m.* (*an Italian word*) impresario, theatrical director *or* manager, showman
Imprescriptibilité, *s.f.* imprescriptibility, indefeasibility [feasible
Imprescriptible, *adj.* imprescriptible, inde-
Imprescriptiblement, *adv.* imprescriptibly, indefeasibly
Impressibilité, *s.f.* impressibility
Impressible, *adj.* impressible
Impressi-f, ve, *adj.* impressive, striking
Impression, *s.f.* impression; mark; trace; printing; print; issue; edition; (*paint.*) priming, dead-colouring. *Faute d'—*, error of the press, typographical error, misprint. *Être à l'—*, to be printing, to be in the printer's hands
Impressionnabilité, *s.f.* impressionability, impressionableness
Impressionnable, *adj.* impressionable, impressible, impressive, sensitive, excitable, nervous
Impressionner, *v.a.* to impress, to make an impression upon, to move, to affect
S'—, *v.r.* to be impressed *or* &c.
Impressivement, *adv.* impressively
Imprévision, *s.f.* want of prevision
Imprévoyable, *adj.* that cannot be foreseen, not to be foreseen [foresight
Imprévoyance, *s.f.* improvidence, want of
Imprévoyant, e, *adj.* improvident, wanting foresight
Imprévu, e, *adj.* unforeseen, unexpected; — *s.m.* unforeseen accidents, unexpected events; adventure, surprise; unexpectedness; sudden determination
Imprimable, *adj.* printable, worth printing
Imprimatur, *s.m.* imprimatur
Imprimé, e, *part. adj.* imprinted, &c. (*V.* **Imprimer**); printed, in print; — *s.m.* printed paper, printed book, printed document, print
Imprimer, *v.a.* to imprint; to impress; to print; to stamp; to letter; to impart; to communicate; to give; (*paint.*) to prime; to stain. *Se faire —*, to appear in print, to set up for an author
S'—, *v.r.* to be printing; to be printed *or* &c.
Imprimerie, *s.f.* printing; printing-office *or* house; press
Imprimeur, *s.m.* printer; pressman
Imprimure, *s.f.* (*paint.*) priming [hood
Improbabilité, *s.f.* improbability, unlikeli-
Improbable, *adj.* improbable, unlikely
Improbablement, *adv.* improbably
Improbance, *s.f.* inconclusiveness

Improbant, e, *adj.* inconclusive, unconvincing [**bateur**
Improba-teur, trice, *adj. s. V.* **Désappro-**
Improbati-f, ve, *adj.*, **Improbation,** *s.f.*, **Improbativement,** *adv. V.* **Désapprobatif,** &c., &c.
Improbe, *adj.* dishonest
Improbité, *s.f.* improbity, dishonesty
Improduc-teur, trice, *adj.* unproducing, unproductive
Improductibilité, *s.f.* unproducibleness
Improductible, *adj.* unproducible
Improducti-f, ve, *adj.* unproductive
Improductivement, *adv.* unproductively
Improductivité, *s.f.* unproductiveness
Improduit, e, *adj.* unproduced
Improfitable, *adj.* unprofitable
Impromptu, e, *adj.* impromptu, extemporary, extemporaneous, extempore, unprepared; — *s.m.* impromptu, extempore, thing unprepared; — *adv.* impromptu, extemporarily, extempore, without preparation
Impromptuaire, *s.m.f.* maker of impromptus
Impromulgué, e, *adj.* unpromulgated
Imprononçable, *adj.* unpronounceable
Impropice, *adj.* unpropitious
Impropre, *adj.* improper; wrong; unfit (for)
Improprement, *adv.* improperly
Impropriété, *s.f.* impropriety; unfitness
Improspère, *adj.* unprosperous
Improtégé, e, *adj.* unprotected
Improuvable, *adj.* unprovable
Improuvé, e, *part. adj.* disapproved, blamed; — *adj.* unproved
Improuver, *v.a.* to disapprove, to blame
Improvisa-teur, trice, *s.m.f.* improvisator, improvisatress, improviser, extemporizer; — *adj.* improvising, extemporizing
Improvisation, *s.f.* improvisation, extemporization, extempore
Improvisé, e, *part. adj.* improvised, &c. (*V.* **Improviser**); extemporaneous, extemporary, extempore, unprepared
Improviser, *v.a.n.* to improvise, to extemporize, to speak *or* deliver extempore
S'—, *v.r.* to be improvised, &c.
Improviste (A l'), *adv.* unexpectedly, unawares; aback; suddenly, on a sudden
Imprudemment, *adv.* imprudently
Imprudence, *s.f.* imprudence; indiscretion; imprudent thing, folly, indiscreet action
Imprudent, e, *adj.* imprudent; indiscreet; heedless; — *s.m.f.* ditto person
Impubère, *adj.* impuberal; — *s.m.f.* child
Impuberté, *s.f.* impuberty
Impubliable, *adj.* unpublishable
Impudemment, *adv.* impudently
Impudence, *s.f.* impudence; piece of impudence
Impudent, e, *adj.* impudent; — *s.m.f.* impudent person *or* fellow, saucy creature, brazenface [dence, shamelessness
Impudeur, *s.f.* immodesty, indecency; impu-
Impudicité, *s.f.* unchastity, lewdness; unchaste *or* lewd act
Impudique, *adj.* immodest, lewd, unchaste
Impudiquement, *adv.* immodestly, lewdly
†Impugner, *v.a.* to impugn
Impuissance, *s.f.* powerlessness; inability; impotency, impotence [effectual; impotent
Impuissant, e, *adj.* powerless; unable; in-
Impulseur, *s.m.* impeller; — *adj.m.* impelling
Impulsi-f, ve, *adj.* impulsive
Impulsion, *s.f.* impulse, impulsion; impetus
Impulvérisé, e, *adj.* unpulverized
Impunément, *adv.* with impunity; harmlessly, without suffering for it; (*old, poet.*) without vengeance
Impuni, e, *adj.* unpunished
Impunité, *s.f.* impunity
Impur, e, *adj.* impure; foul, unclean; unchaste
Impurement, *adv.* impurely; unchastely
Impureté, *s.f.* impurity; obscenity
Impurifié, e, *adj.* unpurified
Imputabilité, *s.f.* imputability, imputableness
Imputable, *adj.* imputable; chargeable
Imputati-f, ve, *adj.* imputative
Imputation, *s.f.* imputation; charge; deduction
Imputer, *v.a.* to impute, to ascribe; to charge; to deduct [imputed *or* &c.
S'—, *v.r.* to impute *or* &c. to oneself; to be
Imputeu-r, se, *s.m.f.* imputer
Imputréfiable, *adj.* unputrefiable
Imputréfié, e, *adj.* unputrefied
Imputrescibilité, *s.f.* imputrescibility
Imputrescible, *adj.* imputrescible
Inabordable, *adj.* inaccessible, unapproachable
Inabordé, e, *adj.* unapproached, unvisited
Inabrité, e, *adj.* unsheltered
Inabrogé, e, *adj.* unabrogated, unrepealed
Inabsou-s, te, *adj.* unabsolved
Inabstinence, *s.f.* inabstinence
Inabstinent, e, *adj.* inabstinent
Inacceptable, *adj.* unacceptable
Inaccepté, e, *adj.* unaccepted, declined
Inaccessibilité, *s.f.* inaccessibility
Inaccessible, *adj.* inaccessible; unattainable
Inacclimatable, *adj.* unacclimatizable
Inacclimaté, e, *adj.* unacclimatized
Inaccommodable, *adj.* unaccommodable, not to be settled *or* arranged *or* made up [attended
†Inaccompagné, e, *adj.* unaccompanied, un-
Inaccomplissement, *s.m.* unaccomplishment
Inaccord, *s.m.* false concord
Inaccordable, *adj.* irreconcilable; ungrantable; unallowable, inadmissible; untunable
Inaccostable, *adj.* inaccessible [unusual
Inaccoutumé, e, *adj.* unaccustomed; unused;
Inachevé, e, *adj.* unfinished, uncompleted
Inacquérable, *adj.* unacquirable
Inacti-f, ve, *adj.* inactive; unemployed
Inaction, *s.f.* inaction; indolence
Inactivement, *adv.* inactively
Inactivité, *s.f.* inactivity
***Inadéquat, e,** *adj.* (*philos.*) inadequate
Inadhérent, e, *adj.* inadherent
Inadmis, e, *adj.* unadmitted
Inadmissibilité, *s.f.* inadmissibility
Inadmissible, *adj.* inadmissible
Inadvertamment, *adv.* inadvertently
Inadvertance, *s.f.* inadvertence, oversight
Inaffectation, *s.f.* inaffectation
Inaffecté, e, *adj.* unaffected
Inaguerri, e, *adj.* untrained *or* uninured to war; undisciplined; uninured, unaccustomed, unused
Inailé, e, *adj.* (*zool.*) unwinged, impennate
Inaliénabilité, *s.f.* inalienability, indefeasibility [untransferable
Inaliénable, *adj.* inalienable, indefeasible,
Inaliéné, e, *adj.* unalienated
Inalliable, *adj.* that cannot be alloyed; unalliable; incompatible
Inalpage, *s.m.* ascent (*in the Alps*)
Inaltérabilité, *s.f.* inalterability, unalterableness; unchangeableness
Inaltérable, *adj.* unalterable; unchangeable; unimpairable; proof (against ...), (...-)proof
Inaltération, *s.f.* unimpairment [impaired
Inaltéré, e, *adj.* unaltered; unchanged; un-
Inamabilité, *s.f.* unamiableness; unkindness
Inamendable, *adj.* unimprovable
Inamical, e, *adj.* unfriendly
Inamicalement, *adv.* in an unfriendly manner
Inamissibilité, *s.f.* inamissibility
Inamissible, *adj.* inamissible [nency
Inamovibilité, *s.f.* irremovability; perma-
Inamovible, *adj.* irremovable; permanent, for life
Inamusable, *adj.* unamusable
Inanimation, *s.f.* inanimation [insensible
Inanimé, e, *adj.* inanimate, lifeless; spiritless;
Inanisation, *s.f.* (*med.*) process of starvation
Inanité, *s.f.* inanity, emptiness
Inanitiation, *s.f. V.* **Inanisation**
Inanition, *s.f.* inanition, starvation
Inapaisable, *adj.* unappeasable
Inapaisé, e, *adj.* unappeased [ceptible
Inapercevable, *adj.* unperceivable, imper-

Inaperçu, e, *adj.* unperceived, unseen
Inapparent, e, *adj.* unapparent
Inappauvri, e, *adj.* unimpoverished
Inappétence, *s.f.* (*med.*) inappetence, inappetency
Inapplicabilité, *s.f.* inapplicability
Inapplicable, *adj.* inapplicable; inapposite; irrelevant; impracticable; unpractical
Inapplication, *s.f.* inapplication, heedlessness
Inappliqué, e, *adj.* unapplied; inattentive, indolent, heedless, careless
Inappréciable, *adj.* inappreciable; inestimable, invaluable; imperceptible
Inappréciablement, *adv.* inappreciably; invaluably; imperceptibly
Inappréciation, *s.f.* inappreciation
Inapprécié, e, *adj.* unappreciated
Inapprenable, *adj.* unlearnable
Inapprêté, e, *adj.* unprepared; uncooked; undressed
Inapprivoisable, *adj.* untamable
Inapprivoisé, e, *adj.* untamed, wild
Inapprouvé, e, *adj.* unapproved
Inapte, *adj.* unfit, inapt; unqualified
Inaptitude, *s.f.* inaptitude, unfitness; disqualification
Inarticulation, *s.f.* inarticulation
Inarticulé, e, *adj.* inarticulate
Inartificiel, le, *adj.* inartificial
Inartificiellement, *adv.* inartificially
Inartificieu-x, se, *adj.* artless, guileless
Inassermenté, e, *adj.* unsworn
Inasservi, e, *adj.* unenslaved, unsubjected, unsubdued, unconquered
Inassiduité, *s.f.* inassiduity
Inassiégeable, *adj.* unbesiegeable
†Inassignable, *adj.* unassignable
Inassisté, e, *adj.* unassisted
Inassorti, e, *adj.* unassorted
Inassoupi, e, *adj.* sleepless
Inassouvi, e, *adj.* unsatiated
Inassujetti, e, *adj.* *V.* **Inasservi**
Inassuré, e, *adj.* uninsured; unsecured; insecure, unsafe; unsteady; uncertain
Inattaquable, *adj.* unassailable; unimpeachable; unobjectionable; unquestionable; unactionable
Inattaqué, e, *adj.* unattacked; unassailed; unaffected
Inattendu, e, *adj.* unexpected; unforeseen
Inattenti-f, ve, *adj.* inattentive; heedless, careless; neglectful
Inattention, *s.f.* inattention; carelessness; neglect; thoughtlessness
Inattesté, e, *adj.* unattested
Inattraction, *s.f.* inattraction
Inaugural, e, *adj.* inaugural
Inaugura-teur, trice, *s.m.f.* inaugurator, inauguratress; — *adj.* inaugurating
Inauguration, *s.f.* inauguration
Inaugurer, *v.a.* to inaugurate
Inauration, *s.f.* inauration
Inauthenticité, *s.f.* inauthenticity
Inauthentique, *adj.* unauthentic
Inautorisé, e, *adj.* unauthorized
Inaverti, e, *adj.* uninformed; unwarned
Inavouable, *adj.* unavowable
Inavoué, e, *adj.* unavowed
Inca, *s.m.* Inca (*of Peru*)
Incalcinable, *adj.* uncalcinable
Incalciné, e, *adj.* uncalcined
Incalculable, *adj.* incalculable; innumerable
Incalculablement, *adv.* incalculably
Incalculé, e, *adj.* uncalculated, untold
Incamérateur, *s.m.* incamerator
Incamération, *s.f.* incameration
Incamérer, *v.a.* to incamerate
Incandescence, *s.f.* incandescence, white heat; burning, ardour, fieriness, overexcitement, violence
Incandescent, e, *adj.* incandescent, white-hot, at a white heat; burning, ardent, fiery, overexcited, violent
Incane, *adj.* (*bot.*) incanous
Incantation, *s.f.* incantation
Incapable, *adj.* incapable, unable, unfit; incompetent; unqualified; inefficient
Incapacité, *s.f.* incapacity, inability, unfitness; incompetence, disability; disablement; disqualification; inefficiency. *Frapper d'—*, to incapacitate; to disqualify
Incarcération, *s.f.* incarceration, imprisonment, confinement; (*surg.*) incarceration
Incarcéré, e, *part. adj.* incarcerated, imprisoned, confined; (*surg.*) incarcerated
Incarcérer, *v.a.* to incarcerate, to imprison, to confine. *S'—*, (*surg.*) to become strangulated
Incarnadin, e, *adj.* **Incarnadin,** *s.m.* *V.* **Incarnat**
Incarnat, e, *adj.* flesh-coloured, rosy; — *s.m.* carnation, flesh-colour, rosy colour
Incarnation, *s.f.* incarnation; (*of nails*) growing in, ingrowing
Incarné, e, *adj.* incarnate; (*surg.*) ingrowing (*nail*)
Incarner (S'), *v.r.* to become incarnate; (*of nails*) to grow in
Incartade, *s.f.* insult; quarrel; blowing-up; prank, freak, frolic; extravagance
Incassable, *adj.* unbreakable
Incélébré, e, *adj.* uncelebrated
Incendiaire, *s.m.f. adj.* incendiary
Incendie, *s.m.* fire; burning; conflagration. — *par malveillance*, — *volontaire*, incendiary fire, arson
Incendié, e, *part. adj.* burnt, &c. (*V.* **Incendier**); — *s.m.f.* sufferer from fire
Incendier, *v.a.* to burn, to burn down; to set fire to, to set on fire, to fire
S'—, *v.r.* to set fire to o.'s own house
Incération, *s.f.* inceration
Incérémonieu-x, se, *adj.* unceremonious
Incertain, e, *adj.* uncertain; doubtful; indistinct; vague; faint; undecided; undetermined; unsettled; unsteady; inconstant
Incertain, *s.m.* uncertainty, uncertain, that which is uncertain; doubtful fact; feeling of uncertainty; (*in Exchange language*) uncertain price
Incertainement, *adv.* uncertainly, with uncertainty, doubtfully
Incertifié, e, *adj.* uncertified
Incertitude, *s.f.* uncertainty, incertitude; doubt; suspense; hesitation; unsettledness; unsteadiness; instability; inconstancy
Incessamment, *adv.* immediately, at once; shortly; incessantly
Incessant, e, *adj.* incessant
Incessibilité, *s.f.* inalienability
Incessible, *adj.* inalienable, untransferable
Inceste, *s.m.* incest; — *s.m.f.* (*obsolete*) incestuous person; — *adj.* incestuous
Incestueusement, *adv.* incestuously
Incestueu-x, se, *adj.* incestuous; — *s.m.f.* incestuous person
Inchangé, e, *adj.* unchanged
Inchantable, *adj.* unsingable
Incharitable, *adj.* uncharitable
Incharitablement, *adv.* uncharitably
Incharité, *s.f.* uncharitableness
Inchasteté, *s.f.* unchastity
Inchâtié, e, *adj.* unchastised; unchastened
Inchavirable, *adj.* uncapsizable
‡Inchoati-f, ve, *adj.* (*gram.*) inchoative, inceptive; — *s.m.* inchoative *or* inceptive verb
‡Inchrétien, ne, *adj.* unchristian
‡Inchrétiennement, *adv.* unchristianly
Incidemment, *adv.* incidentally
Incidence, *s.f.* incidence
Incident, *s.m.* incident; occurrence; difficulty; objection; cavil
Incident, e, *adj.* incidental, incident; (*gram.*) subordinate, incident; (*opt.*) incident
Incidente, *s.f.* (*gram.*) subordinate sentence, incident proposition
Incidentel, le, *adj.* incidental
Incidenter, *v.n.* to raise incidents; to raise difficulties *or* objections, to cavil
Incinération, *s.f.* incineration
Incinérer, *v.a.* to incinerate
Incipit, *s.m.* incipit
Incirconcis, e, *adj. s.* uncircumcised
Incirconcision, *s.f.* uncircumcision
Incirconscrit, e, *adj.* uncircumscribed

Incise, *s.f.* (*gram.*) subordinate sentence
Inciser, *v.a.* to incise, to make an incision in, to cut, to gash; to tap (*a tree*)
Inciseur, *s.m.* (*instr.*) incisor
Incisi-f, ve, *adj.* incisive, cutting, sharp; — *s.f.* incisive tooth, incisor
Incision, *s.f.* incision, cut
Incisivement, *adv.* cuttingly, sharply
Incisure, *s.f.* incisure
Incitabilité, *s.f.* incitability
Incitable, *adj.* incitable
Incitant, e, *adj.*, **Incitant,** *s.m.* incitant
Incita-teur, trice, *s.m.f.* inciter; — *adj.* inciting [ment; instigation; stimulus
Incitation, *s.f.* incitation, incitement; induce-
Incitement, *s.m.* incitement
Inciter, *v.a.* to incite; to induce; to entice; to instigate; to stimulate; to stir up
Incivil, e, *adj.* uncivil
Incivilement, *adv.* uncivilly
Incivilisable, *adj.* uncivilizable
Incivilisé, e, *adj.* uncivilized, barbarous
Incivilité, *s.f.* incivility
Incivique, *adj.* uncivic, unpatriotic
Inciviquement, *adv.* uncivically
Incivisme, *s.m.* incivism
Inclassable, *adj.* unclassifiable, nondescript
Inclémence, *s.f.* inclemency
Inclément, e, *adj.* inclement
Inclinaison, *s.f.* inclination; incline; gradient; slope; dip, dipping
Inclination, *s.f.* inclination; bowing; bow; nodding; nod; stooping; propensity, proneness; passion, love, attachment; lover; lady-love
Incliner, *v.a.n.*, **S'—,** *v.r.* to incline; to bend; to bow; to bow down; to nod; to hang down; to stoop; to tilt; to lower; to depress; to lean; to recline; to slope; to dip; to verge; to border (upon); to be inclined, to be disposed
Inclure, *v.a.* to include; to enclose; to insert; to contain; to imply
Inclus, e, *part. adj.* included, enclosed, &c. (*V.* **Inclure**). *Ci-* —, enclosed; herewith, sent herewith. *Mettre ci-* —, to enclose
Incluse, *s.f.* enclosed letter, enclosed
Inclusi-f, ve, *adj.* inclusive
Inclusion, *s.f.* inclusion
Inclusive, *s.f.* (*eccl.*) admittance
Inclusivement, *adv.* inclusively
Incoagulable, *adj.* uncoagulable
Incoercible, *adj.* incoercible
Incognito, *adv. s.m.* incognito, incognita
Incognoscible, *adj.* incognizable
Incohéremment, *adv.* incoherently
Incohérence, *s.f.* incoherence
Incohérent, e, *adj.* incoherent
Incohésion, *s.f.* incohesion
Incolore, *adj.* colourless
Incoloré, e, *adj.* uncoloured
Incombant, e, *adj.* incumbent [(upon)
Incomber, *v.n.* to be incumbent; to fall, to lie
Incombustibilité, *s.f.* incombustibility
Incombustible, *adj.* incombustible
Incommensurabilité. *V.* page 3, § 1
Incommensurable, *adj.* incommensurable; boundless
Incommerçable, *adj.* unnegotiable
Incommodant, e, *part. adj.* incommoding, troublesome, annoying, tiresome
Incommode, *adj.* incommodious; inconvenient; unhandy; uncomfortable; uneasy; troublesome, annoying, importunate, disagreeable, tiresome
Incommodé, e, *adj.* indisposed, unwell, poorly; (*of ships*) distressed, in distress; — *part.* incommoded, &c. (*V.* **Incommoder**)
Incommodément, *adv.* incommodiously; inconveniently; uncomfortably
Incommoder, *v.a.* to incommode; to inconvenience; to trouble; to annoy; to disturb; to embarrass; to impair; to disable; to make unwell, to disagree with; to interrupt, to intercept, to obstruct, to hinder

Incommodité, *s.f.* incommodity; inconvenience; uncomfortableness; discomfort; trouble; annoyance; embarrassment; ailment, indisposition; infirmity; (*nav.*) distress
Incommuabilité, *s.f.* incommutability
Incommuable, *adj.* incommutable
Incommun, e, *adj.* uncommon
Incommunicabilité, *s.f.* incommunicability
Incommunicable, *adj.* incommunicable
Incommuniqué, e, *adj.* uncommunicated
Incommutabilité, *s.f.* incommutability
Incommutable, *adj.* incommutable, not to be dispossessed, irremovable [irremovably
Incommutablement, *adv.* incommutably,
Incompacité, *s.f.* incompactness
Incomparabilité, *s.f.* incomparableness
Incomparable, *adj.* incomparable, peerless, matchless, without o.'s match, wonderful
Incomparablement, *adv.* incomparably
Incomparé, e, *adj.* uncompared [sistency
Incompatibilité, *s.f.* incompatibility, incon-
Incompatible, *adj.* incompatible, inconsistent
Incompatiblement, *adv.* incompatibly, inconsistently
Incompatissant, e, *adj.* incompassionate
Incompétemment, *adv.* incompetently
Incompétence, *s.f.* incompetence, incompe-
Incompétent, e, *adj.* incompetent [tency
Incompl-et, ète, *adj.* incomplete; unfinished; — *s.m.* incompleteness, incompletion; incomplete book
Incomplètement, *adv.* incompletely
Incomplexe, *adj.* incomplex
Incomplexité, *s.f.* incomplexity [bility
Incompréhensibilité, *s.f.* incomprehensi-
Incompréhensible, *adj.* incomprehensible
Incompréhensiblement, *adv.* incomprehensibly
Incompressibilité, *s.f.* incompressibility
Incompressible, *adj.* incompressible
Incomprimé, e, *adj.* uncompressed [ciated
Incompris, e, *adj.* not understood; unappre-
Inconcevabilité, *s.f.* inconceivableness
Inconcevable, *adj.* inconceivable; extraordinary; wonderful; singular; odd; strange
Inconcevablement, *adv.* inconceivably
Inconciliable, *adj.* irreconcilable
Inconciliablement, *adv.* irreconcilably
Inconciliant, e, *adj.* unconciliating
Inconcilié, e, *adj.* unconciliated; irreconciled
Inconclu, e, *adj.* unconcluded
Inconcluant, e, *adj.* inconclusive
Inconçu, e, *adj.* unconceived
Inconditionnel, le, *adj.* unconditional [ally
Inconditionnellement, *adv.* unconditionally
Inconduc-teur, trice, *adj.* (*phys.*) non-conducting
Inconduite, *s.f.* misconduct, misbehaviour
Inconfessé, e, *adj.* unconfessed
Inconfiance, *s.f.* unconfidence
Inconfiant, e, *adj.* unconfident
Incongelable, *adj.* incongealable
Incongelé, e, *adj.* uncongealed
Incongru, e, *adj.* incongruous, improper; indecent; uncouth, boorish; ungrammatical
Incongruité, *s.f.* incongruity, impropriety; indecency; beastly thing; boorishness
Incongrûment, *adv.* incongruously, improperly; indecently; boorishly; ungrammatically
Inconjugal, e, *adj.* unconjugal [cally
Inconnaissable, *adj.* unknowable, incognizable
Inconnu, e, *adj.* unknown; secret; concealed; strange, unusual; — *s.m.f.* unknown person; stranger; mere nobody, nobody; adventurer, adventuress; — *s.m.* things unknown, (the) unknown; — *s.f.* (*math.*) unknown quantity
Inconquis, e, *adj.* unconquered
Inconscience, *s.f.* (*philos.*) unconsciousness
Inconscient, e, *adj.* (*philos.*) unconscious
Inconséquemment, *adv.* inconsistently; thoughtlessly

Inconséquence, *s.f.* inconsistency; thoughtlessness; inconsistent thing
Inconséquent, e, *adj.* inconsistent; inconsiderate, thoughtless; — *s.m.f.* ditto person
Inconsidération, *s.f.* inconsiderateness, rashness; disrepute; disregard, slight
Inconsidéré, e, *adj.* inconsiderate, rash; — *s.m.f.* ditto person [rashly
Inconsidérément, *adv.* inconsiderately,
Inconsistance, *s.f.* inconsistence, inconsistency, unsteadiness
Inconsistant, e, *adj.* inconsistent
Inconsolable, *adj.* inconsolable, disconsolate
Inconsolablement, *adv.* inconsolably
Inconsolé, e, *adj.* unconsoled, uncomforted
Inconsommable, *adj.* inconsumable
Inconsommé, e, *adj.* unconsumed [steadily
Inconstamment, *adv.* inconstantly; un-
Inconstance, *s.f.* inconstancy; instability; unsettledness; unsteadiness; fickleness
Inconstant, e, *adj.* inconstant; unsteady; unsettled; changeable, variable; fickle; — *s.m.f.* ditto person [ality
Inconstitutionnalité, *s.f.* unconstitution-
Inconstitutionnel, le, *adj.* unconstitutional
Inconstitutionnellement, *adv.* unconsti-
Inconsulté, e, *adj.* unconsulted [tutionally
Inconsumable, *adj.* inconsumable
Inconsumé, e, *adj.* unconsumed
Incontable, *adj.* unrelatable
Incontestabilité. *V.* page 3, § 1
Incontestable, *adj.* incontestable, unquestionable, indisputable
Incontestablement, *adv.* incontestably, unquestionably, indisputably [undisputed
Incontesté, e, *adj.* uncontested, unquestioned,
Incontinemment, *adv.* incontinently
Incontinence, *s.f.* incontinence
Incontinent, e, *adj.* incontinent, unchaste
Incontinent, *adv.* (*old*) incontinently, immediately, forthwith
Incontinu, e, *adj.* uncontinuous
Incontinuité, *s.f.* incontinuity
Incontrôlable, *adj.* uncontrollable
Incontrôlé, e, *adj.* uncontrolled
Incontroversable, *adj.* incontrovertible
Incontroversé, e, *adj.* uncontroverted
Inconvaincu, e, *adj.* unconvinced
Inconvenable, *adj.* unsuitable, unbecoming
Inconvenablement, *adv.* unsuitably, unbecomingly [ness
Inconvenance, *s.f.* impropriety, unbecoming-
Inconvenant, e, *adj.* improper, unbecoming, unseemly, indecorous; ill-behaved
Inconvénient, *s.m.* inconvenience; disadvantage; untoward accident, ill consequence, harm; trouble; difficulty; objection; annoyance; (*pop.*) infirmity [tible
Inconversible, *adj.* inconversible, inconver-
Inconverti, e, *adj.* unconverted [convertible
Inconvertible, Inconvertissable, *adj.* in-
Inconvertiblement, *adv.* inconvertibly
Inconvié, e, *adj.* uninvited [ity
Incorporalité, *s.f.* incorporality, incorporeal-
Incorporation, *s.f.* incorporation; embodi-
Incorporéité, *s.f.* incorporeity [ment
Incorporel, le, *adj.* incorporal, incorporeal
Incorporellement, *adv.* incorporally, incorporeally [embody
Incorporer, *v.a.*, **S'—,** *v.r.* to incorporate; to
Incorrect, e, *adj.* incorrect; inaccurate; wrong [rately; wrongly, wrong
Incorrectement, *adv.* incorrectly; inaccu-
Incorrection, *s.f.* incorrectness; inaccuracy
Incorrigé, e, *adj.* uncorrected
Incorrigibilité, *s.f.* incorrigibility, incorrigibleness; unimprovableness
Incorrigible, *adj.* incorrigible; unimprovable
Incorrigiblement, *adv.* incorrigibly
Incorrodible, *adj.* incorrodible
Incorrompu, e, *adj.* uncorrupted, incorrupt
Incorruptibilité. *V.* page 3, § 1
Incorruptible, *adj.* incorruptible
Incorruptiblement, *adv.* incorruptibly
Incorruption, *s.f.* incorruption
Incourant, e, *adj.* uncurrent [crassative
Incrassant, e, *adj.*, **Incrassant,** *s.m.* in-
Incréable, *adj.* uncreatable
Incrédibilité. *V.* page 3, § 1
Incrédule, *adj.* incredulous; unbelieving; — *s.m.f.* incredulous person, unbeliever, infidel
Incrédulité, *s.f.* incredulity; unbelief
Incréé, e, *adj.* uncreated; eternal
Incrément, *s.m.* increment, increase
Incriminable, *adj.* incriminable, criminable
Incrimination, *s.f.* incrimination, crimina-
Incriminatoire, *adj.* incriminatory [tion
Incriminel, le, *adj.* uncriminal [to accuse
Incriminer, *v.a.* to incriminate, to criminate,
Incristallisable, *adj.* incrystallizable [able
Incritiquable, *adj.* uncriticizable, uncensur-
Incrochetable, *adj.* (*of locks*) unpickable
Incroyable, *adj. s.* incredible; (*obsolete*) swell, exquisite, dandy, dundreary
Incroyablement, *adv.* incredibly
Incroyance, *s.f.* unbelief
Incroyant, e, *adj.* unbelieving
Incrustation, *s.f.* incrustation, inlay, inlaying, inlaidwork; crust, fur, sediment
Incrusté, e, *part. adj.* incrusted; inlaid; — *s.m.* inlay, inlaidwork [over
Incruster, *v.a.* to incrust; to inlay; to lay
S'—, *v.r.* to become (*or* be) incrusted, &c.;
Incubation, *s.f.* incubation [to fur
Incube, *s.m.* incubus
Incuisable, *adj.* uncookable [underdone part
Incuit, e, *adj. s.m.* underdone, underbaked;
Inculcation, *s.f.* inculcation
Inculpable, *adj.* chargeable, accusable
Inculpation, *s.f.* inculpation
Inculpé, e, *part. adj.* inculpated, accused; — *s.m.f.* accused; culprit, prisoner
Inculper, *v.a.* to inculpate
Inculquer, *v.a.* to inculcate, to impress
S'—, *v.r.* to be inculcated *or* impressed; to inculcate *or* impress on o.'s (own) *or* on each other's mind
Inculte, *adj.* uncultivated; waste; uneducated, unpolished, rude, coarse; neglected, rough;
Incultivable, *adj.* uncultivable [wild
Incultivé, e, *adj.* uncultivated
Inculture, *s.f.* unculture, uncultivation
Incunable, *adj.* of early printing; — *s.m.* early printed book (—**s,** *pl.* incunabula)
Incurabilité, *s.f.* incurability, incurableness
Incurable, *adj. s.m.f.* incurable; —**s,** *s.m.pl.* incurables; hospital for incurables
Incurablement, *adv.* incurably
Incurie, *s.f.* carelessness, heedlessness, indifference; negligence; malpractice; dereliction
Incurieusement, *adv.* incuriously [of duty
Incurieu-x, se, *adj.* incurious
Incuriosité, *s.f.* incuriosity
Incursi-f, ve, *adj.* incursive [expedition
Incursion, *s.f.* incursion, inroad; excursion,
Incurvation, *s.f.* incurvation [incurved
Incurvé, e, *part. adj.* incurvated, incurvate,
Incurver, *v.a.* to incurvate, to incurve
Incuse, *adj.f.* imperfectly struck; — *s.f.* ditto
Inde, *s.m.* indigo-blue [medal
†Indébrouillable, *adj.* inextricable, inexplicable, not to be unravelled [opened
Indécachetable, *adj.* not to be unsealed *or*
Indécemment, *adv.* indecently
Indécence, *s.f.* indecency
Indécent, e, *adj.* indecent
Indéchiffrable, *adj.* undecipherable; illegible; unintelligible, inextricable, obscure; inexplicable; unaccountable; incomprehensible; impenetrable, unfathomable
Indéchiffrablement, *adv.* undecipherably; illegibly; unintelligibly; inextricably; inexplicably; unaccountably; impenetrably [out
Indéchiffré, e, *adj.* undeciphered; not made

Indéchirable, *adj.* untearable

Indéchiré, e, *adj.* untorn, unrent

Indécis, e, *adj.* undecided; indeterminate; uncertain; doubtful; indistinct; vague, faint; indecisive, wavering, irresolute

Indécisi-f, ve, *adj.* indecisive

Indécision, *s.f.* indecision, irresolution; indistinctness; doubtful item

Indécisivement, *adv.* indecisively

Indéclinabilité, *s.f.* indeclinableness

Indéclinable, *adj.m.f., s.m.* indeclinable

Indécliné, e, *adj.* undeclined

Indécomposable, *adj.* indecomposable

Indécomposé, e, *adj.* undecomposed

Indécousable, *adj.* unsewable

Indécrit, e, *adj.* undescribed, nondescript

Indécrottable, *adj.* uncleanable; unteachable, unpolishable, incapable of cultivation; intractable; incorrigible

Indéfectibilité. *V.* page 3, § 1

Indéfectible, *adj.* indefectible

Indéfendable, *adj.* indefensible; untenable

Indéfendu, e, *adj.* undefended, defenceless

Indéfiguré, e, *adj.* undisfigured; undeformed, undefaced; undistorted [unlimited

Indéfini, e, *adj.* indefinite; "sine die;" vague;

Indéfiniment, *adv.* indefinitely; (to) an indefinite time, "sine die;" vaguely; unlimitedly; for ever [unaccountable; nondescript

Indéfinissable, *adj.* indefinable; inexplicable,

Indéformable, *adj.* not liable to get out of

Indéfrichable, *adj.* unclearable [shape

Indéfriché, e, *adj.* uncleared

Indéguisé, e, *adj.* undisguised

Indéhiscence, *s.f.* (*bot.*) indehiscence

Indéhiscent, e, *adj.* (*bot.*) indehiscent

Indélébile, *adj.* indelible, ineffaceable

Indélébilité, *s.f.* indelibility, indelibleness

Indélibéré, e, *adj.* indeliberate

Indélibérément, *adv.* indeliberately

Indélicat, e, *adj.* indelicate; unscrupulous; unhandsome [pulously; unhandsomely

Indélicatement, *adv.* indelicately; unscru-

Indélicatesse, *s.f.* indelicacy; unscrupulousness; unhandsomeness; indelicate *or* unscrupulous *or* unhandsome act

Indemandé, e, *adj.* unasked, &c. (*V.* **De-**

Indemne, *adj.* indemnified [**mander**)

Indemnisation, *s.f.* indemnification

Indemniser, *v.a.* to indemnify; to recoup

Indemnitaire, *s.m.f.* claimant to an indemnity

Indemnité, *s.f.* indemnity

Indémontrable, *adj.* indemonstrable

Indémontré, e, *adj.* undemonstrated

Indéniable, *adj.* undeniable

Indentation, *s.f.* indentation

Indenté, e, *adj.* unindented; not toothed

Indenture, *s.f.* indenture, indentation

Indépendamment, *adv.* independently

Indépendance, *s.f.* independence

Indépendant, e, *adj.*, **Indépendant,** *s.m.* independent

Indépendantisme, *s.m.* independentism

Indéracinable, *adj.* ineradicable

Indescriptibilité, *s.f.* indescribableness

Indescriptible, *adj.* indescribable

Indescriptiblement, *adv.* indescribably

Indestituable, *adj.* irremovable [defeasibility

Indestructibilité, *s.f.* indestructibility; in-

Indestructible, *adj.* indestructible; indefeasible [indefeasibly

Indestructiblement, *adv.* indestructibly;

Indéterminable, *adj.* indeterminable

Indétermination, *s.f.* indetermination

Indéterminé, e, *adj.* indeterminate; undetermined; unlimited; undecided; irresolute

Indéterminément, *adv.* indeterminately; vaguely [guessed

Indevinable, *adj.* unguessable, not to be

Indeviné, e, *adj.* unguessed

Indévot, e, *adj.* indevout, not pious, not religious; irreverent; — *s.m.f.* ditto person

Indévotement, *adv.* indevoutly; irreverently

Indévotion, *s.f.* indevotion; irreverence

Index, *s.m.* index; forefinger. *Être à l'—*, to be forbidden. *Mettre à l'—*, to forbid

Indextérité, *s.f.* indexterity

Indian-isme, -iste, -ologie. *V.* page 3, § 1

Indianite, *s.f.* (*min.*) indianite

Indicateur, *s.m.* indicator; informer; forefinger; index; index-plate; gauge; guide; time-bill, time-book; (*bird, kind of cuckoo*) honey-guide, moroc, indicator; — *adj.m.* indicating, indicatory; guide, sign. *Doigt —*, forefinger. — *des chemins de fer*, railway-guide [tive

Indicati-f, ve, *adj.*, **Indicatif,** *s.m.* indica-

Indication, *s.f.* indication; direction; information; sign, mark, proof; declaration

Indicatrice, *s.f.* indicatrix; — *adj.f.* indicating, indicatory

Indice, *s.m.* indication, token, sign, mark, symptom, clue; (*nav.*) landmark; (*obsolete*) index [expressible, indescribable

Indicible, *adj.* unspeakable, unutterable, in-

Indiciblement, *adv.* unspeakably, unutterably, inexpressibly, indescribably [scription

Indiction, *s.f.* indiction; convocation; pre-

Indicule, *s.m.* small index

Indien, ne, *adj. s.m.f.* Indian; — *s.f.* Indian fashion; printed calico *or* cotton, print; (*obsolete*) dressing *or* morning gown

Indienneur, *s.m.* calico-printer, cotton-printer

Indifféremment, *adv.* indifferently; indiscriminately, equally, alike

Indifférence, *s.f.* indifference; unconcern; insensibility; apathy

Indifférent, e, *adj.* indifferent; unconcerned; insensible, cold; indolent; uninteresting; without expression, insignificant; immaterial; of indifference; — *s.m.f.* indifferent person; one who is neither a friend nor an enemy

Indifférent-isme, -iste. *V.* page 3, § 1

Indigenat, *s.m.* nativeness; denizenship; naturalization [indigent, (the) poor, (the) needy

Indigence, *s.f.* indigence, poverty, need; (the)

Indigène, *adj. s.m.f.* indigenous; home-born, home-grown, home-made; native

Indigénéité, *s.f.* nativeness

Indigent, e, *adj. s.* indigent, poor, needy; indigent *or* poor person, pauper

Indigéré, e, *adj.* undigested, indigested [tion

Indigérer (S'), *v.r.* to give oneself an indiges-

Indigeste, *adj.* indigestible; undigested, crude,

Indigestibilité. *V.* page 3, § 1 [raw

Indigestible, *adj.* indigestible

Indigestion, *s.f.* indigestion

Indigète, *adj.* of the country

†Indignation, *s.f.* indignation

†Indigne, *adj.* unworthy; undeserving; worthless; vile, base; infamous, scandalous; (*law*) disqualified; — *s.m.f.* unworthy person, worthless wretch

†Indigné, e, *adj.* indignant, shocked

†Indignement, *adv.* unworthily; infamously

†Indigner, *v.a.* to make indignant, to shock

S'—, *v.r.* to be indignant *or* shocked, to be angry *or* exasperated

†Indignité, *s.f.* unworthiness; worthlessness; vileness, baseness; indignity; infamy; shame; infamous *or* scandalous thing; (*law*) disqualification

Indigo, *s.m.* indigo; indigo-plant; indigo colour

Indigofère, *adj.* indigoferous; — *s.m.* indigofer

Indigomètre, *s.m.* indigometer

Indigotate, *s.m.* (*chem.*) indigotate [tation

Indigoterie, *s.f.* indigo-factory; indigo-plan-

Indigotier, *s.m.* indigo-plant; indigo-manu-

Indigotifère, *adj.* indigoferous [facturer

Indigotine, *s.f.* (*chem.*) indigotine

Indigotique, *adj.* (*chem.*) indigotic

Indiligemment, *adv.* indiligently

Indiligence, *s.f.* indiligence

Indiligent, e, *adj.* indiligent

Indine, *s.f.* (*chem.*) indine

Indiquer, *v.a.* to indicate, to show; to point out; to point to; to direct to; to tell; to inform of, to acquaint with; to recommend; to appoint; to mention; to name; to describe; to sketch out
S'—, *v.r.* to be indicated *or* &c.
Indirect, e, *adj.* indirect; (*of evidence*) indirect, circumstantial, presumptive
Indirectement, *adv.* indirectly
Indirection, *s.f.* indirection
Indiscernabilité, *s.f.* indiscernibleness
Indiscernable, *adj.* indiscernible
Indiscernablement, *adv.* indiscernibly
Indiscerné, e, *adj.* undiscerned [crimination
Indiscernement, *s.m.* indiscernment, indis-
Indisciplinable, *adj.* indisciplinable; unruly
Indiscipline, *s.f.* indiscipline; insubordination
Indiscipliné, e, *adj.* undisciplined
Indiscipliner (S'), *v.r.* to become undisciplined; to run riot
Indiscr-et, ète, *adj.* indiscreet; inconsiderate; unceremonious, free; obtrusive, intrusive; unreasonable; taking advantage of anyone's kindness; unsecret; talkative, blabbing; idle, useless, foolish; inquisitive; — *s.m.f.* ditto person
Indiscrètement, *adv.* indiscreetly; inconsiderately; unceremoniously, freely; obtrusively, intrusively; unreasonably; idly, foolishly; inquisitively
Indiscrétion, *s.f.* indiscretion, imprudence; impertinence, liberty; unreasonableness; inquisitiveness; piece of indiscretion
Indiscutable, *adj.* undebatable; indisputable, unquestionable [questionably
Indiscutablement, *adv.* indisputably, un-
Indiscuté, e, *adj.* undiscussed, undebated
Indisert, e, *adj.* ineloquent
Indisertement, *adv.* ineloquently
Indispensabilité, *s.f.* indispensableness
Indispensable, *adj.* indispensable; — *s.m.* what is indispensable *or* strictly necessary; cicisbeo; (*obsolete*) reticule, bag
Indispensablement, *adv.* indispensably
Indisponibilité, *s.f.* indisposableness; unavailableness
Indisponible, *adj.* indisposable; unavailable
Indisposé, e, *adj.* indisposed, unwell, poorly
Indisposer, *v.a.* to indispose; to disincline; to disaffect, to estrange; to make unwell
S'—, *v.r.* to be indisposed; to make oneself
Indisposition, *s.f.* indisposition [unwell
Indisputabilité, *s.f.* indisputableness
Indisputable, *adj.* indisputable
Indisputablement, *adv.* indisputably
Indisputé, e, *adj.* undisputed
Indissolubilité. *V.* page 3, § 1
Indissoluble, *adj.* indissoluble
Indissolublement, *adv.* indissolubly
Indissou-s, te, *adj.* undissolved
Indistinct, e, *adj.* indistinct; undistinguishable; confused; vague; faint; dim
Indistinctement, *adv.* indistinctly; undistinguishably; confusedly; vaguely; faintly; dimly; indiscriminately; indifferently
Indistinction, *s.f.* indistinction, indistinctness
Indistingué, e, *adj.* undistinguished
Indistinguible, *adj.* undistinguishable
Indium, *s.m.* (*chem.*) indium
Individu, *s.m.* individual, person, man, fellow; self, inside, number one
Individu, e, *adj.* (*theol.*) undivided
Individualisation, *s.f.* individualization
Individualiser, *v.a.* to individualize
S'—, *v.r.* to become individualized
Individualisme, *s.m.* individualism
Individualiste, *s.m.f.* individualist; — *adj.* individualistic
Individualité, *s.f.* individuality; entity
Individuation, *s.f.* individuation
Individuel, le, *adj.* individual
Individuellement, *adv.* individually
Individuer, *v.a.* to individuate
Indivinité, *s.f.* indivinity
Indivis, e, *adj.* undivided. *Par* —, jointly, undivided. *Propriétaire* —, joint tenant
Indivisé, e, *adj.* undivided
Indivisément, *adv.* undividedly, jointly
Indivisibilité. *V.* page 3, § 1
Indivisible, *adj.* indivisible; inseparable
Indivisiblement, *adv.* indivisibly; insepa-
Indivision, *s.f.* joint tenancy [rably
In-dix-huit, *adj. s.m.* 18mo.
Indo-, (*in compounds*) Indo-...
Indocile, *adj.* indocile, intractable, disobedient
Indocilement, *adv.* indocilely, intractably
Indocilité, *s.f.* indocility, intractableness
Indocte, *adj.* unlearned, unlettered, unliterary
Indoctement, *adv.* unlearnedly
Indolemment, *adv.* indolently
Indolence, *s.f.* indolence, idleness
Indolent, e, *adj.* indolent, idle; — *s.m.f.* ditto
Indolore, *adj.* painless [person
Indomptabilité, *s.f.* indomitableness
Indomptable, *adj.* indomitable, untamable; unconquerable; ungovernable
Indomptablement, *adv.* indomitably, untamably; ungovernably
Indompté, e, *adj.* untamed, wild; unsubdued, unconquered; uncontrolled; unbroken
Indou, e, *adj. s.* Hindu, Hindoo
In-douze, *adj. s.m.* duodecimo, 12mo.
Indri, *s.m.* (*zool.*) indri
Indu, e, *adj.* undue; unseasonable; late, improper, unreasonable, bad
Indubitable, *adj.* indubitable, beyond doubt
Indubitablement, *adv.* indubitably, undoubt-
Induc-teur, trice, *adj.* inducing [edly
Inducti-f, ve, *adj.* inductive
Inductile, *adj.* inductile
Inductilité, *s.f.* inductility
Induction, *s.f.* induction; inference
Inductivement, *adv.* inductively
Induire, *v.a.* to induce, to lead; to infer
S'—, *v.r.* to be inferred; to induce *or* lead
Indulgemment, *adv.* indulgently [each other
Indulgence, *s.f.* indulgence
Indulgencier, *v.a.* (*Cath. rel.*) to indulgence
Indulgent, e, *adj.* indulgent
Indult, *s.m.* indult
Indultaire, *s.m.* nominee by virtue of an indult
Indûment, *adv.* unduly, unlawfully
Induplicati-f, ve, *adj.* (*bot.*) induplicative,
Induration, *s.f.* induration [induplicate
Indurer, *v.a.*, **S'—,** *v.r.* to indurate
Induse, Indusie, *s.f.* (*bot., min.*) indusium. *Calcaire à —s*, indusial limestone
Industrialisme, *s.m.* industrialism
Industrialiste, *s.m.f.* industrialist; — *adj.* industrialistic
Industrie, *s.f.* skill; dexterity; talent; ingenuity; invention; trade, business; arts and manufactures, trade and manufactures, industry; husbandry; growing; rearing; breeding; cunning tricks, tricks of trade. *Vivre d'*—, to live by o.'s wits. *V.* **Chevalier**
Industriel, le, *adj.* industrial, manufacturing, commercial; — *s.m.* industrial; manufacturer; commercial man, trader; jobber
Industriellement, *adv.* industrially
Industrier (S'), *v.r.* *V.* **Ingénier (S')**
Industrieusement, *adv.* ingeniously, skilfully; industriously [clever, industrious
Industrieu-x, se, *adj.* ingenious, skilful,
Indut, *s.m.* assistant priest
Induvie, *s.f.* (*bot.*) induviæ
Induvié, e, *adj.* (*bot.*) induviate
Inébranlabilité, *s.f.* unshakableness, immovableness; firmness, steadiness, resolution
Inébranlable, *adj.* unshakable, immovable; unshaken; firm, steady, resolute; fixed
Inébranlablement, *adv.* unshakably, unshakingly, immovably, firmly, steadily, resolutely
Inébranlé, e, *adj.* unshaken, unmoved
Inébriati-f, ve, *adj.* inebriating, inebriant

Inéclairci, e, *adj.* unexplained, not clear
Inécouté, e, *adj.* unlistened to [scribed; new
Inédit, e, *adj.* unpublished; inedited; unde-
Ineffabilité, *s.f.* ineffableness, unspeakableness
Ineffable, *adj.* ineffable, unspeakable
Ineffablement, *adv.* ineffably, unspeakably
Ineffaçable, *adj.* ineffaceable, indelible
Ineffaçablement, *adv.* ineffaceably, indelibly
Ineffacé, e, *adj.* uneffaced, unobliterated
Ineffecti-f, ve, *adj* ineffective
Ineffectué, e, *adj.* uneffected, unperformed, unfulfilled, unaccomplished, unexecuted
Inefficace, *adj.* inefficacious, inefficient
Inefficacement, *adv.* inefficaciously, inefficiently
Inefficacité, *s.f.* inefficacy, inefficiency
Inégal, e, *adj.* unequal; uneven; rough; irregular; capricious
Inégalement, *adv.* unequally; unevenly
Inégalité, *s.f.* inequality; unevenness; roughness; asperity; irregularity; caprice
Inélasticité, *s.f.* inelasticity
Inélastique, *adj.* inelastic
Inélégamment, *adv.* inelegantly
Inélégance, *s.f.* inelegance
Inélégant, e, *adj.* inelegant
Inéligibilité, *s.f.* ineligibility
Inéligible, *adj.* ineligible
Inéligiblement, *adv.* ineligibly
Inéloquemment, *adv.* ineloquently
Inéloquent, e, *adj.* ineloquent
Inéluctable, *adj.* ineluctable; unavoidable, inevitable; indisputable, unquestionable
Inembryonné, e, *adj.* (*bot.*) inembryonate
Inemployé, e, *adj.* unemployed
Inénarrable, *adj.* unspeakable, inexpressible, indescribable [pressibly, indescribably
Inénarrablement, *adv.* unspeakably, inex-
Inentendu, e, *adj.* unheard
Inépanoui, e, *adj.* unexpanded [perienced
Inéprouvé, e, *adj.* untried; unfelt, unex-
Inepte, *adj.* inept, unfit; silly, foolish [ishly
Ineptement, *adv.* ineptly, unfitly; sillily, fool-
Ineptie, *s.f.* ineptness, unfitness; silliness, foolishness, folly, stupidity, absurdity
Inépuisable, *adj.* inexhaustible
Inépuisablement, *adv.* inexhaustibly
Inépuisé, e, *adj.* unexhausted
§**Inéquiangle,** *adj.* inequiangular
§**Inéquilatéral, e, Inéquilatère,** *adj.* in-
Inéquitable, *adj.* inequitable [equilateral
Inéquitablement, *adv.* inequitably
Inerme, *adj.* (*bot.*) inermous, inerm; (*zool.*) unhorned, hornless [lifeless
Inerte, *adj.* inert; inactive; sluggish, dull,
Inertie, *s.f.* inertia; inertness; inactivity; sluggishness, indolence. *Force d'—*, passive resistance, "vis inertiæ" [tered
Inérudit, e, *adj.* inerudite, unlearned, unlet-
Inérudition, *s.f.* inerudition
Inespérable, *adj.* not to be hoped for
Inespéré, e, *adj.* unhoped for; unexpected
Inespérément, *adv.* beyond all hopes, unex-
Inessayé, e, *adj.* untried [pectedly
Inestimable, *adj.* inestimable, invaluable
Inestimé, e, *adj.* unesteemed; unvalued
Inétendu, e, *adj.* unextended; having no
Inétudié, e, *adj.* unstudied [dimensions
Inévidence, *s.f.* inevidence
Inévident, e, *adj.* inevident [unavoidableness
Inévitabilité, *s.f.* inevitability, inevitableness,
Inévitable, *adj.* inevitable, unavoidable
Inévitablement, *adv.* inevitably, unavoidably
Inévité, e, *adj.* unavoided
Inexact, e, *adj.* inexact; inaccurate, incorrect, wrong; unpunctual; negligent
Inexactement, *adv.* inexactly; inaccurately, incorrectly, wrongly, wrong; unpunctually; negligently
Inexactitude, *s.f.* inexactness; inaccuracy, incorrectness; unpunctuality; negligence
Inexaucé, e, *adj.* unheard; ungranted

Inexcitabilité, *s.f.* inexcitability
Inexcitable, *adj.* inexcitable
Inexcusable, *adj.* inexcusable; unjustifiable
Inexcusablement, *adv.* inexcusably; unjustifiably
Inexcusé, e, *adj.* unexcused; unjustified
Inexécutable, *adj.* inexecutable, impracticable
Inexécutablement, *adv.* impracticably
Inexécuté, e, *adj.* unexecuted [ance
Inexécution, *s.f.* inexecution, non-perform-
Inexercé, e, *adj.* unexercised, unpractised; untrained
Inexigé, e, *adj.* unrequired; undemanded
Inexigibilité, *s.f.* inexigibility
Inexigible, *adj.* inexigible, not demandable, not requirable, not due, not payable
Inexistant, e, *adj.* inexistent
Inexistence, *s.f.* inexistence [ness
Inexorabilité, *s.f.* inexorability, inexorable-
Inexorable, *adj.* inexorable, unrelenting
Inexorablement, *adv.* inexorably
Inexpérience, *s.f.* inexperience
Inexpérimenté, e, *adj.* inexperienced; untried, unexperienced
Inexpert, e, *adj.* inexpert, unskilled
Inexpiable, *adj.* inexpiable, unatonable
Inexpié, e, *adj.* unexpiated, unatoned for
Inexplicabilité, *s.f.* inexplicability, inexplicableness [able; unintelligible; singular
Inexplicable, *adj.* inexplicable; unaccount-
Inexplicablement, *adv.* inexplicably, unac-
Inexplicite, *adj.* inexplicit [countably
Inexplicitement, *adv.* inexplicitly
Inexpliqué, e, *adj.* unexplained
Inexploitabilité, *s.f.* unworkableness; uncultivableness
Inexploitable, *adj.* unworkable; uncultivable
Inexploité, e, *adj.* unworked; uncultivated
Inexplorable, *adj.* inexplorable
Inexploré, e, *adj.* unexplored
Inexplosibilité, *s.f.* inexplosiveness [plosive
Inexplosible, Inexplosi-f, ve, *adj.* inex-
Inexpressible, *s.m.* (*jest.*) inexpressibles, unmentionables, trousers, breeches, drawers
Inexpressi-f, ve, *adj.* inexpressive; wanting expression, insignificant
Inexprimable, *adj.* inexpressible, unutterable
Inexprimablement, *adv.* inexpressibly, un-
Inexprimé, e, *adj.* unexpressed [utterably
Inexpugnable, *adj.* inexpugnable, impregnable
Inextensibilité, *s.f.* inextensibility, inextensibleness
Inextensible, *adj.* inextensible, inextendible
Inextinguibilité, *s.f.* inextinguishableness, unquenchableness; irrepressibleness
Inextinguible, *adj.* inextinguishable, unquenchable; irrepressible, uncontrollable
Inextirpable, *adj.* inextirpable
Inextirpé, e, *adj.* unextirpated
Inextricabilité, *s.f.* inextricableness
Inextricable, *adj.* inextricable
Inextricablement, *adv.* inextricably
†**Infaillibilité,** *s.f.* infallibility; certainty
†**Infaillible,** *adj.* infallible; unerring; inevitable, certain, sure [inevitably, certainly
†**Infailliblement,** *adv.* infallibly; unerringly;
Infaisable, *adj.* infeasible, not to be done, impracticable, impossible
Infalsifiable, *adj.* unfalsifiable [disgraceful
Infamant, e, *adj.* infamous; ignominious;
Infamation, *s.f.* (*obsolete*) stamp of infamy; ignominy; disgrace
Infâme, *adj.* infamous; shameful; base; sordid; filthy; of ill fame; — *s.m.f.* infamous person, infamous wretch, villain
Infâmement, *adv.* infamously
Infamer, *v.a.* to disgrace
Infamie, *s.f.* infamy; infamous thing
Infant, *s.m.* Infante [wench; sweetheart
Infante, *s.f.* Infanta; (*jest.*) queen, beauty;
Infanterie, *s.f.* infantry, foot
Infanticide, *s.m.* infanticide, child-murder;

— s.m.f. infanticide, child-murderer *or* murderess; — *adj.* infanticidal
Infatigabilité, *s.f.* indefatigableness
Infatigable, *adj.* indefatigable
Infatigablement, *adv.* indefatigably
Infatigué, e, *adj.* unfatigued, untired
Infatuation, *s.f.* infatuation
Infatuer, *v.a.* to infatuate [(on *or* upon)
S'—, *v.r.* to become *or* be infatuated; to dote
Infavorable, *adj.* unfavourable
Infavorablement, *adv.* unfavourably
Infavorisé, e, *adj.* unfavoured
Infécond, e, *adj.* infecund, unfruitful, infertile, sterile, barren
Infécondité, *s.f.* infecundity, unfruitfulness, infertility, sterility, barrenness
Infect, e, *adj.* infectious, tainted, foul, stinking; most offensive, horrid [ing; infectious
Infectant, e, *adj.* infecting; tainting; stink-
Infecter, *v.a.* to infect; to taint; to corrupt; to pollute; — *v.n.* to stink horridly. *S'—,* to become infectious *or* infected; to infect each
Infectieu-x, se, *adj.* infectious [other
Infection, *s.f.* infection; infectious disease;
Infectioniste, *s.m.* infectionist [horrid stench
Infélicité, *s.f.* infelicity, unhappiness
Inféodation, *s.f.* infeudation, enfeoffment
Inféoder, *v.a.* to enfeoff; (*fig.*) to attach, to
Infère, *adj.* (*bot.*) inferior, lower [appropriate
Inférence, *s.f.* (*log.*) inference
Inférer, *v.a.* to infer. *S'—,* to be inferred
Inférieur, e, *adj. s.* inferior; lower; under; nether; subordinate; subaltern; unequal; petty; below; (*pop.*) worse than indifferent
Inférieurement, *adv.* in an inferior manner *or* degree, in a low degree, inferiorly; below
Infériorité, *s.f.* inferiority [or shut
Infermable, *adj.* unclosable, not to be closed
Infermenté, e, *adj.* unfermented
Infermentescibilité, *s.f.* infermentescibility
Infermentescible, *adj.* infermentescible
Infernal, e, *adj.* infernal; hellish. *V.* **Pierre**
Infernalement, *adv.* infernally
Infernalité, *s.f.* hellishness; fiendish act
Infertile, *adj.* infertile, unfruitful, sterile, barren
Infertilement, *adv.* infertilely, unfruitfully
Infertilisable, *adj.* infertilizable
Infertilisé, e, *adj.* unfertilized
Infertilité, *s.f.* infertility, unfruitfulness, steri-
Infestation, *s.f.* infestation [lity, barrenness
Infester, *v.a.* to infest; to overrun; to harass; to annoy; to plunder; to haunt
Infibulation, *s.f.* infibulation
Infibuler, *v.a.* to infibulate
Infidèle, *adj.* unfaithful, faithless; untrue; false; inaccurate; disloyal; unbelieving, infidel; — *s.m.f.* unfaithful person; unbeliever, infidel
Infidèlement, *adv.* unfaithfully, faithlessly; untruly; falsely; inaccurately; disloyally
Infidélité, *s.f.* unfaithfulness, faithlessness; infidelity; unbelief; disloyalty; inaccuracy; failing. *Faire des —s à,* to be unfaithful to
Infiltration, *s.f.* infiltration
Infiltrer, *v.a.*, **S'—,** *v.r.* to infilter, to infiltrate, to percolate; (*fig.*) to creep
Infime, *adj.* lowest [est condition, abjection
Infimité, *s.f.* lowest degree, lowest depth; low-
Infini, e, *adj.* infinite; endless; numberless; boundless; immense
Infini, *s.m.* infinite; (*math.*) infinite quantity. *A l'—,* infinitely, boundlessly, endlessly, without end; to infinity, indefinitely
Infiniment, *adv.* infinitely; boundlessly; immensely; extremely, exceedingly; very much, ever so much; all; a great deal, a very great amount *or* quantity *or* number. **— petit,** *adj. s.m.* (*math.*) infinitesimal
Infinité, *s.f.* infinity, infiniteness, infinitude; infinite number *or* amount, vast number, multitude, crowd, host, world, no end (of); end-
Infinitésimal, e, *adj.* infinitesimal [lessness
Infinitésimalement, *adv.* infinitesimally
Infinitésime, *adj.m.f., s.f.* infinitesimal
Infinitif, *s.m.* (*gram.*) infinitive mood, infinitive
Infinitude, *s.f.* infinitude
Infirmable, *adj.* that can be invalidated
Infirmati-f, ve, *adj.* invalidating
Infirmation, *s.f.* invalidation
Infirme, *adj. s.* infirm; disabled; invalid; valetudinarian; sickly; weak, feeble; frail; feeble-minded; ditto person; fool
Infirmer, *v.a.* to invalidate; to weaken; to reverse, to annul, to quash
Infirmerie, *s.f.* infirmary, hospital, sick-house, sick-ward, sick-room, sanatorium
Infirmier, *s.m.* hospital attendant
Infirmière, *s.f.* hospital-nurse, sick-nurse, nurse
Infirmité, *s.f.* infirmity; disablement; weak-
Infixer, *v.a.* to infix [ness; failing
Inflammabilité, *s.f.* inflammability
Inflammable, *adj.* inflammable
Inflammation, *s.f.* inflammation
Inflammatoire, *adj.* inflammatory
Inflation, *s.f.* inflation
Infléchir, *v.a.* to inflect, to bend
S'—, *v.r.* to be inflected, to bend
Infléchissable, *adj.* inflexible, unbendable
Inflexe, *adj.* inflexed, inflected
Inflexibilité, *s.f.* inflexibility, inexorability
Inflexible, *adj.* inflexible; unrelenting; stiff
Inflexiblement, *adv.* inflexibly
Inflexion, *s.f.* inflection
Inflexueu-x, se, *adj.* inflexuous
Inflicti-f, ve, *adj.* inflictive
Infliction, *s.f.* infliction
Infliger, *v.a.* to inflict, to impose
S'—, *v.r.* to inflict oneself *or* each other, to impose on oneself *or* on each other; to be in-
Inflorescence, *s.f.* (*bot.*) inflorescence [flicted
Influence, *s.f.* influence; sway; power
Influencer, *v.a.* to influence; to sway
Influent, e, *adj.* influential
Influenza, *s.f.* (*med.*) influenza
Influer, *v.n.* to have *or* exert an influence; to make an impression; (*old*) to inflow; — *v.a.*
Influx, *s.m.* influx [(*old*) to infuse
Influxion, *s.f.* influxion, influx
In-folio, *adj. s.m.* (*book-size*) folio
Infondre, *v.a.* (*old*) to infuse
Inforçable, *adj.* not to be forced [informing
Informa-teur, trice, *s.m.f.* informer; — *adj.*
Information, *s.f.* information; inquiry. *Aller aux —s, prendre des —s,* to make inquiries
Informe, *adj.* shapeless; unformed; misshapen; imperfect, incomplete, undigested, rude, crude; (*law*) informal
Informé, *s.m.* investigation, inquiry; — *m.,* **e,** *f., part. adj.* informed, &c. (*V.* **Informer**)
Informer, *v.a.* to inform, to acquaint; (*philos.*) to inform, to animate; — *v.n.* to make an in-
S'—, *v.r.* to inquire, to ask [quest
Informité, *s.f.* shapelessness
Infortiat, *s.m.* infortiate (*second volume of Justinian's digest*)
Infortifiable, *adj.* unfortifiable
Infortifié, e, *adj.* unfortified
Infortune, *s.f.* misfortune
Infortuné, e, *adj.* unfortunate, unhappy; — *s.m.f.* ditto person *or* creature, poor person, wretch, unfortunate
Infrac-teur, trice, *s.m.f.* infractor, infringer, breaker, violator, transgressor
Infraction, *s.f.* infraction, infringement, breach, violation, transgression, offence
Infranchissable, *adj.* impassable; insuperable, insurmountable
Infrangibilité, *s.f.* infrangibility
Infrangible, *adj.* infrangible
Infraternel, le, *adj.* unfraternal, unbrotherly
Infrayé, e, *adj.* untraced; unbeaten, untrodden
Infréquemment, *adv.* unfrequently, seldom
Infréquence, *s.f.* infrequency; scanty attendance, fewness
Infréquent, e, *adj.* unfrequent, rare

Infréquenté, e, *adj.* unfrequented
Infructueusement, *adv.* fruitlessly, to no purpose, unprofitably, in vain
Infructueu-x, se, *adj.* unfruitful; fruitless; unavailing; unprofitable; vain
Infructuosité, *s.f.* unfruitfulness, fruitlessness, unprofitableness, uselessness
Infundibulé, e, Infundibuliforme, *adj.* infundibulate, infundibuliform, funnel-shaped
Infundibulum, *s.m.* (*nat. hist.*) infundibulum
Infus, e, *adj.* infused, inborn, innate, intuitive
Infusé, *s.m.* (*pharm.*) infusion; — *m.*, **e,** *f.*, *part.* infused, &c. (*V.* **Infuser**)
Infuser, *v.a.n.*, **S'—,** *v.r.* to infuse; to steep; to stand; to draw; to be infused
Infusibilité, *s.f.* infusibility
Infusible, *adj.* infusible
Infusion, *s.f.* infusion; intuition
Infusoire, *s.m.* (*zool.*) infusory (—**s,** *pl.* infusoria, infusories); — *adj.* infusorial, infusory
†Ingagnable, *adj.* ungainable
Ingambe, *adj.* active, nimble, light-footed
Ingaranti, e, *adj.* unguaranteed; unwarranted
Ingénérabilité, *s.f.* ingenerability
Ingénérable, *adj.* ingenerable
Ingénier (S'), *v.r.* to tax o.'s ingenuity, to set o.'s wits to work, to bend o.'s wits (to), to strive, to contrive
Ingénieur, *s.m.* engineer; mathematical instrument maker; optician. — *-constructeur* (*de vaisseaux*), naval architect
Ingénieusement, *adv.* ingeniously, cleverly
Ingénieu-x, se, *adj.* ingenious, clever
Ingéniosité, *s.f.* ingenuity, ingeniousness
Ingénu, e, *adj.* ingenuous, candid, artless, innocent, simple-minded, simple, open, sincere; — *s.m.f.* ditto person (young man, youth, girl, maiden, &c.) [dour, artlessness, simplicity
Ingénuité, *s.f.* ingenuousness, frankness, can-
Ingénument, *adv.* ingenuously, frankly, candidly, fairly
Ingerçable, *adj.* not liable to crack
Ingérence, *s.f.* meddling, intermeddling, inter-
Ingérer, *v.a.* to ingest, to introduce [ference
S'—, *v.r.* to be ingested *or* introduced; to introduce *or* insinuate oneself, to intrude, to meddle, to intermeddle, to interfere (with); to take upon oneself
Ingesta, *s.m.pl.* (*Latin*) ingesta
Ingestion, *s.f.* ingestion
Inglorieusement, *adv.* ingloriously
Inglorieu-x, se, *adj.* inglorious
Inglorifié, e, *adj.* unglorified
Ingouvernable, *adj.* ungovernable, unmanageable, uncontrollable [gracefully
Ingracieusement, *adv.* ungraciously; un-
Ingracieu-x, se, *adj.* ungracious; ungraceful
Ingrammatical, e, *adj.* ungrammatical [cally
Ingrammaticalement, *adv.* ungrammati-
Ingrat, e, *adj.* ungrateful, thankless, unthankful; unprofitable, unproductive, sterile; unpromising; unfavourable; disagreeable, unpleasant; — *s.m.f.* ungrateful person *or* man *or* woman *or* fellow *or* creature *or* wretch
Ingratement, *adv.* ungratefully
Ingratitude, *s.f.* ingratitude, ungratefulness; unproductiveness; unpleasantness; piece of ingratitude
Ingrédient, *s.m.* ingredient
Inguéable, *adj.* unfordable
Inguérissable, *adj.* incurable
Inguinal, e, *adj.* (*anat.*) inguinal
Ingurgitation, *s.f.* ingurgitation
Ingurgiter, *v.a.* to ingurgitate
S'—, *v.r.* to ingurgitate; to be ingurgitated
Inhabile, *adj.* unskilful; incapable, unfit; unqualified, incompetent; disqualified
Inhabilement, *adv.* unskilfully, awkwardly
Inhabileté, *s.f.* unskilfulness; unfitness; inability [disqualification, incompetency
Inhabilité, *s.f.* (*law*) incapacity, disability,
Inhabitable, *adj.* uninhabitable
Inhabitation, *s.f.* non-habitation, inoccupation, non-residence
Inhabité, e, *adj.* uninhabited, unoccupied
Inhabitude, *s.f.* want of habit
Inhabitué, e, *adj.* unaccustomed, unused
Inhabituel, le, *adj.* unusual
Inhalation, *s.f.* inhalation
Inhaler, *v.a.* to inhale [3, § 1
Inharmon-ie, -ique, -iquement. *V.* page
Inharmonieusement, *adv.* inharmoniously
Inharmonieu-x, se, *adj.* inharmonious
Inhérence, *s.f.* inherence, inherency
Inhérent, e, *adj.* inherent
Inhiber, *v.a.* (*old*) to inhibit, to forbid
Inhibition, *s.f.* inhibition, prohibition
Inhibitoire, *adj.* inhibitory
Inhonoré, e, *adj.* unhonoured
Inhospitali-er, ère, *adj.* inhospitable
Inhospitalièrement, *adv.* inhospitably
Inhospitalité, *s.f.* inhospitality
Inhumain, e, *adj.* inhuman, cruel; — *s.m.* cruel man; — *s.f.* cruel woman, cruel beauty, cruel fair one
Inhumainement, *adv.* inhumanly, cruelly
Inhumanité, *s.f.* inhumanity, cruelty [burial
Inhumation, *s.f.* inhumation, interment,
Inhumer, *v.a.* to inhume, to inter, to bury
Inie, *s.m.* (*zool.*) inia [able
Inimaginable, *adj.* unimaginable, inconceiv-
Inimitabilité, *s.f.* inimitability, inimitableness
Inimitable, *adj.* inimitable
Inimitablement, *adv.* inimitably
Inimité, e, *adj.* unimitated [pathy; aversion
Inimitié, *s.f.* enmity, hatred; hostility; anti-
Inimprimable, *adj.* unprintable
Inindustrieu-x, se, *adj.* unindustrious
Ininflammabilité, *s.f.* uninflammability
Ininflammable, *adj.* uninflammable
Ininscription, *s.f.* non-inscription
Inintelligemment, *adv.* unintelligently
Inintelligence, *s.f.* want of intelligence
Inintelligent, e, *adj.* unintelligent
Inintelligibilité, *s.f.* unintelligibility, unintelligibleness
Inintelligible, *adj.* unintelligible
Inintelligiblement, *adv.* unintelligibly
Ininterrompu, e, *adj.* uninterrupted
Inique, *adj.* iniquitous; unrighteous
Iniquement, *adv.* iniquitously; unrighteously
Iniquité, *s.f.* iniquity; unrighteousness; sin
Initial, e, *adj.*, **Initiale,** *s.f.* initial
Initialement, *adv.* initially [— *adj.* initiative
Initia-teur, trice, *s.m.f.* apostle, institutor;
Initiati-f, ve, *adj.* initiative, initiatory
Initiation, *s.f.* initiation
Initiative, *s.f.* initiative; originating power
Initié, e, *part. adj.* initiated; — *s.m.f.* person initiated, initiate, initiated
Initier, *v.a.* to initiate
Injecté, e, *part. adj.* injected; bloodshot; suffused, flushed, red, ruddy. — *de sang*, bloodshot
Injecter, *v.a.* to inject
S'—, *v.r.* to inject into oneself; to be injected; to become filled; to become bloodshot
Injecteur, *s.m.* injector
Injec-teur, trice, *adj.* injecting, injection
Injection, *s.f.* injection; bloodshottenness; suffusion; redness
Injonction, *s.f.* injunction, order [formable
Injouable, *adj.* unplayable; unactable, unper-
Injudicieusement, *adv.* injudiciously
Injudicieu-x, se, *adj.* injudicious
Injure, *s.f.* injury, wrong; insult; abuse; taunt; outrage; slander; injustice. *Dire des —s à*, to abuse, to insult, to call names. *Faire — à*, to injure, to wrong; to do injustice; to offend [taunt; to offend
Injurier, *v.a.* to abuse, to insult, to revile; to
Injurieusement, *adv.* injuriously; insultingly, abusively; outrageously; offensively; unjustly [abusive; outrageous; offensive; unjust
Injurieu-x, se, *adj.* injurious; insulting,

Injuste, *adj.m.f., s.m.* unjust, wrong; unrighteous; unjust man, wrong-doer; what is unjust *or* wrong, wrong, injustice
Injustement, *adv.* unjustly, wrongfully; unrighteously; iniquitously
Injustice, *s.f.* injustice; wrong; wrong-doing; unrighteousness; act of injustice
Injustifiable, *adj.* unjustifiable
Injustifiablement, *adv.* unjustifiably
Injustifié, e, *adj.* unjustified
Inlisible, *adj.* unreadable; illegible
Innavigabilité, *s.f.* innavigability; unseaworthiness [unseaworthy
Innavigable, *adj.* innavigable, unnavigable;
Inné, e, *adj.* innate, inborn, natural
Innégociable, *adj.* unnegotiable
Innéité, *s.f.* innateness
Innervable, *adj.* innervable
Innervation, *s.f.* innervation [sillily, foolishly
Innocemment, *adv.* innocently; harmlessly;
Innocence, *s.f.* innocence; harmlessness; silliness, simplicity; ignorance
Innocent, e, *adj.* innocent; guiltless; not guilty; guileless; pure; harmless; silly, foolish, simple; — *s.m.f.* innocent; innocent man *or* woman *or* &c., innocent creature; simpleton, fool; idiot; young pigeon. *La fête des —s*, Innocents' day. *Faire l'—*, to sham innocence *or* ignorance
Innocenter, *v.a.* to declare innocent; to find not guilty; to exculpate, to acquit; to justify; to declare harmless [noxiousness, harmlessness
Innocuité, *s.f.* innocuity, innocuousness, in-
Innombrable, *adj.* innumerable, numberless
Innombrablement, *adv.* innumerably, without number
Innominé, e, *adj.* (*anat.*) innominate. *Os —*, innominate bone, "os innominatum." *Artère —e*, innominate artery, "arteria innominata"
Innommable, *adj.* innominable; unmentionable; for whom *or* which there is no name
Innommé, e, *adj.* unnamed, nameless, nondescript; of no special denomination
Innova-teur, trice, *s.m.f.* innovator, innovatress; — *adj.* innovating
Innovation, *s.f.* innovation
Innover, *v.a.n.* to innovate
Inobservable, *adj.* inobservable
Inobservance, Inobservation, *s.f.* inobservance, non-observance [overlooked
Inobservé, e, *adj.* unobserved, unnoticed,
Inoccupation, *s.f.* inoccupation
Inoccupé, e, *adj.* unoccupied
In-octavo, *adj. s.m.* octavo, 8vo.
Inoculabilité, *s.f.* inoculability
Inoculable, *adj.* inoculable [*adj.* inoculating
Inocula-teur, trice, *s.m.f.* inoculator; —
Inoculation, *s.f.* inoculation; vaccination
Inoculer, *v.a.* to inoculate; to vaccinate
S'—, *v.r.* to inoculate *or* vaccinate oneself; to take the small pox; to be inoculated
Inoculiste, *s.m.* partisan of inoculation
Inodore, *adj.* inodorous, scentless, without smell, free from smell; **—s,** *s.m.pl.* (*fam.*) water-closets, water-closet. *Cabinet —*, water-closet
Inodorité, *s.f.* inodorousness
Inoffensi-f, ve, *adj.* inoffensive
Inoffensivement, *adv.* inoffensively
Inofficiel, le, *adj.* inofficial
Inofficiellement, *adv.* inofficially
Inofficieusement, *adv.* (*law*) inofficiously
Inofficieu-x, se, *adj.* (*law*) inofficious
Inofficiosité, *s.f.* (*law*) inofficiousness
Inondation, *s.f.* inundation, flood, overflow; deluge; (*agr.*) floating
Inondé, e, *part. adj.* inundated, &c. (*V.* **Inonder**); — *s.m.f.* sufferer from inundation; — *s.m.* (*bird*) sedge-warbler, reed-warbler
Inonder, *v.a.* to inundate, to overflow; to deluge; to drench; to cover; to fill; to overrun; to overspread
Inopérable, *adj.* not to be operated
Inopiné, e, *adj.* unexpected, unforeseen, sudden
Inopinément, *adv.* unexpectedly, unawares, suddenly [able
Inopportun, e, *adj.* inopportune, unseason-
Inopportunément, *adv.* inopportunely, unseasonably [ableness
Inopportunité, *s.f.* inopportunity, unseason-
Inorganique, *adj.* inorganic; unorganized
Inorné, e, *adj.* unadorned
Inosate, *s.m.* (*chem.*) inosate
Inosculation, *s.f.* (*anat.*) inosculation
Inosique, *adj.* (*chem.*) inosic
Inosite, *s.f.* (*chem.*) inosite
Inostensible, *adj.* inostensible
Inostensiblement, *adv.* inostensibly
Inosurie, *s.f.* (*med.*) inosuria [be remembered
Inoubliable, *adj.* never to be forgotten, ever to
Inouï, e, *adj.* unheard of, unprecedented, most singular, extraordinary, excessive [oxydizable
Inoxydable, *adj.* inoxidable, inoxidizable, in-
In-plano, *adj. s.m.* (*print.*) broadside
Inqualifiable, *adj.* unqualifiable, for whom *or* which there is no name, for whom *or* which no name is too bad [**tation**
Inquart, *s.m.*, **Inquartation,** *s.f. V.* **Quar-**
***In-quarto,** *adj. s.m.* (*of books*) quarto, 4to.
Inqui-et, ète, *adj.* uneasy; anxious; restless; fidgety; unquiet [restlessly
Inquiètement, *adv.* uneasily; anxiously;
Inquiéter, *v.a.* to disquiet, to alarm, to make uneasy; to trouble, to disturb, to molest, to annoy, to vex, to harass
S'—, *v.r.* to make oneself uneasy, to alarm oneself; to be uneasy *or* anxious; to trouble *or* concern oneself, to care (about *or* for), to think (of); to inquire; to take notice (of)
Inquiétude, *s.f.* disquietude; uneasiness; anxiety; care, thought; alarm; fear; restlessness; fidget; itching; slight pains
Inquisiteur, *s.m.* inquisitor
Inquisiti-f, ve, *adj.* inquisitive, searching
Inquisition, *s.f.* inquisition
Inquisitorial, e, *adj.* inquisitorial
Insaisissabilité, *s.f.* unseizableness, non-liability to be seized
Insaisissable, *adj.* unseizable, not to be seized; not liable to be seized; not distrainable; not to be caught; indiscernible; imperceptible; inconceivable
Insaisissablement, *adv.* indiscernibly; imperceptibly; inconceivably
Insalivation, *s.f.* insalivation [wholesome
Insalubre, *adj.* insalubrious, unhealthy, un-
Insalubrement, *adv.* insalubriously, unhealthily, unwholesomely [unwholesomeness
Insalubrité, *s.f.* insalubrity, unhealthiness,
Insalutaire, *adj.* insalutary
Insanité, *s.f.* insanity
Insapide, *adj.* insapid
Insapidité, *s.f.* insapidity
Insatiabilité, *s.f.* insatiability, insatiableness
Insatiable, *adj.* insatiable
Insatiablement, *adv.* insatiably
Insaturable, *adj.* insaturable
Insaturé, e, *adj.* unsaturated [unconsciously
Insciemment, *adv.* unknowingly, unwittingly,
Inscriptible, *adj.* inscriptible, inscribable
Inscription, *s.f.* inscription; inscribing; writing; epigraph; notice; registry; entry; enrolment; matriculation; term; scrip; stock-receipt. *— de* or *en faux*, allegation of forgery. *Prendre ses —s*, to enter o.'s name for the terms (*at a school*), to keep o.'s terms
Inscrire, *v.a.* to inscribe; to write down, to write, to put *or* set down; to enter; to register
S'—, *v.r.* to inscribe *or* write *or* enter *or* &c. o.'s name; (*math.*) to be inscribed. *— en faux contre*, to plead the falsity of, to dispute the genuineness *or* truth of, to contest, to protest against, to declare ... to be false, to undertake to prove that ... is false [ableness
Inscrutabilité, *s.f.* inscrutability, unsearch-

Inscrutable, *adj.* inscrutable, unsearchable
Inscrutablement, *adv.* inscrutably, unsearchably
Insécabilité, *s.f.* insecability, indivisibility
Insécable, *adj.* insecable, indivisible
Insecte, *s.m.* insect
Insecticide, *adj.* vermin *or* insect-destroying, insecticidal; — *s.m.* insecticide, vermin *or* insect-destroyer
Insectier, *s.m.* insect-case
Insectifère, *adj.* (*min.*) insectiferous
Insectivore, *adj.* insectivorous; — *s.m.* insectivore (*pl.* insectivora, insectivores)
Insectolog-ie, -ique, -iste. *V.* page 3, § 1
Insécurité, *s.f.* insecurity
In-seize, *adj. s.m.* 16mo.
Insensé, e, *adj.* insane, mad; senseless, foolish; — *s.m.f.* madman, mad woman; fool
Insensément, *adv.* madly, senselessly, foolishly
Insensibilité, *s.f.* insensibility; unconsciousness; unfeelingness; hard-heartedness, heartlessness; unconcern; callousness; apathy
Insensible, *adj.* insensible; unconscious; unfeeling; hard-hearted, heartless; unconcerned; senseless; callous; phlegmatic; apathetic; imperceptible
Insensiblement, *adv.* insensibly; unconsciously; imperceptibly; gradually, by degrees, little by little
Inséparabilité, *s.f.* inseparableness
Inséparable, *adj.* inseparable; —**s,** *s.m.f.pl.* inseparable friends, thick *or* fast friends, chums, cronies
Inséparablement, *adv.* inseparably
Insérable, *adj.* to be inserted
Insérer, *v.a.* to insert, to put in, to wedge in
Insermenté, e, *adj.* unsworn
Insertion, *s.f.* insertion
Inserviable, *adj.* unobliging
Inservilité, *s.f.* inservility
Insexé, e, *adj.* unsexed, unsexual
Insidieusement, *adv.* insidiously
Insidieu-x, se, *adj.* insidious
†Insigne, *adj.* notorious, egregious, arrant, downright; signal; — *s.m.,* — **s,** *s.m.pl.* badge, token, mark, insignia
†Insignifiance, *s.f.* insignificance
†Insignifiant, e, *adj.* insignificant
Insinuant, e, *adj.* insinuating, winning, taking
Insinuati-f, ve, *adj.* insinuative
Insinuation, *s.f.* insinuation; suggestion; hint; innuendo; intrigue
Insinuer, *v.a.* to insinuate; to introduce; to suggest; to hint; to intimate; to instil
S'—, *v.r.* to insinuate *or* introduce oneself, to insinuate; to creep (in, into), to get (into); to worm oneself; to steal (in, into)
Insipide, *adj.* insipid; tasteless; unsavoury; flat; spiritless, dull
Insipidement, *adv.* insipidly; dully, heavily
Insipidité, *s.f.* insipidity; tastelessness; unsavouriness; flatness; dulness
Insistance, *s.f.* insistence, insisting; urgent request
Insistant, e, *adj.* insistent; insisting
Insister, *v.n.* to insist; to dwell; to urge
Insociabilité, *s.f.* unsociability; unsociableness
Insociable, *adj.* unsociable
Insociablement, *adv.* unsociably
Insocial, e, *adj.* unsocial
Insolation, *s.f.* insolation
Insolemment, *adv.* insolently, impudently, impertinently
Insolence, *s.f.* insolence, impudence, impertinence, pertness, rudeness, incivility
Insolent, e, *adj.* insolent, impudent, impertinent, pert, saucy; extraordinary, unheard of, undeserved; — *s.m.f.* insolent person, pert fellow, insolent creature, saucy baggage, saucebox, malapert. *Mademoiselle l'—e,* Miss Impudence
Insoler, *v.a.* to insolate, to sun
Insolidarité, *s.f.* insolidarity
Insolide, *adj.* unsolid
Insolidement, *adv.* unsolidly
Insolidité, *s.f.* insolidity
Insolite, *adj.* unusual, unwonted
Insolitement, *adv.* unusually
Insolubilité, *s.f.* insolubility; insolvability
Insoluble, *adj.* insoluble; insolvable
Insolublement, *adv.* insolubly; insolvably
Insolvabilité, *s.f.* insolvency
Insolvable, *adj. s.* insolvent
Insomnie, *s.f.* sleeplessness, want of sleep, insomnia; fit of sleeplessness
Insondable, *adj.* unfathomable, fathomless
Insonore, *adj.* insonorous
Insonorité, *s.f.* insonorousness
Insouci, *s.m.* carelessness, recklessness
Insouciamment, *adv.* carelessly, heedlessly, thoughtlessly, recklessly
Insouciance, *s.f.* carelessness, heedlessness, recklessness, indifference; apathy; neglect, negligence
Insouciant, e, *adj.* careless, heedless, thoughtless, unmindful, reckless, indifferent; neglectful; — *s.m.f.* ditto person
Insoucieusement, *adv.* free from care, carelessly, heedlessly, thoughtlessly
Insoucieu-x, se, *adj.* free from care, unattended with care, easy, careless, heedless, thoughtless
Insoudable, *adj.* unsolderable
Insouffrable, *adj.* insufferable
Insoumis, e, *adj.* unsubdued, unsubjected; unsubmissive, unruly, refractory; defaulting; — *s.m.* defaulting recruit, defaulter
Insoumission, *s.f.* insubmission, unsubmissiveness, unruliness, refractoriness, insubordination, non-compliance
Insoutenable, *adj.* indefensible, unsustainable, untenable; insupportable, unbearable, intolerable
Insoutenablement, *adv.* indefensibly, untenably; unbearably, intolerably
Inspecter, *v.a.* to inspect; to survey, to examine; to superintend; to supervise
Inspec-teur, trice, *s.m.f.* inspector, inspectress; examiner, surveyor; superintendent; supervisor; overseer; vice-principal
Inspection, *s.f.* inspection; examination, survey; inspectorship; surveyorship; superintendence; supervision; view, sight
Inspira-teur, trice, *adj.* inspiring; infusing; suggesting; (*anat.*) inspiratory; — *s.m.f.* inspirer; — *s.m.* (*anat.*) inspiratory muscle
Inspiration, *s.f.* inspiration; inhaling, breathing; suggestion
Inspiratoire, *adj.* inspiratory
Inspirer, *v.a.* to inspire; to inhale, to breathe in, to breathe; to instil; to suggest; to prompt; to advise
S'—, *v.r.* to draw o.'s inspiration, to be inspired
Instabilité, *s.f.* instability
Instable, *adj.* instable, unstable
Instablement, *adv.* instably, unstably
Installateur, *s.m.* inductor
Installation, *s.f.* installation; induction
Installer, *v.a.* to install; to induct; to establish, to settle; to place, to put; to seat
Instamment, *adv.* earnestly, urgently
Instance, *s.f.* entreaty; solicitation; urgency; earnestness; degree of jurisdiction; suit, action, process of a suit; (*obsolete*) rejoinder. *Avec —,* earnestly, urgently. *En —,* soliciting; suing; on the cause-list, about to be tried *or* considered. *Tribunal de première —,* inferior court, county court. *Faire des —s, prier avec —,* to entreat, to urge, to solicit earnestly
Instant, e, *adj.* earnest, urgent, pressing, instant
Instant, *s.m.* instant, moment; trice; while. *A l'—,* instantly; this *or* that instant; immediately; just now. *Un —!* hold! hold hard! stop *or* wait a bit! not so fast! that won't do!
Instantané, e, *adj.* instantaneous
Instantanéité, *s.f.* instantaneousness
Instantanément, *adv.* instantaneously
Instar (A l'— de), *adv.* like, as, similar to, in imitation of, after the fashion of
Instaura-teur, trice, *s.m.f.* instaurator, instauratress; — *adj.* instaurating

Instauration, *s.f.* instauration
Instaurer, *v.a.* to instaurate
Instiga-teur, trice, *s.m.f.* instigator, inciter; — *adj.* instigating, inciting
Instigation, *s.f.* instigation, incitement
Instiguer, *v.a.* to instigate, to incite
Instillation, *s.f.* instillation
Instiller, *v.a.* to instil. *S'*—, to be instilled
Instinct, *s.m.* instinct; (*rid.*) temper. *D'*—, *par* —, instinctively
Instincti-f, ve, *adj.* instinctive
Instinctivement, *adv.* instinctively [ness
Instinctivité, *s.f.* instinctivity, instinctive-
Instinctuel, le, *adj.* instinctual
Instinctuellement, *adv.* instinctually
Instipulé, e, *adj.* (*bot.*) instipulate
Instituer, *v.a.* to institute; to establish; to settle; to found; to appoint [(*religious*)
Institut, *s.m.* institute; institution; order
Institutes, *s.f.pl.* (*law*) institutes
Institu-teur, trice, *s.m.f.* institutor, institutress; founder, foundress; instructor, instructress; tutor, tutoress *or* tutress; teacher; governess; school-master, school-mistress, master *or* mistress of a school
Institution, *s.f.* institution; establishment; settlement; foundation; appointment; institute; instruction, education; boarding-school, school. *Chef d'*—, *V. Chef. Maîtresse d'*—, school-mistress, lady principal of a school
Instructeur, *s.m.* instructor; drill-instructor, drill-sergeant, sergeant-instructor (*of musketry*); riding-master; — *adj.m.* instructing; examining. *Juge* —, examining magistrate. *Officier* —, drill-officer
Instructi-f, ve, *adj.* instructive
Instruction, *s.f.* instruction; education, tuition; lesson, precept; information, knowledge, learning, attainments; direction; (*law*) preliminary proceeding, examination; proceedings, trial
Instruire, *v.a.* to instruct, to teach, to educate; to train up; to inform, to apprise, to acquaint, to make acquainted (with); (*law*) to examine, to prepare (for trial)
S'—, *v.r.* to instruct *or* improve oneself; to inform oneself, to learn; (*law*) to be under examination, to form the subject of an inquiry; to be being made *or* held
Instruisable, *adj.* teachable
Instruit, e, *part. adj.* instructed, &c. (*V.* **Instruire**); informed, aware; well-informed, learned
Instrument, *s.m.* instrument; tool, implement
Instrumentaire, *adj.* (*law*) instrumentary, to
Instrumental, e, *adj.* instrumental [a deed
Instrumentalement, *adv.* instrumentally
Instrumentation, *s.f.* instrumentation
Instrumenter, *v.n.* to make deeds, to draw up instruments; to serve writs, to proceed; to compose instrumental music; — *v.a.* (*mus.*) to
Instrumentiste, *s.m.f.* instrumentalist [score
Instudieu-x, se, *adj.* unstudious
Insu (A l'— de), unknown to. *A mon, son, &c.* —, without my, his *or* her, &c. knowledge, unknown to me, him *or* her, &c.; unknowingly, unwittingly, unconsciously
Insubmersibilité, *s.f.* insubmergibleness
Insubmersible, *adj.* insubmergible, unsubmergible, unsinkable
Insubordination, *s.f.* insubordination
Insubordonné, e, *adj.* insubordinate
Insubstantiel, le, *adj.* unsubstantial
Insuccès, *s.m.* unsuccessfulness, failure
Insuffisamment, *adv.* insufficiently
Insuffisance, *s.f.* insufficiency; incapacity
Insuffisant, e, *adj.* insufficient; inadequate
Insufflateur, *s.m.* insufflator; inhaler; blower
Insufflation, *s.f.* insufflation; inspiration; inflation breathe in; to inflate
Insuffler, *v.a.* to insufflate; to inspire, to
Insuivi, e, *adj.* unattended
Insulaire, *adj.* insular; — *s.m.f.* islander
Insularité, *s.f.* insularity
Insultable, *adj.* insultable; assailable
Insulte, *s.f.* insult, affront; abuse; attack
Insulter, *v.a.n.* to insult, to affront; to abuse; to attack
Insulteu-r, se, *s.m.f.* insulter [to attack
Insupportable, *adj.* insupportable, unbearable, intolerable [unbearably, intolerably
Insupportablement, *adv.* insupportably,
Insurgé, e, *adj. s.* insurgent
Insurgence, *s.f.* insurgency
Insurgent, *s.m.* (*hist.*) insurgent [tion, to rouse
Insurger, *v.a.* to urge *or* stir up to insurrec-
S'—, *v.r.* to rebel, to revolt, to rise
Insurmontable, *adj.* insurmountable, insuperable, unconquerable
Insurmontablement, *adv.* insurmountably, insuperably, unconquerably
Insurpassable, *adj.* unsurpassable
Insurrec-teur, trice, *adj.* insurrectionary; — *s.m.f.* insurrectionist
Insurrection, *s.f.* insurrection, rising, rebellion
Insurrectionnel, le, *adj.* insurrectionary
Insurrectionnellement, *adv.* insurrection-
Insymétrique, *adj.* unsymmetrical [arily
Insymétriquement, *adv.* unsymmetrically
Intact, e, *adj.* intact, untouched; entire; unimpaired, undamaged, sound; unsullied, unblemished, spotless, pure; honest
Intactile, *adj.* intactible
Intactilité, *s.f.* intactibleness
†**Intaille,** *s.f.* intaglio
Intangibilité. *V.* page 3, § 1
Intangible, *adj.* intangible
Intarissable, *adj.* inexhaustible; endless
Intarissablement, *adv.* inexhaustibly; endlessly
Intégral, e, *adj.*, **Intégrale,** *s.f.* integral
Intégralement, *adv.* integrally, wholly, entirely, in full [ness, entirety; (the) whole
Intégralité, *s.f.* integrality, wholeness, entire-
Intégrant, e, *adj.* integrant
Intégration, *s.f.* (*math.*) integration
Intègre, *adj.* upright, honest, just; pure
Intègrement, *adv.* uprightly, honestly, justly
Intégrer, *v.a.* (*math.*) to integrate
Intégrité, *s.f.* integrity; uprightness, honesty; honour; purity; soundness; entireness, entirety
Intégument, *s.m.* (*obsolete*) *V.* **Tégument**
Intellect, *s.m.* intellect, understanding
Intellecti-f, ve, *adj.* intellective; — *s.f.* intel-
Intellection, *s.f.* intellection [ligence, intellect
Intellectualiser, *v.a.* to intellectualize
Intellectualité, *s.f.* intellectuality
Intellectuel, le, *adj.* intellectual
Intellectuellement, *adv.* intellectually
Intelligemment, *adv.* intelligently, knowingly
Intelligence, *s.f.* intelligence; intellect, understanding; mind; spirit; skill, ability; knowledge; acquaintance; intercourse, correspondence, communication; secret correspondence, means of information; union, harmony; league, compact; collusion. *En bonne — avec*, on good terms with. *Être d'*—, to have a mutual understanding, to go hand in hand
Intelligent, e, *adj.* intelligent; quick; sharp, shrewd; clever; sensible
Intelligibilité. *V.* page 3, § 1
Intelligible, *adj.* intelligible; distinct, clear; audible; (*philos.*) intellectual
Intelligiblement, *adv.* intelligibly; distinctly, clearly; audibly; (*philos.*) intellectually
Intempéramment, *adv.* intemperately
Intempérance, *s.f.* intemperance
Intempérant, e, *adj.* intemperate; — *s.m.f.* ditto person
Intempéré, e, *adj.* intemperate, immoderate
Intempérément, *adv.* intemperately, immoderately
Intempérie, *s.f.* inclemency; intemperance
Intempesti-f, ve, *adj.* unseasonable, untimely
Intempestivement, *adv.* unseasonably

Intempestivité, *s.f.* unseasonableness, untimeliness

Intenable, *adj.* untenable

Intendance, *s.f.* management, direction, administration, superintendence; intendancy, intendance; intendant's house; stewardship; (— *militaire*) commissariat

Intendant, *s.m.* steward; surveyor; director; superintendent; master; chief officer; commissary; commissioner; intendant; lord lieutenant. — *militaire*, commissary of stores, chief of the staff

Intendante, *s.f.* superintendent, directress, superioress; intendant's *or* lord lieutenant's wife

Intense, *adj.* intense; violent, severe; great

Intensi-f, ve, *adj.* intensive; extensive

Intensité, *s.f.* intensity; violence, severity; extensiveness

Intensivement, *adv.* intensively; intensely

Intenter, *v.a.* to enter; to bring; to prefer; to institute, to begin, to commence

S'—, *v.r.* to be entered *or* &c.

Intention, *s.f.* intention; intent; purpose, view; meaning; (*mus.*) subject. *A l'— de*, for the sake of, for, on account of. *A mon* (*votre, &c.*) —, for my (your, &c.) sake, for me (you, &c.), on my (your, &c.) account. *Avec* —, intentionally, on purpose

Intentionné, e, *adj.* ...-intentioned, ...-disposed, ...-meaning, ...-minded; intentional

Intentionnel, le, *adj.* intended; of intention; intentional

Intentionnellement, *adv.* in intention; intentionally

Interarticulaire, *adj.* (*anat.*) interarticular

Intercadence, *s.f.* subsultory motion

Intercadent, e, *adj.* subsultory, irregular

Intercalaire, *adj.* intercalary

Intercalateur, *s.m.* intercalator; interpolator

Intercalation, *s.f.* intercalation; insertion; addition; interpolation; interlineation

Intercaler, *v.a.* to intercalate; to insert; to wedge in; to interpolate

Intercéder, *v.n.* to intercede

Intercellulaire, *adj.* intercellular

Interceptation, *s.f.* *V.* **Interception**

Intercepter, *v.a.* to intercept; to cut off; to interrupt; to stop; to shut out

S'—, *v.r.* to be intercepted *or* &c.

Interception, *s.f.* interception; interruption

Intercesseur, *s.m.* intercessor, interceder, mediator

Intercession, *s.f.* intercession, mediation

Interclaviculaire, *adj.* (*anat.*) interclavicular

Intercolonial, e, *adj.* intercolonial

Intercolonialement, *adv.* intercolonially

Intercommunication, *s.f.* intercommunication

Intercontinental, e, *adj.* intercontinental

Intercostal, e, *adj.* (*anat.*) intercostal

Intercourse, *s.f.* intercourse

Intercurrent, e, *adj.* intercurrent

Intercutané, e, *adj.* intercutaneous

Interdiction, *s.f.* interdiction; inhibition; prohibition; suspension; deprivation; interdict; tabooing; taboo

Interdigital, e, *adj.* interdigital

Interdire, *v.a.* to interdict; to inhibit; to prohibit; to suspend; to declare legally (*a man*) incapable of managing his own affairs; to taboo; to forbid; to preclude from; to deprive of; to amaze, to stun, to bewilder, to confuse, to confound, to nonplus, to abash, to dumbfound, to take aback, to take ...'s breath away

S'—, *v.r.* to become confused, to be bewildered *or* &c.

Interdit, e, *part. adj.* interdicted, &c. (*V.* **Interdire**); speechless; sheepish; — *s.m.* person interdicted; interdict; taboo. *Frapper d'—, mettre en* —, to lay under an interdict; to taboo

Intéressé, e, *part. adj.* interested, &c. (*V.* **Intéresser**); self-interested; selfish; — *s.m.f.* interested party, party concerned; self-interested *or* selfish person

Intéresser, *v.a.* to interest; to concern; to affect; to give a share to; to associate; to engage; to gain over; to prejudice; to appeal to; (*of games*) to stake money on; (*med.*) to injure, to affect; — *v.n.* to be interesting, to excite an interest, to have interest

S'—, *v.r.* to interest *or* concern oneself; to be interested *or* concerned, to have an interest; to take an interest (in)

Intérêt, *s.m.* interest; profit; advantage; good; concern; share; indemnification, indemnity; selfishness. — *composé*, — *des intérêts*, compound interest. — *en dedans*, interest deducted from the loan, discount; (*of stocks*, &c.) interest included in the price. — *en dehors*, interest paid at the end of the year, interest; (*of stocks*, &c.) interest not included in the price. *Mettre hors d'—*, to indemnify, to secure. *Prendre* — (or *de l'—*) *à, se prendre d'— pour*, to take *or* have an interest in

Interférence, *s.f.* (*opt.*) interference

Interférent, e, *adj.* (*opt.*) interfering

Interférer, *v.n.* (*opt.*) to interfere

Interfoliacé, e, *adj.* (*bot.*) interfoliaceous

Interfolier, *v.a.* to interleave

Intérieur, e, *adj.* interior, internal, inward, inner, inside; intrinsic; inland; domestic; home; meditative; — *s.m.* interior; inside; inland; home; home-life; private life; privacy; heart; conscience; soul; Home department. *A l'—*, within, in the inside, inside; internally; in doors; inland; at home. *D'—*, inside; inland; in-door; of home-life, of private life, domestic. *Dans son* —, home, at home; in privacy; in private life. *Ministère de l'—*, Home department. *Ministre de l'—*, Home secretary. *Tableau d'—*, picture *or* scene of home-life. *Ville de l'—*, inland town

Intérieurement, *adv.* internally, inwardly, inwards, within, inside

Intérim, *s.m.* interim. *Par* —, ad interim

Intérimaire, *adj.* ad interim, interim; — *s.m.f.* substitute ad interim, interim functionary

Intérimairement, *adv.* ad interim

Intérimat, *s.m.* interim functions

Intériorité, *s.f.* interiority

Interjecti-f, ve, *adj.* interjectional

Interjection, *s.f.* (*gram.*) interjection; (*law*) lodging (*of an appeal*)

Interjectivement, *adv.* interjectionally

Interjeter, *v.a.* (*law*) to lodge (*an appeal*)

†Interligne, *s.m.* space *or* insertion between two lines, interlineation, interline; (*mus.*) space; — *s.f.* (*print.*) lead

†Interligner, *v.a.* to interline; to space out (*lines*); (*print.*) to lead

Interlinéaire, *adj.* interlinear

Interlinéation, *s.f.* interlineation

Interlinéer, *v.a.* to interline

Interlocu-teur, trice, *s.m.f.* interlocutor, interlocutress, speaker

Interlocution, *s.f.* interlocution; dialogue

Interlocutoire, *adj.* interlocutory; — *s.m.* interlocutory judgment *or* decree

Interlope, *s.m.* interloper; interloping trade; — *adj.* interloping; smuggling; contraband; fraudulent; clandestine; intrusive; flash *or* gay (*society, world*)

Interloquer, *v.a.* to puzzle, to silence, to shut up, to confuse, to confound, to dumbfound, to abash

S'—, *v.r.* to become confused, to be puzzled *or* &c.

Interlunaire, *adj.* (*astr.*) interlunar

Interlune, Interlunium, *s.m.* (*astr.*) interlunium

Intermariage, *s.m.* intermarriage

Intermaxillaire, *adj.* intermaxillary

Intermède, *s.m.* interlude, intermede; medium, intermedium, intermediate; vehicle

Intermédiaire, *adj.* intermediate; intervening; — *s.m.* intermedium, intermediate agent; medium; middleman; — *s.m.f.* medium, go-between

Intermédiairement, *adv.* intermediately
Intermédiarité, *s.f.* intermediateness
Intermédiat, e, *adj.* intermediate
Interminable, *adj.* interminable; endless
Interminé, e, *adj.* unterminated, unfinished; unbounded, boundless, unlimited
Intermission, *s.f.* intermission
Intermittence, *s.f.* intermittent character *or* nature; intermission [mitting
Intermittent, e, *adj.* intermittent; inter-
Intermonde, *s.m.* intermundane space
Intermusculaire, *adj.* intermuscular
Internat, *s.m.* boarding-school; house-surgeonship (*of hospitals*)
International, e, *adj.* international
Internationalement, *adv.* internationally
Interne, *adj.* internal, inward, interior; indoor, in; resident; — *s.m.f.* resident; boarder; (*of hospitals*) house-surgeon. *Élève* —, boarder; house-surgeon [country, confinement
Internement, *s.m.* confinement within the
Interner, *v.a.n.* to confine within the country, to confine; to introduce into the country, to introduce; to reside within the country, to reside
Internissable, *adj.* that cannot be sullied
Internonce, *s.m.* internuncio
Internonciature, *s.f.* internunciature
Interocéanique, *adj.* interoceanic
Interoculaire, *adj.* interocular
Interosseu-x, se, *adj.* (*anat., surg.*) interosseous, interosseal. *Couteau* —, (*surg.*) catlin
Interpella-teur, trice, *s.f.* interpellator; questioner; summoner [summons, call
Interpellation, *s.f.* interpellation; question;
Interpeller, *v.a.* to interpellate; to question, to put a question to; to summon, to call on; to address, to speak to; to appeal to
Interpolateur, *s.m.* interpolator
Interpolation, *s.f.* interpolation
Interpoler, *v.a.* to interpolate, to insert, to foist
Interponctuation, *s.f.* interpunction
Interposer, *v.a.,* **S'**—, *v.r.* to interpose
Interposition, *s.f.* interposition, intervention
Interprétable, *adj.* interpretable
Interpréta-teur, trice, *s.m.f.* interpreter, interpretress, expounder; — *adj.* interpretative
Interprétati-f, ve, *adj.* interpretative [tion
Interprétation, *s.f.* interpretation; construc-
Interprétativement, *adv.* interpretatively
Interprète, *s.m.f.* interpreter, interpretress; translator, translatress; expounder; expositor; augur; (*bird*) turnstone. *Muets* —*s*, eyes, looks, sweet looks
Interpréter, *v.a.* to interpret; to translate; to expound, to explain; to construe; to put a (*good or bad*) construction upon
S'—, *v.r.* to be interpreted *or* &c.
†Interrègne, *s.m.* interregnum
Interrogant, e, *adj.* interrogating, questioning, inquisitive; of interrogation
Interroga-teur, trice, *s.m.f.* interrogator; questioner; querist; inquirer; examiner; — *adj.* interrogating, questioning, inquiring, inquisitive [rogatory; of interrogation
Interrogati-f, ve, *adj.* interrogative, inter-
Interrogation, *s.f.* interrogation; question; examination
Interrogativement, *adv.* interrogatively
Interrogatoire, *s.m.* interrogatory, examination [to examine; to consult
Interroger, *v.a.* to interrogate, to question;
S'—, *v.r.* to examine oneself *or* o.'s own conscience; to question each other
Interroi, *s.m.* interrex, regent
Interrompre, *v.a.* to interrupt; to break off; to break; to stop; to suspend; to leave off; to disturb; (*law*) to bar
S'—, *v.r.* to interrupt oneself *or* each other, to break off, to stop, to leave off; (*of things*) to be interrupted *or* &c.
Interrup-teur, trice, *s.m.f.* interrupter; — *adj.* interrupting, interruptive of interruption
Interruption, *s.f.* interruption; discontinuance; intermission; suspension; (*law*) bar
Interscapulaire, *adj.* (*anat.*) interscapular
Intersecter, *v.a.,* **S'**—, *v.r.* to intersect
Intersection, *s.f.* intersection
Interstellaire, *adj.* (*astr.*) interstellar
Interstice, *s.m.* interstice; interval; opening
Interstitiel, le, *adj.* interstitial
Intertrigineu-x, se, *adj.* (*med.*) intertriginous
Intertrigo, *s.m.* (*med*) intertrigo
Intertropical, e, *adj.* intertropical
Intervalle, *s.m.* interval; distance; space; room; opening
Intervenir, *v.n.* to intervene; to interfere; to interpose; to use o.'s influence; to happen, to occur [tervener; — *adj.* intervening
Interven-teur, trice, *s.m.f.* interventor, in-
Interventi-f, ve, *adj.* interventive
Intervention, *s.f.* intervention, interference
Interversion, *s.f.* inversion
Intervertébral, e, *adj.* (*anat.*) intervertebral
Intervertir, *v.a.* to invert; to reverse; to change [reversing; changing
Intervertissement, *s.m.* inverting, inversion;
Intervertisseur, *s.m.* inverter
Intestable, *adj.* (*law*) intestable
Intestat, *s.m. adj.* intestate. *Ab* —, *V. Letter* **A**
Intestin, e, *adj.* internal, interior; domestic; civil; — *s.m.* intestine, bowel
Intestinal, e, *adj.* intestinal
Intimation, *s.f.* notification; notice
Intime, *adj.* intimate; familiar; inward, inmost; deep; secret; close; — *s.m.f.* intimate friend, intimate; (*theat.*) hired clapper
Intimé, e, *s.m.f.* (*law*) appellee, defendant
Intimement, *adv.* intimately; familiarly; inwardly; deeply; secretly; closely
Intimer, *v.a.* to notify; to give notice; to give notice of appeal; to summon; to convoke, to assemble, to call
Intimidable, *adj.* accessible to intimidation
Intimida-teur, trice, *s.m.f.* intimidator; — *adj.* intimidatory
Intimidation, *s.f.* intimidation
Intimidé, e, *part. adj.* intimidated, frightened, abashed, cowed; nervous [abash, to cow
Intimider, *v.a.* to intimidate, to frighten, to
S'—, *v.r.* to become (*or* be) intimidated *or* &c.; to be nervous; to become confused
Intimité, *s.f.* intimacy; closeness, close connection, connection; inmost recesses
Intinction, *s.f.* (*Cath. lit.*) intinction
Intitulation, *s.f.* entitling; title; inscription
Intitulé, *s.m.* title (*of a deed or book*)
Intituler, *v.a.* to entitle, to call, to name
Intolérabilité, *s.f.* intolerableness
Intolérable, *adj.* intolerable
Intolérablement, *adv.* intolerably
Intolérammment, *adv.* intolerantly
Intolérance, *s.f.* intolerance
Intolérant, e, *adj. s.* intolerant
Intolérantisme, *s.m.* system of intolerance
Intoléré, e, *adj.* intolerated, untolerated
Intonation, *s.f.* intonation
Intorsion, *s.f.* intortion, intorsion
Intouchable, *adj.* untouchable
Intoxicant, e, *adj.* (*med.*) poisonous
Intoxication, *s.f.* (*med.*) poisoning
Intoxiquer, *v.a.* (*med.*) to poison
Intracé, e, *adj.* untraced; not laid out
Intrados, *s.m.* (*arch.*) intrados
Intraduisible, *adj.* untranslatable; inexpressible; indescribable
Intraduit, e, *adj.* untranslated [unreasonable
Intraitable, *adj.* intractable, unmanageable;
Intra-muros, *adv. adj. V.* **Muros**
Intransiti-f, ve, *adj.* intransitive
Intransitivement, *adv.* intransitively
Intransmuable, *adj.* intransmutable
Intransmutabilité, *s.f.* intransmutability
Intransparence, *s.f.* intransparency
Intransparent, e, *adj.* untransparent

Intransportable, *adj.* irremovable [able
Intraversable, *adj.* not to be crossed, impass-
Intraversé, e, *adj.* uncrossed
In-trente-deux, *adj. s.m.* 32mo.
Intrépide, *adj.* intrepid, fearless, dauntless, undaunted; — *s.m.f.* ditto person [dauntedly
Intrépidement, *adv.* intrepidly, fearlessly, un-
Intrépidité, *s.f.* intrepidity, fearlessness, dauntlessness, undauntedness
†**Intrigailler,** *v.n.* to engage in petty intrigues
†**Intrigailleu-r, se,** *s.m.f.* petty *or* mean intriguer
Intrigant, e, *adj.* intriguing; — *s.m.f.* intriguer
Intriguant, *part.* intriguing; puzzling; &c. (*V.* **Intriguer**)
Intrigue, *s.f.* intrigue, plot; intriguery
Intriguer, *v.n.* to intrigue; — *v.a.* to puzzle, to perplex, to disturb, to make uneasy; to lay the plot of, to plot
S'—, *v.r.* to intrigue; to creep in, to worm oneself in; to set o.'s wits to work, to puzzle *or* rack o.'s brains, to strive hard, to take pains; to puzzle *or* &c. each other
Intrigueu-r, se, *s.m.f.* intriguer
Intrinsèque, *adj.* intrinsic
Intrinsèquement, *adv.* intrinsically
Introduc-teur, trice, *s.m.f.* introducer [tory
Introducti-f, ve, *adj.* introductive, introduc-
Introduction, *s.f.* introduction; entrance; beginning; first part; first process
Introductoire, *adj.* introductory
Introduire, *v.a.* to introduce; to conduct in, to show in; to convey in; to slip in; to thrust in; to foist; to put in; to bring in; to let in; to intrude; to begin
S'—, *v.r.* to introduce oneself *or* itself; to get in, to enter, to penetrate; to break in; to intrude; to be introduced *or* &c.; to begin
Introït, *s.m.* (*Cath. rel.*) introit
Intromission, *s.f.* intromission
Intrôner, *v.a.* to enthrone [tion
Intronisation, *s.f.* enthronement, enthroniza-
Introniser, *v.a.* to enthrone, to enthronize; (*fig.*) to establish
Introspecti-f, ve, *adj.* introspective
Introspection, *s.f.* introspection
Introuvable, *adj.* not to be found, undiscoverable; matchless. *V.* **Chambre**
Introuvé, e, *adj.* unfound, undiscovered
Intrure, *v.a.* (*old*) to intrude [*s.m.f.* intruder
Intrus, e, *part. adj.* intruded, intrusive; —
Intrusion, *s.f.* intrusion. *Roche d'—*, intru-
Intuiti-f, ve, *adj.* intuitive [sive rock
Intuition, *s.f.* intuition
Intuitivement, *adv.* intuitively
Intumescence, *s.f.* intumescence
Intumescent, e, *adj.* intumescent
Intussusception, *s.f.* intussusception
Inule, *s.f.* (*bot.*) inula
Inuline, *s.f.* (*chem.*) inuline
Inurbanité, *s.f.* inurbanity
Inusable, *adj.* that will never wear out
Inusé, e, *adj.* not worn out
Inusité, e, *adj.* unusual; unused, not in use;
Inustion, *s.f.* inustion [out of use, obsolete
Inutile, *adj.* useless; of no use; unnecessary; needless; unavailable; idle [purpose
Inutilement, *adv.* uselessly, in vain, to no
Inutilisable, *adj.* inutilizable
Inutilisé, e, *adj.* unutilized [thing; idleness
Inutilité, *s.f.* inutility, uselessness; useless
Invagination, *s.f.* (*surg.*) invagination
Invaginer, *v.a.* (*surg.*) to invaginate
S'—, *v.r.* to become invaginated
Invaincu, e, *adj.* unvanquished, unconquered;
Invalidation, *s.f.* invalidation [unsurpassed
Invalide, *adj. s.m.f.* invalid; infirm; disabled; void; disabled soldier *or* sailor; (military or naval) pensioner; —**s,** *s.m.pl.* invalids, &c.; retiring pension *or* allowance, pension; (*hotel des —s*) Invalides, hospital for disabled soldiers
Invalidement, *adv.* invalidly [*or* sailors
Invalider, *v.a.* (*law*) to invalidate; to vitiate
Invalidité, *s.f.* invalidity
Invariabilité, *s.f.* invariability, invariableness
Invariable, *adj.m.f.*, *s.m.* invariable
Invariablement, *adv.* invariably
Invasi-f, ve, *adj.* invasive
Invasion, *s.f.* invasion; irruption; outbreak
Invecti-f, ve, *adj.*, **Invective,** *s.f.* invective
Invectiver, *v.n.* to inveigh
Invendable, *adj.* unsalable
Invendu, e, *adj.* unsold
Invengé, e, *adj.* unavenged
Inventaire, *s.m.* inventory; stock-taking; (*pop.*) *V.* **Éventaire**; (*obsolete*) auction, sale. *Faire l'—*, to take stock; to take an inventory (of). *Sous bénéfice d'—*, with liability for the debts of the succession only up to the amount of the inventory; (*fig.*) only to a certain point, conditionally [trive; to imagine; to forge; to coin
Inventer, *v.a.* to invent; to find out; to con-
S'—, *v.r.* to be invented, &c.
Inven-teur, trice, *s.m.f.* inventor, inventress; finder; contriver; author
Inventi-f, ve, *adj.* inventive
Invention, *s.f.* invention; discovery; finding; trover; contrivance; fiction; untruth; trick
Inventorier, *v.a.* to inventory, to take an inventory of, to catalogue
Inversable, *adj.* not to be overturned *or* upset
Inverse, *adj.* inverse, inverted; contrary; —
Inversement, *adv.* inversely [*s.f.* reverse
Inversi-f, ve, *adj.* inversive
Inversion, *s.f.* inversion; (*mil.*) inverted order
Invertébré, e, *adj.*, **Invertébré,** *s.m.* inver-
Invertir, *v.a.* to invert, to reverse [tebrate
Investiga-teur, trice, *s.m.f.* investigator, inquirer; — *adj.* investigating, inquiring
Investigation, *s.f.* investigation; inquiry
Investir, *v.a.* to invest; — *v.n.* (*nav.*) to land
Investissement, *s.m.* investment
Investiture, *s.f.* investiture
Invétéré, e, *adj.* inveterate
Invétérer, *v.n.*, **S'—,** *v.r.* to become inveterate
Invigilance, *s.f.* invigilance
Invigoration, *s.f.* (*physiology*) invigoration
Invination, *s.f.* (*theol.*) invination
Invincibilité, *s.f.* invincibility; irresistibleness; unanswerableness
Invincible, *adj.* invincible, unconquerable; irresistbile; unanswerable; inevitable
Invinciblement, *adv.* invincibly, unconquerably; irresistibly; unanswerably; inevitably
In-vingt-quatre, *adj. s.m.* 24mo.
Inviolabilité, *s.f.* inviolability
Inviolable, *adj.* inviolable; inviolate; sacred
Inviolablement, *adv.* inviolably
Inviolé, e, *adj.* inviolate
Inviscation, *s.f.* inviscation
Invisibilité, *s.f.* invisibility
Invisible, *adj.* invisible, not to be seen
Invisiblement, *adv.* invisibly
Invisquer, *v.a.* to inviscate
Invitati-f, ve, *adj.* invitatory
Invitation, *s.f.* invitation; incitement; inducement; advice; request; bidding; exhortation; call; requisition; summons
Invitatoire, *adj.m.f.*, *s.m.* invitatory [Peter
Invite, *s.f.* (*at whist*) signal for trumps, Blue
Invité, e, *part. adj.* invited, &c. (*V.* **Inviter**); — *s.m.f.* person invited, guest
Inviter, *v.a.* to invite; to engage; to tempt, to allure; to incite; to induce; to advise; to ask; to request; to beg of; to bid; to exhort; to call; to summon
Invocabit, *s.m.* first Sunday in Lent [invoking
Invoca-teur, trice, *s.m.f.* invoker; — *adj.*
Invocation, *s.f.* invocation
Invocatoire, *adj.* invocatory
Involontaire, *adj.* involuntary; forced; unintended, unintentional [tentionally
Involontairement, *adv.* involuntarily, unin-
Involucelle, *s.m.* (*bot.*) involucel

Involucellé, e, *adj.* (*bot.*) involucellate
Involucral, e, *adj.* (*bot.*) involucral
Involucre, *s.m.* (*bot.*) involucre, cover, husk
Involucré, e, *adj.* (*bot.*) involucred
Involuté, e, *adj.* (*bot.*) involute, involuted
Involution, *s.f.* involution, involvement, involvedness
Invoquer, *v.a.* to invoke, to call, to call upon; to plead; to appeal to
Invraisemblable, *adj.* unlikely, improbable
Invraisemblablement, *adv.* unlikely, improbably
Invraisemblance, *s.f.* unlikelihood, improbability; improbable thing
Invulnérabilité. *V.* page 3, § 1
Invulnérable, *adj.* invulnerable
Invulnérablement, *adv.* invulnerably
Iodate, *s.m.* (*chem.*) iodate
Iode, *s.m.* (*chem.*) iodine
Ioder, *v.a.* to iodize
Iodeu-x, se, *adj.* (*chem.*) iodous
Iodhydrate, *s.m.* (*chem.*) hydriodate
Iodhydrique, *adj.* (*chem.*) hydriodic
Iodique, *adj.* (*chem.*) iodic
Iodisme, *s.m.* (*med.*) iodism
Iodo-, (*in compounds, chem.*) iodo-...
Iodure, *s.m.* (*chem.*) iodide
Iodurer, *v.a.* to iodidize
Iolithe, *s.m.* (*min.*) iolite
Ionien, ne, Ionique, *adj.* Ionian; Ionic
Ionidium, *s.m.* (*bot.*) cuichunchulli
Iostchik, *s.m.* (*Russian*) sledge-driver, cabman
Iota, *s.m.* iota; jot, tittle
Iotacisme, *s.m.* iotacism
Iouler, *v.n.* to sing in the Swiss *or* Tyrolese manner
Ipécacuana, *s.m.* ipecacuanha
Ipomée, *s.f.* (*bot.*) ipomæa
Ipso facto, *adv.* (*Latin*) ipso facto, in *or* by the fact itself, by the very deed
Irascibilité, *s.f.* irascibility
Irascible, *adj.* irascible
Irato (Ab), *adv.* (*Latin*) in a passion
Ire, *s.f.* ire, wrath, anger
Irène, *s.f.* (*astr.*) Irene
Iriartéa, *s.m.* (*bot.*) iriartea
Iridacées, Iridées, *s.f.pl.* (*bot.*) iridaceæ, irideæ
Iridescence, *s.f.* iridescence
Iridescent, e, *adj.* iridescent
Iridium, *s.m.* (*chem.*) iridium
Iridotomie, *s.f.* (*surg.*) iridotomy
Irien, ne, *adj.* (*anat.*) irian
Iris, *s.m.* iris, rainbow; (*bot., anat.*) iris. *Poudre d'—*, powdered iris-root *or* orris-root
Irisation, *s.f.* irisation
Iriser, *v.a.*, **S'—,** *v.r.* to irisate
Iritis, *s.f.* (*med.*) iritis
Irlandais, e, *adj. s.* Irish; Irishman; Irish boy; Irish woman *or* lady *or* girl; Irish fashion
Iron-ie, -ique, -iquement. *V.* page 3, § 1
Ironiser, *v.n.a.* (*fam.*) to chaff
Iroquois, e, *s.m.f.* Iroquois; eccentric fellow, rum one, odd fish; guy; fool; — *s.m.* unintelligible stuff, double-Dutch; — *adj.m.f.* eccentric, odd, uncouth
Irraccommodable, *adj.* unmendable
Irrachetable, *adj.* unredeemable
Irracheté, e, *adj.* unredeemed
Irracontable, *adj.* unrelatable
Irradiation, *s.f.* irradiation, irradiance
Irradier, *v.n.a.*, **S'—,** *v.r.* to irradiate
Irraisonnable, *adj.* irrational
Irraisonnablement, *adv.* irrationally
Irraisonné, e, *adj.* unreasoned, thoughtless
Irrassasié, e, *adj.* unsatiated
Irratifiable, *adj.* irratifiable
Irrationnel, le, *adj.* irrational
Irrationnellement, *adv.* irrationally
Irréalisable, *adj.* unrealizable
Irrecevable, *adj.* unreceivable; inadmissible
Irréconciliable, *adj.* irreconcilable
Irréconciliablement, *adv.* irreconcilably
Irréconcilié, e, *adj.* unreconciled
Irrecouvrable, *adj.* irrecoverable
Irrécupérable, *adj.* irrecoverable
Irrécusable, *adj.* unexceptionable, unobjectionable, undeniable
Irrécusablement, *adv.* unexceptionably, unobjectionably, undeniably
Irréductibilité, *s.f.* irreducibleness
Irréductible, *adj.* irreducible
Irréel, le, *adj.* unreal
Irréfléchi, e, *adj.* unreflecting, unthinking, thoughtless, inconsiderate, unguarded; unpremeditated
Irréflexion, *s.f.* thoughtlessness
Irréformable, *adj.* unreformable; irreclaimable; irrevocable
Irréfragabilité, *s.f.* irrefragability
Irréfragable, *adj.* irrefragable
Irréfragablement, *adv.* irrefragably
Irréfutabilité. *V.* page 3, § 1
Irréfutable, *adj.* irrefutable
Irréfutablement, *adv.* irrefutably
Irréfuté, e, *adj.* unrefuted
Irrégularité, *s.f.* irregularity
Irréguli-er, ère, *adj.* irregular
Irrégulièrement, *adv.* irregularly
Irrélati-f, ve, *adj.* irrelative
Irréligieusement, *adv.* irreligiously
Irréligieu-x, se, *adj.* irreligious
Irréligion, *s.f.* irreligion
Irreligiosité, *s.f.* irreligiousness
Irremarquable, *adj.* unremarkable
Irremboursable, *adj.* unrepayable; unredeemable
Irrémédiable, *adj.* irremediable, irretrievable, irrecoverable
Irrémédiablement, *adv.* irremediably, irretrievably, irrecoverably
Irrémissible, *adj.* irremissible
Irrémissiblement, *adv.* irremissibly
Irréparabilité, *s.f.* irreparability; irretrievableness
Irréparable, *adj.* irreparable; irretrievable
Irréparablement, *adv.* irreparably; irretrievably
Irréparé, e, *adj.* unrepaired; unretrieved
Irréplicable, *adj.* unanswerable
Irrépréhensibilité, *s.f.* irreprehensibleness
Irrépréhensible, *adj.* irreprehensible
Irrépréhensiblement, *adv.* irreprehensibly
Irrépressible, *adj.* irrepressible
Irrépressiblement, *adv.* irrepressibly
Irréprimable, *adj.* (*old*) *V.* **Irrépressible**
Irréprochabilité, *s.f.* irreproachableness
Irréprochable, *adj.* irreproachable, unexceptionable, blameless, faultless
Irréprochablement, *adv.* irreproachably, unexceptionably, blamelessly, faultlessly
Irreproducti-f, ve, *adj.* irreproductive
Irreproductivement, *adv.* irreproductively
Irrésistibilité, *s.f.* irresistibility
Irrésistible, *adj.* irresistible
Irrésistiblement, *adv.* irresistibly
Irrésolu, e, *adj.* irresolute
Irrésoluble, *adj.* irresoluble; insolvable
Irrésolûment, *adv.* irresolutely
Irrésolution, *s.f.* irresolution
Irrespectueusement, *adv.* disrespectfully
Irrespectueu-x, se, *adj.* disrespectful
Irrespirabilité, *s.f.* irrespirability, unrespirableness
Irrespirable, *adj.* irrespirable, unrespirable
Irresponsabilité, *s.f.* irresponsibility
Irresponsable, *adj.* irresponsible
Irresponsablement, *adv.* irresponsibly
Irrétractable, *adj.* irretractable
Irrétrécissable, *adj.* unshrinkable
Irréussite, *s.f.* (*old*) *V.* **Insuccès**
Irrévéremment, *adv.* irreverently
Irrévérence, *s.f.* irreverence; disrespect
Irrévérencieusement, *adv.* disrespectfully
Irrévérencieu-x, se, *adj.* disrespectful
Irrévérent, e, *adj.* irreverent
Irrévocabilité, *s.f.* irrevocability, irrevocableness, irreversibleness, irrepealableness
Irrévocable, *adj.* irrevocable, irreversible, irrepealable

Irrévocablement, *adv.* irrevocably, irreversibly, irrepealably [repealed
Irrévoqué, e, *adj.* unrevoked, unreversed, un-
Irrigateur, *s.m.* watering-engine, garden-engine, hydropult; injecting-apparatus, enema
Irrigation, *s.f.* irrigation; watering; injection
Irrigatoire, *adj.* irrigating, watering; injecting
Irriguer, *v.a.* to irrigate; to water
Irrision, *s.f.* irrision, derision, laughing
Irritabilité, *s.f.* irritability
Irritable, *adj.* irritable
Irritant, e, *adj.* irritating, irritant; — *s.m.* irritant. *Clause —e,* essential condition
Irritati-f, ve, *adj.* irritative
Irritation, *s.f.* irritation; angry feeling, vexation, exasperation [angry, raging, wroth
Irrité, e, *part. adj.* irritated, &c. (*V.* **Irriter**);
Irriter, *v.a.* to irritate; to excite; to provoke; to incense; to exasperate; to enrage; to inflame; to chafe; to make sore; to sting; to increase, to aggravate

S'—, *v.r.* to become *or* get angry *or* exasperated, to get into a passion; to become *or* get irritated; to rage; to chafe; to become impatient; to increase

Irrorateur, *s.m.* scented fountain
Irroration, *s.f.* irroration, bedewing, watering
Irruption, *s.f.* irruption, inroad. *Faire —,* to make an irruption; to break in *or* out; to pervade
Isabelle, *adj.* isabel-coloured, isabelle-coloured, isabel, isabelle; dove-coloured; (*of horses*) dun; — *s.m.* isabel colour, isabelle colour, isabel, isabelle; dove colour; — *s.m.f.* dun horse *or* mare
Isard, *s.m.* izard (*wild goat of the Pyrenees*)
Isatine, *s.f.* (*chem.*) isatine
Isatis, *s.m.* (*bot.*) woad; (*zool.*) arctic fox
‡**Ischém-ie, -ique,** (*med.*) *V.* page 3, § 1
‡**Ischiagre,** *s.f.* (*med.*) ischiagra
‡**Ischial, e,** *adj.* (*anat.*) ischial
‡**Ischiatique,** *adj.* (*anat.*) ischiatic
‡**Ischio-,** (*in compounds, anat.*) ischio-...
‡**Ischiocèle,** *s.f.* (*med.*) ischiocele
‡**Ischion,** *s.m.* (*anat.*) ischium
‡**Ischurétique,** *adj.* (*med.*) ischuretic
‡**Ischurie,** *s.f.* (*med.*) ischuria, ischury
Isérine, *s.f.* (*min.*) iserine
Isiaque, *adj.* Isiac
Isis, *s.f.* (*myth., astr.*) Isis
Islam, *s.m.* Islam
Islamique, *adj.* Islamitic
Islamisme, *s.m.* Islamism
Islamite, *s.m.f.* Islamite; — *adj.* Islamitic
Islandais, e, *adj. s.* Icelandic; Icelander
Ismaélien, *s.m.* Ismaelian
Ismaélisme, *s.m.* Ismaelism
Ismaélite, *s.m.* Ishmaelite; — *adj.* Ishmaelitish
Iso, (*in compounds*) iso...
Isobarométrique, *adj.* isobarometric
Isocèle, *adj.* (*bad spelling*) *V.* **Isoscèle**
‡**Isochimène,** *adj.* (*meteorology*) isochimenal; — *s.f.* isochimene, isocheim
‡**Isochromatique,** *adj.* isochromatic
‡**Isochrone,** *adj.* isochronal, isochronous
‡**Isochron-ique, -iquement, -isme.** *V.* [page 3, § 1
Isodynamique, *adj.* isodynamic
Isogone, *adj.* (*geom.*) isagonal; — *s.m.* isagon
Isographie, *s.f.* isography
Isolable, *adj.* isolable; insulable
Isolateur, *s.m. V.* **Isoloir**
Isolation, *s.f.* (*phys.*) insulation
Isolé, e, *part. adj.* isolated; insulated; separated, separate; apart; detached; unattached; unconnected; lonely, solitary, retired; alone
Isolement, *s.m.* isolation; insulation; separation; retirement; seclusion; loneliness; solitude
Isolément, *adv.* separately, apart; solitarily
Isoler, *v.a.* to isolate; to insulate; to separate; to seclude; to detach; to keep away

S'—, *v.r.* to isolate oneself; to live lonely *or* retired; to retire; to be solitary; (*of things*) to be isolated *or* insulated *or* &c.

Isologue, *adj.* (*chem.*) isologous
Isoloir, *s.m.* (*phys.*) insulator
Isomère, *adj.* isomeric
Isomér-ie, -ique, -isme. *V.* page 3, § 1
Isométrique. *V.* page 3, § 1
Isomorphe, *adj.* isomorphous
Isomorph-ie, -isme. *V.* page 3, § 1
Isopérimètre, *adj.* (*geom.*) isoperimetrical
Isopétale, *adj.* (*bot.*) isopetalous
Isopode, *adj.* (*zool.*) isopodous, isopod; — *s.m.*
Isoscèle, *adj.* isosceles [isopod
Isothère, *adj.* (*meteorology*) isotheral; — *s.f.*
Isotherme, *adj.* (*phys.*) isothermal [isothere
Israël, *s.m.* Israel
Israélite, *s.m.f.* Israelite, Hebrew, Jew, Jewess; — *adj.* Israelitic, Jewish, Hebrew. *Bon —,* (*obsolete*) sincere guileless man
Issant, e, *adj.* (*her.*) issuant
Isséro, *s.m.* issero (*south-east wind in the Mediterranean*)
Issois, *s.m.* mongrel dog
Issu, e, *adj.* sprung, born, descended
Issue, *s.f.* issue; egress; exit; outlet; way out; escape; way; passage; vent; end; means; expedient; loophole; refuse; offal, garbage, tripes, fry; drainage; (*flour and bran*) pollard. *A l'— de,* on leaving, after
Isthme, *s.m.* isthmus. *— du gosier,* (*anat.*) isthmus of the fauces, posterior fauces
Isthmien, ne, Isthmique, *adj.* Isthmian
Isthmique, *s.f.* (*Gr. liter.*) Isthmic (*Pindar's*)
Istrien, ne, *adj. s.* Istrian
Itac-isme, -iste. *V.* page 3, § 1
Ita est, *adv.* (*Latin*) it is so, so it is
Itague, *s.f.* (*nav.*) tye, runner
Italianiser, *v.a.n.* to italianize [come Italian

S'—, *v.r.* to become *or* be italianized, to be-

Italianisme, Italicisme. *V.* page 3, § 1
Italien, ne, *adj.* Italian; — *s.m.f.* Italian (*man or boy*); Italian woman *or* lady *or* girl; — *s.m.* Italian (*language*); — *s.f.* Italian fashion; Italian sauce. *Les Italiens,* the Italians, the Italian people; the Italian opera
Italique, *adj.* (*of ancient Italy, obsolete, poet.*) Italian, Italic; (*print.*) italic; — *s.m.* italic (*type*); — *s.f.* italic (*letter*)
Italisme, *s.m.* italicism
Italo-gothique, *adj.* Italo-Gothic
Item, *adv.* item, also, likewise, ditto; — *s.m.* item; (*fam.*) thing, matter, story; hitch, rub
Itérati-f, ve, *adj.* iterative, repeated
Itération, *s.f.* iteration, repetition
Itérativement, *adv.* iteratively, iteratedly,
Itérer, *v.a.* to iterate, to repeat [repeatedly
Ithos, *s.m.* (*obsolete*) ethics
Itinéraire, *s.m.* itinerary; line; beat; route; journey; guide-book, guide; — *adj.* itinerary; way, road. *Colonne —,* way-post, guide-post
Itou, *adv.* (*pop., jest.*) also, too, likewise
Iule, *s.m.* (*bot.*) julus, catkin; (*zool.*) julus, iulus, snake milleped, gally-worm
Ive, Ivette, *s.f.* (*bot.*) wall-germander
Ivoire, *s.m.* ivory; (*anat.*) bone (*of the teeth*); (*mollusc*) ivory-shell, eburna; (*fig.*) teeth, (*fam.*) ivories; comb; whiteness. *D'—,* (*adject.*) ivory
Ivoirerie, *s.f.* ivory-working; ivory-works
Ivoirier, *s.m.* ivory-worker
Ivoirin, e, *adj.* ivory, eburnean
Ivraie, *s.f.* (*weed*) tare, tares; (*bot.*) darnel. — *vivace,* ray-grass
Ivre, *adj.* drunk, tipsy, intoxicated. — *-mort,* dead-drunk [rapture; enthusiasm
Ivresse, *s.f.* intoxication; drunkenness; frenzy;
†**Ivrogne,** *adj.* drunken; — *s.m.* drunkard
†**Ivrogner,** *v.n.* to carouse, to booze, to tope, to tipple, to get drunk
†**Ivrognerie,** *s.f.* drunkenness; drinking, topping, tippling; drunken fit
†**Ivrognesse,** *s.f.* drunken woman, drunkard
Ixia, *s.m.,* **Ixie,** *s.f.* (*bot.*) ixia
Ixion, *s.m.* (*astr.*) Ixion
Ixode, *s.m.* (*zool.*) *V.* **Tique**
Izard, *s.m. V.* **Isard**

J

J, *s.m.* (*letter*) j
J', *pron.* (*contraction of* **Je,** *which see*)
Jà, *adv.* (*old*) already, &c. (*V.* **Déjà**); certainly,
Jabiru, *s.m.* (*bird*) jabiru [indeed, forsooth
Jable, *s.m.* (*coop.*) groove
Jabler, *v.a.* (*coop.*) to groove [ing-tool
Jablière, Jabloire, *s.f.* (*coop.*) notcher, notch-
Jabot, *s.m.* (*of birds*) crop, craw, maw; (*pop.*) stomach, inside; breast; (*of shirts*) frill
Jabotage, *s.m.* jabbering, jabber, chattering, chatter
Jaboter, *v.n.* to jabber, to chatter, to talk
Jaboteu-r, se, *s.m.f.* jabberer, chatterer, chatterbox [Guinea goose
Jabotière, *s.f.* frilling; (*bird*) China goose,
Jacamar, *s.m.* (*bird*) jacamar
Jacana, Jacane, *s.m.* (*bird*) jacana
Jacasse, *adj.* chattering; — *s.f.* chatterbox
Jacasser, *v.n.* to chatter, to jabber; to blab
Jacasserie, *s.f.* chattering, jabbering; blabbing
Jacasseu-r, se, *s.m.f.* chatterer, jabberer; blab
Jacée, *s.f.* (*bot.*) knapweed. — *des blés,* bluebottle, corn-flower
Jacent, e, *adj.* (*law*) in abeyance
Jachère, *s.f.* (*agr.*) fallow; fallow land, fallow-
Jachérer, *v.a.* (*agr.*) to fallow [field
Jacinthe, *s.f.* hyacinth. — *des prés* or *des bois,* blue-bell, harebell
Jaco, *s.m.* grey parrot; Poll; Pug
Jacobée, *s.f.* (*bot.*) ragwort [(*revolutionist*)
Jacobin, *s.m.* Jacobine (*monk, bird*); Jacobin
Jacobin, e, *adj.* jacobinic (*revolutionary*)
Jacobine, *s.f.* Jacobine (*nun, bird*)
Jacobinière, *s.f.* club of the Jacobins; revolutionary club *or* meeting
Jacobiniser, *v.a.* to jacobinize
Jacobinisme, *s.m.* jacobinism
Jacobite, *s.m.* jacobite
Jacobus, *s.m.* jacobus (*old coin*)
Jaconas, *s.m.* jaconet
Jacot, *s.m.* *V.* **Jaco**
Jacquart, *s.f.*, *Métier à la —*, *s.m.* Jacquart loom
Jacque, *s.m.* (*pop.*) jay (*bird*); (*slang*) halfpenny, mag; (*obsolete*) jerkin, jacket, coat, jack, jacque of defence [sword; (*slang*) wench
Jacqueline, *s.f.* carboy, jar, can; cavalry-
Jacquerie, *s.f.* jacquerie (*insurrection of peasants*)
Jacques, *s.m.* James; (*Fr. hist.*) Jacques (*insurgent peasant*). — *Bonhomme,* (*old*) (French) peasantry, peasants, peasant
Jacquet, *s.m.* backgammon
Jacquinier, *s.m.* (*bot.*) jacquinia
Jacquot, *s.m.* grey parrot; Poll; Pug; (*pers.*) Jem, Jim; Jack; (*pop.*) ninny, muff; twaddler
Jactance, *s.f.* boasting, boast
Jactancieu-x, se, *adj.* boastful
Jactation, Jactitation, *s.f.* (*med.*) jactation,
Jacter (Se), *v.r.* (*old*) to boast [jactitation
Jaculateur, *s.m.* jaculator; shooting-fish, archer-fish; — *adj.* jaculating, shooting
Jaculation, *s.f.* jaculation
Jaculatoire, *adj.* jaculatory, jaculating, shooting, darting, spouting; ejaculatory
Jade, *s.m.* (*min.*) jade, axe-stone
Jadelle, *s.f.* (*bad spelling*) *V.* **Judelle**
Jadien, ne, *adj.* (*min.*) jadian
Jadis, *adv.* of old, of yore, formerly. *Au temps* —, in times of old, in days of yore, once upon
Jaffe, *s.f.* (*pop.*) *V.* **Gifle** [a time
Jaffet, *s.m.* hook
Jaguar, *s.m.* jaguar, American tiger
Jaïet, *s.m.* (*obsolete*) *V.* **Jais**
†Jaillir, *v.n.* to gush, to gush out; to spout; to splash; to spring; to spirt; to burst out *or* forth; to shoot; to flash; to strike. *Faire* —, to make (...) gush *or* &c.; to splash; to spirt; to throw up; to strike out
†Jaillissement, *s.m.* gushing, gush; spouting out; splashing, splash; springing, spring; spirting; shooting; flashing, flash
Jais, *s.m.* (*min.*) jet
Jalabre, *s.m.* Alpine moorfowl
Jalap, *s.m.* jalap
Jalapine, *s.f.* (*chem.*) jalapine
Jalapique, *adj.* (*chem.*) jalapic
Jale, *s.f.* bowl, tureen, bucket
Jalée, *s.f.* bowlful, bucketful
Jalet, *s.m.* (*obsolete*) pebble, pebble-stone. *Arbalète* or *arc à* —, stone-bow
Jalle, *s.f.* stony subsoil [cation, mark, lineament
Jalon, *s.m.* stake, pole; landmark; (*fig.*) indi-
Jalonnement, *s.m.* staking out, boning; marking out, marking; indicating
Jalonner, *v.a.n.* to stake out; to place landmarks; to mark out, to mark; to indicate
Jalonneur, *s.m.* (*mil.*) marker
Jalousement, *adv.* jealously
Jalouser, *v.a.* to be jealous of, to envy
Jalousie, *s.f.* jealousy; jealousness; enviousness, envy; alarm, uneasiness; window-blind; Venetian blind; lattice; (*hort.*) three-coloured amaranth; sweet William; kind of autumn pear; (*obsolete*) jalousie (*kind of dance*)
Jalou-x, se, *adj.* jealous; envious; anxious; ambitious; (*nav.*) crank, rolling; (*of carriages*) leaning on one side; — *s.m.f.* jealous person *or* fellow *or* creature *or* thing. *Faire des* —, to excite *or* create jealousy
Jamaïcain, e, *adj. s.* Jamaican
Jamaïcine, *s.f.* (*chem.*) jamaicine, jamacina
Jamais, *adv.* ever; never; anyhow. *A* —, *pour* —, *à tout* —, for ever; ever. *Au grand* —, — *de la vie,* never never, no never, never any more
Jambage, *s.m.* (*arch.*) jamb; (*writ.*) down stroke
Jambe, *s.f.* leg; shank; (*of compasses*) foot; —*s*, *pl.* legs, &c.; swiftness, nimbleness, speed, activity. — *arquée,* — *en manche de veste,* bowleg. — *deçà* — *delà,* astride, one leg on each side, one leg on one side and one on the other. — *de force,* (*build.*) principal rafter. —*s de quinze ans,* (o.'s) young legs. — *de vin,* drunkenness. *Os de la* —, shin-bone. *A toutes* —*s*, at full speed. *Par-dessous* (*la*) —, *sous* —, easily; outright; with contempt. *Faire* — *de vin,* to quaff, to fuddle, to get drunk. *Jouer des* —*s*, *prendre ses* —*s à son cou,* to take to o.'s heels, to run away, to run, to cut along. *Rendre la* — *bien* (or *mieux*) *faite, faire une belle* —, (*fig., jest.*) to better (o.'s) position, to benefit, to do good. *Cela lui rend la* — *bien* (or *mieux*) *faite!* he is all the better for it! *En aurai-je la* — *mieux faite?* shall I be any the better for it?
Jambé, e, *adj.* legged
Jambette, *s.f.* small *or* little leg; clasp-knife, pocket-knife, whittle; (*build.*) jamb; (*nav.*) timber of the head; (*obsolete*) tripping up
Jambi-er, ère, *adj.m.f.* (*anat.*) of the leg; — *s.m.* (*anat.*) tibialis; — *s.f.* legging; leg-guard; (*old armour*) jambeux, greave
Jambon, *s.m.* ham [**Pinne**
Jambonneau, *s.m.* small ham; (*mollusc*) *V.*
Jambose, *s.f.* (*bot.*) jambos, jamrosade, rose-apple [apple tree
Jambosier, *s.m.* (*bot.*) jambos, jamrosade, rose-
Jan, *s.m.* (*tricktrack*) table. — *de retour,* outer
Janicule, *s.m.* Janiculum [table
Janissaire, *s.m.* janizary, janissary
Janot, *s.m.* Jack-pudding; fool, tomfool, booby, noodle, gaby [tomfoolery
Janotisme, *s.m.* nonsense, blunder, bull, foolery,
Jansén-isme (*s.m.*), **-iste,** (*s.m.f. adj.*) *V.* page
Jante, *s.f.* (*of wheels*) felly, felloe [3, § 1
Janvier, *s.m.* January
Japhétique, *adj.* Japhetic
Japon, *s.m.* Japan, Japan ware
Japonais, e, *adj. s.* Japanese
Japonner, *v.a.* to hard-bake
Jappe, *s.f.* (*pop.*) gabble, talk
Jappement, *s.m.* yelping

Japper, *v.n.* to yelp; to squall
Jappeu-r, se, *s.m.f.* squaller
Jaque, *s.m. V.* **Jacque;** (*bot.*) bread-fruit
Jaqueline, *s.f. V.* **Jacqueline**
Jaquemart, *s.m.* jack of the clockhouse, minute-jack, jack
Jaquerie, *s.f. V.* **Jacquerie**
Jaquette, *s.f.* jacket; short coat, coat; short clothes; (*boy's*) petticoats, frock; (*pop.*) magpie
Jaquier, *s.m.* (*bot.*) bread-fruit tree
Jarde, *s.f. V.* **Jardon**
Jardin, *s.m.* garden; ground; (*nav.*) quarter-gallery. — *anglais*, ornamental garden, pleasure-garden *or* ground. — *des plantes*, botanical *or* horticultural (and zoological) gardens
Jardinage, *s.m.* gardening; garden-ground; gardens; garden-stuff; specks (*in a diamond*)
Jardiné, e, *adj.* specked, spotty, flawy
Jardiner, *v.n.* to garden
Jardinet, *s.m.* little garden
Jardineu-x, se, *adj.* (*of emeralds*) spotty
Jardinier, *s.m.* gardener; — *adj.m.* of gardens, garden. — *fleuriste*, flower-gardener
Jardinière, *s.f.* (female) gardener; gardener's wife; flower-stand; low ruffle; lace edging; garden-beetle; (*cook.*) mixed carrots and turnips, &c., dish of ditto; — *adj.f.* of gardens, garden. *A la* —, (*cook.*) dressed with various vegetables (*principally carrots and turnips*)
Jardiniste, *s.m.* landscape-gardener
Jardon, *s.m.* (*vet.*) jardes, curbs
Jaret, *s.m.* (kind of plum)
Jargauder, *v.n.a.* (*of ganders*) to cover
Jargon, *s.m.* jargon, lingo, gibberish; slang; small talk; (*jewel.*) jargon, jargoon
Jargonelle, *s.f.* jargonel, jargonelle (*pear*)
Jargonner, *v.a.n.* to jargon, to jabber, to mutter, to talk gibberish; to twaddle; to gabble, to cackle
Jargonnesque, *adj.* of jargon, of gibberish
Jargonneu-r, se, *s.m.f.* jabberer; twaddler
Jarnac, *s.m.* (*old*) dagger, dirk. *Coup de* —, *V.* **Coup**
Jarni, Jarnibleu, Jarnicoton, Jarnidieu, *int.* (*pop.*) zooks! zookers! zounds! by Jingo!
Jarosse, *s.f.* (*bot.*) vetch, chickling-vetch; vetchling
Jarre, *s.f.* jar; can; cistern; bran-tub; — *s.m.* coarse hairs (*of furs*)
Jarré, e, *adj.* (*of furs*) containing coarse hairs
Jarret, *s.m.* ham, hamstring, hock, hough; knuckle (*of veal*); shin *or* leg (*of beef*); (*fig.*) leg, legs, strength *or* elasticity in the legs; (*arch.*) projection, protuberance, unevenness. *Tendon du* —, hamstring. *Tendre le* —, to strain o.'s legs; (*fig.*) to strut
Jarreté, e, *adj.* gartered; knock-kneed; close-hammed, close-hocked; (*arch.*) projecting, protuberant
Jarreter, *v.a.* to garter, to put garters on; — [*v.n.* (*arch.*) to project] **Se** —, *v.r.* to garter oneself, to put o.'s garters on
Jarreti-er, ère, *adj.* close-hammed, close-hocked
Jarretière, *s.f.* garter
Jarreu-x, se, *adj. V.* **Jarré**
Jarron, *s.m.* small jar, can
Jars, *s.m.* (*bird*) gander; (*bad spelling for* "jarre") *V.* **Jarre,** *s.m.* *Entendre le* —, (*old*) to know what is what, to be up to snuff
Jas, *s.m.* (*nav.*) stock (*of an anchor*)
Jaser, *v.n.* to chatter, to prate; to tattle; to blab
Jaseran, *s.m. V.* **Jaseron**
Jaserie, *s.f.* chatter, prate; tittle-tattle
Jaseron, *s.m.* (*jewel.*) belcher-chain; (*bot.*) orange-milked agaric
Jaseu-r, se, *s.m.f.* chatterer, prater, chatter-box; blab; — *s.m.* (*bird*) chatterer, waxwing; — *s.f.* (*bird*) short-tailed paroquet
Jasmin, *s.m.* jasmine, jessamine
Jaspagate, *s.f.* agate jasper
Jaspage, *s.m.* marbling
Jaspe, *s.m.* jasper
Jaspé, e, *part. adj.* jasper-like, jasperated, jaspery, variegated; marbled
Jasper, *v.a.* to marble
†**Jaspiller, Jaspiner,** *v.n.* (*pop.*) to talk, to chatter, to gabble
Jaspoïde, *adj.* jaspoid
Jaspure, *s.f.* marbling
Jatropha, *s.m.* (*bot.*) jatropha
Jatte, *s.f.* bowl; stand (*for cheese*)
Jattée, *s.f.* bowlful
Jauge, *s.f.* gauge; measure; gauging-rod; water-gauge; standard cask; gauging, measurement
Jaugeage, *s.m.* gauging; measurement; tonnage; gauging dues
Jauger, *v.a.n.* (*nav.*, &c.) to gauge, to measure; (*navig.*) to draw (... *feet of water*)
Jaugeur, *s.m.* gauger, measurer
Jaumière, *s.f.* (*nav.*) helm-port
Jaunâtre, *adj.* yellowish; sallow
Jaune, *adj.m.f.*, *s.m.* yellow; sallow; yolk
Jaunet, te, *adj.* yellowish; (*of bread*) whity-brown; — *s.m.* (*flower*) butter-cup, gold-cup; (*gold coin, pop.*) yellow-boy. — *d'eau*, yellow water-lily
Jaunir, *v.a.n.* to make yellow; to yellow; to get *or* turn yellow; to become sallow; to ripen; to wither
Jaunissage, *s.m.* yellowing
Jaunissant, e, *adj.* turning yellow, yellow; golden, ripening; withering; turning sallow
Jaunisse, *s.f.* jaundice; (*vet.*) yellows
Jaunissement, *s.m.* yellowing
Javanais, e, *adj. s.* Javanese
Javart, *s.m.* (*vet.*) quittor-bone
Javeau, *s.m.* sandbank
Javel (Eau de). *V.* **Eau**
Javelage, *s.m.* (*agr.*) laying down in loose sheaves *or* in parcels; price of ditto; drying in the field
Javelé, e, *adj.* (*agr.*) in loose sheaves *or* in parcels; growy
Javeler, *v.a.* (*agr.*) to lay down in loose sheaves *or* in parcels; to deliver in sheaves; — *v.n.* to dry (in the field), to get dry, to turn deeper yellow
Javeleu-r, se, *s.m.f.* (*agr.*) reaper who makes into parcels *or* loose sheaves; — *adj.* sheaf-delivery. *Appareil* —, sheaf-delivery apparatus
Javeline, *s.f.* javelin; (*agr.*) small parcel
Javelle, *s.f.* (*agr.*) parcel, bundle, sheaf (*not bound up*); (*also, collectively*) parcels, sheaves; (*of vine-branches*, &c.) bundle, bundles. *Tomber en* —, (*of a cask*) to come to pieces. *Eau de* —, *V.* **Eau**
Javelot, *s.m.* javelin
Jayet, *s.m.* (*obsolete*) *V.* **Jais**
Je, J', *pron.* I
Jé, *s.m. V.* **Rotin**
Jean, *s.m.* John; Jack; Johnny; fool. — *-farine*, Jack-pudding, merry-andrew, fool, booby. — *-fesse*, — *-foutre*, blackguard. — *-Jean*, raw recruit, recruit; simpleton, muff
Jeanneton, *s.f.* Janet, Jenny; wench
Jeannette, *s.f.* Janet, Jenny; servant-girl; cross worn round the neck; (*obsolete*) spinning-jenny
Jeannot, *s.m.* Johnny, Jack, Jacky; &c. (*V.* **Janot**)
Jeannotisme, *s.m. V.* **Janotisme**
Jécoraire, *adj.* (*anat.*) hepatic; — *s.f.* hepatic vein
Jectigation, *s.f.* (*bad spelling*) *V.* **Jactitation**
Jectisses, *adj.f.pl.* *Terres* —, made earth, loose soil; cleansings, sewage matter, sewage, drainage. *Pierres* —, (*build.*) stones small enough to be laid by hand
†**Jégneux,** *s.m.* (*bad spelling*) *V.* **Génieux**
Jéhovah, *s.m.* Jehovah
Jéhoviste, *s.m.* jehovist; — *adj.* jehovistic
Jéjunum, *s.m.* (*anat.*) jejunum
Jenny, *s.f.* (*spin.*) jenny
Jérémiade, *s.f.* jeremiade, croaking
Jerni, Jerniguienne, *int. V.* **Jarni**
Jérôme, *s.m.* (*pop.*) stick, cudgel
Jérose, *s.f.* (*bot.*) *V.* **Anastatique**
Jérusalem, *s.f.* Jerusalem; the Catholic Church. — *céleste* or *nouvelle*, heavenly city
Jervine, *s.f.* (*chem.*) jervine
Jesse, *s.m.* (*fish*) *V.* **Chevanne**
Jésuite, *s.m.* jesuit; — *adj.* jesuitic, jesuitical
Jésuitesse, *s.f.* jesuitess

Jésuit-ique, -iquement, -isme. *V.* page 3, § 1 [imperial
Jésus, *adj. s.m.* (*paper*) super-royal. *Grand* —,
Jet, *s.m.* throw, throwing; cast, casting; dash, dashing; toss, tossing; haul, catch, take; sketch; stroke; effort; jet; gush; spirt; stream; shoot; sprout; cane; ray; (*of bees*) swarm; (*of earth*) bank; (*of sails*) set, suit; (*of a drapery*) folds; (*agr.*) tiller; (*falc.*) jess; (*nav.*) throwing overboard; jetsam, jettison. — *d'eau*, water-spout, fountain, jet, jet d'eau. *Faire le* —, (*nav.*) to throw overboard
Jetage, *s.m.* throwing, &c. (*V.* **Jeter**); (*vet.*)
Jeté, *s.m.* (*dancing*) jeté [running at the nose
Jeté, e, *part.* thrown, &c. (*V.* **Jeter**)
Jetée, *s.f.* jetty, pier, mole; causeway, bank, embankment; casting; swarm (*of bees*); stoning (*of a road*)
Jeter, *v.a.n.* to throw; to throw away *or* off *or* out *or* down; to cast; to dash; to hurl; to fling; to toss; to put; to drop; to shoot; to take, to strike (*root*); to shed; to spread; to utter; to set up; to heave, to fetch (*sighs*); to lay; to swarm, to breed; to discharge; to give; to suppurate, to run; (*of rivers*) to empty; (*vet.*) to have a running at the nose
  Se —, *v.r.* to throw oneself; to jump; to spring; to rush; to run; to fall; to dash; to break out; to strike out; to launch out; to retire; to be thrown; to be thrown away *or* &c.
Jeton, *s.m.* counter; mark; (*fig.*) brass shilling; (*agr.*) swarm of young bees
Jettice, *adj.f.* refuse *or* coarse (*wool*)
Jeu, *s.m.* play; sport; amusement; game; freak, frolic; trick; jest; gaming; gambling; set; pack (*of cards*); cards; set *or* suit (*of sails*); stop (*of an organ*); working; action; room; performance, acting; execution; motion; animation, life; affair, matter; stakes; ground, court, alley. — *d'esprit*, witticism. — *de hasard*, game of chance. — *du hasard*, freak of fortune. — *de mains*, rough play, horse-play; sparring; romping. —*x de mains* —*x de vilains*, playing with the hands is bad manners, rough play is bad. — *de mots*, play *or* playing on words, conundrum, pun, quibble. — *de théâtre*, stage-trick; clap-trap; attitude. *Beau* —, fair play *or* opportunity; fine sport *or* game. *Bon — bon argent*, in right earnest. *De bon* —, *de franc* —, by fair play, fairly, openly, candidly, in good earnest. *En* —, in jest, for fun; at stake; in question; in *or* into play, in action; in gear. *Donner beau — à*, to give fair play *or* a fair opportunity; to play into . . .'s hands. *Être à deux de* —, to be even *or* quits; to be a match for each other. (*Nous sommes* or *vous êtes* or *&c. à deux de* —, it is a game at which two can play.) *Jouer gros* —, to play high, to stake a good deal, to risk very much. *Jouer petit* —, to play low, to stake little. *Mettre au* —, to stake. *Mettre en* —, to bring out; to bring into play, to bring to bear; to bring into question. *Se faire un — de*, to sport with, to make light of. *Cela n'est pas du* (or *de*) —, that is not fair, that was not agreed on, I did not bargain for that. *Le — ne vaut pas la chandelle*, it is not worth trying, it is not worth powder and shot, it will not pay, it is not worth the while. *A beau — beau retour*, one good turn deserves another
Jeudi, *s.m.* Thursday. — *saint*, Thursday before Easter, Maundy-Thursday
Jeun (A), *adv.* fasting; on *or* with an empty stomach; sober; empty
Jeune, *adj.* young; youthful; younger; junior; recent; new; early; green
Jeûne, *s.m.* fasting; fast; abstinence
Jeunement, *adv.* youngly, youthfully; (*hunt.*)
Jeûner, *v.n.* to fast; to abstain [just, lately
Jeunesse, *s.f.* youth; infancy; young people, young; (*pop.*) lass, young girl
Jeunet, te, *adj.* very young

Jeûneu-r, se, *s.m.f.* faster
Jigler, *v.n.* (*pop.*) to plash, to splash
Jinglard, *s.m.* weak *or* tart wine [trade
†Joaillerie, *s.f.* jewellery, jewelry; jeweller's
†Joailli-er, ère, *s.m.f.* jeweller
Job, *s.m.* Job; trick, take-in, hoax, practical joke; simpleton, muff [gull, muff
Jobard, *s.m.* simpleton, fool, ninny, gudgeon,
Jobarder, *v.a.* to fool, to befool, to gull, to
Jobarderie, *s.f.* foolery [gudgeon
Jober, *v.a. V.* **Jobarder**
Joberie, *s.f.* simplicity, credulity
Jobisme, *s.m.* extreme poverty, penury; simplicity, credulity
Joc, *s.m.* (*of mills*) stop, stand-still
Jocasse, *s.f.* (*bird*) missel thrush
Jockey, *s.m.* jockey, rider; postilion; (*rid.*) dumb jockey. — *-club*, jockey-club
Jocko, *s.m.* long roll (*of bread*); (*zool.*) pongo, black orang
Joconde, *s.m.* lady-killer, gay Lothario
Jocrisse, *s.m.* simpleton, ninny, fool; dupe; henpecked husband
Jodelet, *s.m.* (*obsolete*) wag, buffoon
Johannique, *adj.* Johannic
Johannisberg, *s.m.* johannisberger (*hock wine*)
Joie, *s.f.* joy; joyfulness; exultation; delight; pleasure; mirth; gaiety; cheerfulness
†Joignant, e, *part. adj. prep.* joining, adjoining, adjacent, contiguous, next to, close to
†Joigneur, *s.m.* boot-closer
Joindre, *v.a.* to join; to unite; to connect; to couple; to bind; to fit; to add; to overtake; to reach; to meet; to clasp (*o.'s hands*); to bring close to; to come *or* keep close to; — *v.n.* to join, to close, to fit, to fit *or* shut close
  Se —, *v.r.* to join; to unite; to meet; to couple; to be joined *or* united; to be added; to be contiguous *or* connected
Joint, e, *part. adj.* joined, &c. (*V.* **Joindre**); jointed; close together, close. *Ci-* —, annexed; subjoined; accompanying; herewith [way
Joint, *s.m.* joint; seam; (*fig.*) best means, right
Jointe, *s.f.* (*rid.*) pastern
Jointé, e, *adj.* jointed
Jointée, *s.f.* double-handful
Jointi-f, ve, *adj.* (*tech.*) joined, close
Jointivement, *adv.* closely
Jointoiement, *s.m.* (*mas.*) grouting, pointing
Jointoyer, *v.a.n.* (*mas.*) to grout, to point
Jointure, *s.f.* joint; articulation; knuckle
Joli, e, *adj.* pretty; nice-looking; nice; fine, handsome, beautiful; comfortable, good; — *s.m.* pretty; best; (a) pretty thing; (a) pretty mess. — **-bois,** *s.m.* (*bot.*) mezereon
Joliet, te, *adj.* rather pretty, prettyish, comely
Joliment, *adv.* prettily; nicely; neatly; finely; preciously; soundly; famously; awfully, with a vengeance; very, very much; indeed; a fine *or* nice lot. — *bien*, capitally
Joliveté, *s.f.* (*old*) *V.* **Gentillesse**
Jomarin, *s.m.* (*pop.*) *V.* **Ajonc**
Jombarde, *s.f.* singing-pipe
Jonc, *s.m.* (*bot.*) rush, bulrush; Malacca cane, Malacca; (*jewel.*) hoop-ring. — *épineux*, — *marin*, furze. — *d'Espagne*, rush-broom
Joncer, *v.a.* to rush-bottom (*a chair*)
Jonchaie, *s.f.* bed *or* plantation of rushes
Jonchée, *s.f.* strewing, strewed flowers *or* &c.; heap; cream-cheese; (*obsolete*) slaughter [ing
Jonchement, *s.m.* strewing; scattering; heap-
Joncher, *v.a.* to strew; to scatter; to heap
  Se —, *v.r.* to become (*or* be) strewed, &c.
Jonchère, *s.f. V.* **Jonchaie**
Jonchet, *s.m.* (*pedantic slang for* **Onchet**)
Joncheur, *s.m.* strewer, scatterer
Joncier, *s.m.* (*bot.*) rush-broom
Jonciforme, *adj.* rush-shaped, rush-like
Joncinelle, *s.f.* (*bot.*) pipewort
Jonction, *s.f.* junction, joining, meeting
Jongler, *v.n.* to juggle
Jonglerie, *s.f. V.* **Escamotage**

Jongleu-r, se, *s.m.f.* juggler, juggleress; [wizard, witch
Jonque, *s.f.* junk (*Chinese vessel*)
†Jonquille, *s.f.* (*bot.*) jonquil; — *s.m.* jonquil colour, jonquil yellow, jonquil; — *adj.* jonquil-coloured, jonquil
Jordonner, *v.n.a.* to command, to dictate
Joseph, *adj. Papier* —, tissue paper
Jota, *s.f.* jota (*Spanish dance, tune*)
Jottereau, *s.m.* (*nav.*) cheek
Jouable, *adj.* playable; actable, performable
†Jouailler, Jouasser, *v.n.* to play for a trifle *or* for amusement; (*mus.*) to thrum, to strum, to scrape, to play badly
†Jouaillon, Jouasson, *s.m.f.* bad player
Joubarbe, *s.f.* (*bot.*) house-leek, sengreen
Joue, *s.f.* cheek; (*of a ship*) bow. *Coucher* or *mettre en* —, to aim at, to take aim at, to present at; to aim, to take aim; to watch closely *or* narrowly. *En — ! — !* (*mil.*) present!
Jouée, *s.f.* (*arch.*) reveal
Jouer, *v.n.a.* to play; to play a *or* o.'s game; to sport; to trifle; to wanton; to gamble; to play away; to gamble away; to stake, to venture, to risk, to expose; to expose oneself; to speculate; to pun; to fumble; to move; to work; to warp; to explode; to execute; to act; to perform; to represent; to counterfeit; to feign; to imitate; to mimic; to deceive; to trifle with; to make game of, to ridicule; to outwit, to outdo, to beat. — *de bonheur, de malheur*, to be lucky, unlucky. — *des mains*, to play roughly; to romp; to spar; to scuffle; to pilfer, to pick pockets. — *sur son ancre*, (*nav.*) to be tossed about. *Faire* —, to make (*one*) play *or* &c.; to have (...) played *or* acted *or* &c.; to set going, to set *or* put in motion *or* in action; to move; to try; to work; to play; to bring into play; to bring to bear; to spring; to fire off, to fire

Se —, *v.r.* to play; to sport; to trifle; to wanton; to make a play (of), to make sport (of), to make game (of); to make light (of); to laugh (at); to make a fool (of); to baffle; to set at defiance; to meddle *or* interfere (with); to deceive *or* delude oneself; to be played at; to be acted; to be worked *or* done; to be staked; &c.
Jouereau, *s.m.* (*obsolete*) *V.* **Jouaillon**
Jouet, *s.m.* plaything, toy; sport; laughing-[stock; dupe
Jouette, *s.f.* rabbit-hole
Joueu-r, se, *s.m.f.* player; gamester; gambler; speculator; stock-jobber; performer; — *adj.* playful; given to gaming *or* gambling. *Rude* —, rough player; (*fig.*) rough customer
Joufflu, e, *adj.* chub-faced, chubby, blowzy; — *s.m.f.* chubby child, fat-cheeked fellow *or* woman *or* girl, blowze
Joug, *s.m.* yoke. *Atteler au* —, to yoke [*sluice*)
†Jouillières, Jouières, *s.f.pl.* cheeks (*of a*
Jouir, *v.n.* to enjoy; to possess; to use; to feel *or* have pleasure, to be pleased *or* delighted. *Faire* —, to give pleasure, to please, to delight, to enrapture; to be pleasant *or* delightful. *Cela ne fait pas* —, that is not quite pleasant
Jouissance, *s.f.* enjoyment; gratification; delight; luxury; possession; use, fruition; (*fin.*) payment of interest *or* of dividend, interest *or* dividend payable
Joujou, *s.m.* plaything, toy. *Faire* —, to play
Joujouter, *v.n.* (*pop.*) to play
Jour, *s.m.* day; daylight; light; daytime; aperture, opening, cutting; open-work; window; interval, open *or* clear space; facility, way, means; birth; life; —**s**, *pl.* days, &c.; life. *A* —, open; open-work; through; in order, up to the day. *Au* —, by daylight. *Au — le* —, from hand to mouth; according to o.'s daily wants; without care for the morrow. *De Au premier* —, on the first opportunity. *De* —, by day; daily; day; on duty for the day. *Du* —, of *or* for the day; to-day's; daily; modern; fashionable. *D'un — à l'autre, du — au lendemain*, from day to day; in one day; the same day; any day. *En plein* —, in broad daylight, in broad day, at noonday; openly. *Grand* —, broad daylight. — *pour* —, to a day, exactly. *Le* —, the day; in the day; on the day. *Petit* —, morning twilight, dawn, daybreak. *Tout le* —, *Tous les* —*s*, *V.* **Tout,** *adj. Un* —, a day; one day; some day; some time. *Donner* —, to appoint a day, to make an appointment. *Donner le — à*, to give birth to. *Donner du* —, to let the light in, to give light. *Mettre au* —, to bring to light; to bring out *or* forth; to publish. *Prendre* —, to agree upon a day, to make an appointment. *Recevoir le* —, to be born. *Se faire* —, to make o.'s way, to cut *or* force o.'s way; to find its way; to come to light, to come out. *Voir le* —, to see the light, to come to light; to come into the world, to be born; to come out, to appear. — *de Dieu!* (*obsolete*) bless me! bless my soul! egad! by the Powers! *A chaque — suffit sa peine*, (*Proverb*) sufficient for the day is the evil thereof [paper, paper; (*obsolete*) acre
Journal, *s.m.* journal; diary; day-book; news-
Journali-er, ère, *adj.* daily; inconstant, changeable, variable, fickle, unsteady, irregular, uncertain, not the same every day; capricious; — *s.m.f.* day-labourer; charwoman; — *s.m.* (*nav.*) daily provisions
Journaliser, *v.n.* to journalize
Journalisme, *s.m.* journalism
Journaliste, *s.m.f.* journalist; (*print.*) newspaper-compositor; — *adj.* journalistic
Journée, *s.f.* day; day's occupation; day's work; day's gain *or* pay *or* wages; day's journey; battle; riot, insurrection; work-day. *A la* —, by the day. *A grandes* —*s*, by forced marches, by long stages; fast. *A petites* —*s*, by slow journeys, by short stages. *Aller en* —, to work by the day; to char
Journellement, *adv.* daily, every day
Journoyer, *v.n.* (*pop.*) to take a day's holiday
Joute, *s.f.* joust; tilt; fight, fighting; struggle; match; debate; lists
Jouter, *v.n.* to joust, to tilt; to fight; to wrestle; to struggle; to cope; to contend; to dispute
Jouteur, *s.m.* jouster; tilter; antagonist, combatant, adversary, champion
Jouvence, *s.f.* (*obsolete*) youth. *Fontaine de* —, fountain of youth [fellow, youth, lad, stripling
Jouvenceau, *s.m.* (*old, jest.*) young man, young
Jouvencelle, *s.f.* (*old, jest.*) young girl, lass, damsel
Jouxtant, Jouxte, *prep.* (*old*) close to, near
Jovial, e, *adj.* jovial, jolly, merry
Jovialement, *adv.* jovially, merrily
Jovialité, *s.f.* jovialness, joviality, merriment
Joyau, *s.m.* jewel [ly; cheerfully; gladly
Joyeusement, *adv.* joyfully, joyously; merri-
Joyeuseté, *s.f.* joyfulness, joyousness; merriment; mirth; cheerfulness; gladness; jest, joke
Joyeu-x, se, *adj.* joyful, joyous; jolly; merry; cheerful; glad; delighted [fish, razor-back
Jubarte, *s.f.* (*zool.*) great northern rorqual, fin-
Jubé, *s.m.* (*of churches*) gallery, rood-loft, rood-screen, ambo. *Venir à* —, to submit, to come to terms, to knuckle down *or* under [of Chili
Jubée, *s.f.* (*bot.*) jubæa, coquito, jaggery-palm
Jubilaire, *adj.* of jubilee; (*pers.*) of fifty years' [standing
Jubilant, e, *adj.* jubilant, delighted
Jubilate, *s.m.* (*lit.*) jubilate, 3rd Sunday after Easter [tion, rapture; jollification
Jubilation, *s.f.* jubilation, merriment, exulta-
Jubilé, *s.m.* jubilee; — *adj.m.* of fifty years' standing. *Faire* —, (*at play*) to mix up the cards *or* &c. so that no one loses or wins
Jubiler, *v.n.* to be jubilant *or* delighted, to [exult; to make merry
Jubis, *s.m.* raisins
Juc, *s.m.* (*old*) *V.* **Juchoir**
Juché, e, *part.adj.* at roost, roosting, perching, perched; (*vet.*) *V.* **Bouleté**

Juchér, *v.n.a.*, **Se** —, *v.r.* to roost, to perch, to perch oneself up
Juchoir, *s.m.* roost, perch
Juda-ïque, -ïquement, -ïsme. *V.* page 3, [§ 1
Judaïser, *v.n.a.* to judaize; to jew
Judas, *s.m.* Judas; peep-hole. *De* —, (*adject.*) treacherous, perfidious, of Judas; (*of hair*) red, sandy, carroty. *Marques de* —, freckles. *Point de* —, number 13
Judasser, *v.a.* to give the kiss of Judas; to betray, to deceive
Judasserie, *s.f.* treachery, perfidy, cheat
Judelle, *s.f.* (*bird*) coot
Judicature, *s.f.* magistracy; law
Judiciaire, *adj.* judicial; legal; forensic; judicative; — *s.f.* judgment, sense, discretion
Judiciairement, *adv.* judicially
Judicieusement, *adv.* judiciously, sensibly, discreetly
Judicieu-x, se, *adj.* judicious, sensible, discreet
Juène, *s.m.* (*fish*) *V.* **Chevanne**
Jugal, e, *adj.* (*anat.*) jugal
Juge, *s.m.* judge; justice; adjudicator. — *d'instruction*, examining magistrate. — *de paix*, justice of the peace; magistrate
Jugé, *s.m.* judging, judgment; guessing, guess. *Au* —, at a guess. *Le bien* —, the right judging *or* judgment
Jugeable, *adj.* to be judged; to be tried, amenable to a tribunal
Jugement, *s.m.* judgment; opinion; trial; sentence; decree; (*med.*) crisis, result, termination. — *dernier*, last judgment, day of judgment, doomsday. *Mettre en* —, to try. *Rendre un* —, to give judgment; to pass sentence
Jugeoline, *s.f.* (*bot.*) sesamum, tilseed
Juger, *v.a.n.* to judge; to discern; to deem, to think; to deem *or* think it; to imagine; to conceive; to suppose; to guess; to decide; to try, to bring to trial; to sentence; (*med.*) to end; — *s.m.* judging, judgment; guessing, guess. *A en* —, judging. *Au* —, at a guess. *Faire* —, to try, to put on trial, to bring to trial
Se —, *v.r.* to judge *or* deem *or* think oneself (*or* each other); to be tried *or* heard; (*med.*) to end
Jugeu-r, se, *s.m.f.* judger, judge of things; caviller; — *adj.* judging
Juglandine, *s.f.* (*chem.*) juglandine
Jugulaire, *adj.* (*anat.*) jugular; — *s.f.* (*anat.*) jugular vein, jugular; (*mil.*) chin-strap; — *s.m.* (*class of fishes*) jugular
Juguler, *v.a.* to strangle; to bother; to press, to dun
Jui-f, ve, *adj. s.* Jewish; Jew; Jewess; Jewish
Juifer, *v.a.* (*fam.*) to jew
†Juillet, *s.m.* July; (*polit.*) July 1830 (*French Revolution*)
Juin, *s.m.* June
Juiverie, *s.f.* jewry; set of Jews; Jew's bargain, Jew's trick
Jujube, *s.f.* (*fruit*) jujube, *s.m.* (*extract*) jujube
Jujubier, *s.m.* jujube-tree
Jule, *s.m.* (*zool.*) *V.* **Iule**
Julep, *s.m.* (*pharm.*) julep
Jules, *s.m.* Julius; (*pop.*) jorden
Julien, ne, *adj.* (*chron., geog.*) Julian
Julienne, *s.f.* (*bot.*) dame's-violet, rocket; (*cook.*) vegetable soup, julienne. *Potage* or *soupe à la* —, vegetable soup, julienne
Jumart, *s.m.* jumart
Jum-eau, elle, *adj.* twin; double; — *s.m.* twin; — *s.f.* twin; double opera-glass; (*tech.*) cheek; (*nav.*) fish, clamp; (*her.*) gemel
Jumelé, e, *part. adj.* coupled, &c. (*V.* **Jumeler**); (*her.*) gemelled
Jumeler, *v.a.* to couple, to join, to put *or* tie two by two; (*nav.*) to fish, to clamp
Jument, *s.f.* mare
Jumenterie, *s.f.* breeding-stud
Jumenteu-x, se, *adj.* (*med.*) jumentous
Juncago, *s.m.* (*bot.*) arrow-grass
Jungermannie, *s.f.* (*bot.*) jungermannia
Jungle, *s.f.* jungle
Junon, *s.f.* (*myth., astr.*) Juno
Junte, *s.f.* junta
Jupe, *s.f.* skirt; petticoat; kilt
Jupiter, *s.m.* (*myth., astr.*) Jupiter; (*old chem.*) Jupiter, tin
Jupitérien, ne, *adj.* Jupiterian

Jupon, *s.m.* petticoat; kilt; (*obsolete*) skirt, flap. — *de dessus*, upper-petticoat, slip. — *de dessous*, under-petticoat
Jurande, *s.f.* wardenship; body of wardens
Jurassien, ne, *adj. s.* of Jura; native of Jura
Jurassique, *adj.* (*geol.*) Jurassic, of the Jura mountains
Jurat, *s.m.* (*obsolete*) alderman, warden of a trade, jurat
Juratoire, *adj.* (*law*) by oath, juratory
Juré, e, *part. adj.* sworn; — *s.m.* juryman, juror; (*obsolete*) warden; — **s,** *s.m.pl.* jurymen, jurors, jury; (*obsolete*) wardens. *Messieurs les* —*s*, gentlemen of the jury
Jurement, *s.m.* oath; swearing
Jurer, *v.a.n.* to swear; to swear by; to blaspheme; to declare, to warrant, to assure; to protest; to vow; to promise; to resolve; to contrast; to jar, to clash; to screech. — *comme un charretier* or *comme un grenadier* or *comme un païen* or *comme un crocheteur*, to swear like a trooper
Jureu-r, se, *s.m.f.* swearer
Juri, *s.m.* (*old spelling*) *V.* **Jury**
Juridiction, *s.f.* jurisdiction; magistracy; tribunal; department, province, line
Juridictionnel, le, *adj.* jurisdictional
Juridique, *adj.* juridical, judicial
Juridiquement, *adv.* juridically, judicially
Jurisconsulte, *s.m.* jurisconsult, jurist, lawyer; chamber-counsel
Jurisprudence, *s.f.* jurisprudence, law; statute-law, precedents
Juriste, *s.m.* jurist
Juron, *s.m.* oath
Jury, *s.m.* jury; board, committee; board of examiners. — *d'accusation*, grand jury. — *de jugement*, common *or* petty jury
Jus, *s.m.* juice; liquor; gravy
Jusant, *s.m.* ebb, ebb-tide
Jusée, *s.f.* tan-liquor, ooze
Jusque, *prep.* to, as far as; so far as; until, till; even; very; up to; down to; as high as; as low as; to the level of; to the length of; as much as; as many as. *Jusqu'à ce que*, until, till. *Jusqu'ici*, as far as this, as far as here, to this place; so far; up *or* down to here; hitherto, till now, as yet, up to this time. *Jusque-là*, as far as that, as far as there, to that place; so far; up *or* down to there; till then, up to that time; so much so. *Jusqu'à quand?* till when? till what time? how long? *Jusqu'où?* how far? *Il n'y a* (or *n'est*) *pas jusqu'aux ... qui ne soient, &c.*, the very ... are, &c., even the ... themselves are, &c.
Jusques, *prep.* *V.* **Jusque**
Jusquiame, *s.f.* (*bot.*) henbane
Jussion, *s.f.* (*old*) command
Justaucorps, *s.m.* close coat, jerkin, jacket, vest
Juste, *adj.* just; equitable; legitimate; correct; accurate; exact; true; apt, fit; right; fair; due; moderate; reasonable; sensible; upright, righteous; fitted; fitting; tight; narrow; close; low; — *adv.* just; exactly; right, precisely; accurately; correctly; in tune; — *s.m.* jacket; upright man; what is just *or* right, right, justice. *Au* —, *tout au* —, *tout* —, exactly, precisely; the least; the lowest; just; barely; bare. *Au plus* —, at the lowest. *Comme de* —, as is (*or* was) right *or* reasonable, as it ought to be, rightly enough, of course, naturally
Justement, *adv.* just, precisely, exactly; justly; reasonably
Justesse, *s.f.* justness; accuracy; correctness; exactness; precision; rectitude; propriety; sense
Justice, *s.f.* justice; equity; right; probity; integrity; impartiality; uprightness; righteousness; fairness; reason; judicial authorities; law-officers; jurisdiction; courts *or* court of law *or* of justice; law; laws; punishment; (*obsolete*) execution; gibbet, gallows. — *de paix*, court of the justice of the peace. *Exécuteur de la haute* —, (*obsolete*) executioner, hangman. — *Appeler* or *attaquer* or *citer* or *poursuivre* or *traduire en* —, to sue at law, to proceed against; to prosecute. *Faire* — *à*, to

do justice to. *Faire — de*, to do justice on; to be avenged of; to punish; to expose; to refute, to confute; to do away with. *Se faire — à soi-même*, to do oneself justice; to revenge oneself; to take the law into o.'s own hands. *Mettre* or *porter en —*, to bring into court. *Rendre — à*, to do justice to. *Rendre la —*, to administer justice. *Se faire rendre —*, to obtain justice

Justiciabilité, *s.f.* amenableness

Justiciable, *adj.* amenable (to), under the jurisdiction (of); — *s.m.f.* person amenable to a tribunal, one under the jurisdiction of a court. *Devenir le — de*, to come under the jurisdiction of

Justicie, Justiciée, *s.f.* (*bot.*) justicia

Justicier, *s.m.* justiciary; judge; lover of justice; — *v.a.* to punish, to lash; to execute

Justifiable, *adj.* justifiable; warrantable

Justifiablement, *adv.* justifiably; warrantably [justifying

Justifica-teur, trice, *s.m.f.* justifier; — *adj.*

Justificati-f, ve, *adj.* justificative; documentary. *Pièce —ve*, proof, voucher; illustration

Justification, *s.f.* justification; defence, vindication; proof; (*print.*) length of line (*so many ems wide*); justification [to prove

Justifier, *v.a.* to justify; to clear, to vindicate; **Se —,** *v.r.* to justify *or* &c. oneself; to be

Jute, *s.m.* jute [justified *or* &c.

Juteu-x, se, *adj.* juicy

Juvénile, *adj.* juvenile, youthful, young

Juvénilement, *adv.* juvenilely, youthfully

Juvénilia, *s.m.pl.* juvenile things, youthful

Juvénilité, *s.f.* juvenility [productions

Juxtalinéaire, *adj.* juxtalinear

Juxtaposer, *v.a.* to juxtapose, to juxtaposit, to place side by side [oneself in juxtaposition **Se —,** *v.r.* to be juxtaposed *or* &c., to place

Juxtaposition, *s.f.* juxtaposition

K

K, *s.m.* k

Kabardin, *adj.m.* (*of musk*) Cabardine, Kabar-

Kabbale, *s.f.* cabala, kabbala [dine

Kabyle, *s.m.f. adj.* Kabyle (*African*)

†**Kagne,** *s.f. V.* **Lasagne**

Kahouane, *s.f. V.* **Caouane**

Kaïmac, *s.m.* kaimac (*Turkish sherbet*)

Kaiserlick, *s.m.*(*pop., jest.*) Kaiserlick, Austrian

Kakatoès, *s.m.* cockatoo

Kakerlat, *s.m. V.* **Cancrelas**

Kakodyle, *s.m.* (*chem.*) cacodyle, kakodyle

Kaléidophone, Kaléidoscope, Kalender, &c. *V.* **Caléidophone,** &c.

Kali, *s.m.* (*bot., chem.*) kali

Kalium, *s.m.* (*chem.*) kalium, potassium

Kalmie, *s.f.* (*bot.*) kalmia

Kalmouk, *s.m. V.* **Calmouk**

Kalpack, *s.m.* (*mil.*) busby, kalpack

Kamichi, *s.m.* (*bird*) kamichi, screamer

Kamsin, *s.m. V.* **Khamsin**

Kamtchadale, *s.m.f. adj.* Kamtchatdale, Kam-

Kan, *s.m.* khan [tchadale

Kanaster, *s.m. V.* **Canastre**

Kandjar, Kandjiar, Kangiar, *s.m.* kandjar (*Indian and Turkish poniard*)

Kanguroo, Kangurou, Kangarou, Kangourou, *s.m.* (*zool.*) kangaroo, kanguroo

Kankan, *s.m.* quack (*of ducks*)

Kantien, ne, *adj. s.* Kantian

Kant-isme, -iste. *V.* page 3, § 1

Kaolin, *s.m.* kaolin, china-clay, porcelain-clay

Kaolinisation, *s.f.* kaolinization [kaolinized

Kaoliniser, *v.a.* to kaolinize. *Se —*, to be

Karabé, Karat, &c. *V.* **Carabé, Carat,** &c.

Karatas, *s.m.* (*bot.*) karatas

Karature, Kari, &c. *V.* **Carature, Cari,** &c.

Karmesse, *s.f. V.* **Kermesse**

Katakoua, *s.m. V.* **Kakatoès**

Kauris, *s.m V.* **Cauris**

Kava, *s.m.* kava

Keepsake, *s.m.* keepsake

Kélotomie, *s.f.* (*surg.*) kelotomy

Képi, *s.m.* kepi, (military) cap

Keplérion, ne, *adj.* Keplerian [keratotome

Kératotome, *s.m.* (*surg.*) keratotomy knife,

Kératotomie, *s.f.* (*surg.*) keratotomy

Kermès, *s.m.* (*nat. hist.*) kermes

Kermesse, *s.f.* parish fair (*in the Netherlands*), fair, feast, wake, kermes

Ketch, *s.m.* (*nav.*) ketch [mallow

Ketmie, *s.f.* (*bot.*) ketmia, hibiscus, Syrian

Khamsin, *s.m.* kamsin, khamsin (*hot wind in*

Khan, *s.m.* khan [*Egypt*)

Khandgiar, *s.m. V.* **Kandjar**

Kiliare, *s.m.* (*Fr. meas.*) kiliare (1000 "ares")

Kilo, (*in compounds*) kilo... (*one thousand* times); — *s.m. V.* **Kilogramme**

Kilogramme, (*abbreviated*) **Kilo, Kilog., Kilogr.,** *s.m.* (*Fr. weight*) kilogramme, kilo (1000 "grammes," *somewhat more than two English pounds*)

Kilogrammètre, *s.m.* (*mech.*) kilogrammeter

Kilolitre, *s.m.* kilolitre (1000 "litres")(*See* p.6.)

Kilométrage, *s.m.* measuring by "kilomètres"; distance in "kilomètres"

Kilomètre, *s.m.* (*measure of distance*) kilomètre, kilometer (1000 "mètres"; *about* $\frac{5}{8}$ *of a mile: eight* "kilomètres" *make about five English miles*)

Kilométrer, *v.a.n.* to measure by "kilomètres," to mark distances in "kilomètres" (*on a road*)

Kilométrique, *adj.* (*Fr. meas*) kilometric

Kilométriquement, *adv.* kilometrically, per "kilomètre"

Kilostère, *s.m.* kilostere (1000 "stères")

Kimry, *s.m. V.* **Kymri**

Kina, *s.m.* (*pharm.*) *V.* **Quinquina**

Kinate, *s.m.* (*chem.*) kinate

Kincajou, *s.m. V.* **Kinkajou**

King, *s.m.* king (*sacred book of the Chinese*)

Kinine, *s.f.* (*chem.*) *V.* **Quinine**

Kinique, *adj.* (*chem.*) kinic

Kinkajou, *s.m.* (*zool.*) kinkajou, honey-bear

Kinnor, *s.m. V.* **Cinnor**

Kino, *s.m.* (*pharm.*) kino

Kinserlick, *s.m. V.* **Kaiserlick**

Kiosque, *s.m.* kiosk; news-stall

Kiotome, *s.m.* (*surg.*) kiotome [kirschenwasser

Kirsch, Kirsch-wasser, *s.m.* kirschwasser,

Kislar-aga, *s.m.* kislar-aga (*chief of the black eunuchs in Turkey*)

Kivite, *s.m.* (*bird*) pewet, pewit

Klephte, Kleptomane, Kleptomanie, &c. *V.* **Clephte,** &c.

Klopémanie, *s.f. V.* **Cleptomanie**

Klopémanique, *adj. V.* **Cleptomane**

Knout, *s.m.* knout

Koff, *s.m.* (*nav.*) koff (*Dutch vessel*)

Kokorico. *V.* **Coquerico**

Kola, *s.m.* (*bot.*) kola, cola

Kolao, *s.m.* kolao, high mandarin, Chinese cabinet-minister *or* privy councillor

Kopeck, *s.m. V.* **Copec**

Koran, *s.m. V.* **Coran**

Koréite, *s.m.* (*min.*) koreite

Kouan, *s.m.* (*bot.*) carmine-seed

Koumis, Koumiss, *s.m.* koumiss, kumiss

Kousso, *s.m.* (*bot.*) kosso, cusso, cabotz [*Moscow*)

Kremlin, *s.m.* Kremlin (*palace of the czars at*

Kreutzer, *s.m.* kreutzer (*German and Swiss coin*)

Kussir, *s.m.* (*mus.*) kussir, kussier

Kwas, *s.m.* quass (*Russian drink*)

Kyaniser, *v.a.* to kyanize [Kymric

Kymri, *s.m.*, **Kymrique,** *adj.m.f.*, *s.m.* Cymric,

Kyrié, Kyrié-éléison, *s.m.* (*Cath. lit.*) kyrie, kyrie-eleison; (*mus.*) kyrie

Kyrielle, *s.f.* string; long story; lot; (*old*) litany

Kyste, *s.m.* (*med.*) cyst, cystis

Kystique, *adj.* (*med.*) cystic [&c.

Kystotome, Kystotomie. *V.* **Cystotome,**

L

L, *s.f.* (*letter*) l

L', *contraction of* **Le** *and of* **La,** *art. and pron., which see; — before* " on" *is only euphonic* (*V.* **On**)

La, L', *art.f.* the; a, an; per; at; in the, during the; what a. *A —, V.* **A;** in the ... fashion, after the manner of; in the style of; (*cook.*) with; done in; preserved in; in; flavoured with; in the ... fashion; [*or simply invert, as*] *glace à — crème*, cream ice. *De —*, of the; from

La, L', *pron.f.* her; it; so [the; some; any

La, *s.m.* (*mus.*) la, A; (*fig.*) tune; tone; lead; cue; — *int.* la! tol-de-rol-lol! *V.* **Là,** *int.*

Là, *int.* there! now! now then! come! — —, there there! come come! softly! gently! not so fast! so so; pretty well; tolerably; indifferently. *Oh — —!* oh dear!

Là, *adv.* there; thither; here; then; that; it; in that; to that; to that point; at *or* to that part; away. — *-bas, V.* **Bas.** — *-contre*, against that; hard by. — *-dedans*, within, in *or* into that, in there, in *or* into that place. — *-dehors*, out there; outside there. — *-derrière*, behind that, behind. — *-dessous*, under that, under there; down there; under; below; underneath. — *-dessus*, on that, on there; over that, over there; up there; thereupon, upon that *or* this, upon it, upon which; saying this, with these words; about that *or* this, about it, on *or* to that *or* this subject (*or* matter), on that *or* this point. — *-devant*, there in front; on before; yonder. — *-haut, V.* **Haut.** — *-même*, in that very place. — *où*, where. *De —*, from that, from there, from that place; from that time; thence; hence; whence. *De-ci de- —*, here and there, to and fro, right and left, on all sides. *Par —, V.* **Par.** *C'est —*, it is *or* was there; that is; such is. *Ce sont —*, those are; such are

Labad-isme, -iste. *V.* page 3, § 1

Labarum, *s.m.* labarum (*standard*)

Labbe, *s.m.* (*bird*) skua, skua gull

Labdacisme, *s.m. V.* **Lambdacisme**

Labdanum, *s.m. V.* **Ladanum**

‡Labech, *s.m.* (*nav.*) south-west wind

Labelle, *s.m.* (*bot.*) label, labellum

Labellé, e, *adj.* (*bot.*) labellate

Labéon, *s.m.* (*fish*) labeo [(*print.*) book-work

Labeur, *s.m.* labour; work; toil; cultivation;

Labial, e, *adj.*, **Labiale,** *s.f.* labial

Labié, e, *adj.* (*bot.*) labiate, labiated; — *s.f.* labiate plant; —**s,** *s.f.pl.* labiatæ, mint-tribe

Labile, *adj.* slippery, failing, bad

Lablab, *s.m.* (*bot.*) lablab

Laboratoire, *s.m.* laboratory

Laborieusement, *adv.* laboriously; painfully

Laborieu-x, se, *adj.* laborious; industrious, painstaking, hard-working; hard; difficult; painful; laboured [painstaking; difficulty

Laboriosité, *s.f.* laboriousness; industry;

Labour, *s.m.* tillage; ploughing; dressing. *En —*, ploughed. *Bœuf de —*, plough-ox, yoke-ox. *Terre de —*, plough-land; (*geog.*) Terra di Lavoro. *Mettre en —*, to plough

Labourable, *adj.* arable [farming

Labourage, *s.m.* tillage; ploughing; husbandry,

Labourer, *v.a.n.* to till; to plough; to dress; to dig; to turn up; to furrow; to cultivate; to rip, to rip up; to gully; to toil through; to toil, to drudge; to land, to carry, to draw; (*of anchors*) to drag; (*of ships*) to graze the bottom

Laboureur, *s.m.* husbandman, farmer, tiller; ploughman [felspar *or* stone, labradorite

Labrador, Labradorite, *s.m.* (*min.*) Labrador

Labre, *s.m.* (*fish*) labrus, wrasse, rock-fish; (*of insects*) labrum

Labrusque, *s.f. V.* **Lambrusque**

Labyrinthe, *s.m* labyrinth, maze

Labyrinthique, *adj.* labyrinthic

Lac, *s.m.* lake; (*of rupees*) lac, lack

Laçage, *s.m.* lacing

Laccine, *s.f.* (*chem.*) laccine

Laccique, *adj.* (*chem.*) laccic [braid; beading

Lacé, e, *part. adj.* laced, &c. (*V.* **Lacer**); — *s.m.*

Lacédémonien, ne, *adj. s.* Lacedæmonian

Lacement, *s.m.* lacing [to line

Lacer, *v.a.* to lace; to run through; (*of dogs*)

Se —, *v.r.* to lace oneself; to be laced

Lacérable, *adj.* lacerable, tearable

Lacération, *s.f.* laceration, tearing

Lacérer, *v.a.* to lacerate, to tear

Laceret, *s.m.* small auger

Lacerie, *s.f.* delicate wicker-work

Laceron, *s.m. V.* **Laiteron**

Lacet, *s.m.* lace; braid; springe; snare; sea-weed; (*in Turkey*) bowstring; (*of a lock*) rivet; (*of a road*) winding. *Mouvement de —*, (*rail.*) oscillation, tail-motion [maker

Laceu-r, se, *s.m.f.* lacer; braid-maker; net-

Lâchage, *s.m.* (*navig.*) letting down

Lâche, *adj.* slack; loose; lax; relaxed; flimsy; muggy; slothful, sluggish, indolent; cowardly, dastardly; mean, base; mean-spirited; — *s.m.* coward, dastard; sluggard

Lâché, e, *part. adj.* slackened, loosened, &c. (*V.* **Lâcher**); loose; out; off

Lâchement, *adv.* cowardly; meanly, basely; slothfully; slackly; loosely

Lâcher, *v.a.* to slacken; to unbend; to relax; to loosen, to loose; to loose o.'s hold of; to let loose; to release; to let go; to let drop; to drop; to quit; to leave; to abandon; to part with; to fork out; to let fly; to let slip; to slip; to let *or* send off; to let *or* send out; to utter; to speak out, to speak; to blurt out; to rap out; to shoot; to fire, to discharge (*fire-arms*); to pull (*the trigger*); to turn on; to open; to give (*a blow*); to make (*water*); — *v.n.*, **Se —,** *v.r.* to slacken; to get loose; to slip; to unbend; to give utterance; to go off. — *d'un cran*, (*fam.*) to leave abruptly, to leave, to give the slip

Lâcheté, *s.f.* cowardice; cowardly act; meanness, baseness; mean *or* base action; sloth; laxity, slackness [cowardly *or* shabby friend

Lâcheur, *s.m.* raftsman, wood-floater; (*fam.*)

Lâchure, *s.f. V.* **Éclusée**

Lacier, *s.m.*, **Lacière,** *s.f.* kind of fishing-net; wolf-net; mow (*part of a barn*)

Lacinié, e, *adj.* (*bot.*) laciniate, laciniated,

Laciniure, *s.f.* (*bot.*) lacinia, jag [jagged

Lacis, *s.m.* network, netting, plaiting; (*anat.*)

Lack, *s.m.* (*of rupees*) lac, lack [plexus

Laconien, ne, *adj. s.* Laconian; Laconian fashion [3, § 1

Lacon-ique, -iquement, -isme. *V.* page

Lacryma-christi, *s.m.* lachryma-christi (*wine*)

Lacrymal, e, *adj.* lachrymal [lachrymary

Lacrymatoire, *s.m.* lachrymatory; — *adj.*

Lacs, *s.m.* string; rope; tape; bowstring (*in Turkey*); springe; snare, noose, toils; knot; —, *pl.* strings, &c.; (*pl. of* **Lac**) *V.* **Lac.** — *d'amour*, love-knot; (*her.*) lacs d'amour

Lactaire, *adj.* lactary, milky

Lactate, *s.m.* (*chem.*) lactate

Lactation, *s.f.* lactation

Lacté, e, *adj.* lacteal, lacteous, milky, of milk, milk; (*anat.*) lacteal; (*astr.*) milky

Lactescence, *s.f.* lactescence

Lactescent, e, *adj.* lactescent

Lactifère, *adj.* lactiferous

Lactifique, *adj.* lactific

Lactifuge, *adj.m.f.*, *s.m.* lactifuge

Lactigène, *adj.* lactigenous

Lactine, *s.f.* lactine, lactose, sugar of milk

Lactique, *adj.* (*chem.*) lactic

Lactomètre, *s.m.* lactometer, galactometer

Lactone, *s.f.* (*chem.*) lactone

Lactose, *s.f.* lactose, lactine, sugar of milk

Lactucarium, *s.m.* (*pharm.*) lactucarium, lettuce-opium

Lactucine, *s.f.* (*chem.*) lactucine
Lactucique, *adj.* (*chem.*) lactucic
Lacunaire, *adj.* lacunar, lacunal
Lacune, *s.f.* lacuna; gap, chasm, hiatus, break, blank, omission, deficiency; desideratum
Lacuneu-x, se, *adj.* lacunose, lacunous
Laçure, *s.f.* lacing
Lacustre, *adj.* lacustral, lacustrine
Ladanum, *s.m.* ladanum, labdanum
Ladite, *adj.f.* the said; the same, ditto
Ladre, *adj.* leprous; (*of pigs*) measled, measly; (*fig.*) insensible, unfeeling, dull, thick-skinned; stingy, mean, shabby, niggardly, scurvy. *Lièvre* —, fen-hare
Ladre, sse, *s.m.f.* leper; miser, niggard, curmudgeon; — *s.m.* (*vet.*) hairless spots
Ladrerie, *s.f.* leprosy; leper-hospital, leper-house, leper-asylum; stinginess, meanness; [(*of pigs*) measles
Lady, *s.f.* (*English*) lady
Laemmer-geier, *s.m.* *V.* **Gypaète**
Lætare, *s.m.* fourth Sunday in Lent
Lagerstrémie, *s.f.* (*bot.*) jarool
Laget, *s.m.* (*bot.*) lagetta, lace-bark tree
Lagomys, *s.m.* (*zool.*) lagomys, rat-hare
Lagon, *s.m.* lagoon
Lagope, *s.m.* (*bot.*) harefoot
Lagopède, *s.m.* (*bird*) lagopus, ptarmigan
Lagophthalmie, *s.f.* (*med.*) lagophthalmia
Lagostome, *s.m.* (*surg.*) lagostoma, hare-lip; (*zool.*) lagostomus
Lagothrix, *s.m.* lagothrix (*kind of monkey*)
Lagrimoso, *adv.* (*mus.*) lagrimoso
Lagune, *s.f.* lagoon, lagune
Lai, e, *adj.* lay; — *s.m.* layman; (*poem*) lay
Laiche, *s.f.* (*bot.*) sedge; — *s.m.* (*zool.*) lob-worm, lug-worm
Laid, e, *adj.* ugly; plain; unhandsome, improper; naughty; — *s.m.* ugliness, (the) ugly, what is ugly; ugly part *or* side; ugly man *or* fellow; naughty boy; — *s.f.* ugly woman *or* creature; naughty girl. *En* —, not so good-[looking
Laidement, *adv.* unhandsomely
Laideron, *s.m.f.* ugly creature, ugly woman, fright; homely puss [someness; deformity
Laideur, *s.f.* ugliness; plainness; unhand-
Laidir, *v.n.* (*old*) *V.* **Enlaidir**
Laie, *s.f.* wild sow; stonecutter's hammer; (*obsolete*) pass, path, lane (*in a forest*); (*obsolete*) copse, coppice; wood; forest
Lainage, *s.m.* woollen stuffs, woollen goods, woollens; fleece, wool; teasing, teaseling, teazling
Laine, *s.f.* wool; worsted. — *filée*, worsted. — *à broder*, Berlin wool. *De* —, of *or* from wool *or* worsted; wool, woollen; worsted. *Manger la — sur le dos à*, to deceive, to cheat, to fleece, to make a fool of. *Se laisser manger la — sur le dos*, to be as patient as a sheep, to submit to everything, to suffer oneself to be deceived *or* made a fool of *or* &c.
Lainer, *v.a.* to tease, to teasel, to teazle
Se —, *v.r.* to be teased, &c.
Lainerie, *s.f.* woollen goods, woollens; manufacture of woollens, woollen trade; wool-market; place for sheep-shearing; teaseling-shop [(*machine*) gig
Laineu-r, se, *s.m.f.* teaseler, teazler; — *s.f.*
Laineu-x, se, *adj.* woolly, fleecy
Lainier, *s.m.* wool-worker; (*obsolete*) wool-stapler
Laini-er, ère, *adj.* of wool, wool, woollen
Laïque, *adj. s.m.f.* lay; (*of courts*) civil; lay-[man, lay woman
Laird, *s.m.* (*Scotch*) laird
Lais, *s.m.* staddle, standard tree, standard; alluvium, alluvion, accretion
Laïs, *s.f.* Lais, great courtesan
Laisse, *s.f.* string; leash; slip; silt, slime; beach; sea-ware. *Mener en* —, to lead by a string *or* in a leash; to leash; (*fig.*) to keep in leading-strings; to lead by the nose
Laissées, *s.f.pl.* (*hunt.*) lesses, dung
Laisser, *v.a.* to leave; to quit; to abandon; to desert; to part with; to give up; to bequeath; to leave *or* let alone; to leave off; to cease; to discontinue; to stop; to leave out, to omit; to lay aside; to lose; to let, to allow, to permit, to suffer; to let go; to let have; to spare. *Ne pas* — *de* or *que de*, not to leave off, not to cease, not to discontinue, to continue, nevertheless, however, for all that, yet; not to fail (to); to ... more than one would suppose. — *de côté*, to leave aside *or* &c. (*V.* **Côté**); to lay aside; to leave alone; to leave off. — *là*, to leave there; to leave, to abandon, to give up; to let alone; to leave off; to lay aside. — *aller*, to let go; to let go on; to let loose; to neglect; *s.m.* [*See below*]. — *dire*, to let (*one*) speak *or* say *or* talk *or* &c.; to let people talk; to let (*a thing*) be said. — *faire*, to let alone; to let go on; not to disturb; not to interfere; to humour; to let (*one*) have his own way *or* act as he pleases; to leave the matter to, to leave it to; to let (...) be done, to allow (...) to be committed; *s.m.* [*See below*]. — *tomber*, to let fall; to drop. — *voir*, to allow to see, to let see; to let (...) be seen; to show; to discover; to betray. *Laisse donc! Laissez donc!* leave that alone! leave off! nonsense! never mind (...)! *Laisse* or *laissez-moi donc tranquille!* do leave me alone! stuff! fiddlededee! — *quelqu'un pour ce qu'il est*, to take no notice of a person. *C'est à prendre ou à* —, you may take it or leave it. *Avoir le prendre et le* — (*s.m.*), to have the choice
Se —, *v.r.* to let *or* allow *or* suffer oneself; to be left; to be worth. *Se* — *aller*, to let oneself go; to abandon oneself; not to resist; to give way; to yield; to give oneself up; to indulge; to lose o.'s energy; to go on carelessly; to neglect o.'s person, to be careless of o.'s personal appearance; to be easily influenced; to despond. *Se* — *dire*, to allow oneself to be told. *Se* — *faire*, not to resist, to offer no resistance, to let people have their own way *or* do as they please with us; to put up with it, to submit to it, to stand it. *Se* — *lire*, to be worth reading, to be readable. *Se* — *manger*, (*of things*) to be worth eating, to be eatable *or* palatable. *Se* — *tomber*, to fall (*accidentally*), to happen to fall, to have *or* get a fall; to drop; to sink. (*General construction*) *Se* — *prendre* or *&c.*, to allow (*or* suffer) oneself to be taken *or* &c.; to allow (...) to be taken from one (*oneself*)
Laisser-aller, *s.m.* ease, unconstraint, freedom, easy manner; indulgence; abandonment; indolence, carelessness, negligence; easiness, yieldingness, weak-mindedness
Laisser-courre, *s.m.* (*hunt.*) *V.* **Courre,** *v.a.n.*
Laisser-faire, Laissez-faire, *s.m.* non-interference, non-intervention
Laisser-passer, *s.m.* pass; permit for transit
Lait, *s.m.* milk; milk-diet; (*of eggs*) white. — *de chaux*, milk of lime; lime-water; limewash, whitewash. — *de poule*, mulled egg; egg-flip. *Gros* —, curd. *Petit* —, — *clair*, whey. *A* —, (*adject.*) milk; milky; milch. *De* —, of *or* from milk; (*adject.*) milk; milky; sucking; foster (*brother or sister*)
Laitage, *s.m.* milk-food, milk, milk-diet
Laitance, Laite, *s.f.* soft roe, milt; lime-water, limewash, whitewash [soft-roed
Laité, e, *adj.* having milk; mixed with milk;
Laiterie, *s.f.* dairy, dairy-house; milk-trade; [milk-shop
Laiteron, *s.m.* (*bot.*) sow-thistle
Laiteu-x, se, *adj.* milky; milk
Laitier, *s.m.* milkman; dairy-man; (*bot.*) milk-wort; (*metal.*) slag, dross, clinkers
Laitière, *s.f.* milkwoman, milkmaid; dairy-maid; milch-cow, milch-goat, &c.; milker; — *adj.f.* (*of cows, goats, &c.*) milch [—, brass wire
Laiton, *s.m.* brass, latten; brass wire. *Fil de*
Laitonné, e, *adj.* wired
Laitue, *s.f.* lettuce. — *pommée*, cabbage-lettuce. — *de mer*, oyster-green, laver
Laize, *s.f.* (*of cloth, stuff, sails*) width, breadth

Lak, *s.m. V.* **Lack**
Lakiste, *s.m.* (*Engl. liter.*) poet of the Lake School; **—s,** *pl.* Lake School, poets of ditto
Lallation, *s.f.* lallation [Lama, Llama
Lama, *s.m.* (*zool.*) lama, llama; (*of the Tartars*)
Lama-ïque, -ïsme, -ïste. *V.* page 3, § 1
Lamaïte, *s.m.* Lamaite
Lamanage, *s.m.* coast-pilotage, lodesmanage
Lamaneur, *s.m.* coast-pilot, lodesman; — *adj.m.* coast [cow
Lamantin, *s.m.* (*zool.*) lamantin, manatee, sea-
Lamaserie, *s.f.* lamasery
Lambdacisme, *s.m.* lambdacism
Lambdoïde, *adj.* (*anat.*) lambdoidal
Lambeau, *s.m.* rag, tatter; shred; strip; scrap; fragment; piece; bit; morsel; remains, rem-
Lambel, *s.m.* (*her.*) label [nant, ruins
Lambin, e, *adj. s.m.f.* loitering, dawdling; loiterer, dawdler, trifler, slow coach; — *s.m.* (*zool.*) sloth
Lambiner, *v.n.* to loiter, to dawdle, to trifle, to linger; to lag; to dilly-dally; to shilly-shally, to boggle [*shell used as a horn*)
Lambis, *s.m.* lambis, scorpion-shell (*kind of*
Lambourdage, *s.m.* joisting
Lambourde, *s.f.* joist; (*mas.*) soft-stone
Lambourder, *v.a.* to joist [brequin, mantling
Lambrequin, *s.m.* (*arch.*) scallop; (*her.*) lam-
Lambris, *s.m.* wainscot; panelling; lining; ceiling; canopy; roof, dwelling, abode. — *d'appui*, skirting, base-plinth [lining
Lambrissage, *s.m.* wainscoting; panelling;
Lambrisser, *v.a.* to wainscot; to panel; to
Lambrot, *s.m. V.* **Lambruche** [line
Lambruche, Lambrusque, *s.f.* wild vine
Lame, *s.f.* plate, sheet (*of metal*); flattened wire, foil, spangle (*of gold, silver*); blade; sword; lath; slat; board; (*of water*) sheet; (*nav.*) wave, sea, billow, surge, swell; (*coin.*) fillet, ribbon; (*anat.*, &c.) lamina; (*weav.*) reed; (*obsolete*) tombstone; (*pers.*) swordsman; jade, hussy, blade. — *de fond*, (*nav.*) ground-swell [*silver*) wire, spangled
Lamé, e, *adj.* laminated; worked with (*gold or*
Lamellaire, *adj.* lamellar
Lamellation, *s.f.* lamellation
Lamelle, *s.f.* lamel, lamella
Lamellé, e, *adj.* lamellate, lamellated
Lamelleu-x, se, *adj.* lamellose [branchiate
Lamellibranche, *adj.m.f., s.m.* (*zool.*) lamelli-
Lamellicorne, *adj.m.f., s.m.* (*zool.*) lamellicorn
Lamellifère, *adj.* lamelliferous
Lamelliforme, *adj.* lamelliform
Lamellirostre, *adj.* (*zool.*) lamellirostral; — *s.m.* lamellirostre
Lamentabile, *adj.m.f., s.m.* (*mus.*) lamentabile
Lamentable, *adj.* lamentable, mournful, sad, distressing [fully
Lamentablement, *adv.* lamentably, mourn-
Lamentation, *s.f.* lamentation, bewailing, whining [wail, to mourn, to whine
Lamenter, *v.a.n.*, **Se —,** *v.r.* to lament, to be-
Lamentin, *s.m. V.* **Lamantin**
Lamento, *s.m.* (*mus.*) lamento
Lamette, *s.f.* small plate *or* &c. (*V.* **Lame**)
Lamie, *s.f.* lamia; white shark [archangel
Lamier, *s.m.* foil-maker; (*bot.*) dead-nettle,
Laminabilité, *s.f.* laminability
Laminable, *adj.* laminable
Laminage, *s.m.* laminating, flattening, rolling
Laminaire, *adj.* laminar, laminary; — *s.f.* (*bot.*) laminaria, tangle
Laminer, *v.a.* to laminate, to flatten, to roll
Se —, *v.r.* to be laminated *or* &c.
Laminerie, *s.f. V.* **Laminoir** [rolling
Lamineur, *s.m.* flattener; — *adj.m.* flattening,
Lamineu-x, se, *adj.* laminose, laminous
Laminoir, *s.m.* flatting-mill, rolling-mill
Lamique, Lamiste. *V.* **Lamaïque,** &c.
Lampadaire, *s.m.* sconce; lamp-post; (*anc. hist.*) torch-bearer
Lampadiste, *s.m.* (*Gr. ant.*) lampadist
Lampadophore, *s.m.* torch-bearer; lampadist
Lampant, e, *adj.* (*of oil*) limpid, refined
Lampas, *s.m.* figured silk, silk damask; (*vet.*) lampas, lampass; (*obsolete*) throat, whistle
Lampascope, *s.m.* phantasmagoria-lantern
Lampassé, e, *adj.* (*her.*) langued
Lampate, *s.m.* (*chem.*) lampate [spirit-lamp
Lampe, *s.f.* lamp; light. — *à esprit-de-vin*,
Lampée, *s.f.* (*pop.*) bumper, brimmer, tumbler-ful; spot, stain
Lamper, *v.a.n.* (*pop.*) to quaff; to guzzle
Lamperon, *s.m.* wick-holder
Lampette, *s.f.* (*bot.*) corn-cockle; ragged robin
Lampion, *s.m.* (illumination *or* church) lamp; (*pop.*) three-cornered hat, hat, tile; peeper
Lampique, *adj.* (*chem.*) lampic [(*eye*)
Lampiste, *s.m.f.* lamp-maker; lamp-keeper, lamp-lighter
Lampisterie, *s.f.* lamp-making; lamp-room
Lampon, *s.m.* (*obsolete*) lampoon
Lampotte, *s.f.* (*fish.*) bait
Lampourde, *s.f.* (*bot.*) bur-weed
Lampresse, *s.f.* lamprey-net
Lamprette, *s.f. V.* **Lampette**
†**Lamprillon,** *s.m.* (*fish*) pride, stone-grig
Lamproie, *s.f.* lamprey
Lampromètre, *s.m.* lamprometer
Lamproyon, *s.m. V.* **Lamprillon**
Lampsane, *s.f.* (*bot.*) nipple-wort
Lampyre, *s.m.* (*zool.*) glowworm
Lan, Lanc, *s.m.* (*nav.*) spring, yaw
Lançage, *s.m.* (*nav.*) launching, launch
Lancastérien, ne, *adj.* Lancasterian
Lancastrien, ne, *adj. s.* Lancastrian
Lance, *s.f.* lance, spear; lancer; flag-staff, staff; spike; branch-pipe, branch (*of a hose-pipe*); spout. — *à feu*, portfire, portfire-stick, match
Lancé, e, *part. adj.* darted, &c. (*V.* **Lancer**); darting *or* dashing *or* rushing on, running, flying; launched; started; gone off, off; set up, well off, rising, afloat, making a fortune; tipsy, fresh, tight, far gone; — *s.m. V.* **Lancer,** *s.m.*; (*pop.*) bold step (*in dancing*)
Lancement, *s.m.* darting; throwing; &c. (*V.* **Lancer,** *v.a.*); (*nav.*) launching, launch
Lancéolaire, *adj.* lanceolar, lance-shaped
Lancéolé, e, *adj.* lanceolate, lanceolated, lance-shaped
Lancer, *v.a.* to dart; to throw; to fling; to cast; to hurl; to toss; to shoot; to shoot *or* send forth; to send out, to send; to issue; to fetch, to deal, to give; to push; to drive; to start; (*nav.*, *and fig.*) to launch; — *v.n.* (*nav.*) to gripe; to sheer, to yaw
Se —, *v.r.* to dart, to spring; to rush; to start; to fly; to launch, to launch out; to come out; to enter; to venture, to chance it
Lancer, *s.m.* (*hunt.*) starting; starting-place *or*
Lanceron, *s.m.* (*fish*) jack, pickerel [point
Lancetier, *s.m.* (*surg.*) lancet-case
Lancette, *s.f.* lancet
Lanceur, *s.m.* pushing fellow; pushing publisher; (— *d'affaires*) promoter, speculator,
Lanceuse, *s.f.* go-between, procuress [jobber
Lanche, *s.f.* (kind of French fishing-boat); (*foreign boat*) lantcha
Lancier, *s.m.* lancer; spearman
Lancière, *s.f.* (*of water-mills*) waste-gate [ing
Lancinant, e, *adj.* (*of pain*) lancinating, shoot-
Lanciner, *v.n.* (*of pain*) to lancinate, to shoot
Lançoir, *s.m.* mill-gate
Lançon, *s.m. V.* **Équille** [the Landes
Landais, e, *adj. s.* of the Landes; native of
Landamman, *s.m.* landamman (*Swiss magis-*
Landammanat, *s.m.* landammanship [*trate*)
Landau, *s.m.* landau [waste land; furze
Lande, *s.f.* heath, brake, sandy moor, plain,
Landerira, Landerirète, *int.* tol-de-rol-lol !
Landgrave, *s.m.* landgrave
Landgraviat, *s.m.* landgraviate
Landgravine, *s.f.* landgravine

Landier, *s.m.* andiron, firedog; (*bot.*) *V.* **Ajonc**
Landière, *s.f.* booth, stall
Landsturm, *s.m.* (*in Germany*) landsturm
Landwehr, *s.f.* (*in Germany*) landwehr
Laneret, *s.m.* (*bird*) lanneret
Lanet, *s.m.* shrimp-net; hoop-net
Langage, *s.m.* language; tongue; speech; dialect; lingo; talk; words; style; expression; tone; tune
Langard, *s.m.* (*nav.*) lug-sail
Lange, *s.m.* swathe
Langoureusement, *adv.* languishingly
Langoureu-x, se, *adj.* languishing, pining; melancholy; — *s.m.* languishing lover
Langouste, *s.f.* spiny lobster, sea-crayfish
Langoustier, *s.m.*, **Langoustière,** *s.f.* lobster-net
Langrois, e, *adj. s.* of Langres; native of Langres
Languard, e, *adj.* tonguy, talkative, blabbing, slanderous; — *s.m.f.* talker, blab, slanderer
Langue, *s.f.* tongue; language; expression; (*of land*) neck, strip, tongue; (*nav.*) wedge; (*of a sail*) breadth, width. — *maternelle*, mother *or* native tongue. — *mère*, primitive tongue *or* language. — *verte*, slang. *Mauvaise* or *méchante* —, slanderous tongue. *Enfant* or *jeune de* —, bursar for the Oriental languages. *Avoir la — grasse*, to speak thick, to lisp. *Faire la — à*, to give (*one*) his cue. *Jeter sa — aux chiens*, to give up guessing, to give it up. *Prendre* —, to get intelligence, to learn news
Langué, e, *adj.* (*her.*) langued
Languedocien, ne, *adj. s.* Languedocian
Langueter, *v.a.* (*tech.*) to tongue
Languette, *s.f.* tongue; strip; valve; partition; (*of a balance*) index; (*of mus. instr.*) key; (*jewel.*) assaying-slip; (*rail.*) tongue; (*nav.*) wedge; (*nav.*) slice; (*zool.*) razor-shell, razor-fish; (*local*) tongue-shaped boat
Langueur, *s.f.* languor; debility, weakness, feebleness, faintness; decline; dulness. *Maladie de* —, decline
Langueyage, *s.m.* examination of a pig's tongue
Langueyer, *v.a.* to examine the tongue of (*a pig*)
Langueyeur, *s.m.* examiner of pigs' tongues
Languide, *adj.* (*old*) languid
Languido, *adv.* (*mus.*) languido
Languier, *s.m.* smoked pig's tongue
Languir, *v.n.* to languish; to pine, to pine away; to droop; to decline; to linger; to wither; to flag; to be dull
Languissamment, *adv.* languidly, languishingly, piningly, droopingly, weakly, feebly, faintly
Languissant, e, *adj.* languid, languishing; pining; drooping; declining; lingering; flagging; weak, feeble, faint; slack; flat, dull; spiritless
Laniaire, *adj.m.f.*, *s.f.* (*anat.*) laniary
Lanice, *adj.* of wool
Lanier, *s.m.* (*bird*) lanner
Lanière, *s.f.* thong, lash, narrow strip *or* strap of leather; (*her.*) bend
Lanifère, *adj.* laniferous
Lanigère, *adj.* lanigerous
†Lanille, *s.f.* (Flemish woollen stuff)
Lanion, *s.m.* (*zool.*) butcher-bird
Laniste, *s.m.* (*Rom. ant.*) lanista
Lan laire, Lanlaire, *int.* tol-de-rol-lol! *Envoyer faire* —, *envoyer* —, (*slang*) to send away *or* about o.'s business, to send packing; to throw *or* kick overboard
Lans, *s.m. V.* **Lan**
Lansac, *s.m.* (kind of autumn pear)
Lanson, *s.m. V.* **Équille**
Lansquenet, *s.m.* lansquenet (*German foot-soldier of former times; game at cards*)
Lant, *s.m.* (*zool.*) zebu, Indian ox
Lantanier, *s.m.* (*bot.*) lantana
Lanter, *v.a.* to emboss, to chase (*copper ware*)
Lanterne, *s.f.* lantern; lamp; lamp-post; lantern-tower; lantern-light; skylight; glass case; spy-place; (*of gas*) flash-pipe; (*tech.*) lantern, lantern-wheel, trundle, wallower; roving-frame, slubbing-machine; —**s,** *pl.* lanterns, &c.; (*fam.*) trifles, nonsense, idle stories; (*pop.*) peepers (*eyes*); goggle-eyes. *Mettre à la* —, to hang up at the lamp-post, to lynch. *A la — !* to the lamp-post with him (*or* with ...)! hang him (*or* hang ...) up at the lamp-post!
Lanterneau, *s.m.* lantern-light, skylight
Lanterner, *v.n.a.* to dilly-dally, to dally, to shilly-shally, to boggle, to trifle; to trifle away o.'s time; to talk nonsense; to twaddle; to deceive, to trifle with, to bamboozle, to humbug; to put off; to keep waiting; to bother; to bother with; (*old*) to hang up at the lamp-post, to lynch
Lanternerie, *s.f.* dilly-dallying, dilly-dally, shilly-shallying, shilly-shally, boggling, trifling; trifle; idle story, twaddle, nonsense, stuff; put-off; delay
Lanternier, *s.m.* lantern-maker; lamp-lighter; boggler; trifler; twaddler
Lanternon, *s.m.* (*arch.*) small cupola
Lanthane, Lanthanium, *s.m.* (*chem.*) lanthanium
Lantimèche, *s.m.* (*pop.*) silly Billy, fool, muff
Lantiponnage, *s.m.* nonsense, stuff, rigmarole, twaddle
Lantiponner, *v.n.* to talk nonsense *or* stuff, to twaddle; to boggle; — *v.a.* to talk stuff to; to bother with
Lanture, *s.f.* embossment, embossing, chasing (*on copper ware*)
Lanturelu, Lanturlu, *int.* tol-de-rol-lol! fiddlestick! fudge! — *s.m.* giddy-goose
Lanugineu-x, se, *adj.* lanuginous, downy
Laonnais, e, *adj. s.* of Laon, Laonnese, native of Laon
Laparocèle, *s.f.* (*med.*) laparocele
Laparotomie, *s.f.* (*surg.*) laparotomy
Lapement, *s.m.* lapping
Laper, *v.n.a.* to lap, to lick up
Lapereau, *s.m.* young rabbit
Lapidaire, *s.m. adj.* lapidary
Lapidation, *s.f.* lapidation, stoning
Lapider, *v.a.* to stone to death, to stone; to pelt with stones, to pelt; (*fig.*) to tear to pieces
Lapidescence, *s.f.* lapidescence
Lapidescent, e, *adj.* lapidescent
Lapideu-r, se, *s.m.f.* stoner
Lapidification, *s.f.* lapidification
Lapidifier, *v.a.*, **Se** —, *v.r.* to lapidify
Lapidifique, *adj.* lapidific
Lapilleu-x, se, *adj.* stony, gravelly
Lapin, *s.m.* rabbit, buck rabbit; coney; bunny; (*pop.*) famous fellow, buck, brick, knowing one; apprentice. — *de gouttière*, (*pop.*) cat. *En* —, on the box, by the side of the driver. *Brave comme un* —, as fine as fivepence
Lapine, *s.f.* doe rabbit, rabbit
Lapineau, *s.m.* (*children's slang*) bunny (*rabbit*)
Lapis, Lapis-lazuli, *s.m.* (*min.*) lapis lazuli
Lapithes, *s.m.pl.* (*myth.*) Lapithæ
Lapmude, *s.f.* dress made of reindeer's skin
Lapon, e, *adj. s.* Laplandish; Laplander; (*fig.*) dwarf, shrimp, runt
Laps, *s.m.* (*of time*) lapse, period, space
Laps, e, *adj.* (*can. law*) fallen, lapsed
Lapsus, *s.m.* (*Latin*) slip. — *calami*, slip of the pen. — *linguæ*, slip of the tongue
Laptot, *s.m.* coolie [*Petit* —, foot-boy
Laquais, *s.m.* footman, lackey; flunkey, flunky.
Laque, *s.f. adj.* lac; (*colour*) lake; — *s.m. adj.* lacquer; japan; lacquer-work; lacquered vase *or* piece of furniture, lacquered ware. *Gomme* —, gum-lac. *Vernis* —, japan
Laquelle, *pron.f.* who, which, whom, that
Laquer, *v.a.* to lacquer; to japan
Laquet, *s.m.* lakelet, little lake
Laqueu-x, se, *adj.* of the nature of lac; lake-coloured
Larbin, e, *s.m.f.* (*pop.*) menial
Larcin, *s.m.* larceny; theft; pilfering; robbery; plagiarism
Lard, *s.m.* bacon; pig's fat; (*of whales, &c.*) blubber. *Être gras à* —, to be as fat as a hog. *Faire du* —, to get fat, to sleep oneself fat. *Aller faire du* —, (*pop.*) to go to bed
Lardacé, e, *adj.* lardaceous
Larde, *s.f.* rasher

Larder, *v.a.* to lard; to interlard; to stick; to run through, to pierce, to riddle, to pink; to load, to cover; to overwhelm; (*rid.*) to wound with the spurs; (*nav.*) to thrum
Larderasse, *s.f.* (*nav.*) common rope
Larderon, *s.m.* (*bird*) blue tit, tomtit
Lardiforme, *adj.* lardiform
Lardite, *s.f.* (*min.*) lardite, Chinese figure-stone
Lardivore, *adj.* lardivorous, bacon-eating
Lardoire, *s.f.* larding-needle *or* pin; (*pop.*) sword
Lardon, *s.m.* slip of bacon, lardoon; gibe, jeer, jest, wipe; (*horol.*) pallet; (*play*) false card
Lardonnement, *s.m.* gibing, jeering
Lardonner, *v.a.* to cut into slips *or* lardoons; [to gibe, to jeer
Lardure, *s.f.* defect (*in cloth*)
Lare, *s.m.* (*Rom. antiq.*) lar, household god; **—s,** *pl.* lares, household gods; fireside, paternal house, home, hearth; — (*zool.*) larus, gull
Larenier, *s.m.* *V.* **Rejéteau**
Large, *adj.* broad; wide; large; great; enlarged; extensive; liberal; generous; free; grand; (*of conscience*) accommodating; (*obsolete*) lax, loose; — *s.m.* breadth; width; distance; (*nav.*) open sea, sea, offing; — *adv.* largely; grandly; wide. *Au* —, spaciously; comfortable, comfortably, at o.'s ease; well off; abroad; at a distance, off; (*nav.*) out at sea, out to sea, in the offing, out, off; (*int.*) keep off! *En* —, broadwise. *Courir au* —, *gagner* or *prendre le* —, (*nav.*) to get out to sea, to stand out to sea; (*fig.*) to get away, to run *or* scamper away, to be off. *Passer au* —, to pass at a distance, to keep off. *Porter au* —, (*nav.*) to bear off from the land. *Pousser au* —, (*nav.*) to push off; to sheer off, to put off. *Se mettre au* —, *tenir le* —, to keep off; to take room
Largement, *adv.* broadly; widely; largely; greatly; copiously; abundantly; amply; fully; liberally; freely; boldly; grandly; at least
Largesse, *s.f.* largess; liberality; bounty; munificence; present, gift, donation, gratuity, fee
Largeur, *s.f.* breadth; width; largeness; broadness; wideness; (*rail.*) gauge
Larghetto, *s.m. adv.* (*mus.*) larghetto
Largo, *s.m. adv.* (*mus.*) largo
Largue, *adj.* (*nav.*) slack (*rope*); flowing (*sheets*); — *adv.* (*nav.*) large; — *s.m.* (*nav.*) offing, open sea. *Vent* —, (*nav.*) leading wind, quartering wind; large wind. *Avoir* or *aller vent* —, *courir* —, *porter* —, to sail *or* go large
Larguer, *v.a.* (*nav.*) to let go, to let run, to ease off; to let out (*reefs*); to let fly (*the sheets*), to ease off (*the sheets*); to loosen (*a sail*); to smite (*the mizzen*); — *v.n.* (*nav.*) to bear up; to spring a butt, to be split. *Largue le lof!* up tacks and sheets!
Larice, *s.m.* *V.* **Larix**
Laricine, *s.f.* (*chem.*) laricine
Laridon, *s.m.* (*obsolete*) scullion
Larigot, *s.m.* flute, flageolet. *A tire-* —, hard
Larix, *s.m.* (*bot.*) larch, larch-tree
Larmaire, *adj.* (*bot.*) tear-shaped
Larme, *s.f.* tear; drop. *A chaudes* —*s*, bitterly. *Avoir le don des* —*s*, to have tears at command
Larmette, *s.f.* (*old*) little tear *or* drop
Larmeu-x, se, *adj.* teary, tear-shaped
Larmier, *s.m.* (*arch.*) larmier, corona, dripstone, drip, eaves, coping; weather-board; (*of the deer*) tear-pit; (*of the horse*) eye-vein; (*draw.*) inner angle (of the eye); (*bot.*) *V.* **Coïx**
Larmière, *s.f.* (*of the deer*) tear-pit
†Larmille, *s.f.* (*bot.*) *V.* **Coïx**
Larmoiement, *s.m.* watering of the eyes; [(*med.*) epiphora
Larmoyant, e, *adj. s.m.* weeping, tearful, in tears; whining, whimpering; lachrymose; sentimental; pathetic; tragic
Larmoyer, *v.n.* to shed tears, to weep, to cry; to whine, to whimper; (*of the eyes*) to water
Larmoyeu-r, se, *s.m.f.* weeper; whiner, whimperer
Larose, *s.m.* larose (wine)
Larron, nesse, *s.m.f.* thief; robber; stealer; (*print.*) bite; (*book-bind.*) dog's ear
Larronneau, *s.m.* (*obsolete*) *V.* **Volereau**
Larve, *s.f.* larva, larve, grub, worm, maggot, caterpillar; (*antiq.*) larva, spectre, hobgoblin
Larvé, e, *adj.* larvated
Larvipare, *adj.* (*zool.*) larviparous
Laryngalgie, *s.f.* (*med.*) laryngalgia
Laryngé, e, Laryngien, ne, *adj.* (*anat.*) laryngeal, laryngean
Laryngisme, *s.m.* (*med.*) laryngismus
Laryngite, *s.f.* (*med.*) laryngitis
Laryngo-graphie, -logie, -phonie. *V.* p. 3, § 1
Laryngoscope, *s.m.* laryngoscope
Laryngo-scopie, -tomie, &c. *V.* page 3, § 1
Laryngotome, *s.m.* (*surg.*) laryngotomy-knife
Larynx, *s.m.* (*anat.*) larynx
Las, se, *adj.* tired, fatigued, weary. *Un* — *d'aller*, a lazy fellow
Las, *int.* (*old, poet.*) *V.* **Hélas;** — *s.m.* mow [(*part of a barn*)
†Lasagne, *s.f.* broad vermicelli
Lascar, *s.m.* lascar
Lasci-f, ve, *adj.* lascivious, lewd
Lascivement, *adv.* lasciviously
Lasciveté, *s.f.* lasciviousness, lust, lewdness
Laser, Laserpitium, *s.m.* (*bot.*) laser-wort
Lasionite, *s.m.* (*min.*) lasionite
Lasquette, *s.f.* skin of a young ermine
Lassant, e, *adj.* tiring, fatiguing; tiresome, wearisome
Lasser, *v.a.* to tire, to tire out, to fatigue, to weary; to discourage
Se —, *v.r.* to tire, to weary, to get *or* become (*or* be) tired *or* wearied
Lasseret, Lasserie, Lassier, &c. *V.* **Laceret,** &c.
Lassitude, *s.f.* lassitude, weariness, heaviness
Lasso, *s.m.* lasso
Last, Laste, *s.m.* (*meas.*) last
Lasting, *s.m.* lasting (*stuff*)
Latakia, *s.m.* latakia
Latanier, *s.m.* (*bot.*) latania, fan-palm. *Chapeau* —, chip-hat
Latemment, *adv.* latently
Latent, e, *adj.* latent, hidden, concealed, secret
Latéral, e, *adj.* lateral, side
Latéralement, *adv.* laterally, sideways
Latere (A), *adv.* (*Latin*) a latere
Latérifolié, e, *adj.* (*bot.*) laterifolious
Latérigrade, *adj. s.f.* laterigrade (*spider*)
Latérite, *s.f.* (*geol.*) laterite
Latex, *s.m.* (*bot.*) latex
Lathyrus, *s.m.* (*bot.*) lathyrus
Laticlave, *s.m.* (*Rom. ant.*) laticlave
Laticifère, *adj.* (*bot.*) laticiferous
Latin, e, *adj.* Latin; Roman; (*nav.*) lateen. *Quartier* or *pays* —, students' quarter (*in Paris*), university
Latin, *s.m.* Latin; (*obsolete*) latinist. — *de cuisine*, dog-Latin. *Au bout de son* —, at o.'s wits' end, at a loss, in a fix. *Perdre son* —, to lose o.'s time and trouble, to rack o.'s brains in vain, to be able to make nothing (of it)
Latine, *s.f.* (*pop.*) student's sweetheart
Latinisation, *s.f.* latinization
Latiniser, *v.a.n.* to latinize
Latiniseur, *s.m.* latinizer
Latinisme, *s.m.* latinism
Latiniste, *s.m.* latinist, Latin scholar
Latinité, *s.f.* latinity, Latin. *La basse* —, low Latin
Latitude, *s.f.* latitude; extent; room, space; margin; freedom of action; climate, clime
Latitudinaire, *adj. s.* latitudinarian
Latitudinarien, ne, *adj. s.* latitudinarian
Latitudinarisme, *s.m.* latitudinarianism
Latitudinariste, *s.m.f.* latitudinarian
Latomie, *s.f.* (*anc. hist.*) latomia
Latran, *s.m.* Lateran
Latreutique, *adj.* (*theol.*) latreutical
Latrie, *s.f.* latria (*worship of God alone*)
Latrines, *s.f.pl.* privy, water-closet, conveniences, latrines
Latrobite, *s.f.* (*min.*) latrobite
Lattage, *s.m.* lathing; lath-work
Latte, *s.f.* lath; batten; rod; straight (cavalry-) sword
Latter, *v.a.* to lath
Lattis, *s.m.* lath-work, lathing
Laudanisé, e, *adj.* (*pharm.*) containing laudanum

Laudanum, *s.m.* laudanum; (*fig.*) blarney, soft sawder
Lauda-teur, trice, *s.m.f.* laudator, lauder
Laudati-f, ve, *adj.* laudatory, eulogistic, en-comiastic
Laudes, *s.f.pl.* (*Cath. lit.*) lauds
Laure, *s.f.* laura (*Greek monastery*)
Lauré, e, *adj.* laureated, laurelled
Lauréat, *adj.m.* laureate; prize-holding; — *s.m.* laureate; prize-taker, prize-holder, prize-man
Laurelle, *s.f.* (*bot.*) rose-bay, oleander
Laurentienne, *adj.f. Bibliothèque* —, Laurentian library (*at Florence*)
Lauréole, *s.f.* (*bot.*) spurge-laurel. — *femelle*, mezereon
Laurier, *s.m.* laurel; bay; (*fig.*) laurel, glory, victory, honour. — *-cerise*, cherry-laurel. — *-rose*, rose-bay, oleander. — *-sauce*, sweet bay. — *-tin*, laurustinus, laurustine, laurestine
Laurière, *s.f.* laurel-plantation, laurel-grove
Laurifolié, e, *adj.* (*bot.*) laurifoliate
Laurine, *s.f.* (*chem.*) laurine
Lauriot, *s.m.* (*baker's*) scovel-tub
Laurique, *adj.* (*chem.*) laurostearic
Laurose, *s.m.* (*bot.*) rose-bay, oleander
Laurostéarique, *adj.* (*chem.*) laurostearic
Lavabe, *s.m.* (*theat. slang*) pit-seat at a reduced price
Lavabo, *s.m.* wash-stand, wash-hand stand; (*Cath. rel.*) lavabo; (*ditto*) towel
Lavage, *s.m.* washing; wash; scrubbing; scouring; cleaning; cleansing; bathing; diluting, dilution; (*of ore*) dressing, washing; (*fam.*) plash; slop, slipslop, mess, wash; great loss, ruinous expense, sale at greatly reduced prices, selling off at a ruinous loss. *En* —, (*med.*) diluted
Lavanche, *s.f. V.* **Lavange**
Lavande, *s.f.* lavender
Lavanderie, *s.f.* (*obsolete*) laundry
Lavandier, *s.m.* (*old*) yeoman of the laundry
Lavandière, *s.f.* laundry-maid; laundress, washerwoman; (*local*) barge, boat; (*bird*) dish-washer, wagtail
Lavanèse, *s.f.* (*bot.*) goat's rue
Lavange, *s.f.* (*obsolete form of* "avalanche") *V.* **Avalanche;** (*in the Alps and Pyrenees*) mass of mud and stones falling from the mountains; fall of the portion of a cliff, &c.
Lavaret, *s.m.* (*fish*) coregonus (gwyniad, powan, pollan, vendace, &c.), freshwater herring, herring-salmon
Lavasse, *s.f.* slop, slipslop, wash, washy stuff, wishy-washy stuff, wishy-washy, wish-wash, (*of tea*) water bewitched; (*obsolete*) sudden shower
Lavatère, *s.f.* (*bot.*) lavatera
Lavatérien, ne, *adj. s.* Lavaterian
Lavation, *s.f.* (*fam.*) washing, wash
Lavatoire, *s.m.* lavatory
Lave, *s.f.* lava
Lavé, e, *part. adj.* washed, &c. (*V.* **Laver**); (*of colours*) light
Lave-mains, *s.m.* finger-glass; wash-hand basin and tap
Lavement, *s.m.* washing; (*med.*) injection, enema; (*pers., fam.*) bore
Laver, *v.a.* to wash; to wash away *or* off *or* out; to scrub; to scour; to clean; to cleanse; to clear; to bathe; to dilute; (*of ore*) to dress, to wash; (*draw.*) to wash, to tint; (*fam.*) to sell at a great loss; to spend away
Se —, *v.r.* to wash *or* &c. oneself; to wash (o.'s ...); to wash; to bathe; to clear oneself
Laverie, *s.f.* washing-house; dressing-house
Laveton, *s.m.* flock, short wool
Lavette, *s.f.* dish-cloth, dish-clout; (*pop.*) tongue
Laveu-r, se, *s.m.f.* washer; washerwoman; scourer; scullion. — *de cendres*, metal-refiner. — *de vaisselle*, scullion
†**Lavignon,** *s.m.* (*shell-fish*) gaping-cockle
Lavique, *adj.* lavatic, lavic
Lavis, *s.m.* (*draw.*) wash, tinting; (*engr.*) aquatint
Lavoir, *s.m.* wash-house; washing-room; washing-place; laundry; lavatory; scullery; washer; rubbing-board; (*metal.*) jigging-sieve, sleeping-table, buddle; (*pop.*) confessional; ramrod and rag
Lavure, *s.f.* dish-water, scourings, swill, swillings, hog-wash; washing; (*of gold and silver*) refining; sweepings

Lawsonie, *s.f.* (*bot.*) lawsonia
Laxati-f, ve, *adj.*, **Laxatif,** *s.m.* laxative
Laxiflore, *adj.* (*bot.*) laxiflorous
Laxifolié, e, *adj.* (*bot.*) laxifoliate
Laxité, *s.f.* laxity
Laye, *s.f.* (*obsolete*) *V.* **Laie**
Layer, *v.a.* to open a pass in (*a forest*); to hew (*stones*)
Layetier, *s.m.* box-maker, case-maker, packing-case maker
Layette, *s.f.* baby-linen; (*obsolete*) box; drawer; (*mus.*) drone-peg (*of a bagpipe*)
Layetterie, *s.f.* box *or* case-making *or* trade; boxes, cases
Layeur, *s.m.* forest-surveyor
Layon, *s.m.* tail-board (*of a van*, &c.); (*hunt.*) straight path
†**Lazagne,** *s.f. V.* **Lasagne**
Lazaret, Lazareth, *s.m.* lazaret, lazaretto, lazar-house, pest-house
Lazariste, Lazarite, *s.m.* Lazarist, Lazarite
Lazarone, *s.m. V.* **Lazzarone**
Lazuli, *s.m.* (*min.*) lazuli, lapis lazuli
Lazulite, *s.f.* (*min.*) lazulite
Lazzarone (*pl.* **Lazzaroni**), *s.m.* (*in Naples*) lazzarone, beggar, loafer, cadger
Lazzi, *s.m.* pantomime; trick; buffoonery; jest, joke, pun, epigram
Le, L', *art.m.* the; a, an; per; at; on the; in the, during the; what a; — *pron.m.* him; it; so; one; the matter
Lé, *s.m.* breadth; (*navig.*) tow-path
Léans, *adv.* (*old*) within, in there, there, in that house; that *or* the house, that *or* the place
Léard, *s.m.* black poplar
Lécanore, *s.f.* (*bot.*) lecanora
Lécanorine, *s.f.* (*chem.*) lecanorine
Lécanorique, *adj.* (*chem.*) lecanoric
Lèche, *s.f.* slice, thin slice; — *s.m.f.* (*in compounds*) one who licks, licker. — **-cul,** *s.m.* (*pop.*) lick-spittle, toad-eater, toady. — **-doigts (A),** *adv.* enough to lick o.'s chops *or* smack o.'s lips; just enough to taste, just a taste, sparingly, very little
Lèchefrite, *s.f.* dripping-pan
Lèchement, *s.m.* licking
Lèchepatte, *s.m.* (*zool.*) sloth
Lécher, *v.a.* to lick; to lick up; to smack (*o.'s lips*) *or* lick (*o.'s chops*); (*fig.*) to polish, to finish off, to labour, to elaborate
Lécheu-r, se, *s.m.f.* licker; gormandizer; sponger; kisser
Lécithine, *s.f.* (*chem.*) lecithine
Leçon, *s.f.* lesson; teaching; lecture; advice; reading; version. *Faire la* — *à*, to give (*one*) his cue; to coach up; to lecture
Lécrelet, *s.m.* (*Swiss*) gingerbread
Lec-teur, trice, *s.m.f.* reader; (*old*) lecturer, professor; (*anc.*) lector
Lectionnaire, *s.m.* (*lit.*) lectionary
Lecture, *s.f.* reading; perusal; lecture. *En* —, engaged, in hand; out. *Avoir beaucoup de* —, to be well read. *Donner* — *de, faire la* —, to read
Lécythis, *s.m.* (*bot.*) lecythis, monkey-pot tree
Léda, *s.f.* (*myth., astr.*) Leda
Ledit, *adj.m.* the said; the same, ditto
Lédon, *s.m.* (*bot.*) ledum
Lée, *s.f.* tow-path
Légal, e, *adj.* legal; lawful; (*med.*) forensic
Légalement, *adv.* legally; lawfully
Légalisable, *adj.* legalizable
Légalisation, *s.f.* legalization; authentication
Légaliser, *v.a.* to legalize; to authenticate
Légalité, *s.f.* legality, lawfulness
Légat, *s.m.* legate
Légataire, *s.m.f.* legatee; devisee. — *universel*, sole (*or* universal) legatee; sole devisee; residuary legatee and devisee. — *à titre universel*, residuary legatee or devisee
Léga-teur, trice, *s.m.f.* legator, legatrix, bequeather, devisor
Légation, *s.f.* legateship; legation
Legato, *adj.* (*mus.*) legato
Légatoire, *adj.* legatory
Lége, *adj.* (*nav.*) light
Légendaire, *adj.m.f., s.m.* legendary
Légende, *s.f.* legend; inscription; motto; story; explanatory introduction; (*of medals*) legend

Lég-er, ère, *adj.* light; nimble; swift; fleet; fast; slender; slim; slight; thin; weak; feeble; faint; trifling; frivolous; flimsy; flippant; airy; buoyant; volatile; fickle; thoughtless, inconsiderate; giddy; light-headed. — *à la course,* swift, fleet, nimble-footed. *A la légère,* thoughtlessly, inconsiderately; slightly; lightly; carelessly; light. *De* —, (*old*) *V.* **Légèrement.** — **de main,** *s.m.* (*obsolete*) legerdemain, sleight of hand
Légèrement, *adv.* lightly; nimbly; swiftly; slightly; feebly; faintly; triflingly; frivolously; buoyantly; thoughtlessly, inconsiderately; giddily; carelessly; delicately
Légèreté, *s.f.* lightness; nimbleness; swiftness; fleetness; slenderness; slimness; slightness; thinness; weakness; feebleness; faintness; frivolity; airiness; buoyancy; fickleness; levity; thoughtlessness, inconsiderateness; giddiness; act of levity, giddy act, light fault, trick
Légiférer, *v.n.* to legislate
Légion, *s.f.* legion. — *d'honneur,* Legion of Honour (*a French order of knighthood, military and civil*)
Légionnaire, *adj. s.m.* legionary; knight of the Legion of Honour
Légis, *s.f.* legis (*Persian silk*)
Législa-teur, trice, *s.m.f.* legislator, legislatress, law-maker, law-giver; — *adj.* legislating, law-making, law-giving
Législati-f, ve, *adj.* legislative
Législation, *s.f.* legislation
Législativement, *adv.* legislatively
Législature, *s.f.* legislature; duration of a legislative assembly *or* of a parliament, parliament, legislature
Légiste, *s.m.* legist, lawyer; civilian
Légitimaire, *adj.* (*law*) legitimate
Légitimation, *s.f.* legitimation; recognition
Légitime, *adj.* legitimate; lawful; legal; rightful; just; justifiable; regular; — *s.f.* (*old law*) lawful portion (of a son or daughter), portion secured by law, (*in Scotch law*) legitim, bairn's part; (*fam.*) lawful *or* wedded wife
Légitimement, *adv.* legitimately; lawfully; legally; rightfully; justly; justifiably; regularly
Légitimer, *v.a.* to legitimate, to legitimize; to recognize; to justify
Se —, *v.r.* to be legitimated *or* &c.
Légitim-isme, -iste. *V.* page 3, § 1
Légitimité, *s.f.* legitimacy; lawfulness; legality
Legs, *s.m.* legacy, bequest, devise. — *universel,* legacy and devise of the whole of the estate; residuary legacy and devise. — *à titre universel,* residuary legacy or devise
Léguer, *v.a.* to leave, to bequeath, to devise
Se —, *v.r.* to be bequeathed *or* &c.
Légumage, *s.m.* vegetables, legumes, pulse
Légume, *s.m.* vegetable, kitchen-vegetable, pot-herb, legume, legumen, pulse
Légumi-er, ère, *adj.* of vegetables, vegetable; leguminous; — *s.m.* vegetable-dish; vegetable-garden, kitchen-garden, market-garden
Léguminaire, *adj.* leguminar
Légumine, *s.f.* (*chem.*) legumine
Légumineu-x, se, *adj.* leguminous; — *s.m.* vegetable; — *s.f.* leguminous plant
Léguminivore, *adj.* leguminivorous
Légumiste, *s.m.f.* market-gardener; vegetarian
Leibnitzianisme, *s.m.* Leibnitzianism
Leibnitzien, ne, *adj. s.* Leibnitzian
Leiche, *s.m.* (*zool.*) Greenland shark; (*bad spelling of* "laiche") *V.* **Laiche**
Léiocomme, *s.m.* leiocome, British gum, dextrine
Leipoa, *s.m.* leipoa, Australian pheasant
Léma, *s.m. V.* **Criocère**
Lémanique, *adj.* Lemanic
Lémanite, *s.f.* (*min.*) lemanite
Lemmatique, *adj.* (*geom.*) lemmatic
Lemme, *s.m.* (*geom.*) lemma
Lemming, *s.m.* (*zool.*) lemming
Lemne, *s.f.* (*bot.*) lemna, duckweed
Lemnien, ne, *adj. s.* Lemnian
Lemniscate, *s.f.* (*geom.*) lemniscata, lemniscate
Lemnisque, *s.m.* (*anc.*) lemniscus; (*of diplomas,* &c.) seal-band
Lémur, *s.m.* (*zool.*) lemur, maki
Lémures, *s.m.pl.* (*Rom. ant.*) lemures
Lémuriens, *s.m.pl.* (*zool.*) lemuridæ
Lémuries, *s.f.pl.* (*Rom. ant.*) lemuria
Lencornet, *s.m.* (*bad spelling*) *V.* **Encornet**
Lendemain, *s.m.* following day, next day, day after, morrow. *Le — de ...,* the day after ... *Le — matin,* the next morning. *Le — matin de ...,* the morning after ...
Lendore, *s.m.f.* humdrum
Lénifier, *v.a.* to lenify, to assuage, to soften
Léniti-f, ve, *adj.*, **Lénitif,** *s.m.* lenitive
Lent, e, *adj.* slow; tardy; sluggish; remiss; slack; dull
Lente, *s.f.* nit
Lentement, *adv.* slowly; tardily; sluggishly; remissly
Lenteur, *s.f.* slowness; tardiness; sluggishness; delay, procrastination; indecision; remissness; slackness; dulness; dull part
Lenticelle, *s.f.* (*bot.*) lenticel
Lenticellé, e, *adj.* (*bot.*) lenticellated
Lenticulaire, *adj.* lenticular
Lenticule, *s.f.* (*bot.*) duckweed
Lenticulé, e, *adj.* lenticular
Lentiforme, *adj.* lentiform
Lentigineu-x, se, *adj.* (*med.*) lentiginous, freckly
Lentigo, *s.m.* (*med.*) lentigo
†**Lentillat,** *s.m.* spotted shark
†**Lentille,** *s.f.* lentil; freckle, lenticula; lens; (*horol.*) ball, bob. — *d'eau,* duckweed. *Plat de* —*s,* dish of lentils; (*of Esau's swap*) mess of pottage, pottage of lentils
†**Lentilleu-x, se,** *adj.* freckled, freckly
Lentisque, *s.m.* (*bot.*) lentisk *or* mastic-tree
Lento, *adv.* (*mus.*) lento
Lenzinite, *s.f.* (*min.*) lenzinite
Léonin, e, *adj.* leonine
Léontiasis, *s.m.* (*med.*) leontiasis
Léontodon, *s.m.* (*bot.*) leontodon, lion's-tooth
Léonure, *s.m.* (*bot.*) motherwort
Léopard, *s.m.* leopard
Léopardé, *adj.m.* (*her.*) passant
Léoville, *s.m.* leoville (*claret wine*)
Lépas, *s.m.* (*shell*) limpet
Lépidier, *s.m.* (*bot.*) lepidium
Lépidine, *s.f.* (*chem.*) lepidine
Lépidolithe, *s.m.* (*min.*) lepidolite, lithia-mica
Lépidoptère, *s.m.* (*zool.*) lepidopteran, lepidopter; — *adj.* lepidopteral, lepidopterous
Lépisme, *s.m.* lepisma, book-worm
Lépisostée, *s.m.* (*fish*) lepidosteus, bony pike
Lépontiennes, *adj.f.pl.* (*geogr.*) Lepontian *or* Lepontine (*Alps*)
Léporides, *s.m.pl.* (*zool.*) leporidæ; (*hybrids*) leporides
Lèpre, *s.f.* leprosy; lepra; (*hort.*) canker
Lépreu-x, se, *adj. s.* leprous; leper
Léproserie, *s.f.* leper-hospital, leper-house, leper-asylum
Lepte, *s.m.* (*zool.*) leptus, tick. — *automnal,* harvest-bug
Lequel, *pron.m.* who, which, whom, that
Lernée, *s.f.* (*zool.*) lernæa, lernean
Lernéen, ne, *adj.* Lernean
Lérot, *s.m.* garden-dormouse
Les, *art.m.f.pl.* the; what; — *pron.m.f.pl.* them; so; they [*Sont-ce là vos gants? Oui, ce — sont,* Are those your gloves? Yes, they are ("it is they")]
Lesbiaque, *adj.*, **Lesbien, ne,** *adj. s.* Lesbian
Lesdites, *adj.f.pl.*, **Lesdits,** *adj.m.pl.* the said; the same, ditto
Lèse-..., (*in compounds*) high treason against ... — **-humanité,** *s.f.* high treason against humanity. — **-majesté,** *s.f.* high treason. — **-nation,** *s.f.* high treason against the nation; &c.
Léser, *v.a.* to injure; to wrong; to hurt; to aggrieve; to offend
Lésine, *s.f.* stinginess, niggardliness, meanness
Lésiner, *v.n.* to be stingy *or* mean; to higgle, to haggle, to chaffer
Lésinerie, *s.f.* stinginess, niggardliness, meanness; mean action *or* act

Lésineu-r,se, Lésineu-x, se, *adj. s.* stingy, niggardly, mean; ditto fellow *or* person
Lésion, *s.f.* lesion, injury, hurt, wrong
Lesquelles, *pl. of* **Laquelle**
Lesquels, *pl.* of **Lequel**
Lesse, *s.f. V.* **Laisse**
Lessivage, *s.m.* wash, washing; heavy loss
Lessive, *s.f.* lye; washing, bucking; wash; linen washed; (*chem.*) lixivium; (*fam.*) (heavy) loss; bad spec; sale at a loss; thorough purgation. *Faire la —*, to wash; to sell at a loss
Lessiver, *v.a.* to wash; (*chem.*) to lixiviate; (*fig., fam.*) to whitewash; to sell at a great loss. *Se faire —*, to get *or* be beaten (*at play*), to lose
Lessiveu-r, se, *s.m.f.* lye-washer; — *s.f.* lye-washing machine, lye-washer [woman, laundress
Lessivi-er, ère, *s.m.f.* (*local*) washer, washer-
Lest, *s.m.* (*nav., and of balloons*) ballast
Lestage, *s.m.* (*nav.*) ballasting
Leste, *adj.* nimble, brisk; smart; quick; light; easy; clever; indecorous, improper, free
Lesté, e, *part. adj.* ballasted. *Bien —*, (*fig.*) with a full stomach
Lestement, *adv.* nimbly, briskly; smartly; quickly; lightly; easily; cleverly, neatly; [improperly; freely
Lester, *v.a.* (*nav.*) to ballast
Se —, *v.r.* (*nav.*) to take in ballast; (*fig.*) to take in provisions, to eat and drink, to line o.'s stomach, to take a full meal, to fill o.'s bread-basket; to become steady
Lesteur, *s.m.* (*adj., Bateau —*) ballast-lighter, ballast-boat; (*pers.*) ballast-heaver
Léthalité, *s.f.* deadliness
Létharg-ie, -ique. *V.* page 3, § 1
Léthé, *s.m.* (*myth.*) Lethe
Léthifère, *adj.* lethiferous, deadly
Létitia, *s.f.* (*astr.*) Letitia [verse
†Létrille, *s.f.* (*Spanish*) compliment *or* letter in
Lette, *s.f.* (*local*) pool, puddle
Lettre, *s.f.* letter; note; bill; type; **—s,** *pl.* letters, &c.; patent; literature; learning; (*in university degrees*) arts. — *chargée* or *recommandée*, (*post.*) registered letter. — *close*, sealed letter; close letter; secret. — *moulée*, moulded letter; printed letter, type, print; (*slang*) newspaper. — *refusée* or *tombée en rebut*, (*post.*) dead letter. — *de cachet*, — *de crédit*, &c., *V.* **Cachet, Crédit,** &c. — *de change*, bill of exchange, bill. —*s de mer*, (*nav.*) pass. — *de voiture*, booking-office ticket. *Belles- —s*, polite literature, polite learning, literature, belles-lettres. *Saintes —s*, (*old*) Holy Writ. *A la —*, *au pied de la —*, literally, in a literal sense, to the letter; verbatim. *En toutes —s*, at full length, in full. *Aider* or *ajouter à la —*, *V.* **Aider**
Lettré, e, *adj.* lettered, literate, literary, learned; — *s.m.* learned man, literate, scholar; (*in China*) literate (*pl.* literati), mandarin
†Lettrille, *s.f. V.* **Létrille**
Lettrine, *s.f.* (*print.*) reference; heading, head-lettering; initial heading
Leucadendron, Leucodendron, *s.m.* (*bot.*) leucadendron, leucodendron
Leucine, *s.f.* (*chem.*) leucine
Leucite, *s.f.* (*min.*) leucite
Leucocythémie, *s.f.* (*med.*) leucocythemia
Leucographie, *s.f.* leucography
Leucographite, *s.m.* white-stone
Leucoline, *s.f.* (*chem.*) leucoline
Leucoma, Leucome, *s.m.* (*med.*) leucoma
Leucopathie, *s.f.* leucopathy
Leucophlegmasie, *s.f.* (*med.*) leucophlegmacy
Leucophlegmasique, *adj.* (*med.*) leucophlegmatic [albus, whites
Leucorrhée, *s.f.* (*med.*) leucorrhœa, fluor
Leucorrhéique, Leucorrhoïque, *adj.m.f.*, *s.f.* (*med.*) leucorrhoic
Leucose, *s.f.* (*med.*) leucosis [tion, thane
Leude, *s.m.* (*feud.*) great vassal, leud, antrus-
Leur, *pron.pers.m.f.pl.* to *or* at them; for *or* with *or* in *or* from *or* by *or* on *or* against them; them; — *adj.* (*See top of next column*)

Leur, *adj.poss.m.f.* (*pl.* **Leurs**) their, their own. *Le —, la —, les —s*, theirs, their own; their relations *or* family; their friends; their men; their servants; their people; their subjects; their tricks *or* pranks; &c. *Être des —s*, to be one of them, to belong to their body *or* &c., to join them *or* their party, &c.
Leurre, *s.m.* lure, allurement, enticement, bait, decoy; snare, trap; (*fish.*) artificial bait [decoy
Leurrer, *v.a.* to lure, to allure, to entice, to
Se —, *v.r.* to lure *or* &c. each other; to [delude oneself
Leutrite, *s.f.* leutrite
Levage, *s.m.* raising, lifting; (*pop.*) swindling
Levain, *s.m.* leaven; yeast; ferment; remains; germ. *Sans —*, unleavened [(*nav.*) east wind
Levant, *adj.m.* rising; — *s.m.* East; Levant;
Levantin, e, *adj. s.m.f.* Levantine; — *s.f.* levantine (*silk stuff*)
Levé, e, *part. adj.* raised, lifted up, &c. (*V.* **Lever**); erect; risen, up; rising; leavened (*bread*); at an end, over; (*mus.*) of the rise (*of the hand or foot*); — *s.m.* drawing, taking, plan, survey; (*obsolete*) levee; (*hunt.*) preserve; (*mus.*) rise (*of the hand or foot*), arsis. *V.* **Assis.** — *des plans*, *V.* **Lever,** *s.m.*
Levée, *s.f.* raising; removal; gathering; crop; rising; breaking up; levy; levying; bank, embankment; (*of a boat*) stanch-sheets; (*at cards*) trick; odd trick; (*of stuffs*) cutting off; (*of letters*) collection; (*of letter-boxes*) clearing; (*of the sea*) swell, heaving; (*obsolete form of* "lever") drawing, &c., *V.* **Lever,** *s.m.*
Lève-gazon, *s.m.* turfing-iron
Lève-nez, *s.m.* (*fam.*) inattentive fellow
Lever, *v.a.* to raise; to raise up; to lift; to lift up; to heave; to take up; to pull *or* draw up; to set up; to shrug; to prick up (*o.'s ears*); to hold up; to help up; to get up; to dress; to remove, to take away *or* off; to throw off; to cut off *or* out; to revoke; to break up (*an assembly, a camp*, &c.); to close, to end (*a sitting*); to gather, to get in; to levy; to collect (*letters*); to clear (*letter-boxes*); to draw, to take (*a plan*); to survey, to plot; to embank; to take a copy of; to relieve (*the guard, the sentry*); to weigh (*the anchor*); to unship (*the oars*); (*hunt.*) to start; (*pop.*) to inveigle, to cheat, to swindle; — *v.n.* to come up; to grow; to rise; to spring up. *Faire —*, to call up; to force up; to leaven; to raise; to flush; (*hunt.*) to start
Se —, *v.r.* to rise; to get up; to arise; to stand up; to start up; to break up; to be raised *or* &c.; to be gathered *or* levied *or* collected *or* &c.
Lever, *s.m.* getting up; rising; rise; dawn; levee; drawing, taking, plan, survey. — *des plans*, surveying, survey; (*in land-surveying*) plotting. — *du rideau* or *de la toile*, (*theat.*) rise of the curtain. — *de rideau*, (*theat.*) short play acted first. — **-Dieu,** *s.m.* (*Cath. rel.*) raising of the host [swindler, pickpocket
Leveu-r, se, *s.m.f.* raiser, lifter; (*pop.*) cheat,
Léviathan, *s.m.* leviathan [beam
Levier, *s.m.* lever; handspike; crowbar; prise;
Lévier, *s.m. pop. for* **Évier**
Levière, *s.f.* (*fish.*) thick rope to raise nets
Lévigation, *s.f.* levigation
Léviger, *v.a.* to levigate
Lévirat, *s.m.* leviration
Levis (Pont), *s.m.* drawbridge
Lévite, *s.m.* Levite; priest; — *s.f.* (*obsolete*) long frock-coat; straight dress *or* frock
Lévitique, *adj.* Levitical; — *s.m.* Leviticus
Levrauder, *v.a.* to harry, to worry, to hare, to [badger
Levraut, *s.m.* leveret
Lèvre, *s.f.* lip; labium (*pl.* labia). *Manger, rire du bout des —s*, *V.* **Manger** *and* **Rire**
Lèvreteau, *s.m.* little leveret
Levrette, *s.f.* female greyhound; little *or* small greyhound, lapdog
Levretté, e, *adj.* shaped like a greyhound

Levretter, *v.a.* to hunt with greyhounds; — *v.n.* (*of hares*) to bring forth young, to leveret
Levretteur, *s.m.* greyhound-breeder
Levriche, *s.f.* young female greyhound
Lévrier, *s.m.* greyhound
Levron, ne, *s.m.f.* greyhound pup, young greyhound; little *or* small greyhound [(*of bacon*)
Levure, *s.f.* yeast, barm; leaven; rind *or* sward
Lexicographe, *s.m.* lexicographer [page 3, § 1
Lexicograph-ie, -ique, -iquement. *V.*
Lexicolog-ie, -ique, &c. *V.* page 3, § 1
Lexicologue, *s.m.* lexicologist
Lexique, *s.m.* lexicon, dictionary
Lexovien, ne, *adj. s.* of Lisieux, Lexovian,
Lez, *prep.* (*obsolete*) near, by [native of Lisieux
Lézard, *s.m.* lizard [chink; gimp
Lézarde, *s.f.* female lizard; crevice, crack,
Lézardelle, *s.f.* (*bot.*) lizard-tail [to split
Lézarder, *v.a.* to crevice, to crack, to chink,
Se —, *v.r.* to become creviced *or* cracked, to crack, to split
Li, *s.m.* (*Chinese meas.*) li (*about* 500 *yards*)
Liage, *s.m.* binding; tying; mixing, mixture
Liais, *s.m.* lias, Portland stone
Liaison, *s.f.* junction, joining, joint; binding; union; connection; tie; acquaintance; acquaintanceship; intimacy; correspondence; intercourse; (*cook.*) thickening; (*mus.*) tied note, ligature, slur; (*writ.*) thin *or* fine stroke, up stroke; (*gram.*) connective; (*falc.*) pouncing; pounce
Liaisonner, *v.a.* to join, to bind; to cement
Liane, *s.f.* (*bot.*) liana, tropical climber *or* creeper
Liant, e, *adj.* supple, pliant, flexible; easy; affable; gentle; mild; sociable; attractive; — *s.m.* suppleness, pliability, pliancy, flexibility; affability; gentleness; mildness; sociability
Liard, *s.m.* (*obsolete Fr. coin, the fourth part of a* "sou" *or halfpenny*) liard; (*fig.*) farthing, doit, stiver, rap; (*bot.*) *V.* **Léard**
Liarder, *v.n.* to be stingy; to higgle, to haggle, to chaffer; to pay *or* save by farthings; (*old*) to each contribute a trifle, to club together
Liardeu-r, se, *adj.* penny-wise, stingy, miserly; — *s.m.f.* stingy fellow *or* creature, stingy Jack, miser, higgler, haggler, chafferer
Lias, *s.m.* (*geol.*) lias
Liasique, *adj.* (*geol.*) liassic [band, tape, string
Liasse, *s.f.* (*of papers*) bundle, file; (*for ditto*)
Liassique, *adj. V.* **Liasique**
Libage, *s.m. V.* **Moellon**
Libanis, Libanotis, *s.m.* (*plant*) libanotis
Libation, *s.f.* libation, potation
Libelle, *s.m.* libel; lampoon
Libellé, *s.m.* (*law*) context (*of a deed*)
Libeller, *v.a.* (*law*) to draw up; (*fin.*) to specify
Libelliste, *s.m.* libeller, lampooner [the use of
Libellule, *s.f.* dragon-fly
Liber, *s.m.* (*bot.*) liber [*dead*)
Libera, *s.m.* (*Cath. lit.*) libera (*prayer for the*
Libérable, *adj.* dischargeable, releasable; exemptible [liberal
Libéral, e, *adj.* liberal, free, generous; — *s.m.*
Libéralement, *adv.* liberally; freely; largely
Libéraliser, *v.a.* to liberalize, to render liberal
Se —, *v.r.* to be liberalized, to become liberal
Libéralisme, *s.m.* liberalism; liberals
Libéralité, *s.f.* liberality, generosity; gratuity, present, gift
Libéra-teur, trice, *s.m.f.* liberator, deliverer, rescuer; — *adj.* liberating, delivering, rescuing
Libération, *s.f.* liberation, discharge, release; deliverance; exemption
Libéré, e, *part. adj.* (*V.* **Libérer**) liberated, &c. *Forçat* —, released *or* returned convict *or* transport; ticket-of-leave man
Libérer, *v.a.* to liberate, to discharge, to release; to deliver; to exempt, to free; to clear
Se —, *v.r.* to liberate *or* free oneself; to clear oneself; to clear oneself from debt; to be liberated *or* discharged

Liberté, *s.f.* liberty; freedom; facility, ease; permission, leave; leisure; licence. — *d'esprit*, leisure. *En* —, at liberty; free; with liberty; freely. *Mettre en* —, to set at liberty, to set free, to liberate, to release, to discharge, to enlarge [— *adj.* liberticidal
Liberticide, *s.m.* (*act*), *s.m.f.* (*pers.*) liberticide;
Libertin, e, *adj.* libertine, licentious, rakish, wanton, dissolute; riotous; flighty; fickle; (*old*) free-thinking; incredulous; (*of children*) idle; — *s.m.f.* libertine, rake; (*old*) free-thinker; (*of children*) idler
Libertinage, *s.m.* libertinism, debauchery, licentiousness, rakishness, wantonness, dissoluteness; riotousness; flightiness; fickleness; (*old*) free-thinking; (*of children*) idleness
Libertiner, *v.n.* to lead a rakish *or* licentious *or* dissolute *or* disorderly life; (*of children*) to be idle [derly; (*of children*) to become *or* be idle
Se —, *v.r.* to become *or* be rakish *or* disor-
Libidibi, *s.m.* libidibi, dividivi
Libidineu-x, se, *adj.* libidinous
Libidinosité, *s.f.* libidinousness
Libitum (Ad), *See Letter* **A**
Libouret, *s.m.* mackerel-fishing line
Libraire, *s.m.f.* bookseller; publisher. — **-éditeur,** *s.m.* publisher, bookseller and publisher
Librairie, *s.f.* book-trade; bookselling; bookseller's business *or* stock; bookseller's shop, book-shop, book-repository, library; publish-
Libration, *s.f.* libration [ing-warehouse; books
Libre, *adj.* free; independent; at liberty; exempt; bold; broad, licentious; disengaged; unoccupied; unemployed; leisure; easy; calm; loose; clear; open; unattached; out-door; (*of schools*) free, private; (*of teachers*) private; (*of paper*) unstamped; (*mach.*) out of gear; (*vers.*) irregular, doggrel (*verses*). — *à vous*, you are at liberty (to); as you please. — **-échange,** *s.m.* free-trade. — **-échangiste,** *s.m.f.* free-trader; *adj.* free-trading, of free-trade, free-
Librement, *adv.* freely; boldly; easily [trade
Librettiste, *s.m.f.* librettist, opera-writer, writer [libretto
Libretto (*pl.* **Librettos** *or* **Libretti**), *s.m.*
Liburne, Liburnien, ne, *adj. s.* Liburnian
Libyen, ne, *adj. s.* Libyan
Lice, *s.f.* list, lists, field, arena; circus; tilt-yard; barrier, fence; hand-rail, rail; (*of tapestry*) warp; (*hunt.*) female hound
Licence, *s.f.* licence; licentiousness; liberty; (*writ.*) flourish; (*univers.*) licentiate's degree; master's degree [of arts
Licencié, *s.m.* licentiate. — *ès-lettres*, master
Licenciement, *s.m.* disbandment, disbanding, breaking up, dispersion [perse, to send home
Licencier, *v.a.* to disband, to break up, to dis-
Se —, *v.r.* to take too much liberty, to forget
Licencieusement, *adv.* licentiously [oneself
Licencieu-x, se, *adj.* licentious
Licet, *s.m.* leave, permission, permit
Liceuse, *s.f.* warper [Iceland moss
‡**Lichen,** *s.m.* (*bot., med.*) lichen. — *d'Islande*,
‡**Lichéneu-x, se,** *adj.* (*bot.*) lichenous
‡**Lichénine,** *s.f.* (*chem.*) lichenine
‡**Lichénique,** *adj.* (*chem.*) lichenic
‡**Lichénographe,** *s.m.* lichenographer
‡**Lichénograph-ie, -ique,** &c. *V.* page 3, § 1
‡**Lichénoïde,** *adj.* (*bot., med.*) lichenoid
Licher, *v.a.n.* (*pop.*) to swallow, to gobble up, to swill; to guttle, to guzzle [drop, taste
Lichette, *s.f.* (*pop.*) small quantity, little bit,
Licheu-r, se, *s.m.f.* (*pop.*) guttler, guzzler
Licier, *s.m.* warper
Licitation, *s.f.* (*Vente par* —) sale by auction (of an estate held in joint tenancy)
Licitatoire, *adj.* (*law*) relating to "*licitation*"
Licite, *adj.* lawful, legal, allowable
Licitement, *adv.* lawfully [*joint tenancy*)
Liciter, *v.a.* to sell by auction (*an estate held in*
Licol, *s.m.* (*old spelling, poet.*) *V.* **Licou**

Licorne, *s.f.* unicorn
Licou, *s.m.* halter
Licteur, *s.m.* lictor
Lie, *s.f.* lees; dregs; grounds; scum; refuse
Lie, *adj.* (*obsolete*) gay, merry. *Faire chère* —, (*old*) to feed well, to lead a merry life, to feast, to revel in dainties
Lié, e, *part. adj.* bound, tied, &c. (*V.* **Lier**); continuous; coherent; compact; thick; intimate. *Partie —e, V.* **Partie**
Liége, *s.m.* cork; cork-tree. *Bouchon de* —, cork
Liégeois,e, *adj. s.m.f.* of Liege; native of Liege;
Liéger, *v.a.* to cork (*nets*) [— *s.m.* Liege almanach
Liégeu-x, se, *adj.* corky, like cork
Lien, *s.m.* bond; tie; band; strap; cord; string; ligament; ligature; chain; trammel, fetter, shackle; bondage; union; affection
Lienterie, *s.f.* (*med.*) lienteria, lientery
Lientérique, *adj.* (*med.*) lienteric
Lier, *v.a.* to bind; to tie; to tie up; to tie down; to fasten; to join; to unite; to link; to connect; to engage; to mix up, to mix; to form; to establish; to arrange; to enter into, to engage in; to thicken (*a sauce*, &c.); (*mus.*) to slur; (*falc.*) to pounce
Se —, *v.r.* to bind *or* &c. oneself; to bind; to tie; to mix; to blend together; to combine; (*of sauces*, &c.) to thicken; to be bound *or* fastened *or* connected *or* joined *or* &c.; to associate; to league; to form an intimacy; to become intimate [**vigne**
Lierne, *s.f.* (*arch.*) rail; tie; (*bot.*) *V.* **Aube-**
Lierner, *v.a.* to fasten with rails
Lierre, *s.m.* ivy. — *grimpant*, tree-ivy. — *terrestre*, ground-ivy
Liesse, *s.f.* (*old*) mirth, merriment, joy
Lieu, *s.m.* place; spot; ground; room, stead, lieu; turn; occasion, cause; reason; rise; family; extraction; source; authority; house; home; company; (*geom.*) locus; (*astr.*) point; (*fish*) pollack, lythe; —**x**, *pl.* premises; spot, water-closet, privy. — *commun*, common-place; common topic; common-place subject. —*x à l'anglaise*, water-closet. *Au — de*, instead of. *Au — que*, instead of which, whereas. *En dernier* —, in the last place, lastly, last, last of all, ultimately. *En premier* —, in the first place, at first, first, first of all. *En quelque — que*, wherever. *En quelque — que ce soit*, anywhere. *En aucun* —, nowhere. *En son — et place*, (*lawyers' bad French*) in o.'s place. *En tout* —, everywhere. *État de —x*, inventory of fixtures. *Avoir* —, to take place; to have reason *or* occasion. (*Y avoir* —, there to be *or* there be occasion; there to be *or* there be reason; there to be *or* there be necessity, to be necessary.) *Donner — à*, to give rise to; to be the occasion of. *Tenir — de*, to fill the place of, to supply; to stand *or* do instead of; to be equivalent to; to be as much as, to be as *or* like, to be
Lieue, *s.f.* league (*meas. of distance*)
Lieu-r, se, *s.m.f.* sheaf-binder, binder, band-ster, hay-trusser, tier; — *s.f.* leaf-rolling cater- [pillar
Lieutenance, *s.f.* lieutenancy
Lieutenant, *s.m.* lieutenant
Lieutenante, *s.f.* (*obsolete*) lieutenant's wife. — *-colonelle*, (*obsolete*) lieutenant-colonel's company (*second company of a regiment*)
Lièvre, *s.m.* hare. *Gentilhomme à* —, country squire with a small estate. *C'est là que gît le* —, that is the main point, there is the rub. *Il ne faut pas courir deux —s à la fois*, (*Proverb*) one must not have too many irons in the fire
Lièvreteau, *s.m.* (*bad spelling*) *V.* **Lèvreteau**
Liévrite, *s.f.* (*min.*) lievrite
Ligament, *s.m.* ligament
Ligamenteu-x, se, *adj.* ligamentous; stringy
Ligature, *s.f.* ligature
Lige, *adj.* liege
†Lignage, *s.m.* lineage, race; lining, drawing lines; lignage (*rough Orleans wine*)
†Lignager, *s.m.* (*old*) person of the same lineage, kinsman; — *adj.m.* (*old*) *Retrait* —, re-emption
†Ligne, *s.f.* line; range; path; way; rank; feature; fishing-line, line; troops *or* soldiers of the line. — *de charge* or *de flottaison*, (*nav.*) load water-mark, load water-line. *Fausse* —, — *postiche*, (*mus.*) leger-line. *Grande* —, (*rail.*) great railway, trunk line. *Troupes, vaisseau de* —, troops, ship of the line. *A la* —, with *or* by a line; in a new line, a new line, a new paragraph, a break. *En* —, in a line; *int.* (*mil.*) fall in! *En première* —, in the first rank, foremost. *Hors* —, *hors de* —, out of the common, standing out from the rest, extraordinary, beyond comparison; in the margin. *Se mettre en* —, (*mil.*) to draw up. *Passer la* —, to cross the line *or* the equator. *Venir en première* or *&c.* —, to rank first *or* &c.
†Ligné, e, *part. adj.* lined; lineated, lineate
†Lignée, *s.f.* lineage, issue, race, progeny
†Ligner, *v.a.* to line, to mark with lines, to draw lines on; (*nav.*) to lay out by line
†Lignerolle, *s.f.* (*nav.*) twine
†Lignette, *s.f.* net-twine; small line
†Ligneul, *s.m.* shoemaker's thread, wax-end
†Ligneu-x, se, *adj.* ligneous, woody
†Lignification, *s.f.* lignification
†Lignifier, *v.a.*, **Se** —, *v.r.* to lignify
†Ligniforme, *adj.* ligniform
Lignite, *s.m.* (*min.*) lignite [insect
†Lignivore, *adj.* lignivorous; — *s.m.* ditto
†Lignosité, *s.f.* ligneousness
Ligoriste, *s.m.* Liguorian
Ligue, *s.f.* league; confederacy; plot
Liguer, *v.a.*, **Se** —, *v.r.* to league, to unite in a league, to confederate, to combine, to band
Ligueu-r, se, *s.m.f.* leaguer, confederate [bium
Ligule, *s.f.* (*bot.*) ligula, ligule; (*of insects*) la-
Ligulé, e, *adj.* (*bot.*) ligulate, ligulated
Liguoriste, *s.m.* Liguorian
Ligurien, ne, *adj. s.* Ligurian
Ligustrine, *s.f.* (*chem.*) ligustrine
Lilacine, *s.f.* (*chem.*) lilacine
Lilas, *s.m. adj.* lilac
Liliacé, e, *adj.* (*bot.*) liliaceous; —**e,** *s.f.* liliaceous plant; —**es,** *s.f.pl.* liliaceous plants, [liliaceæ
Lilliput, *s.m.* Lilliput
Lilliputien, ne, *adj. s.* Lilliputian
Lillois, e, *adj. s.* of Lille; native of Lille
Limace, *s.f.* slug; Archimedean screw, water-screw. *En* —, *V.* **Limaçon**
Limacien, ne, *adj.* of the snail, snail; snail-like; (*anat.*) cochlear
Limacine, *s.f.* (*chem.*) limacine
Limaçon, *s.m.* snail; helix; Archimedean screw; (*anat.*) cochlea; (*horol.*) snail. *En* — (*adject.*) snail-like, snail-shaped, snail; spiral, winding, corkscrew, cockle. — *de mer*, *V.* **Vignot**
Limaçonnière, *s.f.* *V.* **Escargotière**
Limage, *s.m.* filing, limature
†Limaille, *s.f.* filings, file-dust, limature
†Limailleuse, *adj.f.* *Fonte* —, grey cast iron
Limaire, *s.m.* (*fish*) young tunny
Limande, *s.f.* (*zool.*) dab, salt-water fluke; (*nav.*) rounding, service; (*tech.*) flat piece of wood, slat; flat ruler
Limander, *v.a.* (*nav.*) to surround, to serve
Limas, *s.m.* (*old*) *V.* **Limaçon** *and* **Limace**
Limbe, *s.m.* (*astr.*, *math.*, *bot.*, &c.) limb; halo; —**s,** *pl.* limbs, &c.; (*theol.*) limbo, limbus
Lime, *s.f.* (*tool*) file; (*hunt.*) tusk; (*zool.*) clam; (*bot.*) lime, sweet lemon; (*fish.*) smooth spot. — *sourde*, dead file; (*pop.*) hypocrite, Joseph
Lime-bois, *s.m.* (*insect*) wood-fretter [Surface
Limer, *v.a.* to file; to file off, to polish, to finish off; to fret, to fray; to dry up (*salt-marshes*, &c.); — *v.n.* (*pop.*) to loiter, to linger
Se —, *v.r.* to be filed *or* &c.
Limette, *s.f.* (*bot.*) lime, sweet lemon [tree)
Limettier, *s.m.* (*bot.*) lime-tree (*kind of lemon-*

Limeu-r, se, *s.m.f.* filer ; — *s.f.* filing-machine, [filer
Limicule, *s.f.* (*bird*) bar-tailed godwit
Limier, *s.m.* stag-hound, buck-hound, blood-hound, hound ; police-officer, detective ; spy
Liminaire, *adj.* (*old*) preliminary, dedicatory
Limitati-f, ve, *adj.* limitative, limiting, re- [strictive ; specific
Limitation, *s.f.* limitation
Limitativement, *adv.* limitatively
Limite, *s.f.* limit ; bound ; boundary ; land-mark ; extremity ; confine ; border ; verge
Limiter, *v.a.* to limit ; to bound ; to confine ; to stint [oneself
Se —, *v.r.* to be limited, &c. ; to confine *or* &c.
Limitrophe, *adj.* bordering ; neighbouring ; frontier [limpet
Limnée, *s.f.* (*zool.*) limnæa, pond-snail, river-
Limnorie, *s.f.* (*zool.*) limnoria
Limon, *s.m.* slime ; ooze ; silt ; mud ; clay, earth ; (*of carts*) shaft, thill ; (*of a staircase*) string-board, notch-board ; (*bot.*) lemon
Limonade, *s.f.* lemonade
Limonadi-er, ère, *s.m.f.* dealer in lemonade, &c., refreshment-room keeper, coffee-house keeper. *Garçon —*, coffee-house waiter
Limone, *s.f.* *V.* **Limonine**
Limonellier, *s.m.* (*bot.*) limonia
Limoner, *v.a.* to cleanse (*fish*)
Limoneu-x, se, *adj.* slimy, oozy, silty, muddy ; — *s.m.* (*fish*) loach. *Plante —se*, ooze-weed
Limoniade, *s.f.* (*myth.*) limoniad, limniad, [nymph of the pools
Limonie, *s.f.* (*bot.*) limonia
Limonier, *s.m.* shaft-horse, thill-horse, thiller, wheel-horse, wheeler ; (*bot.*) lemon-tree
Limonière, *s.f.* shafts ; waggon with shafts ; [shaft-mare
Limonine, *s.f.* (*chem.*) limonine
Limonite, *s.f.* (*min.*) limonite ; (*geol.*) layer of [slime
Limonnier, *s.m.* (*bot.*) lemon-tree
Limoselle, *s.f.* (*bot.*) mudwort
Limosinage, *s.m.* *V.* **Limousinage**
Limousin, e *adj. s.m.f.* of Limousin (*formerly a province of France*) *or* of Limoges (*its capital*) ; native of Limousin *or* of Limoges, Limousin ; Limousin horse *or* mare ; — *s.m.* rough-waller ; (*pop.*) bricklayer, mason ; — *s.f.* (*of waggoners*, &c.) coarse woollen cloak, cloak. *Têtu de —*, strongheaded *or* stubborn Limousin
Limousinage, *s.m.* ashlar-work ; rough-walling
Limousiner, *v.a.n.* to rough-wall [waller
Limousineur, Limousinier, *s.m.* rough-
Limpide, *adj.* limpid, clear
Limpidité, *s.f.* limpidity, clearness
Limule, *s.m.* (*zool.*) limulus, limule, king-crab
Limure, *s.f.* filing, limature, filings
Lin, *s.m.* flax ; linseed ; linen. — *des marais* or *des prés*, cotton-grass. *Graine de —*, linseed
Linacées, *s.f.pl.* (*bot.*) linaceæ, flax-tribe
Linaigrette, *s.f.* (*bot.*) cotton-grass
Linaire, *s.f.* (*bot.*) toadflax
Linceul, *s.m.* shroud, winding-sheet, sheet
Linçoir, *s.m.* (*build.*) ceiling-joist
Lindor, *s.m.* (*game at cards*) Pope Joan
Linéaire, *adj.* linear ; lineal. *Dessin —*, linear drawing ; geometrical drawing
Linéal, e, *adj.* lineal
Linéalement, *adv.* lineally [line ; trace
Linéament, *s.m.* lineament, feature, outline ;
Linées, *s.f.pl.* *V.* **Linacées**
Linette, *s.f.* linseed, flax-seed
Lingard, *s.m.* American salt-cod
Linge, *s.m.* linen ; cloth ; sheet ; rag. — *à barbe*, shaving-cloth
Ling-er, ère, *s.m.f.* ready-made linen dealer ; needlewoman, sempstress, seamstress ; ward-robe-keeper
Lingerie, *s.f.* ready-made linen warehouse ; linen goods ; linen trade ; linen room [slug
Lingot, *s.m.* ingot ; block ; bullion ; (*for guns*)
Lingotière, *s.f.* ingot-mould
Lingre, *s.m.* (*slang*) knife [stab
Lingrer, *v.a.* (*slang*) to stick a knife into, to
Lingrerie, *s.f.* (*slang*) cutlery, knives
Lingual, e, *adj.*, **Linguale,** *s.f.* lingual
Linguard, Lingouard, *s.m.* *V.* **Lingue**
Linguatule, *s.f.* linguatula (*intestinal worm*)
Lingue, *s.f.* (*fish*) ling
Linguet, *s.m.* (*nav.*) pawl
Lingueter, *v.a.* (*carp.*) to rabbet
Linguiforme, *adj.* linguiform, tongue-shaped
Linguiste, *s.m.f.* linguist [tic
Linguistique, *s.f.* linguistics ; — *adj.* linguis-
Lingule, *s.f.* (*mollusc*) lingula
Lini-er, ère, *adj.* of flax, flax ; — *s.f.* flax-field
Liniment, *s.m.* liniment
Linine, *s.f.* (*chem.*) linine
Linnée, *s.f.* (*plant*) linnæa
Linnéen, ne, *adj.* Linnean, Linnæan
Linoléum, *s.m.* linoleum
Linon, *s.m.* lawn (*fine linen*)
Linot, te, *s.m.f.* linnet ; giddy-head. *Tête de —*, giddy-head, harebrained fellow *or* creature. *Siffler la —te*, to tipple ; to be in quod ; to give [(*one*) his cue
Linteau, *s.m.* (*arch.*) lintel
Lion, *s.m.* lion ; man of fashion, swell, dandy, fast man, man about town [little dandy
Lionceau, *s.m.* lion's cub, young lion, lionet ;
Liondent, *s.m.* *V.* **Léontodon**
Lionne, *s.f.* lioness ; gay woman ; (*obsolete*) woman of fashion
Lionné, *adj.m.* (*her.*) rampant
Lionnerie, *s.f.* fashionable *or* gay world
Liparocèle, *s.f.* (*med.*) liparocele
Liparolé, *s.m.* (*pharm.*) pomade
Lipogrammat-ique, -iste. *V.* page 3, § 1
Lipogramme, *s.m.* lipogram
Lipomateu-x, se, *adj.* (*med.*) lipomatous
Lipome, *s.m.* (*med.*) lipoma
Lipothymie, *s.f.* (*med.*) lipothymia, lipothymy
Lippe, *s.f.* pouting under-lip, thick lip ; pouting
Lippée, *s.f.* (*old*) mouthful ; meal, repast, feast. *Franche —*, repast *or* feast free of cost ; hearty meal. *Chercheur de franches —s*, sponger, para- [site
Lipper, *v.n.* to guttle, to guzzle
Lippitude, *s.f.* (*med.*) lippitude, bleared eyes, blear-eye, blear-eyedness, bleeredness
Lippu, e, *adj.* thick-lipped ; thick
***Liquater,** *v.a.* to liquate, to eliquate
***Liquation,** *s.f.* liquation, eliquation
Liquéfaction, *s.f.* liquefaction
Liquéfiable, *adj.* liquefiable
Liquéfier, *v.a.*, **Se —,** *v.r.* to liquefy
Liquet, *s.m.* (kind of small baking pear)
Liqueur, *s.f.* liquor ; liquid ; spirit ; cordial, liqueur ; syrup ; juice ; drink ; dram ; lusciousness, sweetness
Liquidambar, *s.m.* (*bot.*) liquidambar [dating
Liquidateur, *s.m.* liquidator ; — *adj.m.* liqui-
Liquidation, *s.f.* liquidation ; settlement, settling ; winding up ; selling off, clearing off *or* out, clearance. *En —*, in liquidation, in course of liquidation ; being settled ; winding up, in chancery ; selling off
Liquide, *adj.* liquid ; flowing ; watery ; soft ; clear ; net ; unencumbered ; sure ; — *s.m.* liquid ; fluid ; liquor, spirit ; — *s.f.* (*gram.*) liquid. *Clair et —*, net, clear, unencumbered, sure
Liquidement, *adv.* liquidly ; clearly ; clear
Liquider, *v.a.* to liquidate ; to discharge ; to pay off ; to settle ; to wind up ; to sell off, to clear off *or* out [settle *or* wind up o.'s affairs
Se —, *v.r.* to liquidate *or* pay o.'s debts ; to
Liquidité, *s.f.* liquidity
Liquoreu-x, se, *adj.* sweet, luscious
Liquoriste, *s.m.f.* dealer in spirits and liqueurs, [spirit-dealer
Lira, *s.f.* lira (*Italian coin*)
Lire, *v.a.n.* to read ; to read of ; to peruse ; to study [be read ; to read
Se —, *v.r.* to read oneself *or* each other ; to
Lire, *s.f.* lira (*Italian coin*)
Liriodendrine, *s.f.* (*chem.*) liriodendrine
Liriodendron, *s.m.* (*bot.*) liriodendron, tulip- [tree
Liron, *s.m.* *V.* **Lérot**
Lis, *s.m.* lily ; (*fig.*) whiteness
Lisage, *s.m.* (*tech.*) reading ; (*of cloth*) stretching

Lise, *s.f.* quicksand

Liser, *v.a.* (*tech.*) to stretch (*cloth*)

Liserage, *s.m.* embroidered border

Liséré, *s.m.* border; edging; piping; strip

Lisérer, *v.a.* to border, to edge

Liseron, *s.m.* (*bot.*) bindweed

Liset, *s.m.* (*bot.*) bindweed; (*zool.*) vine-fretter

Lisette, *s.f.* (*zool.*) vine-fretter; (*local*) whittle

Liseu-r, se, *s.m.f.* reader; — *s.f.* reading-machine, reader; reading-hook [ness

Lisibilité, *s.f.* legibleness, legibility; readable-

Lisible, *adj.* legible; readable

Lisiblement, *adv.* legibly; readably

Lisier, *s.m.* (*agr.*) liquid manure from stalls and stables, farm-yard manure, ahl

Lisière, *s.f.* list; selvage, selvedge; leading-string; binding, edge; border, skirt, verge, extremity [som-bed

Lisoir, *s.m.* (*of a carriage*) axle-tree bed, tran-

Lissage, *s.m.* smoothing; glossing; glazing; (*nav.*) railing; rails

Lisse, *adj.* smooth; sleek; glossy; smooth-bore; — *s.m.* smoothness; sleekness; gloss; polish; — *s.f.* hand-railing, hand-rail, rail; barrier, fence; (*nav.*) rail, line, riband; (*of tapestry*) warp; (*tech.*) pack-thread, string

Lissé, *s.m.* smoothness; smooth surface; (*of boiled sugar*) ropiness

Lisser, *v.a.* to smooth; to sleek; to gloss; to glaze; to polish; (*nav.*) to rail

Lisseu-r, se, *s.m.f.* glazer; polisher

Lissier, *s.m.* warper

Lissoir, *s.m.* polisher (*tool*) [polish, gloss

Lissure, *s.f.* polishing; glazing; smoothness,

Liste, *s.f.* list; roll; rolls; catalogue; schedule; bill; (*of jurors*) panel; (*old*) band, line

Listeau, *s.m.* *V.* **Listel**

Listel (*pl.* **Listeaux**), *s.m.* (*arch.*) listel, fillet,

Liston, *s.m.* (*her.*) scroll [list, annulet

Lit, *s.m.* bed; bedstead; berth; layer, stratum; channel; direction (*of the wind*); stream (*of a current*); (*fig.*) marriage; (*obsolete*) bed-hangings, valance. — *à* or *en armoire*, press-bed. — *de bourre*, flock-bed. — *de camp*, camp-bed, field-bed. — *de douleur*, sick-bed. — *de justice*, seat of justice, judicial seat, bench; (*Fr. hist.*) king's throne in the parliament of Paris; bed of justice (*sitting of the parliament of Paris in the king's presence*). — *de marée*, tide-way. — *de mort*, death-bed. — *de repos*, couch. — *de sangle*, folding-bed (*with sacking bottom*), trussel-bed. — *de veille*, nurse's bed, pallet. *Au* —, in bed; to bed; into bed; on the *or* o.'s bed; *int.* (*hunt.*) tally-ho! *Mourir au* — *d'honneur*, to die in battle. *Comme on fait son* — *on se couche*, (*Proverb*) as you make your bed, so you must lie [—**s,** *pl.* litany

Litanie, *s.f.* endless story, long-winded story;

Litchi, *s.m.* (*bot.*) litchi, lee-chee, longan-tree

Liteau, *s.m.* stripe (*on table-linen*); (*tech.*) bracket, ledge, border; (*hunt., of wolves*) lair. *A —x*, with stripes, striped

Litée, *s.f.* (*hunt.*) lair, haunt

Liter, *v.a.* to place in layers

Literie, *s.f.* bedding, bed-furniture [lithagogue

Lithagogue, *adj.* (*med.*) lithagogic; — *s.m.*

Litharge, *s.f.* (*chem.*) litharge

Lithargé, e, Lithargyré, e, *adj.* adulter-

Lithate, *s.m.* (*chem.*) lithate [ated with litharge

Lithiase, Lithiasie, *s.f.* (*med.*) lithiasis

Lithiate, *s.m.* (*chem.*) lithiate

Lithine, *s.f.* (*chem.*) lithia

Lithique, *adj.* (*chem.*) lithic

Lithium, *s.m.* (*chem.*) lithium

Litho, (*in compounds*) litho...

Lithocarpe, *s.m.* lithocarp

‡Lithochrom-ie, -ique, -iste. *V.* page 3, § 1

Lithoclaste, *s.m.* (*surg. instr.*) lithoclast

Lithoclastie, *s.f.* (*surg.*) lithoclasty

Lithocolle, *s.f.* lithocolla

Lithoglyphe, *s.m.* lithoglypher

Lithoglyphie, *s.f.* lithoglyphy

Lithoglyphique, *adj.* lithoglyphic; — *s.f.* lithoglyphics

Lithographe, *s.m.* lithographer; — *adj.* lithographic [lithographic printing-office

Lithographie, *s.f.* lithography; lithograph;

Lithographier, *v.a.* to lithograph

Lithograph-ique,-iquement. *V.* page 3, § 1

Lithoïde, *adj.* lithoidal [labe

Litholabe, *s.m.* (*surg.*) lithotomy forceps, litho-

Litholog-ie, -ique, &c. *V.* page 3, § 1

Lithologue, *s.m.* lithologist

Lithomarge, *s.f.* (*geol.*) lithomarge

Lithontriptique. *V.* **Lithotriptique**

Lithophage, *adj.* lithophagous; — *s.m.* lithophagist, stone-borer (*insect*)

Lithophanie, *s.f.* lithophane

Lithophotograph-ie, -ique. *V.* page 3, § 1

Lithophyte, *s.m.* (*nat. hist.*) lithophyte

Lithoscope, *s.m.* (*surg.*) lithoscope [tome

Lithotome, *s.m.* (*surg.*) lithotomy knife, litho-

Lithotom-ie, -ique, -iste. *V.* page 3, § 1

Lithotripsie, *s.f.* (*surg.*) lithotripsy

Lithotriptique, *adj.m.f.*, *s.m.* (*med., surg.*) lithotriptic, lithontriptic

Lithotriteur, *s.m.* (*surg. instr.*) lithotrite

Lithotritie, *s.f.* (*surg.*) lithotrity

Lithoxyle, *s.m.* lithoxyle, lithoxylite

Lithuanien, ne, *adj. s.* Lithuanian; Lithuanian fashion

Litière, *s.f.* litter; straw; (*fam.*) bed. *Faire* — *de*, to waste, to squander, to throw away, to

Litigant, e, *adj. s.* (*obsolete*) litigant [sacrifice

Litige, *s.m.* litigation; issue; contest, contest-

Litigieu-x, se, *adj.* litigious [ation, dispute

Litispendance, *s.f.* (*old*) litispendence, pendency of a lawsuit, "pendente lite"

Litorne, *s.f.* (*bird*) fieldfare

Litote, *s.f.* (*rhet.*) litotes

Litre, *s.m.* (*Fr. meas.*) litre (*a little less than an English quart*), quart, pot; — *s.f.* band of black cloth with hatchment. *Demi-* —, pint

Litron, *s.m.* (*old Fr. meas.*) litron (*somewhat above two pints*); (*pop.*) reputed quart

Littéraire, *adj.* literary

Littérairement, *adv.* literarily

Littéral, e, *adj.* literal

Littéralement, *adv.* literally

Littéralisme, *s.m.* literalism

Littéraliste, *s.m.f.* literalist

Littéralité, *s.f.* literality, literalness

Littéra-teur, trice, *s.m.f.* literary man, literary woman; — *adj.* literary, lettered

Littérature, *s.f.* literature, learning; literati

Littératurier, *s.m.* scribbler

Littoral, e, *adj.* littoral, of the coast, coast, shore, sea-coast, sea-shore; — *s.m.* coast, shore, sea-coast, sea-shore, sea-board, coasts

Littorelle, *s.f.* (*bot.*) pond-weed, shore-weed

Littorine, *s.f.* (*zool.*) littorina, periwinkle

Liturg-ie, -ique, -iste. *V.* page 3, § 1

Lituus, *s.m.* (*Rom. antiq.*) lituus

Liure, *s.f.* rope, cart-rope; (*nav.*) gammoning

Livarde, *s.f.* (*nav.*) sprit

Livarder, *v.a.* (*nav.*) to sprit

Livarot, *s.m.* Livarot cheese

Livèche, *s.f.* (*bot.*) lovage

Livide, *adj.* livid, black and blue

Lividité, *s.f.* lividity, lividness

Livonien, ne, *adj. s.* Livonian

Livournais, e, Livournois, e, Livournien, ne, *adj. s.* Leghornese

Livrable, *adj.* (*com.*) deliverable, to be delivered, ready; — *s.m.* articles to be delivered, goods ready for delivery

Livraison, *s.f.* piece; (*of publications*) part, number; (*com.*) delivery

Livrancier, *s.m.* deliverer (*of goods*)

Livre, *s.m.* book; register; volume. —*journal*, (*com.*) day-book. — *de caisse*, cash-book. — *de consignation*, (*police*) charge-sheet. — *de fonds* or *de sortes*, book published by the vendor, book of the vendor's own publication.

— *d'heures*, (*Cath. rel.*) primer. *Grand* —, large book; great book; (*book-keep.*) ledger; (*fin.*) grand-livre, Great Book of the Public Debt, register of the National Debt. *A — ouvert*, at sight

Livre, *s.f.* (*obsolete French weight*) pound, (*still used familiarly to designate the modern official weight* "demi-kilogramme") pound; (*obsolete French coin*) livre (*about* 10*d.*, *superseded by the* "franc," *which is a little more:* 81 "livres" *make* 80 "francs"), (*still used sometimes, especially by old people, for* "franc," *in computations*) franc; as, *Cinq mille —s de rente*, five thousand francs (£200) a year; (*English coin*) pound. — *sterling*, pound sterling, pound, sovereign. — *parisis*, (*suppressed under Louis XIV.*) Paris livre (*about* 1*s.*). — *tournois*, (*superseded in* 1795) Tours livre (*about* 10*d.*). *A la* —, by the pound. *Cinq francs la* —, five francs (four shillings) a pound

Livrée, *s.f.* livery; livery-men, livery-servants; signs, marks; colours; (*hunt.*) coat (*of animals*) of the first year; (*zool.*) striped caterpillar. — *de la noce*, wedding-favours, bride-favours. *Gens de* —, livery-men, livery-servants, footmen, lackeys, flunkeys. *Grande* —, full livery. *Petite* —, undress livery

Livrer, *v.a.* to deliver; to deliver up *or* over; to give up; to give; to surrender; to hand over; to betray; to commit, to consign; to devote; to abandon; to leave; to trust; to expose; to warrant; to wage; to supply; to sell. — *bataille*, — *combat*, to give battle, to engage, to fight, to struggle. — *une bataille*, — *un combat*, to fight a battle

Se —, *v.r.* to deliver *or* give oneself up; to surrender *or* &c. oneself; to apply *or* devote oneself; to indulge (oneself); to abandon oneself; to yield (to), to give way (to); to trust (oneself); to be communicative *or* unreserved; to give each other; to be fought

Livret, *s.m.* book; memorandum-book; register; handbook; guide-book; catalogue; time-book; certificate; (*workman's* or *servant's* or *soldier's*) book *or* register; (*cabman's*) licence; (*savings-bank*) depositor's book; (*foreman's*) check-book; book of the words, words (*of an opera*), opera-book, libretto; book of a *or* the play; (*anat.*) fold, layer; (*obsolete*) multiplication-table

Lixiviation, *s.f.* (*chem.*) lixiviation

Lixiviel, le, *adj.* (*chem.*) lixivial

Lixivium, *s.m.* (*chem.*) lixivium

Lizarine, Lizarique. *V.* **Alizarine,** &c.

Lize, *s.f.* *V.* **Lise**

Lizée, *s.f.*, **Lizier,** *s.m.* *V.* **Lisier**

Llama, *s.m.* *V.* **Lama**

†**Llanéro,** *s.m.* llanero

†**Llano,** *s.m.* llano

Lloyd, *s.m.* Lloyd

Lo, *s.m.* (*Chinese*) gong

Loam, *s.m.* (*agr.*) loam

Loameu-x, se, *adj.* (*agr.*) loamy

Loase, *s.f.* (*bot.*) Chili nettle

Lobaire, *adj.* (*nat. hist.*) lobar

Lobe, *s.m.* lobe

Lobé, e, *adj.* lobed, lobated, lobate

Lobélie, *s.f.* (*bot.*) lobelia; cardinal flower; [Indian tobacco

Lobéline, *s.f.* (*chem.*) lobeline

Lobélique, *adj.* (*chem.*) lobelic

Lobulaire, *adj.* lobular

Lobule, *s.m.* lobule; (*of the ear*) lobulus

Lobulé, e, *adj.* lobulated

Local, e, *adj.* local; — *s.m.* place; premises; situation; room; apartment; house; habitation; quarters

Localement, *adv.* locally

Localisation, *s.f.* localization

Localiser, *v.a.* to localize

Se —, *v.r.* to become localized

Localité, *s.f.* locality, place; local circumstance

Locar, *s.m.* (*adj.*, *Froment* —) (*bot.*) lesser spelt, one-grained wheat

Locataire, *s.m.f.* tenant; renter; lodger; hirer; lessee. *Principal* —, tenant

Loca-teur, trice, *s.m.f.* hirer, letter, lender; lessor

Locati-f, ve, *adj.* tenantable, tenant's (*repairs, risk*, &c.); letting (*value*); (*gram.*) locative

Location, *s.f.* letting, letting out; lending, lending out; hiring, taking; renting; leasing; location; (*theat.*) ditto of boxes; box-office. *Bureau de* —, (*theat.*) box-office. — *de livres*, lending of books; lending-library, subscription library, circulating-library

Locatis, *s.m.* (*fam.*) hack, jade; hackney-coach, common cab, old cab

‡**Loch,** *s.m.* (*nav.*) log. *De* —, (*adject.*) log. *Bateau de* —, log-ship. *Journal* or *table de* —, log-board. *Jeter le* —, to heave the log [slug

Loche, *s.f.* (*fish*) loach, groundling; (*snail*) grey

Locher, *v.n.* to be loose, to shake. *Quelque fer qui loche*, (*fig.*) a screw loose

Lochet, *s.m.* *V.* **Louchet**

Lochial, e, *adj.* (*med.*) lochial

Lochies, *s.f.pl.* (*med.*) lochia

‡**Lochiorrhagie,** *s.f.* (*med.*) lochiorrhage

Lockiste, *s.m.* Lockist

Locman, *s.m.* *V.* **Lamaneur**

Loco, *adv.* (*mus.*) loco [place cited

Loco citato, *adv.* (*Latin*) loco citato, in the

Locomobile, *adj.* portable, traction; — *s.f.* (*machine à vapeur* —) portable steam-engine, traction engine

Locomobilité, *s.f.* portableness [locomotive

Locomo-teur, trice, *adj.* of locomotion,

Locomoti-f, ve, *adj.* locomotive; — *s.f.* locomotive engine, engine, locomotive

Locomotion, *s.f.* locomotion

Locomotivité, *s.f.* locomotivity, locomotiveness

Locrien, ne, *adj.* *s.* Locrian

Loculaire, *adj.* (*bot.*) locular

Locular, *s.m.* *adj.* *V.* **Locar**

Locuste, *s.f.* (*zool.*) locust; (*scientific slang*) shrimp, prawn; (*bot.*) locusta [warbler

Locustelle, *s.f.* (*bird*) locustelle, grasshopper-

Locution, *s.f.* form *or* mode of speech, form, expression, term, phrase

Locutoire, *s.m.* locutory [nut, double cocoa-nut

Lodoïcée, *s.f.* (*bot.*) lodoicea, Seychelles cocoa-

Lods, *s.m.pl.* — *et ventes*, (*old*) lord's due

Loess, *s.m.* (*geol.*) loess

Lof, *s.m.* (*nav.*) luff; weather-side; windward

Lofer, Loffer, *v.n.* (*nav.*) to luff

Logarithme, *s.m.* (*math.*) logarithm

Logarithmique, *adj.* (*math.*) logarithmic; — *s.f.* logarithmic curve

Loge, *s.f.* lodge; cell; hut; cabin; closet; box; (*of actors*) dressing-room, tiring-room, star-room; booth; stand; stall; kennel; den, cage; bellows-chamber; (*bot.*) loculament; (*obsolete*) gallery; (*obsolete*) factory. — *infernale*, swell's stage-box; chair of the first row. — *d'avant-scène*, stage-box. — *de face*, front-box. *Ouvreur* or *ouvreuse de —s*, box-keeper. *Premières —s*, first tier (of boxes)

Logeable, *adj.* habitable, inhabitable, fit to live in, commodious, convenient; tenantable; lodgeable; that can be housed

Logement, *s.m.* lodging; house-room; room; rooms; apartment; house; residence; inn; lodge; place; quartering; quarters; accommodation; lodgment

Loger, *v.a.n.* to lodge; to quarter, to billet; to stable; to take in, to house; to find room for; to accommodate; to harbour; to stay; to put up; to live; to dwell; to reside. *On loge à pied et à cheval*, accommodation for man and horse, entertainment for man and beast. *V.* **Éclairé**

Se —, *v.r.* to take lodgings, to take up o.'s lodging *or* quarters, to put up, to lodge oneself, to lodge; to sleep; to find o.'s own lodging; to make a lodgment; (*of things*) to lodge itself, to lodge, to fix itself [little box

Logette, *s.f.* little lodge, little cell, little cabin,

Logeu-r, se, *s.m.f.* lodging-house keeper. — *en garni*, lodging-house keeper

Logicien, ne, *s.m.f.* logician
Logique, *s.f.* logic; logicalness; — *adj.* logical
Logiquement, *adv.* logically
Logis, *s.m.* dwelling, habitation, residence; lodging; lodging-house; inn; house; home. *Au* —, at home. *Bon — à pied et à cheval*, good accommodation for man and horse. *La folle du* —, imagination, fancy
Logistique, *adj.* logistic; — *s.f.* logistics
Logogramme, *s.m.* logogram
Logographe, *s.m.* (*old*) logographer
Logograph-ie, -ique. *V.* page 3, § 1
Logogriphe, *s.m.* logogriph, riddle, enigma
Logogriphique, *adj.* enigmatic, obscure
Logomach-ie, -ique. *V.* page 3, § 1
Logorrhée, *s.f.* (*jest.*) logorrhœa, flow of useless words
Loi, *s.f.* law; rule; dominion, power, sway, authority; precept; command; obligation; decree; (*coin.*) standard. *Hors la* —, outlawed. *Faire* —, to be law. *Faire la* —, to give the law; to command; to dictate. *Se faire une* —, to make it a point. *Mettre hors la* —, to outlaw
Loin, *adv.* far; afar; far off; far out; far back; at a distance, distant, remote, a great way off, a great way, a great distance, a long way; away; out; long, a long time, a great while. *Au* —, far, afar, far away, far and wide; abroad. *De* —, from afar, from a distance, from a great distance; at a distance, at a great distance, a great way, a long way off; distantly; distant; a long time ago *or* back. *De — en* —, at distant *or* great *or* long intervals; at long distances; wide apart. — *que*, far from. — *de moi la pensée* (*de*), far be it from me (to). — *des yeux — du cœur*, (*Proverb*) out of sight out of mind
Lointain, e, *adj.* remote, far, distant; — *s.m.* distance; background; distant prospect
Lointaineté, *s.f.* (*old*) longinquity, farness, remoteness, distance
Loir, *s.m.* dormouse
Loisible, *adj.* optional, at o.'s option; easy; lawful, allowable, allowed, right
Loisir, *s.m.* leisure; leisure time, leisure hours *or* moments, spare time; time; rest. *A* —, at leisure, leisurely. *De* —, of *or* from leisure; leisure; free
Lok, *s.m.* (*pharm.*) *V.* **Looch;** (*nav.*) *V.* **Loch**
Lollard, *s.m.* (*eccl. hist.*) Lollard
Lolo, *s.m.* (*children's slang*) milk
Lolotte, *s.f.* (*pop.*) gay woman, harlot, mot
Lom, *s.m.* *V.* **Lumme**
Lombago, *s.m.* *V.* **Lumbago**
Lombaire, *adj.* (*anat.*) lumbar
Lombard, e, *adj.* Lombardic, Lombardian; — *s.m.f.* Lombard; — *s.m.* (*fin.*) Lombardian railway share, Lombard; (*obsolete, Belgian French*) lombard, lombard-house, money-lender, pawnbroker, pawn-shop
Lombardique, *adj. s.* Lombardic
Lombard-vénitien, ne, Lombardo-vénitien, ne, *adj.* Lombard-Venetian, Lombardo-Venetian
Lombes, *s.m.pl.* (*anat.*) lumbar region, loins
Lombo, (*in compounds, anat.*) lombo-...
Lombric, *s.m.* lumbric, earth-worm, dew-worm
Lombrical, e, *adj.* (*zool., anat.*) lumbrical
Lomentacé, e, *adj.* (*bot.*) lomentaceous
Lomm, *s.m.* *V.* **Lumme**
Lompe, *s.m.* (*fish*) lumpsucker, lumpfish
Londinais, e, *adj. s.* (*old*) *V.* **Londonien**
Londonien, ne, *adj. s.* of London, London; Londonish; Londoner
Londrès, *s.m.* regalia (*cigar*)
Londres, *s.m.* London. *Premier-* —, (*of London newspapers*) leading article, leader
Londrin, *s.m.* London-cloth
Long, ue, *adj.* long; great; extensive; distant; prolonged; lengthened; lengthy, diffuse; slow; — *s.m.* length; extent; —**ue,** *s.f.* *V.* **Longue,** *s.f.* (*below*); — *adv.* much, a great deal, a good deal; a great *or* good many things; a long story. *Au* —, *tout au* —, along; alongside; all along; at large, at length, at great length, at full length, in full. *Au — de*, along; alongside. *Au — et au large*, both in length and width, far and wide, on all sides. *De — en large, en — et en large*, up and down, to and fro, backward and forward. *Du — et du large*, (*old*) famously, soundly, with a vengeance, of all sorts. *De son* —, *tout de son* —, at full length. *En* —, lengthways, lengthwise; longitudinally; longitudinal. *Le* —, *le — de*, along, alongside, long, by. *Plus* —, longer; greater; more extensive *or* &c.; longest; greatest; most extensive *or* &c.; longest way; more; most. *Tout le — de, tout du* —, all along, all through, all round. *En savoir* —, to know a good deal, to be knowing, to be a knowing one, to know what is what, to be cunning *or* sharp. *Tirer de* —, (*old*) to scamper away, to fly off; to put off, to protract
†**Longailles,** *s.f.pl.* (*of a cask*) upright pieces, staves
Longanimité, *s.f.* longanimity, forbearance, long-suffering; fortitude
Longchamps, *s.m.* (*obsolete*) Longchamps (*fashionable drive, ride, and walk, along the Champs-Élysées, in Paris, on the Wednesday, Thursday, and Friday before Easter*)
Long-courrier, *s.m.* Ocean ship, Ocean steamer; — *adj.m.* Ocean
Longe, *s.f.* longe, tether, thong; (*falc.*) jess; (*butch.*) loin
Longé, e, *part. adj.* gone along, &c. (*V.* **Longer**); (*her.*) jessed
Longer, *v.a.* to go along *or* alongside; to walk *or* march along; to run along; to sail *or* steam along *or* alongside, to coast along; to skirt; (*hunt.*) to take a long way off
Longeron, *s.m.* (*tech.*) string-piece, sleeper
Longévité, *s.f.* longevity
Longi, (*in compounds*) longi...
Longicorne, *s.m. adj.* (*zool.*) longicorn
Longimètre, *s.m.* longimeter
Longimétr-ie, -ique. *V.* page 3, § 1
Longin, *s.m.* slow coach, lazybones
Longipède, *adj.* (*of birds*) long-legged; — *s.m.* longiped
Longipenne, *adj.m.f., s.m.* (*zool.*) longipennate
Longirostre, *adj.m.f.* (*zool.*) longirostral; — *s.m.* longirostre
Longis, *s.m.* *V.* **Longin**
Longitude, *s.f.* longitude
Longitudinal, e, *adj.* longitudinal
Longitudinalement, *adv.* longitudinally
Longiuscule, *adj.* somewhat elongated
Long-pan, *s.m.* roof-length
Longrine, *s.f.* *V.* **Longuerine**
Longtemps, *adv.* long, a long time *or* while, a great while. *Depuis* —, long since, long ago; long before; for a long time; long
Longue, *s.f.* length *or* course of time; (*gram.*) long, long syllable; — *adj.f.* *V.* **Long.** *A la* —, in the long run, in time, in the end, at last. *Observer les —s et les brèves*, to mind o.'s P's and Q's; to be very punctilious; to stand on ceremony
Longue-langue, *s.f.* (*bird*) long-tongue, wryneck
Longuement, *adv.* long, a long time; at length
Longuerine, *s.f.* (*build.*) girder; (*rail.*) longitudinal sleeper
Longuet, te, *adj.* longish, pretty long, rather long, somewhat elongated, long; lengthy
Longueur, *s.f.* length; extent; slowness; delay; lengthiness, prolixity; dulness; lengthy *or* tedious part *or* passage. *En* —, in length; lengthways, lengthwise; at great length. *Tirer en* —, to spin out, to prolong, to wire-draw. *Trainer en* —, to prolong, to protract, to put off; to linger, to be protracted, to go on very slowly
Longue-vue, *s.f.* telescope; spy-glass, field-glass, glass
Loo, *s.m.* *V.* **Lo**
‡**Looch,** *s.m.* (*pharm.*) emulsion; (— *blanc*) emulsion of almonds, milk of almonds
Lophie, *s.f.* (*fish*) lophius, angler, fishing-frog, frog-fish, toad-fish, sea-devil
Lophophore, *s.m.* (*bird*) impeyan, impeyan pheasant

Lophyre, *s.m.* (*zool.*) lophyrus
Lopin, *s.m.* bit, piece; portion, share
***Loquace,** *adj.* loquacious, talkative
***Loquacement,** *adv.* loquaciously, talkatively
***Loquacité,** *s.f.* loquacity, talkativeness
Loque, *s.f.* rag, tatter
Loqué, e, *adj.* (*of fish*) bitten
§**Loquèle,** *s.f.* small talk, gabble, gift of the gab
Loquet, *s.m.* latch; catch; hasp; clasp
Loqueteau, *s.m.* small latch
Loquette, *s.f.* small rag, small piece, little bit, scrap
Loranthe, *s.m.* (*bot.*) loranthus
Lord, *s.m.* (English) lord
Lordose, *s.f.* (*med.*) lordosis
Lore, *s.m.* *V.* **Lorum**
Loré, e, *adj.* (*her.*) finned
Lorette, *s.f.* lorette, gay woman
†**Lorgnade,** *s.f.* ogle, ogling; side-glance, sly glance, side-look
†**Lorgner,** *v.a.* to look through a glass, to look at; to quiz; to cast a glance at *or* a side-look upon; to look wistfully at; to ogle; to leer; to eye; to have an eye on; to covet, to aim at
†**Lorgnerie,** *s.f.* quizzing; ogling; leering; eying; glancing; side-glance
†**Lorgnette,** *s.f.* glass, spy-glass, opera-glass, field-glass. — *de campagne*, field-glass. — *de spectacle* or *de théâtre*, opera-glass
†**Lorgneu-r, se,** *s.m.f.* ogler
†**Lorgnon,** *s.m.* eye-glass, quizzing-glass
Lori, *s.m.* (*monkey*) loris; (*bird*) lory
Loricaire, *s.m.* (*fish*) loricaria
Loricère, *s.f.* (*insect*) loricera
Loriot, *s.m.* (*bird*) oriole, loriot, golden oriole; (*baker's*) scovel-tub; (*fam.*) *V.* **Compère-loriot**
Loriqué, e, *adj.*, **Loriqué,** *s.m.* loricate
Loris, *s.m.* *V.* **Lori**
Lormerie, *s.f.* (*old*) lorimer's trade *or* work *or* article, bridle-cutter's work
Lormier, *s.m.* (*old*) lorimer, bridle-cutter, bit-maker
Lorrain, e, *adj. s.* of Lorraine; native of Lorraine, Lorrain, Lorrainer
Lorré, e, *adj.* *V.* **Loré**
Lors, *adv.* then. — *de*, at the time of. — *même que*, even when; even though. *Depuis* —, *dès* —, from that moment *or* time, since *or* from then, ever since; thence; in that case; therefore; from the moment (that), as soon (as). *Pour* —, then; at that time, at the time; so; in that case; therefore
Lorsque, *conj.* when, at the time *or* moment
Lorum, *s.m.* (*of birds*) lore
Lory, *s.m.* *V.* **Lori**
Los, *s.m.* (*obsolete*) praise
Losange, *s.m.* lozenge; — *s.f.* (*her.*) lozenge
Losangé, e, *part. adj.* lozenged; (*her.*) lozengy
Losanger, *v.a.* to lozenge
Losangique, *adj.* lozenged, lozenge-shaped
Lose, *s.f.* roofing-stone
Lossan, Losson, *s.m.* corn-weevil
Losse, *s.f.* bung-borer
Lot, *s.m.* lot; portion, share; fate; (*of lotteries*) prize. *Gros* —, first *or* highest prize
Lotalite, *s.f.* (*min.*) lotalite
Lote, *s.f.* *V.* **Lotte**
Loterie, *s.f.* lottery; raffle
Loti, e, *part. adj.* portioned; shared. *Bien* —, well-portioned; favoured, lucky; in a fine plight
Lotier, *s.m.* (*bot.*) lotus
Lotion, *s.f.* lotion, wash
Lotionner, *v.a.* to lotion, to wash
Lotir, *v.a.* to lot; to portion; to share
Lotissage, *s.m.* averaging, assaying; lotting
Lotissement, *s.m.* lotting; portioning; sharing
Loto, *s.m.* loto (*game*)
Lotophage, *adj.* lotophagous, lotus-eating; — *s.m.* lotophagus (*pl.* lotophagi), lotus-eater
Lotos, *s.m.* *V.* **Lotus**
Lotte, *s.f.* burbot, eel-pout
Lotus, *s.m.* lotus, lotos; lote, lote-tree
Louable, *adj.* laudable, praiseworthy, deserving of praise, commendable; honest; honourable; of the right sort, good; right, proper, fit; (*med.*) laudable, healthy
Louablement, *adv.* laudably, praiseworthily, commendably
Louage, *s.m.* letting, letting out; hire; hiring; rent; renting. *A* —, on hire. *De* —, hired; hackney; job; (*paint.*) accessory. *Donner à* —, to let, to let out, to let on *or* for hire, to hire out. *Prendre à* —, to hire; to rent
Louageur, *s.m.* job-master, livery-stable keeper
Louange, *s.f.* praise; commendation; eulogy; glory; credit; merit
Louanger, *v.a.* to praise up, to laud
Louangeu-r, se, *adj. s.* laudatory, eulogistic; praiser, flatterer
Loubine, *s.f.* (*zool.*) sea-pike
Louche, *adj.* squint; squint-eyed; ambiguous; doubtful, dubious; suspicious; not clear; obscure; dim; dark; muddy, foul, thick; — *s.m.* ambiguity; obscurity; suspicious appearance, something suspicious; — *s.f.* soup-ladle; cooking-ladle; liquid manure hand-distributor; (*tech.*) auger
Louchée, *s.f.* ladleful
Louchement, *s.m.* squinting
Loucher, *v.n.* to squint
Loucherie, *s.f.* squinting
Louchet, *s.m.* flat spade
Loucheu-r, se, *s.m.f.* squinter; — *adj.* squinting
Louchir, *v.n.* to become muddy *or* thick
Louchon, *s.m.* (*pop.*) squint-eyed fellow, squinter
Louer, *v.a.* to let, to let out; to lend, to lend out; to let for; to hire out, to let on *or* for hire; to hire; to take; to rent; to lease; to demise. *A* —, to let, to be let; for hire; (*paint.*) accessory
Se —, *v.r.* to hire oneself; to be hired; to be let, to let; to let for
Louer, *v.a.* to praise; to commend; to eulogize; to speak in favour of; to thank
Se —, *v.r.* to praise oneself *or* each other; to rejoice (at); to be satisfied *or* pleased (with); to speak highly (of)
Loueu-r, se, *s.m.f.* letter out, letter (of ...); lender; praiser. — *de voitures*, job-master. — *de chevaux*, job-master, livery-stable keeper. — *en garni*, lodging-house keeper
Loufiat, *s.m.* (*pop.*) dirty fellow, blackguard
Lougre, *s.m.* (*nav.*) lugger
Louis, — **d'or,** *s.m.* louis, louis d'or (*old French gold coin worth about* $4.60)
Louise-bonne, *s.f.* louise-bonne (*pear*)
Loulou, te, *s.m.f.* (*fam.*) duck, ducky, darling, love; — *s.f.* peggy (*child's tooth*)
Loup, *s.m.* wolf; solitary *or* unsociable man; stock-jobber, stag; black velvet mask, domino-mask, mask; packing-stick; burnisher; (*machine*) willy, devil; (*print.*) out (*in the copy*); (*tailors' slang*) misfit; (*old med.*) lupus. — **-cerve,** *s.f.* female lynx. — **-cervier,** *s.m.* lynx; (*pers.*) shark. — **-garou,** *s.m.* werewolf; bugbear; (*pers.*) solitary *or* unsociable man, surly dog, churl; (*toy*) whizgig; *adj.* churlish, bluff. — *marin*, sea-wolf, wolf-fish, cat-fish. — *de mer*, sea-pike; sea-wolf, wolf-fish, cat-fish; (*pers.*) expert seaman, hard-a-weather sailor, tar, Jack-tar, salt. *Au* — ! wolf! *De* —, (*adj.*) wolfish; ravenous; violent; (*of cold weather*) sharp, bitter. *A dents de* —, (*of embroidery*, &c.) indented, vandyked. *Avoir vu le* —, to have seen the world, to be no novice, to know what is what. *Être connu comme le* — *blanc*, to be known by everybody. *Tenir le* — *par les oreilles*, to see peril on all sides, not to know what to do. *Quand on parle du* — *on en voit la queue*, (*Proverb*) talk of the devil and he is sure to appear
Loupe, *s.f.* magnifying-glass; (*med.*) wen; (*of camels*, &c.) hump; (*of trees*, &c.) knob; (*jewel.*) lens; (*of iron-works*) bloom, loop, loup; (*house-painter's*) cradle; (*pop.*) loafer, lazybones; loafing. *Camp de la* —, den of thieves, Alsatia
Louper, *v.n.* (*pop.*) to loaf, to idle
Loupeu-r, se, *s.m.f.* (*pop.*) loafer, idler, lazybones; girl of the town
Loupeu-x, se, *adj.* wenny; knobby

Loupiat, *s.m.* (*pop.*) *V.* **Loupeur**
Lourd, e, *adj.* heavy; weighty; slow; dull; clumsy; gross; (*of weather*) close; muggy; — *adv.* much, a great deal
Lourdaud, e, *s.m.f.* lubber, lout, bumpkin, loggerhead, blockhead, dullard; — *adj* awkward, clumsy, lumpish, dull [clumsily; grossly
Lourdement, *adv.* heavily; plump; dully;
Lourderie, *s.f.* heaviness; slowness; dulness; clumsiness; grossness; gross blunder
Lourdeur, *s.f.* heaviness; weight; slowness;
Lourdise, *s.f. V.* **Lourderie** [dulness
Loure, *s.f.* loure (*dance, tune*)
Lourer, *v.a.* (*mus.*) to join (*notes*)
Lousse, *s.f. V.* **Losse**
Loustic, Loustig, *s.m.* wag [cap *or* muff *or* &c.
Loutre, *s.f.* otter; — *s.m.* (*obsolete*) otter-skin
Loutreur, Loutrier, *s.m.* otter-hunter
Louvard, Louvart, Louvat, *s.m. V.* **Lou-**
Louve, *s.f.* she-wolf; (*tech.*) sling [**veteau**
Louver, *v.a.* (*tech.*) to sling
Louvet, te, *adj.* wolf-coloured, deep yellow-dun
Louvetage, *s.m.* (*manu.*) willying
Louveteau, *s.m.* young wolf, wolf's cub, whelp
Louveter, *v.n.* (*of wolves*) to whelp; — *v.a.*
Louveterie, *s.f.* wolf-hunt [(*manu.*) to willy
Louvetier, *s.m.* wolf-hunter; (*obsolete*) master of the wolf-hounds [*the ghost-moth*) otter
Louvette, *s.f.* (*insect*) dog-tick; (*caterpillar of*
Louviers, *s.m.* Louviers cloth
Louvoyage, *s.m.* (*nav.*) tacking
Louvoyer, *v.n.* (*nav.*) to tack, to ply by boards; (*fig.*) to tack, to manœuvre, to dodge
Louvre, *s.m.* Louvre (*an edifice in Paris, formerly the palace of the French kings, now a national museum, &c.*); (*fig.*) palace
Love, *s.f.* wedge (*of soap*)
Lovelace, *s.m.* Lovelace, Lothario, gay Lothario,
Lover, *v.a.* to coil [lady-killer, rake
Loveur, *s.m.* (*fish.*) coiler
Loxarthre, *s.m.* (*med.*) loxarthrus
Loxodrom-ie, -isme. *V.* page 3, § 1
Loxodromique, *adj.* loxodromic; — *s.f.* loxodromic curb *or* line, rhumb line; loxodromics
Loyal, e, *adj.* honest, fair, fair-dealing, just, true, faithful, honourable, upright, straightforward; genuine; bonâ fide; (*old*) loyal
Loyalement, *adv.* honestly, fairly, faithfully, uprightly, straightforwardly; (*old*) loyally
Loyal-isme, -iste. *V.* page 3, § 1
Loyauté, *s.f.* honesty, fairness, fair-dealing, good faith, fidelity, honourableness, uprightness, probity, integrity; (*old*) loyalty
Loyer, *s.m.* hire; rent; (*old, poet.*) reward, retribution, requital; punishment, chastisement
Loyoliste, *s.m.* Loyolist, jesuit
Loyolitique, *adj.* Loyolitic, jesuitic
Lozange, (*old spelling*) *V.* **Losange**
Lubecquois, e, *adj. s.* of Lubeck; native of Lubeck, Lubecker [whimsical, crotchety
Lubie, *s.f.* whim, crotchet, maggot. *A —s,*
Lubricité, *s.f.* lubricity, lewdness, lechery
Lubrifiant, e, *adj.* lubricating; — *s.m.* lubri-
Lubrification, *s.f.* lubrication [cant, lubricator
Lubrifier, *v.a.* to lubricate
Lubrique, *adj.* lewd, lecherous, wanton
Lubriquement, *adv.* lewdly, lecherously
Lucane, *s.m.* (*zool.*) lucanus, stag-beetle
Lucanides, *s.m.pl.* (*zool.*) lucanidæ
Lucanien, ne, *adj. s.* Lucanian
Lucarne, *s.f.* dormer-window; skylight; attic; (*pop.*) eye-glass, quizzing-glass
Lucernois, e, *adj. s.* of Lucerne, Lucernese,
Lucet, *s.m.* (*bot.*) *V.* **Airelle** [native of Lucerne
Lucide, *adj.* lucid, clear
Lucidement, *adv.* lucidly
Lucidité, *s.f.* lucidity, clearness
Lucifer, *s.m.* Lucifer
Lucifère, *adj.* luciferous
Lucifèrien, ne, *adj.* Luciferian
Lucifuge, *adj.* shunning the light
Lucimètre, *s.m.* lucimeter
Lucine, *s.f.* (*mollusc*) lucina
Luciole, *s.f.* glowworm; fire-fly
Lucquois, e, *adj. s.* Lucchese (*of* **Lucca**)
Lucrati-f, ve, *adj.* lucrative
Lucrativement, *adv.* lucratively
Lucre, *s.m.* lucre, gain
Lucrèce, *s.f.* virtuous woman
Luctueu-x, se, *adj.* (*med.*) luctuous
Lucubration, *s.f. V.* **Élucubration**
Lucule, *s.f.* (*astr.*) lucule
Lucullite, *s.f.* (*min.*) lucullite
Lucullus, *s.m.* Lucullus, splendid entertainer
Lucume, *s.f.* (*bot.*) lucuma
Ludion, *s.m.* hydro-pneumatic toy
Luette, *s.f.* (*anat.*) uvula [spark; glimmering
Lueur, *s.f.* glimmer, light; glimpse, gleam;
Lugubre, *adj.* lugubrious, mournful, dismal; lurid [dismally
Lugubrement, *adv.* lugubriously, mournfully,
Lui, *part.* shone, &c. (*V.* **Luire**)
Lui, *pron.pers.m.f.* him; her; it; to *or* at *or* for *or* with *or* in *or* from *or* by *or* on *or* against him; to *or* at *or* for *or* with *or* in *or* from *or* by *or* on *or* against her; to *or* at it; he; for his part; himself; itself. *A —,* to *or* at *or* with him; to *or* at himself; his, his own; of his, of his own; peculiar; to spare. *A — à, à — de, V.* **A.** *— -même,* himself; itself; alone; too, also, likewise [glisten; to dawn
Luire, *v.n.* to shine; to glitter; to gleam; to
Luisant, e, *adj.* shining; glittering; gleaming; glistening; bright; glossy; — *s.m.* gloss; polish; — *s.f.* (*astr.*) bright star
Lulu, *s.m.* (*bird*) wood-lark
Lumachelle, *s.f.* (*min.*) lumachella, lumachel, shell-marble, fire-marble
Lumbago, *s.m.* (*med.*) lumbago
Lumière, *s.f.* light; lamp; luminary; daylight, day; judgment, sense; wisdom; sagacity, intelligence; knowledge, information; hint, clue; elucidation; (*tech.*) opening; hole; socket; (*artil.*, &c.) vent, (*in vulgar English*) touch-hole; (*of math. instr.*) sight; (*of organ-pipes*) mouth; (*of steam-engines*) steam-port; (*obsolete*) window; (*poet. for* "vue") eye-sight, sight; (*ditto for* "vie") life. *Mettre en —,* to bring to light; to elucidate; to illustrate; to demonstrate; to diffuse; (*obsolete*) to publish [end
†Lumignon, *s.m.* (*of candles, &c.*) snuff; bit,
Luminade, *s.f. A la —,* by torchlight
Luminaire, *s.m.* luminary, light; lights; (*pop.*) sight, eyes, peepers [fitter
Luminariste, *s.m.* (*fam.*) lamp-lighter; gas-
Lumineusement, *adv.* luminously
Lumineu-x, se, *adj.* luminous, shining, bright, clear
Luminosité, *s.f.* luminosity, luminousness
Lumme, Lumm, *s.m.* (*zool.*) black-throated
Lump, *s.m.* (*fish*) *V.* **Lompe** [diver
Lumps, *s.m.* sugar-loaf of inferior quality
Lunaire, *adj.* lunar, lunary, of the moon, moon; — *s.f.* (*bot.*) lunary, moonwort, honesty
Lunaison, *s.f.* lunation
Lunatique, *adj.* moon-struck; whimsical, crotchety; (*of horses*) moon-eyed; (*obsolete*) lunatic, insane, mad; — *s.m.f.* whimsical *or* crotchety person; (*obsolete*) lunatic [snack
Lunch, Luncheon, *s.m.* lunch, luncheon,
Luncher, *v.n.* to lunch, to take a snack
Lundi, *s.m.* Monday. *— gras,* Shrove Monday. *— saint,* Monday before Easter, Monday in Passion-week. *Saint —, la saint- —,* Saint-Monday. *Faire le —, fêter saint —, célébrer la saint- —,* to keep Saint-Monday
Lune, *s.f.* moon; whim, crotchet, fit; moments; (*poet.*) month; (*old chem.*) luna, silver. *— d'août,* harvest-moon. *— d'eau,* white water-lily. *— de miel,* honeymoon. *— rousse,* April moon. *— cornée,* (*old chem.*) luna cornea. *Faire un trou à la —,* to shoot the moon, to bolt, to abscond; to fail. *Vouloir prendre la — avec les dents,* to attempt impossibilities

Luné, e, *adj.* mooned; (*pop.*) disposed
Lunel, *s.m.* lunel (wine); (*her.*) lunel
Lunet, *s.m.* shrimp-net [**Lunettier**
Luneterie, Lunetier. *V.* **Lunetterie,**
Lunette, *s.f.* telescope; spy-glass; glass; (*of water-closets*, &c.) seat; (*of watches*) rim; (*of fowls*) wish-bone, merry-thought; (*for a horse's eye*) blinder, lunette; (*arch., fort., of a horse-shoe*) lunette; **—s,** *pl.* spectacles, glasses; (*rid.*) blinders, lunettes. — *d'approche*, — *de* or *à longue vue*, telescope; spy-glass, field-glass,
Lunetté, e, *adj.* spectacled [glass
Lunetterie, *s.f.* spectacle-making *or* trade *or* business; spectacles, glasses
Lunettier, *s.m.* spectacle-maker
Luniforme, *adj.* luniform
Luni-solaire, *adj.* lunisolar
Lunulaire, *adj.* lunular
Lunule, *s.f.* lunule, lune; (*of a monstrance*) lunula, crescent; (*anat.*) lunula
Lunulé, e, *adj.* lunulate, lunulated
Lunulite, *s.f.* (*fossil*) lunulite
Lupanar, *s.m.* house of ill fame, bawdy house
Lupercales, *s.f.pl.* (*Rom. ant.*) lupercalia
Lupin, *s.m.* (*bot.*) lupine, lupin
Lupinastre, *s.m.* (*bot.*) lupinaster, wild lupine
Lupinelle, *s.f.* (*bot.*) red clover; sainfoin
Lupinine, *s.f.* (*chem.*) lupinine
Lupulin, *s.m.* (*bot.*) lupuline (*powder*)
Lupuline, *s.f.* (*chem.*) lupuline (*principle*); (*plant*) lupuline, black medick
Lupus, *s.m.* (*med.*) lupus
Lurelure (A), *adv.* (*pop.*) at random
Luride, *adj.* lurid
Luridité, *s.f.* luridness, lurid hue
Luron, *s.m.* jolly fellow, brick, smart fellow, buck; determined dog [girl
Luronne, *s.f.* buxom woman, forward *or* fast
Lusiade (La), *s.f.* the Lusiad (*Camoens's poem*)
Lusin, *s.m.* *V.* **Luzin**
Lusitanien, ne, *adj. s.* Lusitanian
Lustrage, *s.m.* glossing; glossiness
Lustral, e, *adj.* lustral
Lustration, *s.f.* lustration
Lustre, *s.m.* lustre; gloss; splendour, brilliancy; foil; (*candlestick*) lustre, chandelier, gaselier; (*fam.*) set of (hired) clappers, clappers (*under the chandelier, in the pit of a theatre*); (*antiquated, poet.*) lustrum, lustre (*space of five years*). — *d'eau*, (*bot.*) *V.* **Chara** *and* **Hottone**
Lustré, e, *adj.* glossy [dress
Lustrer, *v.a.* to gloss; to glaze; to sleek; to
Lustreu-r, se, *s.m.f.* glosser, glazer, dresser
Lustrier, *s.m.* lustre *or* chandelier-maker
Lustrine, *s.f.* lustring *or* lutestring (*silk stuff*); glazed cambric, glazed lining
Lustroir, *s.m.* polisher
Lustucru, *s.m.* (*pop.*) silly Billy, simpleton, fool, muff; guy; what's his name, thingumbob
Lut, *s.m.* (*chem.*) lute, luting
Lutation, *s.f.* lutation
Lutéo-gallique, *adj.* (*chem.*) luteo-gallic
Lutéoléine, *s.f.* (*chem.*) luteoleine
Lutéoline, *s.f.* (*chem.*) luteoline
Luter, *v.a.* (*chem.*) to lute
Lutetia, *s.f.* (*astr.*) Lutetia
Luth, *s.m.* (*mus.*) lute
Luthéranisme, *s.m.* Lutheranism
Lutherie, *s.f.* musical-instrument making *or* manufactory *or* business *or* warehouse; musical
Luthérien, ne, *adj. s.* Lutheran [instruments
Luthier, *s.m.* musical-instrument maker
Lutidine, *s.f.* (*chem.*) lutidine
Lutin, *s.m.* goblin, hobgoblin, spirit, sprite, elf, imp; wild child. *Faire le* —, to play the deuce; to be troublesome [gish
Lutin, e, *adj.* wanton, roguish, sprightly, wag-
Lutiner, *v.a.n.* to plague, to torment, to tease; to agitate; to play the deuce; to make a great
Lutraire, *s.f.* (*mollusc*) lutraria [noise
Lutrin, *s.m.* lectern, choir-desk; choristers,
Lutrone, *s.f.* (*bird*) missel thrush [choir

Lutte, *s.f.* wrestling; scuffle; struggle; struggling; fight; conflict; contest; strife; match. *De bonne* —, by fair means, fairly; fair. *De haute* —, by a violent struggle, by main force; with a high hand
Lutter, *v.n.* to wrestle; to scuffle; to struggle; to fight; to conflict; to contend; to contest; to cope; to strive; to have a match; to vie; to tup
Lutteur, *s.m.* wrestler; struggler; adversary
Luxation, *s.f.* (*surg.*) luxation, dislocation
Luxe, *s.m.* luxury; display; splendour, magnificence; sumptuousness; richness; luxuriance, exuberance; profusion; superfluousness, superfluity; extravagance; excess; fashion; fancy. *De* —, of luxury; luxurious; fashionable, elegant, splendid, sumptuous, rich; fancy; ornamental; superfluous. *C'est du* —, (*fam.*) that is not necessary *or* wanted, that is useless *or* superfluous, that is of no use, that is too much of a good thing
Luxembourg, *s.m.* (*geog.*) Luxemburg; (*in Paris*) Luxembourg (*palace and house of peers or senate-house, with gardens, and a national picture gallery*) [Luxemburger
Luxembourgeois, e, *adj. s.* of Luxemburg;
Luxer, *v.a.* (*surg.*) to luxate, to dislocate
Se —, *v.r.* to become luxated *or* dislocated; to luxate *or* dislocate (o.'s ...)
Luxueusement, *adv.* luxuriously, magnificently, sumptuously, richly [sumptuous, rich
Luxueu-x, se, *adj.* luxurious, magnificent,
Luxure, *s.f.* lust, lewdness
Luxuriance, *s.f.* luxuriance
Luxuriant, e, *adj.* luxuriant
Luxurieusement, *adv.* lustfully, lewdly
Luxurieu-x, se, *adj.* lustful, lewd
Luzerne, *s.f.* (*bot.*) lucerne, lucern. — *-houblon*, black medick, black nonsuch
Luzernière, *s.f.* lucerne-field
Luzin, *s.m.* (*nav.*) house-line
Luzule, *s.f.* (*bot.*) luzula, wood-rush
Ly, *s.m.* *V.* **Li**
Lycanthrope, *s.m.* lycanthrope
Lycanthropie, *s.f.* lycanthropy
Lycée, *s.m.* lyceum; college
Lycéen, *s.m.* collegian, student
‡**Lychnanthe,** *s.m.* (*bot.*) campion
‡**Lychnide,** *s.f.*, **Lychnis,** *s.m.* (*bot.*) lychnis
Lyciet, *s.m.* (*bot.*) box-thorn, tea-plant
Lycope, *s.m.* (*bot.*) lycopus, gypsywort, bugle-
Lycoperdon, *s.m.* (*bot.*) puff-ball [weed
Lycopode, *s.m.* (*plant*) lycopodium, club-moss; (*powder*) lycopode, vegetable brimstone
Lycopodine, *s.f.* (*chem.*) lycopodine
Lycopside, *s.f.* (*bot.*) lycopsis, bugloss
Lycorexie, *s.f.* lycorexy, wolfish hunger, canine
Lycose, *s.f.* (*spider*) lycosa [appetite
Lydien, ne, *adj. s.m.f.* Lydian; — *s.f.* (*min.*) Lydian stone
Lymphangite, *s.f.* (*med.*) lymphangitis
Lymphat-ique, -isme. *V.* page 3, § 1
Lymphe, *s.f.* lymph
Lymphite, *s.f.* (*med.*) lymphitis
Lymphorrhagie, *s.f.* (*med.*) lymphorrhage
Lymphotom-ie, -ique. *V.* page 3, § 1
Lynch. *Loi de* —, Lynch-law
Lyncher, *v.a.* to lynch
Lyncheur, *s.m.* lyncher
Lynx, *s.m.* lynx
Lyon, *s.m.* Lyons (*Fr. town*) [nese, native of Lyons
Lyonais, e, Lyonnais, e, *adj. s.* of Lyons, Lyon-
Lypémaniaque, *adj. s.m.f.* (*med.*) lypemaniac
Lypémanie, *s.f.* (*med.*) lypemania, melancholia
Lyre, *s.f.* yre; (*anat., astr.*) lyra; (*bird*) *V* **Ménure**; (*fish*) *V.* **Trigle**
Lyré, e, *adj.* (*bot.*) lyrate, lyrated
Lyriforme, *adj.* lyriform
Lyrique, *adj.* lyric, lyrical; operatic; — *s.m.* lyric; lyrics, lyricism. *Théâtre* —, opera-house
Lyrisme, *s.m.* lyricism [strife, moneywort
†**Lysimachie, Lysimaque,** *s.f.* (*bot.*) loose-

M

M, *s.f.* (*letter*) m
M', *contraction of* **Me ;** (*obsolete*) my
Ma, *adj.poss.f.* my, my own
Mâ, *s.m.* (*bot.*) China grass
Mabolo, *s.m.* (*bot.*) mabola, date-plum
Macabre, *adj. Danse* —, dance of Death
Macadam, *s.m.* macadam ; macadamizing
Macadamisage, *s.m.* macadamization, macadamizing
Macadamiser, *v.a.* to macadamize
Macaire, *s.m.* swindler, cheat, thief, Jack Sheppard; jobber [to diddle
Macairiser, *v.a.* to swindle, to cheat, to chisel,
Macairisme, *s.m.* swindling, cheating ; cheat ; jobbing, jobbery [macaw (*bird*)
Macao, *s.m.* macao (*game at cards*) ; (*obsolete*)
Macaque, *s.m.* (*zool.*) macacus, baboon
Macaret, *s.m. V.* **Mascaret**
Macareux, *s.m.* (*bird*) puffin [bumbailiff
Macaron, *s.m.* macaroon ; back-comb ; (*pop.*)
Macaroncini, *s.m.* (*cook.*) macaroncini (*small kind of macaroni*)
Macaroné, e, *adj.* macaroon-like
Macaronée, *s.f.* macaronic
Macaroni, *s.m.* macaroni
Macaron-ique, -isme, -iste. *V.* page 3, § 1
Macédoine, *s.f.* medley, miscellany, hotchpotch, olio, jumble [fashion
Macédonien, ne, *adj. s.* Macedonian; ditto
Macération, *s.f.* maceration
Macérer, *v.a.* to macerate ; — *v.a.n.* (*chem.*) to macerate, to soak, to stand
Se —, *v.r.* to macerate o.'s body ; (*chem.*) to soak, to stand; to be macerated
Maceret, *s.m.* (*bot.*) *V.* **Airelle**
Maceron, *s.m.* (*bot.*) alisander, alexanders
Macfarlane, Macferlane, *s.m.* (*Manteau* —) Inverness-cape
‡**Machabées,** *s.m.pl.* Maccabees
Mâche, *s.f.* (*for horses*) mash ; (*bot.*) corn-salad, lamb's-lettuce ; (*tool*) scutcher ; — *s.m.* (*in compounds*) instrument *or* apparatus which presses *or* &c. (*V.* **Mâcher**), presser *or* &c. — **-bouchons,** *s.m.* cork-presser
Mâchecoulis, *s.m. V.* **Mâchicoulis** [clinkers
Mâchefer, *s.m.* hammer-slag, slag, dross,
Macheli-er, ère, *adj.* (*anat.*) maxillary, mandibular, of the jaws. *Dent —ère, —ère, s.f.* jaw-tooth, grinder
Mâchement, *s.m.* chewing, munching
Mâchemoure, *s.f.* (*nav.*) biscuit-dust
Mâcher, *v.a.n.* to chew, to masticate; to munch ; to bite at ; to bite ; to press ; to mince ; to reduce to a pulp ; (*fig.*) to prepare ; (*fig.*) to mince (*matters*); (*rid.*) to champ (*the bit*). — *de haut,* (*fam.*) to chew high, to eat without
Se —, *v.r.* to be chewed *or* &c. [appetite
Mâcheu-r, se, *s.m.f.* chewer; muncher; trencher-man *or* woman
‡**Machiavel,** *s.m.* Machiavel, Machiavelli, unscrupulous statesman, crafty unprincipled politician
Machiavélique, *adj.* Machiavelian, Machiavellian, unscrupulous, unprincipled, crafty, insidious, perfidious [diously
Machiavéliquement, *adv.* craftily, insi-
Machiavéliser, *v.n.* to machiavelize, to machiavellize
Machiavélisme, *s.m.* Machiavelism, Machiavelianism, Machiavellianism, unscrupulousness, craftiness, craft, insidiousness, duplicity, perfidious policy
Machiavéliste, *s.m.f.* Machiavelian, Machiavellian, crafty unprincipled politician, unscrupulous statesman
Mâchicatoire, *s.m.* masticatory
Machicot, *s.m.* (*obsolete*) singer (*in churches*); (*pop.*) novice, bad player
Mâchicoulis, *s.m.* (*fort.*) machicolation
†**Mâchiller,** *v.a. V.* **Mâchonner**
Machin, *s.m.* (*fam.*) thing; what do you call him *or* her *or* it? what is his *or* her *or* its name? thingumbob, thingummy
Machinage, *s.m.* (*coin.*) milling; edging
Machinal, e, *adj.* mechanical; automatic; instinctive ; constitutional
Machinalement, *adv.* mechanically; automatically; instinctively, without thinking
Machina-teur, trice, *s.m.f.* machinator, plotter, contriver [trivance
Machination, *s.f.* machination, plot; con-
Machine, *s.f.* machine ; engine ; implement ; apparatus; appliance; machinery; piece of mechanism; piece of work; work; body; fabric; contrivance; system; plan; spring; machination, plot, intrigue ; (*of carriages*) break, brake ; (*fam.*) thing, thingumbob, thingummy. — *à battre,* &c., thrashing-machine, &c. — *de réserve* or *de recours,* — *-pilote,* (*rail.*) pilot-engine. *La — ronde,* (*old fam. poet.*) the earthly ball, the earth, the globe, the world
Machiner, *v.a.* to machinate, to plot, to concoct; to plan; to dispose; to prepare; to provide with machinery; (*coin.*) to mill; to edge
Se —, *v.r.* to be machinated, &c.
Machinerie, *s.f.* machinery; machine-building, engine-building [machine of
Machiniser, *v.a.* to mechanize; to make a
Machinisme, *s.m.* machinism; mechanism
Machiniste, *s.m.* machinist ; engineer, engineman ; stage-carpenter, carpenter ; scene-shifter
Mâchoire, *s.f.* jaw; jaw-bone; chap; chop; blockhead, stupid fellow; fogy, old fogy; novice, bad player [munching
Mâchonnement, *s.m.* chewing, mumbling,
Mâchonner, *v.a.* to chew about, to mumble, to munch
Mâchonneu-r, se, *s.m.f.* mumbler, muncher
Machurer, *v.a.* to blacken, to daub, to smear,
†**Macigno,** *s.m.* (*geol.*) macigno [to smudge
Macilence, *s.f.* (*med.*) emaciation
Macine, *s.f.* (*chem.*) macine
Macis, *s.m.* mace (*spice*) [tosh
Mackintosh, *s.m.* mackintosh coat, mackin-
Macle, *s.f.* (*bot.*) *V.* **Macre ;** (*min.*) macle, andalusite, chiastolite, hollow spar; (*her.*)
Maclé, e, *adj.* (*her.*) mascled [mascle
Mâcon, *s.m.* mâcon (wine)
Maçon, *s.m.* mason; bricklayer; builder; bungler ; — *m.,* —**ne,** *f., adj.* mason, building
Maçonnage, *s.m.* masonry ; stonework, brickwork
Mâconnais, e, *adj. s.m.f.* of Mâcon, Mâconnese, native of Mâcon ; — *s.m.* Mâcon district
Maçonner, *v.a.* to mason, to build, to build up ; to stone ; to wall, to wall up; to bungle
Maçonnerie, *s.f. V.* **Maçonnage**
Maçonnique, *adj.* masonic
Macouba, *s.m.* Macouba tobacco
Macquage, *s.m.* breaking (*of hemp*)
Macque, *s.f.* brake (*for hemp*)
Macquer, *v.a.* to break (*hemp*)
Macre, *s.f.* (*bot.*) water-caltrop, (*fruit*) water-
Macrée, *s.f. V.* **Mascaret** [chestnut
Macreuse, *s.f.* (*bird*) scoter, sea-duck
Macrocosme, *s.m.* macrocosm [pod
Macropode, *adj.* macropodal; — *s.m.* macro-
Macroure, *adj.* macrourous ; — *s.m.* macrouran
Mactre, *s.f.* (*mollusc*) mactra, trough-shell
Maculage, *s.m.,* **Maculation,** *s.f.* spotting, staining, maculation
Maculature, *s.f.* spot, stain, mackle ; mackled sheet, waste-sheet, waste ; wrapper
Macule, *s.f.* spot, stain, blemish, mackle, macule ; (*astr.*) macula
Maculer, *v.a.* to spot, to stain, to smudge, to mackle, to macule, to maculate ; — *v.n.,* **Se** —, *v.r.* to become spotted *or* &c. ; to set off
Madame, *s.f.* Madam, (*vulgarly*) Ma'am, missus; Mrs. ; Mistress ; this *or* the lady ; my lady,

your *or* her ladyship; lady; dame; Madame. — *la comtesse*, the countess; my lady, your ladyship; her ladyship. — *la duchesse*, the duchess; my lady, your Grace; her Grace. — *votre mère* or *&c.*, your mother *or* &c. — *désire-t-elle* ...? does this lady wish ...? do you wish ..., madam?

Madapolam, *s.m.* long-cloth

Madarose, *s.f.* (*med.*) madarosis

Madécasse, *adj. s.m.f. V.* **Malgache**

Madéfaction, *s.f.* (*pharm.*) madefaction

Madéfier, *v.a.* (*pharm.*) to madefy

Madeleine, *s.f.* Magdalen, Magdalene; Madeline; tea-cake, bun, sally-lunn; kind of pear, of peach, and of grape (ripe towards the end of July)

Madelonnettes, *s.f.pl.* Magdalens; Magdalen hospital *or* asylum, female penitentiary; reformatory

Mademoiselle, *s.f.* Miss; this *or* the young lady; Mademoiselle. — *votre sœur* or *&c.*, your sister *or* &c. — *désire-t-elle* ...? does this young lady wish ...? do you wish ..., miss?

Madère, *s.m.* madeira (wine)

Madi, *s.m.* (*bot.*) madia

Madiaïque, *adj.* (*chem.*) madiaic

Madone, *s.f.* madonna

Madrague, *s.f.* tunny-fishery (*line of nets*)

Madras, *s.m.* Madras handkerchief

Madrate, *s.f.* (*bot.*) *V.* **Clandestine**

Madré, e, *adj.* speckled, spotted, mottled; cunning, sharp, knowing, sly; — *s.m.f.* cunning *or* knowing one, sharp fellow, sly dog, cunning [thing

Madrépore, *s.m.* (*nat. hist.*) madrepore

Madréporique, *adj.* madreporic

Madréporite, *s.f.* (*nat. hist.*) madreporite

Madrer, *v.a.* to speckle, to spot, to mottle

Madrier, *s.m.* joist, plank, board, madrier

Madrigal, *s.m.* madrigal [madrigalic

Madrigalesque, Madrigalique, *adj.*

Madrigalier, *s.m.* madrigalist

†**Madrilègne, Madrilène,** *adj. s.m.f.* of Madrid, Madrilenian, native of Madrid

Madrure, *s.f.* speckling, spotting, mottling, [vein

Maestoso, *adj. adv.* (*mus.*) maestoso

Maëstral, *s.m.* (*old spelling*) *V.* **Mistral**

Maestro, *s.m.* (*Italian*) maestro, composer

Maflé, e, Maflu, e, (*also spelt* **Mafflé, Mafflu, Mafré, Maffré**) *adj.* chubby, chub-faced, chub-cheeked; — *s.m.f.* ditto person

†**Magagne,** *s.m.* short iron

Magasin, *s.m.* warehouse, storehouse; ware-room, storeroom; mart; emporium; shop; magazine; store, provision; stock; (*of coaches*) basket. *Garçon de* —, warehouseman, shop-man, porter [rent; storage

Magasinage, *s.m.* warehousing, warehouse-

Magasiner, *v.a.* to warehouse; to store

Magasinier, *s.m.* warehouseman; store-keeper; (*nav.*) yeoman; (*thing*) stock-book

Magdaléon, *s.m.* (*pharm.*) magdaleon

Mage, *s.m.* magian, magus; —**s**, *pl.* magians, magi; wise men (of the East)

Magenta, *adj.m.f.*, *s.m.* magenta (*colour*)

Magicien, ne, *s.m.f.* magician

Magie, *s.f.* magic. — *blanche* or *naturelle*, natural magic. — *noire*, black art

Magile, *s.m.* (*zool.*) magilus

Magique, *adj.* magic

Magisme, *s.m.* magianism

Magister, *s.m.* (country *or* village) school-master, pedagogue, pedant, (*in Scotland*) dominie

Magistère, *s.m.* grand-mastership (*of the order of Malta*); (*chem., obsolete*) magistery; (*pharm., obsolete*) magistral

Magistral, e, *adj.* magisterial; masterly; (*pharm., engin., fort.*) magistral; — *s.m.* (*metal.*) magistral; — *s.f.* (*engin., fort.*) magistral, magistral line

Magistralement, *adv.* magisterially

Magistrat, *s.m.* magistrate; judge; town-council; government; (*of some rivers*) conservators

Magistrature, *s.f.* magistracy. — *assise*, judicial magistracy, judges. — *debout*, body of public prosecutors

Magma, *s.m.* (*pharm., chem.*) magma

†**Magnan,** *s.m.* (*local*) silkworm

†**Magnanage,** *s.m.* silk-husbandry

†**Magnanerie,** *s.f.* silkworm nursery; silk-breeding, silk-growing, silk-husbandry

†**Magnanier,** *s.m.* silk-breeder, silk-grower

†**Magnanière,** *s.f.* silkworm nursery

†**Magnanime,** *adj.* magnanimous, high-minded, noble

†**Magnanimement,** *adv.* magnanimously

†**Magnanimité,** *s.f.* magnanimity, greatness [of mind

Magnat, *s.m.* magnate

Magnatisme, *s.m.* magnatism

†**Magnésie,** *s.f.* magnesia

†**Magnésié, e,** *adj.* magnesiated

†**Magnésien, ne,** *adj.* magnesian

†**Magnésifère,** *adj.* magnesiferous

†**Magnésique,** *adj.* magnesic. *Lumière* —, [magnesium light

†**Magnésite,** *s.f.* magnesite

†**Magnésium,** *s.m.* magnesium

†**Magnét-ique, -iquement.** *V.* page 3, § 1

†**Magnétisation,** *s.f.* magnetization; mesmerization; mesmeric state

†**Magnétisé, e,** *part. adj.* magnetized; mesmerized; — *s.m.f.* ditto person *or* subject, mesmeree

†**Magnétiser,** *v.a.* to magnetize; to mesmerize

†**Magnétiseu-r, se,** *s.m.f.* magnetizer; mesmerizer, mesmerist; — *s.m.f.* magnetizing; mesmerizing

†**Magnétisme,** *s.m.* magnetism; mesmerism

†**Magnéto-électrique,** *adj.* magneto-electric

†**Magnéto-électricité,** *s.f.* magneto-electricity

†**Magnétographe,** *s.m.* magnetograph

†**Magnétolog-ie, -ique.** *V.* page 3, § 1

†**Magnétomètre,** *s.m.* magnetometer

†**Magnétométr-ie, -ique.** *V.* page 3, § 1

†**Magney,** *s.m.* *V.* **Maguey**

†**Magnier,** *s.m.* (*local*) tinker

Magnificat, *s.m.* (*lit.*) magnificat

†**Magnificence,** *s.f.* magnificence; splendour; grandeur; magnificent *or* splendid thing, great beauty; great expense; largess, bounty

†**Magnifico,** *s.m.* (*Italian*) magnifico

†**Magnifier,** *v.a.* to magnify

†**Magnifique,** *adj.* magnificent; splendid; grand; noble; munificent; extravagant

†**Magnifiquement,** *adv.* magnificently, splendidly, grandly, nobly

†**Magnoc,** *s.m.* (*bot.*) manioc; jatropha

†**Magnole,** *s.f.* nut *or* fruit of the magnolia

†**Magnolia, Magnolier,** *s.m.* (*bot.*) magnolia

Magot, *s.m.* magot, Barbary ape, pygmy ape, baboon, ape; grotesque figure, antic; hoard of money, hoard

Maguey, *s.m.* (*bot.*) maguey (*American aloe*)

Magyar, e, *adj. s.* Magyar

Magzem, *s.m.* (*Arabian*) troop (*of cavalry*)

Mahagoni, *s.m.* mahogany

Mahaleb, *s.m.* (*bot.*) mahaleb

Mahari, *s.m.* mahari (*kind of dromedary*)

Mahométan, e, *adj. s.* Mahometan, Mahomedan, Mahommedan, Mohammedan

Mahométanisme, Mahométisme, *s.m.* Mahometanism, Mahomedanism, Mahommedanism, Mohammedanism

†**Mahonille,** *s.f.* (*bot.*) Virginian stock

Mahonne, *s.f.* mahone (*Turkish galley*)

Mahou, *s.m.* coarse woollen cloth

Mahout, *s.m.* (*in India*) mahout (*elephant-driver or keeper*)

Mahratte, *adj. s.m.f.* Mahratta

Mahute, *s.f.* pinion (*of a bird of prey*)

Mai, *s.m.* May; May-pole

Maïa, *s.m.* (*zool.*) maian, sea-spider, spider-crab

Maïdan, *s.m.* maidan (*market-place in the Levant*)

Maie, *s.f.* bread-bin *or* pan; kneading-trough; [trough, bin

Maïeur, *s.m.* (*obsolete*) mayor

Maigre, *adj.* lean; meagre; thin; spare; skinny; slender; scanty; poor, sorry; dry, barren; shallow; without meat; made without meat; dressed without meat-gravy; vegetable; — *s.m.* lean; thin; fish and vegetable food *or* diet; shallow; (*zool., kind of fish*) maigre; — *adverb.* scantily; closely, close; sharply; dryly. *Au* —, dressed without meat-gravy *or* broth. *Jour* —, fish-day. *Potage* or *soupe* —, butter-soup, soup *or* porridge made without meat. *Repas* —, fish-meal, meal without meat. — *repas*, sorry meal. *Faire* —, *manger* —, to abstain from meat, to eat no flesh. *Faire — chère*, to have poor fare, to live poorly [person

Maigrelet, te, *adj. s.* thinnish, leanish; ditto

Maigrement, *adv.* meagrely, thinly, scantily, sparely, sparingly, poorly, badly

Maigret, te, *adj. V.* **Maigrelet**

Maigreur, *s.f.* leanness; emaciation; meagreness; thinness; spareness; poorness, scantiness; barrenness

Maigrir, *v.n.* to become (*or* grow *or* get) lean *or* thin, to get thinner, to fall away, to waste; — *v.a. V.* **Amincir**

†**Mail,** *s.m.* mallet; mall; pall-mall

†**Maille,** *s.f.* stitch; mesh; ring, link; mail; lattice; web (*in the eye*); (*of partridges*, &c.) speckle, speck, spot; (*nav.*) timber and room; (*obsolete*) bud; (*old Fr. coin*) maille, (*fig.*) farthing, doit, stiver. *Ni sou ni* —, no money at all, not a rap, nothing to bless oneself with. — *à partir*, a quarrel, a crow to pick *or* pluck (with)

†**Maillé, e,** *part. adj.* stitched; meshy; latticed; mailed; speckled, spotted. *Fer* —, wire-lattice, wire-netting [packfong; nickel silver

†**Maillechort,** *s.m.* German silver; albata;

†**Mailler,** *v.a.* to stitch; to make the meshes of; to lattice; to arm with a coat of mail, to mail; to beat with a mallet, to mall; (*nav.*) to lace; — *v.n.*, **Se** —, *v.r.* to become (*or* grow *or* get) speckled; (*old*) to bud [pack-horse

†**Mailler,** *s.m.* sumpter-horse, baggage-horse,

†**Maillet,** *s.m.* mallet, beetle; (*fish*) *V.* **Marteau**

†**Mailletage,** *s.m.* sheathing (*a ship's bottom*) with scupper-nails [with nails

†**Mailleter,** *v.a.* to sheathe (*a ship's bottom*)

†**Mailloche,** *s.f.* beetle [ring; tie

†**Maillon,** *s.m.* stitch; mesh; noose; link,

†**Maillot,** *s.m.* long-clothes, swathe, swaddling-clothes; infancy, babyhood; tights, fleshings; (*of vine*) cutting, slip; (*zool.*) pupa (*kind of snail*)

†**Maillotin,** *s.m.* (*old*) small mallet; (*Fr. hist.*) maillotin (*insurgent*)

†**Maillure,** *s.f.* speckles, spots [ursine baboon

Maimon, *s.m.* (*zool.*) chacma, pig-faced baboon,

Main, *s.f.* hand; handwriting, writing, hand; handle; hook; grapple; body-loop; hand-shovel; quire; (*at cards*) trick; lead; deal; clasper (*in botany*); source; authority; power; execution; touch; assistance, help, succour; choosing; purpose. — **-chaude,** *s.f.* (*game*) hot-cockles. — **-coulante,** *s.f.* (*obsolete*) hand-rail. — **-courante,** *s.f.* hand-rail; (*book-keep.*) waste-book. — **-d'œuvre,** *s.f.* workmanship; making, make; manual *or* hand labour, labour, work. — **-forte,** *s.f.* large *or* strong hand; assistance, aid, help. — **-levée,** *s.f.* (*law*) replevin; withdrawal. — **morte,** (*in two words*) slack hand; (*in one word*) *See below. Double* —, (*of an organ*) coupler. *Haute* —, direction, general management, high authority. *Haut la* —, with a high *or* tight hand, with authority; off-hand, easily, briskly, at once, outright; proud, imperious. *Jeu de —s*, *Jouer de —s*, &c., *V.* **Jeu, Jouer,** &c. *A* —, with a hand, with hands; by hand; for the hand; (*in compounds: of utensils*) hand [Ex.: = *Scie à* —, &c., hand-saw, &c.]. *A la* —, to o.'s hand; ready at hand; handy; by *or* with the hand; by hand; in the *or* o.'s hand; in hand; on the hand; on hand; by guess, without weighing; by private hand. *A — armée*, with arms in hand, armed; by force of arms, by main force, with open force; with violence. *A pleines —s*, *à belles —s*, by handfuls, largely, liberally, abundantly, plentifully, profusely. *A la portée de la* —, within reach; handy. *A deux —s*, with both hands; two-handed; for a double purpose; (*of horses*) *V.* **Cheval.** *A toutes —s*, every way; right and left; fit for anything; of all work; (*of horses*) *V.* **Cheval.** *De — morte*, with a slack hand, slackly, feebly. *De longue* —, of long standing; a long while ago, long ago; a long time since, long since; for a long time; long before, long beforehand; of old. *De toutes —s, de toute* —, from anyone, every way, right and left, by hook and by crook. *En* —, in hand; in o.'s hand; at o.'s disposal; handy. *En — propre*, in *or* into . . .'s own hands; personally. *Hors* —, *hors la* —, (*rid.*) off side, off. *Sous la* —, at hand; under o.'s hand; in *or* into o.'s hands; underhand; (*rid.*) near side, near. *Sous* —, underhand, clandestinely, secretly, by stealth; *s.m. See Letter* **S.** *N'y pas aller de — morte*, to hit hard; to go boldly to work; to do it briskly. *Avoir la* —, to have the lead *or* the deal. *Avoir la — bonne* or *heureuse*, to be a good hand; to be skilful *or* clever; to choose well, to have good taste; to be lucky *or* fortunate *or* successful, to succeed, to have good luck; to bring good luck. *Avoir la — forcée*, to be compelled, not to be free. *Donner la* —, to give o.'s hand; to hand; to shake hands (with); to accompany; to assist, to help, to lend a hand (to), to consent (to); (*at cards*) to give the lead off. *Se donner la* —, to give o.'s hand to each other; to shake hands; to join hands; to go hand in hand; to join. *En venir aux —s*, to come to blows, to fight, to engage, to join battle, to come to close quarters, to close (with). *Être aux —s*, to be fighting. *En mettre la — au feu, en lever la* —, to take o.'s oath of it. *Faire — basse sur*, to put to the sword; to kill, to slaughter; to destroy; to lay hands on, to seize upon, to plunder; to attack unsparingly, not to spare. *Faire — morte*, to let o.'s hand fall inert. *Faire sa* —, (*at cards*) to make the greatest number of tricks; (*fig.*) to make nice pickings, to pilfer, to pocket all one can. *Se faire la* —, to get o.'s hand in; to prepare oneself. *Forcer la — à*, (*fig.*) to compel. *Lâcher la* —, to give the reins, to give head; to give rope, to give more liberty, to relax o.'s strictness; to lower o.'s pretensions. *Lever la* —, to raise o.'s hand; to take o.'s oath (of), to swear (to). *Mettre aux —s*, to bring to a conflict, to set (together) by the ears. *Mettre la* —, to set *or* put *or* lay o.'s hand; to contribute (to). *Mettre la dernière — à*, to give the last touch to, to finish off. *Payer en — brève*, to pay directly to the last creditor. *Se perdre la* —, to be out of practice, o.'s hand to be out. *Tendre la* —, to beg; to hold out o.'s hand *or* a helping hand (to), to succour, to help, to assist. *Tenir la — à*, to attend to; to see *or* look to; to take care that; to see that (...) is done. *Les —s m'en sont tombées*, I was amazed *or* astounded. *De la — à la bouche se perd souvent la soupe*, there is many a slip between the cup [and the lip

Mainate, *s.m.* (*bird*) grackle, grakle

Maine, *s.f.* (*obsolete*) handful. *En avoir pour sa — de fèves*, (*old*) to be done for

Mainmortable, *adj.* (*law*) subject to mortmain

Mainmorte, *s.f.* (*law*) mortmain

Mainotte, *s.f.* (*bot.*) coral club-top

Maint, e, *adj.* many a, many

Maintenant, *adv.* now, now then, at present, this moment, this time; nowadays [preserver

Mainteneur, *s.m.* maintainer; upholder;

Maintenir, *v.a.* to maintain; to sustain; to support; to hold; to uphold; to keep up; to keep back; to enforce; to preserve, to keep; to secure

Se —, *v.r.* to maintain *or* &c. oneself; to keep up; to keep; to be maintained *or* &c.; to maintain o.'s position, to hold o.'s own; to keep *or* stand o.'s ground; to hold out; to subsist; to stand; to obtain; to remain; to continue; to last [**Maintenir**)

Maintenu, e, *part. adj.* maintained, &c. (*V.*

Maintenue, *s.f.*(*law*) confirmation of possession

Maintien, *s.m.* maintenance, preservation, keeping up; support; enforcement; carriage, deportment; bearing; attitude; demeanour; looks, countenance; address

Maïolique, *s.f. V.* **Majolique**

Mairain, *s.m.* (*old spelling*) *V.* **Merrain**

Maire, *s.m.* mayor; (*in Paris*) alderman

Mairerie, *s.f. pop. for* **Mairie**

Mairesse, *s.f.* mayoress

Mairie, *s.f.* mayoralty; mayor's house, mansion-house; town-hall, town-house; parochial offices, registrar's office, &c.; police-office. *Secrétaire de la* —, town-clerk

Mais, *conj. adv.* but; why; well; oh; now; ay and indeed; and ... too, and besides; — *s.m.* but. — *bien,* but indeed, but. — *non!* no! oh no! I say no! — *oui!* — *si!* yes! oh yes! ay! to be sure! I say yes! *Eh —!* why, why! nay then! *N'en pouvoir* —, (*obsolete*) cannot help it; cannot help himself (*or* herself *or* myself *or* &c.); to have (*or* to have had) nothing to do with it [maizena

Maïs, *s.m.* maize, Indian corn; maize meal,

Maison, *s.f.* house; residence; home; family; household; service; establishment; firm; shop; agency. — *d'achat,* merchandise house, broker's business. — *d'arrêt,* jail, gaol, prison, bridewell, house of correction. — *de campagne,* country-house, country-seat, villa. — *centrale,* jail, gaol; female convict establishment, female penitentiary. — *des champs,* farm-house. — *de chasse,* hunting-box, shooting-lodge *or* box. — *de commerce,* commercial *or* mercantile house; firm. — *commune,* town-hall, town-house. — *de correction,* — *d'éducation correctionnelle,* house of correction; reformatory school, reformatory. — *de détention,* jail, gaol, bridewell. — *Dorée,* Maison Dorée ("gilt house," *the name of a fashionable dining-house in Paris*). — *d'éducation,* boarding-school, school. — *de force,* jail, gaol, prison, bridewell, house of correction. — *de fous,* madhouse. — *garnie,* (*obsolete for* — "meublée") *V.* **Meublé.** — *de jeu,* gambling-house, gaming-house. — *de jeunes détenus,* reformatory, reformatory school. — *de justice,* house of detention, prison. — *meublée, V.* **Meublé.** — *de plaisance, V.* **Plaisance.** — *de pret,* loan-office; pawnshop. — *publique,* house of ill fame, brothel. — *religieuse,* convent, monastery. — *rustique,* farm-house, farm. — *de santé,* private hospital *or* asylum, sanatorium. — *seigneuriale,* manorial house, manor-house, manor; noble mansion, mansion. — *de ville,* town-house. *État de* —, establishment. *Petites —s,* (*obsolete*) madhouse, Bedlam. *A la* —, at home; home; in doors. *Par-dessus les —s,* (*fig.*) beyond all reason *or* measure. *Faire — nette,* to turn out all o.'s servants, to clear the house. *Faire — neuve,* to change all o.'s servants. *Garder la* —, to keep the house, to keep *or* remain at home. *Tenir* —, to keep house, to be a householder [ful

Maisonnée, *s.f.* whole house *or* family, house-

Maisonnette, *s.f.* small house, cottage, lodge

Maïssourien, ne, *adj. s. V.* **Mysorien**

Maistrance, *s.f.* (*nav.*) petty officers

Maître, *s.m., adj.m.* master; owner, proprietor; landlord; ruler; keeper; overseer; director; governor; tutor; teacher; head, chief; high; principal; great; main; large; consummate; (*nav.*) boatswain; (*of lawyers*) Mr.; (*of animals in fables*) squire, master; (*fig.*) match; (*obsolete*) trooper; freeman. — *clerc,* (*of lawyers*) head clerk; managing clerk. *Grand* —, great master; grand master; master-general; lord high steward. *Passé* —, proficient, skilled; dabster. *Petit* —, fop, coxcomb; exquisite, beau. — *d'anglais, de français, de danse, d'écriture* or *&c.,* English, French, dancing, writing *or* &c. master. [*The construction* "maître à danser, à écrire," &c., *is obsolete.*] — *de camp,* (*obsolete*) colonel. — *de chapelle,* precentor, choir-master; capelmaster. — *de conférences,* lecturer, professor. — *d'école,* (petty) schoolmaster. — *d'équipage,* (*nav.*) boatswain. — *d'étude,* usher (in a school). — *de forges,* iron-manufacturer, iron-master. — *homme,* superior man. — *d'hôtel,* hotel-keeper, landlord; house-steward; steward; butler; (*A la — d'hôtel,* prepared with a sauce of melted butter, chopped parsley, &c., pepper, salt, and vinegar). — *Jacques,* Jack of all work, factotum. — *mineur,* captain (*of a mine*); deputy-manager (*of ditto*). — *de pension,* schoolmaster (*with a second-class certificate*). *De —, de main de —, en* —, masterly, in a masterly manner, like a master. *Être le — de,* (*before a verb*) to be free (to), to be at liberty (to). *Tel — tel valet,* like master like man

Maîtresse, *s.f., adj.f.* mistress; owner, proprietress; landlady; ruler, lady; directress; governess; teacher; sweetheart, lady-love; principal, chief, head; high; great; main; large; consummate. *Petite* —, foppish woman; belle. — *d'école,* schoolmistress (of a small school). — *femme,* superior woman, notable woman. — *d'hôtel,* landlady, hotel-keeper. — *de pension,* schoolmistress, lady principal of a school

Maîtrisable, *adj.* to be mastered *or* overcome

Maîtrise, *s.f.* mastery; freedom (*of a trade company*), a freeman's right, privilege; mastership (*of an order of knighthood*); precentorship; precentory; singing-school (*for choristers*)

Maîtriser, *v.a.* to master; to govern; to rule; to domineer over, to lord it over; to overcome, to subdue; to command; to have command over; to control; to manage

Se —, *v.r.* to control *or* &c. oneself; (*of things*) [to be overcome *or* &c.

Majat, *s.m.* cowry (*shell*)

Majesté, *s.f.* majesty. *Sa* —, his *or* her Majesty

Majestueusement, *adv.* majestically

Majestueu-x, se, *adj.* majestic

Majeur, e, *adj.* major, greater; superior, higher; main, principal, chief; important, paramount, great; (*pers.*) of age, of full age; (*mus., cards, eccl.*) major; — *s.m.* middle-finger; (*mus.*) major; (*obsolete*) ancestor, forefather, predecessor; — *s.f.* (*log.*) major. *Force —e,* main force, superior force *or* power; absolute necessity; impossibility

Majolica, Majolique, *s.f.* majolica

Major, *adj.m., s.m.* (*mil.*) major. — *général,* (*obsolete*) brigade-major

Majorat, *s.m.* majorat, entailed estate, entail; birthright, primogeniture, eldership

Majorataire, *adj.* possessed of a "majorat"

Majoration, *s.f.* majoration

Majordomat, *s.m.* majordomoship

Majordome, *s.m.* majordomo, house-steward

Majorité, *s.f.* majority; full age

Majuscule, *adj.* (*of letters*) capital, large; — *s.f.* capital letter, capital

Maki, *s.m.* (*zool.*) maki, lemur

Makis, *s.m. V.* **Mâquis**

Mal, *s.m.* evil; ill; harm; hurt; injury; damage; mischief; misfortune; bad thing, thing to be regretted, pity; disadvantage; discomfort, inconvenience; trouble; difficulty; labour, work; pains; hardship; suffering; pain, ache; sore; disease, illness, distemper, complaint; sickness. — *au* or *de cœur, V.* **Cœur.** — *caduc, haut* —, (*pop.*) falling-sickness, epilepsy. — *d'âne,* (*vet.*) scratches. — *de mer,* sea-sickness. — *d'yeux,* sore eyes. *Chaud* —, burning fever. *En* —, amiss, ill; unfavourably; in a bad sense; for the worse. *Avoir — à,* to have a pain *or* pains in ..., to have the ... ache; to have sore *or* a sore ..., to have bad *or* a bad

... *Faire* —, to ache, to be painful, to pain, to hurt; (*pop.*) to bother, to sicken, to be sickening. *Faire le* —, to do ill *or* evil; to do mischief. *Faire du* —, to do an injury, to be injurious, to injure, to do harm, to harm, to hurt, to be painful, to pain. *Mener* or *conduire à* —, to bring to a bad end. *Tourner à* —, to take a bad turn. *Tourner en* —, to misconstrue, to misinterpret. *Aux grands maux les grands remèdes*, desperate diseases require desperate remedies

Mal, *adv.* ill; badly; bad; evil; wrong; the wrong way; amiss; in bad part; uncomfortable; uncomfortably; badly off; at variance, on bad terms, unfriendly; out of favour, in disgrace; with difficulty; bad-looking, ugly, plain; (*in compounds*) mis... *Plus* —, worse; worst; more uncomfortable, &c. *Aller plus* —, to grow worse; to be worse. *Faire* —, to do badly; to do *or* act wrong; to make a mistake; (*of things*) to look badly, to produce a bad effect. *Ne ... pas* —, *pas* —, not badly *or* &c.; not a little, not a few; a tolerable quantity; rather; rather so

Mal, e, *adj.* (*obsolete*) bad, ill, evil, injurious, hurtful, wrong, amiss; wicked

Malabathrum, *s.m.* malabathrum

‡Malachite, *s.f.* (*min.*) malachite

Malacie, *s.f.* (*med.*) malacia, depraved appetite

Malacolog-ie, -ique, -iste. *V.* page 3, § 1

Malacostéose, *s.f.* (*med.*) malacosteon

Malade, *adj.* ill; sick; unwell; poorly; diseased; bad; sore; sickly; infirm; affected; attacked; smitten; disordered; in bad condition, in a sad condition *or* plight, badly off; — *s.m.f.* invalid; patient; sick man *or* woman *or* boy *or* girl, sick person (*pl.* sick)

Maladie, *s.f.* malady, illness, disease, distemper, disorder, complaint; sickness; infirmity; epidemic; sickliness; morbidness; inveterate habit, bad habit, weakness, foible, passion, mania. — *noire*, hypochondria, dismals, blue devils. *Faire une* —, to have an illness, to be ill

Maladi-f, ve, *adj.* sickly, puny, unhealthy, ailing, infirm, morbid

Maladivement, *adv.* unhealthily, morbidly

Maladiveté, *s.f.* sickliness, unhealthiness, morbidness

Maladrerie, *s.f.* *V.* **Léproserie**

Maladresse, *s.f.* awkwardness, clumsiness, unskilfulness, foolishness, stupidity, maladroitness; awkward thing; impolitic *or* unwise thing; blunder

Maladroit, e, *adj.* awkward, clumsy, unhandy, unskilful, foolish, stupid, bungling, maladroit; impolitic, unwise; — *s.m.f.* ditto person, awkward *or* clumsy *or* &c. fellow, stupid creature

Maladroitement, *adv.* awkwardly, clumsily, unskilfully, foolishly, stupidly, maladroitly; impoliticly, unwisely

Malaga, *s.m.* malaga (*wine, grape*), mountain (*wine*)

Mal-à-gauche, *adj. s.m.f.* (*pop. and jest. for* **Maladroit, e**)

Malagma, *s.m.* (*med.*) malagma, emollient

Malaguette, *s.f.* malaguetta pepper, grains of paradise, Guinea pepper, Guinea grains

Malai, e, Malais, e, *adj. s.* Malay

Malaire, *adj.* (*anat.*) malar. *Os* —, malar bone, cheek-bone

Malaisance, *s.f.* (*obsolete*) straitened circumstances, straits, penury

Malaise, *s.m.* uneasiness, uncomfortableness; weariness; indisposition; embarrassment, straits, straitened circumstances

Malaisé, e, *adj.* difficult; hard; rough; toilsome; troublesome; inconvenient; awkward; uneasy; unsociable; embarrassed, in straitened circumstances, hard up

Malaisément, *adv.* *V.* **Difficilement**

Malaisien, ne, *adj. s.* Malayan, Malay

Malambo, *s.m.* (*pharm.*) malambo bark

Malamoque, *s.m.* (*bird*) quaker bird (*kind of albatross*)

Malandre, *s.f.* (*vet.*) malanders, mallenders, grease; (*carp.*) rotten knot

Malandreu-x, se, *adj.* (*of wood*) having rotten knots, with rotten knots; (*pop.*) sickly, infirm, seedy

Malandrin, *s.m.* robber, ruffian, vagabond, villain

Mal-appris, e, *adj.* ill-bred, underbred, halfbred, ill-mannered, unmannerly; — *s.m.f.* churl, cocktail, ill-mannered *or* vulgar fellow *or* creature

Malaquette, *s.f.* *V.* **Malaguette**

Malaria, *s.f.* malaria

Malart, *s.m.* (*bird*) mallard

Malate, *s.m.* (*chem.*) malate

Malavisé, e, *adj. s.* ill-advised, ill-judged, imprudent, rash, silly; ill-informed; ditto person

Malaxation, *s.f.* malaxation, working up

Malaxer, *v.a.* to malaxate, to work up

Malbâti, e, *adj. s.* ill-shaped, gawky; ditto person, gawky fellow *or* creature

Malborough, Malbrouk, *s.m.* kind of serge; knubbly coals, nut-coals, nuts, slack; (*zool.*) malbrouk, dog-tailed baboon

Mal-bouché, e, *adj.* ill-mouthed

Malchance, *s.f.* *V.* **Malechance**

Malcomplaisant, e, *adj.* unobliging

Malcontent, e, *adj. s.* discontented, dissatisfied, displeased, malcontent. *A la malcontent*, (*of o.'s head of hair*) close-shaved, cut close

Mal-denté, e, *adj.* ill-mouthed

Maldisant, e, *adj. s.* (*old*) *V.* **Médisant**

Maldonne, *s.f.* (*at cards*) misdeal

Maldonner, *v.a.n.* (*at cards*) to misdeal

Mâle, *s.m., adj.m.f.* male; he; cock; buck; ram; jack; tom; man; manly; masculine; strong, vigorous; bold; (*of a ship*) stanch; (*of the sea*) rough

Maléate, *s.m.* (*chem.*) maleate

Malebranch-isme, -iste, (*philos.*) *V.* page 3, § 1

Malechance, *s.f.* (*pop.*) mischance, ill luck

Malédiction, *s.f.* malediction, curse

Maléfice, *s.m.* witchcraft; sorcery; spell

Maléficié, e, *adj.* bewitched; (*fam.*) ill-used, badly hurt, badly off, injured, damaged, afflicted, affected; sickly

Maléfique, *adj.* (*old*) malevolent, malignant

Maléique, *adj.* (*chem.*) maleic

Malemort, *s.f.* (*obsolete*) violent death

Malencontre, *s.f.* mishap, mischance, misfortune, ill luck, untoward accident

Malencontreusement, *adv.* unluckily

Malencontreu-x, se, *adj.* unlucky, untoward

Malentendu, *s.m.* misunderstanding; misconception; mistake, error

Malepeste, *int.* (*old*) plague on it! egad!

Mal-être, *s.m.* uneasiness, uncomfortableness, painful sensation; poverty

Malévole, *adj.* malevolent

Malfaçon, *s.f.* defect, bad work; foul play

Malfaire, *v.n.* to do evil, to do mischief *or* harm, to be mischievous

Malfaisance, *s.f.* evil-doing; mischievousness; mischief

Malfaisant, e, *adj.* mischievous; evil; malicious; malevolent; noxious, injurious, hurtful; unhealthy, unwholesome

Malfait, e, *adj.* ill-made, badly done; ill-shaped, deformed; ill-advised; &c. (*V.* **Mal** *and* **Fait**)

Malfai-teur, trice, *s.m.f.* malefactor; evildoer

Malfamé, e, *adj.* *V.* **Mal** *and* **Famé**

Malformation, *s.f.* malformation

Malgache, *adj. s.m.f.* Malagash, Malagasy, Madecass, Madecassee, Madegassy, of Madagascar, native of Madagascar

Malgracieusement, *adv.* rudely

Malgracieu-x, se, *adj.* rude, uncivil

Malgré, *prep.* in spite of; notwithstanding; with. — *cela*, in spite of that, for all that, nevertheless, yet. — *que*, (*old*) *V.* **Quoique**

Malhabile, *adj.* unskilful, awkward

Malhabilement, *adv.* unskilfully, awkwardly

Malhabileté, *s.f.* unskilfulness, awkwardness

Malherbe, *s.f.* (*bot.*) leadwort; spurge-laurel

Malheur, *s.m.* misfortune; unhappiness; mischance, mishap; ill luck; ill success, unsuccessfulness; adversity; poverty; disgrace; woe; unfortunate thing; calamity; disaster; accident; mischief; pity. *De* —, woeful; evil; unlucky; ill-omened. *Par* —, unfortunately; unhappily; unluckily. *A quelque chose — est bon*, it is an ill wind that blows nobody good

Malheureusement, *adv.* unfortunately; unhappily; unluckily; unsuccessfully; unfavourably; miserably; wretchedly

Malheureu-x, se, *adj.* unfortunate; unhappy; unlucky; unsuccessful; ill-favoured; unfavourable; inauspicious; ominous; disadvantageous; unpleasant, disagreeable; sad; disastrous; fatal; in bad circumstances, badly off; poor; pitiful; paltry; miserable; wretched; naughty; amiss, a bad job; — *s.m.f.* ditto person *or* creature, poor person (*pl.* poor people, poor), poor *or* unfortunate *or* wretched man *or* woman *or* boy *or* girl, wretched creature, poor wretch; wretch; unfortunate; naughty child. — *comme les pierres*, extremely unfortunate *or* miserable

Malhonnête, *adj.* dishonest; uncivil, rude, unmannerly; — *s.m.f.* rude fellow *or* creature, pert minx, saucy baggage [civilly, rudely

Malhonnêtement, *adv.* dishonestly; un-

Malhonnêteté, *s.f.* rudeness, incivility; rude thing, rude words; dishonesty; dishonest action *or* proceeding, knavery

Malice, *s.f.* malice; maliciousness; spite; spitefulness; malignity; archness; mischievousness; mischief; harm; sly thing; trick; dodge; jest, joke. *V.* **Entendre**

Malicieusement, *adv.* maliciously; spitefully; malignantly; mischievously; slily, archly; roguishly

Malicieu-x, se, *adj.* malicious; spiteful; malignant; mischievous; sly, arch; roguish; sharp; (*of horses*) jibbing, trickish, tricky, vicious

Malicore, Malicorium, *s.m.* pomegranate-

Maliforme, *adj.* maliform, apple-shaped [rind

†**Malignement**, *adv.* maliciously; malignantly; slily, archly

†**Malignité**, *s.f.* malignity; malignancy; malice; maliciousness; mischievousness

†**Malin**, *m.*, **Maligne**, *f.*, *adj.* malicious; malignant; mischievous; ill-natured; spiteful; evil; ill; sly, arch; sharp-witted, sharp, cunning, knowing; clever; — *s.m.f.* ditto person *or* creature; — *s.m.* evil spirit, fiend

Malin, *m.*, **Maline**, *f.*, *adj. s.* sly, arch; sharp-witted, sharp, cunning; clever; difficult; ditto person, sharp (*or* clever) fellow *or* woman *or* girl, cunning *or* knowing one; dabster

Maline, *s.f.* (*nav.*) spring tide. *Grande* —, equinoctial ditto

Malinement, *adv.* slily, archly

Malines, *s.f.* Mechlin, Mechlin lace

Malingre, *adj.* sickly, weakly, feeble, puny

Malintentionné, e, *adj. s.* *V.* **Mal** *and* **Intentionné**

Malique, *adj.* (*chem.*) malic

Malitorne, *adj.* gawky, awkward, uncouth, clumsy; — *s.m.f.* awkward booby, gawky person *or* fellow *or* thing, gawky, dowdy

Mal-jugé, *s.m.* (*law*) erroneous *or* illegal judgment *or* sentence *or* decree, error in judgment

Mallard, *s.m.* small grindstone

Malle, *s.f.* trunk; box; pedlar's basket; (*post.*) mail. *Faire sa* — or *ses* —*s*, to pack o.'s things, to pack up. — **-poste**, *s.f.* mail (coach)

Malléabilité, *s.f.* malleability, malleableness

Malléable, *adj.* malleable

Malléation, *s.f.* malleation

Malléer, *v.a.* to malleate

Mallemolle, *s.f.* mull-muslin

Malléolaire, *adj.* (*anat.*) malleolar

Malléole, *s.f.* (*anat.*) malleolus, ankle

Malletier, *s.m.* trunk-maker

Mallette, *s.f.* small trunk, portmanteau; (*obsolete*) bag, scrip; (*bot.*) shepherd's-purse

Mallier, *s.m.* shaft-horse, wheeler; (*old spelling for* "mailler") *V.* **Mailler**, *s.m.*

Malmené, e, *part. adj.* abused, &c. (*V.* **Malmener**); greatly damaged, in a bad *or* sad plight, suffering

Malmener, *v.a.* to abuse, to ill-use, to use ill, to maltreat, to handle roughly, to bully; to cut up

Malope, *s.f.* (*bot.*) malope

Malotru, e, *s.m.f.* vulgar fellow *or* thing, lout, churl, scrub, beggar [devil *or* dog *or* creature

†**Malpeigné, e**, *adj. s.* unkempt; dirty; dirty

Malpighie, *s.f.*, **Malpighier**, *s.m.* (*bot.*) malpighia, Barbadoes cherry

Malplaisant, e, *adj.* (*old*) unpleasant, disagreeable

Malpropre, *adj.* dirty, unclean; slovenly; (*obsolete*) unfit; — *s.m.f.* ditto person, sloven, slattern, slut

Malproprement, *adv.* dirtily; slovenly; badly

Malpropreté, *s.f.* dirtiness, uncleanliness; slovenliness; dirt, filth

Malsain, e, *adj.* unhealthy; sickly; unwholesome; injurious; dangerous; bad, not good

Malséance, *s.f.* unbecomingness, impropriety, unseemliness [unseemly

Malséant, e, *adj.* unbecoming, improper,

Malsonnant, e, *adj.* ill-sounding; offensive

Malt, *s.m.* malt

Maltage, *s.m.* malting

Maltais, e, *adj. s.* Maltese

Malter, *v.a.* to malt

Malteur, *s.m.* maltster, maltman

Malthe, *s.f.* maltha, mineral pitch

Malthusien, ne, *adj. s.* Malthusian

Maltôte, *s.f.* (*obsolete*) exaction, extortion; (obnoxious) tax *or* rate; tax-gathering; tax-gatherers

Maltôtier, *s.m.* (*obsolete*) exactor; tax-gatherer

Maltraité, e, *part. adj.* maltreated, &c. (*V.* **Maltraiter**); ill-favoured; damaged, in a bad *or* sad plight, suffering

Maltraiter, *v.a.* to maltreat, to ill-treat, to ill-use, to use ill, to abuse, to handle roughly; to wrong; to injure; to damage; to cut up; to punish

Malvacé, e, *adj.* (*bot.*) malvaceous; — *s.f.* malvaceous plant; —**es**, *s.f.pl.* malvaceous plants, malvaceæ [malice

†**Malveillance**, *s.f.* malevolence, ill-will,

†**Malveillant, e**, *adj. s.* malevolent, ill-disposed, evil-minded, ill-natured, spiteful; ditto person [embezzlement, fraud

Malversation, *s.f.* malversation, malpractice,

Malverser, *v.n.* to commit malversation *or* malpractices, to embezzle, to defraud

Malvoisie, *s.m.* malmsey (wine) [cut

Malvoulu, e, *adj.* disliked, hated; avoided,

Mamamouchi, *s.m.* (*in Molière*) mamamouchi, thingumbob; (*fig.*) functionary dressed in his little brief authority

Maman, *s.f.* mamma; mother; woman. *Bonne* —, good mamma; grandmamma, granny. *Grand'*—, grandmamma. *Grosse* —, fat woman

Mamapian, *s.m.* (*med.*) master *or* mother yaw

Mame, *pop. for* **Madame**

Mamelière, *s.f.* breastplate

Mamelle, *s.f.* breast; udder; pap; (*in scientific Latin slang*) mamma

Mamelon, *s.m.* nipple, pap, teat, dug; (*fig.*) pap, mamelon; (*of percussion-firearms*) nipple

Mamelonné, e, *adj.* mammillated [lump

Mamelouk, *s.m.* Mameluke

Mamelu, e, *adj.* full-breasted

Mameluk, *s.m.* Mameluke

Mamillaire, *adj.* mammillary

Mamillé, e, *adj.* mammillated

Mammaire, *adj.* mammary

Mammalog-ie, -ique, -iste. *V.* page 3, § 1

Mammée, *s.f.* (*bot.*) mammea, mammee, mammee-apple tree, wild apricot-tree

Mammifère, *adj.* mammiferous, mammalian; — *s.m.* mammal, mammifer; —**s**, *s.m.pl.* mammalia, mammals, mammifers

Mammiforme, *adj.* mammiform
Mammite, *s.f.* (*med.*) mammitis, mastitis
Mammologie, &c. *V.* **Mammalogie**
Mammon, *s.m.* Mammon
Mammouth, *s.m.* (*zool.*) mammoth [spinneret
Mammule, *s.f.* (*bot.*) mammule; (*of spiders*)
Mamours, *s.f.pl.* (*fam.*) fawning, coaxing, wheedling, cajolery, soft things, soft sawder, soft nonsense. *Faire des* —, to fawn upon, to coax, to wheedle, to cajole
Mam'selle, *pop. for* **Mademoiselle**
Man, *s.m.* larva of the cockchafer, grub
Manakin, *s.m.* (*bird*) manakin
Manant, *s.m.* rustic, churl; cad
Manate, *s.m. V.* **Lamantin**
Mancando, *adv.* (*mus.*) mancando
Manc-eau, elle, *adj. s.* of Maine (*in France*);
Mancelle, *s.f.* tug, thill-tug [native of Maine
†**Mancenille,** *s.f.* (*bot.*) manchineel
†**Mancenillier,** *s.m.* (*bot.*) manchineel-tree
Manche, *s.m.* handle; haft; helve; stick; stock; shaft; pole; rod; (*of mus. instr.*) neck; (*of ploughs*) tail; (*butch.*) knuckle-bone. — *à balai*, broomstick. — *de couteau*, knife-handle; (*zool.*) razor-shell, razor-fish. — *à gigot*, (*for carving a leg of mutton*) bone-holder. — *de gigot*, knuckle-bone of a leg of mutton. — *de ligne*, (*obsolete*) fishing-rod
Manche, *s.f.* sleeve; channel; (*nav.*) hose; (*fish.*) bag-net; (*at play, in matches*) game; hit; bout; (*her.*) manch, maunch. — *à* —, — *à*, (*at play*) even. — *à gigot*, leg-of-mutton sleeve. — *à vent*, (*nav.*) wind-sail. — *d'Hippocrate*, felt filtering-bag. *Bout de* —, half-sleeve; cuff. *Avoir dans sa* —, to have at o.'s disposal. *Une autre paire de* —*s*, (*fig.*) quite another thing, another pair of shoes
Mancheron, *s.m.* (*of ploughs*) handle; (*of ladies' dresses*) epaulet, epaulette
Manchette, *s.f.* cuff; wrist-band; ruffle; (*of furniture*) trimming; (*print.*) side-note; (*nav.*) span, bridle; (*fig.*) twist of the wrist
Manchon, *s.m.* muff; (*tech.*) cylinder; collar; (*pop.*) mop, shock (*head of hair*)
Manchot, e, *adj. s.m.f.* one-handed; one-armed; maimed; awkward; ditto person; (*s.m.*) impennate (*bird*). *N'être pas* —, (*fig.*) to be no fool; to be skilful; to be light-fingered
Mancienne, *s.f.* (*bot.*) wayfaring-tree
Mandanes, *s.m.pl.* Mississippi settlers
Mandant, e, *s.m.f.* mandant, mandator, constituent, employer, principal, warrantor
Mandarin, *s.m.* mandarin
Mandarin, e, *adj.* mandarin; — *s.f.* mandarin
Mandarinat, *s.m.* mandarinship [orange
Mandarinier, *s.m.* mandarin-orange tree
Mandarin-ique, -isme. *V.* page 3, § 1
Mandat, *s.m.* mandate; commission; charge; instructions; authority; money-order, order; cheque; warrant; (*law*) power of attorney; (*law*) mandate; warrant. — *impératif*, pledge required by electors. — *d'amener* or *d'arrêt*, warrant (*of apprehension*). — *de comparution*, summons. — *de dépôt*, commitment. — *de* (or *sur*) *la banque*, bank post-bill. — *de perquisition*, search-warrant. — *de poste*, — *sur la poste*, post-office (money) order
Mandataire, *s.m.f.* mandatary, mandatory; proxy; attorney; representative
Mandater, *v.a.* to deliver an order *or* a warrant for the payment of, to deliver an order *or* a warrant for, to order (...) to be paid
Mandati-f, ve, *adj.* mandatory
Mandement, *s.m.* mandamus; mandate; order; summons; call; (*of bishops*) charge
Mander, *v.a.* to inform, to acquaint, to let know; to tell; to write; to write to say; to send; to send word; to send for; to summon; to call; to call for; to order
Se —, *v.r.* to be sent *or* &c.
Mandibulaire, *adj.* mandibular
Mandibule, *s.f.* mandible; jaw
Mandibulé, e, *adj.*, **Mandibulé,** *s.m.* (*zool.*) mandibulate [humble garment
†**Mandille,** *s.f.* (*obsolete*) livery coat; (*fig.*)
Mandoline, *s.f.* (*mus. instr.*) mandoline
Mandore, *s.f.* (*mus. instr.*) mandore
Mandragore, *s.f.* (*bot.*) mandragora, mandrake
Mandrerie, *s.f.* plain basket-work
Mandrill, *s.m.* mandrill, rib-nose baboon
Mandrin, *s.m.* mandrel; (*tech.*) mandrel, chuck, punch, strike, former; (*pers.*) robber, ruffian, Jonathan Wild, Jack Sheppard
Manducation, *s.f.* manducation, eating
Manéage, *s.m.* handiwork, hand-work
Manége, *s.m.* training; horsemanship; riding-school, manege; riding; roundabout; merry-go-round; horse-gear; horse-gin; work; trick; manœuvres, intrigue
Manéger, *v.a.n.* to break in, to train, to manege; (*fig.*) to use, to play, to work
Mânes, *s.m.pl.* (*myth.*) manes, ghost, shade, ghosts, shades
Manet, *s.m.* (*fish.*) trawl-net, trawl, drift-net,
Maneton, *s.m.* lever-handle [drift
Manette, *s.f.* (*tech.*) hand-gear, handle; (*hort.*) trowel, dibbler; (*bot.*) manettia (*plant*)
Mangabey, *s.m.* mangabey (*monkey*)
Manganate, *s.m.* (*chem.*) manganate
Manganèse, *s.m.* (*min.*) manganese
Manganésien, ne, *adj.* manganesian
Manganeux, *adj.m.* (*chem.*) manganous
Manganique, *adj.* (*chem.*) manganic
Mangeable, *adj.* eatable
†**Mangeaille,** *s.f.* food, meat; eatables, eating, stuffing, victuals, grub, creature comforts
Mangeoire, *s.f.* manger, crib
Mangeoter, *v.n.a.* to eat little, to pick, to nibble
Manger, *v.a.n.* to eat; to eat up *or* away; to devour; to consume; to take; to absorb; to corrode; to destroy; to ruin; to run through, to spend, to squander; to lose; to chew; to nibble, to gnaw; to bite; to clip (*o.'s words*); to conceal; to bury; to forget; to load (*with caresses*); to taste, to have a taste (of); to eat o.'s food *or* o.'s meals; to feed; (*slang*) to split (upon), to denounce. *A* —, to eat; something to eat, some food, food, o.'s food, victuals. *Donner à* —, to keep an eating-house; to entertain; (*à*) to feed, to give food, to give something to eat. — *du bout des dents* (or *des lèvres*), to pick a bit here and a bit there, to hardly eat anything, to pick, to nibble. — *son bien*, to squander o.'s estate *or* money. *On mange bien dans ce restaurant*, the cooking is good in that dining-house
Se —, *v.r.* to be eaten *or* eatable; to eat (o.'s ...); to destroy each other; to devour each other; to look daggers at each other; to be spent; (*gram.*) to be cut off, not to be pronounced
Manger, *s.m.* eating, food, victuals; dish; fare
Mangerie, *s.f.* eating; exaction, extortion; law expenses
Mange-tout, *s.m.* prodigal, spendthrift; (*hort.*) skinless peas, sugar peas, wyker peas; French beans
Mangeu-r, se, *s.m.f.* eater, feeder, trencherman *or* woman; prodigal, spendthrift; extortioner. — *de charrettes*, *V.* **Avaleur.** — *de livres*, *V.* **Dévoreur** [feeding (*for wild boars*)
Mangeure, *s.f.* nibbling, gnawing, place eaten;
Mangier, *s.m. V.* **Manguier**
Mangle, *s.f.* (*bot.*) fruit of the mangrove
Manglier, *s.m.* (*bot.*) mangrove, mangle
Mangonneau, *s.m.* mangonel, mangon
Mangostan, Mangoustan, *s.m.* (*bot.*) mangosteen (*tree*) [neumon; (*fruit*) mangosteen
Mangouste, *s.f.* (*quadruped*) mangouste, ich-
Mangue, *s.f.* (*fruit*) mango; (*quadruped*) cross-
Manguier, *s.m.* (*bot.*) mango-tree [archus
Maniable, *adj.* easy to handle *or* work, handy, wieldy, workable; manageable; supple, pliable; tractable; gentle; mild; moderate
Maniacal, e, *adj.* maniacal

Maniage, *s.m.* handling, working
Maniaque, *adj. s.m.f.* maniac; mad, furious; eccentric, crotchety, whimsical, systematic; ditto person
Manichéen, ne, *adj. s.* manichean
Maniché-isme, -iste. *V.* page 3, § 1 [chord
‡Manichordion, *s.m.* (*old mus. instr.*) mani-
Manicle, *s.f.* hand-leather; manacle, handcuff, iron, shackle, fetter, bilbo
Manicome, *s.m.* lunatic asylum
Manicorde, *s.m. V.* **Manichordion**
Manicou, *s.m.* (*zool.*) Virginian opossum
Manie, *s.f.* mania; madness, folly; rage, passion; excessive fondness, fancy; eccentricity, crotchet, whim; hobby; inveterate habit
Maniement, *s.m.* handling; wielding; working; use; management; conduct; handling of money, sums of money passing through o.'s hands; (*of silk*) rustling; (*butch.*) fat part
Manier, *v.a.* to touch, to feel; to handle, to wield; to work; to ply; to use; to manage; to conduct. *Au* —, by the touch; by handling
Se —, *v.r.* to be handled *or* &c.
Manière, *s.f.* manner; way, fashion; style; sort, kind; mannerism; affectation; fuss; grimace; attitude; attitudinizing. — *noire,* (*engr.*) mezzotint. — *d'être,* usual way. — *de parler, de penser, V.* **Façon.** — *de voir,* views, opinions. *A la — de; A sa —; De cette —; D'aucune —; De — à; De — que; De toute —; D'une — ou d'autre; En — de; En aucune —: V.* **Façon**
Maniéré, e, *adj.* affected, unnatural, forced; attitudinizing; — *s.m.f.* affected person, mannerist; — *s.m.* affectation, mannerism [natural
Maniérer, *v.a.* to force, to strain, to make un-
Se —, *v.r.* to become unnatural *or* affected;
Maniérisme, *s.m.* mannerism [to attitudinize
Maniériste, *s.m.f.* mannerist
Manieu-r, se, *s.m.f.* handler; manager
Manifestation, *s.f.* manifestation
Manifeste, *adj.* manifest; — *s.m.* manifesto; (*com. nav.*) manifest
Manifestement, *adv.* manifestly
Manifester, *v.a.* to manifest, to display, to show
Maniforme, *adj.* maniform
Manigance, *s.f.* manœuvre, intrigue, contrivance, underhand dealing [trive
Manigancer, *v.a.* to brew, to concoct, to con-
Se —, *v.r.* to be brewing *or* brewed, to be concocting *or* &c. [mania
Manigraphie, *s.f.* manigraphy, treatise on
Maniguette, *s.f. V.* **Malaguette**
Maniguière, *s.f.* weir and bucks (*for catching*
Manihot, *s.m. V.* **Manioc** [*eels*)
†Manillais, e, *adj. s.* Manillese
†Manille, *s.f.* manille; ring; handle; (*geog.*) Manilla; — *s.m.* manilla (cigar). — *à bout coupé,* manilla cheroot
Maniluve, *s.m. V.* **Manuluve** [mandioc
Manioc, Manioque, *s.m.* (*bot.*) manioc,
Manipulateur, *s.m.* manipulator
Manipulation, *s.f.* manipulation
Manipule, *s.m.* handful; (*pharm., Cath. rel., Rom. antiq.*) maniple [manipulated
Manipuler, *v.a.n.* to manipulate. *Se* —, to be
Manipuleur, *s.m.* meddler, handler, manipulator [craft
Manique, *s.f.* hand-leather; (*fig., pop.*) handi-
Maniquette, *s.f. V.* **Maniguette** [**Manicou**
Manitou, *s.m.* (*Indian*) manitou; (*zool.*) *V.*
Maniveau, *s.m.* punnet; ditto of from five to eight mushrooms
Manivelle, *s.f.* handle, winch, crank; lift; (*print.*) rounce; (*nav.*) whipstaff (*of the helm*); (*pop.*) same thing over again, round, drudgery, old story [*marée,* fish-basket. — *d'enfant,* cradle
Manne, *s.f.* manna; basket, hamper. — *à*
Mannée, *s.f.* basketful, hamperful
Mannequin, *s.m.* manikin; dummy; layfigure; puppet; hamper, basket
Mannequinage, *s.m.* (*arch.*) basket-work
Mannequiné, e, *part. adj.* hampered; stiff, unnatural [strain, to make unnatural
Mannequiner, *v.a.* to hamper; to force, to
Mannet, *s.m.* (*zool.*) jumping hare, jumping rat
Manneton, *s.m. V.* **Maneton** [**Manette**
Mannette, *s.f.* small hamper; (*tech.*) *V.*
Mannite, *s.f.* (*chem.*) mannite
Manœuvre, *s.f.* handiwork, handicraft; work, working; operation; practice; manœuvre; move; management; (*mil.*) manœuvre; exercise, drill, drilling, parade; tactics; (*nav.*) manœuvre; working (*a ship*); seamanship; rigging; rope; — *s.m.* handicraftsman, labourer, workman, journeyman; bricklayer's *or* mason's *or* builder's labourer, hodman; bungler, botcher; hack; (*obsolete*) artful fellow. —*s courantes,* running rigging. —*s dormantes,* standing rigging. —*s de gréement,* rigging. *Grandes —s,* (*mil.*) field-practice. *Travail* or *ouvrage de* —, manual labour; work of time and patience; drudgery
Manœuvrer, *v.a.n.* to work; to manœuvre; to manage; to drill; to work the ship; to steer
Manœuvri-er, ère, *s.m.f.* manœuvrer; tactician; able seaman; — *adj.* manœuvring; well-drilled; skilled; skilled in working a ship
Manoir, *s.m.* manor; manor-house; mansion, abode; domain; dominions [steam-gauge
Manomètre, *s.m.* manometer, pressure-gauge
Manométr-ie, -ique. *V.* page 3, § 1
Manoque, *s.f.* bunch *or* bundle of tobacco, (*nav.*) bundle of line
Manoscope, *s.m.* (*phys.*) manoscope
Manote, *s.f. V.* **Mainotte**
Manouvri-er, ère, *s.m.f.* labourer, day-labourer, journeyman, workman, workwoman
Manquant, e, *part. adj.* failing, missing, wanting, &c. (*V.* **Manquer**); defaulting; absent; — *s.m.f.* defaulter; absent; — *s.m.* deficiency; wantage; (*of casks,* &c.) ullage (*empty space*)
Manque, *s.m.* want; lack; need; shortcoming; failure; fail; defect; miss; (*rid.*) stumble; — *s.f.* (*mil.*) default, missing, absence. — *de,* for want of. — *de touche,* (*at billiards*) miss. *De* —, short, wanting, missing
Manqué, e, *adj.* defective, imperfect; abortive; miscarried; off; a failure; spoilt; lost; to no purpose; missed; would-be. *Affaire —e, coup* —, failure, miss
Manquement, *s.m.* omission; shortcoming; oversight; slip; failure, want; failing; fault; missing; miss; breach
Manquer, *v.n.* to fail; to err; to make a mistake; to miss; to give way; to slip; to escape; to be near *or* on the point of, to nearly ...; to want; to be in want; to have need; to fall short; to be wanting *or* deficient; to be out (of), to be without; to lack; there be a lack *or* an absence *or* a deficiency (of); to be missing *or* absent; to disappoint; to die, to be carried off, to be taken *or* taken away (from); to be disrespectful, to be wanting in respect; to break; to commit a breach (of); to infringe; to disregard; to miss fire; to miscarry; — *v.a.* to miss; to fail in; to spoil; to lose. *La — belle,* to lose a fine opportunity; (*old*) to have a narrow escape, to escape narrowly. *Ils me manquent,* I miss them (*feel their absence*). *Il ne manquait plus que cela,* this crowns all *or* is the finishing stroke; what next now? what a bother now!
Se —, *v.r.* to be missed *or* spoilt *or* lost; to fail, to miscarry; to miss oneself *or* each other; to lose command of oneself; to forget what is due to oneself, to be wanting in self-respect; to forfeit o.'s honour; to be disrespectful to each other [(*French town*)
Mans, *s.m.* (*zool.*) *V.* **Man.** *Le* —, le Mans
Mansarde, *s.f.* attic, garret; roof; top; attic-window, garret-window. *Fenêtre en* —, attic-window, garret-window. *Toit en* —, mansard-roof, curb-roof

Mansardé, e, *adj.* with attics, attic, mansard
Manse, *s.f. V.* **Mense**
Mansion, *s.f.* (*obsolete*) stage, halting-place
Mansuétude, *s.f.* mansuetude, gentleness; forbearance [of Mantes
Mantais, e, *adj. s.* of Mantes, Mantese, native
Mante, *s.f.* mantle; (*insect*) mantis. — *religieuse*, praying mantis
Manteau, *s.m.* cloak; mantle; train; cape; pall; pretext; (*arch.*) mantel; (*of shells*) mantle. — *d'arlequin*, (*theat.*) *V.* **Arlequin.** — *de cheminée*, mantelpiece; chimney-piece. *Rôle à* —, —, (*theat.*) serious character. *Sous le* —, secretly, privately, slily, underhand
Mantelé, e, *adj.* mantled; (*of crows*) hooded
Mantelet, *s.m.* short cloak, little *or* small mantle, mantle; (*of a carriage*) leather curtain; (*of a horse*) pad; (*fort.*) mantlet; (*nav.*) lid, port-lid
Mantelle, *s.f.* (*zool.*) hooded crow
Mantelure, *s.f.* mantling
†**Mantille,** *s.f.* mantilla
Mantonnet, *s.m. V.* **Mentonnet**
Mantouan, e, *adj. s.* Mantuan
Manuel, le, *adj.* manual; portable; from hand to hand; — *s.m.* manual, hand-book, text-book
Manuellement, *adv.* manually; from hand to hand
Manufacture, *s.f.* manufacture, making, make; manufactory; factory, mill, works; workshop; workmen, hands
Manufacturer, *v.a.* to manufacture; to work
Se —, *v.r.* to be manufactured *or* worked
Manufacturi-er, ère, *s.m.f.* manufacturer; — *adj.* manufacturing; manufactural; factory
Manufacturièrement, *adv.* manufacturally
Manuluve, *s.m.* (*med.*) manuluvium, hand-bath
Manumis, e, *adj.* manumitted
Manumission, *s.f.* manumission, enfranchisement
Manus (In-), *s.m.* *Dire son* —, to commit o.'s soul to God
Manuscrit, e, *adj.*, **Manuscrit,** *s.m.* manuscript
Manustupration, *s.f.* masturbation
Manutention, *s.f.* management; care; making; working; bread-making; bake-house, bakery; (*cust.*) opening and examining; (*obsolete*) maintenance, upholding
Manutentionnaire, *s.m.* manager
Manutentionner, *v.a.* to manage; to make, to work; to bake; (*cust.*) to open and examine
Manzanilla, *s.m.* manzanilla (wine)
Maori, *s.m.* Maori
Mappe, *s.f.* (*obsolete*) map
Mappemonde, *s.f.* map of the world
Maque, &c. *V.* **Macque,** &c.
Maquereau, *s.m.* (*in English*) scorch, (*in some doctors' dog-Latin slang*) "ephelis ab igne;" (*fish*) mackerel
Maquer-eau, elle, *s.m.f.* go-between, pander, pimp, procurer, procuress, bawd; brothel-keeper; bully
Maquerellage, *s.m.* pandering, panderism, pimping, procuring
Maquereller, *v.n.a.* to pander, to pimp, to procure; to arrange
Maquette, *s.f.* (*sculp.*) small rough model; (*paint.*) layfigure
Maqui, *s.m.* (*bot.*) maqui
†**Maquignon, ne,** *s.m.f.* horse-jockey; jobber; go-between, agent; procurer, procuress, pander, pimp
†**Maquignonnage,** *s.m.* horse-jockeying; bishoping; jobbing, jobbery; panderism, procuring; cheating
†**Maquignonner,** *v.a.n.* to bishop; to make up; to get up; to job; to procure; to arrange; to cheat; to carry on the trade of a horse-jockey
Se —, *v.r.* to be bishoped *or* &c.
†**Maquillage,** *s.m.* painting o.'s face, painting, rouging, ruddling, making-up, make-up
†**Maquillée,** *s.f.* painted *or* made-up woman
†**Maquiller,** *v.a.* to paint the face of, to rouge, to ruddle, to make up
Se —, *v.r.* to paint o.'s face, to paint, to put on rouge, to rouge, to ruddle, to make up
†**Maquilleur,** *s.m.* mackerel-boat
†**Maquilleuse,** *s.f.* face-painter, enameller
Mâquis, *s.m.* (*in Corsica*) maquis, thicket, heath
Marabou, *s.m.* (*zool.*) *V.* **Marabout**
Marabout, *s.m.* (*Arabian*) marabout, marabut; ditto mosque *or* chapel; big-bellied coffee-pot *or* kettle, biggin; ugly fellow; (*zool.*) marabou-stork, marabou, adjutant; marabou-feather; kind of ribbon
Maraîch-er, ère, *s.m.f. adj.* market-gardener; of market-gardens; of market-gardeners. *Jardin* —, market-garden. *Jardinier* —, market-gardener
Maraîchin, *s.m.* marsh-bred ox *or* bullock
Marais, *s.m.* marsh, swamp, fen, bog, moor, morass; market-garden; Marais (*part of Paris, inhabited chiefly by retired tradesmen and old fogies*). — *salant*, salt-marsh. *Chasse au* —, moor-shooting
Maranta, *s.m.* (*bot.*) maranta
Marasca, Marasque, *s.m.* marasca cherry
Marasme, *s.m.* (*med.*) decline, consumption, (*in obsolete English*) marasmus
Marasquin, *s.m.* maraschino
Marâtre, *s.f.* step-mother; (*fig.*) cruel *or* barbarous mother
Maratte. *V.* **Mahratte**
Maraud, *s.m.* knave, rascal
Maraudage, *s.m.* marauding
†**Maraudaille,** *s.f.* knaves, rascals, rabble
Maraude, *s.f.* marauding; knave, rascal; (*cabmen's slang*) plying for hire, crawling
Marauder, *v.n.* to maraud; (*cabmen's slang*) to ply for hire, to crawl; — *v.a.* to plunder
Maraudeur, *s.m.* marauder; (*slang*) cabman plying for hire, crawler
Maravédis, *s.m.* maravedi (*small Spanish coin*)
Marbre, *s.m.* marble; marble slab, slab; marble work; marble statue; marbling; imposing-table, imposing-stone; (*nav.*) barrel. *Sur le* —, (*fig.*) in type, about to be printed
Marbrer, *v.a.* to marble; to vein; to mottle; to beat black and blue
Se —, *v.r.* to become marbled *or* &c.
Marbrerie, *s.f.* marble cutting; marble-mill, marble-yard; marble-work *or* works; marble
Marbreur, *s.m.* marbler
Marbrier, *s.m.* marble-cutter, marble-mason; marble-worker; marble-polisher; marble-merchant; marble-grainer, grainer; — *adj.m.* of marble, marble
Marbrière, *s.f.* marble-quarry; — *adj.f.* of marble, marble
Marbrure, *s.f.* marbling; marble-graining, graining; (*on the skin*) blue marks, black and blue marks, marks of blows, weals
Marc, *s.m.* (*old Fr. weight*) marc (*eight ounces, or half a pound*); residuum, murk, marc, grounds, grout, grouts, grains, skins, husks, rape, refuse. *Au — le franc*, (*obsolescent*) so much in the pound. *Au — la livre*, (*obsolete*) so much in the pound
Marcairerie, Marcairie, *s.f.* (*local*) paddock
Marcassin, *s.m.* young wild boar; little pig; (*her.*) grice, marcassin
Marcassite, *s.f.* (*min.*) marcasite
Marcation, *s.f.* (*obsolete*) demarcation
Marcato, *adv.* (*mus.*) marcato
Marceau, *s.m. V.* **Marsault**
Marceline, *s.f.* marceline (*stuff, and mineral*)
Marcescence, *s.f.* marcescence
Marcescent, e, *adj.* marcescent
Marcescible, *adj.* marcescible
Marchage, *s.m.* treading; pressing
Marchais, *s.m.* shotten herring
Marchand, e, *s.m.f.* dealer, seller; tradesman; trader; shopkeeper; hawker; pedlar; (*of wood, coals,* &c.) merchant; (*obsolete*) customer, purchaser; (*at auctions*) bidder. — *de* ..., ...-dealer, dealer in ...; ...-seller; ...-man; ...-woman; ...-monger; ...-fancier; ...-merchant. — *bonnetier*, — *épicier*, — *drapier*, — *libraire*, &c., hosier, grocer, woollen-draper, bookseller, &c. — *de toiles*, linen-draper. — *tailleur*, clothier, merchant tailor.

— *d'habits*, second-hand clothier, old-clothes-man. — *de vin*, wine-shop keeper, wine and spirit dealer, publican. — *de soupe*, paltry schoolmaster. *En être le mauvais* —, to have a bad bargain of it, to get nothing by the bargain, to be the worse for it, to suffer for it

Marchand, e, *adj.* merchantable; salable; marketable; trading; commercial; mercantile; trade; tradesmanlike; fit for business; navigable. *Marine —e*, mercantile navy, merchant-service. *Prix* —, trade *or* wholesale price. *Vaisseau* or *navire* or *bâtiment* —, merchant-

Marchandage, *s.m.* job-contract [ship *or* man

†**Marchandailler,** *v.n.* to higgle and haggle

†**Marchandailleu-r,se,** *s.m.f.* higgler, haggler

Marchander, *v.a.n.* to ask the price of; to cheapen; to bargain for; to contract for; to beat down; to spare; to grudge; to trouble; to threaten; to bargain, to haggle, to chaffer; to hesitate, to boggle; to mince the matter

Se —, *v.r.* to be cheapened *or* &c.; to spare each other [boggler; job-contractor

Marchandeu-r,se, *s.m.f.* cheapener; haggler;

Marchandise, *s.f.* merchandise, goods, wares, ware, commodity; article; stock-in-trade; trade, traffic; traders

Marchantie, *s.f.* (*bot.*) marchantia

Marche, *s.f.* walk; walking; march; marching; procession; ride; sailing; motion; movement; move; journey; progress; course; way; conduct; arrangement; step; stair; treadle; (*of organs*) pedal-board; (*hunt.*) trail; (*geog.*) marches, march. *Fermer la* —, to close the procession; to bring up the rear; to walk last, to be behind. *Ouvrir la* —, to walk *or* march first *or* foremost, to lead the way, to be in front

Marché, *s.m.* market; market-place; mart; emporium; fair; price; rate; marketing; bargain; purchase; sale; agreement; treaty; (*obsolete*) condition, state, plight, case. — *au poisson*, &c., fish-market, &c. — *d'or*, great *or* capital bargain. *A bon* —, cheap, cheaply. *Bon* —, good bargain; cheapness; cheap. *Cours du* —, market-price. *Meilleur* —, *à meilleur* —, cheaper. *Par-dessus le* —, into the bargain, to boot, besides. *Aller* or *courir sur le* — *de*, to outbid; to tread in ...'s steps, to walk in ...'s shoes. *Avoir bon* — *de*, to outdo *or* manage easily, to easily get over *or* bring down. *Faire bon* — *de*, to hold cheap, to think little of, to make free with, not to spare. *Mettre le* — *à la main*, to offer to break off the bargain; to press (*one*) to decide, to press, to urge, to deal authoritatively with [chef")

Marchef, *s.m.* (*abbrev. of* "maréchal des logis

Marche-palier, *s.f.* landing-step

Marchepied, *s.m.* foot-board; foot-stool; foot-step; step; stepping-stone; foot-path; towing-path; (*of boats*) stretcher; (*nav.*) horse, foot-rope

Marcher, *v.n.* to walk; to tread; to step; to travel; to march; to trudge; to wade; to ride; to drive; to sail; to proceed; to get *or* move on; to advance; to progress; to go; to go on; to come; to come on; to flow, to run; to rank; to be; to act; to behave; — *v.a.* to tread; to press. *Faire* —, to get along; to set going; to march; to place; to humbug, to bamboozle

Marcher, *s.m.* walking; walk; gait; step; pace; treading

Marchette, *s.f.* trap-stick, treadle

Marcheu-r, se, *s.m.f.* walker; pedestrian; treader; (*nav.*) sailer; (*bon* —, —,) good sailer, fast *or* swift *or* fine sailer, fast-going ship *or* boat, fast ship *or* boat; — *s.f.* street-walker, procuress, touter; (*theat.*) figurante; — *adj.* walking; (*nav.*) fast, swift

Marcolières, *s.f.pl.* snares for sea-fowl

Marcottage, *s.m.* (*hort.*) layering

Marcotte, *s.f.* (*hort.*) layer

Marcotter, *v.a.* (*hort.*) to layer

Mardelle, *s.f.* *V.* **Margelle**

Mardi, *s.m.* Tuesday. — *gras*, Shrove Tuesday

Mare, *s.f.* duck-pond, pond; pool; puddle; trough [*voyage*)

Maréage, *s.m.* hire *or* pay (*of a sailor for a*

Marécage, *s.m.* marsh, swamp, fen, bog, moor, morass [swampy, fenny, boggy, moorish, moor

Marécageu-x, se, *adj.* marshy, marsh,

Maréchal, *s.m.* farrier, shoeing-smith; marshal, field-marshal; lord high steward. — *ferrant*, farrier, shoeing-smith. — *de camp*, (*obsolete*) brigadier-general, brigadier. — *de France*, field-marshal. — *des logis*, (*of cavalry*) quartermaster, sergeant. — *des logis chef*, (*of cavalry*) sergeant-major

Maréchalat, *s.m.* marshalship

Maréchale, *s.f.* marshal's wife; caking coal; — *adj.f.* farrier's. *Forge* —, shoeing-forge, farrier's *or* blacksmith's shop, smithery, smithy

Maréchalerie, *s.f.* farriery

Maréchaussée, *s.f.* (*old*) marshalsea; constabulary, mounted police. *Prévôt de la* —, chief constable

Marée, *s.f.* tide, water; sea-fish; (*pop.*) flush, swash, flood, pool. *De* —, (*adject.*) tidal; (*of smell*) fishy. *Grande* —, — *de vive eau*, spring tide. *Haute* —, high tide *or* water *or* flood; spring tide. *Pleine* —, high tide *or* water. *Prendre la* —, to take advantage of the tide

Marégraphe, *s.m.* marigraph, tide-gauge

Marelle, *s.f.* (*game*) hopscotch

Maremmatique, *adj.* maremmatic, malarious

Maremme, *s.f.* maremma

Marène, *s.f.* (*fish*) marena

Marengo, *s.f.* (*cook.*) marengo (*dressing of poultry with mushrooms and olive oil*); *A la* —, dressed ditto; — *s.m.* Oxford grey (*colour*)

Maréographe, Maréomètre, *s. m.* *V.* **Marégraphe**

Mareyeur, *s.m.* fish-salesman, fish-factor

Marfil, *s.m.* *V.* **Morfil**

Margaja, *s.m.* (*obsolete*) *V.* **Calepin**

Margarate, *s.m.* (*chem.*) margarate

Margarine, *s.f.* (*chem.*) margarine

Margarique, *adj.* (*chem.*) margaric

Margaritacé, e, *adj.* margaritaceous; —**es,** *s.f.pl.* margaritaceæ

Margaritate, *s.m.* (*chem.*) margaritate

Margarite, *s.f.* pearl-oyster; (*min.*) margarite

Margaritifère, *adj.* margaritiferous

Margaritique, *adj.* (*chem.*) margaritic

Margarone, *s.f.* (*chem.*) margarone

Margauder, *v.a.* to disparage, to cry down, to traduce, to vilify

Margaux, *s.m.* margaux (*claret wine*)

Margay, *s.m.* margay, tiger-cat

Marge, *s.f.* margin; (*fig.*) time; room [brim

Margelle, *s.f.* kerb-stone, curb-stone, kerb, curb,

Marger, *v.n.a.* to set a margin, to margin

Marginal, e, *adj.* marginal

Marginé, e, *part. adj.* margined; marginated

Marginelle, *s.f.* (*mollusc*) cowry

Marginer, *v.a.* to margin

Margot, *s.m.* (*bird*) gannet; — *s.f.* magpie, mag; chatterbox, gossip; wench

Margotin, *s.m.* small fagot; horse-hair line

Margoton, *s.f.* chatterbox, gossip; wench

Margotter, *v.n.* (*of quails*) to call [thimble

†**Margouillet,** *s.m.* (*nav.*) bull's-eye, wooden

†**Margouillis,** *s.m.* puddle, slush; slop, slip-slop; mess; scrape, lurch [whistle

Margoulette, *s.f.* (*fam.*) mouth, mug, jaw,

Margousier, *s.m.* (*bot.*) margosa-tree, bead-tree, pride of India

Margrave, *s.m.* margrave; — *s.f.* margravine

Margravial, e, *adj.* margravial

Margraviat, *s.m.* margraviate

Margravine, *s.f.* margravine

Marguerite, *s.f.* daisy; (*nav.*) messenger; (*obsolete*) pearl; —**s,** *pl.* daisies, &c.; (*of old horses*) white hairs of the temples; (*pers., pop.*) white hairs of the gills

†**Marguillerie,** *s.f.* churchwardenship

†**Marguillier,** *s.m.* churchwarden

Mari, *s.m.* husband. *Femme en puissance de* —, (*law*) feme-covert, woman under coverture *or* under the control of her husband

Mariable, *adj.* marriageable

Mariage, *s.m.* marriage; matrimony; wedlock; wedding; match; union; joining; marriage-portion, fortune; a game at cards (*also called* "brisque"). — *de convenance* or *de raison*, prudent match. — *d'inclination*, love-match. — *d'intérêt*, interested match

Marie, *s.f.* Mary. — **-bon-bec,** *s.f.* gossip, chatterbox. — **-graillon,** *s.f. V.* **Graillon.** — **-salope,** *s.f.* wench, bitch, harlot; slattern, slut, drab, mopsey; (*nav.*) mud-lighter

Marié, *s.m.* bridegroom; married man. *Nouveau* —, bridegroom. *Nouveaux* —*s*, (*pl.*) new-married (*or* newly married) couple [—, bride

Mariée, *s.f.* bride; married woman. *Nouvelle*

Marier, *v.a.*, **Se** —, *v.r.* to marry; to match; to wed; to get married; to unite; to join; to ally; to blend; to twine; to go together

Mariette, *s.f.* (*bot.*) mariet, Canterbury bell

Marieu-r, se, *s.m.f.* match-maker; (*obsolete*) *V.* **Épouseu-r, se** [pool

Marigot, *s.m.* (*in Western Africa*, &c.) marigot;

Marin, e, *adj.* marine; sea; seafaring; sea-going; seaworthy

Marin, *s.m.* sailor, mariner, seaman, seafaring-man, navigator. — *d'eau douce*, freshwater sailor, landlubber [souse

Marinade, *s.f.* marinade, pickled meat, pickle,

Marinage, *s.m.* curing; sousing; pickling

Marine, *s.f.* navigation; navy; marine; sea-affairs; smell *or* taste of the sea; (*paint.*) sea-piece. *De* —, *de la* —, naval; of the navy, navy; marine; sea. *Soldats* or *troupes de la* —, *infanterie de* —, marines. — *militaire*, — *de l'État*, military marine, vessels of war, navy, royal navy

Mariné, e, *part. adj.* cured, soused, pickled; spoilt *or* damaged by the sea; (*her.*) marined, bearing a fish-tail [jerk

Mariner, *v.a.* to cure; to souse; to pickle; to

Maringouin, *s.m.* mosquito

Marinier, *s.m.* mariner, seaman; bargeman, boatman, waterman. *Maître* —, barge-master. *Officiers* —*s*, petty officers. *A la marinière*, (*cook.*) prepared in "marinière" fashion

Mariolâtre, *s.m.f.* mariolater; — *adj.* mario-

Mariolâtrie, *s.f.* mariolatry [latrous

Marionnette, *s.f.* puppet, marionette; —**s,** *pl.* puppet-show, marionettes

Marisque, *s.f.* large tasteless fig; (*med.*) marisca; — *s.m.* (*bot.*) sedge

Marital, e, *adj.* marital, of the *or* of a husband

Maritalement, *adv.* maritally, like *or* as a husband; like man and wife, like husband and wife

Maritime, *adj.* maritime; naval; nautical; sea

Maritorne, *s.f.* coarse ill-shaped woman, dowdy, slattern, slut, drab, mopsey; scullery-maid *or* servant of all work (*at an inn*)

Marivaudage, *s.m.* writing in the style of Marivaux, excessive refinement, sentimentalism, affected style, mannerism

Marivauder, *v.n.* to imitate the style of Marivaux, to fall into "marivaudage"

Marjolaine, *s.f.* (*bot.*) sweet marjoram

Marjolet, *s.m.* (*obsolete*) coxcomb, fop, jacka-

Markab, *s.m.* (*astr.*) Markab [napes; beau

Marle, &c. *V.* **Marne,** &c. [der; rim

Marli, *s.m.* catgut, Scotch gauze; thread, bor-

Marlite, *s.f.* (*min.*) marlite

Marlou, *s.m.* (*pop.*) bully

†**Marmaille,** *s.f.* brats, lot of brats

Marmatite, *s.f.* (*min.*) marmatite

Marmelade, *s.f.* marmalade; jelly. *En* —, (*fig.*) in a jelly. *Mettre en* —, (*fig.*) to beat to a jelly; to smash

Marmenteau, *adj.m.* (*of trees*) reserved; ornamental; — *s.m.* reserved timber-tree; ornamental tree

Marmite, *s.f.* pot, boiler, kettle, copper; saucepan, pan; digester; potful, kettleful. — *à vapeur*, (*cook.*) steamer. *Nez en pied de* —, pug-nose [pitiful, seedy

Marmiteu-x, se, *adj.* (*pop.*) poor, wretched,

Marmiton, *s.m.* scullion, kitchen drudge

Marmolier, *s.m.* (*bot.*) marmalade-box

Marmolite, *s.f.* (*min.*) marmolite

Marmonner, *v.a.n. V.* **Marmotter**

Marmoréen, ne, *adj.* marmorean, marble, marble-like; cold as marble

Marmoriforme, *adj.* marmoriform

Marmorisation, *s.f.* marmorization

Marmoriser, *v.a.*, **Se** —, *v.r.* to marmorize

Marmose, *s.m.* (*zool.*) marmose, yapock opossum, yapock

Marmot, *s.m.* puppet, grotesque figure; brat, chit; (*obsolete*) ape, monkey. *Croquer le* —, to dance attendance, to wait

Marmottage, Marmottement, *s.m.* muttering, mumbling; grumbling

Marmotterie, *s.f. V.* **Marmottage**

Marmotte, *s.f.* (*zool.*) marmot; (*abusively*) *V.* **Marmose;** (*little girl*) brat, chit; (*fam.*) handkerchief (over the head), kerchief, head-wrapper, wrapper; postman's box; (*in bagmen's slang*) sample-case *or* box; (*nav.*) match-tub; (*bot.*) kind of plum. *Huile de* —, kind of plum-kernel oil. *Dormir comme une* —, to sleep like a dormouse [grumble

Marmotter, *v.a.n.* to mutter, to mumble; to

Marmotteu-r, se, *s.m.f.* mutterer, mumbler; grumbler; — *adj.* muttering, mumbling; grumbling [of plum-tree

Marmottier, *s.m.* (*pop.*) Savoyard; (*bot.*) kind

Marmouset, *s.m.* grotesque figure, antic; ugly little fellow, little monkey; runt; urchin; prig, puppy, fribble; andiron, firedog

Marnage, *s.m.* manuring with marl, marling

Marnais, *s.m.* flat-bottomed boat on the river Marne, Marne barge

Marne, *s.f.* marl, clay, chalk

Marner, *v.a.* (*agr.*) to marl, to clay, to chalk; — *v.n.* (*of the tide*) to run above high-water

Marneron, *s.m.* marl-digger [mark

Marneur, *s.m.* marl-manurer; (*in Normandy*)

Marneu-x, se, *adj.* marly [marl-digger

Marnière, *s.f.* marl-pit

Marocain, e, *adj. s.* of Morocco, Morocco, Moroccan, native of Morocco

Marolles, *s.m.* Marolles cheese

Maronage, *s.m.* right on timber-trees

Maronite, *adj. s.m.f.* Maronite

Maronner, *v.n.a.* to grumble, to murmur, to croak, to mutter, to mumble; to be vexed, to fret. *Faire* —, to make (*one*) grumble; to keep waiting a long time; to tease, to vex, to bother, to plague

Maroquin, *s.m.* morocco-leather, morocco; roan; (*nav.*) guy-rope. *Papier* —, morocco-paper

Maroquinage, *s.m.* dressing in imitation of mo-

Maroquiner, *v.a.* to dress morocco-like [rocco

Maroquinerie, *s.f.* morocco-leather manufacture *or* trade *or* factory *or* articles

Maroquinier, *s.m.* morocco-dresser

Marotique, *adj.* Marotic, in the style of the poet Clément Marot, quaint [to write quaintly

Marotiser, *v.n.* to imitate the style of Marot,

Marotisme, *s.m.* imitation of the style of Marot, Marotic style, quaint style, quaintness

Marotiste, *s.m.f.* imitator of the style of Marot, quaint writer [hobby, fancy, folly, whim

Marotte, *s.f.* fool's bauble, cap and bells;

Marouflage, *s.m.* (*paint.*, *tech.*) lining

Maroufle, *s.m.* blackguard, rascal, scoundrel, caitiff, churl, low *or* vulgar fellow; — *s.f.* paste, lining-paste

Maroufler, *v.a.* (*paint.*, *tech.*) to line, to paste

Maroute, *s.f. V.* **Marute**

Marquant, e, *adj.* marking; remarkable; conspicuous; striking; of note, considerable; — *s.f.* marking card

Marque, *s.f.* mark; token; testimony; sign; proof; brand; pit; score; notch; spot; marker; marque; impression; stamp; note, distinction; badge; (*pl.*) insignia; (*obsolete*) ticket. *Lettres de* —, letters of marque

Marqué, e, *part. adj.* marked, &c. (*V.* **Marquer**); conspicuous, evident, obvious; remarkable; distinct; particular; decided; prominent; great; strong; resolute; elderly. — *à l'A,* — *au B, See* **A** *and* **B**

Marquer, *v.a.* to mark; to mark out; to trace out; to note down; to score, to score up; to imprint; to stamp; to brand; to define; to show; to point out; to indicate; to denote; to bear the stamp of; to testify; to signify; to acquaint; to inform; to tell; to mention; to express; to describe; to announce; to appoint; to fix; to decree; to doom; to single out; — *v.n.* to appear, to show; to be evident *or* obvious; to be conspicuous, to occupy a prominent place; to be of note *or* of distinction; to be remarked; to set off; to be striking *or* remarkable *or* particular; to be marked; to play a conspicuous part; to create a sensation; to show the hour; (*of horses*) to mark

Se —, *v.r.* to mark *or* &c. oneself; to be marked *or* &c. [to checker; to tesselate

Marqueter, *v.a.* to speckle, to spot; to inlay;

Marqueterie, *s.f.* marquetry, inlaid-work; checker-work; inlaying; tesselation; patchwork. *De* —, inlaid; tesselated

Marqueteur, *s.m.* inlayer

Marquette, *s.f.* cake of bees' wax

Marqueu-r, se, *s.m.f.* marker; scorer

Marquis, *s.m.* marquis, marquess

Marquisat, *s.m.* marquisate

Marquise, *s.f.* marchioness; marquee; veranda, verandah; awning; jointed-handle parasol; settee; waist-buckle

Marquoir, *s.m.* bodkin; sampler

Marraine, *s.f.* godmother, sponsor; introducer

Marre, *s.f.* large spade; mattock; hoe

Marrer, *v.a.* to dig; to hoe

Marri, e, *adj.* (*old*) sorry, grieved; sorrowful

Marron, *s.m.* (*large*) chestnut; chestnut-colour, maroon; round curl (*of hair*); cracker, maroon; unlicensed broker *or* printer; work printed clandestinely; (*mil.*) mark; — *adj.* chestnut-coloured, chestnut, maroon; (*of brokers, printers,* &c.) unlicensed. — *d'eau,* water-chestnut. — *d'Inde,* horse-chestnut

Marron, ne, *adj.* (*of slaves*) runaway, fugitive; (*of animals*) that has run wild, wild; — *s.m.f.* runaway *or* fugitive slave, maroon

Marronnage, *s.m.* running away; state of a runaway slave; carrying on the business of a broker *or* of a printer without a licence

Marronner, *v.a.* to do (*hair*) in round curls; to print clandestinely; — *v.n.a.* to grumble, to murmur, to croak, to mutter, to mumble; to be vexed, to fret; to carry on the business of a broker *or* of a printer without a licence. *Faire* —, to make (*one*) grumble; to keep waiting a long time; to tease, to vex, to bother, to plague

Marronnier, *s.m.* chestnut-tree; chestnut-wood, chestnut. — *d'Inde,* horse-chestnut-tree

Marrube, *s.m.* (*bot.*) horehound. — *aquatique,* water-horehound, gypsywort

Mars, *s.m.* March, the month of March; (*poet.*) spring; (*agr.*) spring corn; (*myth., astr.*) Mars; (*poet.*) war; warrior; (*old chem.*) Mars, iron; (*butterfly*) purple emperor. *Bière de* —, beer

Marsage, *s.m.* spring sowing [brewed in March

Marsala, *s.m.* marsala (wine)

Marsault, Marseau, *s.m.* (*bot.*) great round-leaved sallow. *Petit* —, round-eared sallow

†**Marseillais, e,** *adj. s.* of Marseilles, Marseillese, native of Marseilles; — *s.f.* marseillaise (*French national anthem*); Marseillese fashion; short pipe, cutty-pipe, cutty

†**Marseille,** *s.f.* Marseilles (*French town*)

Marsette, *s.f. V.* **Fléole**

Marsilée, *s.f.* (*bot.*) marsilea

Marsouin, *s.m.* porpoise, sea-hog; ugly fellow

Marsupial, e, *adj.*, **Marsupial,** *s.m.* marsupial [lily

Martagon, *s.m.* (*bot.*) martagon, Turk's cap

Marte, *s.f. V.* **Martre**

Marteau, *s.m.* hammer; (*of doors*) knocker, rapper; (*anat.*) malleus, hammer; (*fish*) hammer-fish, hammer-headed shark, hammer-head; (*mollusc*) malleus, hammer-oyster, hammer-shell. *Perruque à trois* —*x,* wig with a long curl between two knots

Martel, *s.m.* uneasiness, care, trouble; (*obsolete*) hammer. *Avoir* — *en tête,* to be very uneasy. *Se mettre* — *en tête,* to make oneself very uneasy, to be very uneasy, to fret oneself, to fret [ing, blazing

Martelage, *s.m.* hammering; (*of trees*) mark-

Marteler, *v.a.* to hammer; to mark, to blaze (*trees*); to labour; to strain; to puzzle, to worry, to plague

Martelet, *s.m.* hammer; (*bird*) black swift

Marteleur, *s.m.* hammerer, hammerman

Marteline, *s.f.* pick, small hammer

Martial, e, *adj.* martial, warlike; (*old chem.*) martial, ferruginous, chalybeate, iron, steel

Martialité, *s.f.* martialness

Martin, *s.m.* Martin; Jack (*ass*); tame bear; (*bird*) pastor. *La Saint-* —, Martinmas. — **-pêcheur,** *s.m.* (*bird*) kingfisher. — **-sec,** *s.m.,* — **-sire,** *s.m.,* — **-sucré,** *s.m.* (various kinds

Martiner, *v.a.* to tilt, to hammer [of pears)

Martinet, *s.m.* tilt-hammer; cat-o'-nine-tails; flat candlestick; (*nav.*) martnet, halyard; (*bird*) martin, swift; (*her.*) martlet

Martineur, *s.m.* (*tech.*) tilter [double or quits

Martingale, *s.f.* (*rid., nav.*) martingale; (*play*)

Martre, *s.f.* marten. — *zibeline,* sable

Martyr, e, *s.m.f.* martyr. *V.* **Commun,** *s.m.*

Martyre, *s.m.* martyrdom

Martyriser, *v.a.* to make (*one*) suffer martyrdom, to make a martyr of, to martyr, to martyrize, to torture, to torment

Martyrologe, *s.m.* martyrology

Martyrologiste, *s.m.f.* martyrologist

Marum, *s.m.* (*bot.*) cat-thyme

Marute, *s.f.* (*bot.*) stinking camomile

Maryland, *s.m.* Maryland tobacco

Mas, *s.m.* (*local*) cottage, villa

†**Mascagnin,** *s.m.* (*min.*) mascagnin [song

Mascarade, *s.f.* masquerade; mask; mask-

Mascaret, *s.m.* eddy of water; (*of harbours*) bar

†**Mascarille,** *s.m.* a delicious kind of mushroom; (*obsolete*) flunkey

Mascaron, *s.m.* (*arch.*) mask

Masculiflore, *adj.* (*bot.*) male-flowered

Masculin, e, *adj.* masculine; male; manly; — *s.m.* (*gram.*) masculine gender, masculine

Masculinement, *adv.* masculinely

Masculiniser, *v.a.* to make masculine

Se —, *v.r.* to be made masculine

Masculinité, *s.f.* masculineness, masculinity

Masourka, Masourque, *s.f. V.* **Masurka**

Masque, *s.m.* mask; masque; masker, masquerader; face-guard; face; phiz; head; cast; disguise; pretence; ugly mug; — *s.f.* hussy, monkey, imp, ugly mug

Masquer, *v.a.* to mask; to disguise; to cloak; to cover; to hide, to conceal, to shade

Se —, *v.r.* to mask, to put on a (*or* o.'s) mask; to disguise *or* &c. oneself; (*of things*) to be disguised *or* &c.

Massacrant, e, *adj.* killing; cross, peevish, surly, dreadful, tormenting, disagreeable

Massacre, *s.m.* massacre, slaughter, carnage, butchery; murder; havoc; waste; squandering; spoiling; bungling, botching; hacking, mangling; bungler, botcher; (*hunt.*) head of the stag newly killed, stag's head; (*her.*) head

Massacrer, *v.a.* to massacre; to slaughter; to slay; to kill; to butcher; to murder; to

half-kill; to smash; to destroy; to waste; to squander; to spoil; to bungle, to botch; to hack, to mangle
Massacreur, *s.m.* slaughterer, slayer; murderer; waster; squanderer; smasher; spoiler; bungler, botcher; hacker, mangler
Massage, *s.m.* shampooing
Massalia, *s.f.* (*astr.*) Massalia
Masse, *s.f.* mass; heap; lump; lot; bulk; stock; stoppages; sum of earnings, earnings; fund; mace; butt-end, butt; body; whole; estate; (heron-)plume; (*tech.*) sledge-hammer. — *d'armes*, mace. *En* —, in a mass; in a body; bodily; at large; a lot
Massement, *s.m.* massing; shampooing
Massepain, *s.m.* almond cake, marchpane
Masser, *v.a.* to mass; to shampoo [muscle
Masséter, *s.m.* (*anat.*) masseter, masseter
Massétérin, e, *adj.* (*anat.*) masseterine, masseteric
Massette, *s.f.* (*bot.*) reed-mace, cat's-tail
Masseur, *s.m.* shampooer
Massicot, *s.m.* (*chem.*) massicot
Massier, *s.m.* mace-bearer, macer
Massi-f, ve, *adj.* massive; massy; bulky; solid; heavy; dull, stupid; — *s.m.* solid mass, block; group, clump, cluster; thickset grove, thicket; (*build.*) wall, backing, pier, solid mass, masonry work; (*carp.*) dead-wood
Massilien, ne, *adj. s.* (*old*) *V.* **Marseillais**
Massivement, *adv.* massively; solidly; heavily; stupidly, dully
Massiveté, *s.f.* massiveness
Massorah, Massore, *s.f.* massorah, masora
Massorète, *s.m.* massorite, masorite
Massorétique, *adj.* massoretic, masoretic
Massue, *s.f.* club; heavy weapon, crowbar
Mastic, *s.m.* mastic; putty; cement; wax; (*print.*) transposition [puttying
Masticage, *s.m.* cementing, cementation;
Mastica-teur, trice, *adj.* masticating, masticatory
Mastication, *s.f.* mastication, chewing
Masticatoire, *adj.m.f., s.m.* masticatory
Masticine, *s.f.* (*chem.*) masticine [ing-bit
Mastigadour, *s.m.* (*vet.*) masticador, slaver-
Mastiquer, *v.a.* to cement; to putty; — *v.n.a.* (*fam.*) to masticate, to chew, to eat, to feed, to grub
Mastiqueu-r, se, *adj.* cementing; puttying
Mastite, *s.f.* (*min.*) mastite; (*med.*) mastitis
Mastoc, *s.m.* (*fam.*) lubber; — *adj.* massive, heavy, lumpish, lubberly
Mastodonte, *s.m.* (*zool.*) mastodon
Mastodynie, *s.f.* (*med.*) mastodynia
Mastoïde, *adj.* (*anat.*) mastoid [mastoideal
Mastoïdien, ne, *adj.* (*anat.*) mastoidean,
Masturbation, *s.f.* masturbation
Masturber, *v.a.* to pollute
Masure, *s.f.* ruinous habitation *or* house, ruins; tumble-down hovel, ramshackle hut
Masurka, *s.f.* mazurka (*dance, tune*)
Mat, e, *adj.* heavy; sodden; dead, dull; flat, insipid; (*at chess*) checkmated
Mat, *s.m.* deadening; deadness, dulness; dead *or* dull colour; dead part (*of a metal*); (*at chess*) mate, checkmate. *Faire* —, to mate, to checkmate
Mât, *s.m.* mast, pole, staff. — *de fortune*, jury-mast. — *de pavillon*, ensign *or* flag-staff. *A —s et à cordes*, ahull; under bare poles
Mata, *s.m.* (*print.*) clicker; overseer; (*fig.*) bigwig, nob, snob [wig, don
Matador, *s.m.* matador, matadore; (*fig.*) big-
Mâtage, *s.m.* (*nav.*) masting
Matamata, *s.f.* matamata (*kind of tortoise*)
Matamore, *s.m.* bully
Matasse, *s.f.* *Soie en* —, raw silk
Matassin, *s.m.* matachin (*old dance, dancer*); buffoon; queer fellow, odd fish, guy
Matassinade, *s.f.* matachin (*old dance*) [**Mat**
Mate, *s.f.* Alsatia, den of thieves; — *adj.f. V.*
Maté, *s.m.* (*bot.*) maté, Paraguay tea
Mateau, *s.m.* *V.* **Matteau**
Matelas, *s.m.* mattress; squab; cushion; pad; wadding. — *à air*, air-bed. — *à eau*, water-bed
Matelasser, *v.a.* to trim, to line (with cushions or squabs); to stuff, to pad; to quilt; to cover with a mattress; to surround with mattresses; to coat [coach-trimmer
Matelassi-er, ère, *s.m.f.* mattress-maker;
Matelassure, *s.f.* lining; padding; wadding; coating
Matelot, *s.m.* sailor; seaman; consort ship; chum, comrade, mate; sailor's dress *or* suit; frock and trowsers
Matelotage, *s.m.* seamanship; sailor's pay
Matelote, *s.f.* sailors' dance; (*cook.*) matelote, stew of fishes, fish-stew, stew. *A la* —, seaman-like. *Sauce —, sauce à la* —, wine *or* cider-sauce
Mater, *v.a.* to subdue; to humble; to mortify, to deaden; to thicken, to make heavy; (*at chess*) to checkmate
Mâter, *v.a.* (*nav.*) to mast; to set up
Matérat, *s.m.* (*bird*) long-tailed titmouse [staff
Mâtereau, *s.m.* (*nav.*) small mast, spar, pole,
Matérialiser, *v.a.* to materialize
Matérialisme, *s.m.* materialism [terialistic
Matérialiste, *s.m.f.* materialist; — *adj.* ma-
Matérialité, *s.f.* materiality
Matériaux, *s.m.pl.* materials
Matériel, le, *adj.* material; corporeal; coarse, rough, rude; lumpish, heavy; thick; dull, stupid; — *s.m.* material part, substance; stock, working-stock, plant; implements; apparatus; furniture; fittings; equipage; articles; stores
Matériellement, *adv.* materially; corporeally; coarsely, roughly, grossly
Maternel, le, *adj.* maternal; motherly; of a *or* of o.'s mother, mother's; on the mother's side; (*of o.'s tongue*) mother, native; (*of land*) native
Maternellement, *adv.* maternally, motherly
Maternité, *s.f.* maternity; motherhood; lying-
Mateur, *s.m.* (*tech.*) deadener [in hospital
Mâteur, *s.m.* mast-maker
Mathématicien, ne, *s.m.f.* mathematician
Mathémat-ique (*adj.*), **-iquement.** *V.* page
Mathématiques, *s.f.pl.* mathematics [3, § 1
Mathiole, *s.f.* *V.* **Matthiole**
Mathurin, *s.m.* Mathurin
Maticine, *s.f.* (*chem.*) maticine
Matico, *s.m.* (*bot.*) matico
Matière, *s.f.* matter; material; substance; stuff; fluid; subject; cause, reason, grounds, motive; occasion; theme; contents. — *brute*, raw material; inorganic substance. — *médicale*, materia medica. — *première*, matter; (*com.*) raw material. —*s d'or et d'argent*, bullion. — *à procès* or *à poursuites*, grounds for a lawsuit *or* for an action, case. *En — de*, in matters of, in point of, in
Matin, *s.m.* morning; forenoon; prime; dawn; — *adv.* (*old*) early in the morning, early. *De grand* or *bon* —, very early. *Le* —, the morning, &c.; in *or* on the morning. *Un beau* —, some fine day. *Un de ces quatre —s*, one of these days
Mâtin, *s.m.* mastiff; mongrel dog; fellow, dog, buck; rascal, cur, confounded fellow. — *!* by Jove! — *de*, wretched, beastly, cursed, confounded [of the morning, morning
Matinal, e, *adj.* early, up early, rising early;
Matinalement, *adv.* early in the morning, early
Mâtine, *s.f.* female mastiff; bold woman, bitch, wench, hussy, creature, thing; confounded ditto. — *de*, wretched, beastly, cursed, confounded
Mâtiné, e, *part. adj.* lined, &c. (*V.* **Mâtiner**);
Mâtineau, *s.m.* little mastiff [mongrel
Matinée, *s.f.* morning; forenoon; morning's occupation; morning's work *or* gain; morn-

ing performance *or* recital *or* lecture; morning meeting. *Dormir la grasse* —, to sleep till late in the day, to lie late in bed (of a morning)
Mâtiner, *v.a.* to cur, to line, to cover; to disparage; to rate, to abuse, to snub, to bully
Matines, *s.f.pl.* (*Cath. rel.*) matins
Matineu-x, se, *adj. s.* early, rising early, up early; early riser
Matini-er, ère, *adj.* of the morning, morning
Matir, *v.a.* (*tech.*) to deaden
Matité, *s.f.* heaviness; deadness, dulness; flatness; deadness *or* dulness of sound; dead *or* dull sound
Matoir, *s.m.* deadening-tool; riveting-hammer
Matois, e, *adj.* cunning, sharp, sly; — *s.m.f.* cunning *or* sly person *or* fellow *or* thing, sly blade, sly dog, sly puss; fellow, blade, dog, puss
Matoisement, *adv.* cunningly, slily
Matoiserie, *s.f.* cunning, sliness; cheat, trick
Maton, *s.m.* clotted milk [buck; (*pers.*) monkey
Matou, *s.m.* tom-cat, tom; (*pers.*) tom, ram,
Matras, *s.m.* (*chem.*) matrass, bolthead; (*old*) square-headed arrow, quarrel [mile, feverfew
Matricaire, *s.f.* (*bot.*) matricaria, wild camo-
Matrice, *s.f.* matrice, matrix; womb; original register; standard weight *or* measure; — *adj.f.* mother, primitive, first, principal; unmixed
Matricide, (*murder*) *s.m.*, (*pers.*) *s.m.f.* matricide; — *adj.* matricidal [tricular
Matriculaire, *s.m.* matriculate; — *adj.* ma-
Matricule, *s.f.* matricula, matriculation-book; register; matriculation; certificate of matriculation
Matrimonial, e, *adj.* matrimonial, conjugal
Matrimonialement, *adv.* matrimonially
Matronal, e, *adj.* matronal
Matrone, *s.f.* matron; midwife; (*fam.*) bawd
Matte, *s.f.* (*metal.*) matte, regulus; (*nav.*) weedy shallow; —**s,** *pl.* clotted milk, curds
Matteau, *s.m.* hank of raw silk
Matter, *v.a.* (*tech.*) to deaden
Matthiole, *s.f.* (*bot.*) stock, stock gillyflower. — *blanchâtre*, wall-flower
Mattoir, *s.m.* *V.* **Matoir**
Matton, *s.m.* paving-brick; oil-cake; knot
Maturati-f, ve, *adj.*, **Maturatif,** *s.m.* matu-
Maturation, *s.f.* maturation, ripening [rative
Mâture, *s.f.* (*nav.*) masts; spars; wood for masts; masting; mast-store, mast-yard, mast-shed; sheer-hulk, sheers
Maturité, *s.f.* maturity, ripeness; completion; consideration. *Avec* —, maturely, with con-
Matutinaire, *s.m.* matins-book [sideration
Matutinal, e, *adj.* matutinal
Maubèche, *s.f.* (*bird*) knot [abandon
Maudire, *v.a.* to curse, to accurse; to rue; to
Maudissable, *adj.* cursable, execrable, detest-
Maudisson, *s.m.* (*old*) curse, malediction [able
Maudit, e, *adj.* cursed; accursed; outcast; confounded, blasted; horrible; wretched; bad; execrable, abominable, detestable. — *soit ...!* cursed be ...! confound ...!
Mauge, Maugère, *s.f.* (*nav.*) cow-hide, scup-
Maugrabin, e, *adj. s.* Maugrabin [per-hose
Maugrebleu, *int.* (*obsolete*) *V.* **Sacrebleu**
Maugréer, *v.n.* to swear, to curse and swear; to fret and fume; to grumble; — *v.a.* to curse
Maugréeu-r, se, *s.m.f.* curser, swearer
Maund, *s.m.* maund (*Indian weight*)
Maure, Mauresque, Mauricaud, *V.* **More, Moresque, Moricaud**
Mauret, *s.m.*, **Maurette,** *s.f.* *V.* **Airelle**
Mausolée, *s.m.* mausoleum
Maussade, *adj.* sulky, sullen, cross, disagreeable; awkward, clumsy; dull; insipid
Maussadement, *adv.* sulkily, sullenly, disagreeably [agreeableness
Maussaderie, *s.f.* sulkiness, sullenness, dis-
Mauvais, e, *adj. adv.* bad; ill; mis...; evil; ill-natured; mischievous; wicked; naughty; nasty; foul; injurious; wrong; amiss; unpleasant; unfavourable, contrary, adverse, against one; unlucky; paltry; — *s.m.* bad, that which is bad; — *s.m.f.* bad person, bad fellow *or* creature *or* thing, naughty ditto, rogue. *Plus* —, worse; worst. *Faire* —, to be bad weather
Mauvaisement, *adv.* badly; ill-naturedly; mischievously; wickedly; naughtily; foully; injuriously; wrongly; unfavourably; unluckily
Mauve, *s.f.* (*bot.*) mallow, mallows; (*zool.*) gull, sea-mew; — *s.m.* mauve colour, mauve; — *adj.* mauve-coloured, mauve
Mauvette, *s.f.* round-leaved geranium
Mauviette, *s.f.* (common) lark, field-lark, skylark; (*pers.*) delicate *or* thin person, lath, poor stick; (*pop.*) ribbon (*order of knighthood*). *Manger comme une* —, to eat very little
Mauvis, *s.m.* (*bird*) redwing
Maux, *pl. of* **Mal,** *s.m.*
Maxillaire, *adj.* (*anat.*) maxillary. *Os* —, maxillary bone, jaw-bone
Maxillé, e, *adj.* dented, denticulated
Maxilliforme, *adj.* maxilliform
Maxillo, (*in compounds, anat.*) maxillo-...
Maxima, *s.m.pl.* maxima
Maxime, *s.f.* maxim
Maximer, *v.a.* to maximize
Maximum, *s.m.* maximum; height
Mayençais, e, *adj. s.* of Mayence *or* Mentz; native of ditto
Mayeux, *s.m.*(*jest.*) Punch, hunchback, monkey
Mayonnaise, *s.f.* (*cook.*) mayonnaise (*sauce, dish*) [coffee in a glass
Mazagran, *s.m.* cold coffee with Seltzer-water;
Mazar, *s.m.* (*local*) grub [Mazarin, Mazarinist
Mazarin, Mazariniste, *s.m.* (*Fr. hist.*)
Mazarinade, *s.f.* (*Fr. hist.*) Mazarinade
Mazarinisme, *s.m.* (*Fr. hist.*) Mazarinism
Mazaro, *s.m.* (*soldiers' slang*) quod
Mazéage, *s.m.* refining, refinery (*of iron*)
Mazer, *v.a.* to refine (*iron*)
Mazerie, *s.f.* refinery (*of iron*)
Mazet, *s.m.* (*local*) cottage, villa
Mazette, *s.f.* tit, little tit (*horse*); runt; milksop, poor stick; novice, bad player, bad shot; raw recruit [*V.* **Masurka**
Mazourka, Mazourque, Mazurka, *s.f.*
Mazzinien, ne, *adj. s.* Mazzinian
Me, M', *pron.pers.* me; to *or* at me; for *or* with *or* in *or* from *or* by *or* on *or* against me; myself; to *or* &c. myself
Meâ culpâ, *s.m.* (*Latin*) meâ culpâ. *Crier* —, *dire* or *faire son* —, to cry peccavi
Méandre, *s.m.* meander, winding
Méandrine, *s.f.* meandrina, brainstone coral
Méandrique, *adj.* meandrian
Méat, *s.m.* (*anat.*) meatus, passage
Mécanicien, *s.m.* mechanician, mechanist; mechanic; engine-builder; engineer, engineman; machinist; — *adj.* mechanical; manufacturing. *Serrurier* —, manufacturing locksmith, lock-maker
Mécanique, *adj.* mechanical, mechanic; machine-made; machine; — *s.f.* mechanics; machinery; mechanism; machine; (*of carriages*) break, brake. *A la* —, *fait à la* —, by machinery, machine-made, made by machinery; by power-loom, made by power-loom
Mécaniquement, *adv.* mechanically
Mécaniser, *v.a.* to mechanize; to make a machine of; (*pop.*) to chaff, to rile, to bother
Mécanisme, *s.m.* mechanism; works; structure; mechanical part
Mécénat, *s.m.* protection, patronage
Mécène, *s.m.* Mæcenas; protector, patron (*of sciences, literature, and arts*)
Méchamment, *adv.* wickedly; maliciously; unkindly; mischievously; ill-naturedly; spitefully; waywardly; naughtily; cruelly
Méchanceté, *s.f.* wickedness; badness; perversity; wicked action; maliciousness, malice; unkindness; unkind act *or* thing; mischievousness; ill nature; spitefulness, spite; ill-

natured remark, reflection, slander; naughtiness; naughty thing; roguish trick; cruelty

Méchant, e, *adj.* (*either alone or after a noun, sometimes before a noun*) wicked; bad; evil; perverse; malicious; unkind; mischievous; ill-natured; bad-tempered; spiteful; vicious; wayward; naughty; cruel; fierce, savage; severe; rough; hurtful, harmful, injurious; unfavourable; (*never after a noun*) wretched, paltry, sorry, scrubby, worthless, poor; troublesome, unpleasant; — *s.m.f.* wicked *or* &c. man *or* person; evil-doer; naughty boy *or* girl. *Un cheval* —, a vicious horse. *Un — cheval*, a sorry horse. *Faire le* —, to bully; to swagger; to bluster; to resist, to kick; to be obstreperous *or* naughty

Mèche, *s.f.* wick; tinder; touch-paper; match; (*of hair*) lock; (*of whips*) lash; (*of wimbles, &c.*) screw; bit; auger; (*surg.*) tent; (*fig.*) secret, plot; (*pop.*) way, means, possibility, chance. — *anglaise*, centre-bit. *Découvrir* or *éventer la* —, (*mil.*) to discover the enemy's match; (*fig.*) to discover the secret *or* the plot. *Vendre la* —, (*pop. for* "éventer la —"). *Il n'y a pas* —, (*pop.*) there is no doing it, it is no use, it is no go. *Et — !* (*pop.*) and something more at the end!

Méchef, *s.m.* (*old*) mischief, harm

Mécher, *v.a.* to smoke (*a cask*) with brimstone, to match, to stum

Mécheu-x, se, *adj.* wicky

Méchoacan, *s.m.* (*bot.*) mechoacan, white jalap

Mecklembourgeois, e, Mecklenbourgeois, e, *adj. s.* of Mecklenburg; Mecklenburger

Mécomètre, *s.m.* (*med.*) mecometer

Mécompte, *s.m.* miscalculation, misreckoning, mistake, error, falling short; disappointment, drawback

Mécompter, *v.n.* (*of clocks*) to strike wrong

Se —, *v.r.* to miscalculate, to misreckon, to be mistaken, to make mistakes *or* a mistake; to be disappointed

Méconate, *s.m.* (*chem.*) meconate

Mécone, Méconine, *s.f.* (*chem.*) meconine

Méconique, *adj.* (*chem.*) meconic

Méconium, *s.m.* (*med., &c.*) meconium

Méconnaissable, *adj.* unrecognizable, not to be recognized

Méconnaissance, *s.f.* unthankfulness, ingratitude; forgetfulness; disregard; blindness

Méconnaissant, e, *adj.* unthankful, ungrateful; regardless, unmindful; forgetful; blind

Méconnaître, *v.a.* not to recognize, not to know again; to fail to recognize; not to acknowledge; to disown; to disregard; to slight; not to notice; to ignore; not to appreciate; not to be thankful for; to forget

Méconnu, e, *part. adj.* unrecognized, disowned, &c. (*V.* **Méconnaître**); unacknowledged; unknown; unappreciated; unheeded; unrequited

†Méconseiller, *v.a.* to misadvise

Mécontent, e, *adj. s.* dissatisfied, discontented; displeased; malcontent. *Faire des —s*, to create discontent

Mécontentement, *s.m.* discontent, dissatisfaction; displeasure; vexation; disaffection

Mécontenter, *v.a.* to discontent, to dissatisfy; to displease; to vex; to disaffect

Se —, *v.r.* to be discontented *or* &c.; to discontent *or* &c. each other

Mécréance, *s.f.* (*old*) misbelief, disbelief

Mécréant, e, *adj.* misbelieving, unbelieving, incredulous, infidel; — *s.m.f.* miscreant, unbeliever, infidel

Mécroire, *v.a.n.* (*old*) to misbelieve, to disbelieve

†Médaille, *s.f.* medal; medalet; medallion; (*of porters, &c.*) badge; licence. — *d'honneur*, medal of honour; prize-medal. — *de Judas*, (*bot.*) *V.* **Lunaire.** *Tourner la* —, to turn the tables. *La — est renversée* or *retournée*, the tables are turned

†Médaillé, e, *part. adj.* with a medal, rewarded (with a medal), prize; (*of porters, &c.*) with a badge, licensed, ticket; — *s.m.f.* medallist; badger; prizeman, prize-taker, prize-holder, prize-exhibitor

†Médailler, *v.a.* to give a medal to, to reward with a medal; to badge, to license (*porters, &c.*); — *s.m. V.* **Médaillier**

†Médailleur, *s.m.* die-sinker [medals

†Médaillier, *s.m.* cabinet *or* collection of medals

†Médailliste, *s.m.f.* medallist, antiquary

†Médaillon, *s.m.* medallion; locket

Médecin, *s.m.* medical man; physician; surgeon and general practitioner; doctor; (*admin.*) medical officer; (*fig.*) healer, curer. — *consultant*, physician. — *d'eau douce*, water-gruel doctor. *De —, des —s*, of a medical man, &c., of medical men, &c.; medical

Médecine, *s.f.* medicine, physic; remedy; draught; pill; bore, nuisance; medicine, medical science; medical men, doctors; Faculty. — *légale*, medical jurisprudence, forensic medicine. — *noire*, black draught. — *opératoire*, operative surgery. *De* —, of medicine, medical

Médeciner, *v.a.* to doctor, to physic

Mèdes, *s.m.pl.* (*hist.*) Medes, Medians

Médiaire, *adj.* middle, intermediate

Médial, e, *adj.*, **Médiale,** *s.f.* medial

Médialement, *adv.* medially

Médian, e, *adj.* middle, median, mesial

Médianoche, *s.m.* (*obsolete*) midnight-supper

Médiante, *s.f.* (*mus.*) mediant

Médiastin, *s.m.* (*anat.*) mediastinum; — *m.*, —**e,** *f., adj.* mediastine

Médiastinite, *s.f.* (*med.*) mediastinitis

Médiat, e, *adj.* mediate

Médiatement, *adv.* mediately, by means

Média-teur, trice, *s.m.f.* mediator; mediatress; — *adj.* mediating; mediatory, mediatorial, of mediation

Médiation, *s.f.* mediation

Médiatisation, *s.f.* mediatization

Médiatiser, *v.a.* to mediatize

Médical, e, *adj.* medical

Médicament, *s.m.* medicament, medicine; (*fig.*) bore, nuisance

Médicamentaire, *adj.* medicamental

Médicamentation, *s.f.* administering medicines, doctoring, physicking

Médicamenter, *v.a.* to medicate; to administer medicines to, to doctor, to physic

Médicamenteu-x, se, *adj.* medicinal; medicated

Médicastre, *s.m.* medicaster, quack

Médica-teur, trice, *adj.* healing

Médication, *s.f.* medication, mode *or* method of treatment, treatment

Médicinal, e, *adj.* medicinal; medicated

Médicinalement, *adv.* medicinally

Médicinier, *s.m.* (*bot.*) jatropha, physic-nut

Médico-, (*in compounds*) medico-...

Médiévisme, *s.m.* mediævalism

Médiéviste, *s.m.* mediævalist

Médin, *s.m.* medin (*Turkish coin*)

Médio, (*in compounds*) medio-...

Médiocre, *adj.* mediocre; middling; moderate; commonplace; ordinary; indifferent; poor; — *s.m.* mediocrity

Médiocrement, *adv.* moderately; but little, not much; indifferently; so so; a small amount *or* quantity

Médiocrité, *s.f.* mediocrity; small competency; very ordinary man *or* thing *or* work *or* performance

Médionner, *v.a.* (*tech.*) to average

Médique, *adj.* (*hist.*) Median

Médire, *v.n.* to speak ill; to slander; to backbite

Médisance, *s.f.* evil-speaking, slander, scandal, backbiting; piece of scandal; slanderers, scandal-mongers

Médisant, e, *adj. s.* slanderous, scandalous; slanderer

Méditati-f, ve, *adj.* meditative; thoughtful, pensive; — *s.m.f.* ditto person

Méditation, *s.f.* meditation

Méditativement, *adv.* meditatively

Méditer, *v.a.n.* to meditate; to consider; to reflect; to think; to contemplate; to project; to plan

Se —, *v.r.* to be meditated *or* &c.

Méditerrané, e, *adj.* mediterranean, midland, inland; — *s.f.* Mediterranean sea, Mediterranean [midland, inland
Méditerranéen, ne, *adj.* mediterranean,
Médium, *s.m.* medium; middle
Médius, *s.m.* (*anat.*) medius, middle finger
Medjidieh, *s.m.* medjidie (*Turkish order*)
Médoc, *s.m.* medoc (wine); Medoc pebble
Médonne, Médonner, *V.* **Maldonne,** &c.
Médullaire, *adj.* medullary
Médulle, *s.f.* (*bot.*) medulla
Médulleu-x, se, *adj.* (*bot.*) medullous
Médulline, *s.f.* (*chem.*) medulline
Médullite, *s.f.* (*med.*) medullitis
Méduse, *s.f.* (*myth.*) Medusa; (*zool.*) medusa, jelly-fish, sea-blubber, sea-nettle
Méduser, *v.a.* to horrify, to stupefy, to petrify
Meeting, *s.m* meeting (*political*) [wrong
Méfaire, *v.n.* (*old*) to do evil, to do harm, to do
Méfait, *s.m.* misdeed, evil doing, crime [caution
Méfiance, *s.f.* mistrust; distrust; suspicion;
Méfiant, e, *adj.* mistrustful; distrustful; suspicious; cautious; — *s.m.f.* ditto person
Méfier (Se), *v.r.* to mistrust; to distrust; to suspect; to be suspicious *or* cautious; to beware; to mind; to look out; to be on o.'s guard
Mégacéphale, *adj.* megacephalous [(against)
Mégachile, *s.f.* (*zool.*) megachile, mason-bee, leaf-cutter
Mégalésien, ne, *adj* (*Rom. antiq.*) Megalesian
Mégalithique, *adj.* megalithic [losaurus
Mégalosaure, Mégalosaurus, *s.m.* mega-
Mégalote, *s.m.* *V.* **Fennec**
Mégamètre, *s.m.* (*astr.*) megameter
Mégapode, *s.m.* (*bird*) megapode, jungle-fowl
Mégarde, *s.f.* *Par* —, by mistake, from *or* through inadvertence, inadvertently, unawares
Mégarien, ne, Mégarique, *adj.* Megarian,
Mégascope, *s.m.* megascope [Megaric
Mégathère, Mégathérium, *s.m.* (*zool.*) megatherium
Mége, *s.m.* (*local*) quack doctor, quack
Mégère, *s.f* (*myth.*) Megæra; (*fig.*) termagant, shrew, vixen, Turk
Mégie, *s.f.* leather-dressing, tawing
Mégir, Mégisser, *v.a.* to taw (*leather*) [tawery
Mégisserie, *s.f.* leather-dressing, tawing;
Mégissier, *s.m.* leather-dresser, tawer
Meige, *s.m.* *V.* **Mége**
†**Meilleur, e,** *adj.* (*comp. of* **Bon**) better; preferable; more comfortable; best; — *s.m.* best; best stuff; best part. *Le — n'en vaut rien,* bad
Méionite, *s.f.* (*min.*) meionite [is the best
Meistre, *s.m.* *Arbre de* —, (*nav.*) main mast (*of*
Méjuger, *v.a.n.* to misjudge [*a galley*)
Mélac, *s.m.* Peruvian tin
Mélæna, *s.m.* *V.* **Méléna**
Mélaïne, *s.f.* melaine
Mélam, *s.m.* (*chem.*) melam
Mélambo, *s.m.* *V.* **Malambo**
Mélamine, *s.f.* (*chem.*) melamine
Mélampyre, *s.m.* (*bot.*) cow-wheat
Mélampyrine, *s.f.* (*chem.*) melampyrine [tive
Mélanagogue, *adj.m.f., s.m.* (*obsolete*) purga-
Mélancolie, *s.f.* melancholy; sadness; (*med.*) melancholia, melancholy
Mélancolique, *adj.* melancholy, melancholic; gloomy, dismal, sad, dull; stern; — *s.m.f.* melancholiac
Mélancoliquement, *adv.* melancholily, with melancholy; gloomily, sadly; sorrowfully; mournfully
Mélandre, Mélandrin, *s.m.* (*fish*) sargus
Mélané, e, *adj.* (*nat. hist.*) black; (*med.*) melanic
Mélanémie, *s.f.* (*med.*) melanæmia
Mélanésien, ne, *adj. s.* Melanesian
Mélange, *s.m.* mixture; mixing; mingling; medley; miscellany; mash; alloy; crossing; **—s,** *pl.* mixtures, &c.; miscellanies, miscellany, miscellaneous works *or* pieces; collection; appendix. *Sans* —, without mixture *or* alloy, unmixed, unalloyed, pure; unblended

Mélanger, *v.a.,* **Se** —, *v.r.* to mix; to intermix; to mingle; to mash; to blend; to temper; to cross; to be mixed *or* &c.
Mélanie, *s.f.* (*mollusc*) melania [ian
Mélanien, ne, *adj.,* **Mélanien,** *s.m.* melan-
Mélanine, *s.f.* melanine
Mélanique, *adj.* melanic
Mélanisme, *s.m.* melanism
Mélanite, *s.f.* (*min.*) melanite
Mélanose, *s.f.* (*med.*) melanosis
Mélanotique, *adj.* (*med.*) melanotic
Mélanthérite, *s.f.* (*min.*) melanterite
Mélasictère, *s.m.* (*med.*) black jaundice
Mélasme, *s.m.* (*med.*) melasma
Mélasse, *s.f.* molasses, melasses, treacle
Mélassique, *adj.* (*chem.*) melassic
Mélastome, *s.m.* (*bot.*) melastoma
‡**Melchior,** *s.m.* (*old spelling*) *V.* **Maillechort**
Mélé, e, *part. adj.* mixed, &c. (*V.* **Méler**); miscellaneous; medley; (*of verses*) irregular, doggrel; (*of rhymes*) mixed
Mêlé, *s.m.* mixed stuff; mixed article
Mêlée, *s.f.* confused fight, close fight, hand-to-hand fight; thick of the fight; fight; conflict; affray; scuffle; (*fig.*) squabble, contest, dispute
Méléguette, *s.f.* *V.* **Malaguette**
Méléna, *s.m.* (*med.*) melæna
Mêler, *v.a.* to mix; to mingle; to shuffle; to mash; to blend; to intersperse; to join, to add; to put in; to temper; to involve, to implicate, to concern, to bring in, to mix up; to cross; to entangle; (*of locks*) to force, to spoil
Se —, *v.r.* to mix, to be mixed; to mingle, to be mingled; to blend, to be blended; to be tempered *or* &c.; to become entangled *or* &c.; to interfere (with, in); to meddle, to intermeddle (with); to mind; to concern oneself; to take part (in); to have something to do (with); to join; to dabble (in); to take (to); to take upon oneself; to presume; to undertake; to engage (in); to set (to); to set oneself to do; to try [herring; sprat
Melet, *s.m.*, **Melette,** *s.f.* Vancouver Island
Mélèze, *s.m.* larch, larch-tree
Mélianthe, *s.m.* (*bot.*) honey-flower
Mélicéris, *s.m.* (*med.*) meliceris
Mélie, *s.f.* (*bot.*) melia, bead-tree
Mélilot, *s.m.* (*bot.*) melilot, honey-lotus
Méli-mêlo, *s.m.* (*pop.*) mishmash, wishwash, slipslop, hotchpotch, jumble
Mélinet, *s.m.* (*bot.*) honeywort [sucker
Méliphage, *s.f.* (*bird*) honey-eater, honey-
Mélique, *s.f.* (*bot.*) melic grass
Mélisse, *s.f.* (*bot.*) balm-mint, balm
Mellate, *s.m.* (*chem.*) mellate
Mellifère, *adj.* melliferous; — *s.m.* ditto **insect**
Mellification, *s.f.* mellification
Mellifique, *adj.* mellific
Melliflu, e, *adj.* mellifluous, honeyed, sweet,
Mellique, *adj.* (*chem.*) mellic [soft
Mellitate, *s.m.* (*chem.*) mellitate [honey-syrup
Mellite, *s.f.* (*min.*) mellite, honey-stone; (*pharm.*)
Mellitique, *adj.* (*chem.*) mellitic
Mellivore, *adj.* mellivorous
Mélocacte, *s.m.* (*bot.*) melocactus, melon-thistle, Turk's-cap, Turk's-head [ness
Mélodie, *s.f.* melody; melodiousness; sweet-
Mélodieusement, *adv.* melodiously, musically, sweetly
Mélodieu-x, se, *adj.* melodious, musical [§ 1
Mélod-ique, -iquement, -iste. *V.* page 3,
Mélodium, *s.m.* (*mus. instr.*) melodeon [§ 1
Mélodramat-ique, -iquement. *V.* page 3,
Mélodramaturge, *s.m.* melodramatist
Mélodrame, *s.m.* melodrama
Méloé, *s.m.* (*zool.*) meloe, oil-beetle, May-beetle
Mélograph-ie, -ique, &c. *V.* page 3, § 1
Mélomane, *s.m.f. adj.* melomaniac
Mélomanie, *s.f.* melomania
Melon, *s.m.* melon; jockey-cap, hunting-cap; simpleton, flat, muff; novice; freshman
Meloné, e, *adj.* melon-shaped

Mélongène, Mélongène, *s.f. V.* **Aubergine**
Melonite, *s.f.* (*min.*) melonite
Melonnée, *s.f.* (*bot.*) musk gourd
Melonnière, *s.f.* melon-bed, melon-pit
Mélopée, *s.f.* melopœia; melody; intonation; chant, song
Mélophage, *s.m.* (*zool.*) sheep-louse, sheep-tick
Mélophare, *s.m.* transparent music-desk
Mélophone, *s.m.* (*mus. instr.*) melophone
Méloplaste, *s.m.* (*mus.*) meloplast
Méloplastie, *s.f.* (*surg.*) meloplasty
Mélose, *s.f.* (*surg.*) melosis
Melpomène, *s.f.* (*myth., astr.*) Melpomene
Melundois, e, Melunois, e, *adj. s.* of Melun; native of Melun
Mélusine, *s.f.* Melusine (*fairy*). *Cri de* —, loud scream *or* shriek
Mémarchure, *s.f.* (*vet.*) sprain
Membranacé, e, *adj.* membranaceous
Membrane, *s.f.* membrane; film; web
Membrané, e, Membraneu-x, se, *adj.* membraneous, membranous; filmy
Membraniforme, *adj.* membraniform
Membranule, *s.f.* membranule
Membre, *s.m.* member; limb; (*nav.*) rib, timber
Membré, e, *adj.* limbed, membered; (*her.*) membered
Membru, e, *adj.* strong-limbed, large-limbed
Membrure, *s.f.* limbs; frame; panel-frame; (*nav.*)ribs,timbers; (*for measuring firewood*) cord
Même, *adj. s.* same; very; own; self; himself; herself; itself; themselves. *La — chose*, the same thing. *La chose* —, the very thing. *La bonté* —, goodness itself. *Les —s*, the same; alike. *Faire au* —, (*at billiards*) to pocket directly. *Faire* or *refaire au* —, (*fig.*) to take in (nicely), to cheat (outright); to pay (*one*) back in his own coin, to give (*one*) as good as he brings. *Revenir au* —, to amount *or* come to the same (*or* to the same thing), to be all the same
Même, *adv.* even; also, likewise. *A* —, able; enabled; close to the thing itself, directly applied to ..., without anything between; directly out of the thing itself; from, out of; in; loose in; right in *or* into; from the piece; out of the bottle; (*old*) in the way (of), within reach (of). *De* —, *tout de* —, the same; in the same way; likewise; so; even so; thus; just the same, all the same, for all that; however, yet, still, though; (*obsolete*) like it, such. *De — que*, as, as well as; with. *Mettre à — de*, to enable
Mêmement, *adv.* (*old*) in the same manner, likewise; even
Mémento, *s.m.* memento, memorandum, reminder, remembrancer, hint; (*Cath. lit.*) memento
Mémoire, *s.f.* memory; remembrance, recollection; fame. *— de lièvre*, short memory. *De* —, from memory, by heart. *De — d'homme*, within the memory of man. *Fille de* —, (*poet.*) Daughter of Memory, Aonian maid, Muse. *Temple de* —, temple of Fame. *Pour* —, to refresh o.'s memory, not to forget it, as a memorandum, for a memorial. *Si j'ai bonne* —, if I remember right
Mémoire, *s.m.* memorandum; memorial; memoir; bill; account. *— d'apothicaire*, exorbitant bill
Mémorable, *adj.* memorable
Mémorablement, *adv.* memorably
Mémorandum, *s.m.* memorandum; memorial; memorandum-book
Mémorati-f, ve, *adj.* mindful, remembering, recollecting
Mémorial, *s.m.* memorial; remembrancer; (*com.*) waste-book; — *m.*, **e,** *f.*, *adj.* memorial
Mémorialiste, *s.m.f.* memorialist; memoirist
Menace, *s.f.* threat, menace
Menacer, *v.a.n.* to threaten, to menace; to impend; to threaten to rain, to be rainy. *— ruine*, to threaten to fall, to totter, to be tottering, to go to ruin *or* decay
Menaceu-r, se, *s.m.f.* threatener, menacer
Ménade, *s.f. V.* **Bacchante**
Ménage, *s.m.* housekeeping; household; house; set of furniture; family; married couple, couple, husband and wife; married state *or* life; economy; house-work; cleaning; (*ironically*) disorder, confusion, mess, ruin. *Petit* —, baby-house. *De* —, household; home-made; home-spun; economical; economically. *Être dans son* —, *tenir* —, to keep house. *Faire bon* or *mauvais* —, to live happily *or* unhappily together. *Mettre en* —, to settle
Menage, *s.m.* leading, driving
Ménagement, *s.m.* regard, consideration; considerateness; tenderness; discretion; measure; caution, care; disposition, arrangement; conduct, management
Ménager, *v.a.* to husband; to manage; to be sparing of, to use sparingly, to spare; to make good use of; to make the most of; to save; to economize; to take care of, to be careful of; to temper; to procure; to bring about; to prepare; to reserve; to lay in store (for); to dispose, to arrange; to contrive; to make; to effect; to treat gently *or* kindly, to treat with regard *or* caution *or* care, to take care not to give offence to (*or* not to hurt), to have regard for, to consider; to humour; to deal cautiously with. *N'avoir rien à — avec*, to have no measures to keep with

Se —, *v.r.* to take care of oneself, to spare *or* &c. oneself *or* each other; to act cautiously; to remain friends, to keep on good terms, to keep fair (with), to keep in (with); to procure, to obtain; to be husbanded *or* spared *or* &c.
Ménag-er, ère, *adj.* economical, saving, thrifty, careful; sparing, chary. *Eaux —ères*, house-slops, sewage of the houses
Ménager, *s.m.* saving *or* sparing man; economist, manager
Ménagère, *s.f.* housewife; economist, saving *or* thrifty woman, manager, housekeeper; (*pop.*) wife, goodwoman, gammer, missus; (*obsolete*) housemaid; (*thing*) cruet-frame, cruet-stand
Ménagerie, *s.f.* menagerie, menagery; poultry-yard, fowl-house, cattle-shed, piggery, &c.
Mendiant, e, *s.m.f.* beggar; beggar-woman; mendicant; — *adj.* begging; mendicant. *Les quatre —s*, (*dessert*) almonds (1) raisins (2) figs (3) and filberts (4)
Mendicité, *s.f.* begging; beggary; mendicity; mendicancy; beggars, vagrants
Mendier, *v.a.n.* to beg; to beg for; to solicit; to implore; to go begging. *— sa vie*, to live by begging
Mendol, *s.m.*, **Mendole,** *s.f.*, **Mène,** *s.f.* mœna (*fish*)
Mené, e, *part. adj.* led, &c. (*V.* **Mener**). — *par sa femme*, henpecked
Meneau, *s.m.* (*arch.*) mullion
‡**Ménechme,** *s.m.* very image, twin. *Les —s*, Menæchmi (*of Plautus*)
Menée, *s.f.* intrigue, underhand dealing *or* practice; trick; (*hunt.*) track
Mener, *v.a.n.* to lead; to conduct; to take; to carry; to bring; to introduce; to drive; to head; to govern; to rule; to sway; to influence; to move; to guide; to direct; to manage; to steer; to treat; to handle; to draw; to deceive, to humbug, to bamboozle

Se —, *v.r.* to be led *or* &c.; (*old*) to drive o.'s own carriage
Menesse, *s.f.* (*slang*) doxy
Ménestrel, *s.m.* minstrel
Ménétrier, *s.m.* fiddler
Meneu-r, se, *s.m.f.* gentleman usher; driver, leader; ringleader; agent for wet-nurses
Menhir, *s.m.* cromlech
Méniane, *s.f.*, *adj.f.* (*in Italy*) veranda, balcony
Ménianthe, *s.m. V.* **Minyanthe**
Ménilite, *s.f.* (*min.*) menilite
†**Ménillette,** *s.f.* (*agr.*) *V.* **Moyette**
Menin, *s.m.* gentleman attached to the person of the dauphin, minion, favourite
Méninge, *s.f.*, **Méninges,** *s.f.pl.* (*anat.*) meninges
Méningé, e, *adj.* (*anat.*) meningeal

Méningite, *s.f.* (*med.*) meningitis
Ménispermine, *s.f.* (*chem.*) menispermine
Ménisque, *s.m.* meniscus; crescent
Ménologe, *s.m.* menology
Ménopause, *s.f.* (*med.*) menopausis
Ménoplanie, *s.f.* (*med.*) menoplania
Ménorrhagie, *s.f.* (*med.*) menorrhagia
Ménorrhagique, *adj.* (*med.*) menorrhagic
Ménorrhée, *s.f.* (*med.*) menorrhœa
Ménostasie, *s.f.* (*med.*) menostasia, menostasis
Menotte, *s.f.* little hand; handcuff, manacle; (*bot.*) *V.* **Mainotte**
Menotter, *v.a.* to handcuff, to manacle
Mense, *s.f.* (*of abbeys*) revenue; (*old*) table; [food, board
Mensole, *s.f.* (*arch.*) key-stone
Mensonge, *s.m.* lie, untruth, falsehood, story, fib; fiction; error; illusion, delusion, vanity
Mensong-er, ère, *adj.* untrue, lying, false; deceitful, illusory, illusive
Mensongèrement, *adv.* untruly, falsely; deceitfully, illusively
Menstruation, *s.f.* (*med.*) menstruation
Menstrue, (**—s,** *pl.*) *s.m.* (*chem., obsolete*) menstruum, solvent; **—s,** *s.f.pl.* (*med.*) catamenia, menses [*or* menses
Menstruée, *adj.f.* (*med.*) having her catamenia
Menstruel, le, *adj.* (*med.*) catamenial, men- [strual
Mensuel, le, *adj.* monthly
Mensuellement, *adv.* monthly
Mensurabilité, *s.f.* mensurability
Mensurable, *adj.* mensurable
Mensurateur, *s.m.* mensurator
Mensuration, *s.f.* mensuration
Mentagre, *s.f.* (*med.*) mentagra, sycosis menti
Mentagrophyte, *s.m.* (*med.*) mentagrophyte
Mental, e, *adj.* mental
Mentalement, *adv.* mentally
Menterie, *s.f.* untruth, story, fib
Menteu-r, se, *adj.* lying, false, deceitful, delusive; — *s.m.f.* liar, story-teller, fibber, fibster
Menthe, *s.f.* mint; peppermint. — *poivrée,* peppermint. — *-coq,* — *de coq,* costmary
Menthène, *s.m.* (*chem.*) menthene
Mention, *s.f.* mention [tion of, to name
Mentionner, *v.a.* to mention, to make men-
Mentir, *v.n.* to lie; not to speak the truth; to conceal the truth (from); to tell a lie *or* an untruth *or* a falsehood *or* a story; to tell lies *or* stories; to speak false; to fib; to be false; to belie; — *s.m.* lying. *Ne pas* —, not to lie; to say *or* tell *or* speak the truth; not to belie *or* &c. *Faire* —, to belie; to cause *or* show *or* prove (...) to be false *or* wrong. *Sans* —, to tell the truth, indeed, truly, really, candidly, without exaggeration. *Tu en as* or *vous en avez menti,* that is a lie, that is not true, you have told a story, you are a liar. *A beau* — *qui vient de loin,* travellers lie by authority
Menton, *s.m.* chin
Mentonnet, *s.m.* (*tech.*) ear; tipper; catch
Mentonni-er, ère, *adj.* of the chin
Mentonnière, *s.f.* chin-band, chin-piece, chin-strap, chin-cloth; bib; (*surg.*) bandage round the chin [adviser, monitor
Mentor, *s.m.* Mentor, guide, tutor, counsellor,
Menu, e, *adj.* minute; slender, thin; small; petty; minor; common; — *adv.* small, fine; minutely; with quick and short steps; — *s.m.* detail; bill of fare; small linen; common folks, lower class. *Par le* —, minutely; in detail [small fry; trash
†Menuaille, *s.f.* small coin; small fish, fry,
Menuet, *s.m.* minuet (*dance, tune*) [shot
Menuise, *s.f.* small wood, small pieces; small
Menuiser, *v.a.n.* to cut, to hew, to do joiner's *or* carpenter's work
Menuiserie, *s.f.* joinery; carpentry; joiner's *or* carpenter's work, woodwork
Menuisier, *s.m.* joiner; carpenter; — *m.,* **-ière,** *f., adj.* (*zool.*) carpenter. — *en bâtiments,* house-carpenter, carpenter [lyre-tail
Ménure, *s.m.* (*zool.*) lyre-bird, lyre-pheasant,

Ményanthe, *s.m.* *V.* **Minyanthe**
Méon, *s.m.* *V.* **Meum** [fiend
Méphistophélès, *s.m.* Mephistopheles, devil,
Méphistophélétique, *adj.* Mephistopheletic, diabolical, fiendish
Méphit-ique, -isme. *V.* page 3, § 1
Méplat, *s.m.* (*paint.,* &c.) flat part; flattish curve; disposition of the bones; — *m.,* **e,** *f., adj.* flat, flatwise
Méprendre (Se), *v.r.* to mistake, to be mistaken; to make a mistake; to be under a mistake; to misapprehend
Mépris, *s.m.* contempt, scorn; disregard. *Au* — *de,* in contempt of, in defiance of, in spite of
Méprisable, *adj.* despicable, contemptible
Méprisablement, *adv.* despicably, contemptibly [fully
Méprisamment, *adv.* contemptuously, scorn-
Méprisant, e, *adj.* contemptuous, scornful
Méprise, *s.f.* mistake, oversight, error, misapprehension
Mépriser, *v.a.* to despise, to contemn, to scorn; to slight; to undervalue; to disregard; to set at naught
Mer, *s.f.* sea; ocean; tide, water. — *glaciale,* Frozen Ocean. — *de glace,* Mer de glace (*glacier in Switzerland*). *Basse* —, low water; shallow sea. *Grande* or *haute* —, main *or* open sea, high sea, high water. *Grosse* —, rough sea. *Pleine* —, open *or* main sea. *La* — *à boire,* an impossibility, an endless business *or* task, impossible, so very difficult. *A la* —, to sea; into the sea; overboard. *De* —, (*adj.*) sea; marine; naval; nautical. *En* —, *sur* —, at sea, on the sea; to sea. *En pleine* —, out at sea, out to sea, on the open sea, on the high seas. *Prendre la* —, *Se mettre en* —, to go to sea. *Reprendre la* —, to go to sea again. *Tenir la* —, to keep at sea
Merangène, *s.f.* *V.* **Melongène**
Mercadet, *s.m.* jobber
Mercandier, *s.m.* (*pop.*) cagmag-dealer
Mercanette, *s.f.* (*bird*) garganey
Mercantile, *adj.* mercantile, commercial; grasping, sordid, venal
Mercantilement, *adv.* like shopkeepers, graspingly, sordidly, venally [ness, venality
Mercantilisme, *s.m.* mercantilism, sordid-
†Mercantille, *s.f.* (*old*) petty trading, small
Mercaptan, *s.m.* (*chem.*) mercaptan [trade
Mercapture, *s.m.* (*chem.*) mercaptide
Mercenaire, *adj. s.m.f.* mercenary; hireling;
Mercenairement, *adv.* mercenarily [hack
Mercerie, *s.f.* mercery; haberdashery; pedlary; mercers, haberdashers, pedlars
Merci, *s.f.* mercy; discretion, pleasure, will and pleasure. — *de moi,* — *de ma vie,* (*old*) indeed, to be sure, sure, faith! zounds!
Merci, *s.m. int.* thank, thanks. — *!* thank you! thanks! no, thank you! I have had quite enough; I had rather not; I had rather be excused; oh, no! no, no! that is a fine thing! indeed! — *bien!* much obliged! *Grand* — *!* (*old*) gramercy! many thanks! much obliged!
Merci-er, ère, *s.m.f.* mercer; haberdasher; [pedlar
Mercredi, *s.m.* Wednesday
Mercure, *s.m.* mercury, quicksilver; (*myth., astr.*) Mercury; (*fig.*) pimp, pander
Mercureu-x, se, *adj.* (*chem.*) mercurous
Mercurey, *s.m.* mercurey (wine)
Mercurial, *adj. s.m.* mercurial
Mercuriale, *s.f.* (*Fr. hist.*) mercuriale; (*law*) speech (on the reopening of the courts); (*fig.*) reprimand, lecture; (*com.*) average prices of grain, averages; (*bot.*) mercury
Mercurialiser, *v.a.* to mercurialize [drargyria
Mercurialisme, *s.m.* (*med.*) mercurialism, hy-
Mercuriaux, *s.m.pl.* (*med.*) mercurials
Mercurico, (*in compounds*) mercurico-...
Mercuriel, le, *adj.* mercurial
Mercurification, *s.f.* mercurification
Mercurique, *adj.* (*chem.*) mercuric

†**Merdaille,** *s.f.* (*pop.*) lot of dirty brats
†**Merdaillon,** *s.m.* (*pop.*) contemptible fellow
Merde, *s.f.* (*fam.*) turd, dung, dirt, shit. — *d'oie*, gosling-green. *De* —, (*adj., pop.*) dirty, beastly
Merdeu-x, se, *adj.* (*fam.*) dirty; — *s.m.f.* dirty fellow *or* creature, beast, blackguard. *Bâton* —, ugly customer
Merdicole, *adj.* (*nat. hist.*) merdicolous
Mère, *s.f.* mother; parent; dam; woman, creature, body, thing; — *adj.* mother; parent; primitive; first; principal; leading; main; pure, genuine. (*V.* **Langue,** &c.) — *goutte*, unpressed wine *or* cider. — *-grand*, (*obsolete, childish, and pop. for* "grand'mère") granny, grandam. — *laine*, finest wool. — *patrie*, mother-country, fatherland. *De* —, of a mother, motherly, maternal. *Notre — commune*, our mother earth
Méreau, *s.m.* counter, ticket, check
Mérendère, *s.f.* (*bot.*) merendera
Mergue, *s.m.* (*bird*) *V.* **Harle**
Mergule, *s.m.* (*bird*) rotche
Méricarpe, *s.m.* (*bot.*) mericarp
Méridien, ne, *adj.* meridian; — *s.m.* meridian; sleeping-chair; — *s.f.* meridian line; noon's nap, midday nap; couch, lounge
Méridional, e, *adj.* meridional, southern, southerly, south; — *s.m.f.* southerner
Mérine, *adj.f.* *Race* —, merino breed
Meringue, *s.f.* (*cook.*) meringue (*sponge cake with whipped cream* or *&c.*) [a meringue-mixture
Meringué, e, *adj.* (*cook.*) covered *or* iced with
Mérinos, *s.m.* merino sheep, merino; merino wool, Spanish wool; (*stuff*) merino
Mérion, *s.m.* (*bird*) malurus
Merise, *s.f.* wild cherry, merry, gean [cherry
Merisier, *s.m.* wild cherry-tree; cherry-wood,
Méritant, e, *adj.* deserving, meritorious, worthy; good, fine [plishment
Mérite, *s.m.* merit; desert; worth; accom-
Mériter, *v.a.n.* to deserve, to merit; to be deserving; to earn; to procure, to gain; to need, to require [worthy of each other
Se —, *v.r.* to be deserved *or* &c.; to be
Méritoire, *adj.* meritorious
Méritoirement, *adv.* meritoriously
Merl, *s.m.* *V.* **Marne**
Merlan, *s.m.* (*fish*) whiting; (*pop.*) hairdresser
Merle, *s.m.* blackbird; ousel, ouzel. — *d'eau*, *V.* **Cincle.** — *blanc*, (*fig., jest.*) white crow; mare's nest. *Fin* —, cunning fellow, knowing
Merleau, *s.m.* young blackbird [one
Merlette, *s.f.* hen-blackbird; (*her.*) martlet
Merlin, *s.m.* cleaver; (*butcher's*) pole-axe; (*nav.*) marline; (*old*) Merlin, wizard
Merline, *s.f.* bird-organ
Merliner, *v.a.* (*nav.*) to marl
Merlon, *s.m.* (*fort.*) merlon [haddock
Merluche, *s.f.*, **Merlus,** *s.m.* hake; salt-cod,
Mérocèle, *s.f.* (*med.*) merocele
Mérovingien, ne, *adj. s.* Merovingian
Merrain, *s.m.* broad lath, planks, stave-wood, staves, clap-boards, clap-board; (*zool.*) horn
Mersion, *s.f.* mersion
Mérule, *s.m.* (*bot.*) merulius (*fungus*)
†**Merveille,** *s.f.* wonder, marvel; prodigy; phenomenon; miracle. *A* —, wonderfully well, marvellously, remarkably well, admirably, capitally; capital
†**Merveilleusement,** *adv.* wonderfully, marvellously, remarkably, admirably, wonderfully well
†**Merveilleu-x, se,** *adj.* wonderful, wondrous, marvellous, remarkable, admirable; remarkably good; strange, odd; — *s.m.* wonderful, marvellous; wonders; wonderful part; (*of poems*, &c.) supernatural agency, machinery, wonderful means *or* shift, "Deus ex machinâ;" — *s.m.f.* (*pers.*) swell, exquisite, dandy, beau, belle, fop, foppish woman
Méryc-ique, -isme, -ologie. *V.* page 3, § 1
Mes, *adj.poss.pl.m.f.* my, my own

Mésair, *s.m.* prancing
Mésaise, *s.m.* (*old*) *V.* **Malaise**
Mésalliance, *s.f.* misalliance, bad *or* unequal match, disparagement
Mésallier, *v.a.* to misally, to mismatch, to marry to one below o.'s station; (*fig.*) to lower, to degrade
Se —, *v.r.* to make a misalliance, to marry below o.'s station *or* below oneself, to disparage oneself; (*fig.*) to lower *or* degrade oneself
Mésange, *s.f.* (*bird*) tit, titmouse, tomtit
Mésangère, *s.f.* (*bird*) great tit
Mésangette, *s.f.* bird-trap
Mésaraïque, *adj.* (*anat.*) mesaraic
Mésarriver, Mésavenir, *v.n.* to happen ill *or* amiss, to turn out ill, to take an ill turn
Mésaventure, *s.f.* misadventure, mischance, mishap
Mesdames, *s.f.pl.* Ladies; the Ladies; Mesdames. — *vos tantes* or *&c.*, your aunts *or* &c.
Mesdemoiselles, *s.f.pl.* young Ladies, Ladies; the Misses. — *vos sœurs* or *&c.*, your sisters *or* &c.
Mésembryanthème, *s.m.* *V.* **Ficoïde**
Mésentendre, *v.a.* to hear wrong; to misunderstand
Mésentendu, *s.m.* (*old*) *V.* **Malentendu**
Mésentente, *s.f.* misunderstanding, disagree-
Mésentère, *s.m.* (*anat.*) mesentery [ment
Mésentérie, *s.f.* (*med.*) tabes mesenterica
Mésentérique, *adj.* (*anat.*) mesenteric
Mésentérite, *s.f.* (*med.*) mesenteritis
Mésestimable, *adj.* unworthy of esteem, unworthy, discreditable, disreputable
Mésestime, *s.f.* disesteem, disfavour, discredit, disrepute, contempt
Mésestimer, *v.a.* to undervalue; to disregard; to disesteem, to despise
Mésintelligence, *s.f.* misunderstanding, disagreement, variance [misconstruction
Mésinterprétation, *s.f.* misinterpretation,
Mésinterpréter, *v.a.* to misinterpret, to misconstrue [mesmerist
Mesmérien, ne, *adj.* mesmeric; — *s.m.f.*
Mesmér-ique, -isme, -iste. *V.* page 3, § 1
Méso, (*in compounds*) meso...
Mésocolon, *s.m.* (*anat.*) mesocolon
Mésoffrir, *v.n.* to offer too little, to underbid
Mésogastre, *s.m.* (*anat.*) mesogastrium
Mésogastrique, *adj.* (*anat.*) mesogastric
Mésopotamien, ne, *adj.* Mesopotamian
Mesquin, e, *adj.* mean; shabby; niggardly; illiberal; narrow; paltry, poor, pitiful
Mesquinement, *adv.* meanly, shabbily
Mesquinerie, *s.f.* meanness, stinginess, shabbiness; paltriness, poorness; mean *or* shabby
Mess, *s.f.* (*mil.*) mess [thing
Message, *s.m.* message; errand
Messag-er, ère, *s.m.f.* messenger; harbinger; carrier; — *s.m.* (*zool.*) carrier pigeon, carrier; secretary bird, serpent-eater
Messagerie, *s.f.* (*rail.*) carriage of goods, goods traffic; goods department; goods; (*nav.*) line of mail steam-packets, liners; (*obsolete*) coach-establishment; coach-office; stage-coach, coach [strumpet
Messaline, *s.f.* Messalina, bitch, harlot,
Messe, *s.f.* (*Cath. rel.*) mass. *Grand'*—, — *en musique*, high mass. — *basse*, *basse* —, *petite* —, low mass. — *de minuit*, mass said on Christmas eve. — *du Saint-Esprit*, invocation, mass at the close of the long vacation, &c. *Livre de* —, mass-book, prayer-book [mass
Messé, e, *adj.* (*fam.*) *Être* —, to have attended
Messéance, *s.f.* unbecomingness
Messéant, e, *adj.* unbecoming
†**Messeigneurs,** *s.m.pl.* my lords; your lordships; the lords, their lordships; lords
Messénien, ne, *adj. s.m.f.* Messenian; — *s.f.* national elegy
Messeoir, *v.n.* to ill become, to be unbecoming
Messer, *s.m.* (*old*) mister, master, squire

Messeyait, Messeyaient, *v.* ill became, was *or* were unbecoming
Messiade, *s.f.* Messiad (*Klopstock's poem*)
Messianique, *adj.* messianic
Messianisme, *s.m.* messianism
Messianité, *s.f.* messiahship
Messidor, *s.m.* Messidor (*tenth month of the calendar of the first French Republic, from June* 19 [*to July* 18)
Messie, *s.m.* messiah
Messied, *v.* ill becomes
Messiéent, *v.* ill become
Messier, *s.m.* keeper of a standing crop
Messiéra, Messiéront, *v.* will ill become, will be unbecoming
Messiérait, Messiéraient, *v.* would ill become, would be unbecoming
Messieurs, *s.m.pl.* gentlemen; sirs; Messieurs, Messrs.; people, folks. — *vos frères* or *&c.*, your brothers *or* &c.
Messin, e, *adj. s.* of Metz; native of Metz
Messinois, e, *adj. s.* Messinese
Messire, *s.m.* (*old*) messire, sir, master, squire, Mr. — **-jean,** *s.m.* messire-jean (*kind of pear*)
Mestrance, *s.f. V.* **Maistrance**
Mestre, *s.m.* (*obsolete*) *V.* **Maitre;** (*nav.*) *V.* **Meistre.** — **-de-camp,** *s.m.* (*mil., obsolete*) commander (*of a regiment*), colonel; (*s.f.*) first company (*of a regiment*)
Mesurable, *adj.* measurable
Mesurage, *s.m.* measurement, measuring; metage; gauging; surveying; mensuration
Mesure, *s.f.* measure; gauge; standard; rule; measurement; proportion; size; dimension; extent; capacity; compass; limit, bound; moderation; prudence; propriety; means; calculation, reckoning; time; metre; foot; (*fenc.*) proper distance, distance. — *à deux temps,* (*mus.*) common *or* simple time. — *à trois temps,* (*mus.*) triple time. — *à quatre temps,* (*mus.*) quadruple *or* compound time. *A* —, in proportion; in succession, successively, one after another; accordingly; according (to). *A* — *que,* in proportion as; according as; as; as . . . gradually; as soon as; as fast as. *A la* —, by measure; on draught. *En* —, in time; in regular time; ready, prepared, able, in a position (to). *Aller en* —, to keep time. *Battre la* —, to beat time. *Se mettre en* —, to get ready, to prepare, to arrange, to manage to be ready. *V.* **Rompre**
Mesuré, e, *part. adj.* measured, &c. (*V.* **Mesurer**); circumspect, cautious, prudent, guarded; moderate; proper; precise; regular; in verse; (*mus.*) crotcheted
Mesurément, *adv.* circumspectly, cautiously, prudently; moderately; properly; regularly
Mesurer, *v.a.n.* to measure; to measure out; to gauge; to survey; to span; to weigh; to consider, to examine; to proportion; to compare; to judge; to appreciate; to calculate; to direct; to regulate; to temper; to range
Se —, *v.r.* to measure *or* &c. oneself; to be measured *or* &c.; to be in proportion; to try o.'s strength; to vie, to struggle, to contend, to cope, to fight, to have a fight; to measure swords
Mesureur, *s.m.* measurer; meter; gauger; [gauge; — *adj.m.* measuring
Mésusage, *s.m.* misuse, abuse
Mésuser, *v.n.* to misuse, to abuse
Métabole, *s.f.* metabola; — *adj* metabolian
Métabol-ique, -isme. *V.* page 3, § 1
Métacarpe, *s.m.* (*anat.*) metacarpus
Métacarpien, ne, *adj.* (*anat.*) metacarpal
Métacentre, *s.m.* metacentre
Métacentrique, *adj.* metacentric
Métacétone, *s.f.* (*chem.*) metacetone [§ 1
‡**Métachro-matisme, -nisme.** *V.* page 3,
Métagénèse, *s.f.* metagenesis
Métairie, *s.f.* metairie (*farm the rent of which consists of half the produce*); small farm, farm; farmhouse
Métal, *s.m.* metal; ore; (*her.*) metal. — *blanc,* — *d'Alger,* German silver; albata; packfong; nickel silver; Britannia metal. — *anglais,* Britannia metal
Métalepse, *s.f.* (*rhet.*) metalepsis
Métalepsie, *s.f.* (*chem.*) metalepsy
Métalléité, *s.f.* metalleity
Métallescence, *s.f.* metallescence
Métallescent, e, *adj.* metallescent
Métallifère, *adj.* metalliferous
Métalliforme, *adj.* metalliform
Métallin, e, *adj.* metalline
Métallique, *adj.* metallic; medallic; —**s,** *s.m.pl.* metallic substances; metallic stocks. *Gaze* or *tissu* or *toile* —, wire-gauze, wire-cloth, gauze
Métalliquement, *adv.* in metal, in specie
Métallisage, *s.m.* plating
Métallisation, *s.f.* metallization
Métalliser, *v.a.* to metallize; to plate
Métallo, (*in compounds*) metallo...
Métallographe, *s.m.* metallographer
Métallograph-ie, -ique. *V.* page 3, § 1
Métalloïde, *adj.m.f., s.m.* metalloid
Métallurge, *s.m.* metallurgist
Métallurg-ie, -ique, -iste. *V.* page 3, § 1
Métamorph-ique, -isme, -iste. *V.* p. 3, § 1
Métamorphose, *s.f.* metamorphosis; transformation; change; new form
Métamorphoser, *v.a.* to metamorphose, to transform; to change
Se —, *v.r.* to metamorphose *or* &c. oneself; to be metamorphosed *or* &c.; to change, to alter
Métamorphosique, *adj.* metamorphosic
Métaphore, *s.f.* metaphor
Métaphor-ique, -iquement. *V.* page 3, § 1
Métaphosphate, *s.m.* (*chem.*) metaphosphate
Métaphosphorique, *adj.* (*chem.*) metaphosphoric
Métaphrase, *s.f.* metaphrase
Métaphraste, *s.m.* metaphrast
Métaphrastique, *adj.* metaphrastic
Métaphysicien, ne, *s m.f.* metaphysician; — *adj.* metaphysical [— *s.f.* metaphysics
Métaphysique, *adj.* metaphysical; abstract;
Métaphysiquement, *adv.* metaphysically
Métaphysiquer, *v.n.* to subtilize [subtlety
Métaphysiquerie, *s.f.* (*fam.*) subtilization,
Métaplasme, *s.m.* (*gram.*) metaplasm
Métaplastique, *adj.* (*gram.*) metaplastic
Métastase, *s.f.* (*med.*) metastasis
Métastatique, *adj.* (*med.*) metastatic
Métatarse, *s.m.* (*anat.*) metatarsus
Métatarsien, ne, *adj.* (*anat.*) metatarsal
Métathèse, *s.f.* (*gram., med.*) metathesis
Métayage, *s m.* metayage (*farming where rent consists of half the produce*)
Métay-er, ère, *s.m.f.* metayer (*farmer who gives half the produce as his rent*); small farmer, [farmer
Métazoïque, *adj.* (*geol.*) metazoic
†**Méteil,** *s.m.* meslin (*mixture of wheat and rye*); — *adj.* mixed with rye
Métempsycose, *s.f.* metempsychosis
Métempsycosiste, *s.m.f.* metempsychosist
Métemptose, *s.f.* (*chron.*) metemptosis
Météore, *s.m.* meteor; fire-ball
Météor-ique, -iquement. *V.* page 3, § 1
Météorisation, *s.f. V.* **Météorisme**
Météorisé, e, *part. adj.* flatulent, distended
Météoriser, *v.a.* (*med.*) to distend with flatus
Se —, *v.r.* to become distended with flatus
Météorisme, *s.m.* (*med.*) meteorism, wind; (*vet.*) hoven, wind
Météorite, *s.f.m.* meteorite
Météorognosie, *s.f.* meteorognosy
Météorographe, *s.m.* meteorographer
Météorograph-ie, -ique. *V.* page 3, § 1
Météorolithe, *s.m.* meteorolite [*V.* page 3, § 1
Météorolog-ie, -ique, -iquement, -iste.
Météorologue, *s.m.* meteorologist
Météoromancie, *s.f.* meteoromancy
Météoromancien, ne, *s.m.f.* meteoromancer
Météoronomie, *s.f.* meteoronomy
Météoroscope, *s.m.* meteoroscope
Météoroscop-ie, -ique. *V.* page 3, § 1

Méthode, *s.f.* method; system; means; way, custom, habit [*V.* page 3, § 1
Méthod-ique, -iquement, -isme, -iste.
Méthodisation, *s.f.* methodization
Méthodiser, *v.a.* to methodize
Méthodologie, *s.f.* methodology
Méthylamine, *s.f.* (*chem.*) methylamine
Méthyle, *s.m.* (*chem.*) methyle, methyl
Méthylène, *s.m.* (*chem.*) methylene
Méthyler, *v.a.* (*chem.*) to methylate
Méthylique, *adj.* (*chem.*) methylic
Méthylure, *s.m.* (*chem.*) methylide
Méticuleusement, *adv.* scrupulously, nicely, fastidiously [ticular, fastidious
Méticuleu-x, se, *adj.* scrupulous, nice, par-
Méticulosité, *s.f.* scrupulosity, fastidiousness
Métier, *s.m.* trade, handicraft, craft; profession, business, employment, occupation; work; condition; knack, skill; loom; frame; (*pastry*) wafer; (*fig., liter.*) stocks, anvil. — *mécanique,* — *à tisser,* power-loom. — *à bas,* stocking-frame. *Bas au* —, woven stockings. — *des armes,* — *de la guerre,* military profession; army. *De son* —, by trade *or* profession, professed; of o.'s own. *Donner* or *servir un plat de son* —, to give a specimen of o.'s skill; to play one of o.'s tricks. *Faire* — *de,* to make a trade of. *Faire au* —, to work on a frame, to weave. *Faire du* —, (*of artists and literary men*) to work
Méti-f, ve, *adj. s* (*old*) *V.* **Métis** [for money
Métis, se, *adj.* of a mixed breed; mongrel, cross-breed, half-bred; hybrid; — *s.m.f.* mestizo (*m.*), mestiza (*f.*); half-breed; mongrel,
Métis, *s.f.* (*astr.*) Metis [cross
Métisage, Métissage, *s.m.* crossing
Métivier, *s.m.* (*old*) *V.* **Moissonneur**
Métonien, Métonique, *adj.m.* (*astr.*) metonic
Métonomasie, *s.f.* metonomasia
Métonymie, *s.f.* (*rhet.*) metonymy
Métope, *s.f.* (*arch.*) metope
Métoposcope, *s.m.f.* metoposcopist
Métoposcop-ie, -ique. *V.* page 3, § 1
Métra, *s.m.* metra [measuring, yard-measure
Métrage, *s.m.* measurement by the metre, yard-
Métralgie, *s.f.* (*med.*) metralgia
Métralgique, *adj.* (*med.*) metralgic
Mètre, *s.m.* (*Fr. meas.*) metre (*French yard,* 39 *English inches*); (*vers.*) metre [measured
Métré, *s.m. V.* **Métrage;** — *m.,* **e,** *f., part. adj.*
Métrer, *v.a.* to measure by the metre, to mea-
Métreur, *s.m.* measurer; meter [sure
Métricien, *s.m.* metrician
Métrique, *adj.* metrical; — *s.f.* prosody, versification, scansion; — *s.m.* metrician
Métrite, *s.f.* (*med.*) metritis
Métrocèle, *s.f.* (*med.*) metrocele
Métrographe, *s. m.* (*pers.*) metrograpne; (*instr.*) metrograph
Métro-graphie, -graphique, -logie, -logique, -logiste. *V.* page 3, § 1
Métrologue, *s.m.* metrologist
Métromane, *adj. s.m.f.* metromaniac
Métromanie, *s.f.* metromania
Métronome, *s.m.* (*mus.*) metronome
Métropole, *s.f.* mother country; metropolitan see, cathedral city *or* town; (*in Church law*) metropolis, mother city; (*in antiquity, obsolete*) metropolis (*mother city, capital city*); — *adj.* metropolitan, mother [*s.m.* metropolitan
Métropolitain, e, *adj.,* **Métropolitain,**
Métropolite, *s.m.* metropolite [uteri
Métroptose, *s.f.* (*med.*) metroptosis, prolapsus
Métrorrhagie, *s.f.* (*med.*) metrorrhagia
Métrorrhexie, *s.f.* (*med.*) metrorrhexis
Métrosidéros, *s.m.* (*bot.*) metrosideros
Métrotomie, *s.f.* (*surg.*) metrotomy
Métroxyle, *s.m.* (*bot.*) metroxylon
Mets, *s.m.* dish, viand, mess, food
Mettable, *adj.* wearable, fit to be worn
Mettage, *s.m.* (*tech.*) putting, setting, laying
Metteu-r, se, *s.m.f.* (*tech.*) putter, setter, layer. — *en œuvre,* worker; setter, mounter; stone-setter. — *en pages,* (*print.*) clicker, maker-up. — *au point,* (sculptor's) carver. — *en scène,* getter-up (of a play)
Mettre, *v.a.n.* to put; to place; to lay; to set; to fix; to thrust; to poke; to turn; to fold; to put on; to wear; to set *or* put *or* lay down; to put up; to put out; to put in; to implicate; to contribute; to devote; to give; to employ; to use; to take; to make; to render; to show; to let; to invest; to lay out; to stake; to bid; to go to; to add; to carry; to bring; to drive; to reduce; to dress; to suppose; to put on o.'s hat. — *à l'eau,* (*nav.*) to launch. — *en pièces* or *en morceaux,* to cut in *or* to pieces, to break *or* dash *or* tear *or* pull to pieces, to tear up, to cut up, to shatter. — *en sang,* to make (...) bleed, to cause (...) to bleed; to cover with blood. — *à tous les jours,* to use every day. *Y* — *du sien,* to contribute of o.'s own; to add something of o.'s own; to contribute from o.'s own pocket, to invest some money in the concern; to be out of pocket by it; to make concessions, to meet one half-way

Se —, *v.r.* to put *or* place *or* set oneself; to be put *or* placed *or* &c.; to move; to form; to make oneself; to stand; to sit down; to sit; to lie down; to lie; to keep; to dress; to begin; to set about; to set; to fall; to apply *or* betake oneself (to); to take (to); to get; to go; to join; to enter; to form a connection, to live (with); to spread; to break out; (*of the weather*) to set in. *Se* — *en route* or *en chemin* or *en marche,* to start, to set forward *or* off *or* out, to leave; to move on. *Se* — *en tête,* to take it into o.'s head. *Se* — *bien,* to dress well. *Se* — *bien avec,* to ingratiate oneself with, to get on good terms with, to stand fair with. *Se* — *mal,* to dress badly. *Se* — *mal avec,* to quarrel with, to get on bad terms with, to fall out with. *Se* — *à tout,* to turn o.'s hand to everything. *S'y* —, to set about it, to begin
Meublant, e, *adj.* for furniture, adapted to *or* fit for furniture; — *s.m.* (*fam.*) keeper. *Bien* —, rich. *Meubles* —*s,* (*law slang*) furniture, movables
Meuble, *adj.* (*law*) movable, personal; (*agr.*) light, mellow; — *s.m.* piece of furniture; suite; thing to carry about, utensil, article; tackle; (*her.*) common charge, subordinary; — **s,** *s.m.pl.* furniture, household furniture; personal estate *or* property, personalty, movables; utensils; (*her.*) common charges. — *à demeure fixe,* fixture. *Être dans ses* —*s,* to have o.'s own furniture, the furniture to be o.'s own. *Mettre* (...) *dans ses* —*s,* to furnish apartments *or* a house for (...)
Meublé, e, *part. adj.* furnished, &c. (*V.* **Meubler**). *Non* —, unfurnished, &c. *Maison* —*e,* furnished house; private hotel
Meubler, *v.a.* to furnish; to stock; to store; to adorn; — *v.n.* to be fit for furniture; (— *bien*) to be rich, to look well; to be ornamental

Se —, *v.r.* to get furniture of o.'s own, to get o.'s furniture, to furnish o.'s lodgings *or* &c.; to make o.'s furniture; to get *or* be furnished
Meuglement, Meugler. *V.* **Beuglement,**
†Meuille, *s.f.* (*fish*) mullet [**Beugler**
Meulard, *s.m.* large grinding-stone
Meularde, *s.f.* middle-size grinding-stone
Meule, *s.f.* millstone, stone; grinding-stone; grindstone; grinder, sharpener, polisher; hoop-cheese; (*agr.*) stack, rick; (*hort.*) mushroom-bed; dung-heap; (*zool.*) moon-fish; (*hunt.*) burr, cabbage. — *de moulin,* millstone; (*pop.*) grinder, mill-tooth. *Pierre à* —*s,* burrstone, [buhrstone
Meuleau, *s.m. V.* **Meularde**
Meulerie, *s.f.* millstone yard, grindstone yard
Meulette, *s.f. V.* **Meulon**
Meulier, *s.m.* millstone *or* grindstone maker
Meulière, *s.f.* (*adj.f., Pierre* —) millstone, grindstone, burrstone, buhrstone; millstone *or* burrstone quarry

Meulon, *s.m.* stubble-stack *or* rick; cock (*of hay or grass*); shock *or* stook (*of corn*); heap (*of salt*)
Méum, *s.m.* (*bot.*) meum, spicknel, spignel
Meunerie, *s.f.* grinding of corn; miller's trade; millers; flour-mill; meal-house; sea-biscuit bakery
Meunier, *s.m.* miller; meal-worm; (*fish*) chub
Meunière, *s.f.* miller's wife, miller; hooded crow; long-tailed tit
Meursault, *s.m.* meursault (wine) [ling
Meurt-de-faim, *s.m.f.* starving wretch, starve-
Meurtre, *s.m.* murder; manslaughter, homicide; slaughter; crime, vandalism, sin, great shame, great pity. *Au —!* murder!
Meurtri-er, ère, *adj.* murderous, murdering, homicidal, killing; deadly; bloody; — *s.m.* murderer; — *s.f.* murderess; (*fort.*) loophole,
Meurtrièrement, *adv.* murderously [loop
Meurtrir, *v.a.* to bruise; to contuse; to mangle; to beat *or* make black and blue; to supple (*leather*); to soften (*colours*); (*obsolete*) to murder, to slaughter, to slay, to kill
Se —, *v.r.* to bruise oneself *or* each other; to become *or* be bruised
Meurtrissure, *s.f.* bruise; contusion
Meute, *s.f.* pack of hounds, pack
Mévendre, *v.a.* (*old*) to undersell
Mévenir, *v.n.* (*old*) *V.* **Mésarriver**
Mévente, *s.f.* (*old*) underselling; dulness of sale, dead sale
Mexicain, e, *adj. s.m.f.* Mexican; — *s.f.* Mexican fashion; kind of woollen cloth
Mézair, *s.m. V.* **Mésair**
Mézéréine, *s.f.* (*chem.*) mezereine
Mézéréon, *s.m.* (*bot.*) mezereon
Mezzanine, *s.f. adj.* (*arch.*) mezzanine
Mezzo, Mezza, *adj.* (*Italian*) mezzo, mezza
Mezzo-termine, *s.m.* middle course, mean
Mezzotinto, *s.m.* mezzotint [term, compromise
Mi, *s.m.* (*mus.*) mi, E; — *adj.* half; equally; middle, mid. — **-bis, e,** *adj.* whity-brown. — **-fin, e,** *adj. V.* **Demi-fin.** — **-parti, e,** *adj.* of two equal parts, half ... and half ...; equally divided. *A — -chemin,* mid-way, half-way. *A — -corps,* in *or* to the middle of the body, up *or* down to the waist; half-length. *A — -côte,* half-way up the hill, half-way up. *A — -jambe,* at *or* to mid-leg. *A — -mât,* half-mast high *or* up, at half-mast. *La — -carême,* mid-lent. *La — -janvier* or *&c.*, the middle of January *or* &c.
Miao, *s.m.* (Chinese) temple, miao
Miaou, *s.m. int.* cat's mew, miaou; puss, pussy
Miasmatique, *adj.* miasmatic, malarious, infectious [nation *or* exhalation, malaria
Miasme, *s.m.* miasm, miasma, infectious ema-
Miaulement, *s.m.* (*of cats*) mewing
Miauler, *v.n.* (*of cats*) to mew
Miauleu-r, se, *adj.* mewing
Mica, *s.m.* (*min.*) mica
Micacé, e, *adj.* micaceous
Micaschiste, *s.m.* (*min.*) mica-schist, mica-slate [ous
Micaschisteu-x, se, *adj.* (*min.*) mica-schist-
Miche, *s.f.* loaf (*of bread*); hunch, lump of
Miché, *s.m.* fool, muff, dupe, gull [crumb
Michel, *s.m.* Michael. — *Morin,* Jack of all trades. *Saint- —,* (*s.m.*) Saint-Michael (*kind of pear*). *La Saint- —,* (*s.f.*) Michaelmas
Micmac, *s.m.* underhand trick *or* dealing, intrigue, jobbery, foul play
Mico, *s.m.* mico (*monkey*)
Micocoulier, *s.m.* (*bot.*) nettle-tree
Microcéphale, *adj.* microcephalous
Microchimie, *s.f.* microchymy
Microchimique, *adj.* microchymical
Microcosme, *s.m.* microcosm
Microcosmique, *adj. V.* page 3, § 1
Micrographe, *s.m.* micrographer
Micrograph-ie, -ique, &c. *V.* page 3, § 1
Micrololog-ie, -ique, &c. *V.* page 3, § 1
Micrologue, *s.m.* micrologist
Micromètre, *s.m.* micrometer [3, § 1
Micrométr-ie, -ique, -iquement. *V.* page
Microphone, Microphonium, *s.m.* microphone [voice
Microphonie, *s.f.* microphony, weakness of
Micropsie, *s.f.* (*med.*) micropsia, micropsy
Microscope, *s.m.* microscope, magnifying glass [*V.* page 3, § 1
Microscop-ie, -ique, -iquement, -iste.
Miction, *s.f.* (*med.*) miction
Micturition, *s.f.* (*med.*) micturition
Midas, *s.m.* Midas; ignoramus, long-ears; very rich man, nabob; (*zool.*) midas, tamarin (*mon-*
Middletonite, *s.f.* middletonite [*key*)
Midi, *s.m.* noon; noontide; noonday; midday; twelve o'clock in the day, twelve o'clock, twelve; south; southern aspect; Southern railway. *Chercher — à quatorze heures,* to run a wild-goose chase, to seek difficulties where there are none, to look for a knot in a bulrush; to go round about; to boggle
Mie, *s.f.* crumb (*of bread*); (*obsolete*) a bit, one jot, at all, in the least; (*obsolete for* "amie") friend, dear friend, dear, darling, love, sweetheart; good woman *or* girl; nurse
Miel, *s.m.* honey
Miélaison, *s.f.* honey-season
Miellat, *s.m.* (*bot.*) honey-dew
Mielle, *s.f.* sandy coast [coloured
Miellé, e, *part. adj.* honeyed; honey; honey-
Miellée, *s.f. V.* **Miellat**
Mieller, *v.a.* to honey, to sweeten with honey
Mielleusement, *adv.* sweetly, blandly, honey-like [mawkish; bland, fair-spoken
Mielleu-x, se, *adj.* honeyed, sweet, luscious,
Miellure, *s.f. V.* **Miellat**
Mien, ne, *pron.poss.* mine, my own; of mine. *Le —, la —ne, les —s, les —nes,* mine, my own. *Les —s,* my relations *or* family; my friends; my men; my servants; my company; my party; my people; my subjects; my dynasty; (*les —nes*) my tricks *or* pranks *or* frolics
Miette, *s.f.* crumb; bit, particle, morsel
Mieu-r, se, *s.m.f.* man *or* woman who raises silkworms on half-profits, silk-growing farmer *or* farmeress
Mieux, *adv. adj.* better; best; more correctly; more properly; rather; more; most; more comfortable *or* comfortably; most comfortable *or* comfortably; on better (*or* ... best) terms; better-looking; best-looking; more (*or* most) gentlemanly *or* ladylike; improved in o.'s manners, improved. *A qui — —, V.* **Envi (A l').** *Aimer —,* to prefer, to like better *or* best, to choose rather. *J'aime —, J'aimerais —,* I prefer, I would *or* had rather, I would *or* had rather have. *Ne demander pas —, V.* **Demander.** *Disons —,* or rather, let us speak more correctly. *On ne peut —, V.* **Pouvoir.** *Vous feriez —,* you had better. *Valoir —,* to be better; to be worth more; to excel. — *vaut, vaudrait,* (it is, it would be) better
Mieux, *s.m.* best; best thing; best plan; best way; improvement; better; something better; anything better. *Au —, le — du monde, le — possible,* as well as possible; for the best; on the best of terms. *De — en —,* better and better. *De son —,* as well as one can *or* could, to the best of o.'s ability. *En —,* for the better; better-looking. *Pour le —,* for the best. *Faire de son —,* to do o.'s best, to do the best one can. *Le — est l'ennemi du bien,* let well alone
Mieux-disant, e, *adj. s.* better-spoken, best-spoken; more *or* most eloquent; finer *or* finest speaker
Mieux-être, *s.m.* better *or* best condition, bettering o.'s condition, improvement in o.'s condition, increase of comfort, greater *or* greatest comfort
Mièvre, *adj.* lively, arch, roguish; quaint
Mièvrement, *adv.* archly, roguishly; quaintly

Mièvrerie, Mièvreté, *s.f.* liveliness, archness, roguishness; roguish trick, prank; [quaintness
Mifin, e, *adj. V.* **Demi-fin**
†**Mignard, e,** *adj.* mincing, affected; delicate, pretty, nice; — *s.m.f.* ditto person; — *s.m.* mincing, affectation, affected manner *or* style
†**Mignardement,** *adv.* mincingly, affectedly; delicately, prettily, nicely [in
†**Mignarder,** *v.a.* to coddle; to affect delicacy
†**Mignardise,** *s.f.* mincing, mincing manner, affectation; pretty way; coaxing way, wheedling; coddling, fondling; delicacy, prettiness; (*bot.*) feathered pink; (*need.*) braid
†**Mignon, ne,** *adj.* delicate, pretty, tiny; favourite; (*of money*) spare. *Argent* —, *écus* —*s*, spare money, pocket money, pocket allowance, money saved up
†**Mignon,** *s.m.* favourite; darling; minion
†**Mignonne,** *s.f.* favourite; darling; (*pear, peach, plum*) mignonne; (*print.*) minion
†**Mignonnement,** *adv.* delicately
†**Mignonnette,** *s.f.* little darling; mignonnette (*lace, stuff, pear*); ground pepper; (*bot.*) [feathered pink
†**Mignoter,** *v.a.* to coddle
Migraine, *s.f.* sick headache, brow-ague, hemicrania, megrim; (*vet.*) megrims
Migra-teur, trice, *adj.* migrating, migrant, [migratory
Migration, *s.f.* migration
Migratoire, *adj.* migratory
Mijaurée, *s.f.* affected woman *or* girl, humbug
Mijoter, *v.n.* to simmer; to be brewing; — *v.a.* to simmer; to coddle; to brew
Se —, *v.r.* to simmer; to be brewing; to [coddle oneself
Mikania, *s.m.* (*bot.*) mikania
Mil, *adj.* one thousand; — *s.m.* (*old and pop. for* "millet") millet; (*gymnastics*) club
Milady, *s.f.* (English) lady (*title*); my lady; [your *or* her ladyship
Milan, *s.m.* (*bird*) kite
Milanais, e, *adj. s.* Milanese; Milanese fashion
Milandre, *s.m.* (*fish*) tope
Milaneau, *s.m.* young kite (*bird*)
Milanière, *s.f.* kitery
Milasse, *s.f. V.* **Miliasse**
Milésiaque, Milésien, ne, *adj. s.* Milesian
Miliaire, *adj.* (*med., anat.,* &c.) miliary; — *s.f.* (*med.*) miliaria, miliary fever [hominy, mush
Miliasse, *s.f.* millet *or* maize hasty-pudding,
Milice, *s.f.* militia; army, body of troops, [host; warfare, war
Milicien, *s.m.* militiaman
Milieu, *s.m. adj.* middle, midst; centre; core; heart; depth; height; medium, mean; something between; means, way, expedient; middle course; sphere, society, company, life; (*phys.*) medium. *Juste* —, just medium, just mean, golden mean; (*polit.*) conservatism; conservative. *Au* —, in the middle *or* midst *or* &c.; between; among; in; into; far in; far into; notwithstanding. *Au beau* —, right in the middle *or* midst; right in; right into. — *de salon*, centre ottoman. *Empire du* —, China
Militaire, *adj.* military; soldierly; warlike; — *s.m.* military man, soldier; military; military service, army; — *s.f.* military style *or* [fashion
Militairement, *adv.* militarily
Militant, e, *adj.* militant; aggressive, pugna- [cious
Militariser, *v.a.* to militarize
Militarisme, *s.m.* militarism
Militer, *v.n.* to militate; to argue; to make
†**Millade,** *s.f.* millet hasty-pudding
Mille, *adj.* thousand; one *or* a thousand; — *s.m.* thousand; one *or* a thousand; (*meas. of distance*) mile; —**s,** *s.m.pl* miles. — *et* —, thousands of. *Les — et Une Nuits*, the Arabian Nights. — **-feuilles,** *s.f.* (*bot.*) milfoil, yarrow, maudlin. — **-fleurs,** *s.f.* all flowers. *Eau de — -fleurs*, elixir of all flowers, mixed perfume. — **-pertuis,** *s.m.* (*bot.*) Saint John's wort. — **-pattes,** — **-pieds,** *s.m.* (*zool.*) milleped
Millénaire, *adj.m.f., s.m.* millenary; millenarian; millennium [nianism
Millénarisme, *s.m.* millenarianism, millen-
Milléniste, *s.m.* millennialist
Millénium, *s.m.* millennium
Millepertuis, *s.m. V.* **Mille**
Millépore, *s.m.* (*nat. hist.*) millepore
Millésime, *s.m.* date (*on coins*, &c.)
†**Millet,** *s.m.* (*bot.*) millet; (*med.*) miliary eruption, sudamen [sandth part)
Milli, (*in Fr. weights and meas.*) milli... (*thou-*
Milliaire, *adj.* miliary (*of miles*), milliary; — *s.m.* mile-stone *or* post. *Borne* or *colonne* —, mile-post. *Pierre* —, mile-stone
Milliard, *s.m.* thousand millions; thousand million francs (£40,000,000) [*part of an* "are")
Milliare, *s.m.* (*Fr. meas.*) milliare (*thousandth*
Milliasse, *s.f.* (*obsolete*) *V.* **Trillion;** (*fam.*) thousands, lots, swarms, crowds, a world; (*duplicate spelling*) *V.* **Miliasse**
Millième, *adj.m.f., s.m.* thousandth [ble, p. 6.)
Millier, *s.m.* thousand; thousandweight (*See* ta-
Milligramme, *s.m.* (*Fr. weight*) milligramme
Millilitre, *s.m.* (*Fr. meas.*) millilitre (*See* p. 6.)
Millime, *s.m.* millime (*tenth part of a* "centime," *or thousandth part of a franc; used only in calculations*) [table, p. 6.)
Millimétre, *s.m.* (*Fr. meas.*) millimetre (*See*
Million, *s.m.* million; million francs $200,000)
Millionième, *adj.m.f., s.m.* millionth
Millionnaire, *s.m.f.* person worth a million *or* millions (*of francs*), millionaire; — *adj.* worth ditto. *Être deux, trois fois* —, to be worth two, three million francs
Millistère, *s.m* (*Fr. meas.*) millistere
†**Millococo,** *s.m.* (*bot.*) sorgho
Millouin, *s.m V.* **Milouin**
Milord, *s.m.* (*English*) lord; my lord; your *or* his lordship; (*French open cab or fly*) milord; (*private*) cab phaeton; (*fig.*) nabob
Milouin, *s.m.* (*bird*) poachard, pochard
Milphose, *s.f.* (*med.*) milphosis
Milréis, *s.m.* milrei (*Portuguese coin*)
Miltonien, ne, *adj.* Miltonian
Mime, *s.m.* (*thing*) mime; — *s.m.f.* (*pers.*) mimic, mime; — *adj.* mimic
Mimer, *v.a.n.* to mimic, to express by pantomime *or* by dumb show, to imitate *or* represent by gestures [(*bot.*) mimosa
Mimeu-x, se, *adj.* (*bot.*) sensitive; — *s.f.*
Mimi, *s.m.f.* darling; puss, pussy; tit; sweet- [heart; minnie
Mimicologie, *s.f.* mimicology
Mimique, *adj.* mimic; — *s.m.* mimographer; — *s.f.* mimic art, mimicry
Mimodrame, *s.m.* mimodrama
Mimographe, *s.m.* mimographer [§ 1
Mimograph-ie, -ique, -isme. *V.* page 3,
Mimolog-ie, -ique, -isme. *V.* page 3, § 1
Mimologue, *s.m.* mimologist
Mimoplastique, *adj.* mimoplastic
Mimosa, *s.m.* (*bot.*) mimosa
Mimule, *s.m.* (*bot.*) mimulus, monkey-flower
Mimusope, *s.m.* (*bot.*) mimusops
Minable, *adj.* miserable-looking, wretched, shabby, seedy
Minage, *s.m.* (*feud.*) corn-due; market
Minahouet, Minaouet, *s m.* (*nav.*) burton
Minaret, *s.m.* minaret; (*mining*) shaft
Minauder, *v.n.* to mince, to simper, to smirk
Minauderie, *s.f.* lackadaisicalness; affected way *or* face; mincing *or* lackadaisical manners; simpering, smirking
Minaudi-er, ère, *adj.* lackadaisical, mincing, simpering, smirking, affected; — *s.m.f.* ditto person, humbug
Mince, *adj.* slender, thin, slight; scanty; small, poor; puny; insignificant; trivial
Mincement, *adv.* slenderly, thinly, slightly; scantily; poorly; insignificantly
Mincer, *v.a* (*cook.*) to mince
Minceur, Mincité, *s.f.* slenderness, thinness, slightness; scantiness; poorness; puniness; insignificance
Mine, *s.f.* countenance, face, mien; look, looks; appearance; air; figure; show; style; sign; grimace, mouth. *De bonne* —, good-looking,

De mauvaise —, ill-looking. *Avoir bonne* —, *mauvaise* —, to look well, ill *or* seedy. *Avoir de la* —, to look decent *or* presentable *or* nice, to look well. *Avoir la* — *de*, to look like *or* as if, to seem; to seem to wish. *Faire* — *de*, to pretend, to feign, to make a show; to seem to be about; to seem; to offer. *Faire la* —, to make faces, to pout, to sulk, to scowl, to look cross. *Faire bonne* — *à*, to give a good reception, to receive well, to look pleasant at; to put a good face on. *Faire mauvaise* or *froide* — *à*, to give a cold reception, to receive coldly, to look black at *or* cold upon. *Faire bonne* — *à mauvais jeu*, to put a good face on the matter

Mine, *s.f.* mine; pit; ore; source, store, mint, well; plot, secret. — *de plomb*, lead mine; black lead; black-lead pencil. *Éventer la* —, (*mil.*) to discover the mine; (*fig.*) to discover the plot *or* the secret, to baffle anyone's design

Minel, *s.m.* Canada cherry-tree

Miner, *v.a.* to mine, to undermine; to excavate; to dig; to hollow; to wear away; to eat away; to consume; to waste; to destroy; to impair; to prey upon; (*agr.*) to dig, to dig up

Se —, *v.r.* to become *or* be undermined, &c.

Minerai, *s.m.* ore; mine

Minéral, e, *adj.*, **Minéral**, *s.m.* mineral

Minéralisable, *adj.* mineralizable

Minéralisa-teur, trice, *adj.* mineralizing; — *s.m.* mineralizer

Minéralisation, *s.f.* mineralization

Minéraliser, *v.a.n.* to mineralize [*V.* p. 3, § 1

Minéralog-ie, -ique, -iquement, -iste.

Minéralurg-ie, -ique, -iste. *V.* page 3, § 1

Minérographe, *s.m.* minerographer

Minérograph-ie, -ique. *V.* page 3, § 1

Minerval, e, Minervien, ne, *adj.* Minerval, Minervian [*colleges*) class-fees, course-fees

Minerval, *s.m.* (*in some German and Dutch*

Minerve, *s.f.* Minerva; head, brain, brains; reason. *Arbre de* —, (*poet.*) olive-tree. *Fruit de* —, (*poet.*) olive. *Oiseau de* —, (*poet.*) owl

Minet, te, *s.m.f.* puss, pussy; darling, ducky, love; — *s.f.* (*bot.*) — *dorée*, black medick, black nonsuch

Mineur, *s.m.* miner; underminer; pitman; (*agr.*) digging-plough, digger, subsoil-plough, subsoiler; — *adj.m.* mining; — *m.*, **-euse**, *f.*, *s.* (*zool.*) digger; *adj.* digging

Mineur, e, *adj.* minor, less, lesser, smaller; inferior, lower; (*pers.*) under age; (*geog.*) minor, lesser; (*mus., eccl.*) minor; — *s.m.f.* minor, person under age; — *s.m.* (*eccl.*) minor order; (*mus.*) minor mode; — *s.f.* minoress, Franciscan nun; (*log.*) minor. *Frère* —, minor, minorite, Franciscan friar. *L'Asie* —*e*, Asia Minor

Miniature, *s.f.* miniature [painter

Miniaturiste, *s.m.f.* miniaturist, miniature-

Mini-er, ère, *adj.* mining; — *s.f.* ore, pit

Minima, *s.m.pl.* minima; — *adj.f.* (*Latin ablative*) minimâ. *Appel à* —, appeal by the crown in criminal cases where the punishment is considered insufficient

Minimal, e, *adj.* minimum, lowest

Minime, *adj.* very small; trifling, trivial; low; — *s.f.* (*old mus.*) minim; — *s.m.* (*monk*) minim

Minimesse, *s.f.* minime, nun of the order of St. Francis of Paula

Minimité, *s.f.* extreme smallness, triflingness

Minimum, *s.m.* minimum; lowest

Ministère, *s.m.* ministry; office; department; board; minister's office; ministers; agency, medium; good offices, services; functions; administration; ministration. — *de la marine*, admiralty. — *public*, (*law*) public prosecutor

Ministérialisme, *s.m.* ministerialism

Ministériel, le, *adj.* ministerial; — *s.m.* ministerialist. *Officier* —, *V.* **Officier**

Ministériellement, *adv.* ministerially

Ministre, *s.m.* minister; secretary of state (for . . .), secretary (for . . ., of . . .); clergyman, vicar, rector, parson. *Premier* —, prime minister, premier. — *du commerce*, president of the board of trade

Minium, *s.m.* minium, red lead

Minnesinger, *s.m.* (*German liter.*) minnesinger

Mino, *s.m.* (*zool.*) mina bird

Minois, *s.m.* face, countenance, looks, air, appearance; pretty face, little face, pretty [little face; pretty girl

Minon, *s.m.* puss, pussy

Minorat, *s.m.* (*eccl.*) being in the minor orders

Minorati-f, ve, *adj.*, **Minoratif**, *s.m.* (*med.*) minorative, gently *or* gentle purgative, laxative, aperient

Minoration, *s.f.* gentle purgation

Minoré, *s.m.* (*eccl.*) person in the minor orders

Minoribus (In), (*eccl.*) in the minor orders

Minorité, *s.f.* minority

Minot, *s.m.* (*old meas.*) (*fig.*) peck; (*nav.*) bumkin. *Farine de* —, flour for export

Minotaure, *s.m.* Minotaur [cuckold

Minotaurisé, *adj. s.m.* deceived by his wife,

Minotauriser, *v.a.* to cuckold

Minoterie, *s.f.* flour-store *or* stores; flour-trade

Minotier, *s.m.* flour-merchant

Minuit, *s.m.* midnight; twelve o'clock at night, twelve o'clock, twelve [small letter

Minuscule, *adj.* small, very small; — *s.f.*

Minute, *s.f.* minute; moment, instant; small hand; rough draught, draught; original; (*nav.*) minute-glass; — ! stop a moment!

Minuter, *v.a.* to minute; to draw up; to make a rough draught of; (*fig.*) to contemplate, to intend, to project [minute-wheels; minutes

Minuterie, *s.f.* (*horol.*) minute-wheelwork,

Minuteur, *s.m.* secretary, registrar [nuteness

Minutie, *s.f.* trifle, minutia (*pl.* minutiæ); mi-

Minutieusement, *adv.* minutely

Minutieu-x, se, *adj.* minute; particular; circumstantial [marsh trefoil

Minyanthe, *s.m.* (*bot.*) buckbean, bogbean,

Minyanthine, *s.f.* (*chem.*) minyanthine

Miocène, *adj.m.f.*, *s.m.* (*geol.*) miocene [runt

Mioche, *s.m.* brat, chit, urchin; baby; dwarf,

Miparti, e, *adj. V.* **Mi**

Miquelet, *s.m.* miquelet (*Spanish soldier*)

Mira, *s.f.* (*astr.*) Mira

Mirabelle, *s.f.* mirabelle (*plum*)

Miracle, *s.m.* miracle; wonder; miracle-play. *A* —, to a miracle, miraculously, wonderfully well, wonderfully, admirably [derfully

Miraculeusement, *adv.* miraculously; won-

Miraculeu-x, se, *adj.* miraculous; wonderful; — *s.m.* miraculousness, miraculous; wonderfulness, wonderful

Miradore, *s.m.* (*Spanish arch.*) mirador

Mirage, *s.m.* mirage, looming; (*fig.*) shadow, outline; delusion; (*of eggs*) candling [tail)

†Miraillé, e, *adj.* (*her.*) eyed (*as the peacock's*

†Miraillet, Miralet, *s.m.* (*fish*) homelyn, spotted ray, sand-ray [bane, nitrobenzole

Mirbane, *s.f.* *Essence de* —, essence of mir-

Mire, *s.f.* sight (*of a gun*, &c.); bead; pole, staff, stake, mark; aim. *Point de* —, point of sight; mark, aim, object of aim, object; sight

Miré, e, *part. adj.* aimed, &c. (*V.* **Mirer**); (*of wild boars*) old, with tusks curved inwards

Mirement, *s.m.* looming

Mirepoix, *s.m.* (*cook.*) catchup-sauce, relish

Mirer, *v.a.n.* to aim; to aim at; to take aim at; to look at; to look; to eye; to hold up to a lighted candle, to hold up to the light, to candle, to look through; to reflect

Se —, *v.r.* to look at oneself (*at o.'s image reflected*); to see o.'s image; to admire oneself; to be reflected [peeper (*eye*)

Mirette, *s.f.* (*bot.*) Venus's looking-glass; (*pop.*)

Mireu-r, se, *s.m.f.* — *d'œufs*, egg-candler

Mirifique, *adj.* (*jest.*) mirific, wonderful

Mirliflore, *s.m.* fop, coxcomb, spark, beau

Mirliton, *s.m.* reed-pipe; bob-wig; cream-cake; tol-de-rol-lol. *Vers* or *poésie de* —, dog- [gerel

Mirmidon, *s.m.* *V.* **Myrmidon**

Mirobolamment, *adv.* mirifically, wonderfully, splendidly, astoundingly, amazingly, [stunningly

Mirobolan, *s.m.* *V.* **Myrobolan**

Mirobolan, *s.m.* *V.* **Myrobolan**
Mirobolant, e, *adj.* (*fam.*) wonderful, stupendous, splendid, astounding, stunning
Miroder, *v.a.* (*old*) to trim up, to dress up
Miroir, *s.m.* mirror; looking-glass, glass; blaze. *A —,* (*of horses*) dapple
Miroité, e, *adj.* dapple; shot; shiny, shining, glistening, glittering; reflected
Miroitement, *s.m.* shining, shine, glistening, glittering, glitter, brightness, radiance; reflection
Miroiter, *v.n.* to shine, to glisten, to glitter, to radiate; to reflect; to be reflected; — *v.a.* to make (...) shine *or* reflect like a mirror; to reflect
Miroiterie, *s.f.* mirror-trade, looking-glass trade *or* business *or* making *or* manufactory; mirrors, looking-glasses
Miroitier, *s.m.* looking-glass maker
Mirontaine, Mironton, tol-de-rol-lol
Miroton, *s.m.* beef collops with onions; (*of fruit*) stew (of ...), stewed (...)
Mis, e, *part. adj.* put, &c. (*V.* **Mettre**); attired, dressed, clad (*with good or bad taste*)
Misaine, *s.f.* (*nav.*) fore-mast; fore-sail. *De —,* (*adject.*) fore(-...)
Misanthrope, *s.m.* misanthrope, misanthropist, hater of mankind, man-hater; — *adj.* misanthropic
Misanthrop-ie, -ique. *V.* page 3, § 1
Miscellanea, Miscellanées, *s.m.pl.* miscellanies
Mischna, *s.m.* Mishna, Mischna
Mischnique, *adj.m.f., s.m.* Mishnic, Mischnic
Miscibilité, *s.f.* miscibility
Miscible, *adj.* miscible, mixable
Mise, *s.f.* putting; laying; setting; dress; deposit; investment; outlay, disbursement, expense; stake; bid, bidding; capital, share of capital; currency, circulation. — *en* **accusation,** impeachment; arraignment, indictment. — *en* **arrestation,** arrest, apprehension. — **-bas,** bringing forth young; (*obsolete*) cast-off clothes *or* garment. — *à* **bord,** shipment. — *en* **bouteilles,** bottling. — *en* **cause,** call to appear, summons; implication in a lawsuit; trial. — *en* **cave,** cellarage, binning. — *en* **couleur,** colouring, painting, staining. — *en* **demeure,** demand of payment *or* of settlement, demand, requisition, summons, call, compulsion, putting in suit. — *à l'eau,* (*nav.*) launch, launching. — *à* **exécution,** execution. — *à* **flot,** floating. — *de* **fonds,** outlay, expense, disbursement, investment of capital, capital invested, share of capital. — **hors,** outlay. — *en* **jugement,** trial. — *en* **justice,** bringing into court. — *en* **liberté,** liberation, release, discharge, enlargement. — *en* **musique,** setting to music. — *en* **œuvre,** working up, preparation; making up; employing, using; setting. — *en* **pages,** (*print.*) making up. — *à* **pied,** withdrawing the licence (*of a cabman*); suspension (*of a functionary,* &c.), discharge, dismissal. — *en* **possession,** putting into possession; taking possession. — *en* **pot,** potting. — *en* **prévention,** (*law*) commitment. — *à* **prix,** setting a price; price set; (*of auctions*) putting up, upset price, lowest price fixed, reserved price, price. — *à la* **retraite,** superannuation. — *en* **scène,** getting up *or* mounting (of a play *or* piece); scenery and costumes; scenic effect, stage effect; show. — **à terre,** putting *or* setting down; landing. — **en terre,** burying, burial. — *en* **terrine,** potting. — *en* **train,** setting to work, starting, start; (*print.*) making ready. — *en* **vente,** putting up for sale. — *en* **vigueur,** putting in force, enforcement. *De —,* admissible; acceptable; agreeable; presentable; decent; sociable; fashionable, in fashion; in season; current, in circulation
Misérable, *adj. s.m.f.* miserable; wretched; wicked; worthless; wretch; villain
Misérablement, *adv.* miserably; wretchedly; wickedly; worthlessly
Misère, *s.f.* misery; distress; wretchedness; calamity; misfortune; poverty, destitution; pain; trouble; mere trifle, trifle, mere nothing; petty vexation; unpleasant thing; bickering; backbiting; meanness, mean thing, shabby trick
Miséréré, *s.m.* (*Cath. lit.*) miserere; (*med.*) iliac passion
Miséricorde, *s.f.* mercy; pity, compassion; clemency; pardon, forgiveness; (*arch.*) miserere, small seat; (*obsolete*) dagger; — *int.* mercy! mercy on me! bless me! Lord have mercy upon us!
Miséricordieusement, *adv.* mercifully
Miséricordieu-x, se, *adj.* merciful; compassionate; clement; forgiving
Misocapnie, *s.m.* "Counterblaste to Tobacco" (*by King James I.*)
Misogame, *s.m.f.* misogamist
Misogamie, *s.f.* misogamy
Misogyne, *s.m.* misogynist, woman-hater
Misogynie, *s.f.* misogyny
Misour, *s.m.* misour (*south wind in the Mediterranean*)
Mispickel, *s.m.* (*min.*) mispickel
Miss, *s.f.* (*English*) miss, young lady
Missel, *s.m.* missal; mass-book
Mission, *s.f.* mission
Missionnaire, *s.m.* missionary
Mississipien, ne, *adj. s.* Mississippian; (*Fr. hist.*) holder of Mississippi stock
Missive, *adj.f., s.f.* missive
Mistenflûte, *s.m.* (*pop.*) Thingumbob
Mistic, Mistique, *s.m.* (*nav.*) lugger
Mistigri, *s.m.* Puss; (*cards*) pam; loo
Mistral, *s.m.* mistral (*north-west wind in the Mediterranean*)
Mistress, Mistriss, *s.f.* (*English*) Mrs.
Mitaine, *s.f.* mitten; (*fig.*) precaution, caution
Mitainerie, *s.f.* mitten trade *or* manufactory
Mitaini-er, ère, *s.m.f.* mitten-maker
Mite, *s.f.* (*insect*) mite, tick; moth; (*pop.*) eye-gum
Mité, e, *adj.* mity; moth-eaten
Miteu-x, se, *adj.* mity; (*pop.*) *V.* **Chassieux**
Mithridate, *s.m.* (*obsolete*) mithridate, antidote; quack medicine, nostrum; blarney, humbug
Mithridatique, *adj.* Mithridatic
Mitigati-f, ve, *adj.* mitigative, mitigatory
Mitigation, *s.f.* mitigation
Mitiger, *v.a.* to mitigate; to alleviate; to soften; to temper; to moderate
Se —, *v.r.* to become *or* be mitigated, &c.
Mitis, *s.m.* (*obsolete*) Puss
Miton, *s.m.* mitten, mitt; Puss. *De l'onguent — mitaine,* a chip in porridge, a useless remedy *or* expedient
Mitonnage, *s.m.* (*cook.*) stock; simmering
Mitonner, *v.a.n.* to simmer, to soak, to stew; to nurse up, to coddle; to pet; to humour; to contrive, to manage, to prepare; to let ripen
Se —, *v.r.* to simmer, to be simmering, to stew; to nurse oneself up, to coddle oneself; to be preparing *or* prepared
Mitouche, *s.f.* (*bad spelling*) *V.* **Nitouche**
Mitoyen, ne, *adj.* middle, intermediate, midway; party; joint-property. *Mur —,* party-wall
Mitoyenneté, *s.f.* middle *or* mean *or* common state; joint property; party-right
†**Mitraillade,** *s.f.* discharge *or* fire of grape-shot (*or* canister *or* case-shot), firing ditto
†**Mitraille,** *s.f.* (*obsolete*) scrap-metal, scrap-iron, old metal, old iron; (*slang*) small coin, coppers, browns, mags; (*tech.*) solder, soldering; (*artil.*) grape-shot, canister *or* case-shot; langrage, langrel. *Tirer à —,* to fire grape-shot *or* &c.
†**Mitrailler,** *v.a.* to fire on (...) with grape-shot
†**Mitrailleu-r, se,** *s.m.f.* wholesale slaughterer; machine-gun, rifled battery, mitrailleur, mitrailleuse
Mitral, e, *adj.* mitral
Mitre, *s.f.* mitre; chimney-pot, chimney-top; (*of a knife*) shoulder; (*of fowls*) hinder part, bishop's mitre, bishop
Mitré, e, *adj.* mitred

Mitriforme, *adj.* mitriform
Mitron, *s.m.* baker's man, journeyman baker *or* pastrycook; paper cap
Mitte, *s.f.* cesspool exhalation, mephitic air, stench; eyesore from ditto [body, compound
Mixte, *adj.* mixed; compound; — *s.m.* mixed
†**Mixtiligne,** *adj.* (*geom.*) mixtilinear
Mixtion, *s.f.* mixing, mixture
Mixtionner, *v.a.* to mix
Mixture, *s.f.* mixture; (*agr.*) meslin [3, § 1
Mnémon-ique (*adj.*), **-iquement.** *V.* page
Mnémonique, *s.f.* mnemonics
Mnémoniser, *v.a.* to mnemonize
Mnémosyne, *s.f.* (*myth.*) Mnemosyne; (*poet.*, *fig.*) *V.* **Mémoire,** *s.f.* [technician
‡**Mnémotechnicien, ne,** *s.m.f.* mnemo-
‡**Mnémotechn-ie, -ique, -iquement.**
Moabite, *s.m.f. adj.* Moabite [*V.* page 3, § 1
Mobile, *adj.* movable; moving; variable; unfixed; unsettled; unsteady; fickle; versatile; sliding (*scale*); mobilized; mobile; — *s.m.* body in motion; mover, moving power; spring, motive, incentive, cause, originator; militiaman; — *s.f.* militia. *Garde* —, (*s.f.*) militia; (*s.m.*) militiaman
Mobili-er, ère, Mobiliaire, *adj.* (*law*) movable, personal, in *or* of personal property
Mobilier, *s.m.* furniture; suite; (*obsolete*) personal property, movables [property
Mobilièrement, *adv.* as (*or* in) personal
Mobilisable, *adj.* mobilizable
Mobilisation, *s.f.* (*law*) conversion into movables, making movable, mobilization; liberation; (*mil.*) mobilization
Mobiliser, *v.a.* (*law*) to convert into movables, to make movable, to mobilize; to liberate; (*mil.*) to mobilize
Mobilité, *s.f.* mobility; variableness; unsteadiness; instability; inconstancy; fickleness; versatility; uncertainty
Moblot, *s.m.* (*jest.*) militiaman [sin
Mocassin, *s.m.* mocassin, moccassin, mocca-
Moche, *s.f.* (*of silk*) package
Mock, *s.m.* amuck. *Courir le* —, to run amuck
Moco, *s.m.* (*zool.*) moco
Modal, e, *adj.* modal
Modalité, *s.f.* modality
Mode, *s.f.* mode; fashion; custom, way, manner; vogue; —**s,** *pl.* modes, &c.; millinery; fashionable articles of dress. *A la* —, according to the fashion; in *or* of fashion; fashionable; fashionably; in vogue; popular; (*of beef*) a-la-mode. *De* —, in fashion, fashionable. *Hors* or *Passé de* —, out of fashion, old-fashioned. *Passer de* —, to get *or* go out of fashion. *Marchande de* —*s*, milliner
Mode, *s.m.* mode; form; method; (*gram.*) mood
Modelage, *s.m.* modelling
Modèle, *s.m.* model; pattern; sample; design; copy *or* slip (*of writing*); sitter
Modelé, *s.m.* modelling; form, shape; — *m.*, **e,** *f.*, *adj.* modelled
Modeler, *v.a.* to model; to shape; to mould
Se — (sur), *v.r.* to take for o.'s model, to
Modeleur, *s.m.* modeller [copy, to imitate
Modénais, e, Modénois, e, *adj.s.* Modenese
Modénature, *s.f.* (*arch.*) members, mouldings
Modérant-isme, -iste. *V.* page 3, § 1
Modéra-teur, trice, *s.m.f.* moderator; moderatrix; — *adj.* moderating; modifying
Modération, *s.f.* moderation; abatement; mitigation; modification
Modérato, *adj.* (*mus.*) moderato
Modéré, e, *adj. s.* moderate; temperate
Modérément, *adv.* moderately, in moderation
Modérer, *v.a.* to moderate; to restrain; to check; to slacken; to abate; to mitigate; to temper; to modify
Se —, *v.r.* to moderate *or* restrain oneself; to keep o.'s temper; to abate, to grow moderate
Moderne, *adj. s.* modern; modern style
Modernement, *adv.* modernly
Moderner, *v.a.* to modernize
Modernisation, *s.f.* modernization
Moderniser, *v.a.* to modernize
Modern-isme, -iste. *V.* page 3, § 1
Modernité, *s.f.* modernness
Modeste, *adj.* modest; unpretending, unassuming; coy; unostentatious, quiet; simple, plain; humble; moderate
Modestement, *adv.* modestly; coyly; unostentatiously, quietly; simply, plainly; humbly; moderately
Modestie, *s.f.* modesty; coyness; simplicity, plainness; humbleness; moderateness; moderation [ness
Modicité, *s.f.* smallness; moderateness; low-
Modifiabilité, *s.f.* modifiability
Modifiable, *adj.* modifiable [*s.m.f.* modifier
Modifica-teur, trice, *adj.* modifying; —
Modificati-f, ve, *adj.* modificatory; — *s.m.* modificative
Modification, *s.f.* modification; restriction
Modifier, *v.a.* to modify. *Se* —, to be modified
†**Modillon,** *s.m.* (*arch.*) modillion; cantalever, cantilever; dentil; corbel
Modique, *adj.* moderate, small
Modiquement, *adv.* moderately, little
Modiste, *s.f.* milliner; — *s.m.* (*obsolete*) man-
Modulaire, *adj.* modular [milliner
Modula-teur, trice, *s.m.f.* modulator
Modulation, *s.f.* modulation
Module, *s.m.* (*arch.*) module; (*fig.*) measure; (*of medals and coins*) diameter; (*math., phys., mech.*) modulus
Moduler, *v.a n.* to modulate; to warble
Mœhringie, *s.f.* (*bot.*) mœhringia
Moelle, *s.f.* marrow; pith; (*of the land*) fat. — *allongée*, (*anat.*) medulla oblongata. — *épinière*, spinal cord, spinal marrow. — *des os*, marrow of the bones. *Os à* —, marrow-bone. *Jusqu'à* (or *Jusque dans*) *la* — *des os*, (*fig.*) to the backbone, every inch [mellowness; easily
Moelleusement, *adv.* pithily; softly; with
Moelleu-x, se, *adj.* marrowy; pithy; soft; full and soft; mellow; easy; (*of wine*) having good body and flavour, rich; — *s.m.* softness; mellowness; easiness, ease
Moellon, *s.m.* (*mas.*) ashlar; shiver; ragstone; rubble, rough stone
Moët, *s.m.* Moët champagne (wine)
Mœurs, *s.f.pl.* manners; customs; habits; way of life; behaviour; morals; morality;
Mofette, *s.f. V.* **Moufette** [principle
Mogol, *s.m.* Mogul
Mograbin, e, *adj. s. V.* **Maugrabin**
Moha, *s.m.* (*bot.*) moha, mohar, German millet
Mohair, *s.m.* mohair
Mohican, *s.m.* Mohican
Moi, *pers.pron.* me; to *or* at me; for *or* with *or* in *or* from me; I; for my part; as for me, as to me; myself; — *s.m.* self; subject. *A* —, *à* — *à*, *à* — *de*, *V.* **A.** *A* — *!* help! — *-même*, myself; alone; too, also, likewise
Moidore, *s.m.* moidore (*old Portuguese coin*)
†**Moignet,** *s.m.* (*bird*) long-tailed tit
†**Moignon,** *s.m.* (*of limbs, trees*) stump. — *de l'épaule*, (*anat.*) shoulder-joint [race
†**Moinaille,** *s.f.* (*in contempt*) monks, monkish
Moindre, *adj.* less; smaller; shorter; lower; inferior; meaner; slighter; least; smallest; shortest; lowest; meanest; slightest
Moindrement, *adv.* (*old*) less. *Le* —, in the least, in the slightest degree. *Pas le* —, not in the least, not a bit (of it)
Moine, *s.m.* monk; friar; foot-warmer, bed-warmer; (*print.*) friar. — *bourru*, bugbear, goblin; (*fig.*) bear, brute. *Gras comme un* —, as fat as a mole. *L'habit ne fait pas le* —, the cowl does not make the friar, it is not the coat that makes the man
Moineau, *s.m.* sparrow; (*jest.*) petty monk; — *adj.m.* (*of horses*) cropped. — *domestique*, — *franc*, house-sparrow

Moinerie, *s.f.* monkery; monkhood; monks
Moinesse, *s.f.* (*jest.*) nun
†Moinillon, *s.m.* (*jest.*) petty monk *or* friar
Moinotin, *s.m.* (*bird*) great tit; cole-tit
Moins, *adv. s.m.* less; not so; not so much; the less; fewer; the fewer; least; fewest; except, but; under; minus; (*of the hour*) to; (*print.*) metal-rule, dash. *A —*, at *or* for *or* with less; under. *A — de*, at *or* for *or* with less than; under; unless; except in case of. *A — que*, unless. *Au* , at least; at the least; however; above all; mind! I should think; I hope; at all events. *Dans — de, en — de*, in less than. *De —*, less; wanting; missing; too little; younger. *De — en —*, less and less; fewer and fewer. *Du —*, at least; at all events, at any rate; however. *En —*, less, as so much less; to be deducted; against. *Le —*, the least; as little *or* as few as. *N'en ... pas —*, ... nevertheless, not less for that, for all that. *Non — que*, not less than, as much as, as well as. *Pour le —*, at least, at the least. *Tout au —*, at the very least. *Six heures — un quart*, (a) quarter to six o'clock. *Il est — vingt, — le quart*, it is twenty minutes to, a quarter to. *— bien*, not so well. *Bien —*, much less
Moirage, *s.m.* watering (*of stuffs*, &c.); mottling [moire. *— antique*, moire antique
Moire, *s.f.* watering, moire; watered silk,
Moiré, *s.m.* watering; — *m.*, **e,** *f.*, *part. adj.* watered; mottled. *— de ...*, watered ... *— métallique*, crystallized tin-plate
Moirer, *v.a.* to water (*stuffs*, &c.); to mottle
Se —, *v.r.* to be watered *or* waved
Moireur, *s.m.* waterer (*of stuffs*, &c.); mottler
Mois, *s.m.* month; month's work; month's (*or* monthly) pay *or* wages *or* salary *or* allowance; (*med.*) course, term. *Au —*, by the month; (*de*) in the month (of) [notched rail
Moise, *s.f.* (*carp.*) brace, couple, binding-piece,
Moiser, *v.a.* (*carp.*) to bridge over, to bind
Moisi, e, *adj.* mouldy, musty, rusty; — *s.m.* mould, mouldiness, mustiness; mouldy part; rustiness
Moisir, *v.a.* to mould, to make mouldy *or* musty *or* rusty; — *v.n.*, **Se —,** *v.r.* to mould, to get *or* grow mouldy *or* musty *or* rusty; (*fig.*) to remain long, to rot [mouldy part; rustiness
Moisissure, *s.f.* mouldiness, mustiness;
Moissine, *s.f.* bundle of vine-branches with hanging grapes
Moisson, *s.f.* harvest; reaping; crop; harvest-time, harvest-home; (*poet.*) year. *Fête de la —*, harvest-festival, harvest-home. *Faire la —*, to reap *or* cut the corn, to reap *or* gather in the harvest
Moissonnage, *s.m.* harvesting, reaping
Moissonner, *v.a.* to reap; to harvest; to gather; to cut off *or* down, to mow down
Se —, *v.r.* to be reaped *or* &c.
Moissonneu-r, se, *s.m.f.* reaper, harvestman, harvest-woman, harvester, gatherer; — *s.f.* reaping-machine, reaper [spiration
Moite, *adj.* moist; damp; covered with per-
Moitement, *adv.* moistly; damply
Moiteur, *s.f.* moisture; dampness; slight perspiration
Moitié, *s.f.* half; moiety; better half, wife, helpmate, rib; — *adv.* half. *A —*, half; on half profits. *De —*, by half; for one half. *Être* or *Se mettre de —*, to go halves. *— guerre — marchandise*, (*of ships*) armed; (*fig.*) partly by fair and partly by foul means, one half honestly and the other not, dubiously; half willingly half compulsorily, reluctantly. *— figue — raisin*, *V.* **Figue**
Moitir, *v.a.* to wet. *Se —*, to get *or* be wet
Moka, *s.m.* Mocha coffee, mocha
Mol, le, *adj.* *V.* **Mou**
Molaire, *adj.* molar; — *s.f.* molar tooth, molar, grinder. *Fausse* or *petite —*, false molar, pre-
Molard, *s.m.* (*pop.*) gob (*spittle*) [molar
Molarder, *v.n.* (*pop.*) to hawk up phlegm, to
Molariforme, *adj.* molariform [hawk, to gob
Molasse, *s.f.* (*geol.*) molasse
Molassique, *adj.* (*geol.*) molassic
Moldave, *adj. s.m.f.* Moldavian
Moldo-Valaque, *s.m.f. adj.* Moldo-Wallachian
Môle, *s.m.* mole, jetty-head, pier; (*Adrian's*) tomb; — *s.f.* (*med.*) mole; (*fish*) mole-bat;
Moléculaire, *adj.* molecular [(*Adrian's*) tomb
Moléculairement, *adv.* molecularly
Molécule, *s.f.* molecule, particle, small part,
Molène, *s.f.* (*bot.*) mullein [atom
Moleskin, Moleskine, *s.m.* moleskin
Molestation, *s.f.* molestation
Molester, *v.a.* to molest, to vex, to annoy
Moleté, *s.m.* printed ornament (*on pottery*, &c.)
Moleter, *v.a.* to print (*pottery*, &c.)
Molette, *s.f.* (*for colours*) muller; (*of spurs*) rowel; (*her.*) mullet; (*tech.*) vertical pulley; (*rope-making*) whirl; (*hort.*) turf-knife, turfing-iron; (*vet.*) windgall; (*of hair*) feather
Molière, *s.f.* (*obsolete*) bog, swamp
Molin-isme, -iste. *V.* page 3, § 1
Molinos-isme, -iste. *V.* page 3, § 1
Molla, Mollah, *s.m.* (*Turkish*) mollah
Mollasse, *adj.* flabby; sodden; flimsy
Mollement, *adv.* softly; slackly; loosely; flabbily; faintly; weakly; feebly; effeminately; indolently; carelessly; gracefully; luxuriously
Mollesse, *s.f.* softness; slackness; looseness; flabbiness; faintness; weakness; feebleness; want of energy; effeminacy; indolence; indulgence; carelessness; gracefulness; luxuriousness [tender
Mollet, te, *adj.* soft; soft-boiled; light, spongy;
Mollet, *s.m.* calf (*of the leg*)
Molletière, *s.f.* legging
Molleton, *s.m.* swanskin; cotton flannel
Molletonné, e, Molletonneu-x, se, *adj.* (*of stuffs*) with a floss back
Mollificati-f, ve, *adj.* mollificative
Mollification, *s.f.* mollification, softening
Mollifier, *v.a.* to mollify, to soften
Se —, *v.r.* to become soft
Mollir, *v.n.* to soften, to get soft; to slacken; to flag; to abate; to yield, to give way; (*nav.*) to slacken; — *v.a.* (*nav.*) to ease away, to ease
Molluscum, *s.m.* (*med.*) molluscum
Mollusque, *s.m.* (*zool.*) mollusc; shell-fish;
‡Moloch, *s.m.* Moloch [(*fig.*) old fogy
Molosse, *s.m.* American bat, monk-bat; (*poet.*) watch-dog; (*anc. vers.*) molossus
Moly, *s.m.* (*bot.*) moly
Molybdate, *s.m.* (*chem.*) molybdate
Molybdène, *s.m.* (*min.*) molybdenum
Molybdénite, *s.f.* (*min.*) molybdenite
Molybdeux, *adj.m.* (*chem.*) molybdous
Molybdique, *adj.* (*chem.*) molybdic
Môme, *s.m.* urchin, brat, chit, cub
Moment, *s.m.* moment; instant; proper time; time; occasion; point; interval; fit; present, present time; (*mech.*) moment; momentum; leverage. *Du — que*, the moment that, as soon as; since; so long as. *D'un — à l'autre*, every moment; at any time. *Par —, Par —s*, at times, at intervals, now and then. *Pour le —*, for the moment *or* time, for the present, for the nonce, at present, just now, just yet
Momentané, e, *adj.* momentary; temporary
Momentanément, *adv.* momentarily; tem-
Momerie, *s.f.* mummery; hypocrisy [porarily
Momie, *s.f.* mummy; sluggard; old fogy; mummy-colour; (*hort.*) mummy
Mômier, *s.m.* (*in Switzerland*) momier
Momification, *s.f.* mummification; extreme
Momifier, *v.a.* to mummify [emaciation
Se —, *v.r.* to become a mummy; to get very thin
Momon, *s.m.* (*old*) masquerade; challenge, bet
Momordique, *s.f.* (*bot.*) momordica; squirting-cucumber, touch-me-not
Momot, *s.m.* (*bird*) motmot, momot

Momus, *s.m.* Momus; merry song
Mon, *adj.poss.* my, my own
†**Monacaille,** *s.f.* (*old*) *V.* **Moinaille**
Monacal, e, *adj.* monachal, monkish
Monacalement, *adv.* monachally
Monachisme, *s.m.* monachism
Monaco, *s.f.* (*dance, tune*) monaco; — *s.m.* (*pop.*) halfpenny, mag; **—s,** *s.m.pl.* mags; [money, tin
Monade, *s.f.* monad
Monadelphe, *adj.* (*bot.*) monadelphous
Monadelphie, *s.f.* (*bot.*) monadelphia
Monad-ique, -isme, -iste. *V.* page 3, § 1
Monadolog-ie, -ique. *V.* page 3, § 1
Monandre, *adj.* (*bot.*) monandrous
Monandrie, *s.f.* (*bot.*) monandria [*V.* page 3, § 1
Monarch-ie, -ique, -iquement, -isme.
Monarchiser, *v.a.n.* to monarchize
Monarchiste, *s.m.f.* monarchist; — *adj.* [monarchistic
Monarde, *s.f.* (*bot.*) horse-mint
Monarque, *s.m.* monarch; (*pop.*) coin
Monastère, *s.m.* monastery, friary
Monastique, *adj.* monastic
Monaul, *s.m.* *V.* **Lophophore**
Monaut, *adj.m.* one-eared
Monbin, *s.m.* (*bot.*) hog-plum
Monceau, *s.m.* heap; pile; drift; mass; lot
Mondain, e, *adj.* worldly, mundane; fast; — *s.m.f.* worldling; fast man *or* woman
Mondainement, *adv.* in a worldly way, worldly, mundanely
Mondaniser, *v.a.* to mundanize
Mondanité, *s.f.* worldliness
Monde, *s.m.* world; universe; globe; mound (*in heraldry*); earth; mankind; men; people; folks; persons; hands; society, company; set; some one; quantity *or* lot of people, lot; crowd; multitude; number; servants; retinue, attendants; customers; (*obsolete*) good manners, manners. *Au* —, in *or* into *or* to the world; alive, living; to people, &c. *Du* —, of *or* in the world; alive; worldly; fashionable; some people, &c. — *fou,* (*fam.*) immense crowd, tremendous lot of people, regular crush. *Le beau* —, the fashionable world, fashionable people *or* society, people of fashion. *Le grand* —, great people; high life. *Peu de* —, *pas grand* —, few people, not many people. *Le moins du* —, ever so little, at all. *Pas le moins du* —, not in the least. *Pour tout au* —, for all the world. *Tout le* —, everybody, everyone, all the people; anybody, anyone; everybody else, everyone else, other people. *Connaitre le* —, to know the world. *Connaitre son* —, to know whom one has to deal with, to know o.'s customers. *Savoir son* —, to know how to behave. *Mettre au* —, to bring forth
Monde, *adj.* (*obsolete*) clean
Monder, *v.a.* to cleanse; to clean, to wash; (*barley, rice,* &c.) to husk, to hull. *V.* **Orge**
Mondificati-f, ve, *adj.* mundificative, cleansing
Mondification, *s.f.* mundification
Mondifier, *v.a.* to mundify, to cleanse, to clean, [to wash
Mondor, *s.m.* man made of money
Mondrain, *s.m.* sand-mound, sand-hill
Mone, *s.f.* mona, varied monkey
Monésia, *s.f.* (*pharm.*) monesia
Monétaire, *adj.* monetary; coining — *s.m.* (*obsolete*) moneyer
Monétisation, *s.f.* monetization
Monétiser, *v.a.* to monetize
Mongol, e, *s.m.f. adj.* Mongol, Mogul, Mongolian
Mongolique, *adj.* Mongolian
Moniteur, *s.m.* monitor; admonitor; prepositor; Gazette
Monition, *s.f.* (*eccl.*) monition
Monitoire, *adj.m.f., s.m.* (*eccl.*) monitory
Monitor, *s.m.* (*zool., nav.*) monitor
Monitorial, e, *adj.* (*eccl.*) monitory
Monitrice, *s.f.* monitress
Monnaie, *s.f.* coin; money; piece of money; currency; change; mint. — *d'appoint,* small change. — *de compte,* money of account, nominal money. — *forte,* higher coin; (*obsolete*) full weight. — *de singe,* sham coin, soft sawder, soft soap, blarney. *Hôtel de la* — or *des* —*s,* Mint. *Battre* —, to coin money; to raise money. *Donner* or *rendre à quelqu'un la* — *de sa pièce,* to pay one back in his own coin, to give a person as good as he brings. *La* — *de vingt francs,* change for a twenty franc piece [*Droit de* —, mintage
Monnayage, *s.m.* coinage, coining, minting.
Monnayer, *v.a.* to mint, to coin, to stamp
Monnayère, *s.f.* (*bot.*) moneywort
Monnayeur, *s.m.* coiner, mintman. *Faux* —, coiner of bad money; forger
Mono, (*in compounds*) mono...
Monocarpe, *adj.* (*bot.*) monocarpous
Monocéros, *s.m.* (*zool., astr.*) monoceros
‡**Monochromatique,** *adj.* monochromatic
‡**Monochrome,** *s.m. adj.* monochrome
‡**Monochromie,** *s.f.* monochromy
Monocle, *s.m.* single eye-glass, monocular glass, monocle; (*zool.*) monocule, monoculus; (*surg.*) monoculus
Monocorde, *s.m.* (*mus.*) monochord
Monocotylédone, *adj.* (*bot.*) monocotyledonous; — *s.f.* monocotyledon
Monocotylédoné, e, *adj.* (*bot.*) monocotyledonous; — *s.f.* monocotyledon
Monoculaire, *adj.* monocular
Monodactyle, *adj.m.f., s.m.* (*zool.*) monodactyle, monodactylous [monodelphic
Monodelphe, *s.m.* (*zool.*) monodelph; — *adj.*
Monodie, *s.f.* monody
Monogame, *adj.* monogamous; — *s.m.f.* monogamist
Monogam-ie, -ique. *V.* page 3, § 1
Monogramm-atique, -ique, -iste. *V.* page 3, § 1
Monogramme, *s.m.* monogram
Monographe, *s.m.* monograph; monographer
Monograph-ie, -ique. *V.* page 3, § 1
Monogyne, *adj.* (*bot.*) monogynous
Monogynie, *s.f.* (*bot.*) monogynia
Monolithe, *s.m.* monolith; — *adj.* monolithic
Monolog-ie, -ique, -iste. *V.* page 3, § 1
Monologue, *s.m.* monologue, soliloquy
Monomachie, *s.f.* monomachy, single combat
Monomane, *adj. s.m.f.* monomaniac
Monomaniaque, *adj. s.m.f.* monomaniac
Monomanie, *s.f.* monomania; mania
Monôme, *s.m. adj.* (*alg.*) monomial
Monomètre, *s.m.* monometer
Monométrique, *adj.* monometric
Monopétale, Monopétalé, e, *adj.* (*bot.*) monopetalous
Monophylle, *adj.* (*bot.*) monophyllous
Monopole, *s.m.* monopoly
Monopoleur, *s.m.* monopolist, monopolizer
Monopolisa-teur, trice, *adj.* monopolizing
Monopolisation, *s.f.* monopolization
Monopoliser, *v.a.* to monopolize
Se —, *v.r.* to be monopolized
Monopse, *adj.* (*anat.*) monops
Monoptère, *s.m. adj.* (*arch., zool.*) monopteral
Monorime, *s.m. adj.* monorhyme
Monosépale, *adj.* (*bot.*) monosepalous
Monospermatique, Monosperme, Monospermique, *adj.* (*bot.*) monospermous
Monostique, *s.m. adj.* monostich
Monostome, *s.m adj.* (*zool.*) monostoma
Monostyle, Monostylé, e, *adj.* (*bot.*) monostylous [monosyllabic
Monosyllabe, *s.m.* monosyllable; — *adj.*
Monosyllab-ique, -isme. *V.* page 3, § 1
Monothéisme, *s.m.* monotheism [notheistic
Monothéiste, *s.m.f.* monotheist; — *adj.* mo-
Monotone, *adj* monotonous
Monotonie, *s.f* monotony, sameness
Monotrème, *s.m.* (*zool.*) monotreme; — *adj.* monotrematous [— *adj.* monotriglyphic
Monotriglyphe, *s.m.* (*arch.*) monotriglyph;
Mons, *s.m.* (*in derision or contempt*) Master (*so-and-so*); (*obsolete*) my lord (*bishop, archbishop*)
†**Monseigneur,** *s.m.* my lord, your lordship; the lord, his lordship; lord; your Grace; his

Grace; the bishop; the archbishop; your *or* his Royal *or* Imperial Highness; (*of thieves*) crowbar, jemmy

†**Monseigneuriser,** *v.a.* (*jest.*) to call (*or* style) my lord, to mylord; (*slang*) to pick *or* break (*a lock*), to prise open, to jemmy

Monsieur, *s.m.* gentleman; this *or* the gentleman; Sir; Mr., Esq.; Master; your Worship; his Worship; (*jest.*) party, man, fellow; (*vulgarly*) mister (*sir*); (*formerly, the king's eldest brother*) Monsieur; (*of bishops, &c., obsolete*) *V.* **Monseigneur;** (*by abbreviation*) Orleans plum. *Ce* —, that gentleman; (*jest.*) that party, that man, that fellow. — *le docteur*, Doctor; the doctor. — *le président*, Mr. President. — *le maire*, Mr. Mayor, your Worship, his Worship the mayor. — *le comte*, the count *or* earl; my lord, your lordship; his lordship. — *le duc*, the duke; my lord duke, my lord, your Grace; his Grace. — *votre père* or *&c.*, your father *or* &c. — *désire-t-il* ...? does this gentleman wish ...? do you wish ..., [sir?

Monsieurs, *s.m.pl.* Orleans plums

Monstre, *s.m. adj.* monster

Monstrueusement, *adv.* monstrously

Monstrueu-x se, *adj.* monstrous; huge, immense; prodigious, stupendous; absurd

Monstruosité, *s.f.* monstrosity

Mont, *s.m.* mount, mountain; (*also, a pop. abbrev. of* "mont-de-piété"); **—s,** *pl.* mounts, &c.; Alps. *—s et merveilles*, wonderful things, wonderful tales *or* stories, wonders. *Par —s et par vaux*, up hill and down dale. — **-de-piété,** *s.m.* Mont-de-piété, pawnbroker's shop, pawnshop. *Commissionnaire au* (or *du*) — *-de-piété*, pawnbroker. *Mettre au — -de-piété*, to pawn

Montage, *s.m.* rising; raising, taking up, bringing up, carrying up; setting, mounting; &c. (*V.* **Monter,** *v.n.a.*)

†**Montagnard, e,** *adj.* mountain; highland; — *s.m.f.* mountaineer; highlander; (*Fr. hist.*) Montagnard (*ultra-revolutionist*)

†**Montagne,** *s.f.* mountain, mount; hill; highland; (*Fr. hist.*) Mountain (*ultra-revolutionist party*). — *de glace*, iceberg. *Pays de —s*, mountainous *or* hilly country, highland

†**Montagneu-x, se,** *adj.* mountainous, hilly

Montaison, *s.f.* (*of trouts, &c.*) season of ascending rivers, spawning-season

Montanine, *s.f.* (*chem.*) montanine

Montan-isme, -iste. *V.* page 3, § 1

Montant, *s.m.* amount, sum total; upright; beam, stone, bar; side-piece (*of a ladder*); jamb, door-post; stalk, stem; rising, rise; rising tide, flood, flowing water; strength; flavour; pungency; energy; pith; smartness; stylo

Montant, e, *part. adj.* ascending, rising, going up, &c. (*V.* **Monter**); upward, up; up-hill; hilly; steep; (*of dress*) high; (*of collars*) stand-up. *Garde —e*, (*mil.*) relieving-guard. *En* —, on ascending *or* going up, &c.; upward; up-hill. *Aller en* —, to go up-hill, to rise

Monte, *s.f.* (*of animals*) covering, serving; covering season; — *s.m.f.* (*in compounds, from* **Monter,** "to ascend," &c.) thing (*m.*) that ascends *or* where one ascends, &c., person (*m.f.*) that ascends, &c. — **-à-regret,** *V.* **Abbaye.** — **-au-ciel,** *s.m.* (*bot.*) persicaria

Monté, e, *part. adj.* ascended, &c. (*V.* **Monter**); high; aloft; mounted; riding; standing; disposed, in a mood *or* humour; ...-legged; (*of wine*) harsh. *Bien* —, well-disposed, in a good mood *or* humour; well-supplied; well-appointed; well-mounted *or* &c.; riding a good horse. *Mal* —, ill-disposed, in a bad mood *or* humour; ill-supplied; ill-appointed; badly mounted *or* &c.; riding a bad horse

Montée, *s.f.* ascent; rising; acclivity; slope; staircase; flight; ladder; step, stair; (*arch.*) height; (*fish.*) eel-fare; young eels

Monténégrin, e, *adj. s.* Montenegrin

Monter, *v.n.a.* to ascend; to mount; to go *or* come up; to rise; to go up-hill; to get up *or* in; to walk *or* step up; to run up; to fly up; to reach; to amount; to ride; to grow up, to shoot; to flush; to flow; to boil up *or* over; (*of drinks*) to get *or* fly (*into o.'s head*); to get; to climb; to climb up; to carry *or* bring up, to take up; to lift up; to raise; to increase; to supply; to equip; to furnish; to stock; to fit out *or* up; to make up; to put up; to put together; to prepare, to get up; to wind up; to set up; to establish; to set; to string; to tune; to command (*a ship*); to embark on (*a ship*); to man (*a ship or boat*); to be in (*a boat*); to cover; to irritate, to incense; to heat; to excite, to work up, to turn. *Faire* —, to make (...) go *or* get *or* come up *or* ascend *or* rise; to fetch up; to send up; to call up; to ask *or* show up; to take up, to bring *or* carry up; to get up; to place; to force up; to raise; to increase; to raise the price of; to swell; to run up; (*pop.*) to tease, to rile, to work up, to aggravate

Se —, *v.r.* to rise, to reach; to amount, to come (to); to provide oneself, to take in a stock *or* supply; to become *or* get excited; to be mounted *or* &c.

Monteu-r, se, *s.m.f.* mounter; setter; fitter; getter-up; (ladies') cap-mounter

Montfaucon, *s.m.* Montfaucon (*near Paris*); the gibbet, the gallows; the knacker's yard; the common sewer [balloon

Montgolfière, *s.f.* fire-balloon, heated-air

Monticole, *adj.* living on mountains, mountain

Monticule, *s.m.* hillock, knoll

Montjoie, *s.f.* (*obsolete*) cairn; — *int.* Montjoie! (*formerly, war-cry of the French*); — *s.m.* (*obsolete*) Montjoie (*first king-at-arms in France*)

Montmartrite, *s.f.* (*min.*) montmartrite

Montmorency, *s.f.* Montmorency cherry; — *s.m.* cavalry-sword

Montoir, *s.m.* mounting; horse-block; near-side. *Côté du* —, near-side. *Côté hors du* — or *hors* —, off-side. *Aisé, difficile au* —, easy, difficult to mount

Montois, e, *adj. s.* of Mons; native of Mons

Montrable, *adj.* showable

Montrachet, *s.m.* montrachet (wine)

Montre, *s.f.* watch; sample, pattern; show; exhibition; parade; display; appearance; show-case; show-glass; show-window, window; place to show horses; horse-show; (*of an organ*) front, outside; (*mil., obsolete*) review; muster; demonstration. — *marine*, chronometer, time-keeper. — *à répétition*, repeating watch, repeater. — *à savonnette*, double-cased watch, hunting watch. *Affiche de* —, show-card. *Boite de* —, watch-case. *En* —, conspicuously; (*com.*) in the window

Montrer, *v.a.* to show; to point out; to exhibit; to point; to let see; to intimate; to prove; to teach; to shake *or* double (*o.'s fist at* ...)

Se —, *v.r.* to appear; to make o.'s appearance; to come out; to show oneself *or* o.'s face; to prove oneself to be; to look; to turn out; to prove; (— *bien*) to show spirit *or* firmness *or* resolution; — *mal*, to show a want of [ditto

†**Montreuil,** *s.f.* Montreuil peach

Montreu-r, se, *s.m.f.* shower, showman

Montueu-x, se, *adj.* hilly; swelling

Montuosité, *s.f.* hilliness

Monture, *s.f.* animal (for riding), beast, horse *or* &c., steed, nag; mounting, mount; setting; frame; stock; foil; (*of bridles*) head-stall; (*of spurs*) leather [grave

Monument, *s.m.* monument; memorial; tomb,

Monumental, e, *adj.* monumental; memorial

Moquable, *adj.* mockable, laughable, ridicu- [lous

Moque, *s.f.* (*local*) mug

Moquer (Se), *v.r.* to deride, to mock, to scoff, to ridicule, to jeer, to sneer, to make game *or*

fun (of), to laugh (at); to trifle (with); to make a fool (of); not to care (for), to disregard, to have *or* show no respect *or* no regard (for); to scorn; to neglect; to set at defiance, to defy, to dare, to brave, to beard; to jest, to joke; to laugh (*or* &c.) at people. *Se faire — de soi*, to get laughed at, to make a fool of oneself. *Je me moque bien de, je me moque pas mal de*, what do I care for

Moquerie, *s.f.* mockery; derision; scoff, jeer, jeering, sneer, sneering; scorn; trifling

Moquette, *s.f.* velvet pile, moquette; call-bird; **—s,** *pl.* roebuck-dung

Moqueu-r, se, *adj.* mocking; deriding; scoffing; jeering; sneering; scornful; — *s.m.f.* mocker; derider; scoffer; jeerer; sneerer; quiz; wag; — *s.m.* mocking bird

†Moraille, *s.f.* horse-twitchers, twitchers, barnacles

†Moraillon, *s.m.* hasp, clasp

Moraine, *s.f.* (*geol., of glaciers*, &c.) moraine, border; (*mas.*) border; (*wool*) mortling, morling, dead wool; — *adj.f.* (*of wool*) dead

Moral, e, *adj.* moral; mental

Moral, *s.m.* mind, moral, mental *or* moral faculties; moral sense; spirits, (*in the language of illiterate people in England*) morale

Morale, *s.f.* ethics, morals; morality; lecture, reprimand, rebuke; (*of fables*, &c.) moral. *Faire de la —*, to moralize; to lecture

Moralement, *adv.* morally

Moralisa-teur, trice, *adj.* moralizing; — *s.m.f.* moralizer

Moralisation, *s.f.* moralization

Moraliser, *v n.a.* to moralize; to lecture

Se —, *v.r.* to become moral

Moraliseur, *s.m.* moralizer

Moraliste, *s.m.* moralist; moralizer

Moralité, *s f.* morality; morals; moral sense, moral responsibility; (*of fables*, &c.) moral

Morate, *s.m.* (*chem.*) morate

Moratoire, *adj. Intérêts —s*, (*law*) interest on a judgment debt

Morave, *adj. s.m.f* Moravian

Morbide, *adj.* morbid; (*paint.*) soft and delicate

Morbidement, *adv.* morbidly; (*paint.*) softly and delicately

Morbidesse, *s.f.* (*paint.*) softness, delicacy, (*Italian*) morbidezza

Morbidité, *s.f.* morbidity, morbidness

Morbifique, *adj.* morbific

Morbilleu-x, se, *adj.* (*med.*) morbillous

Morbleu, *int.* hang it! zounds! s'death!

Morceau, *s m.* piece; bit; morsel; snack; mouthful; lump; plot, patch; scrap; fragment; extract. — *de pain*, piece *or* bit of bread; (*fig*) old song, song, mere nothing. — *trempé*, sop. *Bon —*, good *or* nice piece; tit-bit; good thing

Morceler, *v.a* to parcel out, to parcel; to partition; to divide; to cut up; to mangle

Se —, *v.r.* to be parcelled out *or* &c.

Morcellement, *s.m.* parcelling out, parcelling; partition; dividing, division

Mordache, *s.f.* (*tech.*) tongs; jaw; wood-clam; vice-chops; gag

Mordacité, *s.f.* mordacity, corrosiveness; bitterness, sarcasm

Mordançage, *s.m.* mordanting

Mordancer, *v.a.n.* to mordant

Mordant, e, *adj.* biting; corrosive; mordant; mordacious; cutting; sharp; keen; smart; satirical; sarcastic; poignant; thrilling; — *s.m.* mordant; sharpness; keenness; smartness; sarcasm; pointedness; point; poignancy; thrilling sound; — *s.f.* (*thieves' slang*) saw, file

Mordéhi, *s.m.* (*med.*) mordehi, mordezym, mort-de-chien (*Indian disease*)

Mordelle, *s.f.* (*insect*) mordella

Mordette, *s.f. V.* **Man**

Mordeu-r, se, *s.m.f.* biter; — *adj.* biting

Mordicant, e, *adj.* mordicant, acrid, pungent, &c. (*V.* **Mordant**)

Mordication, *s.f.* mordication

Mordicus, *adv.* tenaciously, obstinately, doggedly, stoutly, through thick and thin

Mordié, *int.* (*old*) *V.* **Mordieu**

Mordienne, *s.f. int.* a plague! hang it! confound ...! zounds! *A la grosse —*, openly, bluntly, unceremoniously

Mordieu, *int.* hang it! confound it! zounds! s'death!

†Mordillage, *s.m.* biting slightly, nibbling

†Mordiller, *v.a.n.* to bite at, to bite slightly, to nibble

Mordoré, e, *adj.*, **Mordoré,** *s.m.* reddish brown

Mordorure, *s.f.* reddish brown colour

Mordre, *v.a.n.* to bite; to bite off; to gnaw; to nip; to corrode; to censure, to carp at; to attack; to take effect; to take; to like, to take to; to get on (with); to come (at); to get a hold (on); to catch; to try; to engage; to hold fast. — *à l'hameçon* or *à la grappe*, to bite at the hook, to take *or* swallow the bait; to jump at a *or* the proposal

Se —, *v.r.* to bite oneself *or* each other; to bite (o.'s ...) *Se — les doigts* or *les pouces* or *les lèvres*, (*fig.*) to repent; to be vexed. *Se — la langue*, to bite o.'s tongue; (*fig.*) to stop short (*in speaking*); to repent (*having said a thing*)

Mords, *s.m.* (*tech.*) jaw; chop

More, *s.m.* Moor; blackamoor

Mor-eau, elle, *adj.* (*of horses*) jet-black; — *s.m.f.* jet-black horse *or* mare

Moreau, *s.m.* nose-bag

Morelle, *s.f.* (*bot.*) nightshade

Morène, *s.f.* (*bot.*) frogbit

Moresque, *adj.* Moorish; moresque; — *s.f.* Mooress; morris-dance, Moorish dance; moresque

Morfil, *s.m.* wire edge; elephant's teeth

Morfondre, *v.a.* to chill

Se —, *v.r.* to be *or* get chilled, to be frozen to death, to shiver with cold; (*of dough*) to spend its heat; (*fig.*) to dance attendance; to wait in vain; to waste o.'s time

Morfondu, e, *part. adj.* chilled, frozen; disappointed; kept waiting; damaged; addled, addle, abortive

Morfondure, *s.f.* (*vet., obsolete*) cold, chill, catarrh

Morganat-ique, -iquement. *V.* page 3, § 1

Morgane, *s.f.* (*fairy*) Morgana, Morgane. *Fée —, château de la fée —*, Fata Morgana

Morgeline, *s.f.* (*bot.*) chickweed, sword-grass

Morgeot, *s.m.* morgeot (wine)

Morgue, *s f.* proud look; haughtiness, arrogance; conceitedness; dead-house; (*of a prison*) inspection-room

Morgué, Morguène, Morguenne, Morguienne, *int.* (*boorish*) dang it!

Morguer, *v a.* (*old*) to brave, to defy, to beard; to ridicule

Moribond, e, *adj. s.* moribund, dying; dying man *or* woman

Moricaud, e, *adj.* blackish; — *s.m.f.* blacky; sambo, nigger; black silkworm

Morigéner, *v.a* to reprimand, to lecture, to tutor; (*old*) to form the morals of, to educate; to reform, to correct

Se —, *v.r.* to reform oneself

†Morille, *s.f.* (*bot.*) morel

†Morillon, *s.m.* black grape; tufted duck; rough emerald

Morin (Michel), *s.m. V.* **Michel**

Morinde, *s.f.* (*bot.*) morinda

Morine, *s.f.* (*chem.*) morine; (*bot.*) morina

Moringe, *s.m.* (*bot.*) moringa

Morion, *s.m.* (*old*) morion (*helmet*); (*jewel.*) morion, black rock crystal

Morique, *adj.* (*chem.*) moric

Mormon, *s.m.* (*baboon*) mandrill; (*bird*) puffin, mormon; (*pers.*) Mormon, Mormonite

Mormon, ne, *adj. s.* Mormonite

Mormonisme, *s.m.* Mormonism

Mormyre, *s.m.* (*fish*) mormyrus

Morne, *adj.* depressed, cast down, dejected, gloomy, dismal, dull; — *s.m.* hill, hillock

Morné, e, *adj.* blunted; (*her.*) morne

Mornement, *adv.* gloomily, dismally, dully

Mornet, *s.m.* hillock, mound

Mornette, *s.f.* ferrule, ring

Mornifle, *s.f.* (*pop.*) slap on the snout, bunch of fives

Morose, *adj.* morose, sullen, peevish, surly

Morosité, *s.f.* moroseness, sullenness, peevishness, surliness [sleep
Morphée, *s.m.* (*myth.*) Morpheus; (*old poet.*)
Morphine, *s.f.* (*chem.*) morphia
Morphique, *adj.* (*chem.*) morphic [page 3, § 1
Morpholog-ie, -ique, -iquement, &c. *V.*
Morpion, *s.m.* crab-louse; (*pers., pop.*) varmint
Morrène, *s.f. V.* **Morène**
Mors, *s.m.* bridle-bit, bit; (*fig.*) bridle, curb, check, restraint. *Prendre le — aux dents,* to run away; (*pers.*) to fly into a passion; to get quite loose *or* wild; to fall desperately to work
Morse, *s.m.* (*zool.*) morse, walrus, sea-horse
Morsure, *s.f.* biting; bite; sting; wound
Mort, *s.f.* death. *— aux mouches,* fly-destroyer, fly-paper *or* powder *or* water. *— aux rats,* rats' bane, rat-destroyer, rat-destroying powder *or* &c. *La petite —,* (*pop.*) the shivers. *A —, A la —,* to death; to the death; to the knife; mortally; terribly, dreadfully, awfully, with a vengeance. *A la vie et à la —,* in life and death, for ever; an eternal friendship. *Donner la —,* to be the death of, to kill, to destroy, to poison. *Être à la —,* to be dying, to be on *or* at the point of death. *Mourir de sa belle —,* to die a natural death
Mort, e, *adj.* dead; lifeless; inanimate; lying dead; dull; slack; faint; stagnant; standing; still; (*of tides*) neap; (*of shot*) spent; (*of fire, light, pers. at play*) out; (*of paper*) unstamped; (*of loads*) excessive; *— part.* died; *— s.m.f.* dead person; dead body, corpse; deceased; (*at whist*) dummy; **—s,** *s.m.pl.* dead. *Fête* or *jour des —s,* All-Souls'-Day. *Tête de —, V.* **Tête.** *Être —,* (*pers.*) to be dead, &c.; to have died. *Il est —,* he is dead; he has died; he died. *Faire le —,* to pretend to be dead. *Faire un —, faire une partie du —,* (*whist*) to play dummy. — **-bois, —e-paye, —e-saison,** &c., *V.* **Bois, Paye, Saison,** &c. — **-gage,** *s.m.* (*law, obsolete*) dead pledge, mortgage. — **-ivre,** *adj.* dead-drunk. — **-né, e,** *adj.* still-born
Mortadelle, *s.f.* (Italian) sausage
†Mortaillable, *adj.* (*feud.*) in servitude
Mortaisage, *s.m.* mortising [—, to mortise
Mortaise, *s.f.* mortise. *Assembler* or *tailler à*
Mortaiser, *v.a.* to mortise
Mortaiseuse, *s.f.* mortising-machine
Mortalité, *s.f.* mortality
Mortel, le, *adj.* mortal; deadly; destructive; grievous; extreme, excessive; dreadful; long and tedious; *— s.m.f.* mortal
Mortellement, *adv.* mortally; deadly; grievously; excessively; dreadfully
Mortellerie, *s.f.* stone-breaking
Mortellier, *s.m.* stone-breaker
Mortier, *s.m.* mortar; (*old*) mortier, cap, coif. *Président à —,* chief justice
Mortifère, *adj.* mortiferous, deadly
Mortification, *s.f.* mortification; keeping (*meat*) till it becomes tender
Mortifier, *v.a.* to mortify; to vex; to humble; to subdue; to make (*meat*) tender
Se —, *v.r.* to mortify oneself *or* o.'s body; to mortify; (*of meat*) to become *or* grow tender
Mortodes, *s.f.pl.* artificial pearls, beads
Mortuaire, *adj.* mortuary; funeral; burial; of death; of the dead; of the deceased; of deaths; of mortality; *— s.f.* table *or* bill of mortality. *Drap —,* pall. *Droit —,* burial fees; mortuary
Moruau, *s.m.* (*fish*) codling
Morue, *s.f.* cod, cod-fish; (*pers., pop.*) slut, mopsey, drab, bitch [fishing vessel
Moruy-er, ère, *adj.* cod-fishing; *— s.m.* cod-
Morvandiot, e, *adj. s.* of Morvan; native of Morvan; Morvan horse *or* mare [rot
Morve, *s.f.* snot, mucus; (*vet.*) glanders; (*hort.*)
Morveau, *s.m.* thick mucus
Morver, *v.n.* (*hort.*) to rot
Morveu-x, se, *adj.* snotty; snotty-nosed; (*vet.*) glandered; (*hort.*) rotting; *— s.m.f.* snotty-nosed boy *or* girl; brat, urchin; despicable fellow *or* creature, slut, drab. *Qui se sent — se mouche,* let him whom the cap fits wear it
Morvolant, *s.m.* silk mixed with floss
Mosaïque, *adj.* Mosaic (*of Moses*); *— s.f.* mosaic, mosaic work; tesselation; tesselated pavement. *En —,* mosaic; tesselated
Mosaïsme, *s.m.* Mosaism
Mosaïste, *s.m.* mosaist [**Mozarabique**
Mosarabe, Mosarabique. *V.* **Mozarabe,**
Mosasaure, Mosasaurus, *s.m. V.* **Mososaure** [chatel
Moscatelle, Moscatelline, *s.f.* (*bot.*) mos-
‡Moschifère, *adj.* moschiferous, musk-bearing
Moscouade, *s.f.* muscovado (*sugar*) [fashion
Moscovite, *adj. s.m.f.* Muscovite; Muscovite
Moselle, *s.m.* moselle (wine)
Mosette, *s.f. V.* **Mozette**
Mosieu, *pop. for* **Monsieur**
Moslem, *s.m.* Moslem [sosaurus, mosasaurus
Mososaure, Mososaurus, *s.m.* (*zool.*) mo-
Mosquée, *s.f.* mosque
†Mosquillon, *s.m.* (*bird*) grey wagtail
Mosquito, *s.m.* (*geog.*) inhabitant of the Mosquito coast, Mosquito
Mot, *s.m.* word; right *or* exact word; expression; term; saying; say; motto; note; memorandum; hint; intimation; cue; instructions; price; quarrel, disagreement; upshot; secret; (*of enigmas,* &c.) answer. *— à —,* word for word, verbatim, literally; literal; verbally; verbal; (*s.m.*) literal translation; particulars; every-day occurrences. *— du guet* (*obsolete*), *— d'ordre,* watch-word, pass-word. *— de passe,* pass-word. *— pour rire,* joke, jest, humour, fun. *Bon —,* smart *or* witty *or* quaint saying, witty expression, witticism, wit; repartee; jest, joke. *Demi- —, V.* **Demi.** *Fin —,* main point; gist; force; upshot; key; secret intention; secret; truth of it; rights. *— fin,* sharp *or* shrewd expression. *Gros —s,* high words, hard words, abuse; oaths, expletives. *Au bas —,* at the lowest; to put it at the lowest; at the least; to say the least of it, to put it in its mildest form. *En un —,* in short, in a word. *Sans — dire,* without saying a word, without a word. *Avoir le —,* to have o.'s cue, to know what one has to say *or* to do; to have been warned; to be in the secret. *Avoir le — pour rire,* to be facetious *or* jocose, to crack a joke. *Prendre quelqu'un au —,* to take one at his word. *Se donner le —,* to have an understanding, to agree. *Tenir le —,* to take the bet. *Trancher le —,* to speak plainly, not to mince the matter. *Qui ne dit — consent,* silence gives consent
Motacille, *s.f.* (*bird*) wagtail
Motelle, *s.f.* (*fish*) rockling, whistle-fish
Motet, *s.m.* (*mus.*) motet
Mo-teur, trice, *s.m.f.* mover, moving power, propeller; author; contriver; originator; cause; motor; *— adj.* moving, motive, propelling, driving; (*anat.*) motor, motory
Motif, *s.m.* motive; reason, cause, ground, account; (*mus., paint., sculp.,* &c.) subject; design, pattern. *Le bon —,* (*jest.*) matrimony, marriage
Motilité, *s.f.* motility
Motion, *s.f.* motion
Motivé, e, *part. adj.* with its motive *or* motives stated, supported by a statement of reasons *or* by arguments alleged; founded (upon); justified; brought on *or* about (by); taken *or* come to in consequence (of); not without a motive *or* a cause; natural, reasonable
Motiver, *v.a.* to state *or* allege *or* assign the motive (*or* motives *or* grounds) of; to found; to justify; to give a reason (*or* reasons) for; to be the motive of; to bring on *or* about, to be the cause of, to cause, to lead to, to give rise to; to find a motive for, to manage judiciously; to render natural
Se —, *v.r.* to be founded *or* justified *or* &c.
Moto, *s.m.* (*mus., Italian*) moto

Motricité, *s.f.* motivity
Motte, *s.f.* clod; turf, peat; ball; tan-ball; hillock; mound; lump; roll (*of butter*). — *de gazon*, sod. — *à brûler*, tan-ball, turf, peat
Motter, *v.a.* to clod
Se —, *v.r.* (*hunt.*) to lurk behind a clod
Mottereau, *s.m.* (*bird*) sand-martin
Motteur, *s.m.* peat *or* turf-maker
Motteux, *s.m.* (*bird*) wheatear, fallow-chat
Mottois, *s.m.* Cantal ox
Motu proprio, Proprio motu, *adv.* (*Latin*) motu proprio, of o.'s own accord, spontaneously; — *s.m.* spontaneous act
Motus, *int.* hush! mum! not a word!
Mou, Mol, *m.*, **Molle,** *f.*, *adj.* soft; mellow; lax; slack; loose; flabby; limp; close, heavy, muggy; faint; weak; feeble; effeminate; indolent; lazy; nerveless; tame; slow; careless; graceful; luxurious [slack
Mou, *s.m.* soft; (*of animals*) lights; (*of ropes*)
Mouchache, *s.f.* *V.* **Moussache**
Mouchage, *s.m.* snuffing (*of candles*)
Moucharaby, *s.m.* moucharaby
Mouchard, *s.m.* spy, police-spy; informer;
Mouchardage, *s.m.* spying [detective; decoy
Moucharde, *s.f.* (*fam.*) spy, informer
Moucharder, *v.a.n.* to spy, to be the spy of, to be a spy, to watch, to inform
Mouche, *s.f.* fly; patch, beauty-spot; (*of beard*) imperial; (*of mud*, &c.) spot; (*of a target*) patch, centre; (*of a fencing-foil*) cap; (*astr.*) musca; (*med.*) patch; (—**s,** *pl.*) first twinges *or* pangs of childbirth; (*cards*) loo; (*nav.*) fly-boat; (*pers.*) *V.* **Mouchard;** — *adj.* (*pop.*) bad, ugly, disagreeable. *Fine* —, (*pers.*) sly blade, sly dog, sly one, sly puss. — *-abeille*, — *-bourdon*, drone-fly. — *à feu*, fire-fly. — *à miel*, honey-bee. — *à viande*, meat-fly, flesh-fly, blow-fly. — *bleue*, blue-bottle. — *-guêpe*, wasp-fly. —*s volantes*, (*med.*) muscæ volitantes, specks. *Pattes* or *pieds de —s*, scrawl; trifle. *Faire d'une — un éléphant*, to make a mountain of a mole-hill. *Prendre la* —, (*fig.*) to take offence *or* huff, to be in a pet. *Tuer les —s au vol*, to have a most foul breath. *Quelle — l'a piqué* (or *le pique*)? what whim has got into his head? what ails him? what is the matter with him?
Moucher, *v.a.* to wipe the nose of; to blow (*the nose*); to discharge (...) in *or* by blowing o.'s nose; to snuff (*candles*); (*tech.*) to crop, to trim; (*old*) to spy; (*pop.*) to catch, to nab; to kill, to settle, to do for; to correct, to box ...'s ears, to whack, to lick, to drub, to knock down; to set down, to give a clincher; — *v.n.* to blow *or* wipe o.'s nose
Se —, *v.r.* to blow *or* wipe o.'s nose. *Ne pas se — du pied* or *du coude* or *sur sa manche*, to be no fool, to be up to snuff, to be up to trap, to be skilful *or* clever; not to be a man to be trifled with, to be a determined dog; to be a great swell, to do things in grand style
Moucherolle, *s.m.* (*bird*) fly-catcher
Moucheron, *s.m.* gnat, midge, small fly; (*of candles*) snuff; (*pop.*) brat, chit, small boy
Mouchet, *s.m.* (*bird*) Alpine warbler, Alpine accentor; (*falc.*) *V.* **Tiercelet**
Moucheter, *v.a.* to spot; to speckle; to fleck, to flecker; to cap (*foils, swords*)
Se —, *v.r.* to be spotted *or* &c.
Mouchettes, *s.f.pl.* snuffers; barnacles; bull-ring; (*pop.*) handkerchief
Moucheture, *s.f.* spot; spottedness; speckle; speckledness; (*surg.*) scarification
Moucheu-r, se, *s.m.f.* (*pers.*) nose-blower;
Mouchoir, *s.m.* handkerchief [candle-snuffer
Mouchure, *s.f.* candle-snuff, snuff; nose-stuff, mucus, snot
Moudre, *v.a.* to grind; to mill; to crush
Se —, *v.r.* to be ground *or* &c.
Moue, *s.f.* pouting, wry *or* sulky face, mouth, mouths. *Faire la* —, to pout, to sulk, to be sulky, to show temper, to make mouths

Mouée, *s.f.* (*hunt.*) reward
Mouette, *s.f.* sea-gull, gull, sea-mew, mew
Mouezzin, *s.m.* *V.* **Muezzin**
Moufétique, *adj.* (*obsolete*) mephitic
Moufette, *s.f.* choke-damp, damp, foul air, malaria; exhalation; (*zool.*) skunk. — *du Cap*, (*zool.*) zoril
Mouflard, e, *s.m.f.* bloated face
Moufle, *s.f.* hand-muffler, mitten; (*chem.*) muffle; (*obsolete*) ruffle; — *s.m.* (*mach.*) tackle, tackle-block, block and fall
Mouflon, *s.m.* moufflon, musmon, wild sheep
Mougick, *s.m.* (*Russian*) peasant
Mougrin, *s.m.* Indian jasmine
†**Mouillade,** *s.f.* wetting
†**Mouillage,** *s.m.* wetting; watering; (*nav.*) anchorage; anchoring-ground; depth. *Droit de* —, harbour-dues, anchorage, keelage. *Être au* —, to be *or* lie at anchor
†**Mouille,** *s.f.* (*navig.*) deep place
†**Mouillé, e,** *part. adj.* wetted; wet; soaked, &c. (*V.* **Mouiller**); watery; moist; (*of letters*) liquid; (*nav.*) moored, anchored, at anchor; (*pop.*) tipsy, tight; — *s.m.* wetness, wet
†**Mouille-bouche,** *s.f.* mouille-bouche (*pear*)
†**Mouillement,** *s.m.* wetting; (*cook.*) slight basting
†**Mouiller,** *v.a.n.* to wet; to water; to soak; to steep; to bathe; to drench: to moisten; to sprinkle; (*gram.*) to soften; (*nav.*) to moor (*a ship*); to cast *or* let go (*the anchor*): — *v.r.* (*nav.*) to anchor, to cast anchor, to let go the anchor; to be at anchor
Se —, *v.r.* to get wet, to get *or* be drenched, to become moist, to be bathed *or* &c.; to guzzle, to drink hard; (*gram.*) to be liquid
†**Mouillette,** *s.f.* sippet (*to eat boiled eggs with*)
†**Mouilloir,** *s.m.* (*tech.*) water-can (*to dip the fingers in*) [ness; watering, sprinkling
†**Mouillure,** *s.f.* wetting, making wet, wet-
Moujik, *s.m.* *V.* **Mougick**
Moulage, *s.m.* moulding; casting; grinding; multure; millstone shaft; (*old*) measuring (*of wood*) [dust
Moulard, *s.m.*, **Moularde,** *s.f.* grindstone-
Moule, *s.f.* mussel; — *s.m.* mould; cast; form: model; netting-rule; (*old*) measure (*for wood*). — *à beurre*, butter-print, butter-pat. — *à blagues*, mouth, gab. — *de bonnet*, head, pate. — *de gant*, hand; slap, cuff, punch. *Bois de* —, best firewood. *Fait au* —, (*fig.*) beautifully shaped
Moulé, e, *part. adj.* moulded; cast; printed, in print; shaped, formed; well-shaped, well-formed; — *s.m.* print, printed letters, type; — *s.f.* grindstone-dust; best firewood. *Chandelle —e*, *Lettre —e*, *V.* **Chandelle** *and* **Lettre**
Mouler, *v.a.* to mould; to cast; to take a cast of; to shape, to form; to print; to grind, to sharpen; (*old*) to measure (*wood*). *Se — sur*, to take for o.'s model [casting-house
Moulerie, *s.f.* moulding-place (*in a foundry*),
Moulette, *s.f.* freshwater-mussel
Mouleur, *s.m.* moulder; (*old*) wood-meter
Moulier, *s.m.* mould-maker [sel-fishery
Moulière, *s.f.* mussel-bed, mussel-scalp, mus-
Moulin, *s.m.* mill; (*of a glacier*) shaft, moulin. — *à blé*, — *à eau*, &c., corn-mill, water-mill, &c. — *à nef*, water-mill built on a boat. — *à paroles*, chatterbox, great talker; tongue, gab. — *à van*, fanning-mill. — *à vent*, wind-mill; moulin-à-vent (*kind of Burgundy wine*). *Faire venir l'eau au* —, (*fig.*) to bring grist to the mill. *Jeter son bonnet par-dessus les —s*, to throw off all sense of propriety; not to care a straw for what people may think; not to care for the consequences
Moulinage, *s.m.* grinding; milling; (*of silk*) throwing; silk-throwing mill
Mouliné, e, *part. adj.* ground, &c. (*V.* **Mouliner**); worm-eaten; crisp, friable
Mouliner, *v.a.* to grind; to mill; to throw (*silk*); to eat away (*wood*)

Moulinet, *s.m.* small mill, mill; drum (*for burdens*), roller, moulinet; turnstile; smoke-jack; chocolate-stick; small wheel; windlass, winch; (*fish.*) winch, reel; (*of cross-bows*) moulinet; (*dancing*) moulinet. *Faire le* —, to twirl, to flourish [silk-thrower, throwster

Moulineu-r, se, Moulini-er, ère, *s.m.f.*

Mouliste, *s.m.f.* mould-maker

Moult, *adv.* (*old*) much; many; very [up, aching

Moulu, e, *part. adj.* ground; bruised; knocked

Moulure, *s.f.* (*arch.*, &c.) moulding; (*mas.*)

Moulurier, *s.m.* moulding-maker [screed

Moumoute, *s.m.f.* puss, pussy; (*jest.*) wig, caxon

Mourant, e, *part. adj.* dying; expiring; dying away *or* out; languishing; languid; faint; pale, fading; going down gradually; gently sloping; — *s.m.f.* dying person, dying man *or* woman *or* boy *or* girl; (—**s,** *pl.*) dying

†**Moureillier,** *s.m.* *V.* **Malpighie**

Mourier, *s.m.* (*bird*) long-tailed tit

Mourine, *s.f.* (*fish*) eagle-ray, miller

Mourir, *v.n.* to die; to be dying; to expire; to perish; to go off; to die away; to die out; to dwindle away; to stop; to drop; (*at play*) to be out. *A* —, to die; to death; dreadfully, exceedingly. — *de faim*, to starve, to die of hunger, to be starving, to be dying with hunger. *Faire* —, to cause to die; to put to death; to kill; to destroy; to be the death of; to bring to the grave. *Faire* — *de faim*, to starve out. *Se faire* —, to make away with oneself. *Se laisser* — *de faim*, to starve oneself

Se —, *v.r.* to be dying *or* expiring; to die away; to be dying out

Mouron, *s.m.* (*bot.*) chickweed; pimpernel; (*zool.*) eft. — *d'eau*, brookweed

Mourre, *s.f.* morra (*Italian game*)

Mousart, *s.m.* pollard oak

Mousquet, *s.m.* (*old*) matchlock, musket [ketry

Mousquetade, *s.f.* (*old*) musket-shot; mus-

Mousquetaire, *s.m.* musketeer [ket-shot

Mousqueterie, *s.f.* musketry; volley of mus-

Mousqueton, *s.m.* carbine; musketoon

Moussa, *s.m.* millet hasty-pudding

Moussache, *s.f.* starch of manioc

Mousse, *adj* blunt; blunt-pointed; dull; — *s.m.* (*nav.*) cabin-boy, ship-boy, younker; — *s.f.* moss; froth; foam; lather

Mousseau, *adj.m.* *Pain* —, oaten bread

Mousseline, *s.f.* muslin; — *adj.* muslin-like, very fine. — *de laine*, mousseline de laine, muslin de laine

Mousselinette, *s.f.* muslinet

Mousselini-er, ère, *s.m.f.* muslin-weaver *or* manufacturer *or* warehouseman

Mousser, *v.n.* to froth, to foam; to lather; to effervesce; to sparkle; to be up; to thrive, to be successful. *Faire* —, to froth; to work up; to puff [room)

Mousseron, *s.m.* mousseron (*kind of mush-*

Mousseronne, *s.f.* (variety of lettuce)

Mousseronnière, *s.f.* mousseron-bed, mushroom-bed

Mousseu-x, se, *adj.* mossy, moss; frothy, foamy; effervescing, effervescent; (*of wine*, &c.) sparkling; (*fig.*) puffy. *Non* —, (*of wine*) still. *Agate* —*se*, moss agate, mocha-stone

Moussier, *s.m.* moss-herbarium

Moussoir, *s.m.* chocolate-stick [soons

Mousson, *s.f.* monsoon; season of the mon-

Moussu, e, *adj.* mossy, moss, moss-grown

Moussure, *s.f.* (*tech.*) bur

Moustache, *s.f.* moustache; (*of animals*) whisker. *Vieille* —, — *grise*, veteran soldier, veteran; old greybeard [tached

Moustachu, e, *adj.* with a moustache, mous-

Moustapha, *s.m.* (*pop.*) fat bearded fellow

†**Moustille,** *s.f.* (*of wine*, &c.) strength, headiness

†**Moustillier,** *s.m.* (*obsolete*) *V.* **Moustiquaire**

Moustiquaire, *s.f.* mosquito-net

Moustique, *s.m.* mosquito

Moût, *s.m.* (*of wine*, &c.) must; wort

Moutan, *s.m.* (*bot.*) moutan, tree pæony, Chinese pæony [youngster

Moutard, *s.m.* brat, chit, urchin, young one,

Moutarde, *s.f.* mustard; trifles; small girl, brat, chit. *Faire monter la* — *au nez*, to make angry, to irritate, to provoke, to aggravate, to work up. *S'amuser à la* —, to trifle away o.'s time, to stand trifling. *C'est de la* — *après le dîner*, it comes a day after the fair

Moutardelle, *s.f.* (*bot.*) horse-radish

Moutardier, *s.m.* mustard-pot; mustard-maker; (*bird*) black martin. *Se croire le premier* — *du pape*, to think oneself a great man

Moûtier, *s.m.* (*old*) monastery, convent, minster

Mouton, *s.m.* sheep; wether; mutton; sheepskin, sheep-leather; (*tech.*) fistuca, ram, rammer, beetle, monkey; beam; (*pers.*) lamb; ninny; prison-spy, decoy; —**s,** *pl.* sheep, wethers, &c.; foaming waves; subject

Mouton, ne, *adj.* sheep-like, sheepish, sheep

†**Moutonnaille,** *s.f.* flock of sheep, people who follow one another like sheep [curved

Moutonné, e, *adj.* fleecy; curled, frizzled;

Moutonnement, *s.m.* (*nav.*) foaming

Moutonner, *v.a.n.* to render fleecy, to curl, to frizzle; (*nav.*) to foam, to whiten; (*pop.*) to split (on), to spy and denounce

Moutonnerie, *s.f.* simplicity, silliness; servile imitation, doing as others do

Moutonneu-x, se, *adj.* fleecy, foaming, foamy, white, rough [like; imitative

Moutonni-er, ère, *adj.* fleecy, woolly; sheep-

Moutonnièrement, *adv.* sheep-like

Mouture, *s.f.* grinding, multure; charge for grinding, miller's pay *or* charge; meslin, mixed corn. *Tirer d'un sac deux* —*s*, to get a double profit out of a thing, to make a thing answer a double purpose

Mouvance, *s.f.* (*feud. law*) tenure

Mouvant, e, *adj.* moving; unstable, unfixed, shifting; animated; (*feud. law*) holding (of), depending (on); (*her.*) issuant; — *s.m.* decoy-bird. *Sable* —, quicksand, drift-sand

Mouvement, *s.m.* motion; movement; moving; progress; advance; march; impulse; accord; activity; animation, life, action, bustle, stir; agitation; commotion; rising, insurrection; attack; emotion; excitement; concern; inducement; impression; feeling; transport; fit; variation; variety; fluctuation; mutation; change, changes, alterations; promotion; undulations; (*of clocks*, &c.) movement, works; (*mus.*) time; (*of eloquence*) burst; (*mil.*) move, movement, manœuvre; (*rail.*, &c.) traffic; business. *Chef du* —, *V.* **Chef.** *Se donner du* —, to bustle, to stir about, to bestir oneself. *Se mettre en* —, to stir; (*mil.*) to move

Mouvementé, e, *part. adj.* agitated; bustling; busy; animated; lively; varied; fluctuating; undulated, undulating

Mouvementer, *v.a.* to agitate; to animate, to give animation to, to throw life into; to vary

Mouver, *v.a.* (*hort.*, *cook.*) to stir, to move

Se —, *v.r.* (*pop.*) to move, to stir; to bestir oneself; to fidget

Mouveron, Mouvet, *s.m.*, **Mouvette,** *s.f.*, **Mouvoir,** *s.m.* (*tech.*) stirring-rod *or* stick, ladle

Mouvoir, *v.a.* to move; to stir; to set in motion; to agitate; to start; to impel; to instigate, to incite, to prompt, to actuate; — *v.n.* (*feud. law*) to be depending. *Se* —, to move; to stir; to act; to be moved. *Faire* —, to set in motion, to move

Moxa, *s.m.* (*surg.*) moxa

Moxibustion, *s.f.* (*surg.*) moxibustion

Moye, *s.f.* soft part (*of a stone*)

Moyen, *s.m.* means, way; power; possibility; medium; (*writ.*) round hand; —**s,** *pl.* means, &c.; fortune, circumstances; resources; abilities, talents, parts; middle-sized boys, middle form; (*law*) plea, grounds, arguments. *Au — de*, by means of, with the help of. *Le — ?* how is it to be done? *Le — de ... ?* how is or was it (*or* will it be) possible to ...? *Avoir le — (de)*, to have the means *or* power, to be able; to be able to afford (*Je n'en ai pas le —*, I cannot afford it). *Trouver —*, to find (the) means, to contrive, to manage

Moyen, ne, *adj.* mean; middling, middle, medium; average; middle-sized; (*feud. law*) mesne. *— terme*, mean, medium; middle course, expedient. *Terme —, chiffre —*, average; on an average; mean, medium; (*math.*) middle term. **— -âge,** *s.m.* *V.* **Âge.** **— -âgisme,** *s.m.* mediævalism. **— -âgiste,** *s.m.* mediævalist

Moyennant, *prep.* by means of; with *or* by the help of; with; on condition of; in consideration of; provided; in return for; for. *— que*, provided that, provided, on condition that

Moyenne, *s.f.* average; (*math.*) mean, medium; (*writ.*) round hand. *En —*, at *or* on an average; (*of writing*) in round hand

Moyennement, *adv.* middlingly

Moyenner, *v.a.* to mediate, to procure, to manage, to contrive, to bring about. *Il n'y a pas moyen de —*, (*pop.*) there is no doing it, it is no use, it is no go

Moyer, *v.a.* to saw (*freestone*)

Moyette, *s.f.* (*agr.*) shock, stook

Moyeu, *s.m.* (*of a wheel*) nave, nave-box, axle-box, box; (*tech.*) centre; (*kind of plum*) moyeu; (*obsolete*) yolk (*of an egg*) [**Mozarabique**

Mozarabe, *s.m.* Mozarab, Muzarab; *— adj.* *V.*

Mozarabique, *adj.* Mozarabic, Mozarabian, Muzarabic, Muzarabian

Mozérien, ne, *adj.* (*phys.*) mozerian

Mozette, *s.f.* mozette (*priest's garment*)

M'sieu, (*pop. for* "monsieur") Sir, mister; Mr., &c. *V.* **Monsieur**

Mû, *m.*, **Mue,** *f.*, *part. of* **Mouvoir**

Muabilité, *s.f.* (*old*) *V.* **Mutabilité**

Muable, *adj.* mutable, changeable

Muablement, *adv.* mutably, changeably

Muance, *s.f.* *En —*, (*of the voice*) breaking

Mucate, *s.m.* (*chem.*) mucate

Muche-pot (A), *adv.* in concealment

Mucilage, *s.m.* mucilage

Mucilagineu-x, se, *adj.* mucilaginous

Mucine, *s.f.* (*chem.*) mucine

Mucique, *adj.* (*chem.*) mucic

Mucosine, *s.f.* (*chem.*) mucusine

Mucosité, *s.f.* mucosity, mucus, phlegm

Mucroné, e, *adj.* (*nat. hist.*) mucronate

Mucuna, *s.m.*, **Mucune,** *s.f.* (*bot.*) mucuna, cowage *or* cowhage plant

Mucus, *s.m.* mucus

Mudar, *s.m.* (*bot.*) mudar

Mudarine, *s.f.* (*chem.*) mudarine

Mue, *s.f.* moulting; moulting-time; slough, cast skin; cast horns; mew (*cage*); coop (*for poultry*); breaking *or* break (*of the voice*), alteration in the voice (*of adults*)

Muer, *v.n.a.* to moult; to cast its skin *or* horns, to shed its coat; to cast, to shed; (*of the voice*) to break, to change; (*old*) to alter, to change

Muet, te, *adj.* dumb; speechless; mute; silent; taciturn; secret; without an inscription; (*of maps*) in outline, outline; (*of evidence*) circumstantial, presumptive; *— s.m.f.* dumb person, dumb, dummy; *— s.m.* (*of the seraglio*) mute; *— s.f.* mew; hunting-lodge *or* box; (*gram.*) silent letter; (*thieves' slang*) conscience; (*old*) private bawdy-house

Muezzin, *s.m.* (*Mahom. rel.*) muezzin

Mufle, *s.m.* muzzle, snout. *— de veau, — de bœuf, — de chien*, (*bot.*) *V.* **Mufleau**

Mufleau, Muflier, *s.m.* (*bot.*) snapdragon, calves'-snout

Mufti, *s.m.* (*Turkish*) mufti

Muge, *s.m.* (*fish*) mullet

Mugir, *v.n.* to low; to roar; to bellow; to groan

Mugissement, *s.m.* lowing; roaring, roar; bellowing; groaning, groan

Muguet, *s.m.* lily of the valley, May lily; (*med.*) thrush; (*obsolete*) spark, beau, dangler. *— des bois*, woodruff

Mugueter, *v.a.n.* (*old*) to court; to covet; to flirt

Muguetterie, *s.f.* (*old*) courting; flirting

Muid, *s.m.* hogshead

Mular, *s.m.* (*zool.*) high-finned cachalot

Mulasse, *s.f.* young mule

Mulasserie, *s.f.* mule-breeding

Mulassi-er, ère, *adj.* of the mule, of *or* from *or* for mules, mulish; mule-breeding. *Bête —ère*, mule, hinny. *Espèce —ère*, mule species. *Étalon —*, mule (*or, more properly*, hinny) -breeding stallion. *Jument —ère*, mule-breeding mare

Mulassi-er, ère, *s.m.f.* mule-breeding stallion *or* mare

Mulâtre, *adj.m.f.*, *s.m.* mulatto; *— s.f.* *V.* **Mulâtresse**

Mulâtresse, *s.f.* mulatta, mulattress

Mulcter, *v.a.* (*old*) to mulct; to maltreat, to abuse

Mule, *s.f.* she-mule, mule; slipper; kibe; chap. *Baiser la — du pape*, to kiss the Pope's toe. **— -jenny,** *s.f.* (*spin.*) mule-jenny, mule

Mulet, *s.m.* he-mule, mule; working-bee, worker; (*fish*) mullet. *Garder le —*, to dance attendance [ditto's wife; *— adj.* for mules, mule

Muleti-er, ère, *s.m.f.* muleteer, mule-driver;

Muleton, *s.m.* young mule [**Moulette**

Mulette, *s.f.* (*agr.*) *V.* **Meulon;** (*zool.*) *V.*

Mulier, *s.m.* (*fish.*) mullet-net [(*inferior madder*)

Mulle, *s.m.* (*fish*) surmullet; *— s.f. adj.* mull

Mullette, *s.f.* gizzard, pannel; (*of ruminants*) rennet, reed; (*shell-fish*) *V.* **Moulette**

Mulon, *s.m.* heap; (*agr.*) *V.* **Meulon**

Mulot, *s.m.* field-mouse. *— volant*, monk-bat

Muloter, *v.n.* (*hunt.*) to scratch the ground

Mulsion, *s.f.* milking [multangular

Multangulaire, Multangulé, e, *adj.*

Multi, (*in compounds*) multi... [loured

Multicolore, *adj.* multicoloured, many-co-

Multifide, *adj.* (*bot.*) multifid [flowered

Multiflore, *adj.* (*bot.*) multiflorous, many-

Multiforme, *adj.* multiform

Multilatère, *adj.* multilateral, many-sided

Multiloculaire, *adj.* multilocular

Multipare, *adj.* multiparous

Multipède, *s.m. adj.* multiped

Multiple, *adj.* multiple; manifold, complex, complicated, intricate; *— s.m.* multiple

Multipliable, *adj.* multipliable

Multipliant, *s.m.* multiplying glass

Multiplicande, *s.m.* multiplicand

Multiplicateur, *s.m.* multiplier, multiplicator; *— m.*, **-trice,** *f.*, *adj.* multiplying

Multiplicati-f, ve, *adj.* multiplicative

Multiplication, *s.f.* multiplication

Multiplicité, *s.f.* multiplicity

Multiplié, e, *part. adj.* multiplied; multifarious; manifold; frequent

Multiplier, *v.a.n.* to multiply [everywhere

Se —, *v.r.* to multiply; to be repeated; to be

Multiplieur, *s.m.* (*pers.*) multiplier

Multitude, *s.f.* multitude

Multivalve, *adj.m.f.*, *s.f.* multivalve

Mundick, *s.m.* (*mining*) mundic

Mungo, *s.m.* mungo (*shoddy*); (*bot.*) mungo, moog, moong (*pulse*)

Mungos, *s.m.* (*bot.*) mungo, snake-root

Muni, e, *part.* supplied, provided, furnished; possessed; armed

Municipal, e, *adj.* municipal; *— s.m.* municipal guard, constable, policeman; municipal officer

Municipalement, *adv.* municipally

Municipaliser, *v.a.* to municipalize

Municipalité, *s.f.* municipality, corporation, town *or* common council; town-hall, town-house, guildhall

Municipe, *s.m.* (*in antiquity*) municipium

Munificence, *s.f.* munificence

Munir, *v.a.* to supply, to provide, to furnish; to arm, to fortify
Munition, *s.f.* ammunition, munition; provisions; stores. *—s de bouche*, provisions, victuals, food. *—s de guerre*, ammunition. *Pain de —*, soldier's bread, ammunition-bread
Munitionnaire, *s.m.* army contractor, victualler, commissary of stores
Munitionner, *v.a.* to supply with ammunition *or* stores, to supply, to store
Muphti, *s.m.* *V.* **Mufti** [membrane
Muqueu-x, se, *adj.* mucous; — *s.f.* mucous
Mur, *s.m.* wall. *— blanc*, dead wall. *— d'appui*, parapet wall, wall breast-high; breast-wall; retaining wall. *— d'enceinte*, encircling wall. *Mettre au pied du —*, (*fig.*) to drive into a corner, to nonplus, to put to a stand, to pose; to compel (*one*) to decide one way or the other
Mûr, e, *adj.* ripe; mature; matured; fit for drinking; of mature age; old; (*of women, jest.*) marriageable; (*of clothes*) worn out, rotten
Murage, *s.m.* walling
†**Muraille,** *s.f.* wall
†**Muraillement,** *s.m.* walling
†**Murailler,** *v.a.* *V.* **Murer** [circle
Mural, e, *adj.* mural, wall; — *s.m.* (*astr.*) mural
Murcien, ne, *adj. s.* Murcian
Mûre, *s.f.* mulberry; blackberry. *— sauvage, — de ronce, — de haie*, blackberry, bramble-
Mûrement, *adv* maturely [berry
Murène, *s.f.* muræna, murry, sea-eel
Murer, *v.a.* to wall; to wall in; to immure; to wall up, to block up, to brick up; to protect against attacks; to screen; to veil; to cloud;
Murer, *s.m.* (*bot.*) wall-flower [to keep secret
Mûreraie, *s.f.* mulberry-grove
Murette, *s.f.* (*pop.*) *V.* **Murer,** *s.m.*
Murex, *s.m.* (*zool.*) murex, rock-shell
Mûrier, *s.m.* mulberry-tree
Mûriforme, *adj.* mulberry-shaped
Mûrir, *v.a.n.*, **Se —**, *v.r.* to ripen, to mature
Murmura-teur, trice, *adj.* murmuring; grumbling; muttering; — *s.m.f.* murmurer; grumbler; mutterer [whisper; purling
Murmure, *s.m.* murmur; grumbling; mutter;
Murmurer, *v.a.n.* to murmur; to grumble; to mumble; to mutter; to whisper; to purl
Se —, *v.r.* to be whispered
Mûron, *s.m.* blackberry; wild raspberry
Muros, (*Latin*) the walls. *Extra —*, extra muros, without *or* beyond the walls, extramural, suburban. *Intra —*, intra muros, within the walls, intra-mural, in the city *or* town
Murrhin, e, *adj.*, **Murrhin,** *s.m.* murrhine
Musagète, *adj.m.* (*myth.*) the leader of the
†**Musaraigne,** *s.f.* shrew-mouse, shrew [Muses
Musard, e, *adj.* loitering, trifling, dawdling; — *s.m.f.* loiterer, trifler, dawdler, saunterer
Musarder, *v.n.* *V.* **Muser** [trifling, dawdling
Musarderie, Musardise, *s.f* loitering,
Musc, *s.m.* musk
Muscade, *s.f.* nutmeg; juggler's ball, thimble-rigger's pea *or* ball; — *adj.f.* musky, musk. *Fleur de —*, mace. *Noix —*, nutmeg. *Rose —*,
Muscadelle, *s.f.* muscadel (*pear*) [musk-rose
Muscadet, *s.m.* muscadet (*wine, vine, cider-*
Muscadier, *s.m.* nutmeg-tree [*apple*)
Muscadin, *s.m.* musk-lozenge *or* pastille; (*obsolete*) scented fop, dandy, spark, beau
Muscardin, *s.m.* muscardine, red dormouse
Muscardine, *s.f.* muscardine, silkworm rot
Muscardinique, *adj.* of muscardine *or* silkworm rot; affected with muscardine
Muscari, *s.m.* (*bot.*) grape-hyacinth
Muscat, *adj.m.*, *s.m.* musky, musk; muscatel *or* muscat (*grape, wine, pear*)
Muscatelline, *s.f.* *V.* **Moscatelle** [lime
Muschelkalk, *s.m.* (*geol.*) muschelkalk, shell-
Muscicape, *s.f.* (*bird*) fly-catcher
Muscivore, *adj.* muscivorous
Muscle, *s.m.* muscle
Muscler, *v.a.* to muscle
Muscolog-ie, -ique, -iste. *V.* page 3, § 1
Musculaire, *adj.* muscular
Musculation, *s.f.* muscular action
Musculature, *s.f.* muscling, muscles
Musculeu-x, se, *adj.* musculous, muscular; — *s.f.* muscular fibres
Musculosité, *s.f.* musculosity, muscularity
Muse, *s.f.* Muse; (*hunt.*) rutting-time
Museau, *s.m.* muzzle; snout; nose; face
Musée, *s.m.* museum; picture-gallery [gag
Museler, *v.a.* to muzzle; (*fig.*) to silence, to
Muselière, *s.f.* muzzle [gagging
Musellement, *s.m.* muzzling; (*fig.*) silencing,
Muséographe, *s.m.* museographer
Muser, *v.n.* to loiter, to trifle, to dawdle, to saunter, to moon; (*hunt.*) to go to rut. *Qui refuse muse*, he who is a refuser may be a loser
Muserolle, *s.f.* noseband, musrole
Musette, *s.f.* bagpipe; air *or* tune for ditto; cheerful instrument; nosebag; brush-bag; (*pop.*) voice, noise, whistle
Muséum, *s.m.* museum
Musical, e, *adj.* musical
Musicalement, *adv.* musically
Musicastre, Musicâtre, *s.m.* musicaster
Musicien, ne, *s.m.f.* musician; bandsman
Musico, *s.m.* low music-hall, gaff
Musicographe, *s.m.* (*pers.*) musicographer; (*instr.*) musicograph
Musicomane, *s.m.f. adj.* musicomaniac
Musicomanie, *s.f.* musicomania
Musi-f, ve, *adj.* mosaic
Musique, *s.f.* music; musicians; band; musical box. *A* or *de —*, (*adject.*) music, musical. *Faire de la —*, to play music. *Mettre en —*, to set to music [— *v.a.* (*old*) to set to music
Musiquer, *v.n.* (*jest.*) to music, to play music;
Musoir, *s.m.* pier-head, point, angle
Musophage, *s.m.* (*bird*) plantain-eater
Musqué, e, *part. adj.* musked; musk; scented, perfumed; affected; flattering [with musk
Musquer, *v.a.* to musk, to scent *or* perfume
Musse, *s.f.* (*hunt.*) pass, way
Musse-pot (A), (*old*) *V.* **Muche-pot**
Musser, *v.a.* (*old*) to conceal, to hide
Mussi-f, ve, *adj.* mosaic
Mussitation, *s.f.* (*med.*) mussitation
Mustelle, *s.f.* *V.* **Motelle** [Mussulmanic
Musulman, e, *s m.f.* Mussulman; — *adj.*
Musulmanisme, *s.m.* Mussulmanism
Mutabilité, *s.f.* mutability, changeableness
Mutacisme, *s.m.* (*med.*) mutacism
Mutage, *s.m.* mutage
Mutation, *s.f.* mutation; change
Muter, *v.a.* *V.* **Mécher** [mutilating
Mutila-teur, trice, *s.m.f. adj.* mutilator;
Mutilation, *s.f.* mutilation; maiming; mangling; garbling; damage, injury
Mutiler, *v.a.* to mutilate; to maim; to mangle; to disfigure; to garble; to injure
Mutin, e, *adj.* stubborn, obstinate; unruly; mutinous, seditious, rebellious, riotous; refractory; roguish; sharp, smart, quick, lively, knowing; — *s.m.f.* obstinate person; refractory child; mutineer, rebel, rioter
Mutiné, e, *adj.* mutinous, seditious, rebellious, riotous; angry, raging
Mutiner, *v.a.* to rouse, to excite
Se —, *v.r.* to mutiny, to rebel, to riot, to be *or* become riotous; to be refractory *or* stubborn
Mutinerie, *s.f.* mutiny, sedition, rebellion; refractoriness, unruliness
Mutisie, *s.f.* (*bot.*) mutisia
Mutisme, *s.m.* mutism, dumbness; speech-
Mutité, *s.f.* (*med.*) dumbness [lessness
Mutual-isme, -iste. *V.* page 3, § 1
Mutualité, *s.f.* mutuality
Mutuel, le, *adj.* mutual, reciprocal. *Association* or *société de secours —s*, *association* or *société —le*, friendly society, benefit society. *V.* **École**
Mutuellement, *adv* mutually, reciprocally

Mutuellisme, *s.m.* unionism
Mutuelliste, *s.m.f.* unionist
Mutule, *s.f.* (*arch.*) mutule
Myalgie, *s.f.* (*med.*) myalgia
Mycélium, *s.m.* (*bot.*) mycelium
Mycéto-graphie, -logie, Mycolog-ie, -ique, &c. *V.* page 3, § 1
Mydas, *s.m.* (*zool.*) teledu
Mydriase, *s.f.* (*med.*) mydriasis
Mye, *s.f.* (*zool.*) mya, gaper, pearl-mussel
Myélite, *s.f.* (*med.*) myelitis
Myélomalacie, *s.f.* (*med.*) myelomalacia
Mygale, *s.f.* mygale (*spider*)
Myiodopsie, *s.f.* (*med.*) muscæ volitantes
Myiologie, *s.f.* myiology
Myitis, *s.f.* (*med.*) myitis
Mylabre, *s.m.* (*zool.*) mylabris
Mylady, *s.f. V.* **Milady**
Myliobate, *s.f. V.* **Mourine**
Mylodon, *s.m.* (*zool.*) mylodon
Mylord, *s.m. V.* **Milord**
Myocardite, *s.f.* (*med.*) myocarditis
Myocèle, *s.f.* (*med.*) myocele
Myograph-ie, -ique. *V.* page 3, § 1
Myolog-ie, -ique, -iste. *V.* page 3, § 1
Myomalacie, *s.f.* (*med.*) myomalacia
Myope, *adj.* short-sighted, near-sighted, myopic; *s.m.f.* ditto person, myope; (*zool.*) myopa. *Vue* —, short sight, near sight
Myopie, *s.f.* short-sightedness, near-sightedness, myopia, myopy
Myopotame, *s.m.* (*zool.*) myopotamus
Myoptère, *s.m.* (*zool.*) monk-bat
Myose, *s.f.* (*med.*) myosis
Myosite, *s.f.* (*med.*) myositis [scorpion-grass
Myosotis, *s.m.* (*bot.*) myosotis, forget-me-not,
Myosurus, *s.m.* (*bot.*) myosurus, mouse-tail
Myotom-ie, -ique. *V.* page 3, § 1
Myria, (*in compounds*) myria... (*ten thousand*)
Myriade, *s.f.* myriad
Myriagramme, *s.m.* (*Fr.weight*) myriagramme
Myrialitre, *s.m.* (*Fr. meas.*) myrialitre
Myriamètre, *s.m.* (*Fr.meas.*) myriametre (*See*
Myriapode, *s.m.* (*zool.*) myriapod [table, p. 6.)
Myriare, *s.m.* (*Fr. meas.*) myriare
Myrica, *s.m.* (*bot.*) myrica, candleberry, gale
Myricine, *s.f.* (*chem.*) myricine
Myrio, (*in compounds*) *V.* **Myria**
Myriopode, &c. *V.* **Myriapode,** &c.
Myriorama, *s.m.* myriorama
Myrmidon, *s.m.* myrmidon; (*jest.*) pygmy; dwarf, shrimp, runt [balan
Myrobalan, Myrobolan, *s.m.* (*bot.*) myro-
Myronate, *s.m.* (*chem.*) myronate
Myronique, *adj.* (*chem.*) myronic
Myrosine, *s.f.* (*chem.*) myrosine
Myrrhe, *s.f.* myrrh
Myrrhé, e, *adj.* myrrhed [sweet cicely
Myrrhide, *s.f.*, **Myrrhis,** *s.m.* (*bot.*) cicely,
Myrrhite, *s.f.* (*min.*) myrrhite
Myrte, *s.m.* (*bot.*) myrtle
Myrtiforme, *adj.* myrtiform
Myrtil, *s.m.*, **Myrtille,** *s.f.* (*bot.*) bilberry
Mysis, *s.m.* (*zool.*) mysis, opossum shrimp
Mysorien, ne, *adj. s.* Mysorian
Mystagog-ie, -ique. *V.* page 3, § 1
Mystagogue, *s.m.* mystagogue [ado; caution
Mystère, *s.m.* mystery; secret; secrecy; fuss,
Mystérieusement, *adv.* mysteriously
Mystérieu-x, se, *adj.* mysterious
Mysticisme, *s.m.* mysticism
Mysticité, *s.f.* mysticalness; mysticism
Mystifica-teur, trice, *s.m.f.* mystifier, mystificator, hoaxer, banterer; — *adj.* mystifying, hoaxing, bantering [hoax
Mystification, *s.f.* mystification, hoaxing,
Mystifier, *v.a.* to mystify, to hoax [mystic
Mystique, *adj.* mystic, mystical; — *s.m.f.*
Mystiquement, *adv.* mystically
Mytacisme, *s.m. V.* **Mutacisme**
Mythe, *s.m.* myth, fable, fiction [page 3, § 1
Myth-ique, -iquement, -ographie. *V.*
Mythisme, *s.m.* mythicism
Mythographe, *s.m.* mythographer [*V.* p. 3, § 1
Mytholog-ie, -ique, -iquement, -iste.
Mythologiser, *v.a.n.* to mythologize
Mythologue, *s.m.* mythologist
Myure, *adj.* (*med.*) sinking (*pulse*)
Myxine, *s.f.* (*zool.*) hag-fish, hag

N

N, *s.f.* (*letter*) n
N', *contraction of* **Ne**
Na, *int.* (*children's slang for* "là") there!
Nabab, *s.m.* nabob
Nababie, *s.f.* nabobship
Nable, *s.m.* (*nav.*) scuttle-hole; plug, stopper
Nabot, e, Nabotin, e, *s.m.f.* manikin, dwarf,
Nacarat, *s.m. adj.* nacarat [shrimp, elf, runt
Nacelle, *s.f.* small boat, boat; wherry; bark; (*of balloons*) car; (*arch.*) scotia [*perles*, ditto
Nacre, *s.f.* mother of pearl, nacre. — *de*
Nacré, e, *adj.* nacreous, nacred, pearly
Nacrer, *v.a.* to nacre [facturer *or* worker
Nacri-er, ère, *s.m.f.* mother-of-pearl manu-
Nacrite, *s.f.* (*min.*) nacrite
Nadir, *s.m.* (*astr.*) nadir
Nadiral, e, *adj.* (*astr.*) nadiral
Nævus, *s.m.* — *maternel*, (*med.*) nævus, nævus maternus, birth-mark, mother-spot, mole
Nafé, *s.m.* (*bot.*) gombo (*fruit*) [water
Naffe (Eau de), *s.f.* (*obsolete*) orange-flower
Nage, *s.f.* rowing; rowlock; swimming; great perspiration. *A la* —, swimming, by swimming; rowing. *Donner la* —, to pull the stroke oar, to give the stroke. *Passer* or *traverser à la* —, to swim over *or* across; to row ditto. *Se jeter à la* —, to jump *or* leap into the water (*in order to swim*)
Nageant, e, *part. adj.* swimming, &c. (*V.* **Nager**); (*her.*) naiant, natant
Nagée, *s.f.* stroke (*in swimming or rowing*)
Nagement, *s.m.* swimming; rowing
Nageoire, *s.f.* fin; flipper; float for swimming, cork, bladders; board (*in a pail of water*); (*pop.*) whisker
Nageoter, *v.n.* to swim a little, to swim about
Nager, *v.n.a.* to swim; to float; to roll, to welter; to row; to pull. — *entre deux eaux*, to swim under water; (*fig.*) to trim, to be a trimmer, to waver between two parties
Nageret, *s.m.* shooting-boat
Nageu-r, se, *adj.* swimming; — *s.m.f.* swim-
Nagor, *s.m.* (*zool.*) nagor [mer; rower, oarsman
Naguère, Naguères, *adv.* but lately, not long ago, not long since, not long before
Naïa. *V.* **Naja**
Naïade, *s.f.* (*myth.*) naiad, water-nymph; (*nat.*
Naïadées, *s.f.pl.* (*bot.*) naiades [*hist.*) naiad
Naï-f, ve, *adj.* artless; ingenuous; natural, unaffected; candid; innocent; simple; simple-minded; naive; — *s.m.* what is ditto; naive style; nature without art
Nain, e, *s.m.f. adj.* dwarf. — *jaune*, (*game at cards*) Pope Joan. *Œuf* —, addled *or* addle egg
Naïre, *s.m.* nair
Naissain, *s.m.* oyster-spat, spat
Naissance, *s.f.* birth; nativity; descent, extraction; beginning, rise; dawn; spring; springing; root; origin; growth. *De* —, by birth; from o.'s birth; (*adject.*) born; birth. *Anniversaire de la* —, *jour de* —, birthday. *Droit de* —, birthright. *Lieu de* —, birthplace. *Prendre* —, to be born; to originate (in)
Naissant, e, *part. adj.* coming into the world; newly born; infant; young; growing; beginning to grow; beginning; rising; springing up; dawning; budding; nascent; incipient; (*her.*) naissant
Naître, *v.n.* to be born; to come into the world; to be produced; to be formed; to

grow; to begin; to rise; to arise; to originate; to spring up; to take its rise; to spring; to issue; to proceed; to come; to dawn; to bud. *Faire* —, to bring to life; to bring forth; to call into existence; to create; to produce; to form; to cause; to raise; to give rise *or* birth to; to start; to excite; to suggest; to propound; to say that (*one*) was born. *Avoir vu — quelqu'un*, to have known someone a baby; to be someone's birthplace

Naïvement, *adv.* artlessly; ingenuously; naturally, unaffectedly; candidly; innocently; plainly; naively

Naïveté, *s.f.* artlessness; ingenuousness; unaffectedness; candour; innocence; simplicity; naïveté; natural style; silly thing

Naja, Naïa, *s.m.* (*serpent*) naja, naia

Nakoda, *s.m.* nacodah, nacodar

Nanan, *s.m.* (*children's slang*) goodies, something nice

Nandou, Nandu, *s.m.* nandu, American ostrich

Nanisme, *s.m.* dwarfism

Nankin, *s.m. adj.* nankeen, nankin

Nanocéphalie, *s.f.* (*med.*) nanocephaly

Nanquinette, *s.f.* nankinet (*stuff*)

Nansouck, Nansouk, *s.m.* nainsook (*muslin*)

Nantais, e, *adj. s.* of Nantes, Nantese, native of Nantes

Nanti, e, *part. adj.* possessed, provided (with), provided for, secured, in possession (of), having in o.'s possession *or* in o.'s hands, holding as security, having a security

Nantir, *v.a.* to secure, to give security *or* a pledge to; to provide; to provide for

Se —, *v.r.* to secure oneself; to have security; to have in hand; to take possession (of), to seize (upon), to secure; to provide oneself; to feather o.'s nest

Nantissement, *s.m.* security, pledge, lien

Nantois, e, *adj. s. V.* **Nantais**

Napée, *s.f.* napæa, wood-nymph

Napel, *s.m.* (*bot.*) wolf's-bane, monk's-hood

Naphtaline, *s.f.* (*chem.*) naphthaline

Naphte, *s.m.* naphtha

Naphtéine, *s.f.* (*chem.*) naphtheine

Napiforme, *adj.* napiform, turnip-shaped

Napiste, *s.m.* napist (*Greek partisan of Russia*)

Napoléon, *s.m.* napoleon (*gold coin*)

Napoléone, *s.f.* (*bot.*) belvisia, napoleona

Napoléonien, ne, *adj.* Napoleonic, Napoleonistic; — *s.m.f.* Napoleonist

Napoléon-isme, -iste. *V.* page 3, § 1

Napoléonite, *s.f.* (*min.*) napoleonite

Napolitain, e, *adj. s.m.f.* Neapolitan; — *s.f.* ditto fashion; kind of woollen cloth

Nappe, *s.f.* table-cloth; cloth; cover; sheet (*of water*, &c.); clap-net; (*math.*) nappe. *Éclair en* —, sheet-lightning

Napperon, *s.m.* (*of dining-tables*) slip, upper-cloth

Narbonnais, e, *adj. s.* of Narbonne, Narbonnese, native of Narbonne

Narbonne, *s.f.* (kind of peach)

Narcéine, *s.f.* (*chem.*) narceia, narceine

Narcine, *s.f.* (*fish*) narcine (*kind of ray*)

Narcisse, *s.m.* (*bot.*) narcissus; (*myth., fig.*) Narcissus. — *des bois* or *des prés*, — *sauvage*, daffodil

Narcotine, *s.f.* (*chem.*) narcotine

Narcotique, *adj.m.f., s.m.* narcotic

Narcotiser, *v.a.* to narcotize

Narcotisme, *s.m.* narcosis, narcotism

Nard, *s.m.* nard; mat-grass; spikenard

Nardet, *s.m.* (*bot.*) couch-grass

Narghilé, Narghileh, *s.m. V.* **Narguilé**

Nargue, *s.f.* disdain, scorn, slight, sneer, fling. — *de* ... ! — *à* ... ! a fig for ... ! hang ... ! *Dire — de*, to snap o.'s fingers at, to laugh to scorn. *Faire — à*, to set at defiance, to beard; to set at naught; to turn up o.'s nose at; (*of things*) to surpass, to beat

Narguer, *v.a.* to set at defiance, to beard, to snap o.'s fingers at

Narguilé, Narguilhé, *s.m.* narghile *or* nargile *or* nargileh (*tobacco-pipe*)

Narine, *s.f.* nostril

Narquois, e, *adj.* cunning, sly, cheating, bantering, chaffing; — *s.m.f.* cunning *or* sly one. cheat, banterer, chaffer, quiz

Narquoisement, *adv.* cunningly, slily, sneeringly

Narra-teur, trice, *s.m.f.* narrator, relater, teller

Narrati-f, ve, *adj.* narrative

Narration, *s.f.* narration, relation, narrative, story

Narré, *s.m.* narrative, account, story; long story; twaddle; tittle-tattle

Narrer, *v.a.* to narrate, to relate, to tell

Narthex, *s.m.* (*arch.*) narthex

Narval, *s.m.* (*fish*) narwhal, sea-unicorn

Nasal, e, *adj. s.m.f.* nasal

Nasalement, *adv.* nasally

Nasalisation, *s.f.* nasalization

Nasaliser, *v.a.n.* to nasalize

Nasalité, *s.f.* nasality

Nasard, e, *adj. V.* **Nasillard;** — *s.m.* (*of an organ*) vox humana stop; — *s.f.* (*old*) fillip on the nose

Nasarder, *v.a.* (*old*) to fillip on the nose; to jeer, to scoff, to make game of

Nase, *s.m.* (*fish*) nasus

Naseau, *s.m.* (*of animals*) nostril

Nasière, *s.f.* bull-ring

†**Nasillard, e,** *adj.* snuffling; — *s.m.f.* snuffler

†**Nasillement,** *s.m.* snuffling, speaking through the nose; snuffling sound; twang

†**Nasiller,** *v.n.* to speak through the nose, to snuffle

†**Nasilleu-r, se,** *s.m.f.* snuffler

†**Nasillonnement,** &c. *V.* **Nasillement,** &c.

Nasique, *s.f.* nasalis, proboscis monkey

Naso, (*in compounds, anat.*) naso-...

Nasse, *s.f.* bow-net, weel, weir; snare; scrape; lurch

Natal, e, *adj.* native, natal, of o.'s birth, birth; vernacular

Natalité, *s.f.* natality; proportion of births

Natation, *s.f.* swimming

Natatoire, *adj.* natatory, swimming

Natice, *s.f.* (*mollusc*) natica

Nati-f, ve, *adj.*, **Natif,** *s.m.* native

Nation, *s.f.* nation; people; race. *La grande* —, "the great (*or* grand) nation" (*France during the first Republic and under Napoleon I.*)

National, e, *adj.* national; native; vernacular

Nationalement, *adv.* nationally

Nationaliser, *v.a.* to nationalize

Se —, *v.r.* to become nationalized

Nationalisme, *s.m.* nationalism

Nationalité, *s.f.* nationality; nation, country

Nationaux, *adj.pl.m.* of **National;** — *s.m.pl.* natives; native subjects *or* citizens; countrymen; nation

Nativement, *adv.* natively

Nativisme, *s.m.* nativism

Nativité, *s.f.* nativity, birth

Natrolite, *s.f.* (*min.*) natrolite

Natromètre, *s.m.* natrometer

Natron, Natrum, *s.m.* (*min.*) natron

Natte, *s.f.* mat; matting; straw-mat; rush-mat; plat; platting; platted hair; plait; plaiting; twist

Se —, *v.r.* to be matted *or* &c.

Natter, *v.a.* to mat; to twist; to plat; to plait.

Natti-er, ère, *s.m.f.* mat-maker

Naturalibus (In), *adv.* (*Latin*) in a state of nudity, naked, stark naked; in o.'s shirt *or* chemise

Naturalisation, *s.f.* naturalization

Naturaliser, *v.a.* to naturalize

Naturalisme, *s.m.* naturalism

Naturaliste, *s.m.f.* naturalist; — *adj.* naturalistic

Naturalité, *s.f.* naturalness; citizenship, denizenship; (*obsolete*) naturalization

Nature, *s.f.* nature; kind; constitution; disposition; temper; life; life-size; — *adject.* natural; (*cook.*) plain, plainly cooked. *Contre* —, unnatural; unnaturally. *D'après* —, after *or* from nature, from the life. *De sa* —, in its nature, by nature, naturally. *De — à*, of a nature to, calculated to. *De* —, (*agr., of oxen*) suited for grazing and fattening

Naturel, le, *adj.* natural; native; artless; genuine; unadulterated; congenial; sincere; unaffected; plain; free, easy; life-size, life; plainly cooked

Naturel, *s.m.* nature; temper, disposition; natural affection, feeling; naturalness, simplicity, freedom from affectation; genuineness; life-size, life; (*pers.*) native. *Au* —, to the life; naturally; unadorned; plain, plainly cooked. *D'un bon* or *mauvais* —, good *or* ill-natured
Naturellement, *adv.* naturally; by nature; genuinely; sincerely, candidly; plainly; freely, easily; of course
Natur-isme, -iste. *V.* page 3, § 1
Nauclèa, *s.m.*, **Nauclée,** *s.f.* (*bot.*) nauclea, grapple-plant
Naufrage, *s.m.* shipwreck; wreck. *Faire* —, to be shipwrecked; to be wrecked
Naufragé, e, *adj. s.* shipwrecked, wrecked; wrecked sailor, wrecked person [wrecked
Naufrager, *v.n.* to be shipwrecked; to be
Naulage, *s.m.* (*nav.*) freight; fare
Naumachie, *s.f.* naumachy, naumachia
Nauscope, *s.m.* nauscope
Nauscop-ie, -ique. *V.* page 3, § 1
Nauséabond, e, *adj.* nauseous, loathsome, disgusting, sickening
Nausée, *s.f.* nausea, sensation of sickness, qualm, retching; loathing, disgust [retching
Nauséeu-x, se, *adj.* nauseous. *Efforts* —,
Nautile, *s.m.* nautilus; life-belt
Nautilier, *s.m.* nautilus (*animal in the shell*)
Nautilite, *s.f.* nautilite, fossil nautilus
Naut-ique, -iquement. *V.* page 3, § 1
Nautomètre, *s.m.* nautometer
Nautoni-er, ère, *s.m.f.* (*poet.*) pilot, steerer; mariner; ferryman, boatman, boatwoman
Naval, e, *adj.* naval, sea; nautical
Navarchie, *s.f.* navarchy
Navarque, *s.m.* navarch [**e,** *adj. s.* Navarrese
Navarrais, e, Navarrin, e, Navarrois,
Navée, *s.f.* boatful, boatload
Navet, *s.m.* turnip; root
Navetier, *s.m.* shuttle-maker
Navetière, *s.f.* turnip-field *or* ground
Navette, *s.f.* rape; navew; (*graine de* —) rapeseed; (*huile de* —) rape-oil, rapeseed-oil; netting-needle; shuttle; incense-box; Indian canoe. *Point de* —, lock-stitch. *Faire la* —, to run *or* go to and fro
Naviculaire, *adj.* navicular
Navicule, *s.f.* (*nat. hist.*) navicula
Naviforme, *adj.* naviform
Navigabilité, *s.f.* navigability; seaworthiness
Navigable, *adj.* navigable; seaworthy
Navigant, e, *adj. s.* navigating; navigant
Navigateur, *s.m.* navigator, mariner, sailor, seaman, seafaring man; aeronaut, balloonist; — *m.*, **-trice,** *f.*, *adj.* navigating, seafaring
Navigation, *s.f.* navigation; sailing; going; voyage. — *de plaisance*, pleasure navigation (boating, yachting, &c.)
Naviguant, *part.* navigating, sailing, going
Naviguer, *v.n.* to navigate, to sail, to go; to voyage; — *v.a.* to navigate; to row, to sail, to go over
†**Naville,** *s.m.* small canal, water-course
Navire, *s.m.* ship, vessel
Navrant, e, *adj.* heartrending, distressing
Navré, e, *adj.* broken-hearted, &c. (*V.* **Navrer**)
Navrer, *v.a.* to break *or* rend the heart of, to distress; to break, to rend; (*old*) to wound
Nazaréen, ne, *adj. s.* Nazarean, Nazarene
Ne, N', *adv.* not; never. — *pas* or *point*, not; never. — *jamais*, never. — *pas parler*, not to speak. *Je* — *sais*, I know not, I do not (*or* don't) know. *Je n'ose*, I dare not. *Vous* — *devez pas*, you must not. *Vous* — *savez pas*, you do not know. *Vous* — *pouvez pas* — *pas le faire*, you cannot but do it, you cannot dispense with doing it. — ... *que*, only, but; nothing but; no more than; no other than; no one but; none but; anything but; anyone but; any but; entirely; merely, simply
Né, e, *part.* born, &c. (*V.* **Naître**); foaled, &c.; descended; produced; by birth; naturally; (*of ladies' names before marriage*) whose maiden name was ..., Miss ..., née ... *Bien* —, of good birth; well-constituted; well-balanced; well-disposed; noble, generous. *Mort-* —, *Nouveau-* —, *V.* **Mort-né** *and* **Nouveau-né.** *Je suis* —, I was born [withstanding, yet
Néanmoins, *adv.* nevertheless, however, not-
Néant, *s.m.* nothing, naught, nil; nothingness; nonentity; emptiness; worthlessness; vacant space, vacancy, space; nay, no. *Mettre au* —, to annul, to set at naught
Néarthrose, *s.f.* (*med.*) nearthrosis
Nèble, *s.m.* (*agr.*) mist, blight; (*vet.*) rot
Nébride, *s.f.* (*of Bacchus*) deer-skin
Nébulé, e, *adj.* (*her.*) nebuly
Nébuleu-x, se, *adj.* nebulous; cloudy; misty, hazy; obscure; dark; gloomy; — *s.f.* (*astr.*) nebula (*pl.* nebulæ)
Nébulosité, *s.f.* nebulosity; cloudiness; obscurity; gloominess, gloom
Nécessaire, *adj.* necessary; needful; requisite; unavoidable; indispensable; — *s.m.* necessaries; necessary, needful; work-box; dressing-case; canteen
Nécessairement, *adv.* necessarily; of course
Nécessitant, e, *adj.* compelling, compulsory; absolute
Nécessité, *s.f.* necessity; need; want; exigency; necessary. *Faire de* — *vertu*, to make a virtue of necessity
Nécessiter, *v.a.* to necessitate; to render *or* make necessary; to compel, to force, to oblige; to imply
Nécessiteu-x, se, *adj. s.* necessitous, needy
Nec plus ultra, *s.m.* (*Latin*) ne plus ultra
Nécro, (*in compounds*) necro... [obituary
Nécrologe, *s.m.* register *or* list of the dead,
Nécrologie, *s.f.* necrology, obituary
Nécrologique, *adj.* necrologic, obituary
Nécrologue, *s.m.* necrologist
Nécroman-cie, -tique. *V.* page 3, § 1
Nécromancien, ne, *s.m.f.* (**Nécromant,** *s.m.*, *obsolete*) necromancer [*s.m.* necrophagan
Nécrophage, *adj.* (*zool.*) necrophagous; —
Nécrophore, *s.m.* (*zool.*) *V.* **Fossoyeur**
Nécropole, *s.f.* necropolis
Nécropsie, Nécroscopie, *s.f.* necropsy, necroscopy, post-mortem examination
Nécroscopique, *adj.* *V.* page 3, § 1
Nécrose, *s.f.* (*med.*) necrosis
Nécroser, *v.a.* (*med.*) to necrose
Se —, *v.r.* to become necrosed
Nécrotom-ie, -ique. *V.* page 3, § 1
Nectaire, *s.m.* (*bot.*) nectary
Nectar, *s.m.* nectar [nectarean, nectareous
Nectaré, e, Nectaréen, ne, *adj.* nectared,
Nectarifère, *adj.* nectariferous
Néerlandais, e, *adj. s.* Netherlandish; Dutch; Netherlander; Dutchman, Dutchwoman
Nef, *s.f.* (*of churches*) nave; (*obsolete, poet., her.*) ship, vessel, boat. — *collatérale* or *latérale*, (*obsolete*) aisle
Néfaste, *adj.* of rest; solemn; of mourning; inauspicious, ill-omened, fatal, unlucky
Nèfle, *s.f.* medlar
Néflier, *s.m.* medlar-tree
Néga, *s.m.* Canada cherry-tree [denier
Néga-teur, trice, *adj.* denying; — *s.m.f.*
Négati-f, ve, *adj.*, **Négative,** *s.f.* negative
Négation, *s.f.* negation, negative [tive
Négativement, *adv.* negatively; in the nega-
Négativité, *s.f.* negativity, negativeness
Négatoire, *adj.* negatory, negative
Négligé, e, *part. adj.* neglected, &c. (*V.* **Négliger**); unnoticed; unadorned; unstudied; careless; slovenly; loose; incorrect; — *s.m.* undress, loose dress, morning dress, negligee; carelessness; unstudied style [worthy of notice
Négligeable, *adj.* trifling, unimportant, un-
Négligement, *s.m.* (*paint.*, &c.) neglect
Négligemment, *adv.* negligently, carelessly

Négligence, *s.f.* neglect, negligence, carelessness, oversight; inaccuracy; slovenliness

Négligent, e, *adj.* negligent, neglectful, careless; dilatory; inaccurate; — *s.m.f.* ditto person [out; to overlook; to slight; to forget

Négliger, *v.a.* to neglect; to omit; to leave
Se —, *v.r.* to neglect oneself *or* o.'s person; to be negligent *or* careless; to be neglected *or* &c.; to neglect each other

Négoce, *s.m.* trade, business, traffic

Négociabilité, *s.f.* negotiability

Négociable, *adj.* negotiable

Négociant, e, *s.m.f.* merchant; trader

Négociantisme, *s.m.* mercantilism

Négocia-teur, trice, *s.m.f.* negotiator, negotiatrix; transactor; mediator, mediatress, mediatrix [treaty; mediation; business

Négociation, *s.f.* negotiation; transaction;

Négocier, *v.a.n.* to negotiate; to trade
Se —, *v.r.* to be negotiating *or* negotiated

Nègre, *s.m., adj.m.f.* negro, black [yard

Nègrerie, *s.f.* barracoon, negro-jail; negro-

Négresse, *s.f.* negress, negro-woman *or* girl; (*pop.*) bug, b flat; bottle of wine; — *adj.f.* negro, black

Négrier, *s.m.* slave-ship, slaver; slave-dealer; — *adj.m.* of slaves, slave. *Bâtiment* or *vaisseau* —, slave-ship, slaver. *Capitaine* —, captain of a slave-ship. *Marchand* —, slave-dealer

Négrière, *adj.f.* relating to negroes *or* to slaves

†**Négrillon, ne,** *s.m.f.* negro-boy, negro-girl, little negro; (*jest.*) blacky, sambo, nigger

Négrone, *s.f.* negrone (*kind of fig; disease of the silkworm, which renders it quite black*)

Négrophile, *s.m.f. adj.* negrophilist; abolitionist; antislavery [boat

Nègue-chien, Nègue-fol, *s.m.* shooting-

Négundo *s.m.* (*bot.*) negundo, ash-leaved maple [*Abyssinia*)

Négus, *s.m.* negus (*liquor*); Negus (*emperor of*

Neige, *s.f.* snow; whiteness. *Boule de* —, *pelote de* —, snowball; (*bot.*) guelder rose

Neiger, *v.n.* to snow

Neigeu-x, se, *adj.* snowy

†**Neille,** *s.f.* oakum

Nélumbo, *s.m.* (*bot.*) nelumbo

Néméen, ne, *adj. s.f.* Nemean

Nemine contradicente, (*Latin*) nemine contradicente, nem. con., no one contradicting, without opposition

Némophile, *s.m.* (*bot.*) nemophila

Némoral, e, *adj.* nemoral

Ne m'oubliez pas, *s.m.* (*bot.*) forget-me-not

Nems, *s.m.* (*zool.*) nems

Nénais, Nénet, *s.m.* bubby

Nénie, *s.f.* (*Rom. ant.*) nænia, funeral dirge

Nenni, *adv.* (*old, boorish*) no, nay; — *s.m.* (*old*) refusal. —*-dà*, no indeed! nay, nay! not so. *Oh, que* —*!* nay, nay!

Nénufar, Nénuphar, *s.m.* water-lily

Néo, (*in compounds*) neo-...

Néo-Calédonien, ne, *s.m.f. adj.* Nova-Scotian

Néo-catholicisme, *s.m.* neo-catholicism

Néo-catholique, *adj. s.m.f.* neo-catholic

‡**Néo-chrétien, ne,** *adj. s.* neo-christian

‡**Néo-christianisme,** *s.m.* neo-christianity

Néocomien, ne, *adj.*, **Néocomien,** *s.m.* (*geol.*) neocomian, lower greensand

Néocore, *s.m.* (*in antiquity*) neocorus [graphical

Néographe, *s.m.f.* neographer; — *adj.* neo-

Néograph-ie, -ique, -isme. *V.* page 3, § 1

Néo-grec, que, *adj.* modern Greek

Néo-latin, e, *adj.* of Latin origin [page 3, § 1

Néolog-ie, -ique, -iquement, -isme. *V.*

Néologiste, Néologue, *s.m.f.* neologist

Néophron, *s.m.* *V.* **Percnoptère**

Néophyte, *s.m.f. adj.* neophyte

Néoplast-ie, -ique. *V.* page 3, § 1

Néoplatonicien, ne, *adj.* neo-Platonic; — *s.m.f.* neo-Platonician, neo-Platonist

Néo-platonisme, *s.m.* neo-Platonism

Néorama, *s.m.* neorama

Néozoïque, *adj.* (*geol.*) neozoic

Nèpe, *s.f.* (*zool.*) water-scorpion

Népenthe, Népenthès, *s.m.* (*bot.*) nepenthes, pitcher-plant; (*in antiquity*) nepenthe,

Népète, *s.f.* (*bot.*) nepeta [nepenthes

Néphélion, *s.m.* (*surg.*) nephelium

Néphélis, *s.f.* (*zool.*) nephelis (*kind of leech*)

Néphélium, *s.m.* (*bot.*) nephelium, litchi, leechee, longan-tree

Néphralgie, *s.f.* (*med.*) nephralgia, nephralgy

Néphrétique, Néphritique, *adj. s.* (*med.*) nephritic [granulated kidney

Néphrie, *s.f.* (*med.*) nephria, Bright's disease,

Néphrite, *s.f.* (*med.*) nephritis; (*min.*) nephrite, jade [page 3, § 1

Néphro, (*in compounds*) nephro..., *and V.*

Néphrocèle, *s.f.* (*med.*) nephrocele

Népide, *s.m.* (*zool.*) water-scorpion

Népot-ique, -isme, -iste. *V.* page 3, § 1

Neptunales, *s.f.pl.* (*Rom. ant.*) neptunalia

Neptune, *s.m.* (*myth., astr.*) Neptune; (*poet.*) the sea; (*nav.*) neptune, nautical atlas

Neptunien, ne, *adj.* Neptunian; — *s.m.* Neptunian, Neptunist

Neptun-isme, -iste. *V.* page 3, § 1

Nérée, *s.m.* (*myth.*) Nereus; (*poet.*) the sea

Néréide, *s.f.* (*myth.*) nereid; (*zool.*) nereis, nereid

Nerf, *s.m.* nerve; sinew; thew; sinews; vigour, strength, stamina; string; cord; band; slip. — *de bœuf*, bull's sinew, lash, scourge. *Attaque de* —*s*, nervous attack, hysteric fit, hysterics. — **-férure,** *s.f.* (*vet.*) overreach [reach

Nerférer *or* **Nerférir (Se),** *v.r.* (*vet.*) to over-

Nérite, *s.f.* nerite

Néroli, *s.m.* neroli

Néron, *s.m.* Nero, cruel man *or* tyrant

Néronien, ne, *adj.* Neronian

Nerprun, *s.m.* (*bot.*) buckthorn

Nerval, e, *adj.* (*med.*) nervine; (*bot.*) nervous

Nervation, *s.f.* nervation

Nervé, e, *adj.* nerved

Nerver, *v.a.* to cover with sinews; to cord

Nerveusement, *adv.* nervously

Nerveu-x, se, *adj.* nervous; neural; sinewy; brawny, muscular; vigorous; strong

Nervifolié, e, *adj.* (*bot.*) nervifoliate

Nervin, *s.m., adj.m.* (*med.*) nervine

Nervosité, *s.f.* nervosity, nervousness

Nervule, *s.m.* (*nat. hist.*) nervule

Nervure, *s.f.* (*arch.*) nerve, moulding, rib, fillet; (*bot.*) nervure, nerve, nerves, nervation, vein, veins, venation; rib; (*of insects*) nervure; (*book-bind.*) cording, band, slip; (*need.*) piping

Nescio vos, (*Latin*) I do not know you

Nestor, *s.m.* Nestor; oldest, senior

Nestorianisme, *s.m.* (*eccl. hist.*) Nestorianism

Nestorien, ne, *adj. s.* (*eccl. hist.*) Nestorian

Net, te, *adj.* clean, neat; pure; unmixed; clear; sharp; empty; perspicuous, plain; frank; flat; point-blank; fair; blameless; free from vice; (*com.*) net; — *s.m.* fair copy; — *adv.* entirely; quite; clean; outright; short; at once; frankly; clearly; plainly; flatly; flat; point-blank; fairly. *Clair et* —, (*adj.*) clear; plain; (*adv.*) clearly; plainly. *Mettre au* —, to make a fair copy of

Nettement, *adv.* cleanly; clean; neatly; clearly; sharply; frankly; plainly; flatly

Netteté, *s.f.* cleanness, cleanliness, neatness; purity; clearness; distinctness; sharpness; perspicuity; plainness; blamelessness

Nettoie-couteaux, *s.m.* knife-cleaner

Nettoiement, *s.m.* cleaning; cleansing; clearing; scouring; sweeping; brushing; wiping; picking

Nettoyable, *adj.* cleanable, cleansable

Nettoyage, *s.m.* *V.* **Nettoiement**

Nettoyer, *v.a.* to clean; to cleanse; to clear; to scour; to sweep; to brush; to wipe; to pick; to free [clean (o.'s ...); to be cleaned *or* &c.
Se —, *v.r.* to clean oneself *or* each other; to

Nettoyeu-r, se, *s.m.f.* cleaner; scourer; picker

Nettoyure, *s.f.* cleansings; scourings; sweepings; pickings; orts
Neuf, *adj.m.f., s.m.* nine; ninth
Neu-f, ve, *adj.* new; fresh; young; raw, green, inexperienced; innocent; (*of wood*) unfloated
Neuf, *s.m.* new; something new, what is new, new materials, new things *or* articles; new clothes. *A* —, anew, again; like new. *Remettre à* —, to do up, to repair thoroughly, to repair, to make as good as new; to do over again
Neufchâtel, *s.m.* Neufchatel cheese
Neufchâtelois, e, *adj. s.* of Neufchatel; native of ditto
Neure, *s.m.* Dutch herring-buss
Neustrien, ne, *adj. s.* Neustrian
Neutralement, *adv.* neutrally
Neutralisation, *s.f.* neutralization
Neutraliser, *v.a.* to neutralize
Se —, *v.r.* to become neutralized; to neutralize each other
Neutralité, *s.f.* neutrality
Neutre, *adj.m.f., s.m.* neutral, neuter
Neutriflore, *adj.* (*bot.*) neutriflorous
Neuvaine, *s.f.* (*Cath. rel.*) neuvaine, nine days' devotion *or* prayers
Neuvième, *adj.m.f., s.m.* ninth; ninth part; ninth day, &c.; — *s.f.* (*mus.*), *s.m.f.* (*pers.*) ninth
Neuvièmement, *adv.* ninthly
Névé, *s.m.* (*of a glacier*) snowy region, névé
Neveu, *s.m.* nephew; (*obsolete*) grandson; —**x,** *pl.* nephews; (*obsolete*) grandsons; (*poet.*) posterity, descendants. — *à la mode de Bretagne,* son of a cousin german
Névralgie, *s.f.* (*med.*) neuralgia, neuralgy
Névralgique, *adj.* (*med.*) neuralgic
Névraxe, *s.m.* (*anat.*) neural axis
Névrilème, Névrilemme, *s.m.* (*anat.*) neurilemma
Névrine, *s.f.* (*chem.*) neurine
Névrite, *s.f.* (*med.*) neuritis
Névritique, *adj.m.f., s.m.* (*med.*) neurotic, nervine
Névro, (*in compounds*) neuro. . .
Névrographe, *s.m.* neurographer
Névrographie, *s.f.* neurography
Névrologie, *s.f.* neurology
Névrologique, *adj.* neurological
Névrologue, *s.m.* neurologist
Névrome, *s.m.* neuroma, nervous tumour
Névropathie, *s.f.* (*med.*) neuropathy
Névropathique, *adj.* (*med.*) neuropathic
Névroptère, *s.m.* (*zool.*) neuropteran; — *adj.* neuropteral
Névrose, *s.f.* (*med.*) neurosis
Névrotome, *s.m.* neurotome, neurotomy-knife
Névrotomie, *s.f.* neurotomy
Newtonianisme, *s.m.* Newtonianism, Newtonian philosophy
Newtonien, ne, *adj. s.* Newtonian
New-Yorkais, e, *adj. s.* of New York; New-Yorker
Nez, *s.m.* nose; nostrils; (*fig.*) face; teeth; eyes; smell; scent. *Au — de,* before *or* in *or* to . . .'s nose *or* face. *Au — et à la barbe de,* under . . .'s very nose. *Avoir bon —, avoir le — fin, V.* **Fin,** *adj. Donner du — en terre,* to fall on o.'s face; to fail. *Donner sur le* —, to give a slap on the face; (*fig.*) to mortify. **Pied-de-** —, *s.m.* balk; sight. *Avoir un pied-de-* —, to come off unsuccessfully, to be baffled; to look foolish. *Faire un pied-de-* — (*à*), to put o.'s finger to o.'s nose (at), to take a sight (at), to bite o.'s (*or* the) thumb (at), to laugh (at) *Jeter au — de,* (*fig.*) to cast in . . .'s teeth, to twit. *Mettre le — dessus,* to guess it. *Se casser le* —, to break o.'s nose; to fail; to be balked *or* disappointed *or* frustrated; to find no one at home, to call to no purpose. *Tirer les vers du — à,* to pump. *Cela lui pend au* —, he may expect that. *Il me rit au* —, he laughed in my face. — **-coupé,** *s.m.* bladder-nut
Ni, *conj.* neither; nor; either; or. — *moi non plus,* nor I either
Niable, *adj.* deniable; (*law*) traversable
Niais, e, *adj. s.* silly, foolish, simple; spoony; simpleton, ninny
Niaisement, *adv.* foolishly, sillily, simply
Niaiser, *v.n.* to trifle, to peddle
Niaiserie, *s.f.* silliness, foolishness, simplicity; nonsense, foolery; trifle
Nicaise, *s.m. V.* **Nicodème**
Niche, *s.f.* niche; recess; alcove; retreat; kennel, house; trick, prank
Nichée, *s.f.* whole nest, nest; brood; gang, crew, set, lot
Nicher, *v.n.* to nestle, to build nests, to build; to lodge; — *v.a.* to nestle; to place, to put, to set, to lodge, to fix, to settle, to thrust; to quod
Se —, *v.r.* to nestle; to place *or* &c. oneself, to lodge *or* hide oneself, to lodge, to lie
Nichet, *s.m.* nest-egg
Nicheu-r, se, *adj.* nest-building
Nichoir, *s.m.* breeding-cage
Nichons, *s.m.pl.* bubbies
Nickel, *s.m.* (*min.*) nickel
Nickélifère, *adj.* nickeliferous
Nicodème, *s.m.* nincompoop, booby, (a) silly Billy *or* simple Simon
Niçois, e, *adj. s.* of Nice, native of Nice
Nicotiane, *s.f.* (*bot.*) nicotiana
Nicotianine, *s.f.* (*chem.*) nicotianine
Nicotine, *s.f.* (*chem.*) nicotine
Nicotique, *adj.* nicotic
Nicotiser, *v.a.* to nicotize
Nictation, Nictitation, *s.f.* nictation, nictitation
Nictitant, e, *adj.* nictitating
Nid, *s.m.* nest; berth. *Petit à petit l'oiseau fait son* —, light strokes fell great oaks. *A chaque oiseau son — est beau,* home is home, be it ever so homely
Nidification, *s.f.* nidification, nest-building
Nidoreu-x, se, *adj.* nidorous, stinking, nauseous
Nidulant, e, *adj.* nidulant; nest-building
Nièce, *s.f.* niece. — *à la mode de Bretagne,* daughter of a cousin german
Nielle, *s.f.* (*agr.*) smut, blight, mildew; ear-cockles, purples, peppercorn; (*bot.*) corn-cockle; fennel-flower; — *s.m.* niello, niello-work, inlaid modelling work
Nieller, *v.a.* to smut, to blight, to mildew; to cut in niello-work, to inlay with niello *or* &c.
Se —, *v.r.* to become smutty, to be blighted
Nielleur, *s.m.* niello-worker; — *adj.m.* niello-working
Niellure, *s.f.* smut, blight; niello-cutting, niello-work
Nier, *v.a.* to deny; to disown; to deny the existence of; (*law*) to traverse
Se —, *v.r.* to be denied, &c.
Nigaud, e, *adj. s.m.f.* silly, foolish; noodle, simpleton, booby, flat; — *s.m.* (*bird*) green cormorant, shag
Nigaudement, *adv.* foolishly, sillily
Nigauder, *v.n.* to trifle, to play the fool
Nigauderie, *s.f.* silliness, foolishness; silly thing, foolery; noodledom
Nigelle, *s.f.* (*bot.*) nigella, fennel-flower
Nigelline, *s.f.* (*chem.*) nigelline
Nigrescent, e, *adj.* nigrescent
Nigrine, *s.f.* (*min.*) nigrine
†Niguedouille, *s.m.f.* (*pop.*) *V.* **Nigaud**
Nihil-isme, -iste (*s.m.f.*), *V.* page 3, § 1
Nihiliste, *adj.* nihilistic
Nilgaut, *s.m.* nyl-ghau (*kind of antelope*)
†Nille, *s.f.,* **Nillée,** *adj.f. V* **Anille** *and* **Anillée**
Nilomètre, *s.m.* nilometer
Nilométrique, Nilotique, &c. *V.* page 3, § 1
Nimbe, *s.m.* nimbus, halo
Nimbus, *s.m.* (*meteorology*) nimbus, rain-cloud
Nîmois, e, *adj. s.* of Nimes; native of Nimes
Niobique, *adj.* (*chem.*) niobic
Niobium, *s.m.* (*chem.*) niobium
Nipper, *v.a.* to fit out, to stock *or* provide (with clothes)
Nippes, *s.f.pl.* (*fam.*) clothes, duds, togs, toggery
Nique, *s.f.* sign of mockery *or* contempt. *Faire la — à,* to laugh at, to make fun of; to slight, to despise; to bite o.'s thumb at; to baffle
Niquetage, *s.m.* nicking (*a horse's tail*)
Niqueter, *v.a.* to nick (*a horse's tail*)
Nisan, *s.m.* Nisan (*Jewish month*)

Nisanne, Ninsin, Ninsi, *s.m.* (*bot.*) ginseng

Nisco, *int.* (*pop.*) nothing! not it! not a bit of it! no use! not I! I cry off!

Nitée, *s.f.* *V.* **Nichée**

Nitouche, *s.f.* *Sainte* —, demure hypocrite, sanctimonious person, dissembler. *Faire la sainte* —, to look as if butter would not melt in

Nitrate, *s.m.* (*chem.*) nitrate [o.'s mouth

Nitraté, e, *adj.* (*chem.*) nitrated

Nitre, *s.m.* (*chem.*) nitre, saltpetre

Nitré, e, *adj.* nitred

Nitreu-x, se, *adj.* (*chem.*) nitrous

Nitrière, *s.f.* nitriary, nitre-bed, saltpetre-bed

Nitrification, *s.f.* (*chem.*) nitrification

Nitrifier, *v.a.*, **Se** —, *v.r.* (*chem.*) to nitrify

Nitrique, *adj.* (*chem.*) nitric

Nitrite, *s.m.* (*chem.*) nitrite

Nitro, (*in compounds, chem.*) nitro...

Nitrobenzine, *s.f.* (*chem.*) nitrobenzole

Nitrogène, *s.m.*(*chem.*) nitrogen; — *adj.* nitroge-

Nitrogéner, *v.a.* (*chem.*) to nitrogenize [nous

Nitroglycérine, *s f.* (*chem.*) nitroglycerine

‡**Nitrohydrochlorique,** *adj.* (*chem.*) nitro-hydrochloric, nitromuriatic

Nitromètre, *s.m.* nitrometer

Nitrure, *s.m.* (*chem.*) nitride [(*bot.*) *V.* **Nivéole**

Nivéal, e, *adj.* nival, winter, snowy; — *s f.*

Niveau, *s.m.* level. — *d'eau*, water-level. — *des eaux*, water-mark. — *à bulle d'air*, spirit-level. — *à perpendicule*, plumb-level. *De* —, *au* — (*de*), level (with), even (with); on a level (with); to the level (of); equal (to)

Niveler, *v.a.* to level, to make even. *Se* —, to be levelled, to be *or* become level *or* even

Nivelette, *s.f.* level indicator

Niveleu-r, se, *s.m.f.* leveller; — *adj.* levelling

Nivellement, *s.m.* levelling

Nivéole, *s.f.* (*bot.*) snowdrop; snow-flake

Nivereau, *s.m.*, **Niverolle,** *s.f.* snow-bird

Nivernaise, *s.f.* (*cook.*) nivernaise, carrot-stew

Nivet, *s.m.* gratuity, douceur, tip

Nivette, *s.f.* (kind of peach)

Nivôse, *s.m.* Nivose (*fourth month of the calendar of the first French Republic, from December* 21 *to January* 19) [— *s.m.* peerage-book

Nobiliaire, *adj.* of the nobility, aristocratic;

Nobilissime, *adj.* most noble

Noble, *adj.* noble, great, high, elevated; — *s.m.* noble, nobleman; (*old gold coin*) noble [somely

Noblement, *adv.* nobly; honourably; hand-

Noblesse, *s.f.* nobility; nobleness; rank

Nobliau, *s.m.* lordling

Noc, *s.m.* channel, gutter

Noce, *s.f.*, **Noces,** *pl.* marriage; wedding, nuptials; wedding-party *or* feast; jollification, drinking-bout; comfortable *or* pleasant situation. *Gâteau de* —, wedding-cake, bride-cake. *Faire la* —, to revel, to have a jollification, to enjoy oneself; to booze, to get drunk

Nocer, *v.n.* *V.* **Noce** (*Faire la* —)

Noceu-r, se, *s.m.f.* reveller, gay man *or* woman

Nocher, *s.m.* (*poet.*) *V.* **Nautonier**

Noctambule, *s.m.f.* noctambulist, night-walker, sleep-walker; — *adj.* noctambulistic, night-walking, sleep-walking

Noctambuler, *v.n.* (*jest.*) to noctambulate

Noctambulisme, *s.m.* noctambulism, night-walking, sleep-walking

Noctiluque, *adj.* noctilucous; — *s.m.* noctiluca, noctilucous animal

Noctuelle, *s.f.* brown owl; cabbage-moth

Noctule, *s.f.* noctule bat

Nocturnal, *s.m.* (*Cath. lit.*) nocturn

Nocturne, *adj.* nocturnal, nightly, night, of night; — *s.m.* (*nat. hist.*) nocturnal; (*mus.*) nocturne; (*Cath. lit.*) nocturn

Nocturnement, *adv.* nocturnally

Nocuité, *s.f.* noxiousness

Nodal, e, *adj.* nodal

Noddi, *s.m.* (*bird*) noddy

Nodosité, *s.f.* nodosity; node

Nodule, *s.m.* nodule

Noduleu-x, se, *adj.* nodulous, nodular

Nodus, *s.m.* (*med.*) node

Noël, *s.m.* Christmas, Yule; Christmas-carol; — *int.* (*old*) hurrah! *A la fête de* —, *à la* —, *à* —, at Christmas

Nœud, *s.m.* knot; tie; bow; knob; node; knuckle; coil; bond; difficulty, rub; main point; spring. — *de la gorge*, Adam's apple

Noffs, *s.m.* (*in Russian*) nose

Noguet, *s.m.* large flat basket

Noie-chien, *s.m.* shooting-boat

Noir, e, *adj.* black; dark; swarthy; dirty; dull; gloomy, dismal; sad; wicked, base, foul, heinous; (*of bread, meat, sauces, &c.*) brown; (*of butter*) burnt, browned; (*of coffee*) strong, without milk; — *s.m.* black; blackness; dark, darkness; black *or* dark spot; smut; smudge; bruise, black and blue; centre (*of a target*); shade; gloom; gloomy thoughts *or* mood, brown study; negro, black man *or* boy, black; dark *or* swarthy man *or* boy; (*agr.*) brown rust, bunt, smut-ball, mildew: — *s.f.* negress, black woman *or* girl; dark *or* swarthy woman *or* girl; black ball; black one; (*mus.*) crotchet. — *animal*, bone-black, animal charcoal. — *de fumée*, lamp-black. — *comme un four*, — *comme dans un four*, dark as pitch, pitch-dark. *En* —, in black; black; on the dark side. *Faire* —, to make black; (*of the night*) to be dark. *Faire* or *broyer du* —, *V.* **Broyer.** *Rendre* —, to make black, to blacken; to defame

Noirâtre, *adj.* blackish

Noiraud, e, *adj.* *s.* swarthy-looking; swarthy-looking man *or* woman, blacky

Noirceur, *s.f.* blackness; darkness; black spot; gloominess, gloom; gloomy thoughts; sadness; wickedness, baseness, foulness, heinousness, atrocity; wicked *or* base *or* foul act *or* thing; base trick

Noircir, *v.a.n.* to blacken; to black; to darken; to gloom; to sadden; to depress; to blot; to traduce, to asperse, to defame, to sully

Se —, *v.r.* to grow (*or* get *or* become *or* turn) black, to blacken; to blacken oneself; to disgrace oneself; to render oneself odious; to dye (o.'s ...) black; to grow gloomy; to get dark *or* cloudy

Noircissement, *s.m.* blackening, blacking

Noircisseur, *s.m.* blackener, dyer in black. — *de papier*, scribbler [blackening

Noircissure, *s.f.* black spot, smudge; black;

Noirot, *s.m.* *V.* **Blatte**

Noise, *s.f.* quarrel, squabble, brawl [tion

Noiseraie, *s.f.* walnut-grove, walnut-planta-

Noisetier, *s.m.* nut-tree, hazel-tree, hazel

Noisette, *s.f.* hazel-nut, nut; — *s.m.* *adj.* hazel-colour, hazel-coloured, hazel, nut-brown, dun, drab

Noix, *s.f.* walnut; nut; (*of a firelock*) tumbler; (*of an umbrella*) wheel; (*of the knee*) cap; (*of meat*) kernel, pope's eye; (*of mills*) cone; (*of a tobacco-pipe*) bowl; (*carp.*) groove. — *de galle*,

Nolane, *s.f.* (*bot.*) nolana [gall-nut

Noli me tangere, *s.m.* (*bot., med.*) noli me

Nolis, *s.m.* (*nav.*) freight; fare [tangere

Nolisateur, *s.m.* (*nav.*) charterer

Noliser, *v.a.* (*nav.*) to charter

Nolisement, *s.m.* (*nav.*) chartering

Nolition, *s.f.* nolition

Nom, *s.m.* name; noun; fame, reputation, renown; title; style. — *de baptême, petit* —, christian name. — *de demoiselle*, maiden name. — *de famille*, surname. — *de guerre*, assumed name, alias, nickname, nom de guerre, (*of authors, in London newspaper fanciful French*) nom de plume. *Au* — *de*, in the name of; for the sake of; on behalf of. *De* —, by name; in name; nominal; nominally. *Sans* —, *qui n'a pas de* —, without a name, nameless; obscure; for which there is no name; for which no name is too bad. *Avoir* —, to be called, o.'s *or* its name to be. — *d'un chien!*

— *d'un* —! — *d'un petit bonhomme!* — *d'une pipe!* — *d'un tonnerre!* (*pop.*) by George! by Jingo! by the Powers! bedad! — *de Dieu!* (*swearing*) by God!

Noma, *s.m.* (*med.*) noma

Nomade, *adj.* nomadic, nomad, wandering, migratory; — *s.m.* nomad

Nomarchie, *s.f.* nomarchy

Nomarque, *s.m.* nomarch

Nombles, *s.m.pl.* nombles, numbles, umbles

Nombrable, *adj.* numerable

Nombrant, *adj.m.* (*math., of numbers*) abstract

Nombre, *s.m.* number; numbers; quantity; variety; quorum; harmony. — *premier* or *simple,* prime *or* primitive number

Nombré, e, *part. adj.* numbered; concrete

Nombrer, *v.a.* to number, to reckon, to count

Se —, *v.r.* to be numbered *or* &c.

Nombreusement, *adv.* numerously

Nombreu-x,se, *adj.* numerous; many; large; harmonious, full. *Peu* —, not numerous, not many, few; small

Nombril, *s.m.* navel; (*her.*) navel point, nombril point, nombril; (*bot.*) eye

Nome, *s.m.* nome; — *s.f.* (*med.*) noma

Nôme, *s.m.* (*old alg.*) nomial [nomenclatress

Nomencla-teur, trice, *s.m.f.* nomenclator,

Nomenclature, *s.f.* nomenclature

Nominal, e, *adj.* nominal; of (the) names; (*philos.*) nominalistic; — *s.m.* (*philos.*) nomin-

Nominalement, *adv.* nominally [alist

Nominal-isme, -iste (*s.m.*). *V.* page 3, § 1

Nominaliste, *adj.* nominalistic [appointee

Nominataire, *s.m.f.* nominee; presentee;

Nomina-teur, trice, *s.m.f.* nominator; presenter, advowee, patron; appointer

Nominati-f, ve, *adj.* nominative; of (the) names; (*of shares,* &c.) personal; — *s.m.* (*gram.*) nominative, nominative case

Nomination, *s.f.* nomination; appointment; gift; advowson; election [name

Nominativement, *adv.* nominatively, by

Nommé,e, *part. adj.* named, &c. (*V.* **Nommer**); designate; elect; said; by name. *Un* — *Blondel, Le* — *Blondel,* a man *or* a person named Blondel, one Blondel; the said Blondel; Blondel [especially

Nommément, *adv.* namely; particularly;

Nommer, *v.a.* to name, to call; to nominate; to appoint; to collate; to designate; to mention; to elect; to nickname; to call out the name of

Se —, *v.r.* to state *or* tell o.'s name; to be named *or* called; o.'s name to be; &c., *V.*

Nomocanon, *s.m.* nomocanon [**Appeler (S')**

Nomographe, *s.m.* nomographer

Nomo-graphie, -logie, &c. *V.* page 3, § 1

Non, *adv.* no; not; (*in compounds*) non-..., un..., in..., im...; — *s.m.* no. — *pas,* — *point,* not; no; not so. — *plus,* no more; no longer; neither; nor; either; or; on the other hand; after all; though, yet, still. *Que* —, no; not; no indeed, dear no; certainly not. *Dire, parier* (or *gager*), *assurer, jurer, &c. que* —, to say, to bet, to assure, to swear, &c. that it is not (so). — **-activité,** *s.f.* non-activity. *En* — *-activité,* unemployed; ineffective, non-effective; not in active service; unattached; on the unattached list; retired. — **-âge,** *s.m.* (*obsolete*) nonage. — **-combattant,** *s.m.* non-combatant. — **-conducteur, trice,** *s.m.f. adj.* (*phys.*) non-conductor; non-conducting. — **-conformiste,** *s.m.f. adj.* nonconformist; nonconforming. — **-conformité,** *s.f.* nonconformity. — **-être,** *s.m.,* — **-existence,** *s. f.* non-existence, nonentity. — **-intervention,** *s.f.* non-intervention. — **-jouissance,** *s.f.* non-use. — **-lieu,** *s.m.* (*law*) no cause, no ground (to prosecute). *Ordonnance de* — *-lieu,* release, discharge. *Rendre une ordonnance de* — *-lieu,* to ignore the bill of indictment. — **-moi,** *s.m.* (*philos.*) non ego, external world, object. — **-pair, e,** *adj. V.* **Impair.** — **-payement,** *s.m.* non-payment. — **-recevoir,** *s.m. Fin de* — *-recevoir, V.* **Fin,** *s.f.* — **-résidence,** *s.f.* non-residence. — **-réussite,** *s.f.,* — **-succès,** *s. m. V.* **Insuccès.** — **-sanglant, e,** *adj.* bloodless. — **-sens,** *s.m.* nonsense. — **-usage,** *s.m.* disuse, non-usance, non-user. — **-valeur,** *s.f.* unproductiveness, deficiency, waste, loss; bad debt; bill of no value. — **-vente,** *s.f.* no sale

Nonagénaire, *adj. s.m.f.* nonagenarian

Nonagésimal, e, *adj.* nonagesimal [agesima

Nonagésime, *adj.* nonagesimal; — *s.f.* non-

Nonante, *adj.* (*old*) ninety

Nonce, *s.m.* nuncio [ly; supinely; sluggishly

Nonchalamment, *adv.* carelessly, heedless-

Nonchalance, *s.f.* carelessness, heedlessness; supineness; sluggishness

Nonchalant, e, *adj.* careless, heedless; supine; sluggish [dence

Nonciature, *s.f.* nunciature; nuncio's resi-

None, *s.f.* (*Cath. lit.*) none; —**s,** *pl.* (*Rom. calendar*) nones

Nonidi, *s.m.* Nonidi (*ninth day of the decade in the calendar of the first French Republic*)

Nonius, *s.m.* (*math. instr.*) nonius

Nonnain, *s.f.* (*jest.*) nun

Nonnat, *s.m.* (*fish*) atherine, sand smelt

Nonne, *s.f.* (*jest.*) nun

Nonnerie, *s.f.* (*jest.*) nunnery

Nonnette, *s.f.* (*jest.*) young nun, nun; gingerbread nut; (*bird*) barnacle. — *blanche,* (*bird*) smew, white nun. — *cendrée,* (*bird*) marsh tit

Nonobstant, *prep.* notwithstanding, in spite of

†**Nonpareil, le,** *adj.* nonpareil, unparalleled, unequalled, matchless

†**Nonpareille,** *s.f.* nonpareil (*narrow ribbon, small sugar-plum, printing type, &c.*); nonsuch, nonesuch, nonpareil (*kind of apple, &c.*)

Nonuple, *s.m. adj.* nonuple, ninefold

Nonupler, *v.a.n.,* **Se** —, *v.r.* to nonuple, to

Nopage, *s.m.* (*manu.*) burling [increase ninefold

Nopal, *s.m.* (*bot.*) nopal, Indian fig

Nopalerie, Nopalière, *s.f.* nopal-plantation

Nope, *s.f.* (*manu.*) burl

Noper, *v.a.* (*manu.*) to burl

Nopeu-r, se, *s.m.f.* (*manu.*) burler

Nord, *s.m.* north; north wind; Great Northern railway; (*department of France*) Nord; — *adj.* north, northern, northerly. *Au* —, to *or* in *or* on *or* &c. the north; north, northward, northerly. *De* —, *du* —, north, northern, northerly. *Vers le* —, northward. *Faire le* —, to sail *or* steer northward

Nordir, *v.n.* (*nav., of the wind*) to turn north

Nordiste, *s.m.* (*American polit.*) Northerner

Noria, *s.f.* chain-pump, chain-buckets, noria

Norine, *s.f.* (*chem.*) norine

Norique, *adj.* (*geog.*) Noric

Norite, *s.f.* (*min.*) norite

Norium, *s.m.* (*chem.*) norium

Normal, e, *adj.,* **Normale,** *s.f.* normal

Normalement, *adv.* normally

Normalien, *s.m.* normal school pupil

Normalité, *s.f.* normality, normalness

Normand, e, *adj. s m.f.* Norman; cunning; cautious; ambiguous, equivocal, evasive, shuffling; feigned; cunning fellow *or* thing, artful dodger; shuffler; — *s.f.* Norman fashion; kind of plough

Normander, *v.a.* (*agr.*) to dress (*corn*)

Normandisme, Normanisme, *s.m.* Normanism

Norme, *s.f.* norm, rule, law [manism

Norse, *s.m.* Norse [Norwegian; ditto fashion

Norvégien, ne, Norwégien, ne, *adj. s.*

Nos, *adj.poss.pl.m.f.* our, our own

Nosocomial, e, *adj.* nosocomial, hospital

Nosocratique, *adj.* (*med.*) nosocratic, specific

Nosogénie, *s.f.* (*med.*) nosogenia, nosogenesis

Noso-graphie, -graphique, -logie, -logique, -logiste. *V.* page 3, § 1

Nosophore, *s.m.* hospital-bed, sick-bed

†Nosseigneurs, *s.m.pl.* our lords, the lords, your *or* their lordships
Nostalgie, *s.f.* nostalgia, home-sickness
Nostalgique, *adj. s.* nostalgic
‡Nostoc, Nostoch, *s.m.* (*bot.*) nostoc, star [jelly
Nostomanie, *s.f.* nostomania
Nota, *s.m.* remark, observation. — *bene*, observe; nota bene
Notabilité, *s.f.* notability; respectability
Notable, *adj.* notable, remarkable; considerable; principal, leading, eminent, of note; respectable, of respectability; — *s.m.* principal *or* leading man, most influential man, notable man, man of note, notability, notable
Notablement, *adv.* notably, remarkably; considerably; principally [veyancer
Notaire, *s.m.* notary, solicitor, attorney, con-
Notalgie, *s.f.* (*med.*) notalgia, notalgy
Notamment, *adv.* specially, especially, par- [ticularly
Notarial, e, *adj.* notarial
Notariat, *s.m.* notary's business
Notarié, e, *adj.* notarial (*done or taken by a* [*notary*)
Notation, *s.f.* notation
Note, *s.f.* note; mark; brand; remark; notice; report; memorandum; bill, account; list; tune; tone
Noter, *v.a.* to note, to note down, to make a memorandum of; to mark; to brand; to remark; to notice; to take notice of; to observe; (*mus.*) to note, to prick down, to prick. *Mal noté*, (*pers.*) of bad character, disreputable, bad
  Se —, *v.r.* to be noted *or* &c.
Noteur, *s.m.* music-copier
Notice, *s.f.* notice, account; review; list
Notification, *s.f.* notification; notice
Notifier, *v.a.* to notify; to give notice of
Notion, *s.f.* notion; idea; information; knowledge; element, rudiment [plain
Notoire, *adj.* notorious; known; well-known;
Notoirement, *adv.* notoriously; clearly
Notonecte, *s.m.* (*zool.*) boat-fly
Notoriété, *s.f.* notoriety; evidence
Notre, *adj.poss.* our, our own
Nôtre, *pron.poss.* ours, our own. *Le —, la —, les —s*, ours, our own; our relations; our family; our friends; our men; our servants; our company *or* party; our people; our subjects; our tricks *or* pranks; &c. *Être des —s*, to be one of us, to belong to our body *or* &c., to join us *or* our party, &c.
Notre-Dame, *s.f.* our Lady, (the) Virgin Mary; our Lady's day; (*church*) Notre-Dame
Noue, *s.f.* pantile; gutter; gutter-lead; pasture-ground; wash; cod-liver and guts; cod-sounds
Noué, e, *part. adj.* knotted, &c. (*V.* **Nouer**); (*of fruits*) set; (*hunt.*) with pup; (*pers.*) rickety; (*her.*) nowed; — *s.m.f.* rickety person
Nouement, *s.m* knotting, tying, &c. (*V.* **Nouer**)
Nouer, *v.a.* to knot; to tie; to join; to connect; to knit; to twist; to clasp; to form; to get up; to enter into; (*nav.*) to hitch; — *v.n.* (*of fruits*) to set
  Se —, *v.r.* to fasten oneself; to knit; to twist; to be tied *or* &c.; to become *or* be twisted, to twist; to grow rickety; (*of fruits*) to set
Nouet, *s.m.* little bag; (*vet.*) *V.* **Mastigadour**
Noueur, *s.m.* tier, binder
Noueu-x, se, *adj.* knotty; gnarled; nodose
Nougat, *s.m.* nougat, almond-cake; (*agr.*) walnut-cake [micelli
†Nouilles, *s.f.pl.* (*cook.*) nouilles, ribbon ver-
Noules, *s.f.pl.* *V.* **Nouilles**
Noulet, *s.m.* gutter; rafter
Noumène, *s.m.* (*philos.*) noumenon
Nounou, *s.f.* (*children's slang*) nursy
Nourrain, *s.m.* *V.* **Alevin**
Nourri, e, *part. adj.* fed, &c. (*V.* **Nourrir**); rich; full; copious; thick-laid; thick; close; seasoned; high-seasoned; (*of firing*) kept up, thick, brisk. *V.* **Éclairé.** *Bien —*, well-fed, &c.; very rich, &c.; (*of limbs*) brawny, muscular

Nourrice, *s.f.* wet-nurse; nurse; foster-mother. *Mère —*, foster-mother. *En —*, at nurse; out at nurse; in arms; a baby, as *or* when a baby. *Mettre en —*, to put out to nurse. *Et les mois de —*, (*fam., jest.*) and a bit more
Nourricerie, *s.f.* grazing-farm; silkworm nursery; (*jest.*) nurseship
Nourricier, *s.m.* foster-father; fosterer
Nourrici-er, ère, *adj.* nutritive, nutritious, nourishing. *Père —*, foster-father; fosterer; support
Nourrir, *v.a.* to feed, to nourish; to suckle, to nurse; to support, to maintain, to keep; to keep up; to supply; to fill; to make full *or* rich; to board; to educate, to rear, to bring up; to breed; to foster; to nurture; to cherish, to entertain, to harbour; to indulge in; — *v.n.* to be nourishing
  Se — (*de*), *v.r.* to feed, to live (upon); to maintain *or* support oneself; to thrive; to delight (in), to feast (on); to find o.'s own [board *or* food
Nourrissable, *adj.* nourishable
Nourrissage, *s.m.* feeding; breeding; nursing
Nourrisseur, *s. m.* feeder; cattle-feeder; grazier; breeder; cow-keeper; — *adj.m.* (*tech.*) feeding, feed [foster-son, foster-daughter; foal
Nourrisson, ne, *s m.f.* nursling, foster-child,
Nourriture, *s.f.* food, nourishment; diet, living; maintenance; board; suckling, nursing; feeding; breeding
Nous, *pers.pron.* we; us; to *or* at us, for *or* with *or* in *or* from *or* by *or* on *or* against us; for our part; ourselves, ourself, to *or* at *or* within ourselves (*or* ourself); each other, one another; to *or* at *or* for *or* with each other (*or* one another). *A —*, to *or* at *or* with us *or* ourselves *or* ourself; ours, our own; of ours, of our own; peculiar; to spare. *A — à, à — de*, *V* **A.** *A — deux*, *V.* **Deux.** — *-même*, ourself; alone; too, also, likewise. — *-mêmes*, ourselves; alone; too, also, likewise
Nouure, *s.f.* knotting, tying, &c. (*V.* **Nouer**); rickets; (*of fruits*) setting
Nouveau, Nouvel, *m.*, **Nouvelle,** *f.*, *adj.* new; recent; novel; fresh; different; other; further; modern; new-fashioned; inexperienced, young, green; — *adv.* newly, new, fresh, lately, recently; — *s.m.* new boy (*at school*); new man; new, something new, what is new, new thing, new things, novelty; (*com.*) new account. *De —*, anew; afresh; again; over again; once more; new, that *or* what is new; also. *Qu'y a-t-il de — ?* what is the news? — **-né, e,** *adj. s.* new-born; new-born child
Nouveauté, *s.f.* newness; novelty; rarity; change; innovation; recency; new thing; new publication, new work; new play *or* piece; newest article, latest fashion; new pattern; fancy articles *or* goods; linendrapery. *Haute —*, latest fashion. *Magasin de —s*, linendraper's shop. *Marchand de —s*, linendraper
Nouvel, le, *adj.* *V.* **Nouveau**
Nouvelle, *s.f.* news; intelligence, tidings; piece of news; novel; tale, story. *—s à la main*, news-letter; short and lively paragraphs, oddities. *Avoir* or *recevoir* or *apprendre des —s de quelqu'un*, to hear from one. *Avoir des —s de quelqu'un* (*par un autre*), to hear of one. *Attendre des —s de*, to expect to hear from *Demander des —s de*, to inquire after *or* for. *Dire des —s de*, to tell something about; to tell what one thinks of *or* how one likes; to tell whether one does not like, to like much, to be highly pleased with. *Donnez-moi de vos —s*, let me hear from you. *Envoyer savoir des —s de*, to send to inquire after. *Savoir des —s de*, to hear *or* have heard of, to know how ... is *or* gets on (*or* what ... has been *or* is doing). *J'en sais des —s*, I know something about it
Nouvellement, *adv.* newly, recently, lately
Nouvelleté, *s.f.* (*law*) trespass; dispossession
Nouvellier, *s.m.* (*obsolete*) novelist

Nouvelliste, *s.m.f.* newsmonger, quidnunc; newsman; intelligencer; novelist. — *à la main*, gazetteer [tithe on ditto
Novale, *s.f.* land newly ploughed, new land;
Nova-teur, trice, *s.m.f. adj. V.* **Innovateur**
Novation, *s.f.* (*law*) substitution
Novelette, *s.f.* young ewe
Novelle, *s.f.* (*Rom. law*) novel
Novembre, *s.m.* November
Novénaire, *adj.* novenary
Nover, *v.a.* (*law*) to substitute
Noves, *s.f.pl.* cod-liver and guts; cod-sounds
Novice, *s.m.f.* novice; probationer; apprentice; younker; — *adj.* raw, green, new, inexperienced, unskilful [ticeship; seminary
Noviciat, *s.m.* novitiate; probation; appren-
Novissimé, *adv.* (*fam.*) quite recently, very lately [(*fig.*) swamping, ruin
Noyade, *s.f.* drowning; (*Fr. hist.*) noyade;
Noyale, Noyalle, *s.f.* sail-cloth, canvas
Noyalière, *s.f.* fruit-stone plot
Noyau, *s.m.* (*of fruit*) stone; kernel; (*in sciences, tech., and fig.*) nucleus; core; (*of a staircase*) newel; (*liquor*) noyau; —**x**, *pl.* stones, &c.; (*game*) pitch and toss; (*pop.*) money, tin. *Eau* or *crème de* —, noyau
Noyé, e, *part. adj.* drowned, &c. (*V.* **Noyer**); drowning; — *s.m.f.* ditto person
Noyer, *s.m.* walnut-tree; walnut-wood, walnut
Noyer, *v.a.* to drown; to drench; to inundate; to deluge; to dilute; to bathe; to sink; to plunge; to swamp; to ruin; to overwhelm; (*at bowls*) to throw out of bounds; (*nav.*) to lay (*a ship*); to settle (*the land*); (*paint.*) to mix, to blend, to confuse (*colours*); (*tech.*) to countersink, to let in
  Se —, *v.r.* to be drowning; to get *or* be drowned; to drown oneself; to be bathed *or* plunged *or* swamped; to wallow, to welter; to go to wreck and ruin
Noyon, *s.m.* (*at bowls*) mark
Noyure, *s.f.* (*tech.*) countersink
Nu, e, *adj.* naked; bare; uncovered; undressed; open; without disguise; unadorned; plain; destitute. — *-jambes*, bare-legged. — *-pieds*, bare-foot, bare-footed. — *-tête*, *tête* —*e*, bareheaded
Nu, *s.m.* naked, naked part, nakedness, nudity, nude, bareness, bare. *A* —, naked; bare; uncovered; open; nakedly, openly; frankly; plainly; bare-back, without a saddle. *Mettre à* —, to lay bare *or* open; to uncover; to strip
Nuage, *s.m.* cloud; (*fig.*) cloud; mist, darkness; gloom, sadness; shadow; veil; doubt, suspicion; misunderstanding, dissension, jar; storm; (*med., astr., her.*) nebula
Nuagé, e, *adj.* clouded, cloudy, nebuly
Nuageu-x, se, *adj.* cloudy; clouded; obscure
Nuaison, *s.f.* (*nav.*) duration *or* continuance of the same wind *or* weather
Nuance, *s.f.* shade; shadowing; hue; tint; cast; difference, distinction; degree; gradation; tincture
Nuancer, *v.a.* to shade; to variegate; to vary; to blend; (*paint.*) to shade, to tint
  Se —, *v.r.* to be variegated *or* &c.
Nubécule, *s.f.* (*med.*) nubecula
Nubien, ne, *adj. s.* Nubian
Nubile, *adj.* marriageable, nubile
Nubilité, *s.f.* marriageable age, nubility
Nucal, e, *adj.* (*anat.*) of the nape [like
Nuciforme, *adj.* nuciform, nut-shaped, nut-
Nucivore, *adj.* nucivorous
Nucléaire, *adj.* nuclear
Nucléal, e, *adj.* nucleal
Nucléé, e, *adj.* nucleate, nucleated
Nuculaine, *s.f.* (*bot.*) nuculanium
Nucule, *s.f.* (*bot.*) nucule
Nudité, *s.f.* nakedness, nudity
Nue, *s.f* cloud; —**s**, *pl.* clouds, skies; air; heavens. *Élever* or *porter jusqu'aux* —*s*, to raise *or* praise to the skies. *Faire sauter aux* —*s*, to drive wild. *Sauter aux* —*s*, to jump to the ceiling. *Tomber des* —*s*, to fall *or* drop from the clouds *or* skies; to be struck with amazement, to be amazed *or* astounded *or* thunderstruck
Nuée, *s.f.* cloud; host; multitude; swarm; (*of arrows*, &c.) flight; shower; (*in flighty style*)
Nuement, *adv. V.* **Nûment** [storm
Nuer, *v.a. V.* **Nuancer**
Nuire, *v.n.* to do harm *or* injury; to hurt, to injure; to wrong; to prejudice; to be noxious *or* injurious *or* prejudicial; to spoil; to hinder, to prevent; to stand *or* be in the way of; to weaken. *Ne pas* —, not to do harm, to do no harm, to be harmless, not to hurt, &c.; to be of use; to help, to assist; to contribute
Nuisance, *s.f.* nuisance [noxious
Nuisible, *adj.* hurtful, injurious, prejudicial;
Nuisiblement, *adv.* hurtfully, injuriously, prejudicially, noxiously
Nuit, *s.f.* night; night-time; darkness, dark; (*paint.*) night-piece; —**s**, *pl.* nights; (*Young's poem*) Night Thoughts. — *blanche*, sleepless night. — *close*, close of day, nightfall; quite dark, dark night. — *noire*, dark night; quite dark, pitch-dark. *Cette* —, to-night; last night. *A la* — *tombante*, at nightfall. *De* —, by night, nightly; night; on duty for the night. *La* —, the night; night; at night, in the night; on the night. *Faire* —, to be night *or* dark. *Se faire* —, to be getting dark. *Faire une bonne* —, to have a good night's rest. *Passer la* —, to spend *or* pass the night; to sit up all night, to sit up; to live the night out
Nuitamment, *adv.* by night, in the night
Nuitée, *s.f.* whole night, night; night's work;
Nuits, *s.m.* nuits (wine) [night's lodging
Nul, le, *adj.* no, not any; null; void; invalid; nil; nothing; wanting; of no worth; none, no one, nobody; any, any one, anybody; (*of games*) drawn. — *homme*, no man. *Homme* —,
Nulle, *s.f.* null [man of no worth, cipher
Nullement, *adv.* by no means, not at all
Nullificateur, *s.m.* (*American polit.*) nullifier
Nullification, *s.f.* (*American polit.*) nullifica-
Nullifier, *v.a.* (*American polit.*) to nullify [tion
Nullité, *s.f.* nullity; incapacity; flaw; (*pers.*)
Numantin, e, *adj. s.* Numantine [cipher
Nûment, *adv.* nakedly, openly, frankly, plainly; (*feud.*) directly, immediately
Numéraire, *adj.* numerary; legal; — *s.m.* cash, specie, coin, bullion
Numéral, e, *adj.* numeral
Numérateur, *s.m.* (*arith.*) numerator
Numérati-f, ve, *adj.*, **Numératif,** *s.m.* nu-
Numération, *s.f.* numeration [meral
Numér-ique, -iquement. *V.* page 3, § 1
Numéro, *s.m.* number; size; sort, kind, quality; ticket. — *un*, *premier* —, number one; (*fam.*) first-rate, A 1; regular. — *cent*, (*fam.*)
Numérotage, *s.m* numbering [privy, W.C.
Numéroter, *v.a.* to number. *Char numéroté*, (*jest., old*) hackney-coach
Numéroteur, *s.m.* numberer
Numismate, *s.m.f.* numismatist [numismatics
Numismatique, *adj.* numismatic; — *s.f.*
Numismatiste, *s.m.f.* numismatist
Numismatographe, *s.m.* numismatographer
Numismatograph-ie, -ique, &c. *V.* p. 3, § 1
Nummulaire, *s.f.* (*bot.*) moneywort; (*fossil*) nummulite
Nummuline, *s.f.* (*zool.*) nummulina
Nummulite, *s.f.* (*fossil*) nummulite
Nuncupati-f, ve, *adj.* (*old*) nuncupative
Nuptial, e, *adj.* nuptial, wedding, bridal
Nuque, *s.f.* (*anat.*) nape; (*of horses*) poll
Nurage, Nuraghe, *s.m.* nuraghe
Nutation, *s.f.* nutation [rishing
Nutriti-f, ve, *adj.* nutritive, nutritious, nou-
Nutrition, *s.f.* nutrition, nourishment
Nutritivité, *s.f.* nutritiveness
Nyctalope, *s.m.f.* (*med.*) nyctalops

Nyctalopie, *s.f.* (*med.*) nyctalopia, nyctalopy
Nyctalopique, *adj.* nyctalopic
Nymphale, *s.m.* (*butterfly*) nymphalis
Nymphe, *s.f.* nymph; (*zool.*) nymph, nympha (*pl.* nymphæ); (*anat.*) nympha (*pl.* nymphæ)
Nymphéacées, *s.f.pl.* (*bot.*) nymphæaceæ
Nympheau, *s.m.* (*bot.*) buckbean, marsh trefoil
Nymphée, Nymphéum, *s.m.* nympheum
Nymphéen, ne, *adj.* nymphean
Nymphomanie, *s.f.* (*med.*) nymphomania
Nyssa, *s.m.* (*bot.*) nyssa, tupelo
Nystagme, *s.f.* (*med.*) nystagmus

O

O (*fifteenth letter of the alphabet*), *s.m.* o
O, *int. s.m.* O! O thou! O you! O ye! oh! *Les — de Noël,* Christmas anthems
Oasien, ne, *adj. s.* of oases, of an oasis, inhabitant of ditto, oasian
Oasis, *s.f.* oasis [cordate
Obcordé, e, Obcordiforme, *adj.* (*bot.*) ob-
Obédience, *s.f.* (*theol.*) obedience; leave of absence, leave of change of residence; functions; consistory; authority; jurisdiction
Obédienciel, le, *adj.* obediential
Obédiencier, *s.m.* obedienciary
Obéir, *v.n.* to obey; to be obedient; to bend; to yield; to give way; to submit; to comply
Obéissamment, *adv.* obediently
Obéissance, *s.f.* obedience; allegiance; submission; compliance; dominion, sway, power, authority
Obéissant, e, *adj.* obedient; obsequious; submissive; dutiful; docile; compliant; flexible, pliant, yielding; manageable
Obéliscal, e, *adj* obeliscal
Obélisque, *s.m.* obelisk [run in *or* into debt
Obérer, *v.a* to involve, to involve in debt, to
Obèse, *adj.* obese, fat, corpulent, big-bellied
Obésité, *s.f.* obesity, corpulence
Obier, *s.m.* guelder rose
Obit, *s.m.* (*Cath. lit.*) obit
Obituaire, *adj.m.f., s.m.* obituary
Objecter, *v.a.n.* to object (to, against); to allege (against); to reproach (with); to demur (to) [&c to each other
S'—, *v.r.* to be objected *or* &c.; to object *or*
Objecti-f, ve, *adj. s.m.* objective; object;
Objection, *s.f.* objection [object-glass; aim
Objectivement, *adv.* objectively
Objectivité, *s.f.* objectivity, objectiveness
Objet, *s.m.* object; subject; matter; aim, end, view; thing; article, goods; work; lady-love, love, sweetheart, woman, person
Objurgation, *s.f.* objurgation
Objurgatoire, *adj.* objurgatory
Oblade, *s.m.* (*fish*) oblada
Oblat, *s.m.* oblate, lay monk
Oblation, *s.f.* oblation, offering
Obligataire, *s.m.f.* obligee, bond-creditor, bond-holder, debenture-holder
Obligation, *s.f.* obligation; duty; bond; debenture, preference share
Obligationnaire, *s.m.f. V.* **Obligataire**
Obligatoire, *adj.* obligatory, compulsory, binding; incumbent [sorily
Obligatoirement, *adv.* obligatorily, compul-
Obligé, e, *part. adj.* obliged, bound, &c. (*V.* **Obliger**); necessary; usual; (*mus.*) obbligato; — *s.m.f.* (*law*) obligor; debtor; — *s.m.* bond, indentures
Obligeamment, *adv.* obligingly, kindly
Obligeance, *s.f.* obligingness, kindness
Obligeant, e, *adj.* obliging, kind
Obliger, *v.a.n.* to oblige; to compel; to force; to bind; to induce; to impose obligations; (*old*) to mortgage, to pledge

Obliquangle, Obliquangulaire, *adj.* (*geom.*) oblique-angled, obliquangular
Oblique, *adj.* oblique; slanting; skew; side; (*fig.*) indirect; unfair
Obliquement, *adv.* obliquely; slantingly; sideways; (*fig.*) indirectly; unfairly [cut
Obliquer, *v.n.* to slant; to swerve; to turn, to
§Obliquité, *s.f.* obliquity; slant; unfairness
Oblitération, *s.f.* obliteration
Oblitérer, *v.a.* to obliterate. *S'—,* to become ob-
Oblong, ue, *adj.* oblong [literated; to disappear
Oboïste, *s.m.f. V.* **Hautboïste**
Obole, *s.f.* (*anc. coin and weight*) obolus, obole; (*fig.*) groat, farthing, doit, stiver, straw, rap; mite; particle [ing
Obombration, *s.f.* obumbration, overshadow-
Obombrer, *v.a.* to obumbrate, to overshadow,
Obreptice, *adj.* obreptitious [to cover
Obrepticement, *adv.* obreptitiously
Obreption, *s.f.* obreption
Obscène, *adj.* obscene
Obscénité, *s.f.* obscenity [—, to be dark
Obscur, e, *adj.* dark; obscure; black. *Faire*
Obscurant, *s.m.* obscurant
Obscurant-isme, -iste. *V.* page 3, § 1
Obscuration, *s.f.* (*astr.*) obscuration
Obscurcir, *v.a.* to darken; to obscure; to throw into the shade; to gloom; to dim; to cloud; to sully, to tarnish
S'—, *v.r.* to darken, to become (*or* grow *or* get) dark *or* obscure *or* dim *or* gloomy; to become *or* be darkened *or* obscured *or* &c.; to get cloudy; to become stern [ration; dimness
Obscurcissement, *s.m.* darkening; obscu-
Obscurément, *adv.* darkly; obscurely; dimly; confusedly [dimness; duplicity
Obscurité, *s.f.* darkness; obscurity; gloom;
Obsécration, *s.f.* obsecration
Obséder, *v.a.* to beset; to importune; to torment; to prey upon; to haunt; to possess
Obsèques, *s.f.pl.* obsequies, funeral
Obséquieusement, *adv.* obsequiously
Obséquieu-x, se, *adj.* obsequious
Obséquiosité, *s.f.* obsequiousness
Observable, *adj.* observable
Observance, *s.f.* observance
Observantin, *s.m.* observantist, observant Franciscan; — *adj.m.* observant
Observa-teur, trice, *s.m.f. adj.* observer; watcher; spy; looker-on, spectator; observant; observing
Observation, *s.f.* observation; look-out; watch; notice; remark; hint; observance; accomplishment, fulfilment, performance; keeping; (*med.*) case; **—s,** *pl.* observations, &c.; (*law*) facts of the case, evidence
Observatoire, *s.m.* observatory
Observer, *v.a.n.* to observe; to examine, to look at; to look on; to watch; to notice; to remark; to practise; to fulfil, to perform; to keep; to make observations. *Faire —,* to observe; to remind; to point out; to call (...'s) attention to
S'—, *v.r.* to be cautious *or* circumspect, to be on o.'s guard; to look at each other, to observe *or* eye *or* watch each other; to be observed *or* &c.
Obsesseur, *s.m.* besetter; — *adj.m.* besetting
Obsession, *s.f.* besetting; obsession
Obsidiane, Obsidienne, *s.f.* obsidian, vol-
Obsidional, e, *adj.* obsidional [canic glass
Obsolète, *adj.* (*nat. hist.*) obsolete
Obstacle, *s.m.* obstacle, hindrance, obstruction, impediment, bar, check; drawback. *Faire — à,* to throw obstacles in the way of; to hinder; to stand *or* be in the way of. *Mettre — à,* to obstruct, to impede, to hinder, to oppose
Obstétrical, e, *adj.* obstetrical, obstetric
Obstétrique, *s.f.* obstetrics, obstetric medicine and surgery, midwifery; — *adj. V.* **Obstétrical**
Obstination, *s.f.* obstinacy; stubbornness, wilfulness, self-will

Obstiné, e, *adj.* obstinate; stubborn, wilful, self-willed; — *s.m.f.* ditto person *or* creature *or* fellow *or* thing [wilfully

Obstinément, *adv.* obstinately; stubbornly,

Obstiner, *v.a.* to make obstinate

S'—, *v.r.* to be obstinate; to persist; to insist

Obstructi-f, ve, *adj.* obstructive, obstruent

Obstruction, *s.f.* obstruction, stoppage

Obstruer, *v.a.* to obstruct; to stop up

S'—, *v.r.* to become *or* be obstructed, &c.

Obtempération, *s.f.* obedience, compliance, submission [mit

Obtempérer, *v.n.* to obey, to comply, to sub-

Obtenir, *v.a.* to obtain, to get; to gain; to obtain leave. *Faire* —, to get, to procure

S'—, *v.r.* to be obtained *or* &c.

Obtenteur, *s.m.* obtainer

Obtention, *s.f.* obtaining, obtainment, getting

Obturant, e, *adj.* obturating, stopping, obstructing

Obturateur, *s.m.* obturator; stopper; — *m.*, **-trice,** *f.*, *adj.* obturating; obturator (*muscle*), pubic (*artery*). — *conique*, (*tech.*) mitre

Obturation, *s.f.* obturation, stopping

Obtus, e, *adj.* obtuse; blunt, dull

Obtusangle, Obtusangulaire, *adj.* (*geom.*) obtuse-angled, obtusangular

Obtusangulé, e, *adj.* (*bot.*) obtuse-angled

Obtusement, *adv.* obtusely [dulness

Obtusion, *s.f.* obtuseness, obtusion, bluntness,

Obus, *s.m.* (*artil.*) shell

Obusier, *s.m.* (*artil.*) howitzer

Obusière, *s.f.* (*nav.*) bomb-vessel

Obvenir, *v.n.* (*law*) to escheat

Obvention, *s.f.* (*can. law*) obvention [face

Obvers, Obverse, *s.m.* (*of medals*) obverse,

Obvier, *v.n.* to obviate; to prevent; to hinder

Oc. *La langue d'*—, (*old*) the Provençal dialect (the old language of Languedoc), the French language south of the Loire, the language of

Oca, *s.m.* (*bot.*) oca [the troubadours

Occase, *adj.f.* (*astr.*) occasive, western, westerly; — *s.f.* (*nav.*) western *or* westerly amplitude; (*pop.*) opportunity

Occasion, *s.f.* opportunity; occasion; cause, reason; behalf, sake; (*obsolete*) action, fight, engagement. *A* or *dans cette* —, on *or* upon this *or* that occasion. *A l'*—, occasionally; when the opportunity comes *or* occurs; in case of need, if need be, if necessary; on *or* upon the occasion (of); on account (of); in behalf (of), for the sake (of). *Dans l'*—, occasionally; occasional; as occasion offers, when occasion serves. *D'*—, second-hand; chance; occasional. *En toute* —, on all occasions, at all times. *Par* —, occasional; occasionally; accidentally; by private hand

Occasionnalisme, *s.m.* (*philos.*) occasionalism

Occasionnel, le, *adj.* occasional

Occasionnellement, *adv.* occasionally

Occasionner, *v.a.* to occasion, to cause, to produce, to bring on [the west, west, western

Occident, *s.m.* west; setting. *D'*—, of *or* from

Occidental, e, *adj.* occidental, western, westerly, west [nations, Occidentals

Occidentaux, *s.m.pl.* Western people *or*

Occipital, e, *adj.* (*anat.*) occipital; — *s.m.* occipital bone

Occipito-, (*in compounds, anat.*) occipito-...

Occiput, *s.m.* (*anat.*) occiput, poll

Occire, *v.a.* (*pop., jest.*) to kill, to settle, to do the job for, to do for [struction

Occision, *s.f.* (*obsolete*) killing, slaughter, de-

Occlure, *v.a.* to occlude, to shut up, to close

Occlusion, *s.f.* occlusion, shutting up, closing

Occultation, *s.f.* occultation

Occulte, *adj.* occult; hidden; secret

Occultement, *adv.* occultly; secretly

Occulter, *v.a.* to occult, to hide, to conceal

S'—, *v.r.* to be occulted, &c.

Occupant, e, *adj.* occupying; engrossing; troublesome; (*law*) concerned as the attorney, concerned; — *s.m.f.* occupier; occupant

Occupa-teur, trice, *s.m.f.* occupier; occupant

Occupation, *s.f.* occupation; occupancy; employment; business; work

Occupé, e, *part. adj.* occupied, &c. (*V.* **Occuper**); engaged; busy

Occuper, *v.a.* to occupy; to take up; to hold; to be in; to fill; to employ; to inhabit; to occupy the thoughts of; to trouble the mind of, to trouble; — *v.n.* (*law*) to be concerned as the attorney, to be concerned, to appear, to sue, to plead

S'—, *v.r.* (*s'— à*) to occupy *or* employ oneself (in); to be busy (with, in); to occupy *or* spend o.'s time (in); to apply oneself (to); to make it o.'s study (to); (*s'— de*) to think (of); to take notice (of); to be employed *or* engaged (on); to mind, to attend (to), to look (after); to trouble oneself (about); to apply oneself (to); to make it o.'s study (to); to try, to endeavour (to)

Occurrence, *s.f.* occurrence; emergency

Occurrent, e, *adj.* occurrent, occurring

Océan, *s.m.* ocean; sea; high seas

Océane, *adj.f.* *Mer* —, (*old*) Ocean Sea [anic

Océanien, ne, *adj. s.* Oceanian; — *adj.* oce-

Océanique, *adj.* oceanic

Ocellation, *s.f.* ocellation

Ocelle, *s.m.* ocellus

Ocellé, e, *adj.* ocellated

Ocelot, *s.m.* ocelot, tiger-cat

‡**Ochlocratie,** *s.f.* ochlocracy

‡**Ochlocrat-ique, -iquement.** *V.* page 3, § 1

‡**Ochracé, e, Ocracé, e,** *adj.* ochraceous

Ocre, *s.f.* (*min.*) ochre

Ocreu-x, se, *adj.* ochry, ochreous [tahedral

Octaèdre, *s.m.* (*geom.*) octahedron; — *adj.* oc-

Octant, *s.m.* (*astr., navig.*) octant

Octante, *adj.* (*old*) eighty

Octastyle, *s.m. adj.* (*arch.*) octastyle, octostyle

Octave, *s.f.* octave; (*mus.*) octave; octave-flute; (*liter.*) piece of poetry *or* stanza of eight lines, octave

Octavier, *v.n.* (*mus.*) to reach an octave

Octavin, *s.m.* octave-flute, piccolo

Octavo. *V.* **In-octavo**

Octavon, ne, *s.m.f.* octoroon, mustee

Octidi, *s.m.* Octidi (*eighth day of the decade in the calendar of the first French Republic*)

Octil, e, *adj.m.f.*, **Octil,** *s.m.* (*astr.*) octile

Octobre, *s.m.* October

Octogénaire, *adj. s.m.f.* octogenarian

Octogonal, e, *adj.* octagonal, octangular

Octogone, *s.m.* (*geom., fort.*) octagon; — *adj.* octagonal, octangular

Octostyle, *s.m. adj.* (*arch.*) *V.* **Octastyle**

Octroi, *s.m.* grant, concession; town-dues, town-due, city toll, toll, duty, octroi; office *or* department of ditto

Octroyer, *v.a.* to grant; to concede; to give

Octuple, *s.m. adj.* octuple, eightfold

Octupler, *v.a.n.*, **S'—,** *v.r.* to octuple, to increase eightfold

Oculaire, *adj.* ocular; eye; — *s.m.* (*opt.*) eye-piece; (*of helmets*) sight-hole. *Témoin* —, eye-witness. *Verre* —, (*opt.*) eye-glass

Oculairement, *adv.* ocularly

Oculariste, *s.m.* ocularist

Oculé, e, *adj.* oculate, oculated

Oculi, *s.m.* third Sunday in Lent

Oculiforme, *adj.* oculiform

Oculiste, *s.m.* oculist

Oculistique, *s.f.* ophthalmiatria

Odalisque, *s.f.* odalisk, odalisque

Ode, *s.f.* ode

Odelette, *s.f.* odelet [*Paris theatres*)

Odéon, *s.m.* odeon; Odeon (*name of one of the*

Odeur, *s.f.* odour; smell; scent; perfume; fragrance; (*fig.*) repute. *En* — *de sainteté*, in the odour of sanctity; in favour [vidiously

Odieusement, *adv.* odiously, hatefully; in-

Odieu-x, se, *adj.* odious, hateful; obnoxious; invidious; — *s.m.* odium; odiousness; invidiousness

Odin, *s.m* Odin
Odinique, *adj.* Odinic
Odomètre, &c. *V.* **Hodomètre,** &c.
Odontalgie, *s.f.* odontalgia, odontalgy, toothache
Odontalgique, *adj.m.f., s.m.* odontalgic
‡**Odontechnie,** *s.f.* (*bad spelling*) *V.* **Odontotechnie**
Odontine, *s.f.* odonto
Odonto-graphie, -graphique, -logie, -logique, -logiste, &c *V.* page 3, § 1
Odontolithe, *s.m.* tartar of the teeth
Odontome, *s.m.* (*surg.*) odontoma
‡**Odontotechnie,** *s f.* dentistry
Odorabilité, *s.f.* odorousness
Odorable, *adj.* odorous
Odorant, e, *adj.* odorous, fragrant, scented, sweet-scented, sweet-smelling, sweet, flavoury, savoury
Odorat, *s.m* smell, sense of smell, smelling
Odoration, *s.f.* odoration, smelling
Odorer, *v.a.n.* to smell [**Odorant**)
Odoriférant, e, *adj.* odoriferous, &c. (*V.*
Odorine, *s.f.* (*chem.*) odorine
Odyssée, *s.f* Odyssey; eventful travels
Œcuménicité, *s.f* œcumenicity
Œcumén-ique, -iquement. *V.* page 3, § 1
Œdémateu-x, se, *adj.* (*med.*) œdematose, œdematous
Œdématie, *s.f.* (*med.*) œdema
Œdématier, *v.a.* (*med.*) to œdematize
S'—, *v.r.* to become œdematized
Œdème, *s.m.* (*med.*) œdema
Œdicnème, *s.m.* (*bird*) thick-knee
†**Œil,** *s.m.* eye; look; hole; bud; lustre, gloss; bubble; (*of letters*) face; (*pop.*) credit, tick. — *-de-bœuf*, bull's eye; round *or* oval window; dial; (*bot.*) ox-eye daisy, ox-eye; (*old*) king's anteroom (at Versailles); courtiers. — *-de-chat*, (*fig.*) agate, cat's eye. — *-de-chèvre*, (*fig.*) wild parsnip. — *-de-perdrix*, (*fig.*) corn between the toes, soft corn; (*adj., of wine*) pale. — *-de-serpent*, (*fig.*) toad-stone. *Coup d'—*, *V.* **Coup.** *A l'—*, with *or* by the eye; at a glance; (*pop.*) on credit, on tick. *Entre deux yeux*, full in the face. *Entre quatre yeux*, face to face, in private. *Par-dessus les yeux*, over head and ears. *Avoir de l'—*, to look well, to be stylish, to have some style. *Avoir l'— à*, to attend to, to mind. *Avoir l'— sur*, to see to; to watch. *Avoir froid aux yeux*, (*pop.*) to funk. *S'en battre l'—*, not to care a fig for it. *Donner* (or *taper*) *dans l'— à*, to take ...'s fancy. *Donner dans les yeux à*, to dazzle; to allure. *Faire de l'—*, *Faire l'—*, to ogle, to leer. *Faire des yeux*, to wink. *Faire les yeux doux à*, to look sweet at. *Faire des yeux furieux* or *&c. à*, to cast furious *or* &c. looks (*or* a furious *or* &c. eye) upon. *Fermer les yeux sur*, to look over, to shut o.'s eyes upon, to wink *or* connive at. *Jeter les yeux sur*, to cast o.'s eyes on, to look on *or* over; to make choice of, to choose, to select; to think of. *Se mettre* (or, fam., *se fourrer* or *se ficher*) *le doigt dans l'—*, (*fig.*) to injure oneself; to play oneself a trick; to make a bad spec; to make a mistake *or* a blunder; to flatter *or* delude oneself. *Ouvrir de grands yeux*, to stand staring, to stare. *Regarder dans le blanc des yeux*, to look *or* stare right in the face of. *Regarder du coin de l'—*, to ogle, to leer, to cast side looks (upon). *Voir de bon* or *de mauvais —*, to look favourably *or* unfavourably on
†**Œillade,** *s.f.* glance, ogle, leer, sweet look, sheep's eye. *Jeter* or *lancer des —s*, to ogle, to leer, to cast glances
†**Œillader,** *v.a.* to ogle
†**Œillé, e,** *adj.* eyed, oculated. *Agate —e*, eye-agate
†**Œillère,** *adj.f.* of the eye, eye; — *s.f.* eye-tooth; blinker, winker; eye-bath, eye-cup, eye-glass; (*of helmets*) visor. *Dent —*, eye-tooth
†**Œillet,** *s.m.* eyelet, eyelet-hole; lace-hole; (*nav.*) eye, thimble; tack; (*bot.*) pink; carnation. — *giroflée*, clove-pink, carnation. — *de poète*, sweet William. — *d'Inde*, African marigold
†**Œilleterie,** *s.f.* bed of pinks, carnation-bed
†**Œilleton,** *s.m.* (*hort.*) sucker, offset; layer; (*of a telescope*) eye-cap
†**Œilletonner,** *v.a.* (*hort.*) to sucker
†**Œillette,** *s.f.* oil-poppy; poppy-oil. *Huile d'—*, poppy-oil
Œnanthal, *s.m.* (*chem.*) œnanthol
Œnanthe, *s.f.* (*bot.*) œnanthe, water-dropwort, water-hemlock
Œnanthine, *s.f.* (*chem.*) œnanthine
Œnanthique, *adj.* (*chem.*) œnanthic
Œnologie, *s.f.* œnology; wine-making
Œnolog-ique, -iste. *V.* page 3, § 1
Œnologue, *s.m.f.* œnologist
Œnomanie, *s.f.* (*med.*) œnomania, oinomania, dipsomania, drinking insanity, delirium tremens
Œnomel, *s.m.* œnomel
Œnomètre, *s.m.* œnometer
Œnométr-ie, -ique. *V.* page 3, § 1
Œnophile, *s.m.f.* œnophilist; — *adj.* œnophilic *Société —*, wine company
Œnophobe, *adj. s.m.f.* œnophobiac
Œnophobie, *s.f.* œnophobia
Œnophore, *s.m.* (*anc.*) wine-vessel; goblet cup; cup-bearer, butler
Œnothère, *s.f.* (*bot.*) œnothera, evening primrose
Œsophage, *s.m.* (*anat.*) œsophagus, gullet
Œsophagien, ne, *adj.* (*anat.*) œsophagean
Œsophagisme, *s.m.* (*med.*) œsophagismus, spasm of the œsophagus
Œsophagite, *s.f.* (*med.*) œsophagitis
Œsophagotomie, *s.f.* (*surg.*) œsophagotomy
Œstre, *s.m.* (*zool.*) œstrum, gad-fly, bot-fly, bot; (*fig.*) œstrum, impetus, impulse, excitement, frenzy
Œstrides, *s.m.pl.* (*zool.*) œstridæ
Œstromanie, *s.f.* (*med.*) œstromania
Œuf, *s.m.* egg; —**s**, *pl.* eggs; hard roe, spawn — *poché* or *en chemise*, poached egg. — *à la coque*, boiled egg (soft-boiled egg in the shell). —*s sur le plat* or —*s au miroir*, fried *or* poached eggs. —*s à la neige*, whisked eggs. —*s rouges*, —*s de Pâques*, Easter eggs, Pasch eggs, hard-boiled eggs stained red; Easter gifts. *Donner un — pour avoir un bœuf*, to give a sprat to catch a herring. *Tondre sur un —*, to skin a flint. *Qui vole un — vole un bœuf*, he that will steal an ounce will steal a pound
Œufrier, *s.m.* egg-boiler
Œuvé, e, *adj.* hard-roed
Œuvre, *s.f.* work; piece of work; production; performance; deed, act; revenue (*of a church*); churchwardens' pew; (*jewel.*) bezel; setting; — *s.m.* **See below.** —*s mortes*, (*nav.*) dead works, upper works, topsides. —*s vives*, (*nav.*) quick works, keel, bottom. *Banc de l'—*, churchwardens' pew. *Clerc de l'—*, parish clerk. *Maître* or *exécuteur des basses —s*, (*jest.*) nightman, goldfinder. *Maître* or *exécuteur des hautes —s*, (*obsolete*) Jack Ketch, the executioner, the hangman. *Mettre en —*, to set to work; to work; to work up; to make up; to employ, to use; to bring to bear; (*jewel.*) to set. *Mettre tout en —*, to use every means, to leave no stone unturned. *A l'— on connait l'ouvrier*, the workman is known by his work. *Bon jour, bonne —*, the better the day, the better the deed
Œuvre, *s.m.* (*obsolete*) work; performance; (*of an engraver or composer*) works; (*build.*) work, works; clear; (*metal.*) lead containing silver. *Gros —*, outer walls. *Le grand —*, the great work, the philosopher's stone. *A pied d'—*, (*build.*) in the neighbourhood, at hand, within range of the works. *Dans —*, (*build.*) apart, in the clear, inside. *Hors d'—*, *V.* **Hors-d'œuvre.** *Sous —*, *V.* **Sous-œuvre**
Œuvrer, *v.a.n.* to work
Offensant, e, *adj.* offensive, abusive
Offense, *s.f.* offence; affront; abuse; insult; injury, wrong; transgression, trespass; (*law*) contempt
Offensé, e, *part. adj. s.* offended; injured; angry; offended party
Offenser, *v.a.* to offend; to give offence to; to offend against; to abuse; to insult; to injure, to hurt; to shock

S'—, *v.r.* to be offended, to take offence, to be angry; to offend *or* &c. oneself *or* each other
Offenseur, *s.m.* offender
Offensi-f, ve, *adj.*, **Offensive**, *s.f.* offensive
Offensivement, *adv.* offensively
Offert, e, *part. of* **Offrir**
Offerte, *s.f.*, **Offertoire**, *s.m.* offertory
Office, *s.m.* office; post; duty; functions; turn; service; worship; church-time; church; prayers; dressing of a dinner; lower servants. *D'—*, official; officially; ex officio; by the court; appointed by the court; of o.'s own accord. *Le saint —*, the Holy Office, the Inquisition. *Livre d'—*, prayer-book
Office, *s.f.* pantry, larder; servants' hall *or* room, housekeeper's room; **—s**, *pl.* dependencies of the kitchen, offices
Official, *s.m.* official (*ecclesiastical judge*)
Officialité, *s.f.* officialty; ecclesiastical court
Officiant, e, *adj.* officiating; — *s.m.f.* officiant
Officiat, *s.m.* surgeoncy
Officiel, le, *adj.* official
Officiellement, *adv.* officially
Officier, *v.n.* to officiate; to play o.'s part
Officier, *s.m.* officer; butler, steward. — *général*, (*mil.*) general officer; (*nav.*) flag-officer. — *supérieur*, (*mil.*) field-officer; (*nav.*) captain. — *de compagnie* or *de corps*, regimental officer. — *de bouche*, cook. — *civil*, — *de justice*, law-officer. —*s ministériels*, public officers (*attorneys, notaries*, &c.). — *de port*, harbour-master. — *de marine*, naval officer. — *marinier*, (*nav.*) petty officer. — *de santé*, medical officer; surgeon [semi-officially
Officieusement, *adv.* officiously; obligingly;
Officieuseté, *s.f.* officiousness
Officieu-x, se, *adj.* officious; obliging; semi-official; — *s.m.f.* busybody
Officinal, e, *adj.* officinal [pensary
Officine, *s.f.* laboratory; chemist's shop, dis-
Officiosité, *s.f.* officiousness
Offrande, *s.f.* offering; present, offer [bidder
Offrant, *s.m.* bidder. *Au plus —*, to the highest
Offre, *s.f.* offer; tender; proposal; bidding; (*in political economy*) supply. *L'— et la demande*,
Offreur, *s.m.* offerer [the demand and supply
Offrir, *v.a.* to offer; to present; to afford; to give; to tender; to propose; to bid
S'—, *v.r.* to offer *or* &c. oneself *or* itself; to offer; to offer *or* &c. to each other; to be
Offuscation, *s.f.* obfuscation [offered *or* &c.
Offusquer, *v.a.* to obfuscate; to obscure; to darken; to cloud; to eclipse; to hide; to prevent seeing; to dazzle; to blind; to offend
S'—, *v.r.* to become *or* be obfuscated *or* &c.; to take offence [lancet, pointed
Ogival, e, Ogive, *adj.* (*arch.*) ogival, ogive,
Ogive, *s.f.* (*arch.*) ogee, ogive, pointed arch. *En —*, ogive, lancet, pointed
Ogivette, *s.f.* (*arch.*) small ogive
†**Ognon**, *s.m.* onion; bulb, bulbous root, root; bunion; (*pop.*) turnip (*old-fashioned watch*); foul play; bother; row, squabble; rhino, mopus. *En rang d'—s*, in a file *or* row, in file
†**Ognonade, Ognonnade**, *s.f.* onion-stew
†**Ognonet, Ognonnet**, *s.m.* (kind of pear)
†**Ognonette, Ognonnette**, *s.f.* onion-seed
†**Ognonière, Ognonnière**, *s.f.* onion-bed
Ogre, *s.m.* ogre; (*pop.*) shark
Ogresse, *s.f.* ogress; (*pop.*) wardrobe-dealer
Oh, *int.* oh! O!
Ohé, *int.* halloo! ho there! hi!
Oïdium, *s.m.* oidium
Oie, *s.f.* goose. *Patte d'—*, goose-foot; (*fig.*) crow's foot; point of junction of several roads, cross. *Petite —*, small *or* little goose; (*obsolete*) giblets of a goose; (*obsolete*) trimmings
†**Oignon**, &c., (*old spelling*) *V.* **Ognon**, &c.
Oïl. *La langue d'—*, (*old*) the French language before the fifteenth century, the French language north of the Loire, the language of the
†**Oille**, *s.f.* (*cook.*) olio [trouveres
Oindre, *v.a.* to anoint
Oing, *s.m.* cart-grease, hog's grease
Oint, *s.m.* anointed
Oiseau, *s.m.* bird; fowl; (*falc.*) hawk; (*pers.*) fellow, chap, bird, fish; (*mas.*) hod — *x de basse-cour*, barn-door fowls, fowls, poultry. — **-mouche**, *s.m.* humming-bird [train (*birds*)
Oiseler, *v.n.* to catch birds, to fowl; — *v.a.* to
Oiselet, *s.m.* little bird
Oiseleur, *s.m.* fowler, bird-catcher; (*abusively for* "oiselier") bird-dealer, bird-seller; — *adj.m.* bird-catching; (*of winds*) Etesian
Oiselier, *s.m.* bird-dealer, bird-seller
Oisellerie, *s.f.* bird-catching; bird-selling, bird-trade; aviary
Oiseusement, *adv.* idly; triflingly
Oiseu-x, se, *adj.* idle; useless; trifling
Oisi-f, ve, *adj. s.* idle; unoccupied; unemployed; useless; lying dead; idler
†**Oisillon**, *s.m.* little bird, fledgling
Oisivement, *adv.* idly
Oisiveté, *s.f.* idleness; ease
Oison, *s.m.* gosling; green goose; ninny
Okra, *s.m.* (*bot.*) okra
Oldenlandie, *s.f.* (*bot.*) chay-root, choya, sayan
Oléagineu-x, se, *adj.* oleaginous, oily, oil; — *s.m.* oily substance
Oléandre, *s.m.* (*bot.*) oleander, rose-bay
Oléate, *s.m.* (*chem.*) oleate
Olécrane, Olécrâne, *s.m.* (*anat.*) olecranon
Olécranien, ne, *adj.* (*anat.*) olecranal
Oléfiant, e, *adj.* (*chem.*) olefiant
Oléifère, *adj.* oleiferous
Oléine, *s.f.* (*chem.*) oleine
Oléique, *adj.* (*chem.*) oleic
Oléograph-ie, -ique, &c. *V.* page 3, § 1
Oléomètre, *s.m.* oleometer
Oléracé, e, *adj.* oleraceous
Olfacti-f, ve, *adj.* olfactory
Olfaction, *s.f.* olfaction
Oliban, *s.m.* olibanum
Olibrius, *s.m.* conceited *or* meddling *or* obtrusive fellow, humbug, quidnunc [*V.* page 3, § 1
Oligarch-ie, -ique, -iquement, -iste.
Oligarchiser, *v.a.n.* to oligarchize
Oligarque, *s.m.* oligarch
Oligiste, *adj. s.m.* (*min.*) oligist
Olim, *s.m.* (*old*) statute-book
Olinde, *s.f.* thin sword-blade
Olinder, *v.n.* (*old*) to draw the sword [*or* yard
Olivaie, *s.f.* olive-plantation *or* grove *or* garden
Olivaire, *adj.* olive-shaped, olivary
Olivaison, *s.f.* olive-season; crop of olives
Olivâtre, *adj.* olive-coloured, olivaster
Olive, *s.f.* olive; olive-button; (*arch.*) olive-moulding, olive-bead; — *s.m.* olive-colour, olive; — *adj.* olive-coloured, olive
Oliverie, *s.f.* olive-oil works *or* mill
Olivète, *s.f.* *V.* **Œillette**
Olivette, *s.f.* olive-plantation *or* grove *or* garden *or* yard; glass bead; **—s**, *pl.* olivettes (*dance after the olive-gathering*)
Olivier, *s.m.* olive-tree, olive; olive-wood
Oliviforme, *adj.* oliviform, olive-shaped
Olivine, *s.f.* (*min., chem.*) olivine [stone
Ollaire, *adj.f.* (*min.*) soft. *Pierre —*, ollite, pot-
Olla-podrida, *s.f.* olla-podrida, hotch-potch
Ollure, *s.f.* leather apron
Oloffe, Oloffée, (*nav.*) *V.* **Auloffe**, &c.
Olographe, &c. *V.* **Holographe**, &c.
Olonier, *s.m.* *V.* **Arbousier**
Olympiade, *s.f.* Olympiad
Olympien, ne, *adj.* Olympian
Olympique, *adj.m.f.*, *s.f.* Olympic
Olynthien, ne, *adj.* Olynthian; — *s.f.* Olynthiac (*of Demosthenes*)
Ombelle, *s.f.* (*bot.*) umbel [umbellar
Ombellé, e, *adj.* (*bot.*) umbellate, umbellated,
Ombellifère, *adj.* (*bot.*) umbelliferous; — *s.f.* umbellifer
Ombelliforme, *adj.* (*bot.*) umbelliform
Ombellule, *s.f.* (*bot.*) umbellule, umbellet

Ombilic, *s.m.* (*anat.*, *bot.*, &c.) umbilicus
Ombilical, e, *adj.* umbilical
Ombiliqué, e, *adj.* umbilicate, umbilicated
Ombon, *s.m.* boss (*of a shield*)
Ombrage, *s.m.* shade; umbrage, suspicion, distrust. *Donner de l'—, faire —, porter —,* to give umbrage
Ombrager, *v.a.* to shade; to cover; to be on; to adorn; to shelter; to hide, to conceal
S'—, *v.r.* to be shaded *or* &c. [suspiciously
Ombrageusement, *adv.* shyly, skittishly;
Ombrageu-x, se, *adj.* shy, skittish; suspicious, distrustful
Ombre, *s.f.* shade; shadow; spirit, ghost; darkness, dark; night; gloom; pretence; protection; (*min.*) umber; — *s.m.* (*fish*) umber, grayling, char *or* charr; (*fish*) umbra, chromis; (*game at cards*) ombre. — *-chevalier,* (*fish*) char *or* charr. *—s chinoises,* dissolving views; fantastic shadows. *A l'—,* in the shade; shady; under the protection; (*pop.*) in prison, in quod; out of the way, under ground, dead. *Terre d'—,* umber. *Faire — à,* to throw into the shade, to eclipse; to give umbrage to. *Mettre à l'—,* to put in the shade; to shade; to shadow; (*pop.*) to put in quod, to quod; to kill, to do for, to settle, to give a quietus
Ombrelle, *s.f.* parasol
Ombrer, *v.a.* to shade
Ombrette, *s.f.* (*bird*) umber
Ombreu-x, se, *adj.* shady, umbrageous
Ombrine, *s.f.* (*fish*) umbrina
Ombromètre, *s.m.* ombrometer, rain-gauge
Ombrométr-ie, -ique. *V.* page 3, § 1
Oméga, *s.m.* omega
Omelette, *s.f.* omelet
Omentite, *s.f.* (*med.*) omentitis
Omettre, *v.a.* to omit; to leave out; to pass over; to forget; to leave undone
S'—, *v.r.* to be omitted, &c.
Omission, *s.f.* omission
Ommastrèphe, *s.m.* (*mollusc*) flying squid
Omnibus, *s.m. adj.* omnibus. *V.* **Train**
Omnicolore, *adj.* omnicoloured
Omnipotence, *s.f.* omnipotence
Omnipotent, e, *adj.* omnipotent
Omniprésence, *s.f.* omnipresence; ubiquity
Omniprésent, e, *adj.* omnipresent; ubiqui- [tous
Omniscience, *s.f.* omniscience
Omniscient, e, *adj.* omniscient
Omnium, *s.m.* (*fin.*) omnium [animal
Omnivore, *adj.* omnivorous; — *s.m.* ditto
Omophage, *adj.* eating raw meat
Omoplate, *s.f.* (*anat.*) scapula, omoplate, shoulder-blade, blade-bone
Omphalocèle, *s.f.* (*med.*) omphalocele
Omphalotomie, *s.f.* (*surg.*) omphalotomy
On, *pron.sing.m.f.* one, a man, a woman, a person, a boy, a girl, a child, some one, somebody, people, persons, they, men, the world, the party, the company, we, you, he, she, I; any one, anybody; (*often construed with a passive verb in English*) it is, &c. — *dit,* one says; people *or* they say; it is said. — **-dit,** *s.m.* report, tattling, mere rumour, idle report. — *m'a dit,* I have been told, I was told. *Que-dira-t-on?* what will people say? *Qu'en-dira-t-on,* (*s.m.*) *V. Letter* **Q**
Onagre, *s.m.* wild ass, onager; (*anc. mil. engine*) onager; — *s.f.* (*bot.*) evening primrose
Onanisme, *s.m.* onanism [**Jamais**
Onc, Oncques, Onques, *adv.* (*old*) *V.*
Once, *s.f.* ounce; (*fig.*) grain; (*zool.*) ounce
Onceau, *s.m.* young *or* little ounce, ounce's cub
Onchet, *s.m.* spellican
Oncial, e, *adj. s.* uncial
Oncle, *s.m.* uncle; (*pop.*) money-lender, usurer. — *à la mode de Bretagne,* father's *or* mother's cousin german
Onction, *s.f.* unction; anointing; grace; impressiveness, impressive eloquence. *L'extrême-—,* (*Cath. rel.*) extreme unction
Onctueusement, *adv.* unctuously; impressively [impressive, moving
Onctueu-x, se, *adj.* unctuous; oily; fat;
Onctuosité, *s.f.* unctuosity, unctuousness;
Ondatra, *s.m.* musquash, musk-rat [oiliness
Onde, *s.f.* wave, billow, surge; water; stream; sea, main. — *noire,* (*poet.*) Stygian pool *or* lake
Ondé, e, *adj.* undulated; watered; waved; curled; grained; (*her.*) undy, wavy
Ondée, *s.f.* shower; fall
Ondin, e, *s.m.f.* water-sprite, undine
Ondoiement, *s.m.* undulation, waving motion; half-baptism [to flow; — *v.a.* to half-baptize
Ondoyer, *v.n.* to undulate; to wave; to surge;
Ondulation, *s.f.* undulation; waving; flowing; (*of the pulse*) flutter
Ondulatoire, *adj.* undulatory
Onduler, *v.n.a.* to undulate; to wave; to curl; to corrugate; to flow; (*of the pulse*) to flutter
Onduleu-x, se, *adj.* undulating; waving, wavy; curly; flowing [critics
Onéirocritie, Onéirocritique, *s.f.* oneiro-
Onéiroman-cie, -tique. *V.* page 3, § 1
Onéiromancien, ne, *s.m.f.* oneiromancer
Onéraire, *adj.* (*old law*) acting
Onéreusement, *adv.* onerously
Onéreu-x, se, *adj.* onerous, burdensome, heavy; expensive. *A titre —,* (*law*) burdened with certain conditions
Onglade, *s.f.* ingrowing nail
Ongle, *s.m.* nail (*of the fingers or toes*); hoof; claw; (*med.*) unguis, pterygium. *Jusqu'aux —s, jusqu'au bout des —s,* to o.'s finger-ends; every inch. *Sur l'—,* perfectly, all right. *Rogner les —s à,* (*fig.*) to clip ...'s wings
Onglé, e, *adj.* clawed; (*her.*) armed
Onglée, *s.f.* hot-ache, numbness in the finger-ends, o.'s finger-ends benumbed with cold; (*vet.*) unguis
Onglet, *s.m.* finger-case; (*bot.*) unguis, ungula; (*engr.*) flat graver; (*book-bind.*) guard; (*print.*) one-leaf cancel; (*build.*) mitre; (*tech.*) thumb-groove, thumb-mark, notch; (*med.*) pterygium; (*geom.*) ungula
Ongleté, e, *adj.* (*bot.*) *V.* **Onguiculé**
Onglette, *s.f.* flat graver [*tortoises*)
Onglon, *s.m.* hoof (*of ruminants*); nail (*of*
Onguent, *s.m.* ointment, salve
Onguicule, *s.m.* unguicule
Onguiculé, e, *adj.* unguiculate, unguiculated
Onguiforme, *adj.* unguiform
Ongulé, e, *adj.* ungulate, hoofed; (*her.*) unguled
Onirocritie, &c. *V.* **Onéirocritie,** &c.
Onocrotale, *s.m.* (*bird*) pelican
Onomatologie, &c. *V.* page 3, § 1
Onomatopée, *s.f.* (*gram.*) onomatopœia, onomatopy; onomatopœian word, onomatope
Onomatopéique, *adj.* onomatopœian, onomatopoetic [*acanthe*) Scotch thistle
Onoporde, *s. m.* (*bot.*) cotton-thistle; (—
Ontolog-ie, -ique, -iquement, -iste. *V.* page 3, § 1
Onyx, *s.m.* (*min.*) onyx; (*med.*) onyx, pterygium
Onyxis, *s.f.* onyxis, ingrowing nail
'Onzaine, *s.f.* eleven or so, about eleven, eleven
'Onze, *adj.m.f.*, *s.m.* eleven; eleventh
'Onzième, *adj.m.f.*, *s.m.* eleventh; eleventh part; — *s.f.* (*mus.*), *s.m.f.* (*pers.*) eleventh
'Onzièmement, *adv.* eleventhly
Oolithe, *s.m.* (*geol.*) oolite, roestone
Oolithique, *adj.* oolitic
Oolog-ie, -ique, -iste. *V.* page 3, § 1
Opacité, *s.f.* opacity; darkness
Opale, *s.f.* (*min.*) opal
Opalescence, *s.f.* opalescence
Opalescent, e, *adj.* opalescent
Opalin, e, *adj.* opaline
Opaliser, *v.a.*, **S'—,** *v.r.* to opalize
Opaque, *adj.* opaque; dark
Ope, *s.f.* putlog-hole
Opéra, *s.m.* opera; opera-house; (*obsolete*) difficult business *or* matter; wonder, masterpiece

Opérable, *adj.* operable
Opéra-teur, trice, *s.m.f.* operator
Opérati-f, ve, *adj.* operative, operating
Opération, *s.f.* operation; performance; effect; working; transaction
Opératoire, *adj.* operative, operating
Operculaire, *adj.* opercular
Opercule, *s.m.* (*nat. hist.*) operculum
Operculé, e, *adj.* operculate, operculated
Opérer, *v.a.n.* to operate; to perform; to do; to effect; to work; to act; to manage. *Se faire* —, to undergo an operation
S'—, *v.r.* to be operated, &c.
Opérette, *s.f.* operetta
Ophicléide, *s.m.* ophicleid, ophicleide
Ophidien, ne, *adj.*, **Ophidien,** *s.m.* ophidian
Ophidium, *s.m.* (*fish*) ophidion
Ophioglosse, *s.f.* (*bot.*) ophioglossum, adder's-tongue, moonwort
Ophio-graphie, -logie, &c. *V.* page 3, § 1
Ophiolithe, *s.m.* (*min.*) ophiolite
Ophisaure, *s.m.* (*zool*) ophisaurus, glass snake
Ophite, *s.m.* (*min.*) ophite
Ophrys, *s.f.* (*bot.*) ophrys, orchis. — *mouche*, fly-orchis, bee-orchis, bee-flower
Ophthalmalgie, *s.f* (*med.*) ophthalmalgia
Ophthalmie, *s.f.* (*med.*) ophthalmia, ophthalmy
Ophthalm-ique, -ographie, -ologie, &c. *V.* page 3, § 1
Ophthalmoscope, *s.m.* (*surg.*) ophthalmoscope
Ophthalmo-scopie, -scopique, -tomie, &c. *V.* page 3, § 1
Opiacé, e, *adj.* (*pharm., med.*) containing opium
Opiacé, *s.m.* (*pharm.*) opiate
Opiacer, *v.a.* (*pharm.*) to prepare with opium
Opianine, *s.f.* (*chem*) opianine
Opianique, *adj.* (*chem.*) opianic
Opiat, *s.m.* (*pharm*) confection, electuary; tooth-paste; (*obsolete*) opiate
Opilati-f, ve, *adj.* (*med.*) obstruent, obstructive
Opilation, *s.f.* (*med.*) obstruction
Opiler, *v.a.* (*med.*) to obstruct. *S'*—, to become *or* be obstructed
Opimes, *adj.f.pl.* *Dépouilles* —, spolia opima
Opinant, e, *adj.* speaking, advising, voting; — *s.m.f.* speaker, adviser, voter
Opiner, *v.n.a.* to opine; to be of opinion; to give o 's opinion; to speak; to say; to advise; to conclude; to vote. — *du bonnet*, to nod assent, to concur entirely
Opineur, *s.m.* opiner
Opiniâtre, *adj. s.* opinionated, obstinate, stubborn
Opiniâtrément, *adv.* obstinately
Opiniâtrer, *v.a.*, **S'**—, *v.r.* *V.* **Obstiner**
Opiniâtreté, *s.f.* obstinacy, stubbornness, self-will, wilfulness
Opinion, *s.f.* opinion; vote; public opinion. *ller aux* —*s*, to put it to the vote
Opiophage, *s.m.f.* opium-eater
Opium, *s.m.* opium
Opobalsamum, *s.m.* (*old*) opobalsam, balm of Mecca
‡**Opodeldoch, Opodeltoch,** *s.m.* (*pharm.*) opodeldoc, soap liniment
Opopanax, Opoponax, *s.m.* opopanax, opoponax
Oporto, *s.m.* port (wine)
Opossum, *s.m.* (*zool*) opossum
Oppienne, *adj.f.* *Loi* —, (*Rom. hist.*) Oppian law
Opportun, e, *adj.* opportune, well-timed, timely, seasonable; expedient; convenient; favourable. *En temps* —, opportunely, timely, seasonably, due *or* proper time
Opportunément, *adv.* opportunely, timely, seasonably
Opportunité, *s.f.* opportuneness, timeliness, seasonableness; expediency; opportunity
Opposable, *adj* opposable
Opposant, e, *adj. s.* opposing, opposite, adverse; opponent, opposer, adversary; dissentient
Opposé, e, *adj.* opposite; facing; opposed; contrary; contradictory
Opposé, *s.m.* opposite, reverse
Opposer, *v.a.* to oppose; to object; to place opposite; to compare; (*law*) to plead
S'—, *v.r.* to oppose; to be opposed; to stand in the way; to object; to check; to oppose each other
Opposite, *s.m.* opposite, reverse. *A l'*—, opposite, facing, over against
Opposition, *s.f.* opposition; contrast; contradistinction; stop, stoppage; attachment, (*in Scotland*) arrestment
Oppresser, *v.a.* to oppress; to depress
S'—, *v.r.* to become *or* be oppressed, &c.
Oppresseur, *s.m.* oppressor; — *adj m.* oppressive
Oppressi-f, ve, *adj.* oppressive
Oppression, *s.f.* oppression
Oppressivement, *adv.* oppressively
Opprimer, *v.a.* to oppress; to overwhelm; to crush
Opprobre, *s.m.* opprobrium, disgrace, shame, reproach
Optati-f, ve, *adj.*, **Optatif,** *s.m.* optative
Optation, *s.f.* (*rhet.*) optation
Optativement, *adv.* optatively
Opter, *v.n.* to choose; to declare
Opticien, *s.m.* optician
Opticographe, *s.m.* optigraph; — *adj.* optigraphic
Optimé, *adv.* very well, bravo, capital
Optim-isme, -iste. *V.* page 3, § 1
Option, *s f.* option, choice
Optique, *s.f.* optics; sight, vision; view; perspective; illusion; show-box; peep-show; — *adj.* optical, optic
Optiquement, *adv.* optically
Optomètre, *s.m.* optometer
Opulemment, *adv.* opulently, wealthily
Opulence, *s.f.* opulence, affluence, wealth, riches
Opulent, e, *adj.* opulent, affluent, wealthy, rich
Opuntia, *s.m.* Indian fig-tree
Opuscule, *s.m.* opuscule, small work, short treatise, essay, pamphlet, tract
Or, *conj.* now; but; well; pray. — *bien*, — *çà*, (*obsolete*) now, now then, well now, come. — *donc*, now
Or, *s.m.* gold; gold colour; (*her.*) or; — *adj.* gold-coloured, gold, golden. *D'*—, of gold; gold; golden; precious, valuable; great, capital, most excellent, fine, beautiful, splendid, admirable; capitally, finely, beautifully, splendidly, admirably. — *moulu*, or-moulu, ormolu. *Dire* or *parler d'*—, to speak as well as possible *or* admirably, to say a most excellent thing, to give capital advice
Oracle, *s.m.* oracle
Orage, *s.m.* storm, tempest; thunder-storm. *A l'*—, stormy. *Faire de l'*—, to be stormy
Orageusement, *adv.* stormily, tempestuously
Orageu-x, se, *adj.* stormy; tempestuous; agitated
Oraison, *s.f.* oration; speech; orison; prayer. — *dominicale*, Lord's prayer
Oral, e, *adj.* oral, verbal, vivâ voce
Oralement, *adv.* orally, verbally, vivâ voce
Orang, *s.m.* orang. — **-outang,** *s.m.* orang-outang
Orange, *s.f.* orange; — *s.m.* orange colour, orange; — *adj.* orange-coloured, orange. — *à cochons*, (*pop.*) potato
Orangé, e, *adj.* orange-coloured, orange
Orangé, *s.m.* orange colour, orange
Orangeade, *s.f.* orangeade
Orangeat, *s.m.* candied orange-peel
Oranger, *s.m.* orange-tree; orange-man. *Fleur d'*—, orange-flower
Oranger, *v.a.* to dye orange, to tinge with orange colour
Orangère, *s.f.* orange-woman *or* girl
Orangerie, *s.f.* orangery, orange-house, orange-grove
Orangette, *s.f.* orange berry
Orangisme, *s.m.* (*polit.*) Orangism
Orangiste, *s.m.* (*polit.*) Orangist, Orangeman; (*hort.*) orange-grower
Orateur, *s.m.* orator; speaker; spokesman; pleader
Oratoire, *adj.* oratorical; of public speaking, of eloquence; — *s.m.* oratory. *Art* —, art of public speaking, oratory. *Lieux* —*s*, common-places
Oratoirement, *adv.* oratorically
Oratorien, *s.m., adj.m.* Oratorian
Oratorio, *s.m.* (*mus.*) oratorio

Orbe, *s.m.* orb; orbit; folds, coils; (*zool.*) orb-fish; — *adj.* (*surg.*) contusing, bruising; (*build.*) dead *or* blind (*wall*)
Orbiculaire, *adj.* orbicular, round, circular
Orbiculairement, *adv.* orbicularly
Orbicule, *s.f.* orbiculus
Orbiculé, e, *adj.* orbiculate, orbiculated
Orbière, *s.f.* (*of mules*) blinker, winker
Orbitaire, *adj.* orbital [socket
Orbite, *s.f.* (*astr.*) orbit; — *s.f.m.* (*anat.*) orbit,
Orcadien, ne, *adj. s.* Orcadian
Orcanète, Orcanette, *s.f.* (*bot.*) orchanet, alkanet, dyer's bugloss; (*dyeing*) alkanet, al- [kanna, henna
‡**Orchestral, e,** *adj.* orchestral
‡**Orchestration,** *s.f.* (*mus.*) scoring, orchestration [orchestra stall; orchestra stalls
‡**Orchestre,** *s.m.* orchestra; band; musicians;
‡**Orchestrer,** *v.a.* (*mus.*) to score
‡**Orchestrino,** *s.m.* (*mus. instr.*) orchestrino
‡**Orchestrion,** *s.m.* (*mus. instr.*) orchestrion
‡**Orchialgie,** *s.f.* (*med.*) orchialgia
‡**Orchide, Orchidée,** *s.f.*, **Orchis,** *s.m.* (*bot.*) orchid, orchis, orchidea, orchidacea
‡**Orchiocèle,** *s.f.* (*med.*) orchiocele
‡**Orchiotomie,** *s.f.* (*surg.*) orchiotomy
‡**Orchite,** *s.f.* (*med.*) orchitis
Orcine, *s.f.* (*chem.*) orcine
Ord, e, *adj.* (*old*) filthy, squalid, loathsome
Ordalie, *s.f.* ordeal (*trial by fire*, &c.)
Ordinaire, *adj.* ordinary, common; usual, customary; (*of public officers*) in ordinary; (*of wine*, &c.) table; — *s.m.* ordinary; custom; common run; ordinary fare; daily allowance; (*old*) post; post-day; courier; (*mil.*) mess; —**s,** *pl.* (*med.*) courses, menses. *A l'—*, as usual; usual. *D'—, pour l'—*, usually; generally; mostly; commonly [generally; commonly
Ordinairement, *adv.* ordinarily; usually;
Ordinal, e, *adj. s.m.* ordinal [nation
Ordinand, *s.m.* ordinand, candidate for ordi-
Ordinant, *s.m.* ordinant, ordainer; — *adj.m.* ordaining [ordaining
Ordina-teur, trice, *s.m.f.* ordainer; — *adj.*
Ordination, *s.f.* ordination
Ordo, *s.m.* ordo, directory, church service-book
Ordonnance, *s.f.* ordinance; ordering; order; disposition; arrangement; regulation; prescription; law, decree, statute; ordonnance; (*mil., pers., s.f.m.*) orderly. *D'—*, (*pers.*) orderly; (*of clothes*, &c.) regimental; regulation. *Habit d'—*, regimentals, uniform
Ordonnancement, *s.m.* order for payment
Ordonnancer, *v.a.* to order the payment of, to pass; to prescribe; to charter
Ordonna-teur, trice, *s.m.f.* orderer; ordainer; — *adj.* ordaining
Ordonnée, *s.f.* (*geom.*) ordinate
Ordonnément, *adv.* (*old*) ordinately
Ordonner, *v.a.n.* to order; to ordain; to dispose; to arrange; to regulate; to prescribe; to direct; to give orders; to appoint; to decree
S'—, *v.r.* to be ordered *or* prescribed *or* &c.
Ordre, *s.m.* order; word; command; mandate; warrant; management; rule; duty; class; tribe; rate; array; —**s,** *pl.* orders, &c.; service. *A l'—!* order! *A —*, (*of bills*) to order. *Dans l'—*, in the order; in order; proper, right; natural. *De premier —*, first-rate, of the highest order. *Mettre — à*, to look to; to settle; to put *or* set in order. *Mettre à l'—*, (*mil.*) to mention in the general orders. *Rappeler à l'—*, to call to order
Ordure, *s.f.* filth; dirt; excrement; sweepings, rubbish, dust; nuisance; corruption; lewdness; ribaldry; filthiness; filthy thing *or* stuff
Orduri-er, ère, *adj.* filthy; — *s.m.f.* filthy blackguard, ribald; — *s.m.* dust-pan
Oréade, *s.f.* (*myth.*) oread, mountain-nymph
Orée, *s.f.* (*obsolete*) border, skirt
Oréide, *s.m.* oreide
†**Oreillard, e,** *adj.* lop-eared, lap-eared; — *s.m.* long-eared bat; (*pop.*) donkey, moke

†**Oreille,** *s.f.* ear; hearing; (*of papers*) dog's-ear; (*of shoes*, &c.) flap; (*of caps*) ear-lap; (*of ploughs*) breast, mould-board; (*of combs*) end-tooth; (*of anchors*) fluke. — *d'ours*, (*bot.*) auricula. — *de mer*, *V.* **Haliotide.** *Mal d'—*, ear-ache. *Par-dessus les —s*, over head and ears. *Avoir de l'—*, to have a good ear. *Avoir l'— dure*, to be hard of hearing. *Avoir l'— basse*, to look downcast *or* chop-fallen. *Avoir mal à l'—*, to have the ear-ache. *Dire* (or *Parler*) *à l'—* or *dans le tuyau de l'—*, to whisper in (...'s) ear, to whisper. *Donner sur les —s à*, to box ...'s ears. *Échauffer les —s à*, to provoke. *Faire la sourde —*, to turn a deaf ear, to pretend to be deaf; to pretend not to hear. *Prêter l'—*, to lend an ear, to give ear, to listen. *Se faire tirer l'—*, to require pressing. *Il n'entend pas de cette — -là*, he won't listen to that, he won't have it, he will not consent. *Autant lui en pend à l'—*, he may expect as much *or* the like
†**Oreillé, e,** *adj.* eared
†**Oreiller,** *s.m.* pillow [oreillet, ear-piece
†**Oreillère,** *s.f.* (*insect*) earwig; (*anc. armour*)
†**Oreillette,** *s.f.* ear-lap (*of a cap*); ear-cap; (*anat., of the heart*) auricle; (*bot.*, &c.) ear; small ear; handle; (*plant*) asarabacca
†**Oreillon,** *s.m.* (*bot.*, &c.) ear; small ear; handle; (*of a plough*) breast, mould-board; (*anc. armour*) oreillet, ear-piece; (*of leather*) paring; (*med.*) mumps; (*fort.*) orillon
Orémus, *int.* let us pray; — *s.m.* oremus, orison, prayer
Oréognos-ie, -tique, &c. *V.* page 3, § 1
Oréographe, *s.m.* oreographer [3, § 1
Oréograph-ie, -ique, -iquement. *V.* page
Oréolog-ie, -ique, -iquement. *V.* p. 3, § 1
Orfèvre, *s.m.* goldsmith; silversmith; (*obsolete*) jeweller. *Vous êtes —, monsieur Josse*, you are a jeweller, Mr. Josse; you are in the trade, my dear Sir; I see, there is nothing like leather!
Orfèvrerie, *s.f.* goldsmith's art *or* trade *or* work, gold working *or* work; silversmith's art *or* trade *or* work, silver working *or* work; gold and silver plate *or* wares; jewellery
Orfévri, e, *adj.* wrought, worked up
Orfraie, *s.f.* (*bird*) osprey, ospray, sea-eagle
Orfroi, *s.m.* orfrey, facing; (*old*) orfrays [muslin
Organdi, *s.m.* organdi, organdi muslin, book-
Organe, *s.m.* organ; voice; means, medium, agency; agent; spokesman, mouthpiece
Organeau, *s.m.* (*nav.*) ring
Organic-isme, -iste. *V.* page 3, § 1
Organier, *s.m.* organ-builder
Organino, *s.m.* barrel-organ
Organ-ique, -iquement. *V.* page 3, § 1
Organisable, *adj.* organizable [*adj.* organizing
Organisa-teur, trice, *s.m.f.* organizer; —
Organisation, *s.f.* organization; formation; arrangement; constitution; nature; being; individual; mind
Organiser, *v.a.* to organize; to form; to arrange, to draw up, to get up; to settle [to settle
S'—, *v.r.* to become organized, to get settled,
Organisme, *s.m.* organism; system; constitution; arrangement
Organiste, *s.m.f.* organist
Organo-génique, -graphie, -graphique, -leptique, -logie, -logique, &c. *V.* p. 3, § 1
Organsin, *s.m.* organzine (*silk*) [ing
Organsinage, *s.m.* organzining, (silk-)throw-
Organsiner, *v.a.* to organzine, to throw (*silk*)
Organsineur, *s.m.* millman, (silk-)throwster
Orgasme, *s.m.* (*med.*) orgasm
Orge, *s.f.* barley. — *mondée*, husked *or* hulled barley, pot barley, Scotch barley. — *perlée*, pearl-barley. *Faire les —s*, to cut down barley. *Faire ses —s*, (*fig., pop.*) to feather o.'s nest. *Grossier comme du* (or *comme un*) *pain d'—*, as coarse as a hop-sack, very rough *or* uncivil
Orgé, e, *adj.* mixed with barley-water
Orgeat, *s.m.* orgeat [sty (*on the eye*), stye
Orgelet, Orgeolet, *s.m.* (*med.*) hordeolum,

Orgie, *s.f.* orgy, orgie, carousal, potations, debauch, drunken revelry, revelry, revel; drinking-bout, drinking; excess
†Orgne, *s.f.* (*agr.*) row of sheaves
Orgue, *s.m.* organ; (*nav.*) scupper-hole; (*mil., obsolete*) orgues. — *à clavier*, finger-organ. — *de Barbarie*, street *or* barrel organ. — *de*
†Orgueil, *s.m.* pride; boast [*mer, V.* **Tubipore**
†Orgueilleusement, *adv.* proudly [son
†Orgueilleu-x, se, *adj. s.* proud; proud per-
‡Orichalque, *s.m.* orichalcum, orichalch
Orient, *s.m.* east; orient; rising; rise; beginning; (*of pearls*) water, orient. *D'*—, of *or* from the east, east, eastern. *Grand* —, Grand Lodge (*of freemasons*)
Oriental, e, *adj. s.m.f.* oriental, eastern, easterly, east; — *s.f.* oriental fashion
Orientaliser, *v.a.* to orientalize
S'—, *v.r.* to become orientalized
Oriental-isme, -iste. *V.* page 3, § 1
Orientation, *s.f.* orientation; position
Orientaux, *s.m.pl.* Eastern people *or* nations, Orientals
Orientement, *s.m.* orientation; (*nav.*) trim
Orienter, *v.a.* to orientate; to orient; to set towards the east; to give the right aspect to; to set; (*nav.*) to trim (*sails*). *Maison bien* or *mal orientée*, house well *or* badly situated, house in a good *or* bad aspect
S'—, *v.r.* to know in what direction the East is; to find out o.'s situation, to see where one is; to see o.'s way; to see what one is about
Orière, *s.f.* border, skirt, fence
Orifice, *s.m.* orifice; aperture, opening, hole; mouth; port; nose-pipe (*of a hose-branch*)
Orifier, Orifiage. *V.* **Aurifier,** &c.
Oriflamme, *s.f.* oriflamme
Oriforme, *adj.* oriform
Origan, *s.m.* (*bot.*) origanum, marjoram
Originaire, *adj.* native (of), originating (in), originally come (from); originary, original; first; primitive
Originairement, *adv.* originally, primitively
Original, e, *adj.* original; first; primitive; eccentric, odd, queer, strange, singular, peculiar; quaint; — *s.m.f.* ditto man *or* fellow *or* person *or* character, character, humourist, oddity; — *s.m.* (*thing*) original; (*animal*) *V.* **Orignal** [oddly
Originalement, *adv.* originally; singularly,
Originalité, *s.f.* originality; eccentricity, oddness, singularity; oddity; quaintness
Origine, *s.f.* origin, beginning, source, spring, derivation, extraction. *Dans l'*—, originally. *Avoir* or *tirer son* —, to originate, to have o.'s
Originel, le, *adj.* original, primitive [origin
Originellement, *adv.* originally, primitively
†Orignal, *s.m.* (*zool.*) Canada elk
†Orillard, Orillon. *V.* **Oreillard, Oreillon**
Orin, *s.m.* (*nav.*) buoy-rope
Orion, *s.m.* (*myth., astr.*) Orion
Oripeau, *s.m.* tinsel; orsidue; tinselled toggery, faded finery
Orle, *s.m.* (*her., arch.*) orle; (*of a crater*) side
Orléanais, e, *adj. s.m.f.* of Orleans; native of ditto; — *s.m.* Orleans district
Orléan-isme, -iste, (*Fr. polit.*) *V.* page 3, § 1
Orléans, *s.m.* Orleans cloth
Orlet, *s.m.* (*arch.*) orlet
Ormaie, *s.f.* elm-grove, elm-plantation
Orme, *s.m.* elm. *Attendre sous l'*—, to wait till doomsday [**Haliotide**
Ormeau, *s.m.* young elm, elm; (*zool.*) *V.*
Ormet, Ormier, *s.m.* *V.* **Haliotide**
Ormière, *s.f.* (*bot.*) meadow-sweet
†Ormille, *s.f.* elm-sapling; young elms; plantation *or* hedgerow of young elms
Ormin, *s.m.* (*bot.*) annual clary
Orne, *s.m.* (*bot.*) manna-ash, flowering ash
Ornemaniste, *s.m.f.* (*bad spelling*) *V.* **Ornementiste**
Ornement, *s.m.* ornament; (*mus.*) grace, grace-note, embellishment. *D'*—, of *or* as *or* &c. ornament; ornamental
Ornemental, e, *adj.* ornamental [tion
Ornementation, *s.f.* ornamentation, decora-
Ornementer, *v.a.* to ornament, to decorate
Ornementiste, *s. m. f.* ornamentist, ornamenter, ornament-worker *or* maker; — *adj.* ornament-working; ornamental, ornament
Orner, *v.a.* to adorn; to ornament; to decorate; to deck; to grace; to trim up
Ornier, *s.m.* *V.* **Orne** [*Chemin à —s*, tram-road
Ornière, *s.f.* rut; (*fig.*) beaten path, track.
Ornithies, *s.m.pl.* Etesian winds
Ornithogale, *s.m.* (*bot.*) star of Bethlehem
Ornitholog-ie, -ique, -iste, &c. *V.* page 3,
Ornithologue, *s.m.f.* ornithologist [§ 1
Ornithope, *s.m.* (*bot.*) bird's-foot
Ornithorhynque, *s.m.* (*zool.*) duck-bill, duck-mole, water-mole
Orobanche, *s.f.* (*bot*) broom-rape
Orobe, *s.f.* (*bot.*) orobus, bitter vetch
Oro-gnosie, -gnostique, -graphie, -graphique, -logie, -logique, -logiste, &c. *V.* page 3, § 1 [—, fly-mushroom
Oronge, *s.f.* (*bot.*) orange-milked agaric. *Fausse*
†Orpailleur, *s.m.* gold-seeker, gold-finder
Orphelin, e, *adj. s.* orphaned; orphan; orphan child, orphan boy *or* girl
Orphelinage, *s.m.* orphanage
Orphelinat, *s.m.* orphan asylum, orphanage
Orphéon, *s.m.* orpheon; choral singing; choral music; singing-school; choral society *or* union
Orphéonique, *adj.* orpheonic, of choral singing *or* music *or* singers
Orphéoniste, *s.m.f.* orpheonist, choral singer
Orphie, *s.f.* garfish, sea-pike
Orphique, *adj. s.* Orphic
Orpiment, *s.m.* (*min.*) orpiment [orpiment
Orpin, *s.m.* (*bot.*) orpine, stone-crop; (*min.*)
Orque, *s.f.* (*zool.*) orc, ork, grampus
Orrery, *s.m.* orrery [(*dyeing*) orchil, archil
†Orseille, *s.f.* (*bot.*) orchella-weed, dyer's moss;
Ort, *adj.* (*com.*) gross weight
†Orteil, *s.m.* toe; great toe. *Gros* —, great toe
Orthodoxe, *adj. s.* orthodox; catholic
Orthodoxement, *adv.* orthodoxly
Ortho-doxie, -dromie, -dromique, -épie, -épique, -épiste, &c. *V.* page 3, § 1
Orthogonal, e, Orthogone, *adj.* orthogonal
Orthogonalement, *adv.* orthogonally
Orthographe, *s.f.* orthography; spelling; dictation. *Faute d'*—, mistake in spelling, misspelling, bad *or* wrong spelling, misspelt word [page 3, § 1
Orthograph-ie, -ique, -iquement. *V.*
Orthographier, *v.a.n.* to spell. *S'*—, to be spelt
Orthographiste, *s.m.f.* orthographer, speller
Ortholog-ie, -ique, &c. *V.* page 3, § 1
Orthopéd-ie, -ique, -iste, &c. *V.* page 3, § 1
Orthopnée, *s.f.* (*med.*) orthopnœa, orthopny
Orthopnoïque, *adj. s.* (*med.*) orthopnoic
Orthopraxie, *s.f.* orthopraxy
Orthoptère, *adj.* (*zool.*) orthopterous; — *s.m.*
Orthotome, *s.m.* (*zool.*) tailor-bird [orthopteran
Ortie, *s.f.* (*bot.*) nettle; (*vet.*) rowel. *Jeter aux —s*, to throw to the dogs, to throw off *or* away, to cast off, to give up, to quit
Ortié, e, *adj.* nettled. *Fièvre —e*, (*med.*) nettle-
Ortier, *v.a.* to nettle [rash
Ortive, *adj.f.* (*astr.*) ortive, eastern, easterly
Ortolan, *s.m.* (*bird*) ortolan
Orvale, *s.f.* (*bot.*) clary, orval
Orvet, *s.m.* slow-worm, blind-worm
Orviétan, *s.m.* (*obsolete*) orvietan; (*fig.*) quack medicine, nostrum. *Marchand* or *vendeur d'*—, quack doctor, Doctor Dulcamara, quack, mountebank, humbug [wolf
Oryctérope, *s.m.* (*zool.*) orycteropus, earth-
Oryctographe, *s.m.* oryctographer
Orycto-graphie, -graphique, -logie, &c.
Oryx, *s.m.* (*zool.*) oryx; gems-boc [*V.* page 3, § 1
Os, *s.m.* bone: (*pop.*) rhino, blunt, dust, mopus.

— *à ronger*, bone to pick; nut to crack; sop. *Mouillé* or *trempé* or *percé jusqu'aux* —, wet to the skin, wet through [(artificial) teeth
Osanore, *adj. Dents —s*, hippopotamus tusk;
Osar, *s.m.* (*geol.*) osar
‡**Oschéite,** *s.f.* (*med.*) oscheitis
‡**Oschéocèle,** *s.f.* (*med.*) oscheocele
Oscillation, *s.f.* oscillation; oscillancy; sweep; swing; vibration; fluctuation; waver-
Oscillatoire, *adj.* oscillatory [ing
Osciller, *v.n.* to oscillate; to sweep; to swing to and fro; to vibrate; to fluctuate; to waver
Oscitant, e, *adj.* (*med.*) oscitant, yawning, gaping [gaping
Oscitation, *s.f.* (*med.*) oscitation, yawning,
Oscula-teur, trice, *adj.* (*geom.*) osculating
Osculation, *s.f.* (*geom.*) osculation
Oscule, *s.m.* (*nat. hist.*) oscule [daring
Osé, e, *part. adj.* ventured, attempted; bold,
†**Oseille,** *s.f.* (*bot.*) sorrel
Oser, *v.a.n.* to dare, to venture, to be bold enough, to presume; to attempt; to take the
Oseraie, *s.f.* osier-ground [liberty; to like; may
Osier, *s.m.* osier; withe; wicker
Osmanli, *s.m.* Osmanli
Osmazôme, *s.m.* osmazome
Osmique, *adj.* (*chem.*) osmic
Osmium, *s.m.* (*chem.*) osmium
Osmonde, *s.f.* (*bot.*) osmund, flowering fern
Ossature, *s.f.* bones; framework, frame
Ossec, *s.m.* (*nav.*) well; well-room, water-way
Osselet, *s.m.* small bone, ossicle; (*for playing*) knuckle-bone; (*vet.*) osselet; —**s**, *pl.* (*game*) knuckle-bones, dibbs, (*in Scotland*) chucks
Ossements, *s.m.pl.* bones (*of dead bodies*)
Osseret, *s.m.* (butcher's) cleaver *or* chopper
Osserie, *s.f.* bone-working; bone-work *or* works
Osset, *s.m. V.* **Ossec**
Osseu-x, se, *adj.* bony
Ossian-ique, -isme. *V.* page 3, § 1
Ossicule, *s.m.* ossicle
Ossiculé, e, *adj.* ossiculated
Ossifère, *adj.* ossiferous
Ossification, *s.f.* ossification
Ossifier, *v.a.*, **S'**—, *v.r.* to ossify
Ossifique, *adj.* ossific
Ossifrage, Ossifrague, *s.m.* (*obsolete*) ossifrage, osprey, erne, sea-eagle
Ossivore, *adj.* ossivorous
Ossu, e, *adj.* bony, large-boned, big-boned
Ossuaire, *s.m.* ossuary, bone-house, charnel-
Ost, *s.m.* (*obsolete*) *V.* **Host** [house
Ostéine, *s.f.* (*chem.*) osteine, osseine
Ostéite, *s.f.* (*med.*) osteitis
Ostendois, e, *adj. s.* of Ostend; Ostender
Ostensible, *adj.* ostensible, visible
Ostensiblement, *adv.* ostensibly
Ostensi-f, ve, *adj.* ostensive
Ostensivement, *adv.* ostensively
Ostensoir, Ostensoire, *s. m.* (*Cath. rel.*) monstrance, remonstrance, ostensory
Ostenta-teur, trice, *s.m.f.* (*old*) ostentator; — *adj.* ostentatious
Ostentation, *s.f.* ostentation, show; boast
Ostéocolle, *s.f.* osteocolla, bone-glue
Ostéocope, *adj.* (*med.*) osteocopous
Ostéo-génie, -graphie, -graphique, &c.
Ostéolithe, *s.m.* osteolite [*V.* page 3, § 1
Ostéolog-ie, -ique, &c. *V.* page 3, § 1
Ostéomalacie, *s.f.* (*med.*) osteomalacia
Ostéosarcome, *s.m.* (*med.*) osteosarcoma
Ostéotome, *s.m.* (*surg.*) osteotomy-knife
Ostéotom-ie, -ique. *V.* page 3, § 1
Ostracé, e, *adj.* ostraceous; — *s.m.* ostracean
Ostraciser, *v.a.* to ostracize
Ostracisme, *s.m.* ostracism
Ostracite, *s.f.* ostracite, petrified oyster-shell
Ostréicole, Ostréicultural, e, *adj.* ostreicultural
Ostréiculteur, *s.m.* oyster-grower, oyster-farmer [ture
Ostréiculture, *s.f.* ostreiculture, oyster-cul-
Ostréite, *s.f.* ostreite, fossil oyster
Ostrogoth, e, *s.m.f.* Ostrogoth, Eastern Goth; (*fig.*) Goth, Vandal, barbarian, savage; fool, muff; bore; — *adj.* outlandish
Osyris, *s.m.* (*bot.*) osyris, casia, poet's casia
Otacoustique, *adj.* otacoustic; — *s.f* ota-
Otage, *s.m.* hostage; pledge [coustics
Otalgie, *s.f.* (*med.*) otalgia, otalgy, ear-ache
Otalgique, *adj.m.f.*, *s.m.* (*med.*) otalgic
Otarie, *s.f.* (*zool.*) otary, eared seal, sea-lion
Ôté, *prep.* except, save, but, barring, bating; — *m.*, **e,** *f.*, *part. adj.* taken away, &c. (*V.* **Ôter**)
Ôter, *v.a.* to take away *or* off *or* out; to remove; to deprive; to strip off; to get out; to pull off; to leave out; to set *or* put aside; to deduct; to cut off; to rid; to relieve
S'—, *v.r.* to remove; to be taken away; to get away *or* out; to stand out; (*s'— de la bouche*) to deprive oneself *or* each other of
Otique, *adj.* (*anat.*, *med.*) otic
Otite, *s.f.* (*med.*) otitis
Oto-graphie, -logie, &c. *V.* page 3, § 1
Otorrhée, *s.f.* (*med.*) otorrhœa
Otoscope, *s.m.* (*surg.*) otoscope
Ototom-ie, -ique. *V.* page 3, § 1 [man (*sofa*)
Ottoman, e, *adj. s.m.f.* Ottoman; — *s.f.* otto-
Ou, *conj.* or; either; else, or else. — *bien*, or else, or
Où, *adv.* where; whither; what place; what part; where ... to; to what; in *or* into *or* at *or* to *or* on *or* through which (*or*, *obsolete*, whom); which; what; when, that; how. *D'*—, whence; where ... from; out of which; of *or* from which *or* what; on which; how; from what place *or* country. — *que*, wherever
†**Ouaille,** *s.f.* (*fig.*) sheep, flock
'**Ouais,** *int.* (*pop.*) halloo! what! how now! why! indeed! dear me! bless me! bless my soul!
Ouanderou, *s.m.* wanderoo monkey
Ouarine, *s.m. V.* **Alouate**
'**Ouatage,** *s.m.* wadding; padding
'**Ouate,** *s.f.* cotton-wool; wadding; padding; floss; (*plant*) Syrian *or* Virginian swallow-wort; (*fig.*) softness; whiteness
'**Ouaté, e,** *part. adj.* wadded; padded; (*fig.*) soft, velvet, velvety; white; (*paint.*) too soft
'**Ouater,** *v.a.* to wad; to pad; to cover; — *v.a.n.* to paint too soft
Oubli, *s.m.* forgetting; forgetfulness; oblivion; neglect; omission; slip; breach; forgiveness; denial. *Mettre en* —, to forget
Oubliance, *s.f.* (*old*) *V.* **Oubli**
Oublie, *s.f.* wafer (*cake*)
Oublier, *v.a.n.* to forget, to leave out, to neglect, to omit; to forgive
S'—, *v.r.* to forget oneself; to be forgotten
Oubliettes, *s.f.pl.* oubliettes (*secret dungeon or cell*); trap-dungeon. *Mettre aux* —, (*fig.*) to consign to oblivion [wafer-man *or* woman
Oublieu-r, se, *s.m.f.* wafer-maker *or* seller,
Oublieusement, *adv.* forgetfully
Oublieu-x, se, *adj.* forgetful; oblivious
Ouest, *s.m.* west; west wind; Great Western railway; — *adj.* west, western, westerly. *A l'*—, to *or* in *or* on *or* &c. the west; west, westward, westerly. *D'*—, *de l'*—, west, western,
Ouf, *int.* oh! O! [westerly. *Vers l'*—, westward
'**Oui,** *adv. s.m.* yes; ay; indeed; eh? — *-dà*, yes indeed, indeed, truly, forsooth, ay. *Que* —, yes; so; yes indeed, dear yes; to be sure. *Dire, parier* (or *gager*), *assurer, jurer*, &c. *que* —, to say, to bet, to assure, to swear, &c. that it is (so). *Langue d'* —, *V.* **Oïl**
Ouï, e, *part.* (*old*) heard. — *dire*, heard it said, heard. — **-dire,** *s.m.* hearsay. — *parler de*, heard of [ay! yes! indeed!
'**Ouiche,** *int.* (*pop.*) pish! pooh! ah! ha! eh!
Ouïcou, *s.m.* ouycou (*drink from manioc, &c.*)
Ouïe, *s.f.* hearing; —**s**, *pl.* gills; (*of some mus. instr.*) holes. *A perte d'*—, out of hearing
†**Ouillage,** *s.m.* (*of casks of wine*) filling up; adding, refreshing

†**Ouiller,** *v.a.* (*of casks of wine*) to fill up; to add to, to refresh
Ouïr, *v.a.n.* (*old*) to hear; to listen to
Ouistiti, *s.m.* (*zool.*) ouistiti, marmoset
Oukase, *s.m.* *V.* **Ukase** [storm; hail-storm
Ouragan, *s.m.* hurricane; tornado; tempest;
Ouralien, ne, *adj.* (*geog.*) Uralian
Ouralite, *s.f.* (*min.*) uralite
Ouraque, *s.m.* (*anat.*) urachus
Ourari, *s.m.* ourari, curari, arrow-poison
Ourdir, *v.a.* to warp; to weave; to twine; to twist; to plat; to plait; to wattle; to plot, to contrive, to brew; to hatch; to form; to
S'—, *v.r.* to be warped *or* &c. [frame; to lay
Ourdissage, *s.m.* warping; warp
Ourdisseu-r, se, *s.m.f.* warper
Ourdissoir, *s.m.* warp-beam; warping-mill *or* machine; (*nav.*) warping-stanchions
Ourdissure, *s.f.* warping, warp; wattling
Ourdri, e, *adj.* (*of linen*) mildewed
Ourler, *v.a.* to hem. — *à jour*, to hemstitch
Ourlet, *s.m.* hem; border. — *à jour*, hemstitch
Ours, *s.m.* bear; bear-skin; solitary *or* unsociable man, bear; very hairy man, bear; (*printers' slang*) pressman; (*soldiers' slang*) dry-room; (*literary slang*) tame production, old play. — *mal léché*, unlicked cub, ill-bred man; ugly ill-shaped fellow. *Prenez mon* —, there is nothing like leather [north
Ourse, *s.f.* she-bear, bear; (*astr.*) Bear; (*poet.*)
Oursin, *s.m.* sea-urchin; bear-skin; bear-skin
Oursin, e, *adj.* ursine [cap
Oursiné, e, *adj.* echinate, echinated, echinulate [American black bear; howling-monkey
Ourson, *s m.* bear's cub; bear-skin cap;
Ourvari, (*bad spelling*) *V.* **Hourvari**
Outarde, *s.f.* (*bird*) bustard
Outardeau, *s.m.* young bustard
Outil, *s.m.* tool, implement; instrument
†**Outillage,** *s.m.* stock of tools *or* of implements, tools, implements, machinery, gear, plant
†**Outillement,** *s.m.* supplying with tools, &c.
†**Outiller,** *v.a.* to supply *or* furnish *or* stock with tools *or* implements; to gear
†**Outilleur,** *s.m.* tool-maker [ravages
Outrage, *s.m.* outrage; insult; abuse; offence;
Outrageant, e, *adj.* outrageous; insulting; abusive [to offend against; to shock
Outrager, *v.a.* to outrage; to insult; to abuse;
Outrageusement, *adv.* outrageously
Outrageu-x, se, *adj.* outrageous
Outrance, *s.f.* excess. *A* —, *à toute* —, to excess, beyond measure, to the utmost; to the last; to the death; to the knife; desperately, furiously; like blazes; most violently; with a vengeance; unmercifully, without mercy; unsparingly, without sparing; out and out; excessive; exaggerated; desperate, furious; mortal, deadly; internecine; unmerciful
Outre, *s.f.* goat's skin, leather bottle
Outre, *prep. adv.* beyond; farther; besides. *D'*—, *en* —, through, through and through. *En* —, moreover, besides. — *que*, besides that. *Passer* —, to go beyond *or* farther; to go on; to pass on; to proceed; to take no notice
Outré, e, *part. adj.* exaggerated, carried to excess, &c. (*V.* **Outrer**); excessive; extreme; over; too great, too high; unreasonable; extravagant; undue; far-fetched; beside oneself; furious; mad
Outrecuidance, *s.f.* presumption, overweening conceit; extravagance [ed; extravagant
Outrecuidant, e, *adj.* overweening, conceit-
Outremarin, e, *adj.* ultramarine [ously
Outrément, *adv.* excessively, to excess, furi-
Outre-mer, *adv. adj.* beyond the sea, across the Channel, ultramarine
Outremer, *s.m.* (*bleu d'*—) ultramarine (*blue*)
Outre-passe, *s.f.* extra-cuttings (*of wood*), trespass [to transgress; to trespass
Outre-passer, *v.a.* to go beyond; to exceed;
Outre-percer, *v.a.* to pierce *or* run through and through
Outrer, *v.a.* to exaggerate; to carry to excess; to exceed; to overdo; to overfill; to overwhelm; to exasperate; to incense; to transport; to strain; to overwork; to exhaust; to jade; to knock up [transrhenane
Outre-Rhin, *adv. adj.* beyond the Rhine,
Outre-tombe, *adv. adj.* beyond the grave, posthumous [*mism for* **Foutu**)
Outu, e, (*genteel slang and hypocritical euphe-*
Ouvarovite, *s.f.* *V.* **Uwarowite**
Ouvert, e, *part.* opened, &c. (*V.* **Ouvrir**); — *adj.* open; free; frank; sincere; declared; bleak; uncovered; exposed; unfortified; un-
Ouvertement, *adv.* openly; freely [decked
Ouverture, *s.f.* opening; aperture, hole; orifice; port; mouth; entrance; chasm; gap; space, distance; vent; overture; beginning, commencement; means, way; hint; confidence; confession; frankness, openness; sagacity; (*arch.*) span; (*of doors*) width; (*of bankruptcy*) adjudication [day, week-day
Ouvrable, *adj.* *Jour* —, working-day, work-
Ouvrage, *s.m.* work; piece of work; ware; article; workmanship; performance. — *à l'aiguille*, needle-work. — *de ville*, (*print.*) jobbing, jobs [figured
Ouvragé, e, *part. adj.* worked, wrought;
Ouvrager, *v.a.* to work; to figure
Ouvraison, *s.f.* working (*of silk*)
Ouvré, e, *adj.* wrought; diapered. *Linge* —, *toile* —*e*, diaper; huckaback
Ouvreau, *s.m.* (*tech.*) peep-hole [diaper; to coin
Ouvrer, *v.a.* to work; to manufacture; to
Ouvreu-r, se, *s.m.f.* opener; (*theat.*) box-keeper. — *de loges*, (*theat.*) box-keeper
Ouvri-er, ère, *s.m.f.* workman; workwoman; worker; labourer; journeyman; mechanic, operative, artisan; hand; maker; — *adj.* working; labouring; operative; trade. *Premier* —, foreman. *Première* —*e*, forewoman
Ouvrir, *v.a.n.* to open; to unclose; to disclose; to unlock; to turn on; to unstop; to break *or* cut open; to rip up, to rip open; to cut; to rend; to unfold; to unfurl; to spread; to expand; to uncork; to begin, to commence; to start; to broach; to propose; (*of the appetite*) to sharpen; (*at dominoes*) to play; (*by ellipsis*) to open the door
S'—, *v.r.* to open; to be opening; to disclose; to make way; to break; to burst; to expand; to open o.'s heart *or* mind, to unbosom oneself; to open *or* cut (for) oneself, to work, to make; to open *or* cut open (o.'s ...); to begin; to be opened. *S'— un chemin* or *un passage*, to make o.'s way [room
Ouvroir, *s.m.* working-place; workshop; work-
Ovaire, *s.m.* (*anat., bot.*) ovary [foramen ovale
Ovalaire, *adj.* (*anat., surg.*) oval. *Trou* —,
Ovale, *adj.m.f., s.m.* oval
Ovalité, *s.f.* ovalness
Ovarien, ne, *adj.* (*anat., bot.*) ovarian, ovarial
Ovariotom-ie, -ique. *V.* page 3, § 1
Ovar-ique, -isme, -iste. *V.* page 3, § 1
Ovarite, *s.f.* (*med.*) ovaritis
Ovation, *s.f.* ovation
Ove, *s.m.* (*arch.*) ovolo
Ové, e, *adj.* ovate, ovated
Ovicule, *s.m.* (*arch.*) small ovolo
Oviducte, *s.m.* (*zool.*) oviduct
Ovifère, *adj.* oviferous
Oviforme, *adj.* oviform, egg-shaped, egg-like
Ovine, *adj.f.* ovine. *Bêtes* —*s*, sheep [animal
Ovipare, *adj.* oviparous; — *s.m.* oviparous
Ov-isme, -iste. *V.* page 3, § 1
Ovivore, *adj.* ovivorous
Ovo (Ab). *See Letter* **A**
Ovoïdal, e, *adj.* ovoidal
Ovoïde, *adj.m.f., s.m.* ovoid
Ovolog-ie, -ique, -iste. *V.* p. 3, § 1 [animal
Ovovivipare, *adj.* ovoviviparous; —*s.m.* ditto

Ovulaire, *adj.* ovular, ovulary
Ovule, *s.m.* ovulum ; (*bot.*) ovule
Owéniste, *s.m.* Owenite
Oxacide, *s.m.* (*chem.*) oxyacid, oxacid
Oxalate, *s.m.* (*chem.*) oxalate
Oxalide, *s.f.* (*bot.*) oxalis
Oxalique, *adj.* (*chem.*) oxalic [diathesis
Oxalurie, *s.f.* (*med.*) oxaluria, the oxalic acid
Oxide, &c. *V.* **Oxyde,** &c.
Oxy, (*in compounds, chem.*) oxy... [and water
Oxycrat, *s.m.* oxycrate, mixture of vinegar
Oxydabilité, *s.f.* (*chem.*) oxidability
Oxydable, *adj.* (*chem.*) oxidable, oxidizable, oxydizable [oxydization
Oxydation, *s.f.* (*chem.*) oxidation, oxidization,
Oxyde, *s.m.* (*chem.*) oxide, oxyde
Oxyder, *v.a.*, **S'—,** *v.r.* (*chem.*) to oxidate, to oxidize, to oxydize
Oxydulé, e, *adj.* (*chem.*) oxidulated [genizable
Oxygénable, *adj.* (*chem.*) oxygenable, oxy-
Oxygénation, *s.f.* (*chem.*) oxygenation, oxy-
Oxygène, *s.m.* (*chem.*) oxygen [genization
Oxygéner, *v.a.*, **S'—,** *v.r.* (*chem.*) to oxygenate,
Oxymel, *s.m.* oxymel [to oxygenize
Oxymétrie, *s.f.* oxymetry
Oxyopie, *s.f.* (*med.*) oxyopia, oxyopy
Oxyphonie, *s.f.* (*med.*) oxyphonia, oxyphony
Oxyrrhodin, *s.m.* (*pharm.*) oxyrrhodine
Oxyrrhynque, *s.m.* (*zool.*) oxyrhynchus
Oxysel, *s.m.* (*chem.*) oxysalt
Oxyure, *s.m.* (*zool.*) oxyuris
Oyant, e, *part. adj.* (*old*) hearing ; — *s.m.f.* (*law*) hearer. — *-compte,* (*law*) hearer
Oyat, *s.f. V.* **Calamagrostide**
Oyez, *v. int.* (*old*) hear ye ! hear ! listen !
Ozène, *s.m.* (*med.*) ozæna, ozena [rite
Ozocérite, Ozokérite, *s.f.* ozocerite, ozoke-
Ozone, *s.m.* (*chem.*) ozone
Ozonisation, *s.f.* (*chem.*) ozonization
Ozoniser, Ozoner, *v.a.* (*chem.*) to ozonize
Ozonomètre, *s.m.* ozonometer
Ozonométr-ie, -ique. *V.* page 3, § 1

P

P, *s.m.* p
Paca, *s.m.* (*zool.*) paca
Pacage, *s.m. V.* **Pâturage** [*v.a.* to feed off
Pacager, *v.n.* to pasture, to graze, to feed; —
Pacant, *s.m.* (*obsolete*) churl, boor, scrub
Pacaret, *s.m.* (*obsolete*) sherry (wine)
Pace (In), *s.m.* (*of monks*) dungeon, black-hole
Pacha, *s.m.* pasha
Pachalik, *s.m.* pashalic
Pachée, *s.f.* Oriental emerald
Pachyderme, *adj.* (*zool.*) pachydermal, pachydermatous ; — *s.m.* pachydermatous animal, pachyderm (*pl.* pachydermata, pachyderms)
Pacifica-teur, trice, *s.m.f.* pacificator, pacifier, peace-maker ; — *adj.* pacificatory, pacifying [peace-making ; appeasement
Pacification, *s.f.* pacification, pacifying,
Pacifier, *v.a.* to pacify ; to appease
 Se —, *v.r.* to become *or* be pacified *or* &c.
Pacifique, *adj.* pacific ; peaceful, peaceable ; placid ; quiet ; mild ; gentle ; — *s.m.* ditto man ; Pacific (Ocean) [placidly ; quietly
Pacifiquement, *adv.* peacefully, peaceably ;
Packfong, Packfond, *s.m.* packfong, German silver, nickel silver [pacos
Paco, *s.m.* (*zool.*) paco, alpaca ; (*min.*) paco,
†Pacotille, *s.f.* (*com.*) venture, adventure ; stock, quantity ; pack ; bale ; trumpery ware, duffers. *Marchandises de* —, goods for exportation, slop-made goods ; trumpery ware, duffers
†Pacotiller, *v.n.* to traffic in small ventures. to take out ditto
†Pacotilleur, *s.m.* sea trader in small ventures
Pacquage, Pacquer, &c. *V.* **Paquage,** &c.

Pacte, *s.m.* pact ; compact ; contract ; agreement ; treaty ; covenant [pact ; to compound
Pactiser, *v.n.* to covenant ; to make a com-
Padichah, Padischah, Padishah, *s. m.* padishah
Padou, *s.m.*, **Padoue,** *s.f.* ferret (*ribbon*) [coin
Padouan, e, *adj. s.m.f.* Paduan ; — *s.f.* Paduan
Paf, *adj.* (*pop.*) drunk, tight ; — *int.* bang ! slap !
Paffer (Se), *v.r.* (*pop.*) to booze, to get drunk
Pagaie, *s.f.* paddle [bulk, unpacked
Pagale (En), *adv.* (*nav.*) hastily ; (*of lading*) in
Paganiser, *v.a.n.* to paganize, to heathenize
Paganisme, *s.m.* paganism, heathenism
Pagayer, *v.a.n.* (*nav.*) to paddle
Pagayeur, *s.m.* paddler
Page, *s.f.* page ; (*bot.*) pagina. *Mettre en —s,* (*print.*) to make up, to make up into pages
Page, *s.m.* page (*boy*) ; dress-holder. *Tour de* —, schoolboy's trick. *Être hors de* —, to have served o.'s time as a page ; (*fig.*) to be free *or* independent, to be o.'s own master. *Se mettre hors de* —, to emancipate oneself
Pagination, *s.f.* pagination, paging
Paginer, *v.a.* to page, to folio [vegetable tissue
†Pagne, *s.m.* (*negro's,* &c.) cotton drawers ;
†Pagnon, *s.m.* black broadcloth
Pagode, *s.f.* pagoda. *Manche* —, pagoda-sleeve
Pagodite, *s.f.* (*min.*) pagodite
Pagre, *s.m.* (*fish*) pagrus [soldier-crab
Pagure, *s. m.* (*zool.*) pagurus, hermit-crab,
Pagurien, *s.m.* (*zool.*) pagurian
Paie, Paiement. *V.* **Paye, Payement**
Païen, ne, *adj. s.* pagan ; heathenish ; heathen
†Paillage, *s.m.* covering *or* stuffing with straw ; mulching
†Paillard, e, *adj.* wanton, lewd ; — *s.m.f.* rake
†Paillarder, *v.n.* to play the rake
†Paillardise, *s.f.* wantonness, lewdness
†Paillasse, *s. f.* straw-mattress, straw-bed, bed-straw, paillasse, palliasse ; ticking, tick ; (*tech.*) bed ; grate ; (*jest.*) body, carcass ; — *s.m.* clown, merry-andrew, Jack-pudding ; trimmer, time-server, weathercock, harlequin, mountebank, quack, humbug. *Crever la* — *à,* to run through the body
†Paillasson, *s.m.* straw-mat, mat ; straw-matting, matting ; door-mat ; window-pad
†Paille, *s.f.* straw ; chaff ; flaw ; mote ; — *s.m.* straw colour ; — *adj.* straw-coloured ; straw. *De* —, of *or* from straw ; (*adject.*) straw ; straw-bottomed. — *d'Italie,* (*of bonnets, hats*) Leghorn *or* Tuscan. *Menue* —, chaff. *Être* (or *en être*) *à la* —, to be miserably poor ; (*pop.*) to be dying. *Mettre de la — dans ses souliers,* to feather o.'s nest. *Rompre la* —, to break off ; to fall out (with). *Tirer à la courte* —, to draw cuts (*or* lots). — **-en-queue, -en-cul,** *s.m.* (*zool.*) tropic-bird
†Paillé, e, *part. adj.* covered *or* &c. with straw (*V.* **Pailler,** *v.a.*) ; straw-coloured ; flawy ;
†Paillée, *s.f. V.* **Airée** [(*her.*) diapered
†Paillement, *s.m. V.* **Paillage**
†Pailler, *s.m.* farmyard ; heap of straw, straw-rick ; dunghill ; straw-loft ; shed ; — *m.,* **-ère,** *f., adj.* farmyard ; (*of fowls*) barn-door
†Pailler, *v.a.* to cover *or* stuff with straw ; to straw-bottom ; (*agr., hort.*) to spread over with straw, to put straw round, to mulch
†Paillet, *adj.m.* (*of wines*) light red, pale ; — *s.m.* heap of straw ; (*nav.*) mat
†Pailleter, *v.a.* to spangle
†Pailleteur, *s.m. V.* **Orpailleur** [dust
†Paillette, *s.f.* spangle ; particle ; scale ; (gold-)
†Pailleu-r, se, *s.m.f.* straw-dealer *or* carrier ; chair-bottomer
†Pailleu-x, se, *adj.* strawy, straw ; flawy
†Paillis, *s.m.* (*hort.*) mulch [piece of solder
†Paillon, *s.m.* wisp of straw ; spangle ; foil ;
Pain, *s.m.* bread ; loaf ; loaf of bread ; (*of colour, soap,* &c.) cake ; biscuit ; roll ; pat. — *au lait,* — *mollet, petit* —, *petit* — *à café,* roll (*of bread*), French roll. — *à cacheter,* wafer. — *à chanter,*

(*Cath. rel.*) wafer for consecration. — *de coucou*, (*bot.*) *V.* **Surelle.** — *de pourceau*, (*bot.*) sow-bread. — *de proposition*, show-bread. *Avoir du — sur la planche*, to have saved money, to have enough to live on. *Avoir son — cuit*, to be well provided for. *Faire passer* (or *Faire perdre*) *le goût du —*, (*pop.*) to kill, to do for, to settle, to give a quietus. *Perdre le goût du —*, (*pop.*) to die, to go off, to kick the bucket. *C'est — bénit*, it serves him *or* her *or* &c. right

Pair, e, *adj.* equal, like; (*of numbers*) even; (*anat.*) double. *Non —*, (*of numbers*) uneven, odd. *— ou non*, odd or even

Pair, *s.m.* peer; equal; par; equality, equal footing; common level; (*of birds*) mate. *Au —*, at par; even; right up to the present time (*with no arrears*); with board and lodging but no salary. *De —*, on a par; on an equality, on an equal footing. *De — à compagnon*, *— et compagnon*, on terms of equality and intimacy, with great familiarity, hail fellow well met. *Hors de* (or *du*) *—*, above o.'s equals, above the level of others; beyond all comparison

Paire, *s.f.* pair; couple; brace. — *d'heures*, prayer-book

Pairement, *adv.* evenly; (*anat.*) doubly

Pairesse, *s.f.* peeress

Pairie, *s.f.* peerage; peer's fief (*feud.*)

Pairle, *s.m.* (*her.*) pall [calm; silent

Paisible, *adj* peaceable, peaceful; quiet; still;

Paisiblement, *adv* peaceably, peacefully; [quietly

Paisseau, *s.m.* prop (*for vines*)

Paisselage, *s.m.* propping (*of vines*)

Paisseler, *v.a.* to prop (*vines*) [(*tech.*) stretcher

Paisson, *s.f.* pasture, feed; mast; — *s. m.*

Paissonni-er, ère, *s.m.f.* herdsman; herdswoman

Paître, *v.a.n.* to graze; to feed upon; to eat; to feed; to tend; to pasture. *Envoyer —*, to send away *or* about o.'s business; to dismiss; to discard; to kick overboard

Paix, *s.f. int.* peace; rest; stillness, quietness; hush! silence! be quiet! quiet! (*of veal or mutton*) blade-bone; (*Cath. rel.*) pax, paten. *Donner* or *ficher* or *laisser la — à*, *laisser en —*, to leave alone, not to bother

Pal, *s.m.* pale; stake; dibbler

Palabre, *s.f.* palaver

Palade, *s.f.* (*rowing*) stroke; pull

Paladin, *s.m.* paladin, knight-errant, champion

Palais, *s.m.* palace; mansion; courts; law-courts; court; law; lawyers; bar; palate; taste. — *-Royal*, (*in Paris*) Palais-Royal. — *de l'industrie*, Exhibition building. — *de justice*, law-courts, courts of law, palace of justice. *Jour de —*, court-day. *Style de* (or *du*) *—*, law-style. *Terme de —*, law-term

Palamédée, *s.f.* (*bird*) screamer

Palan, *s.m.* (*nav.*) tackle

Palanche, *s.f.* yoke (*for carrying pails*)

Palançon, *s.m.* (*mas.*) stake, beam

Palanque, *s.f.* (*fort.*) pales, stakes, stockade; (*obsolete*) palankas [hoist, to set up

Palanquer, *v.a.* (*nav.*) to bowse, to haul, to

Palanquin, *s.m.* palanquin; (*nav.*) small tackle, burton [(*to a boat*)

Palastre, Palâtre, *s.m.* case (*of a lock*); tingle

Palatal, e, *adj.*, **Palatale,** *s.f.* (*gram.*) palatal

Palatial, e, *adj.* palatial

Palatin, e, *adj.* palatine; — *s.m.* palatine, count palatine; (*anat.*) palatine bone, palatine; — *s.f.* palatine's wife; countess palatine; (fur-)tippet, victorine

Palatinat, *s.m.* palatinate

Palatite, *s.f.* (*med.*) palatitis

Palato, (*in compounds, anat.*) palato-...

Pale, *s.f.* pale, stake, pile; blade (*of an oar*); flood-gate; paddle-board; (*bird*) spoon-bill; (*Cath. rel.*) pall [*couleurs*, green sickness

Pâle, *adj.* pale; wan; tame; affrighted. —*s*

Palé, e, *adj.* (*her.*) paly [spangled

Paléacé, e, *adj.* (*bot.*) paleaceous, chaffy,

Paléage, *s.m.* shovelling

Palée, *s.f.* row of pales *or* stakes *or* piles

Palefrenier, *s.m.* groom; ostler

Palefroi, *s.m.* palfrey

Palémon, *s.m.* prawn [paleographic

Paléographe, *s.m.* paleographer; — *adj.*

Paléograph-ie, -ique, -iquement. *V.* page 3, § 1

Paléologue, *s.m.* (*hist.*) Paleologus, Palæologus

Paléonto-graphie, -logie, &c. *V.* page 3, § 1

Paléontologue, *s.m.* paleontologist

Paléosaure, *s.m.* paleosaurus

Paléothérien, ne, *adj.* paleotherian

Paléothérium, *s.m.* (*zool.*) paleotherium

Paléozo-ïque, -ologie. *V.* page 3, § 1

Paleron, *s.m.* shoulder-blade, blade-bone

Palestine, *s.f.* (*print.*) two-line pica

Palestre, *s.f.* palæstra

Palestrique, *adj.* palæstrian; — *s.f.* palæstra

Palet, *s.m.* quoit. *Jouer au —*, to play at quoits

Paletot, *s.m.* great-coat, overcoat, coat, paletot. — *-pilote*, pilot-coat. — *-sac*, sack-coat

Palette, *s.f.* pallet; paddle, paddle-board; float-board; battledore; racket, racquet; bat; basin; (*of a ratchet-wheel*) pallet, pall; (*printer's*) slice; (*paint.*) palette; (*fig.*) colouring, colours; skill, art; manner, style; (*bird*) spoon-bill; (*anc. armour*) palette; (*obsolete*) ferule; (*pop.*) knee-cap; shoulder-blade

Palétuvier, *s.m.* (*bot.*) mangrove-tree

Pâleur, *s.f.* paleness; wanness; tameness

Pâli, Pali, *s.m.*, *adj.m.* (**e,** *f.*) Pâli (*language*)

Pâli, e, *part. adj.* grown pale, &c. (*V.* **Pâlir**); pale

Palier, *s.m.* landing, landing-place, stair-head; flat, floor, story; (*rail.*) level; (*mach.*) pedestal

Palière, *s.f.* (*arch.*) curtail-step

Palification, *s.f.* palification, paling

Palifier, *v.a.* to palify, to pale, to stake

Palikare, *s m.* palikare, palikary (*modern Greek militiaman*)

Palimpseste, *s.m. adj.* palimpsest [dromic

Palindrome, *s.m.* palindrome; — *adj.* palin-

Palingénésie, *s.f.* palingenesia, palingenesy, palingenesis, regeneration

Palingénésique, Palingénésiaque, *adj.* palingenetic, palingenetical

Palinodie, *s.f.* palinode, palinody, recantation, change of political opinion. *Chanter la —*, to recant, to read o.'s recantation [serving

Palinodique, *adj.* palinodial; trimming, time-

Pâlir, *v.n.a.* to grow *or* turn pale; to grow dim; to look *or* seem pale; to pore (*on books*, &c.), to study very hard *or* deeply; to make pale; to make (...) look pale. *Faire —*, to make pale, to pale; to throw into the shade, to eclipse; to frighten

Palis, *s.m.* pale; paling, enclosure, fence

Palissade, *s.f.* paling; palisade; hedgerow of trees; hoarding; (*fort.*) stockade, palisade

Palissadement, *s. m.* palisading, &c. (*V.* **Palissader**)

Palissader, *v.a.* to pale; to palisade; to line with a hedgerow of trees; to enclose, to fence; (*fort.*) to stockade, to palisade [*trees*)

Palissage, *s.m.* nailing up, training (*of wall-*

Palissandre, *s.m.* rosewood

Palisser, *v.a.* to nail up, to train (*wall-trees*)

Paliure, *s.m.* (*bot.*) paliurus

Palladium, *s.m.* (*antiq., fig., chem.*) palladium

Pallas, *s.f.* (*myth., astr.*) Pallas. *Arbre, fruit, oiseau de —*, *V.* **Minerve**

Palle, *s.f.* (*Cath. rel.*) pall [palliating, palliatory

Pallia-teur, trice, *s.m.f.* palliator; — *adj.*

Palliati-f, ve, *adj.*, **Palliatif,** *s.m.* palliative

Palliation, *s.f.* palliation

Pallier, *v.a.* to palliate

Pallium, *s.m.* pallium, pall

‡Palma-christi, *s.m.* *V.* **Ricin**

Palmaire, *adj.* (*anat.*) palmar [*of prizes*)

Palmarès, *s.m* programme (*of a distribution*

Palmature, *s.f.* palmature

Palme, *s.f.* palm, palm-branch; palm-tree, palm; (*fig.*) palm, victory; — *s.m.f.* (*meas.*) palm, hand [webbed, web-footed
Palmé, e, *adj.* palmed; palmate, palmated;
Palmerie, *s.f.*, **Palmerier,** *s.m.* palm-house, palm-plantation
Palmette, *s.f.* (*bot.*) palmetto; (*hort.*) horizontal training (*of wall-trees*); (*arch.*, &c.) palm-
Palmier, *s.m.* palm-tree, palm [leaf
Palmine, *s.f.* (*chem.*) palmine
Palmipède, *s.m. adj.* palmiped
Palmiste, *s.m.* cabbage-tree, cabbage-palm, palmetto; palm-bird; — *adj.* palm
Palmite, *s.m.* palm-sap
Palmitine, *s.f.* (*chem.*) palmitine
Palmitique, *adj.* (*chem.*) palmitic
Palmoule, *s.f.* *V.* **Pamelle**
Palmure, *s.f.* (*of some birds*) web
Palombe, *s.f.* ring-dove; (*nav.*) strop
Palommier, *s.m.* (*bot.*) winter-green, part-
Palon, *s.m.* wooden shovel; spatula [ridge-berry
Palonnier, *s.m.* (*of carriages*) swing-bar, bar; (*agr.*) whippletree; (*of mil. waggons*, &c., *agr.*) swingletree, swing-tree
Palot, *s.m.* spade; boor, rustic, bumpkin
Pâlot, te, *adj.* palish, rather pale
Palourde, *s.f.* cockle (*shell-fish*)
Palpabilité, *s.f.* palpability, palpableness
Palpable, *adj.* palpable
Palpablement, *adv.* palpably
Palpation, *s.f.* palpation
Palpe, *s.m.* (*of insects*) palp, feeler
Palpébral, e, *adj.* (*anat.*) palpebral
Palper, *v.a.n.* to feel; to handle; to finger, to pocket, to receive; to receive money; — *s.m.* palpation. — *l'eau*, to dip the oar
Palpitation, *s.f.* palpitation; throbbing, throb; panting, pant; beating, beat; quivering, quiver; trembling, tremble; thrilling, thrill; fluttering, flutter
Palpiter, *v.n.* to palpitate; to throb; to pant; to beat; to quiver; to tremble; to thrill; to flutter [pile
Palplanche, *s.f.* (*build.*) pile-plank, sheeting-
Palsambleu, Palsandié, Palsangué, Palsanguienne, Palsembleu, *int.* (*old*) by George! by Jingo! by the Powers! zounds!
Paltoquet, *s.m.* churl; mere nobody
Paludamentum, *s.m.* (*Rom. ant.*) paludamentum, paludament [marshes, marsh, bog-land
Paludéen, ne, paludal, paludine, marshy, of
Paludelle, *s.f.* (*bot.*) bog-moss [bog-land
Paludicole, *adj.* living *or* growing in marshes,
Paludier, *s.m.* salt-marsh worker
Paludière, *s.f.* salt marsh [water snail
Paludine, *s.f.* paludina, marsh-snail; fresh-
Palus, *s.m.* (*anc. geog.*) Palus; (*agr.*) bog-earth
Pamelle, *s.f.* two-rowed barley, common barley
Pâmer, *v.n.*, **Se —,** *v.r.* to faint, to faint away, to swoon; to be transported *or* enraptured; (— *de rire*) to be ready to die with laughter, to split o.'s sides with laughing
Pâmoison, *s.f.* swoon, fainting-fit; rapture
Pampa, *s.f.* pampa; — *s.m.* (*zool.*) pampas hare
Pampe, *s.f.* blade *or* flag (*of corn*)
Pampéen, ne, *adj.* pampean
Pampéro, *s.m.* pampero (*wind*)
Pamphile, *s.m.* (*cards*) loo; pam; (*pers.*) low fellow, mere nobody; (*zool.*) pamphila
Pamphlet, *s.m.* (satirical) pamphlet
Pamphlétaire, *s.m.* pamphleteer
Pamplemousse, *s.m.* (*tree*) shaddock; — *s.f.* (*fruit*) shaddock, pompelmoose, pumplemose
Pampre, *s.m.* vine-branch; (*arch.*) pampre
Pan, *s.m.* skirt; tail; flap; leaf; lappet; piece of a wall, piece, wall; partition; part; front; face; side; (*meas.*) span; (*myth.*) Pan; — *int.* bang! slap! smack! one (*or* a) knock! one (*or* a) rap! — *coupé*, cant. *A —s coupés*, canted,
Panacée, *s.f.* panacea, universal remedy [cant
Panache, *s.m.* plume, feathers, panache; tuft; top, cap; (*bot.*) streaks of colours; (*arch.*) panache; (*pop.*) drop too much. — *de mer*, sea-fan. —*s de porcs*, (*cook.*) pigs' ears
Panaché, e, *adj.* plumed; tufted; streaky, streaked, striped; variegated; mixed
Panacher, *v.a.* to plume; to tuft; to streak, to variegate [be) streaked *or* variegated
Se —, *v.r.* to plume oneself; to become (*or*
Panachure, *s.f.* streak; variegation
Panade, *s.f.* panada, porridge; milksop
Panader (Se), *v.r.* (*old*) *V.* **Pavaner (Se)**
Panage, *s.m.* pannage
Panaire, *adj.* panary
Panais, *s.m.* parsnip
Panama, *s.m.* Panama grass; Panama hat
Panard, *adj.* crook-legged
Panaris, *s.m.* whitlow [**Panetela**
Panatella, Panatela, *s.m.* (*bad spelling*) *V.*
Pancarte, *s.f.* tariff; placard; bill; board; written paper, writing, paper; scrawl; rigmarole; visitors' book; paper-case; pancarte, pancharta [resolute doctor
Pancrace, *s.m.* pancratium. *Docteur —*, most
Pancrais, Pancratier, *s.m.* (*bot.*) pancratium. — *maritime*, sea-daffodil
Pancréas, *s.m.* (*anat.*) pancreas; sweetbread
Pancréatine, *s.f.* (*chem.*) pancreatine
Pancréatique, *adj.* (*anat.*) pancreatic
Pancréatite, *s.f.* (*med.*) pancreatitis
Panda, *s.m.* (*zool.*) panda
Pandanées, *s.f.pl.* (*bot.*) pandanaceæ
Pandanus, *s.m.* (*bot.*) pandanus, screw-pine
Pandect, Pandecte, *s.m.* (*old spelling*) *V.*
Pandectes, *s.f.pl.* Pandects [**Pandit**
Pandém-ie, -ique. *V.* page 3, § 1
Pandémonium, *s.m.* Pandemonium
Pandiculation, *s.f.* (*med.*) pandiculation
Pandion, *s.m.* *V.* **Balbuzard**
Pandit, *s.m.* pandit *or* pundit (*learned Brahmin*)
Pandore, *s.f.* (*mus.*) pandore; (*zool.*) pandora
Pandour, Pandoure, *s.m.* pandour; ma-
Pane, *s.f.* (*pop.*) *V.* **Panne** [rauder; savage
Pané, e, *adj.* covered with bread-crumbs; (*pop.*) *V.* **Panné.** *Eau —e*, *V.* **Eau**
Panégyr-ique (*s.m. adj.*), **-iste.** *V.* page 3, § 1
Paner, *v.a.* to cover with bread-crumbs; (*pop.*)
Panerée, *s.f.* basketful, hamperful [*V.* **Panner**
Panetela, *s.m.* panetela (cigar)
Paneterie, *s.f.* bread-room, pantry [keeper
Panetier, *s.m.* pantler; (*nav.*) baker, store-
Panetière, *s.f.* scrip; pouch; (*local*) black beetle, cockroach
Paneton, *s.m.* bread-basket, basket
Pangermanisme, *s.m.* pangermanism
Pangolin, *s.m.* (*zool.*) pangolin, scaly ant-eater
Panharmonicon, *s.m.* (*mus. instr.*) panhar-
Panhellén-ique, -isme. *V.* p. 3, § 1 [monicon
Panic, *s.m.* (*bot.*) panicum, panic, panic-grass,
Panicaut, *s.m.* (*bot.*) eryngo [Guinea grass
Panicule, *s.f.* (*bot.*) panicle [paniculated
Paniculé, e, *adj.* (*bot.*) panicled, paniculate,
Panier, *s.m.* basket; pannier; hamper; punnet; pottle; scuttle; crate; creel; bee-hive; sieve; basket-chaise; hoop-petticoat; basketful. — *percé*, (*fig.*) spendthrift. — *roulant*, go-cart. — *au papier*, waste-paper basket, waste-basket. — *à salade*, (*pop.*, *jest.*) prison-van; basket-chaise. *Le dessus du —*, the choice, the best. *Le fond du —*, the refuse. *Anse* or *danse du —*, *V.* **Anse**
Panière, *s.f.* (*local*) basket, hamper
Panifiable, *adj.* panifiable
Panification, *s.f.* panification, bread-making
Panifier, *v.a.n.* to panify, to make bread (with)
Panique, *adj.m.f.*, *s.f.* panic
Panis, *s.m.* (*bot.*) *V.* **Panic**
Panne, *s.f.* plush, shag; silk plush; (*her.*) pean; (*of a hammer*) pane; (*arch.*) purlin; (*of pigs*, &c.) flead, fat; (*theat. slang*) short part; (*pop.*) straits, misery, beggary. *En —*, (*nav.*) lying to. *Être* or *rester* or *se tenir en —*, (*nav.*) to lie to. *Mettre en —*, (*nav.*) to bring to, to lay to, to heave to

Panné,e, *adj.* (*pop.*) hard up, done up, beggared, beggarly, a beggar, impecunious, miserable, wretched, seedy
Panneau, *s.m.* panel; pane; trap-net, snare; (*part of a saddle*) pannel; (*small saddle*) pilch; (*of a chair*) rail, splat; (*hort.*) glass frame; (*nav.*) hatch. *Donner dans le* —, to fall into the snare, to be taken in [put glass frames
Panneauter, *v.n.* to lay trap-nets; (*hort.*) to
Panneauteur, *s.m.* trap-net layer
Panner, *v.a.* (*pop.*) to beggar, to ruin, to drain; to win all ...'s money [stone
Panneresse, *s.f.* (*mas.*) stretcher, outbond-
Panneton, *s.m.* key-bit, bit; handle (*of a window-fastening*); bread-basket, basket
Pannicule, *s.m.* (*anat.*) pannicule
Pannonien, ne, *adj. s.* Pannonian
Panonceau, *s.m.* escutcheon, scutcheon
Panoplie, *s.f.* panoply; trophy [con
Panoptique, *adj.* panoptical; — *s.m.* panopti-
Panorama, *s.m.* panorama
Panoramique, *adj.* panoramic
Panoufle, *s.f.* (*pop.*) sheep-skin; old rubbish; old hag; wig, caxon
Pansage, *s.m.* dressing; grooming
Panse, *s.f.* paunch; belly; (*of a bell*) sound-bow; (*of the letter a*) oval. *N'avoir pas fait une — d'a*, not to have done the least thing, to have done nothing whatever [ance
Pansement, *s.m.* dressing; grooming; attend-
Panser, *v.a.* to dress; to groom; to take care of. *Être bien pansé*, (*pop.*) to have had o.'s
Panslavisme, *s.m.* panslavism [bellyful
Panstéréorama, *s.m.* panstereorama
Pansu, e, *adj.* big-bellied, swag-bellied, paunchy; bulging; — *s.m.f.* paunchy fellow *or* creature
Pantagruélique, *adj.* of Pantagruel; gluttonous, voracious, ravenous, insatiable; sumptuous, on a grand scale; festive, banqueting, eating and drinking
Pantagruéliser, *v.n.* *V.* **Ripaille** (*Faire*)
Pantagruélisme, *s.m.* Pantagruelism, epicurism, gluttony [glutton
Pantagruéliste, *s.m.* Pantagruelist, epicure,
Pantalon, *s.m.* trousers, pair of trousers; pantaloons, pair of pantaloons; (*for ladies*) drawers, pair of drawers; pantalets; (*pers.*) Pantaloon; (*figure in dancing*) pantalon. — *collant*, tight trousers *or* pantaloons, tights. — *à pieds*, footed pantaloons, stocking-pantaloons. — *rouge*, (*fig.*) (French) soldier
Pantalonnade, *s.f.* pantaloonery, buffoonery; ridiculous excuse, sham, shuffle, make-believe, humbug [palpitate, to throb, to quiver
Panteler, *v.n.* to pant, to gasp for breath; to
Pantellement, *s.m.* breathlessness, panting
Pantène, Pantenne, *s.f.* punnet; draw-net. *En* —, (*nav.*) disabled, displaced, apeak
Panthée, *adj.* (*obsolete*) pantheistic
Panthéisme, *s.m.* pantheism
Panthéiste, *s.m.f.* pantheist; — *adj.* pantheistic, pantheistical
Panthéistique, *adj.* pantheistic, pantheistical
Panthéon, *s.m.* pantheon; (*in Paris*) Pantheon (*burial place for great men, like Westminster*
Panthère, *s.f.* panther [*Abbey in England*)
Panthérin, e, *adj.* pantherine
Pantière, *s.f.* draw-net; shooting-pouch
Pantin, *s.m.* dancing-puppet, puppet, jumping jack; guy; insignificant fellow, regular machine; trimmer, time-server, weathercock,
Pantine, *s.f.* hank [harlequin
Pantiner, *v.a.* to hank [copying-machine
Pantographe, *s.m.* pantograph, pantagraph,
Pantograph-ie, -ique, -iquement. *V.*
Pantoiement, *s.m.* (*falc.*) pantess [page 3, § 1
Pantois, e, *adj.* out of breath, breathless, panting; short-winded; astounded, dumbfounded, sheepish
Pantomètre, *s.m.* pantometer
Pantomime, *s.f.* (*thing*) pantomime, dumb show; — *s.m.f.* (*pers.*) pantomime, pantomimist; — *adj.* pantomime
Pantomimer, *v.a.* *V.* **Mimer**
Pantomim-ique, -iquement. *V.* page 3, § 1
Pantophage, *adj.* pantophagous; — *s.m.f.*
Pantophagie, *s.f.* pantophagy [pantophagist
Pantophobie, *s.f.* (*med.*) pantophobia, panphobia, mania of fear
Pantoscope, *s.m.* pantoscope
Pantoscopique, *adj.* pantoscopic
Pantoufle, *s.f.* slipper; slip-shoe; (*fer à* —) panton, panton-shoe. *En —s*, in slippers; slip-shoe like, slip-shod; (*fig.*) at o.'s ease *Soulier en* —, slip-shoe [manufacturer
Pantoufli-er, ère, *s.m.f.* slipper-maker *or*
Paolo, *s.m.* paolo (*Italian coin*)
Paon, *s.m.* peacock, peafowl; (*astr.*) pavo. — *bleu*, peacock-fish. — *de jour*, peacock's-eye butterfly. — *de nuit, grand* —, peacock-moth, emperor-moth. — *de mer*, (*bird*) ruff (*female*, reeve); (*fish*) peacock-fish
Paonne, *s.f.* peahen
Paonneau, *s.m.* young peacock, peachick
Papa, *s.m.* papa; daddy; father; fellow; old; Jack. *Bon —, grand- —*, grandpapa
Papal, e, *adj.* papal; — *s.m.* papist
Papalin, *s.m.* (*old*) pope's soldier *or* coin
Papas, *s.m.* pope (*Greek priest*)
Papauté, *s.f.* papacy, popedom; pontificate
Papavéracé, e, *adj.* papaveraceous, papaverous [tribe
Papavéracées, *s.f.pl.* papaveraceæ, poppy
Papavérine, *s.f.* (*chem.*) papaverine
Papaye, *s.f.* (*bot.*) papaw (*fruit*)
Papayer, *s.m.* (*bot.*) papaw-tree
Pape, *s.m.* pope; (*bird*) papa
Papegai, Papegaut, *s.m.* popinjay [crite
Papelard, e, *adj. s.* (*old*) hypocritical; hypo-
Papelardise, *s.f.* (*old*) hypocrisy
Paperasse, *s.f.* old paper, waste paper; paper
Paperasser, *v.n.* to turn over papers, to rummage o.'s papers; to scribble away, to scribble, to waste paper
Paperassi-er, ère, *s.m.f.* rummager into old papers, eternal scribbler; — *adj.* fond of rummaging into old papers; given to scribbling
Papesse, *s.f.* papess. *La — Jeanne*, Pope Joan
Papeterie, *s.f.* paper-mill; paper-manufacture; paper-trade; stationery; paper-warehouse; stationery-box *or* case [— *adj.* paper-making
Papeti-er, ère, *s.m.f.* paper-maker; stationer;
Papetto, *s.m.* papetto (*Italian coin*)
Paphien, ne, *adj. s.* Paphian
Paphlagonien, ne, *adj. s.* Paphlagonian
Papier, *s.m.* paper. — *cassé*, outsides. — *-dentelle*, lace-paper, laced paper. — *goudron*, — *goudronné*, brown paper. — *gris*, brown paper, cap-paper. — *mâché*, paper-pulp, papier-mâché. — *ministre* or *tellière*, petition-paper. — *-monnaie*, paper money. — *peint*, paper-hanging. — *à calquer*, tracing-paper. — *à lettres*, note-paper, letter-paper. — *de Chine*, India paper, Indian paper, rice paper. — *de soie*, — *joseph*, tissue-paper. — *de verre*, glass paper, sand paper. *Marchand de* —, wholesale stationer. *Être* (or *être bien*) *dans les —s de*, to be in favour with, to be in ...'s books. *Rayez cela de vos —s*, do not rely on that, strike that out of your books
Papilionacé, e, *adj. s.* *V.* **Papillonacé**
Papillaire, *adj.* papillary, papillous
†Papille, *s.f.* (*anat., bot.*) papilla
†Papillon, *s.m.* butterfly; moth; fickle man; trifler; flirt; (*tech.*) butterfly-valve, damper; (*nav.*) sky-sail, sky-scraper. — *de nuit*, moth. —*s noirs*, blue-devils, blues, dismals, spleen
†Papillonacé, e, *adj.* papilionaceous; — *s.f.* ditto plant [ing; trifling; flirtation
†Papillonnage, *s.m.* fluttering about; hover-
†Papillonner, *v.n.* to flutter about; to hover; to trifle; to flirt
†Papillonneur, *s.m.* (*slang*) laundry-cart robber

†**Papillotage,** *s.m.* twinkling; dazzling, dazzle; glitter, flash, tinsel; (*print.*) slurring, doubling; (*old*) putting (*hair*) in paper; curl-papers, curls

†**Papillote,** *s.f.* curl-paper, curling-paper; curl; sweetmeat *or* chocolate-drop *or* sugar-plum in paper, kiss; (*cook.*) paper; (*obsolete*) spangle. *Côtelette en* —, cutlet fried in paper. *Fer à —s*, curling-irons

†**Papilloter,** *v.n.* to twinkle, to blink; to dazzle; to glitter, to sparkle; (*print.*) to slur, to double; — *v.a.* to put (*hair*) in paper; to put curl-papers to; to curl; to tinsel

Papin, *s.m.* pap

Papion, *s.m.* papion (*baboon*)

Papisme, *s.m.* papism, popery [ical, popish

Papiste, *s.m.f* papist; — *adj.* papistic, papist-

Papistique, *adj.* papistic, papistical, popish

Papotage, *s.m.* prattle, tattle, tittle-tattle

Papoter, *v.n.* to prattle, to tattle

Papou, e, *adj. s.* Papuan

Pappe, *s.m.* (*bot.*) pappus, down

Pappeu-x, se, *adj.* (*bot.*) pappous, pappose,

Pappifère, *adj.* pappiferous [downy

Pappiforme, *adj.* pappiform

Papule, *s.f.* (*med.*, *bot.*) papula

Papuleu-x, se, *adj.* papulous, papulose

Papyracé, e, *adj.* papyraceous; paper

Papyrifère, *adj.* papyriferous

Papyrus, *s.m.* papyrus

Paquage, *s.m.* packing (*of fish*)

Pâque, *s.f.* passover

Pâques, *s.m.f.* Easter. — *closes*, Low Sunday. — *fleuries*, Palm Sunday. *Faire ses* —, to receive the sacrament at Easter

Paquebot, *s.m.* packet-boat, packet-ship, packet, liner, boat; steam-boat. — *-poste*, mail-packet, mail-boat, mail-steamer

Paquer, *v.a.* to pack (*fish*)

Paqueresse, *s.f.* packer (*of fish*)

Pâquerette, *s.f.* (*bot.*) Easter daisy

Pâquerolle, *s.f.* (*bot.*) bellium

Paquet, *s.m.* parcel; bundle; pack; packet; mail; mass, lump; cluster; dowdy; (*print.*) slip; (*pop.*) dismissal, (the) sack; (o.'s) own; (a) clincher; (a) quietus; (a) drop too much; story, scandalous tale, reflection. — *de linge sale*, (*pers.*) slattern, dowdy. *Donner à quelqu'un son* —, to give one a clincher, to give it well to one; to set one down; to settle one; to give one the sack, to dismiss *or* discharge one. *Faire ses —s*, *plier son* —, to pack up; to be off. *Risquer* or *hasarder le* —, to run the risk, to take o.'s chance of it, to chance it

Paquetage, *s.m.* bundling, packing; pack; kit

Paqueter, *v.a.* to bundle, to pack, to pack up

Paqueteu-r, se, *s.m.f.* packer

Paquetier, *s.m.* (*print.*) compositor

Paquette, *s.f.* (*bot.*) ox-eye daisy

Paqueur, *s.m.* packer (*of fish*)

Pâquis, *s.m.* (*hunt.*) pasture-ground

Par, *prep.* by; by means of; through; across; per, a, for every; out at; out of; from; on; about; in; into; with; for; for the sake of; during; by way of; over; at. *De* —, by order *or* in the name of; by virtue of; by; from; about, in. — *ci* — *là*, *V.* **Ci.** — *ici*, this way; through here, through this place; about here. — *là*, that way; through there, through that place; about there; by there; by that, thereby; by that means, in that way. — *où*, which *or* what way; through where, through what place *or* places; through *or* by *or* in what (*or* which); by what means, in what way, how; where; the way; the same way. — *quoi*, by what; how. — *soi-même*, for oneself, without any help, unassisted

Para, *s.m.* para (*Turkish coin*)

Parabole, *s.f.* parable; (*geom.*) parabola

Parabol-ique, -iquement. *V.* page 3, § 1

Paraboloïde, *s.m.* (*geom.*) paraboloid

Paracel, *s.m.* (*nav.*) cluster of islands, keys

Paracels-isme, -iste. *V.* page 3, § 1

Paracentèse, *s.f.* (*surg.*) paracentesis, tapping

Paracentrique, *adj.* (*geom.*) paracentric

Parachèvement, *s.m.* finishing, completion; last touch

Parachever, *v.a.* to finish entirely, to give the last finish *or* touch, to perfect, to complete **Se** —, *v.r.* to be finished entirely, &c.

‡**Parachronisme,** *s.m.* parachronism

Parachute, *s.m.* parachute

Paraclet, *s.m.* Paraclete, Holy Ghost, comforter

Paracousie, *s.f.* (*med.*) noise in the head

Paracrotte, *s.m.* mud-guard; splasher, splash-board, dash-board

Parade, *s.f.* parade, display; show; boast; state; farce; parry, parrying. *A la* —, (*mil.*) on parade. *De* —, (*adject.*) parade; show; state; court; official. *Lit de* —, bed of state, state-bed. *Exposé sur un lit de* —, lying in state [in sight

Parader, *v.n.* to show off; to parade; to cruise

Paradigme, *s.m.* (*gram.*) paradigm

Paradis, *s.m.* paradise; (*theat.*) upper gallery, gods. *Il ne le portera pas en* —, he shall pay for it before he dies, he will suffer for it

Paradisiaque, *adj.* paradisiacal, paradisian

Paradisier, *s.m.* paradisea, bird of paradise

Paradiste, *s.m.* *V.* **Pitre**

Parados, *s.m.* (*fort.*) parados

Paradoxal, e, *adj.* paradoxical

Paradoxalement, *adv.* paradoxically [ical

Paradoxe, *s.m.* paradox; — *adj.* (*old*) paradox-

Parafe, *s.m.* flourish, initials, mark, paraph

Parafer, *v.a.* to sign with a flourish, to put o.'s initials to, to paraph

Paraffine, *s.f. adj.* paraffine [wire

Parafoudre, *s.m.* lightning-conductor, earth-

Parage, *s.m.* parts; quarter; latitude; extraction, birth, rank; (*tech.*, &c.) paring; dressing; (*feud. law*) parage

Paraglace, *s.m.* ice-beam; ice-breaker

Paraglosse, *s.f.* (*med.*) paraglossa

Paragoge, *s.f.* (*gram.*) paragoge

Paragogique, *adj.* paragogic, paragogical

Paragraphe, *s.m.* paragraph

Paragrêle, *s.m.* paragrandine, hail-rod

Paraguante, *s.f.* (*old*) consideration, present, fee, douceur, tip [Paraguayan

Paraguayen, ne, Paraguéen, ne, *adj. s.*

Paraître, *v.n.* to appear; to make o.'s appearance; to come in sight; to come out; to be seen *or* visible; to show oneself *or* o.'s face; to enter; to stand forth; to seem, to look; to show; to show off, to make a show *or* a figure; to shine; to prove to be; — *s.m.* appearance. *Faire* —, to make (. . .) appear; to show, to display; to publish; to bring out; to produce. *Il n'y paraît pas*, there is no appearance of it. *Il n'y paraît plus*, there remains no trace of it, it does not show any more

Parajour, *s.m.* awning (*in a panorama*)

Paralipomènes, *s.m.pl.* Chronicles; (*fig.*) paralipomena, supplement, appendix

Paralipse, *s.f.* (*rhet.*) paralipsis, paraleipsis

Parallactique, *adj.* (*astr.*) parallactic

Parallaxe, *s.f.* (*astr.*) parallax

Parallèle, *adj.* parallel; comparative, compared; — *s.f.* (*geom.*, *fort.*) parallel; — *s.m.* (*astr.*, *geog.*) parallel; (*instr.*) parallel ruler; (*fig.*) parallel, comparison, simile

Parallèlement, *adv.* parallelly, parallel; comparatively [parallelepiped, parallelopiped

Parallélépipède, Parallélipipède, *s.m.*

Parallélique, *adj.* parallelistic

Parallélisme, *s.m.* parallelism; correspondence, similitude

Parallélogrammatique, *adj.* *V.* page 3, § 1

Parallélogramme, *s m.* parallelogram

Parallélographe, *s.m.* parallel ruler

Paralogisme, &c. *V.* page 3, § 1

Paralyser, *v.a.* to paralyze. *Se* —, to become paralyzed; to paralyze each other

Paralysie, *s.f.* paralysis, palsy. *Attaque de —,* paralytic stroke
Paralytique, *adj. s.m.f.* paralytic
Paraménie, *s.f.* (*med.*) paramenia
Paramètre, *s.m.* parameter
Parangon, *s.m.* paragon; comparison; flawless stone; — *adj.* without a flaw, flawless
Parangonner, *v.a.* (*print.*) to range
Parant, e, *adj.* adorning, ornamental, dressy
Parapet, *s.m.* parapet; breastwork
Paraphe, Parapher. *V.* **Parafe, Parafer**
Paraphernal, e, *adj.* (*law*) paraphernal. *Biens paraphernaux,* paraphernal property, paraphernalia [(*law*) paraphernalia
Paraphernal, *s.m.,* **Paraphernaux,** *s.m.pl.*
Paraphernalité, *s.f.* (*law*) paraphernality
Paraphimosis, *s.m.* (*surg.*) paraphimosis
Paraphonie, *s.f.* paraphonia
Paraphrase, *s.f.* paraphrase; commentary; wrong interpretation; amplification; exaggeration [ment; to amplify
Paraphraser, *v.a.n.* to paraphrase; to com-
Paraphraseu-r, se, *s.m.f.* paraphraser; am-
Paraphraste, *s.m.* paraphrast [plifier
Paraphrast-ique, -iquement. *V.* page 3,
Paraplégie, *s.f.* (*med.*) paraplegia [§ 1
Parapluie, *s.m.* umbrella. — *à canne,* umbrella walking-stick. *Canne* or *manche de —,* umbrella-stick [sang
Parasange, *s.f* (*anc. meas. of distance*) para-
Parasélène, *s.f.* (*astr.*) paraselene, mock moon
Parasitaire, *adj.* parasitic
Parasite, *s.m.f.* parasite; hanger-on; sycophant; — *adj.* parasitic; sycophantic; superfluous; redundant [stroying
Parasiticide, *adj.* parasiticidal, parasite-de-
Parasitifère, *adj.* parasitiferous [3, § 1
Parasit-ique, -iquement, -isme. *V.* page
Parasol, †Parasoleil, *s.m.* parasol
Paratonnerre, *s.m.* lightning-conductor
Parâtre, *s.m* (*obsolete*) step-father; cruel *or* barbarous father
Paravent, *s.m.* screen, folding-screen. *Chinois de —,* grotesque figure; guy. *Comédie de —,* amateur theatricals *or* performance
Parbleu, *int.* well! why! now! indeed! to be sure! why to be sure! ay! of course!
Parc, *s.m.* park; pen; fold, coop, cot, sheep-walk, walk; pasture-land; field; ground; vivarium, vivary; preserve; bed, breeding-ground (*for oysters, mussels,* &c.); fishery, fishing-weir, weir, stakes; salt-pit, brine-pit; skittle-ground; (*nav.*) locker; dockyard. — *aux cerfs,* (*Fr. hist.*) King Louis XV.'s harem
Parcage, *s.m.* penning; folding; bedding;
Parceau, *s.m. V.* **Matteau** [parking; walk
Parcellaire, *adj.* in *or* by (small) portions, in detail, detailed; — *s.m.* register of a survey made in detail
Parcelle, *s.f.* portion, part, particle, driblet
Parcellement, *s.m.* parcelling out
Parceller, *v.a.* to parcel out, to parcel
Parce que, *conj. s.m.* because; as
Par ce que, (*in three words*) by that which, by what, from what
Parchasser, *v.a.* to hunt down
Parchemin, *s.m.* parchment; skin; **—s,** *pl.* parchments, deeds, titles of nobility. *Allonger* or *étendre le —,* to lengthen deeds uselessly, to multiply writings
Parcheminé, e, *adj.* parchment-like
Parcheminerie, *s.f.* parchment-making *or* trade *or* works *or* factory
Parcheminier, *s.m.* parchment-maker
Parcimonie, *s.f.* parsimony [sparingly
Parcimonieusement, *adv.* parsimoniously,
Parcimonieu-x, se, *adj.* parsimonious, sparing
Parcourir, *v.a.* to travel over; to go *or* run over; to go through; to run about; (— *des yeux*) to survey; to look *or* glance over; to read over
Se —, *v.r.* to be gone over, &c.
Parcours, *s.m.* line; distance; length; course; journey; road, way; beat; commonage. *Faire le —,* to run, to ply [Portuguese lynx
Pard, *s.m. Chat- —,* serval, bush-cat, tiger-cat,
Parde, *s.m. Chat- —,* panther
Par-delà, Par-derrière, Par-devant, Par-dessous, Par-dessus, &c., (*prep., adv.*) *V.* **Delà, Derrière,** &c., &c.
Pardessus, *s.m.* overcoat, great-coat
Pardi, Pardienne, Pardieu, Pardine, *int. V.* **Parbleu**
Pardon, *s.m.* pardon, forgiveness; indulgence; condonation. — ! excuse me! I beg your pardon! please!
Pardonnable, *adj.* pardonable, excusable
Pardonner, *v.a.n.* to forgive; to pardon; to condone; to excuse; not to grudge; to spare; to be cured. *Dieu me pardonne!* I really believe! really! [to be forgiven *or* &c.
Se —, *v.r.* to forgive oneself *or* each other;
Pardonneu-r, se, *s.m.f.* forgiver; — *adj.* for-
Pare, *s.m. V.* **Mésange** [giving
Paréage, *s.m.* (*feud. law*) parage
Pareaux, *s.m.pl.* weights (*of a fishing-net*)
Parégorique, *adj.m.f., s.m.* (*med.*) paregoric
†Pareil, le, *adj.* alike; like, similar; such; equal; like this, like that, like it; the same; to correspond (with), to match; — *s.m.f.* like; equal; match; peer; fellow; — *s.m. Du —,* the like of it, something *or* anything like it (*or* like this *or* that); — *s.f. La —e,* the like, like treatment, like for like, the same; the same way; **—s, —les,** *s.m.f.pl.* equals; kind. *Sans —, V.* **Égal** (*Sans égal*). *Rendre la —e,* to do the same; to give like for like; to pay (*one*) back in his own coin; to give tit for tat; to retaliate
†Pareillement, *adv.* similarly, in the same manner; likewise, also, too
Parélie, *s.m. V.* **Parhélie**
Parelle, *s.f.* (*bot.*) parella
Parement, *s.m.* ornament; facing; cuff; altar-cloth; cloth, cover; kerb-stone, kerb, curb-stone, curb; (*of fagots*) large stick; (*butch.*) caul [facings *or* cuffs, to ornament
Parementer, *v.a.* to face; to adorn with
Parenchymateu-x, se, *adj.* parenchymatous
Parenchyme, *s.m.* (*anat., bot.*) parenchyma
Parent, e, *s.m.f.* relation, relative; kinsman; kinswoman; **—s,** *s.m.pl.* (male) relations, &c.; parents (*father and mother*); friends, family, kindred; — *adj.m.f.* related. *Grands —s,* heads of the family, nearest relatives; grand-parents
Parentage, *s.m.* parentage, relationship
Parenté, *s.f.* relationship, kindred; consanguinity; relations, family. — *spirituelle,* spiritual paternal relation (*of godfather or godmother*), spiritual paternity *or* maternity
Parenthèse, *s. f.* parenthesis; digression. *Entre —s,* in a parenthesis. *Par —,* parenthetically, by way of parenthesis, by the way
Parer, *v.a.n.* to adorn, to deck, to set off; to dress, to dress out *or* up, to attire; to trim; to pare; to prepare, to get ready; to clear; to ward off; to parry; to screen, to protect, to shelter; to guard (against); to provide (against); to obviate; to meet, to supply, to satisfy; to ripen; (*rid.*) to stop
Se —, *v.r.* to adorn *or* &c. oneself; to boast (of), to make a boast *or* a show (of); to plume oneself (on); to assume, to put on [*commerce*)
Parère, *s.m.* advice, opinion of merchants (*in*
Parésie, *s.f.* (*med.*) paralysis in which motion is lost but sensation remains unimpaired, akinesia
Paresse, *s.f.* idleness, laziness, sloth; sluggishness; slowness; indolence; weakness
Paresser, *v.n.* to idle, to give oneself up to idleness
Paresseusement, *adv.* idly, lazily, slothfully
Paresseu-x, se, *adj.* idle, lazy, slothful; sluggish; slow; indolent; careless; (*of the*

stomach) weak; (*of the bowels*) sluggish; — *s.m.f.* idle *or* lazy *or* &c. person *or* fellow *or* thing *or* creature, idler; sluggard; — *s.m.* [(*zool.*) sloth
Pareur, *s.m.* parer; finisher
Parfaire, *v.a.* to perfect, to complete, to finish
Parfaiseu-r, se, *s.m.f.* perfecter, finisher
Parfait, e, *adj.* perfect; complete; finished; accomplished; full; — *s.m.* perfection; (*gram.*) perfect tense, perfect; (*conf.*) parfait (*kind of ice*) [entirely; fully; altogether, quite; exactly
Parfaitement, *adv.* perfectly; completely,
Parfilage, *s.m.* unravelling, unweaving [weave
Parfiler, *v.a.* to unravel, to ravel out, to un-
Parfilure, *s.f.* ravellings, ravelling
Parfois, *adv.* sometimes, at times, occasionally, now and then
Parfond, *s.m.* (*fish.*) ground-net; ground-line
Parfondre, *v.a.* to fuse. *Se* —, to be fused
Parfum, *s.m.* perfume, scent, odour; fragrance; flavour; sweetness; sweets; incense; disinfectant, deodorizer [flavoury, savoury
Parfumé, e, *part. adj.* perfumed, scented;
Parfumer, *v.a.* to perfume, to scent; to sweeten; to fumigate; to disinfect, to deodorize
Parfumerie, *s.f.* perfumery
Parfumeu-r, se, *s.m.f.* perfumer
Parfumoir, *s.m.* perfuming-pan; fumigator
Pargasite, *s.f.* (*min.*) pargasite
Pargué, Parguenne, Parguienne, *int.* (*boorish*) *V.* **Parbleu**
Parhélie, *s.m.* (*astr.*) parhelion, mock sun
Pari, *s.m.* bet, wager; betting; match; stake. *Faire un* —, to lay a bet *or* wager *Tenir le* —,
Paria, *s.m.* pariah; outcast [to take the bet
Pariade, *s.f.* (*of partridges*) pairing; pairing-
Pariage, *s.m.* (*feud. law*) parage [time; pair
Parien, ne, *adj. s.* Parian
Parier, *v.a.n.* to bet, to lay, to wager; to lay a wager; to undertake to say, to dare say, to undertake to predict, to be almost certain. — *pour quelqu'un*, to back a person. *Il y a à* —, the odds are. *Il y a dix à — contre un, il y a gros à* —, the odds are ten to one, it is ten to one (that) [pellitory
Pariétaire, *s.f.* (*bot.*) parietary, wall-pellitory,
Pariétal, e, *adj.* parietal; — *s.m.* parietal bone
Pariétine, *s.f.* (*chem.*) parietine
Parieu-r, se, *s.m.f.* better, betting man *or* woman, wagerer; — *adj.* betting [lacine
Parigline, *s.f.* (*chem.*) parigline, parilline, smi-
Paripenné, e, Paripinné, e, *adj.* (*bot.*) paripinnate
Paris, *s.m.* Paris. *Monsieur de* —, Jack Ketch. *Premier-* —, (*of Paris newspapers*) leading article, leader. — *ne s'est pas fait en un jour*, (*Proverb*) Rome was not built in a day
Parisette, *s.f.* (*bot.*) true-love, herb-paris, paris
Parisianisme, *s.m.* Parisianism
Parisien, ne, *adj. s.m.f.* Parisian; — *s.f.* Parisian fashion; (*song*) parisienne; (*print. type*) pearl; (*workman's*) overalls (*trousers*)
Parisiole, Parisiolle, *s.f.* (*bot.*) trillium
Parisis, *adj.* (*of coins, obsolete*) of Paris. *V.* **Livre,** *s.f.* [syllabic
Parisyllabe, Parisyllabique, *adj.* pari-
Parité, *s.f.* parity; likeness; equality; evenness; comparison, simile, parallel
Parjure, *s.m.* perjury; — *s.m.f.* perjurer; — *adj.* perjured, forsworn; perfidious
Parjurer, *v.a.* to perjure, to forswear; — *v.n.*, **Se** —, *v.r.* to perjure *or* forswear oneself
Parkie, *s.f.* (*bot.*) parkia, locust-tree
Parkinsonie, *s.f.* (*bot.*) parkinsonia [palaver
Parlage, *s.m.* prattle; talk; twaddle, gabble;
Parlant, e, *adj.* speaking; talkative, chatty; expressive; a speaking likeness; (*her.*) canting — *s.m.f.* one that can speak (*in contradistinction to one that is dumb*)
Parlement, *s.m.* parliament; court
Parlementage, *s.m.* (*old*) parleying, parley
Parlementaire, *adj.* parliamentary; courteous, civil; (*hist.*) parliamentarian; — *s.m.* (bearer of a) flag of truce; (*hist.*) parliamentarian. *Bâtiment* or *vaisseau* —, cartel-ship, cartel, flag of truce. *Pavillon* —, flag of truce
Parlementairement, *adv.* parliamentarily
Parlementarisme, *s.m.* parliamentarism, parliamentarianism [parley; to come to terms
Parlementer, *v.n.* to parley, to come to a
Parler, *v.a.n.* to speak; to talk; to converse; to talk about; to mention; to say, to tell; to apply; to bark. *A* —, to speak; something to say. *Sans — de*, without mentioning, to say nothing of, besides. *Apprendre à* —, to learn *or* teach how to speak *or* how to behave, to learn *or* teach better manners. *Faire — quelqu'un*, to make one speak, to compel one to speak; to let one speak (to ...) *or* see (...); to make one say what he did not say; &c. (*V.* **Faire**). *Trouver à qui* —, to find someone to talk to; to find o.'s match. *Parlez-moi de cela!* that is something! *Ne m'en parlez pas!* I can vouch for that! *Moi qui vous parle*, I myself, now I [other; to be spoken
Se —, *v.r.* to speak to oneself *or* to each
Parler, *s.m.* speaking, speech, language, manner of speaking; accent; talk; dialect. *Franc* —, freedom of speech, liberty of speaking. *Avoir son franc* —, to be free-spoken, to speak freely, to speak o.'s mind; to have the liberty of saying what one thinks
Parlerie, *s.f.* chatter, babbling
Parleu-r, se, *s.m.f.* talker; speaker; — *adj.* talking, talkative; speaking
Parli-er, ère, *adj.* (*obsolete*) talkative
Parloir, *s.m.* parlour
Parlote, *s.f.* resort of gossips; gossiping circle; exercise in pleading, debating-society
Parloter, *v.n.* to chat, to talk; to twaddle; to practise pleading *or* discussion
Parloterie, *s.f.* idle talk, twaddle
Parloteu-r, se, *s.m.f.* talker, twaddler
Parmélie, *s.f.* (*bot.*) parmelia
Parmesan, e, *adj. s.m.f.* Parmesan; — *s.m.* Parmesan cheese [with
Parmi, *prep* among, amongst; amid, amidst;
Parnassides, *s.f.pl.* (*myth.*) Muses [nassus
Parnassie, *s.f.* (*bot.*) parnassia, grass of Par-
Parnassien, ne, *adj. s.m.f.* Parnassian; — *s.m.* parnassius (*butterfly*)
Parod-ie, -ique, -iste. *V.* page 3, § 1
Parodier, *v.a.* to parody. *Se* —, to be parodied
Parodontis, *s.f.* (*surg.*) parodontis
Paroi, *s.f.* side; inner side; casing; wall, partition; (*anat.*) coat; (*vet.*) hoof
Paroir, *s.m.* (*instr.*) parer; scraper
Paroisse, *s.f.* parish; parish-church; parish-
Paroissial, e, *adj.* parochial, parish [ioners
Paroissien, ne, *s.m.f.* parishioner; (*pop.*) fellow, cove, fish, creature; — *s.m.* prayer-book
Parole, *s.f.* word; speech; language; discourse; talk; conversation; voice; tone; manner of speaking; saying; eloquence; right *or* permission (*or* leave) *or* turn to speak; promise; trust; parole. — *d'honneur*, word of honour; upon my word, upon my honour. *Adresser la — à*, to address, to speak to. *Avoir la* —, to be allowed to speak; to speak in o.'s turn; to be speaking. *Avoir le don de la* —, to speak well *or* fluently. *Céder la* —, to give up o.'s turn to speak. *Couper la — à*, to interrupt; to cut short; to silence. *Demander la* —, to ask leave to speak, to ask to speak. *Donner la* —, to grant permission to speak. *Donner sa* —, to give o.'s word. *Être de* —, to be as good as o.'s word, to keep o.'s word. *Être homme de* —, to be a man of o.'s word. *Manquer de* —, *manquer à sa* —, to break *or* forfeit o.'s word. *Ôter* or *retirer la — à* ..., to withdraw from ... the permission to speak. *Perdre la* —, to lose the use of o.'s tongue. *Porter la* —, to speak, to be the spokesman. *Prendre la* —, to begin to speak; to address the (*or* a) meeting *or* the house. *Rendre la — à*, to give back to (...) the

permission to speak. *Rendre à quelqu'un sa* —, to release one from his word. *Reprendre la* —, to speak again, to resume o.'s speech. *Reprendre sa* —, to withdraw *or* recall o.'s word. *Se prendre de* —*s*, to have words. *Tenir* —, to keep o.'s word, to be as good as o.'s word

Paroli, *s.m.* (*at play*) double stake. *Faire* —, to double. *Faire* or *donner* or *rendre le* — *à*, (*fig.*) to outdo [writer, writer

Paroli-er, ère, *s.m.f.* song-writer, opera-

Paronomase, *s.f.* paronomasia [whitlow

‡**Paronychie,** *s.f.* (*med.*) paronychia, onychia,

Paronyme, *adj.* paronymous; — *s.m.* paronym

Paronym-ie, -ique. *V.* page 3, § 1

Paronyque, *s.f.* (*bot.*) whitlow-grass

Parotide, *s.f.* (*anat.*) parotis, parotid; (*med.*) parotid tumour; — *adj.* parotid

Parotidien, ne, *adj.* (*anat.*) parotid. *Canal* —, Stenonian duct

Parotidite, Parotite, *s.f.* (*med.*) parotitis

Paroxyntique, *adj.* (*med.*) paroxysmal

Paroxysme, *s.m.* paroxysm; height

Paroxyste, *s m.f.* sensation novelist [stone

†**Parpaigne,** *adj.f.* *Pierre* —, (*build.*) bond-

†**Parpaillot, e,** *s.m.f.* Calvinist, heretic; miscreant, infidel

Parpaing, *s.m.* (*build.*) bond-stone, perpender

Parque, *s.f.* (*myth.*) Parca, Fate, fatal sister; Death

Parquer, *v.a.* to pen up (*cattle*); to fold (*sheep*); to bed (*oysters, mussels, &c.*); to lodge, to place; to surround, to enclose; to shut up; (*artil.*) to park; — *v.n.*, **Se** —, *v.r.* to lodge; to surround oneself; to be pent up *or* &c.

Parquet, *s.m.* bench, bar (*of a court of justice*); parquet (*office of the public prosecutor in France; also, the public prosecutor and his officers*), body of magistrates, crown-office; enclosure; chancel; (*in the stock-exchange*) reserved enclosure; (*theat., obsolete*) orchestra (*place*); (*of rooms*) parquet, French floor, inlaid floor, floor, flooring; (*of a looking-glass*) back; (*nav.*) locker. *Tenir le* —, (*law*) to hold a sitting in court [French flooring

Parquetage, *s.m.* parquetage, inlaid flooring,

Parqueter, *v.a.* to floor, to board; to inlay

Parqueterie, *s.f.* parquetry, inlaid flooring

Parqueteur, *s.m.* floor-layer

Parqueur, *s.m.* oyster-bed keeper

Parrain, *s.m.* godfather, sponsor; introducer; (*formerly, in duels*) second

Parrainage, *s.m.* parental relation *or* state of godfather *or* godmother

Parricide, (*murder*) *s.m.*, (*pers.*) *s.m.f.* parricide; matricide; murder; — *adj.* parricidal; matri-

Parse, *s. adj.* *V.* **Parsi** [cidal; murderous

Parsemer, *v.a.* to strew; to spread; to sprinkle; to stud; to dot

Se —, *v.r.* to become *or* be strewn, &c.

Parsi, e, *adj. s.* Parsee

Part, *s.f.* part; share, portion; hand; side; place; concern, interest; sense. — *à deux!* halves! *A* —, apart; separate, distinct; separately; aside; by; except; exceptional, peculiar, particular; special. *A — soi*, to *or* within oneself, inwardly; tacitly; secretly. *Autre* —, elsewhere, somewhere else, in another (*or* some other) place; anywhere else. *D'autre* —, from another quarter; on the other hand; besides, moreover. *De — et d'autre*, on both sides; on all sides. *De — en* —, through, through and through, right through; right across. *De toute* —, *de toutes* —*s*, on all sides, in all directions. *De la — de*, on the part of, on ...'s part, in ...'s name, from; of. *De ma* —, from me. *Nulle* —, nowhere; anywhere. *Nulle autre* —, nowhere else; anywhere else. *Quelque* —, somewhere; anywhere. *Quelque — où* or *que*, wherever. *Lettre* or *billet de faire* —, *lettre* or *billet de* —, circular (*note to announce a birth, marriage, or death*), wedding-card, funeral letter; invitation. *Avoir — à*, to have a share in, to share in; to partake of; to participate in; to contribute to. *Entrer en* —, *être de* —, to share (with), to go shares (with), to have a share (in). *Faire — à quelqu'un de*, to share with one; to make one acquainted with, to acquaint one with, to inform *or* apprise one of; to impart *or* communicate to one. *Faire la — de*, to make allowance for, to allow for; to give (...) its due share; to take into consideration *or* into account. *Faire la — du feu*, (*fig.*) to allow for necessary losses. *Mettre de* —, to give a share (*in a business or concern*), to take as a *or* o.'s partner. *Prendre — à*, to participate in, to be concerned in; to partake of. *Prendre en bonne* or *en mauvaise* —, to take in good *or* ill part, to take well *or* amiss; to use in a good *or* in a bad sense. *Tenir* or *savoir de bonne* —, to have from good authority

Part, *s.m.* (*law*) parturition, delivery, birth, child, infant. *Suppression de* —, concealment of birth. *Supposition de* —, passing off one child for another

Partage, *s.m.* division; partition; portioning, portionment; share, portion, lot; gift

Partagé, e, *part. adj.* divided, &c. (*V.* **Partager**); reciprocal, requited. *Bien* —, (*pers.*) well portioned, well treated, well off. *Mal* —, (*pers.*) ill portioned, hardly treated, hard-

Partageable, *adj.* divisible [favoured, badly off

Partageant, e, *s.m.f.* sharer

Partager, *v.a.n.* to divide; to share; to portion; to favour; to split; to partake of; to participate in; to be the partner of

Se —, *v.r.* to divide, to share; to be divided; to divide o.'s time *or* care *or* affection [**tageux**

Partageu-r, se, *s.m.f.* sharer; (*pop.*) *V.* **Par-**

Partageu-x, se, *s.m.f.* (*pop.*) communist, agrarian; kept mistress

Partance, *s.f.* (*nav.*) sailing, departure. *En* —, on the point of sailing *or* of departure, preparing *or* ready to start. *V.* **Coup**

Partant, *part.* departing, starting, &c. (*V.* **Partir**); — *s.m.* departer; — *adv.* (*obsolete*) consequently, hence, therefore, thus, and so, of course

Partenaire, *s.m.f.* partner (*at play, dancing*)

Partènement, *s.m.* brine-pit

Parterre, *s.m.* flower-bed, bed, garden-plot, plot, flower-garden, parterre; (*theat.*) pit; pitful; (*fig.*) audience, public. — *d'eau*, water-compartment. — *de gazon*, grass-plot. *Prendre un billet de* —, to take a ticket for the pit; (*pop.*) to fall on the ground, to fall down

Parthe, *s.m.f. adj.* Parthian

Parthénologie, *s.f.* (*med.*) parthenology

Parthénon, *s.m.* (*Gr. antiq.*) Parthenon

Parthénope, *s.f.* (*myth., astr.*) Parthenope; (*zool.*) parthenope [nopean (*Neapolitan*)

Parthénopéen, ne, *adj. s.* (*obsolete*) Parthe-

Parthique, *adj.* Parthian

Parti, e, *part. adj.* departed, &c. (*V.* **Partir,** *v.n.*); gone; come; coming, proceeding; tipsy; asleep; (*V.* **Partir,** *v.a.*) parted, divided; (*bot.*) partite; (*her.*) party

Parti, *s.m.* party; side; part; resolution, determination; offer, condition; way, means, course; expedient; utility, advantage; profession; (*for marriage*) match; (*obsolete*) contract. — *pris*, settled determination; foregone conclusion; prepossession, prejudice. *De — pris*, deliberately; resolutely. *Faire un mauvais — à quelqu'un*, to do one harm, to ill-use anyone, to be at anyone. *Prendre* —, to enlist; to side (with *or* against); to declare oneself. *Prendre son* —, to make up o.'s mind; to resign oneself; to take o.'s own course; to take o.'s resolution; (*of someone else*) to take his *or* her part. *Prendre un* —, to take a course *or* a resolution. *Tirer — de*, to make something of, to turn to account, to derive advantage from, to take advantage of, to make use of, to use, to utilize

Partiaire, *adj. Colon* or *fermier* —, farmer who gives part of the produce as his rent
Partial, e, *adj.* partial
Partialement, *adv.* partially, with partiality
Partialité, *s.f.* partiality; bias
Partible, *adj.* partible [lium)
Partibus (In), (*of bishops*) in partibus (infide-
Participant, e, *adj. s.* participating; participant; sharer
Participati-f, ve, *adj.* participative
Participation, *s.f.* participation; share; knowledge; partnership
Participativement, *adv.* participatively
Participe, *s.m.* (*gram.*) participle [share
Participer, *v.n.* to participate, to partake, to
Participial, e, *adj.* (*gram.*) participial
Participialement, *adv.* participially [particle
Particulaire, *adj.* (*gram.*) particular, of the
Particularisation, *s.f.* particularization
Particulariser, *v.a.* to particularize
Se —, *v.r.* to become particularized
Particular-isme, -iste. *V* page 3, § 1
Particularité, *s.f.* particular, circumstance; particularity; peculiarity
Particule, *s.f* particle, the word "DE" before o.'s name (*formerly a mark of nobility in France*), title, nobility
Particuli-er, ère, *adj.* particular; peculiar; appropriate; special; specific; express; private; personal; intimate
Particulier, *s.m.* particular; individual, private man, private individual; fellow; civilian. *Simple* —, private individual; private gentleman; privacy; private life. *En* —, in private, privately; in particular. *En son* —, in private; alone; at home; for o.'s part
Particulière, *s.f.* private lady, independent woman; (*fam.*) woman, girl, body, creature; sweetheart [liarly; specially
Particulièrement, *adv.* particularly; pecu-
Partie, *s.f.* part; party; match; game; heat; excursion; trip; line of business, line; business; affair; project, plan, scheme; side; client; adversary; quality; (*com.*) lot; (*old*) sum; article; bill; (*rid.*) start; (*adverb.*) partly, in part. — *carrée*, party of two men and two women, party of four. — *civile*, plaintiff. — *double*, double game, rubber; (*book-keep.*) double-entry. — *fine*, junket. — *liée*, rubber; (*horse-racing*) running heats, heats. — *publique*, public prosecutor, crown side. — *simple*, (*book-keep.*) single-entry. — *d'honneur*, (*play*) winning game, conqueror, rubber. — *de plaisir*, pleasure trip; entertainment. *En* —, partly, in part. *En grande* —, in a great measure. *Faire* — *de*, to form *or* be part of; to make one of; to belong to; to be on. *Faire la* —, to play. *Faire une* — *de*, to play a game at, to have *or* play a ... match; to go on a ... party *or* trip *or* excursion. *Prendre à* —, to sue; to lay the blame on; to turn round upon; to attack, to set on; to take to task. *Se porter* — *contre*, (*law*) to appear against
Partiel, le, *adj.* partial
Partiellement, *adv.* partially, in part
Partir, *v.n.* to depart; to set out; to go, to leave; to start; to go *or* get away; to be off; to go off; to dart; to rise; to spring; to proceed; to flow; to arise; to issue; to come; to begin; to go into the army. *A* — *de*, from; beginning *or* reckoning from. *Faire* —, to send away *or* off; to despatch; to start; to get away; to let off; to spring. *Laisser* —, to let go; to let off. — *d'un éclat de rire*, to burst out laughing, to burst into a fit of laughter
Partir, *v.a.* (*old*) to part, to divide
Partir, *s m.* starting; start; going; leaving
Partisan, e, *s.m.f.* partisan; adherent; stickler; favourer; friend; (*Fr. hist.*) farmer of the revenue, contractor; — *adj.* partial (to), favourable (to), in favour (of)
Partite, *adj.* (*bot.*) partite [partitive
Partiti-f, ve, *adj.*, **Partitif,** *s.m.* (*gram.*)
Partition, *s.f.* partition; division; (*mus.*) partition, score; musical composition; (*her.*)
Partner, *s.m V.* **Partenaire** [partition
Partout, *adv.* everywhere; anywhere, on all sides; all over; about. — *où*, wherever
Parturition, *s.f.* parturition [published, out
Paru, e, *part. adj* appeared, &c. (*V.* **Paraître**);
Parulie, *s.f* (*med*) parulis, gum-boil
Parure, *s.f.* attire, dress, finery; ornament; set-off; trappings; (*of gems*) set; (*tech.*) paring; (*butch.*) suet, rough fat
Parvenir, *v.n.* to arrive; to reach; to attain; to get (at); to come; to gain access; to obtain; to succeed; to manage; to rise; to get on; to make o.'s way in the world, to make o.'s fortune; to come to hand; to come to ...'s ears, to reach the ears of. *Faire* —, to forward, to send
Parvenu, e, *part. adj.* arrived, &c. (*V.* **Parvenir**); risen from obscurity *or* from the ranks; successful; — *s.m.f.* upstart, parvenu; snob
Parviflore, *adj.* (*bot.*) parviflorous
Parvis, *s.m.* parvise, open space (*in front of the door of a church*), area, cathedral-yard, court; (*poet.*) enclosure; hall. *Sacrés* —, — *sacrés*, sacred enclosure; church; temple. *Célestes* [—, Heavens
Parvoline, *s.f.* (*chem.*) parvoline
Pas, *s.m.* step; pace; rate; footstep, foot; footing; foot-pace; foot-print; tramp; yard; stride; walk; march; dance; progress, precedence; preeminence; pains, trouble, labour; threshold; passage; pass, defile, strait, straits; (*of a screw*) furrow, channel. — *seul*, dance by one dancer. — *d'âne*, (*rid*) sharp bridle-bit; (*vet.*) balling-iron; (*bot.*) colt's-foot. — *d'armes*, passage-at-arms, passage of arms. — *de charge*, — *accéléré*, quick pace *or* time, quick march. — *de clerc*, blunder; miss; piece of folly. — *de course*, running pace, double quick pace *or* time. — *de haie*, stile. *A grands* —, with great strides; at a great pace, fast. *A* — *comptés* or *mesurés*, with measured steps; with circumspection, cautiously. *A* — *de loup*, softly, stealthily, without noise. *Au* —, walking, at a walk, at a walking pace, at a foot-pace; keeping time, in time; (*of behaviour*) right, properly, well. *Au petit* —, at a slow pace, slowly. *A petits* —, with short steps. *De ce* —, now, directly, immediately. *Faux* —, false *or* wrong step; stumble; fault, slip; error; mistake. *Mauvais* —, — *difficile*, awkward road; scrape, difficulty, bad plight, awkward *or* dangerous position. *Mauvais* —, (*obsolete*) wrong step. *Aller* or *marcher au* —, to walk; to march at a walk; to ride at a foot-pace; to keep time. *Avoir le* — *sur*, to take *or* have precedence of. *Mettre au* —, to make (...) pace; to bring to o.'s duty, to put on o.'s good behaviour. *Passer* or *sauter* or *franchir le* —, to hop the twig, to kick the bucket; to take the leap; to take a resolution. *Prendre le* —, to slacken to a foot-pace; to keep time, to keep the step. *Prendre le* — *sur*, to take precedence of; to outstrip, to outrun. *Retourner sur ses* —, to retrace o.'s steps, to go back. *Revenir sur ses* —, to retrace o.'s steps, to come back; to return directly; to back out; (*hunt.*) to double
Pas, *adv.* any; not; never; no, not any
Pasan, *s.m.* (*zool.*) gems-boc
Pascal, e, *adj.* paschal
Pascaline, *s.f.* (*adject., Roue* —) pascaline, Pascal's calculating-machine
Pasigraph-ie, -ique. *V.* page 3, § 1
Paspale, *s.m.* (*bot.*) paspalum [lampoon
Pasquin, *s.m.* Pasquin; lampooner; flunkey;
Pasquinade, *s.f.* pasquinade; lampoon
Pasquiniser, *v.a.n.* to pasquinade, to lampoon, to satirize [decent
Passable, *adj.* passable, tolerable, middling;
Passablement, *adv.* passably, tolerably; so so; decently; a tolerable amount *or* quantity
Passade, *s.f.* passage, short stay; passing; fancy, temporary connection; (*fenc., rid.*) passade; (*in swimming*) ducking, dip

Passage, *s.m.* passage; passing; pass; crossing; transit; fare; toll; passage-money; visit; road, way; thoroughfare; gateway; archway; lane; court; arcade; buildings; opening; vent; change; transition; right of way; ferry; (*mus.*) passage; grace. *Lieu de* —, thoroughfare. *Au* —, on o.'s way. *Attendre* or *guetter au* —, to lie in wait for, to waylay, to wait for (*one*) on his way. *Barrer le* —, to stop the passage; to stop; to stand in the way (of). *Céder le* — *à*, to let (...) pass first. *Livrer* —, [to make way

Passager, *v.a.n.* (*rid.*) to passage

Passag-er, ère, *adj.* passing, of passage, migratory, travelling; transient; transitory; fleeting; short-lived; short; momentary; of a day; — *s.m.f.* passenger, traveller; ferryman, ferrywoman [siently

Passagèrement, *adv.* for a short time, tran-

Passant, e, *part. adj.* passing, &c. (*V.* **Passer**); (*her.*) passant; (*of roads*) public, open to the public; frequented; (*of colours*) fading; — *s.m.f.* person walking in the street, passenger, passer-by, wayfarer, traveller. *Chemin* —, *rue* —*e*, thoroughfare. *Ce chemin est très* —, this is a great thoroughfare. *En* —, in passing; going along; when going by; by *or* on the way; temporarily; cursorily, hastily; slightly; incidentally; for once; for the nonce

Passation, *s.f.* (*law*) passing, executing (*of contracts*, &c.)

Passavant, *s.m.* (*cust.*) permit; (*nav.*) gangway

Passe, *s.f.* pass; situation, state, case; odd money; overplus; passage; fancy, temporary connection; channel; (*fenc.*) pass, thrust; (*at play*) stake; (*of certain games*) hoop, arch; (*of bonnets*) front; — *s.m.f.* (*in compounds*) thing *or* person that passes; — (*adverb.*) *V.* **Passer.** *La — du sac*, the price of the money-bag. *En — de, en belle — de*, in a fair way; in a fair way of getting. — **-avant,** *s.m. V.* **Passavant.** — **-campane,** *s.f.* (*vet.*) capellet. — **-carreau,** *s.m.* sleeve-board; (*jest.*) tailor. — **-cheval,** *s.m.* horse ferryboat. — **-cordon,** *s.m.* bodkin. — **-debout,** *s.m.* (*cust.*) permit for transit. — **-droit,** *s.m.* favour; injustice. — **-fleur,** *s.f. V.* **Coquelourde.** — **-lacet,** *s.m.* bodkin. — **-méteil,** *s.m.* meslin (*mixture of wheat and rye*). — **-parole,** *s.m.* pass-parole. — **-partout,** *s.m.* master-key, pass-key; latch-key; skeleton-key; (*fig.*) passport; (*kind of picture-frame, engr.*, &c.) passe-partout; (*brush for carriages*) spoke-brush; (*print.*) factotum; (*tech.*) compass-saw. — **-passe,** *s.m.* sleight of hand; (*game*) threading the tailor's needle; cherry-bob. *Tour de — -passe*, sleight of hand, juggle, juggling, hocus-pocus. — **-perle,** *s.m.* (fine) wire. — **-pied,** *s.m.* passe-pied (*dance, tune*). — **-pierre,** *s.f.* (*bot.*) samphire, sea-samphire, sea-fennel. — **-poil,** *s.m.* (*need.*) piping. —**port,** *s.m.* passport; pass. — **-rose,** *s.f.* (*bot.*) hollyhock. — **-temps,** *s.m.* pastime; sport. — **-thé,** *s.m.* tea-strainer. — **-velours,** *s.m.* (*bot.*) cockscomb, amaranth. — **-vin,** *s.m.* wine-strainer. — **-volant,** *s.m.* (*mil., nav.*) fagot, false muster; (*fig.*) intruder, interloper; parasite, sponger; bird of passage

Passé, e, *part. adj. prep.* passed, &c. (*V.* **Passer**); past; gone; bygone; former; dead; vanished; over; once past, once gone, once over; worn; out of use, disused; withered; faded; last; after; beyond; except

Passé, *s.m.* past; time past; past tense; past life. *Comme par le* —, as formerly, as before, as heretofore

Passée, *s.f.* passing; passage; track

Passefilage, *s.m.* darning

Passefiler, *v.a.* to darn

Passefilure, *s.f.* darning

Passement, *s.m.* lace, braid, trimming

Passementer, *v.a.* to lace, to braid, to trim

Passementerie, *s. f.* lace-work *or* trade, lacing, trimming-trade *or* business, trimming

Passementi-er, ère, *s.m.f.* laceman, trimming-maker *or* seller

Passeport, *s.m. See under* **Passe**

Passer, *v.n.a.* to pass; to pass by *or* on *or* over *or* through; to be a passer-by; to go by *or* over *or* through *or* off *or* on; to get over *or* out; to go; to come; to call; to pass away *or* off; to run over *or* through; to slide *or* glide away; to slip out; to come *or* peep out; to proceed; to turn; to become; to be promoted; to be brought (before) *or* indicted (at) *or* tried (by), to be brought up (for); to go down; to be handed down *or* transmitted; to digest; to be over; to subside; to fade; to die; to be spent; to be considered; to pass muster; to cross; to put; to hand, to give; to hand down; to exceed; to be *or* go beyond; to carry *or* take over; to ferry over; to leave out, to omit, to miss; to look (over), to overlook; to waive; to surpass, to excel; to outstrip; to strain; to sift; to survive, to live out; to last; to allow; to grant; to forgive; to gratify; to set; to thrust; to slip; to put on, to slip on; to run; to draw; to enter into, to make; to vent; to visit; to spend *or* pass (*time*); to while away (*time*); (— *mal son* or *le temps*, to have a bad time of it); (*com.*) to put in, to carry; to endorse (*to another*); to let have, to sell, to charge for; (*tech.*) to dress. — *chez*, to call upon *or* at (...'s). — *là-dessus*, to pass over this *or* that; to forgive *or* overlook this *or* that *or* it; to say nothing about it *or* that. — *pour*, to pass for, to be considered *or* thought *or* reputed. *En — par*, to submit to. *Faire* —, to make (...) pass *or* &c.; to let in, to introduce; to admit; to pass; to pass on; to pass off; to hand round; to forward; to convey; to bring; to infuse; to instil; to get over; to cure; to remove; to do away with; to stop; to while away. *Y* —, to pass by *or* through it (*or* them), &c.; to go for it; to die. *Passe! passe pour cela!* be it so! let that pass! well and good! it may be well enough; never mind. *Passons*, let us pass *or* &c.; I will not insist. *Cela me passe*, that is beyond my comprehension, I can't understand that (*or* it). *On ne passe pas!* no thoroughfare! no admittance! stop there!

Se —, *v.r.* to pass *or* &c. each other *or* to each other; to forgive oneself *or* each other; to be forgiven *or* &c.; to pass, to pass away *or* off; to elapse; to fall off; to fade; to end; to be spent; to go off; to happen, to take place, to be going on; to do (without), to dispense (with); to abstain (from); (*old*) to be satisfied *or* contented (with). *Se — de*, to do without, to dispense with; to forego; to abstain from; (*old*) to be satisfied with

Passerage, *s.f.* (*bot.*) pepper-grass, pepperwort, dittander, garden cress [passerine

Passereau, *s.m.* sparrow; passerine bird,

Passerelle, *s.f.* foot-bridge; (*nav.*) gangway-

†**Passerille,** *s.m.* raisin [ladder

Passerine, *s.f.* (*bot.*) sparrow-wort; (*zool.*) rice-bird, rice-bunting

Passette, *s.f.* band, elastic band; colander

Passeu-r, se, *s.m.f.* ferryman, ferrywoman; (*rail.*) guard [liability

Passibilité, *s.f.* passibility, passibleness;

Passible, *adj.* passible; liable (to), punishable

Passi-f, ve, *adj.* passive [(by)

Passif, *s.m.* debts, liabilities; debtor; (*of the budget*) expenditure; (*gram.*) passive voice

Passiflore, *s.f.* (*bot.*) passion-flower

Passim, *adv.* (*Latin*) passim, here and there, in various places

Passion, *s.f.* passion; love; affection, fondness; prejudice; passing-bell; Passion sermon. *Souffrir mort et* —, to suffer excruciating pains

Passioniste, *s.m. adj.* passionist

Passionnaire, *s.m.* (*book*) passionary; — *s.f.* (*bot.*) passion-flower

Passionné, e, *adj.* impassioned; passionate;

passionately fond (of), doting (on); affectionate, fond, loving; zealous; warm; prejudiced
Passionnel, le, *adj* passional
Passionnément, *adv.* passionately, fondly
Passionner, *v.a.* to impassion; to animate; to interest powerfully
Se —, *v.r.* to become impassioned; to become enamoured *or* madly fond (of); to become vehement *or* animated, to be ardent; to have a strong desire; to take a lively interest; to fall into a passion
Passivement, *adv.* passively [sivity
Passiveté, Passivité, *s.f.* passiveness, pas-
Passoire, *s.f.* colander, cullender, strainer; sieve [—, brownish orange-colour
Pastel, *s.m.* pastel; woad; crayon. *Orangé-*
Pastenague, *s.f.* (*fish*) sting-ray, fire-flaire
Pastèque, *s.f.* water-melon
Pasteur, *s.m.* pastor; shepherd; minister, clergyman, parson; reverend
Pastiche, *s.m.* imitation, (*in Italian*) pasticcio
Pasticher, *v.a.* to imitate [sugar-paste work
†**Pastillage,** *s.m.* (*conf.*) device in sugar-paste,
†**Pastille,** *s.f.* pastille, pastil; lozenge, drop
†**Pastilleur,** *s.m.* paste-worker
Pastisson, *s.m.* (*bot.*) squash
Pastoral, e, *adj. s.* pastoral
Pastoralement, *adv.* pastorally
Pastorat, *s.m.* pastorate, pastorship
Pastoureau, *s.m.* shepherd-boy
Pastourelle, *s.f.* shepherd-girl; (*figure in dancing*) pastourelle [stalemate
Pat, *s.m.* stalemate (*at chess*). *Faire —,* to
Pât, *s.m.* dog's porridge; (*falc.*) food
Patache, *s.f.* stage-waggon, coach; boat, tender
Patafioler, *v.a.* (*fam.*) to confound, (*ironically*) to bless [(*Spanish coin*) pataca, patacoon
Patagon, e, *adj. s.m.f.* Patagonian; — *s.m.*
Patapouf, *s.m.* bloated fellow
Pataque, *s.f.* pataca (*coin of Algeria,* &c.)
Pataquès, Pataqu'est-ce, *s.m.* dreadful slip. *V.* **Cuir**
Patarafe, *s.f.* scrawl, scribbling; flourish, dash
Pataras, *s.m.* (*nav.*) swifter
Patard, *s.m.* (*old, fig.*) farthing, mite, doit
Patate, *s.f.* batatas, sweet potato; (*local, jest.*) potato, "tater"
Patati, Patata, *int.* chat, chat! tut, tut! pooh, pooh! *Monsieur et madame patati et patata,* fussy people
Patatras, *int.* slap! smack! bang!
Pataud, e, *adj. s.m.f.* clumsily made *or* done, clumsy, awkward; clumsy lout; — *s.m.* large-pawed puppy
Patauger, *v.n.* to dabble; to splash; to plunge *or* flounder about; to wade; to muddle; to make a mess *or* muddle (of it)
Patavinité, *s.f.* patavinity
Patchouli, *s.m.* patchouli, patchouly
Pate, *s.f.* (*old spelling*) *V.* **Patte**
Pâte, *s.f.* paste; dough; pulp; (*print.*) pie, pi; (*fig.*) constitution; nature; sort. *Mettre la main à la —,* to set to work oneself; to have a finger in the pie; to lay o.'s shoulder to the wheel
Pâté, *s.m.* pie; pasty; lump; block (*of houses,* &c.); blot (*of ink*); (*print.*) pie, pi; (*fort.*) pate. *Gros —,* (*pers.*) squabby child *or* fellow *or* creature. *Petit —,* patty
Pâtée, *s.f.* paste; hash of cats' and dogs' meat, dog's porridge; mess; (*pop.*) grub, victuals; blowing-up, thrashing
Patelin, e, *s.m.f. adj.* wheedler; wheedling
Patelinage, *s.m.* wheedling [skilfully
Pateliner, *v.n.a.* to wheedle; to manage
Patelinerie, *s.f.* wheedling
Patelineu-r, se, *s.m.f.* wheedler
Patelle, *s.f.* (*shell-fish*) limpet
Patemar, *s.m.* pattemar (*Indian boat*) [dently
Patemment, *adv.* patently, obviously, evi-
Patène, *s.f.* paten
Patenôtre, *s.f.* paternoster, Lord's prayer; prayer; silly words; chaplet, beads; bead; (*fish.*) corks [**Staphylier**
Patenôtrier, *s.m.* bead-maker; (*pop.*) *V.*
Patent, e, *adj.* patent; evident, obvious; —
Patentable, *adj.* licensable [*s.m.* patent axle
Patente, *s.f.* licence; (*nav.*) bill of health, bill; (*obsolete*) patent, letters patent; (*tech.*) patent axle. *— nette,* clean bill (of health). *— brute,* foul ditto
Patenté, e, *adj. s.* licensed; licensed dealer
Patenter, *v.a.* to license [bead (*of a chaplet*)
Pater, *s.m.* paternoster, Lord's prayer; large
Patère, *s.f.* patera; clothes-peg, peg; curtain-rest, curtain-pin, curtain-hook
Paterne, *adj.* (*jest.*) paternal
Paternel, le, *adj.* paternal; fatherly; of a *or* of o.'s father, father's; fostering; on the father's side
Paternellement, *adv.* paternally, fatherly
Paternité, *s.f.* paternity; fatherhood; fathership
Pâteu-x, se, *adj.* pasty; doughy; clammy, sticky; thick; sodden; muddy; greasy; foul
Pathétique, *adj.* pathetic; affecting, moving; — *s.m.* pathetic; pathos
Pathétiquement, *adv.* pathetically
Patho-génie, -génique, -gnomonique, -gnostique. *V.* page 3, § 1 [page 3, § 1
Patholog-ie, -ique, -iquement, -iste. *V.*
Pathopée, *s.f.* (*rhet.*) pathopœia
Pathos, *s.m.* bathos, bombast; (*obsolete*) pathos
Patibulaire, *adj.* patibulary; gallows, hanging, ruffianly; — *s.m.* (*obsolete*) gibbet, gallows.
Patiemment, *adv.* patiently [*V.* **Fourche**
Patience, *s.f.* patience; endurance; forbearance; button-cleaner; (*game*) puzzle; (*bot.*) patience, dock. *Jeu de —,* puzzle. *Prendre —,* to take *or* have patience. *Prendre en —,* to support *or* bear with patience
Patient, e, *adj.* patient; enduring; forbearing; — *s.m.f.* patient; sufferer; culprit *or* criminal (*about to be executed*)
Patienter, *v.n.* to have *or* take patience
Patin, *s.m.* skate; (*of boots*) clump; (*of horses*) patten-shoe; (*obsolete*) patten, clog; high-heeled shoe; snow-shoe; (*carp.*) sill, sole, plate; (*tech.*) slide. *Fer à —,* (*of horses*) patten-shoe. *Faire —,* (*of wheels*) to slide
Patinage, *s.m.* skating; (*of wheels*) sliding
Patine, *s.f.* (*fine arts*) patina
Patiner, *v.n.* to skate; (*of wheels*) to slide; — *v.a.* to handle, to paw, to fumble, to feel about; (*fine arts*) to cover with patina
Se —, *v.r.* to become *or* be covered with patina; (*nav.*) to be quick, to look sharp
Patineu-r, se, *s.m.f.* skater; handler, fumbler
Patinier, *s.m.* skate-maker
Patio, *s.m.* (*a Spanish word*) court
Pâtir, *v.n.* to suffer; to toil, to drudge
Patira, *s.m.* (*zool.*) collared peccary
Pâtira, Pâtiras, *s.m.* (*pop.*) fag; poor stick
Pâtis, *s.m.* pasture, pasture-ground
Pâtissage, *s.m.* pastry-making
Pâtisser, *v.n.* to make pastry
Pâtisserie, *s.f.* pastry; pastry-work *or* making *or* business; biscuit-baking *or* bakery
Pâtissi-er, ère, *s.m.f.* pastrycook; biscuit-baker. *Sale —,* (*fam.*) dirty fellow
Pâtissoire, *s.f.* pastry-board *or* table [boy
Pâtisson, *s.m.* (*bot.*) squash; (*local*) pastrycook's
Patmar, *s.m.* *V.* **Patemar**
Patoche, *s.f.* ferule; (*pop.*) hand, paw
Patois, *s.m.* patois, country *or* peasant's dialect; jargon, lingo, gibberish, rigmarole
Patois, e, *adj.* (*of language*) boorish [in patois
Patoiser, *v.n.* to talk patois; — *v.a.* to express
Pâton, *s.m.* fattening-ball; lump of dough; lump
†**Patouille,** *s.f.* (*metal.*) washing-apparatus
†**Patouiller,** *v.n.* *V.* **Patauger;** — *v.a.* to handle, to feel
†**Patouilleu-x, se,** *adj.* (*nav.*) *V.* **Clapoteux**
Patraque, *s.f.* bad watch; rubbish, duffer,

gimcrack; weakly person, worn-out person, weakling, poor stick; — *adj.* sickly, poorly, not strong, weakly; worn-out

Pâtre, *s.m.* herdsman, shepherd

Patres (Ad), *See Letter* **A**

Patriarcal, e, *adj.* patriarchal

Patriarcalement, *adv.* patriarchally

Patriarcat, *s.m.* patriarchate, patriarchship

Patriarche, *s.m.* patriarch

Patriarch-ie, -isme. *V.* page 3, § 1

Patrice, *s.m.* patrician

Patricial, e, *adj.* patrician

Patriciat, *s.m.* patriciate; order of patricians

Patricien, ne, *adj. s.* patrician, noble

Patrie, *s.f.* (native) country *or* land, fatherland; native place, birthplace; home

Patrimoine, *s.m.* patrimony; inheritance

Patrimonial, e, *adj.* patrimonial

Patrimonialement, *adv.* patrimonially

Patriote, *s.m.f. adj.* patriot; patriotic [3, § 1

Patriot-ique, -iquement, -isme. *V.* page

Patristique, *adj.* patristic [to lecture, to talk

Patrociner, *v.n.* (*old*) to patrocinate; to argue,

Patrolog-ie, -ique. *V.* page 3, § 1

Patron, *s.m.* patron; patron saint; employer; master; principal; governor; captain; coxswain; pattern, model; stencil, stencil-plate. — **-jaquet** *or* **-minet (Dès le),** *adv.* (*pop.*) very early in the morning, at dawn

Patronage, *s.m.* patronage; pattern-work

Patronal, e, *adj.* patronal. *Fête —e,* patron saint's day

Patronat, *s.m.* patronate, patronship

Patronne, *s.f.* patroness; employer; mistress

Patronner, *v.a.* to patronize; to trace with a pattern, to pattern, to stencil

Patronnesse, *s.f.* patroness

Patronnet, *s.m.* pastrycook's boy [maker

Patronneu-r, se, *s.m.f.* pattern-drawer *or*

Patronymique, *adj.* patronymic

†Patrouillage, *s.m.* paddling; mess

†Patrouille, *s.f.* patrol; scovel; (*pop.*) boozing. — *grise,* night-patrol. *Faire la —,* to patrol [paw; (*old*) to patrol

†Patrouiller, *v.n.a.* to paddle; to splash; to

†Patrouillis, *s.m.* puddle, plash, mess

Patte, *s.f.* paw; foot; leg; claw, claws; (*pers., jest.*) paw, hand; trotter, foot; (*fig.*) claws, clutches; (*of clothes,* &c.) flap; tab; band; (*of braces*) end; (*of anchors*) fluke, palm; (*tech.*) foot, cramp, holdfast; meat-hook; (*bot.*) root. — *-d'oie, V.* **Oie.** *A —s,* pawed, footed, &c.; (*pop.*) on foot. *A quatre —s,* on all fours. *Bête à mille —s,* milleped. *Faire — de velours,* to draw in its claws, to touch softly; to speak smoothly; to flatter, to cajole; to use gentle means. — **-fiche,** *s.f.* cramp, holdfast. — **-pelu, e,** *s.m.f.* hypocrite

Patté, e, *adj.* footed; (*her.*) pattee

Pattée, *s.f.* (*mus.*) stave, staff [the feet, to carry

Patter, *v.n.* (*hunt., of hares,* &c.) to get clods on

Pattu, e, *adj.* large-pawed; thick, heavy; (*of birds*) rough-legged, rough-footed, feather- [footed

Pâturable, *adj.* pasturable

Pâturage, *s.m.* pasturage, pasture, pasture-land, pasture-ground, paddock, walk, station, run

Pâture, *s.f.* food; feed; pasture; pasture-ground. *Vaine —,* common of pasture, common pasture, common [to feed off

Pâturer, *v.n.a.* to pasture, to graze, to feed;

Pâtureur, *s.m.* pasturer

Paturin, *s.m.* (*bot.*) meadow-grass

Pâturon, *s.m.* pastern

Paucité, *s.f.* paucity

†Pauillac, *s.m.* pauillac (*claret wine*)

Paul, *s.m.* (*Italian coin*) paul, paolo

Paulinien, ne, *adj.* Pauline

Paullinia, *s.m.* (*bot., pharm.*) paullinia

Paulownia, *s m.* (*bot.*) paulownia

Paume, *s.f.* palm (*of the hand*); (*meas.*) *V.* **Palme;** (*play*) tennis, rackets, racquets; (*pop.*) loss, failure, check, blunder. *Jeu de —,* tennis-court, racket-court, racquet-court

Paumelle, *s.f.* two-rowed barley, common barley; hand-leather, hand-guard; sailmaker's palm

Paumer, *v.a.* to measure with the hand; (*pop.*) to slap, to smack, to punch, to buffet; to grab; to catch; to nab

Paumi-er, ère, *s.m.f.* tennis-court keeper; — *s.m.* sleeping-chair. — *-raquettier,* tennis-racket maker

Paumoyer, *v.a.* (*nav.*) to underrun (*cables*)

Paumure, *s.f.* (*hunt.*) *V.* **Empaumure**

Paupérisme, *s.m.* pauperism

Paupière, *s.f.* eyelid; eyelash; eyes

Paupiettes, *s.f.pl.* (*cook.*) savoury collops

Pause, *s.f.* pause, stop, stand, rest; (*mus.*) semi-breve rest; (*of a bell*) sound-bow

Pauser, *v.n.* (*mus.*) to make a rest

Pauvre, *adj.* poor; needy; destitute; wretched; pitiful, sad; weak, feeble; meagre; scanty; sorry, paltry, mean, scrubby, very indifferent, of little worth; dear; — *s.m.* poor man; pauper; beggar; poor. — *d'esprit,* poor in spirit; weak-headed person. *Taxe des —s,* poor-rates [wretchedly

Pauvrement, *adv.* in poverty; poorly,

Pauvresse, *s.f.* poor woman, beggar-woman

Pauvret, te, *s.m.f.* poor thing, poor creature

Pauvreté, *s.f.* poverty; poorness; need; wretchedness; poor thing; platitude

Pauxi, *s.m.* (*bird*) pauxi

Pavage, *s.m.* paving; pavement

Pavane, *s.f.* pavan (*dance, tune*)

Pavaner (Se), *v.r.* to show off, to make a show of oneself; to strut; to stalk proudly; to flaunt

Pavé, *s.m.* pavement; paving-stone; carriage-way, road, road-way; street, streets; cause-way. *Haut du —,* wall-side; first rank; precedence. *Sur le —,* in (*or* on) the street *or* streets, houseless, without home; without employment; out of work; out of place. *Battre le —,* to ramble about the streets, to ramble *or* rove *or* idle about. *Brûler le —,* to drive *or* ride with the utmost speed. *Mettre sur le —,* to turn into the streets, to turn out of o.'s place *or* house, to deprive of employment, to put out of employment

Pavement, *s.m.* paving; pavement

Paver, *v.a.* to pave

Paveur, *s.m.* pavier

Pavie, *s.m.* clingstone peach

Pavier, *s.m.* (*bot.*) pavia, buck-eye, American horse-chestnut tree

†Pavillon, *s.m.* pavilion; wing; outhouse; lodge, box; summer-house; tent; canopy; veil; flag, colours, standard; (*mus.*) bell (*of a trumpet,* &c.); (*obsolete, Vaisseau —*) flag-ship. — *chinois,* Chinese bells. *Amener son —, baisser —, mettre — bas,* (*nav.*) to strike; (*fig.*) to yield [target; (*nav.*) top armour, waist-cloth

Pavois, *s.m.* (*hist.*) pavise, shield; (*obsolete*)

Pavoisement, *s.m.* (*nav.*) dressing

Pavoiser, *v.a.* to deck with flags, to dress

Se —, *v.r.* to become *or* be decked with flags *or* dressed; to dress

Pavonie, *s.f.* (*bot., zool.*) pavonia

Pavonien, ne, *adj.* pavonine

Pavot, *s.m.* poppy; **—s,** *pl.* poppies; sleep

Payable, *adj.* payable

Payant, e, *s.m.f.* payer, one who pays *or* paid; — *adj.* paying. *Billet —,* paid ticket. *V.* **Carte**

Paye, *s.f.* pay; wages; salary; paymaster, payer. *Haute —,* extra pay. *Morte- —,* people kept in pay without any service; defaulting tax-payer, loss

Payement, *s.m.* payment; pay

Payen, ne, (*old spelling*) *V.* **Païen**

Payer, *v.a.* to pay; to pay for; to pay out *or* away *or* off; to cash; to buy; to treat to *or* with, to stand; to reward, to requite, to repay, to return; to punish; to expiate, to atone for; to indemnify; to satisfy. — *de*, to pay *or* repay *or* requite with *or* for *or* by; to punish *or* &c. for; to satisfy with; to give; to give *or* have only; to show. — *d'audace* or *d'effronterie*, to put a bold face on the matter, to face (*or* brazen) it out. — *de mine*, to be all outside show; to look well; to have a prepossessing appearance. — *de sa personne*, to expose oneself (to danger); to act in person; to take a personal share; to attend personally; to acquit oneself well; to make oneself agreeable. *Se faire* —, to receive *or* take pay; to require *or* enforce payment; to get paid; to make people pay; to charge. *Être payé pour*, to have learnt at o.'s cost, to have good reasons, to have reason. *Je suis payé pour cela*, I know what it costs

Se —, *v.r.* to pay oneself *or* each other; to treat oneself to; to be satisfied; to be paid *or* repaid *or* &c.; to be paid for; to cost; to be bought [paying

Payeu-r, se, *s.m.f.* payer; paymaster; — *adj.*

Pays, *s.m.* country; land; native place, home, fatherland; part of the country, place; district; way, distance. — *légal*, qualified electors, restricted suffrage. *Mal* or *maladie du* —, home-sickness. *Avoir le mal* or *la maladie du* —, to be home-sick. *Battre du* —, to ramble about. *Battre bien du* —, to travel a great distance. *Être bien de son* —, to be a great simpleton. *Faire voir du — à quelqu'un*, to lead a person a dance

Pays, e, *s.m.f.* (*pop.*) (fellow) countryman; (fellow) countrywoman; country-girl

Paysage, *s.m.* landscape; landscape-painting

Paysag-er, ère, *adj.* of landscapes, landscape; rustic

Paysagiste, *s.m.f.* landscape-painter, landscape-paintress; landscape-gardener; — *adj.* of landscapes, landscape; rustic

Paysan, ne, *s.m.f. adj.* peasant, country-man, country-woman; country-boy *or* girl; boor; rustic; countrified; (*dance*) paysanne. *A la —ne*, peasant-like; in country fashion

Paysannerie, *s.f.* peasantry; rusticity; country manners *or* fashions; scene *or* representation of rustic life

Péage, *s.m.* toll; due; toll-gate, toll-house

Péag-er, ère, *s.m.f.* toll-collector; — *adj.*

Péan, *s.m.* pæan, pean [of tolls, toll

Peau, *s.f.* skin; hide; fell; pell; pelt; fur; leather; rind; peel; husk; (*fam.*) skin, own self, carcass, carcase; life; (*pop.*) strumpet, drab, bitch. — *d'âne*, ass's skin; drum; catskin, children's tale, nursery tale. — *de chien*, dog's skin; dog-fish skin, fish-skin; (*pop.*) strumpet, drab, bitch [cutaneous muscle

Peaucier, *adj.m.*, *s.m.* *Muscle* —, —, (*anat.*)

Peausser, *v.a.* (*pop.*) to clothe, to dress, to disguise [skinner's trade *or* business

Peausserie, *s.f.* peltry, pelts, skins, leather;

Peaussier, *s.m.* skinner, fellmonger, leather-seller; — *adj.m.*, *s.m.* (*anat.*) *V.* **Peaucier**

Pébrine, *s.f.* pebrine (*disease of silkworms*)

Pec, *adj.m.* (*of herrings*) pickled, new-salted

Pécaïre, Pécairé, *int.* (*local*) bless me! just fancy! only fancy! indeed! faith!

Pécari, *s.m.* peccary, Mexican hog

Peccable, *adj.* peccable

†Peccadille, *s.f.* peccadillo, slight offence

Peccant, e, *adj.* (*med.*) peccant

Peccavi, *s.m.* peccavi

Pêche, *s.f.* peach; fishing; angling; fishery; catch, take; fish; (*at dominoes*) drawing game, drawing. — *lisse*, freestone nectarine. — *de vigne*, standard peach. — *à la ligne*, rod-fishing, angling. *Ligne de* —, fishing-line

Péché, *s.m.* sin; trespass; offence

Pécher, *v.n.* to sin; to trespass; to offend; to err; to be deficient *or* defective *or* faulty, to fail

Pêcher, *s.m.* peach-tree. *Couleur (de) fleur de* —, peach-colour; peach-coloured

Pêcher, *v.n.a.* to fish; to angle; to drag; to draw; to fish for; to fish up; to catch; to find, to pick up, to get. — *à la ligne*, to angle

Se —, *v.r.* to be fished *or* &c.

Pêcherie, *s.f.* fishery, fishing-place; fish-pond

Pêchette, *s.f.* crayfish-net; leech-net

Péch-eur, eresse, *s. adj.* sinner, transgressor; sinning, sinful, transgressing

Pêcheu-r, se, *s.m.f.* fisherman, fisherwoman, fisher; angler; gatherer; — *adj.* (**Pêcheuse** *and also* **Pêcheresse** *for the feminine*) fishing. — *à la ligne*, rod-fisher, angler

Pécore, *s.f.* animal, creature; blockhead, fool

Pecque, *s.f.* (*obsolete*) silly conceited woman *or*

Pectate, *s.m.* (*chem.*) pectate [girl

Pectine, *s.f.* (*chem.*) pectine

Pectiné, e, *adj.* pectinate, pectinal, comb-

Pectique, *adj.* (*chem.*) pectic [shaped

Pectoral, e, *adj.*, **Pectoral,** *s.m.* pectoral

Pectoralement, *adv.* pectorally

Pectoriloque, *s.m.f.* pectoriloquist; — *adj.* pectoriloquous [quism

§Pectoriloquie, *s.f.* pectoriloquy, pectorilo-

Pectose, *s.f.* (*chem.*) pectose

Péculat, *s.m.* peculation, embezzlement

Péculateur, *s.m.* peculator

Pécule, *s. m.* peculium, earnings, savings, hoard, stock *or* sum of money, money

Pécune, *s.f.* (*slang*) money, cash, tin, chink

Pécuniaire, *adj.* pecuniary

Pécuniairement, *adv.* pecuniarily

Pécunieu-x, se, *adj.* *V.* **Argenteux**

Pédagog-ie, -ique, -iquement, -isme. *V.* page 3, § 1

Pédale, *s.f.* pedal; pedal-stop; pedal-note; (*tech.*) treadle. — *d'expression*, swell

Pédant, e, *s.m.f.* pedant; — *adj.* pedantic

†Pédantaille, *s.f.* pedants; pedant [pedant

Pédanter, *v.n.* to pedantize, to act *or* play the

Pédanterie, *s.f.* pedantry [style

Pédantesque, *adj.* pedantic; — *s.m.* pedantic

Pédantesquement, *adv.* pedantically

Pédantiser, *v.n.* *V.* **Pédanter**

Pédantisme, *s.m.* pedantry

Pédantocratie, *s.f.* pedantocracy [§ 1

Pédantocrat-ique, -iquement. *V.* page 3,

Pédéraste, *s.m.* pederast

Pédérast-ie, -ique. *V.* page 3, § 1 [walk

Pédestre, *adj.* pedestrian; on foot. *Course* —,

Pédestrement, *adv.* on foot

Pédestrianisme, *s.m.* pedestrianism

Pédicelle, *s.m.* (*bot.*, *zool.*) pedicel

Pédicellé, e, *adj.* pedicellate [(*bot.*) lousewort

Pédiculaire, *adj.* pedicular, lousy; — *s.f.*

Pédicule, *s.m.* (*bot.*) pedicle, stipe; (*med.*) neck

Pédiculé, e, *adj.* pediculate, pediculated, stiped; (*med.*) necked [doctor

Pédicure, *s.m.f.* chiropodist, corn-cutter, corn-

Pédieu-x, se, *adj.* (*anat.*) pedial, of the foot

Pédiforme, *adj.* pediform [*or* feet

Pédigree, *s.m.* (*French turf slang*) pedigree

Pédilanthe, *s.m.* (*bot.*) pedilanthus

Pédiluve, *s.m.* (*med.*) pediluvium, foot-bath

Pédimane, *s.m.* pedimane; — *adj.* pedimanous

Pédomètre, Pédométrique, *V.* **Hodomètre,** and page 3, § 1

Pédon, *s.m.* foot-messenger, runner

Pédonculaire, *adj.* peduncular

Pédoncule, *s.m.* peduncle

Pédonculé, e, *adj.* pedunculate, pedunculated

Pédonculeu-x, se, *adj.* pedunculous

Pédotrophie, *s.f.* pedotrophy, pædotrophy

Pégase, *s.m.* (*myth.*, *astr.*, *zool.*) Pegasus

Pégasien, ne, *adj.* Pegasean

Pègle, *s.f.* pitch (*from wood-tar*)

Pegmatite, *s.f.* (*min.*) pegmatite

Pégomancie, *s.f.* pegomancy

Pégot, *s.m.* (*bird*) *V.* **Mouchet**

Pègre, *s.m.* thief; — *s.f.* light-fingered gentry *or* fraternity, thieves, gang (of thieves). *Haute*

—, swell-mob. *Basse* —, low class of thieves, low *or* common thieves

Pégriot, *s.m.* young thief, petty thief

†Peignage, *s.m.* combing

†Peigne, *s.m.* comb; (*shell*) pecten, clam, scollop. — *fin*, small-tooth comb. — *à démêler*, — *à grosses dents*, large-tooth comb. *Sale comme un* —, as dirty as a pig

†Peigné, e, *part. adj.* combed; elaborate, laboured; (*of gardens*) kept; — *s.m.* combed wool, jersey. *Mal* —, (*pers.*) *V.* **Malpeigné**

†Peignée, *s.f.* combful; dressing, trimming, drubbing, brush, fight, set-to

†Peigner, *v.a.* to comb; to comb the hair of; to dress; to elaborate, to labour; to drub

Se —, *v.r.* to comb oneself *or* o.'s hair; to be combed; to fight, to have a fight *or* a set-to

†Peignerie, *s.f.* comb-making; comb-trade; comb-manufactory; combs

†Peigneu-r, se, *s.m.f.* (*pers.*) comber; — *s.f.* combing-machine, comber

†Peignier, *s.m.* comb-maker

†Peignoir, *s.m.* combing-cloth; dressing-gown, wrapper; bathing-gown

†Peignures, *s.f.pl.* combings

†Peille, *s.f.* rag; (*fish.*) gut-line

Peinchebec, *s.m.* pinchbeck

Peindre, *v.a.n.* to paint; to portray; to depict; to describe; to draw; to represent; to express; to characterize; to adorn, to deck; to show; to write. *A* —, *fait à* —, worth painting; a model for a painter; extremely well made; remarkably handsome, extremely beautiful; admirably. *Achever de* —, to finish up, to do up. *Se faire* —, to have o.'s portrait painted, to have o.'s picture *or* likeness drawn *or* taken

Se —, *v.r.* to paint *or* represent *or* &c. oneself *or* to oneself; to paint *or* dye (o.'s ...); to be painted *or* described *or* expressed *or* &c.; to appear; to gleam

Peine, *s.f.* pain; grief; affliction; sorrow; suffering; torment; torture; discomfort; uneasiness; anxiety; hardship; trouble; difficulty; reluctance; labour, pains; fatigue; penalty, punishment. *A* —, hardly, scarcely, no sooner; very little, scarcely any; with difficulty; under *or* on pain (of); at the risk (of). *A grand'*—, with great (*or* much) difficulty *or* labour *or* pains; very reluctantly. *En* —, at a loss; at pains; uneasy; anxious. *Sans* —, without difficulty, easily; readily; painless. *Sous* — *de*, under *or* on pain of; at the risk of. *Homme* or *garçon de* —, labourer; workman; porter; drudge, fag, hard-working man; (*slang*) old offender. *Être la* —, to be worth *or* worth while. *Donner de la* — *à*, to give trouble to, to trouble. *Faire de la* — *à*, *faire* —, to give pain to, to be painful to, to pain, to hurt, to grieve, to vex. *Mourir à la* —, to die at work, to die in harness, to die at the oar. *Se donner* (or *Prendre*) *de la* —, to take pains. *Se donner* (or *Prendre*) *la* — *de* ..., to take the trouble to ...; to have the goodness to ..., to please to ... *Se mettre en* — *de*, to trouble oneself about (*or* to); to take pains to. *Valoir la* —, to be worth *or* worth while. *Donnez-vous la* — *de vous asseoir!* pray, sit down! pray, take a seat! *Toutes les* —*s du monde*, a world of trouble. *Toute* — *mérite salaire*, (*Proverb*) the labourer is worthy of his hire

Peiner, *v.a.n.* to pain, to grieve, to afflict, to distress, to vex; to torment; to give trouble to; to fatigue; to feel pain; to labour, to toil, to work hard; to be reluctant

Se —, *v.r.* to take pains *or* trouble; to trouble oneself; to grieve, to fret, to take on

Peintre, *s.m.f.* painter; paintress. — *d'histoire*, historical painter *or* paintress. — *de marine*, marine-painter *or* paintress. — *en bâtiments*, house-painter

Peintresse, *s.f.* paintress

Peinturage, *s.m.* painting; daubing, daub

Peinture, *s.f.* painting; picture; description; portraiture; paint; colours; appearance; (*obsolete*) court-card, figure-card. — *en bâtiments*, house-painting. — *en décors*, graining, &c. (*V.* **Décor**)

Peinturer, *v.a.* to paint; to colour; to daub

Peintureur, *s.m.* painter; dauber

Peinturlure, *s.f.* daubing; daub

Peinturlurer, *v.a.* to daub, to bedaub

Se —, *v.r.* *V.* **Maquiller (Se)**

Peinturlureur, *s.m.* dauber [pejorative

Péjorati-f, ve, *adj.*, **Péjoratif,** *s.m.* (*gram.*)

Pékan, *s.m.* (*zool.*) pekan, wood-shock, fisher

Pékin, *s.m.* (*silk fabric*) pekin; (*mil. slang*)

Péko, Pékoe, *s.m.* pekoe (*tea*) [civilian, snob

Pelade, *s.f.* skin-wool, pelt-wool; (*med.*) alopecy, fox-evil, scurf

Pelage, *s.m.* (*of animals*) colour of the hair; coat, hair; fur; (*of skins*) stripping off the

Pélagianisme, *s.m.* Pelagianism [hair, hairing

Pélagien, ne, *adj.* pelagian

Pélagique, *adj.* pelagic

Pélagoscope, *s.m.* pelagoscope

Pélamide, *s.f.* (*zool.*) mud-fish

Pelard, *adj.m.* (*of wood*) barked

Pélargonate, *s.m.* (*chem.*) pelargonate

Pélargonique, *adj.* (*chem.*) pelargonic [bill

Pélargonium, *s.m.* (*bot.*) pelargonium, stork's-

Pélasge, *s.m. adj.* (*anc. hist.*) Pelasgian

Pélasgien, ne, Pélasgique, *adj.* (*anc. hist.*) Pelasgian

Pelé, e, *part. adj.* peeled, &c. (*V.* **Peler**); bald; naked, bare; threadbare; napless; — *s.m.* bald-pated man; ragamuffin. *Quatre* —*s et un tondu*, nobody but tag-rag and bobtail

Pêle-mêle, *adv. s.m.* pell-mell, helter-skelter; confusion, disorder; jumble, litter, confused heap; promiscuousness, promiscuity

Pêle-mêler, *v.a.* to confuse, to disorder, to jumble together, to throw pell-mell *or* helter-skelter

Peler, *v.a.* to strip off the hair; to hair; to strip off, to strip; to peel; to pare; to bark; to make bald *or* bare; to scald (*pigs*); to pare the turf off; — *v.n.*, **Se** —, *v.r.* to lose its hair *or* nap *or* skin, to peel off, to come off; to be peeled *or* &c.

Pèlerin, e, *s.m.f.* pilgrim; palmer; traveller; sly blade, fellow, jade; — *s.m.* basking shark, sail-fish; — *s.f.* cape, tippet, pelerine; (*shell*) scollop. — *Saint-Jacques*, scollop

Pèlerinage, *s.m.* pilgrimage; peregrination; resort of pilgrims

Péliade, *s.m.* pelias (*kind of viper*)

Pélican, *s.m.* (*zool.*, *chem.*, *surg.*) pelican; (*tech.*) cramp, holdfast

Péliome, *s.m.* (*med.*) pelioma

Péliose, *s.f.* (*med.*) peliosis

Pelisse, *s.f.* pelisse

Pellage, *s.m.* shovelling

Pellagre, *s.f.* (*med.*) pellagra

Pellagreu-x, se, *adj. s.* (*med.*) pellagrous

Pelle, *s.f.* shovel; scoop; spade; (— *de four*) peel; (*for salt, ice,* &c.) spoon; (*of oars*) blade. *La* — *se moque du fourgon*, the pot calls the kettle black

Pellée, Pellerée, *s.f.* shovelful; spadeful

Peller, *v.a.n.* to shovel

Pelleron, *s.m.* (*baker's*) peel

Pelletage, *s.m.* shovelling

Pelletée, *s.f.* *V.* **Pellée**

Pelleter, *v.a.n.* to shovel

Pelleterie, *s.f.* peltry, pelts, furs; furriery,

Pelleti-er, ère, *s.m.f.* furrier [fur-trade

Pelleversage, *s.m.* spade-tillage

Pelleverser, *v.a.* to till with a spade

Pelliculaire, *adj.* pellicular

Pellicule, *s.f.* pellicle, cuticle, film

Pellucide, *adj.* pellucid

Pellucidité, *s.f.* pellucidity, pellucidness

Pélopium, *s.m.* (*chem.*) pelopium

Pelotage, *s.m.* putting up into balls; playing loosely, loose play; amusement, trifling

Pelote, *s.f.* pincushion; ball; clue; round sum; pickings, savings, hoard; (*of horses*) blaze

Peloter, *v.a n.* to roll round *or* up; to wind; to make up into a ball, to put up into balls; to gather up; to feel about; to handle; to beat; to toss the ball; to play loosely; to line. — *en attendant partie*, to keep o.'s hand in till the game begins, to do small jobs (*or* something unimportant) until something better turns up

Peloteu-r, se, *s.m.f.* ball-winder; — *s.f.* ball-winding machine, ball-winder; — *adj.* ball-winding

Peloton, *s.m.* ball; clue; lump; knot, group, cluster; (*mil.*) half-company, (*formerly*) platoon. *École de* —, platoon-exercise. *Feu de* —, volley-firing, platoon-firing

Pelotonner, *v.a.* to wind, to make up into a ball, to put up into balls; to group, to cluster, to gather up, to gather together; to roll up; (*mil.*) to form *or* range in half-companies

Se —, *v.r.* to roll oneself up *or* &c.; to gather o.'s limbs; to cuddle; to cake; to cluster; to be wound *or* &c.; (*mil.*) to form in half-companies [sward, green, turf

Pelouse, *s.f.* lawn, grass-plot, greensward,

Pelu, e, *adj.* (*obsolete*) hairy

Peluche, *s.f.* plush, shag [shaggy

Peluché, e, Pelucheu-x, se, *adj.* plushy,

Pelucher, *v.n.* to wear rough, to become shaggy

Pelure, *s.f.* peel, paring, rind; (*pop*) wraprascal. — *d'ognon*, onion-peel; thin stuff *or* paper; light red colour (*of wine*). *Papier* — (*d'ognon*), foreign post paper, foreign paper

Pelvien, ne, *adj.* (*anat.*) pelvic

Pelvimètre, *s.m.* (*surg.*) pelvimeter

Pelvimétrie, *s.f.* (*surg.*) pelvimetry

Pemmican, *s.m.* pemmican

Pemphigode, *adj.* (*med.*) pemphigous

Pemphigus, *s.m.* (*med.*) pemphigus

†**Penaille, Penaillerie,** *s.f.* rags; ragamuffins;

†**Penaillon,** *s.m.* rag; monk [monks, monkery

Pénal, e, *adj.* penal [law *or* enactment; penalty

Pénalité, *s.f.* penality; penal legislation, penal

Penard, *s.m.* decrepit old man

Pénates, *s.m.pl.* penates, household gods; fire-side, paternal house, house, home, hearth

Penaud, e, *adj.* abashed, sheepish, chopfallen, chapfallen, down in the mouth, crestfallen, out of countenance, foolish; — *s.m.f.* ditto person

Pence, *s.m.pl.* (*English*) pence

Penchant, *s.m.* declivity; slope; acclivity; decline; brink; verge; inclination, propensity; taste; — *m.*, **e,** *f.*, *part. adj.* inclining, leaning, bending, sloping, declining, decaying, &c. (*V.* **Pencher**); prone, inclined

Penché, e, *part. adj.* inclined, &c. (*V.* **Pencher**); inclining, leaning; bent, bowed down; stooping; sloping; declining. *Airs* —*s*, lolling, finical airs. *Avoir des airs* —*s*, to loll

Penchement, *s.m.* inclination; leaning; bending, bend; stooping, stoop; &c. (*V.* **Pencher**); bowing; nod

Pencher, *v.a.n.*, **Se** —, *v.r.* to incline; to lean; to bend, to bow down; to stoop; to recline; to loll; to tilt; to slope; to verge; to weigh down; to be inclined; to decline, to totter

Pendable, *adj.* deserving hanging, hanging, for hanging, for the gallows; abominable

Pendaison, *s.f.* hanging

Pendant, e, *adj.* pendent; pending; depending; hanging; hanging down; dangling; drooping; in abeyance. *Les fruits* —*s* (or *les récoltes* —*es*) *par* (*les*) *racines*, standing corn *or* crops, growing corn *or* crops

Pendant, *s.m.* pendant; fellow, companion, companion-piece, match, counterpart; (*of a sword-belt*) frog. — *d'oreille*, ear-ring, ear-drop, pendant. *Faire* —, to be the fellow, to match, to correspond [*que*, while, whilst

Pendant, *prep.* during; for; in; pending. —

Pendard, e, *s.m.f.* rogue, rascal

Pendeloque, *s.f.* pendant, drop; ear-drop; hanging decoration *or* ornament; hanging tatters, tatters, shreds [hanging

Pendement, *s.m.*, **Penderie,** *s.f.* (*jest.*)

Pendentif, *s.m.* (*arch.*) pendentive

Pendeur, *s.m.* hangman, hanger; (*nav.*) pendant

†**Pendille,** *s.f.* pendant, drop

†**Pendiller,** *v.n.* to hang loose, to hang, to dangle, to flutter, to swing

Pendoir, *s.m.* cord *or* line to hang on; hook

Pendre, *v.a.* to hang; to hang up, to suspend; — *v.n.* to hang, to hang down *or* up; to be suspended; to dangle; to droop; to sag. *Dire pis que* — *de*, to say all kinds of things against, to fall foul of

Pendu, e, *part. adj.* hanged, hung, &c. (*V.* **Pendre**; hanging; dangling; — *s.m.f.* person hanged. *Bien* —, (*of the tongue*) well-hung, well-oiled, voluble, glib, nimble, flippant. *Avoir de la corde de* — *dans sa poche*, to be very lucky

Pendulaire, *adj.* (*phys.*) pendular

Pendule, *s.m.* pendulum; — *s.f.* clock, time-piece. *Horloge à* —, pendulum clock

Penduliste, *s.m* clock-case maker, watch-case

Pène, Pêne, *s.m.* lock-bolt, bolt [maker

Pénélope, *s.f.* (*zool.*) penelope

Pénétrabilité, *s.f.* penetrability

Pénétrable, *adj.* penetrable, pervious

Pénétramment, *adv.* penetratingly; piercingly; impressively

Pénétrant, e, *adj.* penetrating; piercing; insinuating; sharp; acute, shrewd; impressive

Pénétrati-f, ve, *adj.* penetrative

Pénétration, *s.f.* penetration; sagacity, acuteness, shrewdness; piercingness

Pénétrativement, *adv.* penetratively

Pénétrer, *v.a.n.* to penetrate; to pervade; to go through; to pierce; to dive into, to search, to fathom; to see through; to discover; to impress; to imbue; to convince; to affect; to move; to concern; to enter; to get in; to get; to go [troublesome; fatiguing

Pénible, *adj.* painful; laborious, difficult, hard,

Péniblement, *adv.* painfully; laboriously,

Péniche, *s.f.* (*nav.*) pinnace [with difficulty

Pénicillé, e, *adj.* penicillate, pencil-shaped

Pénicillion, *s.m.* (*bot.*) vinegar-plant

Pénide, *s.m.* barley-sugar twist

Pénil, *s.m.* (*anat.*) mons veneris

Péninsulaire, *adj.* peninsular

Péninsule, *s.f.* peninsula

Pénis, *s.m.* (*anat.*) penis

Pénitence, *s.f.* penitence; repentance; penance; punishment; disgrace. *En* —, undergoing punishment, being punished, punished, in disgrace, disgraced, in the corner. *Mettre en* —, to punish, to disgrace, to put into the corner

Pénitencerie, *s.f.* penitentiary; office of peni-

Pénitencier, *s.m.* penitentiary [tentiary

Pénitent, e, *adj. s.* penitent, repentant

Pénitentiaire, *adj.* penitentiary

Pénitentiaux, *adj.m.pl.* *Psaumes* —, penitential psalms [penitential

Pénitentiel, le, *adj.*, **Pénitentiel,** *s.m.*

Pennache, (*obsolete spelling*) *V.* **Panache**

Pennage, *s.m.* plumage, feathers

Pennatule, *s.f.* (*zool.*) pennatula, sea-pen

Penne, *s.f.* feather

Penné, e, *adj.* pennate, pinnate

Penniforme, *adj.* penniform [Pennine

Pennine, *s.f.* (*min.*) pennine; — *adj.f.* (*geog.*)

Pennon, *s.m.* pennon; (*of arrows*) feather

Penny, *s.m.* (*English coin*) penny

Pénombre, *s.f.* (*astr.*, *paint.*) penumbra; (*fig.*) twilight, subdued light, faint light, faint shadow

Penon, *s.m.* (*nav.*) dog-vane

Pensée, *s.f.* thought; thinking, opinion, sentiment; mind; soul; belief; idea; conception; notion; meaning; project; hope; sketch; (*bot.*) pansy, heart's-ease

Penser, *v.a.n.* to think; to believe; to imagine;

to conceive; to suppose; to reflect; to consider; to bear in mind; to take care (of), to look (to); to intend, to mean; to expect, to hope; to be near, to nearly ... *Faire* —, to make (...) think; to remind (of). — *bien*, to think well; to think right *or* rightly; to quite think; should think; may think; may easily suppose. — *du bien de*, to think well of. *Pensez donc!* just think of it! *J'ai pensé tomber*, I was near falling, I nearly fell

Se —, *v.r.* to be thought *or* &c.

Penser, *s.m.* thinking; thought [thoughtful

Penseu-r, se, *s.m.f. adj.* thinker; thinking,

Pensi-f, ve, *adj.* thoughtful, pensive

Pension, *s.f.* pension, allowance; annuity; board; board and lodging; boarding-house; boarding-school, school; schooling; (*of officers*) mess; (*of animals*) food, keep; home; (*for horses*) livery; (*in Switzerland*) hotel. — *bourgeoise*, — *de famille*, family boarding-house. *Être en* —, to be at school; to board; to be at a boarding-house

Pensionnaire, *s.m.f.* boarder; school-boy, school-girl; pensioner; (*formerly, in Holland*) pensionary. *Grand* —, grand pensionary. — *en chambre*, parlour-boarder

Pensionnat, *s.m.* boarding-school, school

Pensionner, *v.a.* to pension

Pensivement, *adv.* thoughtfully, pensively

Pensum, *s.m.* (*at school*) imposition, task

Pensylvanien, ne, *adj. s.* Pennsylvanian

Pentacorde, *s.m. adj.* pentachord

Pentaèdre, *s.m.* (*geom.*) pentahedron; — *adj.*

Pentagonal, e, *adj.* pentagonal [pentahedral

Pentagone, *s.m.* (*geom., fort*) pentagon; — *adj.* pentagonal

Pentamètre, *s.m. adj.* pentameter

Pentastyle, *s.m. adj.* (*arch.*) pentastyle

Pentasyllabe, *s.m.* pentasyllable; — *adj.* pentasyllabic

Pentasyllabique, *adj.* pentasyllabic

Pentateuque, *s.m.* Pentateuch

Pente, *s.f.* slope; declivity, descent; acclivity, ascent; inclination; incline; gradient; (*of roofs*) pitch; (*of awnings*) side; (*of beds*) valance; (*of book-cases*) hanging; (*tech.*) bend; (*fig.*) propensity, inclination, proneness, turn, bent; (*pop.*) drop too much. *En* —, sloping, inclined, declivous, declivitous, shelving. *Aller en* —, to slope, to incline, to shelve

Pentécostaire, *adj.* pentecostal [Sunday

Pentecôte, *s.f.* Pentecost, Whitsuntide, Whit-

Pentélique, *adj.* Pentelican

Penter, *v.n.* to slope, to incline, to shelve

Pentière, *s.f. V.* **Pantière**

Penture, *s.f.* hinge; iron brace

Pénultième, *s.f. adj.* penultima, penult; penultimate; last but one

Pénurie, *s.f.* penury, want, scarcity, dearth

Péon, *s.m.* peon; pæon, pæan

Péonage, *s.m.* peonage

Péone, *s.f.* (*bot.*) pæony, peony

Péotte, *s.f.* peotta (*Venetian gondola*) [peperino

Péperin, *s.m.*, **Péperine,** *s.f.* (*geol.*) peperine,

Pépiage, *s.m.* chirping, chirp

Pépie, *s.f.* (*disease in birds*) pip, chip, roup; (*fig.*) thirst. *Avoir la* —, (*pers., jest.*) to be thirsty *or* dry. *N'avoir pas la* —, (*ditto*) to drink freely, to be always ready for a glass, to be glad of a tipple; not to be tongue-tied

Pépiement, *s.m. V.* **Pépiage**

Pépier, *v.n.* to chirp, to pip

Pépin, *s.m.* (*of fruit*) pip, kernel, stone, seed; (*pop.*) old umbrella, gamp

Pépinière, *s.f.* (*hort., fig.*) nursery

Pépiniériste, *s.m.* nursery-man

Pépite, *s.f.* nugget [*garment*) peplus

Péplum, Péplon, Péplus, *s.m.* (*ancient*

Pépon, *s.m.* (*bot.*) pumpkin, gourd

Pepsine, *s.f.* (*chem.*) pepsine

Péquin, *s.m.* (*mil. slang*) civilian, snob

Péragration, *s.f.* peragration

Pérat, *s.m.* patent fuel

Perçage, *s.m.* piercing, boring

Percale, *s.f.* long-cloth, cambric muslin

Percaline, *s.f.* glazed calico; (*book-bind.*) cloth

Perçant, e, *adj.* piercing; penetrating, sharp, keen; acute; shrill [buret

Percarbure, *s.m.* (*chem.*) percarbide, percar-

Percarburé, e, *adj.* percarburetted

Perce, *s.f.* piercer, borer, drill, gimlet, fret; hole. *En* —, on tap, abroach, broached. *Mettre en* —, to tap, to broach

Percé, e, *part. adj.* pierced, &c. (*V.* **Percer**); in holes, out (*at elbows*, &c.); wet through; open; struck. *Bas* —, (*pers.*) low in cash

Percé, *s.m.*, **Percée,** *s.f.* opening; cutting; passage, way; vista, glade

Perce-bois, *s.m.* (*insect*) wood-borer, borer; (*ship-worm*) teredo; (*bee*) carpenter-bee, xylo-

Perce-chaussée, *s.m.* teredo, ship-worm [copa

Perce-crâne, *s.m.* (*surg.*) craniotomy perforator

†**Perce-feuille,** *s.f.* (*bot.*) hare's-ear

Percement, *s.m.* piercing; perforation; boring; cutting; opening; &c. (*V.* **Percer**)

†**Perce-muraille,** *s.f.* (*bot.*) pellitory

Perce-neige, *s.f.* (*bot.*) snowdrop; snow-flake

Percentage, *s.m.* percentage [ear-piercer

†**Perce-oreille,** *s.m.* (*insect*) earwig; (*instr.*)

Perce-pierre, *s.f. V.* **Passe-pierre**

Percepteur, *s.m.* collector, tax-collector

Perceptibilité, *s.f.* perceptibility; collectibleness, yielding [collectible

Perceptible, *adj.* perceptible, perceivable;

Perceptiblement, *adv.* perceptibly

Percepti-f, ve, *adj.* perceptive

Perception, *s.f.* perception; collection; receipt; collectorship; collector's office *or* district

Percer, *v.a.n.* to pierce; to perforate; to bore; to drill; to stick; to prod; to stab; to make a hole in; to cut through; to cut; to crack; to tap, to broach; to open; to tunnel; to lance; to go *or* come through; to run through; to wet through; to see through; to grieve, to thrill; to break through; to appear; to show itself, to show; to peep; to penetrate; to make o.'s way; to rise; to come out; to burst; to break; (*hunt.*) to start, to get off. — *de coups*, to cover with wounds

Se —, *v.r.* to pierce *or* &c. oneself *or* each other; to pierce *or* &c. (o.'s *or* each other's ...); to be pierced *or* &c.

Percerette, *s.f.* piercer, borer, drill, gimlet, fret

Perce-roche, *s.f.* (*zool.*) terebella

Perceu-r, se, *s.m.f.* piercer, borer

Percevable, *adj.* collectible; perceivable

Percevoir, *v.a.* to collect (*taxes*); to levy; to charge; to receive; (*philos.*) to perceive

Se —, *v.r.* to be collected *or* &c.

Perchant, *s.m.* decoy-bird

Perche, *s.f.* perch; pole; stick; (*hunt.*) beam, head, horns; (*fish*) perch; — (*Le*), *s.m.* Perche (*old French province*)

Perché, e, *part. adj.* perched, perched up; — *s.m.* being perched. *Au* —, when perched

Percher, *v.n.a.*, **Se** —, *v.r.* to perch, to perch oneself up, to roost

Percheron, ne, *adj.* of Perche; — *s.m.f.* native of Perche; Perche horse *or* mare

Perchette, *s.f.* pole, prop, stay; (*fish.*) *V.* **Péchette** [— *s.f.* titlark

Percheu-r, se, *adj.* perching; — *s.m.* percher;

Perchis, *s.m.* rod-hurdles, fence

‡**Perchlorate,** *s.m.* (*chem.*) perchlorate

‡**Perchlorique,** *adj.* (*chem.*) perchloric

‡**Perchlorure,** *s.m.* (*chem.*) perchloride

Perchoir, *s.m.* perch, roost

Perclure, *v.a.* to cripple, to disable; (*fig.*) to paralyze, to benumb

Perclus, e, *adj.* crippled, disabled, having lost the use of his (*or* her) limbs; (*fig.*) paralyzed, benumbed

Perclusion, *s.f.* disablement

Percnoptère, *s.m.* Egyptian vulture, Pharaoh's hen, Pharaoh's chicken, neophron
Perçoir, *s.m.* piercer, borer, fret; punch
Percussion, *s.f.* percussion
Percutant, e, *part. adj.* percussing, percussive, percutient, percussion
Percuter, *v.a.n.* to percuss, to strike
Percu-teur, trice, *adj.* V. **Percutant;** — *s.m.* percutient, striker; (*of fire-arms*) hammer
Perdable, *adj.* losable
Perdant, e, *s.m.f.* loser; — *adj.* losing
Perdeu-r, se, *s.m.f.* loser
Perdition, *s.f* perdition; destruction; ruin; loss; waste. *En* —, (*of ships*) being lost, sinking, in great distress
Perdre, *v.a.n.* to lose; to be a loser; to waste; to ruin, to undo; to be the death of; to be fatal to; to corrupt; to spoil; to get out of; to cast away; to throw away; to renounce; to abandon; to carry away; (*of the tide*) to ebb, to recede

Se —, *v.r.* to lose or ruin oneself *or* each other; to lose o.'s way; to be (*or* get) lost *or* &c.; to sink; to disappear; to vanish; to evaporate; to blend; to become extinct; to fall into disuse; to get bewildered; to be at a loss; to be wrecked. *S'y* —, to lose oneself *or* be lost *or* &c. in it; to be unable to make it out, to be bewildered [poult
Perdreau, *s.m.* young partridge, partridge-
Perdrigon, *s.m.* perdrigon plum
Perdrix, *s.f* partridge
Perdu, e, *part. adj.* lost; ruined; undone, done for, done up; entirely spoilt; thrown away; wasted; waste; useless; in vain; leisure, spare; distracted; bewildered; wild; remote and desolate; out-of-the-way; random; loose; advanced; forlorn; abandoned; sunk; over head and ears (in); wrecked; gone; vanished; blended; extinct; out of use, obsolete; invisible; dry. *Salle des pas* **s,** outer hall. *Comme un —, comme des —s,* like mad, like a madman, like madmen
Perdurable, *adj.* (*old*) perdurable
Perdurablement, *adv.* (*old*) perdurably
Père, *s.m.* father; parent; sire; man, fellow; old; senior; Jack; **—s,** *pl.* fathers, forefathers. — *la joie,* jolly fellow. — *noble,* (*theat.*) heavy father, respectable old man. *Gros* —, fat fellow, fatty. *Petit* —, daddy, pa; Augustine friar, Austin friar. *De* —, of a father, fatherly, paternal
Pérégrin, e, *adj.,* **Pérégrine,** *s.f.* peregrine
Pérégrinateur, *s.m.* peregrinator
Pérégrination, *s.f.* peregrination
Pérégriner, *v.n.* to peregrinate
Pérégrinité, *s.f.* (*law*) alienage, alienism
Péremption, *s.f.* (*law*) limitation, nonsuit
Péremptoire, *adj.* peremptory
Péremptoirement, *adv.* peremptorily
Pérenne, *adj.* perennial
Pérennité, *s.f.* perennity
***Péréquation,** *s.f.* equal distribution
Perfectibilité, *s.f.* perfectibility
Perfectible, *adj.* perfectible; improvable
Perfectiblement, *adv.* perfectibly
Perfection, *s.f.* perfection; accomplishment; completion
Perfection-isme, -iste. *V.* page 3, § 1
Perfectionné, e, *part. adj.* perfected, brought to perfection, perfect; improved
Perfectionnement, *s.m.* improvement; perfecting; finishing
Perfectionner, *v.a.* to perfect; to bring to perfection; to improve; to improve on *or* upon

Se —, *v.r.* to perfect *or* improve oneself, to
Perfectionneur, *s.m.* improver [improve
Perfide, *adj.* perfidious, treacherous, false, deceitful; — *s.m.f.* ditto person (man, woman, &c.), wretch [ly, falsely
Perfidement, *adv.* perfidiously, treacherous-
Perfidie, *s.f.* perfidiousness, perfidy, treacherousness, treachery; perfidious *or* treacherous action *or* thing, act of perfidy
Perfolié, e, *adj.* perfoliate, perfoliated
Perfora-teur, trice, *adj.* perforating; — *s.m.* perforator
Perforati-f, ve, *adj.* perforative, perforating
Perforation, *s.f.* perforation [rated
Perforer, *v.a.* to perforate. *Se* —, to be perfo-
Performances, *s.f.pl.* (*French turf slang*) performances
Péri, *s.m.f.* (*Persian myth.*) peri
Périanal, e, *adj.* (*anat., med.*) perianal, round the anus
Périanthe, *s.m.* (*bot.*) perianth
Périapte, *s.m.* periapt
Péribole, *s.m.* (*arch.*) peribolos (*space between an edifice and the enclosure which surrounds it*)
Péricarde, *s.m.* (*anat.*) pericardium [cardial
Péricardique, *adj.* (*anat.*) pericardiac, peri-
Péricardite, *s.f.* (*med.*) pericarditis
Péricarpe, *s.m.* (*bot.*) pericarp
Péricarpial, e, Péricarpique, *adj.* (*bot.*) pericarpial, pericarpic
‡Périchondre, *s.m.* (*anat.*) perichondrium
‡Périchondrite, *s.f.* (*med.*) perichondritis
Péricliter, *v.n.* to be in peril *or* danger *or* jeopardy, to threaten ruin, to go to ruin; — *v.a.* (*old*) to periclitate, to imperil, to endanger, to risk
Péricope, *s.f.* pericope
Péricrâne, *s.m.* (*anat.*) pericranium
Péridot, *s.m.* (*min.*) peridot, olivine
Péridrome, *s.m.* (*arch.*) peridrome
Périgée, *s.m.* (*astr.*) perigee [Perigord
Périgourdin, e, *adj. s.* of Perigord; native of
Périgueux, *s. m.* (*geog.*) Perigueux; (*min.*) Perigord stone
Périgyne, *adj.* (*bot.*) perigynous
Périhélie, *s.m.* (*astr.*) perihelion
Péril, *s.m.* peril, danger; risk [ously
†Périlleusement, *adv.* perilously, danger-
†Périlleu-x, se, *adj.* perilous, dangerous
Périmé, e, *part. adj.* barred by limitation; in abeyance; out of use; out of date; lapsed; overdue
Périmer, *v.n.,* **Se** —, *v.r.* to be barred by limitation, to fall into disuse *or* abeyance, to pass out of date, to fall, to drop, to lapse
Périmètre, *s.m.* perimeter
Périmétr-ie, -ique. *V.* page 3, § 1
Périnéal, e, *adj.* (*anat.*) perineal
Périnée, *s.m.* (*anat.*) perineum, perinæum
Période, *s.f.* period; — *s.m.* period, degree, pitch, point. — (*s.f.*) *d'état,* (*med.*) acme
Périodicité, *s.f.* periodicity, periodicalness
Périodique, *adj.* periodic; (*of decimals*) circulating
Périodiquement, *adv.* periodically
Périodiste, *s.m.f.* periodicalist
Périodontite, *s.f.* (*med.*) periodontitis
Périodure, *s.m.* (*chem.*) periodide
Périœciens, *s.m.pl.* (*geog.*) periœcians
Périoste, *s.m.* (*anat.*) periosteum
Périostite, Périostéite, *s.f.* (*med.*) periostitis
Périostome, *s.m.* (*surg.*) periostomy-knife
Périostomie, *s.f.* (*surg.*) periostomy
Périostose, *s.f.* (*med.*) periostosis
Périostraque, *s.m.* (*of shells*) periostrachum
Péripatéticien, ne, *adj. s.,* **Péripatétique,** *adj.* Peripatetic
Péripatétiquement, *adv.* peripatetically
Péripatétisme, *s.m.* peripateticism
Péripétie, *s.f.* revolution, vicissitude; catastrophe, event denouement; incident
Périphér-ie, -ique. *V.* page 3, § 1
Périphrase, *s.f.* periphrasis, circumlocution
Périphraser, *v.n.a.* to periphrase
Périphrast-ique, -iquement. *V.* page 3, § 1
Périple, *s.m.* (*anc. geog.*) periplus, circumnavigation
Périploque, *s.f.* (*bot.*) periploca
Péripneumonie, *s.f.* (*med.*) peripneumonia
Péripneumonique, *adj.* (*med.*) peripneumonic
Périptère, *s.m.* (*arch.*) periptery; — *adj.* peripteral
Périr, *v.n.* to perish; to decay; to die; to sink; to fall; to lapse; to be lost *or* destroyed. *Faire* —, to put to death; to destroy; to carry off; to cause to decay; to do away with

Périsciens, *s.m.pl.* (*geog.*) periscians
Périscopique, *adj.* periscopic
Périsperme, *s.m.* (*bot.*) perisperm
Périssable, *adj.* perishable
Périssoire, *s.f.* water-boat, canoe
Périssolog-ie, -ique. *V.* page 3, § 1
Péristaltique, *adj.* (*anat.*) peristaltic
Péristole, *s.f.* (*anat.*) peristole
Péristome, *s.m.* (*nat. hist.*) peristome
Péristyle, *s. m.* (*arch.*) peristyle ; — *adj.* adorned with a peristyle
Périsystole, *s.f.* (*anat.*) perisystole
Péritoine, *s.m.* (*anat.*) peritoneum
Péritonéal, e, *adj.* (*anat.*) peritoneal
Péritonite, *s.f.* (*med.*) peritonitis
Perlasse, *s.f.* pearlash
Perle, *s.f.* pearl; bead, beading; best; (*insect*) stone-fly. — *fine*, fine pearl, real pearl. — *-tube*, bugle. *Mère* —, mother-of-pearl shell
Perlé, e, *adj.* pearled; pearly; beady; (*of sugar*) boiled twice; (*mus.*, &c.) brilliant; exquisitely done; capital
Perler, *v.a* to pearl; to bead; to boil (*sugar*) twice; to do to perfection; to give a finish to; to polish; to adorn; — *v.n.* to pearl, to bead, to resemble pearls, to form round like a pearl, to form globules, to stand in beads; to glisten, to sparkle
  Se —, *v.r.* to be (*or* become) pearled *or* &c.
Perlette, *s.f.* little pearl
Perli-er, ère, *adj.* of pearl, pearl
Perlimpinpin, *s.m.* *Poudre de* —, quack powder; nostrum; inefficacious stuff, a chip in [porridge
Perlite, *s.f.* (*min.*) pearlite, pearl-stone
Perlure, *s.f.* (*hunt.*) curling (*of horns*)
Permanemment, *adv.* permanently
Permanence, *s.f.* permanence, permanency. *En* —, permanent; permanently
Permanent, e, *adj.* permanent; lasting; constant; standing
Permanganate, *s.m.* (*chem.*) permanganate
Perméabilité, *s.f.* permeability, perviousness
Perméable, *adj.* permeable, pervious
Permettre, *v.a.* to permit, to allow; to suffer; to give leave; to let; to enable; to afford; may. *Permettez !* allow me! excuse me!
  Se —, *v.r.* to allow oneself; to indulge in; to take the liberty; to take the liberty of doing; to take upon oneself, to take, to assume; to dare; to dare to do; (*of things*) to be allowed
Permien, ne, *adj.* (*geol.*) Permian; — *s.m.* [Permian rocks
Permis, e, *part. adj.* permitted, allowed, &c. (*V.* **Permettre**); allowable; lawful; justifiable; given (to), in the power (of); possible; decent. *A vous* — *de*, — *à vous de*, you may. *S'il m'est* — *de*, if I may
Permis, *s.m.* permission, licence; permit; leave; pass. — *de chasse*, shooting-licence, game-licence. — *de circulation*, (*rail.*) pass. — *de séjour*, permission to reside (*or* to remain)
Permissi-f, ve, *adj.* permissive [in the country
Permission, *s.f.* permission, leave; consent; permit; licence
Permissionnaire, *s.m.f.* permittee; grantee
Permissionner, *v.a.* to license
Permixtion, *s.f.* permixtion
Permutabilité, *s.f.* permutability, permutableness, commutability, exchangeability
Permutable, *adj.* permutable, commutable, exchangeable
Permutant, *s.m.* permuter, exchanger
Permutation, *s.f.* permutation, commutation, change, exchange; transposition
Permuter, *v.a.* to permute, to commute, to change, to exchange
  Se —, *v.r.* to be permuted *or* exchanged
Permuteur, *s.m.* permuter, exchanger
Perne, *s.f.* (*mollusc*) perna [ously, mischievously
Pernicieusement, *adv.* perniciously, injuri-
Pernicieu-x, se, *adj.* pernicious, injurious, mischievous
Perniciosité, *s.f.* perniciousness
Péroné, *s.m.* (*anat.*) fibula
Péronéo, (*in compounds, anat.*) peroneo-...
Péroni-er, ère, *adj.* (*anat.*) peroneal; — *s.m.* peroneal muscle [hussy
Péronnelle, *s.f.* silly wench, saucy baggage,
Péroraison, *s.f.* peroration
Pérorer, *v.n.* to harangue, to speechify, to hold forth, to spout [ifier
Péroreu-r, se, *s.m.f.* speech-maker; speech-
Pérot, *s.m.* (*fam.*) poll; gobbler (*turkey*)
Pérou (Le), *s.m.* Peru; (*fig.*) a mint of money, a fortune; a great *or* extraordinary thing, much
Peroxyde, *s.m.* (*chem.*) peroxide [oxidize
Peroxyder, *v.a.* (*chem.*) to peroxidate, to per-
Perpendiculaire, *adj.m.f.*, *s.f.* perpendicular
Perpendiculairement, *adv.* perpendicularly
Perpendicularité, *s.f.* perpendicularity
Perpendicule, *s.m.* plumb-line, perpendicle
Perpétration, *s.f.* perpetration
Perpétrer, *v.a.* to perpetrate, to commit
Perpétualité, *s.f.* perpetualty
Perpétuation, *s.f.* perpetuation
Perpétuel, le, *adj.* perpetual; everlasting; permanent; for life; constant
Perpétuellement, *adv.* perpetually; everlastingly; permanently; constantly
Perpétuer, *v.a.* to perpetuate. *Se* —, to be perpetuated, to last, to endure, to remain, to continue
Perpétuité, *s.f.* perpetuity. *A* —, in perpetuity; for ever; for life; ever; perpetual; perpetually
Perplexe, *adj.* perplexed; perplexing
Perplexité, *s.f.* perplexity [vestigator
Perquisiteur, *s.m.* perquisitor, searcher; in-
Perquisition, *s.f.* perquisition, search; research, investigation
Perré, *s.m.* (*of rivers*) water-wing; (*of the sea*) pebbly shore, shingly beach
Perreyer, *v.a.* to stone
Perron, *s.m.* flight of steps, steps, flight, perron
Perroquet, *s.m.* parrot; (*nav.*) top-mast, top-gallant mast. *Mât de* —, top-mast, top-gallant-mast. *Voile de* —, top-sail, gallant-sail. — *volant* or *royal*, (*nav.*) *V.* **Cacatois**
Perruche, *s.f.* hen-parrot; paroquet; (*nav.*) mizzen top-gallant
Perruque, *s.f.* wig, periwig, peruke; mop, shock; fogy, old fogy; wigging; — *adj.* old-fashioned, antiquated, obsolete, prejudiced. — *ronde*, bobtail-wig, bob-wig, bob. — *à bourse*, bag-wig. — *à nœuds*, tie-wig [thing
Perruquerie, *s.f.* fogyism; antiquated old
Perruqui-er, ère, *s.m.f.* wig-maker, peruke-maker, perruquier; hair-dresser, hair-cutter; barber; ditto's wife
Pers, e, *adj.* (*old*) blue; — *s.m.* blue cloth
Persan, e, Perse, *adj. s.* Persian; Persian [fashion
Perscrutation, *s.f.* perscrutation
Perse, *s.f.* chintz; — (*geog.*, *La* —) Persia
Persécutant, e, *adj. s.* *V.* **Persécuteur**
Persécuter, *v.a.* to persecute; to torment; to worry; to importune; to bore; to trouble; to dun
Persécu-teur, trice, *adj.* persecuting; importunate, troublesome; — *s.m.f.* persecutor, persecutrix; bore; dun
Persécution, *s.f.* persecution; torment; annoyance, trouble, nuisance, bore, bother
Persée, *s.m.* (*myth.*, *astr.*) Perseus
Persévéramment, *adv.* perseveringly
Persévérance, *s.f.* perseverance
Persévérer, *v.n.* to persevere, to persist
Persicaire, *s.f.* (*bot.*) persicaria
Persicot, *s.m.* persicot (*cordial*)
Persienne, *s.f.* louvre shutter-blind, outside shutter-blind, blind, louvred shutter, Venetian shutter. — *fixe*, louvre, louvre-boarding, lufferboard, lufferboarding
Persiflage, *s.m.* quizzing, bantering, banter, chaffing, chaff [chaff
Persifler, *v.a.n.* to quiz, to banter, to rally, to

Persifleu-r, se, *s.m.f.* quiz, banterer; — *adj.* quizzing, bantering, chaffing
Persil, *s.m.* parsley
†**Persillade,** *s.f.* beef dressed with parsley
†**Persillé, e,** *adj.* (*of cheese*) blue-mouldy, blue-vinnewed, blue-vinny; sage *or* green
Persique, *adj.* Persian, Persic
Persistance, *s.f.* persistence
Persistant, e, *part. adj.* persisting, persistent
Persister, *v.n.* to persist
Personnage, *s.m.* personage; great person; somebody; person; fellow; figure; (*theat.*) part, character, "dramatis persona"
Personnalisation, *s.f.* personalization, impersonation
Personnaliser, *v.a.* to personalize, to impersonate; — *v.n.* to deal *or* indulge in personalities [selfishness
Personnalisme, *s.m.* personalism, egotism,
Personnalité, *s.f.* personality; self-love; selfishness; personage, person
Personne, *s.f.* person; creature; body; own self, self; head; exterior, appearance; — *pron.m.* any one, anybody, any; no one, nobody, none; —**s,** *s.f.pl.* persons; people. *Jeune* —, young girl, young lady. *De sa* —, of *or* from *or* &c. (*V.* **De**) o.'s person; in person; personally [— *s.f.* ditto flower
Personnée, *adj.f.* (*bot.*) personate *or* masked;
Personnel, le, *adj.* personal; selfish
Personnel, *s.m.* persons, people employed, officers and men; officers and servants; officials; men; women; girls; hands; staff; at-
Personnellement, *adv.* personally [tendants
Personnifica-teur, trice, *s.m.f.* personifier
Personnification, *s.f.* personification; personation, impersonation [ate
Personnifier, *v.a.* to personify; to imperson-
Se —, *v.r.* to be personified *or* &c.
Perspecti-f, ve, *adj.* perspective
Perspective, *s.f.* perspective; distance; prospect; view; vista; opening
Perspicace, *adj.* perspicacious
Perspicacité, *s.f.* perspicacity
Perspicuité, *s.f.* perspicuity [tion
Perspiration, *s.f.* (*med.*) insensible perspira-
Persuader, *v.a.* to persuade; to convince, to satisfy [to fully believe; to believe, to imagine
Se —, *v.r.* to persuade *or* convince oneself;
Persuadeur, *s.m.* persuader
Persuasible, *adj.* persuasible, persuadable
Persuasi-f, ve, *adj.* persuasive [lief
Persuasion, *s.f.* persuasion; conviction, be-
Persulfure, *s.m.* (*chem.*) persulphide, persulphuret
Persulfuré, e, *adj.* (*chem.*) persulphuretted
Perte, *s.f.* loss; waste; ruin; perdition; destruction; death; fall; (*med.*) flooding. *A* —, at a loss; losing. *En* —, out of pocket, a loser. *En pure* —, to no purpose, useless, uselessly, in vain. *Être en* —, to be out of pocket, to lose, to be a loser [shooting
Pertérébrant, e, *adj.* (*med.*) perterebrant,
Pertinacité, *s.f.* pertinacity
Pertinemment, *adv.* pertinently
Pertinence, *s.f.* pertinence
Pertinent, e, *adj.* pertinent [(*geog.*) straits
Pertuis, *s.m.* hole; bore; opening; pass;
Pertuisane, *s.f.* partisan, halberd [warder
Pertuisanier, *s.m.* halberdier; (*of convicts*)
Perturba-teur, trice, *s.m.f.* disturber; — *adj.* disturbing; (*med.*) substitutive
Perturbation, *s.f.* perturbation, disturbance
Pertus, e, *adj.* (*bot.*) pertuse, pertused
Péruvien, ne, *adj. s.* Peruvian; Peruvian
Pervenche, *s.f.* (*bot.*) periwinkle [fashion
Pervers, e, *adj.* perverse; — *s.m.f.* perverse person, evil-doer
Perversement, *adv.* perversely
Perversion, *s.f.* perversion
Perversité, *s.f.* perversity [verted
Pervertir, *v.a.* to pervert. *Se* —, to be per-
Pervertissable, *adj.* pervertible
Pervertissement, *s.m.* perverting; perver-
Pervertisseu-r, se, *s.m.f.* perverter [sion
Pesade, *s.f.* (*rid.*) pesade
Pesage, *s.m.* weighing; weighing-room
Pesamment, *adv.* heavily; slowly
Pesant, e, *part. adj.* weighing; heavy; weighty; ponderous; burdensome; slow; sluggish; dull; (*of coin*) of full weight; — *s.m.* weight; — *adv.* weight, in weight
Pesanteur, *s.f.* heaviness; weight; ponderousness; burdensomeness; burden; slowness; sluggishness; dulness; gravity; gravitation
Pesat, *s.m.* pea-haulm
Pèse, *s.m.* (*in compounds, from* **Peser,** "to weigh") thing that weighs, weigher, balance, scales, meter, gauge, &c. — **-acides,** *s.m.* acetometer. — **-esprit,** *s.m.* alcoholometer. — **-lait,** *s.m.* lactometer, galactometer. — **-lettres,** *s.m.* letter-weigher, letter-scales *or* balance, postage-scales. — **-liqueurs,** *s.m.* areometer, hydrometer. — **-papier,** *s.m.* paper-weigher. — **-sel,** *s. m.* salt-gauge, salinometer. — **-vin,** *s.m.* œnometer
Pesée, *s.f.* weighing, weigh; weight; prising, prise (*of a lever*); haul, pull
Peser, *v.a.n.* to weigh; to ponder; to consider; to press; to lean; to bear *or* hang (upon); to be heavy; to hang *or* lie heavy; to be a burden; to dwell; to be of weight *or* of full weight [weigh oneself
Se —, *v.r.* to be weighed *or* &c.; (*pers.*) to
Pesette, *s.f.* assay-scales; (*bot.*) vetch
Peseu-r, se, *s.m.f.* weigher [weight
Peson, *s. m.* steelyard, weighing-machine;
Pessaire, *s.m.* (*surg.*) pessary
Pesse, *s.f.* (*bot.*) mare's-tail; picea, pitch-pine
Pessim-isme, -iste. *V.* page 3, § 1
Peste, *s.f.* plague; pestilence; pest; stink, stench; nuisance; torment; roguish *or* mischievous child; — *adj.* (*old*) arch, sly, roguish, mischievous; — *int.* plague! the deuce! hang it! bless me! indeed! forsooth! — *soit de,* a plague on (*or* upon), the deuce take. *Dire — et rage de,* to say all kinds of things against, to fall foul of [veigh, to bluster, to swear (at)
Pester, *v.n.* to fret and fume; to storm, to in-
Pestifère, *adj.* pestiferous, pestilential
Pestiféré, e, *adj.* infected, plague-stricken; — *s.m.f.* person infected with the plague
Pestiférer, *v.a.* (*old*) to plague
Pestilence, *s.f.* pestilence
Pestilent, e, Pestilentiel, le, *adj.* pestilential; infectious, contagious
Pet, *s.m.* fart, wind. — *-de-nonne,* (*pastry*) puff. — *-en-l'air,* short morning-jacket, tub-coat
Pétale, *s.m.* (*bot.*) petal, flower-leaf
Pétalé, e, *adj.* (*bot.*) petaled, petalous
Pétalisme, *s.m.* (*in antiquity*) petalism
Pétalite, *s.f.* (*min.*) petalite
Pétarade, *s.f.* breaking wind; trumpeting with the mouth; snap of the fingers; vain boast; cracking; noise of crackers [exposure
Pétard, *s.m.* petard; cracker; (*pop.*) scandal,
Pétarder, *v.a.* to blow up with a petard [beetle
Pétardier, *s.m.* petardier; (*zool.*) bombardier-
Pétase, *s.m.* petasus
Pétasite, *s.f.* (*bot.*) petasites, butter-bur
Pétaud. *La cour du roi* —, Bedlam broken loose, Dover court, all speakers and no hearers
Pétaudière, *s.f.* bear-garden, confused company
Pétauriste, *s.m.* (*zool.*) petaurist
Pétéchial, e, *adj.* (*med.*) petechial
Pétéchie, *s.f.* (*med.*) petechia, (*pl.*) petechiæ
Péter, *v.n.* to crackle; to crack; to make a loud report; to explode; to burst; to break wind, to fart [fellow *or* thing; milksop
Péteu-r, se, Péteu-x, se, *s.m.f.* farter; dirty
†**Pétillement,** *s.m.* crackling; sparkling
†**Pétiller,** *v.n.* to crackle; to sparkle; to be full; to long, to be boiling *or* eager *or* impa-
Pétiolaire, *adj.* (*bot.*) petiolar [tient

Pétiole, *s.m.* (*bot.*) petiole, leaf-stalk, foot-stalk, [stalk
Pétiolé, e, *adj.* (*bot.*) petioled, petiolate
Petiot, e, *adj. s.* (*pop.*) little one, little fellow *or* thing, kid, darling, ducky
Petit, e, *adj.* little; small; short; young; junior; low; humble; slow; lesser; minor; inferior; petty; inconsiderable, unimportant, slight, trifling; faint; mean; narrow; shallow; dear, darling; (*of descendants*) grand; — *s.m.f.* little one; little boy; little fellow; little girl; child; little thing; small thing *or* things, little dear, darling; sweet; chuck; young one; cub; whelp; kit, kitten; pup, puppy; —**s,** *s m.pl.* young; low people, low; (*at school*) little boys, (—**es,** *f.pl.*) little girls. —*s-enfants*, *V* **Enfant.** — *-fils*, —*e-fille*, *V.* **Fils** *and* **Fille.** — *-gris*, *s.m.* minever. — *-lait*, — *-maitre*, — *-salé*, &c., *V.* **Lait, Maître, Salé,** &c. — *-neveu*, grand-nephew; (*without a hyphen*) little nephew. —*e-nièce*, grand-niece; (*without a hyphen*) little niece. — *à* —, little by little, by little and little, by degrees, gradually. *Du — au grand*, by comparing small things with great ones; with all alike. *En* —, on a small scale; in miniature. *Faire des —s*, to bring forth young, to whelp, to pup, to kitten, &c.
Petitement, *adv.* narrowly, slenderly, sparingly, poorly, meanly, shabbily; indifferently; little, not much
Petitesse, *s.f.* littleness; smallness; shortness; slenderness; pettiness; insignificance; meanness, shabbiness; narrowness; shallowness; mean *or* shabby thing *or* action
Pétition, *s.f.* petition; memorial. — *de principe*, begging the question [applicant
Pétitionnaire, *s.m.f.* petitioner; memorialist;
Pétitionnement, *s.m.* petitioning; memorializing
Pétitionner, *v.a.n.* to petition; to memorialize
Pétitoire, *adj.* (*law*) petitory; — *s.m.* petitory suit *or* action
Pétiverie, *s f.* (*bot.*) petiveria, Guinea-hen weed
Peton, *s.m.* (*jest.*) pettitoe
Pétoncle, *s.f.* (*shell-fish*) scollop
Pétra, Pétras, *s.m.* lout, bumpkin, boor
Pétrée, *adj.f.* (*of Arabia*) Petræa, Petrea, rocky, stony; (*nat. hist.*) petrean
Pétrel, *s.m.* (*bird*) petrel; shearwater
Pétreu-x, se, *adj.* petrous, rocky, stony, gravelly; (*anat.*) petrous [up (of)
Pétri, e, *part. adj.* kneaded; (*fig.*) full, made
Pétricherie, *s.f.* cod-fishing tackle
Pétricole, *adj.* petricolous, living in stones
Pétrification, *s.f.* petrifaction, petrification
Pétrifier, *v.a.*, **Se** —, *v.r.* to petrify
Pétrin, *s.m.* kneading-trough; scrape, mess, hobble, pickle, hot water. — *mécanique*, knead-
Pétrinal, *s.m.* (*obsolete*) petronel [ing-machine
Pétrir, *v.a.* to knead; to work; to rub; to make, to form; to fill. *Se* —, to be kneaded, &c.
Pétrissage, Pétrissement, *s.m.* kneading; working; rubbing; forming
Pétrisseu-r, se, *s.m.f.* kneader; baker's second hand, bread-maker; — *adj.* kneading. — *mecanique*, kneading-machine [3, § 1
Pétro-graphie, -graphique, &c. *V.* page
Pétrole, *s.m.* petroleum, rock-oil
Pétrolerie, *s.f.* petroleum-works
Pétrolifère, *adj.* petroliferous
Pétrosilex, *s.m.* (*min.*) petrosilex
Pétrosiliceu-x, se, *adj.* petrosilicious
Petto (In), *adv.* (*Italian*) in petto, within the breast, inwardly, in secret, secretly, in reserve
Pétulamment, *adv.* petulantly
Pétulance, *s.f.* petulance
Pétulant, e, *adj.* petulant
Pétunia, *s.m.* (*bot.*) petunia
Pétunsé, *s.m.* petunse, china-stone
Peu, *adv.* little; not much, not very; no great; a little; few; not many; a few; short; soon; a short time; not, un..., in..., im...; under...; the other way; — *s.m.* small amount or quantity; bit; small number; little; few; a little; a few; little *or* short time (*or* while); little consequence; little worth; shortness; scarcity; absence, want. — *à* —, little by little, by little and little, by degrees, gradually. *Avant* —, before long. *Dans* —, shortly. *Pour — que*, however little; if ... ever so little; if ... in the least; if only, if at all. *Quelque* —, a little, rather, somewhat, slightly; somewhat of a. *Si — que*, however little; however short a time. *Si — que rien*, very little, next to nothing. *Sous* —, shortly. *Très* or *bien* or *fort* (*adv.*) —, very little. — *fort* (*adj.*), not very strong *or* &c., weak. *Un* —, a little; not much; a few; not many; rather; somewhat of a, somewhat; just; only; I believe you! *Un petit* —, (*fam.*) a small bit, very little; a trifle. *Un — bien*, soundly; freely; rather too much; with a vengeance; and no mistake. *Un* —, *mon neveu!* (*pop.*) I believe you, my boy!
Peucédan, Peucédane, *s.m.* (*bot.*) peucedanum, hog's-fennel, sulphur-wort
Peucédanine, *s.f.* (*chem.*) peucedanine
Peuh, *int.* pooh! [young fish
Peuplade, *s.f.* people; colony; tribe; fry,
Peuple, *s.m.* people; nation; race; tribe; population; multitude; crowd; citizens; working classes; common people, lower class, lower classes, vulgar; fry, young fish; poplar; deal; (*hort.*) sucker; — *adj.* vulgar. *Le bas* —, the mob, the populace, the lower orders. *Le menu* or *petit* —, the common people, the vulgar. *Du* —, of *or* from the people, &c.; common, vulgar, low
Peuplé, e, *part. adj* peopled; populous; full of people; stocked; planted; filled, full
Peuplement, *s.m.* peopling; stocking; planting
Peupler, *v.a.n.* to people, to populate; to fill with people; to stock; to plant; to fill; to multiply; to propagate; to breed
Se —, *v.r.* to be (*or* become) peopled *or* &c., to become populous [grove
Peupleraie, *s.f.* poplar-plantation, poplar-
Peuplier, *s.m.* poplar
Peuplière, *s.f* poplar-mushroom
Peur, *s.f.* fear; fright; dread; terror; timidity; cowardice. *A faire* —, frightfully; frightful. *De — de*, for fear of. *De — que*, for fear, lest. *Avoir* —, to be afraid; to be frightened. *Faire — à*, to frighten; to frighten away; to deter; to cause fear; to make (*one*) afraid; to be frightful to. *Mourir de* —, to die of fright, to be frightened to death, to be terribly afraid. *Faire mourir de* —, to frighten to death
Peureusement, *adv.* timidly, timorously, skittishly, shyly
Peureu-x, se, *adj.* timid, timorous, fearful, skittish, shy, easily frightened; — *s.m.f.* ditto person, coward; boggler
Peut-être, *adv.* perhaps, may be; — *s.m.* perhaps, chance, possibility, supposition
Peutingérienne, *adj.f.* Peutingerian
Pezize, *s.f.* (*bot.*) peziza
Phacochère, *s.m.* (*zool.*) wart-hog
Phaéton, *s.m.* (*carriage, bird*) phaeton; (*jest.*) driver, coachman, Jehu; (*myth.*) Phaeton
Phagédène, *s.f.* (*med.*) phagedæna
Phagédén-ique, -isme, (*med.*) *V.* page 3, § 1
Phalacrose, *s f.* (*med.*) phalacrosis
Phalange, *s.f.* phalanx; band; (*anat.*) phalanx, bone-joint; (*zool.*) phalangium
Phalanger, *s.m.* (*zool.*) phalanger, phalangist
Phalangite, *s.m.* (*antiq.*) phalangite
Phalangose, *s.f.* (*med.*) phalangosis [nism
Phalanstère, *s.m.* phalanstery; phalansteria-
Phalanstérien, ne, *adj. s.* phalansterian
Phalaris, *s.m.* (*bot.*) phalaris, canary-grass
Phalarope, *s.m.* (*bird*) phalarope
Phalène, *s.f.* moth
Phallique, *adj.* phallic
Phallite, *s.f.* (*med.*) phallitis [lorrhagy
Phallorrhagie, *s.f.* (*med.*) phallorrhagia, phal-

Phallus, *s.m.* phallus
Phanérogame, *adj.* (*bot.*) phanerogamous; — *s.m.f.* phanerogam
Phanérogam-ie, -ique. *V.* page 3, § 1
Phantasme. *V.* **Fantasme**
Pharamineu-x,se, *adj.* (*pop.*) *V.* **Mirobolant**
Pharaon, *s.m.* (*hist.*) Pharaoh; (*game*) faro
Pharaonique, *adj.* Pharaonic
Phare, *s.m.* light-house; beacon, light; (*of Messina*) Straits. —*flottant*, beacon-ship, light- [ship
†**Pharillon,** *s.m.* (*fish.*) lantern
Pharisa-ïque, -ïquement, -ïsme. *V.* page 3, § 1 [saical
Pharisien, ne, *s.m.f.* pharisee; — *adj.* phari-
Pharmaceut-ique (*adj.*), **-iquement.** *V.* page 3, § 1
Pharmaceutique, *s.f.* pharmaceutics
Pharmacie, *s.f.* pharmacy; chemist's shop; surgery (*place*); dispensary, medicine-chest; medicines
Pharmacien, *s.m.* (pharmaceutical *or* dispensing) chemist, apothecary; (*in hospitals*, &c) dispenser [wife
Pharmacienne, *s.f.* (dispensing) chemist's
Pharmacolog-ie,-ique,-iste. *V.* page 3, § 1
Pharmacopée, *s.f.* pharmacopœia
Pharmacopole, *s.m.* pharmacopolist
Pharyngé, e, Pharyngien, ne, *adj* (*anat.*) pharyngeal, pharyngean
Pharyngite, *s.f.* (*med.*) pharyngitis
Pharyngocèle, *s.f.* (*med.*) pharyngocele [§ 1
Pharyngo-graphie, -logie, &c. *V.* page 3,
Pharyngoscope, *s.m.* (*surg.*) pharyngoscope
Pharyngo-scopie, -tomie, &c *V.* page 3, § 1
Pharyngotome, *s.m.* (*surg.*) pharyngotomy- [knife
Pharynx, *s.m.* (*anat.*) pharynx
Phascolome, *s.m.* (*zool.*) phascolome, wombat
Phase, *s.f.* phase, phasis; change; stage, turn, [aspect
Phaséole. *V.* **Faséole**
Phasianelle, *s.f* (*mollusc*) pheasant-shell
Phasma, Phasme, *s.m.* (*insect*) phasma, leaf-insect, walking-leaf, spectre-insect, walking- [stick
Phébé, *s.f* Phœbe; (*poet.*) the moon
Phébus, *s.m.* bombast, fustian, rant; fine talker; (*myth.*) Phœbus, Apollo; (*poet.*) the sun; [poetry, poets
Phéci, *s.m.* (*mil. cap*) kepi, fez
Phellandre, *s.m.* (*bot.*) water-hemlock
Phelloplastique, *adj.* phelloplastic; — *s.f.* [phelloplastics
Phénate, *s.m.* (*chem.*) phenate
Phène, *s.f.* *V.* **Gypaète**
Phénicien, ne, *adj. s.* Phœnician
Phénicine, *s.f.* (*chem.*) phenicine
Phénicoptère, *s.m.* phenicopter, flamingo
Phénique, *adj.* (*chem.*) phenic
Phénix, *s.m.* phœnix, phenix
Phénol, *s.m.* (*chem.*) phenol
Phénoménal, e, *adj.* phenomenal
Phénomène, *s.m.* phenomenon
Phénoménologie, *s.f.* phenomenology
Phényle, *s.m.* (*chem.*) phenyl
Philanthrope, *s.m.* philanthropist
Philanthrop-ie,-ique,-iquement,-isme. *V.* page 3, § 1
Philharmonique, *adj* philharmonic
Philhellène, *s.m.f.* philhellene, philhellenist; — *adj.* philhellenic
Philhellénisme, *s.m.* philhellenism
Philinte, *s.m.* Philinte, everybody's friend
Philippique, *s.f.* philippic
Philistin, *s.m.* Philistine; (*German univers. slang*) Philistine, townsman, snob, cockney, vulgar fellow [cockneyism
Philistinisme, *s.m.* Philistinism, snobbism,
Phillyrée, *s.f.* (*bot.*) phillyrea, mock-privet
Philogéniture, *s.f.* philoprogenitiveness
Philogyne, *s.m.* philogynist
Philogynie, *s.f.* philogyny [§ 1
Philolog-ie, -ique, -iquement. *V.* page 3,
Philologue, *s.m.* philologist
Philomath-ie, -ique. *V.* page 3, § 1
Philomèle, *s.f.* (*myth.*) Philomela; (*poet.*) the nightingale

†**Philosophaille,** *s.f.* (*in contempt*) philosophers
†**Philosophailler,** *v n* (*in contempt*) to philosophize [*Pierre —e*, philosopher's stone
Philosophal, e, *adj.* philosopher's, alchemic.
Philosophaliste, *s m.* philosophalist, alchemist
Philosophe, *s.m.* philosopher; upper-form student; — *adj.* philosophical
Philosopher, *v.n.* to philosophize
Philosophie, *s.f.* philosophy; upper *or* highest form (*or* class); (*print.*) small pica
Philosoph-ique,-iquement,-isme,-iste. *V* page 3, § 1
‡**Philotechnique,** *adj.* philotechnic
Philtre, *s.m.* philter
Phimosis, *s m.* (*surg.*) phimosis
Phlébite, *s.f* (*med.*) phlebitis
Phlébolithe, *s.m.* phlebolite, vein-stone
Phlébo-graphie, -logie, -tomie, -tomiste. *V* page 3, § 1 [lancet, lancet
Phlébotome, *s.m.* (*surg*) phlebotome, spring-
Phlébotomiser, *v.a.* to phlebotomize, to bleed
Phlegmasie, Phlegmatique, Phlegme, Phlegmon, &c. *V* **Flegmasie,** &c., &c.
Phléole, *s.f.* *V.* **Fléole**
Phlogistique, *s.m.* (*anc. chem.*) phlogiston
Phlogose, *s.f.* (*med.*) phlogosis
Phlox, *s.m.* (*bot.*) phlox
Phlyctène, *s.f.* (*med.*) phlyctæna, bulla, blister
Phocéa, *s.f* (*astr.*) Phocea [of Marseilles
Phocéen, ne, *s.m.f. adj.* Phocean, Phocæan;
Phocène, *s.f* (*zool.*) phocæna
Phocénine, *s.f* (*chem.*) phocenine
Phœnicure, *s.m.* (*bird*) bluethroat, redstart
Pholade, *s.f.* (*mollusc*) pholas (*pl.* pholades), [piddock
Pholadite, *s f.* pholadite
Phonét-ique (*adj.*), **-iquement, -isme.**
Phonétique, *s f.* phonetics [*V.* page 3, § 1
Phonique, *adj.* phonic; — *s.f.* phonics
Phonographe, *s.m.* phonograph; (*pers*) phonographer
Phonograph-ie, -ique, &c. *V.* page 3, § 1
Phonomètre, *s.m.* phonometer
Phonométr-ie, -ique. *V.* page 3, § 1
Phoque, *s m.* (*zool.*) seal [New-Zealand flax
Phormion, Phormium, *s m.* phormium,
Phosgène, *adj.m.* (*chem.*) *Gaz* —, phosgene gas
Phosphate, *s.m.* (*chem.*) phosphate
Phosphaté, e, *adj.* phosphated
Phosphatique, *adj.* phosphatic
Phosphite, *s.m.* (*chem.*) phosphite
Phosphore, *s.m.* phosphorus
Phosphorer, *v.a.* to phosphorate. *Pâte phosphorée*, phosphorus paste
Phosphorescence, *s.f.* phosphorescence
Phosphorescent, e, *adj.* phosphorescent
Phosphoreu-x, se, *adj.* phosphorous
Phosphorique, *adj.* phosphoric
Phosphorisation, *s.f.* phosphorization
Phosphoriser, *v.a.* to phosphorize
Phosphorisme, *s.m.* phosphorism
Phosphorite, *s.f.* (*min.*) phosphorite
Phosphure, *s.m.* (*chem.*) phosphide, phosphuret
Phosphuré, e, *adj.* phosphuretted
Photo..., (*in compounds*) photo...
Photogène, *s.m.* photogen, illuminating-oil
Photogén-ie, -ique. *V.* page 3, § 1
Photographe, *s.m.* photographer; — *adj.* photographic [photographic studio
Photographie, *s.f.* photography; photograph;
Photographier, *v.a.* to photograph. *Se faire* —, to have o.'s photograph taken. *Se* —, (*things*) to be photographed
Photograph-ique, -iquement. *V.* page 3, § 1
Photolithographie, Photologie, &c. *V.*
Photomètre, *s.m.* (*phys.*) photometer [page 3, § 1
Photométr-ie, -ique. *V.* page 3, § 1
Photomicrograph-ie, -ique. *V.* page 3, § 1
Photophobe, *adj.s.* photophobic; photophobiac
Photophobie, *s.f.* (*med.*) photophobia
Photopsie, *s.f.* (*med.*) photopsia, photopsy
Photoscope, *s.m.* photoscope
Photoscopique, *adj.* photoscopic

Photosculptural, e, *adj.* photosculptural
Photosculpture, *s.f.* photosculpture
Photosphère, *s.f.* (*astr.*) photosphere
Phrasaire, *s.m.* phrase-book
Phrase, *s.f.* phrase, sentence; (*mus.*) phrase; **—s,** *pl.* phrases; sentences; affected language *or* style, empty talk, rigmarole, twaddle. *Membre de —,* (*gram.*) clause
Phrasé, e, *part. adj.* phrased; — *s.m.* phrasing
Phraséolog-ie, -ique. *V.* page 3, § 1
Phraser, *v.a.n.* to phrase
Phraseu-r, se, Phrasi-er, ère, *s. m. f.* phrase-maker, bombastic writer, affected speaker, empty talker, twaddler; — *adj.* bombastic, pompous, affected, empty, twaddling
Phrénique, *adj.* phrenic [the diaphragm
Phrénite, *s.f.* (*med.*) phrenitis, inflammation of
Phrénitis, *s.f.* (*obsolete*) phrenitis, imflammation of the brain, frenzy [*V.* page 3, § 1
Phrénolog-ie, -ique, -iquement, -iste.
Phrénologue, *s.m.* phrenologist
Phrygane, *s.f.* (*zool.*) caddice-fly, caddice
Phrygien, ne, *adj. s.* Phrygian
Phryné, *s.f.* Phryne, great courtesan
Phthiriase, *s.f.*, **Phthiriasis,** *s.m.* (*med., bot.*) phthiriasis [decline
Phthisie, *s.f.* (*med.*) consumption, phthisis,
Phthisiologie, *s.f.* phthisiology
Phthisique, *adj. s.m.f.* consumptive, phthisical
Phthore, *s.m.* (*chem.*) fluorine
Phylactère, *s.m.* phylactery
Phyllosome, *s.m.* (*zool.*) glass crab
Phyllostome, *s.m.* phyllostoma, spectre-bat,
Physale, *s.m.* (*zool.*) rorqual [blood-sucking bat
Physalide, *s.f.* (*bot.*) physalis
Physalie, *s.f.* (*zool.*) physalia, jelly-fish, sea-
Physaline, *s.f.* (*chem.*) physaline [nettle
Physalite, *s.f.* (*min.*) physalite
Physéter, Physétère, *s.m.* physeter, cachalot, sperm-whale
Physicien, *s.m.* natural philosopher, physicist; student of physics; conjurer, wizard
Physico, (*in compounds*) physico-...
Physiocrate, *s.m.* physiocrat
Physiocratie, *s.f.* physiocracy
Physiocratique, *adj.* physiocratic [ognomy
Physiognomonie, *s.f.* physiognomics, physi-
Physiognomonique, *adj.* physiognomical
Physiographe, *s.m.* physiographer
Physiograph-ie, -ique. *V.* page 3, § 1
Physiolog-ie, -ique, -iquement, -iste. *V.* page 3, § 1
Physionomie, *s.f.* physiognomy; look, countenance; expression; aspect, appearance; character
Physionomiste, *s.m.f.* physiognomist
Physionotrace, Physionotype, *s.m.* physiognotype
Physique, *s.f.* physics, physical science, natural philosophy; class of physics; — *s.m.* natural constitution, constitution; body; exterior, personal appearance, person; physical sense; — *adj.* physical; natural; bodily
Physiquement, *adv.* physically; bodily
Phytographe, *s.m.* phytographer
Phyto - graphie, -graphique, -logie, -logique. *V.* page 3, § 1
Phytolithe, *s.m.* (*min.*) phytolite [tophagan
Phytophage, *adj.* phytophagous; — *s.m.* phy-
Phytotom-ie, -ique, -iste. *V.* page 3, § 1
Piaffe, *s.f.* show, dash
Piaffement, *s.m.* pawing the ground; prancing
Piaffer, *v.n.* to paw the ground; to prance; to make a show, to cut a dash
Piaffeu-r, se, *s.m.f.* pawer; prancer; showy *or* dashy person; — *adj.* pawing; prancing; showy, dashy
†**Piaillard, e,** *s.m.f. adj. V.* **Piailleur** [rant
†**Piailler,** *v.n.* to bawl, to squall; to scold; to
†**Piaillerie,** *s f.* bawling, squalling; scolding
†**Piailleu-r, se,** *s.m.f.* bawler, squaller; scolder, scold; — *adj.* bawling, squalling; scolding

Pian, *s.m.* (*med.*) yaws. *Maman —, mère —, V.* **Mamapian** [ly; so so
Piane-piane, *adv.* (*pop.*) softly, gently; slow-
Pianino, *s.m.* (*mus.*) pianino, pianette, studio
Pianissimo, *adv.* (*mus., fig.*) pianissimo [piano
Pianiste, *s.m.f.* pianist
Piano, *s.m.* piano, pianoforte; — *adv.* piano, softly, gently. — *droit,* upright piano, cottage piano. — *à queue,* grand piano. *Petit — droit,* semi-cottage piano, piccolo piano. *Petit — à queue,* semi-grand piano. — *-forté,* (*obsolete*) *V.* **Forté-piano**
Pianoter, *v.n.* to thrum on the piano
Pianoteu-r, se, *s.m.f.* thrummer; — *adj.* thrumming [palm
Piassava, *s.m.* piassava, piassaba, coquilla-nut
Piaste, *s.m.* piast (*old Polish nobleman*)
Piastre, *s.f.* (*coin*) piastre, piaster
Piat, *s.m.* young magpie
Piaulard, e, *s.m.f. adj. V.* **Piauleur**
Piaulement, *s.m.* whining, puling
Piauler, *v.n.* to whine, to pule
Piauleu-r, se, *s.m.f.* whiner; — *adj.* whining, puling [*Mâté à —,* pole-masted
Pible, *s.m.* (*nav.*) pole. *Mât à —,* pole-mast.
‡**Pibroch,** *s.m.* (*Scotch*) pibroch
Pic, *s.m.* pickaxe, pick; gaff; pike; poker; (*geog.*) peak; (*bird*) woodpecker; (*at the game of piquet*) pique (*V.* **Repic**). *A —,* perpendicular, perpendicularly; bluff; (*nav.*) apeak; (*pop.*) in the nick of time. — **-vert,** *s.m. V.* **Pivert** [pika, Alpine lagomys
Pica, *s.m.* (*med.*) pica, depraved appetite; (*zool.*)
Picador, *s.m.* (*in Spanish bull-fights*) picador
†**Picaillon,** *s.m.* (*pop.*) copper, brown, mag (*coin*); dust, tin (*money*)
†**Picaillonnage,** *s.m.* (*pop.*) hard saving
Picamare, *s.f.* (*chem.*) picamar, picamare
Picard, e, *adj. s.m.f.* Picard, native of Picardy; cunning; cautious; cunning fellow *or* thing, artful dodger; — *s.f.* Picard fashion
Piccolo, *s.m.* (*mus.*) piccolo (*flute*)
Picéa, *s.m.* (*bot.*) picea, pitch-pine
Pichenette, *s.f.* fillip
Pichet, *s.m.* jug, pot, quart
‡**Picholine,** *s.f. adj.* picholine (*olive*)
Picoline, *s.f.* (*chem.*) picoline
Picorée, *s.f.* marauding; pilfering; picking; cribbing; plundering, plunder [plunder
Picorer, *v.n.a.* to pilfer; to pick; to crib; to
Picoreu-r, se, *s.m.f.* marauder, picaroon; pilferer; picker; cribber, plagiarist; plunderer; — *adj.* pilfering; cribbing; plundering
Picot, *s.m.* splinter; (*of lace*) purl
Picoté, e, *part. adj.* pricked, &c. (*V.* **Picoter**); dotted; spotted; (*with the small-pox*) pitted,
Picotement, *s.m.* pricking, tingling [marked
Picoter, *v.a.* to prick; to tingle; to peck; to tease, to provoke, to irritate, to torment; to spur slightly, to touch with the spurs
Picoterie, *s.f.* teasing, bickering
Picoteux, *s.m.* (kind of fishing-boat)
Picotin, *s.m.* peck (*of oats*)
Picoture, *s.f.* spot, spots, dots
Picrate, *s.m.* (*chem.*) picrate
Picride, *s.f.* (*bot.*) ox-tongue
Picrine, *s.f.* (*chem.*) picrine
Picrique, *adj.* (*chem.*) picric
Picrotoxine, *s.f.* (*chem.*) picrotoxine
Picucule, *s.m. V.* **Pipicule**
Picumne, *s.m.* (*bird*) piculet
Pie, *s.f.* magpie; — *adj.* pious, charitable; (*of horses*) piebald. *Fromage à la —,* skimmed-milk cheese, new cheese, country cheese, Sussex cheese. *Trouver la — au nid,* (*ironically*) to make a great discovery. — **-grièche,** *s f.* (*bird*) shrike; (*pers.*) shrew, vixen. — *de* **mer,** (*bird*) sea-pie, oyster-catcher. — **-mère,** *s.f.* (*anat.*) pia-mater
Pièce, *s.f.* piece; fragment; part; portion; bit; patch; document, paper; play, performance; trick; piece of ordnance, gun, cannon;

room, apartment; cask; (*measure: in England*) butt, pipe, puncheon, cask, (*in France*) hogshead; (*of meat*) joint; (*of cattle, game, poultry, &c.*) head; (*of prices*) a piece, each; (*pers.*) blade, fellow, creature; (*her.*) charge, ordinary; **—s,** *pl.* pieces, &c.; gear; work, works; (*of fire-arms*) lock. *—s et morceaux*, odds and ends. *— à —*, piece by piece; bit by bit. *— de campagne*, (*artil.*) field-piece, field-gun. *— de canon*, gun, piece of ordnance. *— de vingt-quatre*, (*artil.*) 24-pounder. *— de conviction*, object used *or* that may be used as evidence against a prisoner, material evidence of the crime *or* of guilt; circumstantial evidence. *— d'eau*, piece of ornamental water, ornamental water, sheet of water; reservoir. *— de four*, oven-cake, oven-pastry. *— de résistance*, main piece; principal dish, solid dish, large joint, piece to cut and come again; substantial work. *— de théâtre*, play. *Bonne* or *fine —*, (*pers.*) cunning blade. *Petite —*, little *or* small piece; (*theat.*) short play; after-piece. *A la —*, *aux —s*, by the piece. *De toutes —s*, completely, entirely; bodily; at all points. *En —*, in the piece; in (the) cask, in the wood. *En —s*, in *or* to pieces; in casks. *Par —s*, piecemeal. *Tout d'une —*, all of a piece; (*pers.*) as stiff as a poker. *Accommoder* or *ajuster* or *habiller de toutes —s*, to treat very ill, to abuse, to fall foul of; to play (*one*) a trick. *Armé de toutes —s*, armed at all points. *Donner la —*, to give something (*money*), to give money, to tip. *Faire* (*une*) *—*, to play a trick. *Jouer une —*, to act *or* perform a play

Piécette, *s.f.* piecette (*small Spanish silver coin*)

Pied, *s.m.* foot; leg; trotter; pettitoe; stalk; plant; footing; base; bottom; ground; pace; step; track; terms; stand; pole; staff; (*of masts*) heel. *— bot*, *V.* **Bot.** *— droit*, right foot; (*arch.*) pied droit, pier, square pillar; upright. *— marin*, sea-legs. *— plat*, flat foot; splay-foot; low *or* dirty fellow, wretch. *— d'alouette*, *— de biche*, &c., *V.* **Alouette, Biche,** &c. *— de bœuf*, ox-foot, neat's foot; pied de bœuf (*kind of child's-game*). *— de cochon*, pig's foot, pettitoe; (*fig.*) beastly trick. *— de loup*, (*bot.*) *V.* **Lycope.** *-de-nez*, *V.* **Nez.** *-de-roi*, (*meas.*) foot-rule. *— de veau*, *V.* **Veau.** *Petits —s*, small *or* little feet *or* &c.; (*cook.*) small birds. *Pointe du —* or *des —s*, tiptoe; toes. *— à —*, foot by foot; step by step; inch by inch, by inches; by degrees; slowly and steadily; obstinately. *-à-terre*, (*s.m.*) temporary lodging, resting-place; country box, small box; (*de chasse*) hunting-box, shooting-lodge *or* box. *A —*, on foot; foot; with a foot *or* stand *or* &c., pole; standing; unmounted; dismounted; (*of a cabman*) deprived of his licence; (*of functionaries, &c.*) suspended, discharged, dismissed. *A — ...*, *aux —s ...*, with the feet *or* legs ...; with ... feet *or* legs; ...-footed, ...-legged. *A — sec*, dry-shod. *Au —*, at *or* on the feet, &c.; (*of arms*) grounded. *Au petit —*, with a small foot; (*fig.*) on a small scale; in miniature; in imitation, mock; in *or* to an inferior position. *Au — levé*, starting, going, on the start; at a disadvantage, unfairly; in an unguarded moment; without a moment's notice; at a minute's warning; unprepared; at o.'s word. *De — ferme*, without stirring; unflinchingly, firmly, resolutely. *En —*, standing; in active service; first; (*of portraits*) full length. *Haut le —*, up with the foot; (*of horses*) loose; (*of railway trains*) without passengers; (*int.*) away! off! be off! begone! (*s.m.*) *V.* **Haut.** *Sur —*, on foot, on o.'s feet *or* legs, up, standing; alive; sitting up, watching, awake, without sleep; (*mil.*) out; (*nav.*) afloat. *Sur le — de*, on the footing of; at the rate of; on the terms of. *Sur ce — -là*, on that footing; at that rate; on those terms. *Sur un bon —*, on a good footing; on good terms. *Aller* or *venir à —*, *aller* or *venir de son —*, to go *or* come on foot, to walk; to trudge. *Avoir —*, to be in o.'s depth. *Avoir bon — bon œil*, to be hale and hearty; to be sharp and active; to be watchful, to look sharp. *Faire — neuf*, (*of horses*) to get a new hoof. *Faire haut le —*, *gagner au —*, (*old*) to scamper away. *Lâcher —* or *le —*, to give way, to lose ground; to scamper away. *Lever le —*, to hold up o.'s foot; to take to o.'s heels, to scamper away, to start, to be off, to levant. *Marcher sur le — à*, to tread on ...'s foot *or* toes; (*fig.*) to be disrespectful *or* rude to; to pick a quarrel with. *Mettre à —*, to dismount (*a horseman*); to withdraw the licence of (*a cabman*); (*fig.*) to suspend (*a functionary, &c.*), to discharge, to dismiss. *Mettre sur —*, to set on foot *or* &c.; to set afloat; to raise; to set up; to make (*one*) get up. *Mettre — à terre*, to alight; to dismount; to land. *Perdre —*, to go *or* get out of o.'s depth; (*fig.*) to lose ground. *Prendre —*, to get a footing; to become established. *Tenir —*, to stand firmly. *Le — lui a manqué*, he missed his footing, his foot slipped, he slipped

Piédestal, *s.m.* pedestal; step [stand

Piédouche, *s.m.* piedouche, little pedestal,

Piége, *s.m.* snare; trap [fashion

Piémontais, e, *adj. s.* Piedmontese; ditto

†Pierraille, *s.f.* pebbles, small stones; broken stone *or* stones

Pierre, *s.f.* stone; flint; rock; gem. *— angulaire*, corner-stone. *— infernale*, lunar caustic, caustic. *— à aiguiser*, whetstone. *— à cautère*, lunar caustic. *— à feu* or *à fusil* or *à briquet*, gun-flint, flint. *— à l'huile*, oilstone. *— à laver*, sink-stone. *— à rasoir*, *— à repasser*, hone, whetstone. *— d'appareil*, building-stone. *—s d'arrachement*, toothing-stones, rustic coins. *— d'attente*, toothing-stone, rustic coin; (*fig.*) stepping-stone. *— d'hirondelle*, swallow-stone. *— de lard*, lardite, steatite, soap-stone. *— de taille*, freestone, cut *or* hewn stone. *— de touche*, touchstone; test. *A — fendre*, enough to split a stone *or* a rock, very hard, dreadfully, with a vengeance. *Faire d'une — deux coups*, to kill two birds with one stone. *Jeter la — à*, (*fig.*) to attack; to blame; to accuse. *Jeter des —s dans le jardin de*, (*fig.*) to attack indirectly, to make insinuations against [course; rubble; pebbles, weights

Pierrée, *s.f.* rubble *or* rubbling drain; water-

Pierreries, *s.f.pl.* gems, precious stones, jewels

Pierrette, *s.f.* hen-sparrow; (*female costume*) pierrette; (*obsolete*) little stone

Pierreu-x, se, *adj.* stony; flinty; rocky; gravelly; — *s.m.* (*old*) *V.* **Calculeux;** — *s.f.* low prostitute [mortar; swivel-gun, pivot-gun

Pierrier, *s.m.* stone drain; (*artil.*) stone-

Pierrière, *s.f.* petrary

Pierriste, *s.m.f.* — *en horlogerie*, watch-jeweller

Pierrot, *s.m.* sparrow; clown, Jack-pudding, fool, pierrot; fellow, fish, odd fish

Pierrures, *s.f.pl.* pearls (*of a deer's horns*)

Piété, *s.f.* piety; godliness; religion, worship; love, affection; (*her.*) pelican in her piety

Piéter, *v.n.* (*at bowls*) to foot the mark; (*hunt.*) to move forward; — *v.a.* to mark with feet; to graduate; (*pers.*) to set (against)

Se —, *v.r.* to set oneself (against); to take a firm footing, to stand firm-footed, to stand firm, to make a stand, to resist; to stand on

Piétin, *s.m.* (*vet.*) foot-rot [tiptoe

Piétinage, Piétinement, *s.m.* stamping; treading, trampling; moving the feet about, fidgeting

Piétiner, *v.a.n.* to stamp; to tread, to trample; to paddle; to move o.'s feet about, to kick about, to fidget; (*mil.*) to mark time

Piétisme, *s.m.* pietism

Piétiste, *s.m.f.* pietist; — *adj.* pietistic

Piéton, ne, *s.m.f.* foot-passenger, pedestrian,

walker; — *s.m.* foot-post, rural postman; (*obsolete*) foot-soldier [trudge it

Piétonner, *v.n.* (*jest.*) to foot it, to walk it, to

Piètre, *adj.* poor, sorry, wretched; — *s.m.* vagabond, tramp, loafer, wretch

Piètrement, *adv.* poorly, sorrily, wretchedly

Piètrerie, *s.f.* shabby thing; poor *or* wretched stuff; shabbiness, poorness, wretchedness

Piette, *s.f.* (*bird*) smew

Pieu, *s.m.* stake, pale, post, pile; (*pop.*) bed

Pieusement, *adv.* piously; religiously; im-

Pieuvre, *s.f.* *V.* **Poulpe** [plicitly

Pieu-x, se, *adj.* pious; godly; holy; religious

Piézomètre, *s.m.* (*phys.*) piezometer [bang!

Pif, *s.m.* bottle-nose, nose, nozzle; — *int.* slap!

Piffard, e, *adj.* *s.* (*pop.*) bottle-nosed; copper-nosed; queer-nosed; ditto person

Piffre, sse, *s.m.f.* glutton, stout fellow *or* creature, bouncer, elephant

Piffrer, *v.a.* *V.* **Empiffrer**

Pigamon, *s.m.* (*bot.*) meadow-rue

Pigeon, *s.m.* pigeon. — *culbutant*, tumbler. — *voyageur* or *messager*, carrier-pigeon. — *à grosse gorge*, pouter, cropper

Pigeonnage, *s.m.* (*mas.*) pargeting; parget

Pigeonneau, *s.m.* young pigeon

Pigeonner, *v.a.* to pigeon, (*mas.*) to parget

Pigeonnier, *s.m.* pigeon-house

Piger, *v.a.* (*pop.*) to catch, to seize, to lay *or* get hold of, to apprehend, to nab

Pigmée, *s.m.* *V.* **Pygmée**

Pigment, *s.m.* pigment

Pigmentaire, *adj.* pigmentary, pigmental

Pigmentation, *s.f.* pigmentation

†**Pignade,** *s.f.* (*local*) *V* **Pinière**

†**Pigne,** *s.f.* pena silver, pena gold; (*bot.*) pine-cone, fir-cone, pine-seed, kernel

†**Pignocher,** *v.n.* to pick a bit here and a bit there, to hardly eat anything, to pick, to nibble

†**Pignon,** *s.m.* gable-end, gable; (*tech.*) pinion; (*bot.*) pine-seed, kernel; (*tree*) stone-pine. — *d'Inde*, physic-nut; croton-seed, tilly-seed. *Avoir — sur rue*, to have a house of o.'s own

†**Pignoratif,** *adj.m.* (*old law*) pignorative. *Contrat* —, pignorative contract, sale of property with power of redemption

†**Pignouf, Pignoufle,** *s.m.* (*pop.*) blackguard, cad, churl, vulgar fellow; cobbler; clodhopper

Pika, *s.m.* (*zool.*) pika

Pilage, *s.m.* pounding

Pilaire, *adj.* pilary, pileous, pilous, pilose

Pilastre, *s.m.* pilaster

Pilau, *s.m.* pilaw, pilau; (*zool., local*) periwinkle

Pilchard, *s.m.* pilchard

Pile, *s.f.* pile; heap; pestle; pile of weights; (*of bridges*) pier; (*fish.*) gut-line; (*fam.*) whacking, licking; (*of coins*) reverse, tail. — *ou face* (or *croix ou* —), heads or tails; pitch and toss; chance, hazard, random. *Jouer à — ou face* (or *à croix ou* —), to play at heads or tails; to toss up for; to stake. *N'avoir ni croix ni* —, to have no money at all [—, to be pounded, &c.

Piler, *v.a.* to pound; to crush; to powder. *Se*

Pilerie, *s.f.* pounding-room

Pilet, *s.m.* pintail, pintail duck, sea-pheasant

Pileu-r, se, *s.m.f.* pounder

Pileu-x, se, *adj.* pileous, pilous, pilose

Pilier, *s.m.* pillar; column; post; constant frequenter, fixture; (*pop.*) stump (*leg*)

Pilifère, *adj.* piliferous

Piliforme, *adj.* piliform [cribbing

†**Pillage,** *s.m.* pillage, plunder; pilfering;

†**Pillard, e,** *adj.* *s.* pillaging, plundering; pillager, plunderer

†**Piller,** *v.a.* to pillage, to plunder; to pilfer; to crib; (*of dogs*) to seize, to worry; (*at play*) to take in

†**Pillerie,** *s.f.* pillage; plunder; pilfer [ferer

†**Pilleu-r, se,** *s.m.f.* pillager, plunderer; pil-

Pilon, *s.m.* pestle; crusher; (*of mills*) stamp, stamper; (*of a fowl*) drum-stick. *Mettre au* —, to tear up (*books*)

Pilonner, *v.a.* to stamp; to mill; to ram; to

Pilori, *s.m.* pillory [pug; to full; to press

Pilorier, *v.a.* to pillory; to expose, to show up; to slander, to libel, to traduce, to asperse

Piloris, *s.m.* musk-rat

Piloselle, *s.f.* (*bot.*) mouse-ear

Pilot, *s.m.* (*build.*) pile

Pilotage, *s.m.* (*build.*) piling; pile-work; (*nav.*) piloting; pilotage; steering, steerage

Pilote, *s.m.* *adj.* pilot; guide; (*zool.*) pilot-fish. — *hauturier* or *au long cours*, sea-pilot [show

Piloter, *v.n.a.* to pile; to pilot; to guide, to

Pilotin, *s.m.* pilot's apprentice; (*fish.*) stake

Pilotis, *s.m.* piles, piling, pile-work; pile

Pilulaire, *adj.* pill-shaped; pill; — *s.m.* (*vet.*) balling-gun, balling-probang; — *s.f.* (*bot.*) pill-wort. *Masse* —, pill-mass

Pilule, *s.f.* pill. — *mercurielle*, blue pill

Pilulier, *s.m.* (*pharm.*) pill-machine

Pilum, *s.m.* (*Rom. antiq.*) pilum

Pimarique, *adj.* (*chem.*) pimaric

Pimbèche, *s.f.* pert minx, saucy baggage, fastidious humbug [Cayenne pepper

Piment, *s.m.* pimento, allspice, Jamaica pepper,

Pimentade, *s.f.* pimento sauce

Pimpant, e, *adj.* smart, smug, spruce, natty, stylish, dashy; — *s.m.* smartness, style, dash

Pimpesouée, *s.f.* (*obsolete*) foppish woman

Pimprenelle, *s.f.* (*bot.*) burnet; pimpernel

Pin, *s.m.* pine, pine-tree, fir, fir-tree. *Pomme de*

Pinace, *s.f.* *V.* **Pinasse** [—, pine-cone, fir-cone

Pinacle, *s.m.* pinnacle; finial

Pinasse, *s.f* (*nav.*) pinnace

Pinastre, *s.m.* (*bot.*) pinaster, cluster-pine

Pinçage, *s.m* pinching, nipping [at the toe

Pinçard, e, *adj.* (*of horses*) wearing the shoe

Pince, *s.f.* crowbar, pinch-bar, pinch; tongs; pincers; tweezers; plyers; nippers; forceps; (*fig*) pinch; hold, gripe; seizing, seizure, catching, nabbing, capture, apprehension; (*of lobsters, &c*) claw; (*of certain animals, as the horse, &c.*) toe; (*horse's tooth*) nipper, incisor, cutter; (*of clothes*) plait — *à sucre*, sugar-tongs

Pincé, e, *part. adj.* pinched, &c. (*V* **Pincer**); affected, stiff, prim; thin; tight. *Bouche* — *e*, thin lips. *Lèvres* — *es*, pursed lips

Pinceau, *s.m* paint-brush, camel-hair brush *or* pencil, brush, hair-pencil, pencil; (*fig.*) touch; painter; (*phys.*) pencil. — *à barbe*, shaving-brush

Pinceautage, *s.m.* painting over, colouring

Pinceauter, *v.a.* to paint over, to colour

Pinceauteu-r, se, *s.m.f.* colourer

Pincée, *s.f.* pinch

Pincelier, *s.m.* (*paint.*) dipper

†**Pince-maille,** *s.m.* (*obsolete*) stingy fellow, skin-flint, pinch-penny, screw [ing

Pincement, *s.m.* pinching; nipping; twitch-

Pince-nez, *s.m.* spring double eye-glass; bar-

Pince-poils, *s.m.* tweezers [nacles; bull-ring

Pincer, *v.a.* to pinch; to bite; to nip, to nip off; to squeeze; to catch, to nab; to lay *or* get hold of; to take in; to jeer, to quiz, to cut; to twitch; to purse up (*o.'s lips*); (*rid.*) to spur gently; (*nav.*) to hug, to haul close to (*the wind*); (*obsolete*) to play (*on the harp, guitar, &c.*); (*pop.*) to do, to make, to sing, to play, to perform, to execute, to dance, to deliver; to have some of, to taste; to steal. *Se faire* —, to be caught *or* nabbed; to get taken in

Pince-sans-rire, *s.m.* sly and malicious person; dry joker

Pinceter, *v.a.* to pluck out with tweezers

Pincette, *s.f.*, **Pincettes,** *s.f.pl.* tongs; tweezers; nippers; pincers; (*pop.*) thin shanks

Pinceu-r, se, *s.m.f.* pincher; catcher

Pinchebeck, *s.m.* *V.* **Peinchebec**

Pinçon, *s.m.* pinch-mark, pinch

Pinçoter, *v.a.* to pinch about

Pinçure, *s.f.* pinching; crease

Pindarique, *adj.* Pindaric

Pindariser, *v.n.a.* to Pindarize

Pindariseur, *s.m.* Pindarist
Pindar-isme, -iste. *V.* page 3, § 1
Pinéal, e, *adj.* pineal
Pineau, *s.m.* pineau (*kind of vine, and its grape*)
Pingouin, *s.m.* penguin, auk, razor-bill, murre
Pingre, *adj.m.f.* stingy, close-fisted; — *s.m.* close-fisted fellow, skin-flint; — *s.f.* (*nav.*) *V.* **Pinque**
Pingrerie, *s.f.* stinginess, meanness
Pingresse, *s.f.* close-fisted woman
Pinguin. *V.* **Pingouin**
Pinier, *s.m.* (*bot.*) stone-pine; — *adj.m.* of pines, pine
Pinière, *s.f.* pine-plantation, pine-grove; — *adj.f.* of pines, pine
Pinifère, *adj.* piniferous, piny
Pinique, *adj.* (*chem.*) pinic
Pinne, *s.f.*, — *marine,* (*mollusc*) pinna, wing-shell
Pinné, e, *adj.* (*bot.*) pinnate
Pinnotère, Pinnothère, *s.m.* (*zool.*) pea-crab
Pinnule, *s.f.* (*of an instr.*) pinule, sight-vane; [(*bot.*) pinnule
Pinque, *s.f.* (*nav.*) pink
Pinson, *s.m.* chaffinch; finch. — *des Ardennes,* brambling, bramble finch, mountain finch. *Gai comme un* —, as gay as a lark, as merry as a grig
Pintade, *s.f.* pintado, Guinea-fowl
Pintadeau, *s.m.* pintado chick, young Guinea-fowl
Pintadine, *s.f.* mother-of-pearl shell
Pinte, *s.f.* pint (*English quart in quantity: the French pint, now obsolete, was of the capacity of a quart, or double of the English pint*)
Pinter, *v.n.* (*old*) to tipple, to tope, to guzzle
Piochage, *s.m.* digging; working, fagging
Pioche, *s.f.* pickaxe; mattock; work, hard work
Piocher, *v.a.n.* to dig; to thump, to whack; to work at, to work hard at, to fag at; to work, to work hard, to fag
  Se —, *v.r.* to fight, to have a fight *or* a set-to, to come to blows; to be dug, &c.
Piocheu-r, se, *s.m.f.* digger; hard worker, fag; — *adj.* hard-working, fagging
Piochon, *s.m.* small pickaxe *or* mattock
Piolet, *s.m.* alpenstock, Alpine staff, staff
Pion, *s.m.* (*at chess*) pawn; (*at draughts*) man; (*in India*) peon; (*obsolete*) wretch, beggar; (*jest.*) usher (*in a school*)
Pionce, *s.f.* (*fam.*) snooze, nap, sleep
Pioncer, *v.n.* (*fam.*) to snooze, to snooze away, to have a nap, to sleep
Pionceu-r, se, *s.m.f.* (*fam.*) snoozer, sleeper
Pione, *s.f.* (*bot.*) pæony, peony
Pionnage, *s.m.* pioneering
Pionner, *v.n.* (*at chess*) to take pawns; (*at draughts*) to lose as many men as one takes; [(*mil.*) to pioneer
Pionnier, *s.m.* pioneer
Piot, *s.m.* (*pop. and old*) wine, drink
Pioupiou, Piou, *s.m.* (*jest.*) foot-soldier
Pipa, *s.m.* (*zool.*) pipa
Pipe, *s.f.* pipe; tobacco-pipe. *Casser sa* —, (*fig., pop.*) to die, to kick the bucket. *Fumer sans* —, (*fig.*) to be in a rage, to fume
Pipeau, *s.m.* pipe, shepherd's pipe; bird-call; lime-twig; (*fig.*) snare
Pipée, *s.f.* bird-catching (with a bird-call); (*fig.*) deceit, trickery. *Prendre à la* —, to catch with a bird-call; to cozen, to take in
Pipelet, *s.m.* (*slang*) house-porter
Piper, *v.a.* to catch with a bird-call; to allure, to entice, to decoy, to deceive, to dupe, to cozen, to take in, to diddle, to cheat; to cheat out of; to prepare (*cards*); to load *or* cog (*dice*); — *v.n.* to pip; to pipe, to whistle; (*fam.*) to smoke, to whiff
Pipéracées, *s.f.pl.* (*bot.*) piperaceæ
Piperie, *s.f.* deception, cheating, cheat, trick
Piperin, *s.m.*, **Piperine,** *s.f.* (*chem.*) piperine
Pipérine, *s.f.* *V.* **Péperin**
Pipet, *s.m.* *V.* **Farlouse**
Pipette, *s.f.* (*chem.*) pipette
Pipeu-r, se, *s.m.f.* bird-caller, bird-catcher; card-sharper, sharper, cheat, blackleg; — *adj.* alluring, enticing, decoying, deceitful, cheating
Pipi, *s.m.* (*children's word*) pee, urine, water; (*bot.*) Guinea-hen weed. *Faire* —, to piddle, to pee, to go pee
Pipicule, *s.m.* (*bird*) hook-billed creeper
Pipiement, Pipier (*v.n.*). *V.* **Pépiement, Pépier**
Pipi-er, ère, *adj.* of tobacco-pipes, tobacco-pipe, pipe
Pipistrelle, *s.f.* (*zool.*) pipistrelle bat
Pipit, *s.m.* (*bird*) pipit, titlark, titling, moss-cheeper
Pipoir, *s.m.* owl-call, call
Piquamment, *adv.* keenly, &c. (*V.* **Piquant,** *adj.*)
Piquant, e, *adj.* prickly; stinging; keen; sharp; piercing; pungent; hot; tart; biting; exciting; pleasing; enticing; interesting; lively, smart; satirical; cutting; pointed; piquant
Piquant, *s.m.* prickle; sting; quill (*of a porcupine*); pungency; smartness; interest; pith; best, cream, fun; point; piquancy
Pique, *s.f.* pike (*weapon*); quarrel, bickering, tiff, grudge, spite, animosity, pique; — *s.m.* (*at cards*) spades
-ique, *s.m.f.* (*in compounds, from* **Piquer,** "to prick," &c.) thing (*m.*) *or* animal *or* person (*m.f.*) that pricks *or* &c., pricker, pecker, &c. — **-assiette,** *s.m.f.* sponger, parasite, diner-out, dinner-hunter, trencher-friend. — **-bœufs,** *s.m.* drover; (*bird*) ox-pecker, beef-eater. — **-bois,** *s.m.* (*bird*) black woodpecker. — **-broc,** *s.m.* *V.* **Coupe-bourgeons.** — **-feu,** *s.m.* (*tech.*) poker. — **-mouches,** *s.f.* (*bird*) great tit. — **-nique,** *s.m.* picnic. — **-notes,** *s.m.* bill-file
Piqué, e, *part. adj.* pricked, &c. (*V.* **Piquer**); quilted; worm eaten; fly-blown; (*of wine*) sourish; (*mus., of notes*) short, detached. *Porte* —*e,* baize door. *Cela n'est pas* — *des vers* (or *des hannetons*), that is not to be sneezed at, that is capital *or* spicy *or* famous
Piqué, *s.m.* quilting; piqué. *Goût de* —, (*of wine*) sourish taste
Piquer, *v.a.* to prick; to sting; to puncture; to prod; to pierce; to peck; to goad; to spur; to bite; to nibble, to eat; to cut; to be piquant to; to nettle; to excite; to stimulate; to entice; to interest; to pique; to offend; to wound; to open; to dart, to shoot; to check; to report as absent; (*need.*) to quilt; to stitch; to pink; (*cook.*) to lard; to stick; (*nav.*) to strike; to hug (*the wind*), to haul close to (*the wind*). — *d'honneur,* to awaken (...'s) sense of honour, to put (...) on his *or* her mettle. — *du nez,* to fall headlong. — *l'assiette,* to sponge, to be a sponger *or* parasite. — *un chien,* (*fam.*) to snooze. — *un renard,* (*fam.*) to shoot the cat, to spew. — *un soleil,* (*fam.*) to get red in the face, to blush. — *une tête,* to take a header, to jump down *or* fall *or* plunge head foremost
  Se —, *v.r.* to prick *or* sting oneself *or* o.'s ...; to be worm-eaten; to become mouldy *or* mildewed; to get sour; to be offended, to take offence, to take a pique; to be excited, to get obstinate, to hold out, to persist; to pride *or* plume *or* pique oneself (on, upon), to glory (in), to take a pride (in); to pretend (to); to profess. *Se* — *d'honneur,* to think o.'s honour engaged, to think oneself bound in honour, to stand on the point of honour, to make it a point of honour, to be put on o.'s mettle, to do o.'s best. *Se* — *au jeu,* to grow warm at play, to continue with obstinacy to play although losing; to be excited, to get obstinate, to hold out, to persist
Piquereau, *s.m.* (*bird*) nutcracker
Piquet, *s.m.* picket; peg; stake; post; pole; (*mil.*) picket, piquet; (*game at cards*) piquet; (*at school*) standing up (*punishment*). *De* —, (*mil.*) on picket. *Être au* —, (*mil.*) to be on picket; (*at school*) to be standing up (*as a punishment*). *Lever le* —, to strike the tents, to decamp. *Mettre au* —, (*at school*) to make (...) stand up (*as a punishment*). *Planter le* —, to pitch the tents, to camp; (*fig.*) to pitch o.'s tent, to take up o.'s quarters
Piqueté, e, *adj.* spotted, dotted; — *part.* *V.* **Piqueter**
Piqueter, *v.a.* to mark *or* set with pickets *or* stakes; to mark; to stick; to fix
Piquette, *s.f.* piquette, rape-wine; thin wine, paltry *or* bad wine, sour wine, rough *or* washy stuff, poor stuff, swipes; sloe-wine

Piqueur, *s.m.* outrider; whipper-in, huntsman; horsebreaker, groom; foreman, overseer, task-master, time-keeper; marker; larder; quilter; stitcher. — *d'assiette*, *V.* **Pique-assiette**
Piqueuse, *s.f.* quilter; stitcher. — *d'assiette*, [*V.* **Pique-assiette**
Piquier, *s.m.* pikeman
Piqûre, *s.f.* pricking, prick; sting; puncture; bite; wound; worm-hole; (*of wine*) sourishness; (*need.*) quilting; stitching, stitch; pinking. — *arrêtée*, lock-stitch
Pirate, *s.m.* pirate, rover; corsair; extortioner
Pirater, *v.n.* to pirate, to commit piracy
Piraterie, *s.f.* piracy; act *or* acts of piracy; ex-[tortion
Piratinier, *s.m.* (*bot.*) letter-wood tree
Piratique, *adj.* piratical [—, worse and worse
Pire, *adj.* worse; worst; — *s.m.* worst. *De — en*
Piriforme, *adj.* pyriform, pear-shaped, pear-[like
Pirogue, *s.f.* pirogue, canoe
Pirole, *s.f.* (*bot.*) winter-green
Piroll, Pirolle, *s.m.* (*zool.*) satin-bird
Pironneau, *s.m.* shell-fishing boat
Pirouette, *s.f.* pirouette; rapid whirling upon one foot; whirling *or* turning round; short appearance; whirligig; subterfuge; jest
Pirouettement, *s.m.* pirouetting [round
Pirouetter, *v.n.* to pirouette; to whirl *or* turn
Pis, *adv. adj.* worse; worst; — *s.m.* worst; (*of animals*) udder. *De — en —*, worse and worse. *De mal en —*, from bad to worse; worse and worse. *Qui — est*, what is worse. *Mettre* (or *prendre*) *les choses au —*, to suppose the worst
Pis-aller, *s.m.* (the) worst that can happen, worst; last resource, last shift; loophole left; makeshift; compensation. *Au —*, at the worst; let the worst come to the worst, when the worst comes to the worst, in the event of the worst, when all comes to all
Pisan, e, *adj. s.* Pisan
Piscicole, *adj.* piscicultural
Pisciculteur, *s.m.* pisciculturist
Piscicultural, e, *adj.* piscicultural
Pisciculture, *s.f.* pisciculture, fish-culture
Pisciforme, *adj.* pisciform
Piscine, *s.f.* piscinary; pond; reservoir; wash-house, lavatory; (*biblical*) pool; (*of churches, and in Rom. antiq.*) piscina; (*poet.*) font
Piscivore, *adj.* piscivorous
Pisé, *s.m.* (*build.*) pisé; mud-wall, cob-wall
Piseur, *s.m.* builder in pisé
Pisiforme, *adj.* pisiform
Pisolithe, *s.m.* (*min.*) pisolite, pea-stone
Pisolithique, *adj.* (*min.*) pisolitic
Pissasphalte, *s.m.* pissasphalt, pissasphaltum
Pissasphaltique, *adj.* pissasphaltic
Pissat, *s.m.*, **Pisse,** *s.f.* piss
Pissée, *s.f.* quantity of piss
Pisse-froid, *s.m.* (*fam.*) milksop, dull fellow
Pissement, *s.m.* pissing [pissabed
Pissenlit, *s.m.* (*bot.*) dandelion, pissabed; (*pers.*)
Pisser, *v.n.a.* to piss, to pump-ship
Pisseu-r, se, *s.m.f.* pisser [piss-burnt
Pisseu-x, se, *adj.* piss-like; piss-coloured;
Pisse-vinaigre, *s.m.f.* (*fam.*) miser, hunks
Pissoir, *s.m.* pissing-place, urinal
Pissote, *s.f.* tap; urinal
Pissoter, *v n.* to piss frequently and little at a time, to piddle; to dribble [dribbling spout
Pissotière, *s.f.* pissing-place, urinal; (*jest.*)
Pistache, *s.f.* pistachio, pistachio-nut. — *de terre*, *V.* **Arachide**
Pistachier, *s.m.* pistachio-tree
Piste, *s.f.* trace; track; trail; slot; scent; race-course, course; (*in a riding-school*) piste, pist; longing-ring, ring; wall-side
Pistia, *s.m.* (*bot.*) pistia, water-lettuce
Pistil, *s.m.* (*bot.*) pistil
Pistillaire, *adj.* (*bot.*) pistillar [pistilliferous
Pistillé, e, Pistillifère, *adj.* (*bot.*) pistillate,
Pistolade, *s.f.* (*old*) pistolade, pistol-shot
Pistole, *s.f.* (*coin*) pistole; (*in a prison*) private room, fee for ditto; (*com.*) Brignoles prune; *obsolete*) pistol. *Cousu de —s*, made of money
Pistoler, *v.a.* (*old*) to pistol
Pistolet, *s.m.* pistol; (*fam.*) kind of fellow, fellow, fish, odd fish; (*in Belgium*) breakfast-roll
Pistolier, *s.m.* (*obsolete*) pistolier
Piston, *s.m.* piston; plug; stopper; sucker; forcer; striker; spring-button; embolus; cornopean; cornopeist; (*jest.*) assistant (*to a lecturer on physics or chemistry*)
Pitance, *s.f.* pittance; allowance; portion; dole; modicum; provisions; daily subsistence; (*pop.*) [market
Pitancher, *v.n.a.* (*pop.*) to drink
Pitaud, e, *s.m.f.* lubber, lout, bumpkin; — *adj.* lubberly [thread, aloe-fibre
Pite, *s.f.* pita-hemp; — *s.m.* pita-fibre, pita-
Piteusement, *adv.* piteously
Piteu-x, se, *adj.* piteous
Pithomètre, *s.m.* pithometer
Pithométr-ie, -ique. *V.* page 3, § 1
Pitié, *s.f.* pity; compassion; mercy; disdain, contempt. *Par —*, for pity's sake, for mercy's sake; from pity. *A faire —*, pitifully; wretchedly; pitiful; wretched. *Faire —*, to excite pity, to move o.'s pity; to be absurd; to be a wretched thing. *Regarder en —*, to take pity on; to look on with contempt, to despise
Piton, *s.m.* ring-screw; eye-bolt; (*geog.*) peak; (*pop.*) bottle-nose, copper-nose
Pitoyable, *adj.* piteous, pitiable; pitiful; contemptible; wretched
Pitoyablement, *adv.* piteously, pitiably; pitifully; contemptibly; wretchedly
Pitpit, *s.m. V.* **Pipit** [fool; jester, wag, humbug
Pitre, *s.m.* merry-andrew, Jack-pudding, clown,
Pitron, *s.m.* (*local*) baulk, beam
Pittacale, *s.m.* (*chem.*) pittacal
Pitte. *V.* **Pite**
Pittoresque, *adj.* picturesque; graphic; pictorial, illustrated; — *s.m.* picturesque, picturesqueness [phically; pictorially
Pittoresquement, *adv.* picturesquely; gra-
Pituitaire, *adj.* (*anat.*) pituitary
Pituite, *s.f.* pituite, mucus, phlegm
Pituiteu-x, se, *adj.* pituitous, phlegmatic
Pityriasis, *s.m.* (*med.*) pityriasis [woodpecker
Pivert, *s.m.* (*bird*) woodspite, woodwall, green
Pivite, *s.m.* (*bird*) peewit, pewet
Pivoine, *s.f.* (*bot.*) pæony, peony [tap-root
Pivot, *s.m.* pivot; hinge; spindle, pin; (*bot.*)
Pivotant, e, *adj.* (*bot.*) tap-rooted. *Racine —e*, tap-root
Pivoter, *v.n.a.* to revolve *or* turn on a pivot, to pivot, to turn; (*bot.*) to tap, to form tap-roots
Pizzicato, *s.m. adv.* (*mus.*) pizzicato
Placabilité, *s.f.* placability, placableness
Placable, *adj.* placable
Plaçable, *adj.* placeable; salable
Placage, *s.m.* plating; laying on *or* down; veneering; padding; patchwork; (*hort.*) budding
Plaçage, *s.m.* placing; stalling
Placard, *s.m.* placard, poster, bill; cupboard (*in a wall*); panel; door-leap; (*print.*) slip, broadside
Placarder, *v.a.* to placard, to post up, to bill; to libel; to lampoon; to abuse; to expose, to [show up
Se —, *v.r.* to be placarded, &c.
Place, *s.f.* place; room; spot; ground; square; situation; seat; fare; (*of cabs, &c.*) rank, stand; (*fig.*) room, stead; office, post, employment, berth; patch; (*com.*) market; Change; town; merchants; (*mil.*) place; fortress; parade-ground; town. — *forte*, fortified town, strong place, stronghold, fortress, fastness. — *publique*, public place *or* square; market-place. — *d'armes*, place of arms; parade-ground, parade, square; stronghold; frontier-town. — *de guerre*, fortified town *or* place. *A la — de*, *en — de*, in the place *or* room of, instead of, in lieu of. *A votre —*, in *or* to your place; instead of you; if I were you. *De —*, (*of vehicles*) hackney. *En — !* in your places! *Sur —*, on the premises, on the spot. *Sur la —*, on *or* upon the spot *or* &c.; (*com.*) in the market; on Change. *De-*

meurer or *rester en* —, to remain in one (*or* in o.'s) place; to remain *or* stand *or* sit still. *Demeurer* or *rester sur la* —, to be left dead on the spot, to remain on the ground *or* on the field of battle. *Faire* —, *faire de la* —, to make room *or* way, to give place; to clear the way; to give way. *Faire la* —, (*com.*) to solicit orders about the town, to canvass. *Mettre* or *remettre quelqu'un à sa* —, (*fig.*) to put one in his *or* her place, to set one down, to give one a clincher. *Se faire* —, *se faire faire* —, to make o.'s way. — ! make room! make way! clear the way!

Placé, e, *part. adj.* placed, &c. (*V.* **Placer**); situated. *Bien* —, well placed *or* situated, in a good place *or* situation, in the right place, in o.'s (*or* its) proper place; apposite; well-timed; proper. *Haut* —, in a high place *or* position, high; noble

Placement, *s.m.* placing; putting; setting; laying; settling; investment, putting out; sale. *Bureau de* —, register-office, registry-office

Placenta, *s.m.* (*anat., bot.*) placenta

Placentaire, *adj.* placentary, placental

Placer, *v.a.* to place; to put; to set; to lay; to seat; to fix; to settle; to dispose; to rank; to get *or* procure a situation for; to find a place for; to introduce, to put *or* throw *or* edge in, to say; to bestow; to invest, to put out; to deposit, to lodge; to sell. — *sur l'État*, to invest in the funds

Se —, *v.r.* to place *or* put oneself; to take o.'s stand *or* seat; to get *or* obtain a situation; to be placed *or* &c.; to be sold, to sell

Placer, *s.m.* (*of gold-diggings*) placer

Placet, *s.m.* (*obsolete*) petition; (*arch-obsolete*) *V.* **Tabouret**

Placeu-r, se, *s.m.f.* placer; register-office [keeper; (*com.*) *V.* **Placier**

Placide, *adj.* placid

Placidement, *adv.* placidly

Placidité, *s.f.* placidity, placidness

Placi-er, ère, *s.m.f.* placer; (*com.*) canvasser, town-traveller, out-door clerk, agent

Plafond, *s.m.* ceiling. *Araignée dans le* —, (*pop.*) bee in o.'s bonnet, crack in the upper works

Plafonnage, *s.m.* ceiling

Plafonner, *v.a.* to ceil

Plafonneur, *s.m.* plasterer

Plagal, e, *adj* (*mus.*) plagal

Plage, *s.f.* beach; strand; shore; region; country; climate

Plagiaire, *s.m.* plagiarist, plagiary; — *adj.* plagiary

Plagiat, *s.m.* plagiarism

Plaid, *s.m.* (*old law*) plea; pleading; sitting (of a court), hearing, court; (*garment*) plaid; railway-rug, travelling-rug

Plaidable, *adj.* pleadable

†Plaidailler, *v.n.* to go to law

Plaidant, e, *adj.* pleading; litigant

Plaider, *v.a.n.* to plead; to argue; to allege; to be at law; to go to law; to sue [to be heard

Se —, *v.r.* to be pleaded *or* argued; to come on;

Plaiderie, *s.f.* (*old*) lawsuit, suit, action

Plaideu-r, se, *s.m.f.* litigant, suitor

Plaidoirie, *s.f.* pleading; address, speech; pleadings; bar [speech

Plaidoyer, *s.m.* counsel's address, address,

Plaie, *s.f.* wound; sore; (*fig.*) plague, evil; (*abusively*) scar. *Ne demander* (or *Ne chercher*) *que* — *et bosse*, to be fond of quarrelling *or* of getting into hot water; to be always ready for a row *or* for a lark; to be bent on (*or* to delight in) mischief; to be ready for all comers

†Plaignant (*part. of* **Plaindre**), pitying, &c. *Se* —, complaining

†Plaignant, e, *adj.* (*law*) complaining; — *s.m.f.* (*law*) complainant; plaintiff; prosecutor, prosecutrix

Plain, e, *adj.* plain, even, level, flat; champaign; — *s.m.* high sea. — **-chant,** *s.m.* (*church-music*) plain-song, plain-chant. — **-pied,** *s.m.* level ground, level, floor, flat, suite of rooms on the same level. *De* — *-pied*, on the same floor; on a level; right (in, into, on); without difficulty, as a matter of course; at once

Plaindre, *v.a.* to pity; to grudge; to regret; to be sparing of, to use sparingly, to spare. *A* —, to be pitied

Se —, *v.r.* to complain; to grumble; to whine; to wail; to lament; to moan, to groan; to sigh; to grudge oneself; to pity oneself *or* each other

Plaine, *s.f.* plain, level ground, lea, common, field, heath; lowland; (*Fr. hist.*) Plain (*moderate party*). — *d'eau*, sheet of water

Plainte, *s.f.* complaint; complaining; wailing; lamentation; whine; moan; groan; deep sigh; charge; plaint

Plainti-f, ve, *adj.* plaintive, moanful, doleful, mournful, sad, querulous, complaining

Plaintivement, *adv.* plaintively, moanfully, dolefully, mournfully

Plaire, *v.n.* to please; to be pleasing; to be agreeable; to suit. *A Dieu ne plaise!* God forbid! *Plût à Dieu* or *au ciel!* would to God *or* to Heaven! *Comme il plaît à Dieu*, as it pleases God; but poorly, indifferently, at sixes and sevens. *S'il plaît à Dieu*, please God. *S'il vous plaît*, if you please; pray; by your leave; allow me to ask; allow me to say. *Si cela vous plaît*, if you like (it). *Comme il vous plaira*, as you please *or* like. *Cela vous plaît à dire*, you are pleased to say so. *Plaît-il?* what did you say? what? yes!

Se —, *v.r.* to please oneself *or* each other; to delight *or* take a delight *or* take pleasure (in); to be pleased; to be fond (of), to like; to love; to take (to); to flatter oneself; to thrive

Plaisamment, *adv.* pleasantly; amusingly, funnily, comically; jocularly; humorously; ludicrously, ridiculously; waggishly

Plaisance, *s.f.* pleasure. *De* —, (*adject.*) of *or* for pleasure, pleasure; pleasurable, agreeable; country. *Lieu* or *maison de* —, agreeable retreat, country house, country seat, villa

Plaisant, e, *adj.* pleasant, pleasurable, agreeable; amusing, droll, funny, comical; laughable; jocular, jocose; humorous; ludicrous, ridiculous, odd; impertinent; (*ironically*) pretty; — *s.m.* ludicrous, ludicrousness; humorous; humour; fun; humourist, wag, jester. *Mauvais* —, sorry jester; mischievous wag; trickster; humbug

Plaisanter, *v.a.n.* to joke, to jest; to jeer; to sport; to trifle. *En plaisantant*, in joke, by way of joke, jocularly, jestingly. *C'est un homme qui ne plaisante pas*, he is no joker, he is not a man to be trifled with

Plaisanterie, *s.f.* pleasantry; joking, jesting; joke, jest; raillery; derision, mockery; mere farce. *Mauvaise* —, bad joke; hoax; trick. — *à part*, seriously, without joking, in earnest. *Par* —, in joke, jocularly [jester, fool; wag

Plaisantin, *s.m.* (*old*) merry-andrew, buffoon,

Plaisir, *s.m.* pleasure; delight; sweet; amusement, sport; favour, kindness; excursion; (*at play*) love (*not money*); wafer (*cake*); —**s,** *pl.* pleasures, &c.; gaieties; pleasure-grounds; royal preserves, preserves. *Bon* —, good pleasure, will and pleasure, pleasure; approbation; arbitrariness. *Menus* —*s*, pocket-money; privy purse. *A* —, at o.'s ease; carefully; wantonly; gratuitously; plentifully; freely; designedly. *Au* —, *au* — *de vous revoir*, I hope I shall have the pleasure of seeing you again. *Par* —, by way of trial; for pleasure. *Faire* —, to give pleasure; to please; to be pleasing; to oblige. *Faire un* —, to do a favour. *Se faire un* — *de*, to make a pleasure of; to anticipate the pleasure of. *Fait* or *inventé à* —, gratuitous, idle; feigned; made up

Plamage, *s.m.* (*of hides*) liming

Plamer, *v.a.* to lime (*hides*)

Plan, e, *adj.* plane, plain, flat

Plan, *s.m.* plane; plan; draught, design, model; view; map; scheme; project; policy; means, method, expedient; survey; (*paint.*) ground; (*vulgar spelling for* "plant") *V.* **Plant.** — *géométral*, — *horizontal*, ground-plan. — *d'arri-*

mage, (*nav.*) tier. — *de niveau*, datum-line. — *de terrain*, plot. *Premier* —, foreground
Planage, *s.m.* planing, planishing, smoothing
Planaire, *s.f.* (*zool.*) planaria
Planche, *s.f.* board; plank; shelf; (*engr.*) plate; block; cut; (*of gardens*) bed, flower-bed; —**s**, *pl.* boards, planks, &c.; (*fig.*) boards, stage, theatrical profession. — *à bouteilles*, bottle-rack. — *de salut*, sheet-anchor. *Jour de* —, (*com. nav.*) lay day. *Faire la* —, to float *or* swim on o.'s back; to show *or* lead the way
Planchéiage, Plancheyage, *s.m.* boarding, planking, flooring [plank, to floor
Planchéier, Plancheyer, *v.a.* to board, to
Planchéieur, Plancheyeur, *s.m.* floor-layer
Plancher, *s.m.* floor; flooring; (*obsolete for* "plafond") ceiling; (*nav.*) stage. — *des vaches*, (*pop.*) ground, terra firma, marrow-bone stage
Planchette, *s.f.* small board *or* shelf; slat; lath; (*math.*) plane-table [plank-timber
Plançon, *s.m.* slip, twig, shoot, set, sapling;
Plane, *s.m.* (*bot.*) Norway maple; — *s.f.* (*tech.*) spoke-shave; draw-knife; turning-chisel
Planer, *v.n.* to hover; (*fig.*) to soar; to look down; to tower, to rise; — *v.a.* to plane; to planish; to smooth; to trim; to shave
Planère, *s.f.* (*bot.*) planer-tree, zelkoua-tree
Planétaire, *adj.* planetary; — *s.m.* orrery,
Planète, *s.f.* planet; star [planetarium
Planeur, *s.m.* hoverer; (*pers.*) planer, planisher
Planier, *s.m.* table-land, upland
Planimètre, *s.m.* planimeter
Planimétr-ie, -ique. *V.* page 3, § 1
Planisphère, *s.m.* planisphere
Planisphérique, *adj.* planispheric
Plano. *V.* **In-plano** [snail, marsh-snail
Planorbe, *s.m.* planorbis, water-snail, pond-
Plant, *s.m.* sapling, slip; plantation, set, grove, bed; plant; cane; (*pop.*) pledge, pawn; pawn-shop. *En* —, standing; standing still; at a stand-still; in the lurch; (*pop.*) pawned, in pawn. *Laisser en* —, to leave abruptly, to leave, to give the slip; to leave in the lurch; to disappoint. *Mettre en* —, (*pop.*) to pawn, to put up the spout. *Rester en* —, to remain standing, to stand still
Plantage, *s.m.* planting; plantation
Plantain, *s.m.* plantain (*grass*) [ris
Plantaire, *adj.* (*anat.*) plantar; — *s.m.* planta-
Plantanier, *s.m.* plantain-tree, plantain
Plantard, *s.m. V.* **Plançon**
Plantation, *s.f.* plantation; planting
Plante, *s.f.* plant; weed; (*of the foot*) sole. — *-éponge*, *V.* **Cristatelle**
Planté, e, *part. adj.* planted, &c. (*V.* **Planter**); standing; erect; situated; placed; settled down. *Bien* —, well planted, &c.; standing well; firm; graceful; in a fine attitude; in a fine predicament *or* fix *or* pickle
Plantement, *s.m.* planting
Planter, *v.a.* to plant; to set; to fix; to stick; to drive, to drive in; to set up; to erect; to lay out; to thrust; to place, to put, to clap; to give. — *là*, — *là pour reverdir*, to leave abruptly, to leave, to give the slip; to leave in the lurch; to abandon, to desert; to give up. — ... *au nez de* ..., to cast ... in ...'s teeth, to tell point-blank
Se —, *v.r.* to be planted; to put *or* fix *or* stick oneself; to stand; to station oneself; to
Planteur, *s.m.* planter; settler [settle
Plantigrade, *adj.m.f.*, *s.m.* (*zool.*) plantigrade
Plantis, *s.m. V.* **Plantation**
Plantoir, *s.m.* (*hort.*, *agr.*) planting-tool, dibbler, dibber, dibble; dibbling-machine
Planton, *s.m.* orderly; orderly duty. *De* —, on
Plantule, *s.f.* (*bot.*) plantule [duty (as orderly)
Plantureusement, *adv.* plentifully, abundantly, copiously, luxuriantly
Plantureu-x, se, *adj.* plentiful, abundant, copious, luxuriant, rank, fertile; large; full;
Planure, *s.f.* shavings [succulent, rich

Plaque, *s.f.* plate; slab; patch; veneer; (*of a chimney*) back; register; hob; (*of a sword*) bow; (*of porters*, &c.) badge, ticket; (*of orders of knighthood*) star. — *tournante*, (*rail.*) turn-plate. — *de propreté*, finger-plate
Plaqué, *s.m.* plated metal, plated *or* electro-plated articles *or* goods, electro-silver; plate
Plaqué, e, *part. adj.* plated, &c. (*V.* **Plaquer**). *Colonne* — *e*, (*arch.*) pilaster [plum
Plaqueminier, *s.m.* (*bot.*) ebony-tree; date-
Plaquer, *v.a.* to plate; to electroplate; to lay, to put, to apply, to clap, to lay on *or* down; to patch; to veneer; (*calico-printing*) to pad; (*fig.*) to throw, to cast; to give (*blows*, &c.)
Se —, *v.r.* to be plated *or* &c.
Plaquette, *s.f.* small plate *or* board *or* slab; slat; lath; small copper coin; thin bound book
Plaqueur, *s.m.* plater; veneerer
Plaquis, *s.m.* incrustation
Plasma, *s.m.* (*physiol.*, *min.*) plasma
Plasmatique, *adj.* plasmatic
Plasticité, *s.f.* plasticity [modelling
Plastique, *adj* plastic; — *s.f.* plastic art,
Plastron, *s.m.* breast-piece, breast-plate; fencing-pad, breast-pad, plastron; chest-protector; (*of tortoises, turtles, crabs*, &c.) lower shell, plastron; (*tech.*) breast-plate, drill-plate; (*fig.*) butt, laughing-stock
Plastronner, *v.a.* to put a breast-pad on, to cover *or* protect with a breast-pad; — *v.n.* to practise on the fencing-master's breast-pad
Se —, *v.r.* to put on a breast-pad
Plat, e, *adj.* flat; level; dull; insipid, tasteless; dead; pointless; miserable; mean; low; shallow; empty; thin; (*of hair*) straight, lank; (*of rhymes*) regular, consecutive. *A* —, flat. *A* — *ventre*, flat on o.'s face, flat on the ground; cringing
Plat, *s.m.* dish; flat side, flat part, flat; (*of the hand*) back; (*of glass*) sheet; (*of a balance*) scale; (*of oars*) blade; (*nav.*) mess. — *à barbe*, shaving-dish. *A* —*s couverts*, underhand, secretly. *Donner du* — *de la langue*, to talk; to flatter, to coax, to make empty promises, to blarney. *Faire merveille du* — *de la langue*, to talk big *Mettre les petits* —*s dans les grands*, (*vulgar*) to spare nothing, to make great preparations. *Mettre les pieds dans le* —, (*fam.*) to use no precautions; to keep no measures; to make a desperate attempt; to go the whole hog
Platanaie, *s.f.* plantation of plane-trees
Platane, *s.m.* (*bot.*) plane-tree
Plat-bord, *s.m.* (*nav.*) gunnel, gunwale
Plate, *s.f.* flat-bottomed boat, flat; — *s.m.* (*English word used by French turfites*) plate
Plateau, *s.m.* flat; board; plank; shelf; low table; dish (*of a balance*), scale, wooden basin; tray, waiter, salver, plateau; table-land, upland, plateau; platform; level; (*tech.*) plate; (*of an electric machine*, &c.) glass plate, plate; (*agr.*, *obsolete*) land-presser. — *tournant*, (*rail.*) turn-plate. — *à découper*, butler's tray. — *de carafe*, decanter-stand [flower-bed; (*arch.*) platband
Plate-bande, *s.f.* (*hort.*) platband, border, plot,
Platée, *s.f.* dishful; (*fig.*) lot; (*arch.*) massive foundation under the whole area of a building
Plate-forme, *s.f.* platform; (*rail.*) truck; foot-board, foot-plate. — *tournante*, (*rail.*) turn-plate [leading-rein
Plate-longe, *s.f.* kicking-strap; kicking-longe;
Platement, *adv.* flatly; dully; without animation *or* spirit; plainly
Platine, *s.f.* linen-dryer; (*of fire-arms*) lock-plate; (*abusively for* "pièces" *or* "ressort" *of ditto*) lock; (*abusively, in flint-locks, for* "batterie") hammer; (*of a key-lock*) plate; (*print.*) platen; (*tech.*) plate, covering-plate; apron; (*pop.*) gabble, gab; — *s.m.* platinum
Platiner, *v.a.* to whiten
Platineu-x, se, *adj.* platinous
Platinifère, *adj.* platiniferous
Platinique, *adj.* platinic

Platitude, *s.f.* flatness; dulness; insipidity; tastelessness; meanness; platitude, flat *or* dull *or* insipid thing, senseless thing
Platonicien, ne, *adj.* Platonic; — *s.m.f.* Platonician, Platonist
Platon-ique, -isme. *V.* page 3, § 1
Platoniser, *v.n.a.* to Platonize
Plâtrage, *s.m.* plastering; plaster-work; manuring with plaster
Plâtras, *s.m.* rubbish of plaster, rubbish, old plaster, piece of dried mortar
Plâtre, *s.m.* plaster; plaster figure; plaster cast; plaster ornamentation; (*on the face*) paint. *Battre comme* —, to beat to a mummy. *Essuyer les —s*, to live in a newly-built house; (*fig.*) to experience the disadvantages of a beginning; (*jest.*) to kiss a painted woman
Plâtrer, *v.a* to plaster; to patch up; to palliate; to manure with plaster; (*of the face*) to paint [o.'s face, to make up
Se —, *v.r.* to be plastered *or* &c.; to paint
Plâtreu-r, se, *s.m.f* (*fig.*) patcher
Plâtreu-x, se, *adj.* plastery
Plâtrier, *s.m.* plasterer
Plâtrière, *s.f.* plaster-quarry; plaster-kiln
Plausibilité, *s.f.* plausibility, plausibleness
Plausible, *adj.* plausible
Plausiblement, *adv.* plausibly
Plèbe, *s.f.* common people, lower orders
Plébécule, *s.f.* mob, rabble
Plébéianisme, *s.m.* plebeianism
Plébéien, ne, *adj. s.* plebeian
Plébiscite, *s.m.* plebiscite, plebiscitum
Plectre, Plectrum, *s.m.* (*mus., in antiquity*) [plectrum, lyre-stick
Pléiade, *s.f.* pleiad; pleiads
Pleige, *s.m.* (*old*) pledge, bail, security
Pleiger, *v.a.* (*old*) to pledge, to bail
Plein, e, *adj.* full; solid; (*of doors*) ordinary; plentiful, abundant, abounding; entire, whole; replete; plenary; thorough; complete; open; broad; bright; (*of animals*) big, with young; roed. *—e eau*, main river, main stream; main sea; swimming *or* swimming-party out in the river *or* sea. *En — air*, in the open air. *En —e classe*, during school-hours; before the whole class. *En —e eau*, out in the river *or* sea. *En — été*, in the height of summer. *En — hiver*, in the depth of winter. *En — jour*, *V.* **Jour.** *En — midi*, at noon-day; openly. *En —e paix*, in the midst of peace. *En —e rue*, in the middle of the street. *Tout* —, quite full; quite, very; much, very much; many, a great many, a lot. *— de soi-même*, conceited, self-conceited
Plein, *s.m.* full; full space; full part; solid part; middle; midst; centre; front; full view; plenum; (*writ.*) thick stroke, down stroke. *En* —, *à* —, in the middle *or* midst; right in; quite; fully, completely; to the full; directly
Pleinement, *adv.* fully, entirely, completely, quite [entire
Pléni-er, ère, *adj.* plenary; full; complete;
Plénièrement, *adv.* plenarily; fully; completely; entirely
Plénipotentiaire, *s.m. adj.* plenipotentiary
Plénitude, *s.f.* plenitude, fulness, abundance
Pléonasme, *s.m.* pleonasm
Pléonastique, *adj.* pleonastic
Pléorama, *s.m.* pleorama
Plérose, *s.f.* (*med.*) plerosis
Plérotique, *adj.* (*med.*) plerotic [saur
Plésiosaure, *s.m.* (*zool.*) plesiosaurus, plesio-
Plessigraphe, *s.m.* (*med.*) plexigraph
Plessimètre, *s.m.* (*med.*) pleximeter
Plessimétrie, *s.f.* (*med.*) pleximetry
Plessimétrique, *adj.* (*med.*) pleximetric
Plet, *s.m.* (*nav.*) fake, coil
Pléthore, *s.f.* (*med.*) plethora
Pléthorique, *adj. s.* (*med.*) plethoric
Pleur, *s.m.sing.* (*poet.*) lament. *V.* **Pleurs**
Pleural, e, *adj.* (*anat.*) pleural [ing
Pleurard, e, *s.m.f.* blubberer; — *adj.* blubber-
Pleure-misère, *s.m.f.* grumbler; curmudgeon
Pleure-pain, *s.m.f.* curmudgeon
Pleurer, *v.n.a.* to weep; to cry; to mourn, to lament, to bewail; to weep over *or* for, to mourn over *or* for; to regret; to grudge; (*of the eyes*) to water; (*of vines*) to bleed
Pleurésie, *s.f.* (*med.*) pleurisy
Pleurétique, *adj.* (*med.*) pleuritic
Pleurette, *s.f.* (*fam.*) crying [weeping
Pleureu-r, se, *s.m.f. adj.* weeper, mourner;
Pleureu-x, se, *adj.* weeping, crying
Pleurnichement, *s.m.* whine, whining
Pleurnicher, *v.n.* to whine
Pleurnicherie, *s.f.* whining [whining
Pleurnicheu-r, se, *s.m.f.* whiner; — *adj.*
Pleurodynie, *s.f.* (*med.*) pleurodynia
Pleuronecte, *s.m.* (*zool.*) flat-fish [monia
Pleuropneumonie, *s.f.* (*med.*) pleuro-pneu-
Pleurs, *s.m.pl.* tears; weeping; crying, cries; lament; (*of vines*) bleeding
Pleutre, *s.m.* contemptible fellow, mere nobody, nobody; scrub; curmudgeon
Pleuviner, *v.n.* (*pop.*) to drizzle
Pleuvoir, *v.n.* to rain; to shower, to fall, to pour in *or* down. *Faire* —, to shower down, to pour *or* send in *or* down
Plèvre, *s.f.* (*anat.*) pleura
Plexiforme, *adj.* plexiform
Plexus, *s.m.* (*anat.*) plexus
Pleyon, *s.m.* osier-tie, twig, withe
Pli, *s.m.* fold; plait; crease; rumple; bend; inequality, undulation, wave; tuck; wrinkle; coil; bent, direction, habit; recess; folded paper, paper; cover, envelope; letter; message; communication; difficulty, hitch, objection. *Faux* —, wrong fold, crease; wrinkle. *Mauvais* —, rumple; bad direction. *Sous ce* —, (*of letters*) enclosed. *Cela ne fera* or *ne souffrira pas un* —, there will not be the slightest difficulty [about that
Pliable, *adj.* pliable, pliant, flexible
Pliage, *s.m.* folding
Pliant, e, *adj.* pliant, pliable, flexible, supple, bending, yielding; (*of seats*, &c.) folding
Pliant, *s.m.* camp-stool, folding seat *or* chair; pliantness; sociability, compliance
Plicature, *s.f.* plicature
Plie, *s.f.* (*fish*) plaice; flounder
Plié, e, *part. adj.* folded, bent, &c. (*V.* **Plier**); (*her.*) close; — *s.m.* bend
Pliement, *s.m.* folding
Plier, *v.a.n.* to fold; to fold up; to bend; to bow; to bring under; to manage; to yield, to submit; to give way; to furl (*sails*)
Se —, *v.r.* to be folded *or* bent; to bend; to bow; to comply, to conform (oneself), to yield, [to submit
Plieu-r, se, *s.m.f.* folder
Plinthe, *s.f.* (*arch.*) plinth; (*of rooms*) skirt, skirting; wash-board
Plinthite, *s.f.* (*min.*) plinthite [cene
Pliocène, *adj.m.f.*, *s.m.* (*geol.*) pleiocene, plio-
Plioir, *s.m.* (*thing*) folder; paper-folder
Plique, *s.f.* (*med.*) plica, plica Polonica
Pliquer (Se), *v.r.* (*med.*) to become affected [with plica
Plissage, *s.m.* *V.* **Plissement**
Plissé, e, *part. adj.* plaited, &c. (*V.* **Plisser**); (*bot.*) plicate; — *s.m.* plaits; wrinkles; corrugation [gation
Plissement, *s.m.* plaiting; wrinkling; corru-
Plisser, *v.a.* to plait; to wrinkle; to corrugate; — *v.n.*, **Se** —, *v.r.* to be plaited *or* wrinkled, to form plaits *or* wrinkles, to wrinkle, to take creases; to contract
Plissure, *s.f.* *V.* **Plissement**
Pliure, *s.f.* folding; fold [*or* poake
Ploc, *s.m.* cow-hair; felt; refuse hair, &c., poak
Ploiement, *s.m.* folding; (*mil.*) ploying
Plomb, *s.m.* lead plumb; plummet; sink; shot; leaden seal *or* stamp, seal, stamp; mephitic air, stench; asphyxia *or* eyesore from ditto; (*fig.*) ballast; (*pop.*) pox. — *de chasse*, shot. — *dans la tête*, (*fig.*) ballast. *Fil à* —, plumb-line, plummet-line. *A* —, perpen-

dicularly; perpendicular; uprightly; upright; vertically; vertical; firmly; plump; right down. *De* —, of lead, lead, leaden; heavy; grey

Plombage, *s.m.* lead-work; leading; plumbing; sealing; stopping (*of teeth*); pressing (*of land*)

Plombagine, *s.f.* plumbago, black lead, graphite

Plombate, *s.m.* (*chem.*) plumbate

Plombé, e, *part. adj.* leaded, &c. (*V.* **Plomber**); (*of sticks*) loaded; (*of colour*) leaden, leady; leaden-coloured; (*of complexion*) livid, of a leaden hue, leaden-coloured, leady

Plomber, *v.a.* to lead; to load (*a stick*); (*cust.*, &c.) to seal; to stop (*a tooth*); (*agr.*) to press (*land*); (*mas.*) to plumb; (*of earthenware*) to glaze; (*pop.*) to pox; — *v.n.* (*pop.*) to stink

Se —, *v.r.* to be leaded, &c.; to assume a leaden hue

Plomberie, *s.f.* plumbery; lead-works; lead-manufacture

Plombeu-r, se, *s.m.f.* sealer; — *adj.* sealing; (*agr.*) pressing. *Rouleau* —, field-roller, land-roller, land-presser

Plombier, *s.m.* plumber

Plombière, *s.f.*, *adj.f.* *Glace* —, "plombière" ice (*refreshment*)

Plombifère, *adj.* plumbiferous

Plombique, *adj.* (*chem.*) plumbic

Plomboir, *s.m.* (*dentist's*) plugger (*for stopping teeth*)

Plongé, e, *part. adj.* plunged, &c. (*V.* **Plonger**); weltering; — *s.f.* dip; (*artil.*, *fort.*) plonge, plongée

Plongeant, e, *part. adj.* plunging, &c. (*V.* **Plonger**); downward

Plongement, *s.m.* plunging, plunge; dipping, dip; pitching

Plongeon, *s.m.* ducking, dip, diving, plunging, plunge; (*bird*) diver. *Faire le* —, to take a ducking, to dive; (*fig.*) to duck, to duck o.'s head; to steal away; to give way; to flinch; to back out; to confess at the point of death

Plonger, *v.a.n.* to plunge; to immerse; to dip; to sink; to involve; to wrap; to throw; to dive; to duck; to pitch; to go downward; to rush

Se —, *v.r.* to plunge *or* &c. oneself; to be plunged *or* &c.; to welter

Plongeur, *s.m.* diver; plunger; — *adj.m.* diving; plunging. *Cloche à* or *de* —, diving-bell

Ploquer, *v.a.* (*nav.*) to felt

Ployable, Ployant, e. *V.* **Pliable, Pliant**

Ployer, *v.a.n.* *V.* **Plier**

Se —, *v.r.* *V.* **Plier (Se)**; (*mil.*) to ploy

Ployure, *s.f.* *V.* **Pliure**

Plu, *part. of* **Plaire** *and of* **Pleuvoir**

Pluche, &c. *V.* **Peluche,** &c.

Pluie, *s.f.* rain; shower. *A la* —, in the rain; rainy. *De* —, of *or* from rain; rain; rainy. *Faire* or *tomber de la* —, to rain. *Faire la — et le beau temps*, to have great influence; to be absolute master, to have it all o.'s own way, to rule the roast. *Parler de la — et du beau temps*, to talk of indifferent things. *Le temps est à la* —, it looks rainy

Plumage, *s.m.* plumage, feathers

†**Plumail,** *s.m.* feather-broom; (*old*) *V.* **Plumet**

Plumasseau, *s.m.* feather-broom; feather; quill; (*surg.*) pledget

Plumasserie, *s.f.* feather-trade *or* business

Plumassi-er, ère, *s.m.f.* plumassier, feather-seller *or* dresser

Plume, *s.f.* feather; plume; quill; pen; writer, author, penman; style; (*thieves' slang*) crow-bar, jemmy. — *métallique* or *d'acier* or *de fer*, steel-pen. *Guerre de* —, paper-war. *Une — à son chapeau*, a feather in o.'s cap

Plumeau, *s. m.* feather-broom; pen-tray; (*fish.*) bobber, float

Plumée, *s.f.* (*ink*) penful, dip

Plumée, *s.f.* plucking; plucking feathers; (*of*

Plumer, *v.a.* to plume, to pluck, to pick; to strip; to fleece

Se —, *v.r.* to be plumed *or* &c.; to fleece each other

Plumet, *s.m.* plume, feather, tuft of feathers; (*pop.*) drop too much

Plumetis, *s.m.* satin stitch

Plumeu-r, se, *s.m.f.* plucker

Plumeu-x, se, *adj.* plumose, plumous, feathery, feathered

Plumigère, *adj.* plumigerous; — *s.m.* quill-driver, red-tapist

Plumipède, *adj.m.f.*, *s.m.* (*zool.*) plumiped

Plumitif, *s.m.* minute-book; quill-driver, red-tapist; scribbler

Plumiti-f, ve, *adj.* quill-driving, red-tape; scribbling

Plum-pudding, *s.m.* plum pudding

Plumulaire, *s.f.* (*zool.*) plumularia

Plumule, *s.f.* (*of birds*) down; (*bot.*) plumule

Plupart, *s.f.* most part, greatest part *or* number, most, majority, generality. *Pour la* —, for the most part, mostly. *La — du temps*, mostly, generally

Pluralisation, *s.f.* pluralization

Pluraliser, *v.a.* to pluralize. *Se* —, to be pluralized

Pluralité, *s.f.* plurality

Pluriel, le, *adj.*, **Pluriel,** *s.m.* plural

Plus, *adv. s.m.* more; most; greater; greatest; greater (*or* greatest) number *or* quantity *or* degree *or* thing; the more; the farther; the longer; any more; any longer; no more; no longer; not any more *or* longer; not again; never again; never; not now; now no more; no (*or* not *or* none) ... now; no (*or* not *or* none) ... left; further; rather; also, moreover, besides; above, over, upwards; item; plus; utmost. *Au* —, *tout au* —, at most, at the most, at the outside; at best; the utmost. *Bien* —, much more; more than that; nay more; ay; moreover. *De* —, more; besides; moreover. *De — en* —, more and more. *De — en — mal, de — en — mauvais*, worse and worse. *En* —, more, as so much more, in addition (to), besides; to be added; in favour of. *Le* —, the most; as much as, as many as; as; as ... as. *Ne ... — que*, ... now only, only ... now, ... only, ... only (...) left, ... nothing left but; ... nothing else but. *Ne ... que* —, ... only the more. — *que*, more than; now only, only (...) left. *Ne ... — rien*, ... nothing more; ... nothing left. *Qui — qui moins*, some more some less. *Qui — est*, what is more. *Sans* —, without any more; no more, and no more, not any more; only. *Tant et* —, abundantly; a great deal; very much; ever so much; a great many; ever so many; excessively; over and over again. *Tant — que moins*, nearly, about. *N'être pas* —, not to be more. *N'être* —, to be no more *or* no longer; to be over *or* past. *Deux fois* —, twice as much. *Deux fois de* —, twice more. *Il y a* —, &c., *V.* **Avoir.** *Je n'ai — qu'à vous remercier*, there only remains for me to thank you

Plusieurs, *adj.pl.* several, some; (*obsolete*) many

Plus-payé, *s.m.* over-payment

Plus-pétition, *s.f.* (*law*) exorbitant demand

Plus-que-parfait, *s.m.* (*gram.*) pluperfect

Plus-value, *s.f.* *V.* **Value**

Plutocratie, *s.f.* plutocracy

Plutocratique, *adj.* plutocratic

Plutonien, ne, *adj. s.*, **Plutonique,** *adj.* (*geol.*) Plutonian; Plutonic

Pluton-isme, -iste, -omie. *V.* page 3, § 1

Plutôt, *adv.* rather, sooner, in preference; first; now, just. *Voyez — !* just look now!

Pluvial, e, *adj.* pluvial, of rain, rain, rainy; — *s.m.* (*Cath. rel.*) pluvial. *Eau —e*, rain-water

Pluvier, *s.m.* (*bird*) plover

Pluvieu-x, se, *adj.* rainy; wet; of rain; pluvious

Pluviomètre, *s.m.* rain-gauge, pluviometer, pluviameter

Pluviôse, *s.m.* Pluviose (*fifth month of the calendar of the first French Republic, from January* 20 *to February* 19)

Pnéomètre, *s.m.* pneumatometer

Pneumatique, *adj.* pneumatic; — *s.f.* pneumatics. *Machine* —, pneumatic engine, air-pump

Pneumatocèle, *s.f.* (*med.*) pneumatocele

Pneumatochimique, *adj.* pneumatochymic. *Cuve* —, pneumatic trough

Pneumatolog-ie, -ique, -iste. *V.* p. 3, § 1
Pneumatose, *s.f.* (*med.*) pneumatosis, windy
Pneumocèle, *s.f* (*med.*) pneumocele [swelling
Pneumogastrique, *adj.* (*anat.*) pneumogastric; — *s.m.* pneumogastric nerve
Pneumo-graphie, -logie, &c. *V.* page 3, § 1
Pneumonie, *s.f.* (*med.*) pneumonia
Pneumonique, *adj. s.* (*med.*) pneumonic
Pneumotomie. *V.* page 3, § 1
Poa, *s.m.* *V* **Paturin** [to, mauling
Pochade, *s.f.* (*paint.*) rough sketch; (*slang*) set-
Pochard, e, *adj. s.* (*pop.*) drunk, tight, groggy, boozy; drunkard, boozer, drunken man *or* fellow *or* woman *or* creature
Pocharder, *v.a.* (*pop.*) to make drunk, to fuddle
Se —, *v.r.* to get drunk
Pocharderie, *s.f.* (*pop.*) drunkenness
Poche, *s.f.* pocket; pouch; sack; bag; poke; purse-net; rabbit-net; soup-ladle; crib (*of a coach-box*); wrinkle; pucker; crop *or* pouch (*of a bird*); kit (*fiddle*), (*writ.*) round stroke. *De —,* (*adject.*) pocket. *Mettez cela dans votre — avec votre mouchoir par-dessus,* (*jest.*) put that in your pipe and smoke it. — **-cuiller,** *s.m.* (*bird*) spoonbill
Poché, e, *adj.* poached; (*of writing and printing*) blotted; (*of the eyes*) black, black and blue, bruised, swollen; (*paint.*) roughly sketched
Pochée, *s.f* sackful; bagful; pocketful
Pocher, *v.a.* to poach (*eggs*); to blot (*letters*); to bruise (*the eyes*); (*paint.*) to sketch roughly; — *v.n* to pucker. — *l'œil, les yeux,* to give a black eye, a pair of black eyes. *Se faire — l'œil, les yeux,* to get ditto [other black eyes
Se —, *v.r.* to be poached, &c.; to give each
Pochet, *s.m.* nose-bag
Pocheter, *v.a.* to keep *or* carry in o.'s pocket; — *v.n.* to be kept *or* carried in the pocket
Pochette, *s.f.* little pocket, pocket; bag; purse-net; kit (*fiddle*) [*sur l'œil*) black eye
Pochon, *s.m.* (*of ink*) blot; (*pop.*) punch, (—
Poco, *adv.* (*mus.*) poco
Pococurante, *s.m* pococurante
Pococurantisme, *s.m.* pococurantism
Podagraire, *s.f* *V.* **Égopode**
Podagre, *s.f* podagra, gout in the feet; — *adj.* podagric, gouty; — *s.m.f.* gouty person
Podestat, *s.m.* podesta (*Italian magistrate*)
Podologie, &c. *V.* page 3, § 1
Podure, *s.m.* (*insect*) spring-tail
Poêle, *s.m.* stove; pall; canopy; — *s.f.* pan; frying-pan. — *à frire,* frying-pan
Poêlée, *s.f.* panful; (*local*) harvest-home
Poêlerie, *s.f.* stove-making *or* trade *or* business; stoves, warming-apparatus
Poêlette, *s.f.* small pan, pan
Poêlier, *s.m.* stove-maker
Poêlon, *s.m.* saucepan, pan; pipkin
Poêlonnée, *s.f.* saucepanful
Poème, *s.m.* poem [poem; verse
Poésie, *s.f.* poetry; poesy; piece of poetry,
Poète, *s.m.* poet; poetess; — *adj.* poetical
Poétereau, *s.m.* poetaster
Poétesse, *s.f.* poetess [(*fig.*) poetry
Poétique, *adj.* poetic, poetical; — *s.f.* poetics;
Poétiquement, *adv.* poetically
Poétiser, *v.a.n.* to poetize; to versify
Se —, *v.r.* to be poetized, to become poetical
Poétriau, *s.m.* *V.* **Poétereau** [drumfish
Pogonias, *s.m.* (*bird*) pogonias; (*fish*) pogonias,
Poids, *s.m.* weight; poise; heaviness; gravity; load, burden; moment, importance, consequence; consideration; force. *Au —,* by weight. *Être de —,* to be full weight [sharply
†Poignamment, *adv.* poignantly, keenly,
†Poignant, e, *adj.* poignant, stinging, keen, sharp; painful, sad, melancholy
†Poignard, *s.m.* dagger, poniard; (*of clothes*) gore, inlay; (*fish*) jack, pickerel
†Poignarder, *v.a.* to stab, to poniard; to grieve, to wound to the heart, to kill, to be the
†Poigne, *s.f.* grasp, gripe, clutch [death of
†Poignée, *s.f.* handful; bundle; hank; handle; holder; (*of a gun-stock*) small; (*of swords having no part to protect the hand*) hilt (*handle*); (*of swords having a curved part to protect the hand, which, in those swords, is technically called the "hilt"*) gripe (*handle*). — *de main,* shake of the hand, shaking of hands. *A —,* tightly, by the handful; with a hilt *or* &c. *Donner une* or *la — de main à,* to shake hands with. *Se donner une* or *la — de main,* to shake hands (together). *Prendre à —,* to grasp tightly
†Poignet, *s.m.* wrist; wrist-band; cuff
Poil, *s.m.* hair; beard; nap; pile, wool; coat, fur; colour; (*med.*) mastitis; (*pop.*) pluck, boldness, resolution; (*pop.*) blow-up, jobation. — *de chèvre,* goat's hair; mohair. — *de souris,* (*adject.*) mouse-coloured. *A —, à —s,* haired, hairy; napped; bareback, without a saddle; (*jest.*) naked; (*pop.*) plucky, bold, resolute. *Chercher du — aux œufs,* to split hairs. *Être au — et à la plume,* to be fit for anything. *Faire le — à,* to clip, to trim (*a horse*); to shave; to cut out, to outdo *Reprendre du — de la bête,* to do the same thing over again, to go at it again, to take a hair of the dog that
Poilu, e, *adj.* hairy; shaggy [bit you
†Poinciane, Poincillade, *s.f.* (*bot.*) flower-fence
Poinçon, *s.m.* stiletto; bodkin; awl; point; pointer; punch, puncheon; stamp; die; (*cask*) puncheon; (*build.*) king-post
Poinçonnage, Poinçonnement, *s. m.* stamping; punching
Poinçonner, *v.a.* to stamp; to punch
Poinçonneu-r, se, *s.m.f.* stamper; puncher; — *s.f.* stamping-machine, stamper; punching-machine, puncher; — *adj.* stamping; punching
Poindre, *v.n.* to spring *or* come up; to braird; to come out; to dawn, to peep, to break; to appear; to begin; — *v.a.* (*old*) to sting
Poing, *s.m.* fist; hand
Point, *s.m.* point; dot; mark; note; spot; speck; pip; hole; break, dawn; size; degree, extent, pitch, height; stitch; sight; part; place; quarter; position; situation; condition; state; case; terms; moment, instant; point-lace, point; (*gram.*) full stop, period; (*gram.*) dot; (*gram.*) note (*of exclamation,* &c.). — *arrière,* back-stitch. — *devant,* (*need.*) running. — *d'Angleterre,* — *de Bruxelles,* Brussels point. — *d'arrêt,* sticking-place; stop; (*mus.*) *V.* — *d'orgue.* — *de chainette,* chain-stitch, knotted stitch. — *de côté,* stitch in the side. — *de couture,* stitch. — *de départ,* starting-point, point of departure; starting-post; beginning, origin, source. — *d'honneur,* point of honour; pride; mettle. — *d'orgue,* — *de repos,* — *d'arrêt,* (*mus.*) organ-point, pedal-point, pause, hold, fermata. — *de vue,* point of sight; point of view; prospect; light; opinion. *Deux —s,* (*gram.*) colon. *A —,* in time, just in time; seasonably; to a nicety, to a turn; right in the end. *A — nommé,* in time, just in time, in the nick of time, at the exact *or* stated *or* appointed time, punctually; at the proper time. *Au — de,* at *or* to the point of; so far *or* so much as; till, until. *Au — que,* to such a point *or* degree that; so far that, so much that; so much so that; till, until. *Au dernier —,* in the highest degree. *De — en —,* exactly, in every point *or* particular, in detail. *De tout —,* in every respect, entirely. *Faute d'un —,* for a trifle. *Mal en —,* (*old*) in bad condition, in a sad plight, badly off. *Mettre les —s sur les i,* (*fig.*) to mind o.'s P's and Q's; to be very punctilious *or* precise, to be scrupulously exact. *Il vous rendrait des —s,* he is more than a match for you
Point, *adv.* any; not; no; not any, none; no such thing; not so; not at all
Pointage, *s.m.* pointing; levelling
Pointal, *s.m.* (*carp.*) girder, summer, prop

Pointe, *s.f.* point; tack; brad; head; (— *de terre*) point of land, headland, foreland; nib; tip; top; end; edge; (*of a butt-end*) toe; (*her.*) base (*of a shield*); (*of clothes*) gore; (*of day*) dawn, break, peep; sharpness, tartness, pungency, sharp taste, high flavour, relish, smack; dash; touch; smart saying, witticism, flash of wit; sting; pun; little drop too much; merry mood; neckerchief; (*rid.*) rear; (*mil.*) movement *or* move out of o.'s line of operations, move, march; (*arts*) etching-needle; (*sculp., engr.*) point; (*print.*) bodkin. *Avoir une — de vin, être en — de vin,* to be a little flustered. *Faire* or *pousser une —,* (*mil.*) to deviate from the line, to make a move. *Poursuivre* or *pousser* or *suivre sa —,* to pursue o.'s point, to persist, to go on, to get on; to try o.'s chance

Pointeau, *s.m.* hard steel point

Pointement, *s.m.* pointing; levelling

Pointer, *v.a.n.* to stick; to pierce; to point; to dot; to check; to level; to prick; to stitch; (*print.*) to register; (*engr.*) to stipple; (*of plants*) to spring up, to shoot, to braird; (*of birds*) to soar, to rise; (*fig.*) to peep, to appear, to show itself, to come out; to taper; (*of horses*) to rear

Se —, *v.r.* to be pointed *or* &c.; to turn [er

Pointeur, *s.m.* checker, pricker, marker; pointer

†Pointillage, *s.m.* dotting; (*engr.*) stippling

†Pointillé, e, *part. adj.* dotted, &c. (*V.* **Pointiller**); spotted; — *s.m.* dotting; stippling; dotted drawing; stippled engraving

†Pointiller, *v.n.a.* to dot; to stipple; to cavil; to carp at; to nettle, to tease, to annoy

Se —, *v.r.* to be dotted, &c.; to tease *or* &c. each other; to bicker [tiousness; bickering

†Pointillerie, *s.f.* cavil, hair-splitting, cap-

†Pointilleu-x, se, *adj.* cavilling, captious; punctilious

Pointu, e, *adj.* pointed, sharp; peaked; subtle; — *s.m.* subtilizer; surly fellow, ugly customer; (*slang*) injection, enema [(*nav.*) earing

Pointure, *s.f.* point; sting; (*of boots*) size;

Poire, *s.f.* pear; flask; (*of steelyards*) weight. — *à couteau,* dessert-pear. — *à poudre,* powder-flask, powder-horn. — *d'angoisse,* choke-pear; gag; bitter pill. — *de terre,* Jerusalem artichoke. *Entre la — et le fromage,* at dessert. *Garder une — pour la soif,* to lay by something

Poiré, *s.m.* perry [for a rainy day

Poireau, *s.m.* leek; wart [chard

Poirée, *s.f.* (*bot.*) white beet, Sicilian beet,

Poirier, *s.m.* pear-tree; ditto wood

Pois, *s.m.* pea; — *pl.* peas, pease. — *à cautère,* — *d'iris,* issue pea. — *carré,* marrow-fat. — *chiche,* chick-pea, dwarf pea. — *goulus* or *gourmands,* — *mange-tout,* — *sans cosse* or *sans parchemin,* skinless peas, sugar peas, wyker peas. — *ramés,* stick-peas. — *verts, petits —,* green peas. *Donner un — pour avoir une fève,* to give a sprat to catch a herring. *Rendre — pour fève, V.* **Fève**

Poison, *s.m.* poison; venom; poisoning; — *s.f.* (*pop.*) slut, drab, minx, bitch of a woman, bitch, pest

Poissard, e, *adj.* low, vulgar, Billingsgate; — *s.f.* fish-woman, fish-fag; market-woman; low *or* vulgar woman [to clam

Poisser, *v.a.n.* to pitch; to glue, to make sticky;

Poisseu-x, se, *adj.* pitchy; gluey, viscous, viscid, sticky

Poisson, *s.m.* fish; (*meas.*) quartern, gill. — *-lune,* — *-soleil,* moon-fish, sun-fish. — *rouge,* gold-fish. — *d'avril,* April fool trick, April fool's errand; mackerel. *Donner un — d'avril à,* to make an April fool of

†Poissonnaille, *s.f.* small fish, small fry, fry

Poissonnerie, *s.f.* fish-market

Poissonneu-x, se, *adj.* abounding in fish, full of fish, fishy

Poissonni-er, ère, *s.m.f.* fishmonger; fish-salesman, fish-factor; — *s.f.* fish-kettle

Poitevin, e, *adj. s.* of Poitou (*formerly a province of France*) *or* of Poitiers (*its capital*), Poitevin, native of Poitou *or* of Poitiers

†Poitrail, *s.m.* (*of horses*) breast, chest; (*of harness*) breast-plate, breast-strap; (*build.*) breastsummer

Poitrinaire, *adj. s.m.f.* consumptive

Poitrinal, *s.m. V.* **Pétrinal**

Poitrine, *s.f.* breast; chest; lungs; (*butch.*) breast, brisket. *Maladie* or *affection de —,* disease of the chest; consumption

Poivrade, *s.f.* pepper-sauce

Poivre, *s.m.* pepper. — *d'eau,* water-pepper, culerage, smart-weed. — *en grains,* whole pepper. — *et sel,* (*of the hair or beard*) of pepper and salt colour, grizzly [dear

Poivré, e, *part. adj.* peppered, &c.; awfully

Poivrer, *v.a.* to pepper; to fleece, to overcharge; to swell (*a bill*), to lay it on stiff; (*pop.*) to clap, to pox

Poivrier, *s.m.* pepper-plant; pepper-box, pepper-caster. *Vol au —,* robbery upon drunken people [per-plantation; sentry-box

Poivrière, *s.f.* pepper-box, pepper-caster; pep-

Poivron, *s.m.* pimento-berry

Poix, *s.f.* pitch; (*of shoemakers*) wax

Polacca, *s.f.* (*dance, tune*) polacca, Polonaise. *Alla —,* (*mus.*) alla polacca

Polacre, Polaque, *s.f.* (*nav.*) polacre, polacca; — *s.m.* polack (*Polish horseman*)

Polaque, *s.f.* (*dance, tune*) polacca, Polonaise; (*nav.*) *V.* **Polacre**; — *s.m. V.* **Polacre**

Polaire, *adj.* polar

Polarimètre, *s.m.* (*phys.*) polarimeter

Polarimétr-ie, -ique. *V.* page 3, § 1

Polarisa-teur, trice, *adj.* (*phys.*) polarizing

Polarisation, *s.f.* (*phys.*) polarization

Polariscope, *s.m.* (*phys.*) polariscope

Polariser, *v.a.* (*phys.*) to polarize. *Se —,* to

Polarité, *s.f.* (*phys.*) polarity [be polarized

Polatouche, *s.m.* flying squirrel

Polder, *s.m.* polder (*in the Netherlands*)

Pôle, *s.m.* (*astr., geog., phys.,* &c.) pole

Polémique, *adj.* polemic, polemical; — *s.f.* polemics, controversy, dispute, paper-war, literary quarrel

Polémiste, *s.m.f.* polemic, polemist [ladder

Polémoine, *s.f.* (*bot.*) polemonium, Jacob's

Polémoscope, *s.m.* polemoscope, side opera-glass [pudding, hominy, mush

Polenta, Polente, *s.f.* polenta, maize hasty-

Poli, e, *adj.* polished; bright; glossy; smooth; sleek; polite, civil; refined

Poli, *s.m.* polish; polishing; finish; gloss

Police, *s.f.* police; police office; police court; police regulations; policy, polity, government; civilization; (*of insurance,* &c.) policy; (*print.*) fount-list *or* bill; fount, sorts. — *de chargement,* (*nav.*) bill of lading. *Tribunal de —* or *de simple —,* police court (*for petty offences*). *Faire la —,* to keep order (in) [ing

Policement, *s.m.* governing, civilizing, polish-

Policer, *v.a.* to establish policy *or* a regular government in; to govern; to civilize; to polish, to refine

Se —, *v.r.* to become civilized *or* &c.

Polichinel, Polichinelle, *s.m.* punch, punchinello; puppet; buffoon, wag; odd fish; (*pop.*) baby; (*pop.*) quartern of brandy; — *s.f.* polichinelle (*dance*) [lice-agent

Polici-er, ère, *adj.* police; — *s.m.* (*fam.*) po-

Poli-couteaux, *s.m.* knife-cleaner

Poliment, *s.m.* polishing; brightening; polish; finish; — *adv.* politely, civilly

Polir, *v.a.* to polish; to brighten; to gloss; to smooth; to finish; to refine; to civilize

Se —, *v.r.* to become (*or* be) polished, &c.

Polissable, *adj.* polishable

Polissage, *s.m.* polishing; finishing

Polisseu-r, se, *s.m.f.* polisher; finisher

Polissoir, *s.m.* (*tool*) polisher

Polissoire, *s.f.* shining-brush

Polisson, ne, *s.m.f.* blackguard, scamp, rogue, rake, dirty fellow *or* creature; – *s.m.* (*of dress, obsolete*) bustle; — *adj.* mischievous, idle; lewd; dirty, smutty, broad; blackguardly, blackguard
Polissonner, *v.n.* to play the blackguard *or* the rake; to play the fool; to crack broad jokes; to play about the streets
Polissonnerie, *s.f.* blackguardism; blackguard trick; smutty thing, broad joke; playing about the streets
Polissure, *s.f.* polishing
Politesse, *s.f.* politeness, civility, good breeding; refinement; polite action *or* thing, act of politeness, kind attention
Politico, (*in compounds*) politico-...
Politicomanie, *s.f.* politicomania
Politique, *adj.* political; politic; prudent; wise; shrewd; — *s.m.* politician, statist; politic *or* prudent man; — *s.f.* politics; policy; political principles; statecraft; prudence; artfulness; shrewd way *or* ways; design, designs
Politiquement, *adv.* politically; politicly, shrewdly
Politiquer, *v.n.* to talk politics, to discuss; to meddle with state affairs; to play a shrewd game
Politiqueur, *s.m.* politicaster, politician
Polka, *s.f.* polka (*dance*)
Polker, *v.n.* to polk, to dance the polka
Polkeu-r, se, *s.m.f.* polker
Poll, *s.m.* poll (*at English elections*)
Pollack, *s.m.* (*fish*) pollack, lythe
Pollen, *s.m.* (*bot.*) pollen
Pollénine, *s.f.* (*chem.*) pollenine
Pollicitation, *s.f.* (*law*) pollicitation
Pollinifère, *adj.* (*bot.*) polliniferous
Polluer, *v.a.* to pollute; to defile; to profane
Pollution, *s.f.* pollution; defilement; profanation
Polonais, e, *adj.* Polish; — *s.m.f.* Pole, Polander; — *s.m.* Polonese, Polish language; (*pop.*) drunkard; — *s.f.* Polish fashion; Polonaise (*dress, dance, tune*)
Polonisme, *s.m.* Polonism
Poltron, ne, *adj.* cowardly, dastardly; — *s.m.f.* coward, poltroon; sculker
Poltronnement, *adv.* cowardly
Poltronnerie, *s.f.* cowardice, poltroonery; cowardly act
Poly, (*in compounds*) poly...
Polyadelphe, *adj.* (*bot.*) polyadelphous
Polyadelphie, *s.f.* (*bot.*) polyadelphia
Polyandre, *adj.* polyandrian, polyandrous
Polyandrie, *s.f.* polyandry; (*bot.*) polyandria
Polyarch-ie, -ique, &c. *V.* page 3, § 1
Polycamératique, *adj.* (*horol.*) polycameratic
Polycarpe, *adj.* (*bot.*) polycarpous
‡**Polychroïsme,** *s.m.* polychroism
‡**Polychromatique,** *adj.* polychromatic
‡**Polychrome,** *s.m. adj.* polychrome
‡**Polychromie,** *s.f.* polychromy
Polycotylédone, *adj.* (*bot.*) polycotyledonous; — *s.f.* polycotyledon
Polycotylédoné, e, *adj.* (*bot.*) polycotyledonous; — *s.f.* polycotyledon
Polydipsie, *s.f.* (*med.*) polydipsia
Polyèdre, *s.m.* polyhedron; — *adj.* polyhedral
Polyédrique, *adj.* polyhedral
Polyergue, *s.f.* (*zool.*) polyergus, amazon-ant
Polygala, Polygale, *s.m.* (*bot.*) milkwort
Polygame, *adj.* polygamous; — *s.m.f.* polygamist
Polygam-ie, -ique. *V.* page 3, § 1
Polygarch-ie, -ique, &c. *V.* page 3, § 1
Polygastrique, *adj.* (*zool.*) polygastric
Polyglotte, *adj.m.f., s.m.* (*man*), *s.f.* (*female, bible*) polyglot
Polygonal, e, *adj.* polygonal
Polygone, *s.m.* (*geom., fort.*) polygon; (*artil.*) ordnance-yard, artillery-practice ground, artillery-ground, butt; — *adj.* polygonal
Polygonum, *s.m.* (*bot.*) polygonum
Polygraphe, *s.m.* polygraph, manifold writer
Polygraph-ie, -ique. *V.* page 3, § 1
Polygyne, *adj* polygynian, polygynous
Polygynie, *s.f.* polygyny; (*bot.*) polygynia

Polyhymnie, *s.f. V.* **Polymnie**
Polymathe, *s.m.* polymathist
Polymath-ie, -ique. *V.* page 3, § 1
Polymnie, *s.f.* polyhymnia, polymnia
Polymorphe, *adj.* polymorphous
Polymorph-ie, -isme, &c. *V.* page 3, § 1
Polynème, *s.m.* (*zool.*) polyneme, mango-fish
Polynésien, ne, *adj. s.* Polynesian
Polynôme, *s.m. adj.* (*alg.*) polynomial
Polyopie, Polyopsie, *s.f.* (*med.*) polyopia, polyopsis
Polyoptre, *s.m.* polyoptron, polyoptrum, multiplying glass
Polyorama, *s.m.* polyorama
Polyorexie, *s.f.* (*med.*) polyorexia
Polype, *s.m.* (*zool.*) polype; (*med.*) polypus
Polypétale, Polypétalé, e, *adj.* (*bot.*) polypetalous
Polypeu-x, se, *adj.* (*med.*) polypous
Polyphone, *adj.* polyphonous, polyphonic
Polyphon-ie, -ique. *V.* page 3, § 1
Polyphylle, *adj.* (*bot.*) polyphyllous
Polypier, *s.m.* (*zool.*) polypary, polypier
Polypiforme, *adj.* polypiform
Polypite, *s.f.* (*fossil*) polypite
Polyplectron, *s.m.* (*bird*) *V.* **Éperonnier**
Polypode, *adj.* (*zool.*) polypodal; — *s.m.* (*zool.*) polypode; (*bot.*) polypodium, polypody, polypode
Polyptère, *adj.* (*zool.*) polypteral
Polyscope, *s.m.* polyscope, multiplying glass
Polyscopique, *adj.* polyscopic
Polysépale, *adj.* (*bot.*) polysepalous
Polyspermatique, Polysperme, Polyspermique, *adj.* (*bot.*) polyspermous
Polystome, *s.m. adj.* (*nat. hist.*) polystoma
Polystyle, *s.m. adj.* (*arch.*) polystyle; — *adj.* (*bot.*) polystylous
Polysyllabe, *s.m.* polysyllable; — *adj.* polysyllabic
Polysyllab-ique, -isme. *V.* page 3, § 1
‡**Polytechnicien,** *s. m.* cadet of the Polytechnic military school, Polytechnician
‡**Polytechnique,** *adj.* polytechnic
Polythéisme, *s.m.* polytheism
Polythéiste, *s.m.f.* polytheist; — *adj.* polytheistic
Polytric, *s. m.* (*bot.*) polytrichum, hair-moss, golden maidenhair, goldilocks
Polytypage, *s.m.* polytypage
Polytype, *s.m. adj.* polytype
Polytyper, *v.a.* to polytype
Polytypeur, *s.m.* polytyper
Polyurie, *s.f.* (*med.*) polyuria
Polyurique, *adj.* (*med.*) polyuric
Pomard, *s.m.* pomard (wine)
Poméranien, ne, *adj. s.* Pomeranian
Pomery, *s.m.* pomery (wine)
Pomiculteur, *s.m.* pomiculturist
Pomiculture, *s.f.* pomiculture
Pomifère, *adj.* pomiferous
Pomiforme, *adj.* pomiform, apple-shaped, apple-like
Pommade, *s.f.* pomade; ointment; salve
Pommader, *v.a.* to pomade
Pommadière, *s.f.* antimacassar
Pommage, *s.m.* pommage, pomace; cider-apple estate
Pommard, *s.m. V.* **Pomard**
Pomme, *s.f.* apple; (*of a lettuce, cabbage, walking-stick,* &c.) head; ball, knob; (*of a water-pot*) rose; (*nav.*) truck. — *-poire,* pearmain. — *à couteau,* dessert-apple, table-apple. — *d'Adam,* (*anat.*) Adam's apple. — *de chêne,* oak-apple. — *de pin, V.* **Pin.** — *de rose,* rose apple. — *de terre,* potato. *Bifteck aux —s* (*de terre*), beef-steak with fried potatoes
Pommé, e, *adj.* (*hort.*) grown to a heart, white-headed, headed; cabbaged, cabbage; (*fig.*) downright, egregious
Pommé, *s.m.* apple-sandwich; (*obsolete*) cider
Pommeau, *s.m.* pommel
Pommelé, e, *adj.* dappled, dapple, mottled; covered with sonder-clouds, curled, cloudy
Pommeler, *v.a.* to dapple. **Se —,** *v.r.* to dapple, to become dappled *or* &c. (*V.* **Pommelé**)
Pommelière, *s.f.* (*vet.*) pulmonary consumption
Pommelle, *s.f.* waste-pipe strainer, strainer, grate; (*of carriages*) roller-bolt

Pommer, *v.n.* (*hort.*) to grow to a heart *or* to a head, to heart, to head, to boll; to cabbage

Pommeraie, *s.f.* apple-orchard

Pommette, *s.f.* apple *or* pear-gatherer; azarole (*fruit*); pommel, pomel, ball, knob; cheek-bone

Pommetté, e, *adj.* (*her.*) pommettée, pomel

Pommier, *s.m.* apple-tree; apple-tree wood; apple-roaster. — *cannelle,* (*bot.*) sweet sop

Pomolog-ie, -ique. *V.* page 3, § 1

Pomologue, *s.m.* pomologist

Pomone, *s.f.* (*bot.*) pomona; (*myth., astr.*) Pomona. *Les dons* or *les présents de* —, (*poet.*) fruit [— *s.f.* Pompadour fashion *or* style

Pompadour, *adj.* Pompadour, old-fashioned;

Pompage, *s.m.* swilling, guzzling, boozing

Pompe, *s.f.* pomp, splendour; loftiness; dignity; ceremony; state; stateliness; procession; pump; engine; syringe; (*of wind-instr.,* &c.) slide. — *aspirante,* suction-pump, sucking-pump, lift-pump. — *à air,* air-pump. — *à bière,* beer-engine (*à la* —, on draught). — *à chapelet,* chain-pump. — *à feu,* — *à vapeur,* steam-waterworks. — *à incendie,* fire-engine. — *d'arrosement,* watering-engine, garden-engine. —*s funèbres,* funerals, burials; funeral *or* interment company. *Entreprise de —s funèbres,* funeral *or* interment company. *V.* **Entrepreneur**

Pompéien, ne, *adj. s.* Pompeian

Pompement, *s.m.* pumping, &c. (*V.* **Pomper**)

Pomper, *v.a.n.* to pump; to suck, to imbibe; to drink, to swill, to guzzle, to booze

Se —, *v.r.* to be pumped *or* &c. [ness; pumps

Pomperie, *s.f.* pump-making *or* trade *or* busi-

Pompette, *adj.* (*pop.*) tipsy, tight, boozy. *Nez de* —, drunkard's nose, red nose

Pompeusement, *adv.* pompously

Pompeu-x, se, *adj.* pompous; stately; lofty

Pompholix, Pompholyx, *s.m.* (*chem., med.*) pompholyx [(*pop.*) guzzler, hard-drinker

Pompier, *s.m.* pump-maker; pumper; fireman;

Pompon, *s.m.* top-knot; tuft; (*of horses*) ear-knot; (*fam.*) glory, palm; first rank, lead; (*pop.*) pate, noddle, sconce. *Rose* —, miniature hundred-leaved rose [dress *or* trim up

Pomponner, *v.a.* to adorn, to ornament; to

Ponant, *s.m.* (*obsolete*) west; (*nav.*) west wind; (*nav.*) western Ocean [seaman

Ponantais, Ponantin, *s.m.* western Ocean

Ponçage, *s.m.* pumicing

Ponce, *s.f.* (*min.*) pumice; (*tech.*) pounce. *Pierre* —, pumice-stone

Ponceau, *s.m.* small bridge of a single arch, arch, archway, culvert; (*bot.*) corn-poppy, red poppy; poppy-colour, flame-colour, coquelicot; — *adj.* poppy-coloured, poppy, coquelicot

Poncer, *v.a.* to pumice; to pounce

Poncette, *s.f.* pounce-bag

Ponceu-x, se, *adj.* pumiceous

Ponche, *s.m.* punch (*beverage*) [expression

Poncif, *s.m.* pouncing-paper; (*fig.*) hackneyed

Poncire, *s.m.* (*bot.*) cedra, cedrat, cedrate

Poncis, *s.m.* pounce; pouncing-paper; pounced drawing

Ponction, *s.f.* (*surg.*) punction, puncture, tapping. *Faire la* — *à,* to puncture, to tap

Ponctionner, *v.a.* (*surg.*) to puncture, to tap

Ponctionneur, *s.m.* (*surg.*) trocar

Ponctualité, *s.f.* punctuality

Ponctuation, *s.f.* punctuation, pointing

Ponctuel, le, *adj.* punctual

Ponctuellement, *adv.* punctually

Ponctuer, *v.a.n.* to punctuate, to point, to

Ponctulé, e, *adj.* punctulated [stop, to dot

Poncture, *s.f.* puncture

Pondage, *s.m.* poundage

Pondérabilité, *s.f.* ponderability

Pondérable, *adj.* ponderable

Pondéral, e, *adj.* ponderal

Pondéra-teur, trice, *adj.* poising, balancing

Pondération, *s.f.* ponderation, poising, balan-

Pondérer, *v.a.* to poise, to balance [cing

Pondéreu-x, se, *adj.* ponderous [(*of eggs*)

Pondeuse, *adj.f.* (*of hens*) laying; — *s.f.* layer

Pondoir, *s.m.* (*for hens*) laying-place; (*of insects*) ovipositor

Pondre, *v.a.n.* to lay (*eggs*). *Je t'en ponds!* don't you wish you may get it!

Ponet, Poney, *s.m.* pony, galloway. *Double* —, cob [galloway. *Double* —, cob mare

Ponette, *s.f.* mare pony, pony, mare galloway,

Pongiti-f, ve, *adj.* (*med.*) pungent, sharp

Pongo, *s.m.* (*zool.*) pongo, black orang

Pont, *s.m.* bridge; (*nav.*) deck; stage; (*of old-fashioned trousers*) flap; (*theat.*) *V.* **Gril.** — *-aqueduc,* aqueduct-bridge. — *biais,* skew-bridge. — *coupé,* half-deck. — *-levis,* draw-bridge; (*of old-fashioned trousers*) flap; (*rid.*) pontlevis. — *-neuf,* popular song. — *tournant,* swing-bridge, swivel-bridge. — *-tube,* tubular bridge. — *volant,* flying bridge, hanging stage. —*s et chaussées,* bridges and highways, bridges and roads; civil engineering. *Faux* —, orlop deck; spar-deck. *Premier* —, (*nav.*) lower deck. *Bâtiment* or *vaisseau à trois —s,* three-decker. *Équipage de* —, (*mil.*) pontoon-train

Pontal, *s.m.* depth (*of a ship*)

Ponte, *s.f.* laying eggs, laying; eggs; laying-time; — *s.m.* (*at play*) punto; punter [open

Ponté, e, *adj.* (*nav.*) decked. *Non* —, undecked,

Ponter, *v.a.* to deck; — *v.n.* to punt [tree

Pontet, *s.m.* bow of the trigger-guard; saddle-

Pontife, *s.m.* pontiff; high priest; bishop, prelate. *Frères* —*s, religieux —s,* bridge-building brothers *or* friars

Pontifical, e, *adj.,* **Pontifical,** *s.m.* pontifical

Pontificalement, *adv.* pontifically

Pontificat, *s.m.* pontificate; (*fam.*) state, stateliness [papal troops, Pope's troops

Pontificaux, *s.m.pl.* pontificals, pontifical *or*

Pontin, e, *adj.* (*anc. geog.*) Pontine

Pontique, *adj.* (*anc. geog.*) Pontic

Ponton, *s.m.* pontoon; pontoon-bridge; hulk

Pontonage, *s.m.* pontage, toll [toll-collector

Pontonier, Pontonnier, *s.m.* pontonier;

Pope, *s.m.* pope (*of the Greek Church*)

Popeline, *s.f.* poplin

Poplité, e, *adj.* (*anat.*) popliteal

Popote, Popotte, *s.f.* (*children's slang*) pap; (*pop. slang*) ordinary, &c. (*V.* **Boubouille**); — *adj.* indifferent, so so

Popoter, Popotter, *v.n.* (*slang*) *V.* **Fricoter**

Populace, *s.f.* populace, mob, rabble

Populaci-er, ère, *adj.* low, vulgar

Populage, *s.m.* (*bot.*) marsh-marigold

Populaire, *adj.* popular; vulgar; — *s.m.* mob, populace, rabble

Populairement, *adv.* popularly

Popularisation, *s.f.* popularization

Populariser, *v.a.* to popularize; to make *or* render popular [lar; to become popular

Se —, *v.r.* to make *or* render oneself popu-

Popularité, *s.f.* popularity

Population, *s.f.* population

Populeu-x, se, *adj.* populous

Populicide, *adj.* populicidal; — *s.m.* populicide

Populine, *s.f.* (*chem.*) populine [brats; mob

Populo, *s.m.* plump child, chubby-cheeks;

Populosité, *s.f.* populousness

Poracé, e, *adj.* *V.* **Porracé**

Porc, *s.m.* pig, hog, swine, porker; pork. — *-épic,* *s.m.* (*pl.* —*s-épics*) porcupine

Porcelaine, *s.f. adj.* porcelain, china, china-ware; china vase *or* vases; porcelain-shell, cowry; — *adj.* blue-grey; (*of card-board,* &c.) enamelled. — *de Chine,* china

Porcelaini-er, ère, *s.m.f.* porcelain (*or* china) manufacturer; — *adj.* of porcelain, porcelain, of china, china

Porcelanique, *adj.* porcelaneous

Porcelanite, *s.f.* fossil porcelain-shell

Porcelet, *s.m.* young pig; wood-louse

Porcellane, *s.f.* (*zool.*) porcellana [lain-jasper

Porcellanite, *s.f.* (*min.*) porcellanite, porce-

Porcelle, *s.f.* (*bot.*) cat's-ear
Porcellion, *s.m.* (*insect*) porcellio, hog-louse
Porchaison, *s.f.* (*hunt.*) wild boar season
Porche, *s.m.* porch; portal
Porch-er, ère, *s.m f.* swineherd, pig-driver
Porcherie, *s.f.* piggery
Porcherons, *s.m.pl.* Porcherons (*part of Paris formerly full of wine-shops*); (*fig.*) wine-shop, public-house
Porcine, *adj.f.* porcine. *Bêtes —s*, swine
Pore, *s.m.* pore
Poreu-x, se, *adj.* porous
†Porillon, Porion, *s.m.* daffodil
Porisme, *s.m.* (*geom.*) porism
Pornograph-ie, -ique. *V.* page 3, § 1
Porosité, *s.f.* porosity, porousness
Porphyre, *s.m.* (*min.*) porphyry; (*pharm.*, &c.) slab (*for grinding*)
Porphyré, e, *adj.* porphyraceous
Porphyrion, *s.m.* (*bird*) porphyrio
Porphyrique, *adj.* porphyritic
Porphyrisation, *s.f.* grinding, pulverization, levigation
Porphyriser, *v.a.* to grind, to pound, to powder, to pulverize, to levigate
Porphyrite, *s.f.* (*min.*) porphyrite
Porphyritique, *adj.* porphyritic
Porque, *s.f.* (*nav.*) rider
Porracé, e, *adj.* porraceous, leek green
Porreau, *s.m.* *V.* **Poireau**
Porrection, *s.f.* (*Cath rel.*) presentation of the instruments
Porrigineu-x, se, *adj.* (*med.*) porriginous
Porrigo, *s.m.* (*med.*) porrigo, ringworm, scald-head
Port, *s.m* port; harbour; haven; seaport town; wharf; quay; postage; carriage; carrying; wearing; bearing; gait, walk; (*in the Pyrenees*) pass; (*of the voice*) compass; (*nav.*) burden. — *marchand*, commercial harbour, shipping-port. — *militaire*, harbour for men-of war, naval station, naval arsenal, royal dockyard. — *d'armes*, carrying arms; carrying weapons; shooting-licence. — *de lettre*, postage. — *à marée*, tidal harbour. — *de toute marée*, — *de toutes marées*, harbour accessible at all tides (*or* at all hours of the tide). — *de mer*, seaport; seaport town. — *payé*, *franc de* —, prepaid, post-paid, free from postage, carriage paid. *Arriver à bon* —, to get safe into port, to arrive safe *or* safely *or* in safety; to end happily *or* prosperously. *Conduire* or *mener à bon* —, to bring to a good end *or* to a happy issue. *Être au — d'armes*, (*mil.*) to carry arms. *Prendre* —, *surgir au* —, to land; (*fig.*) to succeed
Portable, *adj.* wearable; portable, carriable, conveyable; payable at a stipulated place
Portage, *s.m.* portage; carriage, conveyance; porterage; contact; point of contact. *Faire* —, to carry a boat overland at waterfalls
†Portail, *s.m.* portal, front-door, front-gate, front; doorway, gateway
Portant, e, *part. adj.* carrying, bearing, &c. (*V.* **Porter**). *Bien* —, in good health, healthy, well. *Mal* —, in bad health, unhealthy, sickly, unwell, ill. *A bout* —, (at me *or* him *or* her *or* it, &c.) close, point-blank; by a point-blank discharge; (*of duels*) breast to breast
Portant, *s.m.* bearer; handle; (*theat.*) ladder, gas-wing, side-light; (*phys.*) magnet-ring
Portati-f, ve, *adj.* portable, hand
Porte, *s.f.* door; gate; doorway; gateway; threshold, doorstep; pass, defile; Porte; (*for hooks*) eye. — **-croisée,** — **-fenêtre,** *s.f.* casement, French casement opening down to the floor, French window. — *d'entrée*, entrance door, street-door, front-door, chief door. — *de sortie*, door for egress, side-door, back-door; (*fort.*) sally-port. — *à* —, next door to each other. *La Sublime* —, the Sublime Porte. *A la* —, outside, out; turn him *or* her *or* them out! out with ...! *De — en* —, from door to door. *Défendre* or *refuser sa* (or *la*) —, to deny *or* refuse admittance, to deny oneself. *Faire défendre* (or *Faire refuser*) *sa* — *à*, to give orders not to admit, not to be at home for. *Mettre à la* —, to put *or* turn out, to turn out of doors, to put outside the door; to shut the (*or* o.'s) door against
Porte, *adj.* (*anat.*) portal. *Veine* —, portal vein, vena porta
Porte, *s.m.f.* (*in compounds, from* **Porter,** "to carry," "to bear," &c.) thing (*m.*) *or* person (*m.f.*) that carries *or* bears *or* &c., ...-carrier, ...-bearer, ...-stand, ...-holder, ...-case, ...-box, ...-frame, ...-rack, ...-rest, ...-handle, &c., port..., porte-... — **-affiches,** *s.m.* bill-frame, advertisement - frame; advertising board-carrier, poster-bearer, boardman. — **-aigle,** *s.m.* colour-sergeant, ensign, eagle-bearer. — **-aiguilles,** *s. m.* needle - case; (*surg.*) needle-holder. — **-aiguillon,** *s m.* (*zool.*) aculeate. — **-allumettes,** *s.m.* match-box, match-holder. — **-amarre,** *s.m.* life-saving *or* ship-saving apparatus, life mortar, life-saving rocket, life-rocket, line-rocket. — **-assiettes,** *s.m.* plate-rack; plate-stand. — **-baguette,** *s.m.* (*of firelocks*) pipe. — **-baïonnette,** *s.m.* bayonet-belt. — **-balance,** *s.m.* scale-holder. — **-balle,** *s.m.* packman, pedlar. — **-barres,** *s.m.* pole-ring. — **-bossoir,** *s.m.* (*nav.*) supporter of the cat-head. — **-bougie,** *s.m.* (*surg.*) bougie-pipe. — **-bouquet,** *s.m.* bouquet-holder. — **-bouteilles,** *s.m.* bottle-rack, wine-bin. — **-broche,** *s.m.* stock, wimble stock. — **-carabine,** *s.m.* carbine-swivel. — **-carafe,** *s.m.* decanter-stand. — **-cartes,** *s.m.* card-case. — **-caustique,** *s.m.* (*surg.*) caustic bougie. — **-chandelier,** *s.m.* candle-bearer. — **-chandelle,** *s.m.* (*zool.*) Chinese lantern-fly. — **-chape,** *s.m.* cope-bearer. — **-chapeau,** *s. m.* (*bot.*) Christ's - thorn. — **-chapeaux,** *s.m.* hat stand. — **-charbon,** *s.m.* (*of electric light*) carbon-rod. — **-choux,** *s.m.* market-gardener's horse. — **-cierge,** *s.m.* candle-bearer. — **-cigare,** *s.m.* cigar-tube, cigar-holder. — **-cigares,** *s.m.* cigar-case; cigar-holder; cigar-box. — **-clefs,** **-clés,** *s. m.* turnkey; key-ring. — **-col,** **-collet,** *s.m.* pad, stiffener. — **-coquetiers,** *s.m.* egg-frame, egg-stand. — **-coton,** *s.m.* (*jest.*) keeper of the privy, groom of the stool; (*fig.*) pander. — **-coussinets,** *s.m.* hanging carriage. — **-couteau,** *s. m.* knife-rest. — **-crayon,** *s.m.* crayon-holder, portcrayon. — **-crayons,** *s.m.* pencil-case. — **-croix,** *s.m.* cross-bearer, crucifer; (*insect*) *V.* **Criocère.** — **-crosse,** *s.m.* crosier-bearer; (*mil.*) carbine-bucket. — **-cure-dents,** *s.m.* toothpick-case; toothpick-holder. — **-Dieu,** *s.m.* (*Cath. rel.*) viaticum-bearer. — **-drapeau,** *s.m.* colour-sergeant, ensign. — **-enseigne,** *s.m.* ensign-bearer. — **-épée,** *s.m.* sword-bearer; sword-belt. — **-éponge,** *s.m.* (*surg.*) sponge-holder. — **-étendard,** *s.m.* standard-bearer; cornet. — **-étrivière,** *s.m.* stirrup-bar, spring-bar. — **-éventail,** *s.m.* fan-carrier. — **faix,** *s.m.* porter, street-porter. — **-fer,** *s.m.* iron-stand; horseshoe - case. —**feuille,** *s.m.* portfolio, portefeuille; pocket-book; bill-case; commercial bills, bills and acceptances; commercial paper presented for discount (*at the Bank of France*); (*polit.*) post of acting cabinet-minister, department, portfolio, portefeuille; (*pop.*) bed; (*bot.*) catch-weed, goose-grass. *En —feuille*, in manuscript, lying by; (*com.*) in bills; (*of bills*) in hand. — **feuilliste,** *s.m.f.* portfolio *or* pocket-book maker. — **-flambeau,** *s.m.* light-bearer, torch-bearer; link-boy. — **-fleurs,** *s.m.* flower-stand. — **-fort,** *s.m.* (*law*) proxy, attorney. — **-fromage,** *s.m.* cheese-tray. — **-fût,** *s.m.* cask-stand, gauntree, stillion, scantling, stollage. — **-gargousses,** *s.m.* *V.* **Gargoussier.** — **-giberne,** *s.m.* (*mil.*) pouch-belt. — **-guidon,** *s.m.* colour-sergeant. — **-guignon,** *s.m.f.* *V.* — **-malheur.** — **-hache,**

s.m. (*mil.*) axe-case; axe-bearer. — **-haillons,** *s.m.f.* ragamuffin, tatterdemalion, ragged fellow *or* creature. — **-haubans,** *s.m.* (*nav.*) chain-wale. — **-lance,** *s.m.* lance-bucket; lancer. — **-lanterne,** *s.m.* (*zool.*) lantern-fly. — **-lettres,** *s.m.* letter-case; (*admin.*) paper-case, wrapper. — **-liqueurs,** *s.m.* liquor-frame. — **-livres,** *s.m.* book-slide. — **-lof,** *s.m.* (*nav.*) bumkin. — **-lyre,** *s.m.* (*zool.*) *V.* **Ménure;** (*jest.*) poet. — **-maillot,** *s.f.m.* (*theat. slang*) figurante. — **-malheur,** *s.m.f.* bringer of ill-luck; *s.m.* (*thing*) ill omen. —**manteau,** *s.m.* portmanteau, valise; cloak-bag; clothes-peg; row of pegs, coat-stand. — **-masse,** *s.m.* mace-bearer. — **-mèche,** *s.m.* wick-holder; (*surg.*) tent-probe; (*anc. artil.*) linstock. — **-mètre,** *s m* (*in French shops*) yard-holder. — **-mine,** *s.m.* propelling pencil. — **-mire,** *s.m.* (*tech.*) staff-holder. — **-mitre,** *s.m.* mitre-bearer. —**monnaie,** *s.m.* portmonnaie, flat purse, purse. — **-montre,** *s.m.* watch-bag, watch-pocket, watch-hook, watch-stand. — **-montres,** *s.m.* (*of watchmakers*) show-case. — **-mors,** *s.m.* (*of a bridle*) head-piece, cheek-piece. — **-mouchettes,** *s.m.* snuffer-tray, snuffer-stand. — **-mousqueton,** *s.m.* carbine-swivel; swivel. — **-moxa,** *s.m.* (*surg.*) porte-moxa — **-musc,** *s.m.* (*zool.*) musk-deer. — **-musique,** *s.m.* canterbury. — **-nitrate,** *s.m.* (*surg.*) caustic-holder. — **-objet,** *s.m.* (*opt.*) object-holder, holder. — **-or,** *V.* **Portor.** — **-page,** *s.m.* (*print.*) page-paper. — **-parapluies,** *s.m.* umbrella-stand. — **-peigne,** *s.m.* comb-case, comb-bag. — **-pierre,** — **-pierre-infernale,** *s.m.* (*surg.*) caustic-case, portcaustic; caustic-holder. — **-pince,** *s.m.* (*zool.*) chelifer, book-scorpion. — **-pipe,** *s.m.* pipe-case. — **-plume,** *s.m.* pen-holder. — **-plumes,** *s.m.* pen-case; (— *-plumes étagère*) pen rack. — **-queue,** *s.m.* train-bearer — **-queues,** *s.m.* (*billiards*) cue-rack. — **-rame,** *s.m.* oar-ring. — **-respect,** *s.m.* formidable weapon, preserver, protector; badge of dignity; imposing appearance *or* exterior, grave appearance; person of imposing appearance (*or* of an imposing exterior), grave (*or* venerable) person. — **-rideau,** *s.m.* curtain-pole. — **-rôties,** *s.m.* toast-rack; toast-stand. — **-scie,** *s. m.* (*tech.*) saw-pad; (*zool.*) saw-fly. — **-serviettes,** *s.m.* towel-horse. — **-tapisserie,** *s.m.* frame for tapestry. — **-tarière,** *s.m* (*zool.*) borer. — **-tolets,** *s m.* (*nav.*) row-lock. — **-traits,** *s.m.* trace-bearer. — **-vent,** *s.m.* (*mus., of an organ*) wind-chest, (*of a bag-pipe*) tube. — **-verge,** *s.m.* verger, beadle. — **-vergue,** *s.m.* (*nav.*) rail of the head. — **-verre,** *s.m.* (*of lamps*) chimney-holder. — **-vis,** *s.m.* side-plate (*of a firelock*). — **-voix,** *s.m.* speaking-trumpet; speaking-pipe; (*fig.*) mouthpiece; interpreter

Porté, e, *part. adj.* carried, &c. (*V.* **Porter**); inclined; disposed; ready; apt; animated; (*of shadows*) projecting. *Être tout* —, to be on the spot, to be there *or* here; to have it quite handy

Porté, *s.m.* wear, look, appearance, style, fashion

Portée, *s.f.* brood, litter; reach; distance; length; compass; capacity; comprehension; ability; means; power; force; extent; bearing; application; import, scope; importance; pitch; shot; range; (*mus.*) staff, stave; (*hunt.*) entry. *A* or *à la — de*, within reach of; within the range of; within (...-)shot; within ...; near enough to; to the level of; adapted to; in a condition *or* position to, able to. *A ma* or *sa* —, within my *or* his reach. *A une — de fusil*, within gun-shot. *A — de trait*, within bow shot

Portement, *s.m.* carrying, bearing

Porter, *s.m. V* **Porté,** *s.m.*; (*English*) porter (*beer*)

Porter, *v.a.n.* to carry; to bear; to wear, to have on; to support; to sustain; to convey, to take; to bring; to yield, to produce; to spread; to drive; to induce, to lead; to prompt, to incite; to move; to show, to manifest; to entertain; to measure, to be; to have; to hold; to cause; to do; to give; to thrust; to pass; to cast, to turn; to direct; to lay, to put; to raise; to project; to enter, to inscribe, to register; to state; to declare; to express; to mention; to contain; to provide, to stipulate; to prescribe; to order; to bid; to propose, to drink; to vote for; to lodge, to prefer (*a complaint, a charge*); to estimate; to admit of; to shoulder; to present; to rest; to lie; to lean; to fall; to reach; to hit, to strike, to fetch; to take effect, to tell; to act (upon); to affect; (*of drinks, &c.*) to get *or* fly (*into o.'s head*); to aim; to tend; to bear young; (*rid., of the horse*) to carry his head; (*nav.*) to stand, to bear off. — *bonheur* or *malheur*, to bring good *or* ill-luck. — (*le nez*) *au vent*, to toss its nose in the wind, to boar; (*pers.*) to carry o.'s head high; to be supercilious. *En* —, (*fam., jest.*) to wear horns, to be (*or* have been) deceived by o.'s wife. *En faire — à*, (*fam., jest.*) to deceive, to be unfaithful to (*o.'s husband*). *Faire* —, to make (...) carry, &c.; to bring to bear

Se —, *v.r.* to carry *or* &c. oneself *or* each other; to be carried *or* &c.; to bear; to move; to go; to advance; to proceed; to resort; to flock; to turn; to be directed; to rush; to fall; to abandon oneself; to be guilty (of), to commit; to stand forward; to stand, to be; to become; to appear as; to be inclined *or* disposed; to behave, to conduct oneself; to be in a state of health, to do, to be; (*of clothing*) to be worn. *Se — bien* or *mal*, to be well *or* unwell, to be in good *or* bad health. *Comment vous portez-vous?* how do you do? how are you? *Portez-vous bien*, keep in good health, farewell, take care of yourself

Fortereau, *s.m.* dam, floodgate

Porteu-r, se, *s.m.f.* carrier, porter, heaver; bearer; basket-woman; (*of chairs*) chairman; (*bank., fin.*) bearer; holder; (*of vehicles*) near horse. — *de chaise*, chairman

Portier, *s.m. V.* **Concierge.** — *de comédie*, (*obsolete*) money-taker; exactor

Portière, *s.f.* (*pers.*) *V.* **Concierge;** (*of carriages*) door; doorway; window; (*furniture*) door-hangings, curtain; — *adj.f.* breeding, brood

Portion, *s.f.* portion; part; share; allowance; pittance

Portique, *s.m.* (*arch.*) portico; piazza; (*anc. philos.*) Porch

Porto, *s.m.* port (wine)

Portor, *s.m.* portor (marble)

Fortraire, *v.a.* (*old*) to portray, to depict, to paint, to draw, to describe, to represent

Portrait, e, (*old*) *part. of* **Portraire**

Fortrait, *s. m.* portrait, likeness; picture, image; description; (*pop.*) face, phiz

Portraitiste, *s.m.f.* portrait-painter

Fortraiture, *s.f.* portraiture, portrait; figure, figures

Portugais, e, *adj. s.* Portuguese; Portuguese fashion

Portulan, *s.m.* book of seaports

Posage, *s.m.* laying, laying on *or* down; (*of bells*) hanging

Pose, *s.f.* posture; attitude; laying, laying on *or* down, setting; (*of bells*) hanging; (*for o.'s likeness*) sitting, posing, pose; (*at dominoes*) pose, deal; (*mil.*) stationing, posting (*sentries, &c.*), relief; (*pop.*) show, sham, make-believe; — *s.m.* (*in compounds*) thing which serves to lay *or* &c., layer. — **-tuyaux,** *s.m.* pipe-layer, apparatus *or* instrument for laying pipes

Posé, e, *part. adj.* placed, &c. (*V.* **Poser**); bearing, resting, leaning, lying; sitting; standing; sedate, staid; grave; sober; quiet; steady; occupying a position, of standing. *Au* —, sitting; not on the wing. *Bien* —, well placed *or* &c.; in a good position, of good standing. *Cela* —, that *or* this being granted

Posée, *s.f.* (*rid.*) appui

Posément, *adv.* sedately, steadily, gravely, quietly, gently, slowly
Poser, *v.a.n.* to place, to put, to lay, to set; to lay *or* put down; to lay on; to cast; to hang (*bells*); to pose (*at dominoes*); to station, to post (*sentries,* &c.); to post up; to give a status *or* standing to; to suppose, to admit, to grant; to state; to ask; to bear, to rest, to lean; to lie; to stand; to sit *or* pose (*for o.'s likeness*); to dance attendance, to wait in vain; to assume attitudes *or* consequential airs, to attitudinize; to sit *or* stand to be looked at; to have pretensions (to), to pretend (to); (*mus.*) to pitch. *Faire —,* (*fam.*) to make (*one*) wait in vain, to hoax, to disappoint, to balk, to bamboozle
Se —, *v.r.* to place *or* &c. oneself (*or* each other); to perch, to pitch, to settle, to alight; to sit; to tread; to settle oneself; to get *or* take a position; to take up o.'s abode; to take o.'s rank; to stand; to stand forward; to show oneself, to appear; to set up (for); to be [placed *or* put *or* laid, &c.
Poser, *s.m.* (*rid.*) appui
Poseu-r, se, *s.m.f.* layer; setter; floor-layer; (*rail.*) plate-layer; (*paint.,* &c.) sitter, poser; (*fig.*) one who assumes attitudes *or* consequential airs, attitudinarian. *— de sonnettes,* bellhanger
Positi-f, ve, *adj.* positive; absolute; real; certain; sure; matter-of-fact; practical. *C'est —!* that's a fact!
Positif, *s.m.* positive, reality, certainty, fact; (*gram.*) positive; (*mus.*) choir-organ
Position, *s.f.* position; situation; place; stand; posture; case; state; status; standing; station; circumstances
Positivement, *adv.* positively; absolutely; certainly; precisely; exactly; quite, altogether; point-blank
Positiveté, Positivité, *s.f.* positiveness
Positiv-isme, -iste. *V.* page 3, § 1
Posnanien, ne, *adj. s.* Posnanian
Posolog-ie, -ique. *V.* page 3, § 1
Pospolite, *s.f.* (*hist. of Poland*) pospolite
Possédé, e, *s.m.f.* person possessed, demoniac
Posséder, *v.a.* to possess; to be possessed of; to have; to enjoy; to know, to be master of *or* conversant with, to understand; to contain
Se —, *v.r.* to be master of oneself; to keep o.'s temper; to be able to contain oneself; to be possessed *or* &c.
Possesseur, *s.m.* possessor; owner; occupier
Possessi-f, ve, *adj.*, **Possessif,** *s.m.* (*gram.*) possessive
Possession, *s.f.* possession; occupation; right, privilege; habit. *Être en — de,* to be in possession of; to be able to; to have the right to *or* the privilege of; to be in the habit of
Possessionnel, le, *adj.* possessional
Possessoire, *adj.* (*law*) possessory; — *s.m.* possessory suit *or* action; possession
Possessoirement, *adv.* (*law*) possessorily
Posset, *s.m.* posset (*drink*)
Possibilité, *s.f.* possibility
Possible, *adj.* possible; — *s.m.* possible, possibility; possibilities, possible things; utmost, best. *Au —,* extremely, in the extreme, exceedingly, amazingly. *C'est —,* that may be, very likely. *Pas —!* you don't say so! no! *Tout son —,* all one can *or* could
Possiblement, *adv.* possibly
Postal, e, *adj.* postal, post, post-office
Postalement, *adv.* postally [munion
Postcommunion, *s.f.* (*Cath. rel.*) postcom-
Postdate, *s.f.* postdate
Postdater, *v.a.* to postdate
Postdiluvien, ne, *adj.* postdiluvian
Poste, *s.f.* post; stage; post-house; post-office; mail; postman; post-boy; post-horses; post-haste; hail-shot; (*arch.*) Vitruvian scroll. *De —, de la —, des —s,* (*adject.*) post. *— aux chevaux,* post-house. *— aux lettres,* post. *— aux paquets,* parcels delivery. *Bureau de —,* post, post-office. *Directeur des —s,* post-master. *Grande —,* General Post-Office. *Petite —,* receiving-house *or* office. *Relais de —,* post-stage. *— pour —,* by return of post. *Courir la —,* to ride *or* travel post; to go post-haste
Poste, *s.m.* post; station; station-house; guard-house; place, employment, office; berth. *— des malades,* (*nav.*) sick-berth, cockpit. *Être à — fixe,* to reside on the spot, to reside; (*jest.*) to be a fixture
Poster, *v.a.* to post, to place, to station
Postérieur, e, *adj.* posterior, subsequent, later; future; after; hinder, hind, back; — *s.m.* posteriors [quently, afterwards, after, since
Postérieurement, *adv.* posteriorly, subse-
Postériori (A), *adv.* a posteriori, from the effect to the cause, from what follows
Postériorité, *s.f.* posteriority
Postérité, *s.f.* posterity; issue
Postface, *s.f.* final address, postface
Postfixe, *s.m.* (*gram.*) postfix
Posthite, *s.f.* (*med.*) posthitis [humous child
Posthume, *adj.* posthumous; — *s.m.f.* post-
Postiche, *adj.* false, artificial, imitation, mock, sham, fictitious; superadded; misplaced, out of place; (*mil.*) provisional, acting. *Caporal —,* acting corporal, lance-corporal
†**Postille,** *s.f.* postil [*paper kite*) messenger
†**Postillon,** *s.m.* postilion; post-boy; (*of a*
Postliminaire, *adj.* postliminiar
Postliminie, *s.f.* postliminy
Post-scriptum, *s.m.* postscript
Postulance, *s.f.* application, canvass
Postulant, e, *adj. s.* candidate, applicant; [postulant
Postulat, *s.m.* postulate
Postulation, *s.f.* (*law*) conducting a suit; (*can.*
Postulatum, *s.m.* postulatum [*law*) postulation
Postuler, *v.a.* to apply for, to solicit, to canvass for, to be a candidate for; — *v.n.* to sue, to conduct a suit, to plead
Posture, *s.f.* posture; attitude; position, situation, condition; footing
Pot, *s.m.* pot; jug; tankard; can; jar; bucket; helmet; (*in childish games*) hole (*in the ground*); (*stat.*) pot (*paper*); foolscap. *— pourri,* hotchpotch; mishmash; medley; olio; jumble. *— à feu,* cresset; (*mil., nav.*) fire-pot; stink-pot. *— -au-feu,* soup with boiled beef; meat to boil; pot; (*fig.*) common necessaries of life, bread and cheese, bread and butter; (*pop.*) bum; (*adject.*) vulgar, homely. *— à l'eau,* water-jug. *— au lait,* milk-can. *— aux roses,* mystery, secret. *— -de-vin,* bonus, premium; gratuity, douceur, tip. *En —,* potted. *Être à — et à feu* (or *à — et à rôt*), (*fam.*) to be intimate *or* thick. *Mettre en —,* to pot. *Payer les —s cassés,* to pay the costs, to pay for the damage. *Tourner autour du —,* to beat about the bush
Potabilité, *s.f.* potableness
Potable, *adj.* potable, drinkable
Potage, *s.m.* soup, pottage, porridge; basin *or* plate of soup. *Pour tout —,* in all, alone, and nothing else
Potager, *s.m.* kitchen-garden, vegetable-garden; cooking-stove; soup-basin; soup-can
Potag-er, ère, *adj.* culinary, cooking, kitchen, vegetable. *Graine —ère,* vegetable seed. *Herbe* or *plante* or *racine —ère,* pot-herb, vegetable. *Jardin —,* kitchen-garden, vegetable-garden
Potamo-graphie, -graphique, -logie, &c.
Potamot, *s.m.* (*bot.*) pondweed [*V.* page 3, § 1
Potasse, *s.f.* (*chem.*) potash
Potassium, *s.m.* (*chem.*) potassium
Pote, *adj.f.* (*of the hand*) big *or* swollen
Poteau, *s.m.* post; stake; pillar; (*fam.*) thick leg *or* stump. *— -guide, — indicateur,* guide-post, sign-post, finger-post. *— d'arrivée,* ending-post, winning-post. *— d'arrosement,* water-post, stand-post. *— d'enseigne,* sign-post
Potée, *s.f.* pot, potful; lot; putty; moulding-clay, luting-loam. *— d'émeri,* emery-dust. *— d'étain,* putty of tin, putty-powder

Potelé, e, *adj.* plump; — *s.m.* plumpness
Potelet, *s.m.* small post, strut, prop
Potence, *s.f.* gibbet, gallows, drop; hanging; crutch; bracket; potence; (*meas.*) standard. *En* —, potence-wise, shaped like a T; (*mil.*) with a flank forming an angle with the line
Potencé, e, *adj.* (*her.*) potent. *Croix* —*e*, [cross potent
Potentat, *s.m.* potentate
Potentialité, *s.f.* potentiality
Potentiel, le, *adj.*, **Potentiel,** *s.m.* potential
Potentiellement, *adv.* potentially
†**Potentille,** *s.f.* (*bot.*) potentilla, cinquefoil
Poterie, *s.f.* pottery; earthenware; waste-pipe. — *d'étain*, pewter ware *or* wares *or* articles. — [*de grès*, stoneware
Poterne, *s.f.* postern
Potestati-f, ve, *adj.* potestative
Potet, *s.m.* (*pop.*) fogy, old fogy
Potiche, *s.m.* Chinese vase; imitation china
Potier, *s.m.* potter. — *d'étain*, pewterer
Potin, *s.m.* pot-metal; (*pop.*) gossip, tittle-tattle
Potine, *s.f.* small sardine
Potiner, *v.n.* (*pop.*) to gossip, to tattle
Potinière, *s.f.* sardine-net
Potion, *s.f.* potion, draught [stool
Potiron, *s.m.* pumpkin; large mushroom, toad-
Potoroo, Potorou, *s.m.* (*zool.*) potoroo, kangaroo rat
Potos, Potot, *s.m.* (*zool.*) potto, kinkajou
Potron-jaquet, Potron-minet. *V.* **Pa-**
Poturon, *pop. for* **Potiron** [**tron-jaquet,** &c.
Pou, *s.m.* louse
Pouacre, *adj. s.* nasty, filthy; beast
Pouah, *int.* ugh! buh! fie! nasty thing!
Pouce, *s.m.* thumb; great toe; inch. *Coup de* —, *V.* **Coup.** *Et le* —*!* and something more at the end! *Jouer du* —, to fork out; to count money. *Manger sur le* —, *manger un morceau sur le* —, to take a snack. *Mettre* or *coucher les* —*s*, to submit, to come to terms, to knuckle down *or* under. *Serrer les* —*s à*, to put the thumb-screw on. — **-pieds,** *s.m.* (*zool.*) barnacle (*mollusc*) [*tale*) Tom Thumb
Poucet, *s.m.* small thumb. *Le petit* —, (*in the*
Poucette, *s.f.* thumb-piece; —**s,** *pl.* manacles, handcuffs [thumb-piece, trigger, lift
Poucier, *s.m.* thumb-stall; (*of a thumb-latch*)
Pouding, *s.m. V.* **Pudding** [stone
Poudingue, *s.m.* (*min.*) conglomerate, pudding-
Poudre, *s.f.* powder; dust; gunpowder; sand, pounce; —**s,** *pl.* powders; gunpowder; powder-magazine. — *-coton*, gun-cotton. — *à canon*, gunpowder. — *de chasse*, — *à tirer*, shooting-powder. — *de succession*, (*obsolete, jest.*) poison. *En* —, in *or* to powder *or* &c.; powdered; ground. *Jeter de la* — *aux yeux*, to throw dust into (people's) eyes, to dazzle, to impose upon. *Il n'a pas inventé la* —, he will never set the Thames on fire, he is no conjurer
Poudrer, *v.a.* to powder; to pounce; to sprinkle; **Se** —, *v.r.* to powder o.'s hair [to dredge
Poudrerie, *s.f.* gunpowder-factory, powder-mill
Poudrette, *s.f.* desiccated *or* dried night-soil, poudrette. *Faire la* —, (*of fowls*) to roll in the dust
Poudreu-x, se, *adj.* dusty; powdery. *Pied* —, vagabond, vagrant, tramp [powder-maker
Poudrier, *s.m.* sand-box; pounce-box; gun-
Poudrière, *s.f.* powder-mill; powder-magazine; powder-flask *or* horn; sand-box; pounce-box
Poudrin, *s.m. V.* **Embrun**
Poudroyer, *v.a.* to fill *or* cover with dust; — *v.n.* to rise into dust; to be dusty; to make *or* raise a dust; to show the dust; to make the dust sparkle [reduced to dust, to be ground **Se** —, *v.r.* to be filled *or* &c. with dust; to be
Pouf, *adv.* plump, bang; — *adj.* crumbling; — *s.m.* puff; puffery; hoax; dash, fuss; ottoman-seat, stool; centre ottoman; (*pop.*) default, non-payment, failure, exit without paying; (*obsolete*) chignon. *A* —, (*pop.*) on credit, on tick
Pouff, *s.m.* ottoman-seat, stool; centre ottoman
Pouffer, *v.n.* to puff; (— *de rire*) to burst out
Poufferie, *s.f.* puffery [(laughing)
Pouffiasse, Poufiasse, *s.f.* bloated woman; wench, drab, trollop, trull
Pouffiste, *s.m.f.* puffer; — *adj.* puffing [revenues
†**Pouille,** *s.m.* register of livings with their
†**Pouiller,** *v.a.* to abuse, to rail at, to revile; to louse [lid hovel; extreme poverty *or* misery
†**Pouillerie,** *s.f.* lousiness, squalidness; squa-
†**Pouilles,** *s.f.pl.* abusive language, abuse. *Chanter* — *à*, to use abusive language to, to abuse, to rail at, to revile
†**Pouilleu-x, se,** *adj.* lousy; squalid, filthy; beggarly; miserable, wretched; mean; low; stingy; (*of land*) poor, barren; — *s.m.f.* lousy *or* &c. fellow *or* creature
†**Pouillot,** *s.m.* (*bird*) willow warbler
†**Pouilly,** *s.m.* pouilly (wine)
†**Poulaille,** *s.f.* (*obsolete*) poultry
†**Poulailler,** *s.m.* hen-house, hen-roost, fowl-house, poultry-house; poultry-cart; egg-cart; hovel; (*theat.*) upper gallery; (*pers.*) poultry salesman, poulterer [slide; (*pop.*) bubo
Poulain, *s.m.* foal, colt-foal, colt; truck, sledge,
Poulaine, *s.f.* (*nav.*) head; (*obsolete*) point. *Souliers à la* —, (*obsolete*) pointed *or* peaked
Poularde, *s.f.* fat pullet, pullet [shoes
Poule, *s.f.* hen; fowl; (*at play*) pool; (*figure in dancing*) poule; (*fam.*) love, dear, darling, duck; — *adj.* (*of steel*) blistered, blister. — *d'eau*, water-hen, moor-hen. — *d'Inde*, turkey-hen, turkey. — *laitée*, — *mouillée*, (*pers.*) milk-sop. *Faire le cul de* —, (*fam., pop.*) to pout
Pouler, *v.n.* to pool
Poulet, *s.m.* chicken; chick, darling; love-letter; fancy note-paper. — *de grain*, corn-fed chicken. — *d'Inde*, young turkey, turkey-poult; (*pop.*) horse, nag, prad; fool, gaby, spoony, lout, clumsy fellow
Poulette, *s.f.* pullet; chick, darling; girl, lass, wench. *A la* —, with white sauce
Pouleur, *s.m.* pooler
Poulevrin, *s.m. V.* **Pulvérin**
Pouliche, *s.f.* foal, filly-foal, filly
Poulie, *s.f.* pulley; (*nav.*) block
Poulier, *v.a.* to lift up with a pulley; — *s.m.*
Poulière, *s.f.* hen-hole [heap of shingle
Poulierie, *s.f.* block-shed *or* manufactory *or* manufacture *or* making; block-machine
Poulieur, *s.m.* pulley-maker; block-maker
Poulin, *s.m. V.* **Poulain**
Pouline, *s.f. V.* **Pouliche**
Poulinement, *s.m.* (*of mares*) foaling
Pouliner, *v.n.* (*of mares*) to foal [breeder
Poulinière, *s.f., adj.f. Jument* —, brood-mare,
Pouliot, *s.m.* (*bot.*) penny-royal [baby
Poulot, te, *s.m.f.* chick, darling, ducky, child,
Poulpe, *s.m.* (*zool.*) poulpe, poulp, devil-fish,
Pouls, *s.m.* pulse [blood-sucker
Poult de soie, *s.m.* poult-de-soie (*stout silk*)
Poumon, *s.m.* lung; lungs
Poumonique, *adj. s.m.f.* (*med.*) pulmonic
Poupard, e, *s.m.f. adj.* babe, baby; baby-doll
Poupart, *s.m.* large edible crab
Poupe, *s.f.* (*nav.*) stern, poop. *Avoir le vent en* —, to sail before the wind; (*fig.*) to be in good luck
Poupée, *s.f.* doll; puppet; dummy; plaster image; milliner's block; finger-stall; bundle of rags; (*spin.*) bundle, bunch. *Enter en* —, to graft
Poupin, e, *adj. s.* spruce, smart, dashy, foppish; fop, beau, belle [darling
Poupon, ne, *s.m.f.* baby, chubby-faced child;
†**Poupouille,** *s.f. V.* **Boubouille**
Poupoule, *s.f.* duck, ducky, darling, love
Pour, *prep.* for; on account of, on ...'s account; from; for the sake of, for ...'s sake; in favour of, in ...'s favour; in the interest of, in ...'s interest; on the side of, on ...'s side; towards; to; in order to; so as to; enough to; about; as; as to, as for; although, though; worth; to recommend; in the opinion of, in ...'s opinion; to last; capable of; per; — *adv.* for it, for them, in favour of it *or* them; — *s.m.*

for, pro. — *ce qui est de*, as regards, as for. — *que*, in order that, that; so that; to allow; to enable; of opinion that, in favour of; however. — *et contre*, for and against, pro and con. *Comme* —, as if, as much as

Pourboire, *s.m.* drink-money, gratuity, fee, tip, a trifle to drink o.'s health, something besides the fare

Pourceau, *s.m.* hog, pig, swine

Pourcelet, *s.m.* *V* **Porcelet**

Pour-cent, *s.m.* percentage

Pourchasse, *s.f.* pursuit; hunt; search

Pourchasser, *v.a.* to pursue; to hunt, to badger; to seek eagerly

Pour-compte, *s.m.* (*among tailors*) misfit

Pourfendeur, *s.m.* splitter; killer; braggart, swaggerer, bully, hector

Pourfendre, *v.a.* to split, to cleave, to cut in two; to kill

Pourlécher, *v.a.* to lick all round; to lick over; (*fig.*) to polish, to labour

Se —, *v.r.* to lick o.'s chops

Pourparler, *s.m.* conference, parley; treaty

Pourpier, *s.m.* (*bot.*) purslain, purslane

Pourpoint, *s.m.* (*obsolete garment*) doublet. *A brûle-* —, *V.* **Brûle-pourpoint (A)**

Pourpre, *s.f.* (*colouring matter, textile fabric, dignity*) purple; — *s.m.* (*colour, shell-fish*) purple; (*her.*) purpure; (*med.*) purpura, (the) purples; — *adj.* purple. — (*s.f.*) *de Tyr*, Tyrian purple. — (*s.m.*) *de Cassius*, (*chem.*) purple of Cassius

Pourpré, e, *adj.* purple

Pourprier, *s.m.* purple (*shell-fish*), purpura

Pourprin, e, *adj.* purplish, purple; — *s.m.* purple

Pourpris, *s.m.* (*old*) purprise, enclosure; abode, home

Pourquoi, *conj. adv.* why, wherefore, for what reason, for what, what . . . for; — *s.m.* reason why, why, wherefore, cause, reason; question. — *cela?* why so? why not? — *donc?* why then? why so? — *non?* — *pas?* why not? *C'est* —, therefore, so, so that, wherefore, for this (*or* that) reason, this (*or* that) is why. *Demandez-moi* —, I should like to know why, how is this now?

Pourri, e, *part.* rotted; — *adj.* rotten; (*of the weather*) damp, muggy; — *s.m.* rotten part; rottenness. — *de cuisson*, (*cook.*) done to rags

Pourrir, *v.a.n.*, **Se** —, *v.r.* to rot, to make *or* get rotten; (*fig.*) to rot; to perish; to remain long; to languish; (*of a cold or abscess*) to ripen

Pourrissage, *s.m.* (*tech.*) rotting

Pourrissoir, *s.m.* (*tech.*) rotting-vat

Pourriture, *s.f.* rot, rottenness; (*agr.*) bunt, smut-ball. — *d'hôpital*, hospital gangrene

Poursuite, *s.f.* pursuit; chase; run; prosecution; persecution; suit, action, proceedings

Poursuivable, *adj.* suable, actionable

Poursuivant, e, *s.m.f.* suitor; applicant, candidate; wooer; pursuer; prosecutor; plaintiff; (— *d'armes*) pursuivant(-at-arms); — *part. adj.* pursuing, &c. (*V.* **Poursuivre**); suing; prosecuting

Poursuivre, *v.a.n.* to pursue; to follow; to carry on *or* out; to go on with, to proceed with *or* in; to follow on *or* up *or* with; to go on; to go after; to seek for; to have *or* keep in view; to solicit; to persecute; to beset, to haunt; to annoy; to prosecute; to proceed against, to sue; to continue

Se —, *v.r.* to be pursued, to be followed up, to be carried *or* pushed on, to be proceeded with *or* continued *or* &c., to go on

Pourtant, *adv.* yet, though, however, still, nevertheless, for all that, for that

Pourtour, *s.m.* circumference; periphery; circuit; circle; compass; enclosure; surroundings; area; (*theat.*) pit-tier

Pourvoi, *s.m.* appeal, application, petition

Pourvoir, *v.a.n.* to provide; to provide for, to make a provision for, to establish, to settle; to supply; to furnish; to endow; to appoint; to see, to look, to attend; to afford

Se —, *v.r.* to provide oneself; to settle; to apply; to appeal; to sue; to petition. *Renvoyer les parties à se* —, (*law*) to declare oneself incompetent

Pourvoirie, *s.f.* store-house; purveyors

Pourvoyant, e, *adj.* providing, provident

Pourvoyeu-r, se, *s.m.f.* purveyor, provider, caterer, cateress; go-between; (*nav.*) powder-monkey

Pourvu, e, *part. adj.* provided, supplied, &c. (*V.* **Pourvoir**). — **que,** *conj.* provided that, provided; it is to be hoped (that), let us hope (that), I hope (that)

Poussa, Poussah, *s.m.* rocking figure; fat fellow

Poussade, *s.f.* pushing; push

Pousse, *s.f.* shoots; shoot, sprout; shooting, growth; (*of the teeth*) cutting; (*vet.*) broken wind, asthma; (*in mines*, &c.) choke-damp, damp, foul air, malaria, exhalation; (*disease of wine*) bitterness; (*com.*) dust; (*obsolete*) bum-bailiffs, police; — *s.m.f.* (*in compounds, from* **Pousser,** "to push," &c.) person (*m.f.*) *or* thing (*m.*) that pushes *or* &c., pusher. — **-café,** *s.m.* (*fam.*) glass of brandy (taken after coffee). — **-cailloux,** *s.m.* (*jest.*) foot-soldier. — **-cul,** *s.m.* (*pop.*) bumbailiff. — **-pied,** *s.m.* small flat-bottomed boat *or* punt. — **-pieds,** *s.m.* (*bad spelling*) *V.* **Pouce-pieds**

Poussé, e, *part. adj.* pushed, &c. (*V.* **Pousser**); crammed; (*of wine*) bitter; (*paint.*) chilled

Poussée, *s.f.* pushing; push; shoving; shove; move; pressure; thrusting; thrust; jutting out; giving out; skin eruption; (*pop.*) chase; funk

Pousser, *v.a.n.* to push; to push on; to push up; to shove; to thrust; to get on; to drive, to drive on; to drift; to impel; to force; to throw; to push open, to open; to push to, to shut; to carry; to carry on; to extend; to induce; to urge, to urge on, to incite; to excite; to provoke; to press, to press on; to attack; to bring *or* push forward; to help on; to bid up; to strike, to hit; to utter; to set up; to fetch, to heave; to make; to give; to cut (*o.'s teeth*); to shoot forth; to shoot; to spring up; to grow up *or* out; to grow; to incline, to tend; to go; to go on; to advance; (*arch.*) to jut out, to bulge; (*of horses*) to pant, to be pursy *or* broken-winded; (*of wine*) to get bitter

Se —, *v.r.* to push oneself forward; to make o.'s way up; to push *or* &c. oneself *or* each other; to cram *or* stuff oneself; (*of things*) to be pushed *or* &c.

Poussette, *s.f.* (*game*) pushpin

Pousseu-r, se, *s.m.f.* pusher; utterer

Poussier, *s.m.* (— *de charbon*) coal-dust; (— *de mottes*) turf-dust; (— *de poudre à canon*) gun-powder-dust; (*tech.*) dust; (*pop.*) dust (*money*). — *de Noël*, snow, sleet

Poussière, *s.f.* dust; powder; (*bot.*) pollen; (*of fruit*) bloom; (*of water*) spray. *Faire de la* —, to make *or* raise *or* kick up a dust; (*imp.*) to be dusty (*on the roads*)

Poussiéreu-x, se, *adj.* dusty

Poussi-f, ve, *adj.* pursy, broken-winded, short-winded, wheezy; — *s.m.f.* ditto fellow *or* creature

Poussin, *s.m.* chickling, squab-chick, chick

Poussinière, *s.f.* chick-room; chicken-coop; (*pop. for* **Pléiades,** *astr.*)

Poussoir, *s.m.* knob, driver, pusher

Poussolane, *s.f.* *V.* **Pouzzolane**

Poutrage, *s.m.* beam-work, beams

Poutre, *s.f.* beam, girder

Poutrelle, *s.f.* small beam; stop-plank

Pouture, *s.f.* stall-food; stall-feeding

Pouvoir, *v.a.n.* to be able, can; to be able to do, can do; to have power; to be allowed; to be possible; may. — *tout sur*, to have great power (*or* influence) over. *N'en* — *plus*, to be exhausted *or* worn out *or* undone, to be quite knocked up; to be overwhelmed. *Se* —, can be; can be done; to be possible, may be; may be done. *Cela se peut, cela peut être, cela peut se faire,* that can be; that can be done; that is possible, that may be, it may be so, very likely; that may be done. *Cela se peut bien,* that may possibly be, it may be so, it is likely enough; it may do so. *Cela ne se peut pas, cela ne peut pas être,* that (*or* it) cannot be, that (*or* it) is impossible. *Cela ne peut pas ne pas être,* that cannot but be, that must necessarily be. *Il se peut que,* it may be that. *S'il se peut* (or *pouvait*), if possible. *Il se peut faire, il peut se faire,* it may happen. *Se peut-il, se peut il faire* (*que*), can it be, is it possible (that). *Je ne puis, je ne peux pas,* I cannot. *Je n'y puis rien,* I cannot help it. *Vous avez pu voir,* you have been able to see; you may have seen. *Je ne vois pas en quoi cela a pu vous choquer,* I don't see how that can have shocked you. *Vous n'avez pas pu voir,* you cannot have seen. *Vous avez pu ne pas voir,* you may not have seen. *Vous aurez pu voir,* you may have seen. *Vous pouviez le faire,* you could (*were able to*) do it; you might (*were allowed to*) do it; you might have done it. *Vous pouviez avoir dix ans,* you might be (*were perhaps*) ten years old. *Vous pouviez ne pas me dire,* you need not have told me. *Vous aviez pu le faire,* you could *or* might have done it. *Vous pourriez le faire,* you could (*would be able to*) do it; you might (*would be allowed to, would possibly*) do it. *Vous auriez pu le faire,* you could *or* might have done it. *Vous pourriez bien,* you could easily; you might perhaps *or* possibly; you would very likely. *Cela se pourrait bien, cela pourrait bien être,* that might possibly be, it might be so, that is not at all unlikely; it might do so. *Il se pourrait* (*bien*) *que,* it might be that, it might happen that. *Il pourrait se faire que; Autant que faire se peut; V.* **Faire (Se).** *Pouvez-vous bien,* how can you. *Puissiez-vous!* may you! *On ne peut* (*pas*) *plus,* most, as . . . as possible, exceedingly; as much as possible; the greatest possible. *On ne peut* (*pas*) *mieux,* as well as possible

Pouvoir, *s.m.* power; authority; might; force; sway; command; influence, interest; government, executive; power of attorney; warrant

Pouzzolane, Pozzolane, *s.f.* (*min.*) pozzuolana, pozzolana

Pradelle, *s.f.* (*local*) meadow, grass-field

Pradier, *s.m.* (*local*) meadow-labourer

Pragmat-ique, -iquement. *V.* page 3, § 1

Prairial, *s.m.* Prairial (*ninth month of the calendar of the first French Republic, from May* 20 *to June* 18)

Prairial, e, *adj.* of meadows, meadow, meadowy

Prairie, *s.f.* meadow, grass-land, grass-field; [prairie

Praline, *s.f.* burnt almond

Praliné, e, *adj.* baked in sugar; crystallized; burnt; with burnt almonds. *Chocolat* —, chocolate almonds [to crystallize, to burn

Praliner, *v.a.* (*conf.*) to bake *or* crust in sugar,

Prame, *s.f.* (*nav.*) praam *or* pram (*boat*)

Prao, *s.m.* (*nav.*) proa (*boat*)

Prase, *s.f.* (*min.*) prase

Praticabilité, *s.f.* practicability

Praticable, *adj.* practicable; feasible; manageable; bearable; passable; accessible; real; — *s.m.* (*theat.*) accessible *or* real object (*mountain, rock, &c., not merely painted, and accessible to the actors*), real *or* passable way *or* road

Praticien, *s.m.* practitioner; (*sculptor's assistant*) figure-carver, bust-carver, carver

Praticien, ne, *adj.* practising; practical

Praticole, *adj.* (*zool.*) living in meadows

Praticulteur, *s.m.* praticulturist

Praticulture, *s.f.* praticulture

Pratique, *s.f.* practice; dealing; way; habit; custom; customer; exercise; experience; practice of the law; Punch's call, call, Punch and Judy's speaker; intrigue, underhand dealing, secret practice; (*nav.*) pratique; (*pop.*) scamp, blackguard; — *s.m.* experienced mariner or pilot; — *adj.* practical; experienced. *Terme de* —, law-term. *Avoir avalé la — de Polichinelle,* to be very hoarse

Pratiquement, *adv.* practically

Pratiquer, *v.a.n.* to practise; to exercise; to frequent, to associate with, to keep company with; to tamper with, to suborn, to bribe; to procure, to obtain; to open; to make; to contrive; to manage; to arrange; to do; (*nav.*) to have free intercourse

Se —, *v.r.* to be practised, &c.; to be customary *or* usual, to be done; to open *or* make *or* &c. (for oneself)

Pré, *s.m.* grass-field, field of grass, green field, field, meadow, pasture-ground, paddock; (*obsolete*) ground (to fight a duel); —, *grand* —, (*in thieves' slang*) penitentiary, hulks, penal servitude (*V.* **Faucher**). — *salé,* salt-marsh; salt-marsh sheep *or* mutton, southdown [ment

Préachat, *s.m.* payment beforehand, prepay-

Préacheter, *v.a.* to pay beforehand, to prepay; to buy beforehand

Préadamisme, *s.m.* preadamism

Préadamite, *s.m.* preadamite; — *adj.* preadamic, preadamitic

Préalable, *adj.* previous, preliminary; — *s.m.* preliminary. *Au* —, previously, first

Préalablement, *adv.* previously, first

Préambulaire, *adj.* preambulary

Préambule, *s.m.* preamble; preface [ground

Préau, *s.m.* yard; green; paddock; close; play-

Prébende, *s.f.* prebend; prebendaryship

Prébendé, e, *adj.* enjoying a prebend; prebendal; — *s.m.* prebendary

Prébendier, *s.m.* prebendary [tenure

Précaire, *adj.* precarious; — *s.m.* precarious

Précairement, *adv.* precariously

Précarité, *s.f.* precariousness

Précati-f, ve, *adj.* precative, precatory

Précation, *s.f.* precation

Précaution, *s.f.* precaution; caution; care

Précautionné, e, *adj.* cautious, wary, guarded

Précautionnel, le, *adj.* precautionary, precautional [warn

Précautionner, *v.a.* to caution, to guard, to

Se —, *v.r.* to take (o.'s) precautions, to guard, to provide *or* steel oneself

Précautionneu-x, se, *adj.* cautious, careful

Précédemment, *adv.* previously, formerly, [before, already

Précédence, *s.f.* precedence

Précédent, e, *adj.* preceding; former; previous; before; — *s.m.* precedent

Précéder, *v.a.n.* to precede; to go before; to go first; to have *or* take precedence (of)

Préceinte, *s.f.* (*nav.*) wale

Préceltique, *adj.* preceltic

Précepte, *s.m.* precept [master

Précepteur, *s.m.* preceptor, tutor, teacher,

Préceptoral, e, *adj.* preceptorial

Préceptorat, *s.m.* preceptorship, tutorship

Préceptorerie, *s.f.* preceptory

Précession, *s.f.* (*astr.*) precession

Prêchable, *adj.* preachable

Préchantre, *s.m.* (*obsolete*) precentor

Préchantrerie, *s.f.* (*obsolete*) precentorship

Prêche, *s.m.* preaching, preachment, sermon; lecture, jobation; meeting-house, Protestant church

Prêcher, *v.a.n.* to preach; to preach to; to lecture; to preach up; to praise; to extol; to announce, to forebode; to publish; to tell; to complain; to cry

Prêcheu-r, se, *s.m.f.* (*fam.*) preacher; sermonizer; lecturer; predicant; — *adj.* preaching; sermonizing; lecturing. *Frère* —, —, preaching friar, predicant, Dominican friar, black-friar [dler

Prêchi-Prêcha, *s.m.* (*pop.*) jawer, scold, twad-

Précieusement, *adv.* preciously; with great care; elaborately; affectedly, finically, euphuistically

Précieu-x, se, *adj.* precious; costly, valuable;

dear; beloved; careful; elaborate; affected, prim, finical, euphuistic; — *s.m.* affected man, euphuist; affectation, euphuism; — *s.f.* affected lady, euphuist
Préciosité, *s.f.* affectation, finicalness, euphuism
Précipice, *s.m.* precipice
Précipitable, *adj.* (*chem.*) precipitable
Précipitamment, *adv.* precipitately, hastily, hurriedly; headlong
Précipitant, *s m.* (*chem.*) precipitant
Précipitation, *s.f.* precipitation; haste, hurry
Précipité, e, *part. adj.* precipitated, hurled, &c. (*V.* **Précipiter**); precipitate; hasty, hurried; headlong; violent; steep, precipitous; — *s.m.* (*chem.*) precipitate
Précipiter, *v a.n.* to precipitate; to throw, to hurl *or* dash down; to throw headlong; to hasten; to hurry; to hurry on; to plunge
Se —, *v.r.* to precipitate *or* throw oneself; to rush; to rush on *or* forward; to spring; to spring forth; to start; to dart; to dart forth; to dash; to burst forth *or* out, to burst; to fall; to run; to hasten; to hurry; (*chem.*) to precipitate, to be precipitated
Précipitueu-x, se, *adj.* precipitous
Préciput, *s.m.* preference legacy; advantage stipulated in the marriage settlement in favour of the survivor; jointure; extra fees
Précis, e, *adj.* precise; exact; strict; just; formal; terse, concise, neat; fixed; precisely; just; just so — *s.m.* epitome, abstract, summary, substance, compendium, precis
Précisément, *adv.* precisely; exactly; quite;
Préciser, *v.a.* to state precisely, to specify; to show precisely; to fix, to determine
Se —, *v.r.* to be stated *or* shown precisely, to be specified; to be fixed *or* determined; to become distinct
Précisien, ne, *s.m.f.* precisian
Précision, *s.f.* precision
Précité, e, *adj.* above-mentioned, aforesaid
Précoce, *adj.* precocious, early, forward; premature
Précocement, *adv.* precociously; prematurely
Précocité, *s.f.* precocity, precociousness
Précompte, *s.m.* previous deduction
Précompter, *v.a.* to deduct previously *or* beforehand
Préconcepti-f, ve, *adj.* preconceptive
Préconception, *s.f.* preconception
Préconcevoir, *v.a.* to preconceive
Préconisation, *s.f.* preconization; praise; commendation
Préconiser, *v.a.* to sanction the appointment of, to admit, to preconize; to extol, to praise; to cry up; to commend; to recommend; to boast
Préconiseu-r, se, *s.m.f.* praiser, commender
Préconnaissance, *s.f.* foreknowledge
Préconnaître, *v.a.* to foreknow
Précordial, e, *adj.* (*anat.*) precordial
Précurseur, *s.m.* precursor, forerunner, harbinger, herald; precursory symptom *or* symptoms, premonitory symptom *or* symptoms; — *adj.m.* precursory, premonitory
Préda-teur, trice, *s.m.f.* preyer, predator; — *adj.* preying, predatory
Prédécéder, *v.n.* (*law*) to predecease
Prédécès, *s.m.* (*law*) predecease
Prédécesseur, *s.m.* predecessor
Prédénommé, e, *adj.* abovenamed, aforesaid, said
Prédestinateur, *s.m.* predestinator
Prédestinatianisme, *s.m.* predestinarianism
Prédestinatien, ne, *adj. s.* predestinarian
Prédestination, *s.f.* predestination
Prédestiné, e, *adj. s.* predestinate, predestinated, elect; (*jest.*) husband doomed to be deceived by his wife. *Visage* or *face de —*, happy countenance
Prédestiner, *v.a.* to predestine, to predestinate; to foredoom, to doom
Prédétermination, *s.f.* predetermination
Prédéterminer, *v.a.* to predetermine
Prédicable, *adj.* (*log.*) predicable
Prédicament, *s.m.*(*log.*) predicament; (*obsolete*) repute
Prédicant, *s m.* Protestant preacher *or* minister
Prédicat, *s.m.* predicate
Prédicateur, *s.m.* preacher; teacher
Prédication, *s.f.* preaching; sermon
Prédicati-f, ve, *adj.* predicative
Prédicatrice, *s.f.* female preacher (*among Protestants*, &c.)
Prédiction, *s f.* prediction; foreboding; forecast
Prédilection, *s.f.* predilection, preference, partiality. *De —*, (*adject.*) favourite
Prédire, *v.a.* to predict; to foretell; to forebode, to presage; to forecast
Se —, *v.r.* to be predicted, &c.
Prédiseu-r, se, *s.m.f.* predictor, foreteller
Prédisposer, *v.a.* to predispose
Prédisposition, *s.f.* predisposition; tendency
Prédominance, *s.f.* predominance; prevalence
Prédominant, e, *adj.* predominant; prevalent, prevailing
Prédomination, *s.f.* predomination
Prédominer, *v.n.* to predominate; to prevail
Prééminence, *s.f.* preeminence
Prééminent, e, *adj.* preeminent
Préempter, *v.a.* to preempt
Préemption, *s.f.* preemption
Préétablir, *v.a.* to preestablish
Préexistant, e, *part. adj.* preexisting, preexistent
Préexistence, *s.f.* preexistence
Préexister, *v.n.* to preexist
Préface, *s.f.* preface; preamble; introduction
Préfectoral, e, *adj.* prefectoral, prefectorial of a (*or* the) prefect *or* sheriff
Préfecture, *s.f.* sheriffship, sheriff's office *or* house, county-hall; county; county-town; prefecture. — *de la Seine*, (*in Paris*) guildhall, mansion-house. — *de police*, office of (the) commissioner of police, chief office ['*Scotland-yard*']
Préférable, *adj.* preferable
Préférablement, *adv.* preferably
Préféré, e, *part. adj. s.* preferred; favourite
Préférence, *s.f.* preference; choice. *De —*, in preference
Préférer, *v.a.* to prefer, to like better *or* best
Préfet, *s.m.* sheriff; prefect; (— *des études*) vice-principal (in a school). — *maritime*, naval commander-in-chief (of a district). — *de la Seine*, lord mayor (of Paris), (*in slipshod English*) "prefect of the Seine." — *de police*, (chief) commissioner of police
Préfette, *s.f.* "préfet"'s wife
Préfigurer, *v.a.* to prefigure
Préfinir, *v.a.* to prefine, to fix, to appoint
Préfix, e, *adj.* prefixed; appointed; determined
Préfixe, *s.m.* (*gram.*) prefix
Préfixer, *v.a.* to prefix; to appoint, to determine
Préfixion, *s.f.* prefixion
Préfloraison, *s.f.* (*bot.*) prefloration
Préfoliation, *s.f.* (*bot.*) prefoliation
†**Prégnant, e,** *adj.* (*old*) pregnant, with young
Préhenseur, *adj.m.* prehensile
Préhensible, *adj.* prehensible
Préhensile, *adj.* prehensile
Préhension, *s.f.* prehension
Préhistorique, *adj.* prehistoric
Frehnite, *s.f.* (*min.*) prehnite
Préjudice, *s.m.* prejudice, injury, detriment, wrong, harm, hurt, damage; loss
Préjudiciable, *adj.* prejudicial, injurious, detrimental, hurtful
Préjudiciaux, *adj.m.pl* *Frais —*, (*law*) previous costs
Préjudiciel, le, *adj.* (*law*) previous, interlocutory
Préjudicier, *v.n.* to be prejudicial *or* injurious *or* hurtful (to), to prejudice, to injure
Préjugé, *s.m.* prejudice, prepossession; appearance, presumption, earnest; (*law*) precedent
Préjugement, *s.m.* prejudgment, prejudication
Préjuger, *v.a.* to prejudge, to prejudicate; to conjecture, to foresee, to guess at
Se —, *v.r.* to be prejudged, &c.
Prélart, *s.m.* tarpaulin; tilt

Prélasser (Se), *v.r.* to strut, to stalk, to flaunt; to parade; to make a great show; to walk with a free and easy step; to loll, to lounge; to take it easy, to take o.'s ease; to indulge oneself
Prélat, *s.m.* prelate; tarpaulin; tilt
Prélation, *s.f.* (*obsolete*) prelation, preference
Prélature, *s.f.* prelacy
Prêle, *s.f.* (*bot.*) shave-grass, horse-tail
Prélecture, *s.f.* (*print.*) first reading
Prélegs, *s.m.* preference legacy
Préléguer, *v.a.* to leave as a preference legacy
Prêler, *v.a.* to rub with shave-grass
Prélèvement, *s.m.* previous deduction; defalcation; raising *or* taking first; levying
Prélever, *v.a.* to deduct previously *or* beforehand; to raise *or* take first; to levy; to spare
Se —, *v.r.* to be deducted previously *or* &c.
Prélibation, *s.f.* prelibation, foretaste [first
Préliber, *v.a.* to taste beforehand, to taste the
Préliminaire, *adj.m.f.*, *s.m.* preliminary
Préliminairement, *adv.* preliminarily
Prélire, *v.a.* (*print.*) to read a first time
Prélude, *s.m.* prelude
Préluder, *v.n.* to prelude
Prématuré, e, *adj.* premature; forward; un-
Prématurément, *adv.* prematurely [timely
Prématurité, *s.f.* prematurity, prematureness, precocity
Préméditation, *s.f.* premeditation; (*law*) malice aforethought. *Avec* —, with premeditation; (*law*) wilful; wilfully, with malice aforethought [premeditated
Préméditer, *v.a.* to premeditate. *Se* —, to be
Prémices, *s.f.pl.* first-fruits; prime; beginning
Premi-er, ère, *adj.* first; opening; former; ancient, old; primitive; pristine; next; early; earliest; prime; primary; raw; front; foremost; leading; chief, in chief, head; senior; first-rate; — *s.m.* first; chief; head; leader; first floor; —**ère,** *s.f.* (—**ères,** *s.f.pl.*) first class; first *or* chief cabin, saloon; (*theat.*) first-tier box (*pl.* first tier of boxes, dress-circle); first performance *or* night; (*print.*) first proof. *Au* —, on *or* to the first floor. *En* —, in the first place; in the first instance; first; in chief; head, chief. *Jeune* —, (*theat.*) lover
Premièrement, *adv.* first, firstly, in the first
Prémisse, *s.f.* (*log.*) premiss [place, first of all
Premme, Premne, *s.f.* (*bot.*) premna
Prémonitoire, *adj.* (*med.*) premonitory
Prémontré, e, *s.m.f.* (*rel. order*) Premonstrant, Premonstratensian, white canon
Prémotion, *s.f.* (*theol.*) premotion
Prémourant, *s.m.* (*law*) one dying first
Prémunir, *v.a.* to forearm, to arm *or* guard *or* strengthen *or* fortify *or* secure beforehand, to provide; to warn; to caution
Prémunition, *s.f.* premunition
Prenable, *adj.* to be taken, takable; pregnable, expugnable; seizable; catchable; to be bribed, corruptible; accessible
Prenant, e, *part. adj.* taking, &c. (*V.* **Prendre**); receiving, having to receive money; (*zool., of the tail*) prehensile. *Partie —e,* recipient; payee; sharers
Prénanthe, *s.m.* (*bot.*) prenanthes
Prendre, *v.a.n.* to take; to seize; to lay *or* take hold of; to catch; to capture; to apprehend; to take up; to take in *or* out; to take away; to retrench; to save; to handle; to manage; to choose; to get; to gain; to obtain; to come over; to overtake; to surprise; to deceive; to smite; to undertake; to carry; to let in; to call for; to fetch; to strike; to attack; to cut; to fix, to appoint, to settle; to assume; to put on; to wear; to contract (*habits, engagements,* &c.); to get into; to conceive; to receive; to accept; to exact; to charge (*money*); to borrow (*money*); to buy; to hire; to engage; to collect; to gather; to suppose; to consider; to hold; to see; to find; to hear; to use; to take possession of; to help oneself to; to eat; to drink; to fit; to convict; to turn; to go; to come; to begin; to take root; to thicken; to coagulate; to set; to freeze, to congeal; to curdle; to burn, to burn up, to begin to burn; to break out; to act; to succeed. *Aller* —, to go and take *or* &c.; to go for. *Faire* —, to make (...) take *or* &c.; to send for. *Venir* —, to come and take *or* &c.; to come for. — *en amitié,* &c., *V.* **Amitié,** &c. — *sur son sommeil,* to retrench from o.'s sleep. — *pour dit,* to take for granted. *A tout* —, everything considered, upon the whole, in the main. *En* —, (*imp.*) to happen, to befall, to betide, to fare. *Bien lui prit* or *lui en prit,* it was well *or* lucky for him. *Ça ne prend pas,* it won't do, it is no use *or* no go. *Je vous y prends,* I catch you at it, now I have caught you. *Je sors d'en* —, (*fam.*) I had rather be excused. *Il me prend ...,* (*imp.*) I am seized with ...; I take ...; I have ... *Qu'est-ce qui vous prend?* what is the matter with you? *Au fait et au* — (*s.m.*), *V.* **Fait,** *s.m.* *Avoir le* — (*s.m.*) *et le laisser,* *V.* **Laisser**
Se —, *v.r.* to take *or* &c. oneself *or* each other; to be taken *or* caught *or* &c.; to take hold (of); to take (to); to catch; to cling; to fix; to thicken; to coagulate; to set; to freeze, to congeal; to curdle; to begin; to set (about); to go to work (about); to apply oneself; to meddle (with); to attack; to impute, to attribute; to make (*one*) the cause (of). *Se* — *d'amitié pour,* to take a liking to. *Se* — *de vin,* to get tipsy *or* drunk. *S'en* — *à,* to blame, to lay the blame on, to lay it at ...'s door, to lay it upon, to impute it to; to find fault with; to come upon; to attack, to make an attack upon, to set upon. *S'y* —, to proceed, to act, to go *or* set about it, to go to work, to do it, to manage it, to manage; to begin
Preneu-r, se, *s.m.f.* taker; catcher; captor; eater; drinker; buyer, purchaser; lessee; — *adj.* taking; catching; capturing [nomen
Prénom, *s.m.* christian name, forename; pre-
Prénommé, e, *part. adj.* forenamed; abovenamed, aforesaid
Prénommer, *v.a.* to prenominate, to forename
Prénotion, *s.f.* prenotion, previous notion; imperfect notion
Préoccupation, *s.f.* preoccupation; prepossession, prejudice; thought; anxiety; absence of mind
Préoccupé, e, *part. adj.* preoccupied, &c. (*V.* **Préoccuper**); pensive, thoughtful; anxious
Préoccuper, *v.a.* to preoccupy; to engage *or* engross the mind of, to absorb the thoughts of, to engage, to engross, to absorb; to trouble; to prepossess, to prejudice
Se —, *v.r.* to be preoccupied *or* &c.; to trouble oneself (about); to be anxious (about); to think (of), to give thought (to); to turn o.'s attention (to) [last speaker
Préopinant, e, *s.m.f.* preceding *or* previous *or*
Préopiner, *v.n.* to give o.'s opinion (*or* to speak) before (another), to vote first
Préopinion, *s.f.* preopinion
Préordination, *s.f.* preordination
Préordonner, *v.a.* to preordinate
Préorganisation, *s.f.* preorganization
Préorganiser, *v.a.* to preorganize
Préparable, *adj.* preparable [ready; dressing
Préparage, *s.m.* (*tech.*) preparing; getting
Prépara-teur, trice, *s.m.f.* preparator, preparer; dresser; assistant; private tutor, crammer, grinder; — *adj.* preparing; dressing
Préparatif *s.m.* preparation, preparative
Préparation, *s.f.* preparation; dressing; breaking (*news*) [parative; preliminary
Préparatoire, *adj.m.f.*, *s.m.* preparatory; pre-
Préparer, *v.a.* to prepare; to dispose; to make *or* get ready; to fit; to dress; to cook; to break (*news*) to; to pave (*the way, fig.*); to mark (*cards*)
Se —, *v.r.* to prepare oneself (*or* for oneself),

to prepare; to be preparing *or* prepared; &c. *V.* **Apprêter (S')**

Prépondérance, *s.f.* preponderance, sway

Prépondérant, e, *adj.* preponderant; prevailing; convincing. *Voix —e,* casting vote

Préposé, e, (*part. of* **Préposer**) set (over), &c.; —*s.m.f.* officer, overseer, superintendent; keeper

Préposer, *v.a.* to set *or* place (over); to charge, to intrust; to appoint, to commit [prepositive

Prépositi-f, ve, *adj.*, **Prépositif,** *s.m.* (*gram.*)

Préposition, *s.f.* (*gram.*) preposition

Prépositivement, *adv.* (*gram.*) prepositively

Prépotence, *s.f.* prepotence, predominance

Prépuce, *s.m.* (*anat.*) prepuce, foreskin

Préputial, e, *adj.* (*anat.*) preputial

Prérectal, e, *adj.* (*anat.*) prerectal

Prérogative, *s.f.* prerogative; privilege; advantage; attribute

Préromain, e, *adj.* preroman

Près, *prep.* near, by, close, by the side; to; with; nearly, almost; about; on the point; in comparison. *Tout —,* very near; close by; at hand. *A ... —,* save *or* except ...; within ..., to ...; with ...; all but ... *A cela —,* save that, except that, with that exception; for the matter of that; for all that; save, except, excepting. *A peu —,* nearly, pretty near, almost, about; pretty much, much about, much; nearly so; about it; thereabouts; much about the same; much about in the same way; (*substant.*) approximation, approach. *A peu de chose —,* nearly, about, within a trifle. *Au plus —,* to the nearest place; (*nav.*) close to the wind. *De —,* close, near; closely, intimately; narrowly

Présage, *s.m.* presage, omen

Présager, *v.a.* to presage, to forebode, to portend; to conjecture. *Se —,* to be presaged, &c.

Pré-salé, *s.m. V.* **Pré**

Présanctifié, e, *adj. s.* presanctified

Presbyopie, *s.f.* long-sightedness, far-sightedness, presbyopia, presbyopy

Presbyte, *adj.* long-sighted, far-sighted, presbytic, presbyopic; — *s m.f.* ditto person, presbyte, presbyope. *Vue —,* long sight, far sight

Presbytéral, e, *adj.* priestly. *Maison —e,* parsonage; vicarage

Presbytéranisme, *s.m.* presbyterianism

Presbytérat. *V.* **Presbytériat** [tery

Presbytère, *s.m.* parsonage; vicarage; presby-

Presbytérianisme, *s.m.* presbyterianism

Presbytériat, *s.m.* presbytership, presbyterate

Presbytérien, ne, *adj. s.* presbyterian

Presbytie, *s.f.* long-sightedness, far-sightedness, presbytia

Presbyt-ique, -isme. *V.* page 3, § 1

Presbytre, *s.m.* presbyter [foresight

Prescience, *s.f.* prescience, foreknowledge,

Prescient, e, *adj.* prescient

Prescript, *s.m.* (*philos.*) prescript

Prescriptible, *adj.* (*law*) prescriptible

Prescription, *s.f.* prescription; (*law*) prescription, limitation of action, limitation

Prescrire, *v.a.n.* to prescribe; to order; to direct; to set; to bar

Se —, *v.r.* to prescribe to oneself *or* to each other; to be prescribed *or* &c.; (*law*) to be lost *or* acquired by prescription *or* limitation, to be

Préséance, *s.f.* precedence [barred by time

Présence, *s.f.* presence; attendance; sight, view; imitation coffin. *En —,* in the presence (of); in each other's presence; in sight, in view; face to face (*Être en —,* to be ditto, to meet); (*things*) in competition [*—!* here!

Présent, e, *adj.* present; (*of the mind*) ready.

Présent, *s.m.* present; gift; present time; present tense. *A —,* at present, now, this moment, this time, the present time, nowadays. *Pour le —, quant à —,* for the present, for the nonce. *Faire — de,* to present with, to make

Présentable, *adj.* presentable [a present of

Présenta-teur, trice, *s.m.f.* presenter; introducer

Présentation, *s.f.* presentation; introduction. *A —,* (*com.*) on presentation; on demand. *En retard de —,* (*com.*) overdue [presents

Présente, *s.f.* present letter, present; **—s,** *pl.*

Présentement, *adv.* at present, now, immediately; with immediate possession

Présenter, *v.a.* to present; to offer; to offer up; to expose; to show; to turn; to bring forward *or* in; to introduce

Se —, *v.r.* to present *or* &c. oneself *or* itself; to appear; to come; to call; to visit; to apply; to put up; to arise; to occur. *Se — bien,* to have a good address *or* appearance, to look well; to promise well

Présenteu-r, se, *s.m.f.* presenter

Préserva-teur, trice, *adj.* preservative; — *s.m.f.* preserver [preservative

Préservati-f, ve, *adj.*, **Préservatif,** *s.m.*

Préservation, *s.f.* preservation

Préserver, *v.a.* to preserve, to keep. *Le ciel m'en* (or *t'en, l'en, nous en,* &c.) *préserve!* Heaven forbid! [convict-station

Préside, *s.m.* presidio, (Spanish) penitentiary,

Présidence, *s.f.* presidency; chairmanship. — *de M. ...,* Mr. ... in the chair [presiding judge

Président, *s.m.* president; chairman; speaker;

Présidental, e, *adj.* (*old*) presidential

Présidente, *s.f.* presidentess, lady president; president's wife

Présidentiel, le, *adj.* presidential

Présider, *v.n.a.* to preside; to preside over; to be in the chair; to govern; to direct

Présidiaire, *s.m.* (Spanish) convict

Présompti-f, ve, *adj.* presumptive; apparent

Présomption, *s.f.* presumption

Présomptivement, *adv.* presumptively

Présomptueusement, *adv.* presumptuously

Présomptueu-x, se, *adj. s.* presumptuous, presuming; ditto person

Presque, *adv.* almost, nearly, all but; next to; scarcely, hardly; very near; almost entire, almost complete. *— jamais,* scarcely ever, hardly ever. *— pas,* scarcely, hardly; scarcely any, hardly any. *— plus de ...,* scarcely *or* hardly any ... left; scarcely *or* hardly ... now. *— rien,* almost nothing, scarcely *or* hardly

Presqu'île, *s.f.* peninsula [anything

Pressage, *s.m.* pressing

Pressamment, *adv.* pressingly; urgently

Pressant, e, *part. adj.* pressing, &c. (*V.* **Presser**); urgent; importunate; rigorous; acute, sharp, violent; concise

Presse, *s.f.* press; printing-press; crowd, throng; urgency; haste; hurry; pressure; anxiety, pain, trouble, difficulty; (*boys' play*) squash; (*nav.*) press; impressment; press-gang; (*hort.*) clingstone peach. *— mécanique,* engine-press, power-press. *Sous —,* in the press. *Mettre sous —,* to send *or* go to press

Presse, *s.m.* (*in compounds, from* **Presser,** "to press," &c.) thing that presses, presser. — **-artères,** *s.m.* (*surg.*) ligature. — **-étoffe,** *s.m.* (*of sewing-mach.*) cloth-presser. — **-papiers,** *s.m.* paper-weight

Pressé, e, *part. adj.* pressed, &c. (*V.* **Presser**); hurried, in haste, in a hurry; urgent; immediate; anxious; quick; oft-repeated, crowding, numerous, thick; close, serried; condensed, brief, concise

Pressée, *s.f.* pressing, pressure; pressful

Pressement, *s.m.* pressing, compression

Pressément, *adv.* hastily, hurriedly; urgently; closely [ing; misgiving; surmise

Pressentiment, *s.m.* presentiment; forebod-

Pressentir, *v.a.* to have a presentiment of, to foresee; to guess; to surmise; to sound

Se —, *v.r.* to be foreseen *or* &c.

Presser, *v.a.n.* to press; to squeeze; to clasp; to oppress; to pull (*a trigger*); to crowd, to throng; to urge; to urge on; to hasten; to hurry; to quicken; to pinch; to condense; to close; to strain; to be urgent; (*of pain*) to be acute. *Rien ne presse, il n'y a rien qui presse*, there is no hurry

Se —, *v.r.* to press; to press close to each other; to sit *or* stand *or* lie close (*or* closer); to crowd, to throng; to make haste, to hasten, to be quick, to hurry; to press *or* &c. each other; to be pressed *or* &c.

Presseur, *s.m.* presser; cloth-presser; pressman; — *adj.m.* pressing

Pressier, *s.m.* (*print.*) pressman

Pression, *s.f.* pressing; pressure

Pressis, *s.m.* juice; gravy

Pressoir, *s.m.* press; wine-press; press-house

Pressurage, *s.m.* pressing, pressure; marc-wine; (*obsolete*) press-fee

Pressurer, *v.a.* to press; to squeeze; (*fig.*) to oppress, to grind, to screw down, to drain, to [exhaust

Se —, *v.r.* to be pressed, &c.

Pressureur, *s.m.* pressman, presser

Prestance, *s.f.* deportment, carriage, gait, presence, look; commanding deportment *or* carriage, portliness, good presence *or* look

Prestant, *s.m.* (*mus.*) diapason (*of an organ*)

Prestation, *s.f.* prestation; taking (*an oath*); swearing (*fidelity*, &c.) [quick, sharp

Preste, *adj.* quick, nimble; sharp; — *adv.*

Prestement, *adv.* quickly, nimbly

Prestesse, *s.f.* agility, nimbleness, quickness; smartness; readiness [gler, prestidigitator

Prestidigitateur, *s.m* conjurer, wizard, jug-

Prestidigitation, *s.f.* sleight of hand, conjuring, juggling, prestidigitation [spell

Prestige, *s.m.* prestige; illusion; fascination;

Prestigiateur, *s.m.* prestigiator [ing; illusive

Prestigieu-x, se, *adj.* prestigious; fascinat-

Prestimonie, *s.f.* (*can. law*) prestimony

Prestissimo, *adv.* (*mus.*) prestissimo

Presto, *adv.* (*mus.*) presto

Prestolet, *s.m.* priestling

Présumable, *adj.* presumable

Présumé, e, *part. adj.* presumed, supposed, reputed, considered [conjecture; to overrate

Présumer, *v.a.n.* to presume; to suppose; to

Se —, *v.r.* to be presumed, &c.

Présupposer, *v.a.* to presuppose

Se —, *v.r.* to be presupposed, &c.

Présupposition, *s.f.* presupposition

Présure, *s.f.* rennet (*for curdling milk*)

Présurer, *v.a.* to curdle (*milk*)

Prêt, e, *adj.* ready; in readiness; prepared; disposed, willing; about (to), on the point (of)

Prêt, *s.m.* loan; (*mil.*) pay. — *sur gage* (or *gages*), money lent on pledge; pawnbroking

Prêtable, *adj.* lendable [gad about

Pretantaine, *s.f.* *Courir la* —, to ramble *or*

Prête, *s.f.* osier twig, withe

Prêté, e, *part. adj.* lent, &c. (*V.* **Prêter**)

Prêté, *s.m.* thing lent, loan. *Un — rendu, un rendu pour un* —, a Rowland for an Oliver, tit for tat

Prétendance, *s.f.* pretendence, pretendership

Prétendant, e, *s.m.f.* claimant; candidate, applicant; suitor, wooer; pretender

Prétendre, *v.a.n.* to pretend; to claim; to lay claim (to); to presume; to solicit; to aspire (to), to aim (at); to say; to assert; to contend; to maintain; to profess; to allege; to mean to say; to intend, to mean; to wish; to expect; to hope; to think of. — *cause de*, to allege, to plead

Prétendu, e, *adj.* pretended, supposed; so-called, so-termed, said to be (...); intended; — *s.m.f.* intended (*future husband or wife*); — *s.m.* suitor, wooer, lover

Prête-nom, *s.m.* person who lends his name, ostensible agent *or* contractor, dummy

Pretentaine, *s.f.* *V.* **Pretantaine** [fectedly

Prétentieusement, *adv.* pretentiously, af-

Prétentieu-x, se, *adj.* pretentious, assuming, affected; — *s.m.f.* ditto person

Prétention, *s.f.* pretension; claim; expectation; wish; affectation; pretentiousness. *Sans* —, unpretending, unassuming, unaffected. *Avoir des —s*, to have pretensions; to entertain high notions of oneself; to have pretensions to beauty

Prêter, *v.a.* to lend; to impart; to give; to afford; to present; to attribute, to ascribe; to give rise; to take; — *v.n.* to lend money, to lend; to stretch; to afford facilities; to give a hold (to); to afford matter (for); to be fertile; — *s.m.* lending; loan

Se —, *v.r.* to lend *or* &c. to each other *or* to oneself; to be lent *or* &c.; to lend oneself; to be accessory (to); to consent; to yield; to submit; to comply; to accept; to humour; to countenance, to favour; to indulge (in); to adapt oneself (to); to enter (into); to enjoy, [to relish

Prétérit, *s.m.* (*gram.*) preterite

Prétérition, *s.f.* (*rhet.*, *law*, &c.) preterition

Prétermission, *s.f.* (*rhet.*) pretermission

Préteur, *s.m.* pretor, prætor

Prêteu-r, se, *s.m.f.* lender; — *adj.* given to (*or* fond of) lending, of a lending disposition. — *sur gages*, pawnbroker, lender on deposits

Prétexte, *s.m.* pretext, pretence, plea; — *s.f.* (*adj.*, *Robe* —) prætexta (*in Rom. hist.*)

Prétexter, *v.a.* to pretend, to feign; to allege, to plead [sory, appendage

†Pretintaille, *s.f.* (*obsolete*) trimming; acces-

†Pretintailler, *v.a.* (*old*) to trim; (*fig.*) to tinsel

Prétoire, *s.m.* pretorium, prætorium; judges' bench; magisterial bench, police court; precincts [*s.m.* pretorian guard

Prétorien, ne, *adj.* pretorian, prætorian; —

†Prêtraille, *s.f.* (*in contempt*) priesthood, priests, parsons [—, high-priest

Prêtre, *s.m.* priest; clergyman; parson. *Grand*

Prêtresse, *s.f.* priestess. *Grande* —, high-priestess [orders, orders

Prêtrise, *s.f.* priesthood; priest's orders, holy

Préture, *s.f.* pretorship, prætorship

Freu, *adj.m.*, *s.m.* (*slang*) first

Freuve, *s.f.* proof; evidence; testimony, token, mark; trial, experiment; ordeal. — *que, à — que*, as a proof that. *Faire — de*, to show, to evince, to show proof of, to give proofs of, to prove o.'s ... *Faire ses —s*, to show what one is made of *or* can do, to show oneself to be a man; to establish o.'s reputation; (*de* ...) to prove (o.'s ...)

Preux, *adj.m.* gallant, doughty; — *s.m.* gallant knight, doughty knight *or* warrior, worthy

Prévalence, *s.f.* prevalence

Prévaloir, *v.n.* to prevail; to stand; to supersede. *Faire* —, to make (...) prevail; to give the preference *or* the advantage to

Se —, *v.r.* to take advantage, to avail oneself; to boast, to make a show, to pride oneself (upon), to pride (in), to be proud (of), to glory (in)

Prévarica-teur, trice, *s.m.f. adj.* prevaricator; prevaricating [trust

Prévarication, *s.f.* prevarication, breach of

Prévariquer, *v.n.* to prevaricate

Prévenance, *s.f.* kind attention, attention; obligingness, kindness

Prévenant, e, *adj.* prepossessing, engaging; attentive, obliging, kind; (*theol.*) preventing, predisposing

Prévenir, *v.a.* to precede; to go *or* come *or* arrive *or* be before; to be beforehand with; to get the start of; to anticipate; to forestall; to meet; to prevent, to hinder; to prepossess; to prejudice; to predispose; to bias; to tell beforehand, to give notice, to warn, to caution; to inform, to apprise, to acquaint, to tell, to let know [be prepossessed *or* prejudiced *or* &c.

Se —, *v.r.* to anticipate *or* &c. each other; to

Préventi-f, ve, *adj.* preventive; presumptive, on suspicion

Prévention, *s.f.* prevention; precedence; prejudice, prepossession, bias; suspicion, presumption; imputation, accusation; imprisonment on suspicion. *État de* —, (*law*) commitment. *En état de* —, (*law*) committed for trial

Préve..ivement, *adv.* preventively; on suspicion, presumptively
Prévenu, e, *part. adj.* preceded, &c. (*V.* **Prévenir**); — *part. adj. s.m.f.* (*law*) accused; prisoner (*before trial*), culprit
Prévertébral, e, *adj.* prevertebral
Prévision, *s.f.* prevision; foreseeing, foresight; foreknowledge; forecast; conjecture; expectation
Prévoir, *v.a.* to foresee; to forecast; to conjecture; to expect; to anticipate; to provide for *or* against; to meet
Se —, *v.r.* to be foreseen *or* &c
Prévôt, *s.m.* provost; marshal; magistrate; chief justice; mayor; warder; (*fencing or dancing-master's*) assistant. — *de salle*, fencing-master's assistant. — *des marchands*, (*obsolete*) mayor of Paris
Prévôtal, e, *adj.* provostal, provost's
Prévôtalement, *adv.* by a provostal court
Prévôté, *s.f.* provostship [to be foreseen
Prévoyable, *adj.* that can *or* may be foreseen,
Prévoyance, *s.f.* foresight, forethought, prudence, care, caution. *De —*, of *or* from foresight; providing; provident; precautionary
Prévoyant, e, *adj.* provident, prudent, careful, cautious, wary
Prévu, e, *part. adj.* foreseen, &c. (*V.* **Prévoir**). — *par la loi* or *par le code*, statutable, statutory
Priapée, *s.f.* obscene poem *or* painting
Priapéen, ne, *adj.* (*vers.*) priapean
Priap-ique, -isme. *V.* page 3, § 1
Prié, e, *part. adj.* prayed; desired, asked, invited, &c. (*V.* **Prier**); (*of repasts*) of ceremony, — *s.m.f.* person invited, guest
Prie-Dieu, *s.m.* devotion-chair, prayer-desk, prie-Dieu; faldstool, fold-stool
Prier, *v.a.n.* to pray; to pray to; to beseech, to entreat; to press; to beg; to beg of; to request; to bid; to desire; to ask; to invite. *Faire —*, to send to request. *Se faire —, aimer à se faire —*, to require pressing. *Se faire — deux fois* or *&c.*, to require to be asked twice *or* &c. *Je vous en prie*, pray, do, please, I pray you, I beg of you, I entreat you [make an effort
Se —, *v.r.* to invite each other; (*fam.*) to
Prière, *s.f.* prayer; entreaty; request; desire; invitation; petition
Prieur, e, *s.m.f.* prior; prioress
Prieural, e, *adj.* of a prior *or* priory, priorial
Prieuré, *s.m.* priory; priorship, priorate
Prima donna, *s.f.* (*Italian*) prima donna (*pl.* prime donne)
Primage, *s.m.* (*com. nav.*) primage, hat-money
Primaire, *adj* primary, elementary, preparatory
Primat, *s m.* primate
Primatial, e, *adj.* primatial, primatical
Primatie, *s.f.* primacy; supremacy
Primauté, *s.f.* supremacy, preeminence, priority, precedence; lead
Prime, *adj.* (*old*) prime, first; early. *De — abord* (or, obsolete, *de — face*), *V.* **Abord.** *De — saut*, spontaneous; spontaneously; off-hand; suddenly, all at once, at once. — **-sautier, ère,** *adj.* spontaneous, off-hand, unpremeditated, impromptu; impulsive; ready; quick; inconsiderate; original
Prime, *s.f.* premium; bounty; bonus; prize; (*cust.*) drawback; (*Cath. lit., fenc.*, &c.) prime; (*jewel.*) pebble; (*of wool*) prime wool; (*cards*) primero. *A —*, (*fin.*) at a premium; (*Change*) with option [prize
Primé, e, *part. adj.* surpassed, &c. (*V.* **Primer**);
Primer, *v.a.n.* to surpass, to excel, to be superior to, to be above, to beat; to override; to take precedence of; to go before; to be the first; to bear the bell; to take the lead; to lead, to play first; to give a premium to; to give a prize to, to reward with a prize, to reward
Primerole, *s.f.* (*local*) *V.* **Primevère**
Primerose, *s.f.* (*bot.*) hollyhock
Primesauti-er, ère, *adj. V.* **Prime,** *adj.*
Primeur, *s.f.* early fruit *or* vegetable *or* flower, first thing of the season; early part of the season; first (*of anything*); early sentiment, first love; young girl. *Dans la —*, in the early part of the season; early, when early; (*of wine*) new, when new
Primevère, *s.f.* primrose; cowslip; oxlip
Primicériat, *s.m.* (*local*) deanery
Primicier, *s.m.* (*local*) dean
Primidi, *s m.* primidi (*first day of a decade in the calendar of the first French Republic*)
Primipare, *adj.* primiparous; — *s.f.* primiparous female, primipara [native; aboriginal
Primiti-f, ve, *adj.* primitive; original; early;
Primitif, *s.m.* (*gram.*) primitive
Primitivement, *adv.* primitively; originally
Primitivité, *s.f.* primitiveness
Primo, *adv.* firstly, in the first place
Primogéniture, *s.f. V.* **Aînesse**
Primordial, e, *adj.* primordial
Primordialement, *adv.* primordially
Primordialité, *s.f.* primordiality
Primuline, *s.f.* (*chem.*) primuline
Prince, *s m.* prince. — *héritier*, — *royal*, prince royal, crown prince. *Bon —*, easy *or* good-natured fellow, good sort of man
Princeps, *adj.* (*of the editions of old works*) first printed, first, earliest, original
Princerie, *s.f.* (*local*) deanery [creature, dear
Princesse, *s.f.* princess; (*jest.*) charmer, dear
Princi-er, ère, *adj.* princely, of a prince; — *s.m.* (*local*) dean
Princièrement, *adv.* in a princely manner
†Princillon, *s.m.* princeling, princelet
Principal, e, *adj.*, **Principal,** *s.m.* principal, chief, head; main; leading; capital; principal thing, main point; head-master; (*of a mil. hospital*) head physician [ship
Principalat, *s.m.* principalship, head-master-
Principalement, *adv.* principally, chiefly
Principat, *s.m.* princedom
Principauté, *s.f.* principality; princedom
Principe, *s.m.* principle; origin; cause; beginning [prince; little prince, baby prince
Principicule, *s.m.* princeling, princelet, petty
Principion, *s.m.* princeling, princelet
Printani-er, ère, *adj.* spring; vernal; spring-like; youthful; early
Printanière, *s.f.* (*gravy-soup with spring vegetables in it*) spring soup; (*of clothing*) spring material, spring stuff
Printemps, *s.m.* (*season*) spring; (*fig.*) prime, bloom; youth; year, summer
Priorat, *s.m.* priorate
Priori (A), *adv.* a priori, from the cause to the effect, from what precedes; without a sufficient
Priorité, *s.f.* priority [knowledge of the facts
Pris, e, *part. adj.* taken, seized, caught, &c. (*V.* **Prendre**); taken up *or* in; occupied; engaged; full; made, formed, shaped, proportioned; set; coagulated; congealed, frozen, frozen over; curdled; cloudy; the worse (for); ...-bound; (*of the nose*) stuffed up. — *de calme*, (*nav.*) becalmed. — *par les glaces*, (*nav.*) ice-bound. — *de vin*, in liquor, in o.'s cups, the worse for drink, tipsy, far gone
Prisable, *adj.* estimable, valuable
Prise, *s.f.* taking; capture; prize; hold; influence; coagulation; congelation, freezing; quarrel; scuffle; dose; (*of snuff*) pinch; **—s,** *pl.* close quarters. — *d'assaut*, storming. — *de bec*, quarrel, words. — *de corps*, arrest; apprehension; writ of arrest, warrant of apprehension. — *d'eau*, borrowed stream, cut to supply water. — *d'habit*, taking the habit *or* the veil, putting on the cowl, pronunciation of o.'s vows. *Aux —s*, on *or* to close quarters, fighting, struggling; at *or* to loggerheads; disputing. *De bonne —*, a lawful prize. *En —*, exposed; in danger of being taken. *Hors de —*, out of reach, out of danger. *Part de —*, prize-money. *Donner — à*, to give a hold *or* a

handle to; to expose oneself to; to afford matter for. *Être aux —s*, to be fighting *or* engaged; to struggle; to be disputing; to clash. *Faire —*, to coagulate, to set. *Faire une —*, to make a prize *or* capture. *Lâcher —*, to let go o.'s hold; to give way. *Mettre aux —s*, to bring to a conflict, to place in conflict; to set (together) by the ears; to bring into a difficulty

Prisée, *s.f.* appraisement, valuation, estimate

Priser, *v.a.n.* to value; to appraise; to rate; to estimate; to esteem, to prize; to praise; to take snuff [oneself; to be appraised *or* &c.

Se —, *v.r.* to prize oneself, to set a value on

Priseu-r, se, *s.m.f.* appraiser, valuer; snuff-taker; — *adj.* appraising, valuing; snuff-taking

Prismatique, *adj.* prismatic

Prismatisation, *s.f.* prismatization

Prismatisé, e, *adj.* prismatized

Prismatoïde, *adj.* prismatoidal

Prisme, *s.m.* prism

Prismé, e, *adj.* prismy

Prismoïde, *adj.* prismoidal; — *s.m.* prismoid

Prison, *s.f.* prison; jail, gaol; imprisonment;

Prisonni-er, ère, *s.m.f.* prisoner [confinement

Privable, *adj.* deprivable; tamable

Privati-f, ve, *adj.*, **Privatif,** *s.m.* privative

Privation, *s.f.* privation, deprivation, want, need; loss; bereavement; hardship

Privativement, *adv.* privatively; exclusively

Privauté, *s.f.* familiarity; liberty

Privé, e, *part. adj.* deprived, &c. (*V.* **Priver**); private; (o.'s) own; tame; privy; intimate, familiar, free; — *s.m.* privy, water-closet; privacy; intimacy [liarly

Privément, *adv.* privately; intimately, fami-

Priver, *v.a.* to deprive; to debar; to bereave; to strip; to tame, to domesticate

Se —, *v.r.* to deprive *or* debar oneself; to restrict *or* stint oneself; to deny oneself; to abstain; to become tame

Privilége, *s.m.* privilege; exemption; immunity; licence; franchise; prerogative; right; gift; grant; favour; preference

Privilégié, e, *part. adj.* privileged; exempt; licensed; gifted; favourite; (*of shares,* &c.) preference, preferential; — *s.m.f.* privileged person; licensee; favourite [license; to gift

Privilégier, *v.a.* to privilege; to exempt; to

Prix, *s.m.* price; term, terms; fare; rate; cost; value; worth; estimation; money; expense; reward, return; prize; premium; stakes. — *coûtant*, cost price, prime cost. — *fait*, regular *or* settled price. — *fort*, full price. — *de fabrique*, manufacturers' price. — *Monthyon*, prize of virtue (*also*, prize for the best essays or works on subjects of general usefulness). *De —*, (*adject.*) precious, valuable. *A — d'argent*, with *or* for money, by paying money. *A — d'or*, with *or* for gold, very dear. *A tout —*, *à quelque — que ce soit*, at any price *or* cost; cost what it may *or* will; at any rate; by all means; absolutely; anyhow; happen (*or* come) what may. *Au — de*, at the cost of; in comparison with. *Hors de —*, uncommonly *or* extravagantly dear, at an extravagant (*or* exorbitant) price, beyond all price. *Sans —*, invaluable; valueless. *Mettre à —*, to set a price on. *N'avoir pas de —*, to be invaluable; to be valueless

Pro, *s.m.* (*nav.*) proa (*boat*)

Probabil-isme, -iste. *V.* page 3, § 1

Probabilité, *s.f.* probability, likelihood

Probable, *adj.* probable, likely; credible

Probablement, *adv.* probably, likely

Probant, e, *adj.* probatory; of evidence; conclusive, convincing; authentic

Probati-f, ve, *adj.* probative, probatory

Probation, *s.f.* probation

Probatoire, *adj.* probatory, probative

Probe, *adj. s.* honest, upright, of probity

Probité, *s.f.* probity, honesty

Problémat-ique, -iquement. *V.* page 3, § 1

Problème, *s.m.* problem; question

Proboscide, *s.f.* proboscis

Proboscidé, e, *adj.* proboscidate [proboscidian

Proboscidien, ne, *adj.*, **Proboscidien,** *s.m.*

Procédé, *s.m.* proceeding; dealing; behaviour, conduct; usage; process; operation; (*billiards*) cue-top, top; —**s,** *pl.* proceedings, &c.; handsome behaviour, gentlemanly *or* ladylike conduct

Procéder, *v.n.* to proceed; to go on; to get on; to arise, to originate; to behave; to act

Procédure, *s.f.* procedure; proceedings; process; practice

Procéduri-er, ère, *adj.* versed in legal procedure; of legal procedure; — *s.m.f.* litigious person

Procellaire, Procellarie, *s.f.* *V.* **Pétrel**

Procès, *s.m.* process; lawsuit, suit, trial, action, proceedings, case at law, case, cause. —**-verbal,** *s.m.* (official) report; information (against); (*formal*) account; (*written*) statement; declaration; certificate; minute, minutes; (*parl.*) journal. *En —*, at law. *Sans autre forme de —*, without further formality *or* ceremony, without any more ado, at once. *Faire le — à*, to try; to prosecute; to accuse; to criminate; to criticize, to censure, to attack, to find fault with; to pass sentence upon, to condemn. *Faire* or *intenter un — à*, to bring an action against, to proceed against, to sue. *Mettre* or *renvoyer hors de cour* (or *hors de cause*) *et de —*, [*V.* **Cour**

Processi-f, ve, *adj.* litigious

Procession, *s.f.* procession

Processioniste, *s.m.f.* processionist

Processionnaire, *adj. s.f.* *Chenille —*, procession caterpillar

Processionnal, *s.m.* processional

Processionnel, le, *adj.*, **Processionnel,** *s.m.* processional [processionally

Processionnellement, *adv.* in procession,

Processus, *s.m.* process; progress

Prochain, e, *adj.* next; nearest; near; neighbouring; not distant, not remote; proximate; approaching; coming; early; — *s.m.* neighbour, fellow-creature; (*com.*) next month, proximo. *Fin —e*, approaching end. *Fin —*, (*com.*) (at the) end of next month

Prochainement, *adv.* shortly, soon

Prochaineté, *s.f.* nearness, proximity

Proche, *adj. prep. adv.* near, close, close to, close by; approaching, at hand; not distant; nearly related; — *s.m.* relation, relative; near object, short distance, foreground. *De — en —*, from place to place; gradually, by degrees

‡**Prochronisme,** *s.m.* prochronism

Procidence, *s.f.* (*med.*) procidence, prolapsus

†**Procillon,** *s.m.* petty lawsuit [proclaiming

Proclama-teur, trice, *s.m.f. adj.* proclaimer;

Proclamation, *s.f.* proclamation

Proclamer, *v.a.* to proclaim; to announce; to publish; to declare [proclaimed *or* &c.

Se —, *v.r.* to proclaim *or* &c. oneself; to be

Proclitique, *adj.m.f.*, *s.m.* (*gram.*) proclitic

Proclive, *adj.* proclivous, inclined

Proclivité, *s.f.* proclivity

Procné, *s.f.* *V.* **Progné**

Procombant, e, *adj.* procumbent

Proconsul, *s.m.* proconsul

Proconsulaire, *adj.* proconsular

Proconsulat, *s.m.* proconsulate; proconsulship

Procréa-teur, trice, *adj.* procreative, pro-

Procréation, *s.f.* procreation [creating

Procréer, *v.a.* to procreate, to beget

Proctalgie, *s.f.* (*med.*) proctalgia

Proctite, *s.f.* (*med.*) proctitis

Proctocèle, *s.f.* (*med.*) proctocele, prolapsus ani

Proctorrhagie, *s.f.* (*med.*) proctorrhagia

Procurateur, *s.m.* procurator; proxy

Procuratie, *s.f.* procuracy; procurator's palace

Procuration, *s.f.* procuration, power; power of attorney; proxy; (*of convents*) purveyor

Procuratorial, e, *adj.* procuratorial; of the

Procuratrice, *s.f.* proxy [attorney-general

Procure, *s.f.* purveyorship; purveyor's house
Procurer, *v.a.n.* to procure, to obtain, to get
Se —, *v.r.* to procure, to obtain, to get; to raise; to be procured *or* obtained *or* got *or* raised
Procureur, *s.m.* proxy; agent; (*law, obsolete*) attorney, solicitor, proctor; procurator; (*of convents*) purveyor. — *général,* attorney-general. — *de la république,* — *du roi,* — *impérial,* public prosecutor
Procureuse, *s.f.* attorney's wife. — *générale,* &c., attorney-general's wife, &c. (*V.* **Procureur**)
Procyon, *s.m.* (*astr.*) Procyon
Prodataire, *s.m.* (*at Rome*) prodatary
Prodiagnose, *s.f.* (*med.*) prodiagnosis
Prodictateur, *s.m.* prodictator
Prodictature, *s.f.* prodictatorship
Prodigalement, *adv.* prodigally, lavishly; profusely [fusion; extravagance
Prodigalité, *s.f.* prodigality, lavishness; pro-
Prodige, *s.m.* prodigy, wonder; miracle
Prodigieusement, *adv.* prodigiously, wonderfully; a prodigious amount *or* quantity
Prodigieu-x, se, *adj.* prodigious, wonderful; stupendous, amazing; huge, enormous; monstrous
Prodigue, *adj.* prodigal, lavish; profuse; wasteful, extravagant; — *s.m.f.* spendthrift, squanderer, prodigal. *L'enfant —,* the prodigal son [profusely
Prodiguement, *adv.* prodigally, lavishly;
Prodiguer, *v.a.* to lavish, to waste, to throw away, to squander, to be prodigal *or* lavish of; to expose
Se —, *v.r.* to be lavished *or* &c.; to make oneself cheap; to expose oneself; to lavish on each other
Prodigueu-r, se, *s.m.f.* lavisher; squanderer
Prodrome, *s.m.* preface, introduction; preliminaries; forerunner, prodrome; (*med.*) premonitory symptom *or* symptoms; (*of clocks*) warning [symptoms; premonitory
Prodromique, *adj.* (*med.*) of premonitory
Produc-teur, trice, *s.m.f. adj.* producer; producing, productive
Productibilité, *s.f.* producibleness
Productible, *adj.* producible
Producti-f, ve, *adj.* productive
Production, *s.f.* production; exhibition; product; work; performance; proof; growth; law
Productivement, *adv.* productively [papers
Productivité, *s.f.* productiveness, productivity
Produire, *v.a.* to produce; to yield, to bear, to be worth; to cause; to create; to breed; to generate; to bring forth *or* in *or* out, to bring; to put forward; to show; to exhibit; to adduce; to introduce; to make known
Se —, *v.r.* to introduce *or* present *or* show oneself, to put oneself forward, to appear, to introduce oneself to notice; to become known; to go forth; to manifest itself; to occur, to happen, to take place; to come; to be produced *or* &c.
Produit, e, (*part. of* **Produire**) produced, &c.
Produit, *s.m.* produce; product; production; proceeds; yield; gain; result; offspring
Proême, *s.m.* proem, preface, introduction, prelude [ance; projection
Proéminence, *s.f.* prominence; protuber-
Proéminent, e, *adj.* prominent; protuberant;
Proemptose, *s.f.* (*astr.*) proemptosis [projecting
Profana-teur, trice, *s.m.f. adj.* profaner; profaning [pollution
Profanation, *s.f.* profanation; desecration;
Profane, *adj.* profane; secular; unworthy; — *s.m.f.* profane man *or* woman; unlearned person, outsider; unworthy person; black sheep; — *s.m.* profane, profane thing *or* things
Profanement, *adv.* profanely
Profaner, *v.a.* to profane; to desecrate; to
Se —, *v.r.* to be profaned *or* &c. [pollute
Proférer, *v.a.* to utter, to speak, to pronounce
Se —, *v.r.* to be uttered, &c.
Prof-ès, esse, *adj.* (*Cath. rel.*) professed; — *s.m.f.* professed monk *or* nun
Professer, *v.a.n.* to profess; to declare; to teach; to lecture; to be a professor *or* a teacher *or* a lecturer; to practise, to exercise
Se —, *v.r.* to be professed, &c.
Professeur, *s.m.* professor; teacher, master; lecturer; professional, practiser
Profession, *s.f.* profession; declaration; calling, business, trade, occupation. *De —,* by profession, by trade; professed; professedly; professional; professionally
Professionnel, le, *adj.* professional
Professo (Ex), *adv.* ex professo, learnedly
Professoral, e, *adj.* professorial
Professorat, *s.m.* professorship; professoriat; teaching; lectureship
Profil, *s.m.* profile, side-front, side-face, side-view; section; outline. *De —,* in profile, sideways [in profile; to show the outline of
Profiler, *v.a.* to profile; to represent *or* show
Se —, *v.r.* to appear *or* be seen in profile; to show its outline, to stand out
Profilure, *s.f.* outline thread
Profit, *s.m.* profit; gain; benefit, advantage; behalf; improvement, progress; good use, use. *Au — de,* for the benefit of; in aid of, in support of; (*com.*) in behalf of. *Faire du —,* to be profitable; to go far. *Faire son — de,* to make the best of, to profit by, to avail oneself of. *Mettre à —,* to profit by, to avail oneself of, to
Profitable, *adj.* profitable [turn to account
Profitablement, *adv.* profitably
Profitant, e, *adj.* that wears well, that goes far
Profiter, *v.n.* to profit (by); to gain; to benefit; to improve; to avail oneself (of); to make the best (of); to bring a profit; to be profitable, to be of use *or* service; to go far; to grow well, to thrive
Profiterole, *s.f.* hearth-cake, gridiron-cake
Profond, e, *adj.* deep; profound; great, considerable; wide, vast, extensive; sound; low; downright, consummate; dark. *Peu —,* of little depth; shallow [ditch, hole, hollow
Profond, *s.m.* depth; profound, abyss; (*pop.*)
Profondément, *adv.* deeply; profoundly; greatly; widely; deep; low; soundly, fast; very low [tion; extent
Profondeur, *s.f.* depth; profundity; penetra-
Profundis (De), *adv. s.m.* de profundis
Profus, e, *adj.* profuse
Profusément, *adv.* profusely [in profusion
Profusion, *s.f.* profusion, profuseness. *A —,*
Progéniture, *s.f.* progeny, offspring [low
†**Progné,** *s.f.* (*myth.*) Procne; (*poet.*) the swal-
Prognose, *s.f.* (*med.*) prognosis
Prognostique, *adj.* (*med.*) prognostic
Programme, *s.m.* programme; bill; list; syllabus
Progrès, *s.m.* progress; course; advancement; improvement; furtherance; proficiency; rise [gress, to improve
Progresser, *v.n.* to progress, to make pro-
Progressi-f, ve, *adj.* progressive
Progression, *s.f.* progression [ism, liberalism
Progressisme, *s.m.* progressism, progression-
Progressiste, *s.m.f. adj.* progressist, progressionist, liberal
Progressivement, *adv.* progressively, by
Prohiber, *v.a.* to prohibit, to forbid [degrees
Prohibeu-r, se, *s.m.f.* prohibiter
Prohibiti-f, ve, *adj.* prohibitive, prohibitory
Prohibition, *s.f.* prohibition
Prohibitioniste, *s.m.f.* prohibitionist
Prohibitivement, *adv.* prohibitively
Proie, *s.f.* prey; prize; booty. *En — à,* a prey to
Projecti-f, ve, *adj.* projective [missile
Projectile, *adj.* projectile; — *s.m.* projectile,
Projection, *s.f.* projection
Projecture, *s.f.* projecture, projection
Projet, *s.m.* project; design, scheme, plan, idea; view, contemplation; rough draught, sketch, design. — *de loi,* (*parl.*) bill

Projeter, *v.a.n.* to project; to scheme; to plan; to intend; to contemplate to make projects [stand out

Se —, *v.r.* to be projected; to project, to

Projeteu-r, se, *s.m.f.* projector schemer

Projettement, *s.m.* projecting, scheming

Prolapsus, *s.m.* (*surg.*) prolapsus

Prolation, *s.f.* (*gram.*) utterance, prolation; (*mus.*) prolation

Prolégomènes, *s.m.pl.* prolegomena

Prolepse, *s.f.* (*rhet.*) prolepsis [leptical

Proleptique, *adj.* (*rhet., med.*) proleptic, pro-

Prolétaire, *s.m.* proletary, poorest of the poor; — *adj.* proletarian [pauperism

Prolétariat, *s.m.* proletariat, proletarianism,

Prolifère, *adj.* proliferous

Prolifique, *adj.* prolific

Prolixe, *adj.* prolix; diffuse

Prolixement, *adv.* prolixly; diffusely

Prolixité, *s.f.* prolixity, prolixness

Prologue, *s.m.* prologue [delay

Prolongation, *s.f.* prolongation; protraction;

Prolonge, *s.f.* (*mil.*) prolonge, binding-rope; artillery-park waggon

Prolongé, e, *part. adj.* prolonged, &c. (*V.* **Prolonger**); elongated; long [tion, extension

Prolongement, *s.m.* prolongation, continua-

Prolonger, *v.a.* to prolong; to lengthen; to continue; to extend; to protract; to draw out; to spin out; to put off; (*nav.*) to bring alongside; to sail along

Se —, *v.r.* to be prolonged, &c.; to extend; to extend o.'s army *or* troops

Promenade, *s.f.* airing; turn-out; turn; walking out *or* about, walking; walk; riding out *or* about, riding; ride; driving out *or* about, driving; drive; excursion, pleasure-trip, pleasure; procession; promenade; promenading. — *à cheval*, riding; ride. — *en bateau*, boating; sail; row. — *à pied*, walking; walk. — *en voiture*, driving, riding; drive, ride. — *à la voile*, sail, cruise. *Bateau* or *canot de —*, pleasure-boat

Promener, *v.a.* to take out; to take *or* lead *or* carry about; to draw about; to parade; to move about; to move; to turn about; to turn; to take for an airing *or* a walk *or* &c. (*V.* **Promenade**); to drive about, to drive; to indulge; to amuse; to humbug, to bamboozle

Se —, *v.r.* to go *or* walk out *or* about; to walk; to take a walk; to walk leisurely; to go for a walk; to ride, to take a ride; to drive out, to take a drive; to take an airing *or* a turn *or* an excursion; to ramble, to wander; to make a procession; to sail about; to cruise; to promenade. *Se — à cheval*, to ride, to ride on horseback, to take a ride. *Se — à pied*, to walk, to take a walk. *Se — en voiture*, to drive out, to ride, to take a drive *or* a ride. *Aller se —*, to go out for a walk *or* &c. (*V.* **Promenade**). *Allez vous —*, go out for a walk *or* &c.; go out; go about your business, go to Bath. *Emmener* or *mener* or *faire —*, to take out for a walk *or* &c. (*V.* **Promenade**); to take about. *Envoyer —*, to send out for a walk *or* &c.; to send away *or* about o.'s business, to send packing; to throw *or* kick overboard. *Venir se —*, to come for a walk *or* &c. *En se promenant*, while walking *or* &c. about; quietly, slowly, leisurely

Promeneu-r, se, *s.m.f.* walker, pedestrian; rider; person taking a drive, person in a carriage; promenader; processionist; person that takes out invalids *or* &c.; bamboozler, humbugging fellow *or* creature, humbug

Promenoir, *s.m.* ambulatory, walk, walking-place, room for walking exercise, gallery; (*of a race-ground*) paddock

Promérops, *s.m.* (*bird*) promerops

Promesse, *s.f.* promise, word; promissory note, note of hand, bond

Promettant, *s.m.* (*law*) promisor, obligor

Prometteu-r, se, *s.m.f.* promiser

Promettre, *v.a.n.* to promise; to be promising; to bid fair; to forebode

Se —, *v.r.* to promise oneself; to resolve, to determine; to intend; to expect, to hope; to promise each other; to be promised

Promis, e, *adj. s.* intended, engaged, promised

Promiscuité, *s.f.* promiscuousness

Promission, *s.f.* promise. *Terre de —*, Land of Promise [(*anat.*) promontorium

Promontoire, *s.m.* promontory, headland;

Promo-teur, trice, *s.m.f.* promoter; — *adj.* promoting, promotive

Promotion, *s.f.* promotion; preferment

Promouvoir, *v.a.* to promote; to raise; to prefer

Prompt, e, *adj.* prompt, quick, speedy; rapid, swift; active; ready; willing; sudden; hasty; passionate

Promptement, *adv.* promptly, quickly, speedily, fast; rapidly, swiftly; actively; readily; willingly; suddenly; hastily; passionately

Promptitude, *s.f.* promptitude, promptness, quickness, speed; rapidity, swiftness; activity; readiness; willingness; suddenness; hastiness; hasty fit [handbook

Promptuaire, *s.m.* promptuary, summary,

Promu, e, *part. adj* promoted; — *s.m.f.* ditto

Promulgateur, *s.m.* promulgator [person

Promulgation, *s.f.* promulgation

Promulguer, *v.a.* to promulgate. *Se —*, to be promulgated

Pronaos, *s.m.* (*anc. arch.*) pronaos

Pronateur, *adj.m., s.m.* (*anat.*) pronator

Pronation, *s.f.* pronation

Prône, *s.m.* sermon; lecture, jobation

Prôner, *v.a.n.* to preach; to praise *or* cry up, to extol; to lecture [preacher; talker

Prôneu-r, se, *s.m.f.* praiser, extoller; lecturer,

Pronom, *s.m.* pronoun

Pronominal, e, *adj.* pronominal

Pronominalement, *adv.* pronominally

Prononçable, *adj.* pronounceable, utterable

Prononcé, e, *part. adj.* pronounced, &c. (*V.* **Prononcer**); marked, strongly marked; decided; decisive; prominent; broad. *Fortement —*, strongly marked, strong; very decided *or* decisive; very prominent; harsh; very broad, broad

Prononcé, *s.m.* (*law*) terms; pronouncing, delivering, giving; sentence, judgment, decree

Prononcement, *s.m.* pronouncing

Prononcer, *v.a.n.* to pronounce; to utter; to say; to speak; to deliver; to pass, to give; to adjudicate; to declare; to proclaim; to decide with authority, to decide; to bid, to order; to mark; to set off; to show; to find (*a verdict*)

Se —, *v.r.* to declare oneself; to speak out; to show o.'s intentions; to give o.'s opinion; to decide; to be pronounced *or* &c.; to be marked; to become evident

Prononceur, *s.m.* pronouncer

Prononciation, *s.f.* pronunciation; pronouncing; utterance; delivering; delivery; giving

Pronostic, *s.m.* prognostic; (*med.*) prognostic; prognosis [tor; — *adj.* prognosticating

Pronostica-teur, trice, *s.m.f.* prognostica-

Pronostication, *s.f.* prognostication

Pronostique, *adj.* prognostic

Pronostiquer, *v.a.* to prognosticate

Pronostiqueu-r, se, *s.m.f.* prognosticator; — *adj.* prognosticating

Pronunciamento, *s.m.* (*Spanish*) pronunciamento, pronunciamiento

Propagande, *s.f.* propaganda

Propagand-isme, -iste. *V.* page 3, § 1

Propaga-teur, trice, *s.m.f. adj.* propagator, spreader; propagating, spreading

Propagation, *s.f.* propagation; diffusion, spreading, spread

Propager, *v.a.,* **Se —,** *v.r.* to propagate; to diffuse; to spread; to extend; to be propagated

Propagule, *s.m.* (*bot.*) propagulum

Propension, *s.f.* propensity, propension, inclination, disposition, tendency

Prophète, *s.m.* prophet

Prophétesse, *s.f.* prophetess

Prophétie, *s.f.* prophecy; prophesying [3, § 1

Prophét-ique, -iquement, -isme. *V.* page

Prophétiser, *v.a.n.* to prophesy, to foretell

Se —, *v.r.* to foretell *or* &c. to oneself *or* to each other; to be foretold *or* &c.

Prophylactère, *s.m.* phylactery

Prophylactique, *adj.m.f., s.m.* (*med.*) prophylactic; — *s.f.* (*med.*) prophylaxis

Prophylaxie, *s.f.* (*med.*) prophylaxis

Propice, *adj.* propitious, favourable; kind

Propicement, *adv.* propitiously, favourably

Propionate, *s.m.* (*chem.*) propionate

Propionique, *adj.* (*chem.*) propionic

Propitia-teur, trice, *s.m.f.* propitiator; — *adj.* propitiating

Propitiation, *s.f.* propitiation

Propitiatoire, *adj.m.f., s.m.* propitiatory

Propitier, *v.a.* to propitiate

Propolis, *s.f.* (*of bees*) propolis, bee-glue

Proportion, *s.f.* proportion; ratio; due share; suitableness. — *gardée, à* or *en* —, in proportion [portionateness

Proportionnalité, *s.f.* proportionality, pro-

Proportionné, e, *part. adj.* proportioned; proportionate; commensurate; suited

Proportionnel, le, *adj.*, **Proportionnelle,** *s.f.* proportional [proportionately

Proportionnellement, *adv.* proportionally,

Proportionnément, *adv.* proportionately, in proportion [to fit; to adjust; to adapt

Proportionner, *v.a.* to proportion; to suit;

Propos, *s.m.* talk; speech, discourse; conversation; words; observation, remark, remarks; insinuation; gossip, tattle; idle talk; design, purpose; resolution; subject, matter. — *interrompus,* cross purposes; desultory talk. *A* —, to the purpose, to the point; proper; properly; apt; aptly; fit, expedient; pertinent; pertinently; apposite; appositely; appropriate; appropriately; opportune, seasonable; timely; opportunely, seasonably, in good time, at the proper *or* right time. *A-* —, (*subst.*) propriety; fitness, expediency; pertinence; appositeness; appropriateness; seasonableness; opportunity; timeliness; design; hit. *A —!* by the bye! talking of that; now I think of it. *A — de,* with regard to, about, in connection with, speaking *or* talking *or* thinking of. *A ce* —, with regard to this, on this matter, upon this; in connection with this. *A tout* —, on every occasion, at every turn, constantly. *A — de quoi? à quel —?* about what? on what account? on what grounds? for what reason? why? *A — de rien* or *de bottes,* about *or* for nothing at all; without any cause *or* reason; not at all to the purpose, without any reference to the subject; without rhyme or reason. *De — délibéré,* purposely, deliberately, on *or* of set purpose. *Hors de* —, not to the purpose, not to the point; irrelevant; irrelevantly; improper; improperly; impertinent; impertinently; out of season, unseasonable, unseasonably; out of its place; without any cause. *Mal à* —, ill-timed; unseasonable; unseasonably; wrongly; badly. *Juger à* —, to deem it expedient, to think proper. *Il est à — de,* it is expedient *or* necessary to [suitable

Proposable, *adj.* proposable, fit to be proposed,

Proposant, e, *s.m.f.* proposer, propounder; — *s.m.* student in divinity (*among French Protestants*); — *adj.* proposing, propounding

Proposer, *v.a.* to propose; to offer; to proffer; to propound; to put; to express; to state; to move; to bid

Se —, *v.r.* to propose *or* offer oneself (*or* to oneself); to come forward; to have in view, to purpose, to intend; to determine, to resolve; to be proposed *or* &c.

Proposeu-r, se, *s.m.f.* proposer, propounder

Proposition, *s.f.* proposition; proposal; offer; motion; thesis

Propre, *adj.* own; very, same; exact; proper; peculiar; separate; appropriate; calculated; fit, suitable, apt; fitted; qualified; clean; neat, tidy; nice; right, accurate, correct; (*fam.*) in a fine mess *or* plight. *—s termes,* exact *or* own *or* very words. *Termes —s,* proper *or* correct expressions

Propre, *s.m.* characteristic; attribute; property; own *or* separate property; (*gram.*) proper sense; (*Cath. lit.*) particular prayers. *Au* —, (*gram.*) in a proper sense. *En* —, of o.'s own; in o.'s own right. *C'est du —!* nasty thing! a fine thing indeed! [fellow *or* creature

Propre-à-rien, *s.m.f.* (*pop.*) good-for-nothing

Proprement, *adv.* properly; cleanly; neatly; nicely. — *dit,* properly so called

Propret, te, *adj.* neat, tidy, natty, spruce

Propreté, *s.f.* cleanliness, cleanness; neatness,

Propréteur, *s.m.* propretor, proprætor [tidiness

Propréture, *s.f.* propretorship, proprætorship

Propriétaire, *s.m.f.* owner, proprietor, proprietress; holder; landlord, landlady; man of property, gentleman, lady of independent property

Propriétairement, *adv.* proprietorially

Propriété, *s.f.* property; ownership; copyright; estate; homestead; house; landed property; landed interest, landlords; peculiarity; quality; virtue; (*of expressions*) propriety, correctness. *Nue* —, (*law*) property the usufruct of which is in another; reversionary interest; bare *or* naked right

Proprio motu. *V.* **Motu proprio**

Proptome, *s.m.,* **Proptose,** *s.f.* (*med.*) proptoma, proptosis

Propulser, *v.a.* to propel

Propulseur, *s.m.* propeller; — *adj.m.* propelling

Propulsi-f, ve, *adj.* propulsive, propelling

Propulsion, *s.f.* propulsion

Propylée, *s.m.* (*anc. arch.*) propylæum

Propylène, *s.m.* (*chem.*) propylene

Propylique, *adj.* (*chem.*) propylic

§Proquesteur, *s.m.* proquestor, proquæstor

§Proquesture, *s.f.* proquestorship, proquæstorship [in proportion

Prorata, *s.m.* quota, share, proportion. *Au* —,

Prorogati-f, ve, *adj.* prorogative

Prorogation, *s.f.* prorogation; prolongation; continuance; adjournment; delay; putting off

Proroger, *v.a.* to prorogue; to prolong; to continue; to adjourn; to delay; to put off

†Prosailleur, *s.m.* (*jest.*) prose-scribbler

Prosaïque, *adj.* prosaic, unpoetical; prosy; vulgar; cold, dull, tedious; matter-of-fact

Prosaïquement, *adv.* prosaically, unpoetically; prosily; vulgarly; coldly, dully, tediously

Prosaïser, *v.a.n.* to prosaize, to prose, to vulgarize [vulgar

Se —, *v.r.* to become prosaic *or* prosy *or*

Prosaïsme, *s.m.* prosaism, prosaicism, prosaicalness, prosaic form; prosiness; vulgarity; coldness, dulness

Prosateur, *s.m.* prose-writer

Proscénium, *s.m.* (*in anc. theatres*) proscenium

Proscripteur, *s.m.* proscriber; banisher

Proscription, *s.f.* proscription; outlawry; banishment; rejection, abolition, doing away (with)

Proscrire, *v.a.* to proscribe; to outlaw; to banish, to exile; to forbid; to reject, to explode, to abolish, to do away with; to destroy

Se —, *v.r.* to proscribe *or* &c. each other; to be proscribed *or* &c.

Proscrit, e, *part. adj.* proscribed, &c. (*V.* **Proscrire**); outcast; obsolete, exploded; — *s.m.f.* outlaw; exile, refugee; outcast; fugitive, runaway [sequence

Prose, *s.f.* prose; (*Cath. lit.*) prose hymn, prose,

Prosecteur, *s.m.* (*pers.*) prosector

Prosélyte, *s.m.f.* proselyte, convert

Prosélyt-ique, -isme. *V.* page 3, § 1
Proser, *v.a.n.* to prose
Proserpine, *s.f.* (*myth., astr.*) Proserpine
Prosier, *s.m.* (*Cath. rel.*) prose-book [page 3, § 1
Prosod-ie, -ique, -iquement, -iste. *V.*
Prosopopée, *s.f.* (*rhet.*) prosopopœia, personification; (*fam.*) oratorical effusion, great speech
Prospectus, *s.m.* prospectus; bill, hand-bill
Prospère, *adj.* prosperous; favourable [ably
Prospèrement, *adv.* prosperously; favour-
Prospérer, *v.n.* to prosper, to be prosperous, to thrive, to succeed [well-being
Prospérité, *s.f.* prosperity, thriving, success;
Prosphyse, *s.f.* (*bot., med.*) prosphysis
Pross, *s.m.* (*nav.*) proa (*boat*)
Prostate, *s.f.* (*anat.*) prostate, prostate gland
Prostatique, *adj.* (*anat.*) prostatic
Prostatite, *s.f.* (*med.*) prostatitis
Prostatocèle, *s.f.* (*med.*) prostatocele
Prostatorrhée, *s.f.* (*med.*) prostatorrhœa
Prosternation, *s.f.*, **Prosternement,** *s.m.* prostration, obeisance [fallen prostrate
Prosterné, e, *part. adj.* prostrated, prostrate,
Prosterner, *v.a.* to prostrate; to bow
Se —, *v.r.* to prostrate oneself, to fall prostrate, to fall down; to bow o.'s head, to bow, to bend the knee [**Prothèse**
Prosthèse, *s.f.* (*gram.*) prosthesis; (*surg.*) *V.*
Prostibule, *s.m.* house of prostitution, brothel, bawdy house [prostitute
Prostitué, e, *part. adj.* prostituted; — *s.f.*
Prostituer, *v.a.* to prostitute
Prostitu-teur, trice, *s.m.f.* prostitutor. prostitutress; — *adj.* prostituting
Prostitution, *s.f.* prostitution
Prostration, *s.f.* prostration
Prostré, e, *adj.* (*med.*) prostrated
Prostyle, *s.m. adj.* (*anc. arch.*) prostyle
Prosyllog-isme, -istique. *V.* page 3, § 1
Protagon, *s.m.* (*chem.*) protagon [protagonist
Protagoniste, *s.m.* (*theat.*) principal character,
Protase, *s.f.* protasis
Protatique, *adj.* protatic
Prote, *s.m.* (*print.*) overseer; (*in some small printing-offices*) overseer and reader; (*abusively*) reader
Protec-teur, trice, *s. adj.* protector, protectress, patron, patroness; protective; patronizing. *Société —trice des animaux,* Society for the prevention of cruelty to animals
Protection, *s.f.* protection; patronage; interest; support; favour; shelter, cover; protector, patron
Protection-isme, -iste. *V.* page 3, § 1
Protectoral, e, *adj.* protectoral, protectorial
Protectorat, *s.m.* protectorate, protectorship
Protectorerie, *s.f.* protectorship
Protée, *s.m.* (*myth., and fig. of pers.*) Proteus; (*zool.*) proteus; — *s.f.* (*bot.*) protea
Protéen, ne, *adj.* Protean
Protégé, e, *part. adj.* protected, &c. (*V.* **Protéger**); — *s.m.f.* person patronized, favourite, creature, dependent, protégé, protégée
Protéger, *v.a.* to protect; to shield, to shelter; to support; to countenance; to favour; to patronize; to keep
Protéiforme, *adj.* proteiform
Protéine, *s.f.* (*chem.*) proteine
Protèle, *s.m.* (*zool.*) proteles, aard-wolf [room
Proterie, *s.f.* (*print.*) overseership; overseer's
Protestant, e, *adj. s.* protestant
Protestantisme, *s.m.* protestantism
Protestation, *s.f.* protestation; protest
Protester, *v.a.n.* to protest. *Faire —,* to protest. *Se —,* to be protested
Protêt, *s.m.* (*com.*) protest
Prothèse, *s.f.* (*surg.*) prothesis, prosthesis; (*Gr. rel.*) prothesis, credence. — *dentaire,* setting of artificial teeth, mechanical dentistry
Prothétique, *adj.* (*surg.*) prothetic; artificial
Proto-, (*in compounds, chem.,* &c.) proto-...

Protococcus, *s.m.* (*bot.*) protococcus
Protocole, *s.m.* protocol; formulary
Protogyne, *s.m.* (*min.*) protogine, protogene
Protonotaire, *s.m.* prothonotary, protonotary
Protonotariat, *s.m.* prothonotaryship
Protoplasma, *s.m.* protoplasm
Protoplasmique, *adj.* protoplasmic
Protopope, *s.m.* (*Gr. Church*) protopope
Prototype, *s.m.* prototype; model
Prototypique, *adj.* prototypic, prototypical
Protoxyde, *s.m.* (*chem.*) protoxide
Protoxydé, e, *adj.* (*chem.*) protoxidized
Protrusion, *s.f.* protrusion
Protubérance, *s.f.* protuberance
Protubérant, e, *adj.* protuberant [ian
Protuteur, *s.m.* (*law*) person acting as guard-
Prou, *adv.* (*obsolete*) much; enough
Proue, *s.f.* prow; stem
Prouesse, *s.f.* prowess; valour; feat
Proustite, *s.f.* (*min.*) proustite, light red ru-
Prouvable, *adj.* provable [silver-ore
Prouver, *v.a.* to prove; to verify; to make good; to show, to evince
Se —, *v.r.* to be proved, &c.
Provéditeur, *s.m.* (*in Italy*) proveditore
Provenance, *s.f.* origin, source; place, country; production; growth; goods proceeding *or* coming (from); produce, goods, articles. *En —* proceeding, coming
Provençal, e, *adj. s.m.f.* of Provence, Provençal, native of Provence; — *s.m.* Provençal language, Provençal; — *s.f.* Provençal fashion; (*cook.*) Provençal sauce, sharp sauce
Provençalisme, *s.m.* Provençalism
Provencialiser, *v.n.* to speak Provençal; to speak with a Provençal accent [food
Provende, *s.f.* provender; provisions, victuals,
Provenir, *v.n.* to proceed, to arise, to come, to spring, to accrue [of Provins
Provénisien, ne, *adj. s.* of Provins; native
Proverbe, *s.m.* proverb
Proverbial, e, *adj.* proverbial
Proverbialement, *adv.* proverbially
Proverbialiser, *v.a.* to proverbialize
Provide, *adj.* (*old*) provident
Providence, *s.f.* Providence
Provident, e, *adj.* (*philos.*) provident
Providentiel, le, *adj.* providential
Providentiellement, *adv.* providentially
†Provignage, Provignement, *s.m.* layering (*of vines*); propagation
†Provigner, *v.a.* to layer (*vines*); to increase; — *v.n.* to increase; to multiply
†Provigneur, *s.m.* layerer (*of vines*)
Provin, *s.m.* (*of vines*) layer
Province, *s.f.* province; shire; (*not the capital*) country place, country places, country. *De —,* provincial; country; countrified
Provincial, e, *adj.* provincial; country-like, country; countrified; — *s.m.f.* provincial; country person (*pl.* country persons, country people); (*of convents*) provincial
Provincialat, *s.m.* (*of convents*) provincialship
Provincialisme, *s.m.* provincialism
Proviseur, *s.m.* principal, head-master
Provision, *s.f.* provision; stock, supply, store; stock on hand; hoard; commission. *—s de bouche,* victuals, eatables, food. *—s de guerre et de bouche,* ammunition and provisions. *Par —,* provisionally, in the meantime; (*law*) by proviso
Provisionnel, le, *adj.* provisional
Provisionnellement, *adv.* provisionally
Provisoire, *adj.m.f.* provisional; temporary; provisory; nisi; — *s.m.* provisional state, provisional; temporariness
Provisoirement, *adv.* provisionally; temporarily; in the meantime [ship
Provisorat, *s.m.* principalship, head-master-
Provocant, e, *adj.* provoking, exciting; provocative, of provocation; defiant, of challenge
Provoca-teur, trice, *adj. s.* provoking; pro-

vocative, of provocation; defiant; instigating; provoker; instigator; abetter; aggressor
Provocati-f, ve, *adj.* provocative
Provocation, *s.f.* provocation; instigation; excitement; incitement; abetment; challenge; defiance; inducement [**quer**)
Provoquant, *part.* provoking, &c. (*V.* **Provo-**
Provoquer, *v.a.* to provoke; to excite; to incite; to instigate; to abet; to urge; to challenge; to defy; to promote, to induce; to call forth; to call for; to cause; to produce; to lead
Proxénète, *s.m.* go-between, pander, pimp [to
Proxénétisme, *s.m.* panderism, pimping
Proximité, *s.f.* proximity; vicinity; nearness; near relationship. *A — de*, in the vicinity of, within a short distance of, near [ing
Proyer, *s.m.* (*bird*) common bunting, corn-bunt-
Prozoïque, *adj.* prozoic
Prrr, *int.* not a bit of it! not I! fish for it! don't you wish you may get it! ay, indeed!
Pruce, *s.f.* spruce-beer
Prude, *adj.m.f.* prudish; — *s.f.* prude
Prudemment, *adv.* prudently; discreetly; wisely; cautiously [caution, cautiousness
Prudence, *s.f.* prudence; discretion; wisdom;
Prudent, e, *adj.* prudent; discreet; wise;
Pruderie, *s.f.* prudery [cautious; safe
Prud'homie, *s.f.* (*old*) probity, honesty; prudence, wisdom
Prud'homme, *s.m.* (*old sense*) honest man, man of honour, good and true man; (*modern senses*) skilful man, expert; umpire, arbitrator; (*jest.*) fool, goose, silly Billy
Pruine, *s.f.* (*of fruit*) bloom
Prune, *s.f.* plum; (*pop.*) bullet, shot. — *de Monsieur*, Orleans plum; (*dyeing*) cudbear, violet colour. *Pour des —s*, for nothing
Pruneau, *s.m.* prune, dried plum, French plum; (*jest.*) dark and shrivelled face, person with ditto; (*pop.*) bullet, shot; (*pop.*) peeper (*eye*). — *cuit*, stewed prune. *Faire cuire des —x*, to stew prunes
Prunelaie, *s.f.* plum-orchard
Prunelet, *s.m.* sloe-wine
Prunelle, *s.f.* pupil, apple, eyeball; (*bot.*) sloe; self-heal, prunella; (*stuff*) prunella, prunello. *Sel de —*, (*chem.*) prunella salt. *Jouer de la —*, to turn up o.'s eyeballs; to ogle, to leer
Prunellier, *s.m.* sloe-tree, blackthorn
Prunier, *s.m.* plum-tree
Prurigineu-x, se, *adj.* (*med.*) pruriginous
Prurigo, *s.m.* (*med.*) prurigo
Prurit, *s.m.* (*med.*) pruritus, pruriency, pruriencee, itching; tickling
Prusse, *s.f.* spruce-beer; (*La —*) Prussia. *De —*, of *or* from Prussia; Prussian. *Pour le roi de —*, to no purpose, uselessly, in vain, for nothing, for a dead horse
Prussianiser, *v.a.* to prussianize
  Se —, *v.r.* to become *or* be prussianized, to become Prussian
Prussiate, *s.m.* (*chem.*) prussiate
Prussien, ne, *adj. s.m.f.* Prussian; — *s.m.* tumbler (*toy*); —**ne,** *s.f.* Prussian fashion. *Cheminée à la —ne*, open-fire stove
Prussique, *adj.* (*chem.*) prussic
Prussophobe, *adj. s.m.f.* prussophobic; person affected with prussophobia, prussophobist, prussophobiac
Prussophobie, *s.f.* prussophobia
Prussophobique, *adj.* prussophobic
Prytane, *s.m.* (*Gr. antiq.*) prytanis (*pl.* prytanes)
Prytanée, *s.m.* prytaneum, prytanæum
Prytanie, *s.f.* prytany
Psalm-ique, -iste, -istique. . page 3, § 1
Psalmodie, *s.f.* psalmody; singsong; humdrum style [sing; to drone out, to drone
Psalmodier, *v.n.a.* to chant *or* sing psalms; to
Psalmod-ique, -iste. *V.* page 3, § 1
Psalmographe, *s.m.* psalmographer
Psalmographie, *s.f.* psalmography
Psaltérion, *s.m.* (*mus. instr.*) psaltery
Psammite, *s.m* (*min.*) psammite
Psaume, *s.m.* psalm
Psautier, *s.m.* psalter; psalm-book; (*nun's*) veil
Pseudo, (*in compounds*) pseudo, false, counterfeit, feigned, spurious, fictitious, mock, imitation
Pseudonyme, *adj.* pseudonymous, under a false *or* feigned *or* fictitious *or* assumed name; — *s.m.* pseudonym, false *or* feigned *or* fictitious *or* assumed name, nom de plume; alias; writer under ditto; pseudonymousness,pseudonymous
Pseudonymement, *adv.* pseudonymously
Pseudonymie, *s.f.* pseudonymousness
Pseudoscope, *s.m.* pseudoscope
Psilomélane, *s.m.* (*min.*) psilomelane
Psit, Psitt, *int.* hi! hey! halloo! here! **hush!** in a second, suddenly, pop!
Psittacisme, *s.m.* psittacism, parrotry
Psittacule, *s.m.* (*zool.*) love-bird
Psoas, *s.m.* (*anat.*) psoas muscle
Psoïte, *s.f.*, **Psoïtis,** *s.m.* (*med.*) psoitis [watch
Psoque, *s.m.* (*insect*) psocus, wood-fretter, death-
Psora, *s.m.*, **Psore,** *s.f.* (*med.*) psora, itch
Psoralier, *s.m.* (*bot.*) psoralea
Psoriasis, *s.m.* (*med.*) psoriasis
Psorique, *adj.* (*med.*) psoric, itchy
Psorophthalmie, *s.f.* (*med.*) psorophthalmia
Ps't, *int. V.* **Psit** [psychagogical
‡**Psychagogique,** *adj.* (*med.*) psychagogic,
Psyché, *s.f.* cheval-glass; (*myth., astr.*) Psyche
Psychiatre, *s.m.* psychiater
Psychiatrie, *s.f.* psychiatry
Psychique, *adj.* psychic, psychical
‡**Psycholog-ie, -ique, -iquement, -iste.**
‡**Psychologue,** *s.m.* psychologist [*V.* p. 3, § 1
‡**Psychoman-cie, -tique.** *V.* page 3, § 1
‡**Psychomancien, ne,** *s.m.f.* psychomancer
‡**Psychophysique,** *adj.* psychophysical; — *s.f.* psychophysics
‡**Psychose,** *s.f.* (*med.*) psychosis
‡**Psychromètre,** *s.m.* (*phys.*) psychrometer
‡**Psychrométr-ie, -ique.** *V.* page 3, § 1
Psylle, *s.m.* snake-charmer; — *s.f.* plant-louse
Psyllion, *s.m.* (*bot.*) fleawort
Ptarmigan, *s.m.* (*bird*) ptarmigan
Ptarmique, *adj.m.f., s.m.* (*med.*) ptarmic; —
Ptélée, *s.f.* (*bot.*) ptelea [*s.f.* (*bot.*) sneezewort
Ptéride, *s.f.* (*bot.*) pteris, brake [pterocarpus
Ptérocarpe, *adj.* (*bot.*) pterocarpous; — *s.m.*
Ptérocère, *s.m.* (*mollusc*) scorpion-shell
Ptérodactyle, *s.m.* (*fossil*) pterodactyl
Ptéromys, *s.m.* (*zool.*) pteromys, flying squirrel
Ptérope, *s.m.* (*bat*) pteropus, kalong, flying fox
Ptérophore, *s.m.* (*zool.*) pterophorus, plumed moth [pteropod
Ptéropode, *adj.* (*zool.*) pteropodous; — *s.m.*
Ptérygion, *s.m.* (*med.*) pterygium
Ptérygoïde, *adj.* (*anat.*) pterygoid
Ptiloride, *s.m.* (*zool.*) rifle-bird [eyelashes
Ptilose, *s.f.* (*med.*) ptilosis, falling off of the
Ptoléméen, ne, *adj.* Ptolemaic
Ptose, *s.f.* (*med.*) ptosis, drooping *or* falling of the upper eyelid [ptyalagogic
Ptyalagogue, *s.m.* (*med.*) ptyalagogue; — *adj.*
Ptyaline, *s.f.* (*chem.*) ptyaline
Ptyalisme, *s.m.* (*med.*) ptyalism, salivation
Pu, e, (*part. of* **Pouvoir**) been able, &c.; (*part. of* **Paître**) grazed, &c.
Puamment, *adv.* stinkingly; fulsomely, nastily, shockingly; grossly, impudently; conceitedly
Puant, e, *part. adj.* stinking; fetid; fulsome, disgusting, nasty, beastly, offensive, shocking; mean, paltry; gross, impudent, barefaced; full of conceit, conceited; foppish; — *s.m.f.* stinkard; beast; skunk; conceited beast, conceited ass; fop
Puanteur, *s.f.* stench, stink; offensiveness
Pubère, *adj.* pubescent; of puberty
Puberté, *s.f.* puberty
Pubescence, *s.f.* pubescence
Pubescent, e, *adj.* pubescent

Pubien, ne, *adj.* (*anat.*) pubic
Pubis, *s.m.* (*anat.*) pubis. *Os* —, os pubis, pubic bone, share-bone
Publi-c, que, *adj.* public; general; common; notorious; national (*debt*); public (*funds*), government (*securities*); (*of men*) public; (*of women*) disorderly, of the town, of bad character; (*of houses*) of ill fame; — *s.m.* public
Publicain, *s.m.* (*in antiquity*) publican; (*fig.*) extortioner [publishing
Publica-teur, trice, *s.m.f.* publisher; — *adj.*
Publication, *s.f.* publication; publishing; proclamation [journalist
Publiciste, *s.m.* publicist; political writer;
Publicité, *s.f.* publicity; publicness; notoriety; advertising; advertisements
Publier, *v.a.* to publish; to make known; to proclaim; to declare; to announce; to give out; to trumpet; to bring out; to issue
Se —, *v.r.* to be publishing; to be published *or* &c.; to proclaim *or* &c. oneself
Publieur, *s.m.* publisher
Publiquement, *adv.* publicly; openly [mildew
Puccinie, *s.f.* (*bot., agr.*) puccinia, corn-mildew,
Puce, *s.f.* flea; — *s.m.* puce colour, puce; — *adj.* puce-coloured, puce. *La — à l'oreille*, a flea in o.'s ear
Puceau, *s.m.* man who has been wise enough to leave women alone, unpolluted *or* chaste man; (*sneering slang*) simpleton, spoony
Pucelage, *s.m.* maidenhead; virginity; cowry; periwinkle (*bot.*)
Pucelle, *s.f.* maid, maiden; virgin; (*fish*) twaite shad. *Les doctes —s*, (*old poet.*) the Muses
Puceron, *s.m.* plant-louse, vine-fretter, aphis,
Puchot, *s.m.* tornado, hurricane [puceron
Pucier, *s.m.*, **Pucière,** *s.f.* (*bot.*) fleawort
Pudding, *s.m.* pudding
Puddlage, *s.m.* (*metal.*) puddling
Puddler, *v.a.* (*metal.*) to puddle
Puddleur, *s.m.* (*metal.*) puddler
Pudeur, *s.f.* modesty, decency, shame; bashfulness; discretion; reserve
Pudibond, e, *adj.* modest, bashful
Pudibondage, *s.m.*, **Pudibonderie,** *s.f.* modesty; bashfulness
Pudicité, *s.f.* pudicity, chastity, modesty
Pudique, *adj.* chaste, modest, pure
Pudiquement, *adv.* chastely
Puer, *v.n.a.* to stink; to stink of; to smell very strong of; to be most offensive; to be full of conceit; to be a downright fop [ish, girlish
Puéril, e, *adj.* puerile, childish, juvenile, boy-
Puérilement, *adv.* childishly
Puérilité, *s.f.* puerility, childishness
Puerpéral, e, *adj.* (*med.*) puerperal
Puff, *s.m.* puff, puffery, &c. (*V.* **Pouf**)
Puffin, *s.m.* (*bird*) puffin petrel, shearwater
Puffiste, *s.m.f.* puffer; — *adj.* puffing
Pugilat, *s.m.* pugilism, boxing
Pugiliste, *s.m.* pugilist, boxer [combativeness
Pugnacité, *s.f.* pugnacity, pugnaciousness,
Puine, *s.m.* (*bot.*) gatten-tree
Puîné, e, *adj. s.* younger, junior; younger brother *or* sister, junior
Puis, *adv.* then, afterwards, next; besides; and. — ... *que*, *V.* **Puisque**
Puisage, *s.m.* drawing water, drawing up
Puisard, *s.m.* drain-well, drain; cesspool; sump
Puisatier, *s.m.* well-sinker
Puiselle, *s.f.* *V.* **Puisette**
Puisement, *s.m.* *V.* **Puisage**
Puiser, *v.a.n.* to draw; to fetch; to take; to imbibe; to let in; (*nav.*) to leak
Se —, *v.r.* to be drawn, &c.
Puisette, *s.f.* (*tech.*) ladle, scoop; tallow-ladle; (*fish.*) *V.* **Épuisette**
Puiseur, *s.m.* (*pers.*) drawer
Puisoir, *s.m.* (*tech.*) ladle [as
Puisque, *conj.* since, as, seeing that, inasmuch
Puissamment, *adv.* powerfully; mightily; forcibly; extremely, greatly, very; capitally
Puissance, *s.f.* power; dominion; authority; control; might; force; strength; ability; faculty; virtue, property; influence; horse-power; influential man, great personage, magnate
Puissant, e, *adj.* powerful; mighty; forcible; strong; influential; very rich; lusty, stout, big, corpulent; — *s.m.* influential man, great personage, magnate [**Pouvoir,** *v.a.n.*
Puissé-je, Puissiez-vous, &c. *V. end of*
Puits, *s.m.* well; (*mining*) pit, shaft. — *d'abondance*, (*fig.*) inexhaustible fountain. — *d'écoulement*, well-drain. — *perdu*, drain-well, blind well. — *de science*, man of deep learning
Pujal, *s.m.* (*local*) baulk (*of timber*)
Pulicaire, *adj.* pulicene, pulicose; — *s.f.* (*bot.*) pulicaria, fleabane
Pulk, *s.m.* (*of Cossacks*) pulk (*body, regiment*)
Pullulation, *s.f.* multiplication; swarming
Pulluler, *v.n.* to multiply; to swarm; to spread
Pulmonaire, *adj.* (*anat., med.*) pulmonary; — *s.f.* (*bot.*) pulmonary, lungwort, Jerusalem cowslip; — *s.m.* (*zool.*) pulmonary [monate
Pulmoné, e, *adj.*, **Pulmoné,** *s.m.* (*zool.*) pul-
Pulmonie, *s.f.* diseases of the lungs, pulmonary consumption, pneumonia
Pulmonique, *adj. s.m.f.* (*med.*) pulmonic
Pulpation, *s.f.* pulpation, pulping
Pulpe, *s.f.* pulp; pap; (*anat.*) substance
Pulper, *v.a.* to pulp, to reduce to pulp
Pulpeu-x, se, *adj.* pulpous, pulpy
Pulque, *s.f.* pulque (*beverage*)
Pulsa-teur, trice, *adj.* pulsatory, pulsative *Scarabée* —, *V.* **Vrillette**
Pulsati-f, ve, *adj.* pulsative, pulsatory
Pulsatile, *adj.* pulsatile; throbbing
†Pulsatille, *s.f.* (*bot.*) pasque-flower
Pulsation, *s.f.* pulsation; throbbing; beat
Pulsimètre, *s.m.* pulsimeter, sphygmometer
Pultacé, e, *adj.* pultaceous
Pulvéra-teur, trice, *adj.* pulverulent
Pulvérin, *s.m.* pulverine; pounded gunpowder, priming-powder; priming-horn; spray, mist
Pulvérisable, *adj.* pulverizable
Pulvérisa-teur, trice, *s.m.f.* pulverizer; — *adj.* pulverizing
Pulvérisation, *s.f.* pulverization
Pulvériser, *v.a.* to pulverize; to grind to dust; to pound; to crush; to reduce to atoms
Se —, *v.r.* to become *or* be pulverized, &c.
Pulvériseur, *s.m.* pulverizer
Pulvérulence, *s.f.* pulverulence
Pulvérulent, e, *adj.* pulverulent
Puma, *s.m.* puma, cougar, American lion
Pumiciforme, *adj.* pumiciform, pumiceous
Pumicin, *s.m.* palm-oil
Pumicite, Pumite, *s.f.* (*min.*) pumice
Punais, e, *adj.* stinking, frowzy; (*med.*) affect-
Punaise, *s.f.* bug; b-flat [ed with ozæna
Punaisie, *s.f.* stink, stench; (*med.*) ozæna
Punaisière, *s.f.* buggy place, place full of
Punch, *s.m.* punch (*beverage*) [bugs
Puncture, *s.f.* (*in compounds*) puncture
Pungo, *s.m.* *V.* **Pongo**
Punicine, *s.f.* (*chem.*) punicine
Punique, *adj.* Punic
Punir, *v.a.* to punish; to avenge
Punissable, *adj.* punishable
Punisseur, *s.m.* punisher, avenger; — *adj.m.* punishing, avenging [(*mil.*) defaulters' book
Punition, *s.f.* punishment. *Registre des —s*,
Pupe, *s.f.* (*zool.*) pupa
Pupillaire, *adj.* pupilary, pupillary [pupilage
Pupillarité, *s.f.* nonage, pupilarity, pupillarity,
Pupille, *s.m.f.* (*pers.*) ward; pupil; — *s.f.* (*anat.*) pupil [stand; book-stand
Pupitre, *s.m.* desk; davenport; music-desk *or*
Pupivore, *adj.* (*zool.*) pupivorous
Puput, *s.m.* (*bird*) hoopoe
Pur, e, *adj.* pure; unmingled, unmixed; unalloyed; entire; genuine, real; true; guiltless, innocent, chaste; spotless; unsullied; clean;

clear; plain; mere, sheer; neat. *A — et à plein*, entirely, fully. *— et simple*, unconditional; unqualified; absolute
Pureau, *s.m.* foot (*of a tile or slate*)
Purée, *s.f.* pulp, sauce, soup; pea-soup; mashed potatoes; &c.
Purement, *adv.* purely; entirely; genuinely; really; truly; clearly; merely, only; honestly. *— et simplement*, unconditionally, without reserve *or* condition; merely
Pureté, *s.f.* purity; pureness; genuineness; innocence; chastity; simplicity
Purette, *s.f.* black sand
Purgati-f, ve, *adj.*, **Purgatif,** *s.m.* purgative
Purgation, *s.f.* purgation, purgative, purge
Purgatoire, *s.m.* purgatory
Purge, *s.f.* purge; cleansing; disinfection; redemption, paying off
Purger, *v.a.* to purge; to expurgate; to clean; to cleanse; to purify; to refine; to clarify; to weed; to rid; to free; to clear; to justify; to redeem, to pay off
Se —, *v.r.* to purge *or* &c. oneself; to take medicine; (*of things*) to be (*or* become) purged *or* &c.
Purifica-teur, trice, *s.m.f.* purificator, purifier; *— adj.* purifying
Purificati-f, ve, *adj.* purificative, purificatory
Purification, *s.f.* purification; purifying; refining; cleansing; Candlemas
Purificatoire, *s.m.* (*Cath. rel.*) purificatory
Purifier, *v.a.* to purify; to refine; to cleanse
Se —, *v.r.* to purify *or* &c. oneself; to be (*or* become) purified, &c.
Puriforme, *adj.* (*med.*) puriform
Purim, *s.m.* Purim (*Jewish feast*)
Purin, *s.m.* patois of Rouen; (*agr.*) ahl, farmyard liquid manure
Puriner, *v.a.* (*agr.*) to apply farmyard liquid manure to
Pur-isme, -iste. *V.* page 3, § 1
Puritain, e, *s.m.f.* puritan; *— adj.* puritan, puritanic, puritanical
Puritanisme, *s.m.* puritanism
Puron, *s.m.* clarified whey
Purot, *s.m.* liquid manure tank
Purpura, *s.m.* (*med.*) purpura
Purpurin, e, *adj.* purplish; ruddy
Purpurine, *s.f.* purple bronze; (*chem.*) purpurine
Purpurique, *adj.* purpuric
Pur-sang, *adj. s.m.f.* thoroughbred; thoroughbred horse *or* mare
Purulence, *s.f.* purulence
Purulent, e, *adj.* purulent
Pus, *s.m.* (*med.*) pus, purulent matter, matter
Puséysme, *s.m.* Puseyism
Puséyste, *s.m.f. adj.* Puseyite
Pusillanime, *adj.* pusillanimous, chicken-hearted, faint-hearted
Pusillanimement, *adv.* pusillanimously
Pusillanimité, *s.f.* pusillanimity; faint-heartedness
Pustulation, *s.f.* pustulation
Pustule, *s.f.* pustule; blotch; blain; pimple; (*bot.*) blister
Pustuleu-x, se, *adj.* pustular, pustulous
Put, *int.* foh! pooh! pish!
Putain, *s.f.* whore, strumpet
Putanisme, *s.m. V.* **Putasserie**
Putasser, *v.n.* to whore
Putasserie, *s.f.* whorishness; whoredom; whoring, wenching
Putassier, *s.m.* whoremaster, whoremonger, wencher
Putassi-er, ère, *adj.* whorish
Putati-f, ve, *adj.* putative, reputed, supposed
Putativement, *adv.* putatively, reputedly
Pute, *s.f.* (*obsolete*) wench, drab, strumpet
Putier, Putiet, *s.m.* (*bot.*) bird-cherry
Putois, *s.m.* polecat, fitchet, fitch, foumart
Putréfacti-f, ve, *adj.* putrefactive
Putréfaction, *s.f.* putrefaction; putrid state
Putréfier, *v.a.*, **Se —,** *v.r.* to putrefy
Putrescence, *s.f.* putrescence
Putrescent, e, *adj.* putrescent
Putrescibilité, *s.f.* putrescibility
Putrescible, *adj.* putrescible, putrefiable
Putride, *adj.* putrid
Putridité, *s.f.* putridity
Putrilage, *s.m.* (*med.*) putrilage
Putrilagineu-x, se, *adj.* (*med.*) putrilaginous
Putrivore, *adj.* (*zool.*) putrivorous
Putt, *int. V.* **Put**
Puy, *s.m.* knoll, hill, peak
Pycnite, *s.f.* (*min.*) pycnite
Pyélite, *s.f.* (*med.*) pyelitis
Pygargue, *s.m.* (*bird*) erne, sea-eagle
Pygmée, *s.m.* pygmy, dwarf
Pygméen, ne, *adj.* pygmean, pygmy
Pyine, *s.f.* (*chem.*) pyine
Pylône, *s.m.* (*anc. arch.*) pylone
Pylore, *s.m.* (*anat.*) pylorus
Pylorique, *adj.* (*anat.*) pyloric
Pyohémie, *s.f.* (*med.*) pyohæmia, pyæmia
Pyophthalmie, *s.f.* (*med.*) pyophthalmia, purulent ophthalmy
Pyracanthe, *s.f.* (*bot.*) pyracanth, evergreen thorn
Pyrale, *s.f.* (*insect*) pyralis. *— des pommes*, codlin-moth
Pyrame, *s.m.* Blenheim dog, Blenheim spaniel, Marlborough dog
Pyramidal, e, *adj.* pyramidal, pyramidical; *— s.f.* (*bot.*) pyramidal bell-flower
Pyramidalement, *adv.* pyramidally, pyramidically
Pyramide, *s.f.* pyramid
Pyramider, *v.n.* to form a pyramid; to taper; to rise like a pyramid; to tower
Pyramidion, *s.m.* pyramidion (*cap of an obelisk*)
Pyramidographie, *s.f.* pyramidography
Pyramidoïde, *s.m.* pyramidoid
Pyrée, *s.m.* fire altar
Pyrélaïne, *s.f.* (*chem.*) pyrelaine
Pyrénaïne, *s.f.* (*chem.*) pyrenaine
Pyrène, *s.m.* (*chem.*) pyrene; *— s.f.* (*bot.*) pyrena
Pyrénéen, ne, *adj.* Pyrenean
Pyrénéite, *s.f.* (*min.*) pyreneite
Pyrèthre, *s.m.* (*bot.*) pyrethrum, pellitory of Spain, feverfew
Pyréthrine, *s.f.* (*chem.*) pyrethrine
Pyrétique, *adj.* (*med.*) pyretic, pyrexial, pyrexical
Pyrétolog-ie, -ique, -iste. *V.* page 3, § 1
Pyrexie, *s.f.* (*med.*) pyrexia
Pyrhéliomètre, *s.m.* (*phys.*) pyrheliometer
Pyridine, *s.f.* (*chem.*) pyridine
Pyriforme, *adj. V.* **Piriforme**
Pyrique, *adj.* pyrotechnic
Pyrite, *s.f.* (*min.*) pyrite, pyrites
Pyriteu-x, se, *adj.* pyritic, pyritous
Pyritifère, *adj.* pyritiferous
Pyritiser, *v.a.* to pyritize
Pyro, (*in compounds*) pyro...
Pyrobalistique, *adj.* pyroballistic; *— s.f.* pyroballistics
Pyrogallique, *adj.* (*chem.*) pyrogallic
Pyrogène, Pyrogéné, e, *adj.* pyrogenous
Pyrolâtre, *adj.* pyrolatrous, fire-worshipping; *— s.m.f.* pyrolater, fire-worshipper
Pyrolâtrie, *s.f.* pyrolatry, fire-worship
Pyrole, *s.f. V.* **Pirole**
†**Pyroligneu-x, se,** *adj.* (*chem.*) pyroligneous
†**Pyrolignite,** *s.m.* (*chem.*) pyrolignite
Pyrolog-ie, -ique, -iste. *V.* page 3, § 1
Pyrolusite, Pyrolysite, *s.f.* (*chem.*) pyrolusite
Pyroman-cie, -tique. *V.* page 3, § 1
Pyromancien, ne, *s.m.f.* pyromancer
Pyromètre, *s.m.* (*phys.*) pyrometer
Pyrométr-ie, -ique. *V.* page 3, § 1
Pyrope, *s.m.* (*min.*) pyrope
Pyrophage, *adj. s.m.f.* fire-eating; fire-eater
Pyrophore, *s.m.* pyrophorus; *— adj.* pyrophorous
Pyrophorique, *adj.* pyrophoric, pyrophorous
Pyropneumatique, *adj.* pyropneumatic
Pyroscaphe, *s.m.* (*scientific slang*) steamboat, steamer
Pyroscope, *s.m.* pyroscope
Pyrose, *s.f.*, **Pyrosis,** *s.m.* (*med.*) pyrosis, waterbrash
Pyrosome, *s.m.* (*mollusc*) pyrosome
Pyrosphère, *s.m.* pyrosphere
‡**Pyrotechnie,** *s.f.* pyrotechnics, pyrotechny
‡**Pyrotechn-ique, -iste.** *V.* page 3, § 1
Pyrotique, *adj.m.f.*, *s.m.* pyrotic
Pyroxène, *s.m.* (*min.*) pyroxene

Pyroxyle, *s.m.*, **Pyroxyline,** *s.f.* pyroxyle, pyroxyline, gun-cotton
Pyroxylique, *adj.* pyroxylic [pyrrhic
Pyrrhique, *adj.m.f.*, (*vers.*) *s.m.*, (*dance*) *s.f.*
Pyrrhonien, ne, *s.m.f.* pyrrhonist; — *adj.*
Pyrrhonisme, *s.m.* pyrrhonism [pyrrhonic
Pyrule, *s.f.* (*shell-fish*) pyrula
Pyruvique, *adj.* (*chem.*) pyruvic
Pythagoricien, ne, *adj. s.*, **Pythagorique,** *adj.* Pythagorean
Pythagoriser, *v.n.* to pythagorize
Pythagor-isme, -iste. *V.* page 3, § 1
Pythiade, *s.f.* pythiad
Pythie, *s.f.* pythia
Pythien, ne, *adj.* Pythian
Pythique, *adj.* Pythian; – *s f.* Pythic (*Pindar's*)
Python, *s.m.* (*zool.*) python, rock-snake, ana-
Pythonisse, *s.f.* pythoness; witch [conda
Pyurie, *s.f.* (*med.*) pyuria
Pyxide, *s.f.* (*bot.*) pyxidium

Q

Q, *s.m.* q
Qu', *contraction of* **Que**
***Quachi,** *s.m.* *V.* **Coati**
***Quadragénaire,** *adj. s.m.f.* quadragenarian
***Quadragésimal, e,** *adj.* quadragesimal
***Quadragésime,** *s.f.* quadragesima; quadragesima Sunday
***Quadrangle,** *s.m.* quadrangle
***Quadrangulaire, Quadrangulé, e,** *adj.* quadrangular, four-angled, four-cornered
***Quadrat, e,** *adj.* quadrate
Quadrat, Quadratin. *V.* **Cadrat, Cadratin**
***Quadrateur,** *s.m.* (*pers.*) squarer (*of the circle*)
***Quadratique,** *adj.* quadratic
***Quadratoriste,** *s.m.* fresco-painter, architectural painter
***Quadratrice,** *s.f.* (*geom.*) quadratrix
***Quadrature,** *s.f.* (*geom., astr.*) quadrature; (*arts*) fresco-painting, architectural painting
Quadrature, *s.f.* (*horol.*) *V.* **Cadrature**
***Quadri,** (*in compounds*) quadri…
***Quadriailé, e,** *adj.* four-winged
***Quadribasique,** *adj.* (*chem.*) quadribasic
***Quadridenté, e,** *adj.* quadridentate
Quadriennal, e, *adj.* *V.* **Quatriennal**
***Quadrifide,** *adj.* (*bot.*) quadrifid
***Quadriflore,** *adj.* (*bot.*) quadriflorate, quadriflorous, four-flowered [leaved
***Quadrifolié, e,** *adj.* (*bot.*) quadrifoliate, four-
***Quadrifoliolé, e,** *adj.* (*bot.*) quadrifoliolate
***Quadrige,** *s.m.* (*Rom. antiq.*) quadriga
***Quadrijugué, e,** *adj.* (*bot.*) quadrijugate
***Quadrijumeaux,** *adj.m.pl.* (*anat.*) *Tubercules* —, tubercula quadrigemina, four double tubercles, nates, testes
***Quadrilatéral, e,** *adj.*, **Quadrilatère,** *adj.m.f., s.m.* quadrilateral
†**Quadrillage,** *s.m.* *V.* **Cadrillage**
†**Quadrille,** *s.m.* quadrille; check, square, lozenge; (*old, and formerly of the feminine gender*) troop of horses for a tournament
†**Quadriller, Quadrilleur.** *V.* **Cadriller,**
***Quadrillion,** *s.m.* thousand billions [&c.
***Quadrilobé, e,** *adj.* quadrilobate, quadrilobed, four-lobed; (*arch.*) four-cusped, quatrefoiled
***Quadriloculaire,** *adj.* (*bot.*) quadrilocular
***Quadrinôme,** *s.m. adj.* (*alg.*) quadrinomial
***Quadriparti, e, Quadripartite,** *adj.* quadripartite
***Quadripartition,** *s.f.* quadripartition
***Quadrirème,** *s.f.* (*anc. nav.*) quadrireme
***Quadrisaïeul, e,** *s.m.f.* ancestor in the fourth degree [quadrisyllabic
***Quadrisyllabe,** *s.m.* quadrisyllable; — *adj.*
***Quadrisyllabique,** *adj.* quadrisyllabic
***Quadrivium,** *s.m.* quadrivium
***Quadrumane,** *s.m.* quadrumane, quadruman, four-handed beast, monkey; — *adj.* quadrumanous, four-handed [ruped
***Quadrupède,** *adj.m.f., s.m.* four-footed; quad-
***Quadruple,** *s.m. adj.* quadruple, fourfold; — *s.m.* double pistole (*Spanish coin worth about* [£3 4*s.*)
***Quadruplement,** *adv.* quadruply
***Quadrupler,** *v.a.n.*, **Se** —, *v.r.* to quadruple, to increase fourfold
***Quadruplication,** *s.f.* quadruplication
Quai, *s.m.* quay; wharf; embankment; (*rail.*) [platform
Quaiage. *V.* **Quayage**
Quaiche, *s.f.* (*nav.*) ketch
***Quaker, Quakre,** *s.m.* quaker
***Quakeresse,** *s.f.* quakeress
***Quakerisme,** *s.m.* quakerism [or term
Qualifiable, *adj.* qualifiable; that one may call
Qualificateur, *s.m.* qualificator
Qualificati-f, ve, *adj.*, **Qualificatif,** *s.m.* qualificative [title, name; character, nature
Qualification, *s.f.* qualification; entitling,
Qualifié, e, *part. adj.* qualified, &c. (*V.* **Qualifier**); titled, noble, of rank; considerable, of note; (*law*) with aggravating circumstances
Qualifier, *v.a.* to qualify; to entitle; to call, to term, to style
Qualitati-f, ve, *adj.* qualitative
Qualité, *s.f.* quality; property; accomplishment; qualification; capacity; title; rank; —**s**, *pl.* qualities, &c.; (o.'s) name, age, and profession. *En — de*, in the capacity of, as. *Avoir — pour*, to be qualified to. *Avoir de la —*, to be of good quality
***Quamoclit,** *s.m.* (*bot.*) quamoclit
Quand, *adv.* when; whenever; what time; what period; what date; at a time when; while, whilst; — *conj.* although, though, even though, even if. — *même*, though, although, even though, even if; even then; notwithstanding; in spite of obstacles; at whatever price; under any (*or* all) circumstances; anyhow; by all means; absolutely; determined; pertinacious; stubborn; uncompromising; systematic; indiscriminate; indiscriminately. — *bien même*, even though, even if. — *je le disais!* *V.* **Dire**
Quant à, *prep.* with regard to, as to, as for, for (my, thy, his, &c.) part. — *à soi*, (*s.m.*) proud reservedness, pride, vanity, self-conceit, conceit. *Se mettre sur son — à soi*, to give oneself airs, to show off. *Tenir son — à soi, se tenir sur son — à soi*, to assume an air of reserve
Quantième, *s.m.* day of the month, day. *Montre à —s*, watch showing the day of the [month
Quantitati-f, ve, *adj.* quantitative
Quantité, *s.f.* quantity; abundance, plenty; deal; multitude; number; lot; many; variety
***Quantum,** *s.m.* quantum; quantity; amount; sum; proportion, share, quota; account, reckoning, bill; money, cash
Quarantaine, *s.f.* forty or so, about forty, some forty, forty; age of forty; fortieth year; (*Cath. rel.*) Lent; (*bot.*) ten-week stock; (*nav.*) quarantine
Quarante, *adj.m.f., s.m.* forty; fortieth. *Les —*, the forty; the (forty) members of the French Academy, the French Academy. *Remettre à l'an —*, to put off till doomsday. *Je m'en moque comme de l'an —*, I don't care a straw about it
Quarantenaire, *adj.* of quarantine, quarantine; (*law*) of forty years; — *s.m.f.* person in quarantine [tribunal of the forty
Quarantie, *s.f.* (*formerly, at Venice*) forty,
Quarantième, *adj. s.* fortieth
Quarantier, *s.m.* (*pop.*) Academician (*one of the forty members of the French Academy*)
Quarderonner, *v.a.* (*build.*) to round off, to quarter-round
Quart, *s.m.* quarter; fourth; quarter-past; (*nav.*) watch; (*nav.*) point of the compass, point; (*cask*) *V.* **Quartaut.** — *d'agent de*

change, shareholder for one fourth in a stock-broker's business. — *d'auteur*, (*theat.*) contributor of one fourth of a play. — *de cercle*, quadrant. -*d'heure*, quarter of an hour; very short duration; moment, time of it; time; present. — -*d'heure de Rabelais*, time to pay at last; trying time; rub. — *de monde*, lower class of fast men and courtesans, low swells, flash society *or* people (*between the* "demi-monde" *and the lowest blackguards*). — *de rond*, quarter-round. — *de vent*, (*nav.*) point of the compass, point. *Trois —s*, three quarters; three fourths; *s.m. V.* **Trois-quarts.** *Les trois —s du temps*, generally, most frequently. ... *et un* —, ... and a quarter; a quarter past ...

Quart, e, *adj.* fourth; (*med.*, *of fever*) quartan

Quartaine, *adj.f.* (*old*, *of fever*) quartan

Quartan, *s.m.* (*of wild boars*) fourth year

Quartanier, *s.m.* four-year old wild boar

Quartation, *s.f.* (*chem.*, *metal.*) quartation

Quartaut, *s.m.* (*quarter of a hogshead*) octave-cask (*of a pipe of wine or of a butt of beer*)

Quarte, *s.f.* (*fenc.*) quarte; (*mus.*) fourth; (*vet.*) wire-heel; (*old meas.*) half-gallon (*two French pints or four English pints*) [quarter of a pound

Quarteron, *s.m.* quarter of a hundred; (*old*)

Quarteron, ne, *s.m.f.* quadroon

***Quartette, Quartetto,** *s.m.* (*mus.*) quartet

***Quartidi,** *s.m.* quartidi (*fourth day of the decade in the calendar of the first French Republic*)

Quartier, *s.m.* quarter; piece; part; block; mass; hunch; (*of bacon*) gammon; (*of saddles*) flap; (*of towns*) ward, district; (*of a large town*) sub-district; (*of any town, &c., loosely speaking*) quarter, part, neighbourhood; (*of schools*) class, form; class-room; hall; ward; (*mil.*) quarter, quarters. *Faire* or *donner* —, to give quarter. — **-général,** *s.m.* head-quarters. — **-maître,** *s.m.* quartermaster [quartile

***Quartil, e,** *adj.m.f.*, **Quartil,** *s.m.* (*astr.*)

***Quarto,** *adv.* fourthly, in the fourth place. **In-** —, *adj. s.m. See Letter* **I**

***Quartz,** *s.m.* (*min.*) quartz [quartzous

***Quartzeu-x, se,** *adj.* quartzy, quartzose,

***Quartzifère,** *adj.* quartziferous

***Quartziforme,** *adj.* quartziform

***Quartzite,** *s.f.* (*min.*) quartzite

***Quas.** *V.* **Kwas**

Quasi, *adv.* (*in compounds*) quasi; (*old*) *V.* **Presque;** — *s.m.* thick end of the loin (*of veal*). — **-délit,** *s.m.* quasi-delict, unintentional offence [&c.; as you would say, as it were

Quasiment, *adv.* (*pop. for* **Presque**) almost,

Quasimodo, *s.f.* Quasimodo, Low Sunday; — *s.m.* (*jest.*) deformed fellow, horrid fellow,

***Quass.** *V.* **Kwas** [monster

***Quassia,** *s.m.* (*pharm.*) quassia

***Quassier,** *s.m.* (*bot.*) quassia [quassite

***Quassine, Quassite,** *s.f.* (*chem.*) quassine,

***Quaternaire,** *adj.* quaternary

Quaterne, *s.m.* series of four numbers, quaternary, quaternion

***Quaterné, e,** *adj.* quaternate

Quatorzaine, *s.f.* (*obsolete*) fortnight

Quatorze, *adj.m.f.*, *s.m.* fourteen; fourteenth

Quatorzième, *adj. s.* fourteenth; fourteenth

Quatorzièmement, *adv.* fourteenthly [day

Quatrain, *s.m.* piece of poetry *or* stanza of four lines, quatrain

Quatre, *adj.m.f.*, *s.m.* four; fourth. — *de* (or *en*) *chiffre*, figure 4; bird-trap. *A* —, with four ...; four together; with great effort. *Comme* —, like four people, like any other four; excessively; lustily; very heartily. — *à* —, four to four; four by four; four abreast; four steps at a time, in great haste; (*in games*) four all. *Se mettre en* —, to do o.'s utmost, to strain every nerve, to go through fire and water. *Se tenir à* —, to make the greatest effort. *Tirer à* —, to draw and quarter. — **-feuilles,** *s.f.* (*arch.*, *her.*) quatrefoil. — **-Temps,** *s.m.pl.* ember-days. — **-vingts,** — **-vingt,** *adj.* eighty, fourscore. — **-vingt-un,** &c. eighty-one, &c. — **-vingt-dix,** *adj.* ninety, fourscore and ten. — **-vingtième,** *adj. s.* eightieth. — **-vingt-dixième,** *adj. s.* ninetieth. — **-vingt-onze,** *adj.* ninety-one, fourscore and eleven. — **-vingt-onzième,** ninety-first. — **-vingt-douze,** &c. ninety-two, &c. — **-neuf,** *adj.* eighty-nine; (*Fr. hist.*) '89 *or* 1789 (*first year of the French Revolution*). — **-treize,** *adj.* ninety-three; (*Fr. hist.*) '93 *or* 1793 (*worst year of the French Revolution*)

Quatrième, *adj.* fourth; — *s.m.* fourth; fourth floor; pupil of the fourth form *or* class; — *s.f.* fourth; fourth form *or* class; (*at piquet*) quart

Quatrièmement, *adv.* fourthly [nial

Quatriennal, e, *adj.* quadrennial, quadrien-

***Quatrillion,** *s.m. V.* **Quadrillion** [centist

***Quattrocentiste,** *s.m.* (*Italian liter.*) quattro-

***Quatuor,** *s.m.* (*mus.*) quartet

***Quatuorvir,** *s.m.* quatuorvir

***Quatuorviral, e,** *adj.* quatuorviral

***Quatuorvirat,** *s.m.* quatuorvirate

Quayage, *s.m.* wharfage, quayage

Que, Qu', *rel. pron.* whom, that; which, that; what; when. *Qu'est-ce que ...?* what is it ...? what ...? what is *or* are ...? *Qu'est-ce qui*, what. *Qu'est-ce que c'est? Qu'est ce?* what is it? what is the matter? how now? what? *Qu'est-ce que c'est que ...?* what is or are ...? — *faire*, what to do. — or *comment faire? V.* **Comment.** — *désirer de plus?* what more can *or* could be desired?

Que, Qu', *conj. adv.* that; as; when; than; than that; how; how much; how many; what; why; till, until; while, whilst; whether; if; may; let; lest, for fear; except, but, unless; before; after; only, nobody but, nothing but; yet, still, notwithstanding; although; without; since; because; in order that.

[*Untranslated sometimes, as: C'est se tromper — de croire*, it is a mistake to believe. *Ce n'est rien — d'avoir fait cela, il faut encore ...*, it is nothing to have done that, we must besides ... *Quel fripon — cet homme-là!* what a rogue that man is! *C'est un digne homme — M. Roy*, a worthy man Mr. Roy is! *Mensonge — tout cela*, that is all a lie. *Le beau pays — la France!* what a fine country France is! *La belle chose — d'être riche!* what a fine thing it is to be rich! *Je sais ce que c'est — d'attendre, ce que c'est — le travail, ce que c'est — les dangers*, I know what it is to wait *or* what waiting is, what work is, what dangers are. *Ce que c'est — la vie!* what a strange *or* &c. thing life is! *Ce que c'est — de nous*, what we are liable to; what wretched creatures we are! oh, for human nature! *Si j'étais — de vous*, if I were you, if I were in your place. *C'est obliger tout le monde — de rendre service à un honnête homme*, rendering an honest man a service is obliging every one. *Voilà ce que c'est* —, *V.* **Être.**]

— *je perde*, that I may *or* should lose; may I lose; let me lose; if I should lose, if I lose. *C'est* —, *V.* **Être.** — *bien* — *mal*, (*obsolete for* "tant bien que mal") *V.* **Tant**

Quel, le, *adj.* what; what a; which; who. — *que*, whatever; whoever

Quelconque, *adj.* whatever, any; (some ..) or other. *D'une façon* or *d'une manière* —, anyhow, in any way whatever [differently, so so

Quellement, *adv. Tellement* —, (*obsolete*) in-

Quelque, *adj.* some; any; a small amount *or* sum of; a few; odd; whatever, what ... soever. — *chose*, (*m.*) something, anything; somebody; some words, a quarrel; some interest *or* value; some relation; (*f.*) whatever. — ... *que ce soit*, any ..., any ... whatever, whatever ... it is

Quelque, *adv.* however; about, some

Quelquefois, *adv.* sometimes, occasionally

Quelqu'un, e, *pron.* somebody, some one, one; anybody, any one, any [few

Quelques-uns, unes, *pron.pl.* some; any; a

Quémander, *v.n.a.* to go begging, to beg; to beg for, to solicit
Quémanderie, *s.f.* begging, solicitation
Quémandeu-r, se, *s.m.f.* beggar, solicitor
Qu'en-dira-t-on, *s.m.* common talk, what people may say, (the) opinion of others
Quenelle, *s.f.* forcemeat-ball [animal)
Quenotte, *s.f.* peggy (*tooth of a child or pet*
†Quenouille, *s.f.* distaff; bed-post, post; pyramid-shaped fruit-tree. *A —s,* (*of bedsteads*) four-post. *Tomber en —,* to fall to the female line, to fall to the petticoat
†Quenouillée, *s.f.* distafful [thistle
†Quenouillette, *s.f.* little distaff; (*bot.*) distaff-
Quérable, *adj.* (*law*) demandable
§Quercine, *s.f.* (*chem.*) quercine
§Quercite, *s.f.* (*chem.*) quercite
Quercitrin, *s.m* (*chem.*) quercitrine
Quercitron, *s.m* quercitron
Querelle, *s.f* quarrel; row; quarrelling; wrangling; the cudgels (for). *— d'Allemand,* groundless *or* trumpery quarrel
Quereller, *v.a.n.,* **Se —,** *v.r.* to quarrel with; to scold; to quarrel; to wrangle
Querelleu-r, se, *adj. s.* quarrelsome; quarreller, wrangler
Quérir, *v.a.* (*old*) *V.* **Chercher** [reller, wrangler
Quésaco, Qu'es-aco, Qu'es-aquo, (*Provençal dialect for* "Qu'est-ce?" "Qu'est-ce à dire?" "Qu'est-ce que cela veut dire?") what is this? what is it? what? how now? what does this *or* that mean?
§Questeur, *s.m.* questor, quæstor
Question, *s.f.* question; interrogation; query; rack, torture; point; issue. *En —,* in question; in hand. *Donner la — à,* to put to the torture, to torture. *Faire une —, des —s,* to ask a question, questions. *Faire —,* to be doubtful (*Cela ne fait pas —,* there is no question *or* doubt about that, that is beyond question). *Mettre à la —,* to put to the torture, to torture. *Mettre en —,* to call in question, to question. *Il est — de,* it is talked of, there is a talk of; it is in contemplation to; the question *or* point is, ... is the question *or* point; ... is mentioned. *De quoi est-il —?* what is the matter? what is on the carpet? what's up?
Questionnaire, *s.m.* book *or* chapter *or* set of questions; examination questions; (*obsolete*) torturer, tormenter [tions
Questionner, *v.a.n.* to question; to ask ques-
Questionneu-r, se, *s.m.f.* questioner; querist; inquirer; — *adj.* inquisitive
§Questure, *s. f.* questorship, quæstorship; questor's office *or* residence
Quête, *s.f.* quest, search; hunt; collection; offertory; gathering; begging; (*nav.*) rake
Quêter, *v.a.n.* to search; to seek out; to seek for, to look out for; to hunt; to solicit, to beg *or* ask for; to beg; to canvass; to collect, to gather; to make a collection
Quêteu-r, se, *s.m.f. adj.* hunter; gatherer, collector, collectress; mendicant (*friar*)
***Quetsche,** *s.f.* (*bot.*) quetsche, mussel-plum. **— -wasser,** *s.m.* quetsche-wasser (*liquor*)
***Quetschier,** *s.m.* quetsche-tree, mussel-plum
Queu, *boorish for* **Quel** [tree
Queue, *s.f.* tail; tail-piece; end; latter end; fag-end; rear; file (*of people at the door of a theatre or &c.*); train; trail; series; handle; (*of buttons,* &c.) shank; (*of flowers and fruits*) stalk, stem; (*billiards*) cue; (*of hair*) tail, pig-tail; (*of documents*) label; cask (*of* $1\frac{1}{2}$ *hogshead*); hone, whetstone, oilstone. *— -de-chat,* (*meteorology*) cirrus, curl-cloud, mare's-tail, cat's-tail. *— de morue,* tail of a cod; (*fig.*) swallow-tail. *— de rat,* rat's tail; small wax taper. *— à —,* one after another. *A —,* tailed; (*of pianos*) grand; (*of letters*) descending. *A la —,* in the rear, behind; in a *or* the file. *A la — leu leu,* one after another. *En —,* in the rear, behind; at o.'s heels. *Faire —,* to stand in file, to stand in a *or* the file; (*fig.*) to flock, to rush; to wait admittance. *Faire la — à,* to take in, to deceive. *Faire fausse —,* (*billiards*) to miss the cue. *Il y a —,* (*fig.*) there is a rush, ... draws *or* has a great run
Queussi-queumi, *adv.* (*old*) just the same
Queuter, *v.n.* (*at billiards*) to strike two balls at once, to strike the two balls together, to make a foul stroke
Queux, *s.m.* hone, whetstone, oilstone; (*obsolete*) cook. *Grand —, maitre —,* head cook
Qui, *pron.* who; whom; which; that; whoever; whomsoever; he who; him who; what; some one; some. *— est-ce —,* who. *— que ce soit,* whoever, whoever it may be, any one; any; nobody, no one; none. *A — est ...?* whose is ...? whose ... is ...? *A — est-ce à ..., à — a ...?* whose turn is it to ...? *C'est à —, C'était à —,* (*see* **A,** *prep.*)
§Quia. *Être à —,* to be nonplussed, to be at a stand *or* at a loss; to be powerless; to be put to o.'s shifts. *Mettre à —,* to nonplus, to pose; to silence; to render powerless; to put to o.'s shifts [perty, wealth
§Quibus, *s.m.* (*slang*) needful, tin, cash; pro-
Quichotte, Quichottisme, (Don-). *V.* **Don-Quichotte,** &c.
Quiconque, *pron.* whoever; whomsoever
Quidam, *s.m.* (*obsolescent*), **Quidane,** *s.f.* (*obsolete*) certain individual *or* person, individual, person, fellow, stranger, some one
§Quiddité, *s.f.* quiddity
§Quiescence, *s.f.* quiescence
§Quiescent, e, *adj.* quiescent
Quiétisme, *s.m.* quietism
Quiétiste, *s.m.f.* quietist; — *adj.* quietistic
Quiétude, *s.f.* quietude
†Quignon, *s.m.* hunch, large piece
Quilboquet, *s.m. V.* **Équilboquet**
†Quillage, *s.m.* (*obsolete*) keelage
†Quille, *s.f.* keel; skittle, ninepin, pin; (*fam.*) shank, stump. *Jeu de —s,* game *or* set of skittles *or* of ninepins; skittle-alley *or* ground. *Recevoir comme un chien dans un jeu de —s,* to give a very bad reception. *Trousser ses —s,* to pack off, to be off
†Quillé, e, *adj.* (*nav.*) keeled [pack off, to be off
†Quiller, *v.n.* (*at skittles*) to throw for partners *or* for first play; — *v.a.* (*pop.*) to aim at, to throw *or* shy stones (*or* &c.) at
†Quillette, *s.f.* (*of osier*) cutting, slip
†Quillier, *s.m.* skittle-alley *or* ground; set of skittles *or* of ninepins, skittles, ninepins
†Quillon, *s.m.* (*of a sword*) cross-bar
Quina, *s.m. V.* **Quinquina**
Quinaire, *adj.* quinary; — *s.m.* quinarius
Quinate, *s.m. V.* **Kinate**
Quinaud, e, *adj.* (*obsolete*) *V.* **Penaud**
Quincajou, *s.m. V.* **Kinkajou**
†Quincaille, *s.f.* ironmongery; hardware; copper coin, coppers; trash; gimcrack
†Quincaillerie, *s.f.* ironmongery; hardware
†Quincaillier, *s.m.* ironmonger; hardwareman
Quinconce, *s.m.* quincunx
Quinconcial, e, *adj.* quincuncial
§Quindécagone, *s.m.* quindecagon; — *adj.* quindecagonal [decimvir, quindecemvir
§Quindécimvir, Quindécemvir, *s.m.* quin-
Quine, *s.m.* series of five numbers; five winning numbers; five prizes; (*at backgammon*) two fives
Quiné, e, *adj.* quinate
Quinétine, *s.f.* (*chem.*) quinetine
Quinicine, *s.f.* (*chem.*) quinicine
Quinidine, *s.f.* (*chem.*) quinidine
Quinine, *s.f.* (*chem.*) quinine
Quinique, *adj.* (*chem., med.*) quinic. *Maladie —,* quininism, cinchonism
Quinoa, *s.m.* (*bot.*) quinoa
Quinoïdine, *s.f.* (*chem.*) quinoidine
Quinola, *s.m.* (*cards*) knave of hearts [narian
§Quin(*)quagénaire, *adj. s.m.f.* quinquage-
§Quin(*)quagésime, *s. f.* quinquagesima, quinquagesima Sunday, Shrove Sunday [degree
§Quin(§)quaïeul, e, *s.m.f.* ancestor in the fifth

§Quin(*)quangulaire, §Quin(*)quangulé, e, *adj.* quinquangular, quinquangulate
§Quin(§)qué, *s.m.* (*obsolete*) *V.* **Quintette** [tate
§Quin(§)quédenté, e, *adj.* (*bot.*) quinqueden-
§Quin(§)quéfide, *adj.* (*bot.*) quinquefid
§Quin(§)quélobé, e, *adj.* quinquelobate, quinquelobed, five-lobed; (*arch.*) five-cusped, cinque-
§Quin(§)quennal, e, *adj.* quinquennial [foiled
§Quin(§)quéparti, e, Quinquépartite, *adj.* quinquepartite
§Quin(§)quérème, *s.f.* (*anc. nav.*) quinquereme
§Quin(§)quésyllabe, *s.m.* quinquesyllable; — *adj.* quinquesyllabic
§Quin(§)quésyllabique, *adj.* quinquesyllabic
Quinquet, *s.m.* Argand lamp, lamp; (*pop.*) peeper (*eye*)
Quinquina, *s.m.* Peruvian bark, bark, quinquina, cinchona-bark, cinchona. *Vin de* —,
Quint, *adj.m.* the fifth [quinine-wine
Quintaine, *s.f.* quintin, quintain
Quintal, *s.m.* hundredweight; stone pitcher. — *métrique*, 50 "kilogrammes," or 110·231 lb. avoirdupois
Quintane, *adj.f.* (*med., of fever*) quintan
Quinte, *s.f.* fit of coughing, fit; whim, freak, crotchet; (*mus.*) fifth; (*mus., obsolete*) alto; (*at piquet*) quint; (*fenc.*) quinte; (*rid.*) dead stop; (*med., obsolete*) *V.* **Quintane.** *Avoir — et quatorze*, (*fig.*) to have the game in o.'s own hands, to have every advantage
†Quintefeuille, *s.f.* cinquefoil
Quintelage, *s.m.* (*nav.*) kentledge
Quinteron, ne, *s.m.f.* quintroon
Quintessence, *s.f.* quintessence
Quintessenciation, *s.f.* refining, subtilization
Quintessenciel, le, *adj.* quintessential
Quintessencier, *v.a.n.* to extract the quintessence from; to refine, to subtilize
§Quintette, Quintetto, *s.m.* (*mus.*) quintet
Quinteu-x, se, *adj.* whimsical, crotchety; fantastic; pettish; freakish, restive, restiff, jibbing; (*med.*) fitful
§Quintidi, *s.m.* quintidi (*fifth day of a decade in the calendar of the first French Republic*)
§Quintil, e, *adj.*, **Quintil,** *s.m.* (*astr.*) quintile; (*liter.*) piece of poetry *or* stanza of five lines
§Quintillion, *s.m.* trillion
§Quinto, *adv.* fifthly, in the fifth place
§Quintuple, *s.m. adj.* quintuple, fivefold
§Quintupler, *v.a.n.*, **Se** —, *v.r.* to quintuple, to increase fivefold
Quinzaine, *s.f.* fifteen or so, about fifteen, some fifteen, fifteen; fortnight
Quinze, *adj.m.f.*, *s.m.* fifteen; fifteenth. — *jours*, (a) fortnight. *D'aujourd'hui* (or *de demain*, &c.) *en* —, this day (*or* to-morrow, &c.) fortnight. *Il y a eu hier — jours*, yesterday fortnight. *Il y a eu lundi — jours*, last Monday fortnight. **—-Vingts,** *s.m.pl.* Quinze-Vingts (*a blind-asylum, in Paris, with* 300 *inmates*); *s.m.sing.* an inmate of Quinze-Vingts
Quinzième, *adj. s.* fifteenth; fifteenth day
Quinzièmement, *adv.* fifteenthly
Quipo, Quipu, *s.m.* quipo, quipu
Quiproquo, *s.m.* quid pro quo, mistake, blunder
§Quirinal, *s.m.* (*Rom. ant.*) Quirinal; **—es,**
Quiscale, *s.m.* (*bird*) quiscalus [*s.f.pl.* Quirinalia
Quittance, *s.f.* receipt, discharge, acquittance,
Quittancer, *v.a.* to receipt [quittance
Quitte, *adj.* discharged; free; clear; rid; safe; quit; — *adv.* quits. *Franc et* —, (*law*) unencumbered. — *à* or *pour*, at the risk of. — *à* —, quits; even; tit for tat. *Être* —*s*, to be quits; to be even. *En être* — (*à* or *pour*), to escape (with), to come off *or* get off (with … only); to be let off (with). *Tenir — de*, to release from, to let off for, to forgive, to dispense with
Quitter, *v.a.* to quit, to leave; to part with *or* from; to forsake; to desert; to abandon; to let go; to tumble off; to slip off; to take *or* pull off; to give up; to resign; to renounce; to desist from; to leave off; to lay down *or* aside; to dismiss; to depart; (*old*) to discharge, to exempt, to release, to dispense. — *des yeux*, to take o.'s eyes off
Se —, *v.r.* to quit *or* &c. each other; to part with *or* from each other, to part; to be left *or* &c.
§Quitus, *s.m.* quietus, final discharge *or* acquittance, receipt in full
Qui-vive, *s.m.* (*mil.*) challenge, challenge-word; (*fig.*) look-out; alert. *V.* **Vivre**
†Quoaille, *s.f.* *V.* **Coaille**
†Quoailler, *v.n.* (*of horses*) to wag the tail
Quodlibétaire, Quodlibétique, *adj.* quodlibetary, quodlibetical
***Quoi,** *pron. adv. int.* which, that; what; how; in fact; in short; to speak plainly; that's all; to be sure. *De* —, of which; of what; what; something, anything; occasion (for); the means (of), what (to …) with *or* upon *or* about *or* for *or* &c., wherewith, wherewithal; something *or* anything (to …) for *or* out of; room *or* space *or* money *or* &c. enough to; money; property; enough. *En* —, in which *or* &c.; what … made of. — *que*, whatever. — *que ce soit*, whatever, whatever it may be; anything whatever, anything; any; nothing; none. — *qu'il en soit*, be that as it may, however, at all events, at any rate. *Il n'y a pas là de — être fier*, there is nothing there to be proud of. *Il n'y a pas de — rire*, there is nothing to laugh at, this is no joking matter, this is no joke. *Il n'y a pas de* — *!* there is no reason to! there is no occasion for it! (*pop.*) don't mention it!
***Quoique,** *conj.* although, though. — *ça*, (*pop.*) in spite of that, for all that, yet, still
Quolibet, *s.m.* low joke, joke, jest, pun
Quote, *s.f.* (*obsolete, though proper, spelling of* **Cote**); — *adj.f.* (*used only in* **Quote-part**)
Quote-part, *s.f.* quota, share, part, portion; contribution; assessment; rating
Quotidien, ne, *adj.* quotidian; daily. *Pain* —, daily bread; custom, every-day habit
Quotidiennement, *adv.* daily
Quotidienneté, *s.f.* dailiness
Quotient, *s.m.* (*math.*) quotient
Quotité, *s.f.* quota, share, part, portion; rating;
Quouette, *s.f.* *V.* **Couette** [assessment

R

R, *s.f.* r
Ra, *s.m.* short roll of the drum, ruffle, ruff
Rabâchage, *s.m.* tautology; continual *or* tiresome repetition, idle twaddle, rigmarole
Rabâcher, *v.a.n.* to repeat over and over
Rabâcherie, *s.f.* *V.* **Rabâchage**
Rabâcheu-r, se, *s.m.f.* tiresome repeater of the same thing, twaddler
Rabais, *s.m.* abatement; diminution, deduction; fall; reduction; reduction of price, reduced price; allowance; discount; lowest bidding; contract for the lowest tender; depreciation, disparagement. *Au* —, with an abatement, at a reduction, at reduced prices, at a discount; for the lowest bidding; by contract for the lowest tender. *Vente au* —, sale at reduced prices; selling off. *Mettre au* —, to sell with an abatement *or* &c.; to put up for the lowest tender; (*fig.*) to depreciate, to undervalue, to disparage, to run down
Rabaissement, *s.m.* lowering; falling; reduction; depreciation; humiliation; contempt
Rabaisser, *v.a.* to lower; to lessen, to abate; to depreciate, to undervalue, to underrate; to disparage; to humble; to bring *or* put down
Raban, *s.m.* (*nav.*) rope-band, gasket, knittle
Rabat, *s.m.* band (*for the neck*); (*hunt.*) beating
Rabat-joie, *s.* (*pers.*) *m.f.*, (*thing*) *m.* surly fellow, mar-joy; damper, wet blanket; balk, disappointment
Rabattage, *s.m.* (*hort.*) lopping, pruning

Rabatteur, *s.m.* (*hunt.*) beater up, beater
Rabattre, *v.a.n.* to beat down; to put down; to pull *or* cut down; to turn down; to press down; to flatten; to level; to drive down; to beat; to lop, to prune; to abate, to lessen; to deduct, to take off; to humble; to bring down; to parry; to turn, to turn off; to come down. *En* —, to deduct *or* take off from it (*or* them); to come down a peg; to alter o.'s opinion
Se —, *v.r.* to turn, to turn off; to deviate, to wander; to turn down; to fall back; to come down; (*of birds*) to alight; (*passive sense*) to be beaten down *or* &c.
Rabattu, e, *part. adj.* beaten down; turned down; &c. (*V.* **Rabattre**); (*of swords*) blunt
Rabattue, *s.f.* (*nav.*) drift rail
Rabbaniste, *s.m.* rabbinist
Rabbi, *s.m. V.* **Rabbin** [rabbi
Rabbin, *s.m.* rabbi, rabbin. *Grand* —, chief
Rabbinage, *s.m.* rabbinism
Rabbinat, *s.m.* rabbiship
Rabbin-ique, -isme, -iste. *V.* page 3, § 1
Rabbiniser, *v.n.* to rabbinize
Rabdo-logie, -logique, -mancie, -mantique, &c. *V.* page 3, § 1
Rabelaisien, ne, *adj.* Rabelaisian, of Rabelais, in the style of Rabelais, after Rabelais' taste *or* fashion; humorous; sneering; Falstaff-like. *Rire* —, sneer
Rabes, *s.f.pl.* hard roe (*of cod*)
Rabêtir, *v.a.n. V.* **Abêtir** *and* **Hébéter**
Rabette, *s.f.* rape; rapeseed
Rabiau, *s.m.* (*pop.*) remainder, remains, leavings
Rabiauter, *v.n.* to eat *or* drink the leavings; to collect ditto, to pick up the scraps
Rabibochage, *s.m.* (*pop.*) reconciliation
Rabibocher, *v.a.* (*pop.*) to reconcile
Rabiéique, Rabique, Rabien, ne, *adj.* (*med.*) rabieic, rabic
Rabiole, *s.f.* turnip; turnip-cabbage
Rabioule, *s.f.* field-turnip
Râble, *s.m.* (*of hares, rabbits,* &c., *and jest. of pers.*) back; (*tech.*) rake, poker, stirrer; (*nav.*) floor-timber [backed, strong, vigorous
Râblé, e, *adj.* backed; thick-backed; strong-
Râbler, *v.a.* to rake, to poke; to scrape
Râblot, *s.m.* (*tech.*) small rake *or* poker
Râblu, e, *adj. V.* **Râblé**
Râblure, *s.f.* (*nav.*) rabbet [to bungle, to botch
Rabobiner, *v.a.* (*pop.*) to patch up, to mend;
Rabonnir, *v.a.n.*, **Se** —, *v.r.* to improve
Rabot, *s.m.* plane; plaster-beater; road-scraper; hard paving-stone. *Passer le* — *sur*, to
Rabotage, *s.m.* planing [plane; (*fig.*) to polish
Rabote, *s.f.* (*local*) apple-dumpling
Rabotement, *s.m.* planing
Raboter, *v.a.* to plane; (*fig.*) to polish
Raboteu-r, se, *s.m.f.* planer; planing-machine; — *adj.* planing. — *mécanique*, planing-machine, planer [knotty
Raboteu-x, se, *adj.* rough; uneven; rugged;
Raboture, *s.f.* planings, shavings
Rabougrir, *v.a.* to stunt; — *v.n.*, **Se** —, *v.r.* to become *or* grow *or* be stunted
Rabougrissement, *s.m.* stuntedness
†Rabouillère, *s.f.* burrow, rabbit's hole
Rabouter, Raboutir, *v.a.* to join *or* sew end to end, to join on, to piece, to patch
Rabouin, *s.m.* (*pop.*) Old Nick, the Devil
Rabouler, *v.a.n.* (*pop.*) to ... (*V.* **Abouler**) again
Rabraquer, *v.a.* (*nav.*) to haul taught again
Rabrouement, *s.m.* snubbing, chiding, scolding, blowing-up [blow up, to take up short
Rabrouer, *v.a.* to snub, to chide, to scold, to
Rabroueu-r, se, *s.m.f.* snubber, scold
Racage, *s.m.* (*nav.*) parrel
Racahout, *s.m.* racahout
†Racaille, *s.f.* rabble, tag-rag; trash, rubbish
Racambeau, *s.m.* (*nav.*) traveller, jib-iron
Racanette, *s.f.* (*bird*) garganey [works
†Racastillage, *s.m.* (*nav.*) repair of the upper
†Racastiller, *v.a.* (*nav.*) to repair the upper works of [**Accointer** *and* **Accoiser**) again
Raccointer, Raccoiser, *v.a.* (*old*) to ... (*V.*
Raccommodable, *adj.* mendable
Raccommodage, *s.m.* mending, repairing, repair; patching; darning; tinkering
Raccommodement, *s.m.* reconciliation
Raccommoder, *v.a.* to mend, to repair; to patch, to piece; to darn; to tinker; to improve; to correct; to restore; to refresh; to put in order; to set right; to adjust; to reconcile [ciled, to make it up
Se —, *v.r.* to be mended *or* &c.; to be recon-
Raccommodeu-r, se, *s.m.f.* mender; patcher; tinker; reconciler
Raccord, *s.m.* joining, fitting; junction; connection; piece; patch; accord, agreement
Raccordement, *s.m.* joining, fitting; junction; union; coupling; connection; levelling; mending; patching
Raccorder, *v.a.* to join, to fit; to unite; to couple; to adjust; to connect; to level; to mend; to piece; to patch; to tune again; to reconcile, to make (...) agree
Raccoupler, *v.a.* to ... (*V.* **Accoupler**) again
Raccourci, e, *part. adj.* shortened, &c. (*V.* **Raccourcir**); shorter; short; too short
Raccourci, *s.m.* abridgment; epitome; short cut; foreshortening; foreshortened view. *En* —, abridged; epitomized; briefly, in a few words; foreshortened; (*fig.*) in miniature
Raccourcir, *v.a.* to shorten, to make shorter; to contract; to bend; to abbreviate, to abridge; to epitomize; to curtail; to foreshorten; (*pop.*) to behead; — *v.n.*, **Se** —, *v.r.* to shorten, to become *or* grow *or* get shorter; to decrease; to contract; to shrink
Raccourcissement, *s.m.* shortening; abridgment; curtailment; decrease, diminution; contraction; shrinking; foreshortening
Raccours, *s.m.* shrinking
Raccoutrement, *s.m.* (*old*) mending
Raccoutrer, *v.a.* (*old*) to mend, to sew up
Raccoutreu-r, se, *s.m.f.* (*old*) mender
Raccoutumer, *v.a.* to accustom *or* use again
Raccroc, *s.m.* fluke. *Coup de* —, fluke, lucky hit, chance hit *or* stroke *or* &c. (*V.* **Coup**)
Raccrocher, *v.a.n.* to hook again; to hang up again; to recover, to get back; to get hold of; to gain over; to pick up; to stop; to stop people; to fluke, to make a fluke, to play by flukes
Se —, *v.r.* to cling; to catch *or* snatch (at); to hang on; to fall back (upon); to take up (with); to recover oneself; to recover *or* retrieve
Raccrocheur, *s.m.* (*at play*) fluker [o.'s losses
Raccrocheuse, *s.f.* street-walker [again
Raccroupir (Se), *v.r.* to ... (*V.* **Accroupir**)
Race, *s.f.* race; species; family; line; ancestry; breed, blood; brood, kind; (*agr.*) variety; (*obsolete*) generation; posterity. *De* —, thoroughbred. *Faire* —, to breed
Racémate, *s.m.* (*chem.*) racemate
Racème, *s.m.* (*bot.*) raceme [mose
Racémeu-x, se, *adj.* (*bot.*) racemous, race-
Racémifère, *adj.* (*bot.*) racemiferous
Racémiforme, *adj.* (*bot.*) racemiform
Racémique, *adj* (*chem.*) racemic
Racer, *v.n.* to breed; to breed in and in; to keep up the breed [again
Rachalander, *v.a.* to ... (*V.* **Achalander**)
Rachat, *s.m.* repurchase; redemption, redeeming, recovery; delivery; ransom. — *de bans*, (marriage) licence
Rachée, *s.f.* stump with new shoots
Rachetable, *adj.* redeemable, recoverable
Racheter, *v.a.* to repurchase, to buy again; to buy off *or* out; to purchase, to buy; to ransom; to redeem; to compensate, to make up for; to atone for [redeemed *or* &c
Se —, *v.r.* to redeem *or* &c. oneself; to be
Racheteu-r, se, *s.m.f.* redeemer
Rachétique, *adj.* (*vulgar for* **Rachitique**)

Racheu-x, se, *adj.* (*of wood, obsolete*) knotty
Rachèvement, *s.m. V.* **Achèvement**
Rachever, *v.a. V.* **Achever**
Racheveu-r, se, *s.m.f.* (*tech.*) finisher
Rachialgie, *s.f.* (*med.*) rachialgia, spine-ache
Rachialgique, *adj.* (*med.*) rachialgic
Rachidien, ne, *adj.* (*anat.*) spinal, vertebral
Rachis, *s.m.* (*anat., bot.*) rachis [stunted
Rachitique, *adj.* rachitic, rickety; knotty,
Rachitis, Rachitisme, *s.m.* rachitis, rickets
Rachitome, *s.m.* (*surg. instr.*) rachitome
Racinage, *s.m.* esculent roots, roots, root-crops; walnut-dye; root-figuring [sole, sill
Racinal, *s.m.* beam, ground-timber, sleeper,
Racine, *s.f.* root; beginning, principle, origin; rise; walnut-dye; (*of a corn*) core; (*fish.*) silk-worm gut
Raciner, *v.n.* to take root; to spring up; — *v.a.* to dye with walnut; to root-figure
Racinien, ne, *adj.* (*liter.*) Racinian, of Racine
Rack, *s.m.* arrack, rack
Râclage, *s.m.* scraping; thinning
Râcle, *s.f.* scraper; — *adj.* strike. — **-boyau,** *s.m.* catgut-scraper [ing, hiding, licking
Râclée, *s.f.* scraping; (*fam.*) thrashing, whack-
Râclement, *s.m.* scraping
Râcler, *v.a.n.* to scrape; to scrape off; to strike (*a measure of corn*); to thin (*woods*); to strum, to thrum
Râclerie, *s.f.* scraping, strumming, thrumming
Râclette, *s.f.* (small) scraper
Râcleur, *s.m.* scraper; strummer, thrummer
Râcloir, *s.m.* scraper [*measures*) strike, strickle
Râcloire, *s.f.* scraper; tongue-scraper; (*of*
Râclon, *s.m.* turf manure; scraped mud
Râclure, *s.f.* scraping, paring, shaving
Racolage, *s.m.* recruiting, enlisting, crimping, impressment [impress; to pick up
Racoler, *v.a.* to recruit, to enlist, to crimp, to
Racoleur, *s.m.* recruiting officer *or* sergeant; recruiting agent, recruiter; crimp
Raconde, *s.f.* (*fur*) racoonda, nutria
Racontable, *adj.* relatable
Racontage, *s.m.* gossip, tittle-tattle, stories; tale-bearing; backbiting
Raconter, *v.a.n.* to relate, to recount, to tell, to narrate; to tell a story
Se —, *v.r.* to be related, &c.
Raconteu-r, se, *s.m.f.* relater, teller, narrator
Racornir, *v.a.*, **Se —,** *v.r.* to make hard *or* horny; to become *or* get ditto; to harden; to shrivel up
Racornissement, *s.m.* hardening, hardness;
Racouet, *s.m. V.* **Vulpin** [shrivelling
Racque, *s.m.* grape husks [back
Racquérir, *v.a.* to ... (*V.* **Acquérir**) again *or*
Racquit, *s.m.* (*at play*) winning back
Racquitter, *v.a.* to win back; to retrieve; to indemnify; to recoup
Se —, *v.r.* to win back, to retrieve o.'s losses, to indemnify *or* recoup oneself
Rade, *s.f.* (*nav.*) road, roadstead
Radeau, *s.m.* raft, float
Rader, *v.a.* to strike (*a measure*); (*nav.*) to bring into a road, to anchor in a road
Radiaire, *adj.m.f., s.m.* radiate
Radial, e, *adj.* radial
Radiance, *s.f.* radiance
Radiant, e, *adj.* radiant
Radiation, *s.f.* radiation, eradiation, irradiation; striking off *or* out, crossing out, erasure, obliteration; disbarring; stroke, cross
Radical, e, *adj.* radical; — *s.m.* radical; root
Radicalement, *adv.* radically
Radicalisme, *s.m.* radicalism
Radicant, e, *adj.* (*bot.*) radicant
Radication, *s.f.* (*bot.*) radication
Radicelle, *s.f.* (*bot.*) radicel
Radiciforme, *adj.* radiciform
Radicivore, *adj.* radicivorous
Radicule, *s.f.* (*bot.*) radicle, radicule, rootlet
Radié, e, *adj.*, **Radié,** *s.m* radiate
Radier, *s.m.* frame of ground-timber; inverted arch; apron; — *v.n.* to radiate, to beam; — *v.a.* to strike off *or* out, to cross out [blazing
Radieu-x, se, *adj.* radiant, beamy, beaming,
Radio, (*in compounds, anat.*) radio-...
Radis, *s m.* radish
Radius, *s.m.* (*anat.*) radius
Radoire, *s.f.* (*of measures*) strike, strickle
Radotage, *s.m.* dotage; raving, twaddle
Radoter, *v.n.* to dote; to rave, to twaddle
Radoterie, *s.f. V.* **Radotage**
Radoteu-r, se, *s.m.f.* dotard; twaddler
Radoub, *s.m.* (*nav.*) refitting, repairing, repair, graving. *En —,* under repair
Radouber, *v.a.* (*nav.*) to refit, to repair
Se —, *v.r.* to be repaired; (*fig.*) to make up o.'s loss, to recruit o.'s health *or* o.'s strength
Radouci, e, *part. adj.* softened, &c. (*V.* **Radoucir**); subdued; milder; mild
Radoucir, *v.a.* to soften; to sweeten; to make milder; to allay; to mitigate; to appease, to pacify, to calm
Se —, *v.r.* to soften; to become *or* get milder; to relent; to subside; to become *or* be appeased, &c.; to become calm
Radoucissement, *s.m.* softening; getting milder; breaking up, giving; allaying; mitigation; appeasement; improvement
Rafale, *s.f.* squall; (*pop.*) misery, need
Rafalé, e, *adj.* (*nav.*) caught in a squall; (*pop.*) needy, hard up, seedy, up a tree
Rafaler, *v.a.* (*pop.*) to bring down, to bring low
Se —, *v.r* to go down in the world, to be-
Raff, *s.m.* fluke fins [come needy *or* seedy
Raffe, *s.f.* stem, stalk; grape-stalk; paring (*of leather*)
Raffermir, *v.a.*, **Se —,** *v.r.* to harden; to strengthen; to fasten; to consolidate; to confirm; to grow stronger; to become firm; to become *or* be consolidated *or* confirmed; to improve
Raffermissement, *s.m.* hardening; strengthening; fastening; consolidation; confirmation; improvement
Raffinade, *s.f.* best refined sugar
Raffinage, *s.m.* refining
Raffiné, e, *adj. s.m.* refined; delicate; sharp, keen, subtle; clever; consummate; subtilizer; fashionable rake; duellist
Raffinement, *s.m.* refinement
Raffiner, *v.a.n.* to refine [sharp
Se —, *v.r.* to become *or* be refined; to grow
Raffinerie, *s.f.* refining; refinery, sugar refinery
Raffineu-r, se, *s.m.f.* refiner; sugar-baker;
Rafflésie, *s.f.* (*bot.*) rafflesia [subtilizer
Raffolé, e, *part. adj V.* **Affolé**
Raffoler, *v.n.* to be exceedingly *or* passionately fond (of), to dote (on, upon)
Raffolir, *v.n. V.* **Affolir**
Raffranchir, *v.a.*, **Raffubler,** *v.a.*, &c. to ... (*V.* **Affranchir, Affubler,** &c.) again
Raffut, *s.m.* (*pop.*) row, shindy
Rafiau, Rafiot, *s.m.* small boat; (*pop.*) trifle; bauble; duffer; trash; hospital attendant
Rafistolage, *s.m.* patching up, mending
Rafistoler, *v.a.* to spruce up again; to make spruce, to trim up; to tie up, to sew up, to patch up, to mend [mender
Rafistoleu-r, se, *s.m.f.* trimmer, patcher,
Râfle, *s.f.* stem, stalk; grape-stalk; raffle-net, sweep-net; trammel-net; sweep, clearing; capture; (*at dice*) pair royal. *Faire —,* to sweep the stakes, to make a clean sweep, to sweep away (*or* carry away *or* off) everything; to capture *or* apprehend the whole
Râfler, *v.a.* to sweep away *or* off, to carry away *or* off; to capture; to take; to pocket; to filch, to prig [&c., &c.
Raflouage, Raflouer, &c. *V.* **Renflouage,**
Rafraîchir, *v.a.n.* to cool; to refresh; to recruit; to revive; to rest; to renew; to renovate; to repair; to do up; to rub up; to crop, to trim, to cut; (*mil.*) to relieve

Se —, *v.r* to cool, to get cool; to refresh oneself; to take refreshment; to recruit o.'s strength; to rest; to bait

Rafraîchissant, e, *part. adj.* refreshing, cooling; refrigerative

Rafraîchissant, *s.m.* (*med.*) refrigerative

Rafraîchissement, *s.m.* cooling, cooling effect, refreshment; refreshing; repairing, repair; (*mil., nav.*) fresh provisions

Rafraîchisseur, *adj.m.* cooling, refrigeratory; — *s.m. V.* **Rafraîchissoir**

Rafraîchissoir, *s.m.* cooler; refrigerator

†**Ragaillardir,** *v.a.*, **Se** —, *v.r.* to enliven, to cheer, to cheer up, to brisk up, to make merry; to revive

Rage, *s.f.* rage; rabidness, madness, rabies, hydrophobia; fit of rage; passion; furore; mania; inveterate habit; violent pain; dreadful things. — *de dents*, (*fam.*) violent toothache; (*pop.*) ravenous hunger. *Avoir la* —, to be mad. *Avoir la* — *de*, to be mad after, to have a passion *or* a mania for; to have the inveterate habit of. *Faire* —, to rage, to make great havoc; to make a great disturbance; to turn everything topsy-turvy; to do o's utmost; to do wonders; to be the rage, to be quite (*or* all) the rage. *Puer la* —, (*pop.*) to stink dreadfully *or* horridly

Ragencer, *v.a.* to ... (*V.* **Agencer**) again

Rager, *v n.* to be in *or* get into a rage, to fume

Rageu-r, se, *adj. s.* passionate; bad-tempered, ill-tempered; ditto fellow *or* creature *or* thing

Rageusement, *adv.* ragingly, with rage

Ragot, e, *adj.* squabby, podgy, dumpy, thickset; — *s.m.f.* ditto person, runt; — *s.m.* thickset-horse; hog-steer

Ragot, *s.m.* tittle-tattle, twaddle, idle talk, idle *or* scandalous story, backbiting, slander

Ragoter, *v.n.* to tattle; to grumble

Ragotin, *s.m.* runt; guy

Ragouminier, *s.m.* Canada cherry-tree

Ragoût, *s.m.* stew, ragout; relish, zest; pleasure. *En* —, stewed. *Accommoder* or *cuire* or *mettre en* —, to stew

Ragoûtant, e, *adj.* relishing, savoury; tempting; pleasing, agreeable; desirable; clean

Ragoûter, *v.a.* to revive the appetite of; to excite the taste of; to take the fancy of; to tempt; to stimulate, to excite, to quicken, to provoke, to stir up

Se —, *v.r* to revive *or* recover o.'s appetite

Ragrafer, *v.a.* to ... (*V.* **Agrafer**) again

Ragrandir, *v.a.* to ... (*V.* **Agrandir**) again

Ragréage, *s.m.* (*nav.*) refitting

Ragréer, *v.a.* to finish off; to do up, to repair; (*nav.*) to refit [pair, doing up

Ragrément, *s.m.* finishing off; repairing, re-

Raguer, *v.a.n.*, **Se** —, *v.r.* (*nav.*) to fret (by rubbing), to chafe, to gall

Raguet, *s.m.* codling [*Turkey*)

Raïa, *s.m.* raia *or* rayah (*foreign subject in*

Raide, *adj.* stiff; rigid; inflexible; tight; steep; rapid, swift; stubborn; pretty strong; quite drunk; — *adv.* quickly, swiftly, fast, hard, sharply, sharp, right, outright, clean, down, on the spot; surely; — *s.m.* (*pop.*) brandy. — *comme une barre de fer* or *comme un bâton* or *comme un piquet*, as stiff as a poker; bolt upright; inflexible. — *comme balle*, slapdash, slap; in no time

Raidement, *adv.* stiffly; rigidly; inflexibly; tightly; quickly, &c. (*V.* **Raide,** *adv.*)

Raideur, *s.f.* stiffness; rigidity; inflexibility; tightness; steepness; swiftness, rapidity; stubbornness [hillock

†**Raidillon,** *s.m.* ascent, acclivity, little hill,

Raidir, *v.a.n.* to stiffen, to make *or* become *or* grow *or* get stiff; to tighten, to make *or* become *or* grow *or* get tight; to stretch out; to render *or* become rigid *or* inflexible; (*pop.*) to die

Se —, *v.r.* to stiffen, to tighten, to become *or* grow *or* get stiff *or* tight; to draw oneself up; to bear up (against), to resist; to steel *or* harden oneself [tightener, tightening-wheel

Raidisseur, *s.m.* stiffener; tightener; (*hort.*)

Raie, *s.f.* line; stroke; dash; stripe; streak; furrow; (*of hair*) parting; (*fish*) ray, skate, thornback. — *bouclée*, thornback. *A —s*, with stripes, striped. *Faire sa* —, to part o.'s hair

Raïer, *v.n. V.* **Réer** [back

Raieteau, Raieton, *s.m.* (*fish*) little thorn-

Raifort, *s.m.* horse-radish

Raiguiser, *v.a.* to ... (*V.* **Aiguiser**) again

†**Rail,** *s.m.* rail. — *à ornière*, tram-rail

Railé, e, *adj.* (*of hounds*) sorted

†**Railler,** *v.a.n.*, **Se** —, *v.r.* to rally; to laugh at; to make game of; to jeer; to jest, to joke; [to sneer

†**Raillère,** *s.f.* steep

†**Raillerie,** *s.f.* raillery, jesting, joking; jeer, jest, joke. — *à part*, seriously, without joking, in earnest

†**Railleu-r, se,** *adj. s.* rallying, jeering, jesting, satirical, sneering; rallier, jeerer, jester, joker, scoffer, sneerer [jeeringly; sneeringly

†**Railleusement,** *adv.* jestingly, jokingly;

Railure, *s.f.* eye-groove (*of a needle*)

Railway, *s.m.* railway

Rain, *s.m.* skirt (*of a wood*)

Rainceau, *s.m. V.* **Rinceau**

Raine, *s.f.* green frog, tree-frog; (*obsolete*) frog

Rainer, *v.a.* to groove

Rainette, *s.f.* green frog, tree-frog; (*carp.*) marking-tool; (*farrier's*) paring-knife; (*saddler's tool*) creese, crease; (*apple*) *V.* **Reinette**

Rainetter, *v.a.* (*tech.*) to mark, to groove, to furrow, to pare; (*leather*) to creese *or* crease

Rainoire, *s.f. V.* **Guillaume**

Rainure, *s.f.* groove

Raiponce, *s.f.* (*bot.*) rampion

Raire, *v.n. V.* **Réer** [*de cœur*, (*arch.*) ogee

Rais, *s.m.* ray, beam; (*of wheels*) spoke. —

Raisin, *s.m.* grape, grapes; raisin, raisins, plum, plums; (*of paper*) royal. — *sec*, raisin, raisins, plum, plums. — *de caisse*, lexias. — *de Corinthe*, currant, currants, Corinthian raisins. — *d'ours*, (*bot.*) bearberry. — *de renard*, (*bot.*) true-love

Raisiné, *s.m.* raisiné, grape and pear jam; (*pop.*) blood. *Faire du* —, (*pop.*) to bleed at the nose

Raisinier, *s.m.* (*bot.*) grape-tree, seaside grape

Raison, *s.f.* reason; sense; senses; judgment; rationality; matter; argument; proof; cause; motive, ground; consideration; discretion; satisfaction; justice; right; excuse; answer; rate; ratio; —, — *sociale*, — *de commerce*, (*com.*) firm; style (*of a firm*). — *d'etre*, reason to exist *or* to be; business to be there; earthly use; condition of existence. — *de plus*, that is one more reason. *Un être de* —, an imaginary being, a creation of the brain. *A* — *de*, at the rate of; in proportion to; on account of. *A plus forte* —, with stronger *or* greater *or* still more reason, with so much the more reason, much more, still more so, à fortiori; much less. *Comme de* —, as in reason, as is (*or* was) reasonable *or* right, as it ought to be, reasonably *or* rightly enough, of course, naturally, as it is (*or* was) reasonable to suppose, as may (*or* might) be expected. *En* — *de*, in consideration of; in proportion to. *Par* — *démonstrative*, (*jest.*) by rules of art. *Plus que de* —, more than is (*or* was) reasonable. *Avoir* —, to be right, to be in the right; to justify oneself; to have satisfaction; to get the better (of), to get (over), to have the mastery (over), to be master (of), to master, to manage; to have reason. *Avoir des —s*, to have words, to dispute, to contest, to wrangle. *Demander* — *de*, to demand satisfaction for. *Donner* — *à*, to say *or* show that ... is (*or* was) right, to decide in ...'s favour, to approve, to side with; to justify; to confirm, to prove; to give satisfaction. *Faire* — *à*, to pledge. *Faire* — *de*, to

give satisfaction for. *Mettre à la* —, to bring to reason *or* to o.'s senses, to set to rights. *Parler* —, to talk reasonably, to reason, to talk sense *or* sensibly. *Rendre — de*, to give an account of; to account for; to give satisfaction for. *Se faire* — (*à soi-même*), to get satisfaction, to take o.'s revenge; to take the law into o.'s own hands. *Se faire une* —, to be guided by reason. *Se rendre à la* —, to yield to reason. *Tirer — de*, to obtain satisfaction for. *Ce n'est pas une* —, that is no reason *or* &c.; that does not follow

Raisonnable, *adj.* reasonable; rational; wise; good; just, right; fair; moderate; tolerable; suitable; decent; competent

Raisonnablement, *adv.* reasonably; rationally; wisely; justly; fairly; moderately; tolerably; rather; pretty well; suitably; decently; sufficiently

Raisonné, e, *part. adj.* reasoned, &c. (*V.* **Raisonner**); rational; analytical; methodical; descriptive and methodized; classified; accurate; deliberate; supported by proofs; with proofs and illustrations; explanatory; with notices; with reflections [answer

Raisonnement, *s.m.* reasoning; argument;

Raisonner, *v.a.n.* to reason; to reason with; to argue; to answer; to murmur, to grumble; to consider, to study, to examine

Se —, *v.r.* to reason with oneself; to be reasoned about; to be considered, &c.; to be discussed

Raisonneu-r, se, *s.m.f.* reasoner; arguer; tiresome speaker; prater, babbler; grumbler; one who gives answers; impertinent answerer; — *adj.* reasoning, arguing, answering, grumbling. *Faire le* —, to answer; to murmur, to

Raja, Rajah, *s.m.* rajah (*in India*) [grumble

Rajeunir, *v.a.n.* to make *or* grow(, become, get,) *or* look (*or* make . . . look) young *or* young again *or* younger; to rejuvenate, to rejuvenize, to restore to youth; to give a young look to; to refresh; to revive; to renew, to renovate; to modernize; to repair; to shave; to prune; to cut; to clip; to mow

Rajeunissement, *s.m.* restoration to youth, rejuvenescence, making *or* growing young again; young look *or* looks; refreshing; revival; renewal, renovation; modernization; repairing, repair; shaving, shave; cutting; clipping; mowing

Rajeunisseur, *s.m.* reviver; modernizer

Rajouter, *v.a.* to add again *or* more, to add

Rajustement, *s.m.* readjustment; setting in order; repairing, repair; reconciliation

Rajuster, *v.a.* to readjust; to set *or* put in order; to repair; to settle; to reconcile; to . . . (*V.* **Ajuster**) again [to be readjusted, &c.

Se —, *v.r.* to readjust oneself *or* o.'s dress;

Rajusteur, *s.m.* readjuster

Râlant, e, *adj.* rattling; wheezing

Râle, *s.m.* rattle (*in the throat*); death-rattle, rattles; (*med.*) rhonchus, rattle; (*bird*) rail, crake. — *sibilant*, wheezing, sibilant *or* hissing rattle, sibilus

Râlement, *s.m.* rattle (*in the throat*), rattles

Ralenti, e, *part. adj.* made slower, &c. (*V.* **Ralentir**); slower; slow; lessened; less; relenting; flagging

Ralentir, *v.a.n.*, **Se** —, *v.r.* to make *or* become (*or* get) slower; to slacken the speed *or* pace of; to slacken o.'s *or* its speed (*or* pace); to slacken; to abate, to lessen; to diminish; to moderate; to relent; to flag; to cool

Ralentissement, *s.m.* slackening speed; slackening; abatement; relenting; cooling

Râler, *v.n.* to rattle in o.'s throat; to whiz; to have the death-rattle

Raleur, *s.m.* (*pop.*) rummager, fumbler

Raleuse, *s.f.* (*pop.*) lady Quiz; touter

Ralingue, *s.f.* (*nav.*) bolt-rope; foot-rope

Ralinguer, *v.a.* (*nav.*) to shiver (*a sail*)

Raliter, *v.a.* to . . . (*V.* **Aliter**) again

Raller, *v.n. V.* **Réer;** (*old*) to go again

Ralliement, *s.m.* rallying, rally. *Mot de* —, (*mil.*) rallying-word; countersign [get near

Rallier, *v.a.*, **Se** —, *v.r.* to rally; to join, to

Rallonge, *s.f.* piece to lengthen; (*of tables*) leaf [lengthened

Rallongement, *s. m.* lengthening; being

Rallonger, *v.a.n.*, **Se** —, *v.r.* to lengthen

Rallumer, *v.a*, **Se** —, *v.r.* to light again, to relight; to rekindle; to revive; to break out

Ramadan, *s.m. V.* **Ramazan** [again

Ramage, *s.m.* warbling, singing, chirping; prattle; rigmarole; (*hunt.*) branches, boughs; (*on stuffs*) flowers, flowering; (*manu.*) tentering

Ramagé, e, *adj.* flowered, with flowers, ornamented

Ramager, *v.n.* to warble, to sing, to chirp

Ramaigrir, *v.a.n.* to make *or* get thin again

Ramaigrissement, *s.m* growing thin again,

Ramaire, *adj.* rameous [emaciation, leanness

Ramas, *s.m. V.* **Ramassis** [ing up

Ramassage, *s.m.* gathering, collecting; pick-

Ramasse, *s.f.* mountain-sledge. *A la* —, on a

Ramasse-couvert, *s.m.* crumb-tray [sledge

Ramassé, e, *part. adj.* gathered, &c. (*V.* **Ramasser**); short and thick; thickset; squat; compact; (*bot.*) clustered

Ramasser, *v.a.* to gather, to collect; to get together; to rake up, to rake; to scrape up, to scrape, to grub; to pick up, to take up; to help up; to belabour; to drive *or* draw in a mountain-sledge; — *s.m.* picking up

Se —, *v.r.* to collect; to be gathered *or* collected *or* &c.; to gather o.'s limbs; to cuddle; to roll oneself up; to pick oneself up, to get up again

Ramassette, *s.f.* cradle *or* bow (*of a scythe*)

Ramasseu-r, se, *s.m.f.* gatherer, collector, collectress, picker, grubber; — *s.m.* sledge-driver

Ramassis, *s.m.* gathering, heap, mass, collection; set, lot, band, troop, gang; scrapings; rakings; sweepings; loppings, chatwood [dan

Ramazan, *s.m.* (*Mahom. rel.*) ramadan, rhama-

Ramberge, *s.f.* (*old nav.*) ramberge (*galley,*

Rambour, *s.m.* rambour (*apple*) [*row-barge*)

Rambuteau, *s.m.* urinal

Rame, *s.f.* oar; (*manu.*) tenter-frame; (*hort.*) stick, pole, prop, support; (*tech.*) paddle; (*of paper*) ream; (*on canals*) train (*of boats*). *A* —*s*, oared; rowing, row. *A la* —, rowing, row; by the ream. *Aller à la* —, to row. *Être* or *tirer à la* —, to tug at the oar; to work hard

Ramé, e, *part. adj.* propped, &c. (*V.* **Ramer**); rowed; oared; oary; horned; (*her.*) attired; (*of shot*) *V.* **Balle** *and* **Boulet;** (*of peas*) *V.* **Pois**

Raméaire, Raméal, e, *adj.* rameous, rameal

Rameau, *s.m.* bough, branch. *Dimanche des* —*s*, Palm Sunday

Ramée, *s.f.* green boughs; branches with their leaves; green arbour, arbour, bower, cover, covert; (*local*) cock (*of hay*)

Ramenable, *adj.* reclaimable

Ramendage, *s.m.* mending

Ramender, *v.a.* to mend; to improve; to manure again; to lower the price of; — *v.n.* to fall (*in price*), to go down

Ramener, *v.a.* to bring again; to bring back; to bring over *or* round; to recall; to reclaim; to appease; to restore; to revive; to retrieve; to reduce

Se —, *v.r.* to concentrate itself; to be reduced *or* brought back *or* &c.; (*of a horse*) to carry its head

Ramentacé, e, *adj.* (*bot.*) ramentaceous

Ramequin, *s.m.* (*cook.*) ramequin, ramekin, ramakin, ramskin

Ramer, *v.a.* to prop; to stick; to pole; (*manu.*) to tenter; — *v.n.* to row; to pull; to ply the oar, to work hard

Se —, *v.r.* to be propped *or* &c.

Ramereau, *s.m.* young ring-dove, stock-dove
Ramette, *s.f.* ream (*of small paper*); (*print.*) job-chase [rowing
Rameu-r, se, *s.m.f.* rower, oarsman; — *adj.*
Rameu-x, se, *adj.* ramous, branchy, branched, branching
Ramicher, *v.a. pop. for* **Réconcilier**
Ramie, *s.f.* (*bot.*) ramee, China-grass plant
Ramier, *s.m.* (*adj., Pigeon* —) ring-dove, wood-pigeon; stock-dove
Ramière, *s.f.* row *or* border of trees
Ramification, *s.f.* ramification; branch
Ramifier, *v.a.,* **Se** —, *v.r.* to ramify, to branch out, to extend
Ramiflore, *adj.* (*bot.*) ramiflorous
Ramiforme, *adj.* ramiform
†**Ramilles,** *s.f.pl.* twigs, spray; chatwood
Raminagrobis, *s.m.* Grimalkin
Ramingue, *adj.* restive, restiff, jibbing
Ramoindrir. *V.* **Amoindrir** [damp
Ramoitir, *v.a.* to make damp. *Se* —, to get
Ramollir, *v.a.n.,* **Se** —, *v.r.* to soften, to make *or* get soft [*s.m.* (*med.*) emollient
Ramollissant, e, *adj.,* **Ramollissant,**
Ramollissement, *s.m.* softening
Ramon, *s.m.* besom, broom; sweep's machine
Ramona, *s.m.* (*jest.*) sweep
Ramonage, *s.m.* sweeping (*chimneys*)
Ramoner, *v.a.* to sweep (*chimneys*); (*pop.*) to scold, to blow up; — *v.n.* (*pop.*) to grumble
Se —, *v.r.* to be swept
Ramoneur, *s.m.* chimney-sweeper, sweep
Rampant, e, *part. adj.* crawling, &c. (*V.* **Ramper**); low, mean, vile, servile; (*her.*) rampant; — *s.m.* coping; slope; flue
Rampe, *s.f.* baluster, banister, handrail; declivity, descent; acclivity, ascent; slope, inclined plane, incline, gradient; row of jets; row of lights, lights; (*theat.*) foot-lights, foot-lamps; (*fig.*) stage; (*obsolete*) flight (of stairs,
Rampement, *s.m.* crawling, creeping [of steps)
Ramper, *v.n.* to crawl; to creep; to cringe, to crouch, to truckle, to fawn; to grovel; to be low *or* mean *or* prosy; to slope
Rampichet, *s.m. V.* **Grimpereau**
Rampin, e, *adj. V.* **Pinçard**
Rampiste, *s.m.* baluster-maker, banister-maker
Ramponeau, *s.m.* (*toy*) tumbling jack, tumbler
Ramponer, *v.n.* (*pop.*) to tipple, to get drunk
Ramule, *s.f.* (*bot.*) ramule [lose
Ramuleu-x, se, *adj.* (*bot.*) ramulous, ramu-
Ramure, *s.f.* branches, boughs; (*of stags,* &c.) horns, antlers, attire
Ramuscule, *s.m.* (*bot., anat.*) ramuscule
Rancart, *s.m. Mettre au* —, to lay *or* put aside, to cast off, to throw away
Rance, *adj.* rancid, rank; rusty; — *s.m.* rancidness. *Sentir le* —, to smell rancid *or* rank
Rancette, *s.f.* sheet-iron
Ranche, *s.f.* peg, round, step; rack
Rancher, *s.m.* peg-ladder, rack-ladder, roost-ladder; rack; rathe, rave, shelving
Ranci, e, *part. adj.* grown rancid, rancid, rank
Rancidité, *s.f.* rancidity, rancidness, rankness; rustiness [get rancid *or* rank
Rancir, *v.n.,* **Se** —, *v.r.* to become *or* grow *or*
Rancissure, *s.f. V.* **Rancidité**
Rançon, *s.f.* ransom
Rançonnement, *s.m.* ransoming; extortion
Rançonner, *v.a.* to ransom; to tax; to fleece, to overcharge
Rançonneu-r, se, *s.m.f.* extortioner
Rancune, *s.f.* rancour; spite; grudge; malice
Rancuneu-x, se, Rancuni-er, ère, *adj.* rancorous, spiteful; — *s.m.f.* ditto person *or*
Randonnée, *s.f.* (*hunt.*) circuit, round [animal
Rang, *s.m.* row; line; range; rank; station; degree; place; turn; class; order; number; rate; tier; list; (*print.*) frame. *Sur deux* (*trois,* &c.) —*s,* (*mil.*) two (three, &c.) deep. *Avoir* or *prendre* —, to rank. *Être sur les* —*s,* to be on the lists; to be a candidate. *Mettre au* — *de,* to rank *or* reckon among, to place in the number of. *Se mettre sur les* —*s,* to enter the lists; to present *or* offer oneself as candidate, to become a candidate, to apply *or* put up (for), to come forward (as)
Rangé, e, *part. adj.* ranged, &c. (*V.* **Ranger**); (*of pers., conduct*) steady, regular; (*of battles*) pitched
Rangée, *s.f.* row; range; file; line; tier; set
Rangement, *s.m.* ranging; arranging; arrangement; arraying; binning; &c. (*V.* **Ranger**)
Ranger, *v.a.* to range; to arrange; to dispose; to set *or* put in order; to set, to place; to array, to marshal; to draw *or* keep back; to put aside *or* by, to put out of the way *or* in its place; to bin (*bottles*); to set to rights; to subject, to subdue, to tame; to bring over, to bring; to rank, to reckon; (*mil.*) to draw up; (*nav.*) to sail *or* run close to
Se —, *v.r.* to place oneself; to draw back; to step *or* move *or* stand aside; to get out of the way; to make way *or* room; to embrace (*another's opinion*); to go *or* come over (to); to side (with); to amend, to become steady; (*mil.*) to draw up; to fall in; (*nav.*) to come alongside; (*of the wind*) to veer
Ranger, Rangier, *s.m.* (*her.*) reindeer
Rangette, *s.f.* sheet-iron
Rangeu-r, se, *s.m.f.* arranger; binner
Ranimer, *v.a.* to reanimate; to revive; to recruit; to cheer up; to stir up
Se —, *v.r.* to revive; to recover; to come to life again; to cheer up
Ranin, e, *adj.* ranine
Ranule, *s.f.* (*med.*) ranula
Ranz, *s.m.* (*in Switzerland*) ranz, round, air, tune. — *des vaches,* ranz des vaches (*melody of Swiss mountaineers*)
Raout, *s.m.* (*obsolete*) rout, party, assembly
Rapace, *adj.* rapacious; (*metal.*) wasting; — *s.m.* rapacious man; —**s,** *s.m.pl.* rapacious men *or* people; (*zool.*) rapaces, raptores, rapacious birds, raveners
Rapacement, *adv.* rapaciously
Rapacité, *s.f.* rapacity, rapaciousness
Râpage, *s.m.* rasping, grating
Rapaisement, *s.m.* reappeasement
Rapaiser, *v.a.* to reappease; to pacify *or* &c. (*V.* **Apaiser**) again
Rapatelle, *s.f.* hair-cloth
Rapatriage, *s.m.* reconciliation
Rapatriement, *s.m.* repatriation; sending *or* bringing back to o.'s (native) country; recalling home; return to o.'s (native) country, return home; (*fam.*) reconciliation
Rapatrier, *v.a.* to repatriate; to send *or* bring back to o.'s (own *or* native) country; to recall home; (*fam.*) to reconcile
Se —, *v.r.* to repatriate oneself; to return to o.'s (native) country, to return home; (*fam.*) to be reconciled, to make it up
Râpe, *s.f.* rasp, grater; stem, stalk; grape-stalk, rape; —**s,** *pl.* (*vet.*) *V.* **Malandre.** — *douce,* (*fam.*) soft sawder, blarney
Râpé, e, *part. adj.* rasped, &c. (*V.* **Râper**); threadbare, shabby, seedy, worn out
Râpé, *s.m.* rape-wine; fresh grapes (*put in to restore wine*), stum; wine-waste. — *de raisin,* — *-raisin,* restored wine, stum. — *de copeaux,* chips *or* shavings (*used to clarify wine*)
Râper, *v.a.* to rasp, to grate; to shave; to wear out
Se —, *v.r.* to be rasped, &c.; to wear out, to become threadbare
Rapetassage, *s.m.* patching; mending; cobbling; botching; patchwork
Rapetasser, *v.a.* to patch up, to piece; to mend; to cobble; to botch
Rapetasseu-r, se, *s.m.f.* patcher; mender; cobbler; botcher; compiler; adapter
Rapetissement, *s.m.* lessening, shortening, &c. (*V.* **Rapetisser**)
Rapetisser, *v.a.n.,* **Se** —, *v.r.* to lessen; to make *or* grow less; to decrease; to diminish; to shorten; to make *or* grow (*or* get) short *or*

small, to make *or* get shorter *or* smaller; to dwarf; to shrink; to humble; to humble *or* lower oneself; to make oneself small *or* little
Râpette, *s.f.* (*bot.*) catch-weed, goose-grass
Râpeu-r, se, *s.m.f.* rasper
Rapeu-x, se, *adj.* rasp-like, grating, rough
Raphaélesque, *adj* Raphaelesque
Raphanie, *s.f.* (*med.*) raphania, ergotism
Raphé, *s.m.* (*anat., bot.*) raphe, rhaphe
Raphidie, *s.f.* (*zool.*) snake-fly
Rapiat, *s. m.* (*pop.*) Auvergnat; Savoyard; grasping fellow; — *adj.* grasping
Rapide, *adj.* rapid; swift; fleet; quick; speedy; hasty; sudden; steep; (*nav.*) fast-sailing, fast, swift; — *s.m.* (*navig.*) rapid; (*rail.*) speed
Rapidement, *adv.* rapidly, swiftly, speedily, fleetly, quickly, fast; suddenly
Rapidité, *s.f.* rapidity, swiftness, fleetness, quickness, speed; suddenness; steepness
Rapiéçage, Rapiècement, *s.m.* piecing, patching; patchwork
Rapiécer, *v.a.* to piece; to patch; to vamp; [to mend
Rapiècetage, *s.m.* patching; patchwork
Rapièceter, *v a. V.* **Rapiécer**
Rapiéceu-r, se, *s.m.f.* patcher; mender
Rapière, *s.f.* rapier, bilbo, sword
Rapin, *s.m.* painter's articled pupil; dauber
Rapine, *s.f.* rapine; plundering; plunder
Rapiner, *v.n.a.* to plunder; to pilfer
Rapineu-r, se, Rapini-er, ère, *s m.f.* plunderer; pilferer; — *adj.* plundering; pilfering
Rapiquer, *v.n.* (*pop.*) to return
†Rappareiller, Rapparier, *v.a.* to match
Rappe, *s.m.* rappen (*Swiss coin worth about one fifth of a halfpenny*)
Rappel, *s.m.* recall; call (*to order*); call to arms, drums beating to arms *or* to quarters; recheat (*in hunt.*); surplus; distribution (*of light, in paint.*); repeal (*of the Union*). *Battre le* —, to beat to arms; to beat to quarters
Rappelable, *adj.* recallable
Rappeler, *v.a.* to call again; to call back; to recall; to call (*to order*); to summon up, to muster; to collect; to recover, to regain; to remind of, to call to mind; to remember; (*paint.*) to distribute (*light*); — *v.n.* (*mil.*) to beat to arms *or* to quarters. *Rappelez-moi au souvenir* (*au bon souvenir*) *de*, remember me (kindly) to

Se —, *v.r.* to recollect, to remember; to call *or* recall to mind; to call up; to recall *or* collect itself; to be recalled, &c.
Rappliquer, *v.a.* to ... (*V.* **Appliquer**) again
Rappointis, *s.m.pl.* light locksmith's work
Rapport, *s.m.* bringing back; removal; material removed; adding, addition; piece added; bearing; produce; revenue; report, statement, account; return; testimony, evidence; rumour; tale; affinity, analogy, resemblance; agreement, conformity; harmony; correspondence; communication; intercourse; relation; respect, regard; connection; reference; ratio; reimbursement; tide wave; (*of the stomach*) rising, eructation, belch. — *à*, (*pop.*) concerning, about; for the sake of; on account of. *Pièces de* —, pieces, fragments, patches; patchwork; checker-work; inlaid-work; mosaic; productive pieces *or* articles. *De* —, of patchwork; of checker-work; of inlaid-work; added; made (*earth*); (*com.*) productive. *En* —, in connection, connected; in harmony; in communication, in correspondence; in proportion (to); in bearing; productive. *Par* — *à*, with regard to; for the sake of; on account of; in comparison with. *Sous ce* —, in this *or* that respect. *Sous le* — *de*, with regard *or* respect to. *Sous tous les* —*s*, in all respects, in every respect. *Avoir* — *à*, to have reference to, to refer *or* relate to; to be connected with. *Faire un* —, to make a report *or* a return. *Faire des* —*s*, to tell tales, to sneak
Rapportable, *adj.* movable; referable; re- [storable
Rapportage, *s.m.* (*land-surveying*) plotting
Rapporté, e, *part. adj.* brought back, &c. (*V.* **Rapporter**); added; made (*earth*). *Pièces* —*es*, pieces added, pieces, fragments, patches; patchwork; checker-work; inlaid-work
Rapporter, *v.a.n.* to bring back; to bring again; to bring home; to carry *or* take back; to carry; to remove; to add, to join, to put; to joint; to fit; to fetch; to fetch and carry; to post (*in the ledger*); to reimburse; to pay; to bear, to yield, to produce, to bring in, to bring; to gain, to acquire, to get; to report; to relate, to state, to give an account of; to tell; to repeat; to quote; to tell tales, to blab, to sneak; to adduce, to allege; to sum up; to indicate, to show; to aim, to direct, to refer; to attribute, to ascribe; to recall, to revoke; to repeal; (*land-surveying*) to plot

Se —, *v.r.* to agree; to correspond; to fit; to refer; to relate; to be related; to be connected; to allude; to concern. *S'en* — *à*, to refer to, to leave to; to trust to, to believe; to abide by; will not contest
Rapporteur, *s.m.* reporter; tale-bearer, telltale, blab, sneak; (*instr.*) protractor; — *adj.m.* reporting; tale-bearing, blabbing, sneaking
Rapporteuse, *s.f.* tale-bearer, tell-tale, blab, sneak; — *adj.f.* tale-bearing, blabbing, sneak- [ing
Rapprendre, *v.a.* to learn again
Rapprêter, *v.a.* to ... (*V.* **Apprêter**) again
Rapprivoiser, *v.a.* to ... (*V.* **Apprivoiser**) [again
Rapprochage, *s.m.* (*hort.*) thinning
Rapproché, e, *part. adj.* drawn near again, &c. (*V.* **Rapprocher**); not far, not distant, near, at hand; short
Rapprochement, *s.m.* drawing *or* bringing *or* placing near *or* nearer; being drawn *or* brought *or* placed near *or* nearer; joining; bringing together; comparing; comparison; closer connection *or* tie; reconciliation; (*hort.*) thinning
Rapprocher, *v.a.* to draw *or* bring *or* place near again; to draw *or* bring *or* place near (*or* close) *or* nearer (*or* closer); to approximate; to bring together; to compare; to connect; to reconcile; (*hort.*) to thin

Se —, *v.r.* to come near again; to come *or* draw near *or* nearer; to approximate; to approach; to resemble, to be something like; to draw towards a reconciliation, to become reconciled; to be drawn *or* &c. near again, &c.; to be brought together, &c. [rights again
Rapproprier, *v.a.* to clean again; to put to
Rapprovisionner, *v a.* to ... (*V.* **Approvisionner**) again
Rapsode, &c. *V.* **Rhapsode,** &c.
Rapt, *s.m.* abduction; rape
Raptus, *s.m.* (*med.*) raptus, seizure
Râpure, *s.f.* raspings; gratings; shavings
Raquet, *s.m. V.* **Imbrim** [maker
Raquetier, *s. m.* racket-maker, battledore-
Raqueton, *s.m.* large racket
Raquette, *s.f.* racket, racquet; battledore, battledoor; snow-shoe; bird-trap; (*bot.*) Indian fig-tree
Rare, *adj.* rare; scarce; uncommon; unusual; curious; singular; scanty; few; sparse; thin; (*of the pulse and breathing*) slow
Raréfaction, *s.f.* rarefaction; rarity
Raréfiable, *adj.* rarefiable
Raréfier, *v.a.,* **Se** —, *v.r.* to rarefy
Rarement, *adv.* seldom, rarely [larity
Rareté, *s.f.* scarcity; rarity; curiosity; singu-
Rarissime, *adj.* very rare, most rare, extremely rare
Ras, e, *adj.* close-shaved, cut close, close; short-haired; short; smooth; shorn, short-nap; open; flat; blank; (*of measure*) strike; (*nav.*) low-built, low, straight-sheered; undecked; flat-bottomed; bare. *Poil* —, short hair; short nap. *Table* —*e*, *V.* **Table.** *Couper* —, to cut close. *A* —*e terre*, level with the ground

Ras, *s.m.* level; short-nap cloth; (*geog.*) race. — *de carène*, —, (*nav.*) floating stage, punt. — *de marée*, tide-way; race, bore, eagre. *A* — (*de*), *au* — (*de*), level (with); close (to). *Plein à*
Rasade, *s.f.* bumper, brimmer [—, brimful
Rasal, *s.m.* (*local*) baulk (*of timber*)
Rasant, e, *part. adj.* shaving, &c. (*V.* **Raser**); grazing, sweeping; horizontal; (*fort.*) rasant. *Vue —e*, view of a flat *or* open country
Rase, *s.f.* (*nav.*) calking-pitch
Rasement, *s.m.* shaving; razing *or* levelling to the ground; (*of horses*) ceasing to mark
Raser, *v.a.* to shave; to shave off; to graze, to brush, to sweep, to skim, to glance over, to pass close to, to touch lightly; to lay flat; to raze *or* rase, to raze to the ground, to demolish, to pull down; to suppress; to destroy, to ruin, to do for; to bore, to plague; to strike (*a measure*); to cut down *or* to razee (*a ship*); to disable (*a ship*); (*of ships*) to run *or* sail close to, to hug (*a coast*); — *v.n.* to shave; (*of horses*) to cease to mark, to be aged. — *l'air*, to hover. — *le tapis*, (*of horses*) to raze the ground
Se —, *v.r.* to shave, to shave oneself; to shave (o.'s ...); to get *or* be shaved, &c.; (*hunt.*, *of game*) to keep close to the ground
Rasette, *s.f.* (*agr.*) skim coulter
Raseur, *s.m.* shaver; (*pop.*) bore, plague
Rasibus, *prep.* (*pop.*) quite close [bore, plague
Rasoir, *s.m.* razor; (*zool.*) razor-fish; (*pop.*)
Rason, *s.m.* (*zool.*) razor-fish
Rassade, *s.f.* glass beads
Rassasiement, *s.m.* satiety; glut; surfeit
Rassasier, *v.a.* to satiate, to fill, to satisfy; to cloy; to glut; to surfeit; to overwhelm; to tire
Se —, *v.r.* to satisfy o.'s hunger *or* appetite; to take o.'s fill (of), to glut oneself (with); to get *or* be cloyed *or* &c.
Rassemblement, *s.m.* assembling, collecting, gathering; assemblage; crowd; mob, riotous meeting; muster, mustering
Rassembler, *v.a.* to reassemble; to assemble, to collect, to gather; to join, to unite; to put together; to summon up; to muster
Se —, *v.r.* to assemble; to congregate; to meet again; to meet; to crowd; to unite; to muster
Rasseoir, *v.a.* to seat again, to reseat; to replace; to calm, to appease, to compose, to settle
Se —, *v.r.* to sit down again; to sit down; to calm, to become (*or* be) calm *or* appeased *or* composed; to settle
Rasséréner, *v.a.* to clear up, to restore serenity to; to calm; to cheer up
Se —, *v.r.* to clear up, to recover o.'s *or* its serenity; to brighten up [again
Rassiéger, *v.a.* to besiege again; to beset
†Rassigner, *v.a.* (*old spelling*) *V.* **Réassigner**
Rassis, e, *part. adj.* reseated, &c. (*V.* **Rasseoir**); calm, quiet, settled, sedate, cool, sober-minded, staid; (*of bread*) stale. *De sens* (or *de sang*) —, cool; quiet; unmoved; coolly; quietly
Rassortiment, *s.m.* matching again, rematching, restocking, &c.; fresh assortment *or* &c. (*V.* **Assortiment**) [again
Rassortir, *v.a.* to match *or* &c. (*V.* **Assortir**)
Rassoter, *v.a.* *V.* **Assoter**
Rassurance, *s.f.* reassurance
Rassurer, *v.a.* to strengthen, to consolidate, to secure; to reassure, to quiet, to tranquillize, to remove the fears of, to restore confidence to; to cheer, to encourage; to satisfy
Se —, *v.r.* to tranquillize oneself, to be tranquillized *or* reassured, to recover oneself, to take confidence *or* courage, to put o.'s mind at rest, not to be uneasy *or* afraid, to cease to fear, to feel safe; (*of the weather*) to settle
Rat, *s.m.* rat; mouse; whim, crotchet; taper; ballet-dancer, ballet-girl; hotel-thief; ducky, darling; (*nav.*) *V.* **Ras,** *s.m.* — *de cave*, taper; exciseman. — *d'eau*, water-rat, water-vole. — *d'église*, church-mouse. — *-taupe*, mole-rat. *Prendre un* —, to miss fire, (*in old English*) to flash in the pan; (*pers.*) to fail
Rata, *s.m.* (*pop.*) victuals, grub, mess
Ratafia, *s.m.* (*liquor*) ratafia. — *de ...*, ...-ratafia, ...-brandy. — *de cerise*, cherry-brandy
Ratanhia, *s.m.* (*bot.*, *pharm.*) rattany, rhatany
Rataplan, *s.m.* drum-beating, drumming
Ratapoil, *s.m.* political martinet
Ratatiner, *v.a.*, **Se** —, *v.r.* to shrivel, to shrink
†Ratatouille, *s.f.* poor stew, bad stuff, mess, cagmag
Rate, *s.f.* spleen, milt; she-rat; shrew, harpy; hussy; ducky, darling. *Désopiler* or *épanouir la* — (*à*), to dispel the spleen, to excite laughter, to make (*one*) laugh heartily, to throw (*one*) into a roar of laughter, to put (*one*) in high spirits, to amuse (*one*), to make merry. *Ne pas se fouler la* —, not to overwork *or* hurry oneself, to take it (*or* things) easy
Raté, e, *part. adj.* missed; failed; a failure; defective, imperfect; abortive; miscarried; off; spoilt; lost; to no purpose; would-be; rat-gnawed; — *s.m.* miss-fire
Râteau, *s.m.* rake; (*horol.*, *nav.*) rack
Ratel, *s.m.* (*zool.*) ratel
Râtelage, *s.m.* raking
Râtelée, *s.f.* rakeful; (*old*) volley, tirade. *Dire sa* —, (*old*) to speak o.'s mind freely
Râteler, *v.a.* to rake
Râteleu-r, se, *s.m.f.* raker
Rateleu-x, se, *adj.* splenetic
Râtelier, *s.m.* rack; arm *or* gun-rack; (*jest.*) set of teeth, grinders; (*obsolete*) *V.* **Dentier**
Ratelle, *s.f.* (*med.*) splenalgia, splenalgy; (*vet.*) disease of pigs; (*butch.*) caul
Ratepenade, *s.f.* *V.* **Pastenague**
Rater, *v.n.a.* to miss fire, (*in old English*) to flash in the pan; to miss; to miscarry; to fail; to fail in; to spoil; to lose
Ratier, *s.m.* rat-catcher; — *adj.m.* whimsical
Ratière, *s.f.* rat-trap; — *adj.f.* whimsical
Ratificati-f, ve, *adj.* ratifying
Ratification, *s.f.* ratification
Ratifier, *v.a.* to ratify. *Se* —, to be ratified
Ratinage, *s.m.* (*manu.*) frizzing, friezing
Ratine, *s.f.* ratteen (*stuff*)
Ratiner, *v.a.* (*manu.*) to frizz, to frieze
Ratineuse, *s.f.* frizzing-machine
Ratiocination, *s.f.* ratiocination, reasoning
Ratiociner, *v.n.* to ratiocinate, to reason
Ration, *s.f.* ration, allowance
Rational, *s.m.* (*Jew. rel.*) breast-plate
Rationalisme, *s.m.* rationalism [alistic
Rationaliste, *s.m.f.* rationalist; — *adj.* ration-
Rationalité, *s.f.* rationality
Rationnel, le, *adj.* rational
Rationnellement, *adv.* rationally
Rationner, *v.a.* to ration, to allowance
Ratis, *s.m.* (*butch.*) scrapings
Ratissage, *s.m.* scraping; raking
Ratisser, *v.a.* to scrape; to rake; (*pop.*) to filch, to bag, to bone; to diddle, to chisel, to cheat; to win; to beat. *Je t'en ratisse*, (*pop.*) I don't care for you; you be blowed; don't you wish you may get it?
Se —, *v.r.* to be scraped, &c.
Ratissoire, *s.f.* scraper; rake
Ratissure, *s.f.* scrapings
Raton, *s.m.* (*zool.*) raccoon, racoon; (*fam.*) little rat; (*pers.*) ducky, darling; (*cat, in fable*) Mouser; (*obsolete*) bun
Ratoncule, *s.f.* (*bot.*) mouse-tail
Rattacher, *v.a.* to reattach; to tie *or* fasten *or* &c. (*V.* **Attacher**) again; to tie; to fasten; to connect
Se —, *v.r.* to be tied *or* fastened; to be connected; to be centred; to attach oneself again
Ratteindre, *v.a.* to catch again, to retake; to overtake
Ratteler, *v.a.* to ... (*V.* **Atteler**) again
Rattendrir, *v.a.* to ... (*V.* **Attendrir**) again
Rattiser, *v.a.* to ... (*V.* **Attiser**) again

Rattraper, *v.a.* to catch *or* take again; to overtake, to catch up; to recover, to retrieve, to get back; to compensate, to make up for, to recoup

Se —, *v.r.* to catch hold (of); to catch hold of something; to catch at things; to compensate *or* &c. oneself; to win back; to get back o.'s outlay, not to lose; (*of things*) to be caught again *or* &c.

Rature, *s.f.* erasure; scraping; streak

Raturer, *v.a.* to erase, to scratch *or* cross out; to cancel; to scrape; to streak

Rauche, *s.f.* (*bot.*) cat's-tail, bulrush [raucity

Raucité, *s.f.* harshness, roughness, hoarseness,

Rauque, *adj.* harsh, rough, hoarse, husky, rusty; shrill; wild

Ravage, *s. m.* ravage; devastation; waste; damage, havoc, mischief; bustle; (*thieves' slang*) swag [lay waste, to plunder

Ravager, *v.a.* to ravage, to spoil, to waste, to

Ravageur, *s.m.* ravager, spoiler; mud-lark

Ravale, *s.f.* land-presser, roller

Ravalé, e, *part. adj.* swallowed again, &c. (*V.* **Ravaler**); down; low; (*of stockings*) down at heel

Ravalement, *s.m.* pulling down; pressing; lowering; debasement; disparagement; humiliation; (*mas.*) roughcasting; (*arch.*) finishing off; recess. *A* —, (*of pianos*) with a double row of keys

Ravaler, *v.a.* to swallow again; to keep in; to pull down; to press (*land*), to roll; to lower; to debase; to degrade; to disparage; to humble; (*hort.*) to cut down; (*mas.*) to roughcast; (*arch.*) to finish off; — *v.n.* to go down, to fall

Se —, *v.r.* to lower oneself; to descend; to fall down [ling; (*obsolete*) twaddle

Ravaudage, *s.m.* mending; botching; bung-

Ravauder, *v.a.n.* to mend; to botch; to tease, to plague; to bully, to abuse, to rate; to bustle; to fumble, to rummage; to dally; to loiter; (*old*) to twaddle

Ravauderie, *s.f.* (*obsolete*) silly thing *or* stuff, nonsense, rigmarole, twaddle; soft nonsense, flirtation; botching; bungling; trash; teasing

Ravaudeu-r, se, *s. m.f.* stocking-mender; mender; botcher; bungler; (*obsolete*) twaddler

Rave, *s.f.* radish; turnip; hard roe (*of cod*)

Ravelin, *s.m.* (*fort.*) ravelin

Ravenala, *s.m.* (*bot.*) ravenala, traveller's tree

Ravenelle, *s.f.* (*bot.*) charlock; wall-flower

Ravet, *s.m.* *V.* **Cancrelas**

Rav tte, *s.f.* *V.* **Rabette**

Ravi, e, *part. adj.* ravished, &c. (*V.* **Ravir**); delighted, enraptured, overjoyed, glad. — *de joie*, overjoyed

Ravier, *s.m.* radish-dish, pickle-dish

Ravière, *s.f.* radish-bed

Ravigote, *s.f.* sharp sauce

Ravigoter, *v.a.* to revive the appetite of; to revive, to refresh; to enliven, to cheer

Ravilir, Ravilissement. *V.* **Avilir, Avilissement**

Ravin, *s.m.* ravine; hollow road

Ravine, *s.f.* torrent; gully, ravine

Ravinement, *s.m.* gullying

Raviner, *v.a.* to gully

Ravineu-x, se, *adj.* ravinous, gullied

Ravioles, *s.m.pl.* ravioles (*an Italian made-dish*)

Ravir, *v.a.* to ravish; to take away, to carry off *or* away; to snatch away, to snatch; to rescue; to steal; to deprive *or* rob of; to charm, to delight, to enrapture, to overjoy, to transport. *A* —, charmingly, delightfully, admirably, wonderfully *or* remarkably well

Se —, *v.r.* to ravish *or* &c. from oneself *or* each other; to be ravished *or* &c.

Ravisement, *s.m.* second thought, after-thought

Raviser (Se), *v.r.* to think better of it, to change o.'s mind

Ravissable, *adj.* ravishable

Ravissant, e, *adj.* ravenous; rapacious; ravishing, charming, delightful, lovely; (*her.*) ravissant

Ravissement, *s.m.* rape; ravishment; delight rapture, transport

Ravisseur, *s.m.* ravisher; spoiler; —**s,** *pl.* (*zool.*) raptores, raveners, rapacious birds

†**Ravitaillement,** *s. m.* revictualling; (*fig.*) recruiting [(*fig.*) to recruit

†**Ravitailler,** *v.a.*, **Se —,** *v.r.* to revictual;

Raviver, *v.a.*, **Se —,** *v.r.* to revive; to rouse; to cheer

Ravoir, *v.a.* (*used in the inf. only*) to have *or* get again; to have *or* get back; to recover

Se —, *v.r.* (*fam.*) to recover o.'s strength, to recruit, to pick up

Ravoir, *s.m.* (*fish.*) stake-net, poke-net

Raya, Rayah, *s.m.* *V.* **Raïa**

Rayer, *v.a.* to scratch; to erase, to scratch out *or* off, to cross off *or* out, to strike off *or* out; to cancel; to stop, to suppress; to disbar; to rule (*paper*); to stripe, to streak; to rifle

Se —, *v.r.* to be scratched *or* &c.

Rayère, *s.f.* loophole

Rayeur, *s.m.* (*instr.*) ruler

Ray-grass, *s.m.* (*bot.*) ray-grass

Rayon, *s.m.* ray; beam; gleam; radius; spoke (*of a wheel*); comb, honey-comb; shelf; bookshelf; furrow; line; (*com.*) department; (*fish*) young ray *or* skate; thornback

Rayonnage, *s.m.* tracing furrows *or* lines

Rayonnant, e, *part. adj.* radiating; radiant; beaming; starry

Rayonné, e, *part. adj.* radiated; radiate; stellate; (*of rooms*) shelved; — *s.m.* (*nat. hist.*) radiate, radiary [beaming

Rayonnement, *s. m.* radiation; radiance;

Rayonner, *v.n.* to radiate; to emit rays; to beam; to shine; to glisten; to spread; to trace furrows *or* lines; — *v.a.* to shelve (*a room*)

Rayonneur, *s.m.* plough with several shares

Rayure, *s.f.* stripe; streak; scratch; groove; grooves, rifling; (*old*) striking off *or* out [*sea*)

Raz, *s.m.* (— *de marée*) race, bore, eagre (*of the*

Razzia, *s.f.* razzia, inroad, raid, foray, plundering, depredation; clean sweep, sweep; capture [away *or* off, to sweep; to capture

Razzier, *v.a.* to plunder, to pillage; to sweep

Ré, *s.m.* (*mus.*) re, D

Réa, *s.m.* (*nav.*) sheave [renew o.'s subscription

Réabonner (Se), *v.r.* to subscribe again, to

Réabsorber, *v.a.* to reabsorb

Réabsorption, *s.f.* reabsorption [again

Réaccommoder, *v.a.* to ... (*V.* **Accommoder**)

Réacquérir, *v.a.* *V.* **Racquérir**

Réac-teur, trice, *adj. s.* (*old*) *V.* **Réactionnaire** [test-paper, litmus-paper

Réacti-f, ve, *adj.* reacting. *Papier* —, (*chem.*)

Réactif, *s.m.* (*chem.*) reagent, test

Réaction, *s.f.* reaction

Réactionnaire, *adj.* reactionary; — *s.m.f*

Réactionnel, le, *adj.* reactionary [reactionist

Réactionner, *v.a.* to sue again; — *v.n.* to react; to go down again

Réadmettre, *v.a.* to readmit, to admit again

Réadmission, *s.f.* readmission, readmittance

Réadopter, *v.a.* to readopt

Réadoption, *s.f.* readoption

Réafficher, *v.a.* to stick *or* post up again

Réaffirmer, *v.a.* to reaffirm [monitory

Réaggrave, *s.f.* (*can. law*) reaggravation, last

Réaggraver, *v.a.* (*can. law*) to reaggravate

Réagir, *v.n.* to react [summons

Réajournement, *s.m.* readjournment; fresh

Réajourner, *v.a.* to readjourn; to summon again

Réal, *s.m.*, **Réale,** *s.f.* real *or* rial (*Spanish coin*)

Réale, *s.f.* (*old*) royal galley

Réalgar, *s.m.* (*min.*) realgar

Réalisable, *adj.* realizable

Réalisa-teur, trice, *adj.s* realizing; realizer

Réalisation, *s.f.* realization; conversion into money

Réaliser, *v.a.* to realize; to convert into money

Se —, *v.r.* to be realized, &c.

Réalisme, *s.m.* realism
Réaliste, *s.m.f.* realist; — *adj.* realistic
Réalité, *s f.* reality; (*theol.*) real presence
Réamarrer, *v a.* to ... (*V.* **Amarrer**) again
Réapparaître, *v.n.* to reappear; to show one-self again
Réapparition, *s.f.* reappearance; return
Réappel, *s.m.* second call
Réappeler, *v.a.* to call again [**Apposer**) again
Réapposer, *v.a.* to reaffix, to affix *or* &c. (*V.*
Réapposition, *s.f.* reaffixing, affixing *or* &c. (*V.* **Apposition**) again; reintroduction, rein-sertion [silver *or* plate again
Réargenter, *v.a.* to resilver, to replate, to
Réargenture, *s.f.* resilvering, replating
Réarmement, *s.m.* rearmament, fresh arma-ment; reequipment, fresh equipment
Réarmer, *v.a.* to rearm, to arm *or* &c. (*V.*
Réarpentage, *s.m.* resurvey [**Armer**) again
Réarpenter, *v.a.* to resurvey
Réasservir, *v.a.* to ... (*V.* **Asservir**) again
†**Réassignation,** *s.f.* reassignment; fresh summons *or* &c. (*V.* **Assignation**)
†**Réassigner,** *v.a.* to reassign; to resummon; to ... (*V.* **Assigner**) again [**Rassortiment**
Réassortir, Réassortiment. *V.* **Rassortir,**
Réassurance, *s.f.* reinsurance
Réassurer, *v.a.* to reinsure
Réatteler, *v.a.* to ... (*V.* **Atteler**) again
Rebadigeonner, *v.a.* to ... (*V.* **Badigeonner**) again
†**Rebaigner,** *v.a.n.* to ... (*V.* **Baigner**) again
†**Rebâiller,** *v.a.*; **Rebailler,** *v.a.* to ... (*V.* **Bâiller** *and* **Bailler**) again
Rebaiser, *v.a.* to kiss again
Rebaisser, *v.a.n.* to ... (*V.* **Baisser**) again
Rébalade, *s.f.* waterfowl-shooting
Rébaleur, *s.m.* waterfowl-shooter
Rebander, *v.a.r.* to ... (*V.* **Bander**) again
Rebannir, *v.a.* to rebanish, to ... (*V.* **Bannir**) again [tizer
Rebaptisant, Rebaptisateur, *s.m.* rebap-
Rebaptisation, *s.f.* rebaptization, rebaptism
Rebaptiser, *v.a.* to rebaptize, to ... (*V.* **Baptiser**) again [cross, ill-looking, repulsive
Rébarbati-f, ve, *adj.* stern, gruff, crabbed,
Rebassiner, *v.a.* to ... (*V.* **Bassiner**) again
Rebâter, *v.a.* to resaddle, to saddle again
Rebâtir, *v.a.* to rebuild, to ... (*V.* **Bâtir**) again
Se —, *v.r.* to be rebuilding; to be rebuilt; to change o.'s own nature
Rebattre, *v.a.* to ... (*V.* **Battre**) again; to stun *or* din (*the ears*), to fatigue, to weary; to repeat over and over, to repeat
Se —, *v.r.* to fight again, to have another fight; to scramble again; to beat (o.'s ...) again
Rebattu, e, (*part. of* **Rebattre**) beaten again, &c.; — *adj.* often-told, old, trite, hackneyed, worn-out, tiresome; fatigued, weary, sick. *Avoir les oreilles —es de,* to be tired of hearing
Rebaudir, *v.a.* (*hunt.*) to caress, to encourage (*dogs*); — *v.n.* to wag the tail
Rebec, *s.m.* (*anc. mus. instr.*) rebec
Rébecca, *s.f.* saucy baggage, pert minx
Rebelle, *adj.* rebellious; disobedient; contu-macious; obstinate; refractory; unfeeling, indifferent; ill-adapted; — *s.m.f.* rebel
Rebeller (Se), *v r.* (*old*) to rebel, to revolt
Rébellion, *s.f* rebellion; resistance; contumacy
Rébellionnaire, *s.m.f.* contumacious person
Rébellionner (Se), *v.r.* to rebel, to revolt
Rebéni, e, *part. adj.* blessed again
Rebénir, *v.a.* to bless again; to reconsecrate, to consecrate anew
Rebénit, e, *part. adj.* reconsecrated [to resist
Rebéquer (Se), *v.r.* to be saucy, to answer,
Rebiffer (Se), *v.r.* to resist, to kick; to hold up the head, to bridle up, to have a soldierlike appearance
Reblanchir, *v.a.* to ... (*V.* **Blanchir**) again
Rèble, *s.m.* *V.* **Rièble**
Reblesser, *v.a.* to wound again

Reboire, *v.a.n.* to drink again
Reboisage, *s.m.* timbering *or* wainscoting again
Reboisement, *s.m.* restocking with woods *or* trees, replanting (*of forests*); timbering again
Reboiser, *v.a.* to restock with woods *or* trees, to replant; to timber again; to wainscot again
Rebond, *s.m.* rebound; bump
Rebondi, e, *adj.* plump; round; chubby; full; swollen; swelling
Rebondir, *v.n.* to rebound; to bump
Se —, *v.r.* to become plump *or* round *or* full
Rebondissement, *s.m.* rebounding, rebound;
Rebondonner, *v.a.* to bung again [bumping
Rebord, *s.m.* brim; rim; edge; ledge; border; hem; flange
Reborder, *v.a.* to border again, to new-border; to new-bind, to rebind; to rehem; to new-line; to tuck in again; to ... (*V.* **Border**) again. *Oreilles rebordées,* thick-hemmed ears
Rebotter, *v.a.* to ... (*V.* **Botter**) again
Se —, *v.r.* to put o.'s boots on again
Rebouchage, Rebouchement, *s.m.* stop-ping up again [(*old*) to blunt, to bend
Reboucher, *v.a.* to ... (*V.* **Boucher**) again,
Se —, *v.r.* to become *or* get (*or* be) stopped *or* &c. (*V.* **Boucher**) again; (*old*) to get blunt, to
†**Rebouil,** *s.m.* skin-wool, pelt-wool [bend
†**Rebouillir,** *v.n.* to ... (*V.* **Bouillir**) again [ing
Rebouisage, *s.m.* (*of hats*) cleaning and polish-
Rebouiser, *v.a.* (*of hats*) to clean and polish
Rebourgeonner, *v.n.* to ... (*V.* **Bourgeonner**) again
Rebours, *s.m.* wrong way, wrong side; reverse, contrary. *A —, au —,* the wrong way; against the grain; backward; the reverse (of); con-trary (to); reversed; cross-grained
Rebours, e, *adj.* cross-grained; crabbed, testy; restive, restiff, jibbing
Reboutage, Reboutement, *s.m.* bone-setting
Rebouter, *v.a.* (*old*) to put again; (*pop.*) to set (*limbs*) [bone-setter
Rebouteu-r, se, Rebouteu-x, se, *s.m.f.*
Reboutonner, *v.a.n.* to ... (*V.* **Boutonner**)
Rebrassé, e, *adj.* (*her.*) bordered [again
Rebrider, *v.a.* to ... (*V.* **Brider**) again
Rebrocher, *v.a.* to stitch *or* sew again (*books*)
Rebroder, *v.a.* to reembroider; to embroider over
†**Rebrouiller,** *v.a.* to ... (*V.* **Brouiller**) again
Rebroussement, *s.m.* turning up *or* back; ruffling; (*geom.*) retrogression
Rebrousse-poil (A), *adv.* against the hair; against the grain, the wrong way
Rebrousser, *v.a.* to turn up *or* back; to ruffle; to go against; to go up, to ascend; to retrace; — *v.n.* to go *or* turn back; to run *or* flow back; to recoil. — *chemin,* to go *or* turn back, to
Se —, *v.r.* to recoil [retrace o.'s steps
Rebroyer, *v.a.* to ... (*V.* **Broyer**) again
Rebrûler, *v.a.n.* to ... (*V.* **Brûler**) again
Rebrunir, *v.a.n.* to ... (*V.* **Brunir**) again
Rebuffade, *s.f.* rebuff; repulse; rebuke; denial
Rébus, *s.m.* rebus; conundrum, pun
Rebut, *s.m.* repulse, rebuff; rejection; refusal; refuse, waste; trash, rubbish; scum; outcast; dead-letter. *De —,* waste, refuse; left off, cast off; trashy. *Bureau des —s,* dead-letter office. *Mettre au —,* to throw aside, to cast off; to send to the dead-letter office
Rebutant, e, *adj.* repulsive, forbidding; dis-couraging; tedious; loathsome; crabbed
Rebuter, *v.a.* to reject; to throw aside, to cast off; to discard; to repel; to repulse; to refuse; to rebuff; to discourage, to dishearten; to disgust; to deter; to shock; to displease
Se —, *v.r.* to be rejected, &c.; to be discou-raged *or* disheartened *or* deterred, to lose courage
Recacher, *v.a.* to hide *or* conceal again
Recacheter, *v.a.* to seal again, to reseal
Récalcitrant, e, *adj.* recalcitrant; refractory, stubborn; restive, restiff; reluctant; averse

Récalcitrer, *v.n.* to recalcitrate, to kick back, to kick; to be obstinate, to resist; to be reluctant
Recalculer, *v.a.* to ... (*V.* **Calculer**) again
Recaler, *v.a.* to ... (*V.* **Caler**) again
Se —, *v.r.* to be wedged up *or* &c. again; (*pop.*) to get a fresh rig-out; to recruit o.'s strength, to pick up
Recalfater, *v.a.* (*nav.*) to calk again, to recalk
Recalfeutrer, *v.a.* to ... (*V.* **Calfeutrer**) again
Récapitulati-f, ve, *adj.* recapitulatory [up
Récapitulation, *s.f.* recapitulation, summing
Récapituler, *v.a.* to recapitulate, to sum up
Recarboniser, *v.a.* to recarbonize
Recarder, *v.a.* to card again [sole
Recarreler, *v.a.* to new-pave; (*boots*) to new-
Recasser, *v.a.* to ... (*V.* **Casser**) again
Recéder, *v.a.* to yield *or* &c. (*V.* **Céder**) again; to recede; to sell back *or* again; to give back, [to restore
Recel, *s.m.* receiving (*stolen goods*)
Recélé, Recèlement, *s.m.* receiving (*stolen goods*); concealment; embezzlement
Receler, *v.a.* to receive (*stolen goods*); to conceal, to hide, to secrete; to harbour; to contain; to embezzle; — *v.n.* (*hunt.*) to remain concealed [intaker; concealer; embezzler
Recéleu-r, se, *s.m.f.* receiver (*of stolen goods*),
Récemment, *adv.* recently, lately
Récence, *s.f.* recency [tion; revisal, revision
Recensement, *s.m.* census; return; verifica-
Recenser, *v.a.* to take the census of; to verify; to revise, to review, to recense
Recenseur, *s.m.* enumerator; recensionist
Recension, *s.f.* recension
Récent, e, *adj.* recent, new, fresh, late
Recépage, *s.m.* cutting down
Recépée, *s.f.* cut part (of a wood)
Recéper, *v.a.* to cut down
Récépissé, *s.m.* receipt, acknowledgment
Réceptacle, *s.m.* receptacle
Réceptaculaire, *adj.* receptacular
Récepteur, *s.m.* recipient, receiver, reservoir; (*of electric telegraphs*) receiving *or* recording instrument
Réception, *s.f.* receipt, receiving; reception; admittance; admission; acceptance; assembly, party; audience; levee; drawing-room; court. *Accuser — de,* to acknowledge the receipt of [receiver, recipient
Réceptionnaire, *adj.* receiving; — *s.m.f.*
Réceptivité, *s.f.* receptivity
Recercelé, e, *adj.* (*her.*) recercelee, cercelee
Recerclage, *s.m.* new-hooping
Recercler, *v.a.* to put new hoops to, to new-hoop, to hoop again, to rehoop
Recès, *s.m.* *V.* **Recez**
Récession, *s.f.* recession
Recette, *s.f.* receipt; receipts; collection; recipe; receiver's *or* collector's office; receivership; collectorship. *Garçon de —,* collecting-clerk [ness; admissibility
Recevabilité, *s.f.* receivability, receivable-
Recevable, *adj.* receivable; admissible; admitted, allowed
Recevant, e, *s.m.f.* recipient, receiver
Receveu-r, se, *s.m.f.* receiver; collector
Recevoir, *v.a.n* to receive; to accept; to admit; to introduce; to take; to take in; to collect; to have; to get; to catch; to meet, to meet with; to submit to; to allow; to approve; to authorize; to harbour; to welcome; to greet; to treat; to entertain; to receive *or* have company; to be at home (*for visitors*); to give audience; to hold a levee *or* drawing-room *or* court
Se —, *v.r.* to receive *or* visit each other; to be received *or* &c.; to catch hold (of); to catch hold of something; to catch at things
Recez, *s.m.* (*hist.*) recess, decrees (*of the Empire*); minutes (*of a congress,* &c.), conventions
Réchabite, *s.m.* Rechabite [off
Réchampir, *v.a.* (*gilding, house-paint.*) to set
Réchampissage, *s.m.* setting off
Rechange, *s.m.* change; spare thing; spare stores; (*com.*) reexchange. *De —,* spare
Rechanger, *v.a.n.* to ... (*V.* **Changer**) again
Se —, *v.r.* to change o.'s linen *or* clothes
Rechanter, *v.a.* to sing again; to repeat
Réchappé, *part. adj.* escaped; recovered; — *adj. s.* runaway; one saved (from). *— de la potence,* regular ruffian, gallows-bird
Réchapper, *v.n.* to escape; to recover
Recharge, *s.f.* fresh charge [restoning
Rechargement, *s.m.* reloading; reballasting;
Recharger, *v.a.n.* to load again, to reload; to charge again, to recharge; to reballast; to re-stone; to ... (*V.* **Charger**) again
Rechasser, *v.a.n.* to drive back; to drive away *or* &c. (*V.* **Chasser**) again
Réchaud, *s.m.* dish-warmer, warmer; hot-water dish *or* plate; warming-apparatus; heater; stove; etna; panakin; (*hort.*) mulch
Réchauffage, *s.m.* heating; getting up the steam
Réchauffé, e, *part. adj.* warmed again, &c. (*V.* **Réchauffer**); stale, old, insipid; — *s.m.* warmed-up dish *or* dinner; stale *or* old stuff; after-thought [again; (*hort.*) mulching; mulch
Réchauffement, *s.m.* warming *or* heating
Réchauffer, *v.a.* to warm again *or* over; to heat again; to warm up; to warm; to chafe; to revive, to stir up; (*hort.*) to mulch
Se —, *v.r.* to get warm, to warm oneself; to warm; to revive
Réchauffoir, *s.m.* stove, dish-warmer
Rechaussement, *s.m.* (*hort.*) earthing up, moulding up
Rechausser, *v.a.* to ... (*V.* **Chausser**) again; (*agr.*) to earth up, to mould up; (*build.*) to [underpin
Rêche, *adj.* rough, harsh
Rechef (De), *adv.* (*obsolete*) *V.* **Derechef**
Recherche, *s.f.* search, seeking; pursuit; inquiry; investigation; research; addresses, courting, courtship; affectation; refinement; elegance; finish; care. *A la — de,* in search *or* quest of; in pursuit of
Recherché, e, *part. adj.* sought after, &c. (*V.* **Rechercher**); in demand, in request; rare; studied; affected; far-fetched; refined; fine; elegant; highly finished; exquisite; particular, nice; careful; — *s.m.* affectation
Rechercher, *v.a.* to seek again; to seek, to seek for *or* after, to look for; to search, to search for *or* after; to pursue; to inquire into; to investigate; to examine; to call to account; to visit; to court, to seek *or* solicit in marriage, to pay o.'s addresses to; (*arts*) to finish off, to polish; (*rid.*) to animate
Se —, *v.r.* to seek *or* &c. each other; to seek each other's society; (*things*) to be sought after *or* &c.; (*old*) to be affected; to overrefine; to be particular
†**Rechigné, e,** *adj.* cross-looking, sour-looking, sour-faced, cross, crabbed, gruff, sulky
†**Rechignement,** *s.m.* crabbedness, crabbed look, sulkiness
†**Rechigner,** *v.n.* to look cross *or* sour *or* crabbed *or* gruff, to have a cross *or* &c. look, to sulk. *En rechignant,* with a cross *or* &c. look, reluctantly, with a bad grace
Rechoir, *v.n.def.* (*old*) to fall again; to relapse
Rechute, *s.f.* relapse
Rechuter, *v.n.* to have a relapse, to relapse
Récidive, *s.f.* relapse, fresh offence, repetition; (*med.*) reappearance
Récidiver, *v.n.* to commit the same offence, to relapse; (*med.*) to reappear
Récidiviste, *s.m.f.* old offender
Récidivité, *s.f.* tendency to relapse; (*med.*) tendency to reappear
Récif, *s.m.* reef, ridge, ledge
Recimenter, *v.a.* to ... (*V.* **Cimenter**) again
Récipé, *s.m.* recipe, receipt [ber
Récipiendaire, *s.m.* member elect, new mem-

Récipient, *s.m.* (*chem., phys.,* &c.) recipient, receiver; cistern; well
Réciprocation, *s.f.* reciprocation
Réciprocité, *s.f.* reciprocity; reciprocation
Réciproque, *adj.* reciprocal; mutual; converse; — *s.m.* (*fam.*) like, same, return; — *s.f.* (*math., log.*) converse
Réciproquement, *adv.* reciprocally; mutually; conversely; vice versâ
Réciproquer, *v.n.a.* to reciprocate; to requite
Recirer, *v.a.* to ... (*V.* **Cirer**) again
Récit, *s.m.* recital; relation, narrative, account, report, statement; tale, story; (*mus.*) solo; (*mus., obsolete*) recitative; (*of the organ*) swell
Récitant, e, *adj.* (*mus.*) solo
Récita-teur, trice, *s.m.f.* reciter
Récitatif, *s.m.* (*mus.*) recitative [recitation
Récitation, *s.f.* recital, rehearsal, repetition;
Réciter, *v.a.n.* to recite, to rehearse, to repeat; to relate; to say; to say o.'s lesson *or* the lessons; (*mus.*) to sing *or* play a recitative
Se —, *v.r.* to be recited, &c.
Réciteu-r, se, *s.m.f.* reciter; story-teller
Réclamable, *adj.* claimable
Réclamant, e, *s.m.f.* claimant; plaintiff
Réclama-teur, trice, *s.m.f.* claimant; complainer
Réclamation, *s.f.* claim; demand; protest, protestation; opposition; objection; observation; representation; complaint; rectification; compensation claim, claim for damages
Réclame, *s.f.* article, advertisement; paragraph-puff, puff; (*print.*) catchword; prima; (*theat.*) catchword, cue; — *s.m.* bird-call
Réclamer, *v.a.n.* to ask back; to reclaim; to claim, to lay claim to; to demand; to require; to call for; to implore, to entreat; to protest; to oppose; to object; to complain; to claim compensation *or* damages
Se —, *v.r.* to be claimed, &c.; (*de*) to make use of the name (of), to mention the name (of) as a reference, to refer (to); to invoke; (*of birds*) to call each other
Reclassement, *s.m.* reclassing
Réclinaison, *s.f.* reclination
Réclinant, e, *part. adj.* reclining, reclinant
Récliné, e, *part. adj.* reclined, reclinate
Récliner, *v.a.n.* to recline
Recloîtrer, *v.a.* to cloister *or* shut up again
Reclouer, *v.a.* to ... (*V.* **Clouer**) again
Reclure, *v.a.* to shut up, to seclude
Reclus, e, *part. adj. s.* shut up, secluded; re-
Recluserie, *s.f.* close cell [cluse
Réclusion, *s.f.* reclusion, seclusion; confinement; (*law*) imprisonment with hard labour, hard labour (*for a minimum term of five years and a maximum of ten, in France*), penal servitude
Réclusionnaire, *s.m.f. adj.* convict
†**Recogner,** *v.a.* to ... (*V.* **Cogner**) again; (*pop.*) to rebuff, to knock on the head
Récogniti-f, ve, *adj.* recognitory
Récognition, *s.f.* recognition
Recoiffer, *v.a.* to ... (*V.* **Coiffer**) again
Recoin, *s.m.* corner, nook; by-place; recess
Récolement, *s.m.* examination; verification
Récoler, *v.a.* to examine; to verify
Récollection, *s.f.* recollection
Recollement, *s.m.* pasting *or* gluing *or* sticking *or* adhering again [again
Recoller, *v.a.n.*, **Se** —, *v.r.* to ... (*V.* **Coller**)
Récollet, te, *s.m.f.* Recollet, Reformed Franciscan friar *or* nun [(Se)
Récolliger (Se), *v.r.* (*pers.*) *V.* **Recueillir**
Recoloration, *s.f.* recoloration, fresh colouring, fresh colour [again
Recolorer, *v.a.* to recolour, to ... (*V.* **Colorer**)
Récolte, *s.f.* crop; harvest; vintage; growth; [collection
Récolter, *v.a.* to reap, to gather
Se —, *v.r.* to be reaped *or* gathered
Recombattre, *v.a.n.* to ... (*V.* **Combattre**) again [again
Recombiner, *v.a.* to recombine; to contrive
Recombler, *v.a.* to ... (*V.* **Combler**) again
Recommandable, *adj.* recommendable, commendable; respectable [ably, commendably
Recommandablement, *adv.* recommend-
Recommandation, *s. f.* recommendation; introduction; reference; esteem
Recommander, *v.a.* to recommend; to commend; to intrust; to enjoin, to bid; to charge; to instruct; to advise; to exhort; to desire, to request, to beg; to pray for
Se —, *v.r.* to recommend oneself; to look for protection; (*de*) to make use of the name (of), to say one is known (to), to refer (to)
Recommandeu-r, se, *s.m.f.* recommender
Recommence, *s.f.* fresh count
Recommencement, *s.m.* recommencement, beginning again, new beginning; repetition; renewal; fresh count
Recommencer, *v.a.n.* to recommence, to begin again; to repeat; to renew; to do again *or* over again; to have again; to do so *or* it again; to do (*or* to be) the same thing again; to renew the attempt, to try again; to occur *or* happen again
Se —, *v.r.* to be recommenced, &c.
Récompense, *s.f.* recompense; reward; return; requital; compensation, amends
Récompenser, *v.a.* to recompense; to reward; to requite, to repay; to compensate; to make amends; to make up for
Se —, *v.r.* to recompense *or* compensate oneself *or* each other; to make amends, to make up for it; to be recompensed *or* &c.
Récompenseur, *s.m.* rewarder; — *adj.m.* re-
Recomposable, *adj.* recomposable [warding
Recomposer, *v.a.* to recompose; to reset
Se —, *v.r.* to recompose itself; to be recomposed; to be reset
Recomposition, *s.f.* recomposition; resetting
Recomptage, *s.m.* counting again, fresh reckoning
Recompter, *v.a.* to count *or* reckon again
Réconciliable, *adj.* reconcilable
Réconcilia-teur, trice, *s.m.f.* reconciler; — *adj.* reconciling, reconciliatory
Réconciliation, *s.f.* reconciliation
Réconciliatoire, *adj.* reconciliatory
Réconcilier, *v.a.* to reconcile
Se —, *v.r.* to reconcile oneself, to be reconciled, to make it up [again
Recondamner, *v.a.* to ... (*V.* **Condamner**)
Réconduction, *s.f.* renewal of a lease, continued tenancy
Reconduire, *v.a.* to reconduct; to lead *or* take back; to accompany; to see out; to show out; to see home
Reconduite, *s. f.* reconducting, seeing *or* showing out, seeing home. *Faire la* —, *V.* **Reconduire**
Reconfesser, *v.a.* to ... (*V.* **Confesser**) again
Reconfiner, *v.a.* to confine *or* shut up again
Reconfirmation, *s.f.* reconfirmation
Reconfirmer, *v.a.* to reconfirm [again
Reconfisquer, *v.a.* to ... (*V.* **Confisquer**)
Reconfort, *s.m.*, **Reconfortation,** *s.f.* strengthening; refreshment; comfort, comforting, consolation
Reconforter, *v.a.* to strengthen; to recruit, to refresh; to revive; to comfort, to cheer up
Se —, *v.r.* to recruit o.'s strength; to be strengthened *or* &c. [confronting again
Reconfrontation, *s.f.* new confrontation,
Reconfronter, *v.a.* to confront again
Reconnaissable, *adj.* recognizable, to be recognized, to be known again easy to be recognized
Reconnaissance, *s.f.* gratitude, thankfulness; recognition; recognizance; examination; verification; confession; acknowledgment; I O U; receipt; pawn-ticket, ticket, duplicate; requital, reward; exploration; (*mil., nav.*) reconnoitring, reconnaissance;

reconnoitring party *or* expedition; (*nav.*) discovery; sea-mark. *Faire de la* —, to make a show *or* a display of gratitude. *Faire* or *pousser une* —, (*mil.*) to reconnoitre

Reconnaissant, e, *adj.* grateful, thankful

Reconnaître, *v.a.* to know again, to know; to recognize; to remember; to identify; to acknowledge; to admit; to allow; to own; to confess; to discover, to find out; to find, to find to be; to see; to be grateful *or* thankful for; to requite, to repay, to reward, to recompense; to explore, to observe; (*mil., nav.*) to reconnoitre; (*of patrols*) to challenge. — *pour*, to acknowledge as; to know *or* find to be. *Je vous reconnais bien là*, that is just like you; it is always the way with you

Se —, *v.r.* to recognize *or* know *or* find *or* see *or* own oneself; to plead (*guilty*); to know one another again; to recognize *or* &c. each other; to understand each other; to know where one is; to find *or* see o.'s way; to know what one is about; to make out; to tell which is which; to look about, to reflect; to recollect oneself; to recover oneself, to come to oneself again; to give *or* take breathing time; to acknowledge o.'s errors, to repent; to be recognized *or* &c. *Je me reconnais bien là*, that is just like me. *Je me reconnais dans cet endroit*, I know where I am here [to regain

Reconquérir, *v.a.* to reconquer; to recover,

Reconsidération, *s.f.* reconsideration

Reconsidérer, *v.a.* to reconsider

Reconsoler, *v.a.* to console anew, to recom-

Reconsolidation, *s.f.* reconsolidation [fort

Reconsolider, *v.a.* to reconsolidate. *Se* —, to become *or* be reconsolidated

Reconstituer, *v.a.* to reconstitute; to reestablish; to reorganize; to reinvigorate; to ... (*V.* **Constituer**) again

Se —, *v.r.* to reconstitute *or* &c. oneself; to become *or* be reconstituted, &c. *Se — prisonnier*, to surrender again

Reconstitution, *s.f.* reconstitution; reorganization; resettlement; (*law*) substitution

Reconstruction, *s.f.* reconstruction, reconstructing, rebuilding

Reconstruire, *v.a.* to reconstruct, to rebuild

Se —, *v.r.* to be reconstructed, &c.

Reconsulter, *v.a.* to consult again

Reconter, *v.a.* to relate *or* tell again

Recontinuer, *v.a.n.* to recontinue, to go on again (with) [again

Recontracter, *v.a.* to ... (*V.* **Contracter**)

Reconvenir, *v.n.a.* (*law*) to enter a cross-suit (against) [action, reconvention

Reconvention, *s.f.* (*law*) cross-suit, cross-

Reconventionnel, le, *adj.* (*law*) cross. *Demande —le*, cross-suit, cross-action; cross-summons [cross-suit

Reconventionnellement, *adv.* (*law*) by a

Reconvertir, *v.a.* to reconvert

Reconvier, *v.a.*, **Reconvoquer,** *v.a.* to ... (*V.* **Convier** *&* **Convoquer**) again

Recopier, *v.a.* to recopy, to copy again

Se —, *v.r.* to be recopied, &c

Recoquer (Se), *v.r.* (*of birds*) to couple again; (*pop.*) to get a fresh rig-out; to recruit o.'s strength *or* health, to pick up

Recoquetage, *s.m.* (*of birds*) second coupling

†**Recoquillement,** *s.m.* curling up, shrinking, shrivelling

†**Recoquiller,** *v.a.* to curl up; to cockle up; to shrink up; to cock; to dog's-ear

Se —, *v.r.* to curl up, to cockle up, to turn up, to shrivel

Recorder, *v.a.* to record; to rehearse, to get by heart, to con; to remind; to give the cue; to cord again; to tie again; to twist again

Se —, *v.r.* to recall to mind; to remember; to remember what one has to say *or* do; to concert (with); to be recorded *or* &c. [to revise

Recorriger, *v.a.* to recorrect, to correct again,

Se —, *v.r.* to recorrect *or* &c. oneself *or* o.'s own work; to be recorrected *or* &c.

Recors, *s.m.* bailiff's man *or* follower, under-bailiff, bumbailiff [**Coucher**) again

Recoucher, *v.a.n.*, **Se** —, *v.r.* to ... (*V.*

Recoudre, *v.a.n.* to ... (*V.* **Coudre**) again

Recouler, *v.n.a.* to ... (*V.* **Couler**) again

Recoupe, *s. f.* cuttings; chippings, chips; scraps; rubble; diluted alcohol; (*of meal*) seconds; (*agr.*) *V.* **Regain** [cess

Recoupement, *s.m.* (*arch.*) offset, set-off, re-

Recouper, *v.a.* to ... (*V.* **Couper**) again

Recoupette, *s.f.*, **Recoupon,** *s.m.* (*of meal*) thirds [recurved, recurvate; crooked; hooked

Recourbé, e, *part. adj.* bent round *or* back,

Recourbement, *s.m.* bending round *or* back, recurvation [recurve, to recurvate; to crook

Recourber, *v.a.* to bend round *or* back, to

Se —, *v.r.* to bend round *or* back; to become crooked [curvature

Recourbure, *s.f.* bending round *or* back, re-

Recourir, *v.n.a.* to run again; to hunt *or* &c. (*V.* **Courir**) again; to have recourse, to apply, to resort; to petition, to sue; to appeal

Recouronner, *v.a.* to recrown, to crown again

Recourre, *v.a.n.* (*hunt.*) to hunt again; (*old*) to rescue, to save

Recours, *s.m.* recourse; resort; refuge; resource; help; redress; remedy; appeal; petition, suit. — *en grâce*, petition for pardon *or* commutation

Recousse, *s.f.* (*old*) rescue; (*nav.*) recapture

Recouvrable, *adj.* recoverable

Recouvrance, *s.f.* (*old*) recovery

Recouvrement, *s.m.* recovery; regaining; payment; collection (*of debts*, &c.); outstanding debt; covering; projection, overlap, lap; (*of watches*, &c.) cap; (*of telescopes*) sun-shade. *Faire un* —, to collect an outstanding debt

Recouvrer, *v.a.* to recover; to regain; to get again *or* back; to get in, to get; to collect

Se —, *v.r.* to be recovered *or* &c.

Recouvrir, *v.a.* to cover again, to recover; to cover up *or* over; to cover; to conceal, to hide, to mask, to cloak; to overlap

Se —, *v.r.* to cover oneself again; to be covered again *or* &c.; to cover each other; to overlap; (*of the sky*) to be overcast again, to become cloudy again

Recracher, *v.n.a.* to spit again; to spit out again; to fork out again; to disgorge

Récréance, *s.f.* (*can. law*) provisional possession; (*dipl.*) recall. *Lettres de* —, letters of recall [verting, entertaining

Récréati-f, ve, *adj.* recreative, amusing, di-

Récréation, *s.f.* recreation, amusement, diversion; play; play-time

Récréativement, *adv.* recreatively

Recréer, *v.a.* to create anew, to recreate

Récréer, *v.a.* to recreate, to amuse, to divert, to entertain, to enliven, to refresh, to relieve

Récrément, *s.m.* recrement

Récrémenteu-x, se, Récrémentitiel, le, *adj.* recremental, recrementitial, recrementitious

Recrêper, *v.a.* to ... (*V.* **Crêper**) again

Recrépiment, *s.m.* *V.* **Recrépissage**

Recrépir, *v.a.* (*mas.*) to roughcast again, to plaster over again; (*fig.*) to paint; to dress up; to patch up; to conceal

Recrépissage, Recrépissement, *s.m.*, **Recrépissure,** *s.f.* new roughcasting

Recreuser, *v.a.* to dig again *or* deeper; to ... (*V.* **Creuser**) again

Recribler, *v.a.* to ... (*V.* **Cribler**) again

Récri, *s.m.* exclamation, outcry, clamour; pro-

Recrier, *v.n.a.* to ... (*V.* **Crier**) again [testation

Récrier (Se), *v.r.* to exclaim, to utter exclamations *or* an exclamation, to cry out; to shout; to clamour; to admire; to protest

Récrimina-teur, trice, *adj. s.* recriminating; recriminator

Récrimination, *s.f.* recrimination
Récriminatoire, *adj.* recriminatory
Récriminer, *v.n.* to recriminate
Récrire, *v.a.n* to rewrite; to write again; to write over again; to write back; to answer
Se —, *v.r.* to write again to (*or* answer) each other; to be rewritten, to be written again *or* over again
†Recrobiller. *V.* **Recoquiller**
Recroiser, *v.a.* to recross, to ... (*V.* **Croiser**) again
Recroiseté, e, *adj.* *Croix —e,* (*her.*) cross crosslet
Recroître, *v.n.* to grow again; to rise again
†Recroqueviller. *V* **Recoquiller**
Recrotter, *v.a.* to .. (*V.* **Crotter**) again
Recru, e, *adj.* worn out, tired out, knocked up, exhausted, spent, jaded
Recrû, *m.,* **Recrue,** *f., part. of* **Recroître,** grown again; risen again
Recru, *s.m.* (*of wood*) new growth
Recrudescence, *s.f* recrudescence
Recrudescent, e, *adj.* recrudescent
Recrue, *s.f.* recruiting; recruit; recruits; year's shoots
Recrutement, *s.m.* recruiting, recruitment
Recruter, *v.a.* to recruit
Recruteur, *s.m.* recruiter; recruiting officer *or* sergeant; — *adj.m.* recruiting
Recta, *adv.* punctually, all right; directly, straight; in full, everything, to the last farthing
Rectal, e, *adj.* (*anat.*) rectal
Rectangle, *s.m.* rectangle
Rectangle, Rectangulaire, *adj.* rectangled, rectangular, right-angled
Rectangularité, *s.f.* rectangularity
Recteur, *s.m.* rector; provost; — *adj.m.* (*old*) aromatic
Rectifiable, *adj.* rectifiable
Rectifica-teur, trice, *s.m.f.* rectifier
Rectificati-f, ve, *adj.* rectificatory; rectified, amended
Rectification, *s.f.* rectification; amendment
Rectifier, *v.a.* to rectify; to correct; to amend
Se —, *v.r.* to rectify *or* &c. oneself *or* each other; to be rectified, &c.
†Rectiligne, *adj.* rectilinear, rectilineal; plane; right, straightforward
†Rectilignement, *adv* rectilinearly; straightforwardly
Rectite, *s.f.* (*med.*) rectitis
Rectitude, *s.f.* rectitude; rightness; uprightness
Recto, *s.m.* right-hand page, first page, odd page; — (*in compounds, anat.*) recto-...
Rectoral, e, *adj.* rectoral, rectorial
Rectorat, *s.m.* rectorate; rectorship; provostship
Rectrice, *s.f., adj.f.* (*of birds*) tail-feather
Rectum, *s.m.* (*anat.*) rectum
Reçu, e, *part. adj.* received; accepted; admitted; allowed; treated, &c. (*V.* **Recevoir**); recognized; usual, customary; current
Reçu, *s.m.* receipt; acknowledgment
†Recueil, *s.m.* collection; selection; miscellany; book. — *choisi,* choice selection, elegant extracts. — *de lieux communs,* commonplace book
†Recueillement, *s.m.* gathering, collecting, collection; collectedness; concentration of thought; self-communing; meditation, contemplation; reflection; composure; abstraction; devout attention, devotion; calmness, stillness
†Recueilleu-r, se, *s.m.f.* gatherer; collector, collectress
†Recueilli, e, *part. adj.* gathered, collected, &c. (*V.* **Recueillir**); concentrated; meditative, contemplative; abstracted, wrapped in contemplation; devout; quiet, placid, calm, still
†Recueillir, *v.a.* to gather, to reap; to collect; to get in; to take up, to pick up; to receive; to shelter; to come into possession of, to inherit; to summon up; (*old*) to sum up
Se —, *v.r.* (*pers.*) to collect oneself, to collect *or* concentrate's o.'s thoughts; to commune with oneself; to meditate; to wrap oneself in contemplation; to reflect; (*things*) to be gathered, &c.
†Recueilloir, *s.m.* (*ropemaker's*) top
Recuire, *v.a.n.* to ... (*V.* **Cuire**) again; to reheat; to anneal
Recuisson, *s.f.* reheating; annealing
Recuit, e, *part. of* **Recuire,** *and adj.* cooked again, &c.; reheated; annealed; overdone; — *s.m.f.* reheating; annealing
Recuiteur, *s.m.* annealer
Recul, *s.m.* recoil; kick
Reculade, *s.f* backing; recoiling; retreat; falling back; drawback; failure
Reculé, e, *part. adj.* put back, &c. (*V.* **Reculer**); remote, distant, far; late; backward
Reculée, *s.f.* recess; moving back; backing-room. *Feu de —,* roasting fire
Reculement, *s.m.* backing; recoiling; moving *or* drawing *or* putting back; putting off; delay; extension; (*of harness*) breeching, breech-band
Reculer, *v.a.* to move *or* put back; to pull *or* draw back; to rein back; to throw back; to carry back; to extend; to put off, to defer, to delay, to retard; — *v.n.* to go *or* draw *or* move *or* step back; to recoil; to kick; to start *or* totter back; to fall back; to stand back; to recede; to retreat; to give way; to shrink; to flinch; to stick (at); to be afraid, to funk; to back; to back out; to shirk it; to refuse
Se —, *v r.* to move *or* go *or* draw back, to go farther off; to be put back *or* put off *or* extended *or* &c.
Reculons (A), *adv.* backward, backwards; the wrong way; worse and worse; with o.'s back to the horses *or* to the engine
Reculotter, *v.a.* to ... (*V.* **Culotter**) again
Recultiver, *v.a.* to ... (*V.* **Cultiver**) again
Récupération, *s.f.* recovery, recuperation
Récupérer, *v.a.* to recover; to retrieve; to recoup
Récurage; Récurer; Récureu-r, se. *V.* **Écurage; Écurer; Écureu-r, se**
Récurrence, *s.f* recurrence
Récurrent, e, *adj.* recurrent
Récursoire, *adj.* (*law*) remedial
Récusable, *adj.* challengeable; exceptionable, objectionable, deniable
Récusant, e, *s.m.f.* (*law*) challenger; (*hist.*) recusant
Récusation, *s.f.* (*law*) challenge, recusation; (*fig.*) exception; objection; denial
Récuser, *v.a.* (*law*) to challenge; (*fig.*) to take exception to; to object to; to deny; to reject
Se —, *v.r.* to excuse oneself, to declare oneself incompetent; to decline
Rédac-teur, trice, *s.m.f.* writer; contributor; contributress; editor; editress; reporter. — *-gerant,* sub-editor
Rédaction, *s.f.* redaction; drawing up; writing; wording; draught; editing; editors, (editorial) staff; editors' room
Redan, *s.m.* (*fort., arch.*) redan
Redanser, *v.n.a.* to dance again
Reddition, *s.f.* returning, giving back, restitution; reddition; surrender; (*of accounts*) giving in
Redditionnaire, *s.m.f.* surrenderer
Redébattre; Redébuter; Redéchausser; Redéclarer; Redécorer; Redécroître; Redédier; &c. to ... (*V.* **Débattre; Débuter;** &c., &c.) again
Redéfaire, *v.a.* to ... (*V.* **Défaire**) again
Redéjeuner; Redélibérer; Redélivrer; &c. to ... (*V.* **Déjeuner,** &c., &c.) again
Redemander, *v.a.* to ask again; to ask back again; to redemand; to encore; to ... (*V.* **Demander**) again
Se —, *v.r.* to be asked again, &c.
Redémettre; Redemeurer; Redémolir; to ... (*V.* **Démettre,** &c.) again
Rédempteur, *s.m.* Redeemer; — *m.,* **-trice,** *f., adj.* redeeming, redemptive, redemptory
Rédemption, *s.f.* redemption; redeeming; ransom
Rédemptoriste, *s.m.* Redemptorist
Redénoncer; Redépêcher; Redépouiller; Redéranger; to ... (*V.* **Dénoncer, Dépêcher,** &c.) again

Redescendre, *v.n.a.* to .. (*V.* **Descendre**) again [&c. to ... (*V.* **Désirer,** &c., &c.) again
Redésirer; Redessiner; Redétruire;
Redevable, *adj.* indebted; owing; beholden; obliged; — *s.m.f.* debtor. *Être — de,* to be indebted *or* &c. for, to owe [service; fine
Redevance, *s.f.* rent; royalty; due; duty;
Redevanci-er, ère, *s.m.f.* tenant; debtor
Redevenir, *v.n.* to become *or* &c. (*V.* **Devenir**)
Redévider, *v.a.* to wind again [again
Redevoir, *v.a.* to owe still; to owe as a per-
Redhibition, *s.f.* (*law*) redhibition [centage
Redhibitoire, *adj.* (*law*) redhibitory; (*fam.*)
Redicter, *v.a.* to dictate again [for dispensation
Rédiger, *v.a.* to draw up *or* out; to draught; to write out; to write; to word; to indite; to
Se —, *v.r.* to be drawn up, &c. [edit
Rédimer, *v.a.* to redeem
Redîner, *v.n.* to dine again
Redingote, *s.f.* frock-coat; riding-coat, over-coat; open dress. — *de voyage,* riding-coat, overcoat. — *à la propriétaire,* buttoned up frock-coat
Rédintégration, *s.f* (*med.*) redintegration
Redire, *v.a.* to repeat; to say *or* tell again; to tell; to say; to report; to relate; to blame, to criticize, to find fault with. *Trouver à* — (*à*), to find fault (with); (*old*) to miss, to find missing. *Il n'y a rien à — à,* no fault can be found with. *Se faire —,* to have (...) repeated, &c.; to require *or* have *or* wait to be told again
Se —, *v.r.* to repeat oneself; to repeat *or* &c. to each other; to be repeated *or* &c. [tell-tale
Rediseu-r, se, *s.m.f.* repeater; tale-bearer,
Redissoudre, *v.a.* to redissolve, to dissolve
Redistillation, *s.f.* redistillation [again
Redistiller, *v.a.* to redistil, to distil again
Redistribuer, *v.a.* to redistribute; to reissue; to ... (*V.* **Distribuer**) again
Redistribution, *s.f.* redistribution; reissue
Redit, e, (*part. of* **Redire**) repeated, &c. [tion
Redit, *s.m.* (*obsolete*) saying over again, repeti-
Redite, *s.f.* repetition; report, gossiping
Rediviser, *v.a.* to ... (*V.* **Diviser**) again
Redompter, *v.a.* to ... (*V.* **Dompter**) again
Redondamment, *adv.* redundantly
Redondance, *s.f.* redundancy
Redondant, e, *adj.* redundant
Redonder, *v.n.* to be redundant
Redonner, *v.a.n.* to give again *or* back; to restore; to return; to redouble; to fall again; to charge again; to ... (*V.* **Donner**) again
Redorer, *v.a.* to regild, to gild *or* &c. (*V.*
Redormir, *v.n.* to sleep again [**Dorer**) again
Redorure, *s.f.* regilding
Redou, *s.m.* *V.* **Roudou** [boy
Redoublant, *s.m.* unpromoted boy, backward
Redoublé, e, *part. adj.* redoubled, &c. (*V.* **Redoubler**); double; (*mil., of pace*) double quick; — *s.m.* (*agr.*) repeated crop
Redoublement, *s.m.* redoubling; reduplication; increase; (*med.*) paroxysm
Redoubler, *v.n.a.* to redouble, to increase; to double, to repeat, to reiterate, to renew; to reduplicate; to new-line, to line *or* &c. (*V.* **Doubler**) again. — *de jambes,* to mend o.'s
Redoul, *s.m.* *V.* **Roudou** [pace
Redoutable, *adj.* redoubtable, formidable, dreadful, terrible [cing-room, assembly-room
Redoute, *s.f.* redoubt, redout; ridotto, dan-
Redouter, *v.a.* to dread, to fear
Rédowa, *s.f.* redowa (*dance, tune*)
Rèdre, *s.m.* *V.* **Manet**
Redressage, *s.m.* straightening
Redresse, *s. f.* (*nav.*) relieving-rope; (*pop.*) loafing. *Chevalier de la —,* loafer, cadger
Redressé, e, *part. adj.* straightened, &c. (*V.* **Redresser**); stiff, high, haughty
Redressement, *s.m.* straightening; redressing, righting; redress, reparation; relief
Redresser, *v.a.* to straighten, to make straight again; to hold up; to draw back; to erect *or* raise again; to raise; to take up; to prick up to set upright; to set up again; to rectify to redress; to correct, to mend, to set right, to right; to chastise; to mortify; (*fam.*) to deceive, to cheat, to take in; (*tech.*) to stretch, to smooth
Se —, *v.r.* to get *or* become *or* grow straight again; to stand erect *or* upright again; to raise oneself; to get up again; to hold oneself straight; to stand *or* sit upright; to hold up o.'s head; to bridle up; to cock; to carry o.'s head high; to correct oneself; to right itself; to be rectified *or* corrected *or* redressed; to be set right
Redresseu-r, se, *s.m.f.* redresser, righter
Redû, *m.*, **Redue,** *f. part. of* **Redevoir**
Redû, *s.m.* balance due [reductor; clove-hitch
Réducteur, *s.m., adj.m.* reducer; reducent;
Réductibilité, *s.f.* reducibleness; resoluble-
Réductible, *adj.* reducible; resoluble [ness
Réducti-f, ve, *adj.* reductive
Réduction, *s.f.* reduction; abatement, allowance; subjugation; (*obsolete*) district, parish,
Réductivement, *adv.* reductively [station
Réduire, *v.a.* to reduce; to abate; to diminish; to curtail; to retrench; to limit, to confine; to restrain; to sum up; to bring; to drive; to compel; to subdue; to break
Se —, *v.r.* to reduce *or* &c. oneself *or* itself *or* each other; to diminish, to abate; to dwindle; to vanish; to be reduced *or* &c.; to come, to amount; to consist
Réduit, e, (*part. of* **Réduire**) reduced, &c.
Réduit, *s.m.* small habitation *or* dwelling *or* lodging; small room, closet, reduct; by-place; recess; nook; retreat; hole, hovel; (*fort.*) reduit, small redoubt; (*obsolete*) place of resort, resort, club
Réduplicable, *adj.* reduplicable [reduplicative
Réduplicati-f, ve, *adj.*, **Réduplicatif,** *s.m.*
Réduplication, *s.f.* reduplication
Réduplicativement, *adv.* reduplicatively
Rédupliqué, e, *adj.* reduplicate
Réduve, *s.m.* (*insect*) reduvius
Ree-bock, *s.m.* (*zool.*) reebok
Réédification, *s.f.* reedification, rebuilding
Réédifier, *v.a.* to rebuild, to reedify
Rééditer, *v.a.* to reedit; to republish [cation
Réédition, *s.f* new edition, reprint; republi-
Réel, le, *adj.* real; true; actual; substantial; — *s.m.* reality; truth
Réélection, *s.f.* reelection
Rééligibilité, *s.f.* reeligibility
Rééligible, *adj.* reeligible
Réélire, *v.a* to reelect [deed
Réellement, *adv.* really, in reality, truly, in-
Réemballage, *s.m.* repacking
Réemballer, *v.a.* to repack [utter
Réémettre, *v.a.* to reissue; to reemit; to re-
Réémigration, *s.f.* reemigration, remigration
Réémigrer, *v.n.* to reemigrate, to remigrate
Réémission, *s. f.* reissue; reemission; re-uttering [**ployer, Rengager,** &c.
Réemployer, Réengager, &c. *V.* **Rem-**
Réensemencement, *s.m.* resowing
Réensemencer, *v.a.* to ... (*V.* **Ensemencer**)
Réentement, *s.m.* regrafting [again, to resow
Réenter, *v.a.* to regraft. *Se —,* to be regrafted
Réenterrement, *s.m.* reburial, reinterment
Réenterrer, *v a.* to bury again, to rebury, to
Réer, *v.n.* to troat [reinter
Réescompte, *s.m.* rediscount
Réescompter, *v.a.* to rediscount
Réexaminer, *v.a.* to reexamine
Réexpédier, *v.a.* to send back *or* again, to return [turn
Réexpédition, *s.f.* sending back *or* again, re-
Réexportation, *s.f.* reexportation; reexport
Réexporter, *v.a.* to reexport
Réexposer, *v.a.* to ... (*V.* **Exposer**) again, to reexpose, to reexhibit
Refâcher, *v.a.* to ... (*V.* **Fâcher**) again

Refaçon, *s.f.* remaking, remake; new dressing
Refaçonner, *v.a.* to ... (*V.* **Façonner**) again, to refashion
Réfaction, *s.f.* remaking, remake; repairing, repairs, repair; (*com.*) allowance; rebate; tret
Refaire, *v.a.n.* to make again, to remake; to do *or* &c. (*V.* **Faire**) again; to remodel; to mend, to repair; to begin again; to refresh; to recruit, to restore; to revive; to do, to fool, to bamboozle, to take in, to cheat, to swindle, to diddle, to dish; (*cards*) to deal again; (*of the weather*) to be again
Se —, *v.r.* to be done *or* made *or* &c. (*V.* **Se Faire**) again; to refresh oneself; to recruit o.'s health *or* strength; to recover, to retrieve o.'s losses *or* fortune; to make oneself again; to change o.'s own nature [cheat
Refaiseu-r, se, *s.m.f.* remaker; restorer;
Refait, e, *part. adj.* made again, remade, &c. (*V.* **Refaire**); done again *or* over again; cheated, swindled, fooled, done, done brown, diddled, dished; paid back in his own coin; (*carp.*) squared, prepared for use [antlers
Refait, *s.m.* drawn game; (*hunt.*) new horns *or*
Refaucher, *v.a.* to mow again
Réfection, *s.f.* refection; repairing, repairs, repair; restoring
Réfectionner, *v.n.* to eat, to refect oneself
Réfectoire, *s.m.* refectory; dining-hall, dining-room
Réfectori-er, ère, *s.m.f.* steward; stewardess
Reféer, *v.a.* (*old*) to reenchant, to recharm
Refend, *s.m.* splitting; sawing; dividing, division; channel; splinter, chip; partition-wall, bearing-wall. *Bois de —*, sawed wood. *Mur de —*, partition-wall, bearing-wall. *Pierre de —*, corner-stone [split, to saw
Refendre, *v.a.* to split *or* cleave again; to
Refente, *s.f.* splitting again; splitting, sawing
Référé, *s.m.* (*law*) application to a judge sitting in chambers; order, judgment, report. *En —*, in chambers; sitting in chambers
Référence, *s.f.* (*bank.*, *fig.*) reference; (*com.*: *of persons*) reference, (*of articles*) reference number, number, duplicate
Référencer, *v.a.* (*com.*) to number, to duplicate
Référendaire, *s.m. adj.* referendary
Référendariat, *s.m.* referendaryship
Référer, *v.a.* to refer; to ascribe; — *v.n.* (*law*) to report, to make a report. *En —*, to refer; to report [*S'en —*, to refer
Se —, *v.r.* to refer; to leave it (to); to trust.
Refermer, *v.a.*, **Se —,** *v.r.* to shut *or* shut up *or* &c. (*V.* **Fermer**) again; to close up
Referrer, *v.a.* to ... (*V.* **Ferrer**) again
Refesser, *v.a.* to whip *or* flog again
Refêter, *v.a.* to ... (*V.* **Fêter**) again
†Refeuiller, *v.a.* to make a double lapping rabbet to; — *v.n.*, **Se —,** *v.r.* to leaf again
†Refeuilleter, *v.a.* to ... (*V.* **Feuilleter**) again
†Refeuillure, *s.f.*, **Refeuillement,** *s.m.* double lapping rabbet [to grout *or* point afresh
Reficher, *v.a.* to ... (*V.* **Ficher**) again; (*mas.*)
Refiger, Refiler, Refiltrer, Refixer, &c. to ... (*V.* **Figer, Filer, Filtrer, Fixer,** &c.)
Refin, *s.m.* finest wool [again
Reflairer, Reflamboyer, Reflatter, &c. to ... (*V.* **Flairer, Flamboyer, Flatter,** &c.) again
Réfléchi, e, *part. adj.* reflected, &c. (*V.* **Réfléchir**) reflective; deliberate; considerate; thoughtful; meditative; profound; circumspect; — *s.m.* reflective verb
Refléchir, *v.a.n.* to ... (*V.* **Fléchir**) again
Réfléchir, *v.a.n.* to reflect; to think; to consider; to meditate
Se —, *v.r.* to reflect; to be reflected
Réfléchissement, *s.m.* reflection
Réfléchisseu-r, se, *s.m.f.* (*pers.*) reflector; — *adj.* reflecting; thoughtful; meditative
Réflecteur, *adj.m.* (*phys.*) reflecting, reflective; — *s.m.* (*phys.*) reflector

Réflecti-f, ve, *adj.* reflective
Réflectivement, *adv.* reflectively
Reflet, *s.m.* reflexion; reflex [be reflected
Refléter, *v.a.n.* to reflect. *Se —*, to reflect; to
Refleuret, *s.m* fine Spanish wool
Refleurir, *v.n.a.* to ... (*V.* **Fleurir**) again, to reflower; to reflourish. *Faire —*, to revive
Refleurissement, *s.m.* reflorescence
Réflexe, *adj.* reflex
Réflexibilité, *s.f.* reflexibility
Réflexible, *adj.* reflexible, reflectible
Réflexi-f, ve, *adj.* reflexive
Réflexion, *s.f.* reflection; consideration; thought; meditation. *— faite, toute — faite,* on *or* upon reflection, after due reflection, on consideration, all things *or* everything considered; upon reconsideration, on second
Réflexivement, *adv.* reflexively [thoughts
Reflorir, *v.n.* to ... (*V.* **Florir**) again, to reflourish. *Faire —*, to revive
Refluer, *v.n.* to ebb; to flow back *or* again, to reflow; to overflow; to flow [back; reflux
Reflux, *s.m.* ebbing; ebb; ebb-tide; flowing
Refomenter, *v.a.* to refoment
Refonçage, *s.m.* rebottoming
Refonder, *v.a.* to refound, to reestablish; (*old*) to refund, to reimburse, to repay
Refondeur, *s.m.* refounder, remodeller
Refondre, *v.a.* to refound, to recast, to melt again; to recoin; to reform, to remould, to remodel; to correct, to improve; to tear up (*old paper*); (*nav.*) to rebuild, to repair (thoroughly)
Se —, *v.r.* to be refounded, &c.; to reform *or* &c. oneself; to change o.'s own nature
Refonte, *s.f.* refounding, recasting, melting down again; recoinage; remoulding; remodelling; tearing up (*old paper*); (*nav.*) (thorough)
Reforer, *v.a.* to ... (*V.* **Forer**) again [repair
Reforger, *v.a.* to reforge, to forge again
Réformable, *adj.* reformable; (*law*) reversible; (*mil.*) invalidable, dischargeable; (*of recruits*) exemptible
Réforma-teur, trice, *s.m.f.* reformer; — *adj.* reforming, reformatory, reformative [ing
Réformation, *s.f.* reformation; (*coin.*) restamp-
Réforme, *s.f.* reform; reformation; amendment; retrenchment, reduction; (*mil., obsolete*) reduction; (*mil.*) invaliding, discharge; (*mil., obsolete*) half-pay; (*mil.*) exemption (*of a recruit*); (*mil.*) selling off (*of horses*); (*mil.*) cast horses. *Cheval de —*, (*mil.*) cast horse. *Congé de —*, (*mil.*) discharge, being invalided. *Traitement de —*, (*mil., obsolete*) half-pay. *Mettre à la —*, (*mil., fig.*) *V.* **Réformer**
Réformé, e, *part. adj.* reformed, &c. (*V.* **Réformer**); Protestant; cast (*horse*); — *s.m.f.* (*hist.*) reformer, Protestant; (*of monks, nuns*) reformist [form
Reformer, *v.a.* to form again *or* anew, to re-
Se —, *v.r.* to form oneself *or* itself again *or* anew, to form again *or* anew, to reform; to be formed again *or* anew
Réformer, *v.a.* to reform, to amend, to correct; to redress; to retrench; to reduce; (*coins*) to restamp; (*law*) to reverse; (*mil.*) to reform; (*mil.*) to invalid, to discharge; (*mil., obsolete*) to put on half-pay; (*mil.*) to exempt (*a recruit*); (*mil.*) to cast (*horses*); (*fig.*) to put (*things*) aside with the intention of either repairing or disposing of (*them*) [formed, &c.
Se —, *v.r.* to reform, to amend; to be re-
Réformiste, *s.m.f.* reformist; — *adj.* reform
Refortifier, Refouetter, †Refouiller, &c. to ... (*V.* **Fortifier, Fouetter, Fouiller,** &c.) again
Refoulement, *s.m.* driving back; compression; suppression; ramming; stemming; flowing back; ebbing; retreat; downward motion; enlargement of the bore (*of a cannon*)
Refouler, *v.a.* to drive back; to force back; to compress; to suppress; to press again; to

ram; (*nav.*) to go *or* run against, to stem (*the tide*); — *v.n.* to flow *or* go back; to ebb; (*pop.*) to hesitate, to boggle, to be reluctant
Refouleur, *s.m.* forcer, presser
Refouloir, *s.m.* (*artil.*) rammer
Refourbir, Refournir, Refourrer, &c. to ... (*V.* **Fourbir, Fournir, Fourrer,** &c.) again
Réfractaire, *adj.* refractory; disobedient; rebellious; stubborn; defaulting; eccentric; fireproof, fire-...; — *s.m.* defaulting recruit, defaulter; — *s.m.f.* refractory *or* eccentric person [ed. *Dose réfractée,* (*med.*) divided dose
Réfracter, *v.a.* to refract. *Se —,* to be refract-
Réfracteur, *s. m.* refractor, refracting tele-
Réfracti-f, ve, *adj.* refractive [scope
Réfraction, *s.f.* refraction. *A —,* refracting
Refrain, *s.m.* burden of a song, burden; (constant) theme *or* topic *or* cry; rolling of the waves, eddy-water
Refranchir, *v.a.* to ... (*V.* **Franchir**) again; (*nav*) to free *or* clear (by means of the pumps)
Se —, *v r* (*nav.*) to get (*or* be) freed *or* cleared
Réfranger, *v.a. V* **Réfracter**
Réfrangibilité, *s.f.* refrangibility
Réfrangible, *adj* refrangible [recoinage
Refrappement, *s.m.* restriking, recoining,
Refrapper, *v.a.n.* to ... (*V* **Frapper**) again
Refrayer, &c. to ... (*V* **Frayer,** &c.) again
Refrénation, *s.f.,* **Refrènement,** *s.m.* refraining, &c. (*V.* **Refréner**)
Refréner, *v a.* to refrain, to restrain, to curb, to bridle, to check [&c.) again
Refréquenter, &c. to ... (*V.* **Fréquenter,**
Réfrigérant, e, *adj.* refrigerant, refrigerating, freezing
Réfrigérant, *s.m* refrigerant; refrigerator
Réfrigérati-f, ve, *adj.,* **Réfrigératif,** *s.m.*
Réfrigération, *s.f.* refrigeration [refrigerative
Réfrigérer, *v.a.* to refrigerate
Réfringence, *s.f.* (*phys.*) refringency
Réfringent, e, *adj.,* **Réfringent,** *s.m.* (*phys.*) refringent; absolute refractive (*power*)
Refrire, *v.a.n.* to fry again
Refriser, *v.a.n.* to ... (*V.* **Friser**) again
†Refrogné, e, *adj.* gruff, surly, sullen, scowling, frowning [of the brow, sullen look
†Refrognement, *s.m.* scowl, frown, knitting
†Refrogner, *v a.* to knit (*o.'s brow*), to give a sullen look to [brow
Se —, *v.r.* to scowl, to frown, to knit o.'s
Refroidi, *s.m.* (*pop.*) corpse, dead body
Refroidir, *v.a.n.,* **Se —,** *v.r.* to cool; to cool down; to make cold; to chill; to damp; to become *or* grow *or* get cold *or* cool; to slacken, to moderate, to relent, to abate; (*pop.*) to kill, to settle, to do for; (*pop.*) to die
Refroidis, *s.m.* (*agr.*) fallow-crops
Refroidissement, *s.m.* cooling; coolness; coldness; chill, cold
Refroidisseur, Refroidissoir, *s.m.* cooler
Refroissé, e, *adj* (*agr.*) unfallowed
Refrotter, *v.a.* to ... (*V.* **Frotter**) again
Refuge, *s.m.* refuge; shelter; asylum; home; resource; protection; excuse, pretence, loop-
Réfugié, e, *s.m.f. adj.* refugee [hole
Réfugier, *v.a.* to shelter, to harbour
Se —, *v.r.* to take refuge *or* shelter, to harbour; to have recourse (to)
Refui, *s.m.* (*hunt.*) shelter, cover
Refuir, *v.n.* (*hunt.*) to double; to fly; — *v.a.* to shun, to avoid [dodge; flight; track, path
Refuite, *s.f.* (*hunt.*) doubling, double, shift,
Refumer, *v.a.n.* to smoke *or* &c. (*V.* **Fumer**) again
Refus, *s.m.* refusal; denial; refuse. *Battre* or *enfoncer jusqu'à — de mouton,* (*of piles*) to set, to drive home. *Cela n'est pas de —,* that is not to be refused, that is very acceptable, that is quite welcome, with pleasure
Refusable, *adj.* refusable
Refusant, e, *s.m.f.* refuser
Refuser, *v.a.n.* to refuse, to deny; to decline; to grudge; to demur; to object (to); to reject; to refuse admittance; to pluck; to refuse to engage; to wince, to jib; to refuse its work; (*nav., of the wind*) to scant
Se —, *v.r.* to refuse *or* deny *or* grudge oneself; to resist; to object; to refuse, not to allow; to grudge; to demur; to shrink (from); to refuse to yield *or* submit; to refuse *or* &c. each other; to be refused *or* &c.
Refuseu-r, se, *s.m.f.* refuser
Réfutable, *adj.* refutable [ting
Réfuta-teur, trice, *s.m.f. adj.* refuter; refu-
Réfutation, *s.f.* refutation, confutation, dis-
Réfutatoire, *adj.* refutatory [proof
Réfuter, *v.a.* to refute, to confute, to disprove
Se —, *v.r.* to refute *or* &c. oneself *or* itself *or* each other; to be refuted, &c.
†Regagner, *v.a.* to regain; to recover, to get back *or* again; to gain *or* win back; to make up for; to retake, to take again; to get back to, to return to; to reach again, to reach, to overtake, to rejoin
Se —, *v.r.* to be regained, &c.
†Regaillardir, *v.a. V.* **Ragaillardir**
Regain, *s.m.* after-grass, aftermath, eddish, second crop; eatage; (*fig.*) revival, return, new lease (*of life*)
Régal, *s.m.* entertainment; feast; treat, luxury; favourite dish; relish; pleasure; fee, gratuity, douceur; coffee with brandy
Régalade, *s.f* treat; treating; brisk *or* rousing fire; gulping. *Boire à la —,* to drink without putting the vessel (*or* glass) to the lips, to
Régalage, *s.m.* (*of ground*) levelling [gulp down
Régalant, e, *adj.* entertaining, amusing, pleasant
Régale, *s.m.* (*of organs*) vox humana stop; (*obsolete mus instr.*) regal; — *s.f* (*hist*) regale *or* regalia (*right*); — *adj.f.* (*Eau —, V.* **Eau**)
Régalec, *s.m.* (*fish*) chimæra, king of the herrings
Régalement, *s.m.* (*of ground*) levelling; (*of ballast*) spreading; (*of taxes*) assessment; (*of shares*) equalization
Régaler, *v.a.* to regale, to entertain, to treat, to feast; to bestow, to favour; to cheer; to please, to gratify; to level (*ground*); to spread (*ballast*); to assess (*taxes*); to equalize (*shares*); (*old*) to indemnify, to reward, to repay
Se —, *v.r.* to regale *or* &c. oneself *or* each other; to enjoy oneself [spreader
Régaleur, *s.m.* entertainer, treater; leveller,
Régalia, *s.m., adj.m.* regalia (cigar)
Régalien, ne, *adj.* (*old*) regal, royal
Regard, *s.m.* look; glance; gaze; eye, eyes; attention, notice; aspect; two portraits looking at each other; (*tech.*) draught-hole; gully-hole; opening, entrance. *En —,* opposite. *Avoir — sur,* to look into, to face. *Avoir un —,* (*pop.*) to be struck [ing at
Regardable, *adj.* to be looked at; worth look-
Regardant, e, *adj* near, close, saving, stingy; particular; looking on; (*her.*) regardant; — *s.m.f.* looker-on, beholder, spectator
Regarder, *v.a n.* to look at *or* on *or* upon *or* to, to gaze at *or* on; to behold; to see; to peep at; to eye; to examine; to consider, to regard; to watch; to concern; to be ...'s business, to face, to be opposite, to look; to look to see (if); to mind. *— faire,* to look at. *Se faire —,* to attract notice. *— quelqu'un de haut en bas* (or *du haut de sa grandeur*), to look on one with contempt, to look down upon one; to eye one from head to foot. *Y —,* to look at it; to consider about it; to care about it. *Y — à deux fois,* to look well first; to think twice; to know a trick worth two of it. *Y — de près,* to look at it close *or* narrowly; to be particular about it, to be particular
Se —, *v.r.* to look at oneself *or* at each other; to look at (*o.'s ...*): to eye *or* &c. each

other; to face each other; to consider oneself or each other; to be looked at or &c.; to be reflected
Regardeu-r, se, *s.m.f.* looker
Regarnir, *v.a.* to ... (*V.* **Garnir**) again
Régate, *s.f.* regatta
Régayer, *v.a.* to ... (*V.* **Égayer**) again
Regazonnement, *s.m.* returfing
Regazonner, *v.a.* to turf again, to returf
†Regazouiller, *v.n.* to ... (*V.* **Gazouiller**) again
Regel, *s.m.*, **Regélation,** *s.f.* new frost, freezing again, refreezing, regelation
Regeler, *v.a.n.*, **Se —,** *v.r.* to freeze again, to refreeze; to be frozen again, to be refrozen
Régence, *s.f.* regency; professorship, mastership; (*obsolete*) town-council; — *adj.* rakish, dissolute, licentious, gay
Régénéra-teur, trice, *adj. s.* regenerating; regenerator
Régénérati-f, ve, *adj.* regenerative
Régénération, *s.f.* regeneration
Régénérer, *v.a.* to regenerate
Se —, *v.r.* to grow again, to be regenerated or renewed
Régent, e, *s.m.f. adj.* regent; (*in a grammar school*) professor, master; (*of the Bank of France*) director
Régentation, *s.f.* domineering
Régenter, *v.n.a.* (*old*) to teach; (*fig.*) to domineer (over), to lord it (over); to lecture
Régenteu-r, se, *s.m.f.* overbearing person
Regermer, *v.n.* to ... (*V.* **Germer**) again
Regeste, *s.m.* (*old*) regest, record
Régicide, (*murder*) *s.m.*, (*pers.*) *s.m.f.* regicide; — *adj.* regicidal
Régie, *s.f.* management, administration; government; excise; excisemen; excise department; excise office. *Employé de la —,* exciseman
Regimbement, *s.m.* kicking; resistance
Regimber, *v.n.*, **Se —,** *v.r.* to kick; to resist
Regimbeu-r, se, *s.m.f.* kicker, refractory person
Régime, *s.m.* regimen; diet; government; administration; system; rule; order of things; (*gram.*) object; (*bot.*) spadix, bunch. *Être au —,* to be on low diet, to diet. *Mettre au —,* to diet. *Vivre de —,* to live by rule
Régiment, *s.m.* regiment; swarm, host
Régimentaire, *adj.* regimental
Régimentairement, *adv.* regimentally
Reginglette, *s.f.* (*obsolete*) bird-trap, gin, snare
Région, *s.f.* region
Régional, e, *adj.* local; agricultural
Régir, *v.a.* to govern; to rule; to manage
Se —, *v.r.* to be governed or &c.
Régisseur, *s.m.* manager; steward
Registrateur, *s.m.* (*at Rome*) registrar, recorder
Registre, *s.m.* register; book; record; account; (*mus., print.,* &c.) register; (*mus.*) drawstop; (*tech.*) register; (*tech.*) damper
Registrer, *v.a.* (*old*) to register, to record
Réglable, *adj.* to be ruled or &c. (*V.* **Régler**)
Réglage, *s.m.* ruling; regulating; settling; setting; timing
Règle, *s.f.* rule; ruler; order; model, pattern; guide; regulation; sum; **—s,** *pl.* rules, &c.; (*med.*) monthly courses, courses, terms, catamenia, menses. — *logarithmique,* — *mobile,* — *à calcul,* slide-rule, sliding rule. — *de société* or *de compagnie,* (*arith.*) fellowship. *En —,* *dans les —s,* in rule; according to rule or rules; in order; right, all right, correct, regular; well-ordered; downright; regularly; in due form
Réglé, e, *part. adj.* ruled, &c. (*V.* **Régler**); regular; orderly; punctual; exact; steady; good; moderate; (*med.*) menstruated. — *comme un papier de musique,* as regular as clock-work
Règlement, *s.m.* regulation; rule; laws; bylaws, bye-laws; standing orders; settlement; (*mil.*) roster. — *de juges,* (*law*) decision on the competency of a court
Réglément, *adv.* regularly; exactly; constantly
Réglementaire, *adj.* regulating, regulative; according to regulations or to law, regulation, allowed, lawful; relating to regulations; worked by regulations
Réglementairement, *adv.* according to regulations
Réglementation, *s.f.* regulating
Réglementer, *v.a.n.* to regulate. *Se —,* to be regulated
Régler, *v.a.* to rule (*paper,* &c.); to regulate; to order; to determine; to fix; to settle; (*clocks,* &c.) to set, to regulate, to time
Se —, *v.r.* to regulate oneself; to become regular; to settle; to be guided (by), to go (by); to follow the example (of), to take example (from); to be ruled or &c.; to be settled or &c.
Réglet, *s.m.* (*arch.*) reglet; (*print.*) rule; (*tech.*) ruler
Réglette, *s.f.* (*print.*) reglet
Régleu-r, se, *s.m.f.* (*pers.*) ruler, paper-ruler
Réglisse, *s.f.* (*plant*) liquorice, *s.m.* (*extract*) liquorice. *Jus de —,* liquorice juice; Spanish liquorice
Reglisser, *v.n.a.* to ... (*V.* **Glisser**) again
Régloir, *s.m.* (*tech.*) ruler, ruling-machine
Réglure, *s.f.* ruling; lines; ruling-shop
Regmate, *s.m.* (*bad spelling*) *V.* **Rhegmate**
†Régnant, e, *adj.* reigning; prevailing, prevalent, predominant; present; chief
†Règne, *s.m.* reign; prevalence; vogue, fashion; (*nat. hist.*) kingdom; (*of the pope*) tiara; (*in churches*) crown (*over the high altar*)
†Régner, *v.n.* to reign; to rule; to govern; to prevail, to be prevalent; to predominate; to be in vogue or fashion; to exist; to subsist, to last; to run, to run along, to extend, to reach
Régnicole, *adj. s.m.f.* native; citizen; naturalized subject or citizen, denizen
Regonflement, *s.m.* new swelling; reinflation; swelling
Regonfler, *v.a.n.* to swell or &c. (*V.* **Gonfler**) again; to swell
Regorgement, *s.m.* overflowing, overflow; superabundance
Regorger, *v.n.a.* to overflow; to run over; to abound, to teem; to be plentiful; to be replete or overstocked or overfull; to be crowded or thronged or crammed (with); to be glutted or surfeited; to disgorge
Regouler, *v.a.* (*pop.*) to snub; to surfeit
Regourmer, *v.a.* to ... (*V.* **Gourmer**) again
Regoûter, *v.a.n.* to taste or &c. (*V.* **Goûter**) again
Regracier, *v.a.* (*law*) to pardon again
†Regradiller, *v. a.* (*hairdressers' slang for* **Friser**)
Regrat, *s.m.* huckstering; huckster's shop or business
Regrattage, *s.m.* (*mas.*) regrating, scraping again
Regratter, *v.a.n.* to scratch again; to scrape again; to regrate; to huckster, to drive a huckster's trade; to higgle, to haggle; to stand upon trifles; to cut down; to nibble, to carp (at)
Regratterie, *s.f.* huckstering, huckster's trade or business; huckster's goods
Regratti-er, ère, *s.m.f.* huckster, huckstress, salesman, broker, dealer in second-hand goods, petty tradesman; (*fig.*) retailer, scribbler, compiler, hack; higgler, haggler
Regraver, *v.a.* to reengrave
Regravir, *v.a.n.* to ... (*V.* **Gravir**) again
Regréer, *v.a.* (*nav.*) to refit
Regreffer, *v.a.* to regraft. *Se —,* to be regrafted
Regrêler, *v.n.a.* to ... (*V.* **Grêler**) again
Regrès, *s.m.* regress
Régressi-f, ve, *adj.* regressive, retrogressive
Régression, *s.f.* regression, retrogression
Régressivement, *adv.* regressively
Regret, *s.m.* regret, grief, sorrow, concern; vexation; repentance; lamentation; knell, tolling, toll. *A —,* with regret; with reluctance, reluctantly; grudgingly. *Au —,* sorry. *Avoir —* or *du —,* to regret; to be sorry
Regrettable, *adj.* regrettable, lamentable, to be regretted or lamented
Regrettablement, *adv.* regrettably, lamentably
Regretter, *v.a.* to regret; to lament; to grieve at; to be sorry for; to be sorry; to repent; to

regret the loss of; to grudge. *Se* —, to be regretted [to be regretted *or* &c.
Se —, *v.r.* to regret oneself *or* each other;
Regretteur, *s.m.* regretter
Regriffer, Regriffonner, †Regriller, Regrimper, Regronder, &c. to ... (*V.* **Griffer, Griffonner, Griller, Grimper, Gronder,** &c.) again
Regros, *s.m.* tanner's bark
Regrossoyer, Reguérir, Reguetter, Reguinder, &c. to ... (*V.* **Grossoyer, Guérir, Guetter, Guinder,** &c) again
Régularisation, *s.f.* regularization; putting in order; settlement
Régulariser, *v.a.* to regularize; to give regularity to; to put in order; to settle [larized
Se —, *v.r.* to become regular; to be regu-
Régularité, *s.f.* regularity; steadiness; strictness; strict observance of rules; ecclesiastical state [lator; standard. — *de tirage*, damper
Régula-teur, trice, *adj. s.* regulating; regu-
Régulation, *s.f.* regulation
Régule, *s.m.* (*obsolete*) regulus, kinglet; (*old chem.*) regulus; (*bird*) regulus, wren
Réguli-er, ère, *adj.* regular; steady; punctual; exact; — *s.m.* (*of monks, and mil.*) regular
Régulièrement, *adv.* regularly; steadily; punctually; exactly
Régulin, e, *adj.* (*old chem.*) reguline
Régulus, *s.m.* (*astr.*) Regulus
Régurgitation, *s.f.* regurgitation
Régurgiter, *v.a.* to regurgitate. *Se* —, to be regurgitated [*rupt's*) discharge
Réhabilitation, *s.f.* rehabilitation; (*bank-*
Réhabilité, e, *s.m.f.* discharged bankrupt
Réhabiliter, *v.a.* to rehabilitate; to reinstate, to restore; to redeem; to set right
Se —, *v.r.* to rehabilitate *or* &c. oneself; to pay twenty shillings in the pound
Réhabiter, *v.a.* to reinhabit [again
Réhabituer, *v.a.* to habituate *or* accustom
Rehacher, Rehanter, Reharceler, Rehasarder, &c. to ... (*V.* **Hacher, Hanter, Harceler, Hasarder,** &c.) again
Rehausse, *s.f.* rise, increase of value
Rehaussement, *s.m.* raising; enhancement; rising, rise, increase; increase of value
Rehausser, *v.a.* to raise; to increase the value of; to enhance; to heighten; to set off; to enrich; to extol; — *v.n.* to rise again
Rehaut, *s.m.* (*paint.*) set-off; —**s,** *pl.* (*paint.*) lightest parts, lights, sky parts
Reheurter, Réhumecter, Rehumer, &c. to ... (*V.* **Heurter, Humecter, Humer,**
Réimplanter, *v.a.* to reimplant [&c.) again
Réimportation, *s.f.* reimportation; reimport
Réimporter, *v.a.* to reimport
Réimportuner, *v.a.* to reimportune
Réimposer, *v.a.* to impose *or* assess *or* tax *or* &c. (*V.* **Imposer**) again, to reimpose, to reassess, to impose a new tax on
Réimposition, *s.f.* reimposition, reassessment, new tax *or* rate; (*print.*) reimposing
Réimpression, *s.f.* reprinting; reprint; reissue [to reprint
Réimprimer, *v.a.* to reimprint; to reimpress;
Se —, *v.r.* to be reimprinted *or* reimpressed; to be reprinted; to be reprinting
Rein, *s.m.* kidney; skirt (*of a wood*); —**s,** *pl.* loins, reins; back; (*build.*) haunches, reins. *Chute des* —*s*, small of the back. *Tour de* —*s*, strain in the back. *Avoir les* —*s forts*, to be strong; to have a long purse
Réinciser, *v.a.* to reincise
Réinciter, *v.a.* to reincite [embodiment
Réincorporation, *s.f.* reincorporation; re-
Réincorporer, *v.a.* to reincorporate; to reembody
Reine, *s.f.* queen. — *des bois*, (*bot.*) sweet woodruff — *des prés*, (*bot.*) meadow-sweet, queen of the meadows. —**-claude,** *s.f.* (*bot.*) greengage. —**-marguerite,** *s.f.* (*bot.*) China aster
Reinette, *s.f.* (*apple*) pippin, rennet, rennett reinette; (*frog*) *V.* **Rainette.** — *grise*, russet
Réinfecter, *v.a.* to reinfect
Réinjurier, *v.a* to abuse *or* insult again
Réinscrire, *v.a.* to reinscribe, to enter *or*
Réinsérer, *v a.* to reinsert [register again
Réinsertion, *s.f.* reinsertion [ment
Réinstallation, *s.f.* reinstallation, reinstal-
Réinstaller, *v.a.* to reinstall
Réinstruire, *v a.* to reinstruct
Réinsurger, *v.a.* to ... (*V.* **Insurger**) again
Reinté, e, *adj.* loined; broad-loined, strong-
Réintégrande, *s.f.* (*law*) restoration [backed
Réintégration, *s.f* reintegration, redintegration; reinstatement
Réintégrer, *v.a.* to reintegrate, to redintegrate; to reinstate; to place *or* put again; to recommit; to rewarehouse
Se —, *v.r.* to be reintegrated, &c.
Réinterpréter, Réinterroger, Réintroduire, Réinventer, &c. to ... (*V.* **Interpréter, Interroger, Introduire, Inventer,**
Réinvention, *s.f.* reinvention [&c.) again
Réinvitation, *s.f.* reinvitation
Réinviter, *v.a.* to reinvite
Reis, *s.m.* (*Turkish official, Turkish master mariner, Portuguese and Brazilian coin*) reis. —**-***effendi*, reis-effendi (*Turkish Foreign Minis-*
Reissole, *s.f.* anchovy-net [*ter*)
Réitérable, *adj.* reiterable
Réitéra-teur, trice, *adj.* reiterating
Réitérati-f, ve, *adj.* reiterative
Réitération, *s.f.* reiteration, repetition
Réitérativement, *adv.* reiteratively, reiteratedly, repeatedly
Réitérer, *v.a.n.* to reiterate, to repeat
Se —, *v.r.* to be reiterated *or* repeated
Reître, *s.m.* reiter (*German trooper of the fourteenth and fifteenth centuries. During the religious wars the* "reîtres" *served in the French armies on the Protestant side*). *Vieux* —, old fox; old buck
†Rejaillir, *v.n* to spout; to gush out; to spirt; to splash; to spring; to rebound, to fly back; to reflect; to be reflected; to flash; to accrue
†Rejaillissement, *s.m.* spouting; gushing out; spirting; splashing; springing; rebounding; reflection; flashing
Rejaser, Rejauger, &c. to ... (*V.* **Jaser, Jauger,** &c.) again
Rejaunir, *v.a.n.* to make *or* grow yellow again
Réjection, *s.f.* rejection
Rejet, *s.m.* rejection; (*agr., hort.*) shooting, shoot, offshoot, sprout, runner; (*fin.*) carrying, transfer; (*mining*) outthrow, trap; (*hunt.*) trap; (*of bees*) swarm
Rejetable, *adj.* rejectable, to be rejected
Rejéteau, *s.m.* (*of a window*) weather-board, weather-bead
Rejeter, *v.a.n.* to throw again *or* back *or* away *or* out *or* up; to send back; to vomit; to throw; to cast; to transfer; to remove; to carry; to reject; to refuse; to deny; to set aside; to negative; to ignore; to overrule; (*of plants*) to shoot, to put forth
Se —, *v.r.* to throw oneself again *or* &c.; to fall back; to excuse oneself; to throw back *or* &c. to each other; to be thrown again *or* &c.
Rejetoir, *s.m.,* **Rejetoire,** *s.f.* (*hunt.*) noose, springe, gin
Rejeton, *s.m.* (*agr., hort.*) shoot, offshoot, sprout, runner; (*fig.*) scion, offspring
Rejetonner, *v.n.* to throw out shoots, to
Rejettement, *s.m.* rejection [sprout
Rejoindre, *v.a.,* **Se** —, *v.r.* to rejoin; to join again; to reunite; to meet again; to go back to; to join; to reach; to overtake, to catch up
Rejointoiement, Rejointoyement, *s.m.* (*mas.*) repointing, rejointing
Rejointoyer, *v.a.* (*mas.*) to repoint, to rejoint
Rejouer, *v.a.n.* to play again
Se —, *v.r.* to be played again

Réjoui, e, *part. adj. s.* rejoiced, &c. (*V.* **Réjouir**); joyous, jovial, jolly, merry; jolly fellow *or* woman. *Gros* —, big jolly fellow. *Grosse* —*e*, buxom woman

Réjouir, *v.a.*, **Se** —, *v.r.* to rejoice; to delight; to gladden; to please; to exhilarate; to cheer; to enliven; to divert, to amuse; to make merry; to be glad; to enjoy oneself

Réjouissance, *s.f.* rejoicing; merry-making; festivity; (*butch.*) bone, bones, coarse meat, makeweight

Réjouissant, e, *adj.* merry, jovial, joyous, gladdening, glad, exhilarating, cheering, cheerful, cheery, enlivening, diverting, amusing, pleasant

Rejouter, Rejuger, Rejurer, &c. to ... (*V.* [**Jouter, Juger, Jurer,** &c.) again

Relabourement, *s.m.* new tillage *or* ploughing

Relabourer, *v.a.* to till *or* plough again

Relâchant, e, *adj.*, **Relâchant,** *s.m.* laxative

Relâche, *s.m.* intermission, remission, respite, discontinuance, ceasing; rest; relaxation; (*theat.*) no performance; — *s.f.* (*nav.*) putting into port, putting in, calling at a port, stay; place to put in, port, harbour. *Sans* —, without intermission *or* &c.; *V.* **Cesse (Sans)**

Relâché, e, *part. adj.* slackened, loosened, relaxed, &c. (*V.* **Relâcher**); slack; loose; lax; remiss

Relâchement, *s. m.* slackening, loosening; slackness, looseness; relaxation; intermission; remission; remissness; laxity; abatement; decay; flagging; decline; concession; release; (*of the weather*) getting milder, giving

Relâcher, *v.a.n.*, **Se** —, *v.r.* to slacken, to loosen; to relax; to release, to set at liberty; to let go; to yield; to give up; to remit; to abate; to flag; to open the bowels; (*nav.*) to put into harbour *or* port, to put in, to touch; (*of the weather*) to get milder, to give

Relais, *s.m.* relay; fresh horses; stage, posting-house; derelict land, derelict; dereliction. *De* —, relay; spare, change; fresh; unemployed, disengaged, at leisure [(*hunt.*) resting

Relaissé, e, *part. adj.* staying; on a visit;

Relaisser (Se), *v.r.* to stay; to take up o.'s abode *or* quarters; (*hunt.*) to rest

Relancer, *v.a.* to dart *or* &c. (*V.* **Lancer**) again; to start anew; to hunt out; to pursue; to rouse; to urge; to trouble, to importune, to intrude upon; to retort on, to take up short, to take up, to snub, to give it to; to outdo

Relaps, e, *adj.* relapsed; — *s.m.f.* relapser

Rélargir, *v.a.n.*, **Se** —, *v.r.* to widen

Rélargissement, *s.m.* widening

Relater, *v.a.* to relate; to state; to mention

Rela-teur, trice, *s.m.f.* relater, relator, relatrix

Relati-f, ve, *adj.*, **Relatif,** *s.m.* relative

Relation, *s. f.* relation; account, narrative; statement; reference, regard; connection; acquaintance; acquaintanceship; intercourse; communication; correspondence; affairs. *Terme de* —, term found in travellers' narratives

Relationnaire, *s.m.f.* relater, narrator

Relativement, *adv.* relatively; comparatively

Relativité, *s.f.* relativity, relativeness

Relatter, *v.a.* to new-lath, to relath

Relaver, *v.a.* to wash again, to rewash

Relaxation, *s.f.* relaxation; abatement; remission; (*of prisoners*) release, enlargement

Relaxer, *v.a.* to relax; (*law*) to release, to enlarge, to set free

Relayer, *v.a.* to relieve; — *v.n.* to change [horses

Se —, *v.r.* to relieve each other; to take [turns

Relayeur, *s.m.* job post-master

Relécher, *v.a.* to lick again

Relecture, *s.f.* new *or* second reading

Relégation, *s.f.* relegation, exile, banishment

Reléguer, *v.a.* to relegate, to exile, to banish; to confine, to shut up; to seclude; to consign; to send off; to put *or* keep away

Relent, *s.m.* mustiness, frowsiness, musty *or* frowsy taste *or* smell. *Sentir le* —, to taste *or* smell musty *or* &c.

Relevage, *s.m.* raising, &c. (*V.* **Relever**); (*post.*) collection (*of letters*), clearing (*of letter-boxes*)

†Relevailles, *s.f.pl.* churching. *Faire ses* —, [to be churched

Relevant, e, *part. adj.* depending, &c. (*V.* **Relever**); dependent, held, being holden; (*old*) relevant

Relevé, e, *part. adj.* raised, &c. (*V.* **Relever**); risen again, up again, up; recovered; erect; elevated; exalted; lofty; high; noble; grand; stately; highly seasoned, rich

Relevé, *s.m.* raising again; abstract; extract; summary; statement; return; list; shifting (*of a horse's shoe*); (*cook.*) remove; (*hunt.*) rising, feeding-time; (*nav.*) bearing

Relevée, *s.f.* (*law, admin.*) afternoon. *De* — in the afternoon

Relèvement, *s.m.* raising again; account, statement, return, list; survey; (*nav.*) rising, sheer; (*nav.*) bearing; (*nav.*) setting

Relève-quartier, *s.m.* shoe-horn

Relever, *v.a.n.* to raise, to raise up again; to take up; to lift up; to turn up; to tuck up; to curl up; to twirl up; to draw up; to set up again; to heighten; to enhance; to relieve, to set off; to trim; to give a relish to; to extol, to exalt; to notice; to point out; to criticize; to reprehend; to retort; to reply to; to be mindful of; to free, to discharge, to release, to absolve; to relieve (*sentries,* &c.); to remove; to collect (*letters*), to clear (*letter-boxes*); to shift (*a horse's shoe*); to replace; to substitute; to set afloat again; to survey; to recover; to be churched; to depend, to be dependent; (*law*) to be amenable; (*feud.*) to hold (of); to be held (of); (*hunt.*) to rise, to feed; (*rid.*) to rein, to gather up; to step high. — *de couches,* to recover from o.'s confinement, to have lately been confined; to be churched. — *de maladie,* to recover from illness. — *une côte,* (*nav.*) to take the bearings of a coast, to draw a view of a coast, to survey a coast. — *le quart,* (*nav.*) to set the watch

Se —, *v.r.* to rise again; to get up again; to rise; to get up; to stand up; to raise oneself; to retrieve o.'s losses; to recover; to relieve each other; to take turns; to release oneself; to be raised *or* &c.; to be relieved *or* &c.; to be noticed *or* &c.; (*nav.*) to right. *Se — d'une côte,* (*nav.*) to stretch from a coast *or* shore

Releveur, *adj.m.*, *s.m.* (*anat.*) levator

Reliage, *s.m.* (*of casks*) hooping

Relicher, *v.a.* (*pop.*) to lick up; to kiss

Relief, *s.m.* (*sculp.,* &c.) relief, relievo; embossing; (*fig.*) relief, foil, set-off; distinction; importance; lustre; quaintness; zest; (*obsolete*) leavings, remains, broken scrap *or* scraps. *En* —, in relief; embossed; raised; conspicuous. *Donner du — à, mettre en* —, to set off; to make conspicuous; to give importance to

Reliement, *s.m.* uniting, union, joining, junction, connecting, connection

Relier, *v.a.* to bind *or* tie *or* &c. (*V.* **Lier**) again; to bind; to tie; to unite; to join; to connect; to make (*one*) acquainted (with); (*books*) to bind; (*casks*) to hoop

Se —, *v.r.* to be bound *or* &c.; to join

Relieu-r, se, *s.m.f.* bookbinder, binder

Religieusement, *adv.* religiously; strictly; scrupulously; conscientiously; faithfully; punctually

Religieu-x, se, *adj.* religious; pious; conventual, monastic; sacred; strict; nice, scrupulous; conscientious; faithful; punctual; exact; — *s.m.* monk, friar, brother; — *s.f.* nun, sister

Religion, *s.f.* religion; creed; faith; piety; Church; religious order, conventual life, monastic state; convent, monastery; sacredness; scrupulousness; scruple; justice; conscientiousness; conscience; (*obsolete*) order of Malta. *Entrer en* —, *V.* **Entrer.** *Mettre en* —, to make (*a girl*) a nun, to shut up in a convent. *Se faire une — de*, to make it a matter of conscience, to make it a duty. *Surprendre* or *tromper la — de*, to impose upon, to deceive [ant

Religionnaire, *s.m.f.* (*hist.*) reformer, Protest-

Religiosité, *s. f.* religiosity, religiousness; scrupulosity, scrupulousness

Relimage, *s.m.* filing again

Relimer, *v.a.* to ... (*V.* **Limer**) again

Reliquaire, *s.m.* reliquary, shrine

Reliquat, *s.m.* balance (*of an account*), (*in law*) reliqua; remains [debtor; (*law*) reliquary

Reliquataire, *s.m.f.* debtor owing a balance,

Relique, *s.f.* relic

Relire, *v.a.n.* to read again

Se —, *v.r.* to read oneself *or* each other again; to be read again

Reliure, *s.f.* bookbinding; binding; full-binding. *Demi-* —, half-binding. *En demi-* —, half-bound [letting; under-lease

Relocation, *s.f.* reletting; new lease; under-

Reloger, *v.a.n.* to ... (*V.* **Loger**) again, to re-lodge

Relouage, *s.m.* (*of herrings*) spawning-time

Relouer, *v.a.* to let *or* hire *or* rent *or* &c. (*V.* **Louer,** No. 1) again, to relet; to underlet; to praise *or* &c. (*V.* **Louer,** No. 2) again

Reluire, *v.n.* to shine; to glitter; to glisten

Reluit, *s.m.* (*pop.*) peeper (*eye*); daylight, sun, shiner

Reluquer, *v.a.* (*fam.*) to ogle, to leer upon *or* at; to covet; to have o.'s eyes on, to have an

Reluqueu-r, se, *s.m.f.* ogler; coveter [eye to

Relustrer, *v.a.* to ... (*V.* **Lustrer**) again

Relute, *s.f.* new reading, second reading; (*print.*) revising, revisal

Relutter, *v.n.* to ... (*V.* **Lutter**) again [chewing

Remâchement, *s.m.* chewing again, second

Remâcher, *v.a.* to chew again, to remasticate; to ruminate; to revolve *or* turn over in o.'s mind [to be repaired

Remaçonner, *v.a.* to repair (*masonry*). *Se* —,

Remaigrir, *v.n.* to get thin again

†Rémailler, *v.a.* to enamel again

Remander, *v.a.* to ... (*V.* **Mander**) again

Remanger, *v.a.n.* to ... (*V.* **Manger**) again

Remaniable, *adj.* alterable

Remaniement, Remanîment, *s.m.* handling again; remodelling; repairing; altering, alteration, changing, change; (*print.*) overrunning

Remanier, *v.a.* to handle *or* touch again; to do over again; to remodel; to repair; to alter considerably, to alter, to change; (*print.*) to overrun; (*print.*) to turn (*the paper*)

Remanieu-r, se, *s.m.f.* remodeller; repairer; corrector, correctress [**der**) again

Remarchander, *v.a.n.* to ... (*V.* **Marchan-**

Remarcher, *v.n.* to ... (*V.* **Marcher**) again

Remariage, *s.m.* remarriage

Remarier, *v.a.*, **Se** —, *v.r.* to marry again, to remarry

Remarquable, *adj.* remarkable; conspicuous

Remarquablement, *adv.* remarkably [note

Remarque, *s.f.* remark; observation; notice;

Remarquer, *v.a.* to remark; to observe, to notice, to mind, to mark; to mark again. *Faire* —, to observe, to remark, to point out; to call (...'s) attention to; to make (...) remarked *or* noticed. *Se faire* —, to make oneself *or* itself noticed, to attract notice

Se —, *v.r.* to remark *or* &c. each other; to be remarked *or* &c.

Remasquer, Remastiquer, &c. to ... (*V.* **Masquer, Mastiquer,** &c.) again

Remballage, *s.m.* repacking

Remballer, *v.a.* to pack up again, to repack

Rembarquement, *s.m.* reembarcation, reimbarking, reimbarkment; reshipping, reshipment [to reship; to embark *or* engage again

Rembarquer, *v.a.*, **Se** —, *v.r.* to reembark;

Rembarrer, *v.a.* to repel, to repulse; to set on; to retort on; to take up short, to set down, to check, to stop at once

Rembellir, *v.a.n.* to reembellish, to ... (*V.* **Embellir**) again

Remblai, *s.m.* embankment; embanking; bank; mound; made earth, rubbish; (*fort.*) remblai; (*mining*) gobbing, gob-stuff [to resow

Remblaver, *v.a.* to ... (*V.* **Emblaver**) again,

Remblavure, *s.f.* resowing; land *or* field sown twice over

Remblayer, *v.a.* to embank, to fill up

Remboîtement, *s.m.* fitting in again; setting into joint again; setting

Remboîter, *v.a.* to fit in again, to put together again; to set into joint again; to set

Rembouger, *v.a.* to refill, to fill up, to add to, to refresh [stuffing; padding

Rembourrage, Rembourrement, *s.m.*

Rembourrer, *v.a.* to stuff; to pad. *Porte rembourrée*, baize door [stuffed *or* &c.

Se —, *v.r.* to stuff *or* cram oneself; to be

Rembourrure, *s.f.* stuffing; padding

Remboursabilité, *s. f.* repayableness; redeemableness [able; redeemable

Remboursable, *adj.* reimbursable, repay-

Remboursement, *s. m.* reimbursement, repayment; redeeming, redemption; funds. *Contre* —, on payment, on remittance, for cash. *Faire suivre en* —, to require payment on delivery, to charge for the goods with the carriage, to charge forward o.'s disbursements, to charge forward

Rembourser, *v.a.* to reimburse, to repay; to refund; to redeem; (*fig., fam.*) to return, to give back; (*old*) to receive, to pocket

Se —, *v.r.* to reimburse *or* &c. oneself *or* each other; to be reimbursed *or* &c.

Rembraser, Rembrasser, Rembrocher, &c. to ... (*V.* **Embraser, Embrasser, Embrocher,** &c.) again [gloomy, cloudy

Rembruni, e, *adj.* browner, darker; dark;

Rembrunir, *v.a.* to make browner *or* darker, to darken; to make gloomy, to cloud, to sadden; — *v.n.*, **Se** —, *v.r.* to become browner *or* darker, to darken; to become (*or* grow *or* get) gloomy *or* cloudy *or* sad [iness

Rembrunissement, *s.m.* darkening; gloom-

Rembûchement, *s.m.* (*hunt.*) return to the lair *or* to covert

Rembûcher, *v.a.* (*hunt.*) to trace back to the lair *or* to covert; — *v.n.*, **Se** —, *v.r.* to go back (*or* return) to the lair *or* to covert

Remède, *s.m.* remedy; medicine; cure; (*obsolete for* "lavement") injection, enema; (*coin., obsolete*) remedy. — *d'amour*, cure for love, very ugly *or* old person, fright. — *de bonne femme*, old woman's remedy. *Sans* —, without a remedy; remediless; past recovery; irremediable, irretrievable; remedilessly; irremediably, irretrievably. *Apporter du* — *à, mettre* —

Remédiable, *adj.* remediable [*à*, to remedy

Remédiement, *s.m.* remedying [to stop

Remédier, *v.n.* to remedy; to cure; to help;

Reméditer, &c. to ... (*V.* **Méditer,** &c.)

Remêler, *v.a.* to ... (*V.* **Mêler**) again [again

Remémorati-f, ve, *adj.* rememorative, reminding [brance

Remémoration, *s.f.* rememoration, remem-

Remémorer, *v.a.* to rememorate, to remember; to remind of; to remind

Se —, *v.r.* to remember, to recollect

Remenacer, *v.a.* to threaten *or* menace again

Remenée, *s.f.* arch (*over a door or window*)

Remener, *v.a.* to lead *or* &c. (*V.* **Mener**) again *or* back

Remerciement, *s.m.* *V.* **Remercîment**

Remercier, *v.a.* to thank; to decline; to dis-

Remercîment, *s.m.* thank, thanks [charge

Réméré, *s.m.* (*law*) redemption, redeeming, repurchase. *A* —, *avec faculté de* —, with power of redemption, on return [redeemed

Réméré, *v.a.* (*law*) to redeem. *Se* —, to be

Remesurage, *s.m.* remeasuring, remeasurement

Remesurer, Remétrer, &c. to . . . (*V.* **Mesurer, Métrer,** &c.(again, to remeasure, &c.

Remetteu-r, se, *s.m.f.* remitter, remittor

Remettre, *v.a.* to put *or* set *or* &c. (*V.* **Mettre**) again; to put back *or* back again; to put on again, to wear again; to give back; to bring back; to replace; to reestablish; to reinstate; to restore; to restore to health; to refresh; to do up; to recover; to right; to set right; to tranquillize, to calm, to quiet; to put; to deliver, to deliver up, to give up, to give; to resign; to hand over; to hand; to present; to delay, to defer, to put off, to adjourn; to pardon, to forgive; to remit; to send; to intrust; to commit; to leave; to refer; to remember, to recollect, to recognize; to draw (*a game*), to make (*a drawn game*); (*surg. of limbs*, &c.) to set, to replace; —*v n.* (*hunt.*) to alight. — *bien ensemble*, to reconcile. *Faire* —, to have (...) delivered, to send, to forward

Se —, *v.r.* to put *or* &c. (*V.* **Se Mettre**) oneself again *or* back; to refresh *or* &c. oneself; to recover oneself, to come to oneself; to recover, to get well again; to rally; to compose oneself; to retrieve o.'s losses; to commit oneself, to apply oneself again; to set again (to), to set about again, to begin again; to return (to ...) again, to return (to ...); to recur; to resume; to remember, to recollect; to remember *or* recognize each other; to leave, to refer; to be put again, &c., &c.; to be reconciled; to be put off *or* &c.; (*surg.*) to be set; (*hunt.*) to alight; (*Se — au beau*) to settle *or* get fine (weather) again, to mend. *S'en — à*, to refer *or* trust to; to leave (it) to

Remeubler, *v.a.* to refurnish, to furnish again

Rémige, *s.f.* (*adj.f., Penne* —) quill-feather of the wing, remige, (— *extérieure*) primary

Reminer, *v.a.* to ... (*V.* **Miner**) again

Réminiscence, *s.f.* reminiscence

Rémipède, *adj.m.f., s.m.* (*zool.*) remiped

Remirer, *v.a.* to ... (*V.* **Mirer**) again

Remis, e, *part. adj.* put again, &c. (*V.* **Remettre**); put off, adjourned; recovered, well again; (*of games*) drawn; (*of the weather*) settled again, fine again; (*old*) calm, quiet, composed, sedate, sober

Remisage, *s. m.* housing; carriage-house, coach-house, house; shed

Remise, *s.m.* first-class cab; fly; job-carriage, hired brougham *or* &c.

Remise, *s.f.* delivery; surrender; delay; adjournment; abatement, deduction, discount; allowance; taking off; remission; release, quitclaim; remittance; carriage-house, coach-house, house; shed; shelter; (*theat.*) new performance, revival; (*hunt.*) place of alighting; thicket, covert. *Voiture de* —, first-class cab; fly; job-carriage, hired brougham *or* &c. *Voiture de grande* —, job-carriage, hired brougham *or* &c. *Sous la* —, in the carriage-house; (*pers., fig.*) on the shelf

Remiser, *v.a.* to put in a carriage-house, to house; to put under shelter; to put by

Se —, *v.r.* (*of partridges*, &c.) to alight

Remisier, *s.m.* (*jest.*) commission-agent

Rémisse, *adj.* (*old*) remiss, weak

Rémissibilité, *s.f.* remissibility

Rémissible, *adj.* remissible, pardonable

Rémission, *s.f.* remission; forgiveness, pardon; mercy [remissionary

Rémissionnaire, *s.m.f.* pardoned criminal,

Rémittence, *s.f.* (*med.*) remittent character *or* nature; remission

Rémittent, e, *adj.* (*med.*) remittent [(*bird*)

Remiz, *s. m.* (*adj., Mésange* —) penduline tit

†**Remmaillage, Remmaillement,** *s.m.* restitching, mending

†**Remmailler,** *v.a.* to stitch again, to restitch, to remake the meshes of, to mend

†**Remmaillotter,** *v.a.* to swathe again, to reswathe

Remmancher, *v.a.* to put a new handle *or* stick to, to new-haft, to haft again; to resume, to get on again with

Se —, *v.r.* to be new-hafted *or* &c.

Remmener, *v.a.* to lead *or* take back; to take away again

Remodelage, *s.m.* remodelling

Remodeler, *v.a.* to remodel

Rémois, e, *adj. s.* of Reims; native of Reims

Rémolade, *s.f.* (*bad spelling*) *V.* **Rémoulade**

Remole, *s.f.* (*nav.*) eddy, whirlpool

Remonder, *v.a.* to ... (*V.* **Monder**) again

Remontage, *s. m.* reascending, ascending, going up; putting together again, fitting up again; winding up; new-stocking, putting a new stock; repairing; (*of boots, shoes*) new-fronting, vamping; (*of brandy*) strengthening

Remontant, e, *adj.* (*hort.*) growing again in the autumn, flowering twice in the year, perpetual-flowering, autumn-bearing

Remonte, *s.f.* going up (*a stream*), ascent, up journey, way up; fish ascending a stream for spawning; repairing; (*mil.*, &c.) remounting, remount; (*in breeding-studs*) further leap. *Cheval de* —, remount horse, remount

Remonté, e, *part. adj.* reascended, &c. (*V.* **Remonter**); (*of gout*) retrocedent

Remontée, *s.f.* (*pop.*) afternoon

Remonter, *v.n.a.* to ascend *or* mount *or* go (*or* come) up *or* get up *or* &c. (*V.* **Monter**) again; to reascend; to remount; to rise again; to ascend; to rise; to go up; to get up; to trace o.'s origin up *or* back; to date (from); to go back; to retrocede; to grow again, to flower *or* bear twice in the year; to put together again, to fit *or* make up again; to raise; to wind up (*clocks*, &c.); to new-mount; to new-stock; to new-front (*boots, shoes*), to vamp; to new-string (*mus. instr.*); to take up again; to set up again; to supply *or* stock again; to refurnish; to repair; to revive; to refresh; to cheer; to strengthen; (*mil.*) to remount (*cavalry*); (*falc.*) to fatten. *Faire* —, to cause to rise; to carry *or* bring up again; to carry up; to bring up; to trace up *or* back, to trace

Se —, *v.r.* to supply *or* stock oneself again, &c.; to be put together again, &c.; to recover o.'s spirits; to recover o.'s strength, to gather new strength [escapement

Remontoir, *s.m.* (*horol.*) remontoir, gravity

Remontrance, *s.f.* remonstrance

Remontrant, *s.m.* remonstrant

Remontrer, *v.a.n.* to show again; to show; to point out; to represent; to teach again; to remonstrate. *En — à quelqu'un*, to teach one something he does not know; to be more than a match for one; to outdo *or* outwit one. *C'est Gros-Jean qui veut en remontrer* (or *qui en remontre* or *qui remontre*) *à son curé*, it is teaching o.'s grandmother how to suck eggs

Remontreur, *s.m.* remonstrator [again

Remoquer (Se), *v.r.* to ... (*V.* **Se Moquer**)

Rémora, *s. m.* (*zool.*) remora, sucking-fish, sucker; (*obsolete*) obstacle, delay

Remordre, *v.a.n.* to ... (*V.* **Mordre**) again

Remords, *s.m.* remorse; compunction

Rémore, *s.f.* (*zool.*) *V.* **Rémora**

Remorquage, *s.m.* towage, towing

Remorque, *s.f.* towing; tow; tow-rope. *Câble* or *grelin de* —, tow-rope. *A la* —, in towing; in tow; (*fig.*) under the influence *or* leadership (of); in the train *or* wake (of) [to lead

Remorquer, *v.a.* to tow, to tug, to drag; (*fig.*)

Remorqueur, *s.m.* towing-boat *or* ship, tow-boat, tugboat, tug; (*rail.*) pilot-engine; — *adj.m.* towing

Remorqueuse, *s.f.* (*rail.*) pilot-engine

Remors, *s.m.* — *du diable*, (*bot.*) devil's-bit scabious

Rémotis (A), *adv.* (*old*) aside, by, away

Remoucher, *v.a.* to ... (*V.* **Moucher**) again; (*fam.*) to take up short, to take up, to set down, to snub, to give a clincher, to give it to
Remoudre, *v.a.* to grind *or* &c. (*V.* **Moudre**) again
Rémoudre, *v.a.* to grind (*V.* **Émoudre**) again, to whet *or* sharpen again; to grind, to whet *or* sharpen
†**Remouiller,** *v.a.n.* to ... (*V.* **Mouiller**) again
Rémoulade, *s.f.* (*cook.*) remoulade (*sauce, dressing*); (*vet.*) *V.* **Charge**
Remoulage, *s.m.* grinding *or* &c. (*V.* **Remoudre** *&* **Remouler**) again; shorts (*coarse flour, bran*)
Remouler, *v.a.* to mould *or* &c. (*V.* **Mouler**) again, to remould
Rémouleur, *s.m.* knife-grinder, grinder [death
Remourir, *v.n.* to die again, to die a double
Remous, *s.m.* back-water, dead-water, eddy-water, eddy, shoot, (— *du courant*) rippling
†**Rempaillage, Rempaillement,** *s.m.* re-covering with straw; repacking; restuffing; new-bottoming, mending (*of straw chairs*, &c.)
†**Rempaillé, e,** *part. adj.* new-bottomed, &c. (*V.* **Rempailler**); with straw bottom
†**Rempailler,** *v.a.* to ... (*V.* **Empailler**) again; to new-bottom (*with straw*), to mend
†**Rempailleu-r, se,** *s.m.f.* chair-mender
Rempaquement, *s.m.* packing (*of fish*)
Rempaquer, *v.a.* to pack (*fish*)
Rempaquetage, *s.m.* repacking [pack
Rempaqueter, *v.a.* to pack up again, to re-
Remparement, *s.m.* fortifying, fortification, intrenchment, retrenchment, fence
Remparer, *v.a.* to rampart; to bulwark; to fortify; to intrench; to fence; to cover
Se —, *v.r.* to fortify *or* &c. (*V.* **Remparer**) oneself; to seize *or* take *or* &c. (*V.* **S'Emparer**)
Rempart, *s.m.* rampart; bulwark [again
Rempêtrer, *v.a.* to ... (*V.* **Empêtrer**) again
Rempiéter, *v.a.* to new-foot, to refoot, to foot; — *v.n.a.* to ... (*V.* **Empiéter**) again
Rempirer, *v.a.n.* to ... (*V.* **Empirer**) again
Remplaçable, *adj.* replaceable
Remplaçant, e, *s.m.f.* substitute
Remplacé, *s.m.* (*mil.*) one that has a substitute; — *m.*, **e,** *f.*, *part. of* **Remplacer** (replaced, &c.
Remplacement, *s.m.* replacement, replacing; being replaced; reinvestment; getting a substitute; system of substitutes; (*of nav. stores*) fresh supply. *Bureau de —*, (*mil.*) office for providing substitutes. *En — de*, in place of, to replace; in succession to, vice
Remplacer, *v.a.* to replace; to take the place of; to supply; to supply the place of; to succeed; to supersede; (*old*) to compensate, to make up for; (*mil.*) to be the substitute of; (*fin.*) to reinvest. *Se faire —*, to get a substitute
Se —, *v.r.* to replace *or* &c. each other; to be replaced *or* &c.; to get a fresh supply
Remplage, *s.m.* (*of casks of wine*) filling up; adding, refreshing; (*build.*) filling in, fillings, rubble
Rempli, e, *part. adj.* filled, &c. (*V.* **Remplir**); full; replete; fraught (with); (*her.*) rempli. — *de soi-même*, self-important, full of self-importance
Rempli, *s.m.* turning in, tuck [portance
Remplier, *v.a.* to take in, to turn in; to tuck up
Remplir, *v.a.* to fill again, to refill; to fill up again; to fill; to fill up; to replenish; to cram, to stuff; to complete; to supply; to occupy, to employ, to take up; to fulfil, to perform, to accomplish; to realize; to satisfy; to keep; to hold; to answer (*expectations*), to answer *or* serve (*a purpose*); to go through *or* over, to go the whole length of; to mend; to refund, to repay; — *v.n.* to be filling *or* cloying
Se —, *v.r.* to be filled *or* &c.; to become full; to fill; to fill oneself; to cram or stuff oneself; to feed oneself; to impress oneself; to be refunded *or* repaid
Remplissage, *s.m.* filling; filling up; (*of casks of wine*) *V.* **Ouillage**; filling-up stuff; filling in; fillings, rubble; makeweight; worthless matter, surplusage, padding, trash, rubbish; accessory; accessory part; (*mus.*) middle parts; (*tech., nav.*) dead-wood [mender
Remplisseuse, *s.f.* (*need.*) filler, filler-in, lace-
Remploi, *s.m.* reemployment; reinvestment
Remployer, *v.a.* to reemploy, to employ *or* use again; to reinvest [feather; to new-quill
Remplumer, *v.a.* to feather again, to new-
Se —, *v.r.* to get new feathers; to retrieve o.'s losses, to mend o.'s affairs, to thrive, to feather o.'s nest; to get fat *or* stout again, to pick up again
Rempocher, *v.a.* to pocket again [again
†**Rempoigner,** *v.a.* to ... (*V.* **Empoigner**)
Rempoisonner, *v.a.* to poison again, to re-poison [fish
Rempoissonnement, *s.m.* restocking with
Rempoissonner, *v.a.* to restock with fish
Remporter, *v.a.* to carry *or* take back; to carry *or* take away; to obtain, to gain, to win, to get, to carry off, to carry, to bear away *or* off
Se —, *v.r.* to be carried back *or* &c.
Remporteu-r, se, *s.m.f.* winner, taker. — *de prix*, prize-taker
Rempotage, *s.m.* repotting [into a fresh pot
Rempoter, *v.a.* to pot again, to repot, to put
Remprisonnement, *s.m.* reimprisonment
Remprisonner, *v.a.* to reimprison
Remprunter, *v.a.n.* to borrow again
Remuable, *adj.* movable [transport
Remuage, *s.m.* stirring, moving; removing,
Remuant, e, *adj.* stirring; restless, unquiet, fidgety; bustling, busy; turbulent, seditious
Remué, e, *part. adj.* moved, &c. (*V.* **Remuer**); made (*earth*)
Remue-ménage, *s. m.* rummage, moving, stir; disturbance, bustle, confusion; bustler, turbulent fellow
Remuement, Remûment, *s.m.* stirring, moving, motion; removing; stir, bustle, disturbance, agitation, commotion, tumult
Remue-queue, *s.m.* (*bird*) wagtail
Remuer, *v.a.n.* to move; to set in motion; to stir; to stir up; to shake; to wag; to agitate; to remove (*earth*); to turn up (*a field*); to dig (*in fort.*); to shuffle (*dominoes*); to rummage; to rouse; to affect; to disturb; to handle; to fidget; (*old*) to change the linen of (*a child*), to change. — *ciel et terre*, to move heaven and earth, to leave no stone unturned
Se —, *v.r.* to move, to stir; to stir about; to bestir oneself; to fidget; to be moved *or* &c.
Remueu-r, se, *s.m.f.* mover, stirrer; — *s.f.* (*obsolete*) under-nursemaid [rative
Rémunérant, e, *adj.* remunerating, remune-
Rémunéra-teur, trice, *s.m.f. adj.* remunerator, rewarder; remunerating, remunerative, rewarding
Rémunérati-f, ve, *adj.* remunerative
Rémunération, *s.f.* remuneration, reward, recompense
Rémunératoire, *adj.* remuneratory
Rémunérer, *v.a.* to remunerate, to reward
Remunir, *v.a.* to ... (*V.* **Munir**) again
Remuseler, *v.a.* to muzzle *or* &c. (*V.* **Museler**) again, to remuzzle
Renâcler, *v.n.* to snuff up, to snort; to show reluctance, to hang back, to demur; to wince; to grumble
Renager, *v.n.* to ... (*V.* **Nager**) again
Renaissance, *s.f.* renascence, renascency, new birth, regeneration; revival; renewal; return; shoddy, mungo; (*hist. of liter. and art*) renaissance. — *des lettres et des arts*, revival of letters and arts
Renaissant, e, *part. adj.* springing up *or* &c. (*V.* **Renaître**) again, reviving, returning, recurring, renascent
Renaître, *v.n.* to be born again; to come to life again; to spring up *or* rise again; to grow

again; to revive; to come again; to return; to reappear; to recur; to be restored; to be regenerated. *Faire* —, to revive, to regenerate

Rénal, e, *adj.* (*anat.*) renal

Renard, *s.m.* fox; reynard; (*fam.*) spew; (*tech., nav.*) leak; dog, cant-hook; traverse-board. *Compère le* —, *maître* —, Reynard the [Fox, Reynard

Renarde, *s.f.* she-fox, vixen

Renardeau, *s.m.* fox's cub

Renarder, *v.n.* to dodge; (*fam.*) to spew, to [shoot the cat

Renardier, *s.m.* fox-catcher; — *adj.m.* of foxes, fox [— *adj.f.* of foxes, fox

Renardière, *s.f.* fox's burrow *or* hole *or* earth;

Renaré, e, *adj. s.* (*pop.*) cunning, knowing; cunning *or* knowing one

Renauder, *v.n.* (*pop.*) to refuse, to hang back, to demur; to wince; to sulk; to complain, to grumble, to croak

Renavigable, *adj.* renavigable

Renaviguer, *v.n.a.* to renavigate

Rencaissage, Rencaissement, *s.m.* collecting again, new (*or* fresh) collection *or* &c. (*V.* **Encaissement**); (*hort.*) retubbing

Rencaisser, *v.a.* to ... (*V.* **Encaisser**) again; (*hort.*) to tub again, to retub

Rencart, *s.m.* *V.* **Rancart**

Renchaîner, *v.a.* to chain *or* chain up again

Renchéri, e, *part. adj.* risen in price; (*pers.*) particular, over nice, fastidious; — *s.m.f.* ditto person *or* creature. *Faire le* — *or la* —*e*, to be particular *or* &c.; to give oneself airs

Renchérir, *v.a.* to raise *or* increase the value *or* price of, to raise, to increase; — *v.n.* to rise *or* increase in value *or* price, to rise, to increase, to grow (*or* get *or* become) dear *or* dearer. — *sur*, to outdo, to surpass, to improve upon, to refine upon, to add to, to go beyond, to go farther in (*a thing*) *or* than (*a person*), to be stronger than

Renchérissement, *s.m.* raising of the value *or* price, rising *or* rise *or* increase of price, raising, rising, rise, advance, increase

Rencloîtrer, *v.a.* *V.* **Reclôitrer**

Renclore, *v.a.* to enclose again; to enclose

Renclouer, *v.a.* to ... (*V.* **Enclouer**) again

†Rencogné, e, *part. adj.* drawn back *or* &c. (*V.* **Rencogner**) into a corner; screwed up *or* crouching in a corner [a corner

†Rencogner, *v.a.* to draw back *or* drive into

Se —, *v.r.* to draw *or* shrink back into a corner, to conceal oneself *or* crouch in a corner; to shut oneself up

Rencontre, *s.f.* meeting; chance; adventure; hit; coincidence; conjunction, junction; conjuncture, juncture; occasion; occurrence; rencounter; encounter; duel; collision, shock; (*obsolete*) witticism, jest; — *s.m.* (*her.*) rencounter. *A la* — *de*, to meet (*A ma* or *&c.* —, to meet me *or* &c.), forward to meet, towards; against. *De* —, second-hand. *Faire la* — *de*, to meet

Rencontrer, *v.a.n.* to meet; to meet with; to hit upon; to find; to rencounter; to encounter; to guess, to hit; to make a hit; to fall. — *bien*, to be well served by chance, to be lucky *or* felicitous, to make a good hit; to guess right. — *mal*, to be ill served by chance, to be unlucky *or* infelicitous, to make a bad hit; to guess wrong

Se —, *v.r.* to meet; to meet together; to encounter; to come in contact *or* into collision, to collide; to fight a duel; to agree; to tally; to find; to have the same idea; to jump together; to be met with; to be found; to occur, to happen; to happen to be; to come; (*hunt.*) to be on the scent. *Les beaux esprits se rencontrent*, (*Proverb*) wits jump together

Rencontreur, *s.m.* meeter, hitter, finder; [guesser

Rencorser, *v.a.* to put a new body to

Rencourager, *v.a.* to reencourage

Rendable, *adj.* renderable [output

Rendage, Rendement, *s.m.* produce; yield;

Rendetter, *v.a.* to ... (*V.* **Endetter**) again

Rendeu-r, se, *s.m.f.* renderer; restorer

Rendez-vous, *s.m.* appointment; place appointed; trysting-place; place of meeting, place of resort, resort; assignation; (*hunt.*) meet; (*in English mil. and other slang*) rendezvous. — *de chasse*, hunting-appointment; meet; hunting-box; shooting-lodge *or* box. *Donner* — (*à*), *prendre* —, to make an appointment (with), to appoint to meet (...); to order (...) to repair. *Se donner* —, to make an appointment, to appoint to meet each other; to come together, to meet, to resort

Rendonnée, *s.f.* *V.* **Randonnée**

Rendormir, *v.a.* to lull *or* send to sleep again; to lay asleep again

Se —, *v.r.* to fall asleep *or* go to sleep again

Rendosser, *v.a.* to ... (*V.* **Endosser**) again

Rendoubler, *v.a.* to fold *or* double up, &c. (*V.* **Remplier**)

Rendre, *v.a.* to render; to return; to give back; to give instead; to give up; to give in; to give; to repay; to repay for; to reciprocate; to restore; to deliver; to deliver up; to surrender; to bring up, to vomit; to evacuate, to void, to pass; to convey, to take; to make; to drive (*mad*); to strike (*dumb*, &c.); to do; to carry; to bear; to yield; to produce; to bring in; to pay; to perform; to represent; to emit, to exhale, to give out *or* forth; to express; to translate; to reproduce, to take off; to repeat; to fetch; to lay down; to give change *or* the difference; (*justice*) to do *or* administer (*V.* **Justice**); to issue (*a decree*); to pass (*a law*); (*law, mil., nav.*) to surrender (*an estate, a town, a ship*, &c.); to return (*a verdict*), to bring in; to pronounce *or* pass (*a sentence*); — *v.n.* (*of roads*) to lead, to go; (*of wounds*) to run; — *s.m.* returning, repayment, refunding, paying again *or* back; return

Se —, *v.r.* to render *or* make *or* &c. oneself (*or* to *or* for oneself) *or* each other (*or* to *or* for each other); to become, to turn; to repair, to proceed, to go, to come, to get; to resort; to run; to wait (on *or* upon); to lead; to yield, to submit, to comply; to give oneself up; to surrender; to give it up; to be rendered *or* returned *or* &c.; to be exhausted *or* spent; to be expressed *or* translated

Rendu, e, *part. adj.* rendered, returned, &c. (*V.* **Rendre**); become; arrived; sent in; delivered; exhausted, spent, tired out, worn out, knocked up. *V.* **Prêté,** *s.m.*

Rendu, *s.m.* thing returned, return, tit for tat (*V.* **Prêté,** *s.m.*); (*paint.*, &c.) reproduction, expression

Renduire, *v.a.* to ... (*V.* **Enduire**) again

Rendurcir, *v.a.* to harden, to make harder

Se —, *v.r.* to harden, to become hardened, to get harder [ness, becoming harder

Rendurcissement, *s.m.* hardening, hard-

Rêne, *s.f.* bearing-rein; rein

René, e, *part of* **Renaître**

Renégat, e, *s.m.f.* renegade [ation

Renégation, *s.f.* renegation, denial; renunci-

Reneiger, *v.n.* to snow again

Rêner, *v.n.* (*rid.*) to bear up; — *v.a.* to rein

Rénette, *s.f.* (*carp., vet.*) *V.* **Rainette**

Rénetter, *v.a.* *V.* **Rainetter**

Renettoyer, *v.a.* to ... (*V.* **Nettoyer**) again

Renfaîtage, *s.m.* new-ridging; new ridge

Renfaîter, *v.a.* to new-ridge

Renfanter, *v.a.* to ... (*V.* **Enfanter**) again

Renfermé, e, *part. adj.* shut up again; shut up, confined, &c. (*V.* **Renfermer**); close

Renfermé, *s.m.* fustiness, close *or* confined air. *Odeur de* —, fusty smell. *Sentir le* —, to smell fusty *or* close

Renfermer, *v.a.* to shut up *or* &c. (*V.* **Enfermer**) again; to shut up; to confine; to enclose; to contain; to comprise; to include; to conceal, to hide; to confine (*a prisoner*) more closely. **Se** —, *v.r* *See over*

Se —, *v.r.* to shut oneself up, &c.; (*of things*) to be shut up, &c. *Se — en soi-même*, to retire within oneself; to collect o.'s thoughts
Renferrer, *v.a.* to ... (**Enferrer**) again
†**Renfeuiller,** *v.n.a.*, **Se** —, *v.r.* to leaf again
Renfiler, *v.a.* to thread again
Renflammer, *v.a.* to set on fire again, to kindle *or* &c. (*V.* **Enflammer**) again, to rekindle
Renflé, e, *part. adj.* swollen; swelled; puffed up; risen; swelling, swelling out; inflated; bossed
Renflement, *s.m.* swelling, swelling out, swell; enlargement; boss; (*arch.*) entasis, swelling; (*bot.*) struma [out; to puff up; to rise
Renfler, *v.n.a.*, **Se** —, *v.r.* to swell, to swell
Renflouage, Renflouement, Renfluement, *s.m.* (*nav.*) setting afloat again, raising
Renflouer, Renfluer, *v.a.* (*nav.*) to set afloat again, to raise [*horses by horse-jockeys*)
Renflure, *s.f.* swelling out the eye-pits (*of old*
Renfoncement, *s.m.* sinking again *or* &c. (*V.* **Renforcer**); hollow, cavity, depression; depth; recess; alcove; break; back; background; (*print.*) indentation; (*fam.*) bonneting; cuff, punch, buffet, blow, thump; bruise, dint. — *de porte*, doorway
Renfoncer, *v.a.* to sink *or* &c. (*V.* **Enfoncer**) again *or* back *or* deeper; to sink; to drive further on (*or* in), to drive deeper; to pull down; to pull over o.'s eyes; (*print.*) to indent; (*of casks*) to new-bottom
Se —, *v.r.* to be sunk *or* &c.
Renforçage, *s.m.* strengthening
Renforcé, e, *part. adj.* strengthened, &c. (*V.* **Renforcer**); (*of animals and things*) strong, stout, thick, substantial; (*pers.*) substantial, well-to-do; (*pers. and things*) thorough, regular, downright [of strength; reinforcement
Renforcement, *s.m.* strengthening; increase
Renforcer, *v.a.* to strengthen; to reinforce; to increase; to raise
Se —, *v.r.* to grow *or* get stronger, to gather strength; to be strengthened *or* reinforced; to gain proficiency
Renforcir, *v.a.n.* *V.* **Enforcir**
Renformir, *v.a.* (*mas.*) to plaster, to dub out
Renformis, *s.m.* (*mas.*) plastering, dubbing out, new coat
Renfort, *s.m.* reinforcement; supply, recruit; addition, increase; swell; (*artil.*) reinforce; (*nav.*) tabling (*of a sail*). *A grand — de*, with plenty of, by *or* with *or* through many (*or* much), by dint of. *De* —, extra; additional; fresh. *Pour — de potage*, to add to the mess, to make the thing quite complete
Renfouir, Renfourcher, Renfourner, &c. to ... (*V.* **Enfouir, Enfourcher, Enfourner,** &c.) again
†**Renfrogner,** &c. *V.* **Refrogner,** &c.
Renfrusquiner, *v.a.* (*pop.*) to stock *or* supply again with toggery [ment
Rengagement, *s.m.* reengagement; reenlist-
Rengager, *v.a.*, **Se** —, *v.r.* to engage *or* &c. (*V.* **Engager**) again, to reengage, to reenlist; to begin again, to renew
Rengaine, *s.f.* (*fam.*) old story, favourite theme, tiresome repetition; common-place, backneyed expression, triviality; well-known dodge
Rengaîner, *v.a.n.* to sheathe, to put up; to reserve; to forbear; to withdraw; to put by; to suppress; to stop; to keep to oneself; not to mention; to sheathe *or* put up o.'s sword. — *son compliment*, to reserve *or* put up o.'s compliment; to hold o.'s tongue; to die, to kick the bucket [again, to reproduce
Rengendrer, *v.a.* to ... (*V.* **Engendrer**)
Rengloutir, Rengluer, &c. to ... (*V.* **Engloutir, Engluer,** &c.) again
Rengorgement, *s.m.* bridling up, cocking, carrying o.'s head high; airs of importance, airs
Rengorger (Se), *v.r.* to bridle up, to cock, to carry it high, to assume airs of importance
Rengouffrer, Rengourdir, &c. to ... (*V.* **Engouffrer, Engourdir,** &c.) again
Rengraisser, *v.a.n.*, **Se** —, *v.r.* to fatten again, to make *or* to grow fat *or* stout again; to fatten [tion
Rengrégement, *s.m.* (*old*) increase, aggrava-
Rengréger, *v.a.*, **Se** —, *v.r.* (*old*) to increase, to aggravate
Rengrènement, *s.m.* recoinage, restamping
Rengrener, *v.a.n.* to ... (*V.* **Engrener**) again; to recoin, to restamp
Renhardir, *v.a.* to ... (*V.* **Enhardir**) again
Reni, *s.m.* renegation, denial
Reniable, *adj.* deniable
Renicher, *v.n.a.* to ... (*V.* **Nicher**) again
Renié, e, *part. adj.* denied, &c. (*V.* **Renier**). *Chrétien* —, renegade. *Moine* —, apostate monk
Reniement, *s.m.* renegation, denial; swearing; oath
Renier, *v.a.n.* to deny; to disown; to disclaim; to renounce; to abjure; to swear, to blaspheme
Renieu-r, se, *s.m.f.* (*obsolete*) swearer, blas-
Reniflard, *s.m.* (*tech.*) blow-valve [phemer
Reniflement, *s.m.* sniffing; snuffing up. — *sur l'avoine*, being off his feed
Renifler, *v.n.a.* to sniff; to snuff, to snuff up; to turn up o.'s nose (at); to demur, to hang back, to wince; (*pop.*) to smell, to suspect; (*pop.*) to drink. — *sur l'avoine*, to refuse his oats, to be off his feed
Reniflerie, *s.f.* sniffing; snuffing up
Renifleu-r, se, *s.m.f.* sniffer
Réniforme, *adj.* reniform, kidney-shaped
Renîment, *s.m.* *V.* **Reniement**
Renipper, *v.a.* to ... (*V.* **Nipper**) again
Rénitence, *s.f.* renitence, renitency
Rénitent, e, *adj.* renitent
Reniveler, *v.a.* to level again
Renivellement, *s.m.* new levelling
Renjamber, *v.a.* to ... (*V.* **Enjamber**) again
Renne, *s.m.* reindeer
Rennois, e, *adj.s.* of Rennes; native of Rennes
Rennuyer, Renoircir, &c. to ... (*V.* **Ennuyer, Noircir,** &c.) again [repute, celebrity
Renom, *s.m.* renown, fame, name, reputation,
Renommé, e, *part. adj.* named again, &c. (*V.* **Renommer**); celebrated, renowned, famous, noted, famed
Renommée, *s.f.* renown, fame, name, reputation, repute; report, rumour; (*myth.*) Fame
Renommer, *v.a.* to name *or* mention again; to reelect; to reappoint; to celebrate, to make famous, to give repute, to speak highly of. *Qu'on renomme*, named again, &c.; whose fame is spread, highly spoken of, renowned. *Se — de*, (*old for* "Se réclamer de") *V.* **Réclamer (Se).** *Se faire* —, to make oneself named again *or* &c.; to make oneself famous; to acquire renown *or* fame
Renonçant, e, *adj. s.* renouncing; renouncer
Renonce, *s.f.* (*at cards*) renounce, revoke
Renoncement, *s.m.* renouncement, renouncing, renunciation, denial; self-denial, abnegation. — *de* or *à soi même*, self-denial, abnegation. *Ordonnance* or *acte de — à soi-même*, (*Engl. hist.*) self-denying ordinance
Renoncer, *v.n.* to renounce, to give up; to deny; (*at cards*) to renounce, to revoke; — *v.a.* to deny, to disown, to disclaim; to forsake
Renonciataire, *s.m.f.* (*law*) relessee
Renoncia-teur, trice, *s.m.f.* renouncer; relessor [ment; self-denial, abnegation
Renonciation, *s.f.* renunciation, renounce-
Renonculacé, e, *adj.* (*bot.*) ranunculaceous
Renonculacées, *s.f.pl.* (*bot.*) ranunculaceæ
Renoncule, *s.f.* (*bot.*) ranunculus, buttercup, crowfoot, spearwort
Renonculier, *s.m.* double-flower cherry-tree
Renoter, *v.a.* to ... (*V.* **Noter**) again
Renouée, *s.f.* (*bot.*) polygonum, knot-grass

Renouement, Renoûment, *s.m.* renewal, renewing; new bond

Renouer, *v.a.n.* to tie again; to tie up, to tie; to join again; to join; to renew; to resume; to renew o.'s acquaintance. *Se —,* to be tied

Renoueu-r, se, *s.m.f. V.* **Rebouteur** [again, &c.

Renouveau, *s m.* (*obsolete*) spring (*season*)

Renouvelable, *adj.* renewable

Renouvelant, e, *s.m.f.* renewer; renewer of the first communion

Renouveler, *v.a.n.* to renew; to change; to alter; to renovate; to revive; to refresh; to repeat; to do again; to reestablish; to reissue; to republish (*a will*); to redouble, to increase; to do it again; to renew the first communion

Se —, *v.r.* to be renewed *or* &c.; to succeed each other; to return; to happen *or* occur again; (*of the moon*) to change

Renouveleu-r, se, *s.m.f.* renewer

Renouvellement, *s.m.* renewal, renewing; change; renovation; revival; repetition, reiteration; recurrence; republication; redoubling, increase; return; renewing of the first communion

Rénova-teur, trice, *adj. s.* renovating; re-

Rénovation, *s.f.* renovation; renewal [novator

†Renseignement, *s.m.* information, intelligence; direction, indication; inquiry; reference. *Bureau de —s,* intelligence-office; inquiry-office. *Aller aux —s, prendre des —s,* to make inquiries

†Renseigner, *v.a.* to inform, to give information, to tell; to direct, to indicate, to show; to teach *or* &c. (*V.* **Enseigner**) again

Se —, *v.r.* to get information *or* intelligence; to make inquiries, to inquire, to ask; to inform *or* &c. each other

Rensemencer, &c. *V.* **Réensemencer,** &c.

Renserrer, Rentamer, Rentasser, &c. to ... (*V.* **Enserrer, Entamer, Entasser,**

Rentassé, e, *adj.* (*pers.*) thickset [&c.) again

Rente, *s.f.* income; rent; interest; pension; annuity; stock, stocks; funds; money. *De —* or *de —s,* a year, income. *— foncière,* ground-rent. *— viagère, — à fonds perdu,* life-annuity, annuity. *— sur l'État,* government annuity; government stock, stock, funds; property in the funds. *Taux de la —,* price of stocks. *Acheter des —s,* to invest money in the funds, to buy stock. *Avoir des —s,* to have independent property *or* an independent income, to have money, to be independent. *Faire une —,* to allow a pension. *Racheter une —,* to redeem an annuity *Vivre de ses —s,* to live on o.'s income *or* property *or* money

Renté, e, *part. adj.* endowed; possessed of *or* having (*or* who has) an income, with an income. *Bien —,* possessed of *or* having a good income, rich, wealthy [(*stockings*) to new-foot

Renter, *v.a.* to endow, to give an income to;

Renterrer, &c. *V.* **Réenterrer,** &c.

Renti-er, ère, *s.m.f.* fund-holder, stock-holder; pensioner; annuitant; independent gentleman *or* lady; man or woman with a competency; gentleman; esquire; (*feud.*) tenant; *— s m.* (*feud.*) rent-roll, rental. *— viager* (m.), *rentière viagère* (f.), life-annuitant, annuitant. *Gros —,* man of large income. *Petit —,* man with a small competency [vas *or* new linen (to)

Rentoilage, *s.m* new-lining, putting new can-

Rentoiler, *v a.* to new-line, to put new canvas *or* new linen to

Rentonner, †Rentortiller, &c. to ... (*V.* **Entonner, Entortiller,** &c.) again

Rentrage, *s.m.* bringing in, taking in, housing

Rentraîner, *v.a.* to ... (*V.* **Entraîner**) again

Rentraire, *v.a.* to fine-draw, to darn, to renter

Rentraiture, *s.f.* fine-drawing, darning, rentering

Rentrant, e, *part. adj.* reentering, returning, &c. (*V.* **Rentrer**); (*geom., fort.*) reentering; *— s.m.* recess; (*at play*) new player

Rentrayeu-r, se, *s m.f.* fine-drawer, darner renterer

Rentré, e, *part. adj.* reentered, returned, &c (*V.* **Rentrer**); (*med*) suppressed, driven in (*of nails*) grown in

Rentrée, *s.f.* reentrance, reentering; reopening; reappearance; return, returns; receipt; taking in; housing, getting in, ingathering (*mus.*) reentrance; (*mus.*) repetition; (*mus.*) answer; (*print.*) indentation; (*nav.*) tumbling home, housing in (*of timbers*)

Rentrer, *v n.* to reenter, to enter again; to return; to go *or* come back; to return home, to come home *or* in again; to come again; to go in (*or* go) again; to reopen; to reappear; to come in; to come; to go; to fit; to grow in; to get again *or* back; to recover; to regain; to resume; to retire; to recede; to fall in (*or* fall) again *or* back; to be restored; to be comprised *or* contained; (*med.*) to be suppressed *or* driven in; (*mus.*) to reenter; (*mus.*) to repeat; (*mus.*) to answer; (*engr.*) to retouch; (*at cards*) to come in, to buy in; *— v.a.* to put (in) again *or* back; to take in *or* back; to draw in; to get in; to bring in; to house; to gather in; to turn in; to strike *or* drive in *or* back; to suppress, to stifle, to check; to conceal; (*print.*) to indent; (*a corruption of* "rentraire") *V.* **Rentraire.** *— en soi-même,* to retire within oneself. *Faire —,* to take in; to send in; to call in; to bring back *or* bring (to); to get in; to drive in *or* back; to suppress; (*print.*) to indent

Se —, *v.r.* to be put (in) again *or* back; to be taken in *or* back; &c. (*V.* **Rentrer,** *v a.*)

Rentr'ouvrir, Renvahir, Renvelopper, Renvenimer, Renverguer, &c. to ... (*V.* **Entr'ouvrir, Envahir, Envelopper, Envenimer, Enverguer,** &c.) again

Renversable, *adj.* liable to be overthrown *or* &c. (*V.* **Renverser**); reversible

Renversant, e, *adj.* (*fam.*) astounding, stunning, overwhelming, amazing, stupendous, extraordinary [—, backward; on o.'s back

Renverse, *s.f.* contrary wind; backing. *A la*

Renversé, e, *part. adj.* thrown down, &c. (*V.* **Renverser**); lolling. *Encolure —e,* (*rid.*) ewe-neck, pliant-neck. *C'est le monde —,* it is the world turned upside down, it is preposterous

Renversement, *s m.* throwing down *or* back; disarrangement, disorder, confusion; overthrow; destruction, ruin; subversion; overturning; upsetting; spilling; inversion; reversing; turning down; turning (*of the brain*), alienation; contrary direction, shifting, change; lolling; (*surg.*) prolapsus, retroversion; (*of the eyelid*) eversion

Renverser, *v.a.n.* to throw down *or* back; to knock *or* beat *or* pull *or* blow *or* lay *or* bear *or* bring down; to overthrow; to overturn; to turn upside down *or* topsy-turvy; to upset; to spill; to subvert; to invert; to reverse; to turn down; to transpose; to shift; to disarrange, to disorder, to confuse; to destroy, to ruin; to carry; to turn (*the brain*); to astound, to stun; to confound, to overpower, to overwhelm, to stupefy, to amaze; to discompose; to rout; (*surg.*) to retrovert; to evert; (*pop.*) to spew. *— la marche de la machine, — la vapeur,* (*rail.*) to reverse the engine

Se —, *v.r.* to turn upside down; to upset; to overturn; to turn down; to fall down; to fall backward; to throw oneself back; to fall back; to lie down on o.'s back; to loll; to throw each other down, &c.; to be thrown down, &c.

Renverseu-r, se, *s.m.f.* overthrower; subverter; overturner; destroyer; inverter; reverser; transposer

Renvi, *s.m.* (*at play*) revy, additional stake

Renvidage, *s.m.* (*spinning*) winding up winding

Renvider, *v.a.* to wind up *or* wind (on the [spindle)
Renvideur, *s.m.* winder
Renvier, *v.n.a.* (*at play*) to revy; (— *sur*) to outdo, &c. (*V.* **Renchérir** *sur*)
Renvoi, *s.m.* sending back, returning, return; dismissal, discharge, sending away; referring; reference; caret; adjournment, putting off, postponement; delay; reflection; reverberation; (*of the stomach*) rising, eructation, belch; (*law*) sending (before another court), reference (to another judge); (*of a case*) adjournment. *De* —, (*adject.*) returnable; (*of carriages and horses*) return
Renvoyer, *v.a.* to send again *or* back; to return; to send away, to dismiss, to discharge; to acquit (*a prisoner*); to refer; to send; to adjourn, to put off, to postpone; to delay; to reflect; to reverberate, to repeat
Se —, *v.r.* to bandy, to send back from one to another; to be sent back *or* returned *or* &c.
Réobtenir, *v.a.* to reobtain
Réoccupation, *s.f.* reoccupation
Réoccuper, *v.a.* to reoccupy [&c.
Réomètre, &c. (*bad spelling*) *V.* **Rhéomètre,**
Réopiner, *v.n.a.* to ... (*V.* **Opiner**) again
‡**Réorchestration,** *s.f.* (*mus.*) new scoring
‡**Réorchestrer,** *v.a.* (*mus.*) to score anew
Réordination, *s.f.* reordination
Réordonner, *v.a.* to reordain; to reorder; to ... (*V.* **Ordonner**) again
Réorganisa-teur, trice, *s.m.f.* reorganizer; — *adj.* reorganizing
Réorganisation, *s.f.* reorganization
Réorganiser, *v.a.* to reorganize, to organize *or* &c. (*V.* **Organiser**) again
Réouverture, *s.f.* reopening
Repaire, *s.m.* retreat; abode; haunt; den; lair; hole; nest; flash-house; (*bad spelling for* "repère," *hunt.*) dung
Répaissir, *v.a.n.*, **Se** —, *v.r.* to thicken again; to thicken, to make *or* become (*or* grow *or* get) thicker
Repaître, *v.n.a.*, **Se** —, *v.r.* to bait; to feed; to feast, to delight; to gloat; to indulge (in)
Repâlir, Repâmer, &c. to ... (*V.* **Pâlir, Pâmer,** &c.) again
Répandre, *v.a.* to spill; to shed; to spread; to scatter; to strew; to sprinkle; to pour, to pour out *or* forth; to diffuse; to exhale; to spread abroad, to propagate; to distribute; to bestow
Se —, *v.r.* to be spilt *or* shed *or* spread *or* scattered *or* &c.; to run out; to overrun; to overflow; to spread *or* extend itself *or* themselves, to spread; to scatter themselves; to get abroad; to break *or* burst *or* fly out, to launch forth; to frequent society, to go *or* get into society, to see company, to go out; to get *or* be known; (*old*) to indulge (in); (*pop.*) to fall down, to sprawl
Répandu, e, *adj.* out, in society, in request, fashionable; — *part. adj.* spilt, shed, spread, scattered, &c. (*V.* **Répandre**); rife, common, rampant, prevalent; admitted, received; used, in use; known. *Être très* (or *fort*) — *dans le monde,* (*pers.*) to go very much into society
†**Repapilloter,** *v.a.* to ... (*V.* **Papilloter**) again; (*fam.*) to mend, to repair, to patch up
Repaquage, Repaquetage, *s.m.* repacking
Repaquer, Repaqueter, *v.a.* to bundle again, [to repack
Réparable, *adj.* reparable; mendable
Réparablement, *adv.* reparably
Réparage, *s.m.* (*tech.*) repairing, mending
Reparaître, *v.n.* to reappear, to appear again; to show oneself *or* o.'s face again; to enter again, to reenter; to come out again; to come back
Répara-teur, trice, *s.m.f.* repairer; restorer; redresser; — *adj.* reparative; restoring, restorative; refreshing
Réparation, *s.f.* repairing; mending; repair; repairs; reparation; satisfaction; amends; atonement; apology; (*law*) relief; (—*s civiles*) damages, indemnity. —*s d'entretien,* keeping in repair. *En* —, under repair
Réparatoire, *adj.* reparative
Répare, *s.f.* margin
Reparer, *v.a.* to ... (*V.* **Parer**) again
Réparer, *v.a.* to repair; to mend; to restore; to reestablish; to refresh; to recruit; to recover; to retrieve; to make reparation *or* amends for; to atone for; to apologize for; to make up for; to redeem; to redress; to regenerate; to reproduce
Se —, *v.r.* to be repaired *or* &c.
Répareur, *s.m.* (*tech.*) repairer, mender
Réparition, *s.f.* (*astr.*) reappearance [again
Reparler, *v.n.a.* to speak *or* &c. (*V.* **Parler**)
Repart, *s.m.* (*obsolete*) *V.* **Repartie**
Repartager, *v.a.* to ... (*V.* **Partager**) again
Répartement, *s. m.* (*admin.*) assessment, [rating
Repartie, *s.f.* repartee, retort, reply
Repartir, *v.n.* to set out again, to go off *or* depart *or* &c. (*V.* **Partir**) again; to go back; — *v.a.n.* to reply
[*This verb, in all the above senses, is irregular, and is conjugated like* **Partir**.]
Répartir, *v.a.* to divide, to distribute; to portion out, to apportion; to allot; (*of taxes*) to assess
[*This verb is regular, and is therefore not conjugated like* "Repartir."]
Se —, *v.r.* to be divided *or* &c.
Répartissable, *adj.* dividable, divisible, distributable; assessable
Répartiteur, *s.m.* distributer; portioner, apportioner; (*of taxes*) assessor; — *adj.m.* distributing; assessing. *Commissaire* —, assessor
Répartition, *s.f.* division, distribution; portioning, portionment, apportionment; allotment; (*of taxes*) assessment
Repas, *s.m.* meal, repast; entertainment, feast
Repassage, *s.m.* repassing, repassage; ironing; setting; grinding; stropping; (*hort.*) raking
Repasse, *s.f.* redistillation; (*flour and bran*) pollard; (*pop.*) water bewitched (*bad coffee*)
Repasser, *v.a.n.* to repass, to recross, to pass *or* cross again, to pass *or* carry over again, to call *or* &c. (*V.* **Passer**) again; to return, to go *or* come back; to pass over; to reexamine; to rehearse, to look *or* go over; to revolve, to turn over; to finish off; to polish; to do up; to dress again; to iron; to smooth; to hone, to whet; to sharpen; to set; to grind; to strop; to redistil; to freshen (*stale bread*); to refresh *or* restore (*wine*); (*hort.*) to rake; (*fam., pop.*) to let have, to give; to curry, to beat, to give it to; to take up; to abuse
Se —, *v.r.* to be repassed, &c.; to be ironed *or* ground *or* &c.; to bear *or* stand ironing, to iron; to grind [mender
Repasseur, *s.m.* grinder; finisher; watch-
Repasseuse, *s.f.* ironer
Repassoir, *s.m.* grinding-stone; pointer
Repatrier, &c. (*old spelling*) *V.* **Rapatrier,** &c.
Repaumer, *v.a.* to ... (*V.* **Paumer**) again
Repavage, Repavement, *s.m.* repaving
Repaver, *v.a.* to repave
Repayer, *v.a.* to pay again, to repay
Repêchage, *s.m.* fishing up again
Repêcher, *v.a.n.* to fish *or* fish up *or* fish out again; to take out of the water; to catch again
†**Repeigner,** *v.a.* to ... (*V.* **Peigner**) again
Repeindre, *v.a.n.* to paint *or* &c. (*V.* **Peindre**) again *or* anew, to repaint; to retouch
Repeint, e, *part. adj.* painted again, &c. (*V.* **Repeindre**); — *s.m.* retouch, part retouched
Repeler, Repeloter, Rependre, &c. to ... (*V.* **Peler, Peloter, Pendre,** &c.) again
Repenelle, *s.f.* bird-trap, gin, snare
Repenser, *v.n.* to think *or* consider *or* &c. (*V.* **Penser**) again, to reconsider

Repentance, *s. f.* repentance; change of resolution
Repentant, e, *adj.* repentant
Repenti, e, *part. adj. s.m.f.* repented; repentant, penitent. *Les filles —es, Les —es,* (the *or* a) Magdalen hospital *or* asylum, (the *or* a) female penitentiary
Repentir (Se), *v.r.* to repent
Repentir, *s.m.* repentance, penitence; regret; sorrow; change of resolution; ringlet; *(paint., draw., engr.)* alteration
Repercer, *v.a.n.* to pierce *or* &c. (*V.* **Percer**) again; to pierce
Reperceu-r, se, *s.m.f.* piercer, gold and silver piercer
Répercussi-f, ve, *adj.*, **Répercussif,** *s.m.* repercussive; repellent
Répercussion, *s.f.* repercussion; reverberation; reflection; repellence
Répercutant, e, *adj.* repercussive
Répercuter, *v.a.* to repercuss, to drive *or* beat back, to drive in, to send back, to reverberate, to reflect, to repel
Se —, *v.r.* to be repercussed *or* &c.
Reperdre, *v.a.n.* to lose *or* &c. (*V.* **Perdre**) again
Repère, *s.m.* (*tech.*) mark; point; bench-mark; joining-mark; datum; (*hunt.*) dung. *Point de —,* guiding-mark, indication, direction
Repérer, *v.a.* to mark, to make a mark *or* put an indication to
Se —, *v.r.* to make a guiding-mark for oneself, to make a memorandum
Répertoire, *s.m.* repertory; index; table; chronicle; journal; collection; stock; (*theat.*) repertory, stock (of plays); (*theat.*) list. *Pièce de —,* (*theat.*) stock-play, stock-piece; (*mus.*) stock-piece
Repeser, *v.a.* to weigh again
†**Répétailler,** *v.a.n.* to repeat over and over again, to drum, to din
Repetasser, *v.a.* (*old spelling*) *V.* **Rapetasser**
Répéter, *v.a.* to repeat; to say *or* tell *or* do *or* begin again; to renew; to reproduce; to re-echo; to reflect; to rehearse; to teach in private; (*law*) to claim back again, to redemand. *Faire —,* to make (*one, people*) repeat *or* &c ; to have (...) repeated *or* &c.; to hear. *Se faire —,* to have (...) repeated *or* &c.; to require *or* have *or* wait to be told again (*or* twice)
Se —, *v.r.* to repeat oneself *or* itself; to repeat to each other; to be repeated *or* &c.
Répétiteur, *s.m.* tutor; private teacher; assistant professor; examiner; pianoforte accompanist at rehearsals; (*nav.*) repeater, repeating ship; — *adj.m.* repeating; assistant (*Cercle —,* repeating circle. *Maître —,* assistant master, usher)
Répétition, *s.f.* repetition; renewal; reproduction; duplicate; replica; rehearsal; private tuition *or* lesson; (*horol.*) repeating-works; (*law*) claiming back again, action for money had and received, (*in Scotch law*) repetition. *A* or *de —,* (*horol.*) repeating
Repétrir, *v.a.* to ... (*V.* **Pétrir**) again
Repeuplement, *s.m.* repeopling; restocking; replanting
Repeupler, *v.a.* to repeople; to restock; to replant
Se —, *v.r.* to be (*or* become) repeopled, &c.; to become populous again
Repic, *s.m.* (*at the game of piquet*) repique. *Faire —; faire — et capot; faire pic et —; faire pic et capot; faire pic, — et capot;* (*fig.*) to puzzle, to nonplus, to pose; to outdo, to outwit
Repiger, *v.a.* to ... (*V.* **Piger**) again
Repiler, †**Repiller, Repincer, Repiocher,** &c. to ... (*V.* **Piler, Piller, Pincer, Piocher,** &c.) again
Repiquage, Repiquement, *s.m.* pricking again; picking up; replacing, replacement; transplanting, transplantation
Repiquer, *v.a.* to prick *or* &c. (*V.* **Piquer**) again; to pick up; to repair; to replace; to transplant; — *v.n.* (*pop.*) to pluck up courage; to get off; to come again, to return. — *sur le rôti,* to cut and come again
Se —, *v.r.* to be pricked again *or* &c.
Répit, *s.m.* respite; delay; reprieve; intermission; breathing-time; rest
Replacement, *s.m.* replacement, replacing, placing again; reinvestment
Replacer, *v.a.* to replace, to place *or* &c. (*V.* **Placer**) again, to put back; to reinvest
Replaider, *v.a.n.* to plead *or* &c. (*V.* **Plaider**) again, to replead
Replanchéier, Replancheyer, *v. a.* to new-floor
Replanir, *v.a.* to plane down
Replant, *s.m.* new plant
Replantable, *adj.* replantable
Replantation, *s.f.*, **Replantement,** *s.m.* replantation, replanting
Replanter, *v.a.* to replant, to plant *or* &c. (*V.* **Planter**) again
Replaquer, *v.a.* to replate, to plate *or* &c. (*V.* **Plaquer**) again
Se —, *v.r.* to be replated *or* &c.
Replâtrage, *s.m.* replastering; plastering; botching up, patching up; palliation; patched up reconciliation *or* quarrel
Replâtrer, *v.a.* to replaster; to plaster up; to botch up, to patch up; to palliate
Se —, *v.r.* to be replastered *or* &c.
Repl-et, ète, *adj.* stout, fat, lusty, corpulent
Réplétí-f, ve, *adj.* repletive
Réplétion, *s.f.* stoutness, corpulence, repletion; surfeit
Réplétivement, *adv.* repletively
Repleurer, *v.a.n.* to ... (*V.* **Pleurer**) again
Repleuvoir, *v.n.* to ... (*V.* **Pleuvoir**) again
Repli, *s.m.* fold; loop; plait; wrinkle; winding; coil; recess
Replicati-f, ve, *adj.* (*bot.*) replicate
Repliement, *s.m.* folding again, folding back, &c. (*V.* **Replier**)
Replier, *v.a.* to fold again *or* back; to turn in *or* up; to tuck; to coil; to force back; to throw back; to recall
Se —, *v.r.* to fold again *or* back; to turn up; to wind; to coil; to wriggle; to turn oneself; to fall back; to retreat. *Se — sur soi-même,* to retire within oneself, to meditate; (*rid.*) to turn suddenly round
Réplique, *s.f.* reply; answer; rejoinder; replication; (*mus.*) replicate; (*mus.*) answer; (*theat.*) catch-word, cue
Répliquer, *v.a.n.* to reply; to answer; to rejoin
Replisser, *v.a.n.* to ... (*V.* **Plisser**) again
Reploiement, *s.m.* folding again; winding; turning; coil; falling back; retreat; reploying, reployment, reploy
Replonger, *v.a.n.* to ... (*V.* **Plonger**) again
Reployer, *v.a.* to fold again *or* back, &c. (*V.* **Replier**); to reploy
Repolir, *v.a.* to polish *or* &c. (*V.* **Polir**) again, to repolish
Repolissage, *s.m.* repolishing
Repompement, *s.m.* repumping
Repomper, *v.a.* to pump again, to repump
Se —, *v.r.* to be pumped again, &c.
Répondant, e, *s.m.f.* answerer; respondent; surety, security, bondsman, bail; reference; lay clerk, clerk
Repondre, *v.a.n.* to lay (*eggs*) again
Répondre, *v.a.n.* to answer; to reply; to respond; to say the responses (to *or* in); to agree; to be according (to) *or* in accordance (with); to correspond; to satisfy; to be equal; to return; to be responsible *or* answerable; to be (a) security; to warrant; to promise; to comply (with); to obey; (*of roads*) to lead; (*of sounds*) to be heard, to reach, to answer; (*of pain*) to be felt, to tingle, to hurt. *J'en réponds, Je vous en réponds, Je t'en réponds,* I will answer for it, I'll be bound (for it), I warrant you, I can tell you, you may be sure of it, and no mistake! I dare say! indeed!
Se —, *v.r.* to answer oneself *or* each other; to correspond with each other, to correspond, to suit, to agree; to sympathize

Répons, *s.m.* (*in church, and print.*) response

Réponse, *s.f.* answer, reply; response. *—s de droit*, judicial decisions, precedents. *Sans —*, without an answer; without answering; unanswered; unanswerable; unanswerably. *—, s'il vous plaît*, an answer will oblige, waiting an [answer

Reponte, *s.f.* laying (*eggs*) again

Repopulation, *s.f.* repopulation

Report, *s.m.* (*com.*) carrying *or* bringing forward *or* over; amount *or* sum brought forward *or* over; brought forward *or* over; (*'Change*) continuation, prolongation; (*'Change*) contango; (*law*) antedate. *Faire un —*, (*com.*) to carry *or* bring forward *or* over

Reporter, *v.a.n.* to carry *or* &c. (*V.* **Porter**) again; to carry back; to take back; to reconvey; to put again; to trace back, to trace; to carry, to place; to convey, to report; to attribute; (*com.*) to carry *or* bring forward *or* over; (*'Change*) to lend on continuation; (*v.n.*) to make a continuation *or* prolongation, to continue, to carry on. *Se faire —*, (*'Change*) to borrow on continuation

Se —, *v.r.* to go back, to return; to transport oneself; to look back; to be carried again *or* &c.

Reporter, *s.m.* (*an anglicism, French newspaper slang*) reporter

Repos, *s.m.* rest; repose; quiet; peace; resting; resting-place; stillness; pause; (*in staircases*) quarter-space; (*mus.*) rest; (*vers.*) pause, rest; (*of fire-arms*) half-cock; (*mil. command*) stand at ease! *A —*, (*adject. of watches*) stop; (*of escapements*) dead-beat. *Au —*, at rest; resting; still, motionless; at (*or* to) half-cock, half-cocked; (*of birds*) sitting, not on the wing. *En —*, at rest; quiet, still, motionless, tranquil; quietly; at ease; alone

Reposé, e, *part. adj.* rested, refreshed, settled, &c. (*V.* **Reposer**); fresh; quiet, calm, cool, sedate. *A tête —e*, quietly, coolly, sedately, leisurely, at leisure, deliberately

Reposée, *s.f.* (*hunt.*) resting-place, lair. *A —s*, with intervals of rest

Reposer, *v.a.n.* to place *or* put *or* &c. (*V.* **Poser**) again; to rest; to repose; to lay; to stand; to refresh; to settle; to abate, to cool down; to ground (*arms, mil.*); to lie; to lie down; to lie fallow

Se —, *v.r.* to put *or* place oneself again; to rest oneself, to rest; to repose; to lie down; to rely, to depend, to trust; to settle; to alight; to lie fallow

Réposition, *s.f.* reposition, repositing

Reposoir, *s.m.* resting-place; pause; (*of procession*) altar; (*tech.*) settling-tub

Reposséder, Reposter, Repoudrer, &c. to … (*V.* **Posséder, Poster, Poudrer,** &c.) again [plaster

Repous, *s.m.* mortar made with brick-dust and

Répouser, *v.a.*, **Se —,** *v.r.* to remarry

Repoussant, e, *adj.* repulsive, forbidding; gruff; shocking

Repoussé, e, *part. adj.* pushed back, &c. (*V.* **Repousser**); regrown; (*of metals*) worked in repoussé, repoussé; *— s.m.* repoussé, repoussé work

Repoussement, *s.m.* repulsion; repulse; detrusion; (*of fire-arms*) recoil, kick

Repousser, *v.a.* to push *or* &c. (*V.* **Pousser**) again; to push *or* thrust back; to push *or* thrust away; to repel; to repulse; to drive back; to force back; to throw back; to drive away; to spurn; to reject; to keep away; to resent; to shoot out again; to work (*metals*) in repoussé; *— v.n.* to shoot *or* bud *or* grow again; to recoil, to kick; to spring, to be elastic; to be repulsive *or* forbidding; (*of colours*) to prevail, to predominate

Se —, *v.r.* to repel *or* &c. each other; to be repelled *or* &c. [worker (*of metals*)

Repousseur, *s.m.* repeller, repulser; repoussé-

Repoussoir, *s.m.* driving-bolt, starting-bolt; (*tech.*) drift; (*of dentists*) punch, elevator; (*paint., fig.*) set-off, contrast, foil

Reprécher, *v.n.a.* to … (*V.* **Prêcher**) again

Répréhenseur, *s.m.* reprehender, reprover

Répréhensibilité, *s. f.* reprehensibleness, reprovableness [ableness

Répréhensible, *adj.* reprehensible, reprov-

Répréhensiblement, *adv.* reprehensibly, reprovably [ing

Répréhensi-f, ve, *adj.* reprehensive, reprov-

Répréhension, *s.f.* reprehension, reproof

Répréhensivement, *adv.* reprehensively reprovingly

Reprendre, *v.a.n.* to take *or* seize *or* catch *or* &c. (*V.* **Prendre**) again; to take back; to retake; to recapture; to resume; to retrace; to renew; to recover; to get back; to fetch back; to regain; to repurchase; to recoup; to acquire, to get; to take; to pluck up; to reprehend, to rebuke, to reprimand, to reprove; to censure, to blame, to find fault with; to correct; to sew up; to take up (*a stitch*); to repair; to underpin; to continue, to say; to reply, to answer; to return; to begin again; to act again; to attack again; to grow again; to set in again; to freeze again; to strike *or* take root again; to get better; to revive; to heal, to close; (*rid.*) to change its pace *or* paces; (*hunt.*) to find the scent again

Se —, *v.r.* to correct oneself; to indulge oneself again (in); to take (to …) again; to reprehend *or* &c. each other; to be taken again *or* &c.; to catch *or* cling *or* &c. (*V.* **Se Prendre**) again; to heal, to close

Repreneu-r, se, *s.m.f.* retaker; recaptor; censurer, critic; *— adj.* retaking; recapturing; censuring

†**Représaille,** *s.f.*, **Représailles,** *s.f.pl.* reprisal, reprisals; retaliation. *User de —*, to retaliate

Représentable, *adj.* representable

Représentant, e, *adj.*, **Représentant,** *s.m.* representative; agent; vicegerent; deputy; member of Parliament, M.P.

Représenta-teur, trice, Représentati-f, ve, *adj.* representative

Représentation, *s.f.* representation; image, likeness; exhibition; production; performance; personation, impersonation; state; display; show; appearances; maintenance of the dignity of o.'s station; official entertainments; presence, look, air; remonstrance; catafalque

Représentativement, *adv.* representatively

Représenter, *v.a.n.* to present again; to represent; to exhibit; to act; to perform; to personate; to depict, to picture, to describe; to remind of; to bring forth; to produce; to show; to keep up appearances; to maintain the dignity of o.'s station; to make a display; to have presence; to have an imposing appearance *or* air *or* look

Se —, *v.r.* to present oneself *or* itself again; to reappear; to occur again; to recur; to revert; to fancy, to imagine, to represent *or* picture to oneself, to call to o.'s mind; to be presented again, &c.

Represser, *v.a.* to .. (*V.* **Presser**) again

Répressibilité, *s.f.* repressibility

Répressible, *adj.* repressible

Répressi-f, ve, *adj.* repressive

Répression, *s.f.* repression

Répressivement, *adv.* repressively

Reprêter, *v a.* to lend again

Reprier, *v.a.n.* to pray *or* &c. (*V.* **Prier**) again; to reinvite, to invite again *or* back *or* in o.'s turn

Réprimable, *adj.* repressible

Réprimande, *s.f.* reprimand, reproof, rebuke

Réprimander, *v.a.* to reprimand, to reprove, to rebuke

Réprimant, e, *adj.* repressive
Réprimer, *v.a.* to repress, to put down, to curb, to check, to restrain
Se —, *v.r,* to repress *or* &c. oneself *or* each other; to be repressed *or* &c.
Réprimeur, *s.m.* represser, checker
Repris, e, *part. adj.* taken again, &c. (*V.* **Reprendre**). *Un homme — de justice,* a man convicted before, an old offender. *Un — de justice,* (*substant.*) a released felon *or* convict, a returned convict
Reprisage, *s.m* darning, fine-drawing
Reprise, *s.f.* taking back; retaking; recapture; resumption; renewal; revival; recovery; return; round; bout; turn; interval; (repeated) time; returns; repurchase; darning, darn; repair; underpinning; (*at play*) game; (*mus.*) repetition; (*mus.*) repeat; (*mus.*) catch; (*mus.*) second part; (*mus.*) burden (*of a song*); (*paint.*) retouch; (*theat.*) revival, new performance, old play acted again; (*fin.*) recoupment; (*law*) renewal; (*law*) reprisal, recaption; (*law*) claims; (*rid.*) lesson; (*hort.*) new roots; (*bot.*) orpine; (*flour and bran*) pollard. — *perdue,* fine-drawing. *A plusieurs —s, A différentes* or *diverses —s,* at different times, several times; repeatedly; at different intervals. *A deux —s,* twice. *A trois, quatre,* &c. *—s,* three, four, &c. times. *Faire des —s,* to darn. *Faire des —s perdues,* to fine-draw
Repriser, *v.a.n.* to darn; to value *or* &c. (*V.* **Priser**) again; to take snuff again
Repriseu-r, se, *s.m.f.* darner, fine-drawer
Réproba-teur, trice, *adj. s.* reprobatory, reprobating; of reprobation; reprobater
Réprobati-f, ve, *adj.* reprobative, reprobating; of reprobation
Réprobation, *s.f.* reprobation [reprobation
Réprobativement, *adv.* reprobatively, with
Reprochable, *adj.* reproachable; challengeable; exceptionable
Reproche, *s.m.* reproach; imputation; expostulation; vituperation; blame; (*law*) objection, exception. *Sans —,* without reproach *or* &c.; blameless; no blame (to), without offence
Reprocher, *v.a.* to reproach; to expostulate; to upbraid; to vituperate; to blame; to taunt; to twit; to cast in the teeth; to grudge; (*law*) to object to, to except to, to take exception to. *— les morceaux a quelqu'un,* to grudge a person what he eats
Se —, *v.r.* to reproach oneself *or* each other (with); to upbraid *or* &c. each other; to grudge oneself; (*things*) to be reproached *or* &c. [braider; taunter; twitter
Reprocheu-r, se, *s.m.f.* reproacher; up-
Reproduc-teur, trice, *adj. s.* reproducing, reproductive; breeding; reproducer; breeder
Reproductibilité, *s.f.* reproducibleness
Reproductible, *adj.* reproducible
Reproducti-f, ve, *adj.* reproductive
Reproduction, *s.f.* reproduction; reprinting; republication
Reproductivement, *adv.* reproductively
Reproductivité, *s.f.* reproductiveness, reproductivity
Reproduire, *v.a.* to reproduce; to produce *or* present again, to show; to represent; to report; to reprint; to republish; to imitate
Se —, *v.r.* to propagate o.'s species; to reproduce oneself *or* itself; to be reproduced *or* &c.; to grow *or* shoot *or* come up again; to show oneself *or* itself again; to reappear; to occur again
Repromener,Repromettre,Reprotéger, &c. to ... (*V.* **Promener, Promettre, Protéger,** &c.) again
Réprouvable, *adj.* reprobatable
Réprouvé, e, *part.* reprobated, &c. (*V.* **Réprouver**); — *adj. s.m.f.* reprobate
Reprouver, *v.a.* to prove again
Réprouver, *v.a.* to reprobate; to condemn; to reject; to disapprove of
†Reprovigner, *v.a.* to ... (*V.* **Provigner**)
Reps, *s.m.* (*kind of silk*) reps, rep [again
Reptation, *s.f.* reptation
Reptatoire, *adj.* reptatory
Reptile, *s.m. adj.* reptile; creeping, crawling
Reptilivore, *adj.* (*zool.*) reptilivorous
Repu, e, *part. adj.* fed, &c. (*V.* **Repaître**); satiated, full; **—e,** *s.f.* [*See below*]
Républicain, e, *adj. s.* republican
Républicainement, *adv.* republicanly
Républicaniser, *v.a.* to republicanize
Républicanisme *s.m.* republicanism
Républicaniste, *s.m f.* republicanist; — *adj.* republicanistic
Republication, *s.f.* republication; reissue
Republier, *v.a.* to republish; to reissue
République, *s.f.* republic; commonwealth
Repuce, *s.m.* bird trap, gin, snare
Répudiable, *adj.* repudiable
Répudiation, *s.f.*, **Répudiement,** *s.m.* repudiation; renunciation
Répudier, *v.a.* to repudiate; to reject, to refuse; to renounce
Repue, *s.f.* feeding, feed, meal [luctance
†Répugnance, *s.f.* repugnance, dislike; re-
†Répugnant, e, *adj.* repugnant; contrary; contradictory, inconsistent; offensive; distasteful; objectionable; reluctant, loath, unwilling
†Répugner, *v.n.* to be repugnant; to imply contradiction, to be contradictory *or* inconsistent *or* contrary; to clash; to inspire with aversion, to be offensive *or* distasteful *or* objectionable; to be *or* feel reluctant *or* loath *or* unwilling, to feel repugnance (at)
Repullulation, *s.f.* new multiplication *or* swarming
Repulluler, *v.n.* to ... (*V.* **Pulluler**) again
Répulsi-f, ve, *adj.* repulsive, repelling, repellent
Répulsion, *s.f.* repulsion; repugnance
Repurger, *v.a.* to ... (*V.* **Purger**) again
Réputation, *s.f.* reputation, repute, fame; name, character
Réputer, *v.a.* to repute, to esteem, to deem, to think, to consider, to account, to hold
Requérable, *adj.* (*law*) demandable
Requérant, e, *s.m.f.* (*law*) applicant; petitioner; plaintiff; — *adj.* suing; (*hunt.*) retrieving
Requérir, *v.a.* to require; to demand; to claim; to summon, to call upon; to call for; to call; to order; (*old*) to request, to ask, to beg; (*law*) to pray; (*obsolete*) to fetch again;
Se —, *v.r.* to be required, &c. [to fetch
Requête, *s.f.* petition; memorial; application, demand, prayer, request; (*hunt.*) new search. — *civile,* appeal by writ of error, procedure in error. *Maitre des —s,* master of requests, referendary (*an officer in France whose duty consists in reporting petitions to the council of state*)
Requêté, *s.m.* (*hunt.*) recheat
Requêter, *v.a.* (*hunt.*) to search again
§Requiem, *s. m.* requiem. *Messe de —,* requiem [bumbailiff
Requin, *s.m.* (*fish*) shark. *— de terre,* (*pop.*)
Requinqué, e, *part. adj.* made spruce, spruce; rigged *or* dressed out
Requinquer, *v.a.* to make spruce, to spruce up; to rig *or* trick *or* dress out
Requinteron, ne, *s.m.f.* offspring of a quintroon and a European
Réquiper, *v.a.* to ... (*V.* **Équiper**) again
Requis, e, *part. adj.* required, &c. (*V.* **Requérir**); requisite; due; — *s.m.* requisite, needful
Réquisition, *s.f.* requisition; application; motion; demand, call; order; levy. — *permanente,* levy in mass

Réquisitionnaire, *s.m.* (*Fr. hist.*) recruit
Réquisitoire, *s.m.* (*law*) requisitory, requisition, address, charge; report
Réquisitorial, e, *adj.* requisitorial
Requitter, Resalir, Resaluer, Resarcler, Resaucer, &c. to . . . (*V.* **Quitter, Salir, Saluer, Sarcler, Saucer,** &c.) again
Rescellement, *s.m.* resealing; refastening
Resceller, *v.a.* to seal *or* &c. (*V.* **Sceller**) again, to reseal
Rescif, *s.m.* *V.* **Récif**
Rescindable, *adj.* rescindable
Rescindant, *s.m.* motion to set aside (*a deed or* &c.)
Rescinder, *v.a.* to rescind, to annul, to cancel
Rescision, *s.f.* (*law*) rescission, rescindment, annulment; (*surg.*) recision
Rescisoire, *adj.* rescissory; — *s.m.* cause for annulment *or* setting aside
Rescontre, *s.m.* bill-book
Rescousse, *s.f.* *V.* **Recousse**
Rescription, *s.f.* rescription; scrip, bond, bill, share, debenture; order; cheque; warrant
Rescrit, *s.m.* rescript
Réseau, *s.m.* network, netting, net; wire-netting; system; section; plexus; (*arch.*) tracery
Resécher, *v.a n.* to ... (*V.* **Sécher**) again
Résection, *s.f.* (*surg.*, &c.) resection
Réséda, *s.m.* (*bot.*) mignonette, weld, reseda. — *gaude*, weld. — *odorant*, mignonette
Reseller, *v.a.* *V.* **Resseller**
Réséquer, *v.a.* (*surg.*, &c.) to resect
Réservation, *s.f.* reservation; reserve
Réserve, *s.f.* reserve; reservation; exception; caution; modesty; stock, store; store-room; (*for game*) preserve; (— *légale*) portion secured by law (to an heir). *A la — de*, with the reservation *or* exception of, except. *De —*, of reserve, reserve; reserved; spare. *En —*, in store; by; spare; in reserve. *Sans —*, without reserve; unreserved; unreservedly; without exception. *Se tenir sur la —*, to be on o.'s guard, to be reserved; to keep back
Réservé, e, *part. adj.* reserved, &c. (*V.* **Réserver**); cautious; guarded; close; modest; shy; coy; distant; — *s.m.f.* ditto person. *Faire le —* or *la —e*, to affect to be reserved
Réservément, *adv.* reservedly; cautiously; modestly; distantly
Réserver, *v.a.* to reserve; to except; to save; to lay *or* put by; to lay in store; to keep; to spare; to reserve the right of
Se —, *v.r.* to reserve *or* &c. oneself *or* to oneself; to wait for an opportunity; to wait; to intend; to reserve to oneself the right of; to be reserved *or* kept *or* &c.
Réservoir, *s.m.* reservoir; tank; pond; cistern, well; holder; steam-chest; (*anat.*) receptacle
Résidant, e, *adj.* resident, residing
Résidence, *s.f.* residence; dwelling, abode; residentship
Résident, e, *s.m.f.* resident
Résider, *v.n.* to reside; to live; to dwell; to lie, to rest
Résidu, *s.m.* sediment, residuum, residue; remainder
Résiduel, le, *adj.* residual, residuary
Resiffler, *v.n.a.* to ... (*V.* **Siffler**) again
†Résignable, *adj.* resignable
†Résignant, e, Résigna-teur, trice, *s.m.f.* resigner
†Résignation, *s.f.* resignation
†Résignataire, *s.m.f.* resignee
†Resigner, *v.a.n.* to . . . (*V.* **Signer**) again
†Résigner, *v.a.* to resign
Se —, *v.r.* to resign oneself, to submit oneself, to submit; to be resigned; to make up o.'s mind; to reconcile oneself (to); to put up with it
Résiliation, *s.f.*, **Résiliement, Résilîment,** *s.m.* cancelling, annulling
Résilier, *v.a.* to cancel, to annul
†Résille, *s.f.* hair-net
Résinage, *s.m.* collecting of resin
Résinate, *s.m.* (*chem.*) resinate
Résine, *s.f.* resin, rosin. — *animé*, gum anime, resin of courbaril
Résinéine, *s.f.* (*chem.*) resineine
Résiner, *v.a.* to rosin; to collect resin from
Résineusement, *adv.* resinously
Résineu-x, se, *adj.* resinous; — *s.m.* resin
Résinier, *s.m.* (*pers.*) resin-collector; steward of a fir-plantation; (*bot.*) bursera
Résinifère, *adj.* resiniferous
Résinification, *s.f.* resinification
Résinifier, *v.a.*, **Se —,** *v.r.* to resinify
Résiniforme, *adj.* resiniform
Résinite, *s.f.* (*min.*) pitchstone
Résino-, (*in compounds*) resino-...
Résipiscence, *s.f.* resipiscence, repentance
Résistance, *s.f.* resistance; opposition; strength; force; power of endurance; (*law*) contumacy; (*med.*) obstinacy; (*polit.*) conservatism. *De —*, of resistance, &c.; solid, substantial, stout, strong, large, great, main, lasting (*V.* **Pièce**)
Résistant, e, *adj.* resistant, resisting; strong, tough
Résister, *v.n.* to resist; to oppose; to withstand; to stand the test (of); to endure; to last; to support, to bear, to stand
Résistibilité, *s.f.* resistibility, resistibleness
Résistible, *adj.* resistible
Résistiblement, *adv.* resistibly
Résolu, e, *part.* (*of* **Résoudre** *in all senses but one* [*V.* **Résous**]), *adj.* resolved; resolved on; solved; settled; determined; decided; induced, persuaded; resolute; stout; bold; firm; (*law*) avoided, cancelled, annulled; — *s.m.f.* resolute *or* determined *or* bold fellow *or* woman *or* creature
Résolubilité, *s.f.* solvability, solvableness; resolvability, resolvableness; (*law*) avoidableness; cancellableness, annulableness
Résoluble, *adj.* solvable; resolvable; (*law*) avoidable, cancellable, annulable
Résolûment, *adv.* resolutely; stoutly; boldly; firmly; fearlessly
Resoluti-f, ve, *adj.*, **Résoluti-f,** *s.m.* (*med.*) resolvent, discutient
Résolution, *s.f.* resolution; resolving, resolve; solution; (*law*) avoidance, cancelling, cancellation, annulment
Résolutoire, *adj.* (*law*) of avoidance *or* cancellation, cancelling, resolutive; — *s.m.* ditto clause *or* condition
Résolvant, e, *adj.*, **Résolvant,** *s.m.* (*med.*) resolvent, discutient
†Resommeiller, *v.n.* to . . . (*V.* **Sommeiller**) again
Résompti-f, ve, *adj.*, **Résomptif,** *s.m.* (*med.*) restorative, resumptive
Résomption, *s.f.* resumption
Resonger, *v.a.n.* to ... (*V.* **Songer**) again
Résonnance, *s.f.* resonance
Résonnant, e, *adj.* resonant, resounding; sonorous, sounding
Résonnement, *s.m.* resounding; resonance; clink; clank; rattling, rattle; reecho
Resonner, *v.a.n.* to ... (*V.* **Sonner**) again
Résonner, *v.n.a.* to resound; to sound; to ring; to clink; to clank; to jingle; to chink; to rattle; to reecho
Résorber, *v.a.* to reabsorb. *Se —*, to be reabsorbed
Résorption, *s.f.* reabsorption
Résoudre, *v.a.n.* to resolve; to melt, to dissolve, to change (into); to solve; to settle; to resolve (on); to determine; to decide; to induce, to persuade, to prevail upon, to bring (to); (*law*) to avoid, to cancel, to annul
Se —, *v.r.* to resolve; to melt, to be dissolved, to dissolve, to be changed (into), to change *or* turn (into); to be resolved *or* solved; to be determined, to determine, to persuade oneself, to make up o.'s mind, to bring oneself (to); to come (to), to amount (to)

Resouffler, *v.a.n.* to ... (*V.* **Souffler**) again
Resouper, *v.n.* to sup again
Résou-s, te, *part.* (*of* **Résoudre** *in one sense only* [*for the others V.* **Résolu**]) resolved, dissolved, melted, changed (into)
Respect, *s.m.* respect; awe; reverence; regard; duty. — *humain*, fear of the world, regard for public opinion; bashfulness. *Sauf —, sauf le —, sauf votre —, sauf* (or *avec*) *le — que je vous dois, parlant par —,* (*fam.*) saving your presence, with due deference to you; with *or* by your leave. *Tenir en —*, to keep in awe
Respectabilité, *s.f.* respectability
Respectable, *adj.* respectable, venerable
Respectablement, *adv.* respectably
Respecter, *v.a.* to respect; to revere, to reverence; to spare
Respecti-f, ve, *adj.* respective
Respectivement, *adv.* respectively
Respectueusement, *adv.* respectfully; reverently; dutifully
Respectueu-x, se, *adj.* respectful; reverential; dutiful
Respirabilité, *s.f.* respirability, respirableness, breathableness
Respirable, *adj.* respirable, breathable
Respirateur, *adj.m.* respiratory; — *s.m.* respirator. *Appareil —*, respirator [breath
Respiration, *s. f.* respiration, breathing,
Respiratoire, *adj.* respiratory
Respirer, *v.a.n.* to breathe; to respire; to draw *or* take breath; to inhale; to betoken, to bespeak, to express; to be apparent *or* conspicuous; to live; to long *or* wish (for); to rest
Se —, *v.r.* to be breathed *or* inhaled
Resplendeur, *s.f.* resplendence
Resplendir, *v.n.* to be resplendent, to shine bright, to shine, to glitter [glittering
Resplendissant, e, *adj.* resplendent, bright,
Resplendissement, *s.m.* resplendence
Responsabilité, *s.f.* responsibility; accountableness; liability [accountable, liable
Responsable, *adj.* responsible, answerable,
Responsi-f, ve, *adj* responsive, responsory
Ressac, *s.m.* (*nav.*) surf
†**Ressaigner,** *v.a.n.* to bleed again
Ressaisir, *v a.,* **Se — (de),** *v.r.* to seize *or* take again, to seize upon again, to reseize; to recover possession of, to recover; (*v.r.*) to be reseized, &c.
Ressaler, Ressalir, Ressaluer, Ressangler, Ressarcler, &c. to ... (*V.* **Saler, Salir, Saluer, Sangler, Sarcler,** &c.) again
Ressasser, *v.a.* to sift *or* &c. (*V.* **Sasser**) again; to sift, to examine carefully, to scrutinize, to criticize; to repeat over and over
Ressasseu-r, se, *s.m.f.* repeater, tiresome repeater
Ressaut, *s.m.* projection; abrupt fall, dip, pitch; irregularity, desultoriness
Ressauter, *v.a.n.* to leap *or* &c. (*V.* **Sauter**) again; to project
Ressayer, *v.a.n.* to ... (*V.* **Essayer**) again
Ressécher, *v.a.n.* to ... (*V.* **Sécher**) again
Resseller, *v.a.* to resaddle, to saddle again
Ressemblance, *s.f.* resemblance, likeness; similitude, similarity; semblance. *Fausse —*, slight resemblance
Ressemblant, e, *adj.* resembling; alike, similar; like, a good likeness; well taken; true; like each other
Ressembler, *v.n.* to resemble, to be *or* look like; to be alike. *— en beau* or *en bien*, to be a handsome likeness. *— en laid* or *en mal*, to be an ugly likeness
Se —, *v.r.* to be alike; to resemble each other, to be *or* look like each other; to resemble oneself; to be uniform, to copy oneself. *Se — comme deux gouttes d'eau*, to be as like (*or* as much alike) as two peas. *Cela ne se ressemble pas*, there is no resemblance between the things. *Qui se ressemble s'assemble*, birds of a feather flock together
Ressemelage, *s.m.* soling, new-soling
Ressemeler, *v.a.* to sole, to new-sole
Se —, *v.r.* to be soled *or* new-soled [resow
Ressemer, *v.a.n.* to ... (*V.* **Semer**) again, to
Ressenti, e, *part. adj.* felt, &c. (*V.* **Ressentir**), strongly marked *or* expressed *or* figured; full of feeling *or* expression; apparent
Ressentiment, *s.m.* resentment; slight return; (*obsolete*) feeling; sense; gratitude; remembrance, recollection
Ressentir, *v a.,* **Se —,** *v.r.* to feel, to experience; to feel the effects of, to perceive, to partake of, to share; not to be free from; to suffer from; to show; to bear marks of, to resent [house
Resserre, *s.f.* depository, repository; tool-
Resserré, e, *part. adj.* tied again, &c (*V* **Resserrer**); narrow; strait; tight, close; compact; strict; limited; confined; small, cramped; bound, costive, constipated
Resserrement, *s.m.* contraction; constriction; stricture; narrowing; narrowness; tightening; tightness; obstruction, stoppage. oppression; scarcity; (*of bowels*) confinement, costiveness, constipation
Resserrer, *v.a.n.,* **Se —,** *v.r.* to tie again; to tighten; to tie tighter; to bind again; to bind faster; to bind; to draw closer *or* tighter, to press *or* squeeze closer; to straiten; to narrow; to contract; to condense; to compress; to shrink, to shrink away; to thicken; to close again; to confine; to shut up; to shut up closer; to put by (*or* in *or* away) again; to withdraw from circulation, to withdraw; to oppress; to constipate, to make costive, to be binding; to become closer *or* narrower *or* tighter; to be oppressed; to confine *or* &c. oneself; to concentrate itself; to be confined; to retrench, to reduce o.'s expenses; to become scarce; (*of the weather*) to get colder
Resservir, *v.a.n.* to ... (*V.* **Servir**) again
Ressif, *s.m. V.* **Récif**
Ressort, *s.m.* spring; lock; bender; elasticity; activity, strength, energy, force; active power; agency; means; motive; spirit, life; effect; jurisdiction; department, province; (*law*) resort. *A —,* (*adject.*) spring, with a spring. *En dernier —*, in the last resort; without appeal. *Faire —*, to spring back, to fly back; to rebound
Ressortir, *v.n.a.* (*irregular, and conjugated like* **Sortir**) to go *or* come out again; to get out again; to walk out *or* &c. (*V.* **Sortir,** *v.n.*) again; to be set off, to show off, to show, to be shown, to appear, to be visible *or* evident, to stand out, to come out; to arise, to result, to spring; to bring *or* &c. (*V.* **Sortir,** *v.a.*) out again; — *v.n.* (*regular, and therefore not conjugated like* **Sortir**) to be in the jurisdiction (of); to depend (on); to refer (to), to be made (for). *Faire —*, to bring forward *or* out; to give relief to, to bring out in relief; to make more conspicuous; to set forth; to set off; to show off; to show
Ressortissant, e, *adj.* under the jurisdiction (of), amenable (to), appealable (to)
Ressouder, *v.a.* to ... (*V.* **Souder**) again
Ressoudure, *s.f.* new *or* second soldering
Ressouffler, Ressouffrir, &c. to ... (*V.* **Souffler, Souffrir,** &c.) again
Ressource, *s.f.* resource; expedient, shift; means; supply; remedy; help. *De —*, full of resources, fertile in expedients. *Sans —*, without resource *or* resources; irretrievable; irretrievably. *Faire —*, to procure resources, to raise the wind, to finance; to sell out
Ressouvenance, *s.f. V.* **Souvenance**
Ressouvenir, (*Se —, v.r.*) *V.* **Souvenir (Se);** — *s.m.* remembrance, recollection; reminder, memorandum; twinge, feeling of pain, touch, return

Ressuage, *s.m.* sweating again; sweating; liquation, eliquation
Ressuer, *v.n.* to perspire *or* sweat *or* &c. (*V.* **Suer**) again; (*tech.*) to sweat; (*chem., metal.*) to liquate, to eliquate
Ressui, *s.m.* (*hunt.*) lair
Ressuiement, *s.m.* drying
Ressuivre, *v.a.n.* to ... (*V.* **Suivre**) again
Ressuscitati-f, ve, *adj.* reviving
Ressuscitation, *s. f.*, **Ressuscitement,** *s.m.* raising the dead, raising; rising from the dead, rising again, rising; resuscitation; reviving, revival
Ressusciter, *v.a.n.* to raise from the dead, to raise (the dead), to bring to life again; to give new life to; to rise from the dead, to rise again, to rise, to come to life again; to resuscitate; to revive [resuscitator
Ressusciteur, *s. m.* raiser (*of the dead*);
Ressuyant, *adj.m.* (*hunt.*) keen dry (*wind*)
Ressuyer, *v.a.n.*, **Se —,** *v.r.* to wipe again; to dry; to get dry; to dry oneself
Restant, e, *adj.* remaining, left. *Bureau —*, (*of parcels*) to be left (at the office) till called for. *Gare —e*, to be left (at the station) till called for. *Poste —e*, poste restante, (office for) letters till called for, (to remain at the) post-office (till called for), to be left till called for [mains. *— de compte*, balance
Restant, *s.m.* remainder, rest, remnant, re-
Restaurage, *s.m.* mending
Restaurant, e, *adj.* restorative
Restaurant, *s.m.* restorative; gravy soup, jelly broth; eating-house, dining-house, dining-rooms, luncheon rooms, refreshment-rooms, restaurant
Restaurateur, *s.m.* restorer; eating-house keeper; *— adj.m.* restoring [restorative
Restaurati-f, ve, *adj.*, **Restauratif,** *s.m.*
Restauration, *s.f.* restoration; reestablishment [storing
Restauratrice, *s.f.* restorer; *— adj.f.* re-
Restaurer, *v.a.* to restore; to reestablish; to to repair; to revive; to refresh
Se —. *v.r.* to take food *or* refreshment, to refresh oneself; to recover o.'s strength; to be restored, &c.
Reste, *s.m.* rest; remainder; remains; remnant; residue; relics; leavings; scraps; change; last stake; remaining time; mortal remains; consequences; finishing-blow, death-blow, quietus; clincher; drubbing. *Au —, du —*, as for the rest; moreover; besides; in all other respects; however, yet, nevertheless, notwithstanding, withal; but; in fact; by the way; finally. *De —*, left; more than enough, enough and to spare, to spare, spare; extra; more than usual; overmuch, too much; too good; only too well, plainly enough; easily enough; at once. *En —*, in arrears, behind, behindhand. *Et le —*, and the rest of it; and so forth, and so on, et cætera. *Demander son —*, to ask for o.'s change; to wait for something more. *Ne pas demander son —, s'en aller sans demander son —, ne pas attendre son —*, not to wait for anything more; to be glad to take oneself off immediately. *Donner son — à*, to give (*one*) his change; to give it to; to beat; to finish, to settle, to give a quietus. *Jouer de son —*, to play o.'s last stake; to employ o.'s last resources, to make o.'s last effort; to be on o.'s last legs; to make the most of o.'s remaining time
Resté, e, *part.* remained, &c. (*V.* **Rester**); staying; left, being left; killed
Rester, *v.n.* to remain; to be left; to stick; to stay; to stay behind; to stop; to keep; to sit; to stand; to be; to continue; to dwell, to reside; to live; (*nav.*) to bear. *En —*, to stop, to leave off, to go *or* proceed no farther than. *Restons-en là*, let us stop there; let us say no more about it. *Il me reste*, I have remaining or left; I have yet *or* still; it (*or* there) remains for me, it remains (to ...)
Restiforme, *adj.* (*anat.*) restiform [payable
Restituable, *adj.* returnable; restorable; re-
Restituer, *v.a.* to return, to give back; to restore, to restitute [be returned *or* &c.
Se —, *v.r.* to return *or* &c. to each other; to
Restituteur, *s.m.* restorer, restitutor
Restitution, *s.f.* restitution; restoration;
Restitutoire, *adj.* restitutory [release
Restreindre, *v.a.* to restrict, to restrain, to confine, to limit; to stint
Se —, *v.r.* to restrict *or* &c. oneself *or* each other; to be restricted *or* &c.
Restricti-f, ve, *adj.* restrictive
Restriction, *s.f.* restriction, restraint; limitation; reservation, reserve
Restringent, e, *adj.*, **Restringent,** *s.m.* astringent, styptic, restringent
Resuivre, *v.a.n.* to ... (*V.* **Suivre**) again
Résultant, e, *part. adj.*, **Résultante,** *s.f.* resulting; resultant
Résultat, *s.m.* result. *En —*, in the result, ultimately, finally, eventually
Résulter, *v.n.* to result (from), to be the result *or* consequence (of), to follow (from), to ensue (from), to arise (from), to come (of); to appear (from). *Qu'en résulte-t-il?* what follows from it?
Résumé, *s.m.* summary; summing up; recapitulation; abstract; compendium; abridgment; epitome; substance; (*law*) summing up; (*law*) charge. *Au —, en —*, on *or* upon the whole, after all
Résumer, *v.a.*, **Se —,** *v.r.* to summarize; to sum up; to recapitulate; to unite; to embody; to comprise; to be summed up *or* recapitulated
Résupination, *s.f.* resupination
Résupiné, e, *adj.* resupinate, resupinated
Résurrecti-f, ve, *adj.* resurrective
Résurrection, *s.f.* resurrection, rising; resuscitation, revival [resurrection-man
Résurrectioniste, *s. m.* resurrectionist,
Résurrectionnel, le, *adj.* resurrectionary
Retable, *s.m.* re-table, reredos, altar-screen; altar-piece
Rétabli, e, *part. adj.* reestablished, &c. (*V.* **Rétablir**); recovered, well again
Rétablir, *v.a.* to reestablish; to repair; to mend; to set right again; to restore; to reinstate; to recover; to retrieve; to revive
Se —, *v.r.* to reestablish *or* &c. oneself; to be reestablished *or* &c.; to recover o.'s health, to recover, to mend, to get better, to get well again; to revive
Rétablissement, *s.m.* reestablishment; repair; restoration; reinstatement; recovery; revival
Rétablisseur, *s.m.* reestablisher, restorer
†**Retaille,** *s.f.* piece cut off, shred, paring; cuttings, shreds, parings, clippings
†**Retaillement,** *s.m.* cutting again
†**Retailler,** *v.a.* to cut *or* &c. (*V.* **Tailler**) again; to mend (*pens, pencils*)
Rétaler, *v.a.* to ... (*V.* **Étaler**) again
Rétamage, *s.m.* tinkering, mending; resilvering
Rétamer, *v.a.* to tin again, to tinker, to mend;
Rétameur, *s.m.* tinker [to resilver
Retancer, *v.a.* to ... (*V.* **Tancer**) again
Retapé, e, *part. adj.* done up, &c. (*V.* **Retaper**); (*pop.*) spruce, smart, natty; — *s.m.* frizz, frizzle; (*pop.*) humbug, quack
Retaper, *v.a.* (*of hats*) to do up; (*of hats, obsolete*) to cock up, to turn up; (*of hair*) to comb up, to frizzle; (*of wigs*) to curl and powder; (*fig.*) to dress out; to dress, to trim, to give it to
Se —, *v.r.* to be done up, &c.; to dress oneself out; to dress *or* trim each other, to fight, to have a fight *or* a set-to
Retard, *s.m.* delay; (*of clocks, watches*) slow-

ness; (*word marked on watches*) slow. *En* —, late, behind o.'s (*or* its) time; behindhand, behind; backward; too slow, slow; in arrears; overdue. *Avoir une patte en* —, (*fam.*) to walk lame

Retardataire, *adj.* in arrears; behind time, behindhand, late; tardy; lagging, loitering; defaulting; — *s.m.f.* one in arrears; late one; lagger, loiterer; defaulter

Retarda-teur, trice, *adj.* retarding

Retardati-f, ve, *adj.* retardative

Retardation, *s.f.* retardation

Retardement, *s.m.* delay; retardment, putting off; (*com. nav.*) overtime, demurrage

Retarder, *v.a.* to delay; to retard; to stop; to hinder; to defer, to put off; to throw *or* put *or* keep back; (*of clocks, watches*) to put back; — *v.n.* to be *or* come *or* rise later; to be behind its time; to go *or* come more slowly; (*of clocks, watches*) to lose, to be *or* go too slow, to be slow

Se —, *v.r.* to throw *or* &c. oneself back *or* each other; to delay each other; to be delayed *or* &c.

Retâter, *v.a.n.* to feel again; to touch again, to retouch, to alter, to mend, to correct; to taste again; to try again

Retaxer, †Reteiller, &c. to ... (*V.* **Taxer, Teiller,** &c.) again

Reteindre, *v.a.* to ... (*V.* **Teindre**) again

Réteindre, *v.a.* to ... (*V.* **Éteindre**) again

Retendre, *v.a.* to ... (*V.* **Tendre**) again

Rétendre, *v.a.* to ... (*V.* **Étendre**) again

Retenir, *v.a.* to get back; to keep back; to detain; to withhold; to retain; to keep; to reserve; to confine; to bind; to hold back *or* up; to hold; to restrain; to check; to contain; to stop; to refrain; to deduct, to take off; to secure; to engage; to book; to bespeak; to order; to remember, to bear in mind; (*arith.*) to carry; — *v.n.* to hold back; to conceive, to breed

Se —, *v.r.* to refrain, to forbear; to restrain *or* check *or* contain oneself; to keep *or* hold back; to stop; to wait; to catch hold (of), to seize; to catch hold of something; to catch at things; to reserve to oneself; to be got back *or* detained *or* retained *or* &c.

Retenter, *v.a.* to reattempt, to try again; to tempt again [retentive

Réten-teur, trice, Rétenti-f, ve, *adj.*

Rétention, *s.f.* retention; retaining; reservation, reserve [detaining

Rétentionnaire, *s.m.f.* detainer; — *adj.*

Retentir, *v.n.* to resound; to reecho; to echo; to clink; to clank; to rattle; to ring; to sound; to make a noise

Retentissant, e, *part. adj.* resounding, &c. (*V.* **Retentir**); sonorous; loud; noisy; famous, celebrated

Retentissement, *s.m.* resounding, resound; resonance; reecho; echo; clink; clank; rattling, rattle; ringing; report; sound; noise; fame, celebrity. *Avoir du* —, to make [a noise

Rétentivité, *s.f.* retentiveness

Retentum, *s.m.* tacit clause; proviso; mental reservation

Retenu, e, *part. adj.* got back, kept back, &c. (*V.* **Retenir**); reserved, cautious; discreet; timid, modest; engaged; kept in

Retenue, *s.f.* reserve; discretion; prudence; modesty; retention, withholding; stoppage; keeping in *or* up, confinement, exclusion from play; pupils kept in; (*of canals*) level; (*of bridges*) fixture; (*nav.*) relieving tackle. *Câble* or *corde de* —, (*nav.*) guy-rope. *Être en* —, (*of schools*) to be kept in. *Faire une — sur*, (*admin., fin.*) to stop. *Mettre en* —, (*of schools*) [to keep in

Rétépore, *s.m.* (*zool.*) retepore

Rétiaire, *s.m.* (*Rom. antiq.*) retiarius

Réticence, *s. f.* reticence; concealment; omission; reserve

Réticulaire, *adj.* reticular [hair-net

Réticule, *s.m.* reticule, reticle, reticulum;

Réticulé, e, *adj.* reticulated, reticulate

Réti-f, ve, *adj.* restive, restiff, stubborn

Rétiforme, *adj.* retiform

Rétinalite, *s.f.* (*min.*) retinalite [tinasphaltum

Rétinasphalte, *s.m.* (*min.*) retinasphalt, re-

Rétine, *s.f.* (*anat.*) retina

Rétinien, ne, *adj.* (*anat.*) retinal

Rétinite, *s.f.* (*med.*) retinitis; (*min.*) retinite

Rétinole, *s.m.* (*chem.*) retinole

Rétipède, *s.m.* (*zool.*) retiped

Retirade, *s.f.* (*old fort.*) retirade

Retiration, *s.f.* (*print.*) retiration

Retiré, e, *part. adj.* drawn back, &c. (*V.* **Retirer**); contracted, shrunk; retired; secluded; solitary; lonely

Retirement, *s. m.* contraction, shrinking; taking back *or* away again

Retirer, *v.a.n.* to draw back *or* again; to draw *or* bring *or* take out again; to draw *or* bring out; to take *or* get out; to pick out, to select; to draw off; to draw up; to draw in; to get in, to house; to take *or* get back; to take away, to pull out; to remove; to recall; to retract; to reclaim; to redeem; to withdraw; to reap, to receive, to get, to derive; to harbour, to shelter; to retire; to pull *or* &c. (*V.* **Tirer**) again; to fire off again; to fire *or* shoot again; to let off again

Se —, *v.r.* to withdraw; to retire; to go off *or* away *or* out; to leave, to quit; to retreat; to recede; to shrink, to shrink away; to contract; to subside; to flow back *or* out; to ebb; to compensate *or* recoup *or* retrieve oneself; to get back o.'s outlay, not to lose; to be drawn back *or* withdrawn *or* &c.

Retisser, *v.a.* to weave again [ness

Rétiveté, Rétivité, *s.f.* restiveness, restiff-

Rétoile, *s. f.* (*fish*) right-whale, Greenland whale

Rétoire, *s.m.* (*vet.*) potential cautery

Retoiser, *v.a.* to ... (*V.* **Toiser**) again

Retombée, *s f.* (*arch.*) springing

Retomber, *v.n.* to fall again, to fall down again; to fall back; to fall, to fall down; to relapse; to lap

Retondre, *v.a.* to shear *or* &c. (*V.* **Tondre**) again; (*arch.*) to clean off

Retorcher, *v.a.* to ... (*V.* **Torcher**) again

Retordage, Retordement, *s.m.* twisting

Retorderie, *s.f.* twisting-house *or* room

Retordeu-r, se, *s.m.f.* (*pers., instr.*) twister

Retordoir, *s.m.* (*instr.*) twister

Retordre, *v.a.* to twist *or* &c. (*V.* **Tordre**) again; to twist

Se —, *v.r.* to be twisted *or* &c. again

Rétorquable, *adj.* retortable

Rétorquer, *v.a.* to retort. *Se* —, to be retorted

Retors, e, *adj.* twisted; hooked; shrewd, cunning, crafty, wily; — *s.m.* cunning fellow, cunning one

Rétorsi-f, ve, *adj.* retortive

Rétorsion, *s.f.* retortion, retorsion; retorting; (*in international law*) retortion, retorsion

Retorte, *s.f.* (*old for* "cornue," *chem.*) retort

†Retortiller, *v.a.* to ... (*V.* **Tortiller**) again; — *v.n.* (*old*) to return *or* advert often

Retorturer, *v.a.* to ... (*V.* **Torturer**) again

Retouchage, *s.m.* retouching

Retouche, *s. f.* retouch, after-touch; retouching

Retoucher, *v.a.n.* to retouch; to touch again; to touch up; to rub up; to correct; to alter; to make alterations

Se —, *v.r.* to be retouched, &c.

Retoucheu-r, se, *s.m.f.* retoucher

Retour, *s.m.* return; returning, going back, coming back; return journey, journey back; recurrence; winding; vicissitude, change;

conversion; reversion; reconciliation; acknowledgment, retribution, reciprocity, reciprocation, requital; compensation; boot, thing given to boot *or* into the bargain, difference; decline; dodge; artifice, trick; luncheon, repast, feast; angle, corner, turning; (*nav.*) home *or* homeward *or* return voyage (*or* passage), voyage home *or* in. — *d'équerre*, right angle. — *sur soi-même*, reflection on o.'s own conduct, self-examination. *Age de* —, — *de l'âge*, declining years, decline of life. *De* —, return; homeward; home-bound; on o.'s return, having returned; returned; back; to boot, over; up *or* back *or* return (*train*). *Sans* —, for ever; irretrievably, irreparably, irrecoverably; irretrievable, irreparable, irrecoverable; absolute; irreconcilable, unforgiving. *Sur le* —, on the decline *or* wane. *Faire* — *à*, to return to; to revert to. *Payer de* —, to return, to repay, to requite (*a person's love, hatred*, &c.), to return *or* repay the like

Retourne, *s.f.* (*cards*) trump-card

Retournement, *s.m.* turning up *or* &c. (*V.* **Retourner**)

Retourner, *v.a.n.* to return; to go again; to go back; to go back again; to turn back; to revert; to recoil, to fall back; to run back; to turn up *or* down *or* over; to turn round *or* about; to turn inside out; to turn; to revolve; to mix (*a salad*); to upset; to be going on, to be about, to be the matter. — *en arrière*, to turn back; to go back. *Savoir* (or *voir*) *de quoi il retourne*, to know (*or* to see) what is going on (*or* what is the matter, *or* how matters stand, *or* the news). *N'y retournez pas*, (*fig.*) don't do that (*or* it) again

Se —, *v.r.* to turn oneself, to turn; to turn oneself round, to turn round; to look behind; to turn over *or* about; to manage; to get on; (*contre*) to turn round (upon); to turn the tables (on, upon, against); (*of things*) to be turned up *or* &c.; to be returned

S'en —, *v.r.* to return, to go back, to go back again [relation

Retracement, *s.m.* retracing; description,

Retracer, *v.a.* to trace *or* draw again; to retrace; to describe, to relate; to bring back, to recall

Se —, *v.r.* to recall to mind, to trace back, to remember; to recur, to return; to be traced again, &c.

Rétractation, *s.f.* retractation; recantation

Rétracter, *v.a.*, **Se** —, *v.r.* to retract; to recant; to contract; to shrink

Rétracteur, *s.m.* retractor

Rétractible, *adj.* retractible, retractile

Rétracti-f, ve, *adj.* retractive

Rétractile, *adj.* retractile, retractible

Rétractilité, *s.f.* retractility, retractibility

Rétraction, *s.f.* retraction, contraction

Retraduction, *s.f.* retranslation, new translation [again

Retraduire, *v.a.* to retranslate, to translate

Retraîner, *v.a.* to ... (*V.* **Trainer**) again

Retraire, *v. a.* to withdraw; to redeem; to milk again [withdrawn; to be redeemed

Se —, *v.r.* to contract; to shrink; to be

Retrait, e, *part. adj.* withdrawn; redeemed; contracted; shrunk; lean, thin; (*her.*) rebated; (*hunt.*) tired out

Retrait, *s.m.* withdrawal; redemption, repurchase; contraction; shrinkage, shrinking; retiring, receding, recession; dereliction; (*build.*) offset; recess; (*flour and bran*) pollard; (*obsolete*) private room, dressing-room; water-closet, privy

Retraite, *s.f.* withdrawal, withdrawing; retreat; retiring, retirement; dereliction; recession; recess; shelter; resource; haunt, resort, den; privacy; contraction; shrinkage, shrinking; pension; superannuation; (*mil.*) retreat; (*mil.*) tattoo; (*artil.*) recoil; (*Cath. rel.*) retirement, retreat, preparation for communion; (*com.*) redraft. *De* —, retiring. *En* —, superannuated, retired, on the retired list; inside. *Caisse* or *fonds de* —, retiring fund, superannuation fund. *Coup de canon de* —, (*mil.*) evening gun. *Pension de* —, retiring pension *or* allowance. *Battre en* —, to retreat; (*fig.*) to give way. *Battre la* —, to beat the tattoo; to beat *or* sound a (*or* the) retreat. *Se battre en* —, to fight while retreating; (*nav.*) to keep up a running fight. *Couper la* — *à*, to cut off ...'s retreat. *Donner* — *à*, to shelter, to harbour. *Donner sa* — *à*, to pension off, to superannuate. *Faire* —, to retreat; to retire; to march off; to recede; to set back; (*com.*) to redraw. *Mettre à la* —, to pension off, to superannuate. *Prendre sa* —, to retire on a pension, to retire. *Sonner la* —, to sound a (*or* the) retreat; (*hunt.*) to call off the hounds

Retraité, e, *part. adj.* treated again; pensioned off, superannuated, retired, on the retired list; — *s.m.* pensioner [to superannuate

Retraiter, *v.a.* to treat again; to pension off,

Retranchement, *s.m.* retrenchment; suppression; stoppage; curtailment; recess; refuge; (*mil.*) intrenchment

Retrancher, *v.a.* to retrench; to cut off *or* out; to suppress; to stop; to stop the allowance of; to strike off, to erase; to curtail; to take off *or* away, to subtract, to deduct; to deprive of; to forbid; (*mil.*) to intrench

Se — *v.r.* to restrain *or* confine oneself; to retrench, to diminish *or* reduce o.'s expenses; to deprive oneself of; to give up; to screen oneself; to fall back (upon), to urge, to plead, to put forward; (*mil.*) to intrench oneself; (*things*) to be retrenched *or* &c.

Retranscrire, *v.a.* to retranscribe, to transcribe *or* copy again [up; to polish, to file

†**Retravailler,** *v.n.a.* to work again; to touch

Retraverser, *v.a.* to recross, to cross again

Retrayant, e, *s.m.f.* repurchaser, redemptor, reemptor; — *adj.* redeeming

Rêtre, *s.m.* *V.* **Reitre**

Rétréci, e, *part. adj.* narrowed, straitened, &c. (*V.* **Rétrécir**); narrower; narrow

Rétrécir, *v.a.n.*, **Se** —, *v.r.* to narrow; to make *or* become narrow *or* narrower *or* closer; to straiten; to take in; to shrink, to shrink away; to contract, to limit, to cramp, to confine; to reduce; to be straitened *or* contracted *or* &c.

Rétrécissement, *s.m.* narrowing; narrowness; straitening; cramping; shrinking, shrinkage; contracting, contraction; stricture

Rétrécissure, *s.f.* straitness, narrowness

Retreindre, *v.a.* to hammer out

Retreinte, *s.f.* hammering out [ing again

Retrempe, *s.f.* new *or* fresh tempering; soak-

Retremper, *v.a.* to dip *or* soak *or* steep again; to temper again; to invigorate, to strengthen; to renovate

Se —, *v.r.* to acquire renewed vigour *or* strength, to recruit o.'s strength, to be strengthened *or* invigorated [again

Retresser, *v.a.* to weave *or* &c. (*V.* **Tresser**)

Rétribuer, *v.a.* to remunerate, to reward, to pay

Rétribu-teur, trice, *s.m.f.* remunerator, remuneratress, retributer, retributress

Rétribution, *s.f.* retribution, remuneration, reward, pay, fee

Retrier, *v.a.* to ... (*V.* **Trier**) again

†**Rétriller,** *v.a.* to ... (*V.* **Étriller**) again

Rétroacti-f, ve, *adj.* retroactive

Rétroactivement, *adv.* retroactively

Rétroactivité, *s.f.* retroactive effect

Rétroagir, *v.n.* to retroact

Rétrocédant, e, *s.m.f.* reconveyer

Rétrocéder, *v.a.* to retrocede, to yield *or* give back, to reassign, to make over again, to reconvey

Rétrocessi-f, ve, *adj.* retroceding, retrocedent
Rétrocession, *s.f.* retrocession, reconveyance
Rétrofléchi, e, *adj.* retroflex, retroflexed
Rétroflexion, *s.f.* retroflexion
Rétrogradation, *s.f.* retrogradation, retrogression
Rétrograde, *adj.* retrograde
Rétrograder, *v.n.* to retrograde, to go backward, to go back
Rétrogressi-f, ve, *adj.* retrogressive
Rétrogression, *s.f.* retrogression
Rétrogressivement, *adv.* retrogressively
Rétrospecti-f, ve, *adj.* retrospective
Rétrospectivement, *adv.* retrospectively
Retrotter, Retroubler, Retrouer, &c. to ... (*V.* **Trotter, Troubler, Trouer,** &c.) again
Retroussement, *s.m.* tucking up; turning up; tying up; cocking up; curling up
Retrousser, *v.a.*, **Se** —, *v.r.* to turn up; to tuck *or* tie up; to cock up; to curl up; to truss up (*sails*); to tuck up o.'s dress
Retroussis, *s.m.* facing; boot-top, top; cock (*of a hat*)
Retrouver, *v.a.* to find again; to find; to recover; to meet again, to meet; to recognize; to retrieve (*game*)
Se —, *v.r.* to find oneself *or* each other again; to recover *or* recognize oneself *or* itself; to meet again; to find o.'s way again; to be again met with; to be again; to be found again; to be found *or* &c.
Rétroversion, *s.f.* retroversion
Rets, *s.m.* net, snare, toil
Retuer, *v.a.* to kill *or* &c. (*V.* **Tuer**) again
Rétudier, *v.a.* to study again
Rétus, e, *adj.* retuse
Réunion, *s.f.* reunion; reuniting; union; concourse; gathering; collection; meeting; assembly; party; body; set
Réunir, *v.a.*, **Se** —, *v.r.* to reunite; to unite, to join; to annex; to collect; to gather; to assemble; to muster; to call *or* bring *or* come together; to combine; to club; to meet again; to meet; to concur; to be reunited *or* &c.
Réussi, e, *adj.* successfully *or* well *or* nicely made *or* done *or* performed or executed, successful; brilliant; accomplished, performed, made, done. *Mal* —, unsuccessfully *or* badly made *or* done, unsuccessful; spoilt; unlucky, unfortunate; unfavourable
Réussir, *v.n.* to succeed; to be successful; to fare; to thrive, to prosper, to get on; to answer; to answer the purpose (of); to agree (with); — *v.a.* to succeed in, to execute well, to accomplish, to perform, to make, to do
Réussite, *s.f.* success; issue, event
Revaccination, *s.f.* revaccination
Revacciner, *v.a.* to revaccinate
†**Rêvailler.** *V.* **Rêvasser**
Revalescière, Revalenta, *s.f.* (*quack pharm.*) revalenta arabica
Revaloir, *v.a.* to return, to pay back for
Revanche, *s.f.* revenge, retaliation; return; turn; return-match, second game, another game. *En* —, in return; by way of retaliation; to make up for it, to make amends; as a compensation (for); on another hand. *Avoir sa* —, to have o.'s revenge *or* o.'s turn. *Prendre sa* —, to take o.'s revenge, to take vengeance; to retaliate, to return like for like; to play the return-match
Revancher, *v.a.* to defend; to revenge; to return
Se —, *v.r.* to defend oneself; to revenge; to return
Rêvasser, *v.n.* to keep dreaming, to dream, to have agitating dreams; to muse
Rêvasserie, *s.f.* broken dream, agitating dream; dream, dreaming; musing
Rêvasseur, *s.m.* dreamer, muser
Rêve, *s.m.* dream; dreaming; fancy, illusion.
— **-creux,** *s.m.* *V.* **Songe-creux**
Revêche, *adj.* harsh, sharp; peevish, cross, crabbed, cantankerous; intractable
†**Réveil,** *s.m.* awaking; waking; revival; alarm-clock, alarm-watch; alarm, alarum; (*mil., nav.*) *V.* **Diane**
†**Réveille-matin,** *s.m.* alarm-clock; alarm-watch; awakener; disturber of sleep; Chanticleer; (*mil., nav.*) *V.* **Diane;** (*bot.*) wartwort
†**Réveiller,** *v.a.* to awake, to wake, to wake up; to call up, to call; to rouse; to stir up; to revive; to rake up
†**Réveilleu-r, se,** *s.m.f.* awakener, waker
†**Réveillon,** *s.m.* supper after midnight, late supper, supper; Christmas-eve feast *or* revel; (*paint.*) strong stroke of light. *Faire le* —, to keep up Christmas-eve
Révéla-teur, trice, *s.m.f.* revealer; detector; informer; — *adj.* revealing, &c.
Révélation, *s.f.* revelation; discovery, disclosure; information
Révéler, *v.a.* to reveal; to discover, to disclose; to inform against
Se —, *v.r.* to reveal *or* &c. oneself *or* itself; to be revealed, &c.
Revenant, e, *adj.* returning; pleasing, prepossessing
Revenant, *s.m.* ghost, apparition
Revenant-bon, *s.m.* perquisite; bonus; emolument; windfall, godsend
Revendage, *s.m.* huckstering, huckster's trade *or* business
Revendeu-r, se, *s.m.f.* retailer; broker; huckster, huckstress; pedlar; salesman. — *à la toilette*, wardrobe dealer
Revendicable, *adj.* claimable
Revendica-teur, trice, *s.m.f.* claimant, claimer
Revendication, *s.f.* claiming, claim, demand
Revendiquer, *v.a.* to claim, to demand
Se —, *v.r.* to be claimed *or* demanded
Revendre, *v.a.* to sell again; to spare. *En avoir à* —, to have some to spare, to have enough (of it, of them) and to spare. *En* — *à*, to outwit, to do, to be more than a match for
Revenez-y, *s.m.* dish *or* piece to cut and come again, nice *or* dainty dish, dainty; return; repetition; doing again, doing it again; beginning again
Revenir, *v.n.* to return; to come back, to come again, to come back again; to come round; to grow again; to reappear; to recover; to get over; to recover o.'s senses, to come to; to awaken; to revert; to recur; to occur; to present oneself *or* itself; to alter; to alter o.'s mind *or* opinion; to reconsider; to retract; to retrieve; to reform; to embrace, to adopt; to dislike; to get rid; to renounce, to abandon; to please, to suit; to accrue, to result, to arise; to fall (to), to be due; to be like, to agree; to amount, to come (to); to cost, to stand in; to be reconciled *or* appeased; to appear, to haunt; (*of food*) to rise (*in the stomach*). — *à soi*, to recover o.'s senses, to come to; to calm oneself; to be reclaimed, to amend, to reform. — *de loin*, (*fig.*) to escape great danger, to have a narrow escape; to recover from severe illness; to retrieve great errors. — *sur l'eau*, to get afloat again. *Son nom ne me revient pas*, I do not recollect his name. *Il me revient que*, I understand *or* I hear *or* I am told that. *Il ne m'en revient rien*, I get nothing by it. *Ne pas* — *de*, to be very much surprised at, to wonder at. *N'en pas* —, not to return *or* recover from it, not to get over it, to be amazed, to be unable to recover from o.'s astonishment. *S'en* —, to return, to come back again. *Y* —, to return to it, &c.; to cut and come again; to do it again. *Faire* —, to make (...) return *or* &c.; to bring back; to call back; to recover; to get back, to have back; to revive; to reclaim; (*cook.*) to half-cook; to parboil
Revente, *s.f.* resale; huckstering, huckster's trade *or* business. *De* —, second-hand

Reventer, Réventer, *v.a.* (*nav.*) to fill again
Revenu, e, *part. adj.* returned, come back, &c. (*V.* **Revenir**); back; having recovered, [&c.
Revenu, *s.m.* revenue; income; profit
Revenue, *s.f.* return; young wood; (*hunt.*) feeding-time
Rêver, *v.a.n.* to dream; to dream of; to rave; to be delirious; to muse; to imagine; to think; to reflect; to consider; to meditate; to [long for
Se —, *v.r.* to be dreamt *or* &c.
Réverbération, *s.f.* reverberation
Réverbératoire, *adj.* reverberatory
Réverbère, *s.m.* reflector; street-lamp. *A —*, reverberatory
Réverbérer, *v.a.n.* to reverberate
Reverdir, *v.n.* to become green again; to grow young again; to revive; — *v.a.* to paint *or* make green again. *Faire —*, to make green; to revive
Reverdissement, *s.m.* growing green again
Révéremment, *adv.* reverently [curtsy
Révérence, *s.f.* reverence; bow; courtesy,
Révérenciel, le, *adj.* reverential
Révérencieusement, *adv.* reverently, reverentially [quious, bowing and scraping
Révérencieu-x, se, *adj.* reverential; obse-
Révérend, e, *adj. s.* reverend
Révérendissime, *adj.* very reverend, right reverend, most reverend [rate
Révérer, *v.a.* to revere, to reverence, to vene-
Rêverie, *s. f.* reverie, dream, idle dream, musing; delirium, raving
Revérifier, *v.a.* to ... (*V.* **Vérifier**) again
Revernir, *v.a.* to revarnish
Revers, *s.m.* back; opposite side, other side; wrong side; back-stroke *or* blow, backhanded blow, backhander; counterpart; reverse; facing; lapel; breast; top (*of boots*); bank. — *de la médaille*, reverse of the medal; (*fig.*) dark side of the picture. *Coup de —*, *V.* **Coup.** *A* or *de —*, (*mil.*) in the rear *or* in flank, not in front [of mutual concessions
Reversal, e, *adj.* confirmatory, confirmative;
Reverseau, *s.m. V.* **Rejéteau**
Reverser, *v.a.* to pour again, to pour out again, to ... (*V.* **Verser**) again; (*com.*) to carry
Reversi, *s.m.* reversis (*game at cards*)
Reversibilité, *s.f.* revertibility [reversible
Reversible, *adj.* revertible, reversionary;
Reversion, *s.f.* reversion
Reversis. *V.* **Reversi**
Reversoir, *s.m.* dam, weir
Revêtement, *s.m.* covering; coating; casing; lining; facing; (*fort.*) revetment, revetement, facing
Revêtir, *v.a.* to clothe; to dress; to cover; to coat; to put on; to invest; to furnish; to confer; to bestow; to endow; to assume; to case; to line; to face; (*fort.*) to revet
Se —, *v.r.* to clothe *or* &c. oneself; to put on; to assume
Rêveu-r, se, *adj. s.* thoughtful, pensive, musing; dreamer; muser; thinker
Revider, *v.a.* to empty again [net cost
Revient, *s.m.* net cost. *Prix de —*, cost price,
Revirement, *s.m.* sudden change; tacking about, tacking; (— *de parties* or *de fonds* or *de deniers*) transfer
Revirer, *v.n.* to tack about; to turn round
Réviser, *v.a.* to revise; to review
Réviseur, *s.m.* reviser, examiner [view
Révision, *s.f.* revision; revising, revisal; re-
Revisiter, *v.a.* to revisit, to reexamine, to visit *or* &c. (*V.* **Visiter**) again
Revivification, *s.f.* revivification [generate
Revivifier, *v.a.* to revivify; to revive; to re-
Reviviscence, *s.f.* reviviscence
Reviviscent, e, *adj.* reviviscent
Reviviscible, *adj.* reviviscible
Revivre, *v.n.* to rise from the dead, to come to life again, to rise again, to return to life, to live again; to revive. *Faire —*, to bring to life again, to raise from the dead; to revive; to restore; to reestablish; to perpetuate
Révocabilité, *s.f.* revocability, revocableness, reversibleness, repealableness
Revocable, *adj.* revocable, reversible, repealable; removable [removal, dismissal
Révocation, *s.f* revocation; repeal; recall;
Révocatoire, *adj.* revocatory, revoking
Revoici, *prep.* here again; here is *or* are ... again; once more; behold again. *Me —*, here am I again
Revoilà, *prep.* there again; there is *or* are ... again; once more; behold again. *Me —*, there am I again
Revoir, *v.a.* to see again; to meet again; to revise; to look over again; to reexamine; to correct; — *s.m.* seeing *or* meeting again, next meeting. *Au —*, *jusqu'au —*, till we meet again, till our next meeting, until I see you again, good-bye for the present, farewell till we meet again
Se —, *v.r.* to see oneself *or* each other again; to meet again; to be seen again, &c.
Revoiturer, *v.a.* to ... (*V.* **Voiturer**) again
Revoler, *v.n.a.* to fly again *or* back; to steal *or* rob again
Revolin, *s.m.* (*nav.*) eddy-wind
Révolte, *s.f.* revolt; rebellion
Révolté, e, *s.m.f.* rebel, revolter; — *part. adj.* revolted, &c. (*V.* **Révolter**); rebellious, rebel
Révolter, *v.a.* to rouse *or* excite *or* urge *or* cause to revolt; to excite, to rouse; to revolt, to shock; to rouse (...'s) indignation; to disgust; to horrify. *Faire —*, to rouse *or* excite to revolt; to cause to rebel; to rouse, to stir up
Se —, *v.r.* to revolt, to rebel; to be shocked
Révolu, e, *adj.* revolved; finished, ended; accomplished, completed, complete, full
Révoluté, e, Révoluti-f, ve, *adj.* revolute
Révolution, *s.f.* revolution
Révolutionisme, *s.m.* revolutionism
Révolutioniste, *s.m.f.* revolutionist; — *adj.* revolutionistic [revolutionist
Révolutionnaire, *adj. s.* revolutionary;
Révolutionnairement, *adv.* revolutionarily
Révolutionner, *v. a.* to revolutionize; to startle, to upset
Se —, *v.r.* to be revolutionized, &c.
Révolver, *s.m.* revolver
Revomir, *v.a.n.* to revomit, to vomit again; to vomit, to bring up, to throw up *or* out *or* back, to cast back; to disgorge
Révoquer, *v.a.* to revoke; to repeal; to recall; to remove, to dismiss
Se —, *v.r.* to be revoked *or* &c. [again
Revouloir, *v.a.* to desire *or* &c. (*V.* **Vouloir**)
Revoyager, *v.n.* to travel again
Revu, e, *part.* seen again, &c. (*V.* **Revoir**)
Revue, *s.f.* review; survey. *Être gens de —*, to meet often; to be likely to meet again. *Faire la — de*, to review; to examine; to survey. *Passer en —*, to review
Révulsi-f, ve, *adj.*, **Révulsif,** *s.m.* revulsive
Révulsion, *s.f.* revulsion
Rez, *prep.* even with, on a level with. — *pied*, — *terre*, on a level with the ground. — *-de-chaussée*, *s.m.* ground-floor; ground-level. *A — -de-chaussée*, level (*or* even) with the ground. *Au — -de-chaussée*, on the ground-floor
Rhabdo-logie, -logique, -mancie, -mantique, &c. *V.* page 3, § 1
†**Rhabillage,** *s.m.* mending, repairing, tinkering; patching up; bone-setting
†**Rhabillement,** *s.m.* dressing again; new-clothing; mending, repairing, patching up
†**Rhabiller,** *v.a.* to dress again; to new-clothe; to mend, to repair, to tinker, to patch up; to set [botcher; bone-setter
†**Rhabilleu-r, se,** *s.m.f.* mender; tinker;
Rhabiter, Rhabituer. *V.* **Réhabiter, Réhabituer**
Rhagade, *s.f.* (*med.*) fissure

Rhaphé. *V.* **Raphé**
Rhapontic, *s.m.* (*bot.*) bastard rhubarb
Rhapsode, *s.m.* rhapsodist
Rhapsoder, *v.a.n.* to rhapsodize; to botch
Rhapsod-ie, -ique, -iste. *V.* page 3, § 1
Rhegmate, *s.m.* (*bot.*) regma
Rhénan, e, *adj.* Rhenish
Rhéomètre, *s.m.* (*phys.*) rheometer
Rhéophore, *s.m.* (*phys.*) rheophore
Rhéoscope, *s.m.* (*phys.*) rheoscope
Rhésus, *s.m.* rhesus monkey
Rhéteur, *s.m.* rhetor, rhetorician
Rhétien, ne, Rhétique, *adj.* (*geog.*) Rhetian, Rhætian; (*geol.*) Rhetic, Rhætic
Rhétoricien, ne, *s.m.f.* rhetorician; student of the highest form but one
Rhétorique, *s.f.* rhetoric; highest form (*or* class) but one. *Faire de la* —, to rhetorize. *Faire sa* —, to study rhetoric, to be in the highest form but one. *Employer toute sa* —, to have recourse to all o.'s eloquence. *Y perdre toute sa* —, to be unable to make it out
Rhin (Le), *s.m.* (the) Rhine. *Vin du* —, Rhine wine, Rhenish wine, hock
Rhinanthe, *s.m.* (*bot.*) cock's-comb
Rhingrave, *s.f.* (*obsolete*) pair of breeches, pair of knickerbockers, breeches, knickerbockers
Rhinocéros, *s.m.* rhinoceros; rhinoceros beetle
Rhino-plastie, -plastique, -scopie, &c. *V.* page 3, § 1
Rhizome, *s.m.* (*bot.*) rhizoma, rhizome, root-stock, root-stalk
Rhizophage, *adj.* rhizophagous
Rhizopode, *s.m.* (*zool.*) rhizopod
Rhodanien, ne, Rhodanique, *adj.* of the Rhône
Rhodien, ne, *adj. s.* Rhodian
Rhodium, *s.m.* (*chem.*) rhodium
Rhododendron, *s.m.* (*bot.*) rhododendron
Rhombe, *s.m.* (*geom.*) rhomb, rhombus; (*fish*) topknot
Rhombiforme, *adj.* rhombiform
Rhombique, *adj.* rhombic
Rhomboèdre, *s.m.* (*geom.*) rhombohedron; — *adj.* rhombohedral
Rhomboédrique, *adj.* rhombohedral
Rhomboïdal, e, *adj.* rhomboidal
Rhomboïde, *s.m., adj.m.f.* rhomboid
‡**Rhonchus, Rhoncus,** *s.m.* (*med.*) rhonchus
Rhotacisme. *V.* **Rotacisme**
Rhubarbe, *s.f.* rhubarb
Rhum, *s.m.* rum
Rhumatalgie, *s.f.* rheumatalgia, chronic rheumatic pain
Rhumatique, *adj.* rheumatic
Rhumatisant, e, *adj.* affected with rheumatism; — *s.m.f.* person affected with rheumatism
Rhumatisé, e, *adj.* affected with rheumatism
Rhumatismal, *adj.* rheumatic
Rhumatismalement, *adv.* rheumatically
Rhumatisme, *s.m.* rheumatism
Rhumb. *V.* **Rumb**
Rhume, *s.m.* cold. *Gros* —, bad *or* severe *or* violent cold. — *de cerveau*, cold in the head
Rhumerie, *s.f.* rum distillery
Rhynchée, *s.f.* (*bird*) shoveller
‡**Rhynchops,** *s.m.* (*bird*) skimmer
Rhythme, *s.m.* rhythm; time
Rhythmique, *adj.* rhythmical; — *s.f.* rhythmics
Ria, *s.m.* (*nav.*) sheave
Riant, e, *part. adj.* laughing, &c. (*V.* **Rire,** *v.n.*); smiling; lively, cheerful; pleasant, pleasing. *En* —, laughing; laughingly; smiling; smilingly; in joke, in jest, in fun
Ribambelle, *s.f.* string; swarm, host, lot
Ribaud, e, *adj. s.* ribald
Ribauderie, *s.f.* ribaldry
Riblette, *s.f.* collop; rasher
Riblons, *s.m.pl.* scrap-iron
Ribord, *s.m.* (*nav.*) garboard strake
Ribordage, *s.m.* (*nav.*) damage by fouling
Riborder, *v.n.* (*nav.*) *V.* **Louvoyer**
Ribote, *s.f.* revel, guzzling, guttling, drunken bout. *Être en* —, to be boozy *or* tipsy *or* drunk *or* tight. *Faire* —, to have a drunken bout
Riboter, *v.n.* to booze, to revel, to carouse, to tipple, to guzzle, to guttle, to get tipsy *or* drunk
Ribote-ur, se, *s.m.f.* boozer, carouser, tippler, drinker, guzzler, guttler
Ricanement, *s.m.* giggling, giggle, tittering, titter; sneering, sneer; chuckling, chuckle
Ricaner, *v.n.* to giggle, to titter, to snigger; to sneer; to chuckle
Ricanerie, *s.f.* *V.* **Ricanement**
Ricaneu-r, se, *adj. s.* giggling, sneering; giggler, sneerer
Ricardeau, Ricardot, *s.m.* scollop
Ric-à-ric, *adv.* by driblets; (*obsolete*) rigorously, strictly, exactly, to a tittle
Richard, *s.m.* moneyed man, rich fellow, capitalist, nabob
Riche, *adj.* rich; wealthy; sumptuous; precious, valuable; abundant, copious; fine; — *s.m.* rich man (*pl.* rich men, rich). *Mauvais* —, Dives, rich man in the Gospel; rich man without compassion for the poor. *Faire le* —, to play the rich man
Richebourg, *s.m.* richebourg (wine)
Richement, *adv.* richly; wealthily; sumptuously; splendidly; abundantly, copiously; preciously
Richesse, *s.f.* riches; wealth; richness; copiousness
Richissime, *adj.* extremely rich
Ricin, *s.m.* castor-oil plant *or* tree. — *d'Amérique*, physic-nut. *Huile de* —, castor-oil
Ricinique, *adj.* (*chem.*) ricinic
Ricochable, *adj.* exposed to ricochet-fire
Ricocher, *v.n.* to ricochet, to rebound. *Faire* —, to ricochet
Ricochet, *s.m.* ricochet; rebound; duck and drake; succession, series. *Feu à* —, ricochet-fire *or* firing. *Par* —, indirectly
Rictus, *s.m.* expansion; grinning, grin
Ride, *s.f.* wrinkle; ripple; (*nav.*) laniard
Rideau, *s.m.* curtain; drop; drop-scene, act-drop; (*fig.*) curtain, sheet, screen, veil; (*of fire-grates*) blower, draw-plate; (*fort.*) rideau. — *d'entr'acte*, act-drop, drop-scene. *Derrière le* —, behind the curtain; behind the scenes
Ridée, *s.f.* clap-net
Ridelle, *s.f.* (*of carts*) staff side, standard-side, rail, rack, rathe, rave, shelving; (*duck*) gadwall
Ridenne, *s.f.* (*duck*) gadwall
Ridement, *s.m.* wrinkling; rippling, ripple; corrugation; contraction
Rider, *v.a.*, **Se** —, *v.r.* to wrinkle; to shrivel; to ripple, to ruffle; to corrugate; to contract
Ridicule, *adj.* ridiculous; — *s.m.* ridicule; ridiculousness; ridiculous thing; reticule, bag. *Avoir des* —*s*, to be ridiculous. *Donner un* — *à*, to bring ridicule upon. *Se donner un* —, to make oneself ridiculous. *Tourner en* —, to ridicule
Ridiculement, *adv.* ridiculously
Ridiculiser, *v.a.* to ridicule
Ridiculissime, *adj.* exceedingly ridiculous
Ridiculité, *s.f.* ridiculousness; ridiculous thing
Rièble, *s.m.* *V.* **Grateron**
Rien, *adv.* anything; nothing, not anything; nobody, no one; no consequence, no importance; no worth; no difference; no result; no interest, no concern; no way, nowise; any way; — *s.m.* nothing, mere nothing; mere trifle, trifle, mite; nonsense, idle talk. — *de* —, nothing at all, nothing whatever. — *autre chose*, nothing else. — *que*, only; alone. — *de moins*, nothing less. — *moins*, nothing less; not in the least, not the least, not at all. — *moins que*, nothing less than; no less than; anything but. *De* —, of nothing *or* &c.; insignificant; don't mention it! *En moins de* —, *En un* — *de temps*, in no time, in a trice. *Moins que* —, less than nothing; next to nothing. *Pour* —, for nothing *or* next to nothing, for a mere trifle; for an old song, for a song; very cheap, dirt cheap; given away; at a gift. *Pas*

plus gros que —, very small, very little. *Comme si de — n'était ; Il n'en est —; V.* **Être.** *Ne — faire, N'en — faire,* &c., *V.* **Faire**
Rieu-r, se, *s.m.f. adj.* laugher; giggler; sneerer; mocker; jeerer; joker; laughing; giggling; grinning; sneering; mocking; jeering; joking
Riflard, *s.m.* jack-plane; paring-chisel; old umbrella, gamp
Rifler, *v.a.* to pare; to file
Rifloir, *s.m.* crooked file
Rigel, *s.m.* (*astr.*) Rigel, Regel
Rigaudon. *V.* **Rigodon**
Rigide, *adj.* rigid; severe; strict; harsh; stiff
Rigidement, *adv* rigidly, strictly; harshly
Rigidité, *s.f.* rigidity; severity; strictness; harshness. — *cadavérique*, cadaveric rigidity, 'rigor mortis'
Rigodon, *s.m.* rigadoon (*dance, tune*)
Rigolade, *s.f.* jollification; rollicking
Rigolage, *s.m.* draining
Rigole, *s.f.* trench; gutter; drain
Rigoler, *v.a.* to drain; — *v.n.* to make merry, to rollic, to revel, to have a jollification *or* a lark *or* a spree
Rigoleu-r, se, *s.m.f.* jolly fellow, boon companion, rollicking fellow, gay woman; — *adj.* merry, jolly, rollicking, gay, fast [ness
Rigorisme, *s.m.* rigorism; austerity; strict-
Rigoriste, *s.m.f* rigorist; rigid moralist; martinet; — *adj.* rigorist, over rigid
Rigoureusement, *adv.* rigorously; severely; strictly; harshly; sternly; closely
Rigoureu-x, se, *adj.* rigorous; severe; strict; harsh, sharp; stern; close
Rigri, *s.m.* (*old, pop.*) churl, curmudgeon
Rigueur, *s.f.* rigour; severity; strictness; harshness, sharpness; sternness; closeness; precision. *A la* —, rigorously; strictly; in a strict sense; for once in a way; in an extreme case; if absolutely necessary. *De* —, indispensable; obligatory; latest; peremptory; (*at play*) the strict game. *En* —, with rigour. *Tenir* —, to be severe (upon); to show spite, to refuse to forgive; to refuse to come round; to remain adverse; to frown (upon)
†**Rillettes,** *s.f.pl.* minced pork
†**Rimaille,** *s.f.* doggrel, doggerel
†**Rimailler,** *v.n.* to make doggrel *or* bad verses, to berhyme; — *v.a.* to put into doggrel, to berhyme
†**Rimailleu-r, se,** *s.m.f.* rhymster
Rimaye, *s.f.* crevasse in a glacier
Rime, *s.f.* rhyme; verse [*prose —e*, doggrel
Rimé, e, *part. adj.* rhymed; versified. *De la*
Rimer, *v.a.n.* to rhyme; (*fig.*) to have connection. *Cela ne rime à rien*, that means nothing, that is nonsense, there is no sense in that. *A quoi cela rime-t-il?* what does it mean? what sense is there in that?
Rimeu-r, se, *s.m.f.* rhymer
Rinçage, *s.m.* rinsing [scroll; (*her.*) bough
Rinceau, *s.m.* foliage; (*arch.*) foliage, foliated
Rince, *s m.* (*in compounds, from* **Rincer,** "to rinse," &c.) thing wherewith to rinse *or* wash, rinser, washer. — **-doigts,** — **-bouche,** *s.m.* finger glass. — **-tasse,** *s.m.* slop-basin
Rincée, *s.f.* whacking, drubbing, hiding, thrashing, dressing; blowing-up; fight, set-to; drenching
Rincement, *s.m.* rinsing; washing
Rincer, *v.a.* to rinse; to wash; to drench; to whack, to drub, to thrash; to blow up; to rifle; to fleece
Rincette, *s.f.* (*fam.*) drop more, extra drop
Rinceu-r, se, *s.m.f.* rinser; washer
Rinçoir, *s.m.* rinsing-vat *or* tub
Rinçure, *s.f.* rinsings, slops
Rinforzando, *adv. s.m.* (*mus.*) rinforzando
Ringard, *s.m.* (*tech.*) fire-iron, poker, iron rake, draw-bar
Rioter. *v.n.* to titter, to giggle, to snigger
Rioteu-r, se, *s.m.f.* titterer, giggler
Ripage, *s.m.* (*tech.*) scraping
†**Ripaille,** *s.f.* feasting, feast, carousal, drinking, guzzling, guttling, debauch, riot, revel, revelry, blow-out, good cheer, extravagant living. *Faire* —, to feast, to carouse, to booze, to guzzle, to guttle, to riot, to revel, to live sumptuously
†**Ripailler,** *v.n. V.* **Ripaille** (*Faire* —)
†**Ripailleu-r, se,** *s.m.f. V.* **Riboteur**
Ripe, *s.f.* (*tech.*) scraper
Ripement, *s.m.* bubbling
Riper, *v.a.* (*tech.*) to scrape; — *v.n.* to bubble
Ripopée, *s.f.* slop; slips op; medley, mishmash
Riposte, *s.f.* repartee; reply; answer; (*fenc.*) return, parry and thrust
Riposter, *v.n.* to make a repartee, to repartee; to reply; to answer; (*fenc.*) to parry and [thrust
Ripuaire, *s.m., adj.m.f.* Ripuarian
Riquet, *s.m.* (*obsolete*) kind of (*lady's*) bonnet. — *à la houpe*, hunchback
Riquiqui, *s.m.* (*pop.*) brandy
Rire, *v.n.* to laugh; to giggle; to chuckle; to sneer; to grin; to be *or* make merry; to amuse oneself; to joke, to jest; to smile; to please; to favour; to be propitious; to gape, to yawn, to be open. — *aux anges*, to be overjoyed; to laugh immoderately; to laugh alone *or* to oneself. — *aux éclats*, to burst out laughing, to roar with laughter. — *à gorge déployée*, — *comme un bossu*, to laugh heartily. — *comme un coffre*, — *comme un fou* or *une folle*, to burst into an immoderate fit of laughter, to laugh immoderately; to laugh heartily. — *dans sa barbe*, — *sous cape*, to laugh in o.'s sleeve. — *du bout des dents* or *lèvres*, to give a faint laugh, to force a laugh. — *jaune*, to laugh the wrong side of o.'s mouth. — *de*, to laugh at; not to care for. *Affaire* or *histoire de* —, *V.* **Histoire.** *En riant*, laughingly; in joke, in jest, for fun. *Pour* —, in joke, in jest, for fun; a joke; funny; laughingly; not in reality; mock, sham. *Faire* —, to make (*one, people*) laugh; to excite laughter; to amuse. *Se tenir les côtes de* —, to split o.'s sides with laughing. *La fortune lui rit*, fortune smiles upon him. *Vous voulez* —, *tu veux* —, you mean this for a joke, you are joking, I suppose! *Rira bien qui rira le dernier*, let them laugh that win. *Tel qui rit vendredi dimanche pleurera*, laugh to-day and cry to-morrow
Se —, *v.r.* to laugh (at), to make game (of); to jest, to trifle (with); not to care (for)
Rire, *s.m.* laughter, laughing; laugh; grin; sneer; smile. — *moqueur*, sneer. *Gros* —, loud laughter, horse-laugh
Ris, *s.m. V.* **Rire,** *s.m.*; — (*nav.*) reef; (*cook.*) sweetbread. — *de veau*, calf's sweetbread, sweetbread. *Prendre un* — *à*, (*nav.*) to reef
Risban, *s.m.* (*fort.*) risband
Risberme, *s.f.* (*fort.*) risberm
Risdale. *V.* **Rixdale**
Risée, *s.f.* laugh; laughter; jeer; derision, mockery; laughing-stock; by-word; (*nav.*) squall, gust, gale, flaw. *Objet de* —, laughing-[stock
Riser, *v.a.* (*nav.*) to reef (*the sails*)
Risette, *s.f.* (*fam.*) pretty laugh, smile
Risibilité, *s.f.* risibility, risibleness; laugh-[ableness
Risible, *adj.* risible; laughable
Risiblement, *adv* risibly, laughably
Risquable, *adj.* hazardous, adventurous; that [may be risked
Risque, *s.m.* risk, hazard, peril
Risqué, e, *adj.* risky, ventured, hazarded, hazardous; bold; broad, free
Risquer, *v.a.n.* to risk, to hazard, to venture, to run the risk (of), to have to fear. *Qui ne risque rien n'a rien*, (*Proverb*) nothing venture nothing have
Se —, *v.r.* to risk, to venture; to take o.'s chance (of it); to be risked *or* &c.
Risque-tout, *s.m.* desperate *or* reckless fellow, desperado, dare-devil

Risse, *s.f.* (*nav.*) *V.* **Saisine**
Risser, *v.a.* (*nav.*) to seize, to lash, to frap
Rissole, *s.f.* (*cook.*) rissole (*small fried pastry*)
Rissolé, *s.m.* outside, browned part, brown, crackling; — *m.*, **e,** *f.*, *part. adj.* browned; brown; sunburnt [brown
Rissoler, *v.a.n.*, **Se —,** *v.r.* to roast brown, to
Ristorne, Ristourne, *s. f.* cancelling *or* modification of a policy of insurance
Ristorner, Ristourner, *v.a.* to cancel *or* modify a policy of insurance
Rit, *s.m. V.* **Rite**
Ritardando, *adv. s.m.* (*mus.*) ritardando
Rite, *s.m.* rite
Ritournelle, *s.f.* ritornelle, ritornello; flourish; burden; tedious repetition, repetition
Ritualisme, *s.m.* ritualism
Ritualiste, *s.m.f.* ritualist; — *adj.* ritualistic
Rituel, le, *adj.*, **Rituel,** *s.m.* ritual [rivetting
Rivage, *s.m.* shore; beach; strand; bank, side;
Rival, e, *adj. s.* rival [compete; to cope
Rivaliser, *v.n.* to rival; to vie (in, with); to
Rivalité, *s.f.* rivalry; competition
Rive, *s.f.* bank, shore; border. *Pain de —*, cottage loaf, Brunswick loaf
Rivement, *s.m.* rivetting
River, *v.a.* to rivet; to clinch; to shut, to close. — *à quelqu'un son clou*, to give one a clincher, to silence one, to pay one off
Riverain, *s.m.* inhabitant of the bank of a river; borderer; owner of river-side property; — *m.*, **e,** *f.*, *adj.* riverain, riparian, (on the river-side, (on the) water-side, river, situated *or* growing on the banks of a river
Rivet, *s.m.* rivet
Riveur, *s.m.* rivetter [stream (*of diamonds*)
Rivière, *s.f.* river; stream; water; (*jewel.*)
Rivoir, Rivois, *s.m.* rivetting-hammer
Rivoyeur, *s.m.* river navigator
Rivulaire, *adj.* growing in rivulets *or* brooks,
Rivure, *s.f.* rivetting; pin [rivulet
Rixdale, *s.f.* rixdollar (*coin*)
Rixe, *s.f.* scuffle, fight, affray; brawl; altercation; conflict
Rixer, *v.n.* to fight, to squabble
Riz, *s.m.* rice; paddy. — *au gras*, rice-soup. — *au lait*, rice-milk. — *au maigre*, boiled rice. *Gâteau de —*, rice-cake; rice-pudding
Rizerie, *s.f.* rice-shelling works
Rizicole, *adj.* rice-growing, rice
Rizière, *s.f.* rice-field, rice-ground, rice-plantation, paddy-field
Rlan, *s.m.* rattle *or* noise of a drum [rubber
Rob, *s.m.* (sweet fluid) extract, rob; (*whist*)
Robe, *s.f.* robe; gown; dress; frock; coat (*of animals*); colour; shell, husk, peel, skin; wrapper, outside leaf (*of a cigar*); law, magistracy; clergy, cloth, orders, church. — *de chambre*, dressing *or* morning gown; (*cook. slang*) skin, jacket (*of a potato*). — *décolletée*, low dress. — *montante*, high dress
Rober, *v.a.* to bark (*madder*)
Rober, *s.m.* (*whist*) rubber
Robert Macaire, *s.m. V.* **Macaire**
Robin, *s.m.* bull; lawyer, limb of the law
Robinet, *s.m.* cock; tap; plug. — *flotteur*,
Robinetier. *V.* **Robinettier** [ball-cock
Robinetterie, *s.f.* tap-making *or* manufactory *or* trade; taps, cocks
Robinettier, *s.m.* tap-maker, cock-maker
Robinier, *s.m.* (*bot.*) robinia, locust-tree
Robinson, *s.m.* (*fam.*) old umbrella, gamp
Robre, *s.m.* (*whist*) rubber [hearty
Robuste, *adj.* robust, strong, vigorous, hardy;
Robustement, *adv.* robustly, stoutly
Robustesse, *s.f.* robustness
Roc, *s.m.* rock; (*bird, in Arabian myth.*) roc, rock; (*at chess, obsolete*) castle, rook. — *vif*,
†**Rocaille,** *s.f. adj.* rock-work [solid rock
†**Rocailleur,** *s.m.* rock-work maker
†**Rocailleu-x, se,** *adj.* rocky; stony, flinty; harsh, rugged

Rocambole, *s.f.* wild garlic, rocambole; pungency, point, zest, cream, best; (*pop.*) gammon, humbug, twaddle; rest of it
Rocantin. *V.* **Roquentin**
Roccelle, *s.f.* (*bot.*) orchil, archil
Roche, *s.f.* rock; quartz; (*fig.*) flint, steel. *De la vieille —*, of the old stock *or* stamp *or* school. *De la bonne —*, true blue. *Eau de —*, spring water
Rochelais,e,Rochellais,e,Rochelois,e, *adj. s.* of la Rochelle; native of ditto
Rocher, *s.m.* rock; cliff; murex, rock-shell. — *artificiel*, rockery
Rocher, *v.n.* (*of beer*) to froth [rock-dove
Rocheraie, *s.f.* wild-rock pigeon, rock-pigeon,
Rochet, *s.m.* rochet (*garment*); (*tech.*) rack, ratch, ratchet, clink
Rocheu-x, se, *adj.* rocky [dog-fish
Rochier, *s.m.* (*bird*) stone-falcon, merlin; (*fish*)
Rock, *s.m.* (*bird, in Arabian myth.*) roc, rock
Rococo, *s.m. adj.* rococo; rococo style; old-fashioned; tasteless; trumpery thing, old-fashioned things [couyer, &c.
Rocou, Rocouyer, &c. *V.* **Roucou, Rou-**
Rôder, *v.n.* to prowl; to ramble, to rove, to roam, to stroll, to wander, to loiter
Rôdeu-r, se, *s.m.f.* prowler; rambler, rover, stroller, wanderer; vagabond, vagrant, tramp; — *adj.* prowling; rambling, roving, strolling, wandering
Rodomont, *s.m.* rodomont, bully, swaggerer, blusterer; — *adj.* rodomont, swaggering, blustering [ing, swagger, bluster
Rodomontade, *s.f.* rodomontade, swagger-
Rodoul, *s.m. V.* **Roudou**
Roffrir, *v.a.* to ... (*V.* **Offrir**) again
Rogations, *s.f.pl.* (*Cath. rel.*) rogation
Rogatoire, *adj.* (*law*) of inquiry, to examine witnesses, judicial [scraps; odds and ends
Rogatons, *s.m.pl.* broken meat; stale stuff;
Roger-bontemps, *s.m.* merry careless fellow
†**Rognage,** *s.m. V.* **Rognement**
†**Rogne,** *s.f.* itch; scab; mange
†**Rognement,** *s.m.* cutting; clipping; paring; pruning; scraping
†**Rogne-pied,** *s.m.* butteris, hoof-parer
†**Rogner,** *v.a.* to cut; to cut off; to cut down; to clip; to pare, to pare away *or* off; to prune; to scrape; to take away, to retrench; to curtail, to cut short; to stint
†**Rogneu-r, se,** *s.m.f.* cutter; clipper; parer
†**Rogneu-x, se,** *adj.* itchy; scabby; mangy
†**Rognoir,** *s.m.* cutting-press; parer, scraper
†**Rognon,** *s.m.* kidney; boulder, cobble, cobstone [gizzard
†**Rognonner,** *v.n.* to grumble *or* growl in o.'s
†**Rognure,** *s.f.* cutting; clipping; paring; cuttings, clippings, parings, scrapings, shavings, shreds, leavings, refuse
Rogomme, *s.m.* liquor, grog, spirits, brandy. *Voix de —*, drunkard's voice, rusty *or* husky voice
Rogue, *adj.* proud, haughty, arrogant; — *s.f*, —**s,** *s.f.pl.* hard roe, spawn
Rogué, e, *adj.* hard-roed [gantly
Roguement, *adv.* proudly, haughtily, arro-
Roguerie, *s.f.* haughtiness, arrogance
Roi, *s.m.* king. — *d'armes*, king-at-arms. *De —*, of *or* from *or* for a king; kingly, royal. *En —*, like a king, kingly, royally. *Gâteau des —s*, Twelfth-cake, Twelfth-night cake. *Jour des —s*, Twelfth-day, Twelfth-night. *Faire* or *tirer les —s*, to celebrate Twelfth-night. *Pour le— de Prusse*, *V.* **Prusse**
Roide, Roideur, Roidir, &c. (*old spellings*) *V.* **Raide, Raideur, Raidir,** &c.
Roitelet, *s.m.* petty king, kinglet; (*bird*) wren
Rôlage, *s.m.* rolling
Rôle, *s.m.* roll; list; part, character; personation, impersonation; (*law*) cause-list. — *de combat*, quarter-bill. — *d'équipage*, list of the crew, muster-roll. — *de quart*, watch-bill

A tour de —, in turn, by turns, in o.'s turn, in *or* by rotation, alternately
Rôlet, *s.m.* little part, part, character. *Au bout de son* —, at the end of o.'s tether
Rôleur, *s.m.* (*pers.*) roller
Roller, *s.m.* roller (*cylinder*)
Rollier, *s.m.* roller (*bird*)
Romaïka, *s.f.* romaika (*modern Greek national dance*)
Romain, e, *adj.m.f., s.m.f.* of Rome; Roman; Romish; —**e,** *adj.f.* (*of lettuce*) cos; — *s.m.* (*in theatres*) (hired) clapper; (*print.*) Roman, primer; —**e,** *s.f.* Roman *or* Romish fashion; steelyard; cos lettuce. *Gros* —, (*print.*) great primer. *Petit* —, (*print.*) long primer
Romaïque, *adj.m.f., s.m.* Romaic; — *s.f. V.* **Romaïka**
Roman, *s.m.* novel; romance; fiction. *De* —, of a novel, of novels, novel; of romance, romantic; of fiction, imaginary
Roman, e, *adj.* Romanic, Romance, Romanesque
Romance, *s.f.* ballad; song
Romancer, *v.a.* to romance
Romancerie, *s.f.* novel *or* romance literature
Romancero, *s.m.* (*Spanish*) romancero
Romanci-er, ère, *s.m.f.* novelist, novel-writer; romancer, romance-writer
Romanciser, *v.a.* to romance
Romand, e, *adj.* (*of Switzerland*) French-speaking
Romanée, *s.m.* romanée (wine)
Romanesque, *adj.m.f., s.m.* romantic; (*arts*) romanesque
Romanesquement, *adv.* romantically
Romaniser, *v.a.n.* to romanize
Roman-isme, -iste. *V.* page 3, § 1
Romantique, *adj.* romantic; — *s.m.* romantic; romanticism; (*pers.*) romanticist
Romantiquement, *adv.* romantically
Romantiser, *v.a.* to romance
Romantisme, *s.m.* romanticism
Romarin, *s.m.* (*bot.*) rosemary
Rominagrobis, *s.m.* Grimalkin
Rompement, *s.m.* breaking. — *de tête,* head-splitting
Rompre, *v.a.n.* to break; to break asunder; to snap; to break off; to break up; to knock up, to harass, to exhaust; to frustrate, to defeat; to split; to stun; to train, to train up, to break in; to use, to accustom, to inure; to divert, to turn off; to interrupt; to disturb; to discontinue; to stop; to annul; to call off; to part; to retreat; (*phys.*) to refract; (*med.*) to rupture; (*colours*) to blend; (*a blow*) to deaden, to break; (*fenc.*) to draw back (a step). — *les chiens,* (*hunt.*) to call off the dogs; (*fig.*) to break up a band of parasites; to break off the conversation. — *la mesure* or *la semelle,* (*fenc.*) to draw back a step, to draw back, to retire in parrying. — *les mesures de,* to defeat ...'s measures *or* purposes. — *la tête a,* to split ...'s head, to turn ...'s brain, to stun ...'s ears, to importune. *A tout* —, extremely; enthusiastically, frantically
Se —, *v.r.* to break; to break asunder; to get *or* be broken; to break (o.'s ...); to rupture; to snap; to break off *or* up, to discontinue; to accustom *or* &c. oneself; to be refracted. *Se — la tête,* to puzzle *or* rack o.'s brains
Rompu, e, *part. adj.* broken, &c. (*V.* **Rompre**); (*of a ship*) broken-backed, hogged; (*her.*) rompu; — *s.m* remaining fraction
Ronce, *s.f.* briar, bramble; blackberry bush; dewberry; cloudberry; (*fig.*) thorn; obstacle
Ronceraie, *s.f.* briary, brake, thorn-bush
Ronceu-x, se, *adj.* briary, brambly, brambled
Ronciné, e, *adj.* (*bot.*) runcinate
Rond, e, *adj.* round; rounded; plain-dealing, straightforward, fair, frank; (*of accounts*) even; (*of thread*) coarse; (*of the voice, hour*) full
Rond, *s.m.* round; circle; ring; orb; disc. *En* —, in a ring, in a circle, in a round; round; circular; circularly
Rondache, *s.f.* round shield *or* buckler
Ronde, *s.f.* round; (*of songs*) round, roundel, roundelay; semibreve; round hand; patrol. *A la* —, round; around. *Chemin de* —, round-way, way of the rounds; (*fort.*) chemin-des-rondes. *En* —, (*mil.*) on the round. *Être de* —, (*mil.*) to be on o.'s round. *Faire la* —, to go the round. *Faire sa* —, to take o.'s round. *Passer à la* —, to hand round
Rondeau, *s.m.* (*poet., mus.*) rondo, rondeau
Ronde-bosse, *s.f. V.* **Bosse**
Rondelet, te, *adj.* roundish, pretty round, stoutish, plump
Rondelette, *s.f.* (*bot.*) ground-ivy; —**s,** *pl.* Brittany sail-cloth
Rondelle, *s.f.* round; round plate *or* slab; washer; round chisel; round shield, roundel, roundelle
Rondement, *adv.* roundly; frankly; fairly; plainly; sharply, briskly, vigorously; quickly, fast; with a high hand
Rondeur, *s.f.* roundness; rotundity; fulness; plain-dealing, candour, frankness
Rondin, *s.m.* billet; cudgel, stick
Rondiner, *v.a.* to cudgel
Rondir, *v.n. V.* **Arrondir (S')**
Rondotte, *s.f.* (*bot.*) winter-cress, yellow rocket
Rond-point, *s.m.* circus; (*arch.*) apsis
Ronflant, e, *adj.* snoring; sonorous; high-sounding; loud; — *s.m.* high-sounding *or* bombastic style
Ronflement, *s.m.* snoring; snore; snorting; rumbling; booming, roaring, roar; peal; humming
Ronfler, *v.n.* to snore; to snort; to rumble; to boom, to roar; to peal; to hum; to sound
Ronfleu-r, se, *s.m.f.* snorer
†**Ronge-maille,** *s.m.* nibble; — *adj.* nibbling
Rongement, *s.m.* gnawing; nibbling, picking; biting; corrosion
Ronger, *v.a.* to gnaw; to nibble; to eat; to pick (*bones*); to bite; to corrode; to fret; to torment, to prey upon; to eat up *or* away; to wear away; to waste away, to waste; to consume, to devour; to undermine; to ruin; (*rid.*) to champ (*the bit*)
Se —, *v.r.* to be gnawed *or* &c.; to gnaw *or* &c. (o.'s ...); to fret oneself. *Se — le cœur,* to fret, to vex oneself; to despond, to yield to despair
Rongeur, *adj.* gnawing; corroding; eating; biting; wasting; (*zool.*) rodent; — *s.m.* gnawer; corrodent, corrosive; (*zool.*) rodent, gnawer. *Ver* —, gnawing worm; never dying worm, remorse; grief; corrosive
Rongeure, *s.f.* gnawing, nibbling; gnawings, nibblings
Ronron, *s.m.* pur, purring, singing of the cat. *Faire* —, to pur, to sing
Ronronner, *v.n.* to pur, to sing
Roquefort, *s.m.* Roquefort cheese
Roquelaure, *s.f.* (*obsolete*) roquelaure
Roquentin, *s.m.* (*obsolete*) dotard, grey-beard; old beau, old buck
Roquer, *v.n.* (*at chess*) to castle
Roquet, *s.m.* pug-dog; (*pers.*) puppy, cur, dog
Roquette, *s.f.* (*bot.*) rocket
†**Roquille,** *s.f.* (*old*) gill, quartern
Rorage, *s.m.* dew-bleaching, dewing
Rorifère, *adj.* roriferous
***Rorqual,** *s.m.* (*zool.*) rorqual
Rosace, *s.f.* (*arch.*) rose; rose-work; rose-window
Rosacé, e, *adj.* rosaceous; —**e,** *s.f.* rosaceous plant; —**es,** *s.f.pl.* rosaceous plants, rose-tribe, rosaceæ
Rosage, *s.m.* (*bot.*) oleander, rose-bay; (*dyeing*) rosing
Rosaire, *s.m.* rosary, beads
Rosaniline, *s.f.* (*chem.*) rosaniline
Rosat, *adj.* of roses, rose
Rosâtre, *adj.* pinkish
Rosbif, *s.m.* roast beef
Rose, *s.f.* rose; rose-colour; rose-diamond

rose-window; (*fig.*) gem; — *adj.* rosy, rose-coloured, rose, pink; — *s.m.* rose-colour, pink. — *mousseuse* or *moussue*, moss-rose. — *-thé*, tea-rose, tea-scented rose. — *de chien*, dog-rose. — *d'Inde*, African marigold. — *de Noël*, black hellebore. — *du Bengale* or *des quatre saisons*, monthly rose. — *des vents*, compass-card, mariner's card. *Aux doigts de* —, rose-fingered. *Couleur de* —, *V.* **Couleur.** *De* —, rosy, rose. *Eau de* —, rose-water. — **-croix,** *s.f.* Rosy Cross; *s.m.* Rosicrucian

Rosé, e, *adj.* rosy, roseate, pink

Roseau, *s.m.* reed. — *des sables*, calamagrostis, small-reed

Rosée, *s.f.* dew; (*vet.*) oozing blood

Roséine, *s.f.* (*chem.*) roseine

Roselet, *s.m.* (*zool.*) stoat

Roseli-er, ère, *adj.* of reeds, reed. *Marais* —, reed-marsh

Roselière, *s.f.* reed-marsh, reed-field [rash

Roséole, *s.f.* (*med.*) roseola, rose rash, scarlet

Roser, *v.a.* to rose. *Se* —, to become rosy

Roseraie, *s.f.* rosary, rosarium, rosetum

Rosette, *s.f.* rosette; rose; bow-knot, bow; red ink; red chalk; rose-diamond

Rosier, *s.m.* rose-tree, rose-bush

Rosière, *s.f.* winner of the rose (*as the best-behaved girl of her village*)

Rosiériste, *s.m.f.* rose-grower

Rosir, *v.n.* to turn rosy *or* pink

Rosolique, *adj.* (*chem.*) rosolic

Roson, *s.m.* *V.* **Rosace**

Rosse, *s.f.* (*horse, mare*) jade, screw; (*man*) milksop; (*woman*) bitch; (*fish*) roach, ide

Rossée, *s.f.* thrashing, beating, drubbing, hiding, licking [trounce, to lick

Rosser, *v.a.* to thrash, to beat, to drub, to
Se —, *v.r.* to fight, to have a fight *or* a set to

†**Rossignol,** *s.m.* nightingale; pipe, whistle-pipe, whistle, call; picklock, skeleton-key; unsalable book; unsalable stuff *or* goods. — *d'Arcadie*, ass, jackass [nightingale

†**Rossignoler,** *v.n.* to imitate the song of the

†**Rossignolet,** *s.m.* young nightingale

†**Rossignolette,** *s.f.* hen-nightingale

Rossinante, *s.f.m.* Rosinante (*Don Quixote's horse*); — *s.f.* (*fig.*) jade

Rossinien, ne, *adj.* Rossinian

Rossin-isme, -iste. *V.* page 3, § 1

Rossolis, *s.m.* rossolis (*kind of liquor*); (*bot.*)

Rostral, e, *adj.* rostral [sun-dew

Rostre, *s.m.* rostrum

Rostré, e, *adj.* rostrate, rostrated

Rostriforme, *adj.* rostriform [—*s*, to belch

Rot, *s.m.* belch, belching. *Faire un* — or *des*

Rôt, *s.m.* (*obsolete*) roast; roast meat; meal, repast, fare. *Menu* or *petit* —, small game, small birds

Rotacé, e, *adj.* rotate, rotated, wheel-shaped

Rotacisme, *s.m.* rotacism, burring, bur, burr

Rotang, *s.m.* rottang, rattan, ratan

Rota-teur, trice, *adj.* rotatory

Rotateur, *s.m.* rotator; (*zool.*) rotatory (*pl.*, rotatories, rotatoria), rotifer, wheel-animalcule

Rotati-f, ve, *adj.* rotative

Rotation, *s.f.* rotation. *A* —, rotating, rotative, rotatory, rotary

Rotatoire, *adj.* rotatory; rotary; — *s.m.* (*zool.*) *V.* **Rotateur**

Rote, *s.f.* rota; (*anc. mus. instr.*) rote, crowd

Roter, *v.n.* to belch

Roteu-r, se, *s.m.f.* belcher

Rôti, e, *part. adj.* roasted, roast

Rôti, *s.m.* roast, roast meat

Rôtie, *s.f.* toast; slice *or* round of toast. — *de* (or *au*) *beurre*, buttered toast. — *au vin*, toast

Rotifère, *s.m.* (*zool.*) *V.* **Rotateur** [in wine

Rotiforme, *adj.* rotiform, wheel-shaped

Rotin, *s.m.* rattan, ratan; (*pop.*) halfpenny, mag

Rôtir, *v.a.n.* to roast; to broil; to toast; to parch, to burn. — *au four*, to bake

Rôtissage, *s.m.* roasting

Rôtisserie, *s.f.* cook-shop

Rôtisseu-r, se, *s.m.f.* cook-shop keeper. — *en blanc*, poulterer [oven

Rôtissoire, *s.f.* roaster; meat-screen; Dutch

Rotonde, *s.f.* rotunda; back compartment (*of a French stage-coach*); (*of a cloak*) cape. *En* —, in the shape of a rotunda, rotund, round, circular, bow

Rotondité, *s.f.* rotundity; plumpness

Rotule, *s.f.* (*anat.*) patella, knee-cap

Rotundifolié, e, *adj.* (*bot.*) rotundifolious, round-leaved

Roture, *s.f.* commonalty; plebeian state

Roturi-er, ère, *adj.* *s.* plebeian; common, vulgar; commoner [vulgarly

Roturièrement, *adv.* in a plebeian manner;

Rouage, *s.m.* wheel-work; machinery. *En* —, (*mil.*) in flank

Rouan, ne, *adj.*, **Rouan,** *s.m.* roan

Rouanne, *s.f.* marking-iron, branding-iron, brand-iron; (*carp.*) *V.* **Rainette;** (*nav.*) boring-tool [bore (*a pump*)

Rouanner, *v.a.* to mark, to brand; (*nav.*) to

Rouannette, *s.f.* (*carp.*) *V.* **Rainette**

Rouant, *adj.m.* (*her., of the peacock*) in his pride (*with his tail expanded*) [of Roubaix

Roubaisien, ne, *adj.* *s.* of Roubaix; native

Rouble, *s.m.* rouble *or* ruble (*Russian coin*)

Rouc, *s.m.* *V.* **Rock** [roucou

Roucou, *s.m.* (*bot., dyeing*) arnotto, arnatto,

Roucouer, *v.a.* to paint *or* dye with arnotto

Roucoulement, *s.m.* cooing

Roucouler, *v.n.* to coo; — *v.a.* to warble, to warble out *or* forth

Roucouyer, *s.m.* (*bot.*) arnotto-tree

Roudou, *s.m.* (*bot.*) tanners' sumach, myrtle-leaved sumach

Roue, *s.f.* wheel; paddle-wheel; (*artil.*) truck; (*punishment*) rack, wheel; (*of cable*) coil. — *à aubes* or *à pales*, paddle-wheel. — *à eau*, water wheel. — *à rochet*, ratchet-wheel. — *hydraulique*, water-wheel. — *de bois*, truck. — *de compte*, notch wheel. — *de minute*, minute-wheel. — *de rencontre*, balance-wheel. *Chemin de la* —, wheel-race. *Faire la* —, to spread its tail; (*pers.*) to strut, to stalk, to flaunt, to show off; to wheel about; to go round on hands and feet like a wheel. *Pousser à la* —, to lay o.'s shoulder to the wheel, to help on. — **-vis,** *s.f.* screw-wheel

Roué, e, *s.m.f. part. adj.* profligate, rake; crafty man, consummate diplomatist; sharp practitioner; roué; crafty, artful, sharp; very deep; knocked up, spent, broken down (*with fatigue*); run over; broken upon the wheel; (— *de coups*) thrashed soundly

Rouelle, *s.f.* round collop *or* slice; round; fillet (*of veal*) [native of Rouen

Rouennais, e, *adj.* *s.* of Rouen, Rouennese,

Rouennerie, *s.f.* (Rouen) printed calico, printed cotton, print, checked and striped cotton, Rouen fabrics [cotton-printer

Rouennier, *s. m.* (Rouen) calico - printer,

Rouer, *v.a.* to break upon the wheel; to run over; (*fig.*) to harass, to jade, to knock up; (*nav.*) to coil; — *v.n.* (*of peacocks*) to spread out *or* expand his tail. — *de coups*, to thrash soundly, to beat unmercifully

Rouerie, *s.f.* piece of knavery; disreputable *or* low practice; sharp practice; deceit, cheat, trickery, trick, take-in; cunning, craft

Rouet, *s. m.* wheel; spinning-wheel; cog-wheel; (*nav.*) sheave. *Mousquet à* —, wheel-lock *Faire le* —, to pur

Rouette, *s.f.* osier-twig, withe, band

Rouge, *adj.* red; blood-red; red-hot; (*of partridges*, &c.) red-legged; — *s.m.* red; redness; blush, colour; red heat, redness; paint, rouge; (*bird*) shoveller; — *s.f.* red ball (*at billiards*, &c.); red one; — *adv.* red. *Se fâcher tout* —, to be flushed with anger, to be very angry, to be in high dudgeon, to get into a

passion, to get into a regular huff. — *d'Angleterre, — de Prusse*, (*chem.*) colcothar of vitriol, crocus. — **-bord,** *s.m.* bumper *or* brimmer (*of red wine*). — **-gorge,** *s.m.* (*bird*) red-breast, robin red-breast. — **-queue,** *s.m.* (*bird*) red-tail
Rougeâtre, *adj.* reddish
Rougeaud, e, *adj.* ruddy, red-faced, blowzy; — *s.m.f.* ditto person
Rougeole, *s.f.* (*med.*) measles; (*bot.*) cow-wheat
Rouget, te, *adj.* reddish
Rouget, *s.m.* harvest-bug; gurnet; red mullet; surmullet; (*of pigs*) measles
Rougette, *s.f.* (*bat*) *V.* **Roussette**
Rougeur, *s.f.* redness; red tint; blush, colour; red spot; red pimple
Rougi, e, *part. adj.* reddened, &c. (*V.* **Rougir**); red-hot. *V.* **Eau**
Rougir, *v.a.n.* to redden, to make red, to grow *or* get *or* become red; to tinge with red *or* with blood *or* with wine; to make *or* get red-hot; to colour; to blush; to be ashamed
Rougissement, *s.m.* heating red-hot
Rougissure, *s.f* red colour, redness, red
Roui, *s.m.* rancidness; retting, steeping; — *m.*, **e,** *f.*, *adj.* rancid; *part.* retted, steeped. *Sentir le* —, to have a rancid taste
†**Rouille,** *s.f.* rust; rustiness; mildew; blight
†**Rouillé, e,** *part. adj.* rusted; rusty; rust, ferruginous (*water*); blighted
†**Rouillement,** *s.m.* rusting; rustiness
†**Rouiller,** *v.a.* to rust, to make rusty; to blight
Se —, *v.r.* to rust, to get *or* grow rusty; to be blighted
†**Rouilleu-x, se,** *adj.* rust-coloured
†**Rouillure,** *s.f.* rustiness, rust
Rouir, *v.a.* to ret, to steep
Rouissage, *s.m.* retting, steeping
Rouissoir, *s.m.* retting-pond *or* pit *or* tank, rettery
Roulable, *adj.* rollable
Roulade, *s.f.* rolling; roll; (*butch.*) collar; (*mus.*) roulade, division, trill, shake
Roulage, *s.m.* rolling; carriage of goods, goods-carriage (*by land*), carriage, conveyance; waggoning; waggon; waggon-office. *Maison de* —, waggon-office. *Voiture de* —, waggon
Roulant, e, *adj.* rolling; easy; (*mil.*) running; (*of presses*) at work; (*surg., of veins*) moving; —**e,** *s.f.* (*pop.*) carriage
Rouleau, *s.m.* roll; roller; rolling-pin; (*for ribbons*) block; (*of rope*) coil; (*of money*) pile; (*of tobacco*) roll, twist, pig-tail; (*butch.*) collar; (*nat. hist.*) volute; (*arch.*) scroll. *Au bout de son* —, at the end of o.'s tether, at o.'s wits' end
Roulée, *s.f.* thrashing, whacking, licking, drubbing; cutting up, slashing
Roulement, *s.m.* roll, rolling; rumbling; rotation. — *de fonds*, circulation of capital. *Fonds de* —, floating capital
Rouler, *v.a.n.* to roll; to wheel; to roll up; to wind, to wind up; to circulate; to roll on, to get on; to pass away, to pass; to turn over, to revolve; to shoot; to thrash, to whack, to lick, to beat to nothing; to ramble; to rove; to stroll; to turn; to hinge; to rest (upon), to depend (upon); to consist (in); to run upon wheels; to succeed by rotation; to be plentiful; to be stirring; to be at work; to rumble; (*butch.*) to collar. *Faire* —, to set *or* keep going; to trundle
Se —, *v.r.* to roll oneself *or* each other; to roll; to tumble; to wallow; to wind; to fight, to have a set-to; to be rolled *or* &c.
Roulette, *s.f.* roller; truckle; caster; truckle-bed; go-cart; Bath chair; (*book-bind.*) fillet; (*game*) roulette; (*obsolete*) calculating-machine. *Comme sur des —s*, as on casters; very smoothly, very easily, swimmingly, of itself, without the least difficulty
Rouleur, *s.m.* roller; (*insect*) *V.* **Coupe-bourgeons**
Rouleuse, *s.f.* leaf-rolling caterpillar; (*pop.*) street-walker
Roulier, *s.m.* waggoner, carrier
Roulière, *s.f.* waggoner's frock
Roulis, *s.m.* (*nav.*) rolling, roll
Rouloir, *s.m.* rolling-board, roller, cylinder
Roulon, *s.m.* rundle, rung, round; (*of a cart*) standard
Roulure, *s.f.* rolling
Roumain, e, Rouman, e, *adj. s.* Roumanian, Rouman
Rouménien, ne, Rouméliote, *adj. s.* of Roumelia, Roumelian, native of Roumelia
Roupe, *s.f.* smockfrock, smock
Roupie, *s.f.* snivel; (*coin*) rupee
Roupieu-x, se, *adj.* snivelly, snivelling
†**Roupiller,** *v.n.* to doze, to snooze
†**Roupilleu-r, se,** *s.m.f.* dozer, snoozer
Rouquet, *s.m.* buck-hare
Roure. *V.* **Rouvre**
Roussâtre, *adj.* reddish, russet
Rousseau, *adj.m.* red-haired; — *s.m.* red-haired fellow; (*duck*) gadwall
Rousselet, *s.m.* (*pear*) rousselet, russet
Rousserolle, *s.f.* (*bird*) sedge-warbler, reed-warbler
Roussette, *s.f.* spotted dog-fish; (*bat*) roussette, pteropus, kalong, flying fox; (*sugar-manu.*) cane-juice
Rousseur, *s.f.* redness, carrotiness; freckle. *Tache de* —, freckle
Roussi, *s.m.* burnt; burning; burnt smell, smell of burning; —**e,** *s.f.* (*agr.*) liquid manure tank, urinarium; — *m.*, **e,** *f.*, *part. of* **Roussir**
†**Roussillon,** *s.m.* roussillon (*wine*)
†**Roussillonnais, e,** *adj. s.* of Roussillon, Roussillonese, native of Roussillon
Roussin, *s.m.* thickset stallion; pack-horse; roadster. — *d'Arcadie*, ass, jackass, donkey, moke
Roussir, *v.a.n.* to redden; to scorch; to singe. [*Faire* —, (*cook.*) to brown
Roussissage, *s.m.* dyeing red
Rouster, *v.a.* (*nav.*) to woold
Rousture, *s.f.* (*nav.*) woolding
Rout, *s.m.* *V.* **Raout**
†**Routailler,** *v.a.* (*hunt.*) to track
Route, *s.f.* road, route; way; journey; track, course; run; path; direction. *Grande* — *grand'*—, main road, high road, high way. *En* —, on the road *or* way; on o.'s way *or* journey; off; on; in progress; all right! go on! *Faire* —, to travel, to go; (*nav.*) to sail, to stand (for), to steer its course (to). *Faire fausse* —, to alter the ship's course; to take a wrong way; to take the wrong step; to make a mistake, to be mistaken
Routier, *s.m.* stager; guide; pilot; shrewd *or* crafty fellow; road-book, tract-chart; sailing-directions, directory
Routi-er, ère, *adj.* of roads, road. *Carte* —*ère*, road-map. *Locomotive* — *ère*, road locomotive, road-engine, road-steamer
Routin, *s.m.* path
Routine, *s.f.* routine; rote
Routiner, *v.a.* to accustom, to use; to teach; to drill
Routini-er, ère, *s.m.f.* person acting by routine; — *adj.* of routine; routine-like
Routinièrement, *adv.* by routine, by rote, in a routine-like way *or* manner
Routoir. *V.* **Rouissoir**
Rouverin, *adj.* hot-short, brittle
Rouvet, *s.m.* (*bot.*) casia, poet's casia
Rouvieu-x, se, *adj.* mangy
Rouvieux, *s.m.* mange
Rouvre, *s.m.* common oak ("*quercus robur*")
Rouvrir, *v.a.*, **Se** —, *v.r.* to reopen, to open again
Rou-x, sse, *adj.* red, sandy, carroty; russet; browned; red-haired; (*hist.*) Rufus. — **-vieux,** *V.* **Rouvieux**
Roux, *s.m.* red; russet; (*cook.*) browned butter, drawn butter, thickening, roux
Royal, e, *adj.* royal; regal, kingly; —**e,** *s.f.* tuft of beard under the lip, imperial

Royalement, *adv.* royally [royalized
Royaliser, *v.a.* to royalize. *Se* —, to become
Royal-isme, -iste. *V.* page 3, § 1
Royaume, *s.m.* kingdom; realm
Royauté, *s.f.* royalty
Ru, *s.m.* channel *or* bed (*of a little stream*)
Ruade, *s.f.* kick; kicking; fling
Rubace, Rubacelle, *s.f.* (*jewel.*) rubasse; rubicel, rubicelle
Ruban, *s.m.* ribbon, riband; tape; band; string. — *d'eau,* (*bot.*) bur-reed. *Canon à* —, twisted barrel [twisted
Rubané, e, *part. adj.* ribboned; ribbon-like;
Rubaner, *v.a.* to ribbon; to twist
Rubanerie, *s.f.* ribbon-weaving; ribbon-trade; ribbons, finery
Rubani-er, ère, *s.m.f.* ribbon-weaver; — *adj.* of ribbons, ribbon; — *s.m.* (*bot.*) bur-reed
Rubarbe, *V.* **Rhubarbe**
Rubasse. *V.* **Rubace**
Rubéfaction, *s.f.* rubefaction, rubification
Rubéfiant, e, *adj.*, **Rubéfiant,** *s.m.* rubefa-
Rubéfier, *v.a.*, **Se** —, *v.r.* to rubify [cient
Rubéole, *s. f.* (*bot.*) cross-wort; (*med.*) *V.* **Roséole** [measly
Rubéolique, *adj.* rubeolic, of the measles,
Rubescent, e, *adj.* rubescent [tribe
Rubiacées, *s.f.pl.* (*bot.*) rubiaceæ, madder-
Rubiacine, *s.f.* (*chem.*) rubiacine
Rubiacique, *adj.* (*chem.*) rubiacic [colour
Rubican, *adj. m.* rubican; — *s.m.* rubican
Rubicelle, *s.f. V.* **Rubace**
Rubicolle, *adj.* (*zool.*) red-breasted; — *s.f.* (*bird*) stonechat
Rubicond, e, *adj.* rubicund, blowzy
Rubidium, *s.m.* (*chem.*) rubidium
Rubigineu-x, se, *adj.* rubiginous
Rubis, *s.m.* ruby; (*horol.*) jewel; (*zool.*) ruby-throated humming-bird; (*fam.*) pimple, grog-blossom. — *sur l'ongle,* exactly, to the last farthing; to the last drop. *Monté sur* —, (*horol.*) jewelled. *Nez de* —, red nose
Rubricaire, *s.m.* rubricist, rubrician
Rubrique, *s.f.* reddle, ruddle, red chalk; rubric; rule, method, practice; heading, head, title; imprint; intelligence; trick, game
Ruche, *s. f.* hive, bee-hive; swarm; (*need.*) quilling, ruche. — *d'abeilles,* bee-hive
Ruchée, *s.f.* hiveful
Rucher, *s.m.* apiary, bee-garden, bee-house; — *v.a.* (*need.*) to quill [churlish
Rudâni-er, ère, *adj.* rough, gruff, surly,
Rude, *adj.* rough; rugged; harsh; hard; steep; blunt; coarse; rude; severe, rigid, strict; difficult; troublesome; disagreeable; painful; fatiguing; dreaded, formidable, terrible; fierce; violent; boisterous; sharp, vigorous; bold, plucky; extreme, famous, remarkable; — *s.m.* (*pop.*) brandy; — *s.f.* (*pop.*) bouncer
Rudement, *adv.* roughly; ruggedly; harshly; hardly; bluntly; coarsely; rudely; severely, strictly; disagreeably; painfully; fiercely; violently; boisterously; formidably; terribly; sharply, vigorously; boldly, pluckily; extremely, famously, remarkably; enormously; with a vengeance
Rudenté, e, *adj.* (*arch.*) cabled
Rudenture, *s.f.* (*arch.*) rudenture, cabling
Rudesse, *s.f.* roughness; ruggedness; harshness; hardness; steepness; bluntness; coarseness; rudeness; rude thing, incivility; severity, strictness; fierceness; violence;
Rudiment, *s.m.* rudiment [boisterousness
Rudimentaire, *adj.* rudimental, rudimentary
Rudoyer, *v.a.* to use *or* treat roughly *or* harshly, to deal roughly *or* harshly with; to speak harshly to; to ill-treat; to bully, to bullirag
Rue, *s.f.* street; (*bot.*) rue. — *barrée!* no thoroughfare! *Grande* —, high-street. *Courir les* —*s,* to run about the streets; to be current, to be in everybody's mouth; to be known to everybody; to be very common. *Les* —*s en sont pavées,* it is as common as mud
Ruée, *s.f.* laystall
Ruelle, *s.f.* lane; by-street; alley; wall-side (*of a bed*); (*obsolete*) bed-chamber, lady's cabinet *or* alcove; lady's private *or* select circle *or* assembly, intimate party, ruelle
Rueller, *v.a.* to mould (*vines*)
Ruellie, *s.f.* (*bot.*) ruellia
Ruer, *v.n.* (*of beasts*) to kick; — *v.a.* (*old*) to throw, to fling, to hurl; to strike
Se —, *v.r* to rush [ing; kicker
Rueu-r, se, *adj. s.* that kicks, given to kick-
Rugine, *s.f.* (*surg.*) rugine, rasp, scalp; (*dentist's*) scaling-instrument, tooth-scaler [scale
Ruginer, *v.a.* (*surg.*) to rasp, to scrape, to
Rugir, *v.n.* to roar; to yell
Rugissement, *s.m.* roar, roaring; yell
Rugosité, *s.f.* rugosity, roughness, unevenness, wrinkle [uneven, wrinkled
Rugueu-x, se, *adj.* rugose, rugous, rough,
Ruilée, *s.f.* (*build.*) jointing, verge
Ruine, *s.f.* ruin; ruination; destruction; disaster; overthrow; fall; downfall; desolation; decay; waste; loss
Ruiner, *v.a.n.* to ruin; to destroy; to spoil; to overthrow; to undo; to be ruinous
Se —, *v.r.* to decay; to be ruined; to ruin oneself; to lose o.'s fortune
Ruineusement, *adv.* ruinously
Ruineu-x, se, *adj.* ruinous; decayed; in ruins
Ruinure, *s.f.* (*carp.*) housing, bearing
Ruisseau, *s.m.* stream; brook, rivulet, runlet, streamlet, rill; (*of streets*) gutter, kennel; (*fig.*) flood, stream, torrent. *Les petits* —*x font les grandes rivières,* many a little makes a mickle [down; to trickle, to trickle down
Ruisseler, *v.n.* to stream; to gush; to run
Ruisselet, *s.m.* rivulet, runlet, streamlet
Rum, *s.m.* rum [rhumb-line
Rumb, *s.m.* (*nav.*) rhumb, rhomb. — *de vent,*
Rumen, *s.m.* (*of ruminants*) rumen, paunch
Rumeur, *s.f.* rumour, report: uproar, clamour; noise; murmur; stir
Rumex, *s.m.* (*bot.*) rumex, dock
Rumicine, *s.f.* (*chem.*) rumicine [ruminant
Ruminant, e, *adj.*, **Ruminant,** *s. m.*
Rumination, *s.f.* rumination
Ruminer, *v.a.n.* to ruminate; to muse (on), to think (over), to turn (over)
Rumpsteak, *s.m.* rumpsteak
Runciné, e, *adj.* (*bot.*) runcinate
Runes, *s.f.pl.* runes
Runique, *adj.* runic
Runologue, *s.m.* runologist
Ruolz, *s.m. V.* **Plaqué,** *s.m.*; (*fig.*) brummagem
Ruotte, *s.f.* (*agr.*) trench
Rupestre, *adj.* growing *or* living on rocks
Rupia, *s.m.* (*med.*) rupia
Rupicole, *adj. V.* **Rupestre;** — *s.m.* (*bird*) rupicola, cock of the rock
Rupin, *s.m.* (*pop.*) swell
Rupture, *s.f.* rupture; breaking; breaking off *or* up; breaking open; bursting; rent; mixing of colours. — *de ban,* escape from banishment
Rural, e, *adj.* rural, country, field, farm
Ruralement, *adv.* rurally
Ruralité, *s.f.* rurality
Ruse, *s.f.* artifice; cunning, craft, deceit; stratagem; plot; trick; trickery; dodge; doubling; ruse
Rusé, e, *adj.* artful, deceitful, cunning, crafty, sly, shrewd, sharp, subtle; — *s.m.f.* artful *or* &c. person, cunning one, knowing one
Ruser, *v.n.* to use artifice *or* deceit *or* cunning; to use stratagems; to shuffle, to shift, to dodge; to double
Ruseu-r, se, *s.m.f.* shuffler, dodger, trickster
Rusma, *s.m.* rusma
Russe, *adj. s.m.f.* Russian; Russian fashion
Russo-, (*in compounds*) Russo-. . .

Rustaud, e, *adj. s.* rustic; coarse; boorish; boor
Rustaudement, *adv. V.* **Rustiquement**
Ruste, *s.m.* (*her.*) *V.* **Rustre**
Rusticage, *s.m.* (*build.*) rustication
Rusticité, *s.f.* rusticity, boorishness
Rustique, *adj.* rustic; rural; country; rude, coarse, boorish; artless; (*arch.*) rustic; — *s.m.*(*arch.*) rustic order; (*obsolete*) rustic, peasant
Rustiquement, *adv.* rustically; roughly, boorishly [cast, to rusticate
Rustiquer, *v.a.* (*build.*) to jag out, to rough-
Rustre, *adj. s.m.f.* boorish; rustic, boor, clodhopper, churl, bumpkin; — *s.m.* (*her.*) rustre
Rut, *s.m.* rut, rutting. *Être en* —, to rut
Rutabaga, *s. m.* rutabaga, Swedish turnip,
Rutacées, *s.f.pl.* (*bot.*) rutaceæ [swede
Ruthénium, *s.m.* (*chem.*) ruthenium
Rutilant, e, *part. adj.* rutilant, shining,
Rutile, *s.m.* (*min.*) rutile [brilliant
Rutiler, *v.n.* to rutilate, to shine
Rutilite, *s.f.* (*min.*) rutilite
Rutoir. *V.* **Routoir**
Ryder, *s.m.* ryder (*Dutch coin*)
Ryott, *s.m.* ryot (*in Hindostan*)
Rythme. *V.* **Rhythme**

S

S, *s.f.* (*letter*) s; (*tech.*) *V.* **Esse.** *Faire des* —, to reel about, to stagger along
S', [*an elision for* **Se,** *and also for* **Si** (if, whether) *before* "il" *or* "ils"]
Sa, *adj. poss.f.* his (own), her (own), its (own), one's (own); their (own)
†**Sabadilline,** *s.f.* (*chem.*) sabadilline
Sabaïsme, *s.m. V.* **Sabéisme**
Sabaye, *s.f.* (*nav.*) mooring-rope; boat-rope
Sabbat, *s.m.* sabbath; nocturnal meeting *or* meetings (*of witches*), nightly revel *or* revels (*of ditto*); witches' work; racket, uproar, row, dust, shindy; scolding, jobation; caterwauling
Sabbataire, *s.m.f. adj.* sabbatarian
Sabbatie, *s.f.* (*bot.*) sabbatia
Sabbatique, *adj.* sabbatic, sabbatical
Sabéen, ne, *adj. s.* Sabæan, Sabian
Sabéisme, *s.m.* Sabæism, Sabeism, Sabaism
Sabin, e, *s.m.f. adj.* Sabine; Sabine woman
Sabine, *s.f.* (*bot.*) savin, savine
Sabisme, *s.m. V.* **Sabéisme** [(*her.*) sable
Sable, *s.m.* sand; gravel; ballast; hour-glass;
Sabler, *v.a.* to gravel; to sand; to toss off, to
Sableu-x, se, *adj.* sandy [quaff
Sablier, *s.m.* sand-glass, hour-glass, glass; egg-glass; sand-box; sandman, dealer in sand; (*bot.*) sand-box tree
Sablière, *s. f.* sand-pit; gravel-pit; (*carp.*) wall-plate; ground-plate
Sabline, *s.f.* (*bot.*) sandwort
Sablon, *s.m.* small sand, fine sand, sand
Sablonner, *v.a.* to scour with sand
Sablonneu-x, se, *adj.* sandy; gravelly; gritty
Sablonnier, *s m.* sandman, dealer in sand
Sablonnière, *s.f.* sand-pit; gravel-pit
Sabord, *s.m.* (*nav.*) port-hole, gun-port, port
Sabordement, *s.m.* (*nav.*) scuttling
Saborder, *v.a.* (*nav.*) to scuttle
Sabot, *s.m.* wooden shoe, clog, sabot; lady's stirrup, foot-stall; hoof; skid, drag; slipper-bath; freezing-pot, ice-mould; whipping-top, top; sorry violin; bad ship, old tub; bad billiard-table; (*tech.*) shoe; ferrule; socket; (*of ploughs*) slade; (*nav.*) heel; (*artil.*) bottom, sabot; (*zool.*) turbo (*shell*) — *littoral,* (*zool.*) periwinkle, winkle. *Dormir comme un* —, to sleep like a top
Sabotage, *s.m.* making of wooden shoes
Saboter, *v.a.* to bungle, to botch; (*tech.*) to shoe; — *v.n.* to whip a top
Saboteu-r, se, *s.m.f.* bungler
Saboti-er, ère, *s.m f.* maker *or* seller of wooden shoes; wearer of wooden shoes; bungler; — *s. f. V.* **Sorbetière;** (*dance*) sabotière
Sabouler, *v.a.* to pull about, to worry; to bully, to bullirag; to tumble; to blow up, to scold; to do badly, to bungle, to botch
Sabre, *s.m.* sabre, broadsword, sword; back-sword. — *de bois!* zooks! zookers! zounds! hang it! bless me! — **-baïonnette,** *s.m.* sabre-bayonet, sword-bayonet, rifle-sword. — **-poignard,** *s.m.* sabre-poniard, dirk
Sabrenas, *s.m.* cobbler, botcher, bungler
Sabrenasser, Sabrenauder, *v.a.* to cobble, to botch, to bungle
Sabrer, *v.a.* to slash about, to cut with a sabre, to cut, to sabre; to bungle, to botch, to hurry
Sabretache, *s.f.* (*mil.*) sabretache [over
Sabreur, *s m.* slasher, hard-fighter; swash-buckler, hector, bully, bloodthirsty soldier; bungler, botcher
Sabulicole, *adj.* growing *or* living in sand
Saburral, e, *adj.* (*med.*) saburral
Saburre, *s f.* (*med.*) saburra, foulness of the stomach, sordes
Sac, *s.m.* bag; sack; knapsack; pouch; crib (*of a coach-box*); poke-net; sac; sack-cloth; sacking, sack, pillage. — *de nuit,* travelling-bag, carpet-bag. — *à ouvrage,* work-bag. — *à papier!* zooks! zookers! zounds! hang it! bless me! — *à plomb,* shot-pouch. — *à* (*or de*) *sable,* — *à* (*or de*) *terre,* sand-bag, earth-bag. — *à vin,* drunkard. *Course en* —, jumping in sacks. *Homme de* — *et de corde,* regular ruffian. *Être dans le* —, to be in a fair way. *Faire le* — *de, Mettre à* —, *V.* **Saccager.** *Mettre au* —, *V.* **Saccager;** (*pers.*) to nonplus. *Prendre or trousser son* — *et ses quilles,* to pack off bag and baggage, to pack off, to be off
Sacatra, *s.m.* man of colour
Saccade, *s f.* jerk; shake; jolt; whim, freak, fit; scolding, blowing-up; (*rid.*) saccade
Saccadé, e, *part. adj.* jerked; by jerks; abrupt; broken; irregular; fitful
Saccader, *v.a.* to jerk; to break, to cut up
Saccage, *s. m.* confusion; confused heap; jumble; havoc
Saccagement, *s.m.* sacking, sack, ransacking, plundering, plunder, pillage
Saccager, *v.a* to sack, to ransack, to plunder; to break and destroy; to overturn; to rum-
Saccageur, *s.m.* sacker [mage
Saccatier, *s.m.* coal-heaver
‡**Saccharate,** *s.m.* saccharate
‡**Sacchareu-x, se,** *adj.* saccharous
‡**Sacchariféré,** *adj.* sacchariferous
‡**Saccharifiable,** *adj.* saccharifiable
‡**Saccharification,** *s.f.* saccharification
‡**Saccharifier,** *v.a.,* **Se** —, *v.r.* to saccharify
‡**Saccharimètre,** *s.m.* saccharometer
‡**Saccharimétr-ie, -ique.** *V.* page 3, § 1
‡**Saccharin, e,** *adj.* saccharine
‡**Saccharique,** *adj.* saccharic
‡**Saccharoïde,** *adj.* saccharoid, saccharoidal
Saccifère, *adj.* sacciferous
Sacciforme, *adj.* sacciform; bagged
Saccomys, *s.m.* (*zool.*) saccomys
Sacerdoce, *s. m.* priesthood; sacerdotal character *or* office; sacred character *or* office; office; mission
Sacerdotal, e, *adj.* sacerdotal, priestly
Sachée, *s.f.* bagful, sackful
Sachem, *s.m.* sachem (*American Indian chief*)
Sachet, *s.m.* satchel; sachet, scent-bag, sweet-bag, perfume-cushion; nose-bag
Sacoche, *s.f.* saddle-bag; money-bag; courier-bag; phial, bottle
Sacraire, *s.m.* sacrarium [sacramentary
Sacramentaire, *s.m. adj.* sacramentarian;
Sacramental, e, *adj.* (*old spelling*) *V.* **Sacramentel** [**Sacramentellement**
Sacramentalement, *adv.* (*old spelling*) *V.*

Sacramentel, le, *adj.* sacramental; formal; solemn; essential, decisive; binding
Sacramentellement, *adv.* sacramentally
Sacre, *s.m.* coronation; consecration; (*bird, anc. cannon*) saker; (*pers.*) blackguard
Sacré, e, *part. adj.* (*generally after the noun*) sacred; holy; inviolable; consecrated; anointed, crowned; (*fam., always before the noun*) cursed, confounded, blasted, damned; (*anat.*) sacral; — *s.m.* sacred, sacred thing *or* things. — **-chien,** *s.m.* (*pop.*) brandy; spirit, fire, genius; humour. — *chien!* — *mâtin!* — *nom!* by Jove! confound it! damn! damn it! — *nom d'un chien,* &c., *V.* **Nom.** — *nom de Dieu!* Goddam! [it! confound ...!
Sacrebleu, *int.* by Jove! dash it! confound
Sacrement, *s.m.* sacrament; (*jest.*) matrimony, marriage. *Saint* —, holy sacrament; (*Cath. rel.*) host; monstrance
Sacrer, *v.a.* to anoint, to crown; to consecrate;
Sacret, *s.m.* sakeret [— *v.n.* to curse, to swear
Sacrifiable, *adj.* sacrificable
Sacrifica-teur, trice, *s.m.f.* sacrificer; — *adj.* sacrificing
Sacrificatoire, *adj.* sacrificatory
Sacrificature, *s.f.* sacrificership
Sacrifice, *s.m.* sacrifice; offering
Sacrifier, *v.a.n.* to sacrifice; to devote
Sacrilége, *adj.* sacrilegious; — *s.m.* sacrilege; — *s.m.f.* sacrilegious person, sacrilegist
Sacrilégement, *adv.* sacrilegiously
Sacripant, *s.m.* bully, fire-eater, swaggerer, hector; scamp, rascal, blackguard
Sacristain, *s.m.* sacristan, sacrist, sexton
Sacristi, *int. V.* **Sapristi**
Sacristie, *s.f.* sacristy, vestry, vestry-room; sacrament-plate, church-plate; church-fees
Sacristine, *s.f.* vestry-nun
Sacro-, (*in compounds, anat.*) sacro-...
Sacrum, *s.m.* (*anat.*) sacrum, os sacrum
Sadder, *s.m.* sadder, sadda [Sadducee
Saducéen, ne, *adj.* Sadducean; — *s.m.f.*
Saducéisme, *s.m.* Sadduceeism, Sadduceism,
Saette. *V.* **Sagette** [Sadducism
Safran, *s.m.* saffron; crocus
Safrané, e, *adj.* saffron
Safraner, *v.a.* to saffron
Safranier, *s.m.* saffron-grower
Safranière, *s.f.* saffron-plantation
Safranum, *s.m.* (*chem.*) safflower
Safre, *s.m.* (*chem.*) zaffer, zaffre, saffre; — *adj.*
Saga, *s.f.* Saga [gluttonous, greedy
Sagace, *adj.* sagacious, acute, shrewd, judi-
Sagacement, *adv.* sagaciously [cious
Sagacité, *s.f.* sagacity, sagaciousness, acuteness, shrewdness
Sagaie. *V.* **Zagaie** [mush
Sagamité, *s.f.* maize hasty-pudding, hominy,
Sagamore, *s.m.* sagamore (*American Indian chief*) [pen
Sagapénum, *s.m.* (*pharm.*) sagapenum, saga-
Sage, *adj.* wise; sensible; judicious; discreet; prudent; cautious; sober; regular, steady; chaste; well-behaved; (*of children*) good; (*of animals*) gentle, quiet; — *s.m.* wise man; prudent man, cautious man; sage. *Femme* —, well-behaved woman. — **-femme,** *s.f.* midwife, accoucheuse
Sagement, *adv.* wisely; sensibly; judiciously; discreetly; prudently; cautiously; soberly; steadily; chastely
Sagesse, *s.f.* wisdom; discretion, prudence; caution; sobriety; steadiness; chastity; propriety; good conduct; (*of children*) goodness, good conduct; (*of animals*) gentleness
Sagette, *s.f.* (*old*) arrow; (*bot.*) arrow-head
Sagination, *s.f.* sagination, fattening, fatting
Sagine, *s.f.* (*bot.*) pearl-grass, pearl-wort
Sagittaire, *s. m.* sagittary, archer; (*astr.*) Sagittarius; — *s.f.* (*bot.*) arrow-head
Sagittal, e, *adj.* sagittal [headed
Sagitté, e, *adj.* sagittate, arrow-shaped, arrow-
Sagou, *s.m.* sago. *Palmier* —, sago-palm, sago-
Sagouier. *V.* **Sagoutier** [tree
Sagouin, *s.m.* (*zool.*) sagouin, squirrel-monkey; (*pers.*) sloven, dirty fellow [mopsey
Sagouine, *s.f.* (*zool.*) she-sagouin; (*pers.*) slut,
Sagoutier, *s.m.* (*bot.*) sago-palm, sago-tree
Sagre, *s.m.* (*insect*) sagra
Sagum, *s.m.* (*Rom. antiq.*) sagum
Saie, *s.f.* sagum, cloak, tunic, frock; goldsmith's
Saietter, *v.a.* (*tech.*) to brush [brush
Saïga, *s.m.* (*zool.*) saiga (*antelope*)
†Saignant, e, *adj.* bleeding; bloody; nearly raw, underdone, (*in America*) rare, rear
†Saignée, *s.f.* bleeding; small of the arm; trench; drain. *Faire une* —, to bleed; to drain
†Saignement, *s.m.* bleeding
†Saigner, *v.a.n.* to bleed; to draw out blood; to drain; to stick; to kill. — *du* (or *au*) *nez,* to bleed at the nose; to want courage, to show the white feather; to retract
Se —, *v.r.* to bleed oneself; to drain oneself; to make a sacrifice; to be bled *or* &c.
†Saigneur, *s.m.* bleeder, blood-letter
†Saigneu-x, se, *adj.* bloody. *Bout* —, scrag end, scrag; scrag of mutton
†Saillant, e, *adj.* projecting; jutting; prominent; high; striking; sharp; salient; — *s.m.* (*fort.*) salient
†Saillie, *s.f.* start; projection; protuberance; jutting, jutting out; relief; seat; fit; sally; flight; flash; witticism; ledge; spindle; leap; (*tech.*) flange. *A* —*s,* flush. *En* —, projecting, jutting, sticking out. *Être en* —, *faire* —, to project; to jut out; to stand out; to stick out
†Saillir, *v.n.* to project, to protrude, to jut, to jut out; to stand out; to gush, to gush out; — *v.a.* to serve, to leap, to cover
Sain, e, *adj.* sound; healthy; wholesome; clean; clear; sane; pure; sound-headed. — *et sauf,* safe, uninjured, safe and sound
Sainbois, *s.m. V.* **Garou**
Saindoux, *s.m.* lard [somely
Sainement, *adv.* soundly; healthily; whole-
Saineté, *s.f. V.* **Sanité** [grass
Sainfoin, *s.m.* (*bot.*) sainfoin, saintfoin, French
Saint, e, *adj. s.* holy; sainted; sacred; consecrated; sanctified; godly; righteous; religious; good; blessed; before Easter, in (*or* of) Passion-week; saint; patron saint. *La* — ..., the day *or* feast of Saint ... *La* —*-Barthélemy,* St. Bartholomew's day. *La* — *-Jean,* St. John's day, Midsummer day, Midsummer. *Le Très* —, the Holy One. —*e journée,* blessed day. *Ne savoir à quel* — *se vouer,* not to know which way to turn. — **-Augustin,** *s.m. V.* **Augustin.** — **-Crépin,** *s.m. V.* **Crépin.** — **-Cyr,** *s.m.* Saint-Cyr (*formerly a convent-school for the daughters of military officers; now, a military school*). — **-cyrien,** *s.m.* cadet of the St. Cyr military school, Saint-Cyrian. — **-cyrien, ne,** *adj.* of St. Cyr. — **e-barbe,** *s.f.* (*nav.*) powder-room, gun-room. — **-Elme.** *Feu* — *Elme, V.* **Feu.** — **-Émilion,** *s.m.* Saint-Émilion (wine). —**e-nitouche,** *s.f. V.* **Nitouche.** —**e-Pélagie,** *s.f.* (*formerly a debtors' prison; now, a political prison*). — **-Estèphe,** *s.m.* Saint-Estèphe (wine). — **-Germain,** *s.m.* Saint-Germain (*town near Paris; kind of pear*) [*V.* **Faubourg**]. — **-Julien,** *s.m.* Saint Julien (wine). — **-Martin,** *V.* **Martin.** — **-Péray,** *s.m.* Saint-Péray (wine). — **-simonien, ne,** *adj. s.* Saint-Simonian, communistic, communist. — **-simonisme,** *s.m.* Saint-Simonianism, communism
Saintement, *adv.* holily; sacredly; saintly; piously; religiously
Sainteté, *s.f.* holiness; sanctity; sacredness; godliness; piety; religion; holy images, &c., articles of devotion
Saintongeois, e, *adj. s.* of Saintonge; native
Saïque, *s.f.* (*nav.*) saic [of ditto
Saisi, e, *adj.* seized, &c. (*V.* **Saisir**); pos-

sessed; struck; impressed; thrilled; burnt; applied to; made cognizant (of); called upon to consider; having (...) put into o.'s hands; (*law*) distrained, distressed; — *s.m.f.* (*law*) party distrained

Saisie, *s.f.* (*law*) seizure; distress; execution. — **-arrêt,** *s.f.* attachment. — **-brandon,** *s.f.* execution on growing crops. — **-exécution,** *s.f.* distress for rent, distress. — **-gagerie,** *s.f.* execution by way of security, distress for rent, distress. — **-revendication,** *s.f.* attachment of goods claimed pending litigation of

Saisine, *s.f.* (*law*) seizin; (*nav.*) gripe [claim

Saisir, *v.a.* to seize; to lay *or* take hold of; to grasp; to catch up; to catch; to snatch; to strike; to seize with fear *or* grief *or* joy, to give a shock to, to shock, to impress, to startle, to thrill; to chill; to avail oneself of; to understand; to perceive; to overhear; to notice, to mark; to distrain, to distress; to attach; to vest; to put in possession (of); to make cognizant (of); to call upon (...) to consider; to put (...) into the hands of; to present (...) to; to have (...) submitted to; to lay (...) before; to bring (...) before (*a court of jus ice*, &c.); (*cook.*) to set; (*nav.*) to span; to bind; to secure. — **-arrêter,** *v.a.*(*law*) to attach. — **-exécuter,** *v.a.* to distrain, to distress

Se —, *v.r.* to seize; to lay hold; to grasp; to snap up; to catch; to arrest; to apprehend; to secure; to take possession; to take cognizance; to consider; to be seized *or* &c.

Saisissable, *adj.* seizable; distrainable; attachable

Saisissant, e, *adj.* impressive; piercing; thrilling; startling; striking; chilling; —*s.m.f.* distrainer, seizer

Saisissement, *s.m.* chill; shock; pang; startling; thrill; (*of criminals*) pinioning

Saison, *s.f.* season; time; weather. — *nouvelle,* spring. *Morte-* —, dead season. *De* —, in season; seasonable; seasonably; timely. *Hors de* —, out of season; unseasonable; unseasonably. *En pleine* —, in its prime. *Marchand des quatre* —*s,* costermonger

Saisonner, *v.n.* to yield an abundant crop

Saisonni-er, ère, *adj.* (*med.*) peculiar to a

Sajou, *s.m. V.* **Sapajou** [season

Saki, *s.m.* (*zool.*) saki, fox-tailed monkey;

Sal, *s.m.* sal (*tree, wood*) [(*Japanese beer*) saki

Salabre, *s.m.* (*fish.*) ground-net; coral-net

Salace, *adj.* salacious

Salacité, *s.f.* salaciousness, salacity

Salade, *s.f.* salad; salading; (*for horses*) mess; (*obsolete*) sallet, helmet

Saladier, *s.m.* salad-bowl; salad-basket

Salage, *s.m.* salting

Salaire, *s.m.* hire; pay; wages; reward, recompense, retribution; punishment; (*not in common use*) salary

Salaison, *s.f.* salting; salt-provisions

Salamalec, *s.m.* low bow

Salamandre, *s.f.* salamander; newt, eft

Salanga, Salangane, *s.f.* (*zool.*) esculent swallow, Chinese swallow, edible nest swallow

Salant, *adj.m.* salt, saline

Salarias, *s.m.* salarias, leaping fish

Salariat, *s.m.* wages system, receiving wages

Salarié, e, *part. adj.* paid, hired; salaried; — *s.m.f.* person receiving pay *or* wages *or* a salary; hired workman *or* labourer; hireling; placeman

Salarier, *v.a.* to give a stipend to, to pay, to hire, to give wages to, to pay wages *or* hire to, to reward; to salary

Salaud, e, *adj. s. V.* **Salop**

Saldo, *s.m.* final settlement; balance

Sale, *adj.* dirty; nasty, filthy; foul; in a mess; coarse, low, loose; unclean; sordid; beastly; (*of colours*) dull; — *s.m.f.* dirty person, sloven, slut; — *s.m.* dirtiness, filthiness; foulness; dirty linen

Salé, e, *adj.* salt, salted; salty; corned; jerked; pickled; pointed, keen, biting, sharp; dirty, loose, coarse; strong, stiff; awfully dear

Salé, *s.m.* salt pork. *Petit-* —, half-salted pork

Salement, *adv.* dirtily; nastily, filthily; foully; slovenly; basely

Salentin, e, *adj. s.* Salentine

Salep, *s.m.* salep

Saler, *v.a.* to salt; to put salt into; to corn; to cure; to pickle; to jerk; to fleece, to overcharge; to swell (*a bill*), to lay it on stiff; to

Se —, *v.r.* to be salted, &c. [scold, to blow up

Saleron, *s.m.* bowl of a salt-cellar

Saleté, *s.f.* dirt; dirtiness; filth; filthiness; soil; obscenity, dirty expression; dirty *or* nasty thing; dirty trick

Saleu-r, se, *s.m.f.* salter; curer

Salicaire, *s.f.* (*bot.*) salicaria, purple willow; (*zool.*) *V.* **Rousserolle**

Salicine, *s.f.* (*chem.*) salicine

Salicole, *adj.* salicultural

Salicoque, *s.f.* shrimp [wort; saltwort

Salicor, *s.m.,* **Salicorne,** *s.f.* (*bot.*) glass-

Saliculture, *s.f.* saliculture

Salicyleux, *adj.m.* (*chem.*) salicylous

Salicylique, *adj.* (*chem.*) salicylic

Salien, ne, *adj. s.* Salian

Salière, *s.f.* salt-cellar; salt-box; salt-holder; (*of horses*) eye-pit; (*pers., pop.*) hollow (*behind*

Salifère, *adj.* saliferous [*the collar-bone*)

Salifiable, *adj.* salifiable

Salification, *s.f.* salification

Salifier, *v.a.* to salify

Saligaud, e, *adj. s. V.* **Salop**

†**Salignon,** *s.m.* salt-cat

Saligot, *s.m* (*bot.*) water caltrop

Salin, e, *adj.* saline, briny

Salin, *s.m.* salt-works, salt-garden, saltern, bay; salt-pan, brine-pan; salt-marsh; raw salt

Saline, *s.f.* salt-fish, salt-meat; salt-works, salt-garden, saltern, bay, saline; salt-pit, brine-

Salique, *adj.* Salic, Salique [pit

Salir, *v.a.* to soil; to make dirty, to dirty; to draggle, to drabble; to foul, to befoul; to stain; to sully; to tarnish; to disgrace

Se —, *v.r.* to dirty *or* soil oneself; to soil, to get soiled *or* dirty; to fade; to sully o.'s reputation, to disgrace oneself [to get dirty

Salissant, e, *adj.* soiling; that soils; liable

Salisson, *s.f.* slut, mopsey

Salissure, *s.f.* spot of dirt; dirt; soil; stain

Salivaire, *adj.* (*anat.*) salivary [salivant

Salivant, e, *adj.* salivating, salivant; — *s.m.*

Salivation, *s.f.* salivation

Salive, *s.f.* saliva, spittle

Saliver, *v.n.* to salivate, to spit

Saliveu-x, se, *adj.* salivous

Salle, *s.f.* hall; room; parlour; ward; chamber; school; fencing-school; practice; bower; (*theat.*) house. — *commune,* (*of inns*) parlour. — *du commun,* servants' hall. — *à manger,* dining-room. — *à manger-galerie,* dining-hall. — *d'armes,* fencing-school, school of arms; armoury. — *d'attente,* waiting-room. — *d'audience,* audience-chamber; court. — *de concert,* concert-room; music-hall, music-room. — *de* (or *du*) *conseil,* council-chamber. — *de danse,* dancing-room; dancing-school. — *d'escrime,* fencing-school. — *d'étude,* school-room. — *des festins,* banqueting-hall. — *de police,* — *de discipline,* (*mil.*) defaulters' room, guard-room, dry-room. — *du rapport,* (*mil.*) orderly-room. — *de récréation,* play-room. — *de réunion,* assembly-room. — *de spectacle,* play-house.

Salmigondis, *s.m.* hotch-potch, hodge-podge, salmagundi, resurrection-pie; mishmash, medley, farrago, olio, jumble [ragout

Salmis, *s.m.* (*cook.*) salmis, salmi, hash, stew,

Salmonés, Salmonidés, *s.m.pl.* (*zool.*) sal-

Saloir, *s.m.* salting-tub; salt-box [monidæ

Salon, *s.m.* drawing-room; saloon; room; divan; sitting-room; parlour; coffee-room;

gallery (*of pictures*); exhibition (*of works of art*); exhibition criticism; first *or* chief cabin; —**s,** *pl.* fashionable circles. — *littéraire*, reading-room, news-room. — *des courses*, betting-club *or* office *or* room. — or *cabinet de lecture*, *V.* **Cabinet.** — *de société* or *particulier*, *V.* **Société.** *Petit* —, small drawing-room; parlour
Salonnier, *s.m.* exhibition critic
Salop, e, *adj.* nasty, dirty, filthy; slovenly; — *s.m.f.* nasty (*or* dirty) fellow *or* creature *or* thing; sloven, slattern, slut, drab, mopsey, trollop; dirty beast, beast; wench, bitch, [harlot
Salopement, *adv. V.* **Salement**
Saloperie, *s.f.* dirtiness, slovenliness, sluttishness; nastiness; beastliness; filth; ribaldry; dirty *or* nasty *or* beastly thing *or* stuff
Salorge, *s.m.* loaf of salt
Salpe, *s.f.* (*mollusc*) salpa
Salpêtrage, *s.m.* saltpetre-making
Salpêtre, *s.m.* saltpetre, nitre; (*fig.*) vivacity, fire, hastiness [petre; to nitrify
Salpêtrer, *v.a.* to cover *or* mix with salt-
Se —, *v.r.* to become *or* be covered with saltpetre; to nitrify
Salpêtrerie, *s.f.* saltpetre-works
Salpêtreu-x, se, *adj.* saltpetrous
Salpêtrier, *s.m.* saltpetre-maker
Salpêtrière, *s.f.* saltpetre-works; Salpêtrière (*asylum for women, in Paris*)
Salpêtrisation, *s.f.* nitrification
Salpicon, *s.m.* (*cook.*) salpicon
Salse, *s.f.* salse (*mud-eruption*)
†**Salsepareille,** *s.f.* (*bot.*) sarsaparilla [rine
Salseparine, *s.f.* (*chem.*) smilacine, salsepa-
Salsifis, *s.m.* (*bot.*) salsify, salsafy; goat's-beard
Salsugineu-x, se, *adj.* salsuginous, saltish
Saltarelle, *s.f.* saltarello (*dance*)
Saltation, *s.f.* saltation
Saltigrade, *adj.m.f.*, *s.f.* (*zool.*) saltigrade
Saltimbanque, *s.m.* mountebank; clown; buffoon, humbug, quack; — *adj.* quackish
Salubre, *adj.* salubrious, healthy, healthful, wholesome [healthfully, wholesomely
Salubrement, *adv.* salubriously, healthily,
Salubrité, *s.f.* salubrity, salubriousness; healthiness, healthfulness; wholesomeness; health. *De* —, of salubrity, &c.; of health; sanitary. *Conseil de* —, board of health. *Inspecteur de* —, sanitary inspector, inspector of nuisances
Saluer, *v.a.n.* to salute; to hail; to greet; to welcome; to bow to; to nod to; to bow; to make a bow; to nod; to take off o.'s hat to; to take off o.'s hat; to cheer; to present o.'s compliments to; (*mil.*) to salute, to fire a salute. *Je vous salue, j'ai l'honneur de vous* —, I am your humble servant, your servant, yours obediently; how do you do? good morning, good day, good evening, I wish you good morning, &c. — *empereur*, to proclaim emperor. — *des voiles*, (*nav.*) to strike the sails
Salure, *s.f.* saltness
Salut, *s.m.* safety; welfare; preservation; recovery; escape; salvation; chance, hope of success, hope; salute; salutation; greeting; bow; nod; cheer; benediction; (*int.*) hail! greeting! (*fish*) *V.* **Glanis**
Salutaire, *adj.* salutary, wholesome; beneficial
Salutairement, *adv.* salutarily, wholesomely; beneficially [compliments
Salutation, *s.f.* salutation; bow; —**s,** *pl.*
Saluth, *s.m. V.* **Glanis**
Salvadore, *s.f.* (*bot.*) salvadora
Salvage, *s.m.* (*old*) *V.* **Sauvetage**
Salvanos, *s.m.* (*nav.*) life-buoy
Salve, *s.f.* (*artil.*) salvo; salute; volley; round; (*of applause*) round
Salvé, *s.m.* (*Cath. rel.*) Salve regina
Samaritain, e, *adj. s.* Samaritan
Sambleu (Par la), *int.* (*old*) *V.* **Palsambleu**
Sambuque, *s.f.* (*anc. mus. instr.. anc. war-engine*) sambuke

Samedi, *s.m.* Saturday. — *saint*, Easter eve
Samien, ne, *adj. s.* Samian
Samis, *s.m.* (*old*) samite (*stuff*)
Samnites, *s.m.pl.* Samnites [brookweed
Samole, *s.m.* (*bot.*) samolus, water pimpernel,
Samoyèdes, *s.m.pl.* Samoyeds, Samoyedes
Sampan, *s.m.* sampan (*Chinese boat*)
San-benito, *s.m.* (*Spanish*) san-benito
Sancir, *v.n.* (*nav.*) to sink, to founder
Sanctifica-teur, trice, *s.m.f.* sanctifier; — *adj.* sanctifying [holy, keeping, observance
Sanctification, *s.f.* sanctification; keeping
Sanctifier, *v.a.* to sanctify; to hallow; to keep holy
Sanction, *s.f.* sanction; approbation; assent. — *pénale*, (*law*) penalty. — *rémunératoire*, [reward
Sanctionner, *v.a.* to sanction
Sanctuaire, *s.m.* sanctuary; chancel; altar
Sanctus, *s.m.* (*Cath. rel.*) sanctus
Sandal, *s.m.* sandal-wood, sandal
Sandale, *s.f.* sandal; fencing-shoe; foot-stall. — *d'armes*, fencing-shoe
Sandaraque, *s.f.* sandarach resin, sandarach; pounce. *Poudre de* —, pounce-powder
Sanderling, *s.m.* (*bird*) sanderling
Sandis, *int.* (*old and local*) by George! by Jingo! bedad! begorra!
Sandjak, Sandjiak. *V.* **Sangiac**
Sandre, *s.m.* (*fish*) pike-perch
Sandwich, *s.f.* sandwich [San-Franciscan
San-franciscain, e, *adj. s.* of San-Francisco,
Sang, *s.m.* blood; kindred; race; nature. *A* — *chaud*, hot-blooded; (*nat. hist.*) warm-blooded. *A* — *froid*, (*nat. hist.*) cold-blooded. *De* —, of blood, blood, bloody. *De pur* — (*adj.*), *pur-* — (*adj. s.*), *V.* **Pur-sang.** *Jusqu'au* —, till the blood comes *or* came, enough (*or* so as) to fetch blood. *Avoir du* — *dans les veines* or *sous les ongles*, to have spirit. *Avoir le* — *chaud*, (*fig.*) to be hasty *or* passionate. *Faire faire du mauvais* — *à*, to annoy, to vex. *Mettre à feu et à* —, *V.* **Feu.** *Mettre en* —, *V.* **Mettre.** *Se battre au premier* —, to fight till the first blood is drawn. *Se faire du mauvais* —, to be annoyed *or* vexed, to fret. *Mon* — *n'a fait qu'un tour*, I was struck all of a heap. — **-de-dragon,** — **-dragon,** *s.m.* dragon's blood, gum dragon. — **-froid,** — **-gris,** *s.m. See below*
Sang-froid, *s.m.* cold blood; cold-bloodedness; coolness, presence of mind, composure, nerve; temper; sobriety. *De* —, cold-blooded; composed; collected; sober; cool; coolly, in [cold blood
Sang-gris, *s.m.* (*drink*) sangaree
Sangiac, *s.m.* sangiac
Sangiacat, *s.m.* sangiacate
Sanglade, *s.f.* lash, cut
Sanglant, e, *adj.* bloody; covered *or* stained with blood, blood-stained; bleeding; attended with bloodshed; outrageous, gross, keen, cutting, deadly; (*of meat*) *V.* **Saignant**
Sangle, *s.f.* strap, band, belt; girth, girt; sacking; (*fish.*) long-line, trawl
Sanglé, e, *part. adj.* strapped, &c. (*V.* **Sangler**); ill-treated; lost, undone, ruined; caught; smitten; tight-fitting, tight
Sangler, *v.a.* to strap; to girth, to girt, to gird; to lash; to beat; to give (*blows*)
Se —, *v.r.* to gird oneself; to lace oneself tightly; to stint *or* pinch oneself, to pinch, to make sacrifices
Sanglier, *s.m.* wild-boar, boar
Sanglon, *s.m.* small strap *or* &c. (*V.* **Sangle**)
Sanglot, *s.m.* sob, sobbing
Sangloter, *v.n.* to sob
Sangsue, *s.f.* leech; bloodsucker
Sanguifère, *adj.* sanguiferous
Sanguification, *s.f.* sanguification
Sanguifier, *v.a.*, **Se** —, *v.r.* to sanguify
Sanguin, e, *adj.* sanguine, sanguineous; full-blooded; of blood; blood-coloured, red; —**e,** *s.f. See below.* *Vaisseau* —, blood-vessel
Sanguinaire, *adj.* sanguinary, bloody; blood

Sanguinaire, *adj.* sanguinary, bloody; bloodthirsty; murderous; — *s.f.* (*bot.*) sanguinaria, blood-root
Sanguinairement, *adv.* sanguinarily, bloodily
Sanguine, *s.f.* red chalk; blood-stone; (*her.*) sanguine, murrey
Sanguinelle, *s.f.* (*bot.*) gatten-tree
Sanguinolent, e, *adj.* sanguinolent
Sanguisorbe, *s.f.* (*bot.*) sanguisorba
Sanhédrin, *s.m.* sanhedrim
Sanicle, *s.f.* (*bot.*) sanicle
Sanie, *s.f.* (*med.*) sanies
Sanieu-x, se, *adj.* (*med.*) sanious
Sanitaire, *adj.* sanitary. *Cordon* —, cordon sanitaire
Sanité, *s.f.* sanity, saneness, soundness, healthiness, wholesomeness
Sans, *prep.* without; free of, free from; were it not for, but for; past; (*in compounds*) ... less (*Sans peur*, &c., fearless, without fear, &c.); — *adv.* without it, without them. — *cela*, otherwise, or else, or, without that. — *que*, without. — *quoi*, otherwise, or else, or
Sans-cœur, *adj.* heartless; — *s.m.f.* heartless wretch
Sanscrit, e, *adj.*, **Sanscrit,** *s.m.* Sanscrit
Sanscrit-ique, -isme, -iste. *V.* page 3, § 1
Sans-culotte, *s.m.* tatterdemalion, ragamuffin, vagabond, cad, sans-culotte
Sans-culotterie, *s.f.*, **Sans-culottisme,** *s.m.* sans-culottism
Sans-dents, *s.f.* toothless old woman
Sansevière, *s.f.* (*bot.*) sanseviera, bowstring hemp
Sans-façon, *s.m.* roughness; bluntness; offhandedness; easy manners; familiarity
Sans-gêne, *s.m.* unceremoniousness, want of ceremony, impudence, coolness; freedom from restraint; carelessness; off-handedness; — *s.m.f.* unceremonious *or* free *or* familiar *or* impudent fellow *or* woman *or* girl *or* creature *or* thing
Sans-soin, *adj.* careless; — *s.m.f.* careless fellow *or* creature *or* thing
Sansonnet, *s.m.* (*bird*) starling
Sans-souci, *s.m.* freedom from care, carelessness; careless jovial fellow; Sans-Souci palace
Sans-terre, *adj.* (*hist.*) Lackland
Santal, *s.m.* sandal-wood, sandal
Santaline, *s.f.* (*chem.*) santaline
Santé, *s.f.* health; healthiness; toast. — *du corps*, (*pop.*) water-cress
Santon, *s.m.* santon; santon's tomb *or* house
Santonine, *s.f.* (*bot.*) santonica, worm-seed; (*chem.*) santonine
Sanve, *s.f.* (*bot.*) charlock
Saoul, Saouler. *V.* **Soûl, Soûler**
Sap, *s.m.* (*pop.*) *V.* **Sapin**
Sapa, *s.m.* grape preserves
Sapajou, *s.m.* (*zool.*) sapajou, cebus; (*pers.*) monkey
Sapan, *s.m.* (*bot.*) sapan; (*bois de* —), sapan-wood
Sape, *s.f.* sap, sapping; mine; trench; (*agr.*) Hainault scythe
Sapement, *s.m.* sapping
Saper, *v.a.* to sap; to mine; to undermine; to shake; to cut off *or* away
Se —, *v.r.* to be sapped *or* &c.
Sapeur, *s.m.* sapper; miner; pioneer. — **-pompier,** *s. m.* fireman. —**s-pompiers,** *s.m.pl.* firemen; fire-brigade. — **porte-hache,** *s.m.* sapper
Saphène, *s.f.* (*anat.*) saphena
Saphique, *adj.m.f.*, *s.m.* sapphic
Saphir, *s.m.* sapphire
Saphirin, e, *adj.*, **Saphirine,** *s.f.* sapphirine
Sapide, *adj.* sapid
Sapidité, *s.f.* sapidity, sapidness
Sapience, *s.f.* (*obsolete*) wisdom. *Pays de* —, Normandy
Sapientiaux, *adj.m.pl.* sapiential
Sapin, *s.m.* fir, fir-tree; fir-wood, fir; deal; hack, cab; coffin. — *blanc*, silver-fir. *Sentir le* —, (*pers.*) to have one foot in the grave. *Une toux qui sent le* —, a churchyard cough
Sapine, *s.f.* fir, fir plank, deal board; scaffold-pole; gin, crane
Sapinette, *s.f.* hemlock spruce; spruce-beer
Sapinière, *s.f.* fir-plantation, fir-grove; deal barge
Saponacé, e, *adj.* saponaceous
Saponaire, *s.f.* (*bot.*) soapwort
Saponifiable, *adj.* saponifiable
Saponification, *s.f.* saponification
Saponifier, *v.a.*, **Se** —, *v.r.* to saponify
Saponine, *s.f.* (*chem.*) saponine
Saponique, *adj.* (*chem.*) saponic
Saponite, *s.m.* (*min.*) saponite, soap-stone
Saponule, *s.m.* (*chem.*) saponule
Saporifique, *adj.* saporific
†**Sapote, Sapotille,** *s.f.* (*bot.*) sapodilla-plum
†**Sapotier, Sapotillier,** *s. m.* (*bot.*) sapodilla-tree, sapodilla
Saprelotte, Sapristi, *int.* by Jingo! hang it! bless your soul! by the Powers! zookers!
Saquebute, *s.f.* (*mus.*, *obsolete*) sackbut
Sarabande, *s.f.* saraband (*dance, tune*)
Sarbacane, *s.f.* trunk, pea-shooter; tube; blowing-tube (*for glass*); speaking-pipe *or* tube; air-cane, air-gun. *Par* —, by proxy
Sarbotière, *s.f.* (*bad spelling*) *V.* **Sorbetière**
Sarcasme, *s.m.* sarcasm
Sarcastique, *adj.* sarcastic
Sarcelle, *s.f.* (*bird*) teal; widgeon; garganey
Sarclage, *s.m.* weeding
Sarcler, *v.a.* to weed
Sarclet, *s.m.* *V.* **Sarcloir**
Sarcleu-r, se, *s.m.f.* weeder
Sarcloir, *s.m.* hoe, weeding-hook *or* fork weeder
Sarclure, *s.f.* weedings
Sarcocarpe, *s.m.* (*bot.*) sarcocarp
Sarcocèle, *s.f.* (*med.*) sarcocele
Sarcocolle, *s.f.* sarcocolla, sarcocol
Sarcocollier, *s.m.* sarcocolla-tree
Sarcolog-ie, -ique, &c. *V.* page 3, § 1
Sarcomateu-x, se, *adj.* (*med.*) sarcomatous
Sarcome, *s.m.* (*med.*) sarcoma
Sarcophage, *s.m.* sarcophagus; coffin; representation of a coffin
Sarcotique, *adj.m.f.*, *s.m.* (*med.*) sarcotic
Sardanapalesque, Sardanapalique, *adj.* of Sardanapalus, Sardanapalic
Sardanapalisme, *s.m.* Sardanapalism
Sarde, *adj. s.m.f.* Sardinian; Sardinian fashion
Sardine, *s.f.* (*fish*) sardine
Sardinerie, *s.f.* sardine-curing establishment
Sardinier, *s.m.* sardine-net; (*adject.*, *Bateau* —) sardine-boat
Sardinière, *s.f.* sardine-net; sardine-curer
Sardoine, *s.f.* (*min.*) sardonyx
Sardonie, *s.f.* (*bot.*) celery-leaved crowfoot, ranunculus sceleratus; sardonica
Sardonien (*adj.m.*), **Sardonique,** *adj.* sardonic
Sardonyx, *s.f* (*min.*) sardonyx
Sarette. *V.* **Sarrette**
Sargasse, *s.f.* (*bot.*) gulfweed. *Mer des* —*s*, Sargasso-Sea
Sarigue, *s.m.f.* (*zool.*) sarigue, opossum
Sarmate, *adj.s.m.f.*, **Sarmatique,** *adj.* Sarmatian
Sarment, *s.m.* vine-branch *or* twig *or* shoot; twig, shoot; (*of climbing plants*) bine
Sarmenteu-x, se, *adj.* branchy; sarmentous; climbing flower
Saronique, *adj.* (*anc. geog.*) Saronic
Sarpejeu, *int.* *V.* **Saprelotte**
Sarracénie, *s.f.* (*bot.*) sarracenia, side-saddle flower
Sarracénique, *adj.* Saracenic, Saracenical
Sarrasin, e, *s.m.f.* Saracen; — *s.m.* buckwheat; — *s.f.* strong-box fastening; (*fort.*) sarrasin, sarrasine; — *adj.* Saracenic, Saracenical. *Blé* —, buck-wheat
Sarrau, *s.m.* smockfrock, smock, frock
Sarrette, *s.f.* (*bot.*) saw-wort
Sarriette, *s.f.* (*bot.*) savory
Sarrot. *V.* **Sarrau**
Sas, *s.m.* sieve; bolt; (*of canal-locks*) chamber. *Passer au* —, to sift. *Passer au gros* —, to bolt; (*fig.*) to examine superficially
Sassafras, *s.m.* (*bot.*) sassafras
Sasse, *s.f.* (*nav.*) scoop
Sassement, *s.m.* sifting; bolting; winnowing
Sassenage, *s.m.* Sassenage cheese
Sasser, *v.a.* to sift; to bolt; to winnow; (*fig.*) to sift, to examine, to scrutinize, to scan
Sasset, *s.m.* small sieve

Sasseu-r, se, *s.m.f.* sifter; bolter, winnower
Satané, e, *adj.* devilish, wretched, confounded
Satanique, *adj.* Satanic, Satanical, diabolical
Satiété, *s.f.* satiety
Sati-f, ve, *adj.* sative
Satin, *s.m.* satin
Satinade, *s.f.* satinet, satteen
Satinage, *s.m.* satining; hot *or* cold pressing
Satiné, e, *adj. s.m.* satin-like, satiny, satin; soft as velvet, velvet; hot *or* cold-pressed, glossed, glazed; satin-like appearance. *Bois* —, [*Cayenne wood, 'ferolia'*]
Satiner, *v.a.* to satin; to press; to gloss, to glaze; — *v.n.* to look like satin. — *à chaud,* to hot-press. — *à froid,* to cold-press
Satinet, *s.m.* satinet [cold-presser
Satineu-r, se, *s.m.f.* presser, hot-presser,
Satire, *s.f.* satire; lampoon
Satirique, *adj.m.f., s.m.* satirical; satirist
Satiriquement, *adv.* satirically
Satiriser, *v.a.n.* to satirize
Satiriste, *s.m.f.* satirist
Satisfaction, *s.f.* satisfaction; gratification, pleasure, comfort; atonement
Satisfactoire, *adj.* satisfactory
Satisfaire, *v.a.n.* to satisfy; to please; to give satisfaction to; to gratify; to soothe; to pay; to indemnify; to answer; to supply; to serve; to meet; to discharge; to perform, to execute; to fulfil; to comply (with), to obey; to atone (for); to be satisfactory
Satisfaisant, e, *adj.* satisfactory
Satisfait, e, *part. adj.* satisfied, &c. (*V.* **Satisfaire**); — *s.m.* (*polit.*) conservative
Satisfecit, *s.m.* good-conduct certificate
Satrape, *s.m.* satrap
Satrapie, *s.f.* satrapy
Satrapique, *adj.* satrapal
Satteau, *s.m.* coral-fishing boat
Saturabilité, *s.f.* saturability
Saturable, *adj.* saturable
Saturant, e, *adj.,* **Saturant,** *s.m.* saturant
Saturateur, *s.m.* saturator
Saturation, *s.f.* saturation [to weary
Saturer, *v.a.* to saturate; to surfeit; to fill;
Se —, *v.r.* to become *or* be saturated *or* &c.
Saturnales, *s.f.pl.* saturnalia
Saturne, *s.m.* (*myth., astr.*) Saturn; (*old chem.*) Saturn, lead. *Extrait de* —, acetate of lead, sugar of lead [lead
Saturner, *v.a.* (*pharm.*) to mix with acetate of
Saturnie, *s.f.* (*zool.*) peacock-moth, emperor-moth [saturnine, grave, heavy, dull, gloomy
Saturnien, ne, *adj.* Saturnian; (*obsolete*)
Saturnin, e, *adj.* (*chem., med.*) of lead, lead,
Saturnite, *s.f.* (*min.*) saturnite [saturnine
Satyre, *s.m.* satyr; — *s.f.* satyric play, satyre
Satyriasis, *s.m.* (*med.*) satyriasis
Satyrion, *s.m.* (*bot.*) satyrion, satyrium
Satyrique, *adj.* satyric
Sauce, *s.f.* sauce; (*fig.*) sauce; pickle; work; blowing-up; (*draw.*) soft crayon. — *blanche,* white sauce; melted butter. — *piquante,* sharp sauce; catchup, ketchup, catsup. — *-Robert,* onion-sauce. *A toute* —, in all manner of ways, on every occasion, to *or* of *or* for all work. *Mettre à toute* — or *à toutes les* —*s,* to use in all manner of ways; to put to all kinds of work; to repeat *or* bring again on all occasions. *Ne savoir à quelle* — *mettre quelqu'un,* not to know what to make of one. *Il n'est* — (or *chère*) *que d'appétit, V.* **Chère,** *s.f.*
Saucer, *v.a.* to dip *or* steep in sauce, to dip, to steep, to sop; to wet through, to drench; to scold, to blow up; (*medals*) to plate
Saucier, *s.m.* saucer (*of a capstan*) [boat
Saucière, *s.f.* sauce-tureen, sauce-boat, butter-
Saucisse, *s.f.* sausage; (*mil.*) saucisson, saucisse [saucisson
Saucisson, *s. m.* sausage; (*mil., fireworks*)
Sau-f, ve, *adj.* safe; spared. *La vie sauve,* o.'s life saved *or* spared, to save *or* spare o.'s life
Sauf, *prep.* save, saving; except, but; reserving; subject to, under; (*à*) at the risk (of). — *erreur de calcul,* — *erreur ou omission,* errors ex-
Sauf-conduit, *s.m.* safe-conduct, pass [cepted
Sauge, *s.f.* (*bot.*) sage [terous, stupid
Saugrenu, e, *adj.* absurd, ridiculous, prepos-
Saugrenuité, *s.f.* absurdity, preposterousness
Saulaie, *s.f.* willow-grove, willow-plantation
Saule, *s.m.* willow, sallow. — *pleureur,* weep-
Saulée, *s.f.* row of willows [ing-willow
Saumâtre, *adj.* briny; brackish
Saumière. *V.* **Jaumière** [(*nav.*) kentledge
Saumon, *s.m.* salmon; (*metal.*) pig; block;
Saumoné, e, *adj.* salmon. *Truite* —*e,* salmon-trout [samlet, grilse, botcher
Saumoneau, *s.m.* young salmon, salmonet,
Saumonerie, *s.f.* salmon-fishery
Saumonerion, *s.m.* grey trout, bull-trout
Saumonière, *s.f.* salmon-kettle
Saumurage, *s.m.* brining, pickling, sousing
Saumure, *s.f.* brine, pickle
Saumurer, *v.a.* to brine, to pickle, to souse
Saumurois, e, *adj. s.* of Saumur; native of
Saunage, *s.m.* salt trade, salt-selling [Saumur
Saunaison, *s.f.* salt-making
Sauner, *v.n.a.* to make salt; to turn into salt
Saunerie, *s.f.* salt-works
Saunier, *s.m.* salter, salt-maker
Saunière, *s.f.* salt-box
Saupe, *s.f.* (*mollusc*) salpa
Saupiquet, *s.m.* (*cook.*) sharp sauce
Saupoudration, *s.f.* salting; besprinkling, sprinkling; dredging
Saupoudrer, *v.a.* to salt, to sprinkle with salt; to besprinkle, to sprinkle; to powder, to dust; to dredge; to intersperse; to strew
Se —, *v.r.* to be salted *or* &c.
Saupoudreu-r, se, *s.m.f.* dredger; caster
Saur, *adj. V.* **Saure**
Saurais [*Conditional mood of* **Savoir**]. *Je* (*tu, &c.*) *ne* —, I should not know; I cannot, I am unable to
Saure, *adj.* yellowish brown; (*of horses*) sorrel; (*of herrings*) red, smoked, bloated
Saurel, *s.m. V.* **Caranx**
Saurer, *v.a.* to smoke, to bloat (*herrings*)
Sauret, *adj.m. V.* **Saure** [saurian
Saurien, ne, *adj.,* **Saurien,** *s.m.* (*zool.*)
Saussaie, *s.f. V.* **Saulaie**
Saussurite, *s.f.* (*min.*) saussurite
Saut, *s.m.* leap; jump; skip; spring; bound; tumble; fall, waterfall; (*rid.*) vault; (*at billiards*) coo. — *périlleux,* — *de carpe,* somerset, somersets; rash act. — *de lit,* bedside-carpet, rug. — *du lit,* o.'s getting out of bed, o.'s getting up, o.'s rising. — *de loup,* sunk fence, ditch, ha-ha. — *de mouton,* (*rid.*) goat's-leap, goat-leap; (*play*) leap-frog. *Au* — *du lit,* at (*or* on) o.'s getting up *or* getting out of bed. *De plein* —, at once, all at once; point-blank. *Par* —*s,* by starts. *Par* —*s et par bonds,* by fits and starts
Sautage, *s.m.* exploding [*the wind*)
Saute, *s.f.* (*nav.*) sudden veering *or* shifting (*of*
Sauté, e, *part. adj.* leapt, &c. (*V.* **Sauter**); (*cook.*) mixed *or* united by shaking, (lightly) fried, stewed, sauté; — *s.m.* (*cook.*) stew,
Saute-en-barque, *s.m.* yachting-jacket [sauté
Sauteler, *v.n. V.* **Sautiller**
Sautelle, *s.f.* vine-plant
Saute-mouton, *s.m* leap-frog
Sauter, *v.n.* to leap; to take a leap; to jump; to skip; to hop; to bound; to bounce; to spring; to tumble; to vault; to explode, to blow up; to break; to be dismissed, to get the sack; to hop the twig, to kick the bucket; to be lost, to go; (*at billiards*) to run a coo; (*nav., of the wind*) to veer, to shift, to fly about; — *v.a.* to leap over; to jump over; to pass over; to leave out, to omit, to skip; to overlook; (*cook.*) to (lightly) fry; to stew; (*of stallions,* &c.) to leap, to cover. — *à la corde,*

to skip with a rope, to skip. — *aux yeux*, to strike the eye; to be conspicuous; to be obvious. *Faire* —, to blow up; to blow *or* dash out; to knock *or* cut off *or* out; to throw; to throw down; to toss; to send up; to draw (*a cork*); to crack *or* drink (*a bottle*); to spring, to blast; to break; to get rid of, to do away with; to get (*one*) dismissed; to ruin; to squander, to spend, to make away with, to [misappropriate

Sautereau, *s.m.* (*mus.*) jack

Sauterelle, *s.f.* grasshopper, locust; leap-frog; trap; (*carp., mas.*) shifting-bevel; (*pop.*) flea, f-sharp. — *de mer*, squilla; shrimp

Sauterie, *s.f.* jumping, skipping, hop

Sauterne, *s.m.* sauterne (wine)

Sauterolle, *s.f.* (*hunt.*) trap

Saute-ruisseau, *s.m.* errand-boy, skip-kennel

Sauteu-r, se, *s.m.f.* leaper; jumper; tumbler; vaulter; mountebank, quack, humbug; trimmer, time-server, weathercock, harlequin; (*rid.*) leaping horse; — *s.f.* sauteuse (*dance*); — *adj.* leaping, jumping [skip

†Sautillement, *s.m.* hopping, skipping, hop,

†Sautiller, *v.n.* to hop, to skip, to jump about

Sautoir, *s.m.* St. Andrew's cross; saltire; scarf, neckerchief; watch-guard, guard-chain; stewpan; (*horol.*) jumper. *En* —, crossways, crosswise; slung across the shoulders *or* over the shoulder; (*her.*) in saltire, saltireways, saltirewise

Sauvage, *adj.* wild; untamed; savage; uncivilized; unsociable; fierce; barbarous; shy, timid; (*of oil*) bitter; — *s.m.f.* savage; unsociable man *or* woman, recluse, bear. *Feu* —, scab [ciably; secludedly

Sauvagement, *adv.* wildly; fiercely; unso-

Sauvageon, *s.m.* (*agr.*) wild stock; seedling

Sauvagerie, *s.f.* unsociableness; shyness; wildness; wild state

Sauvagesse, *s.f.* (*obsolete*) savage (*woman*)

Sauvagin, e, *adj.* fishy; — *s.m.* fishy taste *or* smell; — *s.f.* water-fowl; fishy taste *or* smell; wild-beasts' skins, common furs. *Sentir le* — or *la —e*, to taste fishy; to smell fishy

Sauve, *adj.* (*feminine of* **Sauf**); — *v.* (*V.* **Sauver**)

Sauvegarde, *s.f.* safeguard; protection; safe-keeping; — *s.m.* (*zool.*) salvator, save-guard (*kind of American monitor*)

Sauvegarder, *v.a.* to safeguard, to protect

Sauve qui peut (*save himself who can*), *s.m.* general flight, flight, stampede; panic; alarm

Sauver, *v.a.* to save; to preserve; to rescue; to deliver; to salve; to spare; to ward off; to palliate, to excuse, to justify; to conceal

Se —, *v.r.* to escape; to run away *or* off; to fly *or* &c. away *or* off; to get away *or* out; to abscond; to be off; to take refuge; to work o.'s salvation; to retrieve oneself

Sauvetage, *s.m.* saving, rescuing, rescue, preservation of life (*from shipwreck, drowning, fire,* &c.); preservation of property (*from shipwreck and fire*); salvage. *De* —, for preserving *or* saving life, life-preserving, life-saving, life; life-boat; fire; safety. *Appareil de* —, life-saving apparatus, life-preserver; fire-escape. *Bateau* or *canot de* —, life-boat. *Bouée de* —, life-buoy. *Ceinture de* —, life-belt. *Sac de* —, fire-escape. *Société de — des naufragés*, [life-boat institution

Sauveté, *s.f.* (*old*) safety

Sauveter, *v.a.* to rescue, to salve

Sauveteur, *s.m.* rescuer; salvor; life-preserver; Humane Society man; life-boat man; — *adj.m.* rescuing; salving; life

Sauvette, *s.f.* duck-stone (*game*)

Sauveur, *s.m.* deliverer; rescuer; preserver; salvor; saver; Saviour; — *adj.m.* all-saving, [saving, rescuing

Sauve-vie, *s.f.* (*bot.*) wall-rue

Savacou, *s.m.* (*bird*) boatbill

Savamment, *adv.* learnedly; cleverly; skilfully; knowingly; wittingly

Savane, *s.f.* savanna, savannah

Savant, e, *adj. s.* learned; well-informed; able, clever; skilful; masterly; (the) wiser; scientific man; scholar, learned man, savant. *Femme —e*, learned woman, blue-stocking

Savantasse, *s.m.* smatterer, sciolist, pedant

Savantissime, *adj. s.* (*jest.*) most learned; a prodigy of learning

Savarin, *s.m.* (kind of cake)

Savate, *s.f.* old shoe; slip-shoe; (*game*) hunt-the-slipper; savate (*way of fighting with the feet*); bungled work, bungling, botching; bungler, botcher; (*nav.*) shoe. *En* —, *En —s*, slip-shoe like; down at heels; in old shoes, wretchedly shod. *Chaussé en* —, slipshod. *Tirer la* —, to fight with the feet. *Trainer la* —, to go ragged, to be wretchedly poor

Savater. *V.* **Saveter** [shoe trade

Savaterie, *s.f.* old-shoe shop *or* market, old-

Saveter, *v.a.* to cobble; to bungle, to botch

Savetier, *s.m.* cobbler; bungler, botcher

Saveur, *s.f.* savour; flavour; taste; relish; zest

†Savigny, *s.m.* savigny (wine)

Savinier, *s.m.* (*bot.*) *V.* **Sabine**

Savoir, *v.a.n.* to know; to be aware of; to be acquainted with; to know to be; to understand; to know how; to hear, to be informed of; to learn; can, to be able; to contrive, to manage, to succeed (in); to tell, to say; can tell, can say. *Faire* —, to make (...) known; to let know; to inform, to acquaint, to make (...) acquainted with; to give notice; to notify. — *faire*, to know how to manage, to have skill, to be skilful; *s.m. See below.* — *vivre*, to be well-bred, to have (good) manners; *s.m. See below.* *A* —, —, viz., namely; to wit; that is, that is to say; that remains to be known; perhaps. *En* —, to know; to learn, to hear. *Je ne sache pas que*, I don't know that, I am not aware that. *Que je sache*, to my knowledge, that I know. *Que sais-je?* how do I know? and what not. *Que sais-je, moi?* how can I know? *Je ne saurais*, *V.* **Saurais.** *Autant que je sache*, for aught I know; to the best of my belief. *Je n'en sais rien*, I know nothing about it; I don't know at all. *Je ne sais qui*, I know not who; mere nobody, nobody, thingumbob, low fellow, low creature, abandoned woman. *Je ne sais quoi (de)*, I know not what, something *or* other, something. *Un je ne sais quoi*, a something, an indescribable thing. *C'est à* —, —, it is a question; that remains to be known. *Est-ce que je sais? V. Que sais-je?*

Se —, *v.r.* to know oneself; to know oneself to be; to get *or* be known

Savoir, *s.m.* knowledge, learning, acquirements, talent, skill [agement; contrivance; wits

Savoir-faire, *s.m.* ability; skill; tact; man-

Savoir-vivre, *s.m.* good breeding, good *or* refined manners [native of Savoy

Savoisien, ne, *adj. s.* of Savoy, Savoyard,

Savon, *s.m.* soap; scolding, blowing-up, jobation, wigging, carp-pie. — *noir*, — *vert*, soft soap. — *de montagne*, — *naturel*, rock-soap

Savonnage, *s.m.* soaping; washing; lathering; soap-suds [to scold

Savonner, *v.a.* to soap; to wash; to lather;

Se —, *v.r.* to wash

Savonnerie, *s.f.* soap-factory, soap-works, soapery; soap-trade; soap

Savonnette, *s.f.* soap-ball, wash-ball. *Boite à* —; *Montre à* —. *V.* **Boîte** *and* **Montre**

Savonneu-x, se, *adj.* soapy [soap-berry

Savonnier, *s.m.* soap-boiler; (*bot.*) soap-tree,

Savonnière, *s.f.* (*bot.*) soapwort

Savonule, *s.m.* (*chem.*) saponule [to enjoy

Savourer, *v.a.* to savour; to relish; to taste;

Savouret, *s.m.* (*butch.*) marrow-bone

Savoureusement, *adv.* savourily, with relish

Savoureu-x, se, *adj.* savoury

Savoyard, e, *adj. s.* of Savoy, Savoyard, native of Savoy; chimney-sweeper, sweep; street-porter, errand-porter; churl, low *or* [vulgar fellow

Saxatile, *adj.* saxatile

Saxe, *s.m.* Saxon porcelain
Saxhorn, *s.m.* (*mus. instr.*) saxhorn
Saxicole, *adj.* saxicolous; — *s.f.* (*bird*) chat
Saxifrage, *s.f.* (*bot.*) saxifrage; — *adj.* (*med.*, *obsolete*) saxifragous
Saxon, ne, *adj.s.* Saxon
Saxonique, *adj.* Saxonic
Saxophone, *s.m.* (*mus. instr.*) saxophone
Saxtuba, *s.m.* (*mus. instr.*) saxtuba
Saye, *s.f.* *V.* **Saie**
Sayette, *s.f.* (*stuff*) sayette, sagathy
Saynète, *s.f.* sainete (*Spanish farce*)
Sayon, *s.m.* sagum, cloak, tunic, frock
Sbire, *s.m.* (*Italian*) sbirro (*pl.* sbirri), archer; (*fig.*) myrmidon; bailiff; police-officer; tool of the law
Scabellon, *s.m.* (*arch.*) scabellum, pedestal, stand
Scabieuse, *s.f.* (*bot.*) scabious
Scabieu-x, se, *adj.* (*med.*) scabious
Scabre, *adj.* (*nat. hist.*) scabrous
Scabreu-x, se, *adj.* rugged, rough, scabrous; dangerous; difficult; slippery; delicate; ticklish
Scabrosité, *s.f.* ruggedness, roughness, scabrousness; ticklishness
Scagliola, *s.f.* (*arch.*) scagliola
Scalaire, *s.f.* (*mollusc*) wentletrap
Scalde, *s.m.* Scald *or* Scalder (*poet*)
Scalène, *adj.* (*geom.*) scalene; — *adj. s.m.* (*anat.*) scalenus
Scalope, *s.m.* (*zool.*) shrew-mole
Scalpe, *s.m.* scalp
Scalpel, *s.m.* (*surg.*) scalpel
Scalpement, *s.m.* scalping
Scalper, *v.a.* to scalp
Scalpeur, *s.m.* scalper
Scammonée, *s.f.* (*bot.*, *pharm.*) scammony
Scammonine, *s.f.* (*chem.*) scammonine
Scandale, *s.m.* scandal; offence; shame; exposure
Scandaleusement, *adv.* scandalously
Scandaleu-x, se, *adj.* scandalous
Scandaliser, *v.a.* to scandalize
  Se —, *v.r.* to be scandalized; to take offence
Scander, *v.a.* to scan (*verses*). *Se —*, to be scanned
Scandinave, *adj. s.m.f.* Scandinavian
Scansion, *s.f.* scansion
Scape, *s.m.* (*bot.*) scape, flower-bearing stem
Scaphandre, *s.m.* float for swimming, cork life-jacket, cork jacket, air-jacket, bladders; diving-apparatus, diving-dress
Scaphandreur, Scaphandrier, *s.m.* diver
Scaphoïde, *adj.* (*anat.*) scaphoid; — *s.m.* scaphoid bone
Scapin, *s.m.* knave
Scapolite, *s.f.* (*min.*) scapolite
Scapulaire, *s.m.* (*of monks*, &c.) scapular, scapulary; (*surg.*) shoulder-band *or* strap; — *s.f.* scapular; scapular feather; — *adj.* scapular
Scapulum, *s.m.* (*anat.*) *V.* **Omoplate**
Scarabée, *s.m.* (*zool.*) beetle
Scaramouche, *s.m.* Scaramouch
Scare, *s.m.* (*zool.*) parrot-fish
Scarieu-x, se, *adj.* (*bot.*) scarious
Scarificateur, *s.m.* (*instr.*) scarificator, scarifier; — *m.*, **-trice,** *f.*, *adj.* scarifying
Scarification, *s.f.* scarification
Scarifier, *v.a.* to scarify
Scariole, *s.f.* (*bot.*) endive
Scarlatine, *adj.f.*, *s.f.* (*med.*) scarlet; scarlatina, scarlet fever
Scarole, *s.f.* (*bot.*) endive
Sceau, *s.m.* seal; seal-office; stamp; sanction. *Petit —*, privy seal. *Gardes des —x*, keeper of the seals. *Mettre le — à*, to seal; to sanction; to complete
Scélérat, e, *adj.* villanous, flagitious, vile, infamous; wicked; profligate, unprincipled; — *s.m.f.* villain, scoundrel; wretch
Scélératesse, *s.f.* villany, infamousness, infamy, wickedness, profligacy
Scellé, *s.m.* (*law*) seal
Scellement, *s.m.* sealing; fastening
Sceller, *v.a.* to seal; to seal up; to fasten; to fix; to bind; to cement; to strengthen; to ratify, to confirm
  Se —, *v.r.* to be sealed, &c.
Scelleu-r, se, *s.m.f.* sealer
Scène, *s.f.* scene; stage; scenery; drama; occurrence; uproar, row, quarrel, scene. *Faire une — à*, to get up a scene with, to have a row with, to reproach violently, to blow up, to abuse. *Mettre en —*, to represent *or* bring on the stage; to get up for the stage; to bring forward. *La — est* or *se passe* . . ., the scene is laid . . .
Scénique, *adj.* scenic, scenical
Scénite, *adj.* dwelling in tents
Scénographie, *s.f.* scenography; scene-painting
Scénograph-ique, -iquement. *V.* p. 3, § 1
Scept-icisme, -ique (*adj. s.*), **-iquement.** *V.* page 3, § 1
Sceptre, *s.m.* sceptre; sway; dominion; empire
Schabraque, *s.f.* (*mil.*) shabracque, shabrack
Schah, *s.m.* Shah (*of Persia*)
Schako. *V.* **Shako**
Schamanisme, *s.m.* shamanism
Schamaniste, *s.m.* shamanist
Schapzka, Schapska, *s.m.* (*mil.*) Polish shako, lancer's cap, lance-cap
Scharpenelle, *s.f.* *V.* **Shrapnel**
Scheik, Scheick. *V.* **Cheik**
Schelling, *s.m.* *V.* **Shilling**
‡**Schéma,** *s.m.* schema
‡**Schémat-ique, -iquement.** *V.* page 3, §
‡**Schématiser,** *v.a.* to schematize
‡**Schématisme,** *s.m.* schematism
‡**Schème,** *s.m.* schema
‡**Schène,** *s.m.* schene
Schérif, *s.m.* *V.* **Chérif** *and* **Shérif**
‡**Scherzando,** *adv.* (*mus.*) scherzando
‡**Scherzo,** *s.m.* (*mus.*) scherzo
Schibboleth, *s.m.* shibboleth
Schilling, *s.m.* *V.* **Shilling**
‡**Schine,** *s.m.* (*bot.*) schinus
Schismatique, *adj. s.m.f.* schismatic
Schisme, *s.m.* schism
Schiste, *s.m.* (*min.*) schist; clay-slate, slate-clay, slate; shale; shale-oil. — *argileux*, clay-slate. *Huile de —*, shale-oil
Schisteu-x, se, *adj.* schistous; shaly
Schlague, *s.f.* (*mil.*) flogging
Schli(‡)ch, Schlick, *s.m.* (*metal.*) schlich, slich, slik
Schlittage, *s.m.* sliding down (*felled trees*)
Schlitte, *s.f.* slide (*for felled trees*)
Schlitteur, *s.m.* slider (*of felled trees*)
Schnapan. *V.* **Chenapan**
Schnaps, *s.m.* *V.* **Schnick**
Schnick, *s.m.* (*fam.*) brandy; gin; strong stuff
‡**Schœnus,** *s.m.* (*bot.*) schœnus, bog-rush, sedge
‡**Scholaire, Scholie,** &c. *V.* **Scolaire, Scolie,** &c.
‡**Schooner,** *s.m.* (*nav.*) schooner
Schorl, *s.m.* (*min.*) schorl, shorl
Schottish, Schotisch, *s.f.* (*dance, tune*) schottische, schottish
Sciable, *adj.* sawable
Sciage, *s.m.* sawing
Sciagraph-ie, -ique, -iquement. *V.* page 3, § 1
Sciant, e, *adj.* (*fam.*) bothering, plaguing, annoying; tiresome, tedious
Sciathérique, *adj.* sciatheric
Sciatique, *adj.m.f.*, *s.f.* sciatic, hip; sciatica, hip-gout
Scie, *s.f.* saw; (*fig.*) bore, plague, bother; (*zool.*) saw-fish. — *à découper*, saw-frame. — *de scieur de long*, pit-saw
Sciemment, *adv.* knowingly, wittingly
Science, *s.f.* science; knowledge; learning; information. *De — certaine*, for a certainty, for a positive fact; knowingly
Sciène, *s.f.* (*fish*) maigre
Scientif-ique, -iquement. *V.* page 3, § 1
Scier, *v.a.n.* to saw; to reap; to pull right and left; (*— le dos à*), to bore, to plague, to pester, to bother; to be plaguing *or* bothering; (*nav.*, *— à culer*) to back water, to back astern
  Se —, *v.r.* to be sawn
Scierie, *s.f.* saw-mill; sawing-machine; saw-bench; saw-yard
Scieur, *s.m.* sawyer; reaper. — *de long*, sawyer
Scille, *s.f.* (*bot.*) squill. — *blanche*, sea-daffodil. — *penchée*, harebell
Scillitine, *s.f.* scillitine
Scillitique, *adj.* squillitic

Scindé, e, *part. adj.* divided; (*of books*) *in* parts
Scinder, *v.a.* to divide. *Se* —, to be divided
Scinque, *s.m.* (*zool.*) scink, skink
Scintillant, e, *adj.* scintillant
Scintillation, *s.f.*, **Scintillement,** *s.m.* scintillation, sparkling, twinkling
Scintiller, *v.n.* to scintillate, to sparkle, to emit sparks, to twinkle [3, § 1
Sciograph-ie, -ique, -iquement. *V.* page
Scion, *s.m.* scion, shoot; sprig; (*of a fishing-rod*) top
Scionner, *v.a.* to cane
Scioptique, *adj.* (*opt.*) scioptic
Sciotte, *s.f.* (*tech.*) hand-saw
Scirpe, *s.m.* (*bot.*) scirpus, club-rush; bulrush
Scirrhose, *s.f.* (*med.*) scirrhosis
Scissile, *adj.* scissile, scissible
Scission, *s.f.* scission, division; fission; split; secession; separation
Scissionnaire, *adj.* seceding; — *s.m.f.* seceder
Scissure, *s.f.* scissure; fissure; crack, cleft
Sciure, *s.f.* sawdust
Sclarée, *s.f.* (*bot.*) clary
Sclérème, *s.m.* (*med.*) sclerema
Scléreu-x, se, *adj.* (*med.*) sclerous
Sclériase, *s.f.* (*med.*) scleriasis
Scléromètre, *s.m.* sclerometer
Sclérophthalmie, *s.f.* (*med.*) sclerophthalmia
Sclérose, *s.f.* (*med.*) sclerosis
Sclérostome, *s.m.* (*zool.*) sclerostoma
Sclérotical, e, *adj.* (*anat.*) sclerotic, sclerotical
Sclérotique, *s.f.* (*anat.*) sclerotic, sclerotica
Scolaire, *adj.* school, scholastic, academic
Scolarité, *s.f.* (*formerly*) scholarity; (*now*) course of studies, curriculum
Scolastique, *adj.* scholastic, school, academic; — *s.m.* scholastic, schoolman; — *s.f.* scholasticism
Scolastiquement, *adv.* scholastically
Scoliaste, *s.m.* scholiast
Scolie, (*philology*) *s.f.*, (*geom.*) *s.m.* scholium
Scoliose, *s.f.* (*med.*) scoliosis
Scolopace, *s.f.* (*zool.*) scolopax, snipe
Scolopendre, *s.f.* (*zool.*) scolopendra, centiped; (*bot., pharm.*) scolopendrium, hart's-tongue
Scolyte, *s.m.* (*zool.*) scolytus, bark-beetle, bark-chafer
Scombre, *s.m.* (*fish*) scomber, mackerel
Scombrésoce, *s.m.* (*fish*) saury pike, skipper
Scoparine, *s.f.* (*chem.*) scoparine
Scops, *s.m.* scops-eared owl
Scorbut, *s.m.* scurvy
Scorbutique, *adj. s.* scorbutic
Scordion, Scordium, *s.m.* (*bot.*) scordium, water-germander
Scoriacé, e, *adj.* scoriaceous
Scorie, *s.f.* scoria; dross; slag; clinker
Scorification, *s.f.* scorification
Scorificatoire, *s.m.* scorifier
Scorifier, *v.a.* to scorify
Scoriforme, *adj.* scoriform
Scorpène, *s.f.* (*fish*) scorpæna, hog-fish, scorpion-fish, bergylt
Scorpioïde, *adj.* scorpioid, scorpioidal
Scorpiojelle, *s.f.* scorpion-oil
Scorpion, *s.m.* scorpion
Scorpione, *s.f.* (*bot.*) scorpion-grass
Scorpiure, *s.f.* (*bot.*) caterpillar
Scorsonère, Scorzonère, *s.f.* (*bot.*) scorzonera, viper's grass
Scotie, *s.f.* (*arch.*) scotia
Scot-isme, -iste, -istique. *V.* page 3, § 1
Scotodinie, Scotomie, *s.f.* (*med.*) scotodinia, scotomy
Scottish. *V.* **Schottish**
Scribe, *s.m.* scribe; writer
Scripteur, *s.m.* (*of the Pope*) scriptor
Scripturaire, Scriptural, e, *adj.* scriptural
Scrofulaire, *s.f.* (*bot.*) figwort
Scrofule, *s.f.*, **Scrofules,** *s.f.pl.* (*med.*) scrofula
Scrofuleu-x, se, *adj. s* scrofulous; scrofulous person
Scrofulide, *s.f.* scrofulous disease of the skin
Scrofulose, *s.f.* (*med.*) scrofulosis
Scrotal, e, *adj.* (*anat.*) scrotal
Scrotocèle, *s.f.* (*med.*) scrotocele
Scrotum, *s.m.* (*anat.*) scrotum
Scrupule, *s.m.* scruple, qualm; scrupulousness. *Se faire* — or *un* —, to scruple; to scruple to do
Scrupuleusement, *adv.* scrupulously; nicely, rigorously, strictly, exactly
Scrupuleu-x, se, *adj.* scrupulous; nice, rigorous, strict, exact, precise, particular; — *s.m.f.* scrupler
Scrupulosité, *s.f.* scrupulosity, scrupulousness
Scruta-teur, trice, *s.m.f. adj.* scrutinizer, searcher, investigator; scrutineer, teller; scrutinizing, searching, investigating
Scruter, *v.a.* to scrutinize, to search, to fathom, to investigate, to pry into
Scrutin, *s.m.* ballot, balloting; votes. — *de liste*, vote by ticket. *Au* —, *au — secret*, by ballot
Scrutiner, *v.a.* to ballot
Scubac, *s.m.* usquebaugh (*spirituous liquor*)
Sculptable, *adj.* to be sculptured *or* carved
Sculptage, *s.m.* sculpturing; carving
Sculpter, *v.a.* to sculpture; to carve
Sculp-teur, trice, *s.m.f.* sculptor, sculptress; (ornamental) carver
Sculptural, e, *adj.* sculptural
Sculpture, *s.f.* sculpture; carving; carved work
Scurrilité, *s.f.* scurrility
Scutiforme, *adj.* scutiform
Scybale, *s.f.* (*med.*) scybalum
Scyllare, *s.m.* (*zool.*) scyllarus
Scyllion, *s.m.* (*zool.*) spotted dog-fish
Scyphate, Scyphiforme, *adj.* cup-shaped
Scytale, *s.m.* (*snake*) scytale
Scythe, *adj. s.m.f.* Scythian
Scythique, *adj.* Scythic
Se, S', *pers. pron.* oneself, himself, herself, itself, themselves; each other, one another; to oneself, to himself, to herself, &c.; to *or* at *or* with each other; in *or* within *or* with *or* at *or* for *or* from *or* by *or* on oneself, &c.; between *or* among them *or* themselves
Séance, *s.f.* seat; sitting; meeting; lecture; recital. — *tenante*, forthwith. *En* —, sitting
Séant, e, *part. adj.* (*old*) sitting; fitting, seemly, beseeming, becoming, proper, right
Séant, *s.m.* sitting posture. *Être sur son* —, to be sitting up. *Se lever* or *se mettre* or *se tenir* or *se dresser sur son* —, to sit up
Seau, *s.m.* pail, bucket; scuttle; pailful, bucketful. *Pleuvoir a —x*, to rain in torrents
Sébacé, e, *adj.* sebaceous
Sébacique, *adj.* (*chem.*) sebacic
Sébate, *s.m.* (*chem.*) sebate
Sébeste, *s.m.* (*bot.*) sebesten (*fruit*)
Sébestier, *s.m.* (*bot.*) sebesten-tree
Sébifère, *adj.* sebiferous
Séborrhagie, Séborrhée, *s.f.* (*med.*) seborrhagia
Sébile, *s.f.* wooden bowl
Sec, *m.*, **Sèche,** *f.*, *adj.* dry; lean, thin, spare, skinny, lanky; (*of fruit*, &c.) dried; (*fig.*) dry; unfeeling, hard; tart; sharp; smart; quick; sudden; blunt; severe; harsh; unadorned; stiff; (*of money*) ready; (*of metals*) short-grained, short. — *comme un pendu*, as thin as a lath
Sec, *s.m.* dryness; dry fodder, manger-food; sweetmeats; (*slang*) brandy, liquor; (*pers.*) bony man, lanky fellow. *A* —, dry; drained; exhausted; empty; low; out (of); out of cash, hard up; (*nav.*) ahull; (*nav.*) under bare poles. *A — sur le rivage*, (*nav.*) high and dry. *Mettre a* —, to drain; to exhaust
Sec, *adv.* dryly, sharply; harshly; (*of breaking*) short; (*of drinking*) neat; hard
Sécable, *adj.* divisible
Sécant, e, *adj.*, **Sécante,** *s.f.* (*geom.*) secant
Sécateur, *s.m.* pruning-shears *or* scissors, trimming-shears, hedge-shears
Sécession, *s.f.* secession
Sécessioniste, *s.m.f. adj.* secessionist
Séchage, *s.m.* drying
Sèchard, *s.m.* (*at Geneva*) North-East wind
Sèche, *s.f.* (*zool.*) cuttle-fish, cuttle; (*nav.*) rock *or* sand left dry; (*of a ship*) cross jack yard; — *adj.f. V.* **Sec**

Sèche, *s.m.* (*in compounds, from* **Sécher,** "to dry") thing that dries, dryer. **—-plumes,** [*s.m.* pen-dryer
Séchée, *s.f.* drying
Sèchement, *adv.* dryly; sharply, bluntly; harshly; plainly
Sécher, *v.a.n.* to dry; to dry up; to cure; to wither; to languish, to pine away; to fret; to pore (*on books*). — *sur pied,* to languish, to pine away; to fret; to be extremely dejected; to pine away in single blessedness
Sécheresse, *s.f.* dryness; drought; sharpness; harshness; stiffness; barrenness; aridity; plainness [*or* ground
Sécherie, *s.f.* drying-house *or* room *or* closet
Sécheron, *s.m.* dry meadow; skinny fellow *or* thing [*or* machine
Sécheu-r, se, *s.m.f.* dryer; drying apparatus
Séchoir, *s.m.* drying-room *or* box, drying apparatus *or* place *or* ground; dryer; exsiccator; tenter; clothes-horse; towel-horse
Second, e, *adj.* second; secondary; inferior; junior; other; — *s.m.* second; second floor; assistant; fellow, like, equal, second self; (*nav.*) mate; **—e,** *s.f.* (**—es,** *s.f.pl.*) second; second form *or* class (*highest but one in France, 'fifth' in England*); (*theat.*) second-tier box (*pl.* second tier of boxes); second class (*rail.,* &c.); fore-cabin; (*print.*) second proof, revise; (*fenc.*) segoon. *Au —,* on *or* to the second floor. *En —,* in the second place, in a subordinate capacity; second, under, sub, assistant. *En —e,* in the second class
Secondaire, *adj.* secondary; accessory; (*of schools and instruction*) higher, superior, high-class [sorily
Secondairement, *adv.* secondarily; acces-
Secondement, *adv.* secondly
Seconder, *v.a.* to second, to assist, to help, to support, to back; to promote, to further; to favour [(*med.*) secundines, after-birth
Secondine, *s.f.* (*bot.*) secundine; **—s,** *pl.*
Sécot, *adj.m.* (*pop.*) lean, thin, lanky, bony, skinny; — *s.m.* ditto fellow
Secouade, *s.f.* rating, reprimand, blowing-up
Secouement, *s.m.* shaking; jogging; jolting; shake
Secouer, *v.a.* to shake; to shake off; to give a shake; to toss; to wag; to throw off; to discard; to flick, to flick off; to jog; to jolt; to rouse; to rate, to reprimand, to blow up, to handle roughly. — *les oreilles,* to shake o.'s ears, not to mind it, to demur, to say nay
Se —, *v.r.* to shake oneself; to rouse oneself; to exert oneself; to take exercise; to [move about
Secoueu-r, se, *s.m.f.* shaker
Secoûment. *V.* **Secouement**
Secourable, *adj.* helpful, helping; ready *or* willing to help *or* to assist; benevolent, charitable; relievable [rescuer
Secoureu-r, se, *s.m.f.* succourer, helper,
Secourir, *v.a.* to succour, to relieve, to assist, to help, to aid; to rescue
Secours, *s.m.* succour, relief, assistance, help, aid; rescue, rescuing; preservation of life, restoring suspended animation, appliances for ditto; supply; service, use. "— *contre l'incendie,*" (*on plates in the streets*) F.P. (fire-plug). *Au —! à mon —!* help! *Crier au —,* to call for help. *V.* **Mutuel**
Secousse, *s.f.* shake, shaking; jerk; bump; concussion; shock; toss, tossing; agitation; check; blow; attack
Secr-et, ète, *adj.* secret; hidden; concealed; recondite; mysterious; occult; private; reserved; close; — *s.m.* secret; secrecy; mystery; privacy; close confinement; hidden place; retreat; secret drawer; secret spring. *Le — de la comédie* or *de Polichinelle,* a secret known to everybody, no secret at all. *Au —,* in close confinement. *En —,* in secret, in secrecy, secretly, privately. *Sous le —,* in secret, in secrecy. *Être du —,* to be in the secret

Secreta, *s.m.pl.* (*Latin*) secreta, secretions
Secrétage, *s.m.* secretage
Secrétaire, *s.m.* secretary; clerk; writing-desk; davenport; (*zool.*) secretary, secretary bird, secretary falcon, serpent-eater. — *d'État,* secretary of state. — *général,* (*of a ministry*) under-secretary of state
Secrétairerie, *s.f.* secretary's office
Secrétariat, *s.m.* secretaryship; clerkship; secretary's office [*V.* **Secret,** *adj.*
Secrète, *s.f.* (*Cath. rel.*) secret prayer; — *adj.f.*
Secrètement, *adv.* secretly, in secret; privately, in private; inwardly
Secréter, *v.a.* to secrete (*prepare skins with mercury*) [to be secreted
Sécréter, *v.a.* (*in physiology*) to secrete. *Se —,*
Secréteur, *s.m.* (*of felts*) secreter
Sécré-teur, trice, *adj.* secreting, secretory
Sécrétion, *s.f.* secretion
Secrétiste, *s.m.f.* secretist
Secrétivité, *s.f.* (*in phrenology*) secretiveness
Sécrétoire, *adj.* secretory, secreting
Sectaire, *s.m.f. adj.* sectarian
Secta-teur, trice, *s.m.f.* follower, votary
Secte, *s.f.* sect. *Faire — à part,* to separate [from others
Secteur, *s.m.* sector
Sectile, *adj.* sectile
Section, *s.f.* section; (*of canals*) water-way
Sectionnaire, *s.m.f.* sectionist
Sectionnel, le, *adj.* sectional
Sectionnement, *s.m.* sectionizing
Sectionner, *v.a.* to sectionize
Séculaire, *adj.* secular; a hundred years old, centenary; venerable (*by age*), old
Séculairement, *adv.* secularly
Sécularisation, *s.f.* secularization
Séculariser, *v.a.* to secularize
Sécular-isme, -iste. *V.* page 3, § 1
Sécularité, *s.f.* secularity, secularism; secular [jurisdiction
Séculi-er, ère, *adj. s.* secular
Séculièrement, *adv.* secularly
Secundo, *adv.* secondly, in the second place
Sécurité, *s.f.* security
Sedan, *s.m.* Sedan cloth [tive
Sédati-f, ve, *adj.,* **Sédatif,** *s.m.* (*med.*) seda-
Sédation, *s.f.* (*med.*) sedation
Sédentaire, *adj.* sedentary; stationary; settled; — *s.f.* (*zool.*) sedentary
Sédentairement, *adv.* sedentarily
Sédentarité, *s.f.* sedentariness
Sédiment, *s.m.* sediment, dregs; fur
Sédimentaire, *adj.* sedimentary
Sédimentation, *s.f.* sedimentation
Séditieusement, *adv.* seditiously
Séditieu-x, se, *adj.* seditious; — *s.m.f.* seditionist, seditionary, mutineer
Sédition, *s.f.* sedition
Sedlitz, *s.m.* Sedlitz, Seidlitz
Séduc-teur, trice, *s.m.f. adj.* seducer; enticer; deluder; briber; seductive; enticing; deluding; fascinating; bribing
Séduction, *s.f.* seduction; enticement, allurement; charm, fascination; bribery, bribing; coaxing
Séduire, *v.a.* to seduce; to bribe; to entice, to tempt; to delude; to charm, to beguile; to fascinate, to bewitch, to captivate; to win, to win over, to gain over
Séduisant, e, *part. adj.* seducing, seductive; deluding, delusive; lovely; enticing, &c. (*V.* **Séduire**)
Ségétal, e, *adj.* growing among corn
Segment, *s.m.* segment
Segmentaire, *adj.* segmental
Ségrairie, *s.f.* wood held in common
Ségrais, *s.m.* detached wood
Ségrégati-f, ve, *adj.* segregative
Ségrégation, *s.f.* segregation
Ségrégativement, *adv.* segregatively
†Séguedille, *s.f.* seguidilla (*Spanish tune, song and dance*)
Seiche, *s.f.* (*zool.*) *V.* **Sèche**
Séide, *s.m.* fanatical assassin; fanatic; devoted partisan, blind supporter

Séidisme, *s.m.* fanaticism; devoted partisanship, blind support
Seigle, *s.m.* rye. *Faire les —s,* to cut rye
†Seigneur, *s.m.* lord; squire; mylord; Sir; Mr. *Grand* —, great lord, high personage, nobleman; Grand Seignior (*or* Signior), Sultan. *Petit* —, petty lord, lordling. *En* —, *en grand* —, lordly, lordlike, like a (great) lord. *Faire le* —, to lord, to play the lord. *A tout — tout honneur,* honour to whom honour is due
†Seigneuriage, *s.m.* seigniorage [norial
†Seigneurial, e, *adj.* seigniorial, lordly, ma-
†Seigneurie, *s.f.* lordship; seigniory; manor
Seikh. *V.* **Syke** [bucket
†Seille, *s.f.,* **Seilleau, Seillot,** *s.m.* pail,
Seime, *s.f.* (*vet.*) wire-heel
Sein, *s.m.* bosom; breast; pap; (*fig.*) bosom, womb, heart, midst, middle, depth. *Donner le — à,* to give the breast to, to give suck to, to suckle [drag-net; (*river*) Seine
Seine, *s.f.* (*fish.*) seine-net, seine, trawl-net,
Seiner, *v.n.* to fish with a seine
Seinette, *s.f.* small seine
Seineur, *s.m.* seine-fisherman
Seing, *s.m.* signature; sign manual. *Blanc* —, *See Letter* **B.** — *privé,* private deed. *Sous — privé, V.* **Signature**
Seize, *adj.m.f., s.m.* sixteen; sixteenth
Seizième, *adj. s.* sixteenth; sixteenth day
Seizièmement, *adv.* sixteenthly
Séjour, *s.m.* stay; sojourn; abode, residence, dwelling, habitation, place; regions; continuance; delay [ing, staying, stay
Séjournement, *s.m.* sojournment, sojourn-
Séjourner, *v.n.* to stay; to remain; to reside; to dwell; to sojourn; to tarry; to continue
Sel, *s.m.* salt; sal; (*fig.*) salt, wit, point, poignancy, humour, smartness. — *admirable,* sulphate of soda, Glauber's salt. — *gris,* bay salt. — *de verre,* sandiver. *Au gros* —, served up with coarse salt; (*fig.*) coarse. *Beurre demi-* —, half-salt butter, powdered butter
Selache, *s.m.* (*fish*) *V.* **Pèlerin** [selacian
Sélacien, ne, *adj.,* **Sélacien,** *s.m.* (*zool.*)
Sélage, *s.m.* (*bot.*) selago
Sélaginelle, *s.f.* (*bot.*) selaginella [*in the East*)
Sélam, Sélan, *s.m.* selam (*emblematic nosegay*
Sélecti-f, ve, *adj.* selective
Sélection, *s.f.* selection
Sélectivement, *adv.* selectively
Séléniate, *s.m.* (*chem.*) seleniate
Sélénien, ne, *s.m.f.* lunarian
Sélénieu-x, se, *adj.* (*chem.*) selenious
Sélénifère, *adj.* seleniferous
Sélénique, *adj.* selenic
Sélénite, *s.f.* (*min.*), *s.m.* (*chem.*) selenite
Séléniteu-x, se, *adj.* (*chem.*) selenitic, sele-
Sélénium, *s.m.* (*chem.*) selenium [nitical
Séléniure, *s.m.* (*chem.*) selenide, seleniuret
Sélénocentrique, *adj.* selenocentric
Sélénographe, *s.m.* selenographer
Sélénograph-ie, -ique. *V.* page 3, § 1
Sélénostat, *s.m.* selenostat
Séleucides, *s.m.pl.* (*hist.*) Seleucidæ
Sélictar, *s.m.* (*the Sultan's*) sword. — *aga,* —, crown sword-bearer
Sélin, *s.m.* (*bot.*) selinum, milk-parsley
Séline, *s.f.* (*med.*) spots in the nails
Sellage, *s.m.* saddling
Selle, *s.f.* saddle; washing-board; bench; seat; stool; water-closet; dejection, ejection, evacuation, motion
Seller, *v.a.* to saddle. *Se* —, (*agr.*) to harden
Sellerie, *s.f.* saddlery; harness-room
Sellette, *s.f.* stool; culprit's stool *or* seat; stool of repentance; shoeblack's box; (*house-painter's*) cradle; (*of a carriage-horse*) pad; (*of a plough*) pillow, collar; (*nav.*) calking-box. *Mettre sur la* —, to haul over the coals. *Tenir*
Sellier, *s.m.* saddler [*sur la* —, to cross-question
Selon, *prep.* according to; agreeably to; pursuant to; according to circumstances. — *moi,* in my opinion. — *que,* as, according as. *C'est* —, that depends on circumstances, that
Seltz *or* **Selz (Eau de),** *s.f. V.* **Eau** [depends
Seltzogène, Selzogène, *s.m.* seltzogene
†Semailles, *s.f.pl.* sowing; seed; sowing-time
Semaine, *s.f.* week; week's work; week's (*or* weekly) earnings *or* gain *or* pay *or* wages *or* salary *or* allowance; (weekly *or* week's) pocket-money; week's duty. *A la* —, by the week. *A la petite* —, for a short time and at a high rate of interest. *Par* —, a week. *La — grasse,* Shrovetide. *La — prochaine,* next week. *La — sainte* (or *muette*), the holy week, Passion-week. *La — des quatre jeudis,* when two Sundays come together, Tib's eve, latter Lammas, never. *Être de* —, to be on duty for the week
Semainier, *s.m.* officer of the week, person (*monk,* &c.) on duty for the week, prebendary whose week it is to officiate, manager for the week; weekly diary, date-case; letter-rack; case of seven-day razors; set of seven (*similar things, for every day in the week*) [for the week
Semainière, *s.f.* person (*nun,* &c.) on duty
Semaison, *s.f.* seeding; sowing-time
Sémaphore, *s.m.* semaphore [page 3, § 1
Sémaphor-ique, -iquement, -iste. *V.*
Semaque, *s.m.* smack, fishing-smack
Semblable, *adj.* alike; similar, like; like it; such; — *s.m.* like, fellow, match, equal; fellow-creature, fellow-man, (—**s,** *pl.*) fellow-creatures, fellow-men, kind [manner, too; as much
Semblablement, *adv.* also, likewise, in like
Semblant, *s.m.* appearance, semblance, seeming, air, show, pretence, sham. *Faire* —, to pretend, to feign, to seem, to appear as if. *Ne faire — de rien,* to feign indifference *or* ignorance; to appear to take no notice; to look as if nothing was the matter. *Sans faire — de rien,* without appearing to observe, without seeming to take notice of anything; without seeming to mind it; looking as if nothing was the matter
Sembler, *v.n.* to seem, to appear; to strike. *C'est ce qui me semble,* I think so; I thought so. *Que vous en semble?* what do you think of it? *Il lui sembla reconnaitre,* he thought *or* he fancied (that) he recognized
Semblide, *s.f.* (*insect*) semblis
Semé, e, *part. adj.* sown, &c. (*V.* **Semer**); (*her.*) powdered, aspersed, semé [nut
Sémécarpe, *s.m.* (*tree*) semecarpus, marking-
Séméiographie, &c. *V.* **Sémiographie,** &c.
Sémélé, *s.f.* (*myth., astr.*) Semele
Semelle, *s.f.* sole; sock; foot's length; (*tech.*) sole; sleeper; ground-sill; (*of a gun-butt*) heel-plate; (*of an anchor*) shoe; (*fig.*) step, inch. *Battre la* —, to pad the hoof, to travel on foot, to ramble, to tramp, to be on the tramp; to warm o.'s feet. *Rompre la* —, *V.* **Rompre**
Semence, *s.f.* seed; sowing; cause; (*nails*) sprigs. — *de diamant,* diamond-sparks. — *de perles,* seed-pearl
Semen-contra, *s.m.* semen-contra, worm-seed
Semer, *v.a.n.* to sow; to plant; to scatter; to strew; to sprinkle; to distribute; to cast, to throw; to spread
Se —, *v.r.* to be sown *or* &c.
Semestre, *s.m.* half-year, six months; half-year's duty *or* salary *or* pay *or* income *or* dividends *or* &c.; (*mil.*) six months' furlough; — *adj.* half-yearly. *De* or *par* —, half-yearly
Semestriel, le, *adj.* half-yearly, semi-annual
Semestrier, *s.m.* soldier absent on a six months' furlough
Semeu-r, se, *s.m.f.* sower; spreader
Semi, *adj.* semi, demi, half
†Sémillance, *s.f.* briskness, sprightliness, friskiness; liveliness; quickness
†Sémillant, e, *adj.* brisk, sprightly, frisky; lively; quick [lively *or* quick, to frisk
†Sémiller, *v.n.* to be brisk *or* sprightly *or*

Séminaire, *s.m.* ecclesiastical college, priests' college, seminary
Séminal, e, *adj.* seminal
Séminariste, *s.m.* seminarist
Sémination, *s.f.* semination
Séminifère, *adj.* seminiferous
Sémio-graphie, -graphique, -logie, -logique, &c. *V.* page 3, § 1
Sémiotique, *adj.* semiotic, semeiotic; — *s.f.* semiotics, semeiotics
Semis, *s.m.* seed-plot, seed-bed; sowing
Sémite, *s.m.* Shemite, Semite
Sémitique, *adj.* Shemitic, Semitic
Sémitisme, *s.m.* Shemitism, Semitism
Semnopithèque, *s.m.* (*monkey*) semnopithecus
Semoir, *s.m.* seed-lip; corn-drill, drill
Semonce, *s.f.* reprimand, lecture; summons, invitation, call
Semoncelle, *s.m.* Semoncelle cheese
Semoncer, *v.a.* to reprimand, to scold, to lecture; to summon, to invite, to call
Semondre, *v.a.* (*old*) to invite, to ask
Semoule, *s.f.* semolina; manna-croup
Semoun. *V.* **Simoun**
Semper-virens, *s.m.* (*bot.*) trumpet-honeysuckle, coral-honeysuckle
Sempiternel, le, *adj.* sempiternal, everlasting; — *s.m.f.* antiquated fellow *or* thing
Sempiternellement, *adv.* sempiternally, everlastingly
Sempiternité, *s.f.* sempiternity
Senaire, *adj.* senary
Sénat, *s.m.* senate
Sénateur, *s.m.* senator
Sénatorerie, *s.f.* senatorship
Sénatorial, e, Sénatorien, ne, *adj.* senatorial, senatorian
Sénatrice, *s.f.* senator's wife
Sénatus-consulte, *s.m.* senatus-consultum, decree of the senate
Senau, *s.m.* (*nav.*) snow. *Voile de* —, try-sail
Séné, *s.m.* (*bot.*) senna
Sénebière, *s.f.* (*bot.*) senebiera, wart-cress
Sénéchal, *s.m.* seneschal. *Grand-* —, high-seneschal
Sénéchale, *s.f.* seneschal's wife
Sénéchaussée, *s.f.* seneschal's jurisdiction *or* court
Séneçon, *s.m.* (*bot.*) groundsel; ragwort
Sénéga, *s.m.* (*bot.*) senega, snake-root
Senégré. *V.* **Fenugrec**
Senelle. *V.* **Cenelle**
Sénestre, *adj.* (*obsolete*) left; (*her.*) sinister, left
Sénevé, *s.m.* (*bot.*) charlock; mustard-seed
Sénieur, *s.m.* (*obsolete*) senior
Sénile, *adj.* senile, old
Sénilement, *adv.* senilely
Sénilité, *s.f.* senility
Senne, *s.f.* (*fish.*) *V.* **Seine**
Sens, *s.m.* sense; senses; sensuality; feelings; intellect, understanding; mind; wits; reason; judgment; opinion; meaning, signification; acceptation; side; way; direction. — *commun,* common sense; sense. — *dessus dessous,* upside down, topsy-turvy, in disorder, in confusion, at sixes and sevens. — *devant derrière,* the hind part foremost, the wrong way. — *intime,* consciousness. — *propre,* proper sense. *A double* —, with double meaning. *A mon* —, in my opinion. *Bon* —, good sense; common sense; sense; sensibleness; reason; right senses, senses. *Gros bon* —, plain good sense, good common sense. *Dans le* — *de,* in the direction of; in a way favourable to; conformably to, agreeably to. *Dans tous les* —, in all directions; to and fro. *En tous* —, in every direction. *Abonder* or *donner dans le* — *de, V.* **Abonder.** *N'avoir pas le* — *commun,* to be devoid of sense, to have no sense, to be absurd *or* preposterous. *Reprendre ses* —, to recover o.'s senses, to come to o.'s senses, to come to oneself, to come to. *Se manger les* —, (*vulgar*) to fret oneself to death. *Tomber sous le* (or *les*) —, to be obvious
Sensation, *s.f.* sensation. *A* —, (*adject.*) sensation, sensational. *Faire* —, to create a sensation
Sensé, e, *adj.* sensible, reasonable, of sense
Sensément, *adv.* sensibly, reasonably, judiciously
Sensibilité, *s.f.* sensibility; sensitiveness; feeling; delicacy; tenderness; soreness
Sensible, *adj.* sensible; sensitive; feeling; impressible; lively, keen, acute; painful; tender, sore; perceptible, visible, observable, obvious; — *s.f.* (*mus.*) sensible note
Sensiblement, *adv.* sensibly; feelingly; keenly; vividly; deeply; perceptibly, visibly, obviously; considerably, greatly, much
Sensiblerie, *s.f.* sentimentalism, sentimentality, affected sensibility, maudlin
Sensiti-f, ve, *adj.* sensitive; —**ve,** *s.f.* (*bot.*) sensitive plant
Sensorial, e, *adj.* sensorial
Sensoriel, le, *adj.* sensory
Sensorium, *s.m.* sensorium
Sensualisation, *s.f.* sensualization
Sensualiser, *v.a.* to sensualize
Sensual-isme, -iste (*s.*). *V.* page 3, § 1
Sensualiste, *adj.* sensualistic
Sensualité, *s.f.* sensuality; sensual pleasure
Sensuel, le, *adj. s.* sensual; voluptuous; sensualist
Sensuellement, *adv.* sensually
Sentant, e, *adj.* sentient, feeling
Sente, *s.f. V.* **Sentier**
Sentenay, *s.m.* sentenay (wine)
Sentence, *s.f.* sentence; maxim; judgment; decree; decision; verdict
Sentencier, *v.a.* to sentence
Sentencieusement, *adv.* sententiously
Sentencieu-x, se, *adj.* sententious
Sentène, *s.f.* thread (*that binds a skein*)
Senteur, *s.f.* scent, perfume, fragrance; odour smell. *De* —, odorous, scented, sweet-scented sweet, perfumed; scent. *Pois de* —, sweet pea
Senti, e, *part. adj.* felt, &c. (*V.* **Sentir**); (*bien* or *vivement* —) sensibly felt, heartfelt, feeling; well expressed, expressive
Sentier, *s.m.* footpath, footway, pathway, path, way, track; lane
Sentiment, *s.m.* sensation; perception; sensibility; feeling; sense, consciousness; sentiment; opinion; sentimentality; (*hunt.*) odour, scent. *Faire du* —, to be sentimental, to sentimentalize
Sentimental, e, *adj.* sentimental
Sentimentalement, *adv.* sentimentally
Sentimental-isme, -iste. *V.* page 3, § 1
Sentimentalité, *s.f.* sentimentality
Sentine, *s.f.* (*nav.*) well-room; (*of vice*) sink
Sentinelle, *s.f.* sentinel; sentry; (*pop.*) excrement. — *perdue,* forlorn sentinel. *Être en* —, *faire* —, to be on sentry, to stand *or* keep sentry, to mount guard, to be on duty; to be on the watch, to watch
Sentir, *v.a.n.* to feel; to smell; to scent; to exhale, to emit; to taste; to smell of *or* like, to have a smell of; to taste of *or* like, to have a taste of; to savour of; to look like; to understand; to have a sense (of) *or* feeling (for); to perceive; to experience; to foresee; to guess; to know; to bear the look *or* smell *or* taste of, to bear; to stink. — *bon,* to smell nice *or* sweet. *Ne* — *que l'eau,* to be tasteless. *Ne* — *rien,* to feel *or* smell *or* taste nothing; to have no feeling *or* no smell *or* no taste. *Faire* —, to make (...) feel *or* felt; to make (...) understand *or* understood; to impress with a sense of, to impress with; to make (...) sensible of; to show; to bring home; to pronounce, to sound. *Se faire* —, to make itself felt, to be felt; to be perceptible; to be obvious; to show itself

Se —, *v.r.* to feel oneself; to feel; to know oneself; to be conscious; to feel within oneself; to experience; to feel the effects (of); to be felt, to be sensible; to be smelt, to smell; to be visible *or* perceived. *Ne pas se* — *de joie* (or *d'aise*), to be beside oneself (*or* mad) with joy, to be overjoyed, to be enraptured. *Je ne me sens pas de froid,* I am quite benumbed with cold, I am quite frozen

Seoir, *v.n.* (*old*) to sit, to be sitting; to become, to be becoming, to suit, to fit
Sep, *s.m.* (*of a plough*) frame
Sépale, *s.m.* (*bot.*) sepal
Séparabilité, *s.f.* separableness
Séparable, *adj.* separable
Séparablement, *adv.* separably
Sépara-teur, trice, *s.m.f.* separator, separatress; — *adj.* separating
Séparati-f, ve, *adj.* separative, separatory
Séparation, *s.f.* separation; partition. — *de biens*, separate estate, separate maintenance. — *de corps*, — *de corps et de biens*, judicial separation
Séparatisme, *s.m.* separatism; secession
Séparatiste, *s.m.f.* separatist; secessionist; — *adj.* separatistic; seceding
Séparatoire, *s.m.* separatory
Séparé, e, *part. adj.* separated, &c. (*V.* **Séparer**); separate; apart; distinct. — *de biens*, having a separate estate *or* maintenance. — *de corps*, — *de corps et de biens*, judicially separated [tinctly; asunder
Séparément, *adv.* separately; apart; dis-
Séparer, *v.a.* to separate; to part; to sever; to divide; to disjoin; to disunite; to disconnect; to cut off; to sift; to distinguish. — *de corps et de biens*, to separate judicially
Se —, *v.r.* to separate; to part; to part company; to part with each other; to break up; to secede; to disclaim; to divide; to separate *or* distinguish *or* &c. oneself. *Se — de corps et de biens*, to get a decree of judicial
Sépia, *s.f.* sepia. *A la —*, in sepia [separation
Seps, *s.m.* (*zool.*) seps
Sept, *adj.m.f.*, *s.m.* seven; seventh [lines
Septain, *s.m.* piece of poetry *or* stanza of seven
Septante, *adj. s.* (*old*) seventy. *Version des —*,
Septembre, *s.m.* September [Septuagint
Septembrisade, *s.f.* (*Fr. hist.*) Septembrisade (*massacre, in Paris, September* 2, 1792)
Septembriseur, *s.m.* (*Fr. hist.*) Septembrist (*agent of the massacre, in Paris, September* 2,
Septemvir, *s.m.* septemvir [1792)
Septemviral, e, *adj.* septemviral
Septemvirat, *s.m.* septemvirate
Septénaire, *adj.* septenary; — *s.m.* septenary; seven years; (*med.*) seven days, week
Septennal, e, *adj.* septennial
Septennalité, *s.f.* septennial duration
Septentrion, *s.m.* north; (*astr.*) Lesser Bear
Septentrional, e, *adj.* septentrional, northern, northerly, north; — *s.m.f.* northerner
Septicité, *s.f.* septicity
Septidi, *s.m.* septidi (*seventh day of the decade in the calendar of the first French Republic*)
Septième, *adj.m.f.*, *s.m.* seventh; seventh day; pupil of the seventh form *or* class; — *s.f.* seventh; seventh form *or* class
Septièmement, *adv.* seventhly
Septimo, *adv.* seventhly
Septique, *adj.m.f.*, *s.m.* septic
Septuagénaire, *adj. s.m.f.* septuagenarian
Septuagésime, *s.f.* septuagesima; septuagesima Sunday
Septum, *s.m.* (*anat., bot.*) septum
Septuor, *s.m.* (*mus.*) septet
Septuple, *s.m. adj.* septuple, sevenfold
Septupler, *v.a.n.*, **Se —,** *v.r.* to septuple, to increase sevenfold [cavernous
Sépulcral, e, *adj.* sepulchral; cadaverous;
Sépulcre, *s.m.* sepulchre; grave; tomb
Sépulture, *s.f.* burial, sepulture, interment, entombment; vault [string
Séquelle, *s.f.* gang, set, host, band; series,
Séquence, *s.f.* sequence
Séquestrateur, *s.m.* sequestrator
Séquestration, *s.f.* sequestration
Séquestre, *s.m.* sequestration; deposit; (*pers.*) sequester, sequestrator; depositary; (*med.*) sequestrum. *En —*, sequestered. *Mettre en —*, to sequester

Séquestré, e, *part. adj.* sequestered, &c. (*V.* **Séquestrer**); solitary; retired; lonely
Séquestrer, *v.a.* to sequester, to sequestrate; to separate; to secrete, to set aside, to put away, to remove [solitude
Se —, *v.r.* to sequester oneself; to live in
Sequin, *s.m.* sequin (*gold coin*)
Sequoia, *s.m.* (*bot.*) sequoia
Séracée, *s.f.* curdles
†**Sérail,** *s.m.* seraglio
Seran, *s.m.* hackle, heckle
Serançage, *s.m.* hackling, heckling, dressing
Serancer, *v.a.* to hackle, to heckle, to hatchel, to dress [dresser
Seranceur, *s.m.* hackler, heckler, flax-dresser,
Serançoir, *s.m.* *V.* **Seran**
Sérancolin, *s.m.* Serancolin marble
Séraphin, *s.m.* seraph [phina
Séraphine, *s.f.* (*mus. instr.*) seraphine, sera-
Séraphique, *adj.* seraphic
Sérapias, *s.m.* (*bot.*) helleborine
Séraskier, Sérasquier, *s.m.* seraskier (*Turkish commander*) [rat
Séraskiérat, Sérasquiérat, *s.m.* seraskie-
Serbe, *s.m.f. adj.* Serb, Serbian, Servian
Serein, e, *adj.* serene; placid, calm; happy; — *s.m.* evening dew *or* damp
Sérénade, *s.f.* serenade
Sérénader, *v.n.a.* to serenade
Sérénissime, *adj.* Most Serene, Serene
Sérénité, *s.f.* serenity; calmness, placidness
Séreu-x, se, *adj.* serous; —**se,** *s.f.* serous membrane
Ser-f, ve, *s.m.f.* serf, slave, bondman, bondwoman; — *adj.* of serfs, servile, slavish
Serfouette, *s.f.* hoe
Serfouir, *v.a.* to hoe
Serfouissage, *s.m.* hoeing
Serge, *s.f.* serge
Sergent, *s.m.* (*mil.*) sergeant; (*tool*) cramp. — *de bataille*, (*obsolete*) field-sergeant. — *de ville*, policeman, constable
Sergenter, *v.a.* to dun, to importune
Sergenterie, *s.f.* sergeantship; sergeanty
Serger, *s.m.* serge-maker
Sergerie, *s.f.* serge-manufactory; serge-trade
Sergette, *s.f.* thin and light serge
Sergier, *s.m.* serge-maker
Sériaire, Sérial, e, *adj.* serial
Sériation, *s.f.* seriation [silk-growing, silk
Séricicole, *adj.* sericicultural, sericultural,
Sériciculteur, *s.m.* sericiculturist, sericulturist, silk-grower
Sériciculture, *s.f.* sericiculture, sericulture, silk-culture, silk-growing, silk-breeding, silk-
Série, *s.f.* series [husbandry
Sérié, e, *part. adj.* seriated, seriate
Sérier, *v.a.* to seriate
Sérieusement, *adv.* seriously; gravely; coldly; earnestly, in earnest; for good
Sérieu-x, se, *adj.* serious; grave; earnest; important; real; true; good; solid; substantial; said *or* meant in earnest; thinking; — *s.m.* seriousness; gravity; earnestness; importance, consequence; reality; serious style; serious matters *or* subjects; serious part *or* side. *Au —*, in earnest, seriously, for serious. *Garder son —*, to keep o.'s gravity, to refrain from laughing. *Prendre son —*, to assume (*or* put on) a serious *or* grave look, to begin to look grave. *Reprendre son —*, to assume a serious *or* grave look again, to recover o.'s gravity
Serin, e, *s.m.f.* canary-bird, canary, cock-canary, hen-canary; simpleton, flat, muff; — *adj.* canary yellow; (*pers.*) silly, green. *Queue de —*, (*adject.*) pale canary yellow
Serinage, *s.m.* cramming *or* grinding (*students*)
Serine, *s. adj.f.* *V.* **Serin**
Sérine, *s.f.* (*in physiology*) serine
Seriner, *v.a.* to play on *or* teach with the bird-organ; (*fig.*) to repeat; to teach by rote; to

cram, to coach up, to grind, to prepare; to give (*one*) his cue [power
Serinette, *s.f.* bird-organ; (*pers.*) singer of no
Seringage, *s.m.* syringing, squirting, flushing
Seringa, Seringat, *s.m.* (*bot.*) syringa
Seringue, *s.f.* syringe, squirt; (*pop.*) bore
Seringuement, *s.m. V.* **Seringage**
Seringuer, *v.a.* to syringe, to squirt, to inject,
Sériosité, *s.f.* seriousness [to flush
Serment, *s.m.* oath; swearing; solemn declaration *or* promise; protestation. *Sous la foi du* —, upon oath, under an oath. *Faire* —, to swear. *Faire prêter* — *à*, to put on o.'s oath. *Prêter* —, to take an oath *or* the oath, to be
Sermon, *s.m.* sermon; lecture; jobation [sworn
Sermonnaire, *s.m.* collection of sermons; author of sermons; — *adj.* of sermons
Sermonner, *v.a.* to lecture, to sermonize
Sermonneu-r, se, *s.m.f.* sermonizer
Sermontain, *s.m.* (*bot.*) sermountain
Sérosité, *s.f.* serosity, serum
Sérotine, *s.f.* (*zool.*) serotine (*bat*)
Serpe, *s.f.* bill-hook, hedging-bill, hedge-bill, pruning-bill, pruning-hook
Serpent, *s.m.* serpent; snake; (*mus.*) serpent; serpent-player. — *à lunettes*, spectacled snake. — *à sonnettes*, rattle-snake. *De* —, serpent's; serpentine; snake's; snaky
Serpentaire, *s.f.* (*bot.*) serpentaria, snake-root; — *s.m.* (*astr.*) serpentarius; (*zool.*) *V.* **Secrétaire** [tissue paper
Serpente, *s.f.* (*adject.*, *Papier* —) silver paper,
Serpenteau, *s.m.* young serpent; (*firework*) serpent, squib
Serpenter, *v.n.* to twine; to wind, to meander
Serpentiforme, *adj.* serpentiform
Serpentin, e, *adj.* serpentine
Serpentin, *s.m.* winding pipe; worm (*of a still*); smoke-preventing apparatus, smoke-preventer
Serpentine, *s.f.* (*bot.*) grass-plantain; (*min.*) serpentine-stone, serpentine; serpentine
Serpette, *s.f.* pruning-knife [marble
Serpigineu-x, se, *adj.* (*med.*) serpiginous
†**Serpillière,** *s.f.* packing-cloth, coarse cloth, sarplier, poledavy; awning; (coarse) apron; shroud; (*insect*) mole-cricket
Serpolet, *s.m.* wild thyme
Serpule, *s.f.* (*zool.*) serpula
Serradelle, *s.f.* (*bot.*) serradilla [**Serrer,** *v.a.*)
Serrage, *s.m.* pressing, tightening, &c. (*V.*
Serran, *s.m.* (*fish*) serranus, sea-perch
Serraté, e, *adj.* (*bot.*) serrate, serrated
Serratifolié, e, *adj.* (*bot.*) serratifoliate
Serratiforme, *adj.* serratiform, saw-shaped
Serratule, *s.f.* (*bot.*) saw-wort
Serre, *s.f.* green-house; hot-house; conservatory; pressing, pressure; squeeze; talon, claw, fang; grasp, gripe, clutch, hand; (*nav.*) ship-plank. — *chaude*, hot-house. — *à ananas*, pinery. — *à palmiers*, palm-house. — *à vignes*, vinery. *Avoir la* — *bonne*, to have a strong grasp *or* hand
Serre, *s.m.* (*in compounds, from* **Serrer,** "to squeeze," "to press," "to pinch," "to tie *or* fit tight," "to put away," &c.) thing that squeezes, &c. — **-bosse,** *s.m.* (*nav.*) shank-painter. — **-bras,** *s.m.* arm-bandage. — **-file,** *s.m.* (*mil.*) last man of a file, bringer-up, rear-file, rear-rank; (*nav.*) sternmost ship. *En* — *-file*, at the end of the file, in the rear, behind, last; sternmost. — **-frein,** *s.m.* (*rail.*) breaksman, brakesman. — **-nez,** *s.m.* horse-twitchers, twitchers, twitch. — **-nœud,** *s.m.* (*surg.*) ligature tightener. — **-notes,** — **-papiers,** *s.m.* paper-holder; paper-clip, letter-clip; set of pigeon-holes; (*abusively for* "presse-papiers") paper-weight. — **-tête,** *s.m.* night-cap, head-band
Serré, e, *part. adj.* pressed, &c. (*V.* **Serrer,** *v.a.*); serried; close; tight; fast; compact; crowded; oppressed; clenched; concise; terse; small; stiff; sharp; close-fisted; hard up; hard; cautious; (*bot.*) serrate, serrated; — *adv.* closely, close; hard; much; prudently, cautiously; impudently
Serrement, *s.m.* pressing; clasping; squeezing, squeeze; shake. — *de cœur*, heaviness of
Serrément, *adv.* closely [heart, grief, pang
Serrer, *v.a.* to hold tight; to press; to clasp, to hug; to grasp; to squeeze; to pinch; to tie *or* lace tight; to fit tight; to tighten; to fasten; to bind close, to bind; to confine; to be lashed round; to put close together; to close; to crowd; to screw up; to condense; to lock up; to put by *or* away; to lay up; to put *or* take in; to pocket; to pursue (close); to pass *or* come *or* keep close to; to besiege; to oppress; to shake (*hands*); to clench *or* double (*the fist*, &c.); to draw; to put on, to apply; (*mil.*) to close; (*nav.*) to take in (*sails*); to sail *or* run close to, to hug; (*print.*) to lock, to lock up

Se —, *v.r.* to squeeze *or* &c. oneself *or* each other; to press close to each other, to press *or* come close; to sit *or* stand *or* lie close (*or* closer); to grow tighter; to crowd; to thicken; to tie in; to cuddle; to pinch *or* stint oneself; to pinch (o.'s ...); to tighten *or* squeeze *or* &c. (o.'s ... *or* each other's ...); to lace tight; to be tightened *or* &c.
Serrette. *V.* **Sarrette**
Serricorne, *adj.m.f.*, *s.m.* (*zool.*) serricorn
Serrure, *s.f.* lock
Serrurerie, *s.f.* locksmith's art *or* trade *or* business *or* work; locks, fastenings, iron work
Serrurier, *s.m.* locksmith. — *en voitures*, coachsmith
Sertir, *v.a.* (*jewel.*) to set (in a bezel)
Sertisseu-r, se, *s.m.f.* (*jewel.*) setter
Sertissure, *s.f.* (*jewel.*) setting (in a bezel)
Sertulaire, *s.f.* (*nat. hist.*) sertularia
Sertule, *s.m.* (*bot.*) sertulum
Sertulé, e, *adj.* (*bot.*) sertulated
Sérum, *s.m.* serum
Servable, *adj.* servable; of service, serviceable
Servage, *s.m.* bondage, serfdom
Serval, *s.m.* (*zool.*) serval, bush-cat, tiger-cat
Servant, e, *adj.* serving; in waiting; lay (*brother*) [— *d'amour*, lover
Servant, *s.m.* gunner; assistant priest, clerk.
Servante, *s.f.* servant; maid-servant, servant-maid, maid, servant-girl; dinner-waggon;
Serve, *fem.* of **Serf** [dumb-waiter
Serveur, *s.m.* bowler
Servi, e, *part. adj.* served, &c. (*V.* **Servir**). *Bien* —, well served, &c.; (*of firing*) kept up, thick, brisk, galling. *Le dîner est* —, *Monsieur est* —, *Madame est* —*e*, *On a* —, dinner is ready *or* on the table
Serviabilité, *s.f.* obligingness, serviceableness
Serviable, *adj.* obliging, serviceable
Serviablement, *adv.* obligingly, serviceably
Service, *s.m.* service; attendance; duty; work; household, household matters; administration; department; kindness; plying; use; set; course; line; (*rail.*) traffic; (*theat.*) press order *or* orders, free list. — *foncier*, (*civ. law*) *V.* **Servitude.** — *de table*, dinner-service. *Au* —, (*mil.*) in the service, in the army. *Au* — *de*, at *or* to *or* in *or* into the service of. *De* —, for the servants, servants'; in attendance; in waiting; (*mil.*, &c.) on duty; (*of stairs, paths*, &c.) back; side. *En* —, at service. *Hors de* —, out of use, unfit for service, unserviceable, worn out. *Faire le* — *de*, to perform the service *or* work *or* duty of; to do duty *or* officiate in *or* at, to serve; to serve for; to work; to ply on, to run *or* ply between ... and ..., to run on, to run *or* go to; to meet, to wait on; to connect, to lead to. *Se mettre en* —, to go to service. *Qu'y a-t-il pour votre* —*?* what is your pleasure?
Servien, ne, *s.m.f. adj.* Servian

Serviette, *s.f.* (*— de table*) napkin; (*— de dessert*) doily; (*— de toilette*) towel
Servile, *adj.* servile; slavish, mean
Servilement, *adv.* servilely; slavishly, meanly
Servilisme, *s.m.* servility [cringing
Servilité, *s.f.* servility, servileness; meanness;
Servir, *v.a.n.* to serve; to attend, to wait upon; to be of service *or* use to; to serve up, to bring, to put upon table; to spread; to lay out; to help; to help to; to give; to assist; to avail; to pay; to supply; to minister to; to oblige; to be a servant *or* in service (*mil.*, in the service); to wait; to be used *or* employed; to be useful; to work; to do o.'s work. *— à*, to serve, to be of use to, to be used for; to be subservient. *— de*, to serve as *or* for; to do instead of; to do the office of, to act as a, to be a. *— la messe*, to answer at mass, to assist the priest at mass. *Faire —*, to make use of, to use; to avail oneself of. *Pour vous —*, at your service; if you please, please, with your leave. *A quoi sert ...?* of what use is ...? *A quoi sert de? que sert de?* what is the use of? *Ne — à rien* or *de rien*, to be of no use
Se —, *v.r.* to serve *or* help oneself; to deal (with); to be served up; to serve *or* &c. each other. *Se — de*, to use, to make use of; to employ; to avail oneself of
Servite, *s.m.* servite (*monk*)
Serviteur, *s.m.* servant; *—!* your servant! excuse me! I beg to be excused! farewell! goodbye! nay! no such thing!
Servitude, *s.f.* servitude; slavery; (*law*) servitude, liability, obligation, encumbrance, easement [(own), one's (own); their (own)
Ses, *adj. poss. pl. m.f.* his (own), her (own), its
Sésame, *s.m.* (*bot.*) sesamum, sesame, tilseed. *—, ouvre-toi!* open, Sesame! [sesamoid bone
Sésamoïde, *adj.* (*anat.*) sesamoid; *— s.m.*
Sesban, *s.m.*, **Sesbanée,** *s.f.* (*bot.*) sesbania, sesban, dhunchee [hartwort, lovage
Séséli, *s.m.* (*bot.*) seseli, meadow saxifrage,
§Sesqui, (*in compounds*) sesqui ...
§Sesquialtère, *adj.* sesquialteral
Sessile, *adj.* sessile [term
Session, *s.f.* session; sitting; (*law, univers.*)
Sesterce, *s m.* (*Rom. ant.*) sesterce [shaped
Sétacé, e, *adj.* setaceous, bristle-like, bristle-
Séteu-x, se, *adj.* setose, setous
Setier, *s.m.* (*old meas.*) pint [producing, silk
Sétifère, *adj.* setiferous, bristle-bearing; silk-
Sétiforme, *adj.* setiform, bristle-shaped
Sétigère, *adj.* setigerous, bristly
Séton, *s.m.* (*surg.*) seton
†Seuil, *s.m.* threshold, sill
Seul, e, *adj.* alone; by oneself; lonely; only, one, single; sole, mere, very; *— s.m.f.* one, one alone; only one, only person. *— à, —*, alone, by ourselves *or* yourselves *or* themselves, in private. *Tout —*, all alone, quite alone, alone; by *or* of oneself; of itself; singly; unassisted; easily, without difficulty, as a matter of course. *Un — homme*, one man only, one single man, one man. *Un homme —*, a man alone, a man by himself. *Un —, une —e*, (*substant.*) only one, one only; a single one, one
Seulement, *adv.* only; merely; solely; just; but; even, so much as
Seulet, te, *adj.* alone, lonely, by oneself
Sève, *s.f.* sap; pith; vigour; strength; raciness, fruity taste
Sévère, *adj.* severe; rigid; strict; stern; austere; noble and regular, pure, correct; strong; hard; queer; *— s.f.* (*pop.*) bouncer; queer thing
Sévèrement, *adv.* severely; rigidly; strictly; sternly; austerely; purely, correctly
Sévérite, *s.f.* (*min.*) severite
Sévérité, *s.f.* severity; rigidness; strictness; sternness; austerity; purity, correctness
Séveu-x, se, *adj.* sappy; pithy; vigorous; strong; racy, fruity

Sévice, *s.m.*, **Sévices,** *pl.* (*law*) ill-treatment, cruelty; (*fig.*) persecution
Sévir, *v.n.* to use severity, to be severe, to deal rigorously, to punish; to rage; to be guilty of
Sevrage, *s.m.* weaning [cruelty
Sevrer, *v.a.* to wean; to deprive; to frustrate
Sèvres, *s.m.* Sèvres porcelain, sèvres; Sèvres
Sevreuse, *s.f.* dry-nurse [work of art, sèvres
Sexagénaire, *adj.s.m.f.* sexagenarian
Sexagésimal, e, *adj.* sexagesimal [Sunday
Sexagésime, *s.f.* sexagesima; sexagesima
Sexe, *s.m.* sex; fair sex; womankind; women
Sexennal, e, *adj.* sexennial
Sextant, *s.m.* sextant
Sextil, e, *adj.*, **Sextil,** *s.m.* (*astr.*) sextile
Sextidi, *s.m.* sextidi (*sixth day of a decade in the calendar of the first French Republic*)
Sextillion, *s.m.* thousand trillions
Sexto, *adv.* sixthly, in the sixth place
Sextuor, *s.m.* (*mus.*) sextet
Sextuple, *s.m. adj.* sextuple, sixfold
Sextupler, *v.a.n.*, **Se —**, *v.r.* to sextuple, to increase sixfold
Sexualisme, *s.m.*, **Sexualité,** *s.f.* sexuality
Sexuel, le, *adj.* sexual
Seyait, Seyaient, *v.* became, did become, was *or* were becoming
Seyant, *part. adj.* becoming, suitable
Seyssel, *s.m.* Seyssel asphalte
Sgraffite, *s.m.* (*paint.*) sgraffito
Shah, *s.m.* *V.* **Schah**
Shakespearien, ne, Shakspearien, ne, *adj.* Shakespearean, Shakspearean, Shakspearian
Shako, *s.m.* (*mil.*) shako, cap
Shérif, Shériff, *s.m.* sheriff
Shilling, *s.m.* (*Engl. coin*) shilling
Shrapnel, *s.m.* (*artil.*) shrapnel (*or* shrapnell) shell, shrapnel *or* shrapnell (*shell filled with bullets*)
Si, S', *conj.* if; whether; though; what if, suppose; how much; *— s.m.* if; (*mus.*) si, B. *— ce n'est*, *V.* **Être.** *— tant est que*, *V.* **Tant.** *Que —*, and if, if
Si, *adv.* so; so very; so much; so long; such; though, although; however; yes; indeed. *— bien que*, so much so that, in such a way that, so that. *— fait*, yes, yes indeed, oh yes; excuse me, I beg your pardon; on the contrary. *Que —*, yes; so; to be sure. *Dire, parier* (or *gager*), *assurer, jurer*, &c. *que —*, to say, to bet, to assure, to swear, &c. that it is (so)
Sialagogue, Sialogogue, *s.m.* (*med.*) sialagogue, sialogogue; *— adj.* sialagogic, sialogogic
Sialisme, *s.m.* (*med.*) sialism
Sialologie, *s.f.* (*med.*) sialology
Sialorrhée, *s.f.* (*med.*) sialorrhœa [cotton
Siamois, e, *adj.s.m.f.* Siamese; *— s.f.* Siamese
Sibarite. *V.* **Sybarite**
Sibbens, *s.m.* (*med.*) sibbens
Sibérien, ne, *adj. s.* Siberian
Sibérite, *s.f.* (*min.*) siberite
Sibilance, *s.f.* sibilance [wheezing
Sibilant, e, *adj.* sibilant, hissing; (*med.*)
Sibylle, *s.f.* sibyl
Sibyllin, e, *adj.* sibylline
Sic, *adv.* (*Latin*) sic, thus
Sicaire, *s.m.* hired assassin
Sicamor, *s.m.* (*her.*) *V.* **Orle**
Siccati-f, ve, *adj.*, **Siccatif,** *s.m.* siccative, desiccative, drying; dryer
Siccité, *s.f.* siccity, dryness
Sicilien, ne, *adj. s.m.f.* Sicilian; *— s.f.* (*dance, tune*) siciliana
Sicle, *s.m.* (*Jew. coin*) shekel
Sicomore. *V.* **Sycomore**
Sidéral, e, *adj* sidereal, sideral
Sidération, *s.f.* sideration
Sidérite, *s.f.* (*min.*) siderite
Sidéritis, *s m.* (*bot.*) siderite, ironwort
‡Sidéro-graphie, -technie, &c. *V.* p. 3, § 1
Sidérolithe, *s.m.* siderolite
Sidérolithique, *adj.* siderolitic
Sidéroxyle, *s.m.* (*bot.*) sideroxylon, ironwood

Sidérurg-ie, -ique. *V.* page 3, § 1
Siècle, *s.m.* century, age; time, times; world. *A tous les —s, aux —s des —s,* for ever and ever
Sied, *v.* becomes, suits, fits, is becoming *or* suitable [suitable
Siéent, *v.* become, suit, fit, are becoming *or*
Siége, *s.m.* seat; sedilium; carriage-box, coach-box, box; dicky, rumble; see; bench; offices; siege. *Saint —,* Holy See. *En état de —,* in a state of siege, under martial law. *Équipage de —,* siege train. *Pièce de —,* siege gun. *Faire le — de, mettre le — devant,* to besiege, to lay siege to [to be seated
Siéger, *v.n.* to sit; to hold o.'s see; (*fig.*) to lie,
Sien, ne, *pron. poss.* *Le —, la —ne, les —s, les —nes,* his, his own; hers, her own; its, its own; o.'s own; of his; of hers; o.'s own property. *Les —s,* o.'s (own) relations *or* family *or* friends *or* men *or* servants *or* people *or* subjects *or* dynasty *or* party *or* &c. *Faire des —nes,* to play o.'s tricks *or* pranks
Sienne (Terre de), *s.f.* sienna-earth, sienna, terra di Sienna
Siennois, e, *adj. s.* Siennese [ing
Siéra, Siéront, *v.* will become, will be becom-
Siérait, Siéraient, *v.* would become, would be becoming [to take o.'s siesta
Sieste, *s.f.* siesta, afternoon's nap. *Faire la —,*
Sieur, *s.m.* (*law*) Mr., Mister
Sifflant, e, *part. adj.* whistling, &c. (*V.* **Siffler**); sibilant; **—e,** *s.f.* (*gram.*) sibilant
Sifflasson, *s.m.* (*local*) *V.* **Bécasseau**
Sifflement, *s.m.* whistling, whistle; hissing, hiss, hissing noise *or* sound; wheezing; whizzing, whiz
Siffler, *v.n.a.* to whistle; to hiss; to wheeze; to whiz; to sing, to pipe; to quaff; to spend; to call; to teach to sing; to give (*one*) his cue, to prompt; (*theat.*) to hiss, to damn
Sifflet, *s.m.* whistle; whistle-pipe; cat-call, call; hiss; wind-pipe, weasand, whistle. *Coup de —, V.* **Coup.** *Couper le — à,* to cut ...'s whistle *or* weasand; to silence, to stop ...'s mug, to shut up
Siffleu-r, se, *s.m.f.* whistler; hisser; singer; — *s.m.* wood-wren; widgeon, whew duck, whewer; piping bullfinch; — *adj.* whistling; hissing; singing, piping; (*vet.*) *V.* **Cornard**
Siffloter, *v.n.a.* to whistle
Sigillaire, *adj.* sigillar; — *s.f.* (*fossil*) sigillaria
Sigillé, e, *adj.* sigillated. *Terre —e,* bole
Sigillographie, *s.f.* sigillography
Sigisbée, *s.m.* cicisbeo, lover
Sigisbéisme, *s.m.* cicisbeism
Sigmatisme, *s.m.* sigmatism
Sigmoïdal, e, Sigmoïde, *adj.* (*anat.*) sigmoidal, sigmoid
†Signal, *s.m.* signal [moidal, sigmoid
†Signalé, e, *part. adj.* signalized, &c. (*V.* **Signaler**); signal; remarkable; conspicuous;
†Signalement, *s.m.* description [notorious
†Signaler, *v.a.* to describe, to give the description of; to give a signal of; to signalize; to point out; to notice, to mention; to signal
†Signalétique, *adj.* with a description, with descriptions [woman
†Signaliste, *s.m.f.* signalist, signalman, signal-
†Signataire, *s.m.f. adj.* signer, subscriber; signatary, signatory; signing
†Signature, *s.f.* signature; signing. *Sous — privée,* (*law*) by private deed; private. *Acte* or *contrat* or *écrit sous — privée,* (*law*) private deed
†Signe, *s.m.* sign; token; mark; beck, beckon; nod; wink. *En — de,* as a sign of. *Faire —,* to make signs; to motion; (*de la main*) to beckon; (*de la tête*) to nod; (*de l'œil* or *des yeux*)
†Signer, *v.a.n.* to sign, to subscribe [to wink
Se —, *v.r.* to make the sign of the cross, to cross oneself; (*things*) to be signed
Signet, *s.m.* book-mark, mark, marker, tassel; (*obsolete*) signet, seal; (*bot.*) Solomon's seal
†Signifiance, *s. f.* significance, meaning; sign, mark, token; instance
†Signifiant, e, Significati-f, ve, *adj.* significant, significative, expressive
†Signification, *s.f.* signification, meaning, sense, acceptation; (*law*) notice
†Significativement, *adv.* significantly, significatively, expressively
†Signifier, *v.a.* to signify, to mean; to notify, to declare, to announce, to intimate; (*law*) to serve. *Faire —,* to give notice of
Sil, *s.m.* (*min.*) yellow ochre
Silence, *s.m.* silence; stillness; quietness; secrecy; omission; oblivion; pause; (*mus.*) rest. *En —,* in silence, silently, without noise, quietly; silent. *Sous —,* in silence, silently. *Faire —,* to keep silence, to be silent. *Faire faire —,* to silence; to hush. *Garder* or *observer le —,* to remain silent; to hush. *Imposer — à,* to silence; to hush. *Passer sous —,* to pass over in silence *or* silently. *Réduire au —,* to reduce to silence, to silence
Silencieusement, *adv.* silently, in silence, quietly, without noise
Silencieu-x, se, *adj.* silent; mute; still
Silène, *s.m.* (*myth.*) Silenus; **—** *s.f.* (*bot.*) silene,
Silésien, ne, *adj. s.* Silesian [catchfly
Silex, *s.m.* silex, flint
Silhouette, *s.f.* silhouette, profile, outline,
Silicate, *s.m.* (*chem.*) silicate [shadow
Silicaté, e, *adj.* silicated
Silicatisation, *s.f.* silicatization
Silice, *s.f.* silica, flint
Siliceu-x, se, *adj.* (*min.*) silicious
Silicifère, *adj.* siliciferous
Silicification, *s.f.* silicification
Silicifier, *v.a.,* **Se —,** *v.r.* to silicify
Silicique, *adj.* (*chem.*) silicic
Silicium, *s.m.* (*chem.*) silicon, silicium [pouch
Silicule, *s.f.* (*bot.*) silicule, silicle, seed-pouch,
Siliculeu-x, se, *adj.* (*bot.*) siliculose, siliculous
Silique, *s.f.* (*bot.*) silique, two-valved pod, husk, shell
Siliqueu-x, se, *adj.* (*bot.*) siliquose, siliquous
Siliquiforme, *adj.* (*bot.*) siliquiform
†Sillage, *s.m.* (*nav.*) headway; wake, track
†Sillée, *s.f.* (*agr.*) trench
†Siller, *v.a.* (*old*) to close, to shut; (*falc.*) to blind, to seel; — *v.n.* (*nav.*) to run ahead, to make headway
Sillery, *s.m.* Sillery champagne (wine)
†Sillet, *s.m.* (*of violins,* &c.) turning-peg, turning-pin, nut
†Sillomètre, *s.m.* (*nav.*) sillometer, speed-gauge
†Sillon, *s.m.* furrow; ridge; trench; groove; trace; mark; line; streak; trail, train; flash; wrinkle; (*of ships*) track, wake; **—s,** *pl.* furrows, &c.; fields, land
†Sillonner, *v.a.* to furrow; to ridge; to groove; to streak; to wrinkle; to plough, to cut, to dash *or* flash through; to intersect
†Sillonneur, *s.m.* (*agr.*) horse-hoe
Silo, *s.m.* (*agr.*) silo, pit
Silouette. *V.* **Silhouette**
Silphe. *V* **Sylphe**
Silure, *s.m.* (*fish*) silurus, silure
Silurien, ne, *adj.* (*geol.*) Silurian
Silvain, Silves, Silvestre, Silviculture, &c. *V.* **Sylvain,** &c., &c. (*with* **y**)
Simagrée, *s.f.* grimace; pretence; show; affected way; **—s,** *pl* grimaces; pretence, show; affectation, affected ways; fuss
Simarouba, *s.m.* (*bot.*) simaruba
Simarre, *s.f.* simarre, simare, simar, justices robe, robe, gown
Simbleau, *s.m.* (*carp.*) radius-line
Simien, ne, *adj.* simious, monkey-like; **—s,** *s.m. pl* simia. monkeys, monkey-tribe
Simiesque, *adj. V.* **Simien**
Similaire, *adj.* similar
Similarité, *s.f.* similarity
Similimarbre, *s.m.* imitation marble
Similipierre, *s.m.* imitation stone
Similitude, *s.f.* similitude; simile

Similor, *s.m.* similor, pinchbeck
Simoniaque, *adj.* simoniacal; — *s.m.* simoniac
Simonie, *s.f.* simony
Simoun, *s.m.* simoom, simoon (*burning wind*)
Simple, *adj.* simple; single; one; prime (*number*); single-barrelled; mere; bare; plain; artless; natural; simple-minded; silly; easy; petty; common; private; — *s.m.* simple; (*medicinal plant*) simple; (*mus.*) simple air. *Le double contre le* —, two to one
Simplement, *adv* simply; singly; solely; only; merely; plainly; artlessly; sillily. *Tout* —, merely; that's all
Simplesse, *s.f.* simpleness; simplicity; plainness; artlessness
Simplicité, *s.f.* simplicity; plainness; artlessness; silliness
Simplifiable, *adj.* simplifiable
Simplificateur, *s.m.* simplifier; *adj.m.* simplifying
Simplification, *s.f.* simplification
Simplifier, *v.a.* to simplify. *Se* —, to become *or* be simplified
Simulacre, *s.m.* image; dummy; phantom, spectre; shadow, appearance, semblance; feint; sham; sham fight
Simula-teur, trice, *s.m.f.* simulator, shammer; — *adj.* simulating, shamming
Simulation, *s.f.* simulation; feigning
Simulé, e, *part. adj.* simulated, feigned, &c. (*V.* **Simuler**); fictitious; counterfeit; imitation; sham; "pro formâ"
Simuler, *v.a.* to simulate; to feign, to pretend, to sham; to imitate
Simultané, e, *adj.* simultaneous
Simultanéité, *s.f.* simultaneousness, simultaneity
Simultanément, *adv.* simultaneously, at the same time
Sinapine, *s.f.* (*chem.*) sinapine
Sinapique, *adj.* (*chem.*) sinapic
Sinapisé, e, *adj.* (*pharm., med.*) with mustard *or* flour of mustard
Sinapiser, *v.a.* (*pharm., med.*) to put mustard *or* flour of mustard in
Sinapisine, *s f.* (*chem.*) sinapisine
Sinapisme, *s.m.* sinapism, mustard poultice
Sinapoline, *s.f.* (*chem.*) sinapoline
Sincère, *adj.* sincere; honest, true
Sincèrement, *adv.* sincerely; honestly, truly
Sincérité, *s.f.* sincerity; honesty
Sincipital, e, *adj.* (*anat.*) sincipital
Sinciput, *s.m.* (*anat.*) sinciput
Sindon, *s.m.* (*surg*, &c.) sindon
Sinécure, *s.f.* sinecure
Sinécur-isme, -iste. *V.* page 3, § 1
Singe, *s.m.* ape; monkey; servile imitator; pantograph, pantagraph, copying-machine; — *adj.* apish, mimicking
Singer, *v.a.* to ape, to mimic, to imitate
Singeresse, *adj f* apish, mimicking
Singerie, *s.f.* apish trick, trick; apishness; antic; grimace; mimicry; monkeys
Singeu-r, se, *adj. s.* apish; ape, imitator
Singulariser, *v.a.* to singularize; to make singular *or* odd
Singularité, *s. f.* singularity; peculiarity; oddness; oddity; strangeness; quaintness
Singuli-er, ère, *adj.* singular; peculiar; odd, strange; queer; quaint; (*of combat*) single; — *s.m.* (*gram.*) singular
Singulièrement, *adv.* singularly; peculiarly; particularly; oddly; strangely, in a strange manner; queerly; quaintly
Singultueu-x, se, *adj.* (*med.*) singultuous
Sinistre, *adj* sinister, inauspicious, evil; dismal; lurid; forbidding; — *s.m.* disaster, accident, casualty, loss, damage
Sinistré, e, *adj* wrecked; lost; burnt; damaged
Sinistrement, *adv.* sinisterly, sinistrously, inauspiciously; dismally
Sinologie, *s.f.* sinology, Chinology
Sinologique, *adj.* sinologic, Chinologic
Sinologue, *s.m.* sinologue, sinologist, Chinologist, Chinese scholar
Sinombre, *adj.* shadowless
Sinon, *conj.* otherwise, or else, if not; except, unless
Sinople, *s.m.* (*her., min.*) sinople
Sinué, e, *adj.* sinuate, sinuated
Sinueu-x, se, *adj.* sinuous; winding
Sinuosité, *s.f.* sinuosity; winding
Sinus, *s.m.* sinus; (*math.*) sine
Siphilis, &c. *V.* **Syphilis,** &c.
Siphoïde, *adj.m.f., s.m.* siphoid
Siphon, *s.m.* siphon; bottle of Seltzer water; (*obsolete*) waterspout (*at sea*)
Siphonostome, *s m* (*zool.*) siphonostoma, siphonostome
Siponcle, *s.m.* (*zool.*) sipunculus
Sire, *s.m* sire; (*obsolete*) sir, lord; (*in fables*) squire; (*fam.*) fellow, dog, stick, wight; wretch
Sirène, *s.f.* (*myth.*) siren, mermaid; (*pers., zool.*) siren; (*acoustics*) sirene
Sirien, ne, *adj. s.* (*in Voltaire's fanciful tale,* "*Micromégas*") of Sirius, Sirian, inhabitant of Sirius
Sirius, *s.m.* (*astr.*) Sirius
Siroc, Sirocco, Siroco, *s.m.* sirocco (*wind*)
Sirop, *s.m.* syrup
Siroter, *v.a.n.* to sip; to tipple
Siroteu-r, se, *s.m.f.* sipper; tippler; — *adj.* sipping; tippling
Sirte, *s f.* quicksand
Sirupeu-x, se, *adj.* syrupy
Sirvente, Sirventois, *s.m.* (*old*) sirvente (*poem*)
Sis, e, *adj.* (*law*) situate, situated, seated, lying
Sismal, e, *adj.* sismal, seismal
Sismique, *adj.* sismic, seismic
Sismographe, *s.m* sismograph, seismograph
Sismomètre, *s.m.* sismometer, seismometer
Sismométr-ie, -ique. *V.* page 3, § 1
Sison, *s.m.* (*bot.*) *V.* **Ammi**
Sistre, *s.m.* (*anc. Egyptian mus. instr.*) sistrum; (*more modern*) *V.* **Cistre**
Sisymbre, *s.m.* (*bot.*) sisymbrium
Site, *s.m.* site; scenery
Sitiolog-ie, -ique. *V.* page 3, § 1
Sitiophobie, *s.f.* (*med.*) sitiophobia, sitophobia
Sitôt. *V.* **Aussitôt.** *De* —, so soon; for some time to come
Sittelle, Sittèle, *s.f.* (*bird*) nut-hatch, nut-breaker, nut-pecker
Situation, *s f.* situation; state; position; condition; state of affairs, state of things; (*com., of accounts*) statement; (*nav.*) bearing. *En* —, in a conspicuous situation, conspicuous; in o.'s proper situation *or* place *or* character; in a state *or* position *or* condition (to), able (to)
Situé, e, *adj.* situated, situate; placed; lying; disposed
Situer, *v.a.* to place, to seat
Sium, *s m.* (*bot.*) sium, skirret
Six, *adj.m.f., s.m.* six; sixth
Sixain, *s.m. V.* **Sizain**
Sixième, *adj.* sixth; — *s.m.* sixth; sixth day; sixth floor; pupil of the sixth form *or* class; — *s.f.* sixth; sixth form *or* class; six cards of the same suit
Sixièmement, *adv.* sixthly
Sixte, *s.f.* (*mus.*) sixth
Sixtin, e, *adj.* Sixtine
Sizain, *s.m.* piece of poetry *or* stanza of six lines; (*of cards*) six packs
Sizerin, *s m.* (*bird*) redpole (*kind of linnet*)
Slave, *adj. s.m f.*, **Slavique,** *adj.*, **Slavon, ne,** *adj.m.f.* Slave, Slavon, Slavonian, Sclavonian, Slavonic, Sclavonic, Slavic
Sleeper, *s.m.* (*rail.*) sleeper
Sloop, Sloup, Sloupe, *s.m.* (*nav.*) sloop
Smala, Smalah, *s.f* (*Arabian*) smala; (*fig.*) family, household, troop
Smalt, *s.m.* smalt
Smaltine, *s.f.* (*min.*) smaltine
Smaragdin, e, *adj.* smaragdine
Smaragdite, *s.f.* (*min.*) smaragdite
Smectique, *adj.* smegmatic
Smectite, *s.f.* (*min.*) smectite
Smérinthe, *s.m.* (*zool.*) hawk-moth
Smilace, *s.f.* (*bot.*) smilax
Smilacées, *s.f.pl.* (*bot.*) smilaceæ
Smilacine, *s f.* (*chem*) smilacine
†**Smille,** *s.f.* (*mas.*) scapple-axe
†**Smiller,** *v.a.* (*mas*) to scapple
Smyrnéen, ne, Smyrniote, *adj. s.* Smyrniot, Smyrniote
Sobole, *s.f.* (*bot.*) soboles
Sobolifère, *adj.* (*bot.*) soboliferous

Sobre, *adj.* sober; temperate, abstemious; sparing [stemiously; moderately; sparingly
Sobrement, *adv.* soberly; temperately, ab-
Sobriété, *s.f.* sobriety; soberness; temperance; moderation
Sobriquet, *s.m.* nickname, sobriquet
Soc, *s.m.* share, ploughshare; (*mil.*) bucket
Sochet, *s.m.* swing-plough
Sociabilité, *s. f.* sociability, sociableness; companionableness; good fellowship; intercourse [able; — *s.m.* (*carriage*) sociable
Sociable, *adj.* sociable, social; companion-
Sociablement, *adv.* sociably, socially; companionably [firm *or* company
Social, e, *adj.* social; (*com.*) of the (*or* of a)
Socialement, *adv.* socially [socialized
Socialiser, *v.a.* to socialize. *Se* —, to become
Social-isme, -iste (*s.m.f.*). *V.* page 3, § 1
Socialiste, *adj.* socialistic
Socialité, *s.f.* sociality, socialness
Sociétaire, *s.m.* associate, partner, member of a (*or* of the) society, member; shareholder; (*social philos.*) Fourierist Fourierite; — *adj.* of a (*or* of the) society *or* company
Sociétairement, *adv.* in a society *or* association, in societies *or* associations [associates
Sociétariat, *s.m.* membership; members,
Société, *s.f.* society; company; party; community; club; class; partnership; social life. *Cabinet* or *salon de* —, *salon particulier*, private room (*for parties, in an eating-house*, &c.). *Faire* —, to keep company; to associate
Socinianisme, *s.m.* Socinianism
Socinien, ne, *s.m.f. adj.* Socinian
Sociolog-ie, -ique. *V.* page 3, § 1
Socle, *s.m.* socle, stand, pedestal, base; footing; socket; bracket [trine aloes
Socotrin, e, *adj.s.* Socotrine. *Aloès* —, Soco-
Socque, *s.m.* clog; patten; sock, comedy
Socratique, *adj.* Socratic
Soda, *s.m.* soda; glass of currant-syrup mixed with Seltzer-water; (*med.*) heartburn
Sodé, e, *adj.* (*chem.*) containing soda
Sodique, *adj.* (*chem.*) sodic
Sodium, *s.m.* (*chem.*) sodium
Sodomie, *s.f.* sodomy [guilty of sodomy
Sodomiser, *v.n.* to commit sodomy, to be
Sodomite, *s.m.* sodomite
Sodomitique, *adj.* sodomitical
Sœur, *s.f.* sister; —**s**, *pl.* sisters; sisterhood. — *de mère, de père*, sister on the mother's *or* father's side. *Les neuf —s*, the sacred Nine, the Muses [sister, sissy
Sœurette, *s.f.* (*fam.*) little sister, dear little
Sofa, *s.m.* sofa
Soffite, *s.m.* (*arch.*) soffit [(*of Persia*)
Sofi, *s.m.* dervis *or* dervise, sofi; (*obsolete*) Shah
Soi, *pron.* oneself, o.'s person; itself, it; himself, him; herself, her; themselves, them. *A* —, to *or* at *or* with oneself, &c.; one's own; of o.'s own; peculiar; to spare. *A — à, à — de*, *V.* **A.** — *-même*, oneself; itself; himself; herself; themselves; self; alone; too, also, likewise
Soi-disant, *adj.* professing to be, self-styled, pretended, would-be; supposed, so-called
Soie, *s.f.* silk; bristle; hair; staple; (*of a blade*) tongue; (*vet.*) wire-heel. — *plate*, floss silk. — *végétale*, vegetable silk, silk cotton, mocmain. *De* —, of *or* from silk silk, silky
Soierie, *s.f.* silk; silk stuff, silk stuffs, silk goods; silk trade; silk manufactory. *Marchand de —s*, silk mercer. *Maison de —s*, silk business
Soif, *s.f.* thirst. *Avoir* —, to be thirsty; to thirst (for) [drunk
Soiffer, *v.n.* (*pop.*) to tipple, to tope, to get
Soiffeur, Soiffard, *s.m.* (*pop.*) tippler, toper, drunkard
†**Soigné, e,** *part. adj.* taken care of, &c. (*V.* **Soigner**); carefully done, done *or* executed with care; careful; particular; neat; highly finished, elaborate; well done, nicely got up, nice; capital; proper; sound; sharp; — *s.m.* elaborate style; —**e,** *s.f.* bouncer; whacker; good drubbing; good dose of it
†**Soigner,** *v.a.* to take care of, to look after; to attend to; to attend, to tend, to nurse; to do carefully, to execute *or* finish with care; (*pop.*) to dress, to scold, to blow up, to punish
†**Soigneusement,** *adv* carefully
†**Soigneu-x, se,** *adj.* careful; mindful; studious, diligent
Soin, *s.m.* care; —**s,** *pl.* cares; care; attendance; attentions, attention; pains; trouble; exertions. *Manque de* —, carelessness. *Petits —s*, little *or* minute attentions. *Avec* —, with care, carefully. *Sans* —, careless. *Avoir — de*, to take care of; to attend to; to be careful of; to take charge of. *Donner des —s à*, to attend *Être aux petits —s avec* or *pour*, to be all attention to
Soir, *s.m.* evening; night; afternoon. *Ce* —, this evening, to-night. *Deux heures du* —, two o'clock in the afternoon. *Journal du* —, evening paper. *Le* —, the evening; in *or* on the evening
Soirée, *s.f.* evening; evening's occupation; evening's work *or* gain; evening party, party; evening meeting; evening performance
Soit, *subj.* be, be it, let it be; may be; should be; — *int.* be it so! let it be so! let it be! very good! very well! well! granted; agreed; — *adv.* either, or; either from; whether; whether from; namely, viz., that is; say; suppose, let us suppose. — *dit*, be it said. — *que*, whether, or
Soixantaine, *s.f.* sixty or so, about sixty, some sixty, sixty; age of sixty; sixtieth year
Soixante, *adj. m.f.*, *s.m.* sixty, threescore; sixtieth. — *-dix*, seventy, threescore and ten. — *et onze*, seventy one
Soixantième, *adj. s.* sixtieth
Sol, *s.m.* soil; ground; ground-plot; (*mining*) wall; (*mus.*) sol, G; (*coin, obsolete spelling*) *V.* **Sou** [(*month*)
Solaire, *adj.* solar, of the sun, sun; calendar
Solak, *s.m.* solak, archer, bowman, (*Sultan's*) life-guard [(*bot.*) solandra
Solandre, *s.f.* (*vet.*) solanders, sallenders;
Solanées, *s.f.pl.* (*bot.*) solaneæ, solanaceæ
Solanine, *s.f.* (*chem.*) solanine
Solanum, *s.m.* (*bot.*) solanum, nightshade
Solarien, ne, *s.m.f.* inhabitant of the sun
Solarisation, *s.f.* solarization
Solariser, *v.a.* to solarize
Solbattu, e, Solbatu, e, *adj.* (*vet.*) surbated
Solbatture, Solbature, *s.f.* (*vet.*) quittor, closh, sand-crack [sea-bindweed
Soldanelle, *s.f.* (*bot.*) soldanella, soldanel,
Soldat, *s.m.* soldier; man; private; — *adject.* soldierly, soldier like; —**s,** *s.m.pl.* soldiers, men, soldiery; rank and file. *De* —, soldier's, of a soldier, soldierly. *Se faire* —, to enlist
Soldatesque, *s.f.* soldiery; — *adj.* soldierly
Soldatesquement, *adv.* in a soldierly manner, like a soldier, like soldiers
Solde, *s.f.* pay; — *s.m. See below*
Solde, *s.m.* final settlement; balance; surplus stock; selling off, clearance sale, clearance. — *mort*, (*fin.*) dead weight. *Pour — de tous comptes*, in full of all demands
Solder, *v.a.* to pay; to settle; to discharge; to liquidate; to sell off, to clear off *or* out
Se —, *v.r.* to pay off the balance of o.'s account; (*things*) to be paid *or* settled *or* &c.
Sole, *s.f.* (*fish*) sole; (*of horses*, &c.) sole; (*agr.*) break; allotment; (*of a plough*) frame. — *battue*, *V.* **Solbatture** [soleus muscle, soleus
Soléaire, *adj.m.*, *s.m.* *Muscle* —, —, (*anat.*)
Solécisér, *v.n.* to solecize
Solécisme, *s.m.* solecism
†**Soleil,** *s.m.* sun; sunshine; star; sun-flower; sun-fish; (*firework*) sun, Catherine-wheel; (*Cath. rel.*) monstrance. *Au* —, in the sun *or*

sunshine. *Au grand —*, in the brightest sunshine; at midday. *Il fait du —*, the sun shines [or is out
†Soleillé, e, *adj.* sunned, sunny
Solen, *s.m.* (*zool.*) solen, razor-shell, razor-fish
Solénite, *s.f.* (*fossil*) solenite
Solennel, le, *adj.* solemn
Solennellement, *adv.* solemnly
Solennisation, *s.f.* solemnization
Solenniser, *v.a.* to solemnize [ness
Solennité, *s.f.* solemnity; solemnness, solem-
Solénoïde, *s.m.* (*phys.*) solenoid
Soleret, *s.m.* (*old*) foot-armour
Solfatare, *s.f.* (*geol.*) solfatara
Solfége, *s.m.* (*mus.*) solfeggio
Solfiation, *s.f.* (*mus.*) solfaing
Solfier, *v.a.n.* (*mus.*) to solfa
Solidage, *s.f.* (*bot.*) golden rod
Solidaire, *adj.* solidary, jointly and severally liable, conjointly answerable *or* responsible, joint, answerable, accomplice, (a) party (to); binding upon all parties. *Rendre —*, to render *or* make solidary *or* &c.; to bind
Solidairement, *adv.* solidarily, conjointly
Solidariser, *v.a.* to render *or* make solidary *or* conjointly answerable; to bind; to unite
Se —, *v.r.* to be made solidary *or* &c.; to be bound; to be united *or* connected
Solidarité, *s.f.* solidarity, community of interests, joint and several responsibility *or* liability, responsibility, liability; connection; union
Solide, *adj.* solid; substantial; strong; stout; firm; fast; sound; good; real; sterling; solvent; safe; — *s.m.* solid; reality
Solidement, *adv.* solidly; substantially; stoutly, strongly; firmly; soundly; really; [safely
Solidification, *s.f.* solidification
Solidifier, *v.a.* to solidify, to consolidate
Se —, *v.r.* to solidify, to become solid
Solid-isme, -iste. *V.* page 3, § 1
Solidité, *s.f.* solidity; strength; stoutness; firmness; soundness; reality
Soliloque, *s.m.* soliloquy
Solin, *s.m.* (*arch.*) solin [soliped
Solipède, *adj.* solipedous, soliped; — *s.m.*
Soliste, *s.m.f.* (*mus.*) solist, soloist
Solitaire, *adj.* solitary; lonely; desert; single; — *s.m.* solitary, recluse, hermit; (*bird, game, jewel.*) solitaire; — *s.f.* solitary flower
Solitairement, *adv.* solitarily
Solitude, *s.f.* solitude; solitariness, loneliness; [desert, wilderness
Solive, *s.f.* joist, rafter
Soliveau, *s.m.* small joist; log; King Log
Sollicitation, *s.f.* solicitation; soliciting; entreaty; prosecuting; canvassing, canvass; application
Solliciter, *v.a.n.* to solicit; to ask; to entreat; to beseech; to urge; to incite, to induce; to impel; to push on; to prosecute; to petition; to canvass; to apply for; (*med.*) to induce; (*tech.*) to call into action
Solliciteu-r, se, *s.m.f.* solicitor, solicitress; asker; petitioner; canvasser; applicant
Sollicitude, *s.f.* solicitude, care, anxiety
Solmisation, *s.f.* (*mus.*) solmization
Solmiser, *v.a.n.* (*old*) *V.* **Solfier**
Solo, *s.m.* (*mus.*) solo
†Solognot, e, *adj.s.m.f.* of Sologne; native of Sologne; — *s.m.* Sologne sheep
Solon, *s.m.* Solon, legislator
Solubilité, *s.f.* solubility; solvability; dissolubility; dissolvability
Solstice, *s.m.* (*astr.*) solstice
Solsticial, e, *adj.* (*astr.*) solstitial
Soluble, *adj.* soluble; solvable; dissoluble; dissolvable
Soluti-f, ve, *adj.*, **Solutif,** *s.m.* (*med.*) solutive
Solution, *s.f.* solution; break; dissolution; resolution; (*law*) discharge
Solvabilité, *s.f.* solvency
Solvable, *adj.* solvent [*V.* page 3, § 1
Somat-ique, -iste, -ologie, -ologique.
Somboul, *s.m.* (*pharm.*) sumbul
Sombrage, *s.m.* (*agr.*) first dressing
Sombre, *adj.* dark; dusky; dim; dingy; gloomy; lurid; cloudy; dull; sad, melancholy; sombre. *Les —s bords, les rivages* or *royaumes —s*, (*poet.*) the dark *or* infernal regions. *Faire —*, to be dark
Sombrement, *adv.* gloomily, &c. (*V.* **Sombre**)
Sombrer, *v.n.* (*nav.*) to founder, to sink, to go down; — *v.a.* (*agr.*) to give a first dressing to
Sombrero, *s.m.* (*Spanish*) hat, broad-brimmed [hat
†Sommail, *s.m.* (*nav.*) bank, shoal
Sommaire, *adj.* summary; compendious; — *s.m.* summary, compendium; abridgment; abstract; syllabus. *État —*, abstract
Sommairement, *adv.* summarily; compendiously; briefly
Sommateur, *s.m.* summoner
Sommation, *s.f.* summons; notice; (*math.*) summation. *— respectueuse*, (*law*) respectful summons (*to o.'s parents to consent to o.'s marriage*). *Faire les trois —s*, to summon (*a mob*) three times to disperse, to read the Riot Act
Somme, *s.f.* sum; amount; epitome, abridgment, compendium; burden, load; (*nav.*) bank, shoal, bar; — *s.m.* nap; sleep. *Bête de —*, beast of burden. *— totale*, sum total; altogether. *En —, — toute*, finally; in short; on the whole. *Une — de*, a certain sum of money, a certain sum, a given sum, a stated sum. *Faire la —*, to sum up. *Faire un —*, to take a nap, to have a sleep
†Sommeil, *s.m.* sleep. *Avoir —*, to be *or* get *or* feel sleepy. *Avoir le — dur*, to be a sound sleeper. *Tomber de —, n'en pouvoir plus de —*, to be overcome with sleep, to be dreadfully sleepy [nod; (*fig.*) to lie dormant
†Sommeiller, *v.n.* to slumber; to doze; to
Sommeli-er, ère, *s.m.f.* butler; cellarman
Sommellerie, *s.f.* butlership; buttery, pantry
Sommer, *v.a.* to summon, to call upon; (*math.*) to sum, to sum up, to add up [apex; crown
Sommet, *s.m.* summit, top; height, pinnacle;
Sommier, *s.m.* beast of burden; sumpter-horse, pack-horse; hair-mattress, under-mattress, mattress; (*build.*) breastsummer, beam; (*of carriages*) long bar; (*of organs*) sounding-board, sound-board; (*print.*) winter; (*obsolete*) register-book, account-book; jail-book
Sommité, *s.f.* summit, top, height; extremity, end; head; eminent *or* highest man *or* lady; chief *or* principal point
Somnambule, *s.m.f.* somnambulist, sleep-walker; — *adj* sleep-walking, night-walking, somnambulic, somnambulistic [nambulistic
Somnambulique, *adj.* somnambulic, som-
Somnambulisme, *s.m.* somnambulism, [sleep-walking
Somnial, e, *adj.* somnial
Somnifère, *adj.* somniferous; — *s.m.* narcotic
Somniloque, *s.m.f.* somniloquist; — *adj.* somniloquous
Somniloquie, *s.f.* somniloquy
Somnolence, *s.f.* somnolence, somnolency
Somnolent, e, *adj.* somnolent, sleepy, drowsy
Somptuaire, *adj.* sumptuary [didly
Somptueusement, *adv.* sumptuously, splen-
Somptueu-x, se, *adj.* sumptuous, splendid
Somptuosité, *s.f.* sumptuousness, splendour
Son, *adj. poss.* his (own), her (own), its (own), one's (own); their (own); — *s.m.* sound; ringing; beat; strain; bran; sawdust; freckles. *De —*, branny; freckled. *Gros —*, coarse bran. *Petit —*, pollen. *Tache de —*, [(*fam.*) freckle
Sonate, *s.f.* (*mus.*) sonata
Sonatine, *s.f.* (*mus.*) sonatina
Sondage, *s.m.* sounding; boring; probing
Sonde, *s.f.* fathom-line; sounding-line; sounding-lead, lead; borer, bore; sound, probe; taster; searcher; proof-stick; dipping-rod. *Ligne de —*, lead-line. *Plomb de —*, sounding-lead, lead

Sonder, *v.a.n.* to sound; to fathom; to probe; to bore; to ullage; to taste; to search, to examine; to try; to pump; to test; to explore
Sondeur, *s.m.* sounder; searcher; borer; (*nav.*) leadsman
Songe, *s.m.* dream; dreaming. — **-creux,** *s.m.* dreamer, visionary, fancy-monger
Songer, *v.a.n.* to dream; to think; to reflect; to consider; to cast about (for); to aim (at)
Songerie, *s.f.* dreaming, dream, idle dream, musing
Songeu-r, se, *s.m.f.* dreamer; — *adj.* dreaming
Sonica, *adv.* (*old*) just in time; at once
Sonipède, *adj. s.m.* sonipedous, soniped
Sonna, *s.f.* (*Mahom. rel.*) sunna, sunnah
†Sonnaille, *s.f.* bell (*for animals' necks*)
†Sonnailler, *s.m.* bell-wether; — *v.n.* to ring continually, to keep ringing, to ring away
Sonnant, e, *adj.* sounding; ringing; striking; sonorous; (*gram.*) sonant. *A l'heure —e*, at the precise hour. *A midi —*, as the clock strikes (*or* struck) twelve
Sonné, e, *part. adj.* sounded, rung, struck, &c. (*V.* **Sonner**); come; gone; past; accomplished, completed, full
Sonner, *v.a.n.* to sound; to ring; to ring for; to ring the bell; to toll; to strike; to chink, to jingle; to give; to blow *or* wind (*a horn*, &c.); to strike up *or* sound (*a flourish of trumpet*); to spring (*a rattle*); to say, to speak, to utter. *Faire —*, to sound; to ring; to chink, to jingle; to extol, to trumpet; to boast of; to make a fuss about. *On sonne*, the bell rings. *Midi vient de —*, the clock has just struck twelve
Sonnerie, *s.f.* ringing; ring; bells; striking; striking part, striking-train; sound; airs, flourishes. *Pendule à —*, striking clock
Sonnet, *s.m.* sonnet
Sonnette, *s.f.* small *or* little bell, house-bell, hand-bell, bell; rattle; (*tech.*) pile-driver. *Cordon de —*, bell-pull, bell-rope
Sonnettier, *s.m.* bell-maker
Sonneur, *s.m.* ringer, bell-ringer; blower; fiddler; (*zool.*) bell-bird
Sonnez, *s.m.* (*play*) two sixes
Sonniste, Sonnite, *s.m.* (*Mahom. rel.*) sunnite
Sonomètre, *s.m.* (*phys.*) sonometer
Sonométr-ie, -ique. *V.* page 3, § 1
Sonore, *adj.* sonorous, clear; deep-toned; [(*gram.*) sonant
Sonorement, *adv.* sonorously
Sonorité, *s.f.* sonorousness, sonority
Sopha, Sophi. *V.* **Sofa, Sofi**
Sophisme, *s.m.* sophism; fallacy
Sophiste, *s.m.* sophist; — *adj.* sophistic
Sophisterie, *s.f.* sophistry
Sophistication, *s.f.* sophistication, adultera-[tion
Sophistique, *adj.* sophistic, sophistical; — *s.f.* sophistry
Sophistiquement, *adv.* sophistically
Sophistiquer, *v.a.n.* to sophisticate; to subtilize
Sophistiquerie, *s.f.* sophistry; sophistication
Sophistiqueur, *s.m.* sophisticator; subtilizer
Sophore, *s.m.* (*bot.*) sophora
Sopor, *s.m.* (*med.*) sopor
Soporati-f, ve, *adj.*, **Soporatif,** *s.m.* sopo-[rific
Soporeu-x, se, *adj.* soporous
Soporifère, *adj.* soporiferous; — *s.m.* soporific
Soporifique, *adj.m.f.*, *s.m.* soporific
Sopra, *adv.* (*mus.*) sopra
Sopraniste, *s.m.f.* sopranist
Soprano, *s.m.* (*voice*) soprano; — *s.m.f.* (*pers.*) soprano, sopranist
Sorbe, *s.f.* (*bot.*) sorb-apple, sorb, service-berry
Sorbet, *s.m.* sherbet, ice
Sorbetière, *s.f.* freezing-pot, ice-mould
Sorbier, *s.m.* (*bot.*) service-tree. — *des oiseaux*, rowan-tree, quicken-tree, mountain-ash
Sorbine, *s.f.* (*chem.*) sorbine
Sorbique, *adj.* (*chem.*) sorbic
Sorbonique, *adj.* Sorbonical
Sorboniste, *s.m.* Sorbonist
Sorbonne, *s.f.* Sorbonne, university of Paris; (*pop.*) head, head-piece, brain-pan
Sorcellerie, *s.f.* sorcery, witchcraft
Sorcier, *s.m.* sorcerer; wizard; conjurer; diviner; — *adj.* conjuring; divining; difficult, intricate, mysterious
Sorcière, *s.f.* sorceress; witch; conjurer; diviner; hag; — *adj.* conjuring; divining; difficult, intricate, mysterious
Sordide, *adj.* sordid; filthy; mean
Sordidement, *adv.* sordidly; meanly
Sordidité, *s.f.* sordidness; filthiness; mean-[ness
Sore, *s.m.* (*bot.*) sorus (*pl.* sori)
Sorgho, *s.m.* (*bot.*) sorgho grass, sorgho
Sorgueur, *s.m.* (*pop.*) burglar
Soriciens, *s.m.pl.* (*zool.*) soricidæ, sorecidæ
Sorie, *s.f.* Spanish wool
Sorite, *s.m.* (*log.*) sorites
Sorne, *s.f.* scum, dross, slag
Sornette, *s.f.* trifle; idle story; silly thing idle talk, small talk, nonsense
Sororal, e, Sororial, e, *adj.* sisterly, of a sister, of sisters
Sororicide, (*murder*) *s.m.*, (*pers.*) *s.m.f.* sorori-[cide; — *adj.* sororicidal
Sorose, *s.f.* (*bot.*) sorosis
Sort, *s.m.* fate; lot; fortune; position; condition, state; social condition; life, existence; chance; spell, charm. *Au —, par voie du —*, by lot, by lots. *Faire un — à*, to give a position to, to provide for. *Jeter un —*, to cast a lot. *Jeter un — à* or *sur*, to throw a spell over. *Tirage au —*, drawing by lot, drawing lots. *Tirer au —*, to draw by lot, to draw lots. *Tomber au —*, (*mil.*) to draw a bad number (*at the conscription*). *Le — en est jeté*, the die is [cast
Sortable, *adj.* suitable
Sortablement, *adv.* suitably
Sortant, e, *adj.* going *or* coming out; drawn; leaving office, retiring, outgoing, resigning; — *s.m.* outgoer
Sorte, *s.f.* sort, kind, species; manner, way; —**s**, *pl.* sorts, &c.; stock-books. *D'aucune* or *en aucune —*, in any way; in no wise. *De la —*, of the kind; thus, so, in this (*or* that) way. *De* or *en — que*, so that; so as. *De telle —*, in such a manner. *En quelque —*, in some measure, in a manner; almost. *Faire en — que*, to manage it so that; to see that
Sorteu-r, se, *adj.* much out, fond of going out
Sorti, e, *part. adj.* gone out, &c. (*V.* **Sortir**); out; from home; proceeding; resulting, ensuing
Sortie, *s.f.* going out; coming out; turn-out; departure, leaving; egress; issue; way out; outlet; escape; exportation; sally; exit; holiday, going home; blowing-up; attack, abuse; tirade; (*mil.*) sally, sortie; (*at cards*) low cards. — *de bal*, opera-cloak, opera-mantle. *Fausse —*, (*theat.*) sham exit. *A la — de*, at the end of; on leaving. *Droit de —*, export-duty. *Faire une —*, (*mil.*) to make a sally *or* a sortie, to sally forth. *Faire une — contre quelqu'un*, to abuse *or* attack one, to blow one up
Sortilége, *s.m.* sortilege, sorcery, witchcraft; [spell, charm
Sortir, *v.n.* to go out; to come out *or* off; to walk *or* step out; to go out of the room, to leave the room; to get out *or* off; to go *or* come forth; to go beyond; to issue; to proceed; to come; to emerge; to leave; to quit; to have but just left; to be just out; to rise; to spring; to start *or* rush out; to run out; to start; to gush; to burst; to depart; to deviate; to swerve; to be wide (of); to pass out; to result, to ensue; to recover; to escape; to wander; to project; to stand out; to peep, to peer; to spring up, to come up, to shoot out; to sally forth *or* out, to sally; to make o.'s exit; to go home (*from school*); (*rail.*) to run off; (*steam navig.*) to steam out; (*de*) to have just (*V.* **Venir**); — *v.a.* to bring *or* carry out; to take out; to put out; to get out, to extricate; (*law*) to have, to take, to obtain;

(*com., tech.*) to sort; (*pop.*) to bother. *Faire* —, to make (...) go *or* come out *or* &c.; to bring *or* take *or* get *or* turn *or* send out; to put out; to drive out; to let out; to show out; to call out *or* forth; to squeeze out; to bring to light. *Laisser* —, to let (...) go *or* come out *or* &c.; to let out; to leave out. *Il vient de* —, he is just gone out. *Il va* —, he is going out. *Il va pour* —, he goes towards the door; (*theat.*) going. *Il sort,* (*theat.*) exit. *Ils sortent,* (*theat.*) exeunt. ... *sort,* (*theat.*) exit ... ... *sortent,* (*theat.*) exeunt ...

Sortir, *s.m* going *or* coming out; leaving, quitting; rising, &c. (*V.* **Sortir,** *v.n.*); departure. *Au — de,* on coming out of; on (*or* at o.'s) getting out of; as soon as one is out of; on leaving, on quitting; on emerging from; at o.'s departure from; on rising from; on recovering from; immediately after, after; at the end of; immediately beyond

Sosie, *s.m.* very image, like, twin

Sostenuto, *adj.m.* (*mus.*) sostenuto

Sostère, *s.f.* (*bot.*) wrack-grass, sea wrack-grass

Sot, te, *adj.* foolish, silly; confused, dumbfounded, abashed, sheepish; — *s.m.f.* fool, blockhead, silly fellow *or* thing

Sotie, *s.f.* (*obsolete*) farce

Sot-l'y-laisse, *s.m.* parson's nose (*of a fowl*)

Sotnia, *s.f.* sotnia (*troop of Cossacks*)

Sottement, *adv.* foolishly, sillily, senselessly

Sottise, *s.f.* silliness, foolishness, folly, foolery, nonsense, stupidity; silly *or* foolish thing *or* act *or* trick; indecency; insult; **—s,** *pl.* follies, &c.; abusive language, abuse. *Dire des —s à,* to abuse, to call names

Sottisi-er, ère, *s.m.f. adj.* ribald; — *s.m* collection of loose songs and sayings

Sotto-voce, *adv.* (*mus.*) sotto voce

Sou, *s.m.* sou, halfpenny; copper; halfpennyworth. *Cent —s,* five francs (4 shillings). *Gros* —, penny-piece. *Petit* —, halfpenny-piece, small copper. *Les —s, des —s,* halfpence, pence, coppers. *Deux —s,* two halfpence, a *or* one penny; a pennyworth. *De deux —s,* (*adject.*) penny; paltry, paltry-looking; worthless. *De quatre —s,* (*adject.*) two-penny; paltry, paltry-looking; worthless. *Comme quatre —s,* (*pop.*) wretchedly; shabbily, paltrily, seedily; oddly. *Pour deux —s,* for a penny; a pennyworth; (in) the least. *Sans le* (or *un*) —, penniless. *Vingt —s,* a (*or* one) franc. *N'avoir pas le* (or *un*) —, *être sans le* (or *un*) —, to be penniless, to have no money. *Au — la livre,* (*obsolete*) so much in the pound

Souabe, *adj.s.m.f.* Suabian, Swabian; — (*La*), *s.f.* Suabia, Swabia

Soubarbe, *s.f.* chuck (*under the chin*); hinder part of (*a horse's*) lower jaw; part (*of a bit*) where the curb-chain is fastened; (*nav.*) bobstay

Soubassement, *s.m.* (*of beds, and arch.*) base; [(*of apartments*) painted skirting

Soubredent, *s.f.* supernumerary tooth

Soubrelangue, *s.f.* (*med.*) tongue-tie

Soubresaut, *s.m.* start; jump, leap; jerk; jolt; shock

Soubresauter, *v.n.* to start; to jump, to leap; [to jerk; to jolt

Soubrette, *s.f.* abigail; waiting-maid, maid; intriguing woman, intriguer

Soubreveste, *s.f.* (*old*) jacket without sleeves

Soubuse, *s.f.* (*bird*) buzzard

Souche, *s.f.* stump; stock; stub; stem; log; head; founder; blockhead; block; stack; standard; counterfoil; countertally

Souchet, *s. m.* ragstone; (*bird*) shoveller; (*plant*) cyperus, galingale, rush-nut

Souchong, *s.m. adj.* souchong (*tea*)

Souci, *s.m.* care, solicitude, anxiety, concern, trouble, uneasiness; (*bot.*) marigold. *Sans* —, free from care; careless; carelessly; (*s.m.*) *V.* **Sans-souci,** *s.m.*

Soucier (Se), *v.r.* to care, to mind; to be anxious; to wish, to like, to want

Soucieu-x, se, *adj.* full of care, uneasy, solicitous, anxious, careworn; pensive, melancholy

Soucoupe, *s.f.* saucer; salver

†Soucrillon, *s.m.* kind of winter-barley

Soudable, *adj.* that can be soldered

Soudage, *s.m* soldering; welding

Soudain, e, *adj.* sudden, unexpected; hasty

Soudain, Soudainement, *adv* suddenly, on (*or* of) a sudden, all of a sudden, unexpectedly, at once, immediately

Soudaineté, *s.f.* suddenness, unexpectedness

Soudan, *s.m.* sultan

Soudard, Soudart, *s.m.* soldier, veteran

Soude, *s.f.* (*bot.*) glasswort, saltwort; (*min.*) soda. — *de varech,* kelp

Soudé, e, *part. adj.* soldered, &c. (*V.* **Souder**). *Bien* —, (*of horses*) thickset

Souder, *v.a.* to solder; to weld; to join, to unite

Se —, *v.r.* to be soldered *or* welded; to join, to unite, to consolidate

Soudeu-r, se, *s.m.f.* solderer; welder

Soudi-er, ère, *adj.* of soda, soda

Soudière, *s.f* soda-factory, soda-works

Soudiviser, &c. *V.* **Subdiviser,** &c.

Soudoir, *s.m.* soldering-iron

Soudoyer, *v.a.* to hire, to pay, to keep in pay

Soudure, *s.f.* solder, soldering; welding; joint

Soue, *s.f* pig-sty

Soufflage, *s.m.* blowing; glass-blowing; (*nav.*) [sheathing, furring

Souffle, *s.m.* blowing; breath; breathing; puff; blast; inspiration; (*med.*) souffle, resonance

Soufflé, e, *part. adj.* blown, &c. (*V.* **Souffler**); (*cook.*) soufflé, soufflée, puffed; — *s.m.* (*cook.*) soufflé, puff (*pastry*)

Soufflement, *s.m.* blowing; huffing; spiriting away; suppression

Souffler, *v.a.n.* to blow; to snuffle; to pant; to huff and puff; to puff; to swell; to blow out; to fan; to breathe; to utter; to speak; to whisper; to open o.'s lips *or* o.'s mouth, to utter *or* speak a (*or* one) word, to say anything; to prompt; to insinuate; to suggest; to inspire; to deprive (of), to oust (of), to cheat *or* trick *or* chouse (out of); to spirit away; to suppress; to huff; to avoid serving (*a writ*); to scale (*a gun*); to sheathe *or* fur (*a ship*); (*old*) to quaff. — *le chaud et le froid,* to blow hot and cold with the same mouth

Se —, *v.r.* to be blown *or* &c.

Soufflerie, *s.f.* blowing-apparatus; bellows

Soufflet, *s.m.* bellows; slap on the face, box on the ear; affront, mortification; check, reverse; head *or* hood (*of a carriage*); bag

Souffletade, *s.f.* slapping of (*or* slaps on) the face, boxing of the ears

Souffleter, *v.a.n.* to box the ears of, to slap *or* smack the face of, to slap; to insult, to affront

Souffleteu-r, se, *s.m.f.* slapper, boxer

Souffletier, *s.m.* bellows-maker

Souffleu-r, se, *s.m.f.* blower; panter; prompter; alchemist; (*fish*) blower; — *adj.* blowing; (*of horses*) panting

Soufflure, *s.f.* flaw, bubble; seedy glass

Souffrable, *adj.* sufferable, tolerable

Souffrance, *s.f.* suffering; pain; endurance; suspense; delay; (*law*) sufferance, toleration, permission. *De* —, (*law*) borrowed. *En* —, suffering; neglected; in suspense, suspended; standing over; (*com.*) dull; (*of bills*) dishonoured; (*of accounts*) unliquidated. *Jour de* —, borrowed light

Souffrant, e, *adj.* suffering; enduring, patient; in pain; ailing; sickly; ill; poorly, unwell; (*of things*) of suffering; affected; diseased

Souffre-douleur, *s.m.* drudge, fag; butt, laughing-stock; scapegoat; victim; martyr; (*of things*) one for rough work *or* of all work

Souffreteu-x, se, *adj.* poor, needy, destitute, miserable, wretched; poorly, unwell, sickly, weakly, puny

Souffrir, *v.n.* to suffer; to suffer pain, to be in pain; to have a pain *or* pains; to be pained *or*

grieved, to grieve; to be a sufferer; to be injured; — *v.a.* to suffer; to bear; to endure; to stand; to abide; to sustain; to undergo; to meet with; to encounter; to tolerate; to allow, to let, to permit; to put up with; to admit of, to admit. *Faire* —, to make (...) suffer; to plague; to torture; to pain; to grieve

Se —, *v.r.* to suffer *or* &c. each other; to tolerate oneself; (*of things*) to be suffered *or* &c.

Soufrage, *s. m.* sulphuring; sulphurizing; application of sulphur *or* brimstone; smoking (*a cask*) with brimstone, matching, stumming

Soufre, *s.m.* sulphur, brimstone. *Foie de* —, sulphide of potassium

Soufrer, *v.a.* to sulphur; to sulphurize; to apply sulphur *or* brimstone to; to dip in sulphur *or* brimstone; to smoke (*a cask*) with brimstone, to match, to stum

Soufreur, *s.m.* sulphurer

Soufrière, *s.f.* sulphur-mine; (*geol.*) solfatara

Soufroir, *s.m.* sulphuring-stove

Sougarde, Sougorge. *V.* **Sous-garde, Sous-gorge**

Souhait, *s.m.* wish, desire. *A* —, to o.'s wish, to o.'s mind, according to o.'s desire; as well (*or* as much) as one could wish, perfect, perfectly, all right; in profusion; abundantly

Souhaitable, *adj.* desirable; to be wished for

Souhaiter, *v.a.* to wish; to desire, to wish for; to bid. — *avec ardeur*, to earnestly wish; to long for. — or *vouloir du bien, du mal*, *V.* **Vouloir.** *Je t'en* (or *Je vous en*) *souhaite*, (*fam.*) I wish you may get it! don't you wish you may get it? pooh! nonsense! indeed! forsooth! [be wished *or* wished for

Se —, *v.r.* to wish oneself *or* each other; to

Souhaiteu-r, se, *s.m.f.* (*fam.*) wisher

Soui, *s.m.* soy (*Japanese sauce*). — **-manga,** *s.m.* (*zool.*) sunbird

†**Souillard,** *s.m.* (*carp.*) plate [mud bed, bed

†**Souille,** *s.f.* (*hunt.*) soil; (*nav.*) bed of mud,

†**Souillement,** *s.m.* soiling; defilement

†**Souiller,** *v.a.* to soil; to dirty; to stain; to sully; to defile; to pollute; to profane; to imbrue

†**Souillon,** *s.m.f.* sloven, slut, slattern, dowdy, drab, mopsey, malkin, trollop; scullion

†**Souillonner,** *v.a.* to soil, to dirty

†**Souillure,** *s.f.* spot, stain, soil; contamination, pollution; defilement

Soûl, e, *adj.* drunk; full, surfeited, satiated, glutted; wearied, heartily sick (of). — *comme une grive* or *comme un Polonais*, (as) drunk as a fiddler *or* as a lord

Soûl, *s.m.* fill; bellyfull; heart's content. *Tout son* —, o.'s fill *or* bellyful; to o.'s heart's content; as much *or* as long as one pleases *or* likes; plenty; right out

Soulagement, *s.m.* relief; ease; comfort; assistance, aid, help; alleviation

Soulager, *v.a.* to relieve; to ease; to lighten; to comfort; to assist, to aid, to help; to alleviate; to allay

Se —, *v.r.* to relieve *or* &c. oneself *or* each other; (*things*) to be relieved *or* &c.

Soûlaison, *s.f.* (*pop.*) drunkenness; drinking-

Soûlard, e, *s.m.f.* drunkard [bout, boozing

Soûlée, *s.f.* (*pop.*) drinking-bout, boozing

Soûler, *v.a.* to make drunk, to fuddle, to intoxicate; to cram, to fill; to surfeit; to glut; to satiate; to cloy

Se —, *v.r.* to get drunk; to surfeit *or* &c.

Soûlerie, *s.f.* *V.* **Soûlée** [oneself

Souleur, *s.f.* (*fam.*) fright, start, shake, shock

Soulèvement, *s.m.* heaving; rising; swelling; insurrection, revolt; indignation; (*geol.*) upheaval, upthrow of strata. — *de cœur*, rising of the stomach, qualm

Soulever, *v.a.n.* to lift; to raise; to heave; to upheave; to hold up; to rouse; to stir; to urge; to cause to revolt; to revolt; to start; to turn (*the stomach*); (*agr.*) to turn up. — or *faire* — *le cœur* (*à*), to turn (...'s) stomach, to make (*one*) sick, to be sickening *or* disgusting, to sicken *or* disgust

Se —, *v.r.* to raise oneself; to rise; to rise up; to heave; to swell; to revolt, to rebel; to be lifted *or* &c.

Souleveur, *s.m.* lifter; raiser; heaver; stirrer, agitator; — *adj.m.* lifting; raising; heaving

Soulier, *s.m.* shoe. *Être dans ses petits* —*s*, to be much vexed *or* annoyed, to be very uncomfortable in o.'s mind, to be nonplussed *or* embarrassed, to be in an awkward situation. — **-botte,** *s.m.* Blucher boot [scoring, dashing

†**Soulignement,** *s. m.* underlining, under-

†**Souligner,** *v.a.* to underline, to underscore, to dash; to italicize; to lay a stress upon

†**Souligneur,** *s.m.* hair-splitter

Souliote, *s.m.f.adj.* (*geog.*) Suliot [to use

Souloir, *v.n.* (*old*) to be wont *or* accustomed,

Soulte, *s.f.* (*law, com.*) balance; premium

Soumettre, *v.a.* to subdue; to overcome; to conquer; to subjugate; to subject; to submit; to subordinate; to refer

Se —, *v.r.* to submit; to yield; to give way; to comply; to assent; to refer; to obey; to engage, to undertake

Soumis, e, *part. adj.* subdued, submitted, &c. (*V.* **Soumettre**); submissive; compliant; obedient; humble; respectful; dutiful; subject, liable

Soumission, *s.f.* submission; subjection; submissiveness; compliance; obedience; mark of respect; (*law, admin.*) undertaking; bond; tender; contract

Soumissionnaire, *s.m.f.* tendering party, tenderer [tender

Soumissionner, *v.a.n.* to tender for; to

Soupape, *s.f.* valve; plug. — *à gorge*, throttle-valve. — *de sûreté*, safety-valve. *A* —, with a valve

Soupatoire, *adj.* of supper, supper, cenatory; serving as supper. *Dîner* —, late dinner, supper-dinner

Soupçon, *s. m.* suspicion; surmise; taste, smack, dash, (the) mere name (of it); jot, bit, shade, trifle; slight symptom, touch; appear-

Soupçonnable, *adj.* suspectable [ance

Soupçonner, *v.a.* to suspect; to surmise

Soupçonneu-r, se, *s.m.f.* suspecter

Soupçonneusement, *adv.* suspiciously

Soupçonneu-x, se, *adj.* suspicious

Soupe, *s.f.* soup; porridge; slice of bread, sop; (*fam.*) dinner. — *au lait*, milk-porridge; hasty fellow *or* woman. — *de perroquet*, bread steeped in wine. *Tailler la* —, to cut bread into the soup. *Tremper la* —, to soak the bread in the soup. *Tremper une* — *à*, (*pop.*) to blow up, to give a dressing to, to give it to

Soupé, *part. of* **Souper,** *v.n.*; — *s.m.* (*old spelling*) *V.* **Souper,** *s.m.*

Soupeau, *s.m.* (*of a plough*) ground-wrest

Soupente, *s.f.* loft; brace; strap

Souper, *s.m.* supper; supper-time

Souper, *v.n.* to sup, to have supper, to take *or* eat supper *or* o.'s supper, to be at supper. *A* —, to sup; to *or* at supper; some supper; o.'s supper; a supper [ing

Soupèsement, *s.m.* weighing by hand, weigh-

Soupeser, *v.a.* to weigh by hand, to weigh

Soupette, *s.f.* thin slice of bread, sippet

Soupeu-r, se, *s.m.f.* supper-eater; fast *or* gay man *or* woman; — *adj.* that eats supper,

Soupied, *s.m.* *V.* **Sous-pied** [supper-eating

Soupi-er, ère, *s.m.f.* person fond of soup, soup-eater; — *adj* fond of soup, soup-eating

Soupière, *s.f.* soup-tureen

Soupir, *s.m.* sigh; breath; gasp; wish, longing; (*mus.*) crotchet-rest, rest. *Quart de* —, (*mus.*) semiquaver rest; (*V.* **Demi**). *Rendre le dernier* —, to breathe o.'s last, to give up the ghost

†**Soupirail,** *s.m.* air-hole; vent-hole
Soupirant, *s.m.* lover, suitor, wooer, sigher
Soupirement, *s.m.* sighing
Soupirer, *v.a.n.* to sigh; to breathe; to gasp. — *après,* to long for
Soupireu-r, se, *s.m.f.* sigher
Souple, *adj* supple, flexible, pliant, limber, lissome; soft; tractable, docile; yielding; compliant; nimble [pliantly; submissively
Souplement, *adv.* flexibly, pliantly; com-
Souplesse, *s.f.* suppleness, flexibility; pliantness; facility; compliance; docility, submissiveness; nimbleness; versatility; trick
†**Souquenille,** *s.f.* stable-coat; smockfrock, frock; worn-out coat, old coat
Souquer, *v.a.* (*nav.*) to make fast, to stretch, to seize, to hitch; (*pop.*) to blow up; to drub,
Souquet, *s.m.* (*obsolete kind of tax*) [to whack
Source, *s.f.* spring; source; fountain-head; fountain; rise; authority. *De* —, spring; naturally. *Couler de* —, to flow naturally; to come from the heart
Sourcil, *s.m.* eyebrow, brow
Sourcili-er, ère, *adj.* (*anat.*) superciliary
†**Sourciller,** *v.n.* to knit the brow; to frown; to wince, to flinch; to blench; to move a muscle, to stir; to show the least emotion; to spring, to gush out
†**Sourcilleusement,** *adv.* loftily, haughtily, proudly, superciliously; sadly
†**Sourcilleu-x, se,** *adj.* lofty, cloud-capped, towering, steep; haughty, proud, supercilious; careworn, melancholy, sad
Sourd, e, *adj.* deaf; insensible; secret; underhand; dull; dark (*lantern*); dead (*file*); rumbling; hollow; low; confused; obscure; underground; cloudy; bad for sound; (*old math.*) surd; — *s.m.f.* deaf man *or* boy, deaf woman *or* girl, deaf person (*pl.* deaf); — *s m.* (*zool.*) *V.* **Salamandre;** —**e,** *s.f.* (*zool.*) *V.* **Bécassin.** — *comme un pot,* — *à n'entendre pas Dieu tonner,* deaf as a post. *Frapper comme un* —, to strike very hard *or* knock very loud, to strike unmercifully. *Rendre* —, to make deaf, to deafen. — **-muet,** *adj. s.m.,* —**e-muette,** *f.* deaf and dumb, deaf-mute; ditto person
Sourdaud, e, *adj.* hard of hearing; — *s.m.f.* person hard of hearing
Sourdement, *adv.* deafly; dully; indistinctly; without noise, noiselessly; with a dull *or* rumbling noise; with a hollow *or* in a low voice; secretly; underhand; privately. *Brûler* —, to smoulder
Sourdine, *s.f.* (*mus.*) mute, damper, sordet, sordine; (*horol.*) catch-spring. *A la* —, secretly; in secret; clandestinely; by stealth; slily, on the sly; without noise, noiselessly; silently;
Sourdon, *s m.* (*shell fish*) cockle [privately
Sourdre, *v.n.* (*old*) to spring, to spring up, to gush out *or* forth, to issue; to arise; to rise
Souriceau, *s.m.* young mouse, little mouse
Souricière, *s.f.* mouse-trap; (*fig.*) trap, snare, ambush; scrape; (*pop., jest.*) lock-up; prison-van [murine
Souriquois, e, *adj.* (*old, jest.*) of mice, micy,
Sourire, *v.n.* to smile; to please, to be agreeable, to delight, to take the fancy (of), to tempt, to suit; — *s.m.* smile
Souris, *s.f.* mouse; (*of a leg of mutton*) knuckle; — *s.m.* mouse-colour; (*poet.*) smile; — *adj.* mouse-coloured. *Preneur de* —, mouser
Sournois, e, *adj.* sly, cunning, sneaking; — *s.m.f.* ditto person *or* fellow *or* thing, sly boots. *En* —, slily; sneakingly [ingly
Sournoisement, *adv.* slily, cunningly, sneak-
Sous, *prep.* under; below, beneath; on, upon; with; within, in; by; (*in compounds*) under, sub, deputy, assistant, subordinate, secondary. — *Paris,* outside of Paris (*under its walls*). — **-acétate,** *s.m.* (*chem.*) subacetate. — **-affermer,** *v.a.* to underlet; to underlease; to take an underlease of. — **-agent,** *s.m.* under-agent, sub-agent. — **-aide,** *s.m.f.* under-assistant; under-assistant surgeon. — **-amendement,** *s.m.* amendment on an amendment, additional amendment. — **-amender,** *v.a.* to make an amendment to the amendment of, to make an additional amendment to. — **-arbrisseau,** *s. m.* under-shrub; (*bot.*) suffrutex. — **-aumônier,** *s.m.* under almoner, sub-almoner; under-chaplain. — **-axillaire,** *adj.* subaxillary. — **-bail,** *s. m.* underlease. — **-bailleur, euse,** *s. m. f.* underlessor. — **-barbe,** *s.f.* *V.* **Soubarbe.** — **-berne,** *s.f.* (*nav.*) freshes. — **-bibliothécaire,** *s. m.* under-librarian, sub-librarian, assistant librarian. — **-bois,** *s.m.* underwood, underbrush, undergrowth. — **-brigadier,** *s. m.* second corporal (of cavalry), lance-corporal. — **-cap,** *s.m.* under-foreman, overseer. — **-carbonate,** *s.m.* (*chem.*) subcarbonate. — **-caudal, e,** *adj.* subcaudal. — **-chantre,** *s.m.* sub-chanter, under-chanter. — **-chapelain,** *s.m.* under-chaplain. — **-chaussure,** *s.f.* clog, patten. — **-chef,** *s.m.* chief-assistant, second-class clerk, clerk (*clerk next below the* "chef de bureau" *and the* "chef de division"). — *-chef d'état-major,* (*mil.*) under-brigade-major. — *-chef de train,* (*rail.*) breaksman, brakesman. — **-chevron,** *s.m.* (*carp.*) under rafter. — **-claviculaire,** — **clavier, ière,** *adj.* (*anat.*) subclavian. — **-clerc,** *s.m.* under-clerk. — **-collet,** *s.m.* (*of casks*) last hoop. — **-comité,** *s.m.* sub-committee. — **-commis,** *s.m.* under-clerk, junior clerk. — **-commissaire,** *s.m.* under-commissary *or* &c. (*V.* **Commissaire**); (*nav.*) issuing commissary. — **-commission,** *s f.* sub-commission; sub-committee. — **-contraire,** *adj.* subcontrary. — **-contrefort,** *s.m.* (*of boots, shoes*) stiffener. — **-costal, e,** *adj.* (*anat.*) subcostal. — **-couche,** *s.f.* underlayer, substratum. — **-cutané, e,** *adj.* subcutaneous. — **-décuple,** *adj* sub-decuple. — **-déléguer,** &c. *V.* **Subdéléguer,** &c. — **-diaconat,** *s.m.* subdeaconry. — **-diacre,** *s.m.* subdeacon. — **-directeur, trice,** *s.m.f.* sub-director, sub-directress; sub-manager, sub-manageress; &c. (*V.* **Directeur** *and* **Directrice**). — **-diviser,** &c. *V.* **Subdiviser,** &c. — **-dominante,** *s.f.* (*mus.*) subdominant. — **-double,** *adj.* (*math.*) subduple. — **-doublé, e,** *adj.* (*math.*) subduplicate. — **-doyen,** *s.m.* subdean. — **-doyenné,** *s.m.* subdeanery. — **-économe,** *s.m.f.* sub-manager *or* &c. (*V.* **Économe**). — **-entendre,** *v.a.* not to express fully, to understand; to hint; to imply. *Se* — *-entendre,* to be understood. — **-entendu, e,** *part. adj.* understood; *s.m.* thing understood. — **-entente,** *s.f.* mental reservation. — **-entrepreneur,** *s.m.* sub-contractor. — **-espèce,** *s.f.* subspecies. — **-étage,** *s.m.* undergrowth. — **-ferme,** *s.f.* underlease. — **-fermer,** *v.a.* *V.* — **-affermer.** — **-fermier, ière,** *s.m.f.* under-farmer, under-lessee. — **-fréter,** *v.a.* to under freight, to underlet. — **-garantie,** *s.f.* counter-bond, counter-security. — **-garde,** *s.f.* trigger-guard. — **-générique,** *adj.* subgeneric. — **-genre,** *s.m.* subgenus. — **-gorge,** *s.f.* (*of bridles*) throat-band. — **-gouvernante,** *s. f.* under-governess. — **-gouverneur,** *s. m.* under-governor, sub-governor, deputy-governor; (*law*) subtutor. — **-inspecteur, trice,** *s.m.f.* sub-inspector, sub-inspectress. — **-instructeur,** *s.m.* (*mil.*) fugleman. — **-intendance,** *s.f* under-stewardship; under-wardenship. — **-intendant,** *s.m.* under-steward, farm-bailiff, bailiff; sub-commissioner. — **-jacent, e,** *adj.* subjacent. — **-jupe,** *s.f.* under-skirt. — **lieutenance,** *s.f.* sublieutenancy; second lieutenancy; ensigncy; cornetcy. — **-lieutenant,** *s.m.* sublieutenant; second lieutenant; ensign; cornet. — **-limiter,** *v.a.* to be under, not to reach. — **-lingual, e,** *adj.* *V.* **Sublingual.**

— **-locataire,** *s.m.f.* under-tenant; under-lessee. — **-location,** *s.f.* underletting; under-tenancy; underlease. — **-louer,** *v. a.* to underlet; to underhire. — **-main,** *s.m.* guard-paper, guard-sheet, guard-leaf; writing-pad, blotting-pad, pad. — **-ma tre,** *s.m.* assistant-master, assistant, usher. — **-maîtresse,** *s.f.* governess. — **-marin, e,** *adj.* submarine; submersed; (*of currents*) under, underset. — **-maxillaire,** *adj.* (*anat.*) submaxillary. — **-membre,** *s.m.* *V.* **Incise.** — **-mentonnière,** *s.f.* chin-strap. — **-miner,** *v.a.* to undermine. — **-multiple,** *s.m. adj.* (*arith.*) sub-multiple — **-noix,** *s.f.* (*of beef*) round. — **-normale,** *s.f.* (*geom.*) subnormal. — **-occipital, e,** *adj.* (*anat.*) suboccipital. — **-œuvre,** *s.m.* (*build.*) underpinning, substruction. *Reprendre en — -œuvre,* (*build., and fig.*) to underpin, to alter fundamentally, to alter the groundwork of, to begin all over again on another plan. *Reprise en — -œuvre,* doing ditto. — **-officier,** *s.m.* sub-officer, subordinate officer, non-commissioned officer. — **-ongulaire,** *adj.* subungual. — **-orbitaire,** *adj.* (*anat.*) suborbital. — **-ordre,** *s.m.* subordinate. *En — -ordre,* subordinate; subordinately. — **-oxyde,** *s.m.* (*chem.*) suboxide. — **-perpendiculaire,** *s.f.* (*geom.*) subperpendicular. — **-phosphate,** *s.m.* (*chem.*) subphosphate. — **-pied,** *s.m.* trouser-strap, strap. — **-portier,** *s.m.* under-porter. — **-précepteur,** *s.m.* under-tutor. — **-préfectoral, e,** *adj.* sub-prefectoral, sub-prefectorial. — **-préfecture,** *s. f.* under-sheriffship; sub-prefecture. — **-préfet,** *s.m.* under-sheriff; sub-prefect. — **-préfette,** *s.f.* " sous-préfet "'s wife. — **-pression,** *s.f.* under-pressure. — **-prieur, e,** *s.m.f.* subprior; subprioress. — **-principal,** *s. m.* vice-principal. — **-recteur,** *s.m.* subrector. — **-règne,** *s.m.* (*nat. hist.*) sub-kingdom. — **-sacristain,** *s. m.* under - sacristan, under - sexton. — **-secrétaire,** *s. m.* under - secretary. — **-secrétariat,** *s. m.* under - secretaryship; under-secretary's office. — **-seing,** *s.m.* (*law*) private deed, deed; (*post.*) frank, franking. — **-sel,** *s.m.* (*chem.*) subsalt. — **-signature,** *s.f.* under-signature. — **-sol,** (*geol., agr.*) subsoil, substratum; (*arch.*) basement floor *or* story, basement. *Fossé de — -sol,* area. — **-sulfate,** *s.m.* subsulphate. — **-tangente,** *s.f.* (*geom.*) subtangent. — **-tendante,** *s.f.* (*geom.*) subtense, chord. — **-tendre,** *v.a.* (*geom.*) to subtend. — **-titre,** *s.m.* (*print.*) subhead. — **-trait,** *s.m.* (*agr.*) stack-stand. — **-traitant,** *s.m.* sub-contractor. — **-traité,** *s.m.* subcontract. — **-traiter,** *v.n.* to subcontract, to underfarm. — **-variété,** *s.f.* sub-variety. — **-vendre,** *v.a.* to undersell. — **-vente,** *s.f.* underselling. — **-ventrière,** *s.f.* belly-band. — **-verge,** *s.m.* (*of vehicles*) off-horse. — **-vicaire,** *s.m.* second curate. — **-vicariat,** *s.m.* second curacy

Souscripteur, *s.m.* subscriber; signer; underwriter

Souscription, *s.f.* subscription; signature

Souscrire, *v.a.n.* to subscribe; to sign; to consent, to assent, to agree (to); to approve; to underwrite; to endorse

Se —, *v.r* to be subscribed, &c.

Souscrit, e, *part. adj.* subscribed, &c. (*V.* **Souscrire**); (*Gr. gram.*) subscript

Souscrivant, e, *s.m.f.* signer; endorser; underwriter

Souslic, Souslik, *s.m.* (*zool.*) souslik, suslik, [prairie dog

†Soussigné, e, *adj. s.* undersigned; underwritten. *Je —,* I the undersigned

†Soussigner, *v.a.n.* to undersign, to sign, to underwrite, to subscribe o.'s name to, to sub-[scribe

Soustracti-f, ve, *adj.* subtractive

Soustraction, *s.f.* subtraction; taking away, stealing; abstraction, theft; removal

Soustraire, *v.a.* to subtract; to take away, to steal, to abstract; to remove; to withdraw; to shelter, to preserve, to screen

Se —, *v.r.* to escape, to avoid; to flee; to exempt *or* free oneself, to set oneself free; to withdraw; to be subtracted, &c.

Soutache, *s.f.* braid

Soutacher, *v.a.* to braid

Soutacheu-r, se, *s.m.f.* braider

Soutados, *s.m.* (*pop., slang*) halfpenny-piece, mag; halfpenny cigar

Soutane, *s.f.* cassock; (*fig.*) cloth; priests

Soutanelle, *s.f.* short cassock

Soute, *s.f.* (*nav.*) store room, room; small boat; (*law, com.*) *V.* **Soulte.** — *à* or *au charbon,* coal-bunker, bunker. — *au pain,* bread-room; (*pop.*) bread-basket, stomach. — *aux poudres,* powder-room, powder-magazine, magazine

Soutellas, *s.m.* (*slang*) halfpenny cigar

Soutenable, *adj.* sustainable; maintainable; supportable; tenable

Soutenant, *s.m.* sustainer, mooter, respondent

Soutènement, *s.m.* (*build.*) support, prop; (*law*) written explanation. *Mur de —,* retaining wall; breast-wall

Souteneur, *s.m.* supporter, bully

Soutenir, *v.a.n.* to sustain; to support; to maintain; to stand; to keep up; to bear up, to bear; to hold up; to uphold; to prop, to prop up; to strengthen; to assert, to affirm, to contend; to second, to back; to assist, to help; to favour; to protect; to defend; to abet; to afford; to hold out; to endure, to bear; to answer to; to be strengthening *or* nourishing *or* substantial

Se —, *v.r.* to sustain *or* support *or* &c. oneself *or* each other; to keep oneself up, to keep up; to be sustained *or* &c.; to stand up *or* upright, to stand; to stand firm; to bear up; to be kept up, not to flag *or* fall; to get on; to continue; to last; to subsist; to hold o.'s own; to wear o.'s age. *Se — contre,* to resist, to withstand

Soutenu, e, *part. adj.* sustained, supported, kept up, &c. (*V.* **Soutenir**); unflagging; steady; continued; unremitting; unceasing; constant; permanent; elevated, high, lofty; true

Souterrain, e, *adj.* underground, subterranean; secret, dark, underhand; — *s.m.* underground *or* subterranean place *or* passage; subway; vault, cave; tunnel; underground; **—s,** *s.m.pl.* (*fig.*) secret practices; ins and outs; (*engin.*) tunnels; tunnelling

Souterrainement, *adv.* underground; secretly, underhand

Soutien, *s.m.* support; prop, stay; staff; pillar; maintenance; supporter, sustainer, upholder; defence

Soutirage, *s.m.* drawing off, racking; elutria-[tion

Soutirer, *v.a.* to draw off, to rack off, to rack; to elutriate; (*fig.*) to get (out of), to screw (out of), to extract, to extort

Soutre, *s.m.* paper-case

Souvenance, *s.f.* (*old*) remembrance, recollection. *Avoir —,* to remember, to recollect

Souvenez-vous-de-moi, *s.m.* (*bot.*) forget-me-not

Souvenir (Se), *v.r.* to remember, to recollect; to bear in mind. *Faire —,* to make (...) remember; to remind. *S'en —,* to remember it. *Je me souviens* or *il me souvient,* I remember. *Je m'en souviens* or *il m'en souvient,* I remember it. *Te souviens — tu* or *te souvient — il?* do you remember? *Autant que je puis m'en —,* to the best of my recollection. *Ne plus se — de,* to remember *or* &c. no more, to forget

Souvenir, *s. m.* remembrance, recollection; memory; memorial; keepsake; reminder; remembrancer; memento; memorandum-book; letter-rack; souvenir. *Rappeler quelque chose au — de quelqu'un,* to remind one of a thing. *V.* **Rappeler**

Souvent, *adv.* often, frequently. *Le plus* —, most frequently; most generally; for the most part; as often (as). *Plus — ! Le plus — !* (*pop.*) never! catch me! not I! nay, nay! not at all likely! I dare say! indeed!
Souventefois, *adv.* (*old*) oftentimes, often
Souverain, e, *adj.* sovereign; supreme; highest; extreme; most excellent; infallible; powerful; absolute; final; without appeal; — *s.m.f.* (*pers.*) sovereign; — *s.m.* (*Engl. coin.*) sovereign
Souverainement, *adv.* sovereignly; supremely, superlatively, in the highest degree; extremely, in the extreme, exceedingly; absolutely; finally; without appeal; authoritatively
Souveraineté, *s.f.* sovereignty; supremacy; supreme authority; dominion; dominions
Soy, *s.m.* soy (*Japanese sauce*)
Soy-er, ère, *adj.* of silk, silk-growing, silk-manufacturing, silk
Soyeu-x, se, *adj.* silky, silken; soft; fine
Soyon, *s.m.* (*vet*) wire-heel
Spacieusement, *adv.* spaciously, widely
Spacieu-x, se, *adj.* spacious; wide; large; roomy
Spaciosité, *s.f.* spaciousness
Spadassin, *s.m.* fighter, bully, hector; hired assassin
Spadassiner, *v.n.* to fight, to bully, to hector
Spadice, *s.m.* (*bot.*) spadix
Spadicé, e, *adj.* (*bot.*) spadiceous
†**Spadille,** *s.f.* (*at ombre and quadrille*) spadille
Spagirique, *adj.* spagyric, spagyrical
Spagiriste, *s.m.* spagyrist
Spahi, *s.m.* spahi (*Turkish, & Algerian cavalry-man*)
Spalax, *s.m.* (*zool.*) mole-rat
Spalme, Spalmer. *V.* **Espalme, Espalmer**
Spalt, *s.m.* (*min.*) spalt
Sparadrap, *s.m.* (*pharm.*) soap-plaster, adhesive plaster
Sparcette, *s.f.* *V.* **Sainfoin**
Spare, *s.m.* (*fish*) gilthead
Sparganier, *s.m.* (*bot.*) bur-reed
Sparghetti, *s.m.* Naples vermicelli
Spargose, *s.f.* (*med.*) spargosis
Spargoute. *V.* **Espargoute**
Sparies, *s.f.pl.* (*old*) *V.* **Épaves**
Spart, Sparte, *s.m.* (*bot.*) esparto grass, esparto, Spanish grass, rush, mat-weed; — *s.f.* (*anc. geog.*) Sparta
Sparterie, *s.f.* sparterie, esparto manufacture *or* articles, esparto; rush-matting, mat-making; rush mat, mat-work; rush
Spartiate, *adj. s.m.f.* Spartan; Spartan fashion
Spartier, *s.m.* (*bot.*) Spanish broom
Spartiine, *s.f.* (*chem.*) sparteine
Spartine, *s.f.* (*bot.*) cord-grass
Spasme, *s.m.* spasm
Spasm-odique, -odiquement, -ologie. [*V.* page 3, § 1
Spastique, *adj.* (*med.*) spastic
Spath, *s.m.* (*min.*) spar. — *fluor*, fluor spar. — *perlé*, pearl spar
Spathacé, e, *adj.* (*bot.*) spathaceous
Spathe, *s.f.* (*bot.*) spathe
Spathé, e, *adj.* (*bot.*) spathed
Spathique, *adj.* (*min.*) sparry, spathic
Spatule, *s.f.* spatula; (*bird*) spoonbill
Spatulé, e, *adj.* spatulate
Spécial, e, *adj.* special; peculiar, particular; professional; for particular cases
Spécialement, *adv.* specially, especially; peculiarly, particularly
Spécialisation, *s.f.* specialization
Spécialiser, *v.a.* to specialize
Spécialiste, *s.m. adj.* specialist
Spécialité, *s.f.* speciality; specialty; peculiarity; special study *or* branch *or* trade, department, line; (*fin.*) special expense
Spécieusement, *adv.* speciously; plausibly
Spécieu-x, se, *adj.* specious; plausible
Spécificati-f, ve, *adj.* specificative
Spécification, *s.f.* specification
Spécificité, *s.f.* specificalness
Spécifier, *v.a.* to specify
Spécifique, *adj.m.f.*, *s.m.* specific
Spécifiquement, *adv.* specifically
Spécimen, *s.m.* specimen
Spéciosité, *s.f.* speciousness
Spectacle, *s.m.* spectacle, sight; scene; public view; show; play; theatre; opera; performance; playhouse. *Affiche de* —, play-bill. *Jour de* —, play-night. *Programme de* —, play-bill. *Se donner en* —, to attract notice; to expose oneself
Specta-teur, trice, *s.m.f.* spectator, spectatress; looker-on, by-stander; — *adj.* looking on; —**s,** *s.m.pl.* spectators, &c.; audience
Spectral, e, *adj.* spectral; spectrum
Spectre, *s.m.* spectre, ghost, phantom; spectrum; —**s,** *pl.* spectres, &c.; (*med.*) 'muscæ volitantes.' — *solaire*, solar spectrum. spectrum
Spectrolog-ie, -ique, -iquement. *V.* page 3, § 1
Spectromètre, *s.m.* spectrometer
Spectrométr-ie, -ique, &c. *V.* page 3, § 1
Spectroscope, *s.m.* spectroscope
Spectroscop-ie, -ique, &c. *V.* page 3, § 1
Spéculaire, *adj.* specular; — *s. f.* (*bot.*) Venus's looking-glass
Spécula-teur, trice, *s.m.f. adj.* speculator; investor; speculative
Spéculati-f, ve, *adj.* speculative; — *s.m.* speculative person *or* mind
Spéculation, *s.f.* speculation
Spéculativement, *adv.* speculatively
Spéculer, *v.n.* to speculate
Spéculum, *s.m.* (*surg.*) speculum
Speech, *s.m.* (*slang, jest.*) speech
Speiss, *s.m.* (*metal.*) speiss
Spencer, *s.m.* spencer
Spergule, *s.f.* *V.* **Espargoute**
Spermaceti, *s.m.* spermaceti, sperm
Spermatique, *adj.* spermatic, spermatical
Spermatisé, e, *adj.* spermatized
Spermat-isme, -iste. *V.* page 3, § 1
Spermatocèle, *s.f.* (*med.*) spermatocele
Spermato-graphie, -logie, &c. *V.* p. 3, § 1
Spermatorrhée, *s.f.* (*med.*) spermatorrhœa
Spermatorrhéique, *adj.* (*med.*) spermatorrhœic
Sperme, *s.m.* sperm. — *de baleine*, spermaceti, sperm
Spermophile, *s.m.* (*zool.*) *V.* **Souslic**
Sphacèle, *s.m.* (*med.*) sphacelus
Sphacéler, *v.a.*, **Se** —, *v.r.* (*med.*) to sphacelate
†**Sphaigne,** *s.f.* (*bot.*) sphagnum, bog-moss, peat-moss
Sphège, Sphégien, Sphégide, *s.m.* (*zool.*) sand-wasp
Sphène, *s.m.* (*min.*) sphene
Sphénisque, *s.m.* (*bird*) spheniscan (*kind of penguin*)
Sphéno-, (*in compounds, anat.*) spheno-...
Sphénoïdal, e, *adj.* (*anat.*) sphenoidal
Sphénoïde, *adj. s.m.* (*anat.*) sphenoid; sphenoid bone
Sphère, *s.f.* sphere; orb; globe. *Étude de la* —, use of the globes
Sphéricité, *s.f.* sphericity
Sphér-ique, (*adj.*), **-iquement.** *V.* p. 3, § 1
Sphériques, *s.m.pl.* (*math.*) spherics
Sphérographe, *s.m.* spherograph
Sphéroïdal, e, *adj.* spheroidal
Sphéroïde, *s.m.* (*geom.*) spheroid
Sphéroïdique, *adj.* spheroidic, spheroidical
Sphéromètre, *s.m.* spherometer
Sphérométr-ie, -ique. *V.* page 3, § 1
Sphérule, *s.f.* spherule
Sphincter, *s.m.* (*anat.*) sphincter, sphincter muscle
Sphinx, *s.m.* sphinx; (*zool.*) sphinx, hawk-moth
Sphygmique, *adj* (*med.*) sphygmic
Sphygmographe, *s.m.* (*med.*) sphygmograph
Sphygmomètre, *s.m.* (*med.*) sphygmometer
Sphygmoscope, *s.m.* (*med.*) sphygmoscope
Sphyrène, *s.f.* (*fish*) sphyræna
Spic, *s.m.* (*bot.*) spike, spike-lavender
Spica, *s.m.* (*surg.*) spica-bandage, spica
Spicanard, *s.m.* (*bot.*) spikenard
Spiccato, *adj. adv. s.m.* (*mus.*) spiccato
Spiciforme, *adj.* spiciform, spike-shaped
Spicule, *s.m.* (*bot.*) spicule, spikelet

Spigélie, *s.f.* (*bot.*) spigelia, worm-grass
Spigéline, *s.f.* (*chem.*) spigeline
Spina-bifida, *s.m.* (*med.*) spina bifida
Spinal, e, *adj.* (*anat.*) spinal
Spina-ventosa, *s.m.* (*med.*) spina ventosa
Spinelle, *adj. s.m.* (*jewel.*) spinel, spinelle; — *s.f.* (*bot.*) large bristle
Spinescent, e, *adj.* spinescent
Spinifère, *adj.* spiniferous
Spiniforme, *adj.* spiniform
Spinosisme, *s.m.* Spinozism
Spinosiste, *s.m.f.* Spinozist
Spinule, *s.f.* spinule
Spiral, e, *adj.* spiral; — *s.m.* spiral spring; — *s.f.* spiral; spire. *En —e,* spirally. *Aller en —e,* to wind
Spiralement, *adv.* spirally
Spirant, e, *adj.* (*gram.*) spirant
Spiration, *s.f.* (*theol.*) spiration
Spire, *s.f.* (*arch.*) spire; (*geom.*) helix, screw
Spirée, *s.f.* (*bot.*) spiræa, dropwort, meadow-sweet
Spirite, *s.m.f. adj.* spiritist
Spirit-isme, -iste. *V.* page 3, § 1
Spiritualisation, *s.f.* spiritualization
Spiritualiser, *v.a.* to spiritualize
Se —, *v.r.* to become spiritualized; to become spiritual *or* immaterial
Spiritual-isme, -iste (*s.m.f.*). *V.* page 3, § 1
Spiritualiste, *adj.* spiritualistic
Spiritualité, *s.f.* spirituality, spiritualness
Spirituel, le, *adj.* spiritual; intellectual; intelligent, clever; witty; — *s.m.* spirituality; spiritual matters *or* affairs *or* power
Spirituellement, *adv.* spiritually; cleverly; wittily; ingeniously
Spiritueu-x, se, *adj.* spirituous; — *s.m.* spirit
Spirituosité, *s.f.* spirituousness
Spiromètre, *s.m.* (*med.*) spirometer
Spirométr-ie, -ique. *V.* page 3, § 1
Spirule, *s.f.* (*zool.*) spirula
‡Splanchnique, *adj.* (*anat.*) splanchnic
‡Splanchno-graphie, -logie, -tomie, &c. *V.* page 3, § 1
Spleen, *s.m.* spleen
Splénalgie, *s.f.* (*med.*) splenalgia, splenalgy
Splendeur, *s.f.* splendour; brightness; lustre; brilliancy; magnificence; pomp
Splendide, *adj.* splendid; sumptuous; magnificent
Splendidement, *adv.* splendidly; sumptuously; magnificently
Splénétique, *adj. s.m.f.* splenetic
Splénique, *adj.* (*anat.*) splenic
Splénisation, Splénification, *s.f.* (*med.*) splenization
Splénite, *s.f.* (*med.*) splenitis
Splénocèle, *s.f.* (*med.*) splenocele
Spléno-graphie, -logie, &c. *V.* page 3, § 1
Spolia-teur, trice, *adj. s.* despoiling, spoliatory, of spoliation; spoiler, despoiler, spoliator
Spoliati-f, ve, *adj.* spoliative
Spoliation, *s.f.* spoliation
Spolier, *v.a.* to despoil, to spoliate, to strip, to rob, to plunder
Spondaïque, *adj. s.m.* (*vers.*) spondaic
Spondée, *s.m.* (*vers.*) spondee
Spondias, *s.m.* (*bot.*) spondias, hog-plum
Spondyle, *s.m.* (*zool.*) spondylus
Spongieu-x, se, *adj.* spongy
Spongiforme, *adj.* spongiform
Spongille, *s.f.* (*nat. hist.*) spongilla
Spongiole, *s.f.* (*bot.*) spongiole
Spongiosité, *s.f.* sponginess
Spongite, *s.f.* (*min.*) spongite
Spontané, e, *adj.* spontaneous; voluntary
Spontanéité, *s.f.* spontaneity, spontaneousness
Spontanément, *adv.* spontaneously; of o.'s own accord
Sponton. *V.* **Esponton**
Sporadicité, *s.f.* sporadicity, sporadicalness
Sporad-ique, -iquement. *V.* page 3, § 1
Spore, *s.f.* (*bot.*) spore
Sporée, *s.f.* *V.* **Espargoute**
Sport, *s.m.* sport
Sportman, Sportsman, *s.m.* sportsman
Sportule, *s.f.* sportula, sportum, alms, dole
Sporule, *s.f.* (*bot.*) sporule
Spouliner, *v.a.* to spool
Sprat, *s.m.* sprat
Spume, *s.f.* spume, froth, foam
Spumeu-x, se, *adj.* spumous, spumy, frothy, foamy
Spumosité, *s.f.* spuminess, frothiness
Spure, *s.f.* sea-bream
Spurie, *s.f.* *V.* **Espargoute**
Sputation, *s.f.* spitting, expectoration, sputation; spittle
***Squale,** *s.m.* dog-fish; shark
***Squame, Squamme,** *s.f.* scale
***Squameu-x, se, Squammeu-x, se,** *adj.* scaly, squamous, squamose
***Squamiforme,** *adj.* squamiform
***Square,** *s.m.* square
Squelette, *s.m.* skeleton
Squelettique, *adj.* skeletal
Squelettologie. *s.f.* skeletology
†Squille, *s.f.* (*zool.*) squilla, squill, mantis crab, mantis shrimp, sea-mantis; freshwater-shrimp
Squinancie. *V.* **Esquinancie**
Squine, *s.f.* China-root
Squirrhe, Squirre, *s.m.* (*med.*) scirrhus, schirrhus
Squirrheu-x, se, Squirreu-x, se, *adj.* (*med.*) scirrhous, schirrhous
Squirrhosité, Squirrosité, *s.f.* (*med.*) scirrhosity
S't, *int.* st! hi! hoy! hey! I say! here! hush!
Stabat, Stabat mater, *s.m.* stabat mater
Stabilité, *s.f.* stability; solidity; firmness
Stable, *adj.* stable; solid; firm; steadfast; durable, lasting, permanent
Stablement, *adv.* stably; firmly; durably
Stabulation, *s.f.* stabling, stabulation
Staccato, *adj. adv. s.m.* (*mus.*) staccato
‡Stachyde, *s.f.* (*bot.*) stachys. — *des bois,* — *sylvatique,* hedge-nettle
Stade, *s.m.* stade, stadium; (*med.*) stage, period
Stage, *s.m.* probation, course; terms articles; residence
Stagiaire, *adj.* going through his course, attending terms; of a probation *or* course; of terms; of articles; of residence, residentiary; — *s.m.* [*formerly*] outer barrister, [*now*] student; articled clerk; residentiary, resident
Stagier, *s.m.* residentiary canon
Stagnant, e, *adj.* stagnant; still
Stagnation, *s.f.* stagnation; stagnancy
Stagner, *v.n.* to stagnate, to be *or* remain stagnant
Stagnicole, *adj.* living *or* growing in ponds
†Stagnon. *V.* **Estagnon**
Stahlianisme, *s.m.* Stahlianism
Stahlien, ne, *adj. s.* Stahlian
Stalactite, *s.f.* stalactite
Stalactitique, *adj.* stalactitic
Stalagmite, *s.f.* stalagmite
Stalagmitique, *adj.* stalagmitic
Stalle, *s.f.* stall; box
Staminaire, *adj.* (*bot.*) staminar
Staminal, e, *adj.* (*bot.*) staminal
Staminé, e, *adj.* (*bot.*) staminate
Stamineu-x, se, *adj.* (*bot.*) stamineous
Staminifère, *adj.* (*bot.*) staminiferous
Staminiforme, *adj.* (*bot.*) staminiform
Stampe, *s.f.* (*mining*) [the] country
Stance, *s.f.* stanza
Stannage, *s.m.* tinning
Stannate, *s.m.* (*chem.*) stannate
Stanneu-x, se, *adj.* (*chem.*) stannous
Stannifère, *adj.* stanniferous
Stannine, *s.f.* (*min.*) stannine
Stannique, *adj.* (*chem.*) stannic
Stapélie, *s.f.* (*bot.*) stapelia, carrion flower
Staphisaigre, *s.f.* (*bot.*) stavesacre
Staphylier, *s.m.* (*bot.*) bladder-nut, bladder-tree
Staphylin, *s. m.* (*insect*) staphylinus, rove-beetle, cocktail; — *adj.m.* (*anat.*) staphyline
Staphylôme, *s.m.* (*surg.*) staphyloma
Stappe, *s.f.* (*mining*) stoop, pillar
Starie, *s.f.* (*com. nav.*) running *or* working days
Staroste, *s.m.* starost (*Polish nobleman*
Starter, *s.m.* (*in races*) starter

Stase, *s.f.* (*med.*) stagnation, arrest (*of the blood*, &c.) [and measures
Stathmétique, *s.f.* stathmetic, use of weights
Stathouder, *s.m.* stadtholder
Stathoudérat, *s.m.* stadtholderate
Stathoudérien, ne, *adj. s.* stadtholderian
Statice, *s.f.* (*bot.*) statice, sea-lavender, marsh-rosemary [halt; stoppage
Station, *s.f.* station; standing; stand; stay;
Stationnaire, *adj.* stationary; *s.m.* telegraph-clerk (*nav.*) blockship; guard-ship
Stationnal, e, *adj.* stational
Stationné, e, *part. adj.* stopped, remained; stood; stopping, remaining; standing; on a *or* the stand [page
Stationnement, *s.m.* standing; stand; stop-
Stationner, *v.n.* to make a stay, to stop, to remain; to stand; to lie at rest, to lie
Statique, *s.f.* statics
Statisticien, ne, *s.m.f.* statistician
Statistique, *s.f.* statistics; return; — *adj.* statistical [statuary
Statuaire, *adj. m.f.*, (*pers.*) *s.m.*, (*art*) *s.f.*
Statue, *s.f.* statue, figure; pillar. — *de sel*, pillar of salt
Statuer, *v.a.* to enact; to decide, to decree, to declare, to resolve; — *v.n.* to make laws, to enact, to decree
Statuette, *s.f.* statuette
Statu quo, *s.m.* statu quo, status quo
Stature, *s.f.* stature, size, height
Statut, *s.m.* statute; by-law, bye-law
Statutaire, *adj.* statutory
Statutairement, *adv.* statutorily
Steamer, *s.m.* steamer
Stéaraffine, *s.f.* (*chem.*) stearaffine
Stéarate, *s.m.* (*chem.*) stearate
Stéarine, *s.f.* (*chem.*) stearine
Stéarique, *adj.* (*chem.*) stearic
Stéatite, *s.f.* (*min.*) steatite, soap-stone
Stéatocèle, *s.f.* (*med.*) steatocele
Stéatomateu-x, se, *adj.* (*med.*) steatomatous
Stéatôme, *s.m.* (*med.*) steatoma
Steeple-chase, *s.m.* steeple-chase [nographer
Stéganographe, *s.m.* steganograph; stega-
Stéganograph-ie, -ique, -iquement. *V.* page 3, § 1
Steinbock, *s.m. V.* **Bouquetin**
Stèle, *s.f.* (*arch.*) stela
Stellaire, *adj.* stellar, stellary, starry, star; — *s.f.* (*bot.*) stellaria, stitchwort
Stelliforme, *adj.* stelliform
Stellion, *s.m.* (*zool.*) stellio, stellion
Stellionat, *s.m.* (*law*) stellionate [stellionate
Stellionataire, *s.m.f.* (*law*) person guilty of
Sténographe, *s.m.* stenographer, shorthand-writer; reporter [writing, short-hand
Sténographie, *s.f.* stenography, short-hand
Sténographier, *v.a.* to stenograph, to write down in short-hand; to report
Sténograph-ique, -iquement. *V.* p. 3, § 1
Stenté, e, *adj.* (*paint.*) laboured [voice
Stentor, *s.m.* Stentor. *Voix de* —, Stentorian
Steppe, *s.m.f.* steppe
Steppeur, *s.m.* high-stepper
Stérage, *s.m.* measuring by the "stère"
Stercoraire, *adj.* stercorary, stercoraceous; — *s.m.* (*bird*) skua, skua gull; (*insect*) *V.*
Stercoral, e, *adj.* stercoral [**Bousier**
Stercoration, *s.f.* stercoration
Sterculie, *s.f.*, **Sterculier,** *s.m.* (*bot.*) sterculia, silk-cotton tree
Stère, *s.m.* stere, cubic metre (*See* table, p. 6.)
Stéréo, (*in compounds*) stereo ...
Stéréobate, *s.m.* (*arch.*) stereobate
Stéréo-(‡)chromie, ique, iquement, -graphie, ique, iquement, -métrie, &c. *V.* page 3, § 1
Stéréogramme, *s.m.* stereogram [graph
Stéréographe, *s.m.* stereographer; stereo-
Stéréorama, *s.m.* stereorama
Stéréoscope, *s.m.* stereoscope
Stéréo-scopie,-scopique,-scopiquement, -scopiste, -tomie, -tomique, &c. *V.* page 3, § 1
Stéréotypage, *s.m.* stereotyping
Stéréotype, *adj.* stereotype; — *s.m.* stereotyped work
Stéréotyper, *v.a.* to stereotype [typer
Stéréotypeur, *s.m.* stereotype founder, stereo-
Stéréotypie, *s.f.* stereotypy, stereotyping, stereotype-printing; stereotype-foundry
Stérer, *v.a.* to measure by the "stère"
Stérile, *adj.* sterile, barren; unfruitful, fruitless, vain; of scarcity; farrow
Stérilement, *adv.* barrenly, unfruitfully
Stérilisation, *s.f.* sterilization
Stériliser, *v.a.* to sterilize
  Se —, *v.r.* to become sterile *or* barren
Stérilité, *s.f.* sterility, barrenness; unfruitfulness; dearth, scarcity
Sterlet, *s.m.* (*fish*) sterlet
Sterling, *adj. s.m.* sterling
Sternal, e, *adj.* (*anat.*) sternal
Sternalgie, *s.f.* (*med.*) sternalgia, sternalgy, angina pectoris, heart-stroke
Sterne, *s.m.* (*bird*) tern, sea-swallow
Sterno-, (*in compounds, anat.*) sterno-...
Sternum, *s.m.* (*anat.*) sternum, breast-bone
Sternutati-f, ve, *adj.* sternutative
Sternutation, *s.f.* sternutation
Sternutatoire, *adj.m.f.*, *s.m.* sternutatory
Sterteur, *s.f.* (*med.*) stertor
Stertoreu-x, se, *adj.* (*med.*) stertorous
Stéthomètre, *s.m.* (*med.*) stethometer
Stéthoscope, *s.m.* (*med.*) stethoscope
Stéthoscop-ie, -ique. *V.* page 3, § 1
Steward, *s.m.* steward
Sthénie, *s.f.* (*med.*) sthenia
Sthénique, *adj.* (*med.*) sthenic
Stibial, e, *adj.* (*chem.*) stibial
Stibié, e, *adj.* (*chem.*) stibiated, antimonial
Stigmate, *s.m.* stigma; brand, stain
Stigmatiser, *v.a.* to stigmatize, to brand
Stil de grain, *s.m.* (*paint.*) yellow lake
Stillation, *s.f.* dripping, dropping, dribbling
Stiller, *v.n.* to drip, to drop, to dribble
Stillingie, *s.f.* (*bot.*) stillingia, tallow-tree
Stimulant, e, *adj.* stimulating, stimulant; — *s.m.* stimulant; stimulus
Stimula-teur, trice, *adj. s.* stimulating, stimulative; stimulator, stimulatress
Stimulation, *s.f.* stimulation
Stimuler, *v.a.* to stimulate, to excite
Stimulus, *s.m.* stimulus [feather-grass
Stipe, *s.m.* (*bot.*) stipe; caudex; — *s.f.* (*plant*)
Stipelle, *s.f.* (*bot.*) stipel
Stipendiaire, Stipendié, e, *adj. s.* stipendiary, paid, hired; hireling [pay
Stipendier, *v.a.* to hire, to pay, to keep in o.'s
Stipulation, *s.f.* stipulation
Stipule, *s.f.* (*bot.*) stipule
Stipuler, *v.a.n.* to stipulate
Stock, *s.m.* (*com., fin.*) stock
Stockfisch, *s.m.* stockfish
Stoff, *s.m.* stuff (*woollen*)
Stoïcien, ne, *adj. s.* stoic
Stoïcisme, *s.m.* stoicism
Stoïque, *adj.* (*and s., poet., abusively*) stoic
Stoïquement, *adv.* stoically
Stomacace, *s.f.* (*med.*) stomacace
Stomacal, e, *adj.* stomachal, stomachic, stomach
Stomachique, *adj. m.f.*, *s.m.* stomachic
Stomalgie, *s.f.* (*med.*) stomalgia
Stomate, *s.m.* (*bot.*) stoma (*pl.* stomata), stomate (*pl.* stomates)
Stomatique, *adj.m.f.*, *s.m.* (*med.*) stomatic
Stomatite, *s.f.* (*med.*) stomatitis
Stomatoscope, *s.m.* (*med.*) stomatoscope
Stop, *int.* (*nav.*) stop!
Stopper, *v.a.n.* (*nav.*) to stop
Stoppeur, *s.m.* (*nav., tech.*) stopper
Storax, *s.m.* (*bot., pharm.*) storax

Store, *s.m.* roller-blind, spring-roller blind, spring-blind, blind
Storthing, *s.m.* storthing
Stout, *s.m.* stout (*beer*)
Strabisme, *s.m.* strabismus, strabism, squinting. — *convergent*, convergent squint, squinting inward
Strabite, *adj. s.m.f.* squinting, squint-eyed; [squinter
Strabotom-ie, -iste. *V.* page 3, § 1
Stramoine, *s.f.* (*bot.*) stramony, stramonium, thorn-apple
Stramonine, *s.f.* (*chem.*) stramonine
Stramonium, *s.m.* (*bot.*) stramonium, stramony, thorn-apple
Strangulation, *s.f.* strangulation
Stranguler, *v.a.* to strangle
Strangurie, *s.f.* (*med.*) strangury
Strapasser, *v.a.n.* to rough-sketch, to paint [carelessly
Strapasson, *s.m.* rough-sketcher, careless painter
Strapassonner, *v.a.n. V.* **Strapasser**
Strapontin, *s.m.* bracket-seat
Stras, *s.m.* (*jewel.*) strass, paste
Strasbourgeois, e, *adj. s.* of Strasburg; [Strasburger
Strass, *s.m. V.* **Stras**
Strasse, *s.f.* floss-silk, knubs, husks
Stratagématique, *adj.* stratagemical
Stratagème, *s.m.* stratagem
Strate, *s.f.* (*geol.*) stratum
Stratég-ie, -ique, -iquement, -iste. *V.* [page 3, § 1
Stratification, *s.f.* stratification
Stratifier, *v.a.* to stratify
Stratiforme, *adj.* stratiform
Stratigraph-ie, -ique, -iquement. *V.* [page 3, § 1
Stratiote, *s.m.* (*bot.*) stratiotes. — *faux aloès*, water-aloe, water-soldier
Statocratie, *s.f.* statocracy
Statocrat-ique, -iquement, -isme. *V.* page 3, § 1
Stratograph-ie, -ique, -iquement. *V.* [page 3, § 1
Stratus, *s.m.* (*meteorology*) stratus
Strélitz, *s.m.* strelitz (*Muscovite militia-guard*)
Strélitzie, *s.f.* (*bot.*) strelitzia
Strette, *s.f.* (*mus.*) stretto
Stretto, *adj.m.* (*mus.*) stretto
Striation, *s.f.* striation
Strict, e, *adj.* strict; rigorous; rigid; severe
Strictement, *adv.* strictly; rigorously; rigidly; severely
Striction, *s.f.* striction
Stricture, *s.f.* (*surg.*) stricture
Strident, e, *adj.* strident, harsh, shrill
Strideur, *s.f.* stridor, harsh *or* shrill sound *or* noise, harshness, shrillness
Striduleu-x, se, *adj.* stridulous
Strie, *s.f.* stria (*pl.* striæ)
Strié, e, *adj.* striated
Strige, *s.f.* vampire
Strigueu-x, se, *adj.* (*bot.*) strigose, strigous
Striure, *s.f.* striature
Strobile, *s.m.* (*bot., zool.*) strobile
Strombe, *s.m.* (*mollusc*) strombus, wing-shell, fountain-shell
Strongle, *s.m.* (*zool.*) strongylus
Strontiane, *s.f.* (*chem.*) strontia, strontian
Strontianique, *adj.* (*chem.*) strontianic
Strontianite, *s.f.* (*min.*) strontianite
Strontique, *adj.* (*chem.*) strontitic
Strontium, *s.m.* (*chem.*) strontium
Strophe, *s.f.* strophe
Strophule, Strophulus, *s.m.* (*med.*) strophulus, red gum
Structure, *s.f.* structure, construction, building, form, make
Strume, *s.f.* (*med.*) struma
Strumeu-x, se, *adj.* (*med.*) strumous, strumose
Struthine, *s.f.* (*chem.*) strutheine
Struvite, *s.f.* (*min.*) struvite
‡**Strychnate,** *s.m.* (*chem.*) strychnate
‡**Strychnine,** *s.f.* (*chem.*) strychnia, strychnine
‡**Strychnique,** *adj.* (*chem.*) strychnic
‡**Strychnisme,** *s.m.* (*med.*) strychnism
‡**Strychnos,** *s.m.* (*bot.*) strychnos
Stuc, *s.m.* stucco
Stucateur, *s.m.* stucco plasterer, stuccoer
Stud-book, *s.m.* stud-book
Studieusement, *adv.* studiously
Studieu-x, se, *adj.* studious
Studiosité, *s.f.* studiousness
Stuffing-box, *s.m.* (*tech.*) stuffing-box
Stupéfacti-f, ve, *adj.*, **Stupéfactif,** *s.m.* stupefactive
Stupéfaction, *s.f.* stupefaction
Stupéfait, e, *adj.* stupefied, astonished, astounded, amazed, dumbfounded, thunderstruck
Stupéfiant, e, *adj.*, **Stupéfiant,** *s.m.* stupefying; stupefactive; stupefacient, stupefier
Stupéfier, *v.a.* to stupefy; to astonish, to astound, to amaze, to dumbfound
Stupeur, *s.f.* stupor
Stupide, *adj.* stupid, senseless, dull; — *s.m.f.* stupid fellow *or* creature, stupid, blockhead; — *s.m.* stupidity, stupidness
Stupidement, *adv.* stupidly, senselessly
Stupidité, *s.f.* stupidity, dulness; stupid thing
Stupre, *s.m.* stupration
Stygial, e, Stygien, ne, *adj.* Stygian
Style, *s.m.* style; manner; tone; strain. — *soutenu*, elevated *or* high style. — *de cadran*, style of a dial
Stylé, e, *part. adj.* trained, taught, used; skilful, clever, proficient; stylish, dashing
Styler, *v.a.* to train, to use, to accustom; to teach, to instruct, to bring up, to form; to give (*one*) his cue
Stylet, *s.m.* stiletto, dagger; (*surg.*) style; probe
Styliforme, *adj.* styliform
Styl-isme, -iste. *V.* page 3, § 1
Stylite, *s.m. adj.* (*eccl. hist.*) stylite
Stylobate, *s.m.* (*arch.*) stylobate
Stylographie, &c. *V.* page 3, § 1
Stylomètre, *s.m.* stylometer
Stylométrie, &c. *V.* page 3, § 1
Stypticité, *s.f.* stypticity
Styptique, *adj.m.f., s.m.* styptic
Styracine, *s.f.* (*chem.*) styracine
Styrax, *s.m.* (*bot., pharm.*) storax, styrax
Styrien, ne, *adj. s.* Styrian
Su, (*m.*, **e**, *f.*) *part. of* **Savoir**; — *s.m.* (*old*) knowledge. *Au — de*, to the knowledge of. *Au vu et au — de tout le monde*, in everybody's sight; as everybody knows
Suage, *s.m.* (*of wood*) dampness
Suaire, *s.m.* shroud, winding-sheet
Suant, e, *adj.* perspiring, in a perspiration, sweating, sweaty, in a sweat, moist with sweat
Suave, *adj.* sweet; fragrant; pleasant, agreeable; soft
Suavement, *adv.* sweetly; agreeably, pleasantly
Suavité, *s.f.* suavity; sweetness; fragrance; pleasantness; softness
Subaérien, ne, *adj.* subaerial
Subaigu, ë, *adj.* subacute
Subalaire, *adj.* subalar, under the wings
Subalpin, e, *adj.* subalpine
Subalterne, *adj. s.m.f.* subaltern, inferior, [subordinate
Subalternement, *adv.* subalternately, subordinately
Subalternisation, *s.f. V.* **Subalternité**
Subalterniser, *v.a.* to subalternize, to subalternate, to subordinate
Subalternité, *s.f.* subalternization, subalternation, subordination, inferior position
Subapennin, e, *adj.* subapennine
***Subaquatique,** *adj.* subaquatic
Subdélégation, *s.f.* subdelegation
Subdélégué, e, *s.m.f* subdelegate
Subdéléguer, *v.a.* to subdelegate
Subdiviser, *v.a.* to subdivide. *Se —*, to be [subdivided
Subdivision, *s.f.* subdivision
Subdivisionnaire, *adj.* subdivisional
Subérate, *s.m.* (*chem.*) suberate
Subéreu-x, se, *adj.* suberous, cork-like, corky
Subérine, *s.f.* (*chem.*) suberine
Subérique, *adj.* (*chem.*) suberic
Subfossile, *adj.* subfossil

Subi, e, *part. of* **Subir**
Subinflammation, *s.f.* (*med.*) subinflammation
Subintrant, e, *adj.* (*med.*) subintrans, beginning before the other is over, anticipative quotidian (*fever*)
Subir, *v.a.* to suffer; to undergo, to go through, to endure; to bear; to support; to sustain; to submit to; to put up with; to pass through, to pass; to be under; to feel
Se —, *v.r.* to suffer *or* &c. each other; to be suffered *or* &c.
Subit, e, *adj.* sudden, unexpected
Subitement, *adv.* suddenly, unexpectedly
Subito, *adv.* suddenly, on a sudden
Subjacent, e, *adj.* subjacent
Subjecti-f, ve, *adj. s.m* subjective; subject
Subjection, *s.f.* subjection
Subjectivement, *adv.* subjectively
Subjectiv-isme, -iste. *V.* page 3, § 1
Subjectivité, *s.f.* subjectivity, subjectiveness
Subjonctif, *s.m.* (*gram.*) subjunctive mood, subjunctive
Subjugation, *s.f.* subjugation
Subjuguer, *v.a.* to subjugate; to subject; to subdue; to overcome, to conquer; to captivate; to quell
Subjugueur, *s.m.* subjugator, subduer
Sublapsaire, *adj. s.* sublapsarian
Sublimable, *adj.* (*chem.*) sublimable
Sublimation, *s.f.* (*chem.*) sublimation, subliming
Sublimatoire, *adj. s.m.* sublimatory; subliming-pot
Sublime, *adj.* sublime; — *s.m.* sublime, sublimity
Sublimé, *s.m.* (*chem.*) sublimate
Sublimement, *adv.* sublimely
Sublimer, *v.a.* (*chem.*) to sublimate. *Se* —, to be sublimated
Sublimiser, *v.a.* to make *or* render sublime, to sublimize
Se —, *v.r.* to become sublime
Sublimité, *s.f.* sublimity
Sublingual, e, *adj.* (*anat.*) sublingual
Sublunaire, *adj.* sublunar, sublunary
Submental, e, *adj.* (*anat.*) submental
Submergement, *s.m.* submergence, submersion
Submerger, *v.a.* to submerge, to swamp, to sink; to inundate; to drown; to overwhelm
Submersible, *adj* submergible
Submersion, *s.f.* submersion
Suboculaire, *adj.* (*anat.*) subocular
Subodorer, *v.a.* to smell at a distance
Subordination, *s.f.* subordination
Subordonné, e, *adj. s.* subordinate
Subordonnément, *adv.* subordinately
Subordonner, *v.a.* to subordinate
Subornation, *s.f.*, **Subornement,** *s.m.* subornation; bribery
Suborner, *v.a.* to suborn; to bribe
Suborneu-r, se, *s.m.f.* suborner; briber; — *adj.* suborning; bribing
Subrécargue, *s.m.* (*nav.*) supercargo
Subrécot, *s.m.* after-reckoning; extra expense; fresh demand
Subreptice, *adj.* surreptitious
Subrepticement, *adv* surreptitiously
Subreption, *s.f.* subreption, surreption
Subrogateur, *adj.m.* (*law*) subrogatory, surrogating
Subrogation, *s.f.* (*law*) subrogation
Subrogatoire, *adj.* (*law*) subrogatory
Subrogé, e, *adj.* surrogated. — *tuteur,* deputy-guardian, superior guardian and trustee
Subroger, *v.a.* to surrogate. *Se* —, to be surrogated
Subsécuti-f, ve, *adj.* subsecutive
Subséquemment, *adv.* subsequently
Subséquence, *s.f.* subsequence, subsequency
Subséquent, e, *adj.* subsequent
Subside, *s.m.* subsidy; aid
Subsidiaire, *adj.* subsidiary; collateral; additional
Subsidiairement, *adv.* subsidiarily; collaterally; additionally; likewise, also
Subsistance, *s.f.* subsistence; maintenance; support; food; allowance; —**s,** *pl.* victuals, food, provisions, stores
Subsistant, e, *part. adj.* subsisting, subsistent; existing, existent, extant, being, living
Subsister, *v.n.* to subsist; to exist; to live; to live upon; to continue; to be in force; to hold good
Substance, *s.f.* substance
Substantialiser, *v.a.* to substantialize
Substantiel, le, *adj.* substantial
Substantiellement, *adv.* substantially
Substantif, *s.m.* (*gram.*) substantive
Substanti-f, ve, *adj.* (*gram.*) substantive; substantival
Substantifier. *V.* **Substantiver**
Substantivement, *adv.* (*gram.*) substantively, substantivally
Substantiver, *v.a.* (*gram.*) to make a substantive of, to use substantively
Substituer, *v.a.* to substitute; to change; to replace; (*law*) to appoint; to entail. *Bien substitué* or *propriété substituée,* entailed estate, entail. *Enfant substitué,* changeling
Se —, *v.r.* to substitute oneself; to supersede, to replace
Substitut, *s.m.* substitute; deputy; delegate; surrogate
Substituti-f, ve, *adj.* substitutive
Substitution, *s.f.* substitution; (*law*) entail
Substratum, *s.m.* substratum
Substruction, *s.f.* substruction
Substructure, *s.f.* substructure
Subterfuge, *s.m.* subterfuge, evasion, shift
Subtil, e, *adj.* subtle, subtile; fine, thin; penetrating; dexterous; sharp, quick, keen, acute; shrewd; artful, crafty, cunning
Subtilement, *adv.* subtly, subtilely; finely; dexterously; sharply, quickly, keenly, acutely; shrewdly; artfully, craftily, cunningly; cleverly
Subtilisation, *s.f.* subtilization; abstraction
Subtiliser, *v.n.a.* to subtilize; to refine; to cheat, to chouse, to take in; to abstract, to filch, to prig, to steal; to do (*a person*) out of (*a thing*); to get (*a thing*) out of (*a person*)
Se —, *v.r.* to become *or* be subtilized, &c.; to get sharper; to improve
Subtiliseu-r, se, *s.m.f.* subtilizer
Subtilité, *s.f.* subtleness, subtlety, subtileness, subtility; fineness; refinement; shrewdness, penetration, keenness, acuteness, sharpness; dexterousness, cleverness; artfulness, cunning, craftiness, craft
Subulé, e, *adj.* subulate, subulated, awl-shaped
Suburbain, e, *adj.* suburban
Suburbicain, e, *adj.* suburbican
Subvenir, *v.n.* to supply, to provide, to meet, to afford; to relieve, to assist, to help
Subvention, *s.f.* relief, assistance, help, aid; subsidy, supply, grant, allowance, bounty, subvention
Subventionnel, le, *adj.* subventional, subventionary
Subventionner, *v.a.* to give *or* grant a subvention to, to subvention; to subsidize; to support
Subversi-f, ve, *adj.* subversive
Subversion, *s.f.* subversion, overthrow, destruction, ruin
Subvertir, *v.a.* to subvert, to overthrow, to destroy, to ruin
Subvertissement, *s.m.* *V.* **Subversion**
Subvertisseur, *s.m.* subverter
Suc, *s.m.* juice; substance; essence
Succédané, e, *adj.* succedaneous; — *s.m.* succedaneum, substitute
Succéder, *v.n.* to succeed; to follow; to inherit
Succès, *s.m.* success. — *d'estime,* quiet success, indifferent success
Successeur, *s.m.* successor
Successibilité, *s.f.* right of succession
Successible, *adj.* heritable; capable of inheriting; of succession
Successi-f, ve, *adj.* successive; in succession
Succession, *s.f.* succession; inheritance; estate; inheritors, heirs. *Acte de* —, (*Engl. hist.*) succession Act; Act of settlement. *Droit de* —, right of succession; succession-duty, legacy-duty
Successivement, *adv.* successively, in succession
Successivité, *s.f* successiveness
Successoral, e, *adj.* of successions, of inheritance
Succin, *s.m.* yellow amber

Succinate, *s.m.* (*chem.*) succinate [short
Succinct, e, *adj.* succinct, concise, brief;
Succinctement, *adv.* succinctly, concisely, briefly; sparingly, little
Succinique, *adj.* (*chem.*) succinic
Succinite, *s.f.* (*min.*) succinite
Succion, *s.f.* suction, sucking
Succomber, *v.n.* to succumb; to sink; to fall; to yield, to give way, to give in; to be overcome; to be beaten *or* worsted; to fail; to
Succotrin, *s.m.* Socotrine aloes [die, to perish
Succube, *s.m.* succubus
Succulence, *s.f.* succulence, succulency
Succulemment, *adv.* succulently
Succulent, e, *adj.* succulent, juicy, rich; nutritious, nutritive, nourishing
Succursale, *adj.f.* succursal, additional, branch; — *s.f.* chapel of ease; branch; branch establishment *or* office; branch bank
Succursaliste, *s.m.* incumbent of a chapel of
Succussion, *s.f.* succussion [ease
Sucement, *s.m.* sucking, suck
Sucer, *v.a.* to suck; to suck in *or* out *or* up; to imbibe; to draw; to drain
Se —, *v.r.* to be sucked *or* &c. [er lampern
Sucet, *s.m.* sucking-fish, sucker; lamprel, small-
Suceu-r, se, *s.m.f.* sucker; — *s.m.* (*zool.*) sucker; suctorian; — *adj.* (*zool.*) suctorial
Suçoir, *s.m.* (*of insects*, &c.) sucker
Suçon, *s.m.* spot made by sucking [ing
Suçoter, *v.a.* to suck repeatedly, to keep suck-
Sucre, *s.m.* sugar; —! (*pop. int.*) go to! you be blowed! — *en pain*, loaf-sugar, lump-sugar. *Pain de* —, sugar-loaf, loaf of sugar. *Aller se faire* —, (*pop.*) to go to the deuce, to go and be hanged, to go to. *Envoyer faire* —, (*pop.*) to send to the deuce
Sucré, e, *adj.* sugared; sugary; sweetened; sweet; demure; honeyed, bland. *Eau —e*, sugar and water [to sweeten
Sucrer, *v.a.* to sugar, to put sugar in *or* into,
Se —, *v.r.* (*fam.*) to put some sugar in o.'s coffee *or* tea *or* &c., to take some sugar
Sucrerie, *s.f.* sugar-works, sugar-mill; sugar-refinery; sugar-trade; sweetmeat, sweet. — *de*
Sucreur, *s.m.* sugarer [*cannes*, cane-mill
Sucrier, *s.m.* sugar-basin; sugar-maker
Sucri-er, ère, *adj.* of sugar, sugar; — **ère,** *s.f.* sugar-basin (*for powdered sugar*)
†Sucrillon, Sucrion. *V.* **Soucrillon**
Sucrin, *adj.m.* sugary, sugar, sweet; — *s.m.* sugary melon
Sud, *s.m.* south; south wind; — *adj.* south, southern, southerly. *Au* —, to *or* in *or* on *or* &c. the south; south, southward, southerly. *De* or *du* —, south, southern, southerly. *Vers le* —, southward. *Courir au* —, *faire le* —, to sail *or* steer southward [eruption
Sudamina, *s.m.pl.* (*med.*) sudamina, miliary
Sudation, *s.f.* sudation, sweating, perspiration
Sudatoire, *s.m.* sudatory; — *adj.* sudatory, sweating, perspiring. *Fièvre* —, *V.* **Suette**
Sudatorium, *s.m.* sudatory
Sudiste, *s.m.f. adj.* (*American polit.*) Southerner
Sudoral, e, *adj.* sudorous
Sudorifère, *adj.* sudoriferous
Sudorifique, *adj.m.f.*, *s.m.* sudorific
Sudoripare, *adj.* (*anat.*) sudoriparous
Suède, *s.m.* Swedish skin (*for gloves*); glove made of ditto; — (*La*), *s.f.* Sweden
Suédois, e, *adj. s.* Swedish; Swede; Swedish fashion [pull; blowing-up; crowd, crush
Suée, *s.f.* sweating, sweat; fright, stew, funk;
Suer, *v.n.a.* to sweat; to perspire; to toil, to drudge; to give out humidity, to be damp *or* wet; to ooze; to filter. — *sang et eau*, to toil and moil, to strain every nerve, to do o.'s utmost; to be much pained *or* distressed. *Faire* —, to make (...) sweat *or* perspire; to sweat; to heat; to squeeze *or* extract out of; to tire *or* try o.'s patience, to sicken; to bother; to be very tiresome

Suerie, *s.f.* sweating, sweat; sweating-room; heating-room [fever *or* eruption, miliaria
Suette, *s.f.* (— *miliaire*) sudamina, miliary
Sueur, *s.f.* sweat; perspiration; moisture, dampness; toil, labour
Suèves, *s.m.pl.* (*hist.*) Suevi
Suffètes, *s.m.pl.* (*hist.*) suffetes
Suffire, *v.n.* to suffice, to be sufficient *or* enough; to be adequate; to be equal; to be able to do; to do; to be able oneself; to provide, to supply, to satisfy, to serve, to answer, to meet, to afford. *Il suffit de* ..., ... suffices *or* is enough; it suffices *or* is enough to ...; suffice it to ... *Suffit! cela suffit!* enough! that will do, that is sufficient *or* enough. *Suffit que*, it is enough *or* suffice it to say that, enough that, suffice it that
Se —, *v.r.* to provide for oneself, to support oneself, to do for oneself; to find resources in oneself; to manage to do [adequately
Suffisamment, *adv.* sufficiently, enough;
Suffisance, *s. f.* sufficiency; competency; adequacy, adequateness; capacity; conceitedness, conceit, vanity, consequentialness, bumptiousness
Suffisant, e, *adj. s.* sufficient, enough; competent; adequate; conceited, consequential, bumptious, stuck-up; coxcomb, fop, conceited
Suffit. *V.* **Suffire** [person
Suffixe, *s.m.* (*gram.*) suffix
Suffocant, e, *adj.* suffocating, choking, stifling
Suffocation, *s.f.* suffocation, choking, stifling
Suffoquant, *part.* suffocating, choking, stifling
Suffoquer, *v.a.n.* to suffocate, to choke, to stifle; to burst (*with anger*)
Suffragant, e, *adj. s.* suffragan
Suffrage, *s.m.* suffrage, vote; voice; approbation; support
Suffumigation, *s.f.* suffumigation
Suffusion, *s.f.* suffusion
Sufisme, *s.m.* sufism [intimate, to hint
Suggérer, *v.a.* to suggest; to instigate; to
Se —, *v.r.* to be suggested, &c.
Suggesteur, *s.m.* suggester
Suggestion, *s. f.* suggestion; instigation; intimation, hint; inspiration
Sugillation, *s.f.* suggillation
Sugiller, *v.a.* to suggillate
Suicide, *s.m.* suicide, self-murder, self-destruction; felo de se; — *s.m.f.* suicide, self-murderer, self-murderess, self-destroyer; felo de se; — *adj.* suicidal, self-murderous, self-murdering, self-destroying
Suicidé, e, *s.m.f.* (*pers.*) suicide, self-destroyer
Suicider (Se), *v.r.* to commit suicide
Suie, *s.f.* soot
Suif, *s.m.* tallow; suet, fat; candle-grease; (*pop.*) scolding, blowing-up, jobation, carpie; (*nav.*) *V.* **Courai**
Suifer, *v.a.* to tallow; (*nav.*) *V.* **Courayer**
Suifeu-x, se, *adj.* tallowy; greasy
Sui generis, (*Latin*) sui generis, of its (*or* his *or* &c.) own kind, particular, peculiar
Suint, *s.m.* grease; ooze. — *de verre*, sandiver
Suintement, *s. m.* oozing, ooze, sweating, leaking, running
Suinter, *v.n.* to ooze, to sweat, to leak, to run
Suisse, *s.m.* Swiss; head beadle; hall-porter, porter; Swiss guard; Swiss cheese; — (*La*), *s.f.* Switzerland; (the) Swiss fashion; — *adj. m.f.* Swiss [Swiss
Suissesse, *s.f.* Swiss woman *or* lady *or* girl,
Suite, *s.f.* rest; retinue, train, attendants; continuation; sequel; succession; series; sequence; file, line; set; consequence, result; progress; course; links; connection; order; suite. *A la* —, after; behind; (*mil.*) on half-pay, half-pay. *A la — de*, with; after; behind; in the train of; consequent upon. *Dans la* —, eventually; afterwards. *De* —, one after another, consecutively, following, running, together; immediately, directly, at once. *Par*

—, consequently, in consequence. *Par — de,* in consequence *or* pursuance of. *Par la —,* in the sequel; in the event; in the course of time; afterwards. *Sans —,* unattended; unconnected. *Tout de —,* immediately, directly, at once; (*nav.*) amain. *Avoir des —s,* to have bad consequences. *N'avoir pas de —,* to have no retinue; to have no children *or* near relations; not to be followed up; cannot be followed. *N'avoir pas de —s,* to have no bad consequences. *Donner — à,* to pursue, to proceed with; to follow up; to carry out; to act upon. *Faire — à,* to be a continuation of, to continue; to follow

Suitée, *adj.f.* (*of a mare*) with her foal

Suivant, e, *adj.* following; next; ensuing; — *s.m.f.* follower, attendant, henchman

Suivant, *prep.* according to; agreeably to; conformably to; pursuant to. — *moi,* in my opinion. — *que,* as, according as

Suiver, *v.a.* (*bad spelling for* **Suifer**)

Suiveur, *s.m.* follower

Suivi, e, *part. adj.* followed, &c. (*V.* **Suivre**); connected; consistent; coherent; regular; uninterrupted; constant; sought after, popular; (*of rhymes*) regular, consecutive

Suivre, *v.a.n.* to follow; to go *or* come after; to go *or* come *or* be next (to); to succeed; to pursue; to keep pace with; to keep up; to be forwarded; to go by; to go along; to go with; to accompany; to attend; to frequent; to study; to carry out; to result; to observe; to watch; to indulge; to give way to; to exercise; to run after; to run on; (*nav.*) to run. *A —,* (*of articles in periodicals*) to be continued. *Faire —,* to have (*a person*) followed; to send (*one thing after another*); (*on letters and parcels*) to be forwarded. *Suivez,* or *en suivant,* or *faites —,* (*print.*) run on

Se —, *v.r.* to follow *or* &c. each other; to be continuous; to be consistent *or* connected *or* coherent

Sujet, te, *adj.* subject; dependent; liable; exposed; inclined; addicted, prone, given; apt; — *s.m.f.* subject; person, individual, fellow; — *s.m.* subject; cause, reason, motive, occasion, ground; object; matter; topic; argument; account; case; (*hort.*) stock. *Mauvais —,* rogue, bad *or* worthless fellow, bad character. *Au — de,* about, concerning; for. *A ce —,* on this *or* that subject; on this *or* that account; about *or* for this *or* that

Sujétion, *s.f.* subjection, dependence; attendance; constraint; inconvenience

Sulfate, *s.m.* (*chem.*) sulphate

Sulfaté, e, *part. adj.* sulphated; sulphatic

Sulfater, *v.a.* (*chem.*) to sulphate

Sulfatique, *adj.* (*chem.*) sulphatic

Sulfatisation, *s.f.* (*chem.*) sulphatization

Sulfhydrate, *s.m.* (*chem.*) hydrosulphate

Sulfhydrique, *adj.* (*chem.*) hydrosulphuric

Sulfhydromètre, *s.m.* sulphydrometer

Sulfhydrométrie, *s.f.* sulphydrometry

Sulfhydrométrique, *adj.* sulphydrometric

Sulfhydrure, *s.m.* (*chem.*) hydrosulphide, hydrosulphuret

Sulfite, *s.m.* (*chem.*) sulphite

Sulfo . . ., (*in compounds, chem.*) sulfo . . .

Sulfocyanique, *adj.* (*chem.*) sulphocyanic

Sulfocyanogène, *s.m.* (*chem.*) sulphocyanogen

Sulfocyanure, *s.m.* (*chem.*) sulphocyanide

Sulfuration, *s.f.* (*chem.*) sulphuration, sulphurization

Sulfure, *s.m.* (*chem.*) sulphide, sulphuret

Sulfuré, e, *part. adj.* (*chem.*) sulphurated, sulphurized; sulphuretted

Sulfurer, *v.a.* (*chem.*) to sulphurate, to sulphurize

Sulfureu-x, se, *adj.* sulphurous, sulphureous, sulphury

Sulfurique, *adj.* (*chem.*) sulphuric

Sulfuromètre, *s.m.* sulphurometer

Sultan, *s.m.* sultan; lady's basket

Sultanat, *s.m.* sultanate, sultanship

Sultane, *s.f.* sultana, sultaness; Turkish man-of-war

Sultanin, *s.m.* sultanin (*coin*)

Sumac, *s.m.* (*bot., dyeing*) sumach, sumac

Sumbul, *s.m.* (*pharm.*) sumbul, musk-root

Summum, *s.m.* summum, maximum, highest point *or* degree

Sunna, Sunnite. *V.* **Sonna, Sonnite**

Super, *v.a.* (*nav.*) to aspirate, to suck in; — *v.n.* (*nav.*) to be stopped up

Superbe, *adj.* proud, haughty, supercilious; superb, splendid; magnificent, stately; — *s.f.* vainglory, haughtiness, pride, arrogance, superciliousness

Superbement, *adv.* proudly; superbly, splendidly

Supercherie, *s.f.* deceit, fraud; cunning; trick; artifice

Supercoquentieu-x, se, *adj.* (*pop.*) *V.* **Mirobolant**

Supère, *adj.* (*bot.*) above

Superfétati-f, ve, *adj.* superfetative; superfluous

Superfétation, *s.f.* superfetation, superfœtation; excrescence; superfluity; redundancy

Superficiaire, *adj.* superficiary. *Propriétaire —,* superficiary

Superficialité, *s.f.* superficialness, superficiality

Superficie, *s.f.* superficies; surface; area. *De —,* superficial; areal; (*of measure*) square

Superficiel, le, *adj.* superficial; shallow

Superficiellement, *adv.* superficially

Superfin, e, *adj. s.m. V.* **Surfin**

Superflu, e, *adj.* superfluous; — *s.m.* superfluity

Superfluité, *s.f.* superfluity

Supérieur, e, *adj.* superior; upper, higher; high; top; above; superlative; greater; better; — *s.m.f.* superior; superioress; superintendent; better

Supérieurement, *adv.* in a superior manner *or* degree, in a high degree, superiorly; above; better; capitally, splendidly, uncommonly, very well

Supériorat, *s.m.* superiorship

Supériorité, *s.f.* superiority

Superlati-f, ve, *adj. s.m.* superlative. *Au —,* in the superlative; superlatively

Superlativement, *adv.* superlatively

Supernatural-isme, -iste. *V.* page 3, § 1

Superoxydation, &c. *V.* **Suroxydation,** &c.

Superposer, *v.a.* to superpose, to place over *or* upon, to add

Superposition, *s.f.* superposition

Superpurgation, *s.f.* superpurgation

Superstitieusement, *adv.* superstitiously

Superstitieu-x, se, *adj.* superstitious

Superstition, *s.f.* superstition

Superstitiosité, *s.f.* superstitiousness

Superstruction, *s.f.* superstruction

Superstructure, *s.f.* superstructure

Supin, *s.m.* (*Latin gram.*) supine

Supinateur, *adj.m., s.m.* (*anat.*) supinator

Supination, *s.f.* supination

Supplantateur, *s.m.* supplanter

Supplantation, *s.f.,* **Supplantement,** *s.m.* supplantation

Supplanter, *v.a.* to supplant

Suppléance, *s.f.* substitution; assistantship

Suppléant, e, *s.m.f. adj.* substitute; assistant, deputy; assistant-judge

Suppléer, *v.a.n.* to supply, to make up; to supplement; to fill up; to take the place of

Se —, *v.r.* to complete itself; to be completed *or* supplied

Supplément, *s.m.* supplement; addition; additional price; extra; allowance. — *de solde,* (*mil.*) extra pay; batta. *De —, en —,* extra

Supplémentaire, *adj.* supplementary, supplemental; additional; extra

Suppléti-f, ve, Supplétoire, *adj.* suppletory, completing

Suppliant, e, *adj.* suppliant, supplicating, beseeching, entreating, imploring; — *s.m.f.* suppliant, supplicant, supplicator, beseecher, entreater, implorer

Supplication, *s.f.* supplication, entreaty

Supplicatoire, *adj.* supplicatory

Supplice, *s.m.* punishment; execution; torment; torture; pain; anguish. *Le dernier —,* capital punishment, punishment of death, death. *Être au —*, to be on the rack, to be in torture, to be in great anxiety. *Punir du dernier —*, to inflict the punishment of death on

Supplicié, e, *s.m.f.* one executed, criminal executed [tally; to put *or* plague to death

Supplicier, *v.a.* to execute; to punish capi-

Supplier, *v.a.* to supplicate, to beseech, to entreat, to beg, to pray [quest; prayer

Supplique, *s.f.* petition; supplication; re-

Support, *s.m.* support; rest; stand; prop; stay; pillar; help; (*build.*) bearer; strut; (*her.*) supporter [tolerable

Supportable, *adj.* supportable, bearable,

Supportablement, *adv.* supportably, bearably, tolerably

Supporter, *v.a.* to support; to sustain; to prop; to bear; to suffer; to tolerate; to endure; to bear with; to put up with; to stand

Se —, *v.r.* to support *or* &c. oneself *or* each other; to bear with each other; to be sup-

Supporteur, *s.m.* supporter [ported *or* &c.

Supposable, *adj.* supposable

Supposé, e, *part. adj.* supposed, &c. (*V.* **Supposer**); putative, supposititious; assumed, fictitious; reputed. *— que*, suppose, supposing

Supposer, *v.a.* to suppose; to infer; to imply; to assume; to forge; to feign; to substitute; to change

Se —, *v.r.* to suppose oneself; to be sup-

Supposeur, *s.m.* supposer [posed, &c.

Suppositi-f, ve, *adj.* suppositive

Supposition, *s.f.* supposition; forgery; substitution. *V.* **Part,** *s.m.* [suppository-tube

Suppositoire, *s.m.* (*med.*) suppository; (*surg.*)

Suppôt, *s.m.* agent; instrument, tool; imp

Suppressi f, ve, *adj.* suppressive

Suppression, *s.f.* suppression; concealment (*V.* **Part,** *s.m.*)

Supprimable, *adj.* suppressible

Supprimer, *v.a.* to suppress; to do away with; to stop; to abolish; to omit; to cut off *or* out; to take off *or* out; to retrench; to conceal; to pass over in silence

Se —, *v.r.* to be suppressed *or* &c.

Suppurati-f, ve, *adj.*, **Suppuratif,** *s.m.* (*med.*) suppurative [charge

Suppuration, *s.f.* (*med.*) suppuration, dis-

Suppurer, *v.n.* (*med.*) to suppurate, to discharge [calculation

Supputation, *s.f.* computation, reckoning,

Supputer, *v.a.* to compute, to reckon, to calculate; to guess

Suprajurassique, *adj.* (*geol.*) suprajurassic

Supralapsaire, *adj. s.* (*theol.*) supralapsarian

Supramondain, e, *adj.* supramundane

Supranatural-isme, -iste. *V.* page 3, § 1

Suprématie, *s.f.* supremacy

Suprême, *adj.* supreme, highest; last

Suprêmement, *adv.* supremely

Sur, e, *adj.* sour

Sûr, e, *adj.* sure, certain; safe; secure; firm; steady; unerring; infallible; confident; trusty, trustworthy; *— adv.* surely, certainly, assuredly. *— et certain,* quite sure, positive. *Pour —*, for certain; surely. *Pour le plus —*, (in order) to be on the safe side. *Peu —*, unsafe

Sur, *prep.* on, upon; over; above; more than; according to; after; in; into; to; at; about; for; with; against; towards; by; concerning; on account of, in consequence of; of; from; off; out of; near; close to. *— -le-champ*, *V.* **Champ**

Surabondamment, *adv.* superabundantly

Surabondance, *s.f.* superabundance

Surabondant, e, *adj.* superabundant; *— s.m.* superabundance

Surabonder, *v.n.* to superabound, to over-

Surachat, *s.m.* overpaying [abound

Suracheter, *v.a.* to overpay

Suractivité, *s.f.* overactivity

Suraddition, *s.f.* superaddition

Suraigu, ë, *adj.* very acute, very shrill, very

Surajouter, *v.a.* to superadd [sharp, very high

Sural, e, *adj.* (*anat.*) sural

Suraller, *v.n.* (*hunt.*) to outgo

†**Surandouiller,** *s.m.* (*hunt.*) surantler

Surannation, *s.f.* expiration. *Lettres de —*, letters of renewal

Suranné, e, *adj.* expired, out of date; obsolete; antiquated; old; superannuated

Suranner, *v.n.*, **Se —**, *v.r.* to expire, &c. (*V.*

Surarbitre, *s.m.* (*old*) umpire [**Périmer**)

Surard, Surat, *adj. m.* of elder-flower, elder

Surate, *s.f.* (*Mahom. rel.*) surah, sura (*chapter of the Koran*) [surbased

Surbaissé, e *adj.* (*arch.*) elliptic. elliptical,

Surbaissement, *s.m.* (*arch.*) surbasement, making elliptic

Surbaisser, *v.a* (*arch.*) to make elliptic

Surbasique, *adj.* (*chem.*) surbasic

Surbouchage, *s.m.* overstopping

Surboucher, *v.a.* to overstop

Surcharge, *s.f.* surcharge, overcharge, extra charge; additional burden; extra weight; excess; overplus; superaddition; increase; encumbrance; word written on another

Surcharger, *v.a.* to surcharge, to overcharge; to overburden, to overload; to overtax; to overstock; to overwhelm; to weigh down; to oppress; to encumber; to write on

Surchauffage, *s.m.* overheating; superheating

Surchauffer, *v.a.* to overheat; to superheat

Surchauffure, *s.f.* *V.* **Surchauffage**

Surchoix, *s.m.* first quality

Surcomposé, e, *adj. s.m.* double compound

Surcomposition, *s.f.* double composition

Surcostal, e, *adj.* (*anat.*) supracostal

Surcot, *s.m.* (*old*) surcoat

Surcoupe, *s.f.* (*at cards*) trumping over

Surcouper, *v.a.n.* (*at cards*) to trump over; (*pop.*) to interrupt [excrescence

Surcroissance, *s.f.* overgrowth; outgrowth,

Surcroît, *s.m.* superaddition, addition, increase; aggravation; excess. *De —*, in addition, to boot, additional, extra

Surcroître, *v.n.* to overgrow; to grow out, to outgrow; *— v.a.* to increase beyond measure

Surcuire, *v.a.* (*tech.*) to overbake

Surcuisson, *s.f.* (*tech.*) overbaking [lose

Surculeu-x, se, *adj.* (*bot.*) surculous, surcu-

Surdent, *s.f.* supernumerary tooth; (*of horses*) wolf's tooth [ness

Surdi-mutité, *s.f.* (*med.*) deafness and dumb-

Surdité, *s.f.* deafness

Surdorer, *v.a.* to double-gild

Surdorure, *s.f.* double-gilding

Surdos, *s.m.* loin-strap; porter's-pad

Sureau, *s.m.* elder, elder-tree; elder-flower

Surécot, *s.m.* *V.* **Subrécot** [rise

Surélévation, *s.f.* raising higher; increase,

Surélever, *v.a.* to raise higher; to increase, to raise

Surelle, *s.f.* (*bot.*) sheep's sorrel, wood-sorrel

Sûrement, *adv.* surely, certainly, to be sure; safely, securely

Suréminent, e, *adj.* supereminent

Surémission, *s.f.* (*fin.*) overissue

Surenchère, *s.f.* higher bid, outbidding

Surenchérir, *v.n.* to outbid

Surenchérissement, *s.m.* further rise *or* increase (of price)

Surenchérisseur, *s.m.* outbidder

Surenveloppe, *s.f.* extra envelope *or* wrapper

Surépineu-x, se, *adj.* (*anat.*) supraspinal

Surérogation, *s.f.* supererogation

Surérogatoire, *adj.* supererogatory

Surérogatoirement, *adv.* supererogatorily

Suresnes, *s.m.* Suresnes wine, common wine

Surestarie, *s.f.* (*com. nav.*) demurrage [tion

Surestimation, *s.f.* overestimate, overvalua-

Surestimer, *v.a.* to overestimate, to overvalue

Suret, te, *adj.* sourish

Sûreté, *s.f.* safety; safe-keeping; security; sureness, steadiness; correctness. *De* —, of safety, &c.; safety. *Caisse* or *coffre de* —, safe, iron safe, iron chest. *Police* or *service de* —, detective police. *Ronde de* —, watch-round; police-round
Surette, *s.f.* *V.* **Surelle;** — *adj.f.* *V.* **Suret**
Surévaluation, *s.f.* overvaluation, overestimate
Surévaluer, *v.a.* to overvalue, to overestimate
Surexcitabilité, *s.f.* overexcitability, overexcitableness
Surexcitable, *adj.* overexcitable
Surexcitation, *s.f.* overexcitement, overexcitation
Surexciter, *v.a.* to overexcite
Surexhalation, *s.f.* (*med.*) overexhalation
Surextension, *s.f.* overextension
Surface, *s.f.* surface; outside, appearance, appearances
Surfaire, *v.a.n.* to ask too much for; to overrate; to overcharge; to exaggerate; to overpraise
Surfaix, *s.m.* surcingle
Surfin, e, *adj.* superfine; — *s.m.* superfine quality
Surfleurir, *v.n.* to blossom after bearing fruit
Surforce, *s.f.* (*of spirits*) extra strength
Surge, *s.f.* (*adject., Laine* —) wool in grease
Surgeon, Surgeonner. *V.* **Drageon, Drageonner**
Surgir, *v.n.* to arise; to spring up; to arrive, to land. *Faire* —, to give rise to
Surgissement, *s.m.* arising; springing up; arriving, landing
Surhaussement, *s.m.* raising; overrating
Surhausser, *v.a.* to raise beyond measure; to raise
Surhumain, e, *adj.* superhuman
Surier, *s.m.* cork-tree
Surimposer, *v.a.* to superimpose; to overtax
Surimposition, *s.f.* superimposition; increase of taxes
Surin, *s.m.* (*slang*) knife. — *muet*, loaded stick, life-preserver
Surincombant, e, *adj.* superincumbent
Suriner, *v.a.* (*slang*) to stab, to kill
Surintendance, *s.f.* superintendence
Surintendant, *s.m.* superintendent
Surintendante, *s.f.* superintendent; superintendent's wife
Surir, *v.a.* to make sour, to sour; — *v.n.* to get *or* turn sour, to sour
Surjalé, e, *adj.* (*of anchors*) foul
Surjet, *s.m.* (*need.*) whip, overcasting. *Faire un* —, to whip, to overcast
Surjeter, *v.a.* (*need.*) to whip, to overcast
Surlendemain, *s.m.* second day after, day after the morrow, next day but one
Surlonge, *s.f.* *V.* **Aloyau**
Surlouer, *v.a.* to let at a higher price *or* rent
Surlunaire, *adj.* superlunar, superlunary
Surmarcher (Se), *v.r.* to encroach on each other
Surmener, *v.a.* to override, to overdrive, to overwork; to overtask; to overtax; to overtire, to jade, to knock up, to exhaust
Surmesure, *s.f.* overmeasure
Surmeule, *s.f.* runner-stone, runner, upper mill-stone
Surmontable, *adj.* surmountable, superable
Surmonter, *v.a.n.* to surmount; to overcome, to subdue; to rise above; to excel
Surmoule, *s.m.* cast taken on one of plaster
Surmouler, *v.a.* to make a cast on a figure *or* ornament
Surmoût, *s.m.* new wort
Surmulet, *s.m.* (*fish*) surmullet
Surmulot, *s.m.* (*zool.*) surmulot, brown *or* Norway rat
Surnager, *v.n.* to float, to swim; to survive, to remain
Surnaturalisme, *s.m.* supernaturalism, supranaturalism
Surnaturalité, *s.f.* supernaturalness, preternaturalness
Surnaturel, le, *adj. s.m.* supernatural, preternatural; extraordinary
Surnaturellement, *adv.* supernaturally, preternaturally
Surnom. *s.m.* surname
Surnombre, *s.m.* excess
Surnommer, *v.a.* to surname
Surnuméraire, *adj. m.f., s.m.* supernumerary
Surnumérariat, *s.m.* supernumerary time
Suron, *s.m.* (*com.*) *V.* **Céron;** (*bot.*) earth-nut, pig-nut
Suros, *s.m.* (*vet.*) splint, splinter, knot
Suroxydation, *s.f.* (*chem.*) superoxidation
Suroxyde, *s.m.* (*chem*) superoxide
Suroxyder, *v.a.,* **Se** —, *v.r.* (*chem.*) to superoxidate
Suroxygénation, *s.f.* (*chem.*) superoxygenation
Suroxygéner, *v.a.,* **Se** —, *v.r.* (*chem.*) to superoxygenate
Surpaie. *V.* **Surpaye**
Surpassable, *adj.* surpassable
Surpasser, *v.a.* to surpass; to exceed; to go *or* be beyond; to be taller than; to excel; to outdo; to amaze, to astound
Surpaye, *s.f.* overpayment; extra pay; batta
Surpayer, *v.a.* to overpay, to pay too much, to pay too much for
Surpeau, *s.f.* (*obsolete*) *V.* **Épiderme**
Surplis, *s.m.* surplice
Surplomb, *s.m.* overhanging. *En* —, overhanging. *Être en* —, to overhang
Surplombé, e, *part. adj.* overhanged; overhanging
Surplombement, *s.m.* overhanging
Surplomber, *v.n.a.* to overhang
Surplus, *s.m.* surplus, surplusage, overplus; remainder, rest; difference. *Au* —, moreover; besides; however; yet; but; after all
Surpoids, *s.m.* overweight
Surprendre, *v.a.* to surprise; to take by surprise; to overtake; to catch; to find; to detect; to intercept; to obtain fraudulently *or* surreptitiously; to overreach; to take advantage of, to abuse, to impose upon, to deceive; to beguile; to observe; to overhear; to take aback, to take ...'s breath away
Surpreneur, *s.m.* surpriser
Surpris, e, *part. adj.* surprised, &c. (*V.* **Surprendre**); of surprise
Surprise, *s.f.* surprise; deceit; deception; Jack-in-the-box. *Boite* or *joujou à* —, Jack-in-the-box. *Ménager une* — *à*, to prepare a surprise for
Surproduction, *s.f.* overproduction
Surre, *s.m.* acorn of the cork-tree
Surrénal, e, *adj.* (*anat.*) suprarenal, surrenal
†Sursaillir, *v.n.* to start up; to frisk about
Sursaturation, *s.f.* supersaturation, oversaturation
Sursaturer, *v.a.* to supersaturate, to oversaturate
Sursaut, *s.m.* start. *Éveiller* or *réveiller en* —, to startle (*one*) out of his sleep, to startle up. *S'éveiller* or *se réveiller en* —, to start out of o.'s sleep, to start up
Sursauter, *v.n.* *V.* **Sursaillir**
Surséance, *s.f.* suspension; stop
Sursel, *s.m.* (*chem.*) supersalt
Sursemer, *v.a.* to sow over again
Surseoir, *v.a.n.* to suspend, to put off, to postpone, to defer; to supersede; to respite; to arrest
Sursis, e, *part.* suspended, &c. (*V.* **Surseoir**)
Sursis, *s.m.* delay; respite; reprieve; arrest
Sursolide, *adj.m.f., s.m.* sursolid
Sursomme, *s.f.* excessive burden. *La — abat l'âne*, (*Proverb*) it is the last feather that breaks the camel's back
Surstarie. *V.* **Surestarie**
Surtare, *s.f.* supertare, double tare, extra tare
Surtaux, *s.m.* overassessment, overcharge; overtaxation, excessive taxation
Surtaxe, *s.f.* surtax; overtaxation, excessive taxation; overcharge; extra charge; surcharge; extra postage
Surtaxer, *v.a.* to overtax; to overassess, to overrate, to overcharge; to charge extra
Surtiré, e, *s.m.f.* (*com.*) drawee
Surtout, *adv.* specially, especially, chiefly, particularly, above all; — *s.m.* surtout, overcoat; epergne; truck; (*of a bee-hive*) cap. — *de table*, epergne

Surusage, *s.m.* (*com.*) clough, cloff
Survaleur, *s.f.* overvalue
†Surveillance, *s.f.* superintendence; supervision; inspection; inspectorship; surveying; watching, watch; surveillance
†Surveillant, e, *s.m.f.* superintendent; overseer; inspector, inspectress; supervisor; surveyor; keeper; watchman; attendant; surveillant; — *adj.* vigilant, watchful
†Surveille, *s.f.* *V.* **Avant-veille**
†Surveiller, *v.a.n.* to superintend; to supervise; to inspect; to survey; to watch; to watch over; to look after
Se —, *v.r.* to watch over oneself; to watch each other; (*things*) to be watched
Survenance, *s.f.* unexpected coming, supervention; unforeseen arrival; unexpected birth
Survenant, e, *adj.* coming unexpectedly, supervenient; — *s.m.f.* chance-comer; chance guest; unexpected heir *or* heiress
Survendre, *v.a.n.* to sell too dear, to oversell, to overcharge
Survenir, *v.n.* to supervene; to come unexpectedly, to come up *or* on, to come, to arrive; to drop in; to take place, to happen, to occur, to come upon; to befall; to arise
Survent, *s.m.* (*nav.*) storm, severe gale of wind
Survente, *s.f.* overcharge; (*nav.*) *V.* **Survent**
Surventer, *v.n.* (*nav.*) to overblow, to blow hard, to blow a storm
Survenue, *s.f.* supervention, unexpected coming, unforeseen arrival
Survêtir, *v.a.* to overclothe
Survider, *v.a.* to partly empty, to lighten
Survie, *s.f.* survival, survivorship
Surviner, *v.a.* to overbrandy (*wine*)
Survivance, *s.f.* reversion, survivorship. *De* —, of reversion, &c., reversionary
Survivancier, *s.m.* reversioner
Survivant, e, *adj.* surviving; — *s.m.f.* survivor
Survivre, *v.n.* to survive, to outlive, to outlast
Sus, *prep. adv. int.* upon; above, fore, afore; come! up! *En* —, more, over, extra; over and above; in addition, besides; to boot; additional; after-... *En — de*, above. *Courir — à*, to run at *or* after, to fall upon, to attack
Susceptibilité, *s.f.* susceptibility, susceptibleness; sensitiveness; feelings; oversensitiveness, excitability, excitableness, irritability, irascibility, touchiness
Susceptible, *adj.* susceptible; capable; sensitive; oversensitive, excitable, irritable, irascible, easily offended, touchy, sore; infectious
Susception, *s.f.* susception; (*of holy orders*) taking; (*Cath. rel.*) reception (*of the cross, of the crown*)
Suscitateur, *s.m.* instigator
Suscitation, *s.f.*, **Suscitement,** *s.m.* instigation
Susciter, *v.a.* to raise, to raise up, to stir up, to give rise to, to create, to produce, to make
Suscription, *s.f.* superscription, address, direction
Susdénommé, e, *adj.* abovenamed
Susdit, e, *adj.* aforesaid, said, abovementioned
Sus-énoncé, e, *adj.* abovementioned
Sus-épineu-x, se, *adj.* *V.* **Surépineux**
Sus-hépatique, *adj.* (*anat.*) suprahepatic
Sus-jacent, e, *adj.* superjacent
Sus-maxillaire, *adj.* (*anat.*) supramaxillary; — *s.m.* supramaxillary bone
Susmentionné, e, *adj.* abovementioned, forementioned
Sus-nasal, e, *adj.* (*anat.*) supranasal
Susnommé, e, *adj.* abovenamed, forenamed
Sus-orbitaire, *adj.* (*anat.*) supraorbital
Suspect, e, *adj.* suspicious; suspected
Suspecter, *v.a.* to suspect
Se —, *v.r.* to suspect each other; (*things*) to be suspected
Suspendre, *v.a.* to suspend; to hang, to hang up; to stop; to discontinue; to stay; to delay, to put off, to postpone, to defer
Suspendu, e, *part. adj.* suspended, &c. (*V.* **Suspendre**); hung, hanged; hanging; in suspense; in abeyance; (*of bridges*) suspension; (*of carriages*) spring; (*of steps*) light. *Jardins —s*, hanging gardens. *Jetée —e*, chain-pier. *Non* —, (*of carriages*) without springs, springless
Suspens, *adj.* suspended. *En* —, in suspense; undecided; in abeyance; (*of debts*) outstanding
Suspense, *s.f.* suspension
Suspenseur, *adj.m.* (*anat.*) suspensory
Suspensi-f, ve, *adj.* (*gram.*) of suspension; (*law*) hindering; precedent
Suspension, *s.f.* suspension; suspense; interruption; discontinuance; cessation
Suspensoir, *s.m.* suspensory bandage; suspensory, suspensor
Suspente, *s.f.* (*nav.*) suspending rope
Suspicion, *s.f.* (*law*) suspicion
Sus-pied, *s.m.* upper leather
Suspirieu-x, se, *adj.* (*med.*) suspirious
Susrelaté, e, *adj.* abovementioned
Sus-scapulaire, *adj.* (*anat.*) suprascapular; — *s.m.* suprascapular muscle
Susseyement, *s.m.* pronouncing *j* as *z*, and *ch* as *s*
Susseyer, *v.n.* to pronounce *j* as *z*, and *ch* as *s*
Sustentation, *s.f.* sustentation, sustenance
Sustenter, *v.a.* to sustain; to support, to maintain, to feed, to keep
Sustonique, *adj.m.f.*, *s.f.* (*mus.*) supertonic
Susurration, *s.f.* susurration, whispering, whisper, buzzing, soft murmur
Susurrer, *v.n.* to whisper, to buzz
Susurrus, *s.m.* (*med.*) susurrus
Suttee, Suttie, *s.f.* suttee
Sutural, e, *adj.* sutural
Suture, *s.f.* suture; (*fig.*) junction, join
Suturer, *v.a.* to suture
Suzerain, e, *adj. s.* paramount; sovereign; suzerain, lord paramount
Suzeraineté, *s.f.* suzerainty
Svelte, *adj.* slender, slim
Sveltesse, *s.f.* slenderness, slimness
Swedenborgien, ne, *adj. s.* Swedenborgian
Swedenborgisme, *s.m.* Swedenborgianism
Sweepstakes, *s.m.pl.* (*in horse-racing*) sweepstakes
Sybarite, *s.m.* Sybarite; — *adj.* Sybaritic, Sybaritical
Sybarit-ique, -isme. *V.* page 3, § 1
Sycomore, *s.m.* (*bot.*) sycamore, sycomore
Sycone, *s.m.* (*bot.*) syconium, syconus
Sycophante, *s.m.* sycophant, knave, rogue cheat; impostor; slanderer
Sycophantisme, *s.m.* sycophantism, sycophancy
Sycose, *s.f.*, **Sycosis,** *s.m.* (*med.*) sycosis
Syénite, *s.f.* (*min.*) syenite
Syénitique, *adj.* (*min.*) syenitic
Syke, Sykh, *adj. s.* Seikh, Sikh (*Indian*)
Syllabaire, *s.m.* spelling-book
Syllabation, *s.f.* *V.* **Syllabisation**
Syllabe, *s.f.* syllable
Syllaber, *v.a.* *V.* **Syllabiser**
Syllab-ique, -iquement. *V.* page 3, § 1
Syllabisation, *s.f.* syllabication, syllabification
Syllabiser, *v.a.* to syllabicate, to syllabify
Syllabisme, *s.m.* syllabism
Syllepse, *s.f.* syllepsis
Syllept-ique, -iquement. *V.* page 3, § 1
Syllogiser, *v.n.* to syllogize
Syllog-isme, -istique, -istiquement. *V.* page 3, § 1
Sylphe, *s.m.*, **Sylphide,** *s.f.* sylph, sylphid, elf
Sylvain, *s.m. adj.* sylvan; (*bird*) warbler
Sylvanite, *s.f.* (*min.*) sylvanite
Sylvatique, *adj.* sylvatic, sylvan, wood, woodland, forest
Sylves, *s.f.pl.* (*Rom. liter.*) sylvæ
Sylvestre, *adj.* sylvestrian, sylvan, wood, woodland, forest
Sylvicole, *adj.* sylvicultural
Sylviculteur, *s.m.* sylviculturist
Sylvicultural, e, *adj.* sylvicultural
Sylviculture, *s.f.* sylviculture, forestry
Sylvie, *s.f.* (*bird*) sylvia, warbler
Sylvique, *adj.* (*chem.*) sylvic

Symbole, *s.m.* symbol; creed. — *des Apôtres*, Apostles' creed. — *de saint Athanase*, Athanasian creed. — *de Nicée*, Nicene creed
Symbol-ique, -iquement, -isme. *V.* page 3, § 1
Symbolisation, *s.f.* symbolization
Symboliser, *v.a.n.* to symbolize
Symétrie, *s.f.* symmetry
Symétrique, *adj.* symmetrical
Symétriquement, *adv.* symmetrically
Symétriser, *v.n.a.* to symmetrize
Sympathie, *s.f.* sympathy; (*in physiology*) sympathy, consent
Sympathique, *adj.* sympathetic; congenial; (*med., physiology*) sympathetic, consensual
Sympathiquement, *adv.* sympathetically; congenially
Sympathisant, e, *part. adj.* sympathizing; sympathetic
Sympathiser, *v.n.* to sympathize
Symphon-ie, -ique, -iquement, -iste. *V.* page 3, § 1
Symphoricarpe, *s.m.*, **Symphorine,** *s.f.* (*bot.*) symphoricarpus, symphoria, snowberry
Symphyse, *s.f.* (*anat.*) symphysis. — *pubienne*, symphysis of the pubis
Symphyséotomie, *s.f.* (*surg.*) symphyseotomy
Symphysien, ne, *adj.* (*anat.*) symphyseal
Sympiézomètre, *s.m.* sympiezometer
Symptomat-ique, -ologie. *V.* page 3, § 1
Symptôme, *s.m.* symptom; indication, mark, token, sign
Synagogue, *s.f.* synagogue
Synalèphe, *s.f.* (*gram.*) synalepha
Synallagmatique, *adj.* (*law*) synallagmatic, reciprocal
Synaptase, *s.f.* (*chem.*) synaptase
Synarch-ie, -ique. *V.* page 3, § 1
Synarthrose, *s.f.* (*anat.*) synarthrosis
‡**Synchondrose,** *s.f.* (*anat.*) synchondrosis
‡**Synchondrotomie,** *s.f.* (*surg.*) synchondrotomy
‡**Synchrone,** *adj.* synchronous
‡**Synchron-ique, -iquement, -isme, -ologie.** *V.* page 3, § 1
‡**Synchroniser,** *v.n.a.* to synchronize
‡**Synchise,** *s.f.* (*gram.*) synchisis
‡**Synchisis,** *s.m.* (*med.*) synchisis
Synclinal, e, *adj.* (*geol.*) synclinal
Syncopal, e, *adj.* (*med.*) syncopal
Syncope, *s.f.* (*gram.*) syncope; (*med.*) syncope, swoon, faintness, fainting fit; (*mus.*) syncope; (*mus.*) syncopation
Syncoper, *v.a.* to syncopate; to stupefy; — *v.n.* to syncopate. **Se** —, *v.r.* to swoon, to faint
Syncrét-isme, -iste. *V.* page 3, § 1
Syndérèse, *s.f.* remorse, sting of conscience
Syndic, *s.m.* syndic; councilman, committeeman; assignee
Syndical, e, *adj.* syndical, of a syndic, of syndics. *Chambre —e*, syndical chamber, syndics; council, committee. *Chambre —e des agents de change*, Stock-Exchange Committee
Syndicat, *s.m.* syndicate. — *de faillite*, commission of bankruptcy
Syndicataire, *s.m.* syndic; — *adj.* *V.* **Syndical**
Syndiquer, *v.a.* to syndicate. *Se* —, to form into a syndicate
‡**Synecdoche, Synecdoque,** *s.f.* (*rhet.*) synecdoche
Synérèse, *s.m.* (*gram.*) synæresis, syneresis
Synévrose, *V.* **Synnévrose**
Syngénésie, *s.f.* (*bot.*) syngenesia
Syngnathe, *s.m.* (*zool.*) syngnathus, pipe-fish
Synnévrose, *s.f.* (*anat.*) synneurosis
Synodal, e, *adj.* synadol synodic, synodical
Synodalement, *adv.* synodically
Synode, *s.m.* synod
Synod-ique, -iquement, *V.* page 3, § 1
Synonyme, *adj.* synonymous; —*s.m.* synonym
Synonymie, *s.f.* synonymy
Synonymique, *adj.* synonymic, synonymical; synonymous
Synonymiquement, *adv.* synonymously
Synonymiste, *s.m.* synonymist
Synopse, Synopsis, *s.f.* synopsis
Synopt-ique, -iquement, *V.* page 3, § 1
Synoque, *s.f.* (*med.*) synocha (*fever*)
Synostose, *s.f.* (*anat.*) synosteosis
Synovial, e, *adj.* (*anat.*) synovial
Synovie, *s.f.* (*anat.*) synovia, synovial fluid
Syntact-ique, -iquement. *V.* page 3, § 1
Syntaxe, *s.f.* (*gram.*) syntax
Syntaxique. *V.* **Syntactique**
Synthèse, *s.f.* synthesis
Synthét-ique, -iquement, -isme. *V.* page 3, § 1
Syntonine, *s.f.* syntonine, muscle fibrine
Syphilicome, *s.m.* Lock hospital
Syphilide, *s.f.* syphilitic skin-disease
Syphiligraphe, *s.m.* syphiligrapher
Syphiligraph-ie, -ique. *V.* page 3, § 1
Syphilis, *s.f.* (*med.*) syphilis
Syphilisation, *s.f.* (*med.*) syphilization
Syphiliser, *v.a.* (*med.*) to syphilize
Syphilisme, *s.m.* (*med.*) syphilism
Syphilitique, *adj. s.* (*med.*) syphilitic
Syphiloïde, *adj.* (*med.*) syphiloid
Syphilolog-ie, -ique. *V.* page 3, § 1
Syphon. *V.* **Siphon**
Syracusain, e, *adj. s.* Syracusan
Syriaque, *adj.m.f.*, *s.m.* Syriac
Syrien, ne, *adj. s.* Syrian
Syringe, *s.f.* *V.* **Syringue**
Syringotomie, *s.f.* (*surg.*) syringotomy
Syringue, Syrinx, *s.f.* syrinx, Pandean pipes, mouth-organ
Syro-, (*in compounds*) Syro-...
Syrop, Syrupeux. *V.* **Sirop, Sirupeux**
Syrte. *V.* **Sirte**
Systaltique, *adj.* (*physiology*) systaltic
Systémat-ique, -iquement. *V.* page 3, § 1
Systématisation, *s.f.* systematization
Systématiser, *v.a.* to systematize. *Se* —, to be systematized
Systématiseur, *s.m.* systematizer
Systémat-isme, -iste, -ologie, -ologique. *V.* page 3, § 1
Système, *s.m.* system; plan; policy; set. *Par* —, systematically
Systolaire, *adj.* *V.* **Systolique**
Systole, *s.f.* (*anat.*) systole
Systolique, *adj.* (*anat.*) systolic
Systyle, *s.m.* *adj.* (*arch.*) systyle
Syzygie, *s.f.* (*astr.*) syzygy

T

T, *s.m.* (*letter*) t; anything in the shape of a T; tace; (*tech.*) T iron; (*surg.*) T bandage; (*draw.*) T square; — *between two hyphens, before* "il" "elle," *and* "on," *is only euphonic*
T', *contraction of* **Te**
Ta, *adj. poss.f.* thy, thy own; your, your own; — *int.* tut! now!
Tabac, *s.m.* tobacco; snuff; —**s,** *pl.* tobacco and snuff; manufacture of ditto. — *à fumer*, tobacco, smoking-tobacco. — *à priser*, — *en poudre*, snuff. — *râpé*, rappee. — *à la fève*, snuff scented with Tonka bean. — *de la régie*, tobacco supplied by the government. *Débitant* or *marchand de* —, tobacconist
Tabacique, *adj.* tabacic
Tabacolog-ie, -ique. *V.* page 3, § 1
Tabagie, *s.f.* smoking-room, tap-room, smoking-house, divan; set of smokers; tobacco-box
Tabaïolle. *V.* **Tavaïolle**
Tabaniens, *s.m.pl.* (*zool.*) tabanidæ
Tabar, Tabard, Tabarre, Tabart, *s.m.* tabard
Tabarin, *s.m.* juggler; merry-andrew, Jack-pudding, buffoon, clown
Tabarinage, *s.m.* buffoonery
Tabaschir, *s.m.* tabasheer
Tabati-er, ère, *s.m.f.* (*pers.*) tobacco-worker
Tabatière, *s.f.* snuff-box; (*fusil à* —), snuff-box rifle (*breech-loader*). *Châssis* or *fenêtre à* —, *lucarne en* —, skylight
Tabellaire, *adj.* tabellar
Tabellion, *s.m.* (*obsolete*) (petty) notary, tabellion
Tabellionage, *s.m.* (*obsolete*) notary's office

Tabernacle, *s.m.* tabernacle; tent
Tabes, *s.m.* (*med.*) tabes
Tabide, *adj.* (*med.*) tabid
Tabifique, *adj.* (*med.*) tabific, tabifical
Tabis, *s.m.* tabby (*stuff*)
Tabiser, *v.a.* to tabby
Tablature, *s.f.* (*mus.*) tablature. *Donner de la — à*, to give trouble to; to cut out work for; to outdo. *Entendre la —*, to be sharp *or* cunning, to be a sharp fellow, to be up to snuff, to be up to trap
Table, *s.f.* table; board; index; slab; top; (*of a violin*, &c.) belly; (*of an anvil*) face; (*of eating and drinking*) table, board, food, fare, living, dinner, dinners; (*mil.*, *nav.*) mess. — *à coulisses*, sliding-frame table, telescope-table. — *à écrire*, writing-table. — *à manger*, dining-table. — *à ouvrage*, work-table. — *à rallonges*, telescope-table. — *à volets*, Pembroke table. — *d'attente*, tablet (*for an inscription*); promising youth. — *de canapé*, occasional table. — *de cuisine*, kitchen-table, dresser. — *d'harmonie*, sounding-board. — *de jeu* or *a jouer*, card-table; chess-table; gaming-table, gambling-table; card-party. — *des matières*, table of contents, index. — *de milieu*, centre table, loo-table. — *de multiplication* or *de Pythagore*, multiplication table. — *de nuit*, bedroom pedestal, bedside stand *or* table. — *de salon*, loo-table. — *de travail*, study-table. — *ouverte*, open house. — *-portefeuille*, Sutherland table. — *rase*, 'tabula rasa,' smooth *or* blank tablet, tablet (*for inscriptions*); (*fig.*) blank; clean sweep. *Sainte —*, communion-table. *Aimer la —*, to like good living. *Avoir* or *tenir — ouverte*, to keep open house. *Faire — rase*, to make a clean sweep. *Lever la —*, to remove the cloth. *Se lever de —*, *Sortir de —*, to rise from table. *Mettre la —*, to put the table; to lay the cloth. *Se mettre à —*, to sit down to table. *Vivre a la même —*, (*of officers*) to mess together
Tableau, *s.m.* picture; painting, piece, scene, scenery, view; sight; representation; description; scenic effect; table; list; board; black-board; (*law*) rolls; (*of juries*) panel; (*at horse-races*) telegraph. — *de chevalet*, easel-painting, easel-picture, easel-piece. — *d'histoire*, historical painting *or* piece. — *-annonce*, advertising-board. *—x vivants*, tableaux vivants
Tableautin, *s.m.* small picture
Tablée, *s.f.* tableful; table-length
Tabler, *v.n.* (*old*) to sit at table; to depend (upon)
Tableti-er, ère, *s.m.f.* fancy-stationer; toyman, toywoman, toy-maker *or* dealer
Tablette, *s.f.* tablet; table-book, note-book, book; shelf; (*pharm.*) lozenge, tablet, (*of chocolate*, &c.) cake; (*arch.*) table
Tabletterie, *s. f.* fancy-stationery; fancy goods *or* articles; toy-trade *or* business; toys
Tablier, *s.m.* apron; pinafore; (*of fire-grates*) blower, draw-plate; (*of bridges*) floor; (*fort.*) platform; (*play*) chess-board; draught-board; backgammon-board
Tabou, *s.m.* taboo
Tabouer, *v.a.* to taboo
Tabouret, *s.m.* stool, footstool; (*bot.*) shepherd's purse. — *de piano*, music-stool
Tabourin, *s.m.* chimney-cowl, cowl
Tabulaire, *adj.* tabular
Tac, *s.m.* (*vet.*) rot; (*zool.*) newt, eft
Tacahout, *s.m.* tacahout, mahee (*gall of the tamarisk-tree*)
Tacamaque, *s.m.* tacamahac (*resin*)
Tacaud, *s.m.* (*fish*) bib, pout, whiting-pout, brassy
Tacca, *s.f.* (*bot.*) tacca
Tacet, *s.m.* (*mus.*) tacet, pause; (*fig.*) silence
Tachant, e, *adj* soiling; that soils; liable to get dirty
Tache, *s.f.* spot; stain; speck, speckle; mark; blot, blemish. — *de feu*, tan-spot. — *de naissance*, birth-mark, mother-spot, mother's mark, nævus maternus, nævus, mole
Tâche, *s.f.* task; task-work, job. *A la —*, by the job, by the piece. *Ouvrage à la —*, task-work, jobbing, piece-work. *Ouvrier à la —*, task-worker, jobbing-workman, jobber. *Prendre à —*, to make it a point *or* o.'s business *or* study, to undertake. *Travailler à la —*, to job, to work by the piece
Tacher, *v.a.* to spot; to stain; to soil; to speck; to sully
Se — *v.r.* to soil o.'s clothes; to get soiled *or* dirty
Tâcher, *v.n.* to endeavour, to try, to strive, to seek
Tâcheron, *s.m.* task-worker, jobbing-workman
Tacheté, e, *part. adj.* spotted, &c. (*V.* **Tacheter**); freckled; tabby
Tacheter, *v.a.* to spot; to speckle; to fleck; to flecker
Tacheture, *s.f.* spot; spottedness; speckle; speckledness
Tachygraphe, *s.m.* tachygrapher
Tachygraph-ie, -ique, -iquement. *V.* p. 3, § 1
Tachymètre, *s.m.* tachometer
Tacite, *adj.* tacit, implied
Tacitement, *adv.* tacitly
Taciturne, *adj.* taciturn, silent
Taciturnement, *adv.* taciturnly, silently
Taciturnité, *s.f.* taciturnity
Taconner, &c (*obsolete*) *V.* **Ravauder,** &c
Taconnet, *s.m.* (*bot.*) colt's-foot
Tact, *s.m.* touch, feeling; tact
Tac-tac, *s.m.* tick-tack
Tacticien, *s.m.* tactician
Tacticograph-ie, -ique. *V.* page 3, § 1
Tactile, *adj.* tactile
Tactilité, *s.f.* tactility
Taction, *s.f.* taction
Tactique, *s.f.* tactics; generalship; manœuvre, stratagem; way; move; plan; — *adj.* tactic, tactical
Tadorne, *s.m.* (*bird*) tadorna, shieldrake, sheldrake, shelldrake, bergander
Tænia, *V.* **Ténia**
Taffetas, *s.m.* taffeta, taffety, silk. — *gommé*, oiled silk, oil-silk. — *d'Angleterre*, sticking plaster, court-plaster
Tafia, *s.m.* tafia, inferior rum
†Tafouilleux, *s.m.* mud-lark
Tagète, *s.f.* (*bot.*) African marigold
Taïaut, *int. s.m.* (*hunt*) tally-ho!
Taïcoun, Taïcoune, *s.m.* tycoon (*of Japan*)
Taïcounal, e, *adj.* tycoonal
Taïcounat, *s m.* tycoonate, tycoonship
Taie, *s. f.* pillow-case; (*med.*) speck. — *d'oreiller*, pillow-case
†Taillabilité, *s.f.* taxability, taxableness
†Taillable, *adj.* liable to be taxed, taxable
‡Taillade, *s.f.* cut, slash, gash
†Taillader, *v.a.* to cut, to slash, to scotch, to crimp
†Taillanderie, *s.f.* edge-tool making; edge-tool trade; edge-tools
†Taillandier, *s.m.* edge-tool maker
†Taillant, *s.m.* edge (*of a knife*, &c.)
†Taille, *s.f.* cutting; cut; nick, notch; pruning, dressing; figure, shape; form; waist; size, height, stature; standard; tally (*stick*); taille (*tax*); tallage (*tax*); capitation-tax, poll-tax; coppice-wood; (*engr.*) cut; (*mus.*) tenor part, tenor; (*surg.*) lithotomy, cystotomy; (*obsolete*) edge (*of a sword*, &c.). — *douce*, (*engr.*) copper-plate; copper-plate engraving. — *de bois*, woodcut. *De — à*, big enough to; of a cast to
†Taille, *s.m.f.* (*in compounds, from* **Tailler,** "to cut," &c.) thing (*m.*) *or* person (*m.f.*) that cuts *or* &c., cutter, &c. — **-crayons,** *s.m.* (*instr.*) pencil-pointer. — **-légumes,** *s.m.* (*instr.*) vegetable-cutter. — **-mer,** *s.m.* (*nav.*) cut-water. — **-plumes,** *s.m.* (*instr.*) pen-cutter. — **-pré,** *s.m.* (*insect*) mole-cricket. — **-vent,** *s.m.* (*nav.*) lug main sail
†Tailler, *v.a.n.* to cut; to cut out; to hew; to carve; to shape, to make, to frame; to tally; to prune, to dress; to prepare; to make (*a pen*); (*surg.*) to cut for the stone; (*at cards*) to deal; (*old*) to tax. — *de l'avant*, (*nav.*) to go very fast
Se —, *v.r.* to be cut *or* &c.

†**Tailleresse,** *s.f.* cutter
†**Taillerie,** *s.f.* diamond-cutting, cutting (of diamonds); place for ditto
†**Tailleur,** *s.m.* tailor; cutter; (*surg.*) lithotomist; (*at cards*) dealer, banker, tailleur; (*insect*) crane-fly, daddy-longlegs. — *de pierre* (or *de pierres*), stone-cutter
†**Tailleuse,** *s.f.* tailoress, dress-maker
†**Taillis,** *s.m.* (*adject., Bois* —) copse, coppice; underwood [cus, tailloir
†**Tailloir,** *s.m.* trencher, platter; (*arch.*) aba-
†**Taillon,** *s.m.* nib (of a pen); (*obsolete*) taillon (*kind of tax*) [foil
Tain, *s.m.* quicksilvering, silvering-foil, tin-foil,
Taire, *v.a.* to say nothing of, not to say *or* tell *or* mention, to pass over in silence, to remain silent on; to conceal; to suppress. *Faire* —, to silence; to reduce to silence; to impose silence on; to hush; to make (*one*) hold his tongue *or* keep (*or* be) quiet; to suppress; to lay aside

Se —, *v.r.* to hold o.'s tongue *or* noise *or* peace; to say nothing; to say nothing more; to become *or* be *or* remain *or* keep silent *or* quiet; to keep a secret; to be passed over in silence, not to be mentioned; to be concealed *or* suppressed; to be laid aside

Taisson, *s.m.* (*zool.*) badger
Taissonnière, *s.f.* badger's hole
Taïtien, ne, *adj. s.* Tahitian [poin
Talapoin, *s.m.* (*buddhist priest, and zool.*) tala-
Talc, *s.m.* (*min.*) talc
Talcaire, Talcique, *adj.* talcky
Talcite, *s.m.* (*min.*) talcite
Taled, *s.m.* (*Jew. rel.*) taled
Talégalle, *s.m.* (*zool.*) talegalla, brush-turkey
Talent, *s.m.* talent; ability, skill; faculty, power; art; gift; attainments; knack; man *or* woman of talent; (*old coin*) talent. *A* —, *de* —, of talent; talented
Taler, *s.m.* *V.* **Thaler**
Talève, *s.f.* *V.* **Porphyrion**
Talion, *s.f.* retaliation. *Peine du* —, law of retaliation, retaliation
Talipot, *s.m.* (*bot.*) talipot-tree, fan-palm
Talisman, *s.m.* talisman
Talismanique, *adj.* talismanic
Talitre, *s.m.* (*zool.*) sand-hopper
Talle, Taller. *V.* **Drageon, Drageonner**
Tallevane, *s.f.* butter-jar, jar
Tallipot. *V.* **Talipot**
Talmelier, *s.m.* (*obsolete*) baker
Talmouse, *s.f.* cheese-cake
Talmud, *s.m.* Talmud
Talmud-ique, -iste (*s.*). *V.* page 3, § 1
Talmudiste, *adj.* talmudistic
Talochage, *s.m.* (*mas.*) floating; floated work
Taloche, *s.f.* thump, cuff, punch, rap on the head; (*mas.*) float; darby
Talocher, *v.a.* to thump; (*mas.*) to float
Talon, *s.m.* (*anat., of shoes, razors, tobacco-pipes, keels, gun-butts,* &c., *tech.*) heel; (*of a sword*) shoulder; (*of a rudder*) sole; (*at cards*) stock; (*arch.*) ogee, talon; (*fin.*) talon, certificate of stock; debentures; (*of a saddle*) rest; (*of bread, cheese,* &c.) last piece. — *rouge,* red heel (*formerly a mark of nobility*); aristocrat, nobleman, nob; courtier. *Sur ses —s,* at o.'s heels, close behind one. *Donner un coup* (or *des coups*) *de* —, (*nav.*) to ground, to bump. *Jouer des —s, montrer les —s,* to take to o.'s heels, to skedaddle, to scud off. *Mettre des —s à,* to heel. *Tourner les —s,* to go away
Talonner, *v.a.* to pursue close, to be at the heels of; to press, to urge; to spur; to beset; to dun; — *v.n.* (*nav.*) to touch the ground, to ground, to strike, to bump, to strand
Talonnette, *s.f.* heel-piece
Talonnier, *s.m.* heel-maker
Talonnière, *s.f.* heel-piece; (*of Mercury*) heel-
Talpa, *s.f.* (*surg.*) talpa [wing (*Latin pl.* talaria)
Talpack, *s.m.* (*mil.*) busby
Talqueu-x, se, *adj.* (*min.*) talcous, talcose
Taluer, *v.a.* (*old*) *V.* **Taluter**
Talus, *s.m.* slope, declivity; bank; embankment; heap, mound; talus; — *adj.m.* (*surg.*) *Pied* —, variety of club-foot (upwards with depression of the heel), "talipes calcaneus." *En* —, sloping, shelving. *Aller* or *être en* —, to slope, to shelve
Taluter, *v.a.* to slope, to shelve; to embank
Tamandua, *s.m.* (*zool.*) tamandua (*kind of ant-eater*)
Tamanoir, *s.m.* (*zool.*) great ant-eater, ant-bear
Tamarac, *s.m.* (*bot.*) tamarac, hackmatack, red American larch
Tamaricin, *s.m.* Russian dormouse
Tamarin, *s.m.* (*bot.*) tamarind (*fruit, and tree*); (*zool.*) tamarin (*monkey*) [rind
Tamarinier, *s.m.* (*bot.*) tamarind-tree, tama-
Tamaris, Tamarisc, Tamarisque, Tamarix, *s.m.* (*bot.*) tamarisk
Tamatia, *s.m.* (*bird*) tamatia, puff-bird
Tambour, *s.m.* drum; drummer; lobby; paddle-box; barrel; roller; chest, bin; pillow; tambour; (*fort.*) small redoubt, tambour. — *de basque,* tambourine, tambour. — *de Provence,* tabour. — *-maître,* corporal of the drums, drum-master (*of a battalion*). — *major,* drum-major (*of a regiment*). — *battant,* with the drums beating; with a high hand, with severity, harshly, roundly; openly. *Broderie au* —, tambour-work. *Broder au* —, to do tambour-work [player on ditto
Tambourin, *s.m.* tabour, tabor; timbrel;
Tambourinage, *s.m.* drumming, beating of the drum; crying up, extolling; advertising, puffing
Tambouriner, *v.n.* to drum, to beat the drum; — *v.a.* to drum; to beat; to cry *or* proclaim by beat of drum; to cry up, to extol, to trumpet; to advertise, to puff
Tambourineur, *s.m.* drummer; puffer
Tamias, *s.m.* (*zool.*) ground-squirrel
Tamier. *V.* **Taminier**
Tamije, Tamile. *V.* **Tamoul** [bryony
Taminier, *s.m.* (*bot.*) Indian acacia, black
Tamis, *s.m.* sieve, sifter, tammy. *Passer au* —, to sift; (*fig.*) to be sifted, to be rigorously
Tamisage, *s.m.* sifting; scattering [examined
Tamise, *s.f.* tammy (*stuff*); (*geog.*) Thames
Tamiser, *v.a.* to sift; to scatter
Tamiserie, *s.f.* sieve-making; sieves
Tamiseu-r, se, *s.m.f.* sifter; cinder-sifter
Tamisier, *s.m.* sieve maker
Tamoul, e, *adj.*, **Tamoul,** *s.m.* Tamil
Tampon, *s.m.* plug; stopper; pad; bung; buffer; roller; tampion; (*surg.*) pledget; (*pop.*) fist
Tamponnement, *s.m.* plugging, stopping
Tamponner, *v.a.* to plug, to stop, to stop up; (*of rail. trains*) to strike against

Se —, *v.r.* (*pop.*) to buffet each other, to fight with the fist, to box, to have a set-to

Tam-tam, *s.m.* (*mus.*) tam-tam, tom-tom
Tan, *s.m.* tan; oak-bark
Tanacétique, *adj.* (*chem.*) tanacetic
Tanaisie, *s.f.* (*bot.*) tansy. — *balsamite* or *baumière,* costmary
Tancement, *s.m.* checking, rebuking, scolding
Tancer, *v.a.* to check, to rebuke, to scold
Tanche, *s.f.* (*fish*) tench
Tandem, *s.m.* tandem
Tandis que, *adv.* while, whilst; whereas
Tangage, *s.m.* (*nav.*) pitching
Tangara, *s.m.* (*bird*) tanager
Tangence, *s.f.* (*geom.*) tangency [tangent
Tangent, e, *adj.*, **Tangente,** *s.f.* (*geom.*)
Tangentiel, le, *adj.* tangential
Tanghin, *s.m.*, **Tanghinie,** *s.f.*, **Tanghuin,** *s.m.* (*bot.*) tanghin, tanghinia
Tanghuine, *s.f.* (*chem.*) tanghicine, tanguine
Tangibilité, *s.f.* tangibility
Tangible, *adj.* tangible
Tangon, *s.m.* (*nav.*) fore-sail boom

Tangue, *s.f.* tangue (*kind of sea-sand used as manure*)
Tanguer, *v.n.* (*nav.*) to pitch, to heave
Tangueur, *s.m.* ship liable to pitch, pitcher (*pers.*) lumper, lighterman
Tanguier, *v.a.* to manure with "tangue"
Tanguière, *s.f.* "tangue"-pit
Tanière, *s.f.* den
Tanin. *V.* **Tannin**
Tannage, *s.m.* tanning
Tannant, e, *adj.* tiresome
Tannate, *s.m.* (*chem.*) tannate
Tanne, *s.f.* (*med.*) grub
Tanné, *s.m.* tan-colour
Tanné, e, *adj.* tawny, tan-coloured
Tannée, *s.f.* tan (*that has been used*), waste-tan, tan-waste
Tanner, *v.a.* to tan; to tire, to weary, to bore, to plague, to vex, to tease; to drub, to hide, to beat
Tannerie, *s.f.* tannery, tan-yard, tan-house
Tanneur, *s.m.* tanner
Tannin, *s.m.* (*chem.*) tannin
Tannique, *adj.* (*chem.*) tannic
Tanque. *V.* **Tangue**
Tanrec. *V.* **Tenrec**
Tant, *adv.* so much, as much; so many, as many; so very; so, to such a degree *or* point; so well, as well; so far, as far; so long, as long; so often, as often; so hard, as hard; so loud, as loud; both. — *à* —, (*play*) even. — *et* —, so very much, &c. — *et plus*, *V.* **Plus.** — *soit peu*, ever so little, at all, a very little, very little; a little, rather, somewhat, slightly. — *bien que mal*, partly well and partly ill, indifferently, so so, somehow *or* other, as well as one can. — *bon que mauvais*, both good and bad. — *il est vrai*, so true it is. — (*il*) *y a que*, at all events, at any rate, however that may be, however. — *mieux*, so much the better; that is right. — *pis*, so much the worse. *En* — *que*, as far as, as much as, as. *Si* — *est que*, if it is true that, if; supposing. *Tous* — *que nous sommes* (or *vous êtes*, &c.), every one of us (*or* of you, &c.), all the lot of us (*or* of you, &c.)
Tantalate, *s.m.* (*chem.*) tantalate
Tantale, *s.m.* (*chem.*) tantalum, tantalium; (*bird*) tantalus; (*myth.*) Tantalus. *Vase de* —, Tantalus's cup
Tantaleux, *adj.m.* (*chem.*) tantalous
Tantalique, *adj.* (*chem.*) tantalic
Tantaliser, *v.a.* to tantalize
Tantalite, *s.m.* (*chem.*) tantalite
Tante, *s.f.* aunt; uncle (*pawnbroker*). — *à la mode de Bretagne*, father's or mother's cousin german
Tantet, *s.m.* *V.* **Tantinet**
Tantième, *adj.* proportional; — *s.m.* proportional number *or* quantity, proportion, percentage; bonus [(*adverb.*) somewhat, rather
Tantinet, *s.m.* little bit, snippet; little drop;
Tantôt, *adv.* by and by, presently; soon; this afternoon; this evening, to-night; a little while ago; just now; nearly; sometimes, now
Tanzimat, *s.m.* (*Turkish polit.*) tanzimat
Taon, *s.m.* (*zool.*) breeze, breeze-fly, dun-fly, horse-fly, bull-fly, ox-fly, gad-fly, cleg; (*local*) [*V.* **Man**
Taonner, *v.a.* to bore, to plague
Tapage, *s.m.* racket, noise, uproar, row; bluster; fuss; show, display, gaudiness
Tapageu-r, se, *s.m.f.* noisy fellow *or* creature *or* thing, rioter; roisterer; blusterer; — *adj.* rackety, noisy; riotous; roistering; wild; blustering; fussy; loud; glaring, gaudy, showy, flashy
Tape, *s.f.* slap, pat, tap, thump, chuck; bung, [plug; (*of guns*) tampion, tompion
Tapé, e, *part. adj.* struck, &c. (*V.* **Taper**); (*of fruits*) dried, preserved; (*bien* —) smart, slashing; bold; in style. *Pomme* —*e*, biffin
Tape-cul, Tapecu, *s.m.* swing-gate; see-saw; jolting-carriage
Tapée, *s.f.* lot
Tapement, *s.m.* striking, &c. (*V.* **Taper**)
Taper, *v.a.n.* to strike, to pat, to tap; to beat; to drive; to stamp; to fall, to pitch; to get; to be heady; to thrum, to strum; to frizzle (*hair*); to sketch boldly. — or *donner dans l'œil*, *V.* **Œil.** — *de l'œil*, (*pop.*) to sleep soundly, to be fast asleep, to sleep, to snooze, [to take a nap
Taperelle, *s.f.* (*local*) pop-gun
Tapette, *s.f.* (*engraver's*) dabber; (*cooper's*) bat, cork-driver; [*also, a game at marbles*]
Tapi, e, *part.* crouching, squatting, cowering down; lying hid
Tapin, *s.m.* (*fam.*) rap, knock; (*pop.*) drumstick; drum; drum-beater, drummer
Tapinois (En), *adv.* slily, stealthily, by stealth
Tapioca, *s.m.* tapioca
Tapir, *s.m.* (*zool.*) tapir [down; to lie hid
Tapir (Se), *v.r.* to crouch, to squat, to cower
Tapis, *s.m.* carpet; carpeting; rug; cloth, cover; ground; tapis. — *-brosse*, cocoa-mat. — *de cheminée* or *de foyer*, hearth-rug. — *de gazon*, grass-plot. — *de lit*, bedside carpet, rug. — *de table*, table-cover. — *franc*, pot-house frequented by thieves. — *vert*, grass-plot, green; gaming-table, gambling-table, green cloth, green table; council-board. *Amuser le* —, to talk the time away, to beguile the time; to beat about the bush. *Éclairer le* —, (*gambling slang*) to put down o.'s stake, to put o.'s shiners on the table. *Être sur le* —, to be talked about, to be on the tapis. *Faire* — *net*, *nettoyer le* —, (*fig.*) to sweep the stakes. *Mettre sur le* —, to bring forward, to discuss, to agitate, to move, to bring on the tapis
Tapisser, *v.a.* to carpet; to hang; to paper; to cover; to deck; — *v.n.* to make tapestry, to do fancy work
Tapisserie, *s.f.* tapestry, hangings; fancy needlework, fancy work; wool-work; carpeting, carpet; upholstery; (*jest.*) wall-flowers. *Faire* —, to make only a show, to be a wall-flower. *Faire de la* —, to do fancy work *or* &c.
Tapissier, *s.m.* upholsterer
Tapissière, *s.f.* upholsterer; tapestry-maker; van, spring-van, light cart, tilted cart
Tapon, *s.m.* bundle, heap; (*nav.*) plug, stopper
Tapoter, *v.a.n.* to tap; to slap; to thrum, to strum [thrumming
Tapoteu-r, se, *s.m.f.* thrummer; — *adj.*
Taque, *s.f.* cast-iron plate; back (*of a fireplace*)
Taquer, *v.a.* (*print.*) to plane, to plane down
Taquet, *s.m.* pin; cleat; wedge; kevel
Taquin, e, *adj.* teasing, of a teasing disposition; — *s.m.f.* teasing fellow *or* thing, tease, [torment, plague
Taquinement, *adv.* teasingly
Taquiner, *v.a.n.* to tease, to torment, to plague
Taquinerie, *s.f.* teasing
Taquoir, *s.m.* (*print.*) planer [to vex
Tarabuster, *v.a.* to treat roughly; to pester,
Tararder, *v.a.* to winnow, to dress, to fan
Tarare, *s.m.* winnowing-machine, corn-dressing machine, fan; — *int.* foh! pooh! pish! fiddlestick! [native of Tarare
Tararien, ne, *adj. s.* of Tarare, Tararian,
Taraspic, *s.m.* *V.* **Thlaspi**
Taratantara, *s.m.* flourish (*of a trumpet or &c.*)
Taraud, *s.m.* tap, borer
Taraudage, *s.m.* tapping, boring
Tarauder, *v.a.* to tap, to bore
Taraxacine, *s.f.* (*chem.*) taraxacine
Taraxacum, *s.m.* (*bot.*) taraxacum, dandelion
Taraxis, *s.m.* (*med.*) taraxis
Tarbouch, *s.m.* tarbouch (*Turkish cap*)
Tard, *adv.* late. *Au plus* —, at the latest. *Plus* —, later; afterwards; some time after; at some other time; by and by; in after-life; in after-years; farther back. *Se faire* —, to get *or* grow late. *Il vaut mieux* (or *Mieux vaut*) — *que jamais*, better late than never
Tarder, *v.n.* to delay; to linger, to tarry, to wait, to loiter; to be long; to hesitate; (*imp.*) to long. *Il ne tarda pas à assurer* ..., he (*or* it) was not long before he secured ..., he lost no time in securing ..., he soon secured .. *Il me tarde de*, I long to, I am anxious to
Tardi-f, ve, *adj.* tardy; late; slow; backward; after-...
Tardiflore, *adj.* (*bot.*) late blooming

Tardigrade, *adj.m.f., s.m.* (*zool.*) tardigrade

†**Tardillon,** *s.m.* (*agr.*) late-born *or* backward

Tardivement, *adv.* tardily, slowly [animal

Tardiveté, *s.f.* tardiness; lateness; back-

Tardon, *s.m. V.* **Tardillon** [wardness

Tare, *s.f.* loss, waste; defect, fault, blemish; (*com.*) tare; (*vet.*) defect; (*vet.*) curb

Taré, e, *adj.* damaged; injured; spoilt; vicious; defective; blemished; ill-famed, of bad character, disreputable

Tarentelle, *s.f.* tarantella (*Italian dance, tune*)

Tarentin, e, *adj. s.* Tarantine, Tarentine

Tarentisme, Tarentulisme, *s.m.* (*med.*) tarantism, tarentism [wolf-spider

Tarentule, *s.f.* (*zool.*) tarantula, tarentula,

Tarer, *v.a.* to damage; to injure; to spoil; (*com.*) to tare [to spoil

Se —, *v.r.* to become (*or* be) damaged *or* &c.;

Taret, *s.m.* (*zool.*) cappanus, teredo, ship-worm, pile-worm, boring worm

Targe, *s.f.* (*shield*) targe, target; (*old coin*) targe

Targette, *s.f.* flat bolt, slide-bolt

Targuer (Se), *v.r. V.* **Prévaloir (Se)**

Targum, *s.m.* Targum

Targum-ique, -iste. *V.* page 3, § 1

Tari, *s.m.* tari (*Indian drink*)

Tari, e, *part. of* **Tarir**

Tarier, *s.m.* (*bird*) whinchat

Tarière, *s.f.* auger, wimble; borer; (*of insects*) terebra, borer; (*mollusc*) terebellum

Tarif, *s.m.* tariff, rate, scale, scale *or* list of charges, price-list, list *or* table of fares

Tarifer, *v.a.* to tariff; to price; to rate; to fix

Tarifiable, *adj.* tariffable, ratable

Tarification, *s.f.* tariffing, rating

Tarin, *s.m.* (*bird*) aberdevine, siskin, tarin

Tarir, *v.a.n.,* **Se —,** *v.r.* to dry up; to dry; to drain; to exhaust; to be exhaustible *or* exhausted, to be drained, to cease, to stop, to end; to flag. *Ne pas* (or *point*) —, (*fig.*) to be inexhaustible; to talk incessantly, to descant *or* expatiate endlessly; to have never done; to be endless. *Faire* —, to dry up; to drain; to exhaust

Tarissable, *adj.* exhaustible, that may *or* can be drained *or* dried up [ing up

Tarissement, *s.m.* draining, exhausting, dry-

Tarisseu-r, se, *s.m.f.* drainer, exhauster;

Tarlatane, *s.f.* tarlatan [drinker

Taro, *s.m.* (*bot.*) taro

Taroté, e, *adj.* (*of cards*) spotted

Tarots, *s.m.pl.* spotted cards

Taroupe, *s.f.* hair between the eyebrows

Tarpan, *s.m.* tarpan (*wild horse of Tartary*)

Tarpéien, ne, *adj.* Tarpeian

Tarse, *s.m.* (*anat.*) tarse, tarsus

Tarsien, ne, *adj.* (*anat.*) tarsal

Tarsier, *s.m.* (*zool.*) tarsier

Tartan, *s.m.* tartan, plaid

Tartane, *s.f.* tartan (*ship*)

Tartanelle, *s.f.* linsey-woolsey, linsey, winsey

Tartare, *s.m. adj.* Tartar; (*myth.*) Tartarus. *A la* —, in the Tartar fashion; (*cook.*) with cold mustard-sauce

Tartarelle, *s.f.* (*obsolete*) rattle

Tartareu-x, se, *adj. V.* **Tartreux**

Tartarin, *s.m.* (*zool.*) dog-faced baboon

Tartarique, *adj. V* **Tartrique**

Tartariser, *v.a.* to tartarize

Tartavelle, *s.f.* (*obsolete*) rattle

Tarte, *s.f.* tart

Tartelette, *s.f.* tartlet

Tartine *s.f.* slice of bread (*covered with butter, jam,* &c.), slice; dose; long speech. — *de beurre,* slice of bread and butter. — *de confitures,* slice of bread and jam

†**Tartouillade,** *s.f.* (*paint.*) daub

†**Tartouiller,** *v.a.* (*paint.*) to daub

†**Tartouilleur,** *s.m.* (*paint.*) dauber

Tartrate, *s.m.* (*chem.*) tartrate

Tartre, *adj.* (*chem.*) tartar; argol [eous

Tartreu-x, se, *adj.* (*chem.*) tartarous, tartar-

Tartrifuge, *adj.m.f., s.m.* antitartaric

Tartrique, *adj.* (*chem.*) tartaric

Tartufe, *s.m.f.* tartufe, hypocrite; mawworm; canter; pretender (to); — *adj.* hypocritical, canting; pretending (to)

Tartuferie, *s.f.* hypocrisy; hypocritical act

Tartufier, *v.a.* to wed to Tartufe *or* to a hypocrite; to win over, to cheat, to take in; — *v.n.* to play the hypocrite, to dissemble

Tas, *s.m.* heap; pile; agger; shock; cock; mow; stack; bundle; set, lot, pack, parcel

Tasmanien, ne, *adj s.* Tasmanian

Tasmanite, *s.f.* (*min.*) tasmanite [plant

Tasmannie, *s.f.* (*bot.*) tasmannia, pepper-

Tassart, *s.m.* (*zool.*) seir-fish

Tasse, *s.f.* cup; mug. — *à café,* coffee-cup. — *à thé,* tea-cup. — *de café,* cup of coffee. — *de thé,* cup of tea. *Demi-* — (small) cup of coffee; half-cup [thickset, dumpy

Tassé, e, *part. adj.* heaped up, &c. (*V.* **Tasser**);

Tasseau, *s.m.* bracket; (*arch.*) tassel

Tassée, *s.f.* cupful [dence, settling, settlement

Tassement, *s.m.* sinking, subsiding, subsi-

Tasser, *v.a.n.,* **Se —,** *v.r.* to heap up; to pile up; to ram down; to beat down; to cram; to compress; to press; to sink, to subside, to settle; (*hort.*) to grow thick

Tassette, *s.f.* (*of armour*) tasses

Tata, *s.m.f.* busybody

Tatan, *s.f.* (*children's slang*) aunty

Tatar, e, *adj. s. V.* **Tartare**

Tâté, e, *part. adj.* felt, &c. (*V.* **Tâter**); wanting in boldness, timid

Tâtement, *s.m.* feeling, touching, handling

Tâte-au-pot, Tâte-poule, *s.m.* molly-coddle

Tâter, *v.a.n.* to feel; to touch; to handle; to feel for; to taste; to try; to sound; to examine; to experience; to nurse up; to paint timidly [person, fumbler

Tâteu-r, se, *s.m.f.* feeler; taster; irresolute

Tâte-vin, *s.m.* wine-taster

Tatigué, Tatigoin, *int. V.* **Tétigué**

†**Tatillon, ne,** *s.m.f. adj.* meddler, busybody; meddling, busy

†**Tatillonnage,** *s.m.* meddling

†**Tatillonner,** *v.n.* to meddle, to busy oneself with trifles, to peddle, to potter

†**Tatillonneu-r, se,** *s.m.f. adj. V.* **Tatillon**

Tâtonné, e, *adj.* wanting in boldness, timid

Tâtonnement, *s.m.* groping; fumbling, trying, uncertainty, wavering, hesitation; irresolute attempt. *Méthode de* —, tentative method

Tâtonner, *v.n.* to grope; to fumble, to waver, to hesitate, to tamper

Tâtonneu-r, se, *s.m.f.* groper; fumbler, waverer, irresolute person

Tâtons (A), *adv.* groping; feeling o.'s way; tentatively. *Aller* or *marcher à* —, to grope, to feel o.'s way. *Chercher à* —, to grope for

Tatou, *s.m.* (*animal*) dasypus, tatouay, tatou, tatou-hou, peba

Tatouage, *s m.* tattooing; tattoo

Tatouer, *v.a.* to tattoo

†**Tatouille,** *s.f.* (*pop.*) fight, set-to; beating, thrashing, whacking, hiding, licking

†**Tatouiller,** *v.a.* (*pop.*) to beat, to thrash, to

Tau, *s.m.* (*her.*) tau [whack, to lick

Taud, *s.m.,* **Taude,** *s.f.* (*nav.*) awning

Tauder, *v.a* (*nav.*) to cover with an awning

Taudion, Taudis, *s.m.* hovel, dog-hole, hole

Taule, *s.f.* face (*of an anvil*) [crab-sauce

Taumalin, *s.m.* (*zool.*) *V.* **Pagure;** (*local*)

Taupe, *s f.* (*zool.*) mole; (*fig.*) intriguing person, hypocrite; loose woman; (*surg.*) talpa; (*vet.*) poll-evil. — **-grillon,** *s.f.* mole-cricket

Taupette, *s.f.* mole-cricket

Taupier, *s.m.* mole-catcher; (*pop.*) selfish fellow

Taupière, *s.f.* mole-trap

Taupin, *s.m.* (*insect*) elater, skip-jack, snap, snap-bug, click-beetle; (*fam.*) mathematical student, candidate (to the Polytechnic School, &c.). *Franc-* —, (*obsolete*) militiaman

Taupinée, Taupinière, *s.f.* mole-hill; hillock, knoll; poor little house, little hut
Taure, *s.f.* cow-calf; yearling heifer
Tauréador. *V.* **Toréador**
Taureau, *s.m.* bull; (*astr.*) taurus, bull. *Combat de —x*, bull-fight; bull-baiting
Tauricorne, *adj.* tauricornous [young bull
†Taurillon, *s.m.* bull-calf; yearling bull,
Taurine, *s.f.* (*chem.*) taurine
Taurique, *adj.* (*geog.*) Tauric
Taurobole, *s.m.* (*antiq.*) taurobolium
Tauromachie, *s.f.* tauromachy, bull-fighting
Tauromachique, *adj.* tauromachian
‡Tautochrone, *adj.* tautochronous; — *s.f.* tautochrone
‡Tautochronisme, *s.m.* tautochronism
Tautogrammatique, *adj.* tautogrammatic
Tautogramme, *s.m.* tautogram; — *adj.* tautogrammatic [page 3, § 1
Tauto-logie, -logique, -phonie, &c. *V.*
Taux, *s.m.* rate; rate of interest; price; assessment [secrated bread; antimacassar
Tavaïolle, *s.f.* chrisom-cloth; cloth for con-
Tavelé, e, *part. adj.* spotted; speckled; tabby
Taveler, *v.a.* to spot; to speckle
Tavelle, *s.f.* crown-lace
Tavelure, *s.f.* spots, speckles
Taverne, *s.f.* low public-house, beer-house, beer-shop, pot-house, dram-shop; (*in a good sense*) tavern
Taverni-er, ère, *s.m.f.* publican, tavern-keeper
Taxabilité, *s.f.* taxability, taxableness
Taxable, *adj.* taxable [master
Taxateur, *s.m.* taxer; assessor; (*law*) taxing-
Taxation, *s.f.* taxation; rating; assessment; fixing of prices; fee
Taxe, *s.f.* tax; taxation; rate; assessment; assize; price; charge; postage; toll
Taxer, *v.a.* to tax; to rate; to assess; to fix the price of; to charge; to accuse; to term,
Taxiarque, *s.m.* taxiarch [to call
Taxicorne, *s.m.* (*zool.*) taxicorn
Taxiderm-ie, -ique, -iste. *V.* page 3, § 1
Taxis, *s.m.* (*surg.*) taxis
Tayaut. *V.* **Taïaut**
Tchèque, *s.m.f.* Czech, Czekh; — *adj.* Czechish, Czechian, Czech, Czekh
Te, T', *pers. pron.* thee, you; to thee, to you; at thee *or* you; for thee *or* you; with thee *or* you; in thee *or* you; from thee *or* you; by thee *or* you; on thee *or* you; against thee *or* you; thyself, yourself; to *or* &c. thyself, to *or* &c. yourself
Té, *s.m.* T (*anything in the shape of a T*); tace; (*tech.*) T iron; (*surg.*) T bandage; (*draw.*) T square
‡Technicité, *s.f.* technicalness, technicality
‡Technique, *adj.* technical; — *s.m.* technicality, technicalities; — *s.f.* technics
‡Techniquement, *adv.* technically
‡Techno-graphie, -graphique, -logie, -logique, &c. *V.* page 3, § 1
‡Technologue, *s.m.* technologist
Teck, *s.m.* (*bot.*) teak; teak-wood
Tectrices, *s.f.pl.* (*of birds*) coverts
Te Deum, *s.m.* (*pl.* **Te Deum**) Te Deum
Tégument, *s.m.* tegument, integument
Tégumentaire, *adj.* tegumentary, integu-
†Teignasse. *V.* **Tignasse** [mentary
†Teigne, *s.f.* (*zool.*) moth, clothes-moth; (*med.*) tinea; scurf; scald-head; (*vet.*) thrush; (*bot.*) scald; (*pers.*) tenacious fellow *or* dog *or* thing. — *des grains*, corn-moth
†Teigneu-x, se, *adj. s.* scurfy; ditto person
†Teillage, Teille, Teiller, &c. *V.* **Tillage,** &c.
Teindre, *v.a.* to dye; to tinge; to tincture; to colour; to stain
  Se —, *v.r.* to be dyed *or* &c.; to dye (o.'s . . .)
Teint, e, (*part. of* **Teindre**) dyed, &c.
Teint, *s.m.* dye; tincture; colour; (*pers.*) complexion. *Bon —*, a fast colour. *Faux —*, a bad dye

Teinte, *s.f.* tint; tinge; tincture; colour; hue; dye; shade, cast; smack
Teinter, *v.a.* to tinge; (*arch., paint.*) to tint
Teinture, *s.f.* dye; dyeing; tincture; tinge; smattering [trade
Teinturerie, *s.f.* dye-house, dye-works; dyer's
Teinturi-er, ère, *s.m.f.* dyer; (*fig.*) polisher
Tek. *V.* **Teck**
Tel, le, *adj.* such; like; similar; so; many a, many a man, many; one man; some; certain; this, that; any; so and so. — *que*, such as, such a one as; as; such ... that. — *quel*, such as it is *or* was, such as one is *or* was, as it (*or* one) is *or* was; indifferent, so so. *Un —, une —le*, such a ...; such a one; so and so. — *père — fils*, like father like son
Télagon, *s.m.* (*zool.*) teledu
Télamons, *s.m.pl.* (*arch.*) telamones
Télégramme, *s.m.* telegram
Télégraphe, *s.m.* telegraph. *Faire jouer le —*, to telegraph [*V.* page 3, § 1
Télégraph-ie, -ique, -iquement, -iste.
Télégraphier, *v.a.* to telegraph; — *s.m.*
Télémètre, *s.m.* telemeter [telegraphist
Télémétr-ie, -ique, &c. *V.* page 3, § 1
Téléolog-ie, -ique, &c. *V.* page 3, § 1
Téléphon-ie, -ique. *V.* page 3, § 1
Téléphore, *s.m.* (*insect*) telephorus, soldier-
Télescope, *s.m.* telescope, glass [beetle
Télescop-ie, -ique, -iquement. *V.* p. 3, § 1
Tellement, *adv.* so much, so, in such a way; so far; so many; so well; so hard; so loud
Tellière, *s.m.* (*adject., Papier —*) petition-paper, foolscap (paper)
Telline, *s.f.* (*mollusc*) tellina (*kind of cockle*)
Tellurate, *s.m.* (*chem.*) tellurate
Tellure, *s.m.* (*chem.*) tellurium
Telluré, e, *adj.* (*chem.*) telluretted
Tellureu-x, se, *adj.* (*chem.*) tellurous
Telluride, *s.m.* (*chem.*) telluride
Tellurien, ne, Tellurique, *adj.* tellural, telluric; (*chem.*) telluric
Tellurite, *s.m.* (*chem.*) tellurite
Tellurure, *s.m.* (*chem.*) telluride
Telphuse. *V.* **Thelphuse** [*s.m.f.* ditto person
Téméraire, *adj.* rash; bold; reckless; —
Témérairement, *adv.* rashly; boldly; recklessly [recklessness
Témérité, *s.f.* rashness, temerity; boldness;
Temnodon, *s.m.* (*zool.*) temnodon, bluefish
†Témoignage, *s.m.* testimony; evidence; witness; testimonial; token, mark, proof. *Faux —*, false testimony, false swearing, perjury. *En — de quoi*, in witness *or* in testimony whereof. *Porter* or *rendre —*, to bear witness; to testify; to give evidence
†Témoigner, *v.a.n.* to testify; to bear witness; to attest; to prove; to show, to express; to convey; to intimate; to indicate; to mark; to depose; to give evidence
Témoin, *s. m.* witness; testimony, token, mark, proof; evidence; (*of duels*) second. *Prendre à —*, to call to witness
Tempe, *s.f.* (*anat.*) temple; (*butch.*) belly-set
Tempérament, *s.m.* temperament; constitution; temper, disposition; medium, middle course; equilibrium, balance; (*com.*) tally tally-trade; (*mus.*) temperament; (*fam.* amorous disposition
Tempérance, *s.f.* temperance; sobriety
Tempérant, e, *adj.* temperate, sober; (*med.*) sedative; — *s.m.f.* temperate person; — *s.m.*
Température, *s.f.* temperature [(*med.*) sedative
Tempéré, e, *part. adj.* tempered, &c. (*V.* **Tempérer**); temperate, mild; moderate; mixed; limited; (*of style*) middle, unadorned; — *s.m.* temperate; mild temperature; middle
Tempérément, *adv.* temperately [style
Tempérer, *v.a.* to temper; to moderate; to soften; to assuage, to soothe, to allay, to calm; to cool; to modify; to regulate; to repress; to contain, to check

Se —, *v.r.* to be *or* become tempered, &c.; to soften; to become mild
Tempête, *s.f.* storm, tempest; whirlwind
Tempêter, *v.n.* (*fig.*) to storm, to rage
Tempêtueusement, *adv.* tempestuously, stormily, boisterously [boisterous
Tempêtueu-x, se, *adj.* tempestuous, stormy,
Temple, *s.m.* temple; fane; church; Protestant church; (*tech.*) templet
Templet, *s.m.* (*tech.*) templet
Templier, *s.m.* templar, knight templar
Temploir, Templu, *s.m.* (*tech.*) templet
Tempo, *s.m.* (*mus.*) tempo
Temporaire, *adj.* temporary
Temporairement, *adv.* temporarily
Temporal, e, *adj.* (*anat.*) temporal
Temporalité, *s.f.* temporality; temporal
Temporel, le, *adj.* temporal [jurisdiction
Temporel, *s. m.* temporalities; temporal matters *or* affairs *or* power
Temporellement, *adv.* temporally
Temporisa-teur, trice, *adj. s.* temporizing; temporizer
Temporisation, *s.f.*, **Temporisement,** *s.m.* temporization, temporizing [procrastinate
Temporiser, *v.n.* to temporize; to delay, to
Temporiseur, *s.m.* temporizer; — *adj.* temporizing
Temps, *s.m.* time; period; term; season; while; leisure; weather; (*gram.*) tense; (*mus.*) time. — *de demoiselle,* quiet weather, fair weather. *A* —, in time, in good time; for a time; for a term of years; seasonably. *A deux, trois,* &c. —, (*mus.*) *V.* **Mesure.** *A quelque — de là,* some time after. *Avant le* —, before the time; prematurely. *Avec le* —, in course of time, in time. *Dans le* —, formerly; at the time. *Dans aucun* —, at no time. *De tout* —, at all times. *De — à autre, de — en* —, from time to time, now and then. *Du — de* ..., in the time of ... *Du bon* —, leisure time; enjoyment. *En même* —, at the same time; at once. *En son* —, in time. *En — et lieu,* in due (*or* proper) time and place. *En un rien de* —, *En deux — et trois mouvements,* in no time, in a trice. *Grand* or *grandement* —, high time. *Gros* —, rough *or* stormy *or* foul weather. *Le — qui court,* the present time (*Par* ditto, *V.* **Courir**). *Le — qu'il fait,* the weather we have, such weather as this. *Le — qu'il faisait,* the weather we had, such weather as that. *Peu de* —, a short time; not long. *Quelque* —, some time, a time. *Rien de* —, trice. *Tout d'un* —, at once, straightway. *Tout le* —, all the while; quite time enough, plenty of time. *Avoir fait son* —, to have served o.'s time; to have had o.'s day; to be out of date *or* of repute. *Faire son* —, to serve o.'s time. *Faire beau* or *mauvais* —, to be fine *or* bad weather. *Prendre bien son* —, to choose o.'s time well. *Il n'est plus* —, the time is past, it is too late. *Il fait beau* —, it is fine weather. *Il y a beau* —, *V.* **Beau.** *Il y a peu de* —, a short time ago, not long ago. *Il y a quelque* —, some time ago. *Quel — fait-il?* what sort of weather is it? how is the weather?
Témulence, *s.f.* (*med.*) temulence, temulency
Tenable, *adj.* tenable; bearable, supportable
Tenace, *adj.* tenacious; sticky, adhesive; viscous, viscid; stingy; stubborn; persevering; troublesome [stubbornly; perseveringly
Tenacement, *adv.* tenaciously; stingily;
Ténacité, *s.f.* tenacity, tenaciousness; adhesiveness; avarice, stinginess; obstinacy, stubbornness; perseverance
Ténaculum, *s.m.* (*surg.*) tenaculum
†**Tenaille,** *s.f.* pincers; nippers; tongs; plyers; forceps; (*fort.*) tenaille
†**Tenailler,** *v.a.* to tear off; to hold tight, to squeeze; (*fig.*) to torture, to torment
†**Tenaillon,** *s.m.* (*fort.*) tenaillon
Tenance, *s.f.* (*feud.*) tenancy
Tenanci-er, ère, *s.m.f.* (*feud.*) tenant; holder; under-farmer. *Franc-* —, freeholder
Tenant, e, *part. adj.* holding; having something (of); &c. (*V.* **Tenir**)
Tenant, *s.m.* challenger, champion; defender, supporter; adjacent part *or* land. —*s et aboutissants,* boundaries and abuttals, butts and bounds; particulars, ins and outs; connections; habits. *Tout d'un* —, *tout en un* —, *d'un seul* —, contiguous, adjoining, connected, together, all of a piece
Ténare, *s.m.* Tænarus, hell
Tendance, *s.f.* tendency; leaning; inclination
Tendant, e, *part. adj.* tending, &c. (*V.* **Tendre,** *v.a.n.*); inclined; (*law*) to the effect (that)
Tendelet, *s.m.* awning; tilt; canopy; screen
Tender, *s.m.* (*rail.*) tender
Tenderie, *s.f.* hunting with snares, trapping
Tenderolle, *s.f.* (*nav.*) marquee
Tendeu-r, se, *s.m.f.* stretcher; hanger; spreader; (*of snares*) layer; — *s.m.* (*rail.*) coupling-iron; — *s.f.* retiary (*spider*)
Tendineu-x, se, *adj.* tendinous, sinewy
Tendon, *s.m.* (*anat.*) tendon, sinew; (*vet.*) hamstring. — *d'Achille,* Achilles' tendon
Tendre, *adj.* tender; soft; delicate; sensible, sensitive; affecting, moving; dear; loving, fond, affectionate; early; young; (*of bread*) new; — *s.m.* tenderness, liking, affection, love; Love; inclination; soft part (*of a stone*)
Tendre, *v.a.n.* to stretch; to stretch out; to strain; to tighten; to hold out; to present; to put up; to exert; to bend *or* string (*a bow, a spring,* &c.); to hang (*tapestry*); to pitch (*tents*); to lay (*snares*); to spread (*nets*); to set (*traps*); to lead; to tend; to aim (at); to to draw (to). — *la perche à,* to help, to assist
Se —, *v.r.* to be stretched *or* &c.; to stretch
Tendrelet, te, *adj.* rather tender
Tendrement, *adv.* tenderly; dearly
Tendresse, *s.f.* tenderness, fondness, love, affection; tender caress; delicacy
Tendret, te, *adj.* rather tender
Tendreté, *s.f.* tenderness, softness [**Tendret**
Tendrette, *s.f.* long radish; — *adj.f.* *V.*
Tendron, *s.m.* shoot, tendril; girl, young girl, young lass; (*butch., cook.*) gristle
Tendu, e, *part. adj.* stretched, strained, &c. (*V.* **Tendre,** *v.a.n.*); outstretched; inflated; tight; bent; intent; hung; stiff; studied, affected, far-fetched, unnatural; critical; (*nav.*) taught [gloom; intricacies
Ténèbres, *s.f.pl.* darkness, dark; night;
Ténébreusement, *adv.* darkly; gloomily; secretly, underhand [secret; underhand
Ténébreu-x, se, *adj.* dark; obscure; gloomy;
Ténébrion, *s.m.* (*zool.*) tenebrio, meal-worm
Tènement, *s.m.* tenement; block (of houses)
Ténesme, *s.m.* (*med.*) tenesmus
Tenette, *s.f.*, —**s,** *pl.* (*surg.*) pincers, extractor
Teneur, *s.f.* tenour, terms; text; purport; contents; — *s.m.* holder; keeper. — *de livres,*
Tenez, *v. int. V.* **Tenir** [(*com.*) book-keeper
Ténia, *s.m.* (*zool.*) tænia, tapeworm
Ténioïde, *s.m.* (*zool.*) ribbon-fish
Tenir, *v.a.* to hold; to have hold of; to keep; to contain; to occupy; to possess, to be possessed of; to have; to have inherited; to owe (to); to believe, to think, to consider, to look upon, to esteem; to take; to observe; to keep in order; to manage; to prevent; to restrain; to bind; — *v.n.* to hold; to hold fast; to stick; to adhere; to be fastened *or* attached; to cling; to hang (by, upon); to be contiguous *or* adjacent; to be connected; to hold *or* keep together; to sit; to stand; to lie; to be held; to be contained (in), to go (in, into); to stand, to withstand, to resist; to subsist, to last; to hold good; to result, to proceed; to be owing *or* due (to); to bear, to support; to consider, to be of opinion; to resemble, to be like, to

take (after); to have something (of); to partake, to be of the nature; to belong; to attach importance (to), to value; to be desirous *or* anxious, to care; to be particular (about); to have set o.'s mind *or* heart (upon); to like; to wish; (*of things only, and imp.*) to depend (on, upon); to be the fault (of); (*mil.*) to hold out. *Faire* —, to send, to forward; to convey. *En* —, to be caught; to be in love *or* taken (with); to be fond (of); to feel (for); to be fuddled *or* drunk *or* tight; to have got it. *Y* —, to care about it; to stand *or* bear it; to resist; &c., &c. — *bon*, — *ferme*, to hold fast; to hold out; to stick fast; to stick to it; to keep *or* stand o.'s ground; to resist firmly; to stand firm; to be immovable. — *pour dit*, — *pour fait*, to take for granted; to make *or* be sure (of, that); to depend upon; to remember. *Ne* — *à rien que*, to be very near. *Je n'y tiens plus*, I cannot stand it *or* bear it *or* resist any longer; I don't care for it any more. *Il ne tient qu'à vous de*, it only depends on you to. *Il n'y a (pas d') amitié qui tienne*, friendship has nothing to do with the question, friendship is of no avail, friendship is all very well (, but ...). *A quoi cela tient-il?* what is the cause *or* reason of that? *A quoi tient-il que ...?* how is it that ...? *Cela tient à ce qu'elle est ...*, it comes from her being ... *Qu'à cela ne tienne*, that need be no obstacle, let not that be an obstacle, never mind that, never mind, that makes no difference; be it so; if that's all that is wanted; for the matter of that. *S'il ne tient qu'à cela*, if that is all. *Tenez* or *tiens!* hold! take this! take that! take it! here! hear! there! look! look here! look there! hail! come! now! now then! well! well now! well then! *Tiens!* halloo! oh! indeed! ay! to be sure! *Un Tiens vaut mieux que deux Tu l'auras*, a bird in the hand is worth two in the bush

Se —, *v.r.* to hold; to hold *or* keep *or* &c. oneself *or* each other; to be connected; to lay hold, to cling; to hang; to adhere; to stick; to abide; to stand; to lie; to sit; to keep, to stay, to remain; to be; to stop; to contain oneself; to refrain; to behave; to be held *or* kept *or* &c. *Se* — *debout*, to stand up. *Se* — *pour*, to consider oneself. *Se le* — *pour dit*, to mind what one is *or* was told, to mind it, not to forget it. *S'en* — *à*, to rely on; to keep to, to hold by, to stick to, to abide by; to confine oneself to; to stop with; to content oneself with, to be content with, to rest satisfied with; to rest on *or* upon; to go no farther than. *S'en* — *là*, to stop short; to let it alone; to be satisfied *or* content with that; to stop there; to go *or* proceed no farther. *Savoir à quoi s'en* — *sur*, to know the truth about, to know what to think of, to be settled *or* satisfied [about

Tenon, *s.m.* tenon; loop

Tenonner, *v.a.* to tenon

Ténor, *s.m.* (*mus.*) tenor

Ténotome, *s.m.* (*surg.*) tenotomy-knife

Ténotomie, *s.f.* (*surg.*) tenotomy

Tenrec, *s.m.* (*zool.*) tenrec, tanrec

Tenseur, *adj.m., s.m.* (*anat.*) tensor

Tensi-f, ve, *adj.* tensive

Tension, *s.f.* tension; application; intenseness

Tenson, *s.f.* (*poet.*) tenzon

Tentaculaire, *adj.* tentacular

Tentacule, *s.m.* (*zool.*) tentacle, feeler, horn

Tentaculé, e, *adj.* tentaculated

Tentaculiforme, *adj.* tentaculiform

Tenta-teur, trice, *s.m.f.* tempter, temptress; [— *adj.* tempting

Tentati-f, ve, *adj.* tentative

Tentation, *s.f.* temptation

Tentative, *s.f.* attempt, trial

Tente, *s.f.* tent; awning; pavilion; (*surg.*) tent, roll. — *d'abri*, fixed tent [disposed, inclined

Tenté, e, *part. adj.* attempted, tried; tempted;

Tenter, *v.a.* to attempt, to try; to tempt; to tent

Se —, *v.r.* to be attempted *or* tried; to tempt each other [—, paper-hanging

Tenture, *s.f.* hangings, tapestry. *Papier de*

Tenu, e, *part. adj.* held; kept; reputed, considered, &c. (*V.* **Tenir**); bound, obliged

Ténu, e, *adj.* tenuous, thin; spare; subtle

Tenue, *s.f.* holding; keeping; sitting; session; meeting; attitude; deportment, carriage; manner; behaviour; dress; uniform; appearance; steadiness; (*nav.*) holding, anchor-hold. — *des livres*, book-keeping. *Grande* —, full dress. *Petite* —, undress. *Tout d'une* —, contiguous, all in one piece [tenuirostre

Ténuirostre, *adj.* (*zool.*) tenuirostral; — *s.m.*

Ténuité, *s.f* tenuity, thinness; spareness;

Ténument, *adv.* tenuously [subtlety

Tenure, *s.f.* (*feud.*) tenure, holding

Téorbe, *s.m.* (*mus.*) theorbo, archlute

Téphrosie, *s.f.* (*bot.*) tephrosia

Tépide, *adj.* tepid

Tépidité, *s.f.* tepidity, tepidness

Ter, *adv.* three times; third; B

Téraspic, *s.m.* *V.* **Thlaspi**

Tératolog-ie, -ique, -iste. *V.* page 3, § 1

Tercer, *v.a.* (*agr.*) to give a third dressing to

Tercet, *s.m.* (*vers.*) tiercet

Térébelle, *s.f.* (*zool.*) terebella

Térébène, *s.f.* (*chem.*) terebene

Térébenthine, *s.f.* turpentine

Térébinthe, *s.m.* (*bot.*) turpentine-tree

Térébrants, *s.m.pl.* (*zool.*) terebrantia

Térébra-teur, trice, *adj.* terebrating, boring; — *s.m.f.* perforator, borer

Térébration, *s.f.* terebration, boring [shell

Térébratule, *s.f.* (*mollusc*) terebratula, lamp-

Térédile, *s.m.* (*zool.*) teredo, ship-worm

Tergiversa-teur, trice, *s.m.f.* tergiversator, shuffler; — *adj.* shuffling [shuffle, shuffling

Tergiversation, *s.f.* tergiversation, evasion,

Tergiverser, *v.n.* to shuffle

Terme, *s.m.* limit, bound; goal, post; term; end; stop; time; period; quarter; quarter-day; quarter's rent, rent; account; word, expression; state, condition. *A* —, at o.'s time; (*com., fin.*) on account; for the account; (*law*) for a term of years, for years. *A court* —, for a short time; (*com., of bills*) short-dated. *A long* —, for a long time; (*com. of bills*) long-dated. *Avant* —, premature; prematurely, before o.'s time. *Dans (toute) la force du* —, in the full force of the term

Termès, *s.m.* *V.* **Termite**

Terminaison, *s.f.* termination, end, ending

Terminal, e, *adj.*, **Terminal,** *s.m.* terminal

Terminalier, *s.m.* *V.* **Badamier** [tional

Terminati-f, ve, *adj.* terminative, termina-

Terminationnel, le, *adj.* terminational

Terminé, e, *part. adj.* terminated, finished, ended, &c. (*V.* **Terminer**); done; at an end; over; being over

Terminer, *v.a.*, **Se** —, *v.r.* to terminate, to end; to bound, to limit; to finish; to close, to conclude; to settle; to be bounded *or* limited *or* &c.; to come to a conclusion

Termin-isme, -iste, -ologie. *V.* p. 3, § 1

Termite, *s.m.* (*insect*) termite, white ant

Ternaire, *adj.* ternary

Terne, *adj.* dull; dim; wan; — *s.m.* series of three numbers; three winning numbers; trey; (*at dice*) two threes

Terné, e, *adj.* (*bot.*) ternate [sully, to stain

Ternir, *v.a.* to tarnish; to dull, to dim; to

Se —, *v.r.* to tarnish; to be sullied; to fade

Ternissement, *s.m.* tarnishing; sullying, staining [blemish; spot

Ternissure, *s.f.* dulness; tarnishing; fading;

Téroulle, *s.f.* black earth

‡**Terpsichoréen, ne,** *adj.* Terpsichorean

Terrage, *s.m.* earthing; claying

Terrain, *s.m.* ground; soil; earth; land; piece of ground; ground plot; field; course; stratum; rock. *Sur le* —, on the ground; in the field; at a duel. *Aller sur le* —, to go in the field; to fight a duel. *Céder le* —, to give ground. *Disputer le* —, to stand o.'s ground. *Être sur son* —, to be in o.'s element; to be at home. *Ménager le* —, to act cautiously. *Reconnaître* or *sonder* or *tâter le* —, (*fig.*) to feel o.'s way, to see how matters stand

Terral, *s.m.* (*nav.*) land wind *or* breeze

Terraqué, e, *adj.* terraqueous

Terrasse, *s.f.* terrace; earthwork; flat roof; (*paint.*) foreground

Terrassement, *s.m.* earthwork; embankment; banking; ballasting; throwing down

Terrasser, *v.a.* to throw on the ground; to throw *or* knock down; to floor; to strike with consternation, to dismay; to confound, to nonplus; to crush; to beat; to convince; to terrace; to fill in with earthwork; to embank; to dig [navvy; ballaster

Terrassier, *s.m.* digger; excavator; navigator,

Terre, *s.f.* earth; ground; land; soil; mould; clay; mud; territory; estate; property; homestead; world; (*nav.*) land, shore. — *cuite*, terra cotta. — *ferme*, terra firma, main-land, continent. — *franche*, vegetable mould, mould; free land. — *pourrie*, rotten-stone. — *promise*, land of Promise. — *sacrée*, sacred *or* holy ground. — *sainte*, holy Land; consecrated ground. — *à* or *de pipe*, pipe-clay. *Pipe de* or *en* —, clay pipe. — *à porcelaine*, china-clay. — *à potier*, potter's earth. — *de bruyère*, heath-mould. — *du Japon*, Japan earth. *A* —, to *or* on the ground; on the floor; down; ashore; aground. — *à* —, low; slow; prosy; common-place; in a low state *or* way; slowly; (*s.m.*) prosiness; vulgarity. *De* —, of earth, from the earth, out of the earth, &c.; earthen; earthy; earth; land. *Par* —, on the ground; on the floor; down; by land. *Vers la* —, earthward; landward. *Aller* — *à* —, (*nav.*) to sail *or* run along the coast, to coast; (*fig.*) to go slowly *or* &c.; to be prosy *or* &c.; to grovel. *Mettre en* —, to bury. *Mettre à* —, to put *or* set down; (*nav.*) to land. *Prendre* —, to land, to come ashore; to alight. *Perdre* —, to lose sight of land; to get out of o.'s depth. — **-mérite,** *s.f.* turmeric. — **-neuve,** *s.m.* Newfoundland dog. — **-neuvien, ne,** *adj.* Newfoundland (dog *or* bitch). — **-neuvier,** *s.m.* Newfoundland fisher, banker; Newfoundland dog; *adj.* Newfoundland. — **-noix,** *s.f.* (*bot.*) earth-nut, pig-nut. — **-plein,** — **-plain,** *s.m.* (*pl.* —**s-pleins**) platform; terre-plein [post

Terreau, *s.m.* vegetable mould, mould; com-

Terreaudement, Terreautage, *s. m.* manuring *or* mixing *or* covering with mould *or* compost

Terreauder, Terreauter, *v.a.* to manure *or* mix *or* cover with mould *or* compost

Terrein, *s.m.* (*old spelling*) *V.* **Terrain**

Terrer, *v.a.n.* to earth; to clay; to cover *or* protect with earthwork; to burrow

Se —, *v.r.* to earth oneself; to earth; to burrow; to shelter oneself with earthwork; to be earthed *or* clayed

Terrestre, *adj.* terrestrial; earthly

Terrestréité, *s.f.* terrestrialness; —**s,** *pl.* earthy particles, grounds, sediment

Terrestrement, *adv.* terrestrially

Terrête, Terrette, *s.f.* (*bot.*) ground-ivy

Terreur, *s.f.* terror; dread; awe

Terreu-x, se, *adj.* earthy; cadaverous; dull

Terribilité, *s.f.* terribleness

Terrible, *adj.* terrible, dreadful; awful; (*of children*) wild; blabbing

Terriblement, *adv.* terribly, dreadfully; awfully; with a vengeance

Terricole, *adj.* living on *or* in the earth

Terrien, ne, *s.m.f.* land-holder; —*adj.* of land

Terrier, *s.m.* terrier; burrow, hole; (*feud., adject., Papier* —) court-roll, terrier. *Boule-* —, bull-terrier

Terrifier, *v.a.* to terrify, to dismay

Terrine, *s.f.* earthen vessel, earthen pan, pan; pot; dish; potted meat. *En* —, potted. *Mettre* [*en* —, to pot

Terrinée, *s.f.* panful

Terrir, *v.n.* to lay its eggs in the sand; to come in sight of land; (*of fish*) to come near the land; (*nav.*) *V.* **Atterrir**

Territoire, *s.m.* territory; jurisdiction

Territorial, e, *adj.* territorial, land

Territorialement, *adv.* territorially [taste

Terroir, *s.m.* soil, ground. *Goût de* —, racy

Terroriser, *v.a.n.* to terrorize

Terror-isme, -iste. *V.* page 3, § 1

Terser, *v.a. V.* **Tercer**

Tertiaire, *adj.* tertiary

Tertio, *adv.* thirdly, in the third place

Tertre, *s.m.* hillock, knoll, ridge, mound, eminence, rising ground [own

Tes, *adj. poss.pl. m.f.* thy, thy own; your, your

Tesselle, *s.f.* tessera (*pl.* tesseræ)

Tesseller, *v.a.* to tesselate

Tesson, *s.m.* fragment; broken glass; potsherd

Test, *s.m. V.* **Têt;** (*Engl. hist.*) test

Testacé, e, *adj. s.m.* testaceous; testacean

Testament, *s.m.* testament; will, last will

Testamentaire, *adj.* testamentary; of *or* by *or* under a will

Testamenter, *v.n.* to make o.'s will

Testat, *s.m. adj.* testate [devisor

Testa-teur, trice, *s.m.f.* testator, testatrix;

Tester, *v.n.* to make o.'s will

Testiculaire, *adj.* (*anat.*) testicular

Testicule, *s.m.* (*anat.*) testicle

Testiculé, e, *adj.* (*zool.*) testiculated

Testif, *s.m.* camel's hair

Testimonial, e, *adj.* testimonial, testifying; of testimony; by witness

Testimonialement, *adv.* testimonially

Test-objet, *s.m.* (*anat.*) test-object

Teston, *s.m.* (*old coin*) testoon

Testonner, *v.a.* (*old*) to dress the hair of

Têt, *s.m.* fragment, broken glass, potsherd; sty; (*metal.*) test; (*of shell-fish, tortoises,* &c.) [shell

Tétanique, *adj.* (*med.*) tetanic

Tétanos, *s.m.* (*med.*) tetanus, lock-jaw

Têtard, *s.m.* tadpole; (*fish*) bull-head; (*hort.*) [pollard

Tétasses, *s.f. pl.* hanging breasts

Tête, *s.f.* head; head-piece; head of hair, hair; (*of stags,* &c.) horns; (*of things, and fig.*) head; beginning; top; choice, best; brain, brains, mind, wits, sense, senses, faculties; presence of mind; self-possession; resolution; obstinacy; life; person; block; front; (*swimming*) header; (*of a hammer*) face. — *à perruque*, wig-block; barber's block; blockhead, fogy, old fogy. — *à* —, *en* — *à* —, *See below.* — *d'âne*, ass's-head; (*fish*) *V.* **Chabot.** — *de colonne*, (*mil.*) foremost body (*of troops*). — *-de-loup*, (*brush*) Turk's head, pope's head. — *de mort*, death's head; death's head moth. — *morte*, (*chem.*) caput mortuum. — *de pont*, (*mil.*) bridge-head, tête-de-pont. — *ou pile*, heads or tails. *Homme de* —, *V.* **Homme.** *La* — *la première* or *en avant*, head foremost. *Mal de* —, headache. *Mauvaise* —, bad temper; wrong-headed *or* hot-headed person, obstinate *or* bad *or* quarrelsome fellow. *A la* — *de*, at *or* to the head of; possessed of, possessing, having. *A* — *chaude*, hot-headed. *A* — *chauve*, bald-headed. *De la* — *aux pieds*, from head to foot, from top to toe; head and ears. *En* —, at the head; in front; in *or* into o.'s head. *Par* —, a head, per head; a-piece. *Par-dessus la* —, over o.'s head; over head and ears; more than enough. *Deux* —*s dans un bonnet*, hand and glove together. *Aller la* — *levée*, to carry o.'s head high. *Avoir sa* —, to be in o.'s senses. *Avoir la* — *fêlée*, to be crack-brained. *Avoir la* — *montée*, to be excited. *Avoir la* — *près du bonnet*, to be passionate *or* hasty *or* hot-headed. *Avoir de la* —, to be clever; to be resolute; to have self-possession *or* presence of mind. *Avoir la — qui tourne,* to be giddy. *Avoir mal à la —,* to have a headache. *Avoir mauvaise —,* to be hot-headed *or* obstinate. *Crier à pleine —* or *à tue-tête,* to cry out, to bawl with all o.'s might, to shout at the top of o.'s voice. *Donner à la —,* to get *or* fly into o.'s head, to be heady. *Donner de la —,* to knock *or* run o.'s head (against); (what) to attend to, (which way) to turn. *Donner sa — à couper,* to lay down o.'s life. *En avoir par-dessus la —,* to be heartily sick of it. *Faire — à,* to make head against, to cope with, to oppose, to resist. *Faire sa —,* (*fam.*) to play the important personage; to be cocky; to mince; to turn up o.'s nose; to be a snob, to behave like a snob, to be snobbish; to kick, to resist. *Faire à sa —,* to have o.'s own way, to do as one pleases. *Gager sa —* (or *sa — à couper*), to lay down o.'s life. *Jeter à la —,* to throw at (...'s) head; to be forward in offering *or* proposing; to clap on; to offer to give for nothing *or* for an old song. *Laver la — à,* to scold, to lecture, to give it to, to blow up, to give a wigging, to wig. *Marcher en —* or *à la —,* to walk at the head *or* in front; to lead the way; to take the lead. *Monter* or *porter à la —,* to get *or* fly into o.'s head, to be heady. *Monter la — à,* to excite. *Ne savoir où donner de la —,* not to know what to do *or* which way to turn, to be bewildered. *Perdre la —,* to lose o.'s head *or* o.'s wits; to go mad; to lose o.'s presence of mind. *Rompre la —,* V. **Rompre.** *Tenir — à, V. Faire — à. Tourner la — à,* to turn (...'s) brain. *La — me tourne,* my head is giddy, I feel giddy. *La — me fend,* my head is ready to split. *Ce sont deux —s dans un bonnet* (or *dans le même bonnet*), they are very thick, they are hand and glove together

Tête-à-tête, *s.m.* private interview *or* conversation; (*piece of furniture*) settee; — *adv.* (*En —*) face to face; in private, by ourselves *or* yourselves *or* themselves, alone; together

Têteau, *s.m.* end of a branch

Tête-bêche, *adv.* head against foot, head to feet, top against bottom

Têtebleu, *int.* (*obsolete*) zounds!

Tetée, Tétée, *s.f.* suck, sucking

Teter, Téter, Tetter, *v.a.n.* to suck. *Donner à —,* to suckle

Têtière, *s.f.* baby's cap; (*of bridles*) head-stall; [(*nav.*) head (of a sail)

Tétigué, *int.* (*obsolete*) zounds!

Tétin, *s.m.* nipple, teat

Tétine, *s.f.* udder; (*on a cuirass*) bruise, dent, [dint

Teton, Téton, *s.m.* teat, pap; breast, mamma

Tétonnière, *s.f.* full-breasted woman

Tétracorde, *s.m. adj.* tetrachord

Tétraèdre, *s.m.* (*geom.*) tetrahedron; — *adj.* [tetrahedral

Tétraédrique, *adj.* tetrahedral

Tétragonal, e, *adj.* (*geom.*) tetragonal

Tétragone, *adj.* (*geom.*) tetragonal; — *s.m.* [tetragon

Tétralogie, *s.f.* tetralogy

Tétramètre, *s.m. adj.* (*vers.*) tetrameter

Tétrandrie, *s.f.* (*bot.*) tetrandria

Tétrapétale, Tétrapétalé, e, *adj.* (*bot.*) [tetrapetalous

‡**Tétrarchat,** *s.m.* tetrarchate

Tétrarch-ie, -ique. *V.* page 3, § 1

Tétrarque, *s.m.* tetrarch

Tétras, *s.m.* (*bird*) grouse; capercailzie

Tétrastyle, *s.m. adj.* (*arch.*) tetrastyle

Tétrasyllabe, *s.m.* tetrasyllable; — *adj.* tetrasyllabic

Tétrasyllabique, *adj.* tetrasyllabic

Tette, *s.f.* teat, dug. — **-chèvre,** *s.m. V.* [**Engoulevent**

Tetter, *v.a. V.* **Téter**

Têtu, e, *adj.* obstinate, headstrong, stubborn, self-willed; — *s.m.f.* ditto person; — *s.m. V.* **Grelet;** (*fish*) *V.* **Chevanne**

Teugue, *s.f.* (*nav.*) poop

Teuton, ne, *s.m.f. adj.* Teuton; Teutonic

Teutonique, *adj.* Teutonic

Texte, *s.m.* text; theme; matter; subject; point. *Petit —,* (*print.*) brevier

Textile, *adj.* textile; — *s.m.* textile material

Textilité, *s.f.* textility

Textuaire, *s.m.* text; — *adj.* textuary

Textuel, le, *adj.* textual; word for word, verbatim

Textuellement, *adv.* textually; word for [word, verbatim

Texture, *s.f.* texture; connection

Thaler, *s.m.* thaler (*German dollar*)

Thalle, *s.m.* (*bot.*) thallus

Thallique, *adj.* (*chem.*) thallic

Thallite, *s.f.* (*min.*) thallite

Thallium, *s.m.* (*chem.*) thallium

Thalweg, *s.m.* thalweg

Thapsie, *s.f.* (*bot.*) thapsia, deadly carrot

Thaumatrope, *s.m.* thaumatrope

Thaumaturge, *s.m.* thaumaturgist, thaumaturgus, thaumaturge; — *adj.* thaumaturgic,-al

Thaumaturg-ie, -ique. *V.* page 3, § 1

Thé, *s.m.* tea; tea-party; tea-tree

Théatin, e, *s.m.f.* theatine (*monk* or *nun*)

Théâtral, e, *adj.* theatrical

Théâtralement, *adv.* theatrically

Théâtre, *s.m.* theatre; opera; show; playhouse, house; stage; drama; dramatic works, plays; scenery; scene, seat, field. *De —,* theatrical, stage

Thébaïde, *s.f.* (*liter., geog.*) Thebaid; (*fig.*) deep solitude, desert

Thébain, e, *s.m f. adj.* Theban

Thébaïne, *s.f.* (*chem.*) thebaine

Thébaïque, *adj.* (*chem.*) thebaic

Théière, *s.f.* tea-pot

Théiforme, *adj.* theiform

Théine, *s.f.* (*chem.*) theine

Théisme, *s.m.* theism

Théiste, *s.m.f.* theist; — *adj.* theistic, theist- [ical

Thelphuse, *s.f.* (*zool.*) river-crab

Thématique, *adj.* thematic

Thème, *s.m.* theme, subject, topic; exercise

Thémis, *s.f.* (*myth.*) Themis; (*fig.*) justice

Thénar, *s.m.* (*anat.*) thenar

Théobrome, *s.m.* (*bot.*) theobroma

Théobromine, *s.f.* (*chem.*) theobromine

Théocrate, *s.m.* theocrat

Théocratie, *s.f.* theocracy

Théocrat-ique, -iquement. *V.* page 3, § 1

Théodicée, *s.f.* theodicy, theodicea

Théodolite, *s.m.* theodolite

Théodosien, ne, *adj.* Theodosian

Théogon-ie, -ique, -iste. *V.* page 3, § 1

Théologal, e, *adj.* theological, divine; — *s.m.* lecturer on divinity; — *s.f.* lectureship on divinity

Théologie, *s.f.* theology, divinity

Théologien, *s.m.* theologian, divine

Théolog-ique, -iquement, -isme. *V.* [page 3, § 1

Théologiser, *v.n.a.* to theologize

Théorbe, *s.m.* (*mus.*) theorbo, archlute

Théorème, *s.m.* theorem

Théoricien, ne, *s.m.f.* theorist; — *adj.* [theoretical

Théorie, *s. f.* theory; speculation; drill; (*antiq.*) embassy, sacred embassy, sacred mission; (*fig.*) procession, swarm, crowd, troop

Théorique, *adj.* theoretic,-al; (*antiq.*) theoric

Théoriquement, *adv.* theoretically

Théoriser, *v.n.* to theorize

Théoriste, *s.m.f.* theorist

Théosophe, *s.m.* theosophist

Théosoph-ie, -ique, -isme. *V.* page 3, § 1

Thérapeutes, *s.m.pl.* Therapeutæ, Therapeutics

Thérapeutique, *adj.* therapeutic,-al; — *s.f.* [(*med.*) therapeutics

Thérapeutiste, *s.m.* therapeutist

Thérapie, *s.f.* therapy

Thériacal, e, *adj.* (*pharm.*) theriacal, theriac

Thériaque, *s.f.* (*pharm.*) theriaca, theriac, treacle

Thermal, e, *adj.* thermal. *Eaux —es,* hot [mineral waters

Thermes, *s.m.pl.* hot baths, hot springs, thermæ

Thermidor, *s.m.* Thermidor (*eleventh month of the calendar of the first French Republic, from July 19 to August 17*)

Thermidorien, ne, *adj. s.* (*Fr. hist.*) Thermidorian
Thermique, *adj.* thermic
Thermo, (*in compounds*) thermo ...
Thermo-électricité, *s.f.* thermo-electricity
Thermo-électrique, *adj.* thermo-electric
Thermographe, *s.m.* thermograph
Thermo-graphie, -logie, -logique, &c. *V.* page 3, § 1
†Thermomagnét-ique,-isme. *V.* p. 3, § 1
Thermomètre, *s.m.* thermometer [p. 3, § 1
Thermométr-ie, -ique, -iquement. *V.*
Thermométrographe, *s.m.* thermometrograph
Thermométrographie, *s.f.* thermometrography
Thermopathe, *s.m.* thermopathist, thermopath [*V.* page 3, § 1
Thermopath-ie,-ique, -iquement,-iste.
Thermoscope, *s.m.* thermoscope
Thermoscop-ie, -ique. *V.* page 3, § 1
Thermostat, *s. m.* thermostat, heat-regulator, heat-governor
Thermostatique, *adj.* thermostatic
Thermotique, *s.f.* thermotics; — *adj.* thermotic,-al [ing, hoarding up
Thésaurisation, *s.f.* treasuring up, hoard-
Thésauriser, *v.n.* to treasure up, to hoard, to
Thésauriseu-r, se, *s.m.f.* hoarder [hoard up
Thèse, *s.f.* thesis; theme; argument, discussion; question; case. *En — générale*, as a rule. *Soutenir une —*, to support a thesis; to hold an argument. *Soutenir — pour*, to side
Thessalien, ne, *adj. s.* Thessalian [with
Thessalonicien, ne, *adj. s.* Thessalonian
Thêta, *s.m.* (*Gr. gram.*) theta
Thétis, *s.f.* (*myth., astr.*) Thetis; (*poet.*) the sea
Théurg-ie, -ique, -iste. *V.* page 3, § 1
Thibaude, *s.f.* cow-hair cloth
Thlaspi, *s.m.* (*bot.*) shepherd's-purse
Thomas, *s.m.* Thomas; (*pop.*) jorden
Thom-isme, -iste. *V.* page 3, § 1
Thon, *s.m.* (*fish*) tunny
Thonaire, Thonnaire, *s.f.* tunny-net
Thonine, Thonnine, *s.f.* salt tunny
Thorachique (*bad spelling*), **Thoracique,** *adj.* (*anat.*) thoracic; (*med.*) pectoral
Thorax, *s.m.* (*anat.*) thorax, chest
Thorine, *s.f.* (*chem.*) thorina, thoria
Thorinium, *s.m.* (*chem.*) thorinium, thorium
Thorins, *s.m.* thorins (wine)
Thorique, *adj.* (*chem.*) thoric
Thorite, *s.f.* (*min.*) thorite
Thorium. *V.* **Thorinium**
Thrace, *adj. s.m.f.* Thracian; — (*La*), *s.f.* Thracia; (the) Thracian fashion
Thran, *s.m.* train-oil [lactucarium
Thridace, *s.f.* (*pharm.*) thridace, lettuce-opium,
Thrips, *s.m.* (*insect*) thrips
Thrombose, *s.m.* (*med.*) thrombosis
Thrombus, *s.m.* (*surg.*) thrombus
Thuia, *s.m.* (*bot.*) thuja, thuya, arbor vitæ
Thuriféraire, *s.m.* thurifer, censer-bearer
Thurifère, *adj.* thuriferous
Thuya. *V.* **Thuia**
Thym, *s.m.* (*bot.*) thyme
Thymalle, *s.m.* (*fish*) thymallus, grayling
Thymique, *adj.* (*anat., med.*) thymic [bread
Thymus, *s.m.* (*anat.*) thymus; (*butch.*) sweet-
Thyréoïde, Thyroïde, *adj.* (*anat.*) thyroid
Thyrse, *s.m.* (*myth., bot.*) thyrsus
Tiare, *s.f.* tiara
Tibia, *s.m.* (*anat.*) tibia, shin, shin-bone
Tic, *s.m.* knack, ugly knack, bad *or* vicious habit; habit, way; tic, twitching; crib-biting. — *douloureux*, tic douloureux, (*vulgarly*) tic doloureux, tic doloreux. — **-tac,** *s.m.* tick-tack, tick, ticking, click, clicking, clack, clacking. *Faire — -tac*, to tick, to click, to clack
Tiède, *adj.* lukewarm, tepid; mild, soft; cool
Tièdement, *adv.* lukewarmly; coolly
Tiédeur, *s.f.* lukewarmness, tepidity, tepidness
Tiédir, *v.n.* to become (*or* grow *or* get) lukewarm *or* tepid *or* cool, to cool

Tien, ne, *pron. poss. Le —, les —s; la —ne, les —nes*, thine, thy own; yours, your own. *Les —s*, your relations *or* family; your kindred *or* race; your tribe; your crew; your friends; your men; your servants; your people; your subjects; your tricks *or* pranks; &c.
Tiens, *v., int., s.m. V.* **Tenir**
Tierce, *s.f.* (*of time*) third; (*cards, fenc.*) tierce; (*prayers*) tierce,terce; (*mus.*) tierce,tercet,third; (*print.*) revise for press, press revise, second revise, third proof; — *adj.f. V.* **Tiers,** *adj.* — *majeure*, (*cards*) tierce major; (*mus.*) major third. — *mineure*, (*mus.*) minor third
Tiercelet, *s.m.* (*falc.*) tiercelet, tiercel, tercel
Tiercelin, e, *s.m.f.* Tierceline (*monk* or *nun*)
Tiercement, *s.m.* augmentation of a third (*in prices*) [price *or* prices one third
Tiercer, *v.a. V.* **Tercer;** — *v.n.* to raise the
Tierceron, *s.m.* (*arch.*) tierceron
Tiercet, *s.m.* (*old*) *V.* **Tercet**
Tierçon, *s.m.* (*cask*) tierce
Tiers, *m.*, **Tierce,** *f., adj.* third; of a third person *or* party; (*med., of fever*) tertian. — *-état*, *V.* **État**
Tiers, *s.m.* third; third part; third party *or* person; (*abbrev. of* "Tiers-état") *V.* **État.** — *consolidé*, (*fin.*) reduced consols. — **-point,** *s.m.* (*arch.*) tierce-point; (*tech.*) saw-file. *Le — et le quart*, all kinds of folks,everybody,anybody
Tige, *s.f.* stem, stalk; trunk, body; cane; haulm, haum; straw; (*of a family*) stock; (*of boots*) leg; (*of columns*) shaft; (*tech.*) shank; rod
Tigette, *s.f.* (*arch.*) honeysuckle ornament
†Tignasse, *s.f.* mop, shock-head, shock (*head of hair*); old wig, caxon; (*fig.*) shabby patch
†Tignon, *s.m. V.* **Chignon**
†Tignonner, *v.a.* to arrange the chignon of
Se —, *v.r.* to arrange o.'s chignon; to pull one another's hair, to pull caps, to fight, to have a fight *or* a set-to [**Tigré**
Tigre, *s.m.* tiger; (*geog.*) Tigris; — *adj. V.*
Tigré, e, *adj.* spotted; speckled
Tigrer, *v.a.* to spot; to speckle
Tigresse, *s.f.* tigress
Tigridie, *s.f.* (*bot.*) tiger-flower
Tilbury, *s.m.* tilbury; cart
†Tillac, *s.m.* (*nav., obsolete for* "pont") deck
†Tillage, *s.m.* scutching, breaking, stripping, peeling [(*nav.*) cuddy
†Tille, *s.f.* bast; harl; (*tech.*) hatchet-hammer;
†Tiller, *v.a.* (*hemp*) to scutch, to break, to strip, to peel [lime-tree flowers
†Tilleul, *s.m.* lime-tree, linden; infusion of
†Tilleu-r, se, *s.m.f.* scutcher, breaker, stripper, peeler
Timbale, *s.f.* kettle-drum; cup; mug; battledore, battledoor; (*mus.*) timbal; (*cook.*) mould; timbale (*sort of pie made in a mould*)
Timbalier, *s.m.* kettle-drummer
Timbrage, *s.m.* stamping
Timbre, *s.m.* bell (*with a hammer instead of a clapper*); clock-bell; office-bell, table-bell, call-bell; (*of bells*) ring, sound; (*of drums*) cord; (*pers.*) tone, voice; (*fig.*) head, brain; stamp; stamp-office; stamp-duty; post-mark; postage-stamp; (*her.*) helmet, crest; (*mus.*) timbre. — *sec*, blank stamp; embossing-press. — *de la poste*, post-mark. — **-poste,** *s.m.* postage stamp. *Bureau de —*, stamp-office. *Droit de —*, stamp-duty. *Avoir le — fêlé*, to be crack-brained
Timbré, e, *part. adj.* stamped, &c. (*V.* **Timbrer**); crazy, cracked, crack-brained
Timbrer, *v.a.* to stamp; to post-mark; (*her.*)
Timbreur, *s.m.* stamper [to crest
Timide, *adj.* timid, fearful, timorous; nervous; bashful; shy [rously; bashfully; shyly
Timidement, *adv.* timidly, fearfully, timo-
Timidité, *s.f.* timidity, fearfulness, timorousness; nervousness; bashfulness; shyness
Timocratie, *s.f.* timocracy
Timocratique, *adj.* timocratic

Timon, *s.m.* (*of a carriage*) pole; (*of a plough*) beam; (*nav.*) helm, tiller; (*fig.*) helm. *Tenir le* —, to be at the helm
Timoner, *v.a.* (*nav.*) to steer
Timonerie, *s.f.* (*nav.*) steerage
Timonier, *s.m.* wheel-horse, wheeler; (*nav.*) helmsman, steersman
Timoré, e, *adj.* timorous; scrupulous
Tin, *s.m.* cask-stand; (*nav.*) stock, block
Tincal, Tinkal, *s.m.* (*chem.*) tincal
Tinctorial, e, *adj.* used in dyeing, dye, colouring, tinctorial. *Matière —e,* dye-stuff, dye
Tine, *s.f.* tub; butter-tub *or* firkin
Tinet, *s.m.* (*butch.*) gambrel
Tinette, *s.f.* small tub, kit; butter-tub *or* firkin
Tintamarre, *s.m.* hubbub, racket, hurly-burly, clatter, din, row, uproar, confused *or* thundering noise
Tintement, *s.m.* ringing sound; tingling; tinkling; tolling, toll; jingling, jingle; tingling, noise. — *d'oreilles* or *dans les oreilles,* ringing *or* tingling in the ears, noise in the ears *or* in the head, "tinnitus aurium"
Tintenague, *s.f.* tutenag
Tinter, *v.a.n.* to toll; to ring; to ring for; to jingle; to tinkle; to tingle; (*nav.*) to put upon the stocks, to set on blocks
Tintin, *s.m.* tinkling, jingling, jingle
Tintinnabuler, *v.n.* to tinkle, to jingle, to tintinnabulate, to tintinnate
Tintouin, *s.m.* tingling, noise; trouble; embarrassment; uneasiness, anxiety [*Geneva*)
Tiou-tiou, *s.m.* (*kind of bird of the Lake of*
Tipulaire, *s.m.* (*zool.*) crane-fly; midge
Tipule, *s.f.* (*zool.*) crane-fly, daddy-longlegs
Tique, *s.f.* (*zool.*) tick; dog-tick; harvest-bug
Tiquer, *v.n.* (*vet.*) to have the tic, to be vicious
Tiqueté, e, *adj.* spotted; speckled; variegated
Tiqueture, *s.f.* spottedness, spottiness, spots; speckledness, speckles; variegation
Tiqueu-r, se, *adj. s.* crib-biting, vicious; crib-biter
Tir, *s.m.* shooting; firing, fire; practice; shooting-gallery *or* ground, firing ground, practice-ground, firing-range, rifle-range, range
Tirade, *s.f.* tirade; speech; passage; long string; breath, stretch
Tirage, *s.m.* draught; drawing; towing; tow-path; difficulty, obstacle; (*print.*) working, working off, printing, printing off, impression; pulling; press-work. *V.* **Sort**
†**Tiraillement,** *s.m.* pulling; twitching, twitch; twinge; pain; anxiety, uneasiness; disagreement, jarring, jar
†**Tirailler,** *v.a.n.* to pull about; to tug; to twitch; to tease, to plague, to pester; to fire away, to shoot; to skirmish
†**Tiraillerie,** *s.f.* skirmishing
†**Tirailleur,** *s.m.* bad shot; sharpshooter, skirmisher; rifleman
Tirant, *s.m.* string; strap; tie; brace; tie-beam; holdfast; cramp; gristle; (*nav.*) draught
Tirasse, *s.f.* draw-net; (*bot.*) *V.* **Traînasse**
Tirasser, *v.a.* to catch with a draw-net
Tire, *s.f.* stretch; tug; pull; (*of wings*) quick jerk. *Tout d'une* —, all at one time, at a stretch. *Vol à la* —, pocket-picking. *Voleur* (*m.*, *-euse, f.*) *à la* —, pickpocket. — **-d'aile,** *s.f.* quick jerk of the wing. *A — -d'aile,* at a single flight; as fast as its wings can carry it, at full speed
Tire, *s.m.f.* (*in compounds, from* **Tirer,** "to draw," "to pull," &c.) thing (*m.*) *or* person (*m.f.*) that draws *or* pulls *or* &c., drawer, puller, &c. — **-balle,** *s.m.* (*for guns*) ball-drawer; (*surg.*) bullet-extractor, bullet-forceps. — **-bonde,** *s.m.* bung-drawer. — **-bottes,** *s.m.* boot-jack; boot-hook. — **-bouchon,** *s.m.* cork-screw; (*of hair*) ringlet. — **-bourre,** *s.m.* worm-screw. — **-bouton,** *s.m.* button-hook. — **-clou,** *s.m.* nail-drawer, claw-hammer. — **-feu,** *s.m.* (*artil.*) lanyard. — **-fond,** *s.m.* (*cooper's*) turrel; (*surg.*) elevator. — **-jus,** *s.m.* (*pop.*) pocket-handkerchief. — **-lait,** *s.m.* breast-glass, breast-drawer. — **-larigot (A),** *adv.* hard. — **-ligne,** *s.m.* drawing-pen. — **lire,** *s.f.* money-box; *s.m.* (*of the lark*) song, carol. — **lirer,** *v.n.* to sing, to carol. — **-moelle,** *s.m.* marrow-spoon. — **-pied,** *s.m.* shoemaker's stirrup. — **-plomb,** *s.m.* glazier's vice. — **-point,** *s.m.* saw-file. — **-racine,** *s.m.* (*dentist's*) stump-forceps. — **-sou,** *s.m.* skin-flint, screw; beggar. — **taine,** *s.f.* (*obsolete*) *V.* **Breluche.** — **-tête,** *s.m.* (*surg.*) craniotomy forceps. — **-veille,** *s.f.* (*nav.*) ladder-rope, man rope
Tiré, e, *part. adj.* drawn, &c. (*V.* **Tirer**); wiredrawn; harassed; (*of the face*) emaciated, fagged, seedy; — *s.m.f.* (*com., of bills*) drawee; — *s.m.* shooting; preserve
Tirer, *v.a.n.* to draw; to pull; to drag; to tug; to lug; to haul; to take *or* get out *or* away; to take; to get; to obtain; to put out; to shoot; to fire; to fire at; to fire off; to draw out *or* off; to extract; to extricate; to relieve; to raise; to trace; to receive, to gather; to reap; to derive; to borrow; to infer, to deduce; to make; to draw on, to put on; to let (*blood*); to tap; to milk; to stretch; to tighten; to ring; to work, to work off, to print, to print off, to strike off; to pull off *or* out; to take off; to let off; to cast (*a nativity*); to fence; to border; to approach; to incline; to tend, to verge; to go; to go off. — *l'épée,* to draw the sword; to fence; to be a (*good or bad*) swordsman. — *bien,* to be a good shot *or* a good fencer. — *bien l'epée,* to be a good swordsman. — *gloire* or *vanité de,* to glory *or* pride in, to be proud *or* vain of, to take a pride in, to boast of. — *d'erreur,* to undeceive. — *les cartes,* to tell fortunes. *Bon a*—, (*print.*) order for press; ready for press; press
Se —, *v.r.* to get out (of); to extricate oneself (from); to escape; to get through *or* over; to recover. *S'en* —, to get out of it; to get through *or* over it; to get off; to recover; to come off; to acquit oneself; to manage it, to do it; to rise; to be drawn *or* &c. [ment
Tiret, *s.m.* dash, rule; hyphen; slip of parch-
Tireu-r, se, *s.m.f.* drawer; shooter; shot, marksman; sharpshooter, rifleman; fencer; game-keeper; wire-drawer; pickpocket. — *d'armes,* fencer; fencing-master. — *d'horoscope* or *de cartes,* fortune-teller. *Franc-* —, *V.* **Franc,** *adj.*
Tiroir, *s.m.* drawer; till; slide; strap; (*mil.*) middle rank. *Pièce à* —, comedy of episodes, unconnected scenes
Tironien, ne, *adj.* Tironian
Tisane, *s.f.* infusion, tea; decoction; diluent, tisane. — *de champagne,* light champagne; champagne cup [hell-hound
Tison, *s.m.* brand, firebrand; torch. — *d'enfer,*
Tisonné, e, *adj.* speckled with black spots
Tisonner, *v.n.* to stir *or* poke the fire
Tisonneu-r, se, *s.m.f.* person fond of stirring *or* poking the fire; stoker
Tisonnier, *s.m.* poker; stoker [tissue; texture
Tissage, *s.m.* weaving; twining; plaiting;
Tisser, *v.a.* to weave; to twine; to plait; to
Se —, *v.r.* to be woven *or* &c. [contrive
Tisserand, *s.m.* weaver
Tisseranderie, *s.f.* weaver's trade *or* business, weaving; weaving factory
Tisserin, *s.m.* (*zool.*) weaver-bird
Tisseu-r, se, *s.m.f.* weaver, weaveress
Tissu, e, *part.* (*obsolete form of* "tissé;" *from the old verb* "tistre," now "tisser") woven, spun, made up, &c.; — *s.m.* tissue; texture; contexture; web; fabric; cloth; stuff; material; series
Tissure, *s.f.* texture; contexture
Tissuterie, *s.f. V.* **Tisseranderie**
Tissutier, *s.m.* weaver

Tistre, *v.a.* (*old*) *V.* **Tisser**
Titan, *s.m.* (*myth.*) Titan
Titanate, *s.m.* (*chem.*) titanate
Titan-cotte, *s.m.* (*bot.*) clearing-nut
Titane, *s.m.* *V.* **Titanium**
Titanesque, *adj.* Titanic, Titanian, Titan
Titan-ique, -isme. *V.* page 3, § 1
Titanite, *s.m.* (*min.*) titanite
Titanium, *s.m.* (*chem.*) titanium
Tithymale, *s.m.* (*bot.*) tithymal
Titi, *s.m.* cad; roistering blade [tion, tickling
Titillation, *s.f.*, **Titillement,** *s.m.* titilla-
Titiller, *v.a.* to titillate, to tickle
Titrage, *s.m.* designation; (*chem.*) titration
Titre, *s.m.* title; title-page; capacity; right; claim; reason, cause; respect; way; document, certificate; voucher; title-deed; muniment; indentures, indenture; security; (*of gold, silver*) standard. *Faux* —, false title *or* &c.; falsehood; sham; (*print.*) half-title. *A — de,* by right of; as; on the score of; in virtue of. *A bon* —, *à juste* —, justly; deservedly. *A — gratuit,* gratuitously. *Au* —, (*of gold, silver*) standard. *En* —, on the title, at the head; head, chief; regular
Titrer, *v.a.* to give a title to, to title; to designate; (*chem.*) to titrate
Titrier, *s.m.* forger of titles *or* deeds; (*in monasteries*) curator of the deeds
Titubation, *s.f.* titubation, reeling, staggering, stumbling [stumble
Tituber, *v.n.* to titubate, to reel, to stagger, to
Titulaire, *adj.* titular; head, chief; — *s.m.f.* titulary, titular; incumbent; head
Titulariat, *s.m.* titular office *or* post
Toast, *s.m.* toast, health. *Porter un* —, to propose a toast *or* health, to toast, to drink
Toaster, *v.a.* to toast; to drink; — *v.n.* to drink healths [stop
Toc, *int.* toc; — *s.m.* gentle knock; (*tech.*) dead
Tocade. *V.* **Toquade**
Tocan, *s.m.* (*fish*) grilse
Tocane, *s.f.* unpressed wine
Tocante, *s.f.* (*pop.*) ticker (*watch*)
Toccata, Toccate, *s.f.* (*mus.*) toccata
Tocolog-ie, -ique. *V.* page 3, § 1
Tocsin, *s.m.* alarm-bell, tocsin
Toddi, Toddy, *s.m.* toddy
Todier, *s.m.* (*bird*) tody
Tofacé, e, *adj.* *V.* **Tophacé**
Toge, *s.f.* toga; robe [jumble, medley, chaos
Tohu-bohu, *s.m.* hurly-burly; confusion;
Toi, *pers. pron.* thee, you; thou, you; to *or* at thee, to *or* at you, for *or* with *or* in *or* from *or* by *or* on *or* against thee (*or* you); for thy *or* your part; as for (*or* as to) thee *or* you; thyself, yourself; to *or* at *or* within thyself (*or* yourself). *A* —, to *or* at *or* with thee (*or* you); to *or* at *or* with thyself (*or* yourself); thine, yours, thy own, your own; of thine, of yours, of thy own, of your own; peculiar; to spare. *A — à, à — de,* *V.* **A.** — *-même,* thyself, yourself; alone; too, also, likewise
Toile, *s.f.* cloth; linen, linen-cloth; canvas; sail; curtain; cobweb, web; picture, piece; (*hunt.*) toil. — *cirée,* oil-cloth *or* baize; oil-case; floor-cloth. — *grasse,* tarpaulin. — *peinte,* printed calico *or* cotton, print. — *vernie,* oil-skin. — *à matelas,* tick, ticking, bed-ticking. — *à sacs,* sack-cloth, sacking. — *à voiles,* sail-cloth, canvas. — *d'araignée,* cobweb; spider-work. — *de coton,* cotton-cloth. — *d'emballage,* pack-cloth, packing-cloth, wrapper. — *de Pénélope,* Penelope's web. — *pour chemises,* shirting. — *pour draps* (*de lit*), sheeting. *Chemise de* —, linen shirt
Toilerie, *s.f.* linen-trade *or* goods, linen-drapery
Toilette, *s.f.* toilet; dress, attire; dressing; cleaning; trimming; dressing-table, toilet-table; washstand, wash-hand stand; (*butch.*) caul; (*com.*) wrapper. — *-commode, commode-* —, *V.* **Commode,** *s.f.* *Grande* —, full dress. *Marchande à la* —, *V.* **Revendeuse.** *Seau de* —, toilet-pail, slop-pail. *En* —, dressed up; full-dressed. *En grande* —, in full dress, full-dressed. *Faire* —, to dress oneself up, to dress, to spruce up. *Faire la — à,* to dress; to clean; to trim. *Faire sa* —, to dress (oneself) [— *adj.* of linen, linen
Toili-er, ère, *s.m.f.* linen-weaver *or* merchant;
Toise, *s.f.* fathom, 6 feet, 2 yards
Toisé, *s.m.* measuring, measurement; (*math.*) mensuration
Toiser, *v.a.* to measure; to survey; to examine; to observe; to eye from head to foot; to conclude, to settle; to judge
Toiseur, *s.m.* measurer; surveyor
Toison, *s.f.* fleece; (*pop.*) thick head of hair
Toit, *s.m.* roof; house-top; house, dwelling, home; sty; (*mining*) top. *Sous les —s,* in a garret. *Crier* or *dire par-dessus les —s, prêcher* or *publier sur les —s,* to proclaim on the house- [tops
Toiture, *s.f.* roofing, roof
Tokai, Tokay, *s.m.* tokay (wine)
Tôle, *s.f.* sheet-iron. — *ondulée,* corrugated iron
Tolérable, *adj.* tolerable; supportable, bearable, endurable; middling
Tolérablement, *adv.* tolerably, supportably
Tolérance, *s.f.* toleration; sufferance; endurance; forbearance; indulgence; (*med.*) tolerance; (*coin.*) allowance, deduction. *Maison de* —, house of ill fame
Tolérant, e, *adj.* tolerant [toleration
Tolérantisme, *s.m.* tolerantism, system of
Tolération, *s.f.* toleration
Tolérer, *v.a.* to tolerate; to suffer; to endure; to bear; to allow; to indulge

Se —, *v.r.* to tolerate *or* &c. each other; to be tolerated *or* &c.
Tôlerie, *s.f.* sheet-iron manufacture *or* works
Tolet, *s.m.* (*nav.*) thole [*or* articles
Toletière, *s.f.* (*nav.*) rowlock
Tôlier, *s.m.* sheet-iron worker
Tollé, *s.m.* outcry, hue and cry
Tolu, *s.m.* tolu
Tomahawk, *s.m.* tomahawk
Tomaison, *s.f.* (*print.*) number of a volume
Tomate, *s.f.* (*bot.*) tomato, tomata, love-apple
Tombac, *s.m.* tombac, white copper
Tombal, e, *adj.* tomb. *Pierre —e,* tomb-stone
Tombant, e, *adj.* falling, falling down; drooping; flowing
Tombe, *s.f.* tombstone; tomb, grave
Tombé, e, *part. adj.* fallen, &c. (*V.* **Tomber**); that has failed; unsuccessful
Tombeau, *s.m.* tomb; grave; tombstone
Tombée, *s.f.* fall. — *de la nuit,* — *du jour,*
Tombelier, *s.m.* carter, carman [nightfall
Tombelle, *s.f.* *V.* **Tumulus**
Tomber, *v.n.* to fall; to fall down; to tumble, to tumble down; to sink, to sink down; to drop, to drop down; to droop; to fall off *or* out *or* in; to hit (upon); to have luck; to coincide; to come; to come off *or* out *or* down; to turn; to run, to go; to fall *or* be taken (*ill*); to break, to pine away; to die away; to flag; to abate; to fall down to the level *or* condition (of); (*nav.*) to sag, to incline; — *v.a.* (*pop.*) to knock down, to floor. — *bien* or *mal,* to be lucky *or* unlucky; to come seasonably *or* unseasonably; to go (or come) to the right *or* wrong person *or* man. — *dans l'eau,* to fall into the water; (*fig.*) to fall to the ground, to fall through, to fail, to come to nothing. — *de l'eau,* to rain. *Faire* —, to make (...) fall; to throw *or* push *or* knock down; to shake off *or* down; to trip up; to let fall; to turn; to lead; to betray. *Laisser* —, *Se laisser* —, *V.* **Laisser**
Tombereau, *s.m.* tumbril, cart; dung-cart; mud-cart; dust-cart; ballast-truck; sledge; cartload

Tombeu-r, se, *s.m.f.* tumbler; demolisher; slasher; powerful fighter; bad actor *or* actress
Tombola, *s.f.* tombola, lottery, raffle
Tome, *s.m.* volume [mentous, downy
Tomenteu-x, se, *adj.* (*bot.*) tomentose, to-
Ton, *adj. poss.* thy, thy own; your, your own; — *s.m.*tone; accent, voice; tune, sound; strain; note; manner; style; fashion; breeding, manners; colour, tint, tinge. *Bon* —, good breeding, good manners; fashion. *De bon* —, well-bred, genteel, gentlemanly, ladylike, proper. *Mauvais* —, ill breeding, bad manners, vulgarity. *De mauvais* —, ill-bred, unmannerly, vulgar, low, ungentlemanly, unladylike, improper. *Par* —, to show off. *Donner le* —, to give the tone; to lead; to lead the fashion; (*mus.*) to pitch, to tone. *Mettre au* — (*de*), to attune (with). *Le prendre sur un* —, *Prendre un* —, to assume airs. *Le prendre sur un haut* —, to assume a high tone, to speak haughtily *or* with arrogance, to carry it high
Tonal, e, *adj.* tonal
Tonalement, *adv.* tonally
Tonalité, *s.f.* tonality
Tonca. *V.* **Tonka**
Tondage, *s.m.* shearing
Tondaison, *s.f. V.* **Tonte** [dens
Tondant, e, *adj.* (*med.*) *Teigne —e,* tinea ton-
Tondeu-r, se, *s.m.f.* shearer; shearman; clipper; shearing-machine, shears; mower; mowing-machine. — *de gazon,* lawn-mower, lawn-mowing machine
Tondre, *v.a.* to shear; to fleece; to shave; to crop; to clip; to trim; to mow, to pare; —
Tondure. *V.* **Tonture** [*s.f.* touchwood
Tonga. *V.* **Tonka**
Tonicité, *s.f.* tonicity
Tonifier, *v.a.* to tonify, to invigorate
Tonique, *adj.* tonic; syllabic; — *s.m.* (*med.*) tonic; — *s.f.* (*mus.*) tonic, key-note
Tonka, *s.m.* Tonka, Tonka bean
Tonnage, *s.m.* tonnage. *Droit de* —, tonnage, tonnage-dues
Tonnant, e, *adj.* thundering. *Jupiter* —, Jupiter tonans, Jupiter the thunderer, the Thunderer
Tonne, *s.f.* tun; ton; (— *d'extraction*) (*mining*) corf, corve, tub; (*nav.*) can-buoy
Tonneau, *s.m.* cask; tun; ton; tub; hogshead; butt; barrel; (*play*) tonneau. — *percé,*
Tonnelage, *s.m.* tonnage [(*fig.*) spendthrift
Tonneler, *v.a.* (*hunt.*) to tunnel
Tonnelet, *s.m.* small cask *or* barrel, keg
Tonneleur, *s.m.* (*hunt.*) tunneller
Tonneli-er, ère, *s.m.f.* cooper; cooper's wife
Tonnelle, *s.f.* arbour, green arbour, bower, alcove; tunnel-net, funnel-net; stalking-horse; (*arch.*) semicircular vault
Tonnellerie, *s.f.* cooperage; cooper's trade *or* business; cooper's wares, casks, &c.; cooper's shop *or* shed
Tonner, *v.n.* to thunder; to inveigh
Tonnerre, *s.m.* thunder; thunderbolt; lightning; thundering; (*of applause*) burst; (*poet.*) cannon; (*of fire-arms*) breech-end. — *!* (*int.*) — *de Dieu!* by Jingo! by Jove! bedad! hang it! confound it!
‡**Tonotechn-ie, -ique.** *V.* page 3, § 1
Tonquin, *adj.* Tonquin
Tonsillaire, *adj.* (*anat.*) tonsilar
Tonsille, *s.f.* (*anat.*) tonsil
Tonsure, *s.f.* tonsure; orders; clergy [priest
Tonsuré, e, *adj.* tonsured, shaven; — *s.m.*
Tonsurer, *v.a.* to give tonsure to
Tonte, *s.f.* shearing; fleecing; shaving; cropping; clipping; trimming; shearings; clippings; wool; crop; shearing-time
Tontine, *s.f.* tontine
Tontini-er, ère, *s.m.f.* annuitant of a tontine
Tontisse, *adj.* of shearings; — *s.f.* shearings; hangings. *Bourre* —, cloth-shearings, flocks. *Papier* —, flock-paper

Tonton, *s.m.* teetotum; (*children's slang*) uncle
Tonture, *s.f.* shearings; cloth-shearings; clippings; flock; mowing; (*nav.*) sheer
Toparchie, *s.f.* toparchy
Toparque, *s.m.* toparch
Topaze, *s.f.* (*min.*) topaz
Topazolithe, *s.f.m.* (*min.*) topazolite
Tôpe, *s.m.* tope (*Buddhistic monument*)
Toper, *v.n.* to stake; to agree, to consent. *Tope! Tope là!* agreed! done!
Tophacé, e, *adj.* tophaceous
Tophus, *s.m.* tophus
Topiaire, *adj.m.f., s.f.* topiary
Topinambour, *s.m.* Jerusalem artichoke
Topique, *adj.* topic, topical; — *s.m.* topic
Topographe, *s.m.* topographer
Topo-graphie, -graphique, -logique, &c. *V.* page 3, § 1
Toporama, *s.m.* toporama
Toquade, *s.f.* infatuation, mad fancy; hobby
Toquante. *V.* **Tocante**
Toque, *s.f.* cap. — *à plumes,* cap and feathers
Toqué, e, *adj.* touched, cracked, crazy; infatuated; in love
Toquer, *v.a.n.* to touch; to strike; to knock; to beat; to tick; to offend; to infatuate; to make mad, to turn ...'s brain
Se —, *v.r.* to become *or* be infatuated *or*
Toquet, *s.m.* cap [mad; to fall in love
Torche, *s.f.* torch, link; twist; pad; (*paint.*) rubber; — *s.m.f.* (*in compounds, from* **Torcher,** "to wipe," &c.) thing (*m.*) *or* person (*m.f.*) that wipes *or* &c., wiper, &c. — **-cul,** *s.m.* bumfodder. — **-nez,** *s.m. V.* **Serre-nez.** — **-pinceau,** *s.m.* (*paint.*) rubber. — **-pot,** *s.m. V.* **Sittelle**
Torcher, *v.a.* to wipe; to rub; to clean; to wipe the bottom of; to twist; to cover with loam *or* clay; to knock off *or* do in haste, to do, to work, to get up; to dress up, to dress; to drub, to beat
Se —, *v.r.* to wipe oneself (*or* o.'s ...); to be wiped *or* &c.; to fight, to have a fight *or* a
Torchère, *s.f.* cresset; candelabrum [set-to
Torchette, *s.f.* wisp; twist; fish-basket. *Net comme* —, (*pop.*) clean; outright; and no mistake [wall *or* hut *or* &c.
Torchis, *s.m.* loam, clay, mud; cob-wall, mud-
Torchon, *s.m.* clout, duster, cloth. — *de cuisine,* dish-cloth
Torchonner, *v.a.* (*pop.*) *V.* **Torcher**
Torcol, Torcou, *s.m.* (*bird*) wryneck
Tordage, *s.m.* twisting; twist; torsion; wrest
Tord-boyaux, *s.m.* rotgut, strong brandy
Tordeu-r, se, *s.m.f.* twister; throwster
Tord-nez, *s.m. V.* **Serre-nez**
Tordre, *v.a.,* **Se** —, *v.r.* to twist; to wrench; to wrest; to wring; to writhe; to contort; to distort; to throw; to writhe with laughter, to be convulsed with laughing
Tore, *s.m.* (*arch.*) torus, tore, moulding; (*bot.*) torus, thalamus
Toréador, *s.m.* toreador, bull-fighter [rap
†**Torgniole, Torgnole,** *s.f.* knock, thump,
†**Tormentille,** *s.f.* (*bot.*) tormentil
Torminal, e, Tormineu-x, se, *adj.* (*med.*)
Tornado, *s.m.* tornado [terminal
Toron, *s.m.* (*nav.*) strand; (*arch.*) torus
Torosité, *s.f.* torosity
Torpédo, *s.f.* torpedo
Torpeur, *s.f.* torpor, torpidity, torpidness
†**Torpille,** *s.f.* torpedo
Torquer, *v.a.* to twist
Torquette, *s.f.* basket
Torqueur, *s.m.* twister
Torréfacteur, *s.m.* torrefier, roaster
Torréfaction, *s.f.* torrefaction, roasting
Torréfier, *v.a.* to torrefy, to roast
Torrent, *s.m.* torrent; stream; flood; flow
Torrentiel, le, *adj.* coming down in torrents, pouring; torrent-like [tuous
Torrentueu-x, se, *adj.* torrent-like; impe-

Torride, *adj.* torrid [contorted; wreathed
Tors, e, *adj.* twisted; wrung; wry; crooked;
Torsade, *s.f.* twisted cord, torsel; twist; bul-
Torse, *s.m.* trunk, chest, bust, torso [lion
Torser, *v.a.* to wreathe, to twist
Torsion, *s.f.* torsion, twisting; wrest
Tort, *s.m.* wrong; error, fault; blame; injury, harm, hurt, mischief, offence, prejudice, detriment, tort. *A —*, wrongly; wrongfully; wrong; falsely; unjustly, undeservedly. *A — ou à raison, A — ou* (or *et*) *à droit*, rightly *or* wrongly, right or wrong; whether right or wrong; anyhow, indiscriminately. *A — et à travers*, at random; indiscriminately; inconsiderately, thoughtlessly; madly, ravingly; at cross-purposes. *Dans son —*, wrong, in the wrong. *Avoir —*, to be wrong, to be in the wrong; to be in fault; to be mistaken. *Avoir des —s envers*, to behave badly to. *Donner — à*, to say *or* show that ... is (*or* was) wrong, to decide against, to disapprove, to blame; to lay the blame at ...'s door; to condemn; to side against; to contradict, to disprove. *Se donner des —s*, to do *or* act wrong, to behave badly. *Faire —* (or *du —*) *à*, to wrong; to injure; to do wrong *or* harm. *Se faire —*, to injure oneself. *Mettre (quelqu'un) dans son —*, to leave (a person) no excuse
Tortelle, *s.f. V.* **Vélar**
Torticolis, *s.m.* stiff-neck, wry-neck, torticollis; (*fig.*) hypocrite; — *adj.* stiff-necked, wry-
Tortil, *s.m.* (*her.*) *V.* **Tortis** [necked
Tortile, *adj.* tortile [guage; shuffling
†Tortillage, *s.m.* rigmarole, confused lan-
†Tortillard, Tortillart, *s.m.* common small-leaved elm, English elm; (*pop.*) halter, limper
†Tortille, *s.f.* winding walk
†Tortillement, *s.m.* twisting, twist; wriggle; wrench; wrest; twitching, twitch; shuffling, shuffle
†Tortiller, *v.a.n.*, **Se —,** *v.r.* to twist; to wriggle; to waddle; to wind up; to wreathe; to shuffle, to flinch; (*pop.*) to eat, to gobble up, to swallow. — *bien de la fourchette*, to play a good knife and fork
†Tortillère, *s.f. V.* **Tortille**
†Tortillon, *s.m.* twist; pad; wench
Tortionnaire, *adj.* violent, unjust, wrongful; of torture; — *s.m.* executioner [wrongfully
Tortionnairement, *adv.* violently, unjustly,
Tortionner, *v.a.* to strain, to twist
Tortis, *s.m.* twist; (*obsolete*) wreath, garland; (*her.*) circle of pearls
Tortoir, *s.m.* carter's rack-stick
Tortu, e, *adj.* crooked; tortuous; bandy
Tortue, *s.f.* tortoise; turtle; (*pers.*) snail, slug. *A pas de —*, at a snail's pace; (*adject.*) snail-paced. *Soupe à la —*, turtle soup. *Tête de veau en —*, mock turtle soup
Tortuer, *v.a.*, **Se —,** *v.r.* to crook, to bend
Tortueusement, *adv.* tortuously, crookedly
Tortueu-x, se, *adj.* tortuous; crooked; bending; winding; unfair
Tortuosité, *s. f.* tortuosity, tortuousness, crookedness; crooked way; bending; winding
Torture, *s.f.* torture; rack
Torturer, *v.a.* to torture; to rack; to wrest
Torule, *s.f.* (*bot.*) torula, yeast-plant
Tory, *s.m. adj.* tory
Torysme, *s.m.* toryism
Toscan, e, *adj.* Tuscan; — *s.m.f.* Tuscan (*man or boy*); Tuscan woman *or* lady *or* girl; — *s.m.* (the) Tuscan (language); — *s.f.* (the) Tuscan fashion [Toaster
Toste, *s.m.*; **Toster,** *v.a.n. V.* **Toast** &
Tôt, *adv.* soon; early; in time; promptly, quickly, quick. — *ou tard*, sooner or later. *Plus —*, sooner; earlier; before; soonest; earliest. *Le plus —*, the soonest; the sooner; the earliest; the earlier; as soon as; as early as. *Au plus —, le plus — possible*, at soonest; as soon *or* as early as possible; at once. *Si —, V.* **Sitôt** *and* **Aussitôt.** — **-fait,** *s.m.* light cake
Total, e, *adj. s.m.* total, whole; entire; complete; utter; sum total. *Au —*, on *or* upon the whole; after all [completely; utterly
Totalement, *adv.* totally, wholly, entirely;
Totalisa-teur, trice, *adj.* totalizing; — *s.m.f.* totalizer
Totalisation, *s.f.* totalization, totalizing
Totaliser, *v.a.* to totalize
Totalité, *s.f.* totality, whole
Totane, *s.m.* (*bird*) totanus, gambet; sandpiper
Toto (In), *adv.* (*Latin*) in toto, in the whole, entirely
Toton, *s.m.* (*old spelling for* "tonton") teetotum
Touage, *s.m.* (*nav.*) towage, towing [towel
†Touaille, *s.f.* round towel, roller-towel, jack-
Touareg, Touarik, *s.m.f. adj.* Touareg, Touarik, Tuarick (*African*)
Toucan, *s.m.* (*zool., astr.*) toucan
Touchable, *adj.* touchable
Touchant, e, *adj. s.m.* touching; affecting, moving; impressive; — *prep.* touching, concerning, about
Touchau, Touchaud, *s.m.* touch-needle
Touche, *s.f.* touch; assay, trial; fescue; stick; pen; drove; (*mus.*) key; (*mus.*) finger-board; (*mus.*) fret; (*mus.*) stop; (*fenc.*) hit, touch; (*pop.*) hit, blow, stab; (*pop., fam.*) face, phiz, figure, look, manner, ways
Touché, e, *part. adj.* touched, &c. (*V.* **Toucher**); (*bien —*) well-done; well-written; well-said; well-hit; successful
Touche-à-tout, *s.m.f.* meddler
Touchement, *s.m.* touching
Toucher, *v.a.n.* to touch; to handle; to feel; to try, to assay; (*obsolete*) to play (*the piano, &c.*); to receive (*money*); to beat, to strike; to hit; to whip, to flick; to drive; to drive on; to affect, to move; to impress; to concern, to interest; to express; to paint, to depict; to allude to, to touch on; to mention; to say; to hint; to meddle; to relate; to border; to be near; to have all but reached; to approach, to draw (*near, towards, to*); to reach; to meet; to join; to adjoin each other; to be affected *or* moved; to be related; to stop; (*print.*) to ink; (*nav.*) to touch; (*nav.*) to strike; (*nav.*) to ground; (*nav.*) to call; (*nav.*) to call off; — *s.m.* feeling, touch; contact; (*mus.*) touch. — *dans la main*, to give o.'s hand, to shake hands with. *Touchez là*, give me your hand, shake hands, let us shake hands; agreed. *N'avoir pas l'air d'y —*, to look as if butter would not melt in o.'s mouth
Se —, *v.r.* to touch *or* &c. each other; to touch; to meet; to join; to be adjoining *or*
Toucheur, *s.m.* toucher; drover [contiguous
Toue, *s.f.* barge, ferry-boat; towing, towage
Touée, *s.f.* (*nav.*) tow, tow-line; warp. *Câble de —*, stream-cable
Touer, *v.a.* (*nav.*) to tow, to warp
Toueur, *s.m.* towing-boat, tow-boat
Touffe, *s.f.* tuft; bunch; cluster, clump; wisp; (*bot.*) truss [cluster
Touffer, *v.a.*, **Se —,** *v.r.* to tuft; to bunch; to
Touffeur, *s.f.* suffocating heat
Touffu, e, *adj.* tufted, tufty; bunchy; bushy; branchy; leafy; full; thick
Toujours, *adv.* always; ever; for ever; continually; invariably; usually, usual; still; on; away; again; however; nevertheless, notwithstanding; all the same, just the same; for all that; after all; at least; in the mean time. — *est-il que*, still; the fact is *or* was however that; be that as it may; as it is. *C'est — cela!* that is something!
Touline, *s.f.* (*nav.*) tow-line
Toulonais, e, Toulonnais, e, *adj. s.* of Toulon, Toulonese, native of Toulon
Touloucouna, *s.m.* (*bot.*) touloucouna (*kind of carapa*)

Toulousain, e, *adj. s.* of Toulouse, Toulousan, native of Toulouse
Toupet, *s.m.* tuft; foretop; forelock; scalp; wig; front; toupee, toupet; head; pluck, game; assurance; brass, cheek, impudence, effrontery
Toupie, *s.f.* top, peg-top, spinning-top; (*mollusc*) top-shell, trochus; (*pop.*) trollop, trull, drab, gig. — *d'Allemagne*, humming-top
†**Toupillage,** *s.m.* spinning, whirling about; going to and fro, running up and down *or* about the house
†**Toupiller,** *v.n.* to spin, to whirl about; to go to and fro, to run up and down *or* about the house
†**Toupillon,** *s.m.* tuft (*of hair*); (*of orange-trees*) waste branch
Tour, *s.f.* tower; (*at chess*) castle, rook. — *à feu*, lighthouse. — *à la martello*, martello tower. — *marine*, watch-house
Tour, *s.m.* turn; turning; winding; round; revolution; circumference, circuit; trip, tour; manner; trick; device; feat; frolic; twist; strain; sprain; (*of turners*) lathe, turning-lathe; (*of a nunnery*, &c.) turning-box; (*nav.*) reel, hitch; (*garment*) band, tie, wrapper; (*of garments*) edging, border, lace; (*of beds*) valance, hangings; (*of hair*) foretop, front, tour. — *à* —, in turn, by turns, alternately; successively. — *d'adresse*, legerdemain, sleight-of-hand trick; trick. — *de cheveux*, foretop *or* front of hair. — *de cou*, neck-tie *or* band *or* wrapper, boa, &c. — *de force*, feat of strength *or* skill, feat; wonder. — *de main*, sleight of hand, legerdemain; trice, instant. — *de scrutin*, ballot. — *de tête*, bonnet-front. — *en l'air*, (*tech.*) mandrel-lathe. *A son* —, in o.'s (*or* his *or* her *or* its) turn. *Serrure à double* —, double lock. *Avoir deux mètres de* —, to be two yards round *or* in circumference. *Faire le* — *de*, to go round. *Faire un* — (or *un* — *de promenade*), to take a turn *or* a walk. *Faire le* — *du jardin*, to walk *or* go round the garden. *Faire un* — *de jardin*, to take a turn in the garden. *Fait au* —, made with a lathe, turned; (*fig.*) exquisitely shaped. *Fermer à double* —, to double-lock. *Jouer un* —, to play a trick
Touraco, *s.m.* (*bird*) touraco, hoazin, plantain-eater
†**Touraille,** *s.f.* malt-kiln; malt
†**Touraillon,** *s.m.* malt
Tourang-eau, elle, *adj. s.* of Touraine (*formerly a province of France*) *or* of Tours (*its capital*); native of Touraine *or* of Tours
Touranien, ne, *adj.* (*geog.*) Touranian
Tourbage, *s.m.* turf *or* peat-working
Tourbe, *s.f.* turf; peat; mob, rabble, herd
Tourbeu-x, se, *adj.* turfy, peaty
Tourbi-er, ère, *adj.* of turf *or* peat, turfy, peaty; — *s.m.* peat-worker *or* carrier *or* owner; — *s.f.* turf-pit, peat-bog
†**Tourbillon,** *s.m.* whirl; vortex; whirlpool; eddy; whirlwind; tornado; bustle; mass, volume, cloud. — *de flamme* or *de feu*, rolling flame
†**Tourbillonnement,** *s.m.* whirling; eddying
†**Tourbillonner,** *v.n.* to whirl; to eddy; to wind; to curl
Tourd, *s.m.*, **Tourdelle,** *s.f.* (*bird*) fieldfare
†**Tourdille,** *adj.* (*of grey*) dirty
Tourelé, e, *adj.* turreted
Tourelle, *s.f.* turret
Touret, *s.m.* wheel; reel; drill; ring; spinning-wheel
Tourie, *s.f.* carboy, jar, can
Tourier, *s.m.* (*of convents*) porter [turning-box
Tourière, *s.f.* (*of convents*) attendant of the turning-box
†**Tourillon,** *s.m.* trunnion; pivot; bearing-neck; axle; gudgeon; collar
Tour-isme, -iste. *V.* page 3, § 1
Tourlourou, *s.m.* (*zool.*) land-crab; (*jest.*) foot-soldier, young soldier of the awkward squad, johnny-raw
Tourmaline, *s.f.* (*min.*) tourmaline
Tourment, *s.m.* torment; pain; anguish; pang; anxiety; plague; vexation
Tourmentant, e, *adj.* tormenting, troublesome
Tourmente, *s.f.* storm; tempest; hurricane; agitation; violent commotion; turmoil; trouble
Tourmenté, e, *part. adj.* tormented, &c. (*V.* **Tourmenter**); uneasy; agitated; stormy; boisterous; heavy, rough; irregular
Tourmenter, *v.a.* to torment; to tease; to vex; to annoy; to plague; to pester; to worry; to harass; to distress; to make uneasy; to dun; to toss; to jolt; to work up; to labour, to elaborate; to touch and retouch; to move about upon; to play upon; to fumble at; to twist; to strain; to warp
Se —, *v.r.* to torment *or* worry oneself; to fret; to be uneasy *or* agitated; to move *or* toss about; to be restless; to labour very hard; to twist; to strain; to warp
Tourmenteur, *adj. m.* tormenting; — *s.m.* tormentor
Tourmenteu-x, se, *adj.* (*nav.*) stormy
Tourmentin, *s.m.* (*nav.*) fore-staysail; (*bird*) petrel
Tournage, *s.m.* (*tech.*) turning
†**Tournailler,** *v.n.a.* to turn round *or* about; to hover round, to prowl
Tournant, e, *part. adj.* turning, &c. (*V.* **Tourner**); — *s.m.* turning; turn; bend; corner; winding; turning-room, room to turn; wheel; whirlpool, eddy; indirect means; — *s.f.* runner, upper mill-stone
Tourne, (*in compounds*) *s.m.* — **-à-gauche,** *s.m.* wrench. — **-bouton,** *s.m.* button-hook. — **-bride,** *s.m.* tavern, inn. — **-broche,** *s.m.* kitchen-jack, roasting-jack, jack; turnspit. — **-feuilles,** — **-feuillets,** *s.m.* leaf-turner. — **-fil,** *s.m.* *V.* **Affiloir.** — **-gants,** *s.m.* glove-stretchers. — **main,** *s.m.* trice, instant. — **-mottes,** *s.m.* *V.* **Motteux.** — **-oreille,** *s.m.* (*adject., Charrue* — *-oreille*) turnwrest *or* turnwrist plough. — **-pierres,** *s.m.* (*bird*) turnstone. — **sol,** *s.m.* (*bot.*) sun-flower, turnsole, heliotrope; (*tech.*) turnsole, litmus. *Papier de* — *sol*, (*chem.*) litmus-paper. — **-vent,** *s.m.* chimney-cowl, cowl. — **vire,** *s.f.* (*nav.*) voyal. — **virer,** *v.a.* (*old*) to manage. — **vis,** *s.m.* screw-driver, turn-screw
Tourné, e, *part. adj.* turned, &c. (*V.* **Tourner**); awry; sour; spoilt; nearly ripe; made, shaped; built; contrived; disposed. *Mal* —, badly turned; turned out badly; ill-made, ill-shaped; of an inferior cast; cross-grained
Tournée, *s.f.* round; walk; circuit; visit; visitation; turn; journey; tour; pick, mattock; (*fish.*) trawl-net; stake-net; (*pop.*) bumper all round; drubbing, hiding
Tournelle, *s.f.* (*old*) small tower, turret; Tournelle (*formerly a court of justice*); jurisdiction
Tournement, *s.m.* turning
Tourner, *v.a.n.* to turn; to turn round; to turn up *or* over; to turn out; to turn off; to curl; to twist; to wind, to wind round; to grind; to twirl; to whirl; to wheel; to revolve; to hinge; to translate; to interpret; to question; to go round; to attack indirectly; to come about; to change; to end; to prove; to curdle; (*of the tongue*) to trip, to slip; (*of boots*) to wear on one side. — *de l'œil*, (*pop.*) to fall asleep; to die, to kick the bucket. *Faire* —, to make (...) turn *or* &c.; to turn; to spin; to curdle
Se —, *v.r.* to turn; to turn round *or* about *or* away *or* over; to change, to be changed (into); to be turned *or* &c. *Se* — *en*, to be changed into
Tournette, *s.f.* winding; round; cutter; squirrel's cage; reel, yarn-windle; turning-stand
Tourneur, *s.m.* turner
Tourniole, *s.f.* whitlow
Tourniquet, *s.m.* turnstile; swivel; (*nav.*) roller; (*surg.*) tourniquet; (*insect*) whirligig, weaver

Tournis, *s.m.* (*vet.*) sturdy, turnsick, (the) gid
Tournoi, *s.m.* tournament
Tournoiement, Tournoîment, *s.m.* turning *or* wheeling round, turning, wheeling, whirling, twirling, winding, eddying; (*vet.*) *V.* **Tournis.** — *de tête,* giddiness, swimming in the head
Tournois, *adj.* (*old*) of Tours (*V.* **Livre,** *s.f.*)
Tournoyer, *v.n.* to turn round and round; to wheel round; to whirl; to twirl; to wind; to eddy; to shuffle, to beat about the bush
Tournure, *s.f.* turn; direction, course; cast; shape, figure; look, appearance; curl; peel, rind; (*part of dress*) bustle, tournure; (*tech.*) [turnings
Tourte, *s.f.* tart; pie
Tourteau, *s.m.* (*of seeds*) oil-cake, cake; (*zool.*) [*V.* **Poupart**
Tourtelette, *s.f.* tartlet; patty
Tourtereau, *s.m.* young turtle-dove
Tourterelle, *s.f.* turtle-dove
Tourtière, *s.f.* tart-dish, tart-pan, pie-dish
Tous, *pl.m. of* **Tout,** *adj.*
Touselle, *s.f.* winter wheat
Toussaint, *s.f.* All-Saints'-Day [ing; hemming
Tousser, *v.n.* to cough; to hem; — *s.m.* cough-
Tousserie, *s.f.* coughing; hemming
Tousseu-r, se, *s.m.f.* cougher; — *adj.* coughing; hemming [little; to hem
Toussoter, *v.n.* to cough *or* keep coughing a
Tout, e, *adj.* (*pl.* **Tous,** *m.,* **Toutes,** *f.*) all, whole; the whole of; full; long; every; any; only; sole; (*when used for the adv.*) *V.* **Tout,** *adv.* —*e la famille,* all the family, the whole family. — *le jour,* all day, all day long, the whole day. *Tous les jours, tous les ans,* &c., every day, every year, &c. *Tous les deux jours* or *&c., V.* **Deux.** *Tous les huit jours,* every week, once a week. *Tous les quinze jours,* every fortnight, once a fortnight. *Toutes les fois que,* every time that, as often as, whenever. — *ce qui,* — *ce que,* all that which, all that, whatever. *Tous les trois,* all three of us *or* you *or* them; every three ... *Eux tous, nous tous, vous tous,* all of them, all of us, all of you. *Par* —, all over; all about
Tout, *s.m.* (*pl.* **Touts**) all; whole; the whole; everything; anything; everybody, everyone; chief point; only thing; tout. *Comme* —, exceedingly, extremely, richly, awfully, dreadfully, furiously, like blazes, like one o'clock. *Du* —, not at all. *Du* — *au* —, all in all, entirely, 'toto cœlo.' *En* —, in all, altogether; wholly. *En* — *et pour* —, in everything; entirely. *Le* —, the whole, all. *Pas* or *point du* —, not at all; none at all; no such thing. *Plus du* —, no more now, no longer now, never now; never again; none left at all. *Par-dessus* —, above all. *Propre à* —, fit for anything. *Rien du* —, nothing at all. *Voilà* —, that is all; that was all
Tout, *adv.* wholly, entirely, quite, all; exactly; all over; wide; stark; right; very; much; far; just; however; although, though; ready. — *beau!* — *doux!* gently! softly! stop a little! hold! not so fast! not so quick! stop! enough! take care; nay! (*hunt.*) so-ho! — *comme,* just as *or* like; quite as much as; just the same, all the same, as good as done, as good. — *grand,* wide. — *près, V.* **Près.** — *prêt,* quite ready. — *à coup, V.* **Coup.** — *à fait,* (*adv.*) quite, altogether, wholly, entirely, utterly, exactly. — *fait,* ready made; (*fig.*) cut and dry. — *à l'heure,* — *au long,* — *au moins,* — *au plus,* &c., *V.* **Heure, Long, Moins, Plus,** &c. — *à vous,* yours truly; wholly *or* entirely yours; entirely *or* quite at your service. — *en* (*before a present part.*), while, whilst; while ... still; although, though. — *riche que vous êtes,* rich as you are.—*riche que vous soyez,* however rich you may be
Tout, e, (*in compounds*), all, &c. (*See above*). — **e-bonne,** *s.f.* (*bot.*) clary; all-good; (*pear*) toute-bonne. —**e-bonté,** *s.f.* supreme goodness. —**e-épice,** *s.f.* all-spice. —**-ensemble,** *s.m.* whole, tout-ensemble. — **e-présence,** *s.f.* omnipresence, ubiquity. —**e-puissance,** *s.f.* omnipotence. —**e-puissante,** *adj.f.* all-powerful, omnipotent. —**e-saine,** *s.f.* (*bot.*) tutsan. —**e-science,** *s.f.* omniscience. —**e-table, —es-tables,** *s.m.* (*obsolete*) backgammon. — **-grain,** *s.m.* (kind of Burgundy wine). — **-ou-rien,** *s.m.* all or nothing. — **-puissant,** *adj.m.* (—**e-puissante,** *f.*), *s.m.* all-powerful, omnipotent; Almighty [still
Toutefois, *adv.* however, nevertheless, yet,
Toutenague, *s.f.* tutenag
Toutier, *s.m.* bargeman, ferryman
Toutou, *s.m.* bow-wow, doggy
Toux, *s.f.* cough; coughing. — *de renard,* churchyard cough
Touyou, *s.m.* (*bird*) jabiru
Toxicité, *s.f.* poisonousness
Toxicodendron, *s.m.* (*bot.*) toxicodendron
Toxicolog-ie, -ique, -iquement, -iste. *V.* page 3, § 1
Toxicologue, *s.m.* toxicologist
Toxique, *s.m.* poison; — *adj.* poisonous
Traban, *s.m.* traban (*life-guardsman, in some Northern countries*)
Trabucaire, *s.m.* Spanish robber
Trabuco, *s.m. adj.* trabuco, trabuca (cigar)
Trac, *s.m.* track; trace; (*pop.*) *V.* **Venette**
Traçant, e, *adj.* (*bot., of roots*) running
Tracas, *s. m.* worry; annoyance; bother; bustle, stir; splutter; drudgery; business
Tracasser, *v.a.n.* to worry, to annoy, to trouble, to torment, to plague, to pester, to vex, to tease, to bother; to bustle, to stir; to meddle; to fidget
Tracasserie, *s.f.* cavil, bickering; chicanery; broil, quarrel; annoyance, pester; trickery
Tracassi-er, ère, *s.m.f.* caviller; troublesome body, pesterer; mischief-maker; meddler, busy-body; — *adj.* cavilling; troublesome, annoying, pestering, bothering; vexatious; mischief-making
Trace, *s.f.* trace; print; impression; footstep, step; track; sign, mark; vestige; remains; sketch, draught, outline; laying out; rut; trail; slot [beaten
Tracé, e, *part. adj.* traced, &c. (*V.* **Tracer**);
Tracé, *s.m.* outline, draught, sketch; plan; direction; laying out; (*rail.*) line. *Faire le* — *de,* to lay out
Tracelet, *s.m.* (*instr.*) tracer
Tracement, *s.m.* laying out
Tracer, *v.a.* to trace, to draw out, to draw; to sketch; to chalk out; to lay out; to set out; to mark; to make; to rule (*paper*); — *v.n.* (*of trees*) to run out, to spread about
Se —, *v.r.* to be traced *or* &c.
Traceret, *s.m.* (*instr.*) tracer
Traceu-r, se, *s.m.f.* tracer
Trachéal, e, *adj.* (*anat.*) tracheal
Trachée, *s.f.* (*of plants*) trachea, air-vessel; (*of insects*) trachea, air-tube; (*anat.*) trachea, windpipe. — **-artère,** *s.f.* (*anat.*) trachea,
Trachéen, ne, *adj.* (*zool.*) trachean [windpipe
Trachéite, *s.f.* (*med.*) tracheitis
Trachéocèle, *s.f.* (*med.*) tracheocele
Trachéotome, *s.m.* (*surg.*) tracheotomy-knife
Trachéotomie, *s.f.* (*surg.*) tracheotomy [oma
‡**Trachoma, Trachome,** *s.m.* (*med.*) trach-
Trachyptère, *s.m.* (*zool.*) dealfish
Trachyte, *s.m.* (*min.*) trachyte
Trachytique, *adj.* (*min.*) trachytic
Traçoir, *s.m.* (*instr.*) tracer
Tracquer, *v.n.* (*pop.*) to be funky, to funk, to be in a funk *or* in a stew [or girl
Tracqueu-r, se, *s.m.f.* funky fellow *or* woman
Tractarianisme, *s.m.* tractarianism
Tractarien, *s.m.* tractarian
Tractativement, *adv.* by a treaty
Tracteur, *s.m.* tractor
Tracti-f, ve, *adj.* tractive

Traction, *s.f.* traction, draught
Tractoire, *adj.* tractive, traction; — *s.f.* (*geom.*) tractory, tractrix
Tractrice, *s.f.* *V.* **Tractoire** [wort
Tradescantie, *s.f.* (*bot.*) tradescantia, spider-
Traditeur, *s.m.* traditor
Traditi-f, ve, *adj.* traditive [—, traditional
Tradition, *s.f.* tradition; (*law*) delivery. *De*
Traditional-isme, -iste. *V.* page 3, § 1
Traditionnaire, *s.m. adj.* traditionary
Traditionnel, le, *adj.* traditional
Traditionnellement, *adv.* traditionally
Traduc-teur, trice, *s.m.f.* translator, trans-
Traduction, *s.f* translation [latress
Traduire, *v.a.* to translate; to construe; to interpret; to convey; to express; to describe; to explain; to render; to turn; to convert; to resolve; to show; to manifest; to indicate; to indict; to arraign; to bring

Se —, *v.r.* to be translated *or* construed *or* &c.; to be shown, to be seen, to appear; to show *or* manifest itself; to assume the form (of); to be nothing less (than), to be *or* mean nothing else (but); to become, to turn, to be converted [describable

Traduisible, *adj.* translatable; expressible;
Trafic, *s.m.* traffic, trading, trade; (*rail.*) goods traffic
Traficant, e, *s.m.f.* trafficker, trader, dealer, merchant; — *adj.* trafficking, trading
Trafiquant, *part. pres. of* **Trafiquer**
Trafiquer, *v.n.a.* to traffic, to make a traffic (of), to trade, to deal; to sell; to negotiate

Se —, *v.r.* to be sold *or* &c. [seller; barterer

Trafiqueu-r, se, *s.m.f.* trafficker, dealer,
Tragacanthe, *s.f.* (*bot.*) tragacanth
Tragédie, *s.f.* tragedy
Tragédien, ne, *s.m.f.* tragedian
Tragi-comédie, *s.f.* tragi-comedy [comical
Tragi-comique, *adj.* tragi-comic, tragi-
Tragique, *adj.* tragic; tragical; — *s.m.* tragedy, tragic art *or* style *or* actor *or* character *or* author *or* subjects; tragical part *or* side; tragicalness; something tragical; horror
Tragiquement, *adv.* tragically [sant
Tragopan, *s.m.* (*bird*) tragopan, horned phea-
Trahir, *v.a.* to betray; to discover, to disclose, to reveal; to deceive; to abandon; to fail; to belie; to frustrate
Trahison, *s.f.* treason; treachery, treacherousness; foul dealing, foul play; perfidy; infidelity; breach of faith
Trahisseur, *s.m.* betrayer
†Traille, *s.f.* ferry-boat
Train, *s.m.* train; rate (*of going*); speed; pace; course, way; style of living, style; retinue, attendants, attendance, suite; equipage; establishment; herd, drove; (*of carriages*) skeleton, carriage; (*rail., and of boats*) train; (*of wood*) float, raft; (*artil.*) train of artillery, train, artillery; (*of a horse,* &c.) quarters; (*fam.*) bustle; noise, row, dust, shindy; (*print.*) carriage. — **-train,** *s.m.* regular course, routine, habits. — *direct,* through *or* express train. — *express,* express train. — *mixte,* mixed train. — *omnibus,* third-class train, stopping train, parliamentary train, omnibus train. — *-poste,* mail train — *de poste* (*See below*). — *d'aller,* down train. — *d'artillerie,* train of artillery. — *de derrière,* (*of a carriage*) hind-wheels, after-carriage; (*of a horse,* &c.) hind-quarters. — *de devant,* (*of a carriage*) fore-wheels, fore-carriage; (*of a horse,* &c.) fore-quarters. — *de Jean de Paris, V.* **Équipage.** — *de luxe,* special train. — *de maison,* establishment. — *de marchandises,* luggage *or* goods train. — *de marée,* tidal train. — *de plaisir,* excursion train. — *de poste,* post-haste. — *de retour,* return *or* back *or* up train. — *de transport,* carriage-truck. — *de vie,* way of living, way *or* course of life. — *de grande* or *de petite vitesse, V.* **Vitesse.** — *de voyageurs,* passenger train. *Bon* —, fast; roundly; sharply, vigorously; with a high hand; fair way. *Grand* —, great rate *or* &c.; at a great rate *or* &c., fast. *Équipages de* (or *du*) —, (*mil.*) waggon-train. *Soldats du* —, military train. *A* (or *de*) *ce* —, at this *or* that rate. *A fond de* —, at full speed. *En* —, in good *or* high spirits; enjoying oneself; mellow *or* fresh (*tipsy*); in a right mood, in a humour; disposed; disposed to work; in the act (of), busy; about it, at it; on the way (to); begun; going, working; on foot, afoot; in gear. *Tout d'un* —, all together. *Aller son* —, to go on, to get on; to be *or* keep going on; to go on o.'s own way; to have its course; to go on at the old rate *or* just the same *or* as before *or* as usual. *Mener grand* —, to drive at a great rate; to live in great style. *Mettre en* —, to put in good spirits *or* &c. (*V. En* —); to make mellow *or* fresh *or* &c.; to dispose; to dispose to work; to set going; to set to work; to start; to put in hand; to begin; to throw into gear, to gear; (*print.*) to make ready
Traînage, *s.m.* travelling in sledges, sledging, sleighing; sledges, sleighs
Traînant, e, *part. adj.* dragging, trailing, &c. (*V.* **Traîner**); languid; tiresome; drawling
Traînard, e, *s.m.f.* loiterer; straggler; laggard; — *adj.* loitering; straggling
Traînasse, *s.f.* drag-net; (*hort.*) creeping stalk, runner; (*bot.*) knot-grass; fiorin, fiorin-grass, black couch-grass
Traînasser, *v.a.* to draw out, to spin out, to delay, to protract; — *v.n.* to be dilatory, to linger, to lag behind
Traîne, *s.f.* train; sledge, sleigh; dragging, being dragged *or* drawn; drag-net; brushwood, underwood; shady lane; (*nav.*) cart. *A la* —, (*nav.*) in tow. *En* —, (*of partridges*) unfledged, that cannot fly
Traîneau, *s.m.* sledge, sleigh; truck; trammel-net, drag-net, draw-net [dunnock
Traîne-buissons, *s.m.* (*bird*) hedge-sparrow,
Traîne-charrue, *s.m.* *V.* **Motteux**
Traînée, *s.f.* train; trail; track; line; series; trammel; creeping stalk, runner; (*pop.*) street-walker, harlot, trull
Traîne-malheur, *s.m.f.* wretch [ling
Traînement, *s.m.* dragging; drawing; draw-
Traîne-potence, *s.m.f.* *V.* **Gibier** (— *de potence*)
Traîner, *v.a.n.* to drag; to draw; to trail; to track; to lug; to haul; to attract; to carry *or* bear along; to carry about *or* away; to take about; to lengthen; to protract; to delay, to put off; to drawl, to drawl out; to hang; to lag; to lie about; to linger, to languish; to be protracted; to get on slowly; to remain long; to stay behind; to straggle; to be heavy; to be in suspense *or* in abeyance; to stand over

Se —, *v.r.* to crawl, to creep; to trudge; to lag behind [series; long speech; long piece

Traînerie, *s.f.* dragging; drawling; string,
Traîneu-r, se, *s.m.f. adj.* *V.* **Traînard;** — *s.m.* sledge-driver; trammeller, poacher. — *de sabre,* trooper, swashbuckler, swaggerer,
Traire, *v.a.* to milk; to draw [hector, bully
Trait, e, *adj.* wire-drawn, wire; milked; drawn. *Or* —, gold wire
Trait, *s.m.* shaft, dart, bolt, arrow; bow-shot, shot; thunderbolt; draught; dash; stroke; touch; hit, fling, cut; stricture, reflection; act, action; piece; fact, event; trick; anecdote; incident; particular; point; passage; flash; burst; feature; lineament; line; outline; peculiarity; thought; trait; (*of harness*) trace; (*hunt.*) leash; (*of saws*) kerf; (*of scales*) turn; (*of boats*) train; (*at chess*) first move; (*Cath. rel.*) tract; (*pop.*) infidelity; (*of gold, silver*) wire. — *d'esprit,* flash of wit, witticism. — *d'union,* hyphen; (*fig.*) connecting link. *Bête de* —, beast of draught. *Au* —, (*of a drawing*)

in outline. *A longs —s*, in long draughts, deep. *D'un —, d'un seul—*, at a draught; at a stretch. *Avoir — à*, *V.* **Rapport** (*Avoir—à*). *Boire à longs —s*, to quaff, to drink deep

Traitable, *adj.* tractable, docile, manageable

Traitant, *s.m.* (*Fr. hist.*) farmer of the revenue, contractor; — *adj.m.* practising. *Médecin —*, (medical) practitioner

Traite, *s.f.* journey, stage; conveyance, transport; exportation; trading, commerce; trade with the coast of Africa; slave-trade; milking; banking; (*com.*) draft. — *des nègres*, slave-trade. *Tout d'une —*, without intermission, at a stretch [contract; bargain

Traité, *s.m.* treatise, tract; treaty; agreement;

Traitement, *s.m.* treatment; usage; salary, stipend, emoluments; (*obsolete*) entertainment; honours

Traiter, *v.a.n.* to treat; to use, to deal with; to handle; to treat of; to negotiate; to transact; to paint; to draw; to carve; to execute, to do; to entertain; to board; to buy and sell; to trade; to be in treaty; to come to terms. — *de*, to treat of, &c.; to call; to style, to address by the title of; to consider

Se —, *v.r.* to treat *or* &c. oneself *or* each other; to be o.'s own physician; to live (*well or badly*); (*things*) to be treated *or* &c. [trader

Traiteur, *s.m.* eating-house keeper; Louisiana

Traî-tre, tresse, *adj.* treacherous, traitorous, perfidious; — *s.m.f.* traitor, traitress, treacherous *or* &c. man *or* woman *or* girl *or* creature *or* person. *Pas un — mot*, not a blessed (*or* single) word, not one word. *En —*, treacherously, traitorously. *Prendre en —*, to fall upon or attack treacherously

Traîtrement, *adv.* treacherously, traitorously

Traîtreusement, *adv.* treacherously

Traîtreu-x, se, *adj.* (*old*) *V.* **Traître**

Traîtrise, *s.f.* *V.* **Trahison**

Trajane, *adj.f.* *Colonne —*, Trajan's column

Trajectoire, *s.f.* trajectory, passage, path, curve; — *adj.* trajectory

Trajet, *s.m.* passage; journey; distance, way; course, direction. *Faire le —*, to perform the passage *or* &c.; to run, to ply; to cross over

Tralala, *s.m.* (*pop.*) tol-de-rol-lol; fuss, ado; ceremony; full dress; pomp, pageantry, gaudiness; dancing party; dance, hop; assembly, party; apparatus; rattle-traps, rest of it. *Sur son —*, in o.'s best clothes, in full dress, full-dressed, dressed up, in full feather

†**Tramail,** *s.m.* trammel-net, trammel

†**Tramaillon,** *s.m.* small trammel-net

Trame, *s.f.* woof, weft; (*fig.*) course, progress, thread; plot; (*raw silk*) tram, shute

Tramer, *v.a.* *V.* **Ourdir**

Trameu-r, se, *s.m.f.* weaver

Tramontane, *s.f.* north star; north point; north; north wind, tramontane wind. *Perdre la —*, to lose sight of the north star; not to know where one is; to be put out *or* bewildered, to get confused; to be at o.'s wits' end

Tramway, *s.m.* tramway

Tranchage, *s.m.* cutting

Tranchant, e, *part. adj.* cutting, &c. (*V.* **Trancher**); trenchant; sharp; edged, edge; prominent, salient; strong; glaring; peremptory, decisive; — *s.m.* edge. *Instrument —*, sharp instrument *or* tool, edge-tool. *A deux —s*, two-edged, double-edged

Tranche, *s.f.* slice; rasher; steak; collop; (*butch., of beef*) edge-bone; (*of books, coins*) edge; (*arith.*) period. — *grasse*, (*butch., of beef*) thick flank. — *de filet*, slice of fillet; (*of beef*) fillet-steak. *Doré sur —*, gilt-edged, with gilt edges

Tranche, *s.m.f.* (*in compounds, from* **Trancher,** "to cut," &c.) thing (*m.*) *or* person (*m.f.*) that cuts *or* &c., cutter, &c. — **file,** *s.f.* (*book-bind.*) head-band. — **-gazon,** *s.m.* turf-knife, turfing-iron, breast-plough, paring-spade. — **-lard,** *s.m.* larding-knife, cook's knife, slicing-knife; (*jest.*) short broadsword, dirk. — **-montagnes,** *s.m.* swaggerer, blusterer, braggart. — **-papier,** *s.m.* paper-cutter, paper-knife

Tranchée, *s.f.* trench; ditch; drain; cutting; —**s,** *pl.* trenches, &c.; gripes, colic; pains, throes

Trancher, *v.a.n.* to cut; to cut off; to carve; to strike off; to cut short; to mark; to solve; to decide; to settle; to end, to stop; to speak out; to affect, to play, to set up for; to be glaring; to contrast strongly, to contrast; to clash. — *court*, — *net*, to cut short, to speak plainly. — *du grand*, to affect a great style, to give oneself the airs of a great man *or* of a high personage, to carry it high, to talk big. — *du grand seigneur*, to set up for a (*or* to play the) great lord, to lord it

Tranchet, *s.m.* paring-knife

Trancheur, *s.m.* cutter; carver [trencher, platter

Tranchoir, *s.m.* cutting-machine, cutter;

Tranquille, *adj.* quiet; still; tranquil, calm; at ease, easy; alone. *Sois* or *soyez —*, keep your mind easy, don't be uneasy, never fear; don't trouble yourself about that. *Restez —*, be *or* keep quiet (*or* still). *Laissez-moi —*, leave me alone; stuff! nonsense! [calmly

Tranquillement, *adv.* quietly; tranquilly,

Tranquillisation, *s.f.* tranquillization

Tranquillisé, e, *part. adj.* quieted, stilled; tranquillized; at ease, at rest [quillize

Tranquilliser, *v.a.* to quiet, to still; to tran-

Se —, *v.r.* to make oneself easy; to be tranquillized; to become quiet

Tranquilliseur, *s.m.* tranquillizer

Tranquillité, *s.f.* quiet, stillness; tranquillity, calm, peace [compromise; composition

Transaction, *s.f.* transaction; arrangement;

Transalpin, e, *adj.* transalpine

Transatlantique, *adj.* transatlantic; — *s.m.* transatlantic ship *or* boat [ing

Transbordement, *s.m.* transhipment; shift-

Transborder, *v.a.* to tranship; to shift

Transcaucasien, ne, *adj.* transcaucasian

Transcendance, *s.f.* transcendence, transcendency [cendental; unsurpassed

Transcendant, e, *adj.* transcendent; trans-

Transcendantal, e, *adj.* transcendental

Transcendantalement, *adv.* transcendentally [ism

Transcendantalisme, *s.m.* transcendental-

Transcendantaliste, *s.m.* transcendentalist

Transcontinental, e, *adj.* transcontinental

Transcripteur, *s.m.* transcriber

Transcription, *s.f.* transcription; transcript,

Transcrire, *v.a.* to transcribe; to copy [copy

Transdanubien, ne, *adj.* transdanubian

Transe, *s.f.* apprehension, anxiety, fright,

Transept, *s.m.* (*arch.*) transept [affright; pang

Transférable, *adj.* transferable

Transfèrement, *s.m.* transferment, transference, removal

Transférer, *v.a.* to transfer; to remove, to convey; to shift; to translate (*bishops*); to

Se —, *v.r.* to be transferred, &c. [postpone

Transfert, *s.m.* transfer

Transfiguration, *s.f.* transfiguration

Transfigurer, *v.a.* to transfigure

Se —, *v.r.* to be *or* become transfigured

Transformati-f, ve, *adj.* transformative

Transformation, *s.f.* transformation; conversion [to turn; to convert

Transformer, *v.a.* to transform, to change,

Se —, *v.r.* to be transformed, &c.

Transform-isme,-iste. *V.* page 3, § 1 [rat

Transfuge, *s.m.* fugitive; deserter; turncoat,

Transfuser, *v.a.* to transfuse

Transfuseur, *s.m.* transfuser

Transfusion, *s.f.* transfusion

Transgangétique, *adj.* transgangetic

Transgresser, *v.a.* to transgress, to break, to infringe

Transgresseur, *s.m.* transgressor
Transgressi-f, ve, *adj.* transgressive
Transgression, *s.f.* transgression, violation
Transhumance, *s.f.* grazing in summer on the mountains [mer on the mountains
Transhumer, *v.a.n.* to graze *or* feed in sum-
Transi, e, *part. adj.* chilled, &c. (*V.* **Transir**). *Amoureux* —, bashful lover
Transiger, *v.n.* to compound, to come to terms *or* to an agreement; — *v.a.* to transact
Transir, *v.a.* to chill, to benumb (*with cold*); to overcome, to paralyze; — *v.n.* to be chilled *or* benumbed; to shiver, to tremble, to quake; to be overcome *or* paralyzed
Transissement, *s.m.* chillness, chill; numbness; shivering, trembling; great anxiety
Transit, *s.m.* (*com.*) transit [sender in transit
Transitaire, *adj.* (*com.*) of transit; — *s.m.*
Transiter, *v.a.n.* **Se** —, *v.r.* (*com.*) to pass in
Transiti-f, ve, *adj.* transitive [transit
Transition, *s.f.* transition
Transitivement, *adv.* transitively
Transitoire, *adj.* transitory. transient
Transitoirement, *adv.* transitorily [passage
Transitu (In), *adv.* (*Latin*) in transitu, on the
Translater, *v.a.* (*old*) to translate [**teur**
Transla-teur, trice, *s.m.f.* (*old*) *V.* **Traduc-**
Translati-f, ve, *adj.* translatory, transferring. *Acte — de propriété*, conveyance
Translation, *s.f.* translation; conveyance; removal; shifting; (*of bishops*) translation; (*of festivals*) postponement; (*law*) transfer
Transleithan, e, *adj.* transleithan (*beyond the Leitha river*)
Translucide, *adj.* translucid, translucent
Translucidité, *s.f.* translucidity, translucency
Transmarin, e, *adj.* transmarine
Transmetteur, *s.m.* (*in electric telegraphs*) transmitting key
Transmettre, *v.a.* to transmit; to convey; to forward; to transfer; to hand down
Se —, *v.r.* to be transmitted, &c.
Transmigrant, e, *adj. s.* transmigrant
Transmigration, *s.f.* transmigration
Transmigrer, *v.n.* to transmigrate
Transmissibilité, *s.f.* transmissibility [able
Transmissible, *adj.* transmissible; transfer-
Transmission, *s.f.* transmission; (*com.*) trans-
Transmontain, e, *adj.* transmontane [fer
Transmuable, *adj.* transmutable
Transmuer, *v.a.* to transmute [mutableness
Transmutabilité, *s.f.* transmutability, trans-
Transmutateur, *s.m.* transmuter
Transmutation, *s.f.* transmutation
Transocéanien, ne, Transocéanique, *adj.* transoceanic
Transpacifique, *adj.* transpacific
Transpadan, e, *adj.* transpadane [parent
Transparaître, *v.n.* to transpare, to be trans-
Transparence, *s.f.* transparency
Transparent, e, *adj.* transparent; — *s.m.* black lines, lines; transparent paper; transparency [to run through; to shoot through
Transpercer, *v.a.* to pierce through, to pierce;
Transpirabilité, *s.f.* perspirability; transpirability
Transpirable, *adj.* perspirable; transpirable
Transpiration, *s.f.* perspiration; transpiration
Transpirer, *v.n.* to perspire; to transpire, to
Transplantable, *adj.* transplantable [ooze out
Transplantation, *s. f.*, **Transplantement,** *s.m.* transplantation, transplanting
Transplanter, *v.a.* to transplant. *Se* —, to be transplanted [**toir,** *s.m.* (*thing*) transplanter
Transplanteur, *s.m.* (*pers.*), **Transplan-**
Transpontin, e, *adj.* transpontine
Transport, *s.m.* transport; removal; conveyance; carriage; traffic; attendance; rapture; ecstacy; fit; delirium, light-headedness; (*law*) transfer; (*mil.*) waggon, ammunition waggon, baggage waggon; (*nav.*) transport, transport-ship, storeship. — *au cerveau*, delirium, light-headedness. *Commerce de* —, carrying-trade. *Frais de* —, carriage. *Vaisseau* (*de*) —, transport-ship, troop-ship, storeship
Transportable, *adj.* transportable
Transportation, *s.f.* transportation
Transporté, e, *part. adj.* transported, &c. (*V.* **Transporter**); — *s.m.* transported convict, transport
Transporter, *v.a.* to transport; to remove; to carry; to convey; to transfer; to enrapture
Se —, *v.r.* to transport oneself; to repair, to go
Transporteur, *s.m.* carrier
Transposable, *adj.* transposable [transposed
Transposer, *v.a.* to transpose. *Se* —, to be
Transpositeur, *adj. m.*, *s.m.* transposing; transposer
Transpositi-f, ve, *adj.* transpositive
Transposition, *s.f.* transposition; transposal
Transpyrénéen, ne, *adj.* transpyreneau
Transrhénan, e, *adj.* transrhenane
***Transséquanien, ne,** *adj.* transsequanian (*beyond the Seine*) [tor
Transsubstantiateur, *s.m.* transubstantia-
Transsubstantiation, *s.f.* transubstantiation
Transsubstantier, *v.a.* to transubstantiate
Transsudation, *s.f.* transudation
Transsuder, *v.n.a.* to transude
Transvasation, *s.f.*, **Transvasement,** *s.m.* decantation, decanting
Transvaser, *v.a.* to decant; to pour off *or* out
Transvaseur, *s.m.* decanter [cross
Transversal, e, *adj.* transversal, transverse,
Transversalement, *adv.* transversally, trans-
Transverse, *adj.* transverse [versely, crosswise
Transvider, *v.a.* to empty (*by decanting*)
Transylvain, e, Transylvanien, ne, *adj.s.* Transylvanian
Trantran, *s.m.* *V.* **Train-train**
Trape, *s.f.* (*bot.*) water-caltrop
Trapèze, *s.m.* (*geom.*) trapezoid; (*anat.*) (*adject.*, *Os* —) trapezium, trapezium bone; (*adject.*, *Muscle* —) trapezius muscle, trapezius; (*in gymnastics*) trapeze
Trapézien, ne, *adj.* trapezian
Trapéziforme, *adj.* trapezoidal
Trapéziste, *s.m.f.* trapezist (*acrobat*)
Trapézoïde, *s.m.* (*geom.*) trapezium; (*anat.*) (*adject.*, *Os* —) trapezoidal bone
Trapp, *s.m.* (*geol.*, *min.*) trap. — **-tuf,** *s.m.* trap-tuff, trap-tufa [Trappe (*rel. order, convent*)
Trappe, *s.f.* trap-door; drop; pit-fall; trap;
Trappéen, ne, *adj.* (*min.*) trappean, trappous,
Trappeur, *s.m.* trapper [trappy
†**Trappillon,** *s.m.* (*theat.*) trap-door
Trappiste, *s.m. adj.* trappist
Trappistine, *s.f.* trappistine (*nun, liquor*)
Trappon, *s.m.* trap-door (*over a cellar*)
Trapu, e, *adj.* dumpy, stumpy, stubby, thick-set, squat
Traque, *s.f.* (*hunt.*) beating; enclosing
Traquenard, *s.m.* trap; (*rid.*) racking-pace
Traquer, *v.a.* to beat (*a wood, &c.*); to enclose, to surround, to hem in, to catch [(*bird*) chat
Traquet, *s.m.* trap, snare; (*of mills*) clapper;
Traqueur, *s.m.* (*hunt.*) beater up
Trass, *s.m.* (*min.*) trass
Traumaticine, *s.f.* traumaticine [page 3, § 1
Traumat-ique, -iquement, -isme. *V.*
Travade, *s.f.* (*nav.*) whirlwind, tornado
†**Travail,** *s.m.* labour; toil; pains; trouble; work; working; process; piece of work; workmanship; execution; industry; study; employment; accounts, report, transacting business, business; transaction; travail; (*of farriers*) brake, trave. *Travaux forcés*, (*m. pl.*) penal servitude (*for a minimum term of* 5 *years, in France*)
†**Travaillé, e,** *part. adj.* worked, wrought, laboured, &c. (*V.* **Travailler**); elaborate; well-done; overworked; labouring (under), tormented (by), suffering (from); a prey (to); distracted. — *à jour*, open-worked

†**Travailler,** *v.n.a.* to work; to work at *or* upon; to work up; to be at work; to labour; to toil; to be industrious; to be occupied; to study; to endeavour; to ferment; to warp; to chink; to be invested; to trouble, to disturb; to harass; to beset, to dun; to torment; to distract; to excite; to canvass; to exercise; to overwork, to fatigue; to polish; to sophisticate; to manufacture; to till, to plough; (*cook.*) to stir; (*fam.*) to belabour

Se —, *v.r.* to fret, to work oneself up, to torment oneself; to excite *or* work up (o.'s ...); to endeavour, to study; to torment each other; to be worked, &c.

†**Travailleu-r, se,** *s.m.f.* worker; toiler; labourer; workman, working-man; operative, mechanic, artisan; workwoman; industrious man *or* boy *or* woman *or* girl, hard-working man *or* boy *or* woman *or* girl; pioneer; — *adj.* working; industrious, laborious

Travée, *s.f.* (*arch., tech.*) bay; space, interval; scaffold, trimmer, truss; (*of churches*) triforium

Travers, *s.m.* breadth; (*of a ship*) side; (*in buildings, grounds,* &c.) irregularity; (*fig.*) eccentricity, oddity, whimsicalness; whim, caprice, fancy; fault, defect; bad habits. *A* —, across, athwart; through. *Au* — *de,* through. *De* —, crooked; wry; awry; squinting; cross; wrong; the wrong way; astray; amiss. *En* — across; crosswise; transverse. *Par le* —, across; abreast; off, athwart; midships, amidships. *Avoir l'esprit de* —, to be wrong-headed. *Regarder quelqu'un de* —, to look cross *or* black at anyone

Traverse, *s.f.* traverse; cross-bar; cross-beam, cross-piece, girder; sleeper; cross-road, cross-way, cross-path, cross-cut, cut, cutting, short cut; cross, cross accident. *Chemin de* —, cross-road, cross-way, cross-path, cross-cut, cut, cutting, short cut. *Rue de* —, cross-street; cutting, cut, short cut. *A la* —, in the way, across, untowardly. *De* —, (*adject.*) cross

Traversée, *s.f.* passage, voyage; crossing

Traverser, *v.a.n.* to traverse; to cross; to cross *or* pass over; to go *or* pass *or* run through; to pierce through; to go *or* lie across; to thwart; to agitate, to trouble; (*nav.*) to bring the broadside of. *Faire* —, to get *or* bring *or* send through; to bring *or* get over

Se —, *v.r.* to thwart *or* cross each other; to be traversed *or* crossed *or* &c.; (*rid.*) to traverse; (*nav.*) to turn its broadside

Traversi-er, ère, *adj.* cross, crossing; plying across; favourable for crossing. *Barque* — *e,* passage-boat. *Flûte* — *e,* German flute. *Rue* — *e,* cross-street

Traversin, *s.m.* bolster; (*carp.*) cross-beam, cross-piece, transom; (*of boats*) stretcher

Traversine, *s.f.* cross-beam *or* board; sleeper

Travertin, *s.m.* (*min.*) travertin, travertine

Travestir, *v.a.* to disguise; to misinterpret; to misrepresent; to travesty. *Un travesti,* (*theat.*) a man's part played by a woman

Travestissement, *s.m.* disguise; travesty

Travestisseur, *s.m.* travestier

Trayeu-r, se, *s.m.f.* milker

Trayon, *s.m.* teat, dug, nipple

Trébac, *s.m.* trebac (*Venetian ship*)

Trébuchage, *s.m.* (*coin.*) sorting

Trébuchant, e, *adj.* stumbling; of weight, of full weight, full weight; — *s.m.* full weight

Trébuchement, *s.m.* stumbling; fall; blunder

Trébucher, *v.n.* to stumble; to trip; to err; to fall; to turn down; to weigh down

Trébuchet, *s.m.* bird-trap, trap; assay-scales; [(*old*) trebuchet

Tredame, *int.* (*old*) zounds!

Tréfiler, *v.a.* to wire-draw

Tréfilerie, *s.f.* wire-drawing; wire-mill; wire-drawing machine, draw-bench

Tréfileur, *s.m.* wire-drawer

Trèfle, *s.m.* (*bot.*) trefoil, clover; shamrock; (*at cards*) clubs; (*arch., her.*) trefoil. — *jaune,* black medick, black nonsuch. — *d'eau,* marsh-trefoil, buck-bean

Tréflé, e, *adj.* trefoiled, trefoil; (*her.*) bottony

Tréflière, *s.f.* clover-field

Tréfoncier, *s.m.* owner of the soil and subsoil; — *m.,* **-ière,** *f., adj.* of the soil and subsoil

Tréfonds, *s.m.* (*law*) subsoil; (*fig.*) bottom. *Savoir le fonds et le* — *de,* to be thoroughly acquainted with, to know all about, to know the ins and outs of

Tréhala, *s.m.* trehala, Turkish manna

Tréhalose, *s.f.* (*chem.*) trehalose

†**Treillage,** *s.m.* lattice, lattice-work, trellis; treillage; grating; railing

†**Treillager,** *v.a.* to lattice, to trellis; to grate; [to rail

†**Treillageur,** *s.m.* lattice-maker, trellis-maker

†**Treille,** *s.f.* vine-arbour; vine; (*fish.*) shrimp-net. *Le jus de la* —, the juice of the grape, wine

†**Treillé, e,** *adj.* (*her.*) latticed

†**Treillis,** *s.m.* lattice, lattice-work, trellis; grating; sack-cloth; glazed calico

†**Treillisser,** *v.a.* to lattice, to trellis; to grate

Treizaine, *s.f.* thirteen; long dozen, baker's dozen

Treize, *adj. m.f., s.m.* thirteen; thirteenth. — *à la douzaine,* thirteen for twelve, a long dozen, a baker's dozen

Treizième, *adj. m.f., s.m.* thirteenth; thirteenth part; — *s.f.* (*mus.*), *s.m.f.* (*pers.*) thirteenth

Treizièmement, *adv.* thirteenthly

Trélingage, *s.m.* (*nav.*) cat-harpings

Trélinguer, *v.a.* (*nav.*) to surround

Tréma, *s.m.* (*gram.*) diæresis; — *adj.* with a [diæresis

†**Trémail,** *s.m. V.* **Tramail**

Trémat, *s.m.* sand-bank

Trémater, *v.a.* (*navig.*) to clear; to outrun, to [outstrip

Trématisé, e, *adj.* (*gram.*) marked with a diæresis

Trématode, *s.m.* (*zool.*) trematode worm, fluke

Tremblaie, *s.f.* aspen-grove, aspen-plantation

Tremble, *s.m.* trembling; (*bot.*) aspen, aspen-tree, tremulous *or* trembling poplar

Tremblé, e, *adj.* (*of lines*) waved; (*of writing*) of a trembling *or* shaking hand; (*mus.*) tremulous; — *s.m.* (*print.*) waved rule; — *s.f.* (*vet.*) thwarter

Tremblement, *s.m.* trembling; tremor; trepidation; shaking, shake; quaking, quake; shivering, shiver; fluttering, flutter; quaver; (*pop.*) rest of it, rattle-traps; battle. — *de terre,* earthquake

Trembler, *v.n.* to tremble; to shake; to quake; to shiver; to shudder; to flutter; to quaver; to totter

Trembleu-r, se, *s.m.f.* trembler; quaker

Tremblotement, *s.m.* shivering; quivering; fluttering; flickering; shaking; trembling

Trembloter, *v.n.* to shiver; to quiver; to flutter; to flicker; to shake; to tremble

Tremelle, *s.f.* (*bot.*) tremella

Trémie, *s.f.* mill-hopper, hopper

Trémière, *adj. f.* (*bot.*) *Rose* —, hollyhock, rose-[mallow

Trémolite, *s.f.* (*min.*) tremolite

Tremolo, *s.m.* (*mus., fig.*) tremolo

Trémoussement, *s. m.* fluttering, flutter; flickering; frisking; joggling; hitching

Trémousser, *v.a.* to stir, to bestir, to shake; — *v.n.,* **Se** —, *v.r.* to flutter; to flicker; to frisk; to joggle; to hitch; to bestir oneself

Trémoussoir, *s.m.* swing; riding-chair

Trempage, *s.m.* steeping; soaking; (*print.*) wetting

Trempe, *s.f.* steeping; tempering, temper; wetting; character, stamp, cast; constitution; whacking [ducking; drubbing, whacking

Trempée, *s.f.* steeping; soaking; drenching;

Tremper, *v.a.n.* to steep; to dip; to soak; to drench; to temper; to wet; to wet through; to imbrue; to dilute; to be immersed; to participate, to have a hand (in); to be a party (to), to take part (in), to be concerned (in). — *la soupe,* to put the bread in the soup

Se —, *v.r.* to steep *or* &c. oneself; to be steeped *or* &c.; to become tempered *or* hardened

Tremperie, *s.f.* wetting-room; sink
Trempette, *s.f.* sippet; (*pop.*) shower, rain. *Faire la* —, to soak bread in wine
Trempeur, *s.m.* temperer; wetter
Tremplin, *s.m.* springing-board [trenis,trenisse
Trénis, Trénisse, *s.f.* (*figure in dancing*)
Trentaine, *s.f.* thirty or so, about thirty, some thirty, thirty; age of thirty; thirtieth year
Trente, *adj. m.f., s.m.* thirty; thirtieth. — *et quarante* (*s.m.*), trente et quarante (*game at cards*). — *-et -un, adj. s.m.* thirty-one; thirty-first; trente-et-un (*game at cards*). *Sur son — -et -un, sur son — -six,* in full feather
Trentenaire, *adj.* of thirty years
Trentième, *adj. s.* thirtieth
Tréou, *s.m.* (*nav.*) lug-sail [trephining
Trépan, *s.m.* (*surg.*) trepan, trephine; trepanning,
Trépanation, *s.f.* (*surg.*) trepanning, trephining
Trépaner, *v.a.* (*surg.*) to trepan, to trephine
Trépang, *s.m.* (*zool.*) trepang
Trépas, *s.m.* death, decease [dead; ditto person
Trépassé, e, *part. adj. s.* deceased, departed,
Trépassement, *s.m.* death, decease
Trépasser, *v.n.* to die, to depart this life
Tréphine, *s.f.* (*surg.*) trephine
Trépidation, *s.f.* trepidation
Trépied, *s.m.* trivet; tripod
†**Trépignement,** *s.m.* stamping
†**Trépigner,** *v.n.* to stamp, to stamp o.'s feet
Trépointe, *s.f.* (*tech.*) welt
Très, *adv.* very; very much; much; most; quite; widely; deeply; greatly; great; right. — **-fonds,** *s.m. V.* **Tréfonds.** — **-Haut (Le),** *s.m.* the Most High (*God*)
Trésor, *s.m.* treasure; thesaurus; treasury; exchequer; darling. *Bon du* —, Exchequer bill
Trésorerie, *s.f.* treasury
Trésori-er, ère, *s.m.f.* treasurer; pay-master
Tressage, *s.m.* weaving, &c. (*V.* **Tresser**)
†**Tressaillé, e,** *adj.* cracked, chinked, chipped
†**Tressaillement,** *s.m.* start, starting, startle; thrill; quake; flutter, fluttering; trembling, trepidation; strain, displacement, disturbance
†**Tressailli, e,** *part.* started, &c. (*V.* **Tressaillir**); — *adj.* strained, displaced, disturbed
†**Tressaillir,** *v.n.* to start, to startle; to leap; to thrill; to quake; to tremble; to flutter; to be agitated. *Faire* —, to make (...) start *or* &c., to startle (...); to thrill (...); to agitate
†**Tressaillure,** *s.f.* cracking, chinking, chipping; cracks, chinks, chips
Tressaut, *s.m. V.* **Tressaillement**
Tressauter, *v.n. V.* **Tressaillir**
Tresse, *s.f.* tress; plat; plait; braid; (*carp.*) twist; (*of old rope, nav.*) fox
Tresser, *v.a.* to tress; to weave; to plat; to plait; to braid; to twist; to wreathe; to wattle
Se —, *v.r.* to be tressed, &c.
Tresseu-r, se, *s.m.f.* platter, plaiter; braider
Trest, *s.m.* sail-cloth
Tréteau, *s.m.* (— **x,** *pl.*) trestle, tressel; trestles; (*of a mountebank*) boards, stage, platform. — *de meule,* (*agr.*) stack-stand. *Monter sur les — x,* to tread the boards, to go on the stage, to be a mountebank, to act in shows; to make a mountebank of oneself, to play the quack
†**Treuil** *s.m.* windlass; winch; crane; lift;
†**Treuilles,** *s.f. pl.* herring-guts [wheel and axle
Treuver, *v.a.* (*obsolete and poetical for* **Trouver**)
Trève, *s.f.* truce; enough, no more, stop, away with, let us have no (...)
Trévire, *s.f.* (*nav.*) parbuckle
Trévirer, *v.a.* (*nav.*) to parbuckle
Trézalé, e, *adj. V.* **Tressaillé** [to chink, to chip
Trézaler *or* †**Trézailler (Se),** *v.r.* to crack,
Tri, *s.m. V.* **Triage;** (*game at cards*) tri; (*at whist*) trick; (*in compounds*) tri ...
Triable, *adj.* sortable
Triade, *s.f.* triad [selection
Triage, *s.m.* sorting; picking, choosing; choice,
Triangle, *s.m.* triangle; trivet; — *adj.* triangular
Triangulaire, *adj.* triangular
Triangulairement, *adv.* triangularly

Triangularité, *s.f.* triangularity
Triangulation, *s.f.* triangulation
Triangulé, e, *part. adj.* triangulated; triangled
Trianguler, *v.a.* to triangulate
Trianon, *s.m.* (*arch.*) pavilion
Triarchie, *s.f.* triarchy
Trias, *s.m.* (*geol.*) trias
Triasique, *adj.* (*geol.*) triassic
Tribal, e, *adj.* tribal, tribular
Tribart, *s.m.* clog; yoke
Tribasique, *adj.* (*chem.*) tribasic
Tribomètre, *s.m.* tribometer
Tribord, *s.m.* (*nav.*) starboard
Tribordais, *s.m.* (*nav.*) starboard watch
†**Tribouil,** *s.m.* (*old, pop.*) agitation, turmoil, bustle, fuss, ado
†**Tribouiller,** *v.n.* (*old, pop.*) to be agitated, to be in agitation, to bustle; to start, to leap
Triboulet, *s.m.* fool, jester, buffoon; guy; (*tech.*)
Tribraque, *s.m.* (*vers.*) tribrach [triblet,tribolet
Tribu, *s.f.* tribe; caste; clan
Tribulation, *s.f.* tribulation
Tribule, *s.m.* (*bot.*) caltrop
Tribun, *s.m.* (*pers.*) tribune
Tribunal, *s.m.* tribunal; seat; bench; court of judicature, court of justice, court
Tribunat, *s.m.* tribunate; tribuneship
Tribune, *s.f.* tribune; pulpit; gallery; race-stand, stand; platform; hustings; loft; (*fig.*) parliament; debating; (*Rom. hist.*) rostrum, rostra. — *aux harangues,* rostrum, rostra. — *d'orgues,* organ-loft. *De la* —, (*polit.*) parliamentary [tribunary
Tribunitien, ne, *adj.* tribunitian, tribunitial;
Tribut, *s.m.* tribute; retribution; tax; duty; debt
Tributaire, *adj. s.m.f.* tributary
Tric, *s.m.* (*at whist*) trick
Tricennal, e, *adj.* tricennial
Triceps, *adj. s.m.* (*anat.*) triceps
Tricher, *v.a.n.* to cheat, to trick, to use foul play
Tricherie, *s.f.* cheating, trickery; trick [cheating
Tricheu-r, se, *s.m.f.* cheat, trickster; — *adj.*
‡**Trichiasis,** *s.m.* (*med.*) trichiasis
‡**Trichinal, e,** *adj.* trichinal
‡**Trichine,** *s.f.* (*zool.*) trichina [chinated
‡**Trichiné, e,** *adj.* infested with trichina, tri-
‡**Trichineu-x, se,** *adj.* trichinous
‡**Trichinose,** *s.f.* (*med.*) trichiniasis, trichinosis
‡**Trichiure,** *s.m.* (*fish*) trichiurus, hair-tail
Triclinium, *s.m.* (*Rom. antiq.*) triclinium
Tricoises, *s.f. pl.* (*tech.*) pincers
Tricolor, *s.m.* (*bot.*) tricoloured amaranth
Tricolore, *adj.* tricoloured; three-coloured
Tricorde, *s.m adj.* trichord
Tricorne, *adj.* tricorn, three-horned; three-cornered; — *s.m.* three-cornered hat, shovel hat
Tricot, *s.m.* network, knitting; cudgel, stick,
Tricotage, *s.m.* knitting; weaving [bludgeon
Tricoter, *v.a.n.* to knit; to weave; (*pop.*) to cudgel, to belabour; to dance; to run
Se —, *v.r.* to knit for oneself *or* each other; to be knitted; to cudgel each other
Tricoterie, *s.f.* knitting-manufactory
Tricoteu-r, se, *s.m.f.* knitter
Trictrac, *s.m.* tricktrack, backgammon; trick-track-board, backgammon-board
Tricuspide, *adj.* tricuspid [three-wheeler
Tricycle, *s.m.* tricycle, three-wheeled carriage,
Tridactyle, *adj. m.f., s.m.* (*zool.*) tridactyle, tridactylous [and ready
Tride, *adj.* (*rid.*) tride, quick, swift, fleet, short
Trident, *s.m.* trident; fish-gig, gig, three-pronged spear, eel-spear, spear, leister
Tridenté, e, *adj.* tridented, tridentate, tri-
Tridentin, e, *adj.* Tridentine [dentated
Tridi, *s.m.* tridi (*third day of a decade in the calendar of the first French Republic*)
Trièdre, *s.m.* trihedron; — *adj.* trihedral
Triennal, e, *adj.* triennial
Triennalité, *s.f.* trienniality, term of three years, triennial duration
Triennat, *s.m.* space of three years; triennial charge *or* office *or* probation *or* course, triennium

Trier, *v.a.* to sort; to pick out, to pick; to choose; to cull; to select
Se —, *v.r.* to be sorted, &c.
Triérarchie, *s.f.* trierarchy
Triérarque, *s.m.* trierarch
Trière, *s.f.* (*anc. nav.*) trireme
Trieu-r, se, *s.m.f.* sorter; picker; culler; — [*adj.* sorting; culling
Trifide, *adj.* (*bot.*) trifid
Triflore, *adj.* (*bot.*) triflorous, three-flowered
Trifolié, e, *adj.* (*bot.*) trifoliate, three-leaved
Trifoliolé, e, *adj.* (*bot.*) trifoliolate
Triforium, *s.m.* (*arch.*) triforium, blindstory
Triforme, *adj.* triform, triformed
†Trifouiller, *v.a.n.* *V.* **Farfouiller**
Trifurcation, *s.f.* trifurcation [furcated
Trifurquer (Se), *v.r.* to trifurcate, to be tri-
Trigame, *adj.* trigamous; — *s.m.f.* trigamist
Trigam-ie, -ique. *V.* page 3, § 1
Trigaud, e, *adj.* shuffling, sly, cunning; — [*s.m.f.* shuffler
Trigauder, *v.n.* to shuffle
Trigauderie, *s.f.* shuffling, cunning; artful trick
Trigle, *s.f.m.* (*fish*) gurnard [arrow-grass
Triglochin, *s.m.*, **Triglochine,** *s.f.* (*bot.*)
Triglotte, *adj.* triglot, in three languages
Triglyphe, *s.m.* (*arch.*) triglyph
Trigonal, e, *adj.* trigonal
Trigone, *s.m.* trigon; — *adj.* trigonal
Trigonelle, *s.f.* (*plant*) trigonella
Trigonocéphale, *adj.* trigonocephalous; — *s.m.* (*snake*) copperhead; mocassin, moccassin, mokassin [page 3, § 1
Trigonométr-ie, -ique, -iquement. *V.*
Trigyne, *adj.* (*bot.*) trigynous
Tril. *V.* **Trille** [trilateral
Trilatéral, e, *adj.*, **Trilatère,** *adj. m.f.*, *s.m.*
Trilatéralement, *adv.* trilaterally
Trilingue, *adj.* trilingual
Trilitère, *adj.* (*gram.*) triliteral
Trilithe, *s.m.* trilithon
Trilittère. *V.* **Trilitère**
†Trille, *s.m.* (*mus.*) shake, trill; shaking
†Triller, *v.a.n.* (*mus.*) to shake, to trill
†Trillie, *s.f.* (*bot.*) trillium
Trillion, *s.m.* billion
Trilobé, e, *adj.* trilobate, trilobed, three-lobed; (*arch.*) three-cusped, trefoiled
Triloculaire, *adj.* (*bot.*) trilocular
Trilog-ie, -ique. *V.* page 3 § 1 [about
Trimbaler, *v.a.* to drag *or* lug *or* carry *or* take
Se —, *v.r.* to go about, to go to and fro *or* backward and forward
Trimer, *v.n.* to run about
Trimestre, *s.m.* quarter, three months; quarter's money *or* pay *or* salary *or* rent. *Par —,* [quarterly
Trimestriel, le, *adj.* quarterly
Trimestriellement, *adv.* quarterly, every [quarter
Trimètre, *s.m. adj.* (*vers.*) trimeter
Trin, e, *adj.* trine; trinal
Trinalité, *s.f.* trinality
Tringle, *s.f.* curtain-rod; rod, rail, bar, lath; (*arch.*) tringle, reglet; (*carp.*) mark
Tringler, *v.a.* to chalk
Tringuelte, *s.m.* (*old*) *V.* **Pourboire**
Trinitaire, *s.m.f. adj.* Trinitarian
Trinité, *s.f.* Trinity; Trinity Sunday; (*geog.*) [Trinidad
Trinôme, *s.m. adj.* (*alg.*) trinomial
Trinquart, *s.m.* (*fish.*) herring-buss
Trinquer, *v.n.* to touch glasses, to hobnob, to toast; to drink, to tipple
Trinquet, *s.m.* (*nav.*) foremast
Trinquette, *s.f.* (*nav.*) storm-jib; fore stay-sail
Trinqueu-r, se, *s.m.f.* drinker, tippler
Trio, *s.m.* triplet; (*mus.*, *and fig.*) trio
Triolet, *s.m.* (*poet.*) triolet; (*mus.*) triplet
Triomphal, e, *adj.* triumphal
Triomphalement, *adv.* triumphantly
Triomphant, e, *adj.* triumphant; in triumph, triumphantly; victorious; powerful, decisive
Triompha-teur, trice, *s.m.f. adj.* triumpher; triumphant
Triomphe, *s.m.* triumph; — *s.f.* (*in games at cards*) trump; (*game at cards*) triumph. *De —,* of triumph; triumphal; triumphant. *En —,* in triumph; triumphantly
Triompher, *v.n.* to triumph (*de*, over; *en*, over it, over them); to be triumphant; to exult; to glory; to excel
Triori, *s.m.* triori (*Breton dance and tune*)
Triostée, *s.m.* (*bot.*) feverwort, Tinkar's root
†Tripaille, *s.f.* garbage
Tripan. *V.* **Trépang**
Triparti, e, Tripartite, *adj.* tripartite
Tripartible, *adj.* tripartible
Tripartition, *s.f.* tripartition
Tripe, *s.f.* tripe; bowel; (*of a cigar*) inside. — *de roche*, (*bot.*) tripe de roche. — *de velours*, imitation velvet. — **-madame,** *s.f.* *V.* **Tri-** [**que-madame**
Tripée, *s.f.* garbage
Triperie, *s.f.* tripe-market; tripe-shop; tripe-stall
Tripétale, Tripétalé, e, *adj.* (*bot.*) tripetalous
Tripette, *s.f.* small tripe; (*fig.*) straw, rap, fig
Triphane, *s.f.* (*min.*) triphane
Triphène, *s.m.* (*zool.*) surface grub; great yellow underwing moth
Triphthongue, *s.f.* (*gram.*) triphthong
Triphylle, *adj.* (*bot.*) triphyllous
Tripi-er, ère, *s.m.f.* tripe-man, tripe-woman, tripe-dresser; — *adj.m.* (*falc.*) untamable
Triple, *s.m. adj.* treble, triple; threefold; three; three times as much *or* as many; three times the quantity *or* number *or* value; triplicate
Triplement, *adv.* trebly, triply; — *s.m.* trebling, tripling, triplication; (*mil.*) forming three-deep
Tripler, *v.a.n.* to treble, to triple, to increase threefold; to triplicate; (*mil.*) to form three-deep
Se —, *v.r.* to treble, to triple, to increase threefold, to become treble *or* triple, to be trebled [*or* tripled
Triplet, *s.m.* (*backgammon*) triplet
Tripleter, *v.a.* to treble, to triple
Triplicata, *s.m.* triplicate
Triplicati-f, ve, *adj.* triplicative
Triplication, *s.f.* triplication
Triplicature, *s.f.* triplicature
Triplicité, *s.f.* triplicity
Triplique, *s.f.* triplication
Tripliquer, *v.n.* to triplicate
Triplite, *s.f.* (*min.*) triplite
Tripoléen, ne, *adj.* tripoline
Tripoli, *s.m.* tripoli, rotten stone; (*pop.*) brandy
Tripolir, *v.a.* to polish with tripoli *or* rotten- [stone
Tripolitain, e, *s.m.f. adj.* Tripolitan
Tripot, *s.m.* gambling-house, hell; (*obsolete*) bad house, house of ill fame
Tripotage, *s.m.* medley, mess, mishmash; jumble; intrigue; scandal; jobbery, jobbing; job [ing; lot
Tripotée, *s.f.* (*pop.*) drubbing, hiding, whack-
Tripoter, *v.n.a.* to make a medley *or* a mess; to dabble; to meddle; to intrigue; to slander; to job; to jumble; to huddle; to feel *or* handle about; (*pop.*) to frequent hells *or* bad houses
Tripoteu-r, se, Tripoti-er, ère, *s.m.f.* meddler; intriguer; slanderer; jobber; gambling-house keeper, hell-keeper; — *adj.* meddling; intriguing; slandering; jobbing
Tripsac, Tripsacum, *s.m.* (*bot.*) gama-grass
Triptère, *adj.* (*zool.*) tripterous, tripteral, three-winged [gian (*fish*)
Triptérygien, ne, *adj. s.m.* (*zool.*) triptery-
Triptote, *adj.m.f.*, *s.m.* (*gram.*) triptote
Triptyque, *s.m.* triptych
Trique, *s.f.* cudgel, stick, bludgeon. — **-balle,** *s.f.m.* (*artil.*) truck. — **-madame,** *s.f.* (*bot.*) white stone-crop
Triquer, *v.a.* (*pop.*) to cudgel, to belabour
Triquet, *s.m.* tennis-bat; (*tech.*) trestles
Triquetrac, *s.m.* (*obsolete*) clatter
†Trirègne, *s.m.* tiara, pope's triple crown
Trirème, *s.f.* (*anc. nav.*) trireme
Trirote, *s.f.* three-wheeled self-propelling chair
Trisacramentaire, *s.m.* (*eccl.*) trisacramentarian

Trisagion, *s.m.* (*lit.*) trisagion
Trisaïeul, e, *s.m.f.* great-great-grandfather *or* [mother
Trisannuel, le, *adj.* triennial
Trisection, &c. *V.* **Trissection,** &c.
Trisépale, *adj.* (*bot.*) trisepalous
Trisme, *s.m.* *V.* **Trismus**
Trismégiste, *adj. m.* Trismegistus; — *s.m.* (*print.*) two-line double pica
Trismus, *s.m.* (*med.*) trismus, lock-jaw
Trisoc, *s.m.* *V.* **Trissoc** [past, trispaston
Trispaste, Trispaston, *s.m.* (*mech.*) tris-
Trispermatique, Trisperme, *adj.* (*bot.*) trispermous
‡**Trisplanchnique,** *adj.* (*anat.*) trisplanchnic
Trissec-teur, trice, *adj.* trisecting
Trissection, *s.f.* trisection
Trissement, *s.m.* cry (*of the swallow*)
Trissépale, *adj.* (*bot.*) *V.* **Trisépale**
Trisséquer, *v.a.*, **Se** —, *v.r.* to trisect
Trisser, *v.n.* to cry encore twice; (*of the swallow*) to cry; — *v.a.* to encore twice [row plough
Trissoc, *s.m.* three-shared plough, treble-fur-
Trissotin, *s.m.* conceited fool; wretched author, mere scribbler
Trissyllabe, *s.m* trisyllable; — *adj.* trisyllabic
Trissyllabique, *adj.* trisyllabic
Triste, *adj.m.f., s.m.* sad; melancholy; dull; sorrowful; mournful; dreary; gloomy; dismal; rueful; unhappy; poor, sorry, mean, paltry, wretched; cloudy, overcast; melancholy *or* &c. nature *or* appearance; sadness, dulness, &c. — *comme un bonnet de nuit* (*pers.*) or *comme un enterrement* (*things*), as dull as ditch-water. *Les —s d'Ovide*, Ovid's Tristia. *Le chevalier de la — figure*, the knight of the rueful countenance (Don Quixote)
Tristement, *adv.* sadly; melancholily, with melancholy; dully; sorrowfully; mournfully; drearily; gloomily; dismally; ruefully; unhappily; poorly, sorrily, meanly, paltrily, wretchedly
Tristesse, *s.f.* sadness, melancholy; dulness; sorrowfulness; sorrow, grief; dreariness; gloominess; gloom; dismalness
Tristimanie, *s.f.* (*med.*) tristimania
Tristyle, *adj.* (*bot.*) tristylous [ret
Trisulfure, *s.m.* (*chem.*) trisulphide, trisulphu-
Triterné, e, *adj.* (*bot.*) triternate
Trithé-isme, -iste. *V.* page 3, § 1
Triton, *s.m.* (*myth.*) Triton; (*zool.*) (*mollusc*) triton; (*reptile*) newt, eft, triton; (*tech.*) diving-apparatus; (*mus.*) tritone
Tritonien, ne, *adj.* (*geol.*) tritonian
Tritoxyde, *s.m.* (*chem.*) tritoxide
Triturable, *adj.* triturable
Trituration, *s.f.* trituration
Triture, *s.f.* conversancy, knack, practice, habit
Triturer, *v.a.* to triturate, to grind, to pound, [to masticate
Triumvir, *s.m.* triumvir
Triumviral, e, *adj.* triumviral
Triumvirat, *s.m.* triumvirate
Trivalve, *adj.* (*nat. hist.*) trivalve, trivalved
Trivelin, *s.m.* (*obsolete*) ballet-dancer; merry-andrew, buffoon; (*dentist's instr.*) stump-forceps, forceps [roads meet, junction of three roads
Triviaire, *adj.* *Carrefour* —, place where three
Trivial, e, *adj.* trivial, vulgar, slangy; trite; trifling, light; — *s.m.* triviality, vulgarity; triteness
Trivialement, *adv.* trivially, vulgarly; tritely
Trivialiser, *v.a.* to trivialize, to vulgarize
Trivialité, *s.f.* triviality, vulgarity; triteness;
Trivium, *s.m.* trivium [vulgarism
Trivoie, *s.f.* junction of three roads
Troc, *s.m.* exchange, truck, barter, swap, swop
Trocart, *s.m.* (*surg.*) trocar, trochar; (*bot.*) *V.* **Troscart**
‡**Trochaïque,** *adj. s.m.* (*vers.*) trochaic
‡**Trochanter,** *s.m.* (*anat.*) trochanter [terian
‡**Trochantérien, ne,** *adj.* (*anat.*) trochan-
‡**Trochantin,** *s.m.* (*anat.*) less *or* little trochanter [nian
‡**Trochantinien, ne,** *adj.* (*anat.*) trochanti-
Troche, *s.m.* *V.* **Troque;** —**s,** *s.f.pl.* (*hunt.*) fumet
Trochée, *s.m.* (*vers.*) trochee; — *s.f.* branches (*of a seedling*) [southern pine, Georgia pitch-pine
Trochereau, *s.m.* (*bot.*) long-leaved pine,
Trochet, *s.m.* (*bot.*) cluster; (*tech.*) block. *Pin à —s*, pitch-pine [chilus, trochil
‡**Trochile,** *s.m.* (*arch.*) trochilus; (*bird*) tro-
Trochisque, *s.m.* (*pharm.*) troche; (*of colours*)
‡**Trochoïde,** *adj. s.* trochide [cake
Trochure, *s.f.* (*of deer*) troching, surantler
‡**Trochus,** *s.m.* *V.* **Troque**
Troène, *s.m.* (*bot.*) privet
Troglodyte, *s.m.* troglodyte; (*monkey*) troglodytes; (*bird*) troglodytes, kitty wren
Troglodytique, *adj.* troglodytic, -al [face
†**Trogne,** *s.f.* face, phiz; red face, drunkard's
†**Trognon,** *s.m.* core; stump, stalk; (*fam.*) dear, duck; (*pop.*) head, costard
†**Trognonner,** *v.n.* to look like a core *or* stump [*or* stalk
Trogon, *s.m.* (*bird*) trogon
Trois, *adj. m.f., s.m.* three; third. —**-étoiles,** *s.m.f.* three stars, thingumbob. —**-mâts,** *s.m.* (*nav.*) three-master. —**-pieds,** *s.m.* trivet. —**-ponts,** *s.m.* (*nav.*) three-decker. —**-quarts,** *s.m.* hare nearly full-grown, young buck-hare; (*persp.*) three-fourths, foreshortened side-face; small violin, kit; (*tech.*) triangular *or* three-cornered file; (*admin.*) fly; large cab; (*surg.*) *V.* **Trocart;** *s.m. pl.* three quarters; three fourths; (*of the hour*) three quarters, forty-five (minutes); quarter to ... (*the next hour*). —**-six,** *s.m.* spirits at 36 degrees, raw spirit, common *or* rough brandy
Troisième, *adj.* third; — *s.m.* third; third floor; pupil of the third form *or* class; — *s.f.* (—**s,** *s.f. pl.*) third; third form or class; (*theat.*) third-tier box (*pl.* third tier of boxes); (*rail.*, [&c.) third class
Troisièmement, *adv.* thirdly
Trôler, *v.a.* to lead *or* drag *or* lug about; — *v.n.* to stroll *or* traipse about, to ramble, to rove
Trolle, *s.f.* (*hunt.*) trolling; — *s.m.* wattle, plashoot; (*bot.*) globe-flower
Trombe, *s.f.* waterspout; water-blowing engine *or* machine. — *d'air* or *de vent*, tornado, hurricane
Trombine, *s.f.* (*pop.*) face, phiz; sconce, noddle
Tromblon, *s.m.* blunderbuss, swivel-gun
Trombone, *s.m.* (*mus.*) trombone; trombonist, trombone-player [player
Tromboniste, *s.m.* trombonist, trombone-
‡**Trompable,** *adj.* deceivable, deludable
Trompe, *s.f.* horn; trumpet; Jew's harp; (*of elephants, insects*) trunk, proboscis; (*arch.*) over-hanging; (*tech.*) water-blowing engine *or* machine. — *d'Eustache*, (*anat.*) Eustachian tube. — *de Fallope*, (*anat.*) Fallopian tube
Trompe, *s.m.f.* (*in compounds, from* **Tromper,** "to deceive," &c.) thing (*m.*) *or* person (*m.f.*) that deceives *or* &c., deceiver, &c. —**-la-mort,** *s.m.f.* Death's match (*patient in a desperate case who recovers, soldier fighting desperately who escapes being killed, person grown old contrary to all expectations*, &c.). —**-l'œil,** *s.m.* painting which deceives the eye, deceptive painting of still life, still life deception; (*fig.*) deception, illusion, delusion; sham
Tromper, *v.a.* to deceive; to cheat; to impose upon; to mislead; to put out; to baffle; to disappoint; to betray; to delude; to elude; to beguile; to divert. *Faire* —, to confuse, to put out, to make (...) make a mistake; to mislead. *C'est ce qui vous trompe*, there you are mistaken
Se —, *v.r.* to mistake, to make a mistake, to make mistakes, to be mistaken; to err; to deceive *or* delude oneself; to be deceived; to deceive *or* &c. each other. *Se — de* ..., to mistake the ..., to take the wrong ..., to mistake *or* miss o.'s ... *A s'y* —, enough (*or* so as) to be mistaken about it; enough (*or* so as) to take one for the other
Tromperie, *s.f.* deceit; deception; cheating; cheat; fraud; imposition; trick; illusion, delusion

Trompeter, Trompetter, *v.a.* to proclaim by sound of trumpet; to trumpet; to proclaim, to publish; to divulge; to blab out; — *v.n.* to trumpet; (*of the eagle*) to scream [buccinator
Trompeteur, Trompetteur, *s.m.* (*anat.*)
Trompette, *s.f.* trumpet; gossip, trumpeter; trumpet-shell, — *s.m.* trumpeter. — **-major,** — *s.m.* (*mil.*) trumpet-major. — *marine,* (*obsolete*) trumpet marine. *En* —, turned up. *Sans* —, (*fig.*) without noise, in silence, silently, quietly, privately. *Emboucher la* —, (*of poets*) to soar
Trompettiste, *s.m.* trumpetist, trumpeter
Trompeu-r, se, *adj. s.* deceitful; deceptive; cheating; fallacious, delusive, false; deceiver; cheat; deluder; betrayer [ly, fallaciously, falsely
Trompeusement, *adv.* deceitfully, deceptive-
Tronc, *s.m.* trunk; poor-box, box; (*of trees*) trunk, stock; (*arch.*) trunk, shaft; (*geom.*)
Troncature, *s.f.* truncation [frustum
Tronce, Tronche, *s.f.* Christmas-log, Yule-log
Tronchet, *s.m.* (*tech.*) block
Tronçon, *s.m.* stump; broken piece, fragment; piece; portion, part; (*of a tail*) dock
Tronçonnement, *s.m.* cutting into fragments *or* into pieces, cutting up *or* off
Tronçonner, *v.a.* to cut into fragments *or* into pieces, to cut up *or* off
Trondédious, *int.* (*local*) bedad! begorra!
Trône, *s.m.* throne
Trôner, *v.n.* to sit on a throne *or* in state; to sit in o.'s glory; to be a king *or* a queen; to reign; to predominate, to prevail; to be in the ascendant; to be preeminent, to excel; to lord it
Tronquement, *s.m.* truncating, &c. (*V.* **Tronquer**) [maim; to curtail; to garble
Tronquer, *v.a.* to truncate; to mutilate, to
Tronquette, *s.f.* wee girl, young lass
Trop, *adv.* too much; too much of a, too much of; too many; too long; too often; too well; too far; too; over; very much; very well; very; much; exactly; hardly; — *s.m.* excess; exuberance; superfluity. — *peu,* too little; too few; not enough. — *plein,* too full; (*s.m.*) overflow; surplus water; surplus, overplus, waste; fulness; (*Tuyau de — -plein,* waste-pipe). *De* —, too much; too many; over; not wanted; superfluous; better away than present; intruding; in the way. *Par* —, too; too much; over. *Je ne sais* (*pas*) —, I hardly know; I am not quite sure. — *est* —, *rien de* —, enough is as good as a feast
Trope, *s.m.* (*rhet.*) trope
Trophée, *s.m.* trophy. *Faire — de,* to glory in
Troph-ique,ologie,-ologique,-opathie. [*V.* page 3, § 1
Tropical, e, *adj.* tropical
Tropique, *s.m.* tropic; — *adj.* tropical
Tropolog-ie, -ique. *V.* page 3, § 1
Troque, *s.m.* (*mollusc*) trochus, top-shell
Troquer, *v.a.* to exchange, to truck, to barter, [to swap, to swop
Troqueu-r,se, *s.m.f.* barterer
Troscart, *s.m.* (*bot.*) arrow-grass
Trot, *s.m.* trot. *Grand* —, full trot. *Petit* —, jog-trot, gentle *or* easy trot. *Aller au* —, to trot. *Aller au grand* —, to ride full trot. *Mettre au* —, to bring to a trot
Trotte, *s.f.* distance, way, run, walk, step
Trotte-menu, *adj.* slow-trotting
Trotter, *v.n.* to trot; to walk a great deal; to run about, to run, to take a run; to toddle; to bustle; (*things*) to run (*in o.'s head*)
Trotteu-r, se, *s.m.f.* trotter; — *adj.* trotting
Trottin, *s.m.* errand-boy *or* girl; (*pop.*) foot, trotter [to trot *or* jog along; to toddle
Trottiner, *v.n.* to go a jog-trot; (*pers.*) to trot,
Trottoir, *s.m.* foot-way, foot-path, side-walk, pavement, flag-way. *Faire le* —, to walk the streets
Trou, *s.m.* hole; gap; orifice; cavity; mouth (*of a bottle,* &c.); eye (*of a needle*); hiding-place. — *de la serrure,* key-hole. *Boucher un* —, to stop a hole *or* a gap; to pay a debt; to make up for a loss. — **-de-loup,** *s.m.* (*fort.*) trou-de-loup, wolf-hole. — **d'homme,** (*tech.*) man-hole. — **-madame,** *s.m.* (*game*) pigeon-holes
Troubadour, *s.m.* troubadour, southern bard
Trouble, *adj.* troubled; turbid; not clear; muddy, thick; foul; dim; dull; obscure; confused; cloudy, overcast; hazy; foggy; (*adverb.*) confusedly, dimly; — *s.m.* disturbance; tumult, agitation, confusion; trouble; uneasiness; dissension; turmoil; alteration; —**s,** *pl.* disturbances, troubles, &c., disorder, commotion; — *s.f.* (*fish.*) hoop-net
Trouble, *s.m.f.* (*in compounds, from* **Troubler,** "to disturb," &c.) thing (*m.*) *or* person (*m.f.*) that disturbs *or* &c., disturber, &c. — **-fête,** (*pers.*) *s.m.f.,* (*things*) *s.m.* trouble-feast, disturber of people's pleasure, quarrelsome *or* troublesome guest, mar-joy, damper, wet blanket, untoward incident. — **-ménage,** *s.m.* disturber of married people's happiness
Troublé, e, *part. adj.* disturbed, &c. (*V.* **Troubler**); confused, put out, abashed, bashful,
Troubleau, *s.m.* (*fish.*) hoop-net [nervous
Troublement, *s.m.* disturbing, disturbance; troubling; confusing, confusion
Troubler, *v.a.* to disturb; to agitate; to make thick *or* muddy, to thicken, to muddle; to trouble; to disquiet; to disorder; to ruffle; to distract; to annoy; to confuse; to put out; to discompose; to disconcert; to confound; to flurry, to unsettle; to dim; to dull

Se —, *v.r.* to get thick *or* muddy; to be *or* become *or* get disturbed *or* agitated; to turn, to be *or* get giddy; to become *or* be confused *or* disconcerted *or* confounded; to get muddled; to falter; to get nervous; to become *or* be intimidated; to become *or* be uneasy; to become *or* grow dim; to get cloudy *or* overcast *or* foggy
Troubleu-r, se, *s.m.f.* disturber, troubler; — *adj.* disturbing, troubling
Troué, e, *part. adj.* holed, pierced, bored, full of holes, with holes *or* with a hole in, out (*at elbows,* &c.), torn
Trouée, *s.f.* opening; gap; pass
Trouer, *v.a.* to make *or* bore holes *or* a hole in, to hole, to pierce, to bore, to perforate; to break

Se —, *v.r.* to have holes *or* a hole
†**Troufignon,** *s.m.* (*pop.*) bum
†**Trouille,** *s.f.* (*Pain de* —) oil-cake; walnut-cake; (*pop.*) dowdy, mopsey
Troupe, *s.f.* troop; band; company; party; gang, set, crew; flock, herd; shoal; bevy; multitude, crowd, number; force; soldiery, soldiers; troupe. *Mauvaise* —, (*pop.*) bad lot; bad fellow *or* creature, rogue, vagabond
Troupeau, *s.m.* flock; herd; drove
Troupiale, *s.m.* (*bird*) troopial, troop-bird
Troupier, *s.m.* soldier
Trousse, *s.f.* truss; bundle; quiver; case (*travelling-case, dressing-case, razor-case, case of surgical instruments,* &c.); —**s,** *pl.* trusses, &c.; breeches. *Aux —s de,* in pursuit of; at ...'s heels
Troussé, e, *part. adj.* tucked up, &c. (*V.* **Trousser**). *Bien* —, neat; nice; well-made; well-shaped; well-set; well-turned; well-got-up; well-dressed; dapper
Trousseau, *s.m.* bunch (*of keys*); outfit; bride's outfit, wedding-outfit; trousseau
Trousse-queue, *s.m.* *V.* **Culeron**
Troussequin, *s.m.* (*of a saddle*) cantle; (*tech.*) beam-compass
Trousser, *v.a.* to tuck up; to turn up; to tie up; to pin up; to bundle up, to pack up; to get up; to truss; to carry off; to despatch. — *bagage, V.* **Bagage.** — *ses guenilles,* to be off, to cut it, to hook it [tucked up *or* &c.

Se —, *v.r.* to tuck up o.'s clothes; to be
Troussis, *s.m.* tucking-in, tuck
Trouvable, *adj.* to be found, discoverable
†**Trouvaille,** *s.f.* thing found; godsend; prize; discovery, finding; hit, lucky hit; conception; invention; treasure-trove
Trouvé, e, *part. adj.* found, &c. (*V.* **Trouver**);

(*of words*, &c.) happy; lucky; ingenious; just. *Mot bien* —, happy word

Trouver, *v.a.n.* to find; to find out, to discover; to get; to muster; to have; to meet; to join; to catch; to meet with; to hit upon; to come across; to raise; to like; to think; to deem; to think it, to deem it; to think (...) to be, to think that (...) is; to contrive; to manage; to remember, can remember. *Aller* —, to go to; to go to (*or* and) see; to call *or* wait upon; to visit; to go and meet; to meet, to catch; to join. *Venir* —, to come to; to come to (*or* and) see; to call *or* wait upon; to visit; to come and meet; to join. — *à redire* or *à dire*. *V.* **Redire** *&* **Dire.** — *beau*, to think beautiful, to admire. — *bien*, to like. — *bon*, to like; to think *or* deem good; to think *or* deem proper *or* fit; to approve; to allow; to be pleased *or* glad. — *mal*, to find amiss; to find fault with. — *mauvais*, to dislike; to think *or* deem bad; to disapprove; to blame; to take (it) amiss *or* ill; to be displeased *or* vexed

Se —, *v.r.* to find oneself *or* each other; to meet each other; to be; to be present; to lie; to sit; to stand; to feel oneself; to think oneself; to think one has; to be found, to prove; to happen to be; to happen; to chance; to turn out; to appear; to fare; to come. *Se — avec*, to meet. *Se — bien*, to derive benefit (from), to benefit (by); to feel *or* be comfortable *or* well; to be the better (for); to find (...) to o.'s advantage. *Se — mal*, to faint, to faint away, to swoon; to feel *or* be uncomfortable *or* unwell; to be taken ill; to fare ill; to suffer (from); to be the worse (for). *Il se trouve*, there is *or* are; it happens, it turns out; we find. *Cela se trouve bien*, that is lucky; that will just do

Trouvère, *s.m.* trouvère, northern bard

Trouveu-r, se, *s.m.f.* (*pers.*) finder; — *s.m.* (*astr.*) finder (*glass*); (*poet.*) *V.* **Trouvère;** — *adj.* (*hunt.*) retrieving [Trouville

Trouvillais, e, *adj. s.* of Trouville, native of

Troyen, ne, *adj. s.* Trojan [loafer, cadger

Truand, e, *s.m.f.* vagrant, vagabond, hulker,

†**Truandaille,** *s.f.* vagrants, vagabonds, hulkers, loafers [to hulk, to loaf

Truander, *v.n.* to wander, to ramble, to rove,

Truanderie, *s.f.* vagrancy, hulking, loafing

Truble, *s.f.* (*fish.*) hoop-net

Trubleau, *s.m.* (*fish.*) small hoop-net

Truc, *s.m.* truck; trap, machinery; knack, skill; cunning; artifice, trick, dodge

Trucage, *s.m.* jewing

Trucheman, Truchement, *s. m.* interpreter; spokesman; (*in the East*) dragoman

Truck, *s.m.* truck

Truculent, e, *adj.* truculent

Truelle, *s.f.* trowel; fish-carver, fish-slice

Truellée, *s.f.* trowelful

Truellette, *s.f.* small trowel

Truffe, *s.f.* truffle. *Aux —s*, with truffles, truffled

Truffer, *v.a.* to truffle, to stuff with truffles

Truffi-er, ère, *adj.* of truffles, truffle; — *s.m.* truffle-pig, truffle-dog; — *s.f.* truffle-bed, truf-

Truflier, *s.m.* (*bot.*) privet [fle-ground

Truie, *s.f.* sow

Truisme, *s.m.* truism

Truite, *s.f.* trout [speckled, spotted, mottled

Truité, e, *adj.* trout-coloured, red-spotted, red-

Truitelle, *s.f.*, **Truiton,** *s.m.* young *or* small

Trullisation, *s.f.* (*arch.*) trullization [trout

Trumeau, *s.m.* pier; pier-glass; leg *or* shin

Truquer, *v.n.a.* to dodge, to cheat; to beg [(*of beef*)

Truqueu-r, se, *s.m.f.* dodger, doer, trickster, cheat; cadger; imitator

Trusquin, *s.m.* (*tech.*) *V.* **Troussequin**

Trygon, *s.m.* (*fish*) trygon, sting-ray [**Czar,** &c.

Tsar, Tsarien, &c. (*obsolete spellings*) *V.*

Tu, *pers. pron.* thou; you. *Être à — et à toi*, to be very intimate *or* familiar. — **-autem,** *s.m.*

Tu, e, *part. of* **Taire** [main point; difficulty, rub

Tuable, *adj.* killable, fit for killing

Tuage, *s.m.* killing; slaughter [(*V.* **Assommant**)

Tuant, e, *adj.* killing; toilsome, tedious, &c.

Tubage, *s.m.* tubing

Tubaire, *adj.* (*anat.*) tubal

Tube, *s.m.* tube; pipe; duct

Tubéforme, *adj.* (*bad spelling*) *V.* **Tubiforme**

Tuber, *v.a.* to tube

Tubéracé, e, *adj.* (*bot.*) tuberaceous

Tubercule, *s.m.* tubercle; tuber; truffle

Tuberculé, e, *adj.* tubercled, tuberculated, tuberculate [cular; tubercled

Tuberculeu-x, se, *adj.* tuberculous; tuber-

Tuberculifère, *adj.* tuberculiferous; tuberi-

Tuberculiforme, *adj.* tuberculiform [ferous

Tuberculisation, *s.f.* (*med.*) tuberculization

Tuberculiser, *v.a.* (*med.*) to tuberculize

Se —, *v.r.* to become tubercular

Tuberculose, *s.f.* (*med.*) tuberculosis

Tubéreuse, *s.f.* (*bot.*) tuberose

Tubéreu-x, se, *adj.* (*bot.*) tuberous

Tubérifère, *adj.* tuberiferous

Tubériforme, *adj.* tuberiform

Tubérivore, *adj.* tuberivorous

Tubérosité, *s.f.* tuberosity; tuber

Tubifère, *adj.* tubiferous

Tubiforme, *adj.* tubiform

Tubipore, *s.m.* (*zool.*) tubipore, organ-pipe coral

Tubleu. *V.* **Tudieu**

Tubulaire, *adj.* tubular

Tubule, *s.m.* tubule, small tube

Tubulé, e, *adj.* tubulated, tubulate

Tubuleu-x, se, *adj.* tubulous

Tubulure, *s.f.* tubulure; tubing, tubes; tube

Tudesque, *adj.* Teutonic; rough, coarse, uncouth, Gothic; — *s.m.* Teutonic (*language*);

Tudieu, *int* (*obsolete*) zounds! [Teuton

Tue, *s.m.f.* (*in compounds, from* **Tuer,** "to kill," &c.) person (*m f.*) *or* thing (*m.*) that kills *or* &c., killer, &c. — **-brebis,** *s.m.* (*bot.*) butterwort. — **-chien,** *s.m.* dog-killer, dog-destroyer; (*bot.*) meadow saffron; dog's-bane. — **-loup,** *s.m.* wolf-killer; (*bot.*) wolf's-bane. — **-mouche,** — **-mouches,** *s.m.* fly-destroyer; (*bot.*) fly-agaric, amanita muscaria; *adj.* fly-destroying. — **-tête (A),** *adv.* as loud as one can, with all o.'s might, at the top of o.'s voice. — **-vent,** *s.m. V.* **Abrivent**

Tuer, *v.a.n.* to kill; to slay, to slaughter; to destroy, to do away with; to trifle away, to while away; to be the death of; to be baneful to; to tire to death; to stifle; to prevent; to supersede; to ruin; to put out

Se —, *v.r.* to kill oneself, to commit suicide; to be killed *or* &c.; to take great trouble (in), to wear oneself out (in); never to cease; to kill *or* &c. each other. *Se faire* —, to get *or* be killed; to fall bravely; to expose o.'s life

Tuerie, *s.f.* slaughter, massacre, carnage, butchery; slaughter-house

Tueu-r, se, *s.m.f.* killer; slayer; duellist; (*ironically*) bully, braggart

Tuf, *s.m.* (*min.*) chalky substratum; tuff, tufa

Tufacé, e, *adj.* (*min.*) tufaceous

Tuffeau, *s.m.* (*min.*) tuff, tufa

Tufi-er, ère, *adj.* tufaceous

Tugue, *s.f. V.* **Teugue**

Tuile, *s.f.* tile; (— *sur la tête*) (*fig.*) hard blow, blow; piece of ill luck; unlucky *or* untoward accident, mishap, mischance, awkward thing; —**s**, *pl.* tiles, &c.; tiling

Tuileau, *s.m.* broken tile

Tuilée, *s.f.* skylight; (*shell*) giant tridacna, hippopus; (*zool*) hawkbill turtle

Tuilerie, *s.f.* tile-field, tile-works, tile-kiln; tile-making; tiles; —**s**, *pl.* tile-fields, &c.; Tuileries (*Palace and public garden in Paris*);

Tuilier, *s.m.* tile-maker [court

Tulipe, *s.f.* (*bot.*) tulip

Tulipier, *s.m.* tulipist; (*bot.*) tulip-tree

Tulipomane, *s.m.f.* tulipomaniac

Tulipomanie, *s.f.* tulipomania

Tulle, *s.m.* tulle, net

Tullerie, *s.f.* tulle-making, net-making
Tulli-er, ère, *adj.* of tulle, tulle, of net, net
Tulliste, *s.m.f.* tulle-maker, net-maker
Tuméfaction, *s.f.* tumefaction
Tuméfier, *v.a.*, **Se** —, *v.r.* to tumefy
Tumeur, *s.f.* tumour, swelling
Tumulaire, *adj.* of a *or* of the grave, sepulchral; tomb. *Pierre* —, tomb-stone
Tumulte, *s.m.* tumult; uproar; riot; bustle; agitation; confusion; (*old*) onset
Tumultuaire, *adj.* tumultuary
Tumultuairement, *adv.* tumultuarily
Tumultueusement, *adv.* tumultuously; riotously
Tumultueu-x, se, *adj.* tumultuous; riotous
Tumulus, *s.m.* tumulus, barrow, cairn, sepulchral mound
Tungstate, *s m.* (*chem.*) tungstate
Tungstène, *s.m.* (*chem.*) tungsten
Tungstique, *adj.* (*chem.*) tungstic
Tunique, *s.f.* tunic; tunicle; coat; frock-coat, great-coat
Tuniqué, e, *adj.* tunicated, tunicate
Tunisien, ne, *adj. s.* Tunisian
Tunnel, *s.m.* tunnel; — **s,** *pl.* tunnels; tunnelling
Tuorbe. *V.* **Téorbe**
Tupaia, Tupaya, *s.m.* (*zool.*) banxring
Tupinet, *s.m.* (*bird*) long-tailed tit
Tuque. *V.* **Tugue**
Turanien, ne, *adj. s.* Turanian
Turault, Turo, *s.m.* (*agr.*) raised foot-path
Turban, *s.m.* turban
Turbinage, *s.m.* turbination
Turbine, *s.f.* (*mech.*) turbine; (*of churches*) *V.* **Jubé**
Turbiné, e, Turbiniforme, *adj.* turbinated, turbinate, top-shaped
Turbinelle, *s.f.* (*mollusc*) turbinella, chank-shell, turnip-shell
Turbinite, *s.f.* turbinite
Turbith, *s.m.* (*bot., old chem.*) turpeth, turbith
Turbo, *s.m.* (*mollusc*) turbo
Turbot, *s.m.* (*fish*) turbot
Turbotière, *s.f.* turbot-kettle
Turbotin, *s.m.* young turbot
Turbulemment, *adv.* turbulently; wildly
Turbulence, *s.f.* turbulence; vivacity; wildness
Turbulent, e, *adj.* turbulent; wild
Tur-c, que, *adj. s.* Turkish; Turk; Turkish boy; (the) Turkish language, Turkish; bark-beetle; Turkish woman *or* lady *or* girl; Turkish fashion. *Grand* —, Grand Turk, sultan. *A la turque*, in the Turkish fashion; roughly, cruelly. *S'en soucier comme du Grand* —, not to care a straw for it. *Travailler pour le Grand* —, to work for nothing. *Traiter de — à More*, to treat like a Turk
Turcaret, *s.m.* Turcaret, purse-proud jobber
Turcie, *s.f.* embankment, dike
Turcisme, *s.m.* Turcism, Turkism
Turco, *s.m.* (*soldier*) turco; — *adj.* (*in compounds*) turco- ...
Turcoin, *s.m.* camel's hair; mohair
Turcoman, e, *adj. s.* Turkoman, Turcoman
Turde, *s.m.* (*bird*) turdus
Turelure, *s.f.* tol-de-rol
Turf, *s.m.* turf; horse-racing
Turfiste, *s.m.f.* turfite
Turfol, *s.m.* (*chem.*) turfol
Turgescence, *s.f.* turgescence
Turgescent, e, *adj.* turgescent
Turgide, *adj.* turgid
Turgidité, *s.f.* turgidity, turgidness
Turinois, e, *adj. s.* Turinese
Turion, *s.m.* (*bot.*) turio
Turionifère, *adj.* (*bot.*) turioniferous
Turlupin, *s.m.* punster, scurvy jester; (*Fr. eccl. hist.*) turlupin, lollard
Turlupinade, *s.f.* pun, low joke
Turlupiner, *v.n.* to pun; — *v.a.* to banter, to ridicule; to tease, to provoke, to aggravate
Turlurette, *s.f.* (*old*) kind of guitar; tol-de-rol; gay woman
Turlut, *s.m.* (*bird*) titlark
Turlutaine, *s.f.* (*old*) barrel-organ; hobby, fancy, whim
Turlututaine, *s.f.* burden (*of a song*); constant saying
Turlututu, *s.m.* reed-pipe; tol-de-rol-lol; air, tune; — *int.* hush! tush! tut!

Turnep, *s.m.* field-turnip
Turpitude, *s.f.* turpitude; baseness; shame
Turquerie, *s.f.* harshness, hardness, cruelty
Turquesse, *s.f.* Turkish woman
Turquet, *s.m.* Indian corn; pug-dog
Turquette, *s.f.* (*bot.*) rupture-wort
Turquin, e, *adj.* (*of blue*) dark, deep; dark blue; — *s.m.* dark blue; dark blue marble
Turquoise, *s.f.* (*min.*) turquoise
Turritelle, *s.f.* (*mollusc*) turret-shell
Tusculanes, *s.f. pl.* (*Cicero's*) Tusculanæ
Tussilage, *s.m.* (*bot.*) tussilago, colt's foot, horse-foot
Tussiculation, *s.f.* (*med.*) tussiculation
Tussore, *s.m.* tussore cloth (*Indian silk*)
Tutélaire, *adj.* tutelar, tutelary; protecting; guardian
Tutelle, *s.f.* tutelage; protection; subjection; guardianship; trusteeship; wardship
Tuteur, *s.m.* guardian; trustee; protector; (*hort.*) prop
Tutie, *s.f.* (*chem.*) tutty, tutty-powder
Tutoiement, Tutoîment, *s.m.* thouing
Tutoyer, *v.a.* to thou
Tutoyeu-r, se, *s.m.f.* thouer
Tutrice, *s.f.* guardian, tutrix; trustee; protectress
Tutti, *s.m. pl.* (*mus.*) tutti, all; — *s.m.* tutti, part played by all together. — *quanti*, all of us, all of you, all of them; all such people
Tutu, *s.m.* (*children's slang*) bottom, bum, toby
Tuyau, *s.m.* pipe; tube; nose; nozzle; shaft, flue; funnel; stalk; stem; barrel; shank; gauffer, crimp. —*acoustique*, speaking-pipe. —*alimentaire*, feed-pipe. —*aspirant*, suction-pipe. —*atmosphérique*, vacuum-pipe. — *à cheminée*, funnel-pipe. — *de cheminée*, chimney-flue. — *de la cheminée*, flue of the chimney. — *de décharge*, discharging-pipe; spout. — *de dégagement de la vapeur*, waste steam-pipe. — *d'échappement de vapeur*, steam blow-off pipe. — *d'embranchement*, branch-pipe. — *de mer*, (*zool.*) serpula. — *de poêle*, stove-pipe; chimney-pot hat
Tuyautage, *s.m.* system of pipes, pipes; gauffering, crimping
Tuyauté, e, *part. adj.* gauffered, crimped; — *s.m.* gauffered *or* crimped stuff
Tuyauter, *v.a.* to gauffer, to crimp
Tuyauterie, *s.f.* pipe-making *or* manufactory *or* trade; pipe-store; pipes; system of pipes
Tuyère, *s.f.* (*tech.*) tuyere
Tympan, *s.m.* tympanum; tympan; (*of the ear*) drum; (*of a bridge*) spandrel. *Bruit à briser le* —, stunning noise
Tympanal, e, *adj.* tympanal, tympanic
Tympanique, *adj.* tympanic; — *s.f.* tympanics, drumming
Tympaniser, *v.a.* to defame, to traduce, to expose, to lampoon; to inveigh against, to cry down, to run down
Tympanite, *s.f.* (*med.*) tympanites, tympany, drum-belly; (*vet.*) hoven
Tympanon, *s.m.* (*mus. instr.*) dulcimer
Type, *s.m.* type; model; standard; character; emblem; symbol (*astr.*) plan, drawing
Typha, *s.m.* (*bot.*) typha, reed-mace, cat's-tail
Typhacées, *s.f. pl.* (*bot.*) typhaceæ
Typhique, *adj.* typhic, typhous; — *s.m.f.* person affected with typhus, typhus patient
Typhoïde, *adj.* (*med.*) typhoid
Typhomanie, *s.f.* (*med.*) typhomania
Typhon, *s.m.* (*storm*) typhoon; (*obsolete*) water-spout; (*Egyptian myth.*) Typhon
Typhus, *s.m.* (*med.*) typhus, typhus fever; (*vet.*) — *du gros bétail*, cattle-plague
Typique, *adj.* typic, typical
‡Typochrom-ie, -ique, &c. *V.* page 3, § 1
Typographe, *s.m.* typographer, printer. — *adj.* typographic, printing
Typographie, *s.f.* typography, letter-press printing, printing; printing-office
Typograph-ique, -iquement. *V.* page 3, § 1. *Caractères —iques*, printing-type. *Impression —ique*, letter-press
Typolithe, *s.m.f.* typolite
Typolithograph-ie, -ique, &c. *V.* page 3, § 1
Tyran, *s.m.* tyrant; (*zool.*) tyrant-bird, tyrant-shrike, petchary

Tyranneau, *s.m.* petty tyrant; (*zool.*) *V.* **Tyran**
Tyrannicide, *s.m.* (*act*), *s.m.f.* (*pers.*) tyrannicide; — *adj.* tyrannicidal
Tyrann-ie, -ique, -iquement. *V.* page 3, § 1
Tyranniser, *v.a.n.* to tyrannize
Tyrien, ne, *adj. s.* Tyrian
Tyrolien, ne, *adj. s.m.f.* Tyrolese; — *s.f.* tyrolienne (*dance, tune*)
Tyrrhénien, ne, *adj. s.* Tyrrhenian
Tyrtéen, ne, *adj.* Tyrtæan [&c.
Tzar, Tzarien, &c. (*obsolete spelling*) *V.* **Czar,**
Tzigane, Tzingari, *s.m.* zingari

U

U, *s.m.* u [*adj.* ubiquist, ubiquitary, ubiquitous
§**Ubiquiste,** *s.m.f.* ubiquist; ubiquitarian; —
§**Ubiquitaire,** *s.m.f.* ubiquitarian; — *adj.* ubiquitary, ubiquitous
§**Ubiquité,** *s.f.* ubiquity, omnipresence
Udomètre, *s.m.* udometer, rain-gauge
Udométr-ie, -ique. *V.* page 3, § 1
'**Uhlan,** *s.m.* uhlan
Ukase, *s.m.* ukase
Ulcérable, *adj.* ulcerable
Ulcérati-f, ve, *adj.* ulcerative
Ulcération, *s.f.* ulceration
Ulcère, *s.m.* ulcer
Ulcéré, e, *part. adj.* ulcerated, &c. (*V.* **Ulcérer**); gangrened; cankered; rankling; wounded; sore
Ulcérer, *v.a.* to ulcerate; to embitter, to incense, to exasperate [*or* ulcerous
S' —, *v.r.* to ulcerate, to become ulcerated
Ulcéreu-x, se, *adj.* ulcerous; ulcerated
Uléma, *s.m. pl.* ulema (*Turkish jurists*)
Ulex, *s.m.* (*bot.*) ulex
Uligineu-x, se, *adj.* uliginous [the meadow
Ulmaire, *s.f.* (*bot.*) meadow-sweet, queen of
Ulmine, *s.f.* (*chem.*) ulmine
Ulmique, *adj.* (*chem*) ulmic
Ulnaire, *adj.* (*anat.*) ulnar [after
Ultérieur, e, *adj.* ulterior, further, subsequent,
Ultérieurement, *adv.* ulteriorly; later, subsequently, afterwards, after; further; besides,
Ultième, *adj.* ultimate, last [beyond
Ultimatum, *s.m.* ultimatum
Ultime, *adj.* ultimate; last
Ultimo, *adv.* lastly
Ultra, (*in compounds*) ultra- ...; — *s.m.* ultra
Ultraïsme, *s.m.* ultraism
Ultra-mondain, e, *adj.* ultra-mundane
Ultramontain, e, *adj. s.* ultramontane; Romish, popish; papist [popery
Ultramontanisme, *s. m.* ultramontanism,
Ululation, *s.f.*, **Ululement,** *s.m.* ululation, howling, howl, hooting
Ululer, *v.n.* to ululate, to howl, to hoot
Ulve, *s.f.* (*bot*) ulva, green laver, oyster-green
Umble, *s.m.* (*fish*) *V.* **Ombre,** *s.m.*
Un, e, *s.m. adj. art.* unit; one; a, an; any. — *à* —, one to one; one by one, one after another. *L'*—, the one; one; the former. *L'— l'autre, les —s les autres,* one another, each other. *L'— et l'autre,* both. *Les —s et les autres,* everyone, everybody, all. *L'— ou l'autre,* either. *L'— dans l'autre, l'— portant l'autre,* (taking) one with another, on an average. *Ni l'— ni l'autre,* neither. *Les —s,* some. *N'en faire ni une* (*or ni un*) *ni deux,* to decide at once *or* immediately, to make no more ado, not to hesitate a moment, to make no bones about it. *En donner d' —e à,* to deceive, to take in. *C'est tout* —, it matters not, it is all the same, it is all one
Unanime, *adj.* unanimous
Unanimement, *adv.* unanimously
Unanimité, *s.f.* unanimity. *A l'*—, unanimously
Unau, *s.m.* (*zool.*) unau, two-toed sloth
Uncial, e, *adj. s.* uncial
Undine, *s.f.* (*astr.*) Undine

Unguéal, e, *adj.* ungual, ungueal
Unguifère, *adj.* unguiferous
Unguineu-x, se, *adj.* unguinous
Uni, e, *part. adj.* united, &c. (*V.* **Unir**); — *adj.* even; level; smooth; plain; simple; uniform; regular; ordinary; every-day; — *adv.* evenly; — *s.m.* plain articles; — (*in compounds*) uni ...
Unicapsulaire, *adj.* unicapsular
Unicellulaire, *adj.* unicellular
Unicité, *s.f.* uniqueness
Unicolore, *adj.* unicoloured, single-coloured
Unicorde, *adj.* (*mus.*) unichord
Unicorne, *s.m.* unicorn; — *adj.* unicornous
Unième, *adj.* first
Unièmement, *adj.* firstly
Unification, *s.f.* unification
Unifier, *v.a.*, **S'** —, *v.r.* to unify
Uniflore, *adj.* (*bot.*) uniflorous, single-flowered
Unifolié, e, *adj.* (*bot.*) unifoliate, single-leaved
Uniforme, *adj.* uniform; — *s.m.* uniform; regimentals; dress; military man; (military) service, army. *D'*—, (*adject.*) uniform; regimental. *Grand* —, full dress
Uniformément, *adv.* uniformly
Uniformisation, *s.f.* uniformization
Uniformiser, *v.a.*, **S'**—, *v.r.* to uniformize
Uniformité, *s.f.* uniformity [Unigenitus
Unigenitus. *La bulle* —, (*eccl. hist.*) the Bull
Unijugué, e, *adj.* (*bot.*) unijugate
Unilabié, e, *adj.* (*nat. hist.*) unilabiate
Unilatéral, e, *adj.* unilateral
Unilatéralement, *adv.* unilaterally
Unilingue, *adj.* (*philology*) unilingual
Unilobé, e, *adj.* (*bot.*) unilobate, unilobed
Uniloculaire, *adj.* (*bot.*) unilocular
Uniment, *adv.* evenly; on a level; smoothly; plainly; simply. *Tout* —, plainly, simply, and no more [harmony; agreement
Union, *s.f.* union; junction; unity; concord,
Union-isme, -iste. *V.* page 3, § 1
Unipare, *adj.* uniparous [unipersonal verb
Unipersonnel, le, *adj.* unipersonal; — *s.m.*
Unipersonnellement, *adv.* unipersonally
Unipétale, Unipétalé, e, *adj.* (*bot.*) unipe-
Unipolaire, *adj.* (*phys.*) unipolar [talous
Unipolarité, *s.f.* (*phys.*) unipolarity
Unique, *adj.* only; sole; single; one; unique, alone of the kind, without an equal, matchless; unrivalled; unequalled; unparalleled; unexampled; unprecedented; odd, singular
Uniquement, *adv.* only; solely; alone; above all things, above all the rest; uniquely
Unir, *v.a.*, **S'**—, *v.r.* to unite; to join; to level; to smooth [(*bot.*) unisexual
Unisexuel, le, Unisexué, e, *adj.* unisexuous;
Unisson, *s.m.* unison; concert, keeping, harmony *A l'*—, in unison; in concert
Unissonnance, *s.f.* unisonance
Unissonnant, e, *adj.* unisonant [of unity
Unitaire, *s.m.f.* unitarian; — *adj.* unitarian;
Unitarianisme, Unitarisme, *s.m.* unita-
Unitarien, ne, *s.m.f. adj.* *V.* **Unitaire** [rianism
Unité, *s.f.* unity; unit; digit
Uniti-f, ve, *adj.* unitive; of pure love
Univalve, *adj.* (*nat. hist.*) univalve, univalved;
Univers, *s.m.* universe [— *s.m.* univalve
Universaliser, *v.a.* to universalize
Universal-isme, -iste. *V.* page 3, § 1 [whole
Universalité, *s.f.* universality; generality;
Universaux, *s.m. pl.* (*of the old kings of Poland*) orders, command, writ; — (*pl. of* **Universel,** *s.m.*) (*log.*) universals, predicables
Universel, le, *adj.* universal; of the whole; general; sole; (*of legacies and legatees*) *V.* **Legs** *&* **Légataire**; — *s.m.* (*log.*) universal, predicable
Universellement, *adv.* universally; generally
Universitaire, *adj.* of the (*or* a) university, university, academic, college; — *s.m* univer-
Université, *s.f.* university [sity-man
Univocation, *s.f.* univocation
Univoque, *adj. m.f.*, *s.m.* univocal
Unone, *s.f.* (*bot.*) unona

Upas, *s.m.* (*poison*) upas ; (*bot.*) upas-tree
Uranate, *s.m.* (*chem.*) uranate
Urane, *s.m.* (*chem.*) oxide of uranium
Uraneu-x, se, *adj.* (*chem.*) uranous
Uranie, *s.f.* (*myth., astr.*) Urania ; (*moth*) urania ; (*bot.*) urania, traveller's tree
Uranique, *adj.* (*chem.*) uranic
Uranite, *s.m.* (*min.*) uranite, uran-mica
Uranium, *s.m.* (*chem.*) uranium
Uranographe, *s.m.* uranographer ; uranograph
Urano-graphie, -graphique, -logie, -métrie, -scopie, &c. *V.* page 3, § 1
Uranorama, *s.m.* uranorama
Uranoscope, *s.m.* (*fish*) uranoscopus, star-gazer
Uranus, *s.m.* (*myth., astr.*) Uranus
Urao, *s.m.* (*min.*) urao, trona, natron
Uraque. *V.* **Ouraque**
Urate, *s.m.* (*chem.*) urate
Urbain, e, *adj.* urban ; —**s,** *s.m. pl.* townspeople
Urbaniste, *s.f.* Urbanist (*nun*)
Urbanité, *s.f.* urbanity [urceola
Urcéolaire, *adj.* (*bot.*) urceolate ; — *s.f.* (*plant*)
Urcéole, *s.m.* (*bot.*) urceolus ; — *s.f.* (*plant*)
Urcéolé, e, *adj.* (*bot.*) urceolate [urceola
Ure, *s.m.* urus, (the) wild bull *or* ox [uredineæ
Urédinés, *s.m. pl.*, **Urédinées,** *s.f. pl.* (*bot.*)
Urédo, *s.m.* (*bot.*) uredo (*fungus*)
Urée, *s.f.* (*chem.*) urea
Urémie, *s.f.* (*med.*) uræmia, uremy
Urémique, *adj.* (*med.*) uræmic, uremic
Urène, *s.f.* (*bot.*) urena
Urétéralgie, *s.f.* (*med.*) ureteralgia
Uretère, *s.m.* (*anat.*) ureter
Urétérique, *adj.* (*anat.*) ureteric
Urétérite, *s.f.* (*med.*) ureteritis
Uréthral, e, *adj.* (*anat.*) urethral
Uréthralgie, *s.f.* (*med.*) urethralgia
Urèthre, *s.m.* (*anat.*) urethra
Uréthrite, *s.f.* (*med.*) urethritis
Uréthro, (*in compounds*) urethro- . . .
Uréthrorrhagie, *s.f.* (*med.*) urethrorrhagia
Uréthrorrhée, *s.f.* (*med*) urethrorrhœa
Uréthroscope, *s.m.* (*surg.*) urethroscope
Uréthroscopie, *s.f.* (*surg.*) urethroscopy
Uréthrotome, *s.m.* (*surg.*) urethrotomy-knife
Uréthrotomie, *s.f.* (*surg.*) urethrotomy
Urètre, &c. *V.* **Urèthre,** &c.
Urgemment, *adv.* urgently
Urgence, *s.f.* urgency. *D'—*, of *or* from urgency ; urgent ; urgently ; immediately ; on account *or* in case of urgency
Urgent, e, *adj.* urgent, pressing
Urginée, *s.f.* (*bot.*) urginea, squill
Urinaire, *adj.* urinary ; — *s.f.* (*bot.*) *V.* **Pissenlit**
Urinal, *s.m.* urinal
Urination, *s.f.* urination [*slang*) water
Urine, *s.f.* urine ; stale ; chamber-lye ; (*genteel*
Uriner, *v.n.* to urinate, to stale, to make water
Urineu-x, se, *adj.* urinous
Urinifère, *adj.* uriniferous
Urinipare, *adj.* uriniparous
Urinoir, *s.m.* urinal
Urinomètre, *s.m.* urinometer
Urique, *adj.* (*chem.*) uric [*scrutin*, ballot-box
Urne, *s.f.* urn ; ballot-box. — *électorale*, — *du*
Uro, (*in compounds*) uro . . .
‡**Urochs.** *V.* **Aurochs**
Urolithe, *s.m.* (*med.*) urolithus, urinary calculus
Uroman-cie, -tique. *V.* page 3, § 1
Uromancien, ne, *s.m.f.* uromancer
Uromètre, *s.m.* urometer, urinometer
Uroscop-ie, -ique. *V.* page 3, § 1
Urson, *s.m.* (*zool.*) urson, Canada porcupine
Ursuline, *s.f.* Ursuline (*nun*) ; —**s,** *pl.* Ursulines ; convent of the Ursulines
Urticaire, *s.f.* (*med.*) urticaria, nettle-rash
Urticant, e, *adj.* urticating
Urtication, *s.f.* (*med.*) urtication
Urticées, *s.f. pl.* (*bot.*) urticaceæ, urticeæ
Urus, *s.m.* *V.* **Ure** [and customs
Us, *s.m.* usage, use, way. — *et coutumes*, ways
Us, *s.m.* us (*Latin ending*). *Savant en* —, man learned in Latin words

Usable, *adj.* to be worn out, liable to wear out ; perishable
Usage, *s.m.* use ; usage ; habit, practice, custom ; way ; vogue ; habits of society ; wear ; —**s,** *pl.* uses, &c. ; (*old*) church-books. — *du monde* or *de la vie*, ways of the world, habits of society. *A l'— de*, for the use of. *D'—*, in use ; usual ; customary ; in common use ; of every-day use. *En —*, in use, used ; usual ; common. *Hors d'—*, out of use ; unusual, uncustomary ; obsolete. *Peu en —*, little used ; unused ; unusual ; uncommon. *Avoir de l'—*, to know the habits of society. *Faire — de*, to make use of, to use. *Mettre en —*, to put in use, to make use of, to use, to employ [knowing the habits of society
Usagé, e, *adj.* used to the ways of the world,
Usager, *s.m.* (*law*) commoner
Usance, *s.f.* (*com.*) usance ; usage
Usé, e, *part. adj.* worn out, &c. (*V.* **User**) ; threadbare ; old ; common, trite, hackneyed, stale ; out of use ; broken ; weak
User, *v.n.* to use, to make use ; to employ ; to exercise ; to have ; to avail oneself ; — *v.a.* to use, to consume ; to use up ; to wear ; to wear out *or* away *or* off ; to rub down ; to destroy ; to exhaust ; to waste ; to spend ; to ruin ; to weaken ; to impair ; to blunt ; to cool. *En — avec*, to deal *or* act with, to behave to, to use, to treat. — *bien* or *mal de*, to make a good *or* bad use of
S' —, *v.r.* to be consumed ; to be used up ; to wear oneself out ; to wear out *or* away *or* off ; to be exhausted ; to waste, to be spent ; to decay ; to lose o.'s strength
User, *s.m.* wear, service. *Être d'un bon —*, to wear well. *Être bon a l'—*, (*pers.*) to improve upon acquaintance
Usine, *s.f.* manufactory ; mill ; works
Usini-er, ère, *adj.* manufacturing ; — *s.m.* owner of works, mill-owner, manufacturer
Usité, e, *adj.* in use, used ; usual, customary ;
Usnée, *s.f.* (*bot.*) usnea, beard-moss [common
Usnine, *s.f.* (*chem.*) usnine
Usnique, *adj.* (*chem.*) usnic
Usquebac, *s.m.* *V.* **Scubac**
Ustensile, *s.m.* utensil ; implement ; tool ; tackle
Ustensiler, *v.a.* to supply with utensils *or* implements, to implement
Ustion, *s.f.* ustion, combustion, burning
Usucapion, *s.f.* (*civ. law*) usucaption, usucapion
Usuel, le, *adj.* usual, customary, ordinary, common ; practical [narily, commonly
Usuellement, *adv.* usually, customarily, ordi-
Usufructuaire, *adj.* (*civ. law*) usufructuary
Usufruit, *s.m.* (*civ. law*) usufruct, estate for life, life-estate, life-rent
Usufruiti-er, ère, *s.m.f.* usufructuary, tenant for life, life-renter ; — *adj.* usufructuary
Usuraire, *adj.* usurious
Usurairement, *adv.* usuriously
Usure, *s.f.* usury ; (*fig.*) interest ; wear ; wearing out ; wear and tear. *Faire l'—*, to practise usury, to be a usurer. *Prêter à —*, to lend upon usury. *Rendre avec —*, (*fig.*) to return *or* repay with interest
Usuri-er, ère, *s.m.f. adj.* usurer ; usurious
Usurpa-teur, trice, *s.m.f. adj.* usurper ; encroacher ; intruder ; usurping ; encroaching ; intruding [intrusion
Usurpation, *s.f.* usurpation ; encroachment ;
Usurpatoire, *adj.* usurpatory [trude
Usurper, *v.a.n.* to usurp ; to encroach ; to in-
Ut, *s.m.* (*mus.*) ut, do, C
Utéralgie, *s.f.* (*med.*) uteralgia
Utérin, e, *adj.* uterine ; on the mother's side ; — *s.m.* relation on the mother's side ; (*med.*) uterine medicine. *Fureur —e*, uterine madness, furor uterinus, nymphomania
Utérinité, *s.f.* uterinity
Utéro, (*in compounds, anat.*) utéro- . . .
Utéroscopie, *s.f.* (*med.*) uteroscopy
Utérotome, *s.m.* (*surg.*) uterotomy-knife
Utérotom-ie, -ique. *V.* page 3, § 1

Utérus, *s.m.* (*anat.*) uterus, womb
Utile, *adj.* useful, of use, of utility, of service, serviceable; profitable; beneficial; advantageous; good; advisable, expedient; proper; due; — *s.m.* useful, utility. *En temps* —, in due *or* proper *or* good time
Utilement, *adv.* usefully; serviceably; profitably; beneficially; advantageously
Utilisable, *adj.* utilizable
Utilisation, *s.f.* utilization
Utiliser, *v.a.* to utilize, to make useful, to employ profitably, to turn to account; to make use of, to use; to avail oneself of [*or* &c.
S'—, *v.r.* to make oneself useful; to be utilized
Utilitaire, *adj. s.m.f.* utilitarian [tarianism
Utilitarianisme, Utilitarisme, *s.m.* utili-
Utilité, *s.f.* utility; usefulness; use; service; profit; advantage; benefit; avail; purpose; (*theat.*) common useful part; actor who can perform any common useful part
Utopie, *s.f.* utopia
Utopique, *adj.* utopian
Utopisme, *s.m.* utopianism
Utopiste, *s.m.f.* utopist, dreamer
§**Utraquiste,** *s.m.* (*eccl. hist.*) utraquist [wort
Utriculaire, *adj.* utricular; — *s.f.* (*bot.*) bladder-
Utricule, *s.m.* utricle
Utriculé, e, *adj.* utriculate
Utriculeu-x, se, *adj.* utriculous, utricular
Utriforme, *adj.* utriform
Uva ursi, *s.m.* (*bot.*) uva ursi, bearberry
Uvée, *s.f.* (*anat.*) uvea
Uvette, *s.f.* (*bot.*) sea-grape
Uviforme, *adj.* uviform, grape-shaped
Uvulaire, *adj.* (*anat.*) uvular
Uwarowite, *s.f.* (*min.*) uwarowite

V

V, *s.m.* v
Va, *Imperative of Aller, & int.* well! good! be it so! believe me, &c., *V.* **Aller.** — *pour cela!* I consent to it; agreed! done! — *-t'en, V.* **Aller (S'en).** — **-et-vient,** *s.m.* see-saw; see-saw motion, reciprocating motion, motion to and fro, backward and forward motion; oscillation; alternation; swing, sweep; (*nav.*) communication rope, pass-rope; ferry-boat, wherry. — **-nu-pieds,** *s.m.f.* tatterdemalion, ragamuffin, vagabond, beggar. — **-tout,** *s.m.* staking all one has; (o.'s) last stake, (o.'s) all. *Faire* — *-tout,* to stake o.'s all
Vacance, *s.f.* vacancy; —**s,** *pl.* vacation, holidays, recess. *Entrer en* —, to break up
Vacant, e, *adj.* vacant; unoccupied, empty; in abeyance; unclaimed [turbance; ado
Vacarme, *s.m.* tumult, uproar; hubbub; dis-
Vacation, *s.f.* day's time, time, sitting; fee; vacancy; —**s,** *pl.* sittings, time; fees; vacation, recess [lymph; — *adj.* vaccine
Vaccin, *s.m.* vaccine-matter, vaccine-lymph,
Vaccinal, e, *adj.* vaccinal, vaccine [nating
Vaccinateur, *s.m.* vaccinator; — *adj.* vacci-
Vaccination, *s.f.* vaccination
Vaccine, *s.f.* cow-pox; vaccination. — *du cheval,* — *équine,* horse-pox
Vacciner, *v.a.* to vaccinate
Vaccinier, *s.m.* (*bot.*) *V.* **Airelle** [cinifer
Vaccinifère, *adj.* vacciniferous; — *s.m.* vac-
Vache, *s.f.* cow; cow-hide; tilt; top, outside. — *artificielle,* stalking-horse
Vach-er, ère, *s.m.f.* cow-herd; cow-keeper
Vacherie, *s.f.* cow-house; dairy
Vachette, *s.f.* small cow-hide [**Airelle**
Vaciet, *s.m.* (*bot.*) grape-hyacinth; (*bot.*) *V.*
Vacillation, *s.f.* vacillation; wavering
Vacillatoire, *adj.* vacillatory
Vaciller, *v.n.* to vacillate; to waver; to reel; to stagger; to totter; to flicker; to falter; to shake; to hesitate
Vacuité, *s.f.* vacuity, emptiness
Vacuole, *s.f.* (*nat. hist.*) vacuole
Vacuum, *s.m.* vacuum
Vade, *s.f.* (*at play*) stake, go
Vade-in-pace, *s.m.* vade-in-pace, prison in a monastery, perpetual solitary imprisonment
Vade-mecum, *s.m.* vade-mecum, manual
†**Vadrouille,** *s.f.* (*nav.*) swab; (*pop.*) trollop, trull, drab [wandering
Vagabond, e, *s.m.f. adj.* vagabond; vagrant;
Vagabondage, *s.m.* vagabondage; vagrancy
Vagabonder, *v.n.* to vagabondize; to be a vagabond; to wander
Vagant, *s.m.* wrecker (*plunderer*)
Vagin, *s.m.* (*anat.*) vagina
Vaginal, e, *adj.* (*anat.*) vaginal
Vaginant, e, *adj.* vaginant
Vaginé, e, *adj.* vaginate, vaginated
Vaginelle, *s.f.* (*bot.*) vaginella
Vaginiforme, *adj.* vaginiform
Vaginite, *s.f.* (*med.*) vaginitis
Vagino, (*in compounds, anat.*) vagino-...
Vaginule, *s.f.* (*bot.*) vaginula
Vagir, *v.n.* to cry, to wail, to mewl, to pule
Vagissement, *s.m.* crying, wail, wailing, mewling, puling
Vagon, &c. *V.* **Wagon,** &c.
Vague, *s.f.* wave, billow, surge
Vague, *adj.* vague; loose; uncertain; indistinct; faint; hazy; uncultivated, unbuilt upon, waste; empty; irregular; airy; wandering; — *s.m.* vagueness; looseness; uncertainty; airiness; emptiness; vacancy, void, vacuum, [empty space
Vaguement, *adv.* vaguely
Vaguemestre, *s.m.* (*mil.*) officer in charge of the baggage, baggage-master, waggon-master, [conductor
Vaguer, *v.n.* to wander, to rove
Vaguesse, *s.f.* (*paint.*) airiness
Vaguette, *s.f.* (*tech.*) knee-cap
†**Vaillamment,** *adv.* valiantly, gallantly, courageously, bravely
†**Vaillance,** *s.f.* valour, gallantry, courage, bravery; (*old*) value, worth
†**Vaillant, e,** *adj.* valiant, valorous, gallant, courageous, brave; (*fam.*) in first-rate health, first-rate
†**Vaillant,** *s.m.* what one is worth, whole property; — *adv.* worth. *Tout son* —, all one is worth, all one has, o.'s all. *Avoir cent mille francs* —, to be worth four thousand pounds. *N'avoir pas un sou* —, not to be worth a penny, to be penniless, to have no money
†**Vaillantise,** *s.f.* (*fam.*) prowess; deed, [achievement
†**Vaille.** *V.* **Valoir**
Vain, e, *adj.* vain; conceited; fruitless; useless; empty; idle; frivolous
Vaincre, *v.a.n.* to vanquish, to conquer, to overcome; to subdue; to defeat; to master, to surmount; to beat; to worst; to outdo, to surpass, to excel; to win; to be victorious
Se —, *v.r.* to conquer each other; to conquer oneself, to subdue o.'s passions. *Se laisser* —, to allow oneself to be conquered; to yield, to give way
Vaincu, e, *part.* conquered, vanquished, &c. (*V.* **Vaincre**); — *s.m.* conquered, vanquished, conquered enemy [pose, fruitlessly
Vainement, *adv.* vainly, in vain, to no pur-
Vainqueur, *s.m.* vanquisher; conqueror; victor; subduer; winner; prize-man *or* boy, prize-taker, prize-holder; — *adj.m.* conquering, victorious; winning; triumphant
Vair, *s.m.* (*obsolete, now* "**petit-gris**") vair (*now* "minever"); (*her.*) vair
Vairé, e, *adj.* (*her.*) vairy
Vairon, *adj.* wall-eyed, odd-eyed; — *s.m.* (*fish*) *V.* **Véron.** *Œil* —, wall-eye, glass-eye
Vaisseau, *s.m.* vessel; ship; man; ship of the line, man of war; structure, fabric, pile; (*anat., bot.*) vessel, vein, tube; —**x,** *pl.* ships, &c.; shipping. — *-école,* (*s.m.*) training-ship, school-frigate. — *à hélice,* screw-ship

Vaisselle, *s.f.* plates and dishes; crockery; ware; metal ware; plate (*wrought articles of gold or silver*). — *plate*, — *d'argent*, silver plate. — *d'or*, gold plate. — *de terre*, earthenware — *d'étain*, pewter. — *de poche*, (*pop.*) money, tin [pans
Vaissellerie, *s.f.* household vessels, pots and
Val, *s.m.* valley, vale, dale. *A — de*, at *or* to the bottom (*or* foot) of, down, below
Valable, *adj.* valid; good; receivable, admissible; available; legal; lawful; valuable
Valablement, *adv.* validly; in due form; availably; properly [worth; priced at; valid
Valant, (*part. of* **Valoir**) being worth, &c.;
Valaque, *s.m.f. adj.* Wallachian
Valence, *s.f.* Valencia orange
Valencien, ne, *adj. s.* Valencian
Valenciennes, *s.f.* Valenciennes lace
Valériane, *s.f.* (*bot.*) valerian
Valérianelle, *s.f.* (*bot.*) *V.* **Mâche**
Valérianique, Valérique, *adj.* (*chem.*) valerianic, valeric
Valet, *s.m.* footman; valet; servant, man, boy; flunkey, flunky; (*cards*) knave; (*thing*) door-weight; (*of mirrors*) rest, support, stand; (*of a bench, tech.*) claw, holdfast, cramp; stand. — *de bourreau*, — *du supplice*, assistant executioner. — *de carreau*, (*cards*) knave of diamonds; (*fig.*) nobody, contemptible fellow. — *de chambre*, valet. — *de charrue*, ploughboy. — *de chiens*, dog-keeper, whipper-in. — *de cœur*, (*cards*) knave of hearts; (*fig.*) favoured lover, detrimental. — *de ferme*, farm-servant, hind. — *de pied*, footman, lackey. — *de place*, guide. — *de porte*, door-weight. *Plat* —, toad-eater, toady. *Faire le bon* —, to be over officious. *Faire le bas* or *le plat* —, to crouch and cringe.
Valetage, *s.m.* footman's *or* servant's condition *or* work *or* duty, menial service; drudgery; cringing, servility
†**Valetaille,** *s.f.* pack of footmen, footmen, valets, servants, lackeys, flunkeys, menials
Valeter, *v.n.* to cringe, to play the valet; to drudge; to dance attendance, to wait; to trot
Valétudinaire, *adj. s.m.f.* valetudinarian, valetudinary; invalid
Valeur, *s.f.* value; valuableness; worth; as much (as); importance; meaning, import; valour, bravery, gallantry; (*in races*) stakes; —**s**, *pl.* valuables, anything valuable; (*com.*) paper, bills, moneys, &c.; (*fin.*) stocks, shares, securities —*s mobilières*, transferable securities. — *en espèces*, value in cash. *De* —, valuable. *Être en* —, to bear a good price; (*of land*) to be in good cultivation. *Mettre une terre en* —, to improve a land [valiantly, gallantly
Valeureusement, *adv.* valorously, bravely,
Valeureu-x, se, *adj.* valorous, brave, valiant,
Valhalla. *V.* **Walhalla** [gallant
Validation, *s.f.* validation, rendering valid; ratifying, ratification, confirming
Valide, *adj.* valid; good; in health, healthy, able bodied, sturdy; effective; — *s.m.* healthy person, able-bodied man
Validé, *s.f. Sultane* —, the mother of the Sultan
Validement, *adv.* validly
Valider, *v.a.* to validate, to render *or* make valid; to ratify, to confirm
Validité, *s.f.* validity; availableness
Valise, *s.f.* valise, portmanteau; cloak-bag; mail-bag; parcel
Valisnère, Valisnérie, *s.f. V.* **Vallisnérie**
Valkyrie, *s.f.* (*Scandinavian myth.*) valkyria, valkyr, walkyrie, wish-maiden
Vallaire, *adj. Couronne* —, (*Rom. antiq.*) val-
Vallée, *s.f.* valley, vale [lary crown
Vallisnérie, *s.f.* (*bot.*) vallisneria
Vallon, *s.m.* valley, vale, dale
Vallonée, *s.f. V.* **Avelanède**
Vallonnement, *s.m.* disposition in vales
Vallonner, *v.a.* to dispose in vales
Valoir, *v.n.a.* to be worth; to be of worth; to be *or* to be worth as much as; to be equivalent *or* equal to; to be as good as; to be as bad as; to be good for; to procure, to obtain, to gain; to give; to yield, to bring in, to produce; to have the value of, to stand for. — *bien*, to be well worth; to be as good as. — *mieux*, *V.* **Mieux,** *adv.* — *moins*, to be worth less; to be worse. *A — sur*, (*com.*) on account of; to be deducted from. *Faire* —, to cultivate, to farm; to improve, to make the best *or* the most of, to turn to account; to put out at interest; to employ; to insist upon, to lay great stress on, to enforce; to impress (upon); to maintain; to represent; to establish; to give force to; to give a value to; to object; to raise; to set off; to show; to plead; to set a value on; to praise, to praise up; to exalt; to boast of. *Ne — rien*, to be worth nothing, to be of no value; to be good for nothing; to be bad (for), to disagree, not to agree (with). *Se faire* —, to praise oneself; to boast; to set oneself off to advantage; to put *or* push oneself forward; to maintain o.'s dignity *or* o.'s rights; to keep up o.'s importance. *Vaille que vaille*, whatever it (*or* that) may be worth, for all it may be worth, for what it is worth; at all events; for better for worse. *Rien qui vaille*, nothing good; not
Valonée, *s.f. V.* **Avelanède** [worth having
Valorem (Ad), (*Latin*) ad valorem
Valse, *s.f.* waltz, valse; waltzing
Valser, *v n.a.* to waltz
Valseu-r, se, *s.m.f.* waltzer [**Valoir**)
Valu, e, *part.* been worth, worth, cost, &c. (*V.*
Value, *s.f.* value. *Plus-* —, increased *or* superior value; increase of price; increase; excess. *Moins-* —, decreased *or* inferior value; decrease of price; decrease; deficiency
Valvaire, *adj.* valvate
Valve, *s.f.* valve; trap [valve-shell
Valvé, e, *adj.* valved, valvate; — *s.f.* valvata,
Valvulaire, *adj.* valvular
Valvule, *s.f.* valvule, valve
Valvulé, e, *adj.* valvulate, valved
Vampire, *s.m.* vampire
Vampir-ique, -isme. *V.* page 3, § 1
Van, *s.m.* (*agr.*) winnowing-basket; (*spin.*) fan
Vanadate, *s.m.* (*chem.*) vanadate
Vanadique, *adj.* (*chem.*) vanadic
Vanadium, *s.m.* (*chem.*) vanadium
Vanda, *s.m.* (*bot.*) vanda
Vandale, *s.m. adj.* Vandal
Vandal-ique, -isme. *V.* page 3, § 1
Vandellie, *s.f.* (*bot.*) vandellia
Vandière, *s.f.* (*fish*) gemmeous dragonet, gowdie
Vandoise, *s.f.* (*fish*) dace, dare, dart; graining
Vanesse, *s.f.* (*butterfly*) vanessa (Camberwell beauty, commia, tortoise-shell, peacock, &c.,
Vanga, *s.m.* (*bird*) vanga [butterflies)
†**Vanille,** *s.f.* (*bot.*) vanilla [vanilla
†**Vanillé, e,** *part. adj.* flavoured with vanilla,
†**Vaniller,** *v.a.* to flavour with vanilla
†**Vanillier,** *s.m.* (*bot.*) vanilla-plant, vanilla-tree
Vanité, *s.f.* vanity; self-conceit; vain *or* conceited person. *Sans* —, without vanity; vanity apart. *Tirer* or *faire — de*, *V.* **Tirer**
Vaniteusement, *adv.* vainly, vaingloriously, conceitedly, proudly [ceited; ditto person
Vaniteu-x, se, *adj. s.* vain, vainglorious, con-
Vannage, *s.m.* (*agr.*, &c.) winnowing; (*engin.*) disposition *or* system of paddles, paddles, flood-gates
Vanne, *s.f.* paddle, paddledoor, sluice-gate, flood-gate, gate, shuttle, hatch; dock-gate, gate; (*of a bird*) beam-feather; —**s**, *pl.* paddles, &c.; (*adject.*) *Eaux-* —*s*, waste waters from factories or &c., sewage of the houses, urinous waters, night liquid soil, stale of farm-yards, &c.
Vanneau, *s.m.* (*bird*) lapwing; pewit, pewet; (*of a bird's wing*) beam-feather
Vanner, *v.a.* to winnow; to fan; to husk, to hull; (*engin.*) to furnish with paddles *or* flood-gates

Vannerie, *s.f.* basket-making *or* manufactory *or* trade; basket-work, baskets
Vannet, *s.m.* scollop (*shell-fish*)
Vannette, *s.f.* server, basket, oat-sieve
Vanneu-r, se, *s.m.f.* (*agr.*) winnower
Vannier, *s.m.* basket-maker
Vannure, *s.f.* winnowings, chaff
†Vantail, *s.m.* leaf; folding-door
Vantard, e, *adj. s.* boasting, boastful, bragging, swaggering; boaster, braggart, swaggerer
Vantardise, *s.f. V.* **Vanterie**
Vanter, *v.a.* to boast, to praise, to extol, to exalt, to cry up, to vaunt [to plume oneself
Se —, *v.r.* to boast, to brag, to praise oneself;
Vanterie, *s.f.* boasting, bragging, brag
Vanteu-r, se, *adj. s. V.* **Vantard**
Vantiler *or* **†Vantiller,** *v.a.* to stop the water with planks
Vapeur, *s.f.* vapour; damp; steam; smoke; fume; airiness; engine; — *s.m.* (*nav.*) steamer; —**s,** *s.f. pl.* vapours, &c.; (*med.*) vapours (hypochondria, hysterics, &c.). *A* —, (*adject.*) steam. *A la* —, by steam; (*adject.*) steam. *A toute* —, at full speed. *Bâtiment* or *navire* or *vaisseau à* —, steam-vessel, steam-ship, steamer. *Chaudière, machine, &c., à* —, steam-boiler, steam-engine, &c. *Conduit de la* —, steam-port. *Imperméable à la* —, steam-tight. *Registre de* —, throttle-valve. *Vaisseau de guerre à* —, war-steamer. *Être en* —, to have the steam on. *Être en pleine* —, to have all the steam on. *Jeter* or *donner de la* —, to steam. *Mettre en* —, to put the steam on. *On est en pleine* —, the steam is up. — **-poste,** *s.m.* mail-steamer
Vaporation, *s.f.* vaporation
Vaporeu-x, se, *adj.* vaporous; (*med.*) vapourish;
Vaporisateur, *s.m.* vaporizer [(*paint.*) aerial
Vaporisation, *s.f.* vaporization
Vaporiser, *v.a.*, **Se —,** *v.r.* to vaporize
Vaquer, *v.n.* to be vacant; not to sit; (*of business*) to attend, to apply oneself
Vaquette, *s.f.* (*bot.*) cuckoo-pint, wake-robin
Vaquois, *s.m. V.* **Pandanus**
†Varaigne, *s.f.* tide-gate
Varaire, *s.f.* (*bot.*) white hellebore
Varan, *s.m.* (*zool.*) varan, monitor of the Nile
Varangue, *s.f.* (*nav.*) ribs, floor-timber
‡Varec, Varech, *s.m.* sea-ware; waif; wreck; sea-wrack, wrack; sea-weed; dulse; carrageen, Irish moss; laver; varec, kelp
Varenne, *s.f.* waste land; chase, preserve
Vareuse, *s.f.* Guernsey frock, oil-skin slop, slop; short coat, pea-jacket; yachting-jacket;
Vari, *s.m.* (*zool.*) vari [tunic
Variabilité, *s. f.* variability, variableness, changeableness
Variable, *adj.* variable, changeable; — *s.f.* (*math.*) variable; — *s.m.* (*of the barometer*) change. *Au* —, (*of the weather*) changeable
Variablement, *adv.* variably, changeably
Variant, e, *adj.* changeable, fickle; — *s.f.* various *or* different reading *or* interpretation; various *or* different spelling; difference; mixed
Variation, *s.f.* variation; alteration [pickles
Varice, *s.f.* (*med.*) varicose vein, varix
Varicelle, *s.f.* (*med.*) varicella, chicken-pox
Varicocèle, *s.f.* (*med.*) varicocele
Varier, *v.a.n.* to vary; to alter, to change; to variegate; to diversify; to differ; to disagree
Variété, *s.f.* variety; diversity; difference; change; —**s,** *pl.* varieties, &c.; medley, extracts; miscellanies; literature (*literary articles in a political newspaper*); [*also, the name of a theatre in Paris*] [variolaria
Variolaire, *adj.* (*med.*) variolar; — *s.f.* (*bot.*)
Variole, *s.f.* (*med.*) variola, small-pox. — *des bêtes à laine,* (*vet.*) rot. — *des vaches,* (*vet.*) cow-
Variolette, *s.f. V.* **Varicelle** [pox
Varioleu-x, se, *adj.* (*med.*) variolous
Varioliforme, *adj.* (*med.*) varioliform
Variolique, *adj.* (*med.*) variolic
Variolite, *s.f.* (*min.*) variolite
Varioloïde, *s.f.* (*med.*) varioloid disease, varioloid, modified *or* post-vaccinal small-pox; — *adj.* varioloid [variorum edition
Variorum, (*Latin*) variorum. *Édition* —,
Variqueu-x, se, *adj.* (*med.*) varicose, varicous
Varlet, *s.m.* (*old*) varlet, page [jointer
Varlope, *s.f.* (*tool*) trying-plane, jointing-plane,
Varloper, *v.a.n.* to work with the jointer
Varre, *s.f.* turtle-harpoon
Varrer, *v.a.n.* to harpoon (turtles)
Varreur, *s.m.* turtle-harpooner
Vartigué, *int.* (*old and pop.*) zounds!
Vas (Je), (*pop. for* **Je vais**) I go, I am going
Vasais, *s.m.* brine-pan, salt-pan
Vasard, *adj.m.* (*nav.*) oozy; — *s.m.* oozy ground
Vasculaire, Vasculeu-x, se, *adj.* vascular
Vascularité, *s.f.* vascularity
Vase, *s.f.* mud, slime, mire, ooze, silt; — *s.m.* vase; vessel; cup; urn; (*obsolete*) corolla. — *d'élection,* chosen vessel. — *de nuit,* — *nocturne,* bedroom utensil, urinary vessel
Vaseau, *s.m.* small vase *or* vessel; wooden bowl
Vaseu-x, se, *adj.* muddy, slimy, miry, oozy, silty
Vasière, *s.f.* brine-pan, salt-pan; oozy place *or* spot; oozy hole, holt; mussel-bed, mussel-
Vasiforme, *adj.* vasiform [scalp
Vasistas, *s.m.* casement; (*of a carriage*) Vene-
Vason, *s.m.* lump of tile-clay [tian blind
Vasque, *s.f.* (*of a fountain*) centre basin, basin
Vassal, e, *s.m.f.* (*feud.*) vassal
Vassalité, *s.f.* (*feud.*) vassalage; vassalry
Vasselage, *s.m.* (*feud.*) vassalage
Vastangue, *s.f. V.* **Pastenague**
Vaste, *adj.* vast; spacious; extensive; wide; great; — *s.m. adj.* (*anat.*) vastus (muscle); — *int.* (*nav.*) avast! [greatly
Vastement, *adv.* vastly, extensively, widely,
Vastité, *s.f.* vastness
Vatel, *s.m.* Vatel, great cook
Vatérie, *s.f.* (*bot.*) vateria; sal; tallow-tree
Vatican, *s.m.* Vatican (*at Rome*)
Vaticane, *s.f.* library of the Vatican
Vaticinateur, *s.m.* vaticinator
Vaticination, *s.f.* vaticination
Vaude, *s.f.* (*bot.*) *V.* **Gaude**
Vaudeville, *s.m.* vaudeville, ballad, street-song, song; (*play*) vaudeville, ballad-opera, ballad-farce; (*name of one of the Paris theatres*) Vaudeville [writer
Vaudevilliste, *s.m.f.* vaudeville-writer, ballad-
Vaudois, e, *adj.s.m.f.* of Vaud (*in Switzerland*), native of Vaud, Vaudois; — *s.m. pl.* (*eccl. hist.*) Waldenses, Vaudois; — *s.f.* (*fish*) *V.* **Vandoise**
Vau-l'eau (A), with the current, down the stream; to wreck and ruin; at sixes and sevens; to nothing, into smoke, into thin air
Vaurien, *s.m.* good-for-nothing *or* worthless fellow, vagrant, vagabond, rogue, scamp, scapegrace; — *adj. m.* worthless; roguish, wild
Vautour, *s.m.* vulture; rapacious man; exacting landlord
Vautrait, *s.m.* boar-hunting equipage
Vautré, e, *part.* wallowing, weltering; sprawling
Vautrer, *v.a.* to roll (in mud)
Se —, *v.r.* to wallow, to welter, to roll; to sprawl, to spread oneself
Vau-vent (A), with *or* before the wind
Vaux, (*old pl. of* **Val**) *V.* **Mont**
Vauxhall, *s.m.* Vauxhall [vavasour, valvassor
Vavasseur, *s.m.* (*feud.*) vavassor, vavasor,
Vavassorie, *s.f.* (*feud.*) vavassory, vavasory
Vayvodat, *s.m.* waywodate; waywodeship
Vayvode, *s.m.* waywode
Vayvodie, *s.f.* waywodeship; waywodate
Veau, *s.m.* calf, bull-calf, ox-calf; veal; (*leather*) calf-skin, calf; (*pers.*) lazy dog; stupid fellow; coward; wench. — *marin,* seal, sea-calf; seal-skin. — *de lait,* sucking calf. — *d'or,* golden calf. — *de rivière,* Norman fat calf (*calf fattened in the riverside meadows near Rouen*); land-lubber, fresh-water sailor. — *à la casserole,* stewed veal. *Eau de* —, veal-tea. *Pied de* —,

calf's foot; (*bot.*) *V.* **Gouet.** *Faire le pied de* —, to be servile, to cringe, to bow and scrape, to truckle. *Faire le* —, (*fig.*) to spread oneself out, to sprawl, to loll, to indulge oneself, to be lazy, to go on lazily [vector

Vecteur, *adj. m. Rayon* —, (*math., astr.*) radius

Vécu, e, *part. adj.* lived, &c. (*V.* **Vivre**); (*of*

Véda, *s.m.* (*Hindu rel.*) Veda [*stories*) real

Védanta, *s.m.* (*Hindu rel.*) Vedanta

Védasse, *s.f.* (*dyeing*) weed-ashes

Vedette, *s.f.* (*mil.*) vedette, mounted sentry; (*old*) sentry-box; watch-tower; (*nav.*) scout; (*in writing*) a line by itself; (*on play-bills*)

Védique, *adj.* (*Hindu rel.*) Vedic [large type

Végétable, *adj.* vegetable, capable of vegetation

Végétabilité, *s.f.* vegetability

Végétal, e, *adj.* vegetable; (*in physiology*) vegetal; — *s.m.* vegetable; plant

Végétalité, *s.f.* vegetality [vegetative

Végéta-teur, trice, Végétati-f, ve, *adj.*

Végétation, *s.f.* vegetation; plant

Végéter, *v.n.* to vegetate

Végéto-animal, e, *adj.* vegeto-animal

Végéto-minéral, e, *adj.* vegeto-mineral. *Eau —e*, Goulard's lotion [phuric

Végéto-sulfurique, *adj.* (*chem.*) vegeto sul-

Véhémence, *s.f.* vehemence, vehemency; impetuosity; force; violence

Véhément, e, *adj.* vehement; impetuous; violent; impassioned, passionate

Véhémentement, *adv.* vehemently, strongly,

Véhiculaire, *adj.* vehicular [greatly

Véhicule, *s.m.* vehicle [Vehme, Feme, Fehme

Vehme, *s.f.* (*hist.*) Vehmgerichte, Femgerichte,

Vehmique, *adj.* Vehmic [ful, vigilant; sedulous

†**Veillant, e,** *part. adj.* awake, waking, watch-

†**Veille,** *s.f.* waking; watch; watching; watchfulness; sitting up; day *or* night before; eve; point, verge, brink; —**s,** *pl.* labours, night-labours *or* studies, nights

†**Veillée,** *s.f.* sitting up; watching; night-attendance, night's attendance (*on the sick*); evening (*spent together*), evening meeting *or* company; duration *or* work *or* reading *or* occupation, &c., of ditto

†**Veiller,** *v.n.a.* to be *or* keep awake, to wake, not to go to sleep, not to sleep, not to be asleep; to sit *or* stay up; to watch; to look (after); to see (to); to take care (of, that); to protect; to sit up with; to watch over; to have an eye upon. *Faire — quelqu'un*, to keep one up. — *au grain*, (*fig.*) to look sharp after o.'s servants *or* workpeople (*so as to prevent waste or worse*), to see o.'s property safe

†**Veilleur,** *s.m.* watcher; watchman

†**Veilleuse,** *s.f.* watcher; night-light, night-lamp, watch-light; (*bot.*) meadow-saffron

†**Veillote, Veillotte,** *s.f.* (*agr.*) hay-cock;

Veinage, *s.m.* veining [(*bot.*) meadow-saffron

Veinard, e, *s.m.f.* (*pop.*) lucky fellow *or* woman

Veine, *s.f.* vein; grain; streak; fissure; bosom; humour, mood; strain; luck, run (*of good or ill luck*); run of good luck; underground spring; (*geol.*) vein, seam. — *porte*, *V.* **Porte,** *adj. Je suis en* —, I am in the vein *or* humour (for); my hand is in. *Je ne suis plus en* —, I am no longer in the vein *or* humour (for); my hand is out

Veiné, e, *adj.* veined, veiny

Veiner, *v.a.* to vein [veinous, venose

Veineu-x, se, *adj.* veinv, veined; venous,

Veinule, *s.f.* venule, veinlet, small vein

Vêlage, *s.m.* (*of cows*) calving

Velanède, *s.f.* *V.* **Avelanède** [wild rocket

Vélar, *s.m.* (*bot.*) hedge-mustard, treacle-mustard,

Velarium, *s.m.* (*antiq.*) velarium

Velche, *s.m.* Goth, barbarian, ignoramus

Velcherie, *s.f.* ignorance, stupidity

Vêle, *s.f.* cow-calf

Vélelle, *s.f.* (*zool.*) velella, jelly-fish, sea-nettle

Vêlement, *s.m.* *V.* **Vêlage**

Vêler, *v.n.* (*of cows*) to calve

Vélie, *s.f.* (*insect*) velia

Vélin, *s.m.* vellum; vellum-lace. *Papier* —, vellum-post, wove paper

Vélineuse, *s.f.* vellum-lace maker

Véliote, Véliotte. *V.* **Veillote**

Vélique, *adj.* (*nav.*) of the sails

Vélites, *s.m. pl.* (*Rom. and Fr. mil. hist.*) velites

Vélivole, *adj.* velivolant [(*body of troops*)

Velléité, *s.f.* velleity; slight desire, desire, mind; fancy

Vellosie, Vellozie, *s.f.* (*bot.*) vellozia, tree lily

Véloce, *adj.* swift, rapid

Vélocifère, *s.m.f.* *V.* **Accéléré,** *s.*

Vélocipède, *s.m.* velocipede

Vélocipéder, *v.n.* to go on a velocipede

Vélocipédiste, *s.m.f.* velocipedist

Vélocité, *s.f.* velocity, swiftness, rapidity, speed

Velonée, Velonnée, *s.f.* *V.* **Avelanède**

Velot, *s.m.* still-born calf

Velours, *s.m.* velvet; (*jest., of the nails*) black dirt; (*a euphemism for* **Cuir,** *which See*) soft slip (of the tongue, *s for t*). *De* —, (*adject.*) velvet. — *à côtes*, corduroy. — *de coton*, cotton velvet. — *de coton croisé*, velveteen. — *glacé*, shot velvet. *Habit de* —, *ventre de son*, (*Proverb*) clothe the back and starve the belly, silks and satins put out the kitchen fire

Velouté, e, *adj.* velvet; velveted; velvet-pile; (*fig.*) velvet-like, velvety; velutinous; soft; soft and smooth to the palate, deep-coloured, rich; — *s.m.* velveting; velvet; velvet-down; velvet-pile; velvet-ribbon; velvet-lace; flock-surface; softness [of velvet, to make velvet-like

Velouter, *v.a.* to give (*to a stuff*) the appearance

Veloutier, *s.m.* (*adject., Ouvrier* —) velvet-worker

Velu, e, *adj.* hairy, shaggy, rough; — *s.m.* hairiness, shagginess; hairy part

Veluette, *s.f.* (*bot.*) mouse-ear

Vélum, *s.m.* velum, awning, covering

Velverette, *s.f.* corduroy

Velvet, *s.m.*, **Velvetine,** *s.f.* velveteen

Velvote, *s.f.* (*bot.*) toad-flax

Venaison, *s.f.* venison. *Basse* —, hare and rabbit

Vénal, e, *adj.* venal, mercenary

Vénalement, *adv.* venally

Vénaliser, *v.a.* to venalize, to make *or* render

Vénalité, *s.f.* venality [venal

Venant, e, *adj.* coming; forthcoming; growing, thriving; — *s.m.* comer. *A tout* —, to all comers; to anyone; as the fancy takes (*or* took) one

Vendable, *adj.* salable, vendible, marketable

Vendange, *s.f.* vintage; grape-gathering; picking [gather; to destroy, to sweep away

Vendanger, *v.n.a.* to gather the grapes; to

Vendangeron, *s.m.* (*insect*) harvest-bug

Vendangeu-r, se, *s.m.f.* vintager, grape-

Vendéen, ne, *adj. s.* Vendean [gatherer

Vendémiaire, *s.m.* Vendémiaire (*first month of the calendar of the first French Republic, from September* 22 *to October* 21)

Venderesse, *s.f.* vendor, seller

Vendetta, Vendette, *s.f.* vendetta, private vengeance (*in Corsica*)

Vendeu-r, se, *s.m.f.* vendor, vender, seller, dealer

Vendication, Vendiquer. *V.* **Revendication,** &c. [out. *A* —, to be sold, for sale

Vendre, *v.a.n.* to sell; to sell for; to sell off *or*

Se —, *v.r.* to sell; to sell for; to be sold; to be sold for; to sell oneself *or* each other; to betray oneself

Vendredi, *s.m.* Friday. — *saint*, Good Friday

Vendu, e, *part. adj.* sold, &c. (*V.* **Vendre**); — *s.m.* (*pop.*) military substitute

Vené, e, *adj.* (*of meat*) high

Vénéfice, *s m.* (*old*) venefice, poisoning

Venelle, *s.f.* (*obsolete*) small street, lane, alley. *Enfiler la* —, (*old*) to scamper away, to take flight, to take to o.'s heels

Vénéneu-x, se, *adj.* venomous, poisonous

Vénénifère, *adj.* veneniferous

Vénénifique, *adj.* venenific

Vénénipare, *adj.* veneniparous

Vénénosité, *s.f.* venomousness

Vener, *v.a.* to run (*tame animals, cattle*). *Faire* —, to keep (*meat*) till it gets high
Vénérable, *adj.* venerable
Vénérablement, *adv.* venerably
Vénéra-teur, trice, *s.m.f. adj.* venerator; [venerating
Vénération, *s.f.* veneration
Vénérer, *v.a.* to venerate, to reverence
Vénérides, *s.f. pl.* (*zool.*) veneridæ (*molluscs*)
Vénerie, *s.f.* hunting; hunt; hunting-train; kennel
Vénérien, ne, *adj.* venereal; syphilitic; — *s.m.f.* syphilitic patient. *Hôpital des —s*, Lock [Hospital
Vénésection, *s.f.* (*surg.*) venesection
Venet, *s.m.* (*fish.*) stake-net, poke-net
Venette, *s.f.* (*pop.*) funk, stew. *Avoir la* —, to be funky, to funk, to be in a funk *or* stew. *Donner la — à*, to put in a funk *or* stew, to frighten [the hounds
Veneur, *s.m.* huntsman. *Grand* —, master of
Venez-y-voir, *s.m.* (*jest.*) sight, show, raree-show, puppet-show, pretty thing, catch, cheat
Vengé, e, *part.* revenged, avenged; — *s.m.* (*bot.*) [kino-tree
Vengeance, *s.f.* vengeance, revenge
Venger, *v.a.* to revenge, to avenge; to take revenge for; to resent

Se —, *v.r.* to revenge *or* avenge oneself; to take revenge; to be revenged; to resent

Veng-eur, eresse, *s.m.f. adj.* revenger, avenger; revengeful, avenging
Vénialité, *s.f.* veniality, venialness
Veniat, *s.m.* (*law*) summons
Veni creator, *s.m.* Veni Creator (*hymn*)
Véniel, le, *adj.* venial
Véniellement, *adv.* venially
Veni-mecum, *s.m.* *V.* **Vade-mecum**
Venimeu-x, se, *adj.* venomous, venom, poisonous, poison; malignant
Venimosité, *s.f.* venomousness [malice
Venin, *s.m.* venom; poison; rancour, spite,
Venir, *v.n.* to come; to be coming; to come on *or* along; to come up *or* down *or* in *or* out *or* over *or* round *or* away; to come and; to proceed; to repair; to arrive; to attain; to reach; to fit; to suit; (*of plants*) to grow, to grow up, (*— bien*) to thrive; to succeed; (*of contingencies, ideas*, &c.) to happen; to occur; to chance; to fall out; should, were (to); to strike; to arise, to result; to run, to flow; to issue; to spring; to be descended; — *s.m.* coming. — *de*, to come *or* &c. from; (*before an inf.*) to have *or* be just (*before a past part.*) [*Je viens voir*, I come to see; *Je viens* **de** *voir*, I have just seen; *Il venait* **de** *sortir*, he had *or* was just gone out]. *A* —, to come; coming; future; after- ... *En — à*, to come to; to proceed to; to have recourse to; to bring oneself to; to be reduced to; to at last ...; to come off, to get off; to go so far as; to attain, to reach. *Y*—, to come here *or* there; to come to that; to try. *Faire* —, to make (...) come; to cause to come; to send for; to have (...) brought *or* sent; to call for; to call; to call in; to reduce; to bring; to cause; to produce; to raise, to grow. *S'en* —, to come away *or* along; to come on *or* up; to come. *Se faire bien — de*, to ingratiate oneself with; to get into ...'s favour, to curry favour with. *Voir — quelqu'un*, to see one come *or* coming; to see what one is driving at *or* what one means, to see one's intentions. *Vouloir en — à*, to aim *or* be aiming at, to drive *or* be driving at, to mean, to be up to. *Où voulez-vous en* —, what are you aiming *or* driving at? what do you mean? what is your object? *D'où vient cela?* where does that come from? what is the cause of that? *D'où vient que ...?* how is it that ...? *Il me vient une idée*, an idea occurs to me *or* strikes me, I have an idea. *Viens! Venez! Viens* or *Venez donc!* come! come away! come along!
Vénitien, ne, *adj.s.* Venetian; Venetian fashion
Vent, *s.m.* wind; gale; breeze; air; breath; vent; scent; emptiness; vanity; (*artil.*) windage; (*nav.*) wind, weather; (*nav.*) windward; (*nav.*) weathergage. — *fait*, settled wind. — *roux*, cold dry wind. *Avantage du* —, weather-gage. *A*—, (*adject.*) wind; air. *Au* —, to the wind; (*nav.*) windward. *Côté du* —, windward. *De* or *du* —, (*adject.*) windy; (*nav.*) weather; windward. *En plein* —, in the open air; (*of trees*) standard. *Sous le* —, (*nav.*) leeward; alee. *Aller comme le* —, to go swiftly. *Aller selon le* —, to sail with the wind; (*fig.*) to comply with the times, to be a time-server *or* a weathercock. *Avoir — de*, (*fig.*) to get wind of. *Avoir le — sur*, to be to windward of. *Être au-dessus du* —, (*fig.*) to be safe. *Faire du* —, to be windy; to create wind. *Gagner le — sur*, to get to windward of, to weather. *Prendre le* —, to scent; (*nav.*) to sail near the wind. *Autant en emporte le* —, that is all moonshine; all that is idle talk; there is nothing in that; many words will not fill a bushel. *Il fait du* —, it is windy. *Le — qu'il fait*, the wind which blows, such wind as this, such windy weather. *Le — qu'il faisait*, the wind which blew, such wind as that, such windy weather
Ventage, *s.m.* (*agr.*) fanning [tail, visor
†**Ventail,** *s.m.* *V.* **Vantail;** (*of helmets*) ven-
Ventaison, *s.f.* (*agr.*) wind-blight
Vente, *s.f.* sale; selling; auction; (*of woods*) felling, cutting, cut. — *judiciaire*, sale under warrant. *De bonne* —, salable, that goes off well. *En* —, on sale; for sale; selling; just published, published, now ready. *Mettre en* —, to put up *or* offer for sale; to sell; to publish
Ventelle, *s.f.* (*of lock-gates*) paddle-valve [(*books*)
Venter, *v.n.* to blow, to be windy; — *v.a.* to blow, to drive. *Il vente* (*imp.*) the wind blows
Venteu-x, se, *adj.* windy; flatulent
Ventier, *s.m.* wood-salesman [nightman
Ventilateur, *s.m.* ventilator; fan; bellows;
Ventilation, *s.f.* ventilation; airing; (*law*) valuation
Ventiler, *v.a.* to ventilate; to fan; (*law*) to value
Ventis, *s.m. pl.* wind-fallen wood [the wind
Ventolier, *s.m.* (*falc.*) bird that flies against
Ventôse, *s.m.* Ventose (*sixth month of the calendar of the first French Republic, from February* 19 *to March* 20) [flatulence, flatulency
Ventosité, *s.f.* ventosity, windiness, wind,
Ventousation, *s.f.* (*surg.*) cupping
Ventouse, *s.f.* ventilator; vent-hole; air-hole; (*surg.*) cupping-glass, cup; (*arch.*) ventiduct. *Appliquer des —s*, to cup
Ventouser, *v.a.* (*surg.*) to cup
Ventouseur, *s.m.* (*surg.*) cupper
Ventral, *adj.* ventral
Ventre, *s.m.* belly, abdomen; (*in the slang of those who never call things by their proper name*) stomach; (*ways of speaking, more or less fig. and fam.*) bowels; guts; breast; womb; chest; body; inside; corporation; bulging; victuals, food, eating, grub; (*of bottles*, &c.) belly. *Bas-* —, *See Letter* **B.** — *à terre*, flat on o.'s face; flat on the ground; at full speed. *Dans le* —, in the belly *or* &c.; inside; in one (in me, in thee, in him, &c.); to live upon; to live. *Avoir dans le* —, to have in the belly *or* inside *or* &c.; to be capable of, can do; can yield; to think. *Avoir mal au* —, to have the belly-ache *or* the colic. *Faire le* —, *Faire* —, to bulge, to swell out. *Manger à — déboutonné*, to eat like a glutton. *Passer sur le — à* or *de*, to trample *or* bear down, to rout. *Prendre du* —, to get a corporation, to run to guts. *Se serrer le* —, to tighten o.'s waistband, to buckle o.'s waistband in tightly, to stint *or* pinch oneself. — **bleu,** — **-saint-gris,** *int.* (*old*) zounds!
Ventrée, *s.f.* litter, brood; (*pop.*) bellyful; [blow-out
Ventriculaire, *adj.* ventricular
Ventricule, *s.m.* ventricle; stomach
Ventri-er, ère, *adj.* ventral, abdominal; — *s.f.* girth, girt, belly-band; abdominal belt; sling; (*carp.*) purlin; (*mach.*) brace

Ventriloque, *s.m.f.* ventriloquist; — *adj.* ventriloquous, ventriloquial
Ventriloquer, *v.n.* to ventriloquize
Ventriloquie, *s.f.* ventriloquy, ventriloquism
Ventripotent, e, *adj.* ventripotent
†**Ventrouiller (Se),** *v.r.* to wallow in the mud
Ventru, e, *adj. s.* big-bellied, pot-bellied, tun-bellied, swag-bellied, corpulent; bulging; big-bellied *or* corpulent person; (*polit.*) ministerialist
Venu, e, *part.* (*of* **Venir**), *adj. s.* come, arrived; having come, having arrived; happened; fallen; succeeded; grown, &c.; comer. *Bien* —, welcome; well-received; well-grown; successful; justified; right. *Mal* —, not welcome; ill-received; ill-grown, ill-shaped, stunted; unsuccessful; not justified; wrong. *Le premier* —, *la première* —*e*, the first come *or* arrived; the first comer, the first that comes *or* came; the first person one meets with; no matter who *or* which; anyone. *Le premier* ... —, *la première* ... —*e*, any ...
Venue, *s.f.* coming; arrival; advent; growth; lot. *D'une belle* —, well-grown. *Tout d'une* —, all of a size; all at once, at a stretch
Vénule. *V.* **Veinule**
Vénus, *s.f.* (*myth., astr., mollusc, and fig. of pers.*) Venus; (*old chem.*) Venus, copper
Vénusin, e, *adj. s.* Venusian
Vénusté, *s.f.* (*obsolete*) gracefulness, elegance
Venvole (A la), *adv.* lightly, thoughtlessly
Vêpres, *s.f. pl.* (*Cath. lit.*) vespers
Ver, *s.m.* worm; maggot; mite; grub; gentle; moth. — *blanc, V.* **Man.** — *-coquin*, vine-fretter, vine-grub; cœnurus cerebralis, tapeworm; (*vet.*) *V.* **Tournis**; (*fig.*) maggot, whim. — *luisant*, glowworm. — *rongeur*, gnawing worm, &c. (*V.* **Rongeur**). — *solitaire*, tænia, tapeworm. — *à soie*, silkworm. — *de terre*, earthworm, dewworm; wretch. — *de mer, V.* **Taret.** *Mangé aux* —*s*, *rongé des* —*s*, worm-eaten. *Piqué des* —*s*, worm-eaten; (*fig.*) bad, amiss, &c. (*V.* **Piqué**). *Tuer son* —, (*pop.*) to drink a drop of liquor in the morning on an [empty stomach
Véracité, *s.f.* veracity
Véraison, *s.f.* (*of grapes*) turning, ripening
Véranda, *s.f.* veranda, verandah
Vératre, *s.m.* (*bot.*) veratrum
Vératrine, *s.f.* (*chem.*) veratria, veratrine
Vératrique, *adj.* (*chem.*) veratric
Veratrum, *s.m.* (*bot.*) veratrum [**verbal**
Verbal, e, *adj.* verbal; — *s.m. V.* **Procès-**
Verbalement, *adv.* verbally, by word of mouth
Verbalisation, *s.f.* statement of facts; drawing up an official report; written certification; account
Verbaliser, *v.n.* to state facts, to make a statement of facts; to draw up *or* make an official report; to twaddle, to be verbose *or* long-winded, to make many words; — *v.a.* to certify in writing [tone, voice; words, speech
Verbe, *s.m.* (*gram.*) verb; (*theol.*) Word; (*fam.*)
Verbénacées, *s.f. pl.* (*bot.*) verbenaceæ
Verbération, *s.f.* verberation [words
Verbeusement, *adv.* verbosely, with many
Verbeu-x, se, *adj.* verbose, wordy
Verbiage, *s.m.* verbiage, idle words, empty talk, twaddle, gabble, palaver; jargon
Verbiager, *v.n.* to be verbose *or* wordy; to twaddle, to palaver
Verbiageu-r, se, *s.m.f.* verbose *or* wordy speaker; empty talker, twaddler; — *adj.* wordy, prolix, twaddling, long-winded
Verbosité, *s.f.* verbosity, wordiness; flippancy
†**Verbouillet,** *s.m. V.* **Brusc**
Verd, e, *adj.* (*obsolete spelling*) *V.* **Vert**
Verdal, *s.m.* area-light, cellar-light
Verdâtre, *adj.* greenish
Verdée, *s.f.* verdee (*white wine of Tuscany*)
Verdelet, te, *adj.* (*of wine*) tart, tartish; (*pers.*) vigorous, strong, hale and hearty
Verderame, *s.m.* (*maize disease*) verderame
Verderie, *s.f.* verderer's range *or* jurisdiction
Verdet, *s.m.* (*chem.*) verditer; (*maize disease*) verderame
Verdeur, *s.f.* greenness; briskness, freshness, vigour; unripeness; tartness; roughness; [acrimony
Verdict, *s.m.* verdict
Verdier, *s.m.* (*pers.*) verderer; (*bird*) greenfinch
Verdique, *adj.* (*chem.*) verdic
Verdir, *v.n.*, **Se** —, *v.r.* to become *or* grow *or* turn green, to assume *or* receive a green hue; — *v.a.* to paint *or* make green; to make (...) turn green [making green
Verdissement, *s.m.* growing *or* turning *or*
Verdon, *s.m.* (*bird*) *V.* **Mouchet**
Verdoyant, e, *adj.* verdant, green; greenish
Verdoyer, *v.n.* to be verdant, to become *or* grow *or* turn green; to look green, to show its [verdure
Verdun, *s.m.* long narrow sword
Verdure, *s.f.* verdure; verdancy; greenness, green; greens, green vegetables, pot-herbs, salads; green food; grass; green turf; green branches; forest-work hangings
Verduri-er, ère, *s.m.f.* greengrocer
†**Vérétille,** *s.f.* (*zool.*) veretillum (*kind of polype*)
Véreu-x, se, *adj.* worm-eaten; maggoty; grubby; suspicious, doubtful; unsound, rotten, bad
Verge, *s.f.* rod; wand; stick; tipstaff; verge; whisk; (*of whips*) handle; (*of anchors*) shank; (*obsolete*) rood; (*obsolete meas. for cloth*) yard; —**s,** *pl.* rods, &c.; birch-rod, rod, birch; (*mil.*) gauntlet. — *d'or*, (*bot.*) golden rod. *Faire passer par les* —*s*, (*mil.*) to flog through the line. *Passer* (*v.a.*) *par les* —*s*, (*mil.*) to flog. *Passer* (*v.n.*) *par les* —*s*, *être passé par les* —*s*, (*mil.*) to be flogged, to run the gauntlet
Vergé, e, *adj.* streaky; (*of paper*) laid
Vergée, *s.f.* (*obsolete*) square rood
Verger, *s.m.* orchard, fruit-garden
Vergerette, Vergerolle, *s.f.* (*bot.*) fleabane, fleawort; golden rod
Vergeter, *v.a.* to dust, to beat, to whisk, to brush; to flog, to whip; to streak
Vergetier, *s.m.* brush-maker; rod-maker
Vergette, *s.f.* —**s,** *pl.* dusting-brush, whisk; bundle of rods; (*her.*) vergette
Vergeture, *s.f.* weal; streak; stripe
Vergeure, *s.f.* (*stat.*) wire; wire-mark
Verglacé, e, *part. adj.* coated *or* covered with ice, frozen over
Verglacer, *v. imp. Il verglace*, the rain freezes as it falls; — *v.a.* to coat *or* cover with ice
Verglas, *s.m.* coating of very slippery ice, ice on the roads, ice. *Il fait* (or *il tombe*) *du* —, the rain freezes as it falls
†**Vergne,** *s.m.* (*bot.*) alder
†**Vergogne,** *s.f.* shame [modest; bashful
†**Vergogneu-x, se,** *adj.* shy, coy, reserved,
Vergue, *s.f.* (*nav.*) yard
Véricle, *s.f.* (*jewel.*) paste, imitation
Véridicité, *s.f.* truthfulness, veracity, credibility
Véridique, *adj.* truthful, veracious, of veracity, credible [credibly
Véridiquement, *adv.* truthfully, veraciously,
Vérifiable, *adj.* verifiable, ascertainable
Vérifica-teur, trice, *s.m.f.* verifier; examiner; inspector, inspectress; assizer; reviser; assayer; [auditor
Vérificati-f, ve, *adj.* verificative
Vérification, *s.f.* verification, verifying; examination; inspection; assizing; revising; proving; assaying, assay; auditing, audit; (*of wills*) proving, probate
Vérifier, *v.a.* to verify; to examine; to inspect; to confirm; to ascertain; to prove; to assize; to revise; to assay; to try; to audit; (*law*) to [prove (*a will*)
Se —, *v.r.* to be verified, &c.
Vérin, *s.m.* screw-crane, jack-screw, hand-screw, hand-jack
Vérissime, *adj.* most true, most truthful
Véritable, *adj.* veritable; true; real; actual; genuine; pure; regular, true-bred
Véritablement, *adv.* veritably; verily; truly; really; actually; indeed; in fact

Véritas, *s.m.* *Bureau* —, Lloyd's Rooms
Vérité, *s.f.* verity; truth; truthfulness; **—s,** *pl.* truths; faults; faults told. *A la* —, indeed, it is true. *En* —, indeed, truly, in truth, verily, really. *Toutes —s ne sont pas bonnes à dire,* all truths must not be told at all times
Verjus, *s.m.* verjuice; sour grapes; sour wine. *C'est jus vert et* —, it is six of one and half-a-dozen of the other
Verjuté, e, *adj.* tart; with verjuice
Verjuter, *v.a.* to season with verjuice
†**Vermeil, le,** *adj.* vermilion; (*fig.*) coral, rosy, ruddy; — *s.m.* silver-gilt; (*agr.*) wormy place
Vermicelle, *s.m.* vermicelli; (*potage au* —) vermicelli-soup [warehouseman
Vermicellier, *s.m.* vermicelli-maker; Italian
Vermicide, *adj.* worm-destroying, vermicidal; — *s.m.* vermicide, worm-destroyer
Vermiculaire, *adj.* vermicular; — *s.f.* (*bot.*) white stone-crop
Vermiculation, *s.f.* vermiculation [miculate
Vermiculé, e, *part. adj.* vermiculated; ver-
Vermiculer, *v.a.* (*arch,* &c.) to vermiculate
Vermiculeu-x, se, *adj.* vermiculous
Vermiculures, *s.f.pl.*(*arch.,*&c.) vermiculation
Vermification, *s.f.* vermification [worm-like
Vermiforme, *adj.* vermiform, worm-shaped,
Vermifuge, *adj.* vermifugal, anthelmintic, for worms, worm; — *s.m.* vermifuge, vermicide,
†**Vermille,** *s f. V.* **Cordée** [anthelmintic
†**Vermiller,** *v.n.* to scratch *or* search for worms
†**Vermillon,** *s.m.* vermilion
†**Vermillonner,** *v.a.* to vermilion; — *v.n.* to scratch *or* search for worms
Vermination, *s.f.* vermination
Vermine, *s.f.* vermin; rabble, varmint
Vermineu-x, se, *adj.* verminous; containing worms, wormy; (*med.*) caused by worms
Verminière, *s.f.* worm-pit for poultry: swarm of maggots *or* of vermin
Vermisseau, *s.m.* small worm, grub, vermicule
Vermivore, *adj.* (*zool.*) vermivorous
Vermouler (Se), *v.r.* to grow *or* be worm-eaten
Vermoulu, e, *adj.* worm-eaten; decayed, rotten, crumbling into dust [worm-hole dust
Vermoulure, *s.f.* worm-eating; worm-holes;
Vermout, *s.m.* bitters, vermout
Vernaculaire, *adj.* vernacular
Vernal, e, *adj.* vernal
Vernat, *s.m. V.* **Auvernat**
Vernation, *s.f.* (*bot.*) vernation, prefoliation
Verne, *s.m.* (*bot.*) alder
Verni, e, *part. adj.* varnished, &c. (*V.* **Vernir**); patent; patent-leather. *Cuir* —, varnished leather, patent leather. *Souliers —s,* patent-leather shoes. *Bottes —es,* patent-leather boots
Vernicifère, *adj.* (*bot.*) verniciferous, varnish-
Vernier, *s.m.* (*math. instr.*) vernier [yielding
Vernir, *v.a.* to varnish; to glaze; to lacquer; to japan; to polish
Vernis, *s.m.* varnish; glaze, glazing; japan; polish; gloss. — *de la Chine,* (*bot.*) *V.* **Ailante.** — *du Japon,* (*bot.*) varnish-sumach, Japan varnish-tree [quering; japanning
Vernissage, *s.m.* varnishing; glazing; lac-
Vernisser, *v.a.* to varnish; to glaze; to japan
Vernisseur, *s.m.* varnisher; glazer; lacquerer; japanner; French polisher
Vernissure, *s.f. V.* **Vernissage**
Vernonie, *s f.* (*bot.*) vernonia
Vérole, *s.f.* (*med.*) pox. *Petite* —, small-pox, variola. *Petite — volante,* chicken-pox
Vérolé, e, *adj. s.* (*med.*) poxed, syphilitic
Vérolette, *s f V.* **Varicelle**
Vérolique, *adj.* (*med.*) of the pox, syphilitic
Véroloïde, *s.f.* (*med.*) syphiloid symptoms
Véron, *s.m.* (*fish*) minnow
Véronais, e, *adj. s.* Veronese
Véronique, *s.f.* (*bot.*) veronica, speedwell; (*Cath. lit.*) Veronica [brandlings
Vérotis, *s.m.* (*fish.*) red gentles *or* worms,
†**Verraille,** *s.f.* small glass-wares; old glass
Verrat, *s.m.* boar
Verre, *s.m.* glass; tumbler; glass case; glass frame; glass shade; glass-plate, plate; slide; glass bottle, bottle, glass; chimney (*of a lamp*; illumination-lamp, church-lamp, lamp. *De* —, of *or* from glass; (*adject.*) glass; glass-like, glassy. — *à boire,* drinking-glass, tumbler. — *à facettes,* glass with facets, multiplying glass. — *à patte,* — *à pied,* — *à vin,* wine glass. — *de vin,* glass of wine. — *à vitres,* window-glass. — *de couleur,* coloured *or* stained glass; variegated lamp. — *de montre,* watch-glass. *Demi-* —, half-a-glass; half-a-glass of brandy. *Grand* —, large glass; tumbler. *Petit* —, small
Verrée, *s.f.* glassful, glass [glass; glass of brandy
Verrer, *v.a.* to glass. *Papier verré,* glass-paper
Verrerie, *s.f.* glass-making; glass-trade; glass-manufactory, glass-works; glass-warehouse; glass-house; glass-work, glass-ware, glass-wares, glass, crystal
Verrier, *s.m.* glass-maker *or* founder *or* worker; glass-man; glass-basket; glass-stand; — *adj. m. Peintre* or *artiste* —, glass-painter
Verrière, *s.f.* glass-tub; hand-glass; window; glass frame, glass
†**Verrillon,** *s.m.* (*mus. instr.*) glass harmonicon
Verrin, *s.m. V.* **Vérin**
Verrine, *s.f.* glass frame, glass; hand-glass; glass tube; glass tinsel; (*Cicero's*) Verrine oration (*any one of the seven*)
Verroterie, *s.f.* glass-ware, glass-wares, glass; glass trinkets, glass beads
Verrou, *s.m.* bolt. *Sous les —s,* under lock and key, locked up, shut up, closely confined, in
†**Verrouillement,** *s.m.* bolting [prison
†**Verrouiller,** *v.a.* to bolt; to bolt in, to shut up
Verrucaire, *s.f.* (*bot.*) wart-wort
Verrue, *s.f.* wart
Verruqueu-x, se, *adj.* verrucose, warty
Vers, *s.m.* verse, line (of poetry); — *pl.* verses, poetry. *Grands* —, alexandrines, verses of
Vers, *prep.* towards; about; to [twelve syllables
Versable, *adj.* liable to be overturned *or* upset; apt to overturn
Versade, *s.f.* overturn, overturning, upsetting
Versage, *s.m.* (*agr.*) first dressing
†**Versaillais, e,** *adj. s.* Versaillese, native of
Versant, e, *adj* apt to overturn [Versailles
Versant, *s.m.* watershed, slope, side
Versatile, *adj.* versatile
Versatilité, *s.f.* versatility
Verse, *s.f.* lodging (*of corn,* &c.); coal-basket (*of 35 lb.*); — *adj. m.* (*math.*) versed. *A* —, fast, hard, in torrents. *Pleuvoir à* —, to rain fast *or* in torrents, to pour with rain, to pour
Versé, e, *part. adj.* poured, &c. (*V.* **Verser**); versed, skilled, conversant [bearer
Verseau, *s m.* (*astr.*) Aquarius, (the) Water-
Versement, *s.m.* payment; deposit
Verser, *v.a.n.* to pour, to pour out; to shoot; to discharge; to empty, to put; to spill; to shed; to lay, to lay down; to overturn, to upset; to cast, to throw; to pay; to deposit; (*of corn,* &c.) (*v.a.*) to lodge, to lay, (*v.n.*) to be lodged *or* laid; (*of land*) to dress, to plough, to till
Verset, *s.m.* verse. *Petit* —, versicle
Verseu-r, se, *s.m.f.* pourer
Versicolore, *adj.* versicoloured [verse
Versicule, Versiculet, *s.m.* versicle, little
Versifica-teur, trice, *s.m.f.* versifier
Versification, *s.f.* versification
Versifier, *v.n.a.* to versify. *Se* —, to be versified
Version, *s.f.* version; translation
Verso, *s.m.* left-hand page, second page, even page, back, reverse [wing, turn-furrow
Versoir, *s.m.* (*of a plough*) breast, mould-board,
Verste, *s.f.* (*Russian meas.*) verst
Vert, e, *adj.* green; verdant; evergreen; unripe, sour; tart; sharp; harsh; severe; resolute; rough; raw; fresh; firm; vigorous, robust, strong; brisk; (*of fish*) undried; — *s.m.* green; grass; green food, green meat; (*of wine*) tart-

ness; (*her.*) vert. *Gros* —, cabbage green. — *antique*, — *d'Égypte*, green veined marble. — *tendre*, light green. — **d'eau, — de mer,** sea-green. — **-de-gris,** *s.m.* verdigris. — **-de-grisé, e,** *adj.* covered with verdigris. — **-de-terre,** *s.m.* verditer. — **pomme,** apple-green. *Pomme —e*, green *or* unripe apple. — **-pré,** grass-green, meadow-green. *Employer le — et le sec*, to use every means, to leave no stone unturned. *Mettre au* —, (*of horses*) to turn out to grass. *Ils sont trop —s*, the grapes [are sour

Vertaulet, *s.m.* trout-net

Vertébral, e, *adj.* (*anat.*) vertebral. *Colonne —e*, vertebral *or* spinal column, spine

Vertèbre, *s.f.* (*anat.*) vertebra [*s.m.* vertebrate

Vertébré, e, *adj.* vertebrate, vertebrated; —

Vertement, *adj.* vigorously; smartly, sharply; [severely

Vertex, *s.m.* vertex

Verti, e, *part. adj.* (*old*) inverted

Vertical, e, *adj.* vertical; upright; — *s.m.* vertical; vertical plan; —**e,** *s.f.* vertical line

Verticalement, *adv.* vertically

Verticalité, *s.f.* verticalness, verticality

Verticille, *s.m.* (*bot.*) verticil, whorl

Verticillé, e, *adj.* (*bot.*) verticillate, verti-[cillated, whorled

Verticité, *s.f.* verticity

Vertige, *s.m.* vertigo, giddiness, dizziness, swimming in the head; infatuation, folly; excitement, intoxication, madness; (*vet.*) *V.* **Vertigo.** *Donner le* —, to make giddy, to make . . .'s head turn, to turn . . .'s head

Vertigineu-x, se, *adj.* vertiginous, giddy, dizzy; subject to giddiness

Vertiginosité, *s.f.* vertiginousness

Vertigo, *s.m.* (*vet.*) vertigo, megrims, staggers; (*fig.*) whim, maggot, crotchet

Vertu, *s.f.* virtue; chastity; property, quality; power; force. *En — de*, in *or* by virtue of; in pursuance of. — *de ma vie!* bless me! bless my heart! [bless my heart! zounds!

Vertubleu, Vertuchou, *int.* (*old*) bless me!

Vertueusement, *adv.* virtuously

Vertueu-x, se, *adj.* virtuous

Vertugadin, *s.m.* (*old*) farthingale

Vérue, *s.f.* vine-fretter, vine-grub

Verve, *s.f.* fancy; inspiration; vein; fire, heat; fervour; rapture; animation; life; spirit; humour. — *comique*, vis comica

Verveine, *s.f.* (*bot.*) verbena, vervain

Vervelle, *s.f.* (*falc.*) vervel, varvel

Verveux, Vervier, *s.m.* (*fish.*) hoop-net

Vésanie, *s.f.* (*med.*) vesania

Vesce, *s.f.* (*bot.*) vetch, tare

Vesceron, *s.m.* (*bot.*) vetch, chickling-vetch, tare

Vésical, e, *adj.* (*anat.*) vesical

Vésicant, e, *adj.* (*med.*) vesicant, blistering; — *s.m.* vesicant, blistering agent

Vésication, *s.f.* (*med.*) vesication

Vésicatoire, *adj.* vesicatory, blistering; — *s.m.* blister, vesicatory. *Mouche à* —, blister-fly

Vésiculaire, *adj.* vesicular, bladdery

Vésiculation, *s.f.* (*med.*) vesiculation

Vésicule, *s.f.* (*anat.*, *bot.*, &c.) vesicle, bladder. — *aérienne* or *natatoire*, (*of fishes*) air-bladder, swim [vesiculate, bladdery

Vésiculeu-x, se, *adj.* vesiculous, vesicular,

Vesou, *s.m.* cane-juice, cane-liquor, cane-juice [syrup

Vespasienne, *s.f.* urinal

Vesper, *s.m.* (*astr.*) Vesper [book

Vespéral, *s.m.* vespers-book, evening-prayer

Vespertilion, *s.m.* (*zool.*) vespertilio, noctule [bat

Vespétro, *s.m.* vespetro (*cordial*)

Vesse, *s.f.* noiseless wind, foist, fizzle, fizzling. — **-de-loup,** *s.f.* (*bot.*) puff-ball

Vesser, *v.n.* to let out wind noiselessly, to [foist, to fizzle

Vesseu-r, se, *s.m.f.* fizzler

Vessie, *s.f.* bladder; blister; wind-bag; bubble, trifle, nonsense. — *aérienne* or *natatoire*, (*of fishes*) air-bladder, swim. *Faire croire que des —s sont des lanternes*, to make (. . .) believe that the moon is made of green cheese (*or* of cream-cheese)

Vessigon, *s.m.* (*vet.*) vessignon, wind-gall

Vesta, *s.f.* (*myth.*, *astr.*) Vesta

Vestalat, *s.m.* office of vestal; vestal's period *or* term of service (*thirty years*); vestals

Vestale, *s.f.* vestal, vestal virgin

Veste, *s.f.* jacket; vest

Vestiaire, *s.m.* wardrobe; robing-room, dressing-room, tiring-room; cloak-room; (*of friars, nuns*) clothing-expenses, clothes-money; wardrobe-keeper; — *adj.* vestiarian

Vestibulaire, *adj.* (*anat.*) vestibular

Vestibule, *s.m.* vestibule, entrance hall, hall, passage, lobby, gangway, crush-room; porch; gateway, archway; (*anat.*) vestibule

Vestige, *s.m.* vestige; track; footstep, footprint; sign, mark, trace; remains

Veston, *s.m.* loose jacket, tub-coat

Vésuvien, ne, *adj.* Vesuvian; — *s.f.* (*min.*) vesuvian, idocrase; (*cigar-light*) vesuvian; (*slang*) cynical woman

Vêtement, *s.m.* garment; clothes; dress; clothing, wearing-apparel; vestment; vesture, garb. — *manqué*, misfit

Vétéran, *s.m.* veteran; (old) soldier; pensioner; unpromoted school-boy; — *adj. m.* veteran

Vétérance, *s.f.* veteranship, condition *or* capacity *or* character *or* quality of veteran

Vétérinaire, *s.m.* veterinary surgeon, veterinarian; — *adj.* veterinary

†**Vétillard, e,** *s.m.f.* *V.* **Vétilleur**

†**Vétille,** *s.f.* trifle; puzzle [to split hairs

†**Vétiller,** *v.n.* to trifle, to stand upon trifles,

†**Vétillerie,** *s.f.* hair-splitting

†**Vétilleu-r, se,** *s.m.f.* trifler, person who stands upon trifles, hair-splitter, gnat-strainer

†**Vétilleu-x, se,** *adj.* ticklish; minute; irksome, tedious; trifling; fastidious, over-nice; punctilious; captious

Vêtir, *v.a.* to clothe, to dress; to put on; to vest

Vétiver, *s.m.* (*bot.*) vetiver, cuscus root, cuscus

Veto, *s.m.* veto

Vêtu, e, *part.* clothed, clad, dressed, arrayed

Vêture, *s.f.* taking the monastic habit *or* the veil; vestments, clothing

Vétusté, *s.f.* antiquity, oldness, old age, decay

Vétyver. *V.* **Vétiver**

Veu-f, ve, *adj.* widowed; deprived (of), bereft (of), without; — *s.m.* widower; — *s.f.* widow; (*bird*) widow bird, whydaw bird, whydaw finch; (*pop.*) guillotine, maiden. *Épouser la* —, (*pop.*) to be guillotined *or* beheaded

†**Veuille, Veuillez.** *V.* **Vouloir**

Veule, *adj.* soft, weak; light

Veuvage, *s.m.* widowhood

Vevay, *s.m.* Vevay cigar

Vexa-teur, trice, *s.m.f. adj.* vexer; vexatious

Vexation, *s.f.* vexation, annoyance

Vexatoire, *adj.* vexatious

Vexatoirement, *adv.* vexatiously

Vexer, *v.a.* to vex, to annoy, to provoke, to tease **Se** —, *v.r.* to get vexed; to tease each other

Vexillaire, *s.m. adj.* vexillary

Viâ, *prep.* viâ, by the way of

Viabilité, *s.f.* viability; road-making; good repair, repairs; highways, roads, thorough-[fares; traffic

Viable, *adj.* viable, likely to live

Viaduc, *s.m.* viaduct

Viag-er, ère, *adj.* for life, life; — *s.m.* life-interest, life-income, annuity for life, life-annuity; life-annuities. *Placer en* —, to invest in a life-annuity, to sink

Viagèrement, *adv.* for life, during life [tenure

Viagèreté, *s.f.* life-interest, life-holding, life-

Viande, *s.f.* meat; flesh; food; viand; (*obsolete*) dish. — *blanche*, white meat (*poultry, rabbit, veal*, &c.). — *creuse*, unsubstantial food; frothy matter; idle fancy. — *noire*, brown meat (*hare, woodcock, wild boar, venison*, &c.). — *de boucherie*, butchers' meat. *Basse* —, inferior meat, coarse meat. *Grosse* —, butchers' meat. *Menue* —, poultry, game, &c.

Viander, *v.n.* (*of deer*) to feed

Viandis, *s.m.* (*hunt.*) feeding (*for deer*)
Viatique, *s.m.* viaticum, provisions for a journey, travelling-money; (*fig.*) way to success; (*Cath. rel.*) viaticum
Vibord, *s.m.* (*of a ship*) waist
Vibrant, e, *adj.* vibrating, vibrant; vibratory; (*of the pulse*) vibrating, wiry
Vibratile, *adj.* vibratile
Vibratilité, *s.f.* vibratility
Vibration, *s.f.* vibration
Vibratoire, *adj.* vibratory
Vibrer, *v.n.* to vibrate
Vibrion, *s.m.* (*zool.*) vibrio, microscopic eel
Vibrioniens, *s.m. pl.* (*zool.*) vibrionidæ
Vibrisses, *s.f. pl.* vibrissæ [—, grand vicar
Vicaire, *s.m.* vicar; (*of a parish*) curate. *Grand*
Vicairie, *s.f.* *V.* **Vicariat**
Vicarial, e, *adj.* vicarious, vicarial
Vicariat, *s.m.* vicarship; vicariate; vicarage; (*of a parish*) curacy, curateship; chapel of ease
Vicarier, *v.n.* to do curate's duty; (*fig.*) to do the duty of a subaltern; to hold a subordinate office
Vice, *s.m.* vice; defect; imperfection; flaw; error; (*in compounds*) vice- ... — *de forme*, informality. — **-amiral,** *s.m.* vice-admiral; second ship in a fleet, vice-admiral's ship. — **-amirauté,** *s.f.* vice-admiralty. — **-chambellan,** *s.m.* vice-chamberlain. — **-chancelier,** *s.m.* vice-chancellor. — **-consul,** *s.m.* vice-consul. — **-consulaire,** *adj.* vice-consular. — **-consulat,** *s.m.* vice-consulate; vice-consulship. — **-gérance,** *s.f.* office of deputy-manager *or* manageress; vicegerency. — **-gérant, e,** *s.m.f.* deputy-manager, deputy-manageress; vicegerent. — **-légat,** *s.m.* vice-legate. — **-légation,** *s.f.* vice-legateship. — **-préfet,** *s.m.* vice-prefect. — **-présidence,** *s. f.* vice-presidency; deputy-chairmanship, vice-chairmanship. — **-président, e,** *s.m.f.* vice-president, vice-presidentess; deputy-chairman, vice-chairman. — **-présidentiel, le,** *adj.* vice-presidential. — **-recteur,** *s.m.* vice-rector; vice-provost. — **-reine,** *s.f.* vice-queen; viceroy's wife. — **-roi,** *s.m.* viceroy. — **-royal, e,** *adj.* viceregal. — **-royauté,** *s.f.* viceroyalty. — **versâ,** *adv.* vice versâ, [reciprocally
Vicennal, e, *adj.* vicennial [corruptible
Vicésimal, e, *adj.* vicesimal
Viciable, *adj.* liable to be vitiated *or* corrupted,
Vicia-teur, trice, *adj.* vitiating, corrupting,
Viciation, *s.f.* vitiation, corruption [corruptive
Vicié, e, *part. adj.* vitiated, &c. (*V.* **Vicier**); corrupted, corrupt; foul [spoil; to make foul
Vicier, *v.a.* to vitiate, to corrupt, to taint, to
Se —, *v.r.* to become vitiated *or* corrupt; to become *or* get tainted *or* spoilt; to become *or*
Vicieusement, *adv.* viciously [get foul
Vicieu-x, se, *adj.* vicious; defective, faulty
Vicinal, e, *adj.* (*of roads*) connecting, parish
Vicinalité, *s.f.* (*of roads*) connection, commu-
Vicissitude, *s.f.* vicissitude, change [nication
Vicomtal, e, *adj.* of a viscount *or* viscountess,
Vicomte, *s.m.* viscount [viscount's
Vicomté, *s.m.* viscountship, viscountcy, vis-
Vicomtesse, *s.f.* viscountess [county
Victimaire, *s.m.* (*antiq.*) victimarius; — *adj.* of a victim, of victims
Victime, *s.f.* victim; sufferer
Victimer, *v.a.* to victimize
Victoire, *s.f.* victory; Victoria
Victoria, *s.f.* Victoria phaeton; park phaeton, phaeton; (*pers., planet*) Victoria; (*bot.*) victoria, victoria regia, water-maize
Victorial, e, *adj.* victorial
Victorien, ne, *adj. s.* Victorian
Victorieusement, *adv.* victoriously
Victorieu-x, se, *adj.* victorious; — *s.m.* victor,
Victorin, *s.m.* canon of St. Victor [conqueror
†**Victuaille,** *s.f.* victuals, provisions, creature
Vidage, *s.m.* emptying [comforts; stores
Vidame, *s.m.* (*feud.*) vidame
Vidamé, *s.m.*, **Vidamie,** *s.f.* (*feud.*) vidameship
Vidange, *s.f.* emptying; cleaning; clearing; removing; ullage (*remaining liquor*); (*of a privy*) night-work; (— **s,** *pl.*) night-soil; (*med.*) discharge, discharges, lochia; (*of a road*) trench. *En* —, (*of casks*, &c.) partly empty; (*of liquors*) partly gone, in a cask *or* &c. partly empty, in draught. *Voiture de* —, night-cart
Vidangeur, *s.m.* nightman
Vide, *adj.* empty; void; vacant; blank; vacuous; devoid, destitute; barren; — *s.m.* void; vacuum; vacuity; vacancy; empty *or* vacant space; empty air; empty part; blank; gap; chasm; emptiness, nothingness. *A* —, empty, without anything *or* anybody; hollow; upon nothing; nothing, the air; without producing the required effect *or* attaining o.'s object. *Corde à* —, (*mus.*) open string. — **-bouteilles,** *s.m.* bottle-emptier, siphon; drunkard; small country-house, country-box. — **-poches,** *s.m.* pocket-emptier, carriage-basket *or* bag, basket, bag. — **-pommes,** *s.m.* apple-corer, coring-scoop
Vidé, e, *part. adj.* emptied, &c. (*V.* **Vider**); empty. *Jarrets bien —s*, (*of a horse*) clean hocks
Videlle, *s.f.* paste-jagger, jagging-iron
Videment, *s.m.* emptying
Vider, *v.a.* to empty; to clear; to leave, to quit, to depart from, to vacate, to evacuate; to void; to scoop; to bale; to drain; to draw (*poultry*); to gut (*fish*); to stone (*fruit*); to pink (*cloth, silks*, &c.); to bore (*keys*, &c.); (*fig., an affair, a quarrel*, &c.) to decide, to settle, to terminate [be emptied; to be settled *or* decided
Se —, *v.r.* to empty itself; to get empty; to
Videu-r, se, *s.m.f.* emptier; drainer; drawer; gutter [examine
Vidimer, *v.a.* (*law*) to compare, to collate, to
Viduité, *s.f.* widowhood [work; pinking
Vidure, *s.f.* emptying; drawing; guts; open
Vie, *s.f.* life; existence; being alive; course of life; way of living; morals; character; days, lifetime; vitality; livelihood; living; food; subsistence; (*fig.*) life, spirit, animation; colour; noise, row, set out. *A* —, for life. *A la — et à la mort*, *V.* **Mort,** *s.f.* *Dans la — de l'homme*, in after-life. *De sa* or *la* (*ma*, &c.) —, in o.'s (my, &c.) life; as long as one lives (I live, &c.). *En* —, alive, living. *Sans* —, without life *or* &c., lifeless. *Sa — durant*, during his lifetime. *Sur* or *sous* or *à peine de la* —, under *or* on pain of death. — *future*, — *à venir*, *autre* —, life to come, next world. — *moyenne*, average life, mean life, expectation of life. *Bonnes — et mœurs*, moral conduct, good character. *Avoir la — dure*, to be tenacious of life, to die hard, to have nine lives; to lead a miserable life, to have a hard time of it. *Faire la* —, to live fast; to make merry, to feast, to revel. *Faire — qui dure*, to lead a sober life, to be temperate; to husband well o.'s resources. *Rendre la — à*, to restore life to. *Rendre la — dure à*, to make miserable, to make . . 's life miserable, to make life a burden to. *S'ôter la* —, to make away with oneself. *Tourmenter sa* —, to bestir oneself
Viédase, *s.m.* (*obsolete*) fool, jackass
†**Vieil, le,** *adj.* *V.* **Vieux,** *adj.* [old people
†**Vieillard,** *s.m.* old man; —**s,** *pl.* old men;
†**Vieillarder,** *v.n.* to spoil with age
†**Vieille,** *adj. f.*, *s.f.* *V.* **Vieux,** *adj.* & *s.*
†**Vieillement,** *adv.* in the manner of old people, in an old-fashioned way
†**Vieillerie,** *s.f.* old things; old clothes; old goods; old rubbish, old lumber, old stuff; old trash [old people
†**Vieillesse,** *s.f.* old age; oldness; antiquity;
†**Vieilli, e,** *part. adj.* grown old, &c. (*V.* **Vieillir**); older; looking old *or* older, old-looking; become obsolete, obsolete, antiquated; effete; inveterate; confirmed; hardened
†**Vieillir,** *v.n.* to grow *or* get old *or* older; to

age; to look old *or* older; to become obsolete *or* antiquated; — *v.a.* to make (*one*) old *or* older; to age; to make (*one*) look old *or* older

†**Vieillissant, e,** *adj.* growing old *or* older *or* aged; obsolescent

†**Vieillissement,** *s.m.* growing old *or* aged, creeping old age, senescence; obsolescence

†**Vieillot, te,** *adj.* oldish, somewhat old

Vielle, *s.f.* hurdy-gurdy. — *organisée,* barrel-organ

Vieller, *v.n.* to play on the hurdy-gurdy; (*fig.*) to stand trifling

Vielleu-r, se, *s.m.f.* hurdy-gurdy player

Viennois, e, *s.m.f. adj.* Viennese; Viennese fashion

Vierge, *s.f.* virgin, maid; (*Holy*) Virgin; (*astr.*) Virgin, Virgo; — *adj.* virgin, maiden; pure; virginal; untrodden; unwrought; (*of swords*) unfleshed; (*of metals*) native. *La Sainte —,* the Blessed *or* Holy Virgin

†**Vieux, Vieil,** *m.,* **Vieille,** *f., adj.* old; aged; ancient; antique; obsolete; waste

†**Vieux, Vieille,** *s.m.f.* something old, what is old; old materials *or* things *or* articles, old clothes, old stuff; old man, old fellow, old boy, old one, old crony, old buffer; veteran; old woman, old thing, old girl, old one, old crony; old hag, hag. *Vieux de la vieille,* (*mil.*) veteran of the old guard

Vi-f, ve, *adj.* alive, live, living; quick; vivacious; animated; lively; sprightly; brisk; active; smart; sharp; keen; piercing; acute; vigorous; violent; energetic; strong; great; high; intense; vivid; eager; sanguine; passionate, hasty; spirited, mettlesome, fiery; bright; swift; quickset, green; (*of rock*) solid; (*of water*) spring; — *s.m.* quick; live flesh; solid; (*law*) person living. *Le — de l'eau,* (*nav.*) spring-tide. *De — ve voix,* by word of mouth, verbally, orally, verbal, oral, 'vivâ voce.' — *comme la poudre,* as hot as a peppercorn. *Entre —s,* (*law*) inter vivos. *Le mort saisit le —,* the heir-at-law inherits of course. **— -argent,** *s.m.* quicksilver

Vigeon, *s.m.* (*bird*) American widgeon

Vigésimo, *adv.* vigesimo, twentiethly

Vigie, *s.f.* (*nav.*) look-out; look-out man; rock above water, lurking rock. — *vitrée,* (*rail.*) observatory window. *En —,* on the look-out; on the watch [*or* on the look-out

Vigier, *v.n.* (*nav.*) to watch, to be on the watch

Vigilamment, *adv.* vigilantly, watchfully

Vigilance, *s.f.* vigilance, watchfulness

Vigilant, e, *adj.* vigilant, watchful

Vigile *s.f.* vigil, eve

†**Vigne,** *s.f.* vine; vineyard. — *blanche,* bryony; traveller's joy, sweet virgin's bower. — *noire,* black bryony. — *vierge,* Virginian creeper; wild bryony. *Feuille de —,* vine-leaf; (*sculp., and fig.*) fig-leaf. *Dans les —s, dans les —s du Seigneur,* in o.'s cups, tipsy, tight, in liquor

†**Vigneau,** *s.m. V.* **Vignot**

†**Vigneron, ne,** *s.m.f.* vine-dresser; vine-grower; edible snail; — *adj.* for vine *or* vines, vine; wine-growing, of wine-growers

†**Vignette,** *s.f.* vignette; engraving, cut, picture; mark; (*bot.*) meadow-sweet

†**Vignettiste,** *s.m.f.* vignettist

†**Vignoble,** *s.m.* vineyard, vine-estate; — *adj.* vine-growing; of *or* from the vine-districts. *Propriétaire de —s,* wine-grower

†**Vignon,** *s.m. V.* **Ajonc**

†**Vignot,** *s.m.* (*zool.*) periwinkle, winkle

†**Vigogne,** *s.f.* (*animal*) vicuna, vicugna; (*wool*) vigonia, vicuna-wool; (*cloth*) swan's-down; — *s.m.* vicuna-felt hat, vicuna hat, vigone

Vigoureusement, *adv.* vigorously; strongly; stoutly; energetically; forcibly

Vigoureu-x, se, *adj.* vigorous; strong; stout; robust; hardy; energetic; forcible; determined

Viguerie, *s.f.* (*local*) functions of "viguier" (judgeship)

Vigueur, *s.f.* vigour; strength; stoutness; hardiness; energy; force. *Entrer en —,* to be put in force; to begin to take effect, to take effect. *Mettre en —,* to put in force, to enforce

Viguier, *s.m.* (*local*) viguier (*judge*)

Vil, e, *adj.* vile, base, mean, low; common, vulgar; wretched; swinish. *A — prix,* dirt-cheap, dog-cheap

Vilain, e, *s.m.f.* villain; naughty boy *or* girl, nasty fellow *or* woman *or* girl; miser, niggard; blackguard, cad; — *adj.* ugly; villanous, vile, wretched; vulgar, low; nasty, bad; wicked; naughty; unhandsome, improper; mean, shabby, dirty; miserly, niggardly. — *monsieur,* ugly customer; bad fellow, blackguard

Vilainage, *s.m.* (*feud.*) villanage, villenage

Vilainement, *adv.* villanously; nastily, wretchedly; badly; unhandsomely, improperly; shamefully; meanly, shabbily; dirtily; stingily, niggardly, miserably; uglily; naughtily

Vilayet, *s.m* eyalet, vilayet, Turkish province

Vilebrequin, *s.m.* wimble, drill

Vilement, *adv.* vilely, basely

Vilenie, *s.f.* filth, dirt; shabby trick; meanness, sordidness, niggardliness; mean or dirty action; trash; foul abuse *or* names, abusive words; obscenity, filthiness

Vileté, *s.f.* lowness; cheapness, low price; insignificance; worthlessness; baseness; meanness; abjection

Vilipendement, *s.m.* vilification

Vilipender, *v.a.* to vilify; to undervalue, to despise, to contemn

Vilité, *s.f. V.* **Vileté**

Villa, *s.f.* villa

Villace, *s.f.* large straggling town

Village, *s.m.* village

Villageois, e, *s.m.f.* villager, cottager, rustic, countryman countrywoman; country fashion; — *adj.* village, rustic, country

Villanelle, *s.f.* villanelle (*pastoral ballad, dance, tune*)

Villarsie, *s.f.* (*bot.*) villarsia

Ville, *s.f.* town; city; town-council, corporation. — *de bains,* — *d'eaux,* watering-place. — *de guerre,* fortified town. *A la —,* to the town, to town; in town, in towns. *De —,* town; walking; private. *En —,* in town, in the town, out; town post, town delivery. *Costume de —,* walking-suit *or* dress; private *or* plain clothes. *Habit de —,* private *or* plain clothes; walking-dress *or* suit *or* coat. *Robe* or *toilette de —,* walking-dress *or* attire

Villégiature, *s.f.* villegiature, stay at a country place *or* in the country, holiday-making in the country

Villette, *s.f.* small town, townlet

Villeu-x, se, *adj.* villous, villose

Villifère, *adj.* villiferous

Villiforme, *adj.* villiform

Villosité, *s.f.* villosity

Vimaire, *s.f.* damaged caused by storms (*in forests*

Viminal, *s.m.* (*Rom. antiq.*) Viminal (Hill)

Vin, *s.m.* wine; (*of wine*) strength, vinosity; (*fig.*) drink, liquor, intoxication, drunkenness. *A —,* (*adject.*) wine. *De —,* of wine; from *or* with wine; (*adject.*) wine. (*Bouteille à —,* wine-bottle. *Bouteille de —,* bottle of wine.) *Grand —,* high-class wine. — *brûlé,* — *chaud,* — *cuit,* mulled wine; negus. — *coupé,* mixed wine. — *doux,* unfermented wine. — *ordinaire,* table-wine. — *pur,* neat wine, wine without water. — *de la comète,* wine of the vintage 1811. — *de liqueur,* sweet wine. — *de paille,* wine from grapes dried on straw. — *de Portugal* or *de Porto,* port wine, port. — *du Rhin,* Rhenish wine; hock. *Commerce de —s, V.* **Commerce.** *Marchand de —, V.* **Marchand.** *Négociant en —s,* wine-merchant. *Avoir le — bon* or *mauvais,* to be merry *or* quarrelsome in o.'s cups. *Avoir de bon* or *de mauvais —,* to have good *or* bad wine. *Entre deux —s,* half seas over, three sheets in the wind. *Mettre de l'eau dans son —,* to cool down; to become more moderate *or* reasonable; to lower o.'s pretensions; to mend. *Porter bien son —,* to be a good drinker

Vinage, *s.m.* (*of wine*) brandying, fortifying; (*obsolete*) wine-due

Vinaigre, *s.m.* vinegar. — *de toilette,* toilet-vinegar. — *des quatre voleurs,* thieves' vinegar. *Sel de* —, vinaigrette, smelling-salts
Vinaigrer, *v.a.* to season *or* sprinkle with vinegar, to vinegar; to sharpen, to sour
Vinaigrerie, *s.f.* vinegar-manufactory, vinegar-works; vinegar-trade
Vinaigrette, *s.f.* vinaigrette; vinegar-sauce; meat with vinegar-sauce; Bath-chair, hand-chair [cruet; (*bot.*) *V.* **Roudou**
Vinaigrier, *s.m.* vinegar-maker; (*old*) vinegar-
Vinaire, *adj.* wine, of *or* for wine. *Vaisseaux* or *vases* —*s*, wine-vessels, wine-casks
Vinasse, *s.f.* very weak wine; residuum of
Vinate, *s.m.* (*chem.*) vinate [distillation
Vincibilité, *s.f.* vincibility, vincibleness
Vincible, *adj.* vincible
Vinciblement, *adv.* vincibly
Vindas, *s.m.* windlass
Vindémial, e, *adj.* vindemial
Vindicati-f, ve, *adj.* vindictive, revengeful [fully
Vindicativement, *adv.* vindictively, revenge-
Vindicte, *s.f.* prosecution *or* punishment of
Vinéal, e, *adj.* vineal [crime
Vinée, *s.f.* vintage, wine-harvest
Vinelle, *s.f. V.* **Piquette**
Viner, *v.a.* to brandy, to fortify (*wine*)
Vinerie, *s.f.* wine-press
Vinetier, Vinettier, *s.m.* (*bot.*) barberry
Vinette, *s.f. V.* **Piquette;** (*bird*) *V.* **Becfigue;** (*bot.*) sorrel
Vineu-x, se, *adj.* vinous; winy, wine; wine-like; wine-coloured, red; rich, fruity, strong
Vingeon, *s.m.* (*bird*) American widgeon
Vingt, *adj. m.f., s.m.* twenty; twentieth; score. *Six-* —, (*obsolete*) six-score, one hundred and twenty. — **-et -un,** *adj. s.m.* twenty-one; twenty-first; (*game at cards*) vingt-et-un
Vingtaine, *s.f.* twenty or so, about twenty, some twenty, twenty, score
Vingtième, *adj. s.* twentieth [fold
Vingtupler, *v.a.n.*, **Se** —, *v.r.* to increase twenty-
Vinicole, *adj.* wine-producing, wine-growing, vinicultural
Viniculteur, *s.m.* wine-grower, viniculturist
Viniculture, *s.f.* wine-growing, viniculture
Vinifère, *adj.* viniferous
Vinificateur, *s.m.* vinificator
Vinification, *s.f.* vinification, wine-making *or*
Vinique, *adj.* (*chem.*) vinic [manufacture
Vinomètre, *s.m.* vinometer, œnometer
Vinosité, *s.f.* vinosity, richness, fruity taste
Viol, *s.m.* violation; rape; indecent assault
Viola, *s.f. V* **Viole**
Violabilité, *s.f.* violability
Violable, *adj.* violable
Violacé, e, *adj.* violaceous; (*med.*) purple; —**es,** *s.f. pl.* (*bot.*) violaceæ, violet tribe
Violariées, *s.f. pl. V.* **Violacées**
Violat, *adj. m.* of violets, violet
Viola-teur, trice, *s.m.f.* violator; transgressor; breaker; infringer, infractor; — *adj.* violating; transgressing; breaking; infringing
Violation, *s.f.* violation; transgression; breaking, breach; infringement, infraction
Violâtre, *adj.* purplish, of a purple colour
Viole, *s.f.* (*mus. instr.*) viola, alto viola, tenor violin; (*obsolete*) viol. — *d'amour,* viola d'amore
Violement, *s.m. V.* **Violation** *&* **Viol** [strongly
Violemment, *adv.* violently, with violence;
Violence, *s f.* violence; force; stress. *Faire* — *à,* to offer *or* do violence to; to violate; to strain. *Se faire* —, to force o.'s inclinations
Violent, e, *adj.* violent; strong; too bad
Violenter, *v.a.* to force, to do violence to; to compel; to constrain; to treat with violence, to ill-use [to infringe
Violer, *v.a.* to violate; to transgress; to break;
Violet, te, *adj.* violet, violet-coloured, purple; (*of the skin, lips*) blue
Violet, *s.m.* violet colour, purple; (*jest.*) bishop
Violette, *s.f.* (*bot.*) violet. — *marine,* Canterbury bell, mariet

Violeur, *s.m.* violator, ravisher
Violier, *s.m.* (*bot.*) wall-flower
Violine, *s.f.* (*chem.*) violine; (*bot.*) wall-flower
Violique, *adj.* (*chem.*) violic
Violiste, *s.m.* (*mus.*) violist
Violon, *s.m.* violin; fiddle; violinist; fiddler; fiddle-pattern; (*of a police-station*) lock-up, cell. *Premier* —, first violin, leader. *Payer les* —*s*, (*fig.*) to pay the piper
Violoncelle, *s.m.* violoncello; violoncellist
Violoncelliste, *s.m.* violoncellist
Violoniste, *s.m.f.* violinist
Viorne, *s.f. m.* (*bot.*) viburnum
Vioulte, *s.f.* (*bot.*) *V.* **Cynodon**
Vipère, *s.f.* viper; adder
Vipereau, *s.m.* young viper *or* adder
Vipérides, *s.m. pl.* (*zool.*) viperidæ
Vipérin, e, *adj.* viperine; —**e,** *s.f.* (*bot.*) viper's bugloss, adder-wort
Virage, *s.m.* (*nav.*) veering; heaving
Virago, *s.f.* virago
Virée, *s.f.* veering
Virelai, *s.m.* (*poet.*) virelay
Virement, *s.m.* (*bank., fin.*) transfer, clearing; (*nav.*) veering; turning; tacking about, tacking. — *d'eau,* (*nav.*) turn of the tide. — *de parties,* transfer (*of a debt*), clearing
Virer, *v.n.a.* to turn, to turn about; to twist; (*nav.*) to tack, to tack about; to veer; to heave; (*bank., fin.*) to transfer (*debts*). — *de bord,* — *vent devant,* (*nav.*) to tack, to tack *or* put about; (*fig.*) to turn round, to change sides. *Vire!* [(*nav.*) about!
Virescence, *s.f.* virescence
Virescent, e, *adj.* virescent
Vireton, *s.m.* (*old*) vireton [poisonous
Vireu-x, se, *adj.* virose, fetid, nauseous, noxious,
Virevau, Vireveau, *s.m.* (*nav.*) roller, winch
Virevaude, *s.f. V.* **Virevire**
Virevent, *s.m.* (*bird*) king-fisher
Virevire, *s.f.* (*nav.*) whirlpool
Virevolte, *s.f.* (*rid.*) quick turn
Virevousse, Virevouste, *s.f.* bustle, bustling,
Virgilien, ne, *adj.* Virgilian [moving about
Virgilier, *s.m.* (*bot.*) virgilia
Virginal, e, *adj.* virginal, virgin's, virgin, maiden, maidenly; —**e,** *s.f.* (*old mus. instr.*) virginals. *Lait* —, virgin's milk (*cosmetic*)
Virginalement, *adv.* virginally
Virginéique, Virginique, *adj.* virginic
Virginie, *s.f.* Virginia; — *s.m.* Virginia tobacco
Virginien, ne, *adj. s.* Virginian [head
Virginité, *s.f.* virginity, maidenhood, maiden-
Virgouleuse, *s.f.* virgouleuse (*kind of pear*)
Virgulaire, *adj.* (*gram.*) of a comma, like a comma; — *s.f.* (*bot.*) virgularia
Virgule, *s.f.* (*gram.*) comma; (*mus.*) dash; (*horol.*) hook escapement; (*pop.*) scar; scratch; mark. *Point et* —, (*gram.*) semicolon
Virguler, *v.a.* to mark with a comma *or* with commas; (*fig.*) to scar; to scratch; to mark
Viridine, *s.f.* (*chem.*) viridine
Viridité, *s.f.* viridity, viridness
Viril, e, *adj.* virile; male; manly; masculine. *Age* —, man's estate, manhood. *Portion* —*e*, lot equal with the others
Virilement, *adv.* manly, like a man
Virilité, *s.f.* virility, manhood; man's estate; manliness, vigour, strength, force
Virole, *s.f.* ferrule, iron ring *or* hoop; collar
Viroler, *v.a.* to ferrule; to hoop
Virtualité, *s.f* virtuality, potentiality
Virtuel, le, *adj.* virtual, potential
Virtuellement, *adv.* virtually, potentially
Virtuose, *s.m.f.* virtuoso, artist, artiste
Virtuosité, *s.f.* virtuosity
Virulence, *s.f.* virulence, virulency
Virulent, e, *adj.* virulent
Virure, *s.f.* (*nav.*) streak, strake
Virus, *s.m.* (*med.*) virus
Viry, *s.m.* Viry cheese
Vis, *s.f.* screw; male screw; screw-nail, screw-stud. — *d'Archimède,* Archimedean screw; screw-propeller; water-snail. *A* —, (*adject.*)

screw; spiral, winding, corkscrew. *Escalier à —*, winding *or* corkscrew staircase, vise
Vis (Je), *pres. ind. of* **Vivre,** I live
Vis (Je), *pret. ind. of* **Voir,** I saw
Visa, *s.m.* visa, signature, endorsement
Visage, *s.m.* visage, face; countenance; air, look; reception. *— de bois*, the door shut; no one at home. *Bon —*, good look *or* face, smiling looks, kind reception *or* welcome. *A — découvert*, with o.'s face uncovered, barefaced; open; barefacedly; openly. *A deux —s*, double-faced. *Avoir bon —*, (*obsolete*) to look well. *Changer de —*, to change countenance; to turn pale; to blush; (*fig.*) to put on a new face. *Faire bon* or *mauvais —*, to give a good *or* bad reception
Vis-à-vis, *adv. prep.* opposite; opposite to it *or* to them; face to face; facing, over against; before; towards, to; relatively (to); *— s.m.* vis-à-vis; person seated *or* standing opposite, partner, opposite neighbour; partners, couple
Viscache, Viscaque, *s.f.* (*zool.*) viscacha, lagostomus
Viscéral, e, *adj.* (*anat.*) visceral
Viscère, *s.m.* (*anat.*) viscus, vital organ; **—s,** *pl.* viscera, vital organs, entrails
Viscine, *s.f.* (*chem.*) viscine
Viscivore, *adj.* (*zool.*) viscivorous
Viscosité, *s.f.* viscosity, viscidity, sliminess
Visée, *s.f.* aim; end, design, scheme, plan
Viser, *v.n.a.* to aim; to take aim; to aim at; to drive at; to strike; to refer to; to visa, to sign, to back, to endorse
Viseur, *s.m.* aimer
Visibilité, *s.f.* visibility, visibleness; obviousness, evidence; conspicuousness
Visible, *adj.* visible, to be seen; obvious, evident; conspicuous
Visiblement, *adv.* visibly; obviously; evidently; conspicuously
Visière, *s.f.* visor, sight; shade, peak; (*of fire-arms*) back-sight; (*fam.*) eye-sight, sight; (*her.*) garde-visure. *Rompre en — à*, to break o.'s lance in the visor of o.'s adversary; (*fig.*) to fly in ...'s face; to quarrel abruptly *or* openly with; to insult *or* attack *or* condemn (*one*) openly *or* to his face; to break off with, to fall right out with
Visi-f, ve, *adj.* visive
Visigoth, e, *s.m.f.* Visigoth, Western Goth; (*fig.*) Goth, Vandal, barbarian, savage; *— adj.* Visigothic; (*fig.*) outlandish, barbarous, savage
Visigothique, *adj.* Visigothic; (*fig.*) outlandish, barbarous, savage
Visiomètre, *s.m.* visiometer
Vision, *s.f.* vision; sight; fancy
Visionnaire, *adj.* visionary, fanciful, dreaming; *— s.m.f.* visionary, dreamer, fancy-monger
Visir, &c. *V.* **Vizir,** &c.
Visitandine, *s.f.* Visitandine (*nun*)
Visitant, e, *s.m.f.* visitant
Visita-teur, trice, *s.m.f.* visitor, visiter
Visitation, *s.f.* visitation
Visite, *s.f.* visit, call; visiting; examination, inspection; visitation; search; attendance; (*garment*) visite. *En —*, on a visit; visiting; as a visitor. *Faire* or *rendre —*, to pay a visit, to make *or* give a call, to call (upon); to return a visit. *Rendre sa — à*, to return a visit to
Visiter, *v.a.n.* to visit; to examine, to inspect; to search; to look
Visiteu-r, se, *s.m.f.* visitor; searcher
Vismie, *s.f.* (*bot.*) vismia
Visnage, Visnague, *s.f.* (*bot.*) visnaga
Vison, *s.m.* (*zool.*) mink, vison
Vison-visu, *adv.* opposite, opposite each other
Visorium, *s.m.* (*print.*) copy-holder, catch, jigger
Visqueu-x, se, *adj.* viscous, viscid, slimy, sticky; clammy
Vissage, *s.m.* screwing
Visser, *v.a.* to screw; to screw on; to screw down; to screw up
Se —, *v.r.* to screw; to be screwed
Visserie, *s.f.* screws
Visu (De), *adv.* (*Latin*) from o.'s seeing; with o.'s own eyes
Visuel, le, *adj.* visual
Vitacées, *s.f. pl.* (*bot.*) vitaceæ
Vital, e, *adj.* vital; essential
Vitalement, *adv.* vitally; essentially
Vital-isme, iste. *V.* page 3, § 1
Vitalité, *s.f.* vitality
Vitchoura, *s.m.* vitchoura, furred overcoat
Vite, *adj.* quick; fast; speedy; swift, fleet
Vite, *adv.* quickly, quick, speedily; fast; directly. *Au plus —*, as quickly *or* as fast *or* as soon as possible, instantly, this instant. *Faire —*, to be quick, to make haste
Vitellin, e, *adj.*, **Vitelline,** *s.f.* vitelline
Vitellus, *s.m.* (*zool. bot.*) vitellus
Vitelotte, *s.f.* (red) kidney potato
Vitement, *adv.* quickly, quick
Vitesse, *s.f.* speed, quickness, swiftness; velocity. *Grande —*, great speed; full speed; (*rail.*) fast train *or* trains; passenger train *or* trains. *Petite —*, (*rail.*) slow train *or* trains; goods (*or* luggage) train *or* trains. *A la — de*, at a rate *or* speed of. *A grande —, à toute —*, at full speed. *De grande —*, (*rail.*) fast (*train*); passenger (*train*). *De petite —*, (*rail.*) slow (*train*); goods (*train*), luggage (*train*). *Gagner de —*, to outstrip, to outrun; to overtake
Viticole, *adj.* viticultural, vine-growing
Viticulteur, *s.m.* viticulturist, vine-grower
Viticulture, *s.f.* viticulture, vine-growing
Vitifère, *adj.* vitiferous
Vitiligo, *s.m.* (*med.*) vitiligo
Vitonnière, *s.f.* (*nav.*) limber-hole
Vitrage, *s.m.* glazing; glass partition; glass windows
†Vitrail, *s.m.* glass window, window, church-window
Vitraux, *s.m. pl.* (*pl. of* **Vitrail**)
Vitre, *s.f.* window-glass; pane of glass, glass; glass window, window. *Carreau de —*, pane of glass. *Casser les —s*, to break the windows; (*fig.*) to speak out boldly; not to mince matters; to spare no one; to keep no measure
Vitré, e, *part. adj.* glazed; glass; with a glass door; vitreous. *Porte —e*, glass door; sash-door
Vitrer, *v.a.* to glaze
Vitrerie, *s.f.* glazing; glazier's trade *or* work, glass windows, glass
Vitrescibilité, *s.f.* vitrescibility
Vitrescible, *adj.* vitrescible
Vitreusement, *adv.* vitreously
Vitreu-x, se, *adj.* vitreous, glassy
Vitri-er, ère, *s.m.f.* glazier; glazier's wife
Vitrifiabilité, *s.f.* vitrifiability
Vitrifiable, *adj.* vitrifiable
Vitrification, *s.f.* vitrification
Vitrifier, *v.a.*, **Se —,** *v.r.* to vitrify
Vitrine, *s.f.* glass case; show-case; shop-window; (*zool.*) vitrina
Vitriol, *s.m.* (*chem.*) vitriol
Vitrioler, *v.a.* to vitriolate, to vitriolize
Vitriolerie, *s.f.* vitriol manufactory
Vitriolique, *adj.* (*chem.*) vitriolic
Vitrolisation, *s.f.* vitriolization, vitriolation
Vitrioliser, *v.a.* to vitriolize, to vitriolate
Vitrosité, *s.f.* vitreousness
Vitruvien, ne, *adj.* Vitruvian
Vitulaire, *adj.* vituline
Vivable, *adj.* (*fam.*) fit to live with, sociable
Vivace, *adj.* long-lived; inveterate, deep-rooted, tenacious; (*bot.*) perennial; (*mus.*) vivace
Vivacité, *s.f.* vivacity, liveliness; quickness; activity; mettle; sprightliness; briskness; spirit, life; animation; ardour; hastiness; sally of passion; vividness, brightness
Vivandi-er, ère, *s.m.f.* sutler, canteen-woman
Vivant, e, *s.m.* living, alive, live; quick; lively; animated, animate. *Langue —e*, living language
Vivant, *s.m.* person living; determined character; life, life-time; **—s,** *pl.* living; quick. *Bon* or *joyeux —*, jolly fellow, boon companion. *Du — de*, during *or* in ..'s life-time, during...'s life
Vivat, *int. s.m.* hurrah! cheer. *Pousser des —s*, to cheer
Vive, *s.f.* (*fish*) weever, sting-fish; *— adj. f. V.* **Vif**
Vive! Vivent! *V.* **Vivre**
Vivement, *adv.* livelily, lively; quickly; sharply; smartly; keenly, acutely; deeply; strongly; greatly; much; violently; closely; vigorously; forcibly; sensibly; eagerly; hastily; passion-

ately; hotly; sorely; poignantly; briskly; vividly; suddenly

Viveu-r, se, *s.m.f.* gay man *or* woman, man about town, fast man *or* woman; reveller; man *or* woman of pleasure; — *adj.* gay, fast

Vivier, *s.m.* vivarium, vivary, fish-pond, nurse-pond; well-boat

Vivification, *s.f.* vivification, vivifying, revival

Vivifier, *v.a.* to vivify, to animate; to give life; to quicken; to enliven; to revive; to refresh

Vivifique, *adj.* vivific, vivifying, life-giving

Vivipare, *adj. m.f., s.m.* viviparous; viviparous animal

Viviparie, *s.f.*, **Viviparisme,** *s.m.* viviparism

Vivisecteur, *s.m.* vivisector

Vivisection, *s.f.* vivisection

Vivoter, *v.n.* to live poorly, to live from hand to mouth, to make just shift to live, to keep body and soul together, to rub on

Vivre, *v.n.* to live; to be living *or* alive; to exist; to subsist; to live with *or* on; to board; to take o.'s meals; to behave. *Apprendre à* —, to learn *or* teach manners. *Faire* —, to maintain, to support, to feed, to keep, to keep alive, to enable to live. *Savoir* —, *See Letter* **S.** *Vive! Vivent!* long live! for ever! hurrah for! give me! God save! *Vive la joie*, let us make merry! (*s.m.*) jolly *or* merry fellow. *Vive Dieu!* God be praised! good Heavens! by the Powers! zounds! *Qui vive?* who goes there? (*s.m.*) *See Letter* **Q**

Vivre, *s.m.* living; food; victuals; board; **—s,** *pl.* provisions; victuals; stores. *Faire des* or *ses* **—s**, to get provisions, to victual. **—s-pain,** *s.m.pl.* (*mil.*) bread-stores. **—s-viande,** *s.m.pl.* [(*mil.*) meat-stores

Vivre, *s.f.* (*her.*) *V.* **Guivre**

Vivré, e, *adj. V.* **Guivré**

Vivrier, *s.m.* (*old*) *V.* **Fournisseur**

Vizir, *s.m.* vizier, vizir

Vizirat, Viziriat, *s.m.* vizierate, viziership

Vizirial, e, *adj.* vizierial, vizirial

Vlan, *int.* slap! smack! bang! at once

Vocable, *s.m.* vocable, word, term; name

Vocabulaire, *s.m.* vocabulary, word-book; [expositor

Vocabuliste, *s.m.* vocabulist

Vocal, e, *adj.* vocal, oral; — *s.m.f.* vocal (*voter*)

Vocalement, *adv.* vocally, orally

Vocalique, *adj.* vocalic [vocalizing

Vocalisa-teur, trice, *s.m.f.* vocalizer; — *adj.*

Vocalisation, *s.f.* vocalization

Vocalise, *s.f.* (*mus.*) vowel sound; strain, song

Vocaliser, *v.a.n.* to vocalize

Vocal-isme, iste. *V.* page 3, § 1

Vocatif, *s.m.* (*gram.*) vocative, vocative case

Vocation, *s.f.* vocation; calling; inclination; destination; talent; turn; taste

Vocifèra-teur, trice, *s.m.f.* vociferator, clamourer, brawler; — *adj.* vociferating, clamouring, brawling

Vocifération, *s.f.* vociferation, roar

Vociférer, *v.n.a.* to vociferate, to cry out, to roar, to roar out

Vœu, *s.m.* vow; wish; desire; prayer; will; vote; opinion. *Au comble de ses* **—x**, at the summit of o.'s happiness

Vogue, *s.f.* vogue, credit, favour, repute; fashion; village wake *or* feast; (*nav.*) rowing; sailing; going. *En* —, in vogue *or* &c.; in request. *Avoir la* —, to be in vogue *or* &c.; to be in request. — **-avant,** *s.m.* (*nav.*) foremost rower, strokesman

Voguer, *v.n.* to row; to sail; to go; to be wafted

Vogueur, *s.m.* (*obsolete*) rower; float for swimming, cork, bladders [you are again!

Voi, *int.* (*obsolete*) hush! be quiet! stop! there

Voici, *prep.* behold, see here; look! here! here is *or* comes, here are *or* come; this is, these are; it is. *La* —, here she is; here she comes. *Le* —, here he is; here he comes. *Les* —, here they are; here they come. *Me* —, here I am. *Nous* —, here we are. *Vous* or *te* —, here you are. *Le — qui vient*, here he comes. *L'adresse que* —, this address, the address here. — *que*, now. — *qui*, here *or* this is something which, this. — *venir* ..., here comes *or* come ..., ... is *or* are coming

Voie, *s.f.* way; road; passage; organ; medium, channel; means; resource; course; track; conveyance; (*of wood*, &c.) cartload, load; (*of coal*) sack; (*of water*) two pails; (*rail.*, &c.) line; path; gauge; (*hunt.*) track, trail, scent; (*anat.*) duct, passage; organ; (*nav.*) leak. — *de communication*, thoroughfare, road, street. **—s** *de droit*, due course of law, legal means. — *d'eau*, water-way; two pails of water; (*nav.*) leak. **—s** *de fait*, violence, blows; assault, battery. **—s** *de fait et blessures*, aggravated assault, cutting and wounding. — *de fer*, — *ferrée*, line of rail, railroad, railway. **—s** *et moyens*, ways and means. — *publique*, public way *or* road; highway. *En — de*, in a way to; in a fair way for; in course of. *Être a bout de* —, to lose the scent; (*fig.*) to have exhausted o.'s resources. *Être sur la* —, to be in a fair way; to be on the scent. *Faire une — d'eau*, (*nav.*) to spring a leak. *Mettre sur la* —, to put in the right way *or* path; to put on the right scent. *Sortir de la* —, (*rail.*) to run off the rails. *Il est toujours par — et par chemin*, he is always rambling about

Voilà, *prep.* behold, see there; look! there! lo! there *or* here is *or* goes *or* comes, there *or* here are *or* go *or* come; that is, those are; that was, those were; such is, such are; such was, such were; it is now; there it is; that is the thing; there you are, here you are; here I am; yes! coming! *La* —, look at her, there *or* here she is *or* was, there *or* here she goes *or* comes; she is now. *Le* —, look at him, there *or* here he is *or* was, there *or* here he goes *or* comes; he is now. *Les* —, look at them, there *or* here they are *or* were, there *or* here they go *or* come; they are now. *Me* —, there *or* here I am *or* was; I am now; I have now. *Nous* —, there *or* here we are *or* were; we are *or* have now. *Vous* or *te* —, there *or* here you are *or* were; you are *or* have now. *Le — qui vient*, there he comes. *Le — qui boit!* he is drinking now! he is drinking, look! *Le — qui tombe par terre!* down he falls! *En — -t-il!* there is a lot! *En — assez*, that is enough; that will do. *La personne que* —, that *or* this person, the person there *or* here. *Les personnes que* —, those *or* these persons, the persons there *or* here. *Nous y* —, we have come to it; we have come to the point; that is it. *Vous — bien!* you are now in a fine plight! *Vous — bien! — comme vous êtes!* that is just like you! *Comme vous —!* how ... you are! what a figure you are! what a plight you are in! — *pour!* so much for! *En — pour* ..., that will do for ...; that is for ...; that will last ... — *que*, now; suddenly, all at once; thereupon; see! behold! lo and behold! — *qui*, there *or* that is something which, that. — *dix-huit mois*, it is now eighteen months. — *deux heures qu'il parle*, he has been speaking these two hours. *Ne — -t-il pas* ..., is not that ...? lo and behold ...! *Ne — -t-il pas qu'il pleut!* there now, it is actually raining! I declare it is raining! — *ce que c'est*, *V.* **Être**

Voile, *s.m.* veil; curtain; cloth; cover; crape; (*fig.*) veil; film; mist; cover, pretence, cloak, disguise, colour, show; — *s f.* sail; canvas; (*rhet.*) ship, sail. — (*m.*) *du palais*, (*anat.*) soft palate. — (*f.*) *de fortune*, (*nav.*) lug sail. *A* **—s**, sailing; sail. *A la* —, under sail; by sails; sailing. *A toutes* **—s**, at full speed. *Aller à la* —, *faire* —, to sail. *Mettre à la* —, to sail, to set sail

Voilé, e, *part. adj.* veiled, &c. (*V.* **Voiler**); dull, dim; (*of the eye*) soft, gentle; (*of the voice*) husky; (*nav.*) rigged. *Peu* —, (*of hints*, &c.) broad

Voiler, *v.a.* to veil; to muffle; to cover, to hide, to conceal; to cloud; to disguise, to colour; — *v.n.* to warp

Se —, *v.r.* to veil oneself *or* itself; to wear a veil; to become *or* be veiled *or* &c.; to warp
Voilerie, *s.f.* sail-loft, sail-room; sail-making; sails [lateen sail
Voilette, *s.f.* (small) veil, fall; (*nav.*) small
Voilier, *s.m* sail-maker; sailing-vessel *or* ship *or* boat, sailer; — *adj. m.*, **-ière,** *f.* swift. *Bon* or *fin* —, swift *or* fast sailer, fast-sailing ship *or* boat. *Grand* —, prime sailer; (any) large sea-bird [sails; sail-making; warping
Voilure, *s.f.* set of sails, trim of the sails;
Voir, *v.a.n.* to see; to behold; to look at *or* on; to perceive; to observe; to examine; to inspect; to view; to consider; to witness; to find; to overlook; to visit; to frequent; to keep company with; to attend; to go through; to do; to know; to have connection with; to look. *A* —, to see, to look at, &c.; by o.'s *or* its appearance; by; to be seen; to be seen to; worth seeing. *Aller* —, to go to see; to go and see; to call upon. *Venir* —, to come to see; to come and see; to call upon. — *venir*, *V.* **Venir.** — *faire*, to look at *or* on; to witness. *Faire* —, to show; to let see; to illustrate; to prove. *Se faire* —, to show oneself *or* itself, to be seen, to appear. *N'avoir rien à — à*, to have nothing to do with. *Voyons!* let us see! let me see! come! now then! *Voyez-vous, vois-tu*, do you see? you see; mind you! just fancy; now. *Voyez-vous bien! vois-tu bien!* mind you! *Je n'y vois pas*, I don't see in it; I can't see. *Je vois d'ici*, I see (*or* can see) from here; I foresee; I remember; I fancy I can see, I fancy, I represent to myself
Se —, *v.r.* to see *or* &c. oneself *or* each other; to meet; to visit each other; to find oneself; to be; to be seen *or* witnessed *or* &c.; to show; to be plain; to occur, to happen
Voire, *adv.* — *même*, even, nay even
Voirie, *s.f.* commission of highways; public highways *or* roads; laystall; common sewer; offal, carrion. *Grande* —, commission of public roads, railways, rivers, &c.
Voirine, *s.f.* finest Persian silk
Voisin, e, *adj.* neighbouring; near; next; adjoining, adjacent; bordering; next door; — *s.m.f.* neighbour. *De* —, *en* —, neighbourly, as a neighbour [proximity; analogy; neighbours
Voisinage, *s.m.* neighbourhood; vicinity;
Voisiner, *v.n.* to visit o.'s neighbours; to go to see a neighbour; to neighbour it; to be on a neighbourly footing
Voiturage, *s.m.* conveyance, carriage; cartage
Voiture, *s.f.* vehicle; carriage; coach; cab; omnibus; cart; waggon; van; truck; dray; perambulator; (*bathing-*)machine; conveyance; fare; load. — *d'arrosement*, watering-cart, water-cart. — *de bagages*, luggage van. — *de correspondance*, branch-coach. — *de maître*, private carriage. — *publique*, public vehicle *or* carriage, stage-carriage. — *de place*, street-cab, common cab, cab. *Place* or *station de —s*, cab-stand, cab-rank. *Petite* —, small carriage *or* &c.; (*admin.*) cab. *Bureau de —s*, coach-office
Voiturer, *v.a.* to convey, to carry; to cart, to waggon; to drive; to take
Voiturier, *s.m.* carrier, carman; driver; — *adj. m.*, **-ière,** *f.* carrying
Voiturin, *s.m.* driver; coach
Voix, *s.f.* voice; tone; sound; singing; singer; vote, suffrage; opinion. — *de tête*, falsetto, shrill treble. *A — basse*, in a low voice *or* tone, in an under-tone, in a whisper, softly. *A haute* —, in a loud voice, loudly, loud, aloud, out; audibly. *A haute et intelligible* —, in a loud and distinct voice, aloud and distinctly, audibly. *A portée de la* —, within hearing; within call. *De vive* —, *V.* **Vif.** *D'une seule* —, with one voice *or* consent. *Aller aux* —, to put the question to the vote, to put it to the vote, to come to the vote; to divide. *Mettre aux* —, to put to the vote. *Aux — !* put it to the vote! divide!

Vol, *s.m.* stealing, robbing; theft; robbery; larceny; burglary; extortion; fleecing; stolen goods; (*of birds, insects*, &c.) flight; flying; (*of the wings*) span, distance from tip to tip; (*fig.*) soaring, flight. (*V.* **Effraction.**) — *domestique*, robbery by a servant. *Au* —, flying, on the wing; when flying. *A — d'oiseau*, in a straight line, as the crow flies; from a bird's-eye view, bird's-eye. *Prendre son* —, to take wing; to take its *or* o.'s flight; to soar. — **-au-vent,** *s.m.* (*pl., same spelling*) puff-pie, vol-au-vent
Volable, *adj.* liable to be stolen *or* robbed
Volage, *adj.* fickle, volatile, inconstant; flighty, light; giddy, light-headed; (*nav.*) crank; — *s.m.f.* fickle *or* &c. person. *Feu* —, wildfire
Volagement, *adv.* fickly
Volageté, *s.f.* fickleness [poulterer
†**Volaille,** *s.f.* poultry; fowl. *Marchand de —s*,
†**Volaill-er, ère,** *s.m.f.* poulterer; — *s.m.* poultry-yard
Volant, e, *adj.* flying; loose; floating; movable, portable; (*her.*) volant; — *s.m.* shuttlecock; flounce; (*of a wind-mill*) beam; (*of a machine*, &c.) flier, fly, fly-wheel. *Assiettes —es*, extra dishes [light, airy; —**e,** *s.m.f.* winged animal
Volatil, e, *adj.* winged; (*chem., and fig.*) volatile;
Volatilisable, *adj.* volatilizable
Volatilisation, *s.f.* volatilization
Volatiliser, *v.a.*, **Se —**, *v.r.* to volatilize
Volatilité, *s.f.* volatility
†**Volatille,** *s.f.* small birds, fowls
Volcan, *s.m.* volcano
Volcanicité, *s.f.* volcanicity
Volcan-ique, -isme, -iste. *V.* page 3, § 1
Volcanisation, *s.f.* volcanization [inflamed
Volcanisé, e, *part. adj.* volcanized; volcanic;
Volcaniser, *v.a.* to volcanize; to inflame
Volcanite, *s.f.* (*min.*) volcanite [vole
Vole, *s.f.* (*at cards*) vole. *Faire la* —, to win the
Volée, *s.f.* flight; flock; herd; set; brood; troop, bevy; rank, society; class; rate; discharge; volley; salvo; round; shot; swing; shower; drubbing; (*of stairs, of steps*) flight; (*part of a cannon*) chase, tube; (*of carriages*) splinter-bar; set of swing-bars; set of swingletrees; set of whippletrees; (*agr., of sowing*) cast; (*of bells*) peal; (*tech.*) spell at work. — *de palonniers*, set of swing-bars; set of swingletrees; (*agr.*) set of whippletrees. — *de derrière*, (*of carriages*) splinter-bar. — *de devant*, (*of carriages*) long bar, swing-bars. — *de timon*, (*of carriages*) splinter-bar. *Cheval de* —, *V.* **Cheval.** *Haute* —, high rank; higher classes, dons, nobs, exclusives. *A la* —, flying; in the air; rapidly, quickly; inconsiderately; at random; (*agr.*) broadcast. *A toute* —, at random, random; at full swing; a full peal. *De la haute* —, *de haute* or *de première* —, of high rank, of the first water, tiptop, crack
Voler, *v.n.a.* to fly; to fly about; to hasten, to run; to chase *or* fly *or* fly at (*birds*); to steal, to rob; to take away; to usurp; to fleece; (*fam.*) to deceive, to disappoint, to frustrate, to foil, to balk. *Ne l'avoir pas volé*, to have well earned it; to richly deserve it, to be served right. *Je suis volé!* I am robbed! (*fam.*) I am sold! what a sell! [thief, petty thief, pilferer
Volereau, *s.m.* (*obsolete*) young thief, little
Volerie, *s.f.* robbing, robbery; thievery, theft; pilfering; (*falc.*) flying, chase
Volet, *s.m.* shutter, window-shutter; trap-door; dove-cot, dove-cote, pigeon-house; sorting-board (*for seeds*, &c.); paddle-board; board, sign-board; (*bot.*) water-lily; (*nav.*) boat-compass
Voleter, *v.n.* to flutter; to flicker; to hover
Volette, *s.f.* small hurdle; horse-net
Voleu-r, se, *s.m.f.* flier; thief; robber; burglar; stealer; extortioner; fleecer; — *adj.* thieving, thievish; stealing; robbing; burglarious; exacting, extortionate; fleecing. — *de grand chemin*, highway-robber, highwayman, footpad. — *avec effraction*, housebreaker. — *de nuit*

avec effraction, burglar. *Au —!* stop thief! thief! *Être fait comme un —*, to have o.'s dress all in disorder *or* in tatters

Volière, *s.f.* aviary, volery, large cage; pigeon-house

Volige, *s.f.* (*carp.*) batten, scantling

Voligeage, *s.m.* (*carp.*) battening

Voliger, *v.a.* (*carp.*) to batten

Volition, *s.f.* volition

Volitionnel, le, *adj.* volitional

Volnay, *s.m.* volnay (wine)

Volontaire, *adj.* voluntary; wilful; intended, intentional; willing; spontaneous; free; self-willed, wayward, obstinate, headstrong, stubborn; — *s.m.f.* obstinate person; volunteer

Volontairement, *adv.* voluntarily; willingly; intentionally; spontaneously

Volontariat, *s.m.* volunteering

Volonté, *s.f.* will; mind; pleasure; intention, intentions; inclination; desire, wish; accord; whim, caprice. *A —*, at will; at pleasure; voluntarily; at command. *Bonne —*, good-will; readiness; willingness. *Dernières —s*, last will and testament. *Mauvaise —*, ill-will; unreadiness; unwillingness. *De bonne —*, voluntary; voluntarily; of o.'s free will; ready; readily; willing, earnest; willingly. *De mauvaise —*, unwilling; unwillingly. *Avoir de la bonne —*, to be willing. *Faire ses —s*, to have o.'s own will *or* way

Volontiers, *adv.* willingly; gladly; with pleasure; fain; complacently; readily; easily; freely; commonly, usually, frequently, not unfrequently

Volsque, *adj. s.m.f.* Volscian

Volta-ïque,-ïquement,-ïsme. *V.* page 3 § 1

Voltaire, *s.m.* Voltaire; reclining chair (*V.* **Fauteuil**)

Voltairianisme, *s.m.* Voltairianism, Voltairism

Voltairien, ne, *adj. s.* of Voltaire; Voltairian

Voltamètre, *s.m.* (*phys.*) voltameter

Volte, *s.f.* (*rid., fenc.*) volt. **—-face,** *s.f.* turning of the face, facing about, wheeling round; (*mil. command*) face about! *Faire —, face,* to turn completely round, to wheel round, to wheel about; to turn, to retreat, to turn o.'s back; (*mil.*) to face about

Volter, *v.n.* (*fenc.*) to make a volt, to volt

Voltige, *s.f.* slack rope; vaulting, tumbling; (*rid.*) voltige, vaulting

Voltigement, *s.m.* flying, fluttering, flutter, flickering, flitting; hovering; waving; vaulting, tumbling

Voltiger, *v.n.* to flutter, to flicker, to fly about, to flit; to hover; to wave; to vault, to tumble

Voltigeur, *s.m.* vaulter; tumbler; (*mil.*) voltigeur, rifleman, soldier of a light company; **—s,** *pl.* (*mil.*) voltigeurs, riflemen, rifles, rifle-corps, light companies, light infantry. — *hollandais*, Flying Dutchman

Volubile, *adj.* volubile, volubilate, voluble; — *s.f. V.* **Volubilis**

Volubilis, *s.m.* (*bot.*) bindweed, convolvulus

Volubilité, *s.f.* volubility, rapidity, fluency, glibness, nimbleness

Voluble, *adj.* voluble

Volume, *s.m.* volume; bulk; size; mass; compass

Volumètre, *s.m.* volumeter

Volumétr-ique, -iquement. *V.* page 3, § 1

Volumineusement, *adv.* voluminously

Volumineu-x, se, *adj.* voluminous; large; bulky

Volupté, *s.f.* voluptuousness; delight; pleasure; sensuality; luxury

Voluptuaire, *adj.* luxurious; for embellishment

Voluptueusement, *adv.* voluptuously

Voluptueu-x, se, *adj.* voluptuous; sensual; — *s.m.f.* voluptuary; sensualist; epicure

Voluptuosité, *s.f.* voluptuousness

Volute, *s.f.* (*arch., nat. hist.*) volute

Volva, *s.m.*, **Volve,** *s.f.* (*bot.*) volva, wrapper

Volvoce, *s.m.* (*bot.*) volvox

Volvulus, *s.m.* (*med.*) volvulus

Vomer, *s.m.* (*anat.*) vomer

Vomicine, *s.f.* (*chem.*) vomicine, brucine

Vomique, *adj.* vomic; — *s.f.* (*med.*) vomica. *Noix —*, vomic nut, nux vomica, poison-nut, ratsbane

Vomiquier, *s.m.* (*bot.*) nux vomica tree

Vomir, *v.n.a.* to vomit; to vomit up *or* out; to throw *or* cast up, to bring up; to belch out

Vomissement, *s.m.* vomiting; expectoration: sickness; vomit

Vomiti-f, ve, *adj.* vomitive; — *s.m.* vomit, emetic

Vomitoire, *s.m.* (*anc. arch.*) vomitory

Vomiturition, *s.f.* vomiturition, retching

Vorace, *adj.* voracious, ravenous

Voracement, *adv.* voraciously, ravenously

Voracité, *s.f.* voracity, ravenousness

Vortex, *s.m.* vortex

Vorticelle, *s.f.* (*zool.*) vorticella, bell-flower animalcule

Vos, *adj. poss. pl. m.f.* your, your own

Vosnes, *s.m.* vosnes (wine)

Votant, e, *adj.* voting; — *s.m.f.* voter

Votation, *s.f.* voting; votes

Vote, *s.m* vote; voting

Voter, *v.a.n.* to vote; to poll

Voti-f, ve, *adj.* votive

Voto (Ex), *s.m.* ex voto, ex voto offering, votive offering

Votre, *adj. poss.* your, your own

Vôtre, *pron. poss.* yours, your own. *Le —, la —, les —s*, yours, your own; your relations; your family; your friends; your men; your servants; your company *or* party; your people; your subjects; your dynasty; your tricks *or* pranks, &c. *Être des —s*, to be one of you, to belong to your body *or* &c., to join you *or* your party, &c.

Vouer, *v.a.* to vow; to devote; to consecrate; to doom

Vouge, *s.m.* (*hunt.*) boar-spear; (*agr., hort.*) bill-hook; (*in anc. armour*) voulge

Vougeot, *s.m. V.* **Clos**

Vouloir, *v.a.n.* to will, to be willing; to have a will; to desire; to like; to wish; to wish for; to want; to be inclined; to have a fancy; to be pleased, to please, to choose; ... will have; ... will have it; to intend; to mean; to resolve, to determine; to be resolved *or* determined; to be resolved *or* determined to do; to try, to attempt, to endeavour, to offer; to aim at; to require; to expect; to order; to ask; to consent; to agree; to allow; to admit; to grant; to be intended; — *s.m.* will; pleasure; intention. *Bon —*, good-will; willingness. *Mauvais —*, ill-will; unwillingness. *En — à*, to bear ill-will *or* malice; to have a grudge *or* a spite against; to be angry with; to be against *or* at *or* after; to be hostile to; to set o.'s mind upon; to have a mind for; to have a design upon, to seek; to aim at; to want; to care for. *S'en —*, not to (*or* cannot) forgive oneself (for), to be angry with oneself. — *de*, to wish for, to want, to wish to have, will have. — *dire*, — *parler de*, to mean; to allow; to advert *or* allude to. — *du bien à*, to wish (*one*) well, to bear good-will to; to take an interest in. — *le bien de*, to mean well to. — *bien*, to be quite willing, to be disposed *or* inclined, to will, to be willing *or* pleased, to please; to be glad *or* very glad; to like; to be kind *or* good enough, to have the goodness; to have no objection, not to object (to), not to mind, to consent; to agree; to admit; to grant; to allow. — *du mal à*, to wish (*one*) harm, to bear ill-will *or* malice; to have a grudge *or* a spite against; to be angry with. *Se faire bien, mal — de quelqu'un*, to win a person's affection, to get disliked by a person. *Je veux que cela soit* (or *qu'il en soit ainsi*), I wish it to be so, I will have it so. *Que voulez-vous qu'il fasse?* what will you have him do? *Voulez-vous que je ...?* do you want *or* wish me to ...? shall I ...? *Il voulut sortir*, he would have gone out. *Comment voulez-vous qu'il réussisse?* how can he *or* is he to succeed, pray? *Qui voulez-vous qui vous reconnaisse?* who do you think will know you? *Que me voulez-vous?* what do you want with me? *Que voulez-vous? Que veux-tu?* what do you want? what *or* what more would you have? and what not? what could I do? how could *or* can I help it? how could *or* can it be helped ? it cannot be helped; well, but then, the fact is. *Veuillez*, please; be kind *or* good enough. *En veux-tu en voilà*, as much as you like, plenty of it *or* of them, lots, for the asking. *Tu l'as voulu*, you would have it. *Dieu le veut*, God wills it. *Dieu le veuille!* God grant it!

Voulu, e, *part. adj.* wished, wanted, desired, &c. (*V.* **Vouloir**); requisite, required, due; usual, received. *Bien —*, *V*, **Bienvoulu.** *Mal —*, *V.* **Malvoulu**

Vous, *pers. pron.* you; to *or* at you; for *or* with *or* in *or* from *or* by *or* on *or* against you; for your part; as for you, as to you; yourself; yourselves; to *or* at *or* within yourself *or* yourselves; each other, one another; to *or* at *or* for *or* with each other (*or* one another). *A —*, to *or* at *or* with you *or* yourself *or* yourselves; yours, your own; of yours, of your own; peculiar; to spare. *A — à, à — de, V.* **A.** *De — à moi*, from you to me; between you and me. *—même*, yourself; alone; too, also, likewise. *—mêmes*, yourselves; alone; too, also, likewise

Voussoir, Vousseau, *s.m.* (*arch.*) voussoir, arch-stone, wedge. *— du milieu* (or, *clé de voûte*), middle voussoir, key-stone

Voussoyer, *v.a.* to say 'you' to (*not 'thou'*)

Voussure, *s.f.* (*arch.*) coving; (*anat.*) convexity, round prominence

Voûte, *s.f.* vault, arch; ceiling, roof; (*of a horse-shoe*) hollow; (*fig.*) canopy; sky; **—s,** *pl.* vaults, &c.; vaulting. *— acoustique*, whispering dome *or* gallery

Voûté, e, *adj.* vaulted; arched; crooked; round-shouldered, bent. *Dos —*, round shoulders

Voûter, *v.a.* to vault, to arch; to bend

Se —, *v.r.* to vault, to arch; (*pers.*) to stoop, to bend, to grow round-shouldered, to grow [double

Vouvray, *s.m.* vouvray (wine)

Voyage, *s.m.* travel; travelling, travels; journey; voyage; excursion, trip, tour; progress; ride; run; errand; stay; (*obsolete*) travelling expenses, costs. *Bon —!* a pleasant journey *or* voyage! *De —*, (*adject.*) travelling. *En —*, travelling; on a voyage

Voyageable, *adj.* travellable; voyageable

Voyager, *v.n.* to travel; to journey; to voyage; to sail; to migrate

Voyageu-r, se, *adj.* travelling, migratory; carrier (*pigeon*); *— s.m.f.* traveller; passenger; fare; carrier pigeon, carrier

Voyant, e, *adj.* seeing (*reverse of blind*), that has his (*or* her) eye-sight, that can see; gaudy, showy; (*of horses*) short-sighted; *— s.m.f.* (*in contradistinction to one who is blind*) one who has his (*or* her) eye-sight *or* who sees, one that can see, person who sees; seer, prophet; *— s.m.* (*tech.*) sight, levelling-vane; (*nav.*) buoy- [light

Voyelle, *s.f.* vowel

Voyer, *s.m.* (*adject.*, *Agent* or *inspecteur* or *architecte —*) overseer *or* inspector of the highways, road-surveyor [on

Voyeu-r, se, *s.m.f.* sight-seer, spectator, looker-

Voyou, *s.m.* blackguard-boy, blackguard; street Arab; cad, rough; low *or* vulgar fellow

Vrac, Vrague, *s.m.* *En —*, in bulk, unpacked, loose; (*abusively*) in large packets

Vrai, e, *adj.* true; real; genuine; within the truth; veracious; right; exact; correct; proper; fit; earnest; sincere; true-born; regular, downright, arrant, very; mere; *— s.m.* truth; *— adv. V.* **Vraiment.** *Au —*, truly, in truth; true; really; exactly, precisely. *A — dire, à dire —*, to tell the truth. *Dans le —*, in truth; within the truth, right; true to nature; in character. *Pas —?* (*fam.*) isn't it true? isn't it? isn't that a fact? eh? *Pour de —*, (*pop.*) true, real; truly, really; in earnest

Vraiment, *adv.* truly, really, indeed; in truth; verily; forsooth [likelihood, probability

Vraisemblable, *adj.* likely, probable; *— s.m.*

Vraisemblablement, *adv.* likely, probably

Vraisemblance, *s.f.* likelihood, probability;

Vraque. *V.* **Vrac**

†**Vreille,** *s.f.* (*bot.*) field convolvulus

†**Vrille,** *s.f.* gimlet; (*bot.*) tendril, clasper

†**Vrillé, e,** *part. adj.* gimleted, bored; gimlet-like, spiral; curled; (*bot.*) claspered; **—e,** *s.f.* (*bot.*) bindweed

†**Vriller,** *v.a.* to gimlet, to bore; *— v.n.* to assume a spiral shape; to whirl about, to ascend spirally [factory; gimlets; small tools

†**Vrillerie,** *s.f.* gimlet-making; gimlet-manu-

†**Vrillette,** *s.f.* (*zool.*) wood-fretter, death-watch

†**Vrillier,** *s.m.* gimlet-maker

†**Vrillifère,** *adj.* (*bot.*) claspered

†**Vrillon,** *s.m.* small auger *or* wimble [*prep.*)

Vu, *prep.* seeing, considering, &c. (*V.* **Attendu,**

Vu, e, *part.* seen, looked at *or* on *or* upon, &c. (*V.* **Voir**); examined; read; thought of; liked, received; advised; devised, contrived

Vu, *s.m.* sight, inspection, examination; preamble; contents. *Au — et au su de, V.* **Su**

Vue, *s.f.* sight; eye-sight; eyes, eye; view; prospect; (*stereoscopic*) slide; inspection; presence; light, window; design. *— basse, — courte*, short sight; short-sightedness. *— longue*, long sight; long-sightedness. *Longue-—*, *See Letter* **L.** *A —*, at sight. *A — d'œil*, visibly, by the eye. *A — d'oiseau*, from a bird's-eye view, bird's-eye. *A — de pays*, by guess. *A perte de —*, farther (*or* reaching farther) than the eye can reach *or* see; beyond o.'s view; out of sight; at random; far-fetched; inconclusive. *De —*, of sight, sight; by sight. *En —*, in *or* within sight; conspicuous; conspicuously; in view; in contemplation; in the eye (of); with a view (to). *Avoir la — basse* or *courte*, to be short-sighted *or* near-sighted. *Avoir — sur*, to look into; to have a view of. *Avoir des —s sur*, to have designs upon. *Connaître de —*, to know by sight. *Donner dans la —*, to catch ...'s eye; to take ...'s fancy, to please. *Garder à —*, to watch closely. *Perdre de —*, to lose sight of [**Vider**

Vuide, Vuider, (*obsolete spellings*) *V.* **Vide,**

Vulcain, *s.m.* (*myth.*) Vulcan; (*fig.*) smith, blacksmith; (*butterfly*) vulcan

Vulcanicité. *V.* **Volcanicité**

Vulcanien, ne, *adj. s.* Vulcanian

Vulcanique, *adj.* Vulcanic

Vulcanisation, *s.f.* vulcanization

Vulcaniser, *v.a.* to vulcanize

Vulcan-isme, -iste. *V.* page 3, § 1

Vulcanite, *s.m.* vulcanite

Vulgaire, *adj.* vulgar, common; low; trivial *— s.m.* vulgar, common people; common herd; common run [generally

Vulgairement, *adv.* vulgarly; commonly;

Vulgarisa-teur, trice, *s.m.f.* vulgarizer; *— adj.* vulgarizing

Vulgarisation, *s.f.* vulgarization

Vulgariser, *v.a.* to vulgarize; to popularize

Se —, *v.r.* to be vulgarized *or* popularized

Vulgarisme, *s.m.* vulgarism

Vulgarité, *s.f.* vulgarity; triviality

Vulgate, *s.f.* Vulgate

Vulgivague, *adj.* prostitute, prostituted

Vulnérabilité, *s.f. V.* page 3, § 1

Vulnérable, *adj.* vulnerable

Vulnérablement, *adv.* vulnerably

Vulnéraire, *adj.*, (*med.*) *s.m.*, (*bot.*) *s.f.* vulnerary

Vulnérant, e, *adj.* wounding

Vulnération, *s.f.* wounding, wound, wounds

Vulpin, *s.m.* (*bot.*) foxtail grass

Vulpin, e, *adj.* vulpine, fox-like

Vulpine, Vulpuline, *s.f.* (*chem.*) vulpine

Vulpinique, Vulpique, *adj.* (*chem.*) vulpinic

Vulpinite, *s.f.* (*min.*) vulpinite

Vulselle, *s.f.* (*mollusc*) vulsella

Vultueu-x, se, *adj.* (*med.*) flushed

Vulvaire, *adj.* (*anat.*) vulvar; *— s.f.* (*bot.*) [stinking goosefoot

Vulve, *s.f.* (*anat.*) vulva

Vulvite, *s.f.* (*med.*) vulvitis

W

W, *s.m.* w
Wacaka, *s.m.* wikana
Wacke, Wake, *s.m.* (*min.*) wacke
Wagon, Waggon, *s.m.* carriage; waggon; truck; van. — **-écurie**, *s.m.* (*rail.*) horse-box. — **-poste**, *s.m.* (*rail.*) mail-carriage
Wagonet, Waggonet, *s.m.* small waggon *or* truck *or* van; waggonette
Wagonette, Waggonette, *s.f.* waggonette
Wagonnier, *s.m.* truckman
Wahabi, Wahabite, *s.m. adj.* Wahabi, Wahabee, Wahabite
Wahabitisme, *s.m.* Wahabiism, Wahabitism
Waire, Wairette, *s.f.* pole, staff
Walhalla, *s.m.* walhalla, valhalla
Walida, *s.m.* (*bot.*) wrightia, conessi bark tree
Walkyrie. *V.* **Valkyrie**
Wallon, ne, *adj. s.* Walloon
Warandeur, *s.m.* overseer of herring-salting
Warrant, *s.m.* (*com.*) warrant, certificate
Warranté,e,*adj.*(*com.*) warranted, certificated
Wauxhall, *s.m.* Vauxhall
Weald, *s.m.* (*geol.*) weald-clay
Wealdien, ne, *adj.* (*geol.*) wealden
Wédélia, *s.m.*, **Wédélie**, *s.f.* (*bot.*) wedelia
Wehme, Wehmique, Welche. *V.* **Vehme, Vehmique, Velche**
Wellingtonia, *s.m.* (*bot.*) wellingtonia
Wermouth, Vermuth. *V.* **Vermout**
Wernérite, *s.f.* (*min.*) wernerite
Wesleyanisme, *s.m.* Wesleyanism
Wesleyen, ne, *adj. s.* Wesleyan
Westphalien, ne, *adj. s.*Westphalian; Westphalian fashion
Whig, *s.m. adj.* (*Engl. polit.*) whig
Whiggisme, *s.m.* (*Engl. polit.*) whiggism
Whiskey, Whisky, *s.m.* whiskey, whisky
Whist, *s.m.* (*game at cards*) whist
Wiclefisme, *s.m.* Wicliffism
Wiclefiste, *s.m.* Wicliffite
Wigwam, *s.m.* wigwam
Wiski, *s.m.* (*obsolete*) whisky, tim-whisky [(*carriage*)
Wistérie, *s.f.* (*bot.*) wistaria
Wolfram, *s.m.* (*min.*) wolfram
Wollastonite, *s.f.* (*min.*) wollastonite, tabular spar
Wombat, *s.m.* (*zool.*) wombat
Woorali, Woorari, *s.m.* *V.* **Curare**
Wootz, *s.m.* wootz, Indian steel
Wormien, *adj. m.* *Os —s*, (*anat.*) bones of Wormius, ossa Wormii, ossa triquetra
Wouède, *s.f.* *V.* **Guède**
Wrightie, *s.f.* (*bot.*) wrightia
Wurst, *s.m.* (*obsolete*) ambulance waggon
Wurtembergeois, e, *adj. s.* of Wurtemberg; Wurtemberger

X

X, *s.m.* x
Xanthe, *s.m.* (*zool.*) xantho; (*bot.*) xanthic flower
Xanthine, *s.f.* (*chem.*) xantheine, xanthine of flowers. — *azotée oxyde xanthique*, xanthine, xanthic oxide
Xanthique,*adj.*(*chem.*) xanthic
Xanthophylle, *s.f.* (*chem.*) xanthophyll
Xanthorrhée, *s.f.* (*bot.*) grass-tree
Xanthorrhize, *s.f.* (*bot.*) xanthorrhiza
Xanthoxyle, *s.m.* (*bot.*) xanthoxylum
Xérasie, *s.f.* (*med.*) xerasia
Xérès, *s.m.* sherry (wine)
Xérophagie, *s.f.* xerophagy
Xérophthalmie, *s.f.* (*med.*) xerophthalmia, xerophthalmy
Xiphoïde, *adj.* (*anat.*) xiphoid
Xylocope, *s.m.* (*zool.*) xylocopa, carpenter bee
Xylographe, *s.m.* xylographer, wood-engraver
Xylograph-ie, -ique. *V.* page 3, § 1
Xyloïdine, *s.f.* (*chem.*) xyloidine
Xylolog-ie, -ique. *V.* page 3, § 1
Xylophage, *adj.* (*zool.*) xylophagous; — *s.m.* (*zool.*) xylophagus, xylophagan, wood-eater, wood-fretter, bark-beetle, bark-chafer
Xylophagie, *s.f.* xylophagy
Xylophone, *s.m.* *V.* **Claquebois**
Xyste, *s.m.* (*antiq.*) xyst

Y

Y, *s.m.* (— *grec*) y; — *adv.* there; thither; here; hither; about the place; at home, in, within; — *pers. pron.* to him, him; to her, her; to it, it, to this, to that, this, that; to *or* on the subject; to them, them; in him; in her; in it, in this, in that; in them; into it, into this, into that; into them; through it, through that; through them; on it, on this, on that; on them; by it, by this, by that; by them; at it, at this, at that; at them; about it, about this, about that; about them; of it, of this, of that; of them; for it, for this, for that; for them; with it, with this, with that; with them; against it, against this *or* that; against them; to do it, to do so; to say it, to say so. — *avoir, Il — a*, *V.* **Avoir.** — *être*, *V.* **Être**
Yac, *s.m.* jack, union-jack, union-flag
'Yacht, *s.m.* (*nav.*) yacht
Yacou, *s.m.* (*bird*) yacou, guan
Yack, *s.m.* (*zool.*) yak (*species of ox*)
Yak, *s.m.* *V.* **Yac** *&* **Yack**
Yankee, *s.m.f. adj.* Yankee
Yapock, *s.m.* (*zool.*) yapock
Yard, *s.m.* (*Engl. meas.*) yard; yard-stick
'Yatagan, *s.m.* yataghan, yatagan
Yaws, *s.m.* (*med.*) yaws
Yèble, *s.f.* *V.* **Hièble**
Yénite, *s.f.* (*min.*) yenite
Yeuse, *s.f.* (*bot.*) evergreen oak, holly-oak, holm-oak, holm
Yeux, (*pl. of* **Œil**); eyes, &c. (*V.* **Œil**); (*fam.*) spectacles
'Yole, *s.f.* (*nav.*) yawl
Youyou, *s.m.* youyou, Chinese boat, small boat
Ypréau,*s.m.*(*bot.*) Ypres elm, broad-leaved elm, wych-elm; great round-leaved sallow; white poplar, abele
Ysard. *V.* **Isard**
Yttria, *s.f.* (*chem.*) yttria
Yttrique, *adj.* (*chem.*) yttric
Yttrium, *s.m.* (*chem.*) yttrium
'Yucca, *s.m.* (*bot.*) yucca

Z

Z, *s.m.* z
Zabre, *s.m.* (*zool.*) zabrus, corn ground beetle
Zagaie, *s.f.* assagai, assagay, javelin
Zaïm, *s.m.* zaim (*Turkish soldier*)
Zain, e, *adj.* (*of horses and mares*) zain, whole-coloured, all of one colour
Zambo, *s.m.* zambo, sambo
Zamie, *s.f.* (*bot.*) zamia
Zani, *s.m.* zany
Zapatéado, *s.m.* zapateado (*Spanish dance*)
Zèbre, *s.m.* (*animal*) zebra
Zébré, e, *adj.* zebra-striped, striped
Zébrer, *v.a.* to stripe like the zebra, to stripe
Zébrure, *s.f.* stripe *or* stripes (*like those of the zebra*)
Zébu, *s.m.* (*zool.*) zebu, Indian ox, Brahmin ox
Zédoaire, *s.f.* (*bot.*) zedoary
Zée, *s.m.* (*fish*) zeus. — *forgeron*, John Dory, dory
Zéine, *s.f.* (*chem.*) zeine

Zekkat, *s.m.* zekkat (*income-tax in Algeria,* &c.)
Zélandais, e, *adj. s.* of Zealand, native of Zealand, Zealander [— *adj.* zealous
Zéla-teur,trice,*s.m.f.*zealot; person zealous;
Zèle, *s.m.* zeal; warmth; ardour; devotion
Zélé, e, *adj.* zealous; — *s.m.f.* zealous person,
Zélotisme, *s.m.* zealotry [zealot
Zemni, *s.m.* (*zool.*) zemni, mole-rat
Zend, e, *adj.*, **Zend,** *s.m.* Zend. — **-Avesta,**
Zénith, *s.m.* zenith [*s.m.* Zend-Avesta
Zénithal, e, *adj.* zenithal
Zénon-ique, -isme, -iste. *V.* page 3, § 1
Zéolithe, *s.f.m.* (*min.*) zeolite
Zéolithique, *adj.* (*min.*) zeolitic
Zéphire, *s.m.* (*obsolete spelling*) *V.* **Zéphyr**
Zéphyr, *s.m.* zephyr, gentle breeze
Zerda, *s.m.* (*zool.*) zerda, fennec
Zéphyrien, ne, *adj.* zephyrian, airy, light; (*of eggs*) ungerminated, barren
Zéro,*s.m.*zero; nought, cipher. *Un — en chiffre,*
Zérotage, *s.m.* zeroing [a mere cipher
Zérumbet, *s.m.* (*bot.*) zerumbet, broad-leaved ginger
Zest, Zeste, *int.* pooh! pish! pshaw! nonsense! fiddlestick! ay! upon my word! pop! quick! presto! — *s.m.* (*of oranges, walnuts,* &c.) zest; (*fig.*) straw, fig, rap, rush. *Entre le zist et le —,* in suspense, wavering; middling, so so
Zester, *v.a.* to zest
Zéta, *s.m.* (*Gr. letter*) zeta
Zététique, *adj.* zetetic; — *s.f.* zetetics
Zeugma, Zeugme, *s.m.* (*rhet.*) zeugma
Zézaiement, Zézayement, Zézeyement, *s.m.* lisping, lisp
Zézayer, Zézeyer, *v.n.a.* to lisp [*fur*)
Zibeline, *s.f.* (*adject., Martre —*) sable (*animal,*
Zibet, Zibeth, *s.m.* (*zool.*) zibet
Zig, Zigue, *s.m.* (*fam.*) fellow, chap, cove
Zigzag, *s.m.* zigzag; crankle; (*of lightning*) fork. *En —,* zigzag; winding; forked. *Éclair en —,* forked lightning. *Aller en —, faire des —s,* to go zigzag, to zigzag, to stagger, to go reeling, to reel, to reel about
Zigzaguer, *v.n.* to zigzag
Zimome, *s.f.* (*chem.*) zimome [tutty-powder
Zinc, *s.m.* zinc. *Oxyde de —,* oxide of zinc;
Zincage, *s.m.* zincing; covering with zinc;
Zincifère, *adj.* zinciferous [zinc-plating
Zincique, *adj.* (*chem.*) zincic
Zincite, *s.f.* (*min.*) zincite
Zincographe, *s.m.* zincographer
Zincographie,*s.f.* zincography, zinc-printing
Zincographier, *v.a.* to zincograph
Zincograph-ique,-iquement.*V.*page 3,§ 1
Zingage. *V.* **Zincage**
Zingari, *s.m.* zingari
Zingel, *s.m.* (*fish*) zingel
Zinguer, *v.a.* to zinc, to cover *or* plate with zinc, to lay over with zinc; to galvanize (*iron*)
Zinguerie, *s.f.* zinc-works; zinc-trade; zinc
Zingueur, *s.m.* zinc-worker
Zingueu-x, se, *adj.* (*chem.*) zincous
Zinnia, *s.m.* (*bot.*) zinnia
Zinzolin,e,*adj.***Zinzolin,** *s.m.* reddish violet
Zircon, *s.m.* (*min.*) zircon
Zircone, *s.f.* (*chem.*) zirconia
Zirconien, ne, *adj.* zirconian
Zirconique, *adj.* (*chem.*) zirconic
Zirconite, *s.f.* (*min.*) zirconite
Zirconium, *s.m.* (*chem.*) zirconium
Zist, *s.m.* *V.* **Zest**
Zita, *s.m.* Naples macaroni
Zizanie,*s.f.*(*bot.*) zizania, darnel, tares, Canada rice, wild rice; (*fig.*) discord, dissension
Zizi, *s.m.* (*bird*) cirl bunting
Zoanthe, *s.m.* (*zool.*) zoanthus (*polype*)
Zoanthropie, *s.f.* (*med.*) zoanthropy
Zodiacal, e, *adj.* (*astr.*) zodiacal
Zodiaque, *s.m.* (*astr.*) zodiac
Zoétrope, *s.m.* zoetrope, wheel of life
Zoïle, *s.m.* Zoilus, snarling *or* snappish critic
Zoïodine, *s.f.* (*chem.*) zoiodine
Zoïsme, *s.m.* zoism
Zollverein, *s.m.* zollverein
Zona, *s.m.* (*med.*) shingles
Zone, *s.f.* (*geog., astr., bot.,* &c.) zone; (*fig.*) zone, belt. *A —,* (*bot.*) zoned. *La — glaciale,* the
Zoné, e, *adj.* zoned [frigid zone
Zoniforme, *adj.* zoniform
Zoo, (*in compounds*) zoo ...
Zoogénie, *s.f.* zoogeny
Zoogon-ie, -ique. *V.* page 3, § 1
Zoographe, *s.m.* zoographer
Zoograph-ie, -ique. *V.* page 3, § 1
Zooïde, *s.m. adj.* (*nat. hist.*) zooid
Zoolâtre, *s.m.f.* zoolater, zoolatress; — *adj*
Zoolâtrie, *s.f.* zoolatry [zoolatrous
Zoolâtrique, *adj.* zoolatrous
Zoolithe, *s.m.* zoolite
Zoolithique, *adj.* zoolitic
Zoolog-ie, -ique, -iquement, -iste. *V.*
Zoologue, *s.m.* zoologist [page 3, § 1
†**Zoomagnétisme,** *s.m.* zoomagnetism, animal magnetism
Zoomorphie, *s.f.* zoomorphy
Zoomorphisme, *s.m.* zoomorphism
Zoomorphite, *s.m.* zoomorphite
Zoo-nomie, -nomique, -nosologie, nosologique, -pathologie, -pathologique, &c. *V.* page 3, § 1
Zoonure, *s.m.*(*zool.*) zoonurus [gist, zoophagan
Zoophage, *adj.* zoophagous; — *s.m.f.* zoopha-
Zoophag-ie, -ique. *V.* page 3, § 1
Zoophore, *s.m.* (*arch.*) zoophorus
Zoophorique, *adj.* (*arch.*) zoophoric
Zoophytaire, *adj.* zoophytal
Zoophyte, *s.m.* (*nat. hist.*) zoophyte
Zoophytique, *adj.* zoophytic, zoophytical
Zoophytographe, *s.m.* zoophytographer
Zoophyto-graphie,-logie, &c. *V.* page 3, § 1
Zoophytolithe, *s.m.* zoophytolite
Zoophytologiste, Zoophytologue, *s.m.*
Zoospore, *s.f.* (*bot.*) zoospore [zoophytologist
‡**Zootechnicien,** *s.m.* zootechnist [3, § 1
‡**Zootechn-ie, -ique, -iquement.** *V.* page
Zootom-ie, -ique, -iste. *V.* page 3, § 1
Zopissa, *s.m* (*nav.*) zopissa
†**Zorille,** *s.f.m.* (*zool.*) zoril
Zoroastrien, ne, *adj. s.* Zoroastrian
Zoster, *s.m.* (*med.*) *V.* **Zona**
Zostère,*s.f.*(*bot.*) grasswrack; alva marina, alva
Zouave, *s.m.* zouave (*soldier*)
Zoucet, Zouchet, *s.m.* *V.* **Castagneux**
Zouzou, *s.m.* (*fam. for* **Zouave**) [Zurich
‡**Zurichois, e,** *adj.* of Zurich; native of
Zut, *int.* (*pop.*) you be blowed! hang it! I am not going to do it! not I! stuff! not a bit of it! no use! no go!
Zwinglianisme, *s.m.* Zwinglianism
Zwinglien, *s.m.* Zwinglian
Zygène, *s.m.* (*fish*) hammer-fish, hammer-headed shark, hammer-head, balance-fish
Zygoma, *s.m.* (*anat.*) zygoma
Zygomatique, *adj.* (*anat.*) zygomatic. *Arcade —,* zygomatic arch
Zymase,*s.f.* (*chem.*) zymasis
Zymique, *adj.* (*chem.*) zymic
Zymolog-ie, -ique, -iste. *V.* page 3, § 1
Zymoscope, Zymosimètre, *s.m.* zymoscope, zymosimeter, zymometer
Zymosimétr-ie, -ique. *V.* page 3, § 1
‡**Zymotechn-ie, -ique.** *V.* page 3, § 1
Zymotique, *adj.* zymotic
Zythogale, *s.m.* zythogala

END OF THE FRENCH-ENGLISH DICTIONARY.

FRENCH ABBREVIATIONS.

A., (*mus.*) Alto; (*com.*) Accepté.
A.C., (*com.*) Année courante.
A.C.L., Assuré contre l'incendie.
A.M., Assurance mutuelle.
Am^{al}., Amiral.
A.P., (*com.*) Année passée; (*of bills, &c.*) À protester.
A.R., Altesse Royale. [protêt.
A.S.P., (*com.*) Accepté sous
A.S.P.C., (*com.*) Accepté sous protêt pour à-compte.
B^{on}., Baron.
B^{onne}., Baronne.
B.S.G.D.G., Breveté sans garantie du gouvernement.
C., **Cent.**, (*in accounts*) Centime *or* Centimes (*coin*).
C.-à-d., C'est-à-dire.
C.C., (*com.*) Compte courant.
Ch., **Chap.**, Chapitre.
Ch^{er}., **Ch^{r}.**, Chevalier.
Cie., Compagnie.
C/O., (*com.*) Compte ouvert.
C^{t}., (*com.*) Courant (*instant, inst.*)
Cte., Comte.
Ctesse., Comtesse.
D.M., Docteur-médecin.
D.O.M., (*Latin*) Deo optimo [maximo.
D^{r}., Docteur.
D^{r}.-M^{n}., Docteur-médecin.
E., Est.
etc., et cætera (&c.).
Exc., Excellence.
F., Frère; Franc *or* Francs (*coin*); Feminine (*gender*).
F^{o}., Folio.
Fr., Franc *or* Francs (*coin*).
G^{al}., Général.
ib., **ibid.**, ibidem.
id., idem, ditto.
J.-C., Jésus-Christ.
J^{e}., Jeune (*junior*).
K., **Kil.**, **Kilo.**, **Kilog.**, **Kilogr.**, kilogramme *or* kilogrammes. [kilometres.
Kil., **Kilom.**, kilomètre *or*
LL.AA., Leurs Altesses.
LL.AA.II., Leurs Altesses Impériales. [Royales.
LL.AA.RR., Leurs Altesses
LL.AA.SS., Leurs Altesses Sérénissimes.
LL.EEm., Leurs Éminences.

LL.EExc., Leurs Excellences.
LL.HH., Leurs Hautesses.
LL.MM., Leurs Majestés.
LL.MM.II., Leurs Majestés Impériales. [Royales.
LL.MM.RR., Leurs Majestés
M., Monsieur; Masculine (*gender*).
M.A., Maison assurée.
M.A.C.I. (*or* **L.**), Maison assurée contre l'incendie.
M^{al}., Maréchal.
M^{d}, Marchand.
M^{de}., Marchande.
M^{e}., Maître (*Mr.*).
Melle., Mademoiselle.
Mgr, Monseigneur.
Mis, Marquis.
M^{ise}., Marquise.
MM., Messieurs.
Mme., Madame.
M^{r}., Monsieur.
M^{rs}., Messieurs.
MS., **Msc.**, **Mst.**, Manuscrit.
MSS., Manuscrits.
N., Nord.
N.B., (*Latin*) Nota bene.
N.-D., Notre-Dame.
N.-E., Nord-Est.
Nég^{t}, Négociant.
Nég^{te}., Negociante.
N.-N.-E., Nord-nord-est.
N.-N.-O., Nord-nord-ouest.
NN.SS., Nosseigneurs (Nos
N.-O., Nord-ouest. [Seigneurs).
N^{o}., Numéro.
N.-S., Notre-Seigneur.
N.-S. J.C., Notre-Seigneur [Jésus-Christ.
N^{t}., Négociant.
N^{te}., Négociante.
N.T.C.F., Nos très chers frères.
O., Ouest. [*priest*) Père.
P., (*before the proper name of a*
PP., Pères.
P.P.C., Pour prendre congé.
P.-S., Post-scriptum.
Q.E.D., (*Latin*) Quod erat demonstrandum.
R^{d}., **Rév^{d}**, Révérend.
R.I.P., (*Latin*) Requiescat in
R.P., Révérend père. [pace.
RR.PP., Révérends pères.
R.S.V.P., Réponse s'il vous plait (*An answer will oblige*).

S., Sud.
S.A., Son Altesse.
S.A.I., Son Altesse Impériale.
S.A.R., Son Altesse Royale.
S.A.S., Son Altesse Sérénissime.
S.-E., Sud-est.
S.Em., Son Eminence.
S.Exc., Son Excellence.
S.G., Sa Grandeur.
S.G.D.G., Sans garantie du gouvernement.
S.H., Sa Hautesse.
S.M., Sa Majesté.
S.M.B., Sa Majesté Britannique.
S.M.C., Sa Majesté Catholique.
S.M.I., Sa Majeste Impériale.
S.M.R., Sa Majesté Royale.
S.M.S., Sa Majeste Suédoise.
S.M.T.C., Sa Majesté Très Chrétienne. [Fidèle.
S.M.T.F., Sa Majesté Très
S.-O., Sud-ouest.
S.P., Saint père.
S.P.Q.R., (*Latin*) Senatus populusque Romanus.
SS.PP., Saints pères.
S.S., Sa Sainteté.
S.-S.-E., Sud-sud-est.
S.-S.-O., Sud-sud-ouest.
S^{t}., Saint.
S.V.P., S'il vous plaît.
T.F., Travaux forcés (à temps).
T.P., Travaux forcés à perpétuité. [plait (*Please turn over*).
T.S.V.P., Tournez s'il vous
V., (*French*) Voyez, (*Latin*) Vide.
V/, (*com.*) Votre; (*in church-books*) verset. [Votre Majesté, &c.
V.A., **V.M.**, **&c.**, Votre Altesse,
V/c, (*com.*) Votre compte [lence.
V.E., **V.Exc.**, Votre Excel-
VV.MM., **&c.**, Vos Majestés, &c.

0/0., Pour cent.
In-4o, In-quarto.
In-8o, In-octavo.
In-12, In-douze.
In-18, In-dix-huit.
7bre, **(Sept.)**, Septembre.
8bre, **(Oct.)**, Octobre.
9bre, **(Nov.)**, Novembre.
10bre, **X^{bre}**, **(Déc.)**, Décembre.

GEOGRAPHICAL PROPER NAMES.

Abdère, *f.* Abdera
Abruzze (L'), *f.* Abruzzo. *Les —s,* (*f. pl.*) the Abruzzi
Abyssinie (L'), *f.* Abyssinia
Acadie (L'), *f.* Acadia
Acarnanie (L'), *f.* Acarnania
‡**Achaïe (L'),** *f.* Achaia
Achéron (L'), *m.* the Acheron
Açores (Les), *f. pl.* the Azores
Acre, *m.* (*Saint-Jean d'—*) Acre
Adige (L'), *m.* the Adige
Adour (L'), *m.* the Adour
Afghanistan (L'), *m.* Afghanistan
Afrique (L'), *f.* Africa
Agrigente, *f.* Agrigentum
Albanie (L'), *f.* Albania
Albe, *f.* Alba, Alva
Albion (L'), *f.* Albion
Aléoutes (Les), Aléoutiennes (Les Iles), *f.pl.* the Aleutian Islands
Alep, *m.* Aleppo
Alexandrette, *f.* Alexandretta
Alexandrie, *f.* Alexandria
Algarve (L'), *f.* Algarve
Alger, *m.* Algiers
Algérie (L'), *f.* Algeria
Alicante, *f.* Alicant, Alicante
†**Allemagne (L'),** *f.* Germany
Alpes (Les), *f. pl.* the Alps
Alsace (L'), *f.* Alsace
Altenbourg, *m.* Altenburg
Amadan, *m.* Hamadan
Amazone (L'), *m.* the Amazon. *Le Fleuve des —s,* the Amazon river. *Le Pays des —s,* Amazonia
Amboine, *f.* Amboyna
Amérique (L'), *f.* America
Amirauté (Iles de l'), *f. pl.* Admiralty Islands
Amis (Les Iles des), *f. pl.* the Friendly Islands
Amour (L'), *m.* the Amoor
Anatolie (L'), *f.* Anatolia
Ancône, *f.* Ancona
Andalousie (L'), *f.* Andalusia
Andes (Les), *f. pl.* the Andes
Andorre, *m.* Andorra, Andorre
Andrinople, *f.* Adrianople
Angleterre (L'), *f.* England. *La Nouvelle —,* New England
Antigue, Antigoa, *f.* Antigua
†**Antilles (Les),** *f. pl.* the Antilles, the West Indies
Antioche, *f.* Antioch
Anvers, *m.* Antwerp
Aoste, *f.* Aosta
Aoude, *f.* Oude (*town*)
Aoude (L'), *m.* Oude (*province*)
Apennins (Les), *m. pl.* the Apennines
Apollonie, *f.* Apollonia
Apulie (L'), *f.* Apulia
Aquilée, *f.* Aquileia
Aquitaine (L'), *f.* Aquitania, Aquitaine
Arabie (L'), *f.* Arabia. *L'—Déserte,* Arabia Deserta (the Barren). *L'— Heureuse,* Arabia Felix (the Happy). *L'—Pétrée,* Arabia Petræa
Aragon (L'), *m.* Aragon
Araucanie (L'), *f.* Araucania
Arbelles, Arbèles, *f.* Arbela
Arcadie (L'), *f.* Arcadia
Archipel(L'), *m.* the Archipelago
Ardennes (Les), *f. pl.* the Ardennes
Argolide (L'), *f.* Argolis
Argovie (L'), *f.* Aargau, Argovia
Arkhangel, *m.* Archangel
Arménie (L'), *f.* Armenia
Armorique (L'), *f.* Armorica
Asie (L'), *f.* Asia. *L'—Mineure,* Asia Minor
Assyrie (L'), *f.* Assyria
Asturies (Les), *f. pl.* the Asturias
Athènes, *f.* Athens
Atlantide, *f.* Atlantis
Atlas (L'), *m.* the Atlas
Attique (L'), *f.* Attica
Augsbourg, *m.* Augsburg
Aulide, Aulis, *f.* Aulis
†**Aurigny,** *m.* Alderney
Ausonie (L'), *f.* Ausonia; (*poet.*) Italy
Australasie(L'), *f.* Australasia
Australie (L'), *f.* Australia
Austrasie (L'), *f.* Austrasia
Autriche (L'), *f.* Austria
†**Auvergne (L'),** *f.* Auvergne
Aventin (L'), *m.* the Aventine
Averne (L'), *m.* the Averno; (*anc.*) Avernus, the (lake) Avernus; (*poet.*) hell
†**Avignon,** *m.* Avignon
Azincourt, *m.* Agincourt, Azincourt

Babylone, *f.* Babylon
Babylonie (La), *f.* Babylonia
Bactres, *f.* Bactra
Bactriane (La), *f.* Bactriana, Bactria
Bade, *f.* Baden
Baffin (La Baie *or* Mer de), *f.* Baffin's Bay
Bahama (Les Iles), *f. pl.* the Bahama Islands, the Bahamas
Bâle, *f.* Bâle, Basle, Basel
Baléares (Les Iles), *f. pl.* the Balearic Isles
Barbade (La), *f.* Barbadoes
Barbaresques (Les États), *m pl.* the Barbary States
Barbarie (La), *f.* Barbary
Barboude (La), *f.* Barbuda
Barcelone, Barcelonne, *f.* Barcelona
Batavia, *f.* Batavia (*town*)
Batavie (La), *f.* Batavia (*old name of Holland*)
Bavière (La), *f.* Bavaria
Béarn (Le), *m.* Bearn
Belgique (La), *f.* Belgium
Béloutchistan (Le), *m.* Beloochistan
Belt (Le), *m.* the Belt
Bénévent, *m.* Benevento
Bengale (Le), *m.* Bengal. *Golfe du —,* Bay of Bengal
Béotie (La), *f.* Bœotia
Bergame, *f.* Bergamo
Berg-op-Zoom, *m.* Bergen-op-Zoom
Berlin, *m.* Berlin
Bermudes (Les Iles), *f. pl.* the Bermudas
Berne, (*canton*) *m.*, (*town*) *f.* Berne
Bernbourg, *m.* Bernburg
Berri *or* **Berry (Le),** *m.* Berry
Bessarabie(La), *f.* Bessarabia
Bethléem, *m.* Bethlehem
Bétique (La), *f.* Bætica
Birman (L' Empire), *m.*, **Birmanie (La),** *f.* the Birman Empire, the Empire of Birmah *or* Burmah
Biscaye (La), *f.* Biscay
Bithynie (La), *f.* Bithynia
Blanc(Le Cap), *m.* Cape Bianco
Bohême (La), *f.* Bohemia
Bolivie (La), *f.* Bolivia
†**Bologne,** *f.* Bologna
Bolonais (Le), *m.* the Bolognese
Bone, *f.* Bona
Borromées (Les Iles), *f.pl.* the Borromean Islands
Borysthène (Le), *m.* the Borysthenes
Bosnie (La), *f.* Bosnia
Bothnie *or* **Botnie(La),** *f.* Bothnia
Bougie, *f.* Boujeiah, Bugia
Boukhara, *m.* Bokhara
Boukharest, *m.* Bucharest
Boukharie (La), *f.* Bucharia
†**Boulogne,** *f.* Boulogne
†**Bourgogne (La),** *f.* Burgundy
Brabant (Le), *m.* Brabant
Bragance, *f.* Braganza
Brandebourg (Le), *m.* Brandenburg
Brême, *f.* Bremen
Brésil (Le), *m.* Brazil
†**Bretagne (La),** *f.* Brittany; (*anc.*) Britannia, Britain. *La Grande- —,* Great Britain. *La Nouvelle- —,* New Britain
Brindes, *m.* Brindisi
Brousse, *f.* Broussa, Brussa, Brusa
Bruxelles, *f.* Brussels
‡**Bucharest,** *m.* Bucharest
‡**Bucharie (La),** *f.* Bucharia
Bude, *f.* Buda
Bulgarie (La), *f.* Bulgaria
Byzance, *f.* Byzantium

Caboul, *m.* Cabul
Cachemire (Le), *m.* Cashmere
Cachemire, *f.* (*town*) Cashmere
Cadix, *m.* Cadiz
Cafrerie (La), *f.* Caffraria, Cafferland, Kafirland, Kaffirland
Caire (Le), *m.* Cairo
Calabre (La), *f.* Calabria
Calais, *m.* Calais. *Le Pas-de- —,* the Straits of Dover; (*department of France*) Pas-de-Calais
Calédonie (La), *f.* Caledonia. *La Nouvelle- —,* New Caledonia
Californie (La), *f.* California
Campanie (La), *f.* Campania
Campêche, *m.* Campeachy
Canada (Le), *m.* Canada
Canarie, *f.* Canary. *Les —s,* the Canaries. *Les Iles —s,* the Canary Islands
Candie (L' Ile de), *f.* Candia
Canée (La), *f.* Canea
Cannes, *f.* (*in France*) Cannes, (*in Italy*) Cannæ

Cantorbéry, *m.* Canterbury
Cap (Le), *m.* the Cape ; Cape Town. *Le — de Bonne-Espérance*, the Cape of Good Hope. *La Ville du —*, Cape Town
Capoue, *f.* Capua
Cappadoce (La), *f.* Cappadocia
Caprée, *f.* Capri; (*anc.*) Capreæ
Caraïbes (Les Iles), *f. pl.* the Caribbee Islands. *La Mer des —*, the Caribbean Sea
Caramanie (La), *f.* Caramania
Carélie (La), *f.* Carelia
Carie (La), *f.* Caria
Carinthie (La), *f.* Carinthia
Carlsbourg, *m.* Carlsburg, Karlsburg
†**Carmagnole,** *f.* Carmagnola
Carmanie (La), *f.* Carmania
Carniole (La), *f.* Carniola
Caroline (La), *f.* Carolina
Carpathes (Les Monts), *m.pl.* the Carpathian Mountains
Carrare, *f.* Carrara
Carthage, *f.* Carthage
Carthagène, *f.* Carthagena
Carybde, *m.* Charybdis
†**Castille (La),** *f.* Castile
†**Catalogne (La),** *f.* Catalonia
Catane, *f.* Catania; (*anc.*) Catana
Cattégat (Le), *m.* the Cattegat
Caucase (Le), *m.* Caucasus
Celtibérie (La), *f.* Celtiberia
Céphalonie, *f.* Cephalonia
†**Cerdagne (La),** *f.* Cerdagna
Césarée, *f.* Cæsarea
Cévennes (Les), *f. pl.* the Cevennes
Ceylan, *m.* Ceylon
‡**Chalcédoine,** *f.* Chalcedon
‡**Chalcis,** *m.* Chalcis
‡**Chaldée (La),** *f.* Chaldea
†**Champagne (La),** *f.* Champagne
‡**Chanaan,** *m.* Canaan
‡**Chaonie (La),** *f.* Chaonia
‡**Charybde,** *m.* Charybdis
‡**Chéronée,** *f.* Chæronea, Chæroneia
Chili (Le), *m.* Chili
Chine (La), *f.* China
Chio, *f.* Chios
Chypre, *f.* Cyprus
Cilicie (La), *f.* Cilicia
Circassie (La), *f.* Circassia
Cnide, *f.* Cnidus, Gnidos
Cobourg, *m.* Coburg
Cochinchine (La), *f.* Cochin-China
Cocyte (Le), *m.* Cocytus
Coïmbre, *f.* Coimbra
Colchide (La), *f.* Colchis
†**Cologne,** *f.* Cologne
Colombie (La), *f.* Columbia, Colombia
Colone, *f.* Colonus, Colonos
Come, *f.* Como
Compostelle, *f.* Compostella
Congo (Le), *m.* Congo
Constantine, *f.* Constantina
Constantinople, *f.* Constantinople
Copenhague, *f.* Copenhagen
Corcyre, *f.* Corcyra
†**Cordillères (Les),** *f. pl.* the Cordilleras
Cordoue, *f.* Cordova
Corée (La), *f.* the Corea
Corfou, *m.* Corfu
Corinthe, *f.* Corinth
†**Cornouailles (Le),** *m.* Cornwall
†**Corogne (La),** *f.* Corunna
Coronée, *f.* Coronea
Corse (La), *f.* Corsica
Cortone, *f.* Cortona
Côte-d'Or (La), *f.* (*in Africa*) the Gold Coast; (*in France*) the Côte-d'Or

Courlande (La), *f.* Courland
Cracovie, *f.* Cracow
Crémone, *f.* Cremona
Crète (La), *f.* Crete
Crimée (La), *f.* the Crimea
Croatie (La), *f.* Croatia
Crotone, *f.* Crotona, Croton
Cumes, *f.* Cumæ
Curaçao, *m.* Curaçoa
Cyclades (Les), *f. pl.* the Cyclades
Cynocéphales, *f.* Cynocephalæ
Cypre. *V.* Chypre
Cythère, *f.* Cythera

Dacie (La), *f.* Dacia
Dalécarlie (La), *f.* Dalecarlia
Dalmatie (La), *f.* Dalmatia
Damas, *m.* Damascus
Damiette, *f.* Damietta
Danemark *or* **Danemarck (Le),** *m.* Denmark
Dantzick, Dantzig, *m.* Dantzic
Danube (Le), *m.* the Danube
Dardanelles (Les), *f. pl.* the Dardanelles
Dardanie (La), *f.* Dardania
Daunie (La), *f.* Daunia
Dauphiné (Le), *m.* Dauphiny
Décan *or* **Dekkan (Le),** *m.* Deccan
Delphes, *f.* Delphi
Dendermonde, *m.* Dendermond
Dents (La Côte des), *f.* the Ivory Coast
Désirade (La), *f.* Desirade, Desiderade
Deux-Ponts, *m.* Zwei-Brücken
Diéménie (La), *f.* Tasmania, Van Diemen's Land
Dniéper (Le), *m.* the Dnieper
Dniester (Le), *m.* the Dniester
Dodone, *f.* Dodona
Dominique (La), *f.* Dominica
Don (Le), *m.* the Don
†**Dordogne (La),** *f.* the Dordogne
Doride (La), *f.* Doris
Douro (Le), *m.* the Douro
Douvres, *m.* Dover
Dresde, *f.* Dresden
Dublin, *m.* Dublin
Duna (La), *f.* the Duna
Dunkerque, *m.* Dunkirk
Dwina (La), *f.* the Dwina

Èbre (L'), *m.* the Ebro
Ecbatane, *f.* Ecbatana
Écluse (L'), *f.* Sluys
Écosse (L'), *f.* Scotland. *La Basse —*, the Lowlands. *La Haute —*, the Highlands. *La Nouvelle- —*, Nova-Scotia
Édimbourg, *m.* Edinburgh
Égée (La Mer), *f.* the Ægean Sea
Égine, *f.* Ægina, Egina
Égypte (L'), *f.* Egypt
Elbe (L' Ile d'), *f.* Elba, the Island of Elba
Elbe (L'), *m.* the Elbe
Élée, *f.* Elea
Elseneur, *m.* Elsinore
Éolide *or* **Éolie (L'),** *f.* Æolia
Éphèse, *f.* Ephesus
Épices (Les Iles aux), *f. pl.* the Spice Islands
Épidaure, *f.* Epidaurus
Épire (L'), *f.* Epirus
***Équateur (L'),** *m.* Ecuador, Equator
Érèbe (L'), *m.* Erebus
Érié (Le Lac), *m.* Lake Erie
Escaut (L'), *m.* the Scheldt
Esclave (Le Lac de l'), *m.* Slave Lake

Esclaves (La Côte des), *f.* the Slave Coast
Esclavonie (L'), *f.* Sclavonia
†**Espagne (L'),** *f.* Spain
Esthonie (L'), *f.* Esthonia
Estramadure (L'), *f.* Estremadura
États-Unis (Les), *m. pl.* the United States
Éthiopie (L'), *f.* Ethiopia
Etna (L'), *m.* Etna
Étolie (L'), *f.* Ætolia, Etolia
Étrurie (L'), *f.* Etruria
Eubée (L'), *f.* Eubœa
Euphrate (L'), *m.* the Euphrates
Europe (L'), *f.* Europe
Euxin (L'), *m.* the Euxine

Færoé *or* **Færoer (Les Iles),** *f. pl.* the Faroe Islands
Fernambouc, *m.* Pernambuco
Féroé. *V.* Færoé
Ferrarais (Le), *m.* the Ferrarese
Ferrare, *f.* Ferrara
Finisterre, Finistère, *m. Le —*, (*French department*) Finisterre. *Le Cap —*, (*in Spain*) Cape Finisterra; (*in England*) Land's End
Finlande (La), *f.* Finland
Fionie (La), *f.* Fionia
Flandre (La), *f.* Flanders
Flessingue, *m.* Flushing
Floride (La), *f.* Florida
Fontarabie, *f.* Fontarabia
Formose, *f.* Formosa
Forth (Le Golfe du), *m.* the Frith of Forth
France (La), *f.* France
Francfort, *m.* Frankfort
Franche-Comté (La), *f.* Franche-Comté
Franconie (La), *f.* Franconia
Fribourg, *m.* (*in Germany*) Freiburg; (*in Switzerland*) Friburg, Freiburg
Frioul (Le), *m.* Friuli
Frise (La), *f.* Friesland
†**Frontignan,** *m.* Frontiniac, Frontignac

Gabon (Le), *m.* the Gaboon
Gaète, *f.* Gaeta
Galatie (La), *f.* Galatia
Galice (La), *f.* Galicia (*in Spain*)
Galicie (La), *f.* Galicia (*in Austria*)
Galilée (La), *f.* Galilee
Galles, *f.* Wales. *Le Pays de —*, (*m.*) Wales. *La Nouvelle — du Sud*, New South Wales
Gallicie. *V.* Galicie
Gambie (La), *f.* Gambia
Gand, *m.* Ghent
Gange (Le), *m.* the Ganges
Garonne (La), *f.* the Garonne
†**Gascogne (La),** *f.* Gascony. *Le Golfe de —*, the Bay of Biscay
Gaule (La), *f.* Gaul
Gênes, *f.* Genoa
Genève, *f.* Geneva
Géorgie (La), *f.* Georgia
Germanie (La), *f.* (*anc.*) Germany
Gironde (La), *f.* the Gironde
Glascow, Glasgow, *m.* Glasgow
Gœttingue, *f.* Göttingen
Golconde, *f.* Golconda
Gomorrhe, *f.* Gomorrah
Gorée, *f.* Goree
Gothenbourg, *m.* Gothenburg, Gottenburg
Gothie (La), *f.* Gothland
Gottingue. *V.* Gœttingue
Gottland (L' Ile), *f.* Gottland

Grampians (Les Monts), *m.pl.* the Grampians

Granique (Le), *m.* the Granicus

Grèce (La), *f.* Greece

Grenade, *f.* Granada

Grenade (La), *f.* Grenada, Granada. *La Nouvelle-* —, New Granada

Groënland (Le), *m.* Greenland

Groningue, *f.* Groningen

Guadalquivir (Le), *m.* the Guadalquivir

Guadeloupe (La), *f.* Guadaloupe, Guadeloupe

Guadiana (La), *f.* the Guadiana

Guatemala (Le), *m.* Guatemala

Gueldre (La), *f.* Guelderland

Guernesey, *m.* Guernsey

Guiane *or* **Guyane (La)**, *f.* Guiana *or* Guyana

Guinée (La), *f.* Guinea. *La Nouvelle-* —, New Guinea

'Hainaut (Le), *m.* Hainault

Haïti, *m.* Hayti

Halicarnasse, *f.* Halicarnassus

'Hambourg, *m.* Hamburg, Hambro

'Hanovre (Le), *m.* Hanover

'Hapsbourg, *m.* Hapsburg

'Havane (La), *f.* Havana, Havanna, Havannah

'Havre (Le), *m.* Havre

'Haye (La), *f.* the Hague

Hèbre (L'), *m.* the Hebrus

Hébrides (Les), *f. pl.* the Hebrides

Hécla *or* **Hékla (L')**, *m.* Hecla [or Hekla

Hélicon (L'), *m.* Helicon

Hellespont (L'), *m.* the Hellespont

Helvétie (L'), *f.* Helvetia (*ancient Switzerland*)

Héraclée, *f.* Heraclea, Heracleia

Herculanum, *m.* Herculaneum

Herzégovine (L'), *f.* Herzegovina

Hespérie (L'), *f.* Hesperia

'Hesse (La), *f.* Hesse

Hibernie (L'), *f.* Hibernia

Himalaya (L'), *m.* the Himalaya *or* Himaleh

Hindoustan *or* **Hindostan (L')**, *m.* Hindustan *or* Hindostan

Hispanie (L'), *f.* Hispania

'Hollande (La), *f.* Holland. *La Nouvelle-* —, New Holland

'Holstein (Le), *m.* Holstein

'Hombourg, *m.* Homburg

'Honduras (Le), *m.* Honduras

'Hongrie (La), *f.* Hungary

Hydaspe (L'), *m.* the Hydaspes

Hymette (L'), *m.* Hymettus; Hymet

Hyrcanie (L'), *f.* Hyrcania

Ibérie (L'), *f.* Iberia

Icarie (L'), *f.* Icaria

Idalie, *f.* Idalia

Idumée (L'), *f.* Idumea

Ile. *L'— de France; Les —s; &c. V. General Dictionary*

Illyrie (L'), *f.* Illyria, Illyricum

Inde (L'), *f.* India. *Les —s*, the Indies. *Les Grandes —s, les —s Orientales*, the East Indies. *Les —s Occidentales*, the West Indies. *La Compagnie des —s*, the East India Conpany

Indo-Chine (L'), *f.* Indo-China

Indostan *or* **Indoustan.** *V.* Hindoustan

Indus (L'), *m.* (*anc.*) the Indus

Ingrie (L'), *f.* Ingria

Ionie (L'), *f.* Ionia

Irlande (L'), *f.* Ireland

Islande (L'), *f.* Iceland

Istrie (L'), *f.* Istria

Italie (L'), *f.* Italy

Ithaque, *f.* Ithaca

Ivoire (La Côte d'), *f.* the Ivory Coast

Jagrenat, *m.* Juggernaut

Jamaïque (La), *f.* Jamaica

Japon (Le), *m.* Japan

Jérusalem, *f.* Jerusalem

Jourdain (Le), *m.* the Jordan

Judée (La), *f.* Judæa

Jutland (Le), *m.* Jutland

Kaboul. *V.* Caboul

Kabylie (La), *f.* Kabylia

Kamtchatka (Le), *m.* Kamtchatka

Karnatic (Le), *m.* the Carnatic

Krapacks. *V.* Carpathes

Labouan, *m.* Labuan

Labrador (Le), *m* Labrador

Lacédémone, *f.* Lacedæmon

Laconie (La), *f.* Laconia

Lancastre, *m.* Lancaster

Languedoc (Le), *m.* Languedoc

Laodicée, *f.* Laodicea

Laponie (La), *f.* Lapland

Laquedives (Les Iles), *f. pl.* the Laccadive Islands

Larisse, *f.* Larissa

Larrons (Les Iles des), *f. pl.* the Ladrones *or* Thieves' Islands

Latakieh, *m.* Latakia

Latium (Le), *m.* Latium

Leipsick, Leipsig, *m.* Leipsic

Lépante, *f.* Lepanto

Lerne, *f.* Lerna

Léthé (Le), *m.* Lethe

Leuctres, *f.* Leuctra

Leyde, *f.* Leyden

Liban (Le), *m.* Lebanon

Liberia, *f.* Liberia

Liburnie (La), *f.* Liburnia

Libye (La), *f.* Libya

Liége, *f.* Liege

Ligurie (La), *f.* Liguria

Limbourg, *m.* Limburg

Lisbonne, *f.* Lisbon

Lithuanie (La), *f.* Lithuania

Livadie (La), *f.* Livadia

Livonie (La), *f.* Livonia

Livourne, *f* Leghorn

Locres, *f.* Locri

Locride (La), *f.* Locris

Loir (Le), *m.* the Loir

Loire (La), *f.* the Loire

Loiret (Le), *m.* the Loiret

Lombardie (La), *f.* Lombardy

Lombardo-Vénétie (La), *f.* Lombardo-Venetia

Londres, *m.* London

Lorette, *f.* Loretto

Lorraine (La), *f.* Lorraine

Louisbourg, *m.* Louisburg

Louisiane (La), *f.* Louisiana

Lucanie (La), *f.* Lucania

Lucayes (Les), *f.pl.* the Lucaya Islands, the Bahamas

Luçon, *f.* Luzon

Lucques, *f.* Lucca

Lunebourg, *m.* Luneburg

Lusace (La), *f.* Lusatia

Lusitanie (La), *f.* Lusitania

Lutèce, *f.* Lutetia

Luxembourg, *m.* Luxemburg

Lycaonie (La), *f.* Lycaonia

Lycie (La), *f.* Lycia

Lydie (La), *f.* Lydia

Lyon, *m.* Lyons

Macédoine (La), *f.* Macedonia

Madère, *f.* Madeira

Magdebourg, *m.* Magdeburg

†Magnésie (La), *f.* Magnesia

Maïssour (Le), *m.* Mysore

Majeur (Le Lac), *m.* Lake Maggiore

Majorque, *f.* Majorca

Malaisie (La), *f.* Malaysia

Maldives (Les), *f. pl.* the Maldive Islands, the Maldives

Malines, *f.* Mechlin, Malines

Malouines (Les Iles), *f. pl.* the Falkland Islands, the Falklands

Malte, *f.* Malta

Malvoisie, *f.* Malvasia

Manche (La), *f.* the British Channel, the Channel; (*in France*) La Manche; (*in Spain*) La Mancha. *Les Iles de la* —, the Channel Islands

Mandchourie. *V.* Mantchourie

†Manille, *f.* Manilla

Mantinée, *f.* Mantinea

Mantchourie (La), *f.* Manchooria

Mantoue, *f.* Mantua

Marguerite (L'Ile *or* **La)**, *f.* Margarita

Mariannes (Les Iles), *f. pl.* the Marianne Islands

Marienbourg, *m.* Marienburg

Marmara, *f.* Marmora

Marne (La), *f.* the Marne

Maroc (Le), *m.* Morocco

Marquises (Les Iles), *f. pl.* the Marquesas Isles

†Marseille, *f.* Marseilles

Martinique (La), *f.* Martinique

Maryland (Le), *m.* Maryland

Maurice (L'Ile), *f.* (the) Mauritius

Mauritanie (La), *f.* Mauritania

Mayence, *f.* Mayence, Mentz

Mecklenbourg *or* **Mecklembourg (Le)**, *m.* Mecklenburg

Mecque (La), *f.* Mecca

Médie (La), *f.* Media

Médine, *f.* Medina

Mégare, *f.* Megara

Mein (Le), *m.* the Main

Mélanésie (La), *f.* Melanesia

Menton, Mentone, *m.* Mentone

Méonie (La), *f.* Mæonia

Mer, *f.* Sea; Ocean. *La — Glaciale*, the Frozen Ocean. *La — du Nord* or *d'Allemagne*, the North Sea, the German Ocean. *La — des Antilles*, the Caribbean Sea. *La — des Indes*, the Indian Ocean. *La — d'Irlande*, the Irish Sea

Mersebourg, *m.* Merseburg

Mésie (La), *f.* Mœsia

Mésopotamie (La), *f.* Mesopotamia

Messénie (La), *f.* Messenia

Messine, *f.* Messina. *Le Phare de* —, the Straits of Messina

Meuse (La), *f.* the Meuse, the Maas

Mexico, *m.* Mexico (*town*)

Mexique (Le), *m.* Mexico (*the country*)

Middelbourg, *m.* Middleburg

Milanais (Le), *m.* the Milanese

Milet, *m.* Miletus

Mingrélie (La), *f.* Mingrelia

Minho (Le), *m.* the Minho
Minorque, *f.* Minorca
Minturnes, *f.* Minturnæ
Mirandole, *f.* Mirandola [sippi
Mississipi (Le), *m.* the Missis-
Missouri (Le), *m.* the Missouri
Modénais(Le), *m.* the Modenese
Modène, *f.* Modena
Mœsie. *V.* Mésie
Mogador, *m.* Mogadore
Moka, *m.* Mocha
Moldavie (La), *f.* Moldavia
Moldo-Valachie (La), *f.* Moldo-Wallachia [Moluccas
Moluques (Les), *f. pl.* the
Mongolie(La), *f.* Mongolia [gro
Monténégro (Le), *m.* Montene-
Moravie (La), *f.* Moravia
Morée (La), *f.* the Morea
Morlaquie (La), *f.* Morlachia
Moscou, *m.* Moscow
Moscovie (La), *f.* Muscovy
Moselle (La), *f.* the Moselle
Moskova (La), *f.* the Moskova
Mosoul, Mossoul, *f.* Mosul
Mozambique (Le), *m.* Mozam
‡**Munich,** *m.* Munich [bique
Murcie, *f.* Murcia
Mycènes, *f.* Mycenæ
Mysie (La), *f.* Mysia

Nauplie, *f.* Nauplia
Navarin, *m* Navarino
Navarre (La), *f.* Navarre
Navigateurs (L' Archipel des), *m.* Navigators' Islands
Naxie, Naxos, *f.* Naxia
Nazianze, *f.* Nazianzus [lands
Néerlande (La), *f.* the Nether-
Négrepont, *m.* Negropont
Népâl (Le), *m.* Nepaul
Neubourg, *m.* Neuburg
Neustrie (La), *f.* Neustria
Néva (La), *f.* the Neva
New-York, *m.* New-York
Niagara (Le), *m.* the Niagara
Nice, *f.* Nice (*in France*)
Nicée, *f.* Nicæa, Nice
Nicosie, *f.* Nicosia
Niémen (Le), *m.* the Niemen
Nigritie (La), *f.* Nigritia
Nil (Le), *m.* the Nile
Nimègue, *f.* Nimeguen
Ninive, *f.* Nineveh
Normandie (La), *f.* Normandy
Norvége *or* **Norwége (La),** *f.* Norway [Orleans
Nouvelle-Orléans(La), *f.* New
Nouvelle-Zemble (La), *f.* Nova-Zembla
Novare, *f.* Novara
Nubie (La), *f.* Nubia
Numance, *f.* Numantia
Numidie (La), *f.* Numidia

Océanie (L'), *f.* Oceania
Oder (L'), *m.* the Oder
Ohio (L'), *m.* the Ohio
Oise (L'), *f.* the Oise
Oldenbourg, *m.* Oldenburg
Olympe (L'), *m.* Olympus
Olympie, *f.* Olympia
Olynthe, *f.* Olynthus
Ombrie (L'), *f.* Umbria
Orcades (Les), *f.pl.* the Orkney Islands, the Orkneys, (*anc.*) Orcades
Orénoque (L'), *m.* Orinoco
Osnabruck, *m.* Osnaburg, Osna-
Ostende, *f.* Ostend [bruck
Ostie, *f.* Ostia
Otahiti, *m.* Otaheite, Tahiti
Otrante, *f* Otranto
Ouessant, *m.* Ushant
Oural (L'), *m.* the Ural *or* Oural. *Les Monts —s,* the Ural (*or* Oural) Mountains

Pactole (Le), *m* Pactolus
Padoue, *f.* Padua
Palaos (Les Iles), *f. pl.* the Pelew Islands
Palerme, *f.* Palermo
Palestine (La), *f.* Palestine
Palestrine, *f.* Palestrina
Palmyre, *f.* Palmyra
Palus-Méotides (Les), *m. pl.* the Palus Mæotis
Pampelune, *f.* Pampeluna
Pamphylie (La), *f.* Pamphylia
Pannonie (La), *f.* Pannonia
Paphlagonie (La), *f.* Paphlagonia
Papouasie (La), *f.* Papua
Paraguay (Le), *m.* the Paraguay (*river*); Paraguay (*state*)
Paris, *m.* Paris
Parme, *f.* Parma
Parnasse (Le), *m.* Parnassus
Parthie (La), *f.* Parthia
Patagonie (La), *f.* Patagonia
Pausilippe (Le), *m.* Pausilippo
Pavie, *f.* Pavia
Pays-Bas (Les), *m. pl.* the Netherlands, the Low Countries
Pégou, *m.* Pegu
Péloponèse *or* **Péloponnèse (Le),** *m.* the Peloponnesus
Pénée (Le), *m.* the Peneus
Pensylvanie (La), *f.* Pennsylvania [gamum
Pergame, *m.* Pergamus, Per-
Périgord (Le), *m.* Perigord
Permesse (Le), *m.* Permessus
Pernambouc, *m.* Pernambuco
Pérou (Le), *m.* Peru
Pérouse, *f.* Perugia
Perse (La), *f.* Persia
Pétersbourg, *m.* Petersburg
Pharsale, *f.* Pharsalia
Phénicie (La), *f.* Phœnicia
Philadelphie, *f.* Philadelphia
Philippes, *f.* Philippi
Philippines (Les Iles), *f. pl.* the Philippine Islands
Philippsbourg, *m.* Philipsburg
Phocée, *f.* Phocea, Phocæa
Phocide (La), *f.* Phocis
Phrygie (La), *f.* Phrygia
Picardie (La), *f.* Picardy
Piémont (Le), *m.* Piedmont
Pinde (Le), *m.* Pindus
Pirée (Le), *m.* the Piræus
Pise, *f.* Pisa
Pittsbourg, *m.* Pittsburg
Plaisance, *f.* Placentia
Plata(La), *m.* La Plata, the River
Pô (Le), *m.* the Po [Plate
Podolie (La), *f.* Podolia
†**Pologne (La),** *f.* Poland
Polynésie (La), *f.* Polynesia
Poméranie (La), *f.* Pomerania
Pompéi, Pompéies, *f.* Pompeii
Pondichéry, *m.* Pondicherry
Pont (Le), *m.* Pontus
Pont-Euxin(Le), *m.* the Euxine
Pontins (Les Marais), *m. pl.* the Pontine Marshes
Portugal (Le), *m.* Portugal
Potomac (Le), *m.* the Potomac
†**Pouille (La),** *f.* Apulia
Presbourg, *m.* Presburg [tis
Propontide (La), *f.* the Propon-
Provence (La), *f.* Provence
Provinces-Unies (Les), *f. pl.* the United Provinces
Prusse (La), *f.* Prussia
Pyrénées (Les), *f. pl.* the Pyrenees, the Pyrenean Mountains. *Les Monts —,* ditto

Raguse, *f.* Ragusa
Rangoun, *m.* Rangoon
Ratisbonne, *f.* Ratisbon
Ravenne, *f.* Ravenna
Reims, Rheims, *m.* Rheims
Rhétie (La), *f.* Rhetia
Rhin (Le), *m.* the Rhine
Rhône (Le), *m.* the Rhone
Rio de la Plata (Le), *m.* the River Plate
†**Romagne (La),** *f.* Romagna
Rome, *f.* Rome
Rosette, *f.* Rosetta
Rothenbourg, *m.* Rothenburg
Roumanie (La), *f.* Roumania
Roumélie (La), *f.* Roumelia
Royaume-Uni (Le), *m.* the United Kingdom
Rubicon (Le), *m.* the Rubicon
Russie (La), *f.* Russia

Saba, *f.* Sheba, Saba
Sabée (La), *f.* Sabæa
Sabine (La), *f.* Sabina
Sagonte, *f.* Saguntum
Saint-Ange, *m.* Saint Angelo
Saint-Domingue, *m.* Saint Domingo
Sainte-Hélène, *f.* Saint Helena
Saint-Jacques (de Compostelle), *m.* Saint Iago *or* Santiago (de Compostella) [rence
Saint-Laurent, *m.* Saint Law-
Sainte-Lucie, *f.* Saint Lucia
Saint-Pétersbourg, *m.* Saint Petersburg
Salamanque, *f* Salamanca
Salamine, *f.* Salamis
Salente, *f.* Salentum
Salerne, *f.* Salerno; (*anc.*) Sa-
Salonique, *f.* Salonica [lernum
Saluces, *f* Saluzzo
Salzbourg, *m.* Salzburg
Samarcande, *f.* Samarcand, Samarkand
Samarie, *f.* Samaria
†**Santillane,** *f.* Santillana
Saône (La), *f.* the Saone
Saragosse, *f.* Saragossa
†**Sardaigne (La),** *f.* Sardinia
Sardes (Les États), *m. pl.* the Sardinian States
Sardes, *f.* Sardis
Sarmatie (La), *f.* Sarmatia
Saverne (La), *f.* the Severn
Savoie (La), *f* Savoy
Saxe (La), *f.* Saxony [mander
Scamandre (Le), *m.* the Sca-
Scandinavie (La), *f.* Scandinavia
Schaffouse, *f.* Schaffhausen
Schwarzbourg, *m.* Schwarzburg
Sclavonie (La), *f.* Sclavonia
Scylla, *m.* Scylla
Scythie (La), *f.* Scythia
Ségovie, *f.* Segovia
Seine (La), *f.* the Seine
Séleucide (La), *f.* Seleucis
Séleucie, *f* Seleucia

Sénégal (Le), *m.* Senegal [bia
Sénégambie (La), *f.* Senegam-
Serbie *or* **Servie (La),** *f.* Serbia *or* Servia
Sibérie (La), *f.* Siberia
Sicile (La), *f.* Sicily
Sienne, *f.* Sienna
Silésie (La), *f.* Silesia
Silistrie, *f.* Silistria
Silo, Siloé, *f.* Siloa; Shiloh
Sinaï (Le), *m.* Sinai [(*river*)
Sind (Le), *m.* the Sinde *or* Indus
Sindhy (Le), *m.* Sinde (*province*)
Skager-rak (Le), *m.* the Skagerrack
Slavonie (La), *f.* Slavonia
Societé (Les Iles de la), *f.pl.* the Society Islands
Socotora (L'Ile), *f.* Socotra
Sodome, *f.* Sodom
Soleure, (*canton*) *m.*, (*town*) *f.* Soleure, Solothurn
Solfatare (La), *f* the Solfatara
Solway (Le Golfe de), *m.* the Solway Frith
Solyme, *f.* Solyma
Somme (La), *f.* the Somme
Sonde, *f.* *L' Archipel* or *Les Iles de la* —, the Sunda Islands. *Le Détroit de la* —, Sunda Strait
Sorlingues (Les Iles), *f. pl.* the Scilly Islands
Souabe (La), *f.* Suabia, Swabia
Sparte, *f.* Sparta
Spitzberg (Le), *m.* Spitzbergen
Sporades (Les), *f. pl.* the
Stagire, *f.* Stagira [Sporades
Steinkerque, *m.* Steenkirk
Strasbourg, *m.* Strasburg, Strasbourg
Styrie (La), *f.* Styria
Styx (Le), *m.* the Styx
Suède (La), *f.* Sweden
Suisse (La), *f.* Switzerland
Sund (Le), *m.* the Sound
Supérieur (Le Lac), *m.* Lake
Surate, *f* Surat [Superior
Suse, *f.* Susa
Syrie (La), *f.* Syria

Tabago, *m* Tobago
Table, *f.* *La Baie de la* —, Table Bay. *Le Mont de la* —, Table Mount *or* Mountain
Tage (Le), *m.* the Tagus [hiti
Tahiti, Taïti, *m.* Otaheite, Ta-
Tamise (La), *f.* the Thames
Tanaïs (Le), *m.* the Don
Tanger, *m.* Tangier
Tarente, *f.* Taranto, Tarentum
Tarragone, *f.* Tarragona
Tarse, *f.* Tarsus
Tartare (Le), *m.* Tartarus
Tartarie (La), *f.* Tartary
Tasmanie (La), *f.* Tasmania
Tauride (La), *f.* Taurida; (*anc.*) Tauris
Taurus (Le), *m.* the Taurus
Tendre, *m.* *Le Pays de* —, (*fig.*) the Land of Love, Love
Terceire, *f.* Terceira
Terracine, *f.* Terracina
Terre, *f.* Land. *La — de Feu,* Terra (*or* Tierra) del Fuego. *La — de Van Diemen,* Van Diemen's Land. — *-Neuve,* Newfoundland
Tésin *or* **Tessin (Le),** *m.* the Ticino; (*anc.*) Ticinus
Texas (Le), *m.* Texas [Thebais
Thébaïde (La), *f.* the Thebaid,
Thermopyles (Les), *f. pl.* Thermopylæ
Thessalie (La), *f.* Thessaly
Thessalonique, *f.* Thessalonica
Thibet. *V.* TIBET
Thrace (La), *f.* Thrace
Thurgovie (La), *f.* Thurgau, Thurgovia
Thuringe (La), *f.* Thuringia
Tibet (Le), *m.* Tibet, Thibet
Tibre (Le), *m.* the Tiber
Tigre (Le), *m.* the Tigris
Tolède, *f.* Toledo
Tombouctou, *m.* Timbuctoo,
Tortone, *f.* Tortona [Timbuktu
Tortose, *f.* Tortosa
Toscane (La), *f.* Tuscany
Touraine (La), *f.* Touraine
Transcaucasie (La), *f.* Transcaucasia
Transylvanie (La), *f.* Transylvania
Trasimène, *m.* Trasimenus
Trébie (La), *f.* the Trebia
Trébizonde, *f.* Trebizond
Trente, *f.* Trent
Trévise, *f.* Treviso
Trincomale, Trinquemale, *f.* Trincomalee
Trinité (La), *f.* Trinidad
Troade (La), *f.* Troas
Troie, *f.* Troy
Troyes, *f.* Troyes (*in France*)
Tubingue, *f.* Tubingen
Tunisie (La), *f.* Tunis (*state*)
Turcomanie (La), *f.* Turkomania, Turcomania
Turkestan (Le), *m.* Turkestan
Turques (Les Iles), *f.pl.* Turks'
Turquie (La), *f.* Turkey [Islands
Tyr, *f.* Tyre
Tyrol (Le), *m.* the Tyrol

Ukraine (L'), *f.* the Ukraine
Urbin, *m.* Urbino
Uruguay (L'), *m.* the Uruguay (*river*); Uruguay (*state*)
Utique, *f.* Utica

Valachie (La), *f.* Wallachia
Valence, *f.* Valencia; (*in France*) Valence
Valette (La), *f.* Valetta
Varsovie, *f.* Warsaw
Vendée (La), *f.* Vendee
Vénétie (La), *f.* Venetia
Venise, *f.* Venice
Vénusie, *f.* Venusia, Venusium
†**Verceil,** *m.* Vercelli
†**Vermeille (La Mer),** *f.* the
Vérone, *f.* Verona [VermilionSea
Vert (Le Cap), *m.* Cape Verd
Vésuve (Le), *m.* Vesuvius
Vicence, *f.* Vicenza [Vienne
Vienne, *f.* Vienna; (*in France*)
Vierges (Les Iles), *f. pl.* the Virgin Islands
Virginie (La), *f.* Virginia
Visapour, *m.* Visapore
Vistule (La), *f.* the Vistula
Viterbe, *f.* Viterbo
Vitoria, *f.* Vittoria
Volga (Le), *m.* the Volga
Volhynie (La), *f.* Volhynia
Vosges (Les), *f. pl.* the Vosges

Westphalie (La), *f.* Westphalia
Wurtemberg (Le), *m.* Wurtem-
Wurzbourg, *m.* Wurzburg [berg

Xanthe (Le), *m.* the Xanthus

'**Yucatan (Le),** *m.* Yucatan

[land
Zéeland (La), *f.* Zeeland, Zea-
Zélande (La), *f.* Zeeland, Zealand. *La Nouvelle-* —, New Zealand [rein
Zollverein (Le), *m.* the Zollve-
‡**Zurich,** *m.* Zurich
Zuyderzée (Le), *m.* the Zuyder Zee

PROPER NAMES OF PERSONS AND ANIMALS.

Abdias, *m.* Obadiah
Abigail, *f.* Abigail
Absalon, *m.* Absalom
Acaste, *m.* Acastus
Aceste, *m.* Acestes
‡Achab, *m.* Ahab
‡Achate, *m.* Achates
Achille, *m.* Achilles
Actéon, *m.* Actæon
Adélaide, *f.* Adelaide
Adèle, *f.* Adela
Admète, *m.* Admetus; *f.* Admeta
Adolphe, *m.* Adolphus
Adraste, *m.* Adrastus
Adrien, *m.* Adrian
Adrienne, *f.* Adriana
Agar, *f.* Hagar
Agathe, *f.* Agatha
Agathocle, *m.* Agathocles
Agésilas, *m.* Agesilaus
Aggée, *m.* Haggai
Aglaé, *f.* Aglaia
†Agnès, *f.* Agnes
Agrippine, *f.* Agrippina
Aimée, *f.* Amy
Alain, *m.* Allen
Albane (L'), *m.* Albano
Albertine, *f.* Albertina
Alcée, *m.* Alcæus
Alceste, *m.* Alceste, Alcestis
Alcibiade, *m.* Alcibiades
Alcide, *m.* Alcides
Alcmène, *f.* Alcmena
Alecton, *f.* Alecto
Alexandre, *m.* Alexander
Alexandrin, *m.* Alexandrinus
Alexandrine, *f.* Alexandrina
Aliboron, *m.* Grizzle
Alphée, *m.* Alpheus
Alphonse, *m.* Alphonso
Althée, *f.* Althea
Aluin, *m.* Alwin
Amalthée, *f.* Amalthea
Aman, *m.* Haman
Ambroise, *m.* Ambrose
Amédée, *m.* Amadeus, Amedeus
Amélie, *f.* Amelia [Vespucius
Améric Vespuce, *m.* Americus
Anacréon, *m.* Anacreon
Anastase, *m.* Anastasius
Anastasie, *f.* Anastasia
Anatole, *m.* Anatolius
Anaxagore, *m.* Anaxagoras
Anchise, *m.* Anchises
André, *m.* Andrew
Andromaque, *f.* Andromache
Andromède, *f.* Andromeda
Ange, *m.* Angelus; Angelo
Angèle, *f.* Angela
Angélique, *f.* Angelica
Anna, *f.* Anna, Hannah
Anne, *f.* Ann, Anne; Anna
Annette, *f.* Annie, Nancy
Annibal, *m.* Hannibal
Anselme, *m.* Anselm, Anselmo
Antée, *m.* Antæus
Anthée, *m.* Antheus [Antigone
Antigone, *m.* Antigonus; *f.*
Antinoüs, *m.* Antinous
‡Antiochus, *m.* Antiochus
Antoine, *m.* Anthony; Antony
Antoinette, *f.* Antonia
Antonin, *m.* Antoninus
Antonine, *f.* Antonina
Apollodore, *m.* Apollodorus
Apollon, *m.* Apollo
Appien, *m.* Appian
Aquin, *m.* Aquinas
Arabelle, *f.* Arabella
Archambaud, *m.* Archibald
Archimède, *m.* Archimedes
Aréthuse, *f.* Arethusa
Arétin (L'), *m.* Aretino. *Gui* —, Guido Aretino
Ariane, *f.* Ariadne
Arioste (L'), *m.* Ariosto
Arioviste, *m.* Ariovistus
Aristarque, *m.* Aristarchus, Aristarch
Aristée, *m.* Aristæus
Aristide, *m.* Aristides
Aristippe, *m.* Aristippus
Aristobule, *m.* Aristobulus
Aristodème, *m.* Aristodemus
Aristogiton, *m.* Aristogeiton
Aristophane, *m.* Aristophanes
Aristote, *m.* Aristotle
Arlequin, *m.* Harlequin
Arnaud, *m.* Arnold
Arrien, *m.* Arrian
Arsène, *m.* Arsenius
Artaban, *m.* Artabanus
Artaxerce, *m.* Artaxerxes. — *Longue - Main,* Artaxerxes Longimanus
Artémise, *f.* Artemisia
†Ascagne, *m.* Ascanius
Asmodée, *m.* Asmodeus
Aspasie, *f.* Aspasia
Assuérus, *m.* Ahasuerus
Astaroth, *f.* Ashtaroth
Astarté, *f.* Astarte
Astrée, *f.* Astræa
Astyage, *m.* Astyages
Atalante, *f.* Atalanta, Atalante
Athalie, *f.* Athaliah
Athanase, *m.* Athanasius
Atrée, *m.* Atreus
Augias, *m.* Augeas, Augias
Auguste, *m.* Augustus
Augustin, *m.* Austin; Augustin; Augustine
Augustine, *f.* Augustina
Augustule, *m.* Augustulus
Aulu-Gelle, *m.* Aulus-Gellius
Aurèle, *m.* Aurelius
Aurélie, *f.* Aurelia
Aurélien, *m.* Aurelian
Aurélius, *m.* Aurelius
Aurore, *f.* Aurora
Ausone, *m.* Ausonius
Azor, *m.* Doggy, o.'s dog

Babet, *f.* Betsy, Bess
†Bailleul, *m.* Baliol
Bajazet, *m.* Bajazeth [shazzar
Balthazar, *m.* Balthazar, Bel-
Baptiste, *m.* Baptist
Barbe, *f.* Barbara
Barberousse, *m.* Barbarossa
Barnabé, *m.* Barnaby, Barnabas
Barthélemy, *m.* Bartholomew
‡Baruch, *m.* Baruch
Basile, *m.* Basil
Bathilde, *f.* Batilda
Baudouin, *m.* Baldwin [Beatrix
Béatrice, Béatrix, *f.* Beatrice,
Bélisaire, *m.* Belisarius
Bellone, *f.* Bellona
Belzébuth, *m.* Beelzebub
Bénédict, *m.* Benedict
Bénédicte, *f.* Benedicta
Benoît, *m.* Benedict
Benoîte, *f.* Benedicta
Bérénice, *f.* Berenice
Bernardin, *m.* Bernardine
Bernin (Le), *m.* Bernini
Berthe, *f.* Bertha
Bertrand, *m.* Bertram; Pug
Blaise, *m.* Blase
Blanche, *f.* Blanch, Blanche
Boadicée, *f.* Boadicea
Boccace, *m.* Boccaccio
Boèce, *m.* Boethius
Boleslas, *m.* Boleslaus
†Bolognèse (Le), *m.* Bolognese
Bonaventure, *m.* Bonadventure
Bonne, *f.* Bona
Borée, *m.* Boreas
Briarée, *m.* Briareus
Brigitte, *f.* Bridget
Bucéphale, *m.* Bucephalus

Caïn, *m.* Cain
Caïphe, *m.* Caiaphas. *Renvoyer de — à Pilate,* to send from pillar to post
Caliste, *m.* Calistus
Callimaque, *m.* Callimachus
Cambyse, *m.* Cambyses [milla
†Camille, *m.* Camillus; *f.* Ca-
Canut, *m.* Canute. — *le Hardi,* Hardicanute
Capitolin, *m.* Capitolinus
Carabas (Marquis de), *m.* (*jest.*) man made of money, nabob, Crœsus, Plutus, Dives, great land-owner, marquis of Westminster (*land-monopolizer*)
Caravage, *m.* Caravaggio
Caron, *m.* Charon
Carrache, *m.* Caracci
Cartouche, *m.* Jonathan Wild, Jack Sheppard
Cassandre, *m.* Cassander; Pantaloon; *f.* Cassandra
Catilina, *m.* Catiline
Catin, Catiche, *f.* Kate, Kitty
Caton, *m.* Cato
Catulle, *m.* Catullus
Cécile, *f.* Cecilia, Cecily
Célestin, *m.* Celestine
Célestine, *f.* Celestina
Célie, *f.* Celia
Celse, *m.* Celsus
†Cendrillon, *f.* Cinderella
Cerbère, *m.* Cerberus
Cérès, *f.* Ceres
Césaire, *m.* Cesarius
César, *m.* Cæsar
‡Cham, *m.* Ham
‡Charistie, *f.* Charistia

‡**Charistie,** *f.* Charistia
Charlot, *m.* Charly; Jack Ketch
‡**Charon,** *m.* Charon
‡**Chloé,** *f.* Chloe
‡**Chrétien,** *m.* Christian
‡**Chrétienne,** *f.* Christina
‡**Christ (Le),** *m.* Christ
‡**Christine,** *f.* Christina
‡**Christophe,** *m.* Christopher
‡**Chrysostome,** *m.* Chrysostom
Cicéron, *m.* Cicero
Circé, *f.* Circe
Claire, Clara, *f.* Clara
Clarisse, *f.* Clarissa
Claude, *m.* Claudius, Claud; *f.* Claudia. — *-Lorrain,* (*m.*) Claude Lorraine
Claudie, *f.* Claudia
Claudien, *m.* Claudian
Cléanthe, *m.* Cleanthes
Clémence, *f.* Clementia
Clément, *m.* Clement
Clémentine, *f.* Clementina
Cléopâtre, *f.* Cleopatra
Clotilde, *f.* Clotilda
Clytemnestre, *f.* Clytemnestra
Collatin, *m.* Collatinus
Colomb, *m.* Columbus
Colombine, *f.* Columbine
Come. *V.* Cosme
Commode, *m.* Commodus
Comnène, *m.* Comnenus; *f.* Comnena
Constance, *m.* Constantius; *f.* Constance; Constantia
Constantin, *m.* Constantine
Copernic, *m.* Copernicus
Copronyme, *m.* Copronymus
Corinne, *f.* Corinna
Coriolan, *m.* Coriolanus
Cornélie, *f.* Cornelia
Corrège (Le), *m.* Correggio
Cosme, *m.* Cosmus, Cosmo. — *de Medicis,* Cosmo di Medici
Courte-heuse (Robert), *m.* Curthose (Robert)
Crépin, *m.* Crispin
Crésus, *m.* Crœsus
Créuse, *f.* Creusa
Croquemitaine, *m.* Old Bogy
Crusoé, *m.* Crusoe
Cupidon, *m.* Cupid
Curiace, *m.* Curiatius [Curiatii
Curiaces (Les), *m. pl.* the
Curion, *m.* Curio
Cyaxare, *m.* Cyaxares
Cybèle, *f.* Cybele
Cyprien, *m.* Cyprian
†**Cyrille,** *m.* Cyril
Cythérée, *f.* Cytheræa, Venus

Dalila, *f.* Dalilah, Delilah
Damoclès, *m.* Damocles
Danaé, *f.* Danae
Dante (*or, abusively,* **Le Dante**), *m.* Dante
Débora, *f.* Deborah
Dédale, *m.* Dædalus
Déjanire, *f.* Dejanira
Délie, *f.* Delia
Démocrate, *m.* Democrates
Démocrite, *m.* Democritus
Démonique, *m.* Demonicus
Démosthène, *m.* Demosthenes
Denis, Denys, *m.* Denis; Dionysius
Denise, *f.* Dionysia
Diane, *f.* Diana
Didon, *f.* Dido
Dieudonné, *m.* Deodatus
Dimanche (Monsieur), *m.* a creditor, a dun
Dioclétien, *m.* Diocletian
Diodore, *m.* Diodorus. — *de Sicile,* Diodorus Siculus
Diogène, *m.* Diogenes
Diomède, *m.* Diomedes
Domingue, *m.* Domingo
Dominique, *m.* Dominic
Dominiquin (Le), *m.* Domeni- [chino
Domitien, *m.* Domitian
Donat, *m.* Donatus
Dorothée, *f.* Dorothea, Dorothy
Dracon, *m.* Draco
†**Drusille,** *f.* Drusilla
Dulcinée, *f.* Dulcinea

Éaque, *m.* Æacus, Eacus
Edmond, *m.* Edmund
Édouard, *m.* Edward
Égérie, *f.* Egeria
Électre, *f.* Electra
Éléonore, *f.* Eleanor
Élie, *m.* Elias; Elijah
Élisabeth, *f.* Elizabeth
Élise, Élisa, *f.* Eliza
Élisée, *m.* Elisha
Éloi, *m.* Eloy
Elvire, *f.* Elvira
Émeri, *m.* Emery
Émile, *m.* Emilius, Æmilius
Émilie, *f.* Emily; Æmilia
Émilien, *m.* Emilian, Æmilian
Emmanuel, *m.* Emanuel
Empédocle, *m.* Empedocles
Encelade, *m.* Enceladus
Énée, *m.* Æneas
‡**Énoch,** *m.* Enoch
Éole, *m.* Æolus
Épictète, *m.* Epictetus
Épicure, *m.* Epicurus
Épiménide, *m.* Epimenides
Érasme, *m.* Erasmus
Éraste, *m.* Erastus
Érèbe, *m.* Erebus
Ésaü, *m.* Esau
Eschine, *m.* Æschines
Eschyle, *m.* Æschylus
Esculape, *m.* Æsculapius
Esdras, *m.* Ezra
Ésope, *m.* Æsop
Étéocle, *m.* Eteocles
Étienne, *m.* Stephen
Euclide, *m.* Euclid
Eudème, *m.* Eudemus
Eudoxe, *m.* Eudoxus
Eudoxie, *f.* Eudoxia
Eugène, *m.* Eugene; Eugenius
Eugénie, *f.* Eugenia
Eulalie, *f.* Eulalia
Eumée, *m.* Eumæus
Eumène, *m.* Eumenes
Euphémie, *f.* Euphemia
Euphraise, *m.* Euphrasius
Euphrasie, *f.* Euphrasia
Euphrosyne, *f.* Euphrosyne
Euripide, *m.* Euripides
Europe, *f.* Europa
Euryale, *m.* Euryalus
Eurybiade, *m.* Eurybiades
Eurydice, *f.* Eurydice
Eusèbe, *m.* Eusebius
Eusébie, *f.* Eusebia [chius
Eustache, *m.* Eustace; Eusta-
Eustathe, *m.* Eustathius
Euterpe, *f.* Euterpe
Eutrope, *m.* Eutropius
Évandre, *m.* Evander
Évariste, *m.* Evaristus
Ève, *f.* Eve
Ézéchias, *m.* Hezekiah
Ézéchiel, *m.* Ezekiel

Fabien, *m.* Fabian
Fabrice, *m.* Fabricius
Fagotin, *m.* Pug
Fanchette, Fanchon, *f.* Fanny
Fanny, *f.* Fanny
Fatime, *f.* Fatima
Faune, *m.* Faunus
Faust, *m.* Faustus, Faust
Faustine, *f.* Faustina
Félicie, *f.* Felicia
Félicien, *m.* Felician
Félicité, *f.* Felicity
Félix, *m.* Felix
Fernand, *m.* Fernando
Fifine, *f.* Joey (Josephine)
Flavien, *m.* Flavian
Flore, *f.* Flora
Fortune, *f.* Fortuna
Fortuné, *m.* Fortunatus
Foulque, *m.* Fulk
François, *m.* Francis, Frank
Françoise, *f.* Frances
Frédéric, *m.* Frederick, Frederic
Frédérique, *f.* Frederica
Fulgence, *m.* Fulgentius
Fulvie, *f.* Fulvia

Gabrielle, *f.* Gabriella
Galatée, *f.* Galatea
Galien, *m.* Galen
Galilée, *m.* Galileo
Gallien, *m.* Gallienus
Ganymède, *m.* Ganymedes
Gaspard, *m.* Jasper, Jaspar
Gautier, *m.* Walter, Wat
Gédéon, *m.* Gideon
Gédouin, *m.* Goodwin
Geoffroy, *m.* Geoffrey, Geoffry, [Jeffrey
Georges, *m.* George
Georgette, *f.* Georgetta, Georgey, Georgie
Georgienne, *f.* Georgiana, Georgey, Georgie [Georgie
Georgine, *f.* Georgina, Georgey,
Géralde, *m.* Gerald
Gérard, *m.* Gerard
Germain, *m.* German
Géronte, *m.* Geronteus
Gervais, *m.* Gervase
†**Gigogne (La mère),** *f.* "the old woman who lived in a shoe"
Gille, *m.* Clown
Gilles, *m.* Giles [frey
Godefroi, Godefroy, *m.* God-
Gondebaud, *m.* Gondebald
Gordien, *m.* Gordian
Gorgone, *f.* Gorgon
‡**Gracchus,** *m.* Gracchus
Gracques (Les), *m. pl.* the [Gracchi
Gratien, *m.* Gratian
Grégoire, *m* Gregory
Grippeminaud, *m.* Grimalkin
Griselda, Grisélidis, *f.* Gri- [selda
Gudule, *f.* Gudula, Gudule
Guerchin (Le), *m.* Guercino
Guide (Le), *m.* Guido
†**Guignol,** *m.* Punch and Judy, Punch's show
Guilelmine, *f.* Wilhelmina
†**Guillaume,** *m.* William
†**Guillot,** *m.* Bill, Billy
Gustave, *m.* Gustavus

Habacuc, *m.* Habakkuk
Haggée, *m.* Haggai
Hamilcar, *m.* Hamilcar
Hannibal, *m.* Hannibal
'**Hardi-Canut,** *m.* Hardicanute
'**Harold,** *m.* Harold
Harpocrate, *m.* Harpocrates

Hébé, *f.* Hebe
Hécate, *f.* Hecate
Hector, *m.* Hector
Hécube, *f.* Hecuba
Hégésippe, *m.* Hegesippus
Hélène, *f.* Helen, Ellen; Helena
Héliodore, *m.* Heliodorus
Héliogabale, *m.* Heliogabalus
Héloïse, *f.* Eloisa, Heloisa
Henri, **'Henri**, } Henry, Harry
Henriette, **'Henriette**, } Henrietta, Harriet
Héraclide, *m.* Heraclides
Héraclien, *m.* Heraclian
Héraclite, *m.* Heraclitus
Herbert, *m.* Herbert
Hercule, *m.* Hercules
Hermione, *f.* Hermione
Hérode, *m.* Herod
Hérodien, *m.* Herodian
Hérodote, *m.* Herodotus
Hésiode, *m.* Hesiod
Hiéronyme, *m.* Hieronymus
Hilaire, *m.* Hilary
Hipparque, *m.* Hipparchus
Hippocrate, *m.* Hippocrates
Hippolyte, *m.* Hippolytus
Hippone, *f.* (*myth.*) Hippona (*goddess of horses*)
Hircan, *m.* Hyrcanus
Holopherne, *m.* Holophernes
Homère, *m.* Homer
'Homfroi, *m.* Humphrey
Honoré, *m.* Honoratus; Honorius
Honorée, *f.* Honoria
Horace, *m.* Horatio; Horace
Horaces (Les), *m. pl.* the Horatii
Hortense, *f.* Hortensia
Hubert, *m.* Hubert
'Hugues, *m.* Hugh
Humbert, *m.* Humbert
Hyacinthe, *m.* Hyacinthus
Hygie *or* **Hygiée**. *V. General Dictionary*
Hymen, **Hyménée**, *m.* Hymen
Hyrcan, *m.* Hyrcanus
Hystaspe, *m.* Hystaspes

Icare, *m.* Icarus
Idoménée, *m.* Idomeneus
†**Ignace**, *m.* Ignatius
Ildefonse, *m.* Ildephonso
Iphigénie, *f.* Iphigenia
Irène, *f.* Irene
Irénée, *m.* Irenæus
Isabeau, *f.* (*obsolete*) *V.* ISABELLE
Isabelle, *f.* Isabella, Isabel
Isaïe, *m.* Isaiah
Iscariote, *m.* Iscariot
Isidore, *m.* Isidorus, Isidore
Ismaël, *m.* Ishmael
Isocrate, *m.* Isocrates
Israël, *m.* Israel
Ivanhoé, *m.* Ivanhoe

Jaco, **Jacot**, *m.* Poll
Jacqueau. *V.* JACQUOT
Jacques, *m.* James
Jacquet, *m.* Jem, Jim
Jacquot, *m.* Jemmy, Jem, Jim; Jack; Poll; Pug
Jagrenat, *m.* Juggernaut
Janot, *m.* Jack-Pudding
Jansénius, *m.* Jansenius, Jansen
Janvier, *m.* Januarius
Japet, *m.* Iapetus
Japhet, *m.* Japhet, Japheth
Jean, John, Jack
Jean-Jean. *V. General Dictionary*
Jeanne, *f.* Jane; Joan; Joanna. — *d'Arc*, Joan of Arc
Jeannette, **Jeanneton**, *f.* Janet, Jenny
Jeannot, *m.* Jack, Jacky; Jack-Pudding
‡**Jéchonias**, *m.* Jechoniah
Jéhovah, *m.* Jehovah
Jémima, *f.* Jemima
Jenny, *f.* Jenny
Jephté, *m.* Jephthah
Jérémie, *m.* Jeremy; Jeremiah
Jérôme, *m.* Jerome, Hieronymus
Jésus, *m.* Jesus. — *-Christ*, Jesus-Christ
‡**Joachim**, *m.* Joachim
Jocaste, *f.* Jocasta, Jocaste
Jocrisse, *m.* Jack-Pudding
Joël, *m.* Joel
Jonas, *m.* Jonah, Jonas
Joram, *m.* Jehoram
Josaphat, *m.* Jehoshaphat, Josaphat
Joseph, *m.* Joseph, Joe
Josèphe, *m.* Josephus
Joséphine, *f.* Josephine
Joseppin (Le), *m.* Joseppino
Josias, *m.* Josiah
Josué, *m.* Joshua
Jovien, *m.* Jovian
Juda, *m.* Judah
Judas, *m.* Judas
Jules, *m.* Julius
Julie, *f.* Julia
Julien, *m.* Julian
Julienne, *f.* Juliana
Juliette, *f.* Juliet
Junie, *f.* Junia
Junon, *f.* Juno
Jupin, *m.* Jove, Jupiter
Jupiter, *m.* Jupiter, Jove
Juste, *m.* Justus
Justine, *f.* Justina
Justinien, *m.* Justinian
Juvénal, *m.* Juvenal

‡**Lachésis**, *f.* Lachesis
Ladislas, *m.* Ladislaus
Laërce, *m.* Laertius
Laërte, *m.* Laertes
Lancelot, *m.* Launcelot
Latone, *f.* Latona
Laure, *f.* Laura
Laurent, *m.* Lawrence
Laverne, *f.* Laverna
Lavinie, *f.* Lavinia
Lazare, *m.* Lazarus
Léandre, *m.* Leander
Lélie, *f.* Lælia
Léon, *m.* Leo, Leon
Léonard, *m.* Leonard
Léonce, *m.* Leontius
Léonidas, *m.* Leonidas
Léonore, *m.* Leonorus; *f.* Leonora
Léopold, *m.* Leopold
Lévi, **Lévy**, *m.* Levi, Levy
Lia, *f.* Leah
Linné, **Linnée**, *m.* Linnæus
Lise, **Lisette**, *f.* Lizzie, Lizzy
Livie, *f.* Livia
Longin, *m.* Longinus
Loth, *m.* Lot
Lothaire, *m.* Lothario, Lotharius
Louis, *m.* Lewis, Louis
Louise, **Louison**, *f.* Louisa
Luc, *m.* Luke
Lucain, *m.* Lucan
Lucette, *f.* Lucetta
Lucie, *f.* Lucy
Lucien, *m.* Lucian
Lucile, *f.* Lucilla
Lucinde, *f.* Lucinda
Lucine, *f.* Lucina
Lucrèce, *m.* Lucretius; *f.* Lucretia
Lycurgue, *m.* Lycurgus
Lydie, *f.* Lydia
Lysandre, *m.* Lysander
Lysimaque, *m.* Lysimachus
Lysippe, *m.* Lysippus

Macaire (Robert), *m.* Jack Sheppard
‡**Machabée**, *m.* Maccabeus, Maccabæus
‡**Machabées**, *m. pl.* Maccabees
‡**Machiavel**, *m.* Machiavelli, Machiavel
Macrin, *m.* Macrinus
Macrobe, *m.* Macrobius
Madeleine, *f.* Madeline; Magdalen, Magdalene
Madelon, *f.* Maud
Magon, *m.* Mago
Mainfroi, *m.* Manfred
Malachie, *m.* Malachi; Malachy
Manassé, *m.* Manasseh
Mandrin, *m.* Jonathan Wild, Jack Sheppard
Manon, *f.* Molly
Mantouan (Le), *m.* Mantuan
Marc, *m.* Mark, Marcus. — *-Antoine*, Mark Antony. — *-Aurèle*, Marcus Aurelius
Marcel, *m.* Marcellus
Marcellin, *m.* Marcellinus
Marcelline, *f.* Marcellina
Marcien, *m.* Marcian
Mardochée, *m.* Mardocheus, Mordecai
Margot, *f.* Marget; Mag
Marguerite, *f.* Margaret
Marie, *f.* Mary
Mariette, **Marion**, *f.* Molly
Marthe, *f.* Martha
Martin, *m.* Martin; (*ass*) Jack
Mathieu, *m.* Matthew
Mathilde, *f.* Matilda
Mathusalem, *m.* Methuselah
Matthieu, *m.* Matthew
Mausole, *m.* Mausolus
Maxence, *m.* Maxentius
Maxime, *m.* Maximus
Maximien, *m.* Maximianus, Maximian
Maximilien, *m.* Maximilian
Maximin, *m.* Maximinus
Mayeux, *m.* Punch
Mécène, *m.* Mæcenas
‡**Médée**, *f.* Medea
Médicis, *m.f.* Medici
Méduse, *f.* Medusa
Mégère, *f.* Megæra
Mélanie, *f.* Melania
‡‡**Melchisédech**, *m.* Melchisedek
Mélibée, *m.* Melibœus
Ménandre, *m.* Menander
Ménélas, *m.* Menelaus
Ménippe, *m.* Menippus
Mercure, *m.* Mercury
Mérovée, *m.* Meroveus
Messaline, *f.* Messalina
Métastase, *m.* Metastasio
Michaud, *m.* Mike
Michée, *m.* Micah
Michel, *m.* Michael
‡**Michel-Ange**, *m.* Michael Angelo
Milet, *m.* Miletus
Milon, *m.* Milo
Miltiade, *m.* Miltiades
Mimi, *m.f.* Puss, Pussy
Minerve, *f.* Minerva
Minet, **Minon**, *m.*, **Minette**, *f.* Puss, Pussy
Mithridate, *m.* Mithridates
Mnémosyne, *f.* Mnemosyne
Moïse, *m.* Moses
‡**Moloch**, *m.* Moloch
Molosse, *m.* Molossus

Montaigu, *m.* Montague
Morphée, *m.* Morpheus
Myrtée, *f.* Myrtea
Myrtile, *m.* Myrtilus

‡**Nabuchodonosor,** *m.* Nebuchadnezzar
Nannette, *f.* Nancy, Nanny
Napoléon, *m.* Napoleon
Narcisse, *m.* Narcissus
Nazaire, *m.* Nasarius
Néarque, *m.* Nearchus
Néhémie, *m.* Nehemiah
Némésis, *f.* Nemesis
Nemrod, *m.* Nimrod
Néoptolème, *m.* Neoptolemus
Nérée, *m.* Nereus
Néron, *m.* Nero
Nicaise, *m.* Nicasius
Nicéphore, *m* Nicephorus
Nicodème, *m.* Nicodemus
Nicolas, *m.* Nicholas, Nick
Nicomède, *m.* Nicomedes
Ninon, *f.* Nino
Niobé, *f.* Niobe
Noé, *m.* Noah
Noël, *m.* Noel
Noémi, *f.* Naomi

Océan, *m.* Oceanus
Octave, *m.* Octavius
Octavie, *f.* Octavia
Octavien, *m.* Octavianus
Œdipe, *m.* Œdipus
Olivie, *f.* Olivia
Olivier, *m.* Oliver
Olympe, *m.* Olympus; *f.* Olympia
Onésime, *m.* Onesimus
Ophélie, *f.* Ophelia
Oppien, *m.* Oppian
Oreste, *m.* Orestes
Origène, *m.* Origen
Oronte, *m.* Orontes
Orose, *m.* Orosius
Orphée, *m.* Orpheus
Osée, *m* Hosea
Osmond, *m.* Osmund
Otello, Othello, *m.* Othello
Othon, *m* Otho
Ouen, *m.* Owen
Ovide, *m.* Ovid

Palamède, *m.* Palamedes
Palémon, *m.* Palæmon
Paléologue, *m* Palæologus
Palinure, *m.* Palinurus
Palmyre, *f* Palmyra
Pamphile, *m.* Pamphilus
Pandore, *f.* Pandora
Pantaléon, *m* Pantaleo, Pantaleon
Pantalon, *m.* Pantaloon
Paracelse, *m* Paracelsus
Pâris, *m* Paris
Paris (Monsieur de), *m.* Jack Ketch
Parménide, *m.* Parmenides
Parménion, *m.* Parmenio
Parmesan (Le), *m.* Parmigiano
Parques (Les), *f.pl.* the Parcæ, the Fates
Patrice, *m.* Patrick; Patricius
Patrocle, *m* Patroclus
Paul, *m.* Paul; Paulus
Paule, *f* Paula
Paulin, *m.* Paulinus
Pauline, *f.* Paulina
Pégase, *m.* Pegasus
Pélage, *m.* Pelagius
Pélagie, *f.* Pelagia
Pélée, *m.* Peleus
Pénélope, *f.* Penelope
Penthée, *m.* Pentheus
Pépin, *m.* Pepin
Périandre, *m.* Periander
Périclès, *m.* Pericles
Perse, *m.* Persius
Persée, *m.* Perseus
Pérugin (Le), *m.* Perugino
Pétrarque, *m.* Petrarca
Pétrone, *m.* Petronius
†**Pétronille,** *f.* Pernella
Pharaon, *m* Pharaoh
Phébé, *f.* Phœbe
Phébus, *m.* Phœbus
Phédon, *m.* Phædon
Phèdre, *m.* Phædrus; *f.* Phædra
Philarète, *m.* Philaretus
Philippe, *m.* Philip; *f.* Philippa
Philippine, *f.* Philippina
Philoctète, *m.* Philoctetes
Philomèle, *f.* Philomela
Philon, *m.* Philo, Philon
Philopon, *m.* Philoponus
Phinéas, Phinée, *m.* Phineas
Pie, *m.* Pius
Pierre, *m.* Peter
Pindare, *m.* Pindar
Pisistrate, *m.* Pisistratus
Pison, *m.* Piso
Pizarre, *m.* Pizarro
Placide, *m.* Placidus
Placidie, *f.* Placidia
Planude, *m.* Planudes
Platon, *m.* Plato
Plaute, *m.* Plautus
Pline, *m.* Pliny
Plotin, *m.* Plotinus
Plutarque, *m.* Plutarch
Pluton, *m.* Pluto
Polichinel, Polichinelle, *m.* Punch
Polybe, *m.* Polybius
Polyclète, *m.* Polycletus
Polydore, *m.* Polydorus
Polyeucte, *m.* Polyeuctus
Polynice, *m.* Polynices
Polyphème, *m.* Polyphemus
Polyxène, *f.* Polyxena
Pomone, *f.* Pomona
Pompée, *m.* Pompey
Ponce, *m.* Pontius
Porcie, *f.* Porcia
Porphyre, *m.* Porphyry
Poucet (Le Petit-), *m.* Tom Thumb
Praxitèle, *m.* Praxiteles
Priape, *m.* Priapus
Priscien, *m.* Priscian
Priscille, *f.* Priscilla
Procope, *m.* Procopius
Procruste, Procuste, *m.* Procrustes
†**Progné,** *f.* Procne
Prométhée, *m.* Prometheus
Properce, *m.* Propertius
Protée *m.* Proteus
Prudence, *m.* Prudentius; *f.* Prudence
Psyché, *f.* Psyche
Ptolémée, *m.* Ptolemy
‡**Pulchérie,** *f.* Pulcheria
Putiphar, *m.* Potiphar
Pylade, *m.* Pylades
Pyrame, *m.* Pyramus
Pyrrhon, *m.* Pyrrho
Pythagore, *m.* Pythagoras

Quichotte, *m.* Quixote
§**Quinte-Curce,** *m.* Quintus Curtius
§**Quintilien,** *m.* Quintilian

‡**Rachab,** *f.* Rahab
Radegonde, *f.* Radegund
Raminagrobis, *m.* Grimalkin
Randolphe, *m.* Randolph, Randal
Raoul, *m.* Ralph
Raphaël, *m.* Raphael
Raton, *m.* Mouser, Puss
Raymond, *m.* Raymund
Rébecca, *f.* Rebecca
Remi, Remy, *m.* Remigius
Renaud, *m.* Reynold
†**Réveille-matin (Le),** *m.* Chanticleer
Rhadamanthe, *m.* Rhadamanthus
Rhée, *f.* Rhea
‡**Roch,** *m.* Roque
Rodolphe, *m.* Rodolph
Rodrigue, *m.* Roderick
Roland, *m.* Rowland; Orlando
Romain (Jules), *m.* Romano (Giulio)
Roméo, *m.* Romeo
Rominagrobis, *m.* Grimalkin
†**Ronge-maille,** *m.* Nibble, Squire Nibble
Rosalie, *f.* Rosalia
Rosemonde, *f.* Rosamund
Rosine, *f.* Rosine, Rosina
Roxane, *f.* Roxana
Roxelane, *f.* Roxalana
Ruben, *m.* Reuben

Sabine, *f.* Sabina
Salluste, *m.* Sallust
Salomon, *m.* Solomon
Sapho, *f.* Sappho
Sara, *f.* Sarah, Sally
Sardanapale, *m.* Sardanapalus
Satan, *m.* Satan
Saturne, *m.* Saturn
Saturnin, *m.* Saturninus
Saül, *m.* Saul
Saumaise, *m.* Salmasius
Savinien, *m.* Savinian
Savonarole, *m.* Savonarola
Scipion, *m.* Scipio
Sébastien, *m.* Sebastian
Sébastienne, *f.* Sebastiana
Sédécias, *m.* Zedekiah
Séjan, *m.* Sejanus
Sélène, *f.* Selene
Sem, *m.* Shem
Sémélé, *f.* Semele
Sénèque, *m.* Seneca
‡**Sennachérib,** *m.* Sennacherib
Septime, *m.* Septimius
Sésostris, *m.* Sesostris
Sévère, *m.* Severus
Sidoine, *m.* Sidonius
Sidonie, *f.* Sidonia
Sigismond, *m.* Sigismund
Silène, *m.* Silenus
Silvain, *m.* Silvan
Silvestre, *m.* Silvester
Silvie, *f.* Silvia
Siméon, *m.* Simeon
Simonide, *m.* Simonides
Sisyphe, *m.* Sisyphus
Sixte, *m.* Sixtus
Socin, *m.* Socinus
Socrate, *m.* Socrates
Sophie, *f.* Sophia, Sophy
Sophocle, *m.* Sophocles
Sophonie, *m.* Zephaniah
Sophronie, *f.* Sophronia
Sosie, *m.* Sosia
Stace, *m.* Statius
Stanislas, *m.* Stanislaus
Stéphanie, *f.* Stephania
‡**Stésichore,** *m.* Stesichorus
Strabon, *m* Strabo
Suénon, *m* Sweyn
Suétone, *m.* Suetonius
Sulpice, *m.* Sulpicius
Susanne, Suzanne, *f.* Susan, Susanna, Susannah

Susette, Suzette, Suson, Suzon, *f.* Susy
Sylvain, *m.* Sylvan
Sylvestre, *m.* Sylvester
Sylvie, *f.* Sylvia

Tacite, *m.* Tacitus
Tamerlan, *m.* Tamerlane
Tancrède, *m.* Tancred
Tannegui, *m.* Tanaquil
Tantale, *m.* Tantalus
§**Tarquinie,** *f.* Tarquinia
Tasse (Le), *m.* Tasso
Taxile, *m* Taxiles
Télémaque, *m.* Telemachus
Télèphe, *m.* Telephus
Térée, *m.* Tereus
Térence, *m.* Terence
‡**Terpsichore,** *f.* Terpsichore
Tertullien, *m.* Tertullian
Thalès, *m.* Thales
Thalie, *f.* Thalia
Thémis, *f.* Themis
Thémistocle, *m.* Themistocles
Théocrite, *m.* Theocritus
Théodore, *m.* Theodore; Theodorus; *f.* Theodora
Théodose, *m.* Theodosius
Théodosie, *f.* Theodosia
Théophane, *m.* Theophanes
Théophile, *m.* Theophilus; *f.* Theophila
Théophraste, *m.* Theophrastus
Thérèse, *f.* Theresa
Thersite, *m.* Thersites
Thésée, *m.* Theseus
Thibaut, *m.* Theobald
Thisbé, *f.* Thisbe
Thrasybule, *m.* Thrasybulus
Thucydide, *m.* Thucydides
Thyeste, *m.* Thyestes
Tibère, *m.* Tiberius
Tibulle, *m.* Tibullus
Tiburce, *m.* Tiburtius
Tigrane, *m.* Tigranes
Timante, Timanthe, *m.* Timanthes
Timée, *m.* Timæus
Timothée, *m.* Timothy
Tintoret (Le), *m.* Tintoretto
Tite, *m.* Titus
Tite-Live, *m.* Livy
Titien (Le), *m.* Titian
Titus, *m.* Titus
Tobie, *m.* Tobias, Toby
Toinette, Toinon, *f.* Antonia
Trajan, *m.* Trajan
Tribonien, *m.* Tribonian
Triptolème, *m.* Triptolemus
Trismégiste, *m.* Trismegistus
Trissin, *m.* Trissino
Tubalcaïn, *m.* Tubal-Cain
Tullie, *f.* Tullia
Tullius, *m.* Tully
Tyrtée, *m.* Tyrtæus

Ulpien, *m.* Ulpian
Ulrique, *f.* Ulrica
Ulysse, *m.* Ulysses
Uranie, *f.* Urania
Urbain, *m.* Urban
Urie, *m.* Uriah; Urias
Ursule, *f.* Ursula

Valentin, *m.* Valentine
Valentine, *f.* Valentine
Valentinien, *m.* Valentinian
Valère, *m.* Valerius
Valérie, *f.* Valeria
Valérien, *m.* Valerian
Varron, *m.* Varro
Vautour (Monsieur), *m.* Mr. Landlord
Vautrin, *m.* Jack Sheppard
Venceslas, *m.* Venceslaus
Vénus, *f.* Venus
Véronèse, *m.* Veronese
Véronique, *f.* Veronica
Verrès, *m.* Verres
Vertumne, *m.* Vertumnus
Vespasien, *m.* Vespasian
Vichnou, *m.* Vishnu
Victoire, *f.* Victoria
Victorin, *m.* Victorinus
Victorine, *f.* Victorina
Vidocq, *m.* Jack Sheppard
Virgile, *m.* Virgil
Virginie, *f.* Virginia
Vitruve, *m.* Vitruvius
Vivien, *m.* Vivian
Vulcain, *m.* Vulcan

Wilhelmine, *f.* Wilhelmina

Xanthippe, *m.* Xanthippus; *f.* Xanthippe
Xénocrate, *m.* Xenocrates
Xénophane, *m.* Xenophanes
Xercès, Xerxès, *m.* Xerxes

‡**Zacharie,** *m.* Zachariah, Zac[hary]
Zachée, *m.* Zaccheus
Zébédée, *m.* Zebedee
Zénobie, *f.* Zenobia
Zénon, *m.* Zeno
Zéphyre, *m.* Zephyr, Zephyrus
Zoé, *f.* Zoe
Zoïle, *m.* Zoilus
Zoroastre, *m.* Zoroaster
Zorobabel, *m.* Zerubbabel
Zosime, *m.* Zosimus
Zwingle, Zwingli, *m.* Zwingl[i]

SUPPLEMENT.

☞ The intelligent reader need hardly be told that no perfect dictionary ever was made, or ever can be, or that if one could be written, language would advance beyond it before it could be printed. To issue a dictionary without a supplement is to ignore this fact. Consequently each issue of this dictionary will be accompanied by a supplement containing such new words and uses of words as the editor has noticed in authoritative writings issued since the edition was put to press, as well as those which had escaped his attention in earlier writings.

A

Abbatiat, *s.m.* abbotship
†**Abeillé, e,** *adj.* (*her.*) with bees
Abigaïl, *s.f.* abigail
Abreuver, *v.a.* (*casks,* &c.) to season (*with water*)
Abruption, *s.f.* abruption
Abstentionisme, *s.m.* abstentionism
Abstentioniste, *s.m.f.* abstentionist
Acclimateu-r, se, *s.m.f. V.* **Acclimatateur**
Accouplage, *s.m. V.* **Accouplement**
Accusatoire, *adj.* accusatory
Acétifier, *v.a.*, **S'—,** *v.r.* to acetify
Achopper, *v.n.* to stumble
Acquit, *s.m.* acquittal
Acrobatie, *s.f.*, **Acrobatisme,** *s.m.* acrobatism
Actin-ique, -isme. *V.* page 3, § 1
Actinomètre, *s.m.* (*opt.*) actinometer
Actinométr-ie, -ique, -iquement. *V.* p. 3, § 1
Actionner, *v.a.* to put into action, to set in
Addenda, *s.m.* addenda; addendum [motion
Adjecti-f, ve, *adj.* adjective; adjectival
Afghan, e, Afgan, e, *adj. s.* Afghan
Agalmatolithe, *s.m.* agalmatolite, figure-stone
†**Agenouiller (S'),** *v.r.* (*of horses*) to fall on
Aggloméré, *s.m. V.* **Briquette** [its knees
Agissement, *s.m* doing, dealing, action, act
Agoniste, *s.m.* agonist
Agonist-ique, -iquement. *V.* page 3, § 1
Ahurissement, *s.m.* confusion, perplexity, flurry, bewilderment; amazement
Alaire, *adj.* alar [sible gain or loss
Aléa, *s.m.* (*com.*) chance of profit or loss, pos-
Algolog-ie, -ique, -iste. *V.* page 3, § 1
Algologue, *s.m.* algologist
Allégeage, *s.m.* (*nav.*) lightening (*a ship*); buoying up (*a cable*)
Allitérati-f, ve, *adj.* alliterative
Allumoir, *s.m.* lighter [*or* alluvions
Alluvionnement, *s.m.* formation of alluvia
Altiste, *s.m.* altist
Amativité, *s.f.* amativeness
†**Ambresailles,** *s.f.pl.* (*Swiss for* **Myrtil**)
Ambulanci-er, ère, *s.m.f.* ambulancier
Ammoniacé, e, *adj.* ammoniated
Amodiataire, *s.m.* lessor [dissected
Anatomiser (S'), *v.r.* to be anatomized *or*
Ane, *s.m.* — *salé,* aunt Sally (*game*)
Anecdotiser, *v.a.* to intersperse with anecdotes
Angularité, *s.f.* angularity
Anhinga, *s.m.* (*bird*) anhinga, darter, snake-bird
Animalculaire, *adj* animalcular
Annoncier, *s.m.* advertiser
Anodonte, *adj.* toothless
Antagonique, *adj.* antagonistic
Anticlérical, e, *adj.* anticlerical
Antidoter, *v.a.* to antidote
Antigréviste, *s.m.* non-striker, knobstick
Antilibéral, e, *adj. s.* antiliberal
Antiministériel, le, *adj.* antiministerial; — *s.m.* antiministerialist
Antonyme, *adj.* antonymous; — *s.m.* antonym
Antonymie, *s.f.* antonymy [antonymous
Antonymique, *adj* antonymic, antonymycal;
Antonymiquement, *adv.* antonymously
Antonymiste, *s.m.* antonymist
Aoûtage, *s.m.* harvest time; harvesting, harvest
Apeuré, e, *adj.* affrighted, frightened
Aphis, *s.m.* (*zool.*) aphis
Apicole, *adj.* apicultural
Apion, *s.m.* (*zool.*) clover-weevil
Apnée, *s.f.* (*med.*) apnæa
Apostolicité, *s.f.* apostolicity, apostolicalness
Apothéotique, *adj.* apotheotic
Appas, *s.m.pl.* (*fam.*) bosom
Appétent, e, *adj.* appetent; covetous
Appli, *s.m.* gear
Appointir, *v.a.* to point, to sharpen
Appointissage, *s.m. V.* **Empointage**
Apprivoiseu-r, se, *s.m.f.* tamer
Apron, *s.m.* (*fish*) zingel
§**Aquicole,** *adj.* aquicultural
§**Aquiculteur,** *s.m.* aquiculturist
Arbois, *s.m.* (*bot.*) laburnum
Architecturalement, *adv.* architecturally
Architecturiste, *s.m.f.* monument painter *or*
Argentation, *s.f. V.* **argentage** [paintress
Argentier, *s.m.* money-lender; (*pop.*) moneyed
Argien, ne, *s.m.f. adj.* Argive, of Argos [man
Argumentati-f, ve, *adj.* argumentative
Arme, *s.f. Mettre l' — au pied,* to order arms
Armérie, *s.f.* (*bot.*) thrift, sea-pink
†**Armille,** *s.f.* armilla, armil, ring, circle; (*arch.*) annulet
Arrière-cuisine, *s.f.* back-kitchen
Arrivé, *s.m.* successful man; (*turf*) arrival
Articulaire, *adj. Rhumatisme —,* acute rheumatism, rheumatic fever
Articulés, *s.m.pl.* articulates, articulata
Arundinaire, *s.f.* (*bot.*) arundinaria, cane-brake
Aspidophore, *s.m.* (*fish*) pogge, armed bullhead
Aspirance, *s.f.* candidature, candidateship
Asprêle, *s.f.* (*bot.*) Dutch rush, polishing-rush
Assessoral, e, *adj.* assessorial
Assortisseu-r, se, *s.m.f.* dealer in remnants
Atone, *adj.* (*gram.*) atonic
Atoniser, *v.a.* to atonize
Atte, *s.m. V.* **Corossol;** — *s.f.* ant
†**Attignole,** *s.f.* sausage cake
Auroral, e, *adj.* auroral [amination of
Autopsier, *v.a.* to make a post-mortem ex-
Avaliser, *v.a.* to endorse, to guarantee
Avant-bassin, *s.m.* tide-dock
Aventin, *s.m.* Aventine
Axial, e, *adj.* axial

B

†**Baignant,** *s.m.* bather. *Le — et le baigneur,* the bather and the bathing-man (*attendant*)
†**Baignante,** *s.f.* bather. *La — et la baigneuse,* the bather and the bathing-woman (*attendant*)
†**Bâillonnement,** *s.m.* gagging
Banaliser, *v a.* to vulgarize
Bancable, *adj.* bankable
Banjo, *s.m.* banjo
Bannisseur, *s.m.* banisher
Baquois, *s.m. V.* **Pandanus**
Baracon, *s.m.* barracoon
Barricot, *s.m. V.* **Barriquaut**
Bars, *s.m.* (*fish*) *V.* **Bar**
Barsac, *s.m.* barsac (wine) [*V.* **Hâler**
Basaner, *v.a.* to cover with sheep-leather; (*fig.*)

Baselle, *s.f.* (*bot.*) Malabar nightshade
Bassin, *s.m.* — *d'or,* (*bot.*) *V.* **Bassinet**
Bayette, *s.f.* baize
Béatement, *adv.* sanctimoniously; blissfully
Beau, Bel, *m.,* **Belle,** *f., adj. Beau garçon,* handsome man. *Beau vieillard,* handsome old man. *Bel homme,* fine man. *Belle femme,* fine woman. *Cette femme est belle,* that woman is handsome
Bec-en-fourreau, *s.m.* (*bird*) sheath-bill
Bêchée, *s.f.* spadeful
Becmare, *s.m. V.* **Attélabe**
Bège, *adj. V.* **Beige**
Belligérance, *s.f.* belligerence
Belligérer, *v.n.* to make war
Benturong, *s.m.* (*zool.*) binturong
Betteravi-er, ère, *adj.* of beet-roots, beet-root
Biacide, *adj.* (*chem.*) biacid
Bibasique, *adj.* (*chem.*) bibasic
Biblic-isme, -iste. *V.* page 3, § 1
Bicycliste, *s.m.* bicyclist
Bi-hebdomadaire, *adj.* fortnightly
†Billard, *s.m.* — *anglais,* bagatelle; bagatelle table or board
Bissec-teur, trice, *adj.* bisecting
Bobin, *s.m.* (*adject., Tulle* —) bobbin-net
Bommerang, *s.m.* boomerang
Bonhomme, *s.m. Petit — vit encore* (*old game of forfeits*), Jack's alive
Bonnette, *s.f.* (*of a telescope*) cap
Boucheuse, *s.f.* corking machine
Bouiboui, *s.m.* low theatre; hovel, hole [house
†Bouillon, *s.m.* cook-shop, second-rate dining-
†Bouilloter, Bouillotter, *v.n.* to simmer
Boulange, *s.f.* grinding; baking [hours' Change
Bourse, *s.f. Petite* —, small purse; after-
Boutien, ne, *adj. s. Gros* —, (*in Gulliver's Travels*) Big-endian. *Petit* —, Small-endian
†Braillerie, *s.f. V.* **Braillement**
Brasière, *s.f.* coal-pan, brasier
Brave, *adj.* first-rate
Brichet, *s.m. V.* **Brechet**
†Brillantine, *s.f.* glazed lining; pomade or &c. to give brilliancy to the hair, brillantine,
Bringuer, *v.n.* to skip, to frisk [brilliantine
Brosme, *s.m.* (*fish*) torsk, tusk
†Brugnonier, Brugnonnier, *s.m.* (cling-stone) nectarine-tree
Brûloire, *s.f. V.* **Brûloir,** *s.m.*
Buffeti-er, ère, *s.m.f.* refreshment-room keeper
Bufflone. *V.* **Bufflonne**
Bureaucratiquement, *adv.* bureaucratically
Buttoir, *s.m.* (*rail.*) buffer-stop
Buvette, *s.f.* drinking-fountain

C

Cabalisme. *V.* page 3, § 1
Cache. — **-lumière,** *s.m.* (*of a telescope*) sunshade. — **-misère,** *s.m.* overcoat to conceal old clothes. — **-poussière,** *s.m.* light overcoat to preserve o.'s clothes from the dust
Cagoule, *s.f.* cagoule (*monk's garment without*
Caissette, *s.f.* small case or box [*sleeves*)
Calence, *s.f.* (*pop.*) *En* —, out of work
Calino, *s.m. V.* **Jocrisse**
Calorifiant, e, *adj.* calorifacient, calorifiant
Calou, *s.m.* palm-wine
Camembert, *s.m.* Camembert cheese
†Canaillerie, *s.f.* blackguardism
Canaque, *s.m.f. adj.* New-Caledonian
Canepetière, *s.f.* field-duck
Cannage, *s.m.* caning (*of chairs,* &c.)
Canner, *v.a.* to cane (*chairs,* &c.)
Canneur (**-euse,** *f.*), **Cannier,** *s.m.* caner, chair-caner, cane chair bottomer
Canoter, *v.n.* to go for a row, to go rowing, to row
Canter, *s.m.* (*in horse-racing*) canter [hood
Capoter, *v.a.* (*at play*) to capot; (*a carriage*) to
Capsuler, *v.a.* (*tech.*) to cap
Carafon, *s.m.* quarter-bottle
Carassin, *s.m.* (*fish*) crucian
Carte, *s.f.* — *album, s.f.* (*photo.*) cabinet size. — *de visite, s.f.* visiting-card; (*photo.*) carte de visite. — *postale,* — *-poste, s.f.* post-card
Cartoucherie, *s.f.* cartridge-manufactory
Caserni-er, ère, *adj.* of barracks, barrack
Casser, *v.a.* to reduce to a lower grade or to the ranks [tasis, counterturn
Catastase, *s.f.* (*med.*) catastasis; (*rhet.*) catas-
Céanothe, *s.m.* (*bot.*) red-root
Centennal, e, *adj.* centennial
Céramiste, *s.m.* ceramist
Cérasifère, *adj.* cerasiferous, cherry-bearing
Cercle. — *magique,* — *des fées,* — *des sorciers,*
Céréale, *adj. f.* corn [(*in pastures*) fairy ring
Chabin, *s.m.* cross between the he-goat and
Chaîne, *s.f.* — *de gilet,* Albert chain [the ewe
Chaînier, *s.m. V.* **Chaîniste**
Châle, *s.m.* — *long,* scarf, scarf shawl
Chalef, *s.m.* (*bot.*) elæagnus, oleaster, wild olive
Challis, Chalys, *s.m. V.* **Chaly**
Chamelet, *s.m. V.* **Chamélon**
‡Chamitique, *adj.* Hamitic
†Champagniser, Champaniser, *v.a.* to make champagne-like; to make sham cham-
Champ-fermage, *s.m.* hoarding [pagne of
Champ-fermer, *v.a.* to enclose with a hoarding
Chanteclair, *s.m.* Chanticleer
Chantonnement, *s.m.* humming
Chanvri-er, ère, *adj.* of hemp, hemp [**dage**)
Chapardage, *s.m.* (*soldiers' slang for* **Marau-**
Chaparder, *v.n.* (*soldiers' slang for* **Marauder**)
Chapardeur, *s.m.* (*soldiers' slang for* **Marau-**
Charronnerie, *s.f.* wheelwright's trade [**deur**)
Chasse-café, *s.m. V.* **Pousse-café**
Chavirage, *s.m. V.* **Chavirement**
Chef, *s.m.* — *de bouche,* head cook. — *de comptabilité,* accountant-general
‡Chélifère, *adj.* (*zool.*) cheliferous; — *s.m.* chelifer, book-scorpion
†Chenille, *s.f. Fausse-* —, nigger
†Chenilleu-r, se, *s.m.f.* chenille-maker
Chevalier, *s.m.* — *de la coupe,* knight of the
Chevrelle, *s.f.* she-kid [shears, snip
Chiffler, *pop. and local for* **Siffler**
‡Chlorops, *s.m.* (*zool.*) corn-fly
Chômeur, *s.m.* operative out of work
‡Chromatrope, *s.m.* chromatrope
Cingle, *s.m.* (*fish*) zingel
Cinquantenaire, *s.m.* fiftieth anniversary; — *s.m.f. V.* **Quinquagénaire**
Circonférentiel, le, *adj.* circumferential
Circonspectement, *adv.* circumspectly
Circumméridien. *V.* **Circomméridien**
Cirro-cumulus, *s.m.* (*meteorology*) cirro-cumulus
Cirro-stratus, *s.m.* (*meteorology*) cirro-stratus
Clain, *s.m. V.* **Clin**
Classiquement, *adv.* classically
Cléricalisation, *s.f.* clericalization
Cléricaliser, *v.a.* to clericalize
Cléricalisme, *s.m.* clericalism
Clouure, *s.f.* nailing
Coagulabilité, *s.f.* coagulability
Coétendu, e, *adj.* coextensive
Coïncidemment, *adv.* coincidently
Colis, *s.m.* — *postal* (*sing.*), postal parcel, post-parcel. — *postaux* (*pl.*), postal parcels, post-parcels; parcels post, parcel post. *Service des — postaux,* parcels post, parcel post
Colisa, Colise, *s.m.* rainbow-fish
Collatéralité, *s.f.* collateralness
Collationnement, *s.m. V.* **Collationnage**
Collectivité, *s.f.* collectiveness
Colombar, *s.m.* (*bird*) vinago
Colorado, *s.m.* colorado-beetle
Colossalement, *adv.* colossally
Coltar, *s.m. V.* **Coaltar**
Commercialiser, *v.a.* to commercialize
Concorder, *v.n.* to compound (*with creditors*)
Concubinaire, *adj.m.f., s.m.* concubinary
Concurrencer, *v.a.* to compete with

Concurrentiel, le, *adj.* competing, in competition

Condamna-teur, trice, *s.m.f.adj.* condemner; condemning

Congénial, e, *adj.* congenial

Congénialité, *s.f.* congeniality, congenialness

Congréganiste, *s.m.f.* congregationist

Congressionnel, le, *adj.* congressional

Consciemment, *adv.* consciously

Constabulaire, *adj.* constabulary

Contagionner, *v.a. V.* **Contagier. Se —,** *v.r.* to be affected by contagion, to be infected

Contemporainement, *adv.* contemporaneously

Contre-plainte, *s.f.* counter-charge; cross-action

Conventionalisme, *s.m.* conventionalism

Convolution, *s.f.* convolution

Corégone, *s.m.* (*fish*) coregonus

Coule, *s.f.* (*of monks*) frock

Couleur, *s.m.* *Le — de ...,* the ... colour. *D'un — de ..., — de ...,* of a ... colour, ... colour, ... coloured

Coup, *s.m.* *— du départ,* parting glass *or* cup. *— de force,* violent measure, attempt by force of arms. *— de fouet,* (*nav.*) sudden swell

Coupure, *s.f.* cutting; (*fin.*) bond

Courbe, *s.f.* (*for carrying pails,* &c.) *V.* **Courge**

Courir, Se —, *v.r.* to be run *or* run for *or* &c.

Couronne, *s.f.* circular roll (*of bread*)

Crasserie, *s.f. V.* **Vilenie**

Crédirenti-er, ère, *s.m.f.* holder *or* receiver of an annuity, annuitant

Crêpeline, *s.f.* crepeline (*light stuff*)

Crevettière, *s.f.* (*fish.*) shrimp-net

Cucurbitacées, *s.f.pl.* (*bot.*) cucurbitaceæ

†Cueille-fruits, *s.m.* fruit-gatherer

Curvation, *s.f.* curvation

D

Damar, *s.m.* dammar, damar; (*tree*) dammar-pine. *Gomme —,* dammar, damar

Damarine, *s.f.* dammar, damar

Débirenti-er, ère, *s.m.f.* payer of an annuity

Débourre-pipe, *s.m.* tobacco-pipe cleaner, tobacco-pricker

†Débroussaillement, *s.m.* clearing of brushwood

†Débroussailler, *v.a.* to clear of brushwood

Décaisser, *v.a.* to take out of a cash-box; to withdraw from a capital *or* fund

Décanteur, *s.m.* (*chem.*) decanter

Décimalité, *s.f.* decimality

Décompte, *s.m.* total; account

Décompter, *v.a.* to sum up, to add up

Décrépi, e, *adj.* unplastered

Décrépir, *v.a.* to unplaster

Décrépissage, *s.m.* unplastering

Décrueu-r, se, *s.m.f.* scourer

Dédorage, *s.m.* ungilding

Dédoubler, *v.a.* to reduce one half; to take away one of ... out of two

Défécateur, *s.m.* defecator

Déflagrer, *v.n.* to deflagrate

Déforestation, *s.f.* disafforestation, deforestation, deforesting

Déforester, *v.a.* to disafforest, to deforest

Dégaînement, *s.m. V.* **Dégaîner,** *s.m.*

Délien, ne, *adj. s.* Delian

Démêlures, *s.f. pl.* combings

Démerger, *v.a.* to take out of the water again, to free from the water

Demi-soldier, *s.m.* one on half-pay

Démissionner, *v.n.* to resign

Démontable, *adj.* capable of being taken to pieces

Dentelli-er, ère, *adj.* of lace, lace; — *s.m.f.* laceman, lacewoman, lace-maker

Dentisterie, *s.f.* dentistry

Dépaisselage, *s.m.* unpropping (*of vines*)

Dépaisseler, *v.a.* to unprop (*vines*)

Dépensable, *adj.* spendable; expendible

Dépoétiser, *v.a.* to depoetize

Dérangeu-r, se, *s.m.f.* deranger

Derby, *s.m.* Derby, Derby-day

Dérôlement, *s.m.* striking off the rolls

Dérôler, *v.a.* to strike off the rolls

Désaimantation, *s.f.* unmagnetization

Désargentage, *s.m.* unsilvering

Descenseur, *s.m.* fire-escape

Déséchouage, *s.m. V.* **Déséchouement**

†Désencanailler. *V.* **Décanailler**

Désenclaver, *v.a.* to open, to lay open; to free, to set free

Désenfouir, *v.a.* to unbury, to unearth

Désengouer, *v.a.* to cure of infatuation, to put out of conceit; to deobstruct, to clear, to free

Dessalage, *s.m. V.* **Dessalement**

Dessous, *s.m.* *— de table,* crumb-cloth

Détorsion, *s.f.* detortion, distortion

Dévasement, *s.m.* unsilting

Dévaser, *v.a.* to unsilt

Déveinard, *s.m.* unlucky wight

Déveuver, *v.n.* to remarry

Devinette, *s.f.* puzzling question

Dévoration, *s.f.,* **Dévorement,** *s.m.* devoration, devouring

Diable, *s.m.* *Quand le — y serait,* after all

Dictatorialement, *adv.* dictatorially

Diremption, *s.f.* invalidation, annulment

Discrétionnairement, *adv.* discretionarily

Disparu, e, *part. adj.* (*mil.*) missing

Disposeu-r, se, *s.m.f.* disposer

Dissémina-teur, trice, *adj.* disseminating, spreading; — *s.m.f.* disseminator, spreader

Disséqueur, *adj. m.* dissecting

Dissymétrie, *s.f.* unsymmetricalness, want of symmetry

Distraitement, *adv.* inattentively, listlessly, heedlessly; vacantly; in an absent manner

Domptage, *s.m.* (*bad modern word*) *V.* **Domptement**

Doryphore, *s.m.* doryphora, colorado-beetle

Doterelle, *s.f. V.* **Guignard**

Drageonnement, *s.m.* (*bot.*) shooting suckers

Dressable, *adj.* trainable

Droitier, *s.m.* member of the Right (*in an assembly*)

Duodécennal, e, *adj.* duodecennial

Dynamite, *s.f.* dynamite

E

†Ébouillantage, *s.m.* application of boiling water

†Écaillure, *s.f.* scales

Ecclésiologue, *s.m.* ecclesiologist

Écœurement, *s.m.* sickening, sickness

École, *s.f.* *— libre,* sectarian school

Écume, *s.f.* *— printanière,* cuckoo spit, frog spittle

Édit, e, *adj.* published

Éducationnel, le, *adj.* educational

Effloraison, *s.f. V.* **Fleuraison**

Égarement, *s.m.* losing, loss

Égouti-er, ère, *adj.* of sewers, sewer

Égyptolog-ie, -ique. *V.* page 3, § 1

Égyptologue, *s.m.* Egyptologist

Élaps, *s.m.* (*serpent*) elaps

Électionner, *v.n.* to electioneer

Électivement, *adv.* electively

Électoralement, *adv.* electorally

Éléphanteau, *s.m.* young elephant

Émasculateur, *s.m.* emasculator

Embarriquer, *v.a.* to put into a cask

Embourgeoiser, *v.a.* to make or render vulgar, to vulgarize. **S'—,** *v.r.* to become vulgar

†Embouteillement, *s.m. V.* **Embouteillage**

Embrasure, *s.f.* stoke-hole

Émetteu-r, se, *s.m.f.* emitter; utterer; issuer

Émissible, *adj.* utterable; issuable

Émissionnaire, *s.m.f.* issuer; — *adj.* issuing

Émondoir, *s.m.* (*instr.*) pruner

Émoussement, *s.m.* blunting; bluntness

Empaffer (S'), *v.r. V.* **Paffer (Se)**

Empansement, *s.m. V.* **Météorisme**

†Empapilloter, *v.a. V.* **Papilloter**

Empotement, *s.m. V.* **Empotage**

Emprunt, *s.m.* *Terre d'—,* made earth

Encaisser, *v.a.* to encash

Encanteur, *s.m.* auctioneer
Enchaussement, *s.m.* mulching
Encornure, *s.f.* horns
Encreur, *adj. m.* (*print.*) inking, ink
Enfutage, *s.m.*, **Enfuter,** *v.a. V.* **Enfutaillement, Enfutailler**
Enrayage, *s.m. V.* **Enraiement**
Enrober, *v.a.* to cover, to wrap up
Ensilage, *s.m.* ensilage
†**Ensommeillé, e,** *adj.* sleepy, drowsy
Épinage, *s.m.* thorn covering
Épingle. *Être tiré à quatre —s,* to be dressy, to be dressed up (*or* out) to the nines
Épitaphier, *s.m.* collection of epitaphs
Équarrisseur, *s.m.* squarer
§**Équidés,** *s.m.pl.* equidæ, equine species *or* race, horse species
Équilibration, *s.f.* equilibration
Érotisme, *s.m.* erotism
Escargotage, *s.m.* clearing *or* destruction of snails
Escargoter, *v.a.* to clear of snails
Escomptable, *adj.* discountable
Esprit, *s.m.* — *de bois,* methylated spirit
Essayage, *s.m.* trying; trying on; assaying
Estimatif, *s.m.* estimate
Estompage, *s.m.* (*draw.*) stumping
Étalonnage, *s.m.* stallion-keeping
Étalonnerie, *s.f.* stallion-stable, stud
Étalonnier, *s.m.* stallion-keeper
État-major. *Colonel d'*—, adjutant-general
Étave, *s.f.* trout-net
Étente, *s.f.* (*fish.*) stake-net
Éternisation, *s.f.* eternization
Étouffer (S'), *v.r.* to suffocate *or* &c. oneself *or* each other; to be suffocated *or* &c.
Être, *v.n.* *Voilà ce que c'est,* that's what it is
Évalua-teur, trice, *s.m.f.* valuer; appraiser; — *adj.* valuing; appraising
Évanescence, *s.f.* evanescence
Évangélisateur, *s.m.* evangelizer
Évolutioniste, *s.m.f.* evolutionist
Excusa-teur, trice, *s.m.f.* excuser; exculpator; — *adj.* excusing, exculpating, exculpatory
Excuse, *s.f.* sham sword
Exemplarité, *s.f.* exemplariness
Exertion, *s.f.* exertion
Exhausteur, *s.m.* (*tech.*) exhauster
Exotisme, *s.m.* exoticism
Expansivité, *s.f.* expansiveness
Explosionner, *v.n.* to explode
Exposé, *s.m.* — *des motifs,* explanatory statement
Exposition, *s.f.* — *publique,* (*of sales*) on view
Expropria-teur, trice, *adj.* expropriating
Extincti-f, ve, *adj.* annulling, cancelling

F

Faisandi-er, ère, *adj.* of pheasants, pheasant
Fanfariste, *s.m.* bandsman
Fque, (*abbreviation of* fabrique)
Farais, *s.m.* (*fish.*) coral-net
Faussetier, *s.m.* worker of *or* dealer in imitation stones
Féodalisation, *s.f.* feudalization
Ferme, *adj.* (*com., Exchange*) final and complete, firm
Férocement, *adv.* ferociously
Ferrer, *v.a.* to ring (*a pig*)
Fertilisant, *s.m.* fertilizer; — *m.,* **e,** *f., part. adj.* fertilizing
†**Feuillard,** *s.m.* (*of an iron bedstead*) lath
†**Feuillette,** *s.f.* leaflet
Ficellerie, *s.f.* string-making *or* manufactory *or* business *or* warehouse
Fiévreusement, *adv.* feverishly
Fil, *s.m.* — *de soie,* silk thread; silkworm gut. — *de Florence,* silkworm gut
Filer, *v.a.* to follow at a distance, to follow, to follow up
Fileti-er, ère, *s.m.f.* net-maker
Filialité, *s.f.* filiality, filialness
†**Fille-mère,** *s.f.* unmarried mother
Fin, *s.f.* *Prendre* —, to end
Fleuriste, *s.m.* flower-garden
Floralie, *s.f.* flower-show
Florimane, *s.m.f. adj.* florimaniac
Florimanie, *s.f.* florimania
Fois, *s.f.* *Une seule* —, only once; even once
Foliicole, *adj.* living on leaves
Folkething, *s.m.* folkething
Fonctionarisme, *s.m.* functionarism
Fontainerie, *s.f.* fountain-making *or* trade; cistern-making *or* trade
Fortuité, *s.f* fortuitousness, fortuity
Fosse, *s.f.* — *commune,* common grave. *Être mis dans la — commune,* to be buried by the parish, to have a pauper's funeral
†**Fouaillée,** *s.f. V.* **Fessée**
†**Fouilleuse, Fouillouse,** *s.f.* (*slang*) purse
Foulée, *s.f.* (*in horse-racing*) stride
Four, *s.m.* — *de campagne,* salamander
Fourbissage, *s.m. V.* **Fourbissement**
Fournache, *s.f.* weeds (*burnt in the fields*)
Fous (Je), I put, I throw, I chuck, I pitch; &c. (*V.* **Foutre,** *v.a n.*) ["*Je — le saint-siège au feu,*" **Béranger,** *Chansons,* "*Le fils du pape*"]
Fracasse (le capitaine), *s.m.* Bombastes
Fraisage, *s.m.* (*tech.*) countersinking
Fraiseuse, *s.f.* wimble, drill, countersink (*tool*)
Fraisure, *s.f.* countersink
Frelatation, *s.f. V.* **Frelatage**
Fromag-er, ère, *adj.* of cheese, cheese
Fructiculteur, *s.m.* fructiculturist, fruit-grower
Fructiculture, *s.f.* fructiculture, fruit-culture
†**Fusillement,** *s.m.* shooting
Futilement, *adv.* futilely

G

†**Gailleterie, Gaillette,** *s.f.,* **Gailletin,** *s.m.,* **Galiette,** *s.f.* cobbles, knubbly coals
Gallium, *s.m.* (*chem.*) gallium
Galvaudeux, *s.m.* jobbing porter
Garderie, *s.f.* infant-home
Garniture, *s.f.* — *de rideau,* valance. — *de toilette,* toilet set; toilet ware
Gâteuse, *s.f.* ulster (*garment*)
Gavée, *s.f* (*pop.*) guttle, blow-out
Gavroche, *s.m.* street Arab
Gazi-er, ère, *adj.* of gas, gas
Gécarcin, *s.m.* (*zool.*) land-crab
Gemmage, *s.m.* tapping (*of trees*)
Gemmeur, *s.m.* tapper (*of trees*)
Génial, e, *adj.* genial
Génialement, *adv.* genially
Génialité, *s.f.* geniality
Génie, *s.m.* *Garde du* —, barrack-master
Germanisation, *s.f.* germanization
Gibus, *s.m.* opera-hat
Gicler, *v.a.n.* (*old, pop.*) to spirt, to splash
Gig, *s.m.* gig
Girafeau, *s.m.* young giraffe
Girouetter, *v.n.* to chop round (like a weather-cock)
Glaciériste. *V.* **Glaciairiste**
Gladiatorial, e, *adj. V.* **Gladiatoire**
Glander (Se), *v.r.* (*vet.*) to become glandered
Global, e, *adj.* lump
Globalement, *adv.* in the lump; bodily
Glorifica-teur, trice, *s.m.f.* glorifier
Gommeu-r, se, *s.m.f.* gummer
Gommeux, *s.m. V.* **Gandin**
Gonichon, *s.m.* cap (*of a sugar-loaf*)
Goudronnier, *s.m.* tar-maker
Goudronnière, *s.f.* tar-pit
Grain, *s.m.* *Veiller au —, Avoir l'œil au* —, to look after o.'s interest *or* business, to have an eye to business
Graisin, *s.m. V.* **Casson**
Grandiloquence, *s.f.* grandiloquence
Gravette, *s.f.* native oyster, native
Gravidité, *s.f.* gravidity
Gravimétr-ie, -ique. *V.* page 3, § 1
Greffage, *s.m.* grafting
Greffon, *s.m.* (*hort.*) cutting, slip
Grégal, *s.m.* gregal (*north-west wind in the Mediterranean*)
Grêlasse, *s.f.* large hail

†**Grésillons,** *s.m.pl.* broken *or* pounded glass, cullet; cobbles, knubbly coals
Gréviste, *s.m.* striker; — *adj.* striking
Griffu, e, *adj.* clawed
†**Grillagerie,** *s.f.* wire-working [roaster
†**Grilleu-r, se,** *s.m.f.* griller, broiler, toaster,
Grisollement, *s.m.* carolling, chirping, warbling
†**Groisillons,** *s.m.pl.* *V.* **Grésillons**
Grugeoire, *s.f.* teeth, grinders
Guaner, *v.a.* (*agr.*) to manure with guano
Guelte, *s.f.* (*com.*) commission (*to shopmen*)
Gueulard, *s.m.* gully, gully-hole
†**Guillot,** *s.m.* (*obsolete*) *V.* **Guillemot**
Gynérion, Gynerium (— *argenteum*), *s.m.* (*bot.*) pampas-grass

H

'**Hale,** *s.m.* (*nav.*) tow-line
'**Halibut,** *s.m.* (*fish*) halibut [of cockchafers
'**Hannetonnage,** *s.m.* clearing *or* destruction
'**Hannetonner,** *v.a.* to clear of cockchafers
'**Hantement,** *s.m.* *V.* **Hantise**
'**Hardi-er, ère,** *s.m.f.* (*obsolete, local*) herdsman, shepherd, shepherdess; wardrobe-keeper
'**Harengueux,** *s.m.* herring-boat
'**Haut-le-cœur,** *s.m.* *V.* **Haut-le-corps**
'**Hawaiien, ne,** *s. adj.* Hawaiian
Hayon, *s.m.* *V.* **Ayon**
Heure, *s.f.* — *militaire,* punctually, sharp
Hiérat-ique, -iquement. *V.* page 3, § 1
Hiéroglyph-ique,-isme,-iste. *V.* page 3, § 1
Himalayen, ne, *adj.* Himalayan
Hindouisme, *s.m.* Hindooism, Hinduism
Hindoustaniste, *s.m.* Hindustani scholar, Hindustanist
Historicité, *s.f.* historicity, historicalness
Historien, *s.m.* historical painter
Homme, *s.m.* — *de l'art,* *V.* **Art**
Hommelet, *s.m.* manikin, bit of a man; milksop, poor stick [making
Horlog-er, ère, *adj.* of clocks, clock, clock-
Hospitalisé, e, *adj.* admitted in the (*or* an)
'**Houblonnage,** *s.m.* hopping [hospital
'**Houblonni-er, ère,** *adj.* hop-growing, hop
Huilerie, *s.f.* oil-trade
Huîtrée, *adj.f.* (*of an oyster*) in its shell
'**Hussitisme,** *s.m.* (*eccl. hist.*) Hussitism
Hydrant, Hydrante, *s.m.* hydrant
Hydrauliste, *s.m.* *V.* **Hydraulicien**

I

‡**Ichthyomorphe,** *adj.* ichthyomorphous
Ignifère, *adj.* igniferous
Illisibilité, *s.f.* illegibility, illegibleness
Imbâti, e, *adj.* unbuilt; unbuilt on
Immaniable, *adj.* unmanageable
Immigré, e, *s.m.f.* immigrant
Imparlementaire, *adj.* unparliamentary
Impassable, *adj.* impassable
Impleuré, e, *adj.* unwept
Impoétique, *adj.* unpoetical
Impoétiquement, *adv.* unpoetically
Imprécision, *s.f.* imprecision
Imprimeuse, *s.f.* printing-machine
Improvoqué, e, *adj.* unprovoked
Inaccentué, e, *adj.* unaccented
Inacceptation, *s.f.* non-acceptance
Inadvertant, e, *adj.* inadvertent
Inaliénablement, *adv.* inalienably
Inappris, e, *adj.* untaught
Incensurable, *adj.* incensurable
Incomestible, *adj.* inedible, uneatable
Incommensurablement, *adv.* incommensurably [concilableness
Inconciliabilité, *s.f.* irreconcilability, irre-
Inconquérable, *adj.* unconquerable
Inconsciemment, *adv.* unconsciously
Inconsidérable, *adj.* inconsiderable
Indécouvert, e, *adj.* undiscovered
Indécouvrable, *adj.* undiscoverable
†**Indéraillable,** *adj.* not liable to run off the
Indicatoire, *adj.* indicatory [rails
Indiennerie, *s.f.* calico-printing, cotton-printing; printed calico *or* cotton stuffs, prints; ditto business *or* trade
Inéclairé, e, *adj.* unenlightened
Inécrit, e, *adj.* unwritten
Inégalé, e, *adj.* unequalled [evadible
Inéludable, *adj.* ineludible, inevasible, in-
Inensemencé, e, *adj.* unsowed, unsown
Inescomptable, *adj.* undiscountable
Inexaminable, *adj.* unexaminable
Infantile, *adj.* infantile [— *adj.* infecting
Infec-teur, trice, *s.m.f.* infector, infectress;
Infermenté, e, *adj.* unfermented
Infinitésimalement, *adv.* infinitesimally
Infumable, *adj.* unsmokable
Injuridique, *adj.* injuridical, injudicial
Injuridiquement, *adv.* injuridically, injudi-
Innerver, *v.a.* to innervate, to innerve [cially
Innutriti-f, ve, *adj.* innutritious
Inopérant, e, *adj.* inoperative
Inoublié, e, *adj.* unforgotten
Inrenversable, *adj.* not to be overturned, not liable to be overturned
Insatisfait, e, *adj.* unsatisfied [suspicion
Insoupçonnable, *adj.* unsuspectable, above
Inspectorat, *s.m.* inspectorship; surveyorship
Interjacent, e, *adj.* interjacent
Interminablement, *adv.* interminably
Internationalité, *s.f.* internationality
Interpolaire, *adj.* (*phys.*) interpolary
Intransférable, *adj.* untransferable
Inviteu-r, se, *s.m.f.* inviter
Iridier, *v.a.* (*chem.*) to iridize [reconcilableness
Irréconciliabilité, *s.f.* irreconcilability, ir-
Irréformé, e, *adj.* unreformed
Irréméable, *adj.* irremeable
Irréméablement, *adv.* irremeably
Itinérant, e, *adj.* itinerant

J

Jennérien, ne, *adj.* Jennerian
Jeune, *adj.* *Un — homme,* a young man. *Un homme —,* a man still young
Jointement, *s.m.* jointing
Jointer, *v.a.* to joint
Jonc, *s.m.* cane
Journalier, *s.m.* diary
Jumelage, *s.m.* coupling, joining

K

Kanat, Khanat, *s.m.* khanate
Khédive, *s.m.* khedive (*viceroy of Egypt*)

L

Laboureuse, *s.f.* steam-plough
Laïcat, *s.m.* laics
Laïcité, *s.f.* laicality
Laissez-passer, *s.m.* pass; exeat; permit for
Laïus, *s.m.* (*slang*) speech [transit
Lamperie, *s.f.* *V.* **Lampisterie**
Lampris, *s.m.* (*fish*) opah, king-fish
Lapidairerie, *s.f.* lapidary's work *or* trade *or*
Lapinière, *s.f.* rabbitry [business
Laqueur, *s.m.* lacquerer; japanner
Larronner, *v.n.* to steal; to rob
Larronnerie, *s.f.* stealing; robbing
Lasiocampe, *s.f.* eggar moth
Lasser, *v.a.* to lasso [*ranean*)
Lébèche, *s.m.* south-west wind (*in the Mediter-*
Lénité, *s.f.* lenity, leniency
Lépidope, *s.m.* garter-fish

Lévigateur, *s.m.* levigator
Libyque, *adj.* *V.* **Libyen**
†**Lignard,** *s m.* (*pop.*) soldier of the line
†**Ligneur,** *s.m.* line-fishing boat; — *adj. m.* line-fishing [**phie,** &c.
‡**Lithochromie,** &c. *V.* **Chromolithogra-**
Lithofracteur, *s.m.* lithofracteur
Livrer (Se), *v.r.* (*com.*) to receive (*goods*)
Livreur, *s.m.* *V.* **Livrancier**
Longe, *s.f.* (*nav.*) long-boat
Louchettes, *s.f. pl.* goggles
Lubrifaction, *s.f.* *V.* **Lubrification**
Lustrerie, *s.f.* lustre-making, chandelier-making (*or* manufactory)

M

Macéra-teur, trice, *adj.* macerating
Madrigaliste, *s.m.f.* madrigalist
Magellanique, *adj.* (*geog.*) Magellanic. *Nuées —s,* (*astr.*) Magellanic clouds
Maigrichon, ne, *adj. s.* *V.* **Maigrelet**
Main, *s.f.* *Forcer la — à,* to force the hand of (*or* ...'s hand) [declare of full age
Majorer, *v.a.* to overvalue; to increase; to
Maladministration, *s.f.* maladministration
Malayen, ne, *adj. s.* *V.* **Malai**
Malchanceu-x, se, *adj.* unlucky
Mâlement, *adv.* manfully
Malterie, *s.f.* malt-house
Malthusianisme, *s.m.* Malthusianism
Maniabilité, *s.f.* manageableness, handiness
Maréchal, *s.m.* (*zool.*) *V.* **Taupin**
Maringote, *s.f.* (kind of carriage)
Mariniste, *s.m.f.* marine painter *or* paintress
Marlin, *s.m.* (*nav.*) *V.* **Merlin**
Marnois, *s.m.* *V.* **Marnais**
Marquage, *s.m.* marking
Martello, *s.m.* martello tower
Martine, *s.f.* doe rabbit
Martyrolog-ique, -iste. *V.* page 3, § 1
Mastroquet, *s.m.* (*pop.*) wine-shop keeper, [publican
Matériel, *s.m.* material
Mécénien, ne, *adj.* Mæcenian
Méchage, *s.m.* smoking (*a cask*) with brimstone, sulphuring, matching, stumming
Médicalement, *adv.* medically
Médico-légal, e, *adj.* medico-legal, of medical jurisprudence, of forensic medicine
Médiéval, e, *adj.* mediæval
Mélasser, *v.a.* to treacle
Mélodramatiser, *v.a.* to melodramatize
Mercenarité, *s.f.* mercenariness
Mercurifère, *adj.* mercuriferous
Méthodolog-ique, -iste. *V.* page 3, § 1
Métisation, *s.f.* *V.* **Métissage**
Métisser, *v.a.* (*of animals*) to cross
Meurt-de-soif, *s.m.* (*pop.*) drunkard
Microbe, *s.m.* micro-organism, bacillus (*pl.* [bacilli)
Mikado, *s.m.* mikado (*of Japan*)
Milieu, *s.m.* centre-piece. *— de table,* epergne
Mireu-r, se, *s.m.f.* *— d'œufs,* egg-candler
Mirobolé, e, *adj.* (*pop.*) wonder-struck, [astounded, amazed
Miser, *v.a.* to stake
Missile, *s.m.* (*obsolete*) missile
Moha, *s.m.* (*bot.*) moha, German millet
Môle, *s.m.* (*fish*) *V.* **Poisson-lune**
Molesquine. *V.* **Moleskin**
Monasticité, *s.f.* monasticism
Monétairement, *adv.* monetarily
Monobasique, *adj.* (*chem.*) monobasic
Monolithisme, *s.m.* monolithism
Monologuer, *v.n.* to monologize, to soliloquize
Monologueu-r, se, *s m.f.* monologist
Monopolisa-teur, trice, *s.m.f.* *V.* **Mono-**
Monotonement, *adv.* monotonously [**poleur**
Montdore, *s.m.* Montdore cheese
Monte-charge, *s.m.* lift [*d'affaires*
Monteur, *s.m.* *— d'affaires,* *V.* **Lanceur**
Moriforme, *adj.* moriform, mulberry-shaped
Mouche, *s.f.* river steam-boat
Mouli-er, ère, *adj.* of mussels, mussel
Moustiquière, *s.f.* *V.* **Moustiquaire**
Muette (A la), *adv.* without saying anything, silently, quietly
Municipalisme. *V.* page 3, § 1
Mureu-x, se, *adj.* of *or* for walls, wall
Murrhe, *s.f.* (*min.*) murrha
Muserie, *s.f.* loitering, &c. (*V.* **Muser)**
Mustang, *s.m.* (*zool.*) mustang

N

Naniser, *v.a.* (*hort.*) to dwarf
Narcose, *s.f.* narcosis
Natte, *s.f.* *— de Chine,* Indian matting
Naufrageu-x, se, *adj.* wreckful, wrecky
Néo-celtique, *adj.* of Celtic origin
Népalais, e, *adj. s.* Nepaulese
Nerf, *s.m.* *Donner sur les —s,* to act on the nerves; to irritate; to provoke; to plague; to tease; to annoy
Nickeler, Nickeliser, *v.a.* to nickelize
Nicobar, Nicombar, *s.m.* Nicobar pigeon
Nidifier, *v.n.* to build its nest, to nidificate
Ninivite, *adj.* Ninevite [habitant of Nevers
Nivernais, e, *adj. s.* of Nevers; native *or* in-
Noci-f, ve, *adj.* (*med.*) noxious, hurtful, injurious
Nocivité, *s.f.* noxiousness, hurtfulness, in-
Noctilion, *s m.* noctilio (*bat*) [juriousness
Nom, *s.m.* *Petit — d'amitié,* pet name
Nomadiser, *v.n.* to nomadize
Nomadisme, *s.m.* nomadism
Norrain, e, *adj.* Norwegian [solicitor's wife
Notaresse, Notairesse, *s.f.* notary's *or*
Numérotation, *s.f.* *V.* **Numérotage**
Numide, *s.m.f. adj.,* **Numidique,** *adj.* Numidian

O

Oblivieu-x, se, *adj.* (*old, poet.*) oblivious
Odontite, *s.f.* (*med.*) odontitis
Odynère, *s.m.* (*zool.*) odynerus, mason-wasp
Œil, *s.m.* *Faire les yeux blancs,* to turn up o.'s
Œufrerie, *s.f.* egg-warehouse [eye-balls
Oiseau-cloche, *s.m.* bell-bird
Omnivorité, *s.f.* omnivorousness
Onglier, *s.m.* nail-dressing case
Opportun-isme, -iste. *V.* page 3, § 1
Oratrice, *s.f.* oratress, speaker
Ord, e, *adj.* gross. *Poids —,* gross weight
Ores, Ors, *adv.* *D'— et déjà,* (*old*) henceforth, [thenceforth
Ornithique, *adj.* ornithic
Orthophon-ie, -ique, -iquement. *V.* p. 3, § 1
Osséine, *s.f.* (*chem.*) osseine, osteine
Ostéologue, *s.m.* osteologist
Oudenarde, *s.f.* Oudenarde tapestry *or* carpet
Oût. *V.* **Août**
Outremonts (D'), *adj. adv.* ultramontane
Ovibos, *s.m.* musk-ox [the ewe
Ovicapre, *s.m.* cross between the he-goat and
Ovidien, ne, *adj.* Ovidian
Ovipositeur, *s.m.* (*of insects*) *V.* **Pondoir**
Oxyhydrique, *adj.* (*chem.*) oxyhydric

P

Pairer, *v.n.* (*parliam.*) to pair off
Paissance, *s.f.* grazing
Palestinien, ne, *adj.* Palestinean
Palière, *adj. f.* *Porte —,* door of the landing
Palustre, *adj.* *V.* **Paludéen**
Panasserie, *s.f.* rolls (*of bread*)
Panégyriser, *v.a.* to panegyrize
Panne, *s.f.* pantile
Paraître, *v.n.* *Vient de —,* (*of books*) just published, just out. *Sans que ça paraisse,* though it does (*or* may) not look like it

Paralléliser, *v.a.* to parallel
Parère, *s.m.* (*commercial*) regulation *or* policy; (*med.*) report
Parfiler, *v.a.* to fillet
Pariage, *s.m.* (*feud. law*) parage
Pariétaire, *adj.* of walls, wall, parietal, mural
Parisianiser, *v.a.* to parisianize. *Se* —, to become *or* be parisianized, to become parisian
Parquement, *s.m.* *V.* **Parcage**
Parsisme, *s.m.* Parseeism
Passe-pomme, *s.f.* (*apple*) jenneting
Passet, *s.m.* butter-basket, flat
Pastelliste, *s.m.f.* pastellist
†**Pastillage,** *s.m.* sugar-paste working
†**Pastilleur,** *s.m.* sugar-paste worker
Patachier, *s.m.* stage-waggon *or* coach driver *or* proprietor
Pécan, *s.m.* *V.* **Pékan**
Pêcheraie, *s.f.* peach-orchard
Pelattage, *s.m.* *V.* **Dépilage**
Pelleteur, *s.m.* (*pers.*) shoveller
Peloton, *s.m.* racers (*men and horses running a race*)
Pelotonnement, *s.m.* winding, &c. (*V.* **Pelotonner**)
Pelvan, *s.m.* standing stone
Pénalement, *adv.* penally
Pendule, *s.f.* — *de voyage,* carriage clock
Penne, *s.f.* feather; beam-feather
Pensivité, *s.f.* thoughtfulness, pensiveness
Perceptrice, *s.f.* collector's wife
Percolateur, *s.m.* percolator
Périodique, *s.m.* periodical
†**Perpignan,** *s.m.* whip-handle
Perquisitionner, *v.a.* to search
Persépolitain, e, *adj. s.* Persepolitan
Persuasivement, *adv.* persuasively
Pesable, *adj.* weighable
Pétroler, *v.a.* to set fire to (...) by means of petroleum
Pétroleu-r, se, *s.m.f.* incendiary by means of petroleum
Petun, *s.m.* (*obsolete*) tobacco; snuff
Phonoscope, *s.m.* phonoscope
Phonoscop-ie,-ique, &c. *V.* page 3, § 1
Photogravure, *s.f.* photoengraving
Photolithographier, *v.a.* to photolithograph
Phyllie, *s.f.* (*zool.*) phyllium, leaf-insect, walking-leaf
Phylloxéra, *s.m.* (*zool.*) phylloxera
Phylloxère, *adj.* of the phylloxera
Phylloxéré, e, *adj.* phylloxerated
Phylloxérien, ne, *adj.* phylloxerian
Phylloxérique, *adj.* phylloxeric
Physcie, *s.f.* (*bot.*) Iceland moss
‡**Picholin,** *s.m.* picholin-tree (*olive-tree*)
Piconnier *s.m.* *V.* **Piquonnier**
Picte, *s.m.* Pict
Pictural, e, *adj.* pictorial, pictural
Pied, *s.m.* — *courant,* foot run. *Perdre* —, to be carried off o.'s legs
Pierre, *s.f.* — *levée,* standing stone
Pigeonni-er, ère, *adj.* of pigeons, pigeon
Pinaie, Pinatelle, Pinède, Pinée, Pineraie, *s.f.* *V.* **Pinière**
Piottement, *s.m.* chirping, chirp, chirrup
Piotter, *v.n.* to chirp
Piquage, *s.m.* — *d'once,* breach of trust, robbing o.'s employer, embezzlement. — *de fût,* sucking the monkey
Pique, *s.m.f.* — **-chiffe, -poux,** *s.m.* snip (*tailor*)
Piqueture, *s.f.* mark, spot, dot, point
Piquonnier, *s.m.* dealer in refuse wool
Piscatorial, e, *adj.* piscatorial
Pitch-pin, *s.m.* (*an anglicism*) pitch-pine
Plafonnement, *s.m.* *V.* **Plafonnage**
Planétoïde, *s.m.* planetoid
Planitude, *s.f.* planeness
Plaquemine, *s.f.* date-plum (*fruit*)
Platiniser, *v.a.* to platinize
Plébiscitaire, *adj.s.* plebiscitary, plebiscitarian
Plombeu-x, se, *adj.* leady, leaden; lead
Plumier, *s.m.* pen-case
Pluviométr-ie, -ique, &c. *V.* page 3, § 1
Poids, *s.m.* — *médicinal,* apothecaries' weight
†**Poigne,** *s.f.* *A* —, high-handed
†**Pointille,** *s.f.* *V.* **Pointillerie**
Politicien, *s.m.* politician
Polybasique, *adj.* (*chem.*) polybasic
Pommier, *adj. m.* *Bateau* —, apple-boat
Pondérosité, *s.f.* ponderosity
Pontage, *s.m.* pontage; bridge-building
Pontifier, *v.a.n.* to celebrate *or* officiate pontifically
Portabilité. *V.* page 3, § 1
Porte, *s.f.* *Prendre la* —, to go out, to leave the room
Porte-bouteille, *s.m.* bottle-stand, decanter-stand
Porte-parole, *s.m.* spokesman
Porte-veine, *s.m.* bringer of good luck
Portionner, *v.a.* to portion, to apportion
Portland, *s.m.* Portland cement
Poses plastiques, *s.f.pl.* statuesque attitudes
Posthumement, *adv.* posthumously
Postier, *s.m.* post-horse
Post-méridien, ne, *adj.* postmeridian
Pouponnière, *s.f.* baby-room
Pourcentage, *s.m.* percentage
Pourtourner, *v.a.* to encompass, to enclose, to surround
Préavis, *s.m.* forewarning; preadvice
Préavertir, *v.a.* to forewarn
Préaviser, *v.a.* to preadvise
Précautionneusement, *adv.* cautiously, carefully
†**Prêchailler,** *v.n.* to preach tamely; to preach away
Prêcherie, *s.f.* lecture, jobation
Préélire, *v.a.* to preelect
Préjudicier, *v.a.* to wrong, to defraud
Prélater, *v.a.* to cover with tarpaulin
Prématurer, *v.a.* to make premature, to premature
Prémentionné, e, *adj.* *V.* **Susmentionné**
Prépondérer, *v.n.* to preponderate
Prépositionnel, le, *adj.* prepositional
Préraphaélisme, Préraphaélitisme, *s.m.* pre-Raphaelism
Préraphaélite, *adj. s.* pre-Raphaelite
Prescriptibilité. *V.* page 3, § 1
†**Présignifier,** *v.a.* to presignify
Presse-citrons, *s.m.* lemon-squeezer
Presse-étoupe, *s.m.* (*tech.*) stuffing-box
Primage, *s.m.* premium-giving
Primeuriste, *s.m.* grower of early fruits *or* vegetables *or* flowers
Priorité, *s.f.* *Action de* —, preference share
Privatoire, *adj.* privatory
Proa, *s.m.f.* *V.* **Prao**
Procentuel, le, *adj.* of percentage, percentage, per cent
Processionner, *v.n.* to walk in procession
Procurable, *adj.* procurable
Promenette, *s.f.* go-cart
Promeneuse, *s.f.* flat candlestick
Protesta-teur, trice, *s.m.f.* protester
Ptolémaïque, *adj.* *V.* **Ptoléméen**
Publiable, *adj.* publishable
Pugilistique, *adj.* pugilistic
Puits, *s.m.* — *pleureur,* surface well
Purgeu-r, se, *s.m f.* purger; cleaner; cleanser

Q

Quadrans, Quadrant, *s.m.* quadrant
***Quadrimestre,** *s.m.* space of four months, four months, third of a year
Quartenier, Quartinier, *s.m.* (*old*) district police officer
Quessoy, *s.m.* quessoy (*kind of pear*)
§**Quindécennal, e,** *adj.* quindecennial, of fifteen years
Quinzenaire, *adj.* of fifteen years

R

Rabassaire, Rabassier, *s.m.* truffle-digger
Rabé, e, *adj.* hard-roed
Racineur, *s.m.* root-figurer
Radicicole, *adj.* living on roots
Raidissement, *s.m.* stiffening; tightening; resistance
Râle, *s.m.* — *de genêts,* (*bird*) corn-crake
Ramasse-miettes, *s.m.* crumb-brush; crumb-tray
†**Ramillon,** *s.m.* twig

Rapinade, *s.f.* daub [right
Rarranger, *v.a.* to rearrange. *Se —*, to come
Rasage, *s.m.* *V.* **Rasement**
Rassainir, *v.a.* *Same as* **Assainir;** *also means* **Assainir de nouveau,** to . . . (*V.* **Assainir**) [again
Rat, *s.m.* niggard; — *adj.* niggardly
Râtelures, *s.f.pl.* rakings
Rationaliser, *v.a.* to rationalize
Rationnaire, *s.m.* ration man
Rationnement, *s.m.* rationing, allowancing; rations, allowances [*paper*); rifling
Rayage, *s.m.* striking off *or* out; ruling (*of*
Rebuffer, *v.a.* to rebuff
Récalcitrance, *s.f.* recalcitration
Recapturer, *v.a.* to recapture
Recauser, *v.n.* to talk again
Réclameu-r, se, *s.m.f.* *V.* **Réclamateur**
Recomparaître, *v.n.* to appear again
Reconcourir, *v.n.* to . . . (*V.* **Concourir**) again
Reconsacrer, *v.a.* to . . . (*V.* **Consacrer**) again
Recouvrage, *s.m.* recovering, covering again
Récursoirement, *adv.* (*law*) remedially
Rediscuter, *v.a.* to . . . (*V.* **Discuter**) again
Redoublant, e, *s.m.f.* (*at school*) unpromoted boy *or* girl, backward boy *or* girl
Redoubler, *v.n.* (*at school*) to remain two years in the same class [**boîter, Remparer,** &c.
Réemboîter, Réemparer, &c. *V.* **Rem-**
Réemption, *s.f.* buying in
Réformatoire, *adj.* reformatory
Réfractomètre, *s.m.* (*phys.*) refractometer
Réglementarisme, *s.m.* reglementarism
Rehaussage, *s.m.* (*paint., engr.*) setting off
Réincarcérer, *v.a.* to reincarcerate
Relai, *s.m.* *Titre de —*, fresh title-page (*to an old edition*)
Relaxe, *s.f.* (*law*) giving up of prosecution
Relève, *s.f.* relieving
Relever, *v.n.* (*nav.*) to set off, to depart
Religioniste, *s.m.f.* religionist
Remiseur, *s.m.* job-master
Renardi-er, ère, *adj.* of foxes, fox
Rentrer, *v.n.* to shrink, to contract
Répandage, *s.m.* spreading, scattering
Reparcourir, *v.a.* to . . . (*V.* **Parcourir**) again
Repêche, *s.f.* *V.* **Repêchage**
Répétible, *adj.* (*law*) repeatable, demandable again [teacher
Répétitrice, *s.f.* tutress; governess; private
Réplique, *s.f.* replica
Repousse, *s.f.* fresh growth
Repuiser, *v.a.* to . . . (*V.* **Puiser**) again
Réquisitionnement, *s.m.* requisitioning
Réquisitionner, *v.a.* to requisition
Réserviste, *s.m.* (*mil.*) reservist, reserve-man
Ressence, *s.f.* soap-paste
Ressuscitable, *adj.* resuscitable, revivable
Ressuyage, *s.m.* wiping again; drying
Retoquer, *v.a.* to pluck (*at an exam.*)
Retransférer, Retransplanter, &c. to . . . *V.* **Transférer, Transplanter,** &c.) again
Réum, *s.m.* (*nav.*) capacity; space
†**Réveillonner,** *v.n.* to keep up Christmas eve
Reversoir, *s.m.* dam, weir
Rêveusement, *adv.* thoughtfully, pensively
Revif, *s.m.* revival; return
Révisioniste, *adj.* revisionary, revisory
Révocablement, *adv.* revocably
Rhétoriquement, *adv.* rhetorically
Rhodanthe, *s.f.* (*bot.*) rhodanthus
†**Rimaillerie,** *s.f.* *V.* **Rimaille**
Rivetage, *s.m.* rivetting
Riveter, *v.a.* to rivet
Rizi-er, ère, *adj.* of rice, rice
Robage, *s.m.* (*of cigars*) wrapping
Ronchonner, *v.n.* (*pop.*) to grumble
Roncier, *s.m.*, **Roncière,** *s.f.* *V.* **Ronceraie**
Rongerie, *s.f.* (*fam.*) bone to pick [of roses
Rose, *s.f.* (*fig.*) pleasantness, pleasure, a bed
Roublard, *s.m.* cunning fellow, stager
Rupelle, *s.f.* (*bot.*) ruppia
Russifier, *v.a.* to Russify

S

Sablage, *s.m.* gravelling; sanding
Sablier, *s.m.* sand-dredger [wooden shoes
Saboterie, *s.f.* manufacture *or* manufactory of
Sacerdotalisme, *s.m.* sacerdotalism
Saharien, ne, *adj.* Saharian, of Sahara
Salineur, *s.m.* salt-maker [maker; salt-seller
Salini-er, ère, *adj.* salt-making; — *s.m.* salt-
Salopette, *s.f.* (*garment*) slop; overalls
Sapineau, *s.m.* young fir-tree
Sarge, Sargue, *s.m.* (*fish*) sheep's-head
Sataniquement, *adv.* satanically
Sati, *s.f.* *V.* **Suttee**
Satinette, *s.f.* satinet
Saupoudrage, *s.m.* *V.* **Saupoudration**
Saupoudroir, *s.m.* *V.* **Saupoudreur**
Saute-à-l'œil, *s.m.* show, mere show, dash
Savanterie, *s.f.* pedantry
Schénanthe, *s.m.* (*bot.*) lemon-grass
‡**Schiedam,** *s.m.* schiedam
Scoticisme, *s.m.* scotticism
Sécéder, *v.n.* to secede
Secouage, *s.m.* *V.* **Secouement**
Séductible, *adj.* seducible [half-year
Semestriellement, *adv.* half-yearly, every
Sémitiste, *s.m.* Shemitist, Semitist
Séniorat, *s.m.* seniority
Sennal, *s.m.* *V.* **Anabas**
Septennat, *s.m.* septennate
Séricole, &c. *V.* **Séricicole,** &c.
Sériel, le, *adj.* *V.* **Sérial**
Sérigène, *adj.* serigenous, silk-producing
Serre-bois, *s.m.* wood-house *or* shed *or* hole
Siester, *v.n.* to take o 's siesta
Silphion, *s.m.* (*bot.*) silphium, compass-plant
†**Singe-araignée,** *s.m.* *V.* **Atèle**
Sion, *m.* Zion
Slavisme, *s.m.* Slavism
Smack, *s.m.* (*nav.*) smack
Socrat-ique, -iquement. *V.* **page 3, § 1**
Sodalité, *s.f.* sodality
Soia, *s.m.* *V.* **Soui**
Somno, *s.m.* bedroom locker
Sophocléen, ne, *adj.* Sophoclean
Sorcier, *s.m.* (*toy*) automaton tumbler, tumbler
Sorte, *s.f.* *En —*, (*com.*) whole
Soubise, *s.f.* onion-sauce
Soucieusement, *adv.* solicitously, anxiously
Soufflet, *s.m.* (*in clothes*) inlay
Sourate, *s.f.* *V.* **Surate**
Souricier, *s.m.* mouser
Sourieu-r, se, *s.m.f.* smiler
Sournoiserie, *s.f.* sliness, cunning; sneakingness, sneakiness; sly *or* cunning trick
Sous, *prep.* — **-chef** *de gare, s.m.* (*rail.*) train-starter. — **-cortical, e,** *adj.* subcortical. — **-nappe,** *s.f.* under table-cloth
Spruce, *s.m.* (*bot.*) spruce
***Squatter,** *s.m.* squatter
Sr., (*abbreviation of* "successeur")
Stéariner, *v.a.* to stearinate
Stepper, *v.n.* to step high
Stolon, *s.m.* (*bot.*) creeping stalk runner
Stylographe, *s.m.* stylograph
Subsidier, *v.a.* to subsidize
Subtropical, e, *adj.* subtropical
Subversivement, *adv.* subversively
Sucrage, *s.m* sugaring
Suggesti-f, ve, *adj.* suggestive
Sulfide, *s.m.* *V.* **Sulfure**
Sulfurisation, *s.f.* *V.* **Sulfuration**
Suréminence, *s.f.* supereminence
Surépaisseur, *s.f.* extra thickness
Suro, *s.m.* *V.* **Surier**
Suroffre, *s.f.* higher offer *or* tender *or* proposal *or* bidding [**Remise,** *s.f.*)
Surremise, *s.f.* extra allowance *or* &c. (*V.*
Susurrement, *s.m.* *V.* **Susurration**
Syllabus, *s.m.* (*eccl.*) syllabus

T

Tachymétr-ie, -ique, &c., tachometry, &c.

Tangiblement, *adv.* tangibly

Tant, *adv.* — *mieux*, I am glad of it. — *pis*, I am sorry for it

Tapageusement, *adv.* noisily, riotously, &c. (*V.* **Tapageur,** *adj.*)

Tape-à-l'œil, *s.m. V.* **Saute-à-l'œil**

Téléphone, *s.m.* telephone

Téléphoner, *v.a.* to telephone

Tempérament, *s.m.* *A* —, on the terms of payment by small instalments

Théi-er, ère, *adj.* of tea, tea

Thème, *s.m.* (*gram.*) base, stem, crude form

Thérapeutiquement, *adv.* therapeutically

Tirable, *adj.* drawable

Tire-bouchonné, e, *adj.* corkscrew-like; in ringlets

Tomaison, *s.f.* dividing into volumes

Topette, *s.f.* phial

Tordeuse, *s.f.* (*zool.*) roller moth

†Torpilleur, *s.m. adj.* *Bateau* —, torpedo-boat

Tournade, *s.f. V.* **Tornado**

Tourne-soc, *s.m. V.* **Tourne-oreille**

Tournière, *s.f. V.* **Chaintre**

Tram, *s.m.* tram, tramway

Transformable, *adj.* transformable

Transforma-teur, trice, *adj. s.* transforming; transformer

Transméditerranéen, ne, *adj.* transmediterranean

†Treillagiste, *s.m. V.* **Treillageur**

Trépider, *v.n.* to trepidate

Tricotée, *s.f.* cudgelling, hiding, drubbing

Tridacne, *s.f. V.* **Bénitier** *and* **Tuilée**

Truculence, *s.f.* truculence, truculency

Truculemment, *adv.* truculently

Trufficulteur, *s.m.* truffle-grower

Trufficulture, *s.f.* truffle-growing

Turbané, e, *adj.* turbaned

Turbit, *s.m.* turbit

Tweed, *s.m.* tweed

U

Ubéreu-x, se, *adj.* uberous

Ulster, *s.m.* ulster

Umbo, *s.m. V.* **Ombon**

Undécennal, e, *adj.* undecennial

Universalisation, *s.f.* universalization

V

Vacoa, *s.m. V.* **Vaquois**

†Vanillerie, Vanillière, *s.f.* vanilla-plantation

Vanne, *s.f.* winnowing

Vaticiner, *v.n.a.* to vaticinate

Végétarianisme, *s.m.* vegetarianism

Végétarien, ne, *s.m.f. adj.* vegetarian

Verdière, *s.f. V.* **Zostère**

Vernière, *s.f. V.* **Aunaie**

Verre, *s.m.* — *trempé* — *incassable*, toughened glass

†Versaillais, e, *adj. s.* Versaillese, of Versailles, native of Versailles

Verveu-x, se, *adj.* fiery; hot; fervid; rapturous; animated; lively; spirited; racy; humorous

Vidanger, *v.a.* to empty

Vider, *v a.* to pick (*pockets*)

Videu-r, se, *s m.f.* — *de poches*, pickpocket

Vitriolage, *s.m.* vitriolating, vitriolizing

Vif-gage, *s.m.* (*law*) living pledge, vivum vadium

Voiturée, *s.f.* carriageful; coachful; cabful; cartful, &c. (*V.* **Voiture**)

Voyoucratie, *s.f.* mobocracy, mob-rule

Z

Zélote, *s.m.f.* zealot

Zoulou, e, *adj. s.* Zulu

ENGLISH AND FRENCH

TABLE OF

ENGLISH COINS, MEASURES AND WEIGHTS,

REDUCED TO FRENCH MONEY, MEASURES AND WEIGHTS.

☞ *FOR AMERICAN MONEY SEE TABLE ON PAGE* 6.

	Pounds.*	Shillings.	Pence.		Feet.		Inches.
	Fr.†	fr. c.†	fr.c.		mètres.		centi-mètres.
1	25	1·25	0·10·4166	1	0·30479449	1	2·539954
2	50	2·50	0·20·8233	2	0·60958898	2	5·079908
3	75	3·75	0·31·2399	3	0·91438348	3	7·619862
4	100	5	0·41·6466	4	1·21917796	4	10·159816
5	125	6·25	0·52·0633	5	1·52397245	5	12·699770
6	150	7·50	0·62·4999	6	1·82876694	6	15·239724
7	175	8·75	0·72·9166	7	2·13356143	7	17·779678
8	200	10	0·33·3333	8	2·43836592	8	20·319632
9	225	11·25	0·93·7498	9	2·74315041	9	22·859586
10	250	12·50	1·04·1666	10	3·0479449	10	25·399540
11	275	13·75	1·14·5833	11	3·3527394	11	27·939494
12	300	15	1·25	12	3·6575338	12	30·479449
13	325	16·25					
14	350	17·50					
15	375	18·75					
16	400	20					
17	425	21·25					
18	450	22·50					
19	475	23·75					

lb.	Avoirdupois, kilogrammes.
1	0·4535926
2	0·9071852
3	1·3607778
4	1·8143704
5	2·2679630
6	2·7215556
7	3·1751482
8	3·6287408
9	4·0823334

THERMOMETER.

Fahrenheit 32° = 0° centigrade and Réaumur.

100° centigrades = 212° Fahrenheit = 80° Réaumur.

Numbers of Fahrenheit — 32 × $\frac{5}{9}$ = centigrades.

Numbers of Fahrenheit — 32 × $\frac{4}{9}$ = Réaumur.

TROY WEIGHT.

Grain	0·064798	grammes.
Penny-weight	1·55517	,,
Ounce	31·1035	,,
Pound	0·373242	kilog.

AVOIRDUPOIS WEIGHT.

Dram	1·7718	grammes.
Ounce	28·3495	,,
Pound	0·4535926	kilog.
Quarter	12·6956	,,
Hundred-weight	50·802	,,
Ton (20 hundred weight)	1016·048	,,

* A pound sterling is worth intrinsically Fr. 25·2079.

† Fr., Francs. C., centimes.

LONG MEASURES.

	mètre.
3 feet *or* 1 yard	0·914383
Fathom (2 yards)	1·8287669
	mètres.
Pole *or* perch (5½ yards)	5·02911
Furlong (220 yards)	201·16437
Mile (1,760 yards)	1609·3149

SUPERFICIAL MEASURES.

	centimètres carrés.
Square inch	6·451366
	mètre carré.
Square foot	0·0929
Square yard	0·836097
	mètres carrés.
Rod	25·291939
	ares.
Rood (1,210 square yards)	10·116775
	hectare.
Acre (4,840 square yards)	0·404671
	kilomètres carrés.
Square mile	2·588881

SOLID MEASURES.

	centimètres cubes.
Cubic inch	16·386176
	mètre cube.
Cubic foot	0·028214
Cubic yard	0·764502

MEASURES OF CAPACITY.

	litres.
Pint	0·5679
Quart	1·1359
Gallon	4·543458
Peck (2 gallons)	9·086916
Bushel (8 gallons)	36·34766
	hectolitres.
Sack (3 bushels)	1·0904
Quarter (8 bushels)	2·90781
Chaldron (12 sacks)	13·08516

ENGLISH-FRENCH.

A, (*first letter of the alphabet*), *s.* a, *m.*; (*mus.*) la, *m.*; (*of numbers*) bis. *Number* 1 *A*, numéro 1 bis. *A* 1, de première classe; (*fig.*) de première qualité, marqué à l'A. *Not to know A from B*, ne savoir ni A ni B.

A, An, *art.* (*when it signifies one*) un, *m.*, une, *f.*; (*speaking of weight or measure, &c., for* or *to* or *in one* ...) le, l', *m.*, la, l', *f.*, les, *m.f.pl.*; (*speaking of time, &c., for* or *to* or *in every* ...) par; (*of mere proportion*) au, à l', *m.*, à la, à l', *f.*, aux, *m.f.pl.* *Eight shillings — yard, — bottle*, dix francs le mètre, la bouteille. *Four shillings — ticket*, cinq francs le billet. *Four pounds — day, — month*, cent francs par jour, par mois. *Half-a-guinea — lesson*, treize francs par leçon. *Five pence — head*, cinquante centimes par tête *or* par personne. *Fifty miles — hour*, quatre-vingts kilomètres à l'heure. *I have — book*, (*one book*) j'ai un livre. *I have not — book*, (*not one*) je n'ai pas un livre; (*any book*) je n'ai pas de livre. *Without — book*, (*without one*) sans un livre; (*without any*) sans livre.

Abaca, *s.* abaca, chanvre de Manille, *m.*

Aback, *adv.* en arrière; par derrière, par surprise, à l'improviste, au dépourvu; (*nav.*) sur le mât, coiffé, masqué. *To take* —, prendre à l'improviste *or* &c.; déconcerter, interdire

Abacus, *s.* abaque, *m.*

Abaft, *prep.* en arrière de, derrière; — *adv.* arrière, à l'arrière, en arrière

Abandon, *v.a.* abandonner; délaisser; quitter; renoncer à; se désister de; (*neglect*) laisser à l'abandon

Abandoned, *adj.* abandonné; perdu de débauche, dissolu. — *wretch*, misérable, *m.f.*

Abandoning, Abandonment, *s.* abandon, *m.*; (*fig.*) laisser-aller, *m.*; (*com. nav.*) délaissement, *m.*

Abase, *v.a.* abaisser; (*degrade*) avilir

Abasement, *s.* abaissement, *m.*; (*degradation*) avilissement, *m.*

Abash, *v.a.* confondre, couvrir de confusion, déconcerter, décontenancer, intimider, interdire

Abashed, *part. adj.* confondu, &c. (*V.* **Abash,** *v.a.*); honteux, confus (de)

Abate, *v.a.* (*lessen*) diminuer, rabattre; amoindrir; réduire; (*bring down, lower, depress*) rabaisser, rabattre; abaisser; abattre; (*weaken*) affaiblir, calmer, apaiser, atténuer; (*remit*) faire remise de; (*remove*) abolir, faire cesser; (*annul*) annuler; — *v.n.* diminuer; se calmer, s'apaiser, tomber, baisser; s'abattre; s'affaiblir; perdre de sa force *or* de son effet; s'amortir; céder; cesser

Abatement, *s.* diminution, *f.*; affaiblissement, *m.*; abaissement, *m.*; abolition, *f.*; annulation, *f.*; cessation, *f.*; (*com.*) remise, réduction, *f.*, rabais, *m.*

Abatis, Abattis, *s.* (*fort.*) abattis *m.*

Abature, *s.* abattures, *f.pl.*

Abbacy, *s.* administration d'une abbaye, *f.*; droits abbatiaux, *m.pl.*; abbaye, *f.*; abbatial, *m.*

Abbatial, Abbatical, *adj.* abbatial

Abbé, *s.* abbé, *m.*

Abbess, *s.* abbesse. *f.*

Abbey, *s.* abbaye, *f.*

Abbot, *s.* supérieur d'abbaye, abbé, *m.*

Abbotship, *s.* fonctions de supérieur d'abbaye, *f.pl.*

Abbreviate, *v.a.* abréger; raccourcir

Abbreviation, *s.* abréviation, *f*

Abbreviator, *s.* abréviateur, *m.*

Abbreviatory, *adj.* abréviatif

A B C, *s.* A B C, *m.*

Abderite, *s. adj.* Abdéritain, *m.*, e, *f.*, Abdérite, *m.f.*

Abdicate, *v.a.n.* abdiquer

Abdication, *s.* abdication *f.*

Abdomen, *s.* abdomen, ventre, *m.* *Lower part of the* —, bas-ventre, *m.*

Abdominal, *adj.* abdominal

Abduct, *v.a.* détourner; enlever

Abduction, *s.* (*law*) détournement (de mineur), *m.*; (*law*) enlèvement, *m.*; (*anat., log.*) abduction, *f.*

Abductor, *s.* enleveur, *m.*; (*anat.*) abducteur, *m.*

Abed, *adv.* au lit, sur son lit, couché

Aberdevine, *s.* tarin, *m.*

Abernethy, *s.* biscuit sec, *m.*

Aberrant, *adj.* égaré; irrégulier; anormal

Aberration, *s.* aberration, *f.*; déviation, *f.*; écart, *m.*; erreur, *f.*; égarement, *m.*; éloignement, *m.*

Abet, *v.a.* soutenir, appuyer; favoriser; encourager; pousser; exciter; (*law*) être fauteur de

Abetment, Abetting, *s.* encouragement, appui, *m.*; instigation, *f.*; provocation, *f.*

Abetter, Abettor, *s.* fauteur, *m.*, -trice, *f.*; instigateur, *m.*, -trice, *f.*

Abeyance, *s.* expectative, attente, *f.*; suspension, *f.*; désuétude, *f.*; (*law*) vacance, *f.* *In* —, suspendu, en suspens; pendant; tombé en désuétude; périmé; (*law*) vacant, jacent. *To fall into* —, être suspendu *or* &c. (*V.* **In** —); cesser d'être en vigueur, tomber en désuétude, périmer, se périmer

Abhor, *v.a.* abhorrer, avoir en horreur, avoir horreur de, détester. *Nature —s a vacuum*, la nature a horreur du vide

Abhorrence, *s.* horreur, *f.* *To hold in* —, *V.* **Abhor**

Abhorrent, *adj.* en horreur (à), odieux (à); contraire (à), opposé (à), inconciliable (avec), incompatible (avec); (*horrified*) saisi d'horreur; révolté

Abhorrently, *adv.* avec horreur

Abhorrer, *s.* personne qui abhorre, *f.*, ennemi juré, *m.*

Abide, *v.a.n.* (*bear*) souffrir, supporter; subir; subir les conséquences de; résister à; (*keep to*) s'en tenir à; (*await*) attendre; attendre l'issue de; (*dwell, stay*) demeurer, rester; subsister. *To — by*, (*defend*) soutenir; (*maintain*) maintenir; (*stick to*) s'en tenir à; (*trust to*) s'en rapporter à; (*keep true to*) rester fidèle à; (*o.'s word, a promise*) tenir; (*submit to*) se soumettre à; observer; (*suffer for*) subir les conséquences de; subir

Abiding, *s.* séjour, *m.*; — *adj.* qui subsiste; permanent; constant, ferme, inébranlable; immuable

Abidingly, *adv.* d'une manière permanente, permanemment; en permanence; constamment; fermement; immuablement

Abigail, *s.* suivante, *f.*; soubrette, *f.*

Ability, *s.* pouvoir, *m.*, faculté, force, *f.*; habileté, *f.*, talent, *m.*, capacité, *f.*, moyens, *m. pl.*

Abintestate, *adj.* ab intestat

Abject, *adj.* abject, vil

Abjection, Abjectness, *s.* abjection, bassesse, *f.*, abaissement, avilissement, *m.*

Abjectly, *adv.* abjectement
Abjuration, *s.* abjuration, *f.*
Abjure,*v.a.*abjurer, faire abjuration de [l'ablatif
Ablative, *s.* (– *case*) ablatif, *m.* *In the* —, à
Ablaze, *adv* en feu, en flammes, enflammé; flamboyant; reluisant; brillant; étincelant; resplendissant; (*pers.*) bouillant
Able, *adj.* capable (de), à même (de), en état (de); (*being able to*) pouvant; (*knowing how to*) sachant; (*clever*) habile, capable; (*fit*) propre (à); compétent; (*strong*) robuste, vigoureux, fort; (*good*) excellent. *To be — to*, pouvoir, être à même de, être en état de; avoir la force de; (*to know how to*) savoir. *As one is* —, selon ses moyens. — **bodied,** *adj.* fort, robuste, vigoureux, valide; (*nav.*) expérimenté, bon, [manœuvrier
Ablet, *s.* able, *m.*, ablette, *f.*
Ablution, *s.* ablution, *f.*
Ably, *adv.* habilement, adroitement, avec talent
Abnegation, *s.* abnégation, renonciation, *f.*
Abnormal, *adj.* anormal, irrégulier [ment
Abnormally, *adv.* anormalement, irrégulière-
Aboard, *adv. prep.* (*nav.*) à bord; à bord de ... *To fall — of*, aborder [(*stay*) séjour, *m.*
Abode, *s.* demeure, habitation, *f.*, séjour, *m.*;
Abolish, *v.a.* abolir; détruire; anéantir
Abolishable, *adj.* abolissable
Abolition, *s.* abolition *f.*; destruction, *f.*
Abolition-ism, -ist. *V.* page 3, § 1
Abominable, *adj.* abominable
Abominableness, *s.* nature abominable, *f.*
Abominably, *adv.* abominablement
Abominate, *v.a.* abominer, avoir en abomination *or* en horreur, détester
Abomination, *s.* abomination, horreur, *f.* *To hold in* —, *V.* **Abominate** [aborigène, *m.*
Aboriginal, *adj.* aborigène; primitif; — *s.*
Aborigines, *s. pl.* aborigènes, *m. pl.*
Abort, *v.n.* avorter [avorton, *m.*
Abortion, *s.* (*act*) avortement, *m.*; (*thing*)
Abortive, *adj.* abortif; (*fig.*) avorté, manqué; — *s.* abortif, *m.* *To be* or *prove* —, avorter
Abortively, *adv.* avant terme, en avortant; (*fig.*) prématurément; sans résultat, sans succès
Abortiveness, *s.* avortement, *m.*; insuccès, *m.*
Abound, *v.n.* abonder
About, *prep.* (*round*) autour de; (*near to*) auprès de; (*for*) pour; (*in*) dans; en; par; (*towards*) vers; (*with, on o.'s person*) sur; (*after, engaged in, on*) après; à; (*concerning*) sur, au sujet de, à l'égard de; à propos de; sur le compte de; à; de; — *adv.* autour, tout autour; alentour, à l'entour, aux alentours, dans les environs; (*around oneself*) autour de soi; (*here and there*) çà et là; de côté et d'autre, de tous côtés; partout; (*circularly*) en rond; (*by turns*) à la ronde; (*in compass*) de tour; (*circuitously*) de détour; (*nearly*) environ; à peu près; (*on the point of*) sur le point de, près de. — *it, them* (*things*), en; y; autour: auprès. — *here, somewhere — here*, près d'ici, par ici, dans les environs. — *there, somewhere — there*, près de là, par là, de ce côté-là, dans les environs. — *that*, là-dessus, à ce sujet, à cet égard. — *and* —, de côté et d'autre. — *ship!* (*nav.*) adieu va! *All* —, partout dans ..., dans tout (*or, f.*, toute) ...; (*adverb.*) partout. *To be* —, faire, s'occuper de. *To be — to*, être sur le point de, aller; (*nav.*) virer de bord, faire virer de bord
Above, *prep.* au-dessus de; par-dessus; sur; (*before*) avant; (*more than*) plus de, plus que; de plus que; (*in addition to*) par-dessus; en sus de; (*too proud for*) trop fier pour; (*navig.*) en amont de; — *adv.* en haut; là-haut; au-dessus; (*beyond*) au-delà; au-dessus; (*before*) plus haut, ci-dessus; (*preceding*) précédent, ci-dessus; (*navig.*) en amont. — **all,** surtout; par-dessus tout. — **board,** ouvertement, franchement, à jeu découvert, cartes sur table; (*adject.*) franc et ouvert. — **ground,** sur terre, en vie. — **mentioned,** *adj.* mentionné ci-dessus, ci-dessus mentionné, susmentionné; ci-dessus; susdit; précité. — **named,** *adj.* [susnommé
Abracadabra, *s.* abracadabra, *m.*
Abrade, *v.a.* user; miner; ronger; enlever; écorcher
Abrasion, *s.* frottement, *m.*; (*of coin*) frai, *m.*; (*med.*) abrasion, *f.*; (*of the skin*) écorchure, *f.*
Abraxas, *s.* abraxas, *m.* [(*nav.*) par le travers
Abreast, *adv.* de front, à côté l'un de l'autre;
Abridge, *v.a.* abréger; raccourcir; diminuer, réduire; restreindre; (*deprive*) priver (de); dépouiller (de)
Abridger, *s.* abréviateur, *m*, -trice, *f.*
Abridgment, *s.* abrégement, *m.*; diminution, réduction, *f.*; restriction, *f.*; privation, *f.*; (*epitome, compendium, summary*) abrégé, *m.*
Abroach, *adv.* en perce; (*fig.*) en avant; en œuvre, en train; (*open*) à découvert. *To set* —, mettre en perce; (*fig.*) mettre en avant *or* &c.; répandre; propager
Abroad, *adv.* (*at large*) au large, au loin; (*out*) dehors; sorti; absent; (*in foreign parts*) au dehors, à l'étranger; (*everywhere*) partout. *To be* or *get* —, (*fig.*) courir, se répandre. *The schoolmaster is* —, l'éducation est partout
Abrogate, *v.a.* abroger
Abrogation, *s.* abrogation, *f.*
Abrupt,*adj* (*sudden*) brusque; précipité; subit; (*unconnected, with sudden jerks or transitions*) abrupt, saccadé; (*broken*) brisé; (*craggy*) abrupt; rocailleux; escarpé; (*bot.*) abrupt
Abruptly, *adv.* brusquement; abruptement; subitement, tout à coup; avec précipitation
Abruptness, *s.* brusquerie, rudesse, *f.*; aspérité, *f.*; inégalité, *f.*; escarpement, *m.*; pré- [cipitation, *f.*
Abscess, *s.* abcès, *m.*
Absciss, Abscissa, *s.* abscisse, *f.*
Abscond, *v.n.* s'enfuir; disparaître; se soustraire à des poursuites judiciaires; se cacher
Absence, *s.* absence, *f.*; éloignement, *m.*; (*of mind*) distraction, *f.*; (*want*) manque, *m.*
Absent, *adj.* absent; (*inattentive*) distrait; — *v.a.* éloigner. *To — oneself*, s'absenter
Absentee, *s.* absent, *m.*
Absenteeism, *s.* absentéisme, *m.*
Absenter, *s.* absent, *m.*
Absinthe, *s.* absinthe, *f.*
Absinthiated, *adj.* absinthé
Absis, *s.* abside, apside, *f.*
Absolute, *adj.* absolu; positif; (*downright*) vrai, franc, véritable; (*unlimited*) illimité; — *s.* absolu, *m.* [complètement; vraiment
Absolutely, *adv.* absolument; positivement;
Absolution, *s.* absolution, *f.*; absoute, *f.*
Absolut-ism, ist. *V.* page 3, § 1
Absolutory, *adj.* absolutoire
Absolve, *v.a.* absoudre; (*discharge*) délier, dégager, décharger; (*free*) affranchir
Absorb, *v.a.* absorber; engloutir
Absorbable, *adj.* absorbable [sorbant, *s.m.*
Absorbent, *adj. s.* absorbant, *adj. m.*, e, *f.*, ab-
Absorption, *s.* absorption, *f.*
Absorptive, *adj.* absorptif, absorbant
Absorptivity, *s.* absorptivité, *f.*
Abstain, *v.n.* s'abstenir (de)
Abstainer, *s.* abstenant, *m.*, e, *f.*
Abstaining, *s.* abstinence, *f.*
Abstemious, *adj.* sobre; modéré; abstème
Abstemiously, *adv.* sobrement, avec sobriété
Abstemiousness, *s.* sobriété, tempérance, abstinence, *f.* [privation, *f.*
Abstention, *s.* abstention, *f.*; abstinence, *f.*;
Abstentionist, *s.* abstentioniste, *m.f.*
Absterge, Absterse, *v.a.* absterger
Abstergent, *adj. s.* abstergent, *adj. m.*, e, *f.*, [abstergent, *s.m.*
Abstersion, *s.* abstersion, *f.*
Abstersive, *adj. s.* abstersif, *adj. m.*, -ive, *f.*, abstersif, *s.m.*
Abstinence, *s.* abstinence, *f.*; abstention, *f.*
Abstinent, *adj.* abstinent, sobre
Abstinently, *adv.* avec abstinence, sobrement
Abstract, *v.a.* soustraire (à); (*separate*) séparer (de), détacher (de); (*epitomize*) résumer; (*exclude*)

faire abstraction (de); abstraire; — *adj.* abstrait; —*s.* résumé, abrégé, extrait, *m.*; relevé, *m.*; (*arch.*, *engin.*, &c.) état sommaire, *m.*; (*log.*) abstrait, *m.* *In the* —, abstractivement
Abstracted, *part. adj.* soustrait, &c. (*V.* **Abstract,** *v.a.*); abstrait; séparé (de), détaché (de); purifié; pur; (*excluded*) abstraction faite de; (*in mind*) distrait, préoccupé
Abstractedly, *adv.* abstractivement; par abstraction; abstraitement
Abstractedness, *s.* nature abstraite, *f.*
Abstracter, *s.* abréviateur, *m.*, -trice, *f.*
Abstraction, *s.* abstraction, *f.*; (*stealing*) soustraction, *f.*; (*of mind*) distraction, préoccupation, *f.*
Abstractive, *adj.* abstractif
Abstractively, *adv.* *V.* **Abstractedly**
Abstractly, *adv.* abstraitement, d'une manière abstraite
Abstractness, *s.* nature abstraite, *f.*
Abstruse, *adj.* abstrus; abstrait; caché, secret; obscur
Abstrusely, *adv.* d'une manière abstruse *or* abstraite; obscurément
Abstruseness, *s.* nature abstruse, *f.*; obscurité, *f.*; difficulté, *f.*
Absurd, *adj.* absurde
Absurdity, Absurdness, *s.* absurdité, *f.*
Absurdly, *adv.* absurdement
Abundance, *s.* abondance, *f.*; quantité, *f.*; grand nombre, *m.*; prospérité, *f.*
Abundant, *adj.* abondant; riche
Abundantly, *adv.* abondamment; en abondance; largement
Abuse, *v.a.* (*misuse*) abuser de; (*ill-treat*) maltraiter, malmener; (*revile*) injurier, dire des injures à, insulter, outrager; (*speak ill of*) déblatérer contre; médire de, dire du mal de; (*deceive*) abuser, tromper; —*s.* abus, *m.*; (*reviling*) injures, insultes, *f. pl.*
Abuser, *s.* abuseur, *m.*, -euse, *f.*; insulteur, *m.*, -euse, *f.*, grossier personnage, *m.* [(*pers.*) grossier
Abusive, *adj.* abusif; (*insulting*) injurieux;
Abusively, *adv.* abusivement; (*rudely*) injurieusement
Abusiveness, *s.* nature injurieuse *or* outrageante, *f.*; langage injurieux *or* outrageant, *m.*, injure, insulte, grossièreté, *f.*
Abut, *v.n.* aboutir (à), confiner (à); (*of roads*) s'embrancher (avec)
Abutment, *s.* aboutement, *m.*; about, *m.*; but, *m.*, borne, *f.*; (*build.*) arc-boutant, *m.*; (*of bridges*) culée, *f.* — **pier,** *s.* butée, *f.*
Abuttal, *s.* aboutissant, *m.*
Abutting, *s.* embranchement, *m.*
Abyss, *s.* abîme, gouffre, *m.*; (*her.*) abîme, *m.*
Abyssinian, *s.* Abyssinien, *m.*, -ne, *f.*, Abyssin, *m.*, e, *f.*; (*language*) l'abyssinien, *m.*; — *adj.* abyssinien, abyssin, d'Abyssinie; (*of language*) abyssinien, abyssinique
Acacia, *s.* acacia, *m.*
Academic, -al, *adj.* académique; classique; universitaire; scolaire; scolastique; —*s.* académicien, *m.*
Academically, *adv.* académiquement
Academicals, *s. pl.* costume académique, *m.*, insignes académiques, *m. pl.*
Academician, *s.* académicien, *m.*, -ne, *f.*
Academism, *s.* académie, *f.*
Academist, *s.* académiste, *m.*; académicien, *m.*
Academy, *s.* académie, *f.*; (*school of science or art*) école, *f.*; conservatoire, *m.*; (*common school*) école primaire, *f.*; pension, *f.*, pensionnat, *m.* — **figure,** *s.* académie, étude, *f.*
Acadian, *s.* Acadien, *m.*, -ne, *f.*; — *adj.* acadien, d'Acadie
Acanthine, *adj.* d'acanthe
Acanthus, *s.* acanthe, *f.*
Acarus, *s.* acarus, acare, *m.*
Accede, *v.n.* accéder (à), consentir (à); (*come to*) venir (à), arriver (à), parvenir (à); (*to the throne*) monter (sur)
Accelerate, *v.a.* accélérer; hâter, activer, presser; précipiter
Accelerating, Accelerative, *adj.* accélérateur
Acceleration, *s.* accélération, *f.*
Accelerator, *s.* (*post.*) fourgon des dépêches, *m.*
Accent, *s.* accent, *m.*; — *v.a.* accentuer, articuler
Accenting, *s* accentuation, *f.*
Accentor, *s.* (*bird*) accenteur, *m*
Accentuate, *v.a.* accentuer
Accentuation, *s.* accentuation, *f.*
Accept, *v.a.* accepter; agréer; recevoir; (*understand*) comprendre, entendre. *To — of*, accepter. *To — persons*, (*old*) faire acception de personnes
Acceptable, *adj.* acceptable; agréable
Acceptableness, Acceptability, *s.* acceptabilité, nature acceptable *or* agréable, *f.*
Acceptably, *adv.* agréablement
Acceptance, *s.* acceptation, *f.*; approbation, *f.*; accueil, *m.*; (*of bills*) acceptation, *f.*; (*theol.*) grâce, *f.* *Worthy of* —, digne d'être accepté *or* offert, acceptable. *To be worth* (*your*, &c.) —, mériter de (vous, &c.) être offert. *I request your — (your kind —) of*, je vous prie d'accepter (de vouloir bien accepter)
Acceptation, *s.* accueil, *m.*, réception, *f.*; faveur, *f.*; (*meaning*) acception, *f.*, sens, *m.*
Accepter, Acceptor, *s.* accepteur, *m.*; (*law*) acceptant, *m.*, e, *f.*
Access, *s.* accès, abord, *m.* *Difficult of* —, d'un accès difficile
Accessary. *V.* **Accessory**
Accessibility, Accessibleness, *s.* accessibilité, *f.*
Accessible, *adj.* accessible, abordable
Accession, *s.* accession, *f.*; (*increase*) accroissement, surcroît, *m.*, augmentation, *f.*; addition, *f.*; acquisition, *f.*; (*to the throne*) avénement, *m.*
Accessorial, *adj.* de complicité
Accessorily, *adv.* accessoirement
Accessoriness, *s.* nature accessoire, *f.*; complicité, *f.*
Accessory, *adj. s.* accessoire, *adj. m.f.*, *s.m.*; (*law*) complice, *adj. s.m.f.*
Accidence, *s.* rudiment, *m.*, grammaire, *f.*
Accident, *s.* accident, *m.*; hasard, *m.*; (*of fire and ship-insurance*) sinistre, *m.*
Accidental, *adj.* accidentel; accessoire; —*s.* (*mus. paint.*, &c.) accident, *m.* — *light*, (*paint.*) accident de lumière, *m.*
Accidentally, *adv.* accidentellement, par hasard; accessoirement
Accidentalness, Accidentality, *s.* nature accidentelle *or* accessoire, *f.*
Acclaim, *v.a.* acclamer; — *s.* acclamation, *f.*
Acclamation, *s.* acclamation, *f.*
Acclamatory, *adj.* acclamateur, d'acclamation
Acclimatization, *s.* acclimatation, *f.*
Acclimatize, *v.a.* acclimater
Acclimatizer, *s.* acclimatateur, *m.*, -trice, *f.*
Acclivity, *s.* montée, rampe, *f.*
Acclivous, *adj.* montant, en rampe
Accolade, *s.* accolade, *f.*
Accommodable, *adj.* accommodable
Accommodate, *v.a.* accommoder; ajuster; disposer; (*arrange, suit*) arranger; obliger; (*give*) fournir, procurer, donner; servir; (*lend*) prêter; (*lodge*) loger; (*give a seat to*) donner un siége *or* une place à; (*contain*) contenir; — *oneself*, s'accommoder (à), se prêter (à)
Accommodation, *s.* accommodement, *m.*; ajustement, *m.*; arrangement, *m.*; (*convenience*) commodité, convenance, *f.*; facilité, *f.*; avantage, *m.*; (*comfort*) confortable, *m.*; (*lodgings*) logement, *m.*; (*space, room*) place, *f.*; (*seats*) places, *f. pl.*; (*com.*) facilités, *f. pl.*; (*nav.*) emménagements, *m. pl.* *The — is good in that hotel*, on est bien dans cet hôtel. — *for man and horse*, on loge à pied et à cheval. — **bill,** *s.* billet de complaisance, *m.* — **ladder,** *s.* (*nav.*) échelle de commandement, *f.*
Accompaniment, *s.* accompagnement, *m.*
Accompanist, *s.* accompagnateur, *m.*, -trice, *f.*
Accompany, *v.a.* accompagner ('*with*,' de)
Accompanying, *adj.* (*subjoined*) ci-joint
Accomplice, *s.* complice, *m.f.*
Accomplish, *v.a.* accomplir; achever; perfectionner; former; (*fulfil*) remplir
Accomplished, *adj* accompli; parfait; achevé; émérite
Accomplishment, *s.* accomplissement, *m.*; qualité, *f.*, talent, mérite, *m.*; art d'agrément, *m.*; (*learning*) connaissances, *f. pl.*

Accord, *s.* accord, *m.*; union, *f.*; consentement, *m.*; convention, *f.*, accommodement, *m.*; — *v.a.* accorder; — *v.n.* s'accorder, être d'accord. *In* —, d'accord. *Of o.'s own* —, de son plein gré, de son propre mouvement, de soi-même, de soi, spontanément. *With one* —, d'un commun accord

Accordance, *s.* accord, *m.*, union, *f.*; conformité, *f.*, rapport, *m.* *In* —, d'accord (avec); (*conformably*) conformément (à)

Accordant, *adj.* d'accord (avec), conforme (à)

According, *part. adj.* qui s'accorde, d'accord, conforme; — *adverb.* conformément. — **to,** qui s'accorde avec, d'accord avec, conforme à; (*prep.*) suivant, selon; conformément à; d'après; à. — **as,** selon que, suivant que; comme

Accordingly, *adv.* en conséquence; donc, aussi

Accordion, *s.* accordéon, *m.*

Accordionist, *s.* accordéoniste, *m.f.*

Accost, *v.a.* accoster, aborder

Accouchement, *s.* accouchement, *m.*

Accoucheur, *s.* accoucheur, *m.*

Accoucheuse, *s.* accoucheuse, *f.*

Account, *s.* compte, *m.*; (*narrative*) récit, *m.*, relation, description, *f.*; version, *f.*; rapport, *m.*; (*statement*) exposé, *m.*; (*list*) énumération, *f.*; (*assertion*) dire, *m.*; (*news*) nouvelle, *f.*, avis, *m.*; (*information*) renseignement, *m.*; (*reason*) raison, *f.*, sujet, motif, *m.*; (*value*) cas, *m.*, estime, considération, *f.*, prix, *m.*; profit, *m.*; importance, *f.*, poids, *m.*; (*com.*) compte, *m.*, (*bill*) mémoire, *m.*, note, *f.* — **book,** *s.* livre de comptes, *m.* *As per — rendered,* suivant compte remis. *By all —s,* au dire de tout le monde; de l'aveu de tous. *For the* —, *On* —, (*fin., com.*) à terme; (*as an instalment*) à compte, d'à-compte; (*on o.'s* —) en compte. *On — of,* à cause de; en considération de; par égard pour; (*in consequence of*) pour cause de; (*com.*) pour le compte de; à valoir sur. *On all —s, on every* —, en tout point, sous tous les rapports. *On another* —, d'ailleurs. *On joint* or *mutual* —, (*com.*) de compte à demi. *On my* (*your,* &c.) —, à cause de moi (vous, &c.); par égard pour moi (vous, &c.), à (*or* en) ma (votre, &c.) considération; (*com.*) pour mon (votre, &c.) compte, (*after the verb* '*to put,*' mettre) sur mon (votre, &c.) compte. *On no* —, en aucune manière, pour rien au monde. *On that* —, pour cette raison; à ce sujet. *To call to* —, demander des explications à; demander compte (à quelqu'un) de sa conduite. *To give an* —, *V.* **Give.** *To give an — of oneself,* dire ce qu'on a fait, rendre compte de ses actions; décliner ses qualités; justifier de ses moyens d'existence; rendre compte de ses antécédents. *To make no — of,* ne faire aucun cas de. *To take an — of,* prendre note de. *To take into* —, tenir compte de; mettre en ligne de compte. *To turn to* —, mettre à profit, tirer parti de. *Short —s make long friends, V.* **Reckoning**

Account, *v.a.* compter; estimer, réputer, regarder comme, croire; — *v.n.* ('*for*') rendre compte (de); expliquer, rendre raison (de); être responsable (de); (*understand,* s'expliquer, se rendre compte (de) [explicable

Accountable, *adj.* comptable; responsable;

Accountableness, Accountability, *s.* responsabilité, *f.*

Accountant, *s.* comptable, agent comptable, *m.*; (*book-keeper*) teneur de livres, *m.*; (*computer*) calculateur, *m.* — *-general,* chef de comptabilité, *m.* [de teneur de livres), *f.*

Accountantship, *s.* place de comptable (*or*

Accoutre, *v.a.* habiller; équiper; (*rig out*) accoutrer

Accoutrement, *s.* habillement, *m.*; équipement, *m.*; (*odd dress*) accoutrement, *m.*

Accredit, *v.a.* accréditer

Accretion, *s.* accroissement, *m.*; (*of earth*) atterrissement, lais, *m.*; (*med.*) accrétion, *f*

Accretive, *adj.* croissant

Accrue, *v.n.* (*arise*) provenir (de), résulter (de); s'ensuivre; (*fall to*) revenir (à)

Accumulate, *v.a.* accumuler; entasser; amasser, amonceler; — *v.n.* s'accumuler; s'entasser, s'amasser, s'amonceler

Accumulating, *adj.* croissant

Accumulation, *s.* accumulation, *f.*; entassement, amoncellement, *m.* [lateur

Accumulative, *adj.* qui accumule, accumu-

Accumulator, *s.* accumulateur, *m.*, -trice, *f.*

Accuracy, *s.* exactitude, justesse, fidélité, *f.*; (*care*) soin, *m.*, attention, *f.* [soigneux

Accurate, *adj.* exact, correct, fidèle; (*careful*)

Accurately, *adv.* exactement, avec exactitude, correctement, avec fidélité; (*carefully*) soigneusement, avec soin

Accurateness, *s.* *V.* **Accuracy**

Accurse, *v.a.* maudire

Accursed, *adj.* maudit, exécrable

Accusable, *adj.* accusable

Accusation, *s.* accusation, *f.* [—, à l'accusatif

Accusative, *s.* (— *case*) accusatif, *m.* *In the*

Accusatory, *adj.* accusatoire; accusateur

Accuse, *v.a.* accuser [-trice, *f.*

Accuser, *s.*, **Accusing,** *adj.* accusateur, *m.*,

Accustom, *v.a.* accoutumer (à), habituer (à), faire (à) [ordinaire

Accustomed, *adj.* (*usual*) accoutumé, habituel,

Ace, *s.* (*cards*) as, *m.*; (*fig.*) iota, brin, *m.* *Within an — of,* à deux doigts de

Acephalous, *adj.*, **Acephalan,** *adj. s.* acé-

Acerb, *adj.* acerbe, âpre [phale, *adj. m.f.*, *s.m.*

Acerbity, *s.* acerbité, âpreté, *f.*; (*fig.*) acerbité, âpreté, aigreur, *f.*; dureté, *f*; sévérité, rigueur, *f.*; intensité, *f.*

Acerose, Acerous, *adj.* acéreux, acéré

Acescency, *s.* acescence, *f.*

Acescent, *adj.* acescent

Acetate, *s.* acétate, *m.*

Acetic, *adj.* acétique

Acetification, *s.* acétification, *f.*

Acetify, *v.a.* acétifier; — *v.n.* s'acétifier

Acetimeter, Acetometer, *s.* acétimètre, *m.*

Acetous, *adj.* acéteux

Achæan, Achean, *adj.* achéen

Ache, *v.n.* faire mal; (*fig.*) souffrir ('*for*', de) *My head aches,* j'ai mal à la tête

Ache, *s.* mal, *m.*, douleur, *f.*; souffrance, *f.* *To have a head* —, avoir mal à la tête

Achieve, *v.a.* exécuter, accomplir; obtenir, acquérir, gagner; (*a reputation,* &c.) se faire; (*a victory*) remporter

Achievement, *s.* accomplissement (de), *m.*; exploit, haut-fait, fait d'armes, *m*; production œuvre, *f.*; succès, *m.*; victoire, *f.*; (*discovery*) découverte, *f.*; (*her.*) *V.* **Hatchment**

Achiever, *s.* auteur, exécuteur, *m.*

Aching, *s.* douleur, souffrance, *f.*; — *adj.* douloureux, endolori [croûtes laiteuses, *f. pl.*

Achores, *s. pl.* achores, *m. pl.*, croûtes de lait,

Achromat-ic, -ism. *V.* page 3. § 1

Achromatize, *v.a.* achromatiser

Acicular, *adj* aciculaire

Acid, *adj. s.* acide, *adj. m.f.*, *s.m.*

Acidiferous, *adj.* acidifère

Acidifiable, *adj.* acidifiable

Acidification, *s.* acidification, *f.*

Acidify, *v.a.* acidifier; — *v.n.* s'acidifier

Acidimeter, *s.* acidimètre, *m.*

Acidity, *s.* acidité, *f.*

Acidulate, *v.a.* aciduler

Acidulous, *adj.* acidule

Acknowledge, *v.a.* reconnaître; avouer; annoncer; (— *the receipt of*) accuser réception de; (*answer*) répondre à, faire honneur à

Acknowledgment, *s.* reconnaissance, *f.*; (*confession*) aveu, *m.*; (*apology*) excuse, *f.*; (*of the receipt of missives*) accusé de réception, *m.*; (*receipt given for money or* &c.) reçu, *m.*; (*certificate*) certificat, *m.*, attestation, *f.*; (*of a debt*) reconnaissance, *f.*; (*thanks*) remerciments, *m. pl.*; (*reward*) récompense, *f.*

Acme, *s.* apogée, comble, faite, *m.*; terme, *m.*; (*of a disease*) fort, acmé, *m.*, période d'état, *f.*
Acne, *s.* acné, *m.*, dartre couperose, *f.*
Acolyte, *s.* acolyte, *m.*
Aconite, *s.* aconit, *m.* [balane, gland de mer, *m.*
Acorn, *s.* gland, *m.* — **shell,** — **barnacle,** *s.*
Acotyledon, *s.* acotylédone, acotylédonée, *f.*
Acotyledonous, *adj.* acotylédoné, acotylédone
Acoustic, *adj.* acoustique
Acoustics, *s. pl.* acoustique, *f.*
Acquaint, *v.a.* faire savoir, faire connaître, faire part (de), informer (de), instruire (de), apprendre, annoncer; familiariser (avec). *To be —ed with*, connaître; (*to be aware of, to have learnt*) savoir. *To become* or *get —ed with*, (*pers.*) faire la connaissance de, connaître; (*things*) apprendre; connaître. *To make* (...) *—ed with*, faire connaître (à ...). *To — oneself with, To make oneself —ed with*, (*pers.*) faire la connaissance de; (*things*) apprendre; apprendre à connaître; étudier; prendre connaissance de; se mettre au courant (*or* au fait) de
Acquaintance, *s.* connaissance, *f.*; liaison, *f.*; accointance, *f.* *To make his* or *her —*, faire sa connaissance
Acquaintanceship, *s.* connaissance, *f.*, relations, *f.pl.*, relation, *f.*, liaisons, *f.pl.*, liaison, *f.*
Acquainted, *adj.* (*known*) connu; (*informed*) instruit (de); (*familiar*) familier (avec). *V.* **Acquaint** [se soumettre (à)
Acquiesce, *v.n.* acquiescer (à); consentir (à);
Acquiescence, *s.* acquiescement, *m.*
Acquiescent, *adj.* disposé à acquiescer, facile, pliant, accommodant
Acquirable, *adj* acquérable [apprendre
Acquire, *v.a.* acquérir, obtenir; gagner; (*learn*)
Acquirement, *s.* acquisition, *f.*; (*learning*) acquis, *m.*, connaissance, *f.*; érudition, instruction, *f.*, talent, *m.*
Acquisition, *s.* acquisition, *f.*
Acquit, *v.a.* acquitter; délivrer, délier, dégager, décharger, absoudre; (*law*) acquitter. *To — oneself*, s'acquitter (de); agir; s'en tirer; faire son devoir; se justifier (de)
Acquittable, *adj.* acquittable
Acquittal, Acquitment, *s.* acquittement, *m.*
Acquittance, *s.* acquittement, *m.*; libération, décharge, *f.*; (*receipt*) quittance, *f.*, acquit, *m.*
Acre, *s.* (*English meas.*) acre, *m.*; (*old French meas.*) arpent, *m.*; (*equivalent modern French meas.*) demi-hectare, *m.*
Acrid, *adj.* âcre
Acridity, *s.* âcreté, *f.*
Acridly, *adv.* âcrement
Acrimonious, *adj.* acrimonieux, âcre [aigreur
Acrimoniously, *adv.* avec acrimonie, avec
Acrimony, *s.* acrimonie, âcreté, aigreur, *f.*
Acrobat, *s.* acrobate, *m.f.*
Acrobatic, *adj.* acrobatique
Acroceraunian, *adj* acrocéraunien
Acronycal, *adj.* acronyque
Acronycally, *adv.* acronyquement
Acropolis, *s.* acropole, *f.*
Acrospire, *s.* germe, *m.*
Across, *prep.* (*athwart, quite over, through*) à travers, au travers de; (*intersecting*) en travers de; (*on* or *to the other side of*) de l'autre côté de; (*upon*) sur; par; — *adv.* (*lying crossways*) en travers; (*folded crossways, as the arms*) croisé, *adj.*; (*on* or *to the other side*) de l'autre côté
Acrostic, *s. adj.* acrostiche, *s.m.*, *adj. m.f.*
Acrostically, *adv.* en acrostiche [acrotère, *m.*
Acroter, Acroterion, Acroterium, *s.*
Act, *v.n.* agir; influer (sur); opérer; produire son effet; fonctionner; servir ('*as a*,' '*as*,' de); (*perform*) jouer; (*behave*) se conduire, se comporter, agir; — *v.a.* (*a play*) jouer, représenter; (*a part*) jouer, remplir; faire; (*feign*) faire, contrefaire, feindre; (*functions*) remplir, exercer. *To — upon*, agir *or* influer sur; (*according to*) agir d'après; mettre à exécution; mettre en pratique
Act, *s.* acte, *m.*; (*deed*) acte, *m.*; action, *f.*; fait, *m.*; trait, *m.*; coup, *m.*; (*parliam.*) acte, *m.*, loi, *f.* — *of indemnity*, bill d'indemnité, *m.* *In the —, in the very —*, sur le fait; (*law*) en flagrant délit. *In the — of*, en train de (*with inf.*); (*whilst*) en (*with pres. part.*)
Actable, *adj.* jouable [*charades*, &c.) en action
Acted, *part. adj.* joué, &c. (*V.* **Act,** *v.a.*); (*of*
Acting, *adj.* actif, qui agit; (*of functionaries, mil.*) suppléant, faisant fonctions de, remplissant les fonctions de; de service; (*managing*) gérant; (*of charades*, &c.) en action; (*tech.*) à effet ...; —*s.* action, *f.*; (*theat.*) jeu, *m.*; (*feint*) feinte, *f.*; (*effect, tech.*) effet, *m.* — *corporal* (*mil.*) caporal postiche, élève-caporal, *m.* — *manager*, directeur gérant, *m.* *Double —*, (*adject., tech.*) à double effet. *Single —*, à simple effet
Action, *s.* action, *f.*; (*mil., nav.*) action, bataille, *f.*, combat, *m.*, affaire, *f.*; (*effect, tech.*) effet, *m.*; (*suit*) procès, *m.* *To bring an — against*, intenter un procès à, attaquer en justice, actionner. *To bring* or *call into —*, faire jouer, mettre en jeu, mettre en action, employer
Actionable, *adj.* attaquable en justice, sujet à procès, actionnable, poursuivable, punissable
Active, *adj* actif. — *force*, force vive
Actively, *adv.* activement
Activity, *s.* activité, *f.*
Actor, *s.* acteur, *m.*
Actress, *s.* actrice, *f.*
Actual, *adj.* actuel; réel, véritable, vrai positif; (*of cauteries*) actuel
Actualization, *s.* actualisation, *f.*
Actualize, *v.a.* actualiser
Actuality, *s.* réalité, *f.*; actualité, *f.*
Actually, *adv.* réellement, véritablement effectivement, positivement; actuellement
Actuary, *s.* expert-comptable, *m.*; calculateur, *m.*; (*manager*) gérant, *m.*; secrétaire, *m.*; (*in antiquity*) actuaire, *m.*
Actuate, *v.a.* mouvoir; animer (à), exciter (à), pousser (à); influencer [—*s.* porte-aiguillon, *m.*
Aculeate, *adj.* aiguillonné, pointu, piquant;
Acumen, *s.* pénétration, finesse, *f.*
Acuminate, *v.a.* aiguiser; — *v.n.* se terminer en pointe; — *adj.* *V.* **Acuminated**
Acuminated, *adj.* pointu, aigu; (*bot.*) acuminé
Acupuncturation, Acupuncture, *s.* acuponcture, *f*
Acupressure, *s.* acupression, *f.* [poncture, *f*
Acutangular, *adj.* acutangle
Acute, *adj.* aigu; violent, vif, poignant; subtil, pénétrant, fin; (*witty*) fin, spirituel. — **angled,** *adj.* acutangle [vivement
Acutely, *adv.* subtilement, finement; (*strongly*)
Acuteness, *s.* acuité, aiguité, *f.*; violence, force, intensité, *f.*; subtilité, pénétration, finesse, *f.*; (*of sound*) élévation, *f.*, acuité, *f.*
A.D. (*Anno Domini*) l'an du Seigneur, l'an de grâce, *m.*
Adage, *s.* adage, *m.*
Adagial, *adj.* proverbial, passé en adage
Adagio, *s.* adagio, *m.*
Adamant, *s.* diamant, *m.*
Adamantean, Adamantine, *adj.* de diamant; (*min.*) adamantin
Adamic, *adj.* adamique
Adamite, *s.* adamite, *m.* [pliquer
Adapt, *v.a.* adapter; ajuster, approprier; ap-
Adaptable, *adj.* adaptable
Adaptation, *s.* adaptation, *f.*
Adapted, *part. adj.* adapté (à); propre (à)
Adapter, *s.* adapteur, *m.* -euse, *f.*; (*chem.*) allonge, *f.*
Add, *v.a.* ajouter; joindre; annexer. — **up,** additionner. — *to this*, ajoutez à cela
Addenda, *s. pl.* addenda, *m. pl.*, additions, *f. pl*
Addendum, *s.* addenda, *m.*
Adder, *s.* vipère, *f.*; serpent, *m.* —*'s-tongue*, (*bot.*) ophioglosse, langue de serpent, *f.* — **wort,** *s.* vipérine, *f.*
Addict, *v.* *To — oneself* (*to*), *to be addicted* (*to*). s'adonner (à), se livrer (à), être adonné à
Addictedness, Addiction, *s.* penchant, goût, *m.*, disposition, *f.*; attachement, *m.*

Adding, — up, *s.* addition, *f.*
Addition, *s.* addition, *f.*; supplément, *m.*; augmentation, *f.*, accroissement, *m.*; surcroît, *m.*; acquisition, *f.*; (*title*) titre, *m.*, qualité, *f.* *In —*, en outre, en sus. *In — to*, outre, plus, en sus de. *Revised edition with —s*, édition revue et augmentée
Additional, *adj.* additionnel; supplémentaire; de surcroît; (*another*) nouveau, de plus
Additionally, *adv.* en outre, en sus
Addle, Addled, *adj.* gâté, pourri, couvi; (*fig.*) stérile, vide. *To prove —*, se gâter. **—headed, -pated,** *adj.* qui a le cerveau vide
Address, *v.a.* adresser; (*speak to*) s'adresser à, parler à, adresser la parole à; apostropher; présenter une adresse à; (*accost*) aborder; (*dedicate*) dédier; (*of letters*, &c.) adresser; mettre l'adresse à
Address, *s.* (*speech*) discours, *m.*, allocution, *f.*; (*pleading*) plaidoyer, *m.*; (*to electors*) profession de foi, *f.*; (*to a king*, &c.) adresse, *f.*; supplique, requête, *f.*; (*dedication*) dédicace, épître dédicatoire. *f.*; (*of letters*, &c.) adresse, *f.*; (*invocation*) prière, invocation, *f.*; (*to a lady*) cour, *f.*; (*skill, dexterity*) adresse, *f.*; (*deportment*) tenue, démarche, *f.*, port, *m.*; (*manner of speaking*) abord, *m.* *Style of —*, manière de s'adresser (à quelqu'un), *f.*; titre, *m.* *He is a man of good —*, c'est un homme distingué. *V.* **Pay,** *v.a.*
Addressee, *s.* (*post.*) destinataire, *m.f.*
Addresser, *s.* pétitionnaire, *m.f.*; (*sender*) envoyeur, *m.*, -euse, *f.* [avancer, produire, citer
Adduce, *v.a.* présenter; (*fig.*) alléguer, fournir,
Adducible, *adj.* allégable
Adept, *adj.* habile, versé, expérimenté, émérite; — *s.* adepte, *m.f.*
Adequacy, *s.* suffisance, proportion, *f.*
Adequate, *adj.* proportionné; suffisant; égal; à la hauteur (de); (*philos.*) adéquat
Adequately, *adv.* proportionnément, en juste proportion, justement; suffisamment
Adequateness. *V.* **Adequacy**
Adhere, *v.n.* adhérer (à); s'attacher (à); être attaché (à); tenir (à); se tenir (à); rester fidèle (à); persister (dans); se coller (à)
Adherence, *s.* adhérence, *f.*; adhésion, *f.*; (*fig.*) attachement, *m.*; fidélité, *f.*; persévérance, *f.*
Adherent, *adj.* adhérent (à); attaché (à); collé (à); — *s.* adhérent, *m.*; partisan, *m.*; disciple, *m.* [(*sticking*) adhérence, *f.*
Adhesion, *s.* adhésion, *f.*; attachement, *m.*;
Adhesive, *adj.* qui adhère (à), qui tient (à); tenace; (*sticky*) collant; (*gummed*) gommé; (*pharm.*) adhésif, agglutinatif
Adhesively, *adv.* avec adhérence
Adhesiveness, *s.* adhérence, *f.*; (*fig.*) adhésion, *f.*; ténacité, *f.*
Adiantum, *s.* adiante, *m.*
Adieu. *V.* **Good-bye** *and* **Farewell**
Adipocere, *s.* adipocire, *f.*
Adipose, Adipous, *adj.* adipeux
Adit, *s.* galerie d'écoulement, galerie, *f.*
Adjacency, *s.* proximité, contiguïté, *f.*, voisinage, *m.* [(de), limitrophe (de)
Adjacent, *adj.* adjacent (à), contigu (à), voisin
Adjectival, *adj.* adjectif
Adjectivally, *adv.* adjectivement
Adjective, *s. adj.* adjectif, *s.m.*, adjectif, *adj.*
Adjectively, *adv.* adjectivement [*m.*, (-ive, *f.*)
Adjoin, *v.a.* joindre (à); ajouter (à); (*pers.*) adjoindre (à); — *v.a.n.* (*be contiguous*) attenir (à), être attenant *or* contigu (à); (*fig.*) se joindre (à), s'ajouter (à)
Adjoining, *adj.* attenant (à), adjacent (à), contigu (à), voisin (de), avoisinant, d'à-côté
Adjourn, *v.a.* ajourner; — *v.n.* s'ajourner
Adjournment, *s.* ajournement, *m.*
Adjudge, Adjudicate, *v.a.n.* adjuger; condamner; juger, décider, décréter, arrêter; déclarer
Adjudication, Adjudgment, *s.* adjudication, *f.*; judgment, *m.*, décision, *f.*, décret, arrêt, *m.*, sentence, *f.*; (*in bankruptcy*) déclaration (de faillite), *f.* [-trice, *f.*; juge, *m.*
Adjudica-tor, trix, *s.* adjudicateur, *m.*,
Adjunct, *s.* accessoire, *m.*; accompagnement, *m.*; (*gram.*) adjoint, *m.*; — *adj.* accessoire; joint, lié; adjoint [tion, *f.*
Adjunction, *s.* adjonction, *f.*; jonction, addi-
Adjuration, *s.* adjuration, *f.*; invocation, *f.*
Adjure, *v.a.* adjurer; conjurer
Adjust, *v.a.* ajuster; régler, arranger; fixer,
Adjuster, *s.* ajusteur, *m.* [déterminer
Adjustment, *s.* ajustement, *m.*; règlement, *m.*; arrangement, accommodement, *m.*
Adjutage. *V.* **Ajutage**
Adjutancy, *s.* (*mil.*) grade d'adjudant, *m.*
Adjutant, *s.* (*mil.*) adjudant, *m.*; (*fig.*) second, *m.*; (*bird*) argala, *m.* — *general*, colonel d'état-major, *m.*
Admeasurement, *s.* mesurage, *m.*; mesure, dimension, *f.*; règlement, *m.*; division, *f.*, partage, *m.*
Administer, *v.a.* administrer; (*of affairs*) gérer, régir; (*of oaths*) faire prêter, déférer; (*afford*) fournir, donner (à); (*of justice*) rendre, (*of the law*) appliquer; — *v.n.* contribuer (à); (*provide for*) pourvoir (à), subvenir (à); (*take care of*) soigner
Administration, *s.* administration, *f.*; gouvernement, *m.*; distribution, dispensation, *f.*; (*law*) gestion, *f.*
Administrative, *adj.* administratif
Administratively, *adv.* administrativement
Administrator, *s.* administrateur, *m.*; régent, *m.* [strateur, *m.*
Administratorship, *s.* emploi d'admini-
Administratrix, *s.* administratrice, *f.*
Admirable, *adj.* admirable
Admirableness, *s.* beauté, *f.*
Admirably, *adv.* admirablement, à merveille
Admiral, *s.* amiral, *m.* *High —*, grand amiral, *m.* *—'s ship*, vaisseau-amiral, *m.*
Admiralship, *s.* amiralat, *m.*
Admiralty, *s.* amirauté, *f.*, ministère de la marine, *m.* *First lord of the —*, ministre de la marine, *m.*
Admiration, *s.* admiration, *f.* *To —*, à ravir
Admire, *v.a* admirer, trouver beau; (*to love*) aimer, être épris de; (*to like*) aimer, trouver à son goût
Admirer, *s.* admirateur, *m.*, -trice, *f.*; (*lover*) adorateur, *m.*; (*fancier*) grand amateur (de). *m.*
Admiring, *adj.* dans l'admiration, ravi, émer-
Admiringly, *adv.* avec admiration [veillé
Admissibility, *s.* admissibilité, *f.*
Admissible, *adj.* admissible, recevable, valable
Admissibly, *adv.* d'une manière admissible
Admission, *s.* admission, *f.*; réception, *f.*; (*access*) entrée, *f.*; (*price*) prix d'entrée, *m*; prix des places, *m.*; (*concession*) aveu, *m.*, concession, *f.*; supposition, *f.* *Free —*, entrée libre, *f.*; libre accès, *m.* *Free —, — by an order*, entrée libre, *f.*, entrée de faveur, *f.*, entrée, *f.*, (*regular*) entrées, *f. pl.* *Free — ticket*, billet de faveur, *m.* — **money,** *s* prix d'entrée, *m.*, entrée, *f.*; prix des places, *m.* — **ticket,** *s* billet d'entrée, *m.*, entrée, *f.*
Admit, *v.a.* admettre; recevoir; (*let in*) laisser entrer; (*introduce*) faire entrer; (*procure admission*) donner entrée à, faire admettre; (*admit of*) admettre, comporter; (*confess*) avouer; reconnaître. — *of*, admettre, comporter; souffrir. *This ticket —s the bearer*, ce billet donne entrée au porteur
Admittance, *s.* accès, *m.*; entrée, admission, *f.* *To give —*, admettre, &c. (*V.* **Admit**). *No —!* on n'entre pas, défense d'entrer. *No — except on business*, le public n'entre pas ici, défense d'entrer
Admixture, *s.* mélange, *m.*, admixtion, *f.*
Admonish, *v.a.* avertir (de), prévenir (de); reprendre, réprimander, admonester; exhorter (à)

Admonisher, *s.* admoniteur, *m.*, -trice, *f.*
Admonition, *s.* avertissement, avis, conseil, *m.*; (*reproof*) admonestation, admonition, remontrance, *f.* [conseiller, *m.*
Admonitor, *s.* admoniteur, moniteur, *m.*;
Admonitory, *adj.* avertissant; monitorial
Ado, *s.* (*trouble*) peine, difficulté, *f.*; (*noise*) bruit, *m.*; (*fuss*) affaires, façons, histoires, *f.pl.*, embarras, *m.*, *m.pl.* *Much — about nothing*, beaucoup de bruit pour rien. *Without any more* —, sans plus de façons. *To make no more* —, n'en faire ni une ni deux, n'en pas faire à
Adolescence, *s.* adolescence, *f.* [deux fois
Adolescent, *s. adj.* adolescent, *m.*, e, *f.*
Adopt, *v.a.* adopter
Adoptable, *adj.* adoptable [tion, adopté
Adopted, *adj.* (*pers.*) adoptif; (*things*) d'adop-
Adoptedly, *adv.* par adoption
Adopter, *s.* adoptant, *m.*, e, *f.*; (*chem.*) allonge, *f.*
Adoption, *s.* adoption, *f.*; choix, *m.*
Adoptive, *adj.* *V.* **Adopted**
Adorable, *adj.* adorable
Adorableness, *s.* nature adorable, *f.*
Adorably, *adv.* adorablement
Adoration, *s.* adoration, *f.*
Adore, *v.a.* adorer
Adorer, *s.* adorateur, *m.*, -trice, *f.*
Adorn, *v.a.* orner, parer, embellir; (*fig.*, *of pers.*) faire l'ornement de [bellissement, *m.*
Adornment, *s.* ornement, *m.*, parure, *f.*, em-
Adragant. *V.* **Tragacanth**
Adriatic, *s. adj.* Adriatique, *f.*
Adrift, *adj. adv.* (*nav.*) en dérive; (*fig.*) à l'abandon. *To run* —, dériver, flotter; s'égarer.
Adroit, *adj.* adroit [*To turn* —, abandonner
Adroitly, *adv.* adroitement
Adroitness, *s.* adresse, dextérité, *f.*
Adulate, *v.a.* aduler
Adulation, *s.* adulation, *f.*
Adula-tor, tress, *s.* adulateur, *m.*, -trice, *f.*
Adulatory, *adj.* adulateur
Adult, *adj. s.* adulte, *m.f.*
Adulterate, *v.a.* falsifier, frelater, sophistiquer; (*deteriorate*) altérer, corrompre; (*pharm.*, *law*) adultérer; — *adj.* adultère; (*fig.*) falsifié, frelaté, altéré, sophistiqué
Adulteration, *s.* falsification, altération, sophistication, *f.*, frelatage, *m.*, adultération, *f.*
Adulterator, *s.* frelateur, sophistiqueur, *m.*
Adulterer, Adulteress, *s.* adultère, *m.f.*; femme adultère, *f.*
Adulterine, *adj. s.* adultérin, *m.*, e, *f.*
Adulterous, *adj.* adultère; (*fig.*) faux, corrompu, impur
Adulterously, *adv.* par l'adultère
Adultery, *s.* adultère, *m.*
Advance, *v.a.* avancer; faire avancer; (*move, one step or several*) faire; (*in rank*) élever; (*of prices*) hausser, augmenter, élever; — *v.n.* s'avancer; avancer; se porter en avant; (*to progress*) avancer, faire des progrès; (*in rank*) arriver; (*of prices*) hausser, s'élever
Advance, *s.* mouvement, *m.*, marche, *f.*; approche, *f.*; progrès, *m.*; (*in rank*) avancement, *m.*; (*step*) pas, *m.*; (*first step*) avance, *f.*, premier pas, *m.*; (*payment in advance, loan*) avance, *f.*; (*of prices*) hausse, augmentation, *f.* *In* —, en avant; (*beforehand*) d'avance; en avance. — **guard,** *s.* garde avancée, *f.* — **money,** *s.* avance, *f.*
Advancement, *s.* avancement, *m.*; promotion, *f.*; progrès, *m.*, *m.pl.*; (*of money*) avance, *f.*
Advantage, *s.* avantage, *m.*; supériorité, *f.*; intérêt, *m.*; profit, *m.* *To* —, à son avantage; avec avantage, avantageusement. *To take* — *of*, tirer avantage *or* profit de, profiter de; se servir de; se prévaloir de, se targuer de; abuser de; exploiter. *To turn to* —, tirer parti de, mettre à profit. — **ground,** *s.* *V.* **Vantage-ground**
Advantage, *v.a.* avantager; favoriser; avancer
Advantageous, *adj.* avantageux
Advantageously, *adv.* avantageusement
Advantageousness, *s.* avantage, *m.*, utilité, *f.*
Advent, *s.* venue, arrivée, *f.*; (*season before Christmas*) avent, *m.* *The first Sunday in* —, le premier dimanche de l'avent
Adventitious, *adj.* accidentel, accessoire; (*extrinsic, med., bot.*) adventice
Adventitiously, *adv.* accidentellement
Adventure, *s.* aventure, *f.*; incident, *m.*; hasard, risque, *m.*, chance, *f.*; spéculation, *f.*; (*com.*) pacotille, *f.*; — *v.n.a.* *V.* **Venture**
Adventurer, *s.* aventurier, *m.*; spéculateur, *m.*
Adventuresome, &c. *V.* **Venturesome,** &c.
Adventuress, *s.* aventurière, *f.*
Adventurous, Adventurously. *V.* **Venturous, Venturously**
Adventurousness. *V.* **Venturousness**
Adverb, *s.* adverbe, *m.*
Adverbial, *adj.* adverbial
Adverbialize, *v.a.* adverbialiser
Adverbially, *adv.* adverbialement
Adversary, *s.* adversaire, *m.f.*
Adverse, *adj.* adverse; contraire (à); opposé (à); ennemi (de), hostile (à); défavorable; (*unprosperous*) malheureux; (*bot.*) adverse
Adversely, *adv.* d'une manière hostile; défavorablement; (*unfortunately*) malheureuse-
Adversity, *s.* adversité, *f.* [ment
Advert, *v.n.* parler (de); appeler l'attention (sur); faire observer; faire allusion (à); vouloir parler (de); considérer; observer; faire
Advertenc-e, y, *s.* attention, *f.* [attention (à)
Advertent, *adj.* attentif
Advertently, *adv.* attentivement
Advertise, *v.a.* annoncer, faire annoncer; (*inform*) avertir, informer; (*post up, show up, expose*) afficher
Advertisement, *s.* avertissement, avis, *m.*; (*in public papers and periodicals*) annonce, *f.*; (*inserted among the news*) réclame, *f.*; (*placard, poster*) affiche, *f.*; (*fig.*, *anything to attract notice*) réclame, *f.*; enseigne, *f.* — **agent,** *s.* *V.* **Advertising.** — **frame,** *s.* porte-affiches, *m.* — **office,** *s.* (*of a newspaper*) bureau des annonces, *m.*; (*for newspapers*) bureau d'annonces, *m.*, agence de publicité, *f.* — **sheet,** *s.* feuille d'annonces, *f.*
Advertiser, *s.* personne qui annonce, *f.*; (*paper*) journal d'annonces, *m.*, petites affiches, *f. pl.*
Advertising, *s.* annonces, *f. pl.*, publicité, *f.* — **agent,** *s.* courtier d'annonces, agent de publicité, *m.* — **frame, office, sheet.** *V.* **Advertisement**
Advice, *s.* avis, *m.*; conseil, *m.*; consultation, *f.*; consultations, *f. pl.*; opinion, *f.* *Piece of* —, avis, conseil. *To take* —, prendre conseil (de); consulter. *To take a person's* —, suivre le conseil de quelqu'un, en croire quelqu'un. — **boat,** *s.* *V.* **Despatch-boat**
Advisable, *adj.* conseillable; prudent (de), sage (de), judicieux (de); (*proper*) convenable (de), à propos (de), utile (de)
Advisableness, *s.* prudence, sagesse, *f.*; utilité, convenance, *f.*; opportunité, *f.*
Advisably, *adv.* prudemment, sagement; convenablement, à propos
Advise, *v.a.* conseiller (de); informer (de), instruire (de), donner avis (de), prévenir (de); (*com.*) aviser (de); — *v.n.* délibérer, considérer, réfléchir; prendre conseil, se consulter
Advised, *part.* conseillé, &c. (*V.* **Advise**); — *adj.* avisé, prudent, circonspect; (*deliberate*) réfléchi, prémédité. *Ill* —, mal avisé; (*things*) mal vu, imprudent, irréfléchi. *Well* —, bien avisé; (*things*) bien vu, prudent, sage, judicieux. *Be — by me*, croyez-m'en
Advisedly, *adv.* avec réflexion; avec circonspection; sciemment; de propos délibéré, délibérément, à dessein, exprès, avec préméditation; judicieusement [conspection *f.*
Advisedness, *s.* prudence, sagesse, *f.*; cir-

Adviser, *s.* conseiller, *m.*, -ère, *f.*
Advocacy, *s.* défense, *f.*, appui, soutien, *m.*; intercession, *f.*
Advocate, *s.* avocat, défenseur, *m.*; — *v.a.* plaider; appuyer, soutenir, défendre
Advowee, *s.* patron, collateur, nominateur, *m.*
Advowson, *s.* patronage, *m.*, collation, nomination, *f.*
Adynam-ic, -y. *V.* page 3, § 1
Adze, *s.* herminette, doloire, *f.*; — *v.a.* doler
Ædile, *s.* édile, *m.*
Ædileship, *s.* édilité, *f.*
Ægis, *s.* égide *f.*
Æneid, *s.* Énéide, *f.*
Æolian, *adj.* éolien
Æolic, *adj.* éolique
Æra. *V.* **Era**
Aerate, *v.a.* (*chem.*) aérer
Aerated, *adj.* (*chem.*) aéré; (*commonly*) gazeux
Aeration, *s.* aération, *f.*
Aerial, *adj.* aérien, d'air, de l'air
Aerie, *s.* aire, *f.*
Aerification, *s.* aérification, *f.*
Aeriform, *adj.* aériforme
Aerify, *v.a.* aériser
Aerodynamics, *s. pl.* aérodynamique, *f.*
Aerolite, *s.* aérolithe, *m.*
Aerometer, *s.* aéromètre, *m.*
Aerometry, *s.* aérométrie, *f.*
Aeronaut, *s.* aéronaute, *m.f.*
Aeronautic, -al, *adj.* aéronautique, *m.f.*; —**s,** [*s. pl.* aéronautique, *f.*
Aerostat, *s.* aérostat, *m.*
Aerostatic, -al, *adj.* aérostatique, *m.f.*; —**s,** *s. pl.* aérostatique, *f.*
Aerostation, *s.* aérostation, *f.*
Aerothermal, *adj.* aérotherme
Aery, *s.* aire, *f.*
Æsculapian, *adj.* d'Esculape, médical
Æsopian, *adj.* ésopique, d'Ésope
Æsthetic, -al, *adj.* esthétique; — **s,** *s. pl.* [esthétique, *f.*
Æsthetically, *adv.* esthétiquement
Æstivation, &c. *V.* **Estivation,** &c.
Afar, — **off,** *adv.* loin; au loin; de loin
Affability, *s.* affabilité, *f.*
Affable, *adj.* affable, gracieux
Affably, *adv.* affablement, avec affabilité
Affair, *s.* affaire, *f.*
Affect, *v.a.* affecter (de); (*to move*) toucher, attendrir, émouvoir, affecter; (*to interest*) intéresser; (*aim at*) viser à, aspirer à, prétendre à
Affectation, *s.* affectation, *f.*
Affected, *part. adj.* affecté; (*moved*) touché, attendri, ému, affecté; (*not natural*) affecté, prétentieux; (*disposed*) disposé, intentionné
Affectedly, *adv.* avec affectation
Affectingly, *adv.* d'une manière touchante *or* attendrissante
Affection, *s.* affection, *f.*; attachement, *m.*; inclination, *f.*, penchant, *m*; passion, *f.*; sentiment, *m.*; émotion, *f.*; (*med.*) affection, maladie, *f.*
Affectionate, *adj.* affectueux; affectionné
Affectionately, *adv.* affectueusement, avec affection, affectionnément. *V.* **Yours**
Affectionateness, *s.* affection, tendresse, *f.*
Affective, *adj.* affectif
Affiance, *s.* fiançailles, *f. pl.*; — *v.a.* fiancer
Affidavit, *s.* déclaration sous serment, *f.*
Affiliate, *v.a.* adopter; affilier; (*law*) attribuer (à); (*fig.*) rattacher (à)
Affiliation, *s.* adoption, *f.*; affiliation, *f.*; (*law*) recherche de la paternité, *f.*, reconnaissance légale d'un enfant naturel, *f.*
Affinity, *s.* affinité, *f.*
Affirm, *v.a.n.* affirmer (à), assurer (à); confirmer
Affirmation, *s.* affirmation, *f.*; confirmation, *f.*; (*law*) déclaration, *f.*
Affirmative, *adj.* affirmatif; — *s.* affirmative, *f.* *In the* —, affirmativement
Affirmatively, *adv.* affirmativement
Affix, *v.a.* (*a seal,* &c.) apposer (à); (*add*) ajouter (à); (*attach*) attacher (à), lier (à); (*to fix*) fixer (à); — *s.* (*gram.*) affixe, *m.*

Afflatus, *s.* souffle, *m.*; inspiration, *f.*
Afflict, *v.a.* affliger, chagriner, tourmenter
Affliction, *s.* affliction, *f.*; calamité, *f.*; malheur, *m.*; adversité, *f.*; misère, *f.*
Afflictive, *adj.* affligeant
Afflictively, *adv.* d'une manière affligeante
Affluence, *s.* affluence, *f.*; abondance, *f.*; opulence, *f.*; richesses, *f. pl.*
Affluent, *adj.* affluent; abondant; opulent, riche; — *s.* (*geog*) affluent, *m.*; (*pers.*) personnes qui ont de la fortune, *f. pl.*, riches, *m. pl.*
Affluently, *adv.* abondamment; avec opulence
Afflux, Affluxion, *s.* affluence, *f.*; (*med.*) afflux, *m.*
Afford, *v.a.n.* (*to give*) donner (à), fournir (à), procurer (à), accorder (à); (*communicate*) faire part de (à); (*be able*) pouvoir; être en position (de); (*to have the means*) avoir le moyen (de); être assez riche (pour); se donner, se permettre; (*of time,* &c., *find*) trouver; (*to have time enough*) avoir le temps (de). *I cannot — to keep a horse,* je n'ai pas le moyen d'avoir un cheval. *I cannot — it,* je n'en ai pas le moyen, mes moyens ne me le permettent pas. *He could not — you a minute,* il n'a pas pu vous donner une minute. *I could not — to give so much for it,* je ne pourrais pas en donner tant que cela
Afforest, *v.a.* convertir en forêt; boiser
Afforestation, *s.* conversion en forêt, *f.*; boisement, *m.*
Affray, *s.* échauffourée, querelle, *f.*
Affright, *v.a.* *V.* **Frighten**; — *s.* *V.* **Fright**
Affrightedly, *adv.* avec effroi, avec épouvante
Affront, *v.a.* insulter, outrager, faire un affront à; (*fam.*) blesser, piquer; (*to meet*) affronter; — *s.* affront, *m.*, insulte, injure, *f.*, outrage, *m.* *To give or offer an — to, to put an — upon,* faire [un affront à
Affronter, *s.* offenseur, *m.*
Affronting, Affrontive, *adj.* offensant, insultant, outrageant
Afield, *adv.* dans les champs, aux champs, à la campagne; (*mil.*) en campagne
Afire, *adv.* en feu
Afloat, *adv.* à flot; en mer; (*fig.*) sur pied; en [circulation; en train
Afoot, *adv.* à pied; (*moving*) en chemin; en train
Afore, *prep. adv., conj.* (*old, vulgar*) *V.* **Before**; — *prep.* (*nav.*) devant; — *adv.* (*nav.*) sur le devant, en avant; — *s.* (*nav.*) avant, *m.* — **going,** *adj.* précédent. — **hand,** *adv.* *V.* **Beforehand.** — **mentioned,** *adj.* *V.* **Above-mentioned.** — **named,** *adj.* susnommé. — **said,** *adj.* susdit. — **thought,** *adj.* prémédité
Afraid, *adj.* effrayé; qui a peur; craignant; craintif. *To be — of,* avoir peur de, craindre. *To make* (...) — *of,* faire peur à (...) de, faire craindre (...) à, faire craindre à (...)
Afresh, *adv.* de nouveau
African, *s.* Africain, *m.*, e, *f.*; — *adj.* africain, [d'Afrique
Aft, *adv.* *V.* **Astern.** *The — part,* l'arrière, *m.*
After, *prep.* après; (*before a verb not an inf.*) que; (*in the train of*) à la suite de [à ma, ta, sa *or* &c. suite]; (*in imitation of*) d'après; (*according to*) selon, suivant; à; sur; (*of names*) du nom de; — *adv.* après; ensuite; (*following*) suivant, d'après; — *adj.* ultérieur, postérieur, futur, à venir; tardif; arrière; (*nav.*) de l'arrière, d'arrière. — *it, them* (*things*), après. *What are you — ?* qu'est ce que vous faites? — **ages,** *s. pl.* siècles futurs, siècles à venir, *m.pl.*, postérité, *f.* — **all,** *adv.* après tout; au fond; au résumé; au bout du compte; enfin. — **birth,** *s.* arrière-faix, *m.*; (*med.*) délivre, *m.* — **cabin,** *s.* (*nav.*) chambre d'arrière, première chambre, *f.* — **carriage,** *s.* arrière-train, *m.* — **clap,** *s.* événement *or* coup inattendu, *m.*; contre-coup, second coup, *m.* — **costs,** *s. pl.* frais ultérieurs, *m. pl.*; surcroît de dépense, *m.* — **crop,** *s.* seconde récolte, *f.*; regain, *m.* — **date,** *s.* postdate, *f.*; *v.a.* postdater. — **days,** *s. pl.* jours à venir, *m. pl.*, avenir, *m.* — **dinner,** *s.* après-dîner, *m.*; *adj.* de l'après-

diner, d'après-diner. — **game,** *s.* nouvel expédient, *m.*, dernière ressource, *f.* — **grass. -growth,** *s.* regain, *m.* — **hours,** *s.pl.* heures à venir, *f. pl.*, avenir, *m.*; (*of workmen*, &c.) heures en sus, *f. pl.*; *adv.* après l'heure habituelle. — **life,** *s.* vie à venir, (l') autre vie, *f.*; cours ultérieur de la vie, avenir, *m.* *In — life*, plus tard. — **liver,** *s.* survivant, *m.*; descendant, *m.* — **love,** *s.* second amour, *m.* — **math,** *s.* regain, *m.* — **meeting,** *s.* réunion ultérieure, *f.* — **noon,** *s.* après-midi, *f.*; (*fig.*) déclin, *m.* *Good — noon!* bonjour! — **pains,** *s. pl.* douleurs après l'accouchement, *f. pl.*; (*med.*) tranchées, coliques, *f. pl.* — **part,** *s.* seconde partie, *f.*; dernière partie, *f.* — **piece,** *s.* (*theat.*) petite pièce, *f.* — **proceedings,** *s.pl.* procédures subséquentes, *f.pl.* — **proof,** *s.* preuve ultérieure *or* subséquente, *f.* — **reckoning,** *s.* révision de compte, *f.*; nouveau compte, *m.*; surécot, subrécot, *m.* — **repentance,** *s.* repentir tardif, *m.* — **season,** *s.* arrière-saison, *f.* — **supper,** *s.* après-souper, *m.* — **swarm,** *s.* arrière-essaim, *m.* — **taste,** *s.* arrière-goût, *m.*; (*unpleasant*) déboire, *m.* — **thought,** *s.*réflexion (*or* pensée) tardive, *f.*; autre pensée, *f.*, changement d'avis, ravisement, *m.* — **time,** *s.* (*of workmen*) temps en sus, *m.* — **times,** *s.pl.* temps à venir, avenir, *m.* — **tossing,** *s.* (*of the sea*) agitation (après la tempête), *f.*, clapotage, *m.* — **touch,** *s.* (*paint.*) retouche, *f.* — **ward,** — **wards,** *adv.* après, ensuite, puis; par la suite, depuis, plus tard. — **wise,** *adj.* sage après coup. — **wit,** *s.* sagesse tardive, sagesse après coup, bonne idée qui vient trop tard, *f.* — **years,** *s.pl.* années subséquentes, *f.pl.*; temps, *m.* [*In — years*, plus tard

Aga, *s.* aga, *m.*

Again, *adv.* (*once more*) de nouveau, encore, encore une fois; deux fois; (*further*) ensuite, d'autre part, de plus; (*also, likewise*) aussi, de même; (*in return*) en retour; de retour. — *and —*, (*several times*) plusieurs fois, à plusieurs reprises; (*often*) souvent, bien des fois, mille et mille fois; (*continually*) sans cesse, sans discontinuer, tant et plus; (*of knocking*) à coups redoublés. *As large —*, deux fois aussi grand. *As much —, as many —*, *V.* **Much** *and* **Many.** *Not —*, (*not any more*) ne ... plus. *Never —*, ne ... plus jamais; ne ... plus. [*With many verbs, 'again' is expressed by* **re,** *as* faire, refaire; *or by* **r** *before a vowel, as* ouvrir, rouvrir; *or by* **res** *before another* s, *as* sortir, ressortir]

Against, *prep.* contre; (*towards*) vers; (*for*) pour; (*facing*) vis-à-vis; (*near*) près de; (*until*) *V.* **Until.** — *it, them* (*things*), contre; vis-à-vis; auprès. *Over —*, vis-à-vis, en face

Agama, *s.* agame, *m.*

Agami, *s.* agami, *m.*

Agamous, *adj.* agame

Agape, *adj.* la bouche béante; (*for*) dans l'attente (de); — *s.* (*theol.*) agape, *f.*

Agaric, *s.* agaric, *m.*

Agate, *s.* agate, *f.*

Agaty, *adj.* d'agate

Agave, *s.* agave, *f.*

Age, *s.* âge, *m.*; (*century*) siècle, âge, *m.*; temps, *m.pl.*; (*generation*) génération, *f.*; (*mature age*) âge mûr, *m.*; (*old age*) vieillesse, *f.*, âge, *m.* *In the — of*, (*hist.*) au siècle de. *Of —*, majeur. *Of an — to*, d'âge à. *Under —*, mineur. *Want of —*, défaut d'âge, *m.* *To come of —*, arriver à sa majorité. *To look o.'s —*. paraître son âge. *To bear o.'s — well*, ne pas paraître son âge, porter bien son âge. *What is your —?* quel âge avez-vous? *Ten years of —*. dix ans. *The — of ten*, l'âge de dix ans, dix ans

Age, *v.n.a.* vieillir

Aged, *adj.* âgé; vieux; âgé de; (*of horses*) hors d'âge, âgé; —, *s. pl.* vieillards, *m.pl.*

Agency, *s.* action, *f.*; (*medium*) entremise, *f.*, intermédiaire, *m.*; (*com.*) agence, *f.*; commission, *f.* *Business —*, agence d'affaires, *f.* — **business,** *s.* agence, *f.* — **office,** *s.* agence, *f.*; agence d'affaires, *f.*

Agenda, *s.* agenda, *m.*

Agent, *s.* agent, *m.*, e, *f.*; (*admin.*) homme d'affaires, *m.*; (*com.*) commissionnaire, *m.f.*

Agger, *s.* tas, amas, *m.*; remblai, *m.* [glomérer

Agglomerate, *v.a.* agglomérer; — *v.n.* s'ag-

Agglomeration, *s.* agglomération, *f.*

Agglutinant, *adj.* agglutinant; — *s.* agglutinant, agglutinatif, *m.* [tiner

Agglutinate, *v.a.* agglutiner; — *v.n.* s'agglu-

Agglutination, *s.* agglutination, *f.*

Agglutinative, *adj.* agglutinatif

Aggrandize, *v.a.* agrandir

Aggrandizement, *s.* agrandissement, *m.*

Aggravate, *v.a.* aggraver; exagérer; (*vex*) agacer, taquiner, faire endêver; provoquer; pousser à bout [**gravate**); grave

Aggravated, *part. adj.* aggravé, &c. (*V.* **Ag-**

Aggravation, *s.* aggravation, *f.*; circonstance aggravante, *f.*; exagération, *f.*; provocation, *f.*; agacerie, *f.*; agacement, *m.*

Aggregate, *v.a.* rassembler; réunir; recueillir; — *adj.* rassemblé, réuni; agrégé; total; collectif; — *s.* masse, *f.*; total, *m.*; collection, *f.*; assemblage, *m.*; agrégat, *m.* *In the —*, en masse, en somme, tout ensemble, à tout prendre

Aggregately, *adv.* en masse, collectivement

Aggregation, *s.* réunion, *f.*; assemblage, *m.*; total, *m.*; (*chem.*) agrégation, *f.*

Aggregative, *adj.* agrégatif [teinte (à), *f*

Aggression, *s.* agression, *f.*; (*on, upon*) at-

Aggressive, *adj.* agressif, hostile

Aggressively, *adv.* agressivement

Aggressiveness, *s.* caractère agressif, *m.*

Aggressor, *s.* agresseur, *m.*

Aggrieve, *v.a.* affliger, chagriner, peiner, molester; blesser, offenser, léser

Agha, *s.* aga, *m.* [sterné, épouvanté; ébahi

Aghast, *adj.* saisi d'effroi *or* d'horreur, con-

Agile, *adj.* agile, leste, dispos

Agility, *s.* agilité, légèreté, *f*

Agio, *s.* agio, *m.* [bution

Agist, *v.a.* faire paître moyennant une rétri-

Agitate, *v.a.* agiter; remuer; troubler; discuter; exciter [cussion, *f.*, examen, *m.*

Agitation, *s.* agitation, *f.*, trouble, *m.*; dis-

Agitator, *s.* agitateur, meneur, *m.*

Agnate, *s.* agnat, *m.*; — *adj.* d'agnat

Agnation, *s.* agnation, *f.*

Agnomen, *s.* surnom, *m.*

Ago, *adv.* il y a; il y a eu. *Some time —*, il y a quelque temps. *A short time —*, il n'y a pas longtemps. *Long —, a good while —*, il y a longtemps; depuis longtemps. *Not long —*, il n'y a pas longtemps. *A year —, ten years —*, il y a un an, il y a dix ans. *A year — yesterday*, il y a eu hier un an. *Some years —*, il y a quelques années. *How long —?* combien y a-t-il de temps? *That* (or *it*) *was ten years —*, il y a de cela dix ans

Agog, *adj.* (*active*) dans l'agitation, en émoi, en l'air; (*heated*) excité, enflammé, monté, qui a la tête montée, ivre; en train; (*longing*) bouillant, pétillant. *To be —*, être dans l'agitation *or* &c.; avoir la tête montée. *To set —*, mettre dans l'agitation *or* &c.; exciter, monter, monter la tête à [train, en branle

Agoing, *adj.* en action, en mouvement, en

Agonize, *v.n* souffrir l'agonie, être au supplice; — *v.a.* faire souffrir l'agonie à, mettre au supplice, martyriser, torturer

Agonized, *adj.* qui souffre l'agonie

Agonizing, *adj.* qui souffre cruellement; (*giving pain*) déchirant; cruel

Agonizingly, *adv.* d'une manière déchirante, avec d'affreuses douleurs

Agony, *s.* agonie, angoisse, douleur, *f.* *To suffer —ies*, souffrir l'agonie *or* le martyre, être [au supplice

Agouti, *s.* agouti, *m.*

Agrarian, *adj.* agraire

Agree, *v.n.* s'accorder, être d'accord; (— *in opinion with*) être de l'avis (de); (*settle, admit*) convenir (de); (*engage*) s'engager (à); (*consent*) consentir (à); (*assent*) donner son assentiment (à); (*accept*) accepter; adopter; (*be like*) ressembler (à); (*be like each other*) se ressembler; (*suit*) convenir (à), s'accorder (avec); (*be suited to each other*) se convenir; (*be reconciled*) se réconcilier; (*of the health*) convenir (à), réussir (à), faire du bien (à); bien passer; (*gram.*) s'accorder. *Not to* —, *V.* **Disagree.** *To make* (...) —, accorder (...), mettre (...) d'accord; réconcilier (...); concilier (...); faire consentir *or* &c. *To be* —*d*, (*pers.*) être d'accord; (*things*) être convenu. *That is* —*d on by all*, tout le monde est d'accord là-dessus; tout le monde en convient. *I* — *with you there*, je suis de votre avis. *My dinner* —*d with me*, mon dîner a bien passé

Agreeable, *adj.* agréable; conforme (à); d'accord (avec). *To be* — *to a thing*, vouloir bien quelque chose

Agreeableness, *s.* agrément, *m.*; conformité, harmonie, *f.*; ressemblance, *f.*

Agreeably, *adv.* agréablement; conformément (à)

Agreed, *adj.* d'accord; (*things*) convenu; admis, reconnu; — *int.* d'accord! c'est convenu! va! — *part. and pret. V.* **Agree.** —**on,** *adj.* convenu

Agreement, *s.* accord, *m.*; rapport, *m.*; union, concorde, bonne intelligence, *f.*; ressemblance, *f.*; convention, *f.*, pacte, *m.*; contrat, *m.*; (*bargain*) marché, *m.*; (*gram.*) accord, *m.* *To come to an* —, entrer en accommodement

Agricultural, *adj.* agricole, d'agriculture; aratoire. —*implement maker*, — *engineer*, fabricant de machines d'agriculture, *m.*

Agriculturalist. *V.* **Agriculturist**

Agriculture, *s.* agriculture, *f.*

Agriculturist, *s.* agriculteur, cultivateur, *m.*

Agrimony, *s.* aigremoine, *f.*

Agronom-ic, al, -ically, -y. *V.* page 3, § 1

Agronomist, *s.* agronome, *m.*

Aground, *adv.* (*nav.*) échoué, à terre. *To cast* —, jeter à la côte. *To run* —, *v.n.* s'échouer, échouer; *v.a.* échouer, faire échouer

Ague, *s.* fièvre (intermittente), *f.* — **drops,** *s. pl.* gouttes fébrifuges, *f.pl.* — **fit,** *s.* accès de fièvre, *m.* — **powder,** *s.* poudre fébrifuge, *f.*

Agued, Aguish, *adj.* fébricitant, fiévreux; fébrile; (*fig.*) ardent, brûlant. *Aguish fever*, fièvre intermittente, *f.*

Aguishness, *s.* état fébrile, *m.*

Ah, *int.* ah! hélas!

Ahead, *adv.* en avant, devant; devant soi; (*fig.*) en tête, à la tête. — *of*, en avant de, devant; en tête de, à la tête de; plus avancé que. *Right* —, tout droit. *To get* — *of*, devancer. *To have the wind* —, (*nav.*) avoir vent debout

Ahl, *s.* (*agr.*) purin, *m.*

Ahoy, *int.* (*nav.*) ho!

Ahull, *adv.* (*nav.*) à sec, à mâts et à cordes

Aid, *v.a.* aider, secourir, assister; — *s.* aide, *f.*, secours, *m.*, assistance, *f.*; subside, *m.*; (*pers.*) aide, *m.f.* *By the* — *of*, à l'aide de. *In* — *of*, (*of performances*) au profit de, au bénéfice de. — **major,** *s.* adjudant-major, *m.*

Aide-de-camp, *s.* aide de camp, *m.*

Aider, *s.* aidant, *m.*, complice, *m.f.*

Aidless, *adj.* sans secours, délaissé

Aigret, Aigrette. *V.* **Egret**

Aiguillette, *s.* aiguillette, *f.*

Ail, *v.a.* avoir; faire mal à; chagriner. *What* —*s you?* qu'avez-vous? qu'est-ce qui vous fait mal *or* vous chagrine? *Nothing* —*s me*, je n'ai rien, rien ne me fait mal *or* ne me chagrine. *Something* —*s him*, il a quelque chose

Ailing, *adj.* souffrant, maladif

Ailment, *s.* mal, *m.*, indisposition, *f.*; malaise, *m.*; souffrance, *f.*

Aim, *v.a.* viser, ajuster, diriger; (*to throw*) lancer; (*a blow*) porter; — *v.n.* viser (contre); (*fig.*) viser (à), aspirer (à), tendre (à); chercher (à); avoir pour but; (*to threaten*) menacer; — *s.* but, *m.*; dessein, *m.*, intention, vue, *f.*; prétention, *f.*; (*mark*) point de mire, *m.*; (*sight of a gun*) guidon, *m.*, mire, *f.* *To miss o.'s* —, manquer son but; manquer son coup. *To take* —, viser

Aimless, *adj.*, **Aimlessly,** *adv.* sans but

Air, *s.* air, *m.* *In the* —, dans l'air; (*high up*) en l'air; (*outside*) à l'air. *In the open* —, en plein air; au grand air. *To go out in the open* —, prendre l'air. *To take fresh* —, prendre le frais. *To vanish into thin* —, s'en aller à vau-l'eau; s'en aller *or* tourner en eau de boudin. — **ball,** *s.* petit ballon, *m.* — **balloon,** *s.* ballon, aérostat, *m.* — **bed,** *s.* matelas à air, *m.* — **bladder,** *s.* vessie natatoire, *f.* — **box,** *s.* boîte à air, *f.*, réservoir d'air, *m.* — **bubble,** *s.* bulle d'air, *f.* — **built,** *adj.* en l'air, chimérique, imaginaire. — **cane,** *s.* canne à vent, *f.* — **cell,** *s.* cellule aérienne, *f.* — **current,** *s.* courant d'air, *m.* — **cushion,** *s.* coussin à air, *m.* — **gun,** *s.* fusil à vent, *m.* —**holder,** *s.* tube à air, *m.* — **hole,** *s.* trou pour donner de l'air, *m.*; soupirail, *m.*; ventouse, *f.*; (*of furnaces*) évent, carnau, *m.*; (*in founding*) globule, *m.* — **jacket,** *s.* scaphandre, *m.* — **lamp,** *s.* lampe à courant d'air, *f.* — **mattress,** *s.* matelas à air, *m.* — **passages,** *s.pl.* (*anat.*) voies aériennes, *f.pl.* — **pipe,** *s.* ventilateur, *m.* — **plant,** *s.* épiphyte, *m.* — **pump,** *s.* pompe à air, *f.*; (*phys.*) machine pneumatique, *f.* — **shaft,** *s.* bure d'airage, *f.*, puits d'aérage, *m.* — **slaked, -slacked,** *adj.* (*of lime*) fusé. — **stove,** *s.* calorifère, *m.* — **thermometer,** *s.* thermomètre à air, *m.* — **thread,** *s.* fil de la Vierge, *m.* — **tight,** *adj.* imperméable à l'air. — **tightness,** *s.* imperméabilité à l'air, *f.* — **trap,** *s.* ventilateur, *m.* — **tube,** *s.* conduit aérien, *m.*, voie aérienne, *f.*; (*of insects*) trachée, *f.* — **valve,** *s.* soupape à air, *f.* — **vessel,** *s.* (*bot.*) trachée, *f.*; (*tech.*) réservoir d'air, *m.*

Air, *v.a.* aérer, mettre à l'air, donner de l'air à, éventer; (*of linen*) chauffer; (*of liquids*) faire dégourdir. *To* — *oneself*, prendre l'air

Aired, *adj.* (*of linen*) sec

Airily, *adv.* légèrement; gaiment

Airiness, *s.* exposition à l'air, *f.*; (*fig.*) légèreté, gaieté, *f.*

Airing, *s.* aération, *f.*; aérage, *m.*; exposition à l'air, *f.*, éventage, éventement, *m.*; exposition au feu, *f.*; (*a turn out*) promenade, *f.*, tour de promenade, *m.* *To take an* —, prendre l'air, faire une promenade, se promener. *To give an* —, faire prendre l'air (à), faire faire une promenade (à), faire promener, mener promener, promener

Airless, *adj.* sans air, privé d'air

Airy, *adj.* aérien, de l'air, des airs; (*open*) aéré; (*light*) léger, délicat, aérien; (*lively*) gai, enjoué, folâtre, sémillant; (*idle*) en l'air; vain

Aisle, *s.* bas-côté, *m.*, aile, *f.*

Aisled, *adj.* à bas-côtés

Ait, *s.* îlot, *m.*

Ajar, *adj.* entre-bâillé, entr' ouvert, tout contre; (*not agreed*) en désaccord

Ajutage, *s.* ajutage, ajutoir, *m.*

Akimbo, *adv.* *V.* **Kimbo**

Akin, *adj.* (*pers.*) parent; (*things*) allié (à), voisin (de), qui ressemble (à), qui a du rapport (avec)

Alabaster, *s.* albâtre, *m.*; — *adj.* d'albâtre

Alack, Alackaday, *int.* hélas!

Alacrity, *s.* alacrité, *f.*, allégresse, gaieté, *f.*, plaisir, *m.*, vivacité, ardeur, *f.*; (*eagerness*) empressement, *m.*; promptitude, *f.*

Alamode, *adj. adv.* à la mode

Alar, *adj.* alaire

Alarm, *s.* alarme, *f.*; instrument *or* appareil pour donner l'alarme, *m.*; (*of time-pieces*) réveil, *m.* —**bell,** *s.* cloche *or* sonnette d'alarme, *f.*; tocsin, beffroi, *m.* — **clock,** *s.* réveille-matin, réveil, *m.* — **gun,** *s.* canon d'alarme, *m.* — **post,** *s.* point de ralliement, *m.* — **watch,** *s.* *V.* — **clock**

Alarm, *v.a.* alarmer, donner l'alarme à; faire peur à, effrayer; (*fig.*) réveiller. *Don't be —ed*, ne vous alarmez pas, n'ayez pas peur, soyez sans inquiétude
Alarmingly, *adv.* d'une manière alarmante
Alarmist, *s.* alarmiste, *m.f.*
Alarum, *s. V.* **Alarm**
Alas, *int.* hélas! — *the day!* ô jour malheureux!
Alb, Albe, *s.* aube, *f.*
Albanian, *s. adj.* Albanais, *m.*, e, *f.*
Albata, *s.* métal blanc, maillechort, *m.*
Albatross, *s.* albatros, *m.*
Albeit, *conj. adv.* (*although*) quoique, bien que; (*still*) malgré cela, quoi qu'il en soit, néanmoins, toutefois; (*even*) même
Alberge, *s.* alberge, *f.* — **tree**, *s.* albergier, *m.*
Albigenses, *s. pl.* Albigeois, *m.pl.*
Albina, Albiness, *s.* albina, *f.*
Albinism, Albinoism, *s.* albinisme, *m.*
Albino, *s. adj.* albinos, *s.m.*, *adj. m.f.*
Albugineous, *adj.* albuginé, albugineux
Albugo, *s.* albugo, *m.f.*, taie, *f.*
Album, *s.* album, *m.*
Albumen, *s.* (*chem.*) albumine, *f.*; (*bot.*) albumen, *m.*
Albumenize, *v.a.* albuminer
Albuminous, *adj.* albumineux
Albuminuria, *s.* albuminurie, *f.*
Alburnum, *s.* aubier, *m.*
Alcade, Alcaid, Alcalde, *s.* alcade, alcaïde, *m*
Alcaic, *adj. s.* alcaïque, *adj. m.f.*, *s.m.*
Alcarazza, Alcarraza, *s.* alcarazas, alcarraza, *m.*
Alcazar, *s.* alcazar, *m.*
Alchemic, -al, *adj.* alchimique
Alchemically, *adv.* par l'alchimie
Alchemist, *s.* alchimiste, *m.*
Alchemistic, -al, *adj.* alchimique
Alchemy, *s.* alchimie, *f.*
Alcohol, *s.* alcool, *m.*
Alcoholic, *adj.* alcoolique
Alcoholicity, *s.* alcoolicité, *f.*
Alcoholism, *s.* alcoolisme, *m.*
Alcoholization, *s.* alcoolisation, *f.*
Alcoholize, *v.a.* alcooliser
Alcoholometer, Alcoholmeter, Alcoometer, *s.* alcoolomètre, alcoomètre, *m.*
Alcoran. *V.* **Koran**
Alcove, *s.* renfoncement, *m.*; (*for a bed*) alcôve, *f.*; (*arbour*) tonnelle, *f.*, berceau, *m.*
Alcyon. *V.* **Halcyon**
Aldehyde, *s.* aldéhyde, *m.*
Alder, *s.* aune, *m.* — **tree**, *s.* aune, *m.* — — **grove, -plantation**, *s.* aunaie, *f.*
Alderman, *s.* conseiller municipal, *m.*; adjoint, *m.*; (*in Paris*) maire (d'arrondissement), *m.*; (*in England*) alderman, *m.*
Aldermanic, Aldermanly, *adj.* d'alderman
Aldern, *adj.* d'aune
Aldine, *adj.* aldin. — *edition*, édition aldine, *f.*, alde, *m.*
Ale, *s.* ale, *f.* — **house**, &c. *V.* **Beer.** — **wife**, *s.* cabaretière, *f.*; (*fish*) gasparot, gasperau, *m.*
Alee, *adv.* (*nav.*) sous le vent; — *int.* envoyez!
Alembic, *s.* alambic, *m.*
Alert, *adj.* alerte; vif; vigilant; éveillé; — *s.* alerte, *f.* *On* or *upon the —*, en alerte; sur le qui-vive, sur ses gardes, en éveil
Alertly, *adv.* alertement
Alertness, *s.* promptitude, *f.*; vivacité, *f.*; légèreté, *f.*; vigilance, *f.*
Alexanders, *s.* (*bot.*) maceron, *m.*
Alexandrian, *adj.* (*of Alexander*) d'Alexandre; (*of Alexandria*) alexandrin, d'Alexandrie
Alexandrine, *adj. s.* (*vers.*) alexandrin, *m.*; — *adj.* (*of Alexandria*) alexandrin, d'Alexandrie
Alexipharmic, *adj. s.* alexipharmaque, *adj. m.f.*, *s.m.*
Alga, *s.* (*bot.*) algue, *f.* — *marina*, *V.* **Grass-wrack**
Algebra, *s.* algèbre, *f.*
Algebraic, -al, *adj.* algébrique
Algebraically, *adv.* algébriquement
Algebraist, *s.* algébriste, *m.*
Algerian, Algerine, *s.* Algérien, *m.*, -ne, *f.*; — *adj.* algérien, de l'Algérie, d'Alger
Algid, *adj.* (*med.*) algide
Algor, *s.* (*med.*) algor, froid glacial, *m.*
Algorithm, *s.* algorithme, *m.*
Alguazil, *s.* alguazil, *m.*
Alhambra, *s.* Alhambra, *m.*
Alias, *adv.* dit; autrement dit; connu sous le nom de; — *s.* faux nom, nom de guerre, [pseudonyme, *m.*
Alibi, *s.* alibi, *m.*
Alible, *adj.* alibile
Alicant, *s.* Alicante, *f.*; (*wine*) alicante, *m.*
Alidade, *s.* alidade, *f.*
Alien, *adj.* étranger (à); éloigné (de); — *s.* étranger, *m.*, -ère, *f.* — **act, -bill**, *s.* loi sur les étrangers, *f.* — **office**, bureau des étrangers, *m.*
Alienability, *s.* aliénabilité, *f.*
Alienable, *adj.* aliénable
Alienage, *s.* pérégrinité, *f.*
Alienate, *v.a.* aliéner; (*estrange*) aliéner, s'aliéner; éloigner; — *adj. V.* **Alien**
Alienation, *s.* aliénation, *f.*
Aliena-tor, trix, *s.* aliénateur, *m.*, -trice, *f.*
Alienee, *s.* aliénataire, *m.f.*
Alienism, *s.* pérégrinité, *f.*
Alienist, *s.* médecin aliéniste, aliéniste, *m.*
Alight, *v.n.* descendre (de); mettre pied à terre; (*of birds*) s'abattre; (*fall*) tomber
Alight, *adj.* allumé. *To be —*, être allumé; [brûler
Align, *v a.* aligner; — *v.n.* s'aligner
Alignment, *s.* alignement, *m.*
Alike, *adj.* semblable, pareil; — *adv.* également, aussi; de même; de la même manière; l'un comme l'autre; tout autant; (*at the same time*) à la fois
Aliment, *s.* aliment, *m.*
Alimental, *s.* alimenteux, nutritif
Alimentally, *adv.* d'une manière nutritive
Alimentary, *adj.* alimentaire
Alimentation, *s.* alimentation, *f.*
Alimony, *s.* pension alimentaire, *f.* — *pendente lite*, provision alimentaire, *f.*
Aliquant, *adj.* aliquante
Aliquot, *adj.* aliquote
Alisander, *s.* (*bot.*) maceron, *m.*
Alive, *adj.* (*living*) en vie, vivant; vif; au monde, du monde; (*lively*) vif, gai, animé, éveillé; (*things*) excité; (*of towns, streets*) vivant, animé; (*susceptible*) sensible (à); accessible (à); attentif (à). *To be still —*, être encore en vie, être encore vivant, vivre encore. *To be — again*, revivre; ressusciter. *To burn, bury, flay* or *&c.* —, brûler, enterrer, écorcher or &c. vif. *To take* (...) *dead or —*, prendre (...) mort ou vif. *More dead than —*, plus mort que vif. *To keep —*, faire vivre; (*fig.*) entretenir. *The best man —*, le meilleur homme du monde. *No man —*, personne au monde. *Look — !* remuez-vous un peu! remuez-vous donc!
Alkalescency, *s.* alcalescence, *f.*
Alkalescent, *adj.* alcalescent
Alkali, *s.* alcali, *m.*
Alkalifiable, *adj.* alcalifiable
Alkalify, *v.a.* alcaliser; — *v.n.* s'alcaliser
Alkalimeter, *s.* alcalimètre, *m.*
Alkaline, *adj.* alcalin
Alkalinity, *s.* alcalinité, *f.*
Alkalization, *s.* alcalisation, *f.*
Alkalize. *V.* **Alkalify**
Alkaloid, *s.* alcaloïde, *m.*
Alkanet, *s. V.* **Orchanet**
Alkanna, *s.* alcanna, orcanète, orcanette, *f.*
Alkoran. *V.* **Koran**
All, *adj.* tout, *m.*, toute, *f.*, tous, *m.pl.*, toutes, *f.pl.*; (*all that which*) tout ce que; (*all that*) tout cela; (*all those, followed by "who," "which," "that"*) tous ceux, *m.pl.*, toutes celles, *f.pl.* — *in —*, tout, entièrement; du tout au tout; tel quel. — *of them*, — *of us*, — *of you*, eux tous, nous tous, vous tous. — *at one price*, au choix. — *at 2 francs*, au choix 2 francs. — *that*, tout cela; (*all that which*) tout ce que. *For — that*, malgré tout cela, malgré cela; toutefois; tout de même; n'en ... pas moins. *Four — five —, six —*, &c., (*at play*) quatre

à quatre, cinq à cinq, six à six. *If that be* —, s'il ne tient qu'à cela, si ce n'est que cela. *It is — nonsense*, tout cela est absurde, tout cela n'a pas le sens commun, sottises que tout cela; allons donc! laissez donc! *It is — false*, tout cela est faux; (*it is entirely false*, *V.* **All,** *adv.*) c'est entièrement faux. *That is* —, (*the end*) c'est tout; (*the whole*) voilà tout; c'est tout; (*merely that*) voilà tout; (*no more*) pas davantage. *When — comes to* —, au bout du compte, après tout, au pis aller. — **else,** *V. Everything else* (*under the word* **Else**)

All, *s.* tout, *m.* *My* —, tout mon avoir tout ce que je possède; tout pour moi; mon tout. *To stake o.'s* —, jouer son tout, jouer de son reste, aller de son tout, faire va-tout. *His — is at stake*, il joue son tout, il joue de son reste, il va de son tout, il fait va-tout

All, *adv.* tout, entièrement, tout à fait; absolument; infiniment, souverainement. — *the*, (*before a comp.*) d'autant. *At* —, tant soit peu, le moins du monde; au monde; (faire) tant que de; jamais; tout à fait, entièrement. *No ... at* —, pas de ... du tout, pas du tout de ... *None at* —, aucun, pas un seul, pas du tout, point du tout. *Not at* —, pas du tout, point du tout. *Nothing at* —, rien du tout. — *but*, excepté; (*almost*) presque. *If you go there at — stay some time*, si vous faites tant que d'y aller, restez-y quelque temps

— **abandoned,** *adj.* abandonné de tous. — **absorbing,** *adj.* qui absorbe tout; du plus haut intérêt. — **bearing,** *adj.* qui produit tout. — **bounteous, -bountiful,** *adj.* infiniment bon. — **commanding,** *adj.* qui commande à tout. — **conquering,** *adj.* qui triomphe de tout. — **consuming,** *adj.* qui consume tout. — **dispensing,** *adj.* qui dispose de tout. — **enduring** *adj.* résigné à tout. — **-fools'-Day,** *s.* jour des poissons d'avril, premier avril, *m.* — **giver,** *s.* dispensateur de tous les biens, *m.* — **good,** *adj.* infiniment bon. — **hail,** *int.* salut! — **hallow, -hallows,** *s.* la Toussaint, *f.* — **happy,** *adj.* bienheureux. — **important,** *adj.* de toute importance, de la plus haute importance. — **interesting,** *adj.* du plus haut intérêt. — **judging,** *adj.* juge suprême, juge souverain. — **just,** *adj.* infiniment juste; de toute justice. — **kind,** *adj.* extrêmement bon, de toute bonté. — **knowing,** *adj.* qui sait *or* connaît tout. — **loving,** *adj.* dont l'amour est infini. — **merciful,** *adj.* infiniment miséricordieux. — **powerful,** *adj.* tout-puissant. — **present,** *adj.* présent partout. — **-Saints'-Day,** *s.* jour de la Toussaint, *m.*, la Toussaint, *f.* — **seeing,** *adj.* qui voit tout. — **Souls'-Day,** *s.* jour des morts, *m.*, fête des morts, *f.* — **spice,** *s.* piment, poivre de la Jamaïque, *m.* — **sufficient,** *adj.* suffisant. — **surrounding,** *adj.* tout alentour. — **wise,** *adj.* infiniment sage, d'une sagesse infinie. — **worshipped,** *adj.* adoré de tous. — **worthy,** *adj.* infiniment digne

Allah, *s.* Allah, *m.*

Allay, *v.a.* apaiser, adoucir, calmer, tempérer, soulager, alléger

Allayer, *s.* celui *or* ce qui apaise, *or* adoucit, *or* calme

Allaying, Allayment, *s.* adoucissement, soulagement, *m.*; apaisement, *m.*

Allegation, *s.* allégation, *f.*

Allege, *v.a.* alléguer; prétendre

Allegeable, *adj.* allégable

Alleger, *s.* allégateur, *m.*, -trice, *f.*

Allegiance, *s.* fidélité, *f*; obéissance, soumission, *f.* *Oath of* —, serment de fidélité, *m.*; (*Engl. hist.*) serment d'allégeance, *m.*

Allegoric, -al, *adj.* allégorique

Allegorically, *adv.* allégoriquement

Allegoricalness, *s.* nature allégorique, *f.*

Allegorism, *s.* allégorisme, *m.*

Allegorist, *s.* allégoriste, *m.*

Allegorize, *v.a.n.* allégoriser

Allegorizer, *s.* allégoriseur, *m.*

Allegory, *s.* allégorie, *f.*

Allegretto, *adv. s.* allégretto, *m.*

Allegro, *adv. s.* allégro, *m.*

Alleluia, Alleluiah, Allelujah, *s.* alléluia, *m.*

Alleviate, *v.a.* alléger, adoucir, soulager; atténuer

Alleviation, *s.* allégement, adoucissement, soulagement, *m.*; atténuation, *f.*

Alleviative, *s.* adoucissant, *m.*; palliatif, *m.*

Alley, *s.* allée, *f.*; (*in towns*) ruelle, *f.*

Alliaceous, *adj.* alliacé

Alliance, *s.* alliance, *f.*; (*kindred*) parenté, *f.*

Allied, *adj.* allié, parent

Alligation, *s.* règle d'alliage, *f.*

Alligator, *s.* alligator, caïman, *m.* — **pear,** *s.* — **pear-tree,** *s. V.* **Avocado.** — **tortoise,** *s.* émy-saure, *f.*

Alliteration, *s.* allitération, *f.*

Alliterative, *adj.* allitératif

Allocation, *s.* allocation, *f.*

Allocution, *s.* allocution, *f.*

Allodial, Allodian, *adj.* allodial

Allodium, *s.* alleu, franc alleu, *m.*

Allonge, *s.* (*of horses*) longe, *f.*; (*com.*) allonge, *f.*; (*fenc.*) *V.* **Lunge;** — *v.a.* allonger

Allopath, *s.* allopathe, *m.*

Allopathic, -al, *adj.* allopathique; (*pers.*) allopathe. — *doctor* or *practitioner*, médecin allopathe, *m.*

Allopathically, *adv* allopathiquement

Allopathist, *s.* allopathe, allopathiste, *m.*

Allopathize, *v.a.n.* allopathiser

Allopathy, *s.* allopathie, *f.*

Allot, *v.a.* assigner en partage, départir, donner; diviser par lots; (*grant*) assigner, accorder, répartir, donner; (*appoint*) désigner, destiner, affecter

Allotment, *s.* partage, *m.*, répartition, distribution, *f.*; (*share*) lot, *m.*, part, portion, *f.*; place, *f.*; (*agr.*) sole, *f.*

Allow, *v.a.* permettre; autoriser; souffrir; laisser; admettre, reconnaître, avouer; (*admit of*) comporter; (*grant*) allouer (à), accorder (à), donner (à); (*a discount*) faire; (*of pensions*) faire une pension de *or* une rente de; (*to deduct*) déduire. — **of,** comporter; admettre. — **for,** déduire (...) pour; faire la part de, tenir compte de, avoir égard à; avoir de l'indulgence pour. *To — a thing*, permettre *or* &c. une chose. *To — to*, (*before an inf.*) permettre de. *To — a person* (...), permettre *or* &c. à quelqu'un (...). *To — a person to do a thing*, permettre à quelqu'un de faire quelque chose; autoriser quelqu'un à faire quelque chose; laisser quelqu'un faire quelque chose. *I am allowed* (*to*), il m'est permis (de), on me permet (de); je suis autorisé (à), on m'autorise (à); on me laisse (...). *I am allowed* (*permitted*) *wine*, le vin m'est permis. *We are allowed* (*granted*) *eight shillings a day for our food*, il nous est alloué (on nous alloue *or* accorde *or* donne) dix francs par jour pour notre nourriture. *That is not allowed*, cela n'est pas permis. — *me!* permettez! *To — oneself to be* (*dazzled* or *&c. &c.*), se laisser (éblouir *or* &c. &c.)

Allowable, *adj.* permis; admissible; allouable, accordable; légitime; (*proper*) convenable

Allowableness, *s.* légitimité, *f.*

Allowably, *adv.* légitimement; convenablement

Allowance, *s.* allocation, *f.*; pension, rente, *f.*; ration, *f.*; portion, *f.*; gratification, *f.*; admission, *f.*; sanction, permission, *f.*, consentement, *m.*; indulgence, *f.*; décharge, *f.*; (*com.*) remise, *f.*; — *v.a.* rationner. *Monthly* —, mois, *m.* *Weekly* —, semaine, *f.* *On* —, à la ration; (*med.*) à la diète. *To make — for*, *V. To Allow for*. *To put on short* —, rationner

Alloy, *v.a* allier; altérer; diminuer; —*s.* alliage, *m.*; mélange, *m.*; impureté, *f.*

Alloyage, *s.* alliage, *m.*

Allude, *v.n.* faire allusion (à); vouloir parler (de); (*things*) se rapporter (à), avoir trait (à)

Allure, *v.a.* attirer, amorcer, séduire ; engager (à), inviter (à) [*f.*; (*bait*) amorce, *f.*, appât, *m.*
Allurement, *s.* attrait, charme, *m.*, séduction,
Allurer, *s.* flatteur, tentateur, *m.*
Alluring, *adj.* attrayant, séduisant [séduisante
Alluringly, *adv.* d'une manière attrayante *or*
Allusion, *s.* allusion, *f.*; comparaison, figure, *f.* *In — to*, par allusion à
Allusive, *adj.* allusif, figuré, faisant allusion (à) ; composé d'allusions ; (*her.*) parlant
Allusively, *adv.* par allusion ; figurativement
Alluvial, *adj.* d'alluvion, alluvial, alluvien
Alluvion, Alluvium, *s.* alluvion, *f.*
Ally, *v.a.* allier (à), unir (à), joindre (à) ; —*s.* allié, *m.*, e, *f.* ; confédéré, *m.*, e, *f.*
Almagest, *s.* almageste, *m.*
Almanac, Almanack, *s.* almanach, *m.*
Alme, Almeh, *s.* almée, *f.*
Almightiness, *s.* toute-puissance, *f.*
Almighty, *adj.* tout-puissant ; —*s.* Tout-Puissant, *m.*
Almond, *s.* amande, *f.*; (*tree*) amandier, *m.*; (*anat.*) glande, *f.*, (— *of the ear*) parotide, *f.*, (— *of the throat*) amygdale, *f.* *Bitter* —, amande amère. *Burnt* —, praline, *f.* *Sugared* —, dragée, *f.* *Sweet* —, amande douce. — **cake,** *s.* gâteau d'amandes, *m.*; nougat, *m.*; massepain, *m.* — **flower,** *s.* fleur d'amandier, *f.* — **grove, -plantation,** *s.* amandaie, *f.* — **milk, -emulsion,** *s.* lait d'amandes, amandé, *m.* — **oil,** *s.* huile d'amandes, *f.* — **paste,** *s.* pâte d'amandes (*or* d'amande), *f.* — **tree,** *s.* amandier, *m.*
Almoner, *s.* aumônier, *m.*
Almonry, *s.* aumônerie, *f.*
Almost, *adv.* presque ; (*before a numeral*) près de
Alms, *s. pl.* aumône, *f.* *To give* —, faire *or* donner l'aumône. — **box,** *s.* tronc pour les pauvres, *m.* — **deed,** *s.* œuvre de charité, aumône, *f.* — **giver,** *s.* personne charitable, *f.* — **giving,** *s.* aumône, *f.* — **house,** *s.* hospice, *m.*; maison de secours, *f.*
Almuce, *s.* aumusse, *f.*
Aloe, Aloes, *s.* aloès, *m.* — **wood,** *s.* bois d'aloès, *m.*
Aloetic, (-al), *adj.* *s.* aloétique, *adj. m.f.*, *s.m.*
Aloft, *adv.* en haut, haut, en l'air [*V.* **Let**
Alone, *adj.* seul ; unique. *To let* or *leave* —,
Along, *adv. prep.* le long, au long ; le long de (...), au long de (...) ; sur ... ; sur le côté, de son long ; (*of time*) tout le temps ; (*forward, onward*) en avant, devant soi. *All* —, tout du long ; tout le long de (...) ; tout de son long ; d'un bout à l'autre ; tout le long du chemin ; (*of time*) tout le temps, pendant tout le temps. — *side*, le long, au long ; le long de (...), au long de (...) ; (*nav.*) bord à bord, contre-à-contre. — *side it* or *them* (*things*), le long, au long. — *with*, avec ; ainsi que ; en même temps que. *Go — with you!* allez-vous-en ! allez vous promener ! laissez-moi donc tranquille !
Aloof, *adv.* loin ; au loin, à distance, à l'écart ; éloigné ; sur la réserve ; (*nav.*) au large
Alopecia, Alopecy, *s.* alopécie, pelade, *f.*
Alose. *V.* **Shad**
Aloud, *adv.* *V.* **Loud,** *adv.*
Alpaca, *s.* (*zool.*) alpaca, alpaga, *m.*; (*stuff*) alpaga, *m.*
Alpenstock, *s.* piolet, *m.*
Alpha, *s.* alpha, *m.*
Alphabet, *s.* alphabet, *m.*; — *v.a.* *V.* **Alphabetize**
Alphabetic, -al, *adj.* alphabétique. *In — order*, par ordre alphabétique
Alphabetically, *adv.* alphabétiquement
Alphabetize, *v.a.* ranger alphabétiquement
Alpine, *adj.* des Alpes ; alpestre
Alquifou, *s.* alquifoux, *m.*
Already, *adv.* déjà
Alsacian, Alsatian, *s.* Alsacien, *m.*, -ne, *f.* ; — *adj.* alsacien, d'Alsace
Alsatia, *s.* rendez-vous des gueux, *m.*, (*jest.*) cour des miracles, *f.* ; (*geog.*) l'Alsace, *f.*
Also, *adv.* aussi, également
Altar, *s.* autel, *m.* *High* —, grand *or* maître autel, *m.* — **cloth, -cover,** *s.* nappe d'autel, *f.*, parement d'autel, *m.* — **piece,** *s.* tableau d'autel, *m.* — **screen,** *s.* retable, arrière-dos, *m.* — **wise,** *adv.* en forme d'autel
Altarage, *s.* offrandes, *f.pl.*
Alter, *v.a.* changer ; (*correct*) corriger ; retoucher, retoucher à ; — *v.n.* changer ; se changer
Alterable, *adj.* changeable ; variable, changeant
Alteration, *s.* changement, *m.* ; correction, *f.*
Altercate, *v.n.* se disputer, se quereller, alterquer
Altercation, *s.* altercation, *f.*
Alternate, *adj.* alternatif ; alterné ; (*bot., geom.*) alterne ; (*of rhymes*) croisé ; — *v.a* faire alterner ; (*perform by turns*) exercer *or* faire alternativement, alterner ; — *v.n.* alterner
Alternately, *adv.* alternativement, tour à tour
Alternateness, *s.* alternat, *m.* [tour, *m.*
Alternation, *s.* alternative, succession, *f.*,
Alternative, *s.* alternative, *f.*; choix, *m.*; (*course*) parti, *m.* ; — *adj.* alternatif
Alternatively, *adv.* alternativement
Although, *conj.* quoique, bien que ; (*even if*) [*V.* **Though**
Altimeter, *s.* altimètre, *m.*
Altimetry, *s.* altimétrie, *f.*
Altitude, *s.* élévation, hauteur, *f.*
Alto, *s.* (*mus.*) alto, *m.*
Altogether, *adv.* entièrement, tout à fait ; (*at the same time*) tout à la fois ; (*in all*) en tout
Alto-relievo, Alto-rilievo, Alto-relief, *s.* haut-relief, *m.*
Alum, *s.* alun, *m* ; — *adj.* d'alun, aluminaire, alumineux ; — *v.a.* aluner ; (*med.*) aluminer. — **earth,** *s.* terre d'alun, *f.* — **pit,** *s.* aluminière, alunière, *f.* — **schist, -shale, -slate,** *s.* aluminaire, *f.* — **stone,** *s.* alunite, *f.* — **water,** *s.* eau d'alun, *f.* — **works,** *s. pl.* alunerie, *f.*
Alumina, *s.* alumine, *f.*
Aluming, *s.* alunage, *m.*
Aluminium, Aluminum, *s.* aluminium, *m.*
Aluminite, *s.* aluminite, *f.* [aluneux
Aluminous, Alumish, *adj.* alumineux
Alva, — **marina,** *s.* crin végétal, *m.*
Alveolar, *adj.* alvéolaire
Alveolate, *adj.* alvéolé
Alveole, Alveolus, *s.* alvéole, *f.*
Alvine, *adj.* alvin
Always, *adv.* toujours
A.M. (*Anno Mundi*) l'an du monde, *m.* ; (*Ante Meridiem*) du matin ; (*Artium Magister*) *V.* [**Master of arts**
Amadou, *s.* amadou, *m.*
Amain, *adv.* avec force, de toutes ses forces, vigoureusement
Amalekite, *s.* Amalécite, *m.f.*
Amalgam, *s.* amalgame, *m.*
Amalgamate, *v.a.* amalgamer ; fusionner ; — *v.n.* s'amalgamer ; se fusionner
Amalgamation, *s.* amalgamation, *f.* ; (*fig.*) amalgame, *m.* ; fusionnement, *m.*
Amalgamator, *s.* amalgameur, *m.*
Amanuensis, *s.* secrétaire, *m.*; copiste, *m.*
Amaranth, *s.* (*bot.*) amarante, *f.*; (*colour*) amarante, *m.*
Amaranthine, *adj.* d'amarante
Amaryllis, *s.* amaryllis, *f.*
Amass, *v.a.* amasser
Amateur, *s.* amateur, *m.*; — *adj.* amateur ; (*things*) d'amateur, d'amateurs
Amativeness, *s.* amativité, *f.*
Amatory, *adj.* d'amour, amoureux, érotique
Amaurosis, *s.* amaurose, *f.*
Amaze, *v.a.* étonner, confondre, interdire ; (*dazzle*) émerveiller ; (*frighten*) épouvanter ; —*s.* *V.* **Amazement**
Amazed, *part. adj.* étonné, &c. (*V.* **Amaze,** *v.a.*) ; ébahi
Amazement, *s.* étonnement, *m.* ; stupeur, *f.*; ébahissement, *m.* ; (*fright*) épouvante, *f.*, effroi, *m.*
Amazing, *adj.* étonnant ; (*fam.*) furieux
Amazingly, *adv.* étonnamment ; (*fam.*) furieusement, au possible
Amazon, *s.* amazone, *f.* — **ant,** *s.* polyergue, *f.*
Amazonian, *adj.* d'amazone ; (*bold*) hardi
Ambages, *s. pl.* ambages, *f. pl.*

Ambassador, *s.* ambassadeur, *m.*
Ambassadorial, *adj.* ambassadorial
Ambassadress, *s.* ambassadrice, *f.*
Amber, *s.* ambre, *m.*; — *adj.* d'ambre; — *v.a.* ambrer. — **coloured,** *adj.* ambré. — **gris,** *s.* ambre gris, *m.* — **scented,** *adj.* ambré. — **seed,** *s.* ambrette, *f.* — **tipped,** *adj.* à bout [d'ambre
Ambidexter, *s.* ambidextre, *m.f.*
Ambidexterity, *s.* ambidextérité, *f.*
Ambidextrous, *adj.* ambidextre
Ambient, *adj.* ambiant
Ambiguity, *s.* ambiguïté, équivoque, *f.*
Ambiguous, *adj.* ambigu, équivoque; douteux
Ambiguously, *adv.* ambigument, d'une manière équivoque
Ambiguousness. *V.* **Ambiguity**
Ambit, *s.* circonférence, *f.*, contour, *m.*
Ambition, *s.* ambition, *f.*
Ambitious, *adj.* ambitieux
Ambitiously, *adv.* ambitieusement
Amble, *s.* amble, *m.*; — *v.n.* aller l'amble; (*pers.*) trottiner; aller son train; — *v.a.* faire aller l'amble à [*m.*, -euse, *f.*
Ambler, *s.* cheval qui va l'amble, *m.*, ambleur,
Ambling, *s.* amble, *m.*; — *adj.* ambleur, qui va à l'amble. — **pace,** *s.* amble, *m.*
Amblingly, *adv.* à l'amble
Ambo, *s.* (*arch.*) ambon, *m.*
Ambrosia, *s.* ambroisie, *f.*
Ambrosial, *adj.* ambrosiaque, d'ambroisie
Ambrosian, *adj.* ambrosien
Ambsace, *s.* beset, ambesas, *m.*
Ambulance, *s.* ambulance, *f.*; (*vehicle*) voiture d'ambulance, *f.* — **cart, -waggon,** *s.* voiture d'ambulance, *f.*, caisson d'ambulance, *m.*
Ambulancier, *s.* ambulancier, *m.*
Ambulant, *adj.* ambulant
Ambulatory, *adj.* ambulatoire; ambulant; qui a la faculté de marcher; — *s.* promenoir, *m.*
Ambury, *s.* furoncle, *m.* [quer
Ambuscade, *s.* embuscade, *f.*; — *v.a.* embus-
Ambush, *s.* embûche, *f.*; (*mil.*) embuscade, *f.*; — *v.a.* embusquer; — *v.n.* s'embusquer
Ameliorate, *v.a.* améliorer; — *v.n.* s'améliorer
Amelioration, *s.* amélioration, *f.*
Amen, *adv.* amen, ainsi soit-il; —*s.* amen, *m.*
Amenability. *V.* **Amenableness**
Amenable, *adj.* responsable; (*subject*) soumis (à), sujet (à); disposé à écouter *or* à entendre; (*to a jurisdiction*) justiciable (de). *To make one — to reason,* faire entendre raison à quelqu'un
Amenableness, *s.* responsabilité, *f.*; soumission, *f.*; justiciabilité, *f.*
Amend, *v.a.* amender, améliorer, corriger, réformer; modifier; — *v.n.* s'amender, s'améliorer, se corriger
Amendable, *adj.* amendable
Amendment, *s.* amendement, *m.*; réforme, *f.*
Amends, *s. pl.* dédommagement, *m.*; compensation, *f.*; réparation, *f.* *To make — for,* dédommager de; compenser; réparer
Amenity, *s.* aménité, *f.* [punir
Amerce, *v.a.* mettre *or* condamner à l'amende;
Amerceable. *V.* **Finable**
Amercement, *s.* amende, *f.*; peine, *f.*
American, *s.* Américain, *m.*, e, *f.*; — *adj.* américain, d'Amérique. — *woman* or *lady* or *girl,* Américaine, *f.* — *phaeton,* américaine, *f.*
Americanism, *s.* américanisme, *m.*
Americanization, *s.* américanisation, *f.*
Americanize, *v.a.* américaniser. *To become* [*—d,* s'américaniser
Amess. *V.* **Amice**
Amethyst, *s.* améthyste, *f.*
Amethystine, *adj.* améthystin
Amiability, *s.* amabilité, *f.*
Amiable, *adj.* aimable
Amiableness, *s.* amabilité, *f.*
Amiably, *adv.* avec amabilité, d'une manière aimable, aimablement, gracieusement
Amianth, Amianthus, *s.* amiante, *m.*
Amicable, *adj.* amical; (*of an arrangement*) à l'amiable, (*pers.*) amiable
Amicableness, *s.* nature *or* disposition amicale, cordialité, *f.*
Amicably, *adv.* amicalement; (*of an arrangement*) à l'amiable, amiablement, de gré à gré
Amice, *s.* amict, *m.*
Amid, Amidst, *prep.* au milieu de
Amidships, *adv.* (*nav.*) par le travers, au milieu du vaisseau. *Helm —!* droit la barre!
Amiss, *adj.* mauvais; (*inopportune*) hors de propos; (*unwell*) indisposé; — *adv.* mal; en mal, en mauvaise part; (*inopportunely*) mal à propos. *Nothing comes — to her,* elle s'arrange de tout, tout lui va [(*peace*) paix, *f.*
Amity, *s.* amitié, *f.*; entente cordiale, *f.*;
Ammonia, *s.* ammoniaque, *f.*
Ammoniac, Ammoniacum, *s.* gomme ammoniaque, *f.*, ammoniacum, *m.*
Ammoniac, Ammoniacal, *adj.* ammoniac, ammoniacal
Ammunition, *s.* munitions (de guerre), *f. pl.*, munition, *f.* — **bread,** *s.* pain de munition, *m.* — **waggon, -cart,** *s.* caisson, *m.*
Amnesty, *s.* amnistie, *f.*
Among, Amongst, *prep.* parmi; chez; entre; au milieu de, avec. *From —,* d'entre. — *others, — the rest,* entre autres. — *them,* parmi eux; entre autres. — *the Romans,* chez les Romains. *There is not one — a thousand,* il n'y en a pas un sur mille
Amorous, *adj.* amoureux
Amorously, *adv.* amoureusement
Amorousness, *s.* penchant à l'amour, tempérament amoureux, *m.*; passion, *f.*
Amorphous, *adj.* amorphe
Amortization, Amortizement, *s.* amor-
Amortize, *v.a.* amortir [tissement, *m.*
Amount, *v.n.* monter (à), se monter (à), s'élever (à); (*result in*) se réduire (à), revenir (à). *The sum —s to,* la somme se monte *or* s'élève à. *His speech —s to,* son discours se réduit à. *That —s to the same,* cela revient au même
Amount, *s.* montant, *m.*; total, *m.*, totalité, *f.*; somme, quantité, *f.*; valeur, *f.*; résultat, *m.*
Amour, *s.* intrigue amoureuse, galanterie, *f.*, amourette, *f.*, amour, *m.*, amours, *m. pl.*
Amphibian, *s.* amphibie, *m.*
Amphibious, *adj.* amphibie
Amphibiousness, *s.* nature amphibie, *f.*
Amphibolog-ic, al, -ically, -y. *V.* page [3, § 1
Amphictyonic, *adj.* amphictyonique
Amphictyons, *s. pl.* amphictyons, *m.pl.*
Amphitheatre, *s.* amphithéâtre, *m.*
Amphitheatrical, *adj.* d'amphithéâtre, en amphithéâtre, amphithéâtral
Amphora, *s.* amphore, *f.*
Ample, *adj.* ample; large, vaste; grand
Ampleness, *s.* ampleur, *f.*; (*extent*) grandeur, étendue, *f.*; importance, *f.*
Amplification, *s.* amplification, *f.*
Amplifier, *s.* amplificateur, *m.*
Amplify, *v.a.* amplifier; (*increase*) étendre, augmenter, accroître, grossir; — *v.n.* amplifier; (*on, upon*) s'étendre (sur)
Amplitude, *s.* (*in sciences*) amplitude, *f.*; (*general senses*) étendue, extension, *f.*; largeur, *f.*; grandeur, *f.*; abondance, richesse, *f.*
Amply, *adv.* amplement
Ampulla, *s.* ampoule, *f.*
Amputate, *v.a.* amputer, faire l'amputation de
Amputation, *s.* amputation, *f.*
Amuck, *s. adv.* mock, *m.* *To run — against* or *at,* courir le mock sur; (*fig.*) attaquer en [furieux
Amulet, *s.* amulette, *f.*
Amusable, *adj.* amusable
Amuse, *v.a.* amuser
Amusement, *s.* amusement, divertissement, *m.*, distraction, *f.*, plaisir, *m.*
Amuser, *s.* amuseur, *m.*, -euse, *f.*
Amusingly, *adv.* d'une manière amusante, plaisamment
Amygdalate, *adj.* fait d'amandes, amandé; —*s.* lait d'amandes, amandé, *m.*

Amylaceous, *adj.* amilacé, amylacé
An, *art.* *V.* **A**
Ana, *s.* ana, *m*
Anabapt-ism, -ist. *V.* page 3, § 1
Anabaptistic, -al, *adj.* anabaptiste
Anachoret, Anachorite. *V.* **Anchoret, Anchorite**
Anachronism, *s.* anachronisme, *m.*
Anaconda, *s.* python, boa, *m.*
Anacreontic, *adj.* anacréontique; — *s.* poème anacréontique, *m.*
Anadem, *s.* couronne de fleurs, *f.*
Anæmia, *s.* anémie, *f.*
Anæsthesia, *s.* anesthésie, *f.*
Anæsthetic, *adj.s.* anesthésique, *adj.m.f.*, *s.m.*
Anagram, *s.* anagramme, *f.*
Anagrammat-ic, al, -ically, -ism, -ist. *V.* page 3, § 1
Anagrammatize, *v.a.n.* anagrammatiser
Anal, *adj.* anal
Analemma, *s.* analemme, *m.* [3, § 1
Analog-ical, -ically, -ism, -ist. *V.* page
Analogize, *v.a.* expliquer par analogie
Analogous, *adj.* analogue
Analogously, *adv.* d'une manière analogue
Analogue, *s.* analogue, *m.*
Analogy, *s.* analogie, *f.*
Analysis, *s.* analyse, *f.*
Analyst, *s.* analyste, *m.*
Analytic, -al, *adj.* analytique; raisonné. — *chemist*, expert-chimiste, *m.*
Analytically, *adv.* analytiquement
Analyzable, *adj.* analysable
Analyze, *v.a.* analyser
Analyzer, *s.* analyseur, *m.*
Anamorphosis, *s.* anamorphose, *f.*
Anapest, *s.* anapeste, *m.*
Anapestic, -al, *adj.* anapestique
Anarch-ic,al,-ically,-ist,-y. *V.* page 3, § 1
Anathema, *s.* anathème, *m.* [anathème
Anathematical, *adj.* d'anathème, qui porte
Anathematize, *v.a.* anathématiser
Anathematized, *adj.* anathème
Anatom-ic, al, -ically, -ist. *V.* page 3, § 1
Anatomize, *v.a.* anatomiser
Anatomy, *s.* anatomie, *f.*; (*skeleton*) squelette, *m.*
Anbury, *s.* (*vet.*) furoncle, *m.*
Ancestor, *s.* ancêtre, aïeul, *m.*; **—s,** *pl.* ancêtres, aïeux, *m.pl.*
Ancestral, *adj.* d'ancêtre *or* d'aïeul, d'ancêtres *or* d'aïeux, qui vient des ancêtres; [héréditaire
Ancestress, *s.* ancêtre, aïeule, *f.*
Ancestry, *s.* ancêtres, aïeux, *m.pl.*; race, extraction, *f.*; origine, *f.*; naissance, *f.*; suite d'ancêtres *or* d'aïeux, *f.*; haute extraction, *f.*
Anchor, *s.* ancre, *f.*; — *v.a* (*nav.*) mouiller; (*fig.*) ancrer; — *v.n.* (*nav.*) ancrer, mouiller; (*fig.*) s'ancrer, se fixer, s'arrêter. *Lying at* —, à l'ancre. *To cast (the)* —, jeter l'ancre, mouiller. *To come to an* —, venir au mouillage. *To drag the* —*s*, chasser sur ses ancres. *To lie* or *ride at* —, être à l'ancre. — **ground,** *s* mouillage, *m.* — **hold,** *s.* tenue, *f.* — **smith,** *s.* forgeur d'ancres, *m.*
Anchorage, *s.* mouillage, *m.*; ancrage, *m.*; (*duty*) droit de mouillage *or* d'ancrage, *m.*; (*tackle*) ancres, *f.pl.*
Anchoret, *s.* anachorète, *m.*
Anchoring, *adj.* à l'ancre. — **ground, -place,** *s.* mouillage, *m.*
Anchorite, *s.* anachorète, *m.*
Anchoritical, *adj.* anachorétique
Anchovied, *adj* anchoisé, anchoité
Anchovy, *s.* anchois, *m* — **paste** *or* **butter,** *s.* pâte, (*f.*) *or* beurre (*m.*) d'anchois. — **pear,** *s.* (*tree*) grias, *m.*; (*fruit*) poire d'anchois, *f.* — **sauce,** *s.* sauce aux anchois, *f.*
Anchylose, *v.a.* ankyloser. *To become* —*d*, [s'ankyloser
Anchylosis, *s.* ankylose, *f.*
Ancient, *adj.* ancien; antique; (*old*) vieux; — [*s.* ancien, *m.*
Anciently, *adv.* anciennement
Ancientness, Ancientry, *s.* ancienneté, *f.*
Ancillary, *adj.* *V.* **Subservient**
Ancle. *V.* **Ankle**
And, *conj.* et; (*with 'more' or 'less' or a comp. repeated*) de ... en ...; (*drawn by*) à. *More — more, less — less, better — better, worse — worse*, *V.* **More, Less,** &c. *Fewer — fewer*, de moins en moins, de moins en moins nombreux. *Smaller — smaller* de plus en plus petit. *Carriage — four*, voiture à quatre chevaux. *Two — two*, deux à deux. *One hundred — one*, cent-un. *Five — twenty*, vingt-cinq
Andalusian, *s.* Andalous, *m.*, e, *f.*; — *adj.* andalous, d'Andalousie
Andante, *s.* andante, *m.*
Andean, *adj.* des Andes
Andiron, *s.* chenet, *m.*
Androgyne, *s.* androgyne, *m.*
Androgynous, *adj.* androgyne
Android, *s.* androïde, *m.*
Anecdote, *s.* anecdote, *f.*
Anecdotic, -al, *adj* anecdotique
Anecdotist, *s.* anecdotier, *m.*, -ière, *f.*
Anelectric, *adj.* anélectrique
Anemometer, *s.* anémomètre, *m.*
Anemone, *s.* anémone, *f.*
Anemoscope, *s.* anémoscope, *m.*
An-end, *adv.* debout; guindé
Anent, *prep.* touchant, sur, au sujet de, à propos de; (*opposite*) vis-à-vis de
Aneroid, *adj.* *s.* anéroïde, *adj.m.f.*, *s.m.*
Anet, *s.* aneth, *m.*
Aneurism, *s.* anévrisme, *m.*
Aneurismal, *adj.* anévrismal
Anew, *adv.* de nouveau; (*like new*) à neuf
Anfractuose, Anfractuous, *adj.* anfractueux [**fracture,** *s.* anfractuosité, *f.*
Anfractuosity, Anfractuousness, An-
Angel, *s.* ange, *m.*; — *adj.* d'ange, angélique. — **fish,** *s.* ange de mer, *m.* — **shot,** *s.* boulet ramé, ange, *m.* — **winged,** *adj* aux ailes [d'ange
Angelic, -al, *adj.* angélique; d'ange
Angelica, *s.* angélique, *f.*
Angelically, *adv.* angéliquement
Angelicalness, *s.* nature angélique, *f.*
Angelus, *s.* angélus, *m.*
Anger, *s.* colère, *f.*, courroux, *m.*; — *v.a.* mettre en colère, irriter, provoquer, fâcher
Angina, *s.* angine, *f.*
Angio-graphy, -logy, &c. *V.* page 3, § 1
Angle, *s.* angle, *m.*; (*corner*) coin, *m.*; (*obsolete*) *V.* **Fishing-line;** (*hist.*) Angle, *m.*; — *v.n.* pêcher (à la ligne). — **iron,** *s.* cornière, *f.* — **rod,** *s.* (*obsolete*) *V.* **Fishing-rod.** — **tie,** *s.* [écoinçon, *m.*
Angled, *adj.* à angles
Angler, *s.* (*pers.*) pêcheur (à la ligne), *m.*; (*fish*) baudroie, *f.*, baudreuil, *m.*, lophie, *f.*
Anglican, *adj.* *s.* anglican, *m.*, e, *f.*
Anglicanism, Anglicism. *V.* page 3, § 1
Anglicization, *s.* anglicisation, *f.*
Anglicize, *v.a.* angliciser. *To become* —*d*, [s'angliciser
Angling, *s.* pêche (à la ligne), *f.*
Anglo-, (*in compounds*) anglo- ... — **-Saxon,** *adj.* *s.* anglo-saxon. — **-French,** *adj.* *s.* anglo-français. — **-Indian,** *adj.* *s.* anglo-indien
Anglomania, *s.* anglomanie, *f.*
Anglomaniac, *s.* *adj.* anglomane, *m.f.*
Anglophobia, *s.* anglophobie, *f.*
Anglophobiac, *s.* anglophobe, *m.f.*
Anglophobic, *adj.* anglophobique, anglophobe
Anglophobist, *s.* anglophobe, *m.f.*
Angola, *s.* angola, *m.*; (*stuff*) chaty, *m.*
Angora, *adj.* angora. — **cat,** *s.* chat angora, *m.*
Angrily, *adv.* avec colère; en colère
Angry, *adj.* (*pers.*) en colère fâché, irrité; (*things*) courroucé, en courroux, furieux. *An — word*, une parole vive, *f.*, un mot plus haut que l'autre, *m.* *In an — mood*, en colère, en courroux, courroucé. *To be — with*, être fâché contre, en vouloir à. *To be — at* or *to*, être fâché *or* irrité de. *To get* —, se mettre en colère, se fâcher, s'irriter. *To make* —, mettre en colère, fâcher, irriter

Anguish, *s.* angoisse, *f.*; douleur, *f.*; — *v.a.* angoisser, navrer de douleur
Angular, *adj.* angulaire
Angularity, *s.* angularité, forme angulaire, *f.*
Angularly, *adv.* angulairement
Angulated, *adj.* angulé
Angulous, *adj.* anguleux
Anhydrous, *adj.* anhydre
Anight, Anights, *adv.* de nuit, la nuit
Anil, *s.* anil, *m.*
Anile, *adj.* de vieille femme
Aniline, *s.* aniline, *f.*
Anility, *s.* vieillesse, *f.*, radotage, *m.*
Animadversion, *s.* animadversion, *f.*; blâme, *m.*
Animadvert, *v.n.* (*upon*) censurer (...), blâmer (...), critiquer (...), s'attaquer (à); (*to*) considérer (...)
Animadverter, *s.* critique, *m.*; juge, *m.*; (*fault-finder*) frondeur, *m.*, -euse, *f.*
Animal, *s.* animal, *m.*; — *adj.* animal, *m.*, e, *f.*
Animalcular, *adj.* animalculaire
Animalcule, *s.* animalcule, *m.*
Animal-ism, -ist. *V.* page 3, § 1
Animality, *s.* animalité, *f.*
Animalization, *s.* animalisation, *f.*
Animalize, *v.a.* animaliser. *To become —d,* s'animaliser
Animate, *v.a.* animer ('*with*', de); vivifier; exciter, ranimer; — *adj.* animé; (*of nature*) vivant
Animater, *s.* animateur, *m.*, -trice, *f.*
Animating, *adj.* animateur, qui anime; vivifiant; gai
Animation, *s.* animation, *f.*; (*fig.*) vie, vivacité, *f.*; (*of mind*) chaleur, *f.*, feu, *m.*, verve, *f.* *Suspended —*, léthargie, *f.*; asphyxie, *f.*
Animative. *V.* **Animating**
Animator. *V.* **Animater**
Anime, *s.* (*resin*) animé, *f.*
Animosity, *s.* animosité, *f.*
Animus, *s.* volonté, *f.*; disposition, *f.*; intention, *f.*, but, *m.*; esprit, *m.*; vivacité, humeur *f.*
Anise, *s.* anis, *m.*
Aniseed, *s.* graine d'anis, *f.*, anis, *m.*; (*liquor*) anisette, *f.*
Anisette, *s.* anisette, *f.*
Ankle, *s.* cheville (du pied), *f.* — **bone,** *s.* astragale, *m.* — **deep,** *adj. adv.* jusqu'aux chevilles. — **joint,** *s.* *V.* **Instep**
Ankled, *adj.* (*in compounds*) aux chevilles ...
Anklet, *s.* chevillière, *f.*
Ankylosis, &c. *V.* **Anchylosis,** &c.
Annalist, *s.* annaliste, *m.f.*
Annalize, *v.a.* mettre *or* inscrire dans les annales
Annals, *s. pl.* annales, *f.pl.*; fastes, *m.pl.*; histoire, *f.*
Annamite, *s. adj.* Annamite, *m.f.*
Annates, Annats, *s. pl.* annate, *f.*, annates, *f.pl.*
Annatto. *V.* **Arnotto**
Anneal, *v a.* tempérer; recuire
Annealing, *s.* recuite, recuisson, *f.*
Annelides, *s. pl.* annélides, *m.pl.*
Annex, *v.a.* annexer (à); (*fig.*) joindre (à), attacher (à); — *v.n.* se joindre (à), s'attacher (à); — *s.* annexe, *f.*
Annexation, *s.* annexion, annexation, *f.*
Annexationism, *s.* annexionisme, *m.*
Annexationist, *s. adj.* annexioniste, *m.f.*
Annexed *adj.* ci-joint; — *part. V.* **Annex,** *v.a.n.*
Annexion, *s.* annexion, *f.*
Annexion-ism, -ist. *V.* page 3, § 1
Annihilable, *adj.* annihilable
Annihilate, *v.a.* anéantir, détruire, annihiler
Annihilating, Annihilation, *s.* anéantissement, *m.*, annihilation, *f.*
Annihilator, *s.* destructeur, *m.* *Fire —*, anti-combustible, *m.*; appareil contre l'incendie, extincteur, *m.*
Anniversarily, *adv.* tous les ans, annuellement
Anniversary, *adj.s.* anniversaire, *adj.m.f.*, *s.m.*
Annotate, *v.a.* annoter
Annotation, *s.* annotation, *f.*
Annotator, *s.* annotateur, *m.*, -trice, *f.*
Annotto. *V.* **Arnotto**
Announce, *v.a.* annoncer; proclamer
Announcement, *s.* annonciation, *f.*; annonce, *f.*; avis, *m*; nouvelle, *f.*
Announcer, *s.* personne qui annonce, *f.*, annonceur, *m.*, -euse, *f.*, annonciateur, *m.*, -trice, *f.*, messager, *m.*, -ère, *f.*
Annoy, *v a.* ennuyer, tourmenter, contrarier, tracasser, inquiéter; incommoder, être désagréable à
Annoyance, *s.* ennui, tourment, *m*, contrariété, tracasserie, *f.*, désagrément, déplaisir, *m.*
Annoyer, *s.* tourment, être fatigant, *m.*
Annoying, *adj.* contrariant, vexant; incommode, désagréable
Annual, *adj.* annuel; —*s.* annuaire, *m.*; (*bot.*) plante annuelle, *f.*
Annually, *adv.* annuellement, tous les ans
Annuitant, *s.* rentier viager, *m.*, rentière viagère, *f.*; rentier, *m.*, rentière, *f.*
Annuity, *s.* rente viagère, rente, *f.*; pension, *f.*; (*fin.*) annuité, *f.*
Annul, *v.a.* annuler
Annular, Annulary, *adj.* annulaire
Annulate, Annulated, *adj.* annelé
Annulet, *s.* annelet, *m.*
Annulment, *s.* annulation, *f.*
Annunciation, *s.* annonciation, *f.*
Anodyne, *adj.* anodin; —*s.* anodin, calmant, *m.* — *necklace*, collier anodin, *m.*; (*jest.*) (la) corde au cou
Anoint, *v.a.* oindre; (*a king*) sacrer; (*rub*) frotter
Anointed, *s. adj.* oint, *m.*
Anointing, Anointment, *s.* onction, *f.*
Anomal-ism, -istic, al, -istically. *V.* page 3, § 1
Anomalous, *adj.* anomal; irrégulier; (*odd*) hétéroclite
Anomalously, *adv.* d'une manière anomale; irrégulièrement
Anomaly, *s.* anomalie, *f.*; irrégularité, *f.*
Anon, *adv.* bientôt, tout-à-l'heure; tantôt, quelquefois, parfois; tout de suite, à l'instant, aussitôt. *Ever and —*, de temps en temps, de temps à autre; à tout moment, à chaque instant, à tout bout de champ
Anonymous, *adj. s.* anonyme, *adj. m.f.*, *s.m.*
Anonymously, *adv.* anonymement, sous l'anonyme
Anonymousness, *s.* caractère anonyme, *m.*, anonymie, *f.*; anonyme, *m.*; anonymat, *m.*
Anorexia, Anorexy, *s.* anorexie, *f.*
Anormal, *adj.* *V.* **Abnormal**
Another, *adj.* un autre; (*after* l'un) l'autre, (*after* les uns) les autres; (*one more*) encore un; (*anybody else*) autrui, les autres. *One —, each other*, *V.* **Each.** *One after —*, l'un après l'autre; (*of more than two*) les uns après les autres. *With one —, one with —*, *V.* **One.** *That is — thing*, c'est autre chose, c'est une autre affaire, c'est différent. *That is quite — thing*, c'est tout autre chose, c'est une tout autre affaire, c'est une autre paire de manches
Ansated, *adj.* à anse, à anses, ansé
Anserine, *adj.* d'oie
Answer, *v.a.* (*give in answer*) répondre; (*return an answer to, correspond with*) répondre à, (*satisfy*) satisfaire, remplir, suffire à; (*solve*) résoudre; (*a door*) ouvrir; — *v.n.* répondre; correspondre; (*grumble*) raisonner; (*succeed*) réussir. *To — for*, répondre de *or* pour. *To — my* (*your, &c.*) *purpose*, remplir mon (votre, &c.) but; faire mon (votre, &c.) affaire, me (vous, &c.) convenir; (*succeed*) me (vous, &c.) réussir. *To — several purposes*, servir à plusieurs fins. *To — the bell*, répondre au coup de sonnette
Answer, *s.* réponse, *f.*; (*in a bad sense*) réplique *f.*, raisonnement, *m.*; (*of a problem*, &c.) solution, *f.*; (*mus.*) réponse, rentrée, *f.*; —**s,** *pl.* réponses, &c.; (*grumbling*) raisons, *f.pl.* *An — will oblige, waiting an —*, réponse s'il vous plaît
Answerable, *adj.* susceptible de réponse; réfutable; (*for*) responsable (de); (*correspondent*) conforme (à), correspondant (à), proportionné (à); égal (à)
Answerableness, *s.* conformité, *f.*, rapport, *m.*, proportion, *f.*

Answerably, *adv.* convenablement, proportionnellement, à *or* en proportion (de); conformément (à)
Answerer, *s.* personne qui répond, *f.*, répondant, *m.*, e, *f.*; adversaire, antagoniste, *m.f.*; (*grumbler*) raisonneur, *m.*, -euse, *f.*
Answering, *part. adj.* répondant, correspondant, &c. (*V.* **Answer,** *v.a.n.*); (*grumbling*) raisonneur
Ant, *s.* fourmi, *f.* — **catcher, -thrush,** *s.* (*bird*) fourmilier, *m.* — **eater, -bear,** *s.* (*quadruped*) fourmilier, *m.* — **eggs,** *s. pl.* œufs de fourmis, *m.pl.* — **hill, -hillock, -nest,** *s.* fourmilière, *f.* — **lion,** *s.* (*insect*) fourmi-lion, *m.*
Antacid, *adj.s.* antacide, antiacide, *adj.m.f.*, *s.m.*
Antagon-ism, -ist. *V.* page 3, § 1
Antagonistic, -al, *adj.* antagoniste, opposé, contraire
Antarctic, *adj.* antarctique
Antarthritic, *adj. s.* antigoutteux, *adj. m.*, -euse, *f.*, antigoutteux, *s.m.*
Antecedence, *s.* antécédence, antériorité, priorité, *f.*
Antecedent, *adj.* antécédent, antérieur; —*s.* antécédent, *m.*
Antecedently, *adv.* antécédemment, antérieurement
Antecessor, *s.* prédécesseur, *m.*
Antechamber, *s.* antichambre, *f.*
Antechapel, *s.* avant-corps de chapelle, *m.*
Antecourt, *s.* avant-cour, *f.*
Antecursor. *V.* **Forerunner**
Antedate, *s.* antidate, *f.*; — *v.a.* avancer la date de; antidater; anticiper
Antediluvian, *adj. s.* antédiluvien, *adj. m.*, -ne, *f.*, antédiluvien, *s.m.*
Antelope, *s.* antilope, *f.*
Antemeridian, *adj.* avant midi
Antemetic, *adj. s.* antémétique, *adj. m.f.*, *s.m.*
Antenna, *s.* antenne, *f.*
Antenuptial, *adj.* anténuptial
Antepaschal, *adj.* d'avant Pâques, antérieur à Pâques
Antepenult, Antepenultima, *s.* antépénultième, *f.*
Antepenultimate, *adj. s.* antépénultième
Anteposition, *s.* (*gram.*) inversion, *f.*
Anterior, *adj.* antérieur
Anteriority, *s.* antériorité, *f.*
Anteroom, *s.* antichambre, *f.*
Anthelmintic, *adj. s.* anthelmintique, *adj. m.f.*, *s.m.*
Anthem, *s.* antienne, *f.*; chant, hymne, *m.*
Anther, *s.* anthère, *f.*
Anthology, *s.* flore, *f.*; (*liter.*) anthologie, chrestomathie, *f.*
Anthony's fire, *s.* (*med.*) feu de saint-Antoine
Anthracite, *s.* anthracite, *m.*
Anthrax, *s.* (*med.*) anthrax, charbon, *m.*
Anthropo-graphic, al, -graphy, -logic, al, -logist, -logy, -morphism, &c. *V.* page 3, § 1
Anthropomorphite, *s.* anthropomorphite, *m.f.*
Anthropomorphous, *adj.* anthropomorphe
Anthopopha-gist, -gite, -gus, *s.*, **Anthropopha-gian, -gous,** *adj.* anthropophage, *m.f.*
Anthropophagy. *V.* page 3, § 1
Anti-, (*in compounds*) anti-...
Antiabolition-ism, -ist. *V.* page 3, § 1
Antiacid. *V.* **Antacid**
Antiapoplectic, *adj. s.* antiapoplectique, *adj. m.f.*, *s.m.*
Antiaristocrat, *s.* antiaristocrate, *m.f.*
Antibilious, *adj. s.* antibilieux, *adj. m.*, -euse, *f.*, antibilieux, *s.m.*
Antic, *adj.* grotesque, bouffon; —*s.* bouffon, *m.*; mouvement grotesque, *m.*, bouffonnerie, farce, *f.*; cabriole, *f.*; figure grotesque, *f.*, magot, marmouset, *m.*
Anticatholic, *adj.* anticatholique
Anticholeraic, *adj* anticholérique
Antichrist, *s.* antechrist, *m.*
Antichristian, *adj.* antichrétien
Antichristianism, Antichristianity, *s.* antichristianisme, *m.*
Anticipate, *v a.* anticiper; (*precede*) prévenir, devancer; (*expect*) s'attendre à, prévoir, pressentir; (*hope*) espérer; (*enjoy beforehand*) se promettre, jouir d'avance de; (*suffer*) souffrir d'avance
Anticipated, *part. adj.* anticipé, &c. (*V.* **Anticipate,** *v.a.*); prématuré
Anticipation, *s.* anticipation, *f.*; prévision, appréhension, *f.*; (*hope*) avant-goût, *m.*, espérance, *f.* *By* —, par anticipation, d'avance
Anticipatory, *adj.* par anticipation, anticipé
Anticlimax, *s.* gradation descendante, *f.*
Anticonstitutional, *adj.* anticonstitutionnel
Anticonstitutionally, *adv.* anticonstitutionnellement
Anticorrosive, *adj. s.* anticorrosif, *adj. m.*, -ive, *f.*, anticorrosif, *s.m.*
Antidotarium, *s.* antidotaire, *m.*
Antidote, *s.* antidote, *m.*; — *v.a.* antidoter
Antidramatic, *adj.* antidramatique
Antiemetic, *adj. s.* antiémétique, *adj. m.f.*, *s.m.*
Antiepiscopal, Antiepiscopalian, *adj.* antiépiscopal
Antievangelical, *adj.* antiévangélique
Antifebrile, *adj. s.* antifébrile, fébrifuge, *adj. m.f.*, *s.m.*
Antiherpetic, *adj. s.* antidartreux, *adj. m.*, -euse, *f.*, antidartreux, *s.m.*
Antihysteric, *adj. s.* antihystérique, *adj. m.f.*, *s.m.*
Antilogy, *s.* antilogie, *f.*
Antimacassar, *s.* antimacassar, *m.*, pommadière, *f.*, dessus de fauteuil, *m.*
Antimephitic, *adj. s.* antiméphitique, *adj. m.f.*, *s.m.*
Antiministerial, *adj.*, **Antiministerialist,** *s.* antiministériel
Antimonarch-ic, al, -ist. *V.* page 3, § 1
Antimonial, *adj.* antimonial; antimonié; (*pharm.*) stibié; —*s* antimonial, *m.*
Antimoniated, *adj.* antimonié
Antimony, *s.* antimoine, *m.*
Antinational, *adj.* antinational
Antinomy, *s.* antinomie, *f.*
Antipap-ism, -ist. *V.* page 3, § 1
Antipapistic, -al, *adj.* antipapiste
Antipathetic, -al, *adj.* antipathique
Antipathetically, *adv.* avec (*or* par) antipathie
Antipathy, *s.* antipathie, *f.*
Antipatriotic, *adj.* antipatriotique
Antipestilential, *adj.* antipestilentiel
Antiphilosophic, -al, *adj* antiphilosophique
Antiphlogistic, *adj. s.* antiphlogistique, *adj. m.f.*, *s.m.*
Antiphon, Antiphone, *s.* antiphone, *m.*
Antiphonary, *s.* antiphonaire, antiphonier, *m.*
Antiphon-ic, al, -ically, -y. *V.* page 3, § 1
Antiphrasis, *s.* antiphrase, *f.*
Antipode, *s.* antipode, *m.*
Antipoetic, -al, *adj.* antipoétique
Antipope, *s.* antipape, *m.*
Antipopery, *s.* antipapisme, *m.*
Antipopular, *adj.* antipopulaire
Antiputrefactive, Antiputrescent, *adj.* antiputride
Antiquarian, *adj.* antique; d'antiquaire; —*s.* *V.* **Antiquary**
Antiquary, *s.* antiquaire, *m.*
Antiquate, *v.a.* abolir, abroger; vieillir; (*of dress*) démoder
Antiquated, *adj.* antique; (*obsolete*) suranné, vieilli, vieux; tombé en désuétude; (*out of fashion*) démodé
Antique, *adj.* antique; —*s.* antique, *f.*; antiquité, *f.*
Antiquity, *s.* antiquité, *f.*
Antireform, *adj.* antiréformiste
Antireformist, *s.* antiréformiste, *m.f.*
Antireligious, *adj.* antireligieux
Antirepublican, *s. adj.* antirépublicain, *m.*, e, *f.*
Antirevolutionary, *adj.*, **Antirevolutionist,** *s.* antirévolutionnaire, *m.f.*
Antirheumatic, -al, *adj.* antirhumatismal
Antiscorbutic, *adj. s.* antiscorbutique, *adj. m.f.*, *s.m.*
Antiscrofulous, *adj.* antiscrofuleux, *adj. m.*, -euse, *f.*, antiscrofuleux, *s.m.*
Antiseptic, *adj. s.* antiseptique, *adj. m.f.*, *s.m.*
Antislavery, *s.* antiesclavagisme, abolitionisme, *m.*; — *adj.* antiesclavagiste, abolitioniste
Antisocial, *adj.* antisocial
Antispasmodic, *adj. s.* antispasmodique, *adj. m.f.*, *s.m.*
Antistrophe, *s.* antistrophe, *f.*
Antisyphilitic, *adj. s.* antisyphilitique, *adj. m.f.*, *s.m.*

Antithesis, *s.* antithèse, *f.*
Antithetic, -al, *adj.* antithétique
Antitrinitarian, *s. adj.* antitrinitaire, *m.f.*
Antitype, *s.* antitype, *m.*
Antiunionist, *s. adj.* antiunioniste, *m.f.*
Antivenereal, *adj.* antivénérien
Antler, *s.* andouiller, *m.*; **—s,** *pl.* (*horns*) bois, *m.*
Antlered, *adj.* à andouillers
Antonomasia, *s.* antonomase, *f.*
Antonym, *s.* (*gram.*) antonyme, contraire, *m.*
Antonymous, *adj.* antonyme
Antonymy, *s.* antonymie, *f.*
Antwerper, *s.* Anversois, *m.*, e, *f.*
Anus, *s.* anus, *m.*
Anvil, *s.* enclume, *f.*; (*fig.*) métier, *m.*
Anxiety, *s.* anxiété, inquiétude, *f.*; préoccupation, *f.*; sollicitude, *f.*; impatience, *f.*; curiosité, *f.*; (*eagerness*) empressement, *m.*; désir ardent, *m.*
Anxious, *adj.* inquiet (de, sur), plein d'inquiétude; préoccupé (de); (*careful*) plein de sollicitude (pour); impatient (de), pressé (de); curieux (de); désireux (de), soucieux (de); jaloux (de); (*eager*) empressé; (*distrustful*) défiant; (*med.*) anxieux. *To be* — (*to*), être inquiet *or* &c.; s'inquiéter (de); avoir de la sollicitude (pour); avoir hâte (de); désirer vivement; être jaloux (de), tenir (à)
Anxiously, *adv.* avec anxiété, avec inquiétude; avec sollicitude; avec impatience, impatiemment; (*distrustfully*) avec défiance; (*med.*) anxieusement
Any, *adj.* quelque; (*every*) tout; (*someone*) quelqu'un; (*after a doubt expressed, or inter., or neg.*) aucun; (*whoever, whatever*) qui que ce soit; quelque ... que ce soit; un ... quelconque; le premier ... venu, n'importe quel ...; quoi que ce soit; (*after 'more' or 'less'*) aucun; (*of* ...) n'importe lequel (de ...); aucun (de ...), (*some*) du, *m.*, de la, *f.*, des, *pl.*, (*after* pas, point, *or* plus) de; (*of it, of them*) en. *Have you — hope?* avez-vous quelque espérance? *— man can do it,* tout homme peut le faire, qui que ce soit peut le faire, n'importe qui peut le faire. *If — of you,* si quelqu'un de vous. *I doubt that — of you* . . ., je doute qu'aucun de vous ... *Do you think that — of them* ...? pensez-vous qu'aucun d'eux ...? *Not — of you,* aucun de vous. *I don't know — of those gentlemen,* je ne connais aucun de ces messieurs. *More than — other,* plus qu'aucun autre. *If you have —,* si vous en avez. — **better,** mieux. — **body,** *V.* — **one.** — ... **but,** tout autre ... que. — **farther,** plus loin, plus avant. — **how,** *adv.* de quelque manière (*or* façon) que ce soit, de toute manière, de toute façon; n'importe comment. — **longer,** plus longtemps, davantage. — **more,** encore; (*neg.*) plus; (pas) davantage. — **one,** quelqu'un; (*neg.*) personne; aucun; (*whoever*) quiconque; qui que ce soit; (*the first come*) le premier venu; n'importe qui; n'importe lequel; (*everybody*) tout le monde. — *one but,* tout autre que. — *one you please,* (*pers.*) qui vous voudrez; (*things*) celui que vous voudrez. — **thing,** *s.* quelque chose, *m.*; (*neg.*) rien, *m.*; (*whatever*) quoi que ce soit, n'importe quoi, *m.*; tout, *m.* — *thing but,* tout autre chose que, rien moins que. — *thing good,* — *thing broken,* — *thing more,* quelque chose de bon, quelque chose de cassé, quelque chose de plus (*or* encore quelque chose). *Not — thing,* rien. — **whatever,** quelque ... que ce soit, n'importe quel ...; un ... quelconque; le moindre ... — **when,** n'importe quand. — **where,** partout; en quelque lieu que ce soit; dans le premier endroit venu; n'importe où; (*with an interrog.*) quelque part; (*with a neg.*) nulle part. — **wise,** *V.* — **how**
Aorist, *s.* aoriste, *m.*
Aorta, *s.* aorte, *f.*
Apace, *adv.* à grands pas, rapidement, vite
Apanage. *V.* **Appanage**
Apart, *adv.* à part; de côté; à l'écart; séparé (de); séparément
Apartment, *s.* appartement, *m.*; (*room*) pièce, chambre, *f.*, logement, *m.*; **—s,** *pl* (*one suite*) appartement, *m.*, (*several suites*) appartements, [*m.pl.*
Apathetic, -al, *adj.* apathique
Apathy, *s.* apathie, *f.*
Ape, *s. V.* **Monkey;** — *v.a.* singer
Apeak, Apeek, *adv.* (*nav.*) à pic; en pantenne
Apepsy, *s.* apepsie, *f.* [apéritif, *s.m.*
Aperient, *adj. s.* apéritif, *adj. m.*, -ive, *f.*,
Aperture, *s.* ouverture, *f.*; orifice, *m.*
Apetalous, *adj.* apétale
Apex, *s.* sommet, *m*
Aphelion, *s.* aphélie, *m.*
Aphlogistic, *adj.* aphlogistique
Aphonia, Aphony, *s.* aphonie, *f.* [3, § 1
Aphor-ism, -istic, al, -istically. *V.* page
Aphrodisiac, *adj. s.* aphrodisiaque, *adj. m.f.*, [*s.m.*
Aphtha, *s.* aphthe, *m.*
Aphthous, *adj.* aphtheux
Apiarist, *s.* apiculteur, *m.*
Apiary, *s.* rucher, *m.*
Apiculture, *s.* apiculture, *f.*
Apiece, *adv.* pièce, la pièce, chacun, chaque; (*pers.*) par personne, par tête, chacun; (*cattle*) par tête
Apish, *adj.* de singe; (*jocular*) bouffon; (*foolish*) sot; (*foppish*) affecté, prétentieux. — *trick,* singerie, *f.*
Apishly, *adv.* en singe; (*foppishly*) sottement; prétentieusement, avec prétention, avec affectation [prétention, affectation, *f.*
Apishness, *s.* singerie, *f.*; (*foppery*) sottise, *f.*;
Apitpat. *V.* **Pitapat**
Apocalypse, *s.* apocalypse, *f.*
Apocalypt-ic, al, -ically. *V.* page 3, § 1
Apocope, *s.* apocope, *f.*
Apocrypha, *s. pl.* apocryphes, *m.pl.*
Apocryphal, *adj. s.* apocryphe, *adj. m f.*, *s.m.*
Apodal, *adj.*, **Apode,** *s.* apode, *adj. m.f.*, *s.m.*
Apogee, *s.* apogée, *m.*
Apologetic, -al, *adj.* apologétique, apologique; d'excuse; **—s,** *pl.* (*theol.*) apologétique, *f.*
Apologetically, *adv.* en forme d'apologie *or* [d'excuse
Apologist, *s.* apologiste, *m.*
Apologize, *v.n.* faire une apologie; (*to make excuse*) s'excuser (*to,* auprès de; *for,* de), faire des excuses *or* ses excuses, demander pardon (*to,* à; *for,* de). *To — for a person to another,* excuser une personne auprès d'une autre
Apologue, *s.* apologue, *m.*
Apology, *s.* apologie, *f.*; excuse, *f.* *To make an — for,* faire l'apologie de; faire des excuses [de, s'excuser de
Aponeurosis, *s.* aponévrose, *f.*
Aponeurotic, *adj.* aponévrotique
Apophthegm. *V.* **Apothegm**
Apoplectic, *adj.* apoplectique, d'apoplexie; —*s.* apoplectique, *m.f.* — *fit* or *stroke,* attaque d'apoplexie, *f.* *In an — fit,* frappé d'apoplexie
Apoplexy, *s.* apoplexie, *f.*
Aport, *adv.* (*nav.*) bâbord
Apostasy, *s.* apostasie, *f.*
Apostate, *s. adj.* apostat, *m.*
Apostatize, *v.n.* apostasier; renier, abjurer
Apostle, *s.* apôtre, *m.*
Apostleship, *s.* apostolat, *m.*
Apostol-ic, al, -ically. *V.* page 3, § 1
Apostrophe, *s.* apostrophe, *f.*
Apostrophize, *v.a.* apostropher
Apothecary, *s.* médecin-pharmacien, *m.*; pharmacien, *m.*; (*in contempt*) apothicaire, *m.*
Apothegm, *s.* apophthegme, *m.*
Apotheosis, *s.* apothéose, *f.*
Apotheosize, *v.a.* apothéoser
Appal, *v.a.* épouvanter; consterner; abattre
Appalling, *adj.* épouvantable, effrayant, terrible
Appanage, *s.* apanage, *m.*
Appanagist, *s.* apanagiste, *m.f.*
Apparatus, *s.* appareil, *m.*; attirail, *m.*; matériel, *m.*; instrument, *m.*, machine, *f.*, instru-

ments, *m.pl.*, machines, *f.pl.*; ustensiles, outils, *m.pl.*; objets, articles, *m.pl.*

Apparel, *s.* vêtement, habillement, costume, *m.*, habits, *m.pl.*; (*fig.*) ornement, appareil, *m.*, parure, *f.*, ajustement, *m.*; (*nav.*) apparaux, *m.pl.*, équipement, *m.*; — *v.a.* vêtir, habiller; (*fig.*) revêtir, orner, parer; (*nav.*) équiper

Apparent, *adj.* apparent; visible; évident, clair, manifeste; (*of heirs*) présomptif

Apparently, *adv.* évidemment; (*openly*) ouvertement; (*seemingly*) apparemment, en apparence

Apparition, *s.* apparition, *f.*

Apparitor, *s.* appariteur, *m.*

Appeal, *v.n.* en appeler (à), prendre à témoin; faire appel (à), s'adresser (à); demander (à), supplier; (*law*) appeler, en appeler; — *v.a.* porter à un tribunal supérieur

Appeal, *s.* appel, *m.* *Without* —, en dernier ressort, sans appel

Appealable, *adj.* sujet à appel

Appear, *v.n.* (*make o.'s or its appearance, seem: of pers. and things*) paraître (à); (*make an apparition, start up*) apparaître (à); (*pers only*) se présenter; se montrer; (*law*) comparaître. *To — against*, se présenter contre; (*to sue*) se porter partie contre. *To — for*, se présenter pour; répresenter; répondre pour. *To make* —, faire paraître; (*show*) faire voir, montrer; (*prove*) prouver, démontrer

Appearance, *s.* (*coming into sight*) apparition, *f.*; entrée, *f.*; arrivée, *f.*; présence, *f.*; (*semblance, show*) apparence, *f.*; probabilité, *f.*; air, extérieur, *m.*, figure, *f.*; aspect, *m.*; spectacle, *m.*; perspective, *f.*; (*law*) comparution, *f.* *First* —, (*before the public*) début, *m.* *At first* —, au premier abord, au premier coup d'œil. *In* —, en apparence. *To all —s*, selon toute apparence. *To make o.'s* —, paraître, se montrer, se présenter; faire son entrée; arriver, venir; (*law*) comparaître. *To make o.'s first* —, faire sa première apparition; faire sa première entrée; (*before the public*) faire son début, débuter. *To make o.'s last* —, paraître pour la dernière fois. *To put in* or *enter an* —, faire acte de présence, se présenter; être présent; (*law*) faire acte de comparution, comparaître

Appearer, *s.* (*law*) comparant, *m.*, e, *f.*

Appeasable, *adj.* apaisable

Appease, *v.a.* apaiser, calmer, pacifier; — *v.n.* s'apaiser, se calmer

Appeasement, *s.* apaisement, *m.*

Appeaser, *s.* apaiseur, *m.*

Appellant, *s.* (*law*) appelant, *m.*, e, *f.*; (*challenger*) provocateur, *m.*; — *adj.* (*law*) appelant

Appellate, *adj.* (*law*) d'appel

Appellation, *s.* appellation, *f.*; nom, *m.*; dénomination, *f.*

Appellative, *adj.* appellatif; —*s.* appellation, *f.*; nom, *m.*

Appellee, *s.* (*law*) intimé, *m.*, e, *f.*

Append, *v.a.* apposer; annexer; attacher

Appendage, *s.* dépendance, *f.*, accessoire, *m.*; appendice, *m.*; apanage, *m.*

Appendent, *adj.* suspendu (à); dépendant (de), annexé (à), attaché (à); accessoire

Appendicular, *adj.* appendiculaire

Appendicle, *s.* appendicule, *m.*

Appendix, *s.* appendice, *m.*

Appertain, *v.n.* appartenir (à)

Appertainment, *s.* attribution, *f.*; privilége, *m.*

Appetence, Appetency, *s.* appétence, *f.*; désir, *m.*, envie, inclination, *f.*

Appetent, *adj.* avide (de)

Appetite, *s.* appétit, *m.*; (*fig.*) soif, *f.*, penchant, désir, *m.* *To have, to get, to give an* —, avoir, gagner, donner de l'appétit (*with an adj.*, un appétit ...). *To have a good* —, avoir bon appétit. *A good — to you!* bon appétit!

Appetize, *v.a.* mettre en appétit

Appetizer, *s.* apéritif, *m.*

Appetizing, *adj.* appétissant, apéritif

Appian, *adj.* *The — way*, la voie Appienne, *f.*

Applaud, *v.a.* applaudir, applaudir à

Applauder, *s.* applaudisseur, *m.*, -euse, *f.*

Applause, *s.* applaudissement, *m.*, applaudissements, *m.pl.*

Applausive, *adj.* approbateur, flatteur

Apple, *s.* pomme, *f.*; (*of the eye*) prunelle, *f.*; (— *tree*) pommier, *m.* *Adam's* —, pomme d'Adam. *Baking* or *kitchen* —, pomme à cuire. *Bitter* —, coloquinte, *f.* — **berry,** *s.* billardière, *f.* — **core,** *s.* trognon de pomme, *m.* — **dumpling,** *s.* chausson, *m.* — **fritters,** *s. pl.* beignets de pommes, *m.pl.* — **graft,** *s.* greffe de pommier, *f.* — **green,** *s. adj.* vert pomme, *m.* — **harvest,** *s.* récolte de pommes, *f.* — **jelly,** *s.* gelée de pomme *or* de pommes, *f.* — **juice,** *s.* jus de pomme *or* de pommes, *m.* — **loft,** *s.* fruiterie, *f.*, fruitier, *m.* — **orchard,** *s.* pommeraie, *f.* — **paring, -peel,** *s.* pelure de pommes, *f.* — **pie,** *s.* tourte aux pommes, *f.* — **pudding,** *s.* pudding aux pommes, *m.* — **roaster,** *s.* pommier, *m.* — **sauce,** *s.* compote de pommes, *f.* — **shaped,** *adj.* en forme de pomme, pomiforme, maliforme. — **tart,** *s.* tarte aux pommes, *f.* — **tree,** — **tree wood,** *s.* pommier, *m.* — **woman,** *s.* marchande de pommes, *f.*

Appliable, *adj.* applicable

Appliance, *s.* application, *f.*; moyen, *m.*; secours, *m.*; remède, *m.*; ustensile, instrument, *m.*; machine, *f.*; appareil, *m.*

Applicability, *s.* applicabilité, *f.*

Applicable, *adj.* applicable

Applicableness. *V.* **Applicability**

Applicably, *adv.* d'une manière applicable

Applicant, *s.* postulant, *m.*, e, *f.*; candidat, *m.*, e, *f.*; pétitionnaire, *m.f.*; (*law*) demandeur, *m.*, -eresse, *f.*; requérant, *m.*, e, *f.*

Application, *s.* application, *f.*; (*employment*) emploi, usage, *m.*; (*request*) demande, *f.* *To make an — to*, s'adresser à, faire une demande à

Applique, — **lace,** *s.* application, *f.*

Apply, *v.a.* appliquer (à); (*employ*) employer (à); (*put*) mettre (à), porter (à); (*address*) adresser (à); (*the break, rail.*) serrer; — *v.n.r.* s'appliquer (à); s'attacher (à); se mettre (à); s'adresser (à). *To — for*, solliciter, demander; (*go for*) aller chercher; (*come for*) venir chercher. — *to* or *at* ..., (*at the end of advertisements and bills*) s'adresser à (*or* chez) ...

Applying, *s.* *V.* **Application**

Appoggiatura, *s.* appoggiature, *f.*

Appoint, *v.a.* établir, arrêter; instituer; destiner, assigner; ordonner; désigner, fixer, indiquer, marquer; (— *to meet*) donner rendez-vous à; (*furnish*) meubler; garnir; servir; (*nominate*) nommer (à); préposer (à); (*troops*, &c.) équiper; — *v.n.* arrêter, décréter; —*s.* appoint, *m.*

Appointee, *s.* fonctionnaire nommé, *m.* nominataire, *m.f.*

Appointer, *s.* nominateur, *m.*, -trice, *f.*

Appointment, *s.* établissement, *m.*; (*to an office*) nomination, *f.*; (*office*) emploi, *m.*, place, *f.*; (*decree*) arrêt, décret, *m.*; (*order*) ordre, *m.*; (*of time*) rendez-vous, *m.*; (*salary*) appointements, *m.pl.*, traitement, *m.*; (*furniture*) meuble, ameublement, *m.*; garniture, *f.*; service, *m.*; (*of troops*, &c.) équipement, *m.* *To make an — with*, donner un rendez-vous à, prendre rendez-vous avec. *By* — (*hatter, boot-maker*, &c.) *to His Majesty*, fournisseur breveté de Sa Majesté

Apportion, *v.a.* répartir, partager, distribuer; assigner; proportionner

Apportioner, *s.* répartiteur, distributeur, *m.*

Apportionment, *s.* répartition, *f.*, partage, *m.*

Apposite, *adj.* approprié (à), bien appliqué, à propos; applicable (à); convenable (à); conforme (à)

Appositely, *adv.* convenablement, à propos

Appositeness, *s.* convenance, *f.*, à-propos, *m.*; justesse, *f.*; applicabilité, *f.*

Apposition, *s.* apposition, *f.*

Appraisable, *adj.* estimable, évaluable

Appraise, *v.a.* estimer, évaluer, priser; (*law*) expertiser
Appraisement, *s.* estimation, évaluation, *f.*; (*at auction*) prisée, *f.*; (*law*) expertise, *f.*
Appraiser, *s.* estimateur, *m.*; (*at auction*) commissaire-priseur, *m.*; (*law*) expert, *m.*
Appreciable, *adj.* appréciable
Appreciably, *adv.* appréciablement
Appreciate, *v.a.* apprécier
Appreciating, *adj.* appréciateur
Appreciation, *s.* appréciation, *f.*
Appreciative, *adj.* appréciatif
Apprehend, *v.a.* (*seize*) saisir, empoigner; (*arrest*) arrêter, appréhender au corps; (*conceive*) saisir, comprendre, concevoir; (*think*) croire, penser, présumer; (*fear*) appréhender, craindre [cevable, compréhensible
Apprehensible, *adj.* appréhensible; con-
Apprehension, *s.* (*seizure, power of seizing*) préhension, *f.*; (*arrest*) arrestation, prise de corps, *f.*; (*idea*) conception, *f.*; opinion, *f.*, avis, *m.*; (*fear*) appréhension, crainte, *f.*; inquiétude, *f.*; (*suspicion*) soupçon, *m.* *To be dull of —*, avoir la conception dure. *To be under — of*, être dans l'appréhension de
Apprehensive, *adj.* intelligent; susceptible; (*fearful*) timide, craintif, appréhensif, (*of*) inquiet (de), dans l'appréhension (de). *To be — of*, appréhender, être dans l'appréhension de
Apprehensiveness, *s.* compréhension, conception, *f.*; (*fearfulness*) timidité, *f.*; crainte, *f.*
Apprentice, *s.* apprenti, *m.*, e, *f.*; (*of lawyers*) clerc, *m.*; (*med.*) élève, *m.*; (*nav.*) novice, *m.* *To bind — to*, mettre en apprentissage chez
Apprentice, *v.a.* mettre en apprentissage ('*to*', chez) [apprentissage
Apprenticed, *adj.* ('*to*', chez) apprenti, en
Apprenticeship, *s.* apprentissage, *m.*
Apprise, *v.a.* informer, instruire, prévenir
Approach, *v.n.* approcher (de); s'approcher (de); — *v.a.* (*come near to*) approcher de; s'approcher de; aborder; arriver à; (*bring near*) approcher (de); —*s.* approche, *f.*; accès, *m.*; (*of places*) abord, *m.*; (*fig.*) rapprochement, *m.*; (*step*) pas, *m.*; (*overture*) avance, *f.*; (*fort.*) approche, *f.*; (*math.*) approximation, *f.*
Approachable, *adj.* approchable, abordable,
Approaching, *adj.* prochain [accessible
Approbation, *s.* approbation, *f.*
Approbative, *adj.* approbatif
Approbatively, *adv.* approbativement
Approbatory, *adj.* approbateur
Appropriate, *v.a* s'approprier, approprier (à); affecter (à), destiner (à); attacher (à), attribuer (à); fixer; — *adj.* approprié (à); (*suitable*) convenable (à), propre (à); à propos; juste
Appropriately, *adv.* convenablement; à propos; à juste titre [pos, *m.*; justesse, *f.*
Appropriateness, *s.* convenance, *f.*; à-pro-
Appropriation, *s.* appropriation, *f.*, propriété, *f.*; destination, *f.*, emploi, *m.*, application, *f.*
Approvable, *adj.* approuvable
Approval, *s.* approbation, *f.*
Approve, *v.a.* approuver; être content de; recommander; estimer; (*try*) éprouver; (*show*) montrer. **— of,** approuver; être content de
Approver, *s.* approbateur, *m.*, -trice, *f.*; (*old law*) dénonciateur, *m.*, -trice, *f.*
Approving, *adj.* approbateur, approbatif
Approvingly, *adv.* approbativement
Approximate, *v.a.* rapprocher (de); — *v.n.* se rapprocher (de); approcher (de); — *adj.* approximatif
Approximately, *adv.* approximativement
Approximation, *s.* approximation, *f.*; rapprochement, *m.*
Approximative, *adj.* approximatif
Approximatively, *adv.* approximativement
Appurtenance, *s.* appartenance, *f.*; dépendance, *f.* [dant (de)
Appurtenant, *adj.* appartenant (à); dépen-
Apricot, *s.* abricot, *m.* **— tart,** *s.* tarte *or* tourte aux abricots, *f.* **— tree,** *s.* abricotier, *m.*
April, *s.* avril, *m.* **— fool-day,** *V.* **All fools' Day.** **— fool trick,** **— fool's errand,** *s.* poisson d'avril, *m.* **— shower,** *s.* giboulée de mars, *f.* **— sown,** *adj.* avrillé. *To make an — fool of*, donner un poisson d'avril à
Apron, *s.* tablier, *m.*; (*artil.*) couvre-lumière, *m.*, platine, *f.*, chaperon, *m.*; (*nav.*) contre-étrave, *f.* **— ful (An),** *s.* plein son tablier
Aproned, *adj.* portant tablier, à tablier
A propos, *adv.* à propos
Apse, Apsis, *s.* apside, *f.*
Apt, *adj.* (*liable, inclined*) sujet (à), enclin (à disposé (à), porté (à), prompt (à); (*suitable* convenable; (*fit*) propre (à)
Apter, Apteran, *s.* aptère, *m.*
Apterous, Apteral, *adj.* aptère
Apteryx, *s.* aptéryx, *m.*
Aptha. *V.* **Aphtha**
Aptitude, *s.* aptitude, disposition, *f.* [propos
Aptly, *adv.* convenablement, justement, à
Aptness, *s.* aptitude, *f.*; disposition, *f.*; tendance, *f.*; (*power*) propriété, *f.*; (*suitableness*) convenance, *f.*
Aqua, *s.* eau, *f.* **— fortis,** *s.* eau forte, *f.* **— marina, — marine,** *s.* aigue-marine, *f.* **— regia, — regis,** *s.* eau régale, *f.* **— tint, — tinta,** *s.* aqua-tinta, aquatinte, *f.*
Aquaria, *s. pl.* aquariums, *m.pl.*
Aquarium, *s.* aquarium, *m.*
Aquarius, *s.* le Verseau, *m.*
Aquatic, *adj.* aquatique; —*s.* plante aquatique, *f.*; —**s,** *s. pl.* plantes aquatiques, *f. pl.*; (*sport*) sport nautique, canotage, *m.*
Aquatint. *V.* **Aqua**
Aqueduct, *s.* aqueduc, *m.* **— bridge,** *s.* pont-
Aqueous, *adj.* aqueux [aqueduc, *m.*
Aqueousness, *s.* aquosité, *f.*
Aquila, *s.* aigle, *m.f.*; (*astr.*) aigle, *f.*
Aquiline, *adj.* aquilin, d'aigle, de l'aigle. *— nose*, nez aquilin. *— eye*, regard d'aigle, *m.*
Arab, *s. adj.* Arabe, *m.f.* *Street —*, gamin, voyou, *m.*
Arabesque, *adj. s.* arabesque, *adj. m.f.*, *s.f.*
Arabian, *s.* Arabe, *m.f.*; — *adj.* arabe, d'Arabie. *— Gulf*, Golfe Arabique, *m.* *— Nights*, Mille et une Nuits, *f.pl.*
Arabic, *adj.* arabe; arabique; —*s.* l'arabe, *m.*
Arabism, *s.* arabisme, *m.*
Arabist, *s.* arabisant, *m.*
Arable, *adj.* arable, labourable
Arachnoid, *s.* arachnoïde, *f.*
Arack. *V.* **Arrack** [aragonais, d'Aragon
Aragonese, *s.* Aragonais, *m.*, e, *f.*; — *adj.*
Araneous, *adj.* arané, aranéen, aranéeux
Araucanian, *s. adj.* Araucanien, *m.*, -ne, *f.*
Araucaria, *s.* araucaire, *m.*
Arbalist, *s.* arbalète, *f.*
Arbalister, *s.* arbalétrier, *m.*
Arbiter, *s.* arbitre, *m.*
Arbitral, *adj.* arbitral
Arbitrament. *V.* **Arbitrement**
Arbitrarily, *adv.* arbitrairement
Arbitrariness, *s.* arbitraire, *m.*
Arbitrary, *adj.* arbitraire [noncer (sur)
Arbitrate, *v.a.n.* arbitrer; décider (de), pro-
Arbitration, *s.* arbitrage, *m.*; décision, *f.* **— bond,** *s.* compromis, *m.*
Arbitrator, *s.* arbitre, *m.*
Arbitrement, *s.* décision, *f.*, jugement, *m.*; compromis, *m.*; arbitrage, *m.*; (*law*) jugement arbitral, *m.*, sentence arbitrale, *f.*; (*philos.*)
Arbitress, *s.* arbitre, *f.* [arbitre, *m.*
Arbor, *s.* arbre, *m.* **— vitæ,** *s.* thuia, thuya, arbre de vie, *m.*
Arboreous, *adj.* d'arbre; qui croît *or* vit sur les arbres, arboré; (*woody*) arboré, ligneux
Arborescence, *s.* arborescence, *f.*
Arborescent, *adj.* arborescent
Arboricultural, *adj.* arboricultural, arboricole, d'arboriculture

Arboriculture, *s.* arboriculture, *f.*
Arboriculturist, *s.* arboriculteur, *m.*
Arboriform, *adj.* arboriforme
Arborist, *s.* arboriste, *m.*
Arborization, *s.* arborisation, *f.*
Arborize, *v.a.* arboriser
Arbour, *s.* tonnelle, *f.*, berceau, *m.*
Arbute, Arbutus, *s.* arbousier, *m.* — **berry**, [*s.* arbouse, *f.*
Arc, *s.* arc, *m.*
Arcade, *s.* arcade, *f.*; galerie, *f.*; passage, *m.*
Arcadian, *s.* Arcadien, *m.*, -ne, *f.*; — *adj.* arcadien, d'Arcadie
Arcanum, *s.* arcane, *m.*; secret, *m.*
Arch, *s.* (*arch.*) arche, *f.*; voûte, *f.*; arcade, *f.*; (*build.*) cintre, *m.*; arc, *m.*; arceau, *m.*; (*of the aorta*) crosse, *f.* — **buttress**, *s.* arc-boutant, *m.* — **like**, *adj.* en arche, en voûte. — **stone**, *s.* voussoir, *m.* — **way**, *s.* passage (sous une voûte), *m.*; guichet, *m.*; portail, *m.*; voûte, *f.*, arceau, *m.* — **wise**, *adj.* en forme d'arche *or* de voûte. — **work**, *s.* arcature, *f.* [courber
Arch, *v.a.* voûter, cintrer; (*bend*) arquer; (*fig.*)
Arch, *adj.* (*cunning*) malin; (*roguish*) espiègle; (*in compounds*) grand, insigne, fieffé, archi- ...
Archæological, *adj.* archéologique
Archæologist, *s.* archéologue, *m.*
Archæology, *s.* archéologie, *f.*
Archaic, -al, *adj.* archaïque
Archaism, *s.* archaïsme, *m.*
Archaist, *s.* archaïste, *m.*
Archangel, *s.* archange, *m.*; (*bot.*) lamier, *m.*
Archangelic, *adj.* archangélique, d'archange
Archbishop, *s.* archevêque, *m.* —*'s palace* or *house*, archevêché, *m.*
Archbishopric, *s.* archevêché, *m.*
Archchancellor, *s.* archichancelier, *m.*
Archdeacon, *s.* archidiacre, *m.*
Archdeaconry, *s.* archidiaconat, *m.*; (*the jurisdiction*) archidiaconé, *m.*
Archdiocesan, *adj.* archidiocésain
Archducal, *adj.* archiducal
Archduchess, *s.* archiduchesse, *f.*
Archduchy, *s.* archiduché, *m.*
Archduke, *s.* archiduc, *m.*
Archdukedom, *s.* archiduché, *m.* [acharné, *m.*
Arch-enemy, *s.* grand ennemi, ennemi
Archer, *s.* archer, *m.*; (*astr.*) sagittaire, *m.*
Archeress, *s.* archer, *m.*
Archery, *s.* tir à l'arc, *m.*; art de tirer l'arc, *m.*
Archetypal, Archetypical, *adj.* archétype
Archetype, *s.* archétype, *m.*; (*coin.*) étalon, *m.*
Archidiaconal, *adj.* archidiaconal
Archiepiscopal, *adj.* archiépiscopal. — *city* or *see* or *palace*, archevêché, *m.*
Archiepiscopacy, Archiepiscopate, *s.* [archiépiscopat, *m.*
Archil. *V.* **Orchil**
Archimandrite, *s.* archimandrite, *m.*
Archimedean, *adj.* d'Archimède
Arching, *s.* *V.* **Arch**, *s.*
Archipelago, *s.* archipel, *m.* [auteur, *m.*
Architect, *s.* architecte, *m.*; (*fig.*) artisan,
Architecton-ic,-ography, &c. *V.* page 3, § 1
Architectural, *adj.* architectural, d'architecture
Architecturally, *adv.* architecturalement
Architecture, *s.* architecture, *f.*
Architrave, *s.* architrave, *f.*
Archival, *adj.* d'archives, des archives
Archives, *s. pl.* archives, *f.pl.*
Archivist, *s.* archiviste, *m.*
Archivolt, *s.* archivolte, *f.*
Archlute, *s.* archiluth, *m.*
Archly, *adv.* malicieusement, avec malice, malinement, malignement; d'un air malin; avec espièglerie
Archness, *s.* malice, *f.*; espièglerie, *f.*
Archon, *s.* archonte, *m.*
Archonship, *s.* archontat, *m.*
Archpresbyter, *s.* archiprêtre, *m.*
Archpresbyterial, *adj.* archipresbytéral
Archpresbytery, *s.* archiprêtré, archipresbytérat, *m.*
Archpriest, *s.* archiprêtre, *m.*
Archtreasurer, *s.* architrésorier, *m.*
Archway, Archwise. *V.* **Arch**, *s.*
Arctic, *adj.* arctique
Ardent, *adj.* ardent; brûlant. — *spirit*, esprit ardent, *m.*; (*liquor*) spiritueux, *m.*
Ardently, *adv.* ardemment, avec ardeur
Ardour, *s.* ardeur, *f.*
Arduous, *adj.* ardu, difficile, rude, pénible
Arduously, *adv.* difficilement, rudement, péniblement
Arduousness, *s.* arduité, difficulté, *f.*
Are, *s.* (*meas.*) are, *m.*
Area, *s.* aire, surface, superficie, *f.*; (*extent*) étendue, *f.*; (*enclosure*) enceinte, *f.*; arène, *f.*; (*of music-halls*, &c.) pourtour, *m.*; (*open space*) espace découvert, *m.*, cour, place, *f.*; (*front: of ground-floor*) devant (de maison), *m.*; (*of basement*) fossé de sous-sol, *m.*; (*of churches*) parvis, *m.* — **steps**, *s. pl.* escalier de service, *m.*
Areal, *adj.* de superficie [arec, *m.*
Areca, *s.* arec, *m.* — **nut**, *s.* noix d'arec, *f.*,
Arena, *s.* arène, *f.*
Arenaceous, *adj.* arénacé
Arenation, *s.* arénation, *f.*
Areola, *s.* aréole, *f.*
Areolar, *adj.* aréolaire
Areolate, *adj.* aréolé
Areometer, *s.* aréomètre, *m.*
Areometric, *adj.* aréométrique
Areometry, *s.* aréométrie, *f.*
Areopagite, *s.* aréopagite, *m.*
Areopagitic, *adj* aréopagitique
Areopagus, *s.* aréopage, *m.*
Argal. *V.* **Argol**
Argala, *s.* argala, *m.*
Argali, *s.* argali, *m.*
Argemone, *s.* argémone, *f.* [argenté
Argent, *s.* (*her.*) argent, *m.*; — *adj.* d'argent,
Argentiferous, *adj.* argentifère
Argentine, *adj.* argentin
Argil, *s.* argile, *f.*
Argillaceous, *adj.* argillacé, argilacé
Argilliferous, *adj.* argilifère
Argol, *s.* tartre brut, *m.*
Argonaut, *s.* argonaute, *m.*
Argonautic, *adj.* argonautique
Argosy, *s.* argosil, *m.*; vaisseau, navire, *m.*
Arguable, *adj.* discutable
Argue, *v.n.* argumenter, raisonner (de); arguer (de); (*plead*) plaider; (*affirm*) soutenir, prétendre; — *v.a.* discuter; plaider; dénoter, indiquer, accuser; conclure [-euse, *f.*
Arguer, *s.* argumentateur, *m.*; raisonneur, *m.*,
Arguing, *s.* argumentation, *f.*; raisonnement, *m.*; discussion, *f.*; — *adj.* raisonneur
Argument, *s.* argument, *m.*; raisonnement, *m.*; argumentation, *f.*; discussion, *f.*; thèse, *f.*; (*of poems*, &c.) sujet, *m.*; (*proof*) preuve, *f.*
Argumentation, *s.* argumentation, *f.*
Argumentative, *adj.* argumentatif, d'argumentation; raisonné; (*pers.*) disposé à argumenter. — *declamation*, argumentation oratoire, *f.*
Argumentatively, *adv.* par argument
Argus, *s.* argus, *m.*
Argute, *adj.* subtil, fin; aigu, perçant
Arguteness, *s.* subtilité, finesse, *f.*
Aria, *s.* air, *m.*
Arian, *s. adj.* arien, *m.*, -ne, *f.*
Arianism, *s.* arianisme, *m.*
Arid, *adj.* aride
Aridity, *s.* aridité, *f.*
Aries, *s.* le Bélier, *m.*
Arietta, *s.* ariette, *f.*
Aright, *adv.* *V.* **Right**
Aril, *s.* arille, *m.*
Arise, *v.n.* (*get up*) se lever; (*emerge*) s'élever, surgir; (*appear*) se présenter; (*originate, proceed*) naître (de); venir (de), provenir (de); (*happen, begin*) s'élever, survenir
Aristarch, Aristarchus, *s.* aristarque, *m.*

Aristocracy, *s.* aristocratie, *f.*
Aristocrat, *s.* aristocrate, *m.f.*
Aristocratic, -al, *adj.* (*things*) aristocratique; (*pers.*) aristocrate
Aristocratically, *adv.* aristocratiquement
Aristocraticalness, *s.* caractère (*m.*) *or* nature (*f.*) aristocratique
Aristocratism, *s.* aristocratisme, *m.*
Aristocratize, *v.a.n.* aristocratiser
Aristolochia, *s.* aristoloche, *f.*
Aristotelian, *s. adj.* aristotélicien, *m.*, -ne, *f.*
Aristotelianism, *s.* aristotélisme, *m.*
Aristotelic, *adj.* aristotélique
Arithmetic, *s.* arithmétique, *f.*
Arithmetical, *adj.* arithmétique
Arithmetically, *adv.* arithmétiquement
Arithmetician, *s.* arithméticien, *m*, -ne, *f.*
Ark, *s.* arche, *f.* — *of the covenant*, arche d'alliance
Arm, *s.* arme, *f.*; **—s,** *pl.* (*her.*) armes, armoiries, *f.pl.*; (*limb*) bras, *m.*; (*of a sofa, settee*, &c.) accotoir, bras, *m.*; (*of a chair, and geog., tech., fig., power*, &c.) bras, *m.* *At —s*, d'armes. *Man-at- —s*, homme d'armes, *m.* *Men-at- —s*, hommes *or* gens d'armes, *m.pl.* *Master at —s*, (*nav.*) capitaine d'armes, *m.* *In —s*, en armes; les armes à la main; (*of children*) au maillot, en nourrice. (*Brother, companion in —s*, frère, compagnon d'armes, *m.*) *To —s!* aux armes! *Under —s*, sous les armes. *With folded —s*, les bras croisés. *With open —s*, à bras ouverts. — *in* —, bras dessus bras dessous, en se donnant le bras. *To beat to —s*, (*mil.*) battre le rappel; battre la générale. *To have long —s*, avoir les bras longs. *To take up —s*, prendre les armes. *Ground —s!* (*mil.*) reposez vos armes! descendez armes! *Lodge —s!* haut les armes! *Shoulder —s!* portez armes! *Slope —s!* l'arme à volonté! *Support —s!* arme au bras! *Unpile —s!* rompez les faisceaux! **— bone,** *s.* (*anat.*) humérus, *m.* **— chair,** *s.* fauteuil, *m.* **— chest,** *s.* coffre d'armes, *m.* **— ful,** *s.* brassée, *f.* **— guard,** *s.* garde-bras, brassard, *m.* **— hole,** *s.* aisselle, *f.*; (*of garments*) emmanchure, entournure, *f.* **— less,** *adj.* sans bras; (*of weapons*) sans armes. **— manufactory,** *s.* armurerie, *f.* **— pit,** *s.* aisselle, *f.*, creux de l'aisselle, *m.* **— rack,** *s.* râtelier, *m.* [armer, prendre les armes
Arm, *v.a.* ('*with*', de) armer; — *v.n.* s'armer,
Armada, *s.* armada, *f.*
Armadilla, *s.* (*nav.*) armadille, *f.*
Armadillo, *s.* (*zool.*) armadille, *f.m.*
Armament, *s.* armement, *m.*
Armature, *s.* armature, *f.*; (*armour*) armure, *f.*
Armenian, *s.* Arménien, *m.*, -ne, *f.*; — *adj.* arménien, d'Arménie. — *bole*, bol d'Arménie, *m.*
Armillary, *adj.* armillaire
Armistice, *s.* armistice, *m.*
Armlet, *s.* brassard, *m.*; bracelet, *m.*; (*geog.*) petit bras (de mer), *m.*
Armorer. *V.* **Armourer**
Armorial, *adj.* d'armoirie, armorial. — *bearings*, armes, armoiries, *f.pl.*
Armorican, *adj. s.* armoricain
Armorist, *s.* armoriste, *m.*
Armory. *V.* **Armoury**
Armour, *s.* armure, *f.*; (*nav.*) cuirasse, *f.*; (*nav., ornament*) pavois, *m.* **— bearer,** *s.* écuyer, *m.* **— cased, -clad, -coated, plated,** *s. adj.* (*nav.*) cuirassé, blindé. **— casing,** *s.* blindage, *m.* **— plate,** *s.* cuirasse, plaque de blindage, *f.* **— plating,** *s.* blindage, *m.* **— ship,** *s.* vaisseau (*or* navire *or* bâtiment) cuirassé *or* blindé, *m.*
Armoured, *adj.* (*of ships*) cuirassé, blindé
Armourer, *s.* armurier, *m.*; (*of knights*) écuyer, *m.*
Armoury, *s.* armurerie, *f.*; arsenal, *m.*; musée d'armes, *m.*; (*room*) salle d'armes, *f.*; (*armour*) armure, *f.*; (*arms*) armoiries, *f.pl.*; (*heraldry*) blason, *m.*

Army, *s.* armée, *f.*; (*fig.*) multitude, foule, armée, *f.* *To be in the* —, être à l'armée, être au service, servir, être militaire. **— accoutrement maker, — clothier,** *s.* fabricant d'équipements militaires, *m.* **— contractor,** *s.* fournisseur de l'armée *or* des troupes, munitionnaire, *m.* **— corps,** *s.* corps d'armée, *m.* **— list,** *s.* cadres de l'armée, *m.pl.*, annuaire militaire, *m.* **— purchase,** *s.* achat des grades militaires, *m.*
Arnatto. *V.* **Arnotto**
Arnee, *s.* arni, *m.*
Arnica, *s.* arnica, *f.*
Arnotto, *s.* roucou, *m.* **—tree,** *s.* roucouyer, *m.*
Aroint, *adv. int.* arrière!
Aroma, *s.* arôme, *m.*; (*of wine*) bouquet, *m.*
Aromatic, *s.* aromate, *m.*
Aromatic, Aromatical, *adj.* aromatique
Aromatization, *s.* aromatisation, *f.*
Aromatize, *v.a.* aromatiser; (*perfume*) embaumer
Around, *prep.* autour de, à l'entour de; — *adv.* autour, tout autour; alentour, à l'entour, aux alentours; (*around oneself*) autour de soi; (*of distance* or *by turns*) à la ronde. — *it, them* (*things*), autour, à l'entour
Arouse, *v.a.* *V.* **Rouse**
Aroynt, *adv. int.* arrière!
Arpeggio, *s.* arpége, *m.*
Arquebusade, *s.* arquebusade, *f.* **— water,** *s.* eau d'arquebusade, eau d'arquebuse, *f.*
Arquebuse, Arquebus, *s.* arquebuse, *f.*
Arquebusier, *s.* arquebusier, *m.*
Arrack, *s.* rack, arack, *m.*
Arragonese. *V.* **Aragonese**
Arraign, *v.a.* traduire en justice, traduire, mettre en accusation; accuser ('*for*', de)
Arraigner, *s.* accusateur, *m.*, -trice, *f.*
Arraignment, *s.* mise en accusation, *f.*; accusation, *f.*
Arrange, *v.a.* arranger; disposer; distribuer; ranger; — *v.n.* s'arranger; faire des arrangements
Arrangement, *s.* arrangement, *m.*; disposition, *f.*
Arranger, *s.* arrangeur, *m.*, -euse, *f.*
Arrant, *adj.* vrai, franc, insigne, fieffé, achevé
Arrantly, *adv.* ouvertement, impudemment; furieusement
Array, *s.* ordre, *m.*; revue, *f.*; rang, *m.*, rangée file, suite, *f.*; troupe, *f.*; cortége, *m.*; concours, nombre, *m.*; costume, *m.*, toilette, *f.*, atours, *m.pl.*; pompe, *f.*; appareil, *m.*; (*law*) liste des jurés, *f.*
Array, *v.a.* ranger; arranger, disposer; (*display*) déployer; (*dress*) revêtir (de); orner (de), parer (de); (*law*) dresser (*a list*)
Arrear, *s.*, **Arrears,** *s. pl.* arriéré, *m.*; arrérages, *m.pl.* *In* —, en arrière, arriéré, en retard
Arrearage, *s.* arrérage, arriéré, redû, *m.*
Arrest, *v.a.* arrêter; fixer; (*law*) surseoir à
Arrest, *s.* (*pers.*) arrestation, prise de corps, *f.*; (*hindrance*) empêchement, *m.*; (*stop*) arrêt, repos, *m.*; (*mil.*) arrêts, *m.pl.*; (*law*) sursis, *m.* — *for debt*, (*law*) contrainte par corps, *f.* *Under* —, en état d'arrestation; (*mil.*) aux arrêts
Arrestment, *s.* arrestation, *f.*; (*Scotch law*) opposition, *f.*
Arriere, *V.* **Rear. — ban,** *s.* arrière-ban, *m.*
Arris, *s.* (*arch.*) arête, *f.*
Arrival, *s.* arrivée, *f.*; (*nav., com.*) arrivage, *m.* **— platform,** *s.* (*rail.*) quai d'arrivée, *m.*
Arrive, *v.n.* arriver; (*reach*) parvenir (à)
Arrogance, *s.* arrogance, *f.*
Arrogant, *adj.* arrogant
Arrogantly, *adv.* arrogamment, avec arrogance
Arrogate, *v.a.* s'arroger. *To — to oneself*, s'arroger
Arrogation, *s.* arrogation, *f.*
Arrow, *s.* flèche, *f.*; (*fig.*) trait, *m.* **— grass,** *s.* troscart, *m.* **— head,** *s.* pointe de flèche, *f.*; (*bot.*) fléchière, sagittaire, *f.* **— headed,** *adj.* (*bot.*) sagitté. **— maker,** *s.* fléchier, *m.* **— root,** *s.* arrow-root, *m.*
Arrowy, *adj.* de flèche, de flèches; en flèche; rapide comme la flèche

Arsenal, *s.* arsenal, *m.*
Arseniate, *s.* arséniate, *m.*
Arsenic, *s.* arsenic, *m.*
Arsenic, -al, *adj.* arsénique, arsenical
Arsenicals, *s. pl.* arsenicaux, *m.pl.*
Arsenide, Arseniuret, *s.* arséniure, *m.*
Arsenious, *adj.* arsénieux
Arsenite, *s.* arsénite, *m.*
Arsis, *s.* (*mus.*) levé, *m.*
Arson, *s.* incendie par malveillance, incendie prémédité *or* volontaire, *m.*
Art, *s.* art, *m.*; (*fine arts*) beaux-arts, *m.pl.*; (*cunning*) artifice, *m.* *Black* —, magie, magie noire, *f.* *School of* —, école des beaux-arts, *f.* — **exhibition,** *s.* exposition des beaux-arts, *f.* — **union,** *s.* société des amis des arts, *f.*
Artemisia, *s.* (*bot.*) armoise, *f.*
Arterial, *adj.* artériel
Arterialization, *s.* artérialisation, *f.*
Arterialize, *v.a.* artérialiser
Arterio-graphy, -logy, -tomy, &c., artériographie, &c. *V.* page 3, § 1
Artery, *s.* artère, *f.*
Artesian, *adj.* artésien
Artful, *adj.* (*things*) fait avec art, ingénieux; (*skilful*) adroit, habile; (*not natural*) artificiel; (*crafty*) artificieux, insidieux
Artfully, *adv.* avec art, artistement, ingénieusement, habilement; (*craftily*) artificieusement, insidieusement [artifice, *m.*
Artfulness, *s.* art, *m.*, adresse, habileté, *f.*;
Artichoke, *s.* artichaut, *m.* *Jerusalem* —, topinambour, *m.* — **bed,** *s.* artichautière, *f.* — **bottom,** *s.* fond d'artichaut, *m.* — **kettle,** *s.* artichautière, *f.*
Article, *s.* article, *m.*; point, *m.*; objet, *m.*; (*of packages, luggage*) colis, *m.*; (*com.*) article, *m.*; marchandise, *f.*; (*gram.*) article, *m.*; (*statute*) statut, *m.*; stipulation, *f.*; —**s,** *pl.* articles, &c.; (*of lawyers' clerks*) contrat d'apprentissage, *m.*; apprentissage, stage, *m.*; — *v.a.* articuler; (*of clerks*, &c.) engager; (*of apprentices*) mettre en apprentissage ('*to*', chez); — *v.n.* stipuler
Articled, *adj.* apprenti. — *pupil*, apprenti, *m.*, e, *f.*; (*in a school*) élève-maître, *m.*, élève-maîtresse, institutrice-élève, *f.*
Articular, *adj.* articulaire
Articulate, *adj.* articulé; — *v.a.n.* articuler
Articulately, *adv.* distinctement; (*in detail*) article par article [lation, *f.*
Articulateness, Articulation, *s.* articu-
Artifice, *s.* artifice, *m.*; art, *m.*
Artificer, *s.* artisan, ouvrier, *m.*
Artificial, *adj.* artificiel
Artificiality. *V.* **Artificialness**
Artificially, *adv.* artificiellement; artistement, avec art
Artificialness, *s.* nature artificielle, *f.*
Artillerist, *s.* artilleur, *m.*
Artillery, *s.* artillerie, *f.* — **corps,** *s.* corps de l'artillerie, *m.* — **ground,** *s.* polygone, *m.* — **man,** *s.* artilleur, *m.* — **park,** *s.* parc d'artillerie, *m.* — **practice,** *s.* tir du canon, *m.* — **train,** *s.* équipage d'artillerie, *m.*
Artisan, *s. adj.* artisan, *m.*, e, *f.*
Artist, Artiste, *s.* artiste, *m.f.*
Artistic, *adj.* artistique; (*pers.*) artiste
Artistically, *adv.* artistement
Artless, *adj.* sans art, naturel; (*frank*) naïf, simple, ingénu
Artlessly, *adv.* sans art, naturellement; (*frankly*) naïvement, ingénument
Artlessness, *s.* naïveté, simplicité, ingénuité, *f.*
Aruspice, *s.* aruspice, *m.*
Aryan, *s. adj.* Aryen, *m.*, -ne, *f.*
As, *conj. adv. pron.* comme; de même que; ainsi que; (*because*) parce que; (*since*) puisque; (*for*) car; (*such as*) tel que; (*in the way of, after the manner of*) en (*to be followed by no article*); (*equally*) aussi; (*after a comparative, and after the word "same"*) que; (*as much as*) autant que; (*in proportion*) à mesure que; (*according to*) selon que; (*while*) pendant que, tandis que; (*however*) tout ... que; (*who, which*) qui. — *rich — you*, aussi riche que vous. *Rich — you are*, tout riche que vous êtes. — *for*, quant à, pour. — *it is*, comme il est; tel quel; (*in this case*) dans le cas présent *or* actuel; les choses étant ainsi, vu l'état des choses. — *it is* or *was*, — *they are* or *were*, (*so far*) comme cela, déjà; (*even then*) même alors; (*still*) toujours est-il que. — *it were*, pour ainsi dire, en quelque sorte. — *to*, pour, quant à; sur; (*according to*) selon, suivant
Asafœtida. *V.* **Assafœtida**
Asarabacca, Asarum, *s.* asaret, cabaret, *m.*
Asbestos, Asbestus, *s.* asbeste, *m.*
Ascaris, *s.* ascaride, *m.*
Ascend, *v.a.n.* monter; (*upon*) monter à *or* sur; (*a river*) remonter; (*high mountains*) faire l'ascension de; (*fig.*) remonter; (*rise*) s'élever
Ascendant, *s.* ascendant, *m.*; influence, *f.*; supériorité, *f.*, dessus, *m.*; (*law*) ascendant, *m.*; — *adj.* ascendant; supérieur. *To be in the* —, régner, prédominer, être tout-puissant; (*increase*) s'accroître, aller croissant
Ascendency, *s.* ascendant, *m.*, influence, *f.*
Ascending, *adj.* ascendant
Ascension, *s.* ascension, *f.* — **day,** *s.* le jour de l'Ascension, *m.*, l'Ascension, *f.*
Ascensional, *adj.* ascensionnel
Ascensionist, *s.* ascensioniste, *m.f.*
Ascent, *s.* ascension, *f.*; (*way up*) montée, *f.*; (*acclivity*) montée, rampe, *f.*; (*eminence*) élévation, éminence, colline, *f.*
Ascertain, *v.a.* s'assurer de; s'assurer (que); (*confirm*) constater; vérifier; prouver; (*fix*) fixer, déterminer [vérifiable
Ascertainable, *adj.* dont on peut s'assurer,
Ascertainment, *s.* constatation, *f.*; fixation, *f.*; règle établie, *f.*, principe reconnu, *m.* [*m.f.*
Ascetic, *adj.* ascétique; —*s.* ascétique, ascète,
Asceticism, *s.* ascétisme, *m.*
Ascites, *s.* ascite, *f.*
Ascitic, -al, *adj.* ascitique, ascite
Ascribable, *adj.* attribuable
Ascribe, *v.a.* attribuer (à); accorder (à)
Asexual, *adj.* asexuel
Ash, *s.* cendre, *f.*; cendres, *f.pl.*; (*tree, its wood*) frêne, *m.*; —**es,** *pl.* cendre, *f.*; cendres, *f.pl.*; — *adj.* cendré; de frêne; — *v.a.* cendrer. *To sleep in its* —*es*, couver sous la cendre. — **box,** *s.* cendrier, *m.* — **colour,** *s.* couleur cendrée, *f.* — **coloured,** *adj.* cendré. — **grey,** *adj. s.* gris cendré, *m.* — **grove, -plantation,** *s.* frênaie, *f.* — **hole,** *s.* cendrier, *m.* — **man, -merchant,** *s.* cendrier, *m.* — **pan,** *s.* cendrier, *m.* — **pit,** *s.* trou aux cendres, *m.*, trou aux ordures, *m.*; cendrier, *m.* — **tree,** *s.* frêne, *m.* — **tub,** *s.* cendrier, *m.*; cuvier, baquet, *m.* — **Wednesday,** *s.* mercredi des Cendres, *m.*
Ashamed, *adj.* honteux, confus. *To be — of* (or *to*), être honteux *or* confus de, avoir honte de, rougir de. *To be — of oneself*, avoir honte de sa conduite, rougir. *I am — of you*, vous me faites honte
Ashen, *adj.* de frêne
Ashlar, Ashler, *s.* moellon, *m.* — **work,** *s.* maçonnerie de moellon, *f.*
Ashore, *adv.* à terre; sur le rivage; (*of a ship*) échoué, à la côte. *To come* or *get* —, venir à terre, prendre terre, débarquer. *To bring* —, débarquer. *To run* —, *to be driven* —, faire côte, échouer
Ashy, *adj.* de cendre, de cendres; (*containing ashes*) cendreux; (*of colour*) cendré; gris pâle; [pâle
Asiarch, *s.* asiarque, *m.*
Asiarchy, *s.* asiarchat, *m.* [d'Asie
Asiatic, *s.* Asiatique, *m.f.*; — *adj.* asiatique,
Aside, *adv.* de côté; (*retired*) à l'écart; *separately*) à part; (*theat.*) à part. *Putting* or *setting* —, (*excluding*) abstraction faite de, sans compter. *Putting* or *setting that* —, à part

cela, sans compter cela. *To run —, (v.a.)* détourner; *(v.n.)* se détourner

Asinine, *adj.* d'âne; asine (*adj. f.*). — *species* or *race*, espèce *or* race asine, *f.*

Ask, *v.a.n.* demander; prier (de), inviter (à); interroger; (*a question*) faire. — **after,** s'informer de; demander, demander après. — **for,** demander. — **in,** faire entrer, prier d'entrer. — **up,** faire monter, prier de monter, *To — a person for a thing, to — a thing of a person,* demander une chose à quelqu'un. *To — a person ... (a price) for a thing,* demander à quelqu'un ... (francs *or* centimes) d'une *or* pour une chose. *To — a person to do, to see,* &c. *a thing,* demander à quelqu'un (*or* prier quelqu'un) de faire, de voir, &c. une chose. *To — to do, to see,* &c., (*oneself*) demander à faire, à voir, &c. *To — in church,* publier les bans de mariage de. *To be —ed in church,* faire publier ses bans

Askance, Askant, *adv.* obliquement, de côté; du coin de l'œil; (*in a bad sense*) de travers

Asker, *s.* questionneur, *m.*, -euse, *f.*, demandeur, *m.*, -euse, *f.*; solliciteur, *m.*, -euse, *f.*

Askew, *adv.* de biais, en biais, obliquement, de côté; de travers [quement

Aslant, *adv.* de côté, de biais, en biais, obli-

Asleep, *adj.* endormi. *To be* or *lie —,* dormir. *To fall —,* s'endormir. *To lay —,* endormir

Aslope, *adv.* en pente; obliquement, de *or* en biais

Asp, *s.* aspic, *m.*; (*aspen*) *V.* **Aspen**

Asparagine, *s.* asparagine, *f.*

Asparagus, *s.* asperge, *f.*, asperges, *f.pl.* — **bed,** *s.* aspergière, *f.* — **dish,** *s.* berceau à asperges, *m.* — **knife,** *s.* coupe-asperges, *m.* — **points,** *s. pl.* pointes d'asperges, *f.pl.* — **tongs,** *s. pl.* pince à asperges *f.*

Aspect, *s.* aspect, *m.*; (*situation*) exposition, *f.*; (*view*) point de vue, *m.*; (*anat.*) face, *f.* *To have a northern, a southern —,* être exposé au nord, au midi

Aspen, *s.* tremble, *m.*; — *adj.* de tremble. — **grove, -plantation,** *s.* tremblaie, *f.* — **tree,** [*s.* tremble, *m.*

Aspergeoire, *s.* aspergès, *m.*

Aspergill, *s.* aspergès, aspersoir, goupillon, *m.*

Asperity, *s.* aspérité, *f.*; (*sourness*) âpreté, *f.*; (*of sound, of temper*) rudesse, *f.*; (*sharpness, fig.*) sévérité, *f.* [(*sprinkle*) asperger

Asperse, *v.a.* diffamer, calomnier, noircir;

Asperser, *s.* diffamateur, *m.*, -trice, *f.*, calomniateur, *m.*, -trice, *f.*

Aspersion, *s.* diffamation, calomnie, *f.*; (*sprinkling*) aspersion, *f.*

Aspersive, *adj.* diffamatoire, calomnieux

Aspersively, *adv.* calomnieusement

Aspersorium, *s.* bénitier, *m.* [asphalte, *m.*

Asphalt, Asphalte, Asphaltum, *s.*

Asphalt, *v.a.* asphalter, bitumer [asphaltite

Asphaltic, *adj.* asphaltique, d'asphalte; (*geog.*)

Asphalting, *s.* asphaltage, *m.*

Asphodel, *s.* asphodèle, *m.*

Asphyxia, *s.* asphyxie, *f.*

Asphyxial, *adj* de l'asphyxie

Asphyxiant, *s.* asphyxiant, *m.*

Asphyxiate, *v.a.* asphyxier

Asphyxiated, Asphyxied, *adj.* asphyxié

Asphyxiation, *s.* asphyxie, *f.*

Asphyxy, *s.* asphyxie, *f.*

Aspic, *s.* aspic, *m.*

Aspirant, *s. adj.* aspirant, *m.*, e, *f.*

Aspirate, *v.a.* aspirer; — *v.n.* s'aspirer; — *adj.* aspiré, *m*, e, *f.*; —*s.* aspirée, *f.*; (*Gr. gram.*) esprit rude, *m.* [(*gram.*) aspiration, *f.*

Aspiration, *s.* aspiration, *f.*; désir, élan, *m.*;

Aspirator, *s.* aspirateur, *m.*

Aspiratory, *adj.* aspiratoire [s'élever

Aspire, *v.n.* aspirer (à), prétendre (à); (*rise*)

Aspiring, *adj.* ambitieux; qui a des vues élevées; qui désire faire son chemin; —*s.* *V.* **Aspiration**

Asquint, *adv.* de côté, de travers, en louchant

Ass, *s.* âne, *m.*, ânesse, *f.* *She- ,* ânesse. —*es'* **bridge,** *s.* pont aux ânes, *m.* — **driver,** *s.* ânier, *m.*, ânière, *f.* —*'s* **foal,** *s.* ânon, *m.* —*'s* **load,** *s.* ânée, *f.* —*'s* **milk,** *s.* lait d'ânesse, *m.*

Assafœtida, *s.* assa-fœtida, *f.*

Assagai, Assagay, *s.* zagaie, *f.*

Assail, *v.a.* assaillir; attaquer

Assailable, *adj.* attaquable

Assailant, Assailer, *s.* assaillant, *m.*

Assassin, *s.* assassin, *m.*, e, *f.* —*-like,* d'assassin

Assassinate, *v.a.n.* assassiner

Assassinating, *adj.* assassinant; d'assassinat

Assassination, *s.* assassinat, *m.*

Assassinator, *s.* assassin, *m.*

Assault, *s.* assaut, *m.*; attaque, agression, *f.*; (*law*) voies de fait, *f.pl.*; attaque, *f.*; — *v.a.* donner l'assaut à; assaillir, attaquer; (*law*) commettre des voies de fait sur; attaquer. — *of arms,* assaut d'armes. *Aggravated —,* voies de fait et blessures, coups et blessures. *Indecent —,* tentative de viol, *f.*; viol, *m.*

Assaultable, *adj.* attaquable

Assaulter, *s.* assaillant, agresseur, *m.*

Assay, *v.a.* essayer; —*s.* (*of metals*) essai, *m.*; (*of weights,* &c.) vérification, *f.* — **mark,** *s.* contrôle, *m.* — **master,** *s.* maître essayeur, *m.* — **office,** *s.* bureau d'essai *or* de garantie, *m.*; essayerie, *f.* — **scales,** *s. pl.* trébuchet *m.*, [pesette, *f.*

Assayer, *s.* essayeur, *m.*

Assaying, *s.* essai, *m.*

Assemblage, *s.* assemblage, *m.*; assemblée, *f.*

Assemble, *v.a.* assembler, rassembler, réunir; — *v.n.* s'assembler, se rassembler, se réunir

Assembler, *s.* assembleur, *m.*, -euse, *f.*; chef, meneur, *m.*

Assembling, *s.* rassemblement, *m.*; réunion, *f.*

Assembly, *s.* assemblée, *f.*; réunion, *f.*; (*of voters*) collége, *m.* *To beat* or *sound the —,* (*mil.*) battre la générale, battre l'assemblée. — **room,** *s.* salle de réunion, *f.*; salle d'assemblée, *f.*

Assent, *s.* assentiment, consentement, *m.*; approbation, *f.*; (*law, polit.*) sanction, *f.*; — *v.n.* donner son assentiment (à), consentir (à), acquiescer (à); approuver, convenir (de)

Assenter, *s.* approbateur, *m.*, -trice, *f.*

Assentingly, *adv.* avec assentiment; en signe d'assentiment; approbativement, avec approbation

Assert, *v.a.* soutenir; défendre; déclarer; proclamer; affirmer, assurer, prétendre; (*claim*) réclamer, revendiquer

Asserter, Assertor, *s.* défenseur, soutien, *m.*

Assertion, *s.* assertion, *f.*; défense, *f.*; reven-

Assertive, *adj.* assertif, affirmatif [dication, *f.*

Assertively, *adv.* assertivement, affirmative-

Assertory, *adj.* assertoire, affirmatif [ment

Assess, *v.a.* taxer; coter; imposer, répartir; estimer, évaluer, fixer [évaluable

Assessable, *adj.* imposable; répartissable;

Assessed, *part.* taxé, coté, imposé, &c. (*V.* **Assess,** *v.a.*); — *adj.* (*of taxes*) direct

Assessionary, *adj.* assessorial

Assessment, *s.* recensement, *m.*; (*of landed property*) cadastre, *m.*; (*of taxes*) imposition, *f.*; cote, *f.*; répartition, assiette, *f.*; fixation, *f.*; (*valuing*) expertise, *f.*; (*in ship-insurance*) dispache, *f.*

Assessor, *s.* assesseur, *m.*; (*of taxes*) répartiteur, *m.*; (*valuer*) estimateur, expert, *m.*; (— *of losses, to an insurance-office*) expert, *m.*; (*ship-insurance*) dispacheur, *m.* *Nautical —,* [dispacheur, *m.*

Assessorial, *adj.* assessorial

Assets, *s. pl.* actif, *m.*; masse active, *f.*

Assever, Asseverate, *v.a.* affirmer solennellement

Asseveration, *s.* affirmation solennelle, *f.*

Assiduity, *s.* assiduité, *f.*

Assiduous, *adj.* assidu

Assiduously, *adv.* assidûment

Assiduousness. *V.* **Assiduity**

Assign, *v.a.* assigner (à); destiner (à); désigner

(à), appliquer (à); fixer, déterminer; (*law*) transférer, céder
Assign, *s.* ayant-droit, ayant-cause, *m.*
Assignable, *adj.* assignable; déterminable; [(*law*) transférable
Assignat, *s.* assignat, *m.*
Assignation, *s.* assignation, *f.*; désignation, *f.*; (*of time*) rendez-vous, *m.*; (*law*) cession, *f.*
Assignee, *s.* cessionnaire, *m.f.*; délégué, *m.*, e, *f.*; (*in bankruptcy*) syndic, *m.* [e, *f.*
Assigner, *s.* indicateur, *m.*; (*law*) cédant, *m.*,
Assignment, *s.* assignation, allocation, *f.*; (*law*) transfert, *m.*, cession, *f.*
Assignor. *V.* **Assigner**
Assimilable, *adj.* assimilable
Assimilate, *v.a.n.* assimiler; s'assimiler
Assimilation, *s.* assimilation, *f.*
Assimilative, *adj.* assimilatif, assimilateur
Assist, *v.a.n.* assister; aider (à *or* dans); secourir; (*support*) appuyer
Assistance, *s.* assistance, aide, *f.*, secours, *m.*; (*of writers*) collaboration, *f.*
Assistant, *adj.* qui aide; auxiliaire; — *s. adj.* aide, *m.f.*; assistant, *m.*; adjoint, *m.*; suppléant, *m.*; second, *m.*; sous-...; garçon, *m.*; (*in schools*) sous-maître, *m.*, sous-maîtresse, *f.*; (*of writers*) collaborateur, *m.*, -trice, *f.*; (*to a fencing or dancing-master*) prévôt, *m.*; (*to a chemical lecturer*) préparateur, (*jest.*) piston, *m.* — **engine,** *s.* machine *or* locomotive de renfort, *f.* — **engineer,** *s.* sous-ingénieur, *m.* — **judge,** *s.* assesseur, *m.* — **lecturer,** *s.* professeur adjoint, *m.*; professeur suppléant, *m.* — **master,** *s.* sous-maître, *m.* — **professor,** *s.* professeur suppléant, agrégé, *m.* — **surgeon,** *s.* aide-chirurgien, *m.*
Assister. *V.* **Aider** [(*tax*) taxe, *f.*
Assize, *s.*, **Assizes,** *s. pl.* (*law*) assises, *f.pl.*;
Assize, *v.a.* taxer le prix de, taxer; mesurer; fixer
Assizer, *s.* vérificateur des poids et mesures, *m.*
Associable, *adj.* associable
Associate, *v.a.n.* associer (à *or* avec); unir (avec); joindre (à); (*— oneself*) s'associer (à *or* avec); s'unir (avec); se joindre (à); vivre en société (avec); faire société (avec); fréquenter; — *adj.* associé; — *s.* associé, *m.*, e, *f.*; compagnon, *m.*, compagne, *f.*; camarade, *m.f.*; compère, *m.*, commère, *f.*; (*of societies*) membre, associé, *m.*; (*accomplice*) complice, *m.f.*; —**s,** *s. pl.* (*in a bad sense*) consorts, *m.pl.*; complices, *m.f.pl.*
Association, *s.* association, *f.*; corporation, *f.*; union, *f.*; (*connection*) rapport, *m.*; —**s,** *pl.* (*of the mind*) idées, notions, *f.pl.*; souvenirs, *m.pl.* *Past —s,* souvenirs intimes, souvenirs, *m.pl.* — *of ideas,* (*philos.: general sense*) association des idées, (*partitive sense*) association [d'idées
Assonance, *s.* assonnance, *f.*
Assonant, *adj.* assonnant
Assort, *v.a.* assortir
Assortment, *s.* assortiment, *m.*; assemblage, *m.*
Assuage, *v.a.* calmer, apaiser, adoucir; — *v.n.* s'apaiser, se calmer [ment, *m.*
Assuagement, *s.* adoucissement, soulage-
Assuasive, *adj.* calmant, adoucissant
Assume, *v.a.* prendre; s'arroger; s'attribuer; (*put on*) revêtir; (*the responsibility*) assumer; (*set up for*) faire (le, la, les), se poser (en); (*suppose*) supposer; prétendre; feindre; — *v.n.* faire l'important, agir avec arrogance, être *or* se montrer arrogant, afficher des prétentions
Assumer, *s.* arrogant, prétentieux, présomptueux, *m.*
Assuming, *adj.* arrogant; prétentieux; présomptueux; (*positive*) tranchant
Assumption, *s.* supposition, *f.*; prétention, *f.*; présomption, *f.*; (*log.*) assomption, mineure, *f.*; (*theol.*) Assomption, *f.*
Assumptive, *adj.* assomptif
Assurable, *adj.* assurable [**Insurance**
Assurance, *s.* assurance, *f.*; certitude, *f.* *V.*
Assure, *v.a.* assurer
Assured, *part. adj.* assuré; sûr; — *s.* assuré, *m.*, e, *f.*
Assuredly, *adv.* assurément; certainement. *Most —,* très certainement, certes
Assuredness, *s.* certitude, *f.*
Assurer, *s.* assureur, *m.* [assyrien, d'Assyrie
Assyrian, *s.* Assyrien, *m.*, -ne, *f.*; — *adj.*
Aster, *s.* aster, *m.*
Asteria, Asterias, *s.* astérie, *f.*
Asterisk, *s.* astérisque, *m.*
Asterism, *s.* astérisme, *m.* [poupe; arrière
Astern, *adv.* (*nav.*) à l'arrière, de l'arrière, en
Asteroid, *s.* astéroïde, *m.*
Asthma, *s.* asthme, *m.*; (*vet.*) pousse, *f.*
Asthmatic, -al, *s. adj.* asthmatique, *m.f.*
Astir, *adj.* agité, en émoi, en rumeur, en l'air; agissant, actif, en mouvement; debout
Astonish, *v.a.* étonner, surprendre ('*at,*' '*to,*' de)
Astonishingly, *adv.* étonnamment
Astonishment, *s.* étonnement, *m.*
Astound, *v.a.* étonner, étourdir, abasourdir
Astoundingly, *adv.* étonnamment
Astracan, Astrakhan, *s.* astracan, astra- [kan, *m.*
Astraddle, *adv.* *V.* **Astride**
Astragal, Astragalus, *s.* astragale, *m.*
Astral, *adj.* astral [*and* **Lead**
Astray, *adv.* égaré; (*fig.*) de travers. *V.* **Go**
Astride, *adv.* à cheval, à califourchon; — *prep.* [à cheval sur
Astringency, *s.* astringence, *f.*
Astringent, *adj. s.* astringent, *adj. m.*, e, *f.*, [astringent, *s.m.*
Astrolabe, *s.* astrolabe, *m.*
Astrologer, *s.* astrologue, *m.*
Astrolog-ic, al, -ically, -y. *V.* page 3, § 1
Astrometer, *s.* astromètre, *m.*
Astronomer, *s.* astronome, *m.*
Astronomic, -al, *adj.* astronomique; d'astronomie. — *instruments,* instruments d'astronomie, *m.pl.*
Astronom-ically, -y. *V.* page 3, § 1
Asturian, *s. adj.* Asturien, *m.*, -ne, *f.*
Astute, *adj.* fin, rusé, pénétrant; (*in a bad sense*) astucieux
Astutely, *adv.* avec finesse, avec ruse; (*in a* (*bad sense*) astucieusement
Astuteness, *s.* finesse, ruse, sagacité, *f.*; (*in a bad sense*) astuce, *f.* [en deux
Asunder, *adv.* séparément, séparé; (*in two*)
Asylum, *s.* asile, refuge, *m.*; (*of charity*) hospice, asile, *m.*
Asymptote, *s.* asymptote, *f.*
Asymptotic, -al, *adj.* asymptotique
At, *prep.* à; (*in*) en, dans; (*of, from, on account of*) de; (*by*) par; (*on*) sur; (*against*) contre; après. — ...'s, chez. — *the baker's,* chez le boulanger. — *a* (or *one*) *bound, gulp,* &c., d'un bond, d'un trait, &c. *To be — it,* y être. *To be hard — it,* y travailler ferme. *What are you — ?* qu'est-ce que vous faites ? *What he would be —,* ce qu'il voulait, son but
Ataghan, Atagan. *V.* **Yataghan**
Ataraxy, Atavism, &c. *V.* page 3, § 1
Athanasian, *adj.* de Saint-Athanase. — *creed,* symbole de Saint-Athanase, *m.*
Atheism, *s.* athéisme, *m.*
Atheist, *s.* athée, *m.f.*
Atheistic, -al, *adj.* athée
Atheistically, *adv.* en athée
Athenæum, *s.* athénée, *m.*
Athenian, *s.* Athénien, *m.*, -ne, *f.*; — *adj.* [athénien, d'Athènes
Athirst, *adj.* altéré
Athlete, *s.* athlète, *m.*
Athletic, *adj.* athlétique; —**s,** *s. pl.* athlétique, *f.*
Athletically, *adv.* athlétiquement
Athleticism, Athletism, *s.* athlétique, *f.*
Athwart, *prep.* à travers, au travers de, en travers de; (*opposite*) à l'encontre de; (*nav.*) en travers de, par le travers de; — *adv.* de travers
Atilt, *adv.* en jouteur; en champ clos; (*of a cask*) debout. *To run — against* or *at,* rompre une lance avec, jouter avec
Atlantean, *adj.* d'Atlantide; d'Atlas

Atlantic, *adj.* atlantique; — *s.* Atlantique, *m.*
Atlantis, *s.* Atlantide, *f.*; (*arch.*) atlante, *m.*
Atlas, *s.* atlas, *m.*; (*paper*) grand colombier, *m.*
Atmosphere, *s.* atmosphère, *f.*
Atmospheric, -al, *adj.* atmosphérique
Atom, *s.* atome, *m.* [*V.* page 3, § 1
Atom-ic, al, -ically, -ism, -ist, -istic.
Atone, *v.a.n.* expier; (*redeem*) racheter
Atonement, *s.* expiation, *f.* ('*for*', de)
Atoner, *s.* expiateur, *m.*, -trice, *f.*
Aton-ic, -y. *V.* page 3, § 1
Atop, *adv.* en haut, au sommet
Atrabilarian, Atrabilious, *adj.* atrabilaire
Atrip, *adv.* (*of anchor*) dérapé; (*of top-sails*)
Atrocious, *adj.* atroce [guindé
Atrociously, *adv.* atrocement
Atrociousness, Atrocity, *s* atrocité, *f.*
Atrophied, *adj.* atrophié. *To become* —,
Atrophy, *s.* atrophie, *f.* [s'atrophier
Atropia, Atropine, *s.* atropine, *f.*
Attach, *v.a.* attacher (à); s'attacher (à); arrêter; saisir; contraindre par corps; contraindre (par saisie de biens); mettre opposition à; — *v.n.* s'attacher (à)
Attachable, *adj.* contraignable par corps;
Attaché, *s.* attaché, *m.* [saisissable
Attachment, *s.* attachement, *m.*; (*law*) contrainte par corps, *f.*; (*law*) contrainte (par saisie de biens), saisie, *f.*; (*law*) opposition, *f.*
Attack, *v.a.* attaquer; — *s.* attaque, *f.*; (*fit*) attaque, atteinte, *f.*, accès, *m.*
Attackable, *adj.* attaquable
Attacker, *s.* agresseur, assaillant, *m.*
Attacking, *adj.* (*mil.*) d'attaque
Attain, *v.a.* atteindre; (*arrive*) parvenir à, arriver à; — *v.n.* atteindre (à); parvenir (à), arriver (à) [sible
Attainable, *adj.* qu'on peut atteindre; acces-
Attainableness, *s.* possibilité d'atteindre, *f*
Attainder, *s.* tache, flétrissure, souillure, *f.*; (*law*) dégradation (civique), mort civile, *f.*
Attainment, *s.* acquisition, *f.*; possession, *f.*; talent, *m.*; connaissance, *f.*; progrès, *m.*
Attaint, *v.a.* déclarer faux; (*convict*) convaincre, condamner; (*stain*) flétrir, entacher, souiller; — *s.* tache, flétrissure, souillure; (*law*) inscription en faux, *f.*; (*rid.*) atteinte, *f.*
Attainture, *s.* flétrissure, *f.*
Attar. *V.* **Otto**
Attemper, *v.a.* *V.* **Temper,** *v.a.*
Attempt, *v.a.* tenter (de), essayer (de), tâcher (de), entreprendre (de), chercher (à); vouloir; (*to attack*) attenter à; (*law*) faire une tentative de. *To — to do a thing*, essayer *or* &c. de faire quelque chose. *To — anyone's life*, attenter à la vie de quelqu'un
Attempt, *s.* tentative, *f.*, essai, effort, *m*; (*criminal or illegal*) attentat ('*on*' or '*upon*', contre, à, sur), *m.* *First* —, coup d'essai, *m.*
Attend, *v.a.* faire attention à, écouter, observer; (*hear*) exaucer, écouter; (*assist*) assister; (*be present at*) assister à; (*follow, go regularly to*) suivre ('*with*', de); (*accompany*) accompagner ('*with*', de); (*the sick*) soigner; (*visitors*) recevoir; accompagner, reconduire; (*wait on*) être de service auprès de; (*in a shop*) servir; (*a door*) ouvrir; (*surround*) entourer, environner; (*belong to*) être attaché à; s'attacher à; — *v.n.* faire attention (à), écouter, observer; (*turn o.'s thoughts to, be busy in*) s'occuper (de); s'appliquer (à); (*take care of*) avoir soin (de); être là; (*of business*) vaquer (à); (*be present*) assister (à), être présent (à); veiller (à); (*wait upon*) servir; (*be on duty*) être de service; (*come*) venir; (*have regard*) avoir égard (à); (*comply, obey*) se rendre (à), se conformer (à), obéir (à)
Attendance, *s* attentions, *f.pl.*; soins, *m.pl.*; assistance, *f.*; visites, *f.pl.*; leçons, *f.pl.*; présence, *f.*; assiduité, *f.*; (*waiting upon*) service, *m.*; (*train*) suite, *f.*; cortége, *m*; domestiques, *m.pl.*; accompagnement, *m.*; (*people present*) assistance, assemblée, *f.*, auditoire, *m.*; classe, *f.* *To be in* —, attendre; (*be on duty*) être de service. *To be regular in o.'s — at* (*lectures, lessons, church service*, &c.), suivre régulièrement. *To dance* —, faire antichambre; attendre, se morfondre, faire le pied de grue, croquer le marmot, droguer, poser
Attendant, *adj.* qui suit *or* accompagne; qui dépend (de), dépendant (de); — *s.* assistant, *m.*; compagnon, *m.*, compagne, *f.*; serviteur, *m.*, domestique, *m.f.*, servante, femme, *f.*; personne de la suite, *f.*; personne de service, *f.*; (*overlooker*) surveillant, *m.*; (*on the sick*) garde, *m.f.*, (*in hospitals*) infirmier, *m.*; (*fig.*) suite, conséquence, *f.*; (*nav.*) surveillant, *m.*; —**s,** *pl.* suite, *f.*, cortége, *m.*, escorte, *f.*; personnes attachées (à), *f.pl.* — **path,** *s.* (*rail.*) chemin de service, *m.*
Attention, *s.* attention, *f.*; (*care*) soin, *m.* —*!* (*mil.*) garde à vous! attention au commandement! *To be all — to*, être aux petits soins avec (*or* pour). *To pay — to*, faire attention à; (*to a young lady*) faire la cour à
Attentive, *adj.* attentif (à); (*careful*) soigneux (de); (*kind*) attentionné
Attentively, *adv.* attentivement
Attentiveness, *s.* attention, *f.*
Attenuate, *v.a.* atténuer; (*lessen*) affaiblir, diminuer, amoindrir; (*make thin*) amincir; (*emaciate*) amaigrir, atténuer
Attenuation, *s* atténuation, *f.*; (*lessening*) diminution, *f.*, affaiblissement, *m.*
Attest, *v.a.* attester; (*to show*) témoigner de
Attestation, *s.* témoignage, *m.*; (*in writing*) attestation, *f.*
Attic, *adj.* attique; — *s.* (*pers., dialect*) attique *m.*; (*arch.*) mansarde, *f.*; grenier, *m.*; attique, *m.* — **salt,** *s.* sel attique, *m.* — **window,** *s.* fenêtre en mansarde, *f.*
Attic-ism, -ist. *V.* page 3, § 1
Attire, *v.a.* ('*in*', de) vêtir; (*adorn*) parer, orner; — *s.* (*dress*) vêtement, *m.*; costume, *m.*; (*apparel*) appareil, *m.*; (*ornamental*) parure, *f.*; (*of women*) atours, *m.pl.*; (*her.*) ramure, *f.*
Attired, *part. adj.* vêtu, &c. (*V.* **Attire,** *v.a.*); (*her.*) ramé
Attitude, *s.* attitude, *f.*; posture, *f.*; air, *m.*; (*in dancing, paint., theat.*) pose, *f.*
Attitudinarian, *s.* poseur, *m.*, -euse, *f.*
Attitudinize, *v.n.* poser
Attorney, *s.* avoué, *m.*; notaire, *m.*; (*public functionary*) procureur, *m.*; (*proxy*) fondé de pouvoir (*or* de pouvoirs), mandataire, *m.* *Power* or *warrant* or *letter of* —, procuration, *f.*, mandat, pouvoir, *m.* — **general,** *s.* procureur général, *m.* — **at-law,** *s.* avoué, *m.*; notaire, *m.* [d'avoué, *f.*; procuration, *f.*
Attorneyship, *s.* charge de procureur *or*
Attract, *v.a.* attirer
Attractable, *adj.* attirable
Attractile, *adj.* attracteur
Attractingly, *adv.* par attraction
Attraction, *s.* attraction, *f.*; (*fig.*) attrait, *m.*
Attractive, *adj.* (*alluring*) attrayant; (*drawing to*) attractif
Attractively, *adv.* d'une manière attrayante
Attractiveness, *s.* attrait, *m.*; vertu attrac-
Attributable, *adj.* attribuable [tive, *f.*
Attribute, *v.a.* attribuer (à); — *s.* attribut, *m.*; qualité, *f.* [attribuée, *f.*, attribut, *m.*
Attribution, *s.* action d'attribuer, *f.*; qualité
Attributive, *adj.* attributif
Attrition, *s.* attrition, *f.* [au diapason (de)
Attune, *v.a.* accorder (avec); mettre au ton *or*
Auburn, *adj.* châtain clair
Auction, *s.* enchère, *f.*; vente, *f.*; adjudication, *f.* *By* —, aux enchères; à la criée. *Sale by* —, vente aux enchères *or* à la criée, *f.*; adjudication, *f.* — **mart,** *s.* hôtel des ventes, *m.*; salles de ventes (publiques), *f.pl.* — **room,** *s.* salle de ventes, *f.*
Auctionary, *adj.* des enchères
Auctioneer, *s.* commissaire-priseur, *m.*; directeur de ventes, *m.*

Auctioneering, *adj.* qui vend aux enchères
Audacious, *adj.* audacieux
Audaciously, *adv.* audacieusement
Audaciousness, Audacity, *s.* audace, *f.*
Audible, *adj.* qui peut être entendu, qui s'entend, perceptible; (*of utterance*) intelligible; distinct. *It was scarcely* —, on l'entendait à peine
Audibly, *adv.* de manière à être entendu *or* à se faire entendre, intelligiblement, distinctement, à haute voix, à haute et intelligible voix
Audience, *s.* audience, *f.*; (*hearers*) auditoire, *m.*; assistance, *f.*, assistants, *m.pl.*; assemblée, *f.* — **chamber, -room,** *s.* salle d'audience, *f.*
Audit, *s.* audition, *f.*; (*account*) compte, *m.*; — *v.a.* apurer. — **house,** *s.* sacristie, *f.* — **office,** *s.* cour des comptes, *f.*
Auditing, *s.* apurement, *m.*, audition, *f.*
Auditor, *s.* auditeur, *m.*; censeur, *m.*
Auditorship, *s.* auditorat, *m.*
Auditory, *adj.* auditif; — *s.* auditoire, *m.*; (*of judges*) tribunal, *m.*
Auditress, *s.* auditrice, *f.*
Augæan, Augean, *adj.* d'Augias. *The — stables,* les écuries d'Augias, *f.pl.*
Auger, *s.* tarière, *f.* — **bit,** *s.* mèche de tarière, *f.*
Aught, *pron. s. V.* **Anything.** *For — I care,* peu m'importe. *For — I know,* autant que je sache
Augment, *v.a.* augmenter; — *v.n.* augmenter, s'augmenter; — *s.* augment, *m.*
Augmentable, *adj.* augmentable
Augmentation, *s.* augmentation, *f.*
Augmentative, *adj. s.* augmentatif, *adj. m.*, -ive, *f.*, augmentatif, *s.m.*
Augmenter, *s.* augmentateur, *m.*, -trice, *f.*
Augur, *s.* augure, *m.*; (*tool*) *V.* **Auger;** — *v.n.a.* augurer; présager
Augural, Augurial, *adj.* augural
Augury, *s.* augure, présage, *m.*; (*the art of*) science des augures, *f.*
August, *adj.* auguste; — *s.* août, *m.*
Augustan, *adj.* d'Auguste; (*the confession*) d'Augsbourg. — *age,* siècle d'Auguste, *m.*
Augustine, *s.* augustin, *m.*, e, *f.*
Augustinian, *adj.* augustinien
Augustly, *adv.* augustement
Augustness, *s.* aspect auguste, *m.*, majesté, *f.*
Auk, *s.* pingouin, *m.*
Aulic, *adj.* aulique
Aumuce, *s.* aumusse, *f.*
Aunt, *s.* tante, *f.*
Aura, *s.* (*med.*) aura, *f.*
Aural, *adj.* de l'air; (*of the ear*) aural, de l'oreille. — *surgeon,* auriste, *m.*
Aurated, Aureate, *adj.* semblable à l'or, comme de l'or, d'or, doré
Aureburnean, *adj.* d'or et d'ivoire
Aurelia, *s.* aurélie, *f.*
Aureola, Aureole, *s.* auréole, *f.*
Auricle, *s.* (*of the ear*) auricule, *f.*; (*of the heart*) oreillette, *f.* [(*zool.*) auricule, *f.*
Auricula, *s.* (*bot.*) oreille d'ours, auricule, *f.*;
Auricular, *adj.* auriculaire
Auricularly, *adv.* à l'oreille; secrètement
Auriculate, Auriculated, *adj.* auriculé
Auriferous, *adj.* aurifère
Aurific, *adj.* aurifique
Auriform, *adj.* auriforme
Aurist, *s.* auriste, *m.*
Aurochs, *s.* aurochs, *m.*
Aurora, *s.* aurore, *f.* — *borealis,* aurore boréale, *f.*
Auroral, *adj.* de l'aurore
Auscultate, *v.a.* ausculter
Auscultation, *s.* auscultation, *f.*
Auscultator, *s.* auscultateur, *m.*
Auspice, *s.* auspice, *m.*
Auspicious, *adj.* propice, favorable, heureux, de bon augure
Auspiciously, *adv.* sous d'heureux auspices, favorablement, heureusement
Auspiciousness, *s.* aspect favorable, *m.*, heureux auspices, *m.pl.*
Auster, *s.* auster, vent du midi, *m.*
Austere, *adj.* austère, sévère; (*to the taste*) âpre
Austerely, *adv.* austèrement
Austereness, Austerity, *s.* austérité, *f.*; (*to the taste*) âpreté, *f.*
Austin, *s.* — *friar,* augustin, *m.* — *nun,* augustine, *f.*
Austral, *adj.* austral
Australasian, *s.* Australasien, *m.*, -ne, *f.*; — *adj.* australasien, d'Australasie, de l'Australasie
Australian, *s.* Australien, *m.*, -ne, *f.*; — *adj.* australien, d'Australie, de l'Australie
Austrasian, *s.* Austrasien, *m.*, -ne, *f.*; — *adj.* austrasien, d'Austrasie
Austrian, *s.* Autrichien, *m.*, -ne, *f.*; — *adj.* autrichien, d'Autriche
Authent-ic, al, -ically. *V.* page 3, § 1
Authenticalness, *s.* authenticité, *f.*
Authenticate, *v.a.* authentiquer, établir l'authenticité de, déclarer authentique; constater; (*law*) légaliser
Authentication, *s.* authenticité, *f.*; (*law*) légalisation, *f.*
Authenticity, *s.* authenticité, *f.*
Author, -ess, *s.* auteur, *m.*
Authorial, *adj.* d'auteur
Authoritative, *adj.* revêtu d'autorité; d'autorité, impérieux
Authoritatively, *adv.* avec autorité
Authoritativeness, *s.* air *or* ton d'autorité, *m.*; exigence, *f.*
Authority, *s.* autorité, *f.*; pouvoir, *m.* *To have from good* —, tenir de bonne source
Authorizable, *adj.* autorisable
Authorization, *s.* autorisation, *f.*
Authorize, *v.a.* autoriser (à)
Authorship, *s.* profession d'auteur, *f.*; qualité d'auteur, *f.*; (*jest.*) paternité, *f.* *To own the — of,* avouer qu'on est l'auteur de. *The — is unknown,* l'auteur est inconnu
Autobiographer, *s.* autobiographe, *m.f.*
Autobiograph-ic, al, -ically, -y. *V.* page 3, § 1
Autocracy, *s.* autocratie, *f.*
Autocrat, *s.* autocrate, *m.f.*
Autocrat-ic, al, -ically. *V.* page 3, § 1
Autocratrix, *s.* autocratrice, *f.*
Auto-da-fe, *s.* auto-da-fé, *m.*
Autograph, *s.* autographe, *m.*; — *adj.* autographe; — *v.a.* autographier
Autographer, *s.* autographe, *m.*
Autographic, -al, *adj.* autographique; (*of letters,* &c.) autographe
Autographically, *adv.* autographiquement
Autography, *s.* autographie, *f.*
Automatic, -al, *adj.* automate; automatique
Automat-ically, -ism. *V.* page 3, § 1
Automaton, *s.* automate, *m.*
Autonomic, Autonomous, *adj.* autonome
Autonomy, *s.* autonomie, *f.*
Autopsy, *s.* autopsie, *f.*
Autumn, *s.* automne, *m.*; — *adj.* d'automne, automnal. *In* —, en automne. *In the* —, dans l'automne; en automne
Autumnal, *adj.* automnal, d'automne; — *s.* plante d'automne, plante automnale, *f.*
Auxiliary, *adj. s.* auxiliaire
Avail, *v.a.n.* servir à; profiter à, être utile à. *To — oneself of,* profiter de, se servir de; se prévaloir de; tirer parti de. *To — nothing,* ne servir à rien *or* de rien, être inutile
Avail, *s.* utilité, *f.*, avantage, service, *m.* *To be of no* —, ne servir à rien *or* de rien, être inutile. *Of what — is it?* à quoi sert? que sert?
Available, *adj.* utile (à), avantageux (à), profitable (à); (*valid, holding good*) valable; (*disposable*) disponible
Availableness, *s.* utilité, *f.*; validité, *f.*
Availably, *adv.* utilement, avantageusement valablement
Availing, *adj.* utile (à), profitable (à)
Avalanche, *s.* avalanche, *f.*
Avanturine. *V.* **Aventurine**
Avarice, *s.* avarice, *f.*

Avaricious, *adj.* avare
Avariciously, *adv.* avarement, avec avarice
Avariciousness, *s.* avarice, *f.*
Avast, *adv. int.* (*nav.*) avaste! baste! (*colloquial.*
Avatar, *s.* avatar, *m.* [*jest.*) assez comme ça!
Avaunt, *int.* arrière! loin de moi! loin d'ici! hors d'ici!
Ave, *s.* avé, *m.* — *Maria,* avé Maria, *m.*
Avenaceous, *adj.* avénacé
Avenge, *v.a.* venger
Avenger, *s.* vengeur, *m.*, -eresse, *f.*
Avenging, *adj.* vengeur
Avens. *V.* **Bennet**
Aventine, *s.* Aventin, *m.*
Aventurine, *s. adj.* aventurine, *f.*
Avenue, *s.* avenue, *f.*
Aver, *v.a.* affirmer, assurer, certifier
Average, *s.* moyenne, *f.*, terme moyen, *m.*; (*damage*) avarie, *f.*; (*duty*) droit, *m.*; **—s,** *pl.* (*of grain*) mercuriale, *f.* *On* or *upon an* —, en moyenne, l'un dans l'autre. **— stater,** *s.* dispacheur, *m.*
Average, *adj.* moyen, en moyenne, commun
Average, *v.a.* prendre la moyenne de; (*divide*) répartir; — *v.n.* donner une moyenne de, revenir en moyenne à, être en moyenne de, valoir en moyenne [melle, *f.*
Averment, *s.* affirmation, déclaration for-
Averruncator, *s.* échenilloir, *m.*
Averse, *adj.* éloigné (de); contraire (à), ennemi (de); opposé (à); peu disposé (à)
Aversely, *adv.* avec répugnance, à contre-cœur
Averseness, Aversion, *s.* aversion (*'to'*, pour), *f.*, répugnance, *f.*, éloignement, *m.* *To take an aversion to,* prendre en aversion. *That man is my aversion,* cet homme-là est pour moi un objet d'aversion, cet homme-là est ma bête noire
Avert, *v.a.* détourner (de), éloigner (de), écarter (de); (*prevent*) empêcher. *God —!* à Dieu ne plaise! Dieu en préserve ...!
Avertin, *s.* (*vet.*) avertin, *m.*
Averuncator. *V.* **Averruncator**
Aviary, *s.* volière, *f.*
Avidity, *s.* avidité, *f.*
Avigato, Avocado, (**— pear**) *s.* poire-avocat, *f.* **— pear-tree,** *s.* avocatier, *m.*
Avocation, *s.* occupation, *f.*; métier, *m.*
Avocet, *s.* avocette, *f.*
Avoid, *v.a.* éviter; (*vacate*) laisser vacant; (*annul*) annuler; (*law*) résoudre; — *v.n.* devenir vacant; s'annuler; se résoudre
Avoidable, *adj.* évitable; annulable; (*law*) résoluble
Avoidance, *s.* action d'éviter, *f.*; fuite, *f.*; abstention, *f.*; vacance, *f.*; annulation, *f.*; (*law*) résolution, *f.*
Avoirdupois, *s.* avoir-du-poids, *m.*
Avoset. *V.* **Avocet** [produire, alléguer
Avouch, *v.a.* affirmer, déclarer, maintenir;
Avow, *v.a.* avouer; déclarer
Avowable, *adj.* avouable
Avowal, *s.* aveu, *m.*
Avowedly, *adv.* de son aveu, ouvertement
Avulsion, *s.* avulsion, *f.*
Avuncular, *adj.* avunculaire
Awaft, *adv.* (*nav.*) en berne
Await, *v.a.* attendre
Awake, *adj.* éveillé, vigilant. *V.* **Wide**
Awake, Awaken, *v.a.* éveiller, réveiller; — *v.n.* s'éveiller, se réveiller; (*fig., from illusions,* &c.) revenir (de)
Awakener, *s.* réveilleur, *m.* -euse, *f.*
Awakening, Awaking, *s.* réveil, *m.*
Award, *v.a.* décerner; adjuger; — *v.n.* décréter, décider; — *s.* jugement, arrêt, *m.*,
Awarder, *s.* juge, *m.*, arbitre, *m.f.* [décision, *f.*
Aware, *adj.* instruit (de), informé (de). *To be — of,* être instruit *or* informé (de), avoir connaissance (de), savoir, connaître, ne pas ignorer. *Not to be — of,* ignorer, ne pas savoir. *Not that I am — of,* pas que je sache
Away, *adv.* loin; à distance; à l'écart; absent; (*wholly*) entièrement; (*without stopping*) toujours, sans discontinuer; (*exclam.*) *V.* **Avaunt**; (*go on*) en avant! — *with!* loin de moi (toi, lui, &c.); laissez là! laissons là! fi de! point de! pas de! (*take away*) emportez! emmenez! — *with you!* allez-vous-en!
Awe, *s.* crainte, *f.*; terreur, *f.*; horreur, *f.*; respect, *m.*; — *v.a.* effrayer; inspirer du respect à, tenir en respect, imposer à; (*to dread*) redouter. *To stand in* —, craindre, redouter. **— struck,** *adj.* frappé de terreur; saisi de respect
Aweather, *adv.* (*nav.*) au vent
Aweigh, *adv.* (*nav., of anchor*) pendant
Awful, *adj.* terrible; horrible; imposant
Awfully, *adv.* terriblement; horriblement; respectueusement, avec respect [nité, *f.*
Awfulness, *s.* terreur, *f.*; horreur, *f.*; solen-
Awhile, *adv.* pendant quelque temps, un peu, un instant
Awkward, *adj.* maladroit, gauche; (*things*) incommode, gênant; embarrassant; dangereux; critique; difficile; étrange; (*unfortunate*) malencontreux, fâcheux, désagréable; (*ungraceful*) disgracieux
Awkwardly, *adv.* maladroitement, gauchement; incommodément; dangereusement; malencontreusement, d'une manière malencontreuse, mal à propos, mal; désagréablement; disgracieusement
Awkwardness, *s.* maladresse, gaucherie, *f.*; (*unpleasantness*) embarras, *m.*
Awl, *s.* alène, *f.*; poinçon, *m.*; *Shoemaker's* —, alène, *f.* **— maker,** *s.* alénier, *m.*
Awless, *adj.* sans crainte, courageux, intrépide; audacieux; impudent, effronté
Awn, *s.* barbe, arête, *f.*
Awned, *adj.* barbu, à barbes
Awning, *s.* banne, *f.*; tente, *f.*; (*of carriages*) bâche, *f.*
Awnless, *adj.* sans barbe
Awny, *adj.* barbu, à barbes
Awry, *adj. adv.* de travers, de côté
Axe, *s.* hache, *f.*; (*woodman's*) cognée, *f.* **— bearer, -case,** *s.* porte-hache, *m.*
Axiferous, *adj.* axifère
Axil, Axilla, *s.* aisselle, *f.*
Axillary, *adj.* axillaire
Axiom, *s.* axiome, *m.*
Axiomatic, -al, *adj.* axiomatique
Axis, *s.* axe, *m.*; (*zool., anat.*) axis, *m.*
Axle, *s.* *V.* **— tree.** **— box,** *s.* moyeu, *m.*, boîte d'essieu, *f.*; (*rail.*) boîte à graisse, *f.* **— guard,** *s.* garde-essieu, *m.* **— tree,** *s.* essieu, *m.*; (*arts*) axe, *m.*; (*tech.*) tourillon, *m.*
Axunge, *s.* axonge, *f.*
Ay, *adv. int.* oui; mais oui, mais certainement, oui-dà; c'est vrai; ah! aïe! hein? (*more than that*) bien plus; et même; (*and what is more*) et qui plus est; — *s* voix pour, *f.*; boule blanche, *f.*
Ayah, *s.* ayah, bonne d'enfant *or* femme de chambre indienne, *f.*
Aye. *V.* **Ay**
Aye-aye, *s.* (*zool.*) aye-aye, *m.*
Ayry. *V.* **Aery**
Azalea, *s.* azaléa, *m.*, azalée, *f.*
Azarole, *s.* azerole, *f.* **— tree,** *s.* azerolier, *m.*
Azimuth, *s.* azimut, *m.*; — *adj.* azimutal
Azotate, *s.* azotate, *m.*
Azote, *s.* azote, *m.*
Azotic, *adj.* azotique
Azotize, *v.a.* azoter
Azotous, *adj.* azoteux
Aztec, *s. adj.* aztec, *s.m.*, aztèque, *adj. s.m.f.*
Azure, *s.* azur, *m.*; — *adj.* azuré, d'azur; — *v.a.* azurer. **— stone,** *s* lazulite, *f.*
Azurite, *s.* azurite, *f.*
Azym, Azyme, *s.* azyme, pain azyme, *m.*
Azymite, *s.* azymite *m.*
Azymous, *adj.* azyme

B

B, *s.* (*letter*) b, *m.*; (*mus.*) si, *m.*; (*of numbers*) ter. —*flat*, (*mus.*) bémol, *m.*; (*bug*) punaise, *f.* —*natural*, (*mus.*) si naturel, *m.* —*sharp*, (*mus.*) bécarre, *m.* *Number* 1 *B*, numéro 1 ter
B.A., bachelier ès-lettres, *m.*
Ba, Baa, *s.* bée, bêlement, *m.*; — *v.n.* bêler
Babble, *v.n.* babiller, jaser, bavarder; (*fig.*) murmurer; — *s.* babil, *m.*, jaserie, *f.*, caquet, bavardage, *m.*; (*fig.*) murmure, *m.*
Babbler, *s.* babillard, *m.*, e, *f.*, bavard, *m.*, e, *f.*
Babbling, *s.* babillage, babil, caquet, bavardage, *m.*; (*fig.*) murmure, *m.*; — *adj.* babillard, bavard; (*of streams*) qui murmure
Babe. *V.* **Baby**
Babel, *s.* Babel, *f.*
Baboon, *s.* babouin, *m.*
Baby, *s.* bébé, petit enfant, *m.*; bambin, *m.*; (*jest.*) poupon, poupard, *m.*; (*doll*) bébé, poupard, *m.*, poupée, *f.* *Great* —, grand enfant, *m.* — **doll,** *s.* bébé, poupard, *m.*, poupée, *f.* — **hood,** *s.* première enfance, *f.* — **house,** *s.* petit ménage, *m.* — **linen,** *s.* layette, *f.* — **linen warehouse,** *s.* lingerie, *f.*
Babyish, *adj.* enfantin, d'enfant
Babylonian, *s.* Babylonien, *m.*, -ne, *f.*; — *adj.* babylonien, de Babylone
Babylonic, -al, Babylonish, *adj.* babylonien, de Babylone
Bacca, *s.* (*slang*) tabac, *m.*
Baccalaureate, *s.* baccalauréat, *m.*
Baccarat, *s.* baccarat, *m.*
Bacchanal, *s.* bacchanale, *f.*
Bacchanal, Bacchanalian, *s.* bacchante, *f.*; débauché, *m.*
Bacchanalian, *adj.* bachique
Bacchant, *s.* bacchant, *m.*
Bacchante, *s.* bacchante, *f.*
Bacchic, -al, *adj.* bachique
Bacciferous, *adj.* baccifère
Baccivorous, *adj.* baccivore
Baccy. *V.* **Bacca**
Bachelor, *s.* célibataire, garçon, *m.*; (*univers.*) bachelier, *m.* — *of arts, of sciences*, bachelier ès-lettres, ès-sciences. — *of laws, of medicine, of divinity*, bachelier en droit, en médecine, en théologie. —*'s degree*, grade de bachelier, *m.*; baccalauréat, *m.* —*'s-button*, (*bot.*) bassinet, bouton d'or, *m.*
Bachelorhood, *s.* célibat, *m.*
Bachelorship, *s.* célibat, *m.*; (*univers.*) baccalauréat, *m.* — *of arts*, baccalauréat ès-lettres
Back, *s.* dos, *m.*; (*of things generally, of the head, of a place*) derrière, *m.*; (*loins*) reins, *m.pl.*; (*upper part*) dessus, *m.*; (*of a book, paper, knife, tool, upper garment*) dos, *m.*; (*of a cuirass*) dossière, *f.*; (*of the hand, of a hill, coin*, &c.) revers, *m.*; (*of chairs*) dossier, dos, *m.*; (*of chimneys*) fond, *m.*, plaque, *f.*; (*of theatres, inside of a carriage, background*) fond, *m.*; (*of hares, rabbits*) râble, *m.*; (*vat*) bac, *m.* *At the* —, derrière; au dos. *At the — of*, derrière; au dos de. *At the — of it* or *of them*, derrière; au dos. *To break anyone's* —, casser les reins à quelqu'un. *To fall on o.'s* —, tomber à la renverse. *To turn o.'s* — (*on* or *to*), tourner le dos (à). *When his master's — was turned*, quand son maître avait le dos tourné
Back, *adv.* en arrière; (*returned*) de retour; rentré; (*again*) encore; (*in return*) en retour; (*in arrears*) arriéré, *adj.*; (*ago*) *V.* **Ago.** *And* — ! (*at a rail. ticket-office*) aller et retour! [*With some verbs*, '*back*' *is rendered in the same way as* '*again*': *as*, '*to ask*,' demander; *and* '*to ask back*,' redemander; &c. *V.* **Again.** *As to* '*back again*', *it is simply a vulgar pleonasm.*]
Back, *v.a.* (*mount*) monter; (*put back*) reculer, faire reculer; (*support*, — *up*) soutenir, appuyer, seconder, épauler; (*of bettings*) parier pour; (*of writings*) viser; (*a bill*) endosser; (*line*) doubler; (*of sails*) coiffer; (*of anchors*) empenneler; — *v.n.* reculer. — **out,** (*get off*) se tirer (de); tirer son épingle du jeu; (*retract*) se dédire; (*elude*) reculer
Back, *adj.* de derrière; arrière-...
Back-band, *s.* dossière, *f.*
Back-basket, *s.* hotte, *f.*
Backbite, *v.a.* médire de, calomnier
Backbiter, *s.* médisant, *m*, e, *f.*, calomniateur, *m.*, -trice, *f.*
Backbiting, *s.* médisance, calomnie, *f.*; (*gossip*) cancans, *m.pl.*; — *adj.* médisant
Backbitingly, *adv.* avec médisance
Back-blow, *s.* coup de revers, revers, *m.*
Back-board, *s.* dossier, *m.*; (*pers.*) planche orthopédique, *f.*
Back-bone, *s.* épine dorsale épine du dos, *f.* *To the* —, (*fig.*) jusqu'à la moelle des os
Back-building, *s.* bâtiment sur le derrière, arrière-corps, *m.*
Back-comb, *s.* peigne à chignon, *m.*
Back-court. *V.* **Back-yard**
Back-door, *s.* porte de derrière, porte dérobée, *f.*
Backer, *s.* partisan, second, *m.*; (*of bettings*) parieur pour, *m.*
Back-fare, *s.* course (*f.*, *or* prix, *m.*) de retour
Backgammon, *s.* trictrac *m.*; jacquet, *m.* — **board,** *s.* trictrac, *m.*
Back-garden, *s.* jardin de derrière, *m.*
Back-ground, *s.* terrain de derrière, *m.*; (*fig.*) fond, *m.*; arrière-plan, *m.* *In the* —, (*fig.*) dans l'ombre, à l'écart, à distance, par derrière
Back-hair, *s.* cheveux de derrière, *m.pl.*; chignon, *m.*
Backhanded, *adj.* donné avec le revers de la main; — *adv.* avec le revers de la main. — *blow*, coup de revers, *m.*
Backhander, *s.* *V.* **Back-blow**
Back-house. *V.* **Back-building**
Backing, *s.* reculement, *m.*, reculade, *f.*; (*support*) soutien, appui, *m.*; (*bet*) pari pour, *m.*; (*build.*) massif, *m.*; (*rid.*) dressage, *m.* — **off motion,** *s.* reculement, *m.* — **room,** *s.* reculée, *f.*
Back-kitchen, *s.* arrière-cuisine, *f.*
Back-parlour, *s* petit salon de derrière, *m.*
Back-part, *s.* *V.* **Back,** *s.*
Back-piece, *s.* dossier, *m.*; (*of a cuirass*) dossière, *f.*
Back-plate, *s.* plaque de derrière, *f.*; (*of a cuirass*) dossière, *f.*
Back-premises, *s. pl.* derrières, *m.pl.*
Backroom, *s.* arrière-pièce, pièce du fond, pièce *or* chambre de derrière, *f.*
Back-seat, *s.* siége (*m.*) *or* place (*f.*) de derrière
Back-settlements, *s. pl.* *V.* **Backwoods**
Back-shop, *s.* arrière-boutique, *f.*
Backside, *s.* derrière, *m.*
Back-sight, *s.* (*of fire-arms*) visière, *f.*
Backslide, *v.n.* apostasier; faillir; retomber
Backslider, *s.* apostat, renégat, *m.*; transgresseur, *m.*; relaps, *m.*, e, *f.*
Backsliding, *s.* apostasie, infidélité, *f.*; faute, *f.*; rechute, *f.*; — *adj.* infidèle; coupable; relaps
Backslums, *s.pl.* bas quartiers, faubourgs, *m.pl.*, barrières, *f.pl.*, carrefours, *m.pl.*
Back-staircase, *s.* escalier de dégagement *or* de service, escalier dérobé, *m.*
Backstairs, *s.pl.* escalier dérobé, *m.*; (*fig.*) voies indirectes, *f.pl.* — *influence*, intrigue, intrigue de cour, influence de courtisans, *f.*
Back-stay, *s.* (*nav.*) *V.* **Stay,** *s.*
Back-stitch, *s.* arrière-point, *m.*
Back-stitcher, *s.* arrière-pointeuse, *f.*
Back-stroke, *s.* coup d'arrière, *m.*; coup de revers, revers, *m.*; (*at billiards, tennis*) bricole, *f.*; (*fig.*) coup de patte, *m.*; (*counter-stroke*) contre-coup, *m.*
Backsword, *s.* sabre, *m.*; (*stick*) canne, *f.*, bâton, *m.*; (*game*) jeu de canne, *m.*
Back-train, *s.* train de retour, *m.*
Back-trick, *s.* tour pour attaquer par derrière, coup de Jarnac, *m.*
Backward, Backwards, *adv.* en arrière; à reculons; (*on the back*) à la renverse; (*in the*

wrong way) à rebours. *To walk — and forward*, se promener de long en large. *V.* **Go** *and* **Going.** *Motion — and forward*, (*mach.*) mouvement de va-et-vient, *m.*

Backward, *adj.* en arrière; arriéré; en retard; peu avancé; (*slow*) lent; tardif; (*not eager*) peu empressé, peu disposé; (*reluctant*) rétif. — *and forward*, (*of machines*) de va-et-vient

Backwardation, *s.* déport, *m.*

Backwardly, *adv.* en arrière; (*reluctantly*) à contre-cœur, avec répugnance

Backwardness, *s.* état arriéré, *m.*; retard, *m.*; peu de progrès, *m.*; lenteur, *f.*; tardiveté, *f.*; répugnance, *f.*

Back-water, *s.* remous, *m.*

Backwoods, *s. pl.* terrains défrichés des forêts, *m.pl.*

Back-yard, *s.* cour de derrière, arrière-cour, *f.*

Bacon, *s.* lard, *m.* *To save o.'s —*, (*pop.*) sauver son lard (*or* sa peau). — **beetle,** *s.* dermeste, *m.* — **omelet,** *s.* omelette au lard, *f.*

Baconian, *adj.* baconien

Bactrian, *s. adj.* Bactrien, *m.*, -ne, *f.*

Bad, *adj.* mauvais; (*pers.: wicked, naughty*) méchant, (*undutiful*) mauvais; (*sick, diseased*) malade; (*serious*) grave; (*of colds*) gros, fort; (*of money, notes*) faux. — *is the best*, le meilleur n'en vaut rien. *It is very — of you* (*to ...*), c'est très mal à vous (de ...). *This* (or *that* or *it*) *is too —!* c'est trop fort! c'est par trop fort! *I have a — finger, a bad leg*, &c., j'ai mal au doigt, mal à la jambe, &c.

Badener, *s.* Badois, *m.*, e, *f.*

Badge, *s.* plaque, *f.*; marque, *f.*, signe, *m.*; insigne, *m.*; symbole, emblème, *m.*; caractère, cachet, *m.*; (*of porters*) plaque, médaille, *f.*; (*cross*) croix, *f.*; — *v.a.* marquer; (*porters*) médailler

Badgeless, *adj.* sans marque, sans signe; sans plaque; sans médaille

Badger, *s.* blaireau, *m.*; (*licensed porter*) commissionnaire médaillé, *m.*; — *v.a.* pourchasser; harceler; tarabuster, tanner

Badian, *s.* badiane, *f.*

Badigeon, *s.* badigeon, *m.*

Badly, *adv.* mal; (*greatly*) grandement, fort, beaucoup, bien; (*seriously*) gravement, grièvement

Badness, *s.* mauvaise qualité, *f.*; mauvais état, *m.*; (*wickedness*) méchanceté, *f.*

Baffle, *v.a.* déjouer; déconcerter, dérouter, confondre; se jouer de; frustrer; décevoir; éluder; défier; braver

Bag, *s.* sac, *m.*; (*pouch*) poche, *f.*; (*purse*) bourse, *f.*; (*post.*) sac, *m.*, (*letters*) dépêches, *f.pl.*; (*of animals*) poche, *f.*; (*of a busby*) flamme, chausse, *f.* *With — and baggage*, avec armes et bagage. *To pack up — and baggage*, plier bagage. — **ful,** *s.* sac plein, sac, *m.*, sachée, *f.*, plein un sac. — **man,** *s.* commis voyageur, *m.* — **net,** *s. V.* **Purse-net.** — **pipe,** *s.* musette, cornemuse, *f.* — **piper,** *s.* joueur de musette *or* de cornemuse, cornemuseur, *m.* — **wig,** *s.* perruque à bourse, *f.*

Bag, *v.a.* mettre en sac, ensacher; (*into a game-bag*) mettre dans sa carnassière; (*kill*) tuer; (*purloin*) empocher, chiper; (*swell*) gonfler, enfler; — *v.n.* faire le sac, être gonflé, bouffer

Bagasse, *s.* bagasse, *f.*

Bagatelle, *s.* bagatelle, *f.* — **table** *or* **board,** *s.* table de bagatelle, *f.*

Baggage, *s.* bagage, *m.*; (*luggage*) *V.* **Luggage;** (*pers.*) coquine, *f.* *Saucy —*, insolente, impertinente, péronnelle, *f.* — **master,** *s.* (*mil.*) vaguemestre, *m.* — **waggon,** *s.* (*mil.*) fourgon de bagages, *m.*

Bagged, *adj.* à sac; — *part.* mis en sac, &c. [(*V.* **Bag,** *v.a.n.*)

Bagging, *s.* toile à sacs, *f.*; (*swelling*) gonflement, *m.*, enflure, *f.*; — *adj.* gonflé, bouffant

Baggy, *adj.* en forme de sac, bouffant

Bagnio, *s.* bain, *m.*, bains, *m.pl.*, maison (*f.*) *or* établissement (*m.*) *or* salle (*f.*) de bains; (*for convicts*) bagne, *m.*

Bah, *int.* bah!

Bail, *s.* caution, *f.*; — *v.a.* cautionner; admettre à fournir caution. *On* or *upon —*, sous caution. *To take —*, recevoir une caution

Bailable, *adj.* admis à fournir caution; (*things*) qui admet le cautionnement

Bailiff, *s.* (*law-officer*) huissier, *m.*; garde du commerce, *m.*; (*of an estate*) sous-intendant, *m.*; (*magistrate*) bailli, *m.* —*'s man*, —*'s follower*, recors, *m.*

Bailing, *s.* cautionnement, *m.*

Bailiwick, *s.* bailliage, *m.*

Bailment, *s.* dépôt, nantissement, gage, *m.*

Bain-marie, *s.* bain-marie, *m.*

Bairn, Bairnie, *s.* enfant, petit enfant, *m.*

Bait, *v.a.* (*a hook*, &c.) amorcer, appâter; (*horses*) rafraîchir; (*bulls*, &c.) faire combattre; (*harass*) harceler, tourmenter; — *v.n.* (*on a journey*) se rafraîchir; arrêter; — *s.* amorce, *f.*; appât, *m.*; rafraîchissement, *m.* *To take* or *swallow the —*, mordre à l'hameçon

Baiting, *s.* amorçage, *m.*; rafraîchissement, *m.*; combat, *m.*

Baize, *s.* (*green —*) bayette, *f.* — **door,** *s.* porte piquée, porte rembourrée, contre-porte, *f.*

Bake, *v.a.* cuire au four, cuire; (*cook*) cuire, faire cuire; — *v.n.* cuire; (*make bread*) boulanger, faire du pain; cuire du pain, cuire. *To — in the oven*, cuire au four

Baked, *adj.* cuit au four, cuit. — *apple*, pomme cuite, *f.* — *clay*, terre cuite, *f.*

Bakehouse, *s.* fournil, *m.*; boulangerie, *f.*; (*mil.*) manutention, *f.*

Baker, *s.* boulanger, *m.*, -ère, *f.* —*'s man*, mitron, *m.*; (*kneader*) geindre, *m.* —*'s shop* or *trade* or *business*, boulangerie, *f.* —*'s wife*, boulangère, *f.*

Bakery. *V.* **Bakehouse**

Baking, *s.* cuisson, *f.*; (*batch*) fournée, cuite, *f.*; (*bread-making*) boulangerie, *f.* — **dish, -pan,** *s.* tourtière, *f.* — **pear,** *s.* poire à cuire, *f.* — **powder,** *s.* poudre à boulanger, *f.*

Balance, *s.* balance, *f.*; équilibre, *m.*; contrepoids, *m.*; (*of watches*) balancier, *m.*; (*book-keep., astr.*) balance, *f.*; (*com.*) reliquat de compte, *m.* — *of power*, balance des pouvoirs, balance politique. — *of trade*, balance du commerce. — **beam,** *s.* balancier, *m.* — **handle,** *s.* manche basculant, manche à bascule, *m.* — **knife,** couteau à bascule, *m.* — **maker,** *s.* balancier, *m.* — **sheet,** *s.* bilan, *m.*; balance, *f.* — **weight,** *s.* contre-poids, *m.* — **wheel,** *s.* roue de rencontre, *f.*; (*of a watch*) balancier, *m.*

Balance, *v.a.* balancer; équilibrer, tenir *or* maintenir en équilibre; (*weigh*) peser; (*of accounts*) balancer, arrêter; — *v.n.* se balancer; faire la bascule, basculer; (*hesitate*) balancer, hésiter

Balanced, *part.adj.* balancé, &c. (*V.* **Balance,** *v.a.n.*); équilibré, en équilibre. *Well —*, bien balancé *or* &c.; bien équilibré, bien en équilibre; (*fig.*) juste, droit; rangé; prudent

Balancer, *s.* équilibriste, *m.f.*; (*weigher*) peseur, *m.*, -euse, *f.*; (*of insects*) balancier, haltère, *m.*

Balancing, *s.* balancement, *m.* — **pole,** *s.* balancier, *m.*

Balas ruby, *s.* rubis balais, *m.*

Balausta, *s.* balauste, *f.*

Balaustine, *s.* balaustier, *m.* — *flower*, balauste, *f.*

Balcony, *s.* balcon, *m.*; (*nav.*) galerie de poupe, *f.*

Bald, *adj.* chauve; (*fig.*) nu; découvert; (*of style*) décharné, plat, sec

Baldachin, *s.* baldaquin, *m.*

Balderdash, *s.* galimatias, *m.*

Baldly, *adv.* nûment; platement, sèchement

Baldness, *s.* calvitie, *f.*; (*fig.*) nudité, *f.*; (*in style*) platitude, sécheresse, *f.*

Baldrick, *s.* baudrier, *m.*; (*fig.*) ceinture, *f.*

Bale, *s.* ballot, *m.*, balle, *f.*; (*old*) misère, *f.*, malheur, *m.*; poison, *m.*; — *v.a.* emballer; (*nav.*) écoper, vider. — **fire,** *s.* fanal, feu, *m.*

Baleful, *adj.* malheureux, sinistre, triste, funeste

Balefully, *adv.* malheureusement, tristement, funestement

Balefulness, *s.* nature funeste, *f.*

Balista, *s.* baliste, *f.*

Balk, *s.* (*of land*) entre-deux *m.*: (*of timber*) *V.*

Baulk; (*fig.*) désappointement, pied-de-nez, *m.*; — *v.a.* désappointer, frustrer l'attente de, frustrer, tromper, se jouer de

Ball, *s.* boule, *f.*; globe, *m.*; (*of thread or string*) pelote, *f.*, peloton, *m.*; (*of small arms*) balle, *f.*; (*of cannon*) boulet, *m.*; (*play*) balle, *f.*; (*foot* —) ballon, *m.*; (*of snow*) boule, *f.*; (*billiards*) bille, *f.*; (*of the eye*) prunelle, *f.*, globe, *m.*; (*of the thumb, of the great toe*) gras, *m.*; (*of earth, of fuel*) motte, *f.*; (*of soap*) savonnette, *f.*; (*of a pendulum*) lentille, *f.*; (*cook.*) boulette, *f.*; (*of physic*) bol, *m.*, boulette, *f.*; (*dancing*) bal, *m.*; — *v.n.* s'arrondir en boule; (*of snow*) se peloter; (*of horses*) se botter. — *and socket*, genou, *m.* *To play at* —, jouer à la balle. — **cartridge,** *s.* cartouche à balle, *f.* — **cock,** *s.* robinet flotteur, *m.* — **drawer,** *s.* tire-balle, *m.* — **dress,** *s.* costume de bal, *m.*; (*of ladies*) robe de bal, *f.*; toilette de bal, *f.* — **practice,** *s.* tir à balle, *m.* — **room,** *s.* (*public*) salle de bal, *m.*; (*in a private house*) salon, *m.*; bal, *m.*

Ballad, *s.* ballade, *f.*; romance, *f.*; (*theat.*) vaudeville, *m.* — **farce, -opera,** *s.* vaudeville, *m.* — **singer,** *s.* chanteur (*m.*, -euse, *f.*) de ballades, chansonnier, *m.*, -ière, *f.*; (*street-singer*) chanteur (*m.*, -euse, *f.*) des rues. — **writer,** *s.* auteur de ballades, *m.*, chansonnier, *m.*, -ière, *f.*; vaudevilliste, *m.f.*

Ballast, *s.* ballast, empierrement, ensablement, cailloutis, cailloutage, *m.*, cailloux, *m.pl.*; (*nav.*) lest, *m.*; (*fig.*) lest, plomb dans la tête, *m.*; — *v.a.* ballaster, empierrer, ensabler, caillouter; (*nav.*) lester. — **boat, -lighter,** *s.* bateau lesteur, lesteur, délesteur, *m.* — **heaver,** *s.* lesteur, délesteur, *m.* — **hole, -pit,** *s.* ballastière, *f.* — **stone,** *s.* cailloutis, *m.* — **train (-waggon),** *s.* train (wagon) de ballast, *m.*

Ballaster, *s.* caillouteur, terrassier, *m.*

Ballasting, *s.* ballastage, empierrement, ensablement, cailloutage, terrassement, *m.*; (*nav.*) lestage, *m.*

Ballet, *s.* ballet, *m.* — **dancer, -girl,** *s.* danseuse (d'opéra), ballerine, *f.* — **master,** *s.* maître de ballet, directeur des ballets, *m.*

Ballista, *s.* baliste, *f.*

Ballistic, *adj.* balistique; —**s,** *s.pl.* balistique, *f.*

Balloon, *s.* ballon, *m.*

Balloonist, *s.* (*maker*) aérostatier, aérostier, ballonnier, *m.*; (*aeronaut*) aérostier, aérostatier, *m.*, aéronaute, *m.f.*; (*excursionist*) ascensioniste, excursioniste en ballon, *m.f.*

Balloonry, *s.* aéronautique, *f.*

Ballot, *s.* (*ball*) boule, *f.*; (*ticket*) bulletin, *m.*; (*voting*) scrutin; (*first or second or &c.*) tour de scrutin, *m.* *Second* —, second tour de scrutin, ballottage, scrutin de ballottage, *m.* *By* —, au scrutin, au scrutin secret. — **box,** *s.* urne du scrutin, *f.* — **paper,** *s.* bulletin, *m.*

Ballot, *v.n.* voter au scrutin, scrutiner. *To — a second time*, ballotter

Balloting, *s.* vote au scrutin, scrutin, *m.* *Second* —, *V.* **Ballot,** *s.*

Balm, *s.* baume, *m.*; (*bot.*) mélisse, citronnelle, *f.* — **mint,** *s.* mélisse, citronnelle, *f.* — **tree,** *s.* baumier, *m.*

Balmy, *adj.* balsamique; (*perfumed*) embaumé, parfumé, odoriférant; (*producing balm*) à baume; (*soft*) doux; (*soothing*) adoucissant, calmant

Balsam, *s.* baume, *m.*; (*plant*) balsamine, *f.* — *of Gilead*, baume de Judée. — *of Tolu*, baume de Tolu. — **tree,** *s.* balsamier, baumier, *m.*

Balsamic, *adj.* *s.* balsamique, *adj.* *m.f.*, *s.m.*

Balsamine, *s.* balsamine, *f.*

Balsamodendron, *s.* balsamodendron, *m.*

Baltic, *s.* *adj.* Baltique, *f.*

Baluster, *s.* balustre, *m.*; (*of staircase*) rampe, *f.* — **maker,** *s.* rampiste, *m.*

Balustrade, *s.* balustrade, *f.*

Bamboo, *s.* bambou, *m.*; — *adj.* de bambou

Bamboozle, *v.a.* refaire, mettre dedans, enjôler, enfoncer; promener, faire aller

Bamboozler, *s.* enjôleur, *m.*, -euse, *f.*, promeneur, *m.*, -euse, *f.*

Bamboozling, *s.* enjôlement, *m.*, duperie, *f.*

Ban, *s.* ban, *m.*; malédiction, *f.*; interdiction, *f.*; (*of marriage*) ban, *m.*, publication de mariage, *f.*; — *v.a.n.* maudire. *Under the* —, au ban

Banana, *s.* banane, *f.*; (*tree*) bananier, *m.* — **bird,** *s.* bananiste, *m.* — **plantation,** *s.* bananerie, *f.* — **tree,** *s.* bananier, *m.*

Banco, *adj.* banco, de banque

Band, *s.* bande, *f.*; bandage, *m.*; bandeau, *m.*; (*bond*) lien, *m.*; (*leather* —) courroie, *f.*; (*ribbon*) ruban, *m.*; (*for the waist*) ceinture, *f.*; (*round o.'s hat*) *V.* **Hatband;** (*of clergymen, lawyers*) rabat, *m.*; (*of guns, muskets, and rifles*) capucine, *f.*; (*arch.*) bande, *f.*; (*troop*) bande, *f.*; (*of musicians*) orchestre, *m.*, musique, *f.*; (*mil. mus.*) musique, *f.* *Full* —, (*mus.*) grand orchestre. *Upper* —, (*of muskets*, &c.) première capucine, *f.*, embouchoir, *m.* *Middle* —, deuxième capucine, grenadière, *f.* *Lower* —, troisième capucine, *f.* — **box,** *s.* carton, *m.* — **master,** *s.* (*mil.*) chef de musique, *m.*

Band, *v.a.* bander; (*fig.*) réunir en troupe, réunir, unir, liguer; — *v.n.* se liguer

Bandage, *s.* bandeau, *m.*; (*surg.*) bandage, *m.*; bande, *f.*; — *v.a.* bander. — **maker,** *s.* bandagiste, *m.*

Bandana, Bandanna, Bandanno, Bandannoe, *s.* foulard, *m.* — **handkerchief,** *s.* mouchoir de foulard, foulard, *m.*

Banded, *part. adj.* bandé; ligué; (*streaked, striped*) rayé

Bandelet. *V.* **Bandlet**

Banderole, *s.* banderole, *f.*

Bandit, *s.* bandit, *m.*

Banditti, *s. pl.* bandits, *m.pl.*

Bandlet, *s.* bandelette, *f.*

Bandog, *s.* mâtin, chien d'attache, *m.*

Bandoleer, *s.* bandoulière, *f.*

Bandoline, *s.* bandoline, *f.*

Bandore, *s.* bandore, *f.*

Bandrole. *V.* **Banderole**

Bandsman, *s.* musicien, *m.*

Bandster, *s.* (*agr.*) lieur, botteleur, *m.*

Bandy, *v.a.* renvoyer, se renvoyer; échanger; faire assaut de; (*agitate*) ballotter; discuter; — *v.n.* rivaliser; se disputer

Bandy, *adj.* tortu. — **leg,** *s.* jambe tortue, *f.* —**legged,** *adj.* bancal, bancroche

Bandying, *s.* rivalité, *f.*; dispute, *f.*

Bane, *s.* poison, *m.*; ruine, *f.*; (*death*) mort, *f.*; (*pest*) fléau, *m.*, peste, *f.*; — *v.a.* empoisonner

Baneful, *adj.* vénéneux; (*fig.*) funeste, mortel, empoisonné

Banefully, *adv.* d'une manière funeste

Banefulness, *s.* caractère vénéneux, *m.*, nature vénéneuse *or* funeste, *f.*; poison, *m.*

Bang, *s.* coup, *m.*; battement, *m.*; bruit, *m.*; — *v.a.* frapper, battre, cogner, rosser, étriller; (*a door*) faire battre, fermer bruyamment, pousser violemment *or* avec force; — *v.n.* battre; résonner; — *int.* pan! paf! patatras! vlan!

Banging, *s.* roulée, volée, *f.*; — *adj.* énorme

Bangle, *v.a.* *V.* **Fritter,** *v.a.*

Banian, *s.* banian, *m.* — **day,** *s.* jour maigre, *m.* — **tree,** *s.* arbre des banians, *m.*

Banish, *v.a.* bannir; exiler; proscrire

Banisher, *s.* bannisseur, proscripteur, *m.*

Banishment, *s.* bannissement, exil, *m.*; proscription, *f.*

Banister. *V.* **Baluster**

Banjo, *s.* balafo, *m.*

Bank, *s.* (*of river*) rive (d'un fleuve), *f.*, bord (d'une rivière, d'un fleuve), *m.*, (*steep*) berge, *f.*; (*of earth*) terrasse, *f.*; bord relevé, bord, *m.*; talus, *m.*; berge, *f.*; remblai, *m.*; (*mole*) digue, levée, *f.*; (*of sand, turf*) banc, *m.*; (*of flowers*) planche, *f.*; (*bench*) banc, *m.*; (*com.*) banque, *f.* — *of deposit*, banque de dépôt. — *of issue*, banque de circulation. — **account,** *s.* compte de banque, *m.* — **bill,** *s.* billet de banque, *m.*

— **book,** *s.* carnet de banque, *m.* — **clerk,** *s.* commis de banque, *m.* — **note,** *s.* billet de banque, *m.* — **paper,** *s.* billets de banque, *m.pl.* — **porter,** *s.* garçon de banque, *m.* — **post-bill,** *s.* mandat de (*or* sur) la banque, *m.* — **stock,** *s.* actions de la banque, *f.pl.*

Bank, *v.a.* (*money,* &c.) déposer dans une banque ; (*to embank*) *V.* **Embank ;** — *v.n.* — *with,* avoir pour banquier. *Where do you* —*?* qui est votre banquier ? [comptable

Bankable, *adj.* recevable à la banque; es-

Banker, *s.* banquier, *m.*; (*nav.*) terre-neuvier, banquier, banquais, *m.*

Banking, *s.* banque, *f.*; — *adj.* de banque. — **business,** *s.* banque, *f.* — **house,** *s.* maison de banque, *f.*

Bankrupt, *s.* failli, *m.*, e, *f.*; banqueroutier, *m.*, -ière, *f.*; — *adj.* failli (e, *f.*), en faillite; banqueroutier (-ière, *f.*), en banqueroute; (*fig.*) ruiné. *To be a* —, *to become* —, faire faillite; faire banqueroute. *To be adjudged* or *adjudicated a* —, être déclaré en faillite

Bankruptcy, *s.* faillite, *f.*; banqueroute, *f.* *Fraudulent* —, banqueroute frauduleuse

Banksia, *s.* banksia, *m.*, banksie, *f.*

Bann. *V.* **Ban**

Banner, *s.* bannière, *f.*

Bannered, *adj.* garni de bannières; rangé sous des bannières; pavoisé [bannerette, *f.*

Banneret, *s.* (*pers.*) banneret, *m.*; (*small banner*)

Bannock, *s.* gâteau *or* pain d'orge, *m.*

Banquet, *s.* banquet, festin, *m.*; (*of canals, bridges*) banquette, *f.*; (*rid.*) banquet, *m.*; — *v.n.* banqueter, faire festin ; faire un festin. — **hall, -house, -room,** *s.* salle de banquet *or* de festin, *f.* [teur de banquets, *m.*

Banqueter, *s.* banqueteur, *m.*, -euse, *f.*, ama-

Banqueting, *s.* banquet, festin, *m.* — **hall,**

Banquette, *s.* banquette, *f.* [&c. *V.* **Banquet**

Bantam, *s. adj.* (— *fowl*) bantam, *m.*, e, *f.*

Banter, *v.a.* railler, plaisanter ; — *s.* raillerie, plaisanterie, *f.*

Banterer, *s.* railleur, *m.*, -euse, *f.*

Bantering, *adj.* railleur ; — *s.* raillerie, *f.*

Bantling, *s.* poupon, bambin, marmot, *m.*

Banyan. *V.* **Banian**

Baptism, *s.* baptême, *m.* *Half-* —, ondoiement, *m.*

Baptismal, *adj.* baptismal, du *or* de baptême. — *register,* registre baptistaire, *m.*

Baptist, *s.* anabaptiste, baptiste, *m.f.*

Baptistery, Baptistry, *s.* baptistère, *m.*

Baptize, *v.a.* baptiser. *To half-* —, ondoyer

Baptizer, *s.* baptiseur, *m.*

Baptizing, *s.* baptême, *m.*

Bar, *s.* barre, *f.*; barreau, *m.*; parquet, *m.*; (*fastening, of fire-grates*) barreau, *m.*; (*swing-* —) palonnier, *m.*; (*splinter-* —) volée, *f.*; (*legal profession, body of barristers*) barreau, *m.*; (*barrier*) barrière, *f.*; (*fig.*) barrière, *f.*, obstacle, *m.*, exclusion, *f.*; (*dock for the accused*) banc des accusés *or* des prévenus, *m.*; (*of taverns*) comptoir, *m.*; (*law*) exception, interruption, *f.*; (*nav., her.*) barre, *f.*; (*mus.*) barre, mesure, *f.*; (*of lace*) bride, *f.*; (*rod*) tringle, *f.*; (—**s,** *pl., of a horse's mouth*) barres, *f.pl.*; (*of a horse's bit*) barre, *f.*; (*of stirrups*) porte-étrivières, *m.*; — *adj.* (*of metals, soap,* &c.) en barre, en barres. *Long* —, (*for swing-bars*) sommier, *m.* *Iron* —, barre de fer, *f.* — **iron,** fer en barres, *m.* *To be called to the* —, être reçu au barreau, être reçu avocat. — **maid,** *s.* fille *or* demoiselle de comptoir, *f.* — **man,** *s.* garçon de comptoir, *m.* — **room,** *s.* salon, *m.* — **shot,** *s.* boulet ramé, *m.*

Bar, *v.a.* barrer; exclure; excepter; (*prevent*) empêcher (de), interdire, prohiber, défendre; (*deprive*) priver de, ôter; (*law*) interrompre, empêcher, rendre nul, débouter; (*her., vet.*) barrer; — *prep.* (*except*) *V.* **Barring.** — **out,** *v.a.* écarter, exclure ; *v.n.* se barricader. — **up,** barrer ; (*confine*) enfermer

Barb, *s.* barbe, *f.*; (*of an arrow, of a hook*) barbillon, *m.*; (*fig.*) pointe, *f.*; (*horse armour*) barde, *f.*; (*horse, mare*) barbe, cheval barbe, *m.*, jument barbe, *f.*; (*pigeon*) pigeon de Barbarie, *m.*; — *v.a.* (*an arrow,* &c.) barbeler; (*a horse*)

Barbacan. *V.* **Barbican** [barder

Barbarian, *s.* barbare, *m.f.*; — *adj.* barbare; (*of Barbary*) barbaresque

Barbaric, *adj.* barbare

Barbarism, *s.* barbarie, *f.*; (*gram.*) barbarisme, *m.*

Barbarity, *s.* barbarie, cruauté, *f.*

Barbarize, *v.n.a.* barbariser

Barbarous, *adj.* barbare

Barbarously, *adv.* d'une manière barbare, avec barbarie, barbarement, cruellement

Barbarousness, *s.* barbarie, *f.*

Barbary, *s* (*geog.*) la Barbarie, *f.*; (*horse, mare*) barbe, cheval barbe, *m.*, jument barbe, *f.*; — *adj.* de Barbarie; barbe [*arrows,* &c.) barbelé

Barbate, Barbated, *adj.* barbu, barbé; (*of*

Barbecue, *s.* animal rôti tout entier; — *v.a.* rôtir (un animal) tout entier

Barbel, *s.* (*fish*) barbeau, *m.*; (*her.*) bar, *m.*; (*vet.*) *V.* **Barbles** [perruque, *f.*

Barber, *s.* barbier, *m.* —**'s block,** *s.* tête à

Barberry, *s.* épine-vinette, *f.*

Barbet, *s.* barbet, caniche, *m.*; (*bird*) barbu, *m.*

Barbette, *s.* (*fort.*) barbette, *f.* *In* —, en

Barbican, *s.* barbacane, *f.* [barbette

Barbles, *s. pl.* barbes, *f.pl.*, barbillons, *m.pl.*

Barcarolle, *s.* barcarolle, *f.*

Bard, *s.* barde, *m.*; troubadour, *m.*; trouvère, *m.*; poète, *m.*; (*cook., armour*) barde, *f.*; — *v.a.* barder [de poète

Bardic, Bardish, *adj.* de barde, des bardes;

Bardism, *s.* bardisme, *m.*

Bare, *adj.* nu; à nu; découvert; (*deprived*) privé (de), dénué (de); (*mere*) simple, seul; tout juste; — *s.* (*arts*) nu, *m.*; — *v.a.* mettre à nu dénuder; (*uncover*) découvrir; (*deprive*) dépouiller (de); (*of swords*) tirer du fourreau. *To lay* —, mettre à nu *or* à découvert, découvrir, exposer. — **back,** *adv.* à nu, à poil. — **bone,** *s.* corps décharné, squelette, *m.* — **boned,** *adj.* décharné. — **bones,** *s.* cafard, cagot, tartufe, *m.* — **faced,** *adj.* à visage découvert; (*openly*) sans déguisement, à découvert; (*impudent*) effronté. — **facedly,** *adv.* à découvert, ouvertement; (*impudently*) effrontément. — **facedness,** *s.* effronterie, *f.* — **footed, -foot,** *adj. adv.* nu-pieds, les pieds nus; (*of friars*) déchaussé. — **headed,** *adj.* nu-tête, la tête nue. — **legged,** *adj.* nu-jambes. — **necked,** *adj.* le cou nu, qui a le cou nu

Barege, *s.* barége, *m.*

Barely, *adv.* simplement, seulement; à peine; tout juste; (*poorly*) pauvrement

Bareness, *s.* nudité, *f.*; (*destitution*) dénûment, *m.*; pauvreté, *f.*

Bargain, *s.* marché, *m.*; convention, *f.*; affaire, *f.*; bonne affaire, *f.*; occasion, *f.*; (*purchase*) achat, *m.* *Dead* —, excellent marché. *Great* —, marché d'or. *Into the* —, par-dessus le marché. *To buy* or *have a thing a* —, *a dead* —, acheter *or* avoir quelque chose à bon marché (*or* pour presque rien), à très bon marché (*or* pour rien). *To sell a thing a* —, vendre quelque chose à gros bénéfices. *To sell a thing to a person a* —, vendre quelque chose à quelqu'un à bon marché (*or* à bon compte). *To make the best of a bad* —, se tirer d'affaire le mieux possible. *V.* **Bargainer**

Bargain, *v.n.* marchander; (*sell*) faire marché; (*agree*) convenir (de), faire affaire. — **for,** marchander; faire marché de; traiter de; convenir de [*m.*, -euse, *f.*

Bargainee, *s.* acquéreur, *m.*, -euse, *f.*, acheteur,

Bargainer, *s.* personne qui marchande, *f.*; (*seller*) vendeur, *m.*, -euse *or* -eresse, *f.* *To be a hard* —, *to drive hard bargains,* être serré *or* chien en affaires

Barge, *s.* barque, *f.*, chaland, *m.*, toue, *f.*, bateau, *m.* — **man,** *s.* batelier, canotier, marinier, *m.*

— **master,** *s.* patron de barque, maître marinier, *m.* — **owner,** *s.* propriétaire de bateaux [de transport, *m.*
Barilla, *s.* barille, *f.*
Barium, *s.* barium, baryum, *m.*
Bark, *s.* (*of trees*) écorce, *f.*; (*Peruvian* —) quinquina, *m.*; (*tanners'* —) tan, *m.*; (*boat*) barque, *f.*; (*of dogs*) aboiement, *m.*; — *v.a.n.* (*strip*) écorcer, décortiquer; (*to cover*) recouvrir d'écorce; couvrir; (*like dogs*) aboyer ('*at*,' après). — **beetle, -chafer,** *s.* turc, *m.* — **mill,** *s.* moulin à tan, *m.* — **tree,** *s.* quinquina, *m.* [aboyeur, *m.*, -euse, *f.*
Barker, *s.* (*of trees*) écorceur, *m.*; (*clamourer*)
Barking, *s.* (*of dogs*) aboiement, *m.*; (*of trees*) écorcement, *m.*, décortication, *f.* — **irons,** *s. pl.* décortiqueur, *m.*
Barkless, *adj.* sans écorce
Barky, *adj.* d'écorce
Barley, *s.* orge, *f.*; — *adj.* d'orge. *Husked* or *hulled* —, *pot* —, *Scotch* —, orge mondée. *Pearl* —, orge perlée. — **bread,** *s.* pain d'orge, *m.* — **corn,** *s.* grain d'orge, *m.* — **meal,** *s.* farine d'orge, *f.* — **mow,** *s.* tas d'orge, *m.* — **sugar,** *s.* sucre d'orge, *m.* — **water,** *s.* eau d'orge, *f.*
Barm, *s.* levure, *f.*
Barmy, *adj.* contenant de la levure
Barn, *s.* grange, *f.* — **door fowls,** — **yard fowls,** — **fowls,** *s. pl.* oiseaux de basse-cour, *m.pl.*, volaille, *f.* — **floor,** *s.* aire de grange, *f.* — **ful,** *s.* grangée, *f.* — **owl,** *s.* effraie, *f.*
Barnabite, *s.* barnabite, *m.*
Barnacle, *s.* (*bird, shell-fish*) barnache, bernache, barnacle, bernacle, *f.*; —**s,** *pl.* barnaches, &c.; (*farrier's instr.*) morailles, *f.pl.*; (*spectacles: obsolete*) besicles, *f.pl.*, (*modern*) pince-nez, *m.*
Barometer, *s* baromètre, *m.*
Barometr-ic, al, -ically, barométrique, &c. *V.* page 3, § 1 [*m.pl.*, baron, *m.*
Baron, *s.* baron, *m.*; (*of beef*) deux aloyaux,
Baronage, *s.* baronnage, *m.*
Baroness, *s.* baronne, *f.*
Baronet, *s.* baronnet, *m.* [baronnets, *m.pl.*
Baronetage, *s.* corps des baronnets, *m.*,
Baronetcy, *s.* titre (*m.*) *or* dignité (*f.*) de
Baronial, *adj.* baronnial; de baron [baronnet
Barony, *s.* baronnie, *f.*
Barouch, Barouche, *s.* calèche, *f.*
Barque, *s.* barque, *f.* — **rigged,** *adj.* gréé en
Barracan, *s.* bouracan, *m.* [barque
Barrack, Barracks, *s.* caserne, *f.* — **master,** *s.* intendant de caserne, garde du génie, *m.* — **room,** *s.* chambrée, *f.* — **sergeant,** *s.* garde-magasin, *m.*
Barracoon, *s.* baracon, *m.*, nègrerie, *f.*
Barrage, *s.* barrage, *m.*
Barratry, *s.* baraterie, *f.*
Barred, *part. adj.* barré, &c. (*V.* **Bar,** *v.a.*); (*law*) interrompu, &c.; nul; périmé, caduc. — *teeth,* dents barrées, *f.pl.*
Barrel, *s.* (*cask*) baril, *m.*; (*of machines*) cylindre, *m.*; tambour, *m.*; (*of guns, pistols*) canon, *m.*; (*of cannons*) *V.* **Tube;** (*of drums*) caisse, *f.*; (*of watches,* &c.) cylindre, barillet, *m.*; (*of organs*) cylindre, *m.*; (*of pumps*) corps, *m.*; (*of pens*) tuyau, *m.*; (*of jacks*) fusée, *f.*, tambour, *m.*; (*of tar*) gonne, *f.*; — *v.a.* embariller, mettre en baril; encaquer; (*roads*) bomber. —**bellied,** *adj.* à gros ventre, pansu, ventru. — **loft,** *s.* (*theat.*) cintre, *m.* — **organ,** *s.* orgue à cylindre, orgue de Barbarie, *m.*
Barrelled, *adj.* à baril; (*of machines*) à cylindre; (*of fire-arms*) à canon; (*of roads*) bombé
Barren, *adj.* stérile; improductif. — **wort,** *s.* [épimède, *m.*
Barrenly, *adv.* stérilement
Barrenness, *s.* stérilité, *f.*
Barricade, *s.* barricade, *f.*; — *v.a.* barricader
Barricading, *s.* action de barricader, *f.*
Barrier, *s.* barrière, *f.*
Barring, *prep.* excepté, sauf, à part, à … près. — **out,** *s.* barricades, *f.pl.*
Barrister, *s.* avocat, *m.* — **-at-law,** avocat, *m.*
Barrow, *s.* brouette, *f.*; (*pig*) porc, pourceau, *m.*; (*sepulchral mound*) tumulus, galgal, *m.* — **man,** *s.* brouetteur, brouettier, *m.*
Barse. *V.* **Basse** [troc, *m.*; trafic, *m.*
Barter, *v.a.n.* échanger; troquer; — *s.* échange,
Barterer, *s.* troqueur, *m.*, -euse, *f.*, brocanteur, *m.*, -euse, *f.*; trafiqueur, *m.*, -euse, *f.*
Baryta, Barytes, *s.* baryte, *f.*
Barytone, *s.* baryton, *m.*; — *adj.* de baryton
Barytum, *s.* baryum, barium, *m.*
Basal, *adj.* basal
Basalt, *s.* basalte, *m.*
Basaltic, *adj.* basaltique
Base, *adj.* bas; vil; illégitime; (*of metals*) de peu de valeur, non précieux; (*of coin*) faux; (*voice*) *V.* **Bass.** — **born,** *adj.* bâtard, illégitime, naturel; de basse naissance, de basse extraction; bas, ignoble. — **minded,** *adj.* qui a l'âme basse, bas, vil, méprisable. — **mindedness,** *s.* bassesse d'âme, *f.* — **plinth,** *s.* lambris d'appui, *m.*, plinthe, *f.* — **spirited,** *adj.* lâche, sans cœur, vil
Base, *s.* base, *f.*; (*of a statue*) piédestal, socle, *m.*; (*build.*) soubassement, *m.*; (*play*) barres, *f.pl.*; (*mus.*) *V.* **Bass;** (*her., of a shield*) pointe, *f.* — **line,** *s.* ligne de base, *f.*
Base, *v.a.* baser, asseoir
Baseless, *adj.* sans base, sans fondement
Basely, *adv.* bassement, vilement; lâchement
Basement, *s.* fondation, *f.*, fondement, *m.*; (*story*) sous-sol, *m.* — **floor, -story,** *s.* sous-sol, *m.*
Baseness, *s.* bassesse, abjection, *f.*; (*of metals*) peu de valeur, *m.*; (*of birth*) illégitimité, *f.*; [(*of sound*) gravité, *f.*
Bashaw. *V.* **Pasha**
Bashful, *adj.* timide, modeste; honteux
Bashfully, *adv.* timidement, modestement
Bashfulness, *s.* timidité, modestie, *f.*; (*in a bad sense*) mauvaise honte, *f.* [*V.* **Bevel,** *v.a.*
Basil, *s.* biseau, *m.*; (*bot.*) basilic, *m.*; — *v.a.*
Basilar, Basilary, *adj.* basilaire
Basilic, -al, *adj* basilique
Basilica, *s.* basilique, *f.*
Basilisk, *s.* basilic, *m.*
Basin, *s.* bassin, *m.*; (*cup*) bol, *m.*; (*for washing o.'s face and hands*) cuvette, *f.*; (*barber's*) plat à barbe, *m.* — **ful,** *s.* bol plein, *m.*
Basis, *s.* base, *f.*
Basist, *s.* basse, *f.* [s'endormir
Bask, *v.a.* chauffer; — *v.n.* se chauffer; (*fig.*)
Basket, *s.* panier, *m.*; (*light, open, and elegant*) corbeille, *f.*; (*for game*) bourriche, *f.*; (*for oysters: of 12½ doz. and odd*) bourriche, *f.*, (*of 26 doz.*) cloyère, *f.*; (*of apple-women,* &c.) éventaire, *m.*; (*of carriages*) vide-poches, *m.*; (*of stage-coaches*) magasin, *m.* — **chaise,** *s.* chaise à panier, *f.*, panier-chaise, *m.* — **ful,** *s.* panier plein, *m.*; panerée, *f.* — **hilt,** *s.* garde à coquille, coquille, *f.* — **hilted,** *adj.* muni d'une garde à coquille, à coquille. — **maker,** *s.* vannier, *m.* — **making, -manufactory,** *s.* vannerie, *f.* — **rod,** *s.* osier, *m.* — **trade,** *s.* vannerie, *f.* — **woman,** *s.* porteuse, *f.* — **work,** *s.* vannerie, *f.*; (*tech.*) clayonnage, *m.*
Bason. *V.* **Basin**
Basque, *s. adj.* Basque, *m.f.*
Bas-relief, *s.* bas-relief, *m.*
Bass, *s.* natte, *f.*; paillasson, *m.*; (*bast*) *V.* **Bast;** (*fish*) *V.* **Basse;** (*mus.*) basse, *f.* *Double* —, contre-basse, *f.* *Thorough* or *continued* —, basse continue, *f.* — **clarinet,** *s.* basse-tube, basse-turbe, *f.* — **counter,** *s.* basse-contre, *f.* — **drum,** *s.* grosse caisse, *f.* — **note,** *s.* basse, *f.* — **singer,** *s.* basse, *f.* — **string,** *s.* basse, *f.* — **viol,** *s.* basse de viole, *f.* — **voice,** *s.* voix de basse, basse, *f.* — **wood,** *s.* tilleul, *m.*
Basse, *s.* (*fish*) bar, bars, *m.*
Basset, *s.* (*dog*) basset, *m.*; (*game*) bassette, *f.*; (*mining*) affleurement, *m.* — **horn,** *s.* cor de [basset, *m.*
Bassia, *s.* bassie, *f.*
Bassinet, *s.* berceau, *m.*, barcelonnette, *f.*
Basso, *s.* (*mus.*) basse, *f.* —**relievo, -rilievo,** *s.* (*sculp.*) bas-relief, *m.*

Bassock, *s.* natte, *f.*; paillasson, *m.*
Bassoon, *s.* basson, *m.*
Bassoonist, *s.* bassoniste, basson, *m.*
Bast, *s.* filasse, *f.*; (*of lime-tree*) tille, *f.* — **mat,** *s.* natte de tille, *f.*
Bastard, *s.* bâtard, *m.*, e, *f.*; (*law*) enfant naturel, *m.*; — *adj.* bâtard; (*bot., med.*) faux
Bastardize, *v.a.* déclarer bâtard
Bastardy, *s.* bâtardise, *f.*
Baste, *v.a.* (*beat*) bâtonner; (*meat*) arroser; [(*need.*) bâtir, faufiler
Basterna, *s.* basterne, *f.*
Bastile, Bastille, *s.* bastille, *f.*
Bastinade, Bastinado, *s.* bastonnade, *f.*; — *v.a.* bâtonner, donner la bastonnade à. *To be —d,* recevoir la bastonnade
Basting, *s.* (*beating*) bastonnade, *f.*; (*of meat*) arrosement, *m.*; (*need.*) couture à longs points, *f.*, bâti, *m.*, faufilure, *f.* — **ladle,** *s.* cuiller à arroser, *f.*
Bastion, *s.* bastion, *m.*; — *v.a.* bastionner
Bat, *s.* battoir, *m.*; (*cooper's*) tapette, *f.*; (*of bricks*) éclat, morceau, *m.*; (*animal*) chauve-souris, *f.* — **fowler,** *s.* oiseleur nocturne, *m.* — **fowling,** *s.* chasse aux flambeaux, fouée, *f.* — **horse,** *s.* (*mil.*) cheval de bagage, *m.* — **man,** *s.* (*mil.*) brosseur, *m.* — **wing, -wing burner,** *s.* (*gas-lighting*) bec à éventail, *m.*
Batardeau, *s.* batardeau, *m.*
Batatas, *s.* patate, *f.*
Batavian, *s. adj.* Batave, *m.f.*
Batch, *s.* fournée, *f.*
Bate, *v.n.a.* rabattre, rabaisser, diminuer, réduire; retrancher; excepter; faire remise de
Bath, *s.* bain, *m.*; (*tub*) baignoire, *f.* *To go for a —,* aller prendre un bain. — **chair,** *s.* *V.* **Chair.** — **house,** *s.* établissement de bains, *m.*, bains, *m.pl.* — **keeper, -man, -woman,** *s.* baigneur, *m.*, -euse, *f.* — **room,** *s.* salle de bains, *f.*
Bathe, *v.a.* baigner; (*of wounds,* &c.) bassiner; éponger; — *v.n.* se baigner; — *s.* bain, *m.*, baignade, *f.* *To go for a —,* aller se baigner
Bather, *s.* baigneur, *m.*, -euse, *f.*
Bathing, *s.* bain, *m.*; bains, *m.pl.* — **cap,** *s.* calotte de bain, *f.* — **costume,** *s.* *V.* — **dress.** — **drawers,** *s. pl.* caleçon de bain, *m.* — **dress,** *s.* costume de bain, *m.*, baigneuse, *f.* — **establishment,** *s.* établissement de bains, *m.* — **gown,** *s.* peignoir, *m.* — **machine,** *s.* voiture de bain, voiture-baignoire, *f.* — **man,** *s.* baigneur, *m.* — **place,** *s.* baignoir, *m.* — **room,** *s.* salle de bains, *f.* — **tub,** *s.* baignoire, *f.* — **woman,** *s.* baigneuse, *f.*
Bathos, *s.* pathos, *m.*; galimatias, *m.*
Bating, *prep.* *V.* **Barring**
Batlet, *s.* battoir, *m.*
Baton, *s.* bâton, *m.*
Batrachian, *s.* batracien, *m.*
Batta, *s.* supplément de solde, *m.*, surpaye, *f.*
Battalion, *s.* bataillon, *m.*
Battalioned, *adj.* embataillonné, en bataillons
Batten, *v.a.* engraisser; fertiliser; (*carp.*) voliger; — *v.n.* s'engraisser (de); (*eat*) se bourrer (de), se gorger (de), se repaître (de); — *s.* volige, *f.*
Batter, *s.* pâte, *f.*; — *v.a.* battre; (*dent*) bossuer, bosseler; (— *with ordnance*) canonner, battre en brèche; (*break*) casser; (*wear out*) délabrer, user. — **down,** abattre; (*mil.*) battre en ruine
Batterer, *s.* abatteur, *m.*; (*fig.*) batteur, *m.*
Battering, *s.* — **gun, -piece,** *s.* pièce de siége, *f.* — **ram,** *s.* bélier, *m.* — **train,** *s.* artillerie de siége, *f.*
Battery, *s.* attaque, *f.*; (*artil., phys.*) batterie, *f.*; (*law*) voies de fait, *f.pl.*, coups, *m.pl.*
Battle, *s.* bataille, *f.*; combat, *m.*; — *v.n.a.* combattre; (*fam.*) batailler; (*to embattle*) créneler. *To do —,* combattre. — **array,** *s.* ordre de bataille, *m.* — **axe,** *s.* hache d'armes, *f.* — **field, -ground,** *s.* champ de bataille, *m.* — **piece,** *s.* bataille, *f.*
Battledoor, Battledore, *s.* raquette, *f.*, [battoir, *m.*
Battlement, *s.* créneau, *m.*
Battlemented, *adj.* crénelé
Battling, *s.* lutte, *f.*, combat, *m.*; (*fam.*) [chamaillis, *m.*
Battology, &c. *V* page 3, § 1
Battue, *s.* battue, *f.*
Baubee, *s.* sou, *m.*; — **s,** *pl.* (*money generally*) [écus, *m.pl.*
Bauble, *s.* babiole, bagatelle, *f.*, brimborion, *m.*, fanfreluche, *f.*; hochet, *m.*; (*charm*) breloque, *f.*; (*fool's*) marotte, *f.*
Baulk, *s.* (*of timber*) bille, *f.*; (*tech., beam*) poutre, *f.*; chantier, *m.*
Bavarian, *s.* Bavarois, *m.*, e, *f.*; — *adj.* bavarois, de Bavière. — *beer,* bière de Bavière, *f.*
Bavin, *s.* fagotage, *m.*; cotret, *m.*; (*mil.*) fascine, *f.*
Bawbee, Bawble. *V.* **Baubee, Bauble**
Bawd, *s.* entremetteur, *m.*, -euse, *f.*; — *v.a.n.* procurer
Bawdily, *adv.* d'une manière obscène
Bawdiness, Bawdry, *s.* obscénité, *f.*
Bawdrick. *V.* **Baldrick**
Bawdy, *adj.* obscène, déshonnête. — **house,** lieu de prostitution, *m.*
Bawl, *v.n.* crier, brailler
Bawler, *s.* criard, *m.*, e, *f.*, braillard, *m.*, e, *f.*
Bawling, *s.* cris, *m.pl.*, braillement, *m.*
Bay, *adj. s.* (*colour*) bai, *adj. m.*, e, *f.*, bai, *s.m.*; — *s.* (*geog.*) baie, *f.*; golfe, *m.*; (*of mills*) écluse, *f.*; (*for salt*) salin, *m.*; (*mas.*) baie, ouverture, *f.*; (*arch.*) travée, *f.*; (*bot.*) laurier, *m.*; (*extremities*) abois, *m. pl.*; — *v.n.a.* aboyer, aboyer à; (*pursue*) chasser. *Sweet —,* laurier-sauce, *m.* *At —,* aux abois. *To keep at —,* tenir en échec *or* en respect, mettre aux abois. — **berry,** *s.* baie de laurier, *f.* — **cherry,** — **laurel,** *s.* laurier-cerise, *m.* — **salt,** *s.* sel gris, *m.* — **tree,** *s.* laurier, *m.* — **window,** *s.* fenêtre en saillie, *f.* — **yarn,** *s.* fil de laine, *m.*
Bayadere, *s.* bayadère, *f.*
Bayed, *adj.* à ouvertures
Baying, *s.* aboiement, *m.*
Bayonet, *s.* baïonnette, *f.*; — *v.a.* percer *or* tuer d'un coup (*or* à coups) de baïonnette; charger à la baïonnette. — **belt,** *s.* porte-[baïonnette, *m.*
Bazaar, Bazar, *s.* bazar, *m.*
B.C., (*before Christ*) avant J.-C.
B.D., bachelier en théologie, *m.*
Bdellium, *s.* bdellium, *m.*
Be, *v.n.* être; [*not expressed generally when before a present part.*]; (*to exist*) exister, être; (*to be found*) se trouver; (*to figure*) figurer; (*to be under an agreement to …, have settled or arranged to …, be appointed to …, must*) devoir; falloir (*imp.*); (*concern*) regarder, faire; (*make*) faire; (*of feeling cold, hot, hungry, thirsty,* &c.) avoir; (*of o.'s state of health*) se porter, aller; (*of o.'s years of age, of dimension*) avoir; (*of weather, temperature, daylight, dark,* &c., *if the verb is imp. with 'it'*) faire; (*happen*) se faire, venir; falloir; aller, venir à, arriver; (*get, arrive*) arriver; venir; (*remain, keep*) rester; (*cost*) coûter; (*be the case*) en être (*'with'* de); (*imp. of time or distance*) y avoir, *'it is'* il y a. *I am an Englishman,* je suis Anglais. *I am writing,* j'écris; (*busy writing*) je suis à écrire, je suis en train d'écrire. *I was writing,* j'écrivais; (*busy writing*) j'étais à écrire, j'étais en train d'écrire. *I am to write to him next month,* je dois lui écrire le mois prochain. *He was to have set out yesterday,* il a dû (*or* il avait dû) partir hier. *What am I to do?* que faut-il que je fasse? que faut-il faire? que dois-je faire? *What is to be done?* que faut-il faire? que *or* comment faire? *Is it to be wondered at if …?* faut-il s'étonner si …? *That is nothing to me,* cela ne me regarde pas; cela ne me fait rien. *What is that to you?* qu'est-ce que cela vous fait? *Two and two are four,* deux et deux font quatre. *Union is strength,* l'union fait la force. *To be cold, hot* (or *warm*), (*things*) être froid, chaud; (*of a person's sensations*) avoir froid, chaud (*both invariable*); (*weather*) faire froid, chaud. *Your hands are cold,* (*expressing*

directly that you feel the cold in them yourself) vous avez froid aux mains; (not expressing that directly) vous avez les mains froides. *How are you?* comment vous portez-vous? comment allez-vous? *I am better,* (in better health) je me porte mieux, je vais mieux; (I am relieved) je suis mieux; (for other senses, See **Better**). *He is not well,* il ne se porte pas bien. *What age is he? what is his age? how old is he?* quel âge a-t-il? *He is ten, he is ten years of age, he is ten years old,* il a dix ans. *It is ten* (o'clock), il est dix heures. *This table is two yards long,* cette table a deux mètres de long *or* de longueur. *It is cold, mild, fine,* or &c. (weather), il fait froid, doux, beau *or* &c. *It begins to — cold,* &c., il commence à faire froid, &c. *It is daylight,* il fait jour. *It is comfortable here,* il fait bon ici. *How is it?* comment cela se fait-il? *How is it that ...?* comment se fait-il que ...? d'où vient que ...? *How is that?* comment cela se fait-il? (how so) comment cela? *Why is it that ...?* pourquoi faut-il que ...? *If I were to do so, were I to do so,* si je le faisais, si j'allais le faire, s'il m'arrivait de le faire. *If he were to know it,* s'il le savait, s'il venait à le savoir. *Were I to be killed!* quand je devrais être tué! dussé-je être tué! *Were it only* or *but ...,* quand ce ne serait que ..., ne fût-ce que ... *Were I* (If I were) *in your place,* si j'étais à votre place. *As it were,* V. **As.** *If it is so,* s'il en est ainsi. *Be that* (or this) *as it may,* quoi qu'il en soit. *It is with you as* (the same case as) *with all your family,* il en est de vous comme de toute votre famille. *It is now ten years since he went,* il y a dix ans qu'il est parti. *It is* (or *it may be*) *five miles from here to London,* il y a (*or* il peut y avoir) huit kilomètres d'ici à Londres. *There is* or *there are,* il y a; (look!) voilà. *There was* or *there were,* (imperfect tense) il y avait, (pret.) il y eut. *There is,* (of weather) il fait (du brouillard, du vent, de la gelée, &c.) *There he* (she, &c.) *is,* V. **There.** *There are, there were three of them,* ils sont, ils étaient trois. *There are, there were six of us,* nous sommes, nous étions six. *If there ever was one,* s'il en fut jamais. *There may, must, is going to be,* il peut, doit, va y avoir. *Let it be so,* soit. *Be it so; So be it; So it is:* V. **So.** *Be it said,* soit dit. *If it were not for, were it not for* (or that), si ce n'était (que), sans. *Had it not been for,* sans. *It being 4 o'clock,* comme il est (now) *or* comme il était (then) 4 heures. *It being very cold* comme il fait (*or* faisait) très froid. *There is nothing to be feared, to be done,* il n'y a rien à craindre, à faire. *There is no time to be lost,* il n'y a pas de temps à perdre. *It is to be regretted that ...,* il est à regretter que ... *It were to be wished that ...,* il serait à désirer que ... *This is not to be compared with that,* ceci n'est pas à comparer avec cela. *That is not to be found,* cela ne se trouve pas, cela est introuvable. *That was not to be forgiven,* c'était impardonnable. *The ruins are still to be seen,* on voit encore les ruines. *I think, believe, say, bet it is, it is not,* je pense, crois, dis, parie que oui (que si, *in answer to a question containing a negation, or in contradiction to a negative statement*), que non. *I took him to be ...,* je l'ai pris pour ... *One would take him to be ... years old,* on lui donnerait ... ans. *That house is being built,* cette maison se bâtit, on bâtit cette maison. *It is being written now,* on l'écrit en ce moment. — **in,** (come home) rentrer. — **off,** V. **Off.**

Beach, *s.* rivage, *m.*, plage, grève, *f.*; (shingle) galet, *m.*; — *v.a.* échouer

Beaching, *s.* échouage, *m.*

Beachy, *adj.* bordé de plages

Beacon, *s.* fanal, *m.*; phare, *m.*; (nav.) balise, *f.*; — *v.a.* allumer; baliser. — **ship,** *s.* bâtiment-balise, *m.*, phare flottant, *m.*

Beaconage, *s.* droit de phare *or* de balise, *m.*; balisage, *m.*

Beaconed, *adj.* surmonté d'un fanal *or* d'un phare; balisé

Bead, *s.* grain, *m.*, perle, *f.*; (bubble) bulle, *f.*; goutte, *f.*; (of guns) bouton, *m.*, mire, *f.*, guidon, *m.*; — **s,** *pl.* grains, &c.; chapelet, *m.* *String of —s,* collier, *m.*; chapelet, *m.* — **maker,** *s.* fabricant de perles en verre *or* de chapelets, patenôtrier, *m.* — **proof,** *adj.* (dist.) qui fait chapelet. — **roll,** *s.* liste de ceux pour qui l'on doit prier, *f.* — **tree,** *s.* mélie, *f.*, azédarac, *m.*

Bead, *v.n.* perler

Beadle, *s.* (of churches) bedeau, *m.*; (of courts) huissier, *m.*; (univers.) appariteur, *m.*

Beadleship, *s.* charge de bedeau *or* &c. (*V.* [**Beadle**), *f.*

Beagle, *s.* briquet, bigle, *m.*

Beak, *s.* bec, *m.*; (geog.) pointe, *f.*; pic, *m.*; (of an anvil) bigorne, *f.* (nav.) éperon, *m.*; coltis, *m.* — **ful,** *s.* becquée, *f.* — **head,** *s.* (nav.) éperon, *m.*; coltis, *m.* — **iron,** *s.* bigorne, *f.*

Beaked, *adj.* à bec; en pointe; (her.) becqué

Beaker, *s.* gobelet, *m.*, coupe, *f.*

Beam, *s.* poutre, *f.*; (of ploughs) age, *m.*, flèche, haye, *f.*, timon, *m.*; (of a pair of scales) fléau, *m.*; (of bells) mouton, *m.*, hune, *f.*; (of windmills) volant, *m.*; (of anchors) verge, *f.*; (of a ship) bau, barrot, *m.*; (of machines) balancier, *m.*; (tech.) arbre, *m.*; (of deer) perche, *f.*; (of the sun) rayon, *m.*; (fig.) rayon, éclat, *m.* — **compass,** *s.* compas à verge, trusquin, *m.* — **ends,** *s. pl.* (nav.) côté, *m.* — **feather,** *s.* penne, *f.* — **tree,** *s.* (bot.) poirier sauvage, *m.*

Beam, *v.n.* rayonner; paraître; — *v.a.* envoyer, darder

Beaming, *s.* rayonnement, *m.*; — *adj.* rayon- [nant, radieux

Beamless, *adj.* sans rayons; (fig.) sans éclat

Beamy, *adj.* rayonnant, radieux; (massy) massif

Bean, *s.* fève, *f.*; (kidney —) haricot, *m.* *Broad —,* grosse fève de marais, grosse fève, fève de marais, fève. *French —s,* haricots verts, *m.pl.* *Garden* or *common —,* fève de marais. *Haricot —,* haricot blanc, haricot. *Horse —,* fèverole, *f.* *Kidney —,* haricot blanc, haricot. *Tonka —,* fève de Tonka. *Windsor —,* fève de Windsor, fève ronde d'Angleterre. — **caper,** *s.* fabagelle, *f.*

Bear, *s.* ours, *m.*, (she —) ourse, *f.*; (astr.) Ourse, *f.*; (of stock-jobbing) baissier, *m.* *Great —,* grande Ourse. *Lesser —,* petite Ourse. — **baiting,** *s.* combat de chiens contre un ours, *m.* — **berry,** *s.* raisin d'ours, *m.* — **driver,** *s.* V. — **leader.** — **garden,** *s.* fosse aux ours, *f.*; (fig.) scène de désordre, pétaudière, (la) cour du roi Pétaud, *f.* — **herd,** *s.* V. — **leader.** — **hunt, hunting,** *s.* chasse à l'ours, chasse aux ours, *f.* — — **leader,** *s.* meneur d'ours, *m.*; (fig.) cornac, *m.* — **like,** *adj.* comme un ours, semblable à un ours. — **pit,** *s.* fosse aux ours, *f.* —**'s breech,** *s.* (bot.) branche-ursine, acanthe, *f.* —**'s cub,** *s.* ourson, *m.* —**'s grease,** *s.* graisse d'ours, *f.* — **skin,** *s.* peau d'ours, *f.* — **skin cap,** *s.* bonnet à poil, *m.* —**'s-paw clam,** *s.* hippope maculé, hippope, *m.*

Bear, *v.a.n.* porter; (away or off) emporter; (gain) remporter, gagner; (support, &c.) supporter, soutenir; souffrir, endurer; (undergo) subir; (experience) essuyer, éprouver; (produce) porter, produire; (bring forth) enfanter, mettre au monde; (give) donner (à); (admit) comporter; (have) avoir; (enjoy) jouir de; (assume) prendre; (act) jouer; (pay) payer; (go) se porter, se diriger; (behave) se conduire, se comporter; (weigh) porter, peser. *To — oneself,* se comporter. *To bring to — upon,* faire agir sur *or* pour, mettre en jeu pour; diriger sur. — **away,** emporter; remporter; (bring) ramener; (flee) s'enfuir; (nav.) V. — **off.** — — **down,** renverser; accabler; détruire; entraîner; (upon) fondre (sur); (nav.) courir. — **forward,** pousser en avant. — **off,** emporter; remporter; enlever; (lead) emmener; (bring) amener; ramener; (parry) parer, détourner; (nav.) porter; (from the land) courir au large.

— **out,** soutenir; défendre; confirmer; justifier; prouver. — **through,** traverser; conduire, diriger. — **up,** soutenir; résister (à); (*raise*) soulever. — **upon, on,** porter sur; se porter sur, s'élancer contre; être dirigé sur *or* contre; (*to fire*) tirer sur; (*to check*) contenir. — **with,** supporter; endurer

Bearable, *adj.* supportable

Bearably, *adv.* supportablement

Beard, *s.* barbe, *f.*; (*of an arrow of a hook*) barbillon, *m.*; — *v.a.* défier, braver, narguer; (*an arrow*, &c.) barbeler

Bearded, *adj.* barbu; (*in compounds*) à barbe; (*of arrows*, &c.) barbelé

Beardless, *adj.* imberbe, sans barbe

Beardlessness, *s.* manque de barbe, *m.*

Bearer, *s.* porteur, *m.*, -euse, *f.*; (*of trees*) arbre de rapport, *m.*; (*of buds*) bouton à fruit, *m.*; (*arch., mech., tech., her.*) support, *m.*

Bearing, *s.* rapport, *m.*; portée, *f.*; face, *f.*; aspect, *m.*; (*of persons*) port, maintien, *m.*, attitude, contenance, *f.*, air, *m.*, mine, *f.*; (*conduct*) conduite, *f.*; (*arch.*) support, *m.*; (*mach.*) coussinet, *m.*; (*of land*) gisement, *m.*; (*nav.*) gisement, relèvement, *m.*; (*of a coast*) hauteur, *f.*; (*her.*) armes, armoiries, *f.pl.* — *of the cross*, portement de croix, *m.* *Beyond* —, insupportable. — **block,** *s.* support, *m.* — **neck,** *s.* tourillon, *m.* — **out,** *s.* (*arch.*) avance, saillie, *f.* — **rein,** *s.* rêne, *f.* — **surface,** *s.* point d'appui, *m* — **up,** *s.* (*build.*) étayement, *m.* — **wall,** *s.* mur de refend, *m.*

Bearish, *adj.* d'ours; brutal

Beast, *s.* bête, *f.*, animal, *m.*; quadrupède, *m.*; (*with regard to riding*) monture, *f.*; (*pers.*) bête brute, *f.*, animal, salop, cochon, *m.*; salope, cochonne, *f.*; (*game*) bête, *f.* *Dirty — !* cochon (*m.*)! cochonne (*f.*)! [**Beestings**

Beastings, Beastlings, Beastnings. *V.*

Beastliness, *s.* bestialité, *f.*; brutalité, *f.*; abrutissement, *m.*; (*filthiness*) saloperie, saleté, *f.*; obscénité, *f.*

Beastly, *adj.* bestial; (*dirty*) sale, dégoûtant, cochon de ...; — *adv.* bestialement; salement, dégoûtamment; comme un cochon. — *drunk*, soûl comme un cochon

Beat, *v.a.n.* battre; frapper; (*thrust*) fourrer, cogner; (*fig.*) chasser; (*surpass*) l'emporter sur, surpasser; (*of rain, snow*) battre, fouetter. *To* — (*all*) *to nothing*, battre à plate couture, éreinter, rouler. *That —s all*, cela l'emporte sur tout. *That —s me*, cela me passe. — **about,** *v.n.* chercher partout; (*hunt.*) battre le bois. — **away,** éloigner. — **back,** repousser. — **down,** abattre; renverser; (*crush*) rabattre; (*of price*) faire baisser; (*chaffer*) marchander, barguigner. — **in,** enfoncer; faire entrer. — **off,** repousser; (*drive away*) chasser. — **out,** battre; (*extract*) faire sortir; (*take off*) ôter, enlever. — **up,** battre; (*mortar*) corroyer; (*cook.*) battre; *v.n.* battre le pays; (*for soldiers*) recruter

Beat, *s.* battement, *m.*; (*blow*) coup, *m.*; (*hunt.*) battue, *f.*; (*of postmen*) itinéraire, *m.*; (*of policemen*) itinéraire, ilot, *m.*; (*of rail. watchmen, of sentries*) parcours, *m.*; (*of foresters*) garderie, *f.*; (*resort*) lieu fréquenté, rendez-vous, *m.*

Beaten, *part. adj.* battu, &c (*V.* **Beat,** *v.a.n.*); (*of paths*, &c.) battu, frayé; (*trite*) rebattu

Beater, *s.* (*pers.*) batteur, *m.*, -euse, *f.*; (*hunt.*) batteur, rabatteur, *m.*; (*machine*) batte, *f.*, battoir, *m.*, batteur, *m.*, batteuse, *f.*, machine à battre, *f.* *The —s and the beaten*, les battants et les battus, *m.pl.* — **up,** *s.* (*hunt.*) batteur, rabatteur, *m.*

Beatific, -al, *adj.* béatifique

Beatification, *s.* béatification, *f.*

Beatify, *v.a.* béatifier

Beating, *s.* (*blows*) coups, *m.pl.*; (*knocking*) battement, *m.*; (*tech.*) battage, *m.*; (*of metals*) batte, *f.*; (*of drums*) batterie, *f.*; (*mus.*) batterie, *f.*

Beatitude, *s.* béatitude, *f.*

Beau, *s.* beau, élégant, *m.*; cavalier, *m.*; (*fop*) petit-maître, coquet, gandin, *m.*; (*lover*) prétendant, adorateur, *m.* — *ideal*, beau idéal, *m.* *To set up for a* —, faire le petit-maitre

Beauish, *adj.* élégant, recherché

Beauteous, &c. *V.* **Beautiful,** &c.

Beautifier, *s.* personne *or* chose qui embellit, *f.*

Beautiful, *adj* beau; magnifique; admirable, charmant. ravissant; excellent, délicieux; — *s.* beau, *m.*

Beautifully, *adv.* admirablement

Beautifulness, *s.* beauté, *f.*

Beautify, *v.a.* embellir; — *v.n.* s'embellir, embellir

Beautiless, *adj.* sans beauté

Beauty, *s.* beauté, *f.*; charme, *m.*; (*pers.*) beauté, belle personne, belle, *f.* *To be a* —, être charmant *or* ravissant. *The sleeping* — (*in the woods*), la Belle au bois dormant. *The — and the Beast*, la Belle et la Bête. *That is the — of it*, c'est ce qui en fait le charme. — **spot,** *s.* grain de beauté, *m.*; mouche, *f.* — **wash,** *s.* eau de beauté, *f.*

Beaver, *s.* castor, *m.* — **rat,** *s.* hydromys, *m.*

Becafico. *V.* **Beccafico**

Becalm, *v.a.* calmer; (*nav.*) abrier, abriter

Because, *conj.* parce que. que. — *of*, à cause de

Beccafico, *s.* becfigue, *m.*

Bechance, *v.a.* arriver à

Bêche-de-mer, *s.* bêche de mer, *f.*

Beck, *s.* signe (de tête, de la main), *m.*; (*fig.* ordres. *m.pl.*

Beckon, *v.n.a.* faire signe (à quelqu'un de faire quelque chose); inviter (quelqu'un à faire quelque chose); (*to call*) appeler

Become, *v.n.* devenir; commencer à être; — *v.a.* (*things*) convenir à, aller à; (*pers.*) être digne de. *What will — of me?* que deviendrai-je? que vais-je devenir? qu'est-ce que je vais devenir? *I don't know what has — of him*, je ne sais pas ce qu'il est devenu. [*'To become,' with a past participle, is often rendered in French by the reflective voice: as. To — accustomed*, s'accoutumer; *to — animated*, s'animer; &c.] *To — big, pale, warm* (*and other adjectives*), *V.* **Grow**

Becoming, *adj.* (*proper*) convenable; (*in accordance, graceful, pretty*) qui va bien

Becomingly, *adv.* convenablement

Becomingness, *s.* bienséance, convenance, *f.*

Bed, *s.* lit, *m.*; (*of gardens*) couche, planche, *f.*, carré, *m.*, corbeille, *f.*; (*layer*) couche, *f.*; (*of billiards*) table, *f.*; (*of river*) lit, *m.*; (*of roads*) encaissement, *m.*; (*build.*) lit, *m.*; (*geol., min., mines*) couche, *f.*; gisement, *m.*; gîte, *m.*; (*of oysters*, &c.) banc, *m.*; parc, *m.*; (*artil.*) coussin de mire, *m.*; (*nav.*) souille, *f.*; (*yard*) chantier de bois, *m.* *From — and board*, (*law*) de corps et de biens. *To be in* —, être au lit, être couché. *To be brought to* —, accoucher. *To confine to o.'s* —, retenir au lit. *To get into* —, se mettre au lit, se coucher. *To go to* —, aller se coucher; se coucher. *To keep o.'s* —, garder le lit, être alité. *To lie in* —, rester au lit, se tenir au lit. *To put to* —, coucher, mettre au lit; (*of women*) accoucher. *To take to o.'s* —, se mettre au lit, s'aliter. *To turn down the* —, faire la couverture. *As you make your — so you must lie*, comme on fait son lit on se couche. — **bug,** *s.* punaise des lits, *f.* — **carriage,** *s.* (*rail.*) coupé-lit, *m.* — **chamber,** *s.* *V.* — **room.** — **clothes,** *s. pl.* couvertures, *f.pl.*, couvertures et draps de lit, draps et couvertures, *m.pl.* — **compartment,** *s.* (*rail.*) coupé-lit, *m.* — **cover,** *s.* couvre-lit, *m.* — **curtains,** *s. pl.* rideaux de (*or* du) lit, *m.pl.* — **fellow,** *s.* camarade de lit, *m.*, compagne de lit, *f.* — **furniture,** *s.* literie, *f.* — **hangings,** *s. pl.* tenture de lit, *f.*; rideaux de lit, *m.pl.*; tour de lit, *m.* — **pan,** *s.* bourdalou, *m.* — **post,** *s.* colonne *or* quenouille de lit, *f.* — **rid, -ridden,** *adj.* alité. — **room,** *s.* chambre à coucher, *f.*; chambre, *f.* — **room candlestick,** — **room pedestal,** *s.* *V.* **Candlestick** *and* **Pedestal.** — **room utensil,** *s.* vase de nuit, *m.* — **sacking,** *s.* sangle de lit, *f.* — **side,** *s.* bord du lit, *m.*; (*wall-side*) ruelle, *f.*; (*head*) chevet, *m.*; (*bed itself*) lit, *m.* *By his — side,* à côté de son lit; à son chevet. — **side carpet,** *s.* tapis (*m.*) *or* descente (*f.*) de lit. — **side stand** *or* **table,** *s.* table de nuit, *f.* — **slipper,** *s.* bourdalou, *m.* — **stead,** *s.* couchette, *f.*, lit, *m.*, (*wooden*) bois de lit, *m.* — **steps,** *s. pl.* escabeau (de lit), *m.* — **straw,** *s.* paillasse, *f.* — **tick,** *s.* coutil pour lit, *m.* — **time,** *s.* temps (*m.*) *or* heure (*f.*) de se coucher

Bed, *v.a.* coucher; (*lodge*) loger, nicher; (*to lay in*) fixer, enfoncer; (*shelter*) abriter; (*oysters, mussels,* &c.) parquer; (*build.*) fixer; (*mas.*) sceller; — *v.n* coucher, cohabiter

Bedabble, Bedarken, Bedaub, Bedazzle. *V.* **Dabble, Darken, Daub, Dazzle**

Bedded, *adj.* à ... lit, à ... lits; — *part.* couché, &c. (*V.* **Bed,** *v.a.*). *Double —,* à deux lits

Bedding, *s.* (*bed*) coucher, lit, *m.*; (*furniture*) literie, *f.*; (*fig.*) couche, *f.*

Bedeck, *v.a.* parer, orner, décorer

Bedevil, *v.a.* mettre dans un état du diable; (*bewitch*) ensorceler [arroser, mouiller, baigner

Bedew, *v.a.* humecter de rosée; ('*with*', de)

Bedim, *v.a.* obscurcir

Bedizen, *v.a.* orner, attifer; chamarrer

Bedlam, *s. adj.* hospice d'aliénés, *m.*, maison de fous, *f.*; (*pers.*) aliéné, *m.*, e, *f.*, fou, *m*, folle, *f.*

Bedlamite, *s.* aliéné, *m.*, e, *f.*, fou, *m.*, folle, *f.*

Bedouin, Beduin, *s.* Bédouin, *m.*

Bedraggle, Bedrench, Bedust, &c. *V.* **Draggle, Drench, Dust,** *v.a.*

Bee, *s.* abeille, *f.* — *in o.'s bonnet,* araignée dans le plafond. — **bread,** *s.* pain d'abeilles, *m.* — **eater,** *s.* guêpier, *m.* — **flower, -orchis,** *s.* ophrys mouche, *f.* — **garden,** *s.* rucher, *m.* — **glue,** *s.* propolis, *f.* — **hive,** *s.* ruche d'abeilles, ruche, *f.* — **house,** *s.* rucher, *m.* — **keeper, -master,** *s.* éleveur d'abeilles, apiculteur, *m.* — **moth,** *s.* gallérie, *f.* —**'s wax,** *s.* cire, cire jaune, *f.* — **swing,** *s.* dépôt, *m.*, pellicule, *f.*, pellicules, *f. pl.*, pelure d'ognon, *f.*

Beech, *s.* hêtre, fouteau, *m.* — **grove,** *s.* hêtraie, foutelaie, *f.* — **marten,** *s.* fouine, *f.* — **mast, -nut,** *s.* faîne, *f.* — **nut oil,** — **oil,** *s.* huile de faîne, *f.* — **plantation,** *s.* hêtraie, foutelaie, *f.* — **tree,** *s.* hêtre, fouteau, *m.*

Beech, Beechen, *adj.* de hêtre

Beef, *s* bœuf, *m.*; — *adj.* de bœuf. *Boiled —,* bouilli, *m.* *Roast —,* rosbif, bœuf rôti, *m.* — **eater,** *s.* mangeur (*m.*, -euse, *f.*) de bœuf; (*stout man*) gros plein de soupe, *m.*; (*yeoman*) cent-gardes, *m.*; (*bird*) pique-bœufs, *m.* — **roll,** *s.* cannelon de bœuf, *m.* — **steak,** *s.* bifteck, *m.* — **tea,** *s.* bouillon de bœuf, *m.* — **wood,** *s.* casuarine, *f.*

Beer, *s.* bière, *f.* — **barrel,** *s.* baril à bière, *m.* — **biscuit,** *s.* brèchetelle, *f.* — **drinker,** *s.* buveur (*m.*, -euse, *f.*) de bière. — **engine,** *s.* pompe à bière, *f.* — **house, -shop,** *s.* débit de bière, *m.*, brasserie, *f.*, cabaret, *m.*, taverne, *f.* — **house keeper,** — **shop keeper,** *s.* cabaretier, *m.*, -ière, *f.* — **pot,** *s.* pot à bière, *m.*

Beery, *adj.* de bière, de boisson; plein de bière; (*tipsy*) gris; (*heavy*) lourd [amouille, *f.*

Beestings, Beestlings, Beestnings, *s.pl.*

Beet, *s.* bette, betterave, *f.* *White —,* poirée, carde-poirée, *f.* — **root,** *s.* betterave, *f.* — **root sugar,** *s.* sucre de betterave, *m.*

Beetle, *s.* maillet, *m.*, mailloche, *f.*; (*for piling*) mouton, *m.*; (*of paviers*) demoiselle, hie, *f.*; (*of washerwomen*) battoir, *m.*; (*insect*) escarbot, scarabée, *m.*; — *v.n.* surplomber, avancer, saillir, faire saillie. *Black —,* blatte, *f.*, cafard, *m.* — **brows,** *s. pl.* sourcils épais, *m.pl.* — **browed,** *adj.* à sourcils épais. — **headed,** *adj.* stupide

Befall, *v.a.* arriver à; — *v.n.* arriver

Befeathered, *adj.* couvert de plumes, emplumé

Befit, *v.a.* convenir à

Befitting, *adj.* convenable (à)

Beflour, *v.a* enfariner

Befoam, *v.a.* couvrir d'écume

Befool, *v.a.* infatuer; (*cheat*) *V.* **Fool,** *v.a.*

Before, *prep.* (*of place*) devant; (*of time, order*) avant; (*law*) par devant; — *adv.* (*of place*) devant; (*of time, order*) avant; auparavant; (*above*) plus haut; (*already*) déjà; (*till then*) jusque-là, jusqu'alors; (*till now*) jusqu'ici, jusqu'à présent; (*sooner*) plus tôt; (*formerly*) autrefois; (*beforehand*) d'avance; — *adject.* (*preceding*) d'avant; — *conj.* avant que (*to be followed by the subj.*); (*before an inf.*) avant de; (*rather*) plutôt que de (*to be followed by the inf.*). — *it, them* (*things*), devant; avant. — **hand,** *adv.* d'avance, à l'avance, par avance, en avance; auparavant. *To be — hand with one,* prévenir *or* devancer quelqu'un. *To be — hand in the world,* être au-dessus de ses affaires, avoir de l'argent devant soi

Befoul, *v.a.* souiller, salir

Befriend, *v.a.* traiter en ami, seconder, aider, appuyer, favoriser, protéger

Befringe, *v.a.* franger, garnir d'une frange

Beg, *v.a.n.* mendier; (*ask, request*) demander ('*of,*' à; '*to*,' de), prier ('*of,*' ...; '*to,*' de); (*entreat*) supplier ('*of,*' ...; '*to,*' de); (*in letters*) avoir l'honneur (de); (*the question*) *V.* **Question.** *To go —ging,* mendier, quémander, gueuser, gueusailler, vivre d'aumônes; (*of things*) chercher un possesseur

Beget, *v.a.* engendrer; enfanter; faire naître; produire; causer, amener; entraîner, avoir

Begetter, *s* père, auteur, *m.* [pour effet

Beggar, *s.* mendiant, *m.*, e, *f.*; gueux, *m.*, -euse, *f.*; — *v.a.* réduire à la mendicité; ruiner, appauvrir; (*deprive*) priver (de); (*exhaust*) épuiser. *Poor —,* (*jest.*) pauvre diable, *m.*, pauvre diablesse, *f.* *To be a —,* (*fig.*) être dans la misère. *Set a — on horseback and he will ride to the devil,* il n'y a rien de plus orgueilleux qu'un riche qui a été gueux. — **boy,** *s.* petit mendiant, *m.* — **girl,** *s.* petite *or* jeune mendiante, *f.* — **-my-neighbour,** *s.* (*game*) bataille, *f.* — **woman,** *s.* mendiante, *f.*

Beggarliness, *s.* pauvreté, misère, *f.*

Beggarly, *adj.* pauvre, misérable, malheureux; — *adv.* misérablement

Beggary, *s.* mendicité, misère, *f.*

Begging, *s.* mendicité, *f.* — *the question,* cercle vicieux, *m.*, pétition de principe, *f.* *To live by —,* vivre d'aumônes. — **letter impostor** *or* **writer,** *s.* coups de manche, *m.*

Begin, *v.a.n.* commencer ('*with,*' '*by,*' par; '*with*' [... *in o.'s possession*], avec; *to do, doing,* &c., à faire, &c.); (*set to*) se mettre (à); (*to open or cut, as a bottle, a pie,* &c.) entamer; (*open, fig.*) *v.a.* ouvrir; *v.n.* ouvrir, s'ouvrir; (*start*) débuter; entonner (*a song*); (*be introduced*) s'introduire. *To — again,* recommencer; se renouveler. *To — with,* (*first of all*) pour commencer; d'abord; et d'abord [*m.*, e, *f.*

Beginner, *s.* commençant, *m.*, e, *f.*; débutant,

Beginning, *s.* commencement, *m.*; principe, *m.*, origine, *f.*; début, *m.* *The first —s,* les éléments, *m.pl.* *To make a —,* commencer

Begird, *v.a.* ('*with,*' de) ceindre; entourer, environner, cerner; assiéger

Begone, *int.* va! allez! va-t'en! allez-vous-en! retirez-vous! arrière!

Begrease, *v.a.* graisser, enduire de graisse

Begrime, Begrudge, *v.a.* *V.* **Grime** *and* **Grudge,** *v.a.* [amuser, faire oublier

Beguile, *v.a.* tromper; séduire; charmer;

Beguiler, *s.* trompeur, *m.*, -euse, *f.*

Beguin, *s.* béguin, *m.*

Beguine, *s.* béguine, *f.*

Behalf, *s.* faveur, *f.*; part, *f.*, nom, *m.*; (*com.*) profit, *m.* *In* or *on — of,* en faveur de, pour; de la part de; (*in the name of*) au nom de; (*com.*) au profit de

Behave, — **oneself**, *v.n.r.* se comporter, se conduire; se conduire bien
Behaved, *adj.* *Ill* —, qui se conduit mal, méchant; (*rude*) mal-appris, mal élevé, grossier. *Well* —, qui se conduit bien, sage
Behaviour, *s.* conduite, *f.*; procédé, *m.*; procédés, *m.pl.*; (*manner*) manières, *f.pl.*, tenue, *f.*
Behead, *v.a.* décapiter; (*on the scaffold*) guillotiner [guillotine, *f.*
Beheading, *s.* décapitation, *f.*; (*on the scaffold*)
Behest, *s.* commandement, ordre, *m.*
Behind, *prep.* derrière; en arrière de; (*late*) en retard de; (*after*) après; — *adv.* derrière, par derrière; en arrière; (*behind oneself*) derrière soi; (*after oneself*) après soi; (*late*) en retard; (*of riding on the same beast*) en croupe. — *it, them* (*things*), derrière. *Before and* —, par devant et par derrière. — **hand**, *adv.* en arrière, en retard; en reste
Behold, *v.a.n.* voir; (*observe*) regarder, contempler, considérer; — *int.* voyez! vois! voilà! voilà que! tout à coup; (*here*) voici!
Beholden, *adj.* redevable; obligé
Beholder, *s.* spectateur, *m.*, -trice, *f.*, témoin, *m.*; observateur, *m.*, -trice *f.*
Behoof, *s.* avantage, profit, intérêt, *m.*
Behoove, Behove, *v.a.* convenir à; — *v.n.* convenir
Being, *s.* être, *m.*; existence, *f.*; — *adj.* présent, actuel. *Supreme* —, Être suprême. *The time* —, le temps présent; le moment [abattre
Belabour, *v.a.* battre, frapper, rosser; (*fig.*)
Belated, *adj.* attardé, anuité, surpris par la nuit [genoper, amarrer
Belay, *v.a.* fermer; assiéger; couvrir; (*nav.*)
Belch, *s.* rot, *m.*, éructation, *f.*; — *v.n.* roter; — *v.a.* (— **forth**, **-out**) vomir
Belcher, *s.* roteur, *m.*, -euse, *f.* — **chain**, *s.* (*jewel.*) jaseron, *m.* [ment, *m.*
Belching, *s.* rot, *m.*, éructation, *f.*; vomisse-
Beldam, Beldame, *s.* vieille femme, *f.*; (*hag*) vieille sorcière, *f.*
Beleaguer, *v.a.* assiéger; cerner, entourer
Beleaguerer, *s.* assiégeant, *m.*
Belee, *v.a.* *V.* **Becalm**
Belemnite, *s.* bélemnite, *f.*
Belfry, *s.* beffroi, *m.*; clocher, *m.*
Belgian, *s.* Belge, *m.f.*; — *adj.* belge, de Belgique, des Belges
Belgic, *adj.* belge, de Belgique, des Belges
Belie, *v.a.* démentir, donner un démenti à; (*mimic*) contrefaire; (*slander*) calomnier
Belief, *s.* croyance, foi, *f.*; opinion, *f.*; credo, *m.* *Past all* —, incroyable
Believable, *adj.* croyable
Believe, *v.a.n.* croire ('*in*' ..., à ...; en ...; '*about it*,' '*about that*,' en). *To make anyone* —, faire croire à quelqu'un. *If he is to be believed*, à l'en croire. *I — you*, je vous crois; je crois bien! [croit, *f.*
Believer, *s.* croyant, *m.*, e, *f.*, personne qui
Believing, *adj.* croyant; crédule
Believingly, *adv.* avec foi
Belike, *adv.* peut-être, probablement
Belime, *v.a.* *V.* **Lime**, *v.a.*
Bell, *s.* cloche, *f.*; (*small. hand-bell*) clochette, *f.*; (*smaller still, house-bell*) sonnette, *f.*; (*with a hammer, call-bell*) timbre, *m.*; (*round*) grelot, *m.*; (*of trumpet*, &c.) pavillon, *m.*; (*of clocks*) timbre, *m.*; (*hort.*) *V.* **Hand-glass**; (*flower*) campanule, clochette, *f.*; (*cup of a flower*) calice, *m.*; (*arch.*) campane, *f.* *To bear away* or *bear* or *carry the* —, remporter la palme, primer; l'emporter (sur). *To pull* or *ring* or *touch the* —, sonner, tirer la sonnette. — **bird**, *s.* sonneur, *m.* — **clapper**, *s.* battant de cloche, *m.* — **crowned**, *adj.* (*of hats*) évasé. — **fashioned**, *adj.* en forme de cloche, en cloche; (*bot.*) campanulé. — **flower**, *s.* campanule, clochette, *f.* — **founder**, *s.* fondeur de cloches, *m.* — **foundry**, *s.* fonderie de cloches, *f.* — **glass**, *s.* *V.* **Hand-glass**. — **hanger**, *s.* poseur de sonnettes, *m.* — **hanging**, *s.* pose de sonnettes, *f.* — **man**, *s.* crieur public, *m.* — **metal**, *s.* métal de cloche, *m.* — **mouth**, *s.* évasement, *m.* — **mouthed**, *adj.* évasé. — **pepper**, *s.* poivre de Guinée, *m.* — **pull**, *s.* cordon de sonnette, cordon, *m.* — **ringer**, *s.* sonneur, *m.* — **rope**, *s.* corde de cloche, *f.*; (*of rooms*) cordon de sonnette, *m.* — **shaped**, *adj.* *V.* — **fashioned**. — **tower**, *s.* clocher, *m.* — **turret**, *s.* clocheton, *m.* — **wether**, *s.* sonnailler, *m.*
Bell, *v.n.* (*bot.*) croître *or* fleurir en forme de clochette; (*hunt.*) bramer; — *v.a.* *To — the cat*, attacher le grelot
Belladonna, *s.* belladone, *f.*
Belle, *s.* belle, beauté, *f.*; élégante, belle dame, *f.*
Belled, *adj.* à clochettes; à sonnettes; à grelots; (*her.*) clariné; grilleté
Belles-lettres, *s. pl.* belles-lettres, *f.pl.*
Bellicose, *adj.* belliqueux, guerrier
Bellied, *adj.* à ventre. *Big-* —, à gros ventre, ventru, pansu
Belligerent, *adj.* belligerant; — *s.* puissance belligérante, *f.*, belligérant, *m.*
Belling, *s.* bramement, *m.*
Bellow, *v.n.* beugler; (*of the sea*, &c.) mugir; (*of thunder*) gronder
Bellowing, *s.* beuglement, *m.*; (*of the sea*, &c.) mugissement, *m.*; (*of thunder*) grondement, *m.*
Bellows, *s. pl.* soufflet, *m.*; (*of steam-eng.*) ventilateur, *m.* *A pair of* —, un soufflet, *m.* — **chamber**, *s.* (*of an organ*) loge, *f.* — **fish**, *s.* *V.* **Trumpet-fish**. — **maker**, *s.* souffletier, *m.*
Belluine, *adj.* belluaire
Belly, *s.* ventre, *m.*; (*of a bottle*) ventre, *m.*, panse, *f.*; (*of a violin*, &c.) table, *f.* — *v.n.* faire le ventre, bomber; se gonfler, s'enfler. *The — and the Members*, (*Fable*) les Membres et l'Estomac. — **ache**, *s.* mal au ventre, *m.*, colique, *f.* — **band**, *s.* (*of harness*) sous-ventrière, *f.*; (*of saddles*) sangle, *f.* — **bound**, *adj.* constipé. — **ful**, *s.* soûl, *m.* — **pinched**, *adj.* affamé
Belong, *v.n.* appartenir (à), être (à); (*be a member or native or inhabitant of*) être (de)
Belongings, *s. pl.* effets, *m.pl.*; accessoires, *m.pl.*; dépendances, *f.pl.*
Beloved, *adj.* bien-aimé, chéri, adoré
Below, *prep.* sous; au-dessous de; indigne de; (*later than*) après; (*navig*) en aval de; — *adv.* en bas; (*down there*) là-bas; (*under*) au-dessous, dessous; (*hereafter*) plus bas, ci-dessous; (*following*) suivant, ci-dessous; (*here —, in this world*) ici-bas; (*navig.*) en aval. — *it, them* (*things*), au-dessous, dessous
Belt, *s.* ceinturon, *m.*; ceinture, *f.*; (*fig.*) ceinture, *f.*; (*of shoulders*) baudrier, *m.*; (*of machines*) courroie, *f.*; (*of land*) bande, *f.*; (*surg.*) bandage, *m.*, ceinture, *f.*; (*arch.*) guirlande, *f.*; — *v.a.* ceindre; (*on the shoulders*) attacher *or* passer en sautoir. — **maker**, *s.* ceinturier, *m.* — **strap**, *s.* allonge de ceinturon, *f.*
Belvedere, Belvidere, *s.* belvédère, *m.*
Bemire, *v.a.* embourber; (*cover with mud*) crotter, embouer
Bemoan, *v.a.* gémir sur, déplorer, pleurer
Bemoaning, *s.* lamentation, *f.*
Ben, *s.* ben, *m.* — **nut**, *s.* noix de ben, *f.* — **oil**, *s.* huile de ben, *f.*
Bench, *s.* banc, *m.*; (*with a stuffed seat*) banquette, *f.*; (*in tiers*) gradin, *m.*; (*of justice*) siége, *m.*; (*of judges*) cour, *f.*; (*of artisans*) établi, *m.*; — *v.a.* garnir de bancs; placer sur un banc *or* sur un siége. *King's* or *Queen's* —, (*in England*) banc du roi *or* de la reine, *m.*, cour royale, *f.* *Treasury —es*, bancs ministériels, *m.pl.* *To play to empty —es*, jouer devant (*or* pour) les banquettes. — **shears**, *s. pl.* cisoires, *f.pl.*
Bencher, *s.* conseiller (de l'ordre des avocats), *m.*; conservateur, *m.* [conservateur, *f.pl.*
Benchership, *s.* fonctions de conseiller *or* de
Bend, *v.a.* courber; plier; (*arch*) cambrer; (*out*

of shape) fausser; (*the knee*) fléchir; (*the brow*) froncer; (*stretch*) tendre, bander; (*a bow*) bander, tendre; (*the ear*) tendre; (*to direct*) diriger, appliquer (à), tourner (vers); (*incline*) pencher, incliner; (*a cable, nav.*) entalinguer. — *v n.* se courber; se plier, plier; (*of the knee*) fléchir; (*apply*) s'appliquer (à); (*incline*) se pencher; (*bow*) s'incliner; (*turn*) tourner; (*jut, overhang*) faire saillie, avancer, surplomber. — **away,** s'éloigner (peu à peu). — **back,** recourber; *v.n.* se recourber; (*incline*) se pencher en arrière. — **down,** courber; (*lower*) abaisser; *v.n.* se pencher; s'incliner. — **forward,** se pencher en avant. — **round,** recourber. — **up,** courber; cambrer

Bend, Bending, *s.* courbure, *f.*; flexion, *f.*; (*arching*) cambrure, *f.*; (*of roads, &c.*) coude, *m.*; (*fig.*) inclinaison, *f.*; (*of the back*) chute (des reins), *f.*; (*of the brow*) froncement, *m.*; (*her.*) bande, *f.*

Bendable, *adj.* courbable, flexible

Bender, *s.* (*spring*) ressort, *m.* [*V.* **Bend,** *s.*

Bending, *adj.* courbé; incliné; sinueux; — *s.*

Bendy, *adj.* (*her.*) bandé

Beneath. *V.* **Below**

Benedict, *s.* homme marié, *m.*; nouveau marié, *m.* *To become a* —, se marier, faire une fin

Benedictine, *s. adj* bénédictin, *m.*, e, *f.*

Benediction, *s.* bénédiction, *f.*; (*thanks*) action de grâces, *f.*

Benefaction, *s.* bienfait, *m.*; œuvre de bienfaisance, *f.*; aumône, charité, *f.*; donation, *f.*

Benefactor, *s* bienfaiteur, *m.*

Benefactress, *s.* bienfaitrice, *f.*

Benefice, *s.* bénéfice, *m.*

Beneficed, *adj.* qui a un bénéfice. — **clergyman,** *s.* bénéficier, *m.*

Beneficence, *s.* bienfaisance, *f.*

Beneficent, *adj.* bienfaisant

Beneficently, *adv.* avec bienfaisance

Beneficial, *adj.* bienfaisant, salutaire (à); avantageux, profitable, utile (à)

Beneficially, *adv.* salutairement; avantageusement, utilement

Beneficialness, *s.* utilité, *f.*, bons effets, *m.pl.*

Beneficiary, *s.* bénéficiaire, *m.f.*; (*eccl.*) bénéficier, *m.*, -ière, *f.*; — *adj.* bénéficiaire

Benefit, *s.* bienfait, *m.*; bénéfice, bien, avantage, profit, *m.*; service, secours, *m.*; usage, *m.*; (*theat.*) représentation à bénéfice, *f.*, bénéfice, *m.* *For the — of,* pour le bien de; au profit de; au bénéfice de; dans l'intérêt de; (*theat.*) au bénéfice de. *To give a person the — of,* faire profiter quelqu'un de. —**night, -performance,** *s.* représentation à bénéfice, *f.* — **society,** *s.* association *or* société de secours mutuels, association *or* société mutuelle, *f.*

Benefit, *v.a.* faire du bien à; (*be useful*) profiter à, servir à; — *v.n.* profiter (de); gagner (à); se trouver bien (de)

Benevolence, *s.* bienveillance, bonté, *f.*; bienfaisance, charité, *f.*; aumône, *f.*; bienfait, *m.*

Benevolent, *adj.* bienveillant, bon; bienfaisant, charitable; de bienfaisance, de charité. — *society, institution,* société, institution de bienfaisance, *f.*

Benevolently, *adv.* bénévolement; avec bonté; avec bienfaisance, charitablement

Bengal, *s.* (*geog.*) le Bengale, *m.* — **light** *or* **fire,** *s.* feu de Bengale, *m.* — **stripes,** *s. pl.* cotonnade rayée, *f*

Bengalee, *adj.* bengali (*m.*, e, *f.*); — *s.* bengali, *m.*

Bengalese, *s.* Bengalais, *m.*, e, *f.*; — *adj.* bengalais, du Bengale

Bengali, *adj. s.* *V.* **Bengalee**

Bengaly, *s.* (*bird*) bengali, *m.*

Benighted, *adj.* anuité, surpris par la nuit; (*in darkness*) couvert *or* enveloppé de ténèbres, dans les ténèbres; (*unenlightened*) plongé dans les ténèbres; ignorant; croupissant (*To be* —, croupir dans l'ignorance)

Benign, Benignant, *adj.* bénin, bienfaisant; doux, bon, affable

Benignity, *s.* bénignité, *f.*; bienveillance, bonté, *f.*; (*gentleness*) douceur, *f.*

Benignly, Benignantly, *adv.* bénignement; avec bonté; avec douceur

Benison, *s.* bénédiction, *f.*

Benjamin, *s* (— *tree*) styrax-benjoin, belzof, *m.*; (*gum*) benjoin, *m.*

Bennet, *s.* benoîte, galiote, *f.*

Bent, *part. adj.* courbé, plié, &c. (*V.* **Bend,** *v.a.n.*); (*prone*) porté (à); (*applied*) appliqué (à); (*on*) fixé (sur), déterminé (à), décidé (à); — *s.* courbure, *f.*; (*fig.*) pli, *m.*; (*application*) tension, *f.*; (*inclination*) penchant, *m.*, inclination, *f.*; disposition, *f.*; tendance, *f.*; direction, tournure, *f.*; détermination, résolution, *f.* — **grass,** *s.* agrostide, *f.*

Benumb, *v.a.* engourdir

Benumbedness, Benumbing, Benumbment, *s.* engourdissement, *m.*

Benzine, *s.* benzine, benzole, *f.*

Benzoic, *adj.* benzoïque

Benzoin. *V.* **Benjamin**

Benzole, Benzoline, *s.* benzole, benzine, *f.*

Bepaint, *v.a.* peinturer, barbouiller

Bepepper, Beplaster, &c., *v.a.* *V.* **Pepper, Plaster,** &c., *v.a.*

Beplume, *v.a.* emplumer

Bepowder, *v.a.* *V.* **Powder,** *v.a.*

Bepraise, *v.a.* louanger

Bequeath, *v.a.* léguer, laisser par testament

Bequeather, *s.* légateur, *m.*, -trice, *f.*

Bequeathment, *s.* action de léguer, *f.*; legs, *m.*

Bequest, *s.* legs, *m.*

Berber, *s.* Berbère, *m.*

Berberry, Berbery, *s.* *V.* **Barberry**

Bereave, *v.a* priver (de); (*take away*) enlever (à), ravir (à)

Bereavement, *s.* privation, *f.*; perte, *f.*; vide, *m.*; solitude, *f.*, abandon, *m.* [seur, *m.*

Bereaver, *s.* spoliateur, *m.*, -trice, *f.*; ravis-

Bergamot, *s.* (*pear, citron*) bergamote, *f.*; (*tree*) bergamotier, *m.*; (*scent*) essence de bergamote, *f.*; (*snuff*) tabac à la bergamote, *m.*; (*tapestry*) bergame, *f.*

Bergander, *s.* tadorne, *m.*

Berhyme, *v.a.n.* rimailler

Berlin, *s.* (*geog.*) Berlin, *m.*; (*carriage*) berline, *f.* — **repository, -warehouse,** *s.* magasin de laine à broder, *m.* — **wool,** *s.* laine à broder, *f.* — **work,** *s.* broderie de laine, *f.*

Berliner, Berlinese, *s. adj.* Berlinois, *m.*, e, *f.*

Berm, Berme, *s.* berme, *f.*

Bernardine, *s. adj.* bernardin, *m.*, e, *f.*

Bernese, *s adj.* Bernois, *m.*, e, *f.*

Berried, *adj.* à baies

Berry, *s.* baie. *f.*, grain, *m.*; fève, *f.*; — *v.n.* porter *or* produire des baies. *Avignon —, French —, Persian —, yellow —,* graine d'Avignon, grenette, *f.* *Indian —,* coque du Levant, *f.* *Coffee in —ies,* café en grains. — **bearing,** *adj.* baccifère

Berth, *s.* (*nav.*) poste, *m.*; (*room*) case, *f.*; (*bed*) lit, *m.*; couchette, *f.*; (*place*) place, *f.*, emploi, poste, *m.*; (*ship's station*) évitage, *m.*, évitée, *f.*

Bertha, *s.* berthe, *f.*

Beryl, *s.* béryl, béril, *m.* [bouiller

Bescrawl, Bescribble, *v.a.* griffonner, bar-

Beseech, *v.a.* *V.* **Implore**

Beseecher, *s.* suppliant, *m.*, e, *f.*

Beseeching, *adj.* suppliant; — *s.* supplication, *f.*; supplications, instances, *f.pl.*

Beseechingly, *adv.* d'un air (*or* d'un ton) suppliant, instamment, avec instance

Beseem, *v.a.* convenir à

Beseeming, Beseemly, *adj.* convenable

Beseemingly, *adv.* convenablement

Beseemingness, *s.* bienséance, convenance, *f.*

Beset, *v.a.* obséder; assiéger, entourer; presser, serrer de près; embarrasser

Besetter, *s.* obsesseur, *m.*

Besetting, *adj.* obsesseur; (*usual*) habituel

Beshrew, *v.a.* maudire
Beside, Besides, *prep.* (*at the side of*) à côté de; auprès de; (*distinct from*) outre, en dehors de; (*out of*) hors de; (*except*) hors, excepté; — *adv.* d'ailleurs, de plus, en outre; (*other*) autre; (*beyond*) au-delà. — *it, them* (*things*), à côté, auprès. *To be — oneself with joy*, être fou (*m.*, folle, *f.*) de joie. — **that,** [*conj.* outre que
Besiege, *v.a.* assiéger
Besieged, *s.* assiégé, *m.*; — *part. adj.* assiégé
Besieger, *s.* assiégeant, *m.* [(*m.*, e, *f.*)
Besieging, *adj.* de siége; assiégeant
Besmear, *v.a.* barbouiller; (*soil*) salir, souiller
Besmirch, *v.a.* salir, tacher, souiller
Besmoke, *v.a.* enfumer; fumer
Besmut, *v.a.* noircir de suie
Besom, *s.* balai (de bouleau), *m.*
Besot, *v.a.* infatuer, assoter; abrutir, hébéter
Besottedly, *adv.* sottement, stupidement
Besottedness, *s.* abrutissement, *m.*; stupidité, *f.*
Bespangle, *v.a.* pailleter, orner de paillettes; (*make shine*) faire étinceler (de); (*make showy*) brillanter; (*dot*) parsemer (de) [noircir
Bespatter, *v.a.* éclabousser, crotter; (*blacken*)
Bespeak, *v.a.* annoncer, dénoter, montrer; (*order*) commander; (*ask for*) demander; (*engage*) retenir; (*secure*) s'assurer de; (*speak to*) parler à, s'adresser à
Bespeckle, Bespot, Bespread, Besprinkle, &c., *v.a.* *V.* **Speckle, Spot, Spread, Sprinkle,** &c., *v.a.*
Best, *adj.* meilleur, le meilleur; le mieux, mieux; (*finest*) plus beau; (*greatest*) plus grand; (*strongest*) plus fort; — *s.* mieux, le mieux, *m.*; — *adv.* mieux; le mieux; (*most*) plus. *At —*, au mieux; tout au mieux; au plus, tout au plus; à tout prendre. *The next —*, le meilleur après ... *To do o.'s —, to do the — one can*, faire de son mieux, faire le mieux que l'on peut, faire (tout) son possible. *To have the — of it*, avoir le dessus. *To make the — of*, tirer le meilleur parti de. *To make the — of o.'s way*, ne pas tarder à se rendre, aller en toute hâte, aller droit *or* tout droit. *To the — of o.'s ability*, de son mieux. *To the — of my belief*, à ce que je crois; autant que je sache. *To the — of my remembrance* or *recollection* or *memory*, autant que je puis m'en souvenir
Bestain, *v.a.* *V.* **Stain,** *v.a.*
Bestead, *v.a.* profiter à, servir à; traiter
Bestial, *adj.* bestial
Bestiality, *s.* bestialité, brutalité, *f.*
Bestialize, *v.a.* bestialiser, abrutir
Bestially, *adv.* bestialement
Bestink, *v.a.* empuantir, infecter, empester
Bestir, *v.a.* remuer, mettre en mouvement; agiter; exercer, employer, déployer. — **oneself,** *v.r.* se remuer, se donner du mouvement, agir; s'agiter; s'empresser
Bestow, *v.a.* accorder (à), donner (à); conférer (à), concéder (à); dispenser; employer (à), consacrer (à); diriger; (*hurl*) lancer
Bestowal, *s.* don, *m.*; dispensation, *f.*
Bestower, *s.* donateur, *m.*, -trice, *f.*, dispensa-
Bestrew, *v.a.* *V.* **Strew** [teur, *m.*, -trice, *f.*
Bestride, *v.a.* enjamber; enfourcher
Bestud, *v.a.* *V.* **Stud,** *v.a.*
Bet, *v.a.n.* parier; — *s.* *V.* **Wager,** *s.*
Betake oneself, *v.r.* se livrer (à), s'adonner (à); avoir recours (à), recourir (à); se retirer, se rendre; se réfugier; se mettre (à)
Betel, *s.* bétel, *m.* — **nut,** *s.* noix de bétel, *f.*
Bethink oneself, *v.r.* se rappeler; penser (à), songer (à), réfléchir (à), considérer; s'aviser (de); aviser (à). *To — oneself better*, se raviser
Betide, *v.a.* arriver à
Betimes, *adv.* *V.* **Early,** *adv.*
Betoken, *v.a.* marquer, désigner, indiquer; dénoter; annoncer, présager
Beton, *s.* (*mas.*) *V.* **Concrete**
Betony, *s.* bétoine, *f.*
Betray, *v.a.* trahir; livrer; vendre; (*deceive*) tromper; (*show*) révéler, déceler, accuser, montrer, laisser voir; indiquer; (*mislead*) entraîner, faire tomber
Betrayer, *s.* traître, *m.*, traitresse, *f.*
Betroth, *v.a.* fiancer
Betrothed, *adj. s.* fiancé, *m.*, e, *f.*
Betrothal, Betrothment, *s.* fiançailles, *f.pl.*
Better, *adj.* meilleur; (*finer*) plus beau; (*greater*) plus grand; (*stronger*) plus fort; — *s.* mieux, *m.*; (*pers.*) supérieur, *m.*, e, *f.* (—**s,** *pl.* supérieurs, ceux qui valent mieux que ..., gens au-dessus de ..., *m.pl.*); (*wagerer*) parieur, *m.*, -euse, *f.*; — *adv.* mieux; (*more*) plus; davantage; (*beyond*) au-delà. *A little —*, un peu meilleur; un peu mieux. *Little —*, ne ... guère meilleur; ne ... guère mieux. — *and —*, de mieux en mieux. *All the —*, d'autant mieux (que); tant mieux! *Far —, much —*, (*adj.*) bien meilleur, (*adv.*) beaucoup *or* bien mieux. *For — for worse*, vaille que vaille. *For the —*, en bien, en mieux. *So much the —*, tant mieux. *The — to*, pour mieux. *To be —*, être meilleur *or* &c.; (*better done*) être mieux; (*preferable, of superior quality*) valoir mieux; (*in better health*) se porter mieux, aller mieux; (*to be relieved*) être mieux. *To be the — for*, se trouver bien de. *To be the — for it*, (*ironically*) être bien avancé. *To be none the — for it*, n'en être pas plus avancé. *To get* (or *grow*) —, s'améliorer; (*in health*) aller mieux, se porter mieux; se remettre. *To get the —*, (*of a person*) prendre le dessus (sur); l'emporter (sur); persuader; (*of a thing*) se consoler (de); se rétablir (de); (*to master*) venir à bout (de), triompher (de), vaincre. *It is — (to ...)*, il vaut mieux (...), mieux vaut (...). *I had —*, je ferais mieux (de). *I thought — of it*, je me suis ravisé. *To think the — of*, estimer davantage
Better, *v.a.* améliorer; — *v.n.* s'améliorer. *To — oneself*, améliorer sa position *or* sa condition
Bettering, *s.* amélioration, *f.*
Betting, *s.* pari, *m.*; paris, *m.pl.*; — *adj.* parieur. — **club, -office, -room,** *s.* salon des courses, *m.* — **man,** *s.* parieur, *m.* — **woman,** *s.* [parieuse, *f.*
Bettor, *s.* parieur, *m.*, -euse, *f.*
Between, Betwixt, *prep.* entre; de; à; — *adv.* dans l'intervalle; entre les deux; — *adj.* intermédiaire. *Far —*, à de longs intervalles; à une grande distance. — **decks,** *s.* (*nav.*) entrepont, *m.* — *whiles*, dans l'intervalle; par intervalles. — *this and then*, d'ici là. — *this and to-morrow, and Monday* or &c., d'ici à demain, à lundi *or* &c. — *you and me, — ourselves, — us*, entre nous. *We bought them — us*, nous les avons achetés à nous deux (*or* à nous trois, &c.). *They shared it — them*, ils le partagèrent entre eux. *They ate it — them*, ils le mangèrent à eux deux (*or* à eux trois, &c.)
Beurré, *s.* beurré, *m.*
Bevel, Bevil, *s.* biseau, *m.*; (*instr.*) fausse équerre, *f.*; — *adj.* en biseau, de biais; (*of angles*) qui n'est pas droit; — *v.a.* biseauter, tailler en biseau *or* en biais, équarrir; — *v.n.* biaiser
Bevelling, *adj.* en biseau, de biais; — *s.* biseau, *m.*; (*cutting*) coupe en biseau, *f.*
Beverage, *s.* breuvage, *m.*, boisson, *f.*
Bevy, *s.* compagnie, *f.*; (*fig.*) troupe, *f.*
Bewail. *V.* **Moan**
Beware, *v.n.* se garder (de); (*look out*) prendre garde (à); (*distrust*) se défier (de)
Bewet, *v.a.* humecter, arroser, mouiller
Bewilder, *v.a.* égarer; (*confuse*) ahurir; effarer; embarrasser; (*enrapture*) transporter (de), ravir (de)
Bewilderment, *s.* égarement, *m.*; ahurissement, *m.*; effarement, *m.*; transport, *m.*
Bewitch, *v.a.* ensorceler; enchanter. *Water —ed*, (*weak tea*) lavasse, *f.*
Bewitcher, *s.* ensorceleur, *m.*, -euse, *f.*

Bewitchery, *s.* ensorcellement, *m.*
Bewitching, *adj.* ensorceleur enchanteur, séduisant; — *s.* ensorcellement, *m.*
Bewitchingly, *adv.* à ravir
Bewitchment, *s.* ensorcellement, *m.*
Bewray. *V.* **Betray**
Bey, *s.* bey, *m.*
Beylic, *s.* beylik, *m.*
Beyond, *prep.* au-delà de; (*above*) au-dessus de; (*fig.*) hors de la portée de; (*without*) hors de; sans; (*besides*) outre; (*farther than*) plus loin que; (*too far for*) trop loin (pour); — *adv.* au-delà; plus loin. — *it, them* (*things*), au-delà; plus loin. *To go — one,* aller plus loin que quelqu'un; surpasser quelqu'un; (*deceive*) tromper quelqu'un. *This is — me,* cela me passe
Bezel, *s.* chaton, *m.*; (*slanting edge*) biseau, *m.*
Bezoar, *s.* bézoard, *m.*
Bias, *s.* biais, *m.*; (*slope*) pente, *f.*; (*inclination*) penchant, *m.*, inclination, *f.*; tendance, direction, *f.*; (*aim*) but, objet, *m.*; (*prejudice*) préjugé, *m.*, prévention, *f.*; — *v.a.* faire pencher; influencer, prévenir [— *v.n.* buvoter
Bib, *s.* bavoir, *m.*, bavette, *f.*; (*fish*) tacaud, *m.*;
Bibacious, *adj.* bibace, adonné à la boisson
Bibacity, *s.* bibacité, *f.*
Bibber, *s.* buveur, *m.*, -euse, *f.*, buvoteur, *m.*, -euse, *f.*, biberon, *m.*, -ne, *f.* [babiller
Bibble-babble, *s.* babil, babillage, *m.*; — *v.n.*
Bible, *s.* bible, *f.* — **society,** *s.* société bibli- [que, *f.*
Biblical, *adj.* biblique
Bibliographer, *s.* bibliographe, *m.*
Bibliograph-ic, al, -ically, -y. *V.* page 3 § 1
Bibliolog-ic, al, -ically, -y. *V.* page 3, § 1
Bibliomania, *s.* bibliomanie, *f.*
Bibliomaniac, *s. adj.* bibliomane, *m.f.*
Bibliophile, *s.* bibliophile, *m.*
Bibliophilism, *s* bibliophilie, *f.*
Bibliophilist, *s.* bibliophile, *m.*
Bibliopolist, *s.* bibliopole, *m.*
Biblist, *s.* bibliste, *m.*
Bibulous, *adj.* qui boit; absorbant; spongieux
Bicarbonate, *s.* bicarbonate, *m.*
Bicephalous, *adj.* bicéphale
Biceps, *s.* biceps, *m.*
Bichord, *adj.* bicorde
Bichromate, *s.* bichromate, *m.* [cher
Bicker, *v.n.* se quereller; (*skirmish*) escarmou-
Bickering, *s.* picoterie, bisbille, *f.*; (*skirmishing*)
Bickern, *s.* bigorne, *f.* [escarmouche, *f.*
Bicolor, Bicoloured, *adj.* bicolore
Bicycle, *s.* bicycle, *m.*
Bid, *v.a.* commander (de), ordonner (de), dire (de); inviter (à), prier (de), demander (de); exhorter (à); recommander (de); (*to cause*) faire; (*good morning,* &c.) souhaiter, dire; (*of price*) offrir; mettre; — *v.n.* enchérir; — *s.* enchère, *f.* *Higher* —, surenchère, *f.* *Highest* —, plus forte enchère, *f.* *To — for,* enchérir, offrir un prix de, demander. *To — goodbye* (or *farewell*) *to,* dire adieu à; faire ses adieux à. *To — fair,* promettre (de); être en passe (de); donner des espérances
Bidder, *s.* enchérisseur, *m.*, -euse, *f.* *Highest* or *best* —, plus offrant, *m.*
Bidding, *s.* commandement, ordre, *m.*; invitation, prière, demande, *f.*; exhortation, *f.*; recommandation, *f.*; (*auction*) enchère, *f.*
Biddy, *s.* cocote, *f.*; (*woman*) bonne femme, *f.*
Bide, *v.n.* demeurer, habiter, résider; — *v.a.* endurer, subir, souffrir; (*wait for*) attendre
Bident, *s.* bident, *m.*
Bidental, Bidentate, *adj.* bidenté
Bidet, *s.* bidet, *m.*
Bidon, *s.* bidon, *m.*
Biennial, *adj.* biennal, bisannuel; (*bot.*) bisannuel; — *s.* plante bisannuelle, *f.*
Biennially, *adv.* tous les deux ans
Bier, *s.* bière, *f.*, cercueil, *m.*
Biestings, Biestlings, Biestnings. *V.* [**Beestings**
Biferous, *adj.* bifère
Biffin, *s.* pomme tapée, *f.*
Bifid, Bifidate, *adj.* bifide
Biflorate, Biflorous, *adj.* biflore
Bifold, *adj.* double
Bifurcate, *v.n.* se bifurquer
Bifurcate, Bifurcated, *adj.* bifurqué
Bifurcation, *s.* bifurcation, *f.*
Big, *adj.* gros; (*vast*) grand, vaste; (*tall*) grand; (*proud*) fier, haut; (*with young*) pleine (de); (*with child*) enceinte, grosse (de). — *with* (*fig.*) gros de. *To be — with expectations,* avoir de grandes espérances. *To be — with pride,* être enflé d'orgueil. *To look* —, avoir l'air fier, faire l'important. *To talk* —, débiter de grands mots, parler haut, faire du bruit; trancher du grand; faire l'important; (*haughtily*) parler avec hauteur, le prendre haut, (*threaten*) parler des grosses dents, menacer; (*bluster*) faire le rodomont. — **wig,** *s.* gros bonnet, matador, *m.*
Bigamic, *adj.* bigamique
Bigamist, *s.* bigame, *m.f.*
Bigamous, *adj.* bigame
Bigamy, *s.* bigamie, *f.*
Bigg, *s.* (*barley*) escourgeon, *m.*
Biggin, *s* (*cap*) béguin, *m.*; (*for coffee*) filtre à café, *m*, cafetière, *f.*, marabout, *m.*
Bight, *s.* (*bend*) coude, *m.*; (*bay*) baie, *f.*; (*of a rope*) rouleau, tour, *m.*, (*nav.*) cueille, glène, *f*, balant, double, *m.*
Bigly, *adv.* fièrement, hautainement
Bigness, *s.* grosseur, *f.*; grandeur, *f.*
Bignonia, *s.* bignone, bignonie, *f.*
Bigot, *s.* bigot, *m.*, e, *f.*, cagot, *m.*, e, *f.*; fanatique, *m.f.*
Bigoted, *adj.* bigot, cagot; fanatique
Bigotedly, *adv.* avec bigoterie; en fanatique
Bigotry, *s.* bigoterie, cagoterie, *f.*; fanatisme, *m.*
Bilander, *s.* bélandre, *f.*
Bilateral, *adj.* bilatéral
Bilberry, *s.* airelle, *f.*
Bilbo, *s.* rapière, *f.* —**es,** *pl.* fers, *m.pl.*
Bile, *s.* bile, *f.* — **duct,** *s.* conduit biliaire, *m.*
Bilge, *s.* *V.* **Bulge;** (*nav.*) petits fonds, *m.pl.*; — *v.a.* (*nav.*) crever, défoncer; — *v.n.* (*nav.*) crever, faire eau. — **water,** *s.* eau de la cale, *f.* — **ways,** *s. pl.* anguilles, coites, coittes, [couettes, *f.pl.*
Biliary, *adj.* biliaire
Bilingual, Bilinguous, *adj.* bilingue
Bilious, *adj.* bilieux [bilieuse, *f.*; bile, *f.*
Biliousness, *s.* état bilieux, *m.*; affection
Bilk, *v a.* frustrer; (*deceive*) tromper, flouer; — *s.* attrape, *f.*; flouerie, *f.*
Bill, *s.* (*of birds*) bec, *m.*; (*axe, hatchet*) hache, *f.*; (*hort.*) serpe, *f.*; croissant, *m.*; (*account*) note, *f.*, mémoire, *m.*; facture, *f.*; (*of eating-houses: reckoning*) addition, *f.*, (*paper itself*) carte à payer, carte, *f.*; (*of hotels*) note, *f.*; (*placard*) affiche, *f.*, placard, *m.*; (*for lodgings*) écriteau, *m.*; (*hand* —) prospectus, imprimé, *m.*; (*com.*) billet, effet, *m.*; valeur, *f.*; (— *of exchange*) lettre de change, *f.*; (*invoice*) facture, *f.*; (*theat.*) affiche, *f.*, programme, *m.* *V.* **Play;** (*law*) requête, demande, *f.*; (*parliam.*) projet de loi, *m.*, (*of England*) bill, *m.*; (*nav.*) patente, *f.* — *of costs,* état de frais, cahier des frais, *m.* — *of exchange,* lettre de change, *f.* — *of fare,* menu, *m.*; (*of eating-houses*) carte, *f.*; — *of fare for the day,* carte du jour. — *of health,* patente de santé, *f.* — *of indemnity,* bill d'indemnité, *m.* — *of indictment,* acte d'accusation, *m.* — *of lading,* connaissement, *m.* — *of mortality,* registre mortuaire, état de mortalité, *m.*, table de mortalité, *f.* — *of parcels,* facture, *f.* — *payable,* effet à payer, *m.* — *payable to bearer,* billet au porteur, *m.* — *payable on demand,* billet payable à présentation, *m.* — *payable at sight,* billet à vue, *m.* — *of rights,* déclaration des droits, *f.* *True* —, (*law*) arrêt d'accusation, arrêt de mise en accusation, *m.* *To find a true — against,* (*law*) prononcer la mise en accusation de. — **book,** *s.* carnet d'échéances, *m.* — **broker,** *s.* changeur, *m.*, -euse, *f.* — **case,** *s.*

portefeuille, *m.* — **discounter,** *s.* escompteur de billets, *m.* — **discounting,** *s.* escompte de billets, *m.* — **file,** *s.* pique-notes, *m.* — **frame,** *s.* porte-affiches, *m.* — **ful,** *s.* becquée, *f.* — **head,** *s.* (*com.*) en-tête de facture, *m.*; (*tech.*) bec-de-corbin, *m.* — **hook,** *s.* serpe, *f.*; faucillon, fauchet, *m.* — **poster, -sticker,** colleur d'affiches, afficheur, *m.* — **sticking, -posting,** *s.* affichage, *m.* *Stick no —s!* défense d'afficher [— *v.n.* se becqueter

Bill, *v.a.* afficher, placarder; (*cover*) placarder;

Billed, *adj.* à bec

Billet, *s.* (*note*) billet, *m.*; (*mil.*) billet de logement, *m.*; (*of wood*) bûche, *f.*, rondin, *m.*, billette, *f.*; (*her., arch.*) billette, *f.*; — *v.a.* délivrer des billets de logement à, billeter; loger; — *v.n.* loger — **doux,** *s.* billet doux, *m.*

Billeting, *s.* billetement, *m.*

Billiard, *adj.* de billard; — **s,** *s. pl.* billard, *m.* — **ball,** *s.* bille (de billard), *f.* — **cloth,** *s.* tapis de billard, *m.* — **cue,** *s.* queue de billard, *f.* — **cushion,** *s* bande de billard, *f.* — **maker,** *s.* fabricant de billards, billardier, *m.* — **marker,** *s.* marqueur, *m.*; garçon de billard, *m.* — **room,** *s.* salle de billard, *f.*, billard, *m.* — **stick,** *s.* queue de billard, *f.* — **table,** *s.* [billard, *m.*

Billicock. *V.* **Billycock**

Billingsgate, *s.* langage des halles, langage [grossier, *m.*

Billion, *s.* trillion, *m.*

Billon, *s.* billon, *m.*

Billow, *s.* vague, *f.*, flot, *m.*, houle, *f.*; — *v.n.* s'enfler en vagues

Billowy, *adj.* houleux, agité

Billycock hat, *s.* chapeau classique, *m.*

Billygoat, *s.* bouc, *m.* — **beard,** *s.* barbe de bouc, barbiche, *f.*

Biman, Bimane, *s.* bimane, *m.*

Bimanous, *adj.* bimane

Bimonthly, *adj.* bimensuel, de *or* de la quinzaine; — *adv.* deux fois par mois, tous les quinze jours

Bin, *s.* huche, *f.*, coffre, *m.*; caisse, *f.*; (*wine —*) porte-bouteilles, *m.*; cave, *f.*; — *v.a.* ranger, empiler

Binary, *adj.* binaire; — *s.* nombre binaire, *m.*

Bind, *v.a.* lier, attacher; (*with fetters*) garrotter; (*to bandage*) bander; (*fix*) assujettir; (*fasten*) serrer; (*detain*) retenir; (*hem*) border (de); (*oblige*) obliger, lier, engager; (*an apprentice*) mettre en apprentissage ('*to*,' chez); (*harden*) durcir; (*freeze*) glacer; (*of the bowels*) resserrer, constiper; (*books*) relier; — *v.n.* se lier; durcir; être obligatoire. *To be bound to*, être tenu de, être obligé à *or* de; devoir. *I will be bound!* j'en réponds! — **down,** lier, astreindre. — **from,** empêcher de. — **in,** entourer, resserrer. — **out,** mettre en apprentissage. — **over,** (*law*) contraindre à comparaître. — **up,** lier; enchaîner; (*a wound*) bander; (*fig.*) retenir, engager

Binder, *s.* lieur, *m.*, -euse, *f.*; (*of books*) relieur, *m.*, -euse, *f.*; (*agr.*) lieur, botteleur, *m.*; (*tie*) lien, *m.*, attache, bande, *f.*; (*build.*) attache, *f.*; (*med.*) astringent, *m.*

Bindery, *s.* atelier de reliure, *m.*

Binding, *adj.* obligatoire; (*confining*) assujettissant; (*med.*) astringent; — *s.* action de lier, *f.*; (*tie*) lien, *m.*, attache, *f.*; bandeau, *m.*; (*of books*) reliure, *f.*; (*of clothes*) galon, *m.*; bordure, *f.*; (*of hats*) bordure, *f.*, bord, *m.*; (*arch.*) enchevêtrure, *f.*; (*pers.*) relations, *f.pl.* — **joist,** *s.* solive d'enchevêtrure, *f.*, chevêtre, *m.*

Bindweed, *s.* liseron, *m*

Bine, *s.* sarment, *m.*

Binnacle, *s.* habitacle, *m.*

Binner, *s.* empileur, *m.*, -euse, *f.*

Binning, *s.* rangement, empilage, *m.*

Binocle, *s.* binocle, *m.*

Binocular, *adj.* binoculaire

Binomial, *s. adj.* binôme, *s.m.*, *adj. m.f.*

Biograph, *v.a.* biographier

Biographer, *s.* biographe, *m.*

Biograph-ic, al, -y. *V.* page 3, § 1

Biolog-ic, al, -ist, &c. *V.* page 3, § 1

Biparous, *adj.* bipare

Bipartite, *adj.* biparti, bipartite

Biped, *s. adj.* bipède, *s.m.*, *adj. m.f.*

Bipedal, *adj.* bipédal, bipède

Biphosphate, *s.* biphosphate, *m.*

Birch, *s.* bouleau, *m.*; (*rod*) verges, *f.pl.*, poignée de verges, *f.*; — *adj.* de bouleau; — *v.a.* fouetter, donner le fouet à. *To give the —*, donner des coups de verges à, donner le fouet à, fouetter. — **broom,** *s.* balai de bouleau, *m.* — **grove, -plantation,** *s.* boulaie, bouleraie, *f.* — **rod,** *s.* verges de bouleau, *f.pl.*, poignée de verges, *f.* — **tree,** *s.* bouleau, *m.*

Birchen, *adj.* de bouleau [fouet, *m.*

Birching, *s.* (des) coups de verges, *m.pl.*, (le)

Bird, *s.* oiseau, *m.*; — *v.n.* *V.* **Fowl,** *v.n.* *Newgate —*, *V.* **Gallows bird.** *To kill two —s with one stone*, faire d'une pierre deux coups. *A — in the hand is worth two in the bush*, un Tiens vaut mieux que deux Tu l'auras. *A little — told me*, (*fam.*) mon petit doigt me l'a dit. — **cage,** *s* cage d'oiseau, *f.* — **cake,** *s.* colifichet, biscuit, *m.* — **call,** *s.* appeau, pipeau, *m.* — **catcher,** *s.* oiseleur, *m.* — **catching,** *s.* oisellerie, *f.* — **cherry,** *s.* putiet, putier, *m.* — **dealer,** *s.* *V.* — **seller.** — **eyed,** *adj.* qui a la vue perçante. — **fancier,** *s.* amateur d'oiseaux, *m.*; (*dealer*) oiselier, *m.* — **like,** *adj.* d'oiseau, semblable à un oiseau. — **lime,** *s.* glu, *f.* — **limed,** *adj.* enduit de glu. — **man,** *s.* oiseleur, *m.* — **nester,** *s.* *V.* —**s'-nester.** — **organ,** *s.* serinette, *f.* — **pepper,** *s.* piment enragé, *m.* — **seed,** *s.* graine pour les oiseaux, *f.* — **seller,** *s.* oiselier, marchand d'oiseaux, *m.* — **selling,** *s.* oisellerie, *f.* —**'s-eye,** *adj.* à vue d'oiseau. —**'s-eye view,** *s.* vue à vol d'oiseau, *f.*, plan à vue d'oiseau, *m.*; (*of* ...), ... à vol d'oiseau. —**'s-foot,** *s.* (*bot.*) pied d'oiseau, ornithope, *m.* — **snarer,** *s.* oiseleur, *m.* —**'s nest,** *s.* nid d'oiseau, *m.*; —**s'-nest,** *v.n.* dénicher des oiseaux. *To go —s'-nesting*, dénicher des oiseaux. —**s'-nester,** *s.* dénicheur (*m.*, -euse, *f.*) d'oiseaux. —**'s-tongue,** *s.* (*bot.*) langue d'oiseau, *f.* — **stuffer,** *s.* empailleur, *m.* — **trap,** *s.* piége pour les oiseaux, trébuchet, *m.*, [raquette, *f.*

Birding, *s.* *V.* **Fowling**

Birman, *s. adj.* Birman, *m.*, e, *f.*

Birr. *V.* **Whirr**

Birth, *s.* naissance, *f.*; (*fig.*) enfantement, *m.*, origine, source, *f.*, commencement, *m.*, naissance, *f.*; (*child-bed*) couches, *f.pl.*; (*things born*) fruit, *m.*; (*of animals*) petits, *m.pl.*, portée, *f.*; (*berth*) *V.* **Berth.** *By —*, de naissance. *To have ... at a —*, accoucher de ...; (*of animals*) mettre bas ... *To give — to*, donner naissance à, donner le jour à; (*fig.*) faire naître, donner lieu à, occasionner. — **day,** *s.* jour de naissance, *m.*; anniversaire de la naissance, *m.*; fête, *f.*; *adj.* de fête. — **less,** *adj.* sans naissance. — **mark,** *s.* *V.* **Nævus.** — **night,** *s.* nuit de la naissance, *f.*; nuit (*or* fête) de l'anniversaire de la naissance, *f.* — **place,** *s.* lieu de naissance, *m.* — **right,** *s.* droit de naissance, *m.*; (*of primogeniture*) droit d'aînesse, *m.*; (*patrimony*) patrimoine, *m.* — **star,** *s.* étoile, *f.* — **wort,** *s.* aristoloche, *f.*

Bis, *adv.* bis

Biscayan, *s.adj.* Biscayen, *m.*, -ne, *f.*, Basque, *m f.*

Biscotin, *s.* biscotin, *m.*

Biscuit, *s.* biscuit, *m.* — **baker,** *s.* pâtissier, *m.*, -ière, *f.* — **bakery, -baking,** *s.* biscuiterie, pâtisserie, *f.* — **business, -making, -manufactory, -trade, -works,** *s.* biscuiterie, *f.* — **manufacturer,** *s.* fabricant de biscuits, *m.* — **root,** *s.* camassie, *f.* *Bread and — baker*, boulanger-pâtissier, *m.*

Bisect, *v a.* diviser en deux

Bisection, *s.* bissection, *f.*

Bisexous, Bisexual, *adj.* bissexuel

Bishop, *s.* évêque, *m.*; (*liquor*) bischof, bishop,

m.; (*chess* fou, *m.*; (*of a fowl*) mitre, *f.*, bonnet d'évêque, *m.*; — *v.a.* maquignonner. —*'s palace* or *house*, évêché, *m.*
Bishoping, *s.* maquignonnage, *m.*
Bishopric, *s.* évêché, *m.*
Bisk, *s.* bisque, *f.*
Bismuth, *s.* bismuth, *m.*
Bison, *s.* bison, *m.*
Bissextile, *s.* (*year*) année bissextile, *f.*, an bissextil, *m.*; (*day*) bissexte, *m.*; — *adj.* bissextil
Bisslings, Bissnings, Bisstings. *V.* **Beestings**
Bister. *V.* **Bistre**
Bistort, *s.* bistorte, *f.*
Bistoury, *s.* bistouri, *m.*
Bistre, *s.* bistre, *m.* — **coloured,** *adj.* bistré
Bisulphate, *s.* bisulfate, *m.*
Bisulphide, *s.* bisulfure, *m.*
Bisulphite, *s.* bisulfite, *m.*
Bit, *s.* morceau, *m.*; (*fam.*) brin, bout, *m.*; quantité, *f.*; (*of time*) minute, seconde, *f.*; (*distance*) bout de chemin, *m.*, distance, *f.*; (*of thread*) bout, *m.*; (*a little*) peu, *m.*, tant soit peu, *m.*; (*jot*) idée, *f.*; (*mouthful*) bouchée, *f.*; (*of bridle*) mors, frein, *m.*; (*of wimbles, augers,* &c.) mèche, *f.*; (*of keys*) panneton, *m.*; (*nav.*) *V.* **Bitt**; — *v.a.* emboucher; (*nav.*) *V.* **Bitt.** — *by* —, pièce à pièce. *Every — of it,* en entier. *Not a —, not a — of it,* (*not at all*) pas du tout, pas le moins du monde
Bitartrate, *s.* bitartrate, *m.*
Bitch, *s.* chienne, *f.*; (*in compounds*) femelle, *f.*; (*pers.*) chienne, *f.*; rosse, *f.*
Bite, *v.a.* mordre; (*gnaw*) ronger; (*pinch*) pincer; (*cut*) couper; (*sting*) piquer; (*offend*) piquer, blesser; (*cheat*) attraper, duper, tromper, prendre, mettre dedans; (*catch*) attraper, pincer; (*the cartridge, in the olden mil. fashion*) déchirer (la cartouche); — *s.* morsure, *f.*; coup de dent, *m.*; (*sting*) piqûre, *f.*; (*mouthful*) bouchée, *f.*; (*trick*) attrape, *f.*, piége, *m.* — **away,** *v.a.* ronger. — **off,** *v.a.* emporter *or* arracher *or* déchirer *or* enlever (avec les dents *or* d'un coup de dent)
Biter, *s.* mordeur, *m.*, -euse, *f.*; (*cheat*) trompeur, [*m.*, -euse, *f.*
Biting, *s.* *V.* **Bite,** *s.*; — *part. adj.* mordant; (*cutting, sharp*) coupant; (*stinging*) piquant
Bitingly, *adv.* d'une manière mordante *or* [piquante
Bitt, *s.* (*nav.*) bitte, *f.*; — *v.a.* bitter
Bittacle, *s.* (*nav.*) habitacle, *m.*
Bitter, *adj.* amer; (*sour*) aigre; (*keen*) piquant, mordant; (*cruel*) cruel, acharné; terrible, affreux; rude, rigoureux; (*of wine*) poussé; —**s,** *s. pl.* bitter, *m.*, absinthe, *f.*, vermout, *m.*; (*pharm.*) amers, *m.pl.* *To get* —, devenir amer *or* &c.; (*of wine*) pousser. — **sweet,** *s.* douce-amère, *f.* — **wort,** *s.* gentiane, *f.*
Bitterish, *adj.* un peu amer
Bitterishness, *s.* légère amertume, *f.*
Bitterly, *adv.* amèrement; avec amertume; aigrement; cruellement; (*of the cold*) extrêmement [mère, *f.*
Bittern, *s.* (*bird*) butor, *m.*; (*bitter liquid*) eau
Bitterness, *s.* amertume, *f.*; fiel, *m.*; aigreur, *f.*; sévérité, *f.*; causticité, *f.*; acharnement, *m.*; (*disease of wine*) pousse, *f.*
Bitumen, *s.* bitume, *m.*
Bituminate, *v.a.* bitumer, bituminer
Bituminiferous, *adj.* bituminifère
Bituminization, *s.* bituminisation, *f.*
Bituminize, *v.a.* bituminiser
Bituminous, *adj.* bitumineux
Bivalve, *adj. s.* bivalve, *adj. m.f.*, *s.m.*
Bivalved, *adj.* bivalve
Bivouac, *s.* bivouac, bivac, *m.*; — *v.n.* bivouaquer, bivaquer
Biweekly, *adv.* deux fois par semaine
B.L., bachelier en droit, *m.*
Blab, *v.n.* bavarder, jaser; — *v.a.* conter; répéter; jaser de; divulguer, révéler; — *s.* bavard, *m.*, e, *f.*, jaseur, *m.*, -euse, *f.*
Blabber, *s.* *V.* **Blab,** *s.*
Blabbing, *adj.* bavard; — *s.* bavardage, *m.*
Black, *adj.* noir; obscur; sombre; triste; horrible, atroce; — *s.* noir, *m.*; (*pers.*) noir, *m.*, e, *f.*, nègre, *m.*, négresse, *f.*; —**s,** *pl.* (*smuts, soot*) noirs, *m.pl.*, particules de suie, *f.pl.*, suie, *f.*; (*negroes*) noirs, *m.pl.*; — *v.a.* noircir; (*boots*) cirer. — *and blue,* noir, bleu, meurtri; (*of eyes*) poché; (*s.*) meurtrissure, *f.*, noir, *m.* *In — and white,* (*printed*) imprimé; (*in writing*) par écrit; (*in full*) en toutes lettres. *To beat — and blue,* meurtrir de coups. *To be — and blue all over,* être tout meurtri *or* tout meurtri de coups. *To look* —, (*pers.*) avoir l'air sombre; regarder de travers *or* de mauvais œil. *To make* — noircir. — **amoor,** *s.* nègre, noir, More, *m.*, moricaud, *m.*, e, *f.* — **art,** *s.* *V.* **Art.** — **ball,** *s.* (*of blacking*) boule de cirage, *f.*; (*for voting*) boule noire, *f.*; *v.a.* rejeter; (*fig.*) noircir, diffamer. — **balling,** *s.* rejet, *m.*; diffamation, *f.* — **beetle,** *s.* *V.* **Beetle.** — **berry,** *s.* mûre sauvage, mûre de ronce, mûre de haie, mûre, *f.* — **berry-bush,** *s.* mûrier sauvage, *m.*, ronce, *f.* — **bird,** *s.* merle, *m.* — **blue,** *s.* bleu de roi, *m.* — **board,** *s.* tableau, *m.* — **book,** *s.* (*schools*) cahier de rapports, *m.*; (*mil.*) registre des punitions, *m.*; (*sorcery*) livre de magie, grimoire, *m.* — **cap,** *s.* bonnet noir, *m.*, toque noire, *f.*, &c. (*V.* **Cap**); (*bird*) fauvette à tête noire, *f.*; (*apple*) pomme noircie au feu, *f.* — **cattle,** *s.* gros bétail, *m.* — **cock,** *s.* coq de bruyère, *m.* — **currant, -currants -currant bush** *or* **tree, -currant wine,** cassis, *m.* — **death,** *s.* peste, *f.* — **draught,** *s.* médecine noire, *f.* — **drops,** *s. pl.* gouttes noires, *f.pl.* — **earth,** *s.* terreau, *m.* — **eye,** *s.* œil noir, *m.*; (*bruised*) œil poché, *m.*; pochon (*or* coup de poing) sur l'œil, *m.* (*For phrases, V.* **Eye**). — **eyed,** *adj.* aux yeux noirs. — **faced,** *adj.* au visage noir. — **Forest,** *s.* (la) Forêt-Noire, *f.* — **friar,** *s.* dominicain, *m.* — **game,** *s.* coq de bruyère, *m.* — **grape,** *s.* morillon, *m.* — **guard,** &c. *See below.* — **heart cherry,** *s.* guigne, *f.* — **heart cherry-tree,** *s.* guignier, *m.* — **hearted,** *adj.* au cœur noir. — **hole,** *s.* cul-de-basse-fosse, cachot, cabanon, *m.* — **jack,** *s.* blende, *f.* — **lead,** *s.* mine de plomb, plombagine, *f.* — **leg,** *s.* grec, escroc, *m.* — **letter,** *s.* lettre gothique, *f.*, gothique, *m.* — **lines,** *s. pl.* *V.* **Lines.** — **mail,** *s.* tribut illicite, *m.*, extorsion, *f.*; (*Engl. hist.*) black-mail, *m.*, maille noire, *f.* — **Monday,** *s.* lundi de Pâques, *m.*; (*in schools*) jour de la rentrée, *m.* — **nun,** *s.* dominicaine, *f.* — **rod,** *s.* huissier à verge noire, *m.* — **rust,** *s.* *V.* **Rust.** — **Sea,** *s.* (la) Mer Noire, *f.* — **sheep,** *s.* (*fig.*) brebis galeuse, *f.* — **smith,** *s.* forgeron, *m.* — **smith's shop,** *s.* forge, *f.* — **thorn,** *s.* épine noire, *f.*, prunellier, *m.* — **work,** *s.* fer forgé, *m.*
Blacken, *v.a.* noircir; obscurcir; (*a pipe*) culotter; — *v.n.* noircir, se noircir, devenir [noir; se culotter
Blackey. *V.* **Blacky**
Blackguard, *s.* polisson, *m.*, -ne, *f.*, gredin, *m.*, e, *f.*, drôle, galopin, voyou, goujat, *m.*, canaille, *f.*; arsouille, *m.f.*
Blackguard, Blackguardly, *adj.* ignoble, sale, canaille; arsouille; polisson de …
Blackguardism, *s.* polissonnerie, *f.*
Blacking, *s.* noircissement, *m.*; (*of or for boots,* &c.) cirage, *m.* — **brush,** *s.* brosse à [cirer, *f.*
Blackish, *adj.* noirâtre
Blackishness, *s.* couleur *or* teinte noirâtre, *f.*
Blackly, *adv.* avec noirceur
Blackness, *s.* noirceur, *f.*
Blacky, *s.* noiraud, *m.*, e, *f.*, moricaud, *m.*, e, *f.*, négrillon, *m.*, -ne, *f.*
Bladder, *s.* vessie, *f.*; (*fig.*) bulle, *f.*; ampoule, *f.*; (*bot.*) vésicule, *f.* — **nut, -tree,** *s.* staphylier, *m.* — **senna,** *s.* baguenaudier, *m.* — **senna pod,** *s.* baguenaude, claque, *f.* — **wort,** *s.* utriculaire, *f.*
Bladdered, *adj.* gonflé, enflé
Bladdery, *adj.* vésiculaire, vésiculeux; qui contient des vessies; gonflé, enflé

Blade, *s.* (*of grass*, &c.) brin, *m.*; (*of corn*) feuille, pampe, fiole, *f.*; (*of knives, swords*, &c.) lame, *f.*; (*poet. for 'sword'*) épée, *f.*, fer, *m.*; (*pers.*) gaillard, compère, compagnon, luron, *m.*; (*of oars*) plat, *m.*; — *v.a.* garnir d'une lame, mettre une lame à. — *of the shoulder*, omoplate, *f.* *Cunning* —, rusé compère, fin matois, *m.* *Jolly* —, joyeux compagnon *or* compère. *Old* —, vieux routier, *m.* *Young* —, jeune luron, *m.* — **bone,** *s.* omoplate, *f.*

Bladed, *adj.* à feuilles; (*of knives*, &c.) garni d'une lame, à lame, à lames; (*min.*) lamellé. *Two-* —, à deux lames

Blain, *s.* pustule, tumeur, *f.*

Blamable, *adj.* blâmable

Blamableness, *s.* nature blâmable, *f.*

Blamably, *adv.* d'une manière blâmable

Blame, *v.a.* blâmer; censurer; accuser (de); s'en prendre à; — *s.* blâme, *m.*; faute, *f.*; accusation, *f.* *To lay the* — *on*, rejeter le blâme sur; s'en prendre à. —**less,** *adj.* exempt de blâme, sans reproche, irréprochable, irrépréhensible; innocent; (*pure*) sans tache. —**lessly,** *adv.* irréprochablement. —**worthiness,** *s.* démérite, *m.* — **worthy,** *adj.* digne de blâme, blâmable

Blamer, *s.* désapprobateur, *m.*, -trice, *f.*, censeur, critique, *m.*

Blanch, *v.a.* blanchir; (*make pale*) pâlir, faire pâlir; (*peel*) peler; (*cook.*, *hort.*) blanchir; (*evade*) éviter, éluder; — *v.n.* blanchir; pâlir; biaiser; hésiter

Blancher, *s.* blanchisseur, *m.*, -euse, *f.*

Blanching, *s.* blanchiment, *m.*

Blanc-mange, Blanc-manger, *s.* blanc-manger, *m.*

Bland, *adj.* doux, aimable; (*in a bad sense*) doucereux, mielleux

Blandiloquence, *s.* langage flatteur, *m.*, douces paroles, *f.pl.*

Blandish, *v.a.* caresser, cajoler, flatter

Blandishment, *s.* caresse, *f.*; charme, attrait, *m.*

Blandness, *s.* douceur, affabilité, *f.*

Blank, *adj.* blanc, en blanc; pâle, décontenancé; (*empty*) vide; (*of verse*) blanc; (*of cartridges*) à blanc, à poudre, sans balle; (*of doors, windows*) faux; — *s.* blanc, *m.*; (*blank paper*) papier blanc, *m.*; (*of lotteries*) billet blanc, *m.*; (*gap*) vide, *m.*, lacune, *f.*; (*of the mind*) table rase, *f.*; (*coin.*) flan, *m.* — **cartridge,** *s.* cartouche à blanc, *f.* *To fire with* — *cartridge or cartridges*, tirer à blanc. — **firing,** *s.* tir à blanc, *m.* — **verse,** *s.* vers blanc, *m.*, vers blancs, *m.pl.*

Blanket, *s.* (*of bed*) couverture, *f.*; (*print.*) blanchet, *m.*; (*pear*) blanquet, *m.*, blanquette, *f.*; — *v.a.* (*toss*) berner; (*cover*) envelopper d'une couverture. *Wet* —, (*fig.*) rabat-joie, trouble-fête, *m.* *To toss in a* —, berner. — **maker,** *s.* couverturier, *m.*

Blanketing, *s.* couvertures, *f.pl.*; (*tossing*) bernement, *m.*

Blankness, *s.* blancheur, pâleur; *f.*; vide, *m.*; confusion, *f.*

Blanquette, *s.* blanquette, *f.*

Blare, *v.n.* sonner, retentir; rugir; — *s.* son, bruit, éclat, *m.*; rugissement, *m.*

Blarney, *s.* (*smooth talk*) eau bénite de cour, *f.*; râpe douce, *f.*; monnaie de singe, *f.*; (*flattery*) coups d'encensoir, *m.pl.*, flagornerie, *f.*; (*wonderful tale, idle talk*) blague, *f.*; — *v.a.* donner de l'eau bénite de cour (*or* de la râpe douce) à; payer en monnaie de singe; flagorner; blaguer

Blaspheme, *v.a.n.* blasphémer

Blasphemer, *s.* blasphémateur, *m.*, -trice, *f.*

Blasphemous, *adj.* blasphémateur, blasphématoire

Blasphemously, *adv.* avec blasphème

Blasphemy, *s.* blasphème, *m.*

Blast, *s.* souffle, *m.*; (*of wind, air*) vent, coup de vent, *m.*; courant d'air, *m.*; (*of wind-instruments*) son, *m.*; (*pestilence*) vent pestilentiel, souffle destructeur, *m.*, influence funeste, *f.*; (*blight*) nielle, brouissure, *f.*; (*of powder*) explosion, *f.*; (*mec.*) échappement, *m.* — **engine,** *s.* machine soufflante, *f.* — **furnace,** *s.* haut-fourneau, *m.* — **pipe,** tuyère, *f.*; (*of engines*) tuyau d'échappement, *m.*

Blast, *v.a.* flétrir; (*to dry*) dessécher; brûler; (*fig.*) détruire, ruiner; confondre; frapper; (*with powder*) faire sauter

Blasted, *part. adj.* flétri, &c. (*V.* **Blast,** *v.a.*): (*cursed*) maudit, fichu

Blasting, *adj.* destructeur; — *s.* destruction, ruine, *f.*; explosion, *f.* — **powder,** *s.* poudre de mine, *f.*

Blatant, *adj.* beuglant; bruyant; pompeux, ronflant

Blay, *s.* able, *m.*, ablette, *f.*

Blaze, *s.* flamme, *f.*; (*fig.*) feu, *m.*; (*light*) lumière, *f.*, éclat, *m.*; (*noise*) bruit, *m.*; (*white spot*) étoile, *f.*, (*of horses*) étoile, pelote, *f.* *In a* —, *V.* **Ablaze.** *Like* —*s*, à outrance, furieusement, terriblement. *To go to* —*s*, aller au diable

Blaze, *v.n.* être en flammes; (*to flame*) flamber, flamboyer, jeter des flammes; (*shine*) briller, briller d'un vif éclat, jeter un vif éclat; — *v.a.* faire briller; (*spread*) publier, répandre; (*mark*) blanchir; étoiler. — **forth,** *v.n.* éclater; *v.a.* faire éclater; proclamer. — **out,** éclater. — **up,** s'enflammer

Blazing, *adj.* enflammé; embrasé; flamboyant; (*shining*) brillant, étincelant; éclatant; radieux; — *s.* flamboiement, *m.*

Blazon, *s.* blason, *m.*; (*fig.*) éclat, *m.*; — *v.a.* blasonner; armorier; (*fig.*) peindre; embellir, orner; publier, proclamer; célébrer; exalter. *To* — **forth,** faire briller; publier, proclamer; célébrer; exalter

Blazoner, *s.* blasonneur, armoriste, *m.*

Blazoning, *s.* blasonnement, *m.*

Blazonry, *s.* blason, *m.*; blasonnement, *m.*

Blea, *s.* aubier, *m.*

Bleach, *v.a.n.* blanchir. — **field, -works, -yard,** *s.* blanchisserie, *f.*

Bleached, *part. adj.* blanchi; blanc

Bleacher, *s.* blanchisseur, *m.*, -euse, *f.*

Bleachery, *s.* blanchisserie, *f.*

Bleaching, *s.* blanchiment, blanchissage, *m.* — **ground, -works,** *s.* blanchisserie, *f.* — **liquid,** *s.* eau de javelle, *f.*

Bleak, *adj.* froid; triste; ouvert; désert; — *s.* aubier, *m.*; (*fish*) able, *m.*, ablette, *f.*

Bleakish, *adj.* un peu froid, assez triste *or* &c. (*V.* **Bleak**)

Bleakly, *adv.* froidement; tristement

Bleakness, *s.* froidure, *f.*, froid, *m.*; tristesse, *f.*

Blear, *adj.* chassieux; — *v.a.* rendre chassieux; (*fig.*) troubler. — **eye, -eyedness,** *s.* (*med.*) lippitude, *f.* — **eyed,** *adj.* chassieux

Bleared, *adj.* chassieux

Blearedness, *s.* (*med.*) lippitude, *f.*

Bleat, *v.n.* bêler; — *s.* bêlement, *m.*

Bleating, *adj.* bêlant; — *s.* bêlement, *m.*

Bleb, *s.* (*med.*) bulle, ampoule, *f.*

Bleed, *v.a.n.* saigner; (*die*) périr; (*drop*) couler, dégoutter; (*of vines*) pleurer; (*pay*) cracher

Bleeding, *adj.* saignant; (*broken*) navré; — *s.* saignement, *m.*; (*surg.*) saignée, *f.*

Blemish, *v.a.* défigurer; (*fig.*) tacher, ternir, flétrir; — *s.* défaut, *m.*; (*stain*) tache, *f.*

Blench, *v.n.* reculer; hésiter; sourciller

Blend, *v.a.* fondre; (*mix*) mêler, réunir, confondre, marier, allier (à *or* avec); (*draw., engr.*) grener; — *v.n.* se fondre; (*mix*) se mêler, se confondre, se marier, s'allier (à *or* avec); (*draw., engr.*) grener; — *s.* *V.* **Blending**

Blende, *s.* (*min.*) blende, *f.*

Blender, *s.* (*paint.*) blaireau, *m.*

Blending, *s.* fusion, *f.*; (*mixture*) mélange, *m.*, alliance, *f.*; (*draw., engr.*) grenure, *f.*

Blenheim dog *or* **spaniel,** *s.* pyrame, *m.*

Blennorrhagia, *s.* blennorrhagie, *f.*

Blennorrhœa, *s.* blennorrhée, *f.*

Blenny, *s.* blenne, blennie, *m.*

Bless, *v.a.* bénir; (*make happy*) rendre heureux, faire le bonheur de; (*charm*) charmer, réjouir. *To* — *with*, accorder; douer de; favoriser de. *To be* —*ed with*, avoir le bonheur d'avoir; être doué de; jouir de. — *me!* — *my heart!* —

my soul! — you! — your soul! Dieu! mon Dieu! oh, mon Dieu! par exemple! sapristi! vraiment! *I'm —ed, I'll be —ed,* (*pop.*) que le bon Dieu me patafiole, que le diable me patafiole *or* m'emporte, du diable (si). — *the fellow!* que le bon Dieu (*or* le diable) le patafiole! *God — you!* Dieu vous bénisse!

Blessable, *adj.* bénissable

Blessed, *adj.* béni; saint; (*happy*) heureux; bienheureux; (*beloved*) chéri; (*ironically*) fichu. *V.* **Bless,** *v.a. The — Virgin,* la Sainte Vierge, *f. All the — day,* toute la sainte journée

Blessedly, *adv.* heureusement

Blessedness, *s.* félicité, *f.*; bonheur, *m.*

Blesser, *s.* bénisseur, *m.*, -euse, *f.*

Blessing, *s.* bénédiction, *f.*; (*prayer*) bénédicité, *m.*; (*happiness*) bonheur, *m.*; jouissance, joie, *f.*; (*gift*) grâce, *f.*, bienfait, *m.*; (*advantage*) bien, *m.*; (*offering*) offrande, *f.*

Blest. *V.* **Blessed**

Bleyme, *s.* bleime, *f.*

Blight, *s.* (*of fruit, flowers*) brouissure, *f.*; (*of plants*) nielle, rouille, *f.*; (*fig.*) peste, *f.*, souffle destructeur, mauvais air, *m.*; (*blemish*) flétrissure, tache, *f.*; — *v.a.* brouir, nieller, ravager, brûler; (*of the wind*) flétrir; (*destroy*) détruire, ruiner, anéantir, flétrir; étouffer

Blind, *adj.* aveugle ('*to*,' sur); (*dark*) obscur; (*hidden*) caché; (*closed*) fermé; sans issue; (*imperfect, abortive*) borgne; (*of doors, windows*) faux; (*of walls*) blanc, orbe; (*of wells*) perdu; (*of vessels*) qui n'a qu'une ouverture; (*not lighted*) qui n'est pas allumé; (*of coal*) qui brûle sans flamme. *The —,* les aveugles, *s.m.pl.* — **alley,** *s.* impasse, *f.* — **born,** *adj.* né aveugle; *s.* aveugle-né, *m.*, aveugle-née, *f.* — **gut,** *s.* (*anat.*) cæcum, *m.* — **man** *or* **boy,** *s.* aveugle, *m.* — **man's buff,** *s.* colin-maillard, *m.* — **side,** *s.* (*pers.*) côté faible, faible, *m.* — **story,** *s.* (*arch.*) triforium, *m.* — **woman** *or* **girl,** *s.* aveugle, *f.* — **worm,** *s.* aveugle, envoye, orvet, *m.* — **of one eye,** *adj. s.* borgne, *m.f.* *Born —,* né aveugle. *Child* or *person born —,* aveugle-né, *m.*, aveugle-née, *f.* *To be — to,* être aveugle sur, s'aveugler sur

Blind, *v.a.* aveugler ('*to*,' sur); (*cover the eyes*) bander les yeux à; (*darken*) obscurcir; embrouiller; éclipser; voiler; (*dazzle*) éblouir; (*mil.*) blinder. *To — of one eye,* éborgner

Blind, *s.* (*of windows*) jalousie, *f.*, (*outside shutter-blind*) persienne, *f.*, (*roller-blind*) store, *m.*, (*Spanish —, bonnet —*) abat-jour, *m.*; (*fig.*) voile, *m.*; masque, *m.*; (*fort.*) blinde, *f.* — **maker,** *s.* fabricant de stores, *m.* — **roller,** *s.* rouleau de store, *m.*

Blindage, *s.* blindage, *m.*

Blinder, *s.* (*rid.*) lunette, *f.*

Blindfold, *adj.* les yeux bandés, qui a les yeux bandés, qui a un bandeau sur les yeux; (*fig.*) les yeux fermés, aveuglément; aveugle; — *v.a.* bander les yeux à. *He was —ed,* il avait les yeux bandés; on lui banda les yeux

Blindfolded, *adj. V.* **Blindfold,** *adj.*

Blindly, *adv.* aveuglément, en aveugle

Blindness, *s.* cécité, *f.*; (*fig.*) aveuglement, *m.*; ignorance, *f.*

Blink, *v.n.* cligner, clignoter; (*fig.*) lorgner; (*of light*) vaciller; — *v.a.* offusquer; fermer les yeux sur, refuser de voir, se refuser à, se cacher; (*evade*) éluder; — *s.* clignement, clignotement, *m.*; (*of ice*) blancheur, clarté, *f.*; —**s,** *pl.* (*hunt.*) brisées, *f.pl.* — **eyed,** *adj.* qui [clignote

Blinker, *s.* (*of harness*) œillère, *f.*

Bliss, *s.* félicité, *f.*, bonheur, *m.*; béatitude, *f.*

Blissful, *adj.* heureux; bienheureux; délicieux

Blissfully, *adv.* dans la félicité, dans le bonheur, avec un parfait bonheur

Blissfulness. *V.* **Bliss**

Blissless, *adj.* malheureux, infortuné

Blister, *s.* ampoule, cloche, élevure, *f.*; (*surg.*) vésicatoire, *m.*; (*bot.*) pustule, *f.*; (*tech.*) bulle, *f.*; (*on a loaf of bread*) coquille, *f.*; (*of pottery*) bavure, *f.*; — *adj.* (*surg.*) *V.* **Blistering,** — *v.n.* se former en ampoule or &c.; se couvrir d'ampoules *or* &c.; (*of bread*) coquiller; — *v.a.* faire venir des ampoules *or* &c. à; (*of bread*) coquiller; (*surg.*) appliquer un vésicatoire à. — **fly,** *s.* cantharide, *f.* — **plaster,** *s.* emplâtre vésicatoire, *m.* — **steel,** *s.* acier poule, *m.*

Blistered, *adj.* ampoulé, couvert d'ampoules *or* &c.; pustuleux. — **steel,** *s.* acier poule, *m.*

Blistering, *adj.* à vésicatoire, vésicatoire, épispastique; — *s.* application de vésicatoires, *f.* — **fly,** &c. *V.* **Blister**

Blithe, Blithesome, *adj.* gai, joyeux

Blithely, Blithesomely, *adv.* gaîment, joyeusement

Blithesomeness, *s.* gaieté, joie, *f.*

Bloat, *v.a.n.* enfler, gonfler; bouffir; (*herrings*) fumer, saurer. —*ed herring,* hareng saur, *m.* —*ed aristocrat,* aristo, *m.*

Bloatedness, *s.* bouffissure, enflure, *f.*

Bloater, *s.* hareng saur, *m.*; (*at Dieppe*) hareng [bouffi, *m.*

Blobber, *s. V.* **Blubber**

Block, *s.* bloc, *m.*; (*for chopping, beheading,* &c.) billot, *m.*; (*fig.*) obstacle, *m.*; (*pers.*) bûche, *f.*; (*for hats*) forme, *f.*; (*for hair-dress*) tête à perruque, *f.*; (*of milliners*) poupée, tête, *f.*; (*of woodcuts*) planche de bois, planche, *f.*; (*stereotype plate*) cliché, *m.*; (*for ribbons*) rouleau, *m.*; (*of a pulley*) chape, *f.*; (*nav.*) poulie, *f.*; (*book-bind.*) pierre à battre, *f.*; (*of coopers*) charpi, *m*; (*of printed tissue*) matrice, *f.*; (*of tin*) saumon, *m.*; lingot, *m.*; (*build.*) dé, *m.*; (*of houses*) pâté, *m.*; (*part of a city*) île, *f.*, îlot, *m.*; — *v.a.*, — **up,** *v.a.* bloquer; encombrer; fermer; (*stop up*) boucher, condamner, murer; — **up,** *s.* encombrement, *m.* — *of houses* or *of buildings,* pâté de maisons, corps de bâtiments, *m.* — *and fall.* moufle, *m.* — **head,** *s.* imbécile, *m.f.*, sot, *m.*, sotte, *f.*, bête, *f.*, bûche, *f.*, ganache, *f.* — **house,** *s.* blockaus, *m.* — **like,** *adj.* comme une bûche. — **machine, -machinery,** *s.* poulierie, *f.* — **maker,** *s.* poulieur, *m.* — **making, -manufacture, -manufactory, -shed,** *s.* poulierie, *f.* — **ship,** *s.* (*of ports*) stationnaire, *m.*; (*of coasts*) garde-côtes, *m.*; (*van*) avant-garde, *f.*; (*rear*) vaisseau de l'arrière-garde, *m.* — **tin,** *s.* étain en saumon *or* en lingot, étain fin, *m.*; (*sheet-tin*) ferblanc de qualité supérieure, *m.*

Blockade, *s.* blocus, *m.*; — *v.a.* bloquer, faire [le blocus de

Blockish, *adj.* sot, stupide, bête

Blockishly, *adv.* sottement, stupidement, bêtement

Blockishness, *s.* stupidité, bêtise, *f.*

Blomary. *V.* **Bloomary**

Blond, Blonde, — lace, *s.* blonde, *f.*

Blond, Blonde, *adj.s.* (*of hair and complexion*) blond, *m.*, e, *f.*

Blood, *s.* sang, *m.*; (*kindred*) parenté, *f.*, sang, *m*; (*life*) vie, *f.*; (*temper,* &c.) tempérament, *m.*; passions, *f.pl.*; (*of horses*) race, *f.*; (*bot.*) jus, *m.*; (*fop*) petit-maître, élégant, *m.* — *v.a.* ensanglanter; accoutumer au carnage; exciter au carnage; (*hounds*) mettre en curée; (*to heat*) échauffer, exaspérer. *Bad* or *ill —,* mauvais sang, *m.*; inimitié, animosité, aigreur, *f.* *Cold —,* sang-froid, *m.* *In cold —,* de sang-froid. *To breed ill —,* faire faire du mauvais sang; aigrir les esprits. *To let —,* tirer du sang, saigner. *It makes o.'s — run cold,* cela glace le sang, cela fait frémir. *One cannot draw — out of a stone,* on ne saurait tirer de l'huile d'un mur. — **coloured,** *adj.* de couleur de sang. — **flower,** *s.* hémanthe, *m.* — **guiltiness,** *s.* crime de meurtre, *m.* — **guilty,** *adj.* coupable de meurtre. — **heat,** *s.* température du sang, *f.* — **horse,** *s.* cheval de race, cheval de pur sang, *m.* — **hot,** *adj.* de la chaleur du sang — **hound,** *s.* limier, *m.* — **less,** *adj.* qui n'a point de sang; (*without shedding of blood*) non sanglant; (*fig.*) mort. — **lessly,** *adv.* sans effusion de sang. — **letter,** *s.* saigneur phlébotomiste, *m.* — **letting,** *s.* saignée, phlébotomie, *f.* — **red,** *adj.* rouge comme du sang, d'un rouge de sang. — **root,** *s.* sanguinaire, célandine, *f.* — **shed,** *s.* effusion de sang, *f.*; carnage, *m.* — **shedder,** *s.* meurtrier, *m.*, -ière, *f.* — **shedding,** *s.* effusion de sang, *f.*; massacre, carnage, *m.*; meurtre, *m.* — **shot,** *adj.* injecté de sang; éraillé. — **shottenness,** *s.* injection, *f.* — **stained,** *adj.* souillé de sang, sanglant, ensanglanté. — **stone,** *s.* sanguine, *f.*; héliotrope, *m.* — **sucker,** *s.* suceur *or* buveur de sang, *m.*; sangsue, *f.* — **sucking,** *adj.* qui suce le sang. — **thirstiness,** *s.* soif du sang, *f.* — **thirsty,** *adj.* altéré de sang, sanguinaire. — **vessel,** *s.* vaisseau sanguin, *m.* *To burst* or *break a — vessel,* se rompre un vaisseau sanguin. — **warm,** *adj.* de la chaleur du sang. — **wood,** *s.* *V.* **Logwood.** — **wort,** *s.* *V.* — **root**

Blooded, *part. adj* ensanglanté, &c. (*V.* **Blood,** *v.a.*); (*in compounds*) à sang ...

Bloodily, *adv.* d'une manière sanglante; (*cruelly*) d'une manière sanguinaire, sanguinairement [disposition sanguinaire, *f.*

Bloodiness, *s.* ensanglantement, *m.*; (*cruelty*)

Bloody, *adj.* de sang; (*murderous*) sanglant; (*stained*) ensanglanté; (*cruel*) sanguinaire. — **minded,** *adj.* sanguinaire, cruel

Bloom, *s.* fleur, *f.*; (*fig.*) fleur, fraîcheur, *f.*) (*of iron-works*) loupe, *f.*; — *v.n.* fleurir; (*fig.*) fleurir, briller, être éclatant; — *v.a.* faire fleurir

Bloomary, Bloomery, *s.* fonderie, *f.*

Blooming, *adj.* fleurissant; fleuri, en fleur; (*fig.*) florissant, brillant; éclatant; naissant; dans le premier éclat de la fraîcheur, frais; à la fleur de l'âge; — *s.* fleuraison, *f.*; (*paint*) embu, *m.*

Bloomingly, *adv.* en fleur; dans sa fraîcheur; avec éclat, d'une manière florissante

Bloomy, *adj.* fleuri; dans sa fleur; florissant

Blossom, *s.* fleur, *f.*; — *v.n.* fleurir; — *v.a.* faire fleurir. *In —,* en fleurs

Blossoming, *s.* fleuraison, *f.*; — *adj.* fleurissant

Blossomy, *adj.* fleuri, couvert de fleurs

Blot, *v.a.* (*with a spot of ink*) faire un pâté sur, tacher; (*soil, scribble over*) barbouiller; (*stain*) souiller, ternir; (*darken*) noircir; (*dry*) sécher; (*efface, erase*) effacer, raturer; — *v.n.* boire; — *s.* (*of ink*) pâté, *m.*; (*stain*) tache, *f.*; (*erasure*) effaçure, rature, *f.* — **out,** *v.a.* effacer

Blotch, *s.* pustule, *f.*; (*spot*) tache, *f.*; — *v.a.* couvrir de pustules; (*to spot*) tacher, noircir

Blote, *v.a.* (*herrings*) fumer, saurer

Blotter, *s.* buvard, *m.*; (*waste-book*) brouillard, *m.*

Blotting, *adj.* qui fait des pâtés *or* des taches; (*of paper*) buvard, qui boit; — *s.* barbouillage, *m.* — **book, -case,** *s.* buvard, *m.* — **pad,** *s.* sous-main, buvard, *m.* — **paper,** *s.* papier buvard, papier brouillard, papier qui boit, *m.*

Blouse, *s.* blouse, *f.*

Blow, *s.* coup, *m.*; (*of flies*) *V.* **Fly-blow;** (*breeze*) brise, *f.*; (*of flowers*) épanouissement, *m.* *At a —, at a single —,* d'un coup, d'un seul coup. *In —,* en fleur. *Without striking a —, without a —,* sans coup férir. — *with a stick,* coup de bâton, coup de canne, *m.* *To come to —s,* en venir aux coups *or* aux mains, en venir aux voies de fait

Blow, *v.n.a.* souffler, (*imp.*) faire du vent, venter; (*of storms*) faire, s'élever; (*of trumpets, &c.*) sonner; (*of whistle*) siffler; (*bellows*) faire aller; (*to bloom*) fleurir, s'épanouir; (*make bloom*) faire fleurir, faire épanouir; (*drive*) chasser; (*swell*) enfler, gonfler; (*put out of breath*) essouffler; (*bring*) amener; (*spread*) répandre; (*excite*) soulever, exciter; (*of flies*) piquer. *To — fresh,* fraîchir. *To — hot and cold,* souffler le froid et le chaud. *To — north, south, &c.,* être au nord, au sud, &c. *To — o.'s nose,* se moucher. *It —s hard* or *high,* il fait beaucoup de vent, le vent souffle fort. *I will be —ed if,* je veux que le diable m'emporte si. — **away,** chasser, dissiper; emporter, enlever; (*down*) faire tomber. — **down,** renverser, abattre, faire tomber. — **off,** *V.* — **away.** — **out,** souffler, éteindre; (*the brains*) brûler, faire sauter. — **over,** passer, se dissiper. — **up,** souffler en l'air; (*with powder*) faire sauter; (*neut.*) sauter; éclater; (*quarrel with*) faire une sortie *or* &c. (*V.* **Blowing-up**) à; (*scold*) laver la tête à, donner un savon à, gronder; (*swell*) enfler, gonfler; (*of tempest, &c.*) soulever; (*kindle*) allumer

Blower, *s.* souffleur, *m.*, -euse, *f.*; (*of fire-grates*) tablier, rideau, *m.*; (*fish*) souffleur, *m.*; (*tech.*) souffleur, insufflateur, *m.*

Blow-fly, *s.* mouche à viande, *f.* [*ing*) globule, *m.*

Blow-hole, *s.* (*nat. hist.*) évent, *m.*; (*in found-*

Blowing, *adj.* soufflant, &c. (*V.* **Blow,** *v.n.a.*); — *s.* action de souffler, *f.*; (*of the wind*) action, force, *f.*, souffle, *m.*; (*of wind-instruments*) son, *m.*; (*of glass, &c.*) soufflage, *m.*; (*med.*) souffle, *m.*; (*blooming*) fleuraison, *f.*, épanouissement, *m.* — **apparatus,** *s.* soufflerie, *f.* — **cylinder,** *s.* cylindre soufflant, *m.* — **engine, -machine,** *s.* machine soufflante, *f.* — **up,** *s.* explosion, *f.*; (*removal*) enlèvement, *m.*; (*quarrel*) sortie, algarade, scène, *f.*; (*scolding*) galop, *m.*, chasse, *f.*, savon, *m.* [*m.*, bosse, culotte, *f.*

Blow-out, *s.* bombance, ripaille, *f.*, gueuleton,

Blow-pipe, *s.* chalumeau, *m.* [*In —,* en fleur

Blowth, *s.* fleuraison, *f.*, épanouissement, *m.*

Blow-up, *s.* *V.* **Blowing-up**

Blow-valve, *s.* reniflard, *m.*

Blowy, *adj.* (*windy*) venteux, orageux

Blowze, *s.* fille joufflue, joufflue, grosse joufflue, grosse rougeaude, *f.*

Blowzed, Blowzy, *adj* joufflu; coloré, qui a des couleurs, haut en couleur, rougeaud, rubicond; hâlé; échauffé

Blubber, *s* (*of whales, &c.*) lard, *m.*, graisse, *f.*; (*animal*) méduse, *f.*; — *v.n.* pleurer

Blubberer, *s.* pleurard, *m.*, e, *f.*

Blubbering, *adj.* pleurard; — *s.* larmes, *f.pl.*

Bludgeon, *s.* assommoir, casse-tête, gourdin, *m.*, trique, *f.*

Blue, *adj.* bleu; (*pharm.*) mercuriel; — *s.* bleu, *m.*; azur, *m.*; (*blue-stocking*) bas-bleu, *m.*; — *v.a.* bleuir; (*dye*) mettre *or* teindre en bleu; (*washing*) passer au bleu; — *v.n.* bleuir, devenir bleu; —**s,** *s. pl.* maladie *or* humeur noire, *f.* *True —,* d'un beau bleu; (*fig.*) marqué au bon coin, solide. *To look —,* (*fig.*) faire la grimace; regarder de travers *or* de mauvais œil. — **bell,** *s.* jacinthe des prés, *f.*; campanule, clochette, *f.* — **bird,** *s.* sialia, traquet sialis, *m.* — **black,** *s.* noir bleu, *m.* — **bottle,** *s.* (*corn-flower*) bluet, bleuet, *m.*; (*fly*) mouche bleue, *f.*; (*policeman*) *V* **Bobby.** — **breast,** *s.* gorge-bleue, *m.* — **cake,** *s.* bleu en pâte, *m.* — **devils,** *s. pl.* maladie *or* humeur noire, *f.*, papillons noirs, *m.pl.*, spleen, *m.* — **disease,** *s.* maladie bleue, cyanose, *f.* — **eyed,** *adj.* aux yeux bleus. — **jacket,** *s.* marin, *m.* — **light,** *s.* *V.* **Light,** *s.* — **mouldy,** *adj.* (*of cheese*) persillé. — **ointment,** *s.* onguent mercuriel, *m.* — **pill,** *s.* pilule mercurielle, *f.* — **stocking,** *s.* bas-bleu, *m.* — **throat,** *s.* gorge-bleue, *m.* — **vinnewed, -vinny,** *adj.* (*of cheese*) persillé

Bluely, *adv.* d'une couleur bleue, en bleu

Blueness, *s.* couleur bleue, *f.*

Bluff, *adj.* (*big*) gros, bouffi; (*surly*) rude, brusque, grossier; (*open*) exposé au vent; (*nav.*) escarpé; — *s.* côte escarpée, *f.*; berge, *f.* *To stand —,* tenir ferme [querie, *f.*

Bluffness, *s.* bouffissure, *f.*; (*surliness*) brus-

Bluish, *adj.* bleuâtre. — *black,* noir bleu, *m.*

Bluishness, *s.* couleur *or* teinte bleuâtre, *f.*

Blunder, *s.* bévue, *f.*; étourderie *f.*; gaucherie, *f.*; — *v.n.* se tromper grossièrement, faire une bévue *or* des bévues; tâtonner; — *v.a.* brouiller, embrouiller. — **about,** agir étourdiment,

— **head,** *s. V.* **Blunderer.** — **out,** dire sans y penser, lâcher, laisser échapper; (*jabber*) [bredouiller
Blunderbuss, *s.* espingole, *f.*
Blunderer, *s.* étourdi, *m.*, e, *f.*, maladroit, *m.*, e, *f.*, brouillon, *m.*, -ne, *f.* [**Blunder,** *s.*
Blundering, *adj.* étourdi, brouillon; — *s. V.*
Blunderingly, *adv.* étourdiment, en étourdi
Blunt, *adj.* (*having lost its edge or point*) émoussé; épointé; (*of weapons made without an edge or point*) contondant; (*rude*) brusque, rude; (*coarse*) grossier; (*stupid*) obtus; — *s.* (*money*) quibus, *m.*; — *v.a.* émousser; épointer; (*fig.*) émousser, amortir, calmer. — **topped,** *adj.* épointé. — **witted,** *adj.* stupide, obtus
Blunting, *s.* action d'émousser, *f.*; épointage, *m.*; (*fig.*) affaiblissement, *m.*
Bluntly, *adv.* sans pointe; (*fig.*) brusquement, crûment; (*pointblank*) de but en blanc
Bluntness, *s.* état émoussé, *m.*; épointement, *m.*; (*fig.*) brusquerie, rudesse, *f.*
Blur, *s.* tache, *f.*; — *v.a.* tacher, barbouiller; (*fig.*) souiller, ternir; altérer [échapper, lâcher
Blurt, — **out,** *v.a.* dire étourdiment, laisser
Blush, *s.* rougeur, *f.*, rouge, *m.*; —**es,** *pl.* la rougeur, *f.*; — *v.n.* rougir ('*for,*' pour; '*at,*' '*to,*' de); (*fig.*) avoir honte, rougir. *At the first* —, au premier abord, au premier aspect. *To put one to the* —, faire rougir quelqu'un
Blushless, *adj.* impudent, effronté
Bluster, *s.* bruit, fracas, tapage, *m.*; fanfaronnade, rodomontade, *f.*; (*of anger*) emportement, *m.*; (*of storms,* &c.) fureur, *f.*; — *v.n.* faire du tapage, tempêter, crier ('*at,*' contre); faire le fanfaron *or* le rodomont; (*of storms,* &c.) gronder, mugir [mont, *m.*
Blusterer, *s.* tapageur, *m.*; fanfaron, rodo-
Blustering, *adj.* (*windy*) orageux; (*noisy*) bruyant; (*boasting*) fanfaron; — *s. V.* **Bluster.** — *fellow,* fanfaron, *m.*
Blusteringly, *adv.* bruyamment; en tempêtant, en criant, &c. (*V.* **Bluster,** *v.n.*)
Blusterous, *adj. V.* **Blustering**
Bo, Boh, *int.* hou!
Boa, *s.* boa, *m.* — *constrictor,* boa constricteur, *m.*
Boar, *s.* verrat, cochon, *m.*; (*wild*) sanglier, *m.*; — *v.n.* (*rid.*) porter le nez au vent, porter au vent, éventer, encenser. *Wild* —, sanglier, *m. Young wild* —, marcassin, *m.* — **hound,** *s.* chien pour le sanglier, *m.* — **hunt,** *s.* chasse au sanglier, *f.* — **pig,** *s.* verrat, *m.* — **spear,** *s.* épieu, *m.* — **stag,** *s.* cochon, *m.*
Board, *s.* planche, *f.*; ais, *m.*; (*sign*) écriteau, *m.*; affiche, *f.*; enseigne, *f.*; (*of a road signpost*) volet, *m.*; écriteau, *m.*; (*for writing*) tableau, *m.*; (*table*) table, *f.*; (*food*) table, nourriture, *f.*; (*price of ditto*) pension, *f.*; (*council*) conseil, *m.*; bureau, *m.*; comité, *m.*; (*of paper*) carton, *m.*; (*of tailors,* &c.) établi, *m.*; (*of bellows*) flasque, *f.*; (*nav.*) bord, *m.*; bordée, *f.*; —**s,** *pl.* (*theat.*) planches, *f.pl.*; (*book-bind.*) cartonnage, *m.* — *and lodging,* (la) table et (le) logement, *m.pl.*, (la) pension, *f.* — *of directors,* — *of management,* conseil d'administration, *m.* — *of examination* or *of examiners,* jury d'examen, jury, *m.* — *of health,* conseil de salubrité, *m.* — *of ordnance,* comité de l'artillerie, *m.* — *of trade,* ministère du commerce, *m.* — *of works,* ministère des travaux publics, *m. President of the* — *of trade,* ministre du commerce, *m. In* —*s,* cartonné. *On* —, (*nav.*) à bord; à bord de ... *On* — *ship, on* — *a ship,* à bord d'un vaisseau. *On* — *o.'s ship,* à son bord. *Over* —, *V.* **Overboard** (*Letter* **O**). *To bind in* —*s,* cartonner. *To go on* —, aller à bord, aller à bord de ..., s'embarquer, s'embarquer sur ... *To have o.'s* — *and lodging but no salary,* être au pair. *To put in* —*s,* cartonner. *To put out to* —, mettre en pension. — **man,** *s.* homme-affiche, porte-affiches, *m.* — **wages,** *s.pl.* frais de nourriture, *m.pl.* (*To be on* — *wages,* avoir tant pour sa nourriture)
Board, *v.a.* (*a room*) planchéier; (*feed*) prendre en pension, nourrir; (*to place at board*) mettre en pension; (*a ship*) *V. To go on* —; (*an enemy's ship*) aborder; (*book-bind.*) cartonner; — *v.n.* être en pension; se mettre en pension
Boardable, *adj.* abordable
Boarder, *s.* pensionnaire, *m.f.*; interne, *m.f.*
Boarding, *s.* (*of rooms*) planchéiage, *m.*; (*of food*) table, nourriture, *f.*; (*nav.*) abordage, *m.*; (*book-bind.*) cartonnage, *m.*; (*planks*) planches, *f.pl.*; (*of a bedstead*) enfonçure, *f.*, fonçailles, *f.pl.*; (*tech.*) bordage, *m.* — **axe, -hatchet,** *s.* hache d'armes, *f.* — **house,** *s.* pension de famille, pension bourgeoise, pension, *f.* — **school,** *V.* **School**
Boarish, *adj.* de sanglier; brutal, grossier
Boast, *v.n.* se vanter (de), se glorifier (de); se faire fort (de); — *v.a.* vanter; (*mas.*) dégrossir, ébaucher, bretter; — *s.* vanterie, *f.*; (*pride*) vanité, *f.*, orgueil, *m.*, gloriole, *f.*; (*glory*) gloire, *f.*, honneur, orgueil, *m. To make a* — *of,* se vanter de, tirer vanité de [choir, *m.*
Boaster, *s.* vantard, fanfaron, *m.*; (*tool*) ébau-
Boastful, *adj.* vantard; (*proud*) orgueilleux, [vain
Boastfully. *V.* **Boastingly**
Boasting, *s.* vanterie, jactance, fanfaronnade, forfanterie, *f.*; (*pride*) orgueil, *m.*; vanité, gloriole, *f.*; (*mas.*) dégrossissage, ébauchage, *m.*, bretture, *f.*; — *adj. V.* **Boastful.** — **tool,** *s.* ébauchoir, *m.*
Boastingly, *adv.* avec ostentation *or* jactance
Boat, *s.* bateau, *m.*, barque, *f.*; canot, *m.*, chaloupe, *f.*; — *v.a.* transporter en bateau, bateler; (*the oars*) rentrer (les avirons); — *v.n.* aller *or* se promener en bateau (*or* en canot). *To sail in the same* — *with,* (*fig.*) être du même bord que. — **bill,** *s.* savacou, *m.* — **builder,** *s.* constructeur de bateaux, *m.* — **fly,** *s.* notonecte, *m.* — **ful,** *s.* navée, batelée, *f.* — **hook,** *s.* croc, *m.*, gaffe, *f.* — **house,** *s.* hangar à bateaux, *m.* — **keeper,** *s.* canotier, *m.* — **load,** *s.* batelée, navée, *f.* — **man,** — **sman,** *s.* batelier, *m.*; canotier, *m.* — **oar,** *s.* rame, *f.*, aviron, *m.* — **race, -racing,** *s. V.* **Race.** — **rope,** *s.* câbleau, câblot, *m.* — **shaped,** *adj.* en forme de bateau. — **staff,** *s.* perche, *f.* — **swain,** *s.* maître d'équipage, *m.* — **swain's mate,** *s.* contre-maître, *m.* — **up,** *v.n.a.* remonter en bateau. — **wise,** *adj.* en bateau
Boatable, *adj.* navigable pour les bateaux
Boating, *s.* transport en bateau, batelage, *m.*; promenade en bateau *or* en canot, *f.*, canotage, *m.*
Bob, *s.* (*end*) bout, *m.*; (*tassel*) gland, *m.*; (*of ear,* &c.) pendant, *m.*; (*fishing*) ver, *m.*; (*of clocks*) lentille, *f.*; (*mach.*) balancier, *m.*; (*of songs*) refrain, *m.*; (*of bells*) carillon, *m.*: (*motion*) balancement, *m.*; ballottement, *m.*; branlement, *m.*; mouvement, *m.*; (*slap*) tape, *f.*, coup, *m.*; (*wig*) perruque ronde, *f.*; (*jeer*) lardon, *m.*, trait de raillerie, *m.*; (*unit of silver coin*) balle, *f.* — **tail,** *s.* queue écourtée, *f.*; (*rabble*) canaille, *f.* — **tailed,** *adj.* à queue écourtée. — **tail wig,** — **wig,** *s.* perruque ronde, *f.*
Bob, *v.a.n.* balancer; secouer; ballotter; s'agiter; faire un mouvement; (*down*) baisser; pencher; (*dangle*) pendiller; (*cheat*) escamoter; (*mock*) bafouer; (*beat*) taper, frapper; (*of a tail*) écourter; (*fishing*) amorcer
Bobber, *s.* (*fish.*) bouchon, plumeau, *m.*
Bobbin, *s.* bobine, *f.*; (*for lace-work*) fuseau, *m.*; (*tape*) ganse ronde, *f.* — **lace,** *s.* dentelle au fuseau, *f.* — **net,** *s.* tulle bobin, bobin, *m.* — **work,** *s.* passement au fuseau, *m.*; dentelle au fuseau, *f.* [*m.*
Bobby, *s.* (*policeman*) bigorneau, balai, argousin,
Boblink, Bobolink, *s. V.* **Rice-bird**
Bocasine, *s.* boucassin, *m.*
Boddice. *V.* **Bodice** [bon *or* de mauvais augure
Bode, *v.a.n.* présager. *To* — *well* or *ill,* être de

Bodement, *s. V.* **Boding**
Bodice, *s.* corset, *m.*; corsage de dessous, *m.* — **maker,** *s.* corsetier, *m.*, -ière, *f.*
Bodied, *adj.* (*in compounds*) à corps ... *Big* —, corpulent, gros. *Strong* —, fort, vigoureux. *Weak* —, faible, débile. *V.* **Able, Full,** &c.
Bodiless, *adj.* incorporel; immatériel
Bodily, *adj.* corporel, du corps; physique; réel; matériel; (*of fear*) pour sa personne; — *adv.* corporellement; (*entirely*) entièrement, en son entier, tout entier, tout ensemble, en [masse
Boding, *s.* augure, présage, *m.*
Bodkin, *s.* passe-lacet, *m.*, aiguille à passer, *f.*; (*for the hair*) épingle de tête, *f.*; (*for boring*) poinçon, *m.*; (*print.*) pointe, *f.*
Body, *s.* corps, *m.*; (*fam.*) personne, *f*; gaillard, compère, *m.*, gaillarde, commère, *f.*; (*corpse*) corps, cadavre, *m.*; (*mass*) masse, *f.*; (*centre*) cœur, *m.*; (*principal thing*) fond, *m.*; (*of an army*) corps d'armée principal, gros, *m.*; (*mil.*) corps, *m.*; (*of a tree*) tronc, *m.*; (*of a church*) nef, *f.*; (*of an altar*) coffre, *m.*; (*of a carriage*) caisse, *f.*; (*of a dress*) corsage, *m.*; (*of a hat*) galette, carcasse, *f.*; (*geom.*) solide, *m.*; — *v.a. V.* **Embody.** *Public* —, corporation, *f.* *In a* —, en corps; en masse. *To have* — or *good* —, (*of wine*, &c.) avoir du corps, être corsé. — **clothes,** *s. pl.* (*of horses*) couverture, *f.*; (*of trappings*) housse, *f.* — **clothing,** *s.* vêtement, *m.*, vêtements, *m.pl.* — **colour,** — **colour painting,** *s.* gouache, *f.* — **guard,** *s.* garde du corps, *f.*; (*fig.*) escorte, *f.*; sauvegarde, *f.* — **horse,** *s.* cheval de cheville, chevillier, *m.* — **linen,** *s.* linge de corps, *m.* — **of the place,** *s.* (*fort.*) enceinte, *f.* — **snatcher,** *s.* déterreur, résurrectioniste, *m.* — **snatching,** *s.* déterrement, *m.*
Bœotian, *s. adj.* Béotien, *m.*, -ne, *f.*
Bœotism, *s.* béotisme, *m.*
Bog, *s.* marais, marécage, bourbier, *m.*, fondrière, *f.*; (*privy*) lieux, *m.pl.*, latrines, *f.pl.*; — *v.a.* embourber. — **bean,** *s.* minyanthe, *m.* — **earth,** *s.* palus, *m.* — **land,** *s.* marais, *m.*; *adj.* paludéen, paludicole. — **moss,** *s.* sphaigne, paludelle, mousse aquatique, *f.* — **rush,** *s.* choin, *m.* — **trotter,** *s.* habitant des marais, *m.* — **wood,** *s.* bois pétrifié, *m.*
Bogey. *V.* **Bogie**
Boggle, *v.n.* reculer; hésiter (à); (*haggle*) marchander, barguigner; (*dissemble*) dissimuler; — *v.a.* embarrasser
Boggler, *s.* personne timide *or* irrésolue, *f*, peureux, *m.*, -euse, *f.*; (*haggler*) barguigneur, *m.*, -euse, *f.*
Boggling, *s.* hésitation, irrésolution, *f.*; barguignage, *m.*; dissimulation, *f.*
Boggy, *adj.* marécageux
Boghead, — **coal,** *s.* boghead, *m.*
Bogie, Bogy, Old —, *s.* croquemitaine, *m.*
Bogle, *s.* loup-garou, *m.*
Bohea, *s. adj.* bohéa, bohé, *m.*
Bohemian, *s.* Bohémien, *m.*, -ne, *f.*; — *adj.* bohémien, de Bohême. — *glass*, verre de Bohême, *m.*
Boil, *v.n.* bouillir; (*cook*) cuire; (*bubble*) bouillonner; — *v.a.* faire bouillir; (*cook*) cuire, faire cuire; — *s.* clou, furoncle, *m.* — **away, down,** ébouillir. — **fast,** bouillir (*or* faire bouillir) à gros bouillons. — **gently** *or* **slowly,** bouillir (*or* faire bouillir) à petits bouillons (*or* doucement). — **over,** s'enfuir, s'en aller; déborder; bouillonner. — **up,** monter; (*fig.*) bouillonner
Boiler, *s.* bouilloire, chaudière, *f.*; (*tech.*, *of steam-engines*) chaudière, *f.*; (*pers.*) bouilleur, *m.* — **maker,** *s.* chaudronnier, *m.* — **manufactory,** *s.* chaudronnerie, *f.* — **tube,** [*s.* bouilleur, *m.*
Boilery, *s.* bouillerie, *f.*
Boiling, *s.* ébullition, *f.*; bouillonnement, *m.*; — *part. adj.* bouillant; bouillonnant. — **hot,** *adj.* tout bouillant. — **point,** *s.* point d'ébullition, *m.*
Boisterous, *adj.* orageux, impétueux, furieux, violent; (*noisy*) bruyant, turbulent, tumultueux
Boisterously, *adv.* impétueusement, violemment; (*with noise*) bruyamment, tumultueusement [turbulence, *f.*
Boisterousness, *s.* impétuosité, violence, *f.*,
Bolary, *adj.* bolaire
Bold, *adj.* hardi; brave; audacieux; téméraire; impudent, effronté; assuré; (*showy*) saillant; (*clear*) net; (*steep*) escarpé, accore. *To be* or *make* —, oser, ne pas craindre (de), avoir la hardiesse (de), prendre la liberté (de), se permettre (de); (*to be free*) prendre des libertés (avec), agir cavalièrement (avec). *As* — *as brass*, hardi comme un page. — **face,** *s.* impudence, effronterie, *f.*; (*pers.*) impudent, *m.*, e, *f.*, effronté, *m.*, e, *f.* — **faced,** *adj.* impudent, effronté. — **spirited,** *adj.* hardi. — **spiritedness,** *s.* hardiesse, *f.*
Boldly, *adv.* hardiment; audacieusement; (*clearly*) nettement
Boldness, *s.* hardiesse, *f.*; audace, *f.*; témérité, *f.*; impudence, effronterie, *f.*; assurance, *f.*; (*clearness*) netteté, *f.*; (*steepness*) escarpement, *m.*
Bole, *s.* (*of a tree*) tronc, *m.*; (*min.*) bol, *m.*
Bolero, *s.* boléro, *m.*
Boletic, *adj.* bolétique
Boletus, *s.* bolet, *m.*
Bolis, *s.* bolide, *m.f.*
Bolivian, *s. adj.* Bolivien, *m.*, -ne, *f.* [pommer
Boll, *s.* (*bot.*) balle, *f.*; — *v.n.* monter en graine;
Bolognese. *V.* **Bolognian.** — *school*, école bolonaise, *f.*
Bolognian, *s.* Bolonais, *m.*, e, *f.*; — *adj.* bolonais, de Bologne. — *stone*, pierre de Bologne, *f.*
Bolster, *s.* traversin, *m.*; (*pad*) coussin, *m.*; — *v.a.* mettre un traversin (*or* un coussin) sous, soutenir sur un traversin (*or* un coussin); (*fig.*) soutenir, appuyer. — **up,** rembourrer; (*fig.*) soutenir, étayer [soutien, *m.*
Bolsterer, *s.* personne qui soutient, *f.*, appui,
Bolt, *s.* (*dart*) trait, *m.*; (*of thunder*) foudre, *f.*; (*of doors*) verrou, *m.*; (*of locks*) pène, *m.*; (*of prisoners*) fers, *m.pl.*; (*pin*) boulon, *m.*; cheville, *f.*; (*sieve*) blutoir, sas, *m.*; (*of straw*) botte, *f.*; (*leap*) bond, saut, *m.* — **head,** *s.* matras, *m.* — **rope,** *s.* ralingue, *f.* — **upright,** *adj.* tout droit
Bolt, *v.a.* (*a door*) verrouiller, fermer au verrou; (*fetter*) lier, enchaîner; (*sift*) bluter, sasser; (*fig.*) passer par l'étamine; (*pin*) boulonner, cheviller; — *v.n.* se lancer; (*escape*) s'évader, s'échapper, décamper, filer, prendre la clé des champs; (*fig.*) sortir; (*of horses*) bourrer; s'emporter. — **down,** (*swallow*) avaler. — **in,** enfermer au verrou; (*fig.*) avaler; (*v.n.*) entrer subitement *or* précipitamment. — **off,** sortir précipitamment. — **out,** mettre le verrou contre; (*words*) lâcher; (*throw out*) faire sortir; (*v.n.*) sortir précipitamment, s'élancer. — **up,** (*shut*) fermer; (*confine*) mettre sous les verrous, enfermer; (*fig.*) en- [chaîner
Bolter, *s.* blutoir, sas, *m.*
Bolting, *s.* (*of doors*) verrouillement, *m.*; (*sifting*) blutage, *m.*; (*fig.*) examen soigneux, *m.*; (*with a pin*) chevillage, *m.* — **cloth,** *s.* étamine, *f.* — **house,** *s.* bluterie, *f.* — **hutch,** *s.* huche à bluter, *f.* — **machine,** *s.* blutoir, *m.* — **mill,** *s.* blutoir, *m.*; bluterie, *f.* — [**room,** *s.* bluterie, *f.*
Bolus, *s.* bol, bolus, *m.*
Bomb, *s.* bombe, *f.* — **chest,** *s.* caisse à bombes, *f.* — **foundry,** *s.* bomberie, *f.* — **ketch,** *s.* bombarde, *f.* — **proof,** *adj.* à l'épreuve de la bombe. — **vessel,** *s.* bombarde, *f.*
Bombard, *v.a.* bombarber; — *s.* bombarde, *f.*
Bombardier, *s.* bombardier, *m.* — **beetle,** *s.* bombardier, *m.*
Bombardment, *s.* bombardement, *m.*
Bombardo, Bombardon, *s.* bombarde, *f.*

Bombasin, Bombasine. *V.* Bombazine
Bombast, *s.* pathos, boursouflage, phébus, *m.*, enflure, *f.*
Bombastic, *adj.* ampoulé, boursoufflé, enflé
Bombazine, *s.* bombasin, *m.*, bombasine, *f.*, alépine, *f.*
Bonâ fide, *adj. adv.* de bonne foi; (*com.*, *exchange, of a sale, purchase, or bargain*) ferme
Bonapart-ism, -ist. *V.* page 3, § 1
Bonasia, *s.* gelinotte, *f.*
Bonbon, *s.* bonbon, *m.*
Bon-chrétien, *s.* bon-chrétien, *m.*
Bond, *s.* lien, *m.*; (*union*) liaison, *f.*; (*irons*) chaînes, *f.pl.*, captivité, *f.*; (*promise*) promesse, *f.*, engagement, *m.*, obligation, *f.*; (*bank.*, *fin.*) obligation, *f.*, bon, billet, *m.*; (*law*) obligation, *f.*; (*cust.*) entrepôt, *m.*; — *v.a.* entreposer. — **holder,** *s.* porteur (*m.*, -euse, *f.*) de bon *or* d'obligation. — **maid,** *s.* esclave, *f.* — **man,** *s.* esclave, *m.*; (*feud.*) serf, vilain, *m.* — **servant,** *s.* esclave, *m.f.* — **service,** *s.* esclavage, *m.*; (*feud.*) servage, *m.* — **slave,** *s.* esclave, *m.f.* —**sman,** *s.* esclave, *m.*; (*feud.*) serf, vilain, *m.*; (*law*) caution, *f.*, répondant, *m.* — **stone,** *s.* parpaing, *m.*, pierre parpaigne, *f.* — **store,** *s.* entrepôt, *m.* —**swoman,** — **woman,** *s.* esclave, *f.*; (*feud.*) serve, *f.*
Bondage, *s.* esclavage, *m.*; captivité, *f.*; emprisonnement, *m.*, prison, *f.*; (*feud.*) servage, *m.*
Bonded, *part. adj.* entreposé; en entrepôt, à l'entrepôt. — **port,** *s.* (*nav.*) port à entrepôt, *m.* — **store, -warehouse,** *s.* entrepôt, *m.*
Bonder, *s.* entrepositaire, *m.f.*
Bonding, *s.* entreposage, *m.*; — *adj.* d'entrepôt. — **store, -warehouse,** *s.* entrepôt, *m.*
Bone, *s.* os, *m.*; (*of fish*) arête, *f.*; (*of whale*) baleine, *f.*; (*of the teeth*) ivoire, *f.*; (*bobbin*) bobine, *f.*; fuseau, *m.*; (*die*) dé, *m.*; (*snap*) cliquette, *f.*; (— *of contention*) pomme (de discorde), *f.*; —**s,** *pl.* os, *m.pl.*; arêtes, *f.pl.*; &c.; (*of the dead, and unconnected*) ossements, *m.pl.*, (*poet.*) ossements *or* os, *m.pl.*; (*scruple*) scrupule, *m.* *To make no —s,* ne pas se faire scrupule (de); (*not to hesitate*) n'en faire ni une ni deux. *What is bred in the — will never (come) out of the flesh,* la caque sent toujours le hareng. — **ache,** *s.* douleur dans les os, *f.* — **ash,** *s.* os calcinés, *m.pl.* — **black,** *s.* noir animal, charbon d'os, *m.* — **boiler,** *s.* bouilleur d'os, *m.* — **breaker, -crusher,** *s.* (*instr.*) casse-os, *m.* — **dust,** *s.* poussière *or* poudre d'os, *f.* — **earth,** *s.* os calcinés, *m.pl.* — **glue,** *s.* ostéocolle, *f.* — **holder,** *s.* manche à gigot, *m.* — **house,** *s.* ossuaire, *m.* — **lace,** *s.* dentelle (au fuseau), *f.* — **less,** *adj.* sans os; (*of fish*) sans arêtes. — **oil,** *s.* huile de corne de cerf, huile animale, *f.* — **setter,** *s.* rebouteur, renoueur, *m.* — **setting,** *s.* reboutement, *m.* — **spavin,** *s.* éparvin osseux, *m.* — **turner,** *s.* tourneur en os, *m.* — **work,** *s.* ouvrage en os, *m.* — **working, -works,** *s.* osserie, *f.*
Bone, *v.a.* (*meat*) désosser; (*fish*) ôter les arêtes de; (*to put whalebone into*) garnir de baleine; (*to steal*) chiper, escamoter
Boned, *part. adj.* désossé; (*with whalebone*) garni de baleine, baleiné; (*in compounds*) à os ..., à ... os. *Big —, large —,* à gros os, ossu. *Strong —,* qui a les os solides
Bonfire, *s.* feu de joie, *m.*
Bongar, *s.* bongare, *m.*
Boning, *s.* désossement, *m.*; (*stealing*) escamotage, *m.*; (*in surveying*) jalonnement, *m.*
Bonito, *s.* bonite, *f.*
Bon mot, *s.* bon mot, *m.*
Bonne bouche, *s.* bonne bouche, *f.*
Bonnet, *s.* chapeau, chapeau de femme, *m.*; (*a Scotchman's*) bonnet, béret, *m.*; (*mil.*, *tech.*) bonnet, *m.*; (*fort.*, *nav.*) bonnette, *f.* (— *blind, sun-blind*) abat-jour, *m.*; — *v.a.* enfoncer (à quelqu'un) son chapeau sur la tête *or* sur les yeux, houspiller. — **block,** *s.* poupée, tête, *f.* — **box,** *s.* carton à chapeau, *m.* — **cap,** *s.* dessous de chapeau, *m.* — **front,** *s.* passe de chapeau, *f.*; (*ornament*) tour de tête, *m.* — **sail,** *s.* bonnette, *f.* — **shape,** *s.* forme de chapeau, *f.* — **stand,** *s.* champignon, *m.* — **string,** *s.* bride de chapeau, *f.*
Bonneting, *s.* houspillement, renfoncement, *m.*
Bonnily, *adv.* gaîment; (*handsomely*) joliment
Bonniness, *s.* gaieté, *f.*; gentillesse, *f.*; (*plumpness*) embonpoint, *m.*
Bonny, *adj.* gai, joyeux, enjoué; (*handsome*) joli, gentil; (*plump*) grassouillet, potelé
Bonus, *s.* boni, *m.*; (*premium*) prime, *f.*; (*douceur*) pot-de-vin, *m.*; (*percentage*) tantième, *m.*
Bony, *adj.* osseux; (*stout*) ossu; (*of bone*) d'os; (*of bones of the dead*) d'ossements; (*with fish-bones*) plein d'arêtes
Bonze, *s.* bonze, *m.* — **nun,** *s.* bonzesse, *f.*
Bonzess, *s.* bonzesse, *f.*
Booby, *s.* nigaud, *m.*, e, *f.*, benêt, dadais, *m.*; (*bird*) boubie, *f.*, fou, *m.*
Boobyism, *s.* nigauderie, *f.*
Boobyish, *adj.* nigaud
Book, *s.* livre, *m.*; (*small, hand-book, time-book, guide-book, of depositors in savings banks, of the words of an opera,* &c.) livret, *m.*; (*for writing*) cahier, *m.*; (*note-book, memorandum-book*) carnet, *m.*; livret, *m.*; (*register*) registre, *m.*; — *v.a.* enregistrer, inscrire; (*a place*) retenir. *To be in a person's —s,* avoir un compte ouvert chez quelqu'un; (*fig.*) être bien dans les papiers (*or* dans l'esprit) de quelqu'un. *To — through to London,* prendre un billet direct pour Londres. *To bring to —,* forcer à rendre des comptes *or* à s'expliquer. *To keep —s,* tenir les livres. — **binder,** *s.* relieur, *m.*, -euse, *f.* — **bindery,** *s.* atelier de reliure, *f.* — **binding,** *s.* état de relieur, *m.*; (*art*) reliure, *f.* — **case,** *s.* bibliothèque, *f.* — **collector,** *s.* collectionneur (*or* amateur) de livres, *m.* — **debt,** *s.* créance, dette active, *f.* —**ful,** *adj.* pédant. — **keeper,** *s.* teneur de livres, *m.* — **keeping,** *s.* tenue des livres, comptabilité, *f.* — **knowledge, -learning,** *s.* savoir, *m.*, érudition, *f.* — **learned,** *adj.* qui a de la lecture, érudit, savant, lettré. —**less,** *adj.* sans livres; illettré. — **maker,** *s.* faiseur (*m.*, -euse, *f.*) de livres, écrivailleur, *m.*, -euse, *f.*, écrivassier, *m.*, -ière, *f.* — **making,** *s.* composition des livres, *f.* — **man,** *s.* homme d'étude, savant, *m.* — **mark, -marker,** *s.* signet, *m.* — **market,** *s.* commerce de la librairie, *m.* — **muslin,** *s.* organdi, *m.* — **post,** *s.* service, (*m.*) *or* expédition (*f.*) des imprimés, imprimés, *m.pl.* *By — post,* en imprimés; sous bande. — **repository,** *s.* librairie, *f.* — **rest,** *s.* pupitre, *m.* — **scorpion,** *s.* chélifère, porte-pince, *m.* — **seller,** *s.* libraire, *m.f.*, marchand (*m.*, e, *f.*) de livres. — *seller and publisher,* libraire-éditeur, *m.* — **seller's shop** *or* **business** *or* **stock,** — **selling,** *s.* librairie, *f.* — **selling,** *adj.* de librairie. — **shelf,** *s.* rayon, *m.* — **shelves,** *s.pl.* bibliothèque, *f.* — **shop,** *s.* librairie, *f.* — **slide,** *s.* porte-livres, *m.* — **stall,** *s.* étalage de livres, *m.* — **staller,** *s.* bouquiniste, *m.f.* — **stand,** *s.* bibliothèque, *f.*; (*for reading*) *V.* **Desk.** — **store,** *s.* magasin de livres, *m.* — **trade,** *s.* commerce de la librairie, *m.*, librairie, *f.* — **work,** *s.* (*print.*) labeur, *m.*, librairie, *f.* — **worm,** *s.* (*insect*) lépisme, *m.*; (*fig.*) dévoreur (*m.*, -euse, *f.*) de livres; bouquineur, *m.* — **writer,** *s.* auteur, *m.* — **writing,** *s.* composition des livres, *f.*
Booking, *s.* enregistrement, *m.* — **office,** *s.* bureau d'enregistrement, *m.*; bureau de messagerie, *m.*; bureau de factage, *m.*; bureau des billets, *m.*
Bookish, *adj.* adonné aux livres, passionné pour la lecture; (*learned*) savant
Bookishness, *s.* étude, *f.*; passion pour l'étude *or* pour la lecture, *f.*
Boom, *s.* (*of a ship*) bout-dehors, boute-hors.

arc-boutant, *m.*; (*of harbour*) chaine, estacade, *f.*; (*noise*) *V.* **Booming;** — *v.n.* gronder; (*drone*) bourdonner [ment, *m.*
Booming, *s.* grondement, *m.*; bourdonne-
Boomkin, *s.* (*nav.*) bout de lof, *m.*
Boon, *s.* bienfait, *m.*, faveur, *f.*, don, *m.*; avantage, bien, *m.*; (*of flax*) chènevotte, *f.*; — *adj.* gai, joyeux; (*kind*) bienfaisant, bon
Boor, *s.* paysan, villageois, rustre, *m.*
Boorish, *adj.* rustre; grossier
Boorishly, *adv.* en rustre, grossièrement
Boorishness, *s.* rusticité, grossièreté, *f.*
Boot, *v.a.* botter; (*to avail*) servir à. *What boots it?* à quoi sert? que sert?
Boot, *s.* (*high, Wellington* —, &c.) botte, *f.*; (*low*) bottine, *f.*; (*lace* —) brodequin, *m.*; (*shoe*) soulier, *m.*; (*instr. of torture*) brodequin, *m.*; (*on a horse's foot*) botte, bottine, *f.*; (*of carriages*) coffre, *m.*, cave, *f.*; (*profit*) profit, avantage, *m.*; (*difference*) appoint, *m.*; —**s,** *pl.* bottes, &c.; chaussures, *f.pl.* (*a servant*) décrotteur, *m.* *Blucher* —, soulier-botte, *m.* *Half* —, bottine, *f.* *Side-spring* —, *elastic-side* —, *elastic-spring* —, bottine à élastiques, *f.* *To* —, par-dessus le marché, en sus. — **cleaner,** *s.* décrotteur, *m.* — **closer,** *s.* joigneur, *m.* — **crimp,** *s.* *V.* — **last.** — **hook,** *s.* crochet de bottes, tire-bottes, *m.* — **jack,** *s.* tire-bottes, *m.* — **lace,** *s.* lacet de brodequin, *m.*; (*shoe-string*) cordon de soulier, *m.* — **last,** *s.* embauchoir, embouchoir, *m.* — **leg,** *s.* tige de botte, *f.* —**less,** *adj.* sans bottes, sans chaussures; (*profitless*) inutile, vain. —**lessly,** *adv.* inutilement, vainement. —**lessness,** *s.* inutilité, *f.* — **maker,** *s.* bottier, *m.* — **making, -manufactory, -mart, -room, -shop,** *s.* botterie, *f.* — **sole,** *s.* semelle de botte, *f.* — **strap,** *s.* tirant de botte, *m.* — **top,** *s.* revers de botte, *m.*; (*covering the knee*) genouillère, *f.* — **trade,** *s.* botterie, *f.* — **tree,** *s.* *V.* — **last**
Booted, *adj.* botté, en bottes. — *with leather,* (*of cavalry trousers*) garni de fausses bottes en cuir
Booth, *s.* baraque, *f.*; tente, *f.*; pavillon, *m.*
Booty, *s.* butin, *m.*
Booze, *v.n.* riboter, godailler [*m.*, -euse, *f.*
Boozer, *s.* riboteur, *m.*, -euse, *f.*, godailleur,
Boozy, *adj.* gris, en ribote
Bopeep, *s.* cache-cache, *m.*
Boracic, *adj.* boracique, borique
Borage, *s.* bourrache, *f.*
Borate, *s.* borate, *m.*
Borax, *s.* borax, *m.*
Border, *s.* bord, *m.*; (*edging*) bordure, *f.*; (*flower-bed*) plate-bande, *f.*; (*of countries*) frontière, *f.*; (*of forests*) bord, *m.*, lisière, *f.*; (*of a coin*) carnèle, *f.*; (*frame*) cadre, *m.*; (*her.*) bordure, *f.*; — *v.a.* border; (*coins, her.*) carneler; — *v.n.* — **on,** toucher à, être contigu à, aboutir à, être limitrophe de, confiner à *or* avec; (*fig.*) approcher de, friser. — **country, -land,** *s.* pays limitrophe, *m.* — **shears,** *s.pl.* (*hort.*) fauchette, *f.* — **town,** *s.* ville frontière, *f.*
Bordered, *adj.* bordé; borduré; (*bounded*) limité, borné [voisin, *m.*, e, *f.* ('*upon,*' de)
Borderer, *s.* habitant (*m.*, e, *f.*) des frontières;
Bordering, *adj.* contigu (à), voisin (de); (*geog.*) limitrophe (de); (*fig.*) approchant (de), voisin (de)
Bore, *v.a.n.* percer; forer; (*to hollow*) creuser; (*of mines*) sonder; (*weary, pester*) assommer; agacer, tanner, taonner, canuler; — *s.* (*hole*) trou, *m.*; (*of fire-arms: inner tube*) âme, *f.*, (*diameter of ditto, obsolete for "calibre"*) calibre, *m.*; (*of a pump*) âme, *f.*; (*instr.*) *V.* **Borer;** (*pers.*) être (*or* personnage) assommant, cauchemar, *m.*; (*troublesome thing*) ennui, *m.*, scie, *f.*, chose assommante, *f.*; (*drudgery*) corvée, *f.*; (*of tide*) ras de marée, *m.* — **cole,** *s.* chou
Boreal, *adj.* boréal [vert, *m.*
Boree, *s.* bourrée, *f.*
Borer, *s.* (*instr.*) perçoir, foret, *m.*, tarière, *f.*; coup-de-poing, *m.*; (*of mines*) sonde, *f.*; (*pers.*) foreur, *m.*, perceur, *m.*, -euse, *f.*; (*insect*) perce-bois, *m.*; (*ship-worm*) taret, *m.*
Boride, *s.* borure, *m.*
Boring, *s.* forage, *m.*; (*of mines*) sondage, *m.* — **bit,** *s.* mèche, *f.* — **worm,** *s.* taret, *m.*
Born, *part.* né; (*by birth*) de naissance. — *dead,* mort-né. — *to,* né pour, destiné à. *To be* —, naître, être né. *To have been* —, être né. *I was* — *in* 1870, je suis né en 1870. *Charles* (*now dead*) *was* — *in* 1855, Charles était né en 1855. *Napoleon I. was* — *in* 1769, Napoléon I. naquit (*historical tense*) en 1769
Boron, *s.* bore, *m.* [bourg pourri, *m.*
Borough, *s.* bourg, *m.*; ville, *f.* *Rotten* —,
Borrow, *v.a.* emprunter ('*of*' or '*from*': *pers.*, à; *things, and fig. of pers.*, de, à) [prunt
Borrowed, *adj.* emprunté; (*factitious*) d'em-
Borrower, *s.* emprunteur, *m.*, -euse, *f.*
Borrowing, *s.* emprunt, *m.*
Bort, *s.* carat, *m.*
Boscage, *s.* bocage, *m.*
Bosh, *s.* galimatias *m.*; drogue, *f.*; blague, *f.*, fadaises, calembredaines, *f.pl.* [-ne, *f.*
Bosnian, *s. adj.* Bosniaque, *m.f.*, Bosnien, *m.*,
Bosom, *s.* sein, *m.*; (*heart*) cœur, *m.*; (*adject., in compounds*) du *or* de cœur, intime. — *friend,* ami (*m.*, e, *f.*) de cœur, ami (*m.*, e, *f.*) intime
Bosphorus, Bosporus, *s.* Bosphore, *m.*
Bosquet, *s.* bosquet, *m.*
Boss, *s.* bosse, *f.*; (*of a bridle-bit*) bossette, *f.*; (*of a shield*) ombon, *m.*
Bossage, *s.* bossage, *m.*
Bosset, *s.* (*hunt.*) bosse, *f.*
Bossy, *adj.* en bosse
Boston, *s.* boston, *m.*
Bot, — **fly,** *s.* œstre, *m.*
Botan-ic, al, -ically, -ist. *V.* page 3, § 1
Botanize, *v.n.* botaniser
Botany, *s.* botanique, *f.*
Botargo, *s.* botargue, boutargue, *f.*
Botch, *s.* pustule, *f.*; (*patch*) pièce maladroitement mise, *f.*; (*patchwork, bad work*) rapiéçage, ravaudage, bousillage, *m.*, mauvaise besogne, *f.*, ouvrage mal fait, *m.*; (*of mistakes*) replâtrage, *m.*; — *v.a.* (— **up**) raccommoder, rapiécer, rapetasser, ravauder; (*do hastily*) saveter, saboter, bousiller, gâcher, bâcler, massacrer; (*of mistakes*) replâtrer; (*collect*) coudre ensemble
Botcher, *s.* raccommodeur, *m.*, -euse, *f.*, ravaudeur, *m.*, -euse, *f.*; (*bungler*) savetier, sabotier, bousilleur, *m.*, -euse, *f.*, gâcheur, *m.*, -euse, *f.*; (*grilse*) *V.* **Grilse**
Botching, *s.* raccommodage, rapiéçage, ravaudage, *m.*; replâtrage, *m.*
Botchy, *adj.* couvert de pustules; (*patchy*) de pièces et de morceaux; tacheté, bariolé
Both, *adj.* deux, les deux, tous deux, tous les deux, l'un et l'autre; et (... et), ... (... et), tant (... que); (*at the same time*) à la fois (... et). — *brothers,* les deux frères. — *his hands,* ses deux mains. — *of them,* eux deux, tous deux, tous les deux. — *of us,* nous deux, tous deux, tous les deux. — *of you,* vous deux, tous deux, tous les deux. — *by sea and land,* et par mer et par terre, par mer et par terre, tant par mer que par terre. — *rich and poor,* les riches et les pauvres. — *disadvantageous and dishonourable,* à la fois désavantageux et déshonorant [embêter
Bother, *v.a.* ennuyer, tracasser, tourmenter,
Bother, Botheration, *s.* ennui, tracas, tourment, embêtement, *m.* — *your* ...! vous m'ennuyez avec votre ...! allez vous promener *or* vous coucher avec votre ...!
Bothnian, *s. adj.* Bothniaque, *m.f.*
Bottle, *s.* bouteille, *f.*; (*small*) flacon, *m.*; (*with a wide short neck*) bocal, *m.*; (*chiefly for water and watery drinks*) carafe, *f.*; (*stone* —) cruchon, *m.*; (*of pilgrims*) gourde, *f.*; (*of hay*) botte, *f.*; — *v.a.* mettre en bouteilles *or* en bouteille;

(*fruits, pickles*) mettre en bocal, conserver; (*hay*) botteler. — **brush,** *s.* goupillon, *m.* — **case,** *s.* cantine, *f.* — **companion,** *s.* camarade de bouteille, *m.* — **conjurer,** *s.* escamoteur, *m.* — **flower,** *s.* bluet, bleuet, *m.* — **friend,** *s.* ami de bouteille, *m.* —**ful,** *s.* bouteille pleine, *f.* — **glass,** *s.* verre de bouteilles, *m.* — **gourd,** *s.* gourde, *f.* — **green,** *s. adj.* vert de bouteille, *m.* — **head,** *s.* hyperoodon, *m.* — **holder,** *s.* partisan, second, *m.* — **making,** *s.* bouteillerie, *f.* — **nose,** *s.* gros nez, pif, *m.*; (*zool.*) hyperoodon, *m.* — **nosed,** *adj.* à gros nez. — **rack,** *s.* porte-bouteilles, *m.*; (*of wood*) planche à bouteilles, *f.* — **room,** *s.* bouteillerie, *f.* — **screw,** *s.* tire-bouchon, *m.* — **trade,** *s.* bouteillerie, *f.* — **up,** *v.a. V.* **Bottle,** *v.a.*; (*fig.*) renfermer, contenir, étouffer, rengaîner. — **warehouse,** *s.* bouteillerie, *f.*

Bottled, *adj.* en bouteilles, en bouteille; (*of fruits, pickles*) en bocal, conservé

Bottler, *s.* metteur en bouteilles, *m.*

Bottling, *s.* mise en bouteilles, *f.*; (*of hay*) bottelage, *m.*

Bottom, *s.* (*lowest part*) bas; (*deepest part, ground*) fond, *m.*; (*foundation*) base, *f.*, fondement, *m.*; (*dale, valley, low ground*) bas-fond, *m.*; (*of a ship*) carène, *f.*, fond, *m.*; (*the ship itself*) bâtiment, navire, vaisseau, *m.*; (*of liquids*) sédiment, *m.*, lie, *f.*; (*limit*) borne, limite, *f.*; (*of a street*, &c.) bout, *m.*; (*of the bowl of a tobacco-pipe, of a crucible, of a lamp*) culot, *m.*; (*of a bed, seat, artichoke*) fond, *m.*; (*of thread*) peloton, *m.*; (*of silkworms*) cocon, *m.*; (*stamina*) nerf, *m.*, vigueur, *f.*; (*in horses, power of enduring continued severe exertion*) fond, *m.*; (*buttocks*) derrière, *m.*; — *adj.* inférieur, de *or* du dessous, du bas, d'en bas; — *v.a.* foncer, mettre un fond à; (*to found*) fonder, baser, asseoir; établir; fixer; — *v.n.* se fonder, se baser, s'appuyer, faire fond, compter (sur). *At* —, au fond. *To examine* or *sift to the* —, examiner à fond. *To sink to the* —, couler à fond. —**less,** *adj.* sans fond. — **pieces,** *s.pl.* enfonçure, *f.*, fonçailles, *f.pl.*

Bottomed, *adj.* à fond ...; (*sheathed*) doublé en. *Copper* —, doublé en cuivre. *Double* —, *false* —, à double fond. *Iron* —, doublé en fer. *Wood* —, à fond de bois

Bottomer, *s.* (*of boots*) ouvrier bottier *or* cordonnier, *m.*; (*of chairs*) empailleur, *m.*

Bottoming, *s.* fonçage, *m.*; fondation, *f.*

Bottomry, *s.* grosse aventure, grosse, bomerie, *f.* *On* —, à la grosse. — **bond,** *s.* contrat à la grosse, *m.* — **interest,** *s.* profit maritime, *m.*, bomerie, *f.* — **loan,** *s.* prêt à la grosse, *m.*

Boudoir, *s.* boudoir, *m.*

Bough, *s.* branche, *f.*, rameau, *m.*

Bought, *part.* acheté, &c. (*V.* **Buy**). — **book,** *s.* (*com.*) livre d'achats, *m.*

Bougie, *s.* bougie, *f.*

Boulder, — **stone,** *s.* fragment *or* quartier de roc, bloc erratique, bloc, *m.*, grosse pierre, *f.*; rognon, caillou, galet, *m.* — **wall,** *s.* mur en galet, *m.*

Boulet, *adj.* bouleté; — *s.* cheval bouleté, *m.*, jument bouletée, *f.*

Bounce, *v.n.* (*leap*) bondir, sauter; (*rush*) se précipiter, s'élancer; (*strike*) frapper, battre, heurter; (*make a noise*) faire du bruit, éclater; (*boast*) se vanter, faire le fanfaron *or* le rodomont; — *s.* bond, rebondissement, *m.*; (*blow*) coup sec, grand coup, *m.*; (*noise*) fracas, éclat, bruit, *m.*; (*boast*) vanterie, hâblerie, fanfaronnade; (*lie*) menterie, bourde, craque, colle, blague, *f.*

Bouncer, *s.* (*boaster*) hâbleur, *m.*, -euse, *f.*, vantard, *m.*, e, *f.*, fanfaron, *m.*, -ne, *f.*; (*liar*) menteur, *m.*, -euse, *f.*; (*boast, lie*) *V.* **Bounce,** *s.*; (*big woman*) dondon, grosse dondon, *f.*

Bouncing, *adj.* (*stout*) gros; (*noisy*) éclatant, bruyant. — *lass*, grosse dondon, *f.*

Bouncingly, *adv.* avec jactance; (*noisily*) bruyamment

Bound, *s.* borne, limite, *f.*; (*leap*) bond, saut, *m.*; — *v.a.* borner, limiter; (*fig.*) contenir, retenir; — *v.n.* bondir, sauter ('*with*,' de); — *part. adj.* lié, &c. (*V.* **Bind**); (*indebted*) redevable ('*to*,' à; '*for*,' de); (*of ships*) destiné (pour), allant (à), à *or* en destination (de); (*detained*) retenu (par ...). — **bailiff,** *s. V.* **Bumbailiff.** —**less,** *adj.* sans bornes, illimité, infini, immense. —**lessly,** *adv.* sans bornes, infiniment, immensément. —**lessness,** *s.* infinité, immensité, *f.*

Boundary, *s.* borne, limite, *f.*; frontière, *f.*

Bounden, *adj.* obligatoire, impérieux, rigoureux, indispensable, sacré; (*indebted*) *V.* **Bound**

Bounding, *s.* bondissement, *m.*; — *adj.* bondissant

Bounteous, Bountiful, *adj.* bon, bienfaisant; généreux, libéral; abondant

Bounteously, Bountifully, *adv.* généreusement, libéralement; abondamment

Bounteousness, Bountifulness, *s.* bonté, bienfaisance, *f.*; générosité, libéralité, *f.*, abondance, *f.*

Bounty, *s.* bonté, bienfaisance, *f.*; générosité, libéralité, munificence, *f.*; largesse, gratification, *f.*, don, *m.*; (*premium*) prime, *f.*; prime d'encouragement, *f.*; (*mil.*) prime (d'engagement), *f.* — *on exportation*, prime d'exportation, *f.*

Bouquet, *s.* bouquet, *m.* — **holder,** *s.* porte-bouquet, *m.*

Bouquetin, *s.* bouquetin, *m.*

Bourbonic, *adj.* bourbonien

Bourbon-ism, -ist. *V.* page 3, § 1

Bourdon, *s.* bourdon, *m.*

Bourgeois, *s.* (*print.*) gaillarde, *f.*

Bourn, Bourne, *s.* borne, limite, *f.*; (*goal*) but, terme, *m.*

Bout, *s.* coup, *m.*, fois, *f.*, tour, *m.*, reprise, *f.*; (*of pleasure*) partie, *f.*; (*fight*) peignée, *f.*; (*one out of a game of two*) manche, *f.*; (*fenc., singlestick*, &c.) assaut, *m.*; manche, *f.*; (*second* or *third* or &c. *in a fight*) reprise, *f.* *At one* —, *all at one* —, d'un seul coup. *To have a* —, faire une partie *or* &c.; (*enjoy oneself*) s'en donner; (*fight*) avoir une peignée, en découdre

Bovine, *adj.* bovine, *f.*; de *or* du bœuf. — *species* or *race*, espèce *or* race bovine, *f.*

Bow, *v.a.* courber, plier; fléchir; incliner; baisser; soumettre; — *v.n.* se courber, plier; fléchir; (*with respect*) s'incliner (devant); faire un salut (à), saluer; (*comply*) se plier, céder, se soumettre. — **down,** *v.a.* courber; baisser; incliner; abaisser; (*overwhelm*) accabler; *v.n.* plier, se courber; (*stoop*) se baisser; (*with respect*) s'incliner, se prosterner, s'humilier. — **out,** congédier par un salut, éconduire. — **to,** fléchir *or* s'incliner devant; (*in common courtesy*) faire un salut à, saluer; (*comply*) se plier à, céder à, se soumettre à

Bow, *s.* (*of the head or body*) salut, *m.*; (*servile* —) courbette, *f.*; (*for shooting*) arc, *m.*; (*of a string*) rosette, *f.*; (*of ribbon*) nœud, *m.*; rosette, *f.*; (*of violins*) archet, *m.*; (*of keys*) anneau, *m.*; (*of saddles*) arçon, *m.*; (*of a sword-mount*) branche, plaque, garde, *f.*; (*of a scythe*) ramassette, *f.*; (*of ships*) avant, *m.*; (*math.*) demi-cercle, *m.* *To draw the long* —, en conter, blaguer, exagérer. — **anchor,** *s.* (*nav.*) *V.* **Bower.** — **bent,** *adj.* courbé en arc, courbé, voûté. — **chaser,** *s.* (*nav.*) canon de chasse, coursier, *m.* — **hand,** *s.* archet, *m.* — **knot,** *s.* rosette, *f.* — **leg,** *s.* jambe arquée, *f.* — **legged,** *adj.* à (*or* aux) jambes arquées, bancal. — **line,** *s.* (*nav.*) bouline, *f.* — **maker,** *s.* arctier, *m.* — **man,** *s.* archer, *m.*; (*nav.*) brigadier, *m.* — **net,** *s.* nasse, *f.* — **shot,** *s.* trait d'arc, trait, *m.*; portée de trait, portée d'arc, *f.* *Within* — *shot*, à portée de trait. — **sprit,** *s.* beaupré, *m.* — **sprit sail,** *s.* civadière, *f.* — **string,** *s.* corde d'arc, *f.*; (*for strangling*) cordon, lacet, *m.* — **window,** *s.* fenêtre en rotonde, fenêtre cintrée en plan, *f.*

— **wow,** *s.* (*doggy*) toutou, *m.*; (*barking*) aboiement, bo-ouo, *m.*; — *v.n.* aboyer, faire bo-ouo

Bowels, *s. pl.* intestins, *m.pl.*, entrailles, *f. pl.*; (*depth*) entrailles, *f.pl.*, sein, *m.*; (*tenderness*) entrailles, *f.pl.*, tendresse, *f.* *To open the —,* (*med.*) relâcher, faire aller (à la selle). *To have* or *keep o.'s — open*, avoir *or* se tenir le ventre libre. *Are your — open?* (*med.*) avez-vous le ventre libre? allez-vous à la selle? *How many times have your — been open to day?* combien de fois avez-vous été à la selle aujourd'hui?

Bower, *s.* tonnelle, *f.*, berceau, *m.*; retraite, *f.*; (*nav.*) ancre de bossoir, ancre de poste, *f.*; — *v.a.* enfermer dans un berceau, enfermer, entourer. *Best —,* seconde ancre, *f.* *Small —,* ancre d'affourche, *f.* *Small — cable*, câble d'affourche, *m.* [plein de berceaux

Bower, Bowery, *adj.* en berceau, qui ombrage;

Bowie-knife, *s.* couteau-poignard, *m.*

Bowl, *s.* bol, *m.*; écuelle, *f.*; sébile, *f.*; (*poet.*) coupe, *f.*, vase, *m.*; (*mil.*, *nav.*) gamelle, *f.*; (*of a tobacco-pipe*) fourneau, *m.*; (*of a spoon*) cuilleron, *m.*; (*ball*) boule, *f.*; — *v.a.* rouler, faire rouler, jeter; — *v.n.* jouer à la boule; servir la boule; (*at ball or cricket*) servir la balle; (*roll*) rouler. *To play at —s*, jouer à la boule

Bowlder. *V.* **Boulder**

Bowler, *s.* joueur de boule, *m.*; (*at ball or cricket*, &c.) celui qui sert la balle, serveur, *m.*

Bowling, *s.* jeu de boules, jeu de boule, *m.* — **alley, -green, -ground,** *s.* jeu de boules, jeu de boule, *m.*; boulingrin, *m.*

Bowyer, *s.* archer, *m.*; (*bow-maker*) arctier, *m.*

Box, *s.* (*tree, or its wood*) buis, *m.*; (*object for enclosing things generally*) boîte, *f.*; (*for packing*) caisse, *f.*; (*trunk*) malle, *f.*; (*for hats*) étui, *m.*; (*of pasteboard, for bonnets or hats*) carton, *m.*; (*for money, precious things*) cassette, *f.*, coffre, *m.*, (*small*) coffret, *m.*; (*for jewels*) écrin, *m.*; (*for the poor*) tronc, *m.*; (*of surgical instr.*) boîtier, *m.*; (*snuff —*) tabatière, *f.*; (*cartridge —*) giberne *f.*; (*of ballot*) urne, *f.*; (*theat.*) loge, *f.*; (*of sentries, signalmen*, &c.) guérite, *f.*; (*in the country*) maisonnette, villa, *f.*, pavillon, pied-à-terre, *m.*; (*shooting* or *hunting —*) *V.* **Shooting** *and* **Hunting;** (*private room*) cabinet particulier, cabinet, *m.*; (*compartment*) stalle, *f.*, compartiment, *m.*; (*in stables*) stalle, *f.*, box, *m.*; (*of carriages*) siége, *m.*; (*of a shoe-black*) sellette, *f.*; (*of screws*) écrou, *m.*; (*of locks*) palastre, palâtre, *m.*; (*of pumps*) corps, *m.*; (*of wheels*) moyeu, *m.*; (*of dice*) cornet, *m.*; (*print.*) cassetin, *m.*; (*anat.*) boîte, *f.*; (*slap*) *V.* **Slap.** — *and needle*, boussole, *f.* — *on the ear*, *V.* **Slap.** *In the wrong —*, fourvoyé, loin de compte. *To be in the wrong —*, se fourvoyer, se tromper, n'y être pas, être loin de compte. — **coat,** *s.* carrick, *m.* — **keeper, -opener,** *s.* ouvreur (*m.*, -euse, *f.*) de loges. — **maker,** *s.* layetier, *m.* — **office,** *s.* bureau de location, *m.* — **plantation,** *s.* buissaie, buissière, *f.* — **thorn,** *s.* lyciet, *m.* — **ticket, -order,** *s.* coupon de loge, *m.* — **tree, -wood,** *s.* buis, *m.*

Box, *v.a.* enfermer *or* mettre dans une boîte, encaisser; mettre une boîte à; (*of trees*) inciser; (*fight with the fist*) boxer; (*slap*) souffleter, donner un soufflet (*or* des soufflets) à; — *v.n.* boxer, se boxer, se battre à coups de poing. — [(*...'s*) *ears*, *V.* **Slap**

Boxen, *adj.* de buis

Boxer, *s.* boxeur, pugiliste, *m.*

Boxing, *s.* boxe, *f.*, pugilat, *m.* — **bout,** *s.* combat (*m.*) *or* peignée (*f.*) à coups de poing. — **day, -night,** *s.* lendemain de Noël, *m.* — **glove,** *s.* gant bourré, *m.* — **match,** *s.* combat de boxeurs *or* de pugilistes, assaut de pugilat, *m.*

Boy, *s.* garçon, *m.*; enfant, *m.*; (*pupil at school*) élève, *m.*; (*servant*) petit domestique, *m.*; (*on board ship*) mousse, *m.*; (*post —*) *V.* **Post;** — *adj.* petit, jeune; d'enfant. *Bad* or *naughty —*, enfant méchant, méchant enfant, petit mauvais sujet, *m.* *Good —*, bon garçon, enfant sage, *m.* *Mere —*, enfant, gamin, *m.* *Old —!* vieux! mon vieux! *—'s trick*, espièglerie, *f.* — **like,** *adj. adv.* de garçon, d'enfant, comme un enfant, en enfant

Boyar, Boyard, *s. adj.* boyard, *m.*

Boyau, *s.* boyau, *m.*

Boyhood, *s.* enfance, *f.*; adolescence, *f.*

Boyish, *adj.* d'enfant; enfantin; puéril; d'enfance [enfant

Boyishly, *adv.* d'une manière enfantine, en

Boyishness, Boyism, *s.* enfantillage, *m.*, [puérilité, *f.*

Brabançonne, *s.* brabançonne, *f.*

Brabanter, *s.* Brabançon, *m.*, -ne, *f.*

Brabantine, *adj.* brabançon

Brabble, *v.n.* se chamailler; — *s.* chamaillis, *m.*

Brabbler, *s.* querelleur, *m.*, -euse, *f.*

Brabbling, *s.* chamaillerie, *f.*, chamaillis, *m.*

Brace, *s.* (*of arms*) brassard, *m.*; (*of trousers*) bretelle, *f.*; (*for children*) brassière, *f.*; (*tightness*) tension, *f.*; (*of game*) couple, *f.*; (*pers.*) couple, *m.*; (*of greyhounds*) laisse, *f.*; (*of pistols*) paire, *f.*; (*of carriages*) soupente, *f.*; (*mach.*) attache, *f.*, lien, *m.*; (*cook.*, *print.*, *writ.*, *mus.*) accolade, *f.*; (*arch.*) tirant, *m.*; (*carp.*) ancre, *f.*; moise, *f.*; (*of drums*) tirant, *m.*; (*tool*) vilebrequin, *m.*; (*meas.*) brasse, *f.*; (*nav.*) bras, *m.*; — *v.a.* lier, attacher; (*tighten*) serrer; bander; tendre; (*invigorate*) fortifier, donner du ton à; (*nav.*) brasser, brasseyer. — **band,** *s.* bretelle, *f.* — **end,** *s.* patte de [bretelle, *f.*

Bracelet, *s.* bracelet, *m.*

Bracer, *s.* brassard, *m.*; bandage, *m.*; (*med.*) tonique, astringent, *m.*

Brach, Brack, — hound, *s.* braque, *m.*

Brachial, *adj.* brachial; huméral [(*keen*) vif

Bracing, *adj.* fortifiant; tonique; salutaire;

Bracken, *s.* ptéride, fougère, *f.*

Bracket, *s.* (*print.*) crochet, *m.*; accolade, *f.*; (*carp.*) tasseau, *m.*; applique, *f.*; (*arch.*) console, *f.*; (*for lights*) bras de lumière, bras d'applique, bras, *m.*, applique, *f.*; (*for clocks*) socle, *m.*, console, *f.*; — *v.a.* réunir par une accolade. — **clock,** *s.* pendule de console, *f.* — **seat,** *s.* strapontin, *m.*

Bracketed, *adj.* réunis par une accolade; égaux

Brack-hound, *s.* *V.* **Brach**

Brackish, *adj.* saumâtre

Brackishness, *s.* goût saumâtre, *m.*

Bract, Bractea, *s.* bractée, *f.*

Brad, *s.* pointe, *f.*, clou, *m.* — **awl,** *s.* poinçon, *m.*

Bradshaw, *s.* tableau des heures, *m.*; indicateur des chemins de fer, *m.*

Brag, *v.n.* se vanter; — *s.* vanterie, fanfaronnade, *f.*; (*pride*) orgueil, *m.*

Braggadocio, *s.* (*pers.*) bravache, fanfaron, *m.*; (*thing*) fanfaronnade, *f.* [faron, *m.*

Braggart, Bragger, *s. adj.* vantard, fan-

Bragging, *s.* vanterie, forfanterie, *f.*

Braggingly, *adv.* en fanfaron

Brahman, Brahmin, *s.* brahmane, *m.*

Brahminical, *adj.* brahmanique

Brahminism, *s.* brahmanisme, *m.*

Braid, *v.a.n.* tresser; (*need.*) soutacher; — *s.* tresse, *f.*; (*tissue*) lacet, *m.*; (*need.*) soutache, *f.* — **machine,** *s.* machine à lacets, *f.*

Braider, *s.* tresseur, *m.*, -euse, *f.*; (*need.*) soutacheur, *m.*, -euse, *f.*

Braiding-machine, *s.* machine à lacets, *f.*

Brail, *s.* (*nav.*) cargue, *f.*; — *v.a.* (— **up**) carguer

Brain, *s.* cervelle, *f.*, cerveau, *m.*; (*fig.*) jugement, esprit, *m.*, tête, *f.*, cerveau, *m.*; — *v.a.* faire sauter la cervelle à, écerveler. *To blow anyone's — s out*, brûler (*or* faire sauter) la cervelle à quelqu'un. *To blow o.'s —s out*, se brûler (*or* se faire sauter) la cervelle. *To knock anyone's — out*, faire sauter la cervelle à quelqu'un. *To puzzle* or *rack o.'s —* (or *—s*), s'alambiquer *or* se creuser le cerveau, se creuser *or* se casser la tête, mettre son esprit à la torture. — **box,** *s.* caboche, *f.* — **fever,** *s.* fièvre cérébrale, *f.* —**less,** *adj.* sans cervelle, écervelé. —**lessness,** *s.* absence (*f.*) *or* manque (m.) or défaut (m.) de cervelle, étourderie, f. — **pan,** s. boîte du crâne, f. — **sick,** adj. à cerveau malade; (giddy) étourdi. — **sickness,** s. dérangement du cerveau, m.; (giddiness) étourderie, f. — **stone coral,** s. encéphaloïde, m., méandrine, f. [cervelle ...; à tête ...

Brained, adj. (in compounds) à cerveau ..., à

Braird, v.n. sortir de terre, paraître, poindre, pointer; — s. germe, jeune semis, m.

Braise, v.a. braiser

Braising-pan, s. braisière, f.

Brait, s. diamant brut, m.

Brake, s. (bot.) ptéride, fougère, f.; (waste land) lande, f.; (thicket) fourré, buisson d'épines, m., buissonnaie, épinaie, f., broussailles, f.pl.; (of fern) fougeraie, f.; (of briars) ronceraie, f.; (cane —) cannaie, f.; (fig.) sentier épineux, m.; (for hemp) brisoir, m.; (for bread) pétrin, m., huche, f.; (of farriers) travail, m.; (of bridles) bridon, m.; (of pumps) brimbale, bringuebale, f.; (agr.) grande herse, f.; (of mach., of a carriage and rail.) frein, m. —**sman,** s. (rail.) garde-frein, sous-chef de train, m. — **van,** s. voiture à frein, f. — **wheel,** s. roue d'engrenage, f.

Braky, adj. couvert de broussailles, épineux

Bramble, s. ronce, f. — **berry,** s. V. **Blackberry.** — **bush,** s. broussailles, f.pl. — **finch,** s. V. **Brambling.** — **net,** s. hallier, m.

Brambled, adj ronceux, plein de ronces

Brambling, s. pinson des Ardennes, m.

Brambly. V. **Brambled**

Bramin, &c. V. **Brahmin,** &c.

Bran, s. son, m. — **new,** adj. tout neuf

Branch, s. branche, f.; (of a hose-pipe) lance, f.; (of roads, rail., tech.) embranchement, m.; (admin.) succursale, f.; — adj. à branches; d'embranchement; (admin.) succursale (adj. f.). — **bank,** s. banque succursale, succursale, f., comptoir, m. — **establishment,** s. succursale, f.; comptoir, m. — **line,** s. (rail.) embranchement, m. — **office,** s. succursale, f.; (post.) bureau supplémentaire, m. Principal — office, (post.) bureau principal, m. — **pipe,** s. tuyau d'embranchement, m.; branche de tuyau, f.; (of a hose) lance, f. — **railway,** s. embranchement de chemin de fer, m. — **road,** s. embranchement, m. — **work,** s. branchage, m.

Branch, v.a. brancher; — v.n pousser des branches; (fig.) se ramifier, se diviser, brancher, se brancher. — **off, out,** pousser des branches; (fig.) se ramifier; se diviser; (of roads) s'embrancher; diverger; partir; aller; (pers.) se jeter, se lancer, s'étendre, s'égarer

Branched, adj. à branches; (bot.) branchu, rameux. — work, branchage, m

Brancher, s. arbre qui pousse des branches, m.; (bird) oiseau branchier, m.

Branchiæ, s. pl. branchies, f.pl.

Branchial, adj. branchial

Branchiness, s. abondance de branches, f.

Branching, adj. rameux; (fig.) d'embranchement; — s. ramure, f., branchage, m.; (fig.) branchement, embranchement, m., branche, f. — **off,** s. embranchement, m.

Branchiopod, s. branchiopode, m.

Branchless, adj. sans branches, ébranché

Branchlet, s. petite branche, branchette, [brindille, f.

Branchy, adj. V. **Branched**

Brancursine. V. **Brankursine**

Brand, s. tison, brandon, m.; (mark) marque, f.; (of infamy) flétrissure, f., stigmate, m.; (sword) épée, f., glaive m.; (kind) sorte, qualité, f.; — v.a. marquer; (with infamy) flétrir, stigmatiser; marquer (du sceau de l'infamie). — **dog,** s. chevrette, f., chenet, m. — **goose,** s. V. **Brent-goose.** — **iron,** s. fer à marquer, m.; (of criminals) fer chaud, m.; (trivet) chevrette, f. — **new,** adj. tout neuf

Brandenburger, s. Brandebourgeois, m., e, f.

Brandied, adj. mêlé d'eau-de-vie; (of fruit) à l'eau-de-vie

Branding, s. action de marquer, f.; flétrissure, &c. (V. **Brand,** s.). — **iron,** s. V. **Brand-iron**

Brandish, v.a. brandir

Brandling, s. (worm) branle-queue, bâtard, vérotis, m.; (young salmon) digitale, f.

Brandy, s. eau-de-vie, f.; (ratafia, as in "cherry-brandy," &c.) ratafia (de ...), m.; — v.a. mettre de l'eau-de-vie dans, mêler d'eau-de-vie; (wine) viner (du vin). — and water, eau mêlée d'eau-de-vie, f., grog à l'eau-de-vie, m. — **cherry,** s. cerise à l'eau-de-vie, f. —**fruit,** s. fruit à l'eau-de-vie, m. —**merchant,** s. négociant en eaux-[de-vie, m.

Brandying, s. (of wine) vinage, m.

Brangle. V. **Wrangle** [acanthe, f.

Brankursine, s. branc-ursine, branche-ursine,

Branny, adj. semblable au son; de son

Brant, — **goose,** s. V. **Brent-goose**

Brasier, s. (pan) brasier, m.; (pers.) V. **Brazier**

Brasil-wood. V. **Brazil**

Brass, s. airain, cuivre jaune, cuivre, laiton, m.; fonte, f.; bronze, m.; (coin) monnaie de cuivre, f., cuivre, m.; (impudence) effronterie, f., front, toupet, m.; —**es,** pl. (in the kitchen) batterie de cuisine, f. Red —, tombac, m. — **band,** s. fanfare, musique de fanfare, musique d'instruments en cuivre, f. — **button,** s. bouton de cuivre, m. — **cannon,** s. canon de fonte, m. — **finisher,** s. polisseur en cuivre, m. — **foil,** s. cuivre battu, m.; (tinsel) clinquant, oripeau, m. — **founder,** s. fondeur en cuivre, m. — **foundry,** s. fonderie de cuivre, f. — **instrument,** s. instrument en cuivre, m. — **leaf,** s. V. — **foil.** — **turner,** s. tourneur en cuivre, m. — **visaged,** adj. au or à front d'airain, effronté. — **wares,** s.pl. dinanderie, f. — **wire,** s. fil de laiton, m. — **works,** s. pl. ouvrages en cuivre jaune, m.pl.; (manufactory) usine à cuivre jaune, f.

Brassica, s. chou, m. [blance avec l'airain, f.

Brassiness, s. nature de l'airain, f.; ressem-

Brassy, adj. d'airain; de cuivre jaune, de cuivre, de laiton; de la nature or de la couleur de l'airain (or du laiton); (impudent) effronté, impudent [môme, m.

Brat, s. marmot, bambin, moutard, mioche,

Brattling, s. tumulte, vacarme, tapage, m.

Bravado, s. bravade, f. In —, par bravade

Brave, adj. brave, vaillant, courageux; noble, grand; excellent; beau; — v.a. braver; défier

Bravely, adv. bravement, vaillamment, courageusement; (fam.) fameusement, joliment, bien [m., magnificence, f.

Bravery, s. bravoure, f., courage, m.; éclat,

Bravingly, adv. avec bravade

Bravissimo, int. bravissimo!

Bravo, int. bravo! — s. bravo, m.

Bravoura, Bravura, s. air de bravoure, m.

Brawl, v.n. brailler, clabauder; (fig.) murmurer; — s. V. **Brawling;** (dance, tune) branle, m.

Brawler, s. braillard, m., e, f., brailleur, m., -euse, f., clabaudeur, m., -euse, f.; querelleur, m., -euse, f.

Brawling, s. braillement, m., clabauderie, f., clabaudage, m., tapage, bruit, m.; querelle, f., chamaillis, m.; mêlée, f.; — adj. braillard, brailleur; querelleur [avec tapage

Brawlingly, adv. en criant, en clabaudant,

Brawn, s. fromage de cochon, m.; (of the body) partie charnue, f., muscles, m.pl., chair ferme, f.; (strength) force musculaire, f.

Brawniness, s. nature charnue, nature musculeuse, f.; force musculaire, f.

Brawny, adj. charnu; musculeux; robuste

Bray, v.a. broyer, piler; (to sound) faire résonner, faire retentir; — v.n. (cry) braire; (fig.) résonner, retentir; — s. braiment, braire, m.; (fig.) résonnement, retentissement, bruit, son éclatant, son, m [f., braillard, m., e, f.

Brayer, s. personne qui brait comme un âne,

Braying, adj. qui brait; (fig.) résonnant, retentissant; — s. V. **Bray,** s.

Braze, *v.a.* braser, souder; (*fig.*) endurcir; rendre effronté

Brazen, *adj.* d'airain; de cuivre, de laiton; de bronze; (*fig.*) d'airain, effronté, impudent; — *v.n.* avoir un front d'airain. *To — it out,* payer d'effronterie *or* d'audace. *To put on a — face,* s'armer d'effronterie, avoir du toupet. — **age,** *s.* âge *or* siècle d'airain, *m.* — **face,** *s.,* — **faced,** *adj.* effronté, *m.*, e, *f.*, impudent, *m.*, e, *f.* — **horse,** *s.* cheval de bronze, *m.*

Brazened, *adj.* effronté, impudent

Brazenly, *adv.* effrontément, impudemment

Brazenness, *s.* ressemblance avec l'airain, *f.*; (*fig.*) effronterie, impudence, *f.*

Brazier, *s.* (*pers.*) chaudronnier, *m.*; dinandier, *m.*; (*pan*) *V.* **Brasier**

Brazil, *s.* (*geog.*) le Brésil, *m.* — **nut,** *s.* noix du Brésil, *f.* — **wood,** *s.* brésil, brésillet, bois de Brésil, *m.*

Braziletto-wood, *s.* brésillet, *m.*

Brazilian, *s.* Brésilien, *m.*, -ne, *f.*; — *adj.* brésilien, du Brésil [soudure, *f.*

Brazing, *s.* brasement, soudage, *m.*; brasure,

Breach, *s.* (*opening, gap*) brèche, *f.*; (*breaking*) fracture, *f.*; bris, *m.*; (*fig.*) infraction, violation, atteinte, *f.*; manque, *m.*; (*of trust*) abus (de confiance), *m.*; (*of the peace*) délit (contre l'ordre public), *m.*; (*quarrel*) rupture, *f.*; — *v.a.* faire une brèche à, battre en brèche

Breaching, *adj.* de brèche

Bread, *s.* pain, *m.*; — *adj.* de pain; à pain; au pain. *Grated —,* chapelure, *f.* — *and butter,* — *and cheese,* (*fig., means of living*) subsistance, *f.*; gagne-pain, *m.*; pot-au-feu, *m.* — **basket,** *s.* panier (*m.*) *or* corbeille (*f.*) à (*or* au) pain; (*stomach*) bocal, coffre, panier au pain, *m.* — **corn,** *s.* céréale, *f.*, céréales, *f.pl.* — **crumb,** *s.* mie de pain, *f.*; (*small particle*) miette de pain, *f.* — **fruit,** *s.* fruit à pain, *m.* — **fruit tree,** *s.* arbre à pain, jaquier, *m.* — **grater,** *s.* râpe à pain, *f.* — **kneading machine,** *s.* pétrin mécanique, *m.* —**less,** *adj.* sans pain. — **maker,** *s.* pétrisseur, geindre, *m.* — **making,** *s.* boulangerie, *f.*; manutention, *f.*; fabrication du pain, *f.* — **making machine,** *s.* machine à faire le pain, *f.* — **plant,** *s.* céréale, *f.* — **poultice,** *s.* cataplasme de mie de pain, *m.* — **pudding,** *s.* pudding au pain, *m.* — **raspings,** *s. pl.* chapelure, *f.* — **room,** *s.* (*nav.*) soute au pain, *f.* — **sauce,** *s.* sauce au pain, *f.* — **stuff,** *s.* céréale, *f.* — **tree,** *s. V.* — **fruit tree.** — **winner,** *s.* gagne-pain, *m.*

Breadth, *s.* largeur, *f.*; (*of tissue*) lé, *m.* —**less,** *adj.* sans largeur, étroit

Break, *v.a.* casser; (*asunder, with an effort, and fig. silence, the ice, a spell, o.'s fast, the ranks,* &c.) rompre; (*smash, destroy, ruin, and fig. the heart*) briser; (*pierce, burst*) percer, crever; (*impair*) délabrer; (*open*) ouvrir, enfoncer; (*divide, fig.*) couper; (*interrupt*) interrompre, entrecouper; (*subdue*) dompter, abattre; (*horses,* &c.) rompre, dresser; (*a fall, a blow*) amortir; (*news*) préparer (une personne) à (une nouvelle); (*begin*) entamer; (*o.'s way*) se frayer (un chemin), s'ouvrir (un passage); (*o.'s word,* &c.) manquer à; violer, enfreindre; (*a law*) enfreindre; (*disturb*) troubler; (*bad habits*) corriger (quelqu'un de ...), faire perdre (à quelqu'un ...); (*accustom*) habituer, rompre; (*dismiss*) renvoyer, dissoudre, licencier; (*cause pers. to fail*) faire faire faillite *or* banqueroute à; (— *upon the wheel*) rouer; (*the bank, at play*) faire sauter (la banque); (*pound, crush: agr.*) concasser; (*mil.*) rompre, enfoncer. *To — the journey,* s'arrêter en route. *To — o.'s arm, o.'s neck,* se casser un bras, le cou. — **asunder,** rompre; briser; séparer, désunir. — **down,** abattre; abaisser; abolir; détruire; altérer, délabrer; affaisser. — **in,** (*train*) rompre, dresser, former; (*tame*) rompre, dompter. — **off,** rompre; interrompre; (*stop*) empêcher, arrêter. — **open,** enfoncer, forcer; (*a letter*) décacheter. — **up,** démolir; dépecer; détruire; disperser; licencier; (*an assembly*) dissoudre; (*sittings, a camp*) lever; (*land, roads*) défoncer; (*cease*) cesser, discontinuer

Break, *v.n.* casser, se casser; rompre, se rompre; briser, se briser; (*burst*) éclater; (*of swellings*) percer, crever, aboutir; (*fall, rush*) fondre (sur); se jeter; (*get away*) s'échapper; s'arracher; se séparer; (*get rid*) se défaire (de), renoncer (à); (*grow old*) décliner, baisser, se casser; (*of the day*) poindre, paraître; (*of the weather*) changer; (*fail*) faire faillite *or* banqueroute; (*of the bank, at play*) sauter [*the bank is broken,* la banque a sauté]; (*of the voice*) muer. — **away,** s'arracher; se séparer, se détacher; (*fig.*) se dissoudre; (*of clouds,* &c.) se dissiper. — **down,** (*of carriages*) verser; (*of horses*) s'abattre; (*fail*) manquer, faillir; échouer; ne pas se soutenir; tomber; défaillir; s'altérer, se délabrer; s'affaisser; s'écrouler; (*stop short*) demeurer court, s'arrêter. — **forth,** éclater; (*of water, light*) jaillir, s'échapper. — **in,** s'introduire (dans); pénétrer (dans); entrer (dans); (*invade*) s'emparer (de), envahir. — **into,** éclater en; laisser échapper; (*enter*) entrer *or* pénétrer *or* s'introduire (par force, *or* à l'aide d'effraction) dans; (*fall*) fondre sur; (*fig.*) se jeter dans. — **in upon,** fondre sur, se jeter sur, tomber sur; s'emparer de, envahir; interrompre; se présenter à, s'offrir à. — **loose,** s'échapper, s'évader; s'affranchir; se détacher; se dégager; s'abandonner, se débaucher. — **off,** rompre; (*cease*) cesser; (*stop*) s'arrêter, s'interrompre; (*separate*) s'arracher (à), se séparer (de), se détacher (de); (*get rid*) se défaire (de), renoncer (à). — **out,** (*of wars, quarrels, conflagrations, fig. of persons,* &c.) éclater; (*of diseases, conflagrations*) se déclarer; (*of taking fire*) prendre; (*of the sun*) paraître; (*escape*) s'échapper; sortir; (*of water, light*) jaillir, s'échapper; (*in*) se répandre; (*give oneself up, indulge*) se jeter (dans), se livrer (à), s'abandonner (à); (*of the skin*) avoir une éruption, sortir, se couvrir (de). — **over,** se répandre, déborder. — **through,** se faire jour *or* se frayer un chemin à travers; traverser, percer, fendre; ne pas s'arrêter à; surmonter, renverser; forcer, franchir; s'affranchir de; enfreindre, violer; (*begin*) entamer; (*mil.*) enfoncer. — **up,** (*cease*) cesser; (*separate*) se séparer, se rompre; (*melt*) fondre; (*of assemblies*) se séparer; (*of sittings, camps*) être levé; (*of schools*) entrer en vacances; (*of roads*) se défoncer; (*of clouds, fog*) se dissiper; (*of the weather*) changer. — **with,** rompre avec, se brouiller avec

Break, *s.* cassure, *f.*; rupture, *f.*; (*opening*) trouée, *f.*; percée, *f.*; clairière, *f.*; (*fig.*) pause, interruption, *f.*; suspension, *f.*; (*blank*) lacune, *f.*; (*of continuity*) solution, *f.*; (*of day*) point, *m.*, pointe, *f.*; (*in the weather*) changement, *m.*; (*of the voice*) mue, *f.*, changement, *m.*; (*of a cuirass*) défaut, *m.*; (*print.*) alinéa, *m.*; (*arch.*) renfoncement, *m.*; (*agr.*) sole, *f.*; (*carriage*) breack, break, *m.*; voiture pour dresser les chevaux, *f.*; (*of mach., of a carriage, and rail.*) frein, *m.*; (*of pumps,* &c.) *V.* **Brake.** — **down,** — **neck,** —**sman,** — **up,** — **water,** &c. *See* [*below*

Breakable, *adj.* cassable

Breakage, *s.* cassage, *m.*, casse, cassure, rupture, *f.*, brisement, *m.*; (*com.*) casse, *f.*

Break-down, *s.* déconfiture, débâcle, *f.*; détérioration, *f.*; (*failure*) insuccès, *m.*; accident, *m.*

Breaker, *s.* casseur, *m.*, -euse, *f.*; briseur, *m.*, -euse, *f.*; (*fig.*) violateur, *m.*, -trice, *f.*, infracteur, *m.*, -trice, *f.*, transgresseur, *m.*; (*tamer*) dompteur, *m.*; (*trainer*) dresseur, *m.*; (*nav.: rock,* &c.) brisant, écueil, *m.*; (*wave*) brisant, *m.*; (*of ice*) brise-glace, *m.*; (*agr.*) concasseur, *m.*

Breakfast, *s.* déjeuner, premier déjeuner, *m.*; — *v.n.* déjeuner ('*on*', de, avec). — **cup,** *s.*

grande tasse, *f.*, bol, *m.* —**less,** *adj.* sans déjeuner. — **room,** *s.* petite salle à manger, *f.* — **service,** *s.* déjeuner, *m.* — **table,** *s.* table servie pour le déjeuner, *f.*; table, *f.* — **time, -hour,** *s.* heure du déjeuner, *f.*

Breakfasting, *s.* déjeuner, *m.*

Breaking, *s.* rupture, cassure, *f.*, cassage, brisement, *m.*; bris, *m.*; fracture, *f.*; (*fig.*) violation, infraction, *f.*; (*taming*) domptement, *m.*; (*training*) dressage, *m.*; (*com.*) faillite, banqueroute, *f.*; (*eruption*) éruption, *f.*; (*irruption*) irruption, invasion, *f.*; (*of the day*) pointe, *f.*, point, *m.*; (*of the voice*) mue, *f.*, changement, *m.*; (*of news*) préparation, *f.*; (*of the ground*) *V.* — **up;** (*thaw*) dégel, *m.* — **down,** *s. V.* **Breakdown,** *s.* — **in,** *s.* irruption, *f.*; (*taming*) domptement, *m.*; (*training*) dressage, *m.* — **open,** *s.* effraction, *f.*; bris, *m.* — **out,** *s.* éruption, &c. (*V.* **Outbreak**). — **up,** *s.* dissolution, *f.*; séparation, dispersion, *f.*; fin, *f.*; ruine, *f.*; (*of schools*) commencement des vacances, *m.*; (*of ice*) débâcle, *f.*; (*of the ground: agr.*) première façon, *f.*, (*mil.*) ouverture des tranchées, *f.*

Breakneck, *s.* casse-cou, *m.*; précipice, *m.*; — *adj.* à se casser le cou, dangereux, périlleux; (*steep*) escarpé, à pic [de train, *m.*

Breaksman, *s.* (*rail.*) garde-frein, sous-chef

Break-up, *s. V.* **Breaking-up**

Breakvan, Breakwheel. *V.* **Brake**

Breakwater, *s.* brise-lames, *m.*; éperon, *m.*; digue, *f.*; jetée, *f.*

Breakwind, *s.* abrivent, *m.*

Bream, *s.* (*fish*) brème, *f.*; — *v.a.* (*nav.*) chauffer

Breaming, *s.* (*nav.*) chauffage, *m.*

Breast, *s.* sein, *m.*, poitrine, *f.*; (*of animals*) poitrine, *f.*; estomac, *m.*; (*of a horse*) poitrail, *m.*; (*of females*) mamelle, *f.*, sein, *m.*; (*fig.*) cœur, *m.*, âme, conscience, *f.*, sein, *m.*; (*of a fowl*, &c.) blanc, *m.*; (*of a coat*) revers, *m.pl.*; (*of a plough*) versoir, *m.*; (*of ships*) travers, flanc, *m.*; (*arch.*) tore, *m.*; — *v.a.* opposer la poitrine à; attaquer de front, affronter, braver, lutter contre. — *to* —, (*of duels*) à bout portant. *To make a clean — of it,* avouer tout, faire un aveu complet, dire tout ce qu'on a sur la conscience. — **bone,** *s.* sternum, *m.*; (*fam.*, *of birds*) brechet, *m.* — **button,** *s.* bouton de devant, *m.* — **collar,** *s.* bricole, *f.* — **deep,** *adj. adv.* jusqu'à la poitrine. — **drawer, -glass,** *s.* tire-lait, *m.* — **height,** *s.* hauteur d'appui, *f.* — **high,** *adj. adv.* à hauteur d'appui; jusqu'à la poitrine. — **pin,** *s.* épingle de chemise, épingle de cravate, épingle, *f.* — **pad, -piece,** *s.* plastron, *m.* — **plate,** *s.* cuirasse, *f.*; plaque, *f.*; (*of horses*) poitrail, *m.*, bricole, *f.*; (*drill-plate*) plastron; (*of Jewish priests*) pectoral, rational, *m.* — **plough,** *s.* tranche-gazon, *m.*, écobue, écobueuse, charrue écobueuse, *f.* — **pocket,** *s.* poche de côté, *f.* — **pump,** *s.* pompe à sein, *f.* — **strap,** *s.* bricole, *f.*, poitrail, *m.* — **summer,** *s.* poitrail, sommier, *m.* — **wall,** *s.* mur de soutènement, *m.* — **work,** *s.* (*fort.*) parapet, *m.*; (*nav.*) fronteau, *m.* [*Single* —, droit

Breasted, *adj.* à ... poitrine. *Double* —, croisé.

Breath, *s.* haleine, *f.*; (*fig.*) souffle, *m.*; (*life*) vie, existence, *f.* *Last* —, dernier soupir, *m.* *Shortness of* —, courte haleine. *In a* —, *in the same* —, d'une haleine, tout d'une haleine; au même instant. *In* —, en haleine. *Out of* —, hors d'haleine, essoufflé; à perte d'haleine. *To draw* —, respirer. *To draw a long* —, prendre une longue respiration. *To draw o.'s last* —, rendre le dernier soupir. *To get out of* —, perdre haleine. *To hold o.'s* —, retenir son haleine. *To put out of* —, faire perdre haleine à. *To run oneself out of* —, courir à perte d'haleine. *To take or recover* —, reprendre haleine, respirer un peu, respirer. *To take ...'s — away,* couper (*or* faire perdre) la respiration à, essouffler; surprendre, déconcerter; interdire. *There is not a — of air stirring,* il ne fait pas un souffle de vent

Breathable, *adj.* respirable

Breathableness, *s.* respirabilité, *f.*

Breathe, *v.n.a.* respirer; (*blow*, &c.) souffler; exhaler; inspirer; (*a wish*) soupirer. *To — short,* avoir l'haleine courte. *To — o.'s last,* rendre le dernier soupir. — **after,** soupirer après, souhaiter. — **forth,** — **out,** souffler; exhaler; pousser [**Winded**

Breathed, *adj.* en haleine; (*in compounds*) *V.*

Breathing, *adj.* qui respire; vivant; (*in compounds*) pour respirer; — *s.* respiration, *f.*, souffle, *m.*; (*fig.*) aspiration, *f.*, soupir, *m.*; (*gram.*) aspiration, *f.*; (*Gr. gram.*) esprit, *m.* *Rough* —, esprit rude, *m.* *Smooth* or *soft* —, esprit doux, *m.* — **hole,** *s.* soupirail, *m.* — **place,** *s.* place pour reposer, pause, *f.* — **time,** *s.* (le) temps de respirer, (le) temps de reprendre haleine, temps de repos, relâche, repos, répit, *m.*

Breathless, *adj.* sans haleine; (*out of breath*) haletant, essoufflé, hors d'haleine; (*fig.*) à perte d'haleine; attentif; confondu, interdit; profond; vif, cruel, mortel; inanimé, sans vie [d'haleine, *f.*

Breathlessness, *s.* essoufflement, *m.*, perte

Bred, *adj.* élevé; — *part.* enfanté, &c. (*V.* **Breed**). *Half* —, *High* —, *Ill* —, *Low* —, *Thorough* —, *Well* —, *See* **Half, High,** &c.

Breech, *s.* derrière, fessier, *m.*; (*of fire-arms*) culasse, *f.*; (*of saddles,* — *band*) reculement; — *v.a.* mettre en culotte, culotter; (*to whip*) fesser; (*fire-arms*) enculasser, mettre une culasse à. — **band,** *s.* reculement, *m.* — **loader,** *s.* arme (*f.*) à feu (fusil *or* &c.) se chargeant par la culasse. — **loading,** *adj.* se chargeant *or* qui se charge par la culasse

Breeches, *s. pl.* culotte, *f.*; (*more than one pair*) culottes, *f.pl.* *A pair of* —, une culotte. *To wear the* —, porter la culotte. — **maker,** *s.* culottier, *m.* *O.'s* — **pocket,** *s.* la poche de sa culotte, sa poche, *f.*, son gousset, *m.*

Breeching, *s.* (*whipping*) fessée, *f.*; (*of saddles*) reculement, *m.*; (*nav.*) brague, *f.*

Breed, *s.* race, *f.*; (*of birds*) couvée, *f.*; — *v.a.* enfanter, engendrer; produire, occasionner, causer, faire naître, être la source de; (*rear, educate*) élever; (*an illness*) couver; (*teeth*) faire; — *v.n.* enfanter; (*be born*) naître; multiplier. — *in and in,* racer. — **up,** élever

Breeder, *s.* (*animal, general sense*) reproducteur, *m.*; (*female, particularly*) femelle qui fait des petits, *f.*; (*mare*) poulinière, *f.*; (*woman*) femme qui fait des enfants, *f.*; (*father*) père, auteur, *m.*; (*mother*) mère, *f.*; (*thing*) cause, source, *f.*; (*rearer*) éleveur, *m.* *Good* —, femelle qui fait beaucoup de petits, *f.*; (*woman*) femme qui fait beaucoup d'enfants, *f.*, (*jest.*) mère Gigogne, *f.*; (*mare*) bonne poulinière, *f.*; (*bird*) bonne pondeuse, *f.*

Breeding, *s.* production, génération, *f.*; reproduction, *f.*; gestation, *f.*; (*fig.*) éducation, *f.*; politesse, *f.*, savoir-vivre, *m.*; (*rearing of animals*) élève, *f.*, élevage, *m.*; (*of silkworms, bees*) éducation, *f.*; — *adj.* (*of animals*) reproducteur; (*of mares*) poulinière; (*of women*) qui fait des enfants. — *in and in,* consanguinité, *f.* — *of teeth,* dentition, *f.* *Bad* or *ill* —, mauvaise éducation, *f.*, mauvaises manières, *f.pl.*, mauvais ton, mauvais genre, *m.* *Good* —, bonne éducation, *f.*, bonnes manières, *f.pl.*, bon ton, *m.*, politesse, *f.*, savoir-vivre, *m.*, urbanité, *f.* *To have no* —, ne savoir pas vivre. — **cage,** *s.* nichoir, *m.* — **stud,** *s.* haras, *m.*

Breeze, *s.* brise, *f.*, vent, *m.*; (*wrangle*) altercation, discussion, affaire, *f.*; (*fly*) taon, *m.*; (*coal-dust*) poussier, *m.*; fraisil, *m.*; (*cinders*) escarbilles, *f.pl.*; (*ashes*) cendres, *f.pl.*; (*in a brick-kiln*) charbonnée, *f.* — **fly,** *s.* taon, *m.* —**less,** *adj.* sans un souffle de vent, calme

Breezy, *adj.* rafraîchi par la brise, frais; (*of the breeze*) de la brise

Brent-goose, Brent-barnacle, s. V. **Barnacle** [mer, s. poitrail, sommier, m.
Bressomer, Bressummer, Brestsum-
Brethren, s. pl. frères, m.pl.
Breton, s. adj. Breton, m., -ne, f.
Breve, s. brève, f.; (papal) bref, m.
Brevet, s. brevet, m.; — adj. à brevet; — v.a. [breveter
Breviary, s. bréviaire, m.
Brevier, s. petit texte, m.
Brevity, s. brièveté, f.; concision, f.
Brew, v.a. brasser; (plot) tramer, machiner; — v.n. faire de la bière; (fig.) se préparer, se tramer, se former, s'amasser, couver. — **house,** s. brasserie, f.
Brewage, s. breuvage mélangé, mélange, m.
Brewer, s. brasseur, m., -euse, f.
Brewery, s. brasserie, f. [brassin, m.
Brewing, s. brassage, m.; (quantity brewed)
Brewster, s. V. **Brewer**
Briar, s. ronce, f.; (wild rose) églantier, m. Sweet —, églantier odorant, m. Wild —, églan-
Briarean, adj. de Briarée [tier, m.
Briary, adj. ronceux, plein de ronces; — s. ronceraie, f.
Bribe, s. présent destiné à corrompre, présent, m.; (fig.) moyen de séduction, appât, m.; tentation, f.; — v.a. corrompre, suborner, gagner; (fig.) séduire; persuader; tenter. To take a —, se laisser corrompre
Briber, s. corrupteur, m., -trice, f., suborneur, m., -euse, f.; (fig.) séducteur, m., -trice, f.
Bribery, Bribing, s. corruption, subornation, f.; (fig.) séduction, f.
Brick, s. brique, f.; (pers.) brave garçon, bon enfant, m.; luron, m.; — adj. de (or en) brique, de (or en) briques; à briques; — v.a. briqueter. — **bat,** s. morceau de brique, m.; brique, f. — **built,** adj. bâti or construit en briques. — **burner,** s. cuiseur, m. — **clay,** s. terre à briques, f. — **coloured,** adj. briqueté. — **dust,** s. poussière de briques, f.; (pounded, ground) poudre de briques, f. — **earth,** s. terre à briques, f. — **field, -kiln,** s. briqueterie, f.; four à briques, m. — **layer,** s. maçon en briques, maçon, briqueteur, m.; (for chimneys) fumiste, m. — **maker,** s. briquetier, m. — **making,** s. briqueterie, f. — **red,** adj. briqueté, de brique. — **up,** v.a. murer de briques. — **work,** s. briquetage, m. — **works,** s. pl., — **yard,** s. V. — **field**
Bridal, adj. nuptial; — s. noce, f., mariage, m.
Bride, s. mariée, nouvelle mariée, f.; (betrothed) fiancée, future, prétendue, f. — **bed,** s. lit nuptial, m. — **cake,** s. gâteau de noce, m. — **chamber,** s. chambre nuptiale, f. — **favours,** s. pl. livrée de la noce, f. — **groom,** s. marié, nouveau marié, m.; (betrothed) fiancé, futur, prétendu, m. —**'s-maid,** s. demoiselle d'honneur, f. —**'s-man,** s. garçon d'honneur, m. [tention or de force, f.
Bridewell, s. maison de correction or de dé-
Bridge, s. pont, m.; (of a violin, &c.) chevalet, m.; (of the nose) dos, m.; (of combs) champ, m.; (artil.) hausse, f.; — v.a. (— **over**) jeter or construire un pont sur. London —, Westminster —, &c., le pont de Londres, le pont de Westminster, &c. — **head,** s. tête-de-pont, f.
Bridgeless, adj. sans pont
Bridle, s. bride, f.; (fig.) frein, m.; (nav.) amarre, f.; — v.a. brider; (fig.) mettre un frein à, tenir en bride, réprimer, contenir; — v.n. (— **up**) porter la tête haute, se rengorger. — **bit,** s. mors, frein, m. — **hand,** s. main gauche, f. — **path, -road, -way,** s. route cavalière, f. [de bridon, f.
Bridoon, s. bridon, filet, m. — **rein,** s. rêne
Brief, adj. bref, court; de courte durée, passager; borné, restreint; concis; — s. (of popes) bref, m.; (law) dossier, m. —**less,** adj. sans cause. —**ly,** adv. brièvement, en peu de mots. —**ness,** s. brièveté, f.; concision, f.
Brier, Briery. V. **Briar, Briary**

Brig, s. brick, m.
Brigade, s. (mil.) brigade, f.; (of firemen, &c.) corps, m.; brigade, f.; — v.a. former en brigade or en brigades, embrigader; former en corps. — **major,** s. chef d'état-major, major de brigade, m.
Brigadier, s. général de brigade, m. — **general,** s. général de brigade, m.
Brigading, s. embrigadement, m.
Brigand, s. brigand, m.
Brigandage, s. brigandage, m.
Brigantine, s. brigantin, m., (small) brigantine, f.
Bright, adj. brillant; poli; limpide; clair; lumineux; rayonnant; éclatant; beau; illustre; glorieux; gai; vif; intelligent; (light-coloured) clair. — fire, feu clair, m. —er days, jours plus heureux, m.pl. To see only (or to look at) the — side of things, voir tout en beau, voir tout couleur de rose
Brighten, v.a. faire briller, rendre brillant; (polish) polir; (clear up) éclaircir; (fig.) jeter de l'éclat sur; illustrer; embellir; (enliven) égayer; animer; (sharpen) dégourdir; — v.n. briller, étinceler, devenir brillant, prendre de l'éclat; s'animer, s'illuminer, rayonner; s'égayer, devenir plus gai; (become sharp) se dégourdir; (of the fire) flamber; (of the weather) s'éclaircir [ment
Brightly, adv. avec éclat, brillamment; claire-
Brightness, s. éclat, lustre, brillant, m.; clarté, f.; vivacité, f.; joie, f.
Brill, s. barbue, f.; —**s,** pl. (of a horse) cils, m.pl.
Brilliance, Brilliancy, s. éclat, lustre, brillant, m.
Brilliant, adj. brillant, éclatant; — s. brillant, m.
Brilliantly, adv. brillamment, avec éclat
Brilliantness. V. **Brilliancy**
Brim, s. bord, m.; (of a hat) bords, m.pl., bord, m.; — v.a. remplir jusqu'au bord (or jusqu'aux bords); — v.n. être plein jusqu'au bord (or jusqu'aux bords), être tout plein. —**ful,** adj. plein jusqu'au bord (or jusqu'aux bords), tout plein, rempli (de). —ful of tears, tout plein de larmes, gros de larmes. —**less,** adj. sans bord, sans bords
Brimmed, adj. à bords; à rebords; — part. adj. (filled) rempli jusqu'au bord (or jusqu'aux bords), rempli, tout plein
Brimmer. V. **Bumper**
Brimming, adj. V. **Brimful**
Brimstone, s. soufre, m.
Brimstony, adj. sulfureux
Brinded, Brindled, adj. tavelé, tacheté
Brine, s. saumure, eau salée, f.; (the sea) mer, onde amère, f.; (tears) larmes amères, larmes, f.pl.; — v.a. saumurer, mettre dans la saumure, saler. — **pan,** s. salin, m. — **pit,** s. saline, f., parc, m. — **shrimp,** s. artémie, f. — **spring,** s. source salée, f.
Bring, v.a. (by carrying, and fig. news, &c.) apporter; (without carrying) amener; (fig., lead) conduire; mener; (put, set) mettre; (induce) amener (à); (draw) attirer; (convey, take) transporter; porter; (produce) rapporter; valoir; (reduce) réduire; (accustom) accoutumer; (serve up) servir; (an accusation or charge) porter; (an action at law) intenter; (pers. before a tribunal) traduire; — oneself, se mettre; se résoudre (à). — **about,** amener; venir à bout de, accomplir, effectuer, exécuter, opérer; former. — **again,** (by carrying) rapporter; (without carrying) ramener. — **away,** (by carrying) emporter; (without carrying) emmener. — **back,** (by carrying) rapporter; (without carrying) ramener. — **down,** (things) descendre; (pers., animals) faire descendre; (by striking) abattre; (reduce) réduire; (lower) baisser; (fig.) abaisser, rabaisser; (weaken) affaiblir; (cause to applaud) faire applaudir, entraîner. — **forth** mettre au monde, accoucher de, enfanter; (of animals) mettre bas; (fig.) produire; faire naître; mettre au

jour; (*law*) représenter. —**forward**, amener; (*fig.*) avancer; présenter; produire; (*help on*) pousser, mettre en avant; (*book-keep.*) reporter. (*Brought forward*, à report). —**in**, (*by carrying*, *and fig.*) apporter; entrer; rentrer; (*without carrying*) faire entrer; amener; introduire; réduire; former; alléguer; (*produce*) rapporter; (*serve up*) servir; (*a verdict*) rendre. — **off**, délivrer, tirer d'embarras; (*law*) faire acquitter. —**on**, (*by carrying*) apporter; (*without carrying*) amener; (*fig.*) amener, attirer, occasionner, causer, produire; (*an action at law*) intenter. —**out**, (*by carrying*) apporter; sortir; (*without carrying*) faire sortir; sortir; (*draw out*) tirer; retirer; faire paraître; produire; montrer; mettre en évidence; découvrir; mettre au jour; (*emit*) énoncer; (*books*) publier; (*theat.*) représenter. — **over**, (*by carrying*) apporter; (*without carrying*) amener; faire venir; attirer; convertir; (*across*) faire passer, passer, transporter. — **round**, ramener; concilier; (*make well*) rétablir. —**to**, amener à; (*to consciousness*) faire reprendre connaissance à; (*to reason*) ramener à la raison; (*nav.*) amener, mettre en panne. — **together**, assembler, réunir; réconcilier; rapprocher; (*for a conference*) aboucher. — **under**, soumettre, réduire; maitriser. —**up**, (*by carrying*) monter; apporter; (*without carrying*) faire monter; faire avancer; amener; porter; (*rear, breed, feed*) élever; (*educate*) élever; instruire; former; destiner; (*serve up*) servir; (*vomit*) vomir, rendre; (*pers. before a tribunal*) traduire

Bringer, *s.* porteur, *m.*, -euse, *f.* — **in,** *s.* introducteur, *m.*, -trice, *f.* —**up,** *s.* instituteur, *m.*; (*of the rear*) celui qui ferme la marche, *m.*; dernier rang, *m.*; (*mil.*) serre-file, *m.*

Bringing, *s.* action d'apporter *or* d'amener, *f.* —**in,** *s.* introduction, *f.* —**up,** *s.* éducation, *f.*

Brinish. *V.* **Briny**

Brinishness, *s.* nature saumâtre, salure, *f.*

Brink, *s.* bord, *m.*; (*fig.*) penchant, *m.* *On the — of*, au bord de. *On the — of ruin*, &c., sur le penchant de sa ruine, à la veille de sa ruine; à deux doigts de sa perte, &c.

Briny, *adj.* saumâtre, salé; (*of the sea, tears*) [amer

Briony. *V.* **Bryony**

Brisk, *adj.* vif; frais et dispos; gai; (*of liquors*) piquant; (*com.*) actif; — **(up)** *v.a.* animer, émoustiller; *v.n.* s'animer, s'émoustiller

Brisket, *s.* poitrine, *f.*

Briskly, *adv.* vivement; (*com.*) activement

Briskness, *s.* vivacité, *f.*; (*com.*) activité, *f.*

Bristle, *s.* (*of swine*) soie, *f.*; (*bot.*) poil, *m.*; — **(up)** *v.a.* hérisser ('*with*,' de); *v.n.* se hérisser; être hérissé; (*pers.*) se raidir ('*to*,' contre); se fâcher

Bristliness, Bristling, *s.* hérissement, *m.*

Bristling, Bristly, *adj.* hérissé (de); (*of swine*) couvert de soies; (*bot.*) poilu

Britannia metal, *s.* métal blanc anglais,

Britannic, *adj.* britannique [métal anglais, *m.*

Brite, *v.n.* s'égrener

British, *adj.* britannique, de la Grande-Bretagne; anglais, d'Angleterre, de l'Angleterre. *The — Isles*, les Iles Britanniques, *f.pl.*

Briton, *s. adj.* (*of Britain*) *V.* **English;** (*of Brittany*) *V.* **Breton**

Britska, *s.* briska, *m.*

Brittle, *adj.* fragile, cassant

Brittleness, *s.* fragilité, *f.*

Britzka, Britzska, *s.* briska, *m.*

Broach, *s.* broche, *f.*; — *v.a.* (*a cask*) percer, mettre en perce; (*open, as stores*, &c.) ouvrir; entamer; (*a subject*) entamer, introduire, communiquer; effleurer; (*publish*) publier, répandre; émettre. *To — to*, (*nav.*) faire chapelle

Broacher, *s.* auteur, *m.*

Broad, *adj.* large; grand; gros; vaste; (*full*) plein, entier; (*of words*) gros, grossier, libre; graveleux; (*bold*) hardi, indiscret; (*of accent*) prononcé, fortement prononcé; (*of hints*) assez clair, peu voilé. *As — as it is long*, (*fig.*) tout un, la même chose. *Ten yards —*, *V.* **Wide.** — **breasted,** *adj.* à large poitrine. — **brimmed,** *adj.* à larges bords. — **cast,** *adj. adv.* à la volée; *s.* semis (*m.*) *or* semailles (*f.pl.*) à la volée. — **cloth,** *s.* drap fin, *m.*; (*people*) beau monde, *m.*, élégants, fashionables, *m.pl.* — **humour,** *s.* grosse gaieté, *f.* — **laugh,** *s.* gros rire, *m.* — **leaved,** *adj.* à feuilles larges, à larges feuilles. — **shouldered,** *adj.* à (*or* aux) larges épaules, qui a les épaules larges. — **side,** *s.* (*of naval guns*) bordée, *f.*; (*of ships*) côté, bord, *m.*; (*print.*) feuille, *f.*, placard, in-plano, *m.*; (*bill*) affiche, *f.* *To fire a — side*, tirer une bordée. — **stone,** *s.* pierre de taille, *f.* — **sword,** *s.* sabre, *m.* — **wise,** *adv.* en [large

Broaden. *V.* **Widen**

Broadish, *adj.* un peu large, assez large

Broadly, *adv.* largement; ouvertement, franchement, rondement; trop librement

Broadness, *s.* largeur, *f.*; (*of expressions*) [grossièreté, *f.*

Brocade, *s.* brocart, *m.*

Brocaded, *adj.* de brocart; (*pers.*) vêtu de [brocart

Brocatelle, *s.* brocatelle, *f.*

Broccoli, *s.* brocoli, *m.*

Brochure, *s.* brochure, *f.*

Brocket, *s.* broquart, daguet, *m.*

Brogue, *s.* accent, patois, *m.*; (*shoe*) brogue, *f.*

Broil, *s.* tumulte, trouble, *m.*; querelle, dispute, *f.*; échauffourée, *f.*; (*cook.*) grillade, carbonade, charbonnée, *f.*; — *v.a.* griller, faire griller, rôtir, faire rôtir; — *v.n.* griller, rôtir

Broiler, *s.* gril, *m.*; (*pers.*) boute-feu, *m.*

Broiling, *adj.* brûlant

Broken, *part. adj.* cassé, rompu, brisé, &c. (*V.* **Break**); *of clothes*) déchiré, troué; (*of the heart*) brisé, navré; (*impaired*) délabré; (*of the voice, sobs*, &c.) entrecoupé; (*of sleep*) interrompu; (*of country*) accidenté; (*of moments*) perdu; (*of assemblies*) dissous (-oute, *f.*); (*bankrupt*) en faillite, failli; (*of language*) mauvais, écorché, baragouiné; (*desultory, incoherent*) sans suite, irrégulier; décousu; (*mil.*) rompu. — **backed,** *adj.* qui a le dos cassé; (*of animals*) qui a les reins cassés; (*nav.*) cassé. — **down,** *adj.* (*pers.*) cassé de vieillesse, cassé, caduc. — **hearted,** *adj.* qui a le cœur brisé *or* navré, navré de douleur (*V.* **Die**). — **kneed,** *adj.* qui a les genoux cassés; (*of horses*) couronné. — **knees** *or* **knee,** *s.* (*of horses*) couronnement, *m.* — **meat,** *s.* restes de viande, rogatons, graillons, *m.pl.* —**mouthed,** *adj.* (*things*) égueulé; (*pers.*) brèche-dents. — **victuals,** *s.pl. V.* — **meat.** —**wind,** *s.* (*vet.*) pousse, *f.* — **winded,** *adj.* qui a l'haleine courte; (*vet.*) poussif

Brokenly, *adv.* sans suite, à bâtons rompus

Brokenness, *s.* inégalité, *f.*; brisement de cœur, *m.*

Broker, *s.* courtier, *m.*; (*stock —*) agent de change, *m.*; (*of old things, furniture*, &c.) brocanteur, *m.*; fripier, *m.* —**s' alley,** *s.* friperie, *f.* —**'s business,** *s.* courtage, *m.*; brocantage, *m.* —**'s shop,** *s.* boutique de brocanteur, friperie, *f.* —**'s trade,** *s.* brocantage, *m.*

Brokerage, *s.* courtage, *m.*

Brokership, *s.* charge de courtier, *f.*; charge [d'agent de change, *f.*

Broma, *s.* broma, *m.*

Bromate, *s.* bromate, *m.*

Brome-grass, *s.* brôme, *m.*

Bromic, *adj.* bromique

Bromide, *s.* bromure, *m.*

Bromidize, *v.a.* bromurer

Bromine, *s.* brome, *m.*

Bromize, *v.a.* bromer

Bronchi, Bronchiæ, *s. pl.* bronches, *f.pl.*

Bronchial, *adj.* bronchial, bronchique

Bronchitis, *s.* bronchite, *f.*

Bronchocele, *s.* bronchocèle, *f.*

Broncho-phony, -tomy. *V.* page 3, § 1

Bronze, *s.* bronze, *m.*; — *adj.* de bronze; — *v.a.* bronzer. — **colour, -paint,** *s.* couleur de bronze, *f.* — **powder,** *s.* bronze jaune, *m.*, or en coquille, *m.*

Bronzer, *s.* bronzeur, *m.*
Bronzing, *s.* bronzage, *m.*
Bronzist, *s.* bronzier, *m.*; bronzeur, *m.*
Bronzite, *s.* bronzite, *f.*
Bronzy, *adj.* semblable au bronze, de bronze
Brooch, *s.* broche, épingle, *f.*; (*paint.*) camaieu, *m.*
Brood, *v.a.n.* couver; (*cherish*) chérir, nourrir, entretenir; soigner; (*over*) méditer (sur), rêver (à), songer (à); — *s.* couvée, nichée, *f.*; (*fig.*) race, engeance, *f.*; production, *f.* — **hen,** *s.* poule couveuse, couveuse, *f.* — **mare,** *s.* jument poulinière, poulinière, *f.*
Brooding, *adj.* qui couve, couveuse (*adj.f.*); — *s.*, — **season** *or* **time,** *s.* couvaison, *f.*
Brook, *s.* ruisseau, *m.*; — *v.a.* souffrir, endurer, digérer. — **lime,** *s.* beccabunga, *m.* — **mint,** *s.* menthe aquatique, *f.* — **weed,** *s.* samole, *m.*
Brooklet, *s.* petit ruisseau, *m.*
Brooky, *adj.* abondant en ruisseaux
Broom, *s.* balai, *m.*; (*shrub*) genêt, *m.* *A new — always sweeps clean,* il n'est rien de tel que balai neuf. — **corn,** *s.* houque, *f.* — **land,** *s.* genétière, *f.* — **rape,** *s.* orobanche, *f.* — **stick,** *s.* manche à balai, *m.*
Broomy, *adj.* couvert de genêts
Broth, *s.* bouillon, *m.* *Black —,* brouet noir, *m.*
Brothel, *s.* bordel, *m.*
Brother, *s.* frère, *m.*; (*in professions*) confrère, *m.*; collègue, *m.*; (*fam.*) camarade, *m.* — **in-law,** *s.* beau-frère, *m.* — **in arms,** — **officer,** — **soldier,** *s.* frère d'armes, compagnon d'armes, (*fam.*) camarade, *m.*
Brotherhood, *s.* fraternité, *f.*; (*association*) confrérie, *f.*; (*in professions*) confraternité, *f.*
Brotherless, *adj.* sans frère
Brotherlike, Brotherly, *adj.* fraternel, de frère, d'un frère; — *adv.* fraternellement, en [frère
Brougham, *s.* coupé, *m.*
Brow, *s.* sourcil, *m.*; (*forehead*) front, *m.*; (*top*) sommet, *m.*, croupe, *f.* *To bend* or *knit the —,* froncer le sourcil. *To unbend the —,* dérider le front. *To unbend o.'s —,* se dérider. — **antler,** *s.* premier andouiller, *m.* — **beat,** *v.a.* intimider, déconcerter, décontenancer; traiter avec hauteur. — **beating,** *s.* arrogance, *f.*, air arrogant, ton impérieux, *m.* — **bound,** *adj.* couronné, le front ceint (de)
Brown, *adj.* brun; (*fig.*) sombre, rembruni; (*of the hair*) châtain; brun; (*of bread*) bis; (*of sugar*) brut; (*of onions*) brûlé; (*of paper*) gris; goudronné; (*of fabrics, unbleached*) écru; (*of meat*) rissolé; (*of butter*) noir; — *s.* brun, *m.*; (*of roast meat*) rissolé, *m.*; — *v.a.* brunir; (*v.n.*) se brunir; (*cook.*) gratiner; (*meat*) rissoler; (*v.n.*) se rissoler; (*butter*) faire roussir. — **Bess,** *s.* fusil de munition, *m.* — **holland,** *s.* toile écrue, toile bise, *f.* — **owl,** *s.* chat-huant, *m.*, chouette, hulotte, *f.* — **study,** *s.* sombre rêverie, humeur noire, *f.* — **sugar,** *s.* sucre brut, *m.*, cassonade, *f.*
Browning, *s.* brunissage, *m.*; (*cook.*) gratinage, *m.*; (*burnt sugar*) caramel, *m.*
Brownish, *adj.* brunâtre
Brownishness, *s.* couleur *or* teinte brunâtre, *f.*
Brownness, *s.* couleur *or* teinte brune, *f.*
Browse, *v.a.n.* brouter; — *s.* brout, *m.* — **wood,** *s.* brout, *m.* [broutant
Browsing, *s.* brouture, *f.*; brout, *m.*; — *adj.*
Brucine, *s.* brucine, *f.*
Bruise, *v.a.* meurtrir, contusionner; (*dent, dint*) bossuer, bosseler; (*crush*) écraser; broyer; concasser; (*fig.*) froisser; — *s.* meurtrissure, contusion, *f.*; (*dent, dint*) bosse, *f.*; renfoncement, *m.*
Bruiser, *s.* écraseur, concasseur, *m.*; (*pop.*) boxeur, *m.*; (*fig.*) froisseur, *m.*
Bruising, *s.* meurtrissure, contusion, *f.*; (*crushing*) écrasement, *m.*; broiement, broyage, *m.*; concassage, *m.*; (*pop.*) boxe, *f.*; roulée, volée, *f.*; (*fig.*) froissement, *m.* — **mill,** *s.* moulin à écraser, écraseur, concasseur, *m.*

Bruit, *s.* bruit, *m.*, rumeur, *f.*; — *v.a.* faire courir (le bruit); ébruiter
Brumal, *adj.* brumal, d'hiver [la camelote
Brummagem, *adj.* de mauvais aloi, faux, de
Brunette, *s.* brunette, *f.*
Brunt, *s.* choc, *m.*; coup, *m.*; violence, force, *f.*; fureur, *f.*; (*heat*) fort, *m.*; (*of fire-arms*) feu, *m.*; (*of fortune*) revers, *m.*
Brush, *s.* brosse, *f.*; (*touch with a brush*) coup de brosse, *m.*, brossée, *f.*; (*paint.*) pinceau, *m.*; (*for pastry*) doroir, *m.*; (*broom*) balai, *m.*; (*of foxes*) queue (de renard), *f.*; (*wood*) broussailles, *f.pl.*; broutilles, *f.pl.*; (*attack*) assaut, *m.*, attaque, *f.*; coup, *m.*; escarmouche, rencontre, *f.*; (*fight, fam.*) brossée, peignée, *f.* *Hard —,* brosse dure, *f.*; (*for cleaning boots*) décrottoire, *f.* *Shining —,* polissoire, *f.* *Soft —,* brosse douce, *f.* — **maker, -manufacturer,** *s.* brossier, fabricant de brosses, *m.* — **making, -manufactory, -trade,** *s.* brosserie, *f.* — **turkey,** *s.* talégalle, *m.* — **wood,** *s.* broussailles, *f.pl.*; broutilles, menues branches, *f.pl.*
Brush, *v.a.* brosser; (*sweep*) balayer; emporter, enlever; (*graze*) raser, effleurer, frôler; — *v.n.* passer rapidement. — **away, off,** *v.a.* enlever en brossant, enlever; essuyer; secouer; (*sweep*) balayer, emporter; *v.n.* s'enfuir, décamper, filer. — **up,** *v.a.* brosser, donner un coup de brosse à, nettoyer; (*a subject,* &c.) se remettre à, repasser, rafraîchir
Brusher, *s.* brosseur, *m.*, -euse, *f.*
Brushing, *s.* brossage, *m.*; brossée, *f.*
Brushy, *adj.* semblable à une brosse; (*rough*) rude; (*shaggy*) hérissé
Brusque, *adj.* brusque
Brusqueness, *s.* brusquerie, *f.*
Brussels, *s* Bruxelles, *f.* — **carpet,** *s.* tapis de Bruxelles, *m.* — **lace,** *s.* dentelle, (*f.*) *or* point (*m.*) de Bruxelles. — **sprout,** *s.* chou de Bruxelles, *m.* [*thing,* brutalité, *f.*
Brutal, *adj.* brutal; barbare, inhumain. —
Brutality, *s.* brutalité, *f.*; barbarie, inhumanité, *f.*
Brutalization, *s.* abrutissement, *m.*
Brutalize, *v.a.* abrutir; — *v.n.* s'abrutir
Brutally, *adv.* brutalement
Brute, *s.* brute, bête, *f.*, animal, *m.*; — *adj.* insensible; privé de raison; (*bestial*) des bêtes, des animaux; (*rough*) brutal, grossier; (*savage*) farouche, sauvage; (*of matter*) brut. *The — creation,* les bêtes, *f.pl.*, l'espèce animale, *f.*
Brutify. *V.* **Brutalize**
Brutish, *adj.* de brute; brutal, grossier; bestial; sauvage, farouche; privé de raison; (*stupid*) abruti; ignorant [brutalement
Brutishly, *adv.* en brute, comme une brute,
Brutishness, Brutism, *s.* nature de la brute, *f.*; brutalité, *f.*; (*degradation*) abrutissement, *m.*
Brutus, *s.* toupet, *m.*
Bryony, *s.* bryone, *f.*
Bubalis, Bubalus, *s.* bubale, *m.*
Bubble, *s.* bulle, *f.*; (*fig.*) utopie, chimère, *f.*; jouet, *m.*; dupe, *f.*; duperie, flouerie, *f.*; — *v.n.* (— **up**) bouillonner; (*of wine*) pétiller; (*of brooks*) murmurer; — *v.a.* duper. — **blower,** *s.* floueur, *m.* — **company,** *s.* flouerie, *f.*
Bubbling, *s.* bouillonnement, *m.*; (*of wine*) pétillement, *m.*; (*of brooks*) murmure, *m.*
Bubby, *s.* sein, *m*, (*fam.*) téton, nénet, *m.*
Bubo, *s.* bubon, *m.*
Bubonocele, *s.* bubonocèle, *f.*
Buccal, *adj.* buccal
Buccan, *s.* boucan, *m.*; — *v a.* boucaner
Buccaneer, *s.* boucanier, *m.*; — *v.n.* pirater
Buccaneering, *s.* piraterie, *f.*
Buccaning, *s.* boucanage, *m.*
Buccinator, *s. adj.* buccinateur, *m.*
Bucentaur, *s.* bucentaure, *m.*
Buck, *s.* mâle, *m.*; (*deer*) daim, chevreuil, *m.*; (*pers.*) luron, gaillard, *m.*; beau, élégant, *m.*; (*of linen*) lessive, *f.*; — *v.n a.* (*of deer*) daguer; (*rid.*) faire le saut de mouton; (*of linen*) lessiver, faire la lessive. — **ashes,** *s. pl.* charrée,

f. — **basket,** *s.* panier au linge sale, *m.* — **bean,** *s.* minyanthe, *m.* — **eye,** *s.* (*bot.*) pavier, *m.* — **goat,** *s.* bouc, *m.* — **hare,** *s.* bouquin, *m.* —**'s horn,** *s.* corne de cerf, *f.* — **hound,** *s.* limier, *m.* — **hunting,** *s.* chasse au daim *or* au chevreuil, *f.* — **mast,** *s.* faîne, *f.* — **rabbit,** *s.* lapin, bouquin, *m.* — **shot,** *s.* chevrotine, *f.* — **skin,** *s.* peau de daim, *f.* — **thorn,** *s.* nerprun, *m.* — **wheat,** *s.* sarrasin, blé noir, *m.*

Bucket, *s.* seau, *m.*; baquet, *m.*; (*hydraulics*) auget, godet, *m.*; (*of pumps*) piston, *m.*; (*mil.*) porte-crosse, *m.*, (*of lancers*) porte-lance, *m.* *To kick the* —, (*to die*) passer *or* sauter le pas, claquer. —**ful,** *s.* seau, baquet, *m.*

Bucking, *s.* lessive, *f.*; (*hunt.*) accouplement, *m.* — **cloth,** *s.* charrier, *m.* — **season** *or* **time,** *s.* (*hunt.*) temps du rut, *m.* — **tub,** *s.* cuvier, *m.*

Buckle, *s.* boucle, *f.*; — *v.a.* boucler; (*fig.*) attacher; resserrer; préparer; se joindre à; — *v.n.* plier, se courber. — **in,** *v.a.* resserrer *or* serrer (en bouclant); limiter, borner. — **on,** *v.a.* (*arms*) revêtir, mettre. — **to,** *v.n.* s'appliquer à; se clouer à; (*marry*) s'unir à, épouser. — **up,** *v.a.* boucler, serrer. — **with,** *v.n.* être aux prises avec, combattre corps à corps [bouclier à, protéger

Buckler, *s.* bouclier, *m.*; — *v.a.* servir de

Buckram, *s.* bougran, *m.*; — *adj.* de bougran; (*fig.*) empesé, collet monté. *Man in* —, homme de carton, soldat pour rire, *m.*

Bucolic, *adj.* bucolique; — *s.* (*poem*) bucolique, *f.*; (*poet*) bucoliaste, *m.*

Bud, *s.* (*first shoot, gem*) bourgeon, bouton, *m.*; (*unexpanded flower*) bouton, *m.*; (*fig.*) germe, *m.*, racine, *f.*; — *v.n.* bourgeonner; fleurir, s'épanouir, éclore; naître; — *v.a.* écussonner. — **picker,** *s.* ébourgeonneur, *m.*

Buddhism, *s.* bouddhisme, *m.*

Buddhist, *s. adj.* bouddhiste, *m.f.*

Buddhistic, *adj.* bouddhique

Budding, *s.* bourgeonnement, *m.*; (*fig.*) germe, *m.*; (*grafting*) greffe en écusson, *f.*, placage, *m.* — **knife,** *s.* écussonnoir, *m.*

Budge, *v.n.* bouger, se remuer; (*run*) courir

Budget, *s.* budget, *m.*; (*bag*) sac, *m.*

Buff, *s.* (*leather*) buffle, *m.*, peau de buffle, *f.*; (*colour*) couleur chamois, *f.*, fauve chamois, *m.*; (*med.*) couenne, *f.*; (*slang*) peau, *f.*; (*blow*) coup, *m.*; (*shock*) choc, *m.*; — *adj.* de peau de buffle, de buffle; de couleur chamois, de fauve chamois, chamois; — *v.a.* frapper; —**s,** *s. pl.* buffleterie, *f.* *To stand* —, tenir bon, tenir ferme (contre), tenir tête (à). *In* —, (*slang*) tout nu. — **dresser,** *s.* buffletier, *m.* — **factory,** *s.* buffleterie, *f.* — **leather,** *s.* peau de buffle, *f.*, buffle, *m.*, buffleterie, *f.* — **skin,** *s.* buffleterie, *f.*; peau de buffle chamoisée, *f.*

Buffalo, *s.* buffle, *m.* *Young* —, — **calf,** *s.* buffletin, bufflon, *m.* — **cow,** *s.* buffle, bufflonne, *f.* — **snake,** *s.* boa constricteur, devin, *m.*

Buffer, *s.* tampon, tampon de choc, *m.* *Old* —, (*pers.*) vieux bonhomme, vieux, *m.*

Buffet, *s.* buffet, *m.*; (*blow*) coup de poing, *m.*; — *v.a.* frapper du poing, frapper à coups de poing; battre; (*struggle*) lutter contre; (*muffle, as a bell*) assourdir, étouffer le son de; — *v.n.* se battre à coups de poing, faire le coup de poing; lutter [assaut, coup, *m.*

Buffeting, *s.* bourrade, *f.*; (*fig.*) attaque, *f.*,

Buffing-apparatus, *s.* appareil de ressorts

Buffa, *adj.* bouffe [à boudin, *m.*

Bufflehead, *s.* lourdaud, *m.*

Buffo, *s. adj.* bouffe, *m.*

Buffoon, *s.* bouffon, *m.*, -ne, *f.*

Buffoonery, *s.* bouffonnerie, *f.*

Buffy, *adj.* (*med.*) couenneux. — **coat,** *s.* couenne, *f.*

Bug, *s.* punaise, *f.* — **bear,** *s.* loup-garou, *m.*; épouvantail, *m.* — **wort,** *s.* cimicaire, chasse punaises, *f.* [boguey, *m.*, américaine, *f*

Buggy, *adj.* plein de punaises; — *s.* boghei,

Bugle, *s.* cor de chasse, *m.*; (*mil.*) bugle, clairon, *m.*; (*bot.*) bugle, *f.*; (*bead*) perle-tube, *f.* — **horn,** *s.* cor de chasse, *m.*; (*mil.*) bugle-horn, bugle, clairon, *m.* — **weed,** *s.* lycope, pied-

Bugler, *s.* clairon, *m.* [de-loup, *m.*

Buglos, Bugloss, *s.* buglosse, buglose, *f.*

Buhl, — **work,** *s.* marqueterie de Boule, *f.*; — *adj.* de Boule

Buhrstone. *V.* **Burrstone**

Build, *s.* construction, *f.*; — *v.a.n.* bâtir, construire; (*ships, boats, machines, engines, railways*) construire; (*get built*) faire bâtir; (*be in course of construction*, '*be —ing*') se bâtir; se construire; (*of birds*) bâtir, faire; faire son nid, nicher; (*fig.*) fonder, baser (sur); (*raise*) élever; (*rely on*) se fonder, compter (sur)

Builder, *s.* (*of houses: general sense*) constructeur, *m.*, (*worker*) maçon, *m.*, (*master* —, *tech.*) entrepreneur de bâtiments, entrepreneur, *m.*; (*jest.*) bâtisseur, *m.*; (*of ships, boats, machines, engines,* &c.) constructeur (de ...) *m.*; (*of organs*) facteur, *m.*; (*fig.*) fondateur, créateur, *m.*; architecte, *m.*

Building, *s.* construction, *f.*; bâtiment, *m.*; bâtisse, *f.*; (*public*) édifice, *m.*; (*of birds*) nid, *m.* — **materials,** *s. pl.* matériaux de construction, *m.pl.*; (*from buildings pulled down*) matériaux de démolition, *m.pl.* — **society,** *s.* société pour la construction des maisons, société de constructeurs, *f.* — **stone,** *s.* pierre à bâtir, pierre d'appareil, *f.*

Built, *part. adj.* bâti, construit; (*in compounds*) construit (en ...), de construction (...). *English* or *French* —, de construction anglaise *or* française. *Frigate* —, construit en frégate, frégaté

Bulb, *s.* (*bot.*) bulbe, *f.*; ognon, *m.*; (*anat.*) bulbe, *m.*; (*of thermometers*) boule, *f.*

Bulbiferous, *adj.* bulbifère

Bulbiform, *adj.* bulbiforme

Bulbil, *s.* bulbille, *f.*

Bulbous, *adj.* bulbeux

Bulbul, *s.* bulbul, *m.*

Bulgarian, *s. adj.* Bulgare, *m.f.*

Bulge, *v.n.* (*jut out*) bomber; faire le ventre; — *v.a.n.* (*nav.*) *V.* **Bilge**

Bulge, Bulging, *s.* bombement, *m.*; bosse, *f.*; ventre, *m.*; (*nav.*) *V.* **Bilge**

Bulimia, Bulimy, *s.* boulimie, *f.*

Bulk, *s.* volume, *m.*, grosseur, masse, *f.*; (*heap*) tas, *m.*; (*fig.*) grandeur, *f.*; (*principal part*) gros, *m.*; masse, *f.*; (*of ships*) capacité, *f.*; charge, *f.* *To break* —, (*nav.*) commencer le déchargement. — **head,** *s.* (*nav.*) cloison, *f.*

Bulkiness, *s.* grosseur, *f.*, volume, *m.*, taille, *f.*

Bulky, *adj.* gros, volumineux, massif; grand

Bull, *s.* taureau, *m.*; (*of the pope*) bulle, *f.*; (*blunder*) bévue, bêtise, brioche, boulette, *f.*; (*of stock-jobbing*) haussier, *m.* — **baiting,** *s.* combat de chiens contre un taureau, *m.* — **bee,** *s.* taon, *m.* — **calf,** *s.* veau mâle, *m.*; taurillon, *m.*; (*pers.*) sot, benêt, *m.* — **dog,** *s.* bouledogue, *m.* — **fight,** *s.* combat de taureaux, *m.* — **fighter,** *s.* toréador, *m.* — **finch,** *s.* bouvreuil, *m.* — **fly,** *s.* taon, *m.* — **head,** *s.* (*fish*) cotte, chabot, *m.*; (*pers.*) sot, *m.*, bête, *f.*, lourdaud, *m.* — **hide,** *s.* peau de bœuf, *f.* — **ring,** *s.* nasière, *f.*, pince-nez, *m.*, mouchette, *f.* —**'s eye,** *s.* (*window*) œil-de-bœuf, *m.*; (*lantern*) lanterne sourde, *f.*; (—*'s eye lamp*) fanal, *m.*; (*skylight*) claire-voie, *f.*; (*sweetmeat*) dragée, *f.*; (*defect in glass,* &c.) bouillon, *m.*, boudine, *f.*; (*old-fashioned watch*) ognon, *m.*; (*of targets*) brasse, *f.*; (*block for nav. rigging*) margouillet, *m.*; (*astr.*) œil de taureau, *m.* — **species,** *s.* race bovine, *f.* — **terrier,** *s.* boule-terrier, *m.* — **trout,** *s.* saumonerion, *m.*

Bulla, *s.* bulle, *f.* [nier sauvage, *m.*

Bullace, *s.* prune sauvage, *f.* — **tree,** *s.* pru-

Bullary, *s.* bullaire, *m.*
Bullet, *s.* balle, *f.*; (*horse's fetlock-joint*) boulet, *m.* — **extractor, -forceps,** *s.* (*surg.*) tire-balle, *m.* — **mould,** *s.* moule à balles, *m.* — **proof,** *adj.* à l'épreuve des balles
Bulletin, *s.* bulletin, *m.*
Bullion, *s.* or en lingot, argent en lingot, lingot, *m.*, matières d'or et d'argent, *f.pl.*; (*bank.*) numéraire, *m.*; (*twist*) cannetille, *f.*; (*of epaulets*) torsade, *f.* *Stock of* —, encaisse métallique, *f* — **dealer,** *s.* changeur, *m.*, -euse, *f.* — **office,** *s.* bureau pour l'achat des matières d'or et d'argent, *m.*
Bullirag, *v.a.* *V.* **Bully,** *v.a.*
Bullock, *s.* bœuf, *m.* *Young* —, bouvillon, *m.*
Bully, *s.* fendant, matamore, fanfaron, bravache, fier-à-bras, *m.*; tapageur, *m.*; brutal, *m.*; taquin, *m.*; (*of bad houses*) souteneur, *m.*; — *v.a.* malmener, maltraiter; bousculer; taquiner; intimider par des bravades; — *v.n.* faire le fendant *or* le crâne; faire du tapage
Bullying, *s.* crânerie, *f.*; brutalité, *f.*; — *adj.* [fendant; brutal
Bulrush, *s.* jonc, *m.*
Bulwark, *s.* boulevard, rempart, *m.*; — *v.a.* [fortifier, protéger
Bum, *s.* derrière, *m.*
Bumbailiff, *s.* huissier, recors, *m.*; garde du [commerce, *m.*
Bumble-bee, *s.* bourdon, *m.*
Bumboat, *s.* bateau de provisions, *m.*
Bumkin, *s.* (*nav.*) bout de lof, *m.*
Bump, *s.* (*swelling*) bosse, *f.*; (*blow*, &c.) coup, choc, *m.*; secousse, *f.*; rebond, rebondissement, *m.*; chute (*f.*) *or* bruit (*m.*) de la chute d'un corps lourd (*heavy* —, chute *or* bruit de la chute d'un corps très lourd); — *v.n.* frapper, cogner, heurter; rebondir
Bumper, *s.* rasade, *f.*, rouge-bord, *m.*; (*theat.*) bonne chambrée, *f.*
Bumping, *s.* *V.* **Bump**
Bumpkin, *s.* rustre, *m.f.*, rustaud, *m.*, -e, *f.*, manant, *m.*; lourdaud, *m.*, -e, *f.*
Bumpkinly, *adj.* rustre, rustaud, grossier
Bumptious, *adj.* suffisant, tranchant
Bumptiousness, *s.* suffisance, *f.*, manières tranchantes, *f.pl.*, ton tranchant, *m.*
Bun, *s.* baba, *m.*; brioche, *f.*; madeleine, *f.*
Bunch, *s.* bosse, *f.*; (*of vegetables*) botte, *f.*; (*of flowers*, &c.) bouquet, *m.*; (*of grapes*) grappe, *f.*; (*tuft*) touffe, *f.*; (*of keys*) trousseau, *m.*; (*of ribbon*) nœud, *m.*; (*of birch-twigs*) poignée, *f.* — *of fives*, giroflée à cinq feuilles, *f.*, coup de tampon, *m.* — **backed,** *adj.* bossu
Bunch, *v.a.* lier en botte *or* en bottes; — *v.n.* (— **out**) faire bosse, bomber
Bunchy, *adj.* touffu; (*of fruit*) en grappe
Buncombe, *s.* blague (politique), *f.*
Bundle, *s.* botte, *f.*; faisceau, *m.*; fagot, fagotin, cotret, *m.*; (*parcel*) paquet, *m.*; (*heap*) tas, *m.*; (*of papers*) liasse, *f.*; (*of birch-twigs, of rods*) poignée, *f.*; (*of corn, of vine-branches*) javelle, *f.*; (*of hay, of asparagus, celery*, &c.) botte, *f.*
Bundle, *v.a.* (— **up**) empaqueter, mettre en paquet; mettre en botte *or* &c.; ramasser ensemble; fagoter; (*shove*) fourrer, flanquer. — **in,** fourrer. — **off,** expédier; envoyer promener. — **out,** faire sortir, flanquer à la porte
Bundle, *v.n.* — **in** or **out,** entrer *or* sortir en masse (*or* tous ensemble). — **off,** (— *oneself off*) décamper, filer, s'en aller. — **up,** faire son paquet
Bung, *s.* bondon, *m.*; (*artil.*) tampon, *m.*; — *v.a.* (— **up**) bondonner; (*obstruct*) boucher, obstruer, encombrer. — **hole,** *s.* bonde, *f.*
Bungle, *v.a.* saveter, saboter, massacrer, gâcher, gâter, cochonner, bousiller, sabrer, estropier; — *v.n.* s'y prendre mal; (*work badly*) faire de mauvaise besogne; brouiller; — *s.* faute, bévue, gaucherie, maladresse, *f.*; mauvaise besogne, *f.*
Bungler, *s.* savetier, sabotier, maladroit, *m.*, -e, *f.*, gâcheur, *m.*, -euse, *f.*, bousilleur, *m.*, -euse, *f.*, brouillon, *m.*, -ne, *f.*, gniaf, *m.*, croûte, *f.*
Bungling, *adj.* (*pers.*) maladroit; (*thing*) maladroitement fait, saveté, saboté, &c. (*V.* **Bungle,** *v.a.*). — *person* (*fellow*, &c.), *V.* **Bungler.** — *work*, mauvaise besogne, *f.*
Bunglingly, *adv.* maladroitement, gauchement
Bunion, *s.* ognon (au pied), *m.*
Bunk, *s.* (*nav.*) bancasse, *f.*
Bunker, *s.* (*nav.*) soute à *or* (au) charbon, *f.*
Bunkum. *V.* **Buncombe**
Bunny, *s.* (*fam.*) lapin, lapineau, *m.*
Bunt, *s.* (*agr., bot.*) charbon, noir, *m.*, carbouille, carie du froment, *f.*; (*of glass*) boudine, *f.*; (*nav.*) fond (de voile), *m.*; — *v.n* s'enfler, se gonfler
Bunting, *s.* (*stuff*) étamine, *f.*; (*flag, flags*) drapeau, *m.*, drapeaux, *m.pl.*; (*bird*) bruant, *m.*
Buoy, *s.* bouée, *f.*; balise, *f.*; — *v.a.* soutenir sur l'eau, porter; (*nav.*) baliser; (*support*) soutenir, supporter, appuyer, seconder; (*a cable*) alléger; (*revive*) ranimer; — *v.n.* se soutenir sur l'eau, flotter, surnager; (*fig.*) percer, s'élever. — **rope,** *s.* orin, *m.*
Buoyage, *s.* balisage, *m.*
Buoyancy, *s.* faculté de se soutenir sur l'eau *or* dans l'air, *f.*; légèreté, *f.*; élasticité, *f.*, ressort, *m.*; énergie, activité, *f.*; élan, *m.*; animation, vivacité, *f.*
Buoyant, *adj.* flottant, qui surnage; léger; élastique; énergique, plein de vie; bien soutenu, animé, vif
Buoyantly, *adv.* avec légèreté; avec vivacité
Buprestis *s.* bupreste, *m.*
Bur, *s.* (*plant*) bardane, *f.*, glouteron, *m.*; (*prickly envelope of a chestnut*) hérisson, *m.*, bogue, *f.*; (*metal., engr.*, &c.) balèvre, bavure, *f.*; (*of pottery*) moussure, *f.*; (*of a lance*) arrêt, *m.*; (*pronunciation*) grasseyement, *m.*; — *v.n.* grasseyer. — **parsley,** *s.* caucalide, *f.* — **reed,** *s.* rubanier, *m.*
Burbot, *s.* barbote, lotte, *f.*
Burden, *s.* fardeau, *m.*, charge, *f.*; (*of a song*) refrain, *m.*; (*of ships*) port, *m.*; — *v.a.* charger ('*with*,' de); (*fig.*) surcharger; peser sur; embarrasser. *Beast of* —, bête de somme, *f.* *Ship of* —, gros bâtiment de charge, bâtiment d'un port considérable, *m.* *To be a* — *to*, être à charge à. *The* — *of proof*, la charge de prouver, *f.* *The* — *of proof lies upon him*, c'est à lui que la preuve incombe, c'est à lui de (*or* à) prouver (que ...)
Burdensome, *adj.* pesant, onéreux (à), à charge (à), lourd (pour); (*tiresome*) ennuyeux (pour), fatigant, incommode (à)
Burdensomeness, *s.* poids, fardeau, *m.*; incommodité, *f.*
Burdock, *s.* bardane, *f.*, glouteron, *m.*
Bureau, *s.* bureau, *m.*
Bureaucracy, *s.* bureaucratie, *f.* [crate
Bureaucratic, *adj.* bureaucratique; bureau-
Bureaucratically, *adv.* bureaucratiquement
Burgess, *s.* bourgeois, citoyen, habitant, *m.*; électeur, *m.*; (*in parliament*) représentant de bourg, *m.*
Burgess-ship, *s.* qualité de bourgeois *or* &c. (*V.* **Burgess**), *f.*; droit de bourgeoisie, *m.*
Burgh, *s.* *V.* **Borough**
Burgher, *s.* *V.* **Burgess**
Burghership, *s.* *V.* **Burgess-ship**
Burglar, *s.* auteur de vol de nuit avec effraction, voleur de nuit, voleur, *m.*
Burglarious, *adj.* de vol de nuit avec effraction, de vol de nuit, de nuit avec effraction
Burglariously, *adv.* la nuit avec effraction, la nuit
Burglary, *s.* vol de nuit avec effraction, *m.*
Burgomaster, *s.* bourgmestre, *m.*; (*bird*) [goéland, *m.*
Burgrave, *s.* burgrave, *m.*
Burgraviate, *s.* burgraviat, *m.*
Burgundian, *s.* Bourguignon, *m.*, -ne, *f.*; — *adj.* bourguignon, de Bourgogne
Burgundy, *s.* (*geog.*) la Bourgogne, *f.*; (*wine*)

bourgogne, vin de Bourgogne, *m.* — **pitch,** *s.* poix de Bourgogne, *f.* — **plaster,** *s.* emplâtre de poix de Bourgogne, *m.* — **wine,** *s.* vin de Bourgogne, *m.*

Burial, *s.* enterrement, *m.*; ensevelissement, *m.*; sépulture, *f.*; inhumation, *f.*; funérailles, *f.pl.*; convoi, *m.*; (*of things*) enfouissement, *m.* *Christian* —, sépulture ecclésiastique, *f.* — **ground,** *s.* cimetière, *m.* — **place,** *s.* lieu de sépulture, *m.*; cimetière, *m.* — **service,** *s.* office des morts, *m.*

Burier, *s.* ensevelisseur, *m.*, -euse, *f.*; (*of things*) enfouisseur, *m.*, -euse, *f.*

Burin, *s.* burin, *m.*

Burke, *v.a.* étouffer

Burl, *s.* nope, *f.*; nœud, *m.*; — *v.a.* noper, épinceter, épincer, énouer

Burler, *s.* nopeur, épinceteur, épinceur, ébouqueur, énoueur, *m.*, -euse, *f.*

Burlesque, *adj. s.* burlesque, *adj. m.f.*, *s.m.*; — *v.a.* tourner en ridicule; travestir

Burlesquely, *adv.* burlesquement

Burletta, *s.* burletta, *f.*

Burliness, *s.* corpulence, grosseur, *f.*; emphase, *f.*

Burling, *s.* nopage, épincetage, épinçage, énouage, *m.*

Burly, *adj.* corpulent, grand, gros, solidement bâti; plein; emphatique; bruyant

Burn, *v.a.n.* brûler; (*by conflagration*) incendier; (*to calcine*) calciner; (*to cauterize*) cautériser, brûler; (*in a kiln*) cuire; (*to long*) brûler (de); (*to rage*) faire fureur; — *s.* brûlure, *f.*; (*of kiln*) cuite, *f.* *To — to ashes*, réduire en cendres. *To — daylight*, brûler le jour. — **away, down, out, up,** *v.a.* brûler, consumer; *v.n.* brûler, se consumer. — **bating,** *s.* (*agr.*) écobuage, *m.*

Burner, *s.* brûleur, *m.*, -euse, *f.*; incendiaire, *m.f.*; (*of bricks*, &c.) cuiseur, *m.*; (*furnace*) fourneau, *m.*; (*of gaslight*, &c.) bec, brûleur, *m.*

Burnet, *s.* pimprenelle, *f.*

Burning, *adj.* en feu; brûlant; ardent; allumé; (*recent*) tout récent, tout chaud; (*excessive*) extrême; — *s.* brûlement, brûlage, *m.*; combustion, *f.*; cautérisation, *f.*; (*burn*) brûlure, *f.*; (*flame*) feu, *m.*, flamme, *f.*; (*conflagration*) incendie, *m.*; (*fig.*) ardeur, *f.*; feu, *m.*; chaleur brûlante, *f.*; inflammation, *f.*; (*of lime, bricks*) cuite, *f.*; (*of smell*) brûlé, *m.* *To smell of* —, sentir le brûlé. — **bush,** *s.* buisson ardent, *m.* — **glass,** *s.* verre ardent, *m.*; lentille, *f.* — **hot,** *adj.* tout brûlant. — **mirror,** *s.* miroir ardent, *m.*

Burnish, *v.a.* brunir; polir; — *v.n.* devenir brillant, prendre du brillant *or* de l'éclat; — *s.* bruni, *m.*, brunissure, *f.*, poli, *m.*; lustre, éclat, *m.*

Burnisher, *s.* brunisseur, *m.*, -euse, *f.*; (*tool*) brunissoir, *m.*

Burnishing, *s.* brunissage, *m.*; brunissure, *f.*

Burnoose, Burnous, *s.* burnous, *m.*

Burnt, *part. adj.* brûlé, &c. (*V.* **Burn**); (*of butter*) noir; — *s.* brûlé, *m.* — **coffee,** *s.* gloria, *m.* — **ear,** *s.* (*agr.*) nielle, *f.*, charbon, *m.* — **offering, -sacrifice,** *s.* holocauste, *m.* — **smell,** *s.* odeur de brûlé *or* de roussi, *f.* — **sugar,** *s.* sucre brûlé, caramel, *m.* — **taste,** *s.* goût de brûlé, *m.*

Burr. *V.* **Bur.** — **oak,** *s.* chêne à gros fruits, *m.* — **stone,** *s.* meulière, pierre de meulière, pierre meulière, *f.*; meule (de moulin), *f.*

Burrer, *s.* grasseyeur, *m.*, -euse, *f.*

Burring, *s.* grasseyement, *m.*

Burrow, *s.* terrier, clapier, *m.*; — *v.n.* terrer, se terrer; faire des trous en terre; (*fig.*) habiter dans un réduit; — *v.a.* creuser

Bursar, *s.* économe, *m.*; (*exhibitioner*) boursier, *m.*

Bursarship, *s.* économat, *m.*

Bursary, *s.* économat, *m.*; (*exhibition*) bourse, *f.*

Burst, *v.n.* crever; éclater; (*fig.*) se rompre; se fendre; percer; (*of liquids*) s'échapper, jaillir; (*rush*) s'élancer, fondre (sur), tomber (sur); (*get away*) s'échapper; s'arracher; (*with laughter*) éclater (de rire); (*into tears*) fondre (en larmes); (*present itself*) s'offrir (à); (*open*) s'ouvrir (à); — *v.a.* crever; (*with explosion*) faire éclater; (*break*) rompre; se rompre. *To — with envy*, crever d'envie. — **open,** (*a door*) enfoncer

Burst, Bursting, *s.* explosion, *f.*; rupture, *f.*; fracas, *m.*; éclat, *m.*; mouvement, transport, *m.*; débordement, *m.*; déchaînement, *m.*; (*med.*) rupture, *f.* — *of laughter*, éclat de rire, *m.* — *of thunder*, éclat de tonnerre, *m.* — *of applause*, tonnerre d'applaudissements, *m.* — *of tears*, torrent de larmes, *m.* — *of eloquence*, mouvement d'éloquence, *m.* — *of passion*, transport de colère, *m.*

Burthen. *V.* **Burden**

Bury, *v.a.* enterrer; ensevelir; (*hide*) cacher; (*fix, stick*) plonger, enfoncer

Burying, *s.* *V.* **Burial**

Burying beetle, *s.* nécrophore, fossoyeur, *m.*

Bus, *s.* omnibus, *m.*

Busby, *s.* colback, *m.*; talpack, *m.*

Bush, *s.* buisson, *m.*; arbuste, *m.*; (*a sign*) bouchon, *m.*; (*in colonies*) terre inculte, *f.*; (*of hair*) touffe, *f.*; (*of foxes*) queue (de renard), *f.*; — *v.n.* devenir touffu, buissonner. *To beat about the* —, tourner autour du pot. *Good wine needs no* —, à bon vin point d'enseigne. — **beater,** *s.* batteur de buissons, *m.*

Bushel, *s.* 40 litres [*formerly*, boisseau, *m.*]. *Under the* —, sous le boisseau

Bushet, *s.* buissonnet, *m.*

Bushiness, *s.* état touffu, *m.*, épaisseur, *f.*

Bushy, *adj.* touffu; épais, bien fourni; (*full of bushes*) buissonneux, plein de buissons, fourré

Busiless, *adj.* désœuvré, sans occupation

Busily, *adv.* activement, avec activité; avec empressement; d'un air affairé, curieusement

Business, *s.* affaire, *f.*; occupation, besogne, *f.*; affaires, *f. pl.*; commerce, *m.*; (*matter*) matière, *f.*, sujet, *m.*; (*calling*) état, métier, *m.*; commerce, *m.*; (*stock*) fonds de commerce, fonds, *m.*; (*connection, of a wholesale trader*) clientèle, *f.* *In* —, dans le commerce. *Engaged in* —, en affaire. *On* —, pour affaire. *Man of* —, *V.* — **man.** *House of* —, maison de commerce, *f.* *Old-established* —, ancienne maison, *f.* *To commence* —, *to set up in* —, se mettre dans les affaires; s'établir; débuter. *To do — with*, être en affaire avec. *To have a good* —, faire de bonnes affaires; avoir une bonne clientèle. *To make it o.'s* —, en faire son affaire; (*to* ...), se donner pour mission (de ...), s'appliquer (à ...). *To retire from* —, se retirer du commerce (*or* des affaires). *To send one about his* —, envoyer quelqu'un promener *or* paître. *Go about your — !* mêlez-vous de vos affaires ! allez vous promener ! *Mind your own — !* mêlez-vous de vos affaires ! *This is no — of yours*, cela ne vous regarde pas. *You have no — here*, vous n'avez que faire ici. *What is your — here ?* qu'est-ce que vous venez faire ici ? que venez-vous faire ici ? *What — had you there ?* qu'est-ce que vous alliez faire là ? qu'alliez-vous faire là ? *What — have you to ... ?* qu'avez-vous besoin de ... ? — **agent,** *s.* agent d'affaires, *m.* — **like,** *adj.* propre aux affaires, régulier, ponctuel; positif, pratique; (*things*) franc, droit; positif, pratique. — **man,** *s.* homme d'affaires, *m.*; homme qui entend les affaires, homme pratique, *m.*; commerçant, *m.*

Busk, *s.* busc, *m.* — **case, -casing,** *s.* busquière, *f.*

Buskin, *s.* brodequin, *m.*; (*of ancient actors*) cothurne, *m.*; (*fig.*) tragédie, *f.*

Buskined, *adj.* chaussé du cothurne; tragique

Buss, *s.* baiser, *m.*; (*bus*) omnibus, *m.*; (*nav.*) bûche, *f.*; — *v.a.* baisoter, embrasser

Bust, *s.* buste, *m.*; (*draw., paint.*) bosse, *f.* *From the* —, d'après la bosse

Bustard, *s.* outarde, *f.*

Buster, *s.* affaire, *f.*

Bustle, *v.n.* se donner du mouvement, s'agiter, se remuer ; (*to hurry*) se presser ; — *s.* mouvement, *m.*, agitation, *f.* ; tracas, *m.* ; tourbillon, *m.* ; (*noise*) bruit, tumulte, *m.* ; (*of ladies' dresses*) tournure, *f.*

Bustler, *s.* homme remuant, *m.*, femme remuante, *f.*

Bustling, *adj.* actif, remuant ; affairé ; (*noisy*) bruyant, tumultueux

Busy, *adj.* occupé, affairé ; actif, remuant ; officieux, importun ; — *v.a.* occuper. *To — oneself*, s'occuper (de) ; se mêler (de) ; s'agiter ; intriguer. — **body,** *s.* officieux, *m.*, -euse, *f.* ; tatillon, *m.*, -ne, *f.* ; brouillon, *m.*, -ne, *f.* — **day,** *s.* jour d'affaires, *m.*

But, *conj. adv. prep.* mais ; (*without*) sans que ; (*except*) excepté ; (*less*) moins ; (*that, than*) que ; (*who* or *which ... not*) qui ne ; (*whom* or *which ... not*) que ... ne ; (*only*) seulement, ne ... que, ne fût-ce que ; (*unless*) sinon ; (*not farther back than*) encore, pas plus loin que, pas plus tard que ; (*in a syllogism*) or ; — *s.* mais, *m.* ; (*butt*) *V.* **Butt.** — *for*, (*without*) sans. — *just now*, il n'y a qu'un instant, à l'instant même. — *yesterday*, hier encore, pas plus loin qu'hier, pas plus tard qu'hier. — *that*, si ce n'était que ; (*without*) sans que ; (*that*) que. — *what*, (*that*) que. — *yet*, cependant, néanmoins. *To do* —, ne faire que. *He does — repeat*, il ne fait que répéter. *He is — just gone*, il ne fait que de sortir. *If I could — see him*, si je pouvais seulement le voir. — *for a moment*, ne fût-ce que pour un moment. *It is — a franc*, ce n'est qu'un franc. *That cannot — be*, cela doit être. *I cannot — believe*, il m'est impossible de ne pas croire, je ne peux pas m'empêcher de croire. *He cannot — break*, il ne saurait éviter de faire banqueroute. *I cannot choose — stay*, je ne peux pas faire autrement que de rester

Butcher, *s.* boucher, *m.*, -ère, *f.* ; — *v.a.* égorger, massacrer. — **bird,** *s.* lanion, *m.*, pie-grièche, *f.* — **boy, —'s boy,** *s.* garçon boucher, *m.* —**'s broom,** *s.* (*bot.*) brusc, fragon, *m.* —**'s dog,** *s.* chien de boucher, *m.* —**'s meat,** *s.* viande de boucherie, grosse viande, *f.* —**'s shop,** *s.* boucherie, *f.* —**'s stall,** *s.* étal de boucher, *m.* —**'s trade,** *s.* boucherie, *f.* —**'s wife,** *s.* bouchère, *f.* — **work,** *s.* boucherie, *f.*, carnage, *m.*

Butchering, *s.* massacre, *m.*, boucherie, *f.*

Butcherliness, *s.* barbarie, cruauté, *f.*

Butcherly, *adj.* barbare, sanguinaire

Butchery, *s.* boucherie, *f.*

Butler, *s.* sommelier, maître d'hôtel. *m.* —**'s tray,** *s.* plateau à découper, *m.*

Butlership, *s.* emploi de sommelier, *m.*, sommellerie, *f.*

Butment. *V.* **Abutment**

Butt, *s.* (*end*) bout, gros bout ; (*of guns*) crosse, *f.* ; (*of billiard-cues*) masse, *f.* ; (*handle*) poignée, *f.*, manche, *m.* ; (*object of aim*) but, *m.* ; (*earth-work*) butte, *f.* ; (*for artillery*) polygone, *m.* ; (*target*) cible, *f.* ; (*laughing-stock*) plastron, *m.* ; (*fenc.*) botte, *f.* ; (*of rams*) coup de tête, *m.* ; (*measure*) pipe, *f.* ; pièce (anglaise), *f.* ; (*recipient for water*) tonneau, *m.* ; (*limit*) aboutissant, *m.* ; limite, *f.* ; — *v.n.a.* cosser, donner des coups de tête ; (*fenc.*) porter une botte ; (*shoot*) tirer au but. —*s and bounds*, tenants et aboutissants, *m.pl.* — **end,** *s.* gros bout, bout, *m.* ; (*of guns*) crosse, *f.* ; (*of billiard-cues*) masse, *f.* ; (*handle*) poignée, *f.*, manche, *m.*

Butter, *s.* beurre, *m.* ; — *adj.* de beurre ; beurrier ; — *v.a.* beurrer ; (*flatter*) flagorner. *Burnt* or *browned* —, beurre noir. *Drawn* —, roux, *m.* *Melted* —, (*a primitive kind of white sauce*) sauce blanche, *f.* — **boat,** *s.* petite saucière, *f.* — **cooler,** *s.* beurrier, *m.* — **cup,** *s.* (*bot.*) bouton d'or, bassinet, *m.* — **dairy,** *s.* beurrerie, *f.* — **dish,** *s.* beurrier, *m.* — **fingers,** *s. pl.* mains de beurre, *f.pl.* — **firkin,** *s.* tinette, *f.* — **fish,** *s.* gunnel, *m.* — **flower,** *s.* bouton d'or, bassinet, *m.* — **fly,** *s.* *See below.* — **like,** *adj.* comme le beurre. — **man,** *s.* marchand de beurre, beurrier, *m.* — **milk,** *s.* babeurre, lait de beurre, *m.* — **pat,** *s.* moule à beurre, *m.* — **pear,** *s.* poire de beurré, *f.*, beurré, *m.* — **pot,** *s.* pot à beurre, *m.*, tallevane, *f.* — **print,** *s.* moule à beurre, *m.* — **prover,** *s.* flûte à beurre, *f.* — **room,** *s.* beurrerie, *f.* — **sauce,** *s.* sauce blanche, *f.* — **scotch,** *s.* caramel au beurre, *m.* — **shop,** *s.* boutique de marchand de beurre, *f.* — **stamp,** *s.* moule à beurre, *m.* — **tooth,** *s.* (*jest.*) grande dent de devant, grande pelle, *f.* — **tree,** *s.* bassie butyracée, *f.* — **tub,** *s* tinette, *f.* — **woman,** *s.* marchande de beurre, beurrière, *f.* — **wort,** *s.* grassette, *f.*

Buttered, *part. adj.* beurré ; au beurre. — **roll,** *s.* galette, *f.* ; gâteau feuilleté, *m.* — **toast,** *s.* rôtie beurrée, rôtie de beurre, *f.*

Butterfly, *s.* papillon, *m.* *To break a — on the wheel*, grêler sur le persil

Butteris, *s.* bute, *f.*, boutoir, *m.*

Buttery, *adj.* de beurre, de la nature du beurre, beurré, semblable au beurre, gras, butyreux, butyracé ; — *s.* office, *f.*, garde-manger, *m.*, sommellerie, *f.* ; (*univers.*) buffet, café, *m.*, buvette, *f.*

Buttock, *s.* fesse, *f.* ; (*of beef*) cimier, gîte, *m.*

Button, *s.* bouton, *m.* ; — *v.a.* (— **up**) boutonner ; *v.n.* (*of clothes*) se boutonner. *To — o.'s clothes*, se boutonner. *A coat, a frockcoat to* —, un habit, une redingote qui se boutonne. — **hole,** *s.* boutonnière, *f.* — **hook,** *s.* tire-bouton, tourne-bouton, *m.* — **maker, -manufacturer,** *s.* fabricant de boutons, boutonnier, *m.* — **making, -manufactory, -manufacture,** *s.* boutonnerie, *f.* — **mould,** *s.* moule de bouton, *m.* ; bouton percé, *m.* — **shank,** *s.* queue de bouton, *f.* — **trade,** *s.* boutonnerie, *f.* — **up coat,** *s.* habit qui se boutonne, *m.* — **ware,** *s.* boutonnerie, *f.*

Buttoning, *s.* boutonnement, *m.*

Buttress, *s.* arc-boutant, *m.* ; éperon, *m.* ; contre-fort, *m.* ; (*fig.*) soutien, *m.* ; — *v.a.* arc-bouter, soutenir ; (*fig.*) appuyer, soutenir

Butyraceous, *adj.* butyracé

Butyrate, *s.* butyrate, *m.*

Butyric, *adj.* butyrique

Butyrine, *s.* butyrine, *f.*

Butyrometer, *s.* butyromètre, *m.*

Butyrous, *adj.* butyreux

Buxom, *adj.* enjoué, gai, joyeux, réjoui ; égrillard, gaillard ; vif ; (*pretty*) joli. — *woman*, grosse réjouie, (*pop.*) grosse gaguie, *f.*

Buxomly, *adv.* gaiment, joyeusement ; gaillardement

Buxomness, *s.* enjouement, *m.*, gaieté, *f.* ; gaillardise, *f.*

Buy, *v.a.n.* acheter ('*of*' à) ; (*bribe*) corrompre. — *and sell*, trafiquer ; brocanter. — *dearly*, acheter cher ; (*fig.*) payer cher. — **back,** racheter. — **for** (*a price*), acheter. — **in,** acheter ; *v.n.* (*mil.*) acheter un grade. — **off,** racheter ; (*bribe*) corrompre. — **out,** racheter, libérer du service ; (*com.*) acheter la part de. — **over,** gagner à prix d'argent, gagner, corrompre. — **up,** acheter, enlever, accaparer

Buyer, *s.* acheteur, *m.*, -euse, *f.* ; (*law*) acquéreur, *m.*, -euse, *f.*

Buying, *s.* achat, *m.*

Buzz, *v.n.* bourdonner ; (*whisper*) parler à voix basse, chuchoter ; — *v.a.* chuchoter, dire tout bas ; murmurer ; (*spread*) ébruiter ; — *s.* bourdonnement, *m.* ; (*whisper*) chuchotement, *m.*

Buzzard, *s.* buse, *f.*, busard, *m.*

Buzzer, *s.* chuchoteur, *m.*, -euse, *f.*

Buzzing, *s.* *V.* **Buzz,** *s.*

By, *prep.* par ; de ; à ; en ; (*of place*) auprès de, près de, à côté de ; (*before, in front of, past*) devant ; (*of intervals of time*) d'ici à ; (*of measure*) à ; (*of rising and falling, after a comparative, and after 'too'*) de ; (*in comparing several dimensions*) sur ; (*upon*) sur ; (*in the house*) chez ; (*in o.'s possession*) en (sa) possession, par devers ; (*for*) pour ; (*according to, from*) d'après. —

chance, par hasard. — *day, night*, de *or* le jour, de *or* la nuit. — *daylight, candlelight*, au jour, à la chandelle *or* &c. *I know him — reputation, — name, — sight*, je le connais de réputation, de nom, de vue. *He is known — the name of Smith*, il est connu sous le nom de Smith. *To call one — his name*, appeler quelqu'un par son nom. *I knew him — his voice*, je l'ai reconnu à sa voix. *What time is it — your watch?* quelle heure est-il à votre montre? (*What time is it — you?* quelle heure avez-vous?) — *the end of the month*, à la fin du mois. — *six o'clock*, avant six heures. *One — one*, un à un. — *retail*, en détail. — *me*, (*near*) auprès de moi, près de moi, à côté de moi; (*on the person*) sur moi; (*in the house*) chez moi; en ma possession, par devers moi. — *to-morrow*, d'ici à demain, demain, pour demain. — *that time*, (*then*) alors, déjà; (*between this and then*) d'ici là; dans l'intervalle. — *this time*, alors; dans l'intervalle; (*now*) maintenant, à l'heure qu'il est. — *the time that*, quand (*with the future tense*); d'ici à ce que (*with the subj. mood*). — *measure, weight*, à la mesure, au poids. — *the bottle, dozen*, &c., à la bouteille, à la douzaine, &c. — *the day, week, month, hour*, &c., à la journée, à la semaine, au mois, à l'heure, &c. *The rate of exchange has risen* (or *fallen*) — *2 francs*, le cours du change a haussé (*or* baissé) de 2 francs. *Longer* (or *too long*) — *two yards*, plus long (*or* trop long) de deux mètres. *One yard long — two wide*, un mètre de long sur deux de large. — *oneself*, seul, tout seul; à part

By, Bye, *adv.* (*of place*) près, auprès; par là; (*before, in front*) devant; (*present*) là, présent; (*of time*) passé; (*aside*) de côté; en réserve; (*in compounds*) détourné, écarté, retiré; à part, accessoire. *By and* —, tout à l'heure; bientôt. *By the* —, à propos; en passant, par parenthèse. *To go* —, *V.* **Go.** *To go to bye-bye*, aller faire dodo. — **blow,** *s.* coup de hasard, *m.*; (*gibe*) coup de patte, *m.* — **end,** *s.* intérêt particulier, *m.*; arrière-pensée, *f.* — **gone,** *adj.* passé, ancien, d'autrefois, qui n'est plus; (*obsolete*) suranné. *Let —gones be —gones*, ne revenons pas sur le passé, que le passé soit oublié. — **lane,** *s.* ruelle, *f.* — **law,** *s.* statut, règlement, *m.* — **matter,** *s.* accessoire, objet secondaire, *m.*; incident, *m.* — **name,** *s.* surnom, *m.*; *v.a.* surnommer. — **path,** *s.* sentier détourné, *m.* — **place,** *s.* lieu écarté *or* retiré, *m.*; réduit, *m.*; retraite, *f.* — **play,** *s.* jeu muet, jeu de scène, *m.*; jeu accessoire, *m.* — **road,** *s.* chemin détourné, *m.* — **room,** *s.* pièce écartée, *f.* — **stander,** *s.* assistant, *m.*, e, *f.*, spectateur, *m.*, -trice, *f.* — **street,** *s.* rue détournée *or* écartée, petite rue, ruelle, *f.* — **stroke,** *s.* coup de hasard, *m.*; (*gibe*) coup de patte, *m.* — **way,** *s.* chemin détourné, *m.*; (*fig.*) moyen indirect, *m.* — **word,** *s.* dicton, proverbe, *m.*, maxime, *f.*; (*jest*) risée, fable, *f.* *To have become* (or *to be*) *a* —, être passé en proverbe, être devenu (*or* être) proverbial, être un proverbe *or* &c.; être devenu (*or* être) la risée *or* la fable (de)

Byre, *s.* *V.* **Cow-house**

Byronian, Byronic, *adj.* byronien

Byronism, *s.* byronisme, *m.*

Byssus, *s.* bysse, byssus, *m.*

Byzantine, *s.* Byzantin, *m.*, e, *f.*; — *adj.* byzantin, de Byzance

C

C, *s.* (*letter*) c, *m.*; (*mus.*) ut, do, *m.*

Cab, *s.* (*common cab*) voiture de place, voiture [voiture à deux places (*seats*); voiture à quatre places], *f.*; fiacre, *m.*; (*first-class cab*) voiture de remise, *f.*, remise, *m.* *Hansom* —, voiture découverte, *f.*, cabriolet (de place), *m.*; (*English ditto*) cab, *m.* *To — it*, aller (*or* venir) en voiture; prendre une voiture. — **driver,** *s.* cocher de voiture de place, cocher de place, cocher de fiacre, cocher, *m.* — **fare,** *s.* prix de la course, *m.*; tarif de voiture de place, *m.* — **horse,** *s.* cheval de fiacre, *m.* — **man,** *s.* *V.* — **driver.** — **rank, -stand,** *s.* station (*or* place) de voitures, place, *f.*

Cabal, *s.* cabale, *f.*; — *v.n.* cabaler

Cabala, *s.* cabale, *f.*

Cabaletta, *s.* cabalette, *f.* [page 3, § 1

Cabal-ism, -ist, -istic, al, -ically. *V.*

Caballer, *s.* cabaleur, *m.*, -euse, *f.*

Caballine, *adj.* caballin

Cabaret, *s.* cabaret

Cabbage, *s.* chou, *m.*; (*as a dish*) choux, *m.pl.*; (*shreds of stuff*) gratte, *f.*, chippes, *f.pl.*; — *adj.* de chou; (*cook.*) de choux; aux choux; — *v.n.* (*hort.*) pommer; (*on stuffs*) gratter; — *v.a.* détourner, voler, empocher, garder pour soi. — **head,** *s.* pomme de chou, *f.* — **leaf,** *s.* feuille de chou, *f.* — **lettuce,** *s.* laitue pommée, *f.* — **palm,** *s.* palmiste, *m.* — **rose,** *s.* rose à cent feuilles, *f.* — **stalk, -stump,** *s.* trognon de chou, *m.* — **tree,** *s.* palmiste, *m.*

Cabbaged, Cabbagy, *adj.* (*hort.*) pommé

Cabby, *s.* cocher, automédon, *m.*

Cabiai, *s.* cabiai, *m.*

Cabin, *s.* cabane, *f.*; (*of American negroes*) case, *f.*; (*nav.*) chambre, cabine, *f.*; — *v.n.* vivre dans une cabane, vivre à l'étroit; habiter, se loger; — *v.a.* enfermer dans une cabane *or* dans une chambre, enfermer, renfermer, emprisonner. *After* —, *V.* **After.** *Chief* —, grande chambre. *Fore* —, *See Letter* **F.** — **boy,** *s.* mousse, *m.* — **mate,** *s.* camarade de chambre, *m.* — **passenger,** *s.* passager (*m.*, -ère, *f.*) de première classe

Cabinet, *s.* cabinet, *m.*; (*polit.*) cabinet, *m.*, ministres, *m.pl.*, gouvernement, *m.*; (*collection*) cabinet, *m.*, collection, *f.*; (*piece of furniture, obsolete in France*) cabinet, *m.*; — *v.a.* renfermer. — **carver,** *s.* sculpteur sur meubles, *m.* — **council,** *s.* conseil des ministres, *m.* — **maker,** *s.* ébéniste, *m.* — **making,** *s.* ébénisterie, *f.* — **minister,** *s.* ministre d'état, *m.* — **piano,** *s.* *V.* **Cottage-piano.** — **turner,** *s.* tourneur ébéniste, *m.* — **wood,** *s.* bois d'ébénisterie, *m.* — **work,** *s.* ébénisterie, *f.*

Cable, *s.* câble, *m.*; — *v.a.* (*twist*) câbler; (*fasten*) amarrer. — **laid,** *adj.* câblé. — **length, —'s length,** *s.* encâblure, câblée, *f.*

Cabled, *part. adj.* câblé; amarré; (*arch.*) [câblé, rudenté

Cablet, *s.* câbleau, câblot, *m.*

Cabling, *s.* (*arch.*) rudenture, *f.*

Caboose, *s.* cuisine, *f.*, fourneaux, *m.pl.*

Cabriole, *s.* cabriole, *f.*; — *v.n.* cabrioler

Cabriolet, *s.* cabriolet, *m.*

Cacao, *s.* (*chocolate nut, preparation*) cacao, *m.*; (*tree*) cacaotier, cacaoyer, *m.* — **bean,** *s.* fève de cacao, *f.* — **butter,** *s.* beurre de cacao, *m.* — **nibs,** *s. pl.* cacao en grains, *m.*, cassons, *m.pl.* — **nut,** *s.* cacao, *m.* — **plantation,** *s.* cacaotière, cacaoyère, *f.* — **pod,** *s.* cabosse, *f.* — **tree,** *s.* cacaotier, cacaoyer, *m.*

Cachalot, *s.* cachalot, *m.*

Cach-ectic, al, -exy. *V.* page 3, § 1

Cachinnation, *s.* éclat de rire, fou rire, *m.*

Cachou. *V.* **Cashoo**

Cachuca, *s.* cachucha, *f.*

Cacique, *s.* cacique, *m.*

Cack, *s.* caca, *m.*; — *v.n.* faire caca, caquer

Cackle, *v.n.* (*of hens*) caqueter; (*of geese*) cacarder; (*to talk*) caqueter, babiller; (*to laugh*) ricaner ('*at*,' de); — *s.* caquet, *m.*; (*of geese*) cri, *m.*

Cackler, *s.* (*hen*) poule qui caquette, *f.*; (*goose*) oie qui cacarde, *f.*; (*pers.*) caqueteur, *m.*, -euse, *f.*, babillard, *m.*, e, *f.*

Cackling, *s.* caquetage, *m.*; (*of geese*) cri, *m.*

Cacochymic, -al, *adj.* cacochyme
Cacochymy, *s.* cacochymie, *f.*
Cacodyle, *s.* kakodyle, *m.*
Cacoethes, *s.* mauvaise habitude, démangeaison, rage, *f.* (*'scribendi,'* d'écrire)
Caco-graphy, -logy, -phony. *V.* page 3, § 1
Cacolet, *s.* cacolet, *m.*
Cactus, *s.* cactus, cactier, *m.*
Cad, *s.* conducteur d'omnibus, *m.*; (*vulgar fellow*) voyou, gamin, *m.*; (*churl*) manant, *m.* — **bait,** *s.* caset, ver caset, *m.*
Cadastral, *adj.* cadastral. — *survey,* cadastre, *m.*
Cadastre, *s.* cadastre, *m.*
Cadaveric, *adj.* cadavérique
Cadaverous, *adj.* cadavéreux
Caddice, Caddis, *s.* (— *fly*) phrygane, *f.*; (— *worm*) caset, ver caset, *m.*
Caddy, *s.* boîte à thé, *f.*
Cade, *s.* baril, *m.*; caque, *f.* — **oil,** *s.* huile de cade, *f.* — **worm,** *s.* *V.* **Cad-bait**
Cadence, *s.* (*mus., danc., rid.,* &c.) cadence, *f.*; (*rhet., mus.*) chute, *f.*; — *v.a.* cadencer
Cadet, *s.* cadet, *m.*; (*pupil*) élève (d'une école militaire *or* navale), *m.* *Naval* —, aspirant *or* élève de marine (de seconde classe), *m.*
Cadetship, *s.* emploi de cadet, *m.*
Cadger, *s.* (*egg-merchant, obsolete*) coquetier, *m.*; (*poultry-salesman, obsolete*) poulailler, *m.*; (*trickster, beggar*) chevalier de la redresse, bricoleur, bricolier, *m.*
Cadi, *s.* cadi, *m.*
Cadmean, Cadmian, *adj.* cadméen
Cadmium, *s.* cadmium, *m.*
Caduceus, *s.* caducée, *m.*
Caducity, *s.* caducité, *f.*
Cæcal, *adj.* cæcal
Cæcum, *s.* cæcum, *m.*
Cærulean. *V.* **Cerulean**
Cæsarean, Cæsarian, *adj.* césarien, de César. — *operation* or *section,* (*surg.*) opération césarienne, *f.*
Cæsarism, *s.* césarisme, *m.*
Cæsium, *s.* cæsium, *m.*
Cæsura, *s.* césure, *f.*
Cæsural, *adj.* de césure
Cæteris paribus, (*Latin*) toutes choses égales d'ailleurs
Caffeic, *adj.* caféique
Caffeine, *s.* caféine, *f.*
Caffre, *s. adj.* Cafre, *m.f.*
Caftan, *s.* cafetan, caftan, *m.*
Cag. *V.* **Keg**
Cage, *s.* cage, *f.*; — *v.a.* mettre en cage, encager; (*imprison*) coffrer. — **bird,** *s.* oiseau de cage, *m.* —**ful,** *s.* cagée, *f.* — **maker,** *s.* cagier, *m.*, -ière, *f.*
Cagmag, *s.* carne, *f.*; ratatouille, *f.*
Caïc, *s.* caïc, caïque, *m.*
Caiman, *s.* caïman, *m.*
Caïque, *s.* caïque, caïc, *m.*
Cairn, *s.* borne, *f.*; (*sepulchral*) cairn, tumulus, galgal, *m.*
Caisson, *s.* caisson, *m.*
Caitiff, *s. adj.* gueux, misérable, maroufle, *m.*
Caitively, *adv.* misérablement, bassement
Cajeput, *s.* cajeput, *m.* — **oil,** *s.* huile de cajeput, *f.*
Cajole, *v.a.* cajoler
Cajoler, *s.* cajoleur, *m.*, -euse, *f.*
Cajolery, Cajoling, *s.* cajolerie, *f.*
Cake, *s.* gâteau, *m.*; biscuit, *m.*; (*flat and buttery*) galette, *f.*; (*of soap, wax, salt, crayons,* &c.) pain, *m.*; (*of colours*) pain, *m.*, tablette, *f.*; (*of chocolate*) tablette, *f.*; (*agr.*) tourteau, *m.*; (*heap*) masse, *f.*; (*crust*) croûte, *f.*; — *v.a.* former en gâteau *or* en pain *or* en croûte *or* &c.; coaguler; cailler; coller; durcir; — *v.n.* se coaguler, se prendre; se cailler; se pelotonner; se coller, coller; se durcir; se croûter, se former en croûte, former une croûte. — **man,** *s.* marchand de gâteaux, *m.* — **mould,** *s.* moule à gâteaux, *m.* — **shop,** *s.* boutique de pâtissier, *f.* — **woman,** *s.* marchande de gâteaux, *f.*
Caking. *adj.* (*of coal*) collant. — *coal,* charbon de terre collant, *m.*, houille grasse, maréchale, *f.*

Calabash, *s.* calebasse, *f.*; (*tree*) calebassier, *m.* — **tree,** *s.* calebassier, *m.*
Calabrian, *s.* Calabrais, *m.*, e, *f.*; — *adj.* calabrais, de Calabre
Calamar, Calamary, *s.* calmar, encornet, *m.*
Calamine, *s.* calamine, *f.*
Calamint, *s.* calament, *m.*
Calamitous, *adj.* calamiteux, désastreux, funeste, malheureux
Calamitously, *adv.* calamiteusement, désastreusement
Calamity, *s.* calamité, *f.*, malheur, *m.*
Calandra, Calandre, *s.* calandre, *f.*
Calash, *s.* (*old-fashioned carriage*) calèche (d'ancienne mode), *f.*; (*head-dress*) grande capote, *f.*, (*formerly*) calèche, *f.*
Calcaneal, *adj.* calcanéen
Calcaneum, *s.* calcanéum, *m.*
Calcareous, *adj.* calcaire
Calcedony. *V.* **Chalcedony**
Calceolaria, *s.* calcéolaire, *f.*
Calcinable, *adj.* calcinable
Calcination, *s.* calcination, *f.*
Calcine, *v.a.* calciner; — *v.n.* se calciner
Calcining, *s.* calcination, *f.*
Calcium, *s.* calcium, *m.*
Calcographer, *s.* calcographe, *m.*
Calcograph-ic, -y. *V.* page 3, § 1
Calculable, *adj.* calculable
Calculate, *v.a.* calculer; adapter, ajuster; — *v.n.* calculer; (*rely on*) compter (sur)
Calculated, *adj.* propre (à), adapté (à); fait (pour); destiné (à); favorable (à); de nature (à); capable (de)
Calculating, *adj.* calculateur. — **machine,** *s.* machine à calculer, machine calculatoire, machine arithmétique, *f.*, calculateur mécanique, *m.*
Calculation, *s.* calcul, *m.*
Calculative, *adj.* de calcul
Calculator, *s.* calculateur, *m.*
Calculatory, *adj.* calculatoire
Calculous, *adj.* calculeux
Calculus, *s.* calcul, *m.*
Caldron, *s.* chaudron, *m.*, chaudière, *f.*
Caledonian, *s. adj.* Calédonien, *m.*, -ne, *f.*
Calefaction, *s.* caléfaction, *f.*
Calefactive, Calefactory, *adj.* caléfacteur
Calefactor, *s.* caléfacteur, *m.*
Calefy, *v.a.* échauffer; — *v.n.* s'échauffer
Calendar, *s.* calendrier, almanach, *m.*; (*list*) tableau, *m.*; (*law*) liste, *f.*; — *v.a.* inscrire dans un calendrier *or* sur une liste, inscrire, enregistrer. — **month,** *s.* mois solaire, *m.*
Calender, *s.* calandre, *f.*; (*monk, dervis*) calender, *m.*; — *v.a.* calandrer
Calenderer, *s.* calandreur, *m.*, -euse, *f.*
Calendering, *s.* calandrage, *m.*
Calends, *s. pl.* calendes, *f.pl.*
Calenture, *s.* calenture, fièvre chaude, *f.*; (*fig.*) délire, transport, *m.*
Calf, *s.* (*young of the cow, and leather*) veau, *m.*; (*of stags*) faon; (*of buffaloes*) buffletin, buffion, *m.*; (*of camels*) chamelon, *m.*; (*anat.*) mollet; (*of ice*) glaçon, *m.*; (*theol.*) sacrifice, *m.* — *of the leg,* gras de la jambe, mollet, *m.* *The fatted* —, le veau gras. *In* or *with* —, (*of cows*) pleine; (*book-bind.*) en veau. — **bound,** *adj.* relié en veau. — **like,** *adj.* comme un veau. —**'s foot,** *s.* pied de veau, *m.* —**'s head,** *s.* tête de veau, *f.* — **skin,** *s.* peau de veau, *f.*, veau, *m.* —**'s liver,** *s.* foie de veau, *m.* —**'s snout,** *s.* (*bot.*) mufle de veau, muflier, *m.* —**'s sweetbread,** *s.* ris de veau, *m.*
Calibre, *s.* calibre, *m.*
Calico, *s.* calicot, *m.*; (*printed*) indienne, *f.* — **manufacturer,** *s.* calicotier, *m.*; fabricant d'indiennes, *m.* — **printer,** *s.* imprimeur d'indiennes, indienneur, *m.* — **printing,** *s.* impression d'indiennes, *f.*
Calif, &c. **Caliph,** &c.
Californian, *s.* Californien, *m.*, -ne, *f.*; — *adj.* californien, de Californie [&c
Caligraph-er, -ic, al, -y. *V.* **Calligrapher,**

Calin, *s.* calin, *m.* — **work,** *s.* calinage, *m.*
Calipash, Calipee, *s.* (*cook.*) calapé, *m.*
Caliper compasses, Callipers, *s. pl.* compas d'épaisseur, *m.*; (*artil.*) compas de [calibre, *m.*
Caliph, *s.* calife, *m.*
Caliphal, *adj.* califal
Caliphate, Caliphship, *s.* califat, *m.*
Calisthen-ic, -ics. *V.* **Callisthenic**
Calix. *V.* **Calyx**
Calk, *v.a.* (*nav.*) calfater; (*horses*) ferrer à glace; — *s.* crampon, *m.* [calfatin, *m.*
Calker, *s.* calfat, calfateur, *m.* —**'s boy,** *s.*
Calkin, *s.* crampon, *m.*
Calking, *s.* calfatage, *m.* — **iron,** *s.* calfait, *m.*
Call, *v.a.n.* appeler; crier, annoncer; publier; faire venir, citer; convoquer, assembler; invoquer; évoquer; inviter; (*to name*) appeler, nommer; (*to style, to term*) appeler, traiter de; (*to think*) trouver; (*awake*) éveiller, réveiller; (*admit*) recevoir, admettre; (*appoint*) nommer; (*collect*) rappeler; (*remember*) se rappeler; (*carriages*) faire venir, faire avancer; (*the names*) faire l'appel de; (*into action, into play*) mettre; (*of visits*) passer, entrer; venir; se présenter; (*stop*) s'arrêter; (*of trains, vessels*) passer, s'arrêter; (*nav.*) toucher. *To — oneself,* s'intituler. *To be called,* (*o.'s or its name to be*) s'appeler. *To have called,* (*have come*) être venu; (*be here*) être ici. *To — names, To — in question,* &c., *V.* **Name, Question,** &c. *To — to order,* rappeler à l'ordre — **again,** rappeler; (*come again*) repasser, revenir. — **aside,** prendre à part. — **away,** appeler; faire sortir; attirer; (*the mind, attention*) détourner; (*disturb*) déranger (de). — **back,** rappeler; faire revenir; (*fig.*) rétracter; révoquer. — **down,** appeler; faire descendre; faire tomber; attirer. — **for,** demander; exiger, réclamer; ordonner, commander; provoquer; aller *or* venir prendre, aller *or* venir chercher; (*an actor*) rappeler. — **forth,** appeler; faire sortir; choisir, désigner; (*fig.*) faire naître; provoquer; produire; inspirer; déployer, mettre en action, mettre en jeu. — **in,** appeler; faire entrer; faire rentrer; faire venir; inviter; envoyer chercher; (*collect*) rappeler, rassembler; (*coin*) retirer de la circulation, faire rentrer, démonétiser; (*enter*) entrer; (*visit*) venir *or* aller voir (...). — **off,** rappeler; appeler; détourner, distraire; éloigner; (*disturb*) déranger (de); (*nav.*) toucher à. — **on,** (*a case at law*) appeler (une cause). — **on, upon,** aller *or* venir voir; aller *or* venir trouver; venir; faire visite à; (*on o.'s way*) passer *or* entrer chez; (*solicit,* &c.) sommer (de), exhorter (à), inviter (à); ordonner (de); conjurer (de), adjurer (de), prier instamment (de); invoquer; obliger; (*for*) demander, réclamer. — **out,** appeler; faire sortir; crier; annoncer; appeler en duel; (*mil.*) appeler sous les drapeaux. — **out for,** invoquer; demander. — **over,** appeler; (*the names*) faire l'appel (de); (*to read*) lire. — **to,** crier à; appeler; invoquer; appeler à son secours. — **together,** convoquer, assembler, rassembler. — **up,** appeler; faire monter; faire venir; (*awake*) réveiller; (*recall*) rappeler, évoquer; (*discuss*) mettre en discussion, discuter; (*law*) faire comparaître, appeler, citer. — **upon** *or* **on,** *V.* — **on**
Call, *s.* appel, *m.*; voix, *f.*; inspiration, *f.*; ordres, *m.pl.*, autorité, *f.*; devoir, *m.*, obligation, *f.*; demande, *f.*; invitation, *f.*; nécessité, *f.*, besoin, *m*, exigences, *f.pl.*; prétentions, *f.pl.*; droit, titre, *m.*; convocation, *f.*; vocation, *f.*; profession, *f.*; admission, *f.*; visite, *f.*; (*cry of some animals*) cri, *m.*; (*for birds*) appeau, pipeau, *m.*; (*whistle*) sifflet, *m.*; coup de sifflet, *m.*; (*Punch's* —) pratique (de Polichinelle), *f.*; (*of a bell*) coup (de cloche *or* de sonnette), *m.* — *of the House,* (*parliam.*) appel nominal, *m.*; convocation spéciale, *f.* — *to order,* rappel à l'ordre, *m.* *At* —, sur-le-champ, à commandement. *Within* —, à portée de la voix. *To give* (...) *a* —, (*visit*) faire une visite à; passer chez; venir; (*summon*) appeler; (*awake*) éveiller. — **bell,** *s.* timbre (de table), *m.* — **bird,** *s.* chanterelle, *f.* — **boy,** *s.* (*theat.*) avertisseur, *m.*
Called, *part. adj.* appelé, &c. (*V.* **Call,** *v.a.*); (*styled*) dit. *So* —, dit; prétendu; soi-disant. *To be —, to have* —, &c., *V.* **Call,** *v.a.* — **for,** demandé, &c. (*V.* **Call for**); utile; nécessaire; mérité; juste. *To be left till — for,* (*of letters*) poste restante; (*of parcels*) bureau restant
Calligrapher, *s.* calligraphe, *m.*
Calligraph-ic, al, -y. *V.* page 3, § 1
Calling, *s.* appel, *m.*; convocation, *f.*; profession, *f.*, état, métier, emploi, *m*; vocation, *f.* — **in,** *s.* (*of coin*) retraite, *f.*, démonétisation, *f.* — **out,** *s.* appel, *m.* — **over,** *s.* appel, *m.*
Callipash, Callipee. *V.* **Calipash,** &c.
Calliper. *V.* **Caliper** [callisthénie, *f.*
Callisthenic, *adj.* callisthénique; —**s,** *s. pl.*
Callosity, *s.* callosité, *f.*; (*fig.*) endurcissement, *m.*, insensibilité, *f.*
Callous, *adj.* calleux; (*fig.*) endurci, insensible
Callously, *adv.* avec callosité; (*fig.*) avec endurcissement, avec insensibilité
Callousness. *V.* **Callosity**
Callow, *adj.* sans plumes; (*fig.*) naissant, jeune
Callus, *s.* calus, cal, *m.*
Calm, *adj.* calme; — *s.* calme, *m.*; — *v.a.* calmer. *To become* or *get* or *grow* —, se calmer
Calmer, *s.* calmant, adoucissant, *m.*; consolation, *f.*; (*pers.*) consolateur, *m.*, -trice, *f.*
Calmly, *adv.* avec calme, tranquillement, paisiblement
Calmness, *s.* calme, *m.*; tranquillité, *f.*
Calmuck, *s.* Calmouk, *m.*
Calomel, *s.* calomel, *m.*
Caloric, *s.* calorique, *m.*; — *adj.* de calorique
Caloricity, *s.* caloricité, *f.*
Calorifere, *s.* calorifère, *m.*
Calorific, *adj.* calorifique
Calorification, *s.* calorification, *f.*
Calorimeter, *s.* calorimètre, *m.*
Calorimetr-ic, -y, calorimétr-ique, -ie (*f.*)
Calorimotor, *s.* calorimoteur, *m.*
Calotte, *s.* calotte, *f.*
Calotype, *s.* calotype, *m.*
Caloyer, *s.* caloyer, *m.*, -ère, *f.*
Calque, *v.a.* calquer
Calquing, *s.* calque, *m.* — **point,** *s.* calquoir, *m.*
Calthrop, Caltrop, *s.* chausse-trappe, *f.*; (*bot.*) tribule (terrestre), *m.*, herse, croix de [Malte, *f.*
Calumet, *s.* calumet, *m.*
Calumniate, Calumny, &c. *V.* **Slander,** &c.
Calvary, *s.* calvaire, *m.*
Calve, *v.n.* vêler
Calville, *s.* calville, *m.f.*
Calvin-ism, -ist. *V.* page 3, § 1
Calvinistic, *adj.* calviniste
Calvish, *adj.* de veau
Calyx, *s.* calice, *m.*
Cam, *s.* came, *f.*
Camaieu, *s.* camaïeu, *m.* *Grey* —, grisaille, *f.*
Camail, *s.* camail, *m.*
Camarilla, *s.* camarilla, *f.* [*v.n.* se cambrer
Camber, *s.* cambrure, *f.*; — *v.a.* cambrer; —
Camberer, *s.* cambreur, *m.*, -euse, *f.*
Cambering, *s.* cambrure, *f.*; — *adj.* cambré
Cambist, *s.* changeur, agent de change, *m.*, (*formerly*) cambiste, *m.*
Camboose. *V.* **Caboose**
Cambrian, *s.* *adj.* Cambrien, *m.*, -ne, *f.*
Cambric, *s.* batiste, *f.* — **muslin,** *s.* percale, *f.*
Camel, *s.* chameau, *m.*, (*She* —) chamelle, *f.* — **backed,** *adj* à dos de chameau; bossu. — **calf,** *s.* chamélon, *m.* — **driver,** *s.* chamelier, *m.* — **hair, —'s hair,** *s.* poil de chameau, *m.*; poil de chèvre d'Angora, turcoin, *m.* — **hair brush** *or* **pencil,** *s.* pinceau, *m.* — **load,** *s.* chamelée, *f.*
Cameleon, *s.* caméléon, *m.*
Camelia, Camellia, *s.* camélia, camellia, *m.*

Camelopard, *s.* girafe, *f.*
Cameo, *s.* camée, *m.*
Camera, *s.* chambre, *f.* — **lucida,** *s.* chambre claire, caméra-lucida, *f.* — **obscura,** *s.* chambre obscure, *f.*
Camerate, *v.a.* voûter, arquer
Cameration, *s.* courbure, arcure, *f.*
Camerlingo, *s.* camerlingue, *m.*
Camlet, *s.* camelot, *m.*
Camleted, *adj.* moiré
Cammock, *s.* arrête-bœuf, *m.*, bugrane, *f.*
Camomile, *s.* camomille, *f.*
Camouflet, *s.* camouflet, *m.*
Camp, *s.* camp, *m.*; — *v.a.n.* camper. — **bed** *or* **bedstead,** *s.* lit de camp, *m.* — **equipage,** *s.* effets *or* articles *or* objets de campement, *m.pl.* — **fight,** *s.* combat judiciaire, *m.* — **follower,** *s.* boulineur, *m.* — **kettle,** *s.* bidon, *m.* — **stool,** *s.* pliant, *m.*
Campaign, *s.* campagne, *f.*; — *v.n.* faire une (*or* la) campagne
Campaigner, *s.* vieux soldat, vétéran, *m.*
Campana, *s.* campane, *f.*
Campaniform, *adj.* campaniforme
Campanile, *s.* campanile, *m.*
Campanula, *s.* campanule, *f.*
Campanulate, *adj.* campanulé
Campeachy, *s.* Campêche, *m.* — **wood,** *s.* bois de campêche, *m.*
Campestral, *adj.* champêtre, des champs
Camphene, *s.* camphène, *m.*
Camphine, *s.* camphine, *f.*
Camphogen, *s.* camphogène, *m.*
Camphor, *s.* camphre, *m.* — **tree,** *s.* camphrier, *m.*
Camphorate, *s.* camphorate, *m.*; — *v.a.* camphrer
Camphoric, *adj.* camphorique
Camping, *s.* campement, *m.*; (*play*) balle au camp, *f.*
Can, *v.n.* pouvoir; (*to know how to*) savoir. *I* —, (*present tense*) je peux *or* je puis; (*future*) je pourrai. — *I?* (*present tense*) puis-je? (*future*) pourrai-je? *I do not see how that — shock you,* je ne vois pas en quoi cela peut vous choquer. *I do not see how that — have shocked you,* je ne vois pas en quoi cela a pu vous choquer. — *it be true?* serait-ce vrai? *As ... as — be,* aussi ... que possible
Can, *s.* broc, pot, *m.*; bidon, *m.*; burette, *f.*
Canaanite, *s.* Chananéen, *m.*, -ne, *f.*
Canaanitish, *adj.* chananéen, de Chanaan
Canadian, *s.* Canadien, *m.*, -ne, *f.*; — *adj.* canadien, du Canada
Canal, *s.* canal, *m.*
Canaliculate, *adj.* canaliculé
Canalizable, *adj.* canalisable
Canalization, *s.* canalisation, *f.*
Canalize, *v.a.* canaliser
Cananean, *s. adj.* Cananéen, *m.*, -ne, *f.*
Canary, *s.* (*geog.*) Canarie, *f.*; (*bird*) serin, *m.*, e, *f.*, canari, *m.* — **bird,** *s.* serin, *m.*, e, *f.*, canari, *m.* — **grass,** *s.* alpiste, *m.* — **plant,** *s.* canarine, *f.* — **seed,** *s.* graine des Canaries, *f.* — **wood,** *s.* bois jaune, *m.*
Canaster, *s.* canastre, canasse, *m.*
Cancel, *v.a.* (*erase*) raturer, effacer, biffer; (*annul*) annuler, résoudre, résilier; (*remit*) remettre, faire remise de; (*reprint*) refaire; — *s.* (*print.*) feuillet refait, carton refait, *m.*, (*of one leaf*) onglet refait, onglet, *m.*
Cancellation, Cancelling, *s.* biffage, biffement, *m.*; annulation, *f.*, annulement, *m.*, résolution, résiliation, *f.*
Cancer, *s.* (*astr., med.*) cancer, *m.* — *of the breast,* cancer au sein, *m.*
Cancerate, *v.n.* dégénérer en cancer, devenir cancéreux
Canceration, *s.* dégénération en cancer, *f.*
Canceriform, *adj.* cancériforme
Cancerous, *adj.* cancéreux
Cancerousness, *s.* nature cancéreuse, *f.*, état cancéreux, *m.*
Cancriform, *adj.* cancriforme
Candelabrum, *s.* candélabre, *m.*
Candian, *s. adj.* Candiote, *m.f.*
Candid, *adj.* franc, candide, ingénu; sincère, loyal; impartial; équitable
Candidacy, *s.* candidature, *f.*
Candidate, *s.* candidat, *m.*, e, *f.*; aspirant, *m.*, e, *f.*; prétendant, *m.*, e, *f.*
Candidateship, Candidature, *s.* candidature, *f.*
Candidly, *adv.* franchement, candidement, avec candeur, ingénument, sincèrement, loyalement, de bonne foi; en bonne foi, en conscience; impartialement, avec impartialité; équitablement
Candidness. *V.* **Candour**
Candied, *adj.* candi; confit
Candiot, Candiote. *V.* **Candian**
Candle, *s.* (*general sense*) chandelle, *f.*; (*particular sense, tallow* —) chandelle, *f.*, (*not of tallow*) bougie, *f.*; (*for churches*) cierge, *m.*; (*surg.*) bougie, *f.*; (*fig.*) lumière, *f.*; — *v.a.* (*eggs*) mirer. — **berry tree,** *s.* cirier, arbre à cire, *m.* — **end,** *s.* bout de chandelle, *m.* — **factory,** *s.* fabrique de chandelles *or* de bougies, chandellerie, *f.* — **grease,** *s.* suif, *m.* — **holder,** *s.* personne qui tient la chandelle, *f.* — **light,** *s.* lumière de la chandelle *or* de la bougie, *f.*; chandelle, *f.*; bougie, *f.*; (*supply of candles*) éclairage, *m.* *By — light,* à la lumière de la chandelle *or* des chandelles, à la chandelle, aux chandelles; à la lumière de la bougie *or* des bougies, à la bougie, aux bougies. — **maker, -manufacturer,** *s.* fabricant de chandelles *or* de bougies, *m.* — **mas,** *s.* la Chandeleur, *f.* — **mould,** *s* moule à chandelles, *m.* — **stick,** *s.* chandelier, *m.*; flambeau, *m.*; (*branched*) candélabre, *m.* *Bedroom — stick, flat — stick,* bougeoir, *m.* — **stuff,** *s.* graisses de cuisine, *f.pl.*, suif, *m.* — **wick,** *s.* mèche de (*or* à) chandelle, *f.*; coton à mèche, *m.*
Candour, *s.* candeur, franchise, ingénuité, *f.*; sincérité, bonne foi, loyauté, *f.*; impartialité, *f.*; équité, *f.*
Candy, *v.a.* candir, faire candir; confire; cristalliser; — *v.n.* candir, se candir; — *s.* candi, *m.* — **tuft,** *s.* ibéride, *f.*
Candying, *s.* candisation, *f.* — **pan,** *s.* candissoire, *f.*
Cane, *s.* canne, *f.*; (*stem*) tige, *f.*; (*stock*) plant, *m.*; cep, *m.*; — *v.a.* battre à coups de canne, donner des coups de canne à; (*chairs, &c.*) canner. *Malacca* —, jonc, *m.* — **basket,** *s.* panier de jonc, *m.* — **brake,** *s.* plantation de cannes, cannaie, *f.*; (*plant*) arundinaire, *f.* — **chair, -seated chair, -bottomed chair,** *s.* chaise de canne, *f.*; fauteuil de canne, *m.* — **field,** *s.* plantation de cannes, cannaie, *f.* — **juice, -liquor,** *s.* jus *or* suc de canne, *m.*; vesou, *m.* — **mill,** *s.* moulin à cannes à sucre, *m.*, sucrerie de cannes, *f.* — **sugar,** *s.* sucre de canne, *m.* — **trash,** *s.* bagasse, *f.* — **work,** *s.* ouvrage en canne, *f.* — **worker,** *s.* cannier, *m.*
Canella, *s.* cannelle blanche, *f.*
Caner, *s.* (*of chairs, &c.*) cannier, *m.*
Canescent, *adj.* blanchissant, blanchâtre, canescent
Canicula, Canicule, *s.* canicule, *f.*
Canicular, *adj.* caniculaire
Canine, *adj.* de chien, canin; — *s.* canine, *f.* — *letter,* lettre canine, *f.* — *tooth,* dent canine, canine, *f.*
Caning, *s.* coups de canne, *m.pl.*; (*a sound one*) volée de coups de canne, *f.*; (*of chairs, &c.*) cannage, *m.*
Canis, *s.* (*astr.*) chien, *m.* — *major,* le grand chien. — *minor,* le petit chien
Canister, *s.* boîte de (*or* en) ferblanc, *f.* — **shot,** *s.* *V.* **Case-shot**
Canker, *s.* (*agr., vet.*) chancre, *m.*; (*hort.*) chancre, *m.*, gangrène, lèpre, *f.*; (*fig.*) ver rongeur, fléau, *m.*, plaie, gangrène, *f.*, chancre, *m.*; — *v.a.* gangrener; ronger; dévorer; infecter; envenimer, empoisonner; corrompre; — *v.n.* se gangrener; se ronger; s'infecter;

se corrompre. — **bit,** *adj.* chancreux; gangrené; infecté; envenimé, empoisonné. — **like,** *adj.* qui ronge comme un chancre. — **worm,** *s.* chenille, *f.*; (*fig.*) ver rongeur, *m.*

Cankerous, *adj.* chancreux

Canna, *s.* canna, *f.* [compacte, *f.*

Cannel, — **coal,** *s.* charbon-cannel, *m.*, houille

Cannelon, *s.* cannelon, *m.*

Cannibal, *s.* cannibale, *m.*, anthropophage, *m.f.*; — *adj.* de cannibale, anthropophage

Cannibalism, *s.* cannibalisme, *m.*

Cannie. *V.* **Canny**

Cannily, *adv.* gentiment; (*slily*) finement; adroitement, habilement; prudemment

Cannon, *s.* canon, *m.*; (*at billiards*) carambolage, *m.*; — *v.n.* caramboler. — **ball,** *s.* boulet de canon, boulet, *m.* — **bone,** *s.* canon, *m.* — **proof,** *adj.* à l'épreuve du canon. — **shot,** *s.* boulet de canon, boulet, *m.*; (*discharge*) coup de canon, *m.*; (*distance*) portée de canon, *f.*

Cannonade, *v.a.* canonner; — *v.n.* se canonner

Cannonade, Cannonading, *s.* canonnade, *f.*

Cannoneer, Cannonier, *s.* canonnier, *m.*

Cannoning, *s.* (*at billiards*) carambolage, *m.*

Cannot, *v.n.* *V.* **Can** *and* **Not.** *I* —, je ne peux (*or* puis) pas; je ne sais pas. *You* —, vous ne pouvez pas, &c. *You — have heard that, for I did not say it,* vous n'avez pas pu entendre cela, car je ne l'ai pas dit *It — be,* cela ne peut pas être (...); (*it cannot be true, it is impossible*) cela ne se peut pas. — **but,** devoir; ne pouvoir pas faire autrement que de; (*imp.*) être impossible (*V.* **But**)

Cannular, *adj.* canulé, tubulaire, tubuleux

Canny, *adj.* bon; gentil; (*sly*) fin, rusé; adroit, habile; prudent

Canoe, *s.* pirogue, *f.*; périssoire, *f.*; canot, *m.*

Canon, *s.* canon, *m.*; (*pers.*) chanoine, *m.*; (*print.*) canon, gros canon, *m.*; — *adj.* canonique. — **bone,** *s.* canon, *m.* — **law,** *s.* droit

Canoness, *s.* chanoinesse, *f.* [canon, *m.*

Canonic, -al, *adj.* canonique; (*of hours, of the dignitary called* '*canon*') canonial; — **s,** *s.pl.* vêtements sacerdotaux, *m.pl.* [alement

Canonically, *adv.* canoniquement; canoni-

Canonicalness, Canonicity, *s.* canoni-

Canonist, *s.* canoniste, *m.* [cité, *f.*

Canonization, *s.* canonisation, *f.*

Canonize, *v.a.* canoniser

Canonry, Canonship, *s.* canonicat, *m.*

Canopy, *s.* dais, *m.*; (*arch., sculp., tester*) baldaquin, *m.*; (*of heaven*) voûte, *f.*, (*fam.*) calotte, *f.*; — *v.a.* couvrir d'un dais; (*fig.*) couvrir. — **bed,** *s.* lit à baldaquin, *m.*

Canorous, *adj.* harmonieux, mélodieux

Canorousness, *s.* harmonie, mélodie, *f.*

Cant, *v.a.* (*throw*) jeter, lancer; (*incline*) incliner; (— **over**) renverser sens dessus dessous, renverser, retourner; (*cut: timber*) débillarder, (*stones*) épanneler; (*build.*) chanfreiner; — *v.n.* cafarder, parler d'un ton cafard, faire le cafard; parler un certain jargon; parler avec affectation; (*nav.*) chavirer, capoter, faire capot; — *s.* langage hypocrite, *m.*, cafarderie, hypocrisie, *f.*; affectation, *f.*; jargon, argot, *m.*; (*thrust*) coup sec, *m.*; (*mus.*) dessus, *m.*; (*arch., build., carp.*) chanfrein, *m.*; pan coupé, *m.* — **timbers,** *s. pl.* (*nav.*) couples dévoyés, *m.pl.* — **window,** *s.* fenêtre à pans coupés, *f.* — **word,** *s.* terme d'argot, *m.*

Cantab, *s.* étudiant de l'université de Cam-

Cantabile, *s.* cantabile, *m.* [bridge, *m.*

Cantabrian, *s. adj.* Cantabre, *m.f.*

Cantalever, Cantaliver, *s.* modillon, *m.*

Cantaloup, *s.* cantaloup, *m.*

Cantankerous, *adj.* revêche, acariâtre

Cantankerousness, *s.* nature revêche *or* acariâtre, acariâtreté, *f.*

Cantata, *s.* cantate, *f.*

Cantatilla, *s.* cantatille, *f.*

Cantatrice, *s.* cantatrice, *f.*

Canteen, *s.* cantine, *f.*; (*vessel*) bidon, *m.*; (*travelling-case*) cantine, *f.* — **keeper, -woman,** *s.* cantinier, *m.*, -ière, *f.*

Canteliver. *V.* **Cantalever**

Canter, *s.* cafard, *m.*, e, *f.*, tartufe, *m.*, hypocrite, *m.f.*; personne qui parle avec affectation, *f.*; (*rid.*) petit galop, *m.*; (*in horse-racing*) canter, *m.*; — *v.n.* aller au petit galop; — *v.a.* faire aller (...) au petit galop

Canterbury, *s.* casier à musique, casier, *m.*; (*geog.*) Cantorbéry, *m.* — **bell,** *s.* (*bot.*) violette marine, mariette, campanule, clochette, *f.* — **gallop,** *s.* petit galop, *m.* — **tales,** *s. pl.* contes de Cantorbéry, *m.pl.*

Cantharide, Cantharis, *s.* cantharide, *f.*

Cantharidine, *s.* cantharidine, *f.*

Canticle, *s.* cantique, *m.*; (*fig.*) chant, *m.*; —**s,** *pl.* cantiques, *m.pl.*; (*fig.*) chants, *m.pl.*; (*song of songs*) cantique des cantiques, *m.*

Cantilena, *s.* cantilène, *f.*

Cantilever, Cantiliver. *V.* **Cantalever**

Cantine. *V.* **Canteen**

Cantineer, *s.* cantinier, *m.*, -ière, *f.*

Canting, *adj.* cafard, hypocrite, tartufe; affecté; (*her.*) parlant. — **humbug,** *s.* cafard, *m.* — **wheel,** *s.* hérisson, *m.*

Cantingly, *adv.* d'un air *or* d'un ton cafard; avec affectation

Cantle, *s.* morceau, fragment, *m.*; (*edge*) bord, *m.*; (*of saddles*) troussequin, *m.*; — *v.a.* morceler, couper en morceaux; (*to edge*) border

Cantlet, *s.* petit morceau, fragment, *m.*

Canto, *s.* chant, *m.*; (*mus.*) dessus, *m.*

Canton, *s.* canton, *m.*; — *v.a.* cantonner; (*divide*) diviser en cantons; diviser, partager

Cantonal, *adj.* cantonal

Cantoned, *adj.* (*arch., her., mil.*) cantonné

Cantonese, *s. adj.* Cantonais, *m.*, e, *f.*

Cantoning, Cantonment, *s.* cantonne-

Canula, *s.* canule, *f.* [ment, *m.*

Canvas, Canvass, *s.* canevas, *m.*; (*coarse cloth*) toile de chanvre, grosse toile, toile, *f.*; (*sail-cloth*) toile à voiles, *f.*; (*sail itself, sails*) voile, *f.*, voiles, *f.pl.*; (*tent, tents*) tente, *f.*, tentes, *f.pl.*; (*for painting*) toile, *f.*; (*pictures*) tableaux, portraits, *m.pl.*; (*solicitation*) sollicitation, brigue, *f.*; sollicitation de suffrages, *f.*; candidature, *f.*; (*abstract of votes*) relevé des suffrages, *m.*; (*counting up of votes*) dépouillement du scrutin, *m.*; (*com.*) sollicitation de commandes, *f.*; (*discussion*) discussion, *f.*; — *v.a.n.* examiner, scruter; discuter, débattre; solliciter, briguer, faire; faire un relevé de (suffrages); dépouiller (un scrutin); solliciter les suffrages; solliciter des commandes, faire la place. *Under* —, (*nav.*) sous voiles. — **back,** *s.* (*duck*) milouin, *m.* — **for,** *v.a.* briguer; solliciter

Canvasser, *s.* solliciteur, *m.*; brigueur, *m.*; solliciteur de suffrages, courtier électoral, *m.*; (*com.*) placier, solliciteur de commandes, *m.*; (*examiner*) scrutateur, *m.*

Canvassing, *s.* examen, *m.*; sollicitation, *f.*, sollicitations, *f.pl.*; brigue, *f.*; &c. (*V.* **Canvass,** *s.*)

Cany, *adj.* de canne, de jonc, de roseau; plein de cannes, plein de joncs, plein de roseaux

Canzone, *s.* canzone, *f.*

Canzonet, Canzonetta, *s.* canzonette, *f.*

Caolin. *V.* **Kaolin**

Caoutchouc, *s.* caoutchouc, *m.*

Cap, *s.* bonnet, *m.*; (*with a peak*) casquette, *f.*; (*of lawyers, judges, univers.*) toque, *f.*; (*of jockeys*) toque, *f.*; (*for the skull, to fit close, smoking-* —) calotte, *f.*; (*of cardinals*) barrette, *f.*; (*mil.*) bonnet, *m.*; képi, *m.*; shako, *m.*; (*of bells*) chapeau, *m.*; (*mach.*) chapiteau, couvercle, *m.*; (*of stills*) chapiteau, *m.*; (*of watches*) cuvette, *f.*, recouvrement, *m.*; (*of telescopes*) bonnette, *f.*; (*of sugar-loaves*) gonichon, *m.*; (*of a bee-hive*) surtout, *m.*; (*of an obelisk*) pyramidion, *m.*; (*of the knee*) boîte, noix, *f.*; (*of fire-arms*) capsule, amorce, *f.*; (*of foils*) mouche, *f.*; (*paper cone*) cornet (de papier), *m.*; (*nav.*) chouquet, *m.*; (*bot.*) chapeau, *m.*; (*tech.*) bonnet, *m.*; coiffe, *f.*; chape, *f.*; capsule, *f.*; — *v.a.* coiffer; (*cover*) surmonter; couvrir, couronner; (*complete*) couronner, mettre le comble à; (*surpass*) surpasser; (*in height*) dépasser; (*fire-arms*) amorcer; (*foils, swords*) moucheter; (*tech.*) bonneter; (*of verses*) réciter alternativement; (*to vie in*) faire assaut de. — *and bells*, marotte, *f.* — *of maintenance* or *of dignity*, bonnet ducal, *m.* *To set o.'s — at*, chercher à plaire à, vouloir captiver. *If the — fits, wear it*, (*Proverb*) qui se sent morveux se mouche. — **-a-pie,** *adv.* de pied en cap. — **line,** *s.* (*mil.*) fourragère, *f.* — **paper,** *s.* papier de couverture *or* d'enveloppe, papier gris, *m.*; (*foolscap*) *V.* **Foolscap.** — **peak,** *s.* visière de casquette, *f.* — **sheaf,** *s.* gerbe de dessus, *f.* — **wire,** *s.* (*millinery*) cannetille, *f.*

Capability, *s.* capacité, *f.*

Capable, *adj.* capable (de); susceptible (de)

Capableness, *s.* capacité, *f.*

Capacious, *adj.* vaste, spacieux, grand

Capaciousness, *s.* capacité, *f.*; étendue, *f.*

Capacitate, *v.a.* rendre capable (de) *or* propre (à), mettre en état (de); qualifier, donner qualité (pour)

Capacity, *s.* capacité, *f.*; qualité, *f.*; titre, *m.* *In the — of*, en qualité de. *He is not known in any —*, il n'est connu à aucun titre [çonner

Caparison, *s.* caparaçon, *m.*; — *v.a.* capara-

Cape, *s.* (*for ladies*) pèlerine, *f.*; berthe, *f.*; (*of a cloak*) collet, *m.*; rotonde, *f.*; (*cloak itself*) manteau à collet ample, manteau, carrick, *m.*; (*geog.*) cap, *m.* *Inverness —*, manteau-macfarlane, *m.* — **Town,** *s.* la Ville du Cap, *f.* — **weed,** *s.* orseille du cap Vert, *f.* — **wine,** *s.* vin du Cap, *m.*

Capelan, Capelin, *s.* capelan, *m.*

Capellet, *s.* capelet, *m.*, passe-campane, *f.*

Capelmaster, *s.* maître de chapelle, *m.*

Caper, *s.* cabriole, *f.*; bond, *m.*; (*in dancing*) entrechat, *m.*; (*bot.*) câpre, *f.*; — *v.n.* cabrioler, faire des cabrioles; bondir, sauter; (*in dancing*) faire des entrechats. — **bush, -tree,** *s.* câprier, *m.* — **sauce,** *s.* sauce aux câpres, *f.* — **spurge,** *s.* épurge, *f.*

Capercailzie, *s.* tétras, *m.*

Caperer, *s.* cabrioleur, *m.*, -euse, *f.*

Capetan, Capetian, *adj.* capétien (*m.*, -ne, *f.*); — *s.* Capétien, *m.*

Capias, *s.* contrainte par corps, prise de corps, *f.*; mandat d'amener, *m.*; mandat d'arrêt, *m.*

Capibara, *s.* cabiai, *m.*

Capillaire, *s.* sirop de capillaire, *m.*; sirop de fleurs d'oranger *or* de fleur d'orange, *m.*

Capillarity, *s.* capillarité, *f.*

Capillary, *adj. s.* capillaire, *adj. m.f.*, *s.m.*

Capital, *adj.* capital; principal, essentiel, important, grand; fameux; excellent; parfait; (*of letters*) grand, majuscule, capital; — *s.* (*town*) capitale, *f.*; (*of letters*) majuscule, capitale, *f.*; (*com.*) capital, *m.*; capitaux, *m.pl.*; (*arch.*) chapiteau, *m.* *To make — out of*, exploiter. — **stock,** *s.* capital *or* fonds social, capital, *m.*

Capitalist, *s.* capitaliste, *m.f.*

Capitalizable, *adj.* capitalisable

Capitalization, *s.* capitalisation, *f.*

Capitalize, *v.a.* capitaliser

Capitally, *adv.* capitalement; de (*or* à) la peine capitale; parfaitement, supérieurement, admirablement, à merveille

Capitan-pasha, *s.* capitan-pacha, *m.*

Capitation, *s.* capitation, *f.* — **fee,** *s.* *V.* [**Head-money**

Capitol, *s.* capitole, *m.*

Capitoline, *adj.* capitolin

Capitular, Capitulary, *adj. s.* capitulaire, *adj. m.f.*, *s.m.*; (*pers.*) capitulant, *adj. m.*, *s.m.*, membre d'un chapitre, *s.m.*

Capitularly, *adv.* capitulairement, en chapitre

Capitulate, *v.n.* capituler

Capitulation, *s.* capitulation, *f.*

Capivi. *V.* **Copaiva**

Caplin, *s.* (*fish*) capelan, *m.*

Capon, *s.* chapon, *m.*; — *v.a.* chaponner

Caponet, *s.* chaponneau, *m.*

Caponier, Caponiere, *s.* caponnière, *f.*

Caponize, *v.a.* chaponner

Caponniere, *s.* caponnière, *f.*

Capot, *adj. s.* (*at play*) capot, *adj. m.*, *s.m.*; — [*v.a.* faire capot

Capote, *s.* capote, *f.*

Cappadine, *s.* capiton, *m.*

Cappanus, *s.* taret, *m.*

Capped, *part. adj.* coiffé, &c. (*V.* **Cap,** *v.a.*); (*of watches*) à recouvrement

Capping, *s.* (*of fire-arms*) amorçage, *m.*; (*tech.*) bonnetage, *m.*; —**s,** *pl.* armature, *f.*

Caprice, *s.* caprice, *m.*

Capricious, *adj.* capricieux

Capriciously, *adv.* capricieusement

Capriciousness, *s.* caractère capricieux, *m.*, humeur capricieuse, *f.* [*s.* capricorne, *m.*

Capricorn, -us, *s.* capricorne, *m.* — **beetle,**

Caprification, *s.* caprification, *f.*

Caprine, *adj.* caprin

Capriole, *s.* cabriole, *f.*; — *v.n.* cabrioler

Capriped, *adj. s.* capripède, *adj. m.f.*, *s.m.*

Caprizant, *adj.* caprisant

Capromys, *s.* capromys, *m.*

Capsicum, *s.* piment, *m.* [chavirer

Capsize, *v.n.* chavirer; — *v.a.* faire chavirer,

Capstan, Capstern, *s.* cabestan, *m.*

Capsular, Capsulary, *adj.* capsulaire

Capsulate, Capsulated, *adj.* renfermé [dans une capsule

Capsule, *s.* capsule, *f.*

Capsuliferous, *adj.* capsulifère

Captain, *s.* capitaine, *m.*; (*of a mine*) maître mineur, *m.* — *of a gun*, chef de pièce, *m.* — *of a ship*, *naval —*, (*imperial navy*) capitaine de vaisseau, (*mercantile navy*) capitaine de navire

Captaincy, *s.* grade de capitaine, *m.*; (*district*) [capitainerie, *f.*

Captainry, *s.* capitainerie, *f.*

Captainship, *s.* commandement, *m.*; talent militaire, *m.*; grade de capitaine, *m.*; capitainerie, *f.*, gouvernement d'un district, *m.*

Captation, *s.* captation, *f.* [*things*) saisie, *f.*

Caption, *s.* arrestation, prise de corps, *f.*; (*of*

Captious, *adj.* captieux, insidieux; (*fault-finding*) pointilleux, difficultueux, épineux, chicaneur; (*touchy*) susceptible

Captiously, *adv.* captieusement, insidieusement; (*peevishly*) avec humeur

Captiousness, *s.* nature (*or* humeur) captieuse *or* insidieuse, *f.*; pointillerie, chicanerie, *f.*; (*peevishness*) humeur querelleuse, *f.*; (*touchiness*) susceptibilité, *f.*

Captivate, *v.a.* captiver, charmer, séduire

Captivating, *adj.* qui captive, enchanteur, séduisant [tion, *f.*

Captivation, *s.* assujettissement, *m.*; séduc-

Captive, *s. adj.* captif, *m.*, -ive, *f.*; prisonnier, *m.*, -ière, *f.*; esclave, *m.f.*

Captivity, *s.* captivité, *f.*

Captor, *s.* capteur, captureur, preneur, *m.*

Capture, *s.* capture, prise, *f.*; arrestation, *f.*; — *v.a.* capturer, prendre; arrêter

Capturer, *s.* *V.* **Captor**

Capturing, *adj.* capteur, captureur, preneur; — *s.* *V.* **Capture,** *s.*

Capuan, *s. adj.* Capouan, *m.*, e, *f.*

Capuchin, *s.* (*friar, pigeon, monkey*) capucin, *m.*, (*nun*) capucine, *f.*; (*of dress*) mante à capuchon, capote, *f.*

Capucine, *adj.* (*colour*) capucine

Caput-mortuum, *s.* caput-mortuum, *m.*

Capybara, *s.* cabiai, *m.*

Car, *s.* char, chariot, *m.*; (*cart*) charrette, *f.*; (*chaise*) carriole, *f.*; (*American rail.*) wagon, *m.*, voiture, *f.*; (*of balloons*) nacelle, *f.*; (*astr.*) chariot, *m.* — **load,** *s.* *V.* **Cart.** — **man,** *s.* charretier, *m.*; voiturier, *f.*

Carabine. *V.* **Carbine**

Carabineer, Carabinier, *s.* carabinier, *m.*

Caracal, *s.* caracal, *m.*

Caracara, — **eagle,** *s.* caracara, *m.*
Caracas *or* **Caraccas cocoa,** *s.* cacao caraque, cacao de Caracas, caraque, *m.*
Carack, *s.* (*nav.*) caraque, *f.*
Caracole, *s.* caracole, *f.*; (*arch.*) escalier en caracole, *m.*; — *v.n.* caracoler
Caracoli, *s.* caracoli, *m.*
Caragana, *s.* caragan, *m.*
Carageen. *V.* **Carrageen**
Carambola, Carambole, *s.* carambole, *f.*
Caramel, *s.* caramel, *m.*
Carana, Caranna, *s.* caragne, *f.*
Carapace, *s.* carapace, *f.*
Carat, *s.* carat, *m.*
Caravan, *s.* caravane, *f.*
Caravaneer, *s.* caravanier, *m.*
Caravanist, *s.* caravaniste, *m.f.*
Caravansary, *s.* caravansérail, *m.*
Caravanseraskier, *s.* caravanséraskier, *m.*
Caravel, *s.* caravelle, *f.*
Caraway, *s.* carvi, *m.*; *seed*) graine de carvi, *f.*
Carbazotate, *s.* carbazotate, *m.*
Carbazotic, *adj.* carbazotique
Carbide, *s.* carbure, *m.*
Carbine, *s.* mousqueton, *m.* — **bucket,** *s.* porte-crosse, *m.* — **match,** *s.* concours au [mousqueton, *m.*
Carbineer. *V.* **Carabineer**
Carbolic, *adj.* carbolique
Carbolize, *v.a.* carboliser
Carbon, *s.* carbone, *m.*
Carbonaceous, *adj.* carbone [— *v.a.* hacher
Carbonade, Carbonado, *s.* carbonade, *f.*;
Carbonari, *s. pl.* carbonari, *m.pl.*
Carbonarism, *s.* carbonarisme, *m.*
Carbonaro, *s.* carbonaro, *m.*
Carbonate, *s.* carbonate, *m.*
Carbonated, *adj.* carboné; carbonaté
Carbonic, *adj.* carbonique
Carboniferous, *adj.* carbonifère [ration, *f.*
Carbonization, *s.* carbonisation, *f.*; carbu-
Carbonize, *v.a.* carboniser; charbonner; — *v.n.* se carboniser; se charbonner; (*of lamps*) [charbonner
Carbonous, *adj.* carboneux
Carboy, *s.* tourie, bonbonne, dame-jeanne, *f.*
Carbuncle, *s.* escarboucle, *f.*; (*pimple*) bouton rouge, *m.*; (*med.*) charbon, *m.*
Carbuncled *adj.* orné d'escarboucles; (*pimpled*) plein de boutons rouges, (*of the nose*) bourgeonné; (*med.*) charbonné
Carbuncular, *adj.* d'escarboucle; rouge; (*med.*) charbonneux, charbonné
Carbunculation, *s.* (*agr.*) carbouille, *f.*
Carburet, *s.* carbure, *m.*
Carburetted, *adj.* carburé; carboné
Carcajou, *s.* carcajou, *m.*
Carcan, Carcanet, *s.* carcan, *m.*
Carcase, Carcass, *s.* carcasse, *f.*; (*entire animal*) corps entier, corps, *m.*; (*corpse*) cadavre, corps mort, corps, *m.* — **butcher,** *s.* *V.* **Meat-salesman.** — **shell,** (*mil.*) carcasse, *f.*
Carcinolog-ic, al, -ist, -y. *V.* page 3, § 1
Carcinoma, *s.* carcinome, *m.*
Carcinomatous, *adj.* carcinomateux
Card, *s.* carte, *f.*; (— *of address*) carte, adresse, *f.*; (*of winds*) rose des vents, *f.*; (*for wool*, &c.) carde, *f.*; — *v.a.* carder. — **basket,** *s.* corbeille à cartes, *f.* — **board,** *s.* carte, *f.*, carton fin, carton, *m.* — **box,** *s.* boîte à cartes, boîte de jeu, *f.* — **case,** *s.* porte-cartes, étui à cartes (de visite), *m.* — **factory,** *s.* carterie, *f.*; (*for wool*, &c.) carderie, *f.* — **house,** *s.* château de cartes, *m.* — **maker,** *s.* cartier, *m.*; (*for wool*, &c.) cardier, *m.* — **making, -manufactory, -manufacture,** *s.* carterie, *f.*; (*for wool*, &c.) carderie, *f.* — **paper,** *s.* cartier, *m.* — **party,** *s.* réunion pour faire la partie de cartes, réunion de joueurs de cartes, *f.* — **player,** *s.* joueur (*m.*, -euse, *f.*) de cartes. — **playing,** *s.* jeu de cartes, *m.*; (les) jeux de cartes, *m.pl.*, (les) cartes, *f.pl.* — **room,** *s.* salle de jeu, *f.* — **sharper,** *s.* fileur de cartes, bonneteur, pipeur, *m.*, -euse, *f.*, grec, *m.* — **table,** *s.* table de jeu, *f.* — **tray,** *s.* plateau à cartes, *m.*
Cardamine, *s.* cardamine, *f.*
Cardamom, *s.* cardamome, *m.*
Carder, *s.* cardeur, *m.*, -euse, *f.*; (*mach.*) carde [mécanique, carde, *f.*
Cardia, *s.* cardia, *m.*
Cardiac, *adj. s.* cardiaque, *adj. m.f.*, *s.m.*
Cardialg-ic, -y. *V.* page 3, § 1
Cardinal, *adj. s.* cardinal, *adj. m.*, e, *f.*, cardinal, *s.m.* — **bird, -finch, -grossbeak,** *s.* cardinal, *m.* — **flower,** *s.* cardinale, *f.* [*m.*
Cardinalate, Cardinalship, *s.* cardinalat,
Carding, *s.* cardage, *m.* — **house,** *s.* carderie, *f.* — **machine,** *s.* machine à carder, carde [mécanique, carde, *f.*
Carditis, *s.* cardite, *f.*
Cardoon, *s.* cardon, *m.*
Care, *s.* soin, *m.*; attention, *f.*; précaution, *f.*; (*anxiety*) souci, *m.*, inquiétude, sollicitude, *f.*; (*of souls*) charge (d'âmes) *f.* — **worn,** *adj.* dévoré de soucis, usé par le chagrin; soucieux. — *of J. Smith, Esq.*, aux soins de Monsieur J Smith. *To* or *under the — of*, aux soins de confié aux soins de; soigné par. *With —*, avec soin; (*on packages*) fragile. *With — of souls*, à charge d'âmes. *To take —*, (*beware*) prendre garde; se garder (de); (*be mindful*) avoir *or* prendre soin (de); soigner; (*keep o.'s eyes about*) faire attention. *Take — of that bull!* prenez garde à ce taureau! *Take — not to fall, take — you don't fall*, prenez garde de tomber. *Take — he does not see you*, prenez garde qu'il ne vous voie. *Take* (*great*) *— not to do it*, gardez-vous (bien) de le faire. *Take — of your books*, ayez *or* prenez soin de vos livres. *Take — of yourself*, ayez soin de vous, soignez-vous; (*beware of harm*) prenez garde à vous; (*mind what you are about*) faites attention à vous. *This patient is well taken — of*, ce malade est bien soigné. *He is too drunk to take — of himself*, il est trop ivre pour faire attention à lui. *He is old enough to take — of himself*, il est d'âge à se conduire (*or* à se gouverner). *Good-bye, take — of yourself*, adieu, portez-vous bien. *To place* or *put under the — of*, confier à, confier aux soins de
Care, *v.n.* tenir (à), se soucier (de); se mettre en peine (de), s'inquiéter (de). *I don't —* (*for it*), je n'y tiens pas, je ne m'en soucie pas; je ne m'en mets pas en peine, je ne m'en inquiète pas; je m'en moque, ça m'est égal. *What do I?* que m'importe? qu'est-ce que ça me fait?
Careen, *v.a.* caréner, mettre en carène; — *v.n.* donner de la bande, être à la bande
Careenage, Careening, *s.* carénage, *m.*
Career, *s.* carrière, *f.*; course, *f.*; cours, *m.*; — *v.n.* courir avec vitesse, courir; voler; voyager; (*to bound*) s'élancer
Careful, *adj.* soigneux; (*taken care of*) soigné; (*attentive*) attentif; (*cautious*) prudent, circonspect; (*anxious*) soucieux, inquiet. *To be — (of* or *to)*, *V.* **Care** (*To take —*)
Carefully, *adv.* soigneusement, avec soin; attentivement, avec attention; prudemment, avec prudence, avec circonspection; (*anxiously*) avec souci, avec inquiétude; d'humeur soucieuse
Carefulness, *s.* soin. *m.*, attention, précaution. *f.*; (*anxiety*) inquiétude, *f.*, soucis, *m.pl.*
Careless, *adj.* sans soin (pour); nonchalant, négligent; (*not taken care of*) négligé; (*artless*) fait sans art; (*unconcerned*) insouciant (de), sans souci (de), indifférent (à); (*cheerful*) insoucieux
Carelessly, *adv.* nonchalamment, négligemment, avec négligence, sans soin; avec insouciance, sans souci
Carelessness, *s.* nonchalance, négligence, *f.*, défaut de soin, *m.*; inattention, *f.*; incurie, *f.*; insouciance, indifférence, *f.*
Caress, *s.* caresse, *f.*; — *v.a.* caresser
Caret, *s.* renvoi, *m.*

Careworn. *See under* **Care,** *s.*
Cargo, *s.* cargaison, *f.*, chargement, *m.*
Cargoose, *s.* grèbe huppé, *m.*
Cariatid, &c. *V.* **Caryatid,** &c.
Carib, Caribbee, *s. adj.* Caraïbe, *m.f.*
Caribbean, *adj.* caraïbe
Caribou, *s.* caribou, *m.*
Caricatural, *adj.* caricatural
Caricature, *s.* caricature, *f*; — *v.a.* caricaturer
Caricaturist, *s.* caricaturiste, *m.f.*
Caries, Cariosity, *s.* carie, *f.*
Carious, *adj.* carié. *To make* —, carier. *To* [*become* —, se carier
Carking, *adj.* cuisant
Carline, Carling, *s.* (*nav.*) carlingue, *f.*
Carl-ism, -ist. *V.* page 3, § 1
Carlovingian, *adj.* carlovingien (*m.*, -ne, *f.*); — *s.* Carlovingien, *m.*
Carmagnole, *s.* carmagnole, *f.*
Carmelite, *s.* carme, *m.*, (— *nun*) carmélite, *f.*
Carminate, *v.a.* carminer
Carminative, *adj. s.* carminatif, *adj. m.*, -ive, *f.*, carminatif, *s.m.* [carminé
Carmine, *s.* carmin, *m.*; — *adj.* de carmin;
Carminic acid, *s.* carmine, *f.*
Carnage, *s.* carnage, *m.*
Carnal, *adj.* charnel. — **minded,** *adj.* charnel, sensuel, mondain. — **mindedness,** *s.* charnalité, sensualité, mondanité, *f.*
Carnality, *s.* charnalité, *f.*
Carnally, *adv.* charnellement; par la chair
Carnation, *s.* carnation, *f.*; incarnat, *m.*; (*bot.*) œillet-giroflée, œillet, *m.* — **colour,** *s.* incarnat, *m.*
Carnationed, *adj.* incarnat; (*hort.*) carné
Carnelian, *s.* cornaline, *f.* — **stone,** *s.* [cornaline, *f.*
Carneous, *adj.* charnu
Carnian, Carnic, *adj.* carnique
Carnification, *s.* carnification, *f.*
Carnify, *v.n.* se carnifier
Carnival, *s.* carnaval, *m.*
Carnivore, *s.* (*pl.* **Carnivores** or **Carnivora**) carnivore, carnassier, *m.*
Carnivorous, *adj.* carnivore, carnassier
Carnosity, *s.* carnosité, *f.*
Carnous, *adj.* charnu
Carny, *v.n.* pateliner
Carnying, *adj.* patelin; — *s.* patelinage, *m.*
Carob, *s.* caroube, *f.* — **tree,** *s.* caroubier, *m.*
Carol, *s.* chanson, *f.*, chant, *m.*; cantique, *m.*; — *v.a.n.* chanter; (*of larks*) grisoller
Carotic, *adj.* carotique
Carotid, *adj. s.* carotide, *f.*
Carotidal, *adj.* carotidien
Carousal, *s.* orgie, ripaille, *f.*; festin, *m.*
Carouse, *v.a.* boire; — *v.n.* boire, riboter; — *s. V.* **Carousal**
Carouser, *s.* grand buveur, ripailleur, *m.*, -euse, *f.*, riboteur, *m.*, -euse, *f.*
Carp, *s.* carpe, *f.* *Young* —, carpeau, carpillon, *m.* — **pond,** *s.* carpier, *m.*, carpière, *f.*
Carp, *v.n.* — **at,** critiquer, censurer, épiloguer sur, gloser sur, trouver à redire à
Carpal, *adj.* carpien
Carpenter, *s.* charpentier, *m.*; (*joiner*) menuisier, *m.*; (*theat.*) machiniste, *m.*; — *adj.* (*zool.*) menuisier. — **ant,** *s.* fourmi menuisière, *f.* — **bee,** *s.* abeille menuisière, *f.* — **'s work,** *s.* charpente, charpenterie, *f.*; menuiserie, *f.* [*f.*; (*joinery*) menuiserie, *f.*
Carpentering, Carpentry, *s.* charpenterie,
Carper, *s.* critiqueur, *m.*, -euse, *f.*, épilogueur, *m.*, -euse, *f.*, gloseur, *m.*, -euse, *f.*
Carpet, *s.* tapis, *m.*; tapis de pied, tapis d'appartement, *m.*; — *v.a.* tapisser. — **bag,** *s.* sac de nuit, *m.*; (*descriptively*) sac en tapisserie, *m.* — **broom,** *s.* balai de jonc, *m.* — **knight,** *s.* chevalier de salon, *m.* — **monger,** *s.* héros de salon, *m.* — **walk, -way,** *s.* chemin, *m.*; (*of grass*) allée tapissée de verdure, *f.*, tapis vert, *m.*
Carpeting, *s.* tapis, *m.*, tapisserie, *f.*
Carping, *adj.* pointilleux; caustique; médisant; grondeur; — *s.* critique, *f.*, épilogage, *m.*, épilogation, *f.*
Carpingly, *adv.* en glosant, en épiloguant, d'une manière critique, en critique, malignement
Carpus, *s.* carpe, *m.* [ment
Carrageen, — moss, *s.* varech comestible, *m*
Carrara marble, *s.* marbre de Carrare, carrare, *m.*
Carraway. *V.* **Caraway** [rare, *m.*
Carriable, *adj.* portable, transportable; charriable
Carriage, *s.* (*act of carrying*) transport, *m.*; charroi, *m.*; (*of parcels*) port, *m.*; factage, *m.*; (*of goods*) port, *m.*; camionnage, factage, *m.*; (*vehicle*) voiture, *f.*; équipage, *m.*; (*rail.*) wagon, *m.*, voiture, *f.*; (*of guns*) affût, *m.*; (*of life-boats, pontoons*) chariot, *m.*; (*of carriages*) train, *m.*; (*deportment*) maintien, port, *m.*, démarche, *f.*; conduite, *f.* — **bag, -basket,** *s.* vide-poches, *m.* — **builder,** *s. V.* **Coach-maker.** — **entrance,** *s.* porte cochère, *f.* — **folks,** *s. pl.* gens à équipage, *m.f.pl.* — **free,** *adj. adv.* franc de port. — **ful,** *s.* voiture pleine, *f.* — **horse,** *s.* cheval d'attelage, carrossier, *m.* — **house,** *s. V.* **Coach-house.** — **lamp,** *s.* lanterne de voiture, *f.* — **maker,** *s. V.* **Coach-maker.** — **paid,** *adj. adv.* port payé, franc de port. — **people,** *s. pl. V.* — **folks.** — **road,** *s. V.* — **way.** — **rug,** *s.* couverture de voyage, *f.* — **setter,** *s.* chèvre, *f.* — **truck,** *s.* (*rail.*) traîneau *or* wagon pour les voitures, train de transport, *m.* — **way,** *s.* route (*f.*) *or* chemin (*m.*) carrossable; (*of streets*) chaussée, *f.*, pavé, *m.*
Carriageable, *adj.* (*passable*) carrossable, carrossier; (*conveyable*) charriable
Carrier, *s.* voiturier, camionneur, facteur, *m.*; roulier, *m.*; (*messenger*) messager, *m*; (*bearer, porter, heaver*) porteur, *m.*, -euse, *f.*; (— *pigeon*) pigeon voyageur, pigeon messager, *m.*
Carrigeen. *V.* **Carrageen**
Carrion, *s.* charogne, *f.*; — *adj.* de charogne. — **crow,** *s.* corneille, *f.*
Carronade, *s.* caronade, *f.*
Carrot, *s.* carotte, *f.* — **soup,** *s.* soupe aux carottes, *f.*, potage (*m.*) *or* purée (*f.*) crécy (*or* à la crécy)
Carrotiness, *s.* rousseur, couleur rousse, *f.*
Carroty, *adj.* roux
Carrousel, *s.* carrousel, *m.*
Carry, *v.a.* porter; transporter; (*forcibly, vehemently*) emporter; entraîner; enlever; (*push*) pousser; (*lead*) mener, conduire; (*fetch and bring, of dogs,* &c.) rapporter; (*obtain*) remporter, obtenir; gagner; (*urge*) porter (à), entraîner (à), pousser (à); (*effect*) accomplir; effectuer; exécuter; (*into effect or execution, put*) mettre (à); (*a resolution*) prendre; adopter; (*a motion*) adopter; faire adopter; (*arith.*) retenir; — *v.n.* porter; (*hunt., of hares,* &c.) patter, se botter. — *oneself,* se comporter, se conduire. — *it,* l'emporter. — *it high,* le prendre sur un haut ton, se donner des airs. — **about,** *s.* porter *or* mener de tous côtés, porter *or* mener partout, promener, traîner, trimbaler; (*on o.'s person*) porter sur soi. — **along,** porter; emporter; (*pers., animals*) mener; emmener; entraîner. — **away,** emporter; (*pers., animals*) emmener; enlever de force, enlever; (*fig.*) entraîner; transporter, ravir en extase; (*aside*) détourner (de). — **back,** reporter, remporter; (*lead away back*) remener, remmener; (*bring back*) rapporter; ramener. — **down,** descendre. — **forth,** sortir, tirer. — **forward,** (*book-keep.*) reporter. — **in,** rentrer. — **off,** emporter; (*of prizes,* &c.) remporter; (*fig.*) enlever; tuer, faire mourir. — **it off,** s'en tirer, réussir. — **on,** poursuivre, pousser; continuer; conduire; mener; exécuter; soutenir; exercer; (*business*) faire, exercer. — **out,** porter dehors; emporter; porter; exécuter; mettre à exécution; faire; mener à bonne fin, faire réussir; développer.

— **over,** transporter, faire passer, passer; (*arith.*) retenir; (*book-keep.*) reporter. — **through,** soutenir; mener à bonne fin; faire traverser; faire surmonter; faire triompher. — **up,** porter en haut, monter; (*to lead*) conduire; (*fig.*) reporter; faire remonter

Carrying, *s.* transport, *m.*; port, *m.* — *of arms,* port d'armes, *m.* — (*of*) *the cross,* portement de croix, *m.*

Cart, *s.* charrette, *f.*; voiture, *f.*; (*with boards all round, for carrying sand, dust, muck,* &c.) tombereau, *m.*; (*mil.*) fourgon, *m.*; — *v.a.* charrier, charroyer; voiturer; — *v.n.* faire des charrois. — **away,** — **off,** *v.a.* enlever, emporter. *To put the — before the horse,* mettre la charrue devant les bœufs. — **gate,** *s.* porte charretière, *f.* — **grease,** *s.* oing, *m.*; cambouis, *m.* — **horse,** *s.* cheval de charrette *or* de trait, *m.* — **house,** *s.* hangar, *m.* — **load,** *s.* charretée, *f.*; tombereau, *m.* — **road,** *s. V.* — **way.** — **rut,** *s.* ornière, *f.* — **shed,** *s.* hangar, *m.* — **way,** *s.* chemin de charroi, chemin charretier, *m.*, voie charretière, charrière, *f.* — **wheel,** *s.* roue de charrette, *f.* — **wright,** *s. V.* **Wheelwright**

Cartage, *s.* charroi, charriage, *m.*

Carte, *s.* carte, *f.*; photographie, *f.* — **blanche,** *s.* carte blanche, *f.*; blanc-seing, *m.*

Cartel, *s.* cartel, *m.*; (— *ship*) bâtiment parlementaire, cartel, *m.*

Carter, *s.* charretier, voiturier, charroyeur, *m.*

Cartesian, *s. adj.* cartésien, *m.*, -ne, *f.*

Cartesianism, *s.* cartésianisme, *m.*

Carthaginian, *s.* Carthaginois, *m.*, e, *f.*; — *adj.* carthaginois, de Carthage

Carthamus, *s.* carthame, *m.*

Carthusian, *s.* chartreux, *m.* — **nun,** — **convent** *or* **monastery,** *s.* chartreuse, *f.*

Cartilage, *s.* cartilage, *m.*

Cartilaginous, *adj.* cartilagineux

Carting, *s.* charriage, charroi, *m.*

Cartisane, *s.* cartisane, *f.*

Cartographer, *s.* cartographe, *m.* [§ 1

Cartograph-ic, al, -ically, -y. *V.* page 3,

Cartomancer, *s.* cartomancien, *m.*, -ne, *f.*

Cartoman-cy, -tic. *V.* page 3, § 1

Carton-pierre, *s.* carton-pierre, *m.*

Cartoon, *s.* carton, *m.* [**Cartouche**

Cartouch, *s.* (*mil.*) *V.* **Cartridge;** (*arch.*) *V.*

Cartouche, *s.* (*arch.*) cartouche, *m.*

Cartridge, *s.* cartouche, *f.*; (*artil.*) gargousse, *f.* — **box,** *s.* (*mil.*) giberne, *f.*; (*artil.*) gargoussier, *m.*, gargoussière, caisse à gargousses, *f.*; (*for sportsmen*) cartouchier, *m.*, cartouchière, *f.* — **maker, -manufacturer,** *s.* fabricant de cartouches, *m.* — **manufactory,** *s.* cartoucherie, *f.* — **paper,** *s.* papier à cartouches *or* à gargousses, *m.*; (*stat.*) papier-cartouche, *m.* — **pouch,** *s. V.* — **box**

Cartulary, *s.* cartulaire, *m.*

Caruncle, *s.* caroncule, *f.*

Caruncular, *adj.* caronculaire

Carunculated, *adj.* caronculé

Carunculous, *adj.* caronculeux

Carus, *s.* carus, *m.*

Carve, *v.a.n.* sculpter, graver, ciseler, tailler; (*cut*) couper; (*at table*) découper, dépecer

Carvel, *s.* caravelle, *f.*

Carver, *s.* sculpteur, *m.*; graveur, *m.*; ciseleur, *m.*; (*of meat*) découpeur, *m.*, -euse, *f.*, (*jest.*) écuyer tranchant, *m.*; (*sculptor's assistant*) praticien, *m.*; (*knife*) couteau à découper, *m.*; (*for fish*) truelle, *f.*

Carving, *s.* sculpture, *f.*; gravure, *f.*; ciselure, *f.*; (*at table*) découpage, *m.* — **knife, (-fork),** *s.* couteau (*m.*, fourchette, *f.*) à découper

Caryatid, Caryatis, *s.* caryatide, cariatide, *f.*

Caryatid, Caryatidic, *adj.* caryatidique, [cariatidique

Cascade, *s.* cascade, *f.*

Cascarilla, — **bark,** *s.* cascarille, *f.*

Case, *s.* (*sheath*) étui, *m.*, gaîne, *f.*; fourreau, *m.*; trousse, *f.*; (*wrapper*) enveloppe, *f.*; (*of umbrellas*) fourreau, étui, *m.*; (*for a hat*) étui, *m.*; (*of furniture*) housse, *f.*; (*of a watch, box*) boîte, *f.*; (*for packing*) caisse, *f.*; (*for needles, cards,* &c.) étui, *m.*; (*for surgical instr.*) boîtier, *m.*, trousse, *f.*; (*for jewels*) écrin, *m.*; (*show* —) vitrine, montre, *f.*; (*of a clock*) boîte, caisse, *f.*, cabinet, *m.*; cage, *f.*; (*for a book*) étui, écrin, *m.*; (*for books, book* —), bibliothèque, *f.*; (*of a piano*) caisse, *f.*; (*of an organ*) buffet, *m.*; (*of a stair, of bells, stoves,* &c.) cage, *f.*; (*body*) corps, *m.*; (*of a door*) chambranle, *m.*; (*of a pillow*) taie, *f.*; (*of a cartridge*) enveloppe, douille, *f.*; (*of fireworks*) cartouche, *m.*; (*print.*) casse, *f.*; (*of a lock*) palastre, *m.*; (*mach.*) enveloppe, *f.*, entourage, *m.*, cage, *f.*; (*occurrence or event*) cas, *m.*; circonstance, *f.*; événement, *m.*; (*state,* &c.) état, *m.*; condition, *f.*; situation, *f.*; position, *f.*; place, *f*; (*question*) question, *f.*; chose, *f.*; (*instance*) exemple, *m.*; (*affair, dispute*) affaire, *f.*; (*law*) cause, *f.*; matière à procès *or* à poursuites, *f.*; (*gram., math., med.*) cas, *m.*; — *v.a.* mettre dans un étui *or* &c.; encaisser; serrer, enfermer; couvrir, recouvrir; envelopper; (*to iron*) ferrer; (*build.*) revêtir; (*mines*) cuveler. *The* —, (*things*) les choses, *f.pl.* *As the — may be,* suivant (*or* selon) le cas. *In any* —, en tout cas. *In such a* —, *in that* —, en pareil cas; dans ce cas. *It is a very hard* —, cela est bien dur. *If that is the* —, s'il en est ainsi. *If I were* (or *Were I*) *in your* —, si j'étais à votre place. *Such being the* —, cela étant. —**ful,** *s.* (*print.*) cassetée, *f.* — **harden,** *v.a.* tremper en paquet, cémenter; (*fig.*) endurcir. — **hardening,** *s.* trempe en paquet, cémentation, *f.* — **knife,** *s.* couteau à gaîne, *m.* — **maker,** *s.* gaînier, *m.* — **man,** *s.* (*print.*) compositeur, *m.* — **shot,** *s.* mitraille, boîte de mitraille, charge à mitraille, *f.* — **worm,** *s.* caset, ver caset, *m.*

Cased, *part. adj.* mis dans un étui *or* &c., encaissé, &c. (*V.* **Case,** *v.a.*); (*nav.*) cuirassé. *Double* —, (*of watches*) à double boîte

Caseation, *s.* caséation, *f.*

Caseic, *adj.* caséique

Caseine, *s.* caséine, *f.*

Casemate, *s.* casemate, *f.*; — *v.a.* casemater

Casement, *s.* fenêtre, croisée, *f.*; (*compartment*) vasistas, *m.* — **window,** *s.* fenêtre, croisée, *f.*; fenêtre à vasistas, *f.*

Casemented, *adj.* à vasistas

Caseous, *adj.* caséeux

Caseum, *s.* caséum, *m.*

Cash, *s.* argent comptant, argent, *m.*; espèces, *f.pl.*; numéraire, *m.*; (*cashier's desk, and book-keep.*) caisse, *f.* *Hard* or *solid* —, espèces sonnantes, *f.pl.* *To be in* —, être en fonds. *To be out of* —, n'avoir pas (*or* plus) d'argent; (*by*) perdre (à). *To sell for* —, vendre au comptant. — **account,** *s.* compte de caisse, *m.*; caisse, *f.*; crédit (ouvert à quelqu'un), *m.* — **book,** *s.* livre de caisse, *m.* — **box,** *s.* caisse, *f.*; (*small*) cassette, *f.* — **credit,** *s.* crédit (ouvert par un banquier), *m.* — **down,** argent comptant. — **keeper,** *s.* caissier, *m.* — **office,** *s.* caisse, *f.* — **payment,** *s.* payement en espèces *or* au comptant, *m.*

Cash, *v.a.* payer; changer; (*discount*) escompter. *To get —ed,* faire payer, (*com.*) encaisser; (*changed*) faire changer; (*discounted*) faire escompter

Cashew-nut, *s.* noix (*or* pomme) d'acajou, anacarde, *f.* — **tree,** *s.* acajou à pommes, anacardier, *m.* [**office,** *s.* caisse, *f.*

Cashier, *s.* caissier, *m.*, -ière, *f.* —**'s desk** *or*

Cashier, *v.a.* destituer; (*mil.*) dégrader

Cashiering, *s.* destitution, *f.*; (*mil.*) dé- [gradation, *f.*

Cashmere, *s.* cachemire, *m.*

Cashmerette, *s.* cachemirette, *f.*

Cashoo, *s.* cachou, *m.*

Casing, *s.* (*build.*) revêtement, *m.*; (*of machines*) enveloppe, *f.*, entourage, *m.*, cage, *f.*; (*covering*)

couverture, *f.*; (*of mines*) cuvelage, cuvellement, *m.*

Casino, *s.* casino, *m.*

Cask, *s.* tonneau, *m.*; baril, *m.*; barrique, *f.*; fût, *m.*, futaille, *f.*; (*meas.*) pièce (anglaise), *f.*; — *v.a.* mettre en tonneau *or* en baril *or* &c., enfutailler. — **stand,** *s.* chantier, porte-fût, cric à baril, *m.*

Casket, *s.* cassette, *f.*; (*for jewels*) écrin, *m.*; (*small cask*) barriquaut, *m.*; (*nav.*) *V.* **Gasket;** — *v.a.* renfermer (*or* enfermer *or* serrer) dans une cassette. —**ful,** *s.* cassetée, *f.*

Casking, *s.* enfutaillement, *m.*

Caspian, *adj.* Caspien, *m.*, -ne, *f.*

Casque, *s.* casque, *m.*

Cassava, *s.* cassave, *f.*

Cassia, *s.* casse, *f.* — **tree,** *s.* cassier, canéficier, *m.*

Cassican, *s.* cassique, *m.*

Cassidony, *s.* cassidoine, *f.*

Cassie, *s.* cassie, *f.*

Cassine, Cassioberry, *s.* cassine, *f.*

Cassinette, *s.* castagnette, *f.*

Cassiopeia, *s.* (*astr.*) Cassiopée, *f.*

Cassock, *s.* casaque, *f.*; (*of priests*) soutane, *f.* *Short* —, soutanelle, *f.*

Cassocked, *adj.* vêtu d'une casaque, en casaque; vêtu d'une soutane, en soutane

Cassowary, *s.* casoar, *m.* — **tree,** *s.* casuarine, *f.*

Cassweed, *s.* capselle, *f.*

Cast, *v.a.* (*throw*) jeter; lancer; précipiter; (*sow, scatter*) semer, répandre; (*drop*) laisser tomber, perdre; (*change*) changer; (*turn*) tourner; (*weigh down*) faire pencher (la balance, &c.); (*reject*) rejeter; (*mil., of troop-horses*) réformer; (*baffle*) déjouer; (*defeat in a lawsuit*) débouter; (*metals*) fondre; (*print.*) clicher; (*mould*) mouler; couler; (*reckon*, &c.) compter, calculer, additionner; combiner; imaginer; (*consider*) examiner, juger, considérer; étudier; (*decide*) tirer au sort; (*doom, sentence*) condamner; (*abandon*) abandonner (à); (*theat.*) distribuer; — *v.n.* (*think*) songer, penser; (*of wood*) se déjeter; (*nav.*) abattre. — **about for,** songer à, chercher. — **about how,** songer aux moyens de. — **aside,** jeter *or* mettre de côté, rejeter, écarter. — **away,** jeter; rejeter; renoncer à; bannir; ruiner; prodiguer; (*nav.*) jeter à la côte; (*to be — away*, être jeté à la côte, faire naufrage, être perdu); *adj.* de rebut; perdu; *s.* rebut, *m.*; (*pers.*) réprouvé, *m.*, -e, *f.* — **by,** rejeter, abandonner. — **cannon,** *s.* canon de fonte, *m.* — **clothes,** *s. pl.* habits de rebut, vieux habits, *m.pl.*, défroque, *f.* — **down,** jeter par terre; (*fig.*) abattre; décourager; affliger; (*o.'s eyes*) baisser (les yeux). — **forth,** jeter, rejeter; (*emit*) pousser; éjaculer. — **iron,** *s.* fonte, *f.* — **net,** *s.* épervier, *m.* — **off,** rejeter, mettre de côté, mettre au rebut; abandonner; renvoyer; (*shake off*) secouer, se débarrasser de, se défaire de, se dépouiller de, dépouiller; *adj.* de rebut; abandonné; ancien. — **off clothes,** *V.* — **clothes.** — **out,** rejeter; chasser; prononcer. — **steel,** *s.* acier fondu, *m.* — **up,** rejeter, vomir, rendre; calculer, additionner; (*o.'s eyes*) lever (les yeux)

Cast, *s.* (*throw, distance*) jet, *m.*; (*stroke, touch*) coup, *m.*; (*of metals*) fonte, *f.*; (*fig.*) trempe, *f.*; caractère, *m.*; sorte, *f.*, genre, *m.*; air, *m.*, apparence, *f.*; expression, *f.*; (*shape*) forme, *f.*; tournure, *f.*; (*mould*) moule, *m.*; creux, *m.*; (*plaster — of a face*) masque, *m.*; (*image*) statuette, *f.*; buste, *m.*; bronze, *m.*; plâtre, *m.*; modèle, *m.*; (*shade, tinge*) nuance, *f.*; teinte, *f.*; (*sowing*) volée, *f.*; (*theat.*) distribution (des rôles), *f.*; rôles, acteurs, *m.pl.*; (*in angling, gut-line*) empile, *f.* — *of the eye*, louchement, *m.* *To have a — in the eye*, loucher. *To take a — of a person's face*, mouler la figure d'une personne

Castalia, *s.* Castalie, *f.*

Castalian, *adj.* de Castalie

Castanet, *s.* castagnette, *f.*

Caste, *s.* caste, *f.*; classe, *f.*; (*of things*) ordre, *m.* *To lose* —, se rabaisser, descendre; s'encanailler

Castellan, *s.* châtelain, *m.*

Castellany, *s.* châtellenie, *f.*

Castellated, *adj.* encastré; (*embattled*) crénelé

Caster, *s.* personne qui jette, *f.*, jeteur, *m.*, -euse, *f.*; (*of metals*) fondeur, *m.*; (*reckoner*) calculateur, *m.*, -trice, *f.*; (*fortune-teller*) tireur (*m.*, -euse, *f.*) d'horoscopes *or* de cartes; (*for condiments*) saupoudreur, *m.*; (*of furniture*) roulette, *f.*

Castigate, *v.a.* châtier, punir

Castigation, *s.* châtiment, *m.*, punition, correction, *f.*; discipline, *f.*

Castigator, *s.* châtieur, *m.*

Castigatory, *adj.* de châtiment, qui sert à châtier

Castilian, *s.* Castillan, *m.*, e, *f.*; — *adj.* castillan, de Castille

Casting, *s.* (*throwing*) jet, *m.*; (*of metals*) fonte, *f.*; (*print.*) clichage, *m.*; (*moulding*) moulage, *m.*; (*reckoning*) calcul, *m.*; (*nav.*) abattée, *f.*; — *adj.* décisif. — **house,** *s.* fonderie, *f.* — **line,** *s.* (*fish.*) empile, *f.* — **net,** *s.* épervier, *m.* — **vote,** *s.* voix prépondérante, *f.* — **weight,** *s.* poids qui l'emporte, *m.*

Castle, *s.* château, *m.*; château fort, *m.*; citadelle, *f.*; (*chess*) tour, *f.*; (*nav.*) gaillard, *m.* *To build —s in the air*, faire des châteaux en Espagne; — *v.n.* (*at chess*) roquer. — **builder,** *s.* faiseur (*m.*, -euse, *f.*) de châteaux en Espagne, rêveur, *m.*, -euse, *f.*, visionnaire, *m.f.* — **building,** *s.* action de faire des châteaux en Espagne, *f.*, rêveries extravagantes, *f.pl.* — **crowned,** *adj.* couronné (*or* surmonté) d'un château. — **keep,** *s.* donjon (de château), *m.* — **ward,** *s.* châtellenie, *f.*

Castled, *adj.* couronné d'un château *or* de châteaux; chargé de tours

Castlet, *s.* châtelet, petit château, *m.*

Castling, *s.* avorton, *m.*

Castor, *s.* (*beaver*) castor, *m.*; (*cloth*) castorine, *f.*; (*chem.*) castoréum, *m.*; (*of furniture*) *V.* **Caster;** (*astr.*) Castor, *m.* — **oil,** *s.* huile de ricin, *f.* — **oil plant,** *s.* ricin, *m.* — **oil-seed,** *s.* graines de ricin, *f.pl.*

Castoreum, *s.* castoréum, *m.*

Castorine, *s.* castorine, *f.*

Castrametation, *s.* castramétation, *f.*

Castrate, *v.a.* châtrer, castrer

Castration, *s.* castration, *f.*

Castrato, *s.* castrat, *m.*

Casual, *adj.* casuel, accidentel, fortuit; irrégulier; de passage

Casuality, Casualness, *s.* casualité, *f.*

Casually, *adv.* casuellement, accidentellement, fortuitement, par hasard; irrégulièrement; en passant

Casualty, *s.* cas fortuit, hasard, *m.*; chance, *f.*; accident, *m.*; (*of fire, shipwreck*) sinistre, *m.*; (*mil.*) perte, *f.*

Casuarina, *s.* casuarine, *f.*

Casuist, *s.* casuiste, *m.*

Casuistic, -al, *adj.* de casuiste

Casuistically, *adv.* en casuiste

Casuistry, *s.* casuistique, *f.*

Casus belli, *s.* cas de guerre, *m.*

Cat, *s.* chat, *m.*, chatte, *f.*; (*whip*) fouet, *m.*; (*game*) bâtonnet, *m.*; (*tripod*) trépied double, *m.*; (*nav.*) capon, *m.*; — *v.a.* (*nav.*) caponner. *He —, tom —*, chat, matou, *m.* *She —*, chatte, *f.* *To agree* (or *to live*) *like — and dog*, s'accorder (*or* vivre) comme chien et chat. *To let the — out of the bag*, éventer la mèche *or* la mine; se couper. *To shoot the —*, (*to spew*) piquer un renard. *All —s are grey in the dark*, la nuit tous les chats sont gris. *When the — is away the mice will play*, quand le chat n'y est pas les souris s'ébattent; *or*, absent le chat les souris dansent. — **bird,** *s.* moqueur, *m.* — **block,** *s.* (*nav.*) poulie de capon, *f.* — **call,** *s.* sifflet, *m.* — **eyed,** *adj.* qui a des yeux de chat. — **fall,** *s.* (*nav.*) garant de capon, *m.* — **fish,** *s.* chat marin, loup marin, anarrhique-loup, *m.* — **gut,** *s.* boyau de chat, *m.*; corde à boyau, *f.*, boyau, *m.*; (*canvas*) marli, *m.* — **gut factory,** *s.* boyauderie, *f.* — **gut maker,** *s.* boyaudier, *m.* — **gut scraper,** *s.* râcleur, *m.* — **harpings,** *s. pl.* (*nav.*) trelingage (des haubans), *m.* — **head,** *s.* (*nav.*) bossoir, *m.* — **hole,** *s.* chatière, *f.* — **hook,** *s.* (*nav.*) croc de capon, *m.* — **kin,** *s.* chaton, *m.* — **like,** *adj.* semblable au chat, comme un chat, de chat. — **mint,** *s.* herbe aux chats, cataire, *f.* — **o' nine tails,** *s.* fouet à neuf cordes, martinet, *m.*; (*nav.*) garcette, *f.* — **pipe,** *s.* sifflet, *m.* —**'s eye,** *s.* œil de chat, *m.* —**'s hole,** *s.* chatière, *f.* — **show,** *s.* exposition de chats, *f.* — **silver,** *s.* argent de chat, *m.* — **skin,** *s.* peau de chat, *f.*; (*tale*) peau d'âne, *f.* —**'s litter,** *s.* chattée, *f.* —**s' meat,** *s.* *V.* **Dogs' meat.** —**'s paw,** *s.* patte de chat, *f.*; (*fig.*) dupe, *f.*, instrument, *m.*, patte du chat pour tirer les marrons du feu, *f.*; (*nav.*) fraîcheur, *f.*, petit vent, *m.* *To make one a —'s paw*, se servir de quelqu'un comme de la patte du chat. *You are his —'s paw*, vous êtes sa dupe, vous tirez les marrons du feu pour lui. —**'s pur,** *s.* (*med.*) frémissement cataire, *m.* —**'s tail,** — **tail,** *s.* queue de (*or* du) chat, *f.*; (*bot.*) massette, *f.* —**'s tail grass,** *s.* fléole, *f.* — **thyme,** *s.* marum, *m.* — **trap,** *s.* chatière, *f.* — **tribe,** *s.* félins, *m.pl.*

Catachresis, *s.* catachrèse, *f.*

Catachrest-ic, al, *adj.*, **-ically,** *adv.* par [catachrèse

Cataclysm, *s.* cataclysme, *m.*

Catacombs, *s. pl.* catacombes, *f.pl.*

Catacoustic, *adj.* catacoustique; —**s,** *s. pl.* catacoustique, *f.*

Catadioptric, *adj.* catadioptrique; —**s,** *s. pl.* [catadioptrique, *f.*

Catafalque, *s.* catafalque, *m.*

Catalan, *s. adj.* *V.* **Catalonian**

Catal-ectic, -eptic, -epsy. *V.* page 3, § 1

Catalogue, *s.* catalogue, *m.*; — *v.a.* cataloguer

Cataloguer, *s.* catalogueur, *m.*

Cataloguing, *s.* cataloguement, *m.*

Catalonian, *s.* Catalan, *m.*, e, *f.*; — *adj.* catalan, de Catalogne

Catalpa, *s.* catalpa, *m.*

Catalysis, *s.* catalyse, *f.*

Catalyt-ic, al, -ically. *V.* page 3, § 1

Catamaran, *s.* catimaron, *m.*

Catamenia, *s.pl.* flux menstruel, *m.*, menstrues, [règles, *f.pl.*

Catamenial, *adj.* cataménial, menstruel

Cataplasm, *s.* *V.* **Poultice**

Catapult, Catapulta, *s.* (*ancient engine*) catapulte, *f.*; (*modern toy*) chasse-pierres, *m.*

Cataract, *s.* cataracte, *f.*

Catarrh, *s.* catarrhe, *m.*

Catarrhal, *adj.* catarrhal

Catarrhous, *adj.* catarrheux

Catastrophe, *s.* catastrophe, *f.*; péripétie, *f.*; (*conclusion*) dénoûment, *m.*

Catch, *v.a.* attraper, saisir; prendre; (*as with a hook*) accrocher; s'accrocher à; (*strike against*) s'attraper à; (*words spoken, anyone's meaning*, &c.) saisir; (*anyone falling*) retenir; (*clasp*) serrer; (*surprise*) prendre; surprendre; (*a train, a steamer*) aller trouver, prendre, (*in time*) arriver à temps pour, ne pas manquer; (*of fire*) prendre; (*of the sight*) frapper; attirer; (*see*) apercevoir, voir; (*find out*) découvrir, trouver; (*gain*) gagner; (*captivate*) séduire, tourner la tête à; (*watch*) guetter, être à l'affût de; (*overtake*) atteindre, rattraper; — *v n.* s'accrocher (à); se prendre (à); s'engager (contre); se saisir (de); se communiquer, se gagner; se propager; prendre; gagner; — *s.* prise, capture, *f.*; profit, *m.*; avantage, *m.*; affaire, *f.*; belle affaire, *f.*; (*trick*) attrape, *f.*; (*watch*) guet, affût, *m.*; (*of fish*) pêche, *f.*; quantité, *f.*; (*small portion*) bribe, *f.*, morceau, *m.*; (*slight idea*) idée, *f.*; légère impression, *f.*; faible souvenir, *m.*; (*smattering*) teinture, *f.*; (*motion*) saccade, *f.*; (*mus.*) reprise, *f.*; (*print.*) visorium, *m.*: (*tech.*, *of locks*, &c.) crochet d'arrêt, crochet, crampon, cliquet, loquet, *m.* *By —es*, à diverses reprises, par intervalles; par saccades, à bâtons rompus. *On* or *upon the —*, aux aguets (pour), à l'affût (de). *To — it*, (*be scolded or punished*) en recevoir, en avoir. *His eye caught mine*, nos yeux se rencontrèrent. — **again,** *v.a.* rattraper; reprendre. — **at,** *v.n.* s'accrocher à; saisir; se prendre à; (*hunt*) courir après. — **fly,** *s.* attrape-mouches, gobe-mouches, *m.* — **line,** *s.* (*print.*) ligne perdue, *f.* — **penny,** *s.* attrape-nigauds, *m.*; *adj.* de réclame, de boutique; mauvais. — **poll,** *s.* recors, alguazil, *m.* — **question,** *s.* question embarrassante, question captieuse, *f.* — **spring,** *s.* ressort à cliquet, *m.*; (*of a repeating-watch*) sourdine, *f.* — **up,** *v.a.* saisir; s'emparer de; ramasser; relever; enlever; (*notice, observe*) relever; faire remarquer; (*overtake*) rattraper; *s.* [*See below*]. — **weed,** *s.* râpette, *f.* — **word,** *s.* (*print.*) réclame, *f.*; (*theat.*) réplique, réclame, *f.*

Catcher, *s.* attrapeur, *m.*, -euse, *f.*, preneur, [*m.*, -euse, *f.*

Catching, *adj.* qui saisit; contagieux, qui se gagne; séduisant; — *s.* action d'attraper, *f.*; prise, capture, *f.*; (*of fish*) pêche, *f.*

Catchup, *s* sauce piquante, *f.*; (*mushroom —*) sauce aux champignons, *f.*

Catechetic, -al, *adj.* catéchétique, catéchistique, par demandes et par réponses

Catechetically, *adv.* catéchétiquement, catéchistiquement, par demandes et par réponses

Catechetics, *s. pl.* catéchèse, méthode d'enseignement par demandes et par réponses, *f.*

Catechine, *s.* catéchine, *f.*

Catech-ism, -ist, catéchisme, &c. *V.* page [3, § 1

Catechistic, -al, *adj.* de *or* du catéchisme; de catéchiste; catéchistique, par demandes et par réponses

Catechistically, *adv.* catéchistiquement, par demandes et par réponses

Catechization, *s.* catéchisation, *f.*

Catechize, *v.a.* catéchiser, instruire; interroger, questionner

Catechizer, *s.* catéchiste, *m.*; interrogateur, *m.*

Catechu, *s.* cachou, *m.*

Catechumen, *s.* catéchumène, *m.f.*

Catechumenate, *s.* catéchuménat, *m.*

Catechumenic, -al, *adj.* de catéchumène

Categor-ic, al, -ically, -y, catégorique. &c. *V.* page 3, § 1

Categorize, *v.a.* catégoriser

Catenarian, *adj.* funiculaire

Catenary, *adj.* *V.* **Catenarian;** — *s.* chaînette, funiculaire, courbe funiculaire, *f.*

Catenation, *s.* enchaînement, *m.*

Cater, *v.n.* — **for,** pourvoir aux besoins de; approvisionner; pourvoir à; prendre soin de; (*in o.'s own house*) héberger

Cater-er, ess, *s.* pourvoyeur, *m.*, -euse, *f.*, approvisionneur, *m.*, -euse, *f.*

Caterpillar, *s.* chenille, *f.*; (*bot.*) chenillette, scorpiure, *f.* — **catcher, -destroyer, -eater,** *s.* échenilleur, *m.* — **nest,** *s.* chenillère, *f.*

Caterwaul, *v.n.* crier, faire du tintamarre *or* [du vacarme *or* du sabbat

Caterwauling, *s.* miaulement, sabbat, *m.*; (*any noise*) tintamarre, vacarme, sabbat, *m.*

Cates, *s. pl.* friandises, *f.pl.*

Catharine-wheel. *V.* **Catherine**

Cathartic, -al, *adj.*, **Cathartic,** *s.* cathartique, *adj. m.f.*, *s.m.*

Cathartine, *s.* cathartine, *f.*

Cathedrâ (Ex), *adv.* ex cathedrâ

Cathedral, *s.* cathédrale, *f.*; — *adj.* de cathédrale; cathédrale. — **church,** *s.* église cathédrale, cathédrale, *f.* — **city, -town,** *s.* ville épiscopale, *f.*, évêché, *m.*; ville archiépiscopale, *f.*, archevêché, *m.*, métropole, *f.* — **service,** *s.* service de cathédrale, *m.* — **yard,** *s.* parvis, *m.*

Catheretic, *adj. s.* cathérétique, *adj. m.f.*, *s.m.*

Catherine. — **pear,** *s.* poire de Sainte-Catherine, *f.* — **wheel,** *s.* (*firework*) soleil, *m.*
Catheter, *s.* cathéter, *m.*
Cathetometer, *s.* cathétomètre, *m.*
Catholic, *adj. s.* catholique, *m.f.*
Catholicism, *s.* catholicisme, *m.*; catholicité, *f.*
Catholicity, *s.* catholicité, *f.*
Catholicly, *adv.* catholiquement
Catholicon, *s.* catholicon, *m.*
Catiline, — **oration,** *s.* catilinaire, *f.*
Catkin, *s.* chaton, *m.*
Catlin, Catling, *s.* (*surg.*) couteau (à amputation) interosseux, *m.*
Catonian, *adj.* catonien
Catonism, *s.* catonisme, *m*
Catoptric, -al, *adj.* catoptrique; —**s,** *s. pl.* catoptrique, *f.*
Catsup, *s.* *V.* **Catchup**
Cattle, *s.* bétail, *m. sing.*; bestiaux, *m.pl.* — **breeder,** *s.* éleveur de bestiaux, éleveur, *m.* — **dealer, -salesman,** *s.* marchand de bestiaux, *m.* — **feeder,** *s.* nourrisseur, herbager, *m.* — **house,** *s.* étable, *f.* — **market,** *s.* marché aux bestiaux, *m.* — **pen,** *s.* parc de bestiaux, parc, *m.* — **plague,** *s.* peste bovine, *f.*, typhus contagieux des bêtes à cornes *or* du gros bétail, *m.* — **shed,** *s.* étable, *f.* — **show,** *s.* exposition de bétail, *f.* — **trade,** *s.* commerce des bestiaux, *m.* — **traffic,** *s.* (*rail.*) transport des bestiaux, *m.* — **train,** *s.* convoi de bestiaux, *m.* — **truck,** *s.* (*rail.*) wagon de bestiaux, *m.*
Caucasian, *adj.* caucasien, caucasique
Caucus, *s.* réunion électorale, *f.*; réunion, conférence, *f.*
Caudal, *adj.* caudal
Caudine forks, *s. pl.* fourches caudines, *f. pl.*
Caudle, *s.* boisson chaude, *f.*, chaudeau, *m.*
Cauf, *s.* (*fish.*) banneton, *m.*; (*mining*) *V.* **Corf**
Caul, *s.* (*net*) filet, réseau, *m.*, résille, *f.*; (*of a cap*) fond, *m.*, calotte, *f.*; (*anat.*) coiffe, *f.*; (*butch.*) crépine, ratelle, *f.*, parement, *m.*, toilette, coiffe, *f.*
Cauldron. *V.* **Caldron**
Cauliflower, *s.* chou-fleur, *m.*
Cauline, *adj.* caulinaire
Caulk. *V.* **Calk**
Causal, *adj.* causal; causatif; — *s.* mot causatif, *m.*
Causality, *s.* causalité, *f.*
Causally, *adv.* selon l'ordre des causes
Causation, *s.* causation, *f.*
Causative, *adj.* causatif
Causatively, *adv.* causativement
Cause, *s.* cause, *f.*; raison, *f.*, motif, sujet, *m.*; — *v.a.* causer; être cause de; occasionner; faire naitre; (*before an infinitive*) faire. *To show* —, exposer ses raisons. *There is* — *to believe*, il y a lieu de croire. *To* — *to sleep*, faire dormir. *He —d him to be put to death*, il le fit mettre à mort. *She —d him to do it*, elle le lui fit faire. *He —d the rebels to be arrested*, il fit arrêter les rebelles. *We have —d a ditch to be dug*, nous avous fait creuser un fossé. —**less,** —**lessly,** *adv. adj.* sans cause; sans raison, sans motif, sans sujet; sans fondement, non fondé. —**lessness,** *s.* absence de fondement *or* de motifs, *f.* — **list,** *s.* (*law*) rôle, *m.*
Causer, *s.* auteur, *m.*, cause, *f.*
Causeway, Causey, *s.* chaussée, *f.*
Caustic, *adj.* caustique, *m.f.*; — *s.* (*chem., pharm., surg.*) caustique, *m.*; (*nitrate of silver*, '*lunar* —') pierre infernale, *f.*; (*opt.*) caustique, *f.* — **case, -holder,** *s.* porte-pierre, porte-pierre-infernale, *m.*
Caustically, *adv.* caustiquement
Causticity, *s.* causticité, *f.*
Cauterism, Cauterization, Cauterizing, *s.* cautérisation, *f.*
Cauterize, *v.a.* cautériser
Cautery, *s.* cautère, *m.*
Caution, *s.* prudence, prévoyance, circonspection, précaution, *f.*; (*notice, advice*) avis, avertissement, *m.*; (*security*) garantie, caution, *f.*; — *v.a.* mettre en garde (contre), prémunir (contre), prévenir (de), avertir (de); inviter à prendre garde (à *or* de). — **money,** *s.* cautionnement, *m.*
Cautionary, *adj.* (*warning*) d'avertissement, pour avertir; (*as security*) comme garantie, donné en garantie *or* en otage
Cautious, *adj.* prudent, circonspect, réservé; précautionné; (*of*) en garde (contre); (*watchful*) vigilant, attentif
Cautiously, *adv.* avec précaution, avec circonspection, avec réserve, prudemment
Cautiousness, *s.* prudence, prévoyance, circonspection, *f.*
Cavalcade, *s.* cavalcade, *f.*
Cavalier, *s.* cavalier, *m.*; — *adj.* cavalier (*m.*, -ière, *f.*)
Cavalierly, *adv.* cavalièrement
Cavalierness, *s.* nature cavalière, *f.*; façons cavalières, *f.pl.*; propos cavaliers, *m.pl.*
Cavalry, *s.* cavalerie, *f.*; — *adj.* de cavalerie. — **barracks,** *s. pl.* caserne de cavalerie, *f.* — **man,** *s.* cavalier, soldat de cavalerie, *m.* — **officer,** *s.* officier de cavalerie, *m.*
Cavatina, *s.* cavatine, *f.*
Cave, *s.* caverne, *f.*, souterrain, antre, *m.*; — *v.n.* habiter dans une caverne; (— **in**) (*fall in*) s'affaisser; (*fig.*) s'affaisser; manquer, faillir; échouer; ne pas se soutenir; tomber; (*yield*) céder, mettre les pouces
Caveat, *s.* opposition, *f.*, empêchement, *m.*; (*of patents*) notification de demande future de brevet, *f.*
Cavern, *s.* caverne, *f.*
Caverned, *adj.* caverneux, plein de cavernes; qui habite dans une caverne
Cavernous, *adj.* caverneux
Caveson, Cavesson, *s.* caveçon, *m.*
Cavetto, *s.* cavet, *m.*
Caviar, Caviare, *s.* caviar, *m.*
Cavil, *v.n.* ('*at*,' sur) pointiller, ergoter, chicaner; — *s.* pointillerie, ergoterie, chicane, cavillation, *f.*
Caviller, *s.* chicaneur, *m.*, -euse, *f.*, chicanier, *m.*, -ière, *f.*, ergoteur, *m.*, -euse, *f.*
Cavilling, *s.* *V.* **Cavil**; — *adj.* pointilleux, ergoteur, chicaneur, chicanier
Cavillingly, *adv.* en chicanant, par esprit de chicane
Cavillous, *adj.* *V.* **Cavilling**
Cavillously, *adv.* en chicaneur, par esprit de chicane
Cavillousness, *s.* esprit de chicane, *m.*
Cavin, *s.* cavin, *m.*
Cavity, *s.* cavité, *f.*
Cavy, *s.* cobaye, *m.*
Caw, *v.n. and s.* *V.* **Croak**
Caxon, *s.* gazon, *m.*, tignasse, crinière, *f.*
Cay, *s.* caie, *f.*
Cayenne, — **pepper,** *s.* poivre de Cayenne, *m.*
Cayman, *s.* caïman, *m.*
Cazique, *s.* cacique, *m.*
Cease, *v.a.n.* cesser. — *firing!* (*mil.*) cessez le feu! —**less,** *adj.* incessant, continuel. —**lessly,** *adv.* sans cesse, continuellement
Ceasing, *s.* cessation, *f.* *Without* —, sans discontinuer, sans cesse
Cedar, *s.* cèdre, *m.*; — *adj.* de cèdre. — **bird,** *s.* jaseur d'Amérique, *m.* — **wood,** *s.* bois de cèdre, cèdre, *m.*
Cede, *v.a.n.* céder
Cedilla, *s.* cédille, *f.*
Cedra, Cedrat, Cedrate, *s.* cédrat, *m.*
Cedrine, *adj.* de cèdre
Ceil, *v.a.* plafonner
Ceiling, *s.* plafond, *m.*; plafonnage, *m.*
Celandine, *s.* chélidoine, éclaire, *f.*
Celebrant, *s.* célébrant, *m.*
Celebrate, *v.a.* célébrer
Celebrated, *adj.* célèbre; renommé; fameux
Celebration, *s.* célébration, *f.*; (*praise*) louange, *f.*, éloge, *m.*
Celebrator, *s.* célébrateur, *m*; panégyriste, *m.*
Celebrity, *s.* (*thing, pers.*) célébrité, *f.*
Celerity, *s.* célérité, vitesse, *f.*
Celery, *s.* céleri, *m.*
Celestial, *adj.* céleste; divin; — *s.* habitant du ciel, esprit céleste, *m.*
Celestially, *adv.* d'une manière céleste, divinement
Celestine, *s.* célestin, *m.*, e, *f.*; (*chem., bot.*) célestine, *f*
Celiac, *adj.* céliaque, cœliaque
Celibacy, *s.* célibat, *m.*

Cell, *s.* (*of convents, prisons,* &c.) cellule, *f.*; (*of a police office*) violon, *m.*, (**—s,** *pl.*) dépôt, *m.*; (*in mad-houses*) cellule, loge, *f.*, cabanon, *m.*; (*mil.*) cachot, *m.*; (*compartment*) case, *f.*, compartiment, *m.*; (*of bees*) alvéole, *f.m.*, cellule, *f.*; (*anat., bot.*) cellule, *f.*
Cellar, *s.* cave, *f.*; (*on the ground floor*) cellier, *m.*; (*small*) caveau, *m.*; — *v.a.* encaver. **—ful,** *s.* cave pleine, *f.* — **man,** *s.* garçon de cave, caviste, *m.*; (*butler*) sommelier, *m.*
Cellarage, *s.* caves, *f.pl.*; (*charge*) cavage, *m.*
Cellarer, Cellarist, *s.* cellerier, *m.*, -ière, *f.*
Cellaret, *s.* cave, *f.*
Celled, *adj.* cellulé; à ... cellule *or* cellules
Cellular, *adj.* cellulaire
Cellulated, *adj.* cellulé
Cellulose, *adj.* celluleux; — *s.* cellulose, *f.*
Celt, *s.* Celte, *m.f.*; (*weapon*) hache de pierre, hache, dolabre, *f.* [Celtibère, *m.f.*
Celtiberian, *s. adj.* Celtibérien, *m.*, -ne, *f.*,
Celtic, *adj.* celtique, *m.f.*; — *s.* (le) celtique, *m.*, (le) celte, *m.*, (la) langue celtique, *f.*
Cement, *s.* ciment, *m.*; (*chem., metal., anat.*) cément, *m.*; (*jewel.*) mastic, *m.*; (*fig.*) lien, *m.*; — *v.a.* cimenter; (*chem., metal.*) cémenter; (*jewel.*) mastiquer; — *v.n.* se cimenter; se consolider. *—ed steel,* acier de cémentation, *m.* — **maker,** *s.* cimentier, *m.*
Cementation, *s.* action de cimenter, *f.*; (*chem., metal.*) cémentation, *f.* [cémentatoire
Cementatory, *adj.* qui cimente; (*chem.*)
Cementer, *s.* personne *or* chose qui cimente, *f.*; (*fig.*) lien, *m.*
Cementitious, *adj.* cémenteux
Cemeterial, *adj.* de cimetière, cémétérial
Cemetery, *s.* cimetière, *f.*
Cenatory, *adj.* de (*or* du) souper, soupatoire
Cenobite, *s.* cénobite, *m.* [*V.* page 3, § 1
Cenobit-ic, al, -ism, cénobitique, &c.
Cenotaph, *s.* cénotaphe, *m.*
Cense, *s.* impôt, *m.*; — *v.a.n.* encenser
Censer, *s.* encensoir, *m.*
Censor, *s.* censeur, *m.*
Censorial, *adj.* de censeur, de censure, censorial; critique; sévère
Censorious, *adj.* critique; hargneux; sévère
Censoriously, *adv.* en censeur; en critique; sévèrement
Censoriousness, *s.* disposition à la censure *or* à la critique, manie de critiquer *or* de
Censorship, *s.* censure, *f.* [blâmer, *f.*
Censurable, *adj.* censurable, répréhensible, blâmable [blâme, *m.*
Censurableness, *s.* répréhensibilité, *f.*, tort,
Censurably, *adv.* répréhensiblement, d'une manière blâmable
Censure, *s.* censure, critique, *f.*, blâme, *m.*; — *v.a.* censurer, critiquer, blâmer
Censurer, *s.* censeur, critique, *m.*
Census, *s.* recensement, *m.*; (*Rom.hist.*) cens, *m.*
Cent, *s.* (*com., and American coin*) cent, *m.*
Centaur, *s.* centaure, *m.*
Centaurea, *s.* (*bot.*) centaurée, *f.*
Centaury, *s.* (*bot.*) érythrée, *f.*
Centenarian, *s. adj.* centenaire, *m.f.*
Centenary, *adj.* centenaire; séculaire; — *s.* centaine, *f.*; centième anniversaire, centenaire, *m.* [centenaire
Centennial, *adj.* séculaire; (*of anniversary*)
Center, *s.* (*build.*) cintre, *m.*; — *s.& v.a.n.* (*centre*) *V.* **Centre** [*centreing*) *V.* **Centreing**
Centering, *s.* (*build.*) cintrage, *m.*; cintre, *m.*;
Centesimal, *adj.* centésimal; — *s.* valeur centésimale, *f.*, chiffre centésimal, *m.*
Centesimation, *s.* exécution d'un soldat sur
Centiare, *s.* centiare, *m.* [cent, *f.*
Centifolious, *adj.* à cent feuilles
Centigrade, *adj.* centigrade
Centigramme, *s.* centigramme, *m.*
Centilitre, *s.* centilitre, *m.*
Centime, *s.* centime, *m.*
Centimetre, *s.* centimètre, *m.*
Centipede, *s.* centipède, *m.*, scolopendre, *f.*
Centipedal, *adj.* centipède
Centistere, *s.* centistère, *m.*
Cento, *s.* centon, *m.*
Central, *adj.* central
Centrality, *s.* centralité, *f.*
Centralization, *s.* centralisation, *f.*
Centralize, *v.a.* centraliser
Centralizer, *s.* centralisateur, *m.*, -trice, *f.*
Centralizing, *adj.* centralisateur; — *s.* centralisation, *f.*
Centrally, *adv.* centralement; au centre
Centre, *s.* centre, milieu, *m.*; (*of a target*) noir, *m.*; mouche, *f.*; (*build.*) cintre, *m.*; — *v.a.* placer au centre; (*tech.*) centrer; (*fig.*) concentrer; — *v.n.* être placé au centre; (*jut out*) faire centre; (*fig.*) se concentrer; (*rest on*) reposer (sur). — **bit,** *s.* mèche anglaise, tarière, *f.* — **carpet,** *s.* carpette, *f.* — **ottoman,** *s.* pouf, *m.*, borne (*f.*) *or* milieu (*m.*) de salon, borne, *f.* — **piece,** *s.* pièce du milieu, *f.*, milieu, *m.*; (*epergne*) *V.* **Epergne.** — **table,** *s.* table de milieu, *f.*, guéridon, *m.*
Centreing, *s.* centre, *m.*; concentration, *f.*; (*build.*) *V.* **Centering**
Centr-ic, al, -ically. *V.* **Central, Centrally**
Centricalness, *s.* centralité, *f.*
Centrifugal, *adj.* centrifuge
Centring, *s. V.* **Centreing**
Centripetal, *adj.* centripète
Centumvir, *s.* centumvir, *m.*
Centumviral, *adj.* centumviral
Centumvirate, *s.* centumvirat, *m.*
Centuple, *adj. s.* centuple, *adj. m.f., s.m.*; — *v.a.n.* centupler [centenier, *m.*
Centurion, *s.* centurion, *m.*; (*in Scripture*)
Century, *s.* siècle, *m.*; (*Rom. hist.*) centurie, *f.*
Cephal-algic, -algy, -ic, &c., céphalalgique, &c. *V.* page 3, § 1
Cephalonian, *s. adj.* Céphalonien, *m.*, -ne, *f.*
Cephalopod, *s.* céphalopode, *m.*
Ceramic, *adj.* céramique, *m.f.*; **—s,** *s. pl.*
Cerasine, *s.* cérasine, *f.* [céramique, *f.*
Cerastes, *s.* céraste, *m.*
Cerate, *s.* cérat, *m.*
Cerated, *adj.* ciré, enduit de cire
Cerberean, *adj.* de Cerbère
Cerberus, *s.* Cerbère, cerbère, *m.*
Cere, *s.* cire, *f.*; — *v.a.* cirer. — **cloth, —ment,** *s.* toile gommée, toile d'embaumement, *f.* [*s. pl.* céréales, *f.pl.*
Cereal, *adj. s.* céréale, *adj. f., s.f.* — **grasses,**
Cerebellum, *s.* cervelet, *m.*
Cerebral, *adj.* cérébral
Cerebro-spinal, *adj.* cérébro-spinal
Ceremonial, *adj.* cérémonial, cérémoniel, de cérémonie; — *s.* cérémonial, *m.*, étiquette, *f.*; (*eccl.*) cérémonie, *f.*
Ceremonialism, *s.* cérémonialisme, *m.*
Ceremonially, *adv.* d'après le cérémonial
Ceremonious, *adj.* cérémonieux; de cérémonie; dans les formes
Ceremoniously, *adv.* avec cérémonie; dans les formes; (*in state*) en cérémonie
Ceremoniousness, *s.* nature cérémonieuse, *f.*, formalisme, *m.*
Ceremony, *s.* cérémonie, *f.*; cérémonies, façons, *f.pl.* *Without —,* sans cérémonie, sans façon. *To make —, to stand on* (or *upon*) *—,* faire des cérémonies *or* des façons
Cereous, *adj.* cireux, de cire
Cerine, *s.* cérine, *f.*
Cerise, *adj. s.* cerise, *adj. m.f., s.m.*
Cerite, *s.* cérite, *f.*
Cerium, *s.* cérium, *m.*
Ceroon, *s.* céron, suron, *m.*
Ceroplastic, *adj. s.* céroplastique, *adj. m.f., s.f.*
Certain, *adj.* certain (*m.*, e, *f.*); — *s.* certain, *m.* *A — thing,* (*some thing*) une certaine chose, (*a positive* or *sure thing*) une chose certaine. *For —,* pour certain; comme chose certaine; (*certainly*) pour sûr; à coup sûr. *One thing is*

—, *that* ..., *This much is* —, *that* ..., ce qu'il y a de certain (*or* ce qui est certain), c'est que ...

Certainly, *adv.* certainement; (*at least*) au moins, du moins

Certainty, *s.* certitude, *f.*; chose certaine, *f.* *To* (or *with*) *a* —, certainement; pour sûr et certain; à coup sûr

Certificate, *s.* certificat, *m.*; diplôme, *m.*; (*of birth, marriage, death*) acte, *m.*, (*copy of ditto*) extrait, *m.*; (*of baptism*) extrait, *m.*; (*fin.*) titre, *m.*; (*of bankrupts*) concordat, *m.*; — *v.a.* délivrer un certificat *or* &c. à; breveter. — *of being alive,* certificat de vie, *m.*

Certificated, *adj.* pourvu d'un certificat, qui a un certificat; diplômé; breveté; (*of bankrupts*) concordataire

Certification, Certifying, *s.* certification, *f.*

Certifier, *s.* certificateur, *m.*

Certify, *v.a.n.* certifier; attester, déclarer; rendre témoignage (de); notifier, donner avis à; faire savoir à, avertir, prévenir. *This is to* — *that Mr.* ..., *&c.*, je certifie que M. ..., &c.

Certitude, *s.* certitude, *f.*

Cerulean, Ceruleous, *adj.* bleu, azuré, [cérulé

Cerumen, *s.* cérumen, *m.*

Ceruse, *s.* céruse, *f.*, blanc de céruse, *m.*; — *v.a.* couvrir *or* farder de blanc de céruse

Cervical, *adj.* cervical

Cervine, *adj.* cervin

Cesarean, Cesarian. *V.* **Cæsarean**

Cess, *s.* impôt, *m.*; — *v.a.* imposer

Cessation, *s.* cessation, *f.*; discontinuation, *f.*; interruption, *f.*; suspension, *f.*

Cession, *s.* cession, *f.*

Cesspool, *s.* puisard, *m.*; (*for closets*) fosse [d'aisances, *f.*

Cestus, *s.* ceste, *m.*

Cesura. *V.* **Cæsura**

Cetacean, *s.* cétacé, *m.*

Cetaceous, *adj.* cétacé, cétacéen

Cevadilla, *s.* cévadille, *f.*

Ceylonese, *s.* Ceylanais, *m.*, e, *f.*

Chace. *V.* **Chase**

Chad. *V.* **Shad**

Chafe, *v.a.* chauffer; réchauffer; (*fig.*) échauffer, irriter; (*a cable*) érailler; — *v.n.* s'échauffer, s'irriter, être irrité; (*by rubbing*) frotter, s'écorcher; (*of cables*) s'érailler, se raguer; — *s.* chaleur, *f.*; irritation, *f.*

Chafer, *s.* (*insect*) scarabée, *m.*, (*cock* —) hanneton, *m.*; (*pan*) réchaud, *m.*

Chafery, *s.* (*forge*) chaufferie, *f.*

Chaff, *s.* balle, *f.*, balles, *f.pl.*, menue paille, paille, *f.*; (*cut hay and straw*) paille hachée, *f.*; (*fig., refuse*) rebut, *m.*, paille, *f.*; (*trifles*) bagatelles, frivolités, *f.pl.*; (*jeer*) gosserie, gouaillerie, blague, *f.*; — *v.a.* blaguer, gosser, se gosser de, gouailler, berner, taquiner. — **cutter, -cutting machine,** *s.* hache-paille, *m.*

Chaffer, *v.n.* marchander, barguigner; — *s.* gosseur, *m.*, -euse, *f.*, gouailleur, *m.*, -euse, *f.*, blagueur, *m.*, -euse, *f.*

Chafferer, *s.* barguigneur, *m.*, -euse, *f.*

Chaffering, *s.* barguignage, *m.*

Chaffinch, *s.* pinson, *m.*

Chaffing, *adj.* gosseur, gouailleur; — *s.* gosserie, gouaillerie, *f.*

Chaffron, *s.* chanfrein, *m.*

Chaffy, *adj.* de paille, semblable à la paille; plein de balles *or* de paille; (*fig.*) léger, sans consistance, frivole

Chafing, *s.* échauffement, *m.*; irritation, *f.* — **dish,** *s.* réchaud, *m.* — **pan,** *s.* chaufferette, *f.*

Chagreen. *V.* **Shagreen**

Chagrin, *s.* chagrin, *m.*; — *v.a.* chagriner

Chain, *s.* chaîne, *f.*; (*small*) chaînette, *f.*; (*for keys*) châtelaine, *f.*; (*meas.*) 20 mètres, *m.pl.*; — *v.a.* enchaîner; attacher avec une chaîne *or* avec des chaînes; faire en forme de chaîne; (*shut*) fermer par une chaîne. *Albert* —, chaîne de gilet, *f.* — **bond,** *s.* (*build.*) chaînage, *m.* — **bridge,** *s.* pont suspendu, *m.* — **cable,** *s.* câble-chaîne, *m.* — **course,** *s.* (*build.*) chaîne de pierre, *f.* — **gang,** *s.* chaîne, cadène, *f.* —**less,** *adj.* sans chaînes, libre. — **let,** *s.* chaînette, *f.* — **maker,** *s.* chaînetier, chaîniste, *m.* — **pier,** *s.* jetée suspendue, *f.* — **pump,** *s.* pompe à chapelet, noria, *f.* — **rule,** *s.* (*arith.*) règle conjointe, *f.* — **shot,** *s.* boulet ramé, *m.* — **stitch,** *s.* point de chaînette, *m.*, chaînette, *f.*; broderie au crochet, *f.* — **timbers,** *s. pl.* chaînage, *m.* — **work,** *s.* *V.* — **stitch**

Chained, *part. adj.* enchaîné, à la chaîne, attaché avec une chaîne, &c. (*V.* **Chain,** *v a.*); (*chain-shaped*) chaîné, en forme de chaîne

Chaining, *s.* enchaînement, *m.*

Chair, *s.* (*seat*) chaise, *f.*; fauteuil, *m.*; (*of professors, of the pope*) chaire, *f.*; (*of a president*) fauteuil, *m.*; (*fig.*) présidence, *f.*; président, *m.*; (*of a judge*) siége, *m.*; (*vehicle*) chaise, *f.*; (*sedan*) chaise à porteurs, *f.*; (*rail.*) coussinet, chair, *m.*; (*of wheels*) boîte, *f.*; — *v.a.* porter en triomphe. *Bath* —, vinaigrette, roulette, brouette, *f.* *Devotion* —, prie-Dieu, *m.* *Easy* —, fauteuil, fauteuil confortable, *m.* *Elizabethan* —, *low-seat* —, chauffeuse, *f.* *To be in the* —, *to fill the* —, tenir *or* occuper le fauteuil (de la présidence), présider, être président. *To take the* —, *V.* **Take.** *The* — *is taken,* la séance est ouverte. *Mr. A. in the* —, présidence de Mr. A. *Chair! chair!* à l'ordre! à l'ordre! — **bottom,** *s.* fond de chaise, *m.* — **bottommer,** *s.* empailleur, *m.*, -euse, *f.* — **caner,** *s.* cannier, *m.* — **cover,** *s.* garniture de chaise *or* de fauteuil, *f.*; (*for protection*) housse, *f.* — **letter,** *s.* chaisière, *f.* — **maker,** *s.* chaisier, *m.* — **man,** *s.* président, *m.*; (*of a company*) président du conseil d'administration, *m.*; (*of a Bath chair*) traîneur de vinaigrette *or* de brouette, brouetteur, *m.*; (*of a sedan*) porteur de chaise, *m.* — **manship,** *s.* présidence, *f.* — **mender,** *s.* rempailleur, *m.*, -euse, *f.* — **turner,** *s.* tourneur en chaises, *m.*

Chaise, *s.* chaise, *f.*

Chalcedony, *s.* calcédoine, chalcédoine, *f.*

Chalcis, *s.* chalcide, *m.*

Chalcographer, *s.* chalcographe, *m.*

Chalcograph-ic, -y. *V.* page 3, § 1

Chaldaic, *adj.* chaldaïque; — *s.* (le) chaldéen, *m.*

Chaldaism, *s.* chaldaïsme, *m.*

Chaldean, *s.* (*pers.*) Chaldéen, *m.*, -ne, *f.*; (*language*) (le) chaldéen, *m.*; — *adj.* chaldéen

Chaldee. *V.* **Chaldean**

Chaldron, *s.* 13 hectolitres, *m.pl.*

Chalice, *s.* (*of church*) calice, *m.*; (*cup*) coupe, *f.*

Chalk, *s.* craie, *f.*; (*draw.*) crayon, *m.*; — *v.a.* frotter *or* blanchir avec de la craie; marquer avec de la craie, marquer à la craie; écrire à la craie; crayonner; tracer; (*agr.*) marner. — **cutter,** *s.* ouvrier qui extrait la craie, *m.* — **drawing,** *s.* dessin aux crayons, pastel, *m.* — **line,** *s.* cordeau, *m.* — **out,** *v.a.* tracer. — **pit,** *s.* crayère, *f.* — **stone,** *s.* morceau de craie, *m.*; (*med.*) concrétion tophacée, *f.*

Chalkiness, *s.* nature crayeuse, *f.*

Chalky, *adj.* crayeux, de craie; crayonneux

Challenge, *s.* cartel, défi, *m.*; provocation, *f.*; appel, *m.*; (*match*) concours, *m.*; (*of rights*) prétention, demande, *f.*; (*law*) récusation, *f.*; (*mil.*) qui-vive, *m.*; — *v.a.* défier; provoquer; appeler en duel; (*fig.*) accuser, blâmer; commander; inspirer; (*rights*) réclamer; (*law*) récuser; (*mil.*) crier qui-vive à; reconnaître (une patrouille, une ronde); (*nav.*) héler. — **word,** *s.* (*mil.*) qui-vive, *m.*

Challengeable, *adj.* réclamable; (*law*) récusable

Challenger, *s.* provocateur, *m.*, -trice, *f.*, agresseur, *m.*; réclamant, *m.*, e, *f.*; (*law*) récusant, *m.*, e, *f.*

Challis, *s.* chaly, *m.*

Chalybeate, *adj.* chalybé, ferrugineux, ferré; — *s.* ferrugineux, *m.*; (*water*) eau ferrugineuse, eau ferrée, *f.*; (*spring*) source d'eau ferrugineuse, *f.*

Chamber, *s.* chambre, *f.*; (*bedroom*) *V.* **Bed-**

room; (*office*) bureau, *m.*; cabinet, *m.*; (*of mines, of fire-arms, of the eye, opt., tech.*) chambre, *f.*; (*of the nose*) fosse, *f.*; (*barrel*) canon, *m*; —**s,** *pl.* chambres, &c.; bureaux, *m.pl.*, (*of solicitors*) étude, *f.*; (*of judges, of counsel*) cabinet, *m.*; (*lodgings*) appartement de garçon, *m.*; — *v.a.* chambrer, enfermer. *In* or *at —s, sitting in* or *at —s,* (*of judges*) en référé. — **council,** *s.* conseil secret, *m.* — **counsel,** *s.* avocat consultant, *m.* — **fellow,** *s.* camarade de chambre, *m.* —**ful,** *s.* chambre pleine, chambrée, *f.* — **lye,** *s.* urine, *f.* — **maid,** *s.* fille (*or* femme) de chambre, *f.*; fille de service *or* de ménage, *f.* — **pot,** *s.* pot de chambre, *m.* — **practice,** *s.* consultations, *f.pl.*; clientèle, *f.* [*For other compounds, V.* **Bedroom**]

Chambered, *part. adj.* chambré; (*of fire-arms*) à ... coups. *Six- — revolver,* révolver à six coups, *m.* [*pope*) camérier, *m.*

Chamberlain, *s.* chambellan, *m.*; (*of the*

Chamberlainship, *s.* charge de chambellan, *f.*

Chameleon, *s.* caméléon, *m.*

Chamfer, *s.* chanfrein, *m.*; — *v.a.* chanfreiner

Chamois, *s.* chamois. *m.* — **leather,** *s.* [chamois, *m.*

Chamomile, *s.* camomille, *f.*

Champ, *v.a.n.* ronger, mâcher. *To — the bit,* ronger son (*or* le) frein

Champagne, *s.* (*geog.*) la Champagne, *f.*; (*wine*) champagne, vin de Champagne, *m.* — **cup,** *s.* tisane de champagne, *f.*

Champaign, *s.* campagne, *f.*; plaine, *f.*; — *adj.* de campagne, de plaine; plat; ouvert. — *country,* pays plat, pays ouvert, *m.*, rase campagne, *f.*

Champertor, *s.* acheteur de procès, *m.*

Champerty, *s.* achat de procès, *m.*

Champion, *s.* champion, *m.*; — *v.a.* défier, provoquer; soutenir, défendre

Championess, *s.* championne, *f.*

Championship, *s.* championnat, *m.*

Chance, *s.* chance, *f.*; hasard, *m.*; (*lot*) fortune, *f.*, sort, *m.*; (*law*) cas fortuit, *m.*; — *adj.* accidentel; fortuit; de (*or* du *or* au) hasard; imprévu, inattendu; (*at play*) de raccroc; — *v.n.* arriver par hasard, arriver; venir (à); se rencontrer, se trouver. *By —,* par hasard. *The main —,* le solide, *m.* *To — it,* risquer le paquet. *To look* (or *to have an eye*) *to the main —,* songer *or* viser au solide. *To take o.'s* (or *the*) *—,* courir la chance. *I chanced to meet him,* je le rencontrai par hasard

Chancel, *s.* parquet, *m.*; sanctuaire, *m.*

Chancellor, *s.* chancelier, *m.* *Lord —, Lord high —, High —,* (*in France*) ministre de la justice, *m.*, (*in England*) grand chancelier, *m.* — *of the Exchequer,* (*in France*) ministre des finances, *m.*, (*in England*) chancelier de l'Échiquier, *m.* [(*univers.*) chancellerie, *f.*

Chancellorship, *s.* dignité de chancelier, *f.*;

Chancery, *s.* chancellerie, cour de la chancellerie, *f.* *Master in —,* maître des requêtes à la cour de la chancellerie, *m.*

Chancre, *s.* chancre, *m.*

Chancrous, *adj.* chancreux [lustrier, *m.*

Chandelier, *s.* lustre, *m.* — **maker,** *s.*

Chandler, *s.* fabricant *or* marchand de chandelles (*or* de bougies), *m.*; (*workman*) ouvrier en chandelles, *m.*; (*generally*) marchand (de ...), *m.*; fournisseur (de ...), *m.*; approvisionneur (de ...), *m.* [denrées, *f.pl.*

Chandlery, *s.* chandellerie, *f.*; provisions,

Chanfrin, *s.* chanfrein, *m.*

Change, *v.a.* changer; (*quit*) changer de; — *v.n.* changer; (*be transformed into*) se changer (en); (*of the moon*) se renouveler; — *s.* changement, *m.*; vicissitude, *f.*; (*of money*) monnaie, *f.*; (*Exchange*) Bourse, *f.*; (*of the moon*) phase, *f.*, (*new moon*) nouvelle lune, *f.*; (*in ringing*) sonnerie, *f.*; (*linen*) linge blanc (pour changer), linge de rechange, *m.*; (*math.*) permutation, *f.* *For a —,* pour changer. *On —,* à la Bourse. *To ask, to have, to give — for,* demander, avoir, donner la monnaie de. *To be a gainer* or *a loser by the —, to gain* or *lose by the —,* gagner *or* perdre au change. *To ring the —s,* carillonner; (*fig.*) revenir toujours (sur), rabâcher, chanter (...) sur tous les tons. — **ringing,** *s.* carillon, *m.*; (*fig.*) rabâchage, *m.* — **step,** *s.* (*in drilling*) contre-pas, *m.*

Changeability. *V.* **Changeableness**

Changeable, *adj.* changeant, variable; muable; inconstant; (*susceptible of change*) changeable

Changeableness, *s.* caractère changeant *or* variable, *m.*, variabilité, mutabilité, mobilité, *f.*; humeur changeante, *f.*; inconstance, *f.*

Changeably, *adv.* variablement, d'une manière variable *or* changeante; muablement; inconstamment, avec inconstance

Changeful. *V.* **Changeable**

Changeless, *adj.* qui ne change pas, invariable, immuable, constant

Changeling, *s.* (*child*) enfant changé en nourrice, enfant substitué, *m.*; (*fool*) imbécile, idiot, *m.*; (*waverer*) homme changeant *or* inconstant, esprit changeant, *m.*, girouette, *f.*

Changer, *s.* changeur, *m.*, -euse, *f.*

Changing, *s.* changement, *m.*

Chank, — **shell,** *s.* turbinelle, *f.*

Channel, *s.* canal, *m.*; (*fig.*) voie, *f.*, moyen, *m.*, entremise, *f.*, canal, *m.*; (*of streams*) lit, *m.*; (*of harbours*) passe, *f.*; (*of roads*) rigole, *f.*; (*nav.*) détroit, *m.*; canal, *m.*; (*of a screw*) pas (de vis), *m.*; (*of a pulley*) gorge, *f.*; (*arch.*) cannelure, *f.*; — *v.a.* creuser, sillonner; (*arch.*) canneler. *The* (*British*) —, la Manche, *f.*, le Détroit, *m.* *The — Islands,* les Iles de la Manche, *f.pl.* *The Irish —,* le canal d'Irlande, *m.* *Saint George's —,* le canal de Saint-Georges, *m.*

Channelling, *s.* cannelure, *f.*

Chant, *v.a.n.* chanter; — *s.* chant, *m.*

Chanter, *s.* chantre, *m.*; chanteur, *m.*

Chanticleer, *s.* le réveille-matin, le coq, *m.*; (*in high poetry*) le chantre du jour, *m.*

Chanting, *s.* chant, *m.*; chants, *m.pl.*

Chantress, *s.* chanteuse, *f.*

Chantry, *s.* chapelle, *f.*

Chaos, *s.* chaos, *m.*

Chaotic, *adj.* chaotique, de chaos; confus

Chap, *v.a.* fendre, crevasser, gercer; — *v.n.* se fendre, se crevasser, se gercer; — *s.* fente, crevasse, gerçure, *f.*; (*jaw*) mâchoire, *f.*, (—**s,** *pl.*) bouche, gueule, *f.*; (*of pig*) bajoue, *f.*; (*fellow*) garçon, gaillard, individu, *m.* *Old —,* vieux bonhomme, vieux, *m.* — **book,** *s.* brochure, *f.* — **fallen,** *V.* **Chop**

Chapel, *s.* chapelle, *f.*; — *v.n.* (*nav.*) faire chapelle. — *of ease,* succursale, aide, annexe, chapelle auxiliaire, *f.* — **master,** *s.* maître de chapelle, *m.* [d'une chapelle, *f.*

Chapellany, Chapelry, *s.* circonscription

Chaperon, Chaperone, *s.* chaperon, *m.*; — *v.a.* chaperonner

Chaplain, *s.* chapelain, *m.*; (*of the court, regiments, ships, colleges,* &c.) aumônier, *m.*

Chaplaincy, Chaplainship, *s.* chapellenie, *f.*; aumônerie, *f.*

Chaplet, *s.* chapelet, *m.*; (*arch., rid., nav.*) chapelet, *m.*; (*garland, wreath*) chapeau de fleurs, chapeau, *m.*; (*of a peacock*) aigrette, *f.*

Chapman, *s.* marchand, *m.*

Chapter, *s.* chapitre, *m.* — **house,** *s.* chapitre, *m.*

Chapteral, *adj.* chapitral

Char, *s.* ouvrage à la journée, *m.*, journée, tâche, *f.*; (*fish*) *V.* **Charr;** — *v.a.* réduire en charbon, charbonner; carboniser; purifier; — *v.n.* se charbonner; (*of lamps*) charbonner; (*work*) travailler à la journée, aller en journée. — **woman,** *s.* femme de journée, femme de ménage, journalière, *f.* — **work,** *s.* ouvrage à la journée, *m.*

Character, *s.* caractère, *m.*; (*state*) rang, *m.*; (*part*) rôle, *m.*; (*capacity*) qualité, *f.*; (*person*)

personnage, *m.*; (*peculiar person*) type, *m.*; (*odd man*) original, *m.*; (*description*) portrait, tableau, *m.*, description, *f.*; (*reputation*) réputation, *f.*; honneur, *m.*; (*morality*) moralité, *f.*; (*sort, kind*) genre, *m.*; nature, *f.*; (*of servants*) certificat, *m.*; renseignements, *m.pl.* *Bad* —, (*pers.*) homme (*m.*, femme, *f.*, gens, *pl.*) de mauvaise vie; mauvais sujet, *m.* *In* —, dans son rôle, dans le vrai, naturel. *Of bad* —, (*pers.*) de mauvaise vie. *Out of* —, déplacé, sorti de son rôle. *To bear a good* or *bad* —, avoir (*or* jouir d') une bonne *or* mauvaise réputation

Characteristic, -al, *adj.* caractéristique; — *s.* signe *or* trait caractéristique, caractère distinctif, *m.*, marque distinctive, *f.*, caractère, (le) propre (de ...), *m.*; (*gram., math.*) caractéristique, *f.* [caractéristique

Characteristically, *adv.* d'une manière

Characteristicalness, *s.* nature caractéristique, *f.*; couleur locale, *f.*

Characterize, *v.a.* caractériser

Characterless, *adj.* sans caractère

Charade, *s.* charade, *f.*

Charcoal, *s.* charbon de bois, charbon, *m.* *Animal* —, noir animal, charbon animal, *m.* — **burner, -dealer, -man, -woman,** *s.* charbonnier, *m.*, -ière, *f.* — **dust,** *s.* poussier de charbon de bois, *m.*; fraisil, *m.* — **fire,** *s.* feu de charbon de bois, *m.* — **kiln, -pit,** *s.* charbonnière, *f.* [*beet*) carde-poirée, *f.*

Chard, *s.* (*foot-stalk, midrib*) carde, *f.*; (*white*

Charge, *v.a.* charger (de); (*as price for work, fee, commission*) prendre, demander, faire payer; (*for an article*) demander, faire payer; (*on a bill*) compter, faire payer; (*admin.*) taxer; imposer; grever; percevoir; faire payer; (*order*) ordonner (à), enjoindre (à); sommer (de); (*exhort*) exhorter (à); inviter (à); adjurer (de); (*accuse*) accuser (de); (*impute*) imputer (à); attribuer (à); (*book-keep.*) porter (à); porter au compte (de); (*a metal on another*) appliquer; (*a jury*) faire le résumé des causes *or* des débats à; — *v.n.* charger, faire une charge, attaquer; — *s.* charge, *f.*; (*care*) soin, *m.*; fardeau, *m.*; (*protection*) garde, *f.*; (*management*) direction, *f.*; (*deposit*) dépôt, *m.*; (*order*) ordre, *m.*, injonction, *f.*; (*imputation*) imputation, *f.*; (*accusation*) accusation, *f.*; (*law*) chef d'accusation, *m.*; (*of a judge*) réquisitoire, *m.*; résumé, *m.*; (*of a bishop*) mandement, *m.*; (*expenses*) frais, dépens, *m.pl.*; (*price*) prix, *m.*; (*admin.*) taxe, *f.*; (*of a metal on another*) pièce d'applique, *f.*; (*mil., paint., phys.*, &c.) charge, *f.*; (*her.*) pièce, *f.* *Common* —, (*her.*) meuble, *m.* *In* — *of*, à la charge de; aux soins de; à la garde de. *To bring a* — *against*, porter une accusation contre, accuser. *To give in* —, (*to the police*) faire arrêter, arrêter. *To take in* —, arrêter. *To take* — *of*, se charger de, avoir soin de. — **forward,** *v.a.* (*com.*) faire suivre en remboursement. — **sheet,** *s.* (*of police*) livre de consignation, *m.*

Chargeable, *adj.* à charge (à); à la charge (de); imputable (à); accusable (de); imposable; taxable; imposé, grevé, soumis (à)

Chargé d'affaires, *s.* chargé d'affaires, *m.*

Charger, *s.* cheval de bataille, *m.*; (*dish*) grand plat, bassin, *m.*

Charily, *adv.* soigneusement; avec précaution; avec circonspection, circonspectement; délicatement; sobrement, frugalement

Chariness, *s.* soin, *m.*; précaution, *f.*; circonspection, *f.*; sobriété, frugalité, *f.*

Chariot, *s.* chariot, char, *m.*; (*private*) coupé, *m.*; — *v.a.* conduire. — **race,** *s.* course de chars, *f.* [cocher, charretier, *m.*

Charioteer, *s.* conducteur, cocher, *m*; (*astr.*)

Charitable, *adj.* charitable; (*for a purpose of charity*) de charité; de bienfaisance. — *board,* bureau de bienfaisance, *m.* — *institution,* institution de charité, *f.*, établissement de bienfaisance, *m.* — *society,* société de bien-

Charitableness, *s.* charité, *f.* [faisance, *f.*

Charitably, *adv.* charitablement, d'une manière charitable

Charity, *s.* charité, *f.*; bienfaisance, *f.*; bienfait, *m.*; bienveillance, *f.*; (*alms*) aumône, *f.* *Sister of* —, sœur de charité, *f.* — *begins at home,* charité bien ordonnée commence par soi-même. — **school,** *s.* école de charité, *f.*

Charivari, *s.* charivari, *m.*

Charlatan, *s.* charlatan, *m.*, e, *f.* [latan

Charlatanical, *adj.* charlatanesque, de char-

Charlatanism, *s.* charlatanisme, *m.*

Charlatanry, *s.* charlatanerie, *f.*

Charlock, *s.* (*bot.*) sénevé, *m.*, sanve, *f.*; (*radish*) raifort sauvage, *m.*, ravenelle, *f.*

Charlotte, *s.* (*cook.*) charlotte, *f.* — *russe,* charlotte russe, *f.*

Charm, *s.* charme, *m.*; (*trinket*) breloque, *f.*; — *v.a.n.* charmer; enchanter

Charmer, *s.* charmeur, *m.*, -euse, *f.*, enchanteur, *m.*, -teresse, *f.* [*or* ravissante, à ravir

Charmingly, *adv.* d'une manière charmante

Charmless, *adj.* sans charme

Charnel, *s.* charnier, *m.*; — *adj.* de charnier. — **house,** *s.* charnier, *m.*

Charr, *s.* ombre-chevalier, *m.*

Charry, *adj.* charbonneux

Chart, *s.* carte, carte marine, *f.*

Charter, *s.* charte, *f.*; privilége, *m.*; (*law*) acte, *m.*; — *v.a.* établir par une charte; investir d'un privilége, privilégier; (*nav., to let*) fréter; (*nav., to hire*) affréter, noliser. — **house,** *s.* (*convent*) chartreuse, *f.* — **land,** *s.* tenure concédée par une charte, *f* — **party,** *s.* charte-partie, *f.* [teur, *m.*

Charterer, *s.* (*letter*) fréteur, *m.*; (*hirer*) affré-

Chartering, *s.* (*letting*) frètement, *m.*; (*hiring*) affrètement, *m.*

Chart-ism, -ist. *V.* page 3, § 1

Chartless, *adj.* sans carte

Chartographer, *s.* cartographe, *m.*

Chartography, *s.* cartographie, *f.*

Chartulary, *s.* cartulaire, *m.*

Charwoman, Charwork. *V.* **Char** [sobre

Chary, *adj.* soigneux; circonspect; économe,

Chase, *v.a.* chasser, donner la chasse à; poursuivre; (*metals*) ciseler; — *s.* chasse, *f.*; poursuite, *f.*; (*print.*) châssis, *m.*; (*of a cannon*) volée, *f.*; (*of a cross-bow*) coulisse, *f.*; (*chased ship*) chassé, *m.* — **away,** *v.a.* chasser, faire prendre la fuite. — **gun,** *s.* (*nav.*) canon de chasse, *m.*

Chaser, *s.* chasseur, *m.*; personne qui poursuit, *f.*; (*nav., gun*) canon de chasse, *m.*; (*nav., chasing ship*) chasseur, vaisseau chasseur, *m.*; (*of metals*) ciseleur, *m.*

Chasing, *s.* chasse, *f.*; poursuite, *f.*; (*of metals*) ciselure, *f.*; — *adj.* chasseur

Chasm, *s.* ouverture *f.*, vide, creux, *m.*; lacune, *f.*; abîme, gouffre, *m.*

Chasse, *s.* chasse, *f.*

Chassé, *s.* chassé, *m.*

Chasselas, *s.* chasselas, *m.*

Chasseur, *s.* chasseur, *m.*

Chassis, *s.* châssis, *m.*

Chaste, *adj.* chaste; pudique; (*of language*) pur. — **tree,** *s.* agnus-castus, gattilier, *m.*

Chastely, *adv.* chastement; pudiquement; (*of language*) purement [corriger

Chasten, *v.a.* purifier; réprimer; châtier;

Chastener, *s.* *V.* **Chastiser**

Chasteness, *s.* chasteté, *f.*; pureté, *f.*

Chastening, *s.* châtiment, *m.*

Chastisable, *adj.* châtiable, punissable

Chastise, *v.a.* châtier, punir

Chastisement, *s.* châtiment, *m.*

Chastiser, *s.* personne qui châtie, *f.*, châtieur, *m.*, correcteur, *m.*, -trice, *f.*, punisseur, *m.*

Chastity, *s.* chasteté, *f.*; (*of language*) pureté, *f.*

Chasuble, *s.* chasuble, *f.*

Chat, *v.n.* causer, jaser, s'entretenir; — *s.*

causerie, causette, *f.*, entretien, *m.*; (*bird*) traquet, *m.*, saxicole, *f.*; — *adj.* inférieur, menu, de rebut. *To have a* —, causer, jaser, faire la causette. — **potatoes,** *s. pl.* petites pommes de terre, pommes de terre de rebut, *f.pl.* — **wood,** *s.* menu bois, *m.*, bourrée, *f.*, ramilles, broutilles, *f.pl.*, fagotage, *m.*

Chatoyant, *adj.* chatoyant (*m.*, e, *f.*); — *s.* chatoyante, *f.*

Chatoyment, *s.* chatoiement, *m.*

Chattels, *s. pl.* biens, *m.pl.*; effets, *m.pl.*

Chatter, *v.n.* jaser, babiller, jacasser; (*of teeth*) claquer; — *s.* jaserie, *f.*; caquetage, caquet, babil, bavardage, *m.* — **box,** *s.* moulin à paroles, *m.*, jacasse, *f.*

Chatterer, *s.* jaseur, *m.*, -euse, *f.*, babillard, *m.*, e, *f.*; (*bird*) jaseur, *m.*

Chattering, *s.* jaserie, *f.*; caquetage, *m.*; (*of the teeth*) claquement, *m.*

Chatty, *adj.* causeur, causant; bavard

Chavender, *s.* chevanne, *f.*

Chawbacon. *V.* **Bumpkin**

Cheap, *adj.* à bon marché, bon marché; à bas prix, à bon compte; peu coûteux; économique; (*common*) de peu de valeur. *As — as dirt,* à vil prix, pour rien. *To hold* —, faire bon marché de. *To make* or *render oneself* —, se prodiguer; se décréditer, se déprécier

Cheapen, *v.a.* marchander; (*lessen in value*) diminuer la valeur de; (*lessen in price*) faire baisser de prix; (*discredit*) nuire à la considération de, décréditer

Cheapener, *s.* marchandeur, *m.*, -euse, *f.*

Cheaper, *adj.* (*comp. of* **Cheap**) à meilleur marché, meilleur marché, moins cher; à plus bas prix, à meilleur compte; moins coûteux; plus économique; (*more common*) de moindre valeur. — *and* —, de moins en moins cher; de plus en plus économique

Cheaply, *adv.* à bon marché; à bas prix, à bon compte; économiquement; (*with little expense*) à peu de frais

Cheapness, *s.* bon marché, bas prix, *m.*; (*little value*) peu de valeur, *m.*, vileté, *f.*

Cheat, *v.a.n.* tromper, duper, attraper, voler, filouter, flouer; (*at play*) tricher; — *s.* tromperie, fourberie, friponnerie, filouterie, flouerie, *f.*, (*at play*) tricherie, *f.*; (*pers.*) trompeur, *m.*, -euse, *f.*, fourbe, *m.f.*, fripon, *m.*, -ne, *f.*, filou, *m.*; (*at play*) tricheur, *m.*, -euse, *f.*

Cheater, *s. V.* **Cheat,** *s.* (*pers.*)

Cheating, *s.* tromperie, fourberie, friponnerie, filouterie, flouerie, *f.*; (*at play*) tricherie, *f.*; — *adj.* trompeur, fourbe, fripon; tricheur

Check, *v. a.* réprimer; arrêter, contenir; modérer; maîtriser; réprimander, reprendre, blâmer; contrôler, vérifier, examiner; (*names on a list*) pointer; (*to defeat*) faire éprouver un échec à; (*at chess*) faire échec à, mettre en échec; (*stuffs*, &c.) cadriller, quadriller; — *s.* échec, *m.*; obstacle, *m.*; réprimande, *f.*; (*blow*) coup, *m.*; (*curb*) frein, *m.* (‘*upon*,’ à); (*control*) contrôle, *m.*; (*at chess*) échec, *m.*; (*on stuffs*, &c.) carreau, *m.*; (*stuff itself*) étoffe à carreaux, étoffe cadrillée (*or* quadrillée), *f.*; (*mark*) marque, *f.*, point, *m.*; (*com., bank., admin.*) *V.* **Cheque.** *With —s*, à carreaux, cadrillé, quadrillé. *To hold* or *keep in* —, tenir en échec. — **book,** *s. V.* **Cheque.** — **mate,** *s.* échec et mat, *m.*; (*fig.*) défaite, *f.*; *v.a.* mater, faire échec et mat; (*fig.*) défaire; achever. — **rail,** *s.* (*rail.*) contre-rail, *m.* — **roll,** *s.* état de maison, *m.*; (*mil.*) contre-appel, *m.* — **string,** *s.* cordon, *m.* — **taker,** *s. V.* **Cheque**

Checked, *part. adj.* réprimé, &c. (*V.* **Check,** *v.a.*); (*of stuffs*, &c.) à carreaux, cadrillé, quadrillé

Checker, Checquer, *s.* (*pers.*) contrôleur, *m.*, -euse, *f.*; (*checker-work*) *See below*; (*check*) carreau, *m.*; —**s,** *pl.* carreaux, *m.pl.*, &c.; (*draughts*) dames, *f.pl.*; — *v.a.* marqueter; (*stuffs*, &c.) cadriller, quadriller; (*variegate*) bigarrer, nuancer, varier, diversifier; (*mix*) mélanger. — **board,** *s.* damier, *m.* — **wise,** *adv.* en échiquier. — **work,** *s.* échiquier, *m.*; cadrillage, quadrillage, *m.*, carreaux, *m.pl.*; marqueterie, *f.*

Checkered, Checquered, *part. adj.* marqueté, &c. (*V.* **Checker,** *v.a.*); échiqueté; à carreaux, cadrillé, quadrillé; varié; plein d'accidents. accidenté. — **work,** *s. V.* [**Checker-work**

Checky, *adj.* échiqueté

Cheek, *s.* joue, *f.*; (*of pigs*) bajoue, *f.*; (*of a door*) feuillure, *f.*; (*of a bridle-bit*) branche, *f.*; (*of a press*, &c.) jumelle, *f.*; (*artil.*) flasque, *m.*; (*fam.*) impudence, *f.*, front, toupet, *m.*; —**s,** *pl.* joues, *f.pl.*, &c.; (*of a balance*) châsse, *f.* — *by jowl*, côte à côte, tête à tête; (*fig.*) amis comme cochons. — **bone,** *s.* pommette, *f.* *To have high — bones*, avoir les pommettes saillantes. — **pouch,** *s.* abajoue, *f.* — **tooth,** *s.* dent molaire, *f.*

Cheeked, *adj.* aux joues ...

Cheeky, *adj.* impudent; hardi; peu gêné

Cheer, (— up) *v.a.* réjouir; égayer, dérider; animer, ranimer, encourager; consoler; rassurer; applaudir, acclamer, saluer par des acclamations; — *v.n.* se réjouir; se dérider; se ranimer, prendre courage; se consoler; se rassurer; pousser des acclamations *or* des vivats; — *s.* gaieté, *f.*; courage, *m.*; consolation, *f.*; acclamation, *f.*, applaudissement, vivat, hourra, *m.*; (*food*) chère, *f.*; —**s,** *s. pl.* (*in reports of speeches*) marques d'approbation, *f.pl.* *To be of good* —, avoir bon courage, prendre courage, ne pas perdre courage. — *up!* courage!

Cheerer, *s.* acclamateur, *m.*, -trice, *f.*, applaudisseur, *m.*, -euse, *f.*; celui qui (*or* ce qui) réjouit *or* &c. (*V.* **Cheer,** *v.a.*)

Cheerful, *adj.* gai, joyeux; (*ready*) de bon cœur

Cheerfully, *adv.* gaiment, joyeusement; (*readily*) de bon cœur, avec plaisir

Cheerfulness, *s.* gaieté, joie, bonne humeur, *f.*, contentement, *m.*

Cheerily, *adv.* gaiment

Cheering, *s.* acclamations, *f.pl.*, applaudissements, vivats, hourras, *m.pl.*

Cheerless, *adj.* triste, sombre, morne

Cheery, *adj.* gai, joyeux, réjoui; égayant, réjouissant

Cheese, *s.* fromage, *m.* — **cake,** *s.* talmouse, *f.* — **curds,** *s. pl.* lait caillé, *m.*, caillebotte, *f.* — **dairy,** *s.* fromagerie, *f.* — **dish,** *s. V.* **tray.** — **factor,** *s.* facteur à la halle au fromage, *m.* — **frame,** *s. V.* **mould.** — **knife,** *s.* couteau à fromage, *m.* — **loft,** *s.* magasin à fromage, *m.* — **maker,** *s.* fromager, *m.*, -ère, *f.*, fromagier, *m.*, -ière, *f.* — **making,** *s.* fabrication du fromage, *f.* — **market,** *s.* fromagerie, *f.* — **mite,** *s.* acarus, *m.* — **monger,** *s.* marchand (*m.*, e, *f.*) de fromage, fromager, *m.*, -ère, *f.* — **mould,** *s.* moule à fromages, fromager, caserel, *m.*, caserette, *f.*; (*mouldiness*) moissure de fromage, *f.* — **paring,** *s.* pelure de fromage, *f.* — **paring economy,** *s.* (*fig.*) économie de bouts de chandelles, *f.* — **press,** *s.* presse à fromage, *f.* — **rennet,** *s.* caille-lait, gaillet, *m.* — **rind,** *s.* pelure de fromage, *f.* — **room,** *s.* fromagerie, *f.* — **scoop,** *s.* couteau à fromage, *m.* — **shop,** *s.* fromagerie, *f.* — **stand,** *s.* jatte à fromage, *f.* — **taster,** *s.* sonde à fromage, *f.* — **trade,** *s.* commerce de fromages, *m.*, fromagerie, *f.* — **tray,** *s.* plat à fromage, porte-fromage, *m.* — **vat,** *s.* éclisse à fromage, *f.*

Cheesy, *adj.* fromageux, caséeux

Cheetah, *s.* guépard, *m.*

Cheffonier, *s.* chiffonnier, *m.*

Cheiromancy, &c. *V.* **Chiromancy**

Cheiropter, *s.* chiroptère, *m.*

Chelifer, *s.* chélifère, porte-pince, *m.*

Chelonian, *s.* chélonien, *m.*

Chemic, -al, *adj.* chimique; de chimie; — *s.* produit chimique, *m.* — **works,** *s. pl.* fabrique de produits chimiques, *f.*
Chemically, *adv.* chimiquement
Chemise, *s.* chemise (de femme), *f.*; (*mas., fort.*) chemise, *f.*
Chemisette, *s.* chemisette, *f.*
Chemist, *s.* chimiste, *m.*; (*apothecary*) pharmacien, *m.* *Scientific* —, chimiste, *m.* *Pharmaceutical* or *dispensing* —, — *and druggist*, pharmacien, *m.* *Manufacturing* —, fabricant de produits chimiques, *m.* *V.* **Analytical.** —**'s shop,** pharmacie, *f.*
Chemistry, *s.* chimie, *f.*
Chenille, *s.* chenille, *f.*
Cheque, *s.* mandat, bon, *m.*; ordre, *m.*; coupon, *m.*; (*bank.*) chèque, *m.*; (*ticket*) bulletin, *m.*, (*theat.*, &c.) contre-marque, *f.*; (*of French omnibuses*) bulletin de correspondance, *m.*; correspondance, *f.* — **book,** *s.* carnet de chèques, *m.* — **taker,** *s.* contrôleur, *m.*; donneur de contre-marques, *m.* — **ticket,** *s.* [contre-marque, *f.*
Chequer. *V.* **Checker**
Cheriff, *s.* chérif, *m.*
Cherish, *v.a.* chérir; protéger, favoriser; (*nurse*) soigner, avoir soin de; (*entertain*) entretenir, nourrir, soutenir, (*a hope*) nourrir
Cheroot, *s.* bout coupé, *m.* *Manilla* —, manille à bout coupé, *m.*
Cherry, *s.* (*fruit*) cerise, *f.*; (*wild ditto*) merise, *f.*; (*colour*) cerise, *m.*; (*wood*) merisier, cerisier, *m.*; (*tree*) cerisier, *m.*, (*wild ditto*) merisier, *m.*; (*wine*) vin de cerise, *m.*; — *adj.* de cerise; de cerisier; (*of wood*) de *or* en merisier, de *or* en cerisier; (*of colour*) cerise, de couleur cerise, vermeil. — **bay,** *s.* laurier-cerise, *m.* — **bob,** *s.* bouquet de deux cerises, passe-passe, *m.* — **brandy,** *s.* ratafia de cerise, *m.* — **cheeked,** *adj.* aux joues vermeilles. — **colour,** *s.* couleur cerise, *f.*, cerise, *m.* — **coloured,** *adj.* de couleur cerise, couleur cerise, cerise. — **garden,** *s.* cerisaie, *f.* — **house,** *s.* serre à cerisiers, *f.* — **laurel,** *s.* laurier-cerise, *m.* — **laurel water,** *s.* eau de laurier-cerise, *f.* — **orchard,** *s.* cerisaie, *f.* — **pie,** *s.* tourte aux cerises, *f.* — **pit,** *s.* fossette, *f.* — **red,** *adj. s.* rouge cerise. — **stone,** *s.* noyau de cerise, *m.* — **tree,** *s.* cerisier, *m.*; (*wild*) merisier, *m.* — **water,** *s.* eau de cerise, *f.* — **wine,** *s.* vin de cerise, *m.* — **wood,** *s.* merisier, cerisier, *m.*
Chersonese, Chersonesus, *s.* chersonèse, *f.*
Chert, *s.* cornéenne, *f.*
Cherub, *s.* chérubin, *m.* [chérubins
Cherubic, *adj.* chérubique, de chérubin, de
Cherubim, *s. pl.* chérubins, *m.pl.*
Cherup. *V.* **Chirrup**
Chervil, *s.* cerfeuil, *m.* [Chester, *m.*
Cheshire, — **cheese,** *s.* chester, fromage de
Chesnut. *V.* **Chestnut**
Chess, *s.* échecs, *m.pl.* — **apple,** *s.* alise, *f.*; (*tree*) alisier, *m.* — **board,** *s.* échiquier, *m.* — **man,** *s.* pièce (aux échecs), *f.* *A set of* — *men*, un jeu d'échecs, *m.* — **player,** *s.* joueur (*m.*, -euse, *f.*) d'échecs. — **playing,** *s.* le jeu des échecs, *m.*, les échecs, *m.pl.* — **table,** *s.* table à échiquier, *f.*
Chest, *s.* (*box*) coffre, *m.*; caisse, boîte, *f.*; (*small*) coffret, *m.*; (*pers.*) poitrine, *f.*; torse, *m.*; (*of horses*) poitrail, *m.* — *of drawers*, commode, *f.* — **disease,** *s.* maladie de poitrine, *f.* — **foundered,** *adj.* courbatu. — **foundering,** *s.* courbature, *f.* — **protector,** [*s.* plastron, *m.*
Chested, *adj.* à poitrine
Chestnut, *s.* châtaigne, *f.*; marron, *m.*; (— *tree*, — *wood*) *See below*; — *adj.* de châtaigne; (*of the tree*) de châtaignier; (*of wood*) de *or* en châtaignier; (*of colour*) châtain, (*speaking of horses*) alezan. — **colour,** *s.* châtain, *m.* — **grove, -plantation,** *s.* châtaigneraie, *f.* — **tree,** — **wood,** *s.* châtaignier, *m.*; marron- [nier, *m.*
Chetah, *V.* **Cheetah**

Cheval, *s.* (*frame*) chevalet, *m.* — **-de-frise,** *s.* cheval de frise, *m.* — **dressing-glass,** — **glass,** *s.* psyché, *f.* — **screen,** *s.* écran de [cheminée, *m.*
Chevalier, *s.* chevalier, *m.*
Chevaliere, *s.* chevalière, *f.*
Chevaux-de-frise, *s.pl.* chevaux de frise, *m.pl.*
Cheven, Chevin, *s.* chevanne, *f.*
Cheveril, *s.* chevrotin, chevreau, *m.*
Chevrette, *s.* chevrette, *f.*
Chevron, *s.* chevron; — *v.a.* chevronner. — **work,** *s.* chevronnage, *m.*
Chevrotain, *s.* chevrotain, *m.*
Chevy, *v.a.* ballotter; bousculer
Chew, *v.a.n.* mâcher; (*tobacco*) chiquer; (*fig.*) ruminer, méditer
Chewing, *s.* mastication, *f.*; (*fig.*) méditation, *f.*
Chian, *adj.* de Chio, de Chios, de Scio
Chiaro-oscuro, Chiaroscuro, *s.* clair-obscur, *m.* [*m.*, chibouque, *m.f.*
Chibouk, Chibouque, *s.* chibouck, chibouk,
Chicane, *s.* chicane, *f.*; — *v.n.* chicaner
Chicaner, *s.* chicaneur, *m.*, -euse, *f.*, chicanier, *m.*, -ière, *f.*
Chicanery, *s.* chicanerie, chicane, *f.*
Chicaning, *adj.* chicaneur, chicanier
Chick, *s.* poussin, *m.*; (*pers.*) poulet, *m.*, poulette, *f.*; — *v.n.* germer. — **pea,** *s.* pois chiche, *m.* — **room,** *s.* poussinière, *f.* — **weed,** *s.* mouron, *m.*
Chickabiddy, *s.* cocote, *f.*
Chicken, *s.* poulet, *m.* *Don't count your* —*s before they are hatched*, il ne faut pas vendre la peau de l'ours avant de l'avoir tué. — **bone,** *s.* os de poulet, *m.* — **broth,** *s.* bouillon de poulet, *m.* — **coop,** *s.* poussinière, *f.* — **hearted,** *adj.* timide, poltron, lâche. — **pox,** *s.* petite vérole volante, *f.*
Chickling, *s.* poussin, *m.* — **vetch,** *s.* gesse, *f.*
Chicoraceous, *adj.* chicoracé
Chicory, *s.* chicorée, *f.* — **colour,** *s.* chicorée, *m.* — **coloured,** *adj.* chicorée, *m.f.*
Chide, *v.a.* gronder, réprimander, gourmander; blâmer; — *v.n.* gronder; murmurer (contre); — *s.* murmure, *m.*
Chider, *s.* grondeur, *m.*, -euse, *f.*
Chiding, *adj.* grondeur; — *s.* gronderie, *f.*
Chidingly, *adv.* en grondant
Chief, *s.* chef, *m.*; (*of things*) partie principale, plus grande partie, *f.*; (*her., of a shield*) chef, *m.*; — *adj.* premier, principal; plus grand; suprême; (*leading*) en chef; — *adv.* principalement, surtout. *In* —, en chef
Chiefdom, *s.* souveraineté, *f.*
Chiefless, *adj.* sans chef
Chiefly, *adv.* principalement, surtout
Chiefship, *s.* *V.* **Chieftainship**
Chieftain, *s.* chef, *m.*
Chieftaincy, Chieftainry, Chieftainship, *s.* fonctions (*f.pl.*) *or* dignité (*f.*) *or* rang (*m.*) de chef
Chiffchaff, *s.* grand pouillot, *m.*
Chiffonier, Chiffonnier, *s.* chiffonnier, *m.*
Chignon, *s.* chignon, *m*
Chigoe, Chigre, *s.* chique, *f.*
Chilblain, *s.* engelure, *f.*
Child, *s.* enfant, *m.f.* *From a* —, depuis son enfance; dès l'enfance. *With* —, enceinte, grosse. *To be gone with* —, être enceinte, être grosse. *To be a good, a naughty* —, être sage, méchant. *To be past a* —, n'être plus un enfant. *To get with* —, faire un enfant à. *A burnt* — *dreads the fire*, (*Proverb*) chat échaudé craint l'eau froide. — **bearing,** *s.* travail d'enfant, *m.*, grossesse, *f.* — **bed,** *s.* couches, *f.pl.* — **bed linen,** *s.* layette, *f.* — **birth,** *s.* enfantement, accouchement, *m.* —**ermas day,** *s.* la fête des Innocents, *f.* — **hood,** *s.* enfance, *f.* —**ish,** *adj.* enfant; (*things*) enfantin, d'enfant; (*trifling*) puéril. *To be* —*ish*, (*pers.*) être enfant; (*to play the child*) faire l'enfant. *To get* or *grow* —*ish*, (*of old people*) tomber en enfance. —**ishly,** *adv.* comme un

enfant, d'une manière enfantine; puérilement. —**ishness,** *s.* enfantillage, *m.*; puérilité, *f.*; (*infancy*) enfance, *f.* —**less,** *adj.* sans enfants — **like,** *adj.* comme un enfant, d'enfant, de l'enfance. — **murder,** — **murderer,** *s.* infanticide, *m.* — **murderess,** *s.* infanticide, *f.* —**'s play,** *s.* jeu d'enfant, *m.*; amusette, *f.*; enfantillage, *m.* — **stealing,** *s.* vol d'enfant (*or* d'enfants), *m.*

Chiliad, *s.* chiliade, *f.*

Chilian, *s.* Chilien, *m.*, -ne, *f.*; — *adj.* chilien, [du Chili

Chill, *s.* froid, *m.*; refroidissement, *m.*; frisson, *m.*; sentiment de tristesse, *m.*; — *adj.* froid, glacé; découragé, abattu; — *v.a.* refroidir; transir de froid, transir; glacer, geler; faire frissonner; décourager, abattre; — *v.n.* se glacer. *Cold* —*s*, frisson, *m.* *To take the* — *off* (*liquids*), faire dégourdir

Chilled, *part. adj.* refroidi, transi, saisi par le froid, &c. (*V.* **Chill,** *v.a.*); (*paint.*) embu, poussé

Chilli, Chillies, *s.* poivre de Guinée, *m.*

Chilliness, Chillness, *s.* frisson, *m.*; frissonnement, *m.*; froid, *m.*; froideur, *f.*

Chillingly, *adv.* froidement

Chilly, *adj.* (*pers.*) frileux; (*things*) froid, un peu froid; — *s.* *V.* **Chilli**

Chime, *s.* accord de sons, concert, *m.*; (*fig.*) accord, *m.*, harmonie, *f.*; (— *of bells*) carillon, *m.*; — *v.n.* résonner en harmonie; (*of bells*) carillonner; (*agree*) s'accorder (avec); faire chorus (avec); — *v.a.* faire résonner avec harmonie; (*bells*) mettre en mouvement, battre, [carillonner

Chimer, *s.* carillonneur, *m.*

Chimera, *s.* chimère, *f.*

Chimerical, *adj.* chimérique

Chimerically, *adv.* chimériquement

Chiming, *s.* *V.* **Chime,** *s.*; (*of bells*) carillonnement, *m.*

Chimney, *s.* cheminée, *f.*; (*of a lamp*) verre, *m.*, cheminée, *f.* — *on fire*, feu de cheminée, *m.* — **board,** *s.* devant de cheminée, *m.* — **corner,** *s.* coin de cheminée, *m.*; (*fig.*) coin du feu, *m.* — **cowl,** *s.* tabourin, *m.*, église, gueule-de-loup, *f.* — **doctor,** *s.* fumiste, *m.* — **flue,** *s.* tuyau de cheminée, *m.* — **glass,** *s.* glace de cheminée, *f.* — **holder,** *s.* (*of a lamp*) porte-verre, *m.*, couronne, *f.*, coulant, *m.* — **hook,** *s.* crémaillère, *f.* — **ornament,** *s.* ornement de cheminée, *m.* *Set of* — *ornaments*, garniture de cheminée, *f.* — **piece,** *s.* cheminée, *f.*; (*build.*) chambranle de cheminée, chambranle, *m.* — **pot,** *s.* mitre de cheminée, cheminée, *f.*; (*hat*) tuyau de poêle, *m.* — **shaft,** *s.* tuyau de cheminée, *m.* — **side,** *s.* *V.* — **corner.** — **stack,** *s.* corps de cheminée, *m.* — **stalk,** *s.* tuyau de cheminée, *m.* — **swallow,** *s.* hirondelle de cheminée, *f.* — **sweeper** *or* **sweep,** *s.* ramoneur de cheminées, ramoneur, *m.* — **sweeping,** *s.* ramonage de cheminées, ramonage, *m.* — **sweeping machine,** *s.* hérisson, ramon, *m.* — **top,** *s.* mitre (*f.*) *or* faîte (*m.*) de cheminée; (*mantelpiece*) *V.* **Mantlepiece**

Chimpanzee, *s.* chimpanzé, *m.*

Chin, *s.* menton, *m.* — **band, -cloth, -piece,** *s.* mentonnière, *f.* — **cough,** *s.* coqueluche, *f.* — **strap,** *s.* mentonnière, *f.*; (*mil.*) jugulaire, *f.*

China, *s.* la Chine, *f.*; (*ware*) porcelaine, *f.*; porcelaine de Chine, *f.* —**aster,** *s.* reine-marguerite, *f.* — **clay,** *s.* terre (*or* argile) à porcelaine, *f.*, kaolin, *m.* — **dealer,** *s.* marchand (*m.*, e, *f.*) de porcelaine. — **grass,** *s.* mâ, china-grass, *m.* — **grass plant,** *s.* ramie, *f.* — **ink,** *s.* encre de Chine, *f.* — **man,** *s.* Chinois, *m.*; (*ship*) navire qui fait le commerce avec la Chine, *m.*; (*obsolete for* — *dealer*) *V.* — **dealer.** — **orange,** *s.* orange de la Chine, orange douce, *f.* — **painter,** *s.* peintre sur porcelaine, *m.* — **painting,** *s.* peinture sur porcelaine, *f.* — **rose,** *s.* rose de la Chine, *f.* — **root,** *s.* squine, *f.* — **shop,** *s.* boutique (*f.*) *or* magasin (*m.*) de porcelaine. — **stone,** *s.* pétunsé, *m.* — **ware.** *s.* porcelaine

Chinchilla, *s.* chinchilla, *m.* — **colour,** — **fur,** *s.* chinchilla, *m.* [— **piece,** *s.* échinée, *f.*

Chine, *s.* (*anat.*) échine, *f.*; (*of pork*) échinée, *f.*

Chinese, *s.* Chinois, *m.*, e, *f.*; (*language*) le chinois, *m.*, la langue chinoise, *f.*; — *adj.* chinois, de Chine, de la Chine. — **bells,** *s. pl.* chapeau chinois, *m.* — **figure,** *s.* magot de la Chine, *m.*, chinoiserie, *f.* — **grass,** — **ink,** &c. *V.* **China**

Chink, *s.* fente, crevasse, *f.*; (*sound*) tintement, son, *m.*; (*cash*) pécune, *f.*; — *v.a.* fendre, crevasser; (*jingle*) faire sonner; — *v.n.* se fendre, se crevasser; sonner

Chinky, *adj.* fendu, crevassé

Chinned, *adj.* à menton

Chintz, *s.* perse, *f.*; cretonne, *f.*

Chip, *v.a.* couper; tailler, hacher; écorner; — *v.n.* (— **off**) s'éclater, éclater; s'écorner; (*of china*, &c.) s'écailler; — *s.* (*of wood*) copeau, *m.*; (*of stone*) éclat, fragment, *m.*; petit morceau, petit bout, *m.*; (*disease in birds*) pépie, *f.* *A* — *in porridge*, un cautère sur une jambe de bois. *To be a* — *of the old block*, chasser de race, tenir de famille, être bien fils de son père. — **axe,** *s.* doloire, *f.* — **box,** *s.* boîte en copeau, *f.* — **hat,** *s.* chapeau-latanier, chapeau brésilien, *m.*

Chipping, *s.* éclat, fragment, *m.*; écornure, *f.*; épaufrure, *f.*; (*of china*, &c.) écaille, *f.*

Chiragra, *s.* chiragre, *f.*

Chiragrical, *adj.* chiragrique; (*pers.*) chiragre

Chirolog-ic, -y. *V.* page 3, § 1

Chiromancer, *s.* chiromancien, *m.*, -ne, *f.*

Chiroman-cy, -tic. *V.* page 3, § 1

Chiroplast, *s.* guide-main, chiroplaste, *m.*

Chiropodist, *s.* pédicure, *m.f.*

Chirp, Chirrup, *v.n.* gazouiller; chanter; (*of larks*) chanter, grisoller; (*of insects*) crier; chanter

Chirp, Chirping, Chirrup, *s.* gazouillement, ramage, *m.*; chant, *m.*; (*of insects*) cri, *m.*; chant, *m.*

Chirurgical, &c. *V.* **Surgical,** &c.

Chisel, *s.* ciseau, *m.*; — *v.a.* ciseler; (*cheat*) filouter, flibuster, carotter, enfoncer, affûter

Chiselling, *s.* ciselure, *f.*; (*cheating*) filouterie, *f.*

Chit, *s.* germe, *m.*; (*child*) bambin, *m.*, e, *f.*, marmot, mioche, môme, moutard, gamin, *m.*, enfant, *m.f.*; — *v.n.* germer. — **chat,** *s.* causerie, *f.*; (*tattle*) babil, caquet, *m.*

Chittah. *V.* **Cheetah**

Chitterlings, *s.pl.* boyaux, *m.pl.*, tripes, *f.pl.*; [(*sausage*) andouille, *f.*

Chivalric, Chivalrous, *adj.* chevaleresque; de chevalerie

Chivalrously, *adv.* chevaleresquement

Chivalry, *s.* chevalerie, *f.*

Chives, *s. pl.* ciboulette, civette, *f.*

Chlamyphore, Chlamyphorus, *s.* chlamyphore, *m.*

Chlamys, *s.* chlamyde, *f.*

Chloral, Chloralum, *s.* chloral, *m.*

Chlorate, *s.* chlorate, *m.*

Chlorhydric, *adj.* chlorhydrique

Chloric, *adj.* chlorique

Chloridate, *v.a.* chlorurer

Chloride, *s.* chlorure, *m.*

Chloridize, *v.a.* chlorurer

Chlorinate, *v.a.* chlorer

Chlorine, *s.* chlore, *m.*

Chlorodyne, *s.* chlorodine, *f.*

Chloroform, *s.* chloroforme, *m.*; — *v.a.* chloroformer. *To administer* — *to*, chloroformer

Chlorometer, *s.* chloromètre, *m.*

Chlorometr-ic, -y, chlorométrique, &c. (*V.* page 3, § 1)

Chlorosis, *s.* chlorose, *f.*, pâles couleurs, *f.pl.*

Chlorotic, *adj.* chlorotique

Chlorous, *adj.* chloreux

Chocolate, *s.* chocolat, *m.* — **almonds,** *s.pl.* chocolat praliné, *m.* — **colour,** *s.* couleur chocolat, *f.* — **coloured,** *adj.* de couleur chocolat. — **cracker,** *s.* diablotin, *m.* — **custard,** *s.* crème au chocolat, *f.* — **dealer,** *s.* chocolatier, *m.*, -ière, *f.* — **drop,** *s.* pastille de chocolat, *f.* — **maker, -manufacturer,**

s. chocolatier, *m.*, -ière, *f.* — **making, -manufacture,** *s.* chocolaterie, *f.* — **nut,** *s.* cacao, *m.* — **pot,** *s.* chocolatière, *f.* — **stick,** *s.* moussoir, *m.* *Stick of* —, bâton de chocolat, *m.* — **trade,** *s.* chocolaterie, *f.*
Choice, *s.* choix, *m.*; (*pers.*) élite, *f.*; (*things*) meilleur, plus beau; — *adj.* choisi, de choix; beau; exquis; précieux; (*of wine*) fin; (*pers.*) d'élite; scrupuleux dans le choix, difficile sur le choix; économe, soigneux. *To take o.'s* —, choisir. *To have Hobson's* —, n'avoir pas le choix
Choiceless, *adj.* qui n'a pas le choix
Choicely, *adv.* avec choix, avec goût, avec soin, délicatement
Choiceness, *s.* heureux choix, choix, *m.*; excellence, supériorité, *f.*; délicatesse, *f.*
Choir, *s.* chœur, *m.* — **desk,** *s.* lutrin, *m.* — **master,** *s.* maître de chœur, maître de chapelle, chantre, *m.* — **organ,** *s.* positif, *m.* — **service,** *s.* service en musique, *m.*
Choke, *v.a.n.* (— **up**) suffoquer, étouffer; étrangler; (*obstruct*) engorger, boucher, encombrer; (*be obstructed*) s'engorger, se boucher, s'encombrer; — *s.* foin, *m.* — **damp,** *s.* moufette, *f.* — **full,** *adj.* tout plein, plein comme un œuf. — **pear,** *s.* poire d'angoisse, *f.*
Choker, *s.* (*pers.*) étouffeur, *m.*, -euse, *f.*; étrangleur, *m.*, -euse, *f.*; (*neck-tie*) cravate, *f.*
Choking, *s.* suffocation, *f.*, étouffement, *m.*; étranglement, *m.*; (*of things*) engorgement, encombrement, *m.*; — *adj.* *V.* **Choky**
Choky, *adj.* suffocant, étouffant
Choler, *s.* bile, *f.*; colère, *f.* *Black* —, atrabile, *f.*
Cholera, *s.* choléra, *m.*; — *adj.* du *or* de choléra, cholérique. — **patient,** *s.* cholérique, *m.f.*
Choleraic, *adj.* cholérique, du *or* de choléra
Choleric, *adj.* cholérique, bilieux; (*of anger*) colérique; de colère
Cholerine, *s.* cholérine, *f.*
Cholesterine, *s.* cholestérine, *f.*
Chondrine, *s.* chondrine, *f.*
Choose, *v.a.* choisir; élire; — *v.n.* vouloir; préférer; se décider (à); (*please*) *V.* **Please**
Chooser, *s.* personne qui choisit, *f.*
Choosing, *s.* choix, *m.*
Chop, *v.a.n.* hacher, couper, fendre; (*to truck*) troquer, trafiquer, brocanter; (*altercate*) disputer; (*of the wind*) changer, tourner; (*of the sea*) clapoter. — *and change*, troquer, échanger, changer, brocanter. — **off,** trancher, couper. — **up,** hacher; dévorer
Chop, *s.* côtelette, *f.*; (*jaw*) mâchoire, *f.*; (*barter*) troc, *m.*; (*nav., short wave*) clapot, *m.*; —**s,** *pl.* côtelettes, *f.pl.*; (*jaws*) mâchoires, *f.pl.*; (*mouth*) bouche, gueule, *f.* — *and change*, troc, *m.*; veine et déveine, *f.*, vicissitude, *f.* *To lick o.'s* —*s*, se lécher les babouines. — **fallen,** *adj.* à mâchoire tombante; (*fig.*) abattu; penaud. — **house,** *s.* restaurant, *m.*; gargote, *f.* — **stick,** *s.* aiguille, baguette, *f.*, petit bâton, bâtonnet, *m.*
Chopper, *s.* couperet, *m.*
Chopping, *s.* coupe, *f.*; (*bartering*, — *and changing*) troc, trafic, échange, brocantage, *m.*; (*wrangling*) discussion, dispute, *f.*; (*nav.*) clapotage, clapotement, *m.*; — *adj.* (*pers.*) gros et gras, gros, boulot; (*of the sea*) clapoteux; (*of the wind*) variable. — **board,** *s.* hachoir, *m.* — **block,** *s.* billot, *m.* — **knife,** *s.* couperet, *m.*
Choragic, *adj.* *V.* page 3, § 1
Choral, *adj.* choral; de chœur; en chœur. — *society*, — *union*, société chorale, *f.*, orphéon, *m.* — *singing*, — *music*, orphéon, *m.* — *singer*, orphéoniste, *m.f.*
Choral, Chorale, *s.* choral, *m.*
Choralist, *s.* choriste. *m.f.*
Chorally, *adv.* en chœur
Chord, *s.* (*of mus. instr.*) corde, *f.*; (*mus.*) accord, *m.*; (*geom.*) corde, *f.*; — *v.a.* garnir de cordes, mettre des cordes à
Chorea, *s.* chorée, *f.*
Choregraphy, &c., chorégraphie, &c. (*V.* page 3, § 1)
Chorist, *s.* choriste, *m.f.*
Chorister, *s.* chantre, *m.*; choriste, *m.f.*
Chorographer, *s.* chorographe, *m.*
Chorograph-ic,al,-ically,-y. *V.* page 3, § 1
Choroid, *adj. s.* choroïde, *adj. m.f.*, *s.f.*
Chorus, *s.* chœur, *m.*; (*fig.*) concert, *m.*
Chosen, *adj.* choisi, de choix, d'élite; (*theol.*) élu
Chough, *s.* choucas, *m.*
Chouse, *v.a.* attraper, carotter; — *s.* attrape, carotte, *f.*
Chrestomathy, *s.* chrestomathie, *f.*
Chrism, *s.* chrême, *m.* — **cloth,** *s.* chrémeau, *m.*
Christen, *v.a.* baptiser; (*fig.*) baptiser; baptiser du nom de, appeler
Christendom, *s.* chrétienté, *f.*
Christening, *s.* baptême, *m.*
Christian, *s. adj.* chrétien, *m.*, -ne, *f.* — *friend*, ami, frère en Jésus-Christ, *m.* *V.* **Burial** *and* **Name**
Christianity, *s.* christianisme, *m.*
Christianization, *s.* christianisation, *f.*
Christianize, *v.a.* christianiser
Christianlike, Christianly, *adj.* chrétien, de chrétien, en chrétien
Christianly, *adv.* chrétiennement, en chrétien
Christmas, *s.* Noël, *m.*; la fête de Noël, la Noël, *f.*; — *adj.* de Noël. — **box, -present,** *s.* étrennes, *f.pl.* — **card,** *s.* carte du jour de Noël, *f.*; (*in France*) carte du jour de l'an, *f.* — **carol,** *s.* noël, cantique *or* chant de Noël, *m.* — **day,** *s.* le jour de Noël, *m.*, la fête de Noël, *f.* — **eve,** *s* la veille de Noël, *f.* — **gift,** *s.* étrennes, *f.pl.* — **gift-book,** *s.* livre d'étrennes, *m.* — **holidays,** *s. pl.* fêtes de Noël, *f.pl.*; (*vacation*) vacances de Noël, *f.pl.* — **log,** *s.* bûche de Noël, *f.* — **party,** *s.* réunion de Noël, *f.* — **tree,** *s.* arbre de Noël, *m.*
Chromate, *s.* chromate, *m.*
Chromat-ic, al, *adj.* **-ically,** *adv.* *V.* page 3, § 1
Chromatic, *s.* chromatique, *m.*; —**s,** *pl.* chromatique, *f.*
Chrome, Chromium, *s.* chrôme, *m.*
Chromic, *adj.* chromique
Chromo-, (*in compounds*) chromo- ...
Chromolithograph, *s.* chromolithographie, *f.*; — *v.a.* chromolithographier
Chromolithographer, *s.* chromolithographe, *m.*
Chromolithographic, *adj.* chromolithographique, de chromolithographie; (*of pers.*) chromolithographe
Chromolithography, *s.* chromolithographie, *f.*
Chron-ic, al, -ically. *V.* page 3, § 1
Chronicity, *s.* chronicité, *f.*
Chronicle, *s.* chronique, *f.*; —**s,** *pl.* (*of the Bible*) Paralipomènes, *m.pl.*; — *v.a.* raconter, faire la chronique de; enregistrer, consigner, tenir note de
Chronicler, *s.* chroniqueur, *m.*
Chronogram, *s.* chronogramme, *m.*
Chronogrammat-ic, al, -ically, -ist. *V.* page 3, § 1
Chronograph, Chronographer, *s.* chronographe, *m.*
Chronograph-ic, al, -y. *V.* page 3, § 1
Chronologer, *s.* chronologiste, *m.*
Chronolog-ic, al, -ically, -ist, -y. *V.* page 3, § 1
Chronometer, *s.* chronomètre, *m.*
Chronometr-ic, al, -y, chronométrique, &c. (*V.* page 3, § 1)
Chrysalid, Chrysalis, *s.* chrysalide, *f.*
Chrysanthemum, *s.* chrysanthème, *m.*
Chryselephantine, *adj.* chryséléphantin
Chrysoberyl, *s.* chrysobéril, *m.*
Chrysochlore, *s.* chrysochlore, *m.*
Chrysocolla, *s.* chrysocolle, *f.*
Chrysography, Chrysology, &c. *V.* page 3, § 1
Chrysolite, *s.* chrysolithe, *m.*
Chrysoprase, *s.* chrysoprase, *f.*
Chrysotype, *s.* chrysotype, *m.*
Chub, *s.* chabot, meunier, *m.* — **cheeked, -faced,** *adj.* joufflu
Chubbed, Chubby, *adj.* joufflu
Chuck, *v.n.a.* (*of hens*) glousser; appeler; (*strike*) donner des petites tapes (sous le menton) à, caresser; (*throw*) jeter; — *s.*

gloussement, *m.*; (*gentle blow*) petite tape sous le menton, caresse, *f.*; (*word of endearment*) poulet, *m.*, -te, *f.*, petit, *m.*, e, *f.*; (*tech.*) mandrin, *m.* —, —! (*to a fowl*) petit, petit! — **farthing,** *s.* fossette, *f.* — **ribs,** *s. pl.* (*butch.*) côtes découvertes, *f.pl.*

Chuckle, *v.n.* rire tout bas (de); rire (de); ricaner; — *v.a.n.* (*to chuck*) *V.* **Chuck;** — *s.* rire étouffé, *m.*; ricanement, *m.*

Chuff, *s.* rustre, *m.*

Chuffily, *adv.* grossièrement, brutalement

Chuffiness, *s.* grossièreté, rusticité, *f.*

Chuffy, *adj.* grossier, rustique

Chum, *s.* camarade de chambre, camarade, *m.*; intime, inséparable, *m.*; — *v.n.* être camarades de chambre

Chump, Chunk, *s.* tronçon, gros morceau, *m.*, grosse pièce, *f.*; (*of mutton*) bout de gigot, *m.* — **chop,** *s.* côtelette de gigot, *f.*

Church, *s.* église, *f.*; (*of Protestants*) temple, *m.*; église, *f.*; (*service*) office, service divin, *m.*; (*profession*) état ecclésiastique, *m.*; — *adj.* d'église; de l'église, de l'Église; des églises; ecclésiastique. *Established* —, Église établie *or* dominante, Église, religion dominante, *f.* — *of England*, Église anglicane. — **attire,** *s.* habits sacerdotaux, *m.pl.* — **bell,** *s.* cloche d'église, *f.* — **burial,** *s.* sépulture ecclésiastique, *f.* — **candle,** *s.* cierge, *m.* — **clock,** *s.* horloge d'église, *f.* — **discipline,** *s.* discipline ecclésiastique, *f.* —**dom,** *s.* autorité ecclésiastique, *f.* — **furnisher,** *s.* chasublier, *m.* — **goer,** *s.* personne qui va à l'église, personne qui fréquente les églises, *f.*, (*jest.*, *pop.*) pilier d'église, *m.*, églisier, *m.*, -ière, *f.* — **going,** *adj.* qui va à l'église, qui est toujours à l'église, qui fréquente les églises. — **history,** *s.* histoire ecclésiastique, *f.* — **lamp,** *s.* lampion, verre, *m.* — **land,** *s.* terre d'église, *f.*, bien d'église, *m.* — **law,** *s.* droit canon, *m.* — **man,** *s.* homme d'église, ecclésiastique, *m.*; partisan de la religion dominante, *m.*; membre de l'Église anglicane, anglican, *m.* — **mouse,** *s.* rat d'église, *m.* — **music,** *s.* musique d'église, *f.* — **ornament,** *s.* ornement d'église, *m.* — **ornament maker,** *s.* chasublier, *m.* — **plate,** *s.* argenterie, chapelle, *f.* — **rate,** *s.* taxe pour l'entretien de l'église, *f.* — **service, -time,** *s.* office *or* service divin, *m.* — **warden,** *s.* marguillier, *m.* — *wardens' pew*, banc de l'œuvre, *m.*, œuvre, *f.* — **wardenship,** *s.* marguillerie, *f.* — **yard,** *s.* cimetière, *m.* — **yard cough,** *s.* toux qui sent le sapin, toux de renard, *f.*

Church, *v.a.* bénir (une femme qui fait ses relevailles). *To be —ed*, faire ses relevailles, relever (de couches)

Churching, *s.* relevailles, *f.pl.*

Churl, *s.* rustre, manant, *m.*; (*miser*) ladre, pingre, avare, *m.*; égoïste, *m.*

Churlish, *adj.* grossier, brutal; (*cross-grained*) revêche, maussade, grognon; (*miserly, stingy*) ladre, pingre, avare; égoïste

Churlishly, *adv.* grossièrement, brutalement

Churlishness, *s.* grossièreté, brutalité, *f.*

Churn, *s.* baratte, *f.*; — *v.a.* baratter; (*fig.*) battre, agiter. — **staff,** *s.* batte à beurre, *f.*

Churning, *s.* barattage, *m.*

Chyle, *s.* chyle, *m.*

Chylifaction, Chylification, *s.* chylification, *f.*

Chyliferous, *adj.* chylifère

Chylify, *v.a.* chylifier; — *v.n.* se chylifier

Chylous, *adj.* chyleux

Chyme, *s.* chyme, *m.*

Chym-ic, al, -ically. *V.* **Chemic, al,** &c.

Chymifaction, Chymification, *s.* chymification, *f.*

Chymiferous, *adj.* chymifère

Chymify, *v.a.* chymifier; — *v n.* se chymifier

Chym-ist, -istry. *V.* **Chemist,** &c.

Chymous, *adj.* chymeux

Cibarious, *adj.* alimentaire, nourrissant

Ciborium, *s.* ciboire, *m.*

Cicada, Cicala, *s.* cigale, *f.*

Cicatrice, Cicatrix, *s.* cicatrice, *f.*

Cicatrizable, *adj.* cicatrisable

Cicatrizant, *s.* cicatrisant, *m.*

Cicatrization, *s.* cicatrisation, *f.*

Cicatrize, *v.a.* cicatriser; — *v.n.* se cicatriser

Cicely, *s.* myrrhide, *f.* *Sweet* —, myrrhide odorante, *f.*, cerfeuil musqué, cerfeuil d'Espagne, *m.*

Cicerone, *s.* (*pl.* **Ciceroni**) cicérone, *m.* (*pl.* [cicéroni])

Ciceronian, *adj.* cicéronien

Cicindela, *s.* cicindèle, *f.*

Cicisbeism, *s.* sigisbéisme, *m.*, galanterie, *f.*

Cicisbeo, *s.* sigisbée, cicisbée, *m.*

Cid, *s.* cid, *m.*

Cider, *s.* cidre, *m.* *New* —, cidre doux. — **engine,** *s.* pompe à cidre, *f.* — **farmer, -grower,** *s.* cultivateur de pommes à cidre, *m.* — **house,** *s.* cabaret où l'on vend du cidre, *m.* — **kin,** *s.* petit cidre, *m.*, boisson, *f.* — **maker,** *s.* fabricant de cidre, *m.* — **making,** *s.* fabrication de cidre, cidrerie, *f.* — **mill,** *s.* moulin à pommes, *m.*; pressoir à cidre, *m.*, cidrerie, *f.* — **press,** *s.* pressoir à [cidre, *m.*, cidrerie, *f.*

Cierge, *s.* cierge, *m.*

Cigar, *s.* cigare, *m.* — **ashes,** *s. pl.* cendre (*f.*) *or* cendres (*f.pl.*) de cigare (*or* de cigares). — **box,** *s.* boîte à cigares, *f.* — **case,** *s.* porte-cigares, *m.* — **cutter,** *s.* coupe-cigares, *m.* — **divan,** *s.* salon-fumoir, fumoir, *m.* — **end,** *s.* bout de cigare, *m.* — **holder,** *s.* brûle-cigare, porte-cigare, *m.* — **lamp,** *s.* lampe à cigares, *f.* — **light,** *s.* *V.* **Fusee.** — **maker,** *s.* cigarier, *m.*, -ière, *f.*, cigareur, *m.*, -euse, *f.* — **mouthpiece,** *s.* *V.* — **holder.** — **shop,** *s.* bureau *or* débit de tabac, *m.* — **smoker,** *s.* fumeur (*m.*, -euse, *f.*) de cigares. — **stores,** *s. pl.* *V.* — **shop.** — **stump,** *s.* bout de cigare, *m.* — **tube,** *s.* *V.* — **holder**

Cigarette, *s.* cigarette, *f.* — **paper,** *s.* papier à cigarettes, *m.* — **smoker,** *s.* fumeur (*m.*, [-euse, *f.*) de cigarettes

Ciliary, *adj.* ciliaire

Ciliate, Ciliated, *adj.* cilié

Cimbri, *s. pl.* Cimbres, *m.pl.*

Cimbric, *adj.* cimbrique; — *s.* cimbre, *m.*

Cimeter. *V.* **Scimitar**

Cimmerian, *adj.* cimmérien

Cinchona, *s.* quinquina, *m.*

Cinchonic, *adj.* cinchonique

Cinchonine, *s.* cinchonine, *f.*

Cinchonism. *V.* **Quininism**

Cincture, *s.* ceinture, *f.*

Cinder, *s.* cendre, *f.*; (*of coals*) escarbille, *f.*; fraisil, *m.* — **pail, -sifter,** *s.* tamiseur, [étouffoir, *m.*

Cineraria, *s.* cinéraire, *f.*

Cinerary, *adj.* cinéraire

Cineration, *s.* cinération, *f.*

Cinereous, *adj.* cinériforme, cendré

Cingalese, *s. adj.* Cingalais, *m.*, e, *f.*

Cinnabar, *s.* cinabre, *m.*

Cinnamon, *s.* cannelle, *f.* — **bark,** *s.* cannelle, *f.* — **tree,** *s.* cannellier, *m.*

Cinque, *s.* cinq, *m.* — **foil,** *s.* quintefeuille, *f.* — **Ports,** *s. pl.* Cinq Ports, *m.pl.*

Cipher, *s.* chiffre, *m.*; (*nought*) zéro, *m.*; (*pers.*) zéro, être nul, homme nul, *m.*, nullité, *f.*; — *v.n.a.* chiffrer, calculer, compter. *To stand for a* —, être un vrai zéro. — **key,** *s.* clé de chiffre, *f.* — **writing,** *s.* écriture en chiffre, cryptographie, *f.*

Ciphering, *s.* calcul, *m.*; écriture en chiffre, *f.*, usage d'un chiffre, *m.* — **book,** *s.* cahier [d'arithmétique, *m.*

Cippus, *s.* cippe, *m.*

Circassian, *s. adj.* Circassien, *m.*, -ne, *f.*

Circean, *adj.* de Circé

Circensian, *adj.* du cirque

Circle, *s.* cercle, *m.*; (*log.*) cercle vicieux, *m.*; — *v.a.* former un cercle autour de, se mouvoir autour de, tourner autour de; entourer ('*with,*' de), environner ('*with,*' de), ceindre ('*with,*' de); — *v.n.* former un cercle; (*move round*) faire le tour; tourner, tournoyer; faire un

détour; se mouvoir circulairement; circuler; (*come again*) revenir; (*rid.*) caracoler. — **out,** *v.n.* se répandre
Circled, *adj.* en cercle, circulaire, rond
Circlet, *s.* anneau, cercle, *m.*; (*fig.*) couronne, *f.*
Circling, *adj.* en cercle, circulaire, rond; (*enclosing*) environnant; (*moving round*) tournant, tournoyant; qui circule; (*coming again*) qui revient; — *s.* entourage, environnement, *m.*; tournoiement, mouvement circulaire, *m.*; (*return*) retour, *m.*; (*rid.*) caracole, *f.*
Circuit, *s.* circuit, tour, *m.*; rotation, *f.*; (*out of o.'s way*) détour, *m.*; (*enclosure*) enceinte, *f.*; (*visitation of judges*) tournée, *f.*; (*district of ditto*) circonscription, *f.* *To go the* —, aller en tournée
Circuitous, *adj.* qui forme un circuit; qui fait des détours; détourné; sinueux
Circuitously, *adv.* en circuit; d'une manière détournée, par des détours
Circuity, *s.* circuit, détour, *m.*, circuits, détours, *m.pl.*
Circulable, *adj.* qui peut être mis en circulation
Circular, *adj.* circulaire; (*encircling*) de ceinture; — *s.* circulaire, *f.*; bulletin, *m.* — *-head window,* fenêtre cintrée, fenêtre à plein cintre, fenêtre en arcade, *f.* — *note,* billet circulaire, *m.* — *railway,* chemin de fer de ceinture, *m.*
Circularity, *s.* circularité, forme circulaire, *f.*
Circularly, *adv.* circulairement, en cercle
Circulate, *v.n.* circuler; — *v.a.* mettre en circulation; (*spread*) faire circuler, répandre
Circulating, *adj.* circulant. — *decimal, s.* fraction périodique, *f.* — *library,* cabinet de lecture, *m.* *V.* **Medium**
Circulation, *s.* circulation, *f.*; succession, suite, *f.*
Circulatory, *adj.* circulatoire
Circumambient, *adj.* environnant, ambiant
Circumcise, *v.a.* circoncire
Circumciser, *s.* circonciseur, *m.*
Circumcision, *s.* circoncision, *f.*
Circumference, *s.* circonférence, *f.*
Circumferential, *adj.* de circonférence
Circumferentor, *s.* boussole (d'arpentage), *f.*
Circumflex, *adj.* circonflexe; — *s.* accent circonflexe, circonflexe, *m.*
Circumfluent, Circumfluous, *adj.* environnant, qui coule autour
Circumjacent, *adj.* circonvoisin, circonjacent
Circumlocution, *s.* circonlocution, *f.*
Circumlocutory, *adj.* qui forme une circonlocution; indirect; verbeux
Circummeridian, *adj.* circomméridien
Circumnavigable, *adj.* dont on peut faire le tour en naviguant
Circumnavigate, *v.a.* naviguer autour de, faire le tour de, contourner
Circumnavigation, *s.* circumnavigation, *f.*
Circumnavigator, *s.* circumnavigateur, *m.*
Circumpolar, *adj.* circumpolaire, circompolaire
Circumscribe, *v.a.* circonscrire
Circumscription, *s.* circonscription, *f.*
Circumspect, *adj.* circonspect; mesuré
Circumspection, *s.* circonspection, *f.*
Circumspectly, *adv.* avec circonspection, circonspectement; mesurément
Circumstance, *s.* circonstance, *f.*; détail, *m.*; état, *m.*; **—s,** *pl.* position, condition, *f.*, état, *m.*; affaires, *f.pl.*; cas, *m.*; moyens, *m.pl.*, facultés, *f.pl.*; — *v.a.* (*pers.*) placer dans une certaine condition; (*things*) fournir d'incidents. *Narrow* or *straitened* —*s.* *V.* **Straiten.** *Under any* —*s,* dans tous les cas; (*with a neg.*) en aucun cas; sous aucun prétexte. *To be in bad* or *good* —*s,* être mal *or* bien dans ses affaires. *To be in easy* or *comfortable* —*s,* être à son aise, être dans l'aisance
Circumstanced, *part. adj.* (*pers.*) dans une position; (*things*) fourni d'incidents. *Well* —, dans une bonne position; bien fourni d'incidents. *As they are* —, dans la position (*or* situation) où ils se trouvent. *They are so — that,* ils se trouvent dans une position (*or* situation) telle que
Circumstantial, *adj.* accessoire, secondaire; de circonstance, qui tient aux circonstances, qui dépend des circonstances, circonstanciel; accidentel, fortuit; circonstancié, détaillé; minutieux; (*of evidence*) indirect; muet; par induction; — *s.* accessoire, détail secondaire, *m.*
Circumstantially, *adv.* par (*or* suivant) les circonstances; accidentellement; en détail, d'une manière circonstanciée; minutieusement
Circumstantiate, *v.a.* circonstancier, détailler
Circumvallation, *s.* circonvallation, *f.*
Circumvent, *v.a.* circonvenir
Circumvention, *s.* circonvention, *f.*
Circumvolution, *s.* circonvolution, *f.*
Circus, *s.* cirque, *m.*; (*of thoroughfares*) rond-point, *m.*
Cirrus, *s.* (*bot., zool.*) cirre, *m.*; (*meteorology*) cirrus, *m.*
Cisalpine, *adj.* cisalpin
Cisatlantic, *adj.* cisatlantique
Cisdanubian, *adj.* cisdanubien
Cisgangetic, *adj.* cisgangétique
Cisleithan, *adj.* cisleithan
Cismontane, *adj.* cismontain
Cispadane, *adj.* cispadan
Cispyrenean, *adj.* cispyrénéen
Cisrhenane, *adj.* cisrhénan
Cist, *s.* ciste, *m.*
Cistercian, *s. adj.* cistercien, *s.m.*, cistercien, *adj. m.*, -ne, *adj. f.*
Cistern, *s.* citerne, *f.*; réservoir, *m.*; fontaine, *f.*; récipient, *m.*; cuvette, *f.* — **barometer,** *s.* baromètre à cuvette, *m.* — **maker,** *s.* fontainier, *m.*
Cistus, *s.* ciste, *m.*
Cit, *s.* citadin, *m.*, e, *f.*, bourgeois, *m.*, e, *f.*
Citable, *adj.* citable
Citadel, *s.* citadelle, *f.*
Citation, *s.* citation, *f.*
Citatory, *adj.* citatoire
Cite, *v.a.* citer; (*enjoin*) enjoindre à, sommer
Citer, *s.* citateur, *m.*, -trice, *f.*
Cithara, *s.* cithare, *f.*
Citharist, *s.* citharède, cithariste, *m.f.*
Cithern. *V.* **Cittern**
Citizen, *s.* citoyen, *m.*, -ne, *f.*; bourgeois, *m.*, e, *f.*; habitant, *m.*, e, *f.*; — *adj.* citoyen, de citoyen, bourgeois, de bourgeois. — **like,** *adj.* bourgeois. — **ship,** *s.* citoyenneté, *f.*; droit de cité, *m.*
Citrate, *s.* citrate, *m.*
Citrene, *s.* citrine, citronyle, *f.*
Citric, *adj.* citrique
Citrine, *adj.* citrin; — *s.* citrin, *m.* — **colour,** *s.* citrin, *m.*
Citron, *s.* *V.* **Lemon.** — **water,** *s.* citronnelle, eau d'écorce de citron, *f.*
Citronyl, *s.* citronyle, *f.*
Cittern, *s.* cistre, *m.*
City, *s.* ville, *f.*; cité, *f.*; (*part of Paris, and of London*) cité, *f.*; — *adj.* de la ville; de la cité; municipal. — **article, -intelligence,** *s.* (*in newspapers*) bulletin financier, compte-rendu de la Bourse, *m.* — **court,** *s.* conseil municipal, *m.*
Cives. *V.* **Chives**
Civet, — **cat,** *s.* civette, *f.*
Civic, *adj.* civique
Civil, *adj.* civil; (*courteous*) poli, civil. — *list,* liste civile, *f.* — *service examination,* examen pour les emplois civils, concours d'admission aux emplois civils, *m.*
Civilian, *s.* (*lawyer*) civiliste, *m.*; (*student*) étudiant en droit civil, *m.*; (*not military*) bourgeois, *m.*; (*civil officer*) employé civil, *m.*; — *adj.* civil; bourgeois
Civility, *s.* civilité, politesse, *f.*
Civilizable, *adj.* civilisable
Civilization, *s.* civilisation, *f.*
Civilize, *v.a.* civiliser. *To become* —*d,* se civiliser
Civilizer, *s.*, **Civilizing,** *adj.* civilisateur, *m.*, -trice, *f.*
Civilly, *adv.* civilement; (*courteously*) poliment, civilement
Civism, *s.* civisme, *m.*

Clack, *v.n.* cliqueter, claquer; (*pers.*) caqueter, babiller; — *s.* (*mach.*) clapet, *m.*; (*of mills*) claquet, *m.*; (*pers.*) caquetage, caquet, *m.* — **door, -valve,** *s.* clapet, *m.*

Clacker, *s.* (*mach.*, &c.) *V.* **Clack,** *s.*; (*pers.*) caqueteur, *m.*, -euse, *f.* [caquetage, *m.*

Clacking, *s.* cliquetis, claquement, *m.*; (*pers.*)

Clad, *adj.* habillé (de), vêtu (de), couvert (de); (*of ships*) blindé, cuirassé

Cladium, *s.* cladion, *m.*

Claim, *v.a.* réclamer; exiger; demander; prétendre à; s'attribuer; revendiquer; — *s.* demande, *f.*; (*right*) titre, droit, *m.*; prétention, *f.*; (*debt*) créance, *f.*; (*law*) réclamation, *f.* *To lay* or *lay in* or *make* or *put in a — to,* élever des prétentions à, prétendre à, faire valoir ses droits sur *or* ses titres à, présenter ses titres à, réclamer, revendiquer. *To prove o.'s —,* (*in a bankruptcy case*) affirmer sa [créance

Claimable, *adj.* réclamable

Claimant, *s.* prétendant, *m.*, e, *f.*; réclamateur, *m.*, -trice, *f.*; (*law*) réclamant, *m.*, e, *f.*; (*entitled*) ayant-droit, *m.*

Clair-obscure, *s.* clair-obscur, *m.*

Clairvoyance, *s.* clairvoyance, *f.*

Clairvoyant, *adj. s.* clairvoyant, *m.*, e, *f.*

Clam, *s.* came, chame, *f.*, peigne, *m.*, mollusque, *m.*; — *v.a.* gluer, coller, poisser; — *v.n.* s'attacher, adhérer, coller, poisser; être moite

Clamber (— up), *v.n.a.* grimper; gravir

Clamminess, *s.* viscosité, *f.*; moiteur, *f.*

Clammy, *adj.* visqueux, gluant; pâteux

Clamorous, *adj.* bruyant; tumultueux; (*pers.*) criard, qui vocifère

Clamorously, *adv.* bruyamment; à grands cris

Clamorousness, *s.* nature bruyante, *f.*

Clamour, *s.* clameur, *f.*, cri, *m.*; vocifération, *f.*; bruit, *m.*; — *v.n.* pousser des clameurs; crier; vociférer; (*for*) demander à grands cris; (*against*) se récrier (contre)

Clamourer, *s.* crieur, *m.*, -euse, *f.*, criard, *m.*, e, *f.*; (*dissatisfied*) mécontent. *m.*

Clamp, *s.* crampon, *m.*; (*of wood*) emboîture, clampe, *f.*; (*heap*) tas, *m.*; (*of bricks*) gible, *f.*; (*artil.*) plate-bande, ferrure, *f.*; (*nav.*) clamp, *m.*; (*heavy footstep*) pas lourd, *m.*; — *v.a.* attacher avec des crampons; (*carp.*) emboîter; (*nav.*) acclamper; — *v.n.* marcher lourdement

Clan, *s.* clan, *m.*; race, famille, *f.*; troupe, *f.*; (*association*) clique, camaraderie, coterie, *f.*

Clandestine, *adj.* clandestin

Clandestinely, *adv.* clandestinement

Clandestineness, *s.* nature clandestine, clandestinité, *f.* [résonner

Clang, *v.n.* résonner; sonner; — *v.a.* faire

Clang, Clangor, *s.* bruit, son perçant *or* aigu, son, *m.*, clangueur, *f.*; (*of arms, chains,* &c.) cliquetis, *m.*; (*of animals*) cri perçant, *m*

Clangorous, Clangous, *adj.* résonnant; [perçant, aigu

Clanish. *V.* **Clannish**

Clank. *V.* **Clang**

Clannish, *adj.* de clan; étroitement uni

Clannishness, *s.* union étroite, *f.*

Clanship, *s.* esprit de famille, *m.*, union étroite, *f.*; association sous un chef, *f.*; autorité d'un chef de clan, *f.*

Clansman, *s.* membre d'un clan, *m.*

Clap, *v.a.* frapper; battre; (*the hands*) battre, claquer; applaudir; (*throw*) jeter, lancer; (*thrust*) mettre, flanquer, camper, fourrer; appliquer; (*of doors, windows*) fermer avec bruit, pousser avec force, fermer; — *v.n.* frapper; battre; battre des mains, claquer des mains, applaudir; se fermer avec bruit; (*set to*) se mettre (à). *To — o.'s hands, its wings,* battre *or* claquer des mains, battre des ailes. *To — o.'s sides,* se battre les flancs. — **down** (*a window*), — **to** (*a door,* &c.), fermer avec bruit, fermer. — **up,** conclure avec précipitation; expédier, bâcler; (*shut up*) enfermer, claquemurer, coffrer, emballer

Clap, *s.* coup, *m.*; (*of the hands*) battement. claquement, *m.*; applaudissement, *m.*; (*of thunder*) coup, *m.*; (*slap*) claque, *f.*; (*med.*) chaude-pisse, *f.* — **board,** *s.* douvain, merrain, *m.*; douve, *f.* — **net,** *s.* filet pour les oiseaux, *m.*, nappe, *f.* — **trap,** *s.* coup de théâtre, *m.*; artifice, *m.*; blague, *f.*; attrape-nigauds, *m.*; *adj.* à effet; captieux

Clapper, *s.* (*pers.*) claqueur, *m.*, -euse, *f.*; (*of bells*) battant, *m.*; (*mach.*) clapet, *m.*; (*of mills*) claquet, *m.*; (*of bellows*) âme, *f.*; (*snap*) claquette, *f.*, claquoir, *m.*; cliquette, *f.*; (*tongue*) langue, *f.* — **claw,** *v.a.* crosser, donner des coups de langue à. — **clawing,** *s.* coups de langue, *m.pl.*

Clapping, *s.* battements, *m.pl.*; applaudissements, *m.pl.* [(de place) fermée, *f.*

Clarence, *s.* clarence, *m.* — **cab,** *s.* voiture

Clare-obscure, *s.* clair-obscur, *m.*

Claret, *s.* bordeaux, vin de Bordeaux, *m.*

Clarification, *s.* clarification, *f.*

Clarifier, *s.* clarificateur, *m.*

Clarify, *v.a.* clarifier; — *v.n.* se clarifier

Clarinet, *s.* clarinette, *f.*

Clarinettist, *s.* clarinette, *f.*, clarinettiste, *m.*

Clarion, *s.* clairon, *m.*

Clarion-et, -ettist. *V.* **Clarinet,** &c.

Clary, *s.* sclarée, orvale, *f.*

Clash, *v.n.* résonner; s'entre-choquer, se choquer, se heurter; se contrarier; être en opposition *or* en conflit *or* en désaccord (avec); être contraire (à); s'opposer (à); — *v.a.* faire résonner; choquer, heurter; — *s.* fracas, *m.*; choc, *m.*; conflit, *m.*; opposition, *f.*; contradiction, *f.*; (*blow*) coup, *m.*; (*of arms, chains,* &c.) cliquetis, *m.*

Clashing, *adj.* résonnant; qui se choque; opposé; contraire; contradictoire; en opposition *or* en conflit *or* en désaccord (avec); — *s.* *V.* **Clash,** *s.*

Clasp, *s.* agrafe, *f.*; fermoir, *m.*; crochet, *m.*; (*embrace*) étreinte, *f.*, embrassement, *m.*; — *v.a.* agrafer; fermer; (*to embrace*) étreindre, serrer, presser, embrasser, presser *or* enlacer entre ses bras; (*the hands*) joindre. *To — one round the neck,* sauter *or* se jeter au cou de quelqu'un. *With —ed hands,* les mains jointes. — **knife,** *s.* couteau pliant, couteau de poche, *m.* — **lock,** *s.* houssette, *f.* — **nail,** *s.* clou à bardeaux, *m.*

Clasper, *s.* (*bot.*) vrille, *f.*; main, *f.*

Class, *s.* classe, *f.*; (*kind*) genre, *m.*; catégorie, *f.*; (*course*) cours, *m.*; — *v.a.* classer. — **book,** *s.* livre de classe, *m.*; livre classique, *m.* — **fellow, -mate,** *s.* camarade de classe, *m.* — **room,** *s.* classe, *f.*

Classic, -al, *adj. s.* classique, *adj. m.f.*, *s.m.*

Classically, *adv.* d'une manière classique

Classicism, *s.* (*system, school*) classicisme, *m.*; (*style*) classique, *m.*

Classicist, *s.* classique, *m.*

Classifiable, *adj.* classifiable

Classification, *s.* classification, *f.*

Classifier, *s.* classificateur, *m.*

Classify, *v.a.* classifier

Classing, *s.* classement, *m.*

Clatter, *s.* bruit, fracas, tapage, *m.*; (*talk*) caquetage, babillage, babil, *m.*; — *v.n.* faire du bruit; résonner, retentir; (*to talk*) caqueter, babiller; — *v.a.* faire résonner

Clatterer, *s.* tapageur, *m.*, -euse, *f.*; (*talker*) caqueteur, *m.*, -euse, *f.*, babillard, *m.*, e, *f.*

Clattering, *s.* *V.* **Clatter,** *s.*

Claudian, *adj.* claudien [phrase, *m.*

Clause, *s.* clause, *f.*; (*gram.*) membre de

Claustral, *adj.* claustral

Claviary, Clavier, *s.* clavier, *m.*

Clavicle, *s.* clavicule, *f.*

Clavicular, *adj.* claviculaire

Claw, *s.* griffe, *f.*; (*of crabs,* &c.) pince, *f.*; bras, *m.*; (*of a bench*) valet, *m.*; (*of a hammer*) pied-de-biche, *m.*; (*bot.*) ongle, *m.*; — *v.a.* griffer, égratigner; gratter; (*fig.*) déchirer; flatter, gratter. — **away, off,** *v.a.* déchirer, enlever.

— **back,** *s.* flatteur, *m.*, -euse, *f.* — **foot,** *s.* pied de griffon, *m.* — **footed,** *adj.* à pied de griffon. — **hammer,** *s.* marteau à pied-de-biche, *m.* —**less,** *adj.* sans griffes
Clawed, *adj.* onguiculé, armé de griffes; — *part.* griffé, &c. (*V.* **Claw,** *v.a.*)
Clay, *s.* argile, *f.*; terre glaise, glaise, *f.*; (*mud*) boue, *f.*; limon, *m.*; (*earth*) terre, *f.*; (*slang for a 'tobacco-pipe'*) bouffarde, *f.*; — *v.a.* couvrir d'argile, glaiser; (*sugar*) terrer; (*agr.*) marner. — **cold,** *adj.* glacé, sans vie. — **eater,** &c., *V.* **Dirt-eater,** &c. — **land,** *s.* terre argileuse, *f.* — **marl,** *s.* marne argileuse, *f.* — **pit,** *s.* argilière, glaisière, marnière, *f.* — **slate,** *s.* schiste argileux, *m.* — **soil,** *s.* sol argileux, terrain glaiseux, *m.* — **stone,** *s.* argilolithe, *m.*
Clayey, Clayish, *adj.* argileux, glaiseux
Claymore, *s.* claymore, *f.*
Clean, *adj.* propre; (*fig., in some phrases*) net; (*entire*) net; (*pure*) pur; (*healthy*) sain; (*dexterous*) adroit; (*of linen*) blanc; (*of boots*) ciré; — *adv.* entièrement, tout à fait, complètement; bien; net; droit, raide; adroitement; sans accident, heureusement; — *v.a.* nettoyer; (*pick out*) éplucher; (*with sand*) écurer; (*boots*) décrotter, cirer; (*wells,* &c.) curer; (*wool*) dégraisser. — *bill of health,* — *bill,* (*nav.*) patente nette, *f.* — *hands,* mains propres, *f.pl.*; (*fig.*) mains nettes, *f.pl.* *To make* —, [nettoyer
Cleanable, *adj.* nettoyable
Cleaner, *s.* nettoyeur, *m.*, -euse, *f.*; (*picker*) éplucheur, *m.*, -euse, *f.*; (*with sand*) écureur, *m.*, -euse, *f.*; (*of boots*) décrotteur, *m.*; (*of wells,* &c.) cureur, *m.*
Cleaning, *s.* nettoyage, nettoiement, *m.*; (*picking*) épluchement, épluchage, *m.*; (*with sand*) écurage, *m.*; (*of boots*) décrottage, *m.*; (*of wells,* &c.) curage, *m.*; (*of wool*) dégrais- [sage, *m.*
Cleanliness, *s.* propreté, *f.*
Cleanly, *adj.* propre; de propreté; pur; — *adv.* proprement; nettement
Cleanness, *s.* propreté, *f.*; pureté, innocence, *f.*; (*in style*) netteté, pureté, *f.*
Cleansable, *adj.* nettoyable
Cleanse, *v.a.* nettoyer; (*wash*) laver; (*purify*) purifier; (*with sand*) écurer; (*wells,* &c.) curer
Cleanser, *s.* (*pers.*) nettoyeur, *m.*, -euse, *f.*; (*with sand*) écureur, *m.*, -euse, *f.*; (*of wells,* &c.) cureur, *m.*; (*thing*) chose qui nettoie *or* purifie, *f.*, détersif, *m.*
Cleansing, *s.* nettoyage, nettoiement, *m.*; (*with sand*) écurage, *m.*; (*of wells,* &c.) curage, curement, *m.*; (*fig.*) purification, *f.*; —**s,** *pl.* nettoyure, *f.*, nettoyures, *f.pl.*; curages, *m.pl.*, curures, *f.pl.*; — *adj.* qui nettoie, détersif; purificateur
Clear, *adj.* clair; sûr, certain; pur, net; (*whole*) plein, entier; (*free*) libre (de), dégagé (de); exempt (de); innocent (de); (*of profits*) clair et net. *To get* —, se tirer d'affaire *or* d'embarras. *To get* — *of,* éviter; se débarrasser de; sortir de; se justifier de, se laver de; être acquitté *or* absous de. *To keep* — *of,* éviter; débarrasser. *To stand* —, être hors de danger. *To steer* — *of,* éviter. — **headed,** *adj.* qui a la tête *or* l'esprit libre; qui a l'esprit clair. — **shining,** *adj.* éclatant. — **sighted, -seeing,** *adj.* clairvoyant. — **sightedness, -seeing,** *s.* clairvoyance, *f.* — **starch,** *v.a.* blanchir à neuf. **starcher,** *s.* blanchisseuse de fin, *f.* — **starching,** *s.* blanchissage de fin (*or* à neuf), *m.* — **story,** *s.* cléristère, *m.*
Clear, *adv.* clairement, clair; entièrement; net
Clear, *v.a.* éclaircir; (*liquids*) clarifier; (*clean*) nettoyer; (*earth, rubbish,* &c.) déblayer; (*disengage,* &c.) dégager, débarrasser; faire évacuer, évacuer; (*dispel*) dissiper; (*leap over*) franchir; (*gain*) gagner, avoir *or* tirer un bénéfice net de; (*acquit,*&c.) acquitter; libérer; absoudre; justifier (de), purger (de); (*accounts*) liquider; (*goods*) acquitter les droits de; (*lands*) défricher; (*a letter-box*) faire la levée de, lever, relever; (*nav.*) doubler; (*mil.*) balayer; — *v.n.* (*of the weather*) s'éclaircir; (*get rid*) se libérer (de), se débarrasser (de); (*bank.*) opérer un virement. — **away, off, out,** débarrasser; (*take away*) enlever; ôter; (*earth, rubbish,* &c.) déblayer; (*empty*) vider; évacuer; (*get rid of*) se débarrasser de, se défaire de; (*com.*) liquider, solder; (*dispel*) dissiper; (*be dispelled*) se dissiper; s'éclaircir; (*depart*) filer, décamper; (— **away,** *v.n., at table*) desservir. — *off o.'s arrears,* se mettre au courant. — **up,** *v.a.* éclaircir; (*accounts*) liquider; *v.n.* s'éclaircir; se dissiper
Clearance, *s.* dégagement, débarrassement, *m.*; évacuation, *f.*; (*cleaning*) nettoyage, *m.*; (*of earth, rubbish,* &c.) déblaiement, *m.*; déblai, *m.*; (*of surplus stock*) liquidation, *f.*, solde, *m.*; (*profit*) bénéfice net, *m.*; (*nav.*) congé, *m.* — **sale,** *s.* solde, *m.*, liquidation, *f.*
Clearing, *s.* éclaircissement, *m.*; (*of liquids*) clarification, *f.*; (*cleaning*) nettoyage, *m.*; (*removal,* &c.) enlèvement, dégagement, débarrassement, *m.*; évacuation, *f.*; (*of earth, rubbish,* &c.) déblaiement, *m.*; déblai, *m.*; (*of letter-boxes*) levée, *f*, relevage, *m.*; (*of lands*) défrichement, *m.*; (*land cleared*) terrain défriché, *m.*; (*clear spot in a wood,* &c.) éclaircie, *f.*; (*carrying off*) râfle, *f.*; (*acquitting,* &c.) acquittement, *m.*; paiement, *m.*; liquidation, *f.*; libération, *f.*; justification, *f.*; (*bank.*) virement de parties, virement, *m.* — **away,** *s.* débarrassement, *m.*; (*removal*) enlèvement, *m.*; (*of earth, rubbish,* &c.) déblaiement, *m.* — **house,** *s.* bureau de liquidation, *m.*; (*rail.*) bureau central, *m.*; (*bank.*) comptoir général de virement, comptoir de règlement, *m.* — **nut,** *s.* strychnos des buveurs, titan-cotte, *m.* — **off,** — **out,** *s.* évacuation, *f.*; (*removal*) enlèvement, *m.*; (*forcible*) râfle, *f.*; (*com.*) liquidation, *f.*, solde, *m.* — **up,** *s.* éclaircissement, *m.* [ment; bien; (*of profits*) clair et net
Clearly, *adv.* clairement; nettement; évidem-
Clearness, *s.* clarté, *f.*; netteté, *f.*; pureté, *f.*
Cleat, *s.* taquet, *m.*
Cleavable, *adj.* clivable
Cleavage, *s.* fendage, *m.*; (*min.*) clivage, *m.*
Cleave, *v.a.* fendre; (*jewel., min.*) cliver; — *v.n.* se fendre; (*stick*) se coller (à), coller (à); (*fig.*) s'attacher (à)
Cleaver, *s.* (*tech.*) fendoir, *m.*; (*of butchers*) couperet, *m.*; (*for wood*) merlin, *m.*; (*pers.*) fendeur, *m.*, -euse, *f.*; —**s,** *pl.* (*bot.*) grateron, *m.*, râpette, *f.*
Cleaving, *s.* fendage, *m.*; attachement, *m.*
Clef, *s.* clé, clef, *f.*
Cleft, *s.* fente, ouverture, crevasse, *f.*; (*piece*) morceau, *m.* — **graft,** *v.a.* greffer en fente. — **grafting,** *s.* greffe en fente, *f.*
Cleg, *s.* taon, *m.*
Clematis, *s.* clématite, *f.* [douceur, *f.*
Clemency, *s.* clémence, *f.*; (*of the weather*)
Clement, *adj.* clément; doux
Clementine, *s.* clémentin, *m.*, e, *f.*
Clemently, *adv.* avec clémence
Clench. *V.* **Clinch**
Clepsydra, *s.* clepsydre, *f.*
Cleptomania, *s.* monomanie du vol, cleptomanie, kleptomanie, clopémanie, klopémanie, *f.*
Cleptomaniac, *s. adj.* cleptomane, *m.f.*
Clerestory, *s.* cléristère, *m.*
Clergy, *s.* clergé, *m.* *Benefit of* —, bénéfice de clergie, *m.* — **man,** *s.* (*generally*) ecclésiastique, *m.*; (*protestant*) ministre, pasteur, *m.*; (*catholic*) prêtre, curé, abbé, *m.*
Clerical, *adj.* clérical; du clergé; ecclésiastique; de clerc; (*of errors*) de copiste; — *s.* clérical, ecclésiastique, *m.* — *error,* erreur (*or* faute) de copiste, *f.*; (*law*) vice de clerc, *m.*
Clerically, *adv.* cléricalement
Clerk, *s.* clerc, *m.*; (— *in orders*) ecclésiastique, *m.*; (*lay* —) clerc, *m.*; répondant, *m.*; (*secretary*) secrétaire, *m.*; (*of law courts*) greffier,

m.; (*of lawyers*) clerc, *m.*; (*com.*) commis, employé, *m.*; (*nav.*) comptable, écrivain, *m.* *Articled* —, clerc apprenti (d'avoué), *m.* *Captain's* —, (*nav.*) comptable, écrivain, *m.* *Chief* or *head* —, (*admin.*) chef de division, *m.*; (*of lawyers*) maître clerc, premier *or* principal clerc, *m.*; (*com.*) premier commis, *m.* *Junior* —, (*of lawyers*) petit clerc, *m.*; (*com.*) petit commis, *m.* *Managing* —, (*of lawyers*) maître clerc, *m.*; (*com.*) premier commis, *m.* *Physician's* —, (*in hospitals*) externe, *m.* *Senior* —, *first-class* —, (*admin.*) chef de bureau, *m.* *Ship's* —, comptable, écrivain, *m.*

Clerkship, *s.* fonctions de clerc, *f.pl.*; secrétariat, *m.*; (*eccl.*) état ecclésiastique, *m.*, cléricature, *f.*; (*of law courts*) fonctions de greffier, *f.pl.*; (*of lawyers*) place de clerc, cléricature, *f.*; (*com.*) place de commis, *f.*; (*of the apostolic chamber*) clèricat, *m.*

Clever, *adj.* habile, adroit; fort; intelligent, de mérite, d'esprit; spirituel, ingénieux; savant; (*well done*) bien fait

Cleverly, *adv.* habilement, adroitement; bien

Cleverness, *s.* habileté, adresse, *f.*; dextérité, *f.*; intelligence, *f.*, moyens, *m.pl.*; mérite, *m.*

Clew. *V.* **Clue**

Click, *v.n.* cliqueter, faire tic-tac; — *s.* cliquet, *m.*; (*sound*) cliquetis, tic-tac, *m.* — **beetle,** *s.* taupin, *m.*

Clicker, *s.* (*in shoemaking*) coupeur cordonnier, *m.*; (*print.*) metteur en pages, *m.*

Clicking, *s* tic-tac, *m.*

Client, *s.* client, *m.*, e, *f.* [colline, *f.*

Cliff, *s.* (*bank*) falaise, *f.*; (*rock*) rocher, *m.*; (*hill*)

Cliffy, *adj.* à falaises; (*craggy*) rocailleux; (*steep*) escarpé [année climatérique, *f.*

Climacteric, -al, *adj.* climatérique; — *s.*

Climate, *s.* climat, *m.*

Climatic, -al, *adj.* de (*or* du) climat, particulier à un climat, climatérique

Climato-graphy, -logy, &c. *V.* page 3, § 1

Climax, *s.* gradation, *f.*, climax, *m.*; gradation ascendante, *f.*; (*height*) plus haut point, plus haut degré, comble, *m.*

Climb, *v.a.n.* grimper, gravir; (*ascend*) monter; (*walls*, — **over**) escalader; (*fig.*) s'élever

Climber, *s.* grimpeur, *m.*, -euse, *f.*; personne qui monte, *f.*; ascensioniste, *m.f.*; (*bot.*) plante grimpante, *f.*; (*bird*) grimpeur, *m.*

Climbing, *adj.* grimpant. — *bird*, grimpeur, *m.* — *perch*, anabas, *m.* — *plant*, plante

Clime, *s.* climat, *m.* [grimpante, *f.*

Clinch, *v.a.* tenir à main fermée *or* à poing fermé, serrer dans sa main; (*the fist*) fermer, serrer; (*nails*) river; (*log.*) établir, confirmer; (*a cable, nav.*) entalinguer; — *s.* crampon, *m.*; (*hold*) prise, *f.*; (*nav.*) entalingure, *f.*

Clincher, *s.* crampon, *m.*; (*set-down*) mot sans réplique, *m.* *To give one a* —, river à quelqu'un son clou, donner à quelqu'un son paquet, remettre quelqu'un à sa place. — **built,** *adj.* bordé à clin. — **nail,** *s.* clou à vis, *m.* — **work,** *s.* bordage à clin, clin, *m.*, encouture, *f.*

Cling, *v.n.* se cramponner (à), s'accrocher (à), se coller (à); se tenir (à), tenir (à); s'attacher (à). *To — together*, se tenir ensemble. — **stone,** *adj.* dont la pulpe tient au noyau

Clinic, -al, *adj.* clinique, de clinique; (*of medical men*) clinicien

Clink, *v.n.* tinter, résonner; — *v.a.* faire tinter, tinter, faire résonner; — *s.* tintement, cliquetis, *m.*; (*mach.*) rochet, *m.*; roue à rochet, *f.*

Clinker, *s.* (*slag*) scorie, *f.*, laitier, mâchefer, *m.* — **built,** *adj.* *V.* **Clincher-built**

Clinometer, *s.* clinomètre, *m.*

Clip, *v.a.* couper, rogner; (*horses*, &c.) tondre; (*abridge*) écourter; (*words*) estropier, manger; (*a language*) écorcher; (*coin*) rogner; (*hold of*) tenir; pincer

Clipper, *s.* rogneur, *m.*, -euse, *f.*; (*of horses*, &c.) tondeur, *m.*, -euse, *f.*; (*ship*) clipper, *m.*; —**s,** *pl.* (*shears*) ciseaux à tondre, *m.pl.*, forces, forcettes, *f.pl.* — **built,** *adj.* construit en clipper

Clipping, *s.* rognure, *f.*; action de rogner *or* de tondre, *f.*; tonte, *f.*; —**s,** *pl.* rognures, *f.pl.*

Clips, *s. pl.* *V.* **Clippers**

Clique, *s.* clique, *f.*

Clivers, *s. pl.* (*bot.*) *V.* **Cleavers**

Cloaca, *s.* cloaque, *m.*

Cloak, *s.* manteau, *m.*; (*with a hood*) caban, *m.*; (*mil.*) capote, *f.*; (*fig.*) masque, voile, *m.*; prétexte, *m.*; — *v.a.* couvrir d'un manteau; (*fig.*) masquer, voiler, cacher. — **bag,** *s.* portemanteau, *m.*, valise, *f.* — **room,** *s.* vestiaire, *m.*; (*rail.*) consigne, *f.*, dépôt de bagages, bureau des bagages, *m.*; (*slang for "water-closets"*) cabinets d'aisances, *m.pl.* *In the — room*, (*rail.*) en consigne, en dépôt

Clock, *s.* horloge, *m.*; (*for apartments*) pendule, *f.*; (*of stockings*) coin, *m.*; (*of ships*) ampoulette, *f.* *O'clock*, heure, *f. sing.*, heures, *f.pl.* *What o'— is it? What is it o'—? What's o'—?* quelle heure est-il? *It is one o'—*, il est une heure. *It is two* or *&c. o'—*, il est deux heures *or* &c. (*V.* **Twelve.**) — **case,** *s.* boîte *or* &c. (*V.* **Case**) de pendule, *f.*; cage d'horloge, *f.* — **case maker,** *s.* penduliste, *m.* — **glass,** *s.* verre de pendule *or* d'horloge, *m.* — **maker,** *s.* horloger, *m.* — **making,** *s.* horlogerie, *f.* — **shade,** *s.* cylindre *or* &c. (*V.* **Shade**) de pendule, *m.* — **tower, -turret,** *s.* tour d'horloge *or* de l'horloge, *f.* — **work,** *s.* mouvement (d'horlogerie), *m.*; (*fig.*) ouvrage de précision, *m.* *As regular as — work*, réglé comme un papier de musique

Clod, *s.* motte (de terre), *f.*; (*piece*) morceau, *m.*, masse, *f.*; (*of beef*) collier, *m.*; (*pers.*) lourdaud, *m.*, e, *f.*; (*clot*) *V.* **Clot;** — *v.n.* se coaguler, se grumeler; — *v.a.* jeter des mottes de terre à, motter; agglomérer. — **breaker, -crusher,** *s.* (*instr.*) brise-mottes, émottoir, *m.*; (*pers.*) émotteur, *m.*, -euse, *f.* — **breaking, -crushing,** *s.* émottage, émottement, *m.* — **hopper,** *s.* rustre, rustaud, lourdaud, *m.*, e, *f.* — **pate,** *s.* lourdaud, *m.*, e, *f.* — **pated,** *adj.* stupide. — **poll,** *s.* lourdaud, *m.*, e, *f.*

Cloddish, *adj.* lourdaud, rustaud, grossier

Cloddy, *adj.* de mottes; en mottes; grumeleux; de boue, de limon; lourdaud, rustaud, [grossier

Cloff. *V.* **Clough**

Clog, *v.a.* (*horses*) entraver; (*fig.*) embarrasser, entraver; obstruer; encombrer; arrêter; charger; — *v.n.* s'embarrasser; se charger; s'attacher (à); s'obstruer, se boucher; — *s.* billot, *m.*; (*of horses*) entraves, *f.pl.*, entrave, *f.*; (*fig.*) entrave, *f.*, embarras, obstacle, *m.*; poids, *m.*; charge, *f.*; (*overshoe*) socque, *m.*, claque, galoche, *f.*; (*wooden shoe*) sabot, *m.*

Clogginess, *s.* embarras, *m.*, gêne, *f.*

Cloggy, *adj.* embarrassant

Cloister, *s.* cloître, *m.*; — *v.a.* cloîtrer

Cloisteral, *adj.* claustral [(*things*) claustral

Cloistered, *adj.* (*pers.*) cloîtré; solitaire;

Cloisterer, *s.* cloîtrier, *m.*, -ière, *f.*

Cloistral, *adj.* claustral

Cloistress, *s.* cloîtrière, *f.*

Close, *v.a.* fermer; terminer; conclure; (*an account, a meeting*, &c.) clore; (*to stop*) boucher; (*to cover*) couvrir; (*mil., nav.*) serrer; — *v.n.* se fermer; (*again*) se refermer; (*have its doors closed, be shut*) fermer; (*end*) se terminer, finir; (*settle*) convenir (de), s'arrêter (à); (*agree*) s'accorder, s'entendre (avec); s'arranger (avec); (accede) accéder (à); adhérer (à); s'en tenir (à); accepter; céder (à); (*of assemblies*) clore; (*get near*) s'approcher (de); (*press*) se serrer, se presser; (*unite*) s'unir (à), se joindre (à); (*grapple*) en venir aux mains; se prendre corps à corps. — **in,** *v.a.* clore, enfermer d'une clôture; *v.n.* marcher d'accord (avec); (*get near*) s'approcher (de). — **up,** *v.a.* fermer; refermer; boucher; rapprocher; *v.n.* se fermer; se refermer; se boucher; se rapprocher

Close, *s.* clos, enclos, *m.*; (*of cathedrals*) cloître, *m.*; (*of streets*) cité, *f.*; (*end*) fin, clôture, *f.*; (*of the night*) tombée, *f.*; (*mus.*) cadence, *f.* *To bring to a* —, terminer. *To draw to a* —, tirer *or* toucher à sa fin

Close, *adj.* (*shut*) clos, fermé; (*narrow*) étroit; (*tight*) serré; étroit, juste; (*dense*) compacte; serré; (*of a carriage*) couvert, fermé; (*confined*) enfermé, renfermé; (*of the air*) renfermé; (*of a room*) sans air; (*of the weather*) lourd; (*of prisoners*) au secret; (*of fights*) de près; corps à corps; (*of elections*) contesté, bien contesté; (*near*) près, proche; (*close-cut or shaved*) ras; (*of style*) concis, serré; (*of translations*) fidèle; (*of arguments*) serré; concluant, pressant; (*stingy*) serré, avare, intéressé; (*retired*) retiré, solitaire; (*hidden*) caché; mystérieux; secret; (*discreet*) discret; réservé; secret; (*intimate*) intime; (*of corporations*) exclusif; (*of study*, &c.) appliqué, assidu; suivi; attentif; scrupuleux; minutieux; exact; extrême; (*of a billiard ball*) collé sous bande; (*her.*) plié; — *adv.* de près, près, tout près; (*densely, tightly*) serré, d'une manière serrée; (*of living*) économiquement, avec économie; (*exactly*) exactement; (*of shutting*) bien, tout à fait; (*of sticking*) fortement; (*of study*, &c.) assidûment. — *by*, *by it*, *by them* (*things*), tout près. — *to*, près de, tout près de, contre, tout contre; à fleur de. — *together*, tout près l'un de l'autre (*or* les uns des autres, *if more than two*). — *to the ground*, à fleur de terre, à rase terre. — **banded,** *adj.* serrés les uns contre les autres, en rangs serrés; étroitement unis. — **bodied,** *adj.* juste, collant, qui prend bien la taille. — **burning,** *adj.* *V.* **Caking.** — **fisted, -handed,** *adj.* *V.* **Fisted.** — **fistedness,** *s.* pingrerie, avarice, *f.* — **hauled,** *adj.* (*nav.*) orienté au plus près. — **set,** *adj.* dru, serré. — **shut,** *adj.* bien fermé. — **tongued,** *adj.* discret

Closely, *adv.* de près; assidûment; attentivement; intimement; secrètement; exactement; strictement, rigoureusement; minutieusement; (*narrowly*) étroitement; (*densely, tightly*) serré; (*of shutting*) bien, hermétiquement; (*pressingly*) vivement

Closeness, *s.* compacité, densité, *f.*; étroitesse, *f.*; solidité, *f.*; solitude, retraite, *f.*; avarice, *f.*; discrétion, *f.*; réserve, *f.*; intimité, *f.*; connexion, *f.*; scrupule, *m.*; exactitude *f.*; rigueur, *f.*; fidélité, *f.*; concision, *f.*; logique serrée, *f.*; (*of the air*) manque d'air, air renfermé, *m.*; (*of the weather*) état lourd, *m.*; (*of pursuit*) vigueur, *f.*

Closer, *s.* finisseur, *m.*, -euse, *f.*

Closet, *s.* cabinet, *m.*; (*for clothes*) garde-robe, *f.*; armoire, *f.*; — *v.a.* enfermer dans un cabinet; prendre en particulier; (*fam.*) enfermer, claquemurer, cloîtrer

Closeting, *s.* tête-à-tête, *m.*

Closh, *s.* solbature, *f.*

Closing, clôture, fin, *f.*; conclusion, *f.*; (*shutting up*) fermeture, *f.*; — *adj.* de clôture; (*last*) dernier, final

Closure, *s.* *V.* **Closing** *and* **Enclosure**

Clot, *s.* grumeau, caillot, *m.*; — *v.a.* grumeler, cailler; (*milk, cream*) cailler; — *v.n.* se grumeler, se cailler. — **bur,** *s.* bardane, *f.*

Cloth, *s.* tissu, *m.*, étoffe, *f.*; (*woollen with short nap*) drap, *m.*; (*linen*) toile, *f.*; (*piece of* —) linge, *m.*; (*for meals*) nappe, *f.*; (*for tables*) tapis, *m.*; (*for animals*) couverture, *f.*; (*duster*) torchon, *m.*; (*of clergy*, &c.) habit, *m.*; profession, *f.*; (*book-bind.*) toile, percaline, *f.* — *of gold*, drap d'or, *m.* *Broad* —, &c., *V.* **Broad,** &c. *Long* —, percale, *f.*, madapolam, *m.*; cretonne, *f.* *To lay the* —, mettre le couvert. *To remove* or *take away the* —, desservir. — **merchant,** *s.* marchand de draps, drapier, *m.* — **presser,** *s.* (*pers.*) presseur, *m.*; (*of sewing-mach.*) presse-étoffe, *m.* — **shearer,** *s.* tondeur de draps, *m.* — **shearings,** *s. pl.* bourre tontisse, *f.* — **trade,** *s.* commerce de draps, *m.*, draperie, *f.* — **weaver,** *s.* tisserand en draps, *m.* — **worker,** *s.* ouvrier en draps, *m.*

Clothe, *v.a.* habiller, vêtir; (*adorn, invest*) revêtir (de); (*cover*) couvrir (de), recouvrir (de)

Clothes, *s. pl.* habits, vêtements, *m.pl.*; (*fam.*) hardes, nippes, *f.pl.*; (*costume*) costume, *m.*; (*of bed*) couvertures, *f.pl.*; (*linen*) linge, *m.* *Long* —, maillot, *m.* *Old* —, vieux habits, *m.pl.* *Old* — *man*, marchand de vieux habits, fripier, *m.* *Old* — *woman*, marchande de vieux habits, fripière, *f.* *Plain* —, *Private* —, (*not uniform*) habit civil, *m.*, tenue civile, *f.*, habit bourgeois, *m.*, tenue bourgeoise, *f.*; (*not court or full dress*) habit (*or* costume) de ville, *m.*, tenue de ville, *f.* *Short* —, jaquette, *f.* *Small* —, culotte, culotte courte, *f.* *Suit of* —, *V.* **Suit.** *To put on o's* —, s'habiller. — **basket,** *s.* panier au linge sale, *m.* — **brush,** *s.* brosse à habits, *f.* — **horse,** *s.* séchoir, *m.* — **lines,** *s. pl.* étendage, *m.* — **man,** *s.* marchand d'habits, *m.* — **moth,** *s.* teigne des draps, *f.* — **peg,** *s.* portemanteau, *m.*, patère, *f.*; (*forked, for hanging clothes*) épingle de bois, *f.*, fichoir, *m.* — **pin,** *s.* épingle de bois, *f.*, fichoir, *m.* — **posts, -props,** *s. pl.* étendoir, *m.* — **press,** *s.* armoire à habits, *f.* — **presser,** *s.* presseur, *m.* — **pressing,** *s.* pressage des étoffes, *m.*

Clothier, *s.* fabricant de draps, drapier, *m.*; marchand de draps, drapier, *m.*; (*dealer in new and ready-made clothes*) confectionneur, marchand tailleur, *m.*; (*second-hand*) marchand d'habits, fripier, *m.*

Clothing, *s.* habillement, *m.*; vêtements, *m.pl.*; (*for animals*) couverture, *f.*, couvertures, *f.pl.*

Clotty, *adj.* grumeleux

Cloud, *s.* nuage, *m.*; (*poet.*) nue, *f.*; (*multitude*) nuée, *f.*; (*in a stone*) veine, tache, *f.*; (*astr.*) nébuleuse, *f.*; — *v.a.* couvrir de nuages; (*fig.*) obscurcir; (*of sorrows*) répandre un nuage sur; assombrir; rembrunir; couvrir (de); (*tarnish*) ternir; (*variegate*) veiner; tacher; bigarrer; diversifier; nuancer; moirer; — *v.n.* se couvrir de nuages, se couvrir, s'obscurcir. *To be under a* —, être discrédité. — **ascending,** *adj.* qui s'élève jusqu'aux nues. — **berry,** *s.* ronce faux mûrier, *f.* — **capped, -capt,** *adj.* sourcilleux, qui touche aux nues, qui se perd dans les nues. — **cleaving,** *adj.* qui fend les nues. — **compelling,** *adj.* qui amoncelle les nuages. — **covered,** *adj.* couvert *or* enveloppé de nuages. — **dispelling,** *adj.* qui dissipe les nuages. —**less,** *adj.* sans nuages, sans nuage, pur, serein. — **piercing,** *adj.* qui perce les nuages, qui s'élève au-dessus des nues. — **topped, -topt,** *adj.* dont la cime se perd dans les nues, sourcilleux [ment

Cloudily, *adv.* avec des nuages; (*fig.*) obscurément

Cloudiness, *s.* état nuageux, état nébuleux, *m.*; (*fig.*) obscurité, *f.*; couleur terne, *f.*; air sombre, *m.*; (*sadness*) tristesse, *f.*

Cloudy, *adj.* nuageux, couvert de nuages; (*fig.*) sombre; obscur, ténébreux; terne; (*of liquids*) trouble; (*variegated*) nuancé; bigarré; marbré; (*of marble*) veiné; (*of tissues*) moiré, ondé. — *weather*, temps couvert. *It is* —, le temps est couvert. *It is getting* —, le temps se couvre [(*civ. engin.*) barrage, *m.*

Clough, *s.* précipice, *m.*; (*com.*) surusage, *m.*;

Clout, *s.* torchon, chiffon, *m.*; (*for mending*) pièce, *f.*, morceau, *m.*; (*for infants*) couche, *f.*; (*blow*) tape, claque, *f.*; (*of axletree*) rondelle, *f*; (*nail*) clou à tête plate, *m.*; — *v.a.* rapetasser, rapiécer; (*wrap up*) envelopper d'un linge *or* d'un torchon; (*curdle*) cailler, grumeler; (*strike*) taper, claquer, donner une tape *or* une claque à; (*with nails*) garnir de clous

Clove, *s.* clou de girofle, girofle, *m.*; (*of garlic*) gousse, *f.* *Mother* —, antofle, clou-matrice, *m.* — **bark,** *s.* cannelle giroflée, *f.* — **oil,** *s.*

huile de girofle, *f.* — **pink,** *s.* œillet-giroflée, *m.* — **spice,** *s.* écorce de girofle, *f.* — **stalk,** *s.* griffe de girofle, *f.* — **tree,** *s.* giroflier, *m.*

Cloven, *adj.* fendu ; fourchu. — **foot,** *s.* pied fourchu *or* fendu, *m.* — **footed, -hoofed,** *adj.* qui a le pied fourchu *or* fendu

Clover, *s.* trèfle, *m.* *To be* or *live in* —, vivre dans l'abondance, avoir du foin dans ses bottes. — **field,** *s.* champ de trèfle, *m.*, tréflière, *f.* — **grass,** *s.* trèfle, *m.* — **seed,** *s.* graine de trèfle, *f.* — **weevil,** *s.* apion, *m.*

Clovered, *adj.* couvert de trèfle

Clown, *s.* paillasse, bouffon, clown, *m.*; paradiste, *m.*; pitre, *m.*; (*with Harlequin and Columbine*) Gille, *m.*; (*rustic*) rustre, manant, *m.*; paysan, *m.*

Clownish, *adj.* de paysan, rustique ; (*coarse*) [grossier, rustre

Clownishly, *adv.* grossièrement, en rustre

Clownishness, *s.* grossièreté, rudesse, *f.*

Cloy, *v.a.* affadir ; (*glut*) rassasier

Cloying, *s.* affadissement, *m.*; satiété, *f.*

Club, *s.* (*staff*) bâton, gourdin, *m.*, massue, *f.*; (*society*) cercle, *m.*, (*polit.*) club, *m.*; (*share*) part, *f.*; (*shot*) écot, *m.*; (*clubbing*) cotisation, *f.*; (*of hair*) catogan, *m*; (—**s,** *pl., at cards*) trèfle, *m.*; — *v.n.* se réunir ; s'associer ; (*of expenses*) se cotiser; contribuer (à), concourir (à) ; — *v.a.* payer, fournir, donner ; (*unite*) joindre, réunir ; (*raise*) se cotiser pour ; (*a firelock*) lever (son fusil) la crosse en l'air ; (*the hair*) relever en catogan. — **fist,** *s.* poing énorme, *m.* — **fisted,** *adj.* qui a un poing énorme. — **foot,** *s.*, — **footed,** *adj.* pied bot, *m.*, — **headed,** *adj.* qui a une grosse tête. — **house,** *s.* cercle, *m.*; (*polit.*) club, *m.* — **law,** *s.* loi du plus fort, loi du bâton, *f.*; (*of societies*) statuts de cercle *or* de club, *m.pl.* — **moss,** *s.* lycopode, *m.* — **room,** *s.* salle de réunion, salle d'assemblée, *f.* — **shaped,** *adj.* en forme de massue, claviforme. — **top,** *s.* (*bot.*) [clavaire, *f.*

Clubbing, *s.* cotisation, *f.*

Clubbist, *s.* clubiste, *m.f.*

Cluck, *v.n.* glousser ; — *v.a.* appeler

Clucking, *s.* gloussement, *m.*

Clue, *s.* (*ball*) pelote, *f.*, peloton, *m.*; (*thread*) fil, *m.*; (*fig.*) fil, indice, *m.*; signe, *m.*; guide, *m.*; avis, vent, *m.*; idée, donnée, *f.*; (*nav.*) point (de voile) *m.*; — *v.a.* guider ; (— **up**) (*nav.*) carguer. *To give a — to it,* en donner un indice, mettre sur la voie

Clump, *s.* bloc, *m.*; masse, *f.*; groupe, *m.*; (*of trees*) massif, bouquet, *m.*, touffe, *f.*; (*of earth*) motte, *f.*; (*of boots*) patin, *m.*; (*heavy footstep*) pas lourd, *m.*; — *v.n.* marcher lourdement. — **soles,** *s. pl.* semelles à patins, *f.pl.*

Clumpy, *adj.* massif, lourd

Clumsily, *adv.* grossièrement ; maladroitement, gauchement

Clumsiness, *s.* maladresse, gaucherie, *f.*

Clumsy, *adj.* grossier; maladroit, gauche ; massif, lourd ; disgracieux, laid, mal fait

Clusia, *s.* clusie, *f.*, clusier, *m.*

Cluster, *s.* groupe, amas, *m.*; (*of fruits*) grappe, *f.*, (*cherries*) bouquet, *m.*, (*nuts*) paquet, *m.*; (*of trees*) bouquet, *m*, touffe, *f.*, massif, *m.*; (*of flowers*) bouquet, *m.*; (*of bees*) peloton, *m.*; (*of hair*) boucle, *f.*; (*of diamonds*) attache, *f.*; — *v.n.* croître en grappes ; se former en grappes ; pousser par bouquets ; se grouper, s'amasser, se rassembler ; (*of bees*) se pelotonner ; — *v.a.* réunir en grappe ; grouper, amasser, rassembler. — **pine,** *s.* pinastre, *m.*

Clutch, *s.* griffe, *f.*; (*grasp*) *V.* **Grasp,** *s.*; (*tech.*) dent, *f.*; — *v.a.* empoigner, saisir ; agripper, gripper. *To — the hand* or *the fist,* fermer *or* serrer le poing

Clutter. *V.* **Clatter**

Clyster, *s.* (*old*) clystère, lavement, *m.* — **pipe,** *s.* (*old*) canule, *f.*; clysoir, *m.* — **pump,** *s.* (*vet.*) clysopompe (de cheval), *m.*

Co., *s.* (*com.*) Cie. (compagnie), *f.*

Coach. *s.* voiture, *f.*, (*obsolete*) carrosse. *m.*; (*public*) diligence, voiture, *f.*; (*tutor*) préparateur, *m.*; (*nav.*) chambre de conseil, *f.*; — *v.a.* mener en voiture, voiturer, carrosser ; (*fig.*) atteler ; (— **up**) préparer, pousser ; — *v.n.* aller en voiture ; aller par la diligence. *V.* **Carriage.** *Slow* —, grosse diligence, *f.*; (*pers.*) lambin, *m.*, e, *f.*, clampin, *m.*, e, *f.*, paresseux, *m.*, -euse, *f.*; (*intellectually*) esprit lourd, *m.* — *To — it,* se faire voiturer. — **box,** *s.* siége (du cocher), *m.* — **builder,** — **building,** *V.* — **maker,** — **making.** — **carver,** *s.* sculpteur pour voitures, *m.* — **door,** *s.* portière, *f.* — **driver,** *s.* cocher, *m.* —**ful,** *s.* voiture pleine, carrossée, *f.* — **horse,** *s.* cheval de carrosse, carrossier, cheval d'attelage, *m.* — **house,** *s.* remise, *f.* *In the — house,* sous la remise. — **joiner,** *s.* menuisier en voitures, *m.* — **load,** *s.* *V.* —**ful.** — **man,** *s.* cocher, *m.* — **manship,** *s.* art *or* talent de conduire, *m.*, habileté à conduire, *f.* — **maker,** *s.* carrossier, fabricant de voitures, *m.* **making,** *s.* carrosserie, fabrication de voitures, *f.* — **office,** *s.* bureau de voitures *or* de diligences, *m.* — **painter,** *s.* peintre en voitures, *m.* — **smith,** *s.* ferreur en voitures, *m.*; serrurier en voitures, *m.* — **stand,** *s.* place de voitures, *f.* — **step,** *s.* marchepied, *m.* — **trimmer,** *s.* garnisseur en voitures, *m.*, matelassier, *m.*, -ière, *f.* — **wheel,** *s.* roue de voiture *or* de carrosse, *f.* — **window,** *s.* glace de voiture, *f.*; portière, *f.* — **wrench,** [*s.* clé anglaise, *f.*

Coaching, *s.* préparation, *f.*

Coaction, *s.* coaction, *f.*

Coactive, *adj.* coactif

Coactively, *adv.* coactivement

Coadjutor, *s.* aide, collaborateur, adjoint, *m.*; collègue, *m.*; (*in the church*) coadjuteur, *m.*

Coadjutorship, *s.* aide, assistance, collaboration, *f.*; fonctions d'adjoint, *f.pl.*; (*of the church*) coadjutorerie, *f.*

Coadjutress, Coadjutrix, *s.* aide, collaboratrice, *f.*; (*of nuns*) coadjutrice, *f.*

Coadventurer, *s.* compagnon d'aventure, *m.*

Coadventuress, *s.* compagne d'aventure, *f.*

Coagent, *s.* aide, coopérateur, *m.*

Coagulable, *adj.* coagulable

Coagulant, *s.* coagulant, *m.*

Coagulate, *v.a.* coaguler ; — *v.n.* se coaguler

Coagulation, *s.* coagulation, *f.*

Coagulative, *adj.* coagulant, coagulateur

Coagulum, *s.* coagulum, *m.*; caillot, *m.*

Coak, *s.* (*nav.*) dé, *m.*

Coal, *s.* charbon, *m.*; charbon de terre, *m.*, (*tech.*) houille, *f.*; —**s,** *pl.* charbon, *m.*; charbons, *m.pl.*; — *adj.* de charbon ; à charbon ; (*pertaining to coal-mining, geol.*) houiller ; — *v.a.* charbonner ; — *v.n.* (*of steam-engines*) faire son charbon. *To blow the —s,* attiser le feu. *To call over the —s,* donner un savon à. *To carry —s to Newcastle,* porter de l'eau à la rivière. — **agent,** *s.* agent pour la vente des houilles, *m.* — **barge,** *s.* bateau à charbon, bateau charbonnier, *m.* — **basin,** *s.* bassin houiller, *m.* — **basket,** *s.* panier à charbon, *m.* — **bed,** *s.* couche de houille, *f.* — **black,** *adj.* noir comme du charbon ; *s.* noir de charbon, *m.* — **box,** *s.* boîte à charbon, *f.*; (*rail.*) boîte à feu, *f.* — **bunker,** *s.* soute à (*or* au) charbon, *f.* — **cellar,** *s.* charbonnier, *m.* — **cinders,** *s. pl.* escarbilles, *f.pl.*, fraisil, *m.* — **closet,** *s.* charbonnier, *m.*; (*of steamboats*) soute au charbon, *m.* — **company,** *s.* compagnie houillère, *f.* — **dealer,** *s.* marchand (*m.*, e, *f.*) de charbon, charbonnier, *m.*, -ière, *f.* — **deposit,** *s.* dépôt houiller, *m.* — **district,** *s.* district *or* terrain houiller, *m.* — **dust,** *s.* poussier de charbon, *m.*; fraisil, *m.* — **exchange,** *s.* entrepôt de charbon de terre *or* de houille, *m.* — **factor,** *s.* facteur (*or* commissionnaire) pour la vente de la houille, *m.* — **field,** *s.* terrain houiller, *m.* — **fire,** *s.* feu de charbon de terre, *m.* —

fish, *s.* colin, *m.*, morue noire, *f.* — **gas,** *s.* gaz d'éclairage, *m.* — **heaver,** *s.* porteur de charbon de terre *or* de houille, *m.* — **hole, -house,** *s.* charbonnier, *m.*; (*of steamboats*) soute au charbon, *f.* — **lighter,** *s. V.* — **barge.** — **man,** *s.* charbonnier, *m.* — **master,** *s.* exploitant de houillère, *m.* — **merchant,** *s.* marchand (*m.*, e, *f.*) de charbon. — **mine,** *s.* houillère, mine de houille, *f.* — **miner,** *s.* houilleur, *m.* — **mining,** *s.* exploitation de la houille, *f.*, charbonnage, *m.*; — *adj.* houiller. — **owner, -proprietor,** *s.* propriétaire de houillère, *m.f.* — **pan,** *s.* brasier, *m.* — **pit,** *s.* houillère, *f.*; (*in America*) charbonnière, *f.* — **scoop,** *s.* pelle à charbon, *f.* — **scuttle,** *s.* seau à charbon, *m.* — **seam,** *s.* couche de houille, *f.* — **shed,** *s.* charbonnier, *m.* — **ship,** *s.* charbonnier, bâtiment charbonnier, *m.* — **shoot,** *s.* seau *or* panier à charbon, *m.* — **skip,** *s.* benne, *f.* — **stone,** *s.* anthracite, *m.* — **store,** *s.* dépôt de houille, *m.*, charbonnerie, *f.* — **stratum,** *s. V.* — **bed.** — **tar,** *s.* goudron de houille, goudron minéral, coaltar, *m.* — **vessel,** *s. V.* — **ship.** — **wharf,** *s.* quai à houille, *m.* — **whipper,** *s.* déchargeur de houille, *m.* — **woman,** *s.* charbonnière, *f.* — **work, -working,** *s.* houillère, *f.* [liguer; se fondre, se fusionner

Coalesce, *v.n.* s'unir, se réunir, s'allier, se

Coalescence, *s.* coalescence, union, *f.*; fusion-

Coalescent, *adj.* coalescent [nement, *m.*

Coaling, *s.* approvisionnement de charbon, *m.*

Coalition, *s.* coalition, *f.*; (*mixing*) réunion,

Coalitionist, *s.* coalisé, *m.*, e, *f.* [fusion, *f.*

Coallied, *adj.*, **Coally,** *s.* allié, *m.*, e, *f.*

Coaly, *adj.* charbonneux, de charbon, comme du charbon; houilleux

Coarse, *adj.* gros, grossier; (*rude*) grossier; (— *grained*) *See below;* (*pers.*) grossier. — **grained,** *s.* (*of metals, tissues, leather,* &c.) à gros grain; (*of nappy fabrics*) à gros poil; (*of wood*) à gros fil

Coarsely, *adv.* grossièrement; rudement

Coarseness, *s.* grossièreté, *f.*

Coast, *s.* côte, *f.*, rivage, *m.*; (*extensive*) littoral, *m.*; — *v.n.* ranger *or* suivre la côte, côtoyer le rivage; (*com. nav.*) faire le cabotage, caboter; — *v.a.* naviguer le long de, côtoyer. *To — along,* côtoyer. *The — is clear,* il n'y a personne sur la côte; (*fig.*) il n'y a personne, il n'y a pas de danger. — **guard,** *s.* garde-côtes, *m.* — **line,** *s.* littoral, *m.* — **pilot,** *s.* pilote côtier, côtier, lamaneur, *m.* — **wise,** *adv.* vers la côte; en suivant la côte

Coaster, *s.* côtier, *m.*; (*com. nav.: pers.*) caboteur, *m.*, (*vessel*) cabotier, *m.*

Coasting, *s.* navigation côtière, *f.*; (*com. nav.*) cabotage, *m.* — **pilot,** *s. V.* **Coast-pilot.** — **skip, -vessel,** *s.* cabotier, *m.* — **trade,** *s.* commerce de cabotage, cabotage, *m.*

Coat, *s.* habit, *m.*; (*short*) vareuse, jaquette, *f.*; (*frock* —) redingote, *f.*; (*jacket*) *V.* **Jacket;** (*of soldiers, collegians*) tunique, *f.*; (*of animals*) robe, *f.*, poil, *m.*, fourrure, *f.*; (*of birds*) plumage, *m.*; (*of sheep*) toison, *f.*; (*skin*) peau, *f.*; (*of paint,* &c., *layer*) couche, *f.*; (*anat.*) paroi, tunique, *f.*; (*her.*) armes, armoiries, *f.pl.*; écusson, *m.*; —**s,** *pl.* (*of a child*) jaquette, *f.*; — *v.a.* revêtir, recouvrir, couvrir (de); (*lay over*) enduire (de). — *armour,* — *of arms,* cotte d'armes, *f.*; (*her.*) armes, armoiries, *f.pl.*; écusson, *m.* — *of mail,* cotte de mailles, *f.* —*ed tongue,* (*med.*) langue chargée, *f.* *Great —, over —,* paletot, *m.*; pardessus, *m.*; (*mil.*) capote, *f.* *Long —s,* (*of children*) robe longue, *f.* *Short —s,* robe courte, jaquette, *f.* *To turn —,* tourner casaque. *Cut your — according to your cloth,* selon ta bourse gouverne ta bouche. — **card,** *s.* figure, *f.* — **pocket,** *s.*, — **sleeve,** *s.*, &c. poche d'habit, *f.*, manche d'habit, *f.*, &c. — **stand,** *s.* portemanteau, *m.*

Coati, Coatimondi, *s.* coati, *m.*

Coating, *s.* étoffe pour habits, *f.*; (*of paint,* &c., *layer*) enduit, *m.*; couche, *f.* *Rough —,* [crépi, *m.*

Coax, *v.a.* cajoler, enjôler, amadouer

Coaxer, *s.* cajoleur, *m.*, -euse, *f.*, enjôleur, *m.*, -euse, *f.* [*adj.* cajoleur; caressant

Coaxing, *s.* cajolerie, *f.*, enjôlement, *m.*; —

Coaxingly, *adv.* avec cajolerie, d'un air cajoleur *or* caressant

Cob, *s.* (*bird*) mouette, *f.*; (*horse*) double poney (*or* ponet), *m.*; (*for feeding*) boulette, gobe, *f.*; (*of maize*) balle, *f.*; (*spider*) araignée, *f.*; — *v.a.* (*tech.*) briser. — **coals,** *s. pl.* grêle, *m.* — **iron,** *s.* chenet, *m.* — **loaf,** *s.* gros pain *m.* — **mare,** *s.* double ponette, *f.* — **nut,** *s.* grosse noisette, aveline, *f.* — **stone,** *s.* galet, rognon, *m.*, grosse pierre, *f.* — **wall,** *s. V.* **Mud-wall.** — **web,** *s.* toile d'araignée, *f.*; *adj.* de toile d'araignée; fragile, faible, frêle. — **webbed,** *adj.* couvert de toiles d'araignées

Cobalt, *s.* cobalt, *m.* — **blue,** *s.* bleu de cobalt, *m.*

Cobaltic, *adj.* cobaltique

Cobaltiferous, *adj.* cobaltifère

Cobaltize, *v.a.* cobaltiser

Cobaltizing, *s.* cobaltisage, *m.*

Cobble, *v.a.* raccommoder, rapetasser; (*fig.*) saveter; — *s.* (*boat*) bateau pêcheur, *m.*; (— *stone*) galet, rognon, *m.*, grosse pierre, *f.*; —**s,** *pl.* (*coals*) grêle, *m.* [cordonnier, *f.*

Cobbler, *s.* savetier, *m.* —*'s wax,* poix de

Cobbling, *s.* raccommodage de souliers, ouvrage de savetier, *m.*; (*coals*) *V.* **Cobbles**

Cobelligerent, *s. adj.* cobelligérant, *s.m.*, *adj.*

Coble, *s.* (*boat*) bateau pêcheur, *m.* [*m.* (e, *f.*)

Cobra da (*or* **de**) **capello,** *s.* cobra-de-capello,

Coburg, *s.* cobourg, *m.* [*m.*

Coca, *s.* coca, *m.*

Cocagne, *s.* cocagne, *f.*; pays de cocagne, *m.*

Coccinella, *s.* coccinelle, *f.*

Cocco, *s.* colocase, colocasie, *f.*

Cocculus, *s.* coccule, *m.* — **Indicus,** *s.* coque

Coccyx, *s.* coccyx, *m.* [du Levant, *f.*

Cochin-Chinese, *s. adj.* Cochinchinois, *m.*, e, *f.*

Cochineal, *s.* cochenille, *f.* — **dye, -dyeing,** *s.* cochenillage, *m.* — **tree,** *s.* cochenillier, *m.*

Cochinilline, *s.* cochenilline, *f.*

Cochlea, *s.* (*of the ear*) limaçon, *m.*; (*screw*) vis, *f.*

Cochlear, Cochleary, Cochleate, Cochleated, *adj.* cochléaire, en spirale

Cochlearia, *s.* cochléaria, *m.*

Cock, *s.* coq, *m.*; (*male generally*) mâle, *m.*; (*adject.*) mâle; (*weathercock*) girouette, *f.*; (*spout*) robinet, *m.*; (*of arrows*) coche, *f.*; (*of fire-arms*) chien, *m.*; (*of dials*) style, *m.*; (*of hay, grass*) tas, meulon, *m.*, veillote, *f.*; (*of a balance*) aiguille, *f.*; (*of hats*) retroussis, *m*; (*boat*) coquet, petit bateau, *m.*; — *v.a.* (*erect*) relever, redresser; (*turn up*) retrousser; (*a fire-arm*) armer; (*hay, grass*) mettre en tas, ameulonner, enveilloter; — *v.n.* se pavaner, se rengorger, se redresser; dresser des coqs de combat. *At full —,* armé. *At half- —, on the half- —,* au repos. *To half- —, To place at half- —,* mettre au repos. *To place at full —,* armer. — *and bull story,* coq-à-l'âne, conte à dormir debout, *m.* — *of the walk,* (*fam.*) coq du village, *m.* — **a-doodle-doo,** *s.* coquerico, *m.* — **a-hoop,** *adj.* triomphant. — **bird,** *s.* oiseau mâle, *m.* — **boat,** *s.* coquet, petit bateau, *m.* — **brained,** *adj.* étourdi, écervelé. — **broth,** *s.* bouillon de coq, *m.* — **canary,** *s.* serin, *m.* — **chafer,** *s.* hanneton, *m.* — **crow, -crowing,** *s.* chant du coq, *m.* — **fight, -fighting,** *s.* combat de coqs, *m.* — **horse,** *s.* dada, *m.*; *adj.* à cheval; triomphant. — **loft,** *s.* grenier, galetas, *m.* — **master,** *s.* éleveur de coqs de combat, *m.* — **match,** *s.* combat de coqs, *m.* — **paddle,** *s.* lompe, *m.* — **partridge,** *s.* perdrix mâle, *f.*; (*falc.*) garbon, *m.* — **pheasant,** *s.* faisan, coq faisan, *m.* — **pit,** *s.* arène de combats de coqs, *f.*; (*nav.*) poste des malades, *m.* — **roach,** *s.* blatte, *f.*, cafard, *m.* —**'s comb,** *s.*

crête de coq, *f.*; (*fig.*) *V.* **Coxcomb.** **—'s-foot grass,** *s.* dactyle, *m.* **—'s-head,** *s.* sainfoin, *m.*; plantain, *m.* **— sorrel,** *s.* oseille commune, *f.* **— sparrow,** *s.* moineau mâle, *m.* **—'s spur,** *s.* éperon de coq, ergot, *m.* **—'s spur burner,** *s.* (*of gas-lighting*) simple jet, *m.* **—'s spur thorn,** *s.* alisier, *m.* **— sure,** *adj.* très sûr, sûr et certain. **— swain,** *s. V.* **Coxswain.** **— tail,** *s.* métis, *m.*, -isse, *f.*; (*horse*) cheval demi-sang, *m.*, (*mare*) jument demi-sang, *f.*; (*pers.*) mal-appris, *m.*, e, *f.*; (*insect*) staphylin, *m.*; (*adj.*) métis. **— weed,** *s.* passerage, *f.*

Cockade, *s.* cocarde, *f.*

Cockaded, *adj.* à cocarde, qui porte une cocarde

Cockaigne. *V.* **Cocagne**

Cockatoo, *s.* kakatoès, *m.*

Cockatrice, *s.* basilic, cocatrix, *m.*

Cocked, *part. adj.* relevé, &c. (*V.* **Cock,** *v.a.n.*); (*of fire-arms*) armé; (*of hats*) à cornes. *Half-—*, (*of fire-arms*) au repos

Cocker, *v.a.* **(— up)** choyer, dorloter; — *s.* (*pers.*) amateur de combats de coqs, *m.*; (*dog*) gredin, *m.*, e, *f.*; (*legging*) jambière, *f.*

Cockerel, *s.* cochet, *m.*

Cockering, *s.* soins délicats, *m.pl.*

Cocket, *s.* (*seal*) sceau de la douane, *m.*; (*warrant*) acquit de douane, *m.*

Cockish. *V.* **Cocky**

Cockle, *s.* (*bot.*) (*corn —*) agrostemme, nielle des blés, *f.*; (*shell-fish*) coque, palourde, *f.*, sourdon, *m.*, bucarde, *f.*; — *v.a.* recoquiller; — *v.n.* se recoquiller; (*of the sea*) moutonner. **— stairs,** *s. V.* **Corkscrew staircase**

Cockney, *s.* (*native of London*) Londonien, *m.*, -ne, *f.*; (*townsman, townswoman*) citadin, *m.*, e, *f.*; (*ignorant of country things*) badaud, *m.*, e, *f.*

Cocky, *adj.* suffisant, vaniteux, présomptueux, avantageux, qui fait l'important, qui fait sa tête; — *s. V.* **Ducky**

Coco, *s.* coco, *m.* **— brush,** *s.* brosse de coco, *f.* **— butter,** *s.* beurre de coco, *m.* **— fibre,** *s.* bourre de coco, *f.*, caire, *m.* **— mat, -nut mat,** *s.* tapis-brosse (en coco), *m.* **— nut,** *s.* coco, *m.*, noix de coco, *f.* **— nut fibre,** *s. V.* **— fibre.** **— nut oil,** *s.* huile de coco, *f.* **— nut palm, — nut palm** *or* **tree,** *s.* cocotier, *m.* **— oil,** *s.* huile de coco, *f.* **— palm, -tree,** *s.* cocotier, *m.*

Cocoa, *s.* (*chocolate-nut, preparation: tradesmen's spelling of* '*cacao*') *V.* **Cacao;** (*nut of a palm-tree: wrong spelling for* '*coco*') *V.* **Coco.** **— root,** *s.* colocase, colocasie, *f.*

Cocoon, *s.* cocon, *m.*

Cocoonery, *s.* coconnière, *f.*

Coction, *s.* coction, *f.*

Cod, *s.* (*fish*) morue, *f.*; (*husk*) cosse, *f.*; (*anat.*) bourses, *f.pl.* **— fish,** *s.* morue, *f.* **— fisher,** *s.* (*pers.*) pêcheur de morue, *m.*; (*vessel*) moruyer, *m.* **— fishery,** *s.* pêche de la morue, *f.* **— fishing,** *s.* pêche de la morue, *f.*; *adj.* moruyer, **— fishing vessel,** *s.* moruyer, *m.* **— liver oil,** *s.* huile de foie de morue, *f.* **— sounds,** [*s. pl.* noue, *f.*, noves, *f.pl.*

Coda, *s.* coda, *f.*

Codded, Coddy, *adj.* à cosse, en cosse

Coddle, *v.a.* mitonner, bouillir; (*pers., animals*) [dorloter, câliner

Code, *s.* code, *m.*

Codeia, Codeine, *s.* codéine, *f.*

Codetta, *s.* codetta, *f.*

Codex, *s.* (*foreign pharm.*) codex, *m.*

Codger, *s.* bonhomme, *m.*

Codicil, *s.* codicille, *m.*

Codicillary, *adj.* codicillaire

Codification, *s.* codification, *f.*

Codifier, *s.* codificateur, *m.*

Codify, *v.a.* codifier

Codilla, *s.* codille, *f.*

Codle. *V.* **Coddle** [pyrale des pommes, *f.*

Codlin, *s.* pomme à cuire, *f.* **— moth,** *s.*

Codling, *s.* (*fish*) petite morue, *f.*, moruau, doguet, *m.*; (*apple*) *V.* **Codlin**

Coefficiency, *s.* coopération, *f.*, concours, *m.*

Coefficient, *adj.* coopératif, coopérateur; (*math.*) coefficient; — *s.* (*math.*) coefficient, *m.*

Coefficiently, *adv.* par coopération

Coehorn. *V.* **Cohorn**

Coelector, *s.* coélecteur, *m.*

Cœliac, *adj.* cœliaque

Coemption, *s.* coemption, *f.*

Cœnaculum, *s.* cénacle, *m.*

Cœnobite. *V.* **Cenobite**

Coequal, *adj.* coégal, égal

Coequality, *s.* coégalité, égalité, *f.*

Coerce, *v.a.* contraindre; réprimer

Coercible, *adj.* coercible

Coercion, *s.* coercition, contrainte, *f.*

Coercive, *adj.* coercitif

Coercively, *adv.* de force, par coercition

Coessential, *adj.* de même essence

Coessentiality, *s.* communauté d'essence, *f.*

Coeternal, *adj.* coéternel

Coeternity, *s.* coéternité, *f.*

Coeval, *adj.* du même âge ('*with*,' que); — *adj. s.* contemporain, *m.*, e, *f.* ('*with*,' de)

Coexecut-or, rix, *s.* coexécuteur, *m.*, -trice, *f.*

Coexist, *v.n.* coexister, exister ensemble

Coexistence, *s.* coexistence, *f.*

Coexistent, *adj.* coexistant, qui coexiste

Coextend, *v.a.* étendre *or* prolonger simultanément; — *v.n.* s'étendre *or* se prolonger simul [tanément

Coextension, *s.* extension égale, *f.*

Coextensive, *adj.* coétendu ('*with*,' à), qui a une égale étendue, de même étendue ('*with*,' [que)

Coextensiveness, *s.* égale étendue, *f.*

Coffee, *s.* café, *m.*; — *adj.* de (*or* du) café; à café. — *with milk, with cream,* café au lait, à la crème, *m.* **— bean, -berry,** *s.* fève de café, *f.*, grain de café, *m.* — *in berries, V.* **Berry.** **— broker,** *s.* courtier en cafés, *m.* **— colour,** *s.* couleur de café, *f.* **— cup,** *s.* tasse à café, *f.* **— dealer,** *s.* marchand (*m.*, e, *f.*) de café. **— estate,** *s.* caféière, cafeterie, *f.* **— filter,** *s.* filtre à café, *m.* **— grounds,** *s. pl.* marc de café, *m.* **— grower,** *s.* caféier, *m.*, -ière, *f.* **— house,** *s.* café, *m.*; crèmerie, *f.* **— house keeper,** *s.* cafetier, limonadier, *m.*, -ière, *f.*; crémier, *m.*, -ière, *f.* **— man,** *s.* cafetier, *m.* **— mill,** *s.* moulin à café, *m.* **— plantation,** *s.* caféière, cafeterie, *f.* **— planter,** *s.* caféier, *m.*, -ière, *f.* **— pot,** *s.* cafetière, *f.* **— roaster,** *s.* brûloir à café, *m.* **— room,** *s.* salon, café, *m.* **— service, -set, -things,** *s.* service à café, *m.* **— shop,** *s. V.* **— house.** **— tree,** *s.* caféier, cafier, *m.* **— urn,** *s.* fontaine à café, *f.*

Coffer, *s.* coffre, *m.*; caisse, *f.*; (*treasure*) cassette, *f.*; (*arch.*) coffre, caisson, *m.*; (*fort.*) coffre, *m.*; — *v.a.* encoffrer, encaisser. **— dam,** *s.* batardeau, *m.* **— fish,** *s.* coffre, *m.*

Coffin, *s.* cercueil, *m.*, bière, *f.*; (*print.*) coffre, *m.*; (*vet.*) soulier, sabot, *m.*; — *v.a.* enfermer *or* mettre dans un cercueil

Cog, *v.a.* (*to wheedle*) cajoler, enjôler; (*deceive*) tromper; (*thrust in*) interpoler, introduire; faire passer; (*dice*) piper; (*wheels*) denter, garnir de dents; — *v.n.* faire des cajoleries; — *s.* dent de roue, dent, *f.*, alluchon, cran, *m.*; (*boat*) bateau pêcheur, *m.* **— wheel,** *s.* roue dentée, *f.* [évidence, *f.*

Cogency, *s.* force, puissance, *f.*; urgence, *f.*;

Cogent, *adj.* fort, puissant; péremptoire; convaincant, incontestable; irrésistible

Cogently, *adv.* fortement, avec force, puissamment; d'une manière convaincante, incontestablement; irrésistiblement [pipé

Cogged, *adj.* denté, à dents, à crans; (*of dice*)

Cogger, *s.* cajoleur, *m.*, -euse, *f.*, enjôleur, *m.*, -euse, *f.*

Coggery, Cogging, *s.* cajolerie, *f.*; tromperie, *f.*

Coggle, *s.* bateau pêcheur, *m.*

Cogitate, *v.n.* penser, méditer, réfléchir

Cogitation, *s.* pensée, méditation, réflexion, *f.*

Cogitative, *adj.* capable de penser, capable de réflexion; porté à la méditation, réfléchi, pensif

Cognac, *s.* (*brandy*) cognac, *m.*, eau-de-vie de Cognac, *f.*
Cognate, *adj.* de la même famille, proche, allié ; qui a la même origine, du même genre; analogue (à), qui a du rapport (avec); — *s.* cognat, *m.*
Cognation, *s.* parenté, consanguinité, *f.*; analogie, *f.*, rapport, *m.*; (*law*) cognation, *f.*
Cognition, *s.* cognition, connaissance, *f.*
Cognitive, *adj.* cognitif [de la compétence (de)
Cognizable, *adj.* du ressort (de), du domaine (de),
Cognizance, *s.* connaissance, *f.*; compétence, *f.*; (*her.*) cimier, *m.*; armes, *f.pl.*
Cognizant, *adj.* instruit; (*law*) compétent
Cognomen, *s.* surnom, nom de guerre, *m.*
Cognominal, *adj.* de surnom; du même nom, homonyme
Coguardian, *s.* cotuteur, *m.*, -trice, *f.*
Cohabit, *v.n.* cohabiter
Cohabitation, *s.* cohabitation, *f.*
Coheir, ess, *s.* cohéritier, *m.*, -ière, *f.*
Cohere, *v.n.* adhérer (à), être attaché (à); être en rapport, se lier bien; concorder (avec), s'accorder (avec) rence, liaison, *f.*
Coherenc-e, y, *s.* cohésion, *f.*; (*fig.*) cohé-
Coherent, *adj.* adhérent; lié; (*connected*) cohérent; (*consistent*) conséquent; d'accord
Coherently, *adv.* cohéremment, d'une manière cohérente, avec cohérence, avec liaison
Cohesion, *s.* cohésion, adhérence, *f.*; (*connection*) cohérence, *f.*, rapport, *m.*
Cohesive, *adj.* susceptible d'adhérer; qui tend
Cohesively, *adv.* avec cohésion [à adhérer
Cohesiveness, *s.* cohésion, adhérence, *f.*
Cohobate, *v.a.* cohober
Cohobation, *s.* cohobation, *f.*
Cohorn, — mortar, *s.* mortier à la Cohorn, *m.*
Cohort, *s.* cohorte, *f.* [d'une calotte; coiffer
Coif, *s.* calotte, *f.*; coiffe, *f.*; — *v.a.* coiffer
Coil, *v.a.* replier; rouler; enrouler; (*nav.*) cueillir, rouer, lover, gléner; — *v.n.* se replier s'enrouler; — *s.* rouleau, *m.*; tour, *m.*; (*of serpents*) repli, *m.*; (*nav.*) cueille, glène, *f.*
Coin, *s.* monnaie, *f.*; pièce de monnaie, *f.*; (*print., tech.*) coin, *m.*; (*artil.*) coin de mire, *m.*; (*corner*) coin, *m.*, encognure, *f.*; — *v.a.* monnayer; (*to stamp*) frapper; (*fig.*) fabriquer; forger, inventer. *Base* or *counterfeit* —, fausse monnaie. *Rustic* —, (*build.*) pierre d'attente, *f.* *To — money*, battre monnaie. *To — into money*, monnayer (*—ed money*, argent monnayé, *m.*). *To pay one back in his own* —, rendre à quelqu'un la monnaie de sa pièce, rendre la pareille à quelqu'un
Coinage, *s.* monnayage, *m.*; (*coin*) monnaie, *f.*; (*fig.*) invention, fabrication, *f.*
Coincide, *v.n.* coïncider; (*agree*) s'accorder, être d'accord; (*meet*) se rencontrer
Coincidence, *s.* coïncidence, *f.*; conformité, *f.*; accord, *m.*; (*occurrence*) rencontre, *f.*, hasard, *m.*
Coincident, *adj* coïncident; (*agreeing*) d'accord
Coincidently, Coincidentally, *adv.* coïn-
Coindicant, *adj.* coïndicant [cidemment
Coindicate, *v.n.* coïndiquer
Coindication, *s.* coïndication, *f.*
Coiner, *s.* monnayeur, *m.*; (*— o bad money*) faux-monnayeur, *m.*; (*inventor, inventress*) faiseur, *m.*, -euse, *f.*, inventeur, *m.*, -trice, *f.*
Coining, *s.* *V.* **Coinage;** — *adj.* de monnayage; monétaire. — **engine, -press,** *s.* balancier monétaire, *m.*; presse monétaire, *f.* — **tool,** *s.* outil de monnayeur *m.*
Coir, *s.* caire, *m.*, bourre de coco, *f.*
Coition, *s.* coït, *m.*, copulation, *f.*
Coke, *s.* coke, *m.*; — *adj.* de coke; à coke. *Hard, soft* —, coke bien cuit, peu cuit. — **dust,** *s.* poussier de coke, *m.*; fraisil, *m.* — **oven,** *s.* four à coke, *m.*
Coker-nut. *V.* **Coco-nut**
Colander, *s.* passoire, *f.*
Colchicum, *s.* colchique, *m.*
Cold, *adj.* froid; — *s.* froid, *m.*, froidure, *f.*; (*disease*) rhume, *m.*; refroidissement, *m.*; (*swollen face*) fluxion, *f.*, (*arising from a draught*) coup d'air, *m.*; — *adv.* à froid. — *in the head*, rhume de cerveau. — *on the chest*, rhume de poitrine. *To be* —, *V.* **Be.** *To be* —, (*indifferent*) être froid. *To be — to one*, battre froid à quelqu'un. *To catch* or *take* —, *to get a* —, attraper un rhume (*or* un refroidissement), attraper (*or* prendre) du froid, s'enrhumer. *To get* (or *become* or *grow*) —, *V.* **Grow.** *To give a* —, enrhumer. *To have a* —, être enrhumé, avoir un rhume. *To have a bad* or *a violent* or *a heavy* —, être très enrhumé, avoir un gros *or* un fort rhume. *To have a — in the head*, être enrhumé du cerveau, avoir un rhume de cerveau. *To look — upon*, battre froid à. — **blood,** *s.* *V.* **Blood.** — **blooded,** *adj.* (*of animals*) à sang froid; (*fig.*) de sang-froid; froid, insensible; prémédité, délibéré. — **bloodedness,** *s.* sang-froid, *m.* — **chisel,** *s.* ciseau à froid, *m.* — **cream,** *s.* cold-cream, *m.* — **drawn,** *adj.* (*of metals*) étiré à froid. — **finch,** *s.* bergeronnette, *f.* — **hearted,** *adj.* froid, insensible. — **heartedness,** *s.* froideur, insensibilité, *f.* — **press,** *v.a.* presser *or* satiner à froid. — **pressing,** *s.* satinage à froid, *m.* — **short,** *adj.* (*of metals*) cassant
Coldish, *adj.* un peu froid, frais [(à froid)
Coldly, *adv.* froidement
Coldness, *s.* froid, *m.*, froideur, *f.*
Cole, *s.* chou, *m.* — **perch,** *s.* petite perche, *f.* — **seed,** *s.* graine de chou, *f.*; navette, *f.* — **wort,** *s.* chou vert, *m.*
Colegatee, *s.* colégataire, *m.f.*
Coleopteral, Coleopterous, *adj.* coléoptère
Coleopteran, *s.* coléoptère, *m.*
Colessee, *s.* copreneur, *m.*; colocataire, *m.f.*
Colic, *s.* colique, *f.*; — *adj.* (*anat.*) colique; (*med., colicky*) de colique
Colin, *s.* (*bird*) colin, *m.*
Coliseum. *V.* **Colosseum**
Colitigant, *s.* colitigant, *m.*, e, *f.*
Collaboration, *s.* collaboration, *f.*
Collaborator, *s.* collaborateur, *m.*, -trice, *f.*
Collapse, *v.n.* tomber l'un sur l'autre; (*sink*) s'affaisser; s'écrouler; tomber; tomber en ruine; baisser complètement; s'apaiser; s'aplatir; — *s.* chute de deux corps l'un sur l'autre, *f*; adhésion de deux surfaces, *f.*, rapprochement, aplatissement, *m.*; (*sinking*) affaissement, *m.*; écroulement, *m.*; chute, *f.*; baisse complète, *f.*; ruine, *f.*; débâcle, *f.*; apaisement, *m.*; (*med.*) collapsus, affaissement, *m.*
Collapsion, *s.* *V.* **Collapse,** *s.*
Collar, *s.* collier, *m.*; (*horse* —) bricole, *f.*; (*of coats, &c.*) collet, *m.*; (*of shirts*) col, *m.*; (*for ladies*) col, *m.*; (*tucker*) collerette, *f.*; (*butch.*) roulade, *f.*, rouleau, *m.*; (*arch.*) ceinture, *f.*; (*bot.*) collet, *m.*; — *v.a.* (*seize by the collar*) colleter, prendre au collet; (*nab*) empoigner; (*fig.*) agripper; (*to put a collar on*) mettre un collier à; (*butch.*) faire une roulade *or* un rouleau de, rouler. *Against the* —, avec désavantage; à perte; (*reluctantly*) à contre-cœur. *To seize* or *take by the* —, prendre au collet. — **bone,** *s.* clavicule, *f.* — **pin,** *s.* bouton à clavette, *m.*
Collaret, Collarette, *s.* collerette, *f.*; berthe, *f.*
Collate, *v.a.* collationner ('*with*,' sur); (*of livings*) conférer; (*appoint*) nommer; — *v.n.* conférer un bénéfice, pourvoir à un bénéfice
Collateral, *adj.* collatéral; parallèle; indirect; accessoire; additionnel; — *s* collatéral, *m.*
Collaterally, *adv.* collatéralement, en ligne collatérale; à côté l'un de l'autre, côte à côte; indirectement; accessoirement; incidemment
Collateralness, *s.* collatéralité, *f.*
Collation, *s.* collation, *f.*; (*gift*) don, présent, *m.*
Collative, *adj.* collatif [*livings*) collateur, *m.*
Collator, *s.* personne qui collationne, *f.*; (*of*
Colleague, *s.* collègue, *m.*

Colleagueship, *s.* qualité de collègue, *f.*
Collect, *v.a.* recueillir, rassembler; ramasser; (*works of arts,* &c.) collectionner; (*money*) ramasser; recevoir; (*com., bank.*) recevoir, encaisser; (*taxes*) percevoir; (*debts*) recouvrer, faire le recouvrement de; (*contributions*) recueillir; (*alms*) quêter; (*letters*) faire la levée de, lever, relever; (*infer*) inférer, conclure; — *v.n* s'amasser, s'entasser; — *s.* collecte, *f.* *To — oneself,* se recueillir; se remettre. — **book,** *s.* collectaire, *m.*
Collected, *part. adj.* réuni, rassemblé, &c. (*V.* **Collect**); recueilli, calme; de sang-froid
Collectedly, *adv.* d'un coup d'œil, ensemble; avec recueillement; avec calme, de sang-froid
Collectedness, *s.* recueillement, *m.*; calme, *m.*; sang-froid, *m.* [ceptible
Collectible, *adj.* (*of taxes*) percevable, per-
Collecting, *s. V.* **Collection;** — *adj* collecteur; (*of works of art,* &c.) collectionneur. — **clerk,** *s.* garçon de recette, garçon de caisse, *m.*
Collection, *s.* collection, *f.*; (*compilation*) recueil, *m.*, compilation, *f.*; (*heap*) amas, assemblage, *m.*; (*pers.*) rassemblement, *m.*, réunion, *f.*; (*of money*) recette, *f.*; (*com., bank.*) recette, *f.*, encaissement, *m.*; (*of taxes*) perception, *f.*; (*of debts, rents*) recouvrement, *m.*; (*of contributions*) collecte, *f.*; (*of alms*) quête, *f.*; collecte, *f.*; (*post.*) levée des boîtes *or* des lettres, levée, *f.*, relevage, *m.* [collectif, *s.m.*
Collective, *adj. s.* collectif, *adj. m.*, -ive, *f.*,
Collectively, *adv.* collectivement
Collectiveness, *s.* état collectif, *m.*
Collector, *s.* collecteur, *m.*; receveur, *m.*; (*of works of art,* &c.) collectionneur, *m.*; (*of taxes*) percepteur, receveur, *m.*; (*at church,* &c.) quêteur, *m.*
Collectorship, *s.* place *or* charge de percepteur, perception, *f.*; place *or* charge de receveur, recette, *f.*
Collectress, *s.* collectrice, *f.*; receveuse, *f.*; (*of works of art,* &c.) collectionneuse, *f.*; (*at church,* &c.) quêteuse, *f.*
College, *s.* collége, *m.*; lycée, *m.*; université, *f.*; société, *f.*; (*for priests*) séminaire, *m.*; (*vet., mil., nav.*) école, *f.*; (*med.*) faculté, *f.* — **cap,** *s.* toque universitaire, *f.*
Collegial, *adj.* collégial, de collége
Collegian, *s.* collégien, *m.*; lycéen, *m.*; membre d'un collége, *m.*
Collegiate, *adj.* collégial, de collége; organisé comme un collége. — *church,* église collégiale, collégiale, *f.* — *school,* institution, *f.*
Collet, *s.* collet, *m.*
Collide, *v.n.* heurter; se heurter, se choquer l'un contre l'autre; se rencontrer; (*nav.*) aborder; s'aborder
Colliding, *s.* choc, *m.*, collision, *f.*
Collier, *s.* houilleur, *m.*; (*nav.*) charbonnier, *m.*
Colliery, *s.* houillère, mine de houille, *f.*
Collie, *s.* chien de berger écossais, *m.*
Colligate, *v.a.* lier *or* attacher ensemble
Collision, *s.* collision, *f.*; choc, *m.*; (*nav.*) abordage, *m.*, collision, *f.* *To come into — with,* heurter, rencontrer; (*nav.*) aborder, heurter, [rencontrer
Collodion, *s.* collodion, *m.*
Collodionize, *v.a.* collodionner
Collop, *s.* tranche, *f.*, (*round*) rouelle, *f.*, (*dressed*) escalope, *f.*
Colloquial, *adj.* de *or* de la conversation, du langage de la conversation, qui appartient au langage de la conversation, qui ne s'emploie que dans la conversation; familier
Colloquialism, *s.* expression familière, *f.*
Colloquially, *adv.* dans la conversation, familièrement
Colloquist, *s.* interlocuteur, *m.*, -trice, *f.*
Colloquy, *s.* conversation, *f.*, colloque, entretien, *m.*
Collude, *v.n.* être d'intelligence *or* de connivence, s'entendre, colluder
Colluder, *s.* complice, *m.f.*, compère, *m.*
Collusion, *s.* collusion, *f.*; connivence, *f.*; intelligence, *f.*; compérage, *m.*
Collusive, *adj.* collusoire
Collusively, *adv.* collusoirement
Collusiveness, *s.* nature collusoire, *f.*
Collusory, *adj.* collusoire
Colly. *V.* **Collie**
Collyrium, *s.* collyre, *m.*
Colocynth, *s.* coloquinte, *f.*
Colocynthine, *s.* colocynthine, *f.*
Colombian. *V.* **Columbian** [côlon, *m.*
Colon, *s.* (*gram.*) deux points, *m.pl.*; (*anat.*)
Colonade. *V.* **Colonnade**
Colonel, *s.* colonel, *m.* [nel, *m.*
Colonelcy, Colonelship, *s.* grade de colo-
Colonial, *adj.* colonial; des colonies; de la colonie. — *produce,* denrées coloniales, *f.pl.*
Colonist, *s.* colon, *m.*
Colonizable, *adj.* colonisable
Colonization, *s.* colonisation, *f.*
Colonizationist, *s.* coloniste, *m.* [coloniser
Colonize, *v.a.* coloniser. *To become —d,* se
Colonizer, *s.* colonisateur, *m.*, -trice, *f.*
Colonizing, *s.* colonisation, *f.*; — *adj.* coloni-
Colonnade, *s.* colonnade, *f.* [sateur
Colony, *s.* colonie, *f.*
Colophony, *s.* colophane, *f.*
Coloration, *s.* coloration, *f.*
Colossal, *adj.* colossal
Colossally, *adv.* colossalement
Collosseum, *s.* colisée, *m.*
Colossus, *s.* colosse, *m.*
Colour, *s.* couleur, *f.*; apparence, *f.*; prétexte *m.*; ombre, *f.*; (*house-paint.*) badigeon, *m.*; (*polit.*) couleur, *f.*; (—**s,** *pl.*) (*mil.*) drapeau, *m.*, (*nav.*) pavillon, *m.*; — *v.a.* colorer; (*paint.*) colorier; (*prints,* &c.) colorier, enluminer; (*in photography*) retoucher; (*the hair*) teindre; (*a tobacco-pipe*) culotter; (*house-paint.*) badigeonner; (*palliate*) colorer, pallier; (*of goods*) mettre sous son nom; — *v.n.* (*pers.*) rougir; (*things*) se colorer; (*of tobacco-pipes*) se culotter. — **blindness,** *s.* daltonisme, *m.* — **box,** *s.* boîte de *or* à couleurs, *f.* —**less,** *adj. See below.* — **man,** *s.* marchand de couleurs, *m.* — **sergeant,** *s.* porte-drapeau, *m.*
Colourable, *adj.* plausible, spécieux
Colourableness, *s.* plausibilité, *f.*, nature spécieuse, *f.*, caractère spécieux, *m.*
Colourably, *adv.* plausiblement, spécieusement
Coloured, *part. adj.* coloré, &c. (*V.* **Colour,** *v.a.*); de couleur; (*in compounds*) de couleur ..., couleur ...
Colourer, *s.* coloriste, *m.f.*; (*of prints,* &c.) enlumineur, *m.*, -euse, *f.*; (*house-paint.*) badigeonneur, *m.*; (*of photographs*) *V.* **Colourist**
Colouring, *s.* couleur, *f.*; (*brightness*) coloris, *m.*; (*of prints,* &c.) enluminure, *f.*; (*of photographs*) retouchage, *m.*; (*house-paint.*) badigeonnage, *m.*; (*burnt sugar*) caramel, *m.*; — *adj.* colorant. — *matter,* matière *or* substance colorante, *f.* [retoucheur, *m.*, -euse, *f.*
Colourist, *s.* coloriste, *m.f.*; (*of photographs*)
Colourless, *adj.* sans couleur, incolore; décoloré; terne, pale; transparent
Colt, *s.* poulain, *m.*; (*pers.*) étourdi, étourneau, jeune fou, *m.*; novice, *m.* —**'s-foot,** *s.* tussilage, pas d'âne, *m.* —**'s-tooth,** *s.* dent de lait, *f.*
Colter. *V.* **Coulter**
Coltish, *adj.* folâtre
Colubrine, *adj.* colubrin, couleuvrin, de couleuvre, de serpent; (*cunning*) rusé, astucieux
Columbian, *s. adj* Colombien, *m.*, -ne, *f.*
Columbier, *s.* (*paper*) colombier, *m.*
Columbine, *adj.* colombaire, de pigeon; (*of colour*) colombin, gorge-de-pigeon; — *s.* colombine, *f.*; (*bot.*) ancolie, *f.*
Columbium, *s.* colombium, *m.* [colombelle, *f.*
Column, *s.* colonne, *f.* — **rule,** *s.* (*print.*)
Columnar, *adj.* colomnaire; de colonne; en
Columned, *adj.* à colonnes [colonne
Columniation, *s.* colonnation, *f.*

Colure, *s.* colure, *m.*
Colza, *s.* colza, *m.* — **oil,** *s.* huile de colza, *f.*
Coma, *s.* (*med.*) coma, *m.*; (*bot.*) coma, *m.*, chevelure, *f.*; (*astr.*) chevelure, *f.* [pagnon, *m.*
Comate, *adj.* chevelu; — *s.* camarade, com-
Comatose, Comatous, *adj.* comateux
Comb, *s.* peigne, *m.*; (*for horses*) étrille, *f.*; (*of cocks, of waves*) crête, *f.*; (*of honey*) rayon, *m.*; (*valley*) combe, *f.*; — *v.a.* peigner; (*horses*) étriller; — *v.n.* (*of the sea*) déferler. *Large-tooth* —, démêloir, *m.* *Small-tooth* —, peigne fin, *m.* *To — the hair* or *head of*, peigner. *To — o's hair* or *head, To — oneself*, se peigner. — **bag,** *s.* porte-peigne, *m.* — **brush,** *s.* brosse à peignes, *f.*, décrasse-peignes, *m.* — **case,** *s.* porte-peigne, *m.* — **cutting,** *s.* coupe des peignes, *f.* —**less,** *adj.* sans crête. — **maker, -manufacturer,** *s.* peignier, fabricant de peignes, *m.* — **making, -manufactory, -trade,** *s.* peignerie, *f.*
Combat, *v.a.n.* combattre; — *s.* combat, *m.*
Combatable, *adj.* combattable
Combatant, *s.* combattant, *m.*
Combative, *adj.* guerroyant, guerrier, belliqueux; querelleur, batailleur
Combativeness, *s.* humeur guerroyante, *f.*, esprit guerrier, *m.*; caractère querelleur *or* batailleur, *m.*, pugnacité, *f.*; (*in phrenology*) [combativité, *f.*
Combe, *s.* (*valley*) combe, *f.*
Comber, *s.* peigneur, *m.*, -euse, *f.*; (*machine*) peigneuse, *f.*; (*wave*) vague crêtée, *f.*
Combinable, *adj.* combinable
Combination, *s.* combinaison, *f.*; réunion, *f.*; union, *f.*; alliance, *f.*; association, *f.*; ligue, coalition, *f.*; concours, *m.*; (*math., chem.*) combinaison, *f.*
Combine, *v.a.* combiner; réunir; unir; allier; associer; liguer, coaliser; (*chem.*) combiner; — *v.n.* se combiner; se réunir (à); s'unir (à); s'allier (à); se liguer, se coaliser; (*chem.*) se combiner
Combiner, *s.* combinateur, *m.*, -trice, *f.*
Combing, *s.* action de peigner, *f.*; (*tech.*) peignage, *m.*; —**s,** *pl.* peignures, *f.pl.* — **cloth,** *s.* peignoir, *m.* — **machine,** *s.* peigneuse, *f.* [combinateur
Combining, *s.* *V.* **Combination;** — *adj.*
Combusti-bility, bleness. *V.* page 3, § 1
Combustible, *adj.s.* combustible, *adj.m.f., s.m.*
Combustion, *s.* combustion, *f.* *Supporter of* —, (*chem.*) comburant, *m.*
Come, *v.n.* venir; arriver; se présenter; approcher; avancer; passer; procéder; (*ascend*) monter (sur); (*be produced*) provenir (de), venir (de); (*happen*) se faire; arriver; (*happen to be*) se rencontrer, se trouver; (*amount, recover*) revenir (à); (*of accounts*) se monter (à), s'élever (à); (*to a pass*) en venir (à); (*be reduced*) se réduire, (*pers.*) être réduit (à), en venir (à); (*to fall*) tomber (dans); (*become*) devenir; (*end in*) aboutir (à); résulter (de); (*be about to*) aller; (*go*) aller. *V.* **Coming,** *part. adj.* *To — to the same* or *to the same thing*, revenir au même. *To — to oneself*, revenir à soi. *To — to* (*a person*), venir à; venir trouver. *To — and see, — and play, — and fetch*, &c., venir voir, venir jouer, venir chercher, &c. *To — and go*, venir et s'en aller; ne faire que passer; nous prendre et nous quitter. *To — undone, unsewed*, &c., se défaire, se découdre, &c. —*!* — *along!* — *on!* allons! venez! venez donc! arrivez! marchons! *To* —, (*future*) à venir, futur. *For some time to* —, d'ici à quelque temps. *How —s it that ...?* comment se fait-il que ...? d'où vient que ...? *How —s that?* comment cela se fait-il? d'où cela vient-il? *How came you to leave the college?* comment se fait-il que vous ayez quitté le collége? — *what may*, — *what will*, arrive (*or* advienne), que pourra. *How much does it — to?* à combien cela se monte-t-il? — **about,** arriver, survenir, se passer; changer, tourner: (*succeed*) arriver à terme; (*recover*) se remettre, revenir à soi. — **across,** donner de la tête contre; (*fall upon*) tomber sur; (*meet*) rencontrer; (*to cross*) traverser. — **after,** venir après; suivre, succéder à; (*come for*) venir chercher. — **again,** revenir. — **against,** heurter, frapper. — **along,** s'en venir, venir; marcher.* — **asunder,** se séparer; se détacher; se défaire; s'en aller par morceaux. — **at,** arriver à *or* jusqu'à, atteindre; (*succeed*) parvenir à. — **away,** s'en venir; s'en aller, se retirer, partir. — **back,** — **back again,** revenir. — **between,** intervenir; s'entremettre; s'interposer. — **by,** passer; passer par; venir par; passer devant; passer près de; passer auprès; approcher de; approcher; obtenir, acquérir, se procurer; attraper; (*succeed*) parvenir à. — **down,** descendre; (*fall suddenly*) tomber; (*of prices*, &c., *get lower*) baisser; (*pounce*) fondre (sur), s'abattre (sur); (*fork out*) financer, dégaîner, abouler; (— *from town*) venir. — **down again,** redescendre; retomber; &c. — **down upon** (*one*) **for,** *V.* — **upon** (*one*) **for.** — **for,** venir pour; (*fetch*) venir chercher; (*a walk, a ride, a drive*, &c., *or a turn*) venir faire. — **forth,** — **forward,** s'avancer, avancer, se présenter, venir, arriver, paraître; sortir; se mettre en avant; (*spread*) se répandre. — **from,** venir *or* &c. de. — **in,** entrer; arriver; venir; se présenter; rentrer; (*into a carriage*) monter; (*be in fashion*) s'introduire, devenir (*or* venir) à la mode, être de mode; (*of tide*) monter; (*contribute*) contribuer (à), servir (à); (*submit*) se soumettre (à). — **in again,** rentrer; revenir; se représenter; remonter. — **in for,** entrer pour; entrer pour chercher, entrer pour prendre; se présenter pour; (*property*) acquérir, obtenir, recevoir, avoir; hériter de. — **in and out,** entrer et sortir; aller et venir. — **in to,** venir trouver; venir se joindre à; venir au secours de. — **into,** entrer dans *or* en, &c. (*V.* — **in**); se mettre dans *or* en; tomber dans; prendre part à, concourir à; consentir à, approuver. — **near,** approcher de, s'approcher de; approcher; n'être pas éloigné de; (*to ... nearly*) faillir, être sur le point (de). — **next,** suivre immédiatement. — **of,** résulter de, provenir de, venir de *or* de ce que. — **off,** *v.n.* s'en aller; (*to fall*) tomber, se détacher; (*of spots*, &c.) s'enlever; (*to end*) se terminer, en finir; (*get out of*) se tirer d'affaire, s'en tirer, en sortir, échapper; (*with*) en être quitte (pour); (*take place*) arriver, avoir lieu; se passer; (*show off*) se détacher; se dessiner; ressortir; (*guard, mil.*) descendre. *To — off victorious*, remporter la victoire. — **off,** *s.* faux-fuyant, *m.*, échappatoire, défaite, *f.* — **on,** venir; s'avancer; avancer; approcher; (*happen*) arriver, survenir, avoir lieu; (*law*) attaquer. — **out,** sortir; (*out of a carriage*) descendre; (*appear*) se montrer, paraître; se manifester; se déclarer; (*in society*) débuter; se lancer; (*of books*) paraître, être publié; (*show off*) ressortir; se dessiner; se détacher; (*to be found out*) se découvrir; transpirer; (*to fall*) tomber, se détacher; (*of spots*) s'en aller, s'effacer, disparaître; (*to end*) se terminer, finir. — **out again,** ressortir; (*out of a carriage*) redescendre; (*reappear*) reparaître. — **out with,** sortir avec; se montrer avec; (*to utter*) dire, lâcher, laisser échapper; (*display*) faire parade de, étaler. — **over,** traverser; passer; venir; (*seize*) s'emparer de, saisir, gagner; (*boil over*) s'enfuir, s'en aller; (*overcome*) surmonter, vaincre, venir à bout de; l'emporter sur; (*wheedle*) enjôler. — **past,** passer; passer devant (...); passer à côté de (...) *or* &c. (*V.* **Past,** *prep.*). — **round,** faire le tour de (...); faire le tour; faire un détour; tourner; prendre le plus long; venir; revenir; (*inspect*) venir faire sa ronde; (*recover*) se ré-

tablir, se remettre; (*yield*) céder; consentir; (*surround*) entourer, environner; (*wheedle*) circonvenir; entortiller. — **round again,** revenir; (*recover*) se rétablir; (*from fainting*) revenir à soi. — **to,** venir *or* &c. à (*V. general senses of* **To Come**); (*reach*) atteindre à; atteindre; gagner; (*a decision*) prendre; (*inherit*) hériter de; entrer en possession de; acquérir; (*recover*) se remettre, revenir à soi, recouvrer ses sens; (*be reported*) revenir à; (*yield*) consentir à; céder. — **together,** venir ensemble; se réunir. — **under,** être compris sous; être soumis à. — **up,** monter; venir; s'avancer; (*rise*) s'élever; (*get*) arriver; (*grow*) pousser; (— *to town*) venir. — **up to,** monter à; s'élever à *or* jusqu'à; venir à, s'avancer vers; (— *a person*) venir à, s'avancer vers; venir trouver; (*reach*) atteindre; (*near*) approcher de; (*correspond*) répondre à, satisfaire. — **up with,** atteindre, attraper. — **upon,** s'avancer sur; (*fall upon*) tomber sur, fondre sur; (*be a burden to*) tomber à la charge de; (*surprise*) surprendre, arriver à (quelqu'un) à l'improviste; (*seize*) saisir, attaquer, s'emparer de; (*meet with*) rencontrer, trouver. — **upon** (*one*) **for** ..., s'en prendre à; s'adresser à (quelqu'un) pour ...; réclamer ... (à quelqu'un)

Comedian, *s.* comédien, *m.*, -ne, *f.*, acteur, *m.*, -trice, *f.*; (*author*) auteur comique, comique, *m.*

Comedy, *s.* comédie, *f.*

Comelily, *adv.* avec grâce

Comeliness, *s.* beauté, grâce, bonne mine, *f.*, agréments, *m.pl.*; dignité, *f.*

Comely, *adj.* beau; gracieux; avenant; (*becoming*) convenable; digne; — *adv.* avec grâce

Comer, *s.* venant, *m.*; (*with 'first,' 'last,' 'new' or 'fresh'*) venu, *m.*, e, *f.*; (*person arrived*) arrivant, *m.*, e, *f.*; (*stranger*) étranger, *m.*, -ère, *f.* *Against all —s,* contre n'importe qui. *To all —s,* à tout venant [comète

Comet, *s.* comète, *f.* — **like,** *adj.* comme une

Cometary, *adj.* cométaire

Comfit, *s.* dragée, *f.*

Comfort, *v.a.* reconforter; consoler; encourager; (*relieve*) soulager; — *s.* bien-être, *m.*, aisance, *f.*; confort, comfort, confortable, *m.*; consolation, *f.*, soulagement, *m.*; encouragement, *m.*; (*delight*) jouissance, douceur, *f.*; (*convenience*) commodité, aise, *f.*, agrément, *m.* *To be of good —, to take —,* prendre courage; se consoler; se réjouir

Comfortable, *adj.* confortable, commode; agréable, bon; consolant; suffisant, convenable, honnête; (*pers.*) à son aise; bien. *To make oneself —,* se mettre à son aise; se donner toutes ses aises, se donner du bien-être

Comfortableness, *s.* bien-être, *m.*; bonheur, *m.*; jouissance, *f.*; agrément, *m.*

Comfortably, *adv.* commodément; confortablement; à son aise; bien; agréablement

Comforter, *s.* consolateur, *m.*, -trice, *f.*; (*scarf*) cache-nez, *m.*; (*drink*) consolation, *f.*

Comfortless, *adj.* incommode, gênant; désagréable; sans consolation, triste, malheureux; (*pers.*) mal à son aise; inconsolable

Comfortlessly, *adv.* incommodément; mal à son aise, mal; désagréablement; sans consolation, inconsolablement, tristement

Comfortlessness, *s.* incommodité, *f.*; malaise, *m.*, gêne, *f.*; désagrément, *m.*; (*sadness*)

Comfortress, *s* consolatrice, *f.* [tristesse, *f.*

Comfrey, *s.* consoude, *f.*

Com-ic, al, -ically. *V.* page 3, § 1

Comicalness, *s.* caractère comique, *m.*, nature comique, *f.*; comique, *m.*

Coming, *part. adj.* venant, arrivant, &c., qui vient, qui arrive, &c. (*V.* **Come,** *v.n.*); qui s'approche, prochain, proche; futur, à venir. *He is —,* il vient; il arrive; il approche; (*he will soon come*) il va venir. *— ! I am — !* j'y vais! on y va! voilà! — **in,** *part. adj.* entrant, &c.; (*as income*) de revenu

Coming, *s.* venue, arrivée, *f.*; approche, *f.*; (*to the throne, and of Christ*) avénement, *m.* — **back,** *s.* retour, *m.* — **in,** *s.* entrée, *f.*; venue, arrivée, *f.*; commencement, *m.*; introduction, *f.*; (*income*) revenu, *m.* — **on,** *s.* approche, *f.* — **out,** *s.* sortie, *f.*; départ, *m.* — **in and out,** *s.* allées et venues, *f.pl.* — **together,**

Comitia, *s. pl.* comices, *m.pl.* [*s.* réunion, *f.*

Comitial, *adj.* comitial, comicial [tesse, *f.*

Comity, *s.* courtoisie, urbanité, civilité, poli-

Comma, *s.* (*gram.*) virgule, *f.*; (*mus.*) comma, *m.* *Inverted —,* (*gram.*) guillemet, *m.* *In* or *between inverted —s,* guillemeté

Command, *v.a.* commander, ordonner; (*be at the head of*) commander; (*to master*) commander à, maîtriser; (*overlook*) commander, dominer; (*of money,* &c.) avoir à sa disposition; posséder, avoir; (*of respect,* &c.) commander, inspirer; (*impose*) imposer; (*theol.*) envoyer; — *v.n.* commander; — *s.* commandement, *m.*; ordre, *m.*; ordres, *m.pl.*; autorité, *f.*, pouvoir, empire, *m.*; (*obligation*) loi, exigence, *f.*; (*knowledge*) connaissance, *f.*; (*fluency*) facilité, *f.*; (*hunt.*) créance, *f.* — *of a language,* connaissance d'une langue. — *of language,* facilité d'expressions. *Word of —,* (*mil.*) commandement, *m.* *At —,* à commandement; à sa disposition. *Yours to —,* à vos ordres, votre obéissant serviteur. *To be at anyone's —,* être aux ordres de quelqu'un. *To give the word of —,* (*mil.*) commander. *To — a view of,* dominer. *To be second in —,* commander en second

Commandant, *s.* commandant, *m.*

Commander, *s.* commandant, *m.*; général, *m.*; (*of knights, caliphs*) commandeur, *m.*; (*for paving*) demoiselle, hie, *f.*

Commandery, *s.* commanderie, *f.*

Commanding, *adj.* commandant; (*overlooking*) dominant; (*imposing*) imposant; (*imperious*) de commandement, d'autorité, impérieux. — *officier,* commandant, *m.*

Commandingly, *adv.* avec autorité; d'une manière imposante

Commandment, *s.* commandement, ordre, *m.*; autorité, *f.*; précepte, *m.*; (*theol.*) commandement, *m.*

Commemorate, *v.a.* commémorer; célébrer

Commemoration, *s.* commémoration, *f.*; souvenir, *m.*, mémoire, *f.*; célébration, solennisation, *f.*; (*prayer*) commémoraison, *f.*

Commemorative, *adj.* commémoratif

Commence, Commencement. *V.* **Begin, Beginning**

Commend, *v.a.* recommander; (*praise*) louer; (*remember*) recommander au souvenir de; (*trust*) confier (à), commettre (à), remettre; (*set off*) faire valoir, faire remarquer, faire briller [*worthy*) louable

Commendable, *adj.* recommandable; (*praise-*

Commendableness, *s.* qualité d'être louable, *f.*, mérite, *m.*

Commendably, *adv.* recommandablement, louablement, d'une manière louable *or* recom-

Commendam, *s.* commende, *f.* [mandable

Commendation, *s.* recommandation, *f.*; éloge, *m.*; louange, *f.*; qualité, *f.*

Commendator, *s.* commendataire, *m.*

Commendatory, *adj.* de recommandation; élogieux, d'éloges, flatteur; (*can. law*) com-

Commender, *s.* panégyriste, *m.* [mendataire

Commensal, *s.* commensal, *m.*, e, *f.*

Commensality, *s.* commensalité, *f.*

Commensura-bility, bleness. *V.* page 3, § 1

Commensurable, *adj.* commensurable

Commensurate, *adj.* commensurable; proportionné (à), en rapport (avec); — *v.a.* réduire à une mesure commune; proportionner; mesurer

Commensurately, *adv.* d'une manière commensurable; proportionnément; dans d'égales proportions [proportion, *f.*

Commensuration, *s.* commensuration, *f.*;

Comment, *v.a.n.* commenter
Comment, Commentary, *s.* commentaire, *m.*
Commentator, Commenter, *s.* commentateur, -trice, *f.*
Commerce, *s.* commerce, *m.*
Commercial, *adj.* commercial, de commerce; (*of countries, towns*) commerçant. — *undertaking,* entreprise commerciale, *f.* — *intercourse,* relations commerciales, *f.pl.* — *house, society, traveller, broker, treaty,* maison (*f.*), société (*f.*), voyageur (*m.*), courtier (*m.*), traité (*m.*), de commerce. — *law,* droit commercial, code de commerce, *m.* — *dictionary,* dictionnaire de commerce, *m.* — *directory,* almanach du commerce, *m.* — *man,* homme qui est dans le commerce, *m.*; commerçant, *m.* — *class,* classe commerçante, *f.* — *harbour,* port marchand, port de commerce, *m.* — *navigation,* commerce maritime, *m.*
Commercially, *adv.* commercialement
Commination, *s.* commination, *f.*
Comminatory, *adj.* comminatoire, menaçant
Commingle, *v.a.* mêler, confondre; — *v.n.* se mêler, se confondre
Comminute, *v.a.* comminuer, briser en petits morceaux. —*d fracture,* (*surg.*) fracture comminutive, *f.*
Comminuting, *adj.* comminutif
Comminution, *s.* comminution, *f.*
Commiserable, *adj.* digne de compassion
Commiserate, *v.a.* plaindre, avoir pitié de, avoir compassion de
Commiserating, *adj.* plein de commisération
Commiseration, *s.* commisération, pitié, *f.*
Commiserative, *adj.* plein de commisération
Commiseratively, *adv.* avec commisération
Commiserator, *s.* âme compatissante, *f.*
Commissarial, *adj.* de commissaire; d'intendant
Commissariat, *s.* intendance militaire, intendance, *f.*
Commissary, *s.* commissaire, *m.*; (*mil.,* — *of stores*) intendant militaire, *m.*
Commissaryship, *s.* commissariat, *m.*
Commission, *s.* commission, *f.*; ordre, *m.*; mandat, *m.*; mission, *f.*; (*of faults*) commission, action de commettre, *f.*; (*of crimes*) perpétration, *f.*; (*of officers*) brevet, *m.*; (*body of commissioners*) commission, *f.*; commissariat, *m.*; — *v.a.* commissionner; déléguer; charger (de); autoriser (à); donner pouvoir à ... (de); envoyer en mission; (*mil.*) breveter. *On* —, à commission. *Sin of* —, péché de commission, *m.* *To throw up o.'s* —, donner sa démission. — **agency,** *s.* (*business*) commission, *f.*; (*house*) maison de commission, *f.* — **agent,** *s.* commissionnaire en marchandises, commissionnaire, *m.*; expéditionnaire, expéditeur, *m.* — **merchant,** *s.* négociant commissionnaire, *m.*
Commissionaire, *s.* commissionnaire, *m.*
Commissioned, *part. adj.* commissionné, &c. (*V.* **Commission,** *v.a.*); (*of mil. officers*) breveté, pourvu d'un brevet. — *and non-* — *officers,* (*mil.*) officiers et sous-officiers, *m.pl.*
Commissioner, *s.* commissaire, *m*; —**s,** *pl.* (*nav.,* —*s of the admiralty, naval* —*s*) commissaires, *m.pl.,* commissariat de la marine, commissariat, *m.* — *of bankruptcy,* juge-commissaire de faillite, *m.* *Chief* — *of police,* préfet de police, *m.*
Commissionership, *s.* commissariat, *m.*
Commissure, *s.* commissure, *f.*
Commit, *v.a.* commettre; confier (à); livrer; envoyer en prison, emprisonner, délivrer un mandat de dépôt contre; déposer; compromettre; engager, lier; entraîner; (*parliam.*) renvoyer à une commission. *To* — *to memory,* graver dans sa mémoire; apprendre par cœur. *To* — *for trial, to fully* —, (*law*) envoyer en prison, emprisonner, délivrer un mandat de dépôt contre
Commitment, *s.* emprisonnement, *m.*; mise en prévention, *f.*; (*warrant of* —) mandat de dépôt, *m.*; (*parliam.*) renvoi à une commission, *m.*; (*trust*) action de confier, *f.*; dépôt, *m.*; (*of faults, crimes*) *V.* **Commission**; (*pledging*) engagement, *m.,* mise en gage, *f.*; (*exposing or endangering*) action de compromettre, *f*
Committal, *s.* *V.* **Commitment** *and* **Commission**
Committee, *s.* comité, *m.*; (*parliam.*) commission, *f.*; bureau, *m.*; (*law, pers.*) curateur, *m.,* -trice, *f.* *Private* —, commission. *Select* —, commission d'enquête. *To call a* — *of the whole House,* demander le comité secret. *The House will resolve itself* (or *will go*) *into a* —, la Chambre se formera en comité secret. — **man,** *s.* membre d'un comité, *m.*; (*parliam.*) membre d'une commission, *m.* — **room,** *s.* salle de comité, *f.*; (*parliam.*) salle de commission, *f.*; bureau, *m.*
Committeeship, *s.* curatelle, tutelle, *f.*
Committer, *s.* personne qui commet *or* qui a commis, *f.,* auteur (de), *m.*; criminel, *m.,* coupable, *m.f.*
Commode, *s.* (*night-stool*) chaise percée, *f.*; (*chest of drawers*) commode, *f.*; (*anc. head-dress*) commode, baigneuse, *f.* *Night* —, chaise percée, *f.*
Commodious, *adj.* commode; confortable
Commodiously, *adv.* commodément; confortablement
Commodiousness, *s.* commodité, *f.*; avantage, *m.*
Commodity, *s.* marchandise, denrée; (*polit. econ.*) produit, *m.*
Commodore, *s.* chef de division, *m.,* (*formerly*) chef d'escadre, *m.*; (*in England and America*) commodore, *m.*; (*ship*) bâtiment convoyeur, *m.*
Commodoreship, *s.* grade de chef de division *or* &c. (*V.* **Commodore**)
Common, *adj.* commun; vulgaire; du peuple; trivial; ordinaire; public; (*soldier, sailor*) simple; (*people*) menu, bas; (*of prices*) courant; (*mus.*) à deux temps; — *s.* plaine, *f.,* terrain vague, *m.,* terre vaine et vague, terre inculte, bruyère, *f.,* landes, *f.pl.*; terrain dépendant de la voie publique, *m.*; terrain communal, *m.,* communaux, *m.pl.*; vaine pâture, *f.*; servitude sur la propriété, *f.*; —**s,** *s.pl.* plaines, *f.pl.,* &c.; (*commonalty*) bourgeoisie, *f.*; (*house of* —*s*) Chambre des Communes, *f.,* Communes, *f.pl.,* (*in France*) Assemblée législative, *f.,* Corps législatif, *m.,* Chambre des députés, *f.*; (*food*) ordinaire, *m.*; chère, *f.*; table, *f.* *Doctors'* —, officialité, *f.* *House of* —, Chambre des Communes, *f.* *In* —, en commun. *To have nothing in* — *with,* n'avoir rien de commun avec. *To be on short* —*s,* être réduit à un petit ordinaire *or* à une maigre pitance, avoir peu à manger, faire maigre chère, être à la ration. *To put on short* —*s,* réduire à une maigre pitance, donner peu à manger, mettre à la ration, rationner. — **council,** — **councillor,** — **crier,** — **hall,** *s.* *V.* **Town-council,** &c. — **law,** *s.* droit commun, *m.*; droit coutumier, *m.* — **lawyer,** *s.* jurisconsulte en droit coutumier, *m.* — **people,** *s. pl.* menu *or* bas peuple, *m.,* petites gens, *f.pl.,* gens du peuple, *m.f. pl.* — **place,** *s.* lieu commun, *m.*; note, *f.,* mémento, *m.*; *adj.* banal, commun; trivial; terre à terre; *v.a.* insérer dans un mémento *or* dans un recueil; *v.n.* faire des extraits et prendre des notes. — **place-book,** *s.* cahier de notes, mémento, *m.*; recueil de lieux communs, *m.* — **pleas,** *s. pl.* *V.* **Plea.** — **prayer,** *s.* liturgie anglicane, *f.* — **sailor,** *s.* simple matelot, *m.* — **sense,** *s.* sens commun, *m.*; bon sens, *m.*; *adj.* du sens commun; sensé, raisonnable. *Good* — *sense,* gros bon sens, *m.* — **school,** *s.* école publique, *f.,* collége, *m.* — **sewer,** *s.* égout public, égout, *m.* — **sized,** *adj.* de grosseur *or* de grandeur *or* de taille ordinaire. — **soldier,** *s.* simple soldat, *m.* — **weal,** — **wealth,** *s.* république, *f.,* état, *m.,* nation, *f.* — **wealth's man,** *s.* républicain, *m.*
Commonage, *s.* usage, droit d'usage, *m.*; (*law*) droit de vaine pâture, *m.*

Commonalty, *s.* bourgeoisie, *f.*
Commoner, *s.* bourgeois, *m.*; (*of parliam.*) membre de la Chambre des Communes, *m.*; (*law*) usager, *m.*; (*univers.*) étudiant ordinaire, *m.*
Commonly, *adv.* communément, ordinairement; souvent
Commonness, *s.* nature commune *or* ordinaire, *f.*; fréquence, *f.*; communauté, jouissance en commun, *f.* [rumeur, en l'air
Commotion, *s.* commotion, *f. In* —, agité; en
Communal, *adj.* communal
Commune, *v.n.* conférer, converser, s'entretenir, parler; — *s.* commune, *f.*
Communica-bility, bleness. *V.* page 3, § 1
Communicable, *adj.* communicable
Communicant, *s.* communiant, *m.*, e, *f.*
Communicate, *v.a.n.* communiquer; (*of sacraments*) communier
Communicating, *adj.* communicant, de communication; — *part.* communiquant
Communication, *s.* communication, *f.*; (*conversation*) entretien, *m.*
Communicative, *adj.* communicatif
Communicatively, *adv.* communicativement
Communicativeness, *s.* caractère *or* naturel communicatif, *m.*
Communicator, *s.* communicateur, *m.*
Communion, *s.* communication, *f.*, rapports, *m.pl.*, relations, *f.pl*, commerce, *m.*; (*sacrament, union in faith*) communion, *f.*; (*community*) communauté, *f. To receive the* —, communier. — **cloth,** *s.* nappe de communion, *f.* — **cup,** *s.* calice, *m.* — **office, -service,** *s.* office de la communion, *m.* — **table,** *s.* sainte table, *f.*
Commun-ism, -ist. *V.* page 3, § 1
Communistic, *adj.* communiste
Community, *s.* communauté, *f.*; société, *f.*, public, *m.*; état, *m.*; nation, *f.*; classe, *f.*
Commuta-bility, bleness, *s.* permutabilité, échangeabilité, *f.*; (*law*) commuabilité, *f.*
Commutable, *adj.* permutable, échangeable; changeable; (*law*) commuable
Commutation, *s.* permutation, *f.*, échange, *m.*; changement, *m.*; (*law*) commutation, *f.*
Commutative, *adj.* commutatif
Commutatively, *adv.* par échange
Commute, *v.a.* permuter, échanger; changer; (*law*) commuer; — *v.n.* tenir lieu (de), racheter
Comose, *adj.* chevelu
Compact, *adj.* compacte; (*close*) serré; (*of style*) concis; — *s.* pacte, contrat, *m.*, convention, *f.*; — *v.a.* rendre compacte, condenser; lier, assembler, unir
Compactly, *adv.* d'une manière compacte *or* serrée; (*of style*) avec concision, brièvement
Compactness, *s.* compacité, densité, *f.*
Companion, *s.* compagnon, *m.*, compagne, *f.*, camarade, *m.f.*; (*for ladies*) demoiselle *or* dame de compagnie, *f.*; (*of furniture*, &c.) pendant, *m.*; (*nav.*) capot d'échelle, *m.* — **ladder,** *s.* (*nav.*) échelle de dunette, *f.* —**less,** *adj.* sans compagnon, sans compagne. — **piece,** *s.* pendant, *m.* [agréable
Companionable, *adj.* sociable, d'une société
Companionableness, *s.* sociabilité, *f.*
Companionably, *adv.* sociablement
Companionship, *s.* camaraderie, *f.*; compagnie, société, *f.*
Company, *s.* compagnie, *f.*; société, *f.*; (*people*) monde, *m.*; (*of actors*) troupe, *f.*; (*troop*) bande, *f.*; (*guild*) corporation, *f.*; (*associates*) entourage, *m.*; (*com.*) compagnie, *f.*; société, *f.*; (*mil.*) compagnie, *f.*; (*nav.: crew*) équipage, *m.*, (*convoy*) conserve, *f. To bear* —, tenir compagnie à, accompagner. *To break* or *break off* (or *up*) —, se séparer. *To go into* —, aller dans le monde. *To keep* —, tenir compagnie à; (*receive*) voir du monde; (*with*) faire société (avec), fréquenter; (*to court*) faire la cour à; (*nav., to sail in* —) aller *or* naviguer de conserve. *To keep bad* or *good* —, fréquenter la mauvaise *or* la bonne compagnie. *To part* —, se séparer. *Mr. A. requests the honour* (or *the pleasure, the favour*) *of Mr. B.'s — this evening* (or *at dinner*), M. A. prie M. B. de lui faire l'honneur (*or* le plaisir) de venir passer la soirée chez lui (*or* de venir dîner avec lui)
Comparable, *adj.* comparable
Comparableness, *s.* comparabilité, *f.*
Comparably, *adv.* comparablement, en comparaison; à beaucoup près
Comparates, *s. pl.* choses (*f.pl.*) *or* objets (*m.pl.*) comparables *or* analogues
Comparative, *adj.* comparatif; relatif; (*of sciences*) comparé; — *s.* comparatif, *m.* — *degree*, comparatif, *m. In the* — (*degree*), au comparatif [lativement
Comparatively, *adv.* comparativement; re-
Compare, *v.a.* comparer; (*of accounts*) confronter; — *v.n.* rivaliser (avec), le disputer (à); — *s. V.* **Comparison.** *Compared with*, en comparaison de, auprès de. *Compared with it* or *them* (*things*), en comparaison, auprès
Comparer, *s.* comparateur, *m.*, -trice, *f.*
Comparing, *adj.* comparateur
Comparison, Compare, *s.* comparaison, *f. Beyond* —, sans comparaison, hors de comparaison. *Beyond all* —, au-delà de toute comparaison. *In — of* or *with*, *V.* **Compared with**
Compartment, *s.* compartiment, *m.*
Compass, *s.* cercle, tour, *m.*; étendue, *f.*; espace, *m.*; dimension, *f.*; sphère, *f.*; limites, bornes, *f.pl.*; (*enclosure*) enceinte, *f.*; (*reach*) portée, *f.*; (*mus., of the voice*, &c.) étendue, *f.*; (*instr.*) compas, *m.*; (*surveyor's*) boussole, *f.*; (*nav.*) boussole, *f.*, compas de mer, *m.*; —**es,** *pl.* (*instr.*) compas, *m. A pair of —es*, un compas, *m. To keep within* —, (*v.a.*) renfermer dans un cadre étroit; retenir dans de justes bornes; (*v.n.*) garder les convenances, se renfermer (*or* se tenir) dans de justes limites. *To speak within* —, parler avec modération; ne pas exagérer. — **card,** *s.* rose des vents, *f.* — **saw,** *s.* passe-partout, *m.*
Compass, *v.a.* entourer, environner; faire le tour de; embrasser; traquer; assiéger; bloquer; atteindre, venir à bout de; obtenir; accomplir; comploter, méditer; (*to measure with compasses*) compasser
Compassing, *s.* compassement, *m.*
Compassion, *s.* compassion, pitié, *f.*
Compassionate, *adj.* compatissant; — *v.a.* compatir à; avoir compassion de
Compassionately, *adv.* avec compassion
Compaternity, *s.* compaternité, *f.*; compérage, *m.*
Compati-bility, bleness. *V.* page 3, § 1
Compatible, *adj.* compatible
Compatibly, *adv.* d'une manière compatible
Compatriot, *s.* compatriote, *m.f.*; — *adj.* du même pays (que), compatriote (de)
Compatriotism, *s.* compatriotisme, *m.*
Compeer, *s.* égal, pair, *m.*; compagnon, *m.*, compagne, *f.*, camarade, *m.f.*; (*accomplice*) compère, acolyte, *m.* [*in the passive*, de)
Compel, *v.a.* forcer, contraindre, obliger (à;
Compellable, *adj.* contraignable
Compendious, *adj.* compendieux, abrégé, raccourci, concis, compacte
Compendiously, *adv.* compendieusement, en abrégé, en raccourci
Compendiousness, *s.* brièveté, concision, *f.*
Compendium, *s.* compendium, abrégé, précis, *m.*
Compensable, *adj.* compensable
Compensate, *v.a.n.* compenser; (*reward*) dédommager (de). — **for,** compenser; dédommager de
Compensating, *adj.* compensateur
Compensation, *s.* compensation, *f.*; — *adj.* compensateur. — **balance** *or* **pendulum,** *s.* balancier *or* pendule compensateur, compensateur, m.
Compensative, *adj.* compensateur

Compensator, *s.* compensateur, *m.*
Compensatory, *adj.* compensatoire
Compete, *v.n.* (*with*) faire concurrence (à), être en concurrence (avec), rivaliser (avec), le disputer (à); (*with ... for*) concourir (avec quelqu'un pour un prix *or* une place *or* &c.), disputer (quelque chose à quelqu'un)
Competence, Competency, *s.* capacité, *f.*; qualité, *f.*; (*of a law-court*) compétence, *f.*; (*sufficiency*) suffisance, *f.*; (*of fortune*) aisance, *f.* *To have a —*, avoir de quoi vivre, avoir de l'aisance; vivre dans l'aisance
Competent, *adj.* convenable, suffisant, raisonnable; (*qualified to judge*) compétent; (*efficient, fit*) capable; (*allowed*) permis (à). *To be — for*, être à la hauteur de, être capable de remplir
Competently, *adv.* convenablement, suffisamment, raisonnablement; (*skilfully*) compétemment
Competition, *s.* concurrence, *f.*; (*for a prize, a place,* &c.) concours, *m.* *To come into —*, faire concurrence (à). *To put up for —*, mettre au concours
Competitive, *adj.* de *or* de la concurrence. *— examination*, concours, *m.*
Competit-or, ress, *s.* compétiteur, *m.*, -trice, *f.*, concurrent, *m.*, e, *f.*, rival, *m.*, e, *f.*
Compilation, *s.* compilation, *f.*; recueil, *m.*
Compile, *v.a.* compiler; composer; recueillir
Compiler, *s.* compilateur, *m.*, -trice, *f.*
Complacence, Complacency, *s.* complaisance, satisfaction, joie, *f.*
Complacent, *adj.* complaisant, de complaisance
Complacently, *adv.* complaisamment, avec [complaisance
Complain, *v.n.* se plaindre
Complainant, *s.* plaignant, *m.*, e, *f.*
Complainer, *s.* personne qui se plaint, *f.*; réclamateur, *m.*, -trice, *f.*
Complaining, *s.* plainte, *f.*, plaintes, *f.pl.*
Complaint, *s.* plainte, *f.*; grief, *m.*; (*med.*) maladie, *f.*, mal, *m.*, affection, *f.*; (*admin.*) réclamation, *f.* *Cause of —*, sujet de plainte, *m.*; [grief, *m.*
Complaisance, *s.* complaisance, *f.*
Complaisant, *adj.* complaisant
Complaisantly, *adv.* complaisamment
Complement, *s.* complément, *m.*; ornement, *m.*; (*height*) comble, *m.*; (*mil., nav.*) complet, *m.* *Full —*, (*mil., nav.*) grand complet, *m.* *To have o.'s full —*, être au grand complet
Complementary, *adj.* complémentaire
Complete, *adj.* complet; achevé; parfait; (*at the height*) au comble; *— v.a.* compléter; achever; consommer; accomplir, terminer; combler; mettre le comble à; réaliser
Completely, *adv.* complètement
Completement. *V.* **Completion**
Completeness, *s.* caractère *or* état complet, complet, *m.*; perfection, *f.*
Completing, *adj.* complémentaire
Completion, *s.* complètement, *m.*; achèvement, *m.*; perfection, *f.*; accomplissement, *m.*; (*utmost height*) comble, *m.*; (*mil., nav.*) complètement, *m.* [(*Cath. lit.*) complies, *f.pl.*
Completory, *adj.* complémentaire; *— s.*
Complex, *adj.* complexe; (*arith.*) composé
Complexion, *s.* (*of the face*) teint, *m.*; (*fig.*) couleur, *f.*; (*constitution, natural inclination*) complexion, *f.*, tempérament, *m.*; (*of things*) caractère, *m.*
Complexional, *adj.* de tempérament
Complexionally, *adv.* par tempérament
Complexioned, *adj.* de teint; constitué, complexionné [*f.*; complication, *f.*
Complexity, Complexness, *s.* complexité,
Complexly, *adv.* d'une manière complexe
Compliance, *s.* condescendance ('*with,*' pour), *f.*; acquiescement, consentement, *m.*, adhésion, *f.* ('*with,*' à); docilité, *f.*; soumission, *f.*; complaisance, *f.* *In — with*, conformément à, suivant
Compliant, *adj.* flexible, souple; docile; soumis; facile; accommodant; complaisant
Compliantly, *adv.* complaisamment, avec complaisance
Complicate, *v.a.* compliquer
Complicated, *part. adj.* compliqué. *To become —*, se compliquer
Complication, *s.* complication, *f.*
Complicity, *s.* complicité, *f.*
Complier, *s.* complaisant, *m.*, e, *f.*
Compliment, *s.* compliment, *m.*; (*present*) présent, cadeau, *m.*, galanterie, gracieuseté, *f.*; **—s,** *pl.* compliments, *m.pl.*; salutations, *f.pl.*; *— v.a.* complimenter, féliciter, faire son compliment à; (*to present*) faire présent *or* cadeau à ... ('*with,*' de). *—s of the season,* (*at Christmas*) compliments *or* souhaits *or* vœux de bonne année, *m.pl.* *My best —s*, mes compliments empressés, *m.pl.*, mes salutations empressées, *f.pl.* *With the Author's* (*respectful, &c.*) *—s,* (*on presenting a book*) hommage (respectueux, &c.) de l'auteur [teur
Complimentary, *adj.* complimenteur; flat-
Complimenter, *s.* complimenteur, *m.*,-euse, *f.*
Complin, Compline, *s.* complies, *f.pl.*
Comply, *v.n.* condescendre (à); se soumettre (à), se plier (à), se prêter (à), s'accommoder (à), se conformer (à); se rendre (à); obéir (à); accéder (à); adhérer (à); (*fulfil*) remplir, satisfaire (à); observer
Complying, *adj.* *V.* **Compliant**
Component, *adj.* constituant, composant; — *s.* partie constituante, *f.*, constituant, composant, *m.*; (*math., mec.*) composante, *f.*
Comport, *v n.* s'accorder (avec), convenir (à). *To — oneself*, se comporter.
Comportment, *s.* conduite, *f.*
Compos. **— mentis,** *adj.* sain d'esprit
Compose, *v.a.* composer; écrire, rédiger; arranger; calmer; apaiser; tranquilliser. *To — oneself*, se calmer. *To — o.'s looks*, se composer. *To be —d*, être composé, se composer
Composed, *part.* composé, &c. (*V.* **Compose,** *v.a.*); *— adj.* calme, tranquille
Composedly, *adv.* avec calme, tranquillement, posément
Composedness, *s.* calme, *m.*, tranquillité, *f.*
Composer, *s.* auteur, *m.*; (*mus.*) compositeur, *m.*
Composing, *adj.* (*pharm.*) calmant; (*print.*) à composer; *— s.* composition, *f.* **— draught,** *s.* calmant, *m.* **— frame,** *s.* (*print.*) casier, *m.* **— room,** *s.* (*print.*) atelier de composition, atelier, *m.* **— stick,** *s.* (*print.*) composteur, *m.*
Composite, *adj.* composé; (*arch.*) composite; *— s.* composé, *m.*; (*bot., — flower*) composée, fleur composée, *f.*; (*arch., — order*) composite, ordre composite, *m.*; (*candle*) bougie composée, *f.* **— candle,** *s.* bougie composée, *f.*
Composition, *s.* composition, *f.*; nature, *f.*; accommodement, *m.*; arrangement, *m.*; (*of bankrupts*) concordat, *m.*; (*print., mus., paint., gram., liter.*) composition, *f.*; (*log., math.*) [synthèse, *f.*
Compositor, *s.* compositeur, *m.*
Compost, *s.* compost, *m.*; *— v.a.* composter
Composure, *s.* calme, *m.*, tranquillité, *f.* sang-froid, *m.*
Compound, *v.a.* composer; combiner; arranger; *— v.n.* s'arranger; transiger; entrer en composition; *— adj.* composé; (*surg., of fractures*) compliqué; (*alg.*) complexe; *— s.* composé, *m.*; composition, *f.* *— interest*, intérêt composé, intérêt des intérêts, *m.* *To — a felony*, entrer en composition pour la restitution d'objets volés. *To — o.'s debts*, s'arranger avec ses créanciers
Compounder, *s.* arbitre, *m.f.*, médiateur, *m.*, -trice, *f.*; (*law*) amiable compositeur, *m.*
Compounding, *s.* composition, *f.*; arrangement, accommodement, *m.*
Comprehend, *v.a.* comprendre
Comprehensi-bility, bleness. *V.* page 3, § 1
Comprehensible, *adj.* compréhensible, intelligible
Comprehension, *s.* compréhension, *f.*

Comprehensive, *adj.* vaste, étendu, grand; compréhensif; d'une grande intelligence
Comprehensively, *adv.* avec étendue, largement [brièveté expressive, *f.*
Comprehensiveness, *s.* étendue, portée, *f.*;
Compress, *v.a.* comprimer; (*fig.*) resserrer; — *s.* compresse, *f.*
Compressi-bility, bleness. *V.* page 3, § 1
Compressible, *adj.* compressible, comprimable
Compression, *s.* compression, *f.*; concision, *f.*
Compressive, *adj.* compressif
Compressor, *s.* compresseur, *m.*
Comprise, *v.a.* comprendre, contenir, renfermer
Compromise, *s.* compromis, *m.*; arrangement, accommodement, *m.*, transaction, *f.*: — *v.a.* compromettre; arranger; — *v.n.* transiger
Compromiser, *s.* personne qui fait un compromis, *f.*
Compromissorial, *adj.* compromissoire
Comprovincial, *adj. s.* comprovincial
Comptroll, Comptroller. *V.* **Control, Controller**
Compulsion, *s.* contrainte, *f.*
Compulsive, Compulsory, *adj.* forcé, obligatoire; coercitif
Compulsively, Compulsorily, *adv.* par contrainte, par force, de force, forcément
Compunction, *s.* remords, *m.*; (*theol.*) componction, *f.*
Computable, *adj.* calculable
Computation, *s.* supputation, *f.*, compte, calcul, *m.*; (*chron.*) computation, *f.*, (*eccl.*) comput, *m.* *On* —, de compte fait
Compute, *v.a.* supputer, compter, calculer; estimer, évaluer; (*of the calendar*) computer
Computer, Computist, *s.* calculateur, *m.*, -trice, *f.*; (*of the calendar*) computiste, *m.*
Comrade, *s.* camarade, *m.f.*
Comradeship, *s.* camaraderie, *f.*
Con, *prep. s.* contre, *m.*; — *v.a.* (— **over**) étudier, apprendre, repasser, recorder
Concatenate, *v.a.* enchaîner
Concatenation, *s.* enchaînement, *m.*
Concave, *adj. s.* concave, *adj. m.f., s.m.*
Concavity, Concaveness, *s.* concavité, *f.*
Concavo-concave, *adj.* concavo-concave
Concavo-convex, *adj.* concavo-convexe
Conceal, *v.a.* cacher ('*from*,' à); dérober; dissimuler; taire; (*law*) recéler; ne pas révéler
Concealable, *adj.* déguisable
Concealer, *s.* personne qui cache, *f.*; (*law*) recéleur, *m.*, -euse, *f.*; non-révélateur, *m.*, -trice, *f.*
Concealment, *s.* action de cacher, *f.*; dissimulation, *f.*; secret, *m.*; retraite, cachette, *f.*; (*law*) recèlement, *m.*; non-révélation, *f.* — *of birth*, dissimulation de (la) naissance, suppression de part, *f.* *In* —, en cachette, en secret. *To keep in* —, (*v.a.*) tenir caché; (*v.n.*) se tenir caché
Concede, *v.a.* concéder, accorder; admettre
Conceit, *s.* conception, *f.*; opinion, *f.*; pensée, *f.*, idée, *f.*; imagination, *f.*; idée plaisante, pointe, *f.*; vanité, suffisance, *f.*; —**s**, *pl.* (*rhet.*) concetti, *m.pl.* *Out of — with*, dégoûté de, décoiffé de. *To put out of — with*, dégoûter de, décoiffer de
Conceited, *adj.* vain, suffisant; infatué (de)
Conceitedly, *adv.* avec vanité
Conceitedness, *s.* vanité, suffisance, *f.*
Conceivable, *adj.* concevable [croire; penser
Conceive, *v.a.n.* concevoir; (*think*) imaginer,
Concentrate, *v.a.* concentrer; — *v.n.* se concentrer
Concentration, *s.* concentration, *f.*
Concentrative, *adj.* concentrateur
Concentrator, *s.* concentrateur, *m.*
Concentre. *V.* **Concentrate**
Concentr-ic, al, -ically. *V.* page 3, § 1
Concept, *s.* concept, *m.*
Conceptacle, *s.* réceptacle, *m.*; (*bot.*) conceptacle, *m.*
Conception, *s.* conception, *f.*; idée, notion, *f.*
Concern, *v.a.* concerner, regarder; intéresser ('*with*,' à); toucher; affliger, peiner; importer à (de); impliquer; appartenir à; (*trouble*) inquiéter. — *oneself*, se mêler (de); s'intéresser (à); se mettre en peine (de), s'inquiéter (de). *To be concerned*, être concerné, &c.; prendre part (à); (*at stake, in question*), *V.* **Stake,** *s.*; (*as the attorney in a suit*) occuper. *To all whom it may* —, (*law, admin.*) à tous ceux qu'il appartiendra. *It —s my brother to know*, il importe à mon frère de savoir
Concern, *s.* affaire, *f.*; intérêt, *m.*; importance, *f.*; part, *f.*; participation, *f.*; affection, *f.*; chagrin, *m.*, peine, affliction, *f.*; (*care*) soin, *m.*; (*anxiety*) souci, *m.*, sollicitude, inquiétude, *f.*; (*com.*) entreprise, *f.*, établissement, *m.*, (*jest.*) boutique, *f.*
Concerned, *part. adj.* concerné, &c. (*V.* **Concern,** *v.a.*); inquiet; (*as the attorney in a suit*) occupant
Concernedly, *adv.* avec intérêt; avec affection; avec peine; avec inquiétude
Concerning, *prep.* concernant, touchant, sur, à l'égard de
Concernment, *s.* *V.* **Concern,** *s.*
Concert, *v.a.* concerter; — *v.n.* se concerter; — *s.* concert, *m.* *In* —, de concert; à l'unisson. — **room,** *s.* salle de concerts, *f.*
Concertante, *adj. s.* concertant, *adj. m.*, e, *f.*, concertante, *s.f.*
Concerted, *part. adj.* concerté; (*mus.*) d'ensemble
Concertina, *s.* concertina, *m.*
Concertino, *s.* concertino, *m.*
Concerto, *s.* concerto, *m.*
Concession, *s.* concession, *f.*
Concessionaire, *s.* concessionnaire, *m.f.*
Concetti, *s.* (*pl. of* **Concetto**) concetti, *m.pl.*
Conch, *s.* conque, *f.*
Conchifer, *s.* conchifère, *m.*
Conchiferous, *adj.* conchifère, coquillier
Conchiform, *adj.* conchiforme
Conchite, *s.* conchite, *f.*
Conchoid, *s.* conchoïde, *f.*
Conchoidal, *adj.* conchoïdal, conchoïde
Concholog-ic, al, Conchyliolog-ic, al, -ist, -y. *V.* page 3, § 1
Conciliabule, *s.* conciliabule, *m.*
Conciliar, Conciliary, *adj.* conciliaire
Conciliate, *v.a.* concilier; (*to gain*) se concilier
Conciliation, *s.* conciliation, *f.*
Conciliator, *s.* conciliateur, *m.*, -trice, *f.*
Conciliatory, *adj.* conciliant, conciliateur, conciliatoire
Concise, *adj.* concis
Concisely, *adv.* avec concision, succinctement, brièvement, laconiquement
Conciseness, *s.* concision, *f.*
Conclave, *s.* conclave, *m.*
Conclavist, *s.* conclaviste, *m.*
Conclude, *v.a.* conclure; décider; (*finish*) terminer, finir ('*with*,' par; *before a present part.*, en); (*consider*) juger, estimer; — *v.n.* conclure; (*to end*) se terminer, finir (par; en)
Concluding, *adj.* final, dernier
Concludingly, *adv.* finalement; (*conclusively*) d'une manière concluante
Conclusion, *s.* conclusion, *f.*; décision, *f.*; jugement, *m.*; (*end*) fin, *f.*, dénoûment, *m.* *In* —, enfin, pour conclure, en dernière analyse. *To pursue* or *try* —*s*, faire des expériences
Conclusive, *adj.* concluant; décisif, final; définitif; (*gram.*) conclusif
Conclusively, *adv.* d'une manière concluante *or* décisive, décisivement; définitivement
Conclusiveness, *s.* nature concluante *or* décisive, *f.*
Concoct, *v.a.* digérer; (*fig.*) élaborer, préparer; (*ripen*) mûrir; (*to plot*) tramer, machiner, manigancer
Concoction, *s.* concoction, digestion, *f.*; (*fig.*) élaboration, préparation, *f.*; maturation, *f.*; (*plotting*) machination, manigance, *f.*
Concoctive, *adj.* concocteur
Concomitanc-e, y, *s.* concomitance, *f.*, concours, *m.*
Concomitant, *adj.* concomitant ('*with*,' de);

qui accompagne; — *s.* compagnon, *m.*, compagne, *f.*; accessoire, *m.* [accessoirement

Concomitantly, *adv.* par concomitance;

Concord, *s.* concorde, *f.*; accord, *m.*; harmonie, *f.*; (*gram.*) concordance, *f.*; accord, *m.*; (*mus.*) consonnance, *f.*; — *v.n.* se mettre d'accord

Concordanc-e,y, *s.* concordance, *f.*; accord, *m.*

Concordant, *adj.* concordant, d'accord, en harmonie

Concordantly, *adv.* de concert, d'accord

Concordat, *s.* concordat, *m.*

Concourse, *s.* concours, *m.*

Concrescence, *s.* concrétion, *f.*

Concrescible, *adj.* concrescible

Concrete, *adj.* concret; — *s.* concrétion, *f.*; corps concret, *m.*; terme concret, *m.*; (*log.*) concret, *m.*; (*mas.*) béton, *m.*; — *v.a.* concréter, concréfier, concrétionner; — *v.n.* se concréter, se concréfier, se concrétionner. — **work,** *s.* (*mas.*) bétonnage, *m.*

Concretely, *adv.* d'une manière concrète

Concreteness, *s.* état concret, état de concrétion, *m.*

Concretion, *s.* concrétion, *f.*

Concretionary, *adj.* concrétionnaire

Concubinage, *s.* concubinage, *m.*

Concubinary, *adj.* concubinaire, de concubinage; — *s.* concubinaire, *m.*

Concubine, *s.* concubine, *f.*

Concupiscence, *s.* concupiscence, *f.*

Concupiscent, *adj.* concupiscent

Concupiscible, *adj.* concupiscible

Concur, *v.n.* concourir; s'accorder, être d'accord; (*to share*) partager

Concurrence, *s.* concours, *m.*, coopération, *f.*; combinaison, *f.*; consentement, assentiment, *m.*; (*law*) communauté (de juridiction), *f.*

Concurrent, Concurring, *adj.* concourant, qui concourt (à); qui s'accorde (avec); réuni; unanime; simultané; (*chron.*) concurrent; — *s.* (*chron.*) jour concurrent, concurrent, *m.* — *jurisdiction*, juridiction commune, *f.*

Concurrently, *adv.* concurremment

Concussion, *s.* ébranlement, *m.*; (*shock*) secousse, *f.*, choc, *m.* [siffler

Condemn, *v.a.* condamner; blâmer; (*theat.*)

Condemnable, *adj.* condamnable; blâmable

Condemnation, *s.* condamnation, *f.*

Condemnatory, *adj.* condamnatoire

Condemner, *s.* condamnateur, *m.*, -trice, *f.*, personne qui condamne, *f.*

Condensability. *V.* page 3, § 1

Condensable, *adj.* condensable

Condensation, *s.* condensation, *f.*

Condensative, *adj.* condensatif

Condense, *v.a.* condenser; (*fig.*) resserrer; — *v.n.* se condenser; (*fig.*) se resserrer

Condenser, *s* condenseur, condensateur, *m.*

Condensing, *adj.* condensateur, condenseur; — *s.* condensation, *f.* — **apparatus,** *s.* condenseur, condensateur, *m.* — **engine,** *s.* machine à condenser *or* à condensateur, *f.* — **jet,** *s.* jet d'eau, *m.*

Condescend, *v n* condescendre (à); s'abaisser (à, jusqu'à); daigner; ne pas se faire scrupule (de); se conformer (à), se soumettre (à)

Condescendence, *s.* condescendance, *f.*

Condescending, *adj.* condescendant, de condescendance; complaisant [descendance

Condescendingly, *adv.* par (*or* avec) con-

Condescension, *s.* condescendance *f.*

Condign, *adj* mérité, juste; (*theol.*) condigne

Condignity, *s.* mérite, *m.*; justice, *f.*; (*theol.*) condignité, *f.* [ment

Condignly, *adv.* justement; (*theol.*) condigne-

Condiment, *s.* condiment, *m.*; assaisonne-

Condisciple, *s.* condisciple, *m.* [ment, *m.*

Condition, *s.* condition, *f.*; (*state*) état, *m.* *In —, in good —*, en bon état. *In a — to*, en état de. *On* or *upon —*, à condition. *Out of —*, en mauvais état

Conditional, *adj.* conditionnel; — *s.* conditionnel, *m.* *In the —*, (*Fr. gram.*) au conditionnel

Conditionality, *s.* conditionnalité, *f.*

Conditionally, *adv.* conditionnellement

Conditioned, *adj.* conditionné; placé; (*of rank*) de condition. *Good —*, bien conditionné, en bon état; d'un bon naturel. *V.* **Ill**

Condole, *v.n.* prendre part à la douleur (de), s'affliger (avec); faire ses compliments de condoléance (à) [de condoléance, *m.pl.*

Condolence, *s.* condoléance, *f.*; compliments

Condonation, *s.* pardon, *m.*

Condone, *v.a.* pardonner

Condor, *s.* condor, *m.* [(à), conduire (à)

Conduce, *v.n.* contribuer (à), servir (à), tendre

Conducive, *adj.* contribuant (à), qui contribue *or* sert (à), qui conduit (à), utile (à), avantageux (à). *To be —*, contribuer (à), servir (à), conduire (à)

Conduct, *v.a.* conduire; mener; guider; diriger; introduire; — *v.n.* (*phys.*) conduire; — *s.* conduite, *f.*; direction, *f.*; procédé, *m.*; (*moves*) démarches, *f.pl.*; (*escort*) escorte, *f.* *To — oneself*, se conduire

Conductibility, *s.* conductibilité, *f.*

Conductible, *adj.* conductible

Conducting, *adj.* conducteur

Conduction, *s.* conduction, *f.*

Conductive, *adj.* conducteur

Conductivity, *s.* conduction, *f.*

Conductor, *s.* conducteur, *m.*; guide, *m.*; directeur, *m.*; chef, *m.*; (*mus.*) chef d'orchestre, *m.*; (*of omnibuses, phys., surg.*) conducteur, *m.*; (*for lightning*) paratonnerre, *m.*; (*mil.*) vaguemestre, *m.*

Conductress, *s.* conductrice, *f.*; directrice, *f.*

Conduit, *s.* conduit, *m.*; (*arch.*) couloir, passage, *m.*; (*anat.*) conduit, *m.*

Condyle, *s.* condyle, *m.*

Condyloma, *s.* condylome, *m.*

Condylura, *s.* condylure, *m.*

Cone, *s.* cône, *m.* — **shell,** *s.* cône, *m.*

Coney, *s.* lapin, *m.* — **burrow,** *s.* terrier de lapin, terrier, clapier, *m.* — **wool,** *s.* poil de [lapin, *m.*

Confabulate, *v.n.* confabuler

Confabulation, *s.* confabulation, *f.*

Confection, *s.* conserve, *f.*; confiture, *f.*; sucrerie, *f.*, bonbon, *m.*; pâtisserie, *f.*; (*pharm.*) (*formerly*) confection, *f.*, (*now*) opiat, *m.*; (*obsolete general sense*) composition, *f.*, mélange, *m.*

Confectioner, *s.* confiseur, *m.*, -euse, *f.*

Confectionery, *s.* confiserie, *f.*; sucreries, *f pl.*, bonbons, *m.pl.*

Confederacy, *s.* confédération, *f.*; alliance, association, *f.*; ligue, *f.*; (*for cheating*) compérage, *m.*; complicité, *f.*

Confederate, *v a.* confédérer; liguer; — *v.n.* se confédérer; se liguer; — *s. adj.* confédéré, *m.*, e, *f.*; allié, *m.*, e, *f.*; associé, *m.*, e, *f.*; ligué, *m.*, e, *f.*; (*for cheating*) compère, *m.*; acolyte, *m.f.*; complice, *m.f.*

Confederation, *s.* confédération, *f.*

Confederative, *adj.* confédératif

Confer, *v.a.n.* conférer

Conference, *s.* conférence, *f.*

Conferva, *s.* conferve, *f.*

Confess, *v.a.* confesser, avouer; reconnaître, admettre; montrer, faire voir, accuser, attester; (*of sins*) confesser; — *v.n.* se confesser; (*law*) faire des aveux

Confessedly, *adv.* de son propre aveu; (*undeniably*) de l'aveu de tout le monde, sans contredit, incontestablement; (*openly*) ouvertement

Confession, *s.* confession, *f.*, aveu, *m.*; (*law*) aveu, *m.*, aveux, *m.pl.*; (*of sins, of faith*) con- [fession, *f.*

Confessional, *s.* confessionnal, *m.*

Confessionary, *adj.* confessionnaire, confes-

Confessionist, *s.* confessioniste, *m.* [sionnel

Confessor, *s.* confesseur, *m.*

Confidant, *s.* confident, *m.*

Confidante, *s.* confidente, *f.*

Confide, *v.a.* confier; — *v.n.* se confier (à), avoir confiance (en, dans); se fier (à)

Confidence, *s.* confiance, *f.*; (*of secrets*) confidence, *f.*; (*boldness*) hardiesse, assurance, *f.* *To put* or *place — in*, avoir confiance en
Confident, *adj.* confiant; certain, sûr; (*bold*) hardi, assuré
Confidential, *adj.* (*pers.*) sûr, de confiance; intime; (*things*) confidentiel; (*of a place*) de confiance
Confidentiality, *s.* confidentialité, *f.*
Confidentially, *adv.* confidentiellement; de confiance; intimement
Confidently, *adv.* avec confiance; en toute confiance; positivement; bien; (*boldly*) hardiment, avec assurance
Confiding, *adj.* confiant
Confidingly, *adv.* avec confiance
Configuration, *s.* configuration, *f.*
Configure, Configurate, *v.a.* configurer
Confine, *s.* confins, *m.pl.*; limite, frontière, *f.*; (*fig.*) limite, borne, *f.*, bord, *m.*; — *v.n.* confiner (à), toucher (à); — *v.a.* confiner, reléguer; (*shut up*) enfermer; renfermer; (*imprison*) emprisonner; (*in o.'s bed*) retenir; (*limit*) borner, limiter; (*restrain*) restreindre; (*bind down*) assujettir; (*hinder*) gêner; (*med.*) resserrer, constiper. *To be —d*, (*of women*) faire ses couches, être en couches, être accouchée; accoucher. *To be —d to o.'s room*, être forcé de garder la chambre. (*V.* **Bed**). *—d air*, air renfermé, *m.* **—less,** *adj.* sans bornes
Confinement, *s.* détention, *f.*; emprisonnement, *m.*; prison, *f.*; réclusion, *f.*; vie sédentaire, *f.*; (*restraint*) contrainte, *f.*, assujettissement, *m.*; (*of women*) couches, *f.pl.*; (*mil.*) arrêts, *m.pl.* *Solitary —*, emprisonnement cellulaire. *In —*, en prison. *In close —*, dans une réclusion rigoureuse; au secret
Confirm, *v.a.* confirmer; (*strengthen*) fortifier, affermir; (*harden*) endurcir; (*eccl.*) confirmer
Confirmable, *adj.* confirmable
Confirmation, *s.* confirmation, *f.*; témoignage, *m.*; (*strengthening*) affermissement, *m.*; (*eccl.*) confirmation, *f.* *In — of*, à l'appui de
Confirmative, Confirmatory, *adj.* confirmatif, confirmatoire, qui confirme, en confirmation (de), à l'appui (de)
Confirmatively, *adv.* confirmativement
Confirmed, *part. adj.* confirmé, affermi, &c. (*V.* **Confirm**); positif, certain; fixe; établi; enraciné, invétéré; bien arrêté; bien décidé; déterminé; endurci; incorrigible
Confirmedness, *s.* nature invétérée, *f.*
Confirmer, *s.* confirmateur, *m.*
Confiscable, *adj.* confiscable
Confiscate, *v.a.* confisquer [fisquant
Confiscating, *adj.* confiscant; — *part.* confisquant
Confiscation, *s.* confiscation, *f.*
Confiscator, *s.* confiscateur, *m.*
Confiscatory, *adj.* de confiscation
Confiteor, *s.* confiteor, *m.*
Conflagration, *s.* conflagration, *f.*, embrasement, *m.*; (*fire*) incendie, *m.*
Conflict, *s.* conflit, *m.*; lutte, *f.*; entre-choquement, *m.*; — *v.n.* être en conflit; lutter; s'entre-choquer, se heurter; être en contradiction
Conflicting, *part. adj.* en conflit; qui se heurte, qui s'entre-choque; opposé, contraire, contradictoire (à), en contradiction (avec)
Confluence, *s.* (*of streams*) confluent, *m.*; (*fig.*) affluence, *f.*; concours, *m.*; (*med.*) confluence, *f.*
Confluent, *adj.* (*of streams*) qui conflue; (*med.*, *bot.*) confluent; — *s.m.* confluent, *m.* *To be —*, confluer
Conform, *v.a.* conformer; — *v.n.* se conformer
Conformable, *adj.* conforme (à), d'accord [(avec)
Conformably, *adv.* conformément (à)
Conformation, *s.* conformation, *f.*
Conformist, *s. adj.* conformiste, *m.f.*
Conformity, *s.* conformité, *f.* *In — with*, conformément à
Confound, *v.a.* confondre. *— him!* que le diable l'emporte! *— it!* bigre! fichtre! va te faire fiche! va te promener!
Confounded, *part.* confondu; — *adj.* maudit, sacré; (*adverb.*) *V.* **Confoundedly**
Confoundedly, *adv.* terriblement, furieusement, diablement [fraternité, *f.*
Confraternity, *s.* confrérie, *f.*; (*amity*) confraternité, *f.*
Confront, *v.a.* se présenter de front à, faire face à; se trouver en face (*or* en présence) de; tenir tête à, arrêter; attaquer de front; (*to set face to face, to compare*) confronter
Confrontation, *s.* confrontation, *f.*
Confuse, *v.a.* mettre en désordre, mettre la confusion dans, confondre, mêler, brouiller; (*perplex*) troubler, embrouiller, déconcerter; faire tromper; rendre confus
Confused, *adj.* confus; troublé
Confusedly, *adv.* confusément
Confusedness, *s.* confusion, *f.*; trouble, *m.*
Confusion, *s.* confusion, *f.*, désordre, *m.*; trouble, *m.*; ruine, destruction, perte, *f.*
Confutable, *adj.* réfutable
Confutation, *s.* réfutation, confutation, *f.*
Confute, *v.a.* réfuter, confuter
Confuter, *s.* réfutateur, *m.*, -trice, *f.*
Congeal, *v.a.* congeler, geler, glacer; — *v.n.* se congeler, se geler, se glacer, se prendre
Congealable, *adj.* congelable
Congealableness, *s.* congélabilité, *f.*
Congealment, Congelation, *s.* congélation, *f.*
Congener, *s.* congénère, *m.f.*
Congeneric, *adj.* congénère
Congenial, *adj.* homogène, de la même nature; naturel; conforme (à); propre (à); convenable (à); sympathique (à); favorable (à); (*to a language*) dans le génie (de)
Congeniality, Congenialness, *s.* affinité, analogie, *f.*; conformité, *f.*; sympathie, *f.*
Congenital, *adj.* congénital
Conger, —eel, *s.* congre, *m.*, anguille de mer, *f.*
Congeries, *s.* amas, *m.*, masse informe, *f.*
Congest, *v.a.* entasser, amonceler; (*med.*) congestionner; engorger. *To become —d*, se congestionner; s'engorger
Congestion, *s* amas, amoncellement, *m.*; (*med.*) congestion, *f.*; engorgement, *m.* *— of blood*, congestion sanguine. *— of the brain*, congestion cérébrale
Congestive, *adj.* congestif
Conglobate, *v.a.* conglober; — *adj.* conglobé
Conglobation, *s.* conglobation, *f.*
Conglomerate, *v.a.* conglomérer; — *v.n.* se conglomérer; — *adj.* congloméré; — *s.* conglomérat, *m.*
Conglomeration, *s.* conglomération, *f.*
Conglutinant, *adj.* conglutinant; — *s.* conglutinant, conglutinatif, *m.* [conglutiner
Conglutinate, *v.a.* conglutiner; — *v.n.* se conglutiner
Conglutination, *s.* conglutination, *f.*
Conglutinative, *adj.* conglutinatif
Congou, *s.* (*tea*) congo, *m.*
Congratulate, *v.a.* féliciter, ('*on*,' '*for*,' de), complimenter ('*on*,' de), faire son compliment à ('*on*,' de). *To — oneself*, se féliciter
Congratulating, *adj.* congratulateur
Congratulation, *s.* ('*on*,' de) félicitation, *f.*, compliment, *m.*
Congratulator, *s.* congratulateur, *m.*, -trice, *f.*
Congratulatory, *adj.* de félicitation, congratulatoire
Congregate, *v.a.* rassembler; — *v.n.* se rassembler, s'assembler, se rendre (à, dans)
Congregation, *s.* agrégation, *f.*, assemblage *m.*; (*heap*) amas, *m.*; (*pers.*) congrégation, *f.*, (*of church*) assemblée, *f.*; fidèles, *m.pl.*; paroissiens, *m.pl.*; (*at a sermon*) auditoire, *m.*
Congregational, *adj.* sous forme de congrégation; congréganiste; d'une (*or* de l') assemblée, des fidèles, des paroissiens
Congregationism, *s.* congréganisme, *m.*
Congregationist, *s.* congréganiste, *m.*
Congregational-ism, -ist. *V.* page 3, § 1

Congress, *s.* congrès, *m.* — **man,** *s.* membre du Congrès, *m.*
Congressional, *adj.* de (*or* du congrès)
Congreve, *s.* (— *match*) allumette chimique, *f.*; (— *rocket*, — *war-rocket*) fusée à la Congrève, *f.*
Congruence, *s.* congruence, *f.*
Congruent, *adj.* congruent
Congruity, *s.* convenance, *f.*; conformité, *f.*, rapport, *m.*; (*theol.*) congruité, *f.*; (*geom.*) égalité, *f.*
Congruous, *adj.* convenable (à); conforme (à); (*theol.*, *arith.*) congru; (*geom.*) égal
Congruously, *adv.* convenablement; conformément (à); congrûment
Conic, -al, *adj.* conique, en cône
Conically, *adv.* en forme de cône, en cône
Conicalness, *s.* conicité, *f.*
Conics, *s. pl.* sections coniques, coniques, *f.pl.*
Conifer, *s.* conifère, *m.*
Coniferous, *adj.* conifère
Coniform, *adj.* coniforme, conique
Conirostral, *adj* conirostre
Conirostre, *s.* conirostre, *m.*
Conjectural, *adj.* conjectural, de conjecture
Conjecturally, *adv.* conjecturalement
Conjecture, *s.* conjecture, *f.*; — *v.a.* conjecturer
Conjecturer, *s.* conjectureur, *m.*, -euse, *f.*
Conjoin, *v.a.* unir, réunir, joindre, conjoindre; (*associate*) adjoindre; — *v.n.* s'unir (à), se joindre (à)
Conjoint, *adj.* uni, lié; commun; en commun; [(*mus.*) conjoint
Conjointly, *adv.* conjointement; d'accord, de concert; ensemble
Conjugable, *adj.* conjugable
Conjugal, *adj.* conjugal
Conjugally, *adv.* conjugalement
Conjugate, *v.a.* conjuguer. *To be —d,* être conjugué; se conjuguer
Conjugate, Conjugated, *adj.* conjugué
Conjugation, *s.* conjugaison, *f.*
Conjunction, *s.* union, liaison, *f.*; (*gram.*, *astr.*) conjonction, *f.* *In — with,* conjointement avec
Conjunctiva, *s.* (*anat.*) conjonctive, *f.*
Conjunctive, *adj.* uni, réuni; (*gram.*) conjonctif
Conjunctively, *adv.* conjonctivement
Conjuncture, *s.* concours, *m.*; (*crisis*) conjoncture, *f.*
Conjuration, *s.* conjuration, *f.*; évocation, *f.*; (*sorcery*) sorcellerie, *f.*
Conjure, *v.a.* conjurer; (*enchant*) ensorceler; (*spirits*) évoquer; (*juggle*) escamoter; — *v.n.* faire de la sorcellerie, user de sorcelleries, escamoter. — **away,** exorciser. — **down,** conjurer. — **up,** évoquer
Conjurer, *s.* conjureur, conjurateur, *m.*, sorcier, *m.*, -ière, *f.*, magicien, *m.*, -ne, *f.*; (*juggler*) escamoteur, *m.*, -euse, *f.*, prestidigitateur, *m*; physicien, *m.*; (*cooking apparatus*) fourneau portatif, *m.* *To be no —,* n'être pas sorcier, n'avoir pas inventé la poudre
Conjuring, *s.* sorcellerie, *f.*; (*juggling*) escamotage, *m.*, prestidigitation, *f.* — **book,** *s.* grimoire, *m.* — **trick,** *s.* tour de prestidigitation, *m.*
Conjuror. *V.* **Conjurer**
Connect, *v.a.* joindre (à), lier (à), unir (à), rattacher (à), relier (à); allier (à); (*tech.*) accoupler, rassembler; mettre en communication
Connected, *part. adj.* joint (à), lié (à), &c. (*V.* **Connect**); en rapport (avec); ayant rapport (à), qui a rapport (à); attaché (à); se rattachant (à), qui se rattache (à); continu; cohérent, suivi. *Loosely —,* décousu. *To be — (with),* être joint (à) *or* &c.; se lier (à), se rattacher (à), se rapporter (à)
Connectedly, *adv.* avec suite, sans interruption, continûment
Connecting, *adj.* d'union; (*tech.*) de communication. — **rod,** *s.* bielle, *f.*
Connection, *s.* connexion, *f.*; (*relation*) rapport, *m*, liaison, *f.*; (*coherence*) suite, *f.*; (*intercourse*) relations, *f.pl.*; (*family —*) parent, *m.*; parents, *m.pl.*, famille, *f.*; parenté, *f.*; (*in business*) clientèle, *f.*; (*complicity*) complicité, *f.* *To run in — (with),* (*of trains,* &c.) correspondre (avec), être en correspondance (avec)
Connective, *s.* liaison, *f.*; — *adj.* de liaison
Connectively, *adv.* conjointement
Connexion. *V.* **Connection**
Connivance, *s.* connivence, *f.* *In —,* de connivence
Connive, *v.n.* conniver (à), être de connivence (pour), fermer les yeux (sur), favoriser secrètement, tolérer
Conniving, *s.* connivence, *f.*; — *adj.* de connivence
Connoisseur, *s.* connaisseur, *m.*, -euse, *f.*; (*of wines and good living*) gourmet, *m.*
Connoisseurship, *s.* talent de connaisseur, *m.*
Connubial, *adj.* conjugal, matrimonial
Conoid, *s.* conoïde, *m.*
Conoidal, *adj.* conoïdal, conoïde
Conquer, *v.a.* vaincre; (*a country, and fig.: to gain, to win*) conquérir; — *v.n.* vaincre
Conquerable, *adj.* qui peut être vaincu *or* conquis, domptable
Conqueress, *s.* femme victorieuse, *f.*; conquérante, *f.*
Conquering, *adj.* conquérant, victorieux
Conqueror, *s.* vainqueur, *m.*; (*of countries*) conquérant, *m.*; (*winning game*) belle, *f.*
Conquest, *s.* conquête, *f.*; victoire, *f.*
Consanguineous, *adj.* du même sang
Consanguinity, *s.* parenté, *f.*; (*law*) consanguinité, *f.*
Conscience, *s.* conscience, *f.* *In —,* en conscience. *In all —,* en bonne conscience
Conscientious, *adj.* consciencieux; (*pertaining to conscience, as scruples,* &c.) de conscience
Conscientiously, *adv.* concienciеusement, avec (*or* en) conscience
Conscientiousness, *s.* conscience, délicatesse de conscience, *f.*; droiture, *f.*
Conscionable, *adj.* raisonnable, juste, équitable
Conscionableness, *s.* justice, équité, *f.*
Conscionably, *adv.* raisonnablement, justement, équitablement
Conscious, *adj.* qui a la conscience (de); conscient; sensible; (*not delirious or &c.*) qui a sa connaissance *or* sa tête; (*aware*) instruit (de), qui sait, qui connaît, persuadé, convaincu; (*things*) dont on a la conscience. *To be* or *remain (fully) —,* (*not delirious or &c.*) avoir *or* conserver (toute) sa connaissance *or* sa tête. *To become — again,* reprendre connaissance, reprendre ses sens. *To be — of,* avoir la conscience de; être instruit de, savoir, connaître, être persuadé *or* convaincu de
Consciously, *adv.* sciemment, en parfaite connaissance
Consciousness, *s* (*philos.*) conscience, *f.*; (*med.*) connaissance, *f.* *To lose, to recover —,* perdre, reprendre connaissance
Conscript, *adj. s.* conscrit, *m.*
Conscription, *s.* conscription, *f.*
Conscriptional, *adj.* conscriptionnel
Consecrate, *v.a.* consacrer, bénir; (*bishops, kings*) sacrer; (*saints*) canoniser
Consecrated, *part. adj.* consacré; bénit; sacré; (*holy*) saint. — *bread,* pain bénit, *m.* — *ground,* terre sainte, *f.*
Consecration, *s.* consécration, *f.*; (*of bishops, kings*) sacre, *m.*; (*of saints*) canonisation, *f.*
Consecrator, *s.* consécrateur, consacrant, *m.*
Consecratory, *adj.* de consécration; sacramentel
Consecution, *s.* consécution, *f.*
Consecutive, *adj.* consécutif, de suite
Consecutively, *adv.* consécutivement, de suite
Consensual, *adj.* (*law*) consensuel; (*physiology*) sympathique
Consent, *v.n.* consentir (à); — *s.* consentement, *m.*; accord, *m.*; (*relation*) rapport, *m.*; (*in physiology*) sympathie, *f.* *With one —,* d'un commun accord
Consentaneous, *adj.* conforme (à), d'accord (avec)
Consentaneously, *adv.* conformément (à), d'accord (avec)
Consentaneousness, *s.* conformité, *f.*
Consenter, *s.* personne qui consent, *f.*

Consentient, *adj.* consentant; d'accord; unanime; (*for*) pour
Consequence, *s.* conséquence, suite, *f.*; effet, *m.*; importance, *f.* *In — of*, en conséquence de, par (*or* à la) suite de; des suites de. *Of no —*, d'aucune (*or* de nulle) conséquence, d'aucune (*or* de nulle) importance, sans conséquence, sans importance. *It is of no —*, c'est sans importance *or* &c.; n'importe; cela ne fait rien. *The — is that* . . ., il résulte de là que . . ., il en résulte que . . ., il s'ensuit que . . .
Consequent, *adj.* qui est la conséquence; consécutif; (*gram.*, *phys.*, &c.) conséquent; — *s.* conséquence, suite, *f.*; (*log.*, *gram.*, *math.*) conséquent, *m.* — *upon* or *on*, qui est la conséquence de, qui résulte de, qui suit, qui vient à la suite de, par suite de, en conséquence de, consécutif à
Consequential, *adj.* important, suffisant; qui est la conséquence; logique
Consequentially, *adv.* avec suffisance, d'un air important; consécutivement; logiquement
Consequentialness, *s.* air d'importance, *m.*, importance, suffisance, *f.*; logique, *f.*
Consequently, *adv.* conséquemment, par conséquent; en conséquence
Conservable, *adj.* conservable
Conservancy, Conservation, *s.* conservation, *f.*
Conservatism, *s.* conservatisme, doctrinarisme, *m.*
Conservative, *adj.* conservatif, conservateur; (*polit.*) conservateur; (*law*) conservatoire; — *s.* conservateur, *m.*, -trice, *f.*, doctrinaire, *m.*
Conservator, *s.* conservateur, *m.*
Conservatory, *adj.* conservatoire; — *s.* dépôt, magasin, *m.*; (*for science or art*) conservatoire, *m.*; (*of gardens*) serre, *f.*
Conservatrix, *s.* conservatrice, *f.*
Conserve, *s.* conserve, *f.*; — *v.a.* conserver
Consider, *v.a.* considérer; examiner; avoir égard à; estimer; (*reckon*) considérer comme, regarder comme; tenir pour; (*requite*) reconnaître, récompenser; — *v.n.* considérer, examiner; (*think*) penser; songer; réfléchir; faire attention; (*deem*) être d'avis, juger
Considerable, *adj.* considérable; important; grand
Considerableness, *s.* importance, *f.*; grandeur, *f.*; valeur, *f.*
Considerably, *adv.* considérablement; infiniment; bien; beaucoup
Considerate, *adj.* considéré, réfléchi, prudent; modéré; indulgent; discret; attentionné; attentif (à); prévenant; délicat; bienveillant, bon
Considerately, *adv.* considérément, avec réflexion; avec prudence; avec modération; avec considération, avec égards, avec ménagement; discrètement, avec discrétion; avec attention; avec prévenance; avec bienveillance, avec bonté; délicatement
Considerateness, *s.* caractère réfléchi, *m.*; prudence, *f.*; discrétion, *f.*; attention, *f.*; délicatesse, *f.*
Consideration, *s.* considération, *f.*; examen, *m.*; réflexion, *f.*; égard, *m.*, égards, *m.pl.*; compensation, *f.*, dédommagement, *m.*; récompense, *f.*; prix, *m.*; équivalent, *m.*; (*value*) valeur, *f.*; (*law*) cause, *f.* *In — of*, *out of — to*, en considération de, par considération pour, par égard pour. *On* or *upon —*, *on further —*, tout bien considéré, réflexion faite, décidément. *To be under —*, être soumis à l'examen, être en délibération. *To take into —*, prendre en considération
Considering, *prep.* considérant, attendu, vu, eu égard à
Consign, *v.a.* livrer (à); (*trust*) confier (à), remettre (à); (*com.*) consigner (à)
Consignee, *s.* consignataire, *m.f.*
Consigner, Consignor, *s.* consignateur, *m.*, -trice, *f.*
Consignment, *s.* consignation, *f.*; envoi, *m.*; lettre de consignation, *f.* *On —*, en consignation. *To the — of*, en consignation chez

Consist, *v.n.* (*in*) consister (en, dans; *before a verb*, à); (*of*) se composer (de), être composé (de), consister (en); (*with*) s'accorder (avec), être conforme *or* compatible (avec), convenir (à)
Consistence, Consistency, *s.* consistance, *f.*; suite, *f.*, esprit de suite, *m.*; accord, *m.*, harmonie, *f.*; conformité, *f.*; conséquence, *f.*; stabilité, *f.*; uniformité, *f.*; constance, *f.*
Consistent, *adj.* consistant; solide, ferme; conséquent; qui ne se dément pas, égal, toujours égal; d'accord (avec), conforme (à), compatible (avec). *To be — with oneself*, être d'accord avec soi-même, être conséquent
Consistently, *adv.* conséquemment; (*agreeably*) conformément (à), d'une manière compatible (avec)
Consisting, *part. adj.* consistant (en, dans, à); se composant (de), composé (de); d'accord (avec), conforme (à), convenable (à), compatible (avec)
Consistorial, *adj.* consistorial
Consistory, *s.* consistoire, *m.*
Consolable, *adj.* consolable
Consolation, *s.* consolation, *f.*; dédommagement, *m.* — **stakes,** *s. pl.* omnium, *m.*
Consolatory, *adj.* consolant; de consolation
Console, *v.a.* consoler ('*for*,' de); — *s.* console, *f.* — **table,** *s.* console, *f.*
Consoler, *s.* consolateur, *m.*, -trice, *f.*
Consolidable, *adj.* consolidable
Consolidant, *adj. s.* consolidant, *adj. m.*, e, *f.*, consolidant, *s.m.*
Consolidate, *v.a.* consolider; (*law*) réunir; [— *v.n.* se consolider
Consolidation, *s.* consolidation, *f.*; (*law*) réunion, *f.*
Consoling, *adj.* consolant; consolateur; de consolation
Consols, *s. pl.* consolidés, *m.pl.*
Consonance, *s.* consonnance, *f.*; (*fig.*) accord, *m.*, union, harmonie, *f.*; conformité, *f.*
Consonant, *adj.* consonnant; (*fig.*) conforme (à), d'accord (avec); — *s.* consonne, *f.*
Consonantly, *adv.* d'accord (avec)
Consonous, *adj.* à l'unisson
Consort, *s.* compagnon, *m.*, compagne, *f.*; (*husband* or *wife*) époux, *m.*, épouse, *f.*, mari, *m.*, femme, *f.*; (*of a ship*) conserve, *f.*; —**s,** *pl.* (*law*) conjoints, *m.pl.*; — *v.n.* se joindre (à), s'associer (à), s'unir (à); être le compagnon *or* la compagne (de); — *v.a.* unir. *Prince —*, prince-époux, mari de la reine, *m.* *Queen —*, reine, *f.*
Consound, *s.* (*bot.*) consoude, *f.*
Conspicuous, *adj.* visible, en vue, apparent; (*set off*) en évidence, en relief; (*striking*) frappant; (*eminent*) marquant, éminent, remarquable, grand. *To be — by o.'s absence*, briller par son absence. *To make oneself —*, se mettre en évidence, se faire remarquer
Conspicuously, *adv.* visiblement, d'une manière apparente, en évidence; éminemment, remarquablement
Conspicuousness, *s.* visibilité, *f.*; évidence, *f.*; position, *f.*; distinction, célébrité, réputation, *f.*; éclat, *m.*
Conspiracy, *s.* conspiration, conjuration, *f.*
Conspirator, *s.* conspirateur, *m.*, -trice, *f.*, conjuré, *m.*
Conspire, *v.n.a.* conspirer
Conspiring, *adj.* conjuré
Constable, *s.* (*hist.*) connétable, *m.*; (*governor*) gouverneur, *m.*; (*keeper*) gardien, *m.*; (*policeman*) *V.* **Policeman.** *Chief —*, commissaire de police, *m.* *High —*, (*Fr. hist.*) grand connétable, *m.* *To outrun the —*, dépenser au-delà de ses revenus, s'endetter
Constabulary, *s.* police, *f.*; (*rural*) gendarmerie, *f.*; — *adj.* de (*or* de la) police; de (*or* de la) gendarmerie
Constancy, *s.* constance, persévérance, fermeté, *f.*; stabilité, *f.*
Constant, *adj.* constant; continuel; fidèle; stable; (*math.*) constant; — *s.* (*math.*) constante, *f.*
Constantinopolitan, *s. adj.* Constantinopolitain, *m.*, e, *f.*

Constantly, *adv.* constamment ; continuellement
Constellate, *v.a.* consteller
Constellation, *s.* constellation, *f.*
Consternation, *s.* consternation, *f.*
Constipate, *v.a.* constiper
Constipation, *s.* constipation, *f.*
Constituency, *s.* circonscription électorale, *f.*, district électoral, corps *or* collége électoral, *m.*; commettants, *m pl.*
Constituent, *adj.* constituant ; — *s.* auteur, créateur, *m.* ; élément, *m.*, partie constituante, *f.* ; (*of elections, and com.*) commettant, *m.* ; (*law*) constituant, *m.*, e, *f.*
Constitute, *v.a.* constituer
Constituter, *s.* constituteur, *m.*
Constitution, *s.* constitution, *f.* ; tempérament, *m.*
Constitutional, *adj.* constitutionnel ; — *s.* (*jest.*) promenade pour la santé, *f.* *To go for* (or *to take*) *a* —, faire son petit tour, faire sa petite promenade, prendre l'air
Constitutionalism, *s.* constitutionnalisme, *m.*
Constitutionalist, *s.* constitutionnel, *m.*
Constitutionality, *s.* constitutionnalité, *f.*
Constitutionalize, *v.a.* constitutionnaliser
Constitutionally, *adv.* constitutionnellement
Constitutive, *adj.* constitutif
Constitutress, *s.* constitutrice, *f.*
Constrain, *v.a.* constraindre, forcer ; (*check*) retenir ; (*hinder*) gêner
Constrainable, *adj.* contraignable
Constrainedly, *adv.* par contrainte
Constraint, *s.* contrainte, *f.*
Constrict, *v.a.* resserrer, contracter
Constriction, *s.* constriction, *f.*, resserrement, *m.* ; (*med.*) rétrécissement, *m.*
Constrictive, *adj.* constrictif
Constrictor, *s. adj.* constricteur, *m.*
Constringe, *v.a.* resserrer, contracter
Constringent, *adj.* constringent
Construct, *v.a.* construire ; bâtir ; fabriquer ; former ; composer ; interpréter
Constructer. *V.* **Constructor**
Constructible, *adj.* constructible
Construction, *s.* construction, *f.* ; (*fig.*) interprétation, *f.* ; sens, *m.* *To put the best — on,* donner la meilleure interprétation à
Constructive, *adj.* constructif ; interprétatif ; implicite ; supposé, censé
Constructively, *adv.* par interprétation, interprétativement ; implicitement ; censément
Constructiveness, *s.* constructivité, *f.*
Constructor, *s.* constructeur, *m.*
Construe, *v.a.* construire, faire la construction de ; interpréter ; considérer (comme) ; (*translate*) traduire, expliquer
Consubstantial, *adj.* consubstantiel
Consubstantialist, *s.* consubstantiateur, *m.*, -trice, *f.*
Consubstantiality, *s.* consubstantialité, *f.*
Consubstantially, *adv.* consubstantiellement
Consubstantiate, *v.a.* unir dans une même substance
Consubstantiation, *s.* consubstantiation, *f.*
Consuetudinary, *adj.* coutumier
Consul, *s.* consul, *m.*
Consular, *adj. s.* consulaire, *adj. m.f., s.m.*
Consulate, Consulship, *s.* consulat, *m.*
Consult, *v.a.* consulter ; — *v.n.* se consulter
Consultable, *adj.* consultable
Consultation, *s.* consultation, *f.* — **room,** *s.* cabinet, *m.*
Consultative, *adj.* consultatif
Consulter, *s.* consultant, *m.*, e, *f.* ; (*eccl.*) consulteur, *m.*
Consulting, *adj.* consultant ; — *s.* consultation, *f.* — **room,** *s.* cabinet, *m.*
Consumable, *adj.* consumable ; (*usable*) consommable
Consume, *v.a.* consumer ; dévorer ; dissiper, gaspiller ; perdre ; (*to use*) consommer ; — *v.n.* se consumer
Consumer, *s.* personne *or* chose qui consume, *f.* ; (*fig.*) consommateur, *m.*, -trice, *f.*
Consummate, *v.a.* consommer ; — *adj.* consommé ; achevé, fini, parfait, complet ; plein
Consummately, *adv.* parfaitement, complètement
Consummation, *s.* consommation, *f.*, accomplissement, *m.* ; (*end*) fin, *f.* ; (*highest pitch*) comble, *m.*
Consumption, *s.* consomption, *f.* ; dissipation, *f.*, gaspillage, *m.* ; (*use*) consommation, *f.* ; (*med.*) maladie de poitrine, phthisie, consomption, *f.* *Galloping* or *rapid* —, phthisie galopante. *Pulmonary* —, phthisie pulmonaire. *To be in a* —, être poitrinaire, être phthisique. *To die of* —, mourir de la poitrine
Consumptive, *adj.* (*pers.*) poitrinaire, phthisique ; (*of the lungs*) attaqué ; (*of constitution*) prédisposé à la phthisie ; (*connected with the lungs*) pulmonaire ; (*destructive*) destructeur, dévorant, qui consume ; — *s.* poitrinaire, phthisique, *m.f.*
Consumptively, *adv.* par une prédisposition à la phthisie
Consumptiveness, *s.* prédisposition à la phthisie, *f.*
Contact, *s.* contact, *m.* *To bring into* —, mettre en contact ; rapprocher. *To come in* —, être mis en contact, arriver à être en contact, se rencontrer ; se mettre en rapport
Contagion, *s.* contagion, *f.*
Contagioned, *adj.* contagié
Contagionist, *s.* contagioniste, *m.*
Contagious, *adj.* contagieux
Contagiously, *adv.* par contagion, d'une manière contagieuse
Contagiousness, *s.* contagiosité, nature contagieuse, *f.*
Contain, *v.a.* contenir ; retenir ; renfermer
Containable, *adj.* qui peut être contenu
Container, *s.* contenant, *m.*
Contaminable, *adj.* contaminable
Contaminate, *v.a.* souiller, contaminer ; — *adj.* souillé, contaminé
Contamination, *s.* souillure, contamination, *f.*
Contango, *s.* report, *m.*
Contemn, *v.a.* mépriser, dédaigner ; braver
Contemner, *s.* contempteur, *m.*, -trice, *f.*
Contemplate, *v.a.n.* contempler ; méditer, projeter, avoir en vue ; prévoir, espérer, s'attendre à ; songer à ; envisager
Contemplation, *s.* contemplation, *f.* ; (*thought*) pensée, *f.* ; méditation, *f.* ; (*purpose*) projet, *m.* ; (*view*) vue, *f.* *To have it in — (to)*, avoir en vue (de), se proposer (de), avoir le projet (de). *It was in — (to)*, on avait le projet (de), il était question (de)
Contemplative, *adj. s.* contemplatif ; rêveur
Contemplatively, *adv.* contemplativement
Contemplator, *s.* contemplateur, *m.*, -trice, *f.*
Contemporaneity, Contemporariness, *s.* contemporanéité, *f.*
Contemporaneous, *adj.* contemporain
Contemporaneously, *adv.* contemporainement ('*with,*' avec), du même temps, dans le même temps ('*with,*' que)
Contemporary, *adj. s.* contemporain, *m.*, e, *f.* ; (*in newspaper slang*) confrère, *m.*
Contempt, *s.* mépris, dédain, *m.* ; (*— of court*) offense, *f.* ; désobéissance, *f.* ; refus de comparaître, défaut, *m.* ; contumace, *f.* *In* —, par mépris ; (*law*) par défaut ; par contumace. *In — of,* au mépris de. *To purge o.'s* —, purger sa contumace. *To sink into* —, tomber dans le mépris
Contemptible, *adj.* méprisable ; (*of little value*) à dédaigner
Contemptibleness, *s.* nature méprisable, *f.*
Contemptibly, *adv.* méprisablement, d'une manière méprisable
Contemptuous, *adj.* méprisant, dédaigneux
Contemptuously, *adv.* méprisamment, d'une manière méprisante, avec mépris
Contemptuousness, *s.* mépris, *m.*, humeur dédaigneuse, *f.*
Contend, *v.n.* combattre ; (*struggle*) lutter ; contester ; (— *for*) concourir (pour) ; se disputer ; rechercher à l'envi ; (*affirm*) soutenir, affirmer, prétendre
Contender, *s.* contendant, *m.*, e, *f.*, contestant, *m.*, e, *f.*, compétiteur, *m.*, -trice, *f.*, con-

current, *m.*, e, *f.*, rival, *m.*, e, *f.*; combattant, *m.*; champion, *m.*; belligérant, *m.*

Contending, *adj.* contendant, contestant; en contestation, en lutte, opposé, contraire; concurrent, rival; — *s.* contestation, *f.* *The — parties*, les parties contendantes, *f.pl.*, les contendants, les contestants, *m.pl.*; les belligérants, *m.pl.*

Content, *adj.* content, satisfait; — *v.a.* contenter, satisfaire; — *s.* contentement, *m.*, satisfaction, *f.*; (*parliam.*) voix pour, *f.* **—s,** *s.pl.* (*things contained*) contenu, *m.*; (*table of —s*) table des matières, *f.*; index, *m.* *To be —*, être content (de), se contenter (de); (*to consent*) consentir (à), vouloir bien. *— is beyond riches*, contentement passe richesse. **—less,** *adj.* mécontent

Contented, *adj.* content (de), satisfait (de); résigné (à), soumis (à). *To be — with*, être content de, se contenter de

Contentedly, *adv.* content; avec satisfaction; sans se plaindre; patiemment

Contentedness, *s.* contentement, *m.*

Contention, *s.* contention, *f.*, débat, *m.*, discussion, dispute, querelle, *f.*; combat, *m.*, lutte, *f.*; discorde, *f.*; efforts, *m.pl.*; ardeur, *f.*

Contentious, *adj.* disputeur, querelleur; litigieux, contentieux. *— jurisdiction*, juridiction contentieuse, *f.*

Contentiously, *adv.* en disputant, en querellant; (*law*) contentieusement

Contentiousness, *s.* humeur querelleuse, *f.*; esprit litigieux, *m.*

Contentment, *s.* contentement, *m.*; résignation, soumission, *f.*

Conterminous, *adj.* voisin (de), limitrophe (de), contigu (à)

Contest, *v.a.n.* contester; disputer; (*struggle*) lutter; (*vie*) rivaliser (de); — *s.* contestation, *f.*; dispute, *f.*; débat, *m.*; (*strife*) lutte, *f.*; combat, *m.* **—less,** *adj.* incontestable

Contestable, *adj.* contestable

Contestableness, *s.* contestabilité, nature contestable, *f.*

Contestably, *adv.* contestablement

Contestation, *s.* *V.* **Contest,** *s.*

Contestingly, *adv.* en disputant

Context, *s.* contexte, *m.*; sens, *m.*

Contexture, *s.* contexture, *f.*; tissu, *m.*; (*series*) enchaînement, *m.*, suite, série, *f.*

Contiguity, Contiguousness, *s.* contiguïté, *f.*; proximité, *f.*

Contiguous, *adj.* contigu [en contiguïté

Contiguously, *adv.* d'une manière contiguë,

Continence, Continency, *s.* continence, chasteté, *f.*; retenue, modération, *f.*

Continent, *adj.* continent, chaste; retenu, modéré; — *s.* continent, *m.*

Continental, *adj.* continental

Continently, *adv.* avec continence, chastement, avec chasteté; avec retenue, avec modération

Contingence, Contingency, *s.* contingence, *f.*; éventualité, *f.*; hasard, *m.*; cas fortuit, cas imprévu, cas, *m.*; dépense imprévue, *f.*

Contingent, *adj.* contingent, éventuel, casuel, fortuit, accidentel, aléatoire, incertain; — *s.* événement *or* cas fortuit, *m.*; (*quota, share, of troops*, &c.) contingent, *m.*

Contingently, *adv.* fortuitement, par cas fortuit, par hasard, casuellement, accidentellement, éventuellement, aléatoirement

Contingentness, *s.* nature fortuite *or* casuelle *or* accidentelle, casualité, *f.*

Continual, *adj.* continuel; (*med., law*) continu

Continually, *adv.* continuellement; (*law*) continûment

Continuance, *s.* continuation, *f.*; continuité, *f.*; persévérance, *f.*; durée, *f.*; perpétuation, *f.*; (*abode*) séjour, *m.*; (*law*) ajournement, *m.*, remise, *f.*

Continuation, *s.* continuation, *f.*; suite, *f.*; durée, *f.*; prolongement, *m.*; perpétuation, *f.*; (*'Change*) report, *m.*

Continuator, *s.* continuateur, *m.*

Continue, *v.n.* continuer; persévérer, persister; (*remain*) rester, demeurer; continuer à être, être toujours; subsister; (*last*) durer; — *v.a.* continuer, poursuivre; prolonger; perpétuer; maintenir; conserver; (*'Change*) reporter. *To be —d*, *V.* **Continued**

Continued, *adj.* continu; prolongé; (*fig.*) soutenu, suivi; — *part.* continué, &c. (*V.* **Continue**). *To be —*, (*of articles in periodicals*) à suivre, la suite prochainement. *To be — in our next*, (*of ditto*) la suite au prochain numéro

Continuedly, *adv.* sans interruption, continûment

Continuer, *s.* continuateur, *m.*, -trice, *f.*; personne qui persévère *or* persiste, *f.*

Continuing, *adj.* qui continue *or* &c.; persévérant; permanent

Continuity, *s.* continuité, *f.* *Solution* or *break of —*, solution de continuité, *f.*

Continuous, *adj.* continu

Continuously, *adv.* continûment

Contorsion. *V.* **Contortion**

Contort, *v.a.* tordre; contourner

Contorted, *part. adj.* tordu; contourné; tors

Contortion, *s.* contorsion, *f.*

Contour, *s.* contour, *m.* [*Per —*, par contre

Contra, *prep.* contre; (*com.*) d'autre part.

Contraband, *s.* contrebande, *f.*; — *adj.* de contrebande

Contrabandist, *s.* contrebandier, *m.*, -ière, *f.*

Contrabass, Contrabasso, *s.* contre-basse, *f.*

Contract, *v.a.* contracter; resserrer; rétrécir; raccourcir; (*the brow*, &c.) rider; (*abridge*) abréger; (*a habit*) prendre, contracter; (*betroth*) fiancer, promettre en mariage; (*admin.*) adjuger; — *v.n.* (*shrink*) se contracter, se resserrer, se rétrécir; (*of the brow*) se rider; (*bargain*) traiter, contracter; s'engager (à); entreprendre; — *s.* contrat, *m.*; convention, *f.*; marché, *m.*; (*of marriage*) fiançailles, *f.pl.*, promesse de mariage, *f.*; (*for public works, supplies*) soumission, *f.*; adjudication, *f.*; entreprise à forfait, entreprise, *f.*; forfait, *m.*; — *adj.* de contrat *or* &c.; à forfait. *Conditions of —*, cahier des charges, *m.* *By* or *upon —*, (*com.*) à forfait, à l'entreprise, par entreprise. *By private —*, de gré à gré, à l'amiable. *To put up to —*, mettre à l'entreprise

Contractable, *adj.* contractable

Contracted, *part. adj.* contracté, &c. (*V.* **Contract,** *v.a.*); (*narrow*) étroit

Contractedly, *adv.* d'une manière restreinte

Contractedness, *s.* rétrécissement, resserrement, *m.*; brièveté, *f.*; (*meanness*) mesquinerie, *f.*

Contractibility, Contractibleness, Contractility, *s.* contractilité, *f.*

Contractible, Contractile, *adj.* contractile

Contracting, *adj.* contractant; — *s.* contractation, *f.*

Contraction, *s.* contraction, *f.*; resserrement, rétrécissement, *m.*; (*shortening*) raccourcissement, *m.*; (*math.*) abréviation, *f.*; (*of metals*) retrait, *m.*, retraite, *f.*

Contractive, *adj.* contractif

Contractor, *s.* contractant, *m.*, e, *f.*; (*farmer*) fermier, *m.*, -ière, *f.*; (*of works*) entrepreneur, *m.*; (*of the army or navy*) fournisseur, *m.*; entrepreneur, *m.*; (*admin.*) adjudicataire, *m.f.*

Contractual, *adj.* contractuel

Contradict, *v.a.* contredire; démentir

Contradicter, *s.* contradicteur, *m.* [menti, *m.*

Contradiction, *s.* contradiction, *f.*; (*denial*) dé-

Contradictious, *adj.* contradictoire; qui aime à contredire; opposé, contraire (à)

Contradictorily, *adv.* contradictoirement

Contradictoriness, *s.* nature contradictoire, *f.* [proposition contradictoire, *f.*

Contradictory, *adj.* contradictoire; — *s.*

Contradistinction, *s.* opposition, *f.*, contraste, *m.* *In — to,* par opposition à
Contradistinctive, *adj.* qui distingue, qui contraste
Contradistinguish, *v.a.* distinguer
Contrafissure, *s.* contre-fissure, contre-fente, contre-fracture, *f.*
Contraindicant, *s.* contre-indication, *f.*
Contraindicate, *v.a.* contre-indiquer
Contraindication, *s.* contre-indication, *f.*
Contralto, *s.* contralto, contralte, *m.*; (*pers.*) contraltiste, *m.f.*; — *adj.* de contralto
Contramure, *s.* contre-mur, *m.*; — *v.a.* contre-murer
Contraposition, *s.* contre-position, *f.*
Contrapuntist, *s.* contrapontiste, contrapuntiste, contre-pointiste. *m.*
Contrariety, *s.* contrariété, *f.*; opposition, contradiction, *f.* [traire; différemment
Contrarily, *adv.* contrairement; en sens con-
Contrariness, *s.* contrariété, *f.* [contraire
Contrariwise, *adv.* au contraire, en sens
Contrary, *adj.* contraire (à); opposé (à). — *to,* contraire à; opposé à; (*adv. prep.*) contrairement à, au contraire de; à l'encontre de; contre. — **minded,** *adj.* d'un avis contraire
Contrary, *s.* contraire, *m.*; proposition contraire, *f.* *On the —,* au contraire. *Quite the —,* tout le contraire; bien au contraire. *To the —,* en sens contraire, dans le sens opposé; contre; contraire
Contrast, *s.* contraste, *m.* ('*to,*' avec); — *v.a.* contraster, mettre en contraste, faire contraster; — *v.n.* contraster
Contratenor. *V.* **Counter-tenor**
Contravallation, *s.* contrevallation, *f.*
Contravene, *v.a.* contrevenir à, enfreindre
Contravener, *s.* contrevenant, *m.*, e, *f.*
Contravention, *s.* contravention, infraction, *f.*
Contrayerva, *s.* contrayerva, *m.*, dorstènie, *f.*
Contre-temps, *s.* contre-temps, *m.*
Contributary, *adj.* contributaire
Contribute, *v.a.* payer, fournir, donner; (*fig.*) prêter; (*write*) écrire ('*to,*' pour *or* dans); — *v.n.* contribuer (à); concourir (à)
Contribution, *s.* contribution, *f.*; part, *f.*, contingent, *m.*; écot, *m.*; don, *m.*; souscription, *f.*; (*writing*) article, *m.* *To lay under —,* mettre à contribution [butoire
Contributional, *adj.* contributaire; contri-
Contributive, *adj.* contributif, qui contribue. *To be — to,* contribuer à
Contributor, *s.* personne qui contribue (à), *f.*, contribuant, contributeur, contributaire, *m.*; (*in working*) collaborateur, *m.*; rédacteur, *m.*; correspondant, *m.* *To be a — to,* contribuer à; (*write*) écrire pour (*or* dans)
Contributorily, *adv.* contributoirement
Contributory, *adj.* contributoire. *To be — to,* contribuer à
Contributress, *s.* femme (*or* dame) qui contribue (à), contribuante, contributaire, *f.*; (*in working*) collaboratrice, *f.*; rédactrice, *f.*; correspondante, *f.* *To be a — to,* contribuer à; (*write*) écrire pour (*or* dans)
Contrite, *adj.* contrit; de contrition
Contritely, *adv.* avec contrition
Contrition, *s.* contrition, *f.*
Contrivable, *adj.* imaginable
Contrivance, *s.* invention, *f.*; combinaison, *f.*; idée, *f.*; plan, *m.*; projet, *m.*; moyen, *m.*; artifice, *m.*; machine, *f.*; appareil, *m.*
Contrive, *v.a.* inventer, trouver, imaginer, concevoir; combiner; concerter; machiner, tramer; (*manage*) arranger; ménager; pratiquer; — *v.n.* s'arranger (pour); faire en sorte (que); trouver moyen (de); (*set about*) s'y prendre, faire (pour); (*know how to*) savoir; (*succeed*) parvenir (à), venir à bout (de)
Contriver, *s.* inventeur, *m.*, -trice, *f.*, auteur, *m.*; combinateur, *m.*, -trice, *f.* [*V.* **Contrivance**
Contriving, *adj.* ingénieux; artificieux; — *s.*

Control, *s.* contrôle, *m.*; empire, *m.*, autorité, *f.*; influence, *f.*; contrainte, *f.*; (*check*) frein, *m.*; (*mil.*) intendance (militaire), *f.*; — *v.a.* contrôler; avoir de l'empire sur; réprimer; modérer; gouverner; diriger; régler. — **department,** *s.* (*mil.*) intendance militaire, *f.*
Controllable, *adj.* sujet à contrôle; gouvernable; docile; soumis à l'empire *or* à l'autorité (de)
Controller, *s.* contrôleur, *m.*, -euse, *f.*; (*master*) maître, *m.*; (*mil.*) intendant militaire, *m.*
Controllership, *s.* emploi de contrôleur, contrôle, *m.*
Controlling, Controlment, *s.* contrôlage, contrôlement, *m.*; contrôle, &c. (*V.* **Control,** *s.*)
Controversial, *adj.* de controverse, polémique
Controversialist, *s.* controversiste, *m.f.*
Controversy, *s.* controverse, *f.*; polémique, *f.*; discussion, contestation, dispute, *f.*; différend, *m.*; lutte, résistance, *f.* [battre, agiter
Controvert, *v.a.* controverser, discuter, dé-
Controvertible, *adj.* controversable, sujet à controverse
Controvertist, *s.* controversiste, *m.f.*
Contumacious, *adj.* obstiné, opiniâtre; rebelle, récalcitrant; pervers; (*law*) contumace, contumax
Contumaciously, *adv.* obstinément, avec obstination, opiniâtrément, avec opiniâtreté; (*law*) par contumace
Contumaciousness, *s.* obstination, opiniâtreté, *f.*; perversité, *f.*
Contumacy, *s.* obstination, opiniâtreté, *f.*; (*law*) résistance, désobéissance, *f.*; (*non-appearance*) défaut, *m.*; (*crim. law*) contumace, *f.*
Contumelious, *adj.* injurieux, offensant, outrageant; insolent; (*contemptuous*) méprisant
Contumeliously, *adv.* injurieusement, outrageusement; insolemment; avec mépris
Contumely, *s.* injure, *f.*, outrage, *m.*, insulte, *f.*; (*contempt*) mépris, dédain, *m.*
Contuse, *v.a.* contusionner, contondre, meurtrir
Contused, *part. adj.* contusionné, meurtri; (*surg.*) contus. — *wound,* plaie contuse, contusion, *f.*
Contusion, *s.* contusion, meurtrissure, *f.*
Conundrum, *s.* jeu de mots, *m.*; énigme, *f.*
Convalescence, Convalescency, *s.* convalescence, *f.*
Convalescent, *s. adj.* convalescent, *m.*, e, *f.* — *hospital,* asile de convalescents (*or* de convalescence), *m.*
Convallary, *s.* convallaire, *f.*, muguet, *m.*
Convene, *v.a.* convoquer, réunir, assembler; citer; — *v.n.* se réunir, s'assembler
Convenience, Conveniency, *s.* commodité, convenance, aise, *f.*; chose commode, *f.*, objet de commodité, *m.*; —**s,** *pl.* commodités, *f.pl.*, &c.; (*nav.*) emménagements, *m.pl.* *At your —,* à votre convenance, à votre aise, quand vous le pourrez. *At your earliest —,* aussitôt que vous en aurez le loisir. *To meet the — of,* arranger, accommoder
Convenient, *adj.* commode; convenable. *If it is — to you,* si cela ne vous gêne pas. *If you could make it — to be there,* si vous pouviez vous arranger pour (*or* de manière à) vous y trouver
Conveniently, *adv.* commodément; à son aise, sans se gêner, sans se déranger; aisément, facilement; bien
Convent, *s.* couvent, *m.*
Conventicle, *s.* conventicule, conciliabule, *m.*
Convention, *s.* convention, *f.* [vention
Conventional, *adj.* conventionnel, de con-
Conventionalism, *s.* nature conventionnelle, *f.*, caractère conventionnel, *m.*; phrase de convention, *f.*; affaire (*f.*) *or* usage (*m.*) de convention
Conventionalist, *s.* (*hist.*) conventionnel, *m.*
Conventionality. *V.* **Conventionalism**
Conventionally, *adv.* conventionnellement

Conventioner, *s.* membre d'une convention, *m.*; (*hist.*) conventicnnel, *m.*
Conventionist, *s.* contractant, *m.*, e, *f.*
Conventual, *adj.* conventuel; — *s.* conventuel, *m.*; (*nun*) religieuse, *f.*
Converge, *v.n.* converger [gence, *f.*
Convergence, Convergency, *s.* conver-
Convergent, Converging, *adj.* convergent
Conversable, *adj.* conversable, sociable, d'une société agréable, agréable dans la conversation; (*chatty*) causeur, causant
Conversableness, *s.* sociabilité, *f.*
Conversably, *adv.* d'une manière sociable
Conversancy, *s.* familiarité, grande connaissance *or* habitude, triture, *f.*
Conversant, *adj.* familier, familiarisé (avec); versé (dans), qui connaît bien, au fait (de), au courant (de); relatif (à)
Conversantly, *adv.* familièrement; sciemment
Conversation, *s.* conversation, *f.*; (*colloquy*) entretien, *m.*; (*intercourse*) commerce, *m.*, société, *f.*; (*experience*) pratique, expérience, *f.* *To carry on a* —, faire *or* soutenir une conversation
Conversational, *adj.* de *or* de la conversation. *A person of great — powers,* une personne qui cause très bien [bien, *f.*
Conversationalist, *s.* personne qui cause
Conversationally, *adv.* par *or* pour la conversation
Conversationism, *s.* expression usitée dans la conversation, expression familière, *f.*
Conversationist, *s.* personne qui cause bien, *f.*
Conversative, *adj.* social, de la société, du monde [conférence, *f.*
Conversazione, *s.* réunion, *f.*, cercle, *m.*;
Converse, *v.n.* converser, causer, s'entretenir (avec); fréquenter; être familier (à); — *s.* conversation, *f.*, entretien, *m.*; commerce, *m.*, familiarité, *f.*, relations, *f.pl.*, rapports, *m.pl.*; (*geom., log.*) converse, réciproque, *f.*; — *adj.* convers, réciproque
Conversely, *adv.* réciproquement
Converser, *s.* personne qui cause, *f.*
Conversible, *adj.* conversible
Conversion, *s.* conversion, *f.*; transformation, *f.*; changement, *m.*; (*of fire-arms*) transformation, *f.*
Conversionist, *s. adj.* conversioniste, *m.f.*
Conversive, *adj.* conversif
Convert, *v.a.* convertir; transformer; changer; (*apply*) appliquer; approprier; faire servir (à); (*fire-arms*) transformer; — *v.n.* se convertir; se transformer; se changer; — *s.* converti, *m.*, e, *f.*; (*of convents*) convers, frère convers, *m.*, converse, sœur converse, *f.* *To become a* —, se convertir
Converted, *part. adj.* converti, &c. (*V.* **Convert,** v.a.). — *steel,* acier poule, *m.*
Converter, *s.* convertisseur, *m.*, -euse, *f.*
Converti-bility, bleness. *V.* page 3, § 1
Convertible, *adj.* (*things*) convertible; (*pers.*) convertissable [quement
Convertibly, *adv.* convertiblement; récipro-
Convex, *adj.* convexe; bombé; — *s.* corps convexe, *m.*; convexité, *f.* — **glass maker,** *s.* bombeur, *m.* [bombement, *m.*
Convexity, Convexness, *s.* convexité, *f.*;
Convexly, *adv.* de forme convexe
Convexo-concave, *adj.* convexo-concave
Convexo-convex, *adj.* convexo-convexe
Convey, *v.a.* porter, transporter; conduire; amener; présenter, offrir; transmettre; communiquer; donner; exprimer, rendre; transférer. — **away** *or* **out,** (*carry*) emporter; (*lead*) emmener
Conveyable, *adj.* portable, transportable; charriable; communicable; exprimable; transférable
Conveyance, *s.* transport; (*means*) moyen de transport, *m.*; (*vehicle*) voiture, *f.*; (*way*) voie, *f.*; transmission, *f.*; communication, *f.*; passage, *m.*; (*sending*) envoi, *m.*; (*law*) transfert, *m.* *Deed of* —, acte de vente, *m.*
Conveyancer, *s.* notaire, *m.*
Conveyancing, *s.* rédaction des actes translatifs de propriété, *f.*; transferts, *m.pl.*; notariat, *m.*
Conveyer, *s.* personne qui transporte *or* transmet *or* communique, *f.*; porteur, *m.*, -euse, *f.*; voiturier, *m.*; commissionnaire, *m.*; (*thing*) véhicule, *m.*
Convict, *v.a.* convaincre; déclarer coupable; condamner; — *s.* condamné, *m.*, e, *f.*; forçat, *m.*; détenu, *m.*, e, *f.*; (*transported*) déporté, *m.* — **establishment,** *s.* établissement pénitentiaire, *m.*, colonie pénitentiaire, *f.*; pénitencier, *m.*; bagne, *m.*; (*for women*) maison centrale, *f.* — **keeper,** *s.* garde-chiourme, *m.* — **ship,** *s.* transport des déportés, *m.*
Conviction, *s.* conviction, persuasion, *f.*; condamnation, *f.*; déclaration de culpabilité, *f.*
Convictive, *adj.* convictionnel; (*convincing*) convaincant [d'une manière convaincante
Convictively, *adv.* convictionnellement;
Convince, *v.a.* convaincre, persuader
Convincing, *adj.* convaincant; — *part.* convainquant [cante
Convincingly, *adv.* d'une manière convain-
Convincingness, *s.* nature *or* puissance convaincante, *f.*
Convivial, *adj.* de festin, de fête, convivial; (*pers.*) joyeux, jovial, convivial, sociable
Convivialist, *s.* bon *or* joyeux convive, *m.*
Conviviality, *s.* gaieté franche, gaieté, bonne humeur, convivialité, sociabilité, *f.*; joyeux repas, *m.*, joyeuse réunion, *f.*
Convivially, *adv.* joyeusement, convivialement
Convocable, *adj.* convocable
Convocation, *s.* convocation, *f.*; assemblée, *f.*
Convoke, *v.a.* convoquer
Convoker, *s.* convocateur, *m.*, -trice, *f.*
Convolute, Convoluted, *adj.* convoluté, convolutif
Convolution, *s.* enroulement, *m.*, circonvolution, *f.*; (*winding motion*) tournoiement, *m.*
Convolve, *v.a.* rouler, enrouler
Convolvulus, *s.* convolvulus, volubilis, *m.* *Minor* —, belle-de-jour, *f.* — *major,* ipomée, *f.*
Convoy, *v.a.* convoyer; escorter; — *s.* (*nav.*) convoi, *m.*; (*mil.*) convoi, *m.*; escorte, *f.*; (*fig.*) escorte, *f.* — **ship,** *s.* convoyeur, *m.*
Convoying, *s.* convoiement, *m.*
Convulse, *v.a.* convulser, convulsionner, jeter dans des convulsions, donner des convulsions à; crisper; agiter, ébranler, bouleverser
Convulsed, *part. adj.* convulsé, &c. (*V.* **Convulse**); en convulsions; agité, tremblant; crispé. *To be — with laughing,* se tordre à force de rire, se tordre
Convulsibility, *s.* convulsibilité, *f.*
Convulsible, *adj.* convulsible
Convulsion, *s.* convulsion, *f.*; (*fig.*) convulsion, commotion, *f.*
Convulsionary, *s. adj.* convulsionnaire, *m.f.*
Convulsionist, *s.* convulsioniste, *m.f.*
Convulsive, *adj.* convulsif
Convulsively, *adv.* convulsivement
Cony. *V.* **Coney** [*To run a* —, sauter
Coo, *v.n.* roucouler; — *s.* (*at billiards*) saut, *m.*
Cooing, *s.* roucoulement, *m.*
Cook, *v.a.* cuire, faire cuire, apprêter, cuisiner; (*fig.*) préparer, arranger; (*an account*) falsifier; — *v.n.* cuire; (*pers.*) faire la cuisine, cuisiner; — *s.* cuisinier, *m.*, -ière, *f.*; (*nav.*) coq, *m.* *Man* —, cuisinier, *m.* *Woman* —, cuisinière, *f.* — **house,** *s.* (*nav.*) coquerie, *f.* — **maid,** *s.* cuisinière, *f.* — **room,** *s.* (*nav.*) coquerie, *f.* — **shop,** *s.* restaurant, *m.*; (*in contempt*) gargote, *f.*; (*for roasting*) rôtisserie, *f.* — **shop keeper,** *s.* restaurateur, traiteur, *m.*; (*in contempt*) gargotier, *m.*, -ière, *f.*; (*for roasting*) rôtisseur, *m.*, -euse, *f.* [cuisine, *f.*
Cookery, *s.* cuisine, *f.* — **book,** *s.* livre de

Cooking, *s.* (*the art*) cuisine, *f.*; (*the action*) cuisson, *f.*; — *adj.* de cuisine. — **apparatus,** *s.* caléfacteur, appareil caléfacteur, *m.* — **ladle,** *s.* cuiller à pot, louche, *f.* — **stove,** *s.* fourneau de cuisine, *m.*; potager, *m.* — **tin,** *s.* (*mil.*) bidon, *m.*

Cool, *adj.* frais; tiède; (*of clothing*) léger; (*pers.*) froid; calme, tranquille, de sang-froid; (*fam.*) impudent, hardi; peu gêné; — *s.* frais, *m.*, fraîcheur, *f.*; — *v.a.* rafraîchir; (*fig.*) refroidir, calmer, modérer; — *v.n.* se rafraîchir; refroidir, se refroidir; se calmer. *In the* —, au frais. *To grow* (or *get* or *become*) —, *V.* **Grow.** — **cup,** *s.* boisson rafraîchissante, *f.* — **headed,** *adj.* qui a la tête froide, calme, de sang-froid [sant, *m.*

Cooler, *s.* rafraîchissoir, *m.*; (*med.*) rafraîchis-

Coolie, *s.* cooli, *m.* [fraîchissant

Cooling, *s.* rafraîchissement, *m.*; — *adj.* ra-

Coolish, *adj.* un peu frais

Coolly, *adv.* fraîchement; (*fig.*) froidement; de sang-froid; tranquillement, avec calme; (*fam.*) impudemment, hardiment, sans gêne

Coolness, *s.* fraîcheur, *f.*, frais, *m.*; (*indifference*) froideur, *f.*; (*unfriendliness*) refroidissement, froid, *m.*; (*composure*) sang-froid, calme, *m.*; (*fam.*) impudence, *f.*; sans-gêne, *m.*

Cooly, *s.* *V.* **Coolie** [bouis, *m.*

Coom, *s.* (*valley*) combe, *f.*; (*cart-grease*) cam-

Coomb, Coombe, *s.* (*valley*) combe, *f.*

Coop, *s.* poulailler, *m.*; mue, *f.*; (*for sheep*) parc, *m.*; — *v.a.* enfermer; emprisonner; claquemurer

Cooper, *s.* tonnelier, *m.*; boisselier, *m.*

Cooperage, *s.* tonnellerie, *f.*; boissellerie, *f.*

Cooperate, *v.n.* coopérer (à), concourir (à)

Cooperation, *s.* coopération, *f.*, concours, *m.*

Cooperative, *adj.* coopératif; coopérant. — *society*, société (*or* association) coopérative, *f.*

Cooperator, *s.* coopérateur, m., -trice, *f.*

Coopery. *V.* **Cooperage**

Coordinate, *adj.* coordonné; —**s,** *s. pl.* coordonnées, *f.pl.*; — *v.a.* coordonner

Coordinately, *adv.* avec coordination; au même rang

Coordinateness, Coordination, *s.* coordination, *f.*

Coordinating, *adj.* coordonnateur

Coordinator, *s.* coordonnateur, *m.*, -trice, *f.*

Coot, *s.* foulque, *f.*

Cop, *s.* sommet, *m.*, cime, crête, *f.*; huppe, aigrette, *f.*; (*on a spindle*) fusée, *f.*

Copaiba, Copaiva, *s.* copahu, *m.* — **balsam,** *s.* baume de copahu, *m.* — **tree,** *s.* copayer, *m.*

Copal, *s.* copal, *m.* — **gum,** *s.* gomme copal, *f.*

Coparcenary, Coparceny, *s.* succession par indivis, *f.*

Coparcener, *s.* cohéritier, *m.*, -ière, *f.*

Copartner, *s.* coassocié, *m.*, e, *f.*, associé, *m.*, e, *f.*

Copartnership, Copartnery, *s.* association, société en nom collectif, *f.*

Cope, *s.* (*for the head*) coiffe, *f.*; (*of heaven,* &c.) voûte, *f.*; (*eccl., arch.*) chape, *f.*; — *v.a.* couvrir; (*arch.*) chaperonner; — *v.n.* lutter (contre); rivaliser (avec); observer. — **bearer, -maker,** *s.* chapier, *m.*

Copec, Copeck, Copek, *s.* copec, copeck, *m.*

Copernican, *adj.* copernicien, de Copernic

Copetitioner, *s.* copétitionnaire, *m.f.*

Copier, *s.* copiste, *m.f.*; imitateur, *m.*, -trice, *f.*

Coping, *s.* faîte, *m.*; (*of walls*) chaperon, couronnement, *m.*, crête, *f.*; (*of bridges*) larmier, *m.*

Copious, *adj.* copieux; abondant, riche

Copiously, *adv.* copieusement; abondamment, richement; amplement [fusion, *f.*

Copiousness, *s.* abondance, *f.*; richesse, pro-

Coplaintiff, *s.* codemandeur, *m.*, codemanderesse, *f.* [huppé

Copped, *adj.* qui s'élève en pointe, conique;

Coppel. *V.* **Cupel**

Copper, *s.* cuivre, *m.*; (*boiler*) chaudière, *f.*; chaudron, *m.*; cuve, *f.*; (*coin*) monnaie de cuivre, *f.*; petite monnaie, *f.*, sous, *m.pl.*; —**s,** *pl.* (*coin*) sous, *m.pl.*, petite monnaie, monnaie de cuivre, *f.*; (*kitchen utensils*) batterie de cuisine, *f.*; — *adj.* de (*or* en) cuivre; (*coloured*) cuivré; — *v.a.* cuivrer; (*to line, to sheathe*) doubler en cuivre. — **bottomed,** *adj.* à fond de cuivre, doublé en cuivre. — **colour, -coloured,** *adj.* cuivré, couleur cuivrée, couleur de cuivre. — **head,** *s.* trigonocéphale, *m.* — **mine,** *s.* mine de cuivre, *f.* — **nose,** *s.* nez couperosé, *m.* — **nosed,** *adj.* à nez couperosé. — **plate,** *s.* plaque de cuivre, *f.*; (*engr.*) planche de cuivre, *f.*; taille-douce, *f.* — **plate engraver,** *s.* graveur en taille-douce, *m.* — **plate engraving,** *s.* gravure en taille-douce, *f.* — **plate printer,** *s.* imprimeur en taille-douce, *m.* — **plate printing,** *s.* impression en taille-douce, *f.* — **sheathed,** *adj.* doublé en cuivre. — **sheathing,** *s.* doublage en cuivre, *m.* — **smith,** *s.* chaudronnier, *m.* — **wares,** *s. pl.* cuivrerie, *f.* — **wire,** *s.* fil de cuivre, *m.* — **works,** *s. pl.* usine à cuivre, fonderie de cuivre, *f.*; atelier de chaudronnerie, *m.* — **worm,** *s.* taret, *m.*

Copperas, *s.* couperose, *f.*

Coppering, *s.* cuivrage, *m.*

Copperish, *adj.* un peu cuivré

Coppery, *adj.* cuivreux

Coppice, *s.* taillis, bois taillis, *m.*

Coprolite, *s.* coprolithe, *m.*

Copropriet-or, ress, *s.* copropriétaire, *m.f.*

Copse, *s.* taillis, bois taillis, *m.*; — *v.a.* entretenir en taillis

Copsy, *adj.* qui renferme des taillis

Copt, *s.* Cophte, Copte, *m.*

Coptic, *s.* cophte, copte, *m.*; — *adj.* cophte, copte, cophtique, coptique

Copula, *s.* copule, *f.*

Copulate, *v.a.* accoupler; — *v.n.* **s'accoupler**

Copulation, *s.* copulation, *f.*

Copulative, *adj. s.* copulatif, *adj. m.*, -ive, *f.*, copulative, *s.f.*

Copulatively, *adv.* copulativement

Copy, *s.* copie, *f.*; (*from a common type*) exemplaire, *m.*; (*of newspapers*) numéro, *m.*; (*model*) exemple, modèle d'écriture, *m.*; (*law*) expédition, *f.*; (*print.*) copie, *f.*, manuscrit, *m.*; — *v.a.n.* copier; transcrire; imiter. *A true* —, pour copie conforme, pour ampliation. *Fair* (or *clean*) —, copie au net, *f.* *Rough* —, brouillon, *m.* *To make* or *write a fair* (or *clean*) — *of,* mettre au net. — **book,** *s.* cahier, *m.*; (*of penmanship*) cahier d'exemples, *m.* — **right,** *s.* propriété littéraire, *f.*, droit d'auteur, *m.*; propriété, *f.*

Copying, *s.* action de copier, copie, *f.*; (*law*) expédition, *f.*; — *adj.* à copier; expéditionnaire. — **clerk,** *s.* commis (*or* copiste) expéditionnaire, expéditionnaire, *m.* — **ink,** *s.* encre à copier, *f.* — **machine, -press,** *s.* [presse à copier, *f.*

Copyist. *V.* **Copier**

Coquelicot, *s. adj.* coquelicot, *m.*

Coquet, *s.* *V.* **Coquette** (*male* —, coquet, *m.*); — *v.a.* faire des coquetteries à; — *v.n.* faire le coquet *or* la coquette, user de coquetteries, [coqueter

Coquetry, *s.* coquetterie, *f.*

Coquette, *s.* coquette, *f.*

Coquettish, *adj.* coquet

Coquettishly, *adv* coquettement

Coquettishness, *s.* coquetterie, *f.*

Coracle, *s.* petit bateau pêcheur, *m.*

Corah, *s.* foulard, *m.*

Coral, *s.* corail, *m.*; (*child's*) hochet, *m.*; — *adj.* de corail; (*fig.*) corallin. — **diver, -fisher,** *s.* corailleur, *m.* — **fishery, -fishing,** *s.* pêche du corail, *f.* — **fishing,** *adj.* corailleur. — **fishing boat,** *s.* navire corailleur, *m.*, coraillère, coraline, *f.* — **flower,** *s.* érythrine, *f.* — **island,** *s.* île de corail, *f.* — **net,** *s.* salabre, farais, *m.* — **rag,** *s.* calcaire à polypiers, *m.* — **reef,** *s.* banc de corail, *m.* — **root,** *s.*

V. — **wort.** — **sea,** *s.* mer de corail, *f.* — **tree,** *s.* érythrine, *f.* — **wood,** *s.* bois de corail, *m.* — **wort,** *s.* clandestine, *f.*
Corallaceous, *adj.* corallaire
Coralled, *adj.* coraillé
Coralliferous, *adj.* corallifère
Coralliform, *adj.* coralliforme
Coralligenous, *adj.* coralligène
Coralline, *adj.* corallin; — *s.* (*boat*) coraillère, coraline, *f.*; (*bot., jewel.*) coralline, coraline, *f.*
Coralloid, -al, *adj.* coralloïde
Corbeil, *s.* corbeille, *f.*
Corbel, *s.* corbeau, *m.*, corbeille, *f.*; niche, *f.*
Corbelling, *s.* encorbellement, *m.*
Cord, *s.* corde, *f.*, cordon, *m.*; (*trimming*) ganse, *f.*; (*stuff*) étoffe à côtes, *f.*; (*velvet*) velours (de coton) à côtes, *m.*; (*of wood*) corde, *f.*; (*nav.*) cordage, *m.*; (*fig.*) lien, *m.*; — *v.a.* corder; (*need.*) ganser. *Three-* —, (*twine*) à trois fils. — **grass,** *s.* spartine, *f.* — **maker,** *s.* cordier, *m.* — **wood,** *s.* (*obsolete*) bois de corde, (*now*) bois de stère, *m.* [cordes, *f.pl.*
Cordage, *s.* cordage, *m.*, cordages, *m.pl.*,
Cordate, Cordated, *adj.* cordé
Corded, *adj.* cordé; (*of stuffs*) à côtes
Cordelier, *s.* cordelier, *m.*
Cordial, *adj.* cordial; — *s.* cordial, *m.*; liqueur, *f.*
Cordiality, *s.* cordialité, *f.*
Cordially, *adv.* cordialement
Cordiform, *adj.* cordiforme
Cordon, *s.* cordon, *m.*
Cordovan, *s.* (*leather*) peau maroquinée, *f.*, cordouan, *m.*; (*pers.*) Cordouan, *m.*, e, *f.*; — *adj.* cordouan, de Cordoue
Corduroy, *s.* velours (de coton) à côtes, *m.*
Cordwain, *s.* (*leather*) *V.* **Cordovan**
Cordwainer, *s.* (*shoemaker*) cordonnier, *m.*; (*cordovan dresser*) maroquineur, cordouanier, *m.*
Core, *s.* cœur, *m.*; (*of the heart*) fond, repli, *m.*; (*of an apple*, &c.) trognon, cœur, *m.*; (*of a boil*) bourbillon, *m.*; (*of an abscess*) fond, *m.*; (*of corns*) racine, *f.*; (*metal.*) noyau, *m.*; (*fig.*) cœur. intérieur, milieu, centre, fond, *m.*; — *v.a.* (*an apple*, &c.) enlever le trognon de; (— **out**) enlever; (*a corn*) déraciner, extirper
Corean, *s.* Coréen, *m.*, -ne, *f.*; — *adj.* coréen, [de Corée
Coregency, *s.* corégence, *f.*
Coregent, *s.* corégent, *m.*, e, *f.*
Coreligionist, *s.* coreligionnaire, *m.f.*
Corespondent, *s.* complice, *m.*
Corf, *s.* benne, banne, *f.*, cuveau, cuffat, *m.*, tonne d'extraction, *f.*
Corfiote, Corfute, *s. adj.* Corfiote, *m.f.*
Coriaceous, *adj.* coriacé, coriace, de cuir
Coriander, *s.* coriandre, *f.*
Corinthian, *s.* Corinthien, *m.*, -ne, *f.*; — *adj.* corinthien, de Corinthe
Cork, *s.* liége, *m.*; (*stopper*) bouchon, *m.*; (*float for swimming*) nageoire, *f.*; — *adj.* de (*or* en) liége; — *v.a.* boucher. — **cutter,** *s.* bouchonnier, *m.* — **driver,** *s.* (*of coopers*) tapette, *f.* — **jacket,** *s.* corset de liége, scaphandre, *m.* — **manufacturer, -merchant, -seller,** *s.* bouchonnier, *m.* — **presser,** *s.* (*of coopers*) mâche-bouchons, *m.* — **screw,** *s.* tire-bouchon, *m.* —**screw staircase,** *s.* escalier en limaçon, escalier à vis, *m.* — **sock, -sole,** *s.* semelle de liége, *f.* — **stopper,** *s.* bouchon de liége, *m.* — **tree,** *s.* chêne-liége, surier, *m.*
Corking, *s.* bouchage, *m.*
Corky, *adj.* liégeux, de (*or* en) liége
Cormorant, *s.* cormoran, *m.*; (*pers.*) glouton, *m.*
Corn, *s.* blé, *m.*; (*standing*) blé, *m.*, blés, *m.pl.*; (*in general*) grain, *m.*, grains, *m.pl.*; céréales, *f.pl.*; (*single seed, minute particle*) grain, *m.*; (*on the feet*) cor, *m.*; — *v.a.* grener; (*salt*) saler. *Soft* —, (*on the feet*) œil-de-perdrix, *m.* — **bin,** *s.* coffre à blé, *m.* — **chandler,** *s.* marchand de grains, grainetier, *m.* — **chandlery,** *s.* graineterie, *f.* — **cockle,** *s.* nielle des blés, agrostemme, *f.* — **crops,** *s. pl.* céréales, *f.pl.* — **crake,** *s.* râle de genêts, *m.* — **crusher,** *s.* concasseur de grains, *m.* — **cutter,** *s.* (*pers.*) pédicure, *m.f.*; (*instr.*) coupe-cors, *m.* — **dealer,** *s.* *V.* — **chandler.** — **doctor,** *s.* pédicure, *m.* — **dressing machine,** *s.* machine à nettoyer le blé, *f.*, tarare, *m.* — **drill,** *s.* semoir, *m.* — **exchange,** *s.* halle au blé, *f.* — **factor,** *s.* facteur aux grains, *m.* — **fed chicken,** *s.* poulet de grain, *m.* — **field,** *s.* champ de blé, *m.* — **flag,** *s.* glaïeul, *m.* — **floor,** *s.* grenier à blé, *m.*; (*for thrashing*) aire (de grange), *f.* — **flower,** *s.* fleur des champs, *f.*; (*blue-bottle*) bluet, bleuet, *m.* — **fly,** *s.* chlorops, *m.* — **grasses,** *s. pl.* céréales, *f.pl.* — **ground beetle,** *s.* zabre, *m.* — **knife,** *s.* coupe-cors, *m.* — **land,** *s.* terre à blé, *f.* — **laws,** *s.pl.* lois sur les céréales, *f.pl.* —**less,** *adj.* dépourvu de blé. — **loft,** *s.* grenier à blé, *m.* — **market,** *s.* halle au blé, *f.*; cours des grains, *m.*; commerce des grains, *m.* — **measure,** *s.* mesure pour les grains, *f.* — **merchant,** *s.* marchand de grains, *m.* — **mill,** *s.* moulin à blé, *m.* — **moth,** *s.* teigne des grains, *f.* — **pipe,** *s.* chalumeau, *m.* — **plant,** *s.* céréale, *f.* — — **plaster,** *s.* emplâtre pour les cors, *m.* — **poppy, -rose,** *s.* coquelicot, *m.* — **salad,** *s.* mâche, doucette, *f.* — **sheaf,** *s.* gerbe de blé, *f.* — **stack,** *s.* meule de blé, *f.* — **stalk,** *s.* chaume de blé, *m.*; (*of Indian* —) chaume de maïs, *m.* — **trade,** *s.* commerce des grains *or* des céréales, *m.* — **violet,** *s.* campanule, *f.* — **weevil,** *s.* calandre, *f.*
Cornea, *s.* cornée, *f.*
Cornel, *s.* (*fruit*) cornouille, *f.*; (*tree*) cornouiller, *m.* — **tree,** *s.* cornouiller, *m.*
Cornelian, *s.* (*bot.*) *V.* **Cornel**; (*min.*) *V.* **Carnelian.** — **cherry,** *s.* cornouille, *f.*
Corneous, *adj.* *V.* **Horny**
Corner, *s.* coin, *m.*; encognure, *f.*; angle, *m.*; (*retired place*) réduit, recoin, *m.*; (*end*) extrémité, *f.*; — *v.a.* pousser *or* chasser dans un coin; acculer. — **dish,** *s.* (*ware*) plat d'entrée, plat d'entremets, *m.*; (*of eatables*) *V.* **Side-dish.** — **house,** *s.* maison du coin, maison qui fait le coin, *f.* — **iron,** *s.* cornière, *f.* — **piece,** *s.* (*of furniture*) encognure, *f.*, coin, *m.* — **stone,** *s.* pierre angulaire, *f.* — **tooth,** *s.* (*vet.*) coin, *m.* — **wise,** *adv.* diagonalement, en coin [cornu
Cornered, *adj.* à coins; à angles; à cornes,
Cornet, *s.* (*mus.*) cornet, *m.*; (*mil.*) sous-lieutenant (de cavalerie), *m.*; (*vet.*) *V.* **Coronet**; (*shell, paper cone*) cornet, *m.*
Cornetcy, *s.* grade de sous-lieutenant (de cavalerie) *m.*, sous-lieutenance, *f.*
Corneter, *s.* joueur de cornet, cornet, *m.*
Cornice, *s.* corniche, *f.*; (*for curtains*) galerie (de croisée), *f.*; (*of a carriage*) gouttière, *f.* — **pole,** *s.* bâton de rideau, porte-rideau, *m.*
Cornicle, *s.* cornicule, *f.*, cornichon, *m.*
Cornigerous, *adj.* cornigère
Cornish, *adj.* de Cornouailles; — *s.* (la) langue [de Cornouailles, *f.*
Cornist, *s.* corniste, *m.*
Cornopean, *s.* cornet à pistons, *m.*
Cornopeist, *s.* piston, *m.*
Cornucopia, *s.* corne d'abondance, *f.*
Cornute, Cornuted, *adj.* cornu
Corny, *adj.* (*of horn*) *V.* **Horny**; (*of corn*) de (*or* du) blé; de (*or* des) grains; fertile en blé
Corol, Corolla, *s.* corolle, *f.*
Corollary, *s.* corollaire, *m.*
Corona, *s.* couronne, *f.*
Coronal, *adj.* coronal; — *s.* couronne, guirlande, *f.*; (— *bone*) os coronal, coronal, *m.*
Coronary, *adj.* de couronne; en couronne; (*anat.*) coronaire
Coronation, *s.* couronnement, sacre, *m.*
Coronella cup, *s.* cornet, *m.*
Coroner, *s.* (*in England and America*) coroner, *m.*
Coronet, *s.* couronne, *f.*; (*peculiarly English*) coronet, *m.*; (*lady's head-dress*) ferronnière, *f.*; (*vet.*) couronne, *f.*, bourrelet, *m.*

Coroniform, *adj.* coroniforme
Coronilla, *s.* coronille, *f.*
Coronoid, *adj.* coronoïde [ivoire végétal, *m.*
Corosso, Corozo, Corozzo, *s.* corozo,
Corporal, *s.* caporal, *m.*; (*of cavalry*) brigadier, *m.*; (*nav.*) second capitaine d'armes, *m.*; (*communion cloth*) corporal, *m.*; — *adj.* *V.* **Bodily**
Corporality, *s.* corporalité, matérialité, *f.*
Corporally, *adv.* corporellement ; de corps
Corporate, *adj.* érigé en corporation, qui forme une corporation ; corporatif ; collectif
Corporation, *s.* corporation, *f.*; communauté, société, *f.*; (*of towns*) municipalité, *f.*; (*corpulence*) bedaine, *f.*, (du) ventre, *m.*
Corporeal, &c. *V.* **Corporal,** &c.
Corporeity, *s.* corporéité, *f.* [sation, *f.*
Corporification, *s.* corporification, corpori-
Corporify, *v.a.* corporifier, corporiser
Corposant, *s.* feu saint-Elme, *m.*
Corps, *s.* corps, *m.*
Corpse, *s.* cadavre, corps, corps mort, mort, *m.*
Corpulenc-e, y, *s.* corpulence, *f.*, embon-
Corpulent, *adj.* corpulent [point, *m.*
Corpus-Christi, *s.* la Fête-Dieu, la fête du saint sacrement, *f.*
Corpuscle, Corpuscule, *s.* corpuscule, *m.*
Corpuscular, *adj.* corpusculaire
Corpuscularian, *s.* corpusculiste, *m.*
Correct, *adj.* correct ; exact ; juste ; convenable ; pur ; bon ; régulier, en règle ; — *v.a.* corriger ; (*a person speaking*) reprendre ; (*regulate*) régler
Corrected, *part. adj.* corrigé ; repris ; réglé. — **copy,** *s.* corrigé, *m.* *To stand* —, reconnaître son erreur, avouer qu'on a tort
Correcting, *adj.* correcteur ; — *s.* correction, *f.*
Correction, *s.* correction, *f.* *Under* —, sauf
Correctional, *adj.* correctionnel [correction
Correctionally, *adv.* correctionnellement
Corrective, *adj.* correctif, de correction ; — *s.* correctif, *m.*
Correctively, *adv.* correctivement
Correctly, *adv.* correctement ; exactement ; justement, juste ; convenablement ; purement ; régulièrement ; (*of thinking*) sainement
Correctness, *s.* correction, *f.*; exactitude, *f.*; justesse, *f.*; convenance, *f.*; pureté, *f.*; régularité, *f.*; (*of a copy,* &c.) fidélité, *f.*
Corrector, *s.* correcteur, *m.* — *of the press,* correcteur d'imprimerie
Correctress, *s.* correctrice, *f.*
Correlation, *s.* corrélation, *f.*
Correlative, *adj. s.* corrélatif, *adj. m.*, -ive, *f.*, corrélatif, *s.m.*
Correlatively, *adv.* corrélativement
Correlativeness, *s.* nature corrélative, *f.*
Correspond, *v.n.* correspondre (avec), se rapporter (à), être en rapport (avec) ; convenir (à) ; (*to be equal*) répondre (à), s'accorder (avec), être conforme (à) ; (*by letters*) correspondre. *With* ... *to* — (*to match*), avec ... pareil
Correspondence, *s.* correspondance, *f.*; rapport, *m.*, relation, *f.*; (*intercourse*) intelligence, *f.*; (*by letters*) correspondance, *f.* — **ticket,** *s.* (*of French omnibuses*) bulletin de correspondance, *m.*, correspondance, *f.*
Correspondent, *adj.* correspondant ; (*relating to*) qui se rapporte (à), en rapport (avec) ; (*agreeable*) conforme (à) ; — *s.* correspondant, *m.*, e, *f.*
Correspondently, *adv.* d'une manière correspondante ; conformément ; exactement
Corresponding, *adj.* *V.* **Correspondent**
Correspondingly, *adv.* *V.* **Correspondently**
Corridor, *s.* corridor, *m.*; (*fort.*) chemin couvert, *m.*
Corrigi-bility, bleness. *V.* page 3, § 1
Corrigible, *adj.* corrigible ; punissable
Corroborant, *adj. s.* corroborant, *adj. m.*, e, *f.*, corroborant, *s.m.*
Corroborate, *v.a.* corroborer, fortifier ; confirmer [firmation, *f.*
Corroboration, *s.* corroboration, *f.*; con-
Corroborative, *adj.* corroboratif ; (*fig.*) qui corrobore, confirmatif, qui confirme, à l'appui (de) ; — *s.* corroboratif, corroborant, *m.*
Corroboratory. *V.* **Corroborative**
Corrode, *v.a.* corroder ; (*fig.*) ronger ; miner ;
Corrodent, *s.* corrodant, *m.* [détruire
Corrodible, *adj.* corrodible
Corroding, *adj.* corrodant ; (*fig.*) rongeur
Corrosion, *s.* corrosion, *f.*; (*fig.*) destruction, *f.*
Corrosive, *adj.* corrosif ; (*fig.*) rongeur ; — *s.* corrosif, *m.*; (*fig.*) ver (*or* souci) rongeur, *m.*
Corrosively, *adv.* d'une manière corrosive, comme un corrosif
Corrosiveness, *s.* corrosiveté, mordacité, *f.*
Corrugant, *adj.* qui ride, qui plisse, qui fronce, corrugateur
Corrugate, *v.a.* rider, plisser, froncer, corruguer ; (*to wave*) onduler ; — *v.n.* se rider, se plisser, se froncer, se corruguer ; onduler ; — *adj.*, **—d,** *part. adj.* ridé, plissé, froncé, corrugué ; ondulé. *—d iron,* tôle ondulée *or* ridée, *f.*, fer ridé, *m.* [froncement, *m.*
Corrugation, *s.* corrugation, *f.*, plissement,
Corrugator, *s.* corrugateur, *m.*
Corrugent, *adj.* corrugateur
Corrupt, *v.a.* corrompre ; altérer ; — *v.n.* se corrompre ; se gâter ; — *adj.* corrompu ; gâté ; vicié. *To become* —, se corrompre ; se gâter ; se vicier
Corrupter, *s.* corrupteur, *m.*, -trice, *f.*
Corrupti-bility, bleness. *V.* page 3, § 1
Corruptible, *adj.* corruptible
Corruptibly, *adv.* d'une manière corruptible, de manière à se corrompre
Corrupting, *adj.* corrupteur
Corruption, *s.* corruption, *f.*; altération, *f.*; dégradation, *f.*; (*matter*) pus, *m.* — *of blood,* (*law*) mort civile, *f.* (*now superseded by the* dégradation civique, *f.*)
Corruptive, *adj.* corruptif, qui corrompt
Corruptless, *adj.* incorruptible
Corruptly, *adv.* d'une manière corrompue ; (*by bribery*) par corruption
Corruptness, *s.* corruption, *f.*
Corruptress, *s.* corruptrice, *f.*
Corsac, *s.* corsac, *m.*
Corsair, *s.* corsaire, forban, *m.*
Corselet, *s.* corselet, *m.* [*m.*, -ière, *f.*
Corset, *s.* corset, *m.* — **maker,** *s.* corsetier,
Corsican, *s.* Corse, *m.f.*; — *adj.* corse, de Corse
Cortes, *s. pl.* cortès, *f.pl.*
Cortical, *adj.* cortical
Corundum, *s.* corindon, *m.*
Coruscate, *v.n.* scintiller, briller, éclater
Coruscation, *s.* coruscation, *f.*; (*fig.*) éclair,
Corve. *V.* **Corf** [éclat, *m.*
Corvette, *s.* corvette, *f.*
Corvine, *adj.* corvin
Corvus, *s.* corbeau, *m.*
Corybant, *s.* corybante, *m.*
Corybantic, *adj.* corybantique
Corymb, Corymbus, *s.* corymbe, *m.*
Corymbiferous, *adj.* corymbifère
Corymbose, Corymbous, *adj.* corymbeux
Coryphæus, Corypheus, *s.* coryphée, *m.*
Coryza, *s.* coryza, *m.*
Cos. — *lettuce,* romaine, *f.*
Cosecant, *s.* cosécante, *f.* [taire, *m.f.*
Cosignatary, Cosignatory, *s. adj.* cosigna-
Cosigner, *s.* cosignataire, *m.f.* [ment
Cosily, *adv.* à l'aise, commodément, agréable-
Cosine, *s.* cosinus, *m.*
Cosmetic, *adj. s.* cosmétique, *adj. m.f.*, *s.m.*
Cosm-ic, al, -ically. *V.* page 3, § 1
Cosmo-gonic, al, -gonically, -gony, -graphic, al, -graphically, -graphy, -logic, al, -logically, -logist, -logy, &c. *V.* page 3, § 1
Cosmographer, *s.* cosmographe, *m.*

Cosmopolitan, Cosmopolite, *adj.* s cosmopolite, *m.f.* [cosmopolitisme, *m.*
Cosmopolitism, Cosmopolitanism, *s.*
Cosmorama, *s.* cosmorama, *m.*
Cosmoramic, *adj.* cosmoramique
Cosmos, *s.* Cosmos, *m.*
Coss. — *lettuce*, romaine, *f.*
Cossack, *s. adj.* cosaque, *s.m., adj. m.f.*
Cosset, *s.* agneau élevé à la main, *m.*; favori, *m.*, -te, *f.*; — *v.a.* caresser; dorloter
Cost, *v.n.a.* coûter; — *s.* prix, *m.*; (*com.*) coût, prix, *m.*; (*expense*) *V.* **Expense;** (*detriment*) dépens, *m.pl.*; —**s,** *pl.* (*law*) dépens, *m pl.* — *what it will* (or *may*), coûte que coûte. *At any* —, à tout prix, coûte que coûte. *To carry —s*, entraîner les dépens. — **free,** *adv.* sans frais, gratis, pour rien. —**less,** *adj.* qui ne coûte rien, sans frais. — **price,** *s.* prix coûtant, *m.* *At — price*, au prix coûtant
Costal, *adj.* costal [(*f.*) des quatre saisons
Costermonger, Coster, *s.* marchand (*m.*, e,
Costive, *adj.* constipé; serré
Costiveness, *s.* constipation, *f.*
Costliness, *s.* grande dépense, somptuosité, richesse, *f.*; frais, *m.pl.*; prix élevé, *m.*
Costly, *adj.* coûteux, dispendieux, cher; précieux, de prix, de grand prix; somptueux,
Costmary, *s.* balsamite, *f.* [magnifique, riche
Costume, *s.* costume, *m.* [-ière, *f.*
Costumer, Costumier, *s.* costumier, *m*,
Cosufferer, *s.* compagnon (*m. or* compagne, *f.*) d'infortune *or* de souffrance
Cosurety, *s.* cofidéjusseur, *m.*
Cosy, *adj.* à l'aise; commode, confortable, agréable; (*chatty*) causeur
Cot, *s.* hutte, cabane, maisonnette, chaumière, *f.*; (*for sheep*, &c.) parc, *m.*; (*for infants*) lit d'enfant, *m.*; barcelonnette, *f.*; (*nav.*) cadre, hamac, *m.* — **land,** *s.* clos, *m.*
Cotangent, *s.* cotangente, *f.*
Cote. *V.* **Cot**
Cotemporary. *V.* **Contemporary**
Cotenant, *s.* colocataire, *m.f.*; copropriétaire, *m.f.*; (*feud.*) cotenancier, *m.*, -ière, *f.*
Coterie, *s.* coterie, *f.*
Coterminous. *V.* **Conterminous**
Cothurn, *s.* cothurne, *m.* [de (*or* du) cothurne
Cothurnate, Cothurnated, *adj.* cothurné;
Cotillon, *s.* cotillon, *m.*
Cotoneaster, *s.* cotonéastre, *m.*
Cotquean, *s.* fouille-au-pot, *m.*
Cotrustee, *s.* cotuteur, *m.*, -trice, *f.*; cura-
Cotta, *s.* (*eccl.*) rochet, *m.* [teur, *m.*, -trice, *f.*
Cottage, *s.* cabane, chaumière, *f.*; (*any small house in general*) petite maison, *f.*; petite maison de campagne, villa, *f.*, cottage, *m.* — **farming,** *s.* petite culture, *f.* — **piano,** *s.* piano droit, *m.* [villageois, *m.*, e, *f.*
Cottager, Cotter, *s.* paysan, *m.*, -ne, *f.*,
Cottian, *adj.* (*geog.*) cottiennes, *f.pl.*
Cottier. *V.* **Cottager**
Cotton, *s.* coton, *m.*; (*cloth*) cotonnade, toile de coton, *f.*; (*thread*) fil d'Écosse, *m.*; (*bot.*) cotonnier, *m.*; — *adj.* de coton; (*pertaining to the cotton trade*) cotonnier; — *v n.* cotonner, se cotonner; (*agree*) s'accorder, corder. — **canvas,** *s.* cotonnine, *f.* — **check,** *s.* cotonnade, *f.* — **cloth,** *s.* toile de coton, *f.*, tissu de coton, *m.*, cotonnade, *f.* — **district,** *s.* district cotonnier, centre de fabrication du coton, *m.* — **dressing establishment,** *s.* cotonnerie, *f.* — **fabric,** *s.* tissu de coton, *m.* — **factory,** *s.* filature de coton, *f.* — **famine,** *s.* crise cotonnière, *f.* — **flannel,** *s.* molleton, *m.* — **gin,** *s.* machine à égrener le coton, égreneuse à coton, *f.* — **goods,** *s. pl.* cotonnade, *f.*, cotonnades, *f.pl.* — **grass,** *s.* linaigrette, *f.* — **growing,** *adj.* cotonnier; *s.* cotonnerie. industrie cotonnière, *f.* — **jenny,** *s.* métier à filer le coton, *m.* — **machine,** *s.* machine à filer le coton, *f.* — **manufactory,** *s.* filature de coton, *f.* — **manufacture,** *s.* manufacture de cotons, *f.* — **mill,** *s.* filature de coton, *f.* — **plant,** *s.* cotonnier, *m.* — **plantation,** *s.* cotonnerie, *f.* — **print,** *s.* *V.* **Printed —.** (*Letter* **P**). — **printer, — printing,** *s.* *V.* **Calico printer** *and* **printing.** — **rose,** *s.* cotonnière, *f.* — **shrub,** *s.* cotonnier, *m.* — **spinner,** *s.* filateur de coton, *m.* — **spinning,** *s.* filage du coton, *m.* — **spinning establishment,** *s.* filature de coton, *f.* — **staple,** *s.* soie de coton, *f.* — **stuff,** *s.* cotonnade, *f.* — **thistle,** *s.* onoporde, *m.* — **trade,** *s.* commerce des cotons, *m.* — **tree,** *s.* cotonnier, *m.* — **waste,** *s.* bourre de coton, *f.* — **weed,** *s.* cotonnière *f.* — **wood,** *s.* peuplier du Canada, *m.* — **wool,** *s.* ouate de coton, ouate, *f.* — **works,** *s. pl.* filature de coton, *f.* — **yarn,** *s.* fil de coton, *m.*
Cottonade, *s.* cotonnade, *f.*
Cottony, *adj.* cotonné; cotonneux
Cottrel, *s.* crémaillère, *f.*
Cotyledon, *s.* cotylédon, *m.*
Cotyledonous, *adj.* cotylédoné
Couch, *v.n.* se coucher, coucher; s'étendre; être couché; (*stoop*) se baisser; (*bow*) s'incliner, se courber; (*sink*) s'affaisser; (*surg.*) abaisser la cataracte; — *v.a.* coucher; (*spread*) étendre; (*hide*) cacher; (*in writing*) concevoir, exprimer, rédiger; (*of spears*) tenir en arrêt; (*an eye*) abaisser (la cataracte); — *s.* couche, *f.*; (*lounge*) chaise longue, *f.*, (*formerly*) lit de repos, *m.*; (*nav.*) *V.* **Coach.** — **fellow,** *s.* camarade de lit, *m.f.* — **grass,** *s.* chiendent, *m.*
Couchant, *adj.* couché; (*her.*) couchant
Coucher, *s.* opérateur oculiste (pour la cataracte), *m.* [ment de la cataracte, *m.*
Couching, *s.* courbette, *f.*; (*surg.*) abaisse-
Cougar, *s.* couguar, couguard, *m.*
Cough, *s.* toux, *f.*; — *v.n.* tousser; — *v.a.* (— **up**) expectorer. *To have a* —, avoir la toux, être enrhumé, (*with an adj.*) avoir une toux (...). — **lozenges,** *s. pl.* pastilles contre la
Cougher, *s.* tousseur, *m.*, -euse, *f.* [toux, *f.*pl.
Coughing, *s.* toux, *f.* *Fit of* — quinte, quinte de toux, *f.*
Could. *I* —, (*was able*) je pouvais; je pus; (*should be able*) je pourrais; (*have been able*) j'ai pu; (*after a verb, conj., &c., governing the subjunctive mood*) je pusse. *You — tell him that now*, vous pourriez lui dire cela maintenant *You — have told him that yesterday*, vous auriez pu lui dire cela hier. *If you — have seen him*, si vous aviez pu le voir
Coulter, *s.* coutre, *m.* — **neb,** *s.* *V.* **Puffin**
Council, *s.* conseil, *m.*; (*eccl.*) concile, *m.* — *of state*, conseil d'état, *m.* — **board,** *s.* conseil, *m.* — **book,** *s.* registre de conseil, *m.* — **chamber,** *s.* salle de conseil, *m.* — **man,** *s.* conseiller municipal, *m.* [seiller d'état, *m.*
Councillor, *s.* conseiller, *m.* — *of state*, con-
Counsel, *s.* conseil, *m.*; délibération, *f.*; prudence, *f.*; secret, *m.*, discrétion, *f.*; (*purpose*) dessein, *m.*; (*barrister, pleader*) avocat, défenseur, conseil, *m.*; — *v.a.* conseiller. — **keeper,** *s.* personne discrète, *f.* — **keeping,** *adj.* discret; *s.* discrétion, *f.*
Counsellable, *adj.* conseillable
Counsellor, *s.* conseiller, *m.*, -ère, *f.*; (*lawyer*) avocat, conseil, *m.*
Counsellorship, *s.* charge de conseiller, *f.*
Count, *v.a.n.* compter; — *s.* compte, *m.*; (*civ. law*) motif, *m.*; (*crim. law*) charge, *f.*, chef, chef d'accusation, *m.*; (*pers.*) comte, *m.* — **less,** *adj.* *See below.* — **wheel,** *s.* (*horol.*) roue de la sonnerie, *f.*
Countable, *adj.* nombrable, qui peut se compter
Countenance, *s.* contenance, *f.*; visage, *m.*, figure, physionomie, *f.*, traits, *m.pl.*; air, *m.*, mine, *f.*; appui, *m.*, protection, faveur, *f.*; encouragement, *m.*, approbation, *f.* *Out of* —, décontenancé. *To give* —, appuyer, &c. (*V.* **Countenance,** *v.a.*). *To keep o.'s* —, faire bonne contenance; (*be composed*) garder son

sang-froid; (*not to laugh*) garder son sérieux. *To keep oneself in* —, se donner (*or* se faire) une contenance. *To put in* —, donner une contenance à, donner de l'assurance à, mettre à son aise. *To put out of* —, décontenancer, faire perdre contenance à, déconcerter. *To stare* or *look* (*one*) *out of* —. dévisager (quelqu'un), &c. (*V.* **Stare**)

Countenance, *v.a.* appuyer, soutenir, défendre, protéger; favoriser; encourager; autoriser; approuver, être en faveur de

Counter, *s.* (*pers.*) compteur, *m.*, -euse, *f.*; (*instr.*) compteur, *m.*; (*table or board*) comptoir, *m.*; (*at play*) jeton, *m.*; (*of boots, shoes*) contre-fort, *m.*; (*of horses*) garrot, *m.*; (*nav.*) voûte, *f.*; (*mus.*) *V.* — **tenor;** — *adv.* contrairement (à), en sens contraire (de), en sens inverse (de), à l'encontre (de); (*in compounds*) contre, contraire. *Lower* —, (*nav.*) grande voûte, *f.* *Upper* —, petite voûte, *f.* *Over the* —, (*for ready money*) au comptant. *To run* — *to*, agir contrairement à; aller à l'encontre de, contrarier; heurter. — **accusation,** *s.* contre-accusation, *f.* — **act,** *v.a.* contrarier, contrecarrer, faire obstacle à; combattre; déjouer; neutraliser; balancer, détruire. — **action,** *s.* action contraire, *f.*, effet contraire, mouvement opposé, *m.*, opposition, résistance, *f.*, antagonisme, empêchement, obstacle, *m.* — **approach,** *s.* contre-approche, *f.* — **attraction,** *s.* attraction opposée, *f.* — **balance,** *v.a.* contre-balancer; contre-peser; *s.* contre-poids, *m.* — **bass,** *s.* contre-basse, *f.* — **batter,** *v.a.* contre-battre. — **battery,** contre-batterie, *f.* — **blast to tobacco,** *s.* "Misocapnie," *m.* — **blow,** *s.* contre-coup, *m.* — **bond,** *s.* sous-garantie, *f.* — **brace,** *v.a.* contre-brasser. — **buff,** *s.* contre-coup, *m.*; *v.a.* renvoyer en sens contraire, repousser. — **caster,** *s.* calculateur, *m.* — **change,** *s.* contre-change, *m.*; *v.a.* contre-changer. — **charge,** *s.* contre-accusation, récrimination, *f.* — **charm,** *s.* contre-charme, *m.*; *v.a.* désenchanter. — **check,** *v.a.* faire obstacle à, s'opposer à, contrarier, contrecarrer; *s.* opposition, *f.*; réprimande, *f.*; réplique, repartie, *f.* — **cheer,** *s.* contre-applaudissement, *m.* — **chevron,** *s.* contre-chevron, *m.* — **chevrony,** *adj.* contre-chevronné. — **criticism,** *s.* contre-critique, *f.* — **current,** *s.* contre-courant, *m.* — **date,** *v.a.* contre-dater. — **declaration,** *s.* contre-déclaration, *f.* — **deed,** *s.* contre-lettre, *f.* — **drain,** *s.* contre-fossé, *m.* — **draw,** *v.a.* calquer; contre-tirer. — **drawing,** *s.* calque, *m.* — **evidence,** *s.* contre-preuve, *f.*, témoignage contraire, *m.*, déposition contradictoire, *f.* — **extension,** *s.* contre-extension, *f.* — **feit,** *v.a.* contrefaire; imiter; feindre; *adj.* contrefait; imité; feint, simulé; (*of coin*) faux; *s.* contrefaçon, *f.*; (*bad money*) fausse monnaie, *f.*; fausse pièce, *f.*; (*fig.*) imitation, *f.*; (*pers.*) imposteur, fourbe, *m.* — **feiter,** *s.* faussaire, contrefacteur, *m.*; faux-monnayeur, *m.*; (*fig.*) imitateur, *m.*, -trice, *f.*, personne qui contrefait, *f.* — **feiting,** *s.* contrefaçon, *f.*; (*fig.*) imitation, *f.* — **foil,** *s.* souche, *f.* — **force,** *s.* contre-force, *f.* — **fort,** *s.* contre-fort, *m.* — **fugue,** *s.* contre-fugue, *f.* — **gauge,** *v.a.* contre-jauger. — **guard,** *s.* contre-garde, *f.* — **guarded,** *adj.* contre-gardé. — **influence,** *s.* *V.* — **sway.** — **inquest, -inquiry,** *s.* contre-enquête, *f.* — **irritant,** *s.* dérivatif, *m.* — **irritation,** *s.* dérivation, *f.* — **jumper,** *s.* calicot, *m.* — **lath,** *s.* contre-latte, *f.*; *v.a.* contre-latter. — **light,** *s.* contre-jour, *m.* — **line,** *s.* contre-ligne, *f.* — **mand,** *v.a.* contremander; (*com.*) décommander; *s.* contremandement, *m.*; contre-ordre, *m.* — **manding,** *s.* contre-mandement, *m.* — **manœuvre,** *s.* contre-manœuvre, *f.* — **march,** *s.* contre-marche, *f.*; *v.n.* contre-marcher, faire une contre-marche. — **marching,** *s.* contre-marche, *f.*, contre-marches, *f.pl.* — **mark,** *s.* contre-marque, *f.*; *v.a.* contre-marquer. — **measure,** *s.* (*mus.*) contre-temps, *m.* — **mine,** *s.* contre-mine, *f.*; *v.a.* contre-miner; (*fig.*) détruire; combattre. — **miner,** *s.* contre-mineur, *m.* — **motion,** *s.* contre-mouvement, *m.* — **move,** *s.* défense, *f.* — **movement,** *s.* contre-mouvement, *m.*; contre-marche, *f.* — **mure,** *s.* contre-mur, *m.*; *v.a.* contre-murer. — **natural,** *adj.* contre nature. — **opening,** *s.* contre-ouverture, *f.* — **operation,** *s.* contre-opération, *f.* — **opposition,** *s.* contre-opposition, *f.* — **order,** *s.* contre-ordre, *m.*; contremandement, *m.* — **pace,** *s.* contre-pas, *m.* — **pale,** *s.* contre-pal, *m.* — **paled,** *adj.* contre-palé. — **pane,** *s.* couvre-pieds, *m.* — **parole,** *s.* contre-mot, *m.* — **part,** *s.* contre-partie, *f.*; (*fellow*) pendant, *m.*; (*of a cipher*) clé, *f.*; (*law*) double, duplicata, *m.* — **passant,** *adj.* contre-passant. — **petition,** *s.* contre-pétition, *f.* — **pierce,** *v.a.* contre-percer. — **plate,** *s.* contre-plaque, *f.* — **plea,** *s.* réplique, *f.* — **plead,** *v.a.* contredire. — **plot,** *s.* contre-ruse, *f.* — **point,** *s.* contre-point, *m.* — **poise,** *V.* — **balance.** — **poison,** *s.* contre-poison, *m.* — **pressure,** *s.* contre-pression, *f.* — **project,** *s.* contre-projet, *m.* — **proof,** *s.* contre-épreuve, *f.* — **proposal, -proposition,** *s.* contre-proposition, *f.* — **prove,** *v.a.* contre-épreuver; contre-tirer. — **rail,** *s.* double balustrade, *f.* — **revolution,** *s.* contre-révolution, *f.* — **revolutionary,** *adj.*, — **revolutionist,** *s.* contre-révolutionnaire, *m.f.* — **roll,** *s.* contrôle, *m.* — **round,** *s.* contre-ronde, *f.* — **salient,** *adj.* contre-saillant. — **scarp,** *s.* contrescarpe, *f.*; *v.a.* contrescarper. — **seal,** *s.* contre-scel, *m.*; *v.a.* contre-sceller. — **security,** *s.* contre-sûreté, sous-garantie, *f.* — **sense,** *s.* contre-sens, *m.* — **sign,** *v.a.* contre-signer; *s.* contre-seing, *m.*; (*mil.*) mot de ralliement, *m.*, contre-mot, *m.* — **signal,** *s.* contre-signal, *m.* — **signature,** *s.* contre-seing, *m.* — **signer,** *s.*, — **signing,** *adj.* contre-signataire, *m.f.* — **sink,** *v.a.* noyer; fraiser; *s.* fraisure, *f.*; (*tool*) fraisoir, *m.* — **slope,** *s.* contre-pente, *f.* — **sortie,** *s.* contre-sortie, *f.* — **statement,** *s.* exposition contraire, *f.*; contradiction, *f.* — **statute,** *s.* statut (*m.*) *or* ordonnance (*f.*) contraire. — **steam,** *s.* contre-vapeur, *f.* — **step,** *s.* contre-pas, *m.*; (*fig.*) mesure contraire *or* opposée, *f.* — **stimulant,** *adj.* *s.* contre-stimulant, *adj.* *m.*, e, *f.*, contre-stimulant, *s.m.* — **stock,** *s.* souche, *f.* — **stroke,** *s.* contre-coup, *m.* — **surety,** *s.* sous-garantie, *f.* — **survey,** *s.* contre-expertise, *f.* — **sway,** *s.* influence contraire *or* opposée, *f.* — **tally,** *s.* contre-taille, souche, *f.*; *v.a.* contre-tailler. — **taste,** *s.* faux goût, *m.* — **tenor,** *s.* contraténor, contralto, *m.* — **tide,** *s.* contre-marée, *f.* — **time,** *s.* contre-temps, *m.*; (*fig.*) résistance, opposition, *f.* — **trench,** *s.* contre-tranchée, *f.* — **trick,** *s.* contre-ruse, contre-finesse, *f.* — **turn,** *s.* catastase, *f.* — **vail,** *v.a.* contre-balancer, balancer, équivaloir à, compenser; *s.* contre-poids, *m.*; compensation, *f.*, dédommagement, *m.* ('*for*,' de). — **vair,** *s.* contre-vair, *m.* — **vairy,** *adj.* contre-vairé. — **vallation,** *s.* contrevallation, *f.* — **valuation,** *s.* contre-expertise, *f.* — **view,** *s.* position en face, *f.*; contraste, *m.*; (*opt.*) contre-vue, *f.* — **volt,** *s.* contre-volte, *f.* — **vote,** *v.a.* voter contre; l'emporter sur. — **weigh,** *v.a.* *V.* — **balance.** — **wheel,** *v.a.* faire faire des évolutions contraires à. — **wind,** *s.* vent contraire, *m.* — **work,** *v.a.* travailler contre; contrarier, contrecarrer; déjouer, confondre; contre-miner. — **works,** *s.pl.* (*fort.*) contre-attaque, *f.*

Countess, *s.* comtesse, *f.*

Counting, *s.* action de compter, *f.* — **house, -room,** *s.* bureau, comptoir, *m.*; caisse, *f.*
Countless, *adj.* innombrable, sans nombre
Countrified, *adj.* rustique, campagnard; provincial, de province
Countrify, *v.a.* rendre rustique
Country, *s.* (*in general*) pays, *m.*; (*region*) contrée, *f.*; (*native land*) patrie, *f.*; (*not a town*) campagne, *f.*; (*not the capital*) départements, *m.pl.*, province, *f.*; (*law*) jury, *m.*; (*polit.*) public, *m.*; — *adj.* de (*or* du) pays; de la patrie; de (*or* de la) campagne; campagnard; champêtre, rural; rustique; de province, provincial; départemental. *Part of the* —, pays, département, *m.* *In* or *into the* —, (*a country-place*) à la campagne; (*midst of fields*) dans la campagne, dans les champs; (*not the capital*) dans les départements, en province. — **air,** *s.* air de la campagne, *m.* — **bank,** *s.* banque départementale, banque provinciale, banque de province, *f.* — **box,** *s.* petite maison de campagne, *f.*, pied-à-terre, *m.* — **bred,** *adj.* élevé à la campagne *or* en province. — **dance,** *s.* (*old*) contredanse, *f.* — **doctor,** *s.* médecin de campagne, *m.* — **gentleman,** *s.* propriétaire de campagne, *m.*; monsieur de la province, *m.* — **girl,** *s.* petite (*or* jeune) paysanne *or* villageoise, *f.*; (*fellow ditto, pop.*) payse, *f.* — **house,** *s.* maison de campagne, *f.* — **life,** *s.* (*rural*) vie champêtre, vie de campagne, *f.*; (*in the* —) vie de province, *f.* — **like,** *adj.* campagnard; provincial. — **man,** *s.* compatriote, *m.*, (*pop.*) pays, *m.*; (*peasant*) paysan, campagnard, homme de la campagne, *m.*; (*not of the capital*) provincial, *m.*; (*of any country*) habitant d'un pays, *m.* *What — man is he ?* de quel pays est-il? quel est son pays? — **mansion,** *s.* *V.* — **seat.** — **note,** *s.* (*bank.*) billet de banque de province, *m.* — **parson,** *s.* curé de campagne, curé de village, *m.* — **people,** *s. pl.* gens de la campagne, campagnards, *m.pl.*; gens de la province, *m.f. pl.*, provinciaux, *m.pl.* — **place,** *s.* campagne, *f.*, village, *m.* — **seat,** *s.* maison de campagne, *f.*, château, *m.*, terre, campagne, *f.* — **squire,** *s.* grand propriétaire campagnard, *m.* — **town,** *s.* ville de province, *f.* — **woman,** *s.* compatriote, *f.*, (*pop.*) payse, *f.*; (*peasant*) paysanne, campagnarde, femme de la campagne, *f.*; (*not of the capital*) provinciale, *f.*; (*of any country*) habitante d'un pays, *f.* *What — woman is she ?* de quel pays est-elle? quel est son pays?
County, *s.* comté, *m.*; (*in France*) département, *m.*; — *adj.* de comté; (*in France*) départemental. — **court,** *s.* tribunal de première instance, *m.* — **hall,** *s.* préfecture, *f.*; palais de justice et salle d'assemblée (du comté); cour d'assises, *f.* — **rate,** *s.* impôt départemental, *m.*, centimes additionnels, *m.pl.* — **town,** *s.* chef-lieu, *m.*
Coupé, Coupee, *s.* coupé, *m.*
Couple, *s.* (*of things, dead animals, brace*) couple, *f.*; (*pers., living beings*) couple, *m.*; (*bond, tie, coupler*) couple, *f.*, lien, *m.*, chaîne, *f.*; (*carp.*) moise, *f.*; — *v.a.* coupler, accoupler; attacher; atteler; (*fig.*) joindre; — *v.n.* s'accoupler
Coupler, *s.* couple, *f.*, lien, *m.*, attache, chaîne, *f.*; (*of an organ*) double-main, *f.* [strophe, *f.*
Couplet, *s.* distique, *m.*; (*of songs*) couplet, *m.*;
Coupling, *s.* accouplement, *m.*; (*mec.*) couplage, *m.*; (*bond*) couple, *f.*, lien, *m.*, attache, chaîne, *f.*; —**s,** *pl.* (*rail.*) attelage, *m.* — **chain,** *s.* (*rail.*) chaîne de l'attelage, chaîne de sûreté, *f.* — **iron,** *s.* (*rail.*) tendeur, *m.*
Coupon, *s.* coupon, *m.*
Courage, *s.* courage, *m.*
Courageous, *adj.* courageux
Courageously, *adv.* courageusement
Courageousness, *s.* courage, *m.* [sacoche, *f.*
Courier, *s.* courrier, *m.* — **bag,** *s.* gibecière,
Courlander, *s.* Courlandais, *m.*, e, *f.*
Courlandish, *adj.* courlandais, de Courlande
Course, *s.* cours, *m.*; progrès, *m.pl.*; (*race*) course, *f.*; (*career*) carrière, *f.*; (*for racing*) *V.* **Race-course;** (*of time*) courant, *m.*; (*means, way*) marche, conduite, *f.*, moyen, *m.*; voie, *f.*; parti, *m.*; (*order*) ordre, *m.*; (*succession*) suite, *f.*; (*at table*) service, *m.*; (*turn*) tour, *m.*; (*direction*) direction, *f.*; (*of life*) genre, train, *m.*; (*form*) forme, *f.*; (*stone*) assise, *f.*; (*geol.*) filon, *m.*; (*of a ship*) route, *f.*; (*of sails*) basse voile, *f.*; —**s,** *pl.* (*med.*) règles, époques, *f.pl.*, mois, *m.pl.* *In* —, par ordre. *In — of*, en voie de. *In* (*the*) *— of time*, avec le temps. *In due* —, dans son ordre régulier; en son temps. *In the — of* 10 *days*, dans le courant de 10 jours. *Of* —, naturellement, bien entendu, cela va sans dire; nécessairement; comme de raison; de pure forme; (*law*) de droit. *Matter of* —, chose qui va sans dire, *f.*; conséquence nécessaire, *f.*; chose de droit, *f.* *To take its* —, prendre son cours. *Take your own* —, faites à votre guise, faites ce que vous voudrez
Course, *v.a.n.* chasser, courir; poursuivre; (*cause to run*) faire courir; (*run over*) parcourir; (*run*) courir
Courser, *s.* coursier, *m.*, -ière, *f.*; coureur, *m.*, -euse, *f.*; (*sportsman*) chasseur (à courre), *m.*; (*bird*) court-vite, *m.*
Coursing, *s.* chasse (à courre), *f.*
Court, *s.* cour, *f.*; (*law*) cour, *f.*, tribunal, *m.*; (*meeting*) assemblée, *f.*, conseil, *m.*; (*in America*) législature, *f.*; (*assembling of courtiers*) grande réception, *f.*; (*street*) passage, *m.*, (*without a thoroughfare*) impasse, *f.*; (*of a church*) parvis, *m.*; — *v.a.* faire la cour à, courtiser; (*solicit*) rechercher, briguer, solliciter; (*invite*) prier, inviter; (*seek*) chercher. — *of appeal*, cour d'appel, *f.* — *of assize*, cour d'assises, *f.* — *of parliament*, cour des pairs, *f.* *At* —, à la cour. *In* —, à la cour, au tribunal. *In open* —, en plein tribunal, en pleine audience. *In several* —*s*, dans plusieurs cours. — **ball,** *s.* bal de la cour, *m.* — **baron,** *s.* cour foncière, cour seigneuriale, *f.* — **bred,** *adj.* élevé à la cour. — **breeding,** *s.* éducation de cour, *f.* — **card,** *s.* figure, *f.* — **chaplain,** *s.* aumônier de la cour, *m.* — **day,** *s.* jour de conseil, *m.*; (*law*) jour d'audience, jour de palais, *m.* — **dress,** *s.* habit de cour, *m.* — **fool, -jester,** *s.* fou du roi *or* de la reine, bouffon, *m.* — **hand,** *s.* écriture de chancellerie *or* de palais, *f.* — **house,** salle des réunions, *f.*; palais de justice, *m.* — **like,** *adj.* *V.* **Courtly.** — **martial,** *s.* conseil de guerre, *m.* — **plaster,** *s.* taffetas d'Angleterre, *m.* — **roll,** *s.* terrier, *m.* — **train,** *s.* manteau de cour, *m.* — **yard,** *s.* cour, *f.* — **yard gate,** *s.* porte cochère, *f.*
Courteous, *adj.* courtois, poli; affable
Courteously, *adv.* courtoisement, avec courtoisie, poliment; avec affabilité [affabilité, *f.*
Courteousness, *s.* courtoisie, politesse, *f.*;
Courter, *s.* aspirant, soupirant, prétendant, *m.*; courtisan, *m.*; flatteur, *m.*
Courtesan, *s.* courtisane, *f.*
Courtesanship, *s.* courtisanerie, *f.*
Courtesy, *s.* courtoisie, politesse, *f.*; (*bow*) révérence, *f*; — *v.n.* faire une révérence
Courtier, *s.* homme (*pl.* gens) de *or* de la cour, courtisan, *m.*
Courtliness, *s.* élégance, *f.*, air de cour, *m.*
Courtling, *s.* piètre courtisan, *m.*
Courtly, *adj.* de cour; de courtisan, courtisan, courtisanesque; du grand monde; poli; élégant; distingué; — *adv.* comme à la cour; élégamment, avec élégance, d'une manière [distinguée
Courtship, *s.* cour, *f.*
Couscous, *s.* couscous, couscoussou, *m.*
Cousin, *s.* cousin, *m.*, e, *f.* *First* —, *— german*, cousin germain, *m.*, cousine germaine, *f.* *Second* —, cousin issu de germain, *m.*, cousine issue de germain, *f.*

Cousinhood, Cousinship, *s.* cousinage, *m.*
Cove, *s.* anse, crique, *f.*; (*pers.*) gaillard, zig, *m.*; — *v.a.* cintrer, voûter
Covenant, *s.* convention, *f.*, contrat, *m.*; (*Engl. hist.*) covenant, *m.*; (*theol.*) alliance, *f.*; — *v.n.* convenir (de); (*law*) s'engager (à); — [*v.a.* stipuler
Covenantee, *s.* obligataire, *m.f.*
Covenanter, *s.* partie contractante, *f.*; obligé, *m.*, e, *f.*; (*Engl. hist.*) covenantaire, *m.*
Covendor, *s.* covendeur, *m.*, -euse, *f.*
Coventry. *To send to* —, mettre en quarantaine. *To be sent to* —, être mis en quarantaine, être en quarantaine
Cover, *v.a.* couvrir ('*with*,' de; '*in*,' en); recouvrir; (*hide*) cacher, déguiser; (*the step*) emboîter; (*of animals*) couvrir, saillir; (*incubate, brood on*) couver. *Be —ed!* couvrez-vous! — **again,** — **over,** recouvrir. — **up,** couvrir entièrement
Cover, *s.* couverture, *f.*; (*top*) dessus, *m.*; (*of parcels, of letters*) enveloppe, *f.*; (*lid*) couvercle, *m.*; (*of dishes*, &c.) cloche, *f.*, couvre-plat, *m.*; (*of chairs*, &c.) housse, *f.*; (*of tables*) tapis, *m.*; (*requisites for eating*) couvert, *m.*; (*shelter*) couvert, abri, *m.*, protection, *f.*; (*shady place*) lieu ombragé, couvert, *m.*, ramée, *f.*; (*hiding-place*) fort, gîte, couvert, *m.*; (*disguise*) voile, masque, *m.*; prétexte, *m.* *Under* —, (*of letters*, &c.) sous enveloppe; sous le couvert (de); (*sheltered*) à couvert (de), à l'abri (de), sous la protection (de), couvert *or* protégé (par); (*favoured*) à la faveur (de); (*disguised*) sous le voile (de), sous le masque (de), sous une apparence (de), sous de faux semblants (de). *Dinner of* 50 —*s*, dîner de 50 couverts
Coverer, *s.* couvreur, *m.*
Covering, *s.* couverture, *f.*; enveloppe, *f.*; (*lid*) couvercle, *m.*; (*of chairs*, &c.) housse, *f.*; (*clothing*) habits, vêtements, *m.pl.*; (*shelter*) abri, *m.*
Coverlet, *s.* couvre-pieds, *m.*; couvre-lit, *m.*
Covert, *s.* (*shelter*) couvert, abri, asile, *m.*; (*shady place*) lieu ombragé, couvert, *m.*, ramée, *f.*; (*hiding-place*) fort, gîte, couvert, *m.*; —**s,** *pl.* (*of birds*) tectrices, *f.pl.*; — *adj.* couvert; à l'abri; (*fig.*) caché, secret; (*of women*) en puissance de mari. *Under* —, à couvert, à l'abri [cachette
Covertly, *adv.* secrètement, en secret, en
Coverture, *s.* (*shelter*) abri, *m.*; (*law*) état d'une femme en puissance de mari, *m.* *Under* —, en puissance de mari
Covet, *v.a.n.* convoiter; (*long for*) désirer ardemment, désirer; ambitionner
Covetable, *adj.* convoitable, désirable
Coveter, *s.* convoiteur, *m.*, -euse, *f.*, convoiteux, *m.*, -euse, *f.*; (*fam.*) reluqueur, *m.*, -euse, *f.*
Coveting, *s.* convoitise, *f.*
Covetous, *adj.* convoiteur, convoiteux, de convoitise; avide; cupide, avare
Covetously, *adv.* convoiteusement, avec convoitise; avidement; avec avarice, sordidement
Covetousness, *s.* convoitise, *f.*; avidité, *f.*; cupidité, avarice, *f.*
Covey, *s.* couvée, *f.*; (*flight of birds*) volée, *f.*; (*of game*) compagnie, *f.*; (*fig.*) troupe, bande, [*f.*, groupe, *m.*
Coving, *s* voussure, *f.*
Cow, *s.* vache, *f.*; (*cowl*) *V.* **Cowl;** — *v.a.* dompter; (*depress*) atterrer; intimider. — **bane,** *s.* cicutaire, *f.* — **berry,** *s.* airelle, *f.* — **calf,** *s.* taure, vêle, *f.* — **clover, -grass,** trèfle des prés, *m.* — **dung,** *s.* bouse de vache, *f.* — **hair,** *s.* poil de vache, *m.*, bourre de vache, *f.*, ploc, *m.* — **herd,** *s.* vacher, *m.*, -ère, *f.* — **hide,** *s.* peau de vache, *f.*; (*nav.*) mauge, maugère, *f.* — **house,** *s.* étable à vaches, *f.*; vacherie, *f.* — **keeper,** *s.* vacher, *m.*, -ère, *f.*; (*for milk*) nourrisseur, *m.* — **lick,** *s.* épi de cheveux, *m.* — **like,** *adj.* de vache, semblable à une vache. — **mash,** *s.* buvée, *f.* — **parsnip,** *s.* berce, *f.* — **pen,** *s.* parc à vaches, *m.* — **plant,** *s.* *V.* — **tree.** — **pox,** *s.* vaccine, *f.*, cow-pox, *m.* — **shed,** *s.* *V.* — **house.** — **slip,** *s.* *See below.* — **tree,** *s.* arbre à la vache, *m.* — **weed,** *s.* cerfeuil sauvage, *m.* — **wheat,** *s.* mélampyre, *m.*
Coward, *s. adj.* poltron, *m.*, -ne, *f.*, lâche, *m.*
Cowardice, *s.* poltronnerie, lâcheté, *f.*
Cowardlike, *adj.* *V.* **Cowardly**
Cowardliness, *s.* *V.* **Cowardice**
Cowardly, *adj.* poltron, lâche; — *adv.* en poltron, poltronnement, en lâche, lâchement
Cower, — **down,** *v.n.* se blottir, s'accroupir, se tapir
Cowl, *s.* capuchon, *m.*; (*of chimney-tops*) tabourin, *m.*, église, gueule-de-loup, *f.*; (*vessel*) seau, *m.* [à tabourin
Cowled, *adj.* à capuchon; (*of chimney-tops*)
Coworker, *s.* *V.* **Fellow-labourer**
Cowry, *s.* cauris, coris, couris, *m.*
Cowslip, *s.* coucou, *m.*, brayette, primevère [commune, *f.*
Coxa, *s.* os coxal, *m.*
Coxal, *adj.* coxal
Coxalg-ic, -y. *V.* page 3, § 1
Coxcomb, *s.* (*pers.*) fat, petit-maître, *m.*; (*bot.*) célosie, crête-de-coq, *f.*, passe-velours, *m.*
Coxcombical, *adj.* fat, plein de fatuité; de fat, impertinent [*racing-boat*) barreur, *m.*
Coxswain, *s.* patron de chaloupe, *m.*; (*of a*
Coy, *adj.* modeste; timide; réservé; — *v.n.* se comporter avec réserve; faire des difficultés
Coyly, *adv.* modestement; timidement; avec réserve
Coyness, *s.* modestie, *f.*; timidité, *f.*; réserve, *f.*
Coypu, *s.* coypou, castorin, *m.*
Cozen, *v.a.* tromper, duper
Cozenage, *s.* tromperie, fourberie, duperie, *f.*
Cozener, *s.* trompeur, *m.*, -euse, *f.*, fourbe, *m.f.*
Cozily, Cozy. *V.* **Cosily, Cosy**
Cr., *s.* (*book-keep.*) avoir, *m.*
Crab, *s.* crabe, *m.*, écrevisse (de mer), *f.*; cancre, *m.*; (*apple*) pomme sauvage, *f.*; (*of men*) loup-garou, mauvais coucheur, *m.*; (*of women*) pie-grièche, *f.*; (*machine*) chèvre, *f.*; (*of a carriage-pole*) crapaud, *m.*; (*astr.*) écrevisse, *f.*, cancer, *m.* — **apple,** *s.* pomme sauvage, *f.* — **catcher, -eater,** *s.* crabier, *m.* — **fish,** *s.* crabe, *m.*, écrevisse de mer, *f.* — **like,** *adj.* de crabe, d'écrevisse, comme un crabe, comme une écrevisse. — **louse,** *s.* morpion, *m.* —**'s eyes,** *s. pl.* yeux d'écrevisse, *m.pl.* — **stock,** *s.* sauvageon, *m.* — **tree,** *s.* pommier sauvage, *m.*
Crabbed, *adj.* âpre; difficile; désagréable; rude; dur; (*illegible*) illisible; (*peevish*) chagrin, bourru, acariâtre, revêche
Crabbedly, *adv.* rudement; durement; d'un air chagrin, d'une humeur acariâtre
Crabbedness, *s.* âpreté, *f.*; difficulté, *f.*; rudesse, *f.*; (*peevishness*) air chagrin, *m.*, humeur acariâtre, *f.*
Crabby, *adj.* difficile, épineux
Craber, *s.* rat d'eau, *m.*
Crabite, *s.* crabite, *m.*
Crack, *v.a.* fendre; (*brittle things, glass, bells*, &c.) fêler; (*ice*) fendre; (*the ground, a wall*) crevasser, gercer; lézarder; (*to chink on the surface*) gercer; craqueler; (*nuts*, &c., *someone's head*) casser; (*fig.*) rompre, briser; (*the brain*) fêler, déranger; (*a joke*) faire, dire, lâcher; (*a whip*) faire claquer; (*a bottle, viz. drink it*) faire sauter, décoiffer, étouffer, vider, boire; (*swallow*) avaler; — *v.n.* se fendre; se fêler; se crevasser; se gercer; se lézarder; (*sound*) craquer; (*burst*) péter; (*crackle*) pétiller, craqueter; (*go off*) partir; (*of whips*) claquer; (*of the voice*) muer; (*threaten to fall*) craquer; (*boast*) se vanter, craquer, hâbler; — *s.* fente, *f.*; fissure, *f.*; crevasse, *f.*; gerçure, *f.*; lézarde, *f.*; craquelure, *f.*; (*of brittle things*) fêlure, *f.*; (*noise*) craquement, *m.*; (*of a whip*) claquement, clic-clac, *m.*; (*of fire-arms*) détonation, *f.*; (*an instant*) instant, clin d'œil, *m.*; (*pers.*) fou, cerveau timbré *or* fêlé, *m*;

(*boaster*) craqueur, *m.*, -euse, *f.*, hâbleur, *m.*, -euse, *f.*; (*boast*) craque, craquerie, hâblerie, *f.*; — *adj.* fameux, de première force *or* volée; (le) plus fort; (le) meilleur; d'élite; de haute volée, huppé; en réputation; (— *shot*) fin (tireur, *m.*); — *int.* (*of whips*) clic-clac! — **brained,** *adj.* à cerveau timbré *or* fêlé, timbré, fou. — **up,** *v.a.* (*to extol*) vanter, prôner, exalter, faire mousser [(*pers.*) timbré, fou

Cracked, *part. adj.* fendu, &c. (*V.* **Crack**);

Cracker, *s.* (*firework*) pétard, *m.*; (*sweetmeat*) diablotin, *m.*; (*biscuit*) croquet, craquelin, *m.*; (*boaster*) craqueur, *m.*, -euse, *f.*, hâbleur, *m.*, -euse, *f.*, vantard, *m.*, e, *f.*; (*in compounds*) [casse-..., *m.*

Cracking, *s.* *V.* **Crack,** *s.*

Crackle, *v.n.* craqueter, crépiter, pétiller; — *s.* *V.* **Crackling,** *s.*

Cracklin, *s.* porcelaine craquelée, *f.*

Crackling, *s.* craquètement, crépitement, *m.*, crépitation, *f.*, pétillement, *m.*; (*of roast pork*) croquant, rissolé, *m.*; (*of browned dishes*) gratin, *m.*; —**s,** *pl.* (*cakes*) pains de cretons, cretons, *m.pl.*; — *part. adj.* craquetant, crépitant, pétillant; (*crisp*) croquant

Cracknel, *s.* craquelin, *m.*; échaudé, *m.*; croquignole, *f.*

Cracovian, *s. adj.* Cracovien, *m.*, -ne, *f.*

Cracovienne, *s.* cracovienne, *f.*

Cradle, *s.* berceau, *m.*; (*of house-painters*, &c.) sellette, loupe, *f.*; (*of a ship*) ber, *m.*; (*of a scythe*) ramassette, *f.*; (*engin.*) chariot, *m.*; (*surg.*) éclisse, *f.*; — *v.a.* mettre au berceau; (*to rock*) bercer; (*to lull*) endormir; (*agr.*) faucher et ranger. *From the* —, dès le berceau. *In the* —, au berceau. *To rock the* —, bercer. — **clothes,** *s. pl.* garniture de ber- [ceau, *f.*

Cradling, *s.* cintre, *m.*; grillage, *m.*

Craft, *s.* art, métier, *m.*; talent, *m.*, habileté, adresse, *f.*; (*cunning*) ruse, astuce, *f.*, artifice, *m.*; (*nav.*) embarcation, *f.*, bâtiment, *m.*

Craftily, *adv.* artificieusement, astucieusement

Craftiness, *s.* artifice, *m.*, ruse, astuce, *f.*

Craftsman, *s.* artisan, *m.*

Craftsmaster, *s.* artiste, expert, maître, *m.*

Crafty, *adj.* rusé, astucieux, artificieux

Crag, *s.* roc abrupt, roc, rocher escarpé, rocher à pic, *m.*; pointe de rocher, *f.*; (*geol.*) crag, falun, *m.*; (*butch.*) *V.* **Scrag**

Cragged, *adj.* rocailleux; anfractueux; abrupt

Craggedness, Cragginess, *s.* état rocailleux, *m.*; anfractuosité, *f.*

Craggy. *V.* **Cragged**

Crake, *s.* râle, *m.* — **berry,** *s.* camarine, *f.*

Cram, *v.a.* (*fill*) remplir (de); (*stuff*) farcir (de); (*with food*) bourrer (de), gorger (de); (*to crowd*) encombrer; (*thrust in*) fourrer; faire entrer; (*heap*) entasser; accumuler; (*poultry*) empâter, engraisser; (*to grind or coach up students*) seriner; élever en serre chaude; (*tell stories*) en conter à, en donner à garder à; — *v.n.* se bourrer, se gorger de nourriture; (*study*) se préparer à la hâte, se faire seriner; — *s.* colle, *f.* [rimés, *m.pl.*

Crambo, *s.* jeu de bouts rimés, *m*, bouts

Crammed, *part. adj.* rempli, &c. (*V.* **Cram**); (*with people*) encombré, comble

Crammer, *s.* (*pers.*) préparateur, répétiteur, bachautier, bachotier, professeur (*or* maître) de colles, colleur, *m.*; (*liar*) colleur, *m.*; (*lie*) colle, *f.*

Cramming, *s.* (*for exam.*) (le) four *or* moule à bachau (*or* bachot) (*jest. for* baccalauréat), *m.*, préparation, répétition, *f.*

Cramp, *s.* (*spasm*) crampe, *f.*; (*restraint*) gêne, entrave, *f.*; (*tech.*) crampon, *m.*; sergent, *m.*; — *adj.* biscornu, baroque; — *v.a.* donner des crampes à; courbaturer; engourdir; (*pack, squeeze*) serrer; (*confine*) gêner, entraver; resserrer, forcer; restreindre; rétrécir; (*fasten*) cramponner. — **arm,** *s.* béquille, *f.* — **fish,** *s.* torpille, *f.* — **iron,** *s.* crampon, *m.* — **out,** *v.a.* arracher de force

Crampit, *s.* bouterolle, *f.*

Crampoon, *s.* crampon, *m.*

Cran, *s.* caque, *f.*

Cranage, *s.* droit de grue, *m.*

Cranberry, *s.* canneberge, airelle, *f.*

Cranch. *V.* **Craunch**

Crane, *s.* (*bird*) grue, *f.*; (*tech.*) grue, chèvre, *f.*; siphon, *m.*; (*of a carriage*) flèche, *f.*; — *v.a.* (— **up**) élever au moyen d'une grue. — **fly,** *s.* (*insect*) tipule, mouche couturière, *f.*, tailleur, *m.* — **neck,** *s.* (*of a carriage*) cou de cygne, *m.* — **neck perch,** *s.* (*of a carriage*) arc, *m.* —**'s-bill,** *s.* (*surg.*) bec-de-grue, *m.*; (*bot.*) géra- [nium, *m.*

Cranial, *adj.* crânien

Craniographer, *s.* crâniographe, *m.*

Cranio-graphic, al, -logic, al, -logy. *V.* page 3, § 1

Craniologist, *s.* crâniologue, crâniologiste, *m.*

Craniometer, *s.* crâniomètre, *m.*

Cranio-metric, al, -metry, -scopic, al, -scopy, -tomy, &c. *V.* page 3, § 1

Cranium, *s.* crâne, *m.*

Crank, *s.* (*winking*) détour, coude, *m.*, sinuosité, *f.*; (*of words*) jeu de mots, *m.*; (*machine*) manivelle, *f.*; (*cramp*) crampon, *m.*; — *adj.* dispos, éveillé, vif, allègre; (*nav.*) volage, qui a le côté faible. — **bird,** *s.* épeichette, *f.* — **shaft,** *s.* arbre coudé, *m.*

Cranked, *adj.* coudé

Cranky, *adj.* *V.* **Crank**

Crannied, *adj.* crevassé, gercé, lézardé

Cranny, *s.* crevasse, fente, lézarde, *f.*; (*hole*) trou, *m.*; — *v.a.* crevasser

Crapaudine, *s.* (*vet.*) crapaudine, *f.*

Crape, *s.* crêpe, *m.*; — *v.a.* crêper

Craping, *s.* crépage, *m.*, crépure, *f.*

Crash, *v.a.* fracasser, briser; — *v.n.* faire du fracas; éclater; — *s.* fracas, grand bruit, *m.*

Crashing, *s.* *V.* **Crash,** *s.*

Crate, *s.* caisse à claire-voie, cage, *f.*, panier, *m.*, manne, *f.*; (*for crockery, china, or glass*) charasse, harasse, *f.*; (*for bottles*) panier à bouteilles, *m.*; (*for fish*) cage, *f.*; (*cart-side*) [*V.* **Rathe**

Crater, *s.* cratère, *m.*

Crateriform, *adj.* cratériforme [quer

Craunch, *v.a.* croquer; — *v.n.* croquer; cra-

Cravat, *s.* cravate, *f.*

Cravatted, *adj.* cravaté

Crave, *v.a.* demander avec instance, demander, implorer, solliciter; désirer ardemment, soupirer après [*v.a.* intimider, décourager

Craven, *s. adj.* lâche, poltron, *m.* (-ne, *f.*); —

Craver, *s.* demandeur, solliciteur, *m.*

Craving, *s.* instance, *f.*, instances, *f.pl.*, sollicitation, *f.*; désir ardent, *m.*; aspiration, *f.*; besoin insatiable, *m.*; exigence, *f.*; — *adj.* importun; avide; insatiable [pliant

Cravingly, *adv.* avec instance, d'un ton sup-

Craw, *s.* jabot, *m.*

Crawfish. *V.* **Crayfish**

Crawl, *v.n.* ramper; (*fig.*) se traîner; (*steal in*) se glisser, s'insinuer; (*of cabmen*) marauder; (*to tingle, shudder*) fourmiller, frémir (*V.* **Flesh**); — *s.* rampement, *m.*; (*pen for fish*) bordigue, *f.*, bouchot, *m.*, écluse, *f.* — **down,** descendre, se traîner en bas. — **in,** s'introduire *or* entrer en rampant, entrer. — **up,** grimper, monter

Crawler, *s.* reptile, *m.*; être rampant, *m.*; (*cabman*) maraudeur, *m.*, hirondelle, *f.*

Crawling, *adj.* rampant, reptile; (*with*) couvert (de); — *s.* rampement, *m.*, reptation, *f.*; (*of cabmen*) maraude, *f.*; (*sensation*) *V.* **Creep-** [**ing**

Crawlingly, *adv.* en rampant

Crayfish, *s.* écrevisse, *f.* — **net,** *s.* pêchette, *f.*

Crayon, *s.* crayon, pastel, *m.*; — *v.a.* crayonner, tracer. *In* —, au pastel

Craze, *v.a.* briser; broyer, pulvériser; écraser; (*the mind*) affaiblir, déranger; (*pers.*) rendre fou; — *s.* aberration, hallucination, folie, *f.*; [manie, *f.*

Crazedness. *V.* **Craziness**

Crazily, *adv.* faiblement; follement

Craziness, *s.* caducité, *f.*; (*of the mind*) démence, folie, *f.*
Crazy, *adj.* caduc, décrépit, délabré; en mauvais état, hors de service; faible; dérangé, détraqué; (*mad*) fou, en démence
Creak, *v.n.* crier; craquer [crie, qui craque
Creaking, *s.* cri, craquement, *m.*; — *adj.* qui
Cream, *s.* crème, *f.*; — *v.a.* (— **off**) écrémer; — *v.n.* crémer. — **bowl,** *s.* pot à crème, *m.* — **cake,** *s.* dariole, *f.*; meringue, *f.* — **cheese,** *s.* fromage à la crème, *m.* — **chocolate,** *s.* chocolat à la crème, *m.* — **coloured,** *adj.* couleur café au lait. — **ewer,** *s.* pot à crème, *m.*, crémière, *f.* — **faced,** *adj.* pâle, blême. — **gauge,** *s.* crémomètre, *f.* — **ice,** *s.* glace à la crème, *f.* — **jug,** *s.* *V.* — **ewer.** — **laid,** *adj.* vergé blanc. — **pot,** *s.* pot à crème, *m.* — **sauce,** *s.* béchamel, *f.* — **skimmer,** *s.* écrémoire, *f.* — **tart,** *s.* tarte à la crème, *f.* — **wove,** *adj.* vélin blanc
Creaming, *adj.* à écrémer; (*of Champagne wine*) crémant; — *s.* écrémage, *m.*
Creamy, *adj.* crémeux, de crème
Crease, *s.* pli, *m.*; faux-pli, *m.*; godet, *m.*, godure, *f.*; (*creese*) criss, *m.*; — *v.a.* faire un pli *or* des plis à, plisser; faire des faux-plis à, chiffonner, friper; — *v.n.* goder, grimacer
Creasote, *s.* créosote, *f.*
Creatable, *adj.* créable
Create, *v.a.* créer; produire; engendrer; faire naître; susciter; inspirer; causer, occasionner; constituer; (*make*) faire; (*establish*) établir; (*an appetite*, &c.) exciter (l'appétit, &c.); (*enemies*) se faire
Creation, *s.* création. *f.*
Creative, *adj.* créateur
Creativeness, *s.* faculté de créer, *f.*, pouvoir créateur, puissance créatrice, *f.*
Creator, *s.* créateur, *m.*
Creatress, *s.* créatrice, *f.*
Creature, *s.* créature, *f.*; animal, *m.*, bête, *f.*; personne, *f.*; (*fellow*) être, *m.*; (*little fellow, little thing*) petit, *m.*, e, *f.*; (*drink*) consolation, *f.*; bouteille, *f.* — **comforts,** *s. pl.* vivres, *m.pl.*, mangeaille, boustifaille, consolation, *f.*
Credence, *s.* créance, foi, *f.*; (*dipl.*) créance, *f.*; (*eccl.*) crédence, *f.* *To give — to,* ajouter foi à. — **table,** *s.* crédence, *f.*
Credenda, *s. pl.* articles de foi, *m.pl.*
Credential, *adj.* de créance; —**s,** *s.pl.* lettres de créance, *f.pl.*
Credibility, *s.* crédibilité, *f.*; véridicité, *f.*
Credible, *adj.* croyable; (*pers.*) digne de foi
Credibleness. *V.* **Credibility**
Credibly, *adv.* d'une manière croyable, d'une manière digne de foi; probablement, avec vraisemblance. *To be — informed,* tenir d'une bonne source
Credit, *s.* (*reliance, belief, faith*) croyance, foi, *f.*; confiance, *f.*; (*testimony, faith*) foi, *f.*; (*influence, power, reputation, esteem, consideration, good opinion*) crédit, *m.*; (*honour, glory*) honneur, *m.*; (*com., fin.*) crédit, *m.*; (*book-keep.*) crédit, avoir, *m.*; — *v.a.* croire, croire à, ajouter foi à; se fier à, se confier à; faire honneur à, honorer; (*com.*) vendre *or* donner à crédit, faire crédit de; (*book-keep.*) créditer ('*with,*' de), porter au crédit (*or* à l'avoir) de. — **side,** *s.* (*book-keep.*) crédit, avoir, *m.* *Letter of —,* lettre de crédit, *f.* *On* or *upon —,* à crédit. *To be a — to, to do —,* faire honneur à. *To give — to,* ajouter foi à; faire honneur à; (*com.*) faire crédit à. *I gave him — for more sagacity,* je lui croyais plus de sagacité. *I give him — for his self denial,* je rends justice à son abnégation. *I gave him — for his good intentions,* je lui tiens compte de ses bonnes intentions. *I give him — for learning,* je lui reconnais du savoir, je conviens qu'il est instruit
Creditable, *adj.* honorable, digne d'éloge, qui fait honneur (à) [estime, *f.*
Creditableness, *s.* crédit, honneur, *m.*:
Creditably, *adv.* avec honneur, honorablement, d'une manière digne d'éloge
Creditor, *s.* créancier, *m.*, -ière, *f.*, (*book-keep.*) créditeur, *m.*; crédit, avoir, actif, *m.* — **side,** *s.* crédit, avoir, *m.*
Creditress, Creditrix, *s.* créancière, *f.*
Credo, *s.* credo, *m.*
Credulity, *s.* crédulité, *f.*
Credulous, *adj.* crédule
Credulously, *adv.* crédulement, avec crédulité
Credulousness, *s.* crédulité, *f.*
Creed, *s.* credo, *m.*; symbole, *m.*; (*belief*) croyance, foi, *f.*; (*fig.*) profession de foi, *f.* *Apostles' —,* symbole des apôtres, *m.*
Creek, *s.* crique, anse, *f.*
Creeky, *adj.* garni de criques
Creel, *s.* panier en osier, panier, *m.*
Creep, *v.n.* (*of some animals and plants*) ramper; (*fig.*) ramper, se traîner; (*steal in*) se glisser, s'insinuer; (*seize*) s'emparer (de); (*to tingle, shudder*) fourmiller, frémir (*V.* **Flesh**). — **down,** descendre, se traîner en bas. — **hole,** *s.* trou, *m.*; (*fig.*) subterfuge, *m.*, échappatoire, porte de derrière, *f.*, faux-fuyant, *m.* — **in,** s'introduire *or* entrer en rampant, entrer; (*fig.*) se glisser, s'insinuer, se faufiler; avancer. — **mouse,** *s.* lambin, *m.*, e, *f.* — **on,** s'avancer peu à peu, s'avancer; (*seize*) s'emparer de. — **out,** sortir en rampant *or* en se traînant, sortir, se traîner hors (de); (*steal away*) sortir à l'improviste, s'esquiver. — **over,** ramper par-dessus; (*seize*) s'emparer de, saisir, gagner. — **up,** grimper, monter
Creeper, *s.* reptile, *m.*; insecte reptile, *m.*; plante grimpante, *f.*; (*bird*) grimpereau, *m.* *Virginian —,* vigne vierge, *f.*
Creeping, *adj.* rampant, reptile; (*up*) grimpant; — *s.* rampement, *m.*, reptation, *f.*; marche insensible, *f.*; bassesse, servilité, *f.*; (*sensation*) fourmillement, *m.* — **sensation,** *s.* fourmillement, *m.*
Creepingly, *adv.* en rampant
Creese, *s.* cric, crid, criss, *m.*
Cremation, *s.* crémation, *f.*
Cremometer, *s.* crémomètre, *m.*
Cremona, *s.* (*geog.*) Crémone, *f.*; (— *violin*) crémone, *m.* [crémonais, de Crémone
Cremonese, *s.* Crémonais, *m.*, e, *f.*; — *adj.*
Crenate, Crenated, *adj.* créné
Crenature, *s.* crénelure, *f.*
Crenellate, Crenelate, *v.a.* créneler
Crenellation, Crenelation, *s.* crénelure, *f.*
Crenelle, *s.* créneau, *m.*; (*bot.*) crénelure, *f.*
Crenelled, *adj.* crénelé
Creole, *s. adj.* créole, *m.f.*
Creolean, Creolian, *adj.* créole
Creosote, *s.* créosote, *f.* [crapaudine, *f.*
Crepance, Crepane, *s.* entre-taillure, *f.*;
Crepitate, *v.n.* crépiter
Crepitation, *s.* crépitation, *f.*, crépitement, *m.*
Crepon, *s.* crépon, *m.*
Crepuscular, *adj.* crépusculaire
Crepuscule. *V.* **Twilight**
Cresane, *s.* cresane, *f.*
Crescendo, *adv. s.* crescendo (*s.m.*)
Crescent, *s.* croissant, *m.*; (*place*) demi-lune, *f.*; — *adj.* croissant. — **shaped,** *adj.* en forme de croissant [cressonnière, *f.*
Cress, Cresses, *s.* cresson, *m.* — **bed,** *s.*
Cresset, *s.* pot à feu, feu, falot, *m.*, cassolette, torchère, *f.*; flambeau, *m.*, torche, *f.*
Crest, *s.* (*of cocks, fishes, reptiles, mountains,* &c., *top, arch.*) crête, *f.*; (*nav., of a wave*) crête, houppée, *f.*; (*of helmets*) cimier, *m.*; (*her.*) cimier, *m.*; écusson, *m.*; (*of birds*) huppe, *f.*; (*of peacocks*) aigrette, *f.*; (*pride*) orgueil, *m.*, fierté, *f.* — **fallen,** *adj.* abattu, déconcerté, l'oreille basse, penaud. — **marine,** *s.* crête-marine, *f.*
Crested, *adj.* crêté; huppé; à aigrette; surmonté *or* orné d'un cimier; écussonné
Cretaceous, *adj.* crétacé

Cretan, *s.* Crétois, *m.*, e, *f.* — *adj.* crétois, de [Crète
Cretin, *s.* crétin, *m.*
Cretinism, *s.* crétinisme, *m.*
Crevasse, *s.* crevasse, *f.*
Crevice, *s.* crevasse, lézarde, *f.*; (*chink*) fente, *f.*; — *v.a.* crevasser, lézarder; fendre
Crew, *s.* troupe, *f.*; bande, *f.*; tas, *m.*; clique, *f.*; (*nav.*) équipage, *m.*; (*of a racing-boat*) équipe, *f.* *To perish — and cargo*, périr corps [et biens
Crewel, *s.* laine à broder, *f.*
Crib, *s.* crèche, *f.*; (*for horses*) mangeoire, *f.*; (*stall*) stalle, *f.*; étable, *f.*; (*cottage*) cabane, hutte, chaumière, *f.*; (*lock-up house*) grenier, *m.*; (*bin*) coffre, *m.*; (*for infants*) couchette, *f.*, lit d'enfant, *m.*; (*of coaches*) poche, *f.*, sac, *m.*; (*from a book*) plagiat, *m.*; traduction mot à mot, *f.*, mot-à-mot, *m.*, traduction littérale, traduction, clé, *f.*; — *v.a.* ('*from*,' à) prendre, chiper; copier. — **biter,** *s.* tiqueur, *m.*, -euse, *f.*, cheval tiqueur, *m.*, jument tiqueuse, *f.* — **biting,** *adj.* tiqueur; — *s.* tic, *m.*
Cribber, *s.* chipeur, *m.*, -euse, *f.*; plagiaire, *m.*; (*horse*) *V.* **Crib-biter**
Cribbing, *s.* action de prendre *or* de chiper, *f.*; copie, *f.*; plagiat, *m.*; (*of horses*) tic, *m.*
Cribble, *s.* crible, *m.*; — *v.a.* cribler
Crick, *s.* crampe, *f.*; (*noise*) cric, *m.* — *in the neck*, torticolis, *m.* — **crack,** *s.* cric-crac, *s.m.*, *adv.*, *int.*
Cricket, *s.* (*insect*) grillon, criquet, cri-cri, *m.*; (*stool*) escabeau, tabouret, *m.*; (*game*) cricket, *m.* — **ball,** *s.* balle de cricket, *f.* — **field, -ground,** *s.* champ *or* jeu de cricket, *m.* — **match,** *s.* partie de cricket, *f.*
Cricketer, *s.* joueur de cricket, *m.*
Crier, *s.* crieur, crieur public, *m.*; (*law*) huissier audiencier, audiencier, *m.*
Crim. con., *s.* adultère, *m.*
Crime, *s.* crime, *m.*
Crimean, *s.* Criméen, *m.*, -ne, *f.*; — *adj.* criméen, de Crimée. — *war*, guerre de Crimée, *f.*
Criminal, *adj. s.* criminel, *m.*, -le, *f.* — *conversation*, adultère, *m.*
Criminalist, *s.* criminaliste, *m.*
Criminality, *s.* criminalité, *f.*; culpabilité, *f.*
Criminally, *adv.* criminellement [procès à
Criminate, *v.a.* incriminer, accuser, faire le
Crimination, *s.* incrimination, accusation, *f.*
Criminatory. *V.* **Incriminatory**
Crimp, *v.a.* friser; gaufrer, tuyauter; (*pinch*) pincer, saisir; (*nav.*, *mil.*) embaucher; racoler; (*cook.*) taillader; — *s.* commissionnaire, *m.*; (*nav.*, *mil.*) embaucheur, *m.*; racoleur, *m.*; — *adj.* friable; fragile, faible, sans consistance
Crimper, *s.* gaufreur, *m.*, -euse, *f.*
Crimping, *s.* frisure, *f.*; gaufrage, tuyautage, *m.*, gaufrure, *f.*; (*nav.*, *mil.*) embauchage, *m.*; racolage, *m.* — **iron,** *s.* fer à friser, frisoir, *m.*; fer à gaufrer, *m.* — **machine,** *s.* gaufroir, *m.* — **roller,** *s.* cylindre à gaufrer, *m.*
Crimple, *v.a.* plisser, froncer, rider
Crimson, *s.* cramoisi, *m.*; (*fig.*) rouge, *m.*; incarnat, *m.*; — *adj.* cramoisi; (*fig.*) rouge; incarnat; — *v.a.* teindre en cramoisi; — *v.n.* devenir cramoisi; (*fig.*) rougir
Cringe, *v.a.* contracter; — *v.n.* faire des courbettes, faire le chien couchant, ramper; — *s.* bassesse, courbette, *f.*
Cringer, *s.* homme rampant, chien couchant, *m.*
Cringing, *s.* bassesse, servilité, *f.*, courbettes, [*f.pl.*
Cringingly, *adv.* bassement, servilement
Cringle, *s.* (*nav.*) erseau, *m.*
Crinkle, *v.n.* serpenter, faire des zigzags; — *v.a.* diriger en zigzag; — *s.* sinuosité, *f.*, zigzag, *m.*
Crino, *s.* crinon, *m.*
Crinoline, *s.* crinoline, *f.*
Crinum, *s.* (*bot.*) crinole, *f.*
Cripple, *adj. s.* estropié, *m.*, e, *f.*, perclus, *m.*, e, *f.*; boiteux, *m.*, -euse, *f.*; — *v.a.* estropier; (*to disable*) mettre hors de combat; (*fig.*) [paralyser
Crisis, *s.* crise, *f.*
Crisp, *adj.* frisé, crépu; (*brittle*) cassant, fragile; friable; (*of metals*) aigre; (*of pastry*, &c.) croquant; (*winding*) qui serpente, sinueux; — *v.a.* crêper, friser; onduler; — *v.n.* se crêper, friser; onduler; serpenter. *To eat* —, croquer [sous la dent
Crisper, *s.* friseur, *m.*, -euse, *f.*
Crispin, *s.* crépin, *m.*
Crisping, *s.* crêpage, *m.*, crépure, frisure, *f.* — **iron, -pin,** *s.* fer à friser, *m.*
Crispness, *s.* frisure, *f.*; fragilité, nature cassante, *f.*; friabilité, *f.*; (*of metals*) aigreur, *f.*; (*of pastry*, &c.) croquant, *m.*
Criteria, *s. pl.* critériums, *m.pl.*; marques, *f.pl.*
Criterion, *s.* critérium, *m.*; marque, *f.*
Critic, *s.* critique, *m.*; — *adj.* *V.* **Critical**
Critical, *adj.* critique; judicieux; (*nice*) délicat; (*particular*) difficile
Critically, *adv.* d'une manière critique; (*exactly*) rigoureusement; soigneusement, scrupuleusement; à point nommé
Criticalness, *s.* nature (*f.*) *or* caractère (*m.*) critique; précision, exactitude, *f.*; délicatesse d'appréciation, *f.* [cisme, *m.*
Criticism, *s.* critique, *f.*; (*Kant's system*) criti-
Criticizable, *adj.* critiquable
Criticize, *v.a.n.* critiquer
Criticizer, *s.* critiqueur, *m.*, -euse, *f.*
Critique, *s.* critique, *f.*
Croak, *v.n.* (*as ravens*) croasser; (*as frogs*) coasser; (*grumble*) grogner, marronner; — *s.* (*of ravens*) croassement, *m.*; (*of frogs*) coassement, *m.*; (*pers.*) grognement, *m.*, grognerie, *f.*
Croaker, *s.* grognon, *m.f.*, Jean-qui-grogne, *m.*, faiseur (*m.*, -euse, *f.*) de jérémiades; prophète de malheur, *m.*
Croaking, *s.* *V.* **Croak,** *s.*; — *part. adj.* qui coasse, &c. (*V.* **Croak,** *v.n.*); (*pers.*) qui grogne, grognon
Croat, Croatian, *s. adj.* Croate, *m.f.*
Crochet, *s.* crochet, *m.* — **hook, -needle,** *s.* crochet, *m.* — **work,** *s.* ouvrage au crochet, crochet, *m.*
Crock, *s.* pot de terre, *m.*; cruche, *f.*; (*stool*) escabeau, *m.*; (*soot*) suie, *f.*; — *v.a.* mettre en pot; (*begrime*) noircir de suie
Crockery, *s.* faïence, *f.*; vaisselle, *f.* — **ware,** *s.* faïence, faïencerie, *f.* — **ware factory** *or* **trade,** *s.* faïencerie, *f.* — **ware man** *or* **woman,** *s.* faïencier, *m.*, -ière, *f.*
Crocket, *s.* (*arch.*) crochet, *m.*
Crocodile, *s.* crocodile, *m.*; — *adj.* de crocodile
Crocodilean, Crocodilian, *adj.* crocodiléen, crocodilien; — *s.* crocodilien, *m.*
Crocus, *s.* crocus, safran, *m.*
Croft, *s.* petit clos, courtil, *m.*
Cromlech, *s.* cromlech, cromlek, *m.*
Cromorna, *s.* cromorne, *m.*
Crone, *s.* vieille femme, vieille, *f.* *Old* —, vieille bonne femme, vieille, *f.*
Crony, *s.* vieille connaissance, *f.*, vieux camarade, *m.*, amie intime, *f.*, compère, *m.*, commère, *f.*
Crook, *s.* courbure, *f.*; coude, détour, *m.*, sinuosité, *f.*; croc, crochet, *f.*; (*of shepherds*) houlette, *f.*; (*of bishops*) crosse, *f.*; (*fig.*) détour, *m.*; tour, artifice, *m.*; — *v.a.* courber, recourber, tortuer; pervertir; détourner; contrarier; — *v.n.* se recourber, être recourbé. — **back,** *s.* bosse, *f.*; (*pers.*) bossu, *m.*, e, *f.* — **backed,** *adj.* bossu, voûté. — **kneed,** *adj.* cagneux. — **legged,** *adj.* qui a les jambes tortues. — **shouldered,** *adj.* voûté
Crooked, *adj.* courbe, crochu; recourbé; (*twisted*) tortu, de travers; (*winding*) tortueux, sinueux; détourné; (*oblique*) de travers; (*pers.*) contrefait; (*with age*) courbé; (*perverse*) pervers; (*adverb.*) de travers
Crookedly, *adv.*; en se recourbant; tortueusement; (*fig.*) de travers
Crookedness, *s.* courbure, *f.*; tortuosité, *f.*; détours, *m.pl.*, sinuosités, *f.pl.*; difformité, *f.*; perversité, *f.*
Croon, *v.n.* (*moan*) gémir, geindre; — *v.n.a.*

(*hum*) chantonner, bourdonner, murmurer; — *s.* gémissement, *m.*; chantonnerie, *f.*, bourdonnement, murmure, *m.*

Crop, *s.* (*harvest*) récolte, *f.*; moisson, *f.*; (*of fruits*) cueillette, *f.*; (*hair cut off, jest.*) tonte, *f.*; (*of birds*) jabot, *m.*; — *v.a.* couper; tailler; (*harvest*) moissonner; (*mow*) faucher; (*a lawn*) tondre; (*fruit*) cueillir; (*animals*) tondre; (*the tail or ears*) écourter; (*browse*) brouter. — **off,** *v.a.* couper. — **out,** *v.n.* (*mining, geol.*) affleurer; (*fig.*) apparaître, paraître, se montrer. *Second* —, regain, *m.* — **ear,** *s.* cheval bretaudé, *m.* — **eared,** *adj.* bretaudé. —**ful,** *s.* jabot plein, *m.*; *adj.* qui a le jabot plein, plein jusqu'au gosier, qui a le ventre plein, rassasié. — **sick,** *adj.* malade d'indigestion. — **sickness,** *s.* indigestion, *f.*

Cropper, *s.* pigeon à grosse gorge, *m.*

Cropping, *s.* coupe, *f.*; taille, *f.*; fauchage, *m.*; moisson, récolte, *f.*; cueillette, *f.*; tonte, *f.*; broutement, *m.* — **out,** *s.* (*mining*) affleurement, *m.*

Croquet, *s.* (*game*) croquette, *f.*

Crore, *s.* crore, *m.*

Crosier, *s.* crosse, *f.*; (*astr.*) croix du sud, croix australe, *f.*

Crosiered, *adj.* crossé

Cross, *s.* croix, *f.*; (*trouble*) croix, *f.*, affliction, *f.*; (*obstacle*) traverse, contrariété, *f.*; (*intersection*) croisée, *f.*, carrefour, *m.*; (*of a sword, of an anchor*) croisée, *f.*; (*breed*) race croisée, *f.*; (*animal*) métis, *m.*, -se, *f.*, (le) produit du croisement (de ... avec ...), (le) produit (de ... et de ...), *m.*; (*fig.*) mélange (de), *m.*; milieu (entre ... et ...), *m.*; (*surveying*) équerre d'arpenteur, *f.*; — *adj.* transversal, en travers, en croix, croisé; oblique; de travers; contraire (à), opposé (à); (*vexatious*) contrariant, fâcheux; (*unfortunate*) malheureux; (*peevish*) de mauvaise humeur, maussade, acariâtre, méchant; (*counter*) contre (*in compounds*). *Sign of the* —, (le) signe de la croix, (un) signe de croix, *m.* — **action,** *s.* *V.* — **suit.** — **armed,** *adj.* les bras croisés. — **bar,** *s.* traverse, *f.*; (*of a bedstead*) goberge, *f.* — **bar-shot,** *s.* boulet ramé, *m.* — **battery,** *s.* contre-batterie, *f.* — **beam,** *s.* traverse, *f.*; (*of steam-engine*) balancier, *m.* — **bearer,** *s.* porte-croix, *m.* — **belt,** *s.* baudrier, *m.*, bandoulière, *f.* — **bill,** *s.* (*bird*) bec-croisé, *m.*; (*law*) *V.* — **suit.** — **bones,** *s. pl.* os en croix, *m.pl.* — **bow,** *s.* arbalète, *f.* — **bowman,** *s.* arbalétrier, *m.* — **bred,** *adj.* métis. — **breed,** *s.* race croisée, *f.* — **breeding,** *s.* croisement des races, croisement, *m.* — **bun,** *s.* brioche marquée d'une croix, *f.* — **charge,** *s.* contre-accusation, *f.* — **course,** *s.* (*mining*) croiseur, *m.* — **cut,** *s.* traverse, *f.*, raccourci, *m.*, accourcie, *f.*; (*mining*) galerie de communication, *f.*; *v.a.* couper en travers; (*engr.*) contre-tailler. — **cut-saw,** *s.* scie à deux mains, *f.*, harpon, *m.* — **examination,** *s.* contre-interrogatoire, *m.* — **examine,** *v.a.* faire subir un contre-interrogatoire à. — **examined,** *part. adj.* interrogé par l'avocat adverse *or* par la partie adverse. — **eye,** *s.* strabisme convergent, *m.* — **eyed,** *adj.* affecté de strabisme convergent. — **fire,** *s.* feu croisé, *m.* — **fortune,** *s.* revers de fortune, malheur, *m.* — **grained,** *adj.* dont la venue est à rebours, dont le fil se croise; (*fig.*) revêche, acariâtre. — **hands,** *s. pl.* (*dancing*) chaîne anglaise, *f.* — **hatch,** *v.a.* contre-hacher. — **hatching,** *s.* contre-hachure, *f.* — **keys,** *s. pl.* clés mises en travers, clés en sautoir, *f.pl.* — **legged,** *adj.* les jambes croisées. — **let,** *s.* *See below.* — **like,** *adj.* en forme de croix, cruciforme; (*surg.*) crucial. — **line,** *s.* (*rail.*) croisière, *f.* — **lode,** *s.* croiseur, *m.* — **marriage,** *s.* mariage entre parents, intermariage, *m.* — **patch,** *s.* (*man*) mauvais coucheur, *m.*, (*woman*) pie-grièche, *f.* — **path,** *s.* chemin de traverse, *m.* — **piece,** *s.* traverse, croisille, entretoise, *f.* — **post,** *s.* (*post.*) service de correspondance, *m.* — **purpose,** *s.* système contradictoire, *m.*; projet contraire, *m.*; quiproquo, malentendu, *m.*; énigme, *f.*; (*play*) propos interrompu, *m.* *To be at — purposes,* se contrecarrer. — **question,** *s.* question captieuse, *f.*; *v.a.* interroger captieusement; (*law*) *V.* — **examine.** — **questioning,** *s.* interrogation captieuse, *f.*, questions captieuses, *f.pl.*; (*law*) *V.* — **examination.** — **road,** *s.* *V.* — **way.** — **row,** *s.* alphabet, *m.*, croix de par Dieu, *f.*; rangée transversale, *f.* — **sea,** *s.* mer creuse, *f.* — **section,** *s.* coupe transversale, *f.* — **shaped,** *adj.* en forme de croix, cruciforme. — **street,** *s.* rue de traverse, rue transversale, *f.* — **suit,** *s.*, — **summons,** *s. pl.* (*law*) demande reconventionnelle, reconvention, *f.* — **tie,** *s.* traverse, *f.* — **tining,** *s.* hersage en ligne droite et en travers, *m.* — **tree,** *s.* (*nav.*) barre de hune, *f.* — **way,** *s.* chemin de traverse, *m.*; (*junction*) carrefour, *m.* — **ways,** *adv.* *V.* — **wise.** — **wind,** *s.* vent contraire, *m.* — **wise,** *adv.* en travers, en croix, en sautoir. — **words,** *s. pl.* paroles dures, *f.pl.* — **wort,** *s.* crucianelle, croisette, *f.*

Cross, *v.a.* croiser; (*make a mark*) faire une croix sur; (*rel.*) faire le signe de la croix sur; (*cancel*) biffer, barrer, rayer, raturer, effacer; (*a cheque*) barrer; (*pass through*) traverser, passer par; couper; (*a threshold*) franchir; (*thwart*) contrarier; contrecarrer; (*contradict*) contredire; (*oppose*) s'opposer à, empêcher; (*debar*) exclure (de); (*of the breed*) croiser; — *v.n.* se croiser; être en travers; traverser, passer, faire la traversée; (*theat.*) traverser la scène; s'avancer (vers), se diriger (vers); (*be opposed*) être en opposition (avec), être contraire (à). *To — oneself,* faire le signe de la croix, se signer. — **again,** repasser. — **off, out,** biffer, barrer, rayer, raturer, effacer. — **over,** traverser, passer

Crosse, *s.* crosse, *f.*

Crossette, *s.* crossette, *f.*

Crossing, *s.* croisement, *m.*; croisé, *m.*; (*going across, way across*) passage, *m.*; (*on the sea*) traversée, *f.*; (*of rail. lines*) croisement, *m.*; (*of roads*) croisière, *f.*; (*of streets*) passage d'un trottoir à l'autre, *m.*; (*of stuffs*) croisure, *f.*; (*opposition*) traverse, contrariété, *f.*; (*rel.*) signe de croix, *m.* — **over,** *s.* passage, *m.*; (*by sea*) traversée, *f.* — **sweeper,** *s.* balayeur de rues, *m.*

Crosslet, *s.* petite croix, *f.*; (*her.*) croisette, *f.*

Crossly, *adv.* en travers, en croix; d'une manière contraire, contrairement, de travers; à contre-temps; malheureusement; avec mauvaise humeur, avec humeur, d'un air revêche

Crossness, *s.* position transversale *or* en croix, *f.*; intersection, *f.*; mauvaise humeur, maussaderie, méchanceté, *f.*

Crotch, *s.* (*hook*) croc, *m.*; (*fork*) fourche, *f.*; (*nav.*) *V.* **Crutch**

Crotched, *adj.* crochu; fourchu

Crotchet, *s.* crochet, *m.*; (*build.*) étai, *m.*; (*knitting*) *V.* **Crochet;** (*mus.*) noire, *f.*; (*whim*) lubie, *f.*, caprice, *m.*, manie, *f.* — **rest,** *s.* (*mus.*) soupir, *m.*

Crotcheted, *adj* mesuré

Crotchety, *adj.* à lubies, sujet aux lubies, capricieux, maniaque

Croton, *s.* croton, *m.* — **oil,** *s.* huile de croton, *f.*

Crouch, *v.n.* se tapir, se blottir; (*to fawn*) ramper

Croup, *s.* croupe, *f.*; (*of birds*) croupion, *m.*; (*med.*) croup, *m.*

Croupade, *s.* croupade, *f.*

Croupal, *adj.* croupal, croupeux

Croupier, *s.* croupier, *m.*

Crow, *s.* (*bird*) corbeau, *m.*, corneille, *f*; (*of cocks*) chant, *m.*; (*iron bar*) levier, *m*, pince, *f.*; (*butch.*) fraise, *f.*; — *v.n.* (*of cocks*) chanter; (*pers.*) chanter victoire. *As the — flies,* à vol d'oiseau. *To have a — to pick* or *pluck* (*with*), avoir maille à partir (avec). — **bar,** *s.* pince.

f., levier, *m.*; (*in thieves' slang*) monseigneur, *m.* — **berry,** *s.* camarine, *f.* — **foot,** *s.* (*bot.*) renoncule, *f.*, bassinet, *m.*; (*mil.*) chausse-trappe, *f.*; (*nav.*) araignée, *f.* — **net,** *s.* hallier, tramail, *m.* — **quill,** *s.* plume de corbeau, *f.* —**'s-foot,** *s.* (*wrinkle*) patte d'oie, *f.*, éperon, *m.*; (*bot., mil.*) *V.* — **foot.** — **silk,** *s.* conferve, *f.*

Crowd, *s.* foule, *f.*; (*gathering*) rassemblement, *m.*; (*mob*) cohue, *f.*; (*anc. mus. instr.*) rote, *f.* —*s of*, une foule de. *In a* —, *in* —*s*, en foule

Crowd, *v.a.* ('*with*,' de) presser; fouler; serrer; resserrer; encombrer; surcharger; remplir; fourrer, entasser; (*surround*) entourer en foule; (*populate*) peupler; (*sails*) forcer de, faire force de; — *v.n.* affluer, venir (*or* se présenter) en foule, faire foule, accourir en foule; s'empresser; (*press close*) se presser, se serrer; (*swarm*) fourmiller. — **down,** descendre en foule. — **in,** *v.a.* faire entrer en pressant, fourrer; *v.n.* entrer en foule; se fourrer. — **out,** sortir en foule. — **round,** entourer en foule. — **up,** monter en foule

Crowded, *part. adj.* pressé, &c. (*V.* **Crowd,** *v.a.*); (*numerous*) nombreux; (*full*) rempli de monde, comble

Crowding, *s.* action (*f.*) de presser *or* &c. (*V.* **Crowd,** *v.a.n.*); encombrement, *m.*

Crowdy, *s.* *V.* **Porridge**

Crowing, *s.* chant (*du coq*), *m.*

Crown, *s.* couronne, *f.*; (*height, top*) sommet, *m.*; (*of hats, bonnets*) forme, *f.*; (*of caps*) fond, *m.*; (*of an arch*) clé (de voûte), *f.*; (*of an anchor*) collet, *m.*; (*of deer*) couronnure, *f.*; (*old Fr. coin*) écu, *m.*; (*Eng. coin*) couronne, *f.*; (*arch., astr., bot., anat.*) couronne, *f.*; (*eccl.*) tonsure, *f.*; — *v.a.* couronner; (*to complete*) couronner, compléter, mettre le comble à; (*at draughts*) damer. *To come to the* —, monter sur le trône. *On his coming to the* —, à son avénement au trône. — **glass,** *s.* crown-glass, *m.* — **imperial,** *s.* (*bot.*) couronne impériale, *f.* — **jewels,** *s. pl.* diamants (*or* joyaux) de la couronne, *m.pl.* — **lace,** *s.* tavelle, *f.* — **land,** *s.* domaine de la couronne, *m.* —**less,** *adj.* sans couronne; découronné. — **like,** *adj.* comme une couronne, en forme de couronne. — **office,** *s.* parquet du procureur de la république (*or* du roi or impérial), *m.* — **piece,** *s.* (*old*) écu, *m.*; (*Engl.*) pièce d'une couronne, couronne, pièce de cinq shillings, *f.* — **post,** *s.* (*build.*) poinçon, *m.* — **prince,** *s.* prince royal, *m.*; (*not of a kingdom*) prince héritier, *m.*; prince impérial, *m.*; (*of Russia*) grand-duc héritier, *m.* — **property,** *s.* *V.* — **land.** — **side,** *s.* partie publique, *f.*; cour criminelle, *f.* — **wheel,** *s.* roue de champ, *f.* — **witness,** *s.* témoin à charge, *m.* — **work,** *s.* ouvrage à couronne, *m.*, couronne, *f.*

Crowning, *adj.* final; dernier; suprême; — *s.* couronnement, *m.* — **piece,** *s.* couronnement, *m.*; bouquet, *m.*

Crozier. *V.* **Crosier**

Crucial, *adj.* crucial; (*fig.*) sérieux, grave, important, principal, excessif; cruel, atroce; (*of the crucible*) du creuset

Crucian, *s.* (*fish*) carassin, *m.*

Cruciate, *adj.* en croix

Crucible, *s.* creuset, *m.*

Crucifer, *s.* porte-croix, *m.*; (*bot.*) crucifère, *f.*

Cruciferous, *adj.* crucifère

Crucifix, *s.* crucifix, *m.*

Crucifixion, *s.* crucifiement *m.*

Cruciform, *adj.* cruciforme

Crucify, *v.a.* crucifier

Crude, *adj.* cru; indigeste; informe; (*rough*) brut, grossier; imparfait

Crudely, *adv.* crûment

Crudeness, Crudity, *s.* crudité, *f.*; nature (*f.*) *or* caractère (*m.*) informe

Cruel, *adj.* cruel

Cruelly, *adv.* cruellement

Cruelty, *s.* cruauté, *f.*; inhumanité, *f.*; (*law*) sévices, actes de violence, mauvais traitements, coups, *m.pl*, voies de fait, *f.pl.* *Society for the prevention of — to animals*, société protectrice des animaux, *f.*

Cruet, *s.* burette, *f.* — **frame, -stand,** *s.* ménagère, *f.*; (*for oil and vinegar only*) huilier, *m.*

Cruise, *v.n.* (*nav.*) croiser, être en croisière; (*of privateers*) aller en course, faire la course; — *s.* croisière, *f.*; (*of privateers*) course, *f.* *On a* —, en croisière; (*of privateers*) en course

Cruiser, *s.* croiseur, *m.*

Cruising, *adj.* (*nav.*) en croisière, croiseur; (*of privateers*) en course; — *s.* *V.* **Cruise,** *s.* — **latitude, -party,** *s.* croisière, *f.*

Crumb, *s.* (*soft part of bread*) mie, *f.*; (*small particle*) miette, *f.* — **brush,** *s.* brosse à miettes, brosse de table, *f.* — **cloth,** *s.* dessous de table, *m.* — **tray,** *s.* ramasse-couvert, *m.*

Crumble, *v.a.* émietter; (*break*) broyer, écraser; pulvériser; (*fig.*) réduire (en poussière *or* en poudre); — *v.n.* s'émietter; (*decay*, — **away** *or* **down**) tomber (*or* se réduire) en poussière *or* en poudre, tomber en morceaux *or* en ruines, s'écrouler, crouler, tomber; (*of earth*) s'ébouler

Crumbling, *adj.* friable; (*ruinous*) croulant; (*of earth*) ébouleux; — *s.* émiettement, *m.*; (*breaking*) broiement, écrasement, *m.*; pulvérisation, *f.*; (*decay*) écroulement, croulement, *m.*; (*of earth*) éboulement, *m.*

Crumby, Crummy, *adj.* qui a beaucoup de mie; mou

Crump, *adj.* courbé

Crumpet, *s.* crumpet (*English cake*), *m.*, madeleine, *f.*

Crumple, *v.a.* rider; ratatiner; (*crease*) chiffonner, froisser; — *v.n.* se rider, se contracter; se ratatiner; se chiffonner, se froisser

Crumpling, *s.* (*apple*) pomme ridée, *f.*

Crunch. *V.* **Craunch**

Cruor, *s.* cruor, *m.*

Cruoric, *adj.* cruorique

Crupper, *s.* croupe, *f.*; (*of harness*) croupière, *f.* — **dock, -loop,** *s.* culeron, *m.*

Crural, *adj.* crural

Crusade, *s.* croisade, *f.*; — *v.n.* entreprendre une croisade, se croiser

Crusader, *s.* croisé, *m.*

Crush, *v.a.* écraser, broyer; concasser; briser; (*oppress*) écraser, accabler, opprimer; (*quell*) étouffer; (*destroy*) détruire, anéantir; (*metal.*) écraser, bocarder; — *v.n.* s'écraser, être écrasé; — *s.* écrasement, *m.*; choc, *m.*; (*crowd*) cohue, bagarre, *f.* — **hat,** *s.* claque, *m.* — **in,** *v.a.* enfoncer. — **out,** *v.a.* exprimer, faire sortir (de), tirer (de); extorquer; anéantir. — **room,** *s.* (*theat.*) foyer (du public), *m.*

Crusher, *s.* écraseur, concasseur, *m.*; (*metal.*) bocard, *m.*; (*for sugar, in grog*, &c.) pilon, *m.*

Crushing, *s.* écrasement, *m.*; broiement, broyage, *m.*; concassage, *m.*; oppression, *f.*; (*metal.*) écrasement, bocardage, *m.* — **machine, -mill,** *s.* écraseur, concasseur, moulin à écraser, *m.*; (*metal.*) bocard, *m.*

Crust, *s.* croûte, *f.*; (*bit of crust*) croûton, *m.*; — *v.a.* couvrir (*or* recouvrir) d'une croûte, encroûter; (*fig.*) couvrir (de), recouvrir (de); — *v.n.* se former en croûte, former une croûte, se couvrir (*or* se recouvrir) d'une croûte (*or* de croûte), se croûter, s'encroûter. — **end,** *s.* croûton, *m.*

Crustacean, *adj.* crustacéen; — *s.* crustacé, *m.*

Crustaceous, *adj.* crustacé

Crusted, *adj.* croûté

Crustily, *adv.* d'un air bourru (*or* chagrin), avec humeur, aigrement

Crustiness, *s.* dureté, *f.*; mauvaise humeur, humeur revêche, *f.*, air chagrin, *m.*

Crusty, *adj.* couvert (*or* recouvert) d'une croûte, croûteux; (*of bread*, &c.) qui a beaucoup de croûte, croûteux; (*scabby*) croûteux; (*hard*) dur; (*pers.*) de mauvaise humeur, bourru, chagrin, revêche, morose, maussade

Crutch, *s.* béquille, *f.*; (*nav.*) corne, *f.*, chandelier, fourcat, *m.*; — *v.a.* soutenir avec des béquilles; (*fig.*) soutenir. *On —s,* avec des béquilles [de la croix, *m.*

Crutched, *adj.* à béquilles. — **friar,** *s.* frère

Cry, *v.a.n.* crier; (*weep*) pleurer; (*exclaim*) s'écrier. — **against,** crier contre, se récrier contre *or* sur. — **down,** décrier. — **off,** quitter la partie, n'en être plus, en avoir assez. — **out,** crier; (*exclaim*) s'écrier; (*complain*) se plaindre hautement, se récrier; (*against*) se récrier (contre); blâmer (...). — **to,** invoquer. — **up,** prôner, exalter, vanter

Cry, *s.* cri, *m.*; **Cries,** *pl.* cris, *m.pl.*; (*weeping*) pleurs, *m.pl.* *Much — and little wool,* plus de bruit que de besogne

Crying, *part. adj.* (*pers.*) criant, qui crie; (*weeping*) pleurant, qui pleure; (*things*) criant; — *s.* cri, *m.*; cris, *m.pl.*; (*weeping*) pleurs, *m.pl.*; (*tears*) larmes, *f.pl.* — **down,** *s.* décri, *m.*

Cryolite, *s.* cryolithe, *m.*

Crypt, *s.* crypte, *f.*, (*anat.*) *m.*

Cryptogam, *s.* cryptogame, *m.f.*

Cryptogam-ic, y. *V.* page 3, § 1

Cryptogamous, *adj.* cryptogame

Cryptograph, Cryptographer, *s.* cryptographe, *m.* [3, § 1

Crypto-graphic, al, -graphy, &c. *V.* page

Crystal, *s.* cristal, *m.*; — *adj.* de cristal. — **glass,** *s.* cristal, *m.* — **making,** *s.* cristallerie, *f.* — **mine,** *s.* cristallière, *f.* — **oil,** *s.* naphte pur, *m.* — **Palace,** *s.* Palais de cristal, *m.*

Crystalliferous, *adj.* cristallifère

Crystalline, *adj.* de cristal, cristallin; (*anat.*) cristallin; — *s.* cristallin, *m.*

Crystallizable, *adj.* cristallisable

Crystallization, *s.* cristallisation, *f.*

Crystallize, *v.a.* cristalliser; — *v.n.* cristalliser, se cristalliser

Crystallizer, *s.* cristallisoir, *m.*

Crystallizing, *s.* cristallisation, *f.*

Crystallographer, *s.* cristallographe, *m.*

Crystallo-graphic, al, -graphy, &c. *V.*

Crystalloid, *adj.* cristalloïde [page 3, § 1

Cub, *s.* (*of animals*) petit, *m.*; (*of lions*) lionceau, *m.*; (*of bears*) ourson, *m.*; (*of wolves*) louveteau, *m.*; (*of foxes*) renardeau, *m.*; (*boy*) gamin, *m.*, (*girl*) gamine, *f.*; — *v.a.n.* mettre bas. *Ill-bred* or *unlicked —,* ours mal léché, *m.* —**less,** *adj.* sans petit, sans petits, privé de son petit *or* de ses petits [Cuba

Cuban, *s.* Cubain, *m.*, e, *f.*; — *adj.* cubain, de

Cubature, *s.* cubature, *f.*; cubage, *m.*

Cubbing, *s.* mise-bas, *f.* [racine cubique, *f.*

Cube, *s.* cube, *m.*; — *v.a.* cuber. — **root,** *s.*

Cubebs, *s. pl.* cubèbe, *m.*

Cubic, -al, *adj.* cubique, cube

Cubit, *s.* coudée, *f.*

Cubital, *adj.* cubital

Cuboid, -al, *adj.* cuboïde

Cuckoo, *s.* coucou, *m.* — **bud,** *s.* bouton d'or, *m.* — **clock,** *s.* pendule à coucou, *f.*, coucou, *m.* — **flower,** *s.* coucou, *m.*

Cucumber, *s.* concombre, *m.* — **frame,** *s.* serre à concombres, *f.*

Cucurbit, *s.* cucurbite, *f.*

Cucurbitaceous, *adj.* cucurbitacé

Cud, *s.* nourriture, *f.*, aliments, *m.pl.*; (*quid*) chique, *f.* *To chew the —,* ruminer

Cudbear, *s.* orseille de Suède, *f.*

Cuddle, *v.a.* serrer, presser; embrasser, caresser; — *v.n.* se serrer; se ramasser, se pelotonner, se tapir, se blottir

Cuddy, *s.* cabine, *f.*; (*cooking-room*) cuisine, *f.*; (*coal-fish*) colin, *m.*, morue noire, *f.*

Cudgel, *s.* bâton, gourdin, *m.*, trique, *f.*; — *v.a.* bâtonner, battre à coups de bâton, battre, rosser. *To take up the —s,* prendre les armes; prendre fait et cause (pour), prendre querelle (pour), prendre la défense (de). — **play, -playing,** *s.* jeu du bâton, *m.* — **player,** *s.* bâtoniste, *m.* [coups de bâton, *f.*; bastonnade, *f.*

Cudgelling, *s.* coups de bâton, *m.pl.*, volée de

Cudweed, *s.* cotonnière, *f.*

Cue, *s.* (*hint*) avis, mot, *m.*, instruction, *f.*; (*theat.*) réplique, *f.*; (*part*) rôle, *m.*; (*humour*) veine, disposition, *f.*; (*billiards, tail*) queue, *f.*; — *v.a.* tresser en queue. *To give the —,* donner le mot à, faire la leçon à, endoctriner; (*theat.*) donner la réplique (à). *To miss the —,* faire fausse queue. — **rack,** *s.* porte-queues, *m.* — **top,** *s.* procédé, *m.*

Cuff, *s.* coup de poing, *m.*; (*for the wrist*) manchette, *f.*; (*part of a sleeve*) parement, *m.*; poignet, *m.*; — *v.a.* gourmer, frapper à coups de poing, donner des coups de poing à; battre; — *v.n.* se battre à coups de poing

Cuirass, *s.* cuirasse, *f.*; — *v.a.* cuirasser. — **maker,** *s.* armurier, *m.*

Cuirassier, *s.* cuirassier, *m.*

Cul-de-sac, *s.* cul-de-sac, *m.*

Culerage, *s.* poivre d'eau, *m.*

Culinary, *adj.* (*of cookery*) culinaire; (*of or for the kitchen*) de cuisine; (*plants*) potager

Cull, *v.a.* recueillir; choisir; trier

Cullender. *V.* **Colander**

Culler, *s.* trieur, *m.*, -euse, *f.*

Cullet, *s.* casson, grésil, *m.*

Cullis, *s.* (*cook.*) coulis, *m.*

Culm, *s.* chaume, *m.*; (*min.*) anthracite, *m.*

Culmiferous, *adj.* culmifère

Culminate, *v.n.* culminer [met, *m.*

Culmination, *s.* culmination, *f.*; (*top*) sommet

Culpa-bility, bleness. *V.* page 3, § 1

Culpable, *adj.* coupable [coupable

Culpably, *adv.* coupablement, d'une manière

Culprit, *s.* coupable, *m.f.*; criminel, *m.*, -le, *f.*; accusé, *m.*, e, *f.*, prévenu, *m.*, e, *f.*, inculpé, *m.*, [e, *f.*

Cultivable, *adj.* cultivable

Cultivate, *v.a.* cultiver

Cultivation, *s.* culture, *f.*

Cultivator, *s.* cultivateur, *m.*

Cultural, *adj.* cultural

Culture, *s.* culture, *f.*; — *v.a.* cultiver. —**less,** *adj.* sans culture, inculte

Culverin, *s.* coulevrine, *f.*

Culvert, *s.* rigole, *f.*, ponceau, petit aqueduc, *m.*

Cumber, Cumbrance. *V.* **Encumber,** &c.

Cumbersome, Cumbrous, *adj.* embarrassant, gênant, incommode; (*heavy*) lourd, pesant; (*burdensome*) à charge; (*vexatious*) importun [sante

Cumbrously, *adv.* d'une manière embarras-

Cumin, *s.* cumin, *m.* — **seed,** *s.* graine de [cumin, *f.*

Cumulate, *v.a.* cumuler

Cumulation, *s.* cumulation, *f.*

Cumulative, *adj.* cumulatif

Cumulo-stratus, *s.* cumulo-stratus, *m.*

Cumulus, *s.* cumulus, *m.*

Cuneal, Cuneate, Cuneated, *adj.* cunéaire

Cuneiform, *adj.* cunéiforme

Cunette, *s.* cunette, *f.*

Cunning, *adj.* fin, rusé, astucieux; habile, adroit, expérimenté; — *s.* finesse, ruse, astuce, *f.*; habileté, adresse, *f.*

Cunningly, *adv.* avec finesse, avec ruse, astucieusement; habilement, adroitement

Cunningness, *s.* *V.* **Cunning,** *s.*

Cup, *s.* tasse, *f.*; (*of metal*) timbale, *f.*; gobelet, *m.*; (*of paper*) cornet, *m.*; (*beaker*) coupe, *f.*; (*fig. of afflictions, and bot. of a flower*) calice, *m.*; (*of acorns, nuts,* &c.) cupule, *f.*; (*paint.*) godet, *m.*; (*eccl.*) calice, *m.*; (*surg.*) ventouse, *f.*; (*prize*) prix, *m.*; (*beverage*) breuvage, *m.*, boisson, *f.*; —**s,** *pl.* tasses, &c.; (*potations*) orgies, *f.pl.*; — *v.a.* ventouser, appliquer des ventouses à. *A* (*small*) *— of coffee,* une demi-tasse, *f.* *In o.'s —s,* ivre, pris de vin, dans les vignes. — **and ball,** *s.* bilboquet, *m.* — **bearer,** *s.* échanson, *m.* — **board,** *s.* ar-

moire, *f.*; (*in a wall*) placard, *m.*; (*for food*) buffet, *m.* —**ful,** *s.* tasse, tasse pleine, tassée, *f.*, plein une tasse
Cupel, *s.* coupelle, *f.* — **assay,** *s.* coupellation, *f.*
Cupellation, *s.* coupellation, *f.*
Cupidity, *s.* cupidité, *f.*
Cupola, *s.* coupole, *f.*; (*metal.*) cubilot, *m.*
Cupper, *s.* ventouseur, *m.*
Cupping, *s.* ventousation, application de ventouses, *f.* — **glass,** *s.* ventouse, *f.*
Cuprate, *s.* cuprate, *m.*
Cupreous, *adj.* de cuivre, cuivreux
Cupric, *adj.* cuprique
Cupulate, *adj.* cupulé
Cupule, *s.* cupule, *f.*
Cupuliferous, *adj.* cupulifère
Cupuliform, *adj.* cupuliforme
Cur, *s.* chien dégénéré, chien de rue, *m.*; (*pers.*) vilain chien, chien hargneux, mâtin, animal, *m.*
Cura-bility, bleness. *V.* page 3, § 1
Curable, *adj.* guérissable, curable
Curaçoa, *s.* curaçao, *m.*
Curacy, *s.* vicariat, *m.*
Curare, Curari, *s.* curare, *m.*
Curarine, *s.* curarine, *f.*
Curassow, *s.* hocco, *m.*
Curate, *s.* vicaire, *m.* *Perpetual* —, ministre, pasteur, curé, *m.*
Curateship, *s.* vicariat, *m.*
Curative, *adj.* curatif. — *agent,* curatif, *m.*
Curator, *s.* curateur, *m.*; administrateur, *m.*; (*of museums, libraries,* &c.) conservateur, *m.*
Curb, *s.* gourmette, *f.*; (*fig.*) frein, *m.*; (*vet.*) jarde, *f.*, jardon, *m.*, tare, courbe, *f.*; (*of pavements, wells*) *V.* **Kerb;** — *v.a.* (*horses*) gourmer, mettre la gourmette à; (*check*) réprimer, contenir, mettre un frein à, tenir en bride; abaisser; (*pavements, wells*) *V.* **Kerb.** — **bit,** *s.* mors avec gourmette, *m.* — **chain,** *s.* gourmette, *f.* — **less,** *adj.* sans frein, effréné. — **roof,** *s.* comble brisé *or* coupé, toit en mansarde, *m.* — **stone,** *s.* *V.* **Kerb**
Curbing, *s.* répression, *f.*; frein, *m.*; (*tech.*) frette, bride, *f.*
Curcuma, *s.* curcuma, *m.*
Curd, *s.* caillé, lait caillé, *m.*; grumeau, *m.*; —**s,** *pl.* caillebotte, *f.*, caillebottes, *f.pl.*; — *v.a.* cailler, coaguler; (*congeal*) figer; (*fig.*) faire tourner, tourner, glacer, figer; — *v.n.* se cailler, se coaguler; se figer; (*fig.*) tourner, se glacer
Curdle, *v.a.n.* *V.* **Curd**
Curdy, *adj.* caillé, coagulé; figé
Cure, *s.* cure, guérison, *f.*; remède, *m.*; (*eccl.*) cure, *f.*; (*of souls*) charge (d'âmes), *f.*; (*slang*) caricature, *f.*; — *v.a.* guérir; remédier à; corriger; (*prevent*) empêcher; (*meat, fish*) mariner, saler; (*hay,* &c.) sécher. *Past* —, incurable; sans remède, irrémédiable. *With the — of souls,* à charge d'âmes. —**less,** *adj.* incurable; sans remède, irrémédiable
Curer, *s.* guérisseur, *m.*, -euse, *f.*, médecin, *m.*; (*of meat, fish*) saleur, *m.*, -euse, *f.*
Curette, *s.* (*surg.*) curette, *f.*
Curfew, *s.* couvre-feu, *m.* — **bell,** *s.* couvre-feu, *m.*
Curia, *s.* curie, *f.*
Curing, *s.* guérison, cure, *f.*; (*of meat, fish*) salaison, *f.*
Curio, *s.* curion, *m.*
Curiosity, *s.* curiosité, *f.* *Old* —, antiquaille, *f.*, bric-à-brac, *m.* — **dealer,** *s.* marchand (*m.*, e, *f.*) de curiosités, antiquaire, *m.f.*
Curious, *adj.* curieux; ('*after,*' '*of,*') curieux (de), à la recherche (de); (*exact*) exact; (*nice*) délicat; difficile
Curiously, *adv.* curieusement; singulièrement; par une singulière coïncidence
Curiousness, *s.* curiosité, *f.*; exactitude, *f.*; recherche, *f.*; délicatesse, *f.*
Curl, *v.a.* friser, boucler; tourner; tordre; retrousser; (*of serpents,* &c.) entortiller; (*of plants*) entrelacer; (*waves, smoke*) faire tourbillonner, faire onduler; — *v.n.* friser, boucler; s'entortiller, se replier; s'entrelacer; tourbillonner, onduler, ondoyer; (*cuddle*) se pelotonner, se ramasser, se blottir; (*to form rings, generally*) former des anneaux; — *s.* frisure, *f.*; frisé, *m.*; (*of hair*) boucle, *f.*; crochet, *m.*; (*of the brim of a hat*) tournure, *f.*; (*of a cigar*) bout tourné, *m.*; (*fig.*) ondulation, *f.*; (*coil*) repli, *m.*; (*potato disease*) frisée, *f.* — **cloud,** *s.* cirrus, *m.*, queue-de-chat, *f.* — **headed,** *adj.* qui a les cheveux bouclés, qui a la tête frisée. — **paper,** *s.* papillote, *f.*; papier à papillotes, *m.* — **up,** *v.a.* retrousser; (*revolve*) faire tourbillonner; (*cockle up*) recoquiller; (*wrinkle*) rider; *v.n.* se retrousser; tourbillonner; se recoquiller, se recroqueviller; se rider; (*bot.*) crépu; (*of the sky*) pommelé
Curled, *part. adj.* frisé, bouclé, &c. (*V.* **Curl**);
Curler, *s.* friseur, *m.*, -euse, *f.*
Curlew, *s.* courlis, courlieu, *m.*
Curliness, *s.* frisure, *f.*, frisé, *m.*
Curling, *s.* (*action, tech.*) frisage, *m.*; (*of the hair*) frisure, *f.*; (*of wood*) fibres tortueuses, *f.pl.*; (*of serpents,* &c.) entortillement, *m.*; (*of plants*) entrelacement, *m.*; (*of waves, smoke*) ondulation, *f.* — **irons, -tongs,** *s. pl.* fer à friser, frisoir, *m.* — **paper,** *s.* *V.* **Curl-paper**
Curly, *adj.* frisé, bouclé; (*of waves,* &c.) ondoyant. — **headed,** *adj.* *V.* **Curl-headed**
Curmudgeon, *s.* pingre, *m.*, pingresse, *f.*
Currant, *s.* groseille, *f.*; (*raisin*) raisin de Corinthe, *m.* *Black* —, &c., *V.* **Black.** — **bush,** *s.* groseillier, *m.* — **jam,** *s.* confitures de groseilles, *f.pl.* — **jelly,** *s.* gelée de groseilles, *f.* — **syrup,** *s.* sirop de groseilles, *m.* — **tree,** *s.* groseillier, *m.*
Currency, *s.* cours, *m.*; circulation, *f.*; monnaie, *f.*; vogue, *f.*, crédit, *m.* *To give — to,* donner cours à
Current, *adj.* courant, qui a cours; reçu, admis, généralement reçu; en crédit, accrédité; en vogue; à la mode; du jour; (*of rumours*) qui court. — *account,* compte courant, *m.* — *coin,* monnaie courante, *f.* — *opinion,* opinion reçue, *f.* — *price,* cours, prix courant, *m.* *To pass* —, avoir cours; être cru; être reçu *or* admis. *There is a report — (that),* le bruit court (que)
Current, *s.* courant, *m.*; (*fig.*) cours, courant, *m.*
Currently, *adv.* librement; généralement. *It is — reported (that),* le bruit court partout (que)
Curricle, *s.* voiture à deux roues et à deux chevaux, *f.*; course, *f.*
Curriculum, *s.* course, *f.*, carrière, *f.*; piste, *f.*; (*univers.*) cours d'études, cours, *m.*, études, *f.pl.*, scolarité, *f.*
Currie, *s.* *V.* **Curry,** *s.*
Curried, *part. adj.* corroyé, &c. (*V.* **Curry,** *v.a.*); (*cook.*) au cari
Currier, *s.* corroyeur, *m.*
Currish, *adj.* hargneux; brutal
Currishly, *adv.* d'une manière hargneuse; brutalement
Currishness, *s.* humeur hargneuse, *f.*; brutalité, *f.*
Curry, *s.* (*cook.*) cari, *m.*; — *v.a.* (*leather*) corroyer; (*horses*) étriller; (*pers.*) étriller, rosser; (*cook.*) accommoder au cari. *To — favour,* faire la cour (à), capter la bienveillance (de), tâcher de se faire bien venir (de), se faufiler (avec). — **comb,** *s.* étrille, *f.*
Currying, *s.* (*of leather*) corroyage, *m.*; (*of horses*) étrillage, étrillement, *m.*
Curse, *v.a.* maudire; affliger; — *v.n.* blasphémer, sacrer, jurer; — *s.* malédiction, *f.*; blasphème, *m.*; (*bane*) fléau, *m.*; malheur, *m.* —**d,** (*adj.*) maudit. *To be —d with,* être affligé de, avoir pour son malheur, avoir le malheur d'avoir
Cursedly. *V.* **Confoundedly**
Curser, *s.* personne qui maudit, *f.*
Cursing, *s.* *V.* **Curse,** *s.*
Cursitor, *s.* greffier de la chancellerie, *m.*
Cursive, *adj.* cursif
Cursively, *adv.* cursivement
Cursor, *s.* curseur, *m.*
Cursorily, *adv.* rapidement, à la hâte, en courant; légèrement
Cursoriness, *s.* rapidité, *f.*; légèreté, *f.*
Cursory, *adj.* rapide; (*hasty*) précipité; **fait à** la hâte; (*slight*) léger; (*usual*) ordinaire

Curt, *adj.* bref ; brusque
Curtail, *v.a.* écourter ; (*shorten*) raccourcir ; abréger ; retrancher ; rogner ; amoindrir, diminuer, réduire ; priver (de) ; — *adj.* écourté ; — *s.* (*tech.*) contour, *m.* — **dog,** *s.* chien écourté, *m.* — **step,** *s.* (*arch.*) palière, *f.*
Curtailing, Curtailment, *s.* raccourcissement, *m.* ; abréviation, *f.* ; abrégé, *m.* ; retranchement, *m.* ; réduction, *f.*
Curtain, *s.* rideau, *m.* ; (*theat.*) rideau, *m.*, toile, *f.* ; (*of bonnets*) bavolet, *m.* ; (*fort.*) courtine, *f.* ; — *v.a.* envelopper, voiler, cacher. *To draw the* —, tirer le rideau ; (*theat.*) baisser le rideau *or* la toile. — **band,** *s.* embrasse, *f.* — **hook,** *s.* patère, *f.* — **lecture,** *s.* semonce conjugale, *f.* — **loop,** *s.* embrasse, *f.* — **pin,** *s.* patère, *f.* — **pole,** *s.* bâton de rideau, porte-rideau, *m.* — **rest,** *s.* patère, *f.* — **rod,** *s.* tringle, *f.*
Curtly, *adv.* brièvement ; brusquement
Curtness, *s.* brièveté, *f.* ; brusquerie, *f.*
Curtsey, Curtsy. *V.* **Courtesy**
Curule, *adj.* curule. — *chair,* chaise curule, *f.*
Curvated, *adj.* courbé
Curvation, Curvature. *V.* **Incurvation**
Curve, *adj.* courbe ; — *s.* courbure, *f.* ; (*geom.*) ligne courbe, courbe, *f.* ; — *v.a.* courber ; arquer ; (*build.*) cintrer ; — *v.n.* se courber, courber, décrire une courbe
Curved, *adj.* courbé, courbe ; arqué ; (*of a horse's head*) busqué ; (*build.*) cintré
Curvet, (*of a horse*) courbette, *f.* ; (*prank*) tour, *m.*, fredaine, *f.* ; — *v.n.* courbetter, faire des courbettes ; (*fig.*) faire des sauts, sautiller, folâtrer [bonds, *m.pl.*
Curvetting, *s.* courbettes, *f.pl.* ; (*fig.*) sauts,
Curvilineal, Curvilinear, *adj.* curviligne
Curvirostral, *adj.* curvirostre
Curvirostre, *s.* curvirostre, *m.*
Cuscus. *V.* **Kuskus**
Cushion, *s.* coussin, *m.* ; (*tech.*) coussinet, *m.* ; (*of billiard-tables*) bande, *f.* ; — *v.a.* asseoir (*or* poser) sur un coussin ; garnir de coussins ; (*fig.*) couvrir ; étouffer ; mettre de côté
Cusp, *s.* pointe, cuspide, *f.* ; (*astr.*) corne du croissant, *f.* ; (*arch.*) lobe, *m.*
Cuspidate, Cuspidated, *adj.* cuspidé
Custard, *s.* crème, *f.*, flan, *m.* ; pot de crème, *m.* — **apple,** *s.* anone, *f.*
Custodian, *s.* gardien, *m.*, -ne, *f.*
Custody, *s.* garde, *f.* ; emprisonnement, *m.*, prison, *f.* ; arrestation, *f.* ; détention, *f.* *To give into* —, faire arrêter, arrêter. *To take into* —, arrêter, emprisonner
Custom, *s.* coutume, habitude, *f.* ; (*common practice*) usage, *m.* ; (*of shops*) achalandage, *m.* ; pratique, *f.* ; (*of wholesale trade*) clientèle, *f.* ; (*tax*) douane, *f.*, droit de douane, *m.* —*s inwards,* droits d'entrée, *m.pl.* —*s outwards,* droits de sortie, *m.pl.* — **duty,** *s.* droit de douane, *m.* — **free,** *adj.* franc (*or* exempt) de droits. — **house,** *s.* douane, *f.*, bureau de la douane, *m.* — **house agent,** *s.* commissionnaire de la douane, *m.* — **house officer,** *s.* employé de la douane, *m.* ; douanier, *m.*
Customable, *adj.* soumis à un droit de douane
Customarily, *adv.* de coutume, d'habitude, habituellement, ordinairement, communément
Customariness, *s.* habitude, fréquence, généralité, *f.*
Customary, *adj.* accoutumé, ordinaire, habituel ; (*in common practice*) d'usage ; reçu ; (*law*) coutumier ; — *s.* coutumier, *m.*
Customer, *s.* chaland, *m.*, e, *f.* ; pratique, *f.* ; (*in a large way of business*) client, *m.*, e, *f.* ; (*of a coffee or eating house*) habitué, *m.*, e, *f.*, client, *m.*, e, *f.* ; consommateur, *m.*, -trice, *f.* ; (*fellow*) individu, particulier, *m.* *Ugly* —, (*man*) mauvais coucheur, *m.*, (*woman*) pie-grièche, *f.* *To know o.'s* —*s*, (*jest.*) connaître son monde
Cut, *v.a.* couper ; (*sever*) trancher ; (*shape*) tailler ; (*cleave*) fendre ; (*pierce*) percer ; blesser ; (*open*) ouvrir, fendre ; (*o.'s way*) se frayer (un chemin) ; (*carve*) ciseler, sculpter ; graver ; (*carve meat at table*) découper ; (*an acquaintance*) rompre avec, ne plus connaître, ne plus parler à, passer sans saluer, laisser là ; (*teeth, capers, a figure, a joke*) faire ; (*cards*) couper ; (*a pen or pencil*) tailler ; (*need.*) broder à jour ; (*books*) rogner ; (*surg.*) inciser, (*for the stone*) tailler ; — *v.n.* couper ; (*be cut*) se couper ; se trancher ; se tailler, &c. ; (*of horses*) se couper, s'entre-tailler ; (*of teeth*) percer ; (*surg.*) inciser, (*for the stone*) tailler ; — *s.* (*opening, wound*) coupure, *f.* ; incision, *f.* ; blessure, *f.* ; (*gash*) balafre, *f.* ; (*blow*) coup, *m.* ; (*shape*) coupe, *f.* ; taille, *f.* ; (*piece*) morceau, *m.* ; (*slice*) tranche, *f.* ; (*picture*) gravure estampe, vignette, image, *f.* ; (*figure*) tournure, *f.* ; (*of roads*) chemin de traverse, *m.*, traverse, *f.* ; (*of streets*) rue de traverse, rue transversale, *f.* ; (*build.*) tranchée, *f.* ; (*sarcasm*) coup de bec, coup de patte, trait, *m.* ; (*at cards*) coupe, *f.* *Queer* —, drôle d'individu, *m.* *Short* —, raccourci, *m.*, accourcie, *f.* *To* — *in pieces,* couper en morceaux ; tailler en pièces. *To* — *to pieces,* mettre *or* tailler en pièces ; (*criticize*) abîmer. *To* — *and come again,* revenir *or* retourner au plat, y revenir, y retourner. *To* — *and run, to* — *o.'s stick, to* — *it,* filer, ficher le camp, déguerpir. *To draw* —*s*, tirer à la courte paille. *To take a short* —, prendre un raccourci. *To take a short* — *by* ..., couper court en suivant ... *To take a shorter* —, prendre un chemin plus court. *The shortest* —, le chemin le plus court ; (*of lots*) la courte paille. — **across,** *v.a.* couper en travers ; *v.n.* traverser. — **along,** *v.n.* filer, jouer des jambes ; aller, marcher. — **and dry,** *adj.* tout fait, tout prêt. — **asunder,** *v.a.* couper *or* partager en deux, couper, trancher ; séparer. — **away,** *v.a.* couper ; ôter, retrancher, élaguer ; *v.n.* s'en aller, déguerpir, filer, ficher le camp. — **away -coat,** *s.* habit à la française, *m.* — **down,** *v.a.* couper, abattre ; (*fig.*) moissonner ; (*an army*) tailler en pièces ; (*overpower*) écraser, surpasser ; (*clip*) rogner ; réduire ; abréger ; (*take down*) détacher, décrocher, dépendre ; (*agr.*) recéper. — **off,** *v.a.* couper ; trancher ; retrancher, supprimer ; ôter, enlever ; (*by death*) enlever, moissonner ; (*destroy,* &c.) détruire ; annuler ; interrompre ; intercepter ; séparer ; empêcher, prévenir ; priver (de) ; exclure (de) ; (*get rid*) se défaire (de) ; (*gram.*) élider. *To* — (*one*) *off with a shilling,* ne laisser qu'un shilling à (quelqu'un), déshériter (quelqu'un). — **on,** *v.n.* *V.* — **along.** — **open,** *v.a.* ouvrir, fendre. — **out,** *v.a.* couper ; tailler ; découper ; former, façonner, faire ; adapter ; priver (de), ôter ; retrancher ; exclure ; couper l'herbe sous le pied à, faire la barbe à ; surpasser, éclipser ; (*to scheme*) préparer, tailler ; assigner ; (*a ship*) capturer au port. — **purse,** *s.* coupeur (*m.*, -euse, *f.*) de bourses, filou, *m.* — **throat,** *s.* coupe-jarrets, *m.* — **throat place,** *s.* coupe-gorge, *m.* — **up,** *v.a.* couper en morceaux ; couper, découper ; dépecer ; disséquer ; (*troops*) tailler en pièces, écharper ; (*criticize*) critiquer impitoyablement, abîmer, déchirer ; (*to sap*) saper ; (*grieve*) affliger ; accabler (de). — **water,** *s.* (*upper starling*) avant-bec, *m.* ; (*lower starling*) arrière-bec, *m.* ; (*nav.*) taillemer, *m.* ; guibre, *f.* ; éperon, *m.* ; (*bird*) coupeur d'eau, bec-en-ciseaux, *m.*
Cutaneous, *adj.* cutané
Cutch, *s.* cachou, *m.* [(*liquids*) pellicule, *f.*
Cuticle, *s.* cuticule, *f.*, épiderme, *m.* ; (*of*
Cuticular, *adj.* cuticulaire
Cutlas, Cutlass, *s.* coutelas, *m.*
Cutler, *s.* coutelier, *m.*, -ière, *f.*
Cutlery, *s.* coutellerie, *f.* — **works,** *s. pl.*
Cutlet, *s.* côtelette, *f.* [coutellerie, *f.*
Cutter, *s.* coupeur, *m.*, -euse, *f.* ; (*hewer*) tail-

leur, *m.*; (*tool*) coupoir, *m.*; (*in compounds: pers.*) coupeur (-euse) *or* tailleur de ..., (*tool*) coupe- ..., *m.*; taille- ..., *m.*; (*tooth*) dent incisive incisive, *f.*; (*ship*) cutter, cotre *m.*; (*boat*) canot, *m.*

Cutting, *adj.* tranchant; incisif; piquant; caustique; mordant; poignant; — *s.* taille, *f.*; incision, *f.*; ouverture, *f.*; (*tech.*) coupage, coupement, *m.*, taille, *f.*; (*piece cut*) rognure, *f.*; (*of wood, hair, cards*) coupe, *f.*; (*of the teeth*) pousse, *f.*; (*slip*) bouture, *f.*, greffon, *m.*; (*of wine*) sarment, *m.*; (*of rail., roads, canals, &c.*) tranchée, *f.*; (*road*) chemin de traverse, *m.*, traverse, *f.*; (*street*) rue aboutissante, *f.*; rue de traverse, rue transversale, *f.*; (*of horses*) entre-taillure, *f.* — *and wounding*, (*law*) coups et blessures. — **boot,** *s.* (*for a horse*) botte, bottine, *f.* — **press,** *s.* (*book-bind.*) rognoir, *m.*

Cuttingly, *adv.* incisivement, caustiquement, d'un ton caustique, d'une manière piquante

Cuttle, *s.* sèche, seiche, *f.* — **bone,** *s.* os de sèche, *m.* — **fish,** *s.* sèche, *f.*

Cuvette, *s.* cuvette, *f.*

Cutty, — **pipe,** *s.* brûle-gueule, *m.*

Cwt., (*abbrev.*) *V.* **Hundredweight**

Cyanate, *s.* cyanate, *m.*

Cyanic, *adj.* cyanique

Cyanide, *s.* cyanure *m.*

Cyanite, *s.* cyanite, *f.*

Cyanogen, *s.* cyanogène, *m.*

Cyclamen, *s.* cyclame, cyclamen, *m.*

Cycle, *s.* cycle, *m.*

Cyclic, -al, *adj.* cyclique

Cycloid, *s. adj.* cycloïde, *s.f., adj. m.f.*

Cycloidal, *adj.* cycloïdal

Cyclone, *s.* cyclone, *m.*

Cyclonic, *adj.* cyclonal

Cyclop, *s.* cyclope, *m.*

Cyclopean, *adj.* cyclopéen, de cyclope

Cyclopedia, &c. *V.* **Encyclopædia,** &c.

Cyclopic, *adj.* cyclopéen, de cyclope

Cyclops, *s.* cyclope, *m.*

Cyclorama, *s.* cyclorama, *m.*

Cycloramic, *adj.* cycloramique

Cyder. *V.* **Cider**

Cygnet, *s.* jeune cygne, *m.*

Cylinder, *s.* cylindre, *m.*; (*of pumps*) corps (de pompe), *m.*; (*pharm.*) crayon, *m.* — **watch,** *s.* montre à cylindre, *f.*

Cylindr-ic, al, -ically. *V.* page 3, § 1

Cylindricity, *s.* cylindricité, *f.*

Cylindroid, *s. adj.* cylindroïde, *s.m., adj. m.f.*

Cyma, *s.* cymaise, *f.*; (*bot.*) *V.* **Cyme**

Cymbal, *s.* cymbale, *f.* — **player,** *s. V.* **Cymbalist**

Cymbalist, *s.* cymbalier, cymbaliste, *m.*

Cymbel, *s.* (*of an organ*) cymbale, *f.*

Cyme, *s.* cyme, *f.*; (*arch.*) *V.* **Cyma**

Cymose, Cymous, *adj.* cymeux [kymri, *s.m.*

Cymric, *adj. s.* kymrique, *adj. m.f., s.m.*,

Cynanchum, *s.* cynanche, cynanque, *m.*

Cynic, *s.* cynique, *m.*

Cyn-ic, al, -ically. *V.* page 3, § 1

Cynicalness, Cynicism, *s.* cynisme, *m.*

Cynocephalus, *s.* cynocéphale, *m.*

Cynodon, *s.* cynodon, *m.*

Cynosure, *s.* (*astr.*) petite ourse, cynosure, *f.*; (*fig.*) point d'attraction, ce qui attire, *m.*; guide, *m.* *The — of all eyes*, l'objet de tous les regards

Cypher. *V.* **Cipher**

Cypress, *s.* cyprès, *m.* — **grove,** *s.* cyprière, *f.* — **tree,** *s.* cyprès, *m.* — **wood,** *s.* cyprès, *m.*

Cyprian, Cypriot, Cypriote, *s. adj.* Chypriote, Cypriote, *m.f.*, Cyprien, *m.*, -ne, *f.*

Cyprus (-wine), *s.* vin de Chypre, *m.*

Cyropædeia, *s.* Cyropédie, *f.*

Cyst, Cystis, *s.* kyste, *m.*

Cystic, *adj.* cystique, kystique

Cytherean, *adj.* de Cythère

Cytisus, *s.* cytise, *m.*

Czar, *s.* czar, *m.*

Czarina, *s.* czarine, *f.*

Czarinian, Czarish, *adj.* czarien

Czarowitz, *s.* czarowitz, *m.*

Czech, Czekh, *s. adj.*, **Czechian, Czechish,** *adj.* Tchèque, *m.f.*

D

D, *s.* (*letter*) d, *m.*; (*mus.*) ré, *m.*

Dab, *v.a.* frapper légèrement, taper; (*mop*) éponger; (*foment*) étuver; (*on*) jeter (à); — *v.n.* pêcher à la ligne flottante; — *s.* léger coup, petit coup, *m.*; (*lump*) petit morceau, *m.*; (*of liquid*) flaquée, *f.*; éclaboussure, *f.*; tache, *f.*; (*of paint*) petite couche, *f.*; (*pers.*) expert, *m.*, adepte, *m.f.*; (*fish*) limande, *f.*; — *adj.* expert, habile. — **chick,** *s.* petit grèbe, castagneux, *m.*

Dabber, *s.* (*engr.*) tapette, *f.*

Dabble, *v.a.* mouiller, humecter; (*splash*) éclabousser; (*daub*) barbouiller; — *v.n.* barboter, patauger; (*meddle*) se mêler (de); s'escrimer (de); toucher (à); (*bungle*) *V.* **Bungle**

Dabbler, *s.* barboteur, *m.*, -euse, *f.*; (*bungler*) *V.* **Bungler**

Dabster, *s.* maître, expert, adepte, (*fam.*) malin, *m.*

Dace, *s.* vandoise, vaudoise, *f.*, dard, *m.*

Dacian, *s. adj.* Dace, *m.f.*

Dactyl, Dactyle, *s.* dactyle, *m.*

Dactyl-ic, -iology, -ology, &c. *V.* page 3, § 1

Dad, *s. V.* **Daddy.** *By —*, parbleu! sapristi! fichtre!

Daddy, *s.* papa, père, *m.* — **longlegs,** *s.* (*spider*) faucheux, *m.*; (*fly*) *V.* **Crane-fly**

Dado, *s.* dé, *m.*

Dædalian, *adj.* dédaléen

Daffodil, *s.* asphodèle, *m.*; narcisse des bois *or* des prés, *m.*

Daft, *adj. s.* stupide, sot; fou

Dag, *s.* (*of deer, &c.*) dague, *f.*

Dagger, *s.* poignard, *m.*; dague, *f.*; (*fig.*) coup de poignard, *m.*; (*fenc.*) fleuret, *m.*; (*print.*) croix, *f.*; — *v.a.* poignarder, daguer. *At —s drawn, at —s-drawing*, à couteaux tirés. *To look —s*, lancer des regards foudroyants *or* furieux, faire des yeux terribles. — **knife,** *s.* couteau-poignard, *m.*

Daggle. *V.* **Draggle**

Daguerrean, *adj.* daguerrien

Daguerreotype, *s.* daguerréotype, *m.*; — *v.a.* daguerréotyper

Daguerreotyping, *s.* daguerréotypage, *m.*

Daguerreotypy, *s.* daguerréotypie, *f.*

Dahlia, *s.* dahlia, *m.*

Dailiness, *s.* quotidienneté, *f.*

Daily, *adj.* journalier, de chaque jour; quotidien; (*astr.*) diurne; — *adv.* journellement, tous les jours; quotidiennement; de jour en jour; (*during the day*) le jour, de jour. — *bread*, pain quotidien, pain de chaque jour, *m.* — *paper*, journal quotidien, *m.*

Daintily, *adv.* friandement, délicatement, avec friandise, avec délicatesse

Daintiness, *s.* friandise, *f.*; délicatesse, *f.*

Dainty, *adj.* friand; délicat; — *s.* friandise, *f.*; délicatesse, *f.*

Dairy, *s.* laiterie, *f.* — **farm, -house, -room,** *s.* laiterie, *f.* — **maid, -woman,** *s.* fille de laiterie, laitière, *f.*; (*com.*) crémière, laitière, *f.* — **man,** *s.* garçon de laiterie, laitier, *m.*; (*com.*) crémier, laitier, *m.*

Dais, *s.* dais, *m.*

Daisied, *adj.* parsemé de marguerites

Daisy, *s.* marguerite, pâquerette, *f.*

Dale, *s.* vallon, *m.*, vallée, *f.* —**sman,** *s.* habitant des vallées, *m.*

Dalliance, *s.* caresses, *f.pl.*; embrassement, *m.*; (*play*) badinage, *m.*, folâtrerie, *f.*

Dallier, *s.* personne légère, *f.*

Dally, *v.n.* tarder; (*trifle*) s'amuser, perdre son temps; (*play*) badiner, folâtrer, jouer

Dalmatian, *s. adj.* Dalmate, *m.f.*

Dalmatic, Dalmatica, *s.* dalmatique, *f.*

Daltonism, *s.* daltonisme, *m.*

Dam, *s.* (*of animals*) mère, *f.*; (*mole*) digue, *f.*;

(*of rivers*) barrage, *m.*; batardeau, *m.*; — *v.a.* diguer, endiguer; contenir; arrêter; fermer; (*fill*) remplir

Damage, *s.* dommage, *m.*; dégât, *m.*; mal, *m.*; tort, préjudice, détriment, *m.*; (*nav.*) avarie, *f.*, avaries, *f.pl.*; **—s,** *pl.* (*law*) dommages et intérêts, dommages-intérêts, *m.pl.*; — *v.a.* endommager; faire tort à, nuire à; (*nav.*) avarier; — *v.n.* s'endommager [avariable

Damageable, *adj.* endommageable; (*nav.*)

Damaging, *adj.* pernicieux; nuisible, préjudiciable; compromettant; — *s.* endommagement, *m.* [blement

Damagingly, *adv.* pernicieusement; nuisi-

Daman, *s.* daman, *m.*

Damar. *V.* **Dammar**

Damascene, *v.a.* *V.* **Damaskeen;** — *s.* damasquinure, *f.*; — *adj.* damascène

Damascener, *s.* damasquineur, *m.*

Damascening, *s.* *V.* **Damaskeening**

Damascus blade, *s.* damas, *m.*

Damask, *s.* (*silk*) damas, *m.*; (*linen, wool*) toile damassée, *f.*, damassé, damas, *m.*; — *adj.* damassé; — *v.a.* damasser; (*fig.*) émailler. — **rose,** *s.* rose de Damas, *f.* — **weaver, -worker,** *s.* damasseur, *m.* — **work,** *s.* damassure, *f.*

Damaskeen, *v.a.* damasquiner; — *adj.* damasquiné; — *s.* *V.* **Damaskeening**

Damaskeener. *V.* **Damascener**

Damaskeening, *s.* damasquinage, *m.*; damasquinerie, *f.*; damasquinure, *f.*

Damaskin, *s.* (*blade*) damas, *m.*

Damasking, *s.* damassure, *f.*

Damassin, *s.* damassin, *m.*, damasquette, *f.*

Dame, *s.* dame, *f.* **—'s violet,** *s.* julienne des dames, cassolette, *f.*, damas, *m.* [mara, *m.*

Dammar, *s.* dammar, *m.* — **pine,** *s.* dam-

Damn, *v.a.* damner; condamner, désapprouver; (*fam.*) envoyer au diable, jurer après; (*theat.*) siffler

Damnable, *adj.* damnable; (*fam.*) maudit

Damnably, *adv.* damnablement; odieusement, horriblement, diablement [chute, *f.*, fiasco, *m.*

Damnation, *s.* damnation, *f.*; (*of a play*)

Damnatory. *V.* **Damning**

Damned, *adj.* damné; maudit, odieux, détestable, abominable; (*fam.*) satané, sacré

Damnify, *v.a.* faire du tort à, nuire à, léser

Damning, *adj.* qui condamne, qui perd; accablant, écrasant; condamnatoire; de malédiction; d'infamie

Damoclean, *adj.* de Damoclès; menaçant

Damp, *s.* humidité, *f.*; vapeur, *f.*; exhalaison, *f.*; (*choke* —) moufette, *f.*; (*fig.*) nuage, *m.*; nuage de tristesse, *m.*, tristesse, *f.*, abattement, *m.*; froid, *m.*; — *adj.* humide; moite; (*fig.*) triste; — *v.a.* humecter, rendre humide; (*the spirits*) abattre, décourager; refroidir, glacer; attrister; troubler; obscurcir; (*slacken*) ralentir; calmer; (*deaden*) amortir; (*stifle*) étouffer

Damper, *s.* (*mus.*) étouffoir, *m.*; sourdine, *f.*; (*of furnaces,* &c.) registre, *m.*; plaque, *f.*; (*fig.*) éteignoir, *m.*; voile de tristesse, *m.*; rabat-joie, trouble-fête, *m.f.*

Dampish, *adj.* un peu humide, moite

Dampishness, *s.* légère humidité, moiteur, *f.*

Damply, *adv.* humidement, moitement

Dampness, *s.* humidité, *f.*; moiteur, *f.*

Damsel, *s.* demoiselle, jeune fille, *f.*; (*attendant*) suivante, *f.*

Damson, *s.* prune de Damas, *f.*, damas, *m.* — **tree,** *s.* prunier de damas, *m.*

Danaid, Danaide, *s.* (*machine*) danaïde, *f.*; (*myth.*) Danaïde, *f.*

Dance, *v.n.* danser; — *v.a.* danser; (*to make to dance*) faire danser; — *s.* danse, *f.*; bal, *m.* — *of Death,* danse des morts, danse macabre, *f.* — **music,** *s.* air de danse, *m.*, danse, *f.*, air dansant, *m.*, musique dansante, *f.* [dame, *f.*

Dancer, *s.* danseur, *m.*, -euse, *f.*; cavalier, *m.*,

Dancing, *s.* danse, *f.* — **master (-room, -school** *or* **-academy),** *s.* maître (*m.*, salle, *f.*, école, *f.*) de danse. — **party,** *s.* soirée dansante, *f.* — **shoe,** *s.* soulier de danse (*or* de bal), *m.*

Dandelion, *s.* dent-de-lion, *f.*, pissenlit, *m.*

Dander, *s.* rage, colère, *f.*

Dandle, *v.a.* faire sauter, faire danser, dodiner, dodeliner, bercer, dorloter

Dandriff, Dandruff, *s.* crasse (de la tête), *f.*, pellicules (de la tête), *f.pl*

Dandy, *s.* gandin, dandy, élégant, *m.* — **roll,** *s.* (*tech.*) rouleau à vergeures, *m.*

Dandyism, *s.* gandinisme, *m.*, gandinerie, *f.*, dandysme, *m.*

Dane, *s.* Danois, *m.*, e, *f.* — **wort,** *s.* hièble, *f.*

Danger, *s.* danger, péril, *m.* —! *int.* (*in games*) casse-cou! **—less,** *adj.* sans danger

Dangerous, *adj.* dangereux, périlleux

Dangerously, *adv.* dangereusement

Dangerousness, *s.* nature dangereuse *or* périlleuse, *f.* [(après); — *v.a.* laisser pendre

Dangle, *v.n.* pendiller; (*after*) être pendu

Dangler, *s.* godelureau, *m.*; parasite, *m.*

Danish, *adj.* danois, de Danemark; — *s.* le danois, *m.*, la langue danoise, *f.*

Dank, Dankish, &c. *V.* **Damp,** &c.

Danubian, *adj.* danubien

Dap, *v.n.* *V.* **Dab**

Daphne, *s.* daphné, *m.* [pant, propret

Dapper, *adj.* leste, vif, actif; fringant; pim-

Dapple, *v.a.* pommeler, barioler, tacheter; — *v.n.* se pommeler, se barioler, se tacheter; — *adj.* pommelé, bariolé, tacheté, truité; (*of the bay colour*) miroité. — *bay,* bai miroité. — *grey,* gris pommelé

Dappled, *adj.* *V.* **Dapple,** *adj.*

Darby, *s.* (*mas.*) taloche, *f.*

Dare, *v.n.* oser; — *v.a.* oser; affronter; défier, braver; provoquer; intimider; — *s.* défi, *m.*; audace, *f.*; (*fish*) *V.* **Dace.** *If you — do* (or *to do*) *it,* si vous osez le faire. *If you — me to do it,* si vous me défiez de le faire. *I — say,* j'ose dire (que); je crois bien (que), je suis sûr (que), je réponds (que), il est probable (que), sans doute (que); je parie (que); c'est probable; c'est possible; je crois bien! je le crois bien! je veux bien le croire! j'en réponds! ah bien oui! par exemple! plus souvent! n'est-ce pas? — **devil,** *adj.s.* audacieux, téméraire, désespéré; effréné; casse-cou, risque-tout, brûlot, *m.*

Daring, *adj.* audacieux, hardi; brave, vaillant; intrépide; — *s.* audace, hardiesse, *f.*; bravoure, *f.*; intrépidité, *f.*

Daringly, *adv.* audacieusement, hardiment

Daringness, *s.* *V.* **Daring,** *s.*

Dariol, Dariole, *s.* dariole, *f.*

Dark, *adj.* noir, obscur; sombre; ténébreux, de ténèbres; sinistre; (*night*) nuit; (*of colours*) foncé; (*of the complexion*) brun; (*of eyes, hair*) noir; (*secret*) caché, mystérieux, sourd; (*of lanterns*) sourd; — *s.* obscurité, *f.*, ténèbres, *f.pl.*; ignorance, *f.*; (*night*) nuit, *f.* — *ages,* siècles de ténèbres, *m.pl.* *To see only the — side of things,* voir tout en noir. — **eyed,** *adj.* aux yeux noirs. — **working,** *adj.* ténébreux

Darken, *v.a.* obscurcir; assombrir; (*the complexion*) brunir; (*sadden*) attrister; (*disturb*) troubler; (*paint.*) assourdir; — *v.n.* s'obscurcir; s'assombrir; se brunir, se rembrunir

Darkening, *s.* obscurcissement, *m.*; assombrissement, *m.*; rembrunissement, *m.*; (*paint.*) assourdissement, *m.*

Darkish, *adj.* noirâtre; un peu sombre, un peu obscur; (*of the complexion*) un peu brun

Darkling, *adj. adv.* dans les ténèbres

Darkly, *adv.* dans les ténèbres; (*fig.*) obscurément; (*secretly*) sourdement

Darkness, *s.* obscurité, *f.*, ténèbres, *f.pl*; (*of colours*) teinte foncée, teinte sombre, *f.*; (*of complexion*) couleur brune, *f.*; teint brun, *m.*

Land of —, séjour ténébreux, tombeau, *m.* *Prince of* —, prince des ténèbres, *m.*

Darksome, *adj.* obscur, sombre, ténébreux

Darky, *s* moricaud, *m.*, e, *f.*

Darling, *s. adj.* chéri, *m.*, e, *f.*; favori, *m.*, -te, *f.*; mignon, *m.*, -ne, *f.*

Darn, *v.a.* repriser, raccommoder; (*do in fancy work*) broder en reprise; — *s.* reprise, *f.*

Darnel, *s.* ivraie, *f.*

Darner, *s.* repriseur, *m.*, -euse, *f.*

Darning, *s.* reprisage, *m.*; (*darn, darns*) reprise, *f.*, reprises, *f.pl.*; (*fancy work*) broderie en reprise, *f.* — **cotton,** *s* coton à repriser, coton plat, *m.* — **needle,** *s.* aiguille à repriser (*or* à reprises), *f.*

Daroo, — **tree,** *s.* figuier sycomore, *m.*

Dart, *s.* dard, trait, *m.*; (*fig.*) trait, *m.*; (*fish*) *V.* **Dace;** — *v.a.* darder; (*at*) lancer (contre); — *v.n.* partir comme un trait; s'élancer, fondre (sur); pénétrer; (*glide*) glisser. — **snake,** *s.* acontias, *m.* [hinga, *m*

Darter, *s.* personne qui lance, *f.*; (*bird*) an-

Darting, *adj.* qui darde, qui lance

Dash, *v.a.* frapper; (*knock*) heurter; (*break*) briser; (*throw*) jeter; (*send up or out*) faire jaillir; (*splash*) éclabousser; (*sprinkle*) arroser; (*mix*) mélanger, mêler; (*depress*) abattre; (*destroy*) détruire, renverser; (*confound*) confondre, déconcerter; (*a writing*) souligner; — *v.n.* se heurter; se briser; (*rush*) se précipiter, s'élancer; (*fly up or out*) jaillir. — **away,** jeter. — **down,** jeter; précipiter; renverser. — **off,** ébaucher, esquisser, crayonner; expédier, bâcler, brocher. — **out,** ébaucher, esquisser; (*a writing*) barrer, biffer, rayer; (*send out*) faire sauter, faire jaillir. — **up,** faire sauter, faire jaillir, soulever

Dash, *s.* choc, *m.*; attaque, *f.*; élan, *m.*; (*blow, stroke*) coup, *m.*; (*mixture*) mélange, *m.*, teinte, *f.*; (*of liquids*) goutte, *f.*; (*of vinegar*) filet, *m.*; (*fig.*) pointe, *f.*, grain, *m.*; (*essay*) incursion, *f.*; (*of pens*, &c.) trait, *m.*; (*mettle*) fougue, *f.*; (*boldness*) hardiesse, *f.*; (*mus.*) virgule, *f.*; (*print.*) *V.* **Rule.** *To cut a* —, trancher du grand, faire florès, faire froufrou, faire de l'embarras, faire ses embarras, faire de l'étalage. — **board,** *s.* garde-crotte, para-crotte, *m.*

Dashing, *adj.* brillant, pimpant, élégant; (*bold*) hardi; (*fiery*) fougueux; — *s.* choc, *m.*; brisement, *m.*; jaillissement, *m.*; éclaboussement, *m.*; &c. (*V.* **Dash,** *v.a.n.*)

Dashingly, *adv.* avec éclat, élégamment

Dashy, *adj. V.* **Dashing**

Dastard, &c. *V.* **Coward,** &c.

Dastardy, *s. V.* **Cowardliness**

Dasyure, *s.* dasyure, *m.*

Data, *s.* données, *f.pl.*

Date, *s.* date, *f.*; durée, *f.*; terme, *m.*, échéance, *f.*; (*of coins*) millésime, *m.*; (*fruit*) datte, *f.*; — *v.a.n.* dater. *Bearing — of, under — of,* en date de. *Out of* —, vieilli, suranné, passé; périmé. (*Three months out of* —, périmé de trois mois.) *At twenty days'* —, à vingt jours de date. *To bear the — of,* être daté de. *To grow* or *pass out of* —, vieillir, passer; périmer, se périmer. — **case,** *s.* semainier, *m.* —**less,** *adj.* sans date. — **palm,** *s.* dattier, *m.* — **plum,** *s.* (*fruit*) plaquemine, *f.*; (*tree*) plaqueminier, *m.* — **stamp,** *s.* timbre de la poste, *m.* — **tree,** *s.* dattier, *m.*

Dated, *part. adj.* daté; (*in compounds*) à date

Dative, *s.* (— *case*) datif, *m.* *In the* —, au datif

Datum, *s.* donnée. *f.*; (*mech.*) repère, *m.* — **line,** *s.* plan de niveau, niveau donné, *m.*

Datura, *s.* datura, *m.*

Daturia, Daturine, *s.* daturine, *f.*

Daub, *v.a.* barbouiller; (*do over, cover*) enduire; (*fig.*) surcharger; barioler, chamarrer; cacher, colorer, plâtrer, déguiser, couvrir, pallier; — *v.n.* (*paint badly*) barbouiller, croûtonner; (*flatter*) flagorner; — *s.* barbouillage, *m.*; enduit, *m.*; (*bad picture*) croûte, *f.*, mauvais tableau, *m.*; (*flattery*) flagornerie, *f.*

Dauber, *s.* barbouilleur, *m.*, -euse, *f.*; mauvais peintre, croûton, croûtier, *m.*; (*flatterer*) flagor-

Daubing, *s. V.* **Daub,** *s.* [neur, *m.*, -euse, *f.*

Dauby, *adj.* gluant, visqueux

Daughter, *s.* fille, *f.* —**in-law,** *s.* belle-fille, *f.*

Daughterly, *adj.* de fille, d'une fille, filial; — *adv.* en fille, filialement

Daunt, *v.a.* intimider; effrayer; décourager, abattre. —**less,** —**lessness,** *V.* **Fearless, Fear-**

Dauphin, ess, *s.* dauphin. *m.*, e, *f.* [**lessness**

Davenport, *s.* bureau, secrétaire, *m.*; pupitre, *m.*

Davit, *s.* davier, *m.* [sûreté, *f.*

Davy lamp, *s.* lampe de Davy, lampe de

Daw, *s. V.* **Jackdaw**

Dawdle, *v.n.* flâner, baguenauder, muser, musarder; chipoter; — *s. V.* **Dawdler.** — **away,** *v.a.* perdre

Dawdler, *s.* flâneur, *m.*, -euse, *f.*, musard, *m.*, e, *f.*

Dawdling, *adj.* flâneur, musard; — *s.* flânerie, musarderie, *f.*

Dawn, *v.n.* poindre, commencer à paraitre, paraître; (*fig.*) luire, briller, se lever; naître; percer; — *s. V.* **Dawning,** *s.*

Dawning, *adj.* naissant; — *s.* point du jour, *m.*, pointe du jour, *f.*, aube, aurore, *f.*; (*fig.*) aurore, naissance, *f.*, commencement, *m.*; (*glimpse*) lueur, *f.*

Day, *s.* jour, *m.*; (*whole day, in regard to work, occupation, or weather*) journée, *f.*; (*fig.*) victoire, *f.*; bataille, journée, *f.*; —**s,** *pl.* jours, *m.pl.*; journées, *f.pl.*; (*times*) temps, *m.*; jours, *m.pl.*; (*years*) années, *f.pl.*; (*life*) jours, *m.pl.*; vie, *f.*; — *adj.* de jour. *All —, all — long, the whole* —, toute la journée. *All the blessed* —, toute la sainte journée. *Any* —, n'importe quel jour; d'un jour à l'autre. *At the present* —, aujourd'hui. *Broad* —, plein jour, grand jour. *One — or other, one of these —s, some — or other*, un jour ou l'autre, un de ces jours, un beau jour. *The — after, the following —, the next* —, le lendemain, *m.*; le lendemain de . . ., *m.* *The — after that on which*, &c., le lendemain du jour où, &c. *The — after to-morrow*, *V.* **To-morrow.** *The — before*, la veille, *f.*; la veille de . . ., *f.* *The — before that on which*, &c., la veille du jour où, &c. *The — before yesterday*, *V.* **Yesterday.** *The next — but one, the third — (after)*, le surlendemain (de), *m.* *Two —s before*, deux jours avant, *m.pl.*, l'avant-veille, l'avant-veille de . . ., *f.* *This* —, ce jour; (*to-day*) aujourd'hui. *This — last year*, il y a aujourd'hui un an, l'année dernière (*or* l'an dernier) à pareil jour, il y a un an jour pour jour. *This — next year*, dans un an, jour pour jour. *This — fortnight, this — week*, *V.* **Fortnight** *and* **Week.** *This many a* —, il y a longtemps. — *after* —, un jour après l'autre, chaque jour, tous les jours; de jour en jour, d'un jour à l'autre. — *came after* —, les jours se succédaient. — *by* —, jour par jour; de jour en jour; chaque jour, tous les jours. *By* —, au jour; le jour; de jour. *By the* —, à la journée. *By the — that*, jusqu'au jour où; le jour où (*or* que). *From — to* —, de jour en jour; d'un jour à l'autre, du jour au lendemain; (*from hand to mouth*) au jour le jour. — *In broad* —, en plein jour, au grand jour. *In former —s*, autrefois. *In my — or —s*, de *or* dans mon temps; dans ma vie. *In our —s*, de nos jours, aujourd'hui. *In the* —, (*day-time*) le jour; (*course of the day*) dans la journée. *In the —s of*, du temps de, au temps de. *In the —s of old*, autrefois, jadis, au temps jadis. *In these —s*, de nos jours. *In those —s*, dans ce temps-là. *To a —*, *V.* **To,** *prep.* *To-* —, aujourd'hui. *It is* —, il fait jour. *It is broad* —, il fait grand jour. *The better the —, the better the deed*, bon jour, bonne œuvre. *To carry* or *win the* —, remporter la victoire. *To have o.'s* —, faire son temps. *To have o.'s —s*, avoir ses jours, être journalier. — **bed,** *s. V.* **Couch.** — **blindness,** *s.* (*med.*) nyctalopie, *f.* — **boarder,** *s.* demi-pensionnaire, *m.f.* — **book,** *s.* journal, *m.* — **break,** *s.* point du jour, *m*, pointe du jour, *f.*; aube, aurore, *f.* — **clock,** *s.* horloge *or* pendule qui marche vingt-quatre heures, *f.* — **fly,** *s.* éphémère, *m.f.* — **labour,** *s.* travail à la journée, *m.*, journée, *f.* — **labourer,** *s.* journalier, *m.*, -ière, *f.* — **light,** *s.* jour, *m.* *In broad — light*, au grand jour; en plein jour. — **lily,** *s.* hémérocalle, belle d'un jour, *f.* — **nursery,** *s.* crèche, *f.* — **post,** *s.* poste de jour, *f.* — **pupil -scholar,** *s.* externe, *m.f.* — **sight,** *s.* (*med.*) héméralopie, *f.* — **spring,** *s. V.* — **break.** — **star,** *s.* étoile du matin, *f.* —**'s work,** *s.* journée, *f.* — **ticket,** *s.* billet valable pour un jour, *m.* — **time,** *s.* jour, *m.* — **work,** *s. V.* — **labour**

Daze, Dazzle, *v.a.* éblouir; — *v.n.* être ébloui

Dazzling, *adj.* éblouissant; *s.* éblouissement, *m.*

Dazzlingly, *adv.* d'une manière éblouissante

Deacon, *s.* diacre, *m.*

Deaconess, *s.* diaconesse, *f.*

Deaconry, Deaconship, *s.* diaconat, *m.*

Dead, *adj.* mort; inanimé; insensible; inerte; profond, de mort; complet, entier; parfait, excellent; décidé, déterminé; (*useless*) inutile; (*dull*) lourd, pesant; (*blunt*) émoussé; (*of liquors*) éventé; (*of water*) croupissant; (*of sound*) sourd; mat; (*of weight*) inerte; (*of money*) qui dort, sans emploi; (*jewel.*) mat; (*of colours*) terne; mat; (*of metals*) mat; (*of walls*) blanc, orbe; (*of calms, nav.*) plat; (*of ropes, nav.*) dormant; (*of the wind, nav.*) debout; (*of letters by post*) mis au rebut; (*of coal*) éteint; (*tech.*) fixe, dormant; — *adv.* complètement, entièrement; profondément; décidément; résolûment; — *s.* morts, *m.pl.*; (*of night*) milieu, *m.*; (*of winter*) cœur, fort, *m.* *Lying —*, (*of money*, &c.) qui dort. *To fall down —, to drop —*, tomber raide mort. *To lie —*, (*of money*, &c.) dormir. — **beat,** *adj.* battu à plate couture; (*tired out*) éreinté; *s.* (*escapement*) échappement à repos, *m.* — **body,** *s.* cadavre, corps mort, *m.* — **bolt,** *s.* (*of locks*) pène dormant, *m.* — **born,** *adj.* mort-né. — **colouring,** *s.* empreinte, impression, *f.* — **drunk,** *adj.* ivre-mort. — **fall,** *s.* (*trap*) assommoir, *m.* — **hearted,** *adj.* pusillanime. — **heartedness,** *s.* pusillanimité, *f.* — **heat,** *s.* (*in horse-racing*) deadheat, *m.* — **house,** *s.* morgue, *f.* — **language,** *s.* langue morte, *f.* — **letter,** *s.* lettre morte, *f.*; (*post.*) lettre refusée, lettre tombée en rebut, lettre mise au rebut, *f.* (— *letters*, rebuts, *m.pl.*). — **letter office,** *s.* bureau des rebuts, *m.* — **lift,** *s.* dernière extrémité, *f.*, état desespéré, *m.*, abois, *m.pl.*; effort inutile, *m.* — **lock,** *s.* arrêt forcé, encombrement, *m.*, obstruction, *f.*, embarras, *m.*, bagarre, *f.* — **march,** *s.* marche funèbre, *f.* — **nettle,** *s.* lamier, *m.* — **reckoning,** *s.* (*nav.*) route estimée, *f.* — **sea,** *s.* (la) Mer Morte, *f.* — **season,** *s.* morte saison, *f.* — **set,** *s.* grand effort, *m.*, tentative désespérée, *f.*; vive attaque, *f.* — **shot,** *s.* excellent tireur, *m.* — **stock,** *s. V.* **Stock.** — **stop,** *s.* halte subite, *f.*; (*rid.*) quinte, *f.*; (*tech.*) toc, point de repos, *m.* — **top,** *s.* (*tree disease*) couronnement, *m.*, décurtation, *f.* — **water,** *s.* remous, *m.* — **weight,** *s.* poids inerte, *m.*; fardeau pesant, *m.* — **wood,** *s.* bois mort, *m.*; (*tech.*) bois de remplissage, massif, *m.* — **wools,** *s.pl.* laines mortes, *f.pl.*

Deaden, *v.a.* amortir; (*to blunt*) émousser; (*liquors*) éventer; (*metals*) matir, amatir; (*sound*) assourdir [mat, *m.*

Deadening, *s.* amortissement, *m.*; (*of metals*)

Deadliness, *s.* nature mortelle, léthalité, *f.*

Deadly, *adj.* mortel; (*of a strife*) à mort; — *adv.* mortellement; à mort; comme la mort; extrêmement; profondément; (*fam.*) diablement. — **carrot,** *s.* thapsie, *f.* — **nightshade,** *s.* belladone, *f.*

Deadness, *s.* mort, *f.*; (*fig.*) paralysie, *f.*; engourdissement, *m.*; langueur, *f.*; stagnation, *f.*; froideur, indifférence, *f.*; (*of liquors*) évent, *m.*; (*of sound*) matité, *f.*; (*of metals*) mat, *m.*

Deaf, *adj.* sourd. *As — as a post*, sourd comme un pot. — **dumbness,** *s.* surdi-mutité, *f.*

Deafen, *v.a.* assourdir, rendre sourd

Deafening, *adj.* assourdissant

Deafly, *adv.* sourdement

Deafness, *s.* surdité, *f.*

Deal, *s.* quantité, *f.*; (*at cards*) donne, *f.*; main, *f.*; (*at dominoes*) pose, *f.*; (*wood*) sapin, bois blanc, *m.*; (— *board*, — *end*) planche de sapin, *f.* *A good —, a great —, a —*, beaucoup; bien; une grande quantité *By a good —*, à beaucoup près. *A good — to do*, beaucoup à faire, fort à faire. — **box, -case,** *s.* caisse de bois blanc, *f.* — **fish,** *s.* trachyptère, *m.*

Deal, *v.a.* (— *out*) distribuer, répartir; (*scatter*) répandre; (*throw*) lancer; (*cards*) donner; (*blows*) porter, donner; (*justice*) faire; — *v.n.* (*behave*) agir, en agir, se comporter, se conduire; (*trade*) faire le commerce (de); (*at cards*) donner, faire. — **by,** traiter. — **in,** se mêler de; s'occuper de; faire; faire le commerce de, vendre. — **with,** (*behave*) agir envers, agir à l'égard de, en agir avec, en user avec, traiter; mener; (*com.*) être en relation d'affaires avec; faire des affaires avec; traiter d'affaires avec; avoir des rapports avec; avoir affaire à; (*of shops*) se fournir (*or* se servir) chez; (*contend*) lutter contre, combattre; (*manage*) conduire, diriger, gouverner, mener, traiter, arranger, venir à bout de. *To have to — with*, avoir affaire à

Dealer, *s.* personne qui agit, *f.*; personne qui se mêle *or* s'occupe (de), *f.*; faiseur (de), *m.*, -euse, *f.*; (*seller*) marchand (de ...), *m*, e, *f*; (*at cards*) personne (*f.*) *or* celui (*m.*, celle, *f.*) qui donne

Dealing, *adj.* qui agit; — *s.* conduite, manière d'agir, *f.*; (*treatment*) procédé, *m.*; (*trade*) affaire, *f.*, affaires, *f.pl.*; (*intercourse*) relation *f.*, rapport, *m.*, relations, *f.pl.*, rapports, *m.pl.*

Dean, *s.* doyen, *m.*

Deanery, Deanship, *s.* doyenné, décanat, *m.*

Dear, *adj.* cher; précieux; (*pretty*) joli, gentil, charmant; — *s.* cher, cher ami, ami, *m.*; chère, chère amie, amie, *f.*; — *adv.* cher; — *int.* mon Dieu! — *me!* vraiment! mon Dieu! *Oh —!* aïe! oh, mon Dieu! *Oh — no*, non non, certainement non, oh que non! *To hold —*, aimer, chérir. — **bought,** *adj.* acheté cher, payé cher, qui coûte cher. — **loved,** *adj.* bienaimé, chéri

Dearly, *adv.* chèrement; cher; tendrement, affectueusement; (*much*) bien. — **beloved,** *adj.* bien-aimé, chéri [dresse, *f.*

Dearness, *s.* (*of price*) cherté, *f.*; (*fig.*) ten-

Dearth, *s.* disette, *f.*

Death, *s.* mort, *f.*; (*poet.*) trépas, *m.*; (*law, admin.*) décès, *m.* *To —, to the —*, à mort. *To be the — of*, faire mourir, tuer, causer la mort *or* la perte de. *It will be the — of me*, j'en mourrai. *To be frightened* (or *frozen*, &c.) *to —*, mourir de peur (*or* de froid, &c.). *To beat to —*, assommer. *To bleed to —*, perdre tout son sang. *To catch o.'s —*, s'attirer la mort. *To drink oneself to —*, se tuer à force de boire. *To frighten* (or *terrify*) *to —*, faire mourir de frayeur (*or* de terreur). *To put to —*, mettre à mort, faire mourir. — **bed,** *s.* lit de mort, *m.* *On his — bed*, à son lit de mort, au lit de mort. — **bell,** *s.* glas funèbre, *m.* — **blow,** *s.* coup de la mort, *m.*; coup mortel, *m.*; coup de grâce, *m.* — **boding,** *adj.* qui présage la mort. — **darting,** *adj.* meurtrier. — **ful,** *adj.* de mort, mortel; (*murderous*) meurtrier. — **fulness,** ;

apparence de mort, *f.* — **knell,** *s.* glas funèbre. *m.* —**less,** *adj.* immortel, impérissable. — **like,** *adj.* semblable à la mort, de mort; lugubre; cadavéreux. — **rate,** *s.* proportion des décès, mortalité, *f.* — **rattle,** *s.* râle de la mort *or* de l'agonie, *m.* —**'s door,** *s.* (les) portes de la mort, *f.pl.* —**'s head,** *s.* tête de mort, *f.* —**'s head moth,** *s.* atropos, papillon à tête de mort, *m.*, tête de mort, *f.* —**'s man,** *s.* bourreau, *m.* — **shot,** *s.* coup mortel, *m.* — **song,** *s.* chant de mort, chant funèbre, *m.* — **stroke,** *s. V.* — **blow.** — **struggles,** *s.pl.* agonie, *f.* — **warrant,** *s.* ordre d'exécution, *m.*; (*fig.*) arrêt de mort, *m.* — **watch,** *s.* horloge de la mort, *f.* — **wound,** *s.* blessure mortelle, *f.*

Debar, *v.a.* exclure (de); priver (de); empêcher (de); interdire, défendre; refuser; frustrer (de)

Debarcation, *s.* débarquement, *m.*

Debark, *v.a.n.* débarquer

Debase, *v.a.* abaisser; avilir; dégrader; abâtardir; (*coin*) altérer; (*chem.*) dénaturer

Debasement, *s.* abaissement, *m.*; avilissement, *m.*; dégradation, *f.*; abâtardissement, *m.*; (*of coin*) altération, *f.*; (*chem.*) dénaturation, *f.*

Debasing, *adj.* avilissant, dégradant

Debatable, *adj.* discutable; contestable, sujet à contestation

Debate, *s.* débat, *m.*, débats, *m.pl.*, discussion, *f.*; contestation, dispute, *f.*; délibération, *f.*; — *v.a.n.* débattre, discuter; contester, disputer; délibérer (sur)

Debater, *s.* discuteur, argumentateur, orateur parlementaire, *m.*

Debating, *s.* discussion parlementaire, *f.*; éloquence de la tribune, *f.*; discussion, *f.* — **club, -society,** *s.* société littéraire, conférence, *f.*

Debauch, *s.* débauche, *f.*; — *v.a.* débaucher; (*pervert*) corrompre, pervertir; — *v.n.* faire ripaille

Debauchedly, *adv.* dans la débauche, en débauché

Debauchedness, *s.* débauche, *f.*

Debauchee, *s.* débauché, *m.*, e, *f.*

Debaucher, *s.* débaucheur, *m.*, -euse, *f.*; corrupteur, *m.*, -trice, *f.*

Debauchery, *s.* débauche, *f.*

Debauchment, *s.* corruption, *f.*

Debenture, *s.* reconnaissance, *f.*; obligation, *f.*; (*Cust.*) certificat de prime *or* de drawback, *m.* — **holder,** *s.* porteur (*m.*, -euse, *f.*) d'obligation, obligataire, *m.f.*

Debilitate, *v.a.* débiliter, affaiblir

Debilitation, *s.* débilitation, *f.*, affaiblissement, *m.*

Debility, *s.* débilité, faiblesse, *f.*

Debit, *s.* débit, débet, doit, *m.*; — *v.a.* débiter ('*with*,' de), porter au débit de. — **side,** *s.* débit, doit, *m.*

Debituminization, *s.* débituminisation, *f.*

Debituminize, *v.a.* débituminiser

Deblai, *s.* déblai, *m.*

Debouch, *v.n.* déboucher

Debouching, *s.* débouchement, *m.*

Debris, *s. pl.* débris, *m.pl.*

Debt, *s.* dette, *f.*; (*of creditors*) créance, *f.*; —**s,** *pl.* (*com.*) passif, *m.* *Bad* —, mauvaise créance, créance véreuse, *f.*; non-valeur, *f.* *To be in* —, être endetté, avoir des dettes, devoir. *To be in the — of,* être le débiteur de. *To bring* or *get into —, to involve in —,* faire faire des dettes à, endetter, charger de dettes. *To run* or *get into —,* faire des dettes, s'endetter. *To be out of —,* n'avoir plus de dettes. *To get out of —,* payer *or* acquitter ses dettes, se désendetter. *To pay the — of nature,* payer le tribut à la nature. *I am in your —,* je suis votre débiteur, je vous dois quelque chose. *I am out of your —,* je ne vous dois plus rien. *I wish to get out of your —,* je désire m'acquitter envers vous. *Out of — out of danger,* qui ne doit rien n'a rien à craindre

Debtor, *s.* débiteur, *m.*, -trice, *f.*; (*book-keep.*) débiteur, débit, doit, passif, *m.* — *and creditor,* débiteur et créancier; (*book-keep.*) doit et avoir. — **side,** *s.* débit, doit, *m.* —**s' prison,** *s.* prison pour dettes, *f.*

Debut, *s.* début, *m.*

Debutant, e, *s.* débutant, *m.*, e, *f.*

Decachord, *s. adj.* décacorde, *s.m.*, *adj. m.f.*

Decadal, *adj.* décadaire

Decad, Decade, *s.* décade, *f.*; (*of a chaplet or* (*rosary*) dizain, *m.*

Decadence, Decadency, décadence, *f.*

Decagon, *s.* décagone, *m.*

Decagonal, *adj.* décagonal, décagone

Decagramme, *s.* décagramme, *m.*

Decahedral, *adj.* décaèdre

Decahedron, *s.* décaèdre, *m.*

Decalitre, *s.* décalitre, *m.*

Decalogue, *s.* décalogue, *m.*

Decameron, *s.* Décaméron, *m.*

Decametre, *s.* décamètre, *m.*

Decamp, *v.n.* décamper

Decampment, *s.* décampement, *m.*

Decanal, *adj.* décanal

Decant, *v.a.* décanter, transvaser; verser

Decantation, *s.* décantation, *f.*, transvasement, *m.*

Decanter, *s.* carafe, *f.*, (*small*) carafon, *m.* — **stand,** *s.* porte-carafe, plateau de carafe, *m.*

Decanting, *s.* décantage, transvasement, *m.*

Decapitalization, *s.* décapitalisation, *f.*

Decapitalize, *v.a.* décapitaliser

Decapitate, *v.a.* décapiter

Decapitation, *s.* décapitation, *f.*

Decapod, *s.* décapode, *m.*

Decapodal, Decapodous, *adj.* décapode

Decarbonization, *s.* décarbonisation, *f.*

Decarbonize, *v.a.* décarboniser

Decastere, *s.* décastère, *m.*

Decastich, *s.* dizain, *m.*

Decay, *v.n.* tomber en décadence, déchoir; (*with age*) baisser, décliner, tomber, s'affaiblir; (*of o.'s sight*) faiblir; (*fall to pieces*) se délabrer; tomber en ruine; (*wither*) se flétrir, dépérir; (*wear off*) s'user; (*fall into disuse*) tomber en désuétude; (*vanish*) s'évanouir, se perdre; (*of fruit, &c.*) se gâter; (*of teeth*) se gâter, se carier; (*of bones*) se carier; (*of wood*) pourrir; — *v.a.* détériorer; délabrer; ruiner; affaiblir; flétrir; user; gâter; carier; pourrir; — *s.* décadence, *f.*, déclin, *m.*; affaiblissement, *m.*; (*falling to pieces*) délabrement, *m.*; (*withering*) dépérissement, *m.*; (*ruin*) ruine, *f.*; (*of bones, teeth*) carie, *f.*; (*end*) chute, *f.* *To fall into —, V. to* **Decay,** *v.n.*

Decease, *s.* mort, *f.*; (*law, admin.*) décès, *m.*; — *v.n.* mourir; (*law, admin.*) décéder

Deceased, *adj.* mort; décédé; — *s.* défunt, *m.*, e, *f.*

Deceit, *s.* déception, *f.*; tromperie, fourberie, *f.*; supercherie, *f.*; imposture, *f.*; stratagème, artifice, *m.*, ruse, *f.*; perfidie, *f.*; (*law*) fraude, *f.*, dol, *m.* —**ful,** *adj.* trompeur. —**fully,** *adv.* frauduleusement. —**fulness,** *s.* tromperie, *f.*; (*falseness*) fausseté, *f.* —**less,** *adj.* sans tromperie, loyal, droit, sincère

Deceivable, *adj.* trompable, décevable, facile à tromper

Deceive, *v.a.* tromper; (*disappoint*) décevoir; frustrer; (*into*) faire tomber (dans), entraîner (dans); (*to fail*) faillir à, faire défaut à

Deceiver, *s.* trompeur, *m.*, -euse, *f.*; imposteur, *m.*

December, *s.* décembre, *m.*

Decemvir, *s.* décemvir, *m.*

Decemviral, *adj.* décemviral

Decemvirate, *s.* décemvirat, *m.*

Decency, *s.* décence, *f.*; bienséance, *f.*, convenances, *f.pl.*

Decennary, *adj.* décennaire; — *s.* période de dix années, *f.*

Decennial, *adj.* décennal

Decennially, *adv.* tous les dix ans

Decent, *adj.* décent; convenable, bienséant, honnête; propre, présentable; ordinaire; passable

Decently, *adv.* décemment, convenablement; passablement

Decentralizable, *adj.* décentralisable

Decentralization, *s.* décentralisation, *f.*

Decentralize, *v.a.* décentraliser

Decentralizer, *s.* décentralisateur, *m.*, -trice, *f.*
Decentralizing, *adj.* décentralisateur; — *s.* décentralisation, *f.*
Deception, *s.* déception, *f.*; illusion, *f.*
Deceptive, *adj.* trompeur, décevant, déceptif, mensonger [gèrement
Deceptively, *adv.* déceptivement, menson-
Decharm, *v.a.* décharmer
Decide, *v.a.* décider; — *v.n.* décider; se décider; se prononcer
Decided, *adj.* décidé; prononcé; positif; bien arrêté; résolu, ferme; incontestable
Decidedly, *adv.* décidément; positivement; certainement; résolûment
Decider, *s.* arbitre, juge, *m.*
Deciduous, *adj.* (*bot.*) décidu
Decigramme, *s.* décigramme, *m.*
Decilitre, *s.* décilitre, *m.* [tion décimale, *f.*
Decimal, *adj.* décimal; — *s.* décimale, frac-
Decimally, *adv.* par dizaines; par le moyen
Decimate, *v.a.* décimer [des décimales
Decimation, *s.* décimation, *f.*
Decimetre, *s.* décimètre, *m.*
Decipher, *v.a.* déchiffrer
Decipherable, *adj.* déchiffrable
Decipherer, *s.* déchiffreur, *m.*, -euse, *f.*
Deciphering, *s.* déchiffrement, *m.*
Decision, *s.* décision, *f.*; (*end*) issue, *f.*; (*firmness*) fermeté, *f.* — *of character*, caractère décidé, *m.*, fermeté, *f.* [*To be — of*, décider
Decisive, *adj.* décisif; (*well marked*) prononcé.
Decisively, *adv.* décisivement, d'une manière décisive [décisive, *f.*; ton tranchant, *m.*
Decisiveness, *s.* caractère décisif, *m.*; nature
Decistere, *s.* décistère, *m.*
Deck, *v.a.* orner (de), parer (de); — *s.* pont, *m.* *Lower* —, premier pont, *m.* *Middle* —, second pont, *m.*
Decker, *s.* *Two-* —, bâtiment (*or* vaisseau) à deux ponts, deux-ponts, *m.* *Three-* —, bâtiment (*or* vaisseau) à trois ponts, trois-ponts, *m.*
Decking, *s.* ornement, *m.*
Declaim, *v.a.n.* déclamer [*m.*, -trice, *f.*
Declaimant, Declaimer, *s.* déclamateur,
Declamation, *s.* déclamation, *f.*
Declamatory, *adj.* déclamatoire, déclamateur, de déclamation
Declarable, *adj.* déclarable
Declaration, *s.* déclaration, *f.*; proclamation, *f.*; manifestation, *f.*; (*law*) conclusions, *f.pl.*
Declaratory, *adj.* déclaratif, déclaratoire
Declare, *v.a.* déclarer; affirmer; assurer; annoncer, proclamer; (*of writings*) porter (que); — *v.n.* se déclarer, se prononcer. *I —!* sur ma parole! ma foi! par exemple! — **off,** *s.* *V.* **Cry off**
Declaredly, *adv.* ouvertement, formellement
Declarer, *s.* déclarateur, *m.*, -trice, *f.*
Declension, *s.* décadence, *f.*, déclin, *m.*; abattement, *m.*; pente, inclinaison, *f.*; (*gram.*)
Declimatize, *v.a.* déclimater [déclinaison, *f.*
Declinability, *s.* déclinabilité, *f.*
Declinable, *adj.* déclinable
Declinate, *adj.* décliné
Declination, *s.* déclination, *f.*, déclinement, déclin, *m.*, décadence, *f.*; descente, *f.*; (*astr.*, *phys.*) déclinaison, *f.*
Declinator, *s.* déclinateur, *m.*
Declinatory, *adj.* déclinatoire
Decline, *v.a.n.* pencher, incliner; dévier; (*decay*) décliner; (*fall*) baisser; (*refuse*) ne pas accepter; refuser; s'excuser (de); se récuser; (*avoid*) éviter; décliner; (*gram.*, *astr.*, *phys.*) décliner; — *s.* déclin, *m.*, décadence, *f.*; baisse, *f.*; affaiblissement, *m.*; (*of the day*) déclin, *m.*, chute, *f.*; (*med.*) marasme, *m.* *To be in a* —, être atteint de marasme
Declining, *adj.* penché, incliné; (*falling*) qui décline; (*failing*) défaillant; (*decaying*) en décadence; — *s.* *V.* **Declination.** — *age* or *years*, déclin de l'âge, *m.*, vieillesse, *f.*
Declivitous. *V.* **Declivous**

Declivity, *s.* déclivité, pente, *f.*, penchant, *m.*
Declivous, *adj.* déclive, en pente
Decoct, *v.a.* faire bouillir
Decoction, *s.* décoction, *f.*
Decollate, *v.a.* décoller
Decollation, *s.* décollation, *f.*
Decolorant, *s.* décolorant, *m.*
Decoloration, &c. *V.* **Discoloration,** &c.
Decomposable, *adj.* décomposable
Decompose, *v.a.* décomposer; — *v.n.* se dé-
Decomposite, *adj.* décomposé [composer
Decomposition, *s.* décomposition, *f.*
Decompound, *adj.* décomposé; — *v.a.* décomposer
Decompoundable, *adj.* décomposable
Decorate, *v.a.* décorer (de); orner (de), embellir (de) [bellissement, *m.*
Decoration, *s.* décoration, *f.*; ornement, em-
Decorative, *adj.* décoratif, de décoration. — **painting,** *s.* décor, *m.*
Decorator, *s.* décorateur, *m.*
Decorous, *adj.* convenable, décent, bienséant
Decorously, *adv.* convenablement, décemment
Decorousness. *V.* **Decorum**
Decorticate, *v.a.* décortiquer, écorcer
Decortication, *s.* décortication, *f.*, écorcement, *m.* [décorum, *m.*
Decorum, *s.* bienséance, *f.*, convenances, *f.pl.*,
Decoy, *s.* (*place*) hutte, *f.*; (*for ducks*) canardière, *f.*; (*trap*) piége, *m.*; (*bait*) leurre, appât, *m.*; (*bird*) appeau, *m.*, chanterelle, *f.*; (*pers.*) mouchard, *m.*; mouton, *m.*; — *v.a.* attirer dans un piége, leurrer, amorcer; attirer (dans). — **bird,** *s.* appeau, *m.*, chanterelle, *f.* — **duck,** *s.* canard privé, leurre, *m.* — **man,** *s.* oiseleur, *m.* — **pond,** *s.* canardière, *f.*
Decreasable. *V.* **Diminishable**
Decrease, *v.n.* décroître; diminuer; — *v.a.* diminuer, amoindrir; — *s.* décroissement, *m.*, décroissance, diminution, *f.*; déclin, *m.*; (*of days*) décroissement, *m.*; (*of the moon*) décours, *m.*; (*of waters*) décrue, *f.*; (*com.*, *cust.*) déchet, *m.* [nuant, de moins en moins
Decreasingly, *adv.* en décroissant, en dimi-
Decree, *s.* décret, *m.*; arrêt, *m.*; jugement, *m.*; — *v.a.* décréter; arrêter; juger, décider, statuer; (*order*) ordonner; (*triumph, honours,* &c.) décerner. — *nisi*, jugement provisoire. *Absolute* or *final* —, jugement définitif
Decrement, *s.* *V.* **Decrease,** *s.*
Decrepit, *adj.* décrépit
Decrepitate, *v.n.* décrépiter [pitement, *m.*
Decrepitation, *s.* décrépitation, *f.*, décré-
Decrepitude, *s.* décrépitude, *f.*
Decrescendo, *adv.* *s.* decrescendo (*s.m.*)
Decrescent, *adj.* décroissant
Decretal, *s.* décrétale, *f.*
Decretist, *s.* décrétaliste, décrétiste, *m.*
Decretory, *adj.* décrétoire; décisif, péremp-
Decrial, *s.* décri, *m.* [toire
Decrier, *s.* personne qui décrie, *f.*, détracteur,
Decrown. *V.* **Discrown** [*m.*, -trice, *f.*
Decry, *v.a.* décrier
Decubitus, Decumbency, *s.* décubitus, *m.*
Decumbent, *adj.* décombant [*v.a.n.* décupler
Decuple, *adj.* *s.* décuple, *adj.* *m f.*, *s.m.*; —
Decurion, *s.* décurion, *m.*
Decurrent, *adj.* décurrent, décourant
Decursive, *adj.* décursif
Decury, *s.* décurie, *f.* [cussatif
Decussate, Decussated, *adj.* décussé, dé-
Decussation, *s.* décussation, *f.*
Dedalian. *V.* **Dædalian** [sacrer (à)
Dedicate, *v.a.* dédier (à); dévouer (à); con-
Dedication, *s.* dédicace, *f.* — **day,** *s.* dédi-
Dedicatory, *adj.* dédicatoire [cace, *f.*
Deduce, *v.a.* déduire (de), conclure (de); tirer (de) [être déduit
Deducible, *adj.* qu'on peut déduire, qui peut
Deduct, *v.a.* déduire; rabattre
Deduction, *s.* déduction, *f.*; (*com.*) remise, *f.*
Deductive, *adj.* déductif

Deductively, *adv.* déductivement, par déduction

Deed, *s.* action, *f.*; acte, *m.*; fait, *m.*; exploit, *m.*; réalité, *f.*; (*law*) titre, acte, *m.*; contrat, *m.*

Deem, *v.a.* juger, croire, penser, estimer, considérer comme

Deep, *adj.* profond; (*hollow*) creux; (*low*) bas; (*wide*) large; (*thick*) épais; (*secret*) secret; (*cunning*) rusé, fin; (*great*) grand, extrême; vif; (*of colours*) foncé; (*of sound*) grave; (*of mourning*) grand; (*of play*) gros; — *adv.* profondément; avant; bas; (*strongly*) fortement; (*much*) largement, beaucoup, bien; (*in depth*) de profondeur; (*in thickness*) d'épaisseur; — *s.* profondeur, *f.*; (*middle*) milieu, fort, *m.*; (*sea*) mer, *f.*, océan, *m.*; (*theol.*) abîme, *m.* — *in debt*, *V.* **Deeply.** *Two* (*three*, &c.) —, (*mil.*, *on two*, &c. *ranks or rows*) sur deux (trois, &c.) rangs. *To be ten feet* —, avoir dix pieds de profondeur. *To go — into*, pénétrer, traiter à fond. **— drawing,** *adj.* qui tire beaucoup d'eau. **— drawn,** *adj.* profond. **— fetched,** *adj.* (*of sighs*) profond; (*of groans*) long. **— laid,** *adj.* secret, caché, ténébreux; profond. **— rooted,** *adj.* profondément enraciné, invétéré. **— sea,** *s.* *V.* **Sea. — sea lead** *or* **line,** *s.* (*nav.*) grande sonde, *f.* **— seated,** *adj.* profond; intérieur, intime. **— waisted,** *adj.* (*nav.*) haut accastillé

Deepen, *v.a.* approfondir; creuser; augmenter; obscurcir; assombrir; (*colours*) rendre plus foncé; (*sound*) rendre plus grave; — *v.n.* devenir plus profond; s'augmenter, augmenter; s'obscurcir; s'assombrir; (*of colours*) devenir plus foncé; (*of sound*) devenir plus grave

Deeply, *adv.* profondément; (*strongly*) fortement; vivement; extrêmement; (*of sounds*) gravement; (*cunningly*) avec ruse, finement. — *in debt*, perdu *or* criblé de dettes. — *laid*, [&c., *V.* **Deep**

Deepness. *V.* **Depth**

Deer, *s.* bête fauve, *f.*; (*buck*) daim, *m.*, daine, *f.*; (*stag*) cerf, *m.* *Fallow* —, bête fauve, *f.*; daim, *f.* *Red* —, cerf, *m.* **— hound,** *s.* limier, *m.* **— mouse,** *s.* gerbille, *f.* **— skin,** *s.* peau de daim, *f.* **— stalker (-stalking),** *s.* chasseur (*m.*, chasse, *f.*) de bêtes fauves à l'affût

Deface, *v.a.* défigurer; détériorer, dégrader, gâter; effacer, biffer, rayer

Defacement, *s.* défigurement, *m.*; détérioration, dégradation, *f.*; rature, *f.*

Defacer, *s.* destructeur, *m.*, -trice, *f.*

Defalcate, *v.a.* défalquer

Defalcation, *s.* défalcation, déduction, *f.*, retranchement, *m.*; diminution, *f.*; déficit, *m.*; (*embezzlement*) détournement (de fonds), *m.*

Defamation, *s.* diffamation, *f.*

Defamatory, *adj.* diffamatoire, diffamant

Defame, *v.a.* diffamer

Defamer, *s.* diffamateur, *m.*, -trice, *f.*

Default, *s.* faute, *f.*; défaut, manque, *m.*; (*law*) défaillance, *f.*; (*non-appearance*) défaut, *m.*, (*crim. law*) contumace, *f.* *By* or *in* —, par défaut; par contumace. *In — of*, à défaut de, faute de. *To suffer a* —, faire défaut

Defaulter, *s.*, **Defaulting,** *adj.* celui (*m.*, celle, *f.*) qui manque à son devoir *or* qui ne fait pas honneur à ses engagements; délinquant, *m.*, e, *f.*; (*of recruits*) retardataire, réfractaire, conscrit réfractaire, *m.*; (*soldier undergoing punishment*) consigné, *m.*; (*embezzler*) coupable de détournement de fonds, *m.*; (*of public money*) concussionnaire, *m.*; (*person in arrears*) retardataire, *m.f.*, (*debtor*) débiteur en retard, *m.*, (*tax-payer*) contribuable retardataire, *m.*; (*civ. law*) défaillant, *m.*, e, *f.*; (*crim. law*) contumace, *m.f.* **—s' book,** *s.* (*mil.*) registre des punitions, *m.* **—s' room,** *s.* (*mil.*) salle de police, *f.*

Defeasance, *s.* annulation, abrogation, *f.*; condition résolutoire, *f.*; contre-lettre, *f.* *Deed of* —, contre-lettre, *f.*

Defeasible, *adj.* annulable

Defeat, *s.* défaite, déroute, *f.*; (*check*) échec, *m.*; (*overthrow*) renversement, *m.*; (*failure*) insuccès, *m.*; (*law*) annulation *f.*; — *v.a.* défaire, mettre en déroute; (*fig.*) vaincre; (*repulse*) repousser; (*reject*) rejeter; (*baffle*) déjouer; renverser; frustrer; (*evade*) échapper à, éluder; (*make void*) annuler

Defecate, *v.a.* déféquer; — *adj.* déféqué

Defecation, *s.* défécation, *f.*

Defect, *s.* défaut, *m.*; défectuosité, imperfection, *f.*; faute, erreur, *f.*; (*law*) vice, *m.*

Defection, *s.* défection, *f.*; (*rel.*) apostasie, *f.*

Defectionist, *s.* défectionnaire, *m.f.*

Defective, *adj.* défectueux, vicieux; fautif; imparfait; insuffisant; (*gram.*) défectif, défectueux; (*of the compass, nav.*) affolé [ment

Defectively, *adv.* défectueusement; fautive-

Defectiveness, *s.* état défectueux, *m.*; défectuosité, *f.*; imperfection, *f.*; défaut, *m.*; (*gram.*) défectivité, *f.*

Defence, *s.* défense, *f.* *For the* —, (*of witnesses*) à décharge. *In o.'s* —, pour sa défense. **—less,** *adj.*, **—lessly,** *adv.* sans défense. **—lessness,** *s.* faiblesse, incapacité de se défendre, *f.*

Defend, *v.a.* défendre; protéger; préserver

Defendable. *V.* **Defensible**

Defendant, *s.* défendeur, *m.*, défenderesse, *f.*

Defender, *s.* défenseur, *m.*

Defense. *V.* **Defence**

Defensible, *adj.* défendable; soutenable; excusable, justifiable. *To make* —, mettre en état de défense [*adj. f.*, défensive, *s.f.*

Defensive, *adj. s.* défensif, *adj. m.*, défensive,

Defensively, *adv.* défensivement

Defer, *v.a.n.* différer, remettre, ajourner; (*regard*) déférer à. *To — a judgment, a sentence, a decree*, ajourner le prononcé (*or* la prononciation) d'un jugement, d'une sentence, d'un arrêt

Deference, *s.* déférence, *f.* *In — to, out of — to*, par déférence pour

Deferent, *adj.* qui transporte, conducteur; (*astr., anat.*) déférent; — *s.* véhicule, moyen de transport, *m.*; (*astr.*) cercle déférent, *m.*; (*anat.*) canal déférent, *m.*

Deferential, *adj.* respectueux, de déférence; (*anat.*) déférent, déférentiel

Deferentially, *adv.* avec déférence

Defiance, *s.* défi, *m.* *In* —, par défi. *In — of*, au mépris de; en dépit de. *To bid — to, to set at* —, porter un défi à, mettre au défi, défier; braver; se jouer de

Defiant, *adj.* provocant, provocateur, de défi

Deficiency, *s.* défaut, manque, *m.*; insuffisance, *f.*; imperfection, *f.*; (*unproficiency*) faiblesse, *f.*; (*quantity wanting*) manquant, *m.*; (*of accounts*) déficit, *m.*

Deficient, *adj.* qui manque; défectueux, imparfait, insuffisant; (*unproficient*) faible, peu avancé; peu habile; (*arith.*) déficient; — *s.* (*arith.*) déficient, *m.* *To be — in*, manquer de, ne pas avoir, ne pas posséder, être dépourvu de; ... manquer à; être faible *or* &c. en. *He is not — in good will*, il ne manque pas de bonne volonté. *He is — in those qualities*, ces qualités lui manquent, il lui manque ces qualités

Deficiently, *adv.* défectueusement, imparfaitement, insuffisamment; faiblement; peu [habilement

Deficit, *s.* déficit, *m.*

Defier, *s.* personne qui défie *or* qui brave, *f.*, provocateur, *m.*, -trice, *f.*

Defilade, *v.a.* défiler

Defilading, *s.* défilement, *m.*

Defile, *v.a.* souiller; corrompre; débaucher; violer; (*fort.*) défiler; — *v.n.* défiler; — *s.* défilé, *m.* [(*fort.*) défilement, *m.*

Defilement, *s.* souillure, *f.*; corruption, *f.*;

Defiler, *s.* corrupteur, *m.*, -trice, *f.*; (*thing*) chose qui souille, *f.*

Defiling, *s.* souillure, *f.*; corruption, *f.*; (*filing off*) défilé, défilement, *m.*, défilade, *f.*

Definable, *adj* définissable; déterminable
Define, *v a.* définir; déterminer; (*delineate*) dessiner; découper; (*mark*) accuser; marquer; accentuer; (*math.*) décrire
Definer, *s.* définisseur, *m.*, -euse, *f.*
Definite, *adj.* défini, déterminé; (*gram.*) défini; — *s.* défini, *m.*
Definitely, *adv.* d'une manière déterminée
Definiteness, *s.* nature déterminée *or* définie, *f.*
Definition, *s.* définition, *f.*
Definitive, *adj.* définitif; déterminé, positif, précis; — *s.* (*gram.*) déterminatif, *m.*
Definitively, *adv.* définitivement, en définitive; précisément, expressément, positivement
Definitiveness, *s.* nature déterminée *or* positive *or* précise, *f.*
Deflagrability, *s.* combustibilité, *f.*
Deflagrable, *adj.* combustible
Deflagrate, *v.n.* brûler avec flamme; — *v.a.* consumer avec flamme
Deflagration, *s.* déflagration, *f.*
Deflagrator, *s.* déflagrateur, *m.*
Deflect, *v.a.* défléchir, faire dévier; — *v.n.* défléchir, se défléchir, dévier; (*of the needle*) décliner [*needle*) déclinaison, *f.*
Deflection, *s.* déflexion, déviation, *f.*; (*of the*
Defloration, *s.* défloration, *f.*; (*choice*) fleur, élite, *f.*, choix, *m.*
Deflour, Deflower, *v.a.* déflorer
Deflourer, Deflowerer, *s.* déflorateur, *m.*
Deflux, Defluxion, *s.* écoulement, *m.*
Defoliation, *s.* défoliation, défeuillaison, *f.*, effeuillement, *m.*
Deform, *v.a.* déformer; défigurer [ment, *m.*
Deformation, *s.* déformation, *f.*; défigure-
Deformed, *adj.* difforme, contrefait
Deformedly, *adv.* d'une manière difforme
Deformer, *s.* déformateur, *m.*, -trice, *f.*
Deformity, *s.* difformité, *f.*; (*ugliness*) laideur, *f.*
Defraud, *v.a.* frauder, tromper; frustrer; (*deprive*) priver de; dépouiller (de)
Defrauder, *s.* fraudeur, *m.*, -euse, *f.*
Defrauding, Defraudment, *s.* fraude, tromperie, *f.* [couvrir
Defray, *v.a.* (*pers.*) défrayer; (*expenses*) payer,
Defrayer, *s.* défrayeur, *m.*, -euse, *f.*
Defraying, Defrayment, *s.* défrayement, *m.*
Deft, *adj.* joli, gentil; leste, pimpant; adroit; convenable [adroitement
Deftly, *adv.* joliment, gentiment; lestement,
Deftness, *s.* gentillesse, *f.*; adresse, *f.*
Defunct, *adj* défunt, décédé, trépassé; (*fig.*) mort; — *s.* défunt, *m.*, e, *f.*
Defy, *v.a.* défier; faire *or* porter un défi à; provoquer; braver [ment, *m.*
Degeneracy, *s.* dégénération, *f.*, abâtardisse-
Degenerate, *v.n.* dégénérer, s'abâtardir; — *adj.* dégénéré, abâtardi; indigne
Degenerately, *adv.* d'une manière dégénérée
Degenerateness, Degeneration. *V.* **De-**
Degenerative, *adj.* dégénérateur [**generacy**
Deglutinate, *v.a.* décoller
Deglutition, *s.* déglutition, *f.* [ment, *m.*
Degradation, *s.* dégradation, *f.*; avilisse-
Degrade, *v.a.* dégrader; avilir
Degradingly, *adv.* d'une manière dégradante *or* avilissante; (*disparagingly*) *V.* **Disparagingly**
Degree, *s.* degré, *m.*; rang, *m.*; condition, *f.*; ordre, *m.*, classe, *f.*; (*univers.*) grade, *m.*; (*arith.*) tranche, *f.* *By —s*, par degrés, graduellement, peu à peu. *In a high —*, à un haut degré. *In some —, to a certain —*, jusqu'à un certain point. *Of high —*, de haut rang. *Of low —*, de rang peu élevé, d'un rang inférieur; (*mean*) de bas étage
Dehiscence, *s.* déhiscence, *f.*
Dehiscent, *adj.* déhiscent
Deicide, *s.* déicide, *m.*
Deific, -al, *adj.* déifique
Deification, *s.* déification, *f.*
Deify, *v.a.* déifier, diviniser
Deign, *v.n.* daigner; — *v.a.* accorder, daigner
Deism, *s.* déisme, *m.* [accorder
Deist, *s.* déiste, *m.f.*
Deistic, -al, *adj.* déiste
Deity, *s.* divinité, *f.*
Deject, *v.a.* abattre [abattu
Dejectedly, *adv.* avec abattement, d'un air
Dejectedness, *s.* abattement, *m.*
Dejection, *s.* abattement, *m.*; (*med.*) déjection, *f.*
Dejectory, *adj.* évacuant, évacuatif
Delation, *s.* délation, *f.*
Delay, *v.a.* différer, remettre; retarder; (*stop*) arrêter, retenir; — *v.n.* tarder; s'arrêter; — *s.* délai, retard, *m.*, remise, *f.* *With the least possible —*, dans le plus bref délai. *All is not lost that is —ed*, ce qui est différé n'est pas perdu
Delayer, *s.* temporiseur, *m.*
Del credere, *s.* ducroire, *m.*
Dele, *s.* (*print.*) déléatur, *m.*
Delectable, *adj.* délectable, délicieux [ment
Delectably, *adv.* délectablement, délicieuse-
Delectation, *s.* délectation, *f.*
Delegacy, *s.* délégation, *f.*
Delegate, *v.a.* déléguer; — *s.adj.* délégué, *m.*, e, *f.*
Delegatee, *s.* délégataire, *m.f.*
Delegation, *s.* délégation, *f.* [gant, *m.*, e, *f.*
Delegator, *s.* délégateur, *m.*, -trice, *f.*, délé-
Delegatory, *adj.* délégatoire
Deleterious, *adj.* délétère
Delf, Delft, — ware, *s.* faïence de Delft, *f.*
Deliac, *adj.* déliaque [problème déliaque, *m.*
Delian, *s. adj.* Délien, *m.*, -ne, *f.* — *problem*,
Deliberate, *v.n.* délibérer; — *adj.* réfléchi; (*on purpose*) délibéré; (*slow*) lent
Deliberately, *adv.* délibérément, de propos délibéré, avec réflexion, à dessein, exprès; (*slowly*) lentement
Deliberateness, *s.* délibération, *f.*; réflexion, *f.*; circonspection, prudence, *f.*
Deliberation, *s.* délibération, *f.*; réflexion, *f.*
Deliberative, *adj.* délibératif; (*of assemblies*) délibérant
Deliberatively, *adv.* délibérativement
Deliberator, *s.* délibérant, *m.*
Deliberatory, *adj.* délibératoire
Delible, *adj.* délébile, effaçable
Delicacy, *s.* délicatesse, *f.*; (*dainty*) friandise, délicatesse, *f.*; régal, *m.*
Delicate, *adj.* délicat
Delicately, *adv.* délicatement, avec délicatesse
Delicateness, *s.* délicatesse, *f.*
Delicious, *adj.* délicieux
Deliciously, *adv.* délicieusement
Deliciousness, *s.* nature délicieuse, excellence, *f.*; délices, *m.f.pl.*, volupté, *f.*, charme, *m.*
Delict, *s.* délit, *m.*
Deligation, *s.* déligation, *f.*
Delight, *s.* délices, *m.f. pl.*, délice, *m.*, charme, *m.*, volupté, jouissance, joie, *f.*, bonheur, plaisir, *m.* *To take* or *find — in*, se plaire à, &c. (*V. To* **Delight,** *v.n.*)
Delight, *v.a.* faire les délices de, délecter, enchanter, charmer, ravir, réjouir ('*with*,' '*at*,' de), plaire à; — *v.n.* (*in*) faire ses délices (de); (*take pleasure*) se plaire (dans; *before a verb*, à, *with the inf.*), prendre plaisir (à), se faire un plaisir (de), mettre *or* trouver son bonheur (à, dans), se réjouir (de), être enchanté *or* charmé (de). *To be delighted with* or *to*, être enchanté *or* charmé *or* ravi *or* joyeux de
Delightful, *adj.* délicieux; (*pers.*) charmant, ravissant
Delightfully, *adv.* délicieusement, à ravir
Delightfulness. *V.* **Deliciousness**
Delightless, *adj.* sans charmes, sans agréments
Delineament, *s.* délinéation, *f.*
Delineate, *v.a.* délinéer, tracer, esquisser, dessiner; (*depict*) peindre, décrire
Delineation, *s.* délinéation, esquisse, *f.*; (*fig.*) peinture, description, *f.*, portrait, *m.*
Delineator, *s.* délinéateur, dessinateur, *m.*; [(*fig.*) peintre, *m.*
Delineatory, *adj.* descriptif

Delinquency, *s.* délit, *m.*; faute, *f.*; prévarication, *f.*
Delinquent, *s. adj.* délinquant, *m.*, e, *f.*
Deliquesce, *v.n.* tomber en déliquescence
Deliquescence, *s.* déliquescence, *f.*
Deliquescent, *adj.* déliquescent
Deliquium, *s.* (*chem.*) déliquium, *m.*
Delirious, *adj.* délirant, en délire; de délire. *To be* —, avoir le délire, être en délire, délirer. *To become* (or *get*) —, tomber dans le délire
Deliriousness, *s.* délire, *m.*
Delirium, *s.* délire, *m.* — *tremens,* delirium [tremens, *m.*
Delitescence, *s.* état latent, *m.*; retraite, *f.*; (*med.*) délitescence, *f.*
Delitescent, *adj.* latent, caché, secret
Deliver, *v.a.* (*to free*) délivrer (de); (*rescue*) sauver (de); (*give*) délivrer, livrer, remettre; (*a place*) livrer, rendre; (*return*) rendre; (*goods*) livrer; (*a letter or parcel*) remettre; (*letters by post or parcels from house to house*) distribuer; (*a message,* &c.) délivrer, remettre; s'acquitter de; faire; (*bring*) apporter; (*a ball*) lancer; (*a blow*) donner, appliquer; (*say*) dire; énoncer, exprimer; (*a speech*) prononcer, débiter; (*a lecture*) *V.* **Lecture;** (*a charge to a jury*) faire; (*a judgment*) rendre, prononcer; (*publish*) publier; (*of childbirth*) accoucher, délivrer. *To — oneself of,* accoucher de. *To be —ed,* (*of a child*) accoucher (de). *To be —ed immediately!* (*of letters,* &c.) pressé. *—ed free,* rendu à domicile. — **over, up,** livrer; rendre; (*a message*) délivrer, remettre
Deliverable, *adj.* (*com.*) livrable
Deliverance, *s.* délivrance, *f.*
Deliverer, *s.* libérateur, *m.*, -trice, *f.*, sauveur, *m.*; (*com.*) livrancier, *m.*
Delivering, *s. V.* **Delivery;** (*of a judgment or sentence*) prononciation, *f.*, prononcé, *m.*
Delivery, *s.* délivrance, *f.*; (*surrender*) remise, reddition, *f.*; (*of goods*) livraison, *f.*, (*from a railway station*) factage, *m.*; (*of a letter or parcel*) remise, *f.*, (*from a railway station*) factage, *m.*; (*of letters by post or of parcels from house to house*) distribution, *f*; (*law*) tradition, délivrance, remise, *f.*; (*tech.*) décharge, *f.*; conduite, *f.*; (*of speeches*) débit, *m.*; diction, *f.*; (*of a judgment,* &c.) *V.* **Delivering;** (*childbirth*) accouchement, *m.*, délivrance, *f.* *For* —, (*fin., of stocks*) au comptant
Dell, *s.* creux, vallon, *m.*
Delphian, Delphic, *adj.* delphien, delphique, de Delphes
Delphin, *adj.* dauphine (*f.*). — **classic,** *s.* dauphin, *m.* — **edition,** *s.* édition dauphine, *f.*
Delphinia, *s.* delphine, delphinine, *f.*
Delta, *s.* delta, *m.*
Deltoid, *adj.* deltoïde; — *s.* (— *muscle*) deltoïde, *m.*
Deludable. *V.* **Deceivable**
Delude, *v.a.* tromper, abuser, &c. (*V.* **Deceive**). *To — oneself,* se faire illusion, s'abuser
Deluded, *adj.* dans l'illusion, bercé d'illusions, [aveugle
Deluder. *V.* **Deceiver**
Deluge, *s.* déluge, *m.*; — *v.a.* inonder ('*with,*' de)
Delusion, *s.* déception, illusion, *f.*
Delusive, Delusory, *adj.* trompeur; illusoire
Delusiveness, *s.* nature trompeuse *or* illusoire, *f.*
Delve, *v.a.* bêcher, creuser; (*fig.*) sonder, pénétrer
Demagnetization, *s.* démagnétisation, *f.*
Demagnetize, *v.a.* démagnétiser
Demagogic, -al, *adj.* (*things*) démagogique; (*pers.*) démagogue
Demagogism, *s.* démagogisme, *m.*
Demagogue, *s.* démagogue, *m.f.*
Demagogy, *s.* démagogie, *f.*
Demain. *V.* **Domain**
Demand, *v.a.* demander; (*claim*) réclamer; (*require*) exiger; requérir; — *s.* demande, *f.*; requête, *f.*; (*claim*) réclamation, *f.*; (*appeal*) appel, *m.*; (*com.*) demande, *f.*, débit, *m.*; (*politic. econ.*) demande, *f.*; (*outlet*) débouché, *m.*; (*fig.*) recherche, *f.* *In great* —, très demandé, très recherché. *In little* —, peu demandé, peu recherché. *In full of all —s,* pour solde de tous comptes. *On* —, (*of bills payable*) à présentation
Demandable, *adj.* exigible
Demandant, *s.* demandeur, *m.*, -eresse, *f.*
Demander, *s.* demandeur, *m.*, -euse, *f.*
Demarcation, *s.* démarcation, *f.*
Demean, *v.a.* injurier; (*debase*) abaisser, avilir, dégrader. *To — oneself,* s'abaisser, s'avilir, se dégrader, se ravaler; (*behave*) se comporter, se conduire
Demeanour, *s.* allure, *f.*, allures, *f.pl.*; air, *m.*, manières, *f.pl.*, tenue, *f.*; maintien, *m.*; conduite, *f.*
Demency, *s.* démence, *f.*
Dement, *s. adj.* dément, *m.*, e, *f.*; — *v.a. V.* **Dementate**
Dementate, *adj.* dément, en démence, fou; — *v.a.* déranger l'esprit de, faire perdre l'esprit à, rendre fou, aliéner
Dementation, *s.* démence, folie, aliénation mentale, *f.*
Demented, *adj.* dément, en démence, fou
Dementia, *s.* démence, *f.*
Demerit, *s.* démérite, *m.*; faute, *f.*; — *v.n.* démériter
Demeritorious, *adj.* déméritoire
Demeritoriously, *adv.* déméritoirement
Demesmerize. *V.* **Demagnetize**
Demesne. *V.* **Domain**
Demi, *adj.* demi; à demi. — **bath,** *s.* demi-bain, *m.* — **bastion,** *s.* demi-bastion, *m.* — **brigade,** *s.* demi-brigade, *f.* — **cupola,** *s.* four, cul-de-four, *m.* — **distance,** *s.* demi-distance, *f.* — **ditone,** *s.* tierce mineure, *f.* — **god,** *s.* demi-dieu, *m.* — **goddess,** *s.* demi-déesse, *f.* — **john,** *s.* dame-jeanne, *f.* — **lance,** *s.* demi-pique, *f.* — **lune,** *s.* demi-lune, *f.* — **quaver,** *s. V.* **Semiquaver.** — **relief, -relievo,** *s.* demi-relief, *m.*, demi-bosse, *f.* — **rep,** *s.* demi-vertu, *f.* — **semi-quaver,** *s.* triple croche, *f.* — **tint,** *s.* demi-teinte, *f.* — **tone,** *s.* demi-ton, *m.* — **volt,** *s.* demi-volte, *f.* — **wolf,** *s.* chien-loup, *m.*
Demisable, *adj.* affermable
Demise, *v.a.* affermer, donner à ferme *or* à bail, louer; — *s.* translation, transmission, *f.*; (*death*) décès, *m.*, mort, *f.*
Demising, *s.* affermage, louage, *m.*
Demobilization, *s.* démobilisation, *f.*
Demobilize, *v.a.* démobiliser
Democracy, *s.* démocratie, *f.*
Democrat, *s.* démocrate, *m.f.* [(*pers.*) démocrate
Democratic, -al, *adj.* (*things*) démocratique;
Democratically, *adv.* démocratiquement
Democraticalness, *s.* caractère (*m.*) *or* nature (*f.*) démocratique
Democratism, *s.* démocratisme, *m.*
Democratize, *v.a.n.* démocratiser
Demoiselle, *s.* (*bird*) demoiselle, *f.*
Demolish, *v.a.* démolir
Demolisher, *s.* démolisseur, *m.*
Demolition, Demolishing, Demolishment, *s.* démolition, *f.*
Demon, *s.* démon, diable, *m.*
Demoness, *s.* démon, *m.*
Demonetization, *s.* démonétisation, *f.*
Demonetize, *v.a.* démonétiser
Demoniac, *s.* démoniaque, *m.f.*
Demoniac, -al, Demonian, *adj.* démoniaque, diabolique
Demon-ism, -ist, -ology, &c., démonisme, [&c., &c. *V.* page 3, § 1
Demonstrability, *s.* démontrabilité, *f.*
Demonstrable, *adj.* démontrable
Demonstrableness, *s.* démontrabilité, *f.*
Demonstrably, *adv.* démonstrativement, par démonstration
Demonstrate, *v.a.* démontrer
Demonstration, *s.* démonstration, *f.*
Demonstrative, *adj.* démonstratif
Demonstratively, *adv.* démonstrativement
Demonstrator, *s.* démonstrateur, -trice, *f.*
Demoralization, *s.* démoralisation, *f.*
Demoralize, *v.a.* démoraliser
Demoralizer, *s.* démoralisateur, *m.*, -trice, *f.*
Demoralizing, *adj.* démoralisateur

Demosthenic, *adj.* démosthénique
Demotic, *adj.* démotique
Demulcent, *adj. s.* adoucissant, *adj. m.*, e, *f.*, émollient, *adj. m.*, e, *f.*, adoucissant, *s.m.*, émollient, *s.m.*
Demur, *v.n.* hésiter, balancer; (*delay*) temporiser; (*at*) ne pas faire raison (à); (*law*) produire une exception (contre); — *s.* hésitation, incertitude, *f.*, doute, *m.*; difficulté, objection, *f.* — **to,** s'opposer à; se refuser à; refuser; ne pas admettre, ne pas partager; (*represent*) objecter [prude
Demure, *adj.* grave, posé; modeste; réservé;
Demurely, *adv.* gravement; modestement
Demureness, *s.* gravité, *f.*, air grave, *m.*; modestie, *f.*, air modeste, *m.*; réserve, *f.*, air *or* maintien réservé, *m.*; pruderie, *f.*
Demurrage, *s.* surestarie, *f.*, retardement, *m.*; (*payment*) frais de surestarie, *m.pl.*
Demurrer, *s.* esprit indécis, *m.*, personne irrésolue, *f.*, temporiseur, *m.*; opposant, *m.*, e, *f.*, mécontent, *m.*, e, *f.*; (*law*) exception, *f.*
Demy, *s. adj.* (*paper*) coquille, *f.*, papier coquille, papier carré, *m.*; (*size of a book*) petit format, *m.*; (*half-fellow at Oxford*) boursier, *m.*
Den, *s.* antre, repaire, *m.*, tanière, *f.*; caverne, *f.*; (*of robbers*, &c.) repaire, *m.*, caverne, *f.*; (*fig.*) repaire, *m.*; (*of menageries*) loge, *f.*
Denary, *adj.* dénaire, décimal; — *s.* dix, *m.*, dizaine, *f.*
Denationalization, *s.* dénationalisation, *f.*
Denationalize, *v.a.* dénationaliser
Denaturalization, *s.* dénaturalisation, *f.*
Denaturalize, *v.a.* dénaturaliser
Denaturate, *v.a.* dénaturer
Dendrite, *s.* dendrite, *f.*
Dendritic, *adj.* dendritique
Dendro-graphy, -logy, &c. *V.* page 3, § 1
Dendroid, *adj.* dendroïde
Dendrolite, *s.* dendrolithe, *m.*
Dendrometer, *s.* dendromètre, *m.*
Denegation, *s.* dénégation, *f.*
Dengue, *s.* rhumatisme noueux, *m.*
Deniable, *adj.* niable
Denial, *s.* dénégation, *f.*; refus, *m.*; (*law*) déni, *m.*; (*of St. Peter*) reniement, *m.* *Flat* —, dénégation formelle, *f.*; démenti, *m.*; refus net
Denier, *s.* personne qui nie *or* renie *or* refuse, *f.*; (*old coin*) denier, *m.* [droit de cité, *m.*
Denization, *s.* (*Engl. law*) dénization, *f.*; (*fig.*)
Denizen, *s.* citoyen, habitant, *m.*; — *v.a.* naturaliser
Denominate, *v.a.* dénommer, nommer, appeler
Denomination, *s.* dénomination, *f.*; classe, *f.*; secte, *f.* [de sectaire
Denominational, *adj.* particulier; de secte,
Denominative, *adj.* dénominatif
Denominatively, *adv.* dénominativement
Denominator, *s.* dénominateur, *m.*
Denotation, *s.* dénotation, *f.* [signer, montrer
Denote, *v.a.* dénoter, marquer, indiquer, dé-
Denouement, *s.* dénoûment, denouement, *m.*
Denounce, *v.a.* dénoncer
Denouncement. *V.* **Denunciation**
Denouncer, *s.* dénonciateur, *m.*, -trice, *f.*
Dense, *adj.* (*scientifically*) dense; (*commonly*, *of fog, clouds*, &c.) épais, compacte
Densely, *adv.* d'une manière épaisse; en masse; par une foule *or* une population com-
Denseness. *V.* **Density** [pacte
Denshire, *v.a.* (*agr.*) écobuer
Denshiring, *s.* (*agr.*) écobuage, *m.*
Density, *s.* densité, *f.*; (*of fog*, &c.) épaisseur, *f.*
Dent, *s.* dent, *f.*; (*indentation*) dentelure, *f.*; entaille, coche, *f.*; (*mark*) marque, empreinte, *f.*; (*bruise*) bosse, *f.*, creux, renfoncement, *m.*; (*blow*) coup, *m.*; — *v.a.* denteler; faire une entaille *or* une coche à; marquer; (*to bruise*) bossuer, bosseler
Dental, *adj.* dentaire; (*gram.*) dental; — *s.* dentale, *f.* — *surgeon*, chirurgien-dentiste, *m.* — *surgery*, *V.* **Dentistry**

Dentaria, *s.* dentaire, *f.*
Dentate, Dentated, *adj.* denté; dentelé
Denticle, *s.* denticule, *f.*
Denticulate, -d, *adj.* denticulé; dentelé
Denticulation, *s.* dentelure, *f.* [modillon, *m.*
Denticule, Dentil, *s.* (*arch.*) denticule, *f.*;
Dentiform, *adj.* dentiforme
Dentifrice, *s.* dentifrice, *m.*
Dentine, *s.* dentine, *f.*
Dentirostral, *adj.* dentirostre
Dentirostre, *s.* dentirostre, *m.*
Dentist, *s.* dentiste, *m.* *Mechanical* —, professeur de prothèse dentaire, *m.*
Dentistry, *s.* art du dentiste, *m.*, odontotechnie, *f.*; guérison des dents, *f.*; opérations dentaires, *f.pl.* *Mechanical* —, prothèse den-
Dentition, *s.* dentition, *f.* [taire, *f.*
Denudation, *s.* dénudation, *f.*
Denude, *v.a.* dénuder, dénuer, mettre à nu, dépouiller, dégarnir [tion, *f.*
Denunciation, *s.* dénonciation, *f.*; déclara-
Denunciator. *V.* **Denouncer**
Denunciatory, *adj.* dénonciatif
Deny, *v.a.* nier, démentir; renier; refuser; rejeter; (*law*) dénier; (*of visitors*) dire qu'on n'est pas chez soi. *To — oneself*, faire abnégation de soi-même; se refuser (...); (*contradict*) se démentir; (*of visitors*) faire défendre sa porte. *Not to be denied*, incontestable
Deobstruct, *v.a.* désobstruer, désopiler
Deobstruction, *s.* désobstruction, désopilation, *f.*
Deobstruent, *adj. s.* désobstruant, *adj. m.*, *s.m.* (e, *adj. f.*), désopilatif, *adj. m.*, *s.m.* (-ive,
Deodorization, *s* désinfection, *f.* [(*adj. f.*)
Deodorize, *v.a.* désinfecter
Deodorizer, *s.* désinfectant, désinfecteur, *m.*
Deodorizing, *adj.* désinfectant, désinfecteur; — *s.* désinfection, *f.*
Deoxidate, Deoxidize, *v.a.* désoxyder
Deoxidation, Deoxidization, *s.* désoxy-
Deoxygenate, *v.a.* désoxygéner [dation, *f.*
Deoxygenation, *s.* désoxygénation, *f.*
Depart, *v.n.* partir; se retirer, s'en aller; (*go out*) sortir; (*away*) s'éloigner (de); (*deviate*) s'écarter (de); (*desist*) se départir (de), se désister (de); renoncer (à); (*vanish*) s'évanouir; (*die*) mourir; — *v.a.* quitter. *To — this life*, quitter cette vie *or* cette terre *or* ce monde, mourir
Departed, *part. adj.* parti, &c. (*V.* **Depart**); décédé, mort; qui n'est plus; évanoui; absent; — *s.* mort, *m.*, morts, *m.pl.*
Departer, *s.* partant, *m.*
Departing, *s.* *V.* **Departure**
Department, *s.* département, *m.*; division, *f.*; service, *m.*; (*business*) partie, *f.*; (*of linen-drapers' and some other shops*) rayon, *m.*; (*admin.*, *geog.*) département, *m.*
Departmental, *adj.* départemental
Departmentally, *adv.* départementalement
Departure, *s.* départ, *m.*; séparation, *f.*; déviation, *f.*, écart, éloignement, *m.*; désistement, *m.*; renonciation, *f.*, renoncement, *m.*; abandon, *m.*; infraction, *f.*; (*death*) mort, *f.*, trépas, *m.*; (*nav.*) départ, *m.*, partance, *f.*; (*distance, in navig.*) différence en longitude, *f.* *To take o.'s* —, partir. — **platform,** *s.* (*rail.*) quai de départ, *m.*
Depend, *v.n.* (*hang*) pendre; (*on, upon*) dépendre (de); (*rest on*) reposer (sur); (*rely on*) compter (sur); se fier (à); (*believe in*) croire (à), ajouter foi (à). — *on* or *upon it!* comptez-y, comptez là-dessus, soyez-en sûr, croyez-le bien, allez. *He is not to be —ed upon*, on ne peut pas compter sur lui, il ne faut pas se fier
Dependable. *V.* **Reliable** [à lui
Dependence, Dependency, Dependance, *s.* dépendance ('*on*,' '*upon*,' de), *f.*; (*things*) chose qui dépend, *f.*; confiance ('*on*,' '*upon*,' dans), *f.* *Foreign* —, possession, colonie, *f.*

Dependent, Dependant, *adj. s.* dépendant; (*hanging*) pendant, qui pend. *To be — on,* dépendre de
Dependently, *adv.* dépendamment
Dephlegmate, *v.a.* déflegmer
Dephlegmation, *s.* déflegmation, *f.*
Depict, *v.a.* dépeindre, peindre
Depilate, *v.a.* épiler
Depilation, *s.* épilation, *f.*
Depilator, *s.* épileur, *m.*, -euse, *f.*
Depilatory, *adj.* épilatoire; — *s.* épilateur, épilatoire, *m.*
Deplantation. *V.* **Displantation** [épuiser
Deplete, *v.a.* désemplir, vider; diminuer;
Depletion, *s.* diminution, *f.*; épuisement, *m.*; (*med.*) déplétion, *f.* [déplétif
Depletive, Depletory, *adj.* épuisant; (*med.*)
Deplorability. *V.* **Deplorableness**
Deplorable, *adj.* déplorable; pitoyable
Deplorableness, *s.* nature (*f.*) *or* caractère (*m.*) déplorable; état déplorable, *m.* [ment
Deplorably, *adv.* déplorablement; pitoyable-
Deplore, *v.a.* déplorer, plaindre
Deplorer, *s.* personne qui déplore, *f.*
Deploy, *v.a.* déployer; — *v.n.* se déployer; — *s. V.* **Deploying**
Deploying, Deployment, *s.* déploiement, *m. In — distance,* à distance (*or* à intervalle)
Deplume. *V.* **Unplume** [de déploiement
Depolarization, *s.* dépolarisation, *f.*
Depolarize, *v.a.* dépolariser
Deponent, *adj.* déponent; — *s.* (*gram.*) déponent, *m.*; (*law*) déposant, *m.*, e, *f.*
Depopulate, *v.a.* dépeupler
Depopulating, *adj.* dépopulateur [lation, *f.*
Depopulation, *s.* dépeuplement, *m.*, dépopu-
Depopulator, *s.* dépopulateur, *m.*
Deport, *v.a.* déporter. *To — oneself,* se comporter, se conduire
Deportation, *s.* déportation, *f.*
Deportment, *s.* maintien, *m.*; air, *m.*, manières, *f.pl.*, tenue, *f.*; conduite, *f.*
Deposable, *adj.* déposable
Deposal, *s.* déposition, *f.* [(de, sur)
Depose, *v.a.n.* déposer ('*from,*' de; '*to*' [*a fact*],
Deposer, *s.* déposeur, *m.*
Deposing, *adj.* déposant; — *s.* déposition, *f.*
Deposit, *v.a.* déposer; — *s.* dépôt, *m.*; (*com.*) arrhes, *f.pl.*; (*bank.*) versement, *m.*
Depositary, *s.* dépositaire, *m.f.*
Depositing, *s.* dépôt, *m.* [pôt, *m.*
Deposition, *s.* déposition, *f.*; (*depositing*) dé-
Depositor, *s.* (*bank.*, &c.) déposant, *m.*, e, *f.*; (*com.*) dépositeur, *m.*, -trice, *f.*
Depository, *s.* dépôt, *m.*; (*book*) répertoire, *m.*; (*pers.*) *V.* **Depositary**
Depôt, *s.* dépôt, *m.*
Depravation, *s.* dépravation, *f.* [dépraver
Deprave, *v.a.* dépraver. *To become —d,* se
Depravedly, *adv.* avec dépravation [vation, *f.*
Depravedness, Depravement, *s.* dépra-
Depraver, *s.* dépravateur, *m.*, -trice, *f.*
Depraving, *adj.* dépravateur; — *s.* déprava-
Depravity, *s.* dépravation, *f.* [tion, *f.*
Deprecate, *v.a.* détourner, conjurer; repousser; s'opposer à; désapprouver; regretter
Deprecatingly, *adv.* en suppliant; en s'excusant [tion, *f.*; excuse, *f.*
Deprecation, *s.* déprécation, *f.*; supplica-
Deprecative, Deprecatory, *adj.* déprécatif, déprécatoire; suppliant; d'excuse
Deprecator, *s.* suppliant, *m.*, e, *f.*
Depreciate, *v.a.* déprécier; — *v.n.* se déprécier, tomber, perdre de valeur [préciation, *f.*
Depreciating, *adj.* dépréciateur; — *s.* dé-
Depreciation, *s.* dépréciation, *f.*
Depreciative. *V.* **Depreciatory**
Depreciator, *s.* dépréciateur, *m.*, -trice, *f.*
Depreciatory, *adj.* dépréciatif, dépréciateur
Depredate, *v.a.* piller, saccager; (*fig.*) ravager, détruire [*m.*, destruction, *f.*
Depredation, *s.* déprédation, *f.*; (*fig.*) ravage,
Depredator, *s.* déprédateur, *m.*, -trice, *f.*; pillard, *m.*, e, *f.*, brigand, maraudeur, *m.*
Depredatory, *adj.* déprédateur, déprédatif
Depress, *v.a.* (*lower*) baisser; (*humble*) abaisser, humilier; déprimer; (*deject*) abattre, décourager; (*crush*) accabler; ruiner; (*sink*) incliner; (*flatten*) aplatir; (*hollow*) creuser; (*of trade*) faire languir; (*prices*) faire baisser; (*phys.*, *anat.*, *bot.*) déprimer
Depressed, *part.adj.* baissé, &c. (*V.* **Depress**); (*downcast*) abattu; (*low*) bas; (*flat*) aplati, plat; (*hollow*) creux
Depressible, *adj.* dépressible
Depressingly, *adv.* de manière à faire baisser; de manière à faire languir; d'une manière décourageante *or* accablante *or* ruineuse
Depression, *s.* abaissement, *m.*; (*sinking*) affaissement, *m.*; (*of the mind*) abattement, *m.*; (*flattening*) aplatissement, *m.*; (*hollow*) creux, enfoncement, *m.*; (*astr.*, *phys.*, *anat.*, &c.) dépression, *f.*; (*of trade*) stagnation, *f.*; (*of prices*) baisse, *f.* [courageant
Depressive, *adj.* dépressif; accablant; dé-
Depressor, *s.* oppresseur, *m.*; (*anat.*) abais-
Depriment, *adj.* (*anat.*) abaisseur [seur, *m.*
Deprivable, *adj.* privable; déposable, révocable, amovible
Deprivation, *s.* privation, *f.*; (*loss*) perte, *f.*; (*deposition*) déposition, révocation, *f.*; (*of a priest*) interdiction, *f.*
Deprive, *v.a.* priver (de); (*depose*) déposer, révoquer; (*a priest*) interdire
Depriver, *s.* personne qui prive, *f.*
De profundis, *adv. s.* de profundis (*s.m.*)
Depth, *s.* profondeur, *f.*; (*recess*) enfoncement, *m.*; (*abyss*) abîme, *m.*; (*of night*) milieu, *m.*; (*of winter*, &c.) cœur, fort, *m.*; (*obscurity*) obscurité, *f.*, ténèbres, *f.pl.*; (*of colours*) teinte foncée, *f.*; vigueur, *f.*; (*of sound*) gravité, *f.*; (*cunning*) ruse, *f.*; (*math.*) épaisseur, hauteur, *f.*; (*mil.*) hauteur, profondeur, *f.*; (*nav.*) (*of a ship*) hauteur, *f.*, creux, pontal, *m.*, (*of the keel, of a sail*) chute, *f.*, (*of the hold*) creux, *m. To be five feet in —,* avoir cinq pieds de profondeur. *To be in* (*out of*) *o.'s —,* avoir (n'avoir pas) pied. *To get* or *go in o.'s —,* prendre fond. *To get* or *go beyond o.'s —, to find oneself out of o.'s —,* perdre pied; (*fig.*) parler de ce qu'on ne connait pas. **—less,** *adj.* sans profondeur
Depurate, *v.a.* dépurer
Depuration, *s.* dépuration
Depurative, *adj. s.* dépuratif, *adj. m.*, -ive, *f.*, dépuratif, *s.m.*
Depuratory, *adj.* dépuratoire
Deputation, *s.* députation, *f.*; délégation, *f.*
Depute, *v.a.* députer; déléguer
Deputy, *s.* député, *m.*; délégué, *m.*; (*admin.*) adjoint, *m.*; (*law*) substitut, *m.*; (*in compounds*) vice …, sous …, *m. By —,* par procuration. — **chairman,** *s.* vice-président, *m.* — **governor,** *s.* lieutenant-gouverneur, *m.*; (*bank.*, &c.) sous-gouverneur, *m.* — **guardian,** *s.* subrogé tuteur, *m.* — **judge,** *s.* juge suppléant, *m.* — **manager,** *s.* sous-directeur, *m.*; (*of a mine*) maître mineur, *m.* — **mayor,** *s.* adjoint du maire, adjoint, *m.* — **postmaster,** sous-directeur des postes, *m.*
Derange, *v.a.* déranger; troubler; désorganiser; (*pers.*) troubler l'esprit de, déranger le cerveau de. *To be —d,* (*pers.*) avoir le cerveau dérangé, être fou [*m.*; folie, *f.*
Derangement, *s.* dérangement, *m.*; trouble,
Derelict, *adj.* abandonné; — *s.* (*law*) objet abandonné, *m.*, chose délaissée par le propriétaire, *f.*; (*of lands*) relais, *m.*; (*ship*) navire abandonné, *m.*
Dereliction, *s.* abandon, *m.*; négligence, omission, *f.*, oubli, *m.*; (*of water*) retraite, *f.*; (*of lands*) relais, *m.*
Deride, *v.a.* se rire de, se moquer de, tourner en dérision; (*banter*) railler

Derider, *s.* railleur, *m.*, -euse, *f.*, moqueur, *m.*, -euse, *f.*; bouffon, *m.*
Deridingly, *adv.* dérisoirement [dérision, *m.*
Derision, *s.* dérision, moquerie, *f.*; objet de
Derisive, Derisory, *adj.* dérisoire; moqueur
Derisively, *adv.* dérisoirement
Derivable, *adj.* dérivable; qu'on peut tirer; qu'on peut retirer, à retirer; (*from a source*) à puiser; qu'on peut tenir
Derivate, *s.* dérivé, *m.*
Derivation, *s.* dérivation, *f.*
Derivative, *adj.* dérivé; (*med.*) dérivatif; — *s.* dérivé, *m.*; (*med.*) dérivatif, *m.*; (*mus.*) accord
Derivatively, *adv.* par dérivation [dérivé, *m.*
Derive, *v.a.* dériver (de); (*water, words*) dériver, faire dériver; (*obtain*) tirer (de); retirer (de); recueillir (de); tenir (de); (*to experience*) éprouver; trouver (dans); — *v.n.* dériver (de), venir (de)
Derm, Dermis, *s.* derme, *m.*
Dermal, Dermic, *adj.* dermique
Dermatolog-ic, al, -ist, -y. *V.* page 3, § 1
Dermestes, *s.* dermeste, *m.*
Derogate, *v.n.* déroger (à)
Derogation, *s.* dérogation, *f.*
Derogatory, *adj.* dérogatoire; (*to*) dérogeant (à)
Derrick, — crane, *s.* guindal, *m.*, écoperche, grue, *f.* [dervis, *m.*
Dervis, Dervise, Dervish, *s.* derviche,
Descant, *v.n.* discourir, s'étendre; commenter; — *s.* dissertation, *f.*, discours, *m.*; commentaires, *m.pl.*; (*mus.*) chant, air, morceau d'ensemble, *m.*
Descend, *v.a.n.* descendre; (*fall suddenly*) tomber; (*of inheritance*) passer (à), descendre (à); (*lower oneself*) s'abaisser (à). *To be —ed from,* descendre de
Descendant, *s.* descendant, *m.*, e, *f.*
Descendent, *adj.* descendant; tombant; (*proceeding*) qui descend (de), provenant (de), qui provient *or* vient (de); issu (de)
Descendibility, *s.* transmissibilité, *f.*
Descendible, *adj.* qu'on peut descendre, dont on peut descendre; (*from ancestors*) transmissible
Descension, *s.* descente, *f.*; (*fig.*) abaissement, *m.*, chute, *f.*; (*astr.*) descension, *f.*
Descensional, *adj.* descensionnel
Descent, *s.* descente, *f.*; (*inclination*) pente, *f.*; (*disgrace*) chute, *f.*; (*of lineage*) descendance, *f.*; naissance, origine, extraction, *f.*; postérité, *f.*; génération, *f.*; famille, *f.*; transmission, *f.*, ordre de succession, *m.*; (*stock*) souche, *f.*; (*of pistons*) dépression, *f.* — *of the crown,* succession à la couronne, *f.*
Describable, *adj.* descriptible
Describe, *v.a.* décrire; dépeindre
Describer, *s.* descripteur, *m.*
Descrier, *s.* personne qui découvre, *f.*, auteur d'une découverte, *m.*
Description, *s.* description, *f.*; (*sort*) sorte, espèce, *f.*, genre, *m.*; (*of pers., for police purposes, and nav.*) signalement, *m.*
Descriptive, *adj.* descriptif [description
Descriptively, *adv.* descriptivement, comme
Descriptiveness, *s.* nature descriptive, *f.*
Descry, *v.a.* découvrir; apercevoir; regarder; explorer, reconnaître
Desecrate, *v.a.* profaner
Desecration, *s.* profanation, *f.*
Desert, *adj.* désert; solitaire; du désert; — *s.* (*wilderness*) désert, *m.*; solitude, *f.*; (*merit*) mérite, *m.*; — *v.n.a.* déserter; abandonner; quitter; (*mil.*) déserter
Deserted, *adj.* abandonné; désert
Deserter, *s.* déserteur, *m.* [(*mil.*) désertion, *f.*
Desertion, *s.* désertion, *f.*; abandon, *m.*;
Deserve, *v.a.n.* mériter [bon droit
Deservedly, *adv.* justement, à juste titre, à
Deserver, *s.* personne méritante, personne qui mérite, *f.* [— *s.* mérite, *m.*
Deserving, *adj.* de mérite; (*pers.*) méritant;
Deservingly, *adv.* méritoirement; à juste
Deshabille. *V.* **Dishabille** [titre
Desiccant, *adj.* dessiccant, dessiccatif; — *s.* dessiccatif, *m.*
Desiccate, *v.a.n.* dessécher, sécher [ment, *m.*
Desiccation, *s.* dessiccation, *f.*, dessèche-
Desiccative, *adj.s.* dessiccatif, siccatif, *adj.m.*, -ive, *f.*, dessiccatif, siccatif, *s m.*
Desiccator, *s.* dessiccateur, *m.*
Desiderate, *v.a.* désirer
Desideratum, *s.* chose à désirer, chose qui manque, *f.*, desideratum (*pl.* desiderata), *m.*; (*want*) lacune, *f.*
Design, *v.a.* se proposer de, avoir le dessein de; projeter; concevoir; tracer; préparer; arranger; destiner (à); (*draw*) dessiner; — *s.* dessein, *m.*, intention, *f.*, projet, *m.*; plan, *m.*, idée, *f.*; (*drawing, pattern*) dessin, *m.*; (*of inventions*) modèle, *m.* *By —,* à dessein. *With a — to,* avec *or* dans le dessein de
Designable, *adj.* désignable
Designate, *v.a.* désigner; (*appoint*) nommer; — *adj.* désigné; nommé; (*of prelates*) nommé
Designation, *s.* désignation, *f.*; destination, *f.*
Designative, *adj.* désignatif
Designedly, *adv.* à dessein, avec intention
Designer, *s.* architecte, *m.*; auteur, inventeur, *m.*; (*of plots*) machinateur, *m.*; (*of plans, &c.*) dessinateur, *m.*
Designing, *adj.* artificieux [intention
Designless, *adj.*, **Designessly,** *adv.* sans
Desirability. *V.* **Desirableness**
Desirable, *adj.* désirable, à désirer; agréable; appétissant [(*m.*) désirable; avantage, *m.*
Desirableness, *s.* nature (*f.*) *or* caractère
Desirably, *adv.* désirablement, d'une manière désirable
Desire, *v.a.* désirer, souhaiter; (*request*) prier *or* charger (de); (*order*) ordonner; (*tell*) dire; — *s.* désir, *m.*; envie, *f.*; demande, prière, *f.* *By — of,* sur *or* à la demande de. **—less,** *adj.* exempt de désirs
Desirer, *s.* personne qui désire, *f.*
Desirous, *adj.* qui désire; désireux (de); empressé (de); avide (de); curieux (de). *To be — of,* désirer, avoir envie de; être empressé *or* &c. de
Desist, *v.n.* se désister (de); renoncer (à); abandonner; (*cease*) cesser, arrêter
Desistance, *s.* désistement, *m.*; cessation, *f.*, abandon, *m.*; refus, *m.*
Desk, *s.* pupitre. *m.*; bureau, *m.*; (*master's desk, in schools*) chaire, *f.*; (*cashier's*) caisse, *f.*; (*of churches*) lutrin, *m.*; chaire, *f.*
Desman, *s.* desman, *m.*
Desolate, *adj.* désert, inhabité; solitaire, isolé; abandonné; ravagé; (*afflicted*) désolé; — *v.a.* dévaster, désoler, ravager; dépeupler
Desolating, *adj.* désolateur
Desolation, *s.* désolation, *f.*
Desolator, *s.* désolateur, *m.*, -trice, *f.*
Despair, *v.n.* désespérer (de); (*despond*) se désespérer; — *s.* désespoir, *m.* *In —,* au désespoir, désespéré. *His life is —ed of,* on désespère de sa vie, on désespère de le sauver
Despairer, *s.* désespéré, *m.*, e, *f.*, personne au désespoir, *f.*, personne qui désespère (de), *f.*
Despairingly, *adv.* d'une manière désespérante; d'une façon désespérée, désespérément; avec désespoir
Despatch, *v.a.* expédier, dépêcher; envoyer; — *s.* expédition, *f.*; promptitude, *f.*; diligence, *f.*; envoi, *m.*; (*message*) dépêche, *f.* **— boat,** *s.* aviso, *m.* **— box,** *s.* buvard (*m.*) *or* papeterie (*f.*) de voyage. **— vessel,** *s.* aviso, *m.*
Desperado, *s.* désespéré, *m.*, e, *f.*; enragé, *m.*, e, *f.*; énergumène, *m.f.*; risque-tout, casse-cou, *m.*
Desperate, *adj.* désespéré; sans espoir; furieux; enragé; intraitable; acharné, à outrance; terrible. *— fight,* combat acharné, *m.*
Desperately, *adv.* en désespéré, désespéré-

ment; avec fureur, avec acharnement, à outrance; (*greatly*) terriblement, furieusement; (*passionately*) éperdument, désespérément
Desperateness, Desperation, *s.* désespoir, *m.*; fureur, furie, *f.*, acharnement, *m.*
Despicable, *adj.* méprisable; bas; mesquin
Despicableness, *s.* nature méprisable, bassesse, *f.*
Despicably, *adv.* méprisablement, d'une manière méprisable, bassement
Despisable, *adj.* méprisable; à dédaigner
Despise, *v.a.* mépriser; dédaigner
Despisedness, *s.* avilissement, *m.*
Despiser, *s.* contempteur, *m.*, -trice, *f.*
Despising, *s.* mépris, *m.*; dédain, *m.*
Despisingly. *V.* **Contemptuously**
Despite, *v.a.* & *s.* *V.* **Spite;** — *prep.* en dépit de, malgré
Despiteful, &c. *V.* **Spiteful,** &c.
Despoil, &c. *V.* **Spoil,** &c.
Despond, *v.n.* être abattu *or* découragé, se laisser abattre, se décourager; désespérer (de); se désespérer
Despondenc-e, y, *s.* abattement, découragement, *m.*; désespoir, *m.*; désappointement, *m.*
Despondent, Desponding, *adj.* abattu, découragé; désespéré; désappointé
Despondently, Despondingly, *adv.* dans l'abattement; d'un air abattu; avec découragement; dans le désespoir; avec désespoir
Despot, *s.* despote, *m.* [despote
Despotic, -al, *adj.* (*things*) despotique; (*pers.*)
Despot-ically, -ism. *V.* page 3, § 1
Despoticalness, *s.* nature despotique, *f.*
Despumate, *v.a.* despumer
Despumation, *s.* despumation, *f.* [quamer
Desquamate, *v.a.* desquamer; — *v.n.* se des-
Desquamation, *s.* desquamation, *f.*
Desquamatory, *adj.* de desquamation
Dessert, *s.* dessert, *m.*; — *adj.* de dessert. *At* —, au dessert. — **apple (, -pear),** *s.* pomme (, poire) à couteau, *f.* — **knife (-plate, -service, -spoon, -wine,** &c.), *s.* couteau (*m.*, assiette, *f.*, service, *m.*, cuiller, *f.*, vin, *m.*) de dessert. — *spoon and fork* (*to match*), couvert de dessert, *m.*
Destination, *s.* destination, *f.*
Destine, *v.a.* destiner (à); désigner, marquer, indiquer, fixer; condamner
Destiny, *s.* destinée, *f.*, destin, *m.*
Destitute, *adj.* dépourvu (de); (*needy*) dénué (de), privé (de); dans le dénûment, dans la misère, indigent, malheureux; (*forlorn*) abandonné délaissé; — *s.* indigent, *m.*, e, *f.*, malheureux, *m.*, -euse, *f.*
Destitution, *s.* dénûment, *m.*; privation, *f.*, manque, défaut, besoin, *m.*; indigence, misère, *f.*; (*forlornness*) abandon, délaissement, *m.*
Destroy, *v.a.* détruire; faire périr; exterminer; ravager; ruiner
Destroyable, *adj.* destructible
Destroyer, *s.* destructeur, *m.*, -trice, *f.*
Destroying, *adj.* destructeur, destructif; — *s.* destruction, *f.*
Destructi-bility, bleness. *V.* page 3, § 1
Destructible, *adj.* destructible
Destruction, *s.* destruction, *f.*; meurtre, *m.*; massacre, carnage, *m.*; perte, ruine, *f.*; perdition, *f.* [destructioniste, *m.*
Destructionist, *s.* démolisseur, *m.*; (*theol.*)
Destructive, *adj.* destructif, destructeur; meurtrier; funeste; nuisible; — *s.* démolisseur, *m.* *To be* — *of* or *to*, détruire, ruiner, être funeste *or* nuisible à [tive, destructivement
Destructively, *adv.* d'une manière destruc-
Destructiveness, *s.* pouvoir *or* caractère destructeur, *m.*, nature destructive, *f.*; (*in phrenology* destructivité, *f.*
Desudation, *s.* désudation, *f.*
Desuetude, *s.* désuétude, *f.*
Desulphurate, Desulphurize *v.a.* dessoufrer, désulfurer
Desulphuration, *s.* dessoufrage, *m.*, désulfuration, *f.* [sans suite, à bâtons rompus
Desultorily, *adv.* d'une manière décousue,
Desultoriness, *s.* décousu, défaut de suite *or* de liaison *or* de méthode, *m.*; manque d esprit d'ordre *or* d'esprit de suite, *m.*
Desultory, *adj.* décousu, sans suite, sans méthode; à bâtons rompus; irrégulier; capricieux, inconstant; subit, du moment. *In a* — *manner*, d'une manière décousue, sans
Detach, *v.a.* détacher [suite, sans méthode
Detached, *part. adj.* détaché; isolé; (*of houses*) entre cour et jardin, entouré de jardins, isolé
Detachment, *s.* détachement, *m.*
Detail, *v.a.* détailler; — *s.* détail, *m.*
Detailer, *s.* détailleur, *m.*, -euse, *f.*; (*liter.*) détailliste, *m.f.* [(*fine*) détenir
Detain, *v.a.* retenir, arrêter; empêcher; (*con-*
Detainer, *s.* détenteur, *m.*, -trice, *f.*; déten-
Detainment, *s.* détention, *f.* [tion, *f.*
Detect, *v.a.* découvrir; (*catch*) surprendre
Detecter. *V.* **Detector**
Detectible. *V.* **Discoverable**
Detection, *s.* découverte, *f.*
Detective, *s.* agent de la police secrète, *m.*; (*in contempt*) mouchard, *m.* — **officer, -policeman,** *s.* agent de la police secrète, *m.*; (*in contempt*) mouchard, *m.* — **police,** *s.* police secrète, police de sûreté, *f.*
Detector, *s.* personne qui découvre, *f.*; dénonciateur, *m.*, -trice, *f.*; révélateur, *m.*, -trice, *f.*
Detent, *s.* détente, *f.*
Detention, *s.* détention, *f.*; (*delay*) retard, *m.*
Deter, *v.a.* faire peur à, effrayer, décourager; (*from*) détourner (de); dissuader (de); (*prevent*) empêcher (de); (*to stop*) retenir, arrêter
Deterge, *v.a.* déterger [détergent, *s.m.*
Detergent, *adj.* *s.* détergent, *adj. m.*, e, *f.*,
Deteriorate, *v.a.* détériorer; — *v.n.* se dété-
Deterioration, *s.* détérioration, *f.* [riorer
Determinable, *adj.* déterminable; déterminant; expirant; se terminant
Determinate, *adj.* déterminé; fixé; réglé; arrêté, décidé; résolu; décisif, définitif
Determinately, *adv.* déterminément
Determination, *s.* détermination, *f.*; décision, résolution, *f.*; direction, *f.*; (*law*) expiration, fin, *f.*; (*med.*) détermination, *f.*
Determinative, *adj.* déterminant; (*gram.*) déterminatif; — *s.* déterminatif, *m.*
Determine, *v.a.n.* déterminer; régler; décider; se décider; résoudre; se terminer; (*law*) expirer, finir, se terminer
Determinedly, *adv.* déterminément
Detersion, *s.* détersion, *f.* [détersif, *s.m.*
Detersive, *adj.* *s.* détersif, *adj. m.*, -ive, *f.*,
Detest, *v.a.* détester
Detestable, *adj.* détestable
Detestableness, *s.* nature détestable, *f.*
Detestably, *adv.* détestablement
Detestation, *s.* détestation, haine, exécration, *f.* *To hold in* —, détester
Detester, *s.* personne qui déteste, *f.*, ennemi juré, *m.*, ennemie jurée, *f.*
Dethrone, *v.a.* détrôner
Dethronement, *s.* détrônement, *m.*
Dethroner, *s.* détrôneur, *m.* [en restitution, *f.*
Detinue, *s.* détention, *f.* *Action of* —, action
Detonate, *v.n.* détoner; fulminer; — *v.a.* faire détoner
Detonating, *s.* détonation, *f.*; — *adj.* à détonation; fulminant. — *powder*, poudre fulminante, *f.*
Detonation, *s.* détonation, *f.*; fulmination, *f.*
Detract, *v.a.* ôter (à), enlever (à); (*lessen*) diminuer (de), rabattre (de); (*slander*) dé-
Detracter. *V.* **Detractor** [nigrer, détracter
Detracting, Detractive, Detractory, *adj.* détracteur [nigrement
Detractingly, *adv.* par détraction, par dé-
Detraction, *s.* détraction, *f.*
Detract-or, ress, *s.* détracteur, *m.*, -trice, *f.*

Detriment, *s.* détriment, *m.*; préjudice, *m.*; dommage, *m.* [(à); — *s.* valet de cœur, *m.*
Detrimental, *adj.* préjudiciable (à), nuisible
Detrimentally, *adv.* d'une manière préjudiciable *or* nuisible, nuisiblement
Detrital, *adj.* détritique
Detrition, *s.* détrition, usure, *f.*
Detritus, *s.* détritus, *m.*
Detrude, *v.a.* précipiter; repousser; chasser
Detruncation, *s.* (*surg.*) détroncation, *f.*
Detrusion, *s.* repoussement, *m.*, poussée, *f.*
Deuce, *s* diantre, diable, *m.*; (*at play*) deux, *m.* *Two —s,* double deux, *m.* *The —!* diantre! diable! *What the —!* que diantre! que diable! (*V.* **Devil**)
Deuced, *adj.* *V.* **Devilish**
Deucedly, *adv.* diantrement
Deus ex machinâ, *s.* Deus ex machinâ, *m.*
Deuterogamist, *s.* deutérogame, *m.f.*
Deuterogamy, *s.* deutérogamie, *f.*
Deuteronomy, *s.* Deutéronome, *m.*
Deutoxide, *s.* deutoxyde, *m.*
Devastate, *v.a.* dévaster
Devastating, *adj.* dévastateur
Devastation, *s.* dévastation, *f.*
Develop, Develope, *v.a.* développer
Developable, *adj.* développable
Development, *s.* développement, *m.*
Deviate, *v.n.* dévier (de); s'écarter (de); (*err*) s'égarer, errer
Deviation, *s.* déviation, *f.*; (*fig.*) écart, *m.*; (*error*) égarement, *m.*, erreur, *f.*
Deviatory. *V.* **Devious**
Device, *s.*, plan, projet, dessein, *m.*; moyen, expédient, *m.*; stratagème, artifice, *m.*, finesse, *f.*; (*emblem*) devise, *f.*
Devil, *s.* diable, *m.*; démon, *m.*; (*she* —) diablesse, *f.*; (*print.*) apprenti, *m.*; (*highly seasoned dish*) brûlot, *m.*; (*machine*) effilocheuse, *f.*; diable, loup, *m.*; — *v.a.* (*tear up*) effilocher; (*cook.*) accommoder à la diable. *She —,* diablesse, *f.* *— of a man,* diable d'homme. *The — on two sticks,* le diable boiteux. *The —!* diable! *What the —! how the —,* &c., que diable! comment diable, &c. *The — a bit if,* du diable si. *There is the — of it,* c'est là le diable. *The — is in him,* il a le diable au corps. *The — is in it,* le diable s'en mêle. *The — take ...,* (que) le diable emporte ... *To play the —, the very —,* faire le diable, le diable à quatre. *Talk of the — and he is sure to appear,* quand on parle du loup on en voit la queue. — **fish,** *s.* pieuvre, *f.*
Devilish, *adj.* diabolique; (*fam.*) diable de, du diable, satané, maudit; — *adverb.* *V.* **Devilishly**
Devilishly, *adv.* diaboliquement; (*fam.*) diablement; en diable, comme un diable
Devilishness, *s.* nature diabolique, *f.*
Devilkin, *s.* diablotin, *m.*
Devilled, *adj.* (*cook.*) à la diable
Devilry, *s.* diablerie, *f.*
Devious, *adj.* détourné, écarté; errant, vagabond; égaré; (*false*) faux
Devisable, *adj.* imaginable; (*law*) disponible
Devise, *v.a.n.* imaginer; inventer; trouver; projeter; songer à, considérer, voir, chercher; (*plot*) tramer, machiner; (*law*) léguer, disposer par testament de; — *s.* disposition testamentaire, *f.*; (*property devised*) legs, *m.* [taire, *m.f.*
Devisee, *s.* légataire à titre universel, léga-
Deviser, *s.* inventeur, *m.*, -trice, *f.*, auteur, *m.*
Devisor, *s.* légateur, *m.*, -trice, *f.*
Devitrifiable, *adj.* dévitrifiable
Devitrification, *s.* dévitrification, *f.*
Devitrify, *v.a.* dévitrifier
Devoid, *adj.* privé (de); dépourvu (de), dénué (de); (*free*) exempt (de)
Devolution, *s.* dévolution, *f.*
Devolve, *v.a.* remettre, transmettre; (*roll down*) rouler; — *v.n.* échoir (à); être dévolu (à); passer (à); retomber (sur); rouler. *It —s upon you (to ...),* c'est à vous (à *or* de ...), c'est à vous qu'il appartient (de ...)
Devolved, *adj.* dévolu, échu
Devonport. *V.* **Davenport**
Devote, *v.a.* dévouer (à); consacrer (à); vouer (à); livrer (à); (*curse*) maudire [dévotement
Devotedly, *adv.* avec dévouement; (*devoutly*)
Devotedness, *s.* dévouement, *m.*
Devotee, *s.* dévot, *m.*, e, *f.*; bigot, *m.*, e, *f.*, cagot, *m.*, e, *f.*
Devotion, *s.* dévotion, *f.*; (*devotedness*) dévouement, *m.* — **chair,** *s.* prie-Dieu, *m.*
Devotional, *adj.* religieux; de dévotion
Devotionalist, Devotionist, *s.* bigot, *m.*, e, *f.*
Devour, *v.a.* dévorer
Devourer, *s.* dévoreur, *m.*, -euse, *f.*; gourmand, *m.*, e, *f.*; (*things*) destructeur, *m.* *To be a — of,* dévorer
Devouring, *adj.* dévorant; destructeur
Devouringly, *adv.* d'une manière dévorante, avec voracité
Devout, *adj.* dévot, pieux; fervent; sincère
Devoutly, *adv.* dévotement, pieusement; avec ferveur; sincèrement
Devoutness, *s.* dévotion, piété, *f.*
Dew, *s.* rosée, *f.*; — *v.a.* *V.* **Bedew.** — **berry,** *s.* ronce à fruits bleus, *f.* — **claw,** *s.* ergot. *m.* — **drop,** *s.* goutte de rosée, *f.* — **lap,** *s.* fanon, *m.* — **lapped, -lapt,** *adj.* à fanon. — **worm,** *s.* (*earthworm*) lombric, ver de terre, *m.*; (*lobworm*) *V.* **Lobworm**
Dewy, *adj.* de rosée; humide de rosée
Dexter, *adj.* dextre
Dexterity, *s.* dextérité, *f.*; adresse, *f.*
Dexterous, *adj.* adroit, habile
Dexterously, *adv.* adroitement, avec dextérité, habilement
Dexterousness. *V.* **Dexterity**
Dextrine, *s.* dextrine, *f.*
Dey, *s.* dey, *m.*
Dhoora, Dhura, Dhurra, *s.* doura, dourah, *m.*
Dhudeen, *s.* brûle-gueule, *m.*
Diabetes, *s.* diabète, *m.*
Diabetic, *adj. s.* diabétique (*m.f.*)
Diabol-ic, al, -ically. *V.* page 3, § 1
Diabolicalness, *s.* nature diabolique, *f.*
Diacaustic, *adj. s.* diacaustique, *adj. m.f.*, *s.f.*
Diachylon, Diachylum, *s.* diachylon, diachylum, *m.*
Diacodium, *s.* diacode, *m.*
Diaconal, *adj.* diaconal [coustique, *f.*
Diacoustic, *adj.* diacoustique; —**s,** *s.pl.* dia-
Diadem, *s.* diadème, *m.* — **spider,** *s.* épeire diadème, *f.*
Diademed, *adj.* ceint d'un diadème; couronné
Diæresis, *s.* (*gram.*) tréma, *m.*; (*surg.*) diérèse, *f.*
Diagnose, *v.a.* diagnostiquer
Diagnosis, *s.* diagnostic, *m.*; (*art*) diagnostique, *f.*; diagnose, *f.*
Diagnostic, *adj.* diagnostique; — *s.* signe diagnostique, *m.*; —**s,** *s.pl.* (*art*) diagnostique, *f.*
Diagnosticate, *v.a.* diagnostiquer
Diagonal, *adj. s.* diagonal, *adj. m.*, e, *f.*, diagonale, *s.f.*
Diagonally, *adv.* diagonalement [plan, *m.*
Diagram, *s.* diagramme, *m.*; (*draw.*) figure, *f.*;
Dial, *s.* cadran, *m.*; (*round clock*) œil-de-bœuf, *m.* — **maker,** *s.* cadranier, *m.* — **plate,** *s.* cadran, *m.* — **plate maker,** *s.* cadranier, *m.* — **stone,** *s.* cadran de pierre, *m.* — **works,** *s. pl.* cadrature, *f.* — **work maker,** *s.* cadraturier, *m.*
Dialect, *s.* dialecte, *m.*
Dialect-ic, al, -ically. *V.* page 3, § 1
Dialectician, *s.* dialecticien, *m.*, -ne, *f.*
Dialectics, *s. pl.* dialectique, *f.*
Dialist, *s.* cadranier, *m.*
Diallage, *s.* diallage, *f.*
Dialling, *s.* gnomonique, *f.*
Dialog-ism, -ist. *V.* page 3, § 1
Dialogistic, -al, *adj.* dialogique
Dialogistically, *adv.* dialogiquement
Dialogize, *v.n.* dialoguer [logueur, *m.*
Dialogue, *s.* dialogue, *m.* — **writer,** *s.* dia-

Dialysis, *s.* dialyse, *f.*
Dialyt-ic, al, -ically. *V.* page 3, § 1
Dialyze, *v.a.* dialyser
Dialyzer, *s.* dialyseur, *m.*
Diamagnetic, *adj.* diamagnétique
Diamagnetism, *s.* diamagnétisme, *m.*
Diamantiferous, *adj.* diamantifère
Diameter, *s.* diamètre, *m.*
Diametrical, Diametral, *adj.* diamétral
Diametrically, *adv.* diamétralement
Diamond, *s.* diamant, *m.*; (**—s,** *pl., at cards*) carreau, *m.*; (*geom.*) rhombe, *m.*; — *adj.* de diamant; de diamants. *Cut —*, diamant taillé, *m.* — *cut —*, (*fig.*) fin contre fin; à bon chat bon rat. — **beetle,** *s.* entime, *m.* — **cut,** *adj.* taillé en diamant. — **cutter,** *s.* diamantaire, *m.* — **cutting,** *s.* taille du diamant, *f.* — **dust,** *s.* égrisée, poudre de diamant, *f.* — **edition,** *s.* édition diamant, *f.* — **like,** *adj.* semblable au diamant, comme le diamant, diamantaire. — **mine,** *s.* mine de diamants, *f.* — **necklace,** *s.* collier de diamants, *m.* — **powder,** *s. V.* — **dust.** — **ring,** *s.* bague en diamant, *f.*, diamant, *m.* — **setter,** *s.* monteur (*or* sertisseur) de diamants, *m.* — **shaped,** *adj.* en carreau, en losange. — **sparks,** *s. pl.* semence de diamant, *f.* — **worker,** *s. V.* — **cutter**
Diamondize, *v.a.* diamanter
Diapason, *s.* diapason, *m.*; (*of organs*) prestant, *m.*
Diaper, *s.* toile ouvrée, *f.*; (*made up*) linge ouvré, linge damassé, damassé, damas de table, *m.*; (*arch.*) diapré, *m.*; — *v.a.* diaprer; (*linen*) ouvrer, damasser. — **work,** *s* diapré, *m.*
Diapering, *s.* diaprure, *f.*, diapré, *m.*
Diaphaneity, *s.* diaphanéité, *f.*
Diaphanous, *adj.* diaphane
Diaphoresis, *s.* diaphorèse, *f.*
Diaphoretic, *adj.s.* diaphorétique, *adj m.f., s.m.*
Diaphragm, *s* diaphragme, *m.*
Diaphragmatic, *adj.* diaphragmatique
Diarian, *adj* de journal
Diarist, *s.* personne qui tient un journal, *f.*
Diarrhœa, *s.* diarrhée, *f.*
Diarrhœal, Diarrhœtic, *adj.* diarrhéique
Diary, *s.* journal, *m.*; agenda, *m.* *Weekly —*, semainier, *m.*
Diastase, Diastasis, *s.* diastase, *f.*
Diastole, *s.* diastole, *f.*
Diastolic, *adj.* diastolique
Diaton-ic, -ically. *V.* page 3, § 1
Diatribe, *s.* diatribe, *f.*
Dibber, *s.* plantoir, *m.*
Dibble, *v.a.* planter au plantoir; — *v.n. V.* **Dab**; — *s.* plantoir, *m.*
Dibbler, *s.* plantoir, *m.*
Dibbling-machine, *s.* plantoir, *m.*
Dibbs, *s. pl.* (*game*) osselets, *m.pl.*
Dice, *s. pl.* dés, *m.pl.*; — *v.n.* jouer aux dés. — **box,** *s.* cornet à dés, cornet, *m.* — **maker,** *s.* fabricant de dés, *m.* — **player,** *s.* joueur aux dés, *m.*
Dichotomous, *adj.* dichotome
Dichroism, *s.* dichroisme, *m.*
Dichromatic. *V.* page 3, § 1
Dickens. *V.* **Deuce**
Dickey, Dicky, *s.* (*of carriages*) siége de derrière, siége, *m.*; (*shirt-front*) chemisette, *f.*; (*pet bird*) petit oiseau, oiseau, *m.*; —*!* (*to a bird*) petit!
Dicotyledon, *s.* dicotylédone, dicotylédonée, *f.*
Dicotyledonous, *adj.* dicotylédoné, dicotylédone
Dictate, *v.a.n.* dicter; commander (à), faire la loi (à); — *s.* ordre, *m.*; précepte, *m.*, règle, *f.*; inspiration, impulsion, *f.*; voix, *f.*
Dictation, *s.* dictée, *f.*; prescription, injonction, *f.*
Dictator, *s.* dictateur, *m.*
Dictatorial, *adj.* dictatorial; de dictateur; impérieux; magistral
Dictatorially, *adv.* dictatorialement
Dictatorship, Dictature, *s.* dictature, *f.*
Diction, *s.* diction, *f.*
Dictionary, *s.* dictionnaire, *m.*
Dictum, *s.* mot, *m.*, parole, *f.*, dit, *m.*; maxime, sentence, *f.*; adage, proverbe, dicton, *m.*; (*law*) dictum, dispositif, *m.*
Didact-ic, al, -ically. *V.* page 3, § 1
Didactics, *s. pl.* didactique, *f.*
Didapper, *s. V.* **Dab-chick**
Diddle, *v.a.* flouer, filouter, carotter, enfoncer; — *v.n. V.* **Toddle**
Die, *v.n.* mourir (*'with' a person*, avec; *'with' or 'of' a thing*, de); (*sink, faint*) défaillir, manquer; (*cease*) cesser; (*desire*) soupirer (après), mourir d'envie (de); (*of liquors*) s'éventer. — **away,** se mourir, s'éteindre; (*fig.*) mourir, s'éteindre; s'évanouir, se dissiper; disparaître; cesser; (*of the wind*) tomber. — **out,** s'éteindre; disparaître; s'oublier. *To be dying with*, mourir de, se mourir de. *To — for thirst*, mourir de soif. *To — of a broken heart, to — broken-hearted*, mourir de chagrin. *To — the death of*, mourir de la mort de. *To — a natural death*, mourir de mort naturelle, mourir de sa belle mort. *To — hard*, avoir la vie dure; avoir de la peine à mourir, lutter contre la mort
Die, *s.* dé, dé à jouer, *m.*; (*fig.*) hasard, *m.*, chance, *f.*; (*stamp*) coin, *m.* *A cast of the —, the cast of a —*, un coup de dé, un coup de dés, *m.* *The — is cast*, le dé *or* le sort en est jeté. — **sinker,** *s.* graveur en creux, médailleur, *m.* — **sinking,** *s.* gravure en creux, *f.*, art du médailleur, *m.*
Diet, *s.* diète, *f.*, régime, *m.*; (*food*) nourriture, *f.*; alimentation, *f.*; (*board*) table, *f.*; (*assembly*) diète, *f.*; — *v.a.* mettre à la diète *or* au régime; (*feed*) nourrir; — *v.n.* faire diète, être au régime; (*feed*) se nourrir, manger, vivre. *On low —*, à la diète, au régime. *To — oneself*, vivre de régime. — **drink,** *s.* tisane, *f.*
Dietary, *s.* régime diététique, *m.*; (*allowance*) régime alimentaire, *m.*, nourriture, *f.*; — *adj.* diététique; alimentaire
Dietetic (-al), *adj.* diététique; alimentaire; **—s,** *s. pl.* diététique, *f.*
Dietetically, *adv.* diététiquement
Dietetist, *s.* diététiste, *m.*
Dietine, *s.* diétine, *f.*
Differ, *v.n.* différer (de); différer d'opinion (avec); n'être pas de l'avis (de); être en désaccord (avec); (*wrangle*) avoir différend, disputer, se quereller
Difference, *s.* différence, *f.*; dissidence, *f.*; (*dispute, quarrel*) différend, *m.*; brouille, *f.*; (*of money*) appoint, *m.*; — *v.a.* différencier, distinguer. *To make no —*, être égal, ne faire rien. *To split the —*, partager le différend
Different, *adj.* différent
Differential, *adj. s.* différentiel, *adj. m.*, -le, *f.*, différentielle, *s.f.* [rentier
Differentiate, *v.a.* différencier; (*math.*) différentier
Differentiation, *s.* différenciation, *f.*; (*math.*) différentiation, *f.*
Differently, *adv.* différemment; autrement
Difficult, *adj.* difficile
Difficultly, *adv.* difficilement
Difficulty, *s.* difficulté, *f.*; (*trouble*) peine, *f.*; embarras, *m.*; (*need*) gêne, *f.*; (*dilemma*) impasse, *f.* *In* or *into* (*pecuniary*) *—ies*, dans la gêne, gêné. *With —*, difficilement, avec difficulté, avec peine
Diffidence, *s.* défiance, *f.*
Diffident, *adj.* défiant; qui se défie (de); modeste, réservé. *To be — of*, se défier de, n'avoir pas de confiance en, douter de
Diffidently, *adv.* avec défiance; avec réserve; timidement
Diffract, *v.a.* diffracter
Diffraction, *s.* diffraction, *f.*
Diffractive, *adj.* diffractif
Diffrangibility, *s.* diffrangibilité, *f.*
Diffrangible, *adj.* diffrangible
Diffringency, *s.* diffringence, *f.*
Diffringent, *adj.* diffringent

Diffuse, *v.a.* répandre; — *adj.* répandu; étendu; (*prolix*) diffus
Diffusedly, *adv.* diffusément; (*far*) au loin
Diffusely, *adv.* diffusément
Diffuseness, *s.* diffusion, *f.*
Diffusi-bility, bleness. *V.* page 3, § 1
Diffusible, *adj.* diffusible
Diffusion, *s.* diffusion, *f.*; dispersion, *f.*; propagation, *f.*
Diffusive, *adj.* diffusif; qui se répand *or* s'étend au loin, répandu, étendu; (*of style*) abondant
Diffusively, *adv.* diffusivement
Diffusiveness, *s.* diffusion, *f.*
Dig, *v.a.n.* (*with a spade*) bêcher; (*with a pick-axe*) piocher; (*excavate*) creuser; fouiller; (*mines*) exploiter; (*fig.*) ouvrir. — **down,** abattre. — **in,** percer. — **open,** ouvrir. — **out,** extraire, retirer; déterrer. — **through,** percer, transpercer. — **up,** défoncer; (*out*) déterrer; (*plants*) arracher
Digest, *v.a.n.* digérer; méditer, étudier, élaborer; classer, ranger; — *s.* digeste, *m.*
Digester, *s.* personne qui digère, *f.*; (*fig.*) personne qui classe *or* qui range méthodiquement *or* qui met en ordre, *f.*; (*med.*) digestif, *m.*; (*chem., phys., cook.*) digesteur, *m.*
Digesti-bility, bleness. *V.* page 3, § 1
Digestible, *adj.* digestible, susceptible d'être digéré, qui se digère
Digestion, *s.* digestion, *f.*; classement méthodique, *m.*; mûre délibération, *f.*; maturation, *f.*
Digestive, *adj. s.* digestif, *adj. m.*, -ive, *f.*, digestif, *s.m.*
Digger, *s.* bêcheur, *m.*; piocheur, *m.*; (*of trenches, ditches,* &c.) terrassier, *m.*; (*miner*) ouvrier mineur, *m.*; (*for gold*) chercheur d'or, mineur, *m.*; (*instr.*) piocheuse, défonceuse, *f.*; arracheur, arrachoir, *m.*
Digging, *s.* fouille, *f.*; (*of trenches,* &c.) terrassement, *m*; (*of*) creusement, *m.*; (— *up*) défoncement, *m.*; —**s,** *pl.* mines d'or, *f.pl.*; gîtes aurifères, *m.pl.* — **plough,** *s.* charrue défonceuse, *f.*
Digit, *s.* (*measure*) doigt, *m.*; (*arith.*) nombre exprimé par un seul chiffre, *m.*, unité, *f.*; chiffre, caractère, *m.*
Digital, *adj.* digital
Digitalia, Digitaline, *s.* digitaline, *f.*
Digitalis, *s.* digitale, *f.*
Digitate, Digitated, *adj.* digité
Digitation, *s.* digitation, *f.*
Digitiform, *adj.* digitiforme
Digitigrade, *adj. s.* digitigrade, *adj. m.f., s.m.*
Dignification, *s.* élévation, *f.*
Dignified, *adj.* constitué en dignité, revêtu d'une dignité; (*fig.*) digne, plein de dignité; — *part.* *V.* **Dignify**
Dignify, *v.a.* dignifier; élever à une dignité; illustrer; ennoblir; honorer; (*ironically*) décorer ('*with,*' de)
Dignitary, *s.* dignitaire, *m.*
Dignity, *s.* dignité, *f.*
Digress, *v.n.* digresser, faire une digression; (*from*) s'écarter (de); (*into*) s'égarer (dans)
Digresser, *s.* digresseur, *m.*
Digression, *s.* digression, *f.*
Digressional, *adj.* de digression
Digressive, *adj.* digressif
Digressively, *adv.* digressivement, par digression
Dihedral, *adj.* dièdre
Dike, *s.* digue, *f.*; (*ditch*) fossé, *m.*; — *v.a.* diguer; fossoyer
Dilacerate, *v.a.* dilacérer
Dilaceration, *s.* dilacération, *f.*
Dilapidate, *v.a.* délabrer, dégrader; (*squander*) dilapider; — *v.n.* se délabrer, se dégrader, tomber en ruines
Dilapidation, *s.* (*decay*) délabrement, *m.*; (*waste*) dilapidation, *f.*
Dilapidator, *s.* dilapidateur, *m.*, -trice, *f.*
Dilatability, *s.* dilatabilité, *f.*
Dilatable, *adj.* dilatable
Dilatation, *s.* dilatation, *f.*
Dilatator, *s.* dilatateur, *m.*
Dilate, *v.a.* dilater; — *v.n.* se dilater; (*descant*) s'étendre (sur)
Dilater, *s.* dilateur, *m.*
Dilation, *s.* dilatation, *f.*; (*old*) dilation, *f.*, délai, *m.*
Dilatorily, *adv.* lentement, tardivement; (*law*) dilatoirement
Dilatoriness, *s.* négligence, lenteur, nature tardive, *f.*
Dilatory, *adj.* négligent, lent; tardif; en retard; long; (*law*) dilatoire
Dilemma, *s.* alternative, *f.*; (*log.*) dilemme, *m.*
Dilemmatic, *adj.* dilemmatique
Dilettante, *s.* dilettante, *m.* (*pl.* dilettanti)
Dilettantism, *s.* dilettantisme, *m.*
Diligence, *s.* diligence, *f.*; (*care*) soin, *m.*; assiduité, *f.*
Diligent, *adj.* diligent
Diligently, *adv.* diligemment
Dill, *s.* (*bot.*) aneth, *m.*
Dilly-dally, *v.n.* lanterner, barguigner
Dilly-dally, Dilly-dallying, *s.* lanternerie, *f.*, barguignage, *m.*
Dilogy, *s.* dilogie, *f.*
Diluent, *adj. s.* délayant, *adj. m.*, e, *f.*, délayant, *s.m*
Dilutable, *adj.* délayable
Dilute, *v.a.* délayer, détremper; (*of liquids*) étendre d'eau, diluer; (*weaken*) affaiblir; — *adj.* *V.* **Diluted**
Diluted, *part. adj.* délayé, &c. (*V.* **Dilute,** *v.a.*)
Diluter, *s.* délayant, *m.*
Diluting, Dilution, *s.* délaiement, *m.*; (*of liquids*) dilution, *f.*; (*weakening*) affaiblissement, *m.*
Diluvial, Diluvian, *adj.* diluvien, diluvial
Diluvium, *s.* diluvium, *m.*
Dim, *adj.* obscurci, trouble; confus, indistinct; (*dark*) obscur, sombre; (*dull*) terne, pâle, sans éclat; (*of light*) blafard; (*of the mind*) peu ouvert, obtus; (*faint*) faible; — *v.a.* obscurcir; troubler; (*dazzle*) éblouir; (*prevent from seeing*) offusquer; (*sully*) ternir, ternir l'éclat de; (*surpass*) éclipser. — **sight,** *s.* vue trouble *or* obscurcie, *f.* — **sighted,** *adj.* qui a la vue trouble *or* obscurcie; dénué de pénétration
Dime, *s.* (*American coin*) dime, *m.*
Dimension, *s.* dimension, *f.*; étendue, *f.*
Diminish, *v.a.n.* diminuer; amoindrir; (*take away*) retrancher (de), ôter (de); (*lower*) abaisser
Diminishable, *adj.* susceptible de diminution, diminuable
Diminuendo, *adv. s.* diminuendo (*s.m.*)
Diminution, *s.* diminution, *f.*; amoindrissement, *m.*
Diminutive, *adj.* petit; minime; chétif; (*gram.*) diminutif; — *s.* diminutif, *m.*
Diminutively, *adv.* diminutivement, en diminutif, en petit
Diminutiveness, *s.* petitesse, exiguïté, *f.*
Dimissory, *adj.* dimissorial. *Letter* —, lettre dimissoriale, *f.*, dimissoire, *m.*
Dimity, *s.* basin, *m.*
Dimly, *adv.* obscurément; confusément, indistinctement; faiblement; sans éclat
Dimming, *s.* obscurcissement, *m.*
Dimmish, *adj.* un peu obscur *or* &c. (*V.* **Dim,** *adj.*)
Dimness, *s.* obscurcissement, *m.*; obscurité, *f*; faiblesse, *f.*; couleur terne, *f.*
Dimple, *s.* fossette, *f.*; — *v.a.n.* former des fossettes; (*fig.*) se plisser, se rider
Dimpled, Dimply, *adj.* à fossettes; (*fig.*) plissé, ridé
Din, *s.* bruit, tumulte, fracas, *m.*; (*of arms*) cliquetis, *m.*; — *v.a.* étourdir; rebattre; (*repeat*) corner; — *v.n.* résonner, retentir
Dinaric, *adj.* dinarique
Dine, *v.n.* dîner ('*on,*' de, avec); — *v.a.* donner à dîner à. — **out,** dîner dehors; dîner en ville. *To — with Duke Humphrey,* dîner par cœur
Diner, *s.* dîneur, *m.*, -euse, *f.* — **out,** *s.* habitué (*m.*, e, *f.*) de restaurant; (*sponger*) coureur (*m.*, -euse, *f.*) de dîners, pique-assiette, *m.f.*
Ding, *s.* (*of bells*) drelin, *m.* — **dong,** *s.* carillon, *m*
Dinginess, *s.* aspect *or* air sombre, *m.*; couleur sombre, *f.*; couleur terne, *f.*
Dingle, *s.* vallon, *m.* — **dangle,** *adv.* en pendillant
Dingy, *adj.* sombre; terne; (*dirty*) sale; noirci
Dining, *s.* dîner, *m.* — **hall,** *s.* réfectoire, *m.*;

salle à manger, *f.* — **house,** *s.* restaurant, *m.* — **room,** *s.* salle à manger, *f.*; (*of schools, convents,* &c.) réfectoire, *m.* — **rooms,** *s. pl.* (*public*) salons de restaurant, *m pl.*, restaurant, *m.* — **table,** *s.* table de salle à manger, table à manger, table, *f.*

Dinner, *s.* dîner, *m.* *To play —s,* faire la dînette. — *is ready,* — *is on the table,* le dîner est servi; (*of servants*) madame est servie, monsieur est servi, on a servi. — **bell,** *s.* cloche du dîner, *f.* — **dress,** *s. V.* **Full dress** (*at Letter* **F**). — **hour,** *s. V.* — **time.** — **hunter,** *s. V.* **Diner-out.** — **eater,** *s.* dineur, *m.*, -euse. *f.* — **knife,** *s.* couteau de table, *m.* —**less,** *adj.* sans dîner. — **mat,** *s.* dessous de plat, *m.* — **party,** *s.* dîner, *m.* — **plate,** *s.* assiette plate, *f.* — **service,** *s.* service de table, *m.* — **table,** *s.* table servie pour le dîner, *f.*; table, *f.* — **time,** *s.* temps du dîner, *m.*; (*hour*) heure du dîner, *f.* — **waggon,** *s.* servante, table de décharge, *f.*

Dinosaurian, *s.* dinosaurien, *m.*

Dinotherium, *s.* dinothérium, *m.*

Dint, *s.* force, puissance, *f.*; (*blow*) coup, *m.*; (*indentation,* &c.) *V.* **Dent;** — *v.a.* marquer, faire une marque à *or* sur; (*to bruise*) bossuer, bosseler. *By — of,* à force de

Diocesan, *adj.* diocésain; — *s.* évêque diocésain, *m.*

Diocese, *s.* diocèse, *m.*

Diodon, *s.* diodon, *m.*

Dionæa, *s.* dionée, *f.*

Dioptric, -al, *adj.* dioptrique; —**s,** *s.pl.* dioptrique, *f.*

Diorama, *s.* diorama, *m.*

Dioramic, *adj.* dioramique

Dip, *v.a.n.* tremper; plonger; (*draw out*) puiser; (*engage*) engager; s'engager; (*in books*) parcourir; (*fall*) s'abaisser; incliner, s'incliner, décliner; — *s.* plongement, plongeon, *m.*; immersion, *f.*; (*tech.*) plongée, *f.*, plongement, *m.*; (*fall*) abaissement, *m.*, inclinaison, *f.*; (*of the horizon*) dépression, *f.*; (*of the needle*) inclinaison, déclinaison, *f.*; (*hollow*) enfoncement, creux, bas-fond, *m.*; (*candle*) chandelle plongée, chandelle à la baguette, *f.*; (*of ink*) plumée, *f.* *Dipped candle,* chandelle plongée, chandelle à la baguette, *f.* — **chick,** *s. V.* **Dab-chick**

Diphtheria, *s.* diphthérie, angine couenneuse, *f.*

Diphtheric, Diphtheritic, *adj.* diphthéritique

Diphthong, *s.* diphthongue, *f.*

Diploe, *s.* (*anat.*) diploé, *m.*

Diploma, *s.* diplôme, *m.*

Diplomacy, *s.* diplomatie, *f.*

Diplomat, *s.* diplomate, *m.*

Diplomat-ic, al, -ically. *V.* page 3, § 1

Diplomatics, *s. pl.* diplomatique, *f.*

Diplomatist, *s.* diplomate, *m.*

Dipper, *s.* plongeur, *m.*; (*ladle*) cuiller, *f.*; (*paint.*) pincelier, *m.*; (*bird*) cincle, *m.*

Dipping, *s.* plongement, *m*; immersion, *f.*; (*fall*) abaissement, *m.*, inclinaison, *f.*; (*reading*) lecture rapide, *f.* — **needle,** *s.* aiguille aimantée, *f.* — **rod,** *s.* sonde, *f.*

Dipsas, *s.* dipsade, *f.*

Dipsomania, *s.* dipsomanie, *f.*

Dipsomaniac, *adj. s.* dipsomane, *m.f.*

Dipteral, *adj.* (*zool.*) diptère; (*arch.*) diptérique

Dipteran, *s.* (*zool.*) diptère, *m.*

Dipterous, *adj.* (*zool.*) diptère

Dire, *adj.* terrible, affreux, cruel

Direct, *adj.* direct; (*straight*) droit; (*express*) exprès, formel, positif, clair; (*adverb.*) directement; — *s.* (*mus.*) guidon, *m.*; — *v.a.* diriger; conduire; (*refer*) rapporter; (*o.'s own attention*) porter; (*someone else's attention*) appeler; (*order,* &c.) ordonner, commander, enjoindre, charger (de); conseiller (de); indiquer, enseigner, renseigner; (*letters, parcels*) adresser; mettre l'adresse à

Direction, *s.* direction, *f.*; conduite, *f.*; (*way*) sens, côté, *m.*; (*order,* &c.) ordre, *m.*; instruction, *f.*; indication, *f.*; (*of letters,* &c.) adresse, suscription, *f.* *In all —s,* de tous côtés

Directive, *adj.* qui dirige, directeur, qui guide; qui indique, indicatif

Directly, *adv.* directement; (*at once*) à l'instant, tout de suite, immédiatement; (*as soon as*) aussitôt que

Directness, *s.* direction en droite ligne, *f.*; [(*uprightness*) droiture, *f.*

Director, *s.* directeur, *m.*; (*of the Bank of France*) régent, *m.*; (*head*) chef, *m.*; (*things*) guide, *m.*

Directorate, *s* directorat, *m.*; directeurs, *m.pl.*

Directorial, *adj* directorial, de directeur

Directorship, *s.* direction, *f.*, directorat, *m.*

Directory, *s.* directoire, *m.*; (*com.*) conseil d'administration, conseil des directeurs, *m.*, directeurs, *m.pl.*, direction, *f.*; (*a book*) almanach, annuaire, *m.*; almanach des adresses, *m.*; (*guide*) guide, *m.*; — *adj. V.* **Directive**

Directress, Directrix, *s.* directrice, *f.*

Direful, *adj. V.* **Dire**

Direfully, *adv.* terriblement, affreusement, cruellement

Direfulness, Direness, *s.* horreur, calamité, *f.*

Direly. *V.* **Direfully**

Dirge, *s.* chant funèbre, chant de mort, chant, *m.*

Dirigent, *s.* (*geom.*) directrice, *f.*

Dirk, *s.* sabre-poignard, *m.*, dague, *f.*; poignard, *m.*

Dirt, *s.* (*filth*) saleté, ordure, *f.*; crasse, *f.*; (*mud*) boue, crotte, *f.*; (*earth*) terre, *f.*; — *v.a. V.* **Dirty,** *v.a.* — **cheap,** *adj.* à vil prix, pour rien. — **eater,** *s.* géophage, *m.f.* — **eating,** *s.* géophagie, *f.*; *adj.* géophage. — **pie,** *s.* pâté en terre, *m.*

Dirtily, *adv.* salement, malproprement; bassement

Dirtiness, *s.* saleté, malpropreté, *f.*; (*meanness*) bassesse, vilenie, *f.*

Dirty, *adj.* sale, malpropre; crasseux; (*with mud*) crotté; (*mean*) bas, vilain, sale; — *v.a.* salir; (*with mud*) crotter; (*pollute*) souiller. — *fellow,* saligaud, salop, *m.* — *work,* saleté, *f.* *To be —,* (*on the roads*) faire sale

Disability, *s.* impuissance, *f.*; (*of mind*) incapacité, *f.*; (*law*) incapacité, inhabilité, *f.*

Disable, *v.a.* rendre incapable (de); mettre hors d'état (de); mettre dans l'impuissance (de); empêcher (de); exclure (de); (*destroy*) détruire, mettre hors de service; (*weaken*) affaiblir; (*in battles*) mettre hors de combat; (*a battery*) démonter; (*ships*) désemparer; (*law*) rendre incapable (de), rendre inhabile (à), frapper d'incapacité (pour)

Disabled, *adj.* rendu incapable, incapable (de); hors d'état (de); empêché (de); hors de service; (*in battles*) hors de combat; (*sick*) invalide; impotent; estropié; perclus; (*of ships*) désemparé, hors de service. — *soldier,* invalide, *m.* — *sailor,* invalide de la marine, *m.*

Disablement, *s. V.* **Disability;** (*from work*) incapacité de travail, perclusion, infirmité, *f.*

Disabuse, *v.a.* désabuser

Disabusing, *s.* désabusement, *m.*

Disaccustom, *v.a.* déshabituer, désaccoutumer

Disadvantage, *s.* désavantage, *m.*; inconvénient, *m.*; (*loss*) perte, *f.* *At a —, to —,* avec désavantage, à son désavantage; à perte

Disadvantageous, *adj.* désavantageux

Disadvantageously, *adv.* désavantageusement

Disadvantageousness. *V.* **Disadvantage**

Disaffect, *v.a.* désaffectionner, mécontenter, indisposer, aliéner; (*dislike*) ne pas aimer; (*shun*) éviter; (*disorder*) déranger

Disaffected, *adj.* désaffectionné, mécontent, mal disposé (' *towards,*' pour)

Disaffectedly, *adv.* avec désaffection, avec mécontentement

Disaffection, *s.* désaffection (' *towards,*' pour), *f.*

Disafforest, *v.a.* enlever au régime des lois forestières; (*denude*) déboiser

Disafforestation, *s.* déboisement, *m.*

Disaggregate, *v.a.* désagréger

Disaggregation, *s.* désagrégation, *f.*

Disagree, *v.n.* différer; n'être pas d'accord, ne

pas s'accorder, être en désaccord; (—*in opinion with*) différer d'opinion (avec), n'être pas de l'avis (de); (*to a proposal*, &c.) refuser d'accéder (à); (*quarrel*) se brouiller; (*make ill*) faire mal (à), incommoder, ne valoir rien (à), être contraire (à), être nuisible (à), ne pas réussir (à); ne pas bien passer, mal passer; (*with o.'s stomach, o.'s constitution*) ne pas convenir (à son estomac, à son tempérament). *My dinner—d with me*, mon dîner n'a pas bien passé, mon dîner a mal passé

Disagreeable, *adj.* désagréable. — *thing*, chose désagréable, *f.*; désagrément, *m.*

Disagreeableness, *s.* désagrément, *m.*; nature désagréable, *f.*

Disagreeably, *adv.* désagréablement

Disagreement, *s.* désaccord, *m.*; disconvenance, *f.*; différence, dissemblance, diversité, *f.*; différence d'opinion, *f.*; (*dissent*) dissidence, *f.*; (*quarrel*) brouille, brouillerie, *f.*

Disallow, *v.a.n.* désapprouver; désavouer; rejeter; refuser; (*prohibit*) défendre, interdire

Disallowable, *adj.* défendu, interdit, qui n'est pas permis

Disallowance, *s.* désapprobation, *f.*; refus d'admettre, *m.*; défense, *f.*

Disappear, *v.n.* disparaître

Disappearance, Disappearing, *s.* disparition, *f.*

Disappoint, *v.a.* désappointer; (*of hopes*) tromper, frustrer, trahir; désillusionner; (*fam.*) attraper; (*vex*) contrarier; (*deprive*) priver (de); (*break a promise*) faire faux bond (à), manquer de parole (à); (*defeat*) faire manquer, faire échouer, déjouer, déconcerter

Disappointment, *s.* désappointement, *m.*; déception, frustration, *f.*; désillusion, *f.*; (*annoyance*) contrariété, *f.*; contre-temps, *m.*; mécompte, *m.*; déconvenue, *f.*

Disapprobation, *s.* désapprobation, improbation, *f.*

Disapprobative, *adj.* désapprobatif

Disapprobatively, *adv.* désapprobativement

Disapprobatory, *adj.* désapprobateur

Disapprovable, *adj.* désapprouvable

Disapproval. *V.* **Disapprobation**

Disapprove, *v.a.* (—*of*) désapprouver; blâmer

Disapprover, *s.* désapprobateur, *m.*, -trice, *f.*

Disapproving, *adj.* désapprobateur, désapprobatif

Disapprovingly, *adv.* désapprobativement

Disarm, *v.a.n.* désarmer

Disarmament, Disarming, *s.* désarmement, *m.*

Disarrange, *v.a.* déranger; désajuster

Disarrangement, *s.* dérangement, *m.*; désajustement, *m.*; désordre, *m.*

Disarray, *v.a.* déranger, mettre en désarroi *or* en désordre; mettre en déroute; —*s.* désarroi, désordre, *m.*, confusion, *f.*; déroute, *f.*

Disarticulate, *v.a.* désarticuler

Disarticulation, *s.* désarticulation, *f.*

Disassociate, &c. *V.* **Dissociate,** &c.

Disaster, *s.* désastre, *m.*; malheur, *m.*

Disastrous, *adj.* désastreux

Disastrously, *adv.* désastreusement

Disastrousness, *s.* nature désastreuse, *f.*

Disavow, *v.a.* désavouer

Disavowal, *s.* désaveu, *m.*

Disband, *v.a.* (*mil.*) licencier; (*scatter*) disperser; —*v.n.* se débander; se disperser, se séparer; se dissoudre, se désorganiser; (*mil.*) être licencié. *To — themselves*, se débander

Disbanding, Disbandment, *s.* (*mil.*) licenciement, *m.*; (*fig.*) débandement, *m.*, dispersion, séparation, *f.*

Disbar, *v.a.* rayer du tableau (des avocats)

Disbarment, Disbarring, *s.* radiation (du tableau des avocats), *f.*

Disbelief, *s.* incrédulité, *f.*, refus de croire, manque de foi, *m.*

Disbelieve, *v.a.* ne pas croire. *To — every word of*, ne pas croire un seul mot de

Disbeliever, *s.* incrédule, *m.f.*

Disbud, *v.a.* ébourgeonner

Disbudding, *s.* ébourgeonnage, ébourgeonnement, *m.*

Disburden, *v.a.* décharger; (*fig.*) débarrasser; (*relieve*) soulager.

Disburse, *v.a.* débourser; (*spend*) dépenser

Disbursement, *s.* déboursement, déboursé, *m.*, mise de fonds, *f.*, paiement, *m.*, dépense, *f.*

Disburthen, *V.* **Disburden**

Disc, *s.* disque, *m.*

Discant. *V.* **Descant**

Discard, *v.a.* renvoyer, congédier; (*reject*) écarter, mettre de côté; (*exclude*) exclure éliminer; supprimer; (*at cards*) écarter

Disceptation, *s.* disceptation, *f.*

Discern, *v.a.n.* discerner, distinguer

Discerner, *s.* observateur, *m.*, -trice, *f.*; juge, *m*

Discernible, *adj.* discernable

Discernibly, *adv.* discernablement

Discerning, *adj.* judicieux; éclairé; attentif

Discerningly, *adv.* avec discernement

Discernment, *s.* discernement, *m.*

Discharge, *v.a.n.* décharger; (*exonerate*) débarrasser, décharger; (*fire-arms*) décharger; (*arrows*) décocher, lancer; (*debts*) payer, liquider, acquitter; (*duties*) remplir, accomplir, s'acquitter de; (*dismiss*) renvoyer, congédier, donner congé à; (*from prison*) élargir, libérer, mettre en liberté; (*exempt*) exempter (de); dispenser (de); délier (de); (*absolve*) acquitter, libérer; (*let out*) lâcher, laisser échapper; (*throw off, emit*) lancer, jeter; (*suppurate*) suppurer; (*mil., nav.*) congédier; (*a man-of-war*) désarmer. *To — with ignominy*, (*mil.*) dégrader

Discharge, *s.* décharge, *f.*; (*of fire-arms*) décharge, *f.*; (*of musketry*) décharge, *f.*; (*of cannon*) décharge, *f.*; volée, *f.*; (*of arrows*) décochement, *m.*, décharge, *f.*; (*of a debt, payment*) acquittement, *m.*; (*from a debt: release or receipt*) décharge, *f.*; quittance, *f.*; (*of duties*) accomplissement, *m.*; exécution, *f.*; exercice, *m.*; (*exemption*) exemption, *f.*; exemption de service, *f.*; libération, *f.*; (*acquittal*) acquittement, *m.*; (*dismissal*) congé, *m.*; renvoi, *m.*; (*from prison*) élargissement, *m*, mise en liberté, *f.*; (*of liquids*, &c.) décharge, *f.*; (*of humour, electricity*) écoulement, *m.*; (*from a sore*) suppuration, *f.*; (*from the bowels*) évacuation, *f.*; (*emission*) émission, *f.*; (*fig.*) épanchement, *m.*; (*law*) décharge, *f.*; (*mil.*) congé absolu, congé, *m.* — *with ignominy*, (*mil.*) dégradation, *f.* — **pipe,** *s.* tuyau de décharge, *m.*

Dischargeable, *adj.* (*pers.*) *V.* **Dismissable**

Discharger, *s.* (*phys.*) excitateur, *m.*

Discharging, *s.* *V.* **Discharge,** *s.*; (*of a man-of-war*) désarmement, *m.* — **cock,** *s.* robinet de vidange, *m.* — **pipe,** *s.* tuyau de vidange, *m.* — **rod,** *s.*, — **tongs,** *s. pl.* (*phys.*) excitateur, *m.*

Disciple, *s.* disciple, *m.*; — *v.a.* instruire

Discipleship, *s.* qualité de disciple, *f.*

Disciplinable, *adj.* disciplinable

Disciplinarian, *s.* personne stricte sur la discipline, *f.*; — *adj.* disciplinaire. *To be a good* —, entendre bien la discipline, savoir tenir des élèves *or* une classe

Disciplinarily, *adv.* disciplinairement

Disciplinary, *adj.* disciplinaire

Discipline, *s.* discipline, *f.*; — *v.a.* discipliner

Disciplining, *s.* disciplinement, *m.*

Disclaim, *v.a.* désavouer; renier; nier, se défendre de; répudier, rejeter; décliner; renoncer à

Disclaimer, *s.* désaveu, *m.*; négation, *f.*; renonciation, *f.*; (*pers.*) personne qui désavoue *or* renie *or* nie, personne qui renonce (à), *f.*

Disclose, *v.a.* découvrir; révéler; divulguer

Discloser, *s.* révélateur, *m.*, -trice, *f.*

Disclosure, *s.* découverte, *f.*; révélation, *f.*; divulgation, *f.*; déclaration, *f.*; confidence, *f.*

Discoid, Discoidal, *adj.* discoïde, discoïdal

Discoloration, Discolouring, *s.* décoloration, *f.*

Discolour, *v.a.* décolorer. *To become —ed*, se [décolorer

Discomfit, *v.a.* défaire, mettre en déroute, tailler en pièces; (*fig.*) dérouter
Discomfiture, *s.* défaite, déroute, déconfiture, *f.*
Discomfort, *s.* désagrément, *m.*; incommodité, *f.*; malaise, *m.*; gêne, *f.*; privation, *f.*; affliction, douleur, *f.*; peine, *f.*; — *v.a.* incommoder, gêner; inquiéter; affliger, attrister, désoler
Discommode, &c. *V.* **Incommode,** &c.
Discompose, *v.a.* décomposer; déranger; (*disconcert*) troubler; (*vex*) irriter; chagriner
Discomposure, *s.* décomposition, *f.*; dérangement, *m.*; (*of mind*) désordre, trouble, *m.*
Disconcert, *v.a.* déconcerter
Disconnect, *v.a.* désunir, séparer, diviser; (*mach.*) désembrayer [division, *f.*
Disconnection, *s.* désunion, séparation,
Disconsolate, *adj.* inconsolable; désolé
Disconsolately, *adv.* inconsolablement
Disconsolateness, Disconsolation, *s.* désolation, *f.* [tentement, *m.*
Discontent, *v.a.* mécontenter; — *s.* mécon-
Discontented, *adj.* mécontent [avec chagrin
Discontentedly, *adv.* avec mécontentement,
Discontentedness, Discontentment, *s.* mécontentement, *m.*
Discontinuance, Discontinuation, *s.* discontinuation, *f.*; (*disruption*) discontinuité, *f.*
Discontinue, *v.a.n.* discontinuer
Discontinuity, *s.* discontinuité, *f.*
Discontinuous, *adj.* discontinu
Discord, *s.* discorde, *f.*; (*mus.*) discordance, *f.*
Discordance, Discordancy, *s.* discordance, *f.* [désaccord
Discordant, *adj.* discordant; (*disagreeing*) en
Discordantly, *adv.* discordamment, d'une manière discordante
Discount, *s.* (*deduction*) escompte, *m.*; (*reduction*) remise, réduction, *f.*, rabais, *m.*; (*arith.*) règle d'escompte, *f.*; — *v.a.* escompter; (*deduct*) décompter, déduire, retrancher; (*allow*) faire une remise de; — *v.n.* escompter, faire l'escompte. *At a* —, à escompte, à perte; au rabais; (*fig.*) en défaveur, en discrédit, discrédité, décrédité, tombé. — **bank,** *s.* banque (*f.*) *or* caisse (*f.*) *or* comptoir (*m.*) d'es-
Discountable, *adj.* escomptable [compte
Discountenance, *v.a.* décontenancer; décourager, rebuter; recevoir froidement; s'opposer à, combattre; désapprouver, être contre; — *s.* mauvais accueil, *m.*, froideur, *f.*; défaveur, *f.*; désapprobation, *f.*
Discounter, *s.* escompteur, *m.*
Discounting, *s.* escompte, *m.*
Discourage, *v.a.* décourager; rebuter; détourner; dissuader
Discourageable, *adj.* décourageable
Discouragement, *s.* découragement, *m.*
Discourager, *s.* personne qui décourage, *f.*
Discourse, *s.* discours, *m.*; conversation, *f.*, entretien, *m.*; propos, *m.*; langage, *m.*; (*treatise*) traité, *m.*; — *v.n.* discourir ('*on*,' sur, de); converser, s'entretenir ('*on*,' de); raisonner; traiter (de); parler en public [teur, *m.*
Discourser, *s.* discoureur, *m.*, -euse, *f.*; ora-
Discoursing, *s.* action de discourir, *f.*; conversation, *f.*, entretien, *m.*; raisonnement, *m.*
Discoursive, *adj.* dialogué; (*reasoning*) discursif
Discourteous, *adj.* discourtois, impoli
Discourteously, *adv.* discourtoisement, avec discourtoisie, impoliment
Discourtesy, *s.* discourtoisie, impolitesse, *f.*
Discover, *v.a.* découvrir; voir; apercevoir; s'apercevoir de, s'apercevoir (que); révéler; (*show*) montrer [visible, perceptible
Discoverable, *adj.* qu'on peut découvrir;
Discoverer, *s.* auteur d'une découverte, découvreur, *m.*; révélateur, *m.*, -trice, *f.*; (*scout*) éclaireur, *m.*
Discovery, *s.* découverte, *f.*; déclaration, *f.*; révélation, *f.*; scandale, éclat, *m.*

Discredit, *v.a.* discréditer, décréditer, déconsidérer; déshonorer; (*disbelieve*) ne pas croire; — *s.* discrédit, *m.*, déconsidération, *f.*; déshonneur, *m.*, honte, *f.* *To bring into* —, *V.* **Disrepute** [mettant; déshonorant; honteux
Discreditable, *adj.* peu honorable; compro-
Discrediting, *s.* décréditement, *m.*
Discreet, *adj.* discret, prudent, sage
Discreetly, *adv.* discrètement, prudemment, sagement [*f.*; contradiction, *f.*
Discrepance, Discrepancy, *s.* différence,
Discrepant, *adj.* différent (de); contradictoire; en contradiction (avec)
Discrete, *adj.* discret; (*log.*) disjonctif
Discretion, *s.* discrétion, *f.* *Age* or *years of* —, âge de raison, *m.* *To use o.'s own* —, faire comme on le juge à propos
Discretional, Discretionary, *adj.* discrétionnaire; facultatif
Discretionally, Discretionarily, *adv.* discrétionnairement, à discrétion; facultativement [séparer; — *adj.* distinct
Discriminate, *v.a.n.* distinguer, discerner;
Discriminately, *adv.* distinctement; avec discernement
Discriminating, *adj.* distinctif, particulier; qui sait discerner, qui a du discernement, judicieux; bien entendu
Discrimination, *s.* distinction, *f.*; marque distinctive, *f.*; discernement, jugement, *m.*
Discriminative. *V.* **Discriminating**
Discriminatively, *adv.* avec discernement
Discrown, *v.a.* découronner
Discrowning, *s.* découronnement, *m.*
Disculpate, &c. *V.* **Exculpate,** &c.
Discursive, *adj.* discursif; vagabond; étendu; vague [ment
Discursively, *adv.* discursivement; vague-
Discuss, *v.a.* discuter; débattre
Discusser, *s.* discuteur, *m.*
Discussion, *s.* discussion, *f.*
Discussive, Discutient, *adj.* *s.* résolutif, *adj. m.*, -ive, *f.*, résolutif, *s.m.*
Disdain, *v.a.* dédaigner; — *s.* dédain, *m.*
Disdainful, *adj.* dédaigneux [dédain
Disdainfully, *adv.* dédaigneusement, avec
Disdainfulness, *s.* nature dédaigneuse, *f.*, dédain, *m.* [malade, faire mal à, affecter
Disease, *s.* maladie, *f.*, mal, *m.*; — *v.a.* rendre
Diseased, *adj.* malade
Disedge, *v.a.* émousser
Disembarcation, *s.* débarquement, *m.*
Disembark, *v.a.n.* débarquer
Disembarkation, Disembarking, Disembarkment, *s.* débarquement, *m.*
Disembarrass, *v.a.* débarrasser
Disembarrassment, *s.* débarrassement, *m.*
Disembellish, *v.a.* désembellir
Disembellishment, *s.* désembellissement, *m.*
Disembody, *v.a.* désincorporer; dépouiller de son corps; (*mil.*) désincorporer, licencier
Disembodying, *s.* (*mil.*) désincorporation, décorporation, *f.*, licenciement, *m.*
Disembogue, *v.a.* décharger; — *v.n.* se décharger, se jeter; (*nav.*) débouquer
Disemboguement, *s.* décharge, *f.*; (*nav.*) débouquement, *m.*
Disembowel, *v.a.* éventrer, éviscérer
Disembroil, *v.a.* débrouiller
Disembroiling, *s.* débrouillement, *m.*
Dispark, *v.a.* déparquer
Disenable. *V.* **Disable**
Disenchant, *v.a.* désenchanter [-teresse, *f.*
Disenchant-er, ress, *s.* désenchanteur, *m.*,
Disenchantment, *s.* désenchantement, *m.*
Disenchanting, *adj.* désenchanteur; — *s.* désenchantement, *m.*
Disencharm, *v.a.* décharmer
Disencumber, *v.a.* désencombrer, débarrasser; dégager
Disencumbrance, *s.* désencombrement, débarras, *m.*; dégagement, *m.*; délivrance, *f.*

Disengage, *v.a.* dégager (de); séparer (de); détacher (de); débarrasser (de); délivrer (de); (*mach.*) désembrayer; — *v.n.* se dégager (de); se séparer (de); se détacher (de); &c.
Disengaged, *part. adj.* dégagé, &c. (*V.* **Disengage**); (*not occupied*) libre
Disengagement, *s.* dégagement, *m.*; (*freedom*) affranchissement, *m.*; (*leisure*) loisir, *m.*
Disennoble, *v.a.* dégrader; avilir
Disenroll, *v.a.* désenrôler
Disenrolment, *s.* désenrôlement, *m.*
Disentangle, *v.a.* (*threads*, &c.) démêler; (*the feet*) dépêtrer (de); (*clear up*) débrouiller; (*separate*) dégager; (*free*) débarrasser (de); affranchir (de); (*get out of*) tirer (de)
Disentanglement, *s.* débrouillement, *m.*; dénoûment, *m.*; (*freedom*) affranchissement, *m.*
Disenthrall, &c. *V.* **Disinthrall,** &c.
Disenthrone. *V.* **Dethrone**
Disentitle, *v.a.* priver du droit, ôter le droit
Disentomb, *v.a.* désensevelir, exhumer
Disesteem, *v.a.* mésestimer; — *s.* mésestime, déconsidération, *f.*
Disfavour, *s.* défaveur, *f.*; disgrâce, *f.*; procédé désobligeant, mauvais office, *m.*; — *v.a.* jeter la défaveur sur; traiter avec défaveur; se prononcer contre; désapprouver
Disfavourer, *s.* désapprobateur, *m.*, -trice, *f.*
Disfiguration. *V.* **Disfigurement**
Disfigure, *v.a.* défigurer
Disfigurement, *s.* défigurement, *m.*; difformité, *f.*, enlaidissement, défaut, *m.*
Disfigurer, *s.* personne qui défigure, *f.*
Disforest. *V.* **Disafforest**
Disforestment. *V.* **Disafforestation**
Disfranchise, *v.a.* priver de ses priviléges; priver du droit électoral
Disfranchisement, *s.* privation de ses priviléges, *f.*; privation du droit électoral, *f.*
Disfurnish, Disgarnish, Disgarrison, *v.a.* dégarnir
Disgorge, *v.a.n.* dégorger, regorger
Disgorgement, Disgorging, *s.* dégorgement, *m.*
Disgorger, *s.* dégorgeoir, *m.*
Disgrace, *s.* disgrâce, *f.*; (*shame*) honte ('*to*,' pour), *f.*; déshonneur, *m.*; — *v.a.* disgracier; déshonorer; avilir; décréditer. *In* —, (*of a child*) en pénitence. *He is a* — *to his family*, il est l'opprobre de sa famille
Disgraceful, *adj.* honteux; déshonorant
Disgracefully, *adv.* honteusement
Disgracefulness, *s.* honte, *f.*, déshonneur, *m.*, ignominie, *f.*, opprobre, *m.*
Disguisable, *adj.* déguisable
Disguise, *v.a.* déguiser ('*from*,' à); cacher ('*from*,' à); masquer; contrefaire; défigurer; — *s.* déguisement, *m.*; (*fig.*) masque, *m.* *In* —, déguisé
Disguising, *s.* déguisement, *m.*; mascarade, *f.*
Disgust, *s.* dégoût, *m.*; — *v.a.* dégoûter (de)
Disgustingly, *adv.* dégoûtamment, d'une manière dégoûtante
Dish, *s.* plat, *m.*; (*for vegetables*) casserole, *f.*; (*for fruit*) coupe, *f.*; (*of a balance*) plateau, bassin, *m.*; —**es,** *pl.* plats, *m.pl.*, &c.; vaisselle, *f.*; — *v.a.* (— *up*) mettre dans un plat, dresser, servir; (*pers.*) mettre dedans, attraper, enfoncer; ruiner; — *v.n.* (*of horses*) faucher. *Made* —, plat apprêté. *To wash up the* —*es*, laver la vaisselle. — **cloth, -clout,** *s.* torchon de cuisine, *m.* — **cover,** *s.* cloche de plat, cloche, *f.*, couvre-plat, *m.* —**ful,** *s.* platée, *f.* — **mat,** *s.* dessous de plat, *m.* — **warmer,** *s.* réchaud, *m.* — **washer,** *s.* laveur (*m.*, -euse, *f.*) de vaisselle; (*bird*) lavandière, bergeronnette, *f.* — **water,** *s.* eau *or* lavure de vaisselle, *f.*
Dishabille, *s.* déshabillé, négligé, *m.*
Dishabited, *adj.* déshabité
Disharmonization, *s.* désharmonisation, *f.*
Disharmonize, *v.a.* désharmoniser
Disharmony, *s.* désharmonie, disharmonie, *f.*
Dishearten, *v.a.* décourager; désespérer, désoler; (*deter*) détourner (de)
Dishevel, *v.a.* décheveler, écheveler, mettre en désordre
Dishevelled, *adj.* en désordre, épars. *With* — *hair*, échevelé
Dishing, *adj.* en forme de plat, concave, creux
Dishonest, *adj.* malhonnête, déloyal
Dishonestly, *adv.* malhonnêtement, déloyalement
Dishonesty, *s.* malhonnêteté, improbité, déloyauté, *f.*
Dishonour, *v.a.* déshonorer; (*com.*) ne pas faire honneur à; — *s.* déshonneur, *m.*; (*com.*) non-paiement, non-payement, *m.*
Dishonourable, *adj.* (*pers.*) sans honneur; (*things*) déshonorable, déshonorant, honteux
Dishonourableness, *s.* nature déshonorable, *f.*
Dishonourably, *adv.* déshonorablement, d'une manière déshonorable *or* déshonorante
Dishonoured, *adj.* déshonoré; (*com.*) auquel on n'a pas fait honneur; en souffrance
Dishonourer, *s.* personne qui déshonore, *f.*, profanateur, *m.*, -trice, *f.*
Dishorn, *v.a.* décorner
Disillusion, *s.* désillusion, *f.*, désillusionnement, *m.*; — *v.a.* désillusionner
Disinclination, *s.* ('*to*,' pour) aversion, *f.*, éloignement, *m.*
Disincline, *v.a.* éloigner (de), indisposer (pour)
Disincorporate, *v.a.* désincorporer
Disincorporation, *s.* désincorporation, *f.*
Disinfect, *v.a.* désinfecter
Disinfectant, *s.* désinfectant, désinfecteur, *m.*
Disinfecting, *adj.* désinfectant, désinfecteur; — *s.* désinfection, *f.*
Disinfection, *s.* désinfection, *f.*
Disingenuous, *adj.* dissimulé, faux; de mauvaise foi, déloyal
Disingenuously, *adv.* sans franchise; avec mauvaise foi, déloyalement
Disingenuousness, *s.* manque de franchise, *m.*, dissimulation, fausseté, *f.*; mauvaise foi, déloyauté, *f.*
Disinherison. *V.* **Disinheritance**
Disinherit, *v.a.* déshériter
Disinheritance, *s.* déshéritement, *m.*, exhérédation, *f.*
Disinhume, *v.a.* exhumer
Disinsure, *v.a.* désassurer
Disintegrate, *v.a.* séparer, diviser, désagréger
Disintegration, *s.* séparation, division, désagrégation, *f.*
Disinter, *v.a.* exhumer, déterrer
Disinterested, *adj.* désintéressé
Disinterestedly, *adv.* avec désintéressement
Disinterestedness, *s.* désintéressement, *m.*
Disinterment, *s.* exhumation, *f.*
Disinthrall, *v.a.* affranchir, tirer d'esclavage, mettre en liberté
Disinthralment, *s.* affranchissement, *m.*, délivrance de l'esclavage, *f.*
Disinure, *v.a.* désaccoutumer, déshabituer
Disinvite, *v.a.* désinviter, déprier
Disjoin, *v.a.* déjoindre, disjoindre; séparer; désunir; — *v.n.* se déjoindre, &c.
Disjoint, *v.a.* démettre, disloquer; désarticuler; (*take to pieces*) démonter; (*divide*) démembrer; (*fig.*) désunir. —*ed speech*, discours décousu, discours sans suite, *m.*
Disjointly, *adv.* séparément
Disjunction, *s.* disjonction, séparation, désunion, *f.*
Disjunctive, *adj.* disjonctif
Disjunctively, *adv.* séparément, à part
Disk. *V.* **Disc**
Dislike, *v.a.* ne pas aimer; avoir du dégoût pour; ne pas approuver, désapprouver, trouver mauvais. *To* — *exceedingly*, ne pas aimer du tout, avoir en horreur, détester. *Not to* —, aimer assez; ne pas trouver mauvais; trouver assez bon. *To be* —*d*, n'être pas aimé
Dislike, *s.* ('*of*,' '*to*,' pour) dégoût, *m.*; répugnance, *f.*; aversion, *f.*; éloignement, *m.*; antipathie, *f.* *Likes and* —*s*, goûts et antipathies.

To take a — to, concevoir *or* prendre du dégoût pour, prendre en dégoût *or* en aversion *or* en grippe, se dégoûter de
Disliker, *s.* désapprobateur, *m.*, -trice, *f.*
Dislocate, *v.a.* disloquer, démettre
Dislocation, *s.* dislocation, *f.*
Dislodge, *v.a.n.* déloger (de); faire sortir (de); déplacer; (*hunt.*) débûcher, lancer; (*mil.*) déloger
Dislodging, Dislodgment, *s.* délogement, *m.*
Disloyal, *adj.* infidèle; rebelle; perfide, déloyal
Disloyally, *adv.* infidèlement; perfidement, déloyalement [perfidie, déloyauté, *f.*
Disloyalty, *s.* infidélité, *f.*; défection, *f.*;
Dismal, *adj.* lugubre, sinistre; sombre; triste; horrible, affreux; **—s,** *s. pl.* maladie *or* humeur noire, *f.*
Dismally, *adv.* lugubrement, sinistrement; tristement; horriblement, affreusement
Dismalness, *s.* air lugubre, aspect sinistre, *m.*; tristesse, *f.*; horreur, *f.*
Dismantle, *v.a.* dépouiller (de); (*fort.*) démanteler; (*nav.*) désarmer, dégréer
Dismantlement, Dismantling, *s.* (*fort.*) démantellement, *m.*; (*nav.*) désarmement, dégréage, dégréement, *m.*
Dismask, *v.a.* démasquer
Dismast, *v.a.* démâter
Dismasting, Dismastment, *s.* démâtage, démâtement, *m.*
Dismay, *v.a.* effrayer, épouvanter, consterner; intimider; décourager; — *s.* effroi, *m.*, terreur, épouvante, consternation, *f.*; décourage-
Dismember, *v.a.* démembrer [ment, *m.*
Dismemberment, *s.* démembrement, *m.*
Dismiss, *v.a.* renvoyer; congédier; (*public functionaries*) destituer (de); (*thoughts, feelings*) bannir, chasser; (*considerations,* &c.) écarter; (*a subject*) quitter, abandonner; *get rid of*) se débarrasser de [amovible
Dismissable, Dismissible, *adj.* congéable;
Dismissal, Dismission, *s.* renvoi, *m.*; congé, *m.*; (*of public functionaries*) destitution, *f.*
Dismortgage, *v.a.* dégrever
Dismount, *v.n.* descendre de cheval, mettre pied à terre; descendre (de); — *v.a.* démonter
Disobedience, *s.* désobéissance, *f.*
Disobedient, *adj.* désobéissant
Disobediently, *adv.* avec désobéissance
Disobey, *v.a.* désobéir à
Disoblige, *v.a.* désobliger
Disobligingly, *adv.* désobligeamment
Disobligingness, *s.* désobligeance, *f.*
Disorder, *s.* désordre, *m.*; (*disease*) maladie, indisposition, *f.*; dérangement, *m.*; — *v.a.* mettre en désordre; déranger; troubler; affecter; (*make ill*) incommoder, indisposer, rendre malade, faire mal à, déranger
Disordered, *adj.* en désordre; dérangé; irrégulier; (*unwell*) indisposé, malade; (*diseased*) malade
Disorderly, *adj.* en désordre; (*unruly*) déréglé; désordonné; tumultueux; turbulent; indocile; irrégulier; de débauche; — *adv.* en désordre; (*fig.*) déréglément, désordonnément, d'une manière déréglée *or* désordonnée
Disorganization, *s.* désorganisation, *f.*
Disorganize, *v.a.* désorganiser. *To become —d,* se désorganiser
Disorganizer, *s.* désorganisateur, *m.*, -trice, *f.*
Disorganizing, *adj.* désorganisateur; — *s.* désorganisation, *f.*
Disown, *v.a.* désavouer; renier; nier
Disoxidate, &c. *V.* **Deoxidate,** &c.
Disparage, *v.a* mépriser; dénigrer, déprécier; faire injure à; faire tort à; déshonorer; (*spoil*) déparer; (*by marriage*) mésallier
Disparagement, *s.* dénigrement, *m.*, dépréciation, *f.*; injure, *f.*; déshonneur, *m.*; tache, *f.*; reproche, *m.*; (*by marriage*) mésalliance, *f.*
Disparager, *s.* dénigreur, *m.*, -euse, *f.*
Disparaging, *adj.* de dénigrement, de mépris, dépréciateur, dépréciatif; défavorable, désavantageux; injurieux; déshonorant
Disparagingly, *adv.* avec *or* par dénigrement; défavorablement, désavantageusement; avec mépris; injurieusement; avec déshonneur
Disparate, *adj.* disparate; **—s,** *s. pl.* disparates, choses disparates, *f.pl.*
Disparity, *s.* disparité, *f.*
Dispark, *v.a.* déparquer
Dispassionate, *adj.* exempt de passion, sans passion, calme, froid; modéré; impartial
Dispassionately, *adv.* sans passion, avec calme, froidement; modérément; impartialement, avec impartialité
Dispatch. *V.* **Despatch**
Dispel, *v.a.* dissiper, chasser; — *v.n.* se dissiper
Dispensable, *adj.* dont on peut se dispenser *or* se passer; distribuable [pharmacie, *f.*
Dispensary, *s.* dispensaire, *m.*; (*of hospitals*)
Dispensation, *s.* dispensation, *f.*; distribution, *f.*; don, *m.*; bienfait, *m.*; calamité, *f.*; (*law*) loi, *f.*; (*exemption, licence*) dispense, *f.*
Dispensatory, *s.* dispensaire, *m.*
Dispense, *v.a.* dispenser; distribuer; administrer; appliquer; préparer. *To — anyone from* or *with,* dispenser quelqu'un de. *To — with,* (*abstain from*) se dispenser de; (*do without*) se passer de
Dispenser, *s.* dispensateur, *m.*, -trice, *f.*; distributeur, *m.*, -trice, *f.*; administrateur, *m.*, -trice, *f.*; (*in hospitals,* &c.) pharmacien, *m.*
Dispensing, *adj.* de dispensation; (*of licence*) de dispense. — *power,* droit de grâce. *m. V.*
Dispeople, *v.a.* dépeupler [**Chemist**
Disperse, *v.a.* disperser; dissiper; (*med.*) résoudre; — *v.n.* se disperser; se dissiper; (*med.*) se résoudre
Dispersion, *s.* dispersion, *f.* [(*press*) abattre
Dispirit, *v.a.* décourager; démoraliser; (*de-*
Dispirited, *part. adj.* découragé, &c. (*V.* **Dispirit**); (*of style*) mou, flasque, languissant
Dispiritedly, *adv.* avec découragement; mollement, languissamment
Dispiritedness, *s.* découragement, *m.*; démoralisation, *f.*; (*depression*) abattement, *m.*
Dispiritingly, *adv.* d'une manière décourageante [&c.) destituer (de)
Displace, *v.a.* déplacer; ôter; (*from an office,*
Displacement, *s.* déplacement, *m.*; (*from an office,* &c.) destitution, *f.*
Displant, *v.a.* déplanter [tage, *m.*
Displantation, *s.* déplantation, *f.*, déplan-
Display, *v.a.* déployer; exposer, développer; montrer; manifester; (*ostentatiously*) étaler, faire étalage de, faire parade de; (*mil.*) déployer; — *s.* exposition, *f.*, développement, *m.*; manifestation, *f.*; exemple, *m.*; (*ostentatious show*) étalage, *m.*, parade, *f.*; (*of troops*) déploiement, *m.* *To make a — of,* faire étalage de, faire parade de
Displease, *v.a.* déplaire à; offenser; mécontenter, fâcher, contrarier, vexer; — *v.n.* déplaire [**Displease**); mécontent (de)
Displeased, *part. adj.* offensé (de), &c. (*V.*
Displeasing, *adj.* déplaisant, désagréable
Displeasingly, *adv.* désagréablement
Displeasingness, *s.* nature désagréable, *f.*, désagrément, *m.*
Displeasure, *s.* déplaisir, *m.*; mécontentement, *m.*; peine, *f.*; défaveur, disgrâce, *f.*; (*anger*) colère, *f.*, courroux, *m.*, indignation, *f.*
Displume. *V.* **Unplume**
Disport, *s.* amusement, divertissement, ébat, jeu, passe-temps, *m.*; — *v.n.a.*, — *oneself,* s'amuser, se divertir, s'ébattre, prendre ses ébats, se jouer, jouer, folâtrer
Disposable, *adj.* disponible
Disposableness, *s.* disponibilité, *f.*
Disposal, *s.* disposition, *f.*; pouvoir de disposer, *m.*; (*sale*) vente, *f.*; (*transfer*) cession, *f.*
Dispose, *v.a.* disposer, arranger; préparer (à); (*the mind*) porter (à), disposer (à); — (*of*),

v.n. disposer de; (*sell*) vendre; placer; (*transfer*) céder; (*get rid of*) se défaire de, disposer de; (*give*) donner; (*despatch*) expédier; (*employ, use*) employer; (settle, &c.) régler; faire justice de. *To be —d of!* à vendre!
Disposed, *adj.* disposé (à), enclin (à), porté (à); en train (de); (*in compounds*) intentionné
Disposer, *s.* disposeur, *m.*, -euse, *f.*; distributeur, *m.*, -trice, *f.*, dispensateur, *m.*, -trice, *f.*; ordonnateur, *m.*, -trice, *f.*; arbitre, *m.f.*
Disposition, *s.* disposition, *f.*; (*temper*) caractère, naturel, *m.* [(*law*) exproprier
Dispossess, *v.a.* déposséder (de), priver (de);
Dispossession, *s.* dépossession, *f.*; (*law*) expropriation, *f.*
Dispossessor, *s.* spoliateur, *m.*, -trice, *f.*
Dispraise. *V.* **Blame** [avec blâme
Dispraisingly, *adv.* désavantageusement,
Disproof, *s.* réfutation, *f.* [disproportionner
Disproportion, *s.* disproportion, *f.*; — *v.a.*
Disproportional, *adj.* disproportionnel
Disproportionally, *adv.* disproportionnellement
Disproportionate, *adj.* disproportionné
Disproportionately, *adv.* disproportionnément [portionnée, *f.*; disproportion, *f.*
Disproportionateness, *s.* nature dispro-
Disprovable, *adj.* réfutable
Disprove, *v.a.* réfuter; prouver le contraire de
Disprover, *s.* réfutateur, *m.*, -trice, *f.* [cutable
Disputable, *adj.* disputable, contestable; dis-
Disputant, *s.* disputant, *m.*, e, *f.* [débat, *m.*
Disputation, *s.* disputation, discussion, *f.*,
Disputatious, Disputative, *adj.* disputeur
Dispute, *v.a.n.* disputer, contester; discuter; — *s.* dispute, *f.*; contestation, *f.*; débat, *m.*, discussion, *f.* *Beyond —, beyond all —,* incontestable; incontestablement, sans contredit
Disputer, *s.* disputeur, *m.*, -euse, *f.*
Disqualification, *s.* incapacité, *f.*; chose qui rend incapable, *f.*; (*in horse-racing*) disqualification, *f.*
Disqualified, *adj.* incapable (de); hors d'état (de); (*law*) inhabile (à); (*in horse-racing*) disqualifié
Disqualify, *v.a.* rendre incapable (de); mettre hors d'état (de); (*law*) rendre inhabile (à); (*in horse-racing*) disqualifier
Disquiet, *v.a.* inquiéter; — *s.* *V.* **Disquietude**
Disquieter, *s.* perturbateur, *m.*, -trice, *f.*
Disquietude, *s.* inquiétude, agitation, *f.*
Disquisition, *s.* recherche, *f.*, examen, *m.*, investigation, disquisition, *f.*; dissertation, *f.*
Disregard, *v.a.* mépriser, dédaigner, faire peu de cas de; méconnaître; négliger, ne pas tenir compte de, ne pas avoir égard à; (*reject*) écarter, éloigner; repousser; — *s.* mépris, dédain, *m.*; indifférence, insouciance, *f.*
Disregardful, *adj.* indifférent, insouciant, négligent; dédaigneux
Disregardfully, *adv.* négligemment, insouciamment; dédaigneusement
Disrelish, *s.* dégoût, *m.*; (*fig.*) répugnance, aversion, *f.*; — *v.a.* avoir du dégoût pour; (*fig.*) avoir de la répugnance pour, ne pas goûter, trouver mauvais; (*give a distaste*) donner de la répugnance *or* de l'aversion pour
Disreputable, *adj.* (*pers.*) de mauvaise réputation, taré; (*things*) déshonorant; compro-
Disreputably, *adv.* honteusement [mettant
Disrepute, *s.* discrédit, *m.*, déconsidération, *f.*; mauvaise réputation, *f.*; déshonneur, *m.* *To bring into —,* faire tomber en discrédit, discréditer, décréditer, déconsidérer. *To fall into —,* tomber en (*or* dans le) discrédit, être discrédité *or* décrédité, perdre de sa réputation
Disrespect, *s.* manque de respect *or* d'égards, *m.*; irrévérence, *f.*
Disrespectful, *adj.* irrespectueux, irrévérencieux. *To be — to,* manquer de respect à, manquer à, être irrespectueux envers, n'être pas respectueux envers
Disrespectfully, *adv.* irrespectueusement, irrévérencieusement [*or* irrévérencieuse, *f.*
Disrespectfulness, *s.* nature irrespectueuse
Disrobe, *v.a.* déshabiller; (*strip*) dépouiller (de); — *v.n.* se déshabiller; se dépouiller (de)
Disruption, *s.* rupture, disruption, *f.* [de), *m.*
Dissatisfaction, *s.* mécontentement ('*with,*'
Dissatisfactory. *V.* **Unsatisfactory**
Dissatisfied, *adj.* mécontent (de); non satisfait (de)
Dissatisfy, *v.a.* mécontenter; ne pas satisfaire
Dissect, *v.a.* disséquer
Dissecting, Dissection, *s.* dissection, *f.* — **room,** *s.* amphithéâtre, *m.*
Dissector, Dissecter, *s.* dissecteur, *m.*,
Disseize, *v.a.* déposséder [(*fam.*) disséqueur, *m.*
Dissemble, *v.a.* dissimuler, déguiser, cacher; simuler, feindre; — *v.n.* dissimuler; feindre, user de feinte; faire l'hypocrite
Dissembled, *adj.* dissimulé; faux, hypocrite
Dissembler, *s.* dissimulateur, *m.*, -trice, *f.*, dissimulé, *m.*, e, *f.*; hypocrite, *m.f.*
Dissembling, *adj.* dissimulé, dissimulateur; — *s.* dissimulation, *f.* [hypocritement
Dissemblingly, *adv.* avec dissimulation,
Disseminate, *v.a.* disséminer; (*fig.*) propager, répandre
Dissemination, *s.* dissémination, *f.*
Disseminator, *s.* propagateur, *m.*
Dissension, *s.* dissension, *f.*
Dissent, *v.n.* *V.* **Disagree;** — *s.* dissentiment, *m.*, dissidence, *f.*; (*rel.*) schisme, *m.*
Dissenter, *s.* dissident, *m.*, e, *f.*
Dissenterism, *s.* dissentérisme, *m.*
Dissentient, *adj.* différent; opposant, contraire, contre; — *s.* dissident, *m.*, e, *f.*, opposant, *m.*, e, *f.*
Dissenting, *adj.* dissident; — *s.* *V.* **Dissent**
Dissert, *v.n.* disserter
Dissertation, *s.* dissertation, *f.*
Dissertative, *adj.* dissertatif
Dissertator, *s.* dissertateur, *m.*, -trice, *f.*, disserteur, *m.*, -euse, *f.*
Disserve, *v.a.* desservir, nuire à, faire tort à
Disservice, *s.* mauvais service, tort, *m.*
Disserviceable, *adj.* préjudiciable (à), nuisible (à) [qualité nuisible, *f.*
Disserviceableness, *s.* nature préjudiciable,
Disserviceably, *adv.* nuisiblement
Dissever, *v.a.* séparer (de); diviser; (*by violence*) arracher (de); (*disunite*) désunir
Disseverance, *s.* séparation, *f.*; division, *f.*;
Dissidence, *s.* dissidence, *f.* [désunion, *f.*
Dissident, *adj. s.* dissident, *m.*, e, *f.* [différent
Dissimilar, *adj.* dissemblable, dissimilaire,
Dissimilarity, Dissimilitude, *s.* dissemblance, dissimilarité, dissimilitude, différence, *f.*
Dissimilarly, *adv.* dissemblablement, diffé-
Dissimulation, *s.* dissimulation, *f.* [remment
Dissipate, *v.a.* dissiper; disperser; — *v.n.* se dissiper; se disperser [débauché; dispersé
Dissipated, *part. adj.* dissipé; de dissipation;
Dissipation, *s.* dissipation, *f.*; dispersion, *f.*
Dissociate, *v.a.* séparer, désunir, dissocier, désassocier [sociation, désassociation, *f.*
Dissociation, *s.* séparation, désunion, dis-
Dissolubility, *s.* dissolubilité, *f.*; solubilité, *f.*
Dissoluble, *adj.* dissoluble; soluble
Dissolute, *adj.* dissolu
Dissolutely, *adv.* dissolûment
Dissoluteness, *s.* dissolution, *f.*
Dissolution, *s.* dissolution, *f.*; (*death*) mort, *f.*
Dissolvable. *V.* **Dissoluble**
Dissolve, *v.a.* dissoudre; (*separate*) séparer; (*destroy*) détruire; — *v.n.* se dissoudre; (*break up*) se séparer; (*perish*) périr, mourir; (*waste away*) dépérir; (*into tears*) fondre (en larmes)
Dissolvent, *adj. s.* dissolvant, *adj. m.*, e, *f.*,
Dissolver, *s.* dissolvant, *m.* [dissolvant, *s.m.*
Dissolving views, *s. pl.* fantasmagorie, *f.*
Dissonance, *s.* dissonnance, *f.*; discordance, *f.*; contrariété, *f.*

Dissonant, *adj.* dissonnant; discordant; (*from* contraire (à)
Dissuade, *v.a.* dissuader (de)
Dissuader, *s.* personne qui dissuade, *f.*
Dissuasion, *s.* dissuasion, *f.*
Dissuasive, *adj.* dissuasif; — *s.* moyen de dissuader, motif de dissuasion, *m.*
Dissyllabic,-al, *adj.* dissyllabe, dissyllabique
Dissyllable, *s.* dissyllabe, *m.* [nouillette, *f.*
Distaff, *s.* quenouille, *f.* — **thistle,** *s.* que-
Distance, *s.* distance, *f.*; intervalle, *m.*; (*remoteness*) éloignement, *m.*; (*of perspective*) lointain, *m.*; (*journey*) trajet, *m.*; (*reserve*) réserve, *f.*; (*mus.*) intervalle, *m.*; — *v.a.* éloigner; (*leave behind*) distancer, dépasser, devancer, laisser en arrière. *At a* —, à distance, à quelque distance; (*far*) loin; au loin; (*from afar*) de loin; (*fig.*) dans l'éloignement. *At a — from,* loin de. *In the* —, dans le lointain. *Out of* —, à perte de vue; (*beyond reach*) hors d'atteinte. *To keep o.'s* —, se tenir à une distance convenable, se tenir à distance; se tenir à sa place. *To keep at a* —, tenir à distance; (*oneself*) se tenir à distance. *To run out of* —, courir à perte de vue, s'éloigner rapidement; laisser loin derrière soi, laisser à une grande distance. — **post,** *s.* poteau de distance, *m.*
Distant, *adj.* éloigné (de); (*from the place we are at or speak of*) lointain; éloigné (de), loin (de); distant (de), de distance; (*retired*) retiré, écarté; (*of time*) éloigné, reculé; (*reserved*) réservé, froid; (*slight*) faible, léger
Distantly, *adv.* à distance; loin; au loin; dans l'éloignement; (*from afar*) de loin; (*reservedly*) avec réserve, froidement; (*slightly*) faiblement, légèrement
Distaste. *V.* **Disrelish** *and* **Dislike**
Distasteful, *adj.* dégoûtant; désagréable
Distastefully, *adv.* dégoûtamment; désagréablement [désagréable; désagrément, *m.*
Distastefulness, *s.* nature (*f.*) *or* goût (*m.*)
Distemper, *s.* maladie, *f.*; (*paint.*) détrempe, *f.*; — *v.a.* rendre malade, incommoder, indisposer, déranger; troubler; (*paint.*) peindre en détrempe
Distempering, *s.* peinture en détrempe, *f.*
Distend, *v.a.* distendre; étendre; dilater, enfler, gonfler; élargir; écarter; (*med.*) distendre; — *v.n.* se distendre, s'étendre, &c.
Distension, *s.* distension, *f.*; extension, *f.*; dilatation, *f.*; écartement, *m.*; (*med.*) disten-
Distich, *s.* distique, *m.* [sion, *f.*
Distil, *v.a.n.* distiller; (*to extract*) extraire (de)
Distillable, *adj.* distillable
Distillation, *s.* distillation, *f.*
Distillatory, *adj.* distillatoire
Distiller, *s.* distillateur, *m.*, -trice, *f.*
Distillery, *s.* distillerie, *f.* [tillerie, *f.*
Distilling, *s.* distillation, *f.*; (*art, trade*) dis-
Distinct, *adj.* distinct; différent; spécifié, exprès, catégorique; clair
Distinction, *s.* distinction, *f.*
Distinctive, *adj.* distinctif
Distinctively, *adv.* distinctivement
Distinctiveness, *s.* caractère distinctif, *m.*
Distinctly, *adv.* distinctement; expressément, nettement, catégoriquement; clairement; bien
Distinctness, *s.* netteté, clarté, *f.*; caractère distinct, *m.*; nature distincte, *f.*; différence, *f.*
Distinguish, *v.a.n.* distinguer
Distinguishable, *adj.* qu'on peut distinguer, qui peut être distingué; remarquable
Distinguished, *adj.* distingué. *A — foreigner,* un étranger de distinction, *m.* *A — man,* un homme éminent *or* célèbre, *m.*
Distinguishing, *adj.* distinctif
Distinguishingly, *adv.* avec distinction; avec discernement
Distort, *v.a.* (*twist*) distordre, tordre; (*deform*) contourner; (*alter*) décomposer, altérer; dénaturer; torturer; défigurer; fausser
Distortion, *s.* distortion, *f.*; contournement, *m.*; contorsion, *f.*; altération, *f.*; dénaturation, *f.*; (*of writings*) sens forcé, *m.*
Distract, *v.a.* tourmenter; troubler; déchirer; (*madden*) rendre fou, affoler, mettre hors de soi, bouleverser; (*divert*) distraire (de), détourner (de); (*divide*) diviser; partager
Distracted, *part. adj.* tourmenté, &c. (*V.* **Distract**); éperdu; effaré; fou
Distractedly, *adv.* avec folie, comme un fou, comme une folle; (*passionately*) éperdument
Distractedness, *s.* folie, *f.*
Distracting, *part. adj.* tourmentant, déchirant, &c. (*V.* **Distract**); qui rend fou, à rendre fou; atroce, cruel; dévorant
Distraction, *s.* confusion, *f.*, trouble, *m.*, agitation, *f.*, désordre, *m.*; déchirement, *m.*; transport, délire, *m.*; désespoir, *m.*, angoisse, *f.*; folie, démence, *f.*; (*diversion*) distraction, *f.*; division, *f.*; séparation, *f.* *To drive to* —, mettre hors de soi, rendre fou. *To love to* —, aimer éperdument, aimer à la folie
Distrain, *v.a.* saisir; — *v.n.* faire *or* exécuter une saisie [saisissable
Distrainable, *adj.* saisissable. *Not* —, in-
Distrainer,Distrainor, *s.* saisissant, *m.*, e, *f.*
Distraining, Distraint, *s.* saisie, *f.*
Distress, *s.* détresse, *f.*; misère, pénurie, gêne, *f.*; affliction, peine, *f.*, malheur, *m.*; (*law*) saisie, *f.*; (*nav.*) détresse, *f.*; — *v.a.* affliger, désoler, désespérer; (*law*) saisir
Distressed, *part. adj.* affligé, dans l'affliction, désolé, désespéré; dans la détresse; dans la misère; (*unhappy*) malheureux; (*law*) saisi
Distressful, *adj.* de détresse; de misère; affligeant; cruel; malheureux
Distressing, *adj.* affligeant, désolant, désespérant; douloureux; cruel; pénible
Distributable, *adj.* distribuable
Distribute, *v.a.* distribuer; (*allot*) répartir; (*justice*) administrer [partiteur, *m.*
Distributer, *s.* distributeur, *m.*, -trice, *f.*; ré-
Distribution, *s.* distribution, *f.*; (*allotment*) répartition, *f.*; (*of justice*) administration, *f.*
Distributive, *adj.* distributif
Distributively, *adv.* distributivement
District, *s.* district, *m.*; circonscription, *f.*; localité, *f.*; région, contrée, *f.*; (*part of a French shire*) arrondissement, *m.*; (*part of a town*) quartier, *m.*, (*admin.*) arrondissement, *m.* — **office,** *s.* (*post.*) bureau d'arrondissement, *m.*
Distringas, *s.* mandat de comparution, *m.*; opposition, *f.*
Distrust, *v.a.* se défier de; (*suspect*) se méfier de; — *s.* défiance, *f.*; (*suspicion*) méfiance, *f.* —**ful,** *adj.* défiant; méfiant. —**fully,** *adv.* avec défiance; avec méfiance. —**fulness,** *s.* défiance, *f.*; méfiance, *f.* —**less,** *adj.* exempt de défiance, sans défiance; sans méfiance
Disturb, *v.a.* troubler; (*interrupt*) déranger; (*alter*) changer
Disturbance, *s.* trouble, *m.*; dérangement, *m.*; désordre, *m.*; confusion, *f.*; embarras, *m.*; (*among the people*) trouble, *m.*, émeute, *f.*; (*noise*) bruit, tapage, *m.*; tumulte, *m.*; éclat, *m.*
Disturber, *s.* perturbateur, *m.*, -trice, *f.*
Disunion, *s.* désunion, *f.* [désunir; se séparer
Disunite, *v.a.* désunir; séparer; — *v.n.* se
Disuse, *s.* désuétude, *f.*; non-usage, *m.*; désaccoutumance, *f.*; — *v.a.* cesser de faire usage de; (*disaccustom*) désaccoutumer (de), déshabituer (de). *To fall into* —, *V.* **Abeyance**
Disused, *part. adj.* dont on a cessé de faire usage, dont on ne sert plus; (*of words*) désusité, inusité, vieilli; (*law*) périmé; (*disaccustomed*) désaccoutumé, déshabitué
Ditch, *s.* fossé, *m.*; — *v.a.* fossoyer; (*surround*) entourer d'un fossé; — *v.n.* faire *or* creuser un fossé. — **water,** *s.* eau croupie, *f.*
Ditcher, *s.* terrassier, fossoyeur, *m.*
Ditching, *s.* fossoyage, *m.*
Dithyramb,Dithyrambus, *s.* dithyrambe, *m.*

Dithyrambic, *adj.* dithyrambique; — *s.* [dithyrambe, *m.*
Ditone, *s.* diton, *m.*
Dittander, *s.* cresson alénois, *m.*, passerage, cresse, *f.*
Dittany, *s.* dictamne, (— *of Crete*) dictame, *m.*
Ditto, *adv.* idem; (*com.*) dito; (*the above mentioned*) ledit, *m.*; ladite, *f.*, lesdits, *m.pl.*, lesdites, *f.pl.*
Ditty, *s.* chant, *m.*; chanson, *f.*; chansonnette, *f.*
Diuresis, *s.* diurèse, *f.*
Diuretic, *adj. s.* diurétique, *adj. m.f.*, *s.m.*
Diurnal, *adj.* du jour, de jour; (*of every day*) journalier, quotidien, de chaque jour; (*nat. hist.*, *med.*, *astr.*) diurne; — *s.* (*nat. hist.*) diurne, *m.*
Diurnally, *adv.* de jour, pendant le jour; (*every day*) journellement, chaque jour
Divagation, *s.* divagation, *f.*
Divan, *s.* divan, *m.*; (*smoking-room*) salon-fumoir, fumoir, *m.*
Divaricate, *v.a.* séparer, diviser; — *v.n.* se séparer, se diviser; — *adj.* (*bot.*) divariqué
Divarication, *s.* divarication, séparation, *f.*; (*of roads*) fourche, *f.*
Dive, *v.n.* plonger; pénétrer; s'engager; s'enfoncer; — *s.* plongeon, *m.* — **into,** plonger *or* &c. dans; (*a subject*) pénétrer dans, approfondir
Diver, *s.* plongeur, *m.*; (*bird*) plongeon, *m.*
Diverge, *v.n.* diverger
Divergence, Divergency, *s.* divergence, *f.*
Divergent, *adj.* divergent
Divergingly, *adv.* en divergeant
Divers, *adj.* divers
Diverse, *adj.* divers; différent (de); varié; (*adverb.*) en sens divers
Diversely, *adv.* diversement
Diversicoloured, *adj.* diversicolore
Diversifiable, *adj.* diversifiable
Diversification, *s.* diversification, *f.*; variation, *f.*; variété, diversité, *f.*; changement, *m.*
Diversiform, *adj.* diversiforme [nuancer
Diversify, *v.a.* diversifier; varier; (*of colours*)
Diversion, *s.* diversion, *f.*; détournement, *m.*; (*recreation*) distraction, *f.*, divertissement, *m.*, récréation, *f.*, amusement, *m.*; (*mil.*) diversion, *f.*
Diversity, *s.* diversité, différence, *f.*; variété, *f.*
Diversive, *adj.* diversif
Divert, *v.a.* détourner (de); (*amuse*) divertir, distraire, désennuyer, récréer; (*mil.*) détourner par une diversion [divertit, *f.*
Diverter, *s.* personne *or* chose qui distrait *or*
Diverting, *adj.* divertissant; amusant
Divertingly. *V.* **Amusingly**
Divertisement, *s.* divertissement, *m.*
Divest, *v.a.* dépouiller (de); (*law*) dévêtir. *To — oneself of,* se dépouiller de; (*fig.*) se dépouiller de, se défaire de; abdiquer; s'ôter de l'esprit; (*law*) se dévêtir de
Divestiture, *s.* dépouillement, *m.*; dévestiture, *f.*; déposition, *f.*; dévêtissement, *m.*
Dividable, *adj.* divisible; répartissable
Divide, *v.a.* diviser; couper; (*in shares*) partager; distribuer; (*com.*) donner un dividende de; (*separate*) séparer; (*disunite*) diviser, désunir; (*the mind*) embarrasser; (*of ballot*) faire voter (...), faire aller (...) aux voix; — *v.n.* se diviser; se partager; se séparer; se désunir; (*to vote*) aller aux voix. — *!* aux voix! *They were —d in opinion,* ils différaient d'opinion. *The opinions were —d,* les avis étaient partagés [détaché
Dividend, *s.* dividende, *m.* *Ex- —,* coupon
Divider, *s.* distributeur, *m.*, -trice, *f.*; diviseur, *m.*; —**s,** *pl.* compas, *m.*
Dividivi, *s.* dividivi, *m.*
Divination, *s.* divination, *f.*
Divinatory, *adj.* divinatoire
Divine, *adj.* divin; — *s.* ecclésiastique, *m.*; théologien, *m.*; — *v.a.* deviner; (*predict*) prédire; (*foresee*) pressentir; (*conjecture*) conjecturer; — *v.n.* pratiquer la divination; faire des prédictions; prophétiser; (*to guess*) deviner. — **right,** *s.* droit divin, *m.*
Divinely, *adv.* divinement
Divineness, *s.* divinité, *f.*; perfection, *f.*
Diviner, *s.* devin, *m.*, devineresse, *f.*; (*guesser*) devineur, *m.*, devineuse, *f.*
Divineress, *s.* devineresse, *f.*
Diving, *s.* plongement, *m.*; plongeon, *m.* — **apparatus,** scaphandre, *m.*; (*bell*) cloche à (*or* de) plongeur, *f.* — **bell,** *s.* cloche à (*or* de) plongeur, *f.* — **dress,** *s.* scaphandre, *m.*
Divining, *s.* divination, *f.* — **rod,** *s.* baguette divinatoire, *f.*
Divinity, *s.* divinité, *f.*; (*science*) théologie, *f.* — **student,** *s.* étudiant en théologie, *m.*
Divisi -bility, bleness. *V.* page 3, § i
Divisible, *adj.* divisible
Divisibly, *adv.* divisiblement
Division, *s.* division, *f.*; (*of shares*) partage, *m.*; (*voting*) vote, *m.*; (*mus.*) roulade, *f.* *Compound —,* (*arith.*) division des nombres complexes, *f.* *Simple —,* division des nombres entiers, *f.* *On a —,* (*parliam.*) en allant aux voix. *Without a —,* sans aller aux voix
Divisional, *adj.* divisionnaire; de division
Divisive, *adj.* divisif; (*arith.*) diviseur
Divisor, *s.* diviseur, *m.*
Divorce, *s.* divorce, *m.*; (*fig.*) séparation, *f.*; — *v.a.n.* divorcer ('*from,*' d'avec); (*fig.*) séparer (de)
Divulgation, *s.* divulgation, *f.*
Divulge, *v.a.* divulguer; publier; révéler
Divulger, *s.* divulgateur, *m.*, -trice, *f.*; révélateur, *m.*, -trice, *f.*
Divulsion, *s.* divulsion, *f.*, arrachement, *m.*
Dizziness, *s.* éblouissement, *m.*; étourdissement, *m.*
Dizzy, *adj.* ébloui, étourdi; (*things*) étourdissant, vertigineux; — *v.a.* étourdir
Do, *v.a.* faire; accomplir; finir; achever; commettre; (*a service, justice*) rendre; (*to put*) mettre; (*to cook*) cuire, faire cuire; (*cheat*) refaire, enfoncer, mettre dedans; — *v.n.* faire; (*act*) agir; (*behave*) se conduire, se comporter; (*of the health*) se porter, aller; (*suit, fit, get on*) aller; convenir; être bon; faire l'affaire; (*fare well*) aller bien, réussir; (*take*) prendre; (*get off*) s'en tirer; (*be enough or adequate*) suffire; (*finish*) finir; (*to become of*) devenir; (*to cook*) cuire; — *s.* fait, *m.*; acte, *m.*, action, *f.*; (*cheat*) duperie, flouerie, *f.*; (*mus.*) do, ut, *m.*; — *adv.* (*abbrev. of* "ditto") id., idem, &c. (*V.* **Ditto**); *int.* donc; je vous en prie; faites; (*go on*) allez, va; (*yes*) oui (*Do be quiet!* restez donc tranquille! *Do give it me!* donnez-le-moi, je vous en prie. *Don't!* finissez!). — **again, over again,** refaire. — **it again,** recommencer. *If you — it again you will be punished,* si vous recommencez vous serez puni. *I won't — it again,* je ne le ferai plus, je ne recommencerai plus. — **all,** *s.* factotum, *m.* — **away with,** ôter, enlever, faire disparaître; éloigner (de); faire cesser; abolir, supprimer; détruire; (*kill*) tuer, se défaire de. — **by,** (*deal with*) agir envers, agir à l'égard de, en agir avec, en user avec, traiter. — **for,** (*kill*) tuer, escoffier, occire. *To — for oneself,* se suffire (à soi-même), se tirer d'affaire tout seul. — **little,** *s.* petit faiseur, *m.* — **nothing,** *s.* fainéant, *m.*, e, *f.* — **out of** (...), filouter *or* flibuster *or* voler (...) à. — **over,** enduire (de); recouvrir (de). — **up,** réparer; remettre en état; remettre à neuf; arranger; (*fold*) plier; (*pack*) empaqueter; (*bundle*) emballer; (*pers.*) enfoncer, couler, ruiner; (*fatigue*) éreinter. — **without,** se passer de (— *without it* or *them* [*things*], s'en passer). *To — well,* (*things*) faire bien, faire bon effet; (*pers.*) faire bien; agir *or* &c. bien; (*be happy*) être heureux; (*be in a good way*) être en bonne voie; (*succeed in business*) faire de bonnes affaires; (*enjoy oneself*) s'en donner. *To have to — with,* avoir affaire

de; avoir à voir dans *or* à; (*to be connected*) avoir rapport à (*or* avec), avoir du rapport avec; (*to quarrel*) avoir à démêler avec; (*have to deal with*) avoir affaire à. *To have something to — with*, être pour quelque chose dans, n'être pas étranger à; se mêler de; avoir rapport à, avoir quelque rapport avec. *To have something to — with it*, y être pour quelque chose, n'y être pas étranger; s'en mêler; avoir rapport à (*or* quelque rapport avec) la question. *To have nothing to — with*, n'être pour rien dans, être étranger à; n'avoir rien à voir dans *or* à; n'avoir rien à démêler avec; ne pas se mêler de; n'avoir que faire de; n'avoir pas de (*or* n'avoir aucun) rapport à *or* avec. *To have nothing to — with it*, n'y être pour rien, y être étranger; n'avoir rien à y voir; ne pas s'en mêler; n'avoir pas de (*or* aucun) rapport à *or* avec la question. *To have done with*, n'avoir plus besoin de; (*leave off, be rid*) en finir avec; (*renounce*) renoncer à, avoir assez de; (*an acquaintance*) avoir rompu avec. *To have done with it*, (*leave off*) en finir. *That will* —, c'est bien, c'est bien comme cela, cela suffit; c'est bon; cela va; cela ira; cela fera l'affaire. *That will not —, that won't* —, cela ne va pas; cela n'ira pas; cela ne peut pas aller comme cela; cela ne prend pas; cela ne prendra pas; cela n'est pas convenable; cela n'est pas bon; cela ne vaut rien; il ne faut pas de ça; pas de ça! *That will not* (or *won't*) *— for me*, cela ne me va pas; cela ne me convient pas; cela ne fera pas mon affaire; (*will not succeed*) cela ne réussira pas avec moi, cela (*or* ça) ne prendra (*or* ne prend) pas avec moi. *That will never* —, cela n'ira jamais; cela (*or* ce) n'est pas tolérable (*or* permis). *Will that —?* cela suffit-il? cela va-t-il? est-ce bien comme cela? *I cannot — anything with that child*, je ne puis rien faire de cet enfant. *What will you — with him?* qu'en ferez-vous? *What have you to — with him?* qu'avez-vous à faire *or* à démêler avec lui? *What have you done with your book?* qu'avez-vous fait de votre livre? *What have you done with it?* qu'en avez-vous fait? *I have nothing to — with it*, (*no concern*) cela ne me regarde pas; (*no hand in it*) je n'y suis pour rien. *What does he — with himself?* à quoi s'occupe-t-il? qu'est-ce qu'il fait? *I don't know what to — with myself*, je ne sais à quoi m'occuper, je ne sais que faire; je m'ennuie. *How do you —?* comment vous portez-vous? bonjour. *What shall I —?* (*what will become of me?*) qu'est-ce que je vais devenir? *To be done*, à faire; faisable; praticable; l'affaire (de); (*being done*), se faire (*That is done every day*, cela se fait tous les jours). *V.* **Done.**

[**Do, Did,** *used as signs of another verb, are not expressed in French, as: I* do *think*, je pense. *What* did *he say?* qu'a-t-il dit? *I* do *not know*, je ne sais pas. Do *not do that*, ne faites pas cela. *I do, he does, you don't, I did, &c., are generally rendered by* oui (*or* si, *after a neg.*), non, *or by repeating the verb they stand for; as, Do you like tea? Yes, I do;* aimez-vous le thé? Oui, *or* oui, je l'aime; *No, I don't*, Non, *or* non, je ne l'aime pas. *Does it rain? I think it does* (*does not*), pleut-il? Je crois que oui (que non). *He did not come, did he? Yes, he did; I tell you he did;* il n'est pas venu, n'est-ce pas? Si (*less fam.* Pardon), *or* si, il est venu; je vous dis que si. *I will come, if I can, but if I do not, do not be surprised*, je viendrai si je le peux, mais si je ne viens pas, ne vous en étonnez pas. *You do not know what he means, but I do*, vous ne savez pas ce qu'il veut dire, mais moi je le sais

Doat. *V.* **Dote**

Dobchick. *V.* **Dabchick**

Dobule, *s.* dobule, *m.*

Docile, *adj.* docile

Docility, *s.* docilité, *f.*

Docimacy, *s.* docimasie, *f.* [docimastique, *f.*

Docimastic, *adj.* docimastique. — *art*,

Dock, *s.* (*of a tail*) tronçon, *m.*; (*of a crupper*) culeron, *m.*; (*bot.*) patience, *f.*; (*in courts of justice*) banc des accusés (*or* des prévenus), *m.*; (*for ships*) bassin, *m.*; (*com. nav.*) dock, *m.*; (*dry dock*) chantier, *m.*; (*of rivers*) gare, *f.*; — *v.a.* écourter; (*ships*) mettre dans le bassin, mettre aux docks; (*on rivers*) garer. — **due,** *s.* droit de bassin, *m.*; droit de dock, *m.* — **gate,** *s.* vanne de bassin, *f.* — **house,** *s.* hôtel de la compagnie des docks, *m.* — **master,** *s.* directeur de docks, *m.* — **yard,** *s.* arsenal de marine, *m.*; chantier, *m.*

Docket, *s.* bordereau, *m*; (*label*) étiquette, *f.*; (*of bankruptcy*) ouverture (d'une faillite), *f.*; — *v.a.* étiqueter [queue, *m.*

Docking-knife *or* **machine,** *s.* (*vet.*) coupe-

Doctor, *s.* docteur, *m.*; (*medical man*) médecin, *m.*; — *v.a.* médeciner, médicamenter; droguer. — *of divinity*, docteur en théologie. — *of law* or *laws*, (LL.D., D.C.L.), docteur en droit. — *of medicine*, docteur en médecine, docteur-

Doctoral, *adj.* doctoral [médecin, médecin

Doctorally, *adv.* doctoralement

Doctorate, Doctorship, *s.* doctorat, *m.*

Doctoress, Doctress, *s.* doctoresse, *f.*

Doctrinaire, *s. adj.* doctrinaire, *m.f.*

Doctrinaireism, Doctrinairism, *s.* doc-

Doctrinal, *adj.* doctrinal [trinarisme, *m.*

Doctrinally, *adv.* doctrinalement

Doctrinarian, *s. adj.* doctrinariste, *m.f.*

Doctrinarianism, *s.* doctrinarisme, *m.*

Doctrine, *s.* doctrine, *f.*

Document, *s.* document, *m.*, pièce, *f.*, titre, *m.*

Documentary, *adj.* de documents; authentique. — *evidence*, preuve écrite, preuve

Dodded, *adj.* sans cornes [authentique, *f.*

Dodder, *s.* cuscute, *f.*

Dodecagon, *s.* dodécagone, *m.*

Dodecagonal, *adj.* dodécagonal, dodécagone

Dodecahedral, *adj.* dodécaèdre

Dodecahedron, *s.* dodécaèdre, *m.*

Dodge, *v.n.* biaiser, ruser; (*shift place*) s'esquiver; faire un détour *or* des détours; (*of hearing lessons*) prendre la leçon à rebours, sauter çà et là; — *v.a.* éviter; (*trifle with*) amuser, promener, faire aller, lanterner; (*watch*) épier; (*pose*) tâcher d'embarrasser par des questions; — *s.* biais, *m.*; détour, *m.*; ruse, rubrique, ficelle, *f.*, tour, *m.*; chic, *m.*

Dodger, *s.* biaiseur, *m.*, -euse, *f.*; finaud, *m.*, e, *f.*; intrigant, *m.*, e, *f.*

Dodo, *s.* dronte, dodo, *m.*

Doe, *s.* daine, chevrette, *f.* — **hare,** *s.* hase, *f.* — **rabbit,** *s.* lapine, hase, *f.* — **skin,** *s.* peau de daim, *f.* [auteur, *m.*

Doer, *s.* faiseur, *m.*, -euse, *f.*; (*of an action*)

Doff, *v a.* ôter, tirer; (*a mask*) lever, jeter; (*to strip*) se dépouiller de, se débarrasser de; (*to delay*) remettre

Dog, *s.* chien, *m.*, -ne, *f.*; (*of certain animals*) mâle, *m.*; (*chap*) gaillard, coquin, *m.*; (*firedog*) chenet, *m.*; (*tech.*) valet, *m.*; — *v.a.* suivre à la piste, suivre, guetter, épier; (*worry*) harceler, pourchasser. *Cunning* —, (*pers.*) rusé coquin, *m.* *Old* —, (*pers.*) vieux routier, *m.* *Sad* —, (*pers.*) triste sujet, *m.* *Sly* —, (*pers.*) fin matois, rusé compère, *m.* *Wild* —, (*pers.*) farceur, *m.* *To go to the —s*, se ruiner, s'enfoncer, se couler, prendre le chemin de l'hôpital, se perdre, aller au diable. *To send* or *give* or *throw to the —s*, envoyer promener, envoyer au diable, jeter aux chiens, jeter. *Give a — a bad name and hang him*, quand on veut noyer son chien on dit qu'il est enragé. *The — in the manger*, le chien du jardinier. — **bane,** *s.* apocyn, *m.* — **berry,** *s.* cornouille, *f.* — **berry-tree,** *s.* cornouiller, *m.* — **biscuit,** *s.* *V.* — **cake.** — **brake,** *s.* collier de force, *m.* — **briar,** *s.* églantier, *m.* — **cake,** *s.* pain de cretons, *m.* — **cart,** *s.* dog-cart, docart, *m.*

— **cheap,** *adj.* à vil prix, pour rien. — **collar,** *s.* collier de chien, *m.* — **days,** *s. pl.* canicule, *f.*, jours caniculaires, *m. pl.* — **doctor,** *s.* médecin de chiens, *m.* — **ear,** *V.* —**'s-ear.** — **fancier,** *s.* marchand de chiens, *m.* — **fight,** *s.* combat de chiens, *m.* — **fish,** *s.* chien de mer, *m.* — **fish skin,** *s.* peau de chien, *f.* — **grass,** *s.* chiendent, *m.* — **hole,** *s.* niche de chien, *f.*; (*fig.*) taudis, *m.* — **house,** *s. V.* **Kennel.** — **keeper,** *s.* valet de chiens, *m.* — **kennel,** *s. V.* **Kennel.** — **Latin,** *s.* latin de cuisine, *m.* — **leech,** *s. V.* — **doctor.** — **louse,** *s.* tique, *f.* — **rose,** *s.* églantine, *f.* — **rose-tree,** *s.* églantier, *m.* —**'s bane,** *s. V.* — **bane.** —**'s-ear,** *s.* corne, oreille, *f.*, pli, *m.*; *v.a.* corner, faire une corne *or* des cornes *or* &c. à. —**'s-grass,** *s. V.* — **grass.** — **show,** *s.* exposition de chiens, *f.* — **sick,** *adj.* malade comme un chien. — **skin,** *s. V.* —**'s skin.** —**'s meat,** *s.* mou, *m.*, tripes, *f.pl.*, abats, *m.pl.* —**'s skin,** *s.* peau de chien, *f.*; *adj.* fait de peau de chien. —**'s-tail grass,** *s.* cynosure, *f.*, (*crested*) cretelle, *f.* — **star,** *s.* canicule, *f.* — **tax,** *s.* impôt sur les chiens, *m.* — **tick,** *s.* tique, *f.* — **tooth,** *s.* dent canine, *f.* — **tooth grass,** — **tooth violet,** *s.* cynodon, *m.*, érythrone, *f.* — **trot,** *s.* petit trot, *m.* — **vane,** *s.* penon, *m.* — **violet,** *s.* violette de chien, *f.* — **weary,** *adj.* las comme un chien, harassé, éreinté. — **wood,** *s.* cornouiller, *m.*

Dogate, Dogeate, *s.* dogat, *m.*

Doge, *s.* doge, *m.*

Dogged, *adj.* hargneux, chien; acariâtre, revêche, maussade, bourru; déterminé; (*obstinate*) obstiné, opiniâtre

Doggedly, *adv.* comme un chien; d'une manière revêche, d'un air bourru *or* chien, d'un ton bourru; (*obstinately*) obstinément, opiniâtrément, mordicus

Doggedness, *s.* nature bourrue *or* revêche, *f.*; caractère hargneux, *m.*; humeur de chien, mauvaise humeur, *f.*; (*obstinacy*) opiniâtreté, *f.*

Dogger, — **boat,** *s.* dogre, dogrebot, *m.*

Doggerel. *V.* **Doggrel**

Dogging, *s.* poursuite, *f.*

Doggish, *adj.* de chien; comme un chien; [bourru, brutal

Doggrel, *adj.* mêlé, libre; (*bad*) rimaillé, mauvais; — *s.* (*irregular*) vers mêlés, vers libres, *m.pl.*; (*bad*) rimaille, prose rimée, *f.*, mauvais [(*or* méchants) vers, *m.pl.*

Doggy, *s.* toutou, *m.*

Dogma, *s.* dogme, *m.* [page 3, § 1

Dogmat-ic, al, -ically, -ism, -ist. *V.*

Dogmatics, *s. pl.* dogmatique, *f.*

Dogmatize, *v.n.* dogmatiser

Dogmatizer, *s.* dogmatiseur, *m.*

Doiley, Doily, *s.* serviette de dessert, *f.*; nappe de toilette, petite nappe, *f.*; dessous de lampe *or* de vase, &c. *m.*

Doing, *adj.* actif, occupé; — *s.*, —**s,** *s. pl.* action, *f.*, acte, *m.*, actions, *f.pl.*, actes, *m.pl.*; (*deed, deeds*) fait, exploit, *m.*, faits, exploits, *m.pl.*; (*conduct*) conduite, façon d'agir, *f.*; (*jest.*) faits et gestes, *m.pl.*; (*jobbing*) tripotage, *m.*; (*work*) œuvre, *f.*; ouvrage, *m.*; (*event, events*) événement, *m.*, événements, *m.pl.*; (*thing, things*) chose, affaire, *f.*, choses, affaires, *f.pl.*; (*bustle*, &c.) agitation, *f.*, remue-[ménage, *m.*

Doit, *s.* (*fig.*) centime, *m.*

Dole, *v.a.* — **out,** distribuer chichement, donner, faire l'aumône de; — *s.* distribution, *f.*; part, *f.*; pitance, *f.*; don gratuit, *m.*, aumône, charité, *f.*; (*grief*, &c.) douleur, affliction, *f.*, chagrin, *m.*; doléance, lamentation, *f.*

Doleful, *adj.* plaintif; (*sad*) triste, malheureux

Dolefully, *adv.* plaintivement; (*sadly*) tristement, malheureusement

Dolefulness, *s.* douleur, *f.*; (*sadness*) mélan-[colie, tristesse, *f.*

Doll, *s.* poupée, *f.*

Dollar, *s.* dollar, *m.*; pièce de cinq francs, *f.*

Dolly, *s.* poupée, *f.* — **shop,** *s.* magasin de [chiffons, *m.*

Dolmen, *s.* dolmen, *m.*

Dolorous, *adj.* douloureux, triste

Dolorously, *adv.* douloureusement, tristement

Dolphin, *s.* dauphin, *m.*

Dolt, *s.* benêt, *m.*, bûche, *f.*, lourdaud, *m.*, e, *f.*

Doltish, *adj.* stupide, sot, lourdaud, lourd

Doltishly, *adv.* stupidement, bêtement

Doltishness, *s.* sottise, stupidité, *f.*

Domain, *s.* domaine, *m.*; (*estate*) propriété, *f.*

Domanial, *adj.* domanial

Dome, *s.* dôme, *m.* [terre, *m.*

Domesday-book, *s.* grand cadastre d'Angle-

Domestic, *adj.* domestique; de famille; (*pers.*) casanier; (*of animals*) domestique; (*interior, inland, national*) intérieur; (*native*) indigène; — *s.* domestique, *m.f.* — **servant,** *s.* domestique, *m.f.*

Domestically, *adv.* domestiquement

Domesticate, *v a.* rendre domestique; accoutumer à la vie d'intérieur; rendre casanier; rendre familier; (*to tame*) domestiquer, apprivoiser

Domesticated, *adj.* (*pers.*) casanier; (*of animals*) domestique; (*things*) constant; — *part. V.* **Domesticate,** *v.a.*

Domestication, *s.* (*pers.*) vie casanière, retraite, *f.*; (*of animals*) domestication, *f.*, apprivoisement, *m.*

Domesticity, *s.* domesticité, *f.*

Domicile, *s.* domicile, *m.*

Domiciled, *adj.* domicilié

Domiciliary, *adj.* domiciliaire

Dominance, Dominancy, *s.* dominance, *f.*

Dominant, *adj.* dominant; dominateur; — *s.* (*mus.*) dominante, *f.*

Dominate, *v.a.n.* dominer

Domination, *s.* domination, *f.*

Dominative, *adj.* dominatif; dominateur

Dominator, *s.* dominateur, *m.*, -trice, *f.*

Domineer, *v.n.* dominer, régenter, commander

Domineering, *adj* impérieux, arrogant; — *s.* humeur impérieuse, arrogance, *f.*; domination, régentation, *f.*

Dominical, *adj.* dominical

Dominican, *s. adj.* (— *friar*) dominicain, *m.*, (— *nun*) dominicaine, *f.*

Dominie, *s.* magister, maître d'école, *m.*

Dominion, *s.* domination, *f.*; autorité, *f.*, pouvoir, *m.*; supériorité, *f.*; colonie, *f.*; —**s,** *pl.* états, *m.pl.*, empire, *m.*; colonies, *f.pl.*

Domino, *s.* domino, *m.*

Don, *s.* (*Spanish title*) don, *m.*; (*fig.*) seigneur, *m.*; (*jest.*) gros bonnet, matador, *m.*; — *v.a.* mettre, revêtir, endosser

Donation, *s.* don, *m.*; (*law*) donation, *f.*

Donative, *s.* don, présent, *m.*

Done, *part. adj.* fait, &c. (*V.* **Do**); (*of meat*, &c.) cuit. — *!* c'est fait! ça y est! c'est convenu! bien! va! tope! *Well — !* à merveille! bravo! à la bonne heure! c'est bien! — **brown,** *part. adj.* refait. — **for,** *part. adj.* perdu, flambé, fichu, enfoncé; fini; (*killed*) occis, [escoffié

Donee, *s.* donataire, *m.f.*

Donjon, *s.* donjon, *m.*

Donkey, *s.* âne, baudet, *m.*, bourrique, *f.* *To ride on a* —, monter (*or* aller) à âne. *Riding* (*mounted*) *on a* —, monté sur un âne. — **boy,** *s.* ânier, *m.* — **driver,** *s.* ânier, *m.*, ânière, *f.* — **engine, -pump,** *s.* machine d'alimentation, *f.*, appareil d'alimentation, *m.*, pompe alimentaire, *f.* — **race,** *s.* course d'ânes, *f.* — **ride, -riding,** *s.* promenade *or* partie à âne, *f.* [doctorale, *f.*

Donnism, *s.* suffisance, fatuité, *f.*; morgue

Donor, *s.* donateur, *m.*, -trice, *f.*

Doom, *v.a.* condamner (à); destiner (à); vouer (à); ordonner, commander; juger; — *s.* jugement, arrêt, *m.*, sentence, *f.*; condamnation, *f.*; décision, *f.*; (*fate*) sort, destin, *m.*; (*destruction*) ruine, perte, *f.* *Final* —, jugement dernier, *m.* — **palm,** *s.* cucifère, doum, *m.*

Doomsday, *s.* jour du jugement dernier, *m.* — **book,** *s. V.* **Domesday-book**

Door, *s.* porte, *f.*; (*of a carriage*) portière, *f.* *Next – to,* voisin de, tout près de, à côté de. *Next — to each other,* porte à porte. *Next — neighbour,* plus proche voisin, voisin qui demeure porte à porte (*To be next — neighbours,* demeurer porte à porte). *In —,* à l'intérieur; (*adj.*) interne. *In —s, within —s,* à la maison, dans la maison, au logis, chez soi; (*parliam.*) à la Chambre, dans les Chambres. *Out —,* dehors; (*adj.*) du *or* au dehors, externe. *Out of —s, without —s,* dehors, hors de la maison, hors de chez soi, en plein air; (*parliam.*) hors de la Chambre, hors des Chambres, dans le public. *With closed —s,* (*of trials*) à huis clos. *To close o.'s — against,* fermer sa porte à. *To go out of —s,* sortir, sortir de la maison, sortir de chez soi. *To turn out of —s,* mettre à la porte. *The fault lies at my —,* la faute en est à moi, c'est ma faute. *I will lay it at your —,* je ferai retomber cela sur vous, je le mettrai sur votre compte, je m'en prendrai à vous. *—, please!* (*open the door, pull the string*) le cordon, s'il vous plait! — **bell,** *s.* sonnette de (*or* de la) porte, *f.* — **case, -frame,** chambranle, *m.* — **fastener,** *s.* ferme-porte, *m.* — **hangings,** *s. pl.* portière, *f.* — **keeper,** *s.* concierge, *m.f.*, portier, *m.*, -ière, *f.*, (*of public edifices*) gardien, *m.* — **knob, -handle,** *s.* bouton de (*or* de la) porte, *m.* — **mat,** *s.* paillasson, *m.*; essuie-pieds, *m.* — **plate,** *s.* plaque, *f.*, écusson, *m.* — **porter,** *s.* (*pers.*) *V.* — **keeper;** (*thing*) arrête-porte, *m.* — **post,** *s.* montant, *m.*; dormant de porte, *m.* —**scraper,** *s.* décrottoir, *m.* —**sill,** *s.* seuil de (*or* de la) porte, *m.* — **spring,** *s.* bascule, *f.*; ferme-porte, *m.* — **step,** *s.* pas de (*or* de la) porte, *m.* — **way,** *s.* porte, *f.*, renfoncement de porte, portail, *m.*, entrée de porte, *f.*, passage sous une (*or* la) porte, *m.* *In a — way,* sous une porte, dans le renfoncement d'une [porte

Dor, — beetle, *s.* bousier, *m.*

Dorado, *s.* dorade, *f.*

Doree. *V.* **Dory**

Dorian, *s. adj.* Dorien, *m.*, -ne, *f.*

Doric, *adj. s.* dorique, *adj. m.f., s.m.*

Doris, *s.* (*zool.*) doris, *f.*

Dormancy, *s.* repos, *m.*

Dormant, *adj.* dormant, endormi, assoupi; engourdi; éteint; latent, caché; tombé en désuétude; (*of money*) qui dort, mort; (*of partners*) commanditaire; (*her.*) dormant. *To lie —,* dormir; être endormi *or* &c.

Dormer, — window, *s.* lucarne, *f.*

Dormitive, *adj. s.* dormitif, *adj.m.*, -ive, *f.*, [dormitif, *s.m.*

Dormitory, *s.* dortoir, *m.*

Dormouse, *s.* loir, *m.*

Dornoch, Dornock, *s.* toile d'Écosse, *f.*

Dorr. *V.* **Dor**

Dorsal, *adj.* dorsal

Dorse, *s.* (*fish*) dorsch, *m.*

Dorsel. *V.* **Dosser**

Dory, *s.* *John —,* dorée, *f.*

Dosage, *s.* dosage, *m.*

Dose, *s.* dose, *f.*; — *v.a.* doser; médicamenter

Dosing, *s.* dosage, *m.*

Dosser, *s.* hotte, *f.*, panier, *m.*

Dossil. *V.* **Pledget**

Dot, *s.* point, *m.*; — *v.a.* marquer de points, marquer d'un point, mettre des points *or* un point sur; (*diversify*) parsemer (de); (*of arts*) pointiller [fance, *f.*

Dotage, *s.* radotage, *m.*; (*old age*) seconde en-

Dotal, *adj.* dotal

Dotard, *s.* radoteur, *m.*, -euse, *f.*

Dotation, *s.* dotation, *f.* [raffoler (de)

Dote, *v.n.* radoter; (*on*) aimer éperdument,

Dotingly, *adv.* passionnément, éperdument, [à la folie

Dottard, *s.* arbre étêté, *m.*

Dotterel, *s.* guignard, *m.* [pointillé, *m.*

Dotting, *s.* (*act*) pointillage, *m.*, (*result*)

Double, *adj.* double; (*in two*) en deux; (*deceitful*) faux; — *s.* double, *m.*; (*counterpart*) pendant, *m.*; (*beer*) bière double, *f.*; (*dodge*) détour, *m.*; (*trick*) ruse, *f.*, artifice, *m.*; (*print.*) doublage, doublon, *m.*; (*mus.*) variation, *f.*; (*mil.*) pas redoublé, *m.*; — *v.a.n.* doubler; (*fold*) mettre en double, plier en deux; (*the fist*) fermer, serrer, (*ditto at* ...) montrer; (*contain*) avoir le double de; (*wind, dodge*) faire des détours; s'esquiver; (*play tricks*) user de ruse, ruser. — *that,* (*twice as much or as many*) le double de cela. — *or quits,* quitte ou double. *To grow —,* (*bot.*) être double; (*pers.*) se voûter. — **barrelled,** *adj.* à deux coups, double. — **buttoned,** *adj.* à deux rangs de boutons. — **cased,** &c., *V.* **Cased,** &c. — **chinned,** *adj.* à double menton. — **compasses,** *s. pl.* compas d'épaisseur, *m.* — **dealer,** *s.* homme (*m.*) *or* femme (*f.*) à deux visages. — **dealing,** *s.* duplicité, mauvaise foi, *f.*; artifice, *m.*, fourberie, *f.*; *adj.* à deux visages, à double jeu. — **dye,** *v.a.* teindre deux fois. — **edged,** *adj.* à deux tranchants. — **entente** (*vulgarly* — **entendre**), *s.* mot à double entente, *f.* — **gild,** *v.a.* surdorer. — **gilding,** *s.* surdorure, *f.* — **handed,** *adj.* à deux mains, bimane; (*fig.*) à deux faces, trompeur. — **lock,** *s.* serrure à double tour, *f.*; *v.a.* fermer à double tour. — **milled,** *adj.* croisé. — **milled cloth,** *s.* cuir de laine, *m.* — **minded,** *adj.* irrésolu, indécis, incertain; faux, dissimulé. — **quick,** *adj.* (*of pace*) redoublé; *s.* pas redoublé, *m.* — **seated,** *adj.* à deux places. — **tongued,** *adj.* à deux langues, bilingue; (*fig.*) faux, dissimulé. — **upon,** *v.a.* (*mil.*) prendre entre deux feux

Doubleness, *s.* état double, *m.*; duplicité, *f.*

Doubler, *s.* (*pers.*) doubleur, *m.*, -euse, *f.*; (*phys. instr.*) doubleur, *m.*

Doublet, *s.* (*garment*) pourpoint, *m.*; (*at backgammon, billiards, opt., jewel.*) doublet, *m.*

Doubling, *s.* doublement, *m.*; (*tech.*) doublage, *m.*; (*geom.*) duplication, *f.*; (*dodge, trick*) dé-[tour, *m.*, ruse, *f.*

Doubloon, *s.* doublon, *m.*

Doubly, *adv.* doublement; avec duplicité

Doubt, *v.n.* douter; (*to suspect*) soupçonner; (*to fear*) craindre; — *v.a.* douter de; (*to fear*) craindre; — *s.* doute, *m.*; incertitude, *f.* *Beyond —, beyond all —,* hors de doute, indubitable. *No —,* sans doute; nul doute. *No — that,* nul doute que. *To make no —,* ne pas douter; (*... of it*) n'en pas douter. *There is* (or *there can be*) *no — of it,* cela ne fait pas de (*or* ne fait aucun) doute. —**able,** *adj.* douteux. —**er,** *s.* douteur, *m.*, -euse, *f.* —**ful,** *adj.* (*of things only*) douteux; de doute; (*of things and pers.*) incertain; indécis; (*of debts*) véreux. *To be —ful of,* douter de, avoir des doutes sur. —**fully,** *adv.* douteusement, d'une manière douteuse, avec doute; avec indécision, avec irrésolution; ambigument, d'une manière ambiguë, avec ambiguïté. —**fulness,** *s.* état de doute, doute, *m.*, incertitude, *f.*; ambiguïté, *f.* —**ingly,** *adv.* dubitativement, avec doute, en doutant, d'une manière douteuse; avec défiance; avec indécision. —**less,** —**lessly,** *adv.* sans doute, indubitablement; assurément [vin, *m.*

Douceur, *s.* présent, *m.*, douceur, *f.*; pot-de-

Douche, *s.* douche, *f.*

Dough, *s.* pâte, *f.* — **baked,** *adj.* *V.* **Sodden;** (*fig.*) inachevé, manqué. — **knife,** *s.* coupe-pâte, *m.* — **nut,** *s.* gâteau de pâte, *m.* [ment

Doughtily, *adv.* vaillamment, valeureuse-

Doughtiness, *s.* valeur, vaillance, *f.*

Doughty, *adj.* vaillant, valeureux, preux

Doughy, *adj.* pâteux; (*soft*) mou, mollasse

Doura, Dourra, *s.* doura, *m.*

Douse, *v.a.n.* plonger; enfoncer; inonder, arroser; (*extinguish*) éteindre

Dove, *s.* colombe, *f.* — **colour,** *s.* couleur gorge-de-pigeon, couleur isabelle, *f.*, gorge-de-pigeon, isabelle, *m.* — **coloured,** *adj.* gorge-de-pigeon, isabelle. — **cot, -cote, -house,** *s.*

colombier, *m.* — **tail,** *s.* queue d'aronde, *f.*; *v.a.* assembler à (*or* en) queue d'aronde; réunir, joindre. — **tailed,** *adj.* à (*or* en) queue d'aronde. — **tailing,** *s.* assemblage à (*or* en) queue d'aronde, *m.*
Dowager, *s.* douairière, *f.*
Dowcets, *s. pl.* daintiers, *m.pl.*
Dowdy, *s.* souillon, *f.*, guenillon, *m.*, paquet, *m.*; — *adj.* négligé, débraillé
Dower, *s.* douaire, *m.*; (*abusively for "dowry"*) dot, *f.*; (*gift*) don, présent, *m.*
Dowl, Dowle, *s.* barbe (de plume), *f.*
Down, *s.* duvet, *m.*; (*of sea-coast*) dune, *f.*; — *adj.* baissé; bas; (*of the bottom*) du bas; (*dejected*) abattu, triste; (*of trains*) d'aller, &c. (*V.* **Train**); — *adv.* en bas; (*low*) bas; (*on the ground*) à terre, par terre; à bas; (*at length*) étendu; (*gone or come down*) descendu; (*fallen*) tombé; (*into disrepute*) en défaveur; (*on the decline*) sur le déclin; (*com.*) en baisse; (*of the sun*) couché; (*of the moon*) couché, sous l'horizon; (*of the wind*) apaisé, tombé; bas; (*of the tide*) bas; (*of prices*) bas, en baisse; (*of clocks, &c.*) pas monté, pas remonté; (*open*) ouvert; (*navig.*) en aval; — *prep.* en bas de; au bas de; vers le bas de; jusqu'au bas de; en descendant; — *int.* à bas! (*nav.*) amène! (*come* or *go* — !) descends, descendez; (*sit* —!) asseyez-vous; (*to a dog*) à bas les pattes! couchez! — *v.a.* abaisser; abattre, humilier; — *v.n.* descendre; passer. *The ups and —s, V.* **Up,** *s.* — *from,* en bas de; à bas de; du haut de; (*of time*) depuis. — *there,* — *below,* là, en bas; (*about*) par là-bas; (*lower down*) plus bas; (*underneath*) là-dessous. — *to,* jusqu'à. — *to here,* jusqu'ici. — *to there,* jusque-là. — *upon him!* cours dessus, courez dessus! — *with . . . !* à bas . . . ! — *with it!* à bas! (*swallow* —!) avalez-moi ça! — (*the*) *stream,* — *the river,* en aval; avec le courant. — *in the mouth,* abattu; penaud. — **bed,** *s.* lit de duvet, *m.* — **cast,** *adj.* baissé, baissé vers la terre; (*sad*) abattu, triste. — **fall,** *s.* chute, *f.*; ruine, *f.*; (*decline*) décadence, *f.* — **fallen,** *adj.* tombé, tombé en ruines; ruiné, déchu. — **hearted,** *adj.* découragé, abattu. — **hill,** *s.* descente, pente, *f.*, penchant, *m.*; *adj.* en pente, incliné; facile, doux; *adv.* en descendant. —**less,** *adj.* sans duvet. — **line,** *s.* (*rail.*) ligne d'aller, *f.* — **pour,** *s.* averse, quantité de pluie, pluie, *f.* — **right,** *adv.* de haut en bas, perpendiculairement; complètement, tout à fait; subitement, tout à coup; nettement, net, tout net; *adj.* franc; vrai; positif; direct. — **rightly,** *adv.* tout uniment, sans façon, clair et net. — **rightness,** *s.* franchise, *f.* — **sitting,** *s.* repos, *m.* — **trod, -trodden,** *adj.* foulé aux pieds. — **ward,** *adj.* de haut en bas; descendant; incliné; humilié; inférieur. — **ward, -wards,** *adv.* (*of place*) en bas; en descendant; (*of time*) en descendant; (*to the present time*) jusqu'aujourd'hui; (*navig.*) en aval
Downed, *adj.* couvert de duvet, duveté
Downy, *adj.* de duvet, duveteux; couvert de duvet, duveté; (*soft*) doux; (*slang for 'sly'*) [rusé
Dowry, *s.* dot, *f.*
Dowse. *V.* **Douse**
Doxolog-ical, y. *V.* page 3, § 1
Doxy, *s.* menesse, *f.*
Doze, *v.n.* s'assoupir, s'endormir; sommeiller; — *s.* assoupissement, *m.*; somme, *m.* *To have a* —, faire un somme. *To — away the time,* passer son temps à dormir
Dozen, *s.* douzaine, *f.* *A baker's* —, *a long* —, treize à la douzaine. *A round* —, une bonne [douzaine
Doziness, *s.* envie de dormir, *f.*
Dozing, *s.* assoupissement, *m.*
Dozy, *adj.* qui a envie de dormir, qui s'assoupit; (*fig.*) pesant, lourd
Dr., *s.* docteur, *m.*; (*book-keep.*) doit, *m.*
Drab, *adj.* gris brun, noisette, chamois — *s.* drap gris brun, drap de couleur noisette, *m.*;
Drabble, *v.n.a.* *V.* **Draggle** [(*woman*) *V.* **Slut**
Drachm, Drachma, *s.* drachme, *m.f.*
Draconian, Draconic, *adj.* draconien
Draff, *s.* lie, *f.*; lavure, rinçure, *f.*; (*refuse*) [rebut, *m.*, ordures, *f.pl.*
Draft. *V.* **Draught**
Drag, *v.a.n.* traîner; (*pull*) tirer; (*dredge*) draguer; (*a pond*) pêcher; (*anchors*) chasser sur, draguer; — *v.n.* se traîner; (*hang down*) traîner; (*fish.*) pêcher à la drague, traîner la drague; (*of anchors*) chasser; — *s.* (*hook*) croc, harpon, *m.*; (*net, nav.*) drague, *f.*; (*truck or sledge*) diable, *m.*; (*private carriage*) voiture à quatre chevaux, *f.*, drag, *m.*; (*of carriages, &c.*) enrayure, *f.*, frein, sabot, *m.*; (*pull*) *V.* **Pull,** *s.*; (*obstacle, 'upon,'* pour) entrave, *f.*; (*burden, 'upon,'* pour) charge, *f.*, fardeau, *m.* *To put on the* —, enrayer, mettre le sabot *or* le frein. — **about,** *v.a.* traîner, trimbaler. — **away,** *v.a.* entraîner; arracher (de). — **chain,** *s.* chaîne, *f.* — **man,** *s.* pêcheur à la seine *or* à la drague, *m.* — **net,** *s.* seine, *f.*; drague, *f.* — **off,** *v.a.* *V.* — **away**
Draggle, *v.n.a.* traîner dans la boue, traîner par terre; crotter, salir
Dragoman, *s.* drogman, truchement, *m.*
Dragomanship, *s.* drogmanat, *m.*
Dragon, *s.* dragon, *m.* — **beam,** *s.* contre-fiche, *f.* — **fly,** *s.* demoiselle, libellule, *f.* — **like,** *adj.* en dragon, comme un dragon. —**'s-blood,** *s.* sang-de-dragon, sang-dragon, *m.* —**'s-head,** *s.* (*astr.*) tête du dragon, *f.*; (*bot.*) dracocéphale, *m.* — **tree,** *s.* dragonnier, *m.*
Dragonet, *s.* petit dragon, *m.*; (*fish*) dragonneau, callionyme, *m.*
Dragonnade, *s.* dragonnade, *f.*
Dragoon, *s.* dragon, *m.*; — *v.a.* livrer à la fureur des soldats, livrer au pillage *or* aux dragonnades; (*to harass*) dragonner; (*to compel*) forcer, soumettre par la persécution. — **bird,** *s.* céphaloptère, *m.*
Dragoonade, *s.* dragonnade, *f.*
Drain, *v.a.* faire écouler l'eau de; faire écouler; (*marshes, land*) drainer, saigner, dessécher, assainir; (*filter*) passer; faire égoutter; (*drink*) vider; (*of money*) saigner; (*exhaust*) épuiser, mettre à sec; (*provide with drains*) pourvoir de tuyaux d'écoulement, pourvoir d'égouts; (*mines*) assécher; — *v.n.* (*flow*) s'écouler; (*dry*) égoutter; — *s.* saignée, tranchée, *f.*; (*ditch*) drain, fossé *or* sillon d'écoulement, *m.*; (*sewer*) égout, *m.*; puisard, *m.*; (*tech.*) égouttoir, *m.*; (*exhaustion*) épuisement, *m.* — **gallery,** *s.* galerie d'écoulement, *f.* — **off,** *v.a.* dessécher. — **pipe,** *s.* tuyau *or* conduit d'écoulement, *m.*; (*agr.*) tuyau *or* tube de drainage, *m.* — **tile,** *s.* tuile de drainage, *f.* — **well,** *s.* puisard, *m.*; puits perdu, *m.*
Drainage, *s.* écoulement, *m.*; (*of towns*) écoulement (*or* système d'écoulement) des eaux (*or* des eaux ménagères), *m.*, égouts, *m.pl.*; (*of marshes, land*) drainage, dessèchement, assainissement, *m.*; (*tech.*) égouttage, égouttement, *m.*; (*filth*) immondices des égouts, *f.pl.*, gadoue, *f.* — **gallery,** *V.* **Drain-gallery.** — **tube,** *s.* (*agr.*) *V.* **Drain-pipe;** (*surg.*) tube à drainage, *m.*
Drainer, *s.* égouttoir, *m.*; (*pers.*) draineur, *m.*
Draining, *s.* *V.* **Drainage;** —**s,** *pl.* égoutture, *f.*; — *adj.* de (*or* à) drainage; draineur. — **tile,** *s.* tuile de drainage, *f.* — **well,** *s.* puisard, *m.*
Drake, *s.* canard, *m.*
Dram, *s.* drachme, *m.f.*; (*small quantity*) grain, *m.*; (*of liquor*) goutte, *f.*; (*liquor itself*) spiritueux, *m.*, liqueur spiritueuse, liqueur forte, liqueur, *f.*, (*fam.*) rogomme, *m.*, goutte, *f.* — **drinker,** *s.* buveur (*m.*, -euse, *f.*) de liqueurs fortes, godailleur, *m.*, -euse, *f.*, riboteur, *m.*, -euse, *f.* — **drinking,** *s.* abus des liqueurs fortes, *m.*, godaille, boisson, *f.* — **shop,** *s.* *V.* **Pot-house**
Drama, *s.* drame, *m.*; (*art*) scène, *f.*, théâtre, *m.*

Dramat-ic, al, -ically. *V.* page 3, § 1
Dramatis personæ, *s. pl.* personnages, *m.pl.*
Dramatist, *s.* auteur dramatique, *m.*, dramatiste, *m.f.*
Dramatize, *v.a.* dramatiser
Dramaturg-ic, al, -y. *V.* page 3, § 1
Drape, *v.a.* draper; tendre
Draper, *s.* drapier, marchand de draps, *m.*
Drapery, *s.* draperie, *f.*
Drastic, *adj. s.* drastique, *adj. m.f.*, *s.m.*
Draught, *s.* (*act of drawing*) tirage, *m.*; trait, *m.*; (*of drink*) trait, coup, *m.*; (*drink*) breuvage, *m.*; potion, *f.*; (*delineation*) dessin, *m.*, ébauche, esquisse, *f.*; plan, projet, *m.*; (*rough copy*) brouillon, *m.*; (*fishing: haul*) coup de filet, *m.*, (*catch*) pêche, prise, quantité, *f.*; (*of air*) courant d'air, (*from a chink*) vent coulis, *m.*; (*of weighable goods*) bon poids, *m.*; (*bill*) traite, *f.*, mandat, *m.*; (*of ships*) tirant, tirant d'eau, *m.*; (*of soldiers*) détachement, *m.*; **—s,** *pl.* (*game*) (le) jeu de dames, *m.*, (les) dames, *f.pl.*; — *v.a.* dessiner; (*writings*) rédiger; (*mil.*) détacher, (*into*) incorporer (dans); (*enroll*) enrôler. *A deep* —, un grand coup. *At a* (or *one*) —, d'un seul trait, d'un seul coup. *In long —s, with deep —s,* à longs traits. *On —,* à la mesure [au litre, &c.] *To play at —s,* jouer aux dames. — **beer,** *or* &c., *s.* bière *or* &c. à la mesure, *f.* — **board,** *s.* damier, *m.* — **compasses,** *s. pl.* compas à branches, *m.* — **eye, -hole,** *s.* regard, *m.* — **horse,** *s.* cheval de trait, *m.* — **off,** *v.a.* détacher. — **ox,** *s.* bœuf de trait, *m.* —**sman,** *s.* dessinateur, *m.*
Draw, *v.a.* tirer; (*drag*) traîner; (*pass*) passer; (*a picture,* &c.) dessiner; tracer, représenter, peindre; faire; (*lengthen*) allonger; (*inhale*) respirer, aspirer; (*suck*) sucer; (*a sigh*) pousser; (*attract*) attirer; (*allure*) attirer (à), inviter (à); (*pluck, obtain*) arracher; (*a liquid from a cask, blood from the veins*) tirer; (*water, anything from a store, and fig. information, consolation,* &c.) puiser ('*from,*' dans, à); (*a conclusion*) tirer; (*induce*) entraîner (dans *or* à); (*gain*) gagner; (*extract*) extraire, exprimer; (*a tooth*) arracher; (*derive*) retirer (de), tirer (de); (*a bow, a sword*) tirer; (*a curtain*) *V.* **Curtain;** (*a writing*) rédiger, dresser; (*bills*) tirer; (*o.'s salary*) toucher; (*the reins*) serrer; (*wires,* &c.) étirer; (*poultry*) vider; (*a pond*) pêcher, dépeupler; (*at dominoes*) pêcher; (*fort.*) tirer, tracer; (*of ships*) tirer, jauger, caler (... mètres *or* pieds d'eau). *To — and quarter,* écarteler. *V.* **Drawn,** *part. adj.* — **along,** traîner. — **aside,** tirer à l'écart; tirer; détourner. — **asunder,** séparer, diviser. — **away,** retirer, ôter; (*carry away*) entraîner; (*turn away*) détourner. — **back,** tirer en arrière; reculer; (*take away*) retirer. — **down,** tirer en bas; baisser; rabaisser; rabattre; (*fig.*) attirer. — **forth,** tirer en avant; faire avancer; faire sortir; amener; développer; faire paraître, faire ressortir; (*pull out*) tirer, sortir. — **in,** tirer dedans; rentrer; ramasser, réunir, rassembler; (*the reins*) serrer; (*fig.*) entraîner. — **near, -nearer,** approcher; s'approcher. — **off,** tirer, ôter, retirer; (*water,* &c.) faire écouler; détourner; (*from a cask*) tirer; (*extract*) tirer, extraire; (*print.*) tirer; (*mil.*) retirer; (*fig.*) détourner (de). — **on,** tirer en avant; (*stockings, boots,* &c.) tirer, mettre; (*com.*) tirer sur; (*fig.*) attirer, susciter; amener, occasionner, causer. — **out,** tirer dehors; tirer; retirer; tracer; (*troops*) faire avancer; ranger; (*extract*) extraire; (*force out*) arracher; (*extend,* &c.) étendre, prolonger; (*a pers., in talk*) faire parler. — **over,** entraîner (à), gagner; faire passer. — **together,** rassembler, réunir; rapprocher. — **up,** (*pull*) tirer en haut, tirer; (*raise*) lever; relever, redresser; retrousser; (*bring*) amener, mener; (*take out*) enlever, retirer, sortir; (*a boat*) tirer à terre; (*to offer*) offrir, présenter; (*writings*) rédiger; dresser; (*an army*) ranger; (*a fleet*) aligner

Draw, *v.n.* tirer; (*shrink*) se retirer, se rétrécir, se contracter, se resserrer; (*move*) se mouvoir, se porter, se diriger; s'avancer, s'approcher; (*of swords*) tirer l'épée; (*delineate*) dessiner; (*of tea,* &c.) s'infuser, infuser, se faire; (*of blisters*) tirer; (*of bills*) tirer, faire traite; (*at dominoes*) pêcher; (*attract people*) attirer du monde; prendre; (*of ships*) gagner; (*of sails*) porter, être tendu. *To — for the deal,* (*at dominoes*) tirer la pose. *To — well together,* vivre (*or* être) bien ensemble. — **back,** reculer; se reculer; se retirer. — **in,** se retirer; rentrer dans les rangs; infuser; (*of the day*) baisser. — **near** *or* **nigh, nearer,** s'approcher (de), approcher (de). — **off,** se retirer. — **on,** s'avancer, approcher, s'approcher; puiser dans; (*com.*) tirer sur. — **out,** s'étendre. —**together,** se rassembler, se réunir. — **up,** se ranger, se mettre en ligne; (*of carriages*) s'arrêter
Drawable, *adj.* tirable
Drawback, *s.* drawback, *m.*, prime d'exportation, prime, *f.*; (*fig.*) décompte, mécompte, *m.*; empêchement, obstacle, *m.*, entrave, *f.*; résistance, *f.*; reculade, *f.*, retard, *m.*, perte, *f.*, désavantage, inconvénient, *m.*; défaut, *m.*
Draw-bench, *s.* banc à étirer, *m.*, argue, *f.*
Drawbridge, *s.* pont-levis, *m.*
Drawee, *s.* tiré, *m.*, e, *f.*, surtiré, *m.*, e, *f.*
Drawer, *s.* (*sliding box*) tiroir, *m.*; (*pers.*) tireur, *m.*, -euse, *f.*; (*of water*) puiseur, *m.*, -euse, *f.*; (*puller*) arracheur, *m.*, -euse, *f.*; (*of public-houses*) garçon de cabaret, *m*; (*of bills*) tireur, *m.*, -euse, *f.*; (*of designs, patterns,* &c.) dessinateur, *m.*, -trice, *f.*; (*thing which attracts*) corps attracteur *or* attractif, *m.*; (*print.*) casseau, *m.*; —**s,** *pl.* tiroirs, *m.pl.*, &c.; (*chest of —s*) commode, *f.*; (*garment*) caleçon, *m.*; (*for ladies*) pantalon, *m.*; (*more than one pair*) caleçons, *m.pl.*; pantalons, *m.pl.* *A pair of —,* un caleçon, *m.*; un pantalon, *m.*
Draw-gear, *s.* attelage, *m.*
Drawing, *s.* tirage, *m.*; attraction, *f.*; (*of lots*) tirage, *m.*; (*at dominoes*) pêche, *f.*; (*delineation*) dessin, *m.* — *and quartering,* écartellement, *m.* *Geometrical —,* dessin géométral, dessin linéaire. *Linear —,* dessin linéaire. *Mechanical —,* dessin des machines. — **account,** *s.* crédit ouvert, *m.* — **board,** *s.* planche à dessin, *f.* — **book,** *s.* cahier de dessin, *m.* — **chalk,** *s.* crayon, *m.* — **frame,** *s.* filière, *f.* — **game,** *s.* (*at dominoes*) pêche, *f.* — **knife,** *s.* *V.* **Draw-knife.** — **lesson,** *s.* leçon de dessin, *f.* — **master,** *s.* maître de dessin, *m.* — **paper,** *s.* papier à dessin, *m.* — **pen,** *s.* tire-ligne, *m.* — **pencil,** *s.* crayon à dessiner, crayon de mine de plomb, *m.* — **room,** *s.* salon, *m.*; (*at court*) réception, *f.* *To hold a — room,* recevoir. *There will be a — room on the ...,* il y aura réception à la cour le ... — **room suite,** *s.* ameublement *or* meuble de salon, *m.* — **up,** *s.* (*writing*) rédaction, *f.*
Draw-knife, *s.* couteau à deux manches, *m.*, [plane, *f.*
Drawl, *v.a.n.* (— *out*) traîner; traîner ses paroles, avoir un débit traînant; — *s.* débit traînant, *m.*, voix traînante, voix lente, *f.*; son traînant, *m.*
Drawn, *part. adj.* tiré, &c. (*V.* **Draw**). — *by two* or &c. *horses,* attelé de deux *or* &c. chevaux. — **battle,** *s.* bataille indécise, *f.* — **bonnet,** *s.* capote, *f.* — **butter,** *s.* roux, *m.* — **game,** *s.* partie nulle, partie remise, *f.*, refait, *m.* — **sword,** *s.* épée nue, *f.* [*V.* **Drag-net**
Draw-net, *s.* tirasse, *f.*; pantière, *f.*; (*fish.*)
Draw-plate, *s.* (*tech.*) filière, *f.*; (*of fire-grates*) tablier, rideau, *m.*
Draw-stop, *s.* (*mus.*) registre, *m.*
Dray, — **cart,** *s.* haquet, *m.* — **horse,** *s.* cheval de brasseur *or* de charrette, *m.* — **man,** *s.* haquetier, charretier, *m.*
Dread, *s.* terreur, crainte, *f.*; — *adj.* terrible, épouvantable; redoutable; révéré; auguste,

imposant; — *v.a.* redouter; craindre. *In — of*, de crainte de. *To be in — of*, redouter, craindre. —**ful,** *adj.* terrible, épouvantable, affreux, horrible; redoutable. —**fully,** *adv.* terriblement, épouvantablement, affreusement, horriblement. —**fulness,** *s.* nature terrible, horreur, *f.*, caractère redoutable, *m.* —**less,** *adj.* intrépide. —**lessness,** *s.* intrépidité, *f.* —**nought,** *s.* intrépide, *m.f.*, audacieux, *m.*, -euse, *f.*; (*coat*) vêtement *or* tissu imperméable, *m.*; caban, *m.*

Dream, *s.* rêve, songe, *m.*; (*fancy*) rêve, *m.*; (*waking* —) rêverie, *f.*; — *v.a.n.* rêver ('*of*,' de), songer; (*imagine, think*) songer (*of*, à); s'imaginer ('*that*,' que); (*long for*), rêver ('*of*,' ...). — **away, out, through,** *v.a.* passer (...) à rêver. —**ful,** *adj.* plein de rêves. — **land,** *s.* pays des rêves, *m.* —**less,** *adj.* sans rêves

Dreamer, *s.* (*who dreams at night*) personne qui rêve, *f.*; (*fig.*) rêveur, *m.*, -euse, *f.*, songeur, *m.*, -euse, *f.*; visionnaire, *m.f.*

Dreaming, *adj.* qui rêve, rêveur; visionnaire; — *s.* rêve, songe, *m.*; rêverie, *f.*

Dreamy, *adj.* idéal, chimérique, vain, semblable aux rêves

Drear, *adj.* *V.* **Dreary**

Drearily, *adv.* tristement; (*dismally*) lugubrement

Dreariness. *V.* **Dismalness**

Dreary, *adj.* triste, morne, désert; sombre; (*dismal*) lugubre, affreux

Dredge, *s.* drague, *f.*; — *v.a.* draguer; (*besprinkle*) saupoudrer; (*with flour*) fariner, saupoudrer de farine. — **box,** *s.* (*cook.*) *V.* **Dredger.** — **man,** *s.* dragueur, *m.* — **net,** *s.* drague, *f.*

Dredger, *s.* dragueur, *m.*, -euse, *f.*; (*cook.*) saupoudreur, *m.*; (*flour* —) boîte à farine, *f.*

Dredging, *s.* dragage, *m.*; (*besprinkling*) saupoudration, *f.*; — *adj.* dragueur. — **box,** *s.* (*cook.*) *V.* **Dredger.** — **engine, -machine, -vessel,** *s.* machine à draguer, drague, *f.*, bateau dragueur, dragueur, *m.*

Dregs, *s. pl.* lie, *f.* *To the* —, jusqu'à la lie

Drench, *v.a.* tremper, mouiller; inonder, noyer; (*of drink*) abreuver (de); (*vet.*) administrer (*or* donner) un breuvage à; — *s.* breuvage, *m.*

Dress, *v.a.* habiller, vêtir; arranger; (*adorn*) parer, orner; (*a wound, a horse*) panser; (*victuals*) accommoder, apprêter, préparer; (*salad*) assaisonner; (*leather, stuffs*) apprêter; (*a land*) donner une façon à, labourer; (*manure*) fumer; (*hort.*) dresser; (*a vine*, &c.) tailler; (*flax, hemp*) serancer, apprêter; (*ore*) laver; (*a beam*) dégrossir, dresser; (*a ship*) pavoiser; (*troops, and print.*) aligner; (*tech.*) dresser; (*shroud*) ensevelir; — *v.n.* s'habiller, se mettre, se vêtir; (*for a party*) faire sa toilette; (*be foppish*) s'occuper beaucoup de toilette; (*mil.*, — *up*) s'aligner. *To — oneself*, s'habiller, faire sa toilette. — **out, up,** parer, orner; (*ironically*) fagoter, enharnacher, harnacher, accoutrer, affubler, attifer. *To — the head* or *hair*, *V.* **Hair.** *Dress!* (*mil. command*) alignement!

Dress, *s.* habillement, *m.*; vêtement, *m.*; habit, *m.*; habits, *m.pl.*; costume, *m.*; (*gown*) robe, *f.*; (*for the night*) chemise, *f.*; (*style of dressing*) mise, *f.*; toilette, *f.*; mise élégante, *f.*; (*ornament*) parure, *f.*; (*mil.*) tenue, *f.*; uniforme, *m.*; — (*adj.*), *for* —, *good for* —, (*of clothes, stuffs*) habillé. *Full* —, *V.* **Full.** *Plain* —, *V.* **Clothes.** *In the — of*, sous l'habit de; en costume de; en uniforme de. — **ball,** *s.* bal paré, *m.* — **boots,** *s. pl.* bottes fines, *f.pl.* — **cap,** *s.* bonnet-coiffure, *m.* — **circle,** *s.* premières, *f.pl.* — **coat,** *s.* habit habillé, habit, frac, *m.* — **holder,** *s.* page, *m.* — **maker,** *s.* couturière, *f.* — **making,** *s.* état de couturière, *m.*

Dressed, *part. adj.* habillé, vêtu, &c. (*V.* **Dress,** *v.a.n.*); (*with regard to style of dress*) mis; (*mil.*) en tenue. *Full* —, *V.* **Full**

Dresser, *s.* personne qui habille *or* prépare *or* &c. (*V.* **Dress,** *v.a.*), *f.*; personne qui s'habille *or* se met, *f.*; (*of hair*) coiffeur, *m.*, -euse, *f.*; (*tech.*) apprêteur, *m.*, -euse, *f.*; appareilleur, *m.*, -euse, *f.*; dresseur, *m.*; (*in hospitals*) externe, *m.*; (*agr.*) ouvrier qui taille les arbres, *m.*; (*table*) table de cuisine, *f.* *To be a good* —, s'habiller *or* se mettre bien. *To be a smart* —, s'habiller *or* se mettre élégamment (*or* avec élégance). *To be a great* —, donner les plus grands soins à sa toilette

Dressership, *s.* (*in hospitals*) externat, *m.*

Dressing, *s.* habillement, ajustement, *m.*; toilette, *f.*; (*of wounds, horses*) pansement, *m.*; (*agr.*) labour, *m.*; façon, *f.*; (*manure*) fumure, *f.*; (*of vine*, &c.) taille, *f.*; (*of ore*) lavage, *m.*; (*of flax, hemp*) serançage, *m.*; (*of a beam*) dégrossissage, dégrossissement, dégrossi, dressage, *m.*; (*of leather, stuffs*) apprêtage, *m.*; (*starch, gum*, &c.) apprêt, *m.*; (*of victuals*) apprêt, *m.*, préparation, *f.*; (*of salad*) assaisonnement, *m.*; fourniture, *f.*; (*surg.*) appareil, *m.*; (*mil., and print.*) alignement, *m.*; (*tech.*) dressage, *m.*; habillage, *m.*; (*correction*) danse, correction, *f.* — **case,** *s.* nécessaire (de toilette), *m.* — **closet,** *s.* cabinet de toilette, *m.* — **comb,** *s.* peigne de toilette, *m.* — **glass,** *s.* miroir de toilette, *m.* — **gown,** *s.* (*of a woman*) peignoir, *m.*; (*of a man*) robe de chambre, *f.* — **house,** *s.* (*metal.*) laverie, *f.* — **jacket,** *s.* camisole, *f.* — **room,** *s.* cabinet de toilette, *m.*; (*theat.*) *V.* **Star-room.** — **table,** *s.* table de toilette, toilette, *f.*

Dressy, *adj.* recherché dans sa mise, tiré à quatre épingles; paré; habillé

Dribble, *v.n.* dégoutter, tomber goutte à goutte; (*to slaver*) baver; — *v.a.* laisser dégoutter, laisser tomber goutte à goutte, égoutter; verser (*or* répandre) goutte à goutte, faire dégoutter

Dribblet. *V.* **Driblet**

Dribbling, *part. adj.* goutte à goutte, par gouttes, tombant goutte à goutte; (*fig.*) par petites sommes *or* quantités *or* portions, petit, mesquin, chétif; — *s.* dégouttement, *m.*; dégoutture, *f.*; gouttes, *f.pl.*

Driblet, *s.* petite somme, *f.*; petite quantité *or* partie *or* portion, bagatelle, *f.*

Dried, *part. adj.* séché, &c. (*V.* **Dry,** *v.a.n.*); (*of eatables*) sec; (*apples, pears*) tapé

Drier. *V.* **Dryer**

Drift, *s.* violence, *f.*; impulsion, *f.*; (*aim*) but, objet, *m.*; tendance, *f.*; portée, *f.*; (*heap*) amas, monceau, *m.*; (*moving mass, of dust or sand*) tourbillon, *m.*; (*shower*) grêle, *f.*; (*mining*) *V.* **Adit;** (*engin.*) passage, chemin, *m.*; (*fishing-net*) manet, *m.*; (*nav.*) dérive, *f.*; (*tech.*) chassoir, repoussoir, *m.*; — *v.n.* s'amasser, s'amonceler; (*be driven*) être chassé, être poussé, être emporté; (*nav.*) dériver, aller en dérive; — *v.a.* entasser, amonceler; (*drive*) chasser, pousser, emporter. —*s of ice*, glaces flottantes, *f.pl.* — **ice,** *s.* glace flottante, *f.* — **net,** *s.* manet, *m.* — **sail,** *s.* arceau, *m.* — **sand,** *s.* sable mouvant, *m.* — **way,** *s.* (*of roads*) accotement, *m.*; (*mining*) *V.* **Adit;** (*engin.*) passage, chemin, *m.*; (*nav.*) dérive, *f.* — **wood,** *s.* bois flottant, *m.*

Drifting, *part.* (*active sense*) chassant, poussant, emportant; (*neuter sense*) chassé, poussé, emporté

Drill, *v.a.* percer, forer; (*agr.*) semer au semoir, semer en ligne; (*mil.*) exercer, faire faire l'exercice à, faire manœuvrer; (*fig.*) dresser, rompre; — *v.n.* couler doucement; (*mil.*) faire l'exercice, manœuvrer; — *s.* (*tool*) foret, vilebrequin, *m.*; (*stuff*) coutil, *m.*; (*agr.*) sillon, *m.*; (*sowing-mach.*) semoir, drill, *m.*; (*baboon*) drill, *m.*; (*mil.*) exercice, *m.*, manœuvre, *f.* *Extra* —, exercice correctionnel *or* de punition, *m.* — **bow,** *s.* archet, *m.* — **instructor,** *s.* instructeur, *m.* — **master,** *s.* maître d'exercice, *m.* — **officer,** *s.* officier instructeur, *m.* — **plough,** *s.* semoir, *m.* — **sergeant,** *s.* sergent instructeur, *m.*

Drilling, *s.* (*boring*) forage, *m.*, perforation, *f.*; (*agr.*) semis au semoir, *m.*; (*mil.*) exercice, *m.*, manœuvre, *f.*

Drink, *v.a.n.* boire; (*take*) prendre; — *s.* boisson, *f.*, breuvage, *m.*; (*drunkenness*) ivresse, *f.* *Strong* —, liqueurs fortes, *f.pl.* *The worse for* —, *in* —, ivre. *Give us some* —, donnez-nous à boire. *To — like a fish*, boire comme un trou. — **in,** *v.a.* absorber, imbiber. — **money,** *s.* pourboire, *m.* — **off,** *v.a.* boire tout d'un trait, boire d'un coup, avaler. — **out,** *v.a.* vider. — *out of*, *V.* **Out.** — **to,** *v.a.* boire à; (*the health*) boire à la santé de. — **up,** *v.a.* *V.* — **off**

Drinkable, *adj.* buvable, potable; — *s.* breuvage, *m.*, boisson, chose à boire, *f.*

Drinkableness, *s.* potabilité, *f.*

Drinker, *s.* buveur, *m.*, -euse, *f.*

Drinking, *adj.* qui boit; adonné à la boisson; (*things*) de *or* de la boisson; (*for drinking*) à boire; — *s.* boire, *m.*; (*drunkenness*) boisson, ivrognerie, *f.* — **booth,** *s.* buvette, *f.* — **bout,** *s.* partie de débauche, débauche, orgie, *f.* — **club,** *s.* club de buveurs, *m.* — **companion,** *s.* compagnon de bouteille, *m.* — **cup,** *s.* tasse, *f.*, gobelet, *m.*; (*beaker*) coupe, *f.* — **fountain,** *s.* fontaine publique, *f.* — **glass,** *s.* verre à boire, *m.* — **house,** *s.* cabaret, *m.* — **song,** *s.* chanson à boire, chanson bachique, *f.* — **vessel,** *s.* vase à boire, *m.*

Drip, *v.n.a.* *V.* **Dribble;** — *s.* goutte, *f.*; (*a falling in drops*) égout, *m.*; (*arch.*) larmier, *m.* — **stone,** *s.* filtre, *m.*; (*arch.*) larmier, *m.* *I am dripping wet*, je suis tout trempé

Dripping, *s.* dégout, dégouttement, *m.*; dégoutture, *f.*; (*drops*) gouttes, *f.pl.*; (*fat*) graisse de rôti, *f.*, dégout, *m.* — **pan,** *s.* lèchefrite, *f.* — **wet,** *V.* **Drip**

Drive, *v.a.n.* pousser (à); (*carry or force away*) chasser; (*horses, carriages, &c., persons in a vehicle*) conduire, mener; (*a nail, stake, &c.*) enfoncer, planter; (*a trade, a bargain*) faire; (*compel*) forcer (à), contraindre (à); (*reduce*) réduire (à); (*render*) rendre; (*prosecute*) poursuivre; (*move*) mouvoir, faire aller; (*to be impelled*) être poussé; être emporté; (*rush*) fondre (sur), se jeter (sur), se précipiter (sur); (*to go*) se diriger, aller; (*in a carriage*) être *or* aller *or* venir *or* se promener en voiture; faire ... (*a distance*) en voiture; aller, courir; passer; se faire conduire; (*aim at*) viser (à), tendre (à), vouloir en venir (à); (*of rain, snow*) battre, fouetter; (*nav.*) dériver. — **about,** (*take about*) promener en voiture, promener; (*go about*) se promener en voiture, se promener. — **along,** pousser. — **away,** chasser; (*depart*) partir. — **back,** repousser; refouler; (*go back*) retourner, s'en retourner, se retirer; (*come back*) revenir. — **down,** (*game*) rabattre; (*in a carriage*) descendre. — **in,** faire entrer; faire rentrer; (*a nail, &c.*) enfoncer. — **into,** faire entrer *or* rentrer dans; enfoncer dans; (*in a carriage*) entrer *or* arriver dans (...) en voiture. — **off,** renvoyer, chasser; (*depart*) partir. — **on,** pousser en avant; pousser; entraîner; exciter; continuer sa route; avancer; aller bon train; presser les chevaux. — *on!* en route! — **out,** faire sortir; chasser; exclure; (*go out*) sortir en voiture. — **up,** arriver, venir, s'avancer, venir s'arrêter

Drive, *s.* promenade en voiture, promenade, *f.*; distance en voiture, *f.*; course, *f.*; trajet, *m.*; (*place*) promenade (pour les voitures), *f.*; allée, avenue, *f.*; (*run of a cab*) course, *f.* *By the* —, à la course

Drivel, *v.n.* baver; (*dote*) radoter; — *s.* bave, *f.*

Driveller, *s.* radoteur, *m.*, -euse, *f.*

Drivelling, *s.* radotage, *m.*

Driver, *s.* celui qui conduit, conducteur, *m.*; (*of cattle*) conducteur, *m.*; (*of carriages*) cocher, *m.*; (*of carts*) voiturier, *m.*; (*cooper's tool*) chassoir, *m.*; (*tropic-bird*) paille-en-queue, *m.*; (*nav., sail*) brigantine, *f.*

Driving, *adj.* qui pousse *or* conduit *or* &c. (*V.* **Drive,** *v.a.n.*); moteur; fort, violent; — *s.* action de pousser *or* de conduire *or* &c. (*V.* **Drive,** *v.a.n.*), *f.*; manière de conduire, *f.*; promenade en voiture, *f.* — **axle,** *s.* axe moteur, *m.* — **band, -belt,** *s.* courroie de chasse, *f.* — **shaft,** *s.* arbre moteur, *m.* — **wheel,** *s.* roue motrice, *f.* — **whip,** *s.* fouet, *m.*

Drizzle, *v.n.* bruiner, brouillasser; tomber en petites gouttes; — *s.* bruine, pluie fine, *f.*

Drizzling, *s.* bruinement, *m.* — **rain,** *s.* bruine, pluie fine, *f.*

Drizzly, *adj.* bruineux, de bruine

Drogman. *V.* **Dragoman**

Droll, *adj.* drôle; drolatique; (*odd*) drôle de; (*facetious*) plaisant; — *s.* plaisant, *m.*; farceur, *m.* — *fellow*, drôle de corps, *m.* — *thing*, drôlerie, *f.*; drôle de chose, *f.*

Drollery, *s.* plaisanterie, drôlerie, *f.*; farce, *f.*

Drollish, *adj.* un peu drôle, assez drôle, [plaisant

Dromedary, *s.* dromadaire, *m.*

Drone, *s.* bourdon, *m.*; frelon, *m.*; (*pers.*) fainéant, *m.*; (*humming*) bourdonnement, *m.*; (*mus.*) bourdon, *m.*; — *v.a.n.* bourdonner; psalmodier; (*idle*) fainéanter, vivre dans la fainéantise. — **bee,** *s.* bourdon, faux bourdon, *m.* — **fly,** *s.* mouche-abeille, mouche-bourdon, *f.* — **pipe,** *s.* bourdon, *m.*

Drongo, *s.* drongo, édolie, *m.*

Droning, *adj.* bourdonnant; (*idle*) fainéant; — *s.* bourdonnement, *m.*; (*talk*) débit monotone, *m.*, psalmodie, *f.*; (*idleness*) fainéantise, *f.*

Dronish, *adj.* fainéant

Droop, *v.n.a.* tomber, s'affaiblir, faiblir; languir; (*lean*) baisser, pencher

Drooping, *s.* langueur, *f.*; tristesse, *f.*, accablement, *m.*; — *adj.* tombant; faible; languissant; abattu, découragé; baissé, penché

Droopingly, *adv.* languissamment

Drop, *s.* goutte, *f.*; (*of glass*) larme, *f.*; (*earring*) pendant d'oreille, *m.*; (*cake*) pastille, *f.*; (*of gallows*) trappe, bascule, *f.*; (*gallows itself*) potence, *f.*; (*of a sail*) chute, *f.*; (*act of falling*) chute, *f.*; (*theat.*) rideau, *m.* *Act* —, — **scene,** *s.* rideau d'entr'acte, rideau, *m.* *By —s*, goutte à goutte. — **bars,** *s. pl.* grille à bascule, *f.* — **serene,** *s.* goutte sereine, *f.* — **wort,** *s.* filipendule, *f.*

Drop, *v.a.* distiller, égoutter, verser en gouttes, verser goutte à goutte; (*let fall, &c.*) laisser tomber; lâcher; abandonner, quitter, laisser, laisser là, planter là; renoncer à; (*lower*) baisser; (*the anchor*) jeter; (*a letter*) mettre *or* jeter (à la poste), envoyer; (*a parcel*) déposer, laisser; (*a curtsy*) tirer, faire; (*from a carriage*) descendre; (*liquids*) répandre, verser; (*let escape*) laisser échapper; (*her young*) mettre bas; (*utter*) glisser, souffler; (*neglect*) négliger; (*lose*) perdre; — *v.n.* tomber en gouttes; dégoutter (de); (*fall, &c.*) tomber (de); descendre (de); (*of animals*) s'abattre; (*die*) tomber; succomber; (*come*) arriver inopinément, arriver à l'improviste; (*cease*) en rester là, tomber; (*of words*) échapper. *To — with fatigue*, tomber de fatigue, n'en pouvoir plus. *To — an acquaintance*, cesser de voir quelqu'un. — **astern,** culer. — **away,** tomber l'un après l'autre. — **down,** tomber par terre, tomber. — **in,** entrer inopinément, entrer à l'improviste; faire une visite en passant. — **off,** tomber, se détacher; diminuer, baisser; s'écouler; s'en aller peu à peu; mourir. — **out,** tomber; se dérober, s'esquiver

Droplet, *s.* gouttelette, petite goutte, *f.*

Dropping, *s.* goutte, *f.*; — *part. adj.* tombant, qui tombe, &c. (*V.* **Drop,** *v.a.n.*); — *s.* chute, *f.*; (*drops*) dégouttement, *m.*, dégoutture, *f.*, gouttes qui tombent, *f.pl.* — *fire*, feu roulant, *m.* [d'hydropisie

Dropsical, *adj.* (*pers.*) hydropique; (*things*)

Dropsy, *s.* hydropisie, *f.*
Dross, *s.* (*of metals*) scorie, *f.*; (*rust*) rouille, *f*; (*refuse*) rebut, *m.*, écume, *f.* [pureté, *f.*
Drossiness, *s.* écume, *f.*; rouille, *f.*; im-
Drossy, *adj.* plein d'écume; écumeux; (*fig.*) grossier, impur, sale; de rebut, mauvais
Drought, Droughtiness, Drouth, *s.* sécheresse, *f.*; (*thirst*) soif, *f.*
Droughty, *adj.* sec; aride; (*pers.*) altéré
Drove, *s.* troupeau, *m.*; touche, *f.*; (*crowd*) foule, troupe, *f.* [chand de bestiaux, *m.*
Drover, *s.* conducteur de bestiaux, *m.*; mar-
Droving, *s.* commerce des bestiaux, *m.*
Drown, *v.a.* noyer; submerger; inonder; absorber; (*bury*) ensevelir; (*lose*) perdre; (*surpass*) éclipser; (*any noise*) dominer, couvrir; (*the voice*) couvrir; (*cries*) étouffer; — *v.n.* se noyer. *To — oneself*, se noyer. *To be —ed*, se noyer; être noyé. *To be —ing*, se noyer
Drowning, *adj.* qui se noie; — *s.* noyade, *f.*; inondation, *f.*; (*med.*) asphyxie par submersion, *f.* [*or* endormi; nonchalamment
Drowsily, *adv.* en dormant; d'un air assoupi
Drowsiness, *s.* assoupissement, *m.*; (*fig.*) engourdissement, *m.*; inertie, *f.*
Drowsy, *adj.* assoupi, endormi; (*lulling*) assoupissant, soporifique; (*dull*) lourd. *To be or grow —*, s'assoupir. *To make —*, assoupir, endormir. — **head,** *s.* assoupissement, *m.* — **headed,** *adj.* assoupi, endormi
Drub, *v.a.* rosser, étriller, frotter
Drubbing, *s.* volée, rossée, roulée, frottée, *f.*
Drudge, *v.n.* travailler sans relâche, piocher, s'éreinter, s'échiner; droguer; — *s.* homme de peine, *m.*; (*slave*) esclave, *m.f.*, souffre-douleur, *m.*; (*fig.*) piocheur, *m.*, -euse, *f.*
Drudgery, Drudging, *s.* travail pénible *or* fatigant, *m.*; peine, *f.*, labeur, *m.*; vile besogne, *f.*; occupation servile, *f.*; corvée, *f.*
Drudgingly, *adv.* péniblement, laborieusement
Drug, *s.* drogue, *f.*; — *v.a.n.* droguer; (*fig.*) empoisonner. — **trade,** *s.* droguerie, *f.*
Drugget, *s.* droguet, *m.*; bure, *f.*
Druggist, *s.* droguiste, *m.f.*
Druid, ess, *s.* druide, *m.*, druidesse, *f.*
Druid-ic, al, -ism. *V.* page 3, § 1
Drum, *s.* tambour, *m.*; caisse, *f.*; (*of the ear*) tympan, *m.*; (*of watches, locks*) barillet, *m.*; (*tech.*) tambour, *m.*; (*party*) soirée, *f.* *Big —*, grosse caisse, *f.* *With the —s beating*, tambour battant. — **barrel,** *s.* tambour, *m.* — **head,** *s.* peau de tambour, *f.* — **head court martial,** *s.* conseil de guerre assemblé sur-le-champ, *m.* — **major,** *s.* tambour-major, *m.* — **maker,** *s.* faiseur de tambours, *m.* — **stick,** *s.* baguette de tambour, *f.*; (*of fowls*) pilon, *m.*
Drum, *v.n.* battre le tambour; tambouriner; (*palpitate*) battre; (*tingle*) tinter; — *v.a.* battre; tambouriner; (*to din*) répétailler, corner aux oreilles; (*into the head*) finir par faire entrer; (— **out**) chasser au son du tambour, chasser tambour battant, dégrader; [(*fig.*) chasser
Drummer, *s.* tambour, *m.*
Drumming, *s.* bruit du tambour, *m.*; tambourinage, *m.*; (*tingling*) tintement, bourdonnement, *m.* — **out,** *s.* dégradation militaire, dégradation, *f.*
Drunk, *adj.* ('*with*,' de) ivre, gris, soûl. *To get —*, s'enivrer, se griser, se soûler. *To make —*, enivrer, griser, soûler. — *as a beast*, soûl comme un cochon. — *as a fiddler*, soûl comme une grive [lard, *m.*, e, *f.*
Drunkard, *s.* ivrogne, *m.*, ivrognesse, *f.*, soû-
Drunken, *adj.* (*pers.*) ivre; ivrogne; (*things*) d'ivresse, d'ivrognerie, d'ivrogne
Drunkenly, *adv.* en ivrogne [ivrognerie, *f.*
Drunkenness, *s.* (*state*) ivresse, *f.*; (*habit*)
Drupaceous, *adj.* drupacé
Drupe, *s.* drupe, *m.* [Druse, *m.*
Druse, *s.* (*min.*) druse, *f.*; — *s. adj.* (*geog.*)
Dry, *adj.* sec; aride; (*dried up*) desséché; (*without water, empty*) tari, à sec; (*thirsty*) altéré, qui a soif; (*sarcastic*) sarcastique, caustique, piquant, mordant; (*of blows*) sans blessure; (*of cows*, &c.) qui ne donne pas de lait; (*of wine, bread*) sec; (*of toast*) sans beurre; — *v.a.* sécher; (*marshes*, &c.) dessécher; (*wipe*) essuyer; (*exhaust*) mettre à sec, tarir; (*empty*) vider; (*tech.*) sécher, essorer; *v.n.* sécher. *To — o.'s eyes*, s'essuyer les yeux. *To be —*, être sec *or* &c.; (*thirsty*) être altéré, avoir soif; (*of the weather*) faire sec. *To be kept —*, (*on packages*) craint l'humidité, préserver de l'humidité. — **bread,** *s.* pain sec, *m.* — **dock,** *s.* bassin de construction, chantier, *m.* — **eyed,** *adj.* qui a l'œil sec, sans larmes. — **goods,** *s. pl.* étoffes, *f.pl.*, tissus, *m.pl.* — **harbour,** *s.* port d'échouage, *m.* — **land,** *s.* terre sèche, *f.*; terre ferme, *f.* — **nurse,** *s.* bonne d'enfant, nourrice qui élève (*or* pour élever) un enfant au biberon, sevreuse, *f.*; garde-malade, *f.*; *v.a.* élever au biberon, sevrer. — **point,** *s.* (*engr.*) pointe sèche, *f.* — **room,** *s.* (*mil.*) salle de police, *f.*, (*jest.*) bloc, *m.* — **rot,** *s.* pourriture sèche, *f.* — **rub,** *v.a.* frotter. — **rubber,** *s.* frotteur, *m.* — **rubbing,** *s.* frottage, *m.* — **salter,** *s.* marchand (*m.*, e, *f.*) de salaisons *or* de comestibles; épicier, *m.*, -ière, *f.*; droguiste, *m.f.* — **saltery,** *s.* salaisons, *f.pl.*; épicerie, *f.*; droguerie, *f.* — **shod,** *adj.* à pied sec. — **stove,** *s.* étuve, *f.* — **up,** *v.a.* sécher; dessécher; mettre à sec, tarir, faire tarir; *v.n.* sécher, se dessécher, tarir, se tarir. *To — up o.'s tears*, sécher ses larmes
Dryad, *s.* dryade, *f.*
Dryer, *s.* (*pers.*) sécheur, *m.*, -euse, *f.*; essoreur, *m.*, -euse, *f.*; (*things*) siccatif, dessiccatif, *m.*; (*utensil*) séchoir, *m.*, sécheuse, *f.*; essoreuse, *f.*
Drying, *adj.* siccatif, qui sèche; — *s.* dessèchement, *m.*; (*tech.*) dessiccation, *f.*; essorage, *m.* — **apparatus,** *s.* sécheuse, *f.* — **box, -ground,** *s.* séchoir, *m.* — **closet,** *s.* *V.* — **room.** — **house,** *s.* sécherie, *f.* — **lines,** *s. pl.* étendage, *m.* — **machine,** *s.* sécheuse, *f.*; essoreuse, *f.* — **oil,** *s.* huile siccative, *f.* — **place,** *s.* *V.* — **room.** — **poles,** *s. pl.* étendoir, *m.* — **room,** *s.* essui, *m.*; séchoir, *m.*; étendage, étendoir, *m.* — **stove,** *s.* étuve, *f.* [ment; sévèrement
Dryly, *adv.* sèchement; caustiquement; froide-
Dryness, *s.* sécheresse, *f.*; aridité, *f.*
Dual, *adj.* double; (*Gr. gram.*) du duel; au duel. — *number*, duel, *m.*
Dual-ism, -ist. *V.* page 3, § 1
Dualistic, *adj.* dualistique, dualiste
Duality, *s.* dualité, *f.*
Duarchy, *s.* duarchie, *f.*
Dub, *v.a.* (*a knight*) armer, faire; (*to style*) qualifier de; (*to nickname*) baptiser. — **out,** (*mas.*) renformir [(*mas.*) renformis, *m.*
Dubbing, *s.* (*grease*) dégras, *m.* — **out,** *s.*
Dubious, *adj.* douteux, incertain; indécis
Dubiously, *adv.* d'une manière douteuse *or* incertaine; d'une manière indécise
Dubiousness, *s.* nature douteuse, *f.*; doute, *m.*, incertitude, *f.*; indécision, *f.*
Dubitative, *adj.* dubitatif
Dubitatively, *adv.* dubitativement
Ducal, *adj.* ducal, de duc
Ducat, *s.* ducat, *m.*
Ducatoon, *s.* ducaton, *m.*
Duchess, *s.* duchesse, *f.*
Duchy, *s.* duché, *m.*
Duck, *s.* (*bird*) canard, *m.*; cane, *f.*; (*of the head*) plongeon, *m.*; (*pers.*) poule, poulette, *f.*, poulet, chou, chat, *m.*, chatte, *f.*; (*cloth*) grosse toile, toile à voiles, *f.*, coutil, *m.*; — *v.n.* plonger; (*bow the head*) faire le plongeon; se courber; — *v.a.* plonger dans l'eau, plonger; (*the head*) baisser; (*nav.*) baptiser; donner la cale à. *—s and drakes*, (*play*) ricochets, *m.pl.* — **bill, -mole,** *s.* ornithorhynque, *m.* — **gun,**

s. canardière, *f.* — **hawk,** *s.* harpaye, *m.* — **house,** *s.* canarderie, *f.* — **pond,** *s.* canardière, *f.* —**'s egg,** *s.* œuf de cane, *m.* — **shooting,** *s.* chasse aux canards, *f.* —**'s meat,** *s. V.* — **weed.** — **stone,** *s.* sauvette, *f.* — **weed,** *s.* canillée, lemne, *f.* — **yard,** *s.* canarderie, *f.*

Ducker, *s.* plongeur, *m.*, -euse, *f.*; (*fig.*) faiseur [de courbettes, *m.*

Duckey. *V.* **Ducky**

Ducking, *s.* plongeon, *m.*; immersion, *f.*; trempée, *f.*; (*from one swimmer to another*) passade, *f.*; (*nav.*) baptême, *m.*; baleine, *f.*; (*nav. punishment*) cale, *f.*

Duckling, *s.* caneton, *m.*, canette, *f.*

Ducky, *s.* petit canard, petit, *m.*; (*pers.*) petit chou, petit chat, *m.*

Duct, *s.* conduit, canal, tube, *m.* [*metals*) ductile

Ductile, *adj.* souple, flexible; docile; (*of*

Ductileness, Ductility, *s.* souplesse, flexibilité, *f.*; docilité, *f.*; (*of metals*) ductilité, *f.*

Dudeen, *s.* brûle-gueule, *m.*

Dudgeon, *s.* brouillerie, *f.*; (*ill-will*) mauvaise part, *f.*; (*anger*) colère, *f.* *In high* —, tout en colère. *To take in* —, prendre en mauvaise part, prendre de travers, s'offenser de

Duds, *s. pl.* nippes, frusques, *f.pl.*

Due, *adj.* dû; (*fallen due*) arrivé à échéance, échu; (*of debts*) exigible; (*proper*) convenable, juste; opportun; bon; (*required*) requis, voulu; (*sufficient*) suffisant; — *adv.* droit, directement, en plein; — *s.* dû, *m.*; (*fee*) honoraires, *m.pl.*; rétribution universitaire, *f.*; (*tribute*) tribut, *m.*; (*duty*) devoir, *m.*; (*tax*) droit, impôt, *m.*; redevance, *f.* *In — form,* dans les formes voulues, dans les formes, en bonne forme, en règle, dans les règles. *In — time,* en temps convenable *or* opportun, en temps utile; au moment voulu, à temps. *In — time and place,* en temps et lieu. *To become* or *fall* —, *V.* **Fall.** *To give everyone his* —, donner à chacun ce qui lui est dû. *We must give the devil his* —, il ne faut pas faire le diable plus noir qu'il n'est. *The train is — at* . . ., le train arrive *or* doit arriver à . . .

Duel, *s.* duel, *m.*; (*fig.*) combat, *m.*, lutte, contestation, *f.* *To fight a* —, se battre en duel

Duelling, *s.* (le) duel, *m.*

Duellist, *s.* duelliste, *m.*

Duello, *s.* duel, *m.*

Duenna, *s.* duègne, *f.*

Duet, Duetto, *s.* duo, *m.*

Duettino, *s.* duettino, *m.*

Duffer, *s.* (de la) camelote, *f.*; drogue, *f.*; patraque, *f.*; (*cheat*) attrape, *f.*; (*pers.: pedlar, hawker*) cameloteur, *m.*, (*cheater*) attrapeur, *m.*, -euse, *f.*, (*dolt*) ganache, *f.*, savetier, gniaf,

Dug, *s.* mamelon, trayon, *m.* [croûton, *m.*

Dugong, *s.* dugong, halicore, *m.*

Duke, *s.* duc, *m.* —**dom,** *s.* duché, titre de duc, *m.*, dignité de duc, *f.*

Dulcamara, *s.* (*bot.*) douce-amère, *f.*

Dulcet, *adj.* doux

Dulcification, *s.* dulcification, *f.*

Dulcify, *v.a.* dulcifier

Dulcimer, *s.* dulcimer, tympanon, *m.*

Dull, *adj.* (*stupid*) lourd, borné, stupide; (*without life*) lourd; (*insipid*) fade; (*tiresome*) ennuyeux, assommant; (*slow*) lent; (*sad*) triste, sombre, mélancolique; (*dreary, not lively*) triste; (*blunt*) émoussé; (*not bright*) terne, pâle, blafard; sombre; (*of fire*) triste; (*of weather*) sombre, gris, triste; (*of sound*) sourd, mat; (*of pain*) sourd; (*of hearing*) dur; (*com.*) mort, plat, calme, languissant, qui ne va pas; — *v.a.* (*stupefy*) hébéter, rendre lourd; (*benumb*) engourdir; (*sadden*) attrister, rendre sombre; (*damp*) fatiguer; (*blunt*) émousser; (*impede*) ralentir, arrêter; (*sully*) ternir; (*weaken*) affaiblir; (*a sound*) assourdir; — *v.n.* devenir lourd, devenir hébété, s'hébéter; s'engourdir; s'émousser. *To feel* or *be* —, *to find it* —, (*pers.*) s'ennuyer. *To get* or *become* —, (*pers.*) s'attrister; (*get blunt*) s'émousser; (*get tarnished*) se ternir. — **brained,** *adj.* stupide, qui a l'esprit lourd. — **browed,** *adj.* sombre, au front sombre. — **eyed,** *adj.* au regard terne; au regard sombre. — **head,** *s.* lourdaud, *m.*, e, *f.* — **season** (*of the year*), *s.* morte saison, *f.* — **sighted,** *adj.* myope. — **witted,** *adj. V.* — **brained**

Dullard, *s. adj.* lourdaud, *m.*, e, *f.*

Dullish, *adj.* un peu lourd *or* &c. (*V.* **Dull**)

Dully, *adv.* (*stupidly*) lourdement, sottement; (*insipidly*) fadement; (*wearisomely*) ennuyeusement; (*slowly*) lentement; (*sadly*) tristement; (*bluntly*) d'une manière émoussée; (*not brightly*) d'une manière terne, sans éclat; (*of sound*) sourdement

Dulness, *s.* (*stupidity*) pesanteur, stupidité, *f.*; (*drowsiness*) appesantissement, assoupissement, *m.*, envie de dormir, *f.*; (*weariness*) ennui, *m.*; (*slowness*) lenteur, *f.*; (*sadness, dreariness*) tristesse, *f.*; (*bluntness*) état émoussé, *m.*; (*dimness*) matité, ternissure, *f.*, manque d'éclat, *m.*; (*of sound*) matité, *f.*; (*weakness*) faiblesse, *f.*; (*numbness*) engourdissement, *m.*, torpeur, *f.*; (*of hearing*) dureté, *f.*; (*com.*) [langueur, *f.*

Dulse, *s.* varech comestible, *m.*

Duly, *adv.* dûment; convenablement, justement; exactement; régulièrement; opportunément; bien. *I have — received* . . ., j'ai [bien reçu . . .

Dum, — **palm,** *s. V.* **Doom**

Dumb, *adj.* muet; (*silenced*) réduit au silence. — **animal,** *s. V.* — **creature.** — **bell,** *s.* haltère, *m.* — **born,** *adj.* muet de naissance. — **creature,** *s.* animal, *m.*, bête, *f.* — **found,** *v.a.* confondre, interdire; abasourdir, ébouriffer. — **jockey,** *s.* (*rid.*) jockey (en bois pour dresser les chevaux), *m.* —**ly,** *adv.* en silence, sans parler. —**ness,** *s.* mutisme, *m.*; (*fig.*) silence, *m.* — **show,** *s.* pantomime, *f.*, jeu muet, *m.* — **waiter,** *s.* servante, *f.*

Dummy, *s.* muet, *m.*, muette, *f.*; (*fig.*) homme de paille, prête nom, *m.*; (*figure*) mannequin, *m.*, figure, *f.*; (*puppet*) marionnette, *f.*; (*any sham object*) simulacre, *m.*; (*at whist*) mort, *m.*; — *adj.* muet; simulé, faux [noire, *f.*

Dump, *s.*, —**s,** *pl.* tristesse, mélancolie, humeur

Dumpish, *adj.* triste, morne

Dumpishly, *adv.* tristement

Dumpishness, *s.* morne tristesse, *f.*

Dumpling, *s.* chausson, *m.*

Dumpy, *adj.* gros et court, trapu

Dun, *adj.* (— *coloured*) gris brun, noisette; (*fig.*) sombre; (*of horses*) isabelle; — *s.* gris brun, noisette, *m.*; (*pers.*) créancier importun, aboyeur, *m.*; (*request*) demande pressante, *f.*; (*mound*) éminence, *f.*, tertre, *m.*; — *v.a.* importuner, poursuivre; (*fish*) saler. — **bee, -fly,** *s.* taon, *m.* — **bird,** *s.* milouin, *m.*

Dunce, *s.* lourdaud, *m.*, e, *f.*, cancre, *m.*, cruche, *f.*

Duncery, *s.* ânerie, sottise, *f.*

Dunciad, *s.* Dunciade, *f.*

Dunderhead, *s.* buse, *f.*

Dundreary, *s.* gandin, *m.*

Dune, *s.* dune, *f.*

Dung, *s.* (*of animals, birds*) fiente, *f.*; (*of horses*) crottin, *m.*, fiente, *f.*; (*of cows,* &c.) bouse, fiente, *f.*; (*of sheep, goats, rabbits, mice,* &c.) crotte, *f.*; (*hunt: of deer*) fumées, *f.pl.*, bousard, *m.*, (*of wolves, wild boars,* &c.) laissées, *f.pl.*; (*agr.*) fumier, *m.*; — *v.a.* fumer; *v.n.* fienter. — **beetle,** *s.* bousier, *m.* — **cart,** *s.* tombereau à fumier, tombereau, *m.* — **fork,** *s.* fourche à fumier, *f.* — **hill,** *s.* tas de fumier, fumier, *m.*; *adj.* de fumier; (*fig.*) sale, bas, vil. — **hole, -pit,** *s.* trou au fumier, *m.* — **yard,** *s.* basse cour, *f.*

Dungeon, *s.* cachot, *m.*, prison, *f.*

Dunging, *s.* (*agr.*) fumure, *f.*; (*manu.*) bousage, *m.*

Dungy, *adj.* de fumier; (*fig.*) vil, méprisable

Dunlin, *s.* cocorli, bécasseau, *m.*

Dunnage, *s.* (*nav.*) fardage, *m.*

Dunning, *s.* importunité, *f.*
Dunnish, *adj.* tirant sur le gris brun
Dunnock, *s.* (*bird*) traîne-buissons, *m.*
Duo, *s.* duo, *m.*
Duodecennial, *adj.* duodécennal
Duodecimal, *adj.* duodécimal
Duodecimo, *adj. s.* in-douze, *adj. m.f., s.m.*
Duodenal, *adj.* duodénal
Duodenary, *adj.* duodénaire
Duodenum, *s.* duodénum, *m.*
Duodrama, *s.* dilogie, *f.*
Dupe, *s.* dupe, *f.*; — *v.a.* duper, tromper
Duper, *s.* dupeur, *m.*, -euse, *f.*
Dupery, *s.* duperie, *f.*
Duplicate, *adj.* double; — *s.* double, *m.*; (*of deeds*) duplicata, *m.*; (*of a pawnbroker*) reconnaissance, *f.*; (*reference number, com.*) référence, *f.*; — *v.a.* doubler; (*to ticket, com.*) référencer; (*to fold*) plier en deux
Duplication, *s.* doublement, *m.*; (*geom.*) duplication, *f.*; (*arith.*) multiplication par deux, *f.*
Duplicative, *adj.* duplicatif
Duplicature, *s.* duplicature, *f.*
Duplicity, *s.* duplicité, *f.*
Dura-bility, bleness. *V.* page 3, § 1
Durable, *adj.* durable [durable
Durably, *adv.* durablement, d'une manière
Dura-mater, *s.* dure-mère, *f.*
Durance, *s.* emprisonnement, *m.*, prison, *f.* [*In — vile,* en cage
Duration, *s.* durée, *f.*
Duress, *s.* prison, chartre privée, *f.*; contrainte, *f.*
During, *prep.* pendant, durant
Durra, Durrha, *s.* doura, *m.*
Dusk, *adj.* sombre; obscur; — *s.* commencement d'obscurité, crépuscule, *m.*, brune, *f.*; (*of colours*) teinte sombre, *f.*; — *v.a.* assombrir, obscurcir. *At —, in the — of the evening,* à la brune, sur la brune, à la tombée de la nuit
Duskily, Duskishly, *adv.* obscurément
Duskiness, *s.* obscurité, *f.*; teinte sombre, *f.*
Dusky, Duskish, *adj.* sombre; obscur; (*of colours*) foncé, brunâtre
Dust, *s.* poussière, *f.*; (*of metals, of substances pounded or ground*) poudre, *f.*; (*of coals*) poussier, *m.*; (*pharm.*) grabeau, *m.*, grabeaux, *m.pl.*; (*refuse*) balayures, *f.pl.*; (*of the dead*) cendre, *f.*, cendres, *f.pl.*, poussière, *f.*; (*money*) pécune, *f.*, quibus, *m.*; (*noise*) tapage, train, bousin, boucan, *m.*; — *v.a.* (*brush*) épousseter; (*sweep*) balayer; (*wipe*) essuyer; (*cover with dust*) couvrir de poussière; (*sprinkle*) saupoudrer; (*grind*) broyer. *To make a —,* faire de la poussière (*with an adj.,* faire une poussière ...). *To raise the —,* faire lever la poussière, faire de la poussière. *To raise from the —,* tirer de la poussière. *To throw — into people's eyes,* jeter de la poudre aux yeux. *To trample in the —,* fouler aux pieds. *To trample into —,* réduire en poussière, réduire au néant. — **bin,** *s.* coffre aux ordures, *m.* — **born,** *adj.* né de la poussière. — **brand,** *s.* charbon, *m.*, nielle des blés, *f.* — **brush,** *s.* vergette, *f.* — **cart,** *s.* tombereau, *m.* — **contractor,** *s.* entrepreneur de l'enlèvement des boues, *m.* — **heap,** *s.* tas d'ordures, *m.* — **hole,** *s.* trou aux ordures, *m.* — **man,** *s.* boueur, *m.* — **pan,** *s.* pelle à ordures, *f.*, ordurier, *m.* — **shot,** *s.* cendrée, *f.*
Duster, *s.* torchon, *m.*; (*for horses*) époussette, *f.*
Dustiness, *s.* état poudreux, *m.*
Dusting, *s.* (*brushing*) époussetage, *m.*; (*sweeping*) balayage, *m.*; (*wiping*) essuyage, *m.* — **brush,** *s.* vergette, *f.*
Dusty, *adj.* couvert de poussière, poudreux; (*of colours*) de poussière, cendré. — *white,* blanc sale. *To be —,* (*on the roads*) faire de la poussière (... *very —,* ... beaucoup de poussière). *To get —,* se couvrir de poussière
Dutch, *adj.* hollandais, de Hollande; — *s.* (*people*) (les) Hollandais, *m.pl.*; (*language*) le hollandais, *m.*, la langue hollandaise, *f.* *Double* or *high —,* allemand, haut allemand, *m.* — **auction,** *s.* adjudication au rabais, *f.* — **beef,** *s.* bœuf fumé, *m.* — **blue,** *s.* émail *or* azur de Hollande, *m.* — **boy,** *s.* (petit) Hollandais, *m.* — **cheese,** *s.* fromage de Hollande, *m.* — **foil,** *s.* oripeau, clinquant, *m.* — **girl,** *s.* (petite *or* jeune) Hollandaise, *f.* — **gold,** *s.* *V.* — **foil.** — **lady,** *s.* dame hollandaise, Hollandaise, *f.* — **leaf,** *s.* *V.* — **foil.** — **linen,** *s.* toile de Hollande, *f.* — **man,** *s.* Hollandais, *m.* — **metal,** *s.* *V.* — **foil.** — **oven,** *s.* rôtissoire, cuisinière, *f.* — **pen, -quill,** *s.* plume hollandée, *f.* — **rush,** *s.* (*bot.*) prêle d'hiver, *f.*; (*stem*) asprêle, *f.* — **school,** *s.* (*paint.*) école hollandaise, *f.* — **ship, -vessel,** *s.* navire *or* vaisseau hollandais, *m.* — **woman,** *s.* Hollandaise, *f.*
Duteous. *V.* **Dutiful**
Dutiable. *V.* **Dutyable**
Dutiful, *adj.* qui remplit ses devoirs (envers); soumis, obéissant; respectueux; bon, excellent
Dutifully, *adv.* avec soumission; respectueusement [respect, *m.*
Dutifulness, *s.* soumission, obéissance, *f.*;
Duty, *s.* devoir, *m.*; soumission, obéissance, *f.*; respect, *m.*; service, *m.*; fonctions, *f.pl.*; (*civilities*) devoirs, hommages, *m.pl.*; (*tax*) droit, *m.* — *off,* sans le droit. *Full —,* grand service. *Half- —,* petit service. *Off —,* libre. *On —,* de service; de garde; (*on sentry*) de faction. *To do —,* servir, faire le service; (*eccl.*) officier; desservir (une église, une chapelle). *To do — to, to give* or *pay o.'s — to,* rendre ses devoirs à, présenter ses hommages à. *To do o.'s —,* faire son devoir. *To enter upon o.'s —ies,* entrer en fonctions
Dutyable, *adj.* soumis aux droits
Duumvir, *s.* duumvir, *m.*
Duumviral, *adj.* duumviral
Duumvirate, *s.* duumvirat, *m.*
Dwale, *s.* (*bot.*) belladone, *f.*
Dwarf, *s. adj.* nain, *m.*, e, *f.*; — *v.a.* rapetisser; (*stunt*) empêcher de croître, rabougrir; — *v.n.* se rapetisser, rapetisser; (*grow stunted*) se rabougrir, rabougrir
Dwarfish, *adj.* de nain, rabougri, petit, minime; chétif, misérable
Dwarfishly, *adv.* comme un nain
Dwarfishness, *s.* taille de nain, petitesse de
Dwarfism, *s.* nanisme, *m.* [taille, petitesse, *f.*
Dwell, *v.n.* demeurer, habiter; (*stay*) rester; (*on, upon*) s'arrêter (sur, à), s'étendre (sur); appuyer (sur); s'appesantir (sur); insister (sur)
Dweller, *s.* habitant, *m.*, e, *f.*
Dwelling, — **house, -place,** *s.* habitation, demeure, résidence, *f.*; (*law*) domicile, *m.*; maison habitée, *f.*
Dwindle, *v.a.n.* (— **away, down**) diminuer; (*fall away*) dépérir; s'en aller; dégénérer; (*come to*) se réduire (à)
Dwt. *abbrev. of* **Pennyweight**
Dye, *v.a.* teindre; — *s.* teinture, *f.*; (*tinge*) teinte, *f.*; (*style of dyeing*) teint, *m.*; (*dye-stuff*) matière tinctoriale, *f.*; (*colour*) couleur, *f.*; (*kind*) nature, *f.*; (*atrocity*) noirceur, *f.* *Bad —,* faux teint. *Fast —, good —,* grand teint, bon teint. *Fugitive —,* faux teint. *To — black, red,* &c., teindre en noir, en rouge, &c. *A crime of a deeper —,* un crime plus noir *or* plus atroce. — **house, -mill,** *s.* teinturerie, *f.* — **stuff,** *s.* matière tinctoriale, *f.*, article de teinture, *m.* — **wood,** *s.* bois de teinture, *m.* — **works,** *s. pl.* teinturerie, *f.*
Dyeing, *s.* teinture, *f.*; teinturerie, *f.*
Dyer, *s.* teinturier, *m.*, -ière, *f.* —**'s weed,** *s.* gaude, *f.*
Dying, *adj.* mourant; (*pining*) moribond; (*things*) de la mort; (*last*) dernier; suprême; (*made on o.'s death-bed*) fait au lit de mort. — *man,* mourant, *m.*; moribond, *m.* — *woman,* mourante, *f.*; moribonde, *f.* — *words,* dernières paroles, *f.pl.* *To be —,* être mourant, [se mourir
Dyke. *V.* **Dike**

Dynamic, -al, *adj.* dynamique
Dynamics, *s. pl.* dynamique, *f.*
Dynamite, *s.* dynamite, *f.*
Dynamometer, *s.* dynamomètre, *m.*
Dynast-ic, al, -y. *V.* page 3, § 1
Dysenteric, *adj.* dyssentérique; (*pers.*) atteint de dyssenterie
Dysentery, *s.* dyssenterie, *f.*
Dyspepsia, Dyspepsy, *s.* dyspepsie, *f.*
Dyspeptic, *adj. s.* dyspeptique, *m.f.*
Dyspnœa, *s.* dyspnée, *f.*
Dysuria, Dysury, *s.* dysurie, *f.*
Dysuric, *adj.* dysurique
Dytiscus, *s.* dytique, *m.*

E

E, *s.* (*letter*) e, *m.*; (*mus.*) mi, *m.*
Each, *pron.* (*every*) chaque; (*every one*) chacun, *m.*, e, *f.* — *one*, chacun, *m.*, e, *f.* — *other*, l'un l'autre; se; nous; vous; (*of more than two*) les uns les autres; se; nous; vous. *For — other*, l'un pour l'autre; les uns pour les autres. *Of — other*, l'un de l'autre; les uns des autres. *To — other*, l'un à l'autre; les uns aux autres
Eager, *adj.* ardent, vif (à); impatient (de); désireux (de), curieux (de); avide (de); (*zealous*) empressé (de)
Eagerly, *adv.* ardemment, vivement; passionnément; impatiemment; avidement; précipitamment; (*zealously*) avec empressement
Eagerness, *s.* ardeur, vivacité, *f.*; impétuosité, *f.*; impatience, *f.*; avidité, *f.*; (*zeal*) empressement, *m.*
Eagle, *s.* aigle, *m.f.*; (*coin*) aigle, *m.*; (— *lectern, of churches*) lutrin, aigle, *m.*; (*on medals*) aigle, *m.*; (*orders of knighthood*) aigle, *m.*; (*her., astr., standard*) aigle, *f.* — *displayed*, (*her.*) aigle éployée, *f.* — **eyed, -sighted,** *adj.* qui a un œil d'aigle. — **hawk,** *s.* aigle autour, *m.* — **owl,** *s.* grand-duc, *m.* — **stone,** *s.* aétite, pierre d'aigle, *f.* — **winged,** *adj.* rapide comme l'aigle. — **wood,** *s.* bois [d'aigle, *m.*
Eaglet, *s.* aiglon, *m.*, -ne, *f.*
Eagre, *s.* ras de marée, *m.*
Ear, *s.* oreille, *f.*; (*handle*) anse, *f.*; (*of corn*) épi, *m.*; (*tech.*) oreille, oreillette, *f.*; (*mach.*) oreille, *f.*, mentonnet, *m.*; — *v.n.* monter en épi, épier. *To be by the —s*, être en querelle, être brouillés. *To have a correct —*, avoir l'oreille juste. *To have a good —*, avoir de l'oreille. *To have a quick —*, avoir l'oreille fine. *To listen with both —s*, écouter de toutes ses oreilles. *To set by the —s*, mettre aux prises; brouiller. *To turn a deaf —*, faire la sourde oreille (à); fermer l'oreille (à). — **ache,** *s.* mal d'oreille, *m.* — **cap,** *s.* oreillette, *f.* — **cockles,** *s. pl.* (*agr.*) nielle, *f.* — **cornet,** *s.* cornet acoustique, *m.* — **deafening,** *adj.* étourdissant, assourdissant. — **doctor,** *s.* auriste, *m.* — **drop,** *s.* pendant d'oreille, *m.* — **drum,** *s.* tympan (de l'oreille), *m.* — **finger,** *s.* doigt auriculaire, petit doigt, *m.* — **knot,** *s.* bouffette, *f.*, pompon, *m.*, cocarde, *f.* — **lap,** *s.* (*of the ear*) lobe de l'oreille, *m.*; (*of a cap*) oreille, oreillette, *f.* —**less,** *adj.* sans oreilles; qui n'écoute point. — **pick, -picker,** *s.* cure-oreilles, *m.* — **piercer,** *s.* perce-oreille, *m.* — **plate,** *s.* oreille, *f.* — **ring,** *s.* boucle d'oreille, *f.* — **shaped, -like,** *adj.* en forme d'oreille, auriforme. — **shell,** *s.* haliotide, *f.*, ormet, ormier, *m.* — **shot,** *s.* *Within — shot*, *V.* **Hearing.** — **trumpet,** *s.* cornet acoustique, écoutoir, *m.* — **wax,** *s.* (la) cire des oreilles, (de la) cire d'oreilles, *f.*, (le, du) cérumen, *m.* — **wig,** *s.* perce-oreille, *m.*; *v.a.* souffler aux oreilles de. — **witness,** *s.* témoin auriculaire, *m.*
Eared, *adj.* aux oreilles ..., à l'oreille ...; (*of corn*) garni d'épis, épié; (*bot.*) auriculé. *Full —*, à épis pleins. *Long —*, aux longues oreilles. *One —*, (*of animals*) monaut, *adj. m.* *Quick —*, qui a l'oreille fine
Earing, *s.* (*of corn: agr.*) épiage, *m.*, (*bot.*) épiation, *f.*; (*nav.*) pointure, *f.*, raban de pointure, *m.*
Earl, *s.* comte, *m.* —**dom,** *s.* comté, titre de [comte, *m.*
Earlier, Earliest, *adj.* plus en avance, plus matinal, &c. (*V.* **Early,** *adj.*); premier; plus ancien; — *adv.* de meilleure heure; plus tôt. *To make —*, avancer
Earliness, *s.* arrivée de bonne heure, arrivée prématurée, *f.*; (*of the day, night*) heure peu avancée, *f.*; (*of fruits*, &c.) précocité, hâtiveté, hâtivité, *f.*; (*fig.*) précocité, *f.*
Early, *adj.* (*pers.*) en avance; (*of rising*) matinal; matineux; (*things*) prématuré; précoce; avancé; (*near*) rapproché; prochain; (*of years, first*) premier; (*of the hour*) peu avancé; (*of a child's age*) tendre, bas; (*of fruits*, &c.) précoce, hâtif. — *age*, — *life*, âge tendre, bas âge, *m.*, jeunesse, *f.* — *old age*, vieillesse prématurée, *f.* — *ages* or *times*, premiers âges, premiers temps, *m.pl.* — *Church*, primitive Église, *f.* — **rising,** *s.* habitude de se lever de bonne heure, *f.* — *printed book*, incunable, *m.* — *vegetables* or *fruit* or *flowers*, primeurs, *f.pl.* *At an — age*, de bonne heure. *At an — hour*, à une heure peu avancée, de bonne heure. *To keep — hours*, *V.* **Hour**
Early, *adv.* de bonne heure; au commencement (de); dans les premiers jours (de); (*in time*) à temps; (*soon*) bientôt; tôt. — *in the morning*, de bon matin, de grand matin, de bonne heure le matin. *As — as possible*, aussitôt que possible, le plus tôt possible
Earn, *v.a.* gagner; acquérir, obtenir; mériter
Earnest, *adj.* ardent; vif; empressé, zélé; sérieux; sincère; — *s.* sérieux, *m.*; (*pledge*) gage, *m.*, arrhes, *f.pl.*; (*fig.*) avant-goût, *m.* *In —*, *in good* or *right —*, tout de bon, sérieusement, au sérieux; sérieux; de bonne foi; vrai; (*moved*) ému. *To be in —*, (*pers., not shamming or joking*) être sérieux, agir sérieusement, parler sérieusement. *To give —*, donner des arrhes. — **money,** *s.* arrhes, *f.pl.*
Earnestly, *adv.* ardemment, avec ardeur, avec zèle, chaudement, avec chaleur, vivement, instamment, avec instance, avec empressement; avec attention; sérieusement, tout de bon
Earnestness, *s.* ardeur, chaleur, *f.*, instances, *f.pl.*, instance, *f.*, zèle, empressement, *m.*; sérieux, *m.*, gravité, *f.*; sincérité, *f.*; attention, *f.*; (*anxiety*) sollicitude, inquiétude, *f.*
Earnings, *s. pl.* gain, fruit du travail, *m*; (*labour*) travail, *m.* *Hard —*, fruit du travail, *m.*
Earth, *s.* terre, *f.*; (*fox-hole*) terrier, *m.*; — *v.a.* enterrer, enfouir, cacher en terre; couvrir de terre; (*tech.*) terrer; — *v.n.*, — **oneself,** *v.a.* terrer, se cacher sous terre, se terrer. *Made —*, terre rapportée. *Our mother —*, la terre, notre mère commune, *f.* — **bag,** *s.* sac de *or* à terre, *m.* — **bank,** *s.* jetée de terre, *f.*; talus, *m.* — **board,** *s.* *V.* **Mould-board.** — **born,** *adj.* né de la terre, fils de la terre; (*fig.*) terrestre, d'ici-bas, de ce monde; (*low*) vil, de basse naissance. — **bound,** *adj.* attaché à la terre. — **bred,** *adj.* vil, abject. — **chestnut,** *s.* souchet comestible, *m.* — **eater,** &c., *V.* **Dirt-eater,** &c. — **flax,** *s.* amiante, *m.* — **nut,** *s.* terre-noix, *f.*; arachide, pistache de terre, *f.* — **nut oil,** *s.* huile d'arachide, huile de pistache de terre, *f.* — **quake,** *s.* tremblement de terre, *m.* — **slip,** *s.* éboulement de terre, *m.* — **up,** *v.a.* déterrer; (*agr., hort.*) butter, chausser. — **ward, -s,** *adj. adv.* vers la terre. — **wire,** *s.* parafoudre, *m.* — **work,** *s.* terrassement, *m.*; (*mil.*) ouvrage en terre, *m.* — **work battery,** *s.* batterie en terre, *f.* — **worm,** *s.* ver de terre, *m.*
Earthed, *part. adj.* enterré, &c. (*V.* **Earth;** *v.a.n.*); (*hunt.*) terré, dans son terrier

Earthen, *adj.* de terre, en terre. — **pan,** *s.* terrine, *f.*; jatte, *f.* — **ware,** *s.* poterie, faïence, *f.* [terrestre, *f.*; grossièreté, *f.*
Earthiness, *s.* nature terreuse, *f.*; nature
Earthliness, *s.* nature terrestre, *f.*; grossièreté, *f.*; (*worldliness*) mondanité, *f.*, caractère mondain, *m.*
Earthly, *adj.* terrestre, de la terre, d'ici-bas; matériel, corporel; (*worldly*) mondain, charnel; (*in the world, fam.*) au monde; (*the least*) le moindre. — **minded,** *adj.* mondain. — **mindedness,** *s.* mondanité, *f.* [grossier
Earthy, *adj.* de terre; terreux; terrestre;
Ease, *s.* aise, *f.*; repos, *m.*; tranquillité, *f.*; oisiveté, *f.*; facilité, aisance, *f.*; abandon, *m.*; (*of pain*) soulagement, *m.*; — *v.a.* mettre à l'aise; (*to free*) délivrer, débarrasser; (*from pain,* &c.) soulager, adoucir, alléger; calmer; tranquilliser; (*nav.,* — *off*) larguer; (*a ship*) amener au vent. — *her!* (*nav.*) doucement! *At* —, *at his* —, à l'aise, à son aise; tranquille, en repos, en paix. *At — ! Stand at — !* (*mil.*) repos! *With* —, avec facilité. *To take o.'s* —, prendre ses aises, se mettre à l'aise
Easel, *s.* chevalet, *m.* — **painting, -picture, -piece,** *s.* tableau de chevalet, *m.*
Easement, *s.* soulagement, *m.*; (*civ. law*) aisance, servitude, *f.*
Easily, *adv.* aisément; facilement; sans peine; à l'aise; commodément; tranquillement; sans répugnance, volontiers; avec calme; (*of motion*) doucement, sans secousse
Easiness, *s.* aisance, *f.*; facilité, *f.*; douceur, *f.*; tranquillité, *f.*
East, *s.* est, *m.*; orient, levant, *m.*; — *adj.* de l'est, d'est, est, oriental; (*of Eastern countries*) oriental, d'orient, d'Orient, de l'Orient; — *adv.* à l'est. — **Indiaman,** *s.* navire des Indes Orientales, *m.* — **ward, -s,** *adj. adv.* vers l'est, vers l'orient. — **wind,** *s.* vent d'est, *m.*
Easter, *s.* Pâques, *m.*; (*Jew. rel.*) la pâque, *f.*; — *adj.* de Pâques. *Before* —, (*of the days of Passion week*) saint. — *Monday,* lundi de Pâques, *m. Monday before* —, lundi saint, *m.* — *eve,* veille de Pâques, *f.*, samedi saint, *m.* — *Day,* le jour de Pâques, *m.*
Easterly, *adj.* d'est, de l'est; — *adv.* vers (*or* à) l'est, vers (*or* à) l'orient
Eastern, *adj. V.* **East,** *adj. Great — railway,* chemin de fer de l'est, *m. An — voyage,* un voyage en Orient. *The — question,* la question d'Orient. *The — nations* or *people,* les Orientaux, *m.pl.*, les nations (*f.pl.*) *or* les peuples (*m.pl.*) de l'Orient. — **most,** *adj.* (le) plus à l'est, à l'extrême est
Easy, *adj.* facile, aisé; tranquille; doux; accommodant, complaisant, facile; libre, dégagé; (*not tight*) aisé; (*well off*) à son aise, dans l'aisance; (*free from pain*) à son aise; (*of chairs,* &c.) confortable; (*of stages*) petit; — *adverb. V.* **Easily.** — *of belief,* crédule. *To keep o.'s mind* —, être sans inquiétude, être tranquille. *To make oneself — about,* se tranquilliser sur. *To take things* or *it* —, en prendre à son aise, ne pas se fouler la rate; se donner du bon temps; (*not to fret*) ne pas se tourmenter, ne pas se faire de bile. *As — as kiss my hand,* facile comme tout, facile comme bonjour
Eat, *v.a.n.* manger; (*have, as a dinner,* &c.) faire; (*corrode, gnaw*) ronger; (*consume*) consumer. *To — o.'s dinner,* dîner; manger. *To — anyone* (*else*)*'s dinner,* manger le dîner de quelqu'un, dîner aux frais de quelqu'un, dîner chez quelqu'un. *To — a good dinner,* faire un bon dîner. *To — o.'s words,* se rétracter. *This meat —s hard,* cette viande est dure à manger, cette viande ne se mange pas facilement. — **away, up,** manger; croquer; (*fig.*) dévorer, ronger, consumer. — **into,** ronger; miner; consumer; faire des ravages dans. — **out,** ronger, dévorer; consumer; gruger, ruiner
Eatable, *adj.* mangeable, bon à manger; (*used as food*) comestible; — *s.* comestible, [aliment, *m.*
Eatage, *s.* regain, *m.*
Eater, *s.* mangeur, *m.*, -euse, *f.*; (*fig.*) corrosif, *m.*
Eating, *adj.* mangeant; (*fig.*) dévorant; rongeur; — *s.* action de manger, manducation, *f.*; manger, *m.*; chère, *f.*; (*in contempt*) mangeaille, *f.* — *and drinking,* le boire et le manger. *To be fond of good* —, aimer la bonne chère. — **house,** *s.* restaurant, *m.* — **house keeper,** *s.* restaurateur, traiteur, *m.* [*English part*
Eau de Cologne, &c. *V.* **Eau,** *in the French-*
Eaves, *s. pl.* bords du toit, *m.pl.*, égout, larmier, *m.* — **board, -catch, -lath,** *s.* chanlate, chanlatte, *f.* — **drop,** *v.n.* écouter aux portes; être aux écoutes. — **dropper,** *s.* personne qui écoute aux portes, *f.*, écouteur, *m.*, -euse, *f.*, épieur, *m.*, -euse, *f.* — **dropping,** *s.* action d'écouter aux portes, *f.*
Ebb, *s.* reflux, *m.*; déclin, *m.*, décadence, *f.*; — *v.n.* refluer; (*of the tide*) baisser, descendre; (*to decay*) décliner, baisser, décroître. *The — and flow,* le flux et le reflux. *At a low* —, bas. — **out,** *v.n.* se retirer. — **tide,** *s.* marée descendante, *f.*, reflux, *m.* [sur le déclin
Ebbing, *s. V.* **Ebb;** — *adj.* qui reflue; (*fig.*)
Ebon, *s. V.* **Ebony;** — *adj.* ébénin, d'ébène, noir
Ebonist, *s.* ébéniste, *m.*
Ebonite, *s.* caoutchouc vulcanisé, *m.*
Ebonize, *v.a.* ébéner; (*fig.*) rendre noir comme l'ébène
Ebony, *s.* (*wood*) ébène, *f.m.*; (*colour, work*) ébène, *m.*; — *adj.* d'ébène. — **tree,** *s.* ébénier, *m.* — **work,** *s.* ébène, *m.*
Ebriety, *s.* ivresse, ébriété, *f.* [vescence, *f.*
Ebullienc-e, y, *s.* ébullition, *f.*; (*fig.*) effer-
Ebullient, *adj.* en ébullition; (*fig.*) bouillon-
Ebullioscope, *s.* ébullioscope, *m.* [nant
Ebullition, *s.* ébullition, *f.*; (*fig.*) effervescence, *f.*; violence, *f.*, emportement, *m.*; transport, *m.*; accès, *m.* [ivoirin
Eburnean, *adj.* éburné, éburnéen, éburnin,
Écarté, *s.* écarté, *m.*
Ecce homo, *s.* ecce homo, *m.*
Eccentric, *adj.* excentrique; (*fig.*) excentrique, bizarre, original, singulier; — *s.* (*anc. astr., mach.*) excentrique, *m.*; (*fig.*) chose bizarre, chose excentrique, anomalie, *f.*
Eccentrically, *adv.* excentriquement
Eccentricity, *s.* excentricité, *f.*
Ecchymose, *v.a.* ecchymoser. *To become —d,*
Ecchymosis, *s.* ecchymose, *f.* [s'ecchymoser
Ecchymotic, *adj.* ecchymotique
Ecclesiastes, *s.* Ecclésiaste, *m.* [*adj. m.f.*
Ecclesiastic, -al, *s. adj.* ecclésiastique, *s.m.*,
Ecclesiastically, *adv.* ecclésiastiquement
Ecclesiasticus, *s.* Ecclésiastique, *m.*
Ecclesiolog-ic, al, -ist, -y, ecclésiologique, &c. *V.* page 3, § 1
Echelon, *s.* (*mil.*) échelon; — *v.a.* échelonner
Echidna, *s.* échidné, *m.*
Echinate, Echinated, *adj.* échiné
Echinoderm, *s.* échinoderme, *m.*
Echinus, *s.* (*arch.*) échine, *f.*
Echo, *s.* écho, *m.*; (*myth.*) Écho, *f.*; — *v.n.* résonner, retentir; (*to be repeated*) faire écho; — *v.a.* répéter. —**less,** *adj.* sans écho
Echometer, *s.* échomètre, *m.*
Éclat, *s.* éclat, *m.*
Eclectic, *adj. s.* éclectique
Eclectically, *adv.* éclectiquement
Eclecticism, *s.* éclectisme, *m.*
Eclectize, *v.n.* éclectiser [s'éclipser
Eclipse, *s.* éclipse, *f.*; — *v.a.* éclipser; — *v.n.*
Ecliptic, *s. adj.* écliptique, *s.f.*, *adj. m.f.*
Eclogue, *s.* églogue, *f.*
Ecod, *int.* ma foi! parbleu!
Economic, -al, *adj.* économique; (*pers.*) économe, ménager
Economically, *adv.* économiquement
Economics, *s. pl.* économique, *f.*
Economist, *s.* économe, *m.f.*; (*polit.*) économiste, *m. Political* —, économiste, *m.*

Economization, *s.* économie, *f.*
Economize, *v.a.n.* économiser
Economizer, *s.* personne économe, *f.*
Economy, *s.* économie, *f.* *Political* —, économie politique, *f.*
Écorché, *s.* écorché, *m.*
Écoute, *s.* écoute, *f.*
Ecraseur, *s.* écraseur, *m.*
Ecstasied, *adj.* ravi en extase, extasié
Ecstasy, *s.* extase, *f.*
Ecstatic, -al, *adj.* extatique, d'extase
Ecthyma, ecthyma, *m.*
Ecuadorean, *s. adj.* Équatorien, *m.*, -ne, *f.*
Ecumenic, &c. *V.* **Œcumenic,** &c.
Eczema, *s.* eczéma, *m.*
Eczematous, *adj.* eczémateux
Edacious, *adj.* vorace, gourmand
Edacity, voracité, gourmandise, *f.*
Edda, *s.* Edda, *f.*
Eddish, *s.* regain, *m.*
Eddoes, *s. pl.* colocase, colocasie, *f.*
Eddy, *s.* remous, tourbillon, *m.*; — *adj.* tourbillonnant, tournoyant; — *v.n.* tourbillonner, [tournoyer
Eden, *s.* Éden, *m.*
Edental, Edentate, Edentated, *s. adj.* édenté, *s.m.*, édenté, *adj. m.*, e, *f.*
Edge, *s.* bord, *m.*; (*of tools*) fil, tranchant, *m.*; (*fig.*) pointe, *f.*; (*of a sword*) fil, *m.*; (*of a forest*, &c.) lisière, *f.*; (*of a stone*) angle, *m.*; (*of a book*) tranche, *f.*; (*agr.*) côte, *f.*; (*of coin*) cordon, *m.* *On* —, sur le bord; de champ; (*of the teeth*) agacé. *With gilt —s*, (*book-bind.*) doré sur tranche. *To give an — to*, donner le fil à, aiguiser. *To set on* —, poser de champ; (*the teeth*) agacer. *To take the — off, to dull the — of*, émousser. — **bone,** *s.* (*of beef*) tranche, *f.* —**less,** *adj.* sans tranchant, sans pointe, obtus, émoussé. — **rail,** *s.* rail saillant, *m.* — **tool,** *s.* instrument (*or* outil) tranchant, *m.* — **tool maker,** *s.* taillandier, *m.* — **tool making** *or* **trade,** *s.* taillanderie, *f.* — **ways, -wise,** *adv.* de champ; sur le bord; (*pers.*) de côté, de profil
Edge, *v.a.* aiguiser, affiler; border; (*coins*) cordonner; (*to move*) avancer de côté; — *v.n.* s'avancer de côté. — **away,** *v.n.* s'éloigner. — **in,** *v.a.* faire entrer, introduire; (*fig.*) glisser, couler; placer; adresser. — **upon,** (*the wind*), aller contre (le vent)
Edged, *adj.* tranchant; (*in compounds*) à ... tranchant, à tranchant ...; (*bordered*) bordé
Edging, *s.* bord, *m.*; (*trimming*) bordure, garniture, *f.*; (*hort.*) bordure, *f.*; (*of coin*) cor- [donnage, *m.*
Edible. *V.* **Eatable**
Edibleness, Edibility, *s.* comestibilité, *f.*
Edict, *s.* édit, *m.*
Edictal, *adj.* édictal
Edification, *s.* édification, *f.*
Edifice, *s.* édifice, *m.*
Edify, *v.a.* édifier
Edifyingly, *adv.* d'une manière édifiante
Edile, Edileship, *V.* **Ædile, Ædileship**
Edinburgher, *s.* Édimbourgeois, *m.*, e, *f.*
Edit, *v.a.* éditer; rédiger; diriger
Editing, *s.* rédaction, *f.*; direction, *f.*
Edition, *s.* édition, *f.*
Editor, *s.* éditeur, *m.*; (*of newspapers and periodicals*) rédacteur, *m.*; directeur, *m.*; gérant, *m.* *Chief* —, rédacteur en chef, *m.* —**s' room,** *s.* rédaction, *f.*
Editorial, *adj.* d'éditeur; de *or* du rédacteur; de la rédaction; — *s.* article de fond, *m.* — *article*, article de fond, *m.* — *staff*, rédaction, *f.*
Editorship, *s.* direction, *f.*; gérance, *f.*
Editress, *s.* éditrice, *f.*; (*of newspapers and periodicals*) rédactrice, *f.*; directrice, gérante, *f.*
Educability, *s.* éducabilité, *f.*
Educable, *adj.* éducable
Educate, *v.a.* élever, faire l'éducation de, instruire, (*fam.*) éduquer. *To be —d at*, avoir fait ses études à
Educating, *s.* éducation, *f.*; — *adj.* éducateur
Education, *s.* éducation, *f.*; enseignement, *m.*; instruction, *f.* *Man of no* —, homme sans in- [struction, *m.*
Educational, *adj.* d'éducation
Educationist, *s.* éducationiste, *m.f.*
Educative, *adj.* éducatif, éducateur
Educator, *s.* éducateur, *m.*, -trice, *f.*, instituteur, *m.*, -trice, *f.*, maître, *m.*, maîtresse, *f.*
Educe, *v.a.* tirer, extraire, faire sortir
Educible, *adj.* que l'on peut tirer *or* extraire
Educt, *s.* extrait, *m.*; produit, résultat, *m.*
Eduction, *s.* extraction, *f.*, dégagement, *m.*; émission, sortie, *f.*; (*tech.*) décharge, *f.*
Edulcorate, *v.a.* édulcorer
Edulcoration, *s.* édulcoration, *f.*
Eel, *s.* anguille, *f.* — **basket, -buck,** *s.* anguillère, *f.* — **fare,** *s.* montée, *f.* — **fishing,** *s.* pêche aux anguilles, *f.* — **pie,** *s.* pâté d'anguille, pâté à l'anguille, *m.* — **pond, -pot,** *s.* anguillère, *f.* — **pout,** *s.* barbote, lotte, *f.* — **shaped,** *adj.* anguilliforme. — **spear,** *s.* trident (à anguilles), *m.* — **trap,** *s.* [anguillère, *f.*
Efface, *v.a.* effacer
Effaceable, *adj.* effaçable
Effacement, Effacing, *s.* effacement, *m.*
Effect, *s.* effet, *m.*; —**s,** *pl.* effets, *m.pl.*; (*law*) biens, effets, *m.pl.*; (*of a bill*) provision, *f.*; — *v.a.* effectuer; opérer; exécuter; accomplir; réaliser; produire. *In* —, en effet, effectivement, de fait. *To that* (or *this*) —, à cet effet. *To the same* —, pour le même effet, pour le même but, dans la même intention. *To carry into* —, mettre à exécution, effectuer, accomplir. *To feel the —s of*, se ressentir de. *To take* —, faire effet (sur); faire son effet; être efficace; porter; porter coup; opérer; être mis à exécution; entrer en vigueur
Effective, *adj.* effectif; efficace; (*mil., nav.*) effectif; (*not disabled*) valide; — *s.* (*mil., nav.*) effectif, *m.*; (*specie*) monnaie effective, *f.*, numéraire, *m.*, espèces, *f.pl.* — *force* or *strength*, force effective, *f.*; (*mil., nav.*) effectif, *m.*
Effectively, *adv.* efficacement; effectivement
Effectual, *adj.* efficace
Effectually, *adv.* efficacement
Effectualness, *s.* efficacité, *f.*
Effeminacy, *s.* efféminatíon, mollesse, *f.*
Effeminate, *adj. s.* efféminé, *m.*, e, *f.*; — *v.a.* efféminer, amollir; — *v.n.* s'efféminer, s'amollir
Effeminately, *adv.* efféminément, mollement, avec mollesse
Effeminating, *s.* effémination, *f.*
Effendi, *s.* effendi, *m.*
Effervesce, *v.n.* être en effervescence; mousser
Effervescence, *s.* effervescence, *f.*
Effervescent, *adj.* *V.* **Effervescing**
Effervescible, *adj.* susceptible d'effervescence
Effervescing, *adj.* effervescent; mousseux; (*of common powders and drinks*) gazeux
Effete, *adj.* stérile; sans effet; inutile; (*worn out*, &c.) usé; épuisé; émoussé; éventé
Efficacious, *adj.* efficace
Efficaciously, *adv.* efficacement
Efficaciousness, Efficacy, *s.* efficacité, *f.*
Efficiency, *s.* efficacité, *f.*; (*pers.*) capacité, *f.*
Efficient, *adj.* efficace; (*of causes*) efficient; (*pers.*) capable; — *s.* cause efficiente, *f.*; (*math.*) facteur, *m.*
Efficiently, *adv.* efficacement; bien
Effigial, *adj.* effigial
Effigy, *s.* effigie, *f.*; image, *f.*
Effloresce, *v.n.* s'effleurir
Efflorescenc-e, y, *s.* (*bot.*) fleuraison, floraison, *f.*; (*chem., min., med.*) efflorescence, *f.*
Efflorescent, *adj.* efflorescent
Effluenc-e, y, *s.* effluence, *f.*
Effluent, *adj.s.* effluent, *adj.m.*, e, *f.*, effluent, *s.m.*
Effluvia, *s., pl. of* **Effluvium** [tion, *f.*
Effluvium, *s.* effluve, *m.*, exhalaison, émana-
Efflux, *s.* écoulement, *m.*; sortie, *f.*; effusion, *f.*; émanation, *f.*; émigration, *f.*
Effort, *s.* effort, *m.* *To use every* —, faire tous ses efforts. *It is an* — (*a great* —) *to me to* ...,

il m'en coûte (beaucoup) de ... —**less,** *adj.* [sans effort
Effrontery, *s.* effronterie, *f.*
Effulgence, *s.* éclat, *m.*, splendeur, *f.*
Effulgent, *adj.* éclatant, resplendissant
Effuse, *v.a.* verser, répandre, épancher; (*med.*) épancher; — *v.n.* se répandre, s'épancher; (*med.*) s'épancher
Effusion, *s.* effusion, *f.*; épanchement, *m.*; (*med.*) épanchement, *m.* — *on the brain*, épanchement au cerveau, *m.*
Effusive, *adj.* qui répand
Eft, *s. V.* **Newt**
E. G. (*exempli gratiâ*), par exemple
Egad, *int.* morbleu! parbleu! ma foi!
Egg, *s.* œuf, *m.*; (*arch.*) ove, *m.*; — *v.a. V.* **Urge.** *Beaten —s*, œufs brouillés. *Boiled —*, (*soft, in the shell*) œuf à la coque. *Fried —s*, œufs frits, œufs sur le plat. *Stale —*, œuf vieux. *To lay an —, two —s, large —s*, &c., pondre un œuf, deux œufs, de gros œufs, &c. *To lay —s*, pondre. — **apple,** *s.* aubergine, *f.* — **bird,** *s.* sterne épouvantail, *m.* — **boiler,** *s.* (*vessel*) œufrier, *m.*; (*sand-glass*) sablier, *m.* — **cup,** *s.* coquetier, *m.* — **dealer,** *s.* marchand d'œufs, *m.* — **flip,** *s.* lait de poule, *m.* — **frame,** *s.* porte-coquetiers, *m.* — **glass,** *s.* sablier, *m.* — **like,** *adj.* oviforme, ovale. — **merchant,** *s.* marchand d'œufs, *m.* — **plant,** *s.* aubergine, *f.* — **sauce,** *s.* sauce aux œufs, *f.* — **shaped,** *adj.* oviforme, ovale. — **shell,** *s.* coquille (*or* coque) d'œuf, *f.* — **slice,** *s.* écumoire, *f.* — **spoon,** *s.* cuiller à œufs, *f.* — **stand,** *s.* porte-coquetiers, *m.* — **trade,** *s.* commerce d'œufs, *m.* — **whisk,** *s.* verge (*f.*) *or* fouet (*m.*) à blancs d'œufs. — **yolk,** *s.* jaune d'œuf, *m.*
Eggar moth, *s.* lasiocampe, *f.*
Eglantine, *s.* églantier odorant, églantier, *m.*; (*flower*) églantine, *f.*
Egoism, *s.* égoïsme, *m.*
Egoist, *s.*, **Egoistic, -al,** *adj.* égoïste, *m.f.*
Egoistically, *adv.* égoïstement
Egotism, *s.* égotisme, *m.*
Egotist, *s.*, **Egotistic, -al,** *adj.* égotiste, *m.f.*
Egotize, *v.n.* égoïser [pommé, fieffé
Egregious, *adj.* insigne, énorme, fameux,
Egregiously, *adv.* d'une manière insigne, énormément, fameusement
Egregiousness, *s.* nature insigne, énormité, *f.*
Egress, Egression, *s.* sortie, issue, *f.*
Egret, *s.* (*bird, ornament, bot.*) aigrette, *f.*
Egriot, *s.* griotte, *f.* — **tree,** *s.* griottier, *m.*
Egyptian, *s.* Égyptien, *m.*, -ne, *f.*; — *adj.* égyptien, d'Égypte. — *vulture*, percnoptère, [néophron, *m.*
Eh, *int.* eh! hein! donc
Eider, *s.* eider, *m.* — **down,** — **down quilt** *or* **cushion** *or* **pillow,** *s.* édredon, *m.* — **duck,** *s.* eider, *m.*
Eight, *adj. s.* huit (*adj. m.f., s.m.*); (*elliptically*) (*of the clock*) huit heures, *f.pl.*, (*of o.'s age*) huit ans, *m.pl.* — **day clock,** *s.* horloge *or* pendule qui marche huit jours, *f.* — **fold,** *adj. adv.* octuple, huit fois autant, huit fois
Eighteen, *adj.* dix-huit. 18*mo*, (*of a book*) in-18, *adj. m.f., s.m.*
Eighteenth, *adj. s.* dix-huitième; (*of the month*) dix-huit. *The —*, (*of sovereigns*) dix-huit
Eighth, *adj.* huitième; — *s.* huitième, (*part*) *m.*, (*pers.*) *m.f.*; (*mus.*) octave, *f.*; (*of the month*) huit, *m.* *The —*, (*of sovereigns*) huit
Eighthly, *adv.* huitièmement
Eightieth, *adj.* quatre-vingtième
Eighty, *adj.* quatre-vingts
Either, *pron.* l'un ou l'autre, *m.*, l'une ou l'autre, *f.*; l'un d'eux *m.*, l'une d'elles, *f.*; (*the one*) celui, *m.*, celle, *f.*; (*one*) un, *m.*, une, *f.*; (*each*) *V.* **Each;** (*both*) *V.* **Both;** (*with a neg.*) ni l'un ni l'autre, *m.*, ni l'une ni l'autre, *f.*; aucun (*m.*, e, *f.*) des deux; aucun, *m.*, e, *f.* *I do not see —*, je ne vois ni l'un ni l'autre
Either, *conj.* soit; ou; (*negatively*) ni ... — *you or your brother*, soit vous, soit votre frère; ou vous, ou votre frère; vous ou votre frère. — *you will obey, or you shall be punished*, ou vous obéirez, ou vous serez puni [plus
Either, *adv.* non plus. *Nor I —*, ni moi non
Ejaculate, *v.a.* éjaculer, lancer; s'écrier
Ejaculation, *s* éjaculation, *f.*; émission, *f.*
Ejaculatory, Ejaculating, *adj.* éjaculatoire; (*anat.*) éjaculateur
Eject, *v.a.* jeter; rejeter; expulser
Ejection, *s.* rejet, *m.*; expulsion, *f.*; (*med.*) [éjection, *f.*
Ejectment, *s.* expulsion, *f.*
Ejector, *s.* expulseur, *m.*
Eke, *v.a.* — **out,** allonger; élargir; ajouter à, augmenter; suppléer à; compléter
Eking-piece, *s.* allonge, *f.*; élargissure, *f.*
Elaborate, *v.a.* élaborer; — *adj.* élaboré, travaillé, soigné, fini
Elaborately, *adv.* d'une manière élaborée, laborieusement, soigneusement, avec soin
Elaborateness, *s.* travail, *m.*; fini, *m.*
Elaborating, Elaborative, *adj.* élaborateur
Elaboration, *s.* élaboration, *f.*; travail, *m.*
Eland, *s.* élan du Cap, *m.*
Elanet, *s.* élane, *m.*
Elapse, *v.n.* s'écouler, se passer, passer
Elastic, *adj. s.* élastique, *adj. m.f., s.m.* — *band*, bande élastique, *f.*; tissu élastique, *m.* — *web*, tissu élastique, élastique, *m. V.* **Boot**
Elastically, *adv.* d'une manière élastique, [élastiquement
Elasticity, *s.* élasticité, *f.*
Elate, *adj.* enorgueilli; fier; — *v.a.* élever; (*puff up*) enorgueillir, enfler
Elatedly, *adv.* orgueilleusement
Elater, *s.* (*insect*) élater, taupin, *m.*
Elaterium, *s.* élatérium, *m.*
Elation, *s.* fierté, *f.*; orgueil, *m.*
Elbow, *s.* coude, *m.*; (*of arm-chairs*) *V.* **Arm;** (*angle*) coude, *m.*; — *v.a.* coudoyer; — *v.n.* faire un coude *or* un angle. *To be at anyone's —s*, être aux côtés *or* à côté de quelqu'un. — **chair,** *s.* fauteuil, *m.* — **grease,** *s.* huile de bras, huile de poignet, *f.* — **out,** *v.a.* repousser à coups de coude; (*fig.*) écarter, évincer. — **piece,** *s.* coudière, *f.* — **rest,** *s.* accoudoir, *m.* — **room,** *s.* coudées franches, *f.pl.*, liberté d'action, *f.*
Elbowing, *s.* coudoiement, *m.*
Elder, *adj.* aîné; plus âgé; (*in date*) plus ancien; — *s.* aîné, *m.*, e, *f.*; (*theol.*) ancien, prêtre, *m.*; (*bot.*) sureau, *m.* — **berry,** *s.* baie *or* graine de sureau, *f.* — **bush,** *s.* sureau, *m.* — **flower,** *s.* fleur de sureau, *f.* — **gun,** *s.* canonnière, *f.* — **tree,** *s.* sureau, *m.* — **wine,** *s.* vin de sureau, *m.*
Elderly, *adj.* assez âgé, d'un certain âge
Eldership, *s.* aînesse, *f.*; ancienneté, *f.*; (*theol.*) dignité d'ancien, *f.*; assemblée d'anciens, *f.*
Eldest, *adj. V.* **Elder,** *adj.*
Eldorado, *s.* eldorado, *m.*
Eleatic, *adj. s.* éléatique, *adj. m.f., s.m.*
Elecampane, *s.* aunée, *f.*
Elect, *v.a.* élire; choisir; nommer; préférer, aimer mieux; se décider (à); (*theol.*) élire; — *adj.* élu; choisi; nommé; (*theol.*) élu; — *s.* [élu, *m.*
Electing, *s. V.* **Election**
Election, *s.* élection, *f.*; choix, *m.*; (*theol.*) élection, *f.*
Electioneer, *v.n.* électionner, travailler les électeurs, solliciter des votes, briguer des suffrages
Electioneering, *s.* manœuvres électorales, *f.pl.*; élections, *f.pl.*; — *adj.* d'élections, des élections
Elective, *adj.* électif; électoral; (*chem., physiol.*) électif
Electively, *adv.* électivement, par choix, par élection, au choix, à l'élection
Elector, *s.* électeur, *m.*
Electoral, *adj.* électoral; d'électeur
Electorate, *s.* électorat, *m.*
Electress, *s.* électrice, *f.*
Electric, -al, *adj.* électrique. — *eel*, gymnote, *m.* — *jar* or *phial*, bouteille de Leyde, *f.*
Electrically, *adv.* électriquement

Electrician, *s.* électricien, *m.*; électrographe, *m.*
Electricity, *s.* électricité, *f.*
Electrifiable, *adj.* électrisable
Electrification, *s.* électrisation, *f.*
Electrify, *v.a.* électriser ('*with*,' de); — *v.n.* s'électriser
Electrization, *s.* électrisation, *f.*
Electrize, *v.a.* électriser
Electrizer, *s.* électriseur, *m.*
Electro, (*in compounds*) électro ... — **chemistry,** &c. électro-chimie, *s.f.*, &c. — **gild,** &c., plaquer en or, dorer, &c. *V.* — **plate,** &c. — **magnet,** *s.* électro-aimant, *m.* — **magnetic, -ism,** &c., électro-magnétique (*adj.*), électro-magnétisme (*s.m.*), &c. — **metallurgy,** *s.* placage, *m.*, galvanoplastie, *f.* — **meter,** *s.* électromètre, *m.* — **motive,** *adj.* électromoteur. — **motor,** *s.* électromoteur, *m.* — **phorus,** *s.* électrophore, *m.* — **plate,** *v.a.* plaquer; *s.* galvanoplastie, *f.*; plaqué, *m.*; *adj.* plaqué, en plaqué. — **plater,** *s.* galvanoplaste, *m.* — **plating,** *s.* galvanoplastie, *f.*; *adj.* galvanoplastique. — **scope,** *s.* électroscope, *m.* — **silver,** *v.a.* plaquer en argent, argenter, plaquer; *s.* plaqué, *m.*; *adj.* plaqué, en plaqué. — **silverer,** &c. *V.* — **plater,** &c. — **type,** *v.a.* électrotyper; *s.* électrotype, *m.* — **typer,** *s.* électrotypeur, *m.* — **typic,** *adj.* électrotypique. — **typing,** *s.* électrotypage, *m.*; *adj.* électrotypique. — **typy,** *s.* électrotypie, *f.*
Electrode, *s.* électrode, *f.*
Electuary, *s.* (*formerly*) électuaire, *m.*, (*now*) opiat, *m.*
Eleemosynary, *adj.* de charité; d'aumône; sous forme d'aumône; gratuit; (*pers.*) qui vit d'aumônes *or* de charités
Elegance, *s.* élégance, *f.*
Elegant, *adj.* élégant; beau
Elegantly, *adv.* élégamment, avec élégance
Elegiac,-al, *adj.* élégiaque; — *s.* vers élégiaque
Elegiast, Elegist, *s.* élégiaque, *m.*
Elegy, *s.* élégie, *f.*
Element, *s.* élément, *m.*; (*theol.*) espèce, *f.*
Elemental, *adj.* élémentaire; des éléments
Elementariness, *s.* nature élémentaire, *f.*
Elementary, *adj.* élémentaire; primaire
Elemi, *s.* élémi, *m.*
Elephant, *s.* éléphant, *m.*, e, (*V.* **She**), *f.* *Double* —, (*paper*) grand aigle, *m.* — **beetle,** *s.* goliath, *m.* — **driver,** *s.* cornac, *m.*
Elephantiac, *adj.* éléphantiaque, éléphantique
Elephantiasis, *s.* éléphantiasis, *f.*
Elephantine, *adj.* éléphantin; d'éléphant
Eleusinian, *adj.* d'Éleusis
Elevate, *v.a.* élever; (*with pride*) exalter, enfler; enorgueillir; (*excite*) exciter; —, —**d,** *adj.* élevé, &c.; (*with drink*) en train, lancé
Elevation, *s.* élévation, *f.*
Elevator, *s.* (*anat.*) élévateur, *m.*; (*mech.*) élévateur, éleveur, *m.*; (*surg.*) élévatoire, *m.*; — *adj.* (*anat.*) élévateur
Elevatory, *adj.* élévatoire, élévateur
Eleven, *adj.* *s.* onze (*adj.* *m.f.*, *s.m.*); (*elliptically*) (*of the clock*) onze heures, *f.pl.*, (*of o.'s age*) onze ans, *m. pl.* [*V. at the end of* **Eleventh**]
Eleventh, *adj.* onzième; — *s.* onzième, (*part*) *m.*, (*pers.*) *m.f.*, (*mus.*) *f.*; (*of the month*) onze, *m.* *The* —, (*of sovereigns*) onze [de *instead of* d', le *or* la *instead of* l', *and* du *or* de la *instead of* de l', *must be used before* onze *and* onzième. *Likewise* ma, ta, sa, *in the feminine, instead of* mon, ton, son]
Eleventhly, *adv.* onzièmement
Elf, *s.* (*myth.*) elfe, lutin, follet, *m.*, fée, *f.*; (*evil spirit*) démon, diable, *m.*; (*dwarf*) nain, *m.*, e, *f.*, nabot, *m.*, e, *f.*, pygmée, *m.*
Elfin, *adj.* des elfes, des lutins, des fées, d'elfe, de lutin, de fée, féerique; enchanté; — *s.* *V.* **Elf;** (*child*) marmot, bambin, *m.*
Elfish, *adj.* *V.* **Elfin,** *adj.*
Elicit, *v.a.* faire jaillir; faire sortir; mettre au jour, mettre en lumière; faire voir; déduire; tirer; obtenir, avoir; découvrir; savoir; faire dire (à), faire avouer (à)
Elicitation, *s.* découverte, *f.*
Elide, *v.a.* élider; — *v.n.* s'élider
Eligibility, *s.* éligibilité, *f.*; avantage, *m.*
Eligible, *adj.* choisissable; (*of candidates*) éligible; (*suitable*) convenable (pour), avantageux (à, pour), désirable (pour); préférable (pour); — *s.* (*match*) parti avantageux, *m.*
Eligibleness. *V.* **Eligibility**
Eligibly, *adv.* éligiblement; (*suitably*) convenablement, avantageusement
Eliminate, *v.a.* éliminer
Eliminating, *adj.* éliminateur; — *s.* élimination, *f.*
Elimination, *s.* élimination, *f.*
Eliquate, Eliquation. *V.* **Liquate, Liquation**
Elision, *s.* élision, *f.*
Elite, *s.* élite, *f.*
Elixation, *s.* élixation, *f.*
Elixir, *s.* élixir, *m.*
Elizabethan, *adj.* du temps *or* du règne d'Élisabeth, d'Élisabeth; gothique
Elk, *s.* élan, *m.*
Ell, *s.* aune, *f.*
Ellipse, Ellipsis, *s.* ellipse, *f.* *To supply the* — *is*, suppléer l'ellipse, rétablir les mots ellipsés
Ellipsize, *v.a.* ellipser
Ellipsograph, *s.* ellipsographe, *m.*
Ellipsoid, *s.* ellipsoïde, *m.*
Ellipsoidal, *adj.* ellipsoïdal, ellipsoïde
Ellipt-ic, al, -ically. *V.* page 3, § 1. — *curve*, ellipsoïde, *f.*; (*rail.*) cassinoïde, *f.*
Ellipticity, *s.* ellipticité, *f.*
Elm, *s.* orme, *m.* — **grove, -plantation,** *s.* ormaie, *f.*
Elmo's fire, *s.* feu saint-Elme, *m.*
Elmy, *adj.* planté d'ormes
Elocution, *s.* élocution, *f.*; (*delivery*) débit, *m.*; (*art*) déclamation, *f.* *Teacher of* —, professeur de déclamation, *m.*
Elocutionist, *s.* déclamateur, *m.*, -trice, *f.*; professeur de déclamation, *m.*
Elongate, *v.a.* allonger, prolonger, étendre; [— *adj.* allongé
Elongation, *s.* allongement, prolongement, *m.*, extension, *f.*; (*astr.*, *surg.*) élongation, *f.*
Elope, *v.n.* ('*from*,' de) s'enfuir; ('*with*,' par) se faire enlever
Elopement, *s.* fuite, *f.*; enlèvement, *m.*
Eloquence, *s.* éloquence, *f.*
Eloquent, *adj.* éloquent
Eloquently, *adv.* éloquemment, avec éloquence
Else, *adj.* autre; — *adv.* autrement, ou, ou bien; (*besides*) encore. — **where,** *adv.* autre part, ailleurs. *Anybody* —, *anyone* —, quelque autre; (*whatever*) n'importe qui. *Everybody* —, *every one* —, tout autre, tous les autres. *Nobody* —, *no one* —, nul autre, aucun autre, personne autre, *m.*, nulle autre personne, *f.* *Somebody* —, *someone* —, quelque autre, un autre, une autre personne (*f.*). *Who* — ? qui encore ? *All* —, toute autre chose, *f.* *Anything* —, quelque autre chose, *f.*, autre chose, *m.*; (*whatever*) toute autre chose, *f.*; n'importe quoi. *Everything* —, toute autre chose, *f.*; toutes les autres choses; tout le reste, *m.* *Nothing* —, pas autre chose, *m.*, aucune (*or* nulle) autre chose, *f.*, rien autre, *m.*, rien de plus, *m.* *Something* —, autre chose, *m.*; (*more*) quelque chose de plus, *m.* *What* — ? quoi encore ? quoi de plus ? qu'y a-t-il encore ? quelle autre chose (*f.*) ? *Anywhere* —, autre part, ailleurs; (*whatever*) partout ailleurs, en tout autre lieu. *Everywhere* —, partout ailleurs. *Nowhere* —, pas autre part, nulle autre part, nulle part ailleurs, en aucun autre lieu *or* pays. *Somewhere* —, ailleurs, autre part, quelque autre part. *Where* — ? où encore ?
Elucidate, *v.a.* éclaircir, élucider; expliquer
Elucidation, *s.* éclaircissement, *m.*, élucidation, *f.*; explication, *f.*
Elucidative, *adj.* qui éclaircit; explicatif
Elucidator, *s.* commentateur, *m.*
Elude, *v.a.* éluder, éviter, esquiver, échapper à

Eluder, *s.* éludeur, *m.*, -euse, *f.*
Eludible, *adj.* éludable
Elusion, *s.* réponse évasive, *f.*, subterfuge, artifice, faux-fuyant, *m.* [artificieux
Elusive, *adj.* qui élude; évasif; trompeur,
Elutriate, *v.a.* soutirer
Elutriation, *s.* élutriation, *f.*, soutirage, *m.*
Elydoric, *adj.* éludorique
Elver, *s.* jeune anguille, *f.*
Elvish. *V.* **Elfish** [Élysées, *m.pl.*
Elysian, *adj.* élyséen. — *fields*, Champs-
Elysium, *s.* Élysée, *m.*
Elytron, Elytrum, *s.* élytre, *m.*
Elzevir, *s.* elzévir, *m.*; — *adj.* elzévirien
Elzevirian, *adj.* elzévirien
Emaciate, *v.a.* amaigrir, maigrir; étioler; — *v.n.* maigrir; s'étioler; — *adj.* *V.* **Emaciated**
Emaciated, *adj.* maigre, décharné; étiolé
Emaciation, *s.* maigreur, *f.*; amaigrissement, *m.*; étiolement, *m.*
Emanate, *v.n.* émaner
Emanation, *s.* émanation, *f.* [chir (de)
Emancipate, *v.a.* émanciper; (*fig.*) affran-
Emancipating, *adj.* émancipateur; — *s.* *V.* **Emancipation** [affranchissement, *m.*
Emancipation, *s.* émancipation, *f.*; (*fig.*)
Emancipator, *s.* émancipateur, *m.*, -trice, *f.*, affranchisseur, *m.*
Emarginate, *v.a.* émarger; — *adj.* émarginé
Emargination, *s.* émargement, *m.*
Emasculate, *v.a.* émasculer, châtrer; (*fig.*) efféminer, énerver; — *adj.* (*same as* **Emasculated,** *part.*)
Emasculation, *s.* émasculation, castration, *f.*; (*fig.*) effémination, mollesse, *f.*
Emasculator, *s.* émasculateur, *m.*
Embalm, *v.a.* embaumer
Embalmer, *s.* embaumeur, *m.*
Embalming, *s.* embaumement, *m.*
Embank, *v.a.* terrasser; remblayer; lever, faire une levée à, entourer d'une levée; (*a river*) encaisser, endiguer
Embanking, Embankment, *s.* terrassement, *m.*; remblai, *m.*, levée, *f.*; talus, *m.*; banquette, *f.*; (*of rivers*) levée, digue, *f.*, quai, *m.*, quais, *m.pl.*; encaissement, endiguement, *m.*, construction de quais, *f.*
Embarcation, *s.* embarquement, *m.*
Embargo, *s.* embargo, *m.*; — *v.a.* mettre un (*or* l') embargo sur
Embark, *v.a.* embarquer; (*money*) engager; — *v.n.* s'embarquer; (*fig.*) s'embarquer, s'engager (dans) [**ment,** *s.* embarquement, *m.*
Embarkation, Embarking, Embark-
Embarrass, *v.a.* embarrasser; (*affairs*) déranger; (*pers. pecuniarily*) gêner [barrassante
Embarrassingly, *adv.* d'une manière em-
Embarrassment, *s.* embarras, *m.*; perplexité, *f.*; (*of affairs*) dérangement, *m.*; gêne, *f.*
Embassy, Embassage, *s.* ambassade, *f.*
Embattle, *v.a.* former (*or* ranger) en bataille, embatailler; (*fort.*) créneler
Embattlement, *s.* crénelure, *f.*
Embattling, *s.* (*mil.*) embataillement, *m.*
Embay, *v.a.* (*nav.*) enfermer dans une baie; affaler sur la côte [fixer; incruster
Embed, *v.a.* coucher, poser; enfoncer, enfouir;
Embellish, *v.a.* embellir
Embellisher, *s.* embellisseur, *m.*
Embellishment, *s.* embellissement, *m.*
Ember. — **days,** *s. pl.* Quatre-Temps, *m.pl.* — **goose,** *s.* imbrim, *m.* — **week,** *s.* semaine des Quatre-Temps, *f.* [(*fig.*) étincelle, *f.*
Embers, *s. pl.* cendre, *f.*; (*live coals*) braise, *f.*;
Embezzle, *v.a.* détourner
Embezzlement, *s.* détournement (de fonds), *m.*
Embezzler, *s.* auteur d'un détournement (de fonds), *m.*
Embitter, *v.a.* rendre amer, remplir d'amertume; empoisonner; irriter, aigrir
Emblazon, Emblazoner. *V.* **Blazon, Blazoner**

Emblazonment, Emblazonry, *s.* blasonnement, *m.*; blason, *m.*; armes, armoiries, *f.pl.*
Emblem, *s.* emblème, *m.*
Emblematic, -al, *adj.* emblématique
Emblematically, *adv.* emblématiquement, d'une manière emblématique
Emblematize, *v.a.* représenter par un emblème, représenter
Emblements, *s. pl.* fruits pendants par racines, *m.pl.*, récoltes pendantes par racines, *f.pl.*
Embodiment, *s.* corporification, corporisation, *f.*; (*fig.*) incorporation, *f.*; incarnation, personnification, *f.*; (*mil.*) incorporation, *f.*
Embody, *v.a.* corporifier, corporiser; (*fig.*) incorporer; personnifier; réunir; résumer; comprendre, contenir, renfermer; (*mil.*) incorporer; — *v.n.* s'incorporer
Embolden, *v.a.* enhardir
Embosom, *v.a.* renfermer *or* tenir dans son sein; serrer contre son sein; (*bury*) ensevelir
Emboss, *v.a.* (*metals*, &c.) bosseler; (*sculp.*) travailler en bosse; (*engr.*) graver en relief; (*steel*) damasquiner; (*paper, leather, stuffs*) gaufrer; (*linen*) brocher [reur, *m.*, -euse, *f.*
Embosser, *s.* (*of paper, leather, stuffs*) gauf-
Embossing, *s.* (*of metals*, &c.) bosselage, *m.*; bossage, *m.*; (*sculp.*) relief, *m.*; (*engr.*) gravure en relief, *f.*; (*of steel*) damasquinerie, *f.*; (*of paper, leather, stuffs*) gaufrage, *m.*, gaufrure, *f.*
Embossment, *s.* bosse, protubérance, *f.*; (*in the arts*) bosse, *f.*, relief, *m.*; (*on metals*, &c.) bosselure, *f.*; (*on steel*) damasquinure, *f.*; (*on paper, leather, stuffs*) gaufrure, *f.*; (*on linen*) brochure, *f.*; (*arch.*) bossage, *m.*
Embowel, *v.a.* *V.* **Disembowel**
Embower, *v.a.* *V.* **Bower,** *v.a.*
Embrace, *v.a.* embrasser; (*an opportunity*, &c.) saisir; (*accept*) accepter; adopter; (*comprise*) embrasser, comprendre, renfermer; (*surround*) entourer; — *s.* embrassement, *m.*; étreinte, *f.* [(*follower*) partisan, *m.*
Embracer, *s.* embrasseur, *m.*, -euse, *f.*;
Embrasure, *s.* embrasure, *f.*
Embrocate, *v.a.* fomenter par une embrocation
Embrocation, *s.* embrocation, *f.*
Embroglio. *V.* **Imbroglio**
Embroider, *v.a.* broder
Embroider-er, ess, *s.* brodeur, *m.*, -euse, *f.*
Embroidering, *s.* broderie, *f.* — **frame,** *s.* métier à broder, *m.* — **machine,** *s.* machine à broder, brodeuse (mécanique), *f.*
Embroidery, *s.* broderie, *f.* — **designer,** *s.* dessinateur en broderies, *m.*
Embroil, *v.a.* embrouiller, brouiller; entremêler, mêler; engager; (*disturb*) bouleverser
Embroilment, *s.* embrouillement, *m.*; confusion, *f.*, désordre, *m.*; (*disturbance*) brouille, *f.*
Embronze, *v.a.* couler (*or* frapper *or* représenter) en bronze
Embrown, Embrue. *V.* **Imbrown, Imbrue**
Embryo, *s.* embryon, *m.*; — *adj.* embryonnaire, à l'état d'embryon
Embryo-graphy, -logy, -logic, al, -logist, -tomy, &c. *V.* page 3, § i [naire
Embryonal, Embryonary, *adj.* embryon-
Embryonate, -d, *adj.* embryonné
Embryonic, *adj.* embryonnaire
Emendable, *adj.* émendable, corrigible
Emendation, *s.* émendation, correction, *f.*
Emendator, *s.* émendateur, correcteur, *m.*
Emendatory, *adj.* émendatif
Emerald, *s.* émeraude, *f.*; — *adj.* d'émeraude, vert. — **green,** *s.* vert d'émeraude, *m.*
Emerge, *v.n.* émerger; surgir; sortir; s'élever; se dégager; paraître
Emergence, Emergency, *s.* conjoncture, *f.*; événement imprévu, *m.*, circonstance imprévue, *f.*; occurrence, *f.*; occasion, *f.*; circonstance pressante *or* critique, émergence, *f.*; besoin, *m.*; cas urgent, *m.*; (*appearance*) émergence, apparition, *f.*

Emergent, *adj.* qui surgit, qui sort, émergent; qui s'élève; qui naît, naissant; imprévu; critique, difficile
Emerited, Emeritus, *adj.* émérite
Emersion, *s.* émersion, *f.*; sortie, *f.*
Emery, *s.* émeri, *m.* — **cloth,** *s.* toile émerisée, *f.* — **dust,** *s.* poudre d'émeri, *f.*; (*jewel.*) potée d'émeri, *f.* — **paper,** *s.* papier d'émeri, papier émerisé, *m.* — **powder,** *s.* *V.* — **dust.** — **stone,** *s.* pierre à polir, *f.*
Emetic, *adj. s.* émétique, *adj. m f., s.m.*
Emetine, *s.* émétine, *f.*
Emeu, *s.* émeu, *m.*
Emiction, *s.* miction, *f.* [émigré, *m.*, e, *f.*
Emigrant, *s. adj.* émigrant, *m.*, e, *f.*; (*refugee*)
Emigrate, *v.n.* émigrer
Emigration, *s.* émigration, *f.*
Eminence, Eminency, *s.* éminence, *f.*; réputation, grandeur, distinction, élévation, *f.*, (*title*) éminence, *f.* *By way of —,* par excellence
Eminent, *adj.* éminent, élevé, haut; distingué, remarquable. *Most —,* (*title*) éminentissime [degré; haut
Eminently, *adv.* éminemment, au suprême
Emir, *s.* émir, *m.*
Emissary, *s.* émissaire, *m.*
Emission, *s.* émission, *f.*
Emissive, Emissory, *adj.* émissif
Emit, *v.a.* jeter, lancer; envoyer; donner; exhaler; (*words*) laisser échapper; (*circulate*) émettre; (*decree,* &c.) promulguer; (*chem.*) dégager [emménagogue, *adj. m.f., s.m.*
Emmenagogic, *adj.*, **Emmenagogue,** *s.*
Emmenology, *s.* emménologie, *f.*
Emmet, *s.* fourmi, *f.* [émollient, *s.m.*
Emollient, *adj. s.* émollient, *adj. m.*, e, *f.*,
Emolument, *s.* émolument, *m.*
Emolumental, *adj.* émolumentaire
Emotion, *s.* émotion. *f.* [émotions; à émotions
Emotional, *adj.* d'émotion, d'émotions, des
Empale, Empanel (*or* **Empannel**). *V.*
Empark, *v.a.* parquer [**Impale,** &c. (*with* I)
Empasm, *s.* empasme, *m.* [saturnie, *f.*
Emperor, *s.* empereur, *m.* — **moth,** *s.*
Emphasis, *s.* force, énergie, *f.*; accent, *m.*; accentuation, *f.*; (*in a bad sense*) emphase, *f.* *To lay — on,* appuyer sur
Emphasize, *v.a.* appuyer sur, accentuer; (*affectedly*) dire *or* prononcer avec emphase
Emphatic, -al, *adj.* fort; énergique; expressif; accentué; positif; décidé; (*affected*) emphatique
Emphatically, *adv.* fortement, avec force; énergiquement; expressivement; positivement, formellement, expressément; (*preeminently*) par excellence; (*affectedly*) avec emphase, emphatiquement
Empire, *s.* empire, *m.*
Empir-ic, al, -ically. *V.* page 3, § 1
Empiricism, *s.* empirisme, *m.*
Employ, *v.a.* employer; se servir de, mettre en usage; (*occupy*) employer (à), occuper (à); — *s.* emploi, *m.*; service, *m.* *To — oneself in,* s'occuper à (*or* de), travailler à; (*attend to*)
Employable, *adj.* employable [s'occuper de
Employé, e, Employee, *s.* employé, *m.*, e, *f.*
Employer, *s.* personne qui emploie *or* occupe, *f.*, client, *m.*, e, *f.*; (*of workmen, clerks,* &c.) maître, *m.*, maîtresse, *f.*, patron, *m.*, -ne, *f.*; (*com.*) commettant, *m.*; (*polit. economy*) employeur, *m.*
Employment, *s.* emploi, *m.*; occupation, *f.*; ouvrage, travail, *m.*; activité, *f.*; service, *m.* *Out of —,* sans emploi. *To seek —,* chercher un
Emporium, *s.* entrepôt, marché, *m.* [emploi
Empoverish, &c. *V.* **Impoverish,** &c.
Empower, *v.a.* autoriser; donner pouvoir à; investir du pouvoir (de); (*enable*) mettre à même (de), permettre à ... (de); (*law*) donner plein pouvoir à, donner procuration à
Empress, *s.* impératrice, *f.*
Emptier, *s.* personne *or* chose qui vide, *f.*
Emptiness, *s.* vide, *m.*; (*fig.*) néant, *m.*, vanité, *f.*; (*pers.*) nullité, *f.*
Empty, *adj.* vide; (*fig.*) vain, frivole; (*words*) vide de sens; (*streets*) désert; — *v.a.* vider; décharger; — *v.n.* se vider; se décharger. *To — itself,* se vider; se décharger. se jeter. — **handed,** *adj.* les mains vides, qui a les mains vides. — **headed,** *adj.* sans cervelle
Emptying, *s.* videment, vidage, *m.*
Empurple, *v.a.* empourprer
Empyema, *s.* empyème, *m.*
Empyreal, *adj.* empyréal [céleste
Empyrean, *s.* empyrée, *m.*; — *adj.* empyrée;
Empyreuma, *s.* empyreume, *m.*
Empyreumatic, -al, *adj.* empyreumatique
Emu, *s.* émeu, *m.*
Emulate, *v.a.* rivaliser avec; tâcher d'égaler; égaler; imiter; suivre; ressembler à
Emulation, *s.* émulation, *f.*; rivalité, *f.* *In — of each other,* à l'envi l'un de l'autre (*or* les uns des autres), à l'envi [d'émulation
Emulative, *adj.* émulatif, émulateur; plein
Emula-tor, tress, *s.* émulateur, *m.*, -trice, *f.*, émule, *m.f.*, concurrent, *m.*, e, *f.*, rival, *m.*, e, *f.*
Emulgent, *adj.* émulgent
Emulous, *adj.* rival; jaloux
Emulously, *adv.* avec émulation, à l'envi
Emulsine, *s.* émulsine, *f.*
Emulsion, *s.* émulsion, *f.*, looch, *m.*
Emulsive, *adj. s.* émulsif, *adj. m.*, -ive, *f.*,
Emunctory, *s.* émonctoire, *m.* [émulsif, *s.m.*
Enable, *v.a.* mettre en état (de), mettre à même (de), donner le moyen *or* les moyens (de), rendre capable (de), permettre (de); autoriser (à). *To be —d to,* être en état de, être à même de, avoir le moyen de, pouvoir
Enact, *v.a.* décréter. arrêter, ordonner, statuer; (*a law*) rendre, porter, édicter, faire
Enactive, *adj.* ayant (*or* qui a) force de loi
Enactment, *s.* établissement, *m.*; loi, *f.*, dé-
Enactor, *s.* auteur, *m.* [cret, *m.*
Enamel, *s.* émail, *m.*; — *adj.* d'émail, en émail; — *v.a.* émailler ('*with,*' de); (*leather*) glacer; (*ladies' faces*) maquiller; — *v.n.* peindre en émail. — **painter** *or* **paintress,** *s.* peintre en émail, *m.f.* — **painting,** *s.* peinture en (*or* sur) émail, *f.* — **work,** *s.* émaillure, *f.*
Enamelled, *adj.* émaillé, en émail; (*of cards*) porcelaine; (*of leather*) glacé; (*of ladies' faces*) maquillé
Enameller, Enamellist, *s.* émailleur, *m.*, -euse, *f.*; peintre en émail, *m.*; (*of ladies' faces*) maquilleuse, *f.*
Enamelling, *s.* émaillage, *m.*; émaillerie, *f*; émaillure, *f.*; peinture en émail, *f.*; (*of ladies' faces*) maquillage, *m.*
Enamour, *v.a.* rendre amoureux; (*in a bad sense*) amouracher. *To be —ed,* être amoureux *or* épris (de); (*in a bad sense*) être amouraché. *To become —ed,* devenir amoureux (de), s'éprendre (de); (*in a bad sense*) s'amouracher (de); (*of a thing*) se passionner (pour)
Encage, *v.a.* *V.* **Cage,** *v.a.*
Encamp, *v.a.n.* camper [ment, *m.*
Encamping, Encampment, *s.* campe-
Encase. *V.* **Incase**
Encashment, *s.* encaissement, *m.*
Encaustic, *s. adj.* encaustique, *s.f., adj. m.f.*
Enceinte, *s.* (*fort.*) enceinte, *f.*; — *adj.* (*slang*)
Encephalic, *adj.* encéphalique [enceinte, *f.*
Encephalon, Encephalos, *s.* encéphale, *m.*
Enchain, *v.a.* enchaîner
Enchant, *v.a.* enchanter, ravir ('*with,*' de); (*of sorcery*) enchanter
Enchanter, *s.* enchanteur, *m.*
Enchanting, *adj.* enchanteur; — *s.* enchantement, *m.*
Enchantingly, *adv.* par enchantement; d'une manière ravissante, à ravir
Enchantment, *s.* enchantement, *m.*
Enchantress, *s.* enchanteresse, *f.*

Enchase, *v.a.* enchâsser; incruster; ciseler; graver; tracer

Enchiridion, *s.* enchiridion, manuel, *m.*

Encircle, *v.a.* ('*with,*' de) entourer d'un cercle; entourer, environner; ceindre; embrasser, [serrer dans ses bras

Enclasp. *V.* **Inclasp**

Enclitic, *adj. s.* enclitique, *adj. m.f.*, *s.f.*

Encloister, *v.a.* encloîtrer, cloîtrer

Enclose, *v.a.* clore, enclore; (*surround*) entourer, environner; (*contain*) renfermer, contenir; (*put by*) serrer; (*of letters*, &c.) envoyer *or* mettre ('*in,*' sous, dans); (*herewith*) envoyer (*or* mettre) ci-inclus, mettre sous ce pli, (*therewith*) envoyer (*or* mettre) sous le même pli ('*with,*' que), envoyer (avec), joindre (à), (*one message only*) mettre sous enveloppe, envoyer

Enclosed, *part. V.* **Enclose;** — *adj.* (*of messages*) inclus, ci-inclus, sous ce pli; — *s.* (*letter*) incluse, *f.* — *letter*, incluse, *f.* *The note here* —, le billet ci-inclus, *m.*

Enclosure, *s.* clôture, *f.*; enclos, clos, *m.*, enceinte, *f.*; (*of messages*) contenu, *m.*; in- [clus, *m.*

Encomiast, *s.* panégyriste, *m.*

Encomiastic, -al, *adj. V.* **Eulogistic**

Encomium, *s.* panégyrique, éloge, *m.*, louange, *f.*

Encompass, *v.a.* entourer, environner; embrasser; comprendre, renfermer

Encore, *adv. int.* bis; — *s.* bis, *m.*; — *v.a.* bisser, crier bis à, redemander. *To cry* —, crier bis, bisser

Encounter, *s.* rencontre, *f.*, combat, *m.*; (*fig.*) lutte, *f.*, assaut, *m.*; — *v.a.* rencontrer; supporter la rencontre *or* le choc de; attaquer; combattre; affronter, aborder; (*difficulties*) éprouver, essuyer; — *v.n.* se rencontrer; [s'attaquer

Encourage, *v.a.* encourager

Encouragement, *s.* encouragement, *m.*

Encourager, *s.* personne qui encourage, *f.*; instigateur, *m.*, -trice, *f.*; protecteur, *m.*, -trice, *f.* [courageante, avec encouragement

Encouragingly, *adv.* d'une manière en-

Encrinite, *s.* encrinite, *m.* [abuser (de)

Encroach, *v.n.* empiéter (sur); (*intrude*)

Encroacher, *s.* personne qui empiète, *f.*; usurpateur, *m.*, -trice, *f.*; personne qui abuse (de), *f.*, intrus, *m.*, e, *f.* [**Encroachment**

Encroaching, *adj.* qui empiète; — *s. V.*

Encroachingly, *adv.* en empiétant; par empiètement

Encroachment, *s.* empiètement, *m.*; envahissement, *m.*; usurpation, *f.*; intrusion, *f.*

Encumber, *v.a.* encombrer (de); embarrasser (de), gêner; (*load*) charger (de); (*overwhelm*) accabler (de); (*with debt*) obérer; (*an estate*) grever; hypothéquer

Encumbrance, *s.* encombrement, *m.*; (*fig.*) embarras, obstacle, *m.*; empêchement, *m.*; gêne, *f.*; (*burden*) charge, *f.*, fardeau, *m.*; (*children*) enfants, *m.pl.*; (*law*) servitude, *f.*, service foncier, *m.*, charge, *f.*; (*mortgage*) hypothèque, *f.*

Encyclic, -al, *adj. s.* encyclique, *adj. m.f.*, *s.f.*

Encyclopædia, Encyclopedia, *s.* encyclopédie, *f.* [cyclopédique

Encyclopædic, Encyclopedic, *adj.* en-

Encyclopædism, Encyclopedism, *s.* encyclopédisme, *m.* [cyclopédiste, *m.*

Encyclopædist, Encyclopedist, *s.* en-

Encysted, *adj.* enkysté. *To become* —, s'en- [kyster

Encysting, *s.* enkystement, *m.*

End, *s.* fin, *f.*; terme, *m.*; (*extremity*) bout, *m.*, extrémité, *f.*; (*of an interval*) bout, *m.*; (*bit*) bout, *m.*; (*aim*) but, objet, dessein, *m.*, intention, vue, fin, *f.*; (*interest*) intérêt, *m.*; (*issue*) issue, *f.*; (*piece*) morceau, *m.*; (*of braces*) patte, *f.*; — *v.a.* finir, terminer, achever; — *v.n.* finir, se terminer ('*with,*' par); cesser; aboutir (à); se réduire (à, en); s'en aller (en); expirer. *At an* —, fini, terminé; fait; épuisé; passé; guéri; apaisé, calmé. *From* — *to* —, d'un bout à l'autre; d'une extrémité à l'autre. *In the* —, à la fin; finalement, en fin de compte, au bout du compte; à la longue; (*on the whole*) en somme, somme toute. *No* — *of,* (*plenty*) force, une infinité de. *On* —, debout. *To no* —, sans effet, en vain. *To the* —, jusqu'à la fin; jusqu'au bout. *To the* — *that,* afin que. *To come to an* —, arriver à son terme, finir. *To come to a bad* —, finir mal; faire une mauvaise fin. *To draw to an* — or *near o.'s* —, tirer *or* toucher à sa fin. *To make an* — *of,* en finir avec; achever; (*kill*) tuer; achever. *To make both* —*s meet,* joindre les deux bouts. *To put an* — *to,* mettre fin à, mettre un terme à. *To stand on* —, se dresser, se tenir droit *or* debout. *That is enough to make o.'s hair stand on* —, il y a de quoi faire dresser les cheveux sur (*or* à) la tête. *There is an* — *of it* (or *of the matter*), c'est fini; c'est tout, voilà tout, voilà, tout est dit. *There is an* — *of it all,* tout est fini. *There is no* — *of it* (or *of them*), cela n'en finit pas. —**less,** *adj.* sans fin; infini; perpétuel; interminable; éternel. —**lessly,** *adv.* sans fin; à l'infini; perpétuellement, sans cesse; éternellement. —**lessness,** *s.* infinité, *f.*; perpétuité, *f.* —**piece,** *s.* bout, *m.* —**ways, -wise,** *adv.* perpendiculairement, debout; (*end to end*) bout à bout

Endanger, *v.a.* mettre en danger *or* en péril, exposer; compromettre; hasarder, risquer

Endear, *v.a.* rendre cher (à), faire aimer *or* chérir (à, de)

Endearing, *adj.* propre à faire chérir; attachant, attrayant, séduisant, aimable; tendre; affectueux

Endearment, *s.* attrait, charme, *m.*; tendresse, *f.*, attachement, *m.*; caresse, *f.*

Endeavour, *v.n.* s'efforcer ('*to,*' de), tâcher ('*to,*' de), essayer ('*to,*' de); (*aim at*) chercher (à), viser (à); — *s.* ('*to,*' pour) effort, *m.*; tentative, *f.*; essai, *m.*; (*care*) soin, *m.* *To use* or *exert every* —, faire tous ses efforts

Endecagon, &c. *V.* **Hendecagon,** &c.

Endemic, -al, *adj.* endémique; — *s.* endémie, *f.*

Endemically, *adv.* endémiquement

Endermatic, Endermic, *adj.* endermique

Ending, *s.* fin, *f.*; (*gram.*) terminaison, *f.*; — *adj.* final, dernier. *Never* —, qui ne finit pas, sans fin, interminable, perpétuel, éternel. —**post,** *s.* poteau d'arrivée, but, *m.*

Endive, *s.* chicorée, escarole, *f.* [*s.f.*, *adj. m.f.*

Endogen, *s.* **Endogenous,** *adj.* endogène,

Endorsable, *adj.* transférable

Endorse, *v.a.* écrire au dos; (*of bills*) endosser; (*passports*) viser; (*fig.*) souscrire à; se déclarer pour; appuyer; garantir; ap- [prouver; se ranger à

Endorsee, *s.* porteur, *m.*

Endorsement, *s.* suscription, *f.*; (*of bills*) endossement, endos, *m.*; (*of passports*) visa, *m.*

Endorser, *s.* endosseur, *m.*

Endosmose, Endosmosis, *s.* endosmose, *f.*

Endow, *v.a.* doter (de); (*fig.*) douer (de)

Endowment, *s.* dotation, *f.*; (*fig.*) don, *m.*, [qualité, *f.*, avantage, *m.*

Endue. *V.* **Indue**

Endurable, *adj.* endurable, supportable, tolérable; (*lasting*) durable

Endurance, *s.* patience, endurance, *f.*; persévérance, *f.*; souffrance, *f.*; (*lastingness*) durée, *f.* [(*last*) durer

Endure, *v.a.n.* endurer, supporter, souffrir;

Enduring, *adj.* endurant, patient; (*lasting*) durable [durablement

Enduringly, *adv.* patiemment; (*lastingly*)

Enduringness, *s.* patience, *f.*; (*lastingness*) [durabilité, *f.*

Eneid, *s.* Énéide, *f.*

Enema, *s.* lavement, *m.*; (*apparatus*) irrigateur, clysopompe, *m.*

Enemy, *s.* ennemi, *m.*, e, *f.* ('*to,*' de)

Energetic, -al, *adj.* énergique

Energetically, *adv.* énergiquement

Energumen, énergumène, *m.f.*

Energy, *s.* énergie, force, vigueur, *f.*

Enervate, *v.a.* énerver

Enervate, Enervated, *adj.* énervé. *To become* —, s'énerver [énervement, *m.*

Enervation, *s.* (*act*) énervation, *f.*; (*state*)

Enfeeble, *v.a.* affaiblir, énerver, débiliter

Enfeeblement, *s.* affaiblissement, *m.*

Enfeoff, *v.a.* (*pers.*) investir d'un fief; (*things*) inféoder, fieffer

Enfeoffment, *s.* inféodation, *f.*

Enfilade, *s.* enfilade, *f.*; — *v.a.* enfiler, prendre

Enfold. *V.* **Infold** [d'enfilade

Enforce, *v.a.* donner de la force à; fortifier, appuyer; (*urge*) presser; faire sentir; faire valoir; insister sur; (*impose*) imposer; faire triompher; faire prévaloir; (*a law, an order*) mettre en vigueur, faire exécuter, faire observer, maintenir, appliquer

Enforceable, *adj.* exécutoire

Enforcement, *s.* contrainte, force, *f.*; mise en vigueur, *f.*, maintien, *m.*, exécution, application, *f.*; sanction, *f.*

Enfranchise, *v.a.* affranchir; mettre en liberté; donner le droit de bourgeoisie à; naturaliser; affranchir du cens électoral

Enfranchisement, *s.* affranchissement, *m.*; mise en liberté, *f.*; admission au droit de bourgeoisie, *f.*; naturalisation, *f.*; affranchissement du cens électoral, *m.*

Enfranchiser, *s.* affranchisseur, *m.*

Engage, *v.a.* engager; (*secure, take*) retenir; prendre; (*a servant, an apartment*) arrêter; (*for dancing,* &c.) inviter; (*gain*) gagner, attirer; (*the mind*) occuper; (*attack*) attaquer, combattre; (*tech.*) engrener; — *v.n.* s'engager; se livrer (à); prendre part (à); (*warrant*) garantir; (*bet*) parier; (*mil.*) livrer bataille, livrer combat, engager le combat; en venir aux mains (avec); (*fig.*) engager une discussion (avec)

Engaged, *part.* engagé, &c. (*V.* **Engage**); (*to wed*) promis; (*busy*) occupé; (*fighting*) aux prises; (*of newspapers*) en lecture, en main

Engagement, *s.* engagement, *m.*; invitation, *f.*; occupation, *f.*; attrait, *m.*; attachement, *m.*; partialité, *f.*; (*fight*) engagement, combat, *m.*, action, *f.* *To be under an* — (*to* ...), être lié par un engagement (à *or* de)

Engaging, *adj.* engageant, attrayant

Engagingly, *adv.* d'une manière engageante

Engender, *v.a.* engendrer; faire naître; — *v.n.* s'engendrer; naître

Engine, *s.* machine, *f.*; (*rail.*) locomotive, *f.*; (*pump*) pompe, *f.* (*V.* **Beer** —, **Fire** —, **Garden** —); (*means*) instrument, engin, moyen, agent, *m.*; (*adject.*) mécanique, à la mécanique. — **builder,** *s.* constructeur de machines, mécanicien, *m.* — **building,** *s.* construction de machines, machinerie, *f.* — **driver,** *s.* conducteur de locomotive, mécanicien, *m.* — **house,** *s.* (*for fire —s*), dépôt de pompes à incendie, *m.* — **maker, -making,** *s.* *V.* — **builder, -building.** — **man,** *s.* mécanicien, machiniste, *m.* — **plane,** *s.* plan manœuvre, *m.* — **press,** *s.* presse mécanique, *f.* — **room,** *s.* chambre de la machine (*or* des machines), *f.* — **station,** *s.* *V.* — **house.** — **turn,** *v.a.* guillocher. — **turner,** *s.* guillocheur, *m.* — **turning,** *s.* guillochis, *m.*

Engineer, *s.* ingénieur, *m.*; (*engine-man*) mécanicien, machiniste, *m.*; (— *builder*) mécanicien, constructeur de machines, *m.*; (*mil.*) officier du génie, *m.*; (*soldier*) soldat du génie, *m.*; —**s,** *pl.* (*mil.*) génie, *m.* *Civil* —, ingénieur civil, ingénieur des ponts et chaussées, *m.* *Mechanical* —, mécanicien, machiniste, *m.* *Military* —, ingénieur militaire, *m.* *Naval* —, ingénieur de la marine, *m.* — **officer,** *s.* officier du génie, *m.*

Engineering, *s.* génie, *m.*; — *adj.* du génie. *Civil* —, génie civil, *m.*, (les) ponts et chaussées, *m.pl.* *Military* —, génie militaire, *m.* *Naval* —, génie maritime, *m.*

English, *adj.* anglais, d'Angleterre; (*of the Church*) anglican; — *s.* (*people*) (les) Anglais, *m.pl.*; (*language*) l'anglais, *m.*, la langue anglaise, *f.*; (*print. type*) saint-augustin, *m.*; — *v.a.* rendre *or* traduire en anglais, angliciser. — *coat, hat, book,* &c., habit, chapeau, livre, &c. anglais. — *ambassador, king, queen, coast, history,* &c., ambassadeur, roi, reine, côte, histoire, &c. d'Angleterre. *Old* —, (*black-letter*) gothique, *m.* *Two-line* —, (*print.*) petit canon, *m.* — **boy,** *s.* (petit) Anglais, *m.* — **girl,** *s.* (petite *or* jeune) Anglaise, *f.* — **lady,** *s.* dame anglaise, Anglaise, *f.* — **man,** *s.* Anglais, *m.* — **master** *or* **teacher,** *s.* maître *or* professeur d'anglais, *m.* — **ship, -vessel,** *s.* navire *or* vaisseau anglais, *m.* — **woman,** *s.* Anglaise, *f.* [sier; (*med.*) engorger

Engorge, *v.a.* dévorer, se gorger de; rassa-

Engorgement, *s.* (*med.*) engorgement, *m.*

Engraft. *V.* **Ingraft**

Engrail, *v.a.* (*her.*) engrêler; (*coin.*) cordonner

Engrailing, *s.* (*her.*) engrêlure, *f.*

Engrailment, *s.* (*coin.*) cordon, *m.*

Engrave, *v.a.* graver; sculpter

Engraver, *s.* graveur, *m.*

Engraving, *s.* gravure, *f.*

Engross, *v.a.* accaparer; monopoliser; absorber; — *v.a.n.* (*law*) grossoyer [copiste, *m.*

Engrosser, *s.* accapareur, *m.*, -euse, *f.*; (*law*)

Engrossing, Engrossment, *s.* accaparement, *m.*; (*law*) action de grossoyer, *f.*; grosse, *f.*

Engulf. *V.* **Ingulf**

Enhance, *v.a.* rehausser, relever; augmenter; aggraver; (*in price*) enchérir, renchérir; — *v.n.* augmenter, monter

Enhancement, *s.* rehaussement, *m.*; hausse, *f.*; augmentation, *f.*; aggravation, *f.*; (*in price*) enchérissement, renchérissement, *m.*

Enharmon-ic, al, -ically, -y. *V.* page 3, § 1

Enigma, *s.* énigme, *f.*

Enigmatic, -al, *adj.* énigmatique

Enigmatically, *adv.* énigmatiquement

Enigmatize, *v.a.n.* énigmatiser

Enjoin, *v.a.* ('*on,*' '*to,*' à; '*to,*' *before a verb,* de) enjoindre; prescrire; recommander

Enjoy, *v.a.* jouir de; savourer; goûter; trouver bon; être heureux de; s'amuser de; aimer à faire, aimer. *To* — *oneself,* s'amuser, se divertir; se réjouir; être heureux; se régaler; se donner du bon temps; jouir de la vie. *How did you — yourself?* vous êtes-vous bien amusé? *I —ed that very much,* j'ai trouvé cela très bon; cela m'a fait beaucoup de plaisir. *I —ed my dinner,* j'ai dîné avec plaisir

Enjoyable, *adj.* dont on peut jouir, agréable

Enjoyment, *s.* jouissance, *f.*; plaisir, *m.*; satisfaction, *f.*

Enkindle, *v.a.* allumer, enflammer, exciter

Enlarge, *v.a.* agrandir; augmenter, accroître; étendre; développer; (*the heart*) dilater; (*set free*) élargir, mettre en liberté; — *v.n.* s'agrandir, grandir, s'accroître; se développer; (*of the heart, brain,* &c.: *med.*) s'hypertrophier, (*fig.*) se dilater; (*upon*) s'étendre (sur)

Enlargement, *s.* agrandissement, *m.*; augmentation, *f.*, accroissement, *m.*; extension, *f.*; développement, *m.*; (*of prisoners*) élargissement, *m.*, mise en liberté, *f.*; (*of the heart, brain,* &c.: *med.*) hypertrophie, *f.*, (*fig.*) dilatation, *f.*; (*expatiation*) long discours, *m.*

Enlighten, *v.a.* éclairer

Enlightener, *s.* personne qui éclaire *or* instruit, *f.*, instructeur, *m.* [*f.pl.*

Enlightenment, *s.* instruction, *f.*; lumières,

Enlist, *v.a.* enrôler, inscrire; (*mil.*) enrôler, engager; — *v.n.* s'enrôler, s'engager

Enlister, *s.* enrôlé, *m.*, recrue, *f.*, conscrit, *m.*

Enlistment, *s.* enrôlement, engagement, *m.*

Enliven, *v.a.* vivifier; animer; ranimer; activer; égayer, réjouir

Enlivener, *s.* personne *or* chose qui anime *or* égaye, *f.*, boute-en-train, *m.*

Enmity, *s.* inimitié, hostilité, haine, *f.* *At — with,* ennemi de, en hostilité avec
Enneagon, *s.* ennéagone, *m.*
Enneagonal, *adj.* ennéagonal, ennéagone
Ennoble, *v.a.* anoblir; (*fig.*) ennoblir; illustrer
Ennoblement, *s.* anoblissement, *m.*; élévation, *f.*
Ennui, *s.* ennui, *m.*
Enormity, *s.* énormité, *f.*; atrocité, *f.*
Enormous, *adj.* énorme; atroce; monstrueux
Enormously, *adv.* énormément
Enormousness. *V.* **Enormity**
Enostosis, *s.* énostose, *f.*
Enough, *adv.* ('*to,*' pour) assez; suffisamment; (*suffice it to say*) suffit (que). *Good —,* assez bon. *Patience —,* assez de patience. *More than —,* plus qu'il n'en faut. *To be —,* être assez; suffire
Enquire, Enquiry, &c. *V.* **Inquire, Inquiry,** &c.
Enrage, *v.a.* rendre furieux, irriter, exaspérer; [(*tease*) faire enrager
Enraged, *adj.* furieux, irrité, exaspéré ('*at,*' de)
Enrapture, *v.a.* transporter, ravir
Enregister, *v.a.* enregistrer
Enrich, *v.a.* enrichir
Enricher, *s.* personne *or* chose qui enrichit, *f.*
Enriching, Enrichment, *s.* enrichissement, *m.*
Enrobe, *v.a.* revêtir
Enrock, *v.a.* enrocher
Enrockment, *s.* enrochement, *m.*
Enroll, Enrol, *v.a.* enrôler; enregistrer, [inscrire
Enroller, *s.* personne qui enrôle *or* enregistre, *f.*
Enrolment, *s.* enrôlement, *m.*; enregistrement, *m.*; registre, *m.*
Ensanguine, *v.a.* ensanglanter
Ensconce, *v.a.* couvrir, mettre à couvert, fortifier, retrancher, défendre, cacher
Ensemble, *s.* ensemble, *m.*
Enshrine, *v.a.* enchâsser; enfermer, mettre sous verre; conserver; mettre au rang des [saints
Enshroud, *v.a.* *V.* **Shroud,** *v.a.*
Ensiform, *adj.* ensiforme
Ensign, *s.* (*flag*) enseigne, *f.*, drapeau, *m.*; (*mark*) signe, insigne, *m.*; signal, *m.*; (*nav. flag*) pavillon de poupe, *m.*; (*mil. flag*) drapeau, *m.*; (*mil. officer*) sous-lieutenant (d'infanterie), *m.*; porte-drapeau, *m.*, (*formerly*) enseigne, *m.* **— bearer,** *s.* porte-drapeau, *m.* **— staff,** *s.* (*nav.*) bâton de commandement, *m.*
Ensigncy, *s.* grade de sous-lieutenant (d'infanterie), *m.*, sous-lieutenance, *f.*
Enslave, *v.a.* asservir, réduire à l'esclavage, rendre esclave; (*subject to*) assujettir (à)
Enslavement, *s.* asservissement, esclavage, *m.*, servitude, *f.*
Enslaver, *s.* asservisseur, *m.*
Ensnare, *v.a.* prendre au piége, faire tomber dans un piége, prendre, attraper; séduire, abuser, tromper; surprendre; embarrasser
Ensnarer, *s.* personne qui tend des piéges, *f.*, attrapeur, *m.*, -euse, *f.*
Ensue, *v.n.* s'ensuivre, suivre; résulter
Ensuing, *adj.* suivant; ultérieur; (*coming*) [prochain
Ensure, &c. *V.* **Insure,** &c.
Entablature, Entablement, *s.* entablement, *m.*
Entail, *s.* (*in law*) substitution, *f.*; (*fig.*) transmission, *f.*; (*property*) bien substitué, majorat, *m.*; — *v.a.* (*in law*) substituer (à); léguer (à); (*fig.*) transmettre (à); imposer (à); entraîner; occasionner. *—ed estate,* bien substitué, *m.*
Entailment, *s.* *V.* **Entail,** *s.*
Entangle, *v.a.* emmêler; empêtrer; embarrasser; engager; (*confuse*) embrouiller; (*lose*) perdre
Entanglement, *s.* emmêlement, *m.*; embarras, *m.*, confusion, *f.*; embrouillement, *m.*; (*error*) égarement, *m.*
Entasis, *s.* renflement, *m.*, entasis, *f.*
Enter, *v.a.* entrer dans *or* à; (*admit*) admettre; (*engage*) engager; (*begin*) débuter dans; (*write down*) enregistrer, inscrire, faire inscrire; consigner; insérer; (*book-keep.*) porter, inscrire, entrer, ('*to,*') porter (sur le compte de); (*an action*) intenter; (*a claim*) avancer, mettre en avant (une prétention); faire (une demande, une réclamation); revendiquer (un droit); (*a protest*) faire; (*a profession*) embrasser; (*deposit*) déposer; — *v.n.* entrer; pénétrer. **— into** *or* **upon,** entrer dans *or* en *or* à; pénétrer dans; s'engager dans; entreprendre; entamer, commencer; débuter dans; passer, conclure, faire; contracter, prendre; former; prendre part à; entrer en possession de, prendre possession de. *To — the army,* entrer au service. *To — the church* or *into the church,* entrer dans les ordres, embrasser l'état ecclésiastique. *To — the law,* entrer au barreau. *To — the navy,* entrer au service de la marine. *To — the* (or *into*) *service,* *V.* **Service**
Enterer, *s.* entrant, *m.*; (*beginner*) débutant, [*m.*, e, *f.*
Enteric, *adj.* entérique
Entering, *s.* entrée, *f.*
Enteritis, *s.* entérite, *f.*
Enterprise, *s.* entreprise, *f.*; caractère entreprenant, esprit d'entreprise, *m.*, hardiesse, *f.* *Man of great —,* homme bien entreprenant
Enterpriser, *s.* personne entreprenante, *f.*
Enterprising, *adj.* entreprenant
Enterprisingly, *adv.* hardiment, résolûment, activement
Entertain, *v.a.* traiter (de), régaler (de); accueillir, recevoir; admettre; amuser (de), divertir (de); (*keep up*) entretenir; (*cherish, as hopes*) nourrir; (*an opinion, a thought, fears*) avoir, concevoir; (*a proposal,* &c.) écouter, accueillir, réfléchir sur
Entertainer, *s.* personne qui traite *or* régale, *f.*, hôte, *m.*, hôtesse, *f.*; amphitryon, *m.*; amuseur, *m.*, -euse, *f.*
Entertaining, *adj.* amusant, divertissant; agréable, aimable; — *s.* *V.* **Entertainment**
Entertainingly, *adv.* agréablement; plaisamment
Entertainment, *s.* repas, festin, banquet, *m.*, fête, *f.*; régal, *m.*; partie de plaisir, *f.*; soirée, *f.*, bal, *m.*; société, *f.*; réception, *f.*, accueil, *m.*; hospitalité, *f.*; amusement, divertissement, *m.*; farce, *f.*; spectacle, *m.*, représentation, *f.* *— for man and beast* (or *horse*), on loge à pied et à cheval
Enthrall, &c. *V.* **Inthrall,** &c.
Enthrone, Enthronize, *v.a.* mettre sur le trône, introner; (*bishops, archbishops*) introniser
Enthronement, Enthroning, Enthronization, *s.* intronisation, *f.*
Enthusiasm, *s.* enthousiasme, *m.*
Enthusiast, *s.* enthousiaste, *m.f.*
Enthusiastic, -al, *adj.* enthousiaste; d'enthousiasme
Enthusiastically, *adv.* avec enthousiasme
Enthymem, Enthymeme, *s.* enthymème, *m.*
Entice, *v.a.* exciter (à), pousser (à); (*allure*) attirer; tenter; séduire; entraîner
Enticement, *s.* instigation, *f.*; attrait, appât, charme, *m.*; tentation, *f.*; séduction, *f.*; entraînement, *m.*
Enticer, *s.* instigateur, *m.*, -trice, *f.*; séducteur, *m.*, -trice, *f.*; (*thing*) appât, attrait, *m.*
Enticing, *adj.* séduisant, attrayant, tentant
Enticingly, *adv.* d'une manière séduisante *or* attrayante *or* tentante
Entire, *adj.* entier; complet; parfait; intact; pur, naturel, sans mélange; sincère; (*wholly*) en entier; — *s.* totalité, *f.*; (*beer*) bière naturelle, *f.* *— horse,* cheval entier, *m.*
Entirely, *adv.* entièrement, en entier; tout entier; complètement; tout à fait, tout; sincèrement
Entireness, Entirety, *s.* intégralité, intégrité, *f.*; totalité, *f.*, tout, *m.*; ensemble, entier, *m.*
Entitle, *v.a.* intituler, nommer, appeler; (*give a right*) donner droit (à), (*before a verb*) donner (à quelqu'un) le droit (de faire quelque chose), mettre en droit (de). *To be —d to,* avoir droit à; (*before a verb*) avoir le droit de, être en [droit de
Entity, *s.* entité, *f.*; individualité, *f.*

Entomb, *v.a.* ensevelir
Entombment, *s.* sépulture, *f.*
Entomolog-ic, al, -ist, -y. *V.* page 3, § 1
Entozoal, Entozoic, *adj.*, **Entozoan, Entozoon,** *s.* entozoaire, *adj. m.f.*, *s.m.*
Entr'act, *s.* entr'acte, *m.*
Entrails, *s. pl.* entrailles, *f.pl.*
Entrance, *s.* entrée, *f.*; accès, *m.*; commencement, début, *m.*; initiation, première connaissance, *f.*, premières notions, *f.pl.*; (*law*) *V.* **Entry.** — **door,** *s.* porte d'entrée, *f.* — **fee,** *s. V.* — **money.** — **gate,** *s.* porte d'entrée, porte cochère, *f.* — **hall,** *s.* vestibule, *m.* — **money,** *s.* prix d'entrée, *m.*, entrée, *f.*, entrées, *f.pl.*
Entrance, *v.a.* jeter dans un sommeil léthargique; (*fig.*) ravir, extasier
Entrancement, *s.* sommeil léthargique, *m.*; (*fig.*) ravissement, *m.*, extase, *f.*
Entrap, *v.a. V.* **Ensnare**
Entreat, *v.a.* supplier (de), conjurer (de), adjurer (de), prier instamment (de), prier en grâce (de), prier (de); implorer, solliciter; (*prevail upon*) fléchir
Entreater, Entreating, Entreatingly. *V.* **Beseecher, Beseeching, Beseechingly**
Entreaty, *s.* instance, supplication, prière, *f.*
Entrée, *s.* (*cook.*) entrée, *f.* — **dish,** *s.* plat [d'entrée, *m.*
Entremets, *s.* entremets, *m.*
Entrench. *V.* **Intrench**
Entrepôt, *s.* entrepôt, *m.*
Entresol, *s.* entresol, *m.*
Entrust. *V.* **Intrust**
Entry, *s.* entrée, *f.*; article, *m.*; consignation, *f.*; insertion, *f.*; note, *f.*; (*book-keep.*) enregistrement, *m.*, inscription, entrée, *f.*; (*account*) compte, *m.*; (*law*) prise de possession, entrée en jouissance, *f.*; (*nav.*) déclaration d'entrée, *f.* *By double* —, en partie double. *By single* —, en partie simple. *To make an* — *against*, débiter
Entwine, Entwist, *v.a.* enlacer, entrelacer; entortiller; — *v.n.* s'enlacer, s'entrelacer; [s'entortiller
Enucleate, *v.a.* énucléer
Enucleation, *s.* énucléation, *f.*
Enumerate, *v.a.* énumérer [mération, *f.*
Enumerating, *adj.* énumérateur; — *s.* énu-
Enumeration, *s.* énumération, *f.*
Enumerative, *adj.* énumératif
Enumerator, *s.* énumérateur, *m.*, -trice, *f.*; (*of census*) recenseur, *m.*
Enunciate, *v.a.* énoncer [énoncé, *m.*
Enunciation, *s.* énonciation, *f.*; (*geom.*)
Enunciative, Enunciatory, *adj.* énon-
Enuresis, *s.* énurésie, *f.* [ciatif, qui énonce
Envelop, Envelope, *v.a.* envelopper ('*in,*' dans; '*with,*' de); — *s.* enveloppe, *f.* *In an* —, sous enveloppe [ment, *m.*
Enveloping, Envelopment, *s.* enveloppe-
Envenom, *v.a.* envenimer, empoisonner
Enviable, *adj.* enviable, digne d'envie
Envier, *s.* envieux, *m.*, -euse, *f.*
Envious, *adj.* envieux. — *eyes*, un œil d'envie, *m.*
Enviously, *adv.* avec *or* par envie; d'un œil d'envie
Enviousness, *s.* humeur envieuse, jalousie, *f.*
Environ, *v.a.* environner ('*with,*' de)
Environment, *s.* environnement, *m.*
Environs, *s. pl.* environs, *m.pl.*
Envoy, *s.* envoyé, *m.*; (*liter.*) envoi, *m.*
Envoyship, *s.* fonctions d'envoyé, *f.pl.*
Envy, *v.a.* envier, porter envie à; — *s.* envie, *f.*
Enwrap. *V.* **Inwrap**
Eolian, Eolic. *V.* **Æolian, Æolic**
Epacris, *s.* épacris, *f.*
Epact, *s.* épacte, *f.*
Epactal, *adj.* épactal
Eparch, *s.* éparque, *m.*
Eparchy, *s.* éparchie, *f.*
Epaule, *s.* épaule, *f.*
Epaulet, Epaulette, *s.* épaulette, *f.* — *with large bullion*, épaulette à grosse torsade *or* à graine d'épinards

Epaulment, Epaulement, *s.* épaulement, *m.*
Epergne, *s.* surtout (*or* dormant) de table, surtout, dormant, *m.*
Ephelis, *s.* éphélide, tache de rousseur, *f.*
Ephemera, *s.*, **Ephemeral,** *adj.* éphémère, [*m.f.*
Ephemeris, *s.* éphéméride, *f.*
Ephesian, *s.* Éphésien, *m.*, -ne, *f.*; — *adj.* [éphésien, d'Éphèse
Ephod, *s.* éphode, *m.*
Ephor, *s.* éphore, *m.*
Ephoral, *adj.* éphorique
Ephoralty, *s.* éphorat, *m.*
Epic, *adj.* épique; — *s.* poème épique, *m.*, épopée, *f.*
Epicarp, *s.* épicarpe, *m.*
Epicene, *adj. s.* épicène, *adj. m.f.*, *s.m.*
Epicranium, *s.* épicrâne, *m.*
Epictetian, *adj.* d'Épictète
Epicure, *s.* épicurien, *m.*, -ne, *f.*; friand, *m.*, e, *f.*; gourmand, *m.*, e, *f.*; gourmet, *m*
Epicurean, *s.* épicurien, *m.*; — *adj.* épicurien; d'épicurien; d'Épicure [*m.*
Epicureanism, Epicurism, *s.* épicurisme,
Epicurize, *v.n.* vivre en épicurien
Epicycle, *s.* épicycle, *m.*
Epicycloid, *s.* épicycloïde, *f.*
Epicycloidal, *adj.* épicycloïdal
Epidaurian, *adj.* épidaurien, d'Épidaure
Epidemic, -al, *adj.* épidémique; — *s.* épidémie, *f.*
Epidemically, *adv.* épidémiquement
Epidemiology, &c. épidémiologie, &c. (*V.* p.
Epidermic, -al, *adj.* épidermique [(3, § 1)
Epidermis, Epiderm, *s.* épiderme, *m.*
Epigastric, *adj.* épigastrique
Epigastrium, *s.* épigastre, *m.*
Epiglottic, *adj.* épiglottique
Epiglottis, *s.* épiglotte, *f.*
Epigram, *s.* épigramme, *f.*
Epigrammatic, -al, *adj.* épigrammatique
Epigrammatically, *adv.* épigrammatiquement
Epigrammatist, *s.* épigrammatiste, *m.f.*
Epigrammatize, *v.n.a.* épigrammatiser
Epigraph, *s.* épigraphe, *f.*
Epigraphic, *adj.* épigraphique
Epigraphy, *s.* épigraphie, *f.*
Epilatory. *V.* **Depilatory**
Epilepsy, *s.* épilepsie, *f.*
Epileptic, *adj.* épileptique, d'épilepsie; — *s.* épileptique, *m.f.* — *fit*, attaque d'épilepsie, *f.*
Epilogistic, *adj.* d'épilogue; en forme d'épi- [logue
Epilogue, *s.* épilogue, *m.*
Epiphany, *s.* Épiphanie, *f.*
Epiploon, *s.* épiploon, *m.*
Episcopacy, *s.* épiscopat, *m.*
Episcopal, *adj.* épiscopal. — *city* or *see* or *palace*, évêché, *m.* [épiscopal, *s.m.*
Episcopalian, *adj. s.* épiscopal, *adj. m.*, e, *f.*.
Episcopally, *adv.* épiscopalement
Episcopate, *s.* épiscopat, *m.*
Episode, *s.* épisode, *m.*
Episodic, -al, *adj.* épisodique
Episodically, *adv.* épisodiquement
Epispastic, *adj. s.* épispastique, *adj. m.f.*, *s.m.*
Epistle, *s.* épître, *f.*
Epistolary, *adj.* épistolaire
Epistolize, *v.n.* écrire des lettres
Epistolizer, *s.* épistolier, *m.*, -ière, *f.*
Epitaph, *s.* épitaphe, *f.*
Epithalamium, *s.* épithalame, *m.*
Epithelium, *s.* épithélium, *m.*
Epithet, *s.* épithète, *f.*
Epithetic, *adj.* épithétique
Epitome, *s.* épitomé, précis, abrégé, *m.*
Epitomist, *s.* abréviateur, *m.*, -trice, *f.*
Epitomize, *v.a.* abréger, faire un abrégé *or* un précis de
Epitomizer, *s.* abréviateur, *m.*, -trice, *f.*
Epizoal, Epizoic, *adj.*, **Epizoan, Epizoon,** *s.* épizoaire, *adj. m.f.*, *s.m.*
Epizootic, *adj.* épizootique; — *s.* épizootie, *f.*
Epizootically, *adv.* épizootiquement
Epizooty, *s.* épizootie, *f.*
Epoch, *s.* époque, *f.*

Epode, s. épode, f. [s.m., adj. m.f.
Eponym, s., **Eponymous,** adj. éponyme,
Epopee, s. épopée, f.
Eprouvette, s. éprouvette, f.
Equability, s. égalité, uniformité, f.
Equable, adj. égal, uniforme
Equably, adv. également, uniformément
Equal, adj. égal; uniforme; indifférent: (*pers.: before a verb*) de force (à), en état (de); (*pers.: before a noun*) propre (à); à la hauteur (de); au niveau de; — s. égal, m., e, f.; **—s,** s. pl. égaux, m.pl., égales, f.pl.; (*kind*) pareils, m.pl., pareilles, f.pl.; — v.a. égaler, être égal à. *Other things being* —, toutes choses égales [d'ailleurs
Equality, s. égalité, f.
Equalization, s. égalisation, f.
Equalize, v.a. égaliser
Equally, adv. également
Equanimity, s. égalité d'âme, f.
Equanimous, adj. qui a l'âme égale, d'un caractère égal [du premier degré, f.
Equation, s. équation, f. *Simple* —, équation
Equator, s. équateur, m. [s. équatorial, m.
Equatorial, adj. équatorial, de l'équateur; —
Equerry, s. écuyer, m.
Equestrian, adj. équestre; (*pers.*) qui monte à cheval; — s. promeneur (m., -euse, f.) à cheval; cavalier, m., -ière, f.; écuyer, m., [-ère, f.
Equestrianism. *V.* **Horsemanship**
Equiangular, adj. équiangle
Equibalance, v.a. équilibrer
Equidifference, s. équidifférence, f.
Equidifferent, adj. équidifférent
Equidistance, s. équidistance, égale dis- [tance, f.
Equidistant, adj. équidistant
Equidistantly, adv. à égale distance
Equilateral, adj. équilatéral; équilatère; — s. figure équilatérale, f.
Equilibrate, v.a. équilibrer
Equilibration, s. équilibre, m. [en équilibre
Equilibrious, adj., **Equilibriously,** adv.
Equilibrism, s. équilibrisme, m.
Equilibrist, s. équilibriste, m.f.
Equilibrium, s. équilibre, m.
Equimultiple, adj.s. équimultiple, adj.m.f., s.m.
Equine, adj. chevaline, f.; hippique; de *or* du cheval, de *or* des chevaux. — *species* or *race*, espèce *or* race chevaline, f.
Equinoctial, adj. équinoxial, d'équinoxe, de l'équinoxe, des équinoxes; — s. ligne équinoxiale, f. [l'équinoxe
Equinoctially, adv. dans la direction de
Equinox, s. équinoxe, m.; vent d'équinoxe, m.
Equip, v.a. équiper
Equipage, s. équipage, m.; (*nav.*) équipement, m.
Equipment, s. équipement, m.
Equipoise, s. équilibre, m.; — v.a. équilibrer
Equipollence, &c. *V.* **Equivalence,** &c.
Equiponderanc-e, y, s. équipondérance, f.
Equiponderant, adj. équipondérant
Equiponderate, v.a. contre-balancer; — v.n. être d'un poids égal (à)
Equitable, adj. équitable, juste
Equitableness, s. nature équitable, équité, f.
Equitably, adv. équitablement, justement
Equitant, adj. (*bot.*) équitant, chevauchant
Equitation. *V.* **Horsemanship**
Equity, s. équité, justice, f.
Equivalenc-e, y, s. équivalence, f.
Equivalent, adj. s. équivalent, adj. m., e, f., équivalent, s.m. *To be* —, être équivalent, équivaloir (à) [manière équivalente
Equivalently, adv. équivalemment, d'une
Equivalve, adj. équivalve
Equivocal, adj. équivoque; — s. équivoque, f.
Equivocally, adv. d'une manière équivoque
Equivocalness, s. nature équivoque, f.
Equivocate, v.n. équivoquer, user d'équivoques
Equivocation, s. équivocation, f.; équivoque, f.
Equivocator, s. personne qui équivoque *or* qui use d'équivoques, f.
Era, s. ère, f.; époque, f. *Christian* —, ère chrétienne. *To form* or *mark an* —, faire [époque
Eradiate, v.n. rayonner
Eradiation, s. rayonnement, m., radiation, f.
Eradicable, adj. déracinable, extirpable, destructible [détruire
Eradicate, v.a. déraciner; (*fig.*) extirper,
Eradication, s. éradication, f., déracinement, m., extirpation, f.
Eradicative, adj. éradicatif
Eradicator, s. extirpateur, m.
Erasable, adj. effaçable
Erase, v.a. effacer; raturer, rayer
Erasement, s. effacement, m. [grattoir, m.
Eraser, s. (*pers.*) effaceur, m., -euse, f.; (*thing*)
Erasion, s. effacement, m.
Erasure, s. effaçure, rature, f.; effacement, m.
Ere, prep. avant; — conj. avant que; (*rather than*) plutôt que. — *while*, naguère. — *yet*, avant que
Erect, adj. (*upright*) droit; (*standing*) debout; (*high*) élevé, haut; (*lifted up*) levé; — v.a. ériger; élever; (*set upright*) dresser; (*establish*) établir, fonder; (*mach.*) poser; (*geom.*) élever
Erecter, s. constructeur, m.; fondateur, m., [-trice, f.
Erecting, s. *V.* **Erection**
Erection, s. érection, f.; construction, f.; élévation, f.; établissement, m., fondation, f.; (*of machines*, &c.) posage, m.
Erectly, adv. droit, tout droit [droite, f.
Erectness, s. position perpendiculaire *or*
Erector, s. *V.* **Erecter;** — s. adj. (*anat.*) [érecteur, m.
Ergo, adv. ergo
Ergot, s. ergot, m.
Ergotine, s. ergotine, f.
Ergotism, s. ergotisme, m.
Eriodendron, s. ériodendron, m.
Erl, s. *The* — *king*, le roi des aulnes, m.
Ermine, s. hermine, f.; — adj. d'hermine
Ermined, adj. fourré d'hermine; (*pers.*) revêtu [d'hermine
Erne, s. haliète, m.
Erode, v.a. éroder
Erodent, s. érosif, m.
Erosion, s. érosion, f.
Erosive, adj. érosif
Erotic, -al, adj. s. érotique, adj. m.f., s.m.
Erotically, adv. érotiquement
Erotomania, s. érotomanie, f.
Erpetology, &c. erpétologie, &c. (*V.* p. 3, § 1)
Err, v.n. errer; (*from*) s'égarer (de), s'écarter (de); (*to mistake*) se tromper, errer; faillir
Errand, s. message, m.; commission, f. *On an* —, en commission; en course. *To go on an* —, aller en commission, aller faire une commission. — **boy, -porter,** s. commis- [sionnaire, m.
Errant, adj. errant
Errantry, s. vie errante, f. *Knight* —, [chevalerie errante, f.
Errata, s. errata, m.
Erratic, adj. errant; vagabond; variable; excentrique; (*astr., med., geol.*) erratique
Erratically, adv. sans ordre, irrégulièrement
Erratum, s. errata, m.
Errhine, adj. s. errhin, adj. m., e, f., errhin, s.m.
Erring, adj. égaré
Erroneous, adj. erroné, faux, inexact
Erroneously, adv. erronément, par erreur; faussement, à faux; à tort
Erroneousness, s. fausseté, f.
Error, s. erreur, f.; faute, f. —*s excepted*, sauf erreur, sauf erreur ou omission
Erse, adj. s. erse, adj. m.f., s.m.
Erst, adv. (*first*) d'abord, au commencement; (*formerly*) autrefois, jadis; (*before*) auparavant; (*till then*) jusqu'alors, jusque-là; (*till now*) jusqu'à présent, jusqu'ici; (*already*) déjà
Erubescence, s. érubescence, f.
Erubescent, adj. érubescent
Eructate, v.n.a. éructer; (*fig.*) vomir
Eructation, s. éructation, f., renvoi, m.
Erudite, adj. érudit
Erudition, s. érudition, f.
Eruginous, adj. érugineux
Eruption, s. éruption, f.; (*of troops*, &c.)

irruption, sortie, *f.*; (*of the voice*) éclat de voix, *m.*, exclamation, *f.*; (*med.*) éruption, *f.*
Eruptive, *adj.* qui éclate; (*geol., med.*) éruptif
Eryngo, *s.* panicaut, *m.*, érynge, *f.*
Erysimum, *s.* érysimon, vélar, *m.*
Erysipelas, *s.* érysipèle, *m.*
Erysipelatous, *adj.* érysipélateux
Erythema, *s.* érythème, *m.*
Erythematic, Erythematous, *adj.* érythématique, érythémateux
Escalade, *s.* escalade, *f.*; — *v.a.* escalader
Escapade, *s.* escapade, *f.*
Escape, *v.a.n.* échapper à, éviter; (*get away*) s'échapper, s'enfuir, se sauver; (*from prison*) s'évader; (*issue*) s'échapper, sortir; (*keep clear*) échapper (à); (*with ..., but no harm*) en être quitte (pour). *This word escaped him,* ce mot lui est échappé. *To — narrowly,* l'échapper belle (*you have —d narrowly,* vous l'avez échappé belle); (*before a verb*) faillir (*followed by the inf. in French*); (*before a noun*) être bien près de, être à deux doigts de, friser le *or* la *or* les ...
Escape, *s.* fuite, *f.*; évasion, *f.*; (*means of escape*) issue, *f.*; appareil de sauvetage, *m.*; (*of steam,* &c.) échappement, *m.*; (*of gas,* &c.) fuite, *f.*; (*fig.*) délivrance, *f.* *To have a narrow* or *a hairbreadth —,* échapper d'une manière miraculeuse, (*fam.*) l'échapper belle. *To make* (or *make good*) *o.'s —,* s'échapper, s'enfuir; (*from prison*) s'évader. *You have had a narrow —,* vous l'avez échappé belle
Escapement, *s.* échappement, *m.*
Escarp. *V.* **Scarp**
Escarpment, *s.* escarpement, *m.*
Eschalot. *V.* **Shallot**
Eschar, *s.* eschare, *f.*
Escharification, *s.* escharification, *f.*
Escharify, *v.a.* escharifier
Escharotic, *adj. s.* escharotique, *adj. m.f., s.m.*
Escheat, *s.* déshérence, *f.*; aubaine, *f.*; (*land*) bien en déshérence, *m.*; — *v.n.* tomber en déshérence; échoir (à)
Escheatable, *adj.* susceptible de déshérence
Escheatage, *s.* droit de déshérence, *m.*; [droit d'aubaine, *m.*
Eschew, *v.a.* éviter, fuir
Escort, *s.* escorte, *f.*; — *v.a.* escorter
Escorter, *s.* cavalier, *m.*
Escritoire, *s.* écritoire, *f.*; secrétaire, bureau, *m.*
Esculent. *V.* **Eatable**
Escurial, *s.* Escurial, *m.*
Escutcheon, *s.* écusson, *m.*; (*of a key-hole*) écusson, cache-entrée, *m.*
Escutcheoned, *adj.* écussonné
Esoteric, *adj.* ésotérique; —**s,** *s.pl.* ésotérisme, *m.*
Esoterically, *adv.* ésotériquement
Esotericism, *s.* ésotérisme, *m.*
Espalier, *s.* espalier, *m.*; — *v.a.* mettre en [espalier
Esparto, — grass, *s.* sparte, spart, *m.*
Especial, -ly. *V.* **Special, -ly.**
Espial, *s.* découverte, *f.*; vue, *f.*; observation, *f.*; surveillance, *f.*
Espionage, *s.* espionnage, *m.*
Esplanade, *s.* esplanade, *f.*; (*grass-plot*) [pelouse, *f.*
Espousal, *s.* adoption, adhésion, *f.*; —**s,** *pl.* épousailles, *f.pl.*, mariage, *m.*; fiançailles, *f.pl.*; accords, *m.pl.*, accordailles, *f.pl.*
Espouse, *v.a.* (*take*) épouser; (*give*) marier, fiancer; (*fig.*) épouser, embrasser, adopter
Espouser, *s.* épouseur, *m.*, -euse, *f.*; (*fig.*) défenseur, *m.*
Espy, *v.a.* apercevoir, voir; remarquer; découvrir; reconnaître; (*watch*) épier, observer, surveiller; — *v.n.* épier
Esquimau, *s.* Esquimau, *m.*, e, *f.* (*pl. m.* [(Esquimaux)
Esquire, *s.* écuyer, *m.*; (*common term of courtesy to a gentleman*) Monsieur. *G. Bell, Esq.*, Monsieur G. Bell
Essay, *v.a.* ('*to,*' de) essayer; tenter; éprouver; [— *s.* essai, *m.*
Essayist, *s.* essayiste, *m.f.*
Essence, *s.* essence, *f.*; parfum, *m.*, odeur, *f.*; [— *v.a.* parfumer
Essene, *s.* Essénien, *m.*
Essential, *adj.* essentiel; — *s.* principe essentiel, *m.*; chose essentielle, *f.*, (l') essentiel, (l') important, *m.*
Essentiality, *s.* essentialité, *f.*
Essentially, *adv.* essentiellement
Essentialness, *s.* importance, *f.*
Establish, *v.a.* établir; ériger; fonder; instituer; constituer; affermir; confirmer
Established, *part. adj.* établi, institué, &c. (*V.* **Establish**); (*agreed*) reçu, convenu; (*of churches*) établi, dominant. — *in* 1826, (*com.*) maison fondée en 1826
Establisher, *s.* personne qui établit *or* &c. (*V.* **Establish**), *f.*; fondateur, *m.*, -trice, *f.*
Establishment, *s.* établissement, *m*; institution, *f.*; constitution, *f.*; affermissement, *m.*; confirmation, *f.*; (*footing*) pied, *m.*; (*household*) maison, *f.*, train *or* état de maison, *m.*; (*Church*) Église établie, Église *or* religion dominante, *f.*; (*nav.*) établissement, *m.* *On the —,* (*print.*) à la (*or* en) conscience. — **hands,** *s. pl.* (*print.*) conscience, *f.*
Estafette, *s.* estafette, *f.*
Estate, *s.* état, *m.*; rang, *m.*, qualité, condition, *f.*; (*property*) bien, *m.*, propriété, terre *f.*; fortune, *f.*; succession, *f.*; (*polit.*) état, *m* *Man's —,* l'âge viril, *m.* — **agent,** *s.* agent d'affaires, *m.* — **office,** *s.* bureau de gestion (*or* de gérance) de propriétés, *m.*
Esteem, *v.a.* estimer; regarder *or* considérer comme; — *s.* estime, *f.*
Esteemer, *s.* estimateur, *m.*, -trice, *f.*, appréciateur, *m.*, -trice, *f.*
Estimable, *adj.* estimable [(*m.*) estimable
Estimableness, *s.* nature (*f.*) *or* caractère
Estimate, *v.a.* estimer, évaluer; apprécier; calculer; — *s.* estimation, évaluation, *f.*; appréciation, opinion, *f.*, jugement, *m.*; (*reckoning*) calcul, *m.*; devis, *m.*; état appréciatif, *m.*; aperçu, *m.*
Estimation, *s.* estimation, *f.*; appréciation, opinion, *f.*, jugement, *m.*; estime, *f.*
Estimative, *adj.* estimatif, appréciatif
Estimator, *s.* estimateur, *m.*, -trice, *f.*, appréciateur, *m.*, -trice, *f.*
Estival, *adj.* estival, d'été
Estivate, *v.n.* estiver, passer l'été
Estivation, *s.* estivation, *f.*
Estrade, *s.* estrade, *f.*
Estrange, *v.a.* éloigner (de); aliéner, indisposer
Estrangement, *s.* éloignement, *m.*, aliéna- [tion, *f.*
Estrapade, *s.* estrapade, *f.*
Estreat, *v.a.* enregistrer comme amende à [payer, confisquer
Estuary, *s.* estuaire, *m.*
Etc., etc.
Et cætera, *conj. s.* et cætera (*s.m.*)
Etch, *v.a.n.* graver à l'eau forte; (*to trace*) dessiner, tracer
Etcher, *s.* graveur à l'eau forte, eau-fortier, [*m.*, aquafortiste, *m.f.*
Etching, *s.* gravure à l'eau forte, *f.*; (*fig.*) trace, marque, *f.* — **needle, -point,** *s.* pointe à graver, pointe, *f.*
Eternal, *adj.* éternel (*m.*, -le, *f.*); — *s.* Éternel, *m.*
Eternalize, *v.a.* éterniser
Eternally, *adv.* éternellement
Eternity, *s.* éternité, *f.*
Eternize, *v.a.* éterniser
Etesian, *adj.* étésien
Ether, *s.* éther, *m.*
Etherate, *s.* éthérate, *m.*
Ethereal, *adj.* éthéré; céleste, aérien
Etherealize, *v.a.* rendre éthéré; (*chem.*) [éthérifier
Etheric, *adj.* éthérique
Etherification, *s.* éthérification, *f.*
Etherify, *v.a.* éthérifier
Etherization, *s.* éthérisation, *f.*
Etherize, *v.a.* éthériser
Ethic, -al, *adj.* moral, éthique; —**s,** *s. pl.* morale, éthique, *f.*; (*Aristotle's*) Éthiques, *f.pl.*
Ethically, *adv.* d'après la morale
Ethiopian, *s.* Éthiopien, *m.*, -ne, *f.*; — *adj.* éthiopien, éthiopique, d'Éthiopie

Ethmoid, *adj. s.* ethmoïde, *m.*
Ethmoidal, *adj.* ethmoïdal
Ethnarch, *s.* ethnarque, *m.*
Ethnarch-ic, al, -y. *V.* page 3, § 1
Ethnic, -al, *adj.* ethnique
Ethnographer, *s.* ethnographe, *m.*
Ethnograph-ic, al, -y. *V.* page 3, § 1
Ethnolog-ic, al, -ist, -y. *V.* page 3, § 1
Ethology, &c. éthologie, &c. (*V.* page 3, § 1)
Ethyl, *s.* éthyle, *m.*
Ethylene, *s.* éthérène, *m.*
Etiolate, *v.a.* étioler; — *v.n.* s'étioler
Etiolation, *s.* étiolement, *m.*
Etiology, &c. étiologie, &c. (*V.* page 3, § 1)
Etiquette, *s.* étiquette, *f.*; (*good manners*) [convenances, *f.pl.*
Etna, *s.* réchaud, *m.*
Etonian, *s.* élève du collége d'Eton, *m.*
Etrurian, *s. adj.* Étrurien, *m.*, -ne, *f.*
Etruscan, *adj.* étrusque; — *s.* Étrusque, *m.f.*
Etymological, *adj.* étymologique
Etymologically, *adv.* étymologiquement
Etymologist, *s.* étymologiste, *m.f.*
Etymologize, *v.a.n.* étymologiser
Etymology, *s.* étymologie, *f.*
Etymon, *s.* mot primitif, primitif, *m.*
Eucharist, *s.* eucharistie, *f.*
Eucharistic, -al, *adj.* eucharistique
Euchology, *s.* eucologe, *m.*
Eucrasy, &c. eucrasie, &c. (*V.* page 3, § 1)
Eudiometer, *s.* eudiomètre, *m.*
Eulogic, -al. *V.* **Eulogistic**
Eulogist, *s.* panégyriste, *m.*; élogiste, *m.*
Eulogistic, *adj.* élogieux, flatteur, louangeur; (*rhet.*) laudatif
Eulogistically, *adv.* avec éloge, flatteusement
Eulogium, *s.* éloge, *m.*
Eulogize, *v.a.* faire l'éloge de, élogier, louer
Eulogy, *s.* éloge, *m.*; (*eccl. hist.*) eulogie, *f.*
Eumenides, *s. pl.* Euménides, *f.pl.*
Eunuch, *s.* eunuque, *m.*
Eunuchism, *s.* eunuchisme, *m.*
Euonymus, *s.* fusain, *m.*
Eupatorium, *s.* eupatoire, *f.*
Euphemism, *s.* euphémisme, *m.*
Euphemistic, -al, *adj.* euphémique
Euphemistically, *adv.* euphémiquement, par euphémie [(*mus.*) euphone, *m.*
Euphon, Euphonium, Euphonon, *s.*
Euphon-ic, al, -ically. *V.* page 3, § 1
Euphonious, *adj.* agréable à l'oreille, agréable, mélodieux, harmonieux, euphonique
Euphoniously, *adv.* agréablement, mélodieusement, harmonieusement, euphoniquement
Euphonium, Euphonon, *s.* (*mus.*) euphone, *m.* [par euphonie
Euphony, *s.* euphonie, *f.* *For the sake of* —,
Euphorbia, Euphorbium, *s.* euphorbe, *f.*
Euphuism, *s.* euphuïsme, style précieux, *m.*, préciosité, *f.*
Euphuist, *s.* euphuiste, *m.f.*, précieux *m.*, -euse, *f.*
Euphuistic, *adj.* euphuïstique, précieux, affecté
Eupione, *s.* eupione, *f.*
Eurasian, *s. adj.* Eurasien, *m.*, -ne, *f.*
Eurhythm-ic, al, -y. *V.* page 3, § 1
European, *s.* Européen, *m.*, -ne, *f.*; — *adj.* [européen, d'Europe
Euryale, *s.* euryale, *f.*
Eurythm-ic, al, -y. *V.* page 3, § 1
Eustachian, *adj.* d'Eustache. — *tube*, trompe d'Eustache, *f.*
Euthanasia, Euthanasy, *s.* euthanasie, *f.*
Evacuant, *adj. s.* évacuant, *adj. m.*, e, *f.*, évacuant, *s.m.*, évacuatif, *adj. m.*, -ive, *f.*, éva- [cuatif, *s.m.*
Evacuate, *v.a.n.* évacuer
Evacuating, *adj.* évacuateur; — *s.* évacuation, *f.*
Evacuation, *s.* évacuation, *f.*; sortie, *f.*
Evacuative. *V.* **Evacuant**
Evacuator, *s.* évacuateur, *m.*
Evade, *v.a.* éviter; échapper à, se soustraire à; éluder; — *v.n.* s'échapper, s'évader, s'esquiver; (*fig.*) user de subterfuges, employer des moyens évasifs, biaiser

Evader, *s.* éludeur, *m.*, -euse, *f.*
Evadible, *adj.* éludable
Evanescence, *s.* évanouissement, *m.*, disparition, *f.*; instabilité, *f.*, existence (*f.*) or état (*m.*) éphémère
Evanescent, *adj.* évanescent, qui s'évanouit, passager, fugitif, éphémère; imperceptible
Evangelic, -al, *adj.* évangélique
Evangelically, *adv.* évangéliquement
Evangelism, *s.* évangélisme, *m.*
Evangelist, *s.* évangéliste, *m.* [taire, *m.*
Evangelistary, *s.* évangéliaire, évangelis-
Evangelization, *s.* évangélisation, *f.*
Evangelize, *v.a.n.* évangéliser
Evanish, *v.n.* s'évanouir, se dissiper, disparaître
Evanishment, *s.* évanouissement, *m.*, dis- [parition, *f.*
Evaporable, *adj.* évaporable
Evaporate, *v.n* s'évaporer; — *v.a.* évaporer, faire évaporer; exhaler; — *adj.* évaporé
Evaporating, *s.* évaporation, *f.*; — *adj.* évaporatoire; d'évaporation
Evaporation, *s.* évaporation, *f.*
Evaporative, *adj.* évaporatif
Evasible, *adj.* éludable
Evasion, *s.* défaite, *f.*, subterfuge, faux-fuyant, *m.*
Evasive, *adj.* évasif; (*of*) qui élude
Evasively, *adv.* évasivement [évasif, *m.*
Evasiveness, *s.* nature évasive, *f.*, caractère
Eve, *s.* veille, *f.*; (*evening*) soir, *m.* *At* —, le soir. *On the* — *of*, à la veille de
Evection, *s.* (*astr.*) évection, *f.*
Even, *s.* soir, *m.* — **song,** *s.* chant (*or* hymne) du soir, *m.* — **tide,** *s.* soir, *m.*, soirée, *f.*
Even, *adj.* (*equal*) égal; (*smooth*) uni; (*level with*) de niveau; (*of numbers*) pair; (*of a sum*) rond; (*settled*) réglé; (*owing nothing*) quitte; (*quiet*) tranquille. — *or odd*, pair ou non. — **handed,** *adj.* impartial, équitable. — **handedness,** *s.* impartialité, équité, *f.*
Even, *adv.* même; (*likewise*) aussi bien, également, de même, ainsi; (*so much as, so far as*) jusqu'à, jusque; (*regularly*) régulièrement; (*equally*) également; (*perfectly*) parfaitement, tout. — *as*, tout comme, comme. — *down*, tout en bas. — *now*, à l'instant; en ce moment; dès à présent. — *on*, tout droit. — *so*, ainsi, de même. — *though*, —, (*even if*) quand, quand même, quand bien même (*to be followed by the verb in the Conditional mood*)
Even, *v.a.* (*level*) égaler, niveler, mettre de niveau, unir, aplanir; (*equal*) égaliser; balancer; régler, acquitter
Evening, *s.* soir, *m.*; (*whole evening, in regard to work, occupation, or weather*) soirée, *f.*; (*decline*) déclin, *m.*; — *adj.* du soir. *In the* —, (*evening time*) le soir; (*in the course of the evening*) dans la soirée; (*of the hour*) du soir. *Last* —, hier soir, hier au soir. *This* —, ce soir. *The next* or *following* —, le lendemain soir. *The — after* ..., le lendemain soir de ... *The — after to-morrow*, après-demain soir. *The — before*, la veille au soir (de ...). *The — before yesterday*, avant-hier soir. *Good* —, bonjour; je vous salue; je vous salue bien; j'ai l'honneur de vous saluer; (*on parting, if late*) bonsoir. — **concert,** *s.* soirée musicale, *f.* — **damp, -dew,** *s.* serein, *m.* — **dress,** *s.* *V.* **Full dress** (*at Letter* **F**). — **gun,** *s.* coup de canon de retraite, *m.* — **paper,** *s.* journal du soir, *m.* — **party, -performance,** *s.* soirée, *f.* — **star,** *s.* étoile du soir, *f.*
Evenly, *adv.* également; uniment; de niveau; impartialement; (*quietly*) tranquillement; (*of numbers*) pairement [*m.*; impartialité, *f.*
Evenness, *s.* égalité, *f.*; sérénité, *f.*, calme,
Event, *s.* événement, *m.*; issue, fin, *f.*; dénoûment, *m.*; (*case*) cas, *m.* *At all* —*s*, à tout événement; en tout cas; de toute manière, de toute façon; à tout hasard
Eventful, *adj* plein d'événements, fécond en événements; accidenté; qui fait époque, grand, mémorable

Eventrate, *v.a.* éventrer
Eventration, *s.* éventration, éviscération, *f.*
Eventual, *adj.* éventuel, aléatoire; définitif, final
Eventually, *adv.* éventuellement, aléatoirement; définitivement, finalement; dans la suite; avec le temps; à la longue
Eventuate, *v.n.* se terminer, finir; arriver (à), aboutir (à)
Ever, *adv.* (*always*) toujours; (*at any time*) jamais; (*in anything*) en quoi que ce soit. *For* —, pour toujours, à jamais; éternellement; toujours, constamment; indéfiniment; (*theol.*) éternellement; *int.* (*hurrah for ...!*) vive ...! (*plural*) vivent ...! *For — and —*, pour toujours, à tout jamais; (*theol.*) jusqu'à la fin des siècles. — *after*, après; (*since*) depuis. — *since*, *V.* **Since.** — *so*, quelque ... que, si ... que. *Be they — so strong*, quelque (*or* si) forts qu'ils soient. — *so many*, — *so much*, tant et plus, je ne sais combien. — *so much*, (*by far*) incomparablement, sans comparaison. *Be they — so many*, quelque nombreux qu'ils soient, quelque soit leur nombre. *Be it — so much*, tant que ce soit. — *so little*, tant soit peu, si peu que rien, bien peu. *Be it — so little*, si peu que ce soit. — *so long* (*a time*), un temps infini; indéfiniment. — **green,** *adj.* toujours vert; vert; *s.* arbre vert, arbuste à feuilles persistantes, *m.* — *green oak*, chêne vert, *m.*, yeuse, *f.* — **lasting,** *adj.* éternel; immortel; perpétuel; *s.* éternité, *f.*; immortalité, *f.*; (*God*) Éternel, *m.*; (*bot.*) immortelle, *f.* — *lasting flower*, immortelle, *f.* — *lasting pea*, favonette, gesse tubéreuse, *f.* — **lastingly,** *adv.* éternellement. — **lastingness,** *s.* éternité, *f.* — **more,** *adv.* toujours, éternellement
Eversion, *s.* renversement, *m.*
Eversive, *adj.* éversif
Evert, *v.a.* renverser
Every, *adj.* chaque; tout; tous les ... —*body*, tout le monde. — *day*, tous les jours, chaque jour; (*adject.*) de tous les jours, de chaque jour, journalier; ordinaire; vulgaire. — *one*, chacun, *m.*, e, *f.*; (*all the people*) tout le monde. — *other*, de deux ... l'un, tous les deux. — *two days*, — *second day*, — *other day*, — *alternate day*, tous les deux jours, de deux jours l'un, un jour sur deux. *Once in — week*, une fois par semaine. — **thing,** *s.* tout, *m.*; toute chose, *f.*; (*all that which*) tout ce que. — **where,** *adv.* partout. — *where that*, partout où
Evict, *v.a.* évincer; expulser [preuve, *f.*
Eviction, *s.* éviction, *f.*; expulsion, *f.*; (*proof*)
Evidence, *s.* évidence, *f.*; (*proof*) preuve, *f.*, témoignage, *m.*; déposition, *f.*; (*pers.*) témoin, *m.*; — *v.a.* prouver, démontrer; montrer, témoigner; manifester; attester. *The — of the senses*, le témoignage des sens, *m.* *To bear* or *give* —, déposer; témoigner (de), porter témoignage (de). *To sum up the* —, (*law*) résumer les débats. *To turn* or *become king's* (or *queen's*) —, révéler ses complices
Evident, *adj.* évident
Evidently, *adv.* évidemment
Evil, *adj.* mauvais; méchant, pervers; de méchanceté; (*unhappy*) malheureux, de malheur; funeste; (*of spirits*) malfaisant, malin; — *s.* mal, *m.*; méchanceté, perversité, *f.*; (*misfortune*) malheur, *m.*; — *adv.* mal. *The — one*, l'esprit malin, le malin esprit, le malin, le diable, *m.* *To do* —, faire le mal. *Sufficient for the day is the — thereof*, à chaque jour suffit sa peine. — *be to him that — thinks*, honni soit qui mal y pense. — **disposed,** *adj.* *V.* — **minded.** — **doer,** *s.* méchant, *m.*, e, *f.*, malfaiteur, *m.* — **doing,** *s.* mauvaise action, *f.*, méfait, *m.*; méchanceté, *f.* — **eye,** *s.* mauvais œil, *m.* — **minded,** *adj.* porté au mal, mal intentionné, malveillant. — **speaking,** *s* médisance, *f.* — **wishing,** *adj.* malveillant. — **worker,** *s.* méchant, *m.*, e, *f.*
Evilness, *s.* méchanceté, malignité, *f.*
Evince, *v.a.* montrer, manifester, témoigner, faire preuve de; prouver, démontrer
Eviscerate, *v.a.* éviscérer
Evisceration, *s.* éviscération, *f.*
Evitable, *adj.* évitable
Evocation, *s.* évocation, *f.*
Evokable, *adj.* évocable
Evoke, *v.a.* évoquer
Evolute, *s.* (*geom.*) développée, *f.*
Evolution, *s.* évolution, *f.*; (*alg.*, *arith.*) extraction des racines, *f.*; (*geom.*) développement, *m.*; (*chem.*) dégagement, *m.* [tionnaire
Evolutional, Evolutionary, *adj.* évolu-
Evolve, *v.a.* déployer, développer, dérouler; (*chem.*) dégager; — *v.n.* évoluer, se déployer, se développer, se dérouler; (*chem.*) se dégager
Evolvent, *s.* (*geom.*) développante, *f.*
Evolving, *adj.* évolutif
Evulsion, *s.* évulsion, *f.*
Evulsive, *adj.* évulsif
Ewe, *s.* brebis, *f.* — **lamb,** *s.* agnelle, *f.* — **neck,** *s.* (*of horses*) encolure renversée, *f.*
Ewer, *s.* pot, *m.*, aiguière, *f.* —**ful,** *s.* potée,
Ex, (*Latin prep.*, *prefix*) ex [aiguiérée, *f.*
Exacerbate, *v.a.* aigrir, irriter; aggraver; (*med.*) exaspérer
Exacerbation, *s.* aigreur, irritation, *f.*; aggravation, *f.*; (*med.*) exacerbation, *f.*
Exact, *adj.* exact; (*of the hour*) précis; — *v.a.* exiger; extorquer; — *v.n.* commettre des ex-
Exactable, *adj.* exigible [actions; extorquer
Exacter, *s.* exacteur, *m.*
Exaction, *s.* exaction, extorsion, *f.*
Exactitude, *s.* exactitude, *f.*
Exactly, *adv.* exactement, au juste, juste, tout juste; précisément, justement; tout à fait; (*of the hour*, *of time*, *of number*) juste; (*to a day*) jour pour jour. — *so!* précisément!
Exactness, *s.* exactitude, *f.*; justesse, *f.*
Exactor, *s.* exacteur, *m.*
Exaggerate, *v.a.* exagérer; outrer
Exaggeration, *s.* exagération, *f.*
Exaggerating, Exaggerative, *adj.* exagérateur, exagératif
Exaggerator, *s.* exagérateur, *m.*, -trice, *f.*
Exaggeratory, *adj.* exagératif, exagérateur
Exalt, *v.a.* élever; (*praise*) exalter
Exaltation, *s.* exaltation, *f.*; (*of rank*) élévation, *f.*; (*of the pope*, *of the cross*) exaltation, *f.*
Exaltedness, *s.* élévation, *f.*; position *or* nature élevée, *f.*; caractère élevé, *m.*; hauteur, *f.*
Examination, *s.* examen, *m.*; inspection, *f.*; interrogation, *f.*; (*of schools*, *of candidates*) examen, *m.*; épreuve, *f.*; composition, *f.*; (*admin.*) inspection, *f.*; vérification, *f.*; visite, *f.*; (*law: of witnesses*) audition, *f.*, (*of prisoners*) interrogatoire, *m.*, (*of trials*) instruction, *f.* *Vivâ voce* —, épreuve orale, *f.* *Written* —, épreuve écrite, composition, *f.* *On* or *upon* —, après examen. — **paper,** *s.* matières *or* questions d'examen, *f.pl.*; composition, *f.*
Examine, *v.a.* examiner; inspecter; (*admin.*) inspecter; vérifier; visiter; (*law*) interroger; (*prepare for trial*) instruire (un procès, une affaire); — *v.n.* faire un examen, procéder à un examen. — **into,** examiner; approfondir
Examiner, *s.* examinateur, *m.*, -trice, *f.*; interrogateur, *m.*, -trice, *f.*; inspecteur, *m.*, -trice, *f.*; observateur, *m.*, -trice, *f.*; vérificateur, *m.*; (*law*) juge d'instruction, *m.* — *of plays*, censeur dramatique, censeur, *m.*
Examinership, *s.* poste (*m.*) *or* emploi (*m.*) *or* place (*f.*) *or* fonctions (*f.pl.*) d'examinateur (*or* d'examinatrice, *f.*). — *of plays*, censure dramatique, censure, *f.*
Examining, *adj.* qui examine; d'examen. — *magistrate*, juge d'instruction, *m.*
Example, *s.* exemple, *m.*; — *v.a.* *V.* **Exemplify.** *For* —, par exemple

Exanthema, *s.* (*pl.* **Exanthemata**) exanthème, *m.* (—s, *pl.*) [exanthématique
Exanthemat-ous, -ic, *adj.* exanthémateux,
Exarch, *s.* exarque, *m.*
Exarchate, *s.* exarchat, *m.*
Exasperate, *v.a.* exaspérer, aigrir, irriter
Exasperation, *s.* exaspération, *f.*; irritation,
Excarnate, *v.a.* excarner [*f.*; violence, *f.*
Excarnation, *s.* excarnation, *f.*
Excavate, *v.a.* creuser, excaver
Excavating, Excavation, *s.* excavation, *f.*; fouille, *f.*; déblai, *m.*
Excavator, *s.* excavateur, terrassier, *m.*
Exceed, *v.a.* excéder, dépasser; outre-passer; (*excel*) surpasser [ment
Exceedingly, *adv.* excessivement, extrême-
Excel, *v.n.a.* exceller; surpasser, l'emporter (sur)
Excellence, Excellency, *s.* excellence, *f.*; perfection, *f.*; mérite, *m.*; supériorité, *f.*; (*title*) excellence, *f.*
Excellent, *adj.* excellent; parfait. *Most* —, excellent, (*fam.*) excellentissime; (*title*) excellentissime
Excellently, *adv.* excellemment, parfaitement; éminemment; particulièrement
Excentric, &c. *V.* **Eccentric,** &c.
Except, *v.a.* excepter; exclure (de); — *v.n.* — **against** *or* **to,** faire des objections contre; ne pas admettre, refuser d'admettre; s'opposer à; récuser (un témoignage, un témoin), décliner (un tribunal) [moins de (*with the inf.*)
Except, *conj.* à moins que (*with the subj.*); à
Except, Excepting, *prep.* excepté, à l'exception de; hors, hormis, sauf; si ce n'est, sinon; (ne ...) que
Exception, *s.* exception, *f.*; objection, *f.*; critique, *f.*; (*law*) exception, *f.* *With the* —, à l'exception de. *With this* or *that* —, à cette exception près, à cela près. *To take* — *at* or *to* or *against*, se blesser de, s'offenser de, se formaliser de; désapprouver, trouver mauvais, trouver à redire à
Exceptionable, *adj.* récusable; blâmable, répréhensible; critiquable [critiquable, *f.*
Exceptionableness, *s.* nature blâmable *or*
Exceptional, *adj.* exceptionnel
Exceptionally, *adv.* exceptionnellement
Excerpt, *s.* extrait, *m.*
Excess, *s* excès, *m.*; (*of weight*) excédant, *m.*; (*math.*) excédant, excès, *m.* — **luggage,** *s.* excédant de bagages, *m.*
Excessive, *adj.* excessif; exagéré; outré
Excessively, *adv.* excessivement, à l'excès
Excessiveness, *s.* excessiveté, nature excessive, *f.*
Exchange, *v.a.* échanger ('*for*,' contre); changer ('*for*,' pour); — *v.n.* faire un échange; (*be exchanged*) s'échanger; se changer; — *s.* échange, *m.*; (*com.*) change, *m.*; (*building*) Bourse, *f.* *In* — *for*, en échange de. *To be a gainer* or *a loser by the* —, gagner *or* perdre au change. — **broker,** *s.* changeur, *m.*, -euse, *f.* — **office,** *s.* bureau de change, *m.*
Exchangeability, *s.* nature échangeable, *f.*
Exchangeable, *adj.* échangeable
Exchanger, *s.* personne qui échange, *f.*; (*com.*) banquier qui fait le change, *m.*, changeur, *m.*, -euse, *f.*
Exchequer, *s.* (*court*) échiquier, *m.*; (*treasury*) trésor public, trésor, *m.*; (*department*) finances, *f.pl.* — **bill,** *s.* bon du trésor, *m.*
Excipient, *s.* excipient, *m.*
Excisable, *adj.* sujet aux contributions indirectes; (*in England*) sujet aux droits d'accise
Excise, *s.* contributions indirectes, *f.pl.*; régie, *f.*; (*in England*) accise, excise, *f.*; — *v.a.* soumettre aux contributions indirectes; (*in England*) soumettre à l'accise, imposer un droit d'accise sur; (*to cut off*) exciser. — **duty,** *s.* droit de régie, *m.*; (*in England*) droit d'accise, *m.* — **man,** *s.* employé des contributions indirectes, employé de la régie, *m.*; (*in England*) employé de l'accise, *m.* — **office,** *s.* bureau des contributions indirectes, bureau de la régie, *m.*; (*in England*) bureau de l'accise, *m.* [tion, *f.*
Excision, *s.* (*surg.*) excision, *f.*; (*fig.*) destruc-
Excitability, Excitableness, *s.* excitabilité, *f.*; irritabilité, *f.*; susceptibilité, *f.*; impressionnabilité, *f.* [tible; impressionnable
Excitable, *adj.* excitable; irritable; suscep-
Excitant, *adj. s.* excitant, *adj. m.*, e, *f.*, excitant, *s.m.*
Excitation, *s.* excitation, *f.* [citant, *s.m.*
Excitative, *adj. s.* excitatif, *adj. m.*, -ive, *f.*,
Excitator, *s.* excitateur, *m.* [excitatif, *s.m.*
Excite, *v.a.* exciter; irriter; agiter; émouvoir; animer; encourager; stimuler; provoquer
Excited, *part. adj.* excité, d'excitation; irrité, d'irritation; agité, d'agitation; ému, d'émotion; animé; entraîné; ardent; monté
Excitement, *s.* excitation, *f.*; motif d'excitation, *m.*; irritation, *f.*; agitation, *f.*; rumeur, *f.*; émotion, *f.*; animation, *f.*; encouragement, stimulant, *m.*; plaisirs, *m.pl.*
Exciter, *s.* excitateur, *m.*, -trice, *f.*; (*things*) excitant, stimulant, *m.*; mobile, *m.*
Exciting, *adj.* excitant; stimulant; irritant; extraînant; piquant; émouvant; violent; — *s.* excitation, *f.*
Excitomotory, *adj.* excitomoteur [se récrier
Exclaim, *v.n.* s'écrier, s'exclamer; (*against*)
Exclaimer, *s.* déclamateur, *m.*, -trice, *f.*
Exclamation, *s.* exclamation, *f.*; clameur, *f.*, cri, *m.*, vocifération, *f.*; (*note of* —, — *point*) point d'exclamation, *m.* [clamatif
Exclamative, Exclamatory, *adj.* ex-
Exclamatively, Exclamatorily, *adv.* exclamativement
Exclude, *v.a.* exclure; (*prevent*) empêcher
Excluding, *prep.* non compris, sans compter
Exclusion, *s.* exclusion, *f.*
Exclusionary, *adj.* exclusiviste; chauvinique
Exclusioner, *s.* *V.* **Exclusionist** [nisme, *m.*
Exclusionism, *s.* exclusivisme, *m.*; chauvi-
Exclusionist, *s. adj.* exclusiviste, *m.f.*; chauviniste, chauvin, *m.*
Exclusive, *adj.* exclusif; — *adv.* exclusivement; — *s.* *V.* **Exclusionist.** — *of*, qui exclut; à l'exclusion de; non compris, sans compter
Exclusively, *adv.* exclusivement. — *of*, à l'exclusion de, non compris; abstraction faite de, à l'exception de
Exclusiveness, *s.* nature exclusive, *f.*, caractère exclusif, *m.*; exclusivisme, *m.*; chauvinisme, *m.*
Exclusivism. *V.* **Exclusionism**
Exclusivist. *V.* **Exclusionist**
Excogitate, *v.a.* inventer, imaginer; — *v.n.* réfléchir (à), penser (à), songer (à), méditer (sur)
Excogitation, *s.* invention, *f.*; réflexion, méditation, *f.* [munication
Excommunicable, *adj.* passible d'excom-
Excommunicate, *v.a.* excommunier; — *s. adj.* excommunié, *m.*, e, *f.*
Excommunication, *s.* excommunication, *f.*
Excommunicator, *s.* excommunicateur, *m.*
Excommunicatory, *adj.* excommunicatoire
Excoriate, *v.a.* écorcher, excorier
Excoriation, *s.* (*act*) écorchement, *m.*; (*result*) écorchure, excoriation, *f.*
Excrement, *s.* excrément, *m.* [mentitiel
Excrement-al, -itial, -itious, *adj.* excré-
Excrescence, *s.* excroissance, *f.*
Excrescent, *adj.* qui forme une excroissance; [(*fig.*) superflu
Excreta, *s. pl.* excreta, *m.pl.*
Excrete, *v.a.* excréter
Excretion, *s.* excrétion, *f.*
Excretive, *adj.* excréteur
Excretory, *adj.* excréteur, excrétoire; — *s.* conduit *or* vaisseau excréteur, *m.*
Excruciate, *v.a.* torturer, mettre au supplice, tourmenter horriblement

Excruciating, *adj.* atroce, cruel, déchirant, horrible
Excruciation, *s.* torture, *f.*, supplice, *m.*
Exculpate, *v.a.* disculper, justifier; excuser
Exculpation, *s.* disculpation, justification, *f.*
Exculpatory, *adj.* tendant à disculper, justificatif, apologétique
Excursion, *s.* excursion, *f.*; partie, *f.*; promenade, *f.*; digression, *f.*, écart, *m.* *On an* —, en excursion. — **ticket,** *s.* billet de train de plaisir, *m.* (*V.* **Train**)
Excursionist, *s.* excursioniste, *m.f.*
Excursive, *adj.* errant, divagant, vagabond; (*of style*) décousu
Excursively, *adv.* en errant, en divaguant
Excursiveness, *s.* écart, *m.*, divagation, *f.*
Excusable, *adj.* excusable
Excusableness, *s.* nature excusable, *f.*
Excusably, *adv.* excusablement
Excusatory, *adj.* tendant à excuser, justificatif, apologétique; d'excuse
Excuse, *s.* excuse, *f.*; — *v.a.* excuser; dispenser de, exempter de; (*remit*) faire remise de, faire grâce de. — *me!* pardon! —**less,** *adj.* sans excuse, inexcusable
Excuser, *s.* apologiste, *m.*, personne qui ex- [cuse, *f.*
Exeat, *s.* exeat, *m.*
Execra-bility, bleness, *s.* exécrabilité, *f.*
Execrable, *adj.* exécrable
Execrably, *adv.* exécrablement [détester
Execrate, *v.a.* exécrer, avoir en exécration,
Execration, *s.* exécration, *f.* *To hold in* —,
Execratory, *adj.* exécratoire [*V.* **Execrate**
Executable, *adj.* exécutable
Executant, *s.* exécutant, *m.*, e, *f.*
Execute, *v.a.* exécuter; faire; exercer
Execution, *s.* exécution, *f.*; (*effect*) effet, *m.*; (*of firing*) exécution, *f.*, effet, *m.*; (*of o.'s duty*) exercice (de ses fonctions), *m.*; (*capital punishment*) exécution, *f.*; supplice, *m.*; (*seizure of goods*) saisie-exécution, saisie, *f.*; (*writ of* —) exécutoire, *m.* *Warrant for* —, (*of criminals*) ordre d'exécution, *m.* *Writ of* —, exécutoire, *m.* *To carry into* —, *to put in* —, mettre à exécution
Executioner, *s.* exécuteur, bourreau, *m.*
Executive, *adj.* exécutif; — *s.* pouvoir exécutif, exécutif, *m.*; pouvoir, *m.* [cuteur, *m.*
Executor, *s.* exécuteur testamentaire, exé-
Executorial, *adj.* d'exécuteur testamentaire
Executorship, *s.* office d'exécuteur testamentaire, *m.*
Executory, *adj.* exécutif; (*law*) exécutoire
Executrix, *s.* exécutrice testamentaire, exé- [cutrice, *f.*
Exegesis, *s.* exégèse, *f.*
Exegete, *s.* exégète, *m.*
Exegetical, *adj.* exégétique
Exegetically, *adv.* par exégèse
Exegetics, *s. pl.* exégèse, *f.*
Exegetist, *s.* exégète, *m.*
Exemplar, *s.* modèle, *m.*
Exemplarily, *adv.* exemplairement
Exemplariness, *s.* exemplarité, nature ex- [emplaire, *f.*
Exemplary, *adj.* exemplaire
Exemplification, *s.* démonstration, explication par des exemples, amplification, *f.*; exemple, *m.*; (*copy*) ampliation, *f.*
Exemplify, *v.a.* servir d'exemple à; expliquer, démontrer *or* éclaircir par un exemple; donner un exemple de; copier, faire une copie authentique *or* une ampliation de
Exempt, *v.a.* exempter (de); exonérer (de); dispenser (de); (*from mil. service*) exonérer, libérer; — *adj.* exempt (de)
Exemptible, *adj.* exemptable; dispensable
Exemption, *s.* exemption, *f.*; exonération, *f.*; dispense, *f.*; (*from mil. service*) exonération, [libération, *f.*
Exequatur, *s.* exequatur, *m.*
Exercise, *s.* exercice, *m.*; (*at school, generally*) devoir, *m.*, (*particularly, translation from o.'s own language into another*) thème, *m.*; (*mil.*) exercice, *m.*, manœuvre, *f.* *Course of* —*s*, cours de thèmes, *m.* *To take* —, prendre de l'exercice. — **book,** *s.* livre de thèmes, *m.*; (*to write in*) cahier de devoirs, *m.*; cahier de thèmes, *m.*
Exercise, *v.a.* exercer; (*to use*) user de; employer; (*take out for an airing*) faire prendre de l'exercice à, promener; — *v.n.* s'exercer; (*for health*) prendre de l'exercice; (*mil.*) faire [l'exercice
Exercitation, *s.* exercice, *m.*
Exergue, *s.* exergue, *m.*
Exert, *v.a.* employer, exercer, mettre en jeu, faire agir; déployer. *To — oneself,* faire des efforts *or* ses efforts (pour); s'efforcer (de), tâcher (de); s'employer (à); s'appliquer (à); se remuer, se donner de la peine, travailler, agir. *To — oneself to the utmost,* faire tout son possible
Exertion, *s.* effort, *m.*; emploi, usage, *m.*; exercice, *m.* *To use every* —, faire tous ses [efforts
Exeunt, *v.n.* sortent
Exfoliate, *v.a.* exfolier; — *v.n.* s'exfolier
Exfoliation, *s.* exfoliation, *f.*
Exfoliative, *adj.* exfoliatif
Exhalable, *adj.* sujet à s'exhaler, évaporable
Exhalation, *s.* exhalation, *f.*; (*vapour*) exhalaison, *f.*
Exhale, *v.a.* exhaler; — *v.n.* s'exhaler
Exhaust, *v.a.* épuiser; (*o.'s patience*) mettre à bout, lasser; (*phys.*) aspirer, absorber
Exhausted, *part. adj.* épuisé, &c. (*V.* **Exhaust**); (*of exhaustion*) d'épuisement
Exhauster, *s.* personne *or* chose qui épuise, *f.*; (*tech.*) exhausteur, *m.*; (*of air-pumps*) [aspirateur, *m.*
Exhaustible, *adj.* épuisable
Exhausting, *adj.* épuisant; d'épuisement; (*phys.*) d'aspiration
Exhaustion, *s.* épuisement, *m.*; (*phys.*) aspiration, *f.*; (*phys., math., log.*) exhaustion, *f.*
Exhaustive, *adj.* épuisant; complet; plein; entier; (*liter.*) qui épuise son (*or* le) sujet; (*log.*) d'exhaustion
Exhaustively, *adv.* complètement, pleinement, entièrement; à fond
Exhaustless, *adj.* inépuisable
Exhibit, *v.a.* montrer, faire voir, déployer; présenter, offrir; (*to view*) exposer; (*law, admin.*) exhiber, produire; (*med.*) administrer; — *s.* produit *or* objet exposé, produit, objet, *m.*; (*law*) pièce produite, *f.*; annexe, *f.*
Exhibiter. *V.* **Exhibitor**
Exhibition, *s.* exposition, *f*; (*performance*) représentation, *f.*; (*sight*) spectacle, *m.*; (*law, admin.*) exhibition, production, *f.*; (*of schools*) [bourse, *f.*
Exhibitioner, *s.* boursier, *m.*
Exhibitor, *s.* personne qui montre *or* &c. (*V.* **Exhibit,** *v.a.*), *f.*; (*of exhibitions*) exposant, [*m.*, e, *f.*
Exhibitory, *adj.* exhibitoire
Exhilarant, *adj.* *V.* **Exhilarating** [récréer
Exhilarate, *v.a.* égayer, réjouir; divertir,
Exhilarating, *adj.* qui égaye, divertissant, exhilarant, hilarant
Exhilaration, *s.* hilarité, gaieté, *f.*; égayement, *m.*; réjouissance, *f.* [hortations
Exhort, *v.a.* exhorter (à); — *v.n.* faire des ex-
Exhortation, *s.* exhortation, *f.*
Exhortative, *adj.* exhortatif
Exhortator, *s.* exhortateur, *m.*
Exhortatory, *adj.* exhortatoire
Exhorter, *s.* exhortateur, *m.*, -trice, *f.*
Exhumation, *s.* exhumation, *f.*
Exhume, *v.a.* exhumer, déterrer
Exigence, Exigency, *s.* exigence, *f.*; (*need*) besoin, *m.*, nécessité, *f.*; embarras, *m.*, extrémité, situation critique, *f.* [critique
Exigent, *adj.* exigeant; pressant, urgent;
Exigibility, *s.* exigibilité, *f.*
Exigible, *adj.* exigible
Exiguity, *s.* exiguité, *f.*
Exiguous, *adj.* exigu
Exile, *v.a.* exiler; — *s.* exil, *m.*; (*pers.*) exilé, *m.*, e, *f.*, proscrit, *m.*, e, *f.*; — *adj.* menu, grêle, mince. *To drive into* —, exiler

Exility, *s.* ténuité, minceur, exilité, *f.*
Exist, *v.n.* exister
Existence, *s.* existence, *f.*; (*being*) être, *m.* *To be in* —, exister. *To call into* —, faire naître. *To grow into* —, naître, être produit, se produire [existe; actuel
Existent, Existing, *adj.* existant, qui
Exit, *v.n.* (*theat.*) sort; — *s.* sortie, *f.*; issue, *f.*; départ, *m.*; (*death*) mort, fin, *f.*; (*theat.*) sortie, *f.* *To make o.'s* —, sortir; partir; s'en aller; (*die*) mourir [sortie, *f.*
Exodus, *s.* exode, *m.*; (*fig.*) exode, départ, *m.*,
Exogen, *s.*, **Exogenous,** *adj.* exogène, *s.f.*,
Exomphalos, *s.* exomphale, *f.* [*adj. m.f.*
Exon, *s.* officier des cent-gardes, *m.*
Exonerate, *v.a.* exonérer, décharger, exempter, dispenser; justifier [justification, *f.*
Exoneration, *s.* exonération, décharge,
Exophthalmia, *s.* exophthalmie, *f.*
Exorable, *adj.* exorable [*m.*; dérèglement, *m.*
Exorbitanc-e, y, *s.* exorbitance, *f.*; excès,
Exorbitant, *adj.* exorbitant; excessif; déréglé
Exorbitantly, *adv.* exorbitamment; excessivement; déréglément
Exorcise, *v.a.* exorciser
Exorciser, *s.* exorciseur, *m.*, -euse, *f.*
Exorc-ism, -ist. *V.* page 3, § 1 [ductoire
Exordial, *adj.* d'exorde, de l'exorde, intro-
Exordium, *s.* exorde, *m.*
Exosmose, Exosmosis, *s.* exosmose, *f.*
Exostosis, *s.* exostose, *f.* [isme, *m.*
Exoteric, *adj.* exotérique; **—s,** *s. pl.* exotér-
Exoterically, *adv.* exotériquement
Exotericism, *s.* exotérisme, *m.*
Exotic, *adj.* exotique; — *s.* plante exotique, *f.*; (*word*) terme exotique, *m.*
Exoticism, *s.* exotisme, *m.*
Expand, *v.a.* étendre; déployer; (*of water*) répandre; (*of flowers,* &c.) faire épanouir; (*dilate*) dilater; — *v.n.* s'étendre; se déployer; se répandre; s'épanouir; se dilater
Expanse, *s.* étendue, *f.*
Expansibility, *s.* expansibilité, *f.*
Expansible, *adj.* expansible
Expansion, *s.* expansion, *f.*; extension, *f.*; déploiement, *m.*; (*extent*) étendue, *f.*; (*of flowers,* &c.) épanouissement, *m.* — **valve,** *s.* tiroir de détente, *f.*
Expansive, *adj.* expansif [pansive, *f.*
Expansiveness, *s.* nature *or* propriété ex-
Ex parte, Ex-parte, Exparte. *See Letter* **P**
Expatiate, *v.n.* s'étendre (sur), discourir (sur); (*wander*) errer
Expatiation, *s.* long discours, *m.*
Expatriate, *v.a.* expatrier
Expatriation, *s.* expatriation, *f.*
Expect, *v.a.n.* (*persons, objects, to wait for, to await*) attendre; (*facts, abstract things, to anticipate*) s'attendre à, s'attendre (que), compter sur, compter (que); (*hope*) espérer; se promettre; (*think*) penser, croire; (*demand*) vouloir, exiger. *That must be —ed,* il faut s'attendre à cela, on doit s'y attendre. *He is not —ed to live,* on désespère de sa vie
Expectanc-e, y. *V.* **Expectation**
Expectant, *adj.* qui est dans l'attente *or* dans l'expectative, expectant; (*things*) en expectative; (*med.*) expectant; — *s.* personne qui est dans l'attente *or* dans l'expectative, *f.*; (*for a vacant post*) expectant, aspirant, *m.*; (*law*) donataire, *m.f.*
Expectation, *s.* attente, *f.*; (*hope*) espérance, *f.*; expectative, *f.*, espoir, *m.*; (*claim, demand*) prétention, *f.*; (*med.*) expectation, *f.*; **—s,** *pl.* attente, *f.*, espérances, *f.pl.*, espoir, *m.*; prétentions, *f.pl.*; (*of fortune*) espérances, prétentions, *f.pl.* — *of life,* (*statistics*) vie moyenne, *f.* *Of* —, (*pers., things*) qui donne des espérances. *Of —s,* (*pers.*) qui a des espérances
Expecter, *s.* personne qui attend *or* qui espère, *f.*
Expectingly, *adv.* dans l'attente

Expectorant, *adj. s.* expectorant, *adj. m.*, e, *f.*, expectorant, *s.m.*
Expectorate, *v.a.n.* expectorer
Expectoration, *s.* (*act*) expectoration, *f.*, crachement, *m.*; (*matter*) matière expectorée, *f.*, crachat, *m.*
Expectorative. *V.* **Expectorant**
Expedienc-e, y, *s.* convenance, utilité, *f.*; opportunité, *f.*, à-propos, *m.*
Expedient, *adj.* expédient; convenable, utile, avantageux, bon, à propos; — *s.* expédient, *m.*
Expediently, *adv.* convenablement, à propos
Expedite, *v.a.* expédier; hâter, avancer, accélérer, activer; faciliter
Expedition, *s.* expédition, *f.*; diligence, promptitude, hâte, *f.* *On an* —, en expédition
Expeditionary, *adj.* expéditionnaire
Expeditious, *adj.* expéditif, prompt [ment
Expeditiously, *adv.* expéditivement, prompte-
Expeditiousness, *s.* expédition, prompti-
Expel, *v.a.* expulser; chasser; rejeter [tude, *f.*
Expelling, *adj.* expulseur
Expend, *v.a.* dépenser; (*fig.*) employer, consacrer; (*consume*) consommer
Expenditure, *s.* dépense, *f.*; dépenses, *f.pl.*; (*fig.*) emploi, *m.*; (*consumption*) consommation, *f.*
Expense, *s.* dépense, *f.*; frais, *m.pl.*; dépens, *m.pl.*; (*fig.*) dépens, *m.pl.* *At the — of,* aux frais de; (*fig.*) aux dépens de. *To be at* or *go* or *run to* or *be put to* —, faire des frais *or* des dépenses. *To put to* —, induire en dépense, constituer en frais, faire faire des frais à. *To cover* or *clear o.'s —s,* faire ses frais. *To pay its —s,* couvrir les frais. **—less,** *adj.* sans dépense, sans frais
Expensive, *adj.* dispendieux, coûteux, cher; de dépense; (*pers.*) dépensier, prodigue
Expensively, *adv.* dispendieusement, coûteusement, à grands frais
Expensiveness, *s.* nature dispendieuse *or* coûteuse, *f.*, prix élevé, grand prix, *m.*; frais, *m.pl.*, dépense, *f.*; (*lavishness*) prodigalité, dépense, *f.*; luxe, *m.*
Experience, *s.* expérience, *f.*; essai, *m.*; — *v.a.* éprouver; (*try*) faire l'expérience de; expérimenter [l'expérience
Experienced, *adj.* expérimenté; qui a de
Experiential, *adj.* d'expérience, acquis par l'expérience [*v.a.n.* expérimenter
Experiment, *s.* expérience, *f.*; essai, *m.*; —
Experimental, *adj.* expérimental [-trice, *f.*
Experimentalist, *s.* expérimentateur, *m.*,
Experimentally, *adv.* expérimentalement, par expérience
Experimentation, *s.* expérimentation, *f.*
Experimenter, *s.* expérimentateur, *m.*, -trice, *f.*
Expert, *adj.* expert, habile, adroit; — *s.* expert, *m.*
Expertly, *adv.* expertement, habilement, adroitement
Expertness, *s.* habileté, adresse, *f.*
Expiable, *adj.* expiable
Expiate, *v.a.* expier; réparer
Expiation, *s.* expiation, *f.*
Expiatist, Expiator, *s.* expiateur, *m.*, -trice, *f.*
Expiatory, *adj.* expiatoire, expiateur
Expiration, *s.* expiration, *f.*; cessation, *f.*; (*end*) expiration, fin, *f.*, terme, *m.*, échéance, *f.*; (*last breath*) dernier soupir, *m.*; (*obsolete*) exhalaison, évaporation, *f.*
Expire, *v.n.a.* expirer [échéance, *f.*
Expiry, *s.* expiration, fin, *f.*, terme, *m.*,
Explain, *v.a.* expliquer; (*clear up*) éclaircir; — *v.n.* s'expliquer. — **away,** expliquer; justifier
Explainable, *adj.* explicable [justifier
Explainer, *s.* explicateur, *m.*, -trice, *f.*; interprète, *m.f.*; commentateur, *m.*, -trice, *f.*
Explanation, *s.* explication, *f.*; éclaircissement, *m.* [plication (de), qui explique
Explanatory, *adj.* explicatif; (*of*) en ex-
Expletive, *adj.* explétif; — *s.* explétif, *m.*; (*coarse language*) gros mot, *m.*, gros mots,

m.pl., mot injurieux, *m.*, injure, *f.*; (*oath*) juron, *m.*, jurons, *m.pl.*
Expletively, *adv.* explétivement
Explicable, &c. *V.* **Explainable,** &c.
Explicit, *adj.* explicite; (*pers.*) clair; — *s.* [explicit, *m.*
Explicitly, *adv.* explicitement
Explicitness, *s.* explicité, *f.*
Explode, *v.n.* faire explosion, explosionner; éclater; — *v.a.* faire éclater; (*a mine*) faire sauter; (*fig.*) condamner; proscrire; rejeter, mettre de côté; abandonner
Exploding, *s.* (*of mines*) sautage, *m.*
Exploit, *s.* exploit, haut fait, fait d'armes, *m.*
Explorable, *adj.* explorable
Exploration, *s.* exploration, *f.*
Explorative, Exploratory, *adj.* exploratif; d'exploration
Exploratively, *adv.* explorativement
Explore, *v.a.* explorer; examiner; sonder
Explorer, *s.* explorateur, *m.*, -trice, *f.* [tion, *f.*
Exploring, *adj.* explorateur; — *s.* explora-
Explosion, *s.* explosion, *f.*
Explosive, *adj.* explosif; explosible; — *s.* substance explosible, *f.*
Explosiveness, *s.* explosibilité, *f.*
Exponent, *s.* exposant, *m.*; (*fig.*) interprète, *m.f.*; représentant, *m.*
Exponential, *adj.* exponentiel
Export, *v.a.* exporter; — *s.* *V.* **Exportation**
Exportable, *adj.* exportable
Exportation, *s.* exportation, *f.* — **duty,** *s.* droit de sortie, *m.* — **trade,** *s.* commerce d'exportation, *m.*
Exporter, *s.* exportateur, *m.*, -trice, *f.* (de ...)
Expose, *v.a.* exposer; montrer; découvrir; faire connaître; démasquer; pilorier. *To — oneself*, s'exposer, se montrer, &c.; se donner en spectacle, s'afficher; se rendre ridicule
Exposer, *s.* personne qui expose *or* &c. (*V.* **Expose,** *v.a.*), *f*, exposeur, *m.*
Exposition, *s.* exposition, *f.* [explicatif
Expositive, Expository, *adj.* expositif;
Expositor, *s.* exposeur, *m.*, interprète, *m.f.*, commentateur, *m.*, -trice. *f.*
Ex post facto, *adv. adj.* après coup; (*of a law*) avec effet rétroactif
Expostulate. *V.* **Remonstrate**
Expostulation, *s.* plainte, *f.*; remontrance, *f.*; reproche, *m.*
Expostulator, *s.* remontreur, *m.*
Expostulatory, *adj.* de plainte; de remontrance; de reproche
Exposure, *s.* exposition, *f.*; exposition à l'air, *f.*; exposition au froid, *f.*; danger, péril, *m.*; éclat, scandale, esclandre, *m.*
Expound, *v.a.* exposer; expliquer; interpréter
Expounder, *s.* *V.* **Expositor**
Expounding, *s.* exposition, *f.*; explication, *f.*; interprétation, *f.*
Express, *v.a.* exprimer; représenter; désigner; — *adj.* exprès; précis, exprès; formel; (*of rail. trains*) express, direct; (*adverb.*) exprès, expressément; — *s.* exprès, *m.*; (*rail. train*) express, train express, train direct, *m.*
Expressible, *adj.* exprimable
Expression, *s.* expression, *f.*
Expressive, *adj.* expressif; (*of*) qui exprime. *To be — of*, exprimer
Expressively, *adv.* expressivement, d'une manière expressive, avec expression
Expressiveness, *s.* nature expressive, *f.*; force d'expression, énergie, *f.*
Expressly, *adv.* expressément; formellement
Expropriate, *v.a.* exproprier
Expropriation, *s.* expropriation, *f.*
Expugnable, *adj.* expugnable
Expulsion, *s.* expulsion, *f.*
Expulsive, *adj.* expulsif
Expunction, *s.* exponction, *f.*
Expunge, *v.a.* rayer, effacer, retrancher
Expurgate, *v.a.* expurger, purger
Expurgation, *s.* expurgation, purgation, *f.*
Expurgatorial, Expurgatory, *adj.* expurgatoire
Exquisite, *adj.* exquis; consommé; (*keen*) vif, excessif, extrême; atroce; — *s.* élégant, *m.*, e, *f.*; homme tiré à quatre épingles, *m.*, petit-maître, *m.*, petite-maîtresse, *f.*; (*thing*) exquis, *m.*
Exquisitely, *adv.* exquisement, d'une manière exquise, parfaitement; complètement; (*keenly*) vivement, excessivement
Exquisiteness, *s.* nature exquise, *f.*, exquis, *m.*, excellence, délicatesse, perfection, *f.*; violence, *f.*
Exsiccant, &c. *V.* **Desiccant,** &c.
Exsudation, *s.* exsudation, *f.*
Exsude, *v.n.* exsuder; — *v.a.* faire exsuder
Extant, *adj.* qui existe, existant, qui subsiste, subsistant; actuel
Extemporaneous, Extemporary, *adj.* improvisé, impromptu, extemporané. — *speaker*, improvisateur, *m.*, -trice, *f.* — *speaking*, improvisation, *f.*
Extemporaneously, Extemporarily, *adv.* en improvisant, sans préparation, d'abondance, impromptu, extemporanément
Extemporaneousness, *s.* extemporanéité, *f.*
Extempore, *adv.* *V.* **Extemporaneously;** — *adj.* improvisé, impromptu; — *s.* improvisation, *f.*; impromptu, *m.* *To speak* or *deliver* —, improviser
Extemporization, *s.* improvisation, *f.*
Extemporize, *v.a.n.* improviser
Extemporizer, *s.* improvisateur, *m.*, -trice, *f.*
Extemporizing, *adj.* improvisateur
Extend, *v.a.* étendre; prolonger; continuer; (*time*) prolonger; (*hold out, reach forth*) tendre; — *v.n.* s'étendre; se prolonger
Extendible, *adj.* extensible, susceptible d'extension, qu'on peut étendre, qui peut s'étendre
Extending,—frame, *adj.* (*of tables*) à rallonges
Extensi-bility, bleness. *V.* page 3, § 1
Extensible, *adj.* *V.* **Extendible**
Extension, *s.* extension, *f.*; prolongement, *m.*; (— *of time*) délai, atermoiement, *m.*
Extensive, *adj.* étendu, vaste, grand, considérable, spacieux
Extensively, *adv.* amplement, grandement, considérablement, beaucoup, bien; (*far*) au loin; bien
Extensiveness, *s.* vaste étendue, étendue, *f.*
Extenso (In), *adv.* in extenso
Extensor, *s. adj.* extenseur, *s.m.*, *adj.m.*
Extent, *s.* étendue, *f.*; degré, point, *m.*; (*bearing*) portée, *f.* *To a certain —, to some —*, jusqu'à un certain point. *To a great —*, considérablement, à un haut degré; en grande partie. *To the — of*, jusqu'au bout de; jusqu'à concurrence de; jusqu'à
Extenuate, *v.a.* exténuer; (*lessen*) atténuer
Extenuation, *s.* exténuation, *f.*; (*palliation*) atténuation, *f.*; (*alleviation*) mitigation, *f.*, adoucissement, *m.*
Exterior, *adj.* extérieur; externe; (*to*) en dehors (de); — *s.* extérieur, *m.*; —**s,** *s. pl.* *V.* [**Externals**
Exteriority, *s.* extériorité, *f.*
Exteriorly, *adv.* extérieurement
Exterminate, *v.a.* exterminer; extirper, déraciner; (*alg.*) éliminer
Exterminating, *adj.* exterminateur
Extermination, *s.* extermination, *f.*; extirpation, *f.*; (*alg.*) élimination, *f.* [-trice, *f.*
Extermina-tor, tress, *s.* exterminateur,
Exterminatory, *adj.* exterminateur, d'ex- [termination
Extern, *s. adj.* externe, *m.f.*
External, *adj.* externe; extérieur; extrinsèque; —**s,** *s. pl.* choses extérieures, *f.pl.*, extérieur, *m.*, dehors, *m.pl.*; pratiques extéri- [eures, *f.pl*
Externality, *s* extériorité, *f.*
Externally, *adv.* extérieurement, à l'extérieur, au dehors
Exterraneous, *adj.* étranger
Exterritoriality, *s.* exterritorialité, *f*

Extinct, *adj.* éteint; aboli. *To become* (or *grow*) —, s'éteindre; tomber en désuétude
Extinction, *s.* extinction, *f.*
Extinguish, *v.a.* éteindre; détruire, faire cesser; éclipser, surpasser
Extinguishable, *adj.* extinguible
Extinguisher, *s.* (*pers.*) éteigneur, *m.*, -euse, *f.*; (*thing: for lights*) éteignoir, *m.*, (*for fire*) extincteur, *m.*; (*fig.*) éteignoir, *m.* [tinction, *f.*
Extinguishing, *adj.* extincteur; — *s.* ex-
Extinguishment, *s.* extinction, *f.*; aboli-
Extirpable, *adj.* extirpable [tion, *f.*
Extirpate, *v.a.* extirper; déraciner
Extirpation, *s.* extirpation, *f.*
Extirpator, *s.* extirpateur, *m.* [vanter, prôner
Extol, *v.a.* élever, exalter, louer; célébrer;
Extoller, *s.* panégyriste, *m.*, louangeur, *m.*, -euse, *f.*; prôneur, *m.*, -euse, *f.*
Extorsive, *adj.* *V.* **Extortionate**
Extorsively, *adv.* par extorsion
Extort, *v.a.* extorquer (à); arracher (à); — *v.n.* commettre une extorsion
Extorter. *V.* **Extortioner**
Extortion, *s.* extorsion, exaction, *f.*; violence, *f.*
Extortionary, Extortionate, *adj.* extorsionnaire [acteur, *m.*
Extortioner, *s.* extorqueur, *m.*, -euse, *f.*, ex-
Extra, *adv. adj. prep.* en sus; d'extra; extraordinaire; additionnel; supplémentaire, de supplément, de plus; de surcroît; de renfort; (*before an adj.*) extra; — *s.* extra, *m.*; supplément, *m.* — **charge,** *s.* (*com.*) frais en sus, *m.pl.*; (*admin.*, *print.*) surcharge, *f.*; (*post.*) *V.* — **postage.** — **fine, -refined, -superfine,** *adj.* extrafin. — **horse,** *s.* cheval de renfort, *m.* — **judicial,** &c. [*See below*]. — **pay,** *s.* *V.* **Pay.** — **postage,** *s.* taxe d'affranchissement supplémentaire, taxe supplémentaire, surtaxe, *f.* — **stamp,** *s.* timbre supplémentaire. — **weight,** *s.* excédant, *m.*; (*burden*) surcharge, *f.*
Extract, *v.a.* extraire (de); (*fig.*) retirer (de), recueillir (de), tirer (de); (*a tooth*) arracher (à), extraire (à); — *s.* extrait, *m.* — *of lead*, extrait de saturne, *m.*
Extracting, *adj.* extracteur; — *s.* extraction, *f.*
Extraction, *s.* extraction, *f.* [extractif, *s.m.*
Extractive, *adj. s.* extractif, *adj.m.*, -ive, *f.*,
Extrac-tor, tress, *s.* extracteur, *m.*, -trice, *f.*; arracheur, *m.*, -euse, *f.*; (*surg.*) instrument pour l'extraction (de ...), appareil extracteur, *m.*; curette, *f.*; forceps, *m.*; tenette, *f.*
Extradition, *s.* extradition, *f.*
Extrados, *s.* extrados, *m.*; — *v.a.* extradosser
Extrajudicial, *adj.* extrajudiciaire
Extrajudicially, *adv.* extrajudiciairement
Extralegal, *adj.* extralégal
Extramundane, *adj.* qui se trouve hors du monde matériel, imaginaire [extra-muros
Extramural, *adj.*, **Extra-muros,** *adv.*
Extraneous, *adj.* étranger (à), en dehors (de)
Extraordinaries, *s. pl.* choses extraordinaires, *f.pl.*, cas extraordinaires, *m.pl.*, extraordinaire, *m.*
Extraordinarily, *adv.* extraordinairement
Extraordinariness, *s.* nature extraordinaire, *f.*, extraordinaire, *m.*, rareté, singularité, *f.*
Extraordinary, *adj. s.* extraordinaire, *adj. m.f.*, *s.m.*
Extraparochial, *adj.*, **Extraparochially,** *adv.* (*civil*) hors de la commune; (*eccl.*) hors de la paroisse
Extravaganc-e, y, *s.* extravagance, *f.*; (*of expenses*) folle dépense, *f.*, folles dépenses, folies, *f.pl.*; prodigalité, *f.*; (*waste*) gaspillage, *m.*
Extravagant, *adj.* extravagant; dépensier, prodigue; (*wasteful*) gaspilleur, gâcheur; (*of prices*) exorbitant, fou; — *s.* extravagant, *m.*, e, *f.*
Extravagantly, *adv.* extravagamment, d'une manière extravagante; excessivement; (*of expenses*) prodigalement, follement

Extravaganza, *s* extravagance, *f.*
Extravasate, *v.a.* extravaser, faire extravaser, épancher. *To be —d*, être extravasé, être épanché; s'extravaser, s'épancher
Extravasation, *s.* extravasation, *f.*, épanchement, *m.*
Extreme, *adj.* extrême; — *s.* extrême, *m.*; extrémité, *f.*; (*height*) comble, *m.* *In the* —, extrêmement. *To an* —, à l'extrême, jusqu'à l'extrémité. *To carry to —s*, pousser à l'extrême. *—s meet*, les extrêmes se touchent
Extremely, *adv.* extrêmement; excessivement; infiniment; au possible
Extremis (In), *adv.* in extremis
Extremity, *s.* extrémité, *f.*; bout, *m.*; cas extrême, *m.*; (*height*) comble, *m.* *To drive to* —, pousser à bout [dégager (de)
Extricate, *v.a.* tirer (de); débarrasser (de);
Extrication, *s.* débarrassement, *m.*; dégagement, *m.*; délivrance, *f.*
Extrinsic, -al, *adj.* extrinsèque
Extrinsically, *adv.* extrinsèquement
Extroversion, *s.* extroversion, *f.*
Extrude, *v.a.* expulser; repousser
Extrusion, *s.* expulsion, *f.* [dance, *f.*
Exuberanc-e, y, *s.* exubérance, surabon-
Exuberant, *adj.* exubérant, surabondant
Exuberantly, *adv.* exubéramment, surabondamment
Exuberate, *v.n.* exubérer, surabonder
Exude. *V.* **Exsude**
Exulcerate, *v.a.* (*med.*) exulcérer; (*fig.*) ulcérer; — *v.n.* (*med.*) s'exulcérer; (*fig.*) s'ulcérer [(*fig.*) ulcération, *f.*
Exulceration, *s.* (*med.*) exulcération, *f.*;
Exult, *v.n.* se réjouir (de); triompher ('*over*,' de, sur; '*at*,' de)
Exultant, *adj.* joyeux, triomphant
Exultation, *s.* joie, allégresse, *f.*; triomphe, *m.*
Exulting, *adj.* joyeux, triomphant
Exultingly, *adv.* avec joie; d'un air de
Exutory, *s.* exutoire, *m.* [triomphe
Exuviability, *s* exuviabilité, *f.*
Exuviable, *adj.* exuviable
Exuviæ, *s. pl.* dépouilles, *f.pl.*
Exuviate, *v.n.* changer de peau
Exuviation, *s.* changement de peau, *m.*
Eye, *s.* œil, *m.*; (*eyes*) yeux, *m.pl.*; (*sight*) vue, *f.*; (*look, looks*) regard, *m.*, regards, *m.pl.*; (*of needles, and shuttles*) trou, *m.*; (*of hooks*) porte, *f.*; (*of cheese*, &c.) œil, *m.*; (*of plants*) œil, bouton, *m.*; (*arch.*) œil, *m.*; (*persp.*) point de vue, *m.*; (*wind's*) lit, *m.*; (*nav.*) œillet, *m.*; (*brood*) couvée, nichée, *f.*; — *v.a.* regarder; observer, considérer; (*watch*) avoir l'œil sur, surveiller, suivre des yeux, ne pas perdre de vue; (*ogle*) lorgner. *By the* —, à l'œil, à vue d'œil. *As far as the — can reach*, aussi loin que la vue peut s'étendre. *Farther than the — can reach*, à perte de vue. *In my, your*, &c. — *s*, (*fig.*) à mes, vos, &c. yeux. *With an — of*, d'un œil de. *With an — to*, en vue de. *With the naked* —, à l'œil nu. *To cast o.'s —s on*, jeter les yeux sur. *To cry o.'s —s out*, pleurer à en perdre la vue. *To get a black —, a pair of black —s*, se faire pocher l'œil, les yeux. *To give anyone a black* — (or *a pair of black —s*), pocher l'œil (*or* les yeux) à quelqu'un. *To have an — to*, (*watch*) avoir l'œil à, ne pas perdre de vue; (*have in view*) avoir en vue; (*pay regard*) avoir égard à. *To have* or *keep an — upon, to give an — to*, avoir l'œil sur, surveiller. *To have bad —s*, avoir mal aux yeux; (*a bad sight*) avoir la vue mauvaise. *To have in o.'s* —, avoir dans l'œil; (*fig.*) avoir en vue. *To have o.'s —s about one* (*oneself*), avoir les yeux ouverts. *To put out anyone's —s*, crever les yeux à quelqu'un. *That's all my* —, tout cela est bel et bon. — **ache,** *s.* mal à l'œil, *m.* — **ball,** *s.* globe de l'œil, *m.*, prunelle de l'œil, *f.* — **bath,** *s.* œillère, *f.*, bassin (*m.*) *or* baignoire (*f.*) ocu-

laire. — **bright,** *s.* eufraise, *f.* — **brow,** *s.* sourcil, *m.* — **cap,** *s.* (*of a telescope*) œilleton, *m.* — **cup,** *s.* *V.* — **bath.** — **doctor,** *s.* oculiste, *m.* — **drop,** *s.* larme, *f.* — **flap,** *s.* œillère, *f.* — **glance,** *s.* coup d'œil, regard, *m.*, œillade, *f.* — **glass,** *s.* lunette, *f.*; (*spectacles*) lunettes, *f.pl.*; (*quizzing-glass*) lorgnon, *m.*; (*magnifying*) loupe, *f.*; (*opt.*) verre oculaire; (— *bath*) *V.* — **bath.** *Double — glass*, binocle, *m.* *Folding — glass*, face à main, *f.* *Single — glass*, monocle, *m.* — **hole,** *s.* orbite de l'œil, *m.* — **hospital, -infirmary,** *s.* hôpital pour les maladies des yeux, *m.* — **lash,** *s.* cil, *m.* —**less,** *adj.* sans yeux; (*blind*) aveugle. — **let,** — **let-hole,** *s.* œillet, *m.* — **lid,** *s.* paupière, *f.* — **offending,** *adj.* qui blesse la vue. — **piece,** *s.* (*opt.*) oculaire, *m.* — **pit,** *s.* (*of horses*) salière, *f.* — **pleasing,** *adj.* qui plaît à l'œil. — **preservers,** *s. pl.* conserves pour les yeux, *f.pl.* — **reach,** *s.* portée de la vue, *f.* — **salve,** *s.* collyre, *m.* — **shade,** *s.* garde-vue, abat-jour, *m.* — **shaped,** *adj.* oculiforme. — **shot,** *s.* (*reach*) portée de la vue, *f.*; (*glance*) coup d'œil, *m.* — **sight,** *s.* vue, *f.* — **sore,** *s.* mal d'yeux, mal aux yeux, mal à l'œil, *m.*; (*fig.*) chose (*f.*) *or* objet (*m.*) désagréable à l'œil (*or* à la vue). *That man is an — sore to me*, la vue de cet homme-là me déplaît, je ne peux pas voir cet homme-là. — **string,** *s.* fibre de l'œil, *f.* — **tooth,** *s.* dent œillère, *f.* — **vein,** *s.* (*of horses*) larmier, *m.* — **wash, -water,** *s.* eau pour les yeux, *f.*, collyre, *m.* — **witness,** *s.* témoin oculaire, *m.*

Eyed, *adj.* (*in compounds*) aux yeux ..., qui a les yeux ... *One- —, adj. s.* borgne. *In the kingdom of the blind the one — man is a king*, au royaume des aveugles les borgnes sont rois

Eyot, *s.* îlot, *m.*

Eyre, *s.* tournée, *f.* *Justice in —*, juge qui va en tournée, juge ambulant, *m.*

Eyrie, Eyry, *s.* aire, *f.*

F

F, *s.* (*letter*) f, *f.*; (*mus.*) fa, *m.* — *sharp*, (*mus.*) fa dièse, *m.*; (*flea*) puce, *f.*

Fa, *s.* (*mus.*) fa, *m.*; clé de fa, *f.*

Fabaceous, *adj.* de fève

Fabian, *adj.* temporisateur, de temporisation

Fable, *s.* fable, *f.*; — *v.n.* inventer *or* composer des fables; (*to lie*) conter une fable, faire un mensonge, mentir; — *v.a.* inventer, feindre, imaginer, supposer, prétendre. — **book,** *s.* livre de fables, fablier, *m.*

Fabled, *part. adj.* inventé, &c. (*V.* **Fable,** *v.a.n.*); fabuleux; de la fable; célèbre dans la mythologie

Fabler, *s.* inventeur *or* conteur de fables, *m.*; [fabuliste, *m.*

Fabliau, *s.* fabliau, *m.*

Fabric, *s.* fabrique, *f.*; édifice, *m.*; structure, *f.*; système, *m.*; (*workmanship*) ouvrage, *m.*; (*texture*) tissu, *m.*; étoffe, *f.*

Fabricate, *v.a.* fabriquer; (*build*) construire

Fabrication, *s.* fabrication, *f.*; construction, *f.*

Fabrica-tor, tress, *s.* fabricateur, *m.*, -trice, *f.*

Fabulist, *s.* fabuliste, *m.*

Fabulous, *adj.* fabuleux; — *s.* fabuleux, *m.*

Fabulously, *adv.* fabuleusement

Fabulousness, *s.* fabulosité, nature fabuleuse, *f.*

Façade, *s.* façade, *f.*

Face, *s.* face, *f.*; surface, *f.*; (*pers.*) visage, *m.*; (*fam.*) figure, *f.*; face, *f.*; (*in high style*) face, *f.*, visage, *m.*; (*jest.*) nez, *m.*; (*wry face*) grimace, *f.*; (*boldness*) front, *m.*, audace, hardiesse, impudence, *f.*; (*look*) physionomie, mine, *f.*, air, *m.*; aspect, *m.*, apparence, *f.*; (*of affaires*) face, situation, *f.*, état, *m.*; (*sight*) présence, vue, *f.*; (*front*) face, façade, *f.*, devant, *m.*; (*of diamonds*) facette, *f.*; (*of a watch or clock*) cadran, *m.*; (*of stuffs*,) endroit, *m.*, (*of a hammer*) tête, *f.*; (*of an anvil*) table, *f.*; (*of walls, of stones*) parement, *m.*; (*of a cannon*) tranche, *f.*; (*print.*) œil, *m.* — *to* —, face à face. *Before* or *in* or *to the — of*, à la face de; en face de; en présence de, devant; (*fam.*) à la barbe de, au nez de. *To make —s*, faire des grimaces. *To put on a new —*, changer de visage. *To put a good — on the matter*, faire bonne contenance. *To set o.'s — against*, s'opposer à, se montrer contraire à, repousser. *To show o.'s —*, se montrer, paraître, se présenter. *To wash o.'s —*, se laver la figure, se débarbouiller. *He struck him in the —*, il le frappa au visage. *He spat in his —*, il lui cracha au visage *or* à la figure. *She shut the door* or *laughed in his —*, elle lui ferma la porte *or* lui rit au nez. *Look at me in the —*, regardez-moi en face. *I will tell him so to his —*, je le lui dirai en face. — **ague,** *s.* névralgie faciale, *f.*, tic douloureux, *m.* — **guard,** *s.* masque, *m.* —**less,** *adj.* sans face. — **painter,** *s.* *V.* **Portrait painter;** (*maker-up of ladies' faces*) maquilleuse, *f.* — **painting, -making,** *s.* *V.* **Portrait painting;** (*making up ladies' faces*) maquillage, *m.*

Face, *v.a.* faire face à; affronter, braver; résister à; regarder en face; (*a garment*) mettre un revers *or* &c. (*V.* **Facing,** *s.*) à; (*adorn*) orner, décorer; (*a card*) tourner; — *v.n.* se faire un visage, se donner de faux dehors; (*mil.*) faire front. *To — to the right*, (*mil.*) faire par le flanc droit. *To — about*, faire face; (*mil.*) faire volte-face. *Face about!* (*mil. command*) volte-face! *To — down*, (*a person*) déconcerter à force d'effronterie, dévisager; (*a thing*) soutenir effrontément. *To — it out*, payer d'audace *or* d'effronterie

Faced, *adj.* à visage ..., à figure ...; de visage. *Double —, two —*, à deux visages. *Ugly —*, laid de visage. — *with*, à revers de

Facet, *s.* facette, *f.*

Facetiæ, *s. pl.* facéties, *f.pl.*

Facetious, *adj.* facétieux

Facetiously, *adv.* facétieusement

Facetiousness, *s.* nature *or* humeur facétieuse, facétie, plaisanterie, *f.*

Facetted, *adj.* facetté, à facettes

Facetting, *s.* facettage, *m.*

Facial, *adj.* facial

Facile, *adj.* facile, complaisant

Facileness, *s.* facilité, complaisance, *f.*

Facilitate, *v.a.* faciliter

Facilitation, *s.* action de faciliter, *f.*

Facility, *s.* facilité, *f.*

Facing, *prep.* en face de, vis-à-vis de; — *s.* (*of garments: on the breast*) revers, *m.*, (*on the sleeves*) parement, *m.*, (*on the skirt*) retroussis, *m.*; (*build.*) revêtement, parement, *m.*; (*ornament*) dehors, ornement extérieur, *m.*; (*mil.*) front, *m.*

Fac-similar, *adj.* fac-similaire

Fac-simile, *s.* fac-simile, *m.*; — *v.a.* fac-similer

Fact, *s.* fait, *m.* *Matter of —*, *V.* **Matter.** *In —*, en fait; dans le fait; au fait; par le fait, de fait; en effet, effectivement. *In the —*, *V.* **Act.** *To know for a* (*positive*) —, savoir de science certaine

Faction, *s.* faction, *f.*

Factionist, *s.* factieux, *m.*, -euse, *f.*

Factious, *adj.* factieux; de faction

Factiously, *adv.* factieusement, en factieux

Factiousness, *s.* esprit de faction, *m.*

Factitious, *adj.* factice

Factitiously, *adv.* facticement

Factitiousness, *s.* nature factice, *f.*

Facto (De), *adv.* de fait

Factor, *s.* agent, *m.*; (*com., math.*) facteur, *m.*

Factorage, *s.* factorage, *m.*

Factoress, *s.* factrice, *f.*

Factorship, *s.* factorat, *m.*

Factory, *s.* manufacture, fabrique, *f.*; usine, *f.*; ateliers, *m. pl.*; (*foreign establishment*)

comptoir, *m.* — **act,** *s.* loi sur les manufactures *or* fabriques, *f.*

Factotum, *s.* factotum, *m.*

Facula, *s.* (*astr.*) facule, *f.*

Faculty, *s.* (*power*) faculté, *f.*; (*ability*) talent, m., moyens, *m.pl.*; (*univers., med.*) faculté, *f.*

Faddle, *v.n.* baliverner, baguenauder

Fade, *v.n.* — **away,** se faner, se flétrir, passer; (*fig.*) s'évanouir; s'effacer; (*to waste*) périr, dépérir, mourir; languir; — *v.a.* faner, [flétrir

Fæcal, Fæces. *V.* **Fecal, Feces**

Fag, *v.n.* fatiguer, se lasser; (*work*) piocher, travailler; — *v.a.* fatiguer; faire travailler, faire aller; — *s.* homme de peine, *m.*; (*in schools*) serviteur, souffre-douleur, *m.*; (*of mental work*) piocheur, *m.*, -euse, *f.*; (*of cloth*) nœud, *m.* — **end,** *s.* (*of cloth*) chef, *m.*; (*last end*) queue, *f.*; (*refuse*) rebut, *m.*, queue, *f.*; (*nav.*) bout, *m.*

Fagot, Faggot, *s.* fagot, *m.*; (*engin.*) fascine, *f.*; (*false muster*) passe-volant, *m.*; — *v.a.* fagoter. — **band,** *s.* hart (*f.*) *or* lien (*m.*) de fagot

Fail, *v.n.* faillir, manquer; (*decay*) tomber, défaillir, faiblir; (*not to succeed*) échouer, ne pas réussir; être impuissant (à); (*miss*) manquer (de); (*com.*) faire faillite; — *v.a.* (*disappoint*) manquer à, faire défaut à; (*be wanting to*) faire faute à; (*desert*) abandonner. *I shall not* — (*to do so*), je n'y manquerai pas

Fail, *s.* *V.* **Failure.** *Without* —, sans faute

Failing, *s.* faute, *f.*; défaut, *m.*; imperfection, *f.*; (*weakness*) faiblesse, défaillance, *f.*; (*com.*) faillite, *f.*; — *adj.* qui manque; qui s'affaiblit, défaillant; affaibli; délabré; — *prep.* à (*or* au) défaut de

Failure, *s.* manque, défaut, *m.*; (*decay*) affaiblissement, *m.*; (*of success*) insuccès, *m.*; chute, *f.*; affaire manquée, *f.*; coup manqué, *m.*; échec, *m.*; (*fam.*) fiasco, *m.*, cacade, *f.*; (*com.*) faillite, *f.* *In* or *on* — *of,* à (*or* au) défaut de

Fain, *adj.* fort aise; trop heureux; bien obligé, forcé, contraint; — *adv.* volontiers; bien

Faint, *adj.* faible; languissant; affaibli; défaillant; léger; (*cast down*) abattu; (*indolent*) mou; timide; (*of colours, light, sound*) faible; — *v.n.* — **away,** s'évanouir, se trouver mal, tomber en défaillance, défaillir, perdre connaissance; (*be weak*) faiblir; s'affaiblir; (*be cast down*) perdre courage, se laisser abattre; (*be overfatigued,* &c.) tomber de fatigue, tomber, n'en pouvoir plus; succomber; (*disappear*) disparaître, s'évanouir. — *heart never won fair lady,* jamais honteux n'eut belle amie. — **hearted,** *adj.* timide, pusillanime; abattu, découragé. — **heartedly,** *adv.* pusillanimement, avec pusillanimité; avec découragement. — **heartedness,** *s.* timidité, pusillanimité, *f.*; abattement, découragement, *m.*

Fainting, *adj.* défaillant; — *s.* évanouissement, *m.*, défaillance, faiblesse, *f.*; découragement, abattement, *m.* — *fit,* évanouissement, *m.*, syncope, *f.* *In a — fit,* évanoui, sans con- [naissance

Faintish, *adj.* un peu faible

Faintishness, *s.* légère faiblesse, *f.*

Faintly, *adv.* faiblement; mollement, sans vigueur; languissamment; légèrement, imparfaitement; timidement

Faintness, *s.* faiblesse, *f.*; langueur, *f.*; mollesse, *f.*, manque de vigueur, *m.*; (*depression*) abattement, *m.*

Fair, *adj.* (*handsome, beautiful*) beau; (*of complexion*) blond; (*of the skin*) blanc; (*clear*) clair; pur; net; (*good*) bon; (*favourable*) bon, favorable; (*likely to succeed*) bon, beau; (*just, equal*) juste, honnête; de bonne guerre; bien; (*frank*) loyal, franc; (*tolerable*) raisonnable, honnête, suffisant; assez bon; (*proper*) convenable; (*mild*) doux; de douceur; (*com., of goods*) courant; — *adv.* *V.* **Fairly;** (*friendly*) en bons termes, bien; (*of writing*) au net; — *s.* (*ladies*) dames, femmes, *f.pl.*; (*market*) foire, *f.* — *and softly,* tout beau. — *and square,* rondement. *To bid* or *promise* —, *V.* **Bid.** *To carry it* —, avoir belle apparence. *To stand* —, être en bons termes (avec), être (*or* se mettre) bien (avec); (*be in a fair way*) être en voie (de), être en passe (de); être en passe (d'avoir). *That is not* —, (*at play*) cela n'est pas du jeu. — **complexioned,** *adj.* blond; qui a la peau blanche. — **dealing,** *adj.* loyal, honnête; *s.* loyauté, honnêteté, probité, bonne foi. *f.* — **faced,** *adj.* qui a un beau visage, bien de figure. — **field, -ground, -piece,** *s.* champ de foire, *m.* — **haired,** *adj.* blond. — **one,** *s.* belle, *f.* — **play,** *s.* *V.* **Play.** — **price,** *s.* juste prix, prix raisonnable, *m.* — **show,** *s.* spectacle *or* théâtre forain, théâtre de la foire, *m.* — **spoken,** *adj.* qui s'exprime en bons termes; affable; doucereux, mielleux. — **time,** *s.* temps de foire, *m.*

Fairing, *s.* foire, *f.*

Fairish, *adj.* assez bien, passable

Fairly, *adv.* bien; favorablement; honnêtement; loyalement, de bonne foi; franchement; avec justice; avec impartialité; raisonnablement; assez bien; doucement, avec douceur; agréablement; complètement

Fairness, *s.* beauté, *f.*; (*of the complexion*) blancheur, *f.*; (*of the hair*) couleur blonde, *f.*; (*clearness*) clarté, pureté, netteté, *f.*; (*equity*) équité, impartialité, justice, *f.*; honnêteté, *f.*; (*frankness*) loyauté, bonne foi, franchise, *f.*; (*mildness*) douceur, *f.*

Fairy, *s.* fée, *f.*; — *adj.* féerique; de fée, de *or* des fées. — **circle,** *s.* *V.* — **ring.** — **land,** *s.* pays *or* royaume *or* empire des fées, *m.*, monde (*m.*) *or* terre (*f.*) féerique, féerie, *f.* — **like,** *adj.* comme une fée. — **queen,** *s.* reine des fées, *f.* — **ring,** *s.* (*in pastures*) cercle magique, *m.* — **scene,** *s.* féerie, *f.* — **tale,** *s.* conte de fée, *m.*

Faith, *s.* foi, *f.*; confiance, *f.*; — *int.* ma foi! vraiment! en vérité! parbleu! *In good* —, de bonne foi. *To put* — *in,* avoir foi à, ajouter foi à, croire à. —**ful,** *adj. s.* fidèle; (*of Mahometans*) croyant, *m.* —**fully,** *adv.* fidèlement (*V.* **Yours**). —**fulness,** *s.* fidélité, *f.* —**less,** *adj.* sans foi; incrédule; déloyal; infidèle (à); (*things*) perfide, trompeur. —**lessly,** *adv.* sans foi; infidèlement; déloyalement; perfidement. —**lessness,** *s.* infidélité, incrédulité, *f.*; déloyauté, perfidie, mauvaise foi, *f.*

Fake, *s.* (*nav.*) plet, *m.*, cueille, *f.*

Fakir, Fakeer, *s.* faquir, *m.*

Falcade, *s.* falcade, falque, *f.*

Falcate, Falcated, *adj.* falqué; falciforme

Falchion, *s.* glaive, *m.*; cimeterre, *m.*

Falciform, *adj.* falciforme

Falcon, *s.* (*bird, anc. cannon*) faucon, *m.*

Falconer, *s.* fauconnier, *m.*

Falconet, *s.* fauconneau, *m.*

Falconry, *s.* fauconnerie, *f.*

Faldstool, *s.* prie-Dieu, *m.*; fauteuil épiscopal, *m.*; siége pliant, pliant, *m.*

Falernian wine, Falernian, Falernum, [*s.* falerne, *m.*

Fall, *v.n.* tomber; (*throw oneself*) se jeter; (*of streams*) se jeter; (*of prices, waters*) baisser, diminuer; (*descend*) s'abaisser, descendre; (*be appeased*) s'apaiser, se calmer; (*vanish*) s'évanouir; se dissiper; (*be cast down*) être abattu; (*succumb*) succomber; (*a victim to*) périr (victime de); être (victime de); (*be killed*) être tué; (*die*) mourir, périr; (*happen*) arriver; (*befall*) tomber en partage, échoir; (*as an obligation, responsibility*) incomber (à); (*become*) devenir; (*be*) être; se trouver; (*begin*) se mettre (à); se livrer (à); (*end*) se terminer; (*of the voice*) baisser; (*of words from a speaker*) être dit *or* prononcé (par), (*of observations*) être fait (par), (*of exclamations*) échapper (à); (*into a passion, a rage*) se mettre (en); (*to blows,* &c.) en venir (à). — **again,** retomber. — **astern,**

culer. — **away,** (*lose flesh*) maigrir; (*decline*) dépérir; mourir; (*fade*) se faner, passer; (*rebel, betray*) défectionner; (*from*) se détacher (de), s'éloigner (de); abandonner, quitter; (*to*) passer (à); (*apostatize*) apostasier. — **back,** tomber en arrière; (*fig.*) retomber; se rejeter (sur), se rabattre (sur); recourir (à), avoir recours (à), avoir pour ressource; (*recoil*) reculer; (*mil.*) se replier. — **behind,** rester en arrière. — **down,** tomber par terre; tomber; (*prostrate*) se prosterner; (*crumble*) s'écrouler; s'ébouler. — **due,** arriver (*or* venir) à échéance, échoir (*part. pres.*, échéant; *part. past*, échu). — **from,** tomber de; tomber du haut de; abandonner, quitter; (*depart from*) manquer à; s'écarter de; se départir de; se désister de, renoncer à; (*of words from a speaker*) *See above, in the general senses.* — **in,** tomber dedans; tomber; (*crumble*) s'écrouler, s'affaisser; s'ébouler; s'effondrer; (*happen*) arriver, se présenter; (*mil.*) se ranger, s'aligner. — *in!* (*mil. command*) formez vos rangs! en ligne! — **in with,** s'accorder avec, être d'accord avec; approuver; se conformer à, se plier à, se prêter à; (*come in*) rentrer dans; (*meet*) rencontrer. — **into,** tomber *or* &c. dans (*or* en); entrer dans (*or* en); se conformer à; contracter. — **off,** tomber; se détacher; s'en aller; se retirer, s'éloigner; abandonner; (*decrease*) diminuer; baisser; (*die away*) se perdre, cesser; (*rebel, betray; apostatize*) *V.* — **away;** (*nav.*) faire son abattée, abattre. — **on,** tomber sur; attaquer, fondre (*or* tomber) sur; (*strike*) frapper; (*begin*) se mettre à ..., s'y mettre; (*befall*) échoir à; (*hit upon*) trouver, rencontrer. *To — on a Sunday* or *&c.*, tomber un dimanche *or* &c. — **out,** tomber dehors; tomber; (*quarrel*) se brouiller, se quereller, rompre (avec); (*happen*) arriver. — **over,** tomber par-dessus, tomber de l'autre côté de; (*rebel, betray*) passer (à). — **through,** (*fail*) échouer, tomber dans l'eau. — **to,** tomber sur; (*begin*) se mettre à ..., s'adonner à ...; s'y mettre; (*befall*) arriver à; (*as a share*) échoir à, tomber en partage à; (*devolve*) être dévolu à; (*blows*, &c.) en venir à. — **under,** tomber sous; (*succumb*) succomber à; (*be subjected*) être soumis à; (*incur*) encourir; (*be reckoned*) être compris sous *or* dans, faire partie de. — **upon,** tomber sur, &c. (*V.* — **on**); (*descend*) s'abaisser sur, descendre sur; (*as an obligation*, &c.) incomber à; être à; (*be a burden*) tomber à la charge de; (*apply*) avoir recours à; (*attempt*) essayer; entreprendre. — **with,** rencontrer. — **within,** tomber dans l'intérieur de; entrer (*or* rentrer) dans, être compris dans, faire partie de, appartenir à

Fall, *s.* chute, *f.*; (*of the night, day*) tombée (de la nuit), chute (du jour), *f.*; (*of water*) chute, cascade, *f.*; (*of some large rivers*) cataracte, *f.*; saut, *m.*; (*descent*) descente, *f.*; (*mouth*) embouchure, *f.*; (*of earth*) éboulement, *m.*; (*of snow, rain*, &c.) tombée, *f.*; quantité, *f.*; (*of wood*) coupe, *f.*, abattis, *m.*; (*autumn*) automne, *m.*, chute des feuilles, *f.*; (*declivity*) pente, *f.*; (*decrease*) diminution, *f.*; (*in the level of waters*) décrue, *f.*; (*of the mercury*) *V.* **Falling;** (*of prices*) baisse, *f.*; (*decay*) décadence, *f.*; (*of a town, taking*) prise, *f.*; (*trap*) trappe, *f.*; (*veil*) voilette, *f.* *To be on the —*, (*com.*) être en baisse, fléchir. *To give a —*, faire tomber, renverser. *To have* or *get* or *meet with a —*, faire une chute, tomber. *A heavy — of rain* or *snow*, une pluie *or* neige abondante. *There has been a — of* (*a great — of*) *snow*, il est tombé de la neige (beaucoup de neige). *There was another — of snow*, il tomba encore de la neige. — **out,** *s.* (*quarrel*) brouille, *f.*

Fallacious, *adj.* trompeur, illusoire, fallacieux

Fallaciously, *adv.* d'une manière trompeuse, illusoirement, fallacieusement

Fallaciousness, *s.* nature trompeuse, fausseté, *f.* [déception, *f.*

Fallacy, *s.* fausseté, *f.*; sophisme, *m.*; illusion,

Fallen, *part. adj.* tombé, &c. (*V.* **Fall,** *v.n.*); dévolu; (*ruined*) déchu. — *woman*, femme [perdue, *f.*

Fallibility, *s.* faillibilité, *f.*

Fallible, *adj.* faillible

Falling, *part. adj.* tombant, &c., qui tombe, &c. (*V.* **Fall,** *v.n.*); — *s.* chute, *f.*; (*crumbling*) écroulement, *m.*; (*of earth*) éboulement, *m.*; (*of waters*) décrue, *f.*; (*of the tide*) reflux, *m.*; (*of prices*) baisse, *f.*; (*of the mercury*) descente, *f.*, abaissement, *m.*; (*appeasement*) apaisement, *m.*, cessation, *f.*; (*decline*) déclin, *m.*, décadence, *f.*; (*death*) mort, perte, ruine, *f.*; (*com.*) échéance, *f.*; (*desertion*) désertion, *f.* — **away,** *s.* (*losing flesh*) amaigrissement, *m.*: (*pining*) dépérissement, *m.*; (*decline*) décadence, *f.*; (*apostasy*) apostasie, *f.*; (*desertion*) défection, *f.* — **back,** *s.* reculade, *f.*; manque de parole, *m.*; renonciation, *f.* — **down,** *s.* chute, *f.*; prosternation, *f.*; (*crumbling*) écroulement, *m.*; (*of earth*) éboulement, *m.* — **due,** *s.* échéance, *f.* — **from,** *s.* chute du haut en bas de, *f.*; abandon, *m.*, défection, *f.*; violation, *f.* — **in,** *s.* enfoncement, *m.*, (*crumbling*) écroulement, *m*; (*of earth*) éboulement, *m.*; (*coming*) arrivée, *f.*; échéance, *f.*; (*mil.*) alignement, *m.*; (*with*) adhésion (à), *f.*, assentiment (à), *m.*; approbation (de), *f.*; complaisance (pour), *f.* — **off,** *s.* chute, *f.*; diminution, baisse, *f.*; déclin, *m.*, décadence, *f.*; cessation, *f.*; abandon, *m.*, défection, *f.*; apostasie, *f.*; (*nav.*) abattée, *f.* — **out,** *s.* chute, *f.*; (*quarrel*) brouillerie, querelle, mésintelligence, rupture, *f.* — **short,** *s.* insuffisance, *f.*; état d'infériorité, *m.* — **sickness,** *s.* épilepsie, *f.*, haut mal, *m.* — **star,** *s.* étoile tombante *or* filante, *f.* — **stone,** *s.* aérolithe, *m.*

Fallopian, *adj.* de Fallope. — *tube*, trompe de Fallope, *f.*

Fallow, *adj.* (*colour*) fauve; (*agr.*) en jachère; en friche, inculte; (*fig.*) négligé, mis en suspens, mis de côté; — *s.* (*colour*) fauve, *m.*; (*land*) jachère, *f.*; friche, *f.*; (*rest*) repos, *m.*; — *v.a.* jachérer; laisser en friche *To lie —*, être en jachère; être en friche. *To let lie —*, laisser en jachère; laisser en friche. — **chat, -finch,** *s.* motteux, cul-blanc, *m.* — **crop,** *s.* récolte faite sur jachère, *f.*

Fallowing, *s.* mise en jachère, *f.*; système des jachères, *m.*

False, *adj.* faux; artificiel, postiche; feint; perfide; infidèle; (*of imprisonment*) illégal; — *adv.* faussement, faux; à faux. — **bottom,** *s.* double fond, *m.* — **dealer,** *s.* homme (*m.*) *or* femme (*f.*) de mauvaise foi. — **faced,** *adj.* hypocrite. — **heart, -hearted,** *adj.* qui a le cœur faux, perfide. — **heartedness,** *s.* perfidie, fausseté, *f.* — **imprisonment,** *s.* détention illégale, *f.*; arrestation illégale. *f.* — **swearing,** *s.* faux serments, *m.pl.*, parjure, *m.*; (*law*) faux témoignage, *m.*

Falsehood, *s.* fausseté, *f.*; (*lie*) mensonge, *m.*

Falsely, *adv.* faussement; à faux, à tort; perfidement, déloyalement

Falseness, *s.* fausseté, *f.*; duplicité, *f.*; perfidie, *f.*; infidélité, *f.* [fausset, voix de tête, *f.*

Falset, Falsetto, *s.* fausset, *m.*, voix de

Falsifiable, *adj.* falsifiable

Falsification, *s.* falsification, *f.*; faux, *m.*

Falsificator, Falsifier, *s.* falsificateur, *m.*, -trice, *f.*; (*forger*) faussaire, *m f.*; (*of coin*) faux-monnayeur, *m.*; (*liar*) menteur, *m.*, euse, *f.*, imposteur, *m.*

Falsify, *v.a.* falsifier; altérer; (*violate*) fausser; (*disprove*) prouver la fausseté de, convaincre de fausseté, réfuter, (*in law*) arguer de faux

Falsifying, *adj.* falsificateur; — *s.* falsifica- [tion, *f.*

Falsity, *s.* fausseté, *f.*

Falter, *v.n.* hésiter, balbutier; se troubler; trembler: (*totter*) chanceler

Faltering, *s.* hésitation, *f.*; balbutiement, *m.*, voix tremblante, *f.*; trouble, *m.*, agitation, *f.*; (*tottering*) chancellement, *m.*

Falteringly, *adv.* avec hésitation, en hésitant; en balbutiant, d'une voix tremblante; avec trouble, avec agitation, en tremblant; en chancelant

Falun, *s.* falun, *m.* — **bed,** *s.* falunière, *f.*

Fame, *s.* renommée, *f.*, renom, nom, *m.*, réputation, *f.*; bruit, *m.*; gloire, *f.*; (*myth.*) la Renommée, *f.*; — *v.a.* rendre fameux; répandre le bruit de. *Of ill* —, mal famé; (*of houses*) de débauche, de tolérance, public. —**less,** *adj.* sans renommée, sans nom, obscur

Famed, *adj.* renommé, célèbre, fameux, famé

Familiar, *adj.* familier; de familiarité; intime; de la famille; — *s.* familier, *m.*, intime, *m.f.*, ami (*m.*) *or* amie (*f.*) intime; démon familier, *m.* *To make* —, familiariser. *To make oneself* —, *to grow* or *get* —, se familiariser

Familiarity, *s.* familiarité, *f.* — *breeds contempt*, trop de familiarité engendre le mépris

Familiarize, *v.a.* familiariser (avec), rendre familier (avec)

Familiarly, *adv.* familièrement

Family, *s.* famille, *f.*; (*household*) maison, *f.*; — *adj.* de famille; de la famille; de *or* des familles; familial. *High* —, grande famille. *In the — way*, enceinte. — **likeness,** *s.* air de famille, *m.* — **man,** *s.* père de famille, *m.* — **tree,** *s.* arbre généalogique, *m.*

Famine, *s.* famine, *f.*

Famish, *v.a.* affamer; faire mourir de faim; — *v.n.* être affamé; mourir de faim

Famished, *adj.* affamé, mort de faim

Famous, *adj.* fameux; renommé

Famously, *adv.* avec célébrité, d'une manière éclatante; (*fam.*) fameusement, joliment, furieusement, extrêmement

Famousness, *s.* famosité, célébrité, réputation, *f.*

Fan, *s.* éventail, *m.*; (*for fires*) éventoir, *m.*; (*bellows*) soufflet, *m.*; (*winnowing-machine*) tarare, *m.*; (*spin.*) van, *m.*; (*of a wind-mill*) gouvernail, *m.*; (*ventilator*) ventilateur, *m.*; — *v.a.* éventer; (*corn*) vanner; (*fire*) souffler; activer; (*spin.*) vanner; (*fig.*) exciter, agiter, souffler; (*ventilate*) ventiler; (*refresh*) rafraîchir. — **carrier,** *s.* porte-éventail, *m* — **joint,** *s.* brisée, *f.* — **light,** *s.* fenêtre en éventail, *f.* —**like,** *adj.* en éventail. —**maker, -painter,** *s.* éventailliste, *m.f.* — **palm,** *s.* palmier à éventail, *m.* — **shaped,** *adj.* en éventail. — **stick,** *s.* bâton d'éventail, *m.* —**tail,** *s.* queue en éventail, *f.*; (*of a wind-mill*) gouvernail, *m.*; (*pigeon*) pigeon paon, *m.* — **tailed,** *adj.* (*tech.*) en queue d'aronde. — **tailed pigeon** *or* **shaker,** *s.* pigeon paon, *m.*

Fanariot, *s.* Fanariote, *m.*

Fanatic, -al, *adj.* *s.* fanatique, *m.f.*

Fanatically, *adv.* avec fanatisme, en fanatique, fanatiquement

Fanaticalness, Fanaticism, *s.* fanatisme, *m.*

Fanaticize, *v.a.* fanatiser

Fanaticizer, *s.* fanatiseur, *m.*

Fancied, *adj.* imaginé, imaginaire; supposé

Fancier, *s.* personne qui s'imagine, personne à fantaisies, *f.*, rêveur, *m.*, -euse, *f.*; (*who likes*) amateur (de), *m.*; (*dealer*) marchand (de), *m.*

Fanciful, *adj.* qui a des fantaisies, fantasque, capricieux; qui tient de l'imagination, chimérique, fantastique, fantaisiste, de fantaisie; bizarre, singulier

Fancifully, *adv.* fantastiquement; fantasquement

Fancifulness, *s.* nature fantastique *or* chimérique, *f.*; caractère fantasque *or* capricieux, *m.*; bizarrerie, singularité, *f.*

Fancy, *s.* imagination, *f.*; (*idea*) idée, *f.*; (*liking*) goût, *m.*; (*whim*) fantaisie, envie, *f.*, caprice, *m.*; (*inspiration*) verve, *f.*; (*object*) objet de fantaisie, *m.*; (*chimera*) chimère, *f.*; (*slang*) boxe, *f.*, boxeurs, *m.pl.*; — *adj.* de fantaisie; de luxe; d'agrément; imaginaire; chimérique; (*worked*) façonné; — *v.a.n.* imaginer; s'imaginer, se figurer; croire; supposer; avoir dans l'idée; (*to like*) aimer, avoir du goût pour. *To have a* —, avoir l'idée (que), avoir dans l'idée (que), se figurer (que); avoir envie (de). *To take the — of*, plaire à, sourire à; ragoûter. *To take a — to*, (*pers.*) prendre en affection or en amitié; (*of things*) prendre *or* avoir du goût pour; (*with a verb*) avoir l'idée *or* la fantaisie de, se mettre dans la tête de, prendre fantaisie de (*imp.*), avoir envie de. *She took a — to travel*, il lui prit fantaisie *or* envie de voyager, la fantaisie *or* l'envie lui prit de voyager, elle eut la fantaisie de voyager, elle se mit dans la tête de voyager, elle eut envie de voyager. *Only* (or *just*) —! figurez-vous! par exemple! — **articles,** *s.pl.* objets de fantaisie *or* de luxe, *m.pl.*; (*dress*) nouveautés, *f.pl.*; (*in ivory, tortoiseshell*, &c.) tabletterie, *f.* — **ball,** *s.* bal costumé, *m.* — **bazaar,** *s.* bazar pour les pauvres, *m.*; bazar (au profit de ...), *m.* — **coloured,** *adj.* de couleur de fantaisie. — **dog,** *s.* chien d'agrément, *m.* — **dress,** *s.* costume *or* habit de fantaisie, *m.* — **dress ball,** *s.* bal costumé, *m.* — **fair,** *s.* *V.* — **bazaar.** — **goods,** *s. pl.* *V.* — **articles.** — **monger,** *s.* visionnaire, *m.f.*, songe-creux, *m.* — **sick,** *adj.* malade imaginaire, hypocondriaque. — **stationer,** *s.* papetier de luxe, *m.*, marchand (*m.*, e, *f.*) d'objets de fantaisie; tabletier, *m.*, -ière, *f.* — **stationery,** *s.* papeterie de luxe, *f.*, objets de fantaisie, *m.pl.*; tabletterie, *f.* — **work,** *s.* (*need.*) tapisserie, *f.*; broderie, *f.*, &c.

Fandango, *s.* fandango, *m.*

Fane, *s.* temple, *m.*

Fanfare, *s.* fanfare, *f.*

Fanfaron, *s.* fanfaron, *m.*

Fanfaronade, *s.* fanfaronnade, *f.*

Fang, *s.* (*of animals*) dent canine, *f.*; (*of boars*, &c.) défense, *f.*; (*of dogs*) croc, *m.*; (*of birds*) griffe, serre, *f.*; (*of snakes, and vet.*) crochet, *m.*; (*of teeth*) racine, *f.*; (*tech.*) griffe, *f.* —**less,** *adj.* sans défenses; sans crocs; &c.

Fanged, *adj.* armé de dents *or* de défenses *or* &c. (*V.* **Fang**); (*fig.*) armé (de ...)

Fannel, *s.* fanon, *m.*

Fanner, *s.* personne qui évente, *f.*; (*of corn*) vanneur, *m.*, -euse, *f.*; (*machine*) *V.* **Fan,** *s.*

Fanning, *s.* éventement, *m.*; (*agr.*) vannage, *m.* — **machine,** *s.* *V.* **Fan,** *s.*

Fanon, *s.* fanon, *m.*

Fantasia, *s.* (*mus.*) fantaisie, *f.*; (*Arabian sport*) fantasia, *f.*

Fantasm. *V.* **Phantasm**

Fantastic, -al, *adj.* fantastique; (*odd*) fantasque

Fantastically, *adv.* fantastiquement; (*oddly*) fantasquement

Fantasticalness, *s.* nature fantastique, *f.*; (*oddness*) caractère fantasque, *m.*, bizarrerie, *f.*

Fantasy, *s.* *V.* **Fancy**

Fantoccini, *s. pl.* (— **puppets**) fantoccini, *m.pl.*, marionnettes, *f.pl.*

Faquir, *s.* faquir, *m.*

Far, *adv.* loin; au loin; (*deep, late*) avant; (*greatly, much*) beaucoup, de beaucoup, bien, fort, grandement; (*very*) très, bien, fort; (*mostly*) en grande partie; — *adj.* éloigné; lointain; reculé; (*righthand*) droit, de droite. *As — as*, aussi loin que; (*till, to, up to, down to*) jusqu'à; jusque; (*as much as*) autant que. *As — as it goes*, dans toute son étendue; jusque-là, jusqu'à ce point. *As* (or *so*) — *as that goes*, quant à cela. *By* —, de beaucoup. *How* —, jusqu'où; jusqu'à quel point; (*of distance*) combien; à quelle distance; jusqu'où. *So* —, *thus* —, (*till here*) jusqu'ici; (*till there*) jusque-là; aussi *or* si loin; (*so much*) à un tel point, tellement; (*as it stands* or *stood*) déjà, comme cela. *So — as*, autant que. *So — as to*, jusqu'à. *So — so good*, jusque-là rien de mieux, jusque-là c'est très bien. — *and near*, de loin et de près, de près comme de loin, de tous côtés. — *and wide*, au loin, bien loin, de tous côtés. — *between*, éloignés (*or* loin) l'un de l'autre; éloignés (*or* loin) les uns des autres, rares, à de longs (*or* de rares) intervalles, de loin en loin; çà et là. — *from it*, bien loin de là; tant s'en faut. — *be it from me* (*to*), loin de moi la pensée (de), à Dieu ne plaise (que). — **away,** loin, très loin, bien loin, très *or* bien éloigné (de). — **back,** loin. — **famed,** *adj.* célèbre. — **fetched,** *adj.* recherché; affecté; forcé; tiré par les cheveux. — **gone,** *adj. V.* **Gone.** — **off,** — **out,** *V.* — **away.** — **seeing,** *adj.* clairvoyant, pénétrant; prévoyant. — **sighted,** *adj.* qui a la vue longue, presbyte; (*sagacious*) *V.* — **seeing.** — **sightedness,** *s.* presbytie, vue longue, *f.*; (*fig.*) clairvoyance, pénétration, *f.*; prévoyance, *f.* — **sought,** *adj. V.* — **fetched**

Faradization, *s.* faradisation, *f.*

Farandole, *s.* farandole, *f.*

Farce, *s.* farce, *f.* — **player,** *s.* farceur, *m.*, [-euse, *f.*

Farcical, *adj.* qui tient de la farce, bouffon, burlesque; drôle, risible; illusoire

Farcically, *adv.* burlesquement; drôlement, [d'une manière risible

Farcied, *adj.* farcineux

Farcy, *s.* farcin, *m.*

Fare, *v.n.* aller, se trouver; être; être traité; réussir; se tirer d'affaire; (*of the health*) se porter; (*feed*) manger, se nourrir, vivre; être nourri; (*imp.*) aller; arriver (à); (*old*) aller, passer, voyager; — *s.* (*drive*) course, *f.*; (*price*) prix de la place *or* des places, prix, *m.*; prix du voyage, prix de transport, prix, *m.*; (*of cabs*) prix de la course, prix, *m.*; (*seat*) place, *f.*; (*pers.*) voyageur, *m.* (-euse, *f.*), -s, *pl*; (*food*) chère, nourriture, *f.*; (*dishes*) plats, mets, *m.pl.*; (*of a repast*) menu, *m.* — *by time*, course à l'heure, *f.* *List* or *table of —s*, tarif, *m.* *To pay full —*, payer place entière. *Here is my —*, *here is your —*, (*to a cabman or omnibus conductor*) voici le prix de ma place

Farewell, *adv. s.* adieu (*s.m.*); — *adj.* d'adieu. — *till we meet again*, au revoir. *To take o.'s — of*, *V.* **Bid.** — **visit,** *s.* visite d'adieu, *f.*

Farina, *s.* farine, *f.*; (*fecula*) fécule, *f.*; (*bot.*) pollen, *m.*

Farinaceous, *adj.* farineux; farinacé

Faring, *s.* voyage, *m.*; vie, manière de vivre, [*f.*; nourriture, *f.*

Farinose, *adj.* farineux

Farm, *s.* ferme, *f.*; — *adj.* de ferme. *On —* (*contract*), à ferme. — **buildings,** *s. pl.* bâtiments de ferme, *m.pl.* — **house,** *s.* ferme, *f.* — **labourer,** *s.* ouvrier de ferme, *m.* — **offices,** *s. pl.* bâtiments de ferme, *m.pl.* — **rent,** *s.* fermage, *m.* — **seed,** *s.* semence agricole, *f.* — **servant,** *s.* garçon *or* valet de ferme, *m.*, fille de ferme, *f.* — **stead,** **-steading,** *s.* ferme, *f.* — **yard,** *s.* cour de ferme, basse-cour, *f.*

Farm, *v.a.* affermer; (*cultivate*) faire valoir, exploiter. — **out,** donner à ferme

Farmable, *adj.* affermable

Farmer, *s.* fermier, *m.*, -ière, *f.*; cultivateur, *m.*, -trice, *f.*, agriculteur, *m.* —*'s wife*, fermière, *f.* — **general,** *s.* fermier général, *m.*

Farmeress, *s.* fermière, *f.*; cultivatrice, *f.*

Farmery, *s.* corps de ferme, *m.*, ferme, *f.*

Farming, *s.* exploitation d'une ferme, *f.*; agriculture, *f.*; culture, *f.*; (*contract*) affermage, fermage, *m.*

Farmost, *adj.* le plus éloigné

Farness, *s.* éloignement, *m.*

Far-niente, *s.* far-niente, *m.*

Faro, *s.* (*beer*) faro, *m.*; (*game*) pharaon, *m.*

Farrago, *s.* farrago, salmigondis, fatras, *m.*

Farrier, *s.* maréchal ferrant, maréchal, *m.*; vétérinaire, *m.*

Farriery, *s.* maréchalerie, *f.*; art vétérinaire, *m.*

Farrow, *s.* portée de petits cochons, portée, cochonnée, *f.*; — *v.n.* cochonner; — *v.a.* mettre bas; — *adj.* stérile. *With —*, pleine

Fart, *s.* pet, *m.*; — *v.n.* péter

Farther, *adv.* plus loin; (*beyond*) au-delà; (*besides*) en outre, de plus, encore; (*more*) davantage; — *adj.* plus éloigné; ultérieur; autre; nouveau; plus de ...; ... de plus; — *v.a. V.* **Further.** — **back** *or* **off** *or* **on,** *adv.* plus loin. — **end,** *s.* extrémité, *f.*; fond, *m.*

Fartherance, Farthermore. *V.* **Furtherance,** &c.

Farthest, *adv. adj. super. of* **Far.** *At —*, (*of place*) au plus loin; (*of time*) au plus tard; (*at most*) au plus. *V.* **Furthest**

Farthing, *s.* (*as the smallest copper coin*) centime, *m.*; (*as the name of the English coin*) farthing, *m.*; (*as the equivalent in French coin*) [2 centimes ½

Farthingale, *s.* vertugadin, *m.*

Fasces, *s. pl.* faisceaux, *m.pl.*

Fascia, *s.* bandelette, *f.*; (*anat.*) aponévrose, *f.*, fascia, *m.*; (*arch.*) fasce, face, plate-bande, *f.*; (*of shells, bot.*) fascie, *f.*; (*astr., surg.*) bande, *f.*

Fascial, *adj.* des faisceaux; (*anat.*) fascial

Fascicle, Fasciculus, *s.* fascicule, *m.*

Fascinate, *v.a.* fasciner; séduire

Fascinater, *s.* fascinateur, *m.*, -trice, *f.*

Fascinating, *adj.* fascinateur; séduisant

Fascination, *s.* fascination, *f.*; séduction, *f.*; charme, *m.*

Fascine, *s.* fascine, *f.* — **work,** *s.* fascinage, *m.*

Fascining, *s.* fascinage, *m.*

Fashion, *s.* (*shape*) façon, *f.*; forme, *f.*; (*pattern*) modèle, *m.*; (*manner*) manière, façon, *f.*, genre, *m.*; (*usage*) mode, *f.*; coutume, *f.*, usage, *m.*; (*vogue*) vogue, *f.*; (*tone*) ton, *m.*; (*rank*) condition, *f.*; (*high life*) grand monde, *m.*; — *v.a.* façonner; former; accommoder, adapter, approprier. *Man, woman, people of —*, homme, femme, gens à la mode (*or* de condition). *In —*, à la mode; de mode. *In this —*, de cette manière, de cette façon. *Out of —*, passé de mode, hors de mode, démodé. *To bring into —*, mettre à la mode *or* en vogue. *To come into —*, devenir (*or* venir) à la mode. *To continue in —*, rester de mode. *To get* or *grow* or *go out of —*, passer de mode, se démoder. *To lead the —*, donner le ton. *To put out of —*, mettre hors de mode, démoder. *After* or *in the English, the French*, &c. —, à la mode anglaise *or* française, &c.; à l'anglaise, à la française, &c.

Fashionable, *adj.* à la mode; de mode; de bon ton; de luxe; fashionable; en vogue; (*of the world*) beau, grand, élégant; (*pers.*) à la mode, élégant, du monde, fashionable; — *s.* élégant, *m.*, e, *f.*, fashionable, *m.f.* — *man* or *gentleman*, homme à la mode, élégant, homme du monde, fashionable, *m.* — *woman* or *lady*, femme à la mode, élégante, femme du monde, grande dame, fashionable, *f.* — *people*, gens à la mode, gens du monde, *m.pl.* — *world* or *society* or *life*, beau monde, grand monde, monde élégant, *m.*, fashion, *f.* *To make —*, mettre à la mode; mettre en vogue

Fashionableness, *s.* conformité à la mode, *f.*; élégance, *f.*; vogue, *f.* [fashionablement

Fashionably, *adv.* à la mode, élégamment,

Fast, *v.n.* jeûner; — *s.* jeûne, *m.*; (*adject.*) de jeûne. — **day,** *s.* jour de jeûne, *m.*

Fast, *adj.* (*firm*) ferme, fixe; (*strong*) fort; (*adhering*) fixé (à), attaché (à); (*faithful*) fidèle (à); (*tight*) serré; (*swift*) rapide, léger; vite; (*shut*) fermé; (*extravagant*) égrillard; viveur, dépensier; (*of sleep*) profond; (*of colours*) solide, bon teint; (*of clocks, watches*) en avance; (*rail.*) de grande vitesse; (*nav., swift*) rapide, bon marcheur; (*fastened, nav.*) amarré; — *adv.* (*firmly*) ferme; (*strongly*) fortement, fort; bien; (*of sleep*) profondément; (*swiftly*) vite, rapidement; (*often*) souvent, fréquemment; (*very*) très, fort, bien; tout. — *and loose*, trompeur, traître, double. — *man*, viveur, *m.* — *woman*, viveuse, *f.* *To be —*, (*pers.*) aimer les plaisirs. *To be —* or *too —*, (*of clocks*, &c.) avancer (de ...); être en avance. *To hold* or *stick* —, tenir ferme; (*fig.*) s'attacher (à). *To live* —, faire la vie. *To make* or *set* —, attacher; fixer, assujettir; (*doors*, &c.) fermer; (*boats*, &c.) amarrer. *To play — and loose*, agir avec duplicité, tromper; tergiverser, biaiser

Fasten, *v.a.* (*tie*) attacher; lier; (*fix*) fixer; assujettir; (*tighten*) serrer; (*doors*, &c.) fermer; (*boats*, &c.) amarrer; (*blows*) asséner; (*charge*) mettre sur le dos, imputer (à); imposer (à); (*need.*) arrêter; — *v.n.* (*on*) s'attacher (à), se cramponner (à); se fixer (sur), s'acharner (sur)

Fastening, *s.* attache, *f.*; (*of windows*, &c.) [fermeture, *f.*

Faster, *s.* jeûneur, *m.*, -euse, *f.*

Fasti, *s. pl.* fastes, *m.pl.*

Fastidious, *adj.* dédaigneux; (*over nice*) difficile; difficultueux; exigeant

Fastidiously, *adv.* dédaigneusement, d'un air dégoûté; difficultueusement

Fastidiousness, *s* dédain, *m.*; (*squeamishness*) goût difficile, *m.*; exigence, *f.*

Fasting, *s. V.* **Fast**

Fastness, *s.* fermeté, solidité, *f.*; attachement, *m.*; sûreté, *f.*; (*stronghold*) place forte, *f.*; forteresse, *f.*; fort, *m.*

Fat, *adj.* gras; gros; (*coarse*) grossier; (*dull*) épais, lourd; (*productive*) riche; — *s.* (*of meat*) gras, *m.*; (*grease, and in physiology*) graisse, *f.*; (*fig.*) substance, *f.*; — *v.a.n. V.* **Fatten.** *Rough* —, graisse de boucherie. *The — of the land*, la graisse (*or* la moelle) de la terre. *To get* or *grow* —, engraisser, s'engraisser, devenir gras. *To make* —, engraisser. *To run to* —, engraisser, prendre de l'embonpoint. *As — as a mole*, gras comme un moine

Fatal, *adj.* fatal; funeste; (*deadly*) mortel

Fatal-ism, -ist. *V.* page 3, § 1

Fatalistic, *adj.* fataliste

Fatality, *s.* fatalité, *f.* [tellement

Fatally, *adv.* fatalement; funestement; mor-

Fata Morgana, *s.* Fata Morgana, *f.*

Fate, *s.* destin, *m*, destinée, *f.*, sort, *m.*; (*death*) mort, *f*, trépas, *m.*; (*myth.*) Destin, *m.*; —**s,** *pl.* (*myth.*) Parques, *f.pl.*; — *v.a.* destiner; condamner; décréter, arrêter

Fated, *part. adj.* destiné, &c. (*V.* **Fate,** *v a.*); réglé par le destin; écrit; (*in compounds*) au sort ...

Father, *s.* père, *m.*; — *v.a.* adopter; donner pour père; avoir pour père; (*on, upon*) prêter (à), attribuer (à), imputer (à); gratifier (de). — *of a family*, père de famille. — **in-law,** *s.* beau-père, *m.* — **hood,** *s.* paternité, *f.* — **land,** *s.* pays natal, *m.*, patrie, *f.* — **lasher,** *s.* cotte, *m.* —**less,** *adj.* sans père, orphelin; anonyme. —*less child*, orphelin, *m.*, e, *f.* —**lessness,** *s.* orphelinage, *m.* — **like,** *adj. adv. V.* —**ly.** —**liness,** *s.* tendresse paternelle, *f.* —**longlegs,** *s. V.* **Daddy.** —**ly,** *adj.* paternel; de père; *adv.* paternellement; en père.

Fathom, *s* 2 mètres, *m.pl.*; (*nav.*) brasse, *f.*; (*fig.*) portée, *f.*; — *v.a.* embrasser; sonder; approfondir; pénétrer. —**less,** *s.* sans fond, insondable; (*fig.*) impénétrable. — **line,** *s.* [sonde, *f.*

Fathomable, *adj.* pénétrable

Fatid-ic, al, -ically. *V.* page 3, § 1

Fatigable, *adj.* fatigable

Fatigue, *s.* fatigue, *f.*; (*mil. extra work*) corvée, *f.*; — *v.a.* fatiguer, lasser. *On* —, (*mil.*) en corvée. — **duty, -party,** *s.* (*mil.*) corvée, *f.*

Fatiguing, *adj.* fatigant; — *part.* fatiguant

Fatimite, *s.* fatimite, *m.*

Fatling, *s.* bête grasse, *f.*, animal engraissé, *m.*

Fatly, *adv.* grassement

Fatness, *s.* embonpoint, *m.*, corpulence, *f.*; (*grease*) graisse, *f.*; (*of the earth*) fertilité, *f.*

Fatted, *part. adj.* engraissé; gras

Fatten, *v.a.* ('*on*,' '*upon*,' de) engraisser; — *v.n.* s'engraisser

Fattener, *s.* engraisseur, *m.*, -euse, *f.*

Fattening, Fatti—, *s.* engraissement, *m.*; — *part. adj.* engraissant; (*of animals*) à l'engrais

Fattiness, *s.* nature graisseuse, onctuosité, *f.*

Fatty, *adj.* grasset, grassouillet; (*of things*) graisseux, huileux [stupidité, *f.*

Fatuity, *s.* faiblesse d'esprit, imbécillité,

Fatuous, *adj.* faible d'esprit, imbécile, stupide; [vain

Faucal, *adj.* guttural

Fauces, *s. pl.* gosier, *m.*, gorge, *f. Anterior* —, avant-bouche, *f. Posterior* —, arrière bouche, *f.*, isthme du gosier, *m.*

Faucet, *s.* (*of casks*) *V.* **Tap**

Faugh. *V.* **Foh**

Fault, *s.* faute, *f.*; défaut, *m.*; (*hunt.*) défaut, *m.*; (*mining, geol.*) faille, *f. At* —, en défaut; embarrassé. *To find — with*, trouver à redire à, trouver mal, trouver mauvais, blâmer, s'en prendre à; critiquer. *Whose — is it?* à qui la faute? — **finder,** *s.* frondeur, *m.*, -euse, *f.*, critiqueur, *m.*, -euse, *f.*, critique, censeur, *m.* — **finding,** *s.* critique, censure, *f.*; *adj.* frondeur

Faultily, *adv.* fautivement; à tort

Faultiness, *s.* nature fautive, *f.*; défauts, *m.pl.*; imperfections, *f.pl.*; caractère vicieux, vice, *m.*; culpabilité, *f.*

Faultless, *adj.* exempt de fautes, sans fautes, sans faute; exempt de défauts, sans défauts, sans défaut, irréprochable, parfait [faitement

Faultlessly, *adv.* irréprochablement, par-

Faultlessness, *s.* irréprochabilité, perfection, *f.*

Faulty, *adj.* en faute, fautif; blâmable; erroné; défectueux, fautif; vicieux; mauvais

Faun, *s.* faune, *m.*

Fauna, *s.* faune, *f.*

Fausse-braye, *s.* fausse-braie, *f.*

Fauvette, *s.* fauvette, *f.*

Faux pas, *s.* faux pas, *m.*

Favor, (*old spelling*) *V.* **Favour**

Favose, *adj.* faveux

Favour, *s.* faveur, *f.*; grâce, *f.*; bienfait, *m.*; plaisir, *m.*; permission, *f.*; (*medium*) entremise, *f.*; (*care*) soins, *m.pl.*; (*letter*) lettre, (*com.*) honorée, *f.*; (*order, com.*) commande, *f.*; (*ribbons*) couleurs, faveurs, *f.pl.*; (*features*) traits, *m.pl.*, physionomie, figure, *f.*, visage, *m.*; — *v.a.* favoriser (de); gratifier (de); honorer (de); avoir l'obligeance de donner (...) à. *Out of* —, en défaveur, disgracié. *Under — of*, à la faveur de; aux soins de. *To find* — (*with*), trouver grâce *or* faveur (auprès de); être bien accueilli (de). *To get* (or *grow*) *into* —, prendre faveur, s'accréditer; se faire aimer (de), obtenir les bonnes grâces (de), s'insinuer dans les bonnes grâces (de). *To get* (or *grow*) *out of* —, perdre les bonnes grâces (de). —**less,** *adj.* sans faveur

Favourable, *adj.* favorable [favorable, *f.*

Favourableness, *s.* bienveillance, *f.*; nature

Favourably, *adv.* favorablement

Favoured, *adj.* favorisé. *Hard* or *ill* —, laid, vilain, disgracieux, disgracié de la nature; mal partagé; malheureux. *Well* —, beau, bien fait, agréable; bien partagé; heureux

Favourer, *s.* personne qui favorise, *f.*; protecteur, *m.*, -trice, *f.*; fauteur, *m.*, -trice, *f.*, partisan, *m.*, e, *f.*

Favourite, *adj. s.* favori, *m.*, -te, *f.*; (*sought after*) couru. *To be a great* —, (*fam.*) être très aimé, être très populaire; plaire beaucoup; avoir un grand succès

Favouritism, *s.* favoritisme, *m.*

Fawn, *s.* faon, *m.*; (*colour*) fauve, *m*; (*fawning*) *V.* **Fawning;** — *adj.* fauve; — *v.n.* (*bring forth*) faonner; (*on, upon*) caresser, flatter, cajoler, câliner. — **coloured,** *adj.* de couleur fauve, fauve [-euse, *f.*, câlin, *m.*, e, *f.*

Fawner, *s.* flatteur, *m.*, -euse, *f*, cajoleur, *m.*,

Fawning, *adj.* caressant, flatteur, câlin; servile; — *s.* caresse, flatterie, cajolerie, câlinerie, *f.*

Fawningly, *adv.* d'une manière caressante; flatteusement; servilement, bassement

Fay, *s.* fée, *f.*
Feal, *adj.* féal, fidèle [hommage
Fealty, *s.* fidélité, *f.* — *and homage*, foi et
Fear, *v.a.* craindre; avoir peur de; — *v.n.* craindre (de, que); avoir peur (de, que); — *s.* crainte, *f.*; peur, *f.*; inquiétude, *f.* — *of the world*, respect humain, *m.* *For — of*, de peur de, de crainte de, (*fam.*) crainte de. *For — (that)*, de peur *or* de crainte que ... ne (*with the subj.*). *To be* (or *stand*) *in —*, avoir peur, craindre. *To be in bodily —*, craindre pour sa personne *or* pour sa sûreté personnelle *or* pour ses jours. *To put in — of*, faire peur de; faire craindre pour. *Never —*, n'ayez pas peur, ne craignez rien, soyez tranquille, soyez sans crainte. *There is no —*, il n'y a rien à craindre. *There is no — of*, il n'y a pas de danger de, *or* que (*with the subj.*). *No —!* pas de danger! le plus souvent! *No — of that*, il n'y a pas de danger, soyez tranquille. **—ful,** *adj.* timide, craintif, peureux, qui craint, qui a peur (de); terrible. affreux, effrayant. *To be —ful of*, craindre, redouter. *To be —ful to*, craindre de. *To be —ful that*, craindre que ... ne (*with the subj.*). **—fully,** *adv.* timidement, craintivement, avec crainte, avec effroi; terriblement, effroyablement, d'une manière effrayante. **—fulness,** *s.* timidité, *f.*, naturel craintif, *m.*; crainte, peur, *f.*; terreur, *f.*, effroi, *m.*; nature terrible *or* effrayante, *f.* **—less,** *adj.* sans crainte, sans peur; intrépide. *To be —less of*, ne pas craindre. **—lessly,** *adv.* sans crainte, sans peur; intrépidement. **—lessness,** *s.* intrépidité, *f.*
Feasibility. *V.* **Feasibleness**
Feasible, *adj.* faisable, praticable, exécutable
Feasibleness, *s.* praticabilité, *f.*
Feasibly, *adv.* d'une manière praticable
Feast, *s.* fête, *f.*; (*repast*) festin, *m.*; (*treat*) régal, *m.*; — *v.n.* faire festin, festiner; se régaler (de); (*fig.*) se repaître (de); — *v.a.* faire fête à, fêter, festoyer, régaler, traiter magnifiquement; (*to delight*) charmer, enchanter. — **day,** *s.* jour de fête, *m.* **—ful,** *adj.* de fête; joyeux; somptueux
Feaster, *s.* amateur de bonne chère, *m.*, gastronome, *m.f.*; (*entertainer*) donneur de festins, amphitryon, *m.*; (*guest*) convive, *m.f.*
Feasting, *s.* festin, régal, *m.*
Feat, *s.* fait, *m.*, action, *f.*; exploit, haut fait, fait d'armes, *m.*; (*of skill, strength*, &c.) tour, *m.*
Feather, *s.* plume, *f.*; (*of the wing or tail*) penne, plume, *f.*; (*empty title*) vain titre, ornement, *m.*; (*of horses*) épi, *m.*; (*bot.*) aigrette, *f.*; (*mil.*) plumet, *m.*; (*sort*) espèce, *f.*; — *v.a.* emplumer, couvrir *or* orner *or* garnir de plumes; (*arrows*) empenner; (*fig.*) enrichir, emplumer; (*oars*) mettre à plat. — *in o.'s cap*, plume à son chapeau, *f.*, honneur, triomphe, *m.*, distinction, *f.*; trophée, *m.*, palme, *f.* *In full — (pers.: of men and women)* en grande toilette, (*of women only*) dans ses plus beaux atours, sous les armes, (*fam., of men and women*) sur son trente-et-un, sur son trente-six. *In high —*, triomphant, glorieux. *Birds of a —*, gens de même espèce *or* de même acabit *or* de même farine. *Birds of a — flock together*, qui se ressemble s'assemble. *Bunch of —s*, bouquet de plumes, *m.* *Plume of —s*, panache, plumet, *m.* *To cut a —*, (*nav.*) faire bon *or* grand sillage. *To — o.'s nest*, faire son nid; (*fig.*) s'enrichir, faire sa pelote, mettre du foin dans ses bottes. *To show the white —*, caponner. — **bed,** *s.* lit de plume. *m.* — **broom,** *s.* plumeau, *m.* — **business,** *s.* plumasserie, *f.* — **dresser,** *s.* plumassier, *m.*, -ière, *f.* — **edge,** *s.* biseau, *m.* — **edged,** *adj.* taillé en biseau, en biseau. — **foil,** *s.* hottone, hottonie, *f.* — **footed,** *adj.* pattu, plumipède. — **grass,** *s.* stipe, *f.* **—less,** *adj.* dépourvu de plumes, sans plumes. — **pink,** *s.* mignardise, *f.*, œillet-mignardise, *m.*, mignonette, *f.* — **seller,** *s.* plumassier, *m.*, -ière, *f.* — **trade,** *s.* plumasserie, *f.*
Feathered, *part. adj.* emplumé, &c. (*V.* **Feather,** *v.a.*); (*winged*) ailé; (*swift*) rapide; (*bot.*) plumeux. — *pink*, *V.* **Feather-pink.** *The — race* or *tribe*, les oiseaux, *m.pl.*, la race [ailée, *f.*
Feathering, *s.* (*arch.*) foliation, *f.*
Feathery, *adj.* plumeux; couvert *or* garni de plumes; (*winged*) ailé; (*light*) léger comme une plume
Feature, *s* trait, *m.*; (*fig.*) trait caractéristique, trait, *m.*, partie saillante, *f.*, point particulier, point, *m.*, particularité, *f.*; signe, *m.*, marque, *f.*; point de vue, *m.*; forme, figure, *f.*; beauté, *f.*
Featured, *adj.* qui a des traits ..., aux traits ...; qui a de beaux traits. *Hard —*, aux traits durs. *Ill —*, laid. *Well —*, beau, qui a de beaux traits
Febrifuge, *adj. s.* fébrifuge, *adj. m.f.*, *s.m.*
Febrile, *adj.* fébrile, de fièvre
February, *s.* février, *m.*
Fecal, *adj.* fécal
Feces, *s. pl.* (*chem., pharm.*) fèces, *m.pl.*; (*med.*) matière fécale, *f.*, fèces, *m.pl.*
Fecial, *adj. s.* fécial, *adj. m.*, e, *f.*, fécial, *s.m.*
Fecula, *s.* fécule, *f.* — **maker, -manufacturer,** *s.* féculiste, *m.f.* — **making, -manufacture, -works,** *s.* féculerie, *f.*
Feculenc-e, y, *s.* féculence, *f.*
Feculent, *adj. s.* féculent, *adj. m.*, e, *f.*, [féculent, *s.m.*
Feculous, *adj.* féculeux
Fecund, *adj.* fécond
Fecundate, *v.a.* féconder
Fecundation, *s.* fécondation, *f.*
Fecundity, *s.* fécondité, *f.*
Federal, *adj. s.* fédéral. *adj m.*, e, *f.*, fédéral, *s.m.*
Federalism, *s.* fédéralisme, *m.*
Federalist, *s.* fédéraliste, *m.* [raliser
Federalize, *v.a.* fédéraliser; — *v n.* se fédé-
Federate, *adj. s.* fédéré, *adj. m.*, e, *f.*, fédéré, *s.m.*; — *v.a.* fédérer; — *v.n.* se fédérer
Federation, *s.* fédération, *f.*
Federative, *adj.* fédératif
Fee, *s.* honoraires, *m.pl.*; rétribution, *f.*; (*duty*) droit, *m.*; (*to servants*, &c.) gratification, *f.*; (*drink-money*) pourboire, *m.*, gratification, *f.*; (*surplice —s*) casuel, *m.*; (*feud.*) fief, *m.*; — *v.a.* payer des honoraires à; payer; (*hire*) gager, avoir *or* tenir à ses gages; (*retain*) retenir; (*give drink-money*) donner un pourboire à; (*bribe*) corrompre, suborner, gagner, graisser la patte à. *Late —*, levée exceptionnelle, *f.* — **simple,** *s.* fief simple, *m.*; propriété libre, *f.*
Feeble, *adj.* faible; débile. *To grow* (or *get* or *become*) *—*, s affaiblir. — **minded,** *adj.* faible d'esprit. — **mindedness,** *s.* faiblesse d'es- [prit, *f.*
Feebleness, *s.* faiblesse, *f.*
Feebly, *adv.* faiblement
Feed, *v.a.* nourrir (de); (*give to eat*) donner à manger à; (*graze*) paître, faire paître; (*fatten*) engraisser; (*supply*) alimenter; (*cherish*) nourrir, entretenir; (*delight*) charmer; (*in a bad sense*) repaître; — *v.n.* se nourrir (de), vivre (de); manger; paître; engraisser; s'alimenter; se repaître; — *s.* nourriture, *f.*; pâture, *f.*; chère, *f.*; portion, ration, mesure, *f.*; régal, *m.*, bombance, *f.*; (*supply*) alimentation, *f.* — *of oats*, picotin d'avoine, *m.* — **pipe,** *s.* tuyau d'alimentation, *m.* — **pump,** *s.* pompe alimentaire, *f.*
Feeder, *s.* nourrisseur, *m.*, personne qui nourrit (...), personne qui donne à manger (à ...), *f.*; (*fig.*) personne qui alimente, *f.*, pourvoyeur, *m.*, -euse, *f.*; (*eater*) mangeur, *m.*, -euse, *f.*; (*guest*) convive, *m.f.*; (*bib*) bavette, *f.*; (*of machines*) trémie, *f.*; appareil d'alimentation, *m.*; (*of a thrashing-machine*) engreneur, *m.*
Feeding, *s. V.* **Feed,** *s.*; (*of cattle*) nourrissage, *m.* — **apparatus,** *s.* appareil d'alimentation, *m.* — **bottle,** *s.* biberon, *m.*
Feel, *v.a.n.* sentir; être sensible à; (*touch*) tâter; toucher; palper; (*suffer from*) se res-

sentir de, se sentir de; (*sound*) sonder, tâter; (*search*) fouiller; (*experience*) éprouver; avoir; (*feel oneself*) se sentir; se trouver; aller; (*be*) être; (*cold, warm, hot, of pers.*) avoir; (*be ... to the touch*) être ... au toucher; (*seem*) sembler, paraître, faire l'effet (de), avoir l'air (de). — **for,** chercher; sympathiser avec, souffrir

Feel, *s.* toucher, tact, *m.* [pour, être sensible à

Feeler, *s.* personne qui sent, *f.*; (*zool.*) palpe, *m.*, antenne, *f.*; (*fig.*) sonde, *f.*; ballon d'essai, *m.*

Feeling, *adj.* sensible (à); (*sensibly felt*) senti, bien senti, vivement senti; (*tender*) tendre; (*affecting*) touchant; — *s.* toucher, tact, *m.*; sensation, *f.*; (*of the heart*) sentiment, *m.*; sensibilité, *f.*; cœur, *m.*; tendresse, *f.*; émotion, *f.*; disposition, *f.*; (*touchiness*) susceptibilité, *f.* *Bad* or *ill* —, mauvaise disposition, *f.*, mauvais vouloir, *m.*, rancune, *f.*, ressentiment, *m.*

Feelingly, *adv.* avec sensibilité, sensiblement; d'une manière sentie; d'un ton de conviction; d'une manière tendre, avec tendresse; avec attendrissement; avec intérêt; d'une manière touchante

Feetless, *adj.* (*bad English*) *V.* **Footless**

Feign, *v.a.n.* feindre; inventer, imaginer; dissimuler; déguiser; contrefaire; (*pretend*) faire semblant de; (*sham*) simuler

Feignedly, *adv.* avec feinte

Feigning, *s.* feinte, dissimulation, *f.*

Feigningly, *adv.* avec feinte

Feint, *s.* feinte, *f.*; — *adj.* feint, faux

Feldspar, Feldspath. *V.* **Felspar**

Felicitate, *v.a.* féliciter; (*obsolete*) rendre

Felicitation, *s.* félicitation, *f.* [heureux

Felicitous, *adj.* heureux

Felicitously, *adv.* heureusement, avec bonheur

Felicitousness, Felicity, *s.* félicité, *f.*; bonheur, *m.*

Feline, *adj.* de *or* du chat, de *or* des chats, de chatte, félin; —**s,** *s. pl.* félins, *m.pl.* — *race,* race féline, *f.*

Fell, *v.a.* (*cut*) abattre; (*throw down*) renverser, terrasser, assommer; (*need.*) rabattre; — *adj.* féroce, cruel, barbare; diabolique; — *s.* peau, *f.* — **monger,** *s.* peaussier, *m.*

Fellah, *s.* fellah, *m.*

Feller, *s.* abatteur, *m.*, -euse, *f.*; (*of wood*) bûcheron, *m.*; (*slaughterer*) assommeur, abatteur, *m.*

Felling, *s.* abattage, *m.*; abattis, *m.*; coupe, *f.*

Fellness, *s.* férocité, cruauté, barbarie, *f.*

Felloe, *s.* *V.* **Felly**

Fellow, *s.* compagnon, camarade, *m.*; (*equal*) égal, pareil, *m.*; (*like*) semblable, *m.*; (*brother*) confrère, *m.*; (*man*) homme, garçon, *m.*; (*youth, boy*) garçon, enfant, *m.*; (*mere nobody*) homme de rien, homme vulgaire, *m.*; (*rogue*) drôle, coquin, *m.*; (*in contempt or fam.*) individu, gaillard, compère, personnage, enfant, garçon, diable, *m.*; (*univers.*, &c.) agrégé, *m.*; (*of societies*) membre, *m.*; associé, *m.*; (*of gloves, boots*, &c.) pareil, *m.*, -le, *f.*; (*of pictures*, &c.) pendant, *m.* *Bad* —, mauvais sujet, mauvais garnement, méchant drôle, *m.* *Coarse* —, grossier personnage, *m.* *Cunning* or *deep* —, rusé compère, fin matois, *m.* *Fine* —, brave garçon, *m.*; (*handsome*) beau garçon, *m.* *Good* —, bon enfant, bon garçon, *m.* (*My good* —, mon bonhomme, mon bon; mon brave homme, mon brave). *Good-for-nothing* —, mauvais sujet, vaurien, *m.* *Jolly* —, joyeux compère, bon vivant, *m.* *Little* —, petit garçon, petit bonhomme, *m.* (*My little* —, mon petit homme). *Nice* —, brave homme, *m.*; (*handsome*) beau garçon, *m.* *Odd* —, drôle de corps, original, *m.* *Old* —, vieux bonhomme, vieux, *m.*; mon vieux! *Poor* —, pauvre homme, *m.*; pauvre garçon, *m.*; pauvre diable, *m.* *Poor little* —, pauvre petit, *m.* *Queer* —, drôle de corps, original, *m.* *Sad* —, triste sire, *m.* *Saucy* —, impudent, insolent, *m.* *Sharp* — fin matois, *m.* *Stout* —, gros gaillard, *m.* *Tall* — grand gaillard, *m.* *You* —! vous! l'ami! mon garçon! drôle que vous êtes! *You* —*s!* vous autres! mes amis! *Worthless* —, mauvais sujet, vaurien, *m.* *Young* —, jeune garçon, jeune homme, *m.* — **christian,** *s.* frère, *m.* — **citizen,** *s.* concitoyen, *m.*, -ne, *f.* — **citizenship,** *s.* concitoyenneté, *f.* — **counsellor,** *s.* collègue au conseil, *m.* — **countryman,** *s.* compatriote, *m.*, (*pop.*) pays, *m.* — **countrywoman,** *s.* compatriote, *f.*, (*pop.*) payse, *f.* — **creature,** *s.* semblable, *m.* — **feeling,** *s.* sympathie, *f.*; esprit de corps, *m.* — **helper,** *s.* aide, *m.f.*; complice, *m.f.* — **labourer,** *s.* (*in hand-work*) compagnon (*m.*, -gne, *f.*) de travail, camarade, *m.f.*; (*in head-work*) collaborateur, *m.*, -trice, *f.* — **like,** *adj.* en égal. — **man,** *s.* semblable, *m.* — **member,** *s.* confrère, *m.* — **membership,** *s.* confraternité, *f.* — **minister,** *s.* collègue, *m.* — **partner,** *s.* coassocié, *m.*, e, *f.* — **passenger,** *s.* *V.* **traveller.** — **prisoner,** *s.* compagnon (*m.*, -gne, *f.*) de captivité; (*law*) codétenu, *m.*, e, *f.*; coaccusé, *m.*, e, *f.* — **servant,** *s.* camarade de service, camarade, *m.f.* — **soldier,** *s.* compagnon d'armes, *m.*, (*fam.*) camarade, *m.* — **student,** *s.* camarade d'études, camarade, *m.f.*, condisciple, *m.* — **subject,** *s.* concitoyen, *m.*, -ne, *f.* — **sufferer,** *s.* compagnon (*m.*, -gne, *f.*) de malheur *or* d'infortune. — **townsman,** *s.* concitoyen, *m.* — **tradesman,** *s.* confrère, *m.* — **traveller,** *s.* compagnon (*m.*, -gne, *f.*) de voyage. — **worker,** *s.* *V.* — **labourer**

Fellowship, *s.* (*relations*) société, *f.*; (*friendship*) confraternité, amitié, *f.*; (*theol.*) communion, *f.*; (*of colleges*) agrégation, place d'agrégé, *f.*, fonctions d'agrégé, *f.pl.*; (*arith.*) règle de société, *f.* [férocité, cruellement

Felly, *s.* (*of a wheel*) jante, *f.*; — *adv.* avec

Felo de se, *s.* suicide délibéré, suicide, *m.*

Felon, *s.* criminel, *m.*; (*med.*) panaris, *m.*; — *adj.* *V.* **Felonious** [traître, déloyal

Felonious, *adj.* criminel; scélérat; perfide,

Feloniously, *adv.* avec une intention criminelle, criminellement, avec préméditation; avec scélératesse; en traître, perfidement, avec perfidie

Felony, *s.* crime, *m.*; crime capital, *m.*

Felspar, Felspath, *s.* feldspath, *m.*

Felspathic, *adj.* feldspathique

Felt, *s.* feutre, *m.*; — *v.a.* feutrer. — **cloth,** *s.* feutrière, *f.* — **grain,** *s.* fil du bois, *m.* — **hat,** *s.* chapeau de feutre, *m.* — **maker,** *s.*

Felting, *s.* feutrage, *m.* [feutrier, *m.*

Felucca, *s.* felouque, *f.*

Felwort, *s.* gentiane, *f.*

Female, *s.* (*of animals*) femelle, *f.*; (*pers.*) femme, *f.*; fille, *f.*; dame, *f.*; — *adj.* (*of animals*) femelle; (*pers.*) féminin, des femmes; de femme; (*of rhymes*) féminin; (*bot.*) femelle. ("*Female,*" *together with the noun following it, are often rendered in French by one word, with its feminine ending; as,* — **cat,** chatte, — **companion,** compagne, — **convict,** détenue, — **cousin,** cousine, — **friend,** amie, — **orphan,** orpheline, — **prisoner,** prisonnière, prévenue, détenue, accusée, — **relation,** parente; &c. *V.* **She**) — *convict establishment,* — *penitentiary,* maison centrale, *f.*

Feme, *s.* (*lawyers' slang*) femme, *f.*

Feminality, *s.* nature féminine, *f.*

Feminiform, *adj.* féminiforme

Feminine, *adj. s.* féminin, *adj. m.*, e, *f.*, féminin, *s.m.* *In the* — *gender,* au féminin

Femininely, *adv.* fémininement

Feminineness, Femininity, *s.* fémininité, *f.*

Femme, *s.* (*law*) femme, *f.*

Femoral, *adj.* fémoral

Femur, *s.* fémur, *m.*

Fen, *s.* marais, marécage, *m.* — **born,** *adj.* né dans les marécages. — **cress,** *s.* cresson de marais, *m.* — **cricket,** *s.* taupe-grillon, *f.* — **duck,** *s.* canard sauvage, *m.* — **fowl,** *s.* oiseau de marais, *m.* — **land,** *s.* terre marécageuse, *f.*, pays marécageux, *m.* — **man,** *s.* habitant d'un pays marécageux, habitant des marais, *m.*

Fence, *s.* clôture, *f.*; enceinte, *f.*; balustrade, *f.*; barrière, *f.*; (*of pales*) palissade, *f.*; (*hedge*) haie, *f.*; (*against cattle*) échalier, *m.*; (*fig.*) défense, barrière, *f.*, rempart, *m.*; (*sword-play*) escrime, *f.*; (*buyer or receiver of stolen property, slang*) fourgat, *m.*, attriqueur, *m.*, -euse, *f.*; — *v.a.n.* enclore; entourer; défendre, protéger; (*with foils*) faire des armes; (*fig.*) escrimer; (*be on o.'s guard*) se mettre en garde (contre), se garder (de); (*leap*) sauter; sauter (*or* franchir) une haie *or* des haies. —**less,** *adj.* sans clôture, ouvert; sans défense; sans bornes

Fencer, *s.* tireur d'armes, *m.*; tireur, *m.*; maître d'armes, *m.*; (*horse, mare*) sauteur, *m.*, -euse, *f.*

Fencible, *adj.* capable de défense; défendable; pour la défense du pays; — *s.* milicien, *m.*; —**s,** *s. pl.* miliciens, *m.pl.*, milice, *f.*

Fencing, *s.* clôture, enceinte, *f.*; (*with foils*) escrime, *f.*, armes, *f.pl.* — **academy,** *s. V.* — **school.** — **bout,** *s. V.* — **match.** — **glove,** *s.* gant bourré, *m.* — **jacket,** *s.* gilet d'armes, *m.* — **mask,** *s.* masque pour l'escrime, *m.* — **master,** *s.* maître d'armes *or* d'escrime, *m.* — **match,** *s.* assaut d'armes, *m.* — **pad,** *s.* plastron, *m.* — **school,** *s.* salle d'armes *or* d'escrime, *f.* — **shoe,** *s.* sandale d'armes, *f.*

Fend, *v.a.* (— **off**) se défendre de, se garder de, se préserver de; parer, détourner, écarter

Fender, *s.* garde-cendres, garde-feu, *m.*; (*tech.*, (*nav.*) defense, *f.*

Fenestra, *s.* fenêtre, *f.*

Fenestral, *adj.* de fenêtre, fenestral

Fenestrate, *v.a.* fenêtrer

Fenestration, *s.* fenêtrage, *m.*

Fenian, *s. adj.* fénian, *m.*, e, *f.*

Fenianism, *s.* fénianisme, *m.*

Fenianist, *s.*, **Fenianistic,** *adj.* fénianiste, *m.f.*

Fennec, *s.* fennec, *m.*

Fennel, *s.* fenouil, *m.* — *Giant* —, férule, *f.* — **apple,** *s.* fenouillet, *m.*, fenouillette, *f.* — **flower,** *s.* nigelle, *f.* — **seed,** *s.* fenouil, *m.* — **water,** *s.* fenouillette, *f.*

Fenny, *adj.* marécageux; de marais

Fenugreek, *s.* fenugrec, *m.*

Feoff, *s.* fief, *m.*; — *v.a. V.* **Enfeoff**

Feoffment, *s.* inféodation, *f.*

Feria, *s.* férie, *f.*

Ferial, *adj.* férial; férié

Ferine, *adj.* férin, sauvage, féroce; — *s.* bête sauvage, *f.*

Fermata, *s.* fermata, *f.*, point d'orgue, point d'arrêt, point de repos, *m.*

Ferment, *s.* ferment, *m.*; fermentation, *f.*; — *v.n.* fermenter; — *v.a.* faire fermenter

Fermentability, *s.* fermentabilité, *f.*

Fermentable, *adj.* fermentable

Fermentation, *s.* fermentation, *f.*

Fermentative, *adj.* fermentatif; de fermentation

Fermentescibility, *s.* fermentescibilité, *f.*

Fermentescible, *adj.* fermentescible

Fermentible, *adj.* fermentable

Fermenting, *s.* fermentation, *f.*

Fern, *s.* fougère, *f.* — **bed, -brake, -plot,** *s.* fougeraie, *f.* — **owl,** *s.* engoulevent, *m.* — **stand,** *s.* jardinière à fougères, *f.*

Fernery, *s.* fougeraie, *f.*

Ferny, *adj.* qui abonde en fougère, couvert de fougère

Ferocious, *adj.* féroce

Ferociously, *adv.* avec férocité

Ferociousness, Ferocity, *s.* férocité, *f.*

Feronia, féronie, *f.*

Ferrarese, *s. adj.* Ferrarois, *m.*, e, *f.*

Ferrate, *s.* ferrate, *m.*

Ferreous, *adj.* ferreux

Ferret, *s.* furet, *m.*; (*tape*) padou, *m.*, (*silk* —) fleuret, *m.*; — *v.a.n.* (— **out**) fureter; dépister, dénicher, relancer

Ferreter, *s.* fureteur, *m.*, -euse, *f.*

Ferriage, *s.* prix du passage (en bac), bachotage, *m.*

Ferric, *adj.* ferrique

Ferriferous, *adj.* ferrifère

Ferro, (*in compounds, chem.*) ferro- ...

Ferrocyanate, *s.* ferrocyanate, *m.*

Ferrocyanic, *adj.* ferrocyanique

Ferrocyanide, *s.* ferrocyanure, *m.*

Ferrocyanogen, *s.* ferrocyane, *m.*

Ferrous, *adj.* ferreux

Ferruginosity, *s.* ferruginosité, *f.*

Ferruginous, *adj.* ferrugineux; ferré

Ferrule, *s.* (*ring*) virole, *f.*; (*of a stick*) bout, *m.*

Ferry, *s.* bac, va-et-vient, *m.*; passage, *m.*; — *v.a.n.* (— **over** *or* **across**) passer dans un bac, passer en bac, passer. — **boat,** *s.* bac, *m.* — **man,** *s.* passeur, batelier, *m.*; (*myth.*) nocher, *m.*

Fertile, *adj.* fertile; fécond

Fertilely, *adv.* fertilement, avec fertilité

Fertileness, Fertility, *s.* fertilité, *f.*; fécondité, *f.*

Fertilizable, *adj.* fertilisable

Fertilization, *s.* fertilisation, *f.*

Fertilize, *v.a.* fertiliser

Fertilizer, *s.* fertilisant, *m.*

Ferula, *s.* férule, *f.* [*V.* **Ferrule**

Ferule, *s.* férule, *f.*; (*bad spelling for "ferrule"*)

Fervency, *s.* ardeur, *f.*; (*of devotion*) ferveur, *f.*

Fervent, *adj.* ardent, vif; (*of devotion*) fervent

Fervently, *adv.* ardemment, vivement; (*of devotion*) avec ferveur, fervemment

Fervid, *adj.* ardent, brûlant

Fervidly, *adv.* ardemment, avec chaleur

Fervidness, Fervour, *s.* ferveur, *f.*; ardeur, *f.*; (*heat*) chaleur, *f.*

Fescennine, *adj.* fescennin

Fescue, *s.* touche, *f.*; (— *grass*) fétuque, *f.*

Fess, Fesse, *s.* (*her.*) fasce, *f.*

Festal, *adj. V.* **Festive**

Fester, *v.n.* s'ulcérer; s'envenimer; se corrompre; — *s.* abcès, *m.*, tumeur, *f.*

Festival, *s.* fête, *f.*; (*mus.*) festival, *m.*, fête musicale, *f.*; — *adj. V.* **Festive**

Festive, *adj.* de fête; joyeux, gai

Festively, *adv.* joyeusement, gaiment [joie, *f.*

Festivity, *s.* fête, *f.*; réjouissance, *f.*; gaieté,

Festoon, *s.* feston, *m.*; — *v.a.* festonner ('*with,*' de)

Fetch, *v.a.* aller chercher; (*bring by carrying*) apporter; (*bring without carrying*) amener; (*draw*) puiser; (*reach, attain*) atteindre, arriver à; (*make*) faire; (*breath*) prendre; (*a blow*) porter, allonger; (*sighs*) pousser; (*blood*) faire venir; faire jaillir; (*a pump*) amorcer, engrener; (*of prices*) rapporter, produire; se vendre; valoir; (*to let for*) se louer; — *s.* stratagème, tour, artifice, *m.* *To — and carry,* (*of dogs*) rapporter. *To come and —,* venir chercher. *To go and —,* aller chercher. — **away,** (*by carrying*) emporter; (*without carrying*) emmener. — **back,** (*by carrying*) rapporter; (*without carrying*) ramener. — **down,** faire descendre; (*by carrying*) descendre; (*lead in*) amener; (*strike*) abattre; (*humble*) abaisser, rabattre; humilier. — **in,** faire entrer; (*bring*) apporter; (*lead in*) amener. — **off,** ôter, enlever; emporter; (*lead off*) emmener. — **out,** faire sortir; (*bring*) apporter; (*lead out, away*) emmener; (*to*) amener; (*cause to appear*) faire ressortir. — **up,** faire monter; (*by carrying*) monter; (*lead up*) amener; (*reach*) atteindre, rattraper, rejoindre; (*make up for*) réparer, rattraper; (*stop*) arrêter court; (*raise*) élever (à)

Fête. *V.* **Feast**

Fetich, &c. *V.* **Fetish,** &c.

Fetid, *adj.* fétide

Fetidness, *s.* fétidité, *f.*

Fetish, *s.* fétiche, *m.*

Fetishism, *s.* fétichisme, *m.*

Fetishist, *s. adj.* fétichiste, *m.f.*

Fetlock, *s.* fanon, *m.* — **joint,** *s.* boulet, *m.*

Fetor, *s.* puanteur, *f.*

Fetter, *v.a.* mettre dans les fers, enchaîner;

(*horses and fig.*) entraver; — *s.*, **—s,** *pl.* fers, *m.pl.*, chaînes, *f.pl.*; (*of horses*) entraves, *f.pl.* **—less,** *adj.* libre, sans entraves

Fetus. *V.* **Fœtus**

Fetwah, *s.* fetfa, *m.*

Feud, *s.* querelle, *f.*

Feudal, *adj.* féodal

Feudalism, *s.* féodalisme, *m.*; féodalité, *f.*

Feudalist, *s.* féodaliste, *m.f.*

Feudalistic, *adj.* féodaliste

Feudality, *s.* féodalité, *f.*

Feudalization, *s.* féodalisation, *f.*

Feudalize, *v.a.* féodaliser

Feudally, *adv.* féodalement

Feudatary, Feudatory, *s.adj.* feudataire, *m.f.*

Feudist, *s.* feudiste, *m.*

Feuillea, *s.* feuillée, *f.*

Feuillemort, *adj. s.* feuille-morte, *adj.m.f., s.m.*

Feuilleton, *s.* feuilleton, *m.*

Feuilletonist, Feuilletoniste, *s.* feuilletoniste, *m.f.*

Fever, *s.* fièvre, *f.*; — *v.a.* donner la fièvre à, enfiévrer. *A* —, la fièvre; (*with an adj., or in a particular sense, as when followed by 'which,'* &c.) une fièvre. *To be in a —, to be ill of a —, to be —ed,* avoir la fièvre. *To set in a —,* donner la fièvre à, enfiévrer. — **cooling,** *adj.* qui apaise la fièvre. — **few,** *s.* (*bot.*) pyrèthre, *m.*, matricaire, *f.* — **fit,** *s.* accès de fièvre, *m.* — **patient,** *s.* fiévreux, *m.*, -euse, *f.*, fébricitant, *m.*, e, *f.* — **wort,** *s.* triostée, *m.*

Fevered, *adj.* fiévreux

Feverish, *adj.* fiévreux, qui a la fièvre (*to be* —, avoir la fièvre); fébrile; (*hot*) brûlant; (*fickle*) inconstant, capricieux; (*impatient*) impatient

Feverishly, *adv.* avec une excitation fiévreuse; impatiemment

Feverishness, *s.* état de fièvre, *m.*, affection fébrile, *f.*; impatience, *f.*

Few, *adj.* peu (de); (*small in number*) petit nombre; peu nombreux, en petit nombre; (*some*) quelques; (*few people*) peu de gens, peu de personnes. *A* —, quelques; (*before 'of,' or with 'of them' understood*) quelques-uns; (*a few people*) quelques-uns, quelques individus. *Give me a* —, donnez-m'en quelques-uns. *Not a* —, pas peu, pas mal; bon nombre (de). — *and far between, V.* **Sparse,** *adj.*

Fewer, *adj. comp.* moins; moins nombreux, en plus petit nombre; (*before a noun*) moins de

Fewest, *adj. super.* (le) moins, (le) plus petit nombre (de); (le) moins possible (de)

Fewness, *s.* petit nombre, *m.*, petite quantité, *f.*

Fez, *s.* fez, *m.*

Fiasco, *s.* fiasco, *m.*

Fiat, *s.* commandement, ordre, décret, *m.*

Fib, *s.* conte, mensonge, *m.*, menterie, *f.*; — *v.n.* faire des contes, mentir

Fibber, *s.* faiseur (*m.*, -euse, *f.*) de contes, menteur, *m.*, -euse, *f.*

Fibre, *s.* fibre, *f.*

Fibril, *s.* fibrille, *f.*

Fibrillous, *adj.* fibrilleux

Fibrine, *s.* fibrine, *f.*

Fibrinous, *adj.* fibrineux

Fibrous, *adj.* fibreux

Fibula, *s.* (*anat.*) péroné, *m.*; (*surg.*) suture, *f.*

Fickle, *adj.* volage; inconstant; léger; changeant; incertain

Fickleness, *s.* inconstance, légèreté, humeur volage, *f.*; instabilité, *f.*

Fictile, *adj.* plastique; (*of pottery*) céramique. — *art,* art plastique, *m.*; (*pottery*) céramique, *f.* — *earth,* argile plastique, *f.*; terre à potier, *f.*

Fiction, *s.* fiction, *f.*

Fictitious, *adj.* fictif; imaginaire; faux; supposé

Fictitiously, *adv.* fictivement

Fictitiousness, *s.* nature fictive, *f.*

Ficus, *s.* (*med.*) fic, *m.*

Fiddle, *s.* violon, *m.*; — *v.n.* jouer du violon; (*trifle*) baguenauder, chipoter; — *!* (*int.*) bah! bagatelle! *Scotch* —, démangeaison, *f.* *To play second* —, jouer le second rôle (auprès de); le céder (à). — **bow,** *s.* archet, *m.* — **case,** *s.* boîte à violon, *f.* — **dedee,** *int.* allons donc! quelle blague! — **faddle,** *s.* fadaise, faribole, niaiserie, sornette, *f.*; *v.n.* baguenauder, niaiser. — **pattern,** *adj.* violon. — *pattern spoon and fork,* couvert violon, *m.* — **stick,** *s.* archet, *m.*; (*nonsense*) fadaise, blague, *f.* — **string,** *s.* corde de violon, *f.* — **wood,** *s.* citharexyle, bois de guitare, guitardin, *m.*

Fiddler, *s.* joueur de violon, violon, ménétrier, *m.*

Fiddling, *adj.* frivole

Fidelity, *s.* fidélité, *f.*

Fidget, *v.n.* remuer, se remuer, s'agiter, frétiller, gigotter; se tourmenter; — *s.* agitation, *f.*; inquiétude, impatience, crispation, *f.*, tourment, *m.*; (*pers.*) être remuant, mouvement perpétuel, *m.*

Fidgety, *adj.* remuant; (*uneasy*) inquiet; impatient; (*troublesome*) tracassier, ennuyeux

Fiduciarily, *adv.* fiduciairement

Fiduciary, *adj. s.* fiduciaire, *adj. m.f., s.m.*

Fie, *int.* fi! fi donc! — *on* or *upon!* fi de!

Fief, *s.* fief, *m.*

Field, *s.* champ, *m.*; (— *of grass*) pré, *m.*; (*of ice*) banc, *m.*; (*fields*) campagne, *f.*; (— *of battle*) champ de bataille, *m.*; (*battle*) bataille, *f.*; (*war*) campagne, *f.*; (*hunting, shooting*) chasse, *f.*; (*space*) champ, *m.*; carrière, *f.*; (*paint., her., opt.*) champ, *m.*; (*geol.*) gîte, *m.*; — *adj.* des champs, champêtre; de campagne. — *of view,* (*opt.*) champ de la vision, *m.* *In the* —, sur le terrain; (*mil.*) en campagne. *In the open —s,* en plein champ. *To take the* —, se mettre (*or* entrer) en campagne. — **artillery,** *s.* artillerie de campagne, *f.* — **battery,** *s.* batterie de campagne, *f.* — **bed,** *s.* lit de camp, *m.* — **colours,** *s. pl.* guidon, *m.* — **cricket,** *s.* (*insect*) grillon des champs, *m.* — **day,** *s.* jour de revue, *m.*; revue, *f.*; jour d'exercice, *m.*; exercice, *m.*; jour de gala, gala, *m.*, fête, *f.* — **duck,** *s.* canepetière, *f.* — **equipage,** *s.* équipage de campagne, *m.* — **fare,** *s.* litorne, *f.* — **gardening,** *s.* petite culture, *f.* — **gate,** *s.* barrière, *f.* — **glass,** *s.* lorgnette de campagne, lunette d'approche, longue-vue, *f.* — **gun,** *s.* pièce de campagne, *f.* — **hospital,** *s.* ambulance, *f.* — **marshal,** *s.* maréchal, *m.* — **marshalship,** *s.* maréchalat, *m.* — **mouse,** *s.* rat des champs, mulot, campagnol, *m.* — **officer,** *s.* officier supérieur, *m.* — **oven,** *s.* four de campagne, *m.* — **piece,** *s.* pièce de campagne, *f.* — **poppy,** *s.* coquelicot, *m.* — **practice,** *s.* évolutions de ligne, grandes manœuvres, *f.pl.* — **roller,** *s.* rouleau plombeur, *m.* — **spider,** *s.* faucheux, *m.* — **sports,** *s. pl.* plaisirs de la chasse, *m.pl.*, chasse, *f.* — **train,** *s.* équipage d'artillerie de campagne, *m.* — **turnip,** *s.* turnep, *m.*, rabioule, *f.* — **vole,** *s.* campagnol, *m.* — **works,** *s. pl.* travaux, ouvrages, *m.pl.*

Fiend, *s.* esprit malin, *m.*; démon, *m.* **—ish,** — **like,** *adj.* diabolique, infernal. **—ishness,** *s.* méchanceté infernale, *f.*

Fierce, *adj.* féroce, farouche; furieux; violent; cruel; ardent

Fiercely, *adv.* férocement, avec férocité; furieusement, avec fureur, avec furie, avec rage; violemment; cruellement; ardemment

Fierceness, *s.* férocité, *f.*; fureur, furie, *f.*; violence, *f.*; impétuosité, *f.*; ardeur, *f.*

Fieriness, *s.* ardeur, chaleur, fougue, *f.*, emportement, *m.*

Fiery, *adj.* de feu; enflammé; brûlant; ardent; (*pers.*) bouillant, fougueux, emporté

Fife, *s.* fifre, *m.*; — *v.n.a.* jouer du fifre, fifrer

Fifer, *s.* fifre, joueur de fifre, *m.*

Fifteen, *adj. s.* quinze, *adj. m.f., s.m.*

Fifteenth, *adj.* quinzième; — *s.* quinzième, (*part*) *m.*, (*pers.*) *m.f.*, (*mus.*) *f.*; (*of the month*) quinze, *m.* *The* —, (*of sovereigns*) quinze

Fifteenthly, *adv.* quinzièmement

Fifth, *adj.* cinquième; — *s.* cinquième, (*part*) *m.*, (*pers.*) *m.f.*; (*mus.*) quinte, *f.*; (*of the month*)

cinq. *The* —, (*of sovereigns*) cinq (*V.* **Charles,** *and* **Sixtus,** *at the end of this Vol.*)
Fifthly, *adv.* cinquièmement.
Fiftieth, *adj.* cinquantième
Fifty, *adj.* cinquante. — **fold,** *adj. adv.* cinquante fois autant, cinquante fois
Fig, *s.* figue, *f.*; (*tree*) figuier, *m.*; (*vet.*) fic, *m.* *A — for!* fi de! au diable! *Not to care a — for,* se moquer de. — **eater,** *s.* becfigue, figuier, *m.* — **garden, -ground,** *s.* figuerie, *f.* — **house,** *s.* serre à figuiers, *f.* — **leaf,** *s.* feuille de figuier, *f.*; (*sculp.*; *and fig.*) feuille de vigne, *f.* — **marigold,** ficoïde, *f.* — **orchard,** *s.* figuerie, *f.* — **pecker,** *s.* becfigue, *m.* — **shaped,** *adj.* ficiforme. — **tree,** *s.* figuier, *m.* — **wort,** *s.* scrofulaire, *f.*
Fight, *v.a.* se battre avec; résister à; contester; (*the enemy*) combattre; (*a battle*) livrer; (*a cause,* &c.) défendre; — *v.n.* se battre; (*contend*) combattre; (*struggle*) lutter; (*resist*) résister (à); (*quarrel*) se disputer; — *s.* *V.* **Fighting.** *To — it out,* s'en tirer; soutenir le combat; vider (une querelle) les armes à la main. *To — another man's battles,* prendre la défense de quelqu'un
Fighter, *s.* combattant, *m.*, e, *f.*; (*in a bad sense*) ferrailleur, *m.*; batailleur, *m.*, -euse, *f.*; boxeur, *m.*, -euse, *f.*
Fighting, Fight, *s.* combat, *m.*; lutte, *f.*; (*jest.*) batterie, bataille, *f.*; — *adj.* (*pers.*) qui combat; (*things*) de combat, de bataille. *To have a* —, se battre; lutter. *To show* —, vouloir se battre; montrer les dents; regimber. — **man,** *s.* *V.* **Fighter**
Figment, *s.* fiction, invention, *f.*
Figuline, *s.* figuline, terre figuline, *f.*
Figurability, *s.* figurabilité, *f.*
Figurable, *adj.* figurable
Figurant, e, *s.* figurant, *m.*, e, *f.*
Figurate, *adj.* figuré; (*mus.*) chiffré
Figuration, *s.* figuration, *f.*; (*mus.*) figure, *f.*
Figurative, *adj.* figuratif; (*of a sense*) figuré, métaphorique. *In a — sense,* au figuré
Figuratively, *adv.* figurativement; figurément, au figuré [métaphorique, *m.*
Figurativeness, *s.* nature figurée, *f.*, sens
Figure, *s.* figure, *f.*; (*personal appearance*) tournure, taille, *f.*; mine, *f.*, air, *m.*; (*arith., mus.*) chiffre, *m.*; (*geom., rhet., dancing*) figure, *f.*; (*log.*) forme, *f.*; (*of fabrics*) dessin, *m.*; — *v.a.* former, façonner; figurer, représenter; imaginer; (*of fabrics,* &c.) dessiner, façonner; brocher; gaufrer; (*mus.*) chiffrer; — *v.n.* figurer. — *of speech,* façon de parler, *f.* *Good* —, bonne tournure, belle taille, *f.* *To make* or *cut a* —, faire figure, faire une figure. *To — to oneself,* se figurer. *What a — you are!* comme vous êtes fagoté! comme vous voilà fait! *All prices marked in plain —s,* (*com.*) prix fixe marqué en chiffres connus. — **card,** *s.* figure, *f.* — **caster,** *s.* figuriste, *m.* — **drawing,** *s.* dessin de figure, *m.* — **head,** *s.* figure, *f.* — **stone,** *s.* agalmatolithe, *m.*
Figured, *part. adj.* figuré, &c. (*V.* **Figure,** *v.a.n.*); (*of fabrics,* &c.) à dessin, à dessins; façonné; ouvragé; broché; gaufré
Figur-ism, -ist. *V.* page 3, § 1
Filagree. *V.* **Filigree**
Filament, *s.* filament, *m.*
Filamentous, *adj.* filamenteux
Filbert, *s.* aveline, *f.* — **tree,** *s.* avelinier, *m.*
Filch, *v.a.* filouter, escamoter, voler, dérober, chiper
Filcher, *s.* filou, escroc, *m.*, voleur, *m.*, -euse, *f.*
Filching, *s.* filouterie, *f.*, escamotage, *m.*; vol, *m.*; — *adj.* de filou, de voleur [voleur
Filchingly, *adv.* par filouterie, en filou, en
File, *s.* (*tool*) lime, *f.*; (*string*) liasse, *f.*; (*wire for bills*) pique-notes, *m.*; (*bundle of papers*) liasse, *f.*; dossier, *m.*; collection, *f.*; (*list*) liste, *f.*; (*rank*) file, *f.*, rang, *m.*, rangée, *f.*; queue, *f.*; (*mil.*) file, *f.*; (*pers.*) finaud, *m.*, e, *f.*, rusé, *m.*, e, *f.* *Cunning* —, fin matois, finaud, *m.*, fine matoise, finaude, fine lame, *f.* *In a* (or *the*) —, à la file; à la queue. *On* —, en liasse, conservé, gardé, collectionné. *Last man of a* —, (*mil.*) serre-file, *m.* *Left — !* par file à gauche! *Right — !* par file à droite! *To stand in* —, faire queue. — **cutter,** *s.* tailleur de limes, *m.* — **dust,** *s.* limaille, *f.* — **fire, -firing,** *s.* feu de file, *m.* — **fish,** *s.* baliste, *m.* — **leader,** *s.* chef de file, *m.* — **stroke,** *s.* coup de lime, *m.*
File, *v.a.* (*rub,* &c.) limer; (*papers*) mettre en liasse; faire collection de, collectionner, conserver, garder; (*to string*) enfiler; (*law*) produire, présenter; (*com. law*) déposer; — *v.n.* filer, marcher à la file. — **off,** *v.a.* limer; polir; (*remove*) enlever en limant; *v.n.* (*move on*) défiler. — **past,** défiler, (...) défiler devant (...) [limeuse, *f.*
Filer, *s.* (*pers.*) limeur, *m.*, -euse, *f.*; (*mach.*)
Filial, *adj.* filial
Filially, *adv.* filialement
Filiation, *s.* filiation, *f.*
Filibeg, *s.* *V.* **Kilt**
Filibuster, *s.* flibustier, *m.*; — *v.n.* flibuster
Filibustering, Filibusterism, *s.* flibus-
Filiform, *adj.* filiforme [terie, *f*
Filigree, *s.* filigrane, *m.*; *v.a.* filigraner. — **work,** *s.* filigrane, *m.* — **worker,** *s.* filigraniste, *m.*
Filing, *s.* (*rubbing,* &c.) limage, *m.*; limure, *f.*; (*of papers*) mise en liasse, *f.*, classement, arrangement, *m.*, collection, *f.*; (*law*) production, présentation, *f.*; (*com. law*) dépôt, *m.*; —**s,** *pl.* limaille, *f.* — **machine,** *s.* limeuse, *f.* — **off,** *s.* défilé, défilement, *m.*, défilade, *f.*
Fill, *v.a.* remplir ('*with,*' de); emplir; combler; occuper; tenir; (*satisfy*) rassasier; (*a pipe,* &c., *stuff in*) bourrer, charger; (*duties,* &c.) remplir; — *s* suffisance, quantité suffisante, *f.*; (*bellyful, pop.*) soûl, content, *m.*; (*of a cart*) limonière, *f.*; — *v.n.* se remplir; se rassasier; rassasier; (*of drink*) verser à boire. — **in,** remplir. — **out,** remplir; (*of drink*) verser, verser à boire; (*swell*) enfler, gonfler; s'enfler, se gonfler; (*get stout*) prendre de l'embonpoint. — **up,** remplir; occuper; compléter; (*a measure, a ditch,* &c.) combler; (*neut.*) se remplir; s'encombrer
Filler, *s.* (*pers.*) chargeur, *m.*; (— *in, need.*) remplisseuse, *f.*; (*thing*) remplissage, *m.*, cheville, *f.*
Fillet, *s.* bandeau, *m.*; (*of gold, arch., bot., anat.,* &c.) filet, *m.*; astragale, *m.*; (*of beef, fish,* &c.) filet, *m.*; (*of veal*) rouelle, *f.*; (*coin.*) lame, *f.*; — *v.a.* ceindre d'un bandeau; orner d'un filet. — **steak,** *s* tranche de filet, *f.*
Filling, *adj.* qui remplit; (*of food*) rassasiant; — *s.* remplissage, *m.*; —**s,** *pl.* remplissage, *m.* — **in** *or* **out** *or* **up,** *s.* remplissage, *m.* — **up stuff,** *s.* remplissage, *m.*; (*of shoes*) dresse, *f.*
Fillip, *s.* chiquenaude, croquignole, pichenette, *f.*; — *v.a.* donner une chiquenaude *or* des chiquenaudes *or* &c. à, chiquenauder, croquignoler
Fillister, - **plane,** *s.* guillaume, *m.* [gnoler
Filly, *s.* pouliche, *f.*; (*girl*) coquette, *f.*
Film, *s.* (*anat.*) tunique, *f.*; (*bot.*) pellicule, *f.*; (*fig.*) voile, nuage, *m.*; — *v.a.* couvrir d'une pellicule *or* &c. [neux; (*fig.*) voilé
Filmy, *adj.* composé de pellicules, membra-
Filter, *v.a.n.* filtrer; — *s.* filtre, *m.*
Filterer, *s.* filtrateur, *m.*, -trice, *f.*
Filtering, *adj.* filtrant, filtrateur; — *s.* filtration, *f.*; filtrage, *m.* — **bag,** *s.* chausse d'Hippocrate, chausse, *f.* — **machine,** *s.* filtre, *m.* — **paper,** *s.* papier à filtrer, *m.* — **stone,** *s.* pierre à filtrer, *f.*, filtre, *m.*
Filth, *s.* ordure, *f.*; saleté, *f.*; immondices, *f.pl.*; (*fig.*) impureté, corruption, *f.*
Filthily, *adv.* salement; (*fig.*) impurement,
Filthiness. *V.* **Filth** [d'une manière impure
Filthy, *adj.* sale, dégoûtant; (*fig.*) impur, cor-

rompu ; ordurier ; obscène ; (*of gain*) sordide, [honteux
Filtrate, *v.a.n.* filtrer
Filtration, *s.* filtration, *f.*; filtrage, *m.*
Fimbriate, *v.a.* franger, border
Fin, *s.* nageoire, *f.*; (*of whales*) fanon, *m.*; (*Finn*) *V.* **Finn.** — **fish,** *s.* jubarte, *f.* — **footed, -toed,** *adj.* palmipède, palmé. —**less,** *adj.* sans nageoires. — **like,** *adj.* en forme de nageoire
Finable, *adj.* (*pers.*) passible d'une amende; (*things*) punissable d'une amende [mortel
Final, *adj.* final; dernier; définitif; décisif;
Finale, *s.* (*dancing, and fig.*) finale, *f.*; (*mus.: note,* &c.) finale, *f.*, (*mus.: piece of music*) [finale, *m.*
Finalist, *s.* finaliste, *m.*
Finality, *s.* finalité, *f.*
Finally, *adv.* finalement, enfin, à la fin, en fin de compte; définitivement; complètement, entièrement; (*in short*) bref
Finance, *s.* finance, *f.*, finances, *f.pl.*; — *v.n.* se procurer de l'argent, faire ressource
Financial, *adj.* financier
Financialist, *s.* financier, *m.*
Financially, *adv.* financièrement
Financier, *s.* financier, *m.*
Finch, *s.* pinson, *m.*
Find, *v.a.n.* trouver; (*get back*) retrouver; (*discover*) découvrir, voir, remarquer, reconnaître, s'apercevoir; (*experience*) éprouver; (*surprise*) surprendre; (*catch*) prendre, attraper; (*learn*) apprendre; (*deem*) juger, croire, penser, estimer; (*supply*) fournir (à), pourvoir, munir; (*procure for oneself*) se fournir; (*decide*) décider; (*guilty,* &c.) déclarer; (*a verdict*) rendre, prononcer; (*damages*) adjuger. ... *is to be found,* ... se trouve, on trouve ... *To — it necessary* (*to*), reconnaître (*or* se voir dans) la nécessité (de); être *or* se trouver obligé (de). *Found, a dog* ..., (*on bills*) il a été trouvé un chien ... — **out,** découvrir; trouver; (*guess*) deviner; (*invent*) inventer; (*resolve*) résoudre; (*become aware*) s'apercevoir, reconnaître. *To be found out,* (*in rascality*) être démasqué
Finder, *s.* trouveur, *m.*, -euse, *f.*; inventeur, *m.*, -trice, *f.*; (*seeker*) chercheur, *m.*, -euse, *f.*; (*opt. glass*) chercheur, trouveur, *m.*
Finding, *s.* découverte, *f.*; trouvaille, *f.*; (*law*) verdict, *m.*; jugement, *m.* — **out,** *s.* découverte, *f.*; solution, *f.*
Fine, *adj.* (*handsome, beautiful*) beau; (*small, thin, not coarse*) fin; délicat; (*clear*) clair; (*pure*) pur; (*neat*) propre; (*good*) bon; (*excellent*) excellent; (*refined*) fin; (*subtle*) subtil; (*accomplished*) accompli, élégant; (*affected*) affecté, recherché; (*slang*) joli; précieux. *That is all very —, but* ..., tout cela est bel et bon, mais ... — **arts,** *s. pl.* (les) beaux arts, *m.pl.* — **bred,** (*of horses*) fin. — **draw,** *v.a.* rentraire, faire une reprise perdue à, repriser. — **drawer,** *s.* rentrayeur, *m.*, -euse, *f.*, ouvrier (*m.*, -ière, *f.*) en reprises perdues, repriseur, *m.*, -euse, *f.* — **drawing,** *s.* rentraiture, reprise perdue, *f.*, reprises perdues, *f.pl.*, reprisage, *m.* — **fingered,** *adj.* adroit, habile. — **grained,** *adj.* (*of metals, tissues, leather,* &c.) à grain fin; (*of nappy fabrics*) à poil fin; (*of wood*) à fil fin. — **spoken,** *adj.* qui s'exprime bien; (*in a bad sense*) beau parleur. — **spun,** *adj.* filé fin; (*fig.*) délicat; subtil; recherché
Fine, *s.* amende, *f.*; (*premium*) pot-de-vin, *m.*; (*feud. law*) redevance; (*end*) fin, *f.* **In** —, *adv.* enfin
Fine, *v.a.* mettre à l'amende; (*in the sum of*...) condamner à une amende de..., condamner à ... d'amende; (*refine*) affiner; (*wine,* &c.) coller, clarifier
Finely, *adv.* fin; (*with skill,* &c.) finement; délicatement; élégamment; bien; (*in contempt*) joliment; (*affectedly*) avec recherche, d'une manière recherchée
Fineness, *s.* beauté, *f.*; élégance, *f.*; finesse, *f.*; délicatesse, *f.*; clarté, pureté, *f.*; subtilité, *f.*; (*of gold, silver*) fin, *m.*
Finery, *s.* brillante parure, magnifique toilette, *f.*; ornements recherchés, beaux habits, *m.pl.*; luxe, étalage, *m.*; chiffons, *m.pl.*; colifichets, *m.pl.*; (*of metals*) affinerie, *f.* [finasser
Finesse, *s.* finesse, *f.*; — *v.n.* user de finesse,
Finessing, *s.* finasserie, *f.*, finasseries, *f.pl.*
Finger, *s.* doigt, *m.*; (*fig., hand*) main, *f.*; (*mus.*) doigter, *m.*; — *v.a.* manier avec les doigts, toucher à; toucher; palper; (*to dirty*) salir avec les doigts; (*pilfer*) mettre la main sur, escamoter, soustraire; (*mus.: on an instr.*) jouer de; (*mus.: perform a piece of music*) jouer, exécuter; (*mus.: mark the fingering on*) doigter; — *v.n.* (*mus.*) doigter. —*'s breadth,* travers de doigt, *m.* (*within a —'s breadth of,* à deux doigts de). —*'s end,* bout du doigt, *m.* *To be like — and thumb,* être ensemble comme les deux doigts de la main. *To blow on o.'s —s,* souffler dans ses doigts. *To have a — in,* être pour quelque chose dans. *To have at o.'s — ends,* savoir sur le bout du doigt. *To wear on o.'s —,* porter au doigt. — **biscuit,** *s.* biscuit à la cuiller, *m.* — **board,** *s.* (*of violins,* &c.) touche, *f.*; (*key-board*) clavier, *m.* — **case,** *s.* onglet, *m.* — **end,** *s.* bout du doigt, *m.* *O.'s — ends,* le bout de ses doigts. — **glass,** *s.* rince-doigts, lave-mains, rince-bouche, bol, *m.* — **ling,** *s.* (*young salmon*) digitale, *f.* — **mark,** *s.* marque de doigt; *v.a.* salir avec les doigts. — **nail,** *s.* ongle de la main, *m.* — **organ,** *s.* orgue à clavier, *m.* — **plate,** *s.* plaque de propreté, *f.* — **post,** *s.* poteau indicateur, *m.* — **reading,** *s.* lecture au moyen des doigts, *f.* — **stall,** *s.* doigtier, *m.* — **talking,** *s.* dactylologie, dactylolalie, *f.*
Fingered, *adj.* qui a des doigts; (*in compounds*) qui a les doigts ..., aux doigts ...; (*bot.*) digité; (*mus.*) doigté
Fingering, *s.* maniement, *m.*; (*mus.*) doigter, *m.*; (*mus., play, performance*) jeu, *m.*; exécution, *f.*; (*handiwork*) ouvrage délicat, *m.*; (*pilfering*) escamotage, *m.*
Fingle-fangle, *s.* baliverne, fadaise, *f.*
Finial, *s.* faîtage de pignon, couronnement, pinacle, *m.*
Finical, *adj.* affecté; précieux, prétentieux
Finically, *adv.* avec afféterie, précieusement, prétentieusement [*f.*, précieux, *m.*
Finicalness, *s.* afféterie, fatuité, préciosité,
Finikin, *adj.* *V.* **Finical;** (*trifling*) vétilleux
Fining, *s.* (*refining*) affinage, *m.*; (*of wine,* &c.) collage, *m.*, clarification, *f.*; (*mulcting*) condamnation à une amende, *f.*; —**s,** *pl.* colle, *f.*
Finis, *s.* fin, *f.*
Finish, *v.a.* finir, achever; terminer; accomplir, consommer; — *s.* fini, *m.*; perfection, *f.*; dernière main, *f.* — **off,** *v.a.* mettre la dernière main à, achever, finir
Finished, *part. adj.* fini, &c. (*V.* **Finish**); parfait; (*careful*) soigné
Finisher, *s.* finisseur, *m.*, -euse, *f.*; polisseur, *m.*, -euse, *f.*; (*theol.*) consommateur, *m.*; (*end*) fin, *f.*; (*slang, finishing blow*) coup de grâce, *m.*
Finishing, *adj.* dernier; (*school*) supérieur; (*governess*) pour finir l'éducation; — *s.* achèvement, *m.*; (*last polish*) fini, *m.*; (*of pictures*) dernière touche, *f.*; (*of stuffs,* &c.) apprêtage, *m.*; (*tech.*) finissage, *m.* — **blow,** *s.* coup de grâce, *m.* — **off,** *s.* (*tech.*) finissage, *m.* — **stroke,** *s.* dernière touche, *f.*; (*fig.*) coup de grâce, *m.*; (*completion*) comble, *m.*
Finite, *adj.* fini; borné; — *s.* fini, *m.*
Finitely, *adv.* d'une manière finie *or* bornée
Finiteness, *s.* nature finie *or* bornée, *f.*
Finlander, *s.* Finlandais, *m.*, e, *f.*
Finn, *s.* Finnois, *m.*, e, *f.*, Finlandais, *m.*, e, *f.*
Finned, *adj.* à nageoires, qui a des nageoires;
Finnish, *adj.* finnois, finlandais [(*her.*) loré
Finny, *adj.* *V.* **Finned.** *The — tribe,* les [poissons, *m.pl.*
Fiorin, — grass, *s.* fiorin, *m.*
Fir, *s.* sapin, *m.*; pin, *m.*; (*wood*) sapin, bois de sapin, *m.* *Scotch* —, pin, *m.* — **apple, -cone,**

s. pomme de pin, *f.* — **grove, -plantation,** s. sapinière, *f.* — **tree,** s. sapin, *m.*; pin, *m.* — **tribe,** s. conifères, *m.pl.*

Fire, s. feu, *m.*; (*conflagration*) incendie, *m.* — *!* au feu! *Destructive* —, incendie, *m.* *By the* —, (*pers.*) auprès du feu; (*things*) au feu. *On* —, en feu; (*fig.*) ardent. *On a slow* —, à petit feu. *To be on* —, être en feu; brûler. *To catch* —, prendre feu, s'allumer. *To go through — and water for*, se mettre au feu pour, se mettre en quatre pour. *To hang* —, faire long feu; rater. *To make a* —, faire du feu (*with an adj.*, faire un feu ...). *To miss* —, rater, manquer. *To set — to*, mettre le feu à. *To set on* —, mettre en feu, enflammer; mettre le feu à; incendier. *To take* —, prendre feu. — **alarm,** s. cri 'au feu!' (*bell*) tocsin, *m.* — **annihilating,** *adj.* anticombustible, extincteur. — **annihilator,** s. *V.* **Annihilator.** — **arm,** s. arme à feu, *f.* — **ball,** s. (*mil.*) balle à feu, *f.*; (*meteor*) globe de feu, *m.*; (*fuel*) boule grasse, briquette, *f.*; bûche économique, *f.* — **balloon,** s. montgolfière, *f.* — **bar,** s. barre de foyer *or* de fourneau, *f.* — **blast,** s. nielle, brouissure, *f.* — **board,** s. devant de cheminée, *m.* — **box,** boîte à feu, *f.*; (*furnace*) foyer, *m.* — **brand,** s. tison, brandon, *m.*; (*pers.*) boute-feu, *m.* — **brick,** s. brique réfractaire, *f.* — **brigade,** s. corps de pompiers *or* de sapeurs-pompiers, *m.*, sapeurs-pompiers, *m.pl.* — **brigade station,** caserne de pompiers, *f.* — **brush,** s. balai de cheminée, *m.* — **bucket,** s. seau à incendie, *m.* — **chest,** s. caisse d'artifice, *f.* — **clay,** s. argile réfractaire, *f.* — **cock,** s. *V.* — **plug.** — **company,** s. compagnie de pompiers *or* de sapeurs-pompiers, *f.* — **cracker,** s. pétard, *m.* — **damp,** s. feu grisou, grisou, *m.* — **department,** s. corps des sapeurs-pompiers, *m.* — **dog,** s. chenet, *m.* — **door,** s. porte de fourneau *or* de four, *f.* — **drake,** s. dragon volant, *m.*; flammerole, *f.*, feu follet, *m.*; feu d'artifice, *m.* — **drum,** s. générale, *f.* — **eater,** s. mangeur (*m.*, -euse, *f.*) de feu, pyrophage, *m.f.*; (*fig.*) ferrailleur, fanfaron, sacripant, *m.* — **eating,** *adj.* qui mange du feu, pyrophage; (*fig.*) fanfaron; s. pyrophagie, *f.* — **engine,** s. pompe à incendie, *f.* — **engine station,** s. dépôt de pompes à incendie, *m.*; caserne de pompiers, *f.* — **escape,** s. sac de sauvetage, appareil de sauvetage pour les incendies, *m.* — **exercise,** s. exercice à feu, *m.* — **extinguisher,** s. extincteur, *m.* — **extinguishing,** *adj.* extincteur. — **fan,** s. éventoir, *m.* — **flaire,** s. pastenague, *f.* — **fly,** s. mouche à feu, *f.* — **grate,** s. grille de foyer, *f.* — **guard,** s. garde-feu, *m.* — **insurance,** s. *V.* **Insurance.** — **insurance company** *or* **office,** s. compagnie (*f.*) *or* bureau (*m.*) d'assurance contre l'incendie. — **irons,** *s.pl.* garniture de foyer *or* de feu, *f.*, feu, *m.* — **irons holder,** s. porte-pelle-et-pincettes, croissant de cheminée, croissant, *m.* — **ladder,** s. échelle à incendie, échelle à crochets, *f.* — **less,** *adj.* sans feu. — **lock,** s. fusil, *m.*; arme à feu, *f.* — **main,** s. conduite d'eau pour les incendies, *f.* — **man,** s. pompier, sapeur-pompier, *m.*; (*stoker*) chauffeur, *m.* — **master,** s. (*mil.*) maître artificier, *m.* — **new,** *adj.* qui sort de la forge; (*fig.*) tout neuf; brillant. — **office,** s. bureau d'assurance contre l'incendie, *m.* — **ordeal,** s. épreuve du feu, *f.* — **pan,** s. brasier, réchaud, *m.*; (*of flint-locks*) bassinet, *m.* — **place,** s. cheminée, *f.*; (*hearth*) âtre, foyer, *m.*; (*furnace*) fourneau, *m.* — **plug,** s. bouche de secours (contre l'incendie), *f.*; bouche d'eau, *f.* — **policy,** s. police d'assurance contre l'incendie, *f.* — **pot,** s. pot à feu, *m.* — **proof,** *adj.* à l'épreuve du feu; réfractaire. — **pump,** s. pompe à incendie, *f.* — **raft,** s brûlot, *m.* — **range,** s. fourneau, *m.* — **red,** *adj.* rouge feu. — **screen,** s. écran, *m.* — **set,** s. feu, *m.* — **ship,** s. brûlot, *m.* — **shovel,** s. pelle à feu, *f.* — **side,** s. coin du feu, *m.*; foyer domestique, foyer, *m.*; cheminée, *f.* *By the — side*, au coin du feu. — **station,** s. caserne de pompiers, *f.* — **steel,** s. briquet, *m.* — **stone,** s. pierre réfractaire, *f.*; âtre, *m.* — **stove,** s. *V.* **Stove.** — **tile,** s. tuile réfractaire, *f.* — **wood,** s bois à brûler, bois de chauffage, *m.* — **work,** s. pièce d'artifice, *f.* (**-s,** *pl. See below*). — **worker,** s. artificier, *m.* — **work maker** *or* **manufacturer** *or* **man,** s. artificier, *m.* — **works,** s. *pl.* (*materials*) artifice, *m.*; (*exhibition*) feu d'artifice, *m.* — **worm,** s. ver luisant, *m.* — **worship,** s. culte (*m.*) *or* adoration (*f.*) du feu. — **worshipper,** s. adorateur du feu, *m.*, guèbre, *m.f.*, parse, *m.f.*, parsi, *m.*, e, *f.*

Fire, *v.a.* mettre le feu à; embraser; mettre en feu; incendier; (*fig.*) enflammer; (*guns, pistols, fireworks*) tirer; tirer un coup de; (*horses*) mettre le feu à; — *v.n.* prendre feu; s'enflammer; (*of fire-arms*) faire feu, tirer ('*at,*' sur). — *!* (*mil. command*) feu! *To be —ed at*, recevoir *or* essuyer un coup de feu. — **away,** *v.a.* tirer; consumer; *v.n.* (*fam.*) marchez! marche! en avant! — **off,** *v.a.* tirer; lâcher. — **up,** *v.n.* s'enflammer; prendre feu; s'échauffer

Firer, s. incendiaire, *m.f.*; (*fig.*) boute-feu, *m.*

Firing, s. combustible, *m.*; chauffage, *m.*; (*mil.*) feu, *m.*, décharge, fusillade, canonnade, *f.*; coups de feu, *m.pl.*; (*practice*) tir, *m.*; (*vet.*) cautérisation, *f.* — **ground,** s. tir, *m.* — **iron,** s. fer à cautériser, *m.* — **practice,** s. exercice à feu, *m.* — **range,** s. tir, *m.*

Firkin, s. barillet, *m.*; quartaut, *m.*; (*for butter*) tinette, *f.*

Firm, *adj.* ferme, solide; constant; (*strong*) fort; — s. maison de commerce, maison, *f.*; raison sociale, raison de commerce, raison, *f.*

Firmament, s. firmament, *m.*

Firmamental, *adj.* du firmament

Firman, s. firman, *m.*

Firmly, *adv.* fermement, avec fermeté; solidement, fortement; constamment [force, *f.*

Firmness, s. fermeté, *f.*; solidité, *f.*; (*strength*)

First, *adj.* s. premier; (*after* 20, 30, &c.) et unième, (*after* 80 *and* 100) unième; (*mil., nav.*) en premier; (*of cousins*) germain; — *adv.* (*of order*) premièrement, en premier lieu, avant tout; (*of time*) d'abord; préalablement; au commencement; pour la première fois; (*of place, rank*) le premier, au premier rang, en première ligne. *At* —, *at the* —, — *of all*, d'abord; dans le premier moment; dans les premiers temps; au commencement, dans l'origine. *From the* —, *from the very* —, dès l'abord, dès le début. *The very* —, tout le premier. *The — that comes*, le premier venu. — *and last*, d'un bout à l'autre, entièrement; (*on an average*) en moyenne. — *or last*, tôt ou tard. — *come*, — *served*, le premier arrivé est le premier servi; les premiers vont devant. *Twenty-* —, *Thirty-* —, *V.* **Twenty** *and* **Thirty.** *Forty-* —, quarante et unième. *One hundred Eighty-* —, quatre-vingt-unième. *One hundred and* —, cent-unième. — **begot, -begotten,** *adj.* aîné. — **born,** *adj.* s. premier-né, aîné. — **class** *carriage, ticket*, &c., voiture, billet, &c. de première classe. — **floor,** s. premier étage, premier, *m.* — **fruits,** s. *pl.* prémices, *f.pl.*; (*eccl. due*) annate, *f.*, annates, *f.pl.* — **hand,** *adj. adv.* de la première main, le première main; s. premier ouvrier, *m.*, première ouvrière, *f.*; premier garçon, *m.* — **rate,** [*V.* **Rate**

Firstling, s. *adj.* premier-né, *m.*

Firstly, *adv.* premièrement

Firth, s. *V.* **Frith**

Fisc, s. fisc, *m.*

Fiscal, *adj.* fiscal; — s. fiscal, procureur fiscal, *m.*

Fiscality, *s.* fiscalité, *f.*
Fiscally, *adv.* fiscalement
Fish, *s.* poisson, *m.*; (*at cards,* &c.) fiche, *f.*; (*fellow*) individu, animal, corps, pistolet, *m.*; — *v.a.n.* pêcher; (*fig.*) chercher; attraper; surprendre. *Fried* —, poisson frit, *m.*, friture, *f.* *Neither* —, *flesh, nor fowl,* ni chair ni poisson. *To be —ing,* être à la pêche, pêcher. *To go —ing,* aller à la pêche. *To — in troubled waters,* pêcher en eau trouble. *To have other — to fry,* avoir bien d'autres chats à fouetter. — **basket,** *s.* panier à poisson, *m.*; manne à marée, *f.* — **bone,** *s.* arête (de poisson), *f.* — **cart,** *s.* chasse-marée, *m.* — **carver,** *s.* truelle à poisson, *f.* — **culture,** *s.* pisciculture, *f.* — **culturist,** *s.* pisciculteur, *m.* — **curer,** *s.* saleur, *m.*, -euse, *f.*, caqueur, *m.*, -euse, *f.* — **day,** *s.* jour maigre, *m.* — **dinner,** *s.* dîner de poisson, *m.* — **eater,** *s.* ichthyophage, *m.f.* — **eating,** *adj.* ichthyophage, ichthyophagique; *s.* ichthyophagie, *f.* — **factor,** *s.* *V.* — **salesman.** — **fag,** *s.* *V.* — **woman.** — **for,** *v.a.* pêcher; (*fig.*) chercher, quêter. —**ful,** *adj.* poissonneux. — **garth,** *s.* nasse, *f.*, duit, *m.* — **gig,** *s.* trident, *m.*, foène, fichûre, *f.* — **glue,** *s.* colle de poisson, ichthyocolle, *f.* — **hook,** *s.* hameçon, *m.* — **house,** *s.* vivier, *m.* — **kettle,** *s.* poissonnière, *f.* — **knife, -eating knife,** *s.* couteau à poisson, *m.* — **like,** *s.* semblable à un poisson, de poisson. — **louse,** *s.* caligé, argule, *m.* — **market,** *s.* marché au poisson, *m.*, halle au poisson, poissonnerie, *f.* — **meal,** *s.* repas maigre, *m.* — **monger,** *s.* marchand (*m*, e, *f.*) de poisson, poissonnier, *m.*, -ière, *f.* — **net,** *s.* filet de pêche, *m.* — **out,** *v.a.* découvrir; surprendre. — **pie,** *s.* pâte de poisson, *m.* — **pond,** *s.* étang, vivier, *m.* — **room,** *s.* (*nav.*) soute au poisson, *f.* — **salesman,** *s.* marchand de poisson (aux halles), poissonnier, mareyeur, *m.* — **sauce,** *s.* sauce pour le poisson, *f.* — **skin,** *s.* peau de chien de mer, peau de chien, *f.* — **slice,** *s.* écumoire, *f.*; truelle à poisson, *f.* — **sound,** *s.* noue de poisson, *f.* — **spear,** *s.* harpon, *m.* — **stall,** *s.* étalage de poisson, *m.* — **stew,** *s.* matelote, *f.* — **tail,** *adj.* en queue de poisson. — **tub,** *s.* cuvier. — **up,** *v.a.* pêcher. — **up again,** *v.a.* repêcher. — **weir, -wear,** *s.* nasse, *f.*, duit, *m.* — **wife, -woman,** *s.* marchande de poisson, poissarde, *f.*
Fisher, *s.* pêcheur, *m.* — **boat,** *s.* *V.* **Fishing-boat.** — **boy,** *s.* petit pêcheur, *m.* — **man,** *s.* pêcheur, *m.*; (*vessel*) bateau pêcheur, *m.* — **town,** *s.* *V.* **Fishing-town**
Fishery, *s.* pêche, *f.*; (*place*) pêcherie, *f.*; (*law*) droit de pêche, *m.*
Fishiness, *s.* goût de poisson, *m.*
Fishing, *s.* pêche, *f.*; — *adj.* pêcheur. *Trout* or &c. —, pêche aux truites *or* &c., *f.* — **bird,** *s.* oiseau pêcheur, *m.* — **boat,** *s.* bateau pêcheur, *m.*, bateau de pêche, barque de pêcheur, *f.* — **fly,** *s.* mouche artificielle, *f.* — **frog,** *s.* baudroie, *f.*, baudreuil, *m.*, lophie, *f.* — **gear,** *s.* *V.* — **tackle.** — **hook,** *s.* hameçon, *m.* — **line,** *s.* ligne à pêcher, ligne, *f.* — **net,** *s.* filet de pêche, *m.* — **place,** *s.* pêcherie, *f.* — **rod,** *s.* canne à pêche, *f.* — **tackle,** *s.* articles *or* ustensiles de pêche, *m.pl.* — **town,** *s.* ville de pêche, ville de pêcheurs, *f.*
Fishy, *adj.* de poisson; poissonneux; (*rank*) [puant
Fisk, *s.* *V.* **Fisc**
Fissile, *adj.* fissile
Fissility, *s.* fissilité, *f.*
Fission, *s.* scission, *f.*
Fissiped, *adj.* *s.* fissipède, *adj.* *m.f.*, *s.m.*
Fissirostral, *adj.* fissirostre
Fissirostre, *s.* fissirostre, *m.*
Fissuration, *s.* fissuration, *f.*
Fissure, *s.* fissure, fente, *f.*; (*anat., surg.*) fissure, *f.*; — *v.a.* fissurer

Fist, *s.* poing, *m.* —**ful,** *s.* poignée, *f.*
Fisted, *adj.* au poing ... *Close* —, *hard* —, serré, pingre, avare, dur à la desserre
Fistic, *adj.* de boxe, de la boxe
Fisticuffs, *s.pl.* coups de poing, *m.pl.*; combat [à coups de poing, *m.*
Fistuca, *s.* mouton, *m.*
Fistula, *s.* fistule, *f.*
Fistular, Fistulous, *adj.* fistulaire, fistuleux
Fit, *s.* accès, *m.*, attaque, *f.*; crise, *f.*; attaque de nerfs, *f.*; convulsion, *f.*; (*whim*) boutade, *f.*; (*of garments*) coupe, *f.*; forme, *f.* *Cold* —, frisson, *m.* *Mad* or &c. —, accès de folie *or* &c. *By —s and starts, by —s,* par sauts et par bonds; par accès; par moments; par boutades; par saccades; à bâtons rompus; irrégulièrement
Fit, *adj.* propre (à), bon (à); (*proper*) convenable (de); à propos (de); (*just*) juste, raisonnable; (*capable*) en état (de), capable (de). — *for service,* — *for use,* propre au service; en état de servir. — *to drink,* bon à boire, buvable; (*matured, of wine*) en boite. — *to eat,* bon à manger, mangeable. *In a — state to,* en état de
Fit, *v.a.* convenir à; arranger, accorder; accommoder (à); pourvoir (de); préparer; approprier (à); ajuster (à), adapter (à); rendre propre (à) *or* capable (de); joindre (à); agencer; (*of garments, corks,* &c.) aller à; (*the shape*) prendre; (*as tailors*) habiller; (*as bootmakers*) chausser; (*as hatters or milliners*) coiffer; — *v.n.* convenir (de); s'adapter, s'ajuster; (*in*) s'emboîter; (*shut*) joindre, fermer; (*of garments*) aller; être. *To — tight* or *close,* être juste; (*shut*) joindre bien, joindre. *That coat —s you well,* cet habit vous va bien. *It —s too tight,* il est trop juste. — **in,** *v.a.* emboîter, encastrer; *v.n.* s'emboîter, s'encastrer. — **on,** *v.a.* adapter (à); *v.n.* s'adapter (à). — **out,** préparer, monter, disposer; équiper; (*o.'s children*) donner un trousseau à, monter; (*nav.*) équiper, armer. — **up,** arranger; préparer; ajuster; (*a shop,* &c.) monter, meubler
Fitch, *s.* (*bot.*) *V.* **Vetch;** (*zool.*) *V.* **Fitchet**
Fitchet, *s.* putois, *m.*
Fitful, *adj.* agité; incertain; vacillant; irrégulier; saccadé; capricieux, plein de boutades
Fitfully, *adv.* avec agitation; avec incertitude; irrégulièrement; par accès; par boutades; par saccades; capricieusement; en vacillant
Fitfulness, *s.* agitation, *f.*; incertitude, *f.*; vacillation, *f.*; irrégularité, *f.*; caprice, *m.*
Fitly, *adv.* convenablement, à propos, bien; justement
Fitness, *s.* convenance, propriété, *f.*; à-propos, *m.*; justesse, *f.*; conformité, *f.*; accord, *m.*; capacité, *f.* [arrangé, &c. (*V.* **Fit,** *v.a.n.*)
Fitted, *adj.* propre (à), fait (pour); — *part.*
Fitter, *s.* ajusteur, *m.*; appareilleur, *m.* — **out,** *s.* (*nav.*) armateur, *m.*
Fitting, *adj.* convenable; à propos; juste, raisonnable; — *s.* adaptation, *f.*; ajustement, *m.*; agencement, *m.*; —**s,** *s. pl.* garnitures, *f.pl.*; armature, *f.*; agencements, *m.pl.*, agencement, *m.*; appareil, *m.*; matériel, *m.*; accessoires, *m.pl.*; appliques, *f.pl.*; (*woodwork*) boiseries, *f.pl.*; (*ironwork*) ferrures, *f.pl.* — **in,** *s.* emboîtement, *m.* — **out,** *s.* équipement, *m.*: (*of o.'s children*) trousseau, *m.* — **up,** *s.* arrangement, *m.*; montage, *m.*; ameublement, *m.*
Fittingly, *adv.* convenablement
Fittingness. *V.* **Fitness**
Five, *adj.* *s.* cinq (*adj. m.f.*, *s.m.*); (*elliptically*) (*of the clock*) cinq heures, *f.pl.*; (*of o.'s age*) cinq ans, *m.pl.*; —**s,** *s. pl.* *See below.* — **cornered,** *adj.* à cinq angles, pentagone. — **fold,** *adj. adv.* quintuple, cinq fois autant, cinq fois. — **leaved,** *adj.* à cinq feuilles. — **pence,** *s. pl.* cinquante centimes, *m.pl.*, (un) demi-franc, *m.* — **penny,** *adj.* de cinquante centimes. — **penny piece,** *s.* pièce de cinquante centimes, *f.*, demi-franc, *m.*

Fives, *s. pl.* cinq, *m.pl.*; (*vet.*) avives, *f.pl.*; (*play*) la balle au mur, *f.* — **court,** *s.* jeu de balle, *m.*

Fix, *s.* impasse, *f.*; embarras, *m.*; — *v.a.* fixer; établir; attacher; arrêter; déterminer; captiver; — *v.n.* se fixer; (*on, upon*) s'arrêter (à), se déterminer (à), se fixer (sur); choisir. *To — bayonets,* mettre la baïonnette au canon. *— bayonets!* baïonnette au canon! *With —ed bayonets,* la baïonnette au bout du fusil

Fixation, *s.* fixation, *f.*; fixage, *m.*; fixité, [stabilité, *f.*

Fixature, *s.* bandoline, *f.*

Fixed, *adj.* fixe; (*pers.*) à poste fixe; — *part.* fixé, &c. (*V.* **Fix,** *v.a.*)

Fixedly, *adv.* fixement; fermement

Fixedness, Fixity, *s.* fixité, *f.*

Fixing, *s.* fixage, *m.*; fixation, *f.*; (*laying*) pose, *f.*

Fixture, *s.* (*of houses*) meuble à demeure fixe, *m.*; immeuble, *m.*; (*tie*) attache, *f.* *Inventory of —s,* état de lieux, *m.*

Fiz, Fizz, Fizzle, *v.n.* siffler; — *s.* sifflement, *m.*

Flabbily, *adv.* flasquement, mollement

Flabbiness, *s.* flaccidité, *f.*

Flabby, *adj.* flasque, mollasse

Flaccid, *adj.* flasque

Flaccidity, Flaccidness, *s.* flaccidité, *f.*

Flag, *v.n.* pendre, flotter; (*strike*) battre; (*fig.*) s'affaisser; perdre courage; languir; faiblir; diminuer; se relâcher; se ralentir; (*be flabby*) être flasque; — *v.a.* baisser; détendre; laisser tomber; affaisser; abattre; (*with stones*) daller

Flag, *s.* drapeau, *m.*; (*nav.*) pavillon, *m.*; (*stone*) dalle, *f.*; (*bot.*) glaïeul, iris, *m.*; (*blade of corn*) feuille, pampe, fiole, *f.*; (*turf*) écobuage, *m.* — *of truce,* (*mil.*) drapeau blanc, *m.*; (*nav.*) pavillon parlementaire, pavillon blanc, *m.*, (*vessel*) bâtiment (*or* vaisseau) parlementaire, parlementaire, *m.* *Bearer of a — of truce,* parlementaire, *m.* *To strike o.'s —,* amener son pavillon, amener. — **bearer,** *s.* porte-drapeau, *m.* — **captain,** *s.* capitaine de pavillon, *m.* — **officer,** *s.* officier général de marine, *m.*; (*in command of a squadron*) chef d'escadre, *m.*, (*in France*) contre-amiral, *m.* — **pole,** *s.* *V.* — **staff.** — **ship,** *s.* vaisseau amiral, *m.* — **staff,** *s.* mât de pavillon, mât, *m.* — **stone,** *s.* dalle, *f.* — **way,** *s.* dalles, *f.pl.*, trottoir, *m.*

Flagellate, *v.a.* flageller

Flagellation, *s.* flagellation, *f.*

Flageolet, *s.* flageolet, *m.*

Flageolettist, *s.* flageolet, flageolettiste, *m.*

Flagginess, *s.* flaccidité, *f.*

Flagging, *part. adj.* pendant, qui pend, flottant, qui flotte, &c. (*V.* **Flag,** *v.n.*); (*striking*) qui bat; — *s.* (*with stones*) dallage, *m.*

Flaggy, *adj.* (*hanging*) qui pend, qui flotte; (*flabby*) flasque, mou; languissant, sans force; (*dejected*) abattu; (*insipid*) insipide, fade; (*bot.*) plein de glaïeuls

Flagitious, *adj.* méchant, pervers, scélérat; atroce, noir; infâme, abominable

Flagitiously, *adv.* avec scélératesse, en scélérat; d'une manière infâme

Flagitiousness, *s.* méchanceté, perversité, scélératesse, *f.*; infamie, *f.*

Flagon, *s.* flacon, *m.*; (*in churches*) burette, *f.* — **maker,** *s.* flaconnier, *m.*, -ière, *f.* — **making, -trade,** *s.* flaconnerie, *f.*

Flagrance, Flagrancy, *s.* flagrance, *f.*, éclat, *m.*; énormité, *f.*

Flagrant, *adj.* flagrant; patent

Flagrantly, *adv.* d'une manière flagrante; d'une manière patente

Flail, *s.* fléau, *m.*

Flake, *s.* (*of snow, wool*) flocon, *m.*; (*lamina, scale, as of metals,* &c.) lame, *f.*; écaille, *f.*; (*of pastry, flesh of fish,* &c.) feuille, *f.*; (*of bran*) paillette, *f.*; (*of ice*) glaçon, *m.*; (*of fire*) flammèche, flammette, étincelle, *f.*; (*layer, as of grease*) couche, *f.*; — *v.a.* former en flocon; (*metals*) laminer; — *v.n.* floconner, se floconner; s'écailler. — **white,** *s.* blanc de céruse, *m.*

Flaky, *adj.* floconneux, en flocons, par flocons; (*in layers*) en couches, par couches; (*scaly*) écailleux; (*of pastry, flesh of fish,* &c.) feuilleté. — *paste,* pâte feuilletée, *f.*, feuilletage, feuilleté, *m.*

Flam, *s.* blague, bourde, bricole, *f.*; — *v.a.n.* blaguer. — **new,** *adj.* tout flambant neuf

Flambeau, *s.* flambeau, *m.*

Flamboyant, *adj.* flamboyant

Flame, *s.* flamme, *f.*; feu, *m.*; (*pers.*) passion, *f.*, amours, *f.pl.*; —**s,** *pl.* flammes, *f.pl.*; (*fire*) incendie, *m.*; — *v.a.* enflammer; — *v.n.* flamber, jeter de la flamme; (— *up, get angry*) s'enflammer, s'emporter; (*shine*) flamboyer, briller. — **colour,** *s.* couleur de feu, *f.*, ponceau, *m.* — **coloured,** *adj.* couleur de feu, ponceau. — **eyed,** *adj.* aux yeux enflammés. —**less,** *adj.* sans flamme. — **let,** *s.* flammette, *f.*

Flamen, *s.* flamine, *m.*

Flamer, *s.* (*fusee*) flammigère, *f.*

Flaming, *adj.* flambant; flamboyant; éclatant; ardent; en feu; violent; magnifique; — *s.* flamboiement, *m.* — **fusee,** *s.* flammigère, *f.*

Flamingly, *adv.* avec éclat; magnifiquement

Flamingo, *s.* flamant, *m.*

Flaminian, Flaminical, Flamineous, [*adj.* flaminien

Flammiferous, *adj.* flammifère

Flammigerous, *adj.* flammigère

Flammivomous, *adj.* flammivome

Flamy, *adj.* de flamme; brûlant; enflammé; (*of colours*) de feu, éclatant

Flanconade, *s.* flanconade, *f.* [boudin, *m.*

Flange, *s.* rebord, *m.*, saillie, *f.*; (*of wheels*)

Flank, *s.* flanc, *m.*; côté, *m.*; (*of beef, cod*) flanchet, *m.*; (*mil.*) flanc, *m.*; — *v.a.* flanquer; (*mil.*) prendre (*or* attaquer) en flanc; — *v.n.* toucher (à), border. — **company,** *s.* compagnie de flanc, *f.*

Flanker, *s.* (*fort.*) flanc, *m.*; (*mil.*) flanqueur, *m.*

Flanking, *s.* flanquement, *m.*

Flannel, *s.* flanelle, *f.*; — *adj.* de *or* en flanelle

Flap, *v.a.n.* (*strike*) frapper, battre; (*drive away*) chasser; (*of wings*) frapper de l'aile; battre des ailes; (*of the tail*) donner des coups de queue; (*hang*) pendre, retomber, battre; — *s.* tape, *f.*, coup, *m.*; (*of wings*) coup d'aile, *m.*; (*flapper*) clapet, *m.*; (*of a hat or cap*) bord pendant, bord rabattu, *m.*; (*of a coat, shirt, table*) pan, *m.*; (*of a counter, portfolio,* &c.) abattant, *m.*; (*of pockets*) patte, *f.*; (*of a shoe*) oreille, *f.*; (*of old-fashioned trousers*) pont, *m.*; (*of the ear*) bout, *m.*; (*of a churn*) bat-beurre, *m.*; (*of a saddle*) quartier, *m.* — **eared,** *adj.* aux oreilles pendantes. — **hat,** *s.* chapeau à bords pendants, claque-oreilles, *m.* — **mouthed,** *adj.* aux lèvres pendantes

Flapping, *part. adj.* battant, &c. (*V* **Flap,** *v.a.n.*); (*of hats*) à bords pendants; — *s.* battement, *m.*; battement d'ailes, coup d'aile, *m.*

Flare, *s.* vive clarté, *f.*; éclat, *m.*; flamme, *f.*; — *v.n.* étinceler; flamber; (*of lamps*) filer; (*fig.*) briller; (*pers.*) s'emporter

Flaring, *adj.* étincelant; brillant; éclatant; éblouissant; (*of lamps*) qui file

Flash, *s.* éclat, *m.*; éclair, *m.*; (*of light, water*) jet, *m.*; (*from a fire-arm*) lumière, *f.*, feu, *m.*; (*tinsel*) clinquant, *m.*; (*slang*) argot, *m.*, langue verte, *f.*; — *adj.* faux; de mauvais *or* de bas aloi; équivoque; interlope; (*slangy*) d'argot, bas, trivial; (*pop.*) brillant, beau, magnifique; — *v.n.* briller, étinceler, éclater; flamber; passer comme un éclair; jaillir; s'élancer; — *v.a.* faire jaillir; (*throw*) jeter, lancer, envoyer, porter à l'instant. — *of the eye,* coup d'œil vif, *m.* — *of wit,* trait d'esprit, *m.*, saillie, *f.* — *in the pan,* faux feu, *m.*; (*fig.*) coup d'épée dans l'eau, pas de clerc, *m.* *To — in the pan,* faire faux feu, rater. — **across,** *v.n.a.* traverser. — **house,** *s.* repaire de

voleurs, *m.* — **out,** *v.n.* éclater; jaillir. — **pan,** *s.* bassinet, *m.* — **pipe,** *s.* tube d'allumage, *m.*
Flasher, *s.* homme superficiel, *m.*
Flashily, *adv.* avec un éclat trompeur, superficiellement
Flashy, *adj.* éclatant, brillant, voyant, à effet, tapageur; superficiel, frivole; insipide, fade
Flask, *s.* bouteille, *f.*, flacon, *m.*; (*for powder*) poire à poudre, *f.* — **maker,** &c. *V.* **Flagon**
Flasket, *s.* corbeille, manne, *f.*
Flat, *adj.* plat; (*smooth*) uni; (*become flat*) aplati; (*lying*) étendu; couché; (*positive*) positif, clair, net, franc, formel; (*cast down*) abattu, découragé; (*silly*) simple, nigaud; (*tasteless*) fade, insipide; (*of drink*) éventé, plat; (*of colours*) amorti; (*of sounds*) grave; (*com.*) peu actif, peu animé, calme, languissant, mort; bas; (*gram.*) dur; (*mus.*) bémol; (*mec.*) plane, aplati; — *adverb.* à plat; — *s.* surface plane, *f.*; terrain plat, *m.*; (*plain*) plaine, *f.*; (*the flat part*) plat, *m.*; (*of a house*) étage, *m.*; appartement, *m.*; (*of thought,* &c.) platitude, *f.*; (*simpleton*) nigaud, *m.*, e, *f.*, niais, *m.*, e, *f.*, serin, cornichon, *m.*; (*mus.*) bémol, *m.*; (*nav.*) écueil, bas-fond, *m.*; bordage, *m.*; (*boat*) bateau à fond plat, bateau plat, *m.*, filadière, *f.*; (*butter-basket*) passet, *m.*, manne, *f.*, panier à beurre, *m.*; (*spin.*) plateau, *m.*; — *v.a.* aplatir; rendre insipide; (*metals*) laminer; (*paint.*) lisser; — *v.n.* s'aplatir; (*of drink*) s'éventer. — *and plain*, franc et net. *To beat* —, aplatir. *To get* or *grow* —, s'aplatir; (*of wine,* &c.) s'éventer. *To lay* —, coucher à plat; coucher; renverser; terrasser; raser. *To lie* —, être à plat; être étendu. — **bottomed,** *adj.* à fond plat, plat. — **fish,** *s.* poisson plat, pleuronecte, *m.* — **headed,** *adj.* à tête plate. — **iron,** *s.* fer à repasser, *m.* — **nosed,** *adj.* qui a le nez plat, au nez plat, camus, camard. — **wise,** *adv.* à plat
Flatly, *adv.* à plat; (*evenly*) de niveau; (*dully*) platement; (*positively*) positivement, clairement, nettement, tout net, net; (*completely*) complètement
Flatness, *s.* aplatissement, *m.*; (*evenness*) égalité, *f.*; (*of liquors*) évent, *m.*, insipidité, fadeur, *f.*; (*dulness*) platitude, *f.*; insipidité, *f.*; (*of sound*) gravité, *f.*
Flatten, *v.a.* aplatir; aplanir; (*make vapid*) affadir, éventer; (*depress*) abattre, décourager; (*soften*) adoucir; (*metals*) laminer; — *v.n.* s'aplatir; s'aplanir; (*become vapid*) s'éventer, s'affadir; (*pers.*) s'attrister
Flattening, *s.* aplatissement, *m.*; aplanissement, *m.*; (*of metals*) laminage, *m.*; (*tech.*) aplatissage, *m.*
Flatter, *s.* (*pers.*) aplatisseur, *m.*; (*instr.*) aplatissoir, aplatisseur, *m.*; — *v.a.* ('*with,*' de) flatter
Flatterer, *s.* flatteur, *m.*, -euse, *f.*
Flattering, *adj.* flatteur
Flatteringly, *adv.* flatteusement, d'une manière flatteuse
Flattery, *s.* flatterie, *f.*
Flatting, *s.* *V.* **Flattening.** — **mill,** *s.* laminoir, *m.* — **rollers,** *s. pl.* aplatissoire, *f.*
Flattish, *adj.* un peu plat
Flatulence, Flatulency, *s.* flatulence, flatuosité, *f.*; (*fig.*) vide, néant, *m.*, vanité, *f.*; légèreté, *f.*
Flatulent, *adj.* flatulent, flatueux, venteux; (*fig.*) gonflé d'air; vain, vide, creux; ampoulé; orgueilleux
Flatuosity, *s.* flatuosité
Flatuous, *adj.* flatueux
Flatus, *s.* vent, *m.*, vents, gaz, *m.pl.*; (*fig.*) souffle, *m.*
Flaunt, *v.n.* se pavaner; parader; avoir (*or* prendre) un air insolent; (*flutter*) flotter, voltiger; — *v.a.* étaler, déployer, montrer, promener; — *s.* étalage, *m.*; impertinence, *f.*
Flaunting, *adj.* qui se pavane; (*proud*) fier; (*fluttering*) flottant, voltigeant; (*gaudy*) *V.* **Gaudy;** — *s.* parade, *f.*, étalage, *m.*
Flavine, *s.* flavine, *f.*
Flavorous, *adj.* *V.* **Flavoured**
Flavour, *s.* goût, *m.*; saveur, *f.*; (*of tea, coffee,* &c.) arôme, *m.*; (*of meat*) fumet, goût, *m.*; (*of wine*) bouquet, fumet, *m.*; (*of flowers*) parfum, *m.*; — *v.a.* donner du goût *or* &c. à; assaisonner ('*with,*' de). —**less,** *adj.* sans goût *or* &c.
Flavoured, *adj.* savoureux; odorant; assaisonné. *Full* —, fort. *High* —, (*of wine*) qui a beaucoup de bouquet; (*of meat*) de haut goût; (*of juicy fruit*) d'une bonne eau, d'une eau agréable. *Mild* —, doux
Flavouring, *s.* assaisonnement, *m.*
Flavoury, *adj.* *V.* **Flavoured**
Flaw, *s.* (*crack*) fente, *f.*; fêlure, *f.*; gerçure, crevasse, *f.*; (*breach*) brèche, *f.*; (*defect*) défaut, *m.*; (*of gems*) paille, *f.*; (*blemish*) tache, *f.*; (*hangnail*) envie, *f.*; (*law*) nullité, *f.*, vice, *m.*; (*of wind*) risée de vent, *f.*; — *v.a.* fendre, fendiller, fêler, gercer, crevasser; (*law*) annuler, vicier. —**less,** *adj.* sans fente; sans défaut, sans tache
Flawy, *adj.* plein de fentes, plein de crevasses, fendillé, crevassé; qui a des défauts, défectueux; (*of gems*) paillé, pailleux
Flax, *s.* lin, *m.*; — *adj.* de lin; (*pertaining to the flax trade*) linier. — **bush,** *s.* phormion, *m.* — **comb,** *s.* seran, *m.* — **dresser,** *s.* seranceur de lin, *m.* — **dressing,** *s.* serançage du lin, *m.* — **field,** *s.* linière, *f.* — **lily,** *s.* phormion, *m.* — **mill,** *s.* filature de lin, *f.* — **seed,** *s.* graine de lin, *f.* — **spinner,** *s.* filateur de lin, *m.* — **tribe,** *s.* linacées, *f.pl.*
Flaxen, Flaxy, *adj.* de lin; (*of the hair*) blond
Flay, *v.a.* écorcher; (*the skin,* &c.) enlever
Flayer, *s.* écorcheur, *m.*
Flaying, *s.* écorchement, *m.*; écorchure, *f.*
Flea, *s.* puce, *f.*; — *v.a.* épucer, ôter les puces à. *A — in o.'s ear*, la puce à l'oreille. — **bane,** *s.* pulicaire, *f.*; conyze, *f.* — **bite,** *s.* morsure de puce, *f.*; (*fig.*) petit mal, *m.*, bagatelle, *f.*, rien, *m.* — **bitten,** *adj.* mangé de puces; (*spotted*) moucheté, tacheté. — **bitten grey,** *adj. s.* aubère, *adj. m.f., s.m.* — **wort,** *s.* herbe aux puces, *f.*
Flead, *s.* graisse de porc, panne, *f.*
Fleam, *s.* (*vet.*) flamme, *f.*
Fleck, Flecker, *v.a.* moucheter, tacheter
Fledge, *v.a.* garnir de plumes, emplumer, donner des ailes à, mettre en état de voler
Fledged, *adj.* garni *or* couvert de plumes, emplumé, en état de voler, dru
Fledgling, *s.* petit oiseau assez fort pour voler, petit oiseau dru, oisillon, *m.*
Flee, *v.a.n.* fuir; prendre la fuite; s'enfuir; se réfugier
Fleece, *s.* toison, *f.* — *v.a.* tondre; (*pers.*) écorcher, plumer, rançonner; (*of*) dépouiller (de). — **wool,** *s.* laine de toison, *f.*
Fleecer, *s.* écorcheur, *m.*, -euse, *f.*, exacteur, *m.*, -trice, *f.*, voleur, *m.*, -euse, *f.*
Fleecing, *s.* tonte, *f.*; (*pers.*) écorcherie, exaction, extortion, *f.*, vol, *m.*
Fleecy, *adj.* laineux; (*fig.*) floconneux; (*white*) moutonneux
Fleeing, *s.* fuite, *f.*
Fleer, *v.n.a.* railler; — *s.* raillerie, moquerie, *f.*
Fleerer, *s.* railleur, *m.*, -euse, *f.*, moqueur, *m.*, -euse, *f.*
Fleering, *s.* raillerie, moquerie, *f.*
Fleet, *s.* flotte, *f.*; — *adj.* rapide; (*of animals*) *V.* **Swift;** (*of soil*) léger; — *v.n.* s'envoler; passer rapidement, fuir, passer, s'évanouir, disparaître
Fleeting, *adj.* fugitif, passager; vague; — *s.* fuite rapide, *f.*, passage rapide, *m.*, prompte disparition, *f.*
Fleetly, *adv.* rapidement, vite; légèrement
Fleetness, *s.* rapidité, vitesse, *f.*; légèreté, *f.*
Flegm, &c. *V.* **Phlegm,** &c.
Fleming, *s.* Flamand, *m.*, e, *f.*
Flemish, *adj.* flamand; — *s.* (*language*) le flamand, *m.*, la langue flamande, *f.* — **school,** *s.* (*paint.*) école flamande, *f.*
Flesh, *s.* chair, *f.*; (*meat*) viande, *f.*; (*plumpness*) embonpoint, *m.*; (*paint.*) chairs, *f.pl.*; — *v.a.* (*glut*) repaître, assouvir; (*try*) essayer;

(*inure*) endurcir; accoutumer (à); (*hunt.*) acharner, mettre en curée; (*hides*) écharner. *Hard* —, durillon, *m.* *In* — *and blood*, en chair et en os. *To gather* or *get* or *pick up* —, prendre de l'embonpoint. *To make o.'s* — *creep* or *crawl*, donner la chair de poule. *My* — *creeps* or *crawls*, *I feel my* — *creep* or *crawl*, j'ai la chair de poule. — **broth,** *s.* bouillon de viande, *m.* — **brush,** *s.* brosse à frictions, *f.* — **colour,** *s.* couleur de chair, carnation, *f.*, incarnat, *m.* — **coloured,** *adj.* couleur de chair, incarnat; (*hort.*) carné. — **day,** *s.* jour gras, *m.* — **diet,** *s.* gras, *m.* — **eater,** *s.* carnassier, *m.* — **eating,** *adj.* carnassier. — **fly,** *s.* mouche à viande, mouche carnaire, *f.* — **glove,** *s.* gant à frictions, *m.* — **hook,** *s.* croc, *m.* —**less,** *adj.* décharné, maigre. — **meat,** *s.* viande, *f.* — **pot,** *s.* marmite, *f.*; (*fig.*) abondance de provisions, *f.* — **tint,** *s.* *V.* — **colour.** — **worm,** *s.* ciron, *m.*

Fleshed, *adj.* gras, qui a de l'embonpoint

Flesher, *s.* écharneur, *m.*

Fleshiness, *s.* embonpoint, *m.*; charnure, *f.*

Fleshing, *s.* écharnement, écharnage, *m.*; écharnure, *f.*; —**s,** *pl.* écharnure, *f.*, écharnures, *f.pl.*; (*dress*) maillot (couleur de chair), *m.* — **knife,** *s.* écharnoir, *m.*

Fleshliness, *s.* charnalité, *f.*

Fleshly, *adj.* de chair; charnel, sensuel, de [la chair

Fleshy, *adj.* charnu; (*fig.*) de chair

Fletcher, *s.* fléchier, *m.*

Fleur-de-lis, *s.* fleur de lis, *f.*

Flexi-bility, bleness. *V.* page 3, § 1

Flexible, Flexile, *adj.* flexible

Flexibly, *adv.* d'une manière flexible

Flexion, *s.* flexion, *f.*; courbure, *f.*

Flexor, *s. adj.* fléchisseur, *s.m.*, *adj. m.*

Flexuous, *adj.* flexueux; vacillant, chancelant; sinueux, tortueux

Flexuousness, Flexuosity, *s.* flexuosité, *f.*

Flexure, *s.* *V.* **Flexion**

Flick, *v.a.* donner un coup sec *or* une chiquenaude à; secouer; (*to whip*) toucher (avec le fouet), fouetter légèrement; (*to comb*) donner un coup de peigne à; — *s.* petit coup, coup sec, coup, *m.*; (*fillip*) chiquenaude, *f.*; (*with a comb*) coup de peigne, *m.* — **off,** faire tomber d'un coup sec; secouer

Flicker, *v.n.* trémousser de l'aile, battre des ailes; (*waver*) ondoyer, vaciller; trembler; (*pers.*) voltiger. — **mouse,** *s.* chauve-souris, *f.*

Flickering, *s.* trémoussement, *m.*; voltigement, *m.*; (*fig.*) vacillation, *f.*; — *adj.* voltigeant; vacillant; incertain

Flier, *s.* (*pers.*) fuyard, fugitif, *m.*; (*mach.*) balancier, *m.*; volant, *m.*; (*of a wind-mill*) gouvernail, *m.*

Flight, *s.* fuite, *f.*; (*of birds*) vol, *m.*; (*flock of birds*) volée, bande, *f.*; (*passage of birds*) passage, *m.*; (*fig.*) vol, *m.*; (*of fancy*) essor, élan, *m.*; transport, accès, *m.*; (*wandering*) écart, *m.*; (*of a staircase*) volée, *f.*; (*story*) étage, *m.*; (*of time*) cours, *m.*; (*volley*) volée, nuée, *f.* — *of stairs*, volée d'escalier, *f.*; escalier, *m.*; (*story*) étage, *m.* — *of steps*, volée d'escalier, *f.*; escalier, *m.*; (*outside and uncovered*) perron, *m.* *At one* —, d'une volée. *At a single* —, à tire-d'aile. *In the* —, au vol. *To betake oneself to* —, s'enfuir, se sauver, prendre la fuite. *To put to* —, mettre en fuite. *To take* —, prendre son vol; prendre sa volée; (*run away*) prendre la fuite; (*fig.*) prendre son essor

Flightiness, *s.* légèreté, étourderie, *f.*; délire, *m.*

Flighty, *adj.* fugitif; volage; (*giddy*) étourdi, léger; (*delirious*) délirant, en délire; (*of works*) de pure imagination, peu sérieux

Flimsiness, *s.* légèreté, *f.*; faiblesse, *f.*; frivolité, *f.*; pauvreté, *f.*; mesquinerie, *f.*

Flimsy, *adj.* léger; mollasse; mince; faible; frivole; pauvre

Flinch, *v.n.* reculer (devant); sourciller; hésiter; broncher; se désister (de); (*swerve*) s'écarter (de). *Without* —*ing*, sans sourciller; de pied ferme

Fling, *v.a.* jeter; lancer; (*repulse*) repousser; (*prostrate*) renverser, abattre; (*scatter*) semer, répandre; (*carry about*) promener; (*defeat*) battre; — *v.n.* s'élancer; bondir; (*kick*) ruer; (*fig.*) s'emporter, regimber; invectiver; — *s.* coup, *m.*; (*jeer*) trait, *m.*; coup de patte, *m.* *To have a* — *at*, lancer un trait contre, donner un coup de patte à. *To have o.'s* —, s'en donner à cœur joie; faire ses farces. — **away,** rejeter, jeter de côté, jeter; se défaire de; repousser; prodiguer. — **down,** jeter par terre, jeter en bas, jeter; abattre, renverser. — **off,** rejeter; fermer sa porte à; (*baffle*) dérouter, déjouer. — **open,** ouvrir avec violence, ouvrir brusquement. — **out,** jeter dehors; (*utter*) lancer. — **over,** abandonner; oublier, déshériter. — **up,** jeter en l'air, jeter; renoncer à, abandonner

Flint, *s.* caillou, *m.*; (*to strike a light*) pierre à briquet, *f.*; pierre à fusil, *f.*; (*min.*) silex, *m.*; (*fig.*) pierre, roche, *f.* — **glass,** *s.* flint-glass, *m.* — **gun, -lock musket, -lock,** *s.* fusil à pierre, *m.* — **hearted,** *adj.* qui a un cœur de roche. — **implements,** *s. pl.* outils de pierre, silex taillés, *m.pl.*

Flintiness, *s.* dureté, *f.*

Flinty, *adj.* de caillou; caillouteux; (*hard*) dur, de roche, impitoyable, insensible

Flip. *V.* **Flick**

Flippancy, *s.* légèreté, étourderie, *f.*; air dégagé *or* cavalier, ton tranchant, *m.*, manières lestes, *f.pl.*; (*of speech*) volubilité, *f.*, verbiage, *m.*

Flippant, *adj.* léger; mobile; (*talkative*) bavard; (*of the tongue*) délié; (*of discourse*) vague; (*pert*) dégagé, cavalier, tranchant

Flippantly, *adv.* légèrement; avec volubilité; d'une manière vague; d'un air dégagé, d'un ton tranchant, cavalièrement, lestement

Flipper, *s.* nageoire pectorale, nageoire, *f.*

Flirt, *v.n.* folâtrer, papillonner; (*of women*) faire la coquette; — *v.a.* jeter, lancer; agiter, faire aller; (*jeer*) bafouer; — *s.* coquette, *f.*

Flirtation, *s.* coquetterie, *f.*

Flirtingly, *adv.* avec coquetterie

Flit, *v.n.* fuir; passer; voltiger; (*flutter*) flotter; (*change o.'s residence*) changer de demeure, déménager. — **by,** passer

Flitch, *s.* (*of bacon*) flèche (de lard), *f.*

Flitter, *V.* **Flutter.** — **mouse,** *s.* chauve-souris, *f.*

Flitting, *adj.* fugitif; rapide; — *s.* fuite, *f.*; passage, *m.*; voltigement, *m.*; (*change of residence*) déménagement, *m.*

Float, *v.n.* flotter; surnager; (*in swimming*) faire la planche; — *v.a.* faire flotter; (*launch*) mettre à flot, lancer; (*flood*) inonder; (*mas.*) talocher; — *s.* (*of wood*) train, *m.*; radeau, *m.*; (*for swimming*) nageoire, *f.*, scaphandre, *m.*; (*fish.*) flotte, *f.*, flotteur, *m.*; (*tech.*) flotteur, *m.*; (*of a wheel*) aube, *f.*; (*wave*) flot, *m.*; (*mas.*) taloche, *f.* — **board,** *s.* aube, palette, *f.*

Floatability, *s.* flottabilité, *f.*

Floatable, *adj.* flottable

Floatage, &c. *V.* **Flotage,** &c.

Floater, *s.* flotteur, *m.*; (*swimmer*) nageur, *m.*

Floating, *adj.* flottant; — *s.* flottement, flottage, *m.*; (*launching*) mise à flot, *f.*; (*agr.*) inondation, *f.*; (*mas.*) talochage, *m.* — **battery,** *s.* batterie flottante, *f.* — **bridge,** *s.* pont flottant, *m.* — **capital,** *s.* capital flottant, *m.* — **debt,** *s.* dette flottante, *f.* — — **dock,** *s.* bassin à flot, *m.* — **island,** *s.* île flottante, *f.* — **light,** *s.* veilleuse, *f.*; (*nav.*) bouée de sauvetage pour la nuit, *f.* — **stage,** [*s.* ras de carène, *m.*

Floaty, *adj.* flottant

Floccillation, *s.* carphologie, *f.*

Flocculent, *adj.* floconneux

Flock, *s.* (*of sheep, and rel. fig.*) troupeau, *m.*; (*of birds*) bande, troupe, *f.*; groupe, *m.*; (*crowd*) foule, *f.*; (*of wool*, &c.) flocon, *m.*;

(*of hair, coarse wool,* &c.) bourre, *f.*; (*tuft*) touffe, *f.*; — *v.n.* s'attrouper, aller par troupeaux; (*of birds*) aller par bandes; (*pers.*) s'assembler, se rassembler, se réunir, s'attrouper; se porter en foule, courir *or* accourir en foule, affluer, s'empresser. — **bed,** *s.* lit de bourre, *m.* — **paper,** *s.* papier velouté, papier tontisse, *m.* — **surface,** *s.* velouté, *m.*

Flocky, *adj.* floconneux

Floe, *s.* glaçon flottant, glaçon, *m.*, banquise, *f.*

Flog, *v.a.* fouetter, donner le fouet à; flageller; [fustiger

Flogger, *s.* fouetteur, *m.*, -euse, *f.*

Flogging, *s.* (le) fouet, *m.*; flagellation, *f.*; fustigation, *f.*; correction, *f.*

Flood, *s.* cours d'eau, *m.*; (*river*) fleuve, *m.*; (*wave*) onde, *f.*, flots, *m pl.*; (*the deluge*) déluge, *m.*; (*inundation*) inondation, *f.*; (*of the tide*) flux, *m.*; marée, *f.*; (*of tears*) torrent, *m.*; (*fig.*) flot, *m.*, foule, *f.*; déluge, *m.*; — *v.a.* ('*with,*' de) inonder, submerger; noyer. *High* —, grandes marées, *f.pl.*; (*of rivers*) grandes eaux, *f.pl.* — **gate,** *s.* écluse, vanne, *f.*; (*fig.*) porte, *f.*, passage, *m.* — **mark,** *s.* niveau des hautes eaux, *m.* — **tide,** *s.* marée montante, *f.*, flux, flot, *m.* [utérine, *f.*

Flooding, *s.* inondation, *f.*; (*med.*) hémorrhagie

Flook. *V.* **Fluke**

Floor, *s.* plain-pied, *m.*; (*of boards*) plancher, *m.*; (*inlaid*) parquet, *m.*; (*pavement*) carreau, *m.*; (*story*) étage, *m.*; (*of barns*) aire, *f.*; (*of bridges*) tablier, *m.*; (*nav.*) varangue, *f.*; — *v.a.* planchéier; parqueter; (*throw down*) jeter par terre, terrasser, renverser, abattre; (*silence*) désarçonner. *On the* —. (*down*) par terre. *On the first* —, au premier étage, au premier. *On the same* —, sur le même étage *or* palier; de plain-pied. — **cloth,** *s.* toile cirée, *f.*; tapis de pied, *m.* — **layer,** *s.* planchéieur, parqueteur, poseur, *m.* — **polisher,** *s.* frotteur, *m.* — **tile,** *s.* carreau, *m.* — **timber,** *s.* solive, *f.*; (*nav.*) varangue, *f.* — **weight,** *s.* valet, *m.* [sur la tête, *f.*

Floorer, *s.* atout, coup d'assommoir, *m.*, tuile

Flooring, *s.* plancher, &c. (*V.* **Floor,** *s.*); (*act of* —) planchéiage, *m.*; parquetage, *m.*; (*with tiles,* &c.) carrelage, *m.*; (*of bridges*) tablier, *m.* — **brad,** *s.* clou à planches, *m.* — **tile,** *s.* carreau, *m.* [oreilles, *m.*

Flop-hat, *s.* chapeau à bords pendants, claque-

Flora, *s.* Flore, *f.*; (*bot.*) flore, *f.*

Floral, *adj.* floral. — *beetle,* cétoine, *f.* — *games,* jeux floraux, *m.pl.* [Florence, *m.*

Florence, *s.* (*cloth*) florence, *m.*; (*wine*) vin de

Florentine, *s. adj.* Florentin, *m.*, e, *f.*; (*satin*) [florentine, *f.*

Florescence, *s.* fleuraison, *f.*

Floret, *s.* fleurette, *f.* [floriculture

Floricultural, *adj.* floricultural, floricole, de

Floriculture, *s.* floriculture, *f.*

Floriculturist, *s.* floriculteur, *m.*

Florid, *adj.* coloré; fleuri

Floridity, Floridness, *s.* fraîcheur, *f.*; teint fleuri, *m.*; style fleuri, *m.*

Floridly, *adv.* d'une manière fleurie; en [termes fleuris

Floriferous, *adj.* florifère

Floriform, *adj.* floriforme

Florin, *s.* florin, *m.* (*in French coin,* 2 francs 50 [centimes)

Floriparous, *adj.* floripare

Florist, *s.* fleuriste, *m.f.*; (*writer*) floriste, *m.* *Artificial* —, fleuriste artificiel, *m.*, fleuriste, *f.*

Floss, *s.* bourre, *f.*; (*metal.*) floss, *m.* — **silk,** *s.* filoselle, bourre de soie, *f.*, fleuret, *m.*; (*for fancy work*) soie plate, soie floche, *f.*

Flotage, *s.* flottage, *m.*

Flotant, *adj.* flottant

Flotation, *s.* flottaison, *f.*; flottabilité, *f.*

Flotilla, *s.* flottille, *f.*

Flotsam, *s.* épaves, *f.pl.*

Flounce, *v.n.* (*struggle*) se débattre, s'agiter; (*move*) se trémousser, se démener; (*rush*) se précipiter, s'élancer; — *v.a.* garnir de volants; [— *s.* volant, *m.*

Flounced, *adj.* à volants

Flounder, *s.* carrelet, *m.*; — *v.n.* se débattre, s'agiter, se démener

Flour, *s.* farine, *f.*; (*of potatoes, beans,* &c.) fécule, *f.*; (*flower*) fleur, *f.*; — *v.a.* fariner, enfariner, saupoudrer de farine; (*grind*) moudre, réduire en farine. — **bin,** *s.* farinière, *f.* — **dealer,** *s.* marchand de farine, *m.* — **dredger,** *s.* boîte à farine, *f.* — **factor, -merchant,** *s.* facteur aux farines, minotier, *m.* — **mill,** *s.* moulin à farine, *m.*, minoterie, *f.* — **trade,** *s.* minoterie, *f.* — **tub,** *s.* farinière, *f.*

Flourish, *v.n.a.* être florissant, prospérer, faire florès, florir, fleurir; (*of plants*) profiter, réussir, venir bien; (*in discourse*) faire des phrases, faire des fleurs de rhétorique, s'exprimer en style fleuri; (*in writing*) faire des traits de plume; (*wave*) ondoyer, s'agiter; (*mus.*) préluder; faire des fioritures; (*boast*) se vanter; (*a trumpet*) sonner une fanfare; (*a stick,* &c.) faire le moulinet (avec), faire aller; (*a sword*) brandir; (*a writing*) orner de traits de plume; (*adorn*) orner, embellir; (*embroider*) broder; — *s.* éclat, *m.*; ornement, enjolivement, embellissement, *m.*; (*in rhetoric*) fleur, *f.*; (*in writing*) trait de plume, *m.*; (*of a signature*) parafe, *m.*; (*of a stick,* &c.) tour, *m.*; (*of a trumpet,* &c.) fanfare, *f.*; (*mus.*) prélude, *m.*; fioriture, *f.*; (*print.*) fleuron, *m.*

Flourishing, *adj.* florissant

Flourishingly, *adv.* d'une manière florissante

Floury, *adj.* farineux

Flout, *v.a.* railler, se moquer de; insulter; — *s.* raillerie, moquerie, *f.*; insulte, *f.* [-euse, *f.*

Flouter, *s.* railleur, *m.*, -euse, *f.*, moqueur, *m.*,

Flouting, *adj.* railleur, moqueur; — *s.* raillerie, moquerie insultante, *f.*

Floutingly, *adv.* avec une moquerie insultante

Flow, *v.n.* couler; s'écouler; (*result*) découler, provenir, venir (de); (*be loose*) flotter; (*be full*) déborder; (*of the tide*) monter; (*of the sea*) fluer; (*med.*) couler, fluer; — *v.a.* inonder, submerger; — *s.* écoulement, *m.*; flux, *m.*; abondance, *f.*; (*effusion*) épanchement, *m.*, effusion, *f.*; (*of water*) cours (d'eau), *m.*; (*fluency*) facilité, *f.* — **back,** *v.n.* refluer. — **down,** *v.n.* couler, descendre. — **bog,** *s.* marais mouvant, *m.* — **in,** *v.n.* affluer, arriver en abondance. — **off,** *v.n.* s'écouler. — **out,** *v.n.* se retirer. — **over,** *v.n.* déborder

Flower, *s.* fleur, *f.*; (*in a crown,* &c., *arch., print.*) fleuron, *m.*; — *v.n.* fleurir; — *v.a.* orner de fleurs. — **basket,** *s.* corbeille à fleurs, *f.* — **bed,** *s.* plate-bande, planche, *f.*; corbeille (de fleurs), *f.*; parterre (de fleurs), *m.* — **bud,** *s.* bourgeon à fleur, *m.* — **cup,** *s.* calice, *f.* — **de-luce,** *s.* iris, *m.*; (*her.*) fleur de lis, *f.* — **dust,** *s.* pollen, *m.* — **fence,** *s.* poinciane, poincillade, *f.* — **garden,** *s.* jardin-fleuriste, parterre (de fleurs), *m.* — **gardener,** *s.* jardinier-fleuriste, *m.* — **gentle,** *s.* amarante, *f.* — **girl,** *s.* bouquetière, *f.* — **leaf,** *s.* pétale, *m.* — **less,** *adj.* sans fleur, sans fleurs; (*stripped*) défleuri. — **maker,** *s.* fleuriste, *m.f.* — **man,** *s.* bouquetier, *m.* — **market,** *s.* marché aux fleurs, *m.* — **painter,** *s.* peintre de fleurs, *m.* — **painting, -piece,** *s.* peinture de fleurs, *f.* — **pot,** *s.* (*for flowers*) pot à fleurs, *m.*; (*with flowers*) pot de fleurs, *m.* — **seeds,** *s. pl.* graines de fleurs, *f.pl.* — **show,** *s.* exposition de fleurs, *f.* — **stalk,** *s.* pédoncule, *m.* — **stand,** *s.* jardinière, *f.*; porte-fleurs, *m.* — **vase,** *s.* bouquetier, *m.* — **woman,** *s.* bouquetière, *f.* — **work,** *s.* ouvrage à fleurs, *m.*; fleurons, *m.pl.*

Flowered, *adj.* à fleurs. *Double* —, à fleurs [doubles

Floweret, *s.* fleurette, petite fleur, *f.*

Floweriness, *s.* abondance de fleurs, *f.*, fleurs, *f.pl.*; style fleuri, *m.*

Flowering, *adj.* *V.* **Flowery;** — *s.* fleuraison, *f.*; parure de fleurs, *f.* — **ash,** *s.* orne, frêne à fleurs, *m.* — **fern,** *s.* osmonde royale, *f.* — **rush,** *s.* jonc fleuri, butome, *m.* — **season,** *s.* fleuraison, *f.*

Flowery, *adj.* fleuri; de fleurs; en fleurs; à fleurs
Flowing, *adj.* coulant; naturel; (*over*) qui déborde; (*waving*) flottant; — *s.* cours, écoulement, *m.*; circulation, *f.*; flux, *m.*; épanchement, *m.*, effusion, *f.*; torrent, *m.*; inondation, *f.*; abondance, affluence, *f.*
Flowingly, *adv.* coulamment, avec volubilité, [avec abondance
Flowingness, *s.* facilité, *f.*
Flown, *part. adj.* envolé; (*swollen*) enflé, gonflé, bouffi (*V.* **High**)
Fluctuate, *v.n.* flotter, hésiter; varier
Fluctuating, *adj.* flottant, incertain; irrésolu; variable, changeant; ondoyant
Fluctuation, *s.* fluctuation, *f.*
Flue, *s.* (*of chimney*) tuyau, *m.*; (*of a steam-engine*) carneau, carnau, *m.*; (*down*) duvet, *m.*
Fluency, *s.* facilité, *f.*; abondance, *f.*; douceur, *f.* [(*pers.*) disert
Fluent, *adj.* coulant, aisé, facile; abondant;
Fluently, *adv.* couramment, facilement, avec [facilité
Fluff, *s.* (*of pockets, clothes*) bourre, *f.*
Flugelman. *V.* **Fugleman** [*m.*; liqueur, *f.*
Fluid, *adj.* fluide; liquide; — *s.* fluide, *m.*; liquide,
Fluidity, Fluidness, *s.* fluidité, *f.*
Fluidize, *v.a.* fluidifier
Fluidizing, *s.* fluidification, *f.*
Fluke, *s.* (*fish*) flet, *m.*; (*worm*) douve, fasciole, *f.*; (*of anchors*) patte, *f.*; (*lucky hit*) raccroc, *m.* *By a —*, par raccroc; de *or* par bricole; par la grâce de Dieu et du hasard. — **potato,** *s.* pomme de terre de Hollande, *f.*
Fluker, *s.* raccrocheur, *m.*
Flummery, *s.* bouillie, gelée, *f.* [gruau, semoule, gaude, blanc-manger, &c.]; (*fig.*) fadaise, blague, *f.*; (*flattery*) flagornerie, *f.*
Flunkey, Flunky, *s.* laquais, valet, estafier, *m.*; plat valet, *m.*
Flunkeydom, *s.* régions de la valetaille, *f.pl.*
Flunkeyism, *s.* esprit de la valetaille, *m.*; manières de valet, *f.pl.*
Fluoborate, *s.* fluoborate, *m.*
Fluoboric, *adj.* fluoborique
Fluor, *s.* fluor, *m.* — **albus,** *s.* fleurs blanches, *f.pl.* — **spar,** *s.* spath fluor, *m.*, chaux fluatée, *f.*
Fluorescence, *s.* fluorescence, *f.*
Fluorescent, *adj.* fluorescent
Fluoride, *s.* fluorure, *m.*
Fluorine, *s.* fluorine, *f.*, fluor, *m.*
Flurry, *s.* trouble, émoi, *m.*, agitation, *f.*, ahurissement, *m.*; — *v.a.* troubler, agiter, ahurir
Flush, *v.n.* accourir; (*of a blush*, &c.) monter; (*redden*) rougir; (*shine*) briller; — *v.a.* colorer, rougir, faire rougir; exciter; exalter, enfler; (*heat*) échauffer; (*wash, cleanse*) laver *or* nettoyer à grande eau; (*steep*) tremper; — *adj.* frais; élevé; animé; (*of*) bien pourvu *or* fourni (de), riche (en); prodigue (de); (*level*) à fleur; (*of doors*) à saillie; (*arch.*) affleuré; — *s.* fraîcheur, *f.*, éclat, *m.*, rougeur, *f.*, rouge, *m.*; transport, accès, *m.*; (*at cards*) flux, *m.*; (*flood*) flux, *m.*; abondance, *f.*; (*wash*) *V.* **Flushing.** — **deck,** *s.* pont ras, *m.*
Flushing, *s.* rougeur, *f.*; (*flooding*) flux, *m.*; (*washing, cleansing*) nettoiement à grande eau, *m.*; flaquées d'eau, *f.pl.*
Fluster, *v.a.* exciter, échauffer; troubler, agiter, ahurir; — *s.* excitation, *f.*; trouble, *m.*, agitation, *f.*
Flute, *s.* flûte, *f.*; (*groove*) cannelure, *f.*; — *v.a.* canneler. — **grafting,** *s.* greffe en flûte, *f.*, empeau, *m.* — **mouth,** *s.* fistulaire, *m.* — **player,** *s.* joueur de flûte, *m.* — **stop, -work,** *s.* (*of an organ*) jeu de flûtes, *m.*
Fluted, *adj.* (*arch.*) cannelé; (*mus.*) flûté
Fluter, *s.* flûteur, *m.*
Fluting, *s.* cannelure, *f.*, cannelures, *f.pl.*
Flutist, *s.* flûtiste, *m.*, flûte, *f.*
Flutter, *v.n.* battre des ailes; voltiger; flotter; s'agiter, se trémousser; se débattre; être agité; palpiter; tressaillir; (*of the pulse*) onduler; — *v.a.* faire voltiger; faire flotter; agiter; troubler, ahurir; déconcerter; effaroucher; déranger; (*to play with*) jouer de
Flutter, Fluttering, *s.* battement d'ailes, *m.*; battement, *m.*; voltigement, *m.*; trémoussement, *m.*; vibration, *f.*; agitation, confusion, *f.*, désordre, trouble, émoi, *m.*; palpitation, *f.*; tressaillement, *m.*; (*of the pulse*) ondulation, *f.*; (*of a fan*, &c.) jeu, *m.* *To put in a —*, mettre en émoi
Fluty, *adj.* flûté [vial, fluviatile
Fluvial, Fluviatic, Fluviatile, *adj.* flu-
Flux, *s.* flux, *m.*; (*chem., tech.*) fondant, *m.* *Bloody —*, flux de sang, *m.*, dyssenterie, *f.*
Fluxion, *s.* fluxion, *f.*
Fly, *v.n.* voler; s'envoler; (*wave*) flotter; (*pass away*) fuir, s'enfuir, passer; (*run away*) fuir; (*fade*) passer; (*take refuge*) se réfugier; (*escape*) s'échapper (de); échapper (à); se soustraire (à); (*burst*) éclater ('*into*,' en); (*to o.'s head, of drinks*) monter *or* porter (à la tête); (*jump*) sauter; — *v.a.* faire voler; (*shun*) fuir, éviter; (*quit*) fuir, s'enfuir de, s'éloigner de, abandonner, quitter. *To let —*, lancer. *To — in the face*, sauter au visage; insulter en face, braver, rompre en visière. *To — into pieces*, voler en éclats. — *-the-garter*, (*game*) anguille, *f.* — **about,** voler, voltiger. — **at,** s'élancer sur *or* vers, se jeter sur, sauter sur (*or* à); attaquer. — **away,** s'envoler; s'enfuir. — **back,** revoler; (*draw back*) reculer, faire un saut en arrière; (*things*) faire ressort. — **down,** descendre; s'abattre. — **in,** entrer. — **off,** s'envoler; (*pers.*) s'enfuir; se révolter; déserter. — **open,** s'ouvrir subitement. — **out,** s'envoler, s'échapper précipitamment; (*get angry*) s'emporter; (*into*) éclater (en), se répandre (en); se livrer (à); se lancer (dans). — **up,** voler; monter; sauter; (*of sparks*, &c.) jaillir
Fly, *s.* mouche, *f.*; (*carriage*) voiture (publique) à quatre places, *f.*; remise, *m.*; (*of machines*) volant, *m.*; (*of a vane*) pavillon, *m.*; (*of trousers*) brayette, *f.*; (*of a busby*) flamme, chausse, *f.* *The — on the coach-wheel*, la mouche du coche. — **bane,** *s.* herbe aux mouches, *f.*, attrape-mouches, *m.* — **bitten,** *adj.* piqué des mouches. — **blow,** *s.* œuf de mouche, *m.*; chiure de mouche, *f.* — **blown,** *adj.* plein de vers, gâté, piqué; sali *or* abîmé par les mouches, couvert de chiures de mouches. — **boat,** *s.* mouche, *f.*; (*Dutch vessel*) flibot, *m.* — **catcher,** *s.* attrapeur (*m.*, -euse, *f.*) de mouches; (*bird*) gobe-mouches, *m.* — **destroyer,** *s.* mort aux mouches, *f.* — **dirt,** *s.* chiure de mouches, *f.* — **driver,** *s.* cocher de place, *m.*; cocher de remise, *m.* — **fan,** *s.* chasse-mouches, *m.* — **fish,** *v.a.* pêcher avec des mouches. — **fishing,** *s.* pêche à la ligne avec des mouches, *f.* — **flap,** *s.* émouchoir, chasse-mouches, *m.* — **flapper,** *s.* émoucheur, *m.*, -euse, *f.* — **leaf,** *s.* feuillet blanc, *m.*; (*book-bind.*) feuillet de garde, *m.*, garde, *f.*; (*abusively for* "*flying leaf*") feuille volante, *f.* — **man,** *s.* *V.* — **driver.** — **net,** *s.* émouchette, *f.*, chasse-mouches, *m.* — **paper, -powder,** *s.* mort aux mouches, *f.* — **sheet,** *s.* feuille volante, *f.* — **speck,** *s.* chiure de mouche, *f.* — **trap,** *s.* attrape-mouches, gobe-mouches, *m.*, dionée, *f.* — **water,** *s.* mort aux mouches, *f.* — **wheel,** *s.* volant, *m.*
Flyer. *V.* **Flier**
Flying, *adj.* volant; (*mil.*) de voltigement; — *s.* vol, *m.* — *bridge* (, *camp*, *fish*, &c.), pont (, camp, poisson, &c.) volant, *m.* — *leaf* or *sheet*, feuille volante, *f.* — *squadron*, (*nav.*) escadre légère, escadre d'évolution, *f.* — **Dutchman,** *s.* voltigeur hollandais, *m.* — **jib,** *s.* (*nav.*) clinfoc, *m.* — **jib-boom,** *s.* (*nav.*) bâton de clinfoc, *m.* — **party,** *s.* *V.* **Party.** *With — colours*, enseignes déployées
Foal, *s.* poulain, *m.*, pouliche, *f.*; (*of asses*) ânon, *m.*; — *v.n.* pouliner; (*of asses*) ânonner; — *v.a.* mettre bas. *In* or *with —*, pleine

Foaled, *part. adj.* mis bas, né
Foam, *s.* écume, *f.*; — *v.n.* écumer; (*of the sea*) moutonner
Foamy, *adj.* écumeux; écumant
Fob, *s.* gousset, *m.*; (*trick*) tromperie, attrape, *f.*; — *v.a.* (— **off**) tromper, duper, attraper, [refaire; (*things*) escamoter
Focal, *adj.* focal
Focimeter, *s.* focimètre, *m.*
Focus, *s.* foyer, *m.* *In* —, à portée
Fodder, *s.* fourrage, *m.*; — *adj.* fourrager; — *v.a.* affourrager; (*nav.*) *V.* **Fother.** — **grass,** **-plant,** *s.* plante fourragère, fourragère, *f.*
Foddering, *s.* affourragement, *m.*
Foe, *s.* ennemi, *m.*, e, *f.* ('*to*,' de); adversaire, *m.f.* — **man,** *s.* ennemi, *m.*
Fœtal, *adj.* fœtal, du fœtus
Fœticide, *s.* fœticide, *m.*
Fœtid, *adj.* *V.* **Fetid**
Fœtus, *s.* fœtus, *m.*
Fog, *s.* brouillard, *m.*; brume, *f.* — **signal,** *s.* [signal de brume, *m.*
Fogey, *s.* bonhomme, *m.*, culotte de peau, *f.*, croûton, *m.*, croûte, ganache, perruque, *f.*
Fogginess, *s.* nature brumeuse, *f.*; temps brumeux, *m.*; brouillard épais, *m.*; obscurité, *f.*
Foggy, *adj.* de brouillard; brumeux; épais, obscur, sombre. *To be* —, faire du brouillard
Fogy. *V.* **Fogey**
Foh, *int.* bast! bah!
Foible, *s.* faible, *m.*; —**s,** *pl.* faiblesses, *f.pl.*
Foil, *v.a.* vaincre; (*baffle*) déjouer; dérouter; frustrer; faire échouer; (*to blunt*) émousser, amortir; (*hunt.*) dépister; — *s.* défaite, *f.*, échec, *m.*; (*leaf*) feuille, *f.*; (*of stone*) monture, *f.*; (*of tin*) tain, *m.*; (*in fencing*) fleuret, *m.*; (*relief*) relief, contraste, *m.*, ombre, *f.*; (*gilding*) clinquant, *m.*; (*hunt.*) *V.* **Foiling** [*f.pl.*
Foiling, *s.* (*hunt.*) abattures, foulées, foulures,
Foist, *v.a.* interpoler, insérer; introduire; (*fig.*) glisser, couler, fourrer ('*upon*,' à)
Fold, *v.a.* (— **up**) plier, ployer; envelopper; serrer; (*the arms*) croiser; (*sheep*) parquer; — *v.n.* se plier; — *s.* pli, *m.*; repli, *m.*; (*enclosure*) enclos, *m.*; (*of sheep*) parc, *m.*; bercail, *m.*; bergerie, *f.*; (*flock*) troupeau, *m.*; (*of a door*) battant, *m.*; (*of a screen*) feuille, *f.*; (*in compounds*) fois, *f.* *V.* **Two, Three,** &c.
Foldage, *s.* droit de parcage, *m.*
Folder, *s.* (*pers.*) plieur, *m.*, -euse, *f.*; (*thing*) plioir, *m.*; (*eye-glass*) face à main, *f.*
Folding, *adj.* (*to fold with*) à plier, à ployer; (*doubling*) pliant; (*of doors*) brisé, à battants; (*of ladders*) brisé; (*of screens*) à feuilles; — *s.* pliage, *m.*; (*of sheep*) parcage, *m.* — **bed,** **-bedstead,** *f.* lit pliant, *m.*; (*with sacking bottom*) lit de sangle, *m.* — **chair,** *s.* fauteuil pliant, *m.* — **door,** *s.* porte brisée, porte à battants, porte à deux battants, *f.* — **knife,** *s.* ploir, *m.* — **machine,** *s.* plieuse, *f.* — **screen,** *s.* paravent à feuilles, paravent, *m.* — **stick,** *s.* ploir, *m.* — **stool,** *s.* *V.* **Fald-stool.** — **table,** *s.* table pliante, *f.*
Foliaceous, *adj.* foliacé
Foliage, *s.* feuillage, *m.*; (*paint.*) feuillé, *m.*; — *v.a.* garnir de feuillage
Foliaged, *adj.* à feuillage
Foliar, *adj.* foliaire
Foliate, *v.a.* battre en feuilles; (*of glass*) étamer; — *adj.* *V.* **Foliated**
Foliated, *adj.* en feuilles; feuillé, garni de feuilles; (*chim.*) folié; (*min.*) feuilleté
Foliation, *s.* foliation, *f.*; (*of glass*) étamage, *m.*
Folio, *s.* (*a volume*) in-folio, *m.*; (*print. for 'leaf'*) folio, *m.*; (*book-keep.*) feuillet, *m.*; (*law*) feuille, *f.*; — *v.a.* folioter. — **paper,** *s.* papier en feuille entière, *m.*
Folioing, *s.* foliotage, *m.*
Foliolar, *adj.* foliolaire
Foliolate, *adj.* foliolé
Foliole, *s.* foliole, *f.*
Folk, Folks, *s.* *V.* **People.** — **lore,** *s.* légendes, traditions, croyances populaires, *f.pl.* — **mote,** *s.* assemblée du peuple, *f.*

Follicle, Follicule, *s.* follicule, *m.*
Follicular, *adj.* folliculaire
Folliculous, *adj.* folliculeux
Follow, *v.a.* suivre (*pursue*) poursuivre; (*seek after*) rechercher; — *v.n.* suivre; s'ensuivre. *As follows,* comme il suit, ainsi qu'il suit. *It follows,* il s'ensuit. *That does not* —, ce n'est pas une raison
Follower, *s.* suivant, *m.*, e, *f.*, personne qui suit, *f.*; dépendant, *m.*, e, *f.*; sectateur, *m.*, -trice, *f.*; partisan, *m.*, e, *f.*; disciple, *m.*; imitateur, *m.*, -trice, *f.*; compagnon, *m.*, compagne, *f.*, camarade, *m.f.*; (*sweetheart*) amoureux, *m.*
Following, *adj.* suivant; (*consecutive*) de suite; — *s.* suite, *f.*; profession, vocation, *f.*, état, *m.*; parti, *m.*
Folly, *s.* folie, sottise, *f.*; imprudence, *f.*
Foment, *v.a.* fomenter
Fomentation, *s.* fomentation, *f.*
Fomenter, *s.* fomentateur, *m.*, -trice, *f.*; fauteur, *m.*, -trice, *f.*
Fond, *adj.* (*of*) fou (de), passionné (pour), qui aime; tendre, aimant, affectueux, affectionné; indulgent, bon; (*of hopes,* &c.) doux, cher; favori, chéri; (*ardent*) vif, ardent. — *ways,* manières caressantes, tendresses, *f.pl.* *To be* — *of,* aimer; affectionner. *To be passionately* — *of,* aimer passionnément, aimer à la folie, être fou de; être passionné pour
Fondle, *v.a.* caresser; dorloter; choyer
Fondler, *s.* personne qui caresse *or* dorlote, *f.*
Fondling, *s.* caresses, *f.pl.*; enfant chéri, *m.*; (*fam.*) enfant gâté, *m.*; mignon, *m.*, -ne, *f.*
Fondly, *adv.* follement, passionnément, à la folie; tendrement, avec tendresse, affectueusement; avec amour; vivement, ardemment
Fondness, *s.* tendresse, affection, *f.*, amour, *m.*; passion, inclination, *f.*, penchant, goût, [*m.*; folie, *f.*
Fondue, *s.* fondue, *f.*
Font, *s.* (*of baptism*) fonts, fonts de baptême, fonts baptismaux, *m.pl.*; (*spring*) source, *f.*; [(*print.*) *V.* **Fount**
Fontanel, *s.* fontanelle, *f.*
Food, *s.* nourriture, *f.*, aliment, *m.*; aliments, *m.pl.*; vivres, *m.pl.*; alimentation, *f.*; subsistance, *f.*; (*of animals*) pâture, *f.* *Article of* —, — **product** (**-substance,** &c.), *s.* produit (, *m.*, substance, *f.*, &c.) alimentaire; comestible, *m.*
Fool, *s.* sot, *m.*, -te, *f.*; bête, *f.*, imbécile, *m.f.*; insensé, *m.*, e, *f.*; idiot, *m.*, e, *f.*; dupe, *f.*; (*when in opposition to 'wise man'*, sage) fou, *m.*; (*court-jester*) fou, *m.*; bouffon, *m.*; (*of showmen*) pitre, *m.*; paradiste, *m.*; (*laughing-stock*) plastron, *m.*; — *v.n.* faire la bête, faire l'imbécile; badiner; (*with*) se jouer (de); — *v.a.* duper, tromper, refaire, jouer, se jouer de, se ficher de, jobarder. *To* — (*one*) *out of his money,* soutirer de l'argent à (quelqu'un), plumer (quelqu'un). *Feast of* —*s,* fête des fous, *f.* *No* or *not such a* —, pas si bête. *To make a* — *of,* se jouer de, jouer, se moquer de, mystifier, enfoncer, faire aller, (*fam.*) se ficher de. *To make a* — *of oneself,* se faire moquer de soi. *To play the* —, faire le sot *or* la bête *or* le fou *or* l'imbécile; faire des bouffonneries, faire des sottises. *To play the* — *with,* se ficher de. — **away,** *v.a.* perdre *or* dissiper follement. — **born,** *adj.* idiot. — **hardily,** *adv.* témérairement. — **hardiness,** *s.* témérité, *f.* — **hardy,** *adj.* téméraire. —**'s bauble,** *s.* marotte, *f.* —**'s cap,** —**scap,** *s.* bonnet de fou, bonnet de folie, *m.*; bonnet d'âne, *m.*; (*paper*) papier-pot, pot, *m.*; papier tellière, *m.* —**'s errand,** *s.* chimère, *f.* *To go on a* —*'s errand,* courir après des chimères. —**'s parsley,** *s.* æthuse, petite ciguë, *f.* — **trap,** *s* attrape-nigauds, *m.*, graine de niais, *f.*
Foolery, *s.* sottise, bêtise, *f.*; niaiserie, *f.*; extravagance, folie, *f.*; bouffonnerie, *f.*; (*sport*) badinage, *m.*
Foolish, *adj.* sot, bête; ridicule; (*thoughtless*) fou, insensé; indiscret. — *thing,* sottise,

bêtise, folie, *f.* *To be* —, être sot *or* &c.; (*play the fool*, &c.) faire la bête, faire des bêtises; faire l'enfant; faire du sentiment. *To look* —, être penaud, rester *or* demeurer sot

Foolishly, *adv.* sottement, bêtement; follement; imprudemment

Foolishness. *V.* **Folly**

Foot, *s.* pied, *m.*; (*of animals with nails or claws, birds, reptiles, insects*) patte, *f.*; (*of animals with a hoof*) pied, *m.*; (*of a table*, &c.) pied, *m.*; (*of glasses*) patte, *f.*; (*of compasses*) jambe, *f.*; (*of a pillar*, &c.) base, *f.*; (*the lower part*) pied, bas, *m.*; (*of a page, of an account*) bas, *m.*; (*meas., vers.*) pied, *m.*; (*mil.*) infanterie, *f.*; (*of sails*) fond, *m.*; — *adj.* de (*or* du) pied, de (*or* des) pieds; (*on foot*) à pied; — *v.n.* aller (*or* venir) à pied; marcher; danser; — *v.a.* (*tread*) fouler aux pieds, marcher sur; (*boots*, &c.) mettre un pied (*or* des pieds) à; (*stockings*) rempiéter. — *by* —, pied à pied. *On* —, à pied; (*standing*) sur pied, debout; (*moving*) en chemin; en train. *To set on* —, mettre sur pied; (*begin*) mettre en train; entreprendre; ouvrir; commencer, entamer; établir, fonder; produire. *To set* — *on*, mettre le pied sur. — — **and mouth disease,** *s.* cocote, *f.* — **artillery,** *s.* artillerie à pied, *f.* — **ball,** *s.* ballon, *m.* — **ball maker,** *s.* ballonnier, *m.* — **bath,** *s.* bain de pieds, *m.* — **board,** *s.* marchepied, *m.*; (*of instruments*) pédale, *f.*; (*of a carriage-box*) coquille, *f.*; (*of railway-carriages*) banquette, *f.*; (*of a railway engine*) plate-forme, *f.* — **boy,** *s.* petit laquais, petit groom, *m.* — **bridge,** *s.* pont pour les piétons, *m.*; passerelle, *f.* — **brush,** *s.* essuie-pieds, *m.* — **cloth,** *s.* tapis de pied, *m.*; housse de pied, *f.* — **fall,** *s.* pas, *m.* — **gear,** *s.* chaussure, *f.* — **guard,** *s.* garde à pied, *m.* (— **guards,** *pl.* gardes à pied, *m.pl.*, garde à pied, *f.*) — **hold,** *s.* place pour le pied, *f.*; prise pour le pied, *f.*; résistance sous le pied, *f.* *To get a — hold*, prendre pied. *To lose o.'s — hold*, perdre l'équilibre. — **key,** *s.* pédale, *f.* — **lamps,** *s. pl. V.* — **lights.** —**less,** *adj.* sans pieds; (*zool.*) apode. — **lights,** *s. pl.* (*theat.*) rampe, *f.* — **man,** *s.* valet de pied, laquais, *m.*; (*mil.*) fantassin, *m.*; (*utensil*) servante, *f.* — **mark,** *s. V.* — **print.** — **match,** *s.* course à pied, *f.* — **muff,** *s.* chancelière, *f.* — **note,** *s.* note au bas d'une page, *f.* — **pace,** —**'s pace,** *s.* pas, *m.*; (*arch.*) haut-pas, *m.* *At a — pace* or *—'s pace*, au pas. — **pad,** *s.* voleur de grand chemin, *m.* — **passenger,** *s.* piéton, *m*, -ne, *f.* — **path,** *s.* sentier, *m.*; (*in towns*) trottoir, *m.*; (*of roads*) banquette, *f.* — **pavement,** *s.* trottoir, *m.* — **plate,** *s.* (*rail.*) plate-forme, *f.* — **plough,** *s. V.* **Swing-plough.** — **post,** *s.* piéton, *m.* — **print,** *s.* empreinte du pied, *f.*, pas, *m.* — **race,** *s. V.* **Race.** — **regiment,** *s.* régiment d'infanterie, *m.* — **rope,** *s.* (*nav.*) (*of yards*) marchepied, *m.*; (*of sails*) ralingue, *f.* — **rot,** *s.* (*vet.*) fourchet, *m.*; piétin, *m.* — **rule,** *s.* pied-de-roi, pied, *m.* — **scraper,** *s.* décrottoir, *m.* — **soldier,** *s.* fantassin, *m.* — **sore,** *adj.* qui a mal aux pieds, qui a les pieds endoloris; (*vet.*) qui a la boite; *s.* (*vet.*) boite, *f.* — **stalk,** *s.* pétiole, *m.*; pédoncule, *m.* — **stall,** *s.* sabot, étrier-sabot, étrier de femme, *m.* — **step,** *s.* pas, *m.*; vestige, *m.*, trace, *f.*; (*tech.*) marchepied, *m.* — **stool,** *s.* tabouret de pieds, tabouret, *m.*; marchepied, *m.* — **stove,** **-warmer,** *s.* chauffe-pieds, *m.*; chaufferette, *f.*; bouillote, *f.*; (*for beds*) moine, *m.* — **way,** *s. V.* — **path**

Footed, *adj.* aux pieds ..., à pieds ..., à pied ..., qui a les pieds ..., qui a le pied ...

Footing, *s.* place pour le pied, *f.*; base, *f.*, fondement, *m.*; établissement, *m.*; (*support*) point d'appui, *m.*; (*fig.*) soutien, *m.*; (*condition*) pied, *m.*; (*step*) pas, *m.*; (*dance*) danse, *f.*; (*entrance, fine for initiation*) bienvenue, *f.* *On a war* —, sur le pied de guerre. *To get a* —, prendre pied, s'établir. *He missed his* —, le pied lui manqua

Fop, *s.* fat, gandin, mirliflore, petit-maître, *m.*

Fopling, *s.* petit fat, freluquet, dameret, *m.*

Foppery, *s.* fatuité, *f.*; recherche, *f.*; affectation, *f.*; ostentation, *f.*; folie, *f.*

Foppish, *adj.* fat; sot, vain; recherché; affecté

Foppishly, *adv.* en fat; d'une manière affectée

Foppishness, *s. V.* **Foppery**

For, *prep.* pour; en faveur de, en (ma, ta, &c.) faveur; (*during*) pendant; de; (*before*) avant; d'ici à; (*since*) depuis; (*to*) à; (*of distance*) à *or* jusqu'à la distance de; (*because of*) à cause de; de; (*from, of*) de; (*for the sake of*) pour; (*out of*) par; (*by*) par; (*in*) dans, en; (*for obtaining*) pour avoir; pour gagner; (*for asking*) pour demander; (*for seeking*) pour chercher; (*for finding*) pour trouver; (*for saving*) pour sauver; (*in exchange for*) en échange de, contre; pour; (*in spite of*) malgré; (*as*) comme; (*to be*) à être; (*towards*) vers; (*becoming*) à; (*that*) que, pour que (*with the subj.*). — *charity*, par charité. *It is not — me to say so*, ce n'est pas à moi de le dire; il ne m'appartient pas de le dire. *It is not proper — you to go there*, il n'est pas convenable que vous y alliez. *It is too absurd — me to believe it*, c'est trop absurde pour que je le croie. *I have not seen him — a month*, je ne l'ai pas vu depuis un mois, il y a un mois que je ne l'ai vu. *I will not go there — a month*, je n'irai pas avant un mois, je n'irai que dans un mois. *Were it not* —, *V.* **Be.** *I would not give a farthing — that hat*, je ne donnerais pas un centime de ce chapeau. — *oneself*, (*on o.'s own account*) pour son compte

For, *conj.* car. — **asmuch,** *conj.* d'autant (que), vu (que), attendu (que), considérant (que). — *that*, (*because*) parce que, par la raison que

Forage, *s.* fourrage, *m.*; provisions, *f.pl.*; — *v.n.* fourrager; faire des ravages; (*wander*) errer; — *v.a.* fourrager; ravager, dévaster; (*feed*) affourrager. — **cap,** *s.* bonnet de police, képi de petite tenue, *m.*

Forager, *s.* fourrageur, *m.*

Foraging, *s.* fourrage, *m.*; ravage, pillage, *m.*, déprédation, *f.* — **cap,** *s. V.* **Forage.** — **party,** *s. V.* **Party**

Foray, *s.* ravage, pillage, *m.*, razzia, *f.*; incursion, *f.*; — *v.a.* ravager, piller

Forbear, *v.n.* s'abstenir (de); se garder (de); s'empêcher (de); se défendre (de); se retenir (de); refuser (de); (*be patient*) être patient, patienter; (*delay*) attendre; différer (de); (*cease*) cesser (de); (*stop*) s'arrêter, arrêter; — *v.a.* supporter; s'abstenir de; éviter

Forbearance, *s.* patience, *f.*; résignation, *f.*; indulgence, *f.*; tolérance, *f.*; ménagement, *m.*; clémence, *f.*; (*avoiding*) abstinence, abstention, *f.*; éloignement, *m.*

Forbearingly, *adv.* patiemment, avec patience *or* &c. (*V.* **Forbearance**)

Forbid, *v.a.* défendre (de), interdire (de); exclure; s'opposer à; (*prevent*) empêcher (de). *To — a person* (...), défendre à quelqu'un (...). *To — a thing*, défendre (&c.) une chose. *I am forbidden* (*to*), il m'est défendu (de), on me défend (de). *That is forbidden*, cela est défendu. *God — ! Heaven — !* à Dieu ne plaise! Dieu *or* le ciel m'en préserve *or* m'en garde!

Forbiddance, *s.* défense, interdiction, *f.*

Forbidding, *adj.* repoussant, rebutant; — *s. V.* **Forbiddance**

Force, *s.* force, *f.*; puissance, *f.*; énergie, *f.*; vigueur, *f.*; vertu, *f.*; efficacité, *f.*; validité, *f.*; nécessité, *f.*; (*law*) violence, *f.*; (*mil.*) corps d'armée, *m.*; troupe, *f.*; —**s,** *pl.* forces, troupes, *f.pl.* *In* —, en vigueur; (*mil.*) en force. —**less,** *adj.* sans force

Force, *v.a.* forcer (à); contraindre (à); violenter; (*assault*) prendre de force; (*impose*) imposer (à); (*urge*) presser; insister sur; (*into*) introduire (*or* faire entrer) de force; pousser; enfoncer; entraîner; (*drive away*) chasser (de); (*extort*) arracher (à); (*plants*) forcer, hâter; (*meat*) farcir. *To — o.'s way into*, entrer de force dans. — **away**, chasser, arracher. — **back**, repousser, refouler, faire reculer. — **down**, faire descendre. — **from**, chasser de; arracher à. — **in**, enfoncer; faire entrer de force. — **on**, présenter forcément à; imposer à. — **open**, forcer. — **out**, faire sortir; chasser; arracher. — **over**, faire tourner. — **up**, faire monter

Forced, *adj.* forcé (à; *before a verb*, de)

Forcedly, *adv.* forcément, de force; nécessairement [quenelle, *f.*

Forcemeat, *s.* farce, *f.* — **ball,** *s.* boulette,

Forceps, *s.* forceps, *m.*

Forcer, *s.* personne *or* chose qui force, *f.*, forceur, *m.*; (*dentist's*) davier, *m.*; (*hydraulics*) piston de pompe foulante, refouleur, *m.*

Forcible, *adj.* fort; énergique; impétueux; puissant; pressant; violent; efficace; (*done by force*) forcé; (*law*) par force

Forcibleness, *s.* force, violence, *f.*

Forcibly, *adv.* fortement; énergiquement; impétueusement, avec impétuosité; puissamment; (*by force*) forcément; par force; de force

Forcing, *s.* forcement, *m.*; contrainte, *f.*; (*of plants*) action de forcer, *f.*; (*tech.*) refoulement, *m.* — **engine, -pump,** *s. V.* **Pump.** — **house,** *s.* forcerie, *f.* — **pipe,** *s.* tuyau de refoulement, *m.* — **pit,** *s.* couche sourde, *f.*

Ford, *s.* gué, *m.*; (*stream*) cours d'eau, *m.*, rivière, *f.*; — *v.a.* passer à gué, guéer

Fordable, *adj.* guéable

Fording, *s.* action de passer à gué, *f.*; passage à gué, *m.* — **place,** *s.* gué, *m.*

Fore, *adj.* antérieur; (*being in front*) de devant; (*first*) premier; (*nav.*) de l'avant, d'avant; (*nav.: of mast, sail, stay, top*) de misaine; — *adv.* antérieurement; (*in compounds*) d'avance; (*nav.*) devant, à l'avant. — *and aft*, (*nav.*) de l'avant à l'arrière

Forearm, *v.a.* prémunir; — *s.* (*anat.*) avant-bras, *m.* *Forewarned forearmed*, un bon averti en vaut deux

Forebode, *v.a.* présager; prédire; pressentir

Forebodement, *s.* présage, *m.*; prédiction, *f.*; pressentiment, *m.*

Foreboder, *s.* devin, *m.*; prophète, *m.*

Foreboding, *adj.* prophétique; — *s. V.* **Forebodement**

Fore-cabin, *s.* (*nav.*) chambre d'avant *or* de devant, seconde chambre, *f.* — **passenger,** *s.*, passager (*m.*, -ère, *f.*) de seconde (*or* de

Fore-carriage, *s.* avant-train, *m.* [deuxième)

Forecast, *v.a.n.* calculer d'avance, prévoir, prédire; projeter; concerter; — *s.* calcul, *m.*; prévision, prédiction, *f.*; projet, plan, *m.*; prévoyance, *f.*

Forecastle, *s.* (*nav.*) gaillard d'avant, *m.*

Forecited, *adj.* précité

Forechosen, *adj.* choisi d'avance [clore

Foreclose, *v.a.* arrêter, empêcher; (*law*) for-

Foreclosure, *s.* empêchement, *m.*; (*law*) for-

Fore-deck, *s.* (*nav.*) avant, *m.* [clusion, *f.*

Foredoom, *v.a.* prédestiner; — *s.* sentence portée d'avance, *f.*; prédestination, *f.*

Fore-end, *s.* partie antérieure, partie de devant,

Forefather. *V.* **Ancestor** [*f.*

Forefend, *v.a. V.* **Forbid**

Fore-finger, *s.* index, *m*

Fore-foot, *s.* pied de devant, *m.*

Fore-front, *s.* frontispice, *m.*; façade, *f.*; (*mil.*) premier rang, *m.*

Forego, *v.a.* quitter, abandonner, céder; renoncer à; s'abstenir de, se refuser; sacrifier; (*lose*) perdre; (*forget*) oublier; (*precede*) précéder

Foregoer, *s.* aïeul, ancêtre, *m.*; prédécesseur, *m.*; précurseur, *m.*

Foregoing, *adj.* précédent; antérieur

Foregone, *adj.* passé; anticipé. — *conclusion*, opinion préconçue, *f.*, parti pris, *m.* [plan, *m.*

Foreground, *s.* devant, *m.*; (*paint.*) premier

Forehand, *s.* partie de devant, *f.*; partie principale, *f.*; avantage, *m.*; — *adj.* antérieur; précédent

Forehanded, *adj.* sur le devant; à l'avance, d'avance; opportun, à propos; à son aise

Forehead, *s.* front, *m.*

Foreign, *adj.* étranger; (*nat. hist.*) exotique; (*in foreign parts*) à l'étranger; extérieur; (*of bills of exchange*) sur l'étranger; (*of post-paper*) pelure, pelure d'ognon. *In — parts*, dans les pays étrangers, à l'étranger. — **bill,** *s.* lettre de change sur l'étranger. — **bound,** *adj.* (*nav.*) en destination pour l'étranger. — **built,** *adj.* de construction étrangère. — **cigar,** *s.* cigare étranger, havane, vrai havane, manille, vrai manille, *m.* — **commerce,** *s.* commerce extérieur, *m.* — **department,** *s.* département des affaires étrangères, *m.* — **grown,** *adj.* de provenance étrangère. — **made,** *adj.* fait à l'étranger. — **office,** *s.* ministère des affaires étrangères, *m.* — **wood,** bois exotique, bois des îles, *m.*

Foreigner, *s.* étranger, *m.*, -ère, *f.*

Foreignness, *s.* caractère étranger, *m.*; (*fig.*) éloignement, *m.*; défaut de rapport ('*from*,' [avec), *m.*

Forejudge, *v.a.* juger d'avance

Foreknow, *v.a.* savoir d'avance; préconnaître; prévoir

Foreknowledge, *s.* prescience, préconnaissance, connaissance, prévision, *f.*

Foreland, *s.* pointe de terre, pointe, *f.*, promontoire, cap, *m.*

Fore-leg, *s.* jambe de devant, *f.*

Forelock, *s.* cheveux de devant, *m.pl.*; toupet, *m.* *We must take time by the —*, il faut prendre l'occasion aux cheveux

Foreman, *s.* (*in manufactories*, &c.) contremaître, *m.*; premier ouvrier, *m.*; chef d'atelier, *m.*; chef, *m.*; (*ganger*) chef d'équipe, *m.*; (*of shops*) premier garçon, *m.*; (*of butchers*) étalier, *m.*; (*of juries*) chef, *m.*; (*generally*) chef, *m.* *Butcher's —*, premier garçon boucher, étalier, *m.*

Foremast, *s.* mât de misaine, *m.* — **man,** *s.* gabier de misaine, *m.*

Forementioned, *adj. V.* **Abovementioned**

Foremost, *adj.* le premier; au premier rang; en tête; en avant. *First and —*, en tête; en première ligne; tout d'abord

Forenamed, *adj.* susnommé, déjà nommé

Forenoon, *s.* matin, *m.*, matinée, *f.*

Forensic, *adj.* du barreau; de palais; (*of medicine*) légal

Foreordain, *v.a.* préordonner, régler d'avance

Forepart, *s.* devant, *m.*; partie antérieure, *f.*; première partie, *f.*; commencement, *m.*; (*nav.*) avant, *m.*, proue, *f.* [*m.*; pronostic, *m.*

Forerunner, *s.* avant-coureur, précurseur,

Foresaid, *adj.* susdit

Foresail, *s.* voile de misaine, misaine, *f.*

Foresee, *v.a.* prévoir

Foreseer, *s.* personne qui prévoit, *f.*

Foreshadow, *v.a.* représenter d'avance, annoncer, figurer; faire pressentir

Foreshorten, *v.a.* raccourcir

Foreshortening, *s.* raccourci, *m.*

Foreshow, *v.a.* présager, annoncer; prédire; représenter d'avance

Foreshroud, *s.* (*nav.*) hauban de misaine, *m.*

Foresight, *s.* prévoyance, *f.*; (*theol.*) prescience, *f.*; (*of fire-arms*) guidon, *m.*

Foreskin, *s.* prépuce, *m.*

Foreskirt, *s.* pan de devant, *m.*; devant, *m.*

Forest, *s.* forêt, *f.*; — *adj.* forestier. *Woods and —s*, (*admin.*) eaux et forêts. — **fly,** *s.* hippobosque, *f.* — **laws,** *s. pl.* lois forestières, *f.pl.*, code forestier, *m.* — **oak,** *s.* casuarine, *f.* — **ranger,** *s.* garde forestier, *m.* — **tree,** *s.* arbre forestier, arbre de haute futaie, *m.*

Forestal, *adj.* forestier

Forestall, *v.a.* anticiper; devancer, prévenir; (*buy*) accaparer
Forestaller, *s.* accapareur, *m.*, -euse, *f.*
Forestalling, *s.* accaparement, *m.*
Forestay, *s.* (*nav.*) étai de misaine, *m.* — **sail,** *s.* petit foc, *m.*, trinquette, *f.*, tourmentin, *m.*
Forester, *s.* forestier, garde forestier, *m.*; habitant de forêt, *m* ; (*tree*) arbre forestier, *m.*
Forestry, *s.* sylviculture, *f.*
Foretaste, *s.* avant-goût, *m.*; — *v.a.* avoir un avant-goût de; goûter avant
Foretell, *v.a.n.* prédire; présager; annoncer
Foreteller, *s.* prédiseur, *m.*, -euse, *f.*, prophète, *m.*, prophétesse, *f.*; (*fig.*) avant-coureur, *m.*, avant-courrier, *m.*, -ière, *f.*
Foretelling, *s.* prédiction, *f.* [tion, *f.*
Forethought, *s.* prévoyance, *f.*; prémédita-
Foretooth, *s.* dent de devant, dent incisive, *f.*
Foretop, *s.* toupet, *m* ; (*of ladies' hair*) tour, *m.*; (*nav.*) hune de misaine, *f.* — **mast,** *s.* petit mât de hune, *m.* — **sail,** *s.* petit hunier, *m.* — **stay,** *s.* étai de petit hunier, *m.* — **yard,** *s.* vergue du petit hunier, *f.*
Forewarn, *v.a.* prévenir, avertir
Forewarning, *s.* avertissement, *m.*
Forewheel, *s.* roue de devant, *f.*
Forewoman, *s.* première ouvrière, *f.*
Foreyard, *s.* (*nav.*) vergue de misaine, *f.*
Forfeit, *v.a.* forfaire (à); (*pay*) être passible d'une amende de; (*law*) confisquer, perdre par confiscation; être déchu de; (*lose*) perdre; (*compromise*) compromettre; (*o.'s honour*) forfaire à; (*o.'s word*) manquer à; — *s.* confiscation, *f.*; (*penalty*) peine, *f.*; (*of bargains*) dédit, *m.*; (*a fine*) amende, *f.*; (*play*) gage, *m.*; (*in horse-racing*) forfait, *m.*; — *adj.* confisqué; perdu; (*feud.*) forfait. *To play at —s*, jouer aux petits jeux [*penalty*) passible d'une peine
Forfeitable, *adj.* confiscable; (*liable to a*
Forfeiture, *s.* forfaiture, *f.*; confiscation, *f.*; (*loss*) perte, *f.*; (*fall*) déchéance, *f.*; (*penalty*) peine, *f*; (*of bargains*) dédit, *m.*
Forge, *v.a.* forger; (*invent*) forger, controuver, fabriquer; (*coin, signature*) contrefaire; (*writings*) faire un faux en; (*a will*) supposer; — *s.* forge, *f.*; — *adj.* de forge
Forgeable, *adj.* forgeable [(*false*) faux
Forged, *part. adj.* forgé, &c. (*V.* **Forge,** *v.a.*);
Forger, *s.* forgeur, *m.*; (*fig.*) forgeur, *m.*, fabricateur, *m.*, -trice, *f.*; (*falsifier*) faussaire, *m.f.*; (*— of coin*) faux monnayeur, *m.*
Forgery, *s.* falsification, *f.*; contrefaçon, *f.*; (*thing forged*) pièce fabriquée, *f.*, acte faux, faux, *m.*, contrefaçon, *f.*; (*crime*) faux, crime
Forget, *v.a.* oublier (' *to*,' de) [de faux, *m.*
Forgetful, *adj.* oublieux; (*of*) qui oublie, qui néglige. *To be — of*, oublier, négliger
Forgetfully, *adv.* oublieusement, avec oubli
Forgetfulness, *s.* oubli, *m.*; manque de mémoire, *m.*; négligence, inattention, *f.*
Forget-me-not, *s.* (*bot.*) ne m'oubliez pas, myosotis, *m.*
Forgett, *s.* (*of gloves*) fourchette, *f.*
Forgetter, *s.* personne oublieuse, personne qui oublie, *f.*
Forging, *s.* forgeage, forgement, *m.*
Forgivable, *adj.* pardonnable
Forgive, *v.a.n.* pardonner (à); faire grâce (à); (*debt, penalty,* &c.) remettre, faire remise de, faire grâce de. *To — a thing*, pardonner quelque chose. *To — a person* (*for*), pardonner à quelqu'un (de)
Forgiveness, *s.* pardon, *m.*; rémission, *f.*; clémence, *f.*; (*of debt,* &c.) remise, *f.*
Forgiver, *s.* pardonneur, *m.*, -euse, *f.*
Forgiving, *adj.* pardonneur, qui pardonne volontiers, qui n'est pas rancunier, généreux; indulgent; clément; miséricordieux; — *s. V.* **Forgiveness**
Forgivingness, *s.* disposition à pardonner, *f.*; indulgence, *f.*; clémence, *f.*
Fork, *s.* fourche, *f.*; (*for eating*) fourchette, *f.*; (*of roads*) bifurcation, *f.*; (*anat., and of trousers*) enfourchure, *f.*; (*barb, point*) pointe, *f.*; (*of lightning*) zigzag, *m.* —**ful,** *s.* fourchée, *f.*; (*of table-forks*) fourchettée, fourchetée, *f.* — **head,** *s.* pointe de flèche, *f.*
Fork, *v.n.* fourcher, se fourcher, faire la fourche, se bifurquer; — *v.a.* enlever avec la fourche; (*agr.*) fourcher; (*steal*) gripper. — **out** (*money*), cracher *or* abouler (de l'argent), financer, dégaîner, jouer du pouce
Forked, *adj.* fourchu, en fourche; (*of lightning*) en zigzag, fulminant
Forkedly, *adv.* en fourche, en forme de fourche
Forkedness, *s.* forme fourchue, *f.*
Forky, *adj.* fourchu, en fourche
Forlorn, *adj.* abandonné, délaissé; solitaire; (*lost*) perdu; (*hopeless*) désespéré; (*wretched*) malheureux, misérable. — *hope*, (*mil.*) enfants perdus, *m.pl.*
Forlornness, *s.* abandon, délaissement, *m.*; solitude, *f.*; état désespéré, *m.*; misère, *f.*
Form, *s.* forme, *f.*; formalité, *f.*; cérémonie, *f.*; formule, *f.*; (*bench*) banc, *m.*; (*class*) classe, salle, *f.*; (*of hares*) gîte, *m*, forme, *f.*; — *v.a.* former; (*an idea*) se faire (une idée); (*— part of*) faire (partie de); — *v.n.* se former. *Set —*, formule, *f.*, modèle, *m.* *In due —*, en bonne forme, dans les règles. *In the fifth —*, en cinquième. —**less,** *adj.* sans forme, informe
Formâ (Pro), pour la forme; (*com.*) simulé
Formal, *adj.* de forme; formel; (*pers., manners,* &c.) façonnier, formaliste, cérémonieux; grave; compassé; précis; régulier; méthodique; affecté; de convention; extérieur
Formal-ism, -ist. *V.* page 3, § 1
Formality, *s.* formalité, *f.*; cérémonie, *f.*; bienséance, convenance, *f.*; gravité, *f.*; affectation, *f.*
Formally, *adv.* formellement; avec formalité
Formation, *s.* formation, *f.* [formatif, *m.*
Formative, *adj.* formatif, formateur; — *s.*
Forme, *s.* (*print.*) forme, *f.* [créateur, *m.*
Former, *s.* formateur, *m.*, -trice, *f.*, auteur,
Former, *adj.* premier; ancien; passé; précédent. *The —*, celui-là, *m.*, celle-là, *f.*, ceux-là, *m.pl.*, celles-là, *f.pl.*
Formerly, *adv.* autrefois; auparavant
Formiate, *s.* (*chem.*) formiate, *m.*
Formic, *adj.* (*chem.*) formique
Formicating, *adj.* (*med.*) formicant
Formication, *s.* (*med.*) fourmillement, *m.*,
Formidable, *adj.* formidable [formication, *f.*
Formidableness, *s.* nature formidable, *f.*
Formidably, *adv.* formidablement, d'une manière formidable
Forming, *s.* formation, *f.*
Formula, *s.* formule, *f.*
Formulary, *s.* formulaire, *m.*; — *adj.* consacré, reçu, établi, régle
Formulate, *v.a.* formuler
Formule, *s.* formule, *f.*
Fornicate, *v.n.* forniquer
Fornication, *s.f.* fornication, *f.*
Fornica-tor, tress, *s.* fornicateur, *m.*, -trice, *f.*
Forsake, *v.a.* délaisser; abandonner; quitter; (*fail*) manquer à
Forsaker, *s.* personne qui délaisse *or* abandonne *or* quitte, *f.*; (*of religion*) apostat,
Forsaking, *s.* abandon, *m.* [renégat, *m.*
Forsooth, *adv.* vraiment, en vérité; assurément; ma foi; oui dà
Forswear, *v.a.* abjurer, renier; renoncer à; répudier; (*swear not to* ...) jurer de ne pas ...; — *v.n.* se parjurer. *To — oneself*, se
Forswearer, *s.* parjure, *m.f.* [parjurer
Forswearing, *s.* parjure, *m.*
Fort, *s.* fort, *m.* [(*mus.*) forte
Forte, *s.* fort, *m.*; (*mus.*) forte, *m.*; — *adv.*
Forth, *adv.* en avant; (*abroad*) au loin; (*out*) dehors; au dehors; hors; (*publicly*) en public, au jour; (*hence*) de là; (*thoroughly*) jusqu'à la fin. *And so —*, *V.* **So**

Forthcoming, *adj.* prêt à paraître; qui arrive; tout prêt; qui va se présenter; qui va avoir lieu; prochain; à venir; (*law*) qui va comparaître; — *s.* comparution, *f.*
Forthwith, *adv.* sur-le-champ, aussitôt, immédiatement, à l'instant; séance tenante
Fortieth, *adj.* quarantième
Fortifiable, *adj.* fortifiable [vinage, *m.*
Fortification, *s.* fortification, *f.*; (*of wine*)
Fortifier, *s.* fortificateur, *m.*; défenseur, protecteur, *m.*
Fortify, *v.a.* fortifier; (*fig.*) munir (de), armer (de); (*to confirm*) consolider, renforcer; (*wine*) viner (du vin). —*ied town,* place forte, *f.*
Fortifying, *s.* fortification, *f.*; consolidation, *f.*; (*of wine*) vinage, *m.*
Fortitude, *s.* force d'âme, *f.*; courage, *m.*
Fortlet, *s.* fortin, *m.*
Fortnight, *s.* quinze jours, *m.pl.*, quinzaine, *f.* *A — ago,* il y a quinze jours. *This day —,* d'aujourd'hui (*or* aujourd'hui) en quinze; (*past*) il y a aujourd'hui quinze jours. *To-morrow —,* de demain en quinze. *Yesterday —, a — ago yesterday,* il y a eu hier quinze jours
Fortnightly, *adj.* de tous les quinze jours; (*of reviews,* &c.) paraissant tous les quinze jours, bimensuel, de la quinzaine; — *adv.* tous [les quinze jours
Fortress, *s.* forteresse, *f.*
Fortuitous, *adj.* fortuit
Fortuitously, *adv.* fortuitement, par hasard
Fortuitousness, Fortuity, *s.* hasard, *m.*
Fortunate, *adj.* heureux; fortuné
Fortunately, *adv.* heureusement; par bonheur
Fortunateness, *s.* bonheur, *m.*; succès, *m.*
Fortune, *s.* fortune, *f.*; (*fate*) sort, *m.*; position, *f.*; (*destiny*) bonne aventure, *f.*; (*dowry*) dot, *f.*; **—s,** *pl.* fortune, *f.*; bonne aventure, *f.* *Good —,* bonheur, *m.*, bonne fortune, *f.* *Ill —,* malheur, *m.*, mauvaise fortune, *f.* *To hunt after —,* courir après la fortune. *To make a —,* faire fortune. *To seek o.'s —,* chercher fortune. *To tell —s,* dire la bonne aventure. *To try o.'s —,* tenter la fortune. — **book,** *s.* grimoire, *m.* — **hunter,** *s.* homme qui cherche de riches partis, coureur de dots, *m.* —**less,** *adj.* sans fortune; malheureux. — **teller,** *s.* diseur (*m.*, -euse, *f.*) de bonne aventure. — **telling,** *adj.* qui dit la bonne aventure; *s.* [bonne aventure, *f.*
Forty, *adj.* quarante
Forum, *s.* forum, *m.*
Forward, Forwards, *adv.* en avant; en évidence. *From that time —,* depuis ce temps. *From this time —,* dorénavant
Forward, *adj.* avancé; disposé (à), enclin (à); empressé (de); pressé (de), prompt (à); ardent (à); impatient (à); (*premature*) précoce, avancé; (*of fruit,* &c.) précoce; (*in studies*) avancé, fort; (*bold*) hardi; (*impudent*) effronté; (*free*) libre; (*presumptuous*) présomptueux
Forward, *v.a.* avancer; (*hasten*) hâter; seconder; favoriser; activer; (*pers.*) pousser; (*send*) envoyer (à), faire parvenir (à), transmettre (à); (*com.*) expédier. *To be —ed,* (*on letters and parcels*) faire suivre [teur, *m.*
Forwarder, *s.* promoteur, *m.*; (*com.*) expédi-
Forwardly, *adv.* avec empressement; ardemment; promptement; (*boldly*) hardiment; (*impudently*) effrontément; présomptueusement
Forwardness, *s.* empressement, *m.*, ardeur, *f.*; zèle, *m.*; hardiesse, assurance, *f.*; effronterie, *f.*; présomption, *f.*; avancement, *m.*; état avancé, *m.*; progrès, *m.*; (*of fruit,* &c.) précocité, *f.*
Foss, Fossa, Fosse, *s.* fossé, *m.*; (*anat.*) fosse, *f.* — **road, -way,** *s.* route romaine, *f.*
Fosset, *s.* (*of casks*) *V.* **Tap**
Fossil, *adj. s.* fossile, *adj. m.f., s.m.*
Fossiliferous, *adj.* fossilifère
Fossilification, *s.* fossilisation, *f.*
Fossil-ism, -ist. *V.* page 3, § 1
Fossility, *s.* fossilité, *f.*
Fossilization, *s.* fossilisation, *f.*
Fossilize, *v.a.* fossiliser; — *v.n.* se fossiliser
Fossorial, *adj. s.* fouisseur, *m.*
Foster, *v.a.* élever; nourrir; encourager; favoriser; protéger; — *adj.* nourricier. — **brother,** *s.* frère de lait, *m.* — **child,** *s.* nourrisson, *m.*, -ne, *f.*; enfant adoptif, *m.*, enfant adoptive, *f.* — **daughter,** *s.* nourrissonne, *f.* — **father,** *s.* père nourricier, *m.*; (*fig.*) père adoptif, *m.* — **mother,** *s.* nourrice, *f.*; (*fig.*) mère adoptive, *f.* — **nurse,** *s* nourrice, *f.*; (*fig.*) bienfaiteur, *m.*, -trice, *f* — **sister,** *s.* sœur de lait, *f.* — **son,** *s.* nourrisson, *m.*; (*fig.*) fils adoptif, *m.*; fils chéri, *m.*
Fosterer, *s.* nourricier, *m.*, nourrice, *f.*; (*fig.*) protecteur, *m.*, -trice, *f.*
Fostering, *adj.* maternel; paternel; (*fig.*) protecteur; bienfaisant
Fosterling, *s.* nourrisson, *m.*, -ne, *f.*
Fother, *v.a.* affourrager; (*nav.*) aveugler, boucher
Fougasse, *s.* (*mil.*) fougasse, *f.*
Foul, *adj.* (*dirty*) sale; souillé; (*muddy*) trouble; bourbeux; (*impure*) impur; mauvais; infâme; infect; obscène; (*disgraceful*) honteux; (*wicked*) méchant, mauvais; noir, atroce; abominable; vil; bas; (*unfair*) injuste; déloyal; malhonnête; illicite; (*ugly*) vilain; difforme; (*bad*) mauvais; (*coarse*) grossier; (*dangerous*) dangereux; — *v.a.* crasser, salir; souiller; (*nav.*) aborder (par accident); (*ropes*) mêler, embarrasser. — *air,* air vicié, air impur, mauvais air, *m.* — *bill,* (*nav.*) patente brute, *f.* — *breath,* mauvaise haleine, haleine infecte, *f.* — *copy,* brouillon, *m.* — *dealing,* déloyauté, *f.*; trahison, *f.*; supercherie, *f.* — *mouth,* bouche impure, *f.* — *page,* (*print.*) page chargée, *f.* — *paper,* brouillon, *m.* — *play,* tricherie, *f.*; (*fig.*) manigance, *f.*, tripotage, micmac, *m.*; vilaine affaire, *f.*; vilain tour, *m.*; (*snare*) guet-apens, *m.* — *proof,* (*print.*) épreuve chargée, *f.* — *rope,* corde embarrassée, *f.* — *spirit,* esprit immonde, *m.* — *stomach,* estomac chargé, *m.* — *tongue,* mauvaise langue, langue injurieuse, *f.*; (*med.*) langue chargée, *f.* — *weather,* mauvais temps, vilain temps, *m.*; (*nav.*) gros temps, *m.* — *wind,* vent contraire, *m.* — *words,* mots injurieux, *m.pl.*; (*dirty*) paroles déshonnêtes *or* sales, *f.pl.* *To fall* or *run — of* (or *upon*), déchirer à belles dents, dire pis que pendre (de *or* sur le compte de); attaquer, s'attaquer à, tomber sur, fondre sur; (*of ships*) aborder (par accident); (*of ropes*) se mêler, s'embarrasser
Fouling, *s.* crasse, *f.*
Foully, *adv.* salement; dégoûtamment, d'une manière dégoûtante; méchamment; vilainement; honteusement; odieusement; atrocement, horriblement, affreusement; déloyalement; injustement
Foulness, *s.* saleté, *f.*; impureté, *f.*; turpitude, *f.*; honte, infamie, *f.*; (*wickedness*) noirceur, atrocité, *f.*; (*unfairness*) déloyauté, perfidie, *f.*; (*ugliness*) laideur, *f.*; difformité, *f.*; (*of the tongue*) état chargé, *m.*; (*of the stomach*) mau- [vais état, *m.*
Foumart, *s.* putois, *m.*
Found, *v.a.* fonder; établir; fixer; (*cast*) fondre
Foundation, *s.* fondation, *f.*; fondement, *m.*; (*act of founding*) fondation, création, *f.*; établissement, *m.*; (*cause*) fondement, *m.*; (*origin*) commencement, *m.*; (*endowment*) fondation, dotation, *f.*; bourses, *f.pl.* *To be on the —,* (*of schools*) être boursier. *To get* (*one*) *on the —,* (*of schools*) obtenir une bourse pour ... *To lay the —,* jeter *or* poser les fondements. — **scholar,** *s.* boursier, *m.*, -ière, *f.* — **school,** *s.* lycée, *m.* — **stone,** *s.* première pierre, *f.*; (*fig.*) pierre fondamentale, *f.* *To lay the — stone,* poser la première pierre
Foundationer, *s.* boursier, *m.*, -ière, *f.*
Founder, *s.* fondateur, *m.*; (*of metals*) fondeur, *m.*; (*vet.*) courbature, *f.*; fourbure, *f.*; — *v.a.n.* rendre courbatu; rendre fourbu; (*of ships*)

sombrer, couler à fond, couler bas; (*fig.*)
Foundered, *adj.* courbatu; fourbu [échouer
Foundering, *s.*(*vet.*) courbature, *f.*; fourbure, *f.*
Foundery. *V.* **Foundry** [fonte, *f.*; fonderie, *f.*
Founding, *adj.* fondateur; — *s.* fondation, *f.*;
Foundling, *s.* enfant trouvé, *m.* — **hospital,** *s.* hospice des enfants assistés (*or* trouvés), *m.*
Foundress, *s.* fondatrice, *f.*
Foundry, *s.* fonderie, *f.*; (*print.*) stéréotypie, *f.*
Fount, *s.* (*print.*) fonte, *f.*; œil, *m.*; (*fountain*) *V.* **Fountain.** *Wrong* —, (*print.*) d'un autre œil. — **list,** *s.* police, *f.*
Fountain, *s.* fontaine, *f.*; (*spring*) source, *f.*; (*artificial*) fontaine, *f.*, bassin, jet d'eau, *m.*; —**s,** *pl.* (*artificial*) eaux, *f.pl.* — **head,** *s.* origine, source, *f.* — **maker,** *s.* fontainier, *m.* — **shell,** *s.* strombe géant, *m.*, aile d'aigle, *f.*
Four, *adj.* *s.* quatre (*adj.m.f.*, *s.m.*); (*elliptically*) (*of the clock*) quatre heures, *f.pl.*, (*of o.'s age*) quatre ans, *m.pl.* *Carriage and* —, *V.* **And.** *On all* —*s*, à quatre pattes. — **angled,** *adj.* quadrangulaire. — **cornered,** *adj.* à quatre coins; quadrangulaire. — **fold,** *adj.* *adv.* quadruple, quatre fois autant, quatre fois. — **footed,** *adj.* à quatre pieds, à quatre pattes, qui a quatre pieds, qui a quatre pattes, quadrupède. — **foot way, -foot, -feet,** *s.* (*rail.*) entre-rails, *m.*, voie, ligne, *f.* — **handed,** *adj.* quadrumane. — **-in-hand,** *adv.* à grandes guides; *s.* attelage de quatre chevaux à grandes guides, *m.* — **post bedstead,** *s.* lit à colonnes, *m.* — **score,** *adj.* quatre-vingts. — *score and ten*, quatre-vingt-dix
Fourchette, *s.* fourchette, *f.*
Fourteen, *adj.* quatorze
Fourteenth, *adj.* *s.* quatorzième; (*of the month*) quatorze. *The* —, (*of sovereigns*) quatorze
Fourth, *adj.* quatrième; — *s.* (*pers., things*) quatrième, *m.f.*; (*fourth part*) quart, *m.*; (*mus.*) quarte, *f.*; (*of the month*) quatre, *m.* *The* —, (*of sovereigns*) quatre
Fourthly, *adv.* quatrièmement
Fowl, *s.* oiseau, *m.*; (*barn-door* —) oiseau de basse-cour, *m.*; volaille, *f.*; (*cook., and table*) volaille, *f.*; (*chicken*) poulet, *m.*; (*hen*) poule, *f.*; — *v.n.* (*catch*) oiseler, prendre des oiseaux; (*shoot*) chasser aux oiseaux. *Wild* —, oie sauvage, canard sauvage, &c. — **house,** *s.* poulailler, *m.*
Fowler, *s.* oiseleur, chasseur aux oiseaux, *m.*
Fowling, *s.* (*catching*) oisellerie, *f.*; (*shooting*) chasse aux oiseaux, *f.* — **piece,** *s.* fusil de chasse, *m.*
Fox, *s.* renard, *m.*, e, *f.*; (*fish*) callionyme, *m.*; (*nav.*) tresse (de vieux cordages), *f.* — **catcher,** *s.* renardier, *m.* — **chase,** *s.* chasse au renard, *f.* — **evil,** *s.* alopécie, *f.* — **glove,** *s.* digitale, *f.* — **hound,** *s.* chien pour le renard, *m.* — **hunt, -hunting,** *s.* chasse au renard, *f.* — **hunter,** *s.* chasseur au renard, *m.* — **like,** *adj.* de renard. —**'s burrow,** *s.* renardière, *f.* —**'s cub,** *s.* renardeau, *m.* —**'s earth** *or* **hole,** *s.* renardière, *f.* — **tail,** *s.* queue de renard, *f.* — **tail grass,** *s.* vulpin, *m.* — **trap,** *s.* traquenard, traquet, *m.*
Foxy, *adj.* de renard, vulpin; (*red*) roux
F.P. ('*fire plug*,' bouche d'eau, *f.*) "Secours contre l'incendie" [fracas, *m.*
Fracas, *s.* querelle, bagarre, *f.*, esclandre,
Fraction, *s.* fraction, *f.* *Simple* or *vulgar* —, fraction ordinaire
Fractional, *adj.* fractionnaire
Fractious, *adj.* querelleur, hargneux; de mauvaise humeur, maussade
Fractiously, *adv.* d'une manière querelleuse *or* hargneuse; de mauvaise humeur, d'une manière maussade, maussadement
Fractiousness, *s.* humeur querelleuse *or* hargneuse, mauvaise humeur, humeur maussade, maussaderie, *f.*
Fracture, *s.* rupture, *f.*; (*surg.*) fracture, *f.*; (*min.*) cassure, *f.*; — *v.a.* casser, rompre, briser; (*surg.*) fracturer; — *v.n.* se casser, se rompre, se briser; se fracturer
Frænum, *s.* (*anat.*) frein, filet, *m.*
Fragile, *adj.* fragile; (*weak*) frêle
Fragility, *s.* fragilité, *f.*; (*weakness*) faiblesse, *f.*
Fragment, *s.* fragment, *m.*; morceau, *m.*; éclat, *m.*; débris, *m.* [mentaire
Fragmental, Fragmentary, *adj.* frag-
Fragmentation, *s.* fragmentation, *f.*
Fragmentous, *adj.* fragmenteux
Fragranc-e, y, *s.* bonne odeur, *f.*; parfum, *m.*
Fragrant, *adj.* odoriférant, odorant; parfumé
Fragrantly, *adv.* avec une odeur suave; bon; agréablement
Frail, *adj.* frêle; fragile; — *s.* cabas, *m.*; (*for poultry, game, or fish*) bourriche, *f.*; (*rush*) jonc, roseau, *m.* [faiblesse, *f.*
Frailness, Frailty, *s.* fragilité, *f.*; (*weakness*)
Fraise, *s.* (*fort.*) fraise, *f.*; — *v.a.* fraiser
Fraising, *s.* (*fort.*) fraisement, *m.*
Frame, *v.a.* former; ajuster; disposer; arranger; façonner; composer, faire; (*draw up*) rédiger; (*contrive*) inventer; imaginer; concevoir; (*plot*) tramer; (*forge*) controuver; (*regulate*) régler (sur), conformer (à), modeler (sur); (*pictures, &c.*) encadrer; (*build*) construire, charpenter, faire la charpente de; — *s.* charpente, structure, *f.*; (*the body*) corps, *m.*; (*fig.*) édifice, *m.*; forme, *f.*; système, arrangement, *m.*; invention, *f.*; projet, *m.*; (*of mind*) disposition, *f.*; trempe, *f.*; (*of pictures*) cadre, *m.*; encadrement, *m.*; bordure, *f.*; (*of windows, &c.*) châssis, *m.*; (*of arts*) monture, *f.*; (*need.*) métier, *m.*; (*of a carriage*) caisse, *f.*; (*of clocks, &c.*) cage, *f.*; (*of ploughs*) sep, *m.*, sole, *f.*; (*print.*) rang, *m.*; (*nav.*) couple, *m.* *Glazed* —, *glass* —, *V.* **Glass.** — **maker,** *s.* encadreur, *m.*; ouvrier en métiers, *m.* — **work,** *s.* charpente, *f.*; (*to work on*) métier, *m.*
Framer, *s.* encadreur, *m.*; (*fig.*) auteur, *m.*; artisan, *m.*
Framing, *s.* charpente, *f.*; (*truss*) ferme, *f.*; (*of pictures*) encadrement, *m.*; (*fig.*) *V.* **Frame**
Franc, *s.* (*coin*) franc, *m.*
Franchise, *s.* franchise, *f.*; privilége, *m.*; droit, *m.*; droit électoral, *m.*; (*qualification*) cens, *m.*; (*district*) territoire, *m.*; (*vote*) suf-
Francic. *V.* **Frankish** [frage, *m.*
Franciscan, *s.* *adj.* franciscain, *m.*
Franco, (*in compounds*) franco-...
Francolin, *s.* (*bird*) francolin, *m.*
Frangibility, *s.* frangibilité, *f.*
Frangible, *adj.* frangible
Frangipane, Frangipanni, *s.* frangipane, *f.*
Frank, *adj.* franc, sincère; généreux, libéral; — *s.* Franc, *m.*, Franque, *f.*; (*letter*) lettre affranchie, *f.*; (*privilege*) franchise, *f.*; (*signature*) signature d'affranchissement, *f.*; — *v.a.* affranchir, envoyer franc. — **incense,** *s.* encens, *m.*
Frankforter, *s.* Francfortois, *m.*, e, *f.* [cens, *m.*
Franking, *s.* affranchissement, *m.*; (*privilege*) franchise, *f.*
Frankish, *adj.* franc (*m.*, franque, *f.*)
Frankly, *adv.* franchement; sincèrement; nettement; généreusement, libéralement; librement, à son gré; volontairement, de son plein gré; volontiers
Frankness, *s.* franchise, *f.*; sincérité, *f.*; loyauté, *f.*; générosité, libéralité, *f.*
Frantic, *adj.* frénétique; fou; forcené; effréné
Frantically, *adv.* avec frénésie
Frap, *v.a.* (*nav.*) risser; ceintrer; aiguilleter
Frapping, *s.* (*nav.*) ceintrage, *m.*
Fraternal, *adj.* fraternel
Fraternally, *adv.* fraternellement
Fraternity. *V.* **Brotherhood** [nisation, *f.*
Fraternization, Fraternizing, *s.* frater-
Fraternize, *v.n.* fraterniser
Fratricidal, *adj.* fratricide
Fratricide, *s.* fratricide, (*pers.*) *m.f.*, (*murder*) *m.*
Fraud, *s.* fraude, *f.*; supercherie, *f.*; fourberie, *f.*; imposture, *f.*; (*law*) fraude, *f.*, dol, *m.*

Fraudulenc-e, y, *s.* fraude, *f.*

Fraudulent, *adj.* (*things*) frauduleux ; (*pers.*) trompeur, fourbe

Fraudulently, *adv.* frauduleusement ; en [fraude

Fraught, *adj.* plein (de), rempli (de); chargé (de) ; gros (de); fertile (en) ; riche (en)

Fraxinella, *s.* (*bot.*) fraxinelle, *f.*

Fray, *s.* querelle, *f.* ; combat, *m.* ; rixe, *f.*; bagarre, *f.* ; contestation, *f.*, débat, *m.* ; (*rubbing*) frottement, *m.* ; éraillure, *f.* ; — *v.a.* frotter ; érailler ; effiloquer ; (*hunt.*) frayer ; — *v.n.* s'érailler ; s'effiloquer

Fraying, *s.* éraillure, *f.*, (*hunt.*) frayure, *f.*

Freak, *s.* caprice, *m.*, fantaisie, *f.* ; boutade, *f.*; tour, *m.* ; — *v.a.* barioler (de) ; bigarrer (de) ; tacheter (de). — *of nature*, caprice de la nature, jeu de la nature, *m.*

Freakish, *adj.* capricieux ; bizarre ; fantasque

Freakishly, *adv.* capricieusement ; bizarrement

Freakishness, *s.* humeur *or* nature capricieuse, *f.* ; bizarrerie, *f.*

Freckle, *s.* tache de rousseur, rousseur, *f.* — **faced,** *adj.* couvert de taches de rousseur

Freckled, *adj.* bariolé, bigarré, tacheté ; (*of the face*) plein de taches de rousseur

Freckledness, *s.* taches de rousseur, rousseurs, *f.pl.*

Freckly. *V.* **Freckled**

Free, *adj.* libre ; débarrassé ; indépendant ; franc ; ouvert ; libéral, généreux ; gratuit ; volontaire ; public ; exempt (de) ; (*easy*) dégagé, aisé ; (*unceremonious*) familier ; cavalier ; (*of a horse*) franc du collier ; (*full*) plein ; — *adverb.* gratuitement. gratis, (*prepaid*) franco ; — *v.a.* délivrer (de), affranchir (de) ; débarrasser (de) ; dégager (de) ; exempter (de) ; décharger (de). — *and easy*, sans cérémonie, familier. — *and easy party*, (*drinkers*) goguette, *f.* *To get* —, se débarrasser (de) ; s'affranchir (de). *To make* —, rendre libre, affranchir ; (*with*) prendre des libertés (avec), ne pas se gêner (avec) ; user librement (de). *To set* —, mettre en liberté, délivrer ; affranchir ; dégager. — **booter,** *s.* flibustier, *m.* — **booting,** *s.* flibusterie, *f.* ; *adj.* de flibusterie. — **born,** *adj.* né libre —**dman,** *s.* affranchi, *m.* —**dom,** *s.* liberté, *f.* ; indépendance, *f.* ; facilité, *f.* ; exemption, *f.* ; absence, *f.* ; (*boldness*) hardiesse, *f.* ; (*of a city*) droit de cité, droit de citoyen, *m.* ; bourgeoisie, *f.*, droit de bourgeoisie, *m.* ; (*theat.*) entrée libre, *f.* — **hearted,** *adj.* franc ; généreux, libéral. — **heartedness,** *s.* franchise, *f.* ; générosité, libéralité, *f.* — **hold,** *s.* propriété foncière libre, *f.* ; (*feud.*) franc alleu, *m.* — **holder,** *s.* propriétaire en biens-fonds libres, *m.* ; (*feud.*) franc-tenancier, *m.* —**ly,** *adv.* librement ; franchement ; copieusement ; libéralement, généreusement ; gratuitement ; aisément ; (*willingly*) volontiers ; (*unceremoniously*) familièrement ; cavalièrement. — **man,** *s.* homme libre, *m.* ; citoyen, *m* — **mason,** *s.* franc-maçon, *m.* — **masonry,** *s.* franc-maçonnerie, *f.* — **minded,** *adj.* qui a l'esprit libre, exempt de soucis, sans soucis. —**ness,** *s.* franchise, sincérité, *f.* ; libéralité, générosité, *f.* ; gratuité, *f.* — **port,** *s.* port franc, port libre, *m.* — **school,** *s.* école libre, *f.* ; (*abusively*) école gratuite, *f.* — **shooter,** *s.* franc-tireur, *m.* — **spoken,** *adj.* qui dit librement ce qu'il pense, qui a son franc parler. — **stone,** *s.* pierre de taille, *f.* — **thinker,** *s.* libre penseur, *m.* ; (*jest*) esprit fort, *m.* — **thinking,** *s.* libre examen, *m.* — **ticket,** *s.* billet de faveur, *m.* — **trade,** *s.* libre commerce, *m.* ; (*political economy*) libre échange, *m.* ; *adj.* libre-échangiste. — **trader,** *s.* libre-échangiste, *m.f.* — **will,** *s.* plein gré, *m.* ; (*philos.*) libre arbitre, *m.* *Of his own — will*, de son plein gré

Freer, *s.* affranchisseur, *m*, libérateur, *m.*, [-trice, *f.*

Freeze, *v.a.* (*congeal*) geler ; (*chill*) glacer ; *v.n.* (*congeal*) geler ; se geler ; (*be chilled*) glacer ; se glacer. *To — to death*, faire mourir de froid. *To be frozen to death*, mourir de froid. *It is freezing very hard*, il gèle très fort. *The rain —s as it falls*, il fait du verglas

Freezer, *s.* glacière, *f.*

Freezing, *s.* congélation, *f.* ; gelée, *f.* ; — *adj.* glacial ; réfrigérant. — **machine,** *s.* glacière, *f.* — **mixture,** *s.* mélange réfrigérant, *m.* — **point,** *s.* point de congélation, *m.* ; zéro, *m.* — **pot,** *s.* sorbetière, *f.*

Freight, *v.a.* affréter ; (*to load*) charger ; — *s.* chargement, *m.*, cargaison, *f.* ; (*hire*) fret, *m.*

Freightage, *s.* frais de chargement, *m.pl.*, fret, *m.*

Freighter, *s.* affréteur, *m.*

Freighting, *s.* affrètement, *m.*

French, *adj.* français, de France, des Français ; (*of the Church*) gallican ; — *s.* (*people*) (les) Français, *m.pl.* ; (*language*) le français, *m.*, la langue française, *f.* — *coat, hat, book,* &c., habit, chapeau, livre, &c. français. — *ambassador*, ambassadeur de France. — *emperor, king*, empereur, roi des Français (*formerly*, ... de France). — *coast*, côte de France. — **berries,** *s. pl.* graines d'Avignon, *f.pl.* — **boy,** *s.* (petit) Français, *m.* — **casement,** *s.* croisée, *f.* — **girl,** *s.* (petite *or* jeune) Française, *f.* — **grass,** *s.* sainfoin, *m.* — **history,** *s.* histoire de France, *f.* — **horn,** *s.* *V.* **Horn.** — **lady,** *s.* dame française, Française, *f.* — **leave,** *s.* *V.* **Leave.** — **lesson,** *s.* leçon de français, *f.* — **man,** *s.* Français, *m.* — **master** *or* **teacher,** *s.* maître *or* professeur de français, *m.* — **polish, -polisher,** &c., *V.* **Polish, Polisher,** &c. — **prize,** *s.* prix de français, *m.* — **roll,** *s.* pain mollet, petit pain à café, *m.* — **school,** *s.* (*paint.*) école française, *f.* — **ship, -vessel,** *s* navire *or* vaisseau français, *m.* — **window,** *s.* croisée, *f.* — **woman,** *s.* Française, *f.* *What is the — for ...?* (*say*) comment dit-on ... en français ? (*call*) comment appelle-t-on ... en français ? — *spoken here*, ici on parle français

Frenchification, *s.* francisation, *f.*

Frenchify, *v.a.* franciser. *To become —ied*, se [franciser

Frenchifying, *s.* francisation, *f.*

Frenetic. *V.* **Frantic**

Frenum. *V.* **Frænum**

Frenzied, *adj.* atteint de frénésie ; frénétique ; forcené ; (*fig*) égaré ; délirant

Frenzy, *s.* frénésie, *f.* ; (*fig.*) égarement, *m.* ; délire, *m.*, ivresse, *f.*

Frequence, Frequency, *s.* fréquence, répétition fréquente *f.*, renouvellement fréquent, *m.*

Frequent, *adj.* fréquent ; — *v.a.* fréquenter

Frequentable, *adj.* fréquentable

Frequentation, *s.* fréquentation, *f.*

Frequentative, *adj.* fréquentatif ; — *s.* fréquentatif, *m.*

Frequenter, *s.* personne qui fréquente, *f.* ; [habitué, *m.*, e, *f.*

Frequenting, *s.* fréquentation, *f.*

Frequently, *adv.* fréquemment, souvent

Frequentness. *V.* **Frequency**

Fresco, *s.* fresque, *f.* *In* —, à fresque. *Painting in* —, peinture à fresque, fresque, *f.* — **painter,** *s.* fresquiste, *m.* — **painting,** *s.* peinture à fresque, fresque, *f.*

Fresh, *adj.* frais ; (*recent*) nouveau ; récent ; (*inexperienced*) novice ; (*still young*) vert, jeune ; (*brisk*) rapide ; (*lively*) vif ; (*tipsy*) en train, gai, gaillard ; (*of water*) *See below* ; (*of the wind, of air, provisions,* &c.) frais ; — *adv.* nouvellement, récemment. — **coloured,** *adj.* au teint frais. — **gathered,** *adj.* frais cueilli (*m.*), fraîche-cueillie (*f.*). — **man,** *s.* novice, *m.* ; (*univers.*) nouveau, élève *or* étudiant de première année, *m.* ; conscrit, *m.* — **manship,** *s.* noviciat, *m.* ; (*univers.*) étude de première année, *f.* — **shaved,** *adj.* rasé de frais. — **water,** *s.* eau fraîche, *f.* ; (*not salt or seawater*) eau douce, *f.* ; *adj.* d'eau douce, de rivière. — **water fish,** *s.* poisson d'eau douce, *m.* — **water herring,** *s.* lavaret, *m.*

— **water mussel,** *s.* moulette, mulette, anodonte, *f.* — **water sailor,** *s.* marin d'eau douce, *m.* — **water shrimp,** *s.* squille, *f.* — **water snail,** *s.* paludine, *f.* — **watered,** *adj.* nouvellement arrosé

Freshen, *v.a.n.* rafraîchir; (*stale bread*) repasser; (*take saltness from*) dessaler; (*lose saltness*) se dessaler; (*of the wind*) fraîchir

Freshet, *s.* crue d'eau, *f.*; cours d'eau, *m.*

Freshly, *adv.* fraîchement; nouvellement, récemment; (*anew*) de nouveau [veauté, *f.*

Freshness, *s.* fraîcheur, *f.*; (*newness*) nou-

Fret, *v.a.* (*rub*) frotter; (*wear away*) user; (*gnaw*) ronger, corroder; (*gall*) écorcher; (*fray*) érailler; (*emboss*) travailler en bosse, bosseler; ciseler; (*inlay*) incruster; (*variegate*) nuancer; (*agitate*) agiter; (*tease*) irriter; chagriner, tourmenter; — *v.n.* s'user, se détruire; s'érailler, se couper; s'agiter; se chagriner; se tourmenter; se faire de la bile, se faire du mauvais sang; s'irriter; remuer; — *s.* agitation, *f.*; inquiétude, *f.*; irritation, *f.*; tracas, *m.*; chagrin, *m.*; mauvaise humeur, *f.*; fermentation, *f.*; (*fraying*) éraillure, *f.*; (*borer*) foret, perçoir, *m.*; (*mus.*) touche, *f.*; (*arch.*) grecque, *f.*; (*her.*) frette, *f.*; (*geog.*) *V.* **Frith.** — **work,** *s.* ouvrage en bosse, *m.*; (*arch.*) grecque, *f.* [inquiet, agité; irritable

Fretful, *adj.* chagrin, de mauvaise humeur,

Fretfully, *adv.* de mauvaise humeur, avec humeur, avec chagrin; d'un caractère irritable

Fretfulness, *s.* mauvaise humeur, *f.*, dépit, *m.*; caractère irritable, *m.*, humeur chagrine, *f.*

Fretted, *adj.* (*her.*) fretté; —*part. V.* **Fret,** *v.a.n.*

Fretter, *s.* rongeur, *m.*

Fretting, *s.* agitation, *f.*, chagrin, *m.*; tracas, *m.*; (*fraying*) éraillement, *m.* [fretté

Fretty, *adj.* en bosse; marqué; agité; (*her.*)

Fria-bility, bleness. *V.* page 3, § 1

Friable, *adj.* friable

Friar, *s.* moine, religieux, frère, *m.*; (*print.*) moine, *m.* *V.* **Black, Grey, White,** *and* **Crutched.** —**'s balsam,** *s.* baume des missions, *m.* —**'s lantern,** *s.* feu follet, *m.*

Friary, *s.* couvent, monastère, *m.*; — *adj.* de moine, monastique

Fribble, *s.* freluquet, farceur, *m.*, personne frivole, *f.*; — *adj.* frivole; — *v.n.* s'amuser à des niaiseries, baguenauder. — **away,** *v.a.* perdre, gaspiller

Fribbler, *s.* baguenaudier, *m.*, personne frivole, *f.*

Fribbling, *s.* perte de temps à des bagatelles, *f.*; gaspillage, *m.*

Fricandeau, *s.* fricandeau, *m.*

Fricassee, *s.* fricassée, *f.*; — *v.a.* fricasser

Friction, *s.* frottement, *m.*; (*med.*) friction, *f.* — **gloves,** *s. pl.* gants à frictions, *m.pl.* — **metal,** *s.* métal antifriction, *m.* — **roller,** *s.* galet, *m.* — **tube,** *s.* (*artil.*) étoupille à friction, étoupille fulminante, *f.* [friction

Frictional, *adj.* de frottement; (*med.*) de

Friday, *s.* vendredi, *m.* *Good* —, vendredi saint

Friend, *s.* ami, *m.*, e, *f.*; partisan (de), *m.*; (*in duels*) second, *m.*; (*com.*) correspondant, *m.*; (*quaker*) quaker, *m.*; —**s,** *pl.* amis, *m.pl.*, amies, *f.pl.*, &c.; (*relations*) famille, *f.*, parents, *m.pl.* *To make —s,* se faire des amis; gagner l'amitié (de); (*together*) se réconcilier, se raccommoder, se rapatrier, faire la paix. *A — in need is a — indeed,* on connaît les amis au besoin. *The best of —s must part,* il n'est (*or* il n'y a) si bonne compagnie qui ne se sépare

Friendless, *adj.* sans ami, sans amis; — *s.* celui qui n'a pas d'amis, *m.*

Friendliness, *s.* bienveillance, *f.*; disposition amicale, *f.*; nature bienveillante *or* amicale, *f.*; témoignage de bienveillance, *m.*

Friendly, *adj.* bienveillant (pour); bien disposé (pour); ami (de); (*things*) amical, d'ami; favorable (à), propice (à); salutaire (à); — *adv.* amicalement, en ami. — **society,** *V.* **Benefit-society**

Friendship, *s.* amitié, *f.*; faveur, *f.* [society

Friesic, *adj.*, **Frieslander,** *s.* Frison, *m.*, -ne, *f.*

Frieze, *s.* frise, *f.* — **like,** *adj.* en forme de frise

Frigate, *s.* frégate, *m.* — **bird,** *s.* frégate, *f.* — **built,** *adj.* *V.* **Built**

Frigatoon, *s.* frégaton, *m.*

Fright, *s.* frayeur, *f.*; peur, *f.*; effroi, *m.*; épouvante, *f.*; (*ugly person or thing*) horreur, *f.*; — *v.a.* *V.* **Frighten.** *To give a —,* faire peur à, donner des frayeurs à. *To have a —,* avoir peur. *To put in a —,* effrayer; jeter dans l'épouvante. *To take —,* s'effrayer (de); prendre l'épouvante. *He is a —,* (*ugly*) il est laid à faire peur; (*ill-dressed*) il est affreusement mis, il est mis à faire peur

Frighten, *v.a.* effrayer, épouvanter, faire peur à. *To be —ed,* être effrayé (de); avoir peur (de). *To — to death* or *out of o.'s wits* or *senses* or *from o.'s propriety,* faire mourir de peur; causer une frayeur mortelle à, faire une peur terrible à. *To be —ed to death,* mourir de peur; être saisi d'une frayeur mortelle, avoir une peur terrible. — **away** *or* **off,** effrayer; faire fuir d'épouvante. — **from,** faire fuir de

Frightful, *adj.* effrayant, effroyable, terrible, épouvantable; affreux, horrible

Frightfully, *adv.* d'une manière effrayante, effroyablement, terriblement, épouvantablement; affreusement, horriblement, à faire peur

Frightfulness, *s.* horreur, *f.*

Frigid, *adj.* froid; glacial; (*impotent*) impuissant. — *zone,* zone glaciale, *f.*

Frigidity, *s.* froideur, *f.*; (*med.*) frigidité, *f.*

Frigidly, *adv.* froidement

Frigidness, *s.* froideur, *f.*

Frigorific, *adj.* frigorifique; glaçant

Frill, *s.* (*of shirts*) jabot, *m.*; (*collar*) fraise, *f.*; (*paper*) papier découpé, *m.*; — *v.a.* garnir

Frilling, *s.* garniture, *f.*

Fringe, *s.* frange, *f.*; crépine, *f.*; effilé, *m.*; (*fig.*) bord, *m.*, extrémité, *f.*; — *v.a.* (*decorate*) franger ('*with,*' de), garnir de frange (*or* de franges); garnir de crépine; garnir (de); border (de); (*cut into, fray*) effranger. — **maker,** *s.* frangier, *m.*, -ière, *f.* — **tree,** *s.* chionanthe, arbre de neige, *m.*

Fringy, *adj.* à frange; à crépine

Frippery, *s.* friperie, *f.*

Frisette, *s.* crêpé, *m.*, frisette, *f.*

Frisian, *s. adj.* Frison, *m.*, -ne, *f.*

Frisk, *v.n.* frétiller; se trémousser; s'ébattre; (*gambol*) gambader; folâtrer; sauter; bondir; — *s.* saut, *m.*; gambade, *f.*

Frisket, *s.* (*print.*) frisquette, *f.*

Friskiness, *s.* folâtrerie, gaieté, *f.*

Frisking, *adj.* frétillant; léger; — *s.* frétillement, *m.*; folâtrerie, *f.*; gambade, *f.*, gambades, *f.pl.* [éveillé

Frisky, *adj.* frétillant; fringant; folâtre;

Frit, Fritt, *s.* fritte, *f.* [bouchure, *f.*

Frith, *s.* détroit, golfe, bras de mer, *m.*; em-

Fritillary, *s.* fritillaire, *f.*

Fritter, *s.* (*pastry*) beignet, *m.*; (*mincemeat*) hachis frit, *m.*; (*fragment*) petit morceau, *m.*; — *v.a.* couper en petits morceaux; (*fig.*) morceler, anéantir. — **away, down, out,** réduire à rien; gaspiller, perdre, dissiper

Frivolity, *s.* frivolité, *f.*

Frivolous, *adj.* frivole

Frivolously, *adv.* frivolement

Frivolousness, *s.* frivolité, *f.*

Friz, Frizz, Frizzle, &c. *V.* **Curl,** &c.

Frizette, Frizzet. *V.* **Frisette**

Fro, *adv.* en arrière. *To and —,* çà et là. *To go* or *come to and —,* aller et venir. *To walk to and —,* se promener de long en large. *Going* or *coming to and —,* allées et venues, *s.f. pl.*; (*traffic*) circulation, *f.* *Motion to and —,* mouvement de va-et-vient, va-et-vient, *s.m.*

Frock, *s.* blouse, *f.*; (*of monks*) froc, *m.*; (*of children*) robe, *f.*; jaquette, *f.*; — *v.a.* froquer. — **coat,** *s.* redingote, *f.*; (*mil.*) tunique, *f.*

Frog, *s.* grenouille, *f.*; (*on coats*) brandebourg,

m.; (*of a sword-belt*) pendant, *m.*; (*of horses*) fourchette, *f.*; (*med.*) aphthe, *m.* — **bit,** *s.* (*bot.*) morène, morrène, *f.* — **fish,** *s. V.* **Fishing frog.** — **fly, -hopper,** *s.* cercope, *m.*

Frogged, *adj.* (*of coats*) à brandebourgs

Froggy, *adj.* plein de grenouilles

Frolic, *s.* folie, folâtrerie, *f.*; (*play*) jeu, *m.*, plaisanterie, *f.*, badinage, *m.*; (*prank*) escapade, *f.*; fredaine, *f.*; (*trick*) tour, *m.*, espièglerie, *f.*; — *v.n.* folâtrer; badiner; gambader. *In a* —, en badinant, en folâtrant

Frolicsome, *adj.* gai; badin; folâtre; espiègle

Frolicsomely, *adv.* gaiment; en badinant; folâtrement, en folâtrant; avec espièglerie

Frolicsomeness, *s.* gaieté folle, humeur folâtre, folâtrerie, *f.*; (*playfulness*) badinage, *m.*, plaisanterie, *f.*; (*trickiness*) espièglerie, *f.*

From, *prep.* de; (*far from*) loin de; à distance de; (*differing from*) d'avec; (*down from*) en bas de; à bas de; du haut de; (*from the bottom of*) du fond de; (*of time*) depuis; (*as early as*) dès; (*commencing on*) à partir de; (*after*) d'après; sur; à; (*because of*) à cause de; (*in consequence of*) par suite de; (*through, out of, by*) par; (*at*) à; (*in*) dans; (*taken from*) sur; (*against*) contre; (*on the part of, as coming from, of messages,* &c.) de la part de. — ...'*s*, de chez ... (*I come — the grocer's*, je viens de chez l'épicier). — ... *to* ..., de ... à ...; depuis ... jusqu'à ...; de ... en ... — *childhood*, depuis *or* dès l'enfance. — *this day*, dès aujourd'hui. — *his manner*, d'après sa manière; à son air. — *malice*, par méchanceté. *Tell him — me*, dites-lui de ma part. — *above*, d'en haut. — *afar*, de loin. — *amidst*, — *the midst of*, du milieu de, du sein de. — *among*, d'entre. — *under*, de dessous. — *without*, du dehors

Frond, *s.* fronde, feuille, *f.*, feuillage, *m.*

Front, *s.* front, *m.*; (*forepart*) devant, *m.*; (*of shops*) devanture, *f.*; (*of edifices*) façade, face, *f.*; (*of bridges*) tête, *f.*; (*of bonnets*) passe, *f.*; (*of a shirt*) devant, *m.*, (*dicky*) chemisette, *f.*; (*of hair*) faux toupet, devant *or* tour de cheveux, *m.*; (*of a horse's head-stall*) frontal, fronteau, *m.*; (*persp.*) élévation, *f.*; (*mil.*) front, *m.*; premier rang, *m.*, premiers rangs, *m.pl.*; — *adj.* de devant; de face; premier, avant- . .; — *v.a.* attaquer de front; affronter; (*stand opposite*) faire face à, être en face de; — *v.n.* (*stand first*) être (*or* se tenir) en avant; (*be opposite*) être en face, être vis-à-vis, faire face *Full* —, face, *f.* *Side* —, profil, *m.* *In* —, sur le devant; en face; (*mil.*) de front, par devant. *In — of*, devant; en avant de; (*opposite*) en face de. *In — of it* or *of them*, devant; en avant; en face. *To show anyone a full* —, se présenter à quelqu'un de face. *Eyes — !* (*mil.*) fixe! — **box,** *s.* (*theat.*) loge de face, *f.* — **court,** *s.* cour de devant, avant-cour, *f.* — **door,** *s.* porte de devant, porte d'entrée, *f.* — **gate,** *s.* porte de devant, *f.*; portail, *m.* —**less,** *adj.* effronté, éhonté, impudent. — **line,** *s.* (*mil.*) front de bandière, *m.* — **piece,** *s.* (*of head-stalls*) frontal, fronteau, *m.* — **rank,** *s.* premier rang, *m.* — **view,** *s.* vue de face, *f.* — **yard,** *s. V.* — **court**

Frontage, *s.* façade, *f.*; (*of shops*) devanture, *f.*

Frontal, *s.* bandeau, *m.*; (*arch.*) fronteau, *m.*; (*of an altar*) devant d'autel, *m.*; — *adj.* (*anat.*) frontal

Frontier, *s.* frontière, *f.*; — *adj.* de frontière; (*bordering*) frontière; limitrophe

Frontignac, Frontiniac, *s.* vin de Frontignan, frontignan, *m.*

Fronting, *prep. V.* **Facing,** *prep.*

Frontispiece, *s.* frontispice, *m.*

Frontlet, *s.* bandeau, *m.*; (*Jew. rel.*) fronteau, *m.*

Fronton, *s.* fronton, *m.*

Frost, *s.* gelée, *f.*; (*ice*) glace, *f.*; — *v.a.* geler; glacer; (*fig.*) glacer; (*in cutlery*) damasquiner; (*glass*) dépolir; (*artificial flowers*) diamanter. *Hard* or *sharp* —, forte gelée, *f.* — **bite** *of the finger* or &c., doigt *or* &c. gelé. — **bitten,** *adj.* gelé. — **bound,** *adj.* retenu par la gelée. —**less,** *adj.* sans gelée. — **nail,** *s.* clou à glace, *m.* — **nailed,** *adj.* ferré à glace. — **shoe,** *s.* fer à glace, *m.* — **work,** *s.* glace, *f.*;

Frostily, *adv.* avec un froid glacial [glacé, *m.*

Frostiness, *s.* froid glacial, *m.*; gelée, *f.*

Frosting, *s.* glaçage, *m.*; (*in cutlery*) damasquinage, *m.*

Frosty, *adj.* de gelée; glacé; (*indifferent*) froid. *It is a — morning*, il gèle ce matin

Froth, *s.* écume, *f.*; mousse, *f.*; (*empty words*) crème fouettée, *f.*, paroles en l'air, *f.pl.*; — *v.n.* écumer; mousser; — *v.a.* faire mousser. — **fly, -hopper,** *s.* cercope, *m.*

Frothily, *adv.* en écumant; avec de la mousse; (*fig.*) d'une manière futile

Frothiness, *s.* état écumeux *or* mousseux, *m.*; (*fig.*) futilité, frivolité, *f.*

Frothy, *adj.* écumant; écumeux; mousseux futile, frivole, vide, creux. — *matter*, (*fig.* crème fouettée, viande creuse, *f.*

Frounce, *v.a.* froncer; (*to curl*) friser; — *s.* froncis, *m.*, plis, *m.pl.*

Frousy, Frouzy. *V.* **Frowsy**

Froward, *adj.* indocile, revêche, mutin, intraitable, obstiné, entêté; méchant; chagrin, de mauvaise humeur

Frowardly, *adv.* d'une manière revêche, avec indocilité, avec entêtement; méchamment; de mauvaise humeur, avec chagrin

Frowardness, *s.* humeur revêche, indocilité, *f.*, entêtement, *m.*; méchanceté, *f.*; mauvaise humeur, *f.*

Frown, *v.n.* (*pers.*) froncer le sourcil; se refrogner; (*things*) être contraire (à); (*upon*) regarder d'un mauvais œil; — *s.* froncement de sourcils, *m.*; regard sévère, air *or* regard courroucé, regard menaçant, *m.*; air refrogné, *m.*; (*fig.*) rigueur, *f.*; disgrâce, *f.*; coup, *m.*

Frowning, *adj.* fronçant le sourcil; courroucé, menaçant; refrogné; — *s. V.* **Frown,** *s.*

Frowningly, *adv.* d'un air courroucé *or* menaçant *or* refrogné [rancidité, *f.*, relent, *m.*

Frowsiness, Frowziness, *s.* moisissure,

Frowsy, Frowzy, *adj.* moisi, rance, qui sent le relent, fétide, infect, sale, dégoûtant; nuageux, enfumé, épais

Frozen, *adj.* gelé; (*cold*) glacé; (*indifferent*) froid; (*geog.*) glacial. — **in,** retenu par les glaces. — **out,** privé d'ouvrage par la gelée. — **over, up,** pris, gelé

Fructed, *adj.* (*her.*) fruité

Fructiculture, *s.* fructiculture, *f.*

Fructiculturist, *s.* fructiculteur, *m.*

Fructiferous, *adj.* fructifère [tion, *f.*

Fructification, *s.* fructification, *f.*; féconda-

Fructify, *v.n.* fructifier; — *v.a.* fertiliser,

Fructifying, *adj.* fructificateur [féconder

Fructuous, *adj. V.* **Fruitful**

Frugal, *adj.* frugal; sobre; économe

Frugality, *s.* frugalité, *f.*; sobriété, *f.*; économie, *f.* [économiquement

Frugally, *adv.* frugalement; sobrement;

Frugiferous, *adj.* frugifère

Frugivorous, *adj.* frugivore

Fruit, *s.* fruit, *m.*; (*in compounds*) à fruit, fruitier; — *v.n.* porter des fruits, donner du fruit, fructifier. — **basket,** *s.* panier (*m.*) *or* corbeille (*f.*) à fruit; (*gatherer*) cueilloir, *m.* — **bearer,** *s.* arbre fruitier, *m.* — **branch,** *s.* branche à fruit, *f.* — **culture,** *s.* fructiculture, *f.* — **dish,** *s.* coupe à fruits, *f.* — **garden,** *s.* jardin fruitier, *m.*; verger, *m.* — **grove,** *s.* plantation d'arbres fruitiers, *f.*, verger, *m.* — **knife,** *s.* couteau à fruit, *m.* — **loft,** *s.* fruitier, *m.*, fruiterie, *f.* — **market,** *s.* marché aux fruits, *m.* — **room,** *s. V.* — **loft.** — **salesman,** *s.* fruitier (aux halles), *m.* — **shop,** *s.* fruiterie, *f.* — **show,** *s.* exposition de fruits, *f.* — **shrub,** *s.* arbuste fruitier, *m.*

— **trade,** *s.* fruiterie, *f.* — **tree,** *s.* arbre fruitier, arbre à fruit, *m.* — **wall,** *s.* espalier, *m.* — **woman,** *s.* fruitière, *f.*
Fruitage, *s.* fruitage, fruit, *m.* [fruiterie, *f.*
Fruiterer, *s.* fruitier, *m.*, -ière, *f.* —*'s shop,*
Fruiteress, *s.* fruitière, *f.*
Fruitery, *s.* fruiterie, *f.*
Fruitful, *adj.* fertile, fécond (en); fructueux
Fruitfully, *adv.* avec fertilité, avec fécondité; avec fruit, fructueusement; abondamment
Fruitfulness, *s.* fertilité, *f.*; fécondité, *f.*; fructuosité, *f.*; abondance, *f.*
Fruitiness, *s.* (*of wine*) sève, vinosité, *f.*
Fruition, *s.* jouissance, *f.* [vain, inutile
Fruitless, *adj.* sans fruit; stérile; infructueux;
Fruitlessly, *adv.* vainement, en vain, inutilement; infructueusement; stérilement
Fruitlessness, *s.* vanité, inutilité, *f.*; stérilité, *f.* [— *taste,* (*of wine*) sève, vinosité, *f.*
Fruity, *adj.* qui a de la sève, séveux, vineux.
Frumentaceous, *adj.* fromentacé, frumentacé
Frush, *s.* (*of horses*) fourchette, *f.*
Frustrate, *v.a.* frustrer; trahir, faire échouer, faire manquer; désappointer; déconcerter; tromper l'espoir de; rendre inutile, rendre vain; neutraliser; déjouer; (*law*) annuler
Frustrater, *s.* frustrateur, *m.*, -trice, *f.*
Frustrating, *adj.* frustrateur
Frustration, *s.* frustration, *f.*; insuccès, *m.*; renversement, *m.*; désappointement, *m.*; échec, *m.*; inutilité, *f.*; nullité, *f.*
Frustratorily, *adv.* frustratoirement
Frustatory, *adj.* frustratoire
Frustum, *s.* (*geom.*) tronc, *m.*
Frutescent, *adj.* frutescent
Fry, *s.* (*fish*) frai, *m.*; fretin, alevin, *m.*; (*crowd*) tas, *m.*; (*dish of things fried*) friture, *f.*; (*of lamb,* &c.) issues, *f.pl.*; fressure, *f.*; — *v.a.* frire; faire frire; cuire. *Small* —, menu fretin, fretin, *m.* *To have other fish to* —, (*fig.*) avoir bien d'autres chiens (*or* chats) à fouetter
Frying, *s.* friture, *f.* — **pan,** *s.* poêle à frire, poêle, *f.* *To fall* (or *jump*) *out of the — pan into the fire,* (*Proverb*) tomber de la poêle dans le feu, tomber de fièvre en chaud mal
Fuchsia, *s.* (bot.) fuchsia, *m.*
Fuchsine, *s.* (*chem.*) fuchsine, *f.*
Fuddle, *v.a.* griser; — *v.n.* se griser
Fuddled, *adj.* gris
Fudge, *s.* faribole, blague, craque, *f.*
Fuel, *s.* combustible, *m.*; chauffage, *m.*; (*fig.*) aliment. *m.* *To add — to the fire* (or *to the flame*), jeter de l'huile sur le feu. *To keep in* —, chauffer; tenir chaud, alimenter
Fugacious, *adj.* fugace, fugitif, passager
Fugacity, *s.* fugacité, nature fugitive *or* passagère, *f.*
Fugitive, *adj.* fugitif; passager; peu durable; (*wandering*) errant; (*mil.*) fuyard; — *s*, fugitif, *m.*, -ive, *f.*; transfuge, *m.*; déserteur, *m.*; réfugié, *m.*, e, *f.*; (*mil.*) fuyard, *m.*
Fugitively, *adv.* fugitivement
Fugitiveness. *V.* **Fugacity**
Fugleman, *s.* sous-officier d'exercice, sous-instructeur, chef de peloton *or* de division *or* de section, guide, *m.*; (*in a mob*) chef de révoltés *or* de rébellion, chef, *m.*
Fugue, *s.* fugue, *f.*
Ful, (*in compounds for "full"*) plein (*adj. m.*, e, *f.*). *A hatful,* un chapeau plein, plein son chapeau. *A boxful,* une boîte pleine, une caisse *or* &c. (*V.* **Box**) pleine
Fulcrum, *s.* point d'appui, *m.*
Fulfil, *v.a.* remplir; accomplir; (*satisfy*) combler
Fulfiller, *s* personne qui remplit *or* qui accomplit, *f.* [ment, *m.*; exécution, *f.*
Fulfilling, Fulfilment, *s.* accomplisse-
Fulgural, *adj.* fulgural
Fulgurant, *adj.* fulgurant
Fulgurate, *v.n.* resplendir
Fulguration, *s.* fulguration, *f.*
Fulgurator, *s.* fulgurateur, *m.*
Fulgurite, *s.* fulgurite, *m.*
Fulgurometer, *s.* fulguromètre, *m.*
Fuliginosity, *s.* fuliginosité, *f.*
Fuliginous, *adj.* fuligineux
Full, *adj.* plein; complet, entier, parfait, tout; ample; abondant, copieux; (*great*) grand; bon; (*mature*) mûr; (*satiated*) rassasié (de); repu; (*of the voice, moon, sails*) plein; (*of sorrow*) accablé; (*of business*) surchargé; — *s.* plein, *m.*; mesure complète, *f.*; (*highest degree*) plus haut degré, *m.*; comble, *m.*; (*the whole*) tout, total, *m.*; (*satiety*) satiété, *f.*; — *adv.* pleinement; en plein; entièrement, en entier; complètement; (*quite*) bien; tout à fait; tout; (*at least*) au moins; (*exactly*) exactement; juste; (*directly*) directement, droit; (*very*) très, fort, bien; — *v.a.* fouler. — *as,* tout aussi. — *well,* parfaitement. *At the* —, (*of the moon*) dans son plein. *In* —, en entier; intégralement; (*of words*) en toutes lettres. *To the* —, entièrement, tout à fait. *Its — force,* toute sa force. — **age,** *s.* âge mûr, âge d'homme, *m.* *Of — age,* d'un âge mûr; majeur. — **blooded,** *adj.* sanguin. — **bloomed,** *adj.* tout en fleur; épanoui. — **blown,** *adj.* en pleine fleur; épanoui; dans tout son éclat, éclatant; (*of sails*) gonflé. — **bodied,** *adj.* (*pers.*) replet; (*of wine,* &c.) corsé. — **butt,** *adv.* en se heurtant; droit, raide comme balle; tête baissée; nez à nez. — **compass,** *adj.* (*of pianos*) à sept octaves. — **dress,** *s.* habit habillé, habit, frac, *m.*; (*of ladies*) grande toilette, *f.*; (*of functionaries*) grand uniforme, grand costume, *m.*, grande tenue, *f.*; (*mil.*) grande tenue, *f.* — *dress ball,* bal paré, *m.* — *dress dinner,* dîner de cérémonie, *m.* — **dressed,** *adj.* en habit, en frac; (*of ladies*) en grande toilette; &c. (*V. above, at* — **dress**). — **drive,** *adv.* ventre à terre. — **eared,** *adj.* *V.* **Eared.** — **faced,** *adj.* qui a le visage plein *or* la figure pleine, au visage plein. — **fed,** *adj.* gras, bien nourri. — **gallop,** *s.* grand galop, *m.* *At — gallop,* au grand galop. — **grown,** *adj.* *V.* **Grown.** — **length,** *adj.* *V.* **Length.** — **price,** *s.* prix fort, *m.* — **relief,** *s.* (*sculp.,* &c.) ronde-bosse, *f.*, plein relief, *m.* — **steam,** *adv.* à toute vapeur. — **stop,** *s.* (*gram.*) point, *m.* — **tilt,** *adv.* à toute bride, au grand galop; (*headlong*) tête baissée. *To run — tilt against,* *V.* **Atilt**
Fullage, *s.* prix du foulage, *m.*
Fuller, *s.* foulon, *m.* —*'s earth,* terre à foulon, *f.*
Fullery, *s.* foulerie, *f.*
Fulling, *s.* foulage, *m.* — **machine,** *s.* machine à fouler, *f.* — **mill,** *s.* moulin à foulon, *m.*; foulerie, *f.*
Fully, *adv.* pleinement; complètement; entièrement; parfaitement; amplement; au moins; bien; tout à fait; tout
Fulmar, *s.* (*bird*) fulmar, *m.*
Fulminant, *adj.* fulminant
Fulminate, *v.a.n.* fulminer; — *s.* fulminate, *m.*
Fulmination, *s.* fulmination, *f.*
Fulminatory, *adj.* fulminatoire
Fulmineous, *adj.* fulminaire, fulminal
Fulminic, *adj.* fulminique
Fulness, *s.* trop-plein, *m.*; abondance, *f.*; réplétion, *f.*, rassasiement, *m.*; (*fig.*) plénitude, *f.*; (*of clothes*) ampleur, *f.*; (*of sound*) volume, *m.*
Fulsome, *adj.* nauséabond, dégoûtant; bas, vil, révoltant; servile
Fulsomely, *adv.* dégoûtamment, d'une manière dégoûtante; bassement, vilement; servilement
Fulsomeness, *s.* nature dégoûtante *or* nauséabonde, *f.*; puanteur, *f.*; saleté, grossièreté, *f.*; bassesse, servilité, *f.*
Fumarole, *s.* fumerolle, *f.*
Fumble, *v.n.* fouiller, remuer; (*play*) jouer; (*grope*) tâtonner; — *v.a.* faire maladroitement, faire de travers; arranger maladroitement; (*rumple*) chiffonner; (*throw*) jeter [*m.*, -euse, *f.*
Fumbler, *s.* maladroit, *m.*, e, *f.*; farfouilleur,

Fumblingly, *adv.* en tâtonnant ; gauchement, maladroitement

Fume, *s.* fumée, *f.* ; vapeur, *f.* ; vanité, *f.* ; idée vaine, *f.* ; (*rage*) colère, *f.* ; — *v.n.a.* fumer ; parfumer ; exhaler. — **away,** s'en aller en fumée ; se dissiper en vapeurs, s'évaporer ; (*be angry*) fumer de colère, enrager, rager

Fumet, *s.* (*hunt.*) fumées, *f.pl.*

Fumigate, *v.a* fumiger ; parfumer ; désinfecter

Fumigating, *adj* fumigatoire ; — *s.* fumigation, *f.* — *pastil* or *pastille*, pastille odoriférante, pastille du sérail, pastille, *f.*

Fumigation, *s.* fumigation, *f.*

Fumigator, *s.* fumigateur, *m.*, appareil (*m.*) *or* boîte (*f.*) fumigatoire ; parfumoir, *m.* ; (*pers.*) fumigateur, *m.*

Fumingly, *adv.* en colère, avec rage

Fumitory, *s.* (*bot.*) fumeterre, *f.*

Fumosity, *s.* fumosité, *f.*

Fumous, Fumy, *adj.* fumeux

Fun, *s.* amusement, *m.* ; gaieté, *f.* ; (*joke*) plaisanterie, *f.* ; drôlerie, *f.* ; badinage, *m.* ; (*comical part*) plaisant, *m.* *For* or *in* —, pour rire, en plaisantant. *To be full of* —, être très joueur ; être très drôle ; aimer à rire. *To have good* —, s'amuser bien, s'en donner. *To make* — *of*, se moquer de

Funambulation, *s.* funambulie, *f.*

Funambulatory, *adj.* funambule

Funambulist, *s.* funambule, *m.f.*

Function, *s.* fonction, *f.*

Functional, *adj.* fonctionnel

Functionally, *adv.* fonctionnellement

Functionary, *s.* fonctionnaire, *m.f.*

Fund, *s.* fonds, *m.* ; (*institution*) caisse, *f.* ; — *v.a.* placer dans les fonds publics ; consolider. — **holder,** *s.* rentier, *m.*, -ière, *f.* ; capitaliste, *m.f.* ; (*fin.*) porteur (*m.*, -euse, *f.*) de fonds [publics

Fundament, *s.* fondement, *m.*

Fundamental, *adj.* fondamental ; — *s.* principe fondamental, *m.*

Fundamentally, *adv.* fondamentalement

Funded, *adj.* en rentes sur l'État ; (*fin.*) consolidé

Funding, *s.* placement (de fonds), *m.* ; (*fin.*) consolidation, *f.* — **system,** *s.* système de consolidation, *m.*

Funeral, *s.* funérailles, obsèques, *f.pl.* ; enterrement, *m.* ; convoi, convoi funèbre, *m.* ; — *adj.* des funérailles ; funèbre ; funéraire. — *company*, entreprise de pompes funèbres, *f.* — *expenses*, frais funéraires, *m.pl.* — *letter*, lettre de faire part, lettre de décès, *f.* — *oration*, oraison funèbre, *f.* — *pile*, bûcher, *m.* — *procession*, convoi funèbre, *m.* — *rites*, cérémonies funèbres, *f.pl.* ; service funèbre, *m.* — *service*, office des morts, *m.* — *song*, chant funèbre, *m.* — *torch*, torche funéraire, *f.*

Funerally, *adv.* funèbrement

Funereal, *adj.* funèbre ; funéraire, (*mournful*) lugubre, triste, funèbre, sombre

Funereally, *adv.* funèbrement

Fungate, *s.* fongate, *m.*

Fungible, *adj.* fongible

Fungic, *adj.* fongique

Fungiform, *adj.* fongiforme

Fungine, *s.* fongine, *f.*

Fungite, *s.* fongite, *f.*

Fungoid, *adj.* fongoïde

Fungosity, *s.* fongosité, *f.*

Fungous, *adj* fongueux [(*med.*) fongus, *m.*

Fungus, *s.* (*bot.*) champignon, fongus, *m.* ;

Funicle, Funiculus, *s.* funicule, *m.*

Funicular, *adj.* funiculaire

Funk, *s.* trac, *m.*, venette, *f.* ; — *v.n.* tracquer, avoir le trac *or* la venette ; caponner, caner, reculer, bouder. *To be in a* —, avoir le trac, tracquer, avoir la venette

Funky, *adj.* qui a le trac *or* la venette. — *fellow*, tracqueur, *m.* *To be* —, avoir le trac, tracquer, avoir la venette

Funnel, *s.* entonnoir, *m.* ; (*of chimneys*) tuyau, *m.* ; (*of steamers*) cheminée, *f.* — **net,** *s.* tonnelle, *f.* — **pipe,** *s.* conduit en entonnoir, *m.* — **shaped,** *adj.* en entonnoir, infundibuliforme, infundibulé

Funny, *adj.* comique, drôle, plaisant, bouffon ; drôle de . . . ; — *s.* *V.* **Wherry**

Fur, *s.* fourrure, *f.* ; (*of peaches*) duvet, *m.* ; (*deposit*, &c.) dépôt, sédiment, *m.*, incrustation, crasse, *f.*, champignon, *m.*, barbe, moisissure, *f.* ; (*med.*) enduit, *m.* ; *adj.* de fourrure ; — *v.a.* fourrer ; (*with deposit*) incruster, encrasser ; — *v.n.* s'incruster, s'encrasser. — **cap,** *s.* bonnet en fourrure, *m.* ; (*with a peak*) casquette en fourrure, *f.* — **collarette,** *s.* berthe, *f.* — **trade,** *s.* commerce de fourrures *or* de pelleteries, *m.*, pelleterie, *f.* — **wrought,** *adj.* fait en fourrure

Furbelow, *s.* falbala, *m.* ; — *v.a.* falbalasser

Furbish, *v.a.* fourbir

Furbisher, *s.* fourbisseur, *m.*

Furbishing, *s.* fourbissage, *m.*, fourbissure, *f.*

Furcate, Furcated, *adj.* fourchu

Furcation, *s.* fourchure, *f.*

Furfuraceous, *adj.* furfuracé

Furious, *adj.* furieux ; acharné ; excessif

Furiously, *adv.* avec fureur, avec furie, avec rage ; furieusement ; avec acharnement ; (*of riding and driving*) à bride abattue, à toute bride, au grand galop [acharnement, *m.*

Furiousness, *s.* furie, fureur, rage, *f.* ;

Furl, *v.a.* ployer ; (*nav.*) ferler

Furling, *s.* ploiement, *m.* ; (*nav.*) ferlage, *m.*

Furlong, *s.* huitième d'un mille, *m.*

Furlough, *s.* congé, *m.* ; — *v.a.* donner un congé à. *On* —, en congé. *He was —ed*, il obtint un congé, on lui donna un congé

Furnace, *s.* fournaise, *f.* ; fourneau, *m.* ; (*of engines*) foyer, *m.* *Fiery* —, fournaise ardente, *f.* — **maker,** constructeur de fourneaux, *m.* — **mouth,** *s.* gueulard, *m.*

Furnish, *v.a.* fournir, pourvoir (de) ; (*fit up*) garnir (de) ; (*equip*) équiper (de) ; (*a dwelling*) meubler ; (*adorn*) orner, décorer ; (*offer*) offrir. —*ed apartments*, (*one suite*) appartement meublé, *m.*, (*several suites*) appartements meublés, *m.pl.*

Furnisher, *s.* fournisseur, *m.* ; pourvoyeur, *m.*

Furnishing, *s.* ameublement, *m.* ; garniture, *f.*

Furniture, *s.* (*of houses*) meubles, *m.pl.*, mobilier, ameublement, *m.* ; (*necessary things*) équipement, *m.* ; fourniture, *f.* ; matériel, *m.* ; (*ornament*) garniture, *f.*, ornement, *m.* ; (*of horses*) équipage, *m.* *Piece of* —, meuble, *m.* *To have o.'s own* —, être dans ses meubles. — **broker,** *s.* fripier, *m.*, -ière, *f.*, brocanteur, *m.*, -euse, *f.* — **carrier,** *s.* déménageur, *m.* — **dealer,** *s.* marchand (*m.*, e, *f.*) de meubles. — **depository, -repository, -warehouse,** *s.* garde-meubles, *m.* — **van,** *s.* voiture de déménagement, *f.*

Furred, *part. adj.* fourré, &c. (*V.* **Fur,** *v.a.n.*). — *tongue*, (*med.*) langue chargée, *f.*

Furrier, *s.* fourreur, pelletier, *m.*

Furriery, *s.* pelleterie, *f.*

Furrow, *s.* sillon, *m.* ; (*fig.*) sillon, *m.*, trace, *f.* ; ride, *f.* ; (*groove*) rainure, *f.* ; (*of a screw*) pas (de vis), *m.* ; — *v.a.* sillonner ; (*to groove*) faire des rainures à, rainer ; (*to wrinkle*) rider. — **faced,** *adj.* qui a le visage sillonné de rides, ridé. — **slice,** *s.* bande de terre, *f.*

Furry, *adj.* fourré ; de fourrure ; de dépôt

Further, *adv. adj.* *V.* **Farther ;** — *v.a.* avancer, pousser ; appuyer ; seconder, servir, aider, favoriser ; faciliter

Furtherance, *s.* avancement, progrès, *m.* ; encouragement, *m.* ; protection, *f.* ; aide, *f.*, appui, *m.*

Furtherer, *s.* promoteur, *m.*, -trice, *f.*

Furthermore. *V.* **Moreover**

Furthermost, Furthest, *adj.* (le) plus éloigné, (le) plus reculé, (le) plus lointain ; — *adv.* à la plus grande distance ; le plus loin ; (*of time*) à l'époque la plus éloignée *or* la plus

reculée (V. **Farthest** and **Far**). — **end,** s. extrémité, f., fond, fin fond, m.
Furtive, adj. furtif
Furtively, adv. furtivement
Furuncle, s. furoncle, m.
Furuncular, adj. furonculeux
Fury, s. furie, f.; fureur, f.; acharnement, m.; (myth.) Furie, f. *In* or *into a* —, en furie, en fureur
Furze, s. ajonc, genêt épineux, m. — **brake,** s. genêtière, lande, f. — **bush,** s. buisson d'ajonc, m.
Furzy, adj. couvert d'ajoncs, couvert de genêts
Fuse, v.a.n. fondre; — s. V. **Fuze**
Fusee, s. (horol.) fusée, f.; (*for smokers*) allumette (pour les fumeurs), f.
Fusel oil, s. huile de pomme de terre, f.
Fusibility, s. fusibilité, f.
Fusible, adj. fusible
Fusiform, adj. fusiforme
Fusileer, Fusilier, s. fusilier, m.
Fusillade, s. fusillade, f.; — v.a. fusiller
Fusion, s. fusion, f.
Fusionist, s. adj. fusioniste, m.f.
Fuss, s. bruit, m.; embarras, m., m.pl.; esbrouffe, f.; histoires, f.pl.; cérémonies, façons, f.pl.
Fussily, adv. avec embarras
Fussiness, s. embarras, m.pl., esbrouffe, f.
Fussy, adj. qui fait de l'embarras *or* des embarras; difficultueux [(fig.) moisir
Fust, v.n. sentir mauvais; sentir le renfermé;
Fustet, s. fustet, m.
Fustian, s. (*stuff*) futaine, f., velours de coton, m.; (*bombast*) phébus, galimatias, boursoufflage, m., boursoufflure, f.; — adv. de *or* en futaine; (*bombastic*) ampoulé, boursoufflé. — **jacket,** s. veste de futaine *or* de velours (de coton), f.; (*working-man*) ouvrier, m., blouse, f.
Fustic, s. fustoc, m.
Fustigate, v.a. fustiger
Fustigation, s. fustigation, f.
Fustiness, s. odeur de renfermé, f.; (*mouldi-*
Fustoc, s. fustoc, m. [*ness*) moisissure, f.
Fusty, adj. qui sent le renfermé; (*mouldy*) moisi. — *smell*, odeur de renfermé, f.; odeur
Futchell, s. armon, m. [de moisi, f.
Futile, adj. futile
Futility, s. futilité, f.
Futtock, s. genou, m.; allonge, f.
Future, adj. futur; à venir; (gram.) futur; — s. avenir, m.; (gram.) futur, m. *In* —, *for the* —, à l'avenir. *In the* —, (gram.) au futur. — **husband,** s. futur, m. — **wife,** s. future, f.
Futurely, adv. dans l'avenir
Futurition, s. futurition, f.
Futurity, s. avenir, m.
Fuze, s. fusée (de bombe), f.
Fuzee. V. **Fusee**
Fuzz, s. chose légère, chose sans consistance, f.; parcelle, particule, f.; petit bout, m.; petite touffe, f. — **ball,** s. vesse-de-loup, f.
Fy. V. **Fie**

G

G, s. (*letter*) g, m.; (mus.) sol, m.; clé de sol, f.
Gab, s. maudite langue, f.; langue, f.; — v.n. bavarder. *To have the gift of the* —, avoir la langue bien pendue, avoir de la blague
Gabardine, s. caban, m.
Gabble, v.n. (*of some birds*) crier; (*of geese*) cacarder; (*of storks and cranes*) craqueter; (pers.) criailler; (*talk*) babiller, jaser; — s. (*of some birds*) cri, m.; (*of geese*) cri, m.; (*of storks and cranes*) craquètement, m.; (pers.) criaillement, m.; (*talk*) bavardage, verbiage, bagout, m.
Gabbler, s. bavard, m., e, f., babillard, m., e, f.
Gabbling, s. V. **Gabble,** s.
Gabian oil, s. huile de Gabian, f.
Gabion, s. gabion, m.; — v.a. gabionner. — **man,** s. gabionneur, m.
Gabionade, s. gabionnade, f.
Gabionage, s. gabionnage, m.
Gable, — end, s. pignon, m.
Gaby, s. jeannot, janot, badaud, m., e, f.
Gad, s. pointe, f.; barre de fer, f., baguette, f.; (*wedge*) coin, m.; — v.n. rôder, errer, courir çà et là, battre le pavé, flâner; — int. V. **Egad.** — **about,** v.n. courir çà et là, courir les rues, battre le pavé, rôder, errer, vagabonder, flâner; s. coureur, m., -euse, f., flâneur, m., -euse, f. — **bee, -fly,** s. œstre, m.; taon, m. — **wall,** s. ridenne, f., chipeau, rousseau, m. [-euse, f.
Gadder, s. coureur, m., -euse, f.; flâneur, m.,
Gadding, s. vie errante, f., vagabondage, m.; flânerie, f.
Gaelic, adj. s. gaélique, adj. m.f., s.m.
Gaff, s. (*fish.*) gaffe, f., crochet, croc, breveux,
Gaffer, s. compère, m. [m.; (nav.) pic, m.
Gaffle, s. (*of game-cocks*) éperon, m.
Gag, s. bâillon, m.; — v.a bâillonner
Gage, s. gage, m., caution, f.; (*law*) nantissement, m.; (*gauge*) V. **Gauge;** (*plum*) V. **Greengage;** — v.a. mettre en gage, engager;
Gagger, s. bâillonneur, m. [(*gauge*) V. **Gauge**
Gagging, s. bâillonnement, m.
Gaggle, Gaggling. V. **Gabble, Gabbling**
Gaiety, s. gaieté, gaîté, f.; plaisir, m.; parure, f., faste, m.; éclat, m.
Gaily, adv. gaiment; élégamment
Gain, v.a.n. gagner ('*by*,' à; '*by it*,' y); acquérir; obtenir; (*a victory, a prize*) remporter; (*a prize medal*) être couronné de; (*a reputation*) se faire, acquérir; (*o's point* or *object*) atteindre; (*prevail*) l'emporter (sur), prévaloir, avoir l'avantage; (*of clocks, watches*) avancer; avancer de (...); — s. gain, profit, m.; intérêt, m.; (com.) bénéfice, m. *To — friends*, se faire des amis. *There are no —s without pains*, nul bien sans peine. — **over, upon,** gagner, attirer; (*overtake*) gagner sur; (*encroach*) em-
Gainable, adj. gagnable [piéter sur
Gainer, s. gagneur, m., -euse, f.; (*at play, lotteries*) gagnant, m., e, f. *To be a* — (*by ..., by it*), gagner (à ..., y)
Gainful, adj. avantageux, profitable; lucratif
Gainfully, adv. avantageusement, profitablement, avec profit; lucrativement
Gainfulness, s. nature avantageuse, f., avantage, m. [travail, m.
Gainings, s. pl. gain, m.; profit, m.; fruit du
Gainless, adj. peu avantageux, sans profit, improfitable, inutile [inutilité, f.
Gainlessness, s. nature peu avantageuse,
Gainsay, v.a. contredire; (*deny*) nier
Gainsayer, s. contradicteur, m.; adversaire, m.
Gainsaying, s. contradiction, f.; opposition, f.
Gait, s. marche, f., pas, m.; (*manner of walking*) démarche, allure, f.
Gaiter, s. guêtre, f.; — v.a. guêtrer. — **maker,** s. guêtrier, m., -ière, f.
Gala, s. gala, m. — **day,** s. jour de gala, m.
Galactite, s. galactite, f.
Galacto-graphy, -logy. V. page 3, § 1
Galactometer, s. galactomètre, m.
Galanga, Galangal, Galangale, s. (bot.)
Galantine, s. (cook.) galantine, f. [galanga, m.
Galatian, s. adj. Galate, m.f.
Galaxy, s. voie lactée, galaxie, f.; (fig.) con-
Galbanum, s. galbanum, m. [stellation, f.
Gale, s. tempête, f.; vent, m.; (bot.) galé, m.
Galeas, Galeass, s. galéasse, galéace, f.
Galeate, Galeated, adj. galéiforme
Galega, s. galéga, m.
Galena, s. galène, f.
Galen-ic, -ism, -ist. V. page 3, § 1
Galician, s. adj. Galicien, m., -ne, f.
Galilean, s. adj. Galiléen, m., -ne, f.
Galingale, s. souchet, m.
Galiot, s. galiote, f.
Galipot, s. galipot, m.

Gall, *s.* fiel, *m.*; amer, *m.*; (*anger*) bile, *f.*; (*bot.*) galle, noix de galle, *f.*; (*a scratch*) écorchure, *f.*; — *v.a.* écorcher; (*fig.*) blesser; irriter, tourmenter; piquer; (*the enemy*) incommoder; (*a stuff*) érailler; — *v.n.* s'irriter, se piquer, se blesser. — *of glass*, fiel de verre, *m.* — **bladder,** *s.* vésicule biliaire, *f.* — **fly,** *s.* cynips, *m.* — **insects,** *s. pl.* gallinsectes, *m.pl.* —**less,** *adj.* sans fiel. —**nut,** *s.* noix de galle, *f.* — **stone,** *s.* concrétion (*f.*) *or* calcul (*m.*) biliaire

Gallant, *adj.* vaillant, brave, courageux; noble; élégant, beau; (*to ladies*) galant; — *s.* preux, *m.*; élégant, *m.*; (*of love*) galant, amant; — *v.a.* courtiser, faire des galanteries à. — **sail,** *s.* voile de perroquet, *f.*

Gallantly, *adv.* galamment; élégamment; (*bravely*) vaillamment, bravement, courageusement; noblement

Gallantness, *s.* élégance, *f.*

Gallantry, *s.* noblesse, *f.*; valeur, vaillance, bravoure, *f.*; élégance, magnificence, *f.*; (*civility, love intrigue*) galanterie, *f.*

Gallate, *s.* gallate, *m.*

Galleas, Galleass. *V.* **Galeas**

Galleon, *s.* galion, *m.*

Gallery, *s.* galerie, *f.*; (*parliam.*, &c.) tribune, *f.*

Galley, *s.* galère, *f.*; (*print.*) galée, *f.*; (*caboose*) cuisine, *f.* — **proof,** *s.* (*print.*) épreuve en placard, *f.* — **slave,** *s.* galérien, *m.* — **slice, -slide,** *s.* (*print.*) coulisse de galée, *f.*

Gallic, *adj.* gaulois, gallique; (*chem.*) gallique

Gallican, *adj. s.* gallican, *m*, e, *f.*

Gallicanism, Gallicism. *V.* page 3, § 1

Gallicize, &c. *V.* **Frenchify,** &c.

Gallimaufry, *s.* galimafrée, *f.*

Gallinacean, *s.* gallinacé, *m.*

Gallinaceous, *adj.* gallinacé

Galling, *adj.* qui écorche; (*vexing*) blessant; irritant; piquant; contrariant; douloureux, amer; (*mil., of fire*) bien nourri, bien servi, meurtrier, vif

Gallingale. *V.* **Galingale**

Gallinule, *s.* gallinule, *f.*

Galliot. *V.* **Galiot**

Gallipot, *s.* pot de faïence, *m.*

Gallo-, (*in compounds*) gallo-...

Gallomania, *s.* gallomanie, *f.*

Gallomaniac, *s. adj.* gallomane, *m.f.*

Gallon, *s.* (*Engl. meas.*) gallon, *m.* (4 litres ½)

Galloon, *s.* galon, *m.*; ruban, *m.* — **maker,** *s.* galonnier, *m.*

Gallooned, *adj.* galonné

Gallop, *v.a.n.* galoper; aller au galop; — *s.* galop, *m.*; galopade, *f.* *To go at a* —, aller au galop, galoper. — **away, off,** partir au galop. — **back,** s'en retourner au galop. — **down,** descendre au galop. — **past,** (*mil.*) défiler au galop; (...) défiler au galop devant (...). — **up,** monter au galop

Gallopade, *s.* galopade, *f.*

Gallophobia, *s.* gallophobie, *f.*

Gallophobiac, *s.* gallophobe, *m.f.*

Gallophobic, *adj.* gallophobique, gallophobe

Gallophobist, *s.* gallophobe, *m.f.*

Galloping, *s.* galopade, *f.*; galop, *m.*; — *adj.* (*med.*) — *consumption*, phthisie galopante, *f.*

Gallo-Roman, *s. adj.* Gallo romain, *m.*, e, *f.*

Galloway, *s. V.* **Pony**

Gallows, *s.* potence, *f.*, gibet, *m.* — **bird,** *s.* gibier de potence, homme de sac et de corde, *m.* — **bitts,** *s. pl.* potence, *f.*

Gally, *adj.* de fiel, amer; — *s.* (*print.*) *V.* **Galley.** — **worm,** *s.* iule, *m.*

Galoche, Galosh. *V.* **Golosh**

Galop, *s.* galop, *m.*

Galvan-ic, -ically, -ism, -ist. *V.* p. 3, § 1

Galvanization, *s.* galvanisation, *f.*

Galvanize, *v.a.* galvaniser; (*iron*) galvaniser, zinguer

Galvanizer, *s.* galvaniseur, *m.*

Galvanizing, *s.* galvanisation, *f.*

Galvano-, (*in compounds*) galvano-...

Galvanometer, *s.* galvanomètre, *m.*

Galvanoplastic, *adj.* galvanoplastique

Galvanoscope, *s.* galvanoscope, *m.*

Gama-grass, *s.* tripsacum, *m.*

Gambeer, *s.* gambir, *m.*

Gambet, *s.* (*bird*) gambette, *f.*

Gambier, Gambir, *s.* gambir, *m.*

Gambit, *s.* (*at chess*) gambit, *m.*

Gamble, *v.n.* jouer. *To* — **away,** *v.a.* perdre au jeu

Gambler, *s.* joueur, *m.*, -euse, *f.*

Gambling, *s.* jeu, *m.*; passion du jeu, *f.*; — *adj.* de jeu. — **house (-table),** *s.* maison (table) de jeu, *f.*

Gamboge, *s.* gomme gutte, *f.*

Gambol, *v.n.* gambader, faire des gambades; bondir; s'ébattre, prendre ses ébats, folâtrer, jouer, se divertir; — *s.* gambade, *f.*; bond, *m.*; jeu, amusement, *m.*, ébats, *m.pl.*

Gambrel, *s.* (*of horses*) jambe de derrière, *f.*; (*butch.*) tinet, *m.*

Game, *s.* jeu, *m.*; (*match at play*) partie ('*at*,' de), *f.*; (*either of two in a rubber*) manche, *f.*; (*stratagem*) rubrique, ficelle, *f.*; (*hunt., shoot.*) gibier, *m.*; (*slang*) courage, cœur, toupet, *m.*; — *adj.* de jeu; de gibier, de chasse; courageux, brave; — *adv.* courageusement, bravement; — *v.n.* jouer. *Little* —, (*fam.*) ficelle, *f.* *To have* or *play a* —, *V.* **Play.** *To make* — *of*, se jouer de, se moquer de. *To play a* —, jouer un jeu; (*a match*) *V.* **Play.** *To play a losing* —, jouer un jeu à perdre. — **bag,** *s.* carnassière, *f.*, carnier, *m.* — **birds,** *s. pl.* gibier à plumes, *m.* — **cock,** *s.* coq de combat, *m.* — **fowls,** *s. pl. V.* — **birds.** — **keeper,** *s.* garde-chasse, *m.* — **laws,** *s. pl.* lois sur la chasse, *f.pl.* — **licence,** *s.* permis de chasse, *m.* — **pouch,** *s. V.* — **bag**

Gamely, *adv.* courageusement, bravement

Gamesome, *adj. V.* **Playful**

Gamester, *s.* joueur, *m.*, -euse, *f.*

Gaming, *s. V.* **Gambling**

Gammer, *s.* commère, *f.*

Gammon, *s.* quartier (de lard), *m.*; (*play*) *V.* **Backgammon;** (*humbug*) blague, *f.*; — *v.a.* [*V.* **Humbug,** *v.a.*

Gamut, *s.* gamme, *f.*

Gamy, *adj.* brave, courageux; qui résiste, qui ne se laisse pas prendre facilement; (*cook.*) faisandé

Gander, *s.* jars, *m.*

Gang, *s.* bande, troupe, *f.*; clique, coterie, *f.*; (*of workmen*) brigade, *f.*; équipe, *f.* — **board,** *s.* planche à débarquer. — **way,** *s. See below*

Ganga, *s.* (*bird*) ganga, *m.*

Ganger, *s.* chef de brigade, brigadier, *m.*; chef d'équipe, *m.*

Gangetic, *adj.* gangétique

Gangliform, *adj.* gangliforme

Ganglion, *s.* ganglion, *m.*

Ganglionary, *adj.* ganglionnaire

Ganglionic, *adj.* ganglionné

Gangrene, *s.* gangrène, *f.*; — *v.a.* gangrener; — *v.n.* se gangrener

Gangrenescence, *s.* gangrenescence, *f.*

Gangrenescent, *adj.* gangrenescent

Gangrenous, *adj.* gangreneux

Gangue, *s.* (*min.*) gangue, *f.*

Gangway, *s.* corridor, vestibule, passage, *m.*; (*nav.*) passavant, *m.*; galerie de l'entrepont *or* du faux-pont, *f.*, corridor, *m.* — **ladder,** *s.* échelle (*f.*) *or* escalier (*m.*) (de navire), pont volant, appontement, *m.*, passerelle, *f.*

Gannet, *s.* boubie, *f.*, fou, *m.*

Gantelope, Gantlet. *V.* **Gauntlet**

Gantry, *s. V.* **Gauntree**

Gaol, Gaoler. *V.* **Jail, Jailer**

Gap, *s.* ouverture, *f.*, trou, *m.*; brèche, *f.*; passage, *m.*, entrée, *f.*; intervalle, *m.*; interstice, *m.*; (*vacuity*) vide, *m.*, lacune, *f.*; (*hiatus*) bâillement, *m.*; (*in a forest*, &c.) trouée, *f.*; — *v.a.* ébrécher. *To fill up a* —, remplir une lacune. *To stand in the* —, se tenir sur la brèche, défendre la brèche. *To stop a* —, boucher un trou

Gape, *v.n.* bâiller; avoir la bouche béante; bayer; ouvrir de grands yeux, regarder fixement; (*of birds*) ouvrir le bec; (*open*) s'ouvrir, s'entr'ouvrir; (*gram.*) faire bâillement; — *s.*

bâillement, *m.*; —**s,** *s. pl.* (*disease of birds*) bâillement, *m.* — **after, for,** soupirer après

Gaper, *s.* bâilleur, *m.*, -euse, *f.*; bayeur, *m.*, -euse, *f.*

Gaping, *s.* bâillement, *m.*; ouverture, *f.*; ardent désir, *m.*; (*gram.*) hiatus, *m.*; — *adj.* qui bâille; béant; entr'ouvert; crevassé; ébahi

Garance, *adj.* s garance, *adj. m.f., s.m.*

Garancine, *s.* garancine, *f.*

Garb, *s.* habillement, habit, costume, *m.*; apparence, *f.*, extérieur, *m.*, dehors, *m.pl.*, air, manteau, *m.*; (*her.*) gerbe, *f.* [curée, *f.*

Garbage, *s.* tripaille, *f.*, tripailles, *f.pl.*; (*hunt.*)

Garble, *v.a.* trier; mutiler, tronquer, altérer, dénaturer [*m.*, -trice, *f.*

Garbler, *s.* trieur, *m.*, -euse, *f.*; mutilateur,

Garbles, *s. pl.* grabeaux, *m.pl.*

Garboard, *s.* (*nav.*) gabord, *m.* — **streak** *or* **strake,** *s.* virure de gabord, *f.*

Garboil, *s.* tumulte, grabuge, *m.*

Garden, *s.* jardin, *m.*; — *adj.* de jardin; des jardins; jardinier; (*for gardening*) de jardinage; — *v.n.* jardiner. *Kensington* —*s*, les jardins de Kensington. — **bean,** *s.* fève de marais, *f.* — **beetle,** *s.* jardinière, *f.* — **cress,** *s.* cresson alénois, *m.* — **engine,** *s.* pompe d'arrosement *or* de jardin, *f.*, irrigateur, *m.* — **flower,** *s.* fleur de jardin, *f.* — **ground,** *s.* jardinage, *m.* — **mould,** *s.* terreau, *m.* — **plant,** *s.* plante jardinière, *f.* — **plot,** *s.* parterre, *m.* — **roller,** *s.* rouleau de jardin, *m.* — **seeds,** *s. pl.* graines potagères, *f.pl.* — **steps,** *s. pl.* perron de (*or* du) jardin, *m.* — **stuff,** *s.* jardinage, *m.*, légumes, *m.pl.*, plantes potagères, *f.pl.* — **tools,** *s. pl.* outils de jardinage, *m pl.*

Gardener, *s.* jardinier, *m.*, -ière, *f.*

Gardenia, *s.* (*bot.*) gardénie, *f.*

Gardening, *s.* jardinage, *m.*

Garfish, *s.* orphie, aiguille des pêcheurs, aiguille de mer, *f.*, brochet de mer, *m.* [sette, *f.*

Garganey, *s.* sarcelle d'été, mercanette, gras-

Gargle, *v.a.* gargariser; — *v.n.* se gargariser; — *s.* gargarisme, *m.*

Gargling, *s.* gargarisme, *m.*

Gargoyle, *s.* gargouille, *f.*

Garish, *adj.* éclatant; voyant; extravagant

Garishly, *adv.* d'une manière éclatante *or* voyante; d'une manière extravagante

Garishness, *s.* éclat, *m.*; extravagance, *f.*

Garland, *s.* guirlande, *f.*; (*principal thing*) plus bel ornement, *m.*; (*of writings*) anthologie, *f.*; — *v.a.* guirlander [d'ail, *f.*

Garlic, *s.* ail, *m.* *Clove* or *head of* —, gousse

Garment, *s.* vêtement, habillement, *m.*; toilette, *f.* [grenier; (*fig.*) amasser

Garner, *s.* grenier, *m.*; — *v.a.* mettre en

Garnet, *s.* (*min.*) grenat, *m.*; (*nav.*) bredindin, *m.*

Garnish, *v.a.* garnir (de); (*adorn*) orner (de), embellir (de); (*law*) former saisie-arrêt entre les mains de; — *s.* ornement, embellissement, *m.*; parure, *f.*; (*of dishes*) garniture, *f.* — **money,** *s.* bienvenue, *f.*

Garnishee, *s.* (*law*) tiers saisi, *m.*

Garnishing, Garnishment, Garniture, *s.* ornement, embellissement, *m.*; parure; (*of dishes*) garniture, *f.*; (*law*) saisie-arrêt, opposition, *f.*

Garotte, *s.* (*capital punishment in Spain*) garrotte, *f.*; (*instr. of ditto*) garrot, *m.*; — *v.a.* (*execute, in Spain*) garrotter; (*strangle, in London fashion*) étrangler. — **robbery,** *s.* vol à l'aide d'étranglement, *m.*

Garotter, *s.* étrangleur, *m.*

Garotting, *s.* vol à l'aide d'étranglement, *m.*

Garou, — **bark, -bush,** *s.* garou, *m.*

Garpike. *V.* **Garfish**

Garret, *s.* mansarde, *f.*; galetas, grenier, *m.* — **master,** *s.* chambrelan, *m.* — **window,** *s.* fenêtre en mansarde, *f.*

Garreteer, *s.* habitant d'une mansarde *or* d'un galetas, chambrelan, *m.*

Garrison, *s.* garnison, *f.*; — *v.a.* mettre garnison; (*a town*) mettre garnison dans, pourvoir d'une garnison. — **town,** *s.* ville de garnison, *f.* [en garnison

Garrisoned, *adj.* (*place*) à garnison; (*troops*)

Garrot, *s.* (*bird*) garrot, *m.*

Garrulity, *s.* garrulité, loquacité, *f.*

Garrulous, *adj.* loquace, babillard

Garter, *s.* jarretière, *f.*; — *v.a.* jarreter. — **fish,** *s.* lépidope, *m.*

Garth, *s.* pêcherie, nasse, *f.*, duit, *m.*; cour de derrière, *f.*; clos, courtil, *m.*

Gas, *s.* gaz, *m.*; — *adj.* de gaz; du gaz; à gaz, au gaz. *To light with* —, éclairer au gaz. *To turn off the* —, fermer le robinet de (*or* du) gaz. *To turn on the* —, ouvrir le robinet de (*or* du) gaz. — **apparatus,** *s.* appareil à gaz, *m.* — **bracket,** *s.* bras de lumière pour le gaz, bras à gaz, *m.* — **burner,** *s.* bec de gaz, *m.* — **company,** *s.* compagnie du gaz, *f.*, gaz, *m.* — **fitter,** *s.* gazier, appareilleur de gaz, appareilleur, *m.* — **fittings,** *s. pl.* becs et tuyaux de gaz, *m.pl.* — **holder,** *s.* gazomètre, *m.* — **illumination,** *s.* éclairage au gaz, *m.* — **lamp,** *s.* lampe à gaz, *f.*; (*in the streets*, &c.) bec de gaz, candélabre à gaz, candélabre, *m.* — **light,** *s.* lumière du gaz, *f.*, gaz, *m.*; éclairage au gaz, *m.*; (*burner*) bec de gaz. *By* — *light*, à la lumière du gaz, au gaz. — **lighting,** *s.* éclairage au gaz, gaz, *m.* — **making,** *adj.* gazifère. — **measurer,** *s.* (*instr.*) gazolitre, *m.* — **meter,** *s.* compteur à gaz, compteur, *m.* — **pipe,** *s.* tuyau de gaz, conduit de (*or* du) gaz, *m.* — **stove,** *s.* calorifère à gaz, *m.*; (*for cooking*) fourneau à gaz, *m.* — **tar,** *s.* *V.* **Coal-tar.** — **works,** *s. pl.* usine à gaz, *f.*

Gascon, *s. adj.* Gascon, *m.*, -ne, *f.*

Gasconade, *s.* gasconnade; — *v.n.* gasconner

Gasconading, *adj.* gascon; — *s.* gasconnades,

Gasconism, *s.* gasconisme, *m.* [*f.pl.*

Gaseity, *s.* gazéité, *f.*

Gaselier, *s.* lustre à gaz, *m.*

Gaseous, *adj.* gazeux

Gaseousness, *s.* gazéité, *f.*

Gash, *v.a.* balafrer, faire une balafre à; faire une blessure profonde à; — *s.* balafre, *f.*; blessure profonde, *f.*

Gasifiable, *adj.* gazéifiable

Gasification, *s.* gazéification, *f.*

Gasiform, *adj.* gazéiforme

Gasify, *v.a.* gazéifier; — *v.n.* se gazéifier

Gasket, *s.* (*nav.*) garcette, *f.*; raban, *m.*

Gaskin, *s.* (*of steam-engines*) garniture, *f.*

Gasogene, *s.* gazogène, *m.*

Gasometer, *s.* gazomètre, *m.*

Gasometric, *adj.* gazométrique

Gasometry, *s.* gazométrie, *f.*

Gasoscope, *s.* gazoscope, *m.*

Gasp, *v.a.n.* respirer avec peine; ouvrir la bouche. *To* — *for breath*, faire des efforts pour respirer, haleter. *To* — *for life*, lutter contre la mort. — **after,** soupirer après

Gasp, Gasping, *s.* effort pour respirer, *m.*; (*fig.*) soupir, *m.*

Gasteropod, *s.* gastéropode, *m.*

Gasteropodous, *adj.* gastéropode

Gastralgia, *s.* gastralgie, *f.*

Gastralgic, *adj.* gastralgique

Gastric, *adj.* gastrique

Gastritis, *s.* gastrite, *f.*

Gastrocele, *s.* gastrocèle, *f.*

Gastrodynia, *s.* gastrodynie, *f.* [nome, *m.f.*

Gastronomer, Gastronomist, *s.* gastro-

Gastronom-ic, al, -ically, -y. *V.* page 3, § 1

Gate, *s.* porte, *f.*; grande porte, *f.*; (*of open-work iron*) grille, *f.*; (*large front-door*) portail, *m.*; (*of roads*, &c.) barrière, *f.*; (*of docks*) vanne, *f.*; (*fig.*) porte, entrée, *f.* — **keeper,** *s.* surveillant (*m.*, e, *f.*) de barrière, garde-barrière, *m.f.* — **stop,** *s.* arrête-porte, *m.* — **way,** *s.* chemin de barrière, *m.*; passage, *m.*,

allée, *f.*; porte cochère, porte, *f.*; portail, *m.*; [guichet, *m.*
Gated, *adj.* à portes ...
Gather, *v.a.* rassembler, ramasser; recueillir; (*heap*) amasser, amonceler; (*fruit, flowers*) cueillir; (*harvest*) recueillir, récolter; (*recover*) reprendre; prendre; (*join*) joindre, réunir; (*deduce*) conclure (de), inférer (de); (*pucker*) froncer; (*print., book-bind.*) assembler; — *v.n.* se réunir, se rassembler, s'assembler; (*heap*) s'amasser, s'amonceler; se préparer; (*increase*) grossir; (*of abscess*) abcéder, former un abcès, venir à suppuration; — *s.* (*need.*) fronce, *f.* *To be —ed to o.'s fathers*, aller rejoindre ses pères. — **in,** recueillir, rentrer, récolter; rassembler; réunir. — **up,** *v.a.* ramasser, relever; amasser; *v.n.* s'amasser. *To — oneself up, to — o.'s limbs*, se ramasser, se pelotonner, se peloter
Gatherer, *s.* personne qui recueille *or* cueille, *f.*, recueilleur, *m.*, -euse, *f.*, cueilleur, *m.*, -euse, *f.*; collecteur, *m.*, -trice, *f.*; (*of corn*) moissonneur, *m.*, -euse, *f.*; (*book-bind.*) assembleur, *m.*, -euse, *f.*; (*of taxes*, &c.) percepteur, *m.*; (*instr.*) cueilloir, *m.*
Gathering, *s.* rassemblement, *m.*; réunion, *f.*; (*of fruit*, &c.) récolte, *f.*; cueillette, cueille, *f.*; (*collection*) quête, collecte, *f.*; (*med.*) abcès, *m.*, tumeur, *f.* ('*on*,' à); (*need.*) froncis, *m.*; (*print., book-bind.*) assemblage, *m.*
Gatten-tree, *s.* puine, *m.* [faux brillant, *m.*
Gaud, *s.* ornement, *m.*, parure, *f.*; clinquant,
Gaudery, *s.* parure éclatante, *f.*; faste, *m.*
Gaudily, *adv.* avec éclat; avec faste, fastueusement
Gaudiness, *s.* éclat, *m.*; ostentation, *f.*, faste, *m.*; (*tinsel*) faux brillant, clinquant, *m.*
Gaudy, *adj.* *V.* **Showy** [&c.) tuyauter
Gauffer, *s.* tuyau, *m.*; — *v.a.* gaufrer; (*frills*,
Gaufferer, *s.* gaufreur, *m.*, -euse, *f.*
Gauffering, *s.* gaufrage, *m.*, gaufrure, *f.*; tuyautage, *m.* — **iron, -machine,** *s.* gaufroir, *m.*
Gauge, *v.a.* mesurer; (*ships, casks*) jauger; — *s.* jauge, *f.*; mesure, *f.*; (*tech.*) indicateur, *m.*; (*nav.*) tirant d'eau, *m.*; (*rail.*) largeur, voie, *f.*, entre-rails, *m.* *Broad —*, (*rail.*) voie d'une largeur de sept pieds, *f.*
Gauger, *s.* jaugeur, *m.*
Gauging, *s.* jaugeage, *m.* — **rod,** *s.* jauge, *f.*
Gaul, *s.* (*country*) la Gaule, *f.*; (*pers.*) Gaulois, [*m.*, e, *f.*
Gault, *s.* (*geol.*) gault, *m.*
Gaultheria, *s.* (*bot.*) gaulthérie, *f.*
Gaultherine, *s.* (*chem.*) gaulthérine, *f.*
Gaunt, *adj.* maigre, décharné
Gauntlet, *s.* gantelet, *m.*; (*challenge*) gant, *m.*; (*mil.*) verges, baguettes, *f.pl.* *To run the —*, passer par les verges *or* par les baguettes; (*nav.*) courir la bouline. *To throw down, to take up the —*, jeter, relever le gant
Gauntly, *adv.* avec maigreur; d'une maigreur repoussante
Gauntree, *s.* chantier, porte-fût, *m.*
Gaur, *s.* (*zool.*) gour, *m.*
Gauze, *s.* gaze, *f.*; — *adj.* de gaze; comme de la gaze. — **maker,** *s.* gazier, *m.*, -ière, *f.*
Gavelkind, *s.* partage égal, *m.*
Gavial, *s.* gavial, *m.*
Gavot, Gavotte, *s.* gavotte, *f.* [niais, *m.*, e, *f.*
Gawk, *s.* coucou, *m.*; (*pers.*) sot, *m.*, -te, *f.*,
Gawky, *adj.* *s.* maladroit, gauche, stupide, sot, niais
Gay, *adj.* gai; (*intoxicated*) en train; (*of dress*, &c.) éclatant, voyant; brillant. *To be —*, être gai *or* &c.; s'amuser, faire la vie, être dans les plaisirs. *As — as a lark*, gai comme un pinson. — *man*, viveur, noceur, bambocheur, *m.*; coureur, *m.* — *woman*, viveuse, noceuse, bambocheuse, *f.*; femme galante, *f.*; (*jest.*) cocote, cocodette, *f.* — *life*, vie de plaisirs, *f.*; (*set of people*) monde interlope, demi-monde, *m.* — *world*, monde interlope, demi-monde, *m.*
Gayety *or* **Gayty, Gayly.** *V.* **Gaiety, Gaily**
Gaze, *v.n.* regarder, contempler, fixer, considérer; — *s.* regard, *m.*
Gazelle, *s.* gazelle, *f.*
Gazer, *s.* spectateur, *m.*, -trice, *f.*
Gazette, *s.* gazette, *f.*; — *v.a.* publier (*or* annoncer) officiellement, (*in England*) publier (*or* annoncer) dans la *Gazette*, (*in France*) publier (*or* annoncer) dans le *Moniteur*, insérer au *Moniteur*; (*of bankrupts*) déclarer en faillite
Gazetteer, *s.* dictionnaire géographique, *m.*; nouvelliste, *m.*; journaliste, *m.*
Gazing-stock, *s.* objet des regards, *m.*; objet de mépris, *m.*; spectacle, *m.*
Gazogene, *s.* gazogène, *m.*
Gazon, *s.* gazon, *m.*
Gear, *s.* accoutrement, *m.*; ameublement, *m.*; habillement, *m.*; ornement, *m.*; toilette, *f.*; (*tackle*) attirail, *m.*; (*apparatus*) appareil, *m.*; (*of animals*) harnais, *m.*; (*horse —*) manége, *m.*; (*of machines*) engrenage, *m.*; jeu, *m.*, action, *f.*; (*of a pump*) garniture, *f.*; (*nav.*) drisse, *f.*; — *v.a.* habiller; ajuster; garnir; harnacher; (*mach.*) engrener, agencer, mettre en train. *In —*, engrené, agencé, en train, en mouvement, en jeu, en état. *Out of —*, désengrené, désagencé, arrêté, en repos; hors d'état, dérangé. *To throw into —*, engrener, agencer, mettre en train, mettre en mouvement. *To throw out of —*, désengrener, désagencer, arrêter; déranger
Gearing, *s.* engrenage, *m.*; disposition, *f.* agencement, *m.*, appareil, *m.*
Gecko, *s.* gecko, *m.*
Gee, *int.* huhau! huhaut! — *-ho!* huhau huhaut! — *-up!* hop! houp!
Gehenna, *s.* géhenne, *f.*
Gelable, *adj.* gelable
Gelatine, *s.* gélatine, *f.*
Gelatiniform, *adj.* gélatiniforme
Gelatinization, *s.* gélatinisation, *f.* [niser
Gelatinize, *v.a.* gélatiniser; — *v.n.* se gélati-
Gelatinous, *adj.* gélatineux
Geld, *v.a.* châtrer, castrer, hongrer; (*fig.*) mutiler, tronquer
Gelder, *s.* châtreur, hongreur, *m.*
Gelding, *s.* castration, *f.*; (*animal*) animal châtré, *m.*; (*horse*) cheval hongre, hongre, *m.*
Gelid, *adj.* froid, glacé, gelé
Gem, *s.* pierre précieuse, *f.*; bijou, *m.*; perle, *f.*; (*of a diadem*) fleuron, *m.*; (*bot.*) bourgeon, bouton, *m.*; (*of grafting*) écusson, *m.*; —**s,** *pl.* pierreries, *f.pl.*; — *v.a.* orner de pierreries; (*fig.*) embellir, orner (de); (*strew*) parsemer (de), émailler (de); — *v.n.* bourgeonner; fleurir
Geminate, *adj.* géminé; — *v.a.* doubler
Gemination, *s.* redoublement, *m.*, répétition, *f.*
Gemini, *s.pl.* (*anat.*) jumeaux, *m.pl.*; (*astr.*) les Gémeaux, *m.pl.*
Gemmated, *adj.* gemmé
Gemmation, *s.* gemmation, *f.*, bourgeonnement, *m.* [blable à une pierre précieuse
Gemmeous, *adj.* de pierre précieuse, sem-
Gemmiparous, *adj.* gemmipare [reries)
Gemmy, *adj.* brillant, étincelant (de pier-
Gems-boc, *s.* (*zool.*) pasan, *m.*; oryx, *m.*
Gendarme, *s.* gendarme, *m.*
Gendarmerie, *s.* gendarmerie, *f.*
Gender, *s.* genre, *m.*
Genealogical, *adj.* généalogique
Genealogically, *adv.* généalogiquement
Genealogist, *s.* généalogiste, *m.*
Genealogy, *s.* généalogie, *f.*
Genera, *s.* (*pl. of* **Genus**) genres, *m.pl.*
General, *adj.* général; ordinaire; commun; n'importe quel ..., ... quelconque; — *s.* général, *m.*; généralité, *f.*; (*mil.*) général, *m.*; (*beat of drums*) générale, *f.* — *agency* or *agent*, agence (*f.*) *or* agent (*m.*) d'affaires. — *servant*, domestique (*m.f.*) *or* bonne (*f.*) à tout faire. *The — public*, le public en général, la masse du public. *In —*, en général
Generalissimo, *s.* généralissime, *m.*
Generality, *s.* généralité, *f.*; plupart, masse, *f.*
Generalizable, *adj.* généralisable
Generalization, *s.* généralisation, *f.*
Generalize, *v.a.n.* généraliser

Generalizer, *s.* généralisateur, *m.*, -trice, *f.*
Generalizing, *adj.* généralisateur; — *s.* généralisation, *f.* [(*usually*) ordinairement
Generally, *adv.* généralement, en général;
Generalship, *s.* généralat, *m.*; talent de général, *m.*; tactique, *f.*; stratégie, *f.*
Generate, *v.a.* engendrer; produire [ration
Generating, *adj.* générateur; — *s. V.* **Gene-**
Generation, *s.* génération, *f.*; production, *f.*
Generative, *adj.* génératif; générateur
Generator, *s.* principe générateur, *m.*; (*tech.*)
Generic, -al, *adj.* générique [générateur, *m*
Generically, *adv.* génériquement
Generosity, *s.* générosité, *f.*
Generous, *adj.* généreux; abondant, riche
Generously, *adv.* généreusement; abondam-
Genesis, *s.* Genèse, *f.* [ment, richement
Genet, Genette, *s.* genette, *f.*; (*Spanish horse*) *V.* **Jennet**
Genethliac, *adj. s.* généthliaque, *adj.m.f.*, *s.m.*
Genetic, -al, *adj.* génétique, génésique
Geneva, *s.* (*geog.*) Genève, *f.*; (*liquor*) genièvre, *m.* — **watch,** *s.* montre de Genève, *f.*
Genevan, Genevese, *s. adj.* Genevois, *m.*, e, *f.*
Genial, *adj.* générateur; fécondant; naturel; gai, joyeux; réjouissant; beau; bienfaisant; bon; doux; tiède
Geniality, Genialness, *s.* caractère naturel, *m.*; gaieté, joie, *f.*; douceur, *f.*
Genially, *adv.* naturellement; gaiment
Genipa, *s.* génipa, génipayer, *m.*
Genipap, *s.* génipat, *m.* [tales, *f.pl.*
Genital, *adj.* génital; **—s,** *s. pl.* parties géni-
Genitive, *s.* (— *case*) génitif, *m.* *In the* —, au
Genitor, *s.* géniteur, *m.*; père, *m.* [génitif
Genius, *s.* génie, *m.*
Genoese, *s. adj.* Génois *m.*, e, *f.*
Genouillere, *s* genouillère, *f.*
Genre, *s.* genre, *m.* — **painting,** *s.* genre, *m.* — **painter,** *s* peintre de genre, *m.* — **picture,** *s.* tableau de genre, *m*
Gent, *s.* (*slang for* **Gentleman**)
Genteel, *adj.* distingué; poli; élégant, de bon goût; comme il faut. — *comedy*, haute comédie, *f.*
Genteelly, *adv.* d'une manière distinguée, en personne comme il faut, comme il faut; poliment; élégamment, avec goût; avec grâce
Genteelness, *s.* manières distinguées, *f.pl.*; bon ton, *m.*; bon goût, *m.*; élégance, *f.*; grâce, *f.*
Gentian, *s.* gentiane, *f.*
Gentianella, *s* gentianelle, *f.*
Gentianic, *adj.* gentianique
Gentianine *s.* gentianine, *f.*
Gentile, *s.* gentil, païen, *m.*; — *adj.* gentil, des gentils; (*gram.*) national, de nation. — *nations*, (*s.pl.*) gentilité, *f.* — *noun* or *adjective*, gentilé, *m.* [paganisme, *m.*, idolâtrie, *f.*
Gentilism, *s.* gentilisme, *m*, gentilité, *f.*,
Gentility, *s.* (*of birth*) naissance distinguée, *f.*; (*politeness*) bon ton, bon genre, *m.*; (*gracefulness*) élégance, distinction, *f.*, bon goût, *m.*; (*paganism*) gentilité, *f.*
Gentle, *adj.* (*mild*) doux; aimable; (*slight*) léger; (*well-born*) bien né, de bonne famille; (*of rank*) élevé; — *s.* (*worm*) asticot, *m.* — *means* or *ways*, (la) douceur, *f.* — *reader*, ami lecteur, *m.* *Of — birth*, bien né
Gentlefolks, *s. pl.* gens distingués, *m.pl.*, personnes comme il faut, *f.pl.*
Gentleman, *s* (*term of courtesy*) monsieur, *m.*; (*man*) homme, *m.*; (*well-bred man*) homme bien né, *m*; homme de bon ton, *m.*; homme comme il faut, *m.*; homme bien élevé, *m.*; (*man of honour*) homme d'honneur, *m.*; (*man of property, independent* —) rentier, *m.*; propriétaire, *m.*; bourgeois, *m.*; (*man of rank, title*) gentilhomme, *m.*; (*in dancing, partner*) cavalier, *m.* *Gentlemen*, *pl.* messieurs, *m.pl.*, &c. *Young* —, jeune homme, *m.* *Young gentlemen*, jeunes gens, *m.pl*; messieurs! *A —'s watch*, une montre d'homme. *He is a* —, c'est un homme comme il faut. *He is a perfect* or *thorough* —, c'est un homme très comme il faut. *That* —, ce monsieur. *This* or *the* — (*here present*), monsieur. *These* or *those gentlemen*, ces messieurs. *To play the fine* —, faire le monsieur. — **farmer,** *s.* propriétaire cultivateur, *m.* **—'s son,** *s.* fils de famille, *m.*
Gentlemanlike, Gentlemanly, *adj.* d'homme d'honneur, honorable; distingué, poli; (*pers.*) bien élevé, de bon ton, de bonne société, de manières distinguées, comme il faut; bien
Gentlemanliness, *s.* bon ton, savoir-vivre, *m.*, manières distinguées, *f.pl.*; urbanité, *f.*
Gentleness, *s.* douceur, *f.*
Gentlewoman, *s.* dame, femme bien née, *f.*; femme de bonne famille, *f.*; femme de bon ton, *f.*; femme comme il faut, *f.*; femme bien élevée, *f*; (*woman of property*) rentière, *f.*; propriétaire, *f*; bourgeoise, *f.*; (*waiting-woman*) dame d'honneur, *f.*
Gently, *adv.* doucement, avec douceur
Gentry, *s.* classe élevée, *f.*; haute bourgeoisie, *f*; gens comme il faut, *m.pl.* *Small* —, petite bourgeoisie, bourgeoisie, *f.*
Genuflection, Genuflexion, *s* génuflexion, *f.*
Genuine *adj.* naturel; pur; vrai, véritable; réel; sincère; bon; authentique
Genuinely, *adv.* naturellement; purement; véritablement; réellement
Genuineness, *s.* pureté, *f.*; vérité, *f.*; réalité, *f.*; sincérité, *f.*; authenticité, *f.*
Genus, *s.* genre, *m.*
Geode, *s.* géode, *f.*
Geodesy, *s.* géodésie, *f.*
Geognos-tic, al, -tically, -y. *V.* p. 3, § 1
Geographer, *s.* géographe *m.*
Geograph-ic, al, *adj.* géographique, de géographie
Geographically, *adv.* géographiquement
Geography, *s.* géographie, *f.*
Geological, *adj* géologique
Geologically, *adv.* géologiquement
Geologist, *s.* géologue, *m.*
Geology, *s.* géologie, *f.*
Geometer, *s.* géomètre, *m.*
Geometric, -al, *adj.* géométrique; géométral
Geometrically, *adv.* géométriquement; géométralement
Geometrician, *s.* géomètre, *m.*
Geometrize, *v.n.* géométriser
Geometry, *s.* géométrie, *f.*
Georama, *s.* géorama, *m.*
Georamic, *adj.* géoramique
Georgian, *s. adj.* Géorgien, *m.*, -ne, *f.*
Georgic, *adj. s.* géorgique, *adj* *m.f.*, *s.f.*
George (By), *int.* nom d'un tonnerre! sapristi! sacrebleu!
Georgium Sidus, *s.* Herschel, Uranus, *m.*
Geranium, *s.* géranium, *m.*
Gerbil, *s.* (*zool.*) gerbille, *f.*
Gerfalcon, *s.* gerfaut, *m.*
Germ, *s.* germe, *m.*
German, *adj.* (*of cousins*) germain; (*of modern Germany*) allemand, d'Allemagne; (*of ancient Germany*) germain; germanique; (*of type*) gothique; (*of flute*) traversière, allemande; — *s* (*of modern Germany*) Allemand, *m.*, e, *f.*; (*of ancient Germany*) Germain, *m.*, e, *f.*; (*language*) l'Allemand, *m.*, la langue allemande, *f.* — *master*, maître *or* professeur d'allemand, *m.* — *Ocean*, mer du Nord, mer d'Allemagne, *f.* — *silver*, métal blanc, maillechort, argentan, argenton, *m.* — *tinder*, amadou, *m.*
Germander, *s.* germandrée, *f.*
German-ic, -ism, -ist. *V.* page 3, § 1
Germanize, *v.a.* germaniser
Germinal, *adj.* de germe; (*bot.*) germinal
Germinant, *adj.* qui germe
Germinate, *v.n.* germer; — *v.a.* faire germer, féconder
Germinating, *adj.* germinateur, germinatif

Germination, *s.* germination, *f.*
Germinative, *adj.* germinatif
Gerund, *s.* gérondif, *m.*
Gestation, *s.* gestation, *f.*
Gestatory, *adj.* gestatoire
Gesticulate, *v.n.* gesticuler
Gesticulating, *adj.* gesticulateur
Gesticulation, *s.* gesticulation, *f.*
Gesticulator, *s.* gesticulateur, *m.*; mime, *m.*
Gesticulatory, *adj* de gesticulation; mimique
Gesture, *s.* geste, *m.*; (*of the body*) mouvement, *m.*; — *v.n.* faire des gestes; faire des mouvements; — *v.a.* accompagner de gestes
Get, *v.a.* obtenir, se procurer, trouver, tirer, avoir; (*for others*) procurer, faire avoir; (*receive*) recevoir; (*acquire*) acquérir; (*catch*) attraper; (*fetch*) chercher; (*seize*) saisir, s'emparer de; (*gain*) gagner, retirer, recueillir; (*a victory, a prize*) remporter; (*a connection, a name, friends, &c.*) se faire; (*habits*) prendre; (*by heart*) apprendre; (*by force or persuasion*) arracher; (*into*) faire entrer, mettre; (*put*) mettre; (*make, force, cause to be done*) faire; — *v.n.* aller; arriver; (*reach*) atteindre; parvenir (à); (*within*) s'introduire; (*from*) se garantir (de); (*put oneself*) se mettre; (*find oneself*) se trouver; (*fall*) tomber; (*become*) devenir; commencer à être; (*dark at night, old, late, &c.*) se faire; (*be*) être; (*into habits*) prendre, contracter; (*improve*) gagner; (*of the health*) aller; (*upon*) monter; (*into o.'s head, of drinks*) monter *or* porter (à la tête). *To have got,* (*possess*) avoir; (*have hold of*) tenir. *To — a thing done* or *made,* faire faire quelque chose. *To — a house built,* faire bâtir une maison. *You will never — him to do that,* vous ne lui ferez jamais faire cela, vous n'obtiendrez jamais de lui qu'il fasse cela. *How do you — on?* comment vont les affaires? (*in health*) comment va la santé? comment ça va-t-il? *It is getting cold, warm,* (*weather*) il commence à faire froid, chaud. *It is getting dark,* il se fait nuit. *To — upon a horse,* monter à cheval. *To — sad,* devenir triste. *To — beaten,* se faire battre; être battu. *To — laughed at,* se faire moquer de soi. *To — talked of,* faire parler de soi. *To — married, tired, accustomed, spoilt, &c.*, se marier, se fatiguer, s'accoutumer, se gâter *or* s'abîmer, &c. [*For further examples, V.* **Grow**]. *I wish you may — it!* (*jest.*) je vous en souhaite! attendez-vous-y! — **about,** *v.n. V.* **Go about;** (*recover from illness*) reprendre ses occupations, sortir, se rétablir. — **above,** se mettre au-dessus de, s'élever au-dessus de; surpasser. — **across,** traverser. — **aground,** échouer. — **along,** *v.a.* faire marcher; faire avancer; traîner; *v.n.* marcher; avancer. — *along with you!* allons donc! allez-vous-en! allez vous promener! — **away,** *v.n.* s'en aller; partir; s'enfuir, s'échapper, se sauver; se dissiper; *v.a.* faire partir; faire en aller; (*take away*) ôter, enlever; (*obtain*) se faire donner, arracher. — **back,** *v.a.* faire revenir; (*have again*) ravoir; se faire rendre; recouvrer; retrouver; regagner; rattraper; reprendre; (*o.'s expenses*) rentrer dans (ses fonds); *v.n.* (*come back*) être de retour; revenir; (*go back*) retourner, s'en retourner; (*home*) rentrer chez soi; (*draw back*) reculer. — **down,** *v.a.* faire descendre; (*things*) descendre; (*beat down*) abattre; (*swallow*) avaler; *v.n.* descendre. — **forward,** *v.a.* faire avancer; faire faire des progrès à; pousser; *v.n.* avancer; s'avancer; aller; faire son chemin; faire fortune. — **in,** *v.a.* entrer; faire entrer; rentrer; placer; mettre; (*get horses in harness*) atteler; (*money*) recouvrer; *v.n.* entrer; pénétrer; s'introduire; (*into a carriage*) monter; (*fig.*) s'insinuer. — **near,** *V.* **Come near.** — **off,** *v.n.* partir; s'en aller; s'échapper; échapper; (*of a scrape*) se tirer d'affaire, se tirer d'embarras, s'en tirer; (*with ... only*) en être quitte (pour ...); (*down from*) descendre de dessus; (*things*) se détacher; (*nav.*) prendre le large; (*from a horse or carriage*) descendre; *v.a.* tirer d'affaire; ôter; enlever; faire en aller, faire retirer; (*sell*) faire écouler, disposer de; (*a ship stranded*) déséchouer. — **on,** *v.n.* avancer; s'avancer; faire des progrès; marcher; aller; (*succeed*) réussir, faire son chemin; (*agree*) s'accorder; *v.a.* (*push on*) pousser; faire avancer, faire faire des progrès à; (*clothes*) mettre, passer. — **open,** *v.a.* ouvrir. — **out,** *v.a.* faire sortir; sortir; (*obtain, extricate, draw*) tirer (de); arracher (de); (*prospectuses, &c.*) publier; (*unharness*) dételer; (*remove*) ôter, enlever; *v.n.* sortir; s'échapper; (*oneself from a scrape*) se tirer (de); (*of spots*) s'ôter, s'enlever; (*from a carriage*) descendre. — **over,** passer; traverser; passer par-dessus; surmonter, vaincre, venir à bout de, triompher de; se tirer de; (*an illness*) se rétablir de, se remettre de, se tirer de; (*a loss, &c.*) se consoler de; (*bear*) supporter; (*get rid of*) s'affranchir de, se défaire de; (*coax*) enjôler. — **through,** *v.a.n.* faire traverser, faire passer; passer à travers, passer par, traverser; franchir; (*run through*) parcourir; (*pierce*) percer; (*a task*) finir, accomplir; faire; venir à bout de; (*difficulties*) surmonter; tirer *or* se tirer (d'embarras *or* d'affaire); (*property*) dépenser, manger. — **to,** aller à; arriver à, &c.; (*find*) trouver. — **together,** *v.a.* réunir, rassembler; (*pick up*) ramasser; *v.n.* se rassembler; se trouver ensemble. — **under,** *v.a.* maîtriser, se rendre maître de, dompter; *v.n.* se mettre sous. — **up,** *v.a.n.* (*pers.*) faire lever; (*things*) lever; (*bring up*) faire monter; (*things*) monter; organiser; arranger, disposer, préparer; exécuter; (*rise*) se lever; (*ascend*) monter; (*a lesson*) apprendre, préparer; (*a subscription*) faire; (*linen*) blanchir. — **up again,** *v.n.* se relever. — **up to,** atteindre. — **upon,** monter sur. — **well** *or* **well again,** (*pers.*) se rétablir; (*of diseased parts*) se guérir
Getter, *s.* personne qui obtient *or* procure *or* se procure, *f.*; personne qui engendre, *f.*, créateur, *m.*, -trice, *f.*, auteur, *m.*; (*winner*) gagnant, *m.*, e, *f.*; (*build.*) terrassier, *m.* — **up,** *s.* monteur, *m.*, -euse, *f.*; promoteur, *m.*, -trice, *f.*
Getting, *s.* acquisition, *f.*; gain, profit, *m.*; (*build.*) fouille, *f.* — **up,** *s.* montage, *m.*; (*of a play*) mise en scène, *f.*
Gewgaw, *s.* babiole, *f.*, colifichet, bibelot, *m.*; bagatelle, fanfreluche, *f.*; — *adj.* futile, frivole, [factice
Ghastful. *V.* **Ghastly**
Ghastfully, *adv.* lugubrement
Ghastliness, *s.* aspect (*or* air) lugubre, *m.*; pâleur affreuse, *f.*; horreur, *f.*
Ghastly, *adj.* de spectre; sépulcral; lugubre; sombre; pâle, blême; (pâle) comme la mort, (affreusement) pâle; horrible, affreux
Gherkin, *s.* cornichon, *m.*
Ghibelline, *s.* Gibelin, *m.*
Ghost, *s.* esprit, *m.*; âme, *f.*; fantôme, spectre, revenant, *m.*; ombre, *f.* *To give up the —,* rendre l'âme. *We needed no — to tell us that,* il n'y a pas besoin d'être sorcier pour deviner cela. — **like,** *adj.* semblable à un spectre, de spectre; pâle et défait. — **moth,** *s.* hépiale, *f.*
Ghostliness, *s.* spiritualité, *f.*
Ghostly, *adj.* spirituel; de spectre, de spectres
Ghoul, *s.* goule, *f.*
Ghoulish, *adj.* goulique
Giant, *s.* géant, *m.*; — *adj.* géant; de géant. —*s' Causeway,* Chaussée des géants, *f.* — **killer,** *s.* pourfendeur de géants, *m.* — **like,** *adj.* de géant, gigantesque
Giantess, *s.* géante, *f.*
Giantism, *s.* géantisme, gigantisme, *m.*
Giantly, *adj.* *V.* **Gigantic**
Giaour, *s.* giaour, *m.* [*f.*; — *v.n.* *V.* **Jib**
Gib, *s.* (— *cat*) chat, matou, *m.*; (*tech.*) clavette,

Gibber, *v.n.* baragouiner
Gibberish, *s.* baragouin, *m.*; baragouinage, *m.*; jargon, *m.*; patois, *m.*
Gibbet, *s.* gibet, *m.*, potence, *f.*; — *v.a.* mettre à la potence, attacher au gibet, pendre; (*fig.*) [pilorier
Gibbon, *s.* gibbon, *m.*
Gibbose, Gibbous, *adj.* gibbeux
Gibbosity, Gibbousness, *s.* gibbosité, *f.*
Gibe, *v.a.n.* se moquer de; railler; — *s.* moquerie, [raillerie, *f.*, sarcasme, *m.*
Gibel, *s.* gibèle, *f.*
Giber, *s.* moqueur, *m.*, -euse, *f.*, railleur, *m.*, [-euse, *f.*
Gibing, *adj.* moqueur, railleur
Gibingly, *adv.* avec moquerie, en raillant
Giblets, *s. pl.* abattis, *m.*, *m.pl.*
Gid, *s.* (*vet.*) tournis, *m.*
Giddily, *adv.* étourdiment, en étourdi, à l'étourdie; avec inconstance; avec des vertiges
Giddiness, *s.* vertige, étourdissement, *m.*; (*heedlessness*, &c.) étourderie, *f.*; inconstance, *f.*
Giddy, *adj.* étourdi, écervelé; (*vertiginous*) qui a le vertige; (*making giddy*) qui donne le vertige, étourdissant, vertigineux; (*inconstant*) inconstant, volage. *To be* or *feel* —, se sentir tout étourdi, avoir le vertige, avoir un étourdissement *or* des étourdissements. *To make* —, étourdir, donner le vertige à, faire tourner la tête à. — **brained, -headed,** *adj.*, — **head, -goose,** *s.* étourdi, *m.*, e, *f.*, écervelé, *m.*, e, *f.* *As — as a goose*, étourdi comme un [hanneton
Giff-gaff, *adv.* donnant donnant
Gift, *s.* don, présent, cadeau, *m*; (*oblation*) offrande, *f.*; (*quality*) don, *m.*; talent, *m.*; (*law*) donation, *f*; (*theol.*) grâce, *f.*; (*of livings, posts*) nomination, *f.*; — *v.a.* douer (de). *In the — of*, à la nomination de. — **book,** *s.* livre de cadeau, *m.*; (*new year's*) livre d'étrennes, *m.* — **horse,** *s.* cheval donné, *m.* *One must not look a — horse in the mouth*, à cheval donné on ne regarde point à la bouche (*or* à la bride)
Gifted, *adj.* doué (de); (*talented*) de talent
Gig, *s.* (*top*) toupie, *f.*, sabot, *m.*; (*teetotum*) tonton, *m.*; (*whirligig*) pirouette, *f.*; (*pers.*) toupie, *f.*; (*carriage*) cabriolet, *m.*; (*machine*) laineuse, *f.*; (*boat*) guigue, *f.*; (*pleasure navig.*) gig, *m.*; (*fish* —) *V.* **Fish-gig;** — *v.a.n.* foéner
Gigantic, *adj.* gigantesque, de géant
Gigantically, *adv.* gigantesquement, en géant
Giganto-graphy, -logy, -machy. *V.* p.3, § 1
Gigg, *s.* gigue, *f.* [étouffé, *m.*
Giggle, *v.n.* ricaner; — *s.* ricanement, rire
Giggler, *s.* ricaneur, *m.*, -euse, *f.*
Giggling, *adj.* ricaneur; — *s.* *V.* **Giggle,** *s.*
Gild, — over, *v.a.* dorer; (*fig.*) colorer; — *v.n.* se dorer
Gilder, *s.* doreur, *m.*, -euse, *f.*; (*coin*) *V.* **Guilder**
Gilding, *s.* dorure, *f.*; (*fig.*) dehors trompeurs, *m pl.*
Gill, *s.* (*of fishes*) ouïe, branchie, *f.*; (*of cocks*, &c.) *V.* **Wattle;** (*meas: pop.*) canon, *m.*, (*nav.*) boujarron, *m.*; (*vehicle*) éfourceau, fardier, diable, *m.*; (*bot.*) lierre terrestre, *m.*
Gilliflower, Gillyflower, *s.* giroflée *f.*
Gilt, *part. adj.* doré; (*fig.*) coloré; — *s.* dorure, *f.*; (*fig.*) éclat, *m.*; profit, *m.* — **edged,** (*with*) — **edges,** *adj.* doré sur tranche. — **head,** *s.* (*fish*) daurade, aurade, *f.* — **jeweller,** *s* [bijoutier en doré, *m.*
Gim, *adj.* pimpant
Gimbal, *s.* balancier (de boussole), *m.*
Gimblet. *V.* **Gimlet**
Gimcrack, *s.* patraque, *f.*; quincaille, *f.*; machine grossière, *f.*; (*nicknack*) bibelot, *m.*; — *adj.* mauvais, délabré, décrépit, usé
Gimlet, *s.* vrille, *f.*; — *v.a.* perforer; (*nav.*) cabaner [*f.*; lézarde, *f.*
Gimp, *s.* brandebourg, *m.*; ganse, *f.*; guipure,
Gin, *s.* machine, *f.*, engin, *m.*; (*snare*) trébuchet, *m.*; (*cylinder*) cylindre, *m.*, trappe, *f.*; (*tech.*) chèvre, *f.*; (*for cotton*) machine à égrener, égreneuse, *f.*; (*liquor*) genièvre, *m.*; — *v.a.* prendre au trébuchet; (*cotton*) égrener. — **palace, -shop,** *s.* débit de genièvre, débit de spiritueux, cabaret, *m.*

Ginger, *s.* gingembre, *m.* — **beer,** *s.* (*English liquor*) ginger-beer, *m.* — **bread,** *s.* pain d'épice, *m.* — **bread nut,** *s.* rond de pain d'épice, *m.*; nonnette, *f.*
Gingerly, *adv.* doucement; en tâtonnant
Gingerness, *s.* douceur, délicatesse, précau- [tion, *f.*
Gingery, *adj.* (*jest.*) blond hasardé
Gingham, *s.* guingamp, guingan, *m.*
Gingival, *adj.* gingival
Gingko, Ginko, *s.* gingko, *m.*
Gingle. *V.* **Jingle**
Ginning, *s.* égrenage, *m.*
Ginseng, *s.* ginseng, *m.*
Gipsy, &c. *V.* **Gypsy,** &c.
Giraffe, *s.* girafe, *f.*
Girandole, *s.* girandole, *f.*
Girasol, *s.* girasol, *m.*
Gird, *v.a.* ('*with*,' de) ceindre; entourer; environner; (*put on*) mettre, se revêtir de; (*clothe*) vêtir; (*bind*) lier; (*horses*, &c.) sangler
Girder, *s.* longrine, traverse, solive, *f.*
Girdle, *s.* ceinture, *f*; ceinturon, *f.*; (*jewel.*) guirlande, *f.*; — *v.a.* *V.* **Gird.** — **belt,** *s.* ceinturon, *m.* — **maker,** *s.* ceinturier, *m.*
Girkin. *V.* **Gherkin**
Girl, *s.* fille, *f.*; enfant, *f.*; jeune fille, jeune personne, demoiselle, *f.*; (*pupil at school*) élève, *f.*; (*servant*) *V.* **Servant.** *Good* —, bonne fille, enfant sage, *f.* *Mere* —, enfant, *f.* *Old* —! vieille! ma vieille! *Servant* —, *V.* **Servant.** — **like,** *adj. adv.* *V.* **Girlish, -ly**
Girlhood, *s.* enfance, *f.*; jeunesse, *f.*; adolescence, *f.*
Girlish, *adj.* de jeune fille, d'enfant, enfantin, d'enfance, comme une enfant, en enfant
Girlishly, *adv.* en jeune fille, comme une jeune fille, en enfant, comme une enfant, d'une manière enfantine
Girlishness, Girlism, *s.* caractère de jeune fille, *m.*; enfantillage, *m*, puérilité, *f.*
Gironde, *s.* Gironde, *f.*
Girondist, *s. adj.* Girondin, *m.*, e, *f.*
Girt, Girth, *s.* ceinture, *f.*; enceinte, *f.*; contour, tour, pourtour, *m.*, circonférence, *f.*; (*of saddles*) sangle, *f*; (*mach.*) courroie, *f.*; (*arch.*) bandelette, *f.*; — *v.a.* *V.* **Gird.** — **strap,** *s.* contre-sanglon, *m.*
Gist, *s.* fin mot, *m.*; fin, *m.*; point principal, *m.*; fond, *m.*, substance, *f.*; essentiel, *m.*
Give, *v.a.n.* donner (à); (*render*) rendre (à); (*an account*, compte) rendre; (*an account*, récit, rapport, description) faire; (*an account*, des nouvelles) donner; (*return*) rendre; (*transmit*) remettre (à); (*allow*) permettre (à), laisser (à); (*abandon*) abandonner (à), livrer (à); (*consider*) considérer, regarder; (*apply*) appliquer (à); (*show*) montrer (à); (*an ear*) prêter (l'oreille); (*pleasure, pain, place, an affront, credit, heed, o.'s compliments, regards, a call*, &c.) faire; (*a message*) *V.* **Deliver;** (*offer*) offrir; (*serve*) servir; (*utter*) prononcer; (*a shriek*, &c.) jeter, pousser; (*a sigh, groan*) pousser; (*a sound*) rendre (un son); (*a knock*) frapper; (*a stroke, of clocks*) sonner; (*a blow*) donner; porter; (*healths*) porter; (*damages*) adjuger; (*yield*) céder; plier; fléchir; (*sink*) s'affaisser; (*stretch*) prêter; (*relax*) se relâcher, se ralentir; (*of the weather*) se détendre, se relâcher, s'adoucir; (*of the frost itself*) être moins fort; (*of sores*) suppurer. *To — battle*, livrer *or* donner bataille. *To — o.'s mind to*, appliquer son esprit à, s'appliquer à. *To — oneself to*, s'adonner à, se livrer à. *To be given to*, être adonné à; être porté à, être enclin à. *To — it to*, en donner à; taper sur; arranger; relancer; donner à ... son paquet. — *and take*, donnant donnant. — **again,** redonner (à), donner de nouveau; rendre (à). — **away,** donner; abandonner; (*from*) enlever (de). — **back,** *v.a.* rendre (à); *v.n.* reculer, se retirer. — **forth,** énoncer; émettre; publier, annoncer; répandre. — **in,** donner (à), livrer (à); déposer; (*account*.)

rendre; (*a sentence*, &c.) prononcer, rendre; (*into the bargain*) donner par-dessus le marché; (*sink*) s'affaisser; (*yield, submit*) céder, plier; se rendre; (*adopt*) donner dans, embrasser, adopter. — **off,** cesser, se désister. — **out,** publier, annoncer, répandre; dire; émettre; avancer; donner à entendre, faire entendre; établir, poser; montrer, affecter; distribuer, donner; (*v.n.*) s'affaisser; plier; (*stretch*) prêter. *To — oneself out for*, se donner pour; se dire; se faire passer pour. — **over,** cesser; finir; renoncer à; livrer; abandonner; laisser; désespérer de; (*a patient*) condamner, abandonner; (*law*) céder. — **up,** renoncer à; rendre; abandonner; laisser là, quitter; livrer; céder; remettre; (*a patient*) condamner; (*for*) considérer (comme), croire. — *oneself* **up,** se rendre; se constituer prisonnier. — *oneself* **up to**, se livrer à, s'adonner à; se consacrer à

Given, *part. adj.* donné, &c. (*V.* **Give**); fixé; déterminé; convenu; (*inclined*) enclin (à), porté (à), adonné (à), sujet (à)

Giver, *s.* donneur, *m.*, -euse, *f.*; donateur, *m.*, -trice, *f.*; dispensateur, *m.*, -trice, *f.*

Giving, *s.* don, *m.*; (*of a judgment or sentence*) prononciation, *f.*, prononcé, *m.*; (*of the weather*) relâchement, adoucissement, *m.* — **out,** *s.* allégation, *f.*, dire, *m.*; annonce, *f.*; distribution, *f.* — **way,** *s.* chute, *f.*; relâchement, *m.*

Gizzard, *s.* gésier, *m.*; (*pers.*) cœur, *m.*; fressure, *f.* *That sticks in his —*, cela lui tient au [cœur

Glabrous, *adj.* glabre

Glacial, *adj.* glacial

Glacialist, *s.* glaciairiste, *m.*

Glaciation, *s.* glaciation, *f.*

Glacier, *s.* glacier, *m.*

Glacis, *s.* glacis, *m.*

Glad, *adj.* aise (de), bien aise ('*of*,' '*to*,' de; '*that*,' que, *with the subj.*); content (de, que), charmé (de, que), joyeux (de, que), heureux (de), ravi (de, que); (*things*) agréable, joyeux

Gladden, *v.a.* réjouir, récréer, égayer; rendre heureux; — *v.n.* se réjouir (de)

Glade, *s.* clairière, percée, *f.*; allée, *f.* — **net,** [*s.* hallier, *m.*

Gladiate, *adj.* gladié

Gladiator, *s.* gladiateur, *m.* [*adj.* gladiatoire

Gladiatorial, Gladiatorian, Gladiatory,

Gladiole, Gladiolus, *s.* glaïeul, *m.*

Gladly, *adv.* avec joie, avec plaisir, volontiers

Gladness, *s.* joie, *f*, plaisir, *m.*

Gladsome, *adj.* joyeux, gai

Gladsomely, *adv.* joyeusement, gaiment

Gladsomeness, *s.* joie, *f.*

Glair, Glaire, *s.* glaire, *m.*; — *v.a.* glairer

Glaireous, *adj.* glaireux

Glairine, *s.* glairine, *f.*

Glairing, *s.* glairage, *m.*; —**s,** *pl.* glairure, *f.*

Glairy, *adj.* glaireux

Glamour, *s.* charme, *m.*, fascination, *f.*

Glance, *s.* regard, coup d'œil, *m.*; œillade, *f.*; (*of light*) éclair, trait de lumière, *m.*; — *v.n.* jeter (*or* lancer) un regard *or* un coup d'œil; jeter les yeux (sur); (*ogle*) lancer des œillades; (*shine*) étinceler, briller; (*pass*) passer rapidement, passer; (*over*) parcourir; effleurer; (*off*) glisser, dévier; — *v.a.* lancer, jeter. *At a —*, d'un regard, d'un coup d'œil. — **coal,** *s.* anthracite, *m.*

Glancing, *s.* éclat, *m.*; déviation, *f.*; regard, coup d'œil, *m.*; œillade, *f.*; examen rapide, léger aperçu, *m.* [passant

Glancingly, *adv.* légèrement, rapidement, en

Gland, *s.* glande, *f.*

Glandered, *adj.* atteint de la morve, morveux, glandé, farcineux. *To become —*, se glander

Glanders, *s. pl.* morve, gourme, *f.*, farcin, *m.*

Glandiferous, *adj.* glandifère

Glandiform, *adj.* glandiforme

Glandivorous, *adj.* glandivore

Glandular, *adj.* glandulaire

Glandule, *s.* glandule, *f.*

Glanduliferous, *adj.* glandulifère

Glanduliform, *adj.* glanduliforme

Glandulous, *adj.* glanduleux

Glare, *s.* lumière éblouissante, *f.*; clarté, *f.*; vif éclat, éclat, *m.*; (*look*) regard fixe et prolongé, regard féroce *or* terrible, regard enflammé, regard, *m.*; — *v.n.* éblouir, jeter une lumière éblouissante; briller; être éclairé (par); regarder fixement, regarder d'un air féroce, lancer des regards enflammés

Glaring, *adj.* éblouissant; éclatant; brillant; étincelant; tranchant; manifeste, patent; notoire; choquant; — *s.* vif éclat, *m.*, lumière éblouissante, *f.*

Glaringly, *adv.* manifestement, ouvertement

Glass, *s.* verre, *m.*; (*— goods*) verreries, *f.pl.*; (*of windows*, &c.) vitre, *f.*; glace, *f.*, miroir, *m.*; télescope, *m.*, longue-vue, lunette d'approche, *f.*; baromètre, *m.*; thermomètre, *m.*; microscope, *m.*; (*sand-glass, hour-glass*) sablier, *m.*; (*eye —*) lorgnon, *m.*; (*of a carriage*) glace, *f.*; (*of a watch, and for drinking*) verre, *m.*; (*time of life*) heures, *f.pl.*; —**es,** *pl.* (*spectacles*) lunettes, *f.pl.*; — *adj.* de verre; en verre. — ! —, *with care!* (*on packages*) fragile. *A — of brandy*, un verre d'eau-de-vie, *m.* *A* (*small*) *— of brandy*, (*in taverns*) un petit verre, *m.* *Cut —*, cristal, cristal taillé, *m.* — **basket,** *s.* verrier, *m.* — **bead,** *s.* grain de verre, *m.* — **beads,** *s. pl.* grains de verre, *m.pl.*, rassade, verroterie, *f.* — **bell,** *s.* cloche de verre, cloche, *f.* — **bender,** *s.* bombeur de verre, *m.* — **bending,** *s.* bombage du verre, *m.* — **blower,** *s.* verrier, *m.*; (*tech.*) souffleur (de verre), *m.* — **blowing,** *s.* soufflage du verre, *m.* — **bottle,** *s.* bouteille de verre, *f.* — **bowl,** *s.* bocal, *m.* — **case,** *s.* vitrine, *f.*, verre, *m.*; (*of shops*) montre, vitrine, *f.* [*in a — case*, sous verre]. — **crab,** *s.* phyllosome, *m.* — **cutter,** *s.* cristallier, *m.* — **door,** *s.* porte vitrée, *f.* — **drop,** *s.* larme batavique, *f.* — **engraver,** *s.* graveur sur verres *or* sur cristaux, *m.* — **eye,** *s.* œil de verre, *m.*; (*vet.*) œil vairon, *m.* — **founder,** *s.* verrier, *m.* — **frame,** *s.* (*hort.*) châssis de couches, châssis, *m.*; (*for show*) case de verre, *f.*, verre, *m.* — **ful (A),** *s.* un verre plein, plein un verre, verre, *m.* — **furnace,** *s.* four de verrerie, *m.* — **gall,** *s.* fiel de verre, *m.* — **grinder,** *s.* polisseur de verre *or* de glaces, *m.* — **grinding,** *s.* polissage de verre *or* de glaces, *m.* — **harmonicon,** *s.* verrillon, *m.* — **holder,** *s.* (*of a carriage-window*) bricole, *f.* — **house,** *s.* maison de verre, *f.*; (*greenhouse*) serre, *f.*; (*manu.*) verrerie, *f.* — **like,** *adj.* semblable au verre, de verre; transparent; fragile. — **maker,** -**manufacturer,** -**man,** *s.* verrier, *m.* — **making,** -**manufacture,** *s.* verrerie, *f.* — **metal,** *s.* verre en fusion, *m.* — **painter,** *s.* peintre sur verre, *m.* — **painting,** *s.* peinture sur verre, *f.* — **paper,** *s.* papier de verre, *m.* — **partition,** *s.* vitrage, *m.* — **shade,** *s.* cylindre, verre, globe de verre, globe, *m.* — **shop,** *s.* boutique de verrerie *f.* — **snake,** *s.* ophisaure, serpent de verre, *m.* — **stand,** *s.* verrier, *m.* — **string,** *s. V.* — **holder.** — **tear,** *s.* larme batavique, *f.* — **trade,** *s.* commerce de verrerie, *m.*, verrerie, *f.* — **tub,** *s.* verrière, *f.* — **ware,** *s.* verrerie, *f.*, cristaux, *m.pl.*; (*small*) verroterie, *f.* — **windows,** *s. pl.* *V.* **Window.** — **work,** *s.*, -**works,** *s. pl.* verrerie, *f.* — **worker,** *s.* verrier, *m.* — **wort,** *s.* salicorne, *f.*; soude, *f.*

Glassiness, *s.* nature vitreuse, *f.*; surface polie, *f.*, poli, *m.* [limpide; uni, lisse, poli

Glassy, *adj.* vitreux; fragile; transparent,

Glaucoma, *s.* glaucome, *m.*

Glaucous, *adj.* glauque

Glaze, *v.a.* vitrer; garnir de glaces; (*to cover*) mettre sous verre; (*to varnish*) vernir; vernisser; (*silk, gloves, paper, meat*) glacer; (*stuffs*) lustrer; (*meat-pies, cakes*) dorer; (*fruit-*

tarts) glacer; (paint.) glacer; (to adorn) orner; enjoliver; rendre brillant; — s. vernis, m.; glacé, m.; surface polie, f., poli, m.

Glazer, s. glaceur, m., -euse, f.; vernisseur, m.; (of stuffs) lustreur, m., -euse, f.

Glazier, s. vitrier, m. —'s work, vitrerie, f.

Glazing, s. vitrage, m.; vitrerie, f.; vernissage, m.; vernissure, f.; vernis, m.; (of silks, gloves, paper, meat) glaçage, m., glaçure, f., glacé, m.; (of stuffs) lustrage, lustre, m.; (of meat-pies, cakes) dorage, m., dorure, f.; (of fruit-tarts) glaçage, m., glaçure, f.; (gravy or jelly for glazing meat; sugar, &c., for glazing fruit-tarts) glace, f.; (paint.) glacis, m. — **brush,** s. (for pies, &c.) doroir, m. — **stick,** s. astic, m.

Gleam, s. rayon de lumière, rayon, m.; trait de lumière, m.; (light) lueur, f.; — v.n. rayonner; jeter une lueur; luire; briller

Gleaming, adj. rayonnant, lumineux, brillant, étincelant, éclatant; — s. rayonnement, trait de lumière, m., lueur, f.

Gleamy, adj. V. **Gleaming,** adj.

Glean, v.a.n. glaner; (of grapes) grappiller; (fig.) glaner, recueillir, ramasser; — s. glane, f.

Gleaner, s. glaneur, m., -euse, f.; (of grapes) grappilleur, m., -euse, f.

Gleaning, s. glanage, m.; glane, f.; glanure, f.; (of grapes) grappillage, m.; (collection) recueil, m.; —**s,** pl. glane, glanure, f., glanes, f.pl.

Glebe, s. glèbe, f.; terre, f., sol, m.; terre d'église, f.; motte de terre, f. — **land,** s. terre dépendant de la cure, f.

Glebous, Gleby, adj. plein de mottes

Glee, s. joie, gaîté, f.; (mus.) chanson à plusieurs voix, f., morceau d'ensemble, m.

Gleeful, adj. joyeux, gai

Gleefully, adv. joyeusement, gaiment

Gleet, s. écoulement, m.; goutte militaire, f.; [— v.n. couler

Gleety, adj. ichoreux, sanieux

Glen, s. vallon, m., vallée, f. — ..., val de ..., m.

Glib, adj. glissant; coulant; (of the tongue) délié; — v.a. rendre glissant; rendre coulant; (the tongue) délier. — **tongued,** adj. à langue déliée

Glibly, adv. d'une manière glissante; doucement; coulamment; avec facilité; avec volubilité

Glibness, s. surface glissante, f.; (of the [tongue) volubilité, f.

Glide, v.n. glisser; (flow) couler; (slip in) se glisser; — s. glissement, m. — **away,** s'écouler. — **through,** (cut) fendre

Glidingly, adv. d'une manière glissante; coulamment; doucement

Glim, s. lumière, f.

Glimmer, v.n. entreluire, jeter une faible lueur; briller; (of daybreak) poindre; — s. faible lueur, lueur faible, lueur, f., faible éclat, m.; (min.) mica, m.

Glimmering, s. faible lueur, lueur, f.; légère apparence, f.; — adj. faible

Glimpse, s. trait, m., lueur, f.; rayon, m.; coup d'œil, m.; légère idée, f., aperçu, m.; légère apparence, teinte, f.; éclaircissement, m.; signe, m., marque, f.; (of resemblance) reflet, m.; — v.n. jeter une lueur passagère. To catch or get or have a — of, entrevoir. To have had a — of, n'avoir fait qu'entrevoir

Glint. V. **Glance**

Glisten, Glister, v.n. étinceler, briller, luire, reluire, scintiller, rayonner

Glitter, v.n. briller, reluire, étinceler; — s. éclat, brillant, lustre, m.; (in contempt) clinquant, m. All that —s is not gold, tout ce qui reluit n'est pas or

Glittering, part. adj. brillant, étincelant, éclatant; — s. V. **Glitter,** s.

Glitteringly, adv. avec éclat

Gloat, v.n. — **over, on, upon,** couver des yeux, dévorer des yeux; repaître ses yeux de; (fig.) se réjouir de, triompher de

Globard, s. lampyre, ver luisant, m.

Globate, Globated, adj. en globe, globeux, sphérique

Globe, s. globe, m.; sphère, f.; (pers.) cercle, m.; (of glass, for fish, &c.) bocal, m.; (for lamps) globe, m.; — v.a. mettre en globe; (pers.) réunir en cercle. Use of the —s, étude de la sphère, f., usage des globes, m. — **amaranth,** s. amarantine, gomphrène, f. — **fish,** s. diodon, m. — **flower,** s. trolle, m. — **shaped,** adj. en forme de globe, en globe, sphérique. — **thistle,** s. échinope, m.

Globose, Globous, adj. globeux, sphérique

Globosity, s. sphéricité, f.

Globular, Globulous, adj. globulaire, [globuleux, sphérique

Globule, s. globule, m.

Gloom, Gloominess, s. obscurité, f., ténèbres, f.pl.; (sadness) air sombre, m.; tristesse, mélancolie, f.; sentiment or voile de tristesse, m.; — v.a. obscurcir, assombrir; attrister; — v.n. s'obscurcir, s'assombrir; être sombre, avoir l'air sombre; s'attrister, être mélancolique. To throw a — over, assombrir, attrister, jeter un voile de tristesse sur

Gloomily, adv. obscurément; avec tristesse, tristement; d'un air sombre

Gloomy, s. obscur; sombre; lugubre; triste, mélancolique. To be —, (of the weather) faire [un temps sombre

Glorifiable, adj. glorifiable

Glorification, s. glorification, f.

Glorify, v.a. glorifier; célébrer, exalter, louer

Glorious, adj. glorieux; beau, magnifique; admirable

Gloriously, adv. glorieusement, avec gloire; magnifiquement; admirablement

Glory, s. gloire, f.; — v.n. se glorifier (de), se [faire gloire (de)

Glose. V. **Gloze**

Gloss, s. (of stuffs) lustre, luisant, apprêt, m.; (fig.) vernis, éclat, lustre, apprêt, m.; palliation, f., déguisement, m.; (comment) glose, f., commentaire, m.; — v.a.n. (stuffs) lustrer, apprêter; (fig.) donner de l'éclat à, donner du lustre à; colorer, donner un vernis à, déguiser; (explain) gloser, commenter. — **over,** v.a. colorer; masquer; déguiser; pallier

Glossarial, adj. de glose, explicatif; de glos-[saire

Glossarist, s. glossateur, m.; commentateur, m.

Glossary, s. glossaire, m.

Glossator, Glosser, s. glossateur, m.; commentateur, m.; (of stuffs, &c.) apprêteur, m.; vernisseur, m.

Glossiness, s. lustre, apprêt, luisant, m.

Glossitis, s. glossite, f.

Glossographer, s. glossographe, m.

Glossograph-ic, al, -y. V. page 3, § 1

Glossolog-ic, al, -y. V. page 3, § 1

Glossologist, s. glossologue, m.

Glossy, adj. luisant, poli; (of stuffs) lustré; [(fig.) poli

Glottis, s. glotte, f.

Glove, s. gant, m.; — v.a. ganter. — **maker,** s. gantier, m., -ière, f. — **making,** s. ganterie, f. — **stretchers,** s. pl. baguettes à gants, f.pl. — **shop, -trade, -warehouse,** s. gan-[terie, f.

Glover, s. gantier, m., -ière, f.

Glow, v.n. briller; (burn) brûler; (get animated) s'animer; s'échauffer; s'enflammer, s'embraser; — v.a. brûler; — s. éclat, m.; (heat) chaleur, f.; ardeur, f., feu, m.; (redness) rouge, m. — of heat, chaleur, f. To be in a —, avoir chaud; être embrasé. To set in a —, donner de la chaleur; échauffer; allumer; enflammer; embraser; transporter. — **worm,** s. ver luisant, lampyre, m.

Glowing, adj. brillant, éclatant; brûlant; ardent; chaleureux; animé; (red) rouge

Glowingly, adv. avec éclat; avec chaleur, chaleureusement, avec feu; passionnément; vivement [V. **Gloss**

Gloze, v.n.a. flatter, cajoler, caresser; (gloss)

Glozer, s. flatteur, m., -euse, f., cajoleur, m., -euse, f.

Glozing, adj. flatteur, cajoleur; — s. flatt

Glucose, s. glucose, f.

Glue, *s.* colle forte, colle, *f.*; (*bot.*, *nav.*) glu, *f.*; — *v.a.* coller; (*to tie*) attacher
Gluer, *s.* colleur, *m.*
Gluey, *adj.* gluant, collant, visqueux, glutineux
Glueyness, *s.* viscosité, *f.*
Glum, *adj.* *V.* **Sullen**
Glume, *s.* (*bot.*) glume, balle, *f.*
Glut, *v.a.* gorger; rassasier; assouvir; repaître; dégoûter; encombrer; — *s.* surabondance, *f.*; excès, *m.*; rassasiement, *m*; assouvissement, *m.*; satiété, *f.*; encombrement, *m.*
Gluten, *s.* gluten, *m.*
Glutination, *s.* glutination, *f.*
Glutinative, *adj.* glutinatif, glutinant
Glutine, *s.* glutine, *f.*
Glutinosity, Glutinousness, *s.* glutinosité, *f.*
Glutinous, *adj.* glutineux
Glutton, *s.* glouton, *m.*, -ne, *f.*, gourmand, *m.*, e, *f.*; (*animal*) glouton, *m.*
Gluttonize, *v.n.* manger en glouton, manger avec excès, se livrer aux plaisirs de la table
Gluttonous, *adj.* glouton, gourmand
Gluttonously, *adv.* gloutonnement, avec gloutonnerie, en glouton
Gluttony, *s.* gloutonnerie, gourmandise, *f.*; [(*med.*) boulimie, *f.*
Glycerine, *s.* glycérine, *f.*
Glyceric, *adj.* glycérique, glycérinien
Glycine, *s.* glycine, *f.*
Glycol, *s.* glycol, *m.*
Glycose, *s.* glycose, glucose, *f.*
Glycosuria, *s.* glycosurie, *f.*
Glyph, *s.* glyphe, *m.*
Glyptics, *s. pl.* glyptique, *f.*
Glypto-graphy, -logy. *V.* page 3, § 1
Gmelinia, *s.* gmelin, *m.*, gmelinie, *f.*
Gnarled, Gnarly, *adj.* noueux
Gnash, *v.a.* grincer; — *v.n.* grincer des dents
Gnashing, *s.* grincement, *m.*
Gnashingly, *adv.* en grinçant les (*or* des) dents
Gnat, *s.* cousin, moucheron, *m.* *To strain at the — and swallow the camel*, rejeter le moucheron et avaler le chameau. — **snapper,** *s.* gobe-moucherons, *m.* — **strainer,** *s.* personne vétilleuse *or* façonnière, *f.*, vétilleur, *m.*, -euse, *f.*
Gnaw, *v.a.n.* ronger; (*o.'s lips*) se mordre (les lèvres)
Gnawer, *s.* rongeur, *m.*, -euse, *f.*
Gnawing, *adj.* rongeur; — *s.* rongement, *m.*; (*fig.*) déchirement, *m.*; (*of the stomach*) tiraillement, *m.*; (*place gnawed*) rongeure, *f.*
Gneiss, *s.* gneiss, *m.*
Gnome, *s.* gnome, *m.*, gnomide, *f.*
Gnomic, -al, *adj.* gnomique
Gnomon, *s.* gnomon, *m.*
Gnomonic, -al, *adj.* gnomonique; **—s,** *s. pl.* [gnomonique, *f.*
Gnomonist, *s.* gnomoniste, *m.*
Gnost-ic, -icism. *V.* page 3, § 1
Gnu, *s.* (*zool.*) gnou, *m.*
Go, *v.n.a.* aller; se rendre; (*walk*) marcher; (*pass*) passer; (*depart*) partir; s'en aller; (*die*) mourir; (*accomplish, as a certain distance, a round, journey, trip, party*) faire; (*a certain way or road: take*) aller par, prendre, (*follow*) suivre; (*the chance*) tenter (l'aventure); (*escape*) échapper; (*of time*) passer, s'écouler; (*disappear*) disparaître; (*be*) être; (*be pregnant*) porter; (*be contained in*) tenir (dans); (*take a good, bad turn*) tourner; (*contribute*) contribuer (à); tendre (à); (*reckon*) compter; (*sell*) se vendre; (*set oneself*) se mettre. (*V.* **Going,** *and* **Gone**). *To be —ing*, aller, &c.; (*be dying*) se mourir. *To — and see, — and play, — and fetch* (or *get*), &c., aller voir, aller jouer, aller chercher, &c. *To — o.'s way*, passer son chemin. *How —es it?* comment cela va-t-il? *As times —*, par le temps qui court. *How —es the time?* quelle heure est-il? *Who —es there?* qui vive? qui va là? *— it!* en avant! tape dessus! allez donc! allez-y! marche! — **about,** aller çà et là, aller et venir, se promener; circuler; aller; courir; (*get out*) sortir; (*go round*) faire le tour (de); faire un détour; faire le tour; (*begin*) entreprendre, se mettre à; (*endeavour*) tâcher (de), chercher (à); (*meddle with*) se mêler (de); (*do*) faire; (*nav.*) virer de bord. — **about it,** (*to proceed*) y aller; s'y prendre. — **abroad,** se répandre; (*from home*) sortir; (*in foreign parts*) aller à l'étranger; voyager. — **across,** aller à travers; traverser. — **again,** retourner; aller de nouveau, aller encore. — **against,** aller contre; marcher contre; être contraire à, s'opposer à; répugner à; tourner contre. — **along,** passer *or* poursuivre son chemin; s'en aller; marcher; aller. — **along with,** aller avec; accompagner; suivre; (*be equal*) aller de pair avec; (*V.* **Along**). — **aside,** se mettre de côté; se retirer; s'écarter. — **astray,** s'égarer; (*fig.*) aller de travers; se déranger. — **asunder,** s'écarter (de), s'éloigner (de). — **at it,** y aller; s'y mettre. — **away,** s'en aller; partir; s'éloigner. — **away with,** enlever; emporter. — **back,** retourner; s'en retourner; (*move back*) reculer; rétrograder; s'éloigner; (*to the source*) remonter; (*to past times*) se reporter. — **back again,** retourner sur ses pas, retourner, rebrousser chemin. — **backward,** aller à reculons, aller en arrière; (*fig.*) reculer, rétrograder. — **backward and forward,** aller et venir. — **before,** aller *or* marcher devant; précéder; devancer. — **between,** aller entre; (*interpose*) s'entremettre, s'interposer, servir de médiateur entre. — **by,** aller par; passer; (*near*) passer auprès de; passer devant; (*of time*) passer, s'écouler; (*judge from*) juger d'après; s'en rapporter à; se guider sur; se régler sur; (*follow*) suivre; (*of names*) être connu sous (le nom de), prendre *or* porter (le nom de). *To — by steam*, marcher à la vapeur. — **down,** descendre; aller en bas; (*— from town*) aller; (*fall suddenly*) tomber; (*pass*) passer; (*decline*) baisser; (*decrease*) diminuer; (*of the wind, of the fire*) tomber; (*of the sun, moon*) se coucher; (*in water*, &c.) s'enfoncer; couler à fond, sombrer. — **down again,** redescendre; retomber. — **far,** aller loin; (*of eatables*) faire du profit, profiter; (*with a person*) faire un grand effet (sur); avoir grande influence (sur); être d'un grand poids (auprès de); (*contribute*) contribuer beaucoup (à). — **for,** aller pour; (*fetch*) aller chercher; (*a walk, a ride, a drive*, &c., *or a turn, a round*, &c.) aller faire; (*a bath*, &c.) aller prendre; (*be considered*) passer pour; compter pour, compter comme; (*be favourable*) être favorable à; (*be spent*) être dépensé en, passer à. — **forth,** avancer; sortir; paraître; se produire. — **forward,** avancer; marcher; (*be continued*) se poursuivre; (*take place*) se passer, se faire, avoir lieu. — **from,** quitter, abandonner, se séparer de; (*deviate*) s'écarter de; se départir de; s'éloigner de; (*o.'s word*) manquer à. — **in,** entrer; (*into a carriage*) monter; (*compete*) concourir. — **in again,** rentrer; se représenter; remonter. — **in for,** entrer pour; (*fetch*) entrer pour chercher, entrer pour prendre; (*fig.*) concourir pour; rechercher; proposer de, être d'avis que; se décider pour; être pour; (*to attempt*) essayer, tenter. — **in and out,** entrer et sortir; aller et venir. — **near,** *V.* **Come near.** — **off,** partir; s'en aller; (*die*) mourir; passer; s'éteindre; (*of fire-arms*, &c.) partir; (*of beauty*, &c., *fade*) passer; (*of goods*) s'écouler, se vendre; (*happen, take place*) se passer. — **on,** aller en avant; avancer; aller; aller toujours; continuer; poursuivre, procéder; marcher, aller son train; (*be proceeded with*) se poursuivre; (*go beyond*) passer outre; (*to ..., with a verb*) ... ensuite; (*take place*) se passer; (*behave*) se comporter, se conduire; (*to quarrel*) tempêter; (*of clothes*) aller; (*of hats*) entrer. — **on with,** continuer, poursuivre; commencer,

procéder à. — **out,** sortir; (*abroad,* '*to,*' à, en) aller; s'en aller; (*out of a carriage*) descendre; (*against the enemy*) marcher, se mettre en campagne; (*of visits*) aller dans le monde; (*of fire, light,* &c.) s'éteindre. — **over,** passer sur; passer par-dessus; (*end*) passer; (*change sides*) passer (à); (*cross*) passer, traverser; (*peruse, and of distance*) parcourir; (*beyond a time*) passer; (*rehearse, review*) repasser; (*examine*) vérifier. — **past,** passer; passer devant *or* &c. (...) (*V.* **Past**). — **round,** *V.* **Round.** — **through,** passer à travers; passer par; passer; traverser; fendre; percer; parcourir; exécuter; faire; venir à bout de; achever; remplir; (*suffer, undergo*) essuyer, subir, éprouver, endurer, supporter, souffrir. — **through with,** venir à bout de, mener à bonne fin. — **to,** aller à *or* &c. (*V.* **To,** *prep.*); se rendre à; se diriger vers; s'avancer vers; s'approcher de; (*a person*) aller à; aller trouver; se rendre auprès de, se rendre chez, aller chez; (*to appeal*) en appeler (à); (*a certain price, put it in a purchase*) y mettre; *int.* va! allez! allons donc! — **under,** aller *or* passer sous; (*the name of*) être connu sous (le nom de), passer (pour), s'appeler (...). — **up,** monter; aller en haut; (*a river, and fig.*) remonter; (*rise*) s'élever; (*of prices*) hausser, monter; (*go away*) s'en aller; (— *to town*) aller; (*for exam.*) se présenter (à). — **up to,** (— *a person*) aller à; aller trouver; (*accost*) aborder. — **up and down,** monter et descendre; (*here and there*) courir de côté et d'autre, courir çà et là. — **upon,** aller sur, marcher sur; (*rely*) se fonder sur, compter sur. — **with,** aller avec; accompagner; suivre; (*yield*) se laisser aller à, aller au gré de; (*be pregnant*) porter. — **without,** aller sans; (*do without*) se passer de

Go, *s.* mode, vogue, *f.*; force, vigueur, *f.*; entrain, *m.*; brio, *m.*; utilité, *f.*; valeur, *f.*; (*sport*) jeu, *m.*; (*time*) coup, *m.*; (*glass*) verre de rogomme, *m.*, goutte, *f.* *Little* —, (*univers.*) examen préliminaire, *m.*; colle, *f.* *To be all the* —, faire fureur. *It is no* —, il n'y a pas mèche; cela ne sert à rien; cela ne vaut rien; ça ne va pas; ça ne prend pas. — **between,** *s.* médiateur, *m.*, -trice, *f.*; entremetteur, *m.*, -euse, *f.* — **by,** *s.* ruse, évasion, *f.*; omission, *f.* *To give the* — *by,* échapper à; faire faux bond à; écarter, mettre de côté. — **cart,** *s.* chariot d'enfant, *m.*, roulette, *f.*

Goad, *s.* aiguillon, *m.*; — *v.a.* aiguillonner, piquer; exciter, stimuler, pousser; (*of the conscience*) bourreler

Go-ahead, *adj.* entreprenant; (*bold*) hardi

Goal, *s.* (*of races,* &c.) but, *m.*; (*starting-place*) point de départ, *m.*; (*end*) but, terme, *m.*

Goat, *s.* (*he-*) bouc, *m.*; (*she-*) chèvre, *f.*; (*astr.*) Capricorne, *m.* *Young* —, chevreau, *m.* — **chafer,** *s.* capricorne, *m.* — **fig,** *s.* caprifiguier, *m.* — **footed,** *adj.* chèvre-pieds. — **herd, -keeper,** *s.* chevrier, *m.*, -ière, *f.* — **moth,** *s.* cosse, *m.* —**'s beard,** *s.* (*bot.*) salsifis, *m.*, barbe de bouc, *f.* —**'s hair,** *s.* poil de chèvre, *m.* — **skin,** *s.* *V.* —**'s skin.** —**'s milk,** *s.* lait de chèvre, *m.* —**s'-rue,** *s.* (*bot.*) galéga, *m.* —**'s skin,** *s.* peau de bouc, peau de chèvre, *f.*; (*bottle*) outre, *f.* — **sucker,** *s.* engoulevent, tette-chèvre, *m.* — **weed,** *s.* [capraire, *f.*

Goatish, *adj.* de bouc, de chèvre

Gob, *s.* bouchée, *f.*, morceau, gobet, *m.*; (*spittle*) glaviot, graillon, *m.*; — *v.a.* (— **up**) avaler goulument; — *v.n.* (*spit*) glaviotter, graillonner

Gobber, *s.* (*spitter*) glaviotteur, *m.*, -euse, *f.*, [graillonneur, *m.*, -euse, *f.*

Gobbet, *s.* gobet, *m.*

Gobble, *v.a.* (— **up** *or* **down**) gober, avaler goulument, avaler; — *v.n.* (*of turkeys*) glouglouter, glouglotter; — *s.* (*of turkeys*) glouglou, *m.*

Gobbler, *s.* gobeur, *m.*, -euse, *f.*, goulu, *m.*, e, *f.*, glouton, *m.*, -ne, *f.*; (*turkey*) dindon, pérot, *m.*

Goblet, *s.* gobelet, *m.*

Goblin, *s.* lutin, follet, gobelin, *m.*

Goby, *s.* (*fish*) gobie, *m.*

God, *s.* Dieu, *m.*; —**s,** *pl.* dieux, *m.pl.*; (*theat.*) paradis, *m.* — **child,** *s.* filleul, *m.*, e, *f.* — **daughter,** *s.* filleule, *f.* — **father,** *s.* parrain, *m.* — **head,** *s.* divinité, *f.* —**less,** *adj.* athée, impie; (*without God*) sans Dieu. —**lessly,** *adv.* irréligieusement. —**lessness,** *s.* impiété, irréligion, *f.* — **like,** *adj.* divin. —**lily,** *adv.* pieusement, dévotement. —**liness,** *s.* piété, dévotion, *f.* —**ly,** *adj.* pieux, dévot; de Dieu; *adv.* pieusement, dévotement. — **mother,** *s.* marraine, *f.* — **send,** *s.* bonne aubaine, *f.*; trouvaille, *f.* —**ship,** *s.* divinité, *f.* — **son,** *s.* filleul, *m.* — **wit,** *s.* barge, *f.*

Goddess, *s.* déesse, *f.*

Godroon, *s.* godron, *m.*; — *v.a.* godronner

Godrooner, *s.* godronneur, *m.*, -euse, *f.*

Godrooning, *s* godronnage, *m.*

Goer, *s.* marcheur, *m.*, -euse, *f.*; coureur, *m.*; allant, *m.* —*s and comers,* allants et venants, *m pl.*

Goffer. *V.* **Gauffer**

Goggle, *v.n.* rouler les yeux, faire de grands yeux; — *s.* roulement d'yeux, *m.*; —**s,** *s. pl.* lunettes mistraliennes, lunettes, *f.pl.*; (*against squinting*) lunettes à strabisme, louchettes, *f.pl.*; (*of saddles*) œillères, *f.pl.*; — *adj.* grand, gros, roulant, à fleur de tête. — **eye,** *s.* œil roulant, œil à fleur de tête, *m.* — **eyed,** *adj.* qui a de grands yeux roulants, qui a les yeux à fleur de tête

Going, *part. adj.* allant, qui va, &c. (*V.* **Go**); (*at auctions*) une fois, deux fois, trois fois! *To be* —, aller, &c. (*V.* **Go**); (*be dying*) être mourant; se mourir; mourir. *To set* —, *V.* **Set.** *I am* — *out,* je sors; (*presently*) je vais sortir. — **in,** *part. adj.* entrant, qui entre, &c. (*V.* **Go in**). — **out,** sortant, qui sort, &c. (*V.* **Go out**); &c. &c.

Going, *s.* allée, *f.*; marche, *f.*; départ, *m.*; (*proceeding*) démarche, *f.* — **back,** *s.* retour, *m.* — **backward and forward,** *s.* allées et venues, *f.pl.* — **down,** *s.* descente, *f.*; (*of the sun, moon*) coucher, *m.*; (*of waters*) baisse, *f.* — **forward,** *s* progrès, *m.* — **in,** *s.* entrée, *f.* — **out,** *s.* sortie, *f.*; (*of fire, light*) extinction, *f.*; (*expense*) dépense, *f.* — **in and out,** *s.* allées et venues, *f.pl.* — **up,** *s.* montée, *f.*; ascension, *f.*

Goitre, *s.* goître, *m.*

Goitrous, *adj.* goitreux

Gola, *s.* cymaise, *f.*

Gold, *s.* or, *m.*; — *adj.* d'or; en or. — **beater,** *s.* batteur d'or, *m.* — **beater's skin,** *s.* baudruche, *f.* — **beating,** *s.* battage de l'or, *m.* — **bound,** *adj.* entouré d'or. — **colour,** *s.* couleur d'or, *f.* — **cup,** *s.* (*bot.*) bouton d'or, bassinet, jaunet, *m.* — **digger,** *s.* chercheur d'or, *m.* — **drawer,** *s.* tireur d'or, *m.* — **dust,** *s.* poudre d'or, *f.* — **fields,** *s. pl.* *V.* **Diggings.** — **finch,** *s.* chardonneret, *m.* — **finder,** *s.* orpailleur, *m.*; (*nightman*) vidangeur, *m.* — **finer,** *s.* affineur d'or, *m.* — **finny,** *s.* crénilabre, *m.* — **fish,** *s.* poisson rouge, *m.*, dorade, *f.*, cyprin doré, *m.* — **hammer,** *s.* bruant, *m.* — **headed,** *adj.* à pomme d'or. — **hilted,** *adj.* à poignée d'or, à garde d'or. — **lace,** *s.* galon (*m.*) *or* broderie (*f.*) d'or. — **laced,** *adj.* bordé d'un galon d'or; brodé d'or. — **leaf,** *s.* feuille d'or, *f.*; or en feuilles, *m.* —**less,** *adj.* sans or. — **lettered,** *adj.* en lettres d'or. — **lettering,** *s.* lettres d'or, *f.pl.* — **mine,** *s.* mine d'or, *f.* — **mounted,** *adj.* monté en or. — **paint,** *s.* couleur d'or, *f.*; couleur de bronze, *f.* — *of* **pleasure,** *s.* (*bot.*) caméline, *f.* — **powder,** *s.* poudre d'or, *f.* — **proof,** *adj.* incorruptible. — **quartz,** *s.* quartz aurifère, *m.* — **ring,** *s.* bague d'or, bague en or, *f.* — **searcher, -seeker,** *s.* chercheur d'or, *m.*; orpailleur, *m.* — **seed,** *s.* cynosure, *f.* — **sinny,** *s.* crénilabre, *m.* — **size,** *s.* colle à brunir les dorures, batture, *f.* — **smith,** *s.* orfèvre, *m.* — *smith's art, trade, work,* orfèvrerie, *f.* — **thread,** *s.* fil d'or, or filé, *m.* — **watch,** *s.* montre d'or, montre en or, *f* — **weight,** *s.* pesant d'or, *m.* — **wire,** *s.* or trait, *m.* — **wire drawer,** *s.* tireur d'or, *m.* — **work,** *s.* orfèvrerie, *f.* — **worked,** *adj.* tissu d or; broché d'or. — **working,** *s.* orfèvrerie, *f.*

Golden, *adj.* d'or; (*fig.*) doré; précieux; heureux; excellent; (*chron.*) d'or. — **age,** *s.* âge d'or, *m.* — **cup,** *s.* (*bot.*) *V.* **Gold-cup.** — **eagle,** *s.* aigle royal, *m.* — **eye,** *s.* (*bird*) garrot, *m.* — **eye fly,** *s.* hémérobe, *m.* — **fleece,** *s.* toison d'or, *f.* — **mean,** *s.* juste milieu, *m.* — **number,** *s.* nombre d'or, *m.* — **oriole,** *s.* loriot d'Europe, *m.* — **pheasant,** *s.* faisan doré, *m.* — **plover,** *s.* pluvier doré, *m.* — **purple,** *s.* pourpre de Cassius, *m.* — **rule,** *s.* règle de trois, règle de proportion, *f.* — **tailed fly,** — **wasp,** *s.* guêpe dorée, chrysides, chrysis, *f.* — **wedding,** *s.* noces d'or, *f.pl.*, jubilé, *m.* [— **maker,** *s.* galochier, *m.*

Golosh, *s.* galoche, claque, *f.*; — *v a.* claquer.

Gome, *s.* cambouis. *m.*

Gomorrhean, *s. adj* Gomorrhéen, *m.*, -ne, *f.*

Gondola, *s.* gondole, *f.*

Gondolier, *s* gondolier, *m.*

Gone, *part. adj.* allé, parti, &c. (*V.* **Go**); (*of time*) passé; écoulé; (*advanced*) avancé; (*of things, no longer there*) disparu; ne ... plus là, n'y ... plus; (*dispelled*) évanoui; (*lost*) perdu; (*dead*) mort; (*drunk*) ivre; (*done away with*) aboli, supprimé; (*ended*) fini; (*worn out*) usé; (*exhausted*) épuisé; (*expended*) dépensé; (*of auction*) adjugé. *Far* —, avancé; (*nearly dead*) bas, près de mourir; (*tipsy*) pris de vin, lancé. — **bad,** gâté. — **by,** passé, écoulé. — **in,** entré, &c.; (*sent*) rendu. — **in years,** avancé en âge. — **out,** sorti, &c.; (*sent*) rendu. *To be* —, être allé *or* parti *or* &c.; n'exister plus; n'y être plus; avoir disparu. *It is — six,* il est six heures passées. *It is all* —, (*none is left*) il n'y en a plus. *It is nearly all* —, il n'y en a presque plus. *To be — only one moment,* ne faire qu'aller et venir

Gonfalon, *s.* gonfalon, *m.*

Gonfalonier, *s.* gonfalonier, *m.*

Gong, *s.* gong, *m.*

Goniometer, *s.* goniomètre, *m.*

Goniometry, *s.* goniométrie, *f.*

Gonorrhœa, *s.* gonorrhée, *f.*

Gonorrhœal, *adj.* gonorrhéique

Good, *adj.* bon; (*fine*) beau; (*honest*) de bien; sage, vertueux; (*fit*) favorable, convenable; propice; avantageux; (*well done or made*) bien fait; bien; (*safe*) sûr; (*solvent*) solide, solvable; (*valid*) valide, valable. *As* —, tout comme. *As — as,* aussi bon que; comme, autant que, presque. *For* —, *for — and all,* sérieusement, tout de bon, pour de bon; (*for ever*) pour toujours. — *and well,* c'est bon, bon, c'est bien, bien. — *for nothing,* bon à rien; mauvais. *Not — for much,* pas bon à grand'chose. — *man,* homme de bien, *m.*; brave homme, *m.*; (*husband*) mari, homme, *m.* *To be* —, (*of children*) être sage. *To be a — child,* être sage. *To be so — as to, V.* **Kind,** *adj.* *To be — for nothing,* (*useless*) n'être bon à rien; (*worthless*) ne valoir rien. *To hold* —, *V* **Hold.** *To make* —, suppléer à, compenser; tenir compte de; combler; couvrir; remplacer; rembourser; restituer, rendre; réparer; dédommager de, indemniser de; prouver; justifier; soutenir; appuyer; établir; exécuter, effectuer, opérer; accomplir, remplir; (*o.'s word*) tenir. *To stand* —, *V.* **Stand**

Good, *s.* (*reverse of evil or of harm*) bien, *m.*; avantage, *m.*; utilité, *f.*; (*reverse of bad, good things*) bon, *m.*; —**s,** *pl.* effets, biens, *m.pl.*; objets, *m.pl.*; (*com.*) marchandises, *f.pl.*; objets, *m.pl.*; articles, *m.pl.*; (*fabrics*) tissus, *m pl.* —*s and chattels,* biens et effets, *m.pl.* *For your* —, pour votre bien. *Stolen —s,* objets volés, *m pl.* *To be of no* —, (*of no use*) *V.* **Use.** *To come to no* —, n'aboutir à rien de bon. *To do* —, (*generally, act rightly*) faire le bien; (*in particular cases*) faire du bien. *To do no* —, ne faire aucun bien; (*nothing good*) ne faire rien de bon *or* rien qui vaille. *Much — may it do you!* grand bien vous fasse! *What — is it to say ...?* à quoi sert-il de dire ...? *What is the — of ...?* à quoi bon ...? *What is the — of that?* à quoi bon? *What — would that do you?* à quoi cela vous avancerait-il? —**s-carriage, -department,** *s.* roulage, *m.*; (*rail.*) messagerie, *f.* —**s-delivery,** *s.* factage, *m.* —**s-manager,** *s.* (*rail.*) chef du trafic, chef du service commercial, *m.* —**s-office,** *s.* (*rail.*) bureau de messagerie, *m.*; bureau de factage, *m.* —**s-station,** *s.* dépôt de marchandises, *m.*; (*rail.*) gare de marchandises. *f.* —**s-traffic,** *s.* roulage, *m.*; (*rail.*) transport des marchandises, trafic, *m.*; messagerie, *f.* —**s-train,** *s. V.* **Train.** —**s-truck, -van,** *s.* (*rail.*) wagon de marchandises, *m.* [bien. *Very* —! très bien!

Good, *adv.* très. bien; — *int.* bon! bien! c'est

Good-bye, *adv.* adieu! — *for the present,* au revoir. — *till this evening, to-morrow, Monday,* &c., à ce soir, à demain, à lundi, &c. *I won't say* —, sans adieu, *To say* or *bid* —, *V.* **Bid**

Goodies, *s pl.* nanan, *m.*

Goodish, *adj.* assez bon

Goodliness, *s.* beauté, grâce, *f.*

Goodly, *adj.* beau, gracieux; (*large*) bon, fort; [(*happy*) heureux

Goodman, *s. V* **Good,** *adj*

Goodness, *s.* bonne qualité, *f.*; (*kindness*) bonté ('*to,*' pour; '*to,*' *before a verb,* de), *f.*; bien, *m.* — *knows,* Dieu sait; en vérité. *For — sake,* pour Dieu. *My* —! mon Dieu! Dieu! *Thank* —, Dieu merci!

Goodwill, *s. V.* **Will**

Goosander, *s* harle, *m.*

Goose, *s.* oie, *f.*; (*pers.*) oie, *f.*, oison, nigaud, *m.*; (*of tailors*) carreau, *m.* *Green* —, oison, *m.* — **berry,** *s.* groseille à maquereau, groseille, *f.* — **berry bush** *or* **tree,** *s.* groseillier à maquereau, groseillier, *m.* — **berry wine,** *s.* vin de groseilles, *m.* — **flesh,** *s.* (*fig.*) chair de poule, *f.* — **foot,** *s.* (*bot.*) ansérine, patte d'oie, *f.* — **grass,** *s. V.* **Cleavers.** — **liver pie,** *s.* pâté de foie gras, *m.* — **quill,** *s.* plume d'oie, *f.* — **skin,** *s.* (*fig.*) chair de poule. *f* — **step,** *s.* cadence, *f.* — **wing,** *s.* (*nav.*) [point, *m.*

Goramy, *s.* gourami, gouramy, *m.*

Gordian, *adj.* gordien. — **knot,** *s.* nœud gordien, *m.*

Gore, *s.* sang, sang caillé, *m.*; (*need.*) pointe, *f.*; — *v.a.* piquer, percer, percer de coups de corne, corner, donner un coup de corne à, blesser avec les cornes

Gorge, *s.* gorge, *f.*, gosier, *m.*; (*feeling*) cœur, *m.*; (*arch. fort.*) gorge, *f.*; (*narrow passage*) gorge, *f.*; — *v.a.* gorger; (*swallow*) ingurgiter, avaler, gober; — *v.n.* se gorger (de), se repaître (de) [fique, splendide

Gorgeous, *adj.* somptueux, fastueux, magni-

Gorgeously, *adv.* somptueusement, fastueusement, magnifiquement, splendidement

Gorgeousness, *s.* somptuosité, faste, *m.*, magnificence, pompe, splendeur, *f.*, éclat, *m.*

Gorgerin, *s.* (*arch.*) gorgerin, *m.*

Gorget, *s.* (*mil.*) hausse-col, *m.*; (*of armour*) gorgerin, *m.*; (*surg.*) gorgeret, *m.*; (*lady's ruff*) [gorgerette, *f.*

Gorgon, *s.* Gorgone, *f.*

Gorgonia, *s.* gorgone, *f.*

Gorgonian, *adj.* de Gorgone

Gorilla, *s.* gorille, *m.*

Gormand, *s. adj.* gourmand, *m.*, e, *f.*

Gormandize, *v.n.* gourmander, goinfrer

Gormandizer, *s.* gourmand, *m.*, e, *f.*, goinfre, goulu, glouton, *m.* [gloutonnerie, *f.*

Gormandizing, *s.* gourmandise, goinfrerie,

Gorse, *s. V.* **Furze**

Gory, *adj.* sanglant, ensanglanté

Goshawk. *s.* autour, *m.*

Gosling, *s.* oison, *m.*
Gospel, *s.* Évangile, *m.* *To accept* or *take as* (or *for*) —, prendre pour parole d'évangile
Gossamer, *s.* (*threads*) fils de la Vierge, *m.pl.*, filandres, *f.pl.*; (*gauze*) gaze, *f.*; — *adj.* de gaze; (*fig.*) ténu, fin; léger; sans consistance
Gossamery, *adj.* filandreux; de gaze, &c. (*V.* **Gossamer,** *adj.*)
Gossip, *s.* commère, *f.*; causeur, *m.*, -euse, *f.*; (*talk*) bavardage, *m.*; commérage, *m.*; cancans, *m.pl.*; (*in a good sense*) causerie, *f.*, entretien, *m.*; — *v.n.* bavarder, commérer
Gossiping, *s.* commérage, bavardage, *m.*; [causerie, *f.*
Gossipred, *s.* compérage, *m.*
Goth, *s.* Goth, *m.*
Gothic, *adj. s.* gothique, *adj. m.f.*, *s.m.*
Gothicism, *s.* gothicité, *f.*
Gouge, *s.* gouge, *f.*; — *v.a.* (— **out**) gouger; (*fig.*, *of eyes*, &c.) arracher (en pressant en rond avec le doigt) [lard, eau blanche, *f.*
Goulard water *or* **lotion,** *s.* eau de Gou-
Gour, *s.* (*zool.*) gour, *m.*
Goura, *s.* goura, *m.*, colombi-galline, *f.*
Gourami, *s.* gourami, gouramy, *m.*
Gourd, *s.* gourde, calebasse, *f.* — **plant, -tree,** *s.* calebassier, *m.*
Gourdiness, *s.* enflure aux jambes, *f.*
Gourdy, *adj.* enflé aux jambes
Gourmand, &c. *V.* **Gormand,** &c.
Gout, *s.* goutte, *f.* — **swelled, -swollen,** *adj.* enflé par la goutte. — **weed, -wort,** *s.* égopode, *m.*, podagraire, *f.*
Goutiness, *s.* état goutteux, *m.*
Gouty, *adj.* goutteux
Govern, *v.a.n.* gouverner, régir; diriger; conduire. *To — oneself* or *o.'s temper*, avoir de l'empire sur soi-même, être maître de soi; se contenir [ciplinable
Governable, *adj.* gouvernable, docile, dis-
Governess, *s.* gouvernante, institutrice, *f.*; (*of schools*) maîtresse, *f.*; institutrice, sous-maîtresse, *f.* — **pupil,** *s.* élève-maîtresse, *f.*
Governing, *adj* gouvernant; dominant; régulateur
Government, *s.* gouvernement, *m.*; régime, *m.*; empire, *m.*; direction, *f.*; État, *m.*; (*of self*) empire (sur), *m.*; (*gram.*) régime, *m.* — **annuity,** *s.* rente sur l'État, *f.* — **house,** *s.* hôtel du gouverneur (*or* du gouvernement), gouvernement, *m.* — **securities,** *s. pl.* effets publics, *m.pl.*
Governmental, *adj.* gouvernemental
Governor, *s.* gouverneur, *m.*; (*polit.*) gouvernant, *m.*; (*of a prison*, &c.) directeur, *m.*; (*regulator, mach.*) régulateur, *m.*; (*employer, master*) patron, bourgeois, *m*; (*father*) papa, *m.*
Governorship, *s.* gouvernement, *m.*; direction, *f.*
Gown, *s.* robe, *f.*; (*for the night*) chemise, *f.* —**sman,** *s.* homme de robe, *m.*; étudiant, *m.* —**smen,** *s.pl.* gens de robe, *m.pl.*; étudiants, *m.pl.*
Gowned, *adj.* en robe, à robe
Grab, *v.a.*, — **at,** empoigner, saisir, se saisir de; agripper; attraper
Grabble, *v.n.* tâtonner
Grace, *s.* grâce, *f.*; (*title of archbishops*) grandeur, *f.*; (*of dukes, duchesses*) *V.* **Lord (my), Lordship (your), Lady (my), Ladyship (your);** (*before meal*) (le) bénédicité, *m.*; (*after meal*) (les) grâces, *f.pl.*; (*com.*) grâce, *f.*; (*mus.*) agrément, ornement, *m.*, fioriture, *f.*, fleuretis, *m.*; (*myth.*) Grâce, *f.*; — *v.a.* orner, embellir ('*with*,' de); faire l'ornement de, illustrer; favoriser, honorer ('*with*,' de); accorder ses grâces à. *With a bad* —, de mauvaise grâce. *With a good* —, de bonne grâce. — **cup,** *s.* dernière santé, *f.* —**ful,** *adj.* gracieux, plein de grâce, élégant. —**fully,** *adv.* gracieusement, avec grâce, élégamment. —**fulness,** *s.* grâce, *f.* —**less,** *adj.* sans grâce; disgracieux; pervers; méchant; dépravé, perdu. —**lessly,** *adv.* sans grâce, disgracieusement. —**lessness,** *s.* manque de grâce, *m.*; dérèglement, *m.* — **note,** *s.* note d'agrément, *f.*, ornement, *m.*, fioriture. *f.*, fleuretis, *m.*
Gracious, *adj.* gracieux; bienveillant; favorable, bon, propice; clément, miséricordieux; condescendant ('*to*,' pour, envers). — *goodness! Good —!* bonté divine! bonté du ciel!
Graciously, *adv.* gracieusement; avec bienveillance, avec bonté; favorablement; avec clémence, miséricordieusement; avec condescendance. *To be — pleased to* .... daigner ...
Graciousness, *s.* nature gracieuse, grâce, *f*; bonté, bienveillance, gracieuseté, *f.*; clémence, miséricorde, *f.*; condescendance, *f.*
Grackle, *s.* mainate, *m.*
Gradation, *s.* gradation, *f.*; degré, *m.*
Gradatory, *adj.* gradatif, progressif; par degrés
Grade, *s.* grade, *m.*; degré, *m.*; rang, *m.*
Gradient, *s.* pente, rampe, inclinaison, *f.*, plan incliné, *m.*
Gradual, *adj.* graduel; — *s.* graduel, *m.*
Graduale, *s.* graduel, *m.*
Graduality, *s.* gradualité, *f.*
Gradually, *adv.* graduellement, par degrés, peu à peu, progressivement
Graduate, *v.a.* graduer; — *v.n.* prendre ses grades; — *s.* gradué, *m.*, e, *f.*; diplômé, *m.*, e, *f.*
Graduated, *adj.* gradué; diplômé
Graduation, *s.* gradation, *f.*; (*division*) graduation, *f.*; (*univers.*) rang, *m.*
Graduator, *s.* graduateur, *m.*
Graft, *s.* greffe, ente, *f.*; — *v.a.n.* greffer, enter
Grafter, *s.* greffeur, *m.*
Grafting, *s.* greffe, *f.* — **knife,** *s.* greffoir, *m.*
Graian, *adj.* (*geog.*) grecques, *f.pl.*
Grain, *s.* grain, *m.*; (*seed*) graine, *f.*; (*corn*) grains, *m.pl.*, céréales, *f.pl.*; (*of wood*) fil, grain, *m.*; —**s,** *pl.* (*residuum*) marc, *m.*; (*of malt*) marc de drèche, *m.*, drèche, *f.*; — *v.a.* grener, greneter; (*leather*) greneler, grener; (*paint.*) peindre en décors. *Against the* —, (*of wood*) contre le fil, à contre-fil; (*fig.*) à contre-poil, à rebrousse-poil; à rebours; (*pers.*) à contre-cœur. *With the* —, (*of wood*) dans le sens du fil; (*fig.*) dans le sens du poil; (*pers.*) de bon cœur. — **eating,** *adj.* (*zool.*) granaire. — **tin,** *s.* étain en larmes, *m.*
Grained, *adj.* grenu, grené, grenelé; (*rough*) rude; (*of colours*) indélébile; (*paint.*) peint en décors; (*bot.*) granuleux; (*in compounds*) à grain ..., à ... grain, &c. *Coarse —, Fine —, V.* **Coarse** *and* **Fine**
Grainer, *s.* peintre décorateur, peintre en décors, peintre marbrier, marbrier, *m.*
Graining, *s.* grenure, *f.*; (*paint.*) peinture en décors, *f.*; marbrure, *f.*; (*fish*) *V.* **Dace.** — **tool,** *s.* grenetoir, *m.*; (*paint.*) peigne, *m.*
Grainy, *adj.* grenu
Grakle. *V.* **Grackle**
Grallæ, Gallatores, *s. pl.* échassiers, *m.pl.*
Gramercy, *int.* grand merci! [*f.pl.*
Graminaceæ, Gramineæ, *s.pl.* graminées,
Gramineal, Gramineous, *adj.* graminé
Graminivorous, *adj.* graminivore, herbivore
Grammar, *s.* grammaire, *f.*; — *adj.* de grammaire; grammatical; correct; (*adverb.*) grammaticalement, correctement. *That is bad* —, c'est incorrect. — **school,** *s.* collége, *m.*
Grammarian, *s.* grammairien, *m.*, -ne, *f.*
Grammatical, *adj.* grammatical; de grammaire
Grammatically, *adv.* grammaticalement
Grammaticalness, *s.* correction grammaticale, *f.*
Grammat-ist,-ologic,al,-ology. *V.* p. 3, § 1
Gramme, *s.* gramme, *m.*
Grampus, *s.* épaulard, *m.*
Granadilla, *s.* grenadille, *f.*
Granary, *s.* grenier, *m.*
Grand, *adj.* grand; magnifique, splendide, superbe, grandiose; (*of staircases*) d'honneur;

(*of titles*) grand; (*of relations: ascendants*) grand, (*descendants*) petit. — **almoner,** *s.* grand-aumônier, *m.* — **aunt,** *s.* grand' tante, *f.* — **child,** *s.* petit-fils, *m.*, petite-fille, *f.* — **children,** *s. pl.* petits-enfants, *m.pl.* *Great — children,* arrière-petits-enfants, *m.pl.* — **Cordon,** *s.* grand-cordon, *m.* — **Cross,** *s.* grand' croix, *f.*, (*knight*) *m.* — **daughter,** *s.* petite-fille, *f.* *Great — daughter,* arrière petite-fille, *f.* — **ducal,** *adj.* grand-ducal. — **duchess,** *s* grande-duchesse, *f.* — **duchy,** *s.* grand-duché, *m.* — **duke,** *s.* grand-duc, *m.* — **father, -sire,** *s.* grand-père, aïeul, *m.* *Great — father,* bisaïeul, *m.* *Great-great — father,* trisaïeul, *m.* — **guard,** *s.* grand' garde, *f.* — **jury,** *s.* *V.* **Jury.** — **mamma,** *s.* grand' maman, grand' mère, *f.* — **master,** *s.* grand-maître, *m.* — **mother,** *s.* grand' mère, aïeule, *f.* *Great — mother,* bisaïeule, *f.* *Great-great — mother,* trisaïeule, *f.* — **nephew,** *s.* petit-neveu, arrière-neveu, *m.* — **niece,** *s.* petite-nièce, arrière nièce, *f.* — **papa,** *s.* grand-papa, grand-père, *m.* — **sire,** *s.* *V.* — **father.** — **son,** *s.* petit-fils, *m.* *Great — son,* arrière-petit-fils, *m.* — **uncle,** *s.* grand-oncle, *m.* — **vizier,** *s.* grand-vizir, *m.* — **vi iership,** *s.* grand-vizirat, *m* [vieille femme, *f.*

Grandam, *s.* grand' mère, *f.*; (*old woman*)

Grandee, *s.* grand d'Espagne, grand, grand

Grandeeship, *s.* grandesse, *f.* [seigneur, *m.*

Grandesse, *s.* grandesse, *f.*, grands (d'Espagne), *m.pl.*

Grandeur, *s.* grandeur, *f.*; magnificence, pompe, *f.*, éclat, *m.*, splendeur, *f.*; grandiose, *m.*; élévation, *f.* [de langage, emphase, *f.*

Grandiloquence, *s.* grandiloquence, pompe

Grandiloquent *adj.* pompeux, emphatique

Grandly, *adv.* grandement, avec grandeur, avec pompe, avec magnificence, magnifiquement, splendidement

Grandness. *V.* **Grandeur**

Grange, *s.* ferme, métairie, *f.*

Granger, *s.* régisseur, intendant, *m.*

Graniferous, *adj.* granifère

Graniform, *adj.* graniforme

Granite, *s.* granit, *m.* — **like,** *adj.* granitellé

Granitel, *s.* granitelle, *m.*

Granitic, -al, *adj.* granitique

Granitous, *adj.* graniteux

Granivoræ, *s. pl.* granivores, *m.pl.*

Granivorous, *adj.* granivore

Granny, *s.* (*grandmamma*) bonne maman, *f.*; (*old woman*) vieille femme, vieille, *f.*

Grant, *v.a.* accorder (à); concéder (à); céder (à); octroyer (à); (*money*) allouer (à); (*a prayer*) exaucer; (*confess*) avouer, reconnaître, convenir de; (*suppose*) supposer; — *s.* concession, *f.*; octroi, *m.*; don, *m.*, faveur, grâce, *f.*; (*of money*) allocation, *f.*; (*subsidy*) subvention, *f.*; (*law*) cession, *f.* —*ed!* d'accord! soit! — *that, —ed that,* supposez que; admettant que. — *it be so,* supposez que cela soit. *God — !* Dieu veuille! *God — it!* Dieu le veuille! *To take for —ed,* prendre pour avéré; prendre *or* tenir pour dit; tenir pour fait; supposer; être persuadé *or* bien sûr, croire bien, croire

Grantable, *adj.* accordable; allouable

Grantee, *s.* concessionnaire, *m.f.*; (*law*) cessionnaire, *m.f.*

Granter, Grantor, *s.* concédant, *m.*, e, *f.*; cédant, *m.*, e, *f.*; donateur, *m.*, -trice, *f.*

Granular, *adj.* granulaire, granuleux

Granulate, *v.a.* grener; (*metals*) granuler; — *v.n.* se réduire en grains; se granuler

Granulated, *adj.* en grains; (*bot.*) grenu

Granulation, *s.* granulation, *f.*

Granule, *s.* granule, *m.*

Granuliform, *adj.* granuliforme

Granulosity, *s.* granulosité, *f.*

Granulous, *adj.* granuleux

Grape, *s.* raisin, *m.*; (*single berry*) grain de raisin, *m.*; (*of horses*) grappe, *f.*; **—s,** *pl.* raisin, *m.*; raisins, *m.pl.* *Bunch of —s,* grappe de raisin, *f.* *Cluster* (or *small bunch*) *of —s,* grappillon, *m.* *To glean —s,* grappiller. — **berry,** *s.* grain de raisin, *m.* — **gatherer,** *s.* vendangeur, *m.*, -euse, *f.* — **gathering,** *s.* vendange, *f.* — **gleaner,** *s.* grappilleur, *m.*, -euse, *f.* — **gleaning,** *s.* grappillage, *m.* — **hyacinth,** *s.* muscari, *m.* — **juice,** *s.* jus de la treille, *m.* — **shot,** *s.* mitraille, *f.* — **stalk,** *s.* râfle, *f.* — **stone,** *s.* pépin de raisin, *m.* — **sugar,** *s.* sucre de raisin, *m.*, glucose, *f.* — **tree,** *s.* raisinier, *m.* — **vine,** *s.* vigne cultivée, *f.* — **wine,** *s.* vin de raisin, vin, *m.* [animé

Graphic, -al, *adj* graphique; (*fig.*) pittoresque;

Graphically, *adv.* graphiquement; (*fig.*) pittoresquement, d'une manière pittoresque; avec beaucoup d'animation

Graphite, *s.* graphite, *m.*

Graphitic, *adj.* graphitique, graphiteux

Grapholite, *s.* grapholithe, *m.*

Graphometer, *s.* graphomètre, *m.*

Graphometric, -al, *adj.* graphométrique

Graphoscope, *s.* graphoscope, *m.*

Graphotype, *s.* graphotype, *m.* [raisin, *m.*

Grapiness, *s.* nature du raisin, *f.*; goût de

Grapnel, *s.* grappin, *m.*

Grapple, *v.a.* (*pers.*) saisir à bras-le-corps; (*things*) accrocher; (*nav.*) accrocher, jeter le grappin sur; grappiner; — *v.n.* en venir aux prises, être aux prises, combattre corps à corps; (*nav.*) en venir à l'abordage, se battre à l'abordage; (*struggle*) lutter ('*with,*' *a person,* avec; *a thing,* contre); (*with a subject*) manier, traiter; — *s.* étreinte, *f.*; combat corps à corps, *m.*, lutte, *f.*; (*hook*) grappin, *m.* — **plant,** *s.* nauclée, *m.*, nauclée, *f.* [grappin, *m.*

Grappling, *s.* *V.* **Grapple,** *s.* — **iron,** *s.*

Grapy, *adj.* de raisin; qui a un goût de raisin; en grappes, comme des grappes; (*full of grapes*) grappu

Grasp, *v.a.* saisir, se saisir de; empoigner; tenir; serrer; comprendre, embrasser; — *v.n.* tâcher de saisir, chercher à s'emparer (de); tâcher d'atteindre; tâcher de parvenir (à), aspirer (à); — *s.* prise, *f.*; étreinte, *f.*; (*strength of hand*) poigne, *f.*; (*power*) pouvoir, *m.*; (*hand*) main, *f.*; (*reach*) portée, atteinte, *f.* *Within o.'s —,* à sa portée; entre ses mains; en son pouvoir. *To loose o.'s —,* lâcher prise. — *all lose all,* (*Proverb*) qui trop embrasse mal étreint. — **all,** *s.* fesse-mathieu, *m.*, pingre, *m.*, pingresse, *f.* [vaste

Grasping, *adj.* avide, cupide; (*comprehensive*)

Graspingly, *adv.* avidement, cupidement

Graspingness, *s.* avidité, cupidité, *f.*

Grass, *s.* herbe, *f.*, gazon, *m.*; herbage, *m.*; verdure, *f.*; (*of horses*) vert, *m.*; (*asparagus*) asperges, *f.pl.*; **—es,** *s pl.* (*bot.*) graminées, *f.pl.*; — *v.a.* couvrir d'herbe *or* de gazon; (*bleach*) herber; — *v.n.* se couvrir d'herbe; produire de l'herbe. — *of Parnassus,* parnassie, *f.* *To turn* or *put* (*a horse*) *out to —,* mettre (un cheval) au vert. — **blade,** *s.* brin d'herbe, *m.* — **cloth,** *s.* grass-cloth, *m.* — **field,** *s.* pré, *m.*, prairie, *f.* — **green,** *adj.* vert comme l'herbe, vert pré (*m.*); *s.* vert d'herbe, vert pré, *m.* — **grown,** *adj.* herbu, couvert d'herbe. — **hopper,** *s.* sauterelle, *f.*; cigale, *f.* — **land,** *s.* prairie, *f.* **—less,** *adj.* sans herbe, sans verdure, dénué de verdure. — **moth,** *s.* crambe, crambé, *m.* — **mower,** *s.* faucheur, *m.*; (*machine*) faucheuse, *f.* — **plot,** *s.* boulingrin, *m.*, pelouse, *f.*, gazon, parterre de gazon, tapis vert, *m.* — **shed,** *s.* herbier, *m.* — **tree,** *s.* xanthorrhée, *f.* — **tribe,** *s.* graminées, *f.pl.* — **wrack,** *s.* zostère, *f.*, crin végétal, *m.* [herbu, *m.*

Grassiness, *s.* abondance d'herbe, *f.*; état

Grassy, *adj.* herbeux, herbu, couvert d'herbe; (*green*) vert comme l'herbe. — *turf,* gazon, *m.*

Grate, *s.* grille, *f.*, grillage, *m.*; (*hearth*) foyer, *m.*;

(*of rivers*) gril, *m.*; (*of ponds*) écrille, *f.*, grillage, *m* ; — *v.a.n.* (*enclose*) griller, grillager ; (*rub*) frotter, râper; (*bread*) chapeler; (*of the teeth*) crisser, grincer; (*the ear*) écorcher, déchirer; (*the heart*) déchirer; (*offend*) choquer, blesser, froisser, offenser; (*make resound*) faire résonner, faire crier, faire grincer; (*resound*) résonner, crier, grincer. — **maker,** *s.* grilletier, *m.* [able; délicieux, excellent

Grateful, *adj.* reconnaissant ('*for*,' de); agré-

Gratefully, *adv.* avec reconnaissance; agréablement [*f.*; (*pleasantness*) agrément, *m.*

Gratefulness, *s.* reconnaissance, gratitude,

Grater, *s.* râpe, *f.*

Graticulate, *v.a.* graticuler

Graticulation, *s.* graticulation, *f.*

Graticule, *s.* graticule, *f.*

Gratification, *s.* satisfaction, *f.*; plaisir, *m.*; agrément, *m.*; jouissance, *f.*

Gratify, *v.a.* satisfaire, contenter, faire plaisir à, charmer; flatter [teur

Gratifying, *adj.* satisfaisant; agréable; flat-

Grating, *s.* grille, *f.*, grillage, *m.*; (*nav.*) caillebotis, *m.*; (*rubbing*) frottement, *m.*; râpage, *m.*; (*of the teeth*) crissement, grincement, *m.*; (*sound*) grincement, *m.*; —**s,** *pl.* râpure, *f.*; (*of bread*) chapelure, *f.*; — *adj.* discordant, dur, rude; désagréable, choquant, blessant

Gratingly, *adv.* d'une manière discordante, durement, rudement; désagréablement, d'une manière désagréable *or* choquante *or* blessante

Gratis, *adv.* gratis, gratuitement

Gratitude, *s.* reconnaissance, gratitude, *f.*

Gratuitous, *adj.* gratuit

Gratuitously, *adv.* gratuitement

Gratuitousness, *s.* gratuité, *f.*

Gratuity, *s.* don gratuit, présent, *m.*; gratification, gracieuseté, *f.*; (*douceur*) pot-de-vin, *m.*; (*drink-money*) pourboire, *m.*

Gratulate, &c. *V.* **Congratulate,** &c.

Gravamen, *s.* plainte, *f.*, grief, *m.*; (*burden*) poids, *m.*

Grave, *s.* (*hole*) fosse, *f.*, (*slab or hole*) tombe, *f.*, (*memorial over the slab*) tombeau, *m.*; (*fig.*) tombeau, *m.* — **clothes,** *s.pl.* drap mortuaire, linceul, *m.* — **digger,** *s.* fossoyeur, *m.* — **digging,** *s.* fossoyage, *m.* —**less,** *adj.* sans sépulture, sans tombeau. — **stone,** *s.* pierre sépulcrale *or* tumulaire, pierre, tombe, *f.* — **yard,** *s.* cimetière, *m.* [(*gram., mus.*) grave

Grave, *adj.* grave, sérieux; (*not showy*) sévère;

Grave, *v.a.n.* graver; tailler, ciseler; sculpter; (*a ship*) espalmer

Gravel, *s.* gravier, *m.*; sable, *m.*; (*med., concretions*) gravelles, *f.pl.*, (*disease*) gravelle, *f.*; — *v.a.* graveler; sabler; (*stick in the sand*) enfoncer dans le sable, ensabler; (*offend,* &c.) offenser, piquer; embarrasser, vexer, inquiéter; — *v.n.* s'ensabler. — **pit,** *s.* sablière, sablonnière, *f.* — **walk,** *s.* allée sablée, *f.*

Gravelling, *s.* gravelage, *m.*; ensablement, *m.*

Gravelly, *adj.* graveleux, sablonneux

Gravely, *adv.* gravement; sérieusement; (*without show*) sévèrement

Graveness. *V.* **Gravity**

Graver, *s.* graveur, *m.*; sculpteur, ciseleur, *m.*; (*tool*) burin, *m.*, (*round*) échoppe, *f.*

Graves, *s. pl.* (*of tallow*) cretons, *m.pl.*; pains de cretons, *m.pl.*; (*pl. of* **Grave**) *V.* **Grave**

Gravid, *adj.* (*med.*) gravide

Gravidity, *s* grossesse, *f.*

Graving, *s.* gravure, *f.*; sculpture, ciselure, *f.*; empreinte, impression, *f.*; (*nav.*) œuvres de marée, *f.pl.* — **dock,** *s.* bassin de radoub, *m.* — **slip,** *s.* cale de radoub, *f.* — **tool,** *s.* burin, *m.*

Gravitate, *v.n.* graviter ('*to*,' '*towards*,' vers)

Gravitation, *s.* gravitation, *f.*

Gravity, *s.* gravité, *f.*, sérieux, *m.*; (*importance*) gravité, *f.*; (*weight*) poids, *m.*; (*phys.*) gravité, pesanteur, *f.*; (*of sound*) gravité, *f.* *Specific* —, poids spécifique, *m.*; pesanteur spécifique, *f.* *Centre of* —, centre de gravité, *m.*

Gravy, *s.* jus, *m.*; sauce, *f.* — **beef,** *s.* bœuf (*m.*) *or* viande (*f.*) pour faire du jus. — **soup,** *s.* consommé, *m.* — **spoon,** *s.* cuiller à ragoût, *f.*

Gray, *adj.* gris; (*old*) vieux; — *s.* gris, *m.* *Dappled* or *mottled* —, gris pommelé. *Oxford* —, marengo, *m.* *To grow* or *get* —, grisonner, blanchir. — **beard,** *s.* barbe grise, *f* ; vieillard, *m.*; (*jest.*) barbon, *m.* — **eyed,** *adj.* aux yeux gris. — **hair,** *s.* cheveux gris, *m.pl.*; (*of old age, white hair*) cheveux blancs, *m.pl.* — **haired, -headed,** *adj.* aux cheveux gris; aux (*or* à *or* en) cheveux blancs. — **hen,** *s.* poule de bruyère, *f.* *V.* **Grey**

Grayish, *adj.* grisâtre

Grayishness, *s.* couleur *or* teinte grisâtre, *f.*

Grayling, *s.* ombre, *m.*

Grayness, *s.* couleur grise, *f.*, gris, *m.*

Graze, *v.a.n.* paître; faire paître, mener paître; (*rear*) élever; (*touch lightly*) raser, effleurer, friser, frôler; (*tear*) écorcher, enlever; — *s.* (*excoriation*) écorchure, *f.*

Grazier, *s.* herbager, *m.*

Grazing, *s.* action de paître, *f.*; (*rearing*) élève, *f.*, élevage, *m.*; (*excoriation*) écorchure, *f.*; — *adj.* qui paît; herbivore. — **farm,** *s.* ferme où l'on élève du bétail, *f.* — **ground, -land,** *s.* pâturage, herbage, *m.*

Grease, *s.* graisse, *f.*; (*vet.*) malandre, *f.*; — *v.a.* graisser. — **box,** *s.* boîte à graisse, *f.* — **merchant** *or* **dealer,** *s.* graissier, *m.*, -ière, *f.* — **pot,** *s.* pot à graisse, *m.* — **shop** *or* **trade,** *s.* graisserie, *f.*

Greaser, *s.* graisseur, *m.*, -euse, *f.*

Greasily, *adv.* avec de la graisse; salement

Greasiness, *s.* nature graisseuse *or* huileuse, graisse, *f.*; saleté, *f.*

Greasing, *s.* graissage, *m.*

Greasy, *adj.* graisseux; gras; huileux; (*spotted*) couvert *or* taché de graisse, sale. — *pole,* mât de cocagne, *m.*

Great, *adj.* grand; principal; vaste; considérable; important; sublime; magnifique; (*keen, sharp*) vif; (*powerful*) puissant; (*skilful*) habile, fort; (*intimate*) intime; (*of time*) long; (*pregnant: pers.*) enceinte, grosse, (*animals*) pleine, (*things, fig.*) gros (*m.*), grosse (*f.*); (*of grand-children*) arrière (*V.* **Grand**). — **aunt,** &c. *V.* **Grand.** — **grand-children,** &c. *V.* **Grand**

Greater, *adj.* plus grand *or* &c. (*V.* **Great**), (*geog., astr., bot., zool.*) grand. *To make* —, agrandir

Greatly, *adv.* grandement; considérablement; (*much, very*) fort, très, beaucoup, bien; (*keenly, sharply*) vivement; (*powerfully*) puissamment; (*nobly*) noblement

Greatness, *s.* grandeur, *f.*; puissance, *f.*; magnificence, splendeur, *f.*; intensité, force, *f.*; sublimité, *f.*; énormité, *f.*

Greaves, *s. pl.* jambières, grèves, *f.pl.*; (*of* [*tallow*) *V.* **Graves**

Grebe, *s.* grèbe, *m.*

Grecian, *adj.s.* *V.* **Greek**; (*scholar*) helléniste, *m.*

Grecianize, *v.a.n.* gréciser

Grecism, *s.* grécisme, hellénisme, *m.*

Grecist, *s.* gréciste, helléniste, *m.*

Grecity, *s.* grécité, *f.*

Grecize, *v.a.n.* gréciser

Greco-Roman, *adj.* gréco-romain

Greed, *s.* avidité, *f.*; cupidité, *f.*; avarice, *f.*; gourmandise, *f.*; voracité, *f.* [goulument

Greedily, *adv.* avidement, avec voracité,

Greediness, *s.* gourmandise, *f.*; voracité, *f.*; avidité, *f.*

Greedy, *adj.* gourmand, goulu, glouton; vorace; avide; cupide. — **gut, -guts,** *s.* goinfre, *m.*, gouliafre, *m.f.*, gueulard, *m.*, e, *f.*, goulu, *m.*, e, *f.*, glouton, *m.*, -ne, *f.*

Greek, *adj.* grec, de Grèce, de la Grèce; — *s.* Grec, *m.*, Grecque, *f.*; (*language*) le grec, *m.*, la langue grecque, *f.* — *fire,* feu grégeois, *m.*

Green, *adj.* vert; frais, nouveau, récent; novice, neuf, inexpérimenté, naïf, serin; (*of*

age) jeune; (*pale*) blême, pâle; (*of cheese*) persillé; — *s.* vert, *m.*; (*verdure*) verdure, *f.*; (*grass*) herbe, *f.*; (*grass plot*) pelouse, *f.*, gazon, tapis vert, *m.*; (*meadow*) prairie, *f.*; (*green leaves*) feuillage, *m.*; **—s,** *s. pl.* plantes, *f pl.*; (*on table*) légumes verts, *m.pl.*; (*cabbage*) choux, *m.pl.* — *old age*, verte vieillesse, *f.* — **broom,** *s* genêt des teinturiers, *m.* — **cloth,** *s.* tapis vert, *m.* — **crop,** *s.* récolte des prairies artificielles, *f.*; (*vegetables*) légumes verts, *m.pl.* — **earth,** *s.* vert de montagne, *m.* — **eyed,** *adj.* aux yeux verts, qui a les yeux verts. — **finch,** *s.* verdier, *m.* — **fly,** *s.* puceron, *m.* — **food,** *s.* (*of horses*, &c.) (le) vert, *m* — **gage,** *s.* reine-claude, *f.* — **goose,** *s.* oison, *m.* — **grocer,** *s.* fruitier, *m.*, -ière, *f.* — **grocery,** *s.* fruiterie, *f.* — **horn,** *s.* blanc-bec, conscrit, novice, niais, cornichon, *m.* — **house,** *s.* serre, *f.* — **meat,** *s. V.* — **food.** — **peas,** *s. pl.* pois verts, petits pois, *m.pl.* — **room,** *s.* foyer des acteurs, foyer, *m.* — **shank,** *s.* (*bird*) aboyeur, *m.* — **sickness,** *s.* pâles couleurs, *f.pl.*, chlorose, *f.* — **stall,** *s.* étalage de fruitier, *m.* — **stone,** *s.* diorite, *m.* —**sward,** *s.* pelouse, *f.*, gazon, tapis vert, *m.* — **weed,** *s. V.* — **broom.** — **wood,** *s* bois vert, *m.* — **yard,** *s.* fourrière, *f.* *To bring* or *take to the — yard*, mettre en fourrière, conduire à la fourrière

Greenish, *adj.* verdâtre

Greenishness, *s.* couleur *or* teinte verdâtre, *f.*

Greenlander, *s.* Groenlandais, *m.*, e, *f.*

Greenly, *adv.* de couleur verte, en vert; (*fig.*) fraîchement, nouvellement, récemment; (*ironically*) sans expérience, naïvement, avec innocence

Greenness, *s.* couleur verte, *f.*; verdure, *f.*; (*unripeness*) verdeur, *f.*, défaut de maturité, *m.*; (*vigour*) verdeur, fraîcheur, *f.*; (*inexperience*, &c.) inexpérience, simplicité, naïveté, *f.*; (*newness*) nouveauté, *f.*

Greet, *v.a.n.* saluer; accueillir

Greeting, *s.* salut, *m.*; salutation, *f.*; accueil, *m.*, réception, *f.*; félicitations, *f.pl.*, compliments, *m.pl.*; (*recognition*) reconnaissance, *f.*

Gregarious, *adj.* qui vit en troupes, grégaire

Gregariously, *adv.* en troupes, par bandes

Gregariousness, *s.* nature grégaire, *f.*

Gregorian, *adj.* grégorien

Gremial, *s.* grémial, *m.*

Grenade, *s.* grenade, *f.*

Grenadier, *s.* grenadier, *m.*

Grenadine, *s.* grenadine, *f.*

Grey, &c. *V.* **Gray,** &c. — **friar,** *s.* franciscain, *m.* — **hound,** *s.* lévrier, *m.*, levrette, *f.* — **trout,** *s.* saumonerion, *m.*

Grice, *s.* marcassin, *m.*

Gridelin, *s. adj.* gris de lin, *m.*

Gridiron, *s.* gril, *m.*; (*for toast*) grille-pain, *m.* — **pendulum,** *s. V.* **Compensation-pendulum**

Grief, *s.* chagrin, *m.*, douleur, peine, affliction, *f.*; (*bad end*) mauvaise fin, *f.* *To come to —*, finir mal, mourir sur la paille; (*be killed*) être tué, trouver la mort; (*fail*) faire fiasco; aller à vau-l'eau; (*get spoilt*) s'abîmer; être perdu

Grievance, *s.* grief, *m.*

Grieve, *v.a.* ('*at*,' '*for*,' '*to*,' de) chagriner, affliger, peiner, attrister; — *v.n.* se chagriner, s'affliger, s'attrister, se désoler, gémir, souffrir

Grievingly, *adv.* avec chagrin, avec douleur

Grievous, *adj.* (*heavy*) grave, lourd, pesant, accablant; (*serious*) grave; (*distressing*, &c.) affligeant, douloureux, pénible, cruel; triste, fâcheux; affreux, énorme; (*provoking*) offensant, blessant

Grievously, *adv.* péniblement, douloureusement; cruellement; gravement, grièvement

Grievousness, *s.* pesanteur accablante, *f.*; nature affligeante, *f.*; affliction, calamité, *f.*, malheur, *m.*; gravité, grièveté, énormité, *f.*

Griffin, Griffon, *s.* griffon, *m.*

Grig, *s.* (*fish*) anguille, *f.*; (*pers.*) égrillard, *m.*, e, *f.* *As merry as a —*, gai comme un pinson

Grill, *v.a.* griller, faire griller; (*torment*) mettre à la torture; (*horrify*) *V.* **Horrify;** — *v.n.* griller; — *s.* grillade, *f.* [sur les charbons

Grillade, *s.* grillade, *f.*

Grilled, *adj.* grillé; à la torture, sur le gril,

Grilling, *s.* grillade, *f.*

Grilse, *s.* saumoneau, tocan, gril, *m.*

Grim, *adj.* horrible, affreux, effrayant, hideux; laid; (*fierce, savage*) farouche; (*cross*) refrogné. — **faced, -visaged,** *adj.* au visage hideux, aux traits horribles; au visage refrogné; à l'air *or* au visage farouche. — **grinning,** *adj.* au rire affreux

Grimace, *s.* grimace, *f.*; — *v.n.* grimacer

Grimaced, *adj.* au visage grimaçant, aux traits grimaçants

Grimacer, *s.* grimacier, *m.*, -ière, *f.*

Grimacing, *adj.* grimacier

Grimalkin, *s.* Grippeminaud, Raminagrobis, *m.*

Grime, *s.* suie, *f.*, noir, *m.*, saleté, crasse, *f.*; — *v.a.* noircir, salir, barbouiller

Grimly, *adv.* horriblement, affreusement, hideusement; (*fiercely, savagely*) d'un air farouche; (*sullenly*) d'un air refrogné

Grimness, *s.* aspect horrible *or* affreux *or* effrayant, *m.*; air farouche, *m.*; air refrogné, *m.*

Grimy, *adj.* noir, noirci, sale, crasseux, barbouillé

Grin, *v.n.* rire, ricaner; grimacer; montrer les dents; grincer des dents; — *s.* rire, ricanement, *m.*; grimace, *f.*; grincement de dents, *m.* *Broad —*, rire satanique, *m.* — **at,** faire des grimaces à; se moquer de

Grind, *v.a.n.* moudre; broyer; ('*to*,' '*into*') réduire (en); (*sharpen*) repasser, émoudre; (*polish*) polir; (*rub*) frotter; (*the teeth*) grincer; (*an organ*) jouer (de), tourner la manivelle, tourner; (*students*) préparer, pousser; (*oppress*) opprimer, pressurer, écraser. *To — corn*, moudre le blé. *To — into meal*, réduire en farine. *To — colours*, broyer des couleurs. *To — with the teeth*, broyer avec les dents. *To — the teeth*, grincer les dents. — **off,** *v.a.* (*wear*) user. — **stone,** *s.* meule, *f.*; (*for tools*) meule, pierre à aiguiser, *f.*; (*for pounding*) pierre à broyer, *f.*

Grinder, *s.* (*of knives*, &c.) repasseur, rémouleur, *m.*; (*of colours*, &c.) broyeur, *m.*; (*tutor*) *V.* **Crammer;** (*player*) joueur, *m.*; (*oppressor*) oppresseur, *m.*; (*stone*) meule, *f.*; (*tooth*) dent molaire, molaire, *f.*; (*of animals*) mâchelière, *f.*; **—s,** *pl.* (*teeth, jest.*) dents, *f.pl.*, râtelier, *m.*

Grindery, *s.* crépins, *m pl.*

Grinding, *adj.* atroce; douloureux, cuisant; écrasant, qui oppresse; — *s.* (*of corn*) mouture, *f.*; (*pulverizing*) broiement, *m.*; (*of knives*, &c.) repassage, *m.*; (*polishing*) polissement, *m.*; (*rubbing*) frottement, *m.*; (*of the teeth*) grincement, *m.*; (*oppressing*) oppression, *f.*

Grinner, *s.* grimacier, *m.*, -ière, *f.*; ricaneur, *m.*, -euse, *f.*

Grinning, *adj.* grimacier; (*laughing*) qui rit; — *s.* grimaces, *f.pl.*; ricanement, *m.*; grincement de dents, *m.*

Grinningly, *adv.* en grimaçant; en riant, en ricanant; en grinçant des dents

Grip. *V.* **Gripe**

Gripe, *v.a.n.* saisir, empoigner; gripper, agripper; (*pinch, squeeze*) serrer, fermer; presser, étreindre; (*give pain*) donner des tranchées à; — *s.* prise, *f.*; serrement, *m.*, étreinte, *f.*; griffe, *f*; (*strength of hand*) poigne, *f.*; (*reach*) atteinte, *f.*; affliction, *f.*, tourment, *m.*; (*part of a sword-mount*) poignée, *f.*; **—s,** *s. pl.* tranchées, *f.pl.*, colique, *f.* [juif, *m.*

Griper, *s.* oppresseur, *m.*; grippe-sou, usurier,

Griping, *adj.* poignant, cuisant; affreux, atroce; (*miserly*) avare, rapace; sordide; (*med.*) de colique; — *s.* (*med.*) colique, *f.*, tranchées, *f.pl.*

Grisaille, *s.* grisaille, *f.*

Grisette, *s.* grisette, *f.*
Griskin, *s.* échinée, *f.*
Grisly, *adj.* affreux, hideux, horrible
Grison, *s.* (*geog.*) Grison, *m.*, -ne, *f.*; (*zool.*) [grison, *m.*
Gris-perle, *s* gris-perle, *m.*
Grist, *s.* (*corn*) blé à moudre, *m.*; (*meal*) farine, *f.*; (*fig.*) approvisionnement, *m.*, provision, *f.*; profit, gain, *m.* *To bring — to the mill,* faire venir l'eau au moulin. — **mill,** *s.* moulin à blé, *m.* — **tax,** *s.* impôt sur la mouture, *m.*
Gristle, *s.* cartilage, *m.*; —**s,** *pl* (*cook.*) tendrons, *m.pl.*
Gristly, *adj.* cartilagineux
Grit, *s.* (*coarse meal*) issues, *f.pl.*; (*oats*) gruau d'avoine, *m.*; (*gravel*) gravier, sable, *m.*; (*min.*) grès, *m.*; — *v.n.* craquer. — **stone,** *s.* grès, *m.*
Grittiness, *s.* nature graveleuse, *f.*
Gritty, *adj.* graveleux; plein de graviers
Grizzle, *s.* (*donkey*) Aliboron, *m.*; (*grey colour*) gris, *m.*, couleur grise, *f.*
Grizzled, Grizzly, *adj.* gris; grisonnant; grisâtre. — *bear,* ours d'Amérique, ours féroce, *m.*
Groan, *v.n.* gémir; (*growl*) grogner; (*pant from violent efforts*) ahaner; — *s.* gémissement, *m.*; grognement, *m.*; ahanement, ahan, *m.*
Groaning, *s.* *V.* **Groan,** *s.*
Groat, *s.* sou, *m.* *Not to be worth a —,* n'avoir [pas le sou
Groats, *s. pl.* gruau d'avoine, *m.*
Grocer, *s.* épicier, *m.*, -ière, *f.*
Grocery, *s.* épicerie, *f.* — **business** *or* **trade,** *s.* épicerie, *f.*
Grog, *s.* grog, *m.* — **blossoms,** *s. pl.* bourgeons, *m.pl.*, couperose, *f.*, trogne bourgeonnée [*or* couperosée, *f.*
Groggy, *adj.* gris, pochard
Groin, *s.* aine, *f.*; (*break-water*) *V.* **Groyne;** [(*build.*) épi, *m.*
Grommet, *s.* erseau, *m.*
Gromwell, *s.* grémil, *m.*
Groom, *s.* palefrenier, groom, valet d'écurie, garçon d'écurie, *m.*; domestique (à cheval), groom, valet, *m.*; (*equerry*) écuyer, *m.*; (*bridegroom*) *V.* **Bridegroom;** — *v.a.* panser. — *of the bedchamber,* gentilhomme de la chambre, *m.* —**'s-man,** *s.* *V.* **Bride's-man**
Grooming, *s.* pansement, *m.*
Groove, *s.* rainure, *f.*; (*slide*) coulisse, *f.*; (*flute*) cannelure, *f.*; (*of a pulley, of a wheel*) gorge, *f.*; (*notch*) entaille, *f.*; (*anat.*) sillon, *m.*; — *v.a.* rainer; (*to hollow*) creuser; (*to flute*) canneler; (*to furrow*) sillonner
Grooving-plane, *s.* bouvet, *m.*
Grope, *v.n.a.* tâtonner; aller (*or* marcher *or* avancer) à tâtons; (*for*) chercher à tâtons *or* en tâtonnant
Groper, *s.* tâtonneur, *m.*, -euse, *f.*
Groping, Gropingly, *adv.* à tâtons
Gros, *adj.* gros; — *s.* gros, *m.* — **beak,** *s.* gros-bec, *m.* — **grain,** *s.* gros, *m.*
Gross, *adj.* grossier; (*bulky*) gros; (*thick*) épais; (*rude*) rude; (*dull*) lourd; (*whole*) total; général; (*com.*) brut; — *s.* gros, *m.*; (12 *dozen*) grosse, *f.* *By the —, in the —,* en gros; en bloc; en masse; en somme; en général; (*com.*) à la grosse. — **beak,** *s.* gros-bec, *m.* — **headed,** *adj.* lourd, stupide
Grossly, *adv.* grossièrement
Grossness, *s.* grossièreté, *f.*
Grot, *s.* grotte, *f.*
Grotesque, *adj.* grotesque; — *s.* grotesque, [(*style*) *m.*, (*ornament*) *f.*
Grotesquely, *adv.* grotesquement
Grotesqueness, *s.* grotesquerie, *f.*, grotesque, [*m.*
Grotto, *s.* grotte, *f.* *Please remember the —!* pour la petite chapelle, s'il vous plaît!
Ground, *s.* terre, *f.*; sol, *m.*; terrain, *m.*; territoire, *m.*; position, *f.*; fondement, *m.*; motif, *m.*, raison, cause, *f.*, sujet, *m.*; principe, *m.*, origine, *f.*; espace, *m.*, distance, *f.*; (*paint.*) plan, *m.*; (*of colours*) fond, *m.*; (*mus.*) motif, *m.*; (*nav.*) fond, *m.*; —**s,** *pl.*, (*dregs*) lie, *f.*, marc, *m.*; (*of a house*) jardins, *m.pl.*, parc, *m.*; terrains, *m.pl.*; — *v.a.* (*fig.*) fonder, baser; (*teach*) enseigner les premiers principes à; (*lay down*) asseoir, poser à terre; (*mil.*) reposer; (*nav.*) échouer; — *v n.* toucher, échouer, faire côte; — *part.* moulu, &c. (*V.* **Grind**); (*pepper, bones,* &c.) en poudre. — *rice, V.* **Rice.** *On* or *upon* or *to the —,* par terre; à terre. *Under —,* sous terre; en terre; souterrain. *To bite the —,* mordre la poussière. *To break —,* ouvrir des tranchées; creuser la terre. *To burn to the —,* brûler de fond en comble. *To fall to the —,* tomber par terre; (*fig.*) tomber à plat, tomber dans l'eau. *To gain —,* gagner du terrain; s'accréditer. *To give —,* lâcher pied, céder le terrain, reculer; (*give cause to*) donner cause (à). *To go upon sure —,* être sûr de son fait, aller à coup sûr. *To hold* or *keep* or *stand o.'s —,* se maintenir, tenir bon, tenir ferme; se défendre. *To lose —,* perdre du terrain; (*yield*) lâcher pied, reculer, faiblir. *To raze with the —,* raser de fond en comble. — **angling,** *s.* pêche à la ligne de fond, *f.* — **ash,** *s.* rejeton de frêne, *m.* — **floor,** *s.* rez-de-chaussée, *m.* — **ivy,** *s.* lierre terrestre, *m.* — **line,** *s.* ligne de terre, *f.*; (*fish.*) ligne de fond, *f.* — **net,** *s.* salabre, parfond, *m.* — **nut,** *s.* *V.* **Earth-nut.** — **oak,** *s.* rejeton de chêne, *m.* — **plan,** *s.* (*geom.*) plan horizontal, *m.*; (*persp.*) plan géométral, *m.* — **plate,** *s.* (*carp.*) sablière, *f.* — **plot,** *s.* sol, terrain, *m.*; plan, *m.*; (*fig.*) base, *f.*, fondement, *m.*; (*arch.*) ichnographie, *f.* — **rent,** *s.* rente foncière, *f.* — **sill,** *s.* seuil, *m.* — **squirrel,** *s.* tamias, *m.* — **swell,** *s.* (*nav.*) lame de fond, *f.* — **work,** *s.* fondement, *m.*, fondation, *f.*; (*fig.*) base, *f.*, fondement, canevas, *m.* — **worm,** *s.* ver de [terre, *m.*
Groundage, *s.* droit d'ancrage, *m.*
Groundless, *adj.* mal fondé, dénué de fondement, sans fondement. —**ly,** *adv.* sans fondement, sans raison. —**ness,** *s.* défaut de fondement, *m.*, frivolité, futilité, *f.*
Groundling, *s.* loche de rivière, *f.*; (*black goby*) boulereau noir, *m.*; (*pers.*) pleutre, pal-[toquet, *m.*
Groundsel, *s.* (*bot.*) séneçon, *m.*
Group, *s.* groupe, *m.*; (*of trees*) massif, bouquet, *m.*, touffe, *f.*; — *v.a.* grouper; — *v.n.* se [grouper
Grouping, *s.* groupement, *m.*
Grouse, *s.* coq de bruyère, *m.* *Black —,* petit coq de bruyère, *m.*
Grout, *s.* (*meal*) grosse farine, farine grossière, *f.*; (*dregs*) marc, *m.*, lie, *f.*; fond, sédiment, *m.*, effondrilles, *f.pl.*; (*mortar*) coulis, *m.*; — *v.a.n.* (*mas.*) jointoyer
Grouting, *s.* (*mas.*) jointoiement, *m.*
Grove, *s.* bosquet, bocage, *m.*; petit bois, *m.*; plantation, *f.*; (*avenue*) allée couverte, *f.*
Grovel, *v.n.* ramper, se traîner; se vautrer
Groveller, *s.* être rampant, *m.*
Grovelling, *adj.* rampant; bas, vil, abject
Grow, *v.n.* croître, pousser; venir; (*pers., animals*) grandir; (*become*) devenir; commencer à être; (*dark at night, old, late,* &c.) se faire; (*increase, fig.*) s'accroître, s'augmenter; (*to*) parvenir (à); (*proceed*) venir (de), provenir (de); (*near*) approcher; — *v.a.* cultiver. *To — alarmed,* s'alarmer, commencer à s'alarmer. *To — animated,* s'animer. — *better, V.* **Better.** — *big,* grossir, devenir gros. — *cold,* (*pers.*) se refroidir; commencer à avoir froid; (*things*) refroidir, se refroidir; (*of the weather*) se refroidir, (*imp, with 'it,'*) commencer à faire froid. — *confused,* se troubler. — *cool,* (*things*) rafraîchir; refroidir; (*of the weather*) se mettre au frais, fraîchir; (*pers.*) se refroidir; se calmer. — *extinct fat, feeble, gray,* &c. *V.* **Extinct, Fat, Feeble, Gray,** &c. — *handsome,* (*pers.*) embellir; (*things*) s'embellir, embellir. — *hard,* durcir, se durcir; (*fig.*) s'endurcir. — *hot* or *high,* (*pers.*) s'échauffer; commencer à avoir chaud; (*things*) s'échauffer; chauffer. — *in years,* avancer en âge. — *mild* or *soft,* s'adoucir. — *old,* vieillir, se faire vieux. — *pale, V.* **Pale.** — *poor,* s'appauvrir. — *tall* or *great,* grandir. — *thick,* &c. *V.*

Thick,&c. — *warm*, (*pers.*) se réchauffer; commencer à avoir chaud; (*things*) chauffer; (*fig.*) s'échauffer; (*of the weather*) devenir chaud, (*imp.*, *with 'it,'*) commencer à faire chaud. — *weak*, *worse*, &c. *V.* **Weak, Worse**, &c. — *wise*, devenir sage. — *young again*, rajeunir. *To — into favour, out of favour*, *V.* **Favour.** *To — out of use, out of fashion*, &c., *V.* **Use, Fashion**, &c. — **again**, repousser; (*fig.*) reprendre; (*become again*) redevenir. — **in**, (*of nails*) s'incarner. — **into**, (*become*) devenir; passer en. — **out**, pousser; (*spread*) s'étendre. *You will — out of your clothes*, vos habits vous deviendront trop petits. — **up**, croître; pousser; monter; (*pers.*) grandir. — **upon**, s'enraciner dans (*or* en)

Grower, *s.* chose qui croît, *f.*; être qui grandit, *m.*; (*pers.*, *agr.*, &c.) producteur, *m.*, -trice, *f.*; cultivateur, *m.*, -trice, *f.* *To be a good —*, *a quick —*, (*of plants*) pousser (*or* croître) bien, pousser (*or* croître) vite

Growing, *part. adj.* croissant, &c. (*V.* **Grow**); (*of animals*, *pers.*) qui grandit; (*rising*) naissant; — *s.* croissance, *f.*; production, culture, *f.* — *corn*, — *crops*, récolte (*f.*) *or* récoltes (*f.pl.*) sur pied; (*law*) fruits pendants par (les) racines, *m.pl.*, récoltes pendantes par (les) racines, *f.pl.*

Growl, *v.n.* gronder, grogner, grommeler, murmurer; — *s.* grondement, grognement, *m.*; murmure, *m.* [grognard, *m.*, e, *f.*

Growler, *s.* (*dog*) chien hargneux, *m.*; (*pers.*)

Growling, *s.* *V.* **Growl**, *s.*

Grown, *part.* crû, poussé; grandi, &c. (*V.* **Grow**); — *adj.* fait; (*in compounds*) de provenance ... *English —*, de provenance anglaise. *Full- —*, fait; (*of animals*, *things*) parvenu à (*or* qui à pris) toute sa croissance. *Well —*, de belle venue. — **over with**, couvert de. — **up**, grand; fait; élevé. — *up people*, grandes personnes, *f.pl.* — *up man*, homme fait, *m.* *Several children, all — up*, plusieurs enfants, tous élevés

Growth, *s.* croissance, *f.*; crue, venue, *f.*; pousse, *f.*; (*produce*) cru, *m.*; récolte, *f.*; produit, fruit, *m.*; production, *f.*; (*increase*) accroissement, développement, *m.*, extension, *f.*, progrès, *m.*; (*origin*) origine, naissance, *f.*; (*com.*) provenance, *f.*

Groyne, *s.* guideau, brise-lames, *m.*

Grub, *v.a.n.* (— **up**) arracher, déraciner, extirper, essarter; défricher; piocher, bêcher; (*scrape up*) ramasser; (*eat*) bouffer; — *s.* larve, *f.*, ver, *m.*; (*pers.*) petit bout d'homme, *m.*; (*food*) mangeaille, boustifaille, *f.*, fricot, *m.*, vivres, *m.pl.*; (*med.*) tanne, *f.* — **axe**, *s.* hoyau, *m.* — **street**, *adj.* de carrefour

Grubber, *s.* (*pers.*) ramasseur, *m.*, -euse, *f.*; (*agr.*) essarteur, *m.*, -euse, *f.*; (*tool*) extirpa-

Grubbing, — **up**, *s.* essartement, *m.* [teur, *m.*

Grubby, *adj.* véreux

Grudge, *v.a.* envier (à); regretter, donner à contre-cœur; plaindre, pleurer; refuser (à); marchander (à); reprocher (à); — *v.n.* porter envie (à), être envieux (de); murmurer, se plaindre (de); se refuser (à), avoir de la répugnance (à), rechigner (à); — *s.* rancune, *f.*; haine, *f.*; animosité, *f.*; envie, *f.* *To owe a —*, *to have a — against*, garder rancune à, avoir une dent contre, en vouloir à

Grudging, *s.* envie, *f.*; répugnance, mauvaise volonté, *f.*; ressentiment, *m.*

Grudgingly, *adv.* à contre-cœur, contre son gré, à regret, avec répugnance, de mauvaise grâce; (*with spite*) avec rancune, avec res-

Gruel, *s.* gruau, *m.* [sentiment

Gruff, *adj.* rechigné, refrogné; (*rough*) brusque, rude, bourru; (*harsh*) aigre, âpre

Gruffly, *adv.* d'un air rechigné *or* refrogné; brusquement, rudement, d'un ton bourru; aigrement

Gruffness, *s.* air rechigné, *m.*, mine refrognée, *f.*; brusquerie, rudesse, *f.*, ton bourru, *m.*

Grum, *adj.* *V.* **Gruff**

Grumble, *v.n.* murmurer; gronder; grommeler, grogner, marronner, bougonner

Grumbler, *s.* grondeur, *m.*, -euse, *f.*; grogneur, *m.*, -euse, *f.*, grognard, *m.*, e, *f.*, grognon, *m.f.*

Grumbling, *adj.* grondeur; (*fam.*) grognon; — *s.* murmure, *m.*; (*fam.*) grognement, *m.*

Grumblingly, *adv.* en grondant, en grognant, en grommelant

Grumly, *adv.* *V.* **Gruffly**

Grumpy, *adj.* *V.* **Surly**

Grunt, *v.n.* grogner; (*pers.*) gémir; — *s.* grognement, *m.*; (*pers.*) gémissement, *m.*

Grunter, *s.* grogneur, *m.*, -euse, *f.*, grognard, *m.*, e, *f.*, grognon, *m.f.*; personne qui gémit, *f.*; (*pig*) cochon, pourceau, *m.*

Grunting, *s.* *V.* **Grunt**, *s.*

Gruntling, *s.* petit cochon, goret, *m.*

Guaiac, Guaiacum, *s.* gaïac, *m.*

Guaiacic, *adj.* gaïacique

Guaiacine, *s.* gaïacine, *f.*

Guan, *s.* (*bird*) guan, yacou, *m.*

Guanine, *s.* guanine, *f.*

Guano, *s.* guano, *m.*

Guarana, — **bread**, *s.* guarana, *f.*

Guarantee, *s.* garantie, *f.*; garant, *m.*, e, *f.*; caution, *f.*; — *v.a.* garantir

Guarantor, *s.* garant, *m.*, e, *f.*

Guard, *v.a.* garder; défendre, protéger; mettre en garde (contre); — *v.n.* se mettre en garde (contre); se garder (de); se tenir (*or* être) sur ses gardes (contre); (*provide*) se prémunir (contre); — *s.* garde, *f.*; (*pers.*) garde, *m.*; (*caution*) réserve, *f.*; (*of swords*, *carving-forks*, &c.) garde, *f.*; (*trigger —*) sous-garde, *f.*; (*of a watch*) chaîne longue, *f.*, sautoir, *m.*; (*fire —*, *hat —*) *V.* **Fire, Hat**; (— *iron*, *of a locomotive engine*) chasse-pierres, *m.*; (*fenc.*) garde, *f.*; (*soldier*) garde, *m.*; (*body of soldiers*, *—s*) garde, *f.*; (*of a stage-coach*) conducteur, *m.*; (*of a railway train*) chef (de train), conducteur (de train) *m.* *On —*, de garde; (*fenc.*) en garde. *To be on —*, être de garde. *To be on o.'s —*, être sur ses gardes. *To be off o.'s —*, n'être pas sur ses gardes. *To be thrown off o.'s —*, être pris au dépourvu. *To come off —*, descendre la garde. *To go on —*, *to mount —*, monter la garde. — **boat**, *s.* canot de ronde, *m.*; stationnaire, *m.* — **chain**, *s.* chaîne longue, *f.*, sautoir, *m.* — **coat**, *s.* capote, *f.* — **house**, *s.* corps de garde, *m.* — **iron**, *s.* chasse-roues, *m.*; (*rail.*) chasse-pierres, *m.* — **less**, *adj.* sans garde; sans gardien; sans défense; sans protection. — **room**, *s.* corps de garde, *m.*; (*as a place of confinement*) salle de police, *f.* — **ship**, *s.* amiral, *m.*; garde-côtes, *m.*; stationnaire, *m.* —**sman**, *s.* garde, *m.* [dent, circonspect

Guarded, *adj.* gardé; mesuré, réservé, pru-

Guardedly, *adv.* avec circonspection, avec réserve

Guardedness, *s.* réserve, circonspection, *f.*

Guardian, *s.* gardien, *m.*, -ne, *f.*; (*of orphans*) tuteur, *m.*, -trice, *f.*; curateur, *m.*, -trice, *f.*; (*of the poor*) administrateur, *m.*; — *adj.* gar-

Guardianship, *s.* tutelle, *f.* [dien; tutélaire

Guava, *s.* goyave, *f.*; (— *tree*) goyavier, *m.*

Gudgeon, *s.* (*fish*) goujon, *m.*; (*pers.*) jobard, *m.*, dupe, *f.*; (*bait*) amorce, *f.*, appât, *m.*; (*iron pin*) goujon, tourillon, *m.*, broche, *f.*; — *v.a.* goujonner, duper, flouer, jobarder

Guebre, *s.* guèbre, *m.f.* [Gueldre, *f.*

Guelder-rose, *s.* boule-de-neige, rose de

Guelf, Guelph, *s.* Guelfe, *m.*

Guerdon, *s.* récompense, *f.*; — *v.a.* récompenser

Guerilla, Guerrilla, *s.* guérilla, *f.*, (*soldier*) *m.*

Guerillero, Guerrillero, *s.* guérillero, *m.*

Guerite, *s.* guérite, *f.*

Guernsey, *s.* vareuse, *f.*

Guess, *v.a.n.* deviner, conjecturer; — *s.* conjecture, *f.*; estimation, *f.* *At a —*, en devinant. *At a rough —*, par approximation, approximativement, par estimation, à peu près.

To give a — at, deviner. *To make a happy —,* deviner juste. *It is a good —,* c'est bien deviné. — **work,** *s.* conjecture, *f.*, conjectures, *f.pl.*, supposition, *f.*, suppositions, *f.pl.*; affaire de hasard, *f.*

Guesser, *s.* devineur, *m.*, -euse, *f.* *To be a good* or *a bad —,* deviner bien *or* mal

Guessingly, *adv.* par conjecture, en conjecturant, en devinant

Guest, *s.* (*of repasts*) convive, *m.f.*, convié, *m.*, e, *f.*; (*visitor*) hôte, *m.*, hôtesse, *f.*; invité, *m.*, e, *f.* — **chamber,** *s.* cénacle, *m.*

Guffaw, *s.* éclat (*m.*, éclats, *m.pl.*) de rire, fou rire, gros rire, *m.*, grosse gaieté, *f.*

Guidable, *adj.* docile

Guidance, *s.* conduite, direction, *f.*; gouverne, *f.*

Guide, *v.a.* guider, conduire, diriger; gouverner; régler; — *s.* guide, *m.*; (*rail.*) indicateur, livret, *m.* — **book,** *s.* guide, *m.*; livret, *m.*; (*rail.*) indicateur, livret, *m.* —**less,** *adj.* sans guide. — **post,** *s.* *V.* **Sign-post**

Guidon, *s.* guidon, *m.*

Guild, *s.* corporation, *f.* — **hall,** *s.* hôtel de [ville, *m.*

Guilder, *s.* florin, *m.*

Guile, *s.* artifice, *m.*, ruse, astuce, fourberie, *f.* —**ful,** *adj.* artificieux, astucieux, rusé; trompeur, fourbe, perfide. —**fully,** *adv.* artificieusement, astucieusement; perfidement. —**fulness,** *s.* *V.* **Guile.** —**less,** *adj.* sans artifice, sincère, loyal, franc, simple, ingénu, naïf. —**lessness,** *s.* sincérité, loyauté, franchise, simplicité, ingénuité, naïveté, *f.*

Guillemot, *s.* guillemot, *m.*

Guilloche, *s.* guillochis, *m.*

Guillochee, *v.a.* guillocher

Guillotine, *s.* guillotine, *f.*; — *v.a.* guillotiner

Guillotiner, Guillotinist, *s.* guillotineur, *m.*

Guillotining, *s.* guillotinement, *m.*

Guilt, *s.* culpabilité, *f.*; crime, *m.*; faute, *f.*

Guiltily, *adv.* coupablement; criminellement, [en criminel

Guiltiness, *s.* *V.* **Guilt**

Guiltless, *adj.* innocent. *To hold —,* tenir pour innocent. —**ly,** *adv.* innocemment. —**ness,** *s.* innocence, *f.*

Guilty, *adj.* coupable; criminel; méchant. *The — party,* le coupable, *m.* *To find —, to bring in —,* déclarer coupable. *To plead —* or *not —,* *V.* **Plead.** — **like,** *adv.* en criminel

Guimp. *V.* **Gimp**

Guinea, *s.* guinée, *f.*; (*geog.*) la Guinée, *f.* — **fowl, -hen,** *s.* pintade, *f.* — **grass,** *s.* panic, *m.* — **pepper,** *s.* poivre de Guinée, *m.* — **pig,** *s.* cochon d'Inde, cochon de Barbarie, *m.* — **worm,** *s.* dragonneau, *m.*, filaire, *m.f.*

Guipure, *s.* — **lace,** *s.* guipure, *f.*

Guise, *s.* costume, *m*; apparence, forme, *f.*, dehors, *m.pl.*; masque, manteau, *m.*; (*manner*) [guise, manière, façon, *f.*

Guitar, *s.* guitare, *f.*

Guitarist, *s.* guitariste, *m.f.*

Gules, *s.* (*her.*) gueules, *m.*

Gulf, *s.* (*geog.*) golfe, *m.*; (*fig.*) gouffre, abîme, *m.* — **Stream,** *s.* gulf-stream, *m.* — **weed,** *s.* sargasse, *f.* [goufres *or* d'abîmes

Gulfy, *adj.* plein de golfes; (*fig.*) plein de

Gull, *s.* (*bird*) mouette, *f.*, goéland, *m.*; (*fish*) chabot, *m.*; (*cheat*) duperie, *f.*; (*pers.*) dupe, *f.*, gobe-mouches, jobard, serin, *m.*; — *v.a.* duper, flouer, jobarder

Guller, *s.* fourbe, trompeur, imposteur, filou, *m.*

Gullet, *s.* gosier, *m.*, gorge, *f.*; (*anat.*) œsophage, *m.*; (*narrow pass*) goulet, *m.* [moucherie, *f.*

Gullibility, *s.* crédulité, jobarderie, gobe-

Gullible, *adj.* crédule, serin, jobard

Gully, *s.* ravine, *f.*, ravin, *m.*; (*— hole*) *See below;* — *v.a.* raviner, creuser; — *v.n.* couler avec bruit. — **hole,** *s.* bouche *or* chute (d'égout), *f.*

Gulp, (— **down**) *v.a.* gober, avaler goulument, avaler; — *s.* goulée, *f.*; gorgée, *f.*; trait, *m.* *At a —,* d'un trait

Gum, *s.* gomme, *f.*; (*of the teeth*) gencive, *f.*; (*of the eyes*) chassie, *f.*; — *v.a.* gommer. — **acacia,** *s.* gommier, *m.* — **arabic,** *s.* gomme arabique, *f.* — **boil,** *s.* abcès aux gencives, *m.*, parulie, épulie, épulide, *f.* — **dammar,** *s.* dammar, *m.* — **dragon,** *s.* adragant, *m.*, gomme adragant, gomme adragante, *f.* — **lancet,** *s.* déchaussoir, *m.* — **resin,** *s.* gomme résine, *f.* — **ring,** *s.* anneau de dentition, *m.* — **tragacanth,** *s.* *V.* — **dragon.** — **tree,** *s.* gommier, *m.*

Gummate, *s* gommate, *m.*

Gummic, *adj.* gommique

Gummiferous, *adj.* gommifère [gomme, *f.*

Gumminess, *s.* viscosité, *f.*; abondance de

Gumming, *s.* gommage, gommement, *m.*; (*disease in hort.*) gomme, *f.*

Gummo-resinous, *adj.* gommo-résineux

Gummous, Gummy, *adj.* gommeux

Gumption, *s.* adresse, intelligence, *f.*, esprit, *m.*

Gun, *s.* (*hand-gun*) fusil, *m.*; (*great gun*) canon, *m.*; (*shot*) coup de fusil, *m.*; coup de canon, *m.*; —**s,** *pl.* (*artillery*) artillerie, *f.*, canons, *m.pl.* *Great —,* canon, *m.* *Heavy —s,* grosse artillerie, *f.* *Son of a —,* scélérat, coquin, *m.* *To blow great —s,* souffler avec violence. — **barrel,** *s.* canon de fusil, *m.* — **boat,** *s.* canonnière, chaloupe canonnière, *f.* — **carriage,** *s.* affût de canon, *m.* — **cotton,** *s.* coton-poudre, *m.*, poudre-coton, *f.*, fulmicoton, *m.* — **deck,** *s.* batterie, *f.* — **factory,** *s.* *V.* — **foundry.** — **fire,** *s.* (*evening —*) *V.* **Evening;** (*morning —*) *V.* **Morning.** — **flint,** *s.* pierre à fusil, *f.* — **foundry,** *s.* fonderie de canons, canonnerie, *f.* — **maker, -manufacturer,** *s.* armurier, *m.* — **making,** *s.* armurerie, arquebuserie, *f.* — **metal,** *s.* métal de fonte, *m.*, fonte, *f.* — **port,** *s.* sabord, *m.* — **powder,** *s.* poudre à canon, *f.* — **powder plot,** *s.* (*hist.*) conspiration des poudres, *f.* — **powder room, mill, works,** &c. *V.* **Powder room,** &c. (*at Letter* **P**). — **powder tea,** *s.* thé poudre à canon, *m.* — **practice,** *s.* tir du canon, *m.* — **rack,** *s.* râtelier, *m.* — **room,** *s.* sainte-barbe, *f.* — **shot,** *s.* (*generally*) coup de feu, *m.*; (*particularly*) coup de fusil, *m.*; coup de canon, *m.*; (*distance*) portée de fusil, *f.*; portée de canon, *f.* — **shot wound,** *s.* blessure (*or* plaie) d'arme à feu, *f.* — **smith,** *s.* armurier, *m.* — **smithery,** *s.* *V.* — **making.** — **stick,** *s.* baguette (de fusil), *f.*; refouloir (de canon), *m.* — **stock,** *s.* bois *or* fût de fusil, *m.* — **tackle,** *s.* drosse, *f.*, palan à canon, *m.* — **tier,** *s.* batterie, *f.* — **trade,** *s.* *V.* — **making.** — **vessel,** *s.* *V.* — **boat.** — **wale,** *s.* plat-bord, *m.*

Gunnage, *s.* canons, *m.pl.*

Gunnel, *s.* (*nav.*) plat-bord, *m.*; (*fish*) gunnel, *m.*

Gunner, *s.* canonnier, *m.*; (*officer in a ship of war*) maître canonnier, *m.* [*f.*, canonnage, *m.*

Gunnery, *s.* science de l'artillerie, artillerie,

Gunny, *s.* (*— cloth*) toile d'emballage indienne, *f.*

Gunter's scale, *s.* échelle anglaise, *f.*

Gurgle, *v.n.* faire glouglou; (*of rivulets*) murmurer, gazouiller; — *s.* *V.* **Gurgling,** *s.*

Gurgling, *adj.* qui fait glouglou; (*of rivulets*) murmurant, gazouillant; — *s.* glouglou, *m.*; (*of rivulets*) murmure, gazouillement, *m.*; (*med.*) gargouillement, *m.*

Gurgoyle. *V.* **Gargoyle**

Gurnard, Gurnet, *s.* rouget, *m.* *Grey —,* gurnard, gurneau, *m.* *Flying —,* poisson volant, *m.* [— **out,** jaillir; bouillonner

Gush, *v.n.* jaillir, ruisseler; — *s.* *V.* **Gushing.**

Gushing, *s.* (— **out**) jaillissement, *m.*; saillie, *f.*; bouillonnement, *m.*; (*fig.*) enthousiasme, *m.*

Gusset, *s.* gousset, *m.*

Gust, *s.* (*of wind*) coup (de vent), *m.*; bouffée, *f.*; (*nav.*) risée, *f.*; (*of passion*) accès, transport, *m.*; (*relish*) goût, plaisir, *m.*, jouissance, *f.*

Gustation, *s.* gustation, *f.* [gustatif, *m.*

Gustatory, *adj.* du goût. — *nerve,* nerf

Gusto, *s.* goût, *m.*; plaisir, *m.*; piquant, *m.*

Gusty, *adj.* orageux

Gut, *s.* boyau, intestin, *m.*; —**s,** *pl.* (*gluttony,* *stomach*) gueule, *f.*, ventre, *m.*, panse, *f.*; — *v.a.* vider; (*fig.*) vider, dépouiller; dévaliser; détruire à l'intérieur. *They entirely —ted the house*, ils ne laissèrent que les (quatre) murs (*or* murailles). *The house is completely —ed*, il ne reste que les (quatre) murs (*or* murailles). — **line,** *s.* (*fish.*) empile, *f.* — **manufacture, -work, -works, -working,** *s.* boyauderie, *f.* — **worker, -spinner,** *s.* boyaudier, *m.*

Gutta, *s.* goutte, *f.* — **percha,** *s.* gutta-percha, *f.* — **rosea,** *s.* goutte rose, *f.* — **serena,** *s.* goutte sereine, *f.*

Gutter, *s.* (*of roofs*) gouttière, *f.*; chéneau, *m.*; (*of streets*) ruisseau, *m.*; (*groove*) sillon, *m.*; cannelure, *f.*; (*of a crossbow*) coulisse, *f.*; (*nav.*) gouttière, *f.*; — *v.a.n.* sillonner; creuser; canneler; (*to run*) couler; (*fall in drops*) dégoutter. — **spout,** *s.* gargouille, *f.* — **tile,** *s.* faîtière, tuile creuse, *f.*

Guttering, *s.* (*of roofs*) gouttières, *f.pl.*; chéneaux, *m.pl.*; (*of streets*) ruisseaux, *m.pl.*

Guttiform, *adj.* guttiforme

Guttle, *v.n.* bâfrer; riboter, faire ripaille; — *v.a.* bâfrer, avaler, gober [-euse, *f.*

Guttler, *s.* bâfreur, *m.*, -euse, *f.*; riboteur, *m.*,

Guttling, *s.* bâfre, bâfrerie, *f.*; ribote, *f.*

Guttural, *adj. s.* guttural, *adj. m.*, e, *f.*, gutturale, *s.f.* [gutturale

Gutturally, *adv.* gutturalement, d'une manière

Gutturalness, *s.* nature gutturale, *f.*; son

Gutty, *adj.* (*her.*) goutté [guttural, *m.*

Guy, *s.* effigie de Guy Fawkes, *f.*, mannequin, *m.*; (*pers.*) pantin, *m.*, caricature, *f.*; chienlit, *m.*; (*rope*) corde de retenue, *f.*, maroquin, *m.* *Here's a —, here comes* (or *there goes*) *another —*, à la chienlit!

Guzzle, *v.a.n.* lamper, pomper; riboter

Guzzler, *s.* biberon, *m.*, -ne, *f.*; riboteur, *m.*,

Guzzling, *s.* ribote, *f.* [-euse, *f.*

Gwyniad, *s.* lavaret, *m.*

Gymnasiarch, *s.* gymnasiarque, *m.*

Gymnasium, *s.* gymnase, *m.* [*m.*; athlète, *m.*

Gymnast, *s.* gymnaste, *m.f.*; gymnasiarque,

Gymnastic, *adj.* gymnastique; —**s,** *s. pl.* gymnastique, *f.* [gymnique, *f.*

Gymnic, -al, *adj.* gymnique; —**s,** *s. pl.*

Gynæceum, *s.* gynécée, *m.*

Gypseous, *adj.* gypseux

Gypsiferous, *adj.* gypsifère

Gypsum, *s.* gypse, *m.*

Gypsy, *s.* bohémien, *m.*, -ne, *f.*, égyptien, *m.*, -ne, *f.*, bohème, *m.f.*; moricaud, *m.*, e, *f.*; (*to a child, in fun*) coquin, *m.*, e, *f.*; (*language*) langage des bohémiens, *m.*; — *adj.* de bohémien. — **wort,** *s.* lycope, pied de loup, *m.*, herbe des bohémiens, *f.*

Gypsyism, *s.* état de bohémien, *m.*

Gyral, *adj.* giratoire, gyratoire

Gyrate, *v.n.* tourner [ment giratoire, *m.*

Gyration, *s.* giration, gyration, *f.*, mouve-

Gyratory, *adj.* giratoire, gyratoire

Gyre, *s.* cercle, *m.*

Gyrfalcon, *s.* gerfaut, *m.*

Gyromancer, *s.* gyromancien, *m.*, -ne, *f.*

Gyroman-cy, -tic. *V.* page 3, § 1

Gyrometer, *s.* gyromètre, *m.*

Gyroscope, *s.* gyroscope, *m.*

Gyve, *s.* fer; — *v.a.* enchaîner, charger de fers

H

H, *s.* (*letter*) h, *f.*

Ha, *int.* ha! ah!

Habeas corpus, *s.* habeas corpus, *m.*

Haberdasher, *s.* mercier, *m.*, -ière, *f.*

Haberdashery, *s.* mercerie, *f.*

Habergeon, *s.* haubergeon, *m.*

Habiliment, *s.* habillement, *m.*, vêtements, *m.pl.*; équipage, attirail, *m.*

Habit, *s.* (*custom*) habitude, *f.*; coutume, *f.*; (*of the body*) disposition, *f.*; (*clothing*) habit, habillement, vêtement, costume, *m.*; (*for riding*) amazone, *f.m.* *Full —* (*of body*), disposition à la corpulence, *f.* *To be in the — of*, être dans l'habitude de, avoir pour habitude de, avoir coutume de. *To get* (or *fall*) *into a —*, prendre *or* contracter une habitude. — **shirt,** *s.* corps de fichu, *m.*

Habitable, *adj.* habitable

Habita-bleness, bility. *V.* page 3, § 1

Habitant, *s.* habitant, *m.*, e, *f.*

Habitat, *s.* habitat, *m.*

Habitation, *s.* habitation, demeure, *f.*

Habitual, *adj.* habituel, ordinaire

Habitually, *adv.* habituellement, d'habitude, ordinairement

Habituate, *v.a.* habituer, accoutumer

Habitude, *s.* habitude, coutume, *f.*

Habitus, *s.* habitus, *m*

Habnab, *adv.* au hasard

Hack, *v.a.* hacher (' *to*,' en); (*notch*) ébrécher; (*kill*) tuer, massacrer; (*a language*) écorcher, estropier, massacrer; — *s.* (*notch*) entaille, coche, brèche, *f.*; (*horse*) cheval de louage, *m.*; cheval de service *or* de fatigue, *m.*; (*jade*) rosse, *f.*; (*pad horse*) hack, *m.*; (*carriage*) *V.* **Hackney-carriage;** (*pers.*) homme de peine, *m.*, mercenaire, *m.f.*, (*literary*) écrivassier à gages, *m.*; — *adj.* de louage

Hacking-knife, *s.* hachette, *f.*

Hackle, *v.a.* (*hemp*, &c.) serancer, peigner; (*to tear*) déchirer; — *s.* soie écrue, soie crue, filasse, *f.*; (*instrument*) seran, serançoir, *m.*; (*fish.*) mouche, *f.*

Hackney, *s.* *V.* **Hack;** — *adj.* *V.* **Hackneyed;** — *v.a.* rompre, exercer, habituer. — **carriage, -coach,** *s.* voiture de louage, *f.*; voiture de place, *f.*; fiacre, *m.* — **coachman,** *s.* cocher de voiture de place, cocher de fiacre, *m.* — **man,** *s.* *V.* **Job-master**

Hackneyed, *adj.* (*for hire*) de louage; (*pers.*) à gages, mercenaire, stipendié; (*common*) commun, banal, trivial, rebattu; — *part.* exercé (dans), rompu (à), habitué (à), accoutumé (à), fait (à) [merluche, *f.*

Haddock, *s.* èglefin, ègrefin, *m.*; (*smoked*)

Hæma ..., Hæmo ..., *V.* **Hema ..., Hemo ...**

Haft, *s.* manche, *m.*; poignée, *f.*; — *v.a.* emmancher; mettre une poignée à

Hafter, *s.* emmancheur, *m.*

Hag, *s.* vieille sorcière, *f.*; (*fury*) furie, *f.*; (*zool.* — *fish*) gastrobranche, *m.*; myxine, *f.*; — *v.a.* tourmenter, obséder

Haggard, *adj.* hagard; égaré; sauvage, farouche

Haggardly, *adv.* d'un air hagard, hagardement

Haggish, *adj.* de sorcière; laid, hideux; difforme

Haggle, *v.a.* *V.* **Hack;** — *v.n.* marchander; hésiter, barguigner [guigneur, *m.*, -euse, *f.*

Haggler, *s.* marchandeur, *m.*, -euse, *f.*; bar-

Haggling, *s.* barguignage, *m.*

Hagiographal, *adj.* hagiographe

Hagiographer, *s.* hagiographe, *m.*

Hagio-graphic, al, -graphy, -logy, &c.

Hah, *int.* ha! [*V.* page 3, § 1

Ha-ha, *s.* saut de loup, haha, *m.*

Hail, *s.* (*frozen rain*) grêle, *f.*; (*salutation*) salut, *m.*; accueil, *m.*; (*nav.*) portée de voix, *f.*; — *int.* salut! — *v.n.* grêler; — *v.a.* (*pour down*) faire pleuvoir; (*salute*) saluer; accueillir; (*call*) appeler; (*a ship*) héler; (*a cab*) appeler, arrêter, héler. — *fellow well met*, familier, de pair à compagnon. *Within —*, (*nav.*) à portée de voix. — **rod,** *s.* paragrêle, *m.* — **stone,** *s.* grêlon, *m.* — **storm, -shower,** *s.* grêlée, grêle, *f.*

Hair, *s.* (*single —*) cheveu, *m.*; (*head of hair*) cheveux, *m.pl.*, chevelure, *f.*; (*of the body or animals, and bot.*) poil, *m.*; (*of horses' main and tail*) crin, *m.*; (*of boars*) soie, *f.* *Soft* or *downy —*, poil follet, *m.* *To a —*, à un cheveu près, exactement. *To dress anyone's —*, coiffer quelqu'un. *To dress o.'s (own) —*, arranger ses cheveux, se coiffer. *To have o.'s — cut*, se faire couper les cheveux. *To part o.'s —*, faire une raie dans ses cheveux, faire sa raie. *To split —s* or *a —*, *V.* **Split.** *To tear o.'s —*, s'arracher les cheveux. — **bag,** *s.* bourse à cheveux, *f.* — **bell,** *s. V.* **Harebell.** — **brained,** *adj. V.* **Harebrained.** — **breadth,** *s.* épaisseur d'un cheveu, *f.*, peu de chose, *m.*; *adj.* qui tient à un fil *or* à un cheveu (*V.* **Escape**). — **broom,** *s.* balai de crin, *m.* — **brush,** *s.* brosse à tête *or* à cheveux, *f.* — **cloth,** *s.* cilice, *m.*; (*for furniture*, &c.) tissu de crin, crin, *m.* — **cutter,** *s.* coiffeur, *m.* — **cutting,** *s.* coupe de cheveux, *f.* — **cutting room** *or* **saloon,** *s.* salon de coiffure, *m.* — **destroyer,** *s.* épilateur, épilatoire, *m.* — **dresser,** *s.* coiffeur, *m.*, -euse, *f.* — **dresser's assistant,** *s.* garçon coiffeur, *m.* — **dressing,** *s.* coiffure, *f.* — **dye,** *s.* teinture pour les cheveux, *f.* — **eel,** *s.* gordie, *f.* — **grass,** *s.* canche, *f.* —**less,** *adj.* sans poils; (*of the head*) chauve, sans cheveux; (*beardless*) imberbe. — **mattress,** *s.* sommier de crin, sommier, *m.* — **net,** *s.* filet à cheveux, *m.*, résille, *f.* — **pencil,** *s.* pinceau, *m.* — **pin,** *s.* épingle à cheveux, *f.* — **powder,** *s.* poudre pour les cheveux, *f.* — **restorer,** *s.* pommade *or* eau régénératrice (*or* réparatrice) des cheveux, *f.*, rénovateur des cheveux (*or* de la chevelure), *m.* — **shirt,** *s.* haire, *f.* — **sieve,** *s.* tamis de crin, *m.* — **splitter,** *s.* épilogueur, *m.*, -euse, *f.*, ergoteur, *m.*, -euse, *f.* — **splitting,** *s.* pointillerie, argutie, ergoterie, *f.*, épilogage, *m.* — **spring,** *s.* (*horol.*) ressort spiral, *m.* — **tail,** *s.* (*fish*) trichiure, *m.* — **trigger,** *s.* double détente, *f.* — **wash,** *s.* eau pour les cheveux, *f.* — **work,** *s.* ouvrage en cheveux, *m.*; (*of horse-hair*) ouvrage en crin, *m.* — **worker,** *s.* artiste en cheveux, *m.f.*, crinier, *m.* — **worm,** *s.* gordie, *f.*

Haired, *adj.* chevelu; (*in compounds*) aux cheveux ..., qui a les cheveux ...; au poil ..., qui a le poil ...

Hairiness, *s.* quantité *or* épaisseur de cheveux, *f.*; épaisseur de poils, *f.*; nature velue, *f.*

Hairy, *adj.* poilu, velu, chevelu; (*astr.*) chevelu

Hake, *s.* merluche, *f.*, merlus, *m.*

Halberd, *s.* hallebarde, *f.*

Halberdier, *s.* hallebardier, m.

Halcyon, *s.* alcyon, *m.*; — *adj.* alcyonien; (*fig.*) serein, heureux

Hale, *adj.* robuste, vigoureux, bien portant; — *v.a. V.* **Haul.** *To be — and hearty*, être frais et dispos, être frais et gaillard, être gaillard et dispos; avoir bon pied bon œil

Half, *s.* moitié, *f.*; demie, *f.*; — *adj.* demi; semi; — *adv.* (*with a noun or adj.*) à moitié; à mi; (*with a part. or verb*) à demi, à moitié; imparfaitement; (*almost*) presque. *... and a —*, ... et demi (... et demie, *after a substantive feminine*); (*of the numbers of houses*) ... bis. — *a loaf*, la moitié d'un pain. — *a bottle*, une demi-bouteille. — *an hour*, une demi-heure. *An hour and a —*, une heure et demie. *Two — bottles*, deux demi-bouteilles. *Two — circles*, deux demi-cercles. *Two hours and a —*, deux heures et demie. *Two yards and a —*, deux mètres et demi. *No.* 17½. (*of houses*) No. (numéro) 17 bis. — *as much*, la moitié autant. — *as much again*, la moitié plus. *By —*, de moitié; (*of dividing*) par moitié. *By halves*, à demi; (*of dividing*) par moitiés. *Too much by —*, la moitié trop. *Too long by —*, trop long de moitié. *In* or *into halves*, en deux. — *and —*, moitié de l'un et moitié de l'autre; (*of beer*) moitié ale et moitié porter. *Better —*, (*wife*) moitié, chère moitié, *f.* *To go halves*, être de moitié. *Halves! int.* part à deux! *She — started up in terror*, elle se dressa à demi (*or* à moitié) d'effarement. — **allowance,** *s.* demi-ration, *f.* — **baptism,** -**baptize,** *V.* **Baptism,** &c. — **binding,** *s.* demi-reliure, *f.* — **blood,** *s.* demi-sang, *m.* — **board,** *s.* demi-pension, *f.* — **boarder,** *s.* demi-pensionnaire, *m.f.* — **bound,** *adj.* (*of books*) en demi-reliure. — **bred,** *adj.* croisé, métis; (*of horses*) demi-sang, de demi-sang; (*fig.*) mal-appris. — **breed,** *s.* demi-sang, *m.* — **brother,** *s.* demi-frère, *m.* — **case,** *s.* (*print.*) casseau, *m.* — **cock,** *V.* **Cock.** — **crown,** *s.* (*old French coin*) petit écu, *m.*; (*English coin*) demi-couronne, *f.* — **dead,** *adj.* à demi mort, à moitié mort. — **deck,** *s.* pont coupé, *m.* — **done,** *adj.* à moitié fait; (*cooked*) à moitié cuit. — **door,** *s.* porte coupée, *f.* — **empty,** *adj.* à moitié vide; *v.a.* vider à moitié. — **fare,** *s.* demi-place, *f.* — **finished,** *adj.* imparfait, ébauché. — **holiday,** *s.* demi-congé, *m.* — **hour,** *s.* demie, *f.* — **length,** *adj. V.* **Length.** — **life-size,** *s.* demi-nature, *f.* — **mast,** — **mast high,** *adv.* à mi-mât. — **measure,** *s.* demi-mesure, *f.* — **moon,** *s.* demi-lune, *f.* — **mourning,** *s.* demi-deuil, petit deuil, *m.* — **open,** *v.a.* entr'ouvrir; *v.n.* s'entr'ouvrir; *adj.* entr'ouvert. — **pay,** *s. V.* **Pay.** — **penny,** *s.* sou, *m.*, cinq centimes, *m.pl.*; *adj.* d'un sou, de cinq centimes. — **pint,** *s. V.* **Pint.** — **price,** *s.* moitié prix; (*of seats*) demi-place, *f.* — **sister,** *s.* demi-sœur, *f.* — **sleeve,** *s.* bout de manche, *m.* — **sole,** *s.* demi-semelle, *f.*; *v.a.* mettre des demi-semelles à. — **tide,** *s. V.* **Tide.** — **tint,** *s.* demi-teinte, *f.* — **way,** *adv.* à moitié chemin, à mi-chemin; au milieu. — *way up the hill*, à mi-côte. — **witted,** *adj.* à moitié fou. — **year,** — **a year,** six mois, *m.pl.*; semestre, *m.* — **yearly,** *adj.* semestriel; *adv.* par semestre, tous les six mois, deux fois par an

Haliard. *V.* **Halyard**

Halibut, *s.* flétan, halibut, hellebut, *m.*

Haliotis, *s.* haliotide, *f.*

Hall, *s.* (*entrance*) vestibule, *m.*; (*room*) salle, *f.*; (*dining-room*) réfectoire, *m.*; (*manor*) château, *m.*; (*public building*) hôtel, *m.*; (*of corporations*) maison, *f.*, hôtel, *m.*; (*univers.*) collège, *m.*; (*courts of justice*) palais de justice, palais, *m.* *Servants' —*, office, *f.* — **keeper,** *s.* concierge, *m.f.*, suisse, *m.* — **lamp,** -**lantern,** *s.* lampe *or* lanterne de vestibule, *f.* — **mark,** *s.* poinçon du contrôle, contrôle, *m.*; *v.a.* contrôler. — **marking,** *s.* contrôlage, *m.* — **porter,** *s. V.* — **keeper**

Hallelujah, Halleluiah, *s.* alléluia, *m.*

Halliard. *V.* **Halyard**

Hallo, Halloo, *s.* cri, *m.*, huée, *f.*; — *v.n.* crier, huer; — *int. adv.* holà! holà ho! hé! ohé! tiens! ah! — *there!* hé là-bas!

Hallow, *v.a.* sanctifier; consacrer

Hallucinate, *v.a.* halluciner

Hallucination, *s.* hallucination, *f.*

Halo, *s.* (*astr.*) halo, *m.*, aréole, *f.*; (*fig.*) cercle lumineux, *m.*; (*glory*) auréole, *f.* — *of glory*, [auréole, *f.*

Haloscope, *s.* haloscope, *m.*

Halt, *v.n.* boiter, clocher; (*fig.*) hésiter, balancer; (*mil.*) faire halte; — *v.a.* faire faire halte à; — *adj.* boiteux, estropié; — *s.* (*mil.*) halte, *f.*; (*limping*) boitement, *m.*

Halter, *s.* (*pers.*) boiteux, *m.*, -euse, *f.*; (*rope*) corde, *f.*; (*of horses*) licou, *m.*; — *v.a.* (*horses*) mettre le licou à; (*to tie*) lier; (*pers.*) mettre la corde au cou à. — **cast,** *s.* enchevêtrure, *f.*

Halting, *s.* boitement, clochement, *m.* — **place,** *s.* halte, *f.* [lentement

Haltingly, *adv.* en boitant, en clochant,

Halve, *v.a.* partager en deux

Halyard, *s.* (*nav.*) drisse, *f.*

Ham, *s.* jarret, *m.*; (*of pork*) jambon, *m.* — **string,** *See below*

Hamadryad, *s.* hamadryade, *f.*

Hamburger, *s.* Hambourgeois, *m.*, e, *f.*

Hame, *s.* attelle, *f.*, attel, *m.*

Hamlet, *s.* hameau, *m.*

Hammer, *s.* marteau, *m.*; (*of auction*) enchère, *f.*, enchères, *f.pl.*; (*cock of a gun*, &c.) chien, marteau, *m.*; (*of flint-locks*) batterie, *f.*; — *v.a.* marteler, forger; (*leather*) battre; (*drive in*) faire entrer (à coups de marteau), enfoncer; — *v.n.* travailler au marteau; (*be busy*) travailler (à), travailler; (*recur*) revenir toujours (sur). *To* (or *by* or *under*) *the* —, à l'enchère, aux enchères. — **away,** *v.n.* travailler d'arrache-pied. — **cloth,** *s.* housse, *f.* — **fish,** *s.* marteau, *m.* — **harden,** *s.* écrouir. — **hardening,** *s.* écrouissage, écrouissement, *m.* — **head,** *s.* tête de marteau, *f.*; (*fish*) marteau, *m.* — **man,** *s. V.* **Hammerer.** — **up,** *v.a.* travailler au marteau

Hammerer, *s.* marteleur, forgeron, *m.*

Hammering, *s.* martelage, *m.*; (*noise*) bruit [de marteau, *m.*

Hammock, *s.* hamac, *m.*

Hamper, *s.* manne, *f.*, mannequin, panier, *m.*; hotte, *f.*; — *v.a.* empêtrer, entraver, embarrasser; entortiller

Hamster, *s.* (*zool.*) hamster, *m.*

Hamstring, *s.* jarret, *m.*; (*vet.*) tendon du jarret, *m.*; — *v.a.* couper les jarrets à; (*incapacitate*) couper bras et jambes à, paralyser

Hand, *s.* main, *f.*; (*a person*) homme, bras, *m.*; ouvrier, *m.*,-ière, *f.*; garçon, *m.*; employé, *m.*, e, *f.*; (*writing*) écriture, *f.*; signature, *f.*; (*side*) côté, *m.*; part, *f.*; (*talent*) talent, *m.*; (*of dials*) aiguille, *f.*; (*of cards*) jeu, *m.*, partie, *f.*; (*meas.*) main, palme, *f.*; (*of birds*) serre, *f.*; — *adj.* (*of tools*) à main; (*heavy*) à bras. *At* —, *ready* or *close at* —, sous la main, tout près, près, proche, à portée de la main; (*in readiness*) tout prêt. *At the —s of*, de la part de; de. *Bound — and foot*, pieds et poings liés. *By* —, à la main; à bras; (*of bringing up: children*) au biberon, (*birds*) à la brochette, (*other animals*) à la cuiller. *From — to* —, de main en main. *From — to mouth*, au jour le jour. — *in* —, se tenant par la main; (*agreeing*) d'accord, de concert, ensemble; (*in a bad sense*) d'intelligence. — *to* —, corps à corps. — *over head*, étourdiment. *In* —, en main; à la main; en train; en question; (*of cash, com.*) en caisse; (*of bills*, &c.) en portefeuille; (*of goods*) en magasin; (*of newspapers*) en main, en lecture. *Large* —, *V.* **Large.** *Off* —, *V.* **Off.** *On* —, entre les mains; sur les bras; (*com.*) en magasin. *On all —s*, de tous côtés, de toutes parts, partout. *On o.'s —s*, (*fig.*) sur les bras. *On the one* —, d'un côté, d'une part. *On the other* —, de l'autre côté, d'autre part; au contraire. *Out of* —, (*adject.*) fini; libre; (*adverb.*) immédiatement, sur-le-champ, tout de suite. *Right* —, main droite, *f.*; (*fig.*) bras droit, *m.* *Round* —, (*writ.*) écriture moyenne, *f.* *Running* —, coulée, écriture expédiée, *f.* *Second —; Short —; Small —: See Letter* **S.** *Under —; Upper —: See Letter* **U.** *Under the —s of*, dans les mains de. *With a high* —, haut la main, d'autorité, rondement, tambour battant; de haute lutte. *With both —s*, à deux mains. *With his —s behind him*, les mains (*or* les bras) derrière le dos. *To be a good — at*, être bon pour. *To be an old* —, n'être pas novice. *To be — and glove together*, être ensemble comme les deux doigts de la main. *To be near* or *nigh at* —, s'approcher, approcher; être *or* se trouver tout près *or* sous la main; se tenir à portée de la voix. *To come to* —, parvenir, arriver. *To get o.'s — in*, se faire la main. *To get the better* or *upper* —, avoir le dessus. *To go — in* —, se tenir par la main; (*agree*) marcher d'accord *or* de concert, aller ensemble; (*in a bad sense*) être d'intelligence. *To have a — in*, contribuer à, être pour quelque chose dans; (*in a bad sense*) tremper dans. *To have no — in*, n'être pour rien dans. *To keep a strict — on*, tenir la main haute à, tenir en bride. *To keep o.'s — in*, s'entretenir la main. *To lay violent —s on* (or *upon*) attenter à; violenter, maltraiter, attaquer; (*carry away*) faire main basse sur. *To lay violent —s on oneself*, attenter à ses jours, se donner la mort, se suicider. *To lend a* —, prêter la main à; donner un coup de main à, aider. *To play into ...'s —s*, donner beau jeu à ... *To play into each other's —s*, être d'intelligence. *To put* or *set o.'s — to*, mettre la main à. *To shake —s with*, *V.* **Shake.** *To take in* —, prendre en main; s'occuper de; se charger de; entreprendre; (*help*) mettre la main à. *To take o.'s — off* ..., ôter la main de ... *To take* (...) *off his —s*, le débarrasser de ... *To try o.'s* —, s'essayer. *To write a good* —, avoir une bonne écriture. *Keep off your —s*, ne touchez pas. *—s off!* ne touchez pas! à bas les mains! ôtez vos mains! *My — is in*, je suis en train *or* en veine, j'y suis. *My — is out*, je ne suis plus en train, je n'y suis plus. — **barrow,** *s.* civière, *f.*, brancard, *m.* — **basket,** *s.* panier à anse, *m.* — **bell,** *s.* clochette, sonnette, *f.* — **bill,** *s.* avis à la main, prospectus, imprimé, *m.*; (*poster*) affiche, *f.* — **book,** *s.* manuel, *m.*; livret, *m.*; guide, *m.* — **cart,** *s.* charrette à bras, *f.* — **chair,** *s.* vinaigrette, brouette, *f.* — **cuff,** *s.* menotte, *f.*; *v.a.* emmenotter, menotter, mettre les menottes à, garrotter. —**ful,** *s.* poignée, *f.* *A double —ful*, deux poignées, *f.pl.* — **gallop,** *s.* petit galop, *m.* — **gear,** *s.* manette, mannette, *f.* — **glass,** *s.* cloche à jardin, cloche, *f.* — **grenade,** *s.* grenade à la main, *f.* — **guard,** *s.* garde-main, *m.f.* — **guide,** *s.* guide-main, *m.* — **gun,** *s.* fusil, *m.* — **jack,** *s.* vérin, *m.* —**kerchief,** *s.* mouchoir, *m.*; (*of silk*) foulard, *m.*; (*for the neck: of men*) cravate, *f.*, (*of women*) fichu, *m.* *Pocket —kerchief, Silk —kerchief*, *V.* **Pocket** *and* **Silk.** — **lead,** *s.* (*nav.*) petite sonde, *f.* — **leather,** *s.* manique, *f.* —**less,** *adj.* manchot. — **light,** *s.* cloche, *f.* — **loom,** *s.* métier à la main, *m.* — **made,** *adj.* fait *or* fabriqué à la main. — **maid, -maiden,** *s.* servante, *f.* — **mill,** *s.* moulin à bras, *m.* — **organ,** *s.* orgue portatif, orgue de Barbarie, *m.* — **press,** *s.* presse à bras, *f.* — **rail,** *s.* garde-fou, *m.*; rampe, *f.*; (*build.*) lisse, main courante, *f.*; (*of a steam-engine or train*) main courante, *f.*; (*of the piano*) guide-main, *m.* — **railing,** *s.* (*build.*) lisse, *f.* — **rake,** *s.* râteau à bras, *m.* — **rest,** *s.* appui-main, *m.* — **saw,** *s.* scie à main, *f.* — **screen,** *s.* écran à main, *m.* — **screw,** *s.* vérin, *m.* — **shaking,** *s.* serrement de main, *m.* — **shovel,** *s.* pelle à main, main, *f.* — **spike,** *s.* levier, *m.*; (*nav.*) anspect, *m.* — **vice,** *s.* étau à main, *m.* — **work,** *s.* travail (*or* ouvrage) manuel, *m.* — **writing,** *s.* écriture, main, *f.*

Hand, *v.a.* passer, donner; (*help, lead*) donner la main *or* le bras à. — **about,** passer de main en main. — **down,** descendre; transmettre; (*a person*) donner la main *or* le bras à (... pour descendre *or* pour aider à descendre), aider à descendre. — **in, over,** remettre, livrer. (— *in, a pers. into a carriage*) donner la main à (pour monter), aider à monter, (*into anything else*) donner la main à (pour entrer), aider à entrer. — **out,** (*a person*) donner la main à (pour sortir *or* descendre). — **round,** faire circuler, faire passer. — **up,** donner la main à (pour monter), aider à monter

Handed, *adj.* (*in compounds*) aux mains ..., qui a les mains ..., les mains ...

Handicap, *s.* handicap, *m.*; — *v.a.n.* handicaper

Handicapper, *s.* handicapeur, *m.*

Handicraft, *s.* main-d'œuvre, *f.*; (*trade*) métier, *m.*; (*pers.*) artisan, ouvrier, manœuvre, *m.* —**sman,** *s.* artisan, ouvrier, manœuvre, *m.*

Handily, *adv.* adroitement, habilement; (*with ease*) commodément

Handiness, *s.* adresse, habileté, dextérité, *f.*; [(*ease*) commodité, *f.*

Handiwork, *s.* main-d'œuvre, *f.*; ouvrage, *m.*; travail des mains, travail (*or* ouvrage) manuel, *m.*

Handle, *v.a.* manier; (*feel*) toucher; (*treat*) traiter; (*practise*) exercer, pratiquer; — *s.* (*of brushes, knives,* &c.) manche, *m.*; (*of swords,* &c.) poignée, *f.*; (*of baskets, pots,* &c.) anse, *f.*; (*of doors*) bouton, *m.*; (*end*) bout, *m.*; côté, *m.*; (*of a barrow*) bras, *m.*; (*of frying-pans*) queue, *f.*; (*of ploughs*) mancheron, *m.*; (*of pumps*) bras, *m.*, brimbale, *f.*; (*winch*) manivelle, *f.*; (*fig.*) prise, *f.*; instrument, *m.*; armes, *f.pl.* *To make a — of,* tourner à son avantage

Handled, *adj.* (*in compounds*) à manche ...

Handling, *s.* maniement, *m.*

Handsel, *s.* étrenne, *f.*; — *v.a.* étrenner

Handsome, *adj.* beau; joli; élégant; bon; généreux; honnête; honorable; flatteur

Handsomely, *adv.* joliment, élégamment, bien; généreusement, grandement; (*of behaviour*) galamment, délicatement; (*nav.*) doucement

Handsomeness, *s.* beauté, *f.*; grâce, élégance, *f.*; (*of behaviour*) délicatesse, générosité, libéralité, *f.*

Handy, *adj.* (*pers.*) adroit, habile; (*things*) commode; utile; (*near*) sous la main, à la portée de la main

Hang, *v.a.n.* pendre; suspendre; (*a room*) tapisser, tendre ('*with,*' de); (*let fall*) baisser, pencher, laisser tomber; (*bells,* &c.) poser; (*lean*) se pencher, s'incliner; (*cling*) s'accrocher (à); être attaché (à); (*stick, as doors,* &c.) tenir; (*remain*) rester; (*rest*) reposer; dépendre (de); (*be burdensome*) peser (sur), être à charge (à). *To go and be —ed,* (*fam.*) aller se faire fiche, aller se faire sucre, aller se promener. — ...*!* au diable ...! que le diable emporte ...! — *it!* au diable! zut! sapristi! fichtre! bigre! — **about,** *v.n.* s'attacher à, être suspendu à; traîner; stationner. — **back,** *v.n.* rester en arrière, reculer. — **by,** *v.n.* appendre; ne tenir qu'à. — **dog,** *adj.* patibulaire. — *dog face* or *look,* mine patibulaire, *f.* — **down,** *v.a.n.* baisser, pencher; (*flabbily*) tomber, pendre; s'avachir. — **heavy,** *v.n. V.* **Heavy.** — **loose,** *v.n.* pendiller; flotter. — **man,** *s.* bourreau, *m.* — **nail,** *s.* envie, *f.* — **on, upon,** (*a thread*) ne tenir qu'à (un fil). — **out,** *v.n.a.* pendre (à); être suspendu (à); déployer; (*to dry,* &c.) étendre; (*hoist*) arborer, élever. — **over,** *V.* **Overhang.** — **together,** *v.n.* tenir; (*agree*) s'accorder; être uni; faire la paire; être de la même pâte. — **up,** *v.a.* pendre, suspendre; accrocher; (*to dry,* &c.) étendre; (*keep undecided*) tenir en suspens; *v.n.* pendre (à), être suspendu (à)

Hanger, *s.* (*hook*) crochet, *m.*; (*of belts,* &c.) pendant, *m.*; (*knife*) couteau de chasse, *m.*; (*pers.*) personne qui pend, *f.* — **on,** *s.* importun, *m.*, e, *f.*; dépendant, *m.*, e, *f.*, parasite, *m.f.*, écornifleur, *m.*, -euse, *f.*

Hanging, *part. adj.* (*down*) pendant, tombant; (*suspended*) suspendu (à); pendu (à); (*resting*) appuyé; (*punishable*) pendable; (*forbidding*) patibulaire; (*nav.*) vertical; — *s.* (*death*) corde, pendaison, *f.*; (*of bells,* &c.) pose, *f.*; (*of rooms*) tenture, tapisserie, *f.*; (*of book-cases*) pente, *f.*; (*of trees*) branchage, *m.* — *bridge,* pont suspendu, *m.* — *face* or *look,* mine patibulaire, *f.* — *garden,* jardin suspendu, *m.* — *matter,* cas pendable, *m.* — *stage,* pont volant, *m.*

Hank, *s.* (*of skeins*) botte, poignée, pantine, *f.*; — *v.a.* mettre en bottes, pantiner

Hanker, *v.n.* soupirer (après), désirer ardemment, avoir grande envie (de)

Hankering, *s.* vif désir, *m.*, grande envie. *f.*

Hanoverian, *s. adj.* Hanovrien, *m.*, -ne, *f.*

Hanse, Hanseatic, *adj.* hanséatique

Hansom, *s.* cabriolet (de place), *m.*; (*English ditto*) cab, *m.*

Hap, *s.* hasard, *m.*; (*misfortune*) accident, *m.*, mauvaise fortune, *f.*; — *v.n. V.* **Happen.** — **hazard,** *s.* hasard, accident, *m.* *At — hazard,* au hasard. —**less,** *adj.* malheureux, infortuné. —**lessly,** *adv.* malheureusement. —**lessness,** *s.* malheur, *m.*, mauvaise fortune, infortune, *f.* —**ly,** *adv.* peut-être; par hasard, par accident; (*unfortunately*) par malheur

Happen, *v.n.* arriver; se passer; (*to be found, to be, to be so situated as to* ...) se trouver par hasard, se trouver; être; (*be seen*) se voir; (*fall*) tomber; (*arise, supervene*) survenir. *To — to somebody to* ..., arriver à quelqu'un de ... *An accident has —ed,* un accident est arrivé, il est arrivé un accident. *If he —s to come,* s'il arrive qu'il vienne. *If you — to see him,* s'il vous arrive de le voir. *If he should — to see you,* s'il venait à vous voir, s'il vous voyait par hasard. *A carriage —ed to pass by,* une voiture vint à passer. *If you — to stand in need of* ..., si vous vous trouvez avoir besoin de ... *You don't — to have* ...? vous n'auriez pas par hasard ...? *As if nothing had —ed,* comme si de rien n'était. — *what may,* — *what will,* arrive (*or* advienne) que pourra. — **again,** arriver encore, se renouveler (*won't — again,* n'arrivera plus)

Happily, *adv.* heureusement, par bonheur

Happiness, *s.* bonheur, *m.*; (*blessedness*) félicité, *f.*

Happy, *adj.* heureux ('*to,*' de)

Harangue, *s.* harangue, *f.*, discours, *m.*; — *v.a.n.* haranguer, faire un discours

Haranguer, *s.* harangueur, *m.*, -euse, *f.*, orateur, *m.*

Harass, *v.a.* harasser; tourmenter; lasser, fatiguer; excéder; accabler ('*with,*' de); (*mil.*) harceler

Harbinger, *s.* avant-coureur, précurseur, *m.*

Harbour, *s.* (*lodging*) logement, logis, gîte, *m.*; (*of sea, river*) port, *m.*; (*shelter*) asile, refuge, abri, *m.*, retraite, *f.*, port, *m.*; — *v.a.* héberger, loger, recevoir, accueillir, recueillir, donner un asile à, donner l'hospitalité à; (*entertain*) entretenir, nourrir; — *v.n.* loger, séjourner; se réfugier, trouver un asile. — *of refuge,* port de refuge, *m.* *Inner —,* arrière-port. *m.* *Outer —,* avant-port, *m.* — **dues,** *s. pl.* droit de mouillage, *m.* —**less,** *adj.* sans port; (*fig.*) sans asile. — **master,** *s.* capitaine *or* officier de port, *m.*

Harbourer, *s.* hôte, *m.*

Hard, *adj.* dur; (*firm*) ferme; (*rough*) rude; difficile; pénible; sévère, rigoureux, cruel; (*bad*) mauvais; (*great*) grand; fort; (*of frost, rain,* &c.) fort; (*of winter*) rigoureux, rude; (*of blows,* &c.) grand, rude, violent; (*of fights*) rude, opiniâtre; (*of the hands*) calleux; (*of water*) cru, dur; (*close-fisted, stingy*) dur à la desserre; — *adv.* dur; durement; rudement; difficilement, péniblement; sévèrement, rigoureusement; (*strongly, much*) fort; ferme, fort et ferme; bien; vigoureusement; vivement; (*of drinking*) sec; (*earnestly*) instamment; (*swiftly*) vite, raide, rondement; (*heavily*) lourdement; (*badly*) mal; (*of staring*) fixement; (*nav.*) tout. — *by* (or *upon*), *by it, by them* (*things*), tout près. — *of belief,* peu crédule, incrédule. — *to deal with,* intraitable, peu sociable. — *to please,* difficile à contenter, difficile. — *a-lee!* lof tout! — *aport!* bâbord tout! — *-a-weather!* arrive tout! *To die —,* *V.* **Die.** *To get* or *grow —,* *V.* **Grow.** *To hold —,* tenir bien; arrêter. — **bake,** *v.a.* (*china*) japonner; *s.* (*conf.*) caramel, *m.* — **boiled,** *adj.* (*of eggs*) dur. — **drinker,** *s.* *To be a — drinker,* boire sec. — **earned,** *adj.* gagné avec peine. — **fought,** *adj.* opiniâtre, acharné. — **headed,** *adj.* sage. — **hearted,** *adj.* au cœur dur, qui a le cœur dur, dur, insensible, inhumain. — **heartedness,** *s.* dureté de cœur, dureté, insensibilité, *f.* — **lines,** *s. pl.* dur, pénible; une chose dure, *f.* — **mouthed,** *adj.* qui a la bouche dure, qui n'a pas de bouche, pesant à la main. — **pointed,** *adj.* (*of pens*) à bec dur. — **reader,** *s.* dévoreur (*m.*, -euse, *f.*) de livres. — **set,** *adj.* fort embarrassé, aux expédients, aux abois, serré de près, pressé. — **up,** *adv.* vivement pressé; aux abois; (*of money*) gêné, dans la débine, à sec, à court (de); aux abois. — **visaged,** *adj.* qui a les traits durs, qui a le visage rude, qui a la mine désagréable. — **ware,** *s.* quincaillerie, *f.* — **wareman,** *s.* quincaillier, *m.* — **wood,** *s.* bois dur, *m.* — **words,** *s. pl. V.* **Word.** — **worker,** *s.* grand travailleur, *m.*, grande travailleuse, *f.*, (*fam.*) piocheur, *m.*, -euse, *f.* — **working,** *adj.* laborieux, (*fam.*) piocheur

Harden, *v.a.* durcir; (*fig.*) endurcir; affermir, raffermir; (*steel*) tremper; — *v.n. V.* **Grow hard**

Hardening, *s.* durcissement, *m.*; (*pers.*) endurcissement, *m.*; (*of steel*) trempe, *f.*

Hardihood, *s. V.* **Hardiness**

Hardily, *adv.* à la dure; durement, péniblement; (*boldly*) hardiment, audacieusement, intrépidement, avec intrépidité; (*severely*) sévèrement

Hardiness, *s.* force, vigueur, *f.*; hardiesse, audace, intrépidité, *f.*; effronterie, impudence, assurance, *f.*

Hardish, *adj.* un peu dur *or* &c. (*V.* **Hard**)

Hardly, *adv.* durement; (*roughly*) rudement; (*severely*) sévèrement, rigoureusement; (*with difficulty*) difficilement, péniblement, avec peine; (*badly*) mal; (*scarcely*) *V.* **Scarcely**

Hardness, *s.* dureté, *f.*; (*roughness*) rudesse, *f.*; (*severity*) rigueur, sévérité, *f.*; (*difficulty*) difficulté, *f.*; (*of the heart*) endurcissement, *m.*; (*of steel*) trempe, *f.*; (*of water*) crudité, *f.*

Hardship, *s.* peine, chose pénible, *f.*; fatigue, *f.*; tribulation, *f.*; souffrance, *f.*; privation, *f.*; rigueur, *f.*; difficulté, *f.*; injustice, *f.*

Hardy, *adj.* robuste, vigoureux; endurci à la fatigue; hardi, audacieux, intrépide; effronté, impudent, plein d'assurance; (*plant*) rustique; (*ferns, shrubs, annuals,* &c.) de pleine terre

Hare, *s.* lièvre, *m.*, hase, *f.*; — *v.a.* levrauder. *Young* —, levraut, *m. Jugged* or *stewed* —, civet de lièvre, *m. To run with the — and hold with the hounds,* ménager la chèvre et le chou. — **bell,** *s.* campanule, clochette, *f.*; jacinthe des prés, *f.* — **brained,** *adj.* écervelé, étourdi. — **foot,** *s.* pied-de-lièvre, *m.* — **hearted,** *adj.* timide, craintif, poltron. — **hound,** *s. V.* **Harrier.** — **hunting,** *s.* chasse au lièvre, *f.* — **lip,** *s.* bec-de-lièvre, *m.* — **lipped,** *adj.* à bec-de-lièvre. — **ragout,** *s.* civet de lièvre, *m.* —**'s-ear,** *s.* (*bot.*) perce-feuille, *f.*

Harem, *s.* harem, *m.*

Harfang, *s.* harfang, *m.*

Haricot, *s.* haricot, *m.*

Harier. *V.* **Harrier**

Hark, *v.n.* écouter; — *int.* écoutez! écoute!

Harl, *s.* filasse, *f.*

Harlequin, *s.* arlequin, *m.*; — *v.n.* faire des arlequinades

Harlequinade, *s.* arlequinade, *f.*

Harlot, *s.* prostituée, fille de joie, catin, *f.*

Harlotry, *s.* catinerie, *f.*

Harm, *s.* mal, *m.*; malheur, *m.*; (*wrong*) tort, préjudice, dommage, *m.*; inconvénient, *m.*; — *v.a.* nuire à, faire du mal à, faire du tort à. *Bodily* —, (*law*) voies de fait, *f.pl. Grievous bodily* —, (*law*) voies de fait et blessures, *f.pl. Out of —'s way,* en sûreté. *There is no — in her,* elle n'est pas méchante; elle n'y entend pas malice. *There is no — in that,* il n'y a pas de mal à cela. —**ful,** &c. *V.* **Hurtful,** &c. —**less,** *adj.* innocent, inoffensif; (*unhurt*) sain et sauf. *To bear* or *hold* or *save —less,* mettre à couvert, protéger. —**lessly,** *adv.* innocemment; (*without hurt*) sain et sauf. —**lessness,** *s.* innocence, *f.*

Harmonic, -al, *adj.* harmonique; — *s.* harmonique, *m.*; —**s,** *s. pl.* harmonie, *f.*; (*sounds*) harmoniques, *m.pl.*

Harmonica, Harmonicon, *s.* harmonica, *m.*; verrillon, *m.*

Harmonically, *adv.* harmoniquement

Harmonichord, *s.* harmonicorde, *m.*

Harmonicon, *s.* harmonicon, *m.*

Harmonious, *adj.* harmonieux; (*pers.*) en harmonie, d'accord, en bon accord

Harmoniously, *adv.* harmonieusement, avec harmonie; (*pers.*) en harmonie, en bon accord

Harmoniousness, *s.* harmonie, *f.*

Harmonist, *s.* harmoniste, *m.f.*

Harmonium, *s.* harmonium, *m.*

Harmonization, *s.* harmonisation, *f.*

Harmonize, *v.n.* être en harmonie; s'harmoniser, s'accorder; — *v.a.* harmoniser, mettre en harmonie, mettre d'accord

Harmonizer, *s.* conciliateur, *m.*, -trice, *f.*; (*mus.*) harmonisateur, *m.*, -trice, *f.*

Harmonizing, *adj.* harmonisateur

Harmony, *s.* harmonie, *f.*; accord, *m.*

Harness, *s.* harnais, *m.*; (*of cavalry*) harnachement, *m.*; — *v.a.* harnacher, enharnacher; (*to a carriage*) atteler. *Goes well in* —, est bon à la voiture. *Good for saddle and* —, à deux fins. *To die in* —, mourir à la peine. — **horse,** *s.* cheval d'attelage, cheval de harnais, *m.* — **maker,** *s.* harnacheur, bourrelier, *m.* — **making,** *s.* bourrellerie, *f.* — **room,** *s.* sellerie, *f.*

Harnesser, *s.* harnacheur, *m*

Harnessing, *s.* harnachement, *m.* — **groom,** *s.* harnacheur, *m.*

Harp, *s.* harpe, *f.*; — *v.n.* jouer de la harpe; (*dwell on*) revenir (sur), répéter, rabâcher. *To — upon one string,* chanter toujours la même chanson *or* la même antienne, rabâcher toujours la même chose. — **player,** *s.* joueur (*m.*, -euse, *f.*) de harpe. — **shaped,** *adj.* harpé. — **shell,** *s.* harpe, *f.* — **string,** *s.* corde de harpe, *f.*

Harper, *s.* harpeur, *m.*

Harping, *s.* musique de harpe, *f.*; (*dwelling on*) rabâchage, *m.*, répétition, *f.*

Harpist, *s.* harpiste, *m.f.*

Harpoon, *s.* harpon, *m.*; — *v.a.* harponner

Harpooner, *s.* harponneur, *m.*

Harpooning, *s.* harponnage, harponnement, *m.*

Harpsichord, *s.* clavecin, *m.*

Harpy, *s.* harpie, *f.* — **eagle,** *s.* harpie, *f.*

Harridan, *s.* vieille rosse, vieille garce, *f.*

Harrier, *s.* briquet pour la chasse au lièvre, chien courant (pour le lièvre), *m.*; (*bird*) busard, *m.*

Harrow, *s.* herse, *f.*; — *v.a.* herser; (*torment*) déchirer, torturer; agiter, troubler

Harrower, *s.* herseur, *m.*

Harrowing, *s.* hersage, *m.*; (*fig.*) déchirement, *m.*; — *adj.* déchirant, navrant

Harry, *v.a.* harasser; harceler; maltraiter; tourmenter; (*pillage*) piller, dépouiller, dévaster

Harsh, *adj.* dur; rude; sévère; (*offensive*) blessant; (*of taste*) âpre; (*crabbed*) aigre. —**ly,** *adv.* durement; rudement; sévèrement; aigrement. — **ness,** *s.* dureté, *f.*; rudesse, *f.*; sévérité, *f.*; âpreté, *f.*; aigreur, *f.*

Harslet, *s.* fressure (de cochon), *f.*

Hart, *s.* cerf, *m.* — **shorn,** *s.* corne de cerf, *f.* — **stongue,** *s.* scolopendre, *f.* — **wort,** *s.* séséli, *m.*

Harum-scarum, *adj.* écervelé, braque, étourdi, brouillon; (*things*) en l'air; — *adv.* bredi-breda; pêle-mêle

Haruspice, *s* aruspice, *m.*

Harvest, *s.* (*of grain*) moisson, *f.*; (*crop, of fruits, vegetables,* &c.) récolte, *f.*; (*fig.*) moisson, *f.*; fruit, *m.*, fruits, *m.pl.*; — *v.a.* moissonner; (*gather*) récolter. *To get in the* —, faire la moisson. — **bug,** *s.* lepte automnal, rouget, vendangeron, *m.*, tique, *f.* — **fly,** *s.* cigale, *f.* — **home, -feast, -festival,** *s.* temps de la moisson, *m.*; fête de la moisson, *f*; chant de la moisson, *m.* — **lord,** *s.* chef des moissonneurs, *m.* — **man,** *s.* moissonneur, *m.*; (*spider*) faucheux, *m.* — **moon,** *s.* lune d'août, *f.* — **queen,** *s.* reine de la moisson, reine des moissonneurs, *f.* — **time,** *s.* temps de la moisson, *m* — **woman,** *s.* moissonneuse, *f.*

Harvester, *s.* moissonneur, *m.*, -euse *f.*

Harvesting, *s.* moissonnage, *m.*
Haschish. *V.* **Hashish**
Hash, *v.a.* hacher; — *s.* hachis, *m.*
Hasheesh, Hashish, *s.* hachich, hachisch, *m.*
Haslet, *s.* fressure (de cochon), *f.*
Hasp, *s.* loquet, *m.*; moraillon, m.; — *v.a.* fermer au loquet; fermer au moraillon
Hassock, *s.* agenouilloir, carreau, *m.*; coussin, *m.*
Hastate, Hastated, *adj.* hasté
Haste, *s.* hâte, diligence, *f.*; précipitation, *f.*; (*passion*) vivacité, impatience, *f.*, emportement, *m.*; — *v.a.n.* *V.* **Hasten.** *In* —, en hâte, à la hâte; pressé. *In great* —, en grande hâte; très pressé. *To be in* —, avoir hâte (de), être pressé (de). *To make* —, se dépêcher, se hâter; se presser, se diligenter, faire diligence. *To make — back*, se dépêcher de revenir, revenir vite. *To make — down*, se dépêcher de descendre, descendre vite. *Most — worst speed; More — less speed;* hâtez-vous lentement
Hasten, *v.a.* hâter, presser; précipiter; — *v.n.* se hâter (de), se dépêcher (de); s'empresser (de); (*run*) accourir (à), courir (à); hâter le pas (vers). — **away,** s'éloigner à la hâte; s'enfuir précipitamment. — **back,** revenir à la hâte; retourner à la hâte; s'en retourner précipitamment. — **on,** se hâter; presser le pas, allonger le pas; courir, accourir. — **out,** sortir précipitamment (de); s'élancer hors (de). — **up,** monter précipitamment
Hastily, *adv.* à la hâte; précipitamment; (*passionately*) avec vivacité, avec emportement, avec colère
Hastiness, *s.* hâte, diligence, promptitude, *f.*; précipitation, *f.*; (*passion*) vivacité, impatience, *f.*, emportement, *m.*
Hasting, *s.* (— *pea*, — *pear*) hâtiveau, *m.*
Hasty, *adj.* prompt, rapide; précipité; irréfléchi; (*passionate*) vif, emporté, violent; (*of fruit*) précoce, hâtif. — **pudding,** *s.* bouillie, *f.*; (*of maize*) gaude, *f.*
Hat, *s.* chapeau, chapeau d'homme, *m.* —*s off!* à bas les chapeaux! — **band,** *s.* galon *or* ruban de chapeau, *m.*; (*com.*) bourdalou, *m.*; (*mourning*) crêpe, *m.* — **box, -case,** *s.* carton à chapeau, *m.*, (*of leather*) étui à chapeau, *m.* — **brush,** *s.* brosse à chapeau, *f.* — **guard,** *s.* caoutchouc (de chapeau), *m.* — **lining,** *s.* doublure de chapeau, *f.* — **making, -manufactory,** *s.* chapellerie, *f.* — **manufacturer,** *s.* chapelier, *m.*, -ière, *f.* — **money,** *s.* (*nav.*) primage, *m.* — **stand,** *s.* porte-chapeaux, *m.* — **trade,** *s.* chapellerie, *f.*
Hatch, *v.n.* éclore; — *v.a.* faire éclore; couver; (*plot*) tramer, couver, former, préparer; (*draw., engr.*) hacher; — *s.* (*brood*) couvée, *f.*; (*hatching*) éclosion, *f.*; (*discovery*) découverte, *f.*; (*a door*) porte coupée, *f.*; (*of a canal*) vanne, *f.*; (*nav.*) écoutille, *f.* — **way,** *s.* écoutille, *f.*
Hatchel. *V.* **Hackle**
Hatchet, *s.* hache, hachette, cognée, *f.*
Hatching, *s.* hachure, *f.*; (*of eggs*) éclosion, *f.*
Hatchment, *s.* écusson (funèbre) *m.*, armes, armoiries, *f.pl.*
Hate, *v.a.* haïr, détester, avoir en horreur; ne pas aimer; — *s.* haine, *f.* — **ful,** *adj.* haïssable, odieux, détestable; haineux, de haine. — **fully,** *adv.* odieusement, d'une manière odieuse, détestablement; haineusement, avec haine. — **fulness,** *s.* nature odieuse *or* détestable, *f.*; énormité, *f.*; odieux, *m.*
Hater, *s.* personne qui hait, *f.*, ennemi, *m.*, e. *f.* *To be a — of*, hair. *To be a good* —, savoir [haïr
Hatred, *s.* haine, *f.*
Hatter, *s.* chapelier, *m.*, -ière, *f.*
Hatting, *s.* chapellerie, *f.*
Hauberk, *s.* haubert, *m.*
Haughtily, *adv.* d'une manière hautaine, avec hauteur, arrogamment, fièrement
Haughtiness, *s.* hauteur, arrogance, *f.*
Haughty, *adj.* hautain, altier, arrogant, fier
Haul, *v.a.* tirer, traîner; (*in a bad sense*) tirailler; (*nav.*) haler; — *s.* action de tirer, *f.*; (*in a bad sense*) tiraillement, *m.*; (*fish.*) coup de filet, *m.* *At a* —, d'un coup de filet. *To — the wind*, aller contre le vent, bouter au lof. — **down,** amener. — **in,** haler à bord. — **out, up,** [hisser
Haulier, *s.* camionneur, *m.*
Hauling, *s.* tiraillement, *m.*; (*carting*) camionnage, *m.*
Haulm, Haum, *s.* chaume, *m.*; (*stem*) tige, *f.*
Haunch, *s.* hanche, *f.*; (*of venison*) cuissot, quartier, *m.*; (*of mutton*) quartier, *m.* — **bone,** *s.* os coxal, *m.*
Haunt, *v.a.* fréquenter, hanter; importuner, obséder, poursuivre; (*of spirits*) visiter; — *s.* lieu fréquenté (par . . .), *m.*; rendez-vous, *m.*; retraite, *f.*; (*in a bad sense*) repaire, *m.*
Haunted, *part. adj.* fréquenté, &c. (*V.* **Haunt,** *v.a.*); (*by spirits*) visité par des revenants, où il y a des revenants, où il revient des esprits, fréquenté par les esprits *or* par les fées, hanté. *That house is* —, il revient des esprits dans cette maison, des esprits reviennent dans cette maison, il y a des revenants dans cette maison
Haunter, *s.* personne qui fréquente *or* qui hante, *f.*, hanteur, *m.*, -euse, *f.*, habitué, *m.*, e. *f.*; (*in a bad sense*) pilier, *m.*
Haunting, *s.* fréquentation, hantise, *f.*
Hautboy, *s.* (*mus. instr.*) hautbois, *m.*; (*strawberry: fruit*) capron, *m.*, (*plant*) capronier, *m.*
Hautboyist, *s.* hautbois, *m.*, hautboïste, *m.f.*
Havana, Havanna, Havannah, *s.* (*geog.*) la Havane, *f.*; (*a cigar*) havane, cigare de la Havane, *m.*
Havanese, *s. adj.* Havanais, *m.* e, *f.*
Have, *v.a.* avoir; posséder; contenir; (*hold*) tenir; (*a bath, &c., take*) prendre; (*eat*) manger; (*drink*) boire; (*a meal, fare, walk, run, ride, drive, nap, fall, journey, illness, &c.*) faire; (*a night*) passer; (*cause anything to be done*) faire; (*know*) savoir; (*send for*) faire venir. *To — from*, tenir de. *To — a coat made*, faire faire un habit. *To — a house built*, faire bâtir une maison. *To — it*, (*say*) dire; (*hit it*) y être. *Will you* —, voulez-vous avoir; (*do you wish for*) voulez-vous. *I will not* (or *I won't*) — *it*, (*I object*) je ne le veux pas, (*reject*) je n'en veux pas. *She will not — him*, elle ne veut pas de lui. *He will — it to be so*, il veut que ce soit ainsi. *How will you — that coat made*, comment voulez-vous que cet habit soit fait? *I will not — you do that*, je ne veux pas que vous fassiez cela. *We — to contend*, nous avons à lutter. *I — to be there*, je dois y être, il faut que j'y sois. *To — sleep*, *V.* **Sleep,** *s.* *To — breakfast* or *lunch*, *to — o.'s breakfast* or *o.'s lunch*, déjeuner. *To — dinner* or *o.'s dinner*, dîner. *To — supper* or *o.'s supper*, souper. *To — a good breakfast or* &c., faire un bon déjeuner *or* &c., *To — a walk*, faire une promenade, se promener. *Had I known that*, *if I had known that*, si j'avais (*or* si j'eusse) su cela. *May be had at*, (*com.*) en vente chez. — **about** *one*, avoir sur soi — **away,** (*pers.*) emmener; (*things*) emporter. — **back,** (*pers.*) faire revenir; (*things*) faire rendre. *Let me — it back*, renvoyez-le-moi, rapportez-le-moi, rendez-le-moi. — **down,** faire descendre. — **in,** faire entrer. — **on,** porter, avoir sur soi, avoir, être vêtu de. — **out,** faire sortir. — **up,** faire monter; (*things*) monter. — **with** *one*, posséder; garder [*m.*, retraite, *f.*
Haven, *s.* havre, port, *m.*; (*fig.*) asile, refuge,
Haver, *s.* possesseur, *m.*
Haversack, Havresack. *V.* **Knapsack**
Havoc, *s.* ravage, dégât, *m.*, dévastation, *f.*; — *v.a.* ravager, dévaster. *To play — with*, faire du dégât de
Haw, *s.* (*bot.*) cenelle, *f.*; (*a field*) clos, *m.*; (*in the eye*) maille, *f.*; — *v.n.* (*to hem* or *hum and* —) ânonner. — **ditch,** *s.* *V.* — **haw.** — **finch,** *s.* dur-bec, *m.* — **haw,** *s.* haha, saut

de loup, *m.* — **thorn,** *s.* aubépine, épine blanche, *f.* [nement, *m.*
Hawing, *s. Hemming* or *humming and* —, ânon-
Hawk, *s.* faucon, *m.*; épervier, *m.*; — *v.n.* chasser au faucon; (*fly at*) voler; (*fig.*) attaquer; (*to spit*) hemmer, (*fam.*) graillonner; — *v.a.* colporter. — **bill turtle,** *s.* caret, carrec, *m.* — **eyed,** *adj.* aux yeux de faucon, qui a la vue perçante. — **moth,** *s.* smérinthe, *m.*; sphinx, *m.* — **nosed,** *adj.* qui a le nez aquilin. — **owl,** *s.* harfang, *m.* — **pouch,** *s.* fauconnière, gibecière, *f.* —**'s bell,** *s.* grelot, *m.*; (*her.*) grillet, *m.*, grillette, *f.* — **weed,** *s.*
Hawked, *adj.* crochu [épervière, *f.*
Hawker, *s.* colporteur, *m.*, -euse, *f.*, marchand ambulant, *m.*, marchande ambulante, *f.*; (*of birds*) fauconnier, *m.*
Hawking, *s.* fauconnerie, *f.*; (*selling*) colportage, *m.*; (*spitting*) expectoration bruyante, *f.*, hem, *m.*, (*fam.*) graillonnement, *m.* *To go* —, chasser au faucon. — **bag, -pouch,** *s.* fauconnière, gibecière, *f.*
Hawse-hole, *s.* écubier, *m.*
Hawser, *s.* aussière, *f.*
Hay, *s.* foin, *m.* *To make* —, faire les foins. *To make — while the sun shines,* battre le fer pendant qu'il est chaud. — **asthma,** *s. V.* — **fever.** — **bird,** *s.* grand pouillot, *m.* — **cock,** *s.* veillote, *f.*, tas de foin, *m.* — **drying apparatus,** *s.* fanoir, *m.* — **fever,** *s.* asthme de foin, catarrhe d'été, chortasthme, *m.* — **field,** *s.* champ de foin, *m.* — **harvest,** *s.* fenaison, *f.* — **knife,** *s.* coupe-foin, *m.* — **loft,** *s.* grenier à foin, fenil, *m.* fenière, *f.* — — **maker,** *s.* faneur, *m.*, -euse, *f.*; (*mower*) faucheur, *m.*; (*machine*) faneuse, *f.* — **making** *s.* fenaison, *f.* — **making machine,** *s.* faneuse, *f.* — **making time,** *s.* temps de la fenaison, *m.* — **market,** *s.* marché au foin, *m.* — **mow,** *s.* tas de foin, *m.* — **rake,** *s.* fauchet, *m.* — **rick, -stack,** *s.* meule de foin, *f.* — **time,** *s.* fanaison, *f.* — **trusser,** *s.* botteleur, *m.* — **trussing apparatus,** *s.* botteleur mécanique, botteloir, *m.*
Haytian, *s. adj.* Haïtien, *m.*, -ne, *f.*
Hazard, *s.* hasard, *m.*; risque, *m.*; (*at dice*) chance, *f.*; — *v.a.* hasarder, risquer, aventurer, exposer; — *v.n.* se hasarder, se risquer, s'aventurer, s'exposer (à)
Hazardous, *adj.* hasardeux, chanceux
Hazardously, *adv.* hasardeusement
Hazardousness, *s.* nature hasardeuse, *f.*
Haze, *s.* vapeur, brume, *f.*, brouillard, *m.*; (*fig.*) obscurité, *f.*, ténèbres, *f.pl.*
Hazel, *s.* noisetier, coudrier, *m.*; (— *nut*) noisette, *f.*; (*colour*) noisette, *m.*; — *adj.* de noisetier, de coudrier; (*of colour*) de couleur noisette, noisette. — **colour,** *s.* couleur noisette, *f.* (noisette, *m.* — **copse,** *s.* coudraie, *f.* — **earth,** *s.* terreau, *m.* — **grouse, -hen,** *s.* gelinotte, *f.* — **nut,** *s.* noisette, *f.* — **tree,** *s.* noisetier, coudrier, *m.*
Hazelly, *adj. V.* **Hazel,** *adj.*
Haziness. *V* **Haze**
Hazy, *adj.* vaporeux, brumeux
He, *pron. adj.* il, *m.*; (*when neither directly connected with nor placed immediately before a following verb*) lui, *m.*; (*the one, anyone, before 'who,' 'whom,' 'that,' or 'whose'*) celui, *m.*; (*before the verb* être *followed by* un *and* a *noun*) ce, c'; (*of animals*) mâle; — *s.* (*of animals*) mâle, *m.* — *reads,* il lit. — *and I,* lui et moi. *As tall as* —, aussi grand que lui. *It is — who reads,* c'est lui qui lit. — *who reads,* celui qui lit. — *will be* or — *is a great man,* ce sera *or* c'est un grand homme. *A — elephant,* un éléphant mâle, *m.* *A — mouse,* une souris mâle, *f.* *A — bear,* un ours, *m.* *A — goat,* un bouc, *m.* *A* —, un mâle. *The* —, le mâle, *m.*
Head, *s.* (*anat.*) tête, *f.*; (*fig.*) tête, *f.*; chef, *m.*; directeur, *m.*, -trice, *f.*; principal, *m.*; sujet, *m.*; point principal, point, *m.*; degré, *m.*; (*title*) titre, *m.*; rubrique, *f.*; (*of bills, &c.*) en-tête, *m.*; (*chapter*) chapitre, *m.*; (*mind*) esprit, *m.*, tête, *f.*; (*of rivers*) source, *f.*; (*of arrows, lances, &c.*) pointe, *f.*; (*of hatchets*) fer, *m.*; (*of a lute*) manche, *m.*; (*of sticks, of cabbages*) pomme, *f.*; (*of wild boars, salmon*) hure, *f.*; (*number of game or poultry*) pièce, *f.*, pièces, *f.pl.*; (*of beds*) chevet, *m.*, tête, *f.*; (*of tables*) haut bout, *m.*; (*of carriages*) capote, *f.*, soufflet, *m.*; (*of casks*) fond, *m.*; (*of bridges*) tête, *f.*; (*of stairs*) haut, *m.*; (*of stags*) bois, *m.*; (*of beer*) mousse, écume, *f.*; (*of water*) colonne, *f.*; chute (d'eau), *f.*; (*of a bay, &c.*) entrée, ouverture, *f.*; (*of ships*) avant, *m.*; éperon, *m.*; poulaine, *f.*; — *adj.* principal; premier; en chef; — *v.a.* conduire; diriger; commander; se mettre à la tête de; être à la tête de, être en tête de; (*get ahead of*) devancer; (*to make a head*) faire une tête à; (*pins, nails, &c.*) entêter; (— **down,** *hort.*) étêter; (*casks*) mettre un fond à, foncer; (*nav.*) naviguer contre; — *v.n.* (*hort.*) pommer. — *foremost,* la tête en avant, la tête la première. —*s or tails,* pile ou face. — *of hair,* chevelure, *f.*, cheveux, *m.pl.* — *over heels,* en faisant la culbute, en culbutant. *A* —, *per* —, par tête; par personne. *At the — of* (*a writing*), en tête de. *From — to foot,* des pieds à la tête, de la tête aux pieds. *Of o.'s* (or *its*) *own* —, de son chef, de soi-même, tout seul. *Over — and ears,* par-dessus la tête *or* les oreilles; (*in love*) affolé (d'amour); (*in debt*) criblé *or* perdu (de dettes). *Over — and heels,* en faisant la culbute, en culbutant. *To bring to a* —, faire mûrir, faire aboutir. *To come* or *draw to a* —, commencer à suppurer, suppurer, aboutir, percer, crever. *To get into* (or *fly to*) *o.'s* —, porter *or* monter à la tête. *To give* —, lâcher la bride. *To hold up o.'s* —, lever la tête; se tenir droit. *To lay their —s together,* s'entendre, se concerter. *To make* —, avancer, faire des progrès. *To make — against,* tenir tête à, résister à, s'opposer à. *To run into o.'s* —, trotter dans la tête. *To run o.'s — against,* donner de la tête contre. *To take into o.'s* —, se mettre dans la tête. *To trouble o.'s — about,* se mêler de, s'inquiéter de, s'embarrasser de. *I can't make — or tail of it,* je n'y comprends rien du tout, je n'y vois que du feu; je ne m'y reconnais plus. — **ache,** *s.* mal de tête, *m.*, migraine, *f.* *To have a — ache,* avoir mal à la tête; (*with an adjective*) avoir un mal de tête. — **attire,** *s.* coiffure, *f.* — **band,** *s.* bandeau, *m.*, bande, *f.*; (*of books*) tranchefile, *f.* — **board,** *s.* dossier, *m.* — **clerk,** *s. V.* **Clerk.** — **cook,** *s.* chef de cuisine, chef, *m.* — **dress, -gear,** *s.* coiffure, *f.* — **land,** *s.* pointe de terre, *f.*, cap, promontoire, *m.*; (*agr.*) guéret, *m.* —**less,** *adj.* sans tête; (*fig.*) sans chef. — **lettering,** *s.* (*print.*) lettrine, *f.* — **light,** *s.* fanal, *m.* — **long,** *adv.* la tête la première; (*rashly*) tête baissée, à corps perdu, aveuglément; de gaieté de cœur; précipitamment, à la hâte, inconsidérément, en étourdi; *adj.* (*steep*) escarpé; (*impetuous, &c.*) impétueux; imprudent, inconsidéré, irréfléchi, précipité, aveugle. — **man,** *s.* chef, meneur. *m.* — **master,** *s.* chef, directeur, *m.*; (*of a college*) principal, *m.*; proviseur, *m.* — **mastership,** *s.* principalat, *m.*; provisorat, *m.* — **money,** *s.* rétribution par tête, capitation, *f.* — **most,** *adj.* en tête, à la tête, premier. — **piece,** *s.* (*helmet*) casque, *m.*; (*of anc. armour*) armure de tête, *f.*, armet, *m.*; (*understanding*) tête, caboche, *f.* — **professor,** *s.* professeur titulaire *or* en titre, *m.* — **quarters,** *s. pl.* quartier-général, *m.*; état-major, *m.*; siége, centre, *m.* *General — quarters,* état-major général, *m.* — **ship,** *s.* autorité suprême, *f.*, premier rang, *m.*, primauté, *f.* —**sman,** *s.* bourreau, exécuteur, *m.* — **spring,** *s.* source, origine, *f.* — **stall,** *s.* têtière, *f.* — **stone,** *s.* pierre principale,

pierre angulaire, *f.*; (*tomb*) pierre tumulaire, tombe, *f.* — **strong,** *adj.* entêté, têtu; opiniâtre, obstiné. — **way,** *s.* (*nav.*) sillage, *m.*; (*fig.*) chemin en avant, *m.* *To make — way,* aller de l'avant. — **wind,** *s.* vent de bout, vent debout, *m.* — **work,** *s.* travail (*or* ouvrage) de tête, *m.* — **workman,** *s.* maître ouvrier, contre-maître, chef d'atelier, *m.* — **workwoman,** *s.* première ouvrière, *f.* — **wrapper,** *s.* fanchon, marmotte, *f.*

Headed, *adj.* à tête ..., qui a la tête ...; à esprit ..., qui a l'esprit ...; (*of books*) intitulé; (*hort.*) pommé; (*of carriages*) à capote, à soufflet; (*for other senses*) *V.* **Head**

Header, *s.* chef, *m.*; (*of pins, nails*) entêteur, *m.*, -euse, *f.*; (*swimming*) tête, *f.* *To take a —,* piquer une tête

Headiness, *s.* emportement, *m.*, violence, *f.*; obstination, *f.*; (*giddiness*) étourderie, *f.*; (*of wine,* &c.) nature capiteuse, *f.*

Heading, *s.* en-tête, *m.*; titre, *m.*; rubrique, *f.*; (*letter —, of a dictionary,* &c.) lettrine, *f.*; (*of casks*) fond, *m.*

Heady, *adj.* emporté, violent; impétueux; (*of odours*) qui porte à la tête; (*of wine,* &c.) capiteux

Heal, *v.a.* (— **up**) guérir; cicatriser; remédier à; apaiser, étouffer; — *v.n.* guérir, se guérir; se cicatriser. *Physician, — thyself,* médecin, guéris-toi toi-même

Healable, *adj.* guérissable

Healer, *s.* personne *or* chose qui guérit, *f.*; médecin, guérisseur, *m.*

Healing, *adj.* curatif; de guérir; (*mild*) doux, salutaire; conciliateur, de paix; — *s.* guérison, *f.*

Health, *s.* santé, *f.*; salubrité, *f.*; hygiène, *f.* *Public —,* salubrité publique, *f.* *The laws of —,* les lois de l'hygiène, *f.pl.* *The art* or *preservation of —,* l'hygiène, *f.* *In —, in good —,* en bonne santé. *Out of —, in poor —,* malade. *To drink any o.'s —,* boire à la santé de quelqu'un. *To drink —s,* porter des santés. *Your —!* à votre santé! —**ful,** &c. *V.* **Healthy,** &c. —**less,** *adj.* sans santé, infirme; insalubre. — **officer,** *s.* inspecteur de salubrité, *m.*

Healthily, *adv.* en bonne santé; sainement; salutairement; dans un endroit salubre

Healthiness, *s.* sanité, *f.*, état de santé, *m.*, santé, bonne santé, *f.*; bon état, *m.*; (*of the public*) salubrité, *f.*

Healthy, *adj.* en bonne santé, bien portant; (*sound, wholesome*) sain; (*air,* &c.) salubre; (*exercise,* &c.) salutaire (à); (*good*) bon

Heap, *s.* tas, amas, monceau, *m.*; (*pers.*) tas, *m.*; — *v.a.* (— **up**) entasser, amonceler; encombrer; (*fig.*) amasser, accumuler; (*a measure*) combler [*v.a.*); (*of measures*) comble

Heaped, *part. adj.* entassé, &c. (*V.* **Heap,**

Hear, *v.a.n.* entendre; (*hear say*) entendre dire; (*listen to*) écouter; (*grant*) exaucer; (*learn*) apprendre. *To — from* (*a person*), recevoir *or* avoir des nouvelles de. *To — of* (*a person*), avoir des nouvelles de; (*pers. or things*) entendre parler de; (*things*) apprendre. *To — one his lesson,* faire répéter à quelqu'un sa leçon. *Let me —,* dites, voyons. *Let me — from you,* donnez-moi de vos nouvelles. —, —! très bien!

Hearer, *s.* auditeur, *m.*, -trice, *f.*, assistant, *m.*, e, *f.*

Hearing, *s.* (*sense*) ouïe, *f.*; (*ear*) oreille, *f.*; (*act of —*) audition, *f.*; (*audience*) audience, *f.* *In my —,* assez haut pour que j'entende; devant moi. *Out of —,* trop loin pour entendre; à perte d'ouïe. *Within —,* (*to hear*) à portée d'entendre; (*to be heard*) à portée de se faire entendre; à portée de la voix. *To be hard* or *dull of —,* avoir l'oreille dure, être dur d'oreille, être un peu sourd. *To condemn without a —,* condamner sans entendre. *To give a —,* donner audience; écouter, entendre. *To obtain* or *get a —,* obtenir audience; obtenir d'être entendu; se faire écouter. — **trumpet,** *s.* cornet acoustique, écoutoir, *m.*

Hearken, *v.n.* écouter

Hearsay, *s.* ouï-dire, *m.*; — *adj.* d'ouï-dire

Hearse, *s.* corbillard, char funèbre, *m.*; (*herse*) herse, *f.*

Heart, *s.* cœur, *m.*; courage, *m.*; conscience, *f.*; affection, *f.*; (*friend*) ami, *m.*, e, *f.*; (*chief point*) fond, *m.*; —**s,** *pl.* (*cards*) cœur, *m.*; — *v.n.* (*hort.*) pommer. *Against o.'s —,* à contre-cœur. *At —,* à cœur; au fond du cœur. *By —,* par cœur. *For my —,* s'il y allait de ma vie. *In the — of,* au cœur de, au fort de. *Out of —,* découragé. *To o.'s —'s content,* à cœur joie, au gré de ses désirs, à souhait. *With all o.'s —,* de tout son cœur. *With open —,* à cœur ouvert. *To be* or *get out of —,* être découragé, perdre courage, se décourager. *To do o.'s — good,* être un vrai plaisir, être plaisir, faire plaisir, réjouir le cœur. *To find it in o.'s — (to),* trouver le courage (de). *To have at —,* avoir à cœur. *To have the — (to),* avoir le courage (de). *To lay to —,* prendre à cœur; graver dans son cœur. *To set o.'s — on,* avoir à cœur; prendre en affection; vouloir absolument avoir (*or* faire), tenir à avoir, tenir à; avoir en vue; convoiter. *To take —,* prendre courage. *To take to —,* prendre à cœur. *Faint — never won fair lady,* jamais honteux n'eut belle amie. — **ache,** *s.* chagrin, *m.*, affliction, peine de cœur, *f.* — **blood,** *s.* le plus pur de son sang, *m.*; (*fig.*) sources de la vie, *f.pl.*; essence, *f.* — **break,** *s.* chagrin du cœur, crève-cœur, *m.* — **breaker,** *s.* accroche-cœur, *m.*; (*pers.*) casse-cœur, *m.* — **breaking,** *s.* *V.* — **break;** *adj.* accablant, déchirant, navrant. — **broken,** *adj.* *V.* **Broken-hearted.** — **burn,** *s.* (*med.*) fer chaud, *m.*, cardialgie, *f.*, mal d'estomac, *m.*; aigreurs, *f.pl.*; (*fig.*) serrement de cœur, *m.*; rancune, haine, animosité, *f.* — **burning,** *adj.* qui aigrit le cœur; *s.* *V.* — **burn.** — **consuming, -corroding,** *adj.* dévorant, rongeur. — **discouraging,** *adj.* désespérant. — **disease,** *s.* maladie de cœur, *f.* — **ease,** *s.* paix du cœur, *f.* — **felt,** *adj.* profondément senti; vif; qui va au cœur. — **grief,** *s.* chagrin du cœur, *m.* — **hardened,** *adj.* endurci. — **hardening,** *adj.* qui endurcit le cœur. — **heaviness,** *s.* abattement, *m.* —**less,** *adj.* sans cœur; sans courage, sans énergie, pusillanime, timide; dur; cruel; lâche; languissant. —**lessly,** *adv.* sans cœur; sans courage, sans énergie; durement; cruellement; sans pitié; lâchement; languissamment. —**lessness,** *s.* manque de cœur, *m.*; manque de courage, *m.*, pusillanimité, *f.*; dureté, cruauté, *f.*; lâcheté, *f.*; insensibilité, *f.*; langueur, *f.* — **oak,** *s.* cœur de chêne, *m.* — **rending,** *adj.* déchirant, navrant. — **searching,** *adj.* qui sonde le cœur. —**'s-ease,** *s.* paix du cœur, *f.*; (*flower*) pensée, *f.* — **shaped,** *adj.* en forme de cœur, en cœur, cordiforme, cordé. — **shell,** *s.* bucarde, *f.* — **sick,** *adj.* navré, qui a la mort dans l'âme, rongé de chagrins; soucieux. — **sickening,** *adj.* navrant, qui met la mort dans l'âme. — **sore,** *s.* crève-cœur, *m.*, désolation, *f.*; *adj.* blessé au cœur. — **sorrowing,** *adj.* profondément affligé. — **stirring,** *adj.* qui remue le cœur. — **string,** *s.* fibre du cœur, *f.* — **struck,** *adj.* frappé au cœur; qui perce le cœur. — **wheel,** *s.* courbes en cœur, *f.pl.* — **whole,** *adj.* qui a le cœur libre; indomptable. — **wood,** *s.* duramen, *m.* — **wounded,** *adj.* blessé au cœur. — **wounding,** *adj.* qui blesse *or* fend *or* navre le cœur. — **wringing,** *adj.* qui déchire le cœur

Hearted, *adj.* (*in compounds*) au cœur ..., qui a le cœur ... *Good —,* qui a bon cœur

Heartedness, *s.* (*in compounds*) ... de cœur. *Good —,* bonté de cœur, *f.*

Hearth, *s.* âtre, *m.*; foyer, *m.*; (*feud.*) feu, *m.*; (*oven*) fourneau, *m.* — **broom, -brush,** *s.* balai de cheminée, *m.* — **money,** *s.* fouage, *m.* — **rug,** *s.* tapis de foyer *or* de cheminée, *m.* — **stone,** *s.* pierre de cheminée, *f.*; âtre, *m.*; foyer, *m.*

Heartily, *adv.* de cœur, de bon cœur, cordialement; sincèrement; activement, vigoureusement; (*of eating*) de bon appétit, bien. *To be — sick of,* avoir par-dessus la tête de, avoir plein le dos de

Heartiness, *s.* cordialité, *f.*; sincérité, *f.*; zèle, *m.*, ardeur, chaleur, *f.*; empressement, *m.*; (*of appetite*) force, *f.*

Hearty, *adj.* cordial, du cœur; sincère; joyeux; zélé, plein d'ardeur; empressé; (*healthy*) bien portant; (*strong*) vigoureux; sain; (*of eating, pers.*) fort, de bon appétit; (*of meals*) copieux, bon

Heat, *s.* chaleur, *f.*, chaud, *m.*; ardeur, *f.*; calorique, *m.*; (*fig.*) chaleur, ardeur, *f.*, feu, *m.*; vivacité, *f.*; véhémence, *f.*; fougue, *f.*; (*passion*) colère, *f.*; animosité, *f.*; dissension, *f.*; (*med.*) échauffement, *m.*; (*pimple*) échauffure, *f.*; (*redness*) rougeur, *f.*; (*of races*) épreuve, *f.*; partie, *f.*; — *v.a.* chauffer; échauffer; allumer; (*agitate*) échauffer; enflammer; *v.n.* chauffer; s'échauffer. *Dead —,* *V.* **Dead.** *Running —s, —s,* (*in a race*) partie liée, *f.*; (*race itself*) course en partie liée, *f.* *The deciding —,* (*in a race*) la belle *f.* *To get into a —,* se mettre en colère, s'échauffer. — **lightning,** *s.* éclair de chaleur, *m.* — **regulator,** *s.* thermostat, *m.*

Heater, *s.* (*iron*) fer chaud, fer rouge, fer à chauffer, fer, *m.*; réchaud, *m.*

Heath, *s.* bruyère, *f.*; (*uncultivated land*) lande, *f.*; friche, *f.*; plaine, *f.* — **cock,** *s.* coq de [bruyère, *m.*

Heathen, *s. adj.* païen, *m.*, -ne, *f.*

Heathenish, *adj.* de païen, païen; barbare, cruel; sauvage [barbare

Heathenishly, *adv.* en païen; d'une manière

Heathenism, *s.* paganisme, *m.*; barbarie, *f.*

Heather, *s.* bruyère, *f.*

Heathy, *adj.* couvert de bruyère [ment, *m.*

Heating, *s.* *V.* **Warming;** (*med.*) échauffe-

Heave, *v.a.* lever; élever; soulever; (*a sigh*) pousser; (*throw*) jeter, lancer; (*nav.*) haler; (*nav.*) jeter; (*nav.*) virer; — *v.n.* (*pant*) haleter; (*of the heart*) palpiter, battre; (*rise*) se soulever; (*to sigh*) soupirer; (*retch*) faire des haut-le-corps; (*ferment*) fermenter, travailler; (*nav.*) haler; (*nav.*) virer; (*nav.*) lever; — *s.* élévation, *f.*; coup, *m.*; effort, *m.*; (*rising*) soulèvement, *m.*; (*agitation*) agitation, secousse, *f.*; (*of the heart*) palpitation, *f.*, battement, *m.*; (*sigh*) soupir, *m.*; (*retching*) haut-le-corps, *m.*; (*nav.*) levée, *f.*; **—s,** *s.pl.* (*vet.*) pousse, *f.* *To — down,* (*nav.*) abattre. *To — short,* (*nav.*) virer à pic. *To — in sight,* (*nav.*) être en vue. *To — to,* (*nav.*) mettre en panne. *Give us a — !* donnez un coup de main! — **offering,** *s.* oblation des prémices, *f.*

Heaven, *s.* ciel, *m.*, cieux, *m.pl.* *Good —s!* juste ciel! grand Dieu! Dieu! mon Dieu! *In* or *to —,* au ciel. — **begotten, -born, -bred,** *adj.* fils du ciel, *m.*, fille du ciel, *f.*, enfant du ciel, *m.f.*, céleste, divin. — **descended** *or* **fallen,** *adj.* descendu *or* tombé du ciel. — **gifted,** *adj.* (*pers.*) doué par le ciel; (*things*) donné par le ciel. — **inspired,** *adj.* inspiré par le ciel. — **liness,** *s.* nature céleste, *f.* — **loved,** *adj.* aimé *or* chéri du ciel. — **ly,** *adj.* céleste, divin; *adv.* divinement, d'une manière céleste; par le ciel. — **ly-guided** *or* **minded,** *adj* guidé *or* inspiré par le ciel. — **ward,** *adj. adv.* vers le ciel. — **warring,** *adj.* qui fait la guerre au ciel

Heaver, *s.* chargeur, porteur, *m.*

Heavily, *adv.* lourdement, pesamment; (*fast, strongly*) fort; (*with grief*) avec chagrin, avec peine, avec tristesse; (*laboriously*) avec fatigue; (*tediously*) avec ennui, ennuyeusement. *To fall* or &c. *—,* tomber lourdement, &c. (*V.* **Heavy**)

Heaviness, *s.* poids, *m.*, pesanteur, f.; (*fig.*) lourdeur, *f.*; appesantissement, *m.*; gravité, *f.*; abattement, *m.*; langueur, *f.*; inactivité, *f.*; (*drowsiness*) assoupissement, *m.*; (*sorrow*) chagrin, *m.*, tristesse, affliction, *f.*; (*tediousness*) ennui, *m.*; (*of roads*) difficulté, *f.*, mauvais état, *m.* [agité

Heaving, *s.* *V.* **Heave,** *s.*; — *adj.* soulevé,

Heavy, *adj.* lourd, pesant; grand; fort; grave; sévère; (*big*) gros; (*loaded*) chargé; (*sad*) triste; (*weary*) fatigué; (*dull*) languissant; inactif; ennuyeux; (*slow*) lent; (*laborious*) pénible, dur, rude; (*burdensome*) à charge (à); (*of rain, snow*) abondant; (*of showers*) fort; (*of the sea, artil., cavalry*) gros; (*of roads*) mauvais; (*adverb.*) *V.* **Heavily.** — *father,* (*theat.*) père noble, *m.* *To fall* or *hang* or *lie* or *press — upon,* être à charge à, peser lourdement sur, peser sur, s'appesantir sur; accabler; gêner. — **hearted,** *adj.* le cœur gros, qui a le cœur gros, triste, affligé, abattu

Hebdomadal, *adj.* hebdomadaire

Hebdomadally, *adv.* hebdomadairement

Hebdomadary, *adj.* hebdomadaire; — *s. adj.* (*Cath. rel.*) hebdomadier, *m.*, -ière, *f.*

Hebetate, *v.a.* hébéter [hébétude, *f.*

Hebetation, Hebetude, *s.* hébétement, *m.*,

Hebraic, *adj.* des Hébreux; hébraïque, hébreu;

Hebraically, *adv.* hébraïquement [israélite

Hebraism, *s.* hébraïsme, *m.*

Hebraist, *s.* hébraïsant, hébraïste, *m.*

Hebraize, *v.n.a.* hébraïser

Hebrew, *s.* Hébreu, *m.*; Israélite, *m.*; (*language*) l'hébreu, *m.*, la langue hébraïque, *f.*; — *adj.* des Hébreux; israélite, juif; (*of language*) hé- [braïque

Hebrewess, *s* Israélite, Juive, *f.*

Hebridian, *adj.* des Hébrides

Hecatomb, *s.* hécatombe, *f.*

Heckle. *V.* **Hackle**

Hectare, *s.* hectare, m. [hectique, *f.*

Hectic, -al, *adj.* hectique, étique; — *s.* fièvre

Hectogramme, *s.* hectogramme, *m.*

Hectolitre, *s.* hectolitre, *m.*

Hectometre, *s.* hectomètre, *m.*

Hectometric -al, *adj.* hectométrique

Hector. *V.* **Bully**

Hectoring, Hectorly, *adj.* de fendant, de matamore, de fier-à-bras, impérieux, insolent

Hedge, *s.* haie, *f.*; — *v.a.n.* fermer *or* entourer d'une haie, hayer; (*to border*) border; (*fig.*) entourer. — **bill,** *s.* serpe, *f.*; faucillon, fauchet, *m.* — **creeper,** *s.* vagabond, *m.* — **garlic,** *s.* alliaire, *f.*, vélar, *m.* — **hog,** *s.* hérisson, *m.* — **hyssop,** *s.* gratiole, *f.* — **in,** *v.a.* enfermer; renfermer; entourer. — **knife,** *s.* serpette, *f.* — **mustard,** *s.* vélar, *m.* — **nettle,** *s.* stachyde des bois, *f.* — **pig,** *s.* jeune hérisson, *m.* — **row,** *s.* haie, *f.* — **school,** *s.* école buissonnière, *f.* — **shears,** *s. pl.* sécateur, *m.* — **sparrow,** *s.* traîne- [buissons, *m.*

Hedger, *s.* faiseur de haies, *m.*

Hedging-bill, &c. *V.* **Hedgebill,** &c.

Heed, *v.a.* faire attention à, observer, remarquer; écouter; — *s.* attention, *f.*; soin, *m.*; précaution, *f.* *To give — to,* faire attention à, observer, remarquer; écouter. *To take — of,* prendre garde à. **—ful,** *adj.* attentif (à), soigneux (de); vigilant, prudent, circonspect. — **fully,** *adv.* attentivement, avec attention, soigneusement, avec soin; avec vigilance, avec circonspection, prudemment. — **fulness,** *s.* attention, *f.*, soin, *m.*; vigilance, circonspection, *f.* — **less,** *adj.* peu soigneux, inattentif, étourdi, insouciant, négligent. — **lessly,** *adv.* inattentivement, étourdiment, à l'étourdie, inconsidérément; négligemment; (*by mistake*) par mégarde. **—lessness,** *s.* inattention, étourderie, insouciance, négligence, *f.*; inadvertance, *f.*

Heel, *s.* talon, *m.*; (*spur*) éperon, *m.*; (*the end*)

fin, *f.*; (*tech.*, *of a razor, of a tobacco-pipe, of a butt-end, of a ship's keel*) talon, *m.*; (*of masts*) pied, *m.*; (*of anchors*) sabot, *m.*; — *v.a.* mettre un talon *or* des talons à; — *v.n.* (*nav.*) donner de la bande, être à la bande, plier. *Down at the* —, (*of shoes*) éculé. *To be at the —s of*, être sur les talons de, être aux trousses de. *To lay by the —s*, mettre aux fers. *To take to o.'s —s*, jouer des talons *or* des jambes, prendre ses jambes à son cou. *To trip up anyone's —s*, donner un croc-en-jambe à quelqu'un. — **bone,** *s.* os du talon, *m.* — **piece,** *s.* talon, *m.*; *v.a.* mettre un talon *or* des talons à. — **plate,** *s.* (*of a gun-butt*) plaque de couche, *f.* — **tap,** *s.* verre à demi vidé, fond de verre, *m.*

Heeled, *adj.* à talons . . .

Hegemony, *s.* hégémonie, *f.*

Hegira, *s.* hégire, *f.*

Heifer, *s.* génisse, *f.* — **calf,** *s. V.* **Cow-calf**

Heigh-ho, *int.* ah! ha!

Height, *s.* hauteur, élévation, *f.*; degré, *m.*; (*summit*) comble, faîte, apogée, *m.*; (*intensity*) fort, *m.*; (*middle*) cœur, *m.*; (*stature*) taille, *f.*; (*geog.*) latitude, *f.*

Heighten, *v.a.* relever, rehausser; augmenter, accroître; perfectionner; aggraver; embellir, orner

Heightening, *s.* élévation, *f.*; rehaussement, *m.*; augmentation, *f.*, accroissement, *m.*; perfectionnement, *m.*; aggravation, *s.*; embellissement, ornement, *m.*

Heinous, *adj.* odieux, détestable, atroce, horrible

Heinously, *adv.* odieusement, horriblement

Heinousness, *s.* nature odieuse, atrocité, énormité

Heir, *s.* héritier, *m.* — **-at-law,** héritier légitime, *m.* — **dom,** *s.* héritage, *m.*, succession, *f.* — **less,** *adj.* sans héritier. — **loom,** *s.* meuble de famille, *m.* — **ship,** *s.* hérédité, qualité d'héritier, *f.*

Heiress, *s.* héritière, *f.*

Heliacal, *adj.* héliaque

Heliacally, *adv.* héliaquement

Helical, *adj.* hélicé, en hélice, en spirale

Heliocentric, -al, &c. héliocentrique, &c. (*V.* page 3, § 1)

Heliograph, *s.* (*instr.*) héliographe, *m.*; (*picture*) héliographie, *f.*

Heliography, &c., héliographie, &c. (*V.* p.3, § 1)

Heliometer, *s.* héliomètre, *m.*

Helioscope, *s.* hélioscope, *m.*

Heliostat, *s.* héliostat, *m.*

Heliotrope, *s.* héliotrope, *m.*

Helio-tropy, -typography, &c., héliotropie, &c. (*V.* page 3, § 1)

Helix, *s.* hélice, *f.*; (*anat.*) hélix, limaçon, *m.*

Hell, *s.* enfer, *m.*; (*gambling-house*) tripot, *m.* — **born, -bred,** *adj.* infernal. — **cat,** *s.* furie, sorcière, *f.* — **fire,** *s.* feu d'enfer, *m.* — **hound,** *s.* chien de l'enfer, *m.*; Cerbère, *m.*; (*fig.*) suppôt de Satan, *m.*; tison d'enfer, *m.* — **ward,** *adj. adv.* vers l'enfer

Hellebore, *s.* ellébore, *m.*

Hellene, *s.* Hellène, *m.*

Hellenian, Hellenic, *adj.* hellénique

Hellenism, *s.* hellénisme, *m.*

Hellenist, *s.* helléniste, *m*

Hellenistic, -al, *adj.* hellénistique

Hellenize, *v.n.a.* helléniser

Hellish, *adj.* infernal, d'enfer

Hellishly, *adv.* infernalement

Hellishness, *s.* méchanceté infernale, *f.*

Helm, gouvernail, timon, *m.*; barre, *f.*; — *v.a.* diriger, gouverner. *To be at the* —, tenir le gouvernail *or* le timon. *The man at the* —, l'homme à la barre. *She would not* (*did not*) *answer her* —, le vaisseau ne gouvernait plus. — **less,** *adj.* sans gouvernail. — **port,** *s.* jaumière, *f.* — **sman,** *s.* timonier, *m.*

Helmet, *s.* casque, *m.*; (*her.*) heaume, timbre, *m.* — **shell,** *s.* casque, *m.*

Helmeted, *adj.* portant un casque, casqué

Helminth-ic, -ologic, -ologist, -ology. *V.* page 3, § 1

Helot, *s.* ilote, *m.*

Helotism, *s.* ilotisme, *m.*

Helotry, *s.* ilotes, *m. pl.*

Help, *v.a.n.* aider, assister, secourir; rendre service à, être utile à, servir; servir à; contribuer (à); (*at table*) servir, offrir à; (*forward*) avancer; (*procure*) obtenir, procurer, faire avoir; (*remedy*) remédier à; (*prevent*) empêcher; éviter; (*forbear*) s'empêcher (de), s'abstenir (de); se défendre (de); éviter (de); se dispenser (de); faire autrement (que de). *To — oneself*, s'aider (de); se servir (de); faire autrement; se suffire à soi-même; s'arranger; (*to*) se servir; prendre. *To — each other* or *one another*, s'aider l'un l'autre (*or* les uns les autres), s'entr'aider. *I cannot — it*, je n'y peux rien, je ne saurais qu'y faire; ce n'est pas ma faute; je ne peux pas faire autrement; (*of feelings*) c'est plus fort que moi. *I cannot — laughing*, je ne peux pas m'empêcher de rire. *It cannot be —ed*, on n'y peut rien, on ne saurait qu'y faire, il n'y a rien à faire, c'est inévitable. *How can I — it?* que voulez-vous que j'y fasse? *How can it be —ed?* qu'y faire? que voulez-vous? *That won't — you*, cela ne vous servira à rien. *That won't — you much*, cela ne vous servira (*or* ne vous avancera) pas à grand' chose. *God — thee*, Dieu t'assiste! Dieu te soit en aide! — *yourself, and God will — you*, aide-toi, le ciel t'aidera. — **down,** aider à descendre. — **forward,** *V.* — **on.** — **in,** aider à entrer, faire entrer; (*into a carriage*) aider à monter. — **on,** aider à avancer; avancer, pousser. — **out,** aider à sortir; (*of a carriage*) aider à descendre; (*of a difficulty*) tirer; tirer d'affaire *or* d'embarras. — **over,** aider à passer; (*a difficulty*) aider à surmonter. — **to** (*a thing*), obtenir, procurer, faire avoir; (*at table*) servir; offrir. — **up,** aider à monter; (*to rise again*) aider à se relever

Help, *s.* aide, *f.*, secours, *m.*, assistance, *f.*; remède, *m.*; ressource, *f.* — ! au secours! *With* (or *by*) *the — of*, à l'aide de; par le moyen de. *To call* (or *cry out*) *for* —, crier au secours, appeler à son secours. *There is no — for it*, il n'y a pas de remède; c'est inévitable

Helper, *s.* aide, *m.f.*; auxiliaire, *m.*; coopérateur, *m.*, -trice, *f.*; secoureur, *m.*, -euse, *f.*

Helpful, Helping, *adj.* utile, secourable, salutaire. *To lend a — hand to*, secourir, aider, venir en aide à

Helpfulness, *s.* aide, *f.*, secours, *m.*; utilité, *f.*

Helpless, *adj.* sans secours; faible; abandonné, délaissé; sans remède, irrémédiable; sans ressource; sans défense; impuissant

Helplessly, *adv.* sans secours; sans force, sans pouvoir, faiblement; sans remède, irrémédiablement; sans ressource

Helplessness, *s.* faiblesse, incapacité, impuissance, *f.*; abandon, délaissement, *m.*

Helpmate, Helpmeet, *s.* aide, *m.f.*, compagnon, *m.*, compagne, *f.*; (*wife*) femme, *f.*

Helter-skelter, *adv.* pêle-mêle; sens dessus dessous

Helve. *V.* **Haft.** *To throw the — after the hatchet*, jeter le manche après la cognée

Helved, *adj.* à manche

Helvetian, *s. adj.* Helvétien, *m.*, -ne, *f.*; (*of the Alps*) helvétique

Helvetic, *adj.* helvétique

Helvetism, *s.* helvétisme, *m.*

Hem, *v.a.n.* border; (*need.*) ourler; — *v.n.* toussoter, (*med.*) hemmer; — *s.* bord, *m.*; (*need.*) ourlet, *m.*; (*exclam., int.*) hem, *m.* *False* —, faux ourlet, *m.* — **in,** ('*with*,' de) enfermer, entourer; cerner. — **stitch,** *v.a.* ourler à jour; *s.* ourlet à jour, *m.*

Hematine, *s.* hématine, *f.*

Hematite, *s.* hématite, *f.*

Hematosine, *s.* hématosine, *f.*

Hematosis, *s.* hématose, *f.*

Hemicycle, *s.* hémicycle, *m.*

Hemisphere, *s.* hémisphère, *m.*
Hemispheric, -al, *adj.* hémisphérique
Hemistich, *s.* hémistiche, *m.*
Hemlock, *s.* ciguë, *f.*
Hemoptic, *adj.* hémoptyique
Hemoptysis, *s.* hémoptysie, *f.*
Hemorrhage, *s.* hémorrhagie, hémorragie, *f.*
Hemorrhagic, *adj.* hémorrhagique, hémorragique [roidal
Hemorrhoidal, *adj.* hémorrhoidal, hémor-
Hemorrhoids, *s. pl.* hémorrhoides, hémorroides, *f.pl.*
Hemp, *s.* chanvre, *m.* — **cloth,** *s.* toile de chanvre, *f.* — **comb,** *s.* seran, *m.* — **dresser,** *s.* chanvrier, *m.*, -ière, *f.* — **field,** *s.* chènevière, *f.* — **seed,** *s.* chènevis, *m.* — **weed,**
Hempen, *adj.* de chanvre [*s.* aigremoine, *f.*
Hen, *s.* poule, *f.*; (*female generally*) femelle, *f.*; (*adject.*) femelle. — **bane,** *s.* jusquiame, *f.* — **bird,** *s.* oiseau femelle, *m.* — **blackbird,** *s.* merlette, *f.* — **canary,** *s.* serine, *f.* — **coop,** *s.* cage à poulets, *f.* — **hearted,** *adj.* au cœur de poule, pusillanime, poltron. — **hole,** *s.* poulière, *f.* — **house,** *s.* poulailler, *m.* — **parrot,** *s.* perruche, *f.* — **partridge,** *s.* perdrix femelle, *f.* — **pecked,** *adj.* (*of husbands*) qui se laisse mener par sa femme, encotillonné, soumis; jocrisse, *m.* — **pheasant,** *s.* faisane, poule faisane, *f.* — **roost,** *s.* juchoir, *m.* — **sparrow,** *s.* moineau femelle, *m.*, pierrette, *f.*
Hence, *adv.* (*of place*) d'ici; de là; (*of time*) d'ici, dans ... d'ici, dans; (*henceforth*) dorénavant; (*from this reason*) de là. *Ten years* —, dans dix ans d'ici, dans dix ans. *A fortnight* —, dans quinze jours
Henceforth, Henceforward, *adv.* désormais, dorénavant, à l'avenir
Henchboy, Henchman, *s.* page, suivant, serviteur, écuyer, *m.*
Hendecagon, *s.* hendécagone, *m.*
Hendecagonal, *adj.* hendécagonal, hendé-
Henna. *V.* **Alkanna** [cagone
Hepatic, -al, *adj.* hépatique
Hepatite, Hepatitis, *s.* hépatite, *f.*
Hepatization, *s.* hépatisation, *f.* [s'hépatiser
Hepatize, *v.a.* hépatiser. *To become —d,*
Heptachord, *s.* heptacorde, *m.*
Heptagon, *s.* heptagone, *m.*
Heptagonal, *adj.* heptagonal, heptagone
Heptahedral, *adj.*, **Heptahedron,** *s.* heptaèdre, *adj. m.f.*, *s.m.*
Heptarch-ic, -y. *V.* page 3, § 1
Her, *pron. pers.* elle; (*obj. of a verb*) la; (*to her*) lui; (*possessive*) son, sa, ses; (*demonstrative*) celle
Herald, *s.* héraut, *m.*; avant-coureur, précurseur, messager, *m.*, -ère, *f.*; — *v.a.* annoncer; proclamer; introduire
Heraldic, *adj.* héraldique
Heraldry, *s.* blason, *m.*, science héraldique, *f.* *Book of* —, armorial, *m.*
Heraldship, *s.* charge de héraut, *f.*
Herb, *s.* herbe, *f.* — **doctor,** *s.* herboriste, *m.* —**less,** *adj.* sans herbe. — **room, -shop, -trade,** *s.* herboristerie, *f.* — **woman,** *s.*
Herbaceous, *adj.* herbacé [herbière, *f.*
Herbage, *s.* herbage, pâturage, *m.*; (*law*) droit de pâture, *m.*
Herbal, *s.* herbier, *m.*; — *adj.* des herbes; d'herbe
Herbalist, *s.* herboriste, *m.f.*
Herbarium, *s.* herbier, *m.* [*s.m.*, *adj.m.f.*
Herbivore, *s.*, **Herbivorous,** *adj.* herbivore,
Herborist. *V.* **Herbalist**
Herborization, *s.* herborisation, *f.*
Herborize, *v.n.* herboriser
Herborizer, *s.* herborisateur, *m.*, -trice, *f.*
Herbous, Herby, *adj.* herbeux
Herculean, *adj.* herculéen, d'Hercule
Herd, *s.* troupeau, *m.*; troupe, *f.*; — *v.n.* vivre en troupes; (*pers.*) s'associer, vivre; — *v.a.* mettre en troupeau. *The common* or *vulgar* —, le commun, le commun des martyrs, le vulgaire, *m.* — **boy,** *s.* petit pâtre, *m.* — **man,** —**sman,** *s.* pâtre, *m.*
Here, *adv.* ici; ici présent, que voici; (*here below*) ici-bas; (*there*) là; y; (*on this point*) en ceci, en cela; (*in answer to a call over of names*) présent! (*take this, look,* &c.) tenez! tiens! — *below,* ici-bas. — *and there,* çà et là. — *is,* — *are,* voici; voilà. — *he is,* le voici; le voilà. — *he comes,* le voici *or* le voilà qui vient, le voici, le voilà. — *she is,* la voici; la voilà. — *they are,* les voici; les voilà. — *I am,* — *am I,* me voici; me voilà. — *we are,* nous voici; nous voilà. — *you are,* vous voici; vous voilà; (*there it is*) voilà! — *they are,* les voici; les voilà. *About* —, *V.* **About.** *Down* —, *in* —, *out* —, *over* —, *up* —, ici [d'ici, ici près
Hereabout, Hereabouts, *adv.* par ici, près
Hereafter, *adv.* désormais, dorénavant, à l'avenir; (*later*) plus tard; ci-après; (*below*) ci-dessous, plus bas; (*in future life*) dans la vie future; pour l'éternité; — *s.* vie future, vie à venir, *f.*, autre monde, *m.*
Hereat, *adv.* à ceci, à cela; de ceci, de cela
Hereby, *adv.* par ceci; par là, par ce moyen, ainsi; (*law*) par les présentes, par le présent
Hereditable, *adj.* héritable [acte
Hereditably, *adv.* par droit de succession
Hereditament, *s.* héritage, bien, *m.*; hérédité, *f.* [héritage
Hereditarily, *adv.* héréditairement, par
Hereditariness, *s.* hérédité, *f.*
Hereditary, *adj.* héréditaire
Heredity, *s.* hérédité, *f.*
Herein, *adv.* ici, en ceci; ci-inclus
Hereof, *adv.* de ceci, de cela, en, d'où
Hereon, *adv.* sur ceci, sur cela, là-dessus
Heresiarch, *s.* hérésiarque, *m.*
Heresy, *s.* hérésie, *f.*
Heretic, *s.* hérétique, *m.f.*
Heretical, *adj.* hérétique
Heretically, *adv.* hérétiquement
Hereticalness, *s.* héréticité, *f.*
Hereto, *adv.* à ceci, à cela, y
Heretofore, *adv.* jusqu'à présent, jusqu'ici
Hereunto. *V.* **Hereto**
Hereupon, *adv.* là-dessus [en; là-dessus
Herewith, *adv.* avec ceci, avec cela; ci-joint;
Herisson, *s.* hérisson, *m.*
Heritable, *adj.* héritable
Heritage, *s.* héritage, *m.*
Hermandad, *s.* (la sainte) Hermandad, *f.*
Hermaphrodism. *V.* **Hermaphroditism**
Hermaphrodite, *s. adj.* hermaphrodite, *s.m.*, *adj.m.f.*
Hermaphroditic, -al, *adj.* hermaphrodite
Hermaphroditism, *s.* hermaphrodisme, *m.*,
Hermes, *s.* hermès, *m.* [hermaphrodie, *f.*
Hermetic, -al, *adj.* hermétique
Hermetically, *adv.* hermétiquement
Hermeticalness, *s.* herméticité, *f.*
Hermit, *s.* ermite, *m.* — **crab,** *s.* pagure, bernard-l'ermite, *m.* [l'Hermitage, *m.*
Hermitage, *s.* ermitage, *m.*; (*wine*) vin de
Hermitess, *s.* recluse, *f.*
Hermitical, *adj.* érémitique, d'ermite
Hernia, *s.* hernie, *f.*
Hernial, *adj.* herniaire
Hernious, *adj.* hernieux
Hero, *s.* héros, *m.* — **worship,** *s.* culte des héros, *m.* — **worshipper,** *s.* adorateur (*m.*, -trice, *f.*) des héros
Herodian, *s.* hérodien, *m.*
Heroic, -al, *adj.* héroique
Heroically, *adv.* héroiquement
Heroicalness, *s.* héroicité, *f.*
Heroicomic, -al, *adj.* héroi-comique
Heroine, *s.* héroine, *f.*
Heroism, *s.* héroisme, *m.*
Heron, *s.* héron, *m.* *Young* —, héronneau, *m.* — **like,** *adj.* héronnier. — **plume,** *s.* masse de héron, *f.* —**'s-bill,** *s.* (*bot.*) érodium, *m.*
Heronry, *s.* héronnière, *f.*

Herpes, *s.* herpès, *m.*, dartre, *f.*
Herpetic, Herpetology, &c. herpétique, herpétologie, &c. (*V.* page 3, § 1)
Herring, *s.* hareng, *m.* — **bone,** *s.* arête de hareng, *f.*; (— *bone work, arch.*) arête de poisson, *f.* — **fishery,** *s.* pêche aux harengs, harengaison, *f.* — **market,** *s.* harengerie, *f.* — **net,** *s.* harenguière, harengade, *f.*, aplet, *m.* — **season,** *s.* harengaison, *f.* — **stick,** *s.* aine, ainette, alignette, alinette, broche, *f.* — **time,** *s.* harengaison, *f.* — **woman,** *s.* harengère, *f.*
Hers, *pron. poss.* le sien, la sienne, les siens, les siennes; ses; (*pron. pers.*) à elle, d'elle. *This drawing is* —, (*belongs to her*) ce dessin est à elle; (*comes from her; she is the author of it*) ce dessin est d'elle. *A friend of* —, un de ses amis, *m.*, une de ses amies, *f.*
Herse, *s.* (*of churches, fort.*) herse, *f.*
Herself, *pron.* elle-même; elle; soi-même; soi; (*in a reflect. verb*) se
Hersillon, *s.* hersillon, *m.*
Hesitancy, *s.* hésitation, *f.*
Hesitant, *adj.* qui hésite
Hesitate, *v.n.* hésiter, balancer [hésitation, *f.*
Hesitating, *adj.* qui hésite, incertain; — *s.*
Hesitatingly, *adv.* en hésitant, avec hésitation
Hesitation, *s.* hésitation, *f.*
Hesperides, *s. pl.* Hespérides, *f.pl.*
Hessian, *s. adj.* Hessois, *m.*, e, *f.* — **boot,** *s.* botte à l'écuyère, *f.*
Heteroclite, *s.* personne *or* chose hétéroclite, *f.*; (*gram.*) mot hétéroclite, *m.* [roclite
Heteroclite, Heteroclitic, -al, *adj.* hété-
Heterodox, *adj.* hétérodoxe
Heterodoxy, *s.* hétérodoxie, *f.* [hétérogène
Heterogeneal, Heterogeneous, *adj.*
Heterogeneity, Heterogeneousness, *s.*
Hetman, *s.* hetman, *m.* [hétérogénéité, *f.*
Hew, *v.a.* couper, tailler. — **down,** abattre; renverser [bois), bûcheron, *m.*
Hewer, *s.* tailleur, *m.*; (*of wood*) fendeur (de
Hewing, *s.* coupe, taille, *f.*
Hexachord, *s.* hexacorde, *m.*
Hexagon, *s.* hexagone, *m.*
Hexagonal, *adj.* hexagonal, hexagone
Hexahedral, *adj.* hexaèdre
Hexahedron, *s.* hexaèdre, *m.*
Hexameter, *s.* hexamètre, *m.* [mètre
Hexameter, Hexametric, -al, *adj.* hexa-
Hey, *int.* hé! hein!
Heyday, *s.* beaux jours, *m.pl.*; apogée, *m.*; folie, extravagance, *f.*; boutades, *f.pl.*; joie, *f.*; ardeur, *f.*, feu, *m.*, fougue, force, *f.*; — *adj.* glorieux; heureux; joyeux; — *int.* hé! ouais!
Hi, *int.* hi! hé! holà! psit! ps't! s't!
Hiatus, *s.* ouverture, brèche, *f.*; (*fig.*) lacune, *f.*; (*gram.*) hiatus, *m.*
Hibernacle, *s.* hibernacle, *m.*
Hibernal, *adj.* hivernal, hibernal, d'hiver
Hibernate, *v.n.* hiverner, hiberner
Hibernation, *s.* hivernation, hibernation, *f.*
Hibernian, *s. adj.* Hibernien, *m.*, -ne, *f.*
Hibernianism, Hibernicism, *s.* hiber-
Hibernicize, *v.a.n.* hiberniser [nisme, *m.*
Hibiscus, *s.* hibiscus, *m.*, ketmie, *f.*
Hiccough, Hiccup, *s.* hoquet, *m.*; — *v.n.* avoir le hoquet
Hickory, *s.* hickory, carya, caryer, *m.*
Hickwall, *s.* épeichette, *f.*
Hidalgo, *s.* hidalgo, *m.* [latent
Hidden, *adj.* caché; secret; mystérieux;
Hiddenly, *adv.* secrètement, en cachette
Hide, *v.a.* cacher ('*from*,' à); couvrir; masquer, dérober à la vue; (*to beat*) rosser, tanner le cuir à; — *v.n.* se cacher, se tenir caché; — *s.* peau, *f.*, cuir, *m.* — **and seek,** *s.* (*game*) cache-cache, *m.* — **bound,** *adj.* (*of animals*) dont la peau adhère aux flancs; (*of trees*) serré dans son écorce; (*fig.*) intraitable; (*stingy*) dur à la desserre. — **stick,** *s.* (*game*) cache-tampon, *m.*
Hideous, *adj.* hideux, affreux, horrible
Hideously, *adv.* hideusement, affreusement, horriblement [hideur, *f.*; nature hideuse, *f.*
Hideousness, *s.* laideur affreuse, horreur,
Hider, *s.* personne qui cache *or* qui se cache, *f.*
Hiding, *s.* action de cacher *or* de se cacher, *f.*; (*blows*) râclée, *f.* — **place,** *s.* cachette, retraite cachée, *f.*
Hie, *v.n.* se hâter, se presser, courir
Hiemal. *V.* **Hyemal**
Hierarchic, -al, *adj.* hiérarchique
Hierarchically, *adv.* hiérarchiquement
Hierarchy, *s.* hiérarchie, *f.*
Hieroglyph, *s.* hiéroglyphe, *m.*
Hieroglyphic, -al, *adj.* hiéroglyphique; *s.* hiéroglyphe, *m.* [en hiéroglyphe
Hieroglyphically, *adv.* par hiéroglyphes,
Hierography, &c., hiérographie, &c. (*V.* p. 3, § 1)
Hierophant, *s.* hiérophante, *m.*
Higgle, *v.n.* revendre; (*chaffer*) barguigner, marchander, marchandailler; lésiner, liarder
Higgledy-piggledy, *adv.* sens dessus dessous; pêle-mêle, à la diable, va comme je te pousse
Higgler, *s.* revendeur, *m.*, -euse, *f.*, regrattier, *m.*, -ière, *f.*; (*chafferer*) barguigneur, *m.*, -euse, *f.*, marchandailleur, *m.*, -euse, *f.*
High, *adj.* haut; élevé; haut placé; grand; supérieur; illustre, sublime; (*salient*) saillant, proéminent; (*proud*) fier, orgueilleux, altier, superbe; (*powerful*) puissant; (*formal*) apprêté, prétentieux; (*severe*) sévère; (*violent*) fort, violent; (*of compliments*) flatteur; (*of colours*) vif; (*of prices*) élevé, cher; (*of the sea*) haut, gros; (*of hats*) haut de forme, grand; (*of dress*) montant; (*of cheek-bones*) saillant; (*of meat*) faisandé; (*seasoned*) de haut goût, relevé; (*of diet*) substantiel, fortifiant; — *s.* haut, ciel, *m.*; (*God*) Haut, *m.*; — *adv.* haut; hautement; (*greatly*) grandement, fortement, fort, très, bien; (*deeply*) profondément; (*powerfully*) puissamment. *The Most* —, le Très-Haut, le Tout-Puissant, *m.* *Ten feet* —, haut de dix pieds, de dix pieds de haut *or* de hauteur. *A house three stories* —, une maison de trois étages, *f.* *It is* — *time*, il est grand *or* grandement temps. — *and dry*, à sec sur le rivage. — *and low*, grands et petits; (*adverb.*) du haut en bas. *From* —, d'en haut. *On* —, en haut, dans les airs, en l'air; au ciel. — **bailiff,** *s.* grand bailli, *m.* — **born,** *adj.* de haute naissance. — **bred,** *adj.* de haute éducation, parfaitement élevé. — **built,** *adj.* (*nav.*) de haut bord. — **Church,** *s.* haute Église, *f.*; *adj.* de la haute Église. — **coloured,** *adj.* d'une couleur éclatante, vivement coloré; (*of the face*) haut en couleur. — **crowned,** *adj.* (*of hats*) haut de forme, grand. — **fed,** *adj.* bien nourri, nourri avec luxe. — **flown,** *adj.* haut, élevé, superbe; (*proud*) fier, altier; (*exaggerated*) outré, ampoulé. — **land,** *s.* pays montagneux *or* de montagnes, *m.*; montagne, haute terre, *f.* — **lander,** *s.* montagnard, *m.*, e, *f.* — **landish,** *adj.* de montagnes, montagneux. — **low,** *s.* (*shoe*) soulier à recouvrement, *m.* — **mass,** *s.* *V.* **Mass.** — **mettled,** *adj.* fougueux, ardent, plein d'ardeur, plein de feu. — **minded,** *adj.* à esprit élevé; magnanime, noble; honorable; (*proud*) fier, altier, arrogant, présomptueux. — **mindedness,** *s.* hauteur d'âme, *f.*; magnanimité, noblesse, *f.*; (*pride*) fierté, arrogance, présomption, *f.* — **pressure,** *s.* haute pression, *f.*; *adj.* à haute pression. — **price,** *s.* prix élevé, *m.* — **priced,** *adj.* cher. — **priest,** *s.* grand-prêtre, *m.* — **priestess,** *s.* grande-prêtresse, *f.* — **relief,** *s.* haut-relief, *m.* — **road,** *s.* *V.* — **way.** — **school,** *s.* grande école, école supérieure, *f.*, collège, *m.* — **seasoned,** *adj.* fort assaisonné; de haut goût, relevé; piquant. — **souled,** *adj.* qui a l'âme grande *or* noble *or* élevée. — **sounding,**

adj pompeux, ronflant. — **spirited,** *adj.* plein de courage *or* de cœur; fier; plein d'ardeur, plein de feu, plein d'énergie, fougueux; vif; irascible; audacieux; noble. — **spiritedness,** *s.* courage, cœur, *m.*; fierté, *f.*; feu, *m.*, énergie, fougue, *f.*; audace, *f.* — **stepper,** *s.* steppeur, *m.* — **stomached,** *adj.* irrité, courroucé, en colère; hautain. — **street,** *s.* grande rue, *f.* — **swoln,** *adj.* enflé; (*proud*) fier. — **tasted,** *adj.* piquant. — **treason,** *s.* *V.* **Treason.** — **treasurer,** *s.* grand trésorier, *m.* — **water,** *s* *V.* **Water** — **water-mark,** *s.* niveau des hautes eaux, *m.* — **way,** *s.* grand chemin, *m.*, grande route, *f.*; (*admin.*) voie publique, *f.* — **way board,** *s.* bureau des voies publiques, *m.* — **wayman,** *s.* voleur de grand chemin, *m.* — **way robber,** *s.* voleur de grand chemin, *m.* — **way robbery,** *s.* vol de grand chemin, *m.*; vol sur la voie publique, *m.* — **way rate,** *s.* taxe pour l'entretien des routes, *f.* — **way surveyor,** *s.* inspecteur des routes, *m.* — **wrought,** *adj.* fait d'une manière exquise, d'un travail exquis; fortement agité; violent

Higher, *adj.* plus haut, plus élevé, &c. (*V.* **High**); supérieur; haut; de *or* du dessus, du haut; d'en haut. — **up,** *adv.* plus haut

Highest, *adj.* (le) plus haut, &c. *V.* **High;** — *s.* comble, *m.*; (*God*) Très-Haut, Tout-Puissant, *m.*

Highly, *adv.* hautement; grandement; considérablement; extrêmement; infiniment; fortement; éminemment; parfaitement, dans la perfection; très, fort, bien; beaucoup; en termes flatteurs, avantageusement; fièrement, orgueilleusement; avec prétention; sévèrement. (*V.* **Think.**) — *seasoned,* &c., *V.* **High-seasoned,** &c.

Highness, *s.* hauteur, élévation, *f.*; grandeur, *f.*; force, violence, intensité, *f.*; (*title*) Altesse, *f.*; (*of the sultan*) Hautesse, *f.*

Hight, *adj.* nommé, appelé

Hilarity, *s.* hilarité, *f.*

Hill, *s.* colline, *f.*, coteau, *m.*, côte, butte, montagne, *f.*, mont, *m.*, hauteur, éminence, élévation, *f.*; — *v.a.* (*agr.*) chausser. *Up* —, *See Letter* **U.** *Up — and down dale,* par monts et par vaux. — **side,** *s.* penchant *or* versant d'une colline, coteau, *m.* — **top,** *s.* sommet d'une colline, *m.*

Hilled, *adj.* qui a des collines, à *or* aux collines. *Seven* —, aux sept collines

Hilliness, *s.* montuosité, *f.*

Hillock, *s.* monticule, coteau, tertre, *m.*, butte, petite colline, *f.*; éminence, hauteur, élévation, *f.*

Hilly, *adj.* montagneux, montueux

Hilt, *s.* (*of a sword,* &c., *handle*) poignée, *f.*, (*part protecting the hand*) garde, *f.* *To put o.'s hand on the — of o.'s sword,* (*as a threat,* &c.) porter la main sur la garde de son épée. *He ran his sword into him up to the* —, il lui enfonça son épée dans le corps jusqu'à la garde

Hilted, *adj.* à poignée ...; à garde ..., garni d'une garde ...

Him, *pron. pers.* le; lui; (*demonstrative*) celui

Himalayan, *adj.* himalayen

Himself, *pron.* lui-même; lui; soi-même; soi; (*in a reflect. verb*) se

Hind, *s.* biche, *f.*; (*pers.*) garçon *or* valet de ferme, *m.*; rustre, *m.*

Hind, Hinder, *adj.* de derrière; postérieur; arrière. — *legs,* jambes de derrière, *f.pl.*

Hinder, *v.a.* empêcher (de); détourner (de); embarrasser, gêner, entraver, arrêter; nuire à; (*delay*) retarder

Hinderance. *V.* **Hindrance**

Hindermost, Hindmost, *adj.* dernier

Hindoo. *V.* **Hindu**

Hindrance, *s.* empêchement, obstacle, *m.*

Hindu, *s. adj.* Hindou, *m.*, e, *f.*, Indou, *m.*, e, *f.*

Hindustani, *s.* l'hindoustani, *m.*; — *adj.* hindoustani

Hinge, *s.* gond, *m.*; (*of boxes*) charnière, *f.*; (*fig.*) pivot, *m.*, base, *f.*; point principal, *m*; — *v.a.* gonder, garnir (*or* munir) de gonds; (*of boxes*) garnir (*or* munir) de charnières; (*fig.*) courber, — *v.n.* tourner, rouler, porter, reposer. — **joint,** *s.* ginglyme. *m.*

Hinna. *V.* **Henna**

Hinny, *s.* bardot, *m.*

Hint, *v.a.* donner à entendre, faire entendre, indiquer à mots couverts, exprimer à demi-mot, insinuer; suggérer; — *v.n.* faire des allusions; (— **at**) faire allusion (à); faire entendre; faire entrevoir; — *s.* avis, mot, *m.*; demi-mot, *m.*, mots couverts, *m.pl.*; allusion indirecte, *f.*; suggestion, *f.*; insinuation, *f.*; idée, donnée, *f.*, aperçu, *m.*; signe, *m.* *To take the* —, comprendre. *To understand at a* —, entendre à demi-mot

Hip, *s.* hanche, *f.*; (*arch.*) arêtier, *m.*; (*bot.*) gratte-cul, *m.*; — *v.a.* déhancher, démettre *or* disloquer la hanche à; (*hyp*) *V.* **Hyp.** — **bath,** *s.* bain de siége, *m.* — **bone,** *s.* os de la hanche, *m.* — **gout,** *s.* sciatique, goutte sciatique, *f.* — **hop,** *adv.* clopin-clopant. — **joint,** *s.* articulation coxo-fémorale, *f.* — **roof,** *s.* croupe, *f.* — **shot,** *adj.* déhanché. — **tree,** *s.* églantier, *m.*

Hipped, *adj.* déhanché; (*hypped*) *V.* **Hypped**

Hippian, *adj.* hippien

Hippic, *adj.* hippique

Hippocamp, Hippocampus, *s.* hippocampe, *m.*

Hippocentaur, *s.* hippocentaure, *m.*

Hippocras, *s.* hippocras, *m.*

Hippocrat-ic, -ism, -ist. *V.* page 3, § 1

Hippocrene, *s.* l'Hippocrène, *f.*

Hippodrome, *s.* hippodrome, *m.*

Hippogriff, Hippogryph, *s.* hippogriffe, *m.*

Hippolith, *s.* hippolithe, *m.*

Hippolog-ic, al, -y. *V.* page 3, § 1

Hippologist, *s.* hippologue, *m.*

Hippomane, *s.* hippomane, *f.*

Hippomania, *s.* hippomanie, *f.*

Hippomaniac, *s.* hippomane, *m.f.*

Hippopatholog-ic, al, -ist, -y. *V.* p. 3, § 1

Hippophag-ic, al, -y. *V.* page 3 § 1

Hippophagian, *adj.* hippophage

Hippophagist, *s.* hippophage, *m.f.*

Hippophagous, *adj.*, **Hippophagus,** *s.* hippophage, *m.f.*

Hippopotamus, *s.* hippopotame, *m.*

Hippuric, *adj.* hippurique

Hircine, *adj. s.* hircin, *adj.m.*, e, *f.*, hircine, *s.f.*

Hire, *v.a.* louer, prendre à louage; (*pers.*) prendre à son service, prendre, louer; engager; embaucher; employer; (*bribe*) gagner à prix d'argent, gagner, soudoyer, acheter, corrompre; — *s.* louage, *m.*; (*price*) prix de louage *or* de location, *m.*; (*wages*) salaire, *m.*, gages, *m.pl.*; — *adj.* de louage. *For* —, à louer. *On* —, à louage. *To let on* or *for* —, donner à louage, louer. *The labourer is worthy of his* —, toute peine mérite salaire. — **out,** *v.a.* louer, donner à louage. — *oneself out,* se louer (à), se mettre aux gages (de)

Hired, *adj.* loué, de louage; (*pers.*) à gages; mercenaire

Hireling, *adj. s.* mercenaire, *m.f.*

Hirer, *s.* loueur, *m.*, -euse, *f.*

Hiring, *s.* louage, *m.*

Hirsute, *adj.* hérissé; velu; (*coarse*) grossier

His, *pron. poss.* (*before a noun*) son, sa, ses; (*not before a noun*) le sien, la sienne, les siens, les siennes; ses; (*pron. pers.*) à lui, de lui. *This drawing is* —, (*belongs to him*) ce dessin est à lui; (*comes from him; he is the author of it*) ce dessin est de lui. *A friend of* —, un de ses amis

Hispanian, *adj.* hispanique

Hispanicism, *s.* hispanisme, *m.*

Hispid, *adj.* velu; (*bot.*) hispide

Hispidity, *s.* hispidité, *f.*

Hiss, *v.a.n.* siffler; — *s.* sifflement, *m.*; (*whistling*) coup de sifflet, sifflet, *m.* — **at,** *v.a.* siffler

Hissing, *adj.* sifflant; de sifflement; — *s.* *V.* **Hiss.** — *noise* or *sound,* sifflement, *m.*

Hissingly, *adv.* en sifflant

Hist, *int.* psit! ps't! s't! chut!
Histolog-ic, al, -y. *V.* page 3, § 1
Historian, *s.* historien, *m.*, -ne, *f.*
Historic, -al, *adj.* historique; d'histoire. — *painter, piece,* peintre, tableau d'histoire, *m.* — *painting,* peinture historique *or* d'histoire, *f.*; tableau d'histoire, *m.* — *subject,* sujet historique, *m.*
Historically, *adv.* historiquement [ricité, *f.*
Historicalness, Historicity, *s.* histo-
Historiette, *s.* historiette, *f.*
Historiographer, *s.* historiographe, *m.*
Historiograph-ic, al, -y. *V.* page 3, § 1
History, *s.* histoire, *f.*; (*relation*) historique, *m.*
Histrion, *s.* comédien, *m.*; (*in a bad sense*) histrion, *m.*
Histrionic, -al, *adj.* du comédien, de la comédie, du théâtre, théâtral, de la scène, scénique; (*in a bad sense*) histrionique, d'histrion
Histrionically, *adv.* en comédien; (*in a bad sense*) histrioniquement, en histrion
Histrionism, *s.* représentation scénique, *f.*, jeux de théâtre, *m.pl.*, théâtre, *m.*; (*jest.*) histrionie, *f.*, histrionage, *m.*
Hit, *v.a.n.* frapper; heurter; donner un coup *or* des coups à; (*a blow*) donner, porter, asséner, frapper; (*a mark*) atteindre, toucher, attraper; (*guess*) tomber sur, deviner; saisir; (*succeed*) réussir, atteindre le but; (*together*) se rencontrer, s'accorder; (*upon*) trouver, rencontrer; (*fenc.*) toucher; — *s.* coup, *m.*; chance, *f.*, hasard, *m.*; heureux hasard, *m.*; trouvaille, *f.*; idée, *f.*; invention, *f.*; grand effet, *m.*, sensation, *f.*, succès, *m.*; (*apposite thought*) à-propos, *m.*; (*fenc.*) touche, *f.*, (*considered as a game*) manche, *f.* *Decisive* or *odd* or *last* —, (*fenc.*) belle, *f.* — *or miss,* à tout hasard. *To have — it,* avoir mis le doigt dessus, avoir deviné, y être. — **off,** *v.a.* saisir, attraper, trouver; représenter; déterminer. — **out,** *v.a.* porter, donner, asséner
Hitch, *v.n.* se démener, se trémousser, sautiller; (*get entangled*) s'embarrasser, s'accrocher, se nouer; (*of horses*) se couper; — *v.a.* accrocher; (*tie*) attacher; (*knot*) nouer; — *s.* empêchement, obstacle, *m.*, entrave, *f.*; anicroche, *f.*, accroc, *m.*; (*knot*) nœud, *m.* *To have a* —, avoir quelque chose qui cloche
Hither, *adv.* ici, y; par ici; — *adj.* citérieur. — *and thither,* çà et là. —**to,** *adv.* jusqu'ici, jusqu'à présent; jusqu'alors. — **ward, -wards,** *adv.* de ce côté-ci, par ici
Hive, *s.* ruche, *f.*; (*a swarm*) essaim, *m.*; —**s,** *pl.* ruches, &c.; (*swine-pox*) varicelle pustuleuse globuleuse, *f.*; — *v.a.* mettre *or* rassembler dans une ruche; (*contain*) renfermer; — *v.n.* vivre dans la même ruche; (*pers.*) vivre ensemble. — **bee,** *s.* abeille de ruche, abeille
Ho, Hoa, *int.* ho! holà! hé! [domestique, *f.*
Hoar, *adj. s. V.* **White**
Hoard, *s.* amas, monceau, tas, *m.*; provision, *f.*; (*of money*) trésor, magot, *m.*; (*fig.*) somme, *f.*; — *v.a.* (— *up*) amasser; entasser, accumuler; — *v.n.* amasser, faire des provisions, thésauriser
Hoarder, *s.* accumulateur, *m.*, -trice, *f.*, amasseur, *m.*, -euse, *f.*, thésauriseur, *m.*, -euse, *f.*; accapareur, *m.*, -euse, *f.*
Hoarding, *adj.* qui amasse, qui thésaurise, accumulateur; — *s.* accumulation, *f.*; (*fence*) clôture de (*or* en) planches, palissade en
Hoarhound, *s.* marrube, *m.* [planches, *f.*
Hoariness, *s.* blancheur, *f.*
Hoarse, *adj.* enroué; (*voice*) rauque, enroué. *To get* or *grow* or *make oneself* —, s'enrouer
Hoarsely, *adv.* d'une voix rauque *or* enrouée
Hoarseness, *s.* enrouement, *m.*; raucité, *f.*
Hoary, *adj.* blanc; (*with age*) blanchi, aux cheveux blancs; chenu; (*with frost*) couvert de frimas; (*old*) vieux. — **headed,** *adj.* qui a les cheveux blancs; (*fig.*) couvert de frimas
Hoax, *v.a.* mystifier, attraper; — *s.* mystification, mauvaise plaisanterie, *f.*, tour, *m.*, farce, attrape, *f.*; (*false news*) canard, *m.*
Hoaxer, *s.* mystificateur, *m.*, -trice, *f.*
Hoaxing, *adj.* mystificateur; — *s.* mystifica-
Hoazin, *s.* hoazin, *m.* [tion, *f.*
Hob, *s.* paysan, rustre, *m.*; (*elf*) lutin, *m.*; (*of fire-places*) plaque, *f.*; (*of wheels*) moyeu, *m.*
Hobble, *s.* clochement, *m.*; (*difficulty*) pétrin, *m.*; — **s,** *pl.* entraves, *f.pl.*; — *v.n.* clocher, clopiner; — *v.a.* mettre dans l'embarras; (*shackle*) entraver. *To get into a* —, se mettre dans le pétrin *or* dans l'embarras
Hobblingly, *adv.* clopin-clopant
Hobby, *s.* (*bird*) hobereau, *m.*; (— *horse*) dada, bidet, cheval de bois, *m.*; (*whim*) marotte, *f.*, dada, *m.* *To ride o.'s* —, être sur son dada; [caresser sa marotte
Hobgoblin, *s.* lutin, *m.*
Hobnail, *s.* clou à grosse tête, clou, *m.*; (*pers.*) rustre, *m.* [à clous
Hobnailed, *adj.* garni de clous à grosse tête;
Hobnob, *v.n.* trinquer; — *adv.* à prendre ou à
Hobson's choice, *s.* choix forcé, *m.* [laisser
Hocco, *s.* hocco, *m.*
Hock, *s.* vin du Rhin, *m.*; (*of horses*) jarret, m.
Hock, Hockle, *v.a.* couper le jarret (*or* les jarrets) à [*m.* — **stick,** *s.* crosse, *f.*
Hockey, *s.* crosse, *f.* — **player,** *s* crosseur,
Hocus, *v.a.* filouter, attraper
Hocus-pocus, *s.* tour de passe-passe, tour de gobelet, *m.*, jonglerie, *f.*; filouterie, duperie, *f.*; — *v.a.* escamoter, filouter, attraper, duper
Hocussing, *s.* filouterie, *f.*
Hod, *s.* oiseau, *m.*, auge, *f.* —**man,** *s.* manœuvre, aide-maçon, *m.*
Hodge-podge. *V.* **Hotch-potch**
Hodograph, *s.* hodographe, *m.*
Hodograph-ic, al, -y. *V.* page 3, § 1
Hodometer, *s.* hodomètre, compte-pas, *m.*
Hoe, *s.* (*agr.*) houe, *f.*; (*hort.*) binette, *f.*; — *v.a.n.* (*agr.*) houer; (*hort.*) biner
Hoer, *s.* houeur, *m.*
Hoeing, *s.* houage, houement, *m.*
Hog, *s.* cochon, porc, pourceau, *m.*; (*pers.*) cochon, *m.*; — *v.a.*(*nav.*) goreter; — *v.n.* (*of a ship,* &c.) se casser. *Wild* —, sanglier, *m.* *To go the whole* —, aller jusqu'au bout. — **cote,** *s. V.* **Piggery.** — **fish,** *s.* scorpène, *f.* — **herd,** *s.* porcher, *m.* — **louse,** *s.* porcellion, *m.* —**mane,** *s.* crinière en brosse, *f.* — **market,** *s.* marché aux cochons, *m.* —**pen,** *s. V.* **Piggery.** — **plum,** *s.* monbin, spondias, *m.* — **rat,** *s.* capromys, houtias, *m.* — **ringer,** *s.* anneleur de porcs, *m.* —**'s cheek,** *s.* bajoue, *f.* —**shead,** *s. See below.* —**'s lard,** *s.* saindoux, *m.*, axonge, *f.* — **steer,** *s.* ragot, *m.* —**sty,** *s. V.* **Piggery.** — **wash,** *s.* lavure, *f.*
Hogged, *adj.* (*of a ship,* &c.) cassé
Hoggerel, Hogget, *s.* antenois, *m.*, e, *f.*
Hogging, *s.* (*of a ship,* &c.) cassure, *f.*
Hoggish, *adj.* de cochon, de pourceau, grossier; glouton
Hoggishly, *adv.* comme un cochon, en cochon, en pourceau, grossièrement
Hoggishness, *s.* cochonnerie, *f.*; grossièreté, *f.*; brutalité, *f.*; gloutonnerie, *f.*
Hogshead, *s.* grand tonneau, tonneau, muid, *m.*; (*English meas., half of a butt or pipe*) demi-pièce (anglaise), *f.*; (*of French wine*) pièce, *f.*
Hoi, *int.* dia! (*to the left*)
Hoiden, *s.* garçonnière, gamine, *f.*; — *adj.* garçonnier, grossier, mal-appris; — *v.n.* garçonner, gaminer
Hoist, *v.a.* hisser, guinder; (*to lift*) lever, élever, hausser; (*nav.*) (*a sail*) hisser, (*a flag*) arborer, (*a mast*) guinder; — *s.* effort, *m.*; (*machine*) guindal, *m.*; (*in a warehouse*) élévatoire *m.*; (*in mines*) ascenseur, *m.*; (*nav.*) drisse, *f.*, guindant, *m.*
Hoity-toity, *int.* bah! vraiment! allons donc; prrr! eh bien! — *adj.* étourdi, écervelé
Hold, *v.a.* tenir; retenir, arrêter, suspendre; cesser, finir; soutenir, maintenir; contenir;

prendre; considérer comme, regarder comme, tenir pour, estimer, croire; persévérer dans, persister dans, continuer; poursuivre; suivre; posséder, avoir, occuper, jouir de; contraindre (à), astreindre (à); détenir; empêcher (de); célébrer; (*a review*) faire, passer; (*to bet*) parier; (*feud.*) relever (de); — *v.n.* tenir; adhérer, s'attacher; arrêter, s'arrêter; se maintenir, se soutenir; être vrai, être juste, être bon; durer, continuer; supporter; se retenir, se contenir; relever, dépendre; (*to bet*) faire un pari, parier; (*to be of opinion*) tenir, être d'avis. — *!* tenez! attendez! arrêtez! — **back,** *v.a.* retenir, arrêter; s'abstenir de produire; cacher; *v.n.* s'éloigner, se tenir en arrière; résister, tenir ferme; s'abstenir; *s.* empêchement, obstacle, *m.*, entrave, *f.*; (*of harness*) reculement, *m.* — **down,** baisser; retenir; contenir; maintenir. —**fast,** *v.a. V.* **Fast;** *s. See below.* — **forth,** tendre; avancer; présenter, offrir; mettre en avant; proposer; promettre; (*speak*) pérorer; haranguer; prêcher. — **from,** se retenir (de), s'empêcher (de). —**good,** être vrai, être juste, être bon, être applicable, s'appliquer, se vérifier; être valable; subsister; tenir. — **in,** retenir; se retenir, se contenir; continuer. — **off,** tenir à distance, tenir éloigné; se tenir à distance, s'éloigner. — **on,** continuer de tenir, tenir toujours; tenir bon, résister; s'arrêter, arrêter, attendre; (*keep on*) poursuivre. — **out,** tendre; offrir, présenter; promettre; tenir bon, tenir ferme, résister (à); soutenir; continuer; (*to last*) durer. — **together,** tenir ensemble; unir; être uni. — **up,** lever; tenir droit; exposer; offrir, présenter; maintenir, soutenir; se soutenir; (*of rain*) cesser; (*of weather*) s'éclaircir. — **with,** être du parti de, tenir pour; être de l'avis de, penser comme, être pour

Hold, *s.* (*power of seizing*) prise, *f.*; (*hand, claw*) main, serre, *f.*; (*custody*) garde, *f.*; (*support*) soutien, appui, *m.*; (*influence*) influence, *f.*, pouvoir, *m*; (*place*) place, *f.*; (*fortress*) place forte, *f.*; fort, *m.*; (*of a ship*) cale, *f.*; (*mus.*) point d'orgue, *m.*; (*of wild beasts*) fort, *m.* *To catch, get, lay, seize,* or *take — of* (*on, upon*), prendre, empoigner, mettre la main sur, se saisir de, saisir, s'emparer de; tenir; s'accrocher à; profiter de; trouver, découvrir; surprendre; obtenir; parvenir à. *To have a — on,* avoir prise sur. *To have — of,* tenir. *To let go* or *release o.'s —, to loose* or *quit o.'s —,* lâcher prise; (*of* . . .) lâcher

Holder, *s.* (*handle*) manche, *m.*, poignée, *f.*; anse, *f.*; (*for liquids*) réservoir, *m.*; (*pers.*) personne qui tient, *f.*; possesseur, *m.*; détenteur, *m.*, -trice, *f.*; porteur, *m.*; dépositaire, *m.f.*; (*of land*) propriétaire, *m.f.*; (*tenant*) locataire, *m.f.*; fermier, *m.*, -ière, *f.*; (*in compounds generally*) porte- . . ., *m.* — **forth,** *s.* harangueur, *m.*, -euse, *f.*, péroreur, *m.*, -euse, *f.*

Holdfast, *s.* (*hook*) crampon, *m.*; main de fer, *f.*; esse, *f.*; (*build.*) tirant, *m.*; (*carpenter's*) valet, *m.*

Holding, *s.* possession, *f.*; influence, *f.*, pouvoir, *m.*, prise, *f.*; (*of assemblies, and writ.*) tenue, *f.*; (*law*) détention, *f.*; (*farm*) tenure, ferme, *f.*

Hole, *s.* trou, *m.*; brèche, *f.*; caverne, *f.*, antre, *m.*; orifice, *m.*, ouverture, *f.*; (*mean habitation*) trou, *m.*; (*in a paved road*) flache, *f.*; — *v.a.* trouer; (*at billiards*) blouser, bloquer, faire. *To pick a — in a person's coat,* critiquer quel- [qu'un

Holibut. *V.* **Halibut**

Holiday, *s.* jour de fête, *m.*, fête, *f.*; (*of schools*) congé, *m.*; jour de congé, *m.* —**s,** *pl.* (*vacation*) vacances, *f. pl.*; — *adj.* de fête; (*of schools*) de congé; de vacances; (*pers.*) en vacances. *To go home for the —s,* aller en vacances. — **maker,** *s.* personne en vacances, *f.* — **makers,** *s. pl.* gens en vacances, *m. pl.*

Holily, *adv.* saintement

Holiness, *s,* sainteté, *f.* *His —,* Sa Sainteté

Holland, *s.* (*geog.*) la Hollande, *f.*; (*linen*) toile de Hollande, *f.*; —**s,** *pl.* (*gin*) genièvre de Hollande, *m.*

Hollander, *s.*,**Hollandish,** *adj.* Hollandais, [*m.*, e, *f.*

Hollo, Holloa. *V.* **Hallo**

Hollow, *adj.* creux; (*empty*) vide; (*of sound*) sourd; (*false*) faux, trompeur, perfide; — *adverb.* à plate couture, complètement; — *s.* creux, *m.*; cavité, *f.*; caverne, *f.*, antre, *m.*; canal, passage, *m.*; (*pit*) fosse, *f.*; (*abyss*) gouffre, abîme, *m.*; — *v.a.* creuser; évider; canneler; — *v.n. V.* **Hollo.** — **cheeked,** *adj.* qui a les joues creuses, aux joues creuses. — — **eyed,** *adj.* aux yeux creux *or* enfoncés, à l'œil cave. — **hearted,** *adj.* au cœur perfide *or* faux

Hollowly, *adv.* en creux; faussement, per- [fidement

Hollowness, *s.* creux, *m.*; (*deceitfulness*) fausseté, perfidie, *f.*, manque de sincérité, *m.*

Holly, *s.* houx, *m.* — **grove,** *s.* houssaie, *f.* —**hock,** *s.* rose trémière, passe-rose, *f.* — **oak,** *s.* yeuse, *f.* — **stick, -tree,** *s.* houx, *m.*

Holm, Holme, *s.* îlot, *m.*; rive plate et fertile, terre riveraine, *f.*; (*bot.*) yeuse, *f.* — **oak,** *s.* yeuse, *f.*

Holocaust, *s.* holocauste, *m.*

Holograph, *s. adj.* holographe, *s.m.*, *adj. m.f.*

Holographic, -al, *adj.* holographe

Holster, *s.* fonte, *f.* — **cap,** *s.* couvre-fonte, [chaperon, *m.*

Holstered, *adj.* garni de fontes

Holy, *adj.* saint, sacré; (*consecrated*) bénit; — *s.* Très-Saint, *m.* *The — One,* le Très-Saint, *m.* *The — of Holies,* le Saint des Saints, *m.*; le sanctuaire, *m.* *To make* or *keep —,* sanctifier; consacrer. — **Alliance,** *s.* sainte alliance, *f.* — **bread,** *s.* pain bénit, *m.* — **cross,** *s. V.* — **rood.** — **day,** *s. V.* **Holiday.** — **empire,** *s.* saint empire, *m.* — **family,** *s.* sainte famille, *f.* — **Father,** *s.* Saint-Père, *m.* — **Ghost, -Spirit,** *s.* Saint-Esprit, *m.* — **ground,** *s.* terre sacrée, *f.* — **Land,** *s.* Terre sainte, *f.* — **man,** *s.* saint homme, homme pieux, *m.* — **Office,** *s.* Saint Office, *m.* — **orders,** *s. pl.* ordres sacrés, *m.pl.* — **phial,** *s.* sainte ampoule, *f.* — **places,** *s. pl.* lieux saints, saints lieux, *m.pl.* —**rood,** *s.* sainte croix, *f.* —**rood day,** *s.* exaltation de la sainte croix, *f.* — **sacrament,** *s.* saint sacrement, *m.* — **see,** *s.* saint-siége, *m.* — **Sepulchre,** *s.* Saint Sépulcre, *m.* — **table,** *s.* sainte table, *f.* — **Thursday,** *s.* l'Ascension, *f.*, le jour de l'Ascension, *m.* — **vessel,** *s.* vase sacré, *m.* — **Virgin,** *s.* sainte Vierge, *f.* — **war,** *s.* guerre sainte, *f.* — **water,** *s.* eau bénite, *f.* — **water basin** *or* **font** *or* **pot** *or* **vessel,** *s.* bénitier, *m.* — **water sprinkler,** *s.* aspersoir, aspergès, goupillon, *m.* — **week,** *s.* semaine sainte, *f.* — **wood,** *s.* gaïac, bois saint, *m.* — **Writ,** *s.* Écriture Sainte, *f.*

Homage, *s.* hommage, *m.*; hommages, *m.pl.*; — *v.a.* rendre hommage à

Homager, *s.* hommager, *m.*

Home, *s.* chez soi, *m.*, maison *f.*, logis, *m.*, demeure, *f.*, domicile, *m.*; intérieur, foyer domestique, foyer, *m.*; famille, *f.*; maison paternelle, *f.*; ménage, *m.*; (*o.'s own country*) pays, *m.*, patrie, *f.*; (*fig*) asile, refuge, *m.*; demeure, *f.*, séjour, *m.*; — *adj.* domestique, de la maison; (*fig.*) intérieur, de l'intérieur, du pays; indigène; (*severe*) qui porte; (*of jests*) mordant; (*of proofs*) convaincant; (*nav.*) de retour; — *adv.* chez soi, à la maison, au logis; (*in o.'s country*) à *or* dans son pays; au dedans, à l'intérieur; (*to the point*) droit au but, au fait; à son adresse; ad hominem; à propos; comme il faut; (*near*) de près; (*to the heart*) au cœur; (*to the last extremity*) à bout; (*directly*) directement; (*entirely*) entièrement, tout à fait, complètement; vigoureusement; (*nav.*) à poste; (*of an anchor*) à bord. *Long* or *last —,* dernière demeure, tombe, *f.*; terre, *f.* *At —,* chez soi (*my, your,* &c., *house,* chez moi, chez vous, &c.), à la maison, au logis, y; dans son intérieur; dans la famille; en famille; à domicile; (*in o.'s own country*) dans son pays; (*in the country*) au dedans, à l'intérieur; (*at ease*) sans gêne, sans cérémonie; à son aise; (*well acquainted with*) dans son élément; sur son terrain; en pays de connaissance; familier. *From —, away from —, gone from —,* absent de chez soi, absent; en voyage; (*gone out*) sorti. *To bring —,* ramener; rapporter; (*a charge,* &c.) prouver ('*to,*' contre). *To come —,* rentrer chez soi, rentrer; (*from abroad*) rentrer dans son pays; revenir; (*to interest*) toucher de près, toucher au vif, intéresser vivement; (*fall upon*) retomber sur; (*of anchors*) chasser. *Come — with me,* venez chez moi. *To come — to our interest,* toucher de près nos intérêts. *To come — to the point,* venir au fait. *To go —,* (*from school, on a holiday*) sortir (*V.* **Holidays**). *To go from —,* s'absenter (de chez soi). *To go to o.'s long* or *last —,* mourir, aller ad patres. *To hit* or *strike —,* frapper juste; frapper en plein; porter coup. *To make oneself at —,* faire comme si l'on était chez soi, faire comme chez soi; se mettre à son aise, ne pas se gêner. *To press —,* pousser à bout. *To take to o.'s long —,* conduire à sa dernière demeure, porter en terre. *I have no — of my own,* je n'ai pas de chez moi. *He has no —,* il est sans asile. *Make my house your —,* considérez ma maison comme la vôtre. *— is —, be it ever so homely,* il n'y a pas (or il n'est pas) de petit chez-soi; à chaque oiseau son nid est beau. — **born, -bred,** *adj.* naturel; indigène; domestique. — **bound,** *adj.* retournant au port, en retour. — **department,** *s.* département *or* ministère de l'intérieur, *m.* — **felt,** *adj.* profondément senti, intime. — **grown,** *adj.* indigène. — **keeping,** *adj.* qui se tient chez lui, sédentaire, casanier. —**less,** *adj. V* **Houseless.** — **life,** *s.* vie de famille, vie d'intérieur, *f.*; intérieur, *m.* —**liness,** *s.* grossièreté, *f.*; simplicité, *f.*; familiarité, *f.* —**ly,** *adj.* domestique; simple, modeste, ordinaire; sans façon; bourgeois; grossier; commun; familier; *adv.* bourgeoisement; grossièrement. —**made,** *adj.* fait à la maison; (*bread*) de ménage; (*wine*) du cru; (*in the country*) fait dans le pays, de fabrication indigène. — **magazine,** *s.* magasin du foyer, *m.* — **minister, -secretary,** *s.* ministre de l'intérieur, *m.* — **office,** *s* ministère de l'intérieur, *m.* — **passage,** *s. V.* — **voyage.** — **sick,** *adj.* qui a le mal du pays. — **sickness,** *s.* mal du pays, *m.* —**spun,** *adj.* fait à la maison; de ménage; (*in the country*) fait dans le pays; (*plain*) simple; (*coarse*) grossier; sans façon, simple. —**stead,** *s.* château, manoir, *m.*; demeure, *f.*; terre, propriété, *f.*; domaine, *m.*; (*farm*) ferme, *f.* — **thrust,** *s.* coup bien appliqué, coup qui porte *or* qui va droit au but, *m.*; (*fenc.*) coup de fond, *m.* — **voyage,** *s.* voyage de retour, retour, *m.* —**ward, -s,** *adj. adv.* vers la maison; chez soi; (*of the country*) vers son pays; (*nav.*) au retour. — **ward bound,** *V.* — **bound**

Homelin, Homelyn, *s.* miraillet, miralet, *m.*

Homeo . . ., *V.* **Homœo . . .**

Homerian, *s.* homérique, *m.*

Homeric, *adj.* homérique

Homicidal, *adj.* homicide

Homicide, *s.* homicide, (*pers.*) *m.f.*, (*murder*) *m.*

Homiletic, -al, *adj.* homilétique; **- s,** *s.pl.* homilétique, *f.*

Homiliarium, *s.* homiliaire, *m.*

Homilist, *s.* homiliaste, *m.*

Homily, *s.* homélie, *f.*

Hominy, *s.* gaude, *f.*

Homocentr-ic, al, -ically. *V.* page 3, § 1

Homœopath, *s.* homœopathe, *m.*

Homœopathic, -al, *adj.* homœopathique; (*pers.*) homœopathe. — *doctor* or *practitioner,* médecin homœopathe, *m.*

Homœopathically, *adv.* homœopathiquement

Homœopathist, *s.* homœopathe, homœopathiste, *m.*

Homœopathize, *v.a.n.* homœopathiser

Homœopathy, *s.* homœopathie, *f.*

Homogeneal, Homogeneous, *adj.* homogène

Homogeneity, Homogeneousness, *s.* homogénéité, *f.*

Homogeneously, *adv.* homogènement

Homologate, *v.a.* homologuer

Homologation, *s.* homologation, *f.*

Homolog-ic, al, -ically, -y. *V.* page 3, § 1

Homologous, *adj.* homologue

Homologue, *s.* homologue, *m.*

Homomorphous, *adj.* homomorphe

Homonym, *s.* homonyme, *m.*

Homonymous, *adj.* homonyme

Homo-nymy, -phony, &c. *V.* page 3, § 1

Hone, *s.* pierre à repasser, pierre à rasoir, *f.*; — *v.a.* repasser, affiler. — **wort,** *s.* sison, *m.*

Honest, *adj.* honnête, probe, loyal, intègre, brave; de bonne foi; franc, sincère. — *fellow,* honnête *or* brave garçon. — *man,* honnête homme, homme de bien

Honestly, *adv.* honnêtement, avec probité, loyalement, de bonne foi; franchement, sincèrement

Honesty, *s.* honnêteté, probité, loyauté, intégrité, *f.*; bonne foi, *f.*; franchise, sincérité, *f.*; (*bot.*) lunaire, *f.*

Honey, *s.* miel, *m.*; (*pers.*) doux ami, *m.*, douce amie, *f.*, (mon) cœur, *m.*; — *v.a.* mieller, emmieller, adoucir avec du miel. — **bag,** *s.* sac à miel, *m.* — **bee,** *s.* mouche à miel, *f.* — **buzzard,** *s.* bondrée, *f.* — **comb,** *s.* gâteau de miel, rayon de miel, *m.*; (*of arms*) chambre, *f.* — **comb bag** *or* **stomach,** *s.* (*of ruminants*) bonnet, *m.* — **comb moth,** *s.* gallérie, *f.* —**combed,** *adj.* criblé (de trous); (*of arms*) chambré. — **cup,** *s.* nectaire, *m.* — **dew,** *s.* miellat, *m.* — **eater,** *s.* méliphage, *f.* — **flower,** *s.* mélianthe, *m.* — **guide,** *s.* indicateur, *m.* — **lotus,** *s.* mélilot, *m.* —**moon,** *s.* lune de miel, *f.* — **mouthed,** *adj.* mielleux. — **pot,** *s.* pot à miel, *m.* — **stone,** *s.* mellite, *f.* — **sucker,** *s.* méliphage, *f.* —**suckle,** *s.* chèvrefeuille, *m.* *French —suckle,* sainfoin, *m.* — **suckled,** *adj.* garni de chèvrefeuille. — **sweet,** *adj.* doux comme du miel. —**tongued,** *adj.* qui a la langue mielleuse, mielleux. — **wort,** *s.* mélinet, *m.*

Honeyed, Honied, *adj.* emmiellé; (*sweet*) mielleux, doux

Honiton, *s.* — **lace,** *s.* application d'Angleterre, *f.*

Honorarium, *s.* honoraires, *m.pl.*

Honorary, *adj.* honorifique; (*without pay*) honoraire; — *s.* honoraires, *m.pl.*

Honour, *v.a.* honorer ('*with,*' de); (*com.*) faire honneur à; (*of God*) glorifier; (*a toast*) boire; — *s.* honneur, *m.* *Sense of —,* loyauté, *f.* — **less,** *adj.* sans honneur

Honourable, *adj.* honorable

Honourableness, *s.* honorabilité, *f.*

Honourably, *adv.* honorablement

Hood, *s.* capuchon, *m.*; (*for ladies*) capeline, *f.*; (*for horses*) béguin, *m.*; (*for a hawk*) chaperon, *m.*; (*of carriages*) capote, *f.*, soufflet, *m.*; (*nav.*) capot, *m.*; — *v.a.* encapuchonner; (*to cover*) couvrir; (*the eyes*) bander; (*a hawk*) chaperonner. —**wink,** *v.a.* bander les yeux à; (*deceive*) tromper, aveugler; (*cover*) cacher

Hooded, *part. adj.* encapuchonné, en capuchon; (*of the eyes*) bandé; (*of hawks*) chaperonné; (*of crows*) mantelé, emmantelé. — *crow,* corneille mantelée, mantelle, *f.* — *snake,* vipère à lunettes, *f.*

Hoof, *s.* sabot, *m.*, corne du pied, corne, *f.*, ongle, *m.* — **bound,** *adj.* encastelé

Hoofed, *adj.* à sabot, ongulé

Hook, *s.* crochet, croc, *m*; crampon, *m.*; (*of dress*) agrafe, *f.*; (*fish.*) hameçon, *m.*; (*snare*)

amorce, *f.*, appât, *m.*; (*of shepherds*) houlette, *f.*; (*of a boat*) gaffe, *f.*; — *v.a.* accrocher; (*a dress*) agrafer; (*fish.*) prendre à l'hameçon; (*entrap*) attraper, amorcer; (*steal*) gripper; — *v.n.* se courber. — *and eye*, agrafe et porte, agrafe. *f.* *By — and* (or *or*) *by —*, de bric et de broc. *On o.'s own —*, à son compte. *To — it*, filer, décamper. *To — on*, accrocher. — **nosed,** *adj.* au nez aquilin; (*in contempt*) au nez crochu

Hookah, *s.* houka, *m.*

Hooked, *part. adj.* accroché, &c. (*V.* **Hook,** *v.a.*); (*bent*) crochu, recourbé; fourchu; (*nose*) aquilin

Hookedness, *s.* forme crochue, forme recourbée, *f.*

Hooker, *s.* (*nav.*) hourque, *f.*

Hooky, *adj.* garni de crochets *or* de crocs

Hoop, *s.* cercle, *m.*; (*for children*) cerceau, *m.*; (*of wheels*) jante, *f.*; (*of iron*) frette, *f.*; (*of dresses*) panier, *m.*; (*shout*) cri, *m.*, vocifération, huée, *f.*; (*bird*) huppe, *f.*; — *v.a.* cercler; (*wheels*) mettre des jantes à; (*with iron*) fretter; (*gird*) entourer; (*call*) appeler par des cris; (*drive away*) chasser par des cris; — *v.n.* crier, vociférer, huer, hurler. — **cheese,** *s.* meule, *f.* — **iron,** *s.* feuillard de fer, *m.* — **maker,** *s.* cerclier, *m.* — **net,** *s.* épuisette, *f.*, verveux, *m.*, truble, *f.* — **petticoat,** *s.* panier, *m.* — **ring,** *s.* (*with or without stones*) bague-jonc, *f.*, jonc, *m.*; (*with stones*) bague-collier, *m.*

Hooper, *s.* cercleur, *m.*; (*swan*) cygne sauvage, *m.*

Hooping, *s.* *V.* **Hooting.** — **cough,** *s.* coqueluche, *f.*

Hoopoe, Hoopoo, *s.* huppe, *f.*

Hoora, Hoorah, Hooray. *V.* **Hurra**

Hoot, *v.a.n.* huer, crier; (*of night birds*) houhouler, huer, crier; — *s.* *V.* **Hooting.** *To — at*, huer

Hooting, *s.* huée, *f.*, huées, vociférations, *f.pl.*, cris, *m.pl.*; (*of night birds*) houhoulement, *m.*, huée, *f.*, cri, *m.*

Hop, *v.n.* sautiller; sauter à cloche-pied; (*to frisk*) gambader; — *v.a.* houblonner; — *s.* sautillement, saut, *m.*; danse, *f.*; bal, *m.*; (*on one leg*) saut à cloche-pied, *m.*; (*lameness*) clochement, *m.*; (*a plant*) houblon, *m.*; —**s,** *s. pl.* (*com.*) houblon, *m.*, houblons, *m.pl.* *To — on one leg*, sauter à cloche-pied. — **bine,** *s.* sarment de houblon, *m.* — **garden, -ground, -plantation, -yard,** *s.* houblonnière, *f.* — **gatherer, -picker,** *s.* houblonneur, *m.*, -euse, *f.* — **gathering, -picking,** *s.* cueillette du houblon *or* des houblons, *f.* — **pole, -prop,** *s.* perche à houblon, *f.*, échalas, *m.* — **race,** *s.* course à cloche-pied, *f.*, cloche-pied, *m.* — **scotch,** *s.* marelle, *f.*

Hope, *s.* (*general sense*) espérance, *f.*; (*particular sense*) espoir, *m.*; espérance, *f.*; (*promise*) espérance, *f.*, espérances, *f.pl.*, avenir, *m.*; (*expectation*) attente, *f.*; —**s,** *pl.* espérances, *f.pl.*; espoir, *m.*; — *v.a.n.* espérer; (*trust*) aimer à croire. *To be in —s that*, avoir l'espoir que, espérer que. *I do —*, j'espère bien. — **for,** *v.a.* espérer. —**ful,** *adj.* de grande espérance, qui donne de grandes espérances, qui promet bien *or* beaucoup; encourageant, rassurant; riant; plein d'espoir, qui espère, qui ne désespère pas (de), qui ne se décourage pas. *To be —ful of*, espérer. *To be —ful that*, espérer que. **fully,** *adv.* avec chance de succès; avec espoir, avec confiance; bien. —**fulness,** *s.* bon espoir, espoir, *m.*, confiance, *f.*; belle apparence, *f.*, belles dispositions, *f.pl.* —**less,** *adj.* sans espoir, désespéré; désespérant; inutile. —**lessly,** *adv.* sans espoir; sans retour. —**lessness,** *s.* désespoir, *m.*; état désespéré, *m.*; nature désespérante, *f.* *The —lessness of his situation*, sa situation désespérée, son état désespéré

Hoper, *s.* personne qui espère, *f.*

Hopingly, *adv.* avec espoir

Hopper, *s.* sauteur, *m.*, -euse, *f.*; (*of mills*) trémie, *f.*; (*agr.*) semoir, *m.*; —**s,** *pl.* (*game*) marelle, *f.*

Hopping, *s.* *V.* **Hop,** *s.*

Hoppy, *adj.* de houblon; houblonné

Horal, Horary, *adj.* horaire

Horatian, *adj.* horatien

Horde, *s.* horde, *f.*

Horehound, *s.* marrube, *m.*

Horizon, *s.* horizon, *m.*

Horizontal, *adj.* horizontal

Horizontally, *adv.* horizontalement

Horizontalness, Horizontality, *s.* horizontalité, *f.*

Horn, *s.* corne, *f.*; (*of deer*) bois, *m.*; (*of insects*) antenne, corne, *f.*; (*in music*) cor, *m.*; cornet, *m.*; (*cup*) coupe, *f.*; (*of the moon*) corne, *f.* — *of plenty*, corne d'abondance, *f.* *French —*, cor d'harmonie, *m.* — **beam,** *s.* charme, *m.*; charmille, *f.* — **beam grove** *or* **plantation,** *s.* charmoie, *f.* — **beetle,** *s.* cerf-volant, *m.* — **bill,** *s.* calao, *m.* — **blende,** *s.* hornblende, *f.m.* — **blower,** *s.* sonneur de cor, *m.*, corneur, *m.*, -euse, *f.* — **book,** *s.* abécédaire, *m.* — **dresser,** *s.* cornetier, *m.* — **fish,** *s.* *V.* **Garfish.** —**less,** *adj.* sans cornes. — **owl,** *s.* duc, *m.* *Great — owl*, grand duc, *m.* — **pipe,** *s.* cornemuse, *f.*; (*dance*) anglaise, *f.* — **stone,** *s.* cornéenne, *f.* — **turner,** *s.* tourneur en corne, *m.* — **work,** *s.* ouvrage en corne, *m.*; (*fort*) ouvrage à corne, *m.* — **worker,** *s.* cornetier, *m.*

Horned, *adj.* cornu; (*of cattle*) à cornes; (*of rye*) ergoté. — *beetle*, — *owl*, *V.* **Horn.** — *cattle*, bêtes à cornes, *f.pl.*

Horner, *s.* cornetier, *m.*

Hornet, *s.* frelon, *m.*

Horny, *adj.* corné, de corne, comme la corne; (*callous*) calleux

Horograph-ic, al, -y. *V.* page 3, § 1

Horologic, -al, *adj.* d'horloge; d'horlogerie

Horology, *s.* horlogerie, *f.*

Horoscope, *s.* horoscope, *m.*

Horoscop-ic, al, -y. *V.* page 3, § 1

Horoscopize, *v.n.* horoscopiser

Horrible, *adj.* horrible, affreux, effroyable

Horribleness, *s.* horreur, nature horrible, *f.*, aspect affreux, *m.*

Horribly, *adv.* horriblement, affreusement, effroyablement

Horrid, *adj.* horrible, affreux, effroyable. *To look —*, être horrible à voir. — *thing*, horreur (*fam.*), *f.* — *man*, *woman*, horreur d'homme, horreur de femme

Horridly, *adv.* *V.* **Horribly**

Horridness. *V.* **Horribleness**

Horrific, *adj.* effroyable, qui fait horreur, horrifique

Horrify, *v.a.* épouvanter, saisir d'horreur, faire horreur à, horripiler; révolter

Horripilation, *s.* horripilation, *f.*

Horror, *s.* horreur, *f.* — **struck,** *adj.* saisi d'horreur

Horse, *s.* cheval, *m.*; (*cavalry*) cavalerie, *f.*; (*wooden frame*) chevalet, bourriquet, *m.*; (*for towels, clothes*) séchoir, *m.*; (*mil. punishment*) cheval de bois, *m.*; (*nav.*) marchepied, *m.*; — *adj.* de cheval; de chevaux; à cheval; — *v.a.* monter. *To ride the high —*, monter sur ses grands chevaux. *To take —*, monter à cheval. *It is a good — that never stumbles*, il n'est (*or* il n'y a) si bon cheval qui ne bronche. — **artillery,** *s.* artillerie à cheval, *f.* — **back,** *adv.* *On — back*, à cheval. *To get on — back*, monter à cheval. *To ride on — back*, aller à cheval. — **barracks,** *s. pl.* caserne de cavalerie, *f.* — **bean,** *s.* féverole, *f.* — **bee,** *s.* taon, *m.* — **block,** *s.* montoir, *m.* — **boat,** *s.* bac, *m.* — **box,** *s.* (*rail.*) wagon-écurie, *m.* — **boy,** *s.* garçon d'écurie, *m.* — **breaker,** *s.* dresseur de chevaux, *m.*; (*tamer*) dompteur de chevaux, *m.*; (*rid.*) écuyer, piqueur, *m.* — **chestnut,** *s* (*fruit*) marron d'Inde, *m.*; (*tree*) marronnier d'Inde, *m.* — **cloth,** *s.* couverture de cheval, *f.*; (*of trappings*) housse, *f.* — **clothing,** *s.* couverture de cheval, *f.*, couvertures de chevaux. *f.pl.* — **comb,** *s.* étrille, *f.* — **courser,** *s.* personne qui fait courir des chevaux, *f.* — **dealer,** *s.* marchand de chevaux, *m.* — **doctor,** *s.* vétérinaire, *m.* — **drench,** *s.*

breuvage de cheval, *m.* — **dung,** *s.* crottin de cheval, *m.*; (*agr.*) fumier, *m.* — **exercise,** *s.* équitation, *f.* — **fair,** *s.* foire aux chevaux, *f.* — **family,** *s.* *V.* — **species.** — **flesh,** *s.* viande de cheval, *f.*, cheval, *m.* — **fly,** *s.* taon, *m.*, hippobosque, *f.* — **foot,** *s.* (*bot.*) tussilage, pas d'âne, *m.* — **gear, -gin,** *s.* manége, *m.* — **guard,** *s.* garde à cheval, *m.*; garde du corps, *m.*; — **guards,** *s. pl.* garde à cheval, *f.*; gardes du corps, *m.pl.*; (*office*) bureaux de l'état-major général (de l'armée), *m.pl.* — **hair,** *s.* crin, *m.* — **hair plume** *or* **tail,** *s.* (*of a helmet*) crinière, *f.* — **hair worker,** *s.* crinier, *m.* — **hoe,** *s.* houe à cheval, *f.* — **jockey,** *s.* maquignon, *m.* — **jockeying, -jockeyship,** *s.* maquignonnage, *m.* — **keeper,** *s.* personne qui tient des chevaux, *f.* — **laugh,** *s.* gros rire, *m.* — **leech,** *s.* sangsue du cheval, hippobdelle, grosse sangsue, *f.*; (*surgeon*) artiste vétérinaire, *m.*; (*farrier*) maréchal ferrant, *m* — **litter,** *s.* litière, *f.* — **load,** *s.* charge d'un cheval, *f.* — **lock,** *s.* entrave, *f.* — **mackerel,** *s.* saurel, caranx, *m.* — **man,** *s.* cavalier, écuyer, *m.*; (*mil.*) cavalier, soldat de cavalerie, *m.* —**manship,** *s.* équitation, *f.*, manége, *m.*; adresse à monter à cheval, *f.*, talent d'écuyer, *m.* — **meat,** *s.* fourrage, *m.* — **mill,** *s.* moulin à manége, *m.* — **mint,** *s.* monarde, *f.* — **net,** *s.* émouchette, *f.*, chasse-mouches, *m.* — **path,** *s.* chemin de halage, *m.* — **picker,** *s.* cure-pieds, *m.* — **piss,** *s.* pissat de cheval, *m.* — **pistol,** *s.* pistolet d'arçon, *m.* — **play,** *s.* jeu grossier, jeu de mains, *m.* — **pond,** *s.* abreuvoir, *m.* — **power,** *s.* force de ... chevaux, *f.* — **pox,** *s.* vaccine du cheval, vaccine équine, *f.* — **quarter,** *s.* quartier de cavalerie, *f.* — **race, -racing,** *s.* *V.* **Race** *and* **Racing.** — **radish,** *s.* raifort, *m.* — **rake,** *s.* râteau à cheval, *m.* — **road,** *s.* route cavalière, *f.*; (*of streets*) chaussée, *f.*, pavé, *m.* — **run,** *s.* manége en va-et-vient, *m.* — **scraper,** *s.* couteau de chaleur, *m.* — **shoe,** *s.* fer de cheval, *m.*; fer à cheval, *m.*; *adject.* en fer à cheval. — **shoeing,** *s.* ferrage des chevaux, *m.*; (*shoes*) fers à cheval, *m.pl.*, ferrure, *f.* — **show,** *s.* exposition de chevaux, *f.* — **slaughterer,** *s.* abatteur de chevaux, équarrisseur, *m.* — **soldier,** *s.* cavalier, *m.* — **species,** *s.* espèce *or* race chevaline, *f.* — **stealer,** *s.* voleur (*m.*, -euse, *f.*) de chevaux. — **stealing,** *s.* vol d'un cheval *or* de chevaux, *m.* — **stinger,** *s.* taon, *m.* — **tail,** *s.* queue de cheval, *f.*; (*bot.*) prêle, queue de cheval, *f.* — **tamer,** *s.* dompteur de chevaux, *m.* — **trainer,** *s.* dresseur de chevaux, *m.*; (*of race-horses*) entraîneur (de chevaux), *m.* — **trappings,** *s. pl.* harnais, caparaçon, *m.* — **twitchers,** *s. pl.* morailles, *f.pl.* — **way,** *s.* *V.* — **road.** — **whip,** *s.* fouet, *m.*; (*for riding*) cravache, *f.*; *v.a.* donner des coups de fouet à, fouetter; (*with a riding-whip*) donner des coups de cravache à, cravacher. — **whipping,** *s.* coups de fouet, *m.pl.*; coups de cravache, *m.pl.* — **woman,** *s.* écuyère, *f.*; cavalière, *f.*

Hortative, Hortatory, *adj.* *V.* **Exhortative,** &c.

Hortensia, *s.* (*bot.*) hortensia, *m.*

Horticultural, *adj.* horticultural, horticole, d'horticulture

Horticulture, *s.* horticulture, *f.*

Horticulturist, *s.* horticulteur, *m.*

Hosanna, *s.* hosanna, *m.*

Hose, *s.* bas, *m.*, bas, *m.pl.*; (*socket*) douille, *f.*; (*pipe*) boyau, *m.*; (*nav.*) manche, *f.* *Half* —, chaussette, *f.*, chaussettes, *f.pl.* — **pipe,** *s.* boyau, *m.*

Hosier, *s.* bonnetier, *m.* —*'s business,* bonneterie, *f.*

Hosiery, *s.* bonneterie, *f.*

Hospitable, *adj.* hospitalier

Hospitableness, *s.* hospitalité, *f.*

Hospitably, *adv.* hospitalièrement, avec hospitalité, d'une manière hospitalière

Hospital, *s.* hôpital, *m.*; (*for incurables, children, infirm or old people*) hospice, *m.*; (*for disabled soldiers or sailors*) Invalides, *m.pl.*, Hôtel des Invalides, *m.* — **attendant,** *s.* infirmier, *m.* — **gangrene,** *s.* pourriture d'hôpital, *f.* — **nurse,** *s.* infirmière, *f.* — **ship,** *s.* vaisseau-hôpital, *m.*

Hospitality, *s.* hospitalité, *f.*

Hospitaller, *s.* hospitalier, *m.*

Hospodar, *s.* hospodar, *m.* —*'s palace* hospodarat, *m.*

Hospodarship, *s.* hospodarat, *m.*

Host, *s.* (*entertainer*) hôte, *m.*; (*number*) armée, *f.*; troupe, *f.*; multitude, foule, *f.*; (*consecrated wafer*) hostie, *f.*, saint sacrement, *m.*

Hostage, *s.* otage, *m.*; (*fig.*) gage, *m.*

Hostelry, *s.* hôtellerie, *f.*

Hostess, *s.* hôtesse, *f.*

Hostile, *adj.* hostile, ennemi; contraire; opposé

Hostilely, *adv.* hostilement

Hostility, *s.* hostilité, *f.*

Hostler. *V.* **Ostler**

Hot, *adj.* chaud; brûlant; ardent; vif, bouillant, violent; (*of spices*) épicé, piquant, brûlant. *To be* —, *V.* **Be.** *To get* —, (or *become* or *grow*) —, *V.* **Grow.** *To make* —, (*pers.*) échauffer; (*things*) chauffer, faire chauffer. *There is* — *work*, il y fait chaud. *As* — *as a peppercorn,* (*pers.*) vif comme la poudre. — **air bath,** *s.* étuve sèche, *f.* — **air hole,** *s.* bouche de chaleur, *f.* — **air stove,** *s.* calorifère, *m.* — **air tube,** *s.* carnau, *m.* — **bed,** *s.* (*hort.*) couche, *f.*; (*fig.*) foyer, *m.* — **blooded,** *adj.* à (*or* au) sang chaud. — **brained,** *adj.* à tête chaude, emporté. — **cockles,** *s. pl.* la main chaude, *f.* — **headed,** *adj.* à tête chaude, qui a la tête chaude, emporté, violent, vif. — **house,** *s.* serre chaude, *f.* — **press,** *v.a.* presser *or* satiner à chaud. — **pressing,** *s.* satinage à chaud, *m.* — **short,** *adj.* (*of metals*) cassant (à chaud). — **spring,** *s.* *V.* **Spring.** — **spur,** *s.* homme violent *or* emporté, *m.*, tête chaude, *f.*; (*pea*) hâtiveau, *m.* — **tempered,** *adj.* vif, violent, emporté. — **water,** *s.* eau chaude, eau bouillante, *f.*; (*fig.*) pétrin, imbroglio, *m.* (*To get into* — *water*, *V.* **Water**). — **water bottle,** *s.* (*for the feet*) boule d'eau chaude, *f.* — **water dish** *or* **plate,** *s.* réchaud, *m.* — **water pipes,** *s. pl.* calorifère à eau chaude, *f.*

Hotch-pot, Hotch-potch, *s.* hochepot, salmigondis, pot-pourri, *m.*; confusion, *f.*

Hotel, *s.* hôtel, *m.* — **keeper,** *s.* maître d'hôtel, *m.*, maîtresse d'hôtel, *f.*, hôtelier, *m.*, -ière, *f.*

Hotly, *adv.* chaudement, ardemment; vivement

Hotness, *s.* chaleur, *f.*

Hottentot, *s. adj.* Hottentot, *m.*, e, *f.*

Hottonia, *s.* hottone, hottonie, *f.*

Hough. *V.* **Hock**

Hound, *s.* chien courant, chien, *m.*; limier, *m.*; (*pers.*) animal; — *v.a.* chasser; (*to set on*) lâcher. — **bitch,** *s.* lice, *f.* —**'s tongue,** *s.* cynoglosse, *f.*

Hounded on, *part.* poussé ('*to*,' a)

Hour, *s.* heure, *f.*; —**s,** *pl.* heures, *f.pl.*; temps, *m.*; (*prayers*) heures canoniales, *f.pl.* *At the eleventh* —, au dernier moment. *To keep bad* (or *late*) —*s*, se retirer *or* se coucher tard, avoir des heures irrégulières, rentrer ordinairement tard, rentrer à des heures indues. *To keep good* (or *early*) —*s*, se retirer *or* se coucher de bonne heure, avoir des heures régulières, rentrer ordinairement de bonne heure. — **glass,** *s.* sablier, *m.* — **hand,** *s.* aiguille des heures, petite aiguille, *f.* — **plate,** *s.* cadran, *m* — **wheel,** *s.* (*horol.*) roue de canon, *f.*

Houri, *s.* houri, *f.*

Hourly, *adj.* de chaque heure; d'heure en heure; d'un instant à l'autre, d'une minute à l'autre; de tous les instants, continuel; — *adv.* d'heure en heure; à toute heure, à tout moment, à chaque instant, d'un moment à l'autre

Housage, *s.* *V.* **Warehousing**

House, *s.* maison, *f.*; habitation, *f.*; logis, *m.*;

demeure, *f.*; (*mansion*) hôtel, *m.*; (*household*) ménage, *m.*; (*of representatives, senate*) chambre, *f.*; (*theat.*) salle, *f.*; (*quantity of spectators*) chambrée, *f.*; (*for dogs*) niche, cabane, *f.*; (*shed*) hangar, *m.*; pavillon, *m.*; remise, *f.*; — (*hot —, green —*) serre, *f.*; (*family*) famillé, *f.*; race, *f.*; — *adj.* de maison, de maisons; de la maison; domestique; — *v.a.* loger; héberger; (*put by*) serrer; (*shelter*) mettre à l'abri, abriter; (*the harvest,* &c.) rentrer; engranger; (*cattle*) faire rentrer; (*a carriage*) remiser; (*hort.*) enserrer, mettre en serre; (*com.*) emmagasiner, magasiner; — *v.n.* loger, habiter. — *of cards,* château de cartes, *m. Full —,* (*theat.*) salle comble, bonne chambrée, *f. In* or *at* or *to the —* (*dwelling*) *of,* chez (... *my, his, your,* &c. —, chez moi, chez lui, chez vous, &c.) *From the — dwelling of,* de chez (*from my, his, your,* &c. —, de chez moi, de chez lui, de chez vous, &c.) *To keep —,* tenir maison. *To keep the —,* garder la maison. *To keep in the —,* rester à la maison, garder la maison, ne pas sortir. *To keep open—, a good —,* avoir *or* tenir table ouverte, bonne table. *A man's — is his castle,* charbonnier est maître chez soi. — **agent,** *s.* agent de location, agent d'affaires, *m.* — **bell,** *s.* sonnette, *f.* — **breaker,** *s.* auteur de vol avec effraction, voleur avec effraction, *m.* — **breaking,** *s.* vol avec effraction, *m.*; effraction, *f.* — **carpenter,** *s.* menuisier en bâtiments, *m.* — **cricket,** *s.* grillon domestique, *m.* — **decorator,** *s.* décorateur, peintre en décors, *m.* — **dog,** *s.* chien de basse-cour, *m.*; chien de garde, *m.* — **fly,** *s.* mouche domestique, *f.* — **ful,** *s.* maisonnée, *f.*; (*theat.*) salle comble, bonne chambrée, *f.* —**hold,** *s.* maison, famille, *f.*; ménage, *m.*; *adj.* de la maison, de ménage, domestique; familier; mobilier. —*hold bread,* pain de ménage, *m.* —*hold establishment,* maison, *f.* —*hold furniture, V.* —*hold goods.* —*hold gods,* pénates, lares, dieux domestiques, *m.pl.* —*hold goods* or *stuff,* meubles, *m.pl.,* ameublement, mobilier, *m.*; ustensiles de ménage, *m.pl.* —*hold removal,* déménagement, *m.* —*hold suffrage,* suffrage à condition de domicile, *m.* —*hold utensils,* ustensiles de ménage, *m.pl.* —**holder,** *s.* chef de maison, *m.*; homme établi, *m.*; patenté, *m.* —**joiner,** *s.* menuisier en bâtiments *m.* —**keeper,** *s.* chef de maison, *m.*; (*servant*) femme de charge, gouvernante, *f.*; (*economist*) ménagère, *f.* —**keeping,** *s.* ménage, *m. To begin — keeping,* se mettre *or* entrer en ménage. —**leek,** *s.* joubarbe, *f.* —**less,** *adj.* sans abri, sans asile. — **maid,** *s.* fille de service, *f.* — **painter,** *s.* peintre en bâtiments, *m.* — **painting,** *s.* peinture en bâtiments, *f.* — **porter,** *s.* concierge, portier, *m.* — **rent,** *s.* loyer d'une (*or* de la) maison, loyer, *m.* — **room,** *s.* place, *f.*, espace, logement, *m.* — **sparrow,** moineau domestique, moineau franc, pierrot, *m.* — **steward,** *s.* maître d'hôtel, *m.* — **surgeon,** *s.* élève interne, interne, *m.* — **surgeonship, -surgeoncy,** *s.* internat, *m.* — **tax,** *s.* impôt personnel et mobilier, *m.* —**top,** *s.* toit, *m. To proclaim on the —tops,* publier *or* prêcher sur les toits, crier par-dessus les toits. — **warming,** *s.* repas pour pendre la crémaillère, *m. To give a* (*to go to a*) *— warming,* pendre (aller pendre) la crémaillère. —**wife,** *s.* maîtresse de maison, *f.*; (*economist*) ménagère, *f.*; (*a case*) ménagère, *f.* —**wifely,** *adj.* de ménage; de ménagère. —**wifery,** *s.* économie domestique, *f.*; ménage, *m.* — **work,** *s.* ménage, *m.*

Housing, *s.* logement, abri, asile, *m.*; (*com.*) *V.* **Warehousing**; (*of carriages*) remisage, *m.*; (*of corn*) rentrage, *m.*; (*horse-cloth*) housse, *f.*; (*arch.*) cage, *f.*, châssis, *m.*

Hovel, *s.* hutte, cahute, cabane, *f.*; (*shed*) hangar, *m.*; (*mean house*) bicoque, baraque, *f.*, taudis, trou, *m.*; — *v.a.* abriter

Hoven, *s.* (*vet.*) ballonnement, météorisme, *m.*, tympanite, *f.*

Hover, *v.n.* voltiger; planer; errer; rôder; papillonner; (*waver*) hésiter, balancer, être suspendu

How, *adv.* comment; (*as*) comme; (*in what*) comme quoi, en quoi; (*how much*) combien, jusqu'à quel point; (*exclam.*) combien, que, comme. — *much,* — *many, V.* **Much** *and* **Many.** — *little,* — *few,* combien peu. — *so?* comment cela? — *now?* qu'est-ce que c'est? qu'est-ce donc? eh bien? comment! — *beautiful!* comme *or* que c'est beau! — *beautiful the sea is!* comme la mer est belle! — *kind you are!* comme *or* que vous êtes bon! — *big?* de quelle grosseur? — *high?* de *or* à quelle hauteur? — *often,* — *far,* — *long,* &c., *V.* **Often, Far Long,** &c. — *is it,* &c.?

Howbeit. *V.* **Although** *and* **However** [*V.* **Be**

However, *adv* (*yet*) cependant, toutefois, pourtant, quoi qu'il en soit; du reste; mais enfin; c'est égal; (*before a verb*) de quelque manière que; (*before an adj. or adv.*) quelque ... que, si ... que. — *he may do it,* de quelque manière qu'il le fasse. — *great* (*he may be, he is*), quelque grand *or* si grand qu'il soit. — *unimportant* ..., si peu important que ... — *wisely you may act,* quelque sagement *or* si sagement que vous agissiez

Howitzer, *s.* obusier, *m.*

Howker. *V.* **Hooker**

Howl, *v.n.* ('*at,*' contre, après; '*with,*' de) hurler; (*wail*) se lamenter, crier; (*roar*) mugir, gronder; — *s.* hurlement, *m.*; (*moan*) cri, *m.*; (*roar*) mugissement, grondement, *m.*

Howler, *s.* hurleur, *m.*, -euse, *f.*; (*zool.*) hurleur, alouate, *m.*

Howlet, *s. V.* **Owlet**

Howling, *s. V.* **Howl,** *s.*; —*part. adj.* hurlant, &c. — *monkey, V.* **Howler**

Howsoever. *V.* **However**

Hoy, *s.* heu, vaisseau côtier, *m.*; — *int.* hé! holà;

Hoyden. *V.* **Hoiden**

Hub. *V.* **Hob**

Hubbub, *s.* vacarme, brouhaha, tintamarre, bruit, *m.*; bagarre, *f.*

Huckaback, *s.* grosse toile ouvrée, *f.*

Huckle, *s.* hanche, *f.* — **backed,** *adj* voûté, bossu. — **berry,** *s.* airelle, *f.* — **bone,** *s.* hanche, *f.*

Huckster, *s.* regrattier, revendeur, *m.*; (*cheat*) fripon, *m.*; — *v.n.a.* regratter; (*haggle*) barguigner, marchander. —*'s shop* or *trade* or *business, V.* **Huckstering.** —*'s wares* or *goods,* regratterie, *f.*

Huckstering, *s.* regratterie, *f.*, regrat, revendage, *m.*; — *adj.* petit

Huckstress, *s.* regrattière, revendeuse, *f.*

Huddle, *v.n.* se coudoyer; se presser; (*fig.*) se précipiter; (*mingle*) se confondre; — *v.a.* coudoyer; presser; (*throw*) jeter pêle-mêle, entasser; (*mingle*) brouiller, confondre; — *s.* foule, *f.*; (*hurry*) précipitation, *f.*; (*confusion*) confusion, *f.*, pêle-mêle, désordre, *m.* — **on,** *v.a.* passer; pousser. — **up,** *v.a.* jeter pêle-mêle; (*botch*) bâcler; (*dress out*) affubler

Hue, *s.* couleur, teinte, *f.*; (*shade*) nuance, *f.*; (*clamour*) cri, *m.* — *and cry,* cri, *m.*, clameur, huée, *f.*; gazette des tribunaux, *f.* —**less,** *adj.* décoloré, sans couleur

Huff, *s.* accès de colère, emportement, *m.*; mouvement d'arrogance, *m.*; — *v.a.* enfler, gonfler; traiter avec arrogance, brusquer; (*at play*) souffler; — *v.n.* s'enfler, gonfler; (*bluster*) tempêter; pester, s'emporter. *To — and puff,* être essoufflé, être hors d'haleine, souffler, haleter, souffler comme un bœuf. *To take —,* s'offenser (de), se formaliser (de)

Huffiness, *s.* fanfaronnerie, *f.*; arrogance, *f.*; pétulance, *f.*

Huffish, *adj.* fanfaron; arrogant; insolent; pétulant; blessé, vexé, de mauvaise humeur, en colère

Huffishly, *adv.* avec fanfaronnerie, en fanfaron; avec arrogance, arrogamment; avec humeur, avec colère, en colère

Huffishness. *V.* **Huffiness**
Huffy. *V.* **Huffish**
Hug, *v.a.* serrer, presser, étreindre; (*fig.*) caresser, chérir; — *s.* étreinte, *f.*, embrassement, *m.* *To — the land* (or *the shore* or *the coast*), serrer (*or* raser) la terre *or* la côte. *To — the wind*, chicaner *or* pincer *or* serrer le vent, tenir le lit du vent. *To — oneself*, s'applaudir (de); se flatter de l'idée (de, que)
Huge, *adj.* grand, énorme, immense, vaste, monstre [extrêmement, fortement, fort
Hugely, *adv.* énormément, immensément;
Hugeness, *s.* grandeur énorme, *f.*; grosseur énorme, *f.*; volume énorme, *m.* [*m.*, cachette, *f.*
Hugger-mugger, *s.* lieu étroit, *m.*; secret,
Huguenot, *s. adj.* huguenot, *m.*, e, *f.*
Huguenotism, *s.* huguenotisme, *m.*
Hulk, *s.* (*of a ship*) carcasse, *f.*; (*old ship*) ponton, *m.*; **—s,** *pl.* (*prison-ships*) pontons, *m.pl.*; (*for convicts*) bagne, *m.*; — *v.n.* fainéanter, flâner, gouêper, gouepper, gouaper
Hulker, *s.* fainéant, *m.*, e, *f.*, flâneur, *m.*, -euse, *f.*, gouêpeur, goueppeur, gouapeur, *m.*, -euse, *f.*
Hulking, *adj.* fainéant, flâneur, gouêpeur, goueppeur, gouapeur; — *s.* fainéantise, flânerie, gouêpe, goueppe, gouape, *f.*
Hull, *s.* *V.* **Husk,** *s.*; (*of a ship*) coque, *f.*; — *v.a.* *V.* **Husk,** *v.a.*; (*nav.*) percer la coque de; — *v.n.* flotter à mâts et à cordes, flotter au gré du vent. *A —, See Letter* **A.** *To — to,*
Hullo. *V.* **Hallo** [(*nav.*) mettre à sec
Hum, *v.a.n.* bourdonner; (*pers.*) fredonner, chantonner; (*in speaking*) barbouiller; (*of brooks*, &c.) murmurer; (*of tops*) ronfler; (*to deceive*) mystifier, tromper, attraper; — *s.* bourdonnement, *m.*; murmure, *m.*; bruit, *m.*; hem, *m.*; (*hoax*) attrape, *f.*, tour, *m.*; — *int.* hum! hem! holà!
Human, *adj.* humain; de l'homme
Humane, *adj.* humain; d'humanité. *Royal —e society*, société humaine, société de secours aux noyés, *f.*
Humanely, *adv.* humainement, avec humanité
Humaneness, *s.* humanité, *f.*
Humanist, *s.* humaniste, *m.*
Humanitarian, *adj. s.* humanitaire
Humanitarianism, *s.* humanitarisme, *m.*
Humanity, *s.* humanité, *f.*
Humanization, *s.* humanisation, *f.*
Humanize, *v.a.* humaniser, adoucir
Humankind. *V.* **Mankind**
Humanly, *adv.* humainement
Humble, *adj.* humble; modeste; — *v.a.* humilier; abaisser. — **bee,** *s.* bourdon, *m.* — **plant,** *s.* sensitive, *f.*
Humbleness, *s.* humilité, *f.*; modestie, *f.*
Humbly, *adv.* humblement; modestement
Humbug, *s.* blague, farce, *f.*; hâblerie, *f.*, conte, *m.*; charlatanisme, *m.*, charlatanerie, *f.*; (*pers.*) blagueur, *m.*, -euse, *f.*, hâbleur, *m.*, -euse, *f.*, farceur, -euse, *f.*, mauvais plaisant, sauteur, charlatan, *m.*; promeneur, *m.*, -euse, *f.*; — *v.a.* blaguer, en conter à; se ficher de; faire aller, promener. *That is all —*, tout cela est de la blague. *He —ged me out of* 20 *francs*, il m'a carotté 20 francs [(*V.* **Humbug,** *pers.*)
Humbugger, *s.* promeneur, *m.*, -euse, *f.*, &c.
Humbugging, *s.* *V.* **Humbug,** *s.*
Humdrum, *adj.* monotone; assoupissant, endormant; ennuyeux, assommant; (*pers.*) lourd, stupide, fatigant; — *s.* monotonie, *f.*; ennui, *m.*, scie, *f.*; (*pers.*) lourdaud, *m.*, e, *f.*, personnage assommant, *m.*, personne assommante, *f.*; — *v.n.* s'ennuyer [humectant, *s.m.*
Humectant, *adj. s.* humectant, *adj. m.*, e, *f.*,
Humectate, *v.a.* humecter, arroser
Humectation, *s.* humectation, *f.*, arrose-
Humeral, *adj.* huméral [ment, *m.*
Humerus, *s.* (*anat.*) humérus, *m.*
Humic, *adj.* (*chem.*) humique
Humid, *adj.* humide
Humidity, Humidness, *s.* humidité, *f.*
Humiliate, *v.a.* humilier; abaisser
Humiliation, *s.* humiliation, *f.*; abaisse-
Humility, *s.* humilité, *f.* [ment, *m.*
Humming, *s.* bourdonnement, fredonnement, *m.*; murmure, *m.*; (*in speaking*) hem, *m.*; (*of tops*) ronflement, *m.*; (*trick*) tour, *m.*, attrape, *f.* — **bird,** *s.* oiseau-mouche, colibri, *m.* — **bird moth,** *s.* sphinx du caille-lait, *m.* — **top,** *s.* toupie d'Allemagne, *f.*
Hummock, *s.* petite colline, *f.*
Humoral, *adj.* humoral
Humoric, *adj.* humorique
Humorist, &c. *V.* **Humourist,** &c.
Humorous, *adj.* (*odd*) capricieux, bizarre, fantasque; (*witty*) plaisant, spirituel; badin, enjoué
Humorously, *adv.* capricieusement, bizarrement; (*wittily*) plaisamment, spirituellement
Humorousness, *s.* caractère bizarre *or* fantasque, *m.*, bizarrerie, originalité, *f.*; (*jocularity*) caractère plaisant, *m.*, nature plaisante, fine gaieté, *f.*
Humour, *s.* humeur, *f.*; (*temper*) caractère, naturel, *m.*, disposition, humeur, *f*; (*will*) volonté, *f.*; (*wit*) gaieté, *f.*, enjouement, *m.*, plaisanterie, verve comique, *f.*, esprit, *m.*; (*whim*) fantaisie, *f.*, caprice, goût, *m.*; — *v.a.* complaire à; chercher à plaire à; laisser faire ses volontés à; laisser faire; (*accommodate oneself to*) se prêter à; flatter; ménager; (*a part*, &c.) faire valoir. *In good* or *bad —*, de bonne *or* de mauvaise humeur. *Out of —*, de mauvaise humeur. *To be in — for*, être en veine de *or* en train de, être disposé à, être d'humeur à
Humoured, *adj.* de ... humeur. *Bad* or *ill —*, de mauvaise humeur. *Good —*, de bonne humeur, d'un bon caractère, gai, joyeux
Humouredly, *adv.* (*in compounds*) de ... humeur. *Good —*, de bonne humeur, gaiment, avec bonhomie
Humourism, *s.* humorisme, *m.*
Humourist, *s.* original, capricieux, *m.*, femme originale, capricieuse, *f.*; (*witty*) personne spirituelle, *f.*; (*droll*) plaisant, comique, *m.*; (*liter., med.*) humoriste, *m.f.*; — *adj.* humoriste, humoristique
Humouristic, *adj.* humoristique
Humourous, &c. *V.* **Humorous,** &c.
Humoursome, Humoursomely. *V.* **Humorous, Humorously**
Hump, *s.* bosse, *f.* — **back,** *s.* bosse au dos, *f.*; (*pers.*) bossu, *m.*, e, *f.* — **backed,** *adj.*
Humped, *adj.* qui a une bosse [bossu
Humph, *int.* hein!
Humus, *s.* humus, *m.*
Hun, *s.* Hun, *m.*
Hunch, *s.* bosse, *f.*; (*lump*) morceau, quartier, chanteau, *m.*; (*a push*) coup de coude, *m.* — **back, -backed,** *V.* **Humpback,** &c.
Hundred, *adj.* cent; — *s.* cent, *m.*, centaine, *f.*; (*district*) canton, district, *m.*, centurie, *f.*; (*weight*) *V.* — **weight,** *s.* *A — eggs*, cent œufs, un cent d'œufs. *—s of people*, des centaines de personnes. *One — and one, one — and two*, &c., cent-un, cent-deux, &c. *In —s*, par centaines. — **fold,** *adj. adv.* centuple, cent fois autant, cent fois. — **voiced Fame,** *s.* la Renommée aux cent bouches, *f.* — **weight,** *s.* quintal, *m.*, (*in modern French measures*) 50 kilogrammes, *m.pl.*
Hundreder, *s.* centenier, *m.*
Hundredth, *adj.* centième; — *s.* centième, (*part*) *m.*, (*pers.*) *m.f.*
Hungarian, *s.* Hongrois, *m.*, e, *f.*; (*language*) le hongrois, *m.*, la langue hongroise, *f.*; — *adj.* hongrois, de Hongrie
Hungary-water, *s.* eau de la reine de
Hung-beef, *s.* bœuf fumé, *m.* [Hongrie, *f.*
Hunger, *s.* faim, *f.*; (*eager desire*) soif, *f.*; — *v.n.* avoir faim; être affamé; (*long for*) avoir soif (de), être altéré (de), désirer ardemment.

— *is the best sauce*, il n'est chère que d'appétit. — **bitten,** *adj.* pressé par la faim [dévorant

Hungrily, *adv.* avidement, avec un appétit

Hungry, *adj.* affamé, qui a faim; (*emaciated*) famélique; (*barren*) stérile, maigre. *To be* or *feel* —, avoir faim; (*fig.*) avoir soif (de), désirer ardemment. *To make* —, donner de l'appétit à. *To feed the* —, donner à manger à (*or* nourrir) ceux qui ont faim, procurer des

Hunk, *s.* (*lump*) *V.* **Hunch** [subsistances

Hunks, *s.* (*pers.*) ladre, avare, *m.*

Hunt, *v.a.n.* chasser; aller à la chasse à; chasser à courre; courir; poursuivre; chercher; rechercher; (*to use dogs*) faire chasser, faire courir; — *s.* chasse, *f.*; chasse à courre, *f.*; poursuite, *f.*; (*pack*) meute, *f.* — **after,** *v.a.* chercher; courir après, rechercher, poursuivre. — **down,** *v.a.* (*an animal*) forcer; (*fig.*) abîmer, accabler, écraser. — **for,** *v.a.* chasser à; (*fig.*) *V.* — **after.** — **out,** *v.a.* découvrir, déterrer

Hunter, *s.* chasseur, *m.*; (*dog*) chien de chasse, *m.*; (*horse*) cheval de chasse, *m.*; (*after*) coureur (de), *m.*

Hunting, *s.* chasse, *f.*; chasse à courre, *f.*; (*pursuit*) poursuite, recherche, *f.*; — *adj.* de chasse. *To go a* —, aller à la chasse. — **boots,** *s. pl.* bottes de chasse, bottes molles, *f.pl.* — **box,** *s.* rendez-vous de chasse (à courre), *m.*, maison de chasse, *f.*, pavillon de chasse, *m.*, muette, *f.* — **dog,** *s.* chien de chasse, *m.* — **dress,** *s.* habit de chasse, *m.* — **ground,** *s.* chasse, *f.* — **horn,** *s.* cor de chasse, *m.* — **knife,** *s.* couteau de chasse, *m.* — **lodge, -seat,** *s. V.* — **box.** — **party,** *s.* (des) chasseurs, *m.pl.* — **season,** *s.* saison de la chasse, chasse, *f.* — **train,** *s.* équipage de chasse, *m.*, vénerie, *f.* — **watch,** *s.* montre de chasse, montre à savonnette, *f.*

Huntress, *s.* chasseuse, *f.*; chasseresse, *f.*; (*mare*) jument de chasse, *f.*

Huntsman, *s.* chasseur, *m.*; (*manager*) veneur, *m.*; piqueur, *m.* — **ship,** *s.* chasse, *f.*; talent de chasseur, *m.*

Hurdle, *s.* claie, *f.*; échalier, *m.*; (*mil.*) fascine, *f.*; — *v.a.* fermer de claies. — **race,** *s.* [*V.* **Race**

Hurdy-gurdy, *s.* vielle, *f.*

Hurl, *v.a.* lancer, jeter, précipiter. — **bone,** *s.* fémur, *m.*

Hurly, — **burly,** *s.* tohu-bohu, brouhaha, vacarme, tintamarre, *m.*; — *adj.* tumultueux

Huron, *s.* Huron, *m.*, -ne, *f.*

Hurra, Hurrah, Hurray, *s.* houra, *m.*; vivat, *m.*; acclamation, *f.*; — *v.n.* pousser des houras *or* des vivats; — *int.* houra! bravo! (*for* ...) vive ...! vivent ...!

Hurricane, *s.* ouragan, *m.*; tempête, *f.*

Hurried, *adj.* précipité, pressé; rapide; à la hâte, au galop, fait à la hâte; écrit à la hâte

Hurriedly, *adv.* précipitamment, à la hâte

Hurry, *v.a.* presser, hâter, précipiter; bousculer; (*drive or drag*) entraîner; — *v.n.* se presser, se hâter, se dépêcher; (*run*) courir, accourir. — **away, off,** *v.a.* emmener *or* entraîner précipitamment, emmener, entraîner; renvoyer précipitamment; *v.n.* se retirer *or* s'éloigner *or* s'enfuir précipitamment, s'en aller à la hâte, se sauver. — **back,** *v.a.* hâter le retour de; *v.n.* revenir *or* retourner précipitamment. — **in,** *v.a.* faire entrer précipitamment; *v.n.* entrer précipitamment. — **on,** *v.a.* presser, pousser, hâter; (*drive*) entraîner; *v.n.* se presser, se hâter; s'élancer, courir. — **out,** *v.a.* faire sortir précipitamment, entraîner; *v.n.* sortir précipitamment. — **over, through,** faire à la hâte, hâter, parcourir, expédier, bâcler, brocher

Hurry, *s.* précipitation, hâte, *f.*; presse, *f.*; tumulte, bruit, *m.*; confusion, *f.*; embarras, *m.* *In a* —, à la hâte, avec précipitation, au galop. *In a great* —, en grande hâte, en toute hâte. *To be in a* —, être pressé. *To be in a great* —, être très pressé. *There is no* —, il n'y a pas de presse, il n'y a rien qui presse, rien ne presse, cela ne presse pas. *There is no* — *about that* (or *it*), cela ne presse pas. — **skurry,** *s.* désordre, *m.*, confusion, *f.*; *adv.* en désordre, pêle-mêle

Hurt, *v.a.* faire mal à, faire du mal à; (*wound*) blesser; (*wrong*) nuire à, faire tort à, porter préjudice à, léser; (*damage*) endommager, gâter, altérer; (*strike*) frapper, atteindre; (*offend*) offenser, blesser, choquer, froisser; (*med.*) léser; — *v.n.* faire du mal, faire mal; — *s.* mal, *m.*; blessure, *f.*; (*wrong*) tort, dommage, préjudice, *m.* *To* — *o.'s* (*own*) ..., se faire mal au *or* à la *or* aux ... *You* — *my arm*, vous me faites mal au bras. *Have you* — *your head?* vous êtes-vous fait mal à la tête? — **ful,** *adj.* nuisible (à), malfaisant (pour), préjudiciable (à), pernicieux (à). —**fully,** *adv.* nuisiblement, d'une manière nuisible *or* préjudiciable. —**fulness,** *s.* tort, préjudice, *m.*; caractère nuisible, *m.*, nature nuisible *or* pernicieuse, propriété malfaisante, *f.*

Hurtle, *v.a.n.* heurter, frapper; pousser; tirer; se heurter, se choquer; (*resound*) retentir. — **berry,** *s.* airelle, *f.*

Hurtling, *s.* choc, *m.*; retentissement, bruit, *m.*

Husband, *s.* mari, époux, *m*; homme marié, *m.*; économe, ménager, *m.*; cultivateur, *m.*; — *v.a.* ménager, économiser; cultiver, labourer. *Ship's* —, gérant à bord, *m.* *Like* — *and wife*, maritalement. —**man,** *s.* laboureur, cultivateur, *m.* [culture, *f.*; économie, frugalité, *f.*

Husbandry, *s.* labourage, *m.*, agriculture, *f.*;

Hush, *v.n.* se taire, garder le silence; — *v.a.* imposer silence à, faire taire; calmer, apaiser; tranquilliser; — *s.* silence, calme, *m.*; — *adj.* silencieux, calme; — *int.* chut! paix! silence! motus! — **money,** *s.* argent (donné *or* reçu) pour se taire, *m.*; chantage, *m.* — **up,** *v.a.* étouffer

Husk, *s.* cosse, gousse, *f.*; (*of walnuts, almonds,* &c.) brou, *m.*, écale, *f.*; (*of grapes*) peau, *m.*; (*of grain*) balle, *f.*; pellicule, *f.*; (*of chestnuts*) *V.* **Bur**; — *v.a.* écaler; écosser; (*seeds*) vanner; (*barley, rice*) monder [ment, *m.*

Huskiness, *s.* rudesse, *f.*; (*of voice*) enroue-

Husky, *adj.* cossu; (*rough*) rude; (*hoarse*) enroué, rauque, éraillé; voilé

Hussar, *s.* hussard, *m.*

Hussite, *s.* hussite, *m.*

Hussey, Hussy, *s.* coquine, friponne, drôlesse, gueuse, *f.*; péronelle, *f.*

Hustings, *s. pl.* tribune des élections, estrade, assemblée électorale, *f.*, hustings, *m.pl.*

Hustle, *v.a.* bousculer; pousser; — *v.n.* se presser, se pousser

Hustling, *s.* bousculade, *f.*

Hut, *s.* hutte, baraque, cabane, *f.*; (*mil.*) baraque, *f.*; — *v.a.* baraquer; — *v.n.* se baraquer

Hutch, *s.* huche, *f.*; (*for rabbits*) clapier, *m.*, cage (à lapins), *f.*; (*for rats*) ratière, *f.*; (*mining*) benne, banne, *f.* — **rabbit,** *s.* lapin de [clapier, *m.*

Hutia, *s.* houtias, *m.*

Hutting, *s.* (*mil.*) baraquement, *m.*

Huzza, Huzzah. *V.* **Hurra** [cinthe, *f.*

Hyacinth, *s.* (*bot.*) jacinthe, *f.*; (*min.*) hya-

Hyades, *s. pl.* hyades, *f.pl.*

Hyæna. *V.* **Hyena**

Hybernate, &c. *V.* **Hibernate,** &c.

Hybrid, *adj. s.* hybride, *m.f.*

Hybridism, *s.* hybridisme, *m.*

Hybridity, *s.* hybridité, *f.*

Hybridization, *s.* hybridation, *f.*

Hydatid, *s.* hydatide, *f.*

Hydra, *s.* hydre, *f.*

Hydrangea, *s.* hydrangée, *f.*, hortensia, *m.*

Hydrant, *s. V.* **Water-plug**

Hydrate, *s.* hydrate, *m.*

Hydrated, *adj.* hydraté [hydraulique, *f.*

Hydraulic, *adj.* hydraulique; —**s,** *s. pl.*

Hydraulist, *s.* hydraulicien, hydrauliste, *m.*

Hydride, *s.* hydrure, *m.*
Hydro, (*in compounds*) hydro ...
Hydrocele, *s.* hydrocèle, *f.*
Hydrocephalic, *adj.* hydrocéphale [phalie, *f.*
Hydrocephalus, *s.* hydrocéphale, hydrocé-
Hydrochlorate, *s.* chlorhydrate, *m.*
Hydrochloric, *adj.* chlorhydrique
Hydrochloride, *s.* chlorhydrure, *m.*
Hydrocyanic, *adj.* cyanhydrique
Hydrodynamic, *adj.* hydrodynamique; **—s,** *s. pl.* hydrodynamique, *f.*
Hydrofluoric, *adj.* fluorhydrique
Hydrogen, *s.* hydrogène, *m.*
Hydrogenate, Hydrogenize, *v.a.* hydrogéner; — *v.n.* s'hydrogéner [hydrogénation, *f.*
Hydrogenation, Hydrogenization, *s.*
Hydrographer, *s.* hydrographe, *m.*
Hydrographic, -al, *adj.* hydrographique; (*pers.*) hydrographe
Hydrography, *s.* hydrographie, *f.*
Hydrolog-ic, al, -y. *V.* page 3, § 1
Hydrologist, *s.* hydrologue, *m.*
Hydromel, *s.* hydromel, *m.*
Hydrometer, *s.* hydromètre, *m.*
Hydrometric, -al, *adj.* hydrométrique
Hydrometry, *s.* hydrométrie, *f.*
Hydropath, *s.* hydropathe, *m.*
Hydropathic, -al, *adj.* hydrothérapique, hydropathique; (*pers.*) hydropathe
Hydropathically, *adv.* hydropathiquement
Hydropathist, *s.* hydropathe, *m.*
Hydropathize, *v.a.n.* hydropathiser
Hydropathy, *s.* hydrothérapie, hydropathie, *f.*
Hydrophobia, *s.* hydrophobie, rage, *f.*
Hydrophobiac, *s. adj.* hydrophobe, *m.f.*
Hydrophobic, *adj.* hydrophobique
Hydropic, -al, &c. *V.* **Dropsical,** &c.
Hydropult, *s.* hydropulte, *f.*
Hydrostat-ic, al, -ically. *V.* page 3, § 1
Hydrostatics, *s. pl.* hydrostatique, *f.*
Hydrosulphate, *s.* sulfhydrate, *m.*
Hydrosulphide, *s.* sulfhydrure, *m.*
Hydrosulphuric, *adj.* sulfhydrique
Hydrothorax, *s.* hydrothorax, *m.*
Hyemal, *adj.* hiémal, hyémal, d'hiver
Hyemation, *s.* hiémation, hyémation, *f.*
Hyena, *s.* hyène, *f.*
Hygeia, Hygieia, *s.* Hygie, *f.*
Hygeian, Hygieian, *adj.* d'Hygie
Hygeist, *s.* hygiéniste, *m.*
Hygiene, *s.* hygiène, *f.*
Hygienic (-al), *adj.* hygiénique; **—s,** *s. pl.* hygiène, *f.*; hygiénique, *f.*
Hygienically, *adv.* hygiéniquement
Hygienist, *s.* hygiéniste, *m.*
Hygrometer, *s.* hygromètre, *m.*
Hygrometr-ic, al, -ically, hygrométrique, &c. *V.* page 3, § 1
Hygroscope, *s.* hygroscope, *m.*
Hygroscop-ic, al, -y. *V.* page 3, § 1
Hymen, *s.* hymen, hyménée, *m.*
Hymeneal, Hymenean, *adj.* de l'hymen, de l'hyménée, d'hyménée, du mariage, nuptial; — *s.* chant nuptial, épithalame, *m.*
Hymenopter, Hymenopteran, *s.* hyménoptère, *m.* [hyménoptère
Hymenopteral, Hymenopterous, *adj.*
Hymn, *s.* hymne, *m.*; — *v.n.* chanter des hymnes; — *v.a.* célébrer par des hymnes. — **book,** *s.* hymnaire, *m.*
Hymnic, *adj.* hymnique
Hymnographer, *s.* hymnographe, *m.*
Hymno-graphy, -logy, &c. *V.* page 3, § 1
Hymnologist, *s.* hymnologue, *m.*
Hyoid, *adj.* (*anat.*) hyoide
Hyp, *s.* hypocondrie, *f.*; — *v.a.* rendre hypocondriaque, rendre triste
Hypallage, *s.* hypallage, *f.*
Hyper, (*in compounds*) hyper ...
Hyperbola, Hyperbole, *s.* hyperbole, *f.*
Hyperbol-ic, al, -ically. *V.* page 3, § 1
Hyperbolism, *s.* hyperbolisme, *m.*
Hyperbolize, *v.n.* hyperboliser
Hyperborean, *adj. s.* hyperboréen
Hypercritic, *s.* hypercritique, *m.*
Hypercritical, *adj.* hypercritique, critique jusqu'à l'excès. *To be* —, épiloguer, chercher du poil aux œufs
Hypercriticism, *s.* hypercritique, *f.*
Hypertrophic, *adj.* hypertrophique
Hypertrophied, *adj.* hypertrophié. *To become* —, s'hypertrophier
Hypertrophy, *s.* hypertrophie, *f.*
Hyphen, *s.* trait d'union, *m.*; (*print., at the end of a line*) division, *f.*
Hypo, (*in compounds*) hypo ...
Hypochonder, *s.* hypocondre, *m.*
Hypochondria, *s.* hypocondrie, *f.*
Hypochondriac,-al, *adj.s.* hypocondriaque, hypocondre, *m.f.*
Hypochondriasis, *s.* hypocondrie, *f.*
Hypochondrium, *s.* hypocondre, *m.*
Hypocrisy, *s.* hypocrisie, *f.*
Hypocrite, *s.* hypocrite, *m.f.*
Hypocritic, -al, *adj.* hypocrite
Hypocritically, *adv.* hypocritement, en hypocrite, avec hypocrisie
Hypogastric, *adj.* hypogastrique
Hypogastrium, *s.* hypogastre, *m.*
Hypostasis, *s.* hypostase, *f.*
Hypostat-ic, al, -ically. *V.* page 3, § 1
Hypotenuse, Hypothenuse, *s.* hypoténuse, *f.*
Hypothesis, *s.* hypothèse, *f.*
Hypothetic, -al, *adj.* hypothétique
Hypothetically, *adv.* hypothétiquement
Hypped, *adj.* abattu, triste, sombre, hypocondre; (*annoyed*) piqué (de)
Hyrcanian, *s. adj.* Hyrcanien, *m.*, -ne, *f.*
Hyson, *s.* hysson, thé hysson, *m.*
Hyssop, *s.* hysope, hyssope, *f.*
Hysteralgia, *s.* hystéralgie, *f.*
Hysteric, (-al), *adj.* hystérique; **—s,** *s. pl.* attaque de nerfs, *f.*; (*med.*) hystérie, *f.* — *fit*, attaque de nerfs, *f.* *To fall* or *go into* —*s*, avoir une attaque de nerfs
Hysteritis, *s.* hystérite, *f.*
Hysteromania, *s.* hystéromanie, *f.*
Hysterotomy, *s.* hystérotomie, *f.*

I

I, *s.* (*letter*) i, *m.*; *pron. pers.* je; (*when neither directly connected with nor placed immediately before a following verb*) moi. — *speak*, je parle. *You and* —, vous et moi. *It is — who speak*, c'est moi qui parle
Iambic, *adj.* iambique; — *s.* iambe, *m.*
Iambus, *s.* iambe, *m.*
Iberian, Iberic, *s. adj.* Ibérien, *m.*, -ne, *f.*
Ibex, *s.* bouquetin, *m.*
Ibidem, *adv. s.* ibidem (*s.m.*)
Ibis, *s.* ibis, *m.*
Icarian, *adj.* icarien
Ice, *s.* glace, *f.*; — *adj.* de glace; (*with ice*) à la glace, glacé; — *v.a.* glacer; (*wine*, &c.) frapper de glace, frapper; (*with sugar*) glacer. *To drink with* —, boire à la glace. — **berg,** *s.* montagne de glace, *f.*; banc de glace, *m.*; banquise, *f.* — **boat,** *s.* canot à glace, *m.* — **bound,** *adj.* pris par (*or* retenu dans) les glaces; fermé par les glaces. — **box,** *s.* glacière, *f.* — **breaker,** *s.* brise-glace, *m.* — **cave,** *s.* glacière, *f.* — **cream,** *s.* crème à la glace, crème glacée, *f.* — **field,** *s.* banc de glace, *m* — **float, -floe,** *s.* glaçon flottant, glaçon, *m.*, banquise, *f.* — **house,** *s.* glacière, *f.* — **lemonade,** *s.* limonade à la glace, *f.* — **machine,** *s.* congélateur, *m.* — **maker,** *s.* glacier, *m.* — **making,** *s.* glacerie, *f.* — **man,** *s.* sauveteur (sur la glace), *m.* — **mould,** *s.* moule à glaces, *m.* — **pack,** *s.*

embâcle, *m.* — **pail,** *s.* seau à glace, *m.* — **plant,** *s.* glaciale, *f.* — **safe,** *s.* glacière, *f.* — **spoon,** *s.* pelle à glace, *f.* — **tongs,** *s. pl.* pince à glace, *f.* — **trade,** *s.* glacerie, *f.* — **well,** *s.* glacière, *f.*; seau à glace, *m.* — **work,** *s.* glace, *f.*

Iced, *part. adj.* glacé; à la glace; (*of wine,* &c.) frappé de glace, frappé; (*with sugar*) glacé

Iceland moss, *s.* mousse d'Islande, physcie, *f.*

Icelander, *s.*, **Icelandic,** *adj.* Islandais, *m.*, e, *f.*

Ichneumon, *s.* ichneumon, *m.* — **fly,** *s.* ichneumon, *m.*

Ichnographer, *s.* ichnographe, *m.*

Ichnograph-ic, al, -ically, -y. *V.* p. 3, § 1

Ichnolog-ic, al, -ically, -y. *V.* page 3, § 1

Ichor, *s.* ichor, *m.*

Ichorous, *adj.* ichoreux

Ichthyographer, *s.* ichthyographe, *m.*

Ichthyo-graphy, -logy, -logic, al, -logist, &c. *V.* page 3, § 1

Ichthyophag-ic, al, -y. *V.* page 3, § 1

Ichthyophagist, *s.*, **Ichthyophagous,** *adj.* ichthyophage, *m.f.*

Ichthyosaur, -us, *s.* ichthyosaure, *m.*

Ichthyosis, *s.* ichthyose, *f.*

Icicle, *s.* glaçon, *m.*

Iciness, *s.* froid glacial, *m.*

Icing, *s.* (*process*) glaçage, *m.*; (*of wine*) frappage, *m.*; (*sugar,* &c., *for icing pastry*) glace, *f.*

Iconoclasm, *s.* iconoclasme, *m.*

Iconoclast, *s.*, **Iconoclastic,** *adj.* iconoclaste

Icono-graphy, -logy, &c. *V.* page 3, § 1

Icosahedral, *adj.*, **Icosahedron,** *s.* icosaèdre, *adj. m.f.*, *s.m.* [la glace

Icy, *adj.* de glace; glacé, glacial; (*with ice*) à

Ide, *s.* (*fish*) gardon, ide, *m.*; **—s,** *pl.* (*Rom. antiq.*) ides, *f.pl.*

Idea, *s.* idée, *f.* *To have no — that,* ne pas savoir que, ne pas se douter que. *An — strikes me,* il me vient une idée. *The —! the* (*very*) *— of such a thing!* par exemple! ah bien, par exemple! on n'a pas d'idée de cela! a-t-on jamais vu! [— *s.* idéal, *m.*

Ideal, *adj.* idéal; (*philos.*) mental, intellectuel;

Idealism, *s.* idéalisme, *m.*

Idealist, *s.*, **Idealistic,** *adj.* idéaliste, *m.f.*

Ideality, *s.* idéalité, *f.*, idéal, *m.*

Idealization, *s.* idéalisation, *f.* [idées

Idealize, *v.a.* idéaliser; — *v.n.* concevoir des

Ideally, *adv.* idéalement, en idée, mentalement

Idem, *adv.* idem

Identic, -al, *adj.* identique; même

Identically, *adv.* identiquement

Identifiable, *adj.* identifiable; reconnaissable

Identification, *s.* identification, *f.*; reconnaissance, *f.*

Identify, *v.a.* identifier; établir (*or* constater) l'identité de; reconnaître; — *v.n.* s'identifier. *To — oneself,* s'identifier

Identity, *s.* identité, *f.*

Ideologic, -al, *adj.* idéologique

Ideologist, *s.* idéologue, *m.*

Ideology, *s.* idéologie, *f.*

Idiocy, *s.* idiotie, *f.* [*m.*; (*dialect*) idiome, *m.*

Idiom, *s.* idiotisme, *m.*; (*genius*) génie, caractère,

Idiomatic, -al, *adj.* idiomatique, pur, conforme au génie de la langue. — *turn* or *expression* or *phrase,* idiotisme, *m.* [ment

Idiomatically, *adv.* idiomatiquement, pure-

Idiopath-ic, al, -ically, -y. *V.* page 3 § 1

Idiosyncrasy, *s.* idiosyncrasie, *f.*

Idiosyncratic, *adj.* idiosyncrasique

Idiot, *s.* idiot, *m.*, e, *f.*; imbécile, *m.f.*; — *adj.*

Idiotcy. *V.* **Idiocy** [*V.* **Idiotic**

Idiotic, -al, *adj.* idiotique; idiot; d'idiot; imbécile; d'imbécile

Idiotically, *adv.* idiotiquement

Idiotism, *s.* idiotisme, *m.*

Idle, *adj.* oisif, désœuvré, inoccupé; (*lazy*) paresseux, fainéant; indolent, nonchalant; (*vain*) oiseux, frivole, inutile, vain, en l'air; (*of time*) de loisir, perdu, inoccupé; (*without power*) impuissant, vain; (*manu.*) arrêté, suspendu, en chômage; — *v.n.* (*pers.*) paresser, faire le paresseux, fainéanter, flâner; (*things*) se jouer; — *v.a.* (— **away**) perdre, dissiper. — *boy,* (petit) paresseux, *m.* — *girl,* (petite) paresseuse, *f.* — *man* or *fellow,* paresseux, fainéant, *m.* — *woman* or *thing,* paresseuse, *f.* — *project,* projet en l'air, *m.* — *story* or *tale,* conte oiseux, conte bleu, conte à dormir debout, *m.* — *talk,* sornettes, *f.pl.*, verbiage, *m.* — *words,* paroles en l'air, *f.pl.*

Idleness, *s.* (*inaction*) oisiveté, *f.*; désœuvrement, *m.*; (*laziness,* &c.) paresse, fainéantise, *f.*; indolence, nonchalance, *f.*; (*emptiness,* &c.) frivolité, *f.*; inutilité, *f.*

Idler, *s.* oisif, m., -ive, *f.*, désœuvré, *m.*, e, *f.*; (*lazy*) paresseux, *m.*, -euse, *f.*, fainéant, *m.*, e, *f.*,

Idling, *s.* *V.* **Idleness** [flâneur, *m.*, -euse, *f.*

Idly, *adv.* dans l'oisiveté, dans le désœuvrement; (*lazily*) dans la paresse, dans la fainéantise; (*carelessly*) avec indolence; nonchalamment; (*vainly*) vainement, en vain, inutilement, oiseusement; (*foolishly*) follement

Idocrase, *s.* idocrase, *f.*

Idol, *s.* idole, *f.* — **worship,** *s.* culte des idoles, *m.* — **worshipper,** *s.* adorateur (*m.*, -trice, *f.*) d'idoles

Idolater, *s.* idolâtre, *m.*

Idolatress, *s.* idolâtre, *f.*

Idolatrous, *adj.* idolâtre

Idolatrously, *adv.* idolâtrement, avec idolâ-

Idolatry, *s.* idolâtrie, *f.* [trie, en idolâtre

Idolize, *v.a.* idolâtrer

Idolizer, *s.*, **Idolizing,** *adj.* idolâtre, *m.f.*

Idyl, *s.* idylle, *f.*

Idyllic, *adj.* idyllique, *f.*

I. E., (*abbrev. of* "*id est*") c.à.d., c'est-à-dire

If, *conj.* si; (*though*) quand, quand même; (*provided*) pourvu que; — *s.* si, *m.* *As —,* comme si; (*before an inf.*) comme pour; (*not before a verb*) comme. — *not,* sinon, si ce n'est; pour ne pas dire. — *possible,* s'il est *or* si cela est possible, s'il se peut, si cela se peut; (*past tense*) s'il était *or* si cela était possible, s'il se pouvait, si cela se pouvait. — *necessary,* s'il est *or* si cela est nécessaire, s'il le faut, au besoin; (*past tense*) s'il était *or* si cela était nécessaire, s'il le fallait, au besoin. *To look as —,* avoir l'air de (*with the inf.*) — *ever there was one,* s'il en fut jamais, s'il en fut. — *anything, I am rather before the time than behind,* s'il y a une différence, je suis plutôt en avance qu'en retard. *Little, — any,* peu, si même il

Igneous, *adj.* igné; de feu [y en a

Ignescence, *s.* ignescence, *f.*

Ignescent, *adj.* ignescent

Ignis fatuus, *s* feu follet, *m.*

Ignitable, *adj.* inflammable

Ignite, *v.a.* enflammer; allumer; mettre le feu à; — *v.n.* s'enflammer, s'allumer, prendre feu

Ignited, *adj.* enflammé, en ignition

Ignition, *s.* ignition, *f.*; inflammation, *f.*

Ignoble, *adj.* ignoble, vil, bas; (*pers.*) roturier, de basse extraction; (*of little value*) de peu de valeur [*birth*) roture, *f.*

Ignobleness, *s.* ignobilité, bassesse, *f.*; (*of*

Ignobly, *adv.* ignoblement, d'une manière ignoble, bassement; (*of low birth*) dans la roture, de basse extraction

Ignominious, *adj.* (*of things*) ignominieux; (*pers.*) indigne, méprisable; (*law*) infamant

Ignominiously, *adv.* ignominieusement, avec ignominie; (*law*) d'une manière infamante

Ignominy, *s.* ignominie, *f.*; (*law*) infamie, *f.*

Ignoramus, *s.* ignorant, *m.*, e, *f.*, ignare, *m.f.*

Ignorance, *s.* ignorance, *f.*

Ignorant, *adj.* ignorant. *An — fellow,* un ignorant, *m.* *To be — of,* ignorer

Ignorantine, *s.* ignorantin, frère ignorantin, *m.*

Ignorantly, *adv.* ignoramment, par ignorance, avec ignorance

Ignore, *v.a.* méconnaître; ne pas reconnaître;

prétendre ne pas connaître; faire semblant de ne pas connaître; ne pas connaître; ne pas faire attention à; négliger, ne pas compter, ne pas tenir compte de; (*not to mention*) passer sous silence; (*omit*) passer; (*reject, repudiate*) rejeter. *To — the bill of indictment*, rendre [une ordonnance de non-lieu

Iguana, *s.* iguane, *m.*

Ileum, *s.* iléon, iléum, *m.*

Ileus, *s.* iléus, *m.*

Ilia, *s. pl.* (*anat.*) iles, *m.pl.* [iliaque, *f.*, iléus, *m.*

Iliac, -al, *adj.* iliaque. — *passion*, passion

Iliad, *s.* Iliade, *f.*

Ilk. *Of that* —, du même nom

Ill, *s.* mal, *m.*; — *adj.* (*sick*) malade; (*bad*) mauvais; méchant; (*unhappy*) malheureux; — *adv.* mal; difficilement; (*little*) peu, ne ... guère. *To fall* or *get* —, tomber malade. *To be taken* —, tomber malade; être pris de malaise. *To take it* —, prendre mal; trouver mauvais. —**advised,**—**behaved,**&c. *V.* **Advised, Behaved,** &c. —**bred,** *adj.* mal élevé. —**conditioned,** *adj.* mal conditionné, en mauvais état. —**considered,** *adj.* peu réfléchi, irréfléchi. —**contrived, -devised,** *adj.* mal imaginé, mal arrangé, mal concerté. —**deserved,** *adj.* peu mérité. —**disposed,** *adj.* mal disposé; mal intentionné. —**famed,** *adj.* mal famé. —**fated,** *adj.* infortuné, dont le sort est malheureux. —**favoured,** *adj.* *V.* **Favoured.** —**favouredly,** *adv.* disgracieusement; désagréablement; mal. — —**favouredness,** *s.* laideur, *f.*; aspect désagréable, air disgracieux, *m.* —**founded,** *adj.* mal fondé. —**gotten,** *adj.* mal acquis. —**grounded**, *adj.* mal fondé. —**judged,** *adj.* mal entendu, mal vu, malavisé, imprudent. —**mannered,** *adj.* grossier, mal-appris. —**meaning,** *adj.* *V.* **Meaning,** *adj.* —**minded,** *adj.* mal intentionné, mal disposé. —**natured,** *adj.* *V.* **Natured.** —**omened,** *adj.* de mauvais augure, de mauvais présage, de malheur, néfaste. —**pleased,** *adj.* mécontent. —**proportioned,** *adj.* mal proportionné. —**requited,** *adj.* mal récompensé. —**seeming,** *adj.* d'un aspect peu agréable. —**shaped,** *adj.* *V.* **Shaped.** —**sounding,** *adj.* mal sonnant, malsonnant. —**spent,** *adj.* mal employé. —**starred,** *adj.* né sous une mauvaise étoile. —**suiting,** *adj.* malséant. —**timed,** *adj.* *V.* **Timed.** —**treat, -use,** *v.a.* maltraiter. —**visaged,** *adj.* laid. —**will,** [*s.* *V.* **Will**

Illaudable, *adj.* peu louable

Illaudably, *adv.* d'une manière peu louable

Illegal, *adj.* illégal; illicite

Illegality, *s.* illégalité, *f.*

Illegally, *adv.* illégalement

Illegi-bility, bleness, *s.* nature illisible, *f.*

Illegible, *adj.* illisible

Illegibly, *adv.* illisiblement

Illegitimacy, *s.* illégitimité, *f.*

Illegitimate, *adj.* illégitime; non autorisé

Illegitimately, *adv.* illégitimement

Illiberal, *adj.* illibéral; (*stingy*) peu généreux, mesquin; (*not becoming*) peu convenable, peu digne; (*stunted*) borné, étroit; petit; (*of professions*, &c.) peu relevé

Illiberalism, *s.* illibéralisme, *m.*

Illiberality, *s.* illibéralité, *f.*; (*stinginess*) manque de générosité, *m.*, mesquinerie, *f.*; (*narrowness of mind*) petitesse, *f.*, manque de dignité, *m.*

Illiberally, *adv.* illibéralement, sans libéralité; (*stingily*) sans générosité, mesquinement; (*narrowly*) étroitement, petitement, sans [dignité

Illicit, *adj* illicite

Illicitly, *adv.* illicitement

Illicitness, *s.* nature illicite, *f.*

Illimitable, *adj.* illimitable

Illimitably, *adv.* illimitablement

Illimited, *V.* **Unlimited**

Illiteracy. *V.* **Illiterateness** [rant

Illiterate, *adj.* illettré, sans instruction, igno-

Illiterately, *adv.* en homme illettré

Illiterateness, *s.* illittérature, *f.*, défaut d'instruction, *m.*, ignorance, *f.*

Illness, *s.* maladie, *f.*, mal, *m.*; indisposition, *f.*; (*ill state*) mauvais état, *m.*

Illog-ical, -ically, -ism. *V.* page 3, § 1

Illogicalness, *s.* illogicité, *f.*

Illude, *v.a.* décevoir, tromper, faire illusion à

Illume, *v.a.* *V.* **Illumine**

Illuminable, *adj.* illuminable

Illuminate, *v.a.* éclairer; (*of rejoicings*, &c.) illuminer; (*fig., a subject*, &c.) éclaircir; (*colour*) enluminer ('*with*,' *de*); colorier; — *s.* illuminé, *m.*, e, *f.*

Illuminati, *s. pl.* illuminés, *m.pl.*

Illuminating, *adj.* qui éclaire, à éclairer, d'éclairage; illuminateur; — *s.* éclairage, *m.*; (*painting*) enluminure, *f.* — *gas*, gaz d'éclairage, *m.* — *artist*, *V.* **Illuminator**

Illumination, *s.* illumination, *f.*; éclairage, *m.*; éclat, *m.*, splendeur, *f.*; lumière, *f.*; inspiration, *f.*; (*painting*) enluminure, *f.* —**lamp,** *s.* verre, lampion, *m.*

Illuminative, *adj.* illuminatif

Illuminator, *s.* illuminateur, *m.*, -trice, *f.*; (*painter*) enlumineur, *m.*, -euse, *f.*, coloriste, *m.f.*

Illumine, *v.a.* éclairer; illuminer; répandre une vive clarté sur

Illuminee, *s.* illuminé, *m.*, e, *f.*

Illuminer, *s.* illuminateur, *m.*, -trice, *f.*

Illumin-ism, -ist. *V.* page 3, § 1

Illusion, *s.* illusion, *f.*

Illusionist, *s.* illusioniste, *m.f.*

Illusive, *adj.* illusoire

Illusively, *adv.* illusoirement

Illusiveness, *s.* nature illusoire, *f.*

Illusory, *adj.* illusoire

Illustrable, *adj.* illustrable

Illustrate, *v.a.* éclaircir; démontrer, expliquer; faire comprendre; prouver; montrer, faire voir; (*adorn*) orner, embellir; (*books*, &c., *make illustrious*) illustrer

Illustration, *s.* éclaircissement, *m.*, explication, *f.*; exposition, *f.*; exemple, *m.*; échantillon, spécimen, modèle, *m.*; image, *f.*; comparaison, *f.*; (*engraving*, &c.) illustration, *f.*

Illustrative, *adj.* qui éclaircit, qui explique, explicatif; (*with glory*) qui illustre

Illustratively, *adv.* de manière à éclaircir, comme explication

Illustrator, *s.* illustrateur, *m.*; explicateur, *m.*; interprète, *m.*; commentateur, *m.*

Illustrious, *adj.* illustre, célèbre; grand, beau; glorieux

Illustriously, *adv.* illustrement, d'une manière illustre; glorieusement

Illustriousness, *s.* illustration, *f.*; éclat, *m.*

Illyrian, *s. adj.* Illyrien, *m.*, -ne, *f.*

Image, *s.* image, *f.*; statuette, *f.*; (*likeness*) portrait, *m.*; — *v.a.* imager; représenter, figurer, peindre; (*to fancy*) se représenter, se figurer, s'imaginer. *Italian — boy*, petit marchand de figures de plâtre, *m.* *To be the very — of*, être tout le portrait de. —**breaker,** *s.* briseur d'images, *m.* —**maker,** *s.* mouleur de statuettes, *m.* —**making,** *s.* imagerie, *f.*, moulage de statuettes, *m.* —**trade,** *s.* imagerie, *f.* —**monger, -vendor,** *s.* marchand (*m.*, e, *f.*) d'images *or* de statuettes. —**worship,** *s.* idolâtrie, *f.*, culte des images, *m.*

Imagery, *s.* images, *f.pl.* (*fig.*) image, *f.*, tableau, *m.*, peinture, représentation, *f.*; (*of fancy*), vision, chimère, *f.*, fantôme, *m.*, visions, chimères, *f.pl.*, fantômes, *m.pl.*; apparence, *f.*

Imaginable, *adj.* imaginable

Imaginary, *adj.* imaginaire

Imagination, *s.* imagination, *f.*; idée, conception, pensée, *f.*; invention, *f.*; machina- [tion, *f.*

Imaginative, *adj.* imaginatif

Imagine, *v.a.n.* imaginer; s'imaginer; se figurer; avoir idée; se faire une idée (de)

Imaginer, *s.* personne qui imagine, *f.*

Imagining, *s. V.* **Imagination**
Imago, *s.* (*zool.*) insecte parfait, *m.*
Imam, Iman, Imaum, *s.* iman, imam, *m.*
Imbalm, Imbank, Imbattle, &c. *V.* **Em-**
Imbecile, *adj. s.* imbécile, *m.f.* [**balm,** &c.
Imbecility, *s.* imbécillité, *f.*; (*weakness*) fai-
Imbed, *v.a. V.* **Embed** [blesse, *f.*
Imbibe, *v.a.* absorber, s'imbiber de; (*fig.*) puiser, prendre, recevoir
Imbiber, *s.* absorbant, *m.*
Imbibition, *s.* imbibition, *f.*
Imbitter, Imbody, Imbolden, Imbosom.
Imbower, *v.a. V.* **Embower** [*V.* **Embitter,** &c.
Imbricant, *adj.* imbriquant
Imbricated, *adj.* imbriqué
Imbrication, *s.* imbrication, *f.*
Imbroglio, *s.* imbroglio, *m.*
Imbronze, *v.a. V.* **Embronze**
Imbrown, *v.a.* rembrunir; (*fig.*) assombrir, obscurcir; — *v.n.* se rembrunir; (*fig.*) s'assombrir, s'obscurcir
Imbrue, *v.a.* tremper, souiller
Imbue, *v.a.* imbiber; (*to dye*) teindre; (*the mind*) inspirer, pénétrer, remplir ('*with,*' de)
Imbued, *part. adj.* imbibé, &c. (*V.* **Imbue**); (*fig.*) imbu (de), pénétré (de)
Imitable, *adj.* imitable [faire
Imitate, *v.a.* imiter; (*to counterfeit*) contre-
Imitation, *s.* imitation, *f.*; (*paint.*) pastiche, *m.*; (*com.*) contrefaçon, *f.*; — *adj.* d'imitation; artificiel; faux. *In — of,* à l'imitation de, à l'exemple de [(*pers.*) imitateur
Imitative, *adj.* imitatif; (*imitated*) imité;
Imitativeness, *s.* faculté d'imiter, *f.*
Imitator, Imitatress, *s.* imitateur, *m.*, -trice, *f.*; contrefaiseur, *m.*, -euse, *f.*; (*com.*) contrefacteur, *m.* [immaculé
Immaculate, *adj.* sans tache; pur; (*theol.*)
Immaculately, *adv.* sans tache, sans souillure
Immaculateness, *s.* pureté sans tache, pureté parfaite, *f.*
Immane, *adj.* énorme, démesuré; atroce
Immanely, *adv.* énormément; atrocement, avec atrocité, cruellement
Immanent, *adj.* immanent
Immanity, *s.* barbarie, atrocité, *f.*
Immaterial, *adj.* immatériel; peu important, sans conséquence; indifférent, égal
Immateriality, *s.* immatérialité, *f.*
Immaterialize, *v.a.* immatérialiser
Immaterially, *adv.* immatériellement; sans importance
Immature, *adj.* pas mûr; prématuré
Immaturely, *adv.* avant la maturité; prématurément
Immatureness, Immaturity, *s.* immaturité, *f.*, défaut de maturité, *m.*; prématurité, *f.*, état prématuré, *m.*
Immeasurable, *adj.* immesurable, incommensurable, immense, infini; incomparable
Immeasurably, *adv.* immensément, sans mesure, outre mesure, démesurément, infiniment, sans limites; incomparablement
Immediate, *adj.* immédiat; instantané; pressant, urgent; (*on letters*) pressé; — *adverb. V.* **Immediately**
Immediately, *adv.* immédiatement; aussitôt; tout de suite; incessamment; sur-le-champ; (*as soon as*) aussitôt que [titude, *f.*
Immediateness, *s.* immédiateté, *f.*; promp-
Immemorable, *adj.* immémorable
Immemorial, *adj.* immémorial; de temps immémorial [temps immémorial
Immemorially, *adv.* immémorialement, de
Immense, *adj.* immense
Immensely, *adv.* immensément
Immensity, *s.* immensité, *f.*
Immerge, *v.a.* immerger, plonger, enfoncer
Immer-goose, *s.* imbrim, *m.*
Immerse, *v.a. V.* **Immerge**
Immersion, *s.* immersion, *f.*
Immesh, *v.a.* envelopper, prendre

Immethodical, &c. *V.* **Unmethodical,** &c.
Immigrant, *s. adj.* immigrant, *m.*, e, *f.*
Immigrate, *v.n.* immigrer
Immigration, *s.* immigration, *f.*
Imminence, *s.* imminence, *f.*
Imminent, *adj.* imminent
Imminently, *adv.* imminemment
Immission, *s.* immission, *f.*
Immitigable. *V.* **Unmitigable**
Immobility, *s.* immobilité, *f.*
Immoderate, *adj.* immodéré; fou
Immoderately, *adv.* immodérément; comme un fou, comme une folle
Immoderateness, Immoderation, *s.* immodération, *f.*, défaut de modération, *m.*
Immodest, *adj.* immodeste, indécent, déshonnête [nêtement, sans modestie
Immodestly, *adv.* immodestement, déshon-
Immodesty, *s.* immodestie, *f.*, défaut de
Immolate, *v.a.* immoler [modestie, *m.*
Immolation, *s.* immolation, *f.*; sacrifice, *m.*
Immolator, *s.* immolateur, *m.*
Immoral, *adj.* immoral
Immorality, *s.* immoralité, *f.*
Immorally, *adv.* immoralement, sans moralité
Immortal, *adj. s.* immortel, *m.*, -le, *f.*
Immortality, *s.* immortalité, *f.*
Immortalization, *s.* immortalisation, *f.*
Immortalize, *v.a.* immortaliser [ment
Immortally, *adv.* immortellement, éternelle-
Immortelle, *s.* immortelle, *f.*
Immovability, *s.* immobilité, *f.*
Immovable, *adj.* immobile; inébranlable; inaltérable; insensible; (*build.*) à demeure; (*law*) immeuble, immobilier; —**s,** *s. pl.* immeubles, biens immeubles, biens immobiliers, *m.pl.* [bilité, *f.*; insensibilité, *f.*
Immovableness, *s.* immobilité, *f.*; inaltéra-
Immovably, *adv.* immobilement; inébranlablement; d'une manière inaltérable, inaltérablement; avec insensibilité, insensiblement [privilége, *m.*
Immunity, *s.* immunité, *f.*; exemption, *f.*;
Immure, *v.a.* enfermer, claquemurer; cloîtrer; (*with walls*) entourer de murs *or* de murailles; (*fig.*) renfermer
Immurement, Immuring, *s.* immuration, *f.*
Immutability, Immutableness, *s.* immutabilité, *f.*
Immutable, *adj.* immuable; irrévocable
Immutably, *adv.* immuablement; irrévocablement [petit drôle, *m.*
Imp, *s.* démon, diablotin, lutin, *m.*; (*child*)
Impact, *s.* impression, empreinte, *f.*; contact, *m.*; (*mec., phys.*) choc, *m.*; impact, *m.*
Impair, *v.a.* détériorer; altérer; endommager; gâter; délabrer; nuire à; affaiblir; diminuer; — *v.n.* se détériorer; s'altérer; se gâter; se délabrer; s'affaiblir
Impairment, *s.* détérioration, altération, *f.*; délabrement, *m.*; affaiblissement, *m.*; diminution, *f.*
Impale, *v.a.* palissader; (*surround*) entourer; environner; enfermer; (*of punishment*) empaler
Impalement, *s.* palissade, *f.*; (*punishment*) empalement, *m.*; (*her.*) pal, *m.*
Impaler, *s.* empaleur, *m.*
Impalpa-bility, bleness. *V.* page 3, § 1
Impalpable, *adj.* impalpable; subtil
Impanation, *s.* impanation, *f.*
Impanel, Impannel, *v.a.* inscrire, former
Imparity, *s.* imparité, *f.*; disparité, dispro-
Impark. *V.* **Empark** [portion, *f.*; inégalité, *f.*
Impart, *v.a.* donner (à); prêter (à); communiquer (à); faire part de (à); imprimer (à)
Impartial, *adj.* impartial
Impartiality, *s.* impartialité, *f.* [partialité
Impartially, *adv.* impartialement, avec im-
Impassable, *adj.* impraticable; infranchissable; encombré
Impassi-bility, bleness. *V.* page 3, § 1
Impassible, *adj.* impassible

Impassion, *v.a.* passionner; enflammer
Impassive, *adj.* impassible; insensible
Impassively, *adv.* impassiblement
Impassiveness, *s.* impassibilité, *f.*
Impastation, *s.* impastation, *f.*
Impaste, *v.a.* (*paint.*) empâter
Impasting, *s.* (*paint.*) empâtement, *m.*
Impatience, *s.* impatience, *f.*
Impatient, *adj.* impatient; (*hasty*) emporté; furieux. *To grow* or *get* —, s'impatienter
Impatiently, *adv.* impatiemment
Impatronization, *s.* impatronisation, *f.*
Impatronize, *v.a.* impatroniser
Impeach, *v.a.* mettre en accusation; (*fig.*) accuser, attaquer; dénoncer; blâmer, censurer
Impeachable, *adj.* accusable; attaquable; blâmable, répréhensible
Impeacher, *s.* accusateur, *m.*, -trice, *f.*; dénonciateur, *m.*, -trice, *f.*; censeur, *m.*
Impeachment, *s.* mise en accusation, *f.*; accusation, *f.*; blâme, reproche, *m.*
Impeccability, *s.* impeccabilité, *f.*
Impeccable, *adj.* impeccable
Impeccancy, *s.* impeccance, *f.* [pauvreté, *f.*
Impecuniosity, *s.* besoin, *m.*, indigence,
Impecunious, *adj.* besoigneux, nécessiteux, indigent, pauvre
Impede, *v.a.* empêcher, arrêter, gêner, entraver, mettre obstacle à; obstruer; retarder
Impediment, *s.* empêchement, obstacle, *m.*; (*in o.'s speech*) embarras (dans la parole), bégaiement, *m.* *To have an — in o.'s speech*, avoir la parole embarrassée, bégayer
Impel, *v.a.* pousser (à); porter (à); engager (à); exciter (à); forcer (à; *in the passive*, de)
Impellent, Impeller, *s.* impulseur, moteur, *m.*
Impelling, *adj.* impulseur (*m.*), moteur (*m.*, -trice, *f.*)
Impend, *v.n.* être suspendu (sur); être imminent; menacer, être prêt à fondre (sur); s'ap-
Impendenc-e, y, *s.* imminence, *f.* [procher
Impendent, Impending, *adj.* suspendu; imminent; menaçant; qui s'approche
Impenetra-bility, bleness, *s.* impénétrabilité, *f.* [sible; insensible; inepte
Impenetrable, *adj.* impénétrable; inacces-
Impenetrably, *adv.* impénétrablement
Impenitenc-e, y, *s.* impénitence, *f.*
Impenitent, *adj. s.* impénitent, *m.*, e, *f.*
Impenitently, *adv.* dans l'impénitence
Impennate, *adj. s.* impenné, *adj. m.*, e, *f.*, impenné, *s.m.* [impératif, *s.m.*
Imperative, *adj. s.* impératif, *adj. m.*, -ive, *f.*,
Imperatively, *adv.* impérativement
Impercepti-bility, bleness. *V.* page 3, § 1
Imperceptible, *adj.* imperceptible
Imperceptibly, *adv.* imperceptiblement
Imperfect, *adj. s.* imparfait, *adj. m.*, e, *f.*, imparfait, *s.m.* — *tense*, imparfait, *m.* *In the — tense*, à l'imparfait
Imperfecti-bility, bleness. *V.* page 3, § 1
Imperfectible, *adj.* imperfectible
Imperfectibly, *adv.* imperfectiblement
Imperfection, *s.* imperfection, *f.*
Imperfectly, *adv.* imparfaitement
Imperfectness, *s.* état imparfait, *m.*
Imperforate, -d, *adj.* imperforé
Imperforation, *s.* imperforation, *f.*
Imperial, *adj.* impérial, d'empereur, de l'empereur, de l'empire; (*princely*) royal, de roi, princier; souverain; (*stat.*) grand jésus; — *s.* (*beard*) impériale, *f.*; (*paper*) grand jésus, *m.*; (*of a French stage-coach*) impériale, *f.*
Imperialism, *s.* impérialisme, *m.*
Imperialist, *s. adj.* impérialiste, *m.f.*; (*soldier*) impérial, *m.* (*pl.* impériaux)
Imperialistic, *adj.* impérialiste
Imperialize, *v.a.* impérialiser [en roi
Imperially, *adv.* impérialement; royalement,
Imperil, *v.a.* *V.* **Endanger**
Imperious, *adj.* impérieux; puissant
Imperiously, *adv.* impérieusement
Imperiousness, *s.* impériosité, *f.*, caractère impérieux, *m.*, humeur impérieuse, fierté, arrogance, hauteur, *f.*
Imperishable, *adj.* impérissable
Imperishableness, *s.* impérissabilité, *f.*
Imperishably, *adv.* impérissablement
Impermeability, *s.* imperméabilité, *f.*
Impermeable, *adj.* imperméable
Impermeably, *adv.* imperméablement
Impersonal, *adj.* impersonnel
Impersonality, *s.* impersonnalité, *f.*
Impersonally, *adv.* impersonnellement
Impersonate, *v.a.* personnifier, personnaliser; représenter
Impersonation, *s.* personnification, personnalisation, *f.*; (*of actors*) rôle, *m.*; représenta-
Impersuasible, *adj.* impersuasible [tion, *f.*
Impertinenc-e, y, *s.* impertinence, *f.*; (*irrelevant matter*) chose étrangère (à la question), *f.*; (*trifle*) bagatelle, niaiserie, futilité, *f.*
Impertinent, *adj.* impertinent; (*unseasonable*) hors de propos, déplacé; (*irrelevant*) étranger (à); (*trifling*) futile; — *s.* impertinent, *m.*, e, *f.*
Impertinently, *adv.* impertinemment; (*unseasonably*) hors de propos
Imperturba-bility, bleness. *V.* p. 3, § 1
Imperturbable, *adj.* imperturbable
Imperturbably, *adv.* imperturbablement
Impervious, *adj.* imperméable (à); impénétrable (à); inaccessible (à); impraticable
Imperviously, *adv.* imperméablemant; impénétrablement
Imperviousness, *s.* imperméabilité, *f.*; impénétrabilité, *f.*; impraticabilité, *f.*
Impetiginous, *adj.* impétigineux
Impetigo, *s.* impétigo, *m.* [tuosité, *f.*
Impetuosity, Impetuousness, *s.* impé-
Impetuous, *adj.* impétueux
Impetuously, *adv.* impétueusement
Impetus, *s.* impulsion, *f.*; force impulsive, *f.*; impétuosité, *f.*; (*fig.*) essor, *m.*
Impeyan- pheasant, *s.* lophophore, impey, *m.*
Impiety, *s.* impiété, *f.* [se heurter, se choquer
Impinge, *v.n.* ('*on*,' contre) heurter, frapper;
Impious, *adj.* impie
Impiously, *adv.* avec impiété, en impie
Impiousness, *s.* impiété, *f.*
Impish, *adj.* de démon, de lutin
Implaca-bility, bleness. *V.* page 3, § 1
Implacable, *adj.* implacable
Implacably, *adv.* implacablement [culquer
Implant, *v.a.* implanter, imprimer, graver, in-
Implantation, *s.* implantation, *f.*
Implement, *s.* instrument, *m.*; outil, *m.*; ustensile, *m.*; machine, *f.*; article, objet, *m.*; — **s,** *pl.* instruments, &c.; attirail, *m.*
Implicate, *v.a.* impliquer; compromettre
Implication, *s.* implication, *f.*; induction, *f.* *By* —, implicitement
Implicit, *adj.* implicite; (*entire*) aveugle; (*of obedience*) absolue, passive
Implicitly, *adv.* implicitement, d'une manière implicite; aveuglément; absolument; passivement; avec une foi implicite, avec une confiance aveugle
Implicitness, *s.* nature implicite, *f.*; foi implicite, confiance aveugle, *f.*
Implied, *part. adj.* impliqué, &c. (*V.* **Imply**); implicite, tacite; sous-entendu qui va sans dire
Impliedly, *adv.* implicitement; tacitement
Implorable, *adj.* implorable
Imploration, *s.* imploration, *f.*
Implore, *v.a.n.* (*a person*) supplier (de), conjurer (de), adjurer (de); (*a thing, as o.'s clemency, mercy*, &c.) implorer
Implorer, *s.* imploreur, *m.*, -euse, *f.*, implorateur, *m.*, -trice, *f.*, suppliant, *m.*, e, *f.*
Imploring, Imploringly. *V.* **Beseeching, Beseechingly**
Imply, *v.a.* impliquer, supposer; contenir, comprendre; inférer; signifier, vouloir dire; (*to hint*) donner à entendre

Impolicy, *s.* impolitique, mauvaise politique, *f.*; imprudence, *f.*; maladresse, *f.* [**civilly**

Impolite, Impolitely. *V.* **Uncivil, Un-**

Impoliteness, *s.* impolitesse, *f.* [droit

Impolitic, *adj.* impolitique; imprudent; mala-

Impoliticly, *adv.* impolitiquement; imprudemment; maladroitement [rabilité, *f.*

Impondera-bility, bleness, *s.* impondé-

Imponderable, Imponderous, *adj.* im-

Imporosity, *s.* imporosité, *f.* [pondérable

Imporous, *adj.* imporeux

Import, *v.a.* (*introduce*) importer; (*mean,* &c.) signifier, dénoter, indiquer; impliquer, supposer; (*imp.*) importer à; — *s.* (*meaning*) portée, signification, *f.*, sens, *m.*; valeur, *f.*; importance, *f.*; (*of goods*) *V.* **Importation. —less,** *adj.* sans importance

Importable, *adj.* importable

Importance, *s.* importance, *f.*

Important, *adj.* important

Importantly, *adv.* avec importance, d'une manière importante

Importation, *s.* importation, *f.* — **duty,** *s.* droit d'entrée, *m.* — **trade,** *s.* commerce d'importation, *m.*

Importer, *s.* importateur, *m.*, -trice, *f.* (de . . .)

Importunate, *adj.* importun; pressant

Importunately, *adv.* importunément, d'une manière importune, avec importunité

Importunateness, Importuneness, *s.* importunité, *f.*

Importune, *v.a.* importuner

Importuner, *s.* importun, *m.*, e, *f.*

Importunity, *s.* importunité, *f.*

Imposable, *adj.* imposable

Impose, *v.a.* ('*on*,' '*upon*,' à) imposer; — *v.n.* — **on, upon,** (*deceive*) en imposer à, tromper, duper, abuser, en faire accroire à

Imposer, *s.* personne qui impose, *f.*, imposeur, *m.*; trompeur, *m.*, -euse, *f.*

Imposing, *adj.* imposant; — *s.* imposition, *f.* — **stone, -table,** *s.* (*print.*) marbre, *m.*

Imposingly, *adv.* d'une manière imposante

Imposition, *s.* imposition, *f.*; (*tax*) impôt, *m.*; (*punishment*) pensum, *m.*; (*cheat*) supercherie, fraude, tromperie, imposture, *f.*; extorsion, *f.*

Impossibility, *s.* impossibilité, *f.*; impossible, *m.*

Impossible, *adj.* impossible. *To find it* — (*to*), se trouver dans l'impossibilité (de); reconnaître l'impossibilité (de)

Impossibly, *adv.* impossiblement, d'une manière impossible

Impost, *s.* impôt, *m.*, imposition, *f.*; (*duty*) droit, *m.*; (*arch.*) imposte, *f.*

Impostor, *s.* imposteur, *m.*

Imposture, *s.* imposture, *f.*

Impotable, *adj.* impotable [faiblesse, *f.*

Impotenc-e, y, *s.* impuissance, *f.*; (*weakness*)

Impotent, *adj.* impuissant; (*weak*) faible, débile; (*crippled*) impotent, perclus; (*not master of*) qui n'est pas maître de, qui ne peut contenir

Impotently, *adv.* avec impuissance; (*weakly*) avec faiblesse, faiblement, sans force; vainement, en vain [fourrière; (*fig.*) enfermer

Impound, *v.a.* confisquer; (*beasts*) mettre en

Impoverish, *v.a.* appauvrir, réduire à la pauvreté [pauvrit, *f.*

Impoverisher, *s.* personne *or* chose qui ap-

Impoverishment, *s.* appauvrissement, *m.*

Impractica-bility, bleness, *s.* impraticabilité, *f.*; impossibilité, *f.*; insociabilité, *f.*

Impracticable, *adj.* impraticable; impossible; (*pers.*) intraitable, insociable

Impracticably, *adv.* d'une manière impraticable, impraticablement

Imprecate, *v.a.* maudire, faire des imprécations contre, charger d'imprécations

Imprecation, *s.* imprécation, *f.*

Imprecator, *s.* imprécateur, *m.*, -trice, *f.*

Imprecatory, *adj.* imprécatoire

Impregnable, *adj.* imprenable, inexpugnable; (*pers.*) inébranlable [prenable

Impregnably, *adv.* de manière à être im-

Impregnate, *v.a.* imprégner; féconder

Impregnate, Impregnated, *adj.* imprégné; fécondé [dation, *f.*

Impregnation, *s.* imprégnation, *f.*; fécon-

Imprescriptibility, *s.* imprescriptibilité, *f.*

Imprescriptible, *adj.* imprescriptible

Imprescriptibly, *adv.* imprescriptiblement

Impress, *v.a.* imprimer, empreindre; graver; inculquer; (*move*) impressionner; pénétrer (de); faire sentir (à); inspirer (à); (*strike*) frapper (de); (*for public service*) mettre en réquisition, enrôler; (*mil.*) racoler; (*nav.*) presser; — *s.* empreinte, impression, *f.*; (*nav.*) presse, *f.*

Impressi-bility, bleness. *V.* page 3, § 1

Impressible, *adj.* impressible, impressionnable [effet, *m.*; idée, *f.*

Impression, *s.* impression, *f.*; empreinte, *f.*;

Impressionability, *s.* impressionnabilité, *f.*

Impressionable, *adj.* impressionnable [*f.*

Impressionableness, *s.* impressionnabilité,

Impressive, *adj.* impressif, frappant; touchant, pénétrant; (*pers.*) impressionnable

Impressively, *adv.* impressivement, d'une manière frappante *or* touchante, fortement

Impressiveness, *s.* propriété de faire impression, *f.*; nature touchante, *f.*; force, *f.*; grandeur, *f.*, grandiose, *m.*

Impressment, *s.* réquisition, *f.*; (*mil.*) racolage, *m.*; (*nav.*) presse, *f.* primer, *m.*

Imprimatur, *s.* imprimatur, permis d'im-

Imprimis, *adv.* d'abord, avant tout, premièrement

Imprint, *v.a.* imprimer, empreindre; graver; inculquer; — *s.* nom de l'imprimeur, *m.*, rubrique, *f.*

Imprison, *v.a.* emprisonner, mettre en prison

Imprisonment, *s.* emprisonnement, *m.*; prison, *f.*; détention, *f.* *One month's* —, un mois de prison [blance, *f.*

Improbability *s.* improbabilité, invraisem-

Improbable, *adj.* invraisemblable, improbable

Improbably, *adv.* improbablement, invrai-

Improbity, *s.* improbité, *f.* [semblablement

Impromptu, *adj. adv. s.* impromptu (*s.m.*)

Improper, *adj.* inconvenant; (*incorrect*) impropre; (*unfit*) peu propre (à), impropre (à), peu convenable (à); (*pers.*) peu propre (à), impropre (à), qui ne convient pas (à), peu fait (pour)

Improperly, *adv.* d'une manière inconvenante; (*incorrectly*) improprement, mal; abusivement, mal à propos; (*wrongfully*) à tort

Impropriate, *v.a.* approprier; (*to oneself*) s'approprier; (*can. law*) séculariser; (*feud.*) inféoder

Impropriation, *s.* appropriation, *f.*; (*can. law*) sécularisation, *f.*; (*feud.*) inféodation, *f.*

Impropriator, *s.* (*can. law.*) possesseur d'un bénéfice sécularisé, possesseur, *m.*

Impropriety, *s.* inconvenance, *f.*; (*incorrectness*) impropriété, *f.*

Improva-bility, bleness, *s.* perfectibilité, *f.*

Improvable, *adj.* susceptible d'amélioration *or* de perfectionnement; (*of land*) exploitable

Improve, *v.a.* améliorer, rendre meilleur; perfectionner; embellir; rehausser; relever; former; développer; (*land, wine,* &c.) bonifier; (*money,* &c.) faire valoir; (*cultivate*) cultiver; (*increase*) accroître, augmenter; (*to turn to account, to profit by*) profiter de, mettre à profit, utiliser; faire valoir; (*strengthen*) fortifier; — *v.n.* s'améliorer, devenir meilleur; se perfectionner; se bonifier; gagner, profiter; embellir, s'embellir; croître, s'accroître, augmenter; se fortifier; (*of prices*) augmenter, hausser; (*make progress*) faire des progrès, avancer; (*outdo*) renchérir (sur), enchérir (sur). *To* — *upon* (or *on*) *acquaintance*, gagner à être connu

Improvement, *s.* amélioration, *f.*; perfectionnement, *m.*; embellissement, *m.*; culture, *f.*; emploi, *m.*; instruction, *f.*; progrès, avancement, *m.*; utilité, *f.*, profit, avantage, *m.*; (*of land, wine,* &c.) bonification, *f.* [fectionneur, *m.*
Improver, *s.* améliorateur, *m.*, -trice, *f.*; per-
Improvidence, *s.* imprévoyance, *f.*
Improvident, *adj.* imprévoyant
Improvidently, *adv.* avec imprévoyance
Improvisation, *s.* improvisation, *f.*
Improvisa-tor, tress, *s.* improvisateur, *m.*,
Improvise, *v.a.n.* improviser [-trice, *f.*
Improviser, *s.* improvisateur, *m.*, -trice, *f.*
Imprudence, *s.* imprudence, *f.*
Imprudent, *adj.* imprudent
Imprudently, *adv.* imprudemment
Impuberal, *adj.* impubère
Impuberty, *s.* impuberté, *f.* [impertinence, *f.*
Impudence, *s.* impudence, *f.*; effronterie, *f.*;
Impudent, *adj.* impudent; effronté; impertinent [ment
Impudently, *adv.* impudemment; effronté-
Impudicity, *s.* impudicité, *f.*
Impugn, *v.a.* attaquer; combattre; contester; mettre en doute [contestable
Impugnable, *adj.* attaquable; combattable;
Impugner, *s.* adversaire, antagoniste, *m.f.*; négateur, *m.*, -trice, *f.*
Impulse, Impulsion, *s.* impulsion, *f.*; mouvement, *m.*; motif, *m.*; instinct, *m.*; élan, *m.*; besoin, *m.*, envie, *f.*; entraînement, *m.*
Impulsive, *adj.* impulsif; fougueux
Impulsively, *adv.* par impulsion; par un mouvement involontaire
Impunity, *s.* impunité, *f.* *With —*, avec impunité, impunément
Impure, *adj.* impur; (*lewd*) impudique; obscène; (*unclean*) immonde
Impurely, *adv.* impurement, avec impureté; (*lewdly*) impudiquement; avec obscénité
Impureness, Impurity, *s.* impureté, *f.*; (*lewdness*) impudicité, *f.*; obscénité, *f.*
Impurple, *v.a.* empourprer
Imputa-bility, bleness. *V.* page 3, § 1
Imputable, *adj.* imputable; (*in a good sense*) attribuable
Imputation, *s.* imputation, *f.*; accusation, *f.*
Imputative, *adj.* imputatif
Imputatively, *adv.* par imputation
Impute, *v.a.* imputer (à); (*in a good sense*) attribuer (à)
Imputer, *s.* personne qui impute *or* attribue, *f.*
Imputrescibility, *s.* imputrescibilité, *f.*
Imputrescible, *adj.* imputrescible
In, *prep.* dans; en; à; chez; entre; (*out of*) sur; (*by, through*) par; (*of*) de; (*on*) sur; (*under*) sous; (*about*) sur, après; (*during*) pendant; (*for*) pour; (*with*) avec; (*of weather*) par; (*after a superlative, and after 'all the'* ...) de; (*with the words 'manner,' 'voice,' 'tone,'* &c.) de; (*cooked — or with*) au, à la, aux, à. — *it, them* (*things*), dedans; y; (*with it or them on, of clothes*) avec. — *the room,* dans la chambre. — *a box,* dans une boîte. — *good health,* en bonne santé. — *a white dress,* en robe blanche. — *a blue coat,* en habit bleu. — *France,* en France. — *London,* (*at*) à Londres, (*within*) dans Londres. — *two days,* (*two days hence*) dans deux jours; (*within the space of two days*) en deux jours; (*at the end of two days*) au bout de deux jours. — *the door,* (*of keys*) sur *or* après *or* à la porte. — *-door,* — *-doors, V.* **Door.** — *o.'s hand,* à la main, (*if entirely inside*) dans la main. *To hold — o.'s hand,* tenir à la main; tenir dans la main, tenir en main. *To hold — one hand,* tenir d'une main. *Nine — ten,* neuf sur dix. *A letter — which,* (*among other matters*) une lettre dans laquelle; (*the sole object of which*) une lettre par laquelle
In, *adv. adj. s.* dedans, en dedans, y; (*at home*) *V.* **Within,** *adv.*; (*housed, of corn,* &c.) rentré; (*harnessed*) attelé; (*of the sun*) caché; (*of fire*) allumé, ne ... pas éteint; (*of a key, in the door*) dessus, après; (*in power*) au pouvoir; en place; (*into the bargain*) par-dessus le marché; (*adject., in-door*) interne; (*way in*) entrée, *s.f.* — *for it,* dedans, pris, attrapé, pincé. — *with it!* entrez-le! —**s and outs,** *s. pl.* coins et recoins, êtres, *m.pl.*, aides, *f.pl.*; (*fig.*) détails, tenants et aboutissants, *m.pl.* *To be — for,* (*to lose*) en être pour. *To be — and out,* aller et venir. *To go — and out,* entrer et sortir. *All —!* (*at school*) rentrez! en classe! *I have had my coals —,* j'ai fait ma provision de charbon de terre
Inability, *s.* impuissance, *f.*; (*of the mind*) incapacité, *f.*; inhabileté, *f.*; (*want of means*) manque de moyens, *m.*
Inabstinence, *s.* inabstinence, *f.*
Inabstinent, *adj.* inabstinent
Inaccessi-bility, bleness. *V.* page 3, § 1
Inaccessible, *adj.* inaccessible; inabordable
Inaccessibly, *adv.* d'une manière inaccessible *or* inabordable
Inaccuracy, *s.* inexactitude, *f.*; erreur, *f.*
Inaccurate, *adj.* inexact; incorrect
Inaccurately, *adv.* inexactement
Inaction, *s.* inaction, *f.*; repos, *m.* [action
Inactive, *adj.* inactif; (*of things*) inerte, sans
Inactively, *adv.* inactivement, dans l'inactivité
Inactivity, *s.* inactivité, *f.*; (*of things*) inertie, *f.*, manque d'action, *m.* [*f.*; disproportion, *f.*
Inadequacy, *s.* insuffisance, *f.*; imperfection,
Inadequate, *adj.* insuffisant; imparfait, incomplet; défectueux; disproportionné; inégal; au-dessous (de); (*philos.*) inadéquat
Inadequately, *adv.* insuffisamment; imparfaitement; disproportionnément
Inadequateness. *V.* **Inadequacy**
Inadherent, *adj.* inadhérent
Inadmissibility, *s.* inadmissibilité, *f.*
Inadmissible, *adj.* inadmissible
Inadvertenc-e, y, *s.* inadvertance, *f.*
Inadvertent, *adj.* inadvertant, négligent, inattentif, étourdi [mégarde
Inadvertently, *adv.* par inadvertance, par
Inaffectation, *s.* inaffectation, *f.*
Inaliena-bility, bleness, *s.* inaliénabilité, *f.*
Inalienable, *adj.* inaliénable
Inalienably, *adv.* d'une manière inaliénable
Inalterability, *s.* inaltérabilité, *f.*
Inalterable, *adj.* inaltérable
Inane, *adj.* vide; vain
Inanimate, *adj.* inanimé; (*of nature*) mort
Inanimation, *s.* inanimation, *f.*
Inanition, *s.* inanition, *f.* [nité, vanité, *f.*
Inanity, *s.* vide, espace vide, *m.*; (*fig.*) ina-
Inappetenc-e, y, *s.* inappétence, *f.* [lité, *f.*
Inapplica-bility, bleness, *s.* inapplicabi-
Inapplicable, *adj.* inapplicable
Inapplication, *s.* inapplication, *f.*
Inapposite, *adj.* inapplicable, sans rapport; déplacé, peu convenable
Inappreciable, *adj.* inappréciable
Inappreciably, *adv.* inappréciablement
Inappreciation, *s.* inappréciation, *f.*
Inappropriate, *adj.* peu approprié
Inapt, *adj.* inapte
Inaptitude, *s.* inaptitude, *f.*
Inarch, *v.a.* greffer par approche
Inarching, *s.* greffe par approche, *f.*
Inarticulate, *adj.* inarticulé
Inarticulately, *adv.* d'une manière inarticulée, indistinctement
Inarticulation, *s.* inarticulation, *f.*
Inartificial, *adj.* inartificiel
Inartificially, *adv.* inartificiellement
Inasmuch, *adv.* vu (que), attendu (que), car, puisque; d'autant plus (que)
Inattention, *s.* inattention, *f.*; distraction, *f.*; indifférence, *f.* [différent
Inattentive, *adj.* inattentif; distrait; in-
Inattentively, *adv.* inattentivement, avec

inattention; avec distraction, distraitement; avec indifférence; négligemment
Inattraction, *s.* inattraction, *f.*
Inaudible, *adj.* qu'on ne peut entendre, qui ne peut être entendu; silencieux
Inaudibly, *adv.* de manière à ne pas être en-
Inaugural, *adj.* inaugural [tendu
Inaugurate, *v.a.* inaugurer [inaugurateur
Inaugurating, *s.* inauguration, *f.*; — *adj.*
Inauguration, *s.* inauguration, *f.* [-trice, *f.*
Inaugura-tor, tress, *s.* inaugurateur, *m.*,
Inauguratory, *adj.* d'inauguration [mauvais
Inauspicious, *adj.* malheureux; funeste;
Inauspiciously, *adv.* sous de mauvais auspices; malheureusement; d'une manière funeste
Inauspiciousness, *s.* mauvais auspices, *m.pl.*; nature malheureuse *or* funeste, *f.*
Inauthenticity, *s.* inauthenticité, *f.*
Inbeing, *s.* inhérence, *f.*
Inborn, Inbred, *adj.* inné; naturel; intérieur
Inca, *s.* Inca, *m.*
Incage, *v.a.* *V.* **Cage,** *v.a.*
Incalculable, *adj.* incalculable
Incalculably, *adv.* incalculablement
Incandescence, *s.* incandescence, *f.*
Incandescent, *adj.* incandescent
Incantation, *s.* incantation, *f.*
Incapability, *s.* incapacité, *f.* [tible (de)
Incapable, *adj.* incapable (de); non suscep-
Incapacious, *adj.* de peu de capacité; (*narrow*) étroit [(*narrowness*) étroitesse, *f.*
Incapaciousness, *s.* défaut d'espace, *m.*;
Incapacitate, *v.a.* *V.* **Disable**
Incapacitation, *s.* défaut de capacité, *m.*
Incapacity, *s.* incapacité, *f.*; (*law*) incapacité,
Incarcerate, *v.a.* incarcérer [inhabilité, *f.*
Incarceration, *s.* incarcération, *f.*
Incarnadine, *adj. s.* incarnadin, *adj. m.*, e, *f.*, incarnadin, *s.m.* [corps; — *adj.* incarné
Incarnate, *v.a.* revêtir de chair; revêtir d'un
Incarnation, *s.* incarnation, *f.* [châsser
Incase, *v.a.* encaisser; couvrir, enfermer; en-
Incautious, *adj.* imprudent, inconsidéré
Incautiously, *adv.* imprudemment, inconsidérément; par mégarde [ration, *f.*
Incautiousness, *s.* imprudence, inconsidé-
Incendiarism, *s.* *V.* **Arson** [*V.* **Arson**
Incendiary, *adj. s.* incendiaire, *m.f.* — *fire,*
Incense, *s.* encens, *m.*; — *v.a.* (*perfume*) encenser; (*irritate*) irriter, courroucer, exaspérer
Incentive, *s.* encouragement, stimulant, aiguillon, *m.*; mobile, motif, *m.*; — *adj.* excitant, encourageant [commencement
Inceptive, *adj.* qui commence; qui marque le
Inceration, *s.* incération, *f.*
Incertitude, *s.* incertitude, *f.*
Incessant, *adj.* incessant, continuel
Incessantly, *adv.* sans cesse, sans relâche,
Incest, *s.* inceste, *m.* [continuellement
Incestuous, *adj.* incestueux
Incestuously, *adv.* incestueusement
Incestuousness, *s.* nature incestueuse, *f.*
Inch, *s.* pouce, *m.*; (*in modern Fr. meas.*) 3 centimètres, *m.pl.*; (*small quantity*) rien, *m.* *By —es, — by —,* pouce par pouce; (*fig.*) pied à pied; peu à peu, petit à petit; (*in a bad sense*) à petit feu; à coups d'épingle. *By — of candle,* à l'extinction des feux. *Every —,* (*fig.*) jusqu'à la moelle des os, jusqu'aux ongles, dans l'âme; dans toute la force du terme. *Within an — of,* à deux doigts de
Inchain, *v.a.* *V.* **Enchain** [pouces
Inched, *adj.* (*in compounds*) à ... pouces, de ...
Inchoate, *adj.* commencé; ébauché, inachevé,
Incidenc-e, y, *s.* incidence, *f.* [imparfait
Incident, *adj.* incident; qui appartient (à), qui fait partie (de), particulier (à); — *s.* incident, *m.*
Incidental, *adj.* incidentel; incident; accessoire; accidentel, fortuit. — *expenses,* —*s,* faux frais, *m.pl.*
Incidentally, *adv.* incidemment; accessoirement; accidentellement, par hasard, fortuite-
Incinerate, *v.a.* incinérer [ment
Incineration, *s.* incinération, *f.*
Incipiency, *s.* commencement, *m.*
Incipient, *adj.* commençant, qui commence *or* débute; naissant; premier
Incipit, *s.* incipit, *m.*
Incise, *v.a.* inciser; couper, tailler. —*d wound,* plaie par instrument tranchant, coupure. in-
Incision, *s.* incision, *f.* [cision, *f.*
Incisive, Incisory, *adj.* incisif. — *tooth,* dent incisive, incisive, *f.* [(*instr.*) inciseur, *m.*
Incisor, *s.* (*tooth*) dent incisive, incisive, *f.*;
Incitability *s.* incitabilité, *f.*
Incitable, *adj.* incitable
Incitant, *adj.s.* incitant, *adj.m.*, e, *f.*, incitant, *s.m.*
Incitation, *s.* *V.* **Incitement**
Incite, *v.a.* exciter, inciter, pousser, porter, encourager, animer (à)
Incitement, incitation, *f.*; &c. (*V.* **Incentive**)
Inciter, *s.* incitateur, *m.*, -trice, *f.*; instigateur, *m.*, -trice, *f.*
Incivil, -ly. *V.* **Uncivil, -ly** [èreté, *f.*
Incivility, *s.* incivilité, impolitesse, grossi-
Incivism *s.* incivisme, *m.* [brasser, étreindre
Inclasp, *v.a.* serrer étroitement, serrer, em-
Inclemency, *s.* inclémence, *f.*; (*pers.*) sévérité, dureté, *f.*; (*of weather*) intempérie, rigueur, inclémence, *f.*
Inclement, *adj.* inclément; dur, impitoyable, inexorable; (*of weather*) rigoureux, inclément
Inclinable, *adj.* enclin (à), porté (à); (*tending*) qui tend (à)
Inclination, *s.* (*slope*) inclinaison, pente, *f.*; (*propensity*) inclination, *f.*, penchant, *m.*, pente, *f.*; (*liking*) goût, *m.*; (*of the head or body*) inclination, *f.*; (*of the magnetic needle*) décli-
Inclinatory, *adj.* qui incline [naison, *f.*
Incline, *v.n.a.* incliner, pencher; être porté *or* disposé (à); porter, disposer (à); (*of colours*) tirer (sur le ...); — *s.* inclinaison, pente, rampe, *f.*
Inclined, *adj.* incliné; (*fig.*) enclin (à), porté (à), disposé (à). — *plane,* plan incliné, *m.*
Inclining, *adj.* incliné. — *to,* (*of colours*) tirant sur (le ...) [**Enclose,** &c.
Incloister, Inclose, &c. *V.* **Encloister,**
Include, *v.a.* renfermer, comprendre
Included, *adj.* renfermé, compris; (*together, with*) y compris. *This room —,* y compris cette chambre, cette chambre comprise *or* y comprise [compris, sans compter
Including, *prep.* y compris. *Not —,* non
Inclusion, *s.* inclusion, *f.*
Inclusive, *adj.* inclusif; (*of ...*) qui renferme, qui comprend; (*adverb.*) inclusivement; (*prep.*) — *of,* y compris. *Not — of,* (*prep.*) non compris, sans compter
Inclusively, *adv.* inclusivement
Incog., Incognita, Incognito, *adv. s.* incognito (*s.m.*)
Incoherenc-e, y, *s.* incohérence, *f.*
Incoherent, *adj.* incohérent
Incoherently, *adv.* incohéremment, d'une manière incohérente, sans cohérence, sans liaison
Incombusti-bility, bleness. *V.* p. 3, § 1
Incombustible, *adj.* incombustible
Income, *s.* revenu, *m.*, rentes, *f.pl.*; recettes, *f.pl.* — **tax,** *s.* impôt sur le revenu, *m.*
Incomer, *s.* entrant, *m*; nouveau propriétaire *or* locataire, *m.*
Incoming, *adj.* entrant, qui entre; nouveau; (*accruing*) qui revient, de revenu, acquis; qui rentre; — *s.* entrée, *f.*; —**s,** *s. pl.* rentrées, *f.pl.*; recettes, *f.pl.*
Incommensurability. *V.* page 3, § 1
Incommensurable, *adj.* incommensurable
Incommensurate, *adj.* disproportionné
Incommensurately, *adv.* d'une manière disproportionnée

Incommode, *v.a.* incommoder, gêner, embarrasser, déranger
Incommodious, -ly. *V.* **Inconvenient,-ly**
Incommodiousness, Incommodity. *V.* **Inconvenience**
Incommunica-bility, bleness. *V* p. 3, § 1
Incommunicable, *adj.* incommunicable
Incommunicably, *adv.* d'une manière incommunicable
Incommunicative, *adj.* peu communicatif
Incommutability, *s.* incommuabilité, incommutabilité, *f.* [mutable
Incommutable, *adj.* incommuable, incom-
Incompactness, *s.* incompacité, *f.*
Incomparable, *adj.* incomparable
Incomparableness, *s.* incomparabilité, *f.*
Incomparably, *adv.* incomparablement, sans comparaison [compassion
Incompassionate, *adj.* incompatissant, sans
Incompassionately, *adv.* sans compassion
Incompati-bility, bleness, *s.* incompati-
Incompatible, *adj.* incompatible [bilité, *f.*
Incompatibly, *adv.* incompatiblement
Incompetenc-e, y, *s.* incompétence, *f.*; insuffisance, *f.*; (*want of strength*) impuissance, *f.*; (*law*) incapacité, inhabilité, *f.*; (*of a court*) incompétence, *f.*
Incompetent, *adj.* incompétent; insuffisant; (*unable*) impuissant; (*law*) incapable, inhabile; (*of a court*) incompétent [suffisamment
Incompetently, *adv.* incompétemment; in-
Incomplete, *adj.* incomplet; imparfait; (*not done*) inachevé [faitement
Incompletely, *adv.* incomplètement; impar-
Incompleteness, Incompletion, *s.* état incomplet, *m.*, imperfection, *f.*
Incomplex, *adj.* incomplexe
Incomplexity, *s.* incomplexité, *f.*
Incompliance, *s.* manque de complaisance, *m.*; (*stiffness*) raideur, *f.*; indocilité, *f.*; sévérité, *f.* [raide, inflexible, opiniâtre
Incompliant, *adj.* peu complaisant; (*stiff*)
Incomposite, *adj.* simple. — *number*, (*arith.*) nombre premier, *m.* [compréhensibilité, *f.*
Incomprehensi-bility, bleness, *s.* in-
Incomprehensible, *adj.* incompréhensible
Incomprehensibly, *adv.* incompréhensiblement [sion, *m.*
Incomprehension, *s.* défaut de compréhen-
Incomprehensive, *adj.* peu étendu, borné
Incomprehensiveness, *s.* peu d'étendue, *m.*
Incompressi-bility, bleness, *V.* p. 3, § 1
Incompressible, *adj.* incompressible
Inconcealable, *adj.* impossible à cacher, qu'on ne peut cacher, qui ne peut se cacher
Inconceiva-bility, bleness, *s.* inconceva-
Inconceivable, *adj.* inconcevable [bilité, *f.*
Inconceivably, *adv.* inconcevablement, d'une manière inconcevable, au-delà de toute
Inconclusive, *adj.* inconcluant [conception
Inconclusively, *adv.* d'une manière inconcluante; sans preuve concluante
Inconclusiveness, *s.* nature inconcluante, *f.*
Inconcocted, *adj.* mal digéré, indigeste
Incondensability. *V.* page 3, § 1 [densable
Incondensable, *adj.* incondensable, non con-
Inconformity, *s.* *V.* **Non-conformity**
Incongealable, *adj.* incongelable
Incongruity, *s.* incongruité, *f.*; disconvenance, *f.*; inconvenance, *f.*
Incongruous, *adj.* incongru, impropre; inconvenant; hétérogène [inconvenance
Incongruously, *adv.* incongrûment; avec
Inconsequent, &c., (*obsolete*) *V.* **Inconsistent,** &c.
Inconsiderable, *adj.* peu considérable; sans importance; petit, insignifiant; peu de chose
Inconsiderableness, *s.* peu d'importance, *m.*; peu de valeur, *m.*; nature insignifiante, insignifiance, *f.*
Inconsiderably, *adv.* sans importance; très peu; faiblement; d'une manière insignifiante
Inconsiderate, *adj.* inconsidéré, irréfléchi; imprudent; inattentif
Inconsiderately, *adv.* inconsidérément, sans réflexion; imprudemment
Inconsiderateness, Inconsideration, *s.* inconsidération, irréflexion, *f.*; imprudence, *f.*
Inconsistenc-e, y, *s.* inconsistance, *f.*; incompatibilité, *f.*; contradiction, *f.*; inconséquence, *f.*; inconstance, *f.*
Inconsistent, *adj.* inconsistant; incompatible; contradictoire; inconséquent
Inconsistently, *adv.* incompatiblement; contradictoirement; inconséquemment
Inconsolable, *adj.* inconsolable
Inconsolably, *adv.* inconsolablement
Inconsonanc-e, y, *s.* discordance, *f.*; défaut de conformité, *m.*; désaccord, *m.*; incompatibilité, *f.*
Inconsonant, *adj.* discordant; en désaccord (avec); incompatible (avec); contraire (à)
Inconsonantly, *adv.* discordamment; en désaccord (avec); incompatiblement; contrairement (à)
Inconspicuous, *adj.* qu'on ne peut apercevoir, qui n'est pas en vue; peu remarquable
Inconstancy, *s* inconstance, *f.*
Inconstant, *adj.* inconstant [constance
Inconstantly, *adv.* inconstamment, avec in-
Inconsumable, *adj.* inconsumable; (*not usable*) inconsommable
Incontesta-bility, bleness. *V.* page 3, § 1
Incontestable, *adj.* incontestable
Incontestably, *adv.* incontestablement
Incontinenc-e, y, *s.* incontinence, *f.*
Incontinent, *adj.* incontinent
Incontinently, *adv.* incontinemment, avec (*or* par) incontinence; (*obsolete for* "*immediately*") sur-le-champ, aussitôt, immédiatement, incontinent
Incontinuity, *s.* incontinuité, *f.*
Incontrovertible, &c. *V.* **Incontestable,** &c.
Inconvenienc-e, y, *s.* incommodité, *f.*; dérangement, *m.*, gêne, *f.*; embarras, *m.*; inconvénient, *m.*; désagrément, *m.* *To put to* — or *to any* —, *V. To* —, *v.a.* (*below*) [gêner
Inconvenience, *v.a.* incommoder, déranger,
Inconvenient, *adj.* incommode, gênant. *If it is* — *to you*, si cela vous gêne *or* vous dérange. *At an* — *hour*, dans un mauvais moment
Inconveniently, *adv.* incommodément; dans un mauvais moment, mal. — *small*, fort exigu, beaucoup trop petit
Inconversable, *adj.* réservé, insociable
Inconverti-bility, bleness. *V.* page 3, § 1
Inconvertible, *adj.* (*things*) non convertible, inconvertible; non transformable; (*pers.*) inconvertissable
Inconvertibly, *adv.* inconvertiblement
Inconvincible, *adj.* impossible à convaincre
Incorporal, *adj.* incorporel
Incorporality, *s.* incorporalité, *f.*
Incorporally, *adv.* incorporellement
Incorporate, *adj.* incorporé; — *v.a.* incorporer; former *or* constituer en corps; établir en corporation; autoriser à se constituer en compagnie *or* en société; — *v.n.* s'incorporer
Incorporation, *s.* incorporation, *f.*
Incorporeal, &c. *V.* **Incorporal,** &c.
Incorporeity, *s.* incorporéité, *f.*
Incorrect, *adj.* incorrect; inexact [ment
Incorrectly, *adv.* incorrectement; inexacte-
Incorrectness, *s.* incorrection, inexactitude, *f.*
Incorrigi-bility, bleness, *s.* incorrigibilité, *f.*
Incorrigible, *adj.* incorrigible
Incorrigibly, *adv.* incorrigiblement
Incorrodible, *adj* incorrodible [pur; intègre
Incorrupt, *adj.* incorrompu, non corrompu;
Incorrupti-bility, bleness. *V.* page 3, § 1
Incorruptible, *adj.* incorruptible
Incorruptibly, *adv.* incorruptiblement
Incorruption, Incorruptness, *s.* incorruption, *f.*; pureté, *f.*; intégrité, *f.*

Incrassate, *v.a.* épaissir; — *v.n.* s'épaissir; — *adj.* épaissi; engraissé
Incrassation, *s.* épaississement, *m.*
Incrassative, *adj. s.* incrassant, *adj. m.*, e, *f.*, incrassant, *s.m.*
Increase, *v.a.* accroître; augmenter; agrandir; grossir; (*to*) porter (à); — *v.n.* s'accroître, accroître, s'augmenter, augmenter, croître; s'agrandir; grossir; multiplier; — *s.* accroissement, *m.*; augmentation, *f.*, surcroît, *m.*; progrès, *m.pl.*; (*of rivers*) crue, *f.*; (*produce*) produit, fruit, *m.*; (*offspring*) rejeton, enfant, *m.*; (*of the moon*) croissant, *m.*
Increasable, *adj.* augmentable, susceptible d'augmentation [qui augmente, *f.*
Increaser, *s.* personne *or* chose qui accroît *or*
Increasing, *adj.* croissant
Increasingly, *adv.* en croissant, en augmentant, de plus en plus
Incredi-bility, bleness, *s.* incrédibilité, *f.*
Incredible, *adj.* incroyable
Incredibly, *adv.* incroyablement
Incredu-lity, lousness, *s.* incrédulité, *f.*
Incredulous, *adj.* incrédule
Incredulously, *adv.* avec incrédulité
Increment, *s.* accroissement, *m.*, augmentation, *f.*; produit, fruit, *m.*; (*math.*) quantité différentielle, *f.*
Incriminable, *adj.* incriminable
Incriminate, *v.a. V.* **Criminate**
Incriminating, *adj. V.* **Incriminatory**
Incrimination, *s. V.* **Crimination**
Incriminatory, *adj.* incriminatoire; com-
Incrust, *v.a.* incruster ('*with*,' de) [promettant
Incrustation, *s.* incrustation, *f.*
Incrystallizable, *adj.* incristallisable
Incubate, *v.n.* couver
Incubation, *s.* incubation, *f.*
Incubator, *s.* couveuse (artificielle), *f.*, facteur-couvoir, couvoir, four d'incubation, *m.*
Incubus, *s.* (*demon*) incube, *m.*; (*nightmare*) cauchemar, *m.*; (*fig.*) grand poids, lourd fardeau, *m.*; oppression, *f.*; péril, *m.*
Inculcate, *v.a.* inculquer ('*on*,' à) [ment, *m.*
Inculcation, *s.* inculcation, *f.*; enseigne-
Inculpate, *v.a.* inculper
Inculpation, *s.* inculpation, *f.* [mettant
Inculpatory, *adj.* accusateur; compro-
Incumbency, *s.* possession, *f.*; (*eccl.*) possession *or* jouissance de bénéfice, *f.*
Incumbent, *adj.* (*lying*) posé, couché; (*supported*) appuyé; (*imposed*) imposé, enjoint, obligatoire, du devoir (de); (*bot.*) incombant; — *s.* titulaire, *m.*; (*eccl.*) bénéficier, *m.* *To make it — on . . .* (*to*), faire un devoir à . . . (de)
Incumber, &c. *V.* **Encumber,** &c.
Incunabula, *s. pl.* incunables, *m.pl.*
Incur, *v.a.* encourir, s'attirer, s'exposer à; (*expenses*) faire; (*debts*) contracter, se créer,
Incura-bility, bleness. *V.* p. 3, § 1 [faire
Incurable, *adj. s.* incurable, *m.f.*
Incurably, *adv.* incurablement, sans remède; incorrigiblement
Incuriosity, *s.* incuriosité, *f.*
Incurious, *adj.* incurieux
Incuriously, *adv.* incurieusement
Incursion, *s.* incursion, *f.*
Incursive, *adj.* incursif [curvé, courbé
Incurvate, *v.a.* incurver, courber; — *adj.* in-
Incurvation, *s.* incurvation, courbure, *f.*; (*of the body*) inflexion, *f.*
Incurve, *v.a.* incurver, courber
Incus, *s.* (*anat.*) enclume, *f.*
Indebted, *adj.* endetté; (*fig.*) redevable ('*for*,' de); obligé ('*for*,' de). *To be — for,* devoir; (*fig.*) être redevable de; être obligé de; devoir
Indebtedness, *s.* état de dette, *m.*, dettes, *f.pl.*
Indecency, *s.* indécence, *f.*
Indecent, *adj.* indécent [cence
Indecently, *adv.* indécemment, avec indé-
Indeciduous, *adj.* (*bot.*) persistant
Indecision, *s.* indécision, *f.*
Indecisive, *adj.* indécisif; (*wavering*) indécis
Indecisively, *adv.* indécisivement
Indecisiveness, *s.* nature indécisive, *f.*; état
Indeclinable, *adj.* indéclinable [indécis, *m.*
Indeclinableness, *s.* indéclinabilité, *f.*
Indecomposable, *adj.* indécomposable
Indecomposableness, *s.* nature indécomposable, *f.*
Indecorous, *adj.* inconvenant, indécent
Indecorously, *adv.* avec inconvenance, d'une manière inconvenante
Indecorousness, Indecorum, *s.* inconvenance, indécence, *f.*, manque de décorum, *m.*
Indeed, *adv.* (*it is true*) à la vérité, bien; (*really*) en vérité; vraiment; certes; en effet; réellement; absolument; bien; — *int.* vraiment! bah! ah bah! tiens! par exemple! *Very fine —,* bien beau. *Very well —,* parfaitement, admirablement; parfait, admirable
Indefatigability. *V.* **Indefatigableness**
Indefatigable, *adj.* infatigable [sistance, *f.*
Indefatigableness, *s.* infatigabilité, *f.*; per-
Indefatigably, *adv.* infatigablement
Indefeasibility, *s.* inaliénabilité, inviolabilité, imprescriptibilité, indestructibilité, *f.*
Indefeasible, *adj.* inaliénable, inviolable, imprescriptible, indestructible
Indefeasibly, *adv.* inaliénablement, inviolablement, imprescriptiblement, indestructible-
Indefectibility, *s.* indéfectibilité, *f.* [ment
Indefectible, *adj.* indéfectible
Indefendable, Indefensible, *adj.* indéfendable; insoutenable; inexcusable, injustifiable [fiablement
Indefensibly, *adv.* inexcusablement; injusti-
Indefinable, *adj.* indéfinissable
Indefinite, *adj.* indéfini; vague
Indefinitely, *adv.* indéfiniment; vaguement
Indefiniteness, *s.* nature indéfinie, *f.*; vague,
Indehiscence, *s.* indéhiscence, *f.* [*m.*
Indehiscent, *adj.* indéhiscent
Indeliberate, *adj.* indélibéré
Indeliberately, *adv.* indélibérément
Indeli-bility, bleness, *s.* indélébilité, *f.*
Indelible, *adj.* indélébile, ineffaçable
Indelibly, *adv.* en caractères ineffaçables, ineffaçablement
Indelicacy, *s.* indélicatesse, *f.*; grossièreté, *f.*
Indelicate, *adj.* indélicat; grossier
Indelicately, *adv.* indélicatement
Indemnification, *s.* indemnisation, *f.*; indemnité, *f.*; dédommagement, *m.*
Indemnify, *v.a.* indemniser, dédommager
Indemnity, *s.* indemnité, *f.*; dédommagement, *m.*; amnistie, *f.* [montrabilité, *f.*
Indemonstra-bility, bleness, *s.* indé-
Indemonstrable, *adj.* indémontrable
Indent, *v.a.* (*shape*) denteler; échancrer; (*break off*) ébrécher; (*make hollows in*) bossuer, bosseler; (*print.*) renfoncer, rentrer; — *v.n.* passer contrat; — *s.* (*stamp*) empreinte, impression, *f.*; (*notch*) dentelure, *f.*
Indentation, Indentment, *s.* dentelure, *f.*; échancrure, *f.*; (*print.*) renfoncement, *m.*, rentrée, *f.* [prentissage, *m.*; (*law*) titre, *m.*
Indenture, *s.*, **Indentures,** *pl.* contrat d'ap-
Independenc-e, y, *s.* indépendance, *f.*; fortune, *f.*; position indépendante, *f.*
Independent, *adj.* indépendant; — *s.* indépendant, *m.*; (*adverb.*) indépendamment (de). — *gentleman,* rentier, propriétaire, bourgeois, *m.* — *lady,* rentière, propriétaire, *f.*
Independentism, *s.* indépendantisme, *m.*
Independently, *adv.* indépendamment; dans l'indépendance
Indescribable, *adj.* indescriptible; indicible
Indescribableness, *s.* indescriptibilité, *f.*
Indescribably, *adv.* indescriptiblement; in-
Indestructibility. *V.* p. 3, § 1 [diciblement
Indestructible, *adj.* indestructible
Indeterminable, *adj.* indéterminable [vague
Indeterminate, *adj.* indéterminé; indécis;

Indeterminately, *adv.* indéterminément; vaguement
Indeterminateness, Indetermination, *s.* nature indéterminée, indétermination, *f.*; [indécision, *f.*
Indevotion, *s.* indévotion, *f.*
Indevout, *adj.* indévot
Indevoutly, *adv.* indévotement
Index, *s.* indice, *m.*; (*guide, pointing hand*) indicateur, *m.*; (*of books*) table des matières, *f.*, index, *m.*; (*of a ledger*, &c.) répertoire, *m.*; (*of a dial*, &c.) aiguille, *f.*; (*forefinger*) index, doigt indicateur, *m.*; (*Pope's list*) index, *m.*; (*math.*) exposant, *m.* — **hand,** *s.* indicateur, *m.* — **plate,** *s.* indicateur, *m.*
Indexterity, *s.* indextérité, maladresse, *f.*
India, *s.* l'Inde, *f.*; les Indes, *f.pl.* —**man,** *s.* navire des Indes, *m.* — **paper,** *s.* papier de Chine, *m.* — **pickles,** *s. pl.* achars, *m.pl.* — —**rubber,** *s.* caoutchouc, *m.*, gomme élastique, *f.*; élastique, *m.* —**rubber ball,** *s.* balle élastique, *f.* —**rubber band,** *s.* bande élastique, *f.*, élastique, *m.*
Indian, *adj.* indien, de l'Inde, des Indes; — *s.* Indien, *m.*, -ne, *f.* *West* —, (*adj.*) des Indes Occidentales, de l'Amérique; (*s.*) créole, *m.f.* — **berry,** *s.* coque du Levant, *f.* — **corn,** *s.* blé de Turquie, maïs, *m.* — **corn meal,** *s.* farine de maïs, *f.* — **ink,** *s.* encre de Chine, *f.* — **meal,** *s.* farine de maïs, *f.* — **paper,** *s.* papier de Chine, *m.* — **pepper,** *s.* poivre d'Inde, *m.* — **potato,** *s.* igname, *f.* — **tobacco,** *s.* lobélie, *f.*
Indian-ism, -ist, -ology. *V.* p. 3, § 1
Indicate, *v.a.* indiquer; marquer; désigner; montrer
Indicating, *adj.* indicateur; — *s.* indication, *f.*
Indication, *s.* indication, *f.*; marque, *f.*, signe, *m.*; (*information*) indice, renseignement, *m.*
Indicative, *adj. s.* indicatif, *adj. m.*, -ive, *f.*, qui indique, indicatif, *s.m.* —*mood*, indicatif, *m.* *In the* —, à l'indicatif. *To be* — *of*, indiquer.
Indicator, *s.* (*pers., bird*) indicateur, *m.*; (*things*) indice, *m.*; (*tech.*) indicateur, *m.*; compteur, *m.*
Indicatory, *adj.* indicateur, qui indique. *To be of* —, indiquer
Indict, *v.a.* (*civ. law*) poursuivre, attaquer; (*crim. law*) traduire, mettre en accusation ('*for*,' pour crime *or* cause de)
Indictable, *adj.* (*pers.*) qui peut être mis en accusation; (*things*) qualifié crime ou délit
Indicter, *s.* accusateur, *m.*, -trice, *f.*, poursuivant, *m.*, e, *f.*
Indiction, *s.* indiction, *f.*
Indictment, *s.* mise en accusation, *f.*; (*bill*) acte d'accusation, *m.*; (*charge*) accusation, *f.*; plainte, *f.*
Indifference, *s.* indifférence, *f*; impartialité, *f.*
Indifferent, *adj.* indifférent; impartial; (*middling*) médiocre, assez mauvais
Indifferentism, *s.* indifférentisme, *m.*
Indifferentist, *s. adj.* indifférentiste, *m.f.*
Indifferently, *adv.* indifféremment; médiocrement, assez mal, pas trop bien, doucement
Indigence, *s.* indigence, *f.*
Indigenous, *adj.* indigène
Indigent, *adj.* indigent
Indigest, Indigested, *adj.* *V.* **Undigested**
Indigesti-bility, bleness. *V.* page 3, § 1
Indigestible, *adj.* indigeste, indigestible
Indigestion, *s.* indigestion, *f.*
Indignant, *adj.* indigné (de); d'indignation; plein d'indignation; irrité. *To make* or *render* —, indigner
Indignantly, *adv.* avec indignation
Indignation, *s.* indignation, *f.*; courroux, *m.*
Indignity, *s.* indignité, *f.*; affront, outrage, *m.*
Indigo, *s.* indigo, *m.* —**blue,** *s.* bleu d'indigo, *m.* — **factory, -manufactory,** *s.* indigoterie, *f.* —**manufacturer,** *s.* indigotier, *m.* — **plant, -tree,** *s.* indigotier, indigo, *m.* — **plantation,** *s.* indigoterie, *f.*
Indigoferous, *adj.* indigofère
Indigotic, *adj.* indigotique
Indigotine, *s.* indigotine

Indiligence, *s.* indiligence, *f.*
Indiligent, *adj.* indiligent
Indiligently, *adv.* indiligemment
Indirect, *adj.* indirect; (*fig.*) indirect, détourné oblique; (*unfair*) déloyal, insidieux
Indirection, *s.* indirection, *f.*
Indirectly, *adv.* indirectement; (*unfairly*) déloyalement
Indirectness, *s.* nature indirecte, *f.*, détours, *m.pl.*; obliquité, *f.*; (*unfairness*) déloyauté, *f.*
Indiscerni-bility, bleness, *s.* indiscernabilité, *f.*
Indiscernible, *adj.* indiscernable
Indiscernibly, *adv.* indiscernablement
Indisciplinable, *adj.* indisciplinable
Indiscipline, *s.* indiscipline, *f.*
Indiscoverable, *adj.* qui ne peut se découvrir
Indiscreet, *adj.* indiscret, imprudent, inconsidéré
Indiscreetly, *adv.* indiscrètement, imprudemment, inconsidérément
Indiscretion, *s.* indiscrétion, inconséquence, imprudence, *f.*
Indiscriminate, *adj.* qui ne fait pas de distinction, peu éclairé, aveugle, quand même confus; indistinct
Indiscriminately, *adv.* sans distinction, indistinctement, indifféremment, également; aveuglément, quand même
Indiscriminating, *adj.* qui ne fait pas de distinction, peu éclairé, aveugle
Indiscrimination, *s.* défaut de distinction, *m.*
Indispensa-bility, bleness. *V.* page 3, § 1
Indispensable, *adj.* indispensable
Indispensably, *adv.* indispensablement
Indisposable, *adj.* indisponible
Indisposableness, *s.* indisponibilité, *f.*
Indispose, *v.a.* indisposer; éloigner (de); incommoder, déranger
Indisposed, *part. adj.* indisposé, &c. (*V.* **Indispose**); contraire. *Not to be* — *to* ..., être assez disposé à ...
Indisposedness, Indisposition, *s.* indisposition, *f.*; dérangement, *m.*; (*aversion*) éloignement, *m.*; répugnance, *f.*
Indisputable, *adj.* indisputable, incontestable, indiscutable
Indisputableness, *s.* indisputabilité, incontestabilité, *f.*
Indisputably, *adv.* indisputablement, incontestablement, indiscutablement, sans contredit
Indissolu-bility, bleness. *V.* page 3, § 1
Indissoluble, *adj.* indissoluble
Indissolubly, *adv.* indissolublement
Indissolvable. *V.* **Indissoluble**
Indistinct, *adj.* indistinct; confus
Indistinction, *s.* *V.* **Indistinctness**
Indistinctly, *adv.* indistinctement; confusément
Indistinctness, *s.* indistinction, confusion, *f.*, défaut de distinction, défaut de netteté, *m.*
Indistinguishable. *V.* **Undistinguishable**
Indite, *v.a.* rédiger, composer; dicter
Inditement, *s.* rédaction, composition, *f.*; dictée, *f.*
Individual, *adj.* individuel; (*only*) seul, unique; — *s.* individu, *m.*; particulier, *m.*; personne, *f.*
Individual-ism, -ist. *V.* p. 3, § 1
Individualistic, *adj.* individualiste
Individuality, *s.* individualité, *f.*
Individualization, *s.* individualisation, *f.*
Individualize, *v.a.* individualiser
Individually, *adv.* individuellement; isolément; séparément
Individuate, *v.a.* individuer
Individuation, *s.* individuation, *f.*
Indivinity, *s.* indivinité, *f.*
Indivisi-bility, bleness. *V.* page 3, § 1
Indivisible, *adj.* indivisible
Indivisibly, *adv.* indivisiblement
Indo-, (*in compounds*) Indo- ...
Indocile, *adj.* indocile
Indocilely, *adv.* indocilement
Indocility, *s.* indocilité, *f.*
Indoctrinate, *v.a.* endoctriner, instruire
Indoctrination, *s.* endoctrinement, *m.*, instruction, *f.*
Indolence, *s.* indolence, *f.*
Indolent, *adj.* indolent

Indolently, *adv.* indolemment, avec indolence
Indomitable, *adj.* indomptable
Indomitableness, *s.* indomptabilité, *f.*
Indomitably, *adv.* indomptablement
Indoor. *V.* **Door.** — *and outdoor games,* jeux de société et de jardin, *m.pl.*
Indorse, &c. *V.* **Endorse,** &c.
Indubitable, *adj.* indubitable
Indubitably, *adv.* indubitablement
Induce, *v a.* porter, décider, engager, inviter; induire; (*to cause*) causer, amener; produire; déterminer, provoquer. *To — the belief,* porter à croire, faire croire, donner lieu de penser. *To — the hope,* donner l'espoir, faire espérer, donner lieu d'espérer [tentation, *f.*
Inducement, *s.* encouragement, motif, *m.*;
Inducible, *adj.* qui peut être induit *or* &c. (*V.* **Induce**)
Induct, *v.a.* installer, établir, introduire
Inductile, *adj.* inductile
Inductility, *s.* inductilité, *f.*
Induction, *s.* induction, *f.*; installation, *f.*; prise de possession, *f.*
Inductive, *adj.* inductif; par induction. — *sciences,* sciences physiques et naturelles, *f.pl.*
Inductively, *adv.* inductivement, par induction
Inductor, *s.* installateur, *m.*
Indue, *v.a.* revêtir (de); (*endow*) douer (de)
Indulge, *v.a.n.* être indulgent envers; permettre; accorder; favoriser; satisfaire; contenter; avoir trop d'indulgence pour. ne refuser rien à, être trop bon envers; flatter; caresser, câliner; (*oneself*) s'abandonner (à), se livrer (à), se laisser aller (à); se permettre (...); (*take o.'s ease*) prendre ses aises; s'écouter trop; se dorloter; s'oublier. *To — a hope,* se bercer d'un espoir, concevoir *or* avoir une espérance; se flatter d'un espoir, se flatter
Indulgence, *s.* indulgence, *f.*; complaisance, *f.*; abandon, *m.*; mollesse, *f.*; faveur, *f.*; facilité, *f.*; douceur, *f.*; plaisir, *m.*; (*Cath. rel.*) indulgence, *f.*; — *v.a.* indulgencier
Indulgent, *adj.* indulgent; complaisant; facile; qui s'abandonne (à), qui se livre (à); doux [dulgence; avec douceur
Indulgently, *adv.* indulgemment, avec in-
Indurate, *v.a.* indurer, durcir; (*fig.*) endurcir; — *v.n.* s'indurer, durcir; (*fig.*) s'endurcir
Induration, *s.* induration, *f.*; durcissement, *m.*; (*fig.*) endurcissement, *m.*
Indusial, *adj.* — *limestone,* calcaire à induses, *m.*
Indusium, *s.* induse, indusie, *f.*
Industrial, *adj.* industriel; de l'industrie; — *s.* industriel, *m.* — *exhibition,* exposition de
Industrial-ism, -ist. *V.* p.3, § 1 [l'industrie, *f.*
Industrialistic, *adj.* industrialiste
Industrially, *adv.* industriellement
Industrious, *adj.* laborieux; travailleur; diligent, actif, industrieux; assidu; zélé; (*eager*) empressé
Industriously, *adv.* laborieusement; diligemment; activement; assidûment; soigneusement, avec soin
Industry, *s.* travail, *m.*; application, assiduité, *f.*; activité, *f.*; zèle, *m.*; (*eagerness*) empressement, *m.*; (*arts and manu.*) industrie, *f.*
Indweller, *s.* habitant, *m.*, e, *f.*
Indwelling, *adj.* intérieur
Inebriate, &c. *V.* **Intoxicate,** &c.; — *adj.* ivre; — *s.* ivrogne, *m.*, ivrognesse, *f.*
Inedited, *adj.* inédit
Ineffable, &c. *V.* **Unspeakable,** &c.
Ineffaceable, *adj.* ineffaçable, indélébile
Ineffaceably, *adv.* ineffaçablement
Ineffective, Ineffectual, *adj.* inefficace, ineffectif, sans effet, vain, inutile
Ineffectively, Ineffectually, *adv.* inefficacement, sans efficacité, sans effet, en vain, inutilement [efficacité, *f.*
Ineffectiveness, Ineffectualness, *s.* in-
Inefficacious, *adj.* inefficace
Inefficaciously, *adv.* *V.* **Ineffectually**
Inefficaciousness, Inefficacy, Inefficiency, *s.* inefficacité, *f.*; (*pers.*) incapacité, *f.*
Inefficient, *adj.* inefficace; impuissant; insuffisant, (*pers.*) incapable
Inefficiently, *adv.* *V.* **Ineffectually**
Inelastic, *adj.* inélastique
Inelasticity, *s.* inélasticité, *f.*
Inelegance, *s.* inélégance, *f.*
Inelegant, *adj.* inélégant, sans élégance; sans goût, commun, grossier
Inelegantly, *adv.* inélégamment, sans élégance
Ineligibility, *s.* inéligibilité, *f.*; (*of choice*) inconvenance, *f.*; désavantage, *m.*
Ineligible, *adj.* inéligible; (*not suitable*) peu convenable; désavantageux
Ineloquent, *adj.* inéloquent, indisert
Ineloquently, *adv.* inéloquemment. indisertement [inconvenant
Inept, *adj.* inepte, sot, absurde; (*of things*)
Ineptitude, Ineptness, *s.* ineptie, inaptitude, *f.* [ment
Ineptly, *adv.* ineptement, avec ineptie, sotte-
Inequality, *s.* inégalité, *f.*; disproportion, disparité, *f.*; insuffisance, *f.*
Inequiangular, *adj.* inéquiangle
Inequilateral, *adj.* inéquilatéral, inéquilatère
Inequitable, *adj.* inéquitable
Inequitably, *adv.* inéquitablement
Ineradicable, *adj.* indéracinable, inextirpable, indestructible
Inerm, Inermous, *adj.* inerme
Inerrable, &c. *V.* **Infallible,** &c.
Inert, *adj.* inerte
Inertia, Inertion, Inertitude, *s.* inertie, *f.*
Inertly, *adv.* d'une manière inerte, inertement
Inertness, *s.* inertie, *f.*
Inerudite, *adj.* inérudit
Inerudition, *s.* inérudition, *f.*
In esse, *adj.* positif, réel
Inestimable, *adj.* inestimable; incalculable
Inestimably, *adv.* d'une manière inestimable; incalculablement
Inevidence, *s.* inévidence, *f.*
Inevident, *adj.* inévident
Inevitable, &c. *V.* **Unavoidable,** &c.
Inexact, *adj.* inexact
Inexactitude, *s.* inexactitude, *f.*
Inexactly, *adv.* inexactement
Inexactness, *s.* inexactitude, *f.*
Inexcitability, *s.* inexcitabilité, *f.*
Inexcitable, *adj.* inexcitable
Inexcusable, *adj.* inexcusable
Inexcusableness, *s.* nature inexcusable, *f.*; tort inexcusable, *m.*
Inexcusably, *adv.* inexcusablement, d'une manière inexcusable, sans excuse
Inexecutable, *adj.* inexécutable
Inexecution, *s.* inexécution, *f.*
Inexhausted, *adj.* inépuisé
Inexhaustible, *adj.* inépuisable, intarissable
Inexhaustibleness, Inexhaustibility, *s.* nature inépuisable, *f.* [tarissablement
Inexhaustibly, *adv.* inépuisablement, in-
Inexigibility, *s.* inexigibilité, *f.*
Inexigible, *adj.* inexigible
Inexistence, *s.* inexistence, *f.*
Inexistent, *adj.* inexistant
Inexora-bility, bleness. *V.* page 3, § 1
Inexorable, *adj.* inexorable impitoyable
Inexorably, *adv.* inexorablement, impitoyablement [d'à-propos, *m.*
Inexpedienc-e, y, *s.* inopportunité, *f.*, défaut
Inexpedient, *adj.* inopportun, mal à propos
Inexpediently, *adv.* mal à propos, inopportunément [coûteux, pas cher, bon marché
Inexpensive, *adj.* peu dispendieux, peu
Inexpensively, *adv.* à peu de frais, à bon
Inexperience, *s.* inexpérience, *f.* [marché
Inexperienced, *adj.* inexpérimenté, sans expérience
Inexpert, *adj.* (*not skilled*) inexpert, inhabile, maladroit; (*without experience*) inexpérimenté

Inexpiable, *adj.* inexpiable
Inexplica-bility, bleness. *V.* page 3, § 1
Inexplicable, *adj.* inexplicable
Inexplicably, *adv.* inexplicablement
Inexplicit, *adj.* inexplicite
Inexplicitly, *adv.* inexplicitement
Inexplorable, *adj* inexplorable
Inexplosive, *adj.* inexplosif; inexplosible
Inexplosiveness, *s.* inexplosibilité, *f.*
Inexpressible, &c. *V.* **Unspeakable,** &c.; **—s,** *s. pl.* (*trousers*) inexpressible, *m.*
Inexpressive, *adj.* inexpressif, sans expression
Inexpressively, *adv.* d'une manière inexpressive, sans expression
Inexpressiveness, *s.* nature inexpressive, *f.*, défaut d'expression, *m.*
Inexpugnable, *adj.* inexpugnable
Inextendible, *adj.* inextensible
Inextensi-bility, bleness. *V.* page 3, § 1
Inextensible, *adj.* inextensible
Inextension, *s.* défaut d'étendue, *m.*
Inextinct, *adj.* non éteint
Inextinguishable, *adj.* inextinguible
Inextinguishableness, *s.* inextinguibilité, *f.*
Inextirpable, *adj.* inextirpable
Inextricable, *adj.* inextricable; indébrouillable
Inextricableness, *s.* inextricabilité, *f.*
Inextricably, *adv.* inextricablement
Ineye, *v.a.* greffer en écusson
Infallibility, Infallibleness, *s.* infaillibilité, *f.*
Infallible, *adj.* infaillible; immanquable, sûr
Infallibly, *adv.* infailliblement; immanquablement
Infamous, *adj.* infâme; indigne; (*law*) infamant
Infamously, *adv.* d'une manière infâme, avec infamie; indignement; horriblement, affreusement
Infamousness, Infamy, *s.* infamie, *f.*
Infancy, *s.* enfance, *f.*; (*law*) minorité, *f.*
Infant, *s.* enfant, *m.f.*; (*law*) mineur, *m.*, e, *f.*; — *adj.* en bas âge; petit; naissant. — **asylum, -home,** *s.* crèche, garderie, *f.* — **like,** *adj.* *V.* **Infantine.** — **school,** *s.* *V.* [School
Infanta, *s.* infante, *f.*
Infante, *s.* infant, *m.*
Infanticidal, *adj.* infanticide
Infanticide, *s.* infanticide, (*pers.*) *m.f.*, (*murder*) *m.*
Infantile, Infantine, Infantly, *adj.* enfantin, d'enfant, des enfants, de l'enfance; (*fig.*) premier, naissant
Infantry, *s.* infanterie, *f.*; — *adj.* d'infanterie. — **barracks,** *s. pl.* caserne d'infanterie, *f.* — **man,** *s.* fantassin, soldat d'infanterie, *m.* — **officer,** *s.* officier d'infanterie, *m.*
Infatuate, *v.a.* infatuer (de), engouer (de), entêter (de); tourner la tête à, rendre fou, affoler, enivrer. *To become —d with,* s'engouer de, s'enticher de, s'infatuer de
Infatuation, *s.* folie, *f.*, vertige, enivrement, *m.*; engouement, *m.*, infatuation, *f.*
Infeasi-bility, bleness, *s.* impraticabilité, *f.*
Infeasible, *adj.* infaisable, impraticable
Infect, *v.a.* infecter ('*with,*' de), empester; gâter, corrompre
Infecter, *s.* infecteur, *m.*, -trice, *f.*, personne *or* chose qui infecte, *f.*; corrupteur, *m.*, -trice, *f.*
Infection, *s.* infection, *f.*; (*fig.*) contagion, corruption, *f.*
Infectionist, *s.* infectioniste, *m.*
Infectious, *adj.* infect; infectant; pestilentiel; contagieux; corrupteur; (*med.*) infectieux
Infectiously, *adv.* par infection; (*fig.*) par contagion
Infectiousness, *s.* *V.* **Infection**
Infective. *V.* **Infectious**
Infecund, *adj.* infécond, stérile
Infecundity, *s.* infécondité, stérilité, *f.*
Infelicitous, *adj.* malheureux
Infelicity, *s.* infélicité, *f.*, malheur, *m.*, infortune, *f.*
Infer, *v.a.* inférer, conclure, déduire; supposer
Inferable, *adj.* qu'on peut inférer, qui peut se déduire
Inference, *s.* conséquence, *f.*; conclusion, *f.*; déduction, *f.*
Inferential, *adj.* déductif
Inferentially, *adv.* déductivement, par déduction
Inferior, *adj. s.* inférieur, *m.*, e, *f.*
Inferiority, *s.* infériorité, *f.*
Inferiorly, *adv.* inférieurement
Infermentescibility, infermentescibilité, *f.*
Infermentescible, *adj.* infermentescible
Infernal, *adj.* infernal, de l'enfer, d'enfer; — *s.* habitant (*m.*, e, *f.*) de l'enfer
Infernally, *adv.* infernalement, furieusement, abominablement, atrocement
Infertile, *adj.* infertile, stérile
Infertilely, *adv.* infertilement, stérilement
Infertility, *s.* infertilité, *f.*
Infertilizable, *adj.* infertilisable
Infest, *v.a.* infester; tourmenter, incommoder
Infestation, *s.* infestation, *f.*
Infeudation, *s.* inféodation, *f.*
Infibulate, *v.a.* infibuler
Infibulation, *s.* infibulation, *f.*
Infidel, *adj. s.* infidèle, *m.f.*; (*deist*) incrédule, impie, *m.f.*
Infidelity, *s.* infidélité; (*unbelief*) incrédulité, *f.*
Infilter, Infiltrate, *v.a.* infiltrer; — *v.n.* s'infiltrer
Infiltration, *s.* infiltration, *f.*
Infinite, *adj. s.* infini, *adj. m.*, e, *f.*, infini, *s.m.*
Infinitely, *adv.* infiniment; à l'infini
Infiniteness. *V.* **Infinitude**
Infinitesimal, *adj.* infinitésimal, infiniment petit; —*s.* infiniment petit, *m.* — *calculus,* calcul infinitésimal, calcul des infiniment petits, *m.*
Infinitive, *adj. s.* infinitif, *m.* — *mood,* infinitif, *m.* *In the —,* à l'infinitif
Infinitude, Infinity, *s.* infinité, *f.*; immensité, *f.*
Infirm, *adj.* infirme; (*weak*) faible, débile. — *state,* état d'infirmité, *m.*; faiblesse, *f.*
Infirmarian, *s.* infirmier, *m.*, -ière, *f.*
Infirmary, *s.* infirmerie, *f.*
Infirmity, Infirmness, *s.* infirmité, *f.*; (*weakness*) faiblesse, *f.*; (*weak point*) faible, défaut, *m.*
Infirmly, *adv.* faiblement, débilement
Infix, *v.a.* fixer, infixer, enfoncer, planter; (*fig.*) fixer, graver, imprimer, inculquer
Inflame, *v.a.* enflammer; allumer; irriter; exciter; exagérer, grossir, aggraver; — *v.n.* s'enflammer
Inflamma-bility, bleness. *V.* page 3, § 1
Inflammable, *adj.* inflammable
Inflammation, *s.* inflammation, *f.* — *of the lungs* or *of the chest,* fluxion de poitrine, *f.*
Inflammatory, *adj.* inflammatoire; (*of speeches,* &c.) incendiaire (*style*) boursouflé
Inflate, *v.a.* ('*with*', de) gonfler, enfler; (*o.'s style*) boursoufler
Inflation, *s.* gonflement, *m.*, enflure, *f.*
Inflect, *v.a.* fléchir; (*gram.*) (*a noun*) décliner, (*a verb*) conjuguer; (*the voice*) moduler
Inflection, Inflexion, *s.* inflexion, *f.*
Inflexed, *adj.* inflexe
Inflexi-bility, bleness. *V.* page 3, § 1
Inflexible, *adj.* inflexible
Inflexibly, *adv.* inflexiblement
Inflexuous, *adj.* inflexueux
Inflict, *v.a.* infliger ('*on,*' à); imposer (à); faire (à), causer (à), occasionner (à)
Inflicter, *s.* personne qui inflige, *f.*; auteur, *m.*
Infliction, *s.* infliction, *f.*; (*punishment*) peine, *f.*, châtiment, *m.*
Inflictive, *adj.* inflictif
Inflorescence, *s.* inflorescence, *f.*
Influence, *s.* influence ('*over,*' '*with,*' sur), *f.*; — *v.a.* influer sur; (*induce*) influencer; porter (à), entraîner (à). *Undue —,* (*law*) captation, *f.* *To exercise undue — over,* (*law*) capter
Influential, *adj.* influent
Influentially, *adv.* avec influence
Influenza, *s.* grippe, influenza, *f.*
Influx, *s.* influx, *m.*; affluence, abondance, *f.*
Influxion, *s.* influxion, *f.*
Infold, *v.a.* envelopper; entourer
Inform, *v.a.n.* informer, instruire, avertir, apprendre à faire savoir à, faire connaître à, renseigner; (*instruct*) instruire, éclairer; (*ani-*

mate) animer, informer; (*against*) dénoncer, accuser [règle; (*unusual*) insolite
Informal, *adj.* informe, irrégulier, non en
Informality, *s.* vice de forme, *m.*
Informally, *adv.* sans les formalités requises (*or* voulues), irrégulièrement
Informant, *s.* informateur, *m.*, -trice, *f.*; garant, *m.*, e, *f.*; auteur, correspondant, *m.*, e, *f.*; (*law*) dénonciateur, *m.*, -trice, *f.*
Information, *s.* avis, *m.*; nouvelle, *f.*, nouvelles, *f.pl.*; renseignement, *m.*, renseignements, *m.pl.*; information, *f.*; instruction, *f.*; connaissances, *f.pl.*; (*law*) dénonciation, délation, *f.*; révélation, *f.*; (*charge*) plainte, accusation, *f.*; procès-verbal, *m.*; (*inquest*) enquête, *f.*; (*proceedings*) poursuites, *f.pl.* *To lodge an — against,* dénoncer; porter plainte contre
Informer, *s.* informateur, *m.*, -trice, *f.*, dénonciateur, *m.*, -trice, *f.*, délateur, *m.*, -trice, *f.*, révélateur, *m.*, -trice, *f.*
Infraction, *s.* infraction, violation, transgression, *f.*; contravention, *f.*
Infractor. *V.* **Infringer**
Infrangi-bility, bleness. *V.* page 3 § 1
Infrangible, *adj.* infrangible
Infrequenc-e, y, *s.* infréquence, rareté, *f.*
Infrequent, -ly. *V.* **Unfrequent, -ly**
Infringe, *v.a.* enfreindre, transgresser, violer; (*counterfeit*) contrefaire; —*v.n.* (*on*) empiéter (sur), porter atteinte (à)
Infringement, *s.* infraction, transgression, violation, *f.*; (*encroachment*) empiètement, *m.*; atteinte (à), *f.*; (*of a patent*) contrefaçon, *f.*
Infringer, *s.* infracteur, *m.*, -trice, *f.*; violateur, *m.*, -trice, *f.*; transgresseur, *m.*; contrevenant, *m.*, e, *f.*; (*counterfeiter*) contrefacteur, *m.*
Infundibular, Infundibulate, Infundibuliform, *adj.* infundibulé, infundibuliforme
Infuriate, *v.a.* rendre furieux, mettre en fureur
Infuriate, Infuriated, *adj.* furieux, en fureur, furibond
Infuse, *v.a.* infuser, faire infuser; (*pour in*) verser; (*instil*) inspirer (à), inculquer (à), communiquer (à); (*introduce*) introduire, faire entrer; — *v.n.* infuser, s'infuser
Infusibility, *s.* infusibilité, *f.*
Infusible, *adj.* infusible; (*fig.*) qui peut être communiqué *or* inspiré *or* inculqué; qu'on peut introduire *or* faire entrer
Infusion, *s.* infusion, *f.*; introduction, *f.*; inspiration, *f.*; suggestion, *f.*
Infusoria, *s.pl.* infusoires, *m.pl.*
Infusorial, *adj.* infusoire
Infusory, *adj. s.* infusoire, *adj. m.f.*, *s.m.*
Ingathering, *s.* rentrée (de la moisson), *f.*
Ingenious, *adj.* ingénieux; (*witty*) spirituel; (*learned*) de talent, de mérite [spirituellement
Ingeniously, *adv.* ingénieusement; (*wittily*)
Ingeniousness, Ingenuity, *s.* ingéniosité, *f.*; habileté, *f.*, art, *m.*; combinaison, *f.*; (*genius*) esprit, génie, *m.*; talent, mérite, *m.*
Ingenuous, *adj.* ingénu, naïf, candide, généreux, noble; (*of birth*) honorable, de bonne famille
Ingenuously, *adv.* ingénument, naïvement
Ingenuousness, *s.* ingénuité, naïveté, can-
Ingest, *v.a.* ingérer [deur, *f.*
Ingesta, *s.pl.* ingesta, *m.pl.*
Ingestion, *s.* ingestion, *f.*
Inglorious, *adj.* inglorieux, sans gloire; (*disgraceful*) honteux, déshonorant
Ingloriously, *adv.* inglorieusement, sans gloire; (*dishonourably*) honteusement, ignominieusement
Ingloriousness, *s.* absence de gloire *or* d'éclat, *f.*; obscurité, bassesse, *f.*
Ingoer, *s.* entrant, *m.*
Ingoing, *s.* entrée, *f.*; — *adj.* entrant; nouveau
Ingot, *s.* lingot, *m.* — **mould,** *s.* lingotière, *f.*
Ingraft, *v.a.* greffer, enter; (*fix*) graver, im-
Ingraftment, *s.* greffe, ente, *f.* [primer

Ingrail, &c. *V.* **Engrail,** &c.
Ingrained, *adj.* enraciné, invétéré
Ingratiate oneself (with), *v.r.* se concilier la faveur (de), gagner (*or* s'insinuer dans) les bonnes grâces (de), se mettre bien dans l'esprit (de), se faire bien venir (de)
Ingratitude, *s.* ingratitude, *f.*
Ingredient, *s.* ingrédient, *m.*
Ingress, *s.* entrée, *f.*
Ingrowing, *adj.* (*of nails*) incarné; — *s.* incarnation, *f.* — **nail,** *s.* ongle incarné, *m.*,
Inguinal, *adj.* inguinal [onglade, onyxis, *f.*
Ingulf, *v.a.* engouffrer, engloutir [gurgiter
Ingurgitate, *v.a.* ingurgiter; — *v.n.* s'in-
Ingurgitation, *s.* ingurgitation, *f.*
Inhabit, *v.a.* habiter, habiter dans
Inhabitable, *adj.* habitable
Inhabitant, *s.* habitant, *m.*, e, *f.*; (*poet.*) hôte, *m.*; (*law*) personne domiciliée, *f.*
Inhabitativeness, Inhabitiveness, *s.* habitativité, *f.*
Inhalation, *s.* inhalation, inspiration, *f.*
Inhale, *v.a.* inhaler, aspirer, respirer
Inharmon-ic, al, -ically, -y. *V.* p. 3, § 1
Inharmonious, *adj.* inharmonieux, sans harmonie [sans harmonie
Inharmoniously, *adv.* inharmonieusement,
Inharmoniousness, *s.* inharmonie, *f.*, défaut d'harmonie, *m.* [tenir (à)
Inhere, *v.n.* s'attacher (à), être inhérent (à),
Inherenc-e, y, *s.* inhérence, *f.*
Inherent, *adj.* inhérent (à)
Inherently, *adv.* par *or* avec inhérence, d'une manière inhérente
Inherit, *v.a.* hériter de, hériter; — *v.n.* hériter, recueillir un héritage, recueillir une succession. *To — some property,* faire un héritage
Inheritable, *adj.* héritable
Inheritance, *s.* héritage, *m.*, succession, *f.*; patrimoine, *m.*; hérédité, *f.* [-ière, *f.*
Inherit-or, ress, *or* **rix,** *s.* héritier, *m.*,
Inhesion, *s.* inhérence, *f.*
Inhibit, *v.a.* empêcher, arrêter; (*forbid*) défendre, prohiber, interdire [interdiction, *f.*
Inhibition, *s.* défense, prohibition, inhibition,
Inhibitory, *adj.* inhibitoire
Inhospitable, *adj.* inhospitalier
Inhospitableness, *s.* inhospitalité, *f.*
Inhospitably, *adv.* inhospitalièrement
Inhospitality *s.* inhospitalité, *f.*
Inhuman, *adj.* inhumain
Inhumanity, *s.* inhumanité, *f.*
Inhumanly, *adv.* inhumainement
Inhumation, *s.* inhumation, *f.*, enterrement, *m.*
Inhume, *v.a.* inhumer, enterrer
Inia, *s.* (*zool.*) inie, *f.*
Inimical, *adj.* ennemi, hostile
Inimically, *adv.* hostilement, en ennemi
Inimita-bility, bleness, *s.* inimitabilité, *f.*
Inimitable, *adj.* inimitable
Inimitably, *adv.* inimitablement
Iniquitous, *adj.* inique
Iniquity, *s.* iniquité, *f.*
Initial, *adj. s.* initial, *adj. m.*, e, *f.*, initiale, *s.f.*; — **s,** *s.pl.* initiales, *f.pl.*; (*signature*) parafe, *m.*; — *v.a.* mettre ses initiales à; (*to sign*)
Initially, *adv.* initialement [parafer
Initiate, *v.a.* initier; — *s.* initié, *m.*, e, *f.*
Initiation, *s.* initiation, *f.*
Initiative, *adj.* initiatif, initiateur, d'initiation; — *s.* initiative, *f.*
Initiatory, *adj.* *V.* **Initiative**
Inject, *v.a.* injecter; seringuer
Injection, *s.* injection, *f.*; (*enema*) lavement, *m.*, (*jest.*) clystère, *m.* — **apparatus,** *s.* irrigateur, clysopompe, *m.* — **pipe,** *s.* canule, *f.*; (*tech.*) tuyau d'injection, *m.* — **tube,** *s.* clysoir, *m.*
Injector, *s.* injecteur, *m.* [imprudent
Injudicious, *adj.* injudicieux, peu judicieux;
Injudiciously, *adv.* injudicieusement, peu judicieusement, imprudemment

Injudiciousness, *s.* nature injudicieuse, *f.*, défaut de jugement, *m.* [sursis, *m.*
Injunction, *s.* injonction, *f.*; (*law*) arrêt de
Injure, *v.a.* *V.* **Hurt,** *v.a.*
Injurer, *s.* personne qui nuit *or* qui offense *or* &c., *f.*; auteur d'un tort, *m.*
Injurious, *adj.* nuisible (à), qui fait tort (à), préjudiciable (à); (*offensive*) injurieux, offensant, outrageant; (*hurting*) qui fait mal (à)
Injuriously, *adv.* nuisiblement, d'une manière nuisible; pernicieusement; injustement, à tort; injurieusement, outrageusement
Injuriousness, *s.* nature nuisible, *f.*; effets nuisibles, *m.pl.*; injustice, *f.*
Injury, *s.* injure, *f.*, tort, mal, *m.*; préjudice, *m.*; outrage, *m.*, offense, *f.*; injustice, *f.*; (*wound*) mal, *m.*, blessure, *f.*; (*damage*) dommage, *m.*; dégât, *m.*; (*med.*) lésion, *f.*; (*nav.*) avaries, *f.pl.*
Injustice, *s.* injustice, *f.*; (*offence*) injure, *f.*
Ink, *s.* encre, *f.*; — *v.a.* tacher *or* barbouiller d'encre; (*print.*) encrer, toucher. *In blue, red* —, à l'encre bleue, rouge. — **bottle,** *s.* bouteille à encre (*or* à l'encre), *f.*; encrier, *m.* — **box,** *s.* encrier, *m.* — **case,** *s.* écritoire, *f.* — **glass, -horn,** *s.* encrier, *m.* — **maker, -manufacturer,** *s.* fabricant d'encre, *m.* — **stand,** *s.* encrier, *m.*, écritoire, *f.* — **trough,** [*s.* encrier, *m.*
Inkiness, *s.* noirceur d'encre, *f.*
Inking-pad, *s.* tampon à impression, *m.*
Inkling, *s.* avis, vent, *m.*; désir, *m.*, envie, *f.*
Inky, *adj.* d'encre; (*spotted*) taché d'encre; (*black*) noir comme de l'encre
Inlaid, *adj.* marqueté; incrusté. —*floor*, parquet, *m.* — *flooring*, parqueterie, *f.*; parquetage, *m.* — *work*, marqueterie, *f.*; incrustation, *f.*
Inland, *adj.* de l'intérieur; intérieur; — *adv.* à l'intérieur; dans l'intérieur, dans l'intérieur des terres *or* du pays; — *s.* intérieur, *m.* — *bill*, (*com.*) lettre de change sur l'intérieur, *f.*
Inlay, *v.a.* marqueter; (*of stone*) incruster (de); (*scatter*) parsemer (de); — *s.* marqueterie, *f.*; incrustation, *f.*; (*in clothes*) élargissure, *f.*
Inlayer, *s.* (*cabinet* —) marqueteur, *m.*; (*floor-layer*) parqueteur, *m.*
Inlaying, *s.* marqueterie, *f.*; incrustation, *f.*
Inlet, *s.* entrée, *f.*, passage, *m.*; (*fig.*) voie, *f.*; (*nav.*) bras de mer, *m.*; petite baie, anse, *f.*; (*of harbours*) entrée, *f.*; goulet, *m.*; (*tech.*) conduite pour les eaux, *f.*, aqueduc, *m.* — **pipe,** *s.* tuyau d'entrée, *m.*
Inmate, *s.* habitant, *m.*, e, *f.*; (*lodger*) locataire, *m.f.*; (*boarder*) pensionnaire, *m.f.*; (*guest*) hôte, *m.*, hôtesse, *f.*; (*resident, indoor*) interne, *m.f.*
Inmost, (*adj.*) (le) plus intérieur; intime; (le) plus profond; (le) plus secret; (*remotest*) (le) plus reculé, (le) plus éloigné
Inn, *s.* auberge, hôtellerie, *f.*; (*block of buildings enclosed*) cité, *f.* — *of court*, collège d'avocats *or* de jurisconsultes, *m.*; école de droit, *f.* — **keeper,** *s.* aubergiste, *m.f.*, hô-
Innate, *adj.* inné, naturel [telier, *m.*, -ière, *f.*
Innately, *adv.* naturellement
Innateness, *s.* innéité, *f.*
Innavigability. *V.* page 3, § 1
Innavigable, *adj.* innavigable
Inner, *adj.* intérieur, du dedans; interne; [(*under*) de dessous
Innermost. *V.* **Inmost**
Innervable, *adj.* innervable
Innervate, *v.a.* innerver
Innervation, *s.* innervation, *f.*
Innerve, *v.a.* innerver; (*fig.*) donner du nerf à
Inning, *s.* (*of grain*) rentrée, *f.*; (*at cricket*) [tour, *m.*
Innocence, *s.* innocence, *f.*
Innocent, *adj.* innocent; (*lawful*) légitime, permis; — *s.* innocent, *m.*, e, *f.* —*s' day*, la fête des Innocents, *f.* [(*lawfully*) légitimement
Innocently, *adv.* innocemment; bonnement;
Innocuity, *s.* innocuité, *f.*
Innocuous, *adj.* innocent, inoffensif
Innocuously, *adv.* innocemment
Innocuousness, *s.* innocuité, *f.*
Innominable, *adj.* innommable
Innominate, *adj.* innominé
Innovate, *v.n.a.* innover
Innovation, *s.* innovation, *f.*
Innova-tor, tress, *s.* innovateur, *m.*, -trice, *f.*, novateur, *m.*, -trice, *f.*
Innoxious, &c. *V.* **Innocuous,** &c.
Innuendo, *s.* allusion, insinuation, *f.*
Innumera-bility, bleness, *s.* état innombrable, *m.*, quantité innombrable, *f.*
Innumerable, *adj.* innombrable
Innumerably, *adv.* innombrablement, sans [nombre
Innutritious, *adj.* innutritif
Inobedience, *s.* désobéissance, *f.*
Inobedient, *adj.* désobéissant
Inobservable, *adj.* inobservable
Inobservance, Inobservation, *s.* inobservation, *f.*
Inoccupation, *s.* inoccupation, *f.*
Inoculability. *V.* page 3, § 1
Inoculable, *adj.* inoculable [inoculer
Inoculate, *v.a.n.* (*hort.*) écussonner; (*med.*)
Inoculating, *adj.* inoculateur
Inoculation, *s.* (*hort.*) greffe en écusson, *f.*; (*med.*) inoculation, *f.* [(*med.*) inoculateur, *m.*
Inoculator, *s.* (*hort.*) greffeur en écusson, *m.*;
Inodorous, *adj.* inodore
Inodorousness, *s.* inodorité, *f.*
Inoffensive, *adj.* inoffensif; inoffensant
Inoffensively, *adv.* inoffensivement
Inoffensiveness, *s.* nature inoffensive, *f.*
Inofficial, *adj.* inofficiel
Inofficially, *adv.* inofficiellement
Inofficious, *adj.* inofficieux
Inofficiously, *adv.* inofficieusement
Inofficiousness, *s.* inofficiosité, *f.*
Inoperative, *adj.* inefficace, sans effet
Inopportune, *adj.* inopportun, mal à propos
Inopportunely, *adv.* inopportunément, mal à propos [portunité, *f.*
Inopportuneness, Inopportunity, *s.* inop-
Inordinacy, *s.* dérèglement, *m.*; désordre, *m.*; irrégularité, *f.*; excès, *m.*; intempérance, *f.*
Inordinate, *adj.* désordonné, déréglé, démesuré
Inordinately, *adv.* désordonnément, d'une manière désordonnée *or* déréglée, irrégulièrement; démesurément [**dinacy**
Inordinateness, Inordination. *V.* **Inor-**
Inorgan-ic, al, -ically. *V.* page 3, § 1
Inorganized. *V.* **Unorganized**
Inosculate, *v.a.* aboucher; unir; — *v.n.* s'aboucher, s'anastomoser; s'unir
Inosculation, *s.* inosculation, anastomose, *f.*, abouchement, *m.*
Inostensible, *adj.* inostensible
Inostensibly, *adv.* inostensiblement
Inoxidable, Inoxidizable, Inoxydiz- [**able,** *adj.* inoxydable
In posse, *adj.* éventuel
Inquest, *s.* enquête, *f.* *To hold an — on the body*, faire une enquête en présence du cadavre
Inquietude, *s.* inquiétude, *f.*
Inquirable, *adj.* dont on peut s'enquérir *or* s'informer; sujet à enquête
Inquire, *v.a.n.* s'informer (de), demander; (*into*) prendre des informations (sur); rechercher; examiner; s'enquérir (de); (*after*) demander des nouvelles (de); (*apply*) s'adresser ('*to*,' '*at*,' à; '*at* ...'*s*,' chez ...); (*law*) faire une enquête. *To — for* (*a pers.*), demander après, demander. *To send to — after one*, envoyer savoir des nouvelles de quelqu'un. — *within!* s'adresser ici
Inquirer, *s.* personne qui s'informe *or* qui demande, *f.*; (*fig.*) investigateur, *m.*, -trice, *f.*; examinateur, *m.*, -trice, *f.*; chercheur, *m.*, -euse, *f.*
Inquiring, *adj.* investigateur; scrutateur
Inquiringly, *adv.* d'un air scrutateur; sous forme d'interrogation
Inquiry, *s.* question, demande, *f.*; recherche,

investigation, *f.*; examen, *m.*; information, *f.*; (*law, parl.*) enquête, *f.* *On* —, après informations prises. *To make —ies after*, s'informer de, prendre des informations (*or* des renseignements) sur; demander d s nouvelles de. — **office,** *s.* bureau de renseignements *or* d'adresses, *m.*; bureau de placement, *m.*
Inquisition, *s.* recherche, *f.*; examen, *m.*, investigation, *f.*; (*in a bad sense*) inquisition, *f.*; (*a tribunal*) inquisition, *f.*; (*law*) enquête, *f.*
Inquisitional, *adj.* assidu dans ses recherches; (*in a bad sense*) inquisitorial
Inquisitive, *adj.* curieux; investigateur; (*in a bad sense*) curieux, indiscret
Inquisitively, *adv.* curieusement, avec curiosité; (*in a bad sense*) indiscrètement
Inquisitiveness, *s.* curiosité, *f.*; (*in a bad sense*) curiosité, indiscrétion, *f.*
Inquisitor, *s.* inquisiteur, *m.*; (*law*) personne qui fait une enquête, *f.* [quête
Inquisitorial, *adj.* inquisitorial; (*law*) d'en-
Inquisitorially, *adv.* d'une manière inquisitoriale [(*encroachment*) empiètement, *m.*
Inroad, *s.* incursion, irruption, invasion, *f.*;
Insalivation, *s.* insalivation, *f.*
Insalubrious, *adj.* insalubre
Insalubriously, *adv.* insalubrement
Insalubrity, *s* insalubrité, *f.*
Insalutary, *adj.* insalutaire
Insane, *adj. s.* insensé, fou, aliéné
Insanely, *adv.* en insensé, en aliéné, follement, comme un fou, comme une folle
Insaneness, Insanity, *s.* folie, démence,
Insapid, *adj.* insapide [aliénation mentale, *f.*
Insapidity, *s.* insapidité, *f.*
Insatia-bility, bleness. *V.* page 3, § 1
Insatiable, *adj.* insatiable
Insatiableness, *s.* insatiabilité, *f.*
Insatiably, *adv.* insatiablement
Insatiate, *adj. V.* **Insatiable**
Insaturable, *adj.* insaturable
Inscribable, *adj.* inscriptible [*dicate*) dédier
Inscribe, *v.a.* inscrire; (*imprint*) graver; (*de-*
Inscribing, *s.* inscription, *f.*
Inscriptible, *adj.* inscriptible
Inscription, *s.* inscription, *f.*; (*title*) titre, *m.*; (*dedication*) dédicace, épître dédicatoire, *f.*
Inscriptive, *adj.* qui porte une inscription
Inscruta-bility, bleness. *V.* page 3, § 1
Inscrutable, &c. *V.* **Unsearchable,** &c.
Insect, *s.* insecte, *m.* — **case,** *s.* insectier, *m.* — **destroyer,** *s*, — **destroying,** *adj. V.*
Insecticidal, *adj.* insecticide [**Vermin**
Insecticide, *s.* insecticide, *m.*
Insectivore, *s.* insectivore, *m.*
Insectivorous, *adj.* insectivore
Insectolog-ic, al, -ist, -y. *V.* page 3, § 1
Insecure, *adj.* sans sécurité; (*unsafe*) *V.* **Unsafe**
Insecurely, *adv.* sans sécurité; (*unsafely*) *V.* **Unsafely**
Insecurity, *s.* insécurité, *f.*; manque de sûreté, danger, péril, hasard, *m.*, incertitude, *f.*
Insensate, *adj.* insensé
Insensibility, Insensibleness, *s.* insensibilité, *f.*; (*swoon*) évanouissement, *m.*
Insensible, *adj.* insensible ('*of*,' à); (*senseless, unconscious*) sans connaissance. *To become* —, *to be* —, (*senseless, unconscious*) *V.* **Uncon-**
Insensibly, *adv.* insensiblement [**scious**
Insepara-bility, bleness, *s.* inséparabilité, nature inséparable, *f.*
Inseparable, *adj.* inséparable
Inseparably, *adv.* inséparablement
Insert, *v.a.* insérer [entre-deux, *m.*
Insertion, *s.* insertion, *f.*; (*of lace-work,* &c.)
Inshrine. *V.* **Enshrine**
Inside, *s.* dedans, intérieur, *m.*; (*of a coach*) intérieur, *m.*; (*stomach*) estomac, *m.*; (*health*) santé, *f.*; — *adj.* intérieur; du (*or* de) dedans, de l'intérieur, d'intérieur; — *adv.* en dedans, dedans, dans (*or* à) l'intérieur; — *prep.* dans l'intérieur de, dans. — *out*, à l'envers. *To turn — out*, mettre sens dessus dessous; (*of clothes, stuffs*) retourner. *To put on a coat — out*, mettre un habit à l'envers [traître
Insidious, *adj.* insidieux; (*pers.*) perfide,
Insidiously, *adv.* insidieusement; perfidement [perfidie, astuce, *f.*
Insidiousness, *s.* nature insidieuse, *f.*; (*pers.*)
Insight, *s.* inspection, *f.*; connaissance approfondie, *f.*; (*information*) éclaircissement, *m.*
Insignia, *s.pl.* insignes, *m.pl.*
Insignificanc-e, y, *s.* insignifiance, peu d'importance, peu de valeur, *m.*; légèreté, frivolité, futilité, *f.* *To sink into* —, se réduire à rien; perdre son importance *or* sa valeur; devenir bien petit [chose; nul
Insignificant, *adj.* insignifiant; peu de
Insignificantly, *adv.* d'une manière insignifiante; sans importance [trompeur
Insincere, *adj.* peu sincère, dissimulé, faux,
Insincerely, *adv.* sans sincérité, avec fausseté, faussement [simulation, fausseté, *f.*
Insincerity, *s.* manque de sincérité, *m.*, dis-
Insinuate, *v.a.* insinuer; (*hint*) donner à entendre; — *v.n.* s'insinuer; se glisser
Insinuation, *s.* insinuation, *f.*
Insinuative, *adj.* insinuatif
Insipid, *adj.* insipide, fade [deur, *f.*
Insipidity, Insipidness, *s.* insipidité, fa-
Insipidly, *adv.* insipidement, fadement
Insist, *v.n.* insister (sur); persister (à), s'obstiner (à); exiger, vouloir absolument, vouloir; s'arrêter (sur)
Insistence, Insisting, *s.* insistance, *f.*
Insistent, Insisting, *adj.* insistant
Inslave, Insnare. *V.* **Enslave, Ensnare**
Insobriety, *s.* intempérance, *f.*
Insociable, &c. *V.* **Unsociable,** &c.
Insolate, *v.a.* insoler, exposer au soleil
Insolation, *s.* insolation, *f.*; (*sunstroke*) insolation, *f.*, coup de soleil, *m.*
Insolence, *s.* insolence, *f.*
Insolent, *adj.* insolent
Insolently, *adv.* insolemment
Insolidarity, *s.* insolidarité, *f.*
Insolidity, *s.* insolidité, *f.*
Insolu-bility, bleness, *s.* insolubilité, *f.*
Insoluble, Insolvable, *adj.* insoluble; irrésoluble; indissoluble
Insolvency, *s.* insolvabilité, *f.*; faillite, *f.*; déconfiture, *f.*; (*things*) insuffisance, *f.*
Insolvent, *adj.* insolvable; failli, en faillite; (*things*) insuffisant; — *s.* débiteur (*m.*, -trice, *f.*) insolvable; failli, *m.*, e, *f.* *To become* —, faire faillite
Insomnia, *s.* insomnie, *f.*, insomnies, *f.pl.*
Insomnious, *adj.* sujet à des insomnies, atteint d'insomnie
Insomuch, *adv.* à un tel point (que), au point (que), tellement (que), si bien (que)
Insonorous, *adj.* insonore
Insonorousness, *s.* insonorité, *f.*
Inspect, *v.a.n.* inspecter; examiner; visiter; vérifier; surveiller
Inspection, *s.* inspection, *f.*; examen, *m.*; visite, *f.*; vérification, *f.*; (*watch*) surveillance, *f.*
Inspector, *s.* inspecteur, *m.*; examinateur, *m.*; vérificateur, *m.*; (*superintendent*) surveillant, *m.* — *general*, inspecteur général, *m.*
Inspectorship, *s.* inspectorat, *m.*, inspection, *f.*; surveillance, *f.*
Inspectress, *s.* inspectrice, *f.*; surveillante, *f.*
Inspirable, *adj.* respirable
Inspiration, *s.* inspiration, *f.*; aspiration, *f.*; respiration, *f.*; (*of a poet*) inspiration, verve, *f.*
Inspiratory, *adj.* inspiratoire; (*anat.*) inspirateur
Inspire, *v.a.* inspirer; animer; (*inhale*) aspirer; respirer; (*blow*) souffler. *To — a person with a thing*, inspirer quelque chose à quelqu'un. *To be —d with*, être inspiré de
Inspirer, *s.* inspirateur, *m.*, -trice, *f.*

Inspiring, *adj.* inspirateur [flammer
Inspirit, *v.a.* animer, encourager, exciter, en-
Inspissate, *v.a.* épaissir
Inspissation, *s.* épaississement, *m.*
Insta-bility, bleness, *s.* instabilité, *f.*
Instable, Instably. *V.* **Unstable, Unstably**
Install, Instal, *v.a.* installer
Installation, *s.* installation, *f.*
Instalment, *s.* installation, *f.*; (*payment*) à-compte, acompte, *m.*; versement partiel, *m.*; (*in bankruptcy*) dividende, *m.*
Instance, *s.* instance, *f.*; demande, *f.*; exemple, *m.*; circonstance, *f.*; cas, *m.*; (*law*) instance, *f.*; demande, *f.*; — *v.a.* prendre *or* citer *or* donner pour exemple. *Court of first* —, (*law*) tribunal de première instance, *m.* *For* —, par exemple. *In the first* —, d'abord; dès le début
Instant, *adj.* pressant, urgent; immédiat, instantané; présent; (*of the date*) courant, du courant, de ce mois; (*adverb.*) à l'instant; — *s.* instant, moment, *m.* *This* —, (*directly*) à l'instant, sur-le-champ, tout de suite. *The* — (*that*), (*as soon as*) aussitôt que, dès que
Instantaneity, *s.* instantanéité, *f.*
Instantaneous, *adj.* instantané. **—ly,** *adv.* instantanément. **—ness,** *s.* instantanéité, *f.*
Instanter, *adv.* à l'instant, sur-le- champ, immédiatement, sans délai, séance tenante
Instantly, *adv.* à l'instant, aussitôt, sur-le-champ, tout de suite, sur le coup; (*earnestly*) instamment, avec instance
Instaurate, *v.a.* instaurer
Instauration, *s.* instauration, *f.* [-trice, *f.*
Instaura-tor, tress, *s.* instaurateur, *m.*,
Instead, *adv.* en place, à la place. — *of,* au lieu de. *To be* or *stand* or *do* — *of,* tenir lieu de, remplacer
Instep, *s.* cou-de-pied, *m.*; (*of horses*) canon, *m.*
Instigate, *v.a.* exciter, pousser, inciter, instiguer [tion, *f.*
Instigating, *adj.* instigateur; — *s.* instiga-
Instigation, *s.* instigation, *f.*
Instigator, *s.* instigateur, *m.*, -trice, *f.*
Instil, *v.a.* instiller; (*fig.*) répandre, inculquer, imprimer, inspirer
Instillation, *s.* instillation, *f.*; (*fig.*) inspiration, *f.*; (*liquor*) infusion, *f.*
Instinct, *s.* instinct, *m.*; — *adj.* animé (de)
Instinctive, *adj.* instinctif [stinct
Instinctively, *adv.* instinctivement, par in-
Instinctiveness, Instinctivity, *s.* in-
Instinctual, *adj.* instinctuel [stinctivité, *f.*
Instinctually, *adv.* instinctuellement
Institute, *v.a.* instituer, établir, fonder; commencer; (*a lawsuit*) intenter; — *s.* institut, *m.*; principe, précepte, *m.*
Institution, *s.* institution, *f.*; établissement, *m.*
Institutive, *adj.* d'institution; (*of* ...) qui institue
Institu-tor, tress, instituteur, *m.*, -trice, *f.*
Instruct, *v.a.* instruire; (*give directions*) donner des instructions à, donner l'ordre à ('*to*, de), enjoindre à (de); charger (de); recommander à (de)
Instruction, *s.* instruction, *f.*; enseignement, *m.*; éducation, *f.*; leçon, *f.*; ordre, *m.*
Instructive, *adj.* instructif [tive
Instructively, *adv.* d'une manière instruc-
Instructor, *s.* instituteur, précepteur, maître, *m.*; (*mil.*) instructeur, *m.*
Instructress, *s.* institutrice, maîtresse, *f*
Instrument, *s.* instrument, *m.*; (*fig.*) agent, organe, moyen, instrument, *m.*; (*law*) acte, *m.*, pièce, *f.*, document, *m*
Instrumental, *adj* instrumental; (*of sound*) d'instrument; (*fig.*) qui sert d'instrument; contribuant (à), qui contribue (à), qui sert (à); utile. — *performer,* instrumentiste, *m.f.* *To be* — *in,* contribuer à, servir à
Instrumentalist, *s.* instrumentiste, *m.f.*
Instrumentality, Instrumentalness, *s.* moyen, *m.*; agence, *f.*; cause, *f.*; action, *f.*; coopération, *f.*, concours, *m.*
Instrumentally, *adv.* instrumentalement; (*fig.*) comme instrument, comme moyen
Instrumentary, *adj.* instrumentaire
Instrumentation, *s.* instrumentation, *f.*
Instrumentist. *V.* **Instrumentalist**
Insubjection, *s.* insoumission, *f.*
Insubmergible, *adj.* insubmersible
Insubmergibleness, *s.* insubmersibilité, *f.*
Insubmission, *s.* insoumission, *f.*
Insubordinate, *adj.* insubordonné
Insubordination, *s.* insubordination, *f.*
Insufferable, *adj.* insouffrable, insupportable, intolérable; détestable
Insufferably, *adv.* insupportablement, intolérablement; détestablement
Insufficiency, *s.* insuffisance, *f.*; incapacité, *f.*
Insufficient, *adj.* insuffisant; incapable
Insufficiently, *adv* insuffisamment
Insufflate, *v.a.* insuffler
Insufflation, *s.* insufflation, *f.*
Insufflator, *s.* insufflateur, *m.*
Insulable, *adj.* isolable
Insular, *adj.* insulaire
Insularity, *s.* insularité, *f.*
Insulate, *v.a.* isoler
Insulation, *s.* isolement, *m.*, isolation, *f.*
Insulator, *s.* isoloir, isolateur, *m.*
Insult, *v a.* insulter, injurier; outrager; — *v.n.* triompher insolemment; — *s.* insulte, injure, *f.*; affront, *m.* *Gross* —, outrage, *m.*
Insulter, *s.* insulteur, *m.*, -euse, *f.*
Insultingly, *adv.* d'une manière insultante, d'un air insultant, avec insulte, avec insolence
Insuperable, *adj.* insurmontable, invincible
Insupera-bleness, bility, *s.* nature insurmontable, *f.* [vinciblement
Insuperably, *adv.* insurmontablement, in-
Insupportable, *adj.* insupportable, intolérable [table, *f.*
Insupportableness, *s.* nature insuppor-
Insupportably, *adv.* insupportablement, intolérablement
Insuppressible, *adj.* qu'on ne peut supprimer *or* contenir; (*of laughter*) inextinguible
Insurable, *adj.* assurable
Insurance, *s.* assurance, *f.* *Life* —, assurance sur la vie. *Fire* —, assurance contre l'incendie. *Ship* or *Lloyd's* —, assurance maritime. — **broker,** *s.* courtier d'assurances, *m.* — **company,** *s.* compagnie d'assurances, *f.* — **office,** *s.* bureau d'assurances, *m.*; compagnie d'assurances, *f.* — **ticket,** *s.* bulletin d'assurance, *m.* [— *v.n.* assurer
Insure, *v.a.* assurer; faire assurer; garantir;
Insured, *part. adj. s.* assuré, *m.*, e, *f.*
Insurer, *s.* assureur, *m.*
Insurgency, *s.* insurgence, *f.*
Insurgent, *adj. s.* insurgé, *m.*, e, *f.*
Insurmountable, &c *V.* **Insuperable,** &c.
Insurrection, *s.* insurrection, *f.*, soulèvement, *m.* *To rise in* —, s'insurger, se soulever
Insurrectionarily, *adv.* insurrectionnellement
Insurrectionary, *adj.* insurrectionnel
Insurrectionist, *s.* insurrecteur, *m.*, -trice, *f.*, émeutier, agitateur, *m.*
Insusceptibility, *s.* insensibilité (à)
Insusceptible, *adj.* non susceptible (de); in-
Intact, *adj.* intact [capable (de); insensible (à)
Intactible, *adj.* intactile
Intactibleness, *s.* intactilité, *f.*
Intagliated, *adj.* gravé en creux
Intaglio, *s.* gravure en creux, intaille, *f.*
Intaker, *s.* recéleur, *m.*, -euse, *f.*
Intangi-bility, bleness. *V.* page 3, § 1
Intangible, *adj.* intangible
Integer, *s.* entier, tout, *m.*, totalité, *f.*; (*arith.*) entier, nombre entier, *m.*
Integral, *adj.* entier; intégral; (*arith.*) entier; (*alg.*) intégral; — *s.* totalité, *f.*, tout, ensemble,

m.; intégrité, *f.*; (*math.*) intégrale, *f.* — *calculus*, calcul intégral, *m.*
Integrality, *s.* intégralité, *f.*
Integrally, *adv.* intégralement
Integrant, *adj.* intégrant
Integrate, *v.a.* compléter; (*math.*) intégrer
Integration, *s.* complètement, *m.*; (*math.*) intégration, *f.*
Integrity, *s.* intégrité, *f.*; pureté, *f.*
Integument, *s.* tégument, *m.*
Intellect, *s.* intellect, *m.*, intelligence, *f.*, [esprit, *m.*
Intellection, *s.* intellection, *f.*
Intellective, *adj.* intellectif
Intellectual, *adj.* intellectuel; idéal; (*pers.*) intelligent, d'intelligence
Intellectuality, *s.* intellectualité, *f.*
Intellectualize, *v.a.* intellectualiser
Intellectually, *adv.* intellectuellement
Intelligence, *s.* intelligence, *f.*; esprit, *m.*; (*news*) nouvelle, *f.*, nouvelles, *f.pl.*, avis, *m.*, communication, correspondance, *f.*; (*information*) renseignements, *m.p.*; (*agreement*) accord, *m.*, intelligence, *f.* *Piece of* —, nouvelle, *f.* *Latest* —, dernières nouvelles. *Literary* —, chronique littéraire, *f.* *To give* — *of*, donner avis de, avertir de. *To receive* — *that* ..., apprendre que ... — **office,** *s.* *V.* **Inquiry-office**
Intelligencer, *s.* donneur (*m.*, -euse, *f.*) de nouvelles; messager, *m.*, -ère, *f.*, interprète, *m.f.*; (*of newspapers*) nouvelliste, *m.*, gazette, *f.*
Intelligent, *adj.* intelligent; (*of*) qui a l'intelligence (de)
Intelligently, *adv.* intelligemment, avec in- [telligence
Intelligi-bility, bleness. *V.* page 3, § 1
Intelligible, *adj.* intelligible
Intelligibly, *adv.* intelligiblement
Intemperance, *s.* intempérance, *f.*; excès, *m.*
Intemperate, *adj.* intempéré, immodéré, démesuré, déréglé, désordonné; excessif; (*of eating and drinking*) intempérant; (*passionate*) emporté, colère, violent; (*of language*) peu mesuré; (*of climates*) excessif
Intemperately, *adv* intempérément, immodérément, démesurément, déréglément; excessivement, avec excès, à l'excès; (*of eating and drinking*) intempéramment, avec intempérance; (*angrily*) avec colère, avec aigreur
Intemperateness, *s.* dérèglement, *m.*; excès, *m.*; (*of the weather*) intempérie, *f.*
Intend, *v.a.* se proposer (de), avoir l'intention (de), avoir dessein (de), projeter (de), compter; (*be determined*) vouloir, entendre; (*destine*) destiner (à). *To* — *something*, avoir des des- [seins
Intendanc-e, y, *s.* intendance, *f.*
Intendant, *s.* intendant, *m.*
Intended, *part. adj. s.* destiné, &c. (*V.* **Intend**); projeté; (*with intention*) intentionnel; volontaire; prémédité; (*future husband, wife*) prétendu, *m.*, e, *f.*, futur, *m.*, e, *f.* *To be* —, être destiné *or* &c.; avoir pour but [exprès
Intendedly, *adv.* avec intention, à dessein,
Intense, *adj.* intense, excessif; fort, vif, violent; aigu; ardent, véhément; (*obstinate*) opiniâtre, acharné
Intensely, *adv.* avec intensité, excessivement, au plus haut point; (*strongly*) fortement, vivement; vigoureusement; (*with obstinacy*) avec opiniâtreté, avec acharnement
Intenseness. *V.* **Intensity**
Intensify, *v.a.* rendre plus vif *or* plus fort, augmenter, accroître; aggraver; — *v.n.* devenir plus vif *or* plus fort, s'augmenter, augmenter, s'accroître; s'aggraver
Intensity, *s.* intensité, *f.*; force, violence, *f.*; vigueur, *f.*; ardeur, *f.*, acharnement, *m.*; opiniâtreté, *f.*; (*of the mind*) contention, *f.*
Intensive, *adj.* intensif
Intensively, *adv.* intensivement
Intent, *adj.* très attentif, très appliqué, très attaché; déterminé
Intent, Intention, *s.* intention, *f.*; dessein, but, *m.*, vue, *f.* *To all* —*s and purposes*, à tous égards, sous tous les rapports, de toute manière
Intentional, *adj.* fait avec intention, intentionnel, intentionné, volontaire
Intentionally, *adv.* à dessein, avec intention, intentionnellement, volontairement
Intentioned, *adj.* intentionné
Intently, *adv.* très attentivement; avec ardeur
Intentness, *s.* application sérieuse, forte attention, *f.*
Inter, *v.a.* inhumer, ensevelir, enterrer
Interact, *s.* entr'acte, *m.*
Intercalar, -y, *adj.* intercalaire
Intercalate, *v.a.* intercaler
Intercalation, *s.* intercalation, *f.*
Intercede, *v.n.* intercéder [*m.*, **-trice,** *f.*
Interceder, *s.* intercesseur, *m.*, médiateur,
Interceding, *s.* intercession, *f.*
Intercept, *v.a.* intercepter; arrêter; interrompre; (*the sight*) dérober; (*math.*) comprendre
Interception, *s.* interception, *f.*; interrup- [tion, *f.*
Intercession, *s.* intercession, *f.*
Intercessor, *s.* intercesseur, *m.*
Intercessory, *adj.* d'intercession
Interchange, *v.a.* échanger; — *s.* échange, *m.*; succession, suite, alternative, *f.*; variété, *f.*
Interchange-ability, bleness, *s.* succession, alternative, *f.* [proque
Interchangeable, *adj.* échangeable; réci-
Interchangeably, *adv.* alternativement, réciproquement
Intercolonial, *adj.* intercolonial
Intercolonially, *adv.* intercolonialement
Intercolumniation, *s.* entre-colonnes, entre-colonnement, *m.* [semble
Intercommunicate, *v.n.* communiquer en-
Intercommunication, Intercommunity, *s.* intercommunication, *f.*
Intercontinental, *adj.* intercontinental
Intercostal, *adj.* intercostal
Intercourse, *s.* commerce, *m.*, relations, *f.pl.*; rapports, *m.pl.*; communication, *f.*, communications, *f.pl.*; correspondance, *f.*; échange, *m.*
Intercross, *v.n.* s'entre-croiser
Interdict, *v.a.* interdire; — *s.* interdiction, *f.*; (*can. law*) interdit, *m.*
Interdiction, *s.* interdiction, *f.* [diction
Interdictive, Interdictory, *adj.* d'inter-
Interest, *v.a.* intéresser; — *s.* intérêt, *m.*; influence, *f.*, crédit, *m.*; protection, *f.*, protections, *f.pl.* *On* or *upon* —, à intérêt. *To* — *oneself in*, s'intéresser à, prendre intérêt à. *To be* —*ed in*, (*com.*) être intéressé dans; (*fig.*) être intéressé à, avoir intérêt à; s'intéresser à. *To make* — *with*, mettre dans ses intérêts, gagner l'intérêt de, user du crédit de. *To pay with* —, (*fig.*) payer avec usure. *To repay* or *return with*, (*fig.*) rendre avec usure. *To take an* — *in*, prendre intérêt à, s'intéresser à
Interestingly, *adv.* d'une manière intéressante, avec intérêt
Interfere, *v.n.* intervenir; (*meddle*) se mêler (de), s'immiscer (dans); s'ingérer (de, dans); se frotter (à), s'attaquer (à); (*oppose*) s'opposer (à), mettre obstacle (à); (*injure*) nuire (à); (*clash together*) se gêner, s'entre-choquer, se croiser; (— *with, thwart*) contrarier, entraver, gêner, déranger; (*of horses*) s'entre-tailler, se couper; (*opt.*) interférer
Interference, *s.* intervention, *f.*; ingérence, *f.*; obstacle, *m.*; choc, *m.*, collision, *f.*; (*rid.*) entre-taillure, atteinte, *f.*; (*opt.*) interférence, *f.*
Interfering, *adj.* (*opt.*) interférent; — *s.* *V.* **Interference**
Interim, *s.* intérim, *m.*; intervalle, *m.*; — *adj.* par intérim, intérimaire. *Ad* —, par intérim, intérimairement. *In the* —, dans l'intérim; dans l'intervalle; en attendant; sur ces entrefaites. — **functions,** *s. pl.* intérimat, *m.*
Interior, *adj.* intérieur; interne; (*to*) en de-

dans (de); — *s.* intérieur, *m.*; —**s,** *s. pl.* intérieur, *m.*
Interiority, *s.* intériorité, *f.*
Interiorly, *adv.* intérieurement
Interjacent, *adj.* placé entre, interposé
Interjection, *s.* interjection, *f.*
Interjectional, *adj.* interjectif
Interjectionally, *adv.* interjectivement
Interjoin, *v.a.* unir, réunir
Interlace, *v.a.* entrelacer, entremêler; intercaler
Interlacing, *s.* entrelacement, *m*
Interlard, *v.a.* entrelarder ('*with*,' de)
Interlarding, *s.* entrelardement, *m.*
Interleaf, *s.* feuillet intercalé, feuillet blanc, *m.*
Interleave, *v.a.* interfolier ('*with*,' de)
Interline, *v.a.* interlinéer, interligner ('*with*,' de); — *s.* interligne, entre-lignes, *m.*; (*engr.*) entre-taille, *f.*
Interlineal, Interlinear, -y, *adj.* interlinéaire
Interlineation, *s.* interlinéation, *f.*; intercalation, *f.*
Interlink, *v.a.* enchaîner, lier, joindre
Interlocution, *s.* interlocution, *f.*, dialogue, *m.*
Interlocu-tor, tress, *s.* interlocuteur, *m.*, -trice, *f.*
Interlocutory, *adj.* interlocutoire
Interlope, *v.n.* faire le commerce interlope; (*fig.*) être de contrebande, s'introduire
Interloper, *s.* intrus, *m.*, e, *f.*; (*com.*) interlope, *m.*
Interloping, *adj.* interlope
Interlude, *s.* intermède, *m.*
Interlunar, -y, *adj.* interlunaire
Interlunium, *s.* interlune, interlunium, *m.*
Intermarriage, *s.* intermariage, *m.*; double mariage, *m.*
Intermarry, *v.n.* faire un double mariage; s'allier par un double mariage; contracter un second mariage; s'allier par des mariages mixtes; — *v.a.* contracter un second mariage avec
Intermeddle, *v.n.* se mêler (de), s'immiscer (dans), s'ingérer (de, dans)
Intermeddler, *s.* personne qui se mêle des affaires des autres, *f.*; (*mediator*) médiateur, *m.*, -trice, *f.*, entremetteur, *m.*, -euse, *f.*, officieux, *m.*, -euse, *f.*
Intermeddling, *s.* intervention, ingérence, *f.*
Intermede, *s.* intermède, *m.*
Intermediary, *s. adj.* intermédiaire, *m.f.*
Intermediate, *adj.* intermédiaire
Intermediately, *adv.* intermédiairement, par intermédiaire
Intermediateness, *s.* intermédiarité, *f.*
Intermediation, *s.* intervention, médiation, *f.*
Intermedium, *s.* intermédiaire, *m.*
Interment, *s.* inhumation, *f.*, ensevelissement, *m.*, sépulture, *f.*, enterrement, *m.* — *company*, entreprise de pompes funèbres, *f.*
Interminable, *adj.* interminable; perpétuel. — *annuity*, rente perpétuelle, *f.*
Interminableness, *s.* nature interminable, *f.*
Interminably, *adv.* sans fin; perpétuellement
Intermingle, *v.a.* entremêler, mêler, mélanger; — *v.n.* s'entremêler, se mêler, se mélanger
Intermission, *s.* intermission, intermittence, interruption, *f.*, relâche, *m.*; intervalle, *m.*
Intermit, *v.a.n.* interrompre, discontinuer, cesser
Intermittent, Intermitting, *adj.* intermittent
Intermittingly, *adv.* avec intermission, par intervalles
Intermix. *V.* **Intermingle**
Intermixture, *s.* entremêlement, *m.*, mélange, *m.*
Intern, *s. adj.* interne, *m.f.*; — *v.a.* interner
Internal, *adj.* interne; intérieur; intrinsèque; essentiel; intestin; domestique; — **s,** *s. pl.* intérieur, dedans, *m.*
Internality, *s.* intériorité, *f.*
Internally, *adv.* intérieurement, à l'intérieur, au dedans
International, *adj.* international
Internationally, *adv.* internationalement
Internecine, *adj.* meurtrier; mortel; à outrance
Internment, *s.* internement, *m.*
Internunciature, *s.* internonciature, *f.*
Internuncio, *s.* internonce, *m.*
Interpellate, *v.a.* interpeller
Interpellation, *s.* interpellation, *f.*
Interpellator, *s.* interpellateur, *m.*, -trice, *f.*
Interpolate, *v.a.* interpoler; intercaler
Interpolation, *s.* interpolation, *f.*; intercalation, *f.*
Interpolator, *s.* interpolateur, *m.*
Interpose, *v.a.* interposer; faire intervenir; offrir; faire pénétrer; — *v.n.* s'interposer; intervenir
Interposer, *s.* médiateur, *m.*, -trice, *f.*
Interposition, *s.* interposition, intervention, médiation, *f.*; situation, position, *f.*; objet interposé, *m.*
Interpret, *v.a.* interpréter; expliquer; traduire
Interpretable, *adj.* interprétable; explicable; traduisible
Interpretation, *s.* interprétation, *f.*
Interpretative, *adj.* interprétatif
Interpretatively, *adv.* interprétativement
Interpreter, *s.* interprète, *m.f.*
Interpretership, *s.* charge (*f.*) *or* emploi (*m.*) d'interprète
Interpretress, *s.* interprète, *f.*
Interregnum, *s.* interrègne, *m.*
Interrex, *s.* interroi, régent, *m.*
Interrogate, *v.a.n.* interroger
Interrogating, *adj.* interrogateur
Interrogation, *s.* interrogation, *f.*; question, *f.*; (*note of* —, *gram.*) point d'interrogation, *m.*
Interrogative, *adj.* interrogatif
Interrogatively, *adv.* interrogativement, avec interrogation
Interrogator, *s.* interrogateur, *m.*, -trice, *f.*
Interrogatory, *adj.* interrogatif; — *s.* interrogatoire, *m.*
Interrupt, *v.a.* interrompre
Interruptedly, *adv.* avec interruption
Interrupter, *s.* interrupteur, *m.*, -trice, *f.*
Interrupt-ing, ive, *adj.* interrupteur
Interruption, *s.* interruption, *f.*; intervention, *f.*; intermission, *f.*
Intersect, *v.a.* entrecouper; couper, croiser; — *v.n.* se couper, se croiser, s'entre-croiser
Intersecting, *adj.* d'intersection
Intersection, *s.* intersection, *f.*, croisement, *m.*
Interspace, *s.* intervalle, *m.*; espacement, *m.*
Intersperse, *v.a.* parsemer (de); entremêler (de)
Interstice, *s.* interstice, *m.*
Interstitial, *adj* interstitiel
Intertexture, *s.* entrelacement, *m.*
Intertropical, *adj.* intertropical
Intertwine, Intertwist, *v.a.* entrelacer; — *v.n.* s'entrelacer
Interval, *s.* intervalle, *m.* *At* —*s*, par intervalles. *At short* or *at long* —*s*, à de courts *or* à de longs intervalles. — *between the acts*, (*theat.*) entr'acte, *m.*
Intervene, *v.n.* (*be between*) se trouver, être; (*happen*) survenir, arriver; (*interpose*) intervenir, s'interposer
Intervening, *adj.* intermédiaire; de l'intervalle; (*pers.*) intervenant
Intervention, *s.* intervention, médiation, entremise, *f.*; interposition, *f.*; action, opération, *f.*
Interview, *s.* entrevue, *f.*
Inter vivos. *Donation* or *gift* —, donation entre-vifs, *f.*
Interweave, *v.a.* entrelacer; entremêler
Interweaving, *s.* entrelacement, *m.*
Intestacy, *s.* succession ab intestat, *f.*
Intestate, *adj.* intestat; ab intestat; — *s.* intestat, *m.*
Intestinal, *adj.* intestinal
Intestine, *adj. s.* intestin, *adj. m.*, e, *f.*, intestin, *s.m.*
Inthrall, Inthralment. *V.* **Enslave, Enslavement**
Inthrone, &c. *V.* **Enthrone,** &c.
Intimacy, *s.* intimité, *f.*
Intimate, *adj. s.* intime, *m.f.*; — *v.a.* faire entendre, donner à entendre (à); faire comprendre (à); annoncer (à); déclarer (à); signifier (à)
Intimately, *adv.* intimement
Intimation, *s.* avis, *m.*; idée, *f.*
Intimidate, *v.a.* intimider

Intimidation, *s.* intimidation, *f.*
Into, *prep.* dans, en; à; entre; (*of changing, converting, forming,* &c.) en; (*at ...'s*) chez (...). — *it, them* (*things*), dedans; y
Intolerable, *adj.* intolérable, insupportable
Intolerableness, *s.* intolérabilité, nature intolérable, *f.*
Intolerably, *adv.* intolérablement, insupportablement
Intolerance, *s.* intolérance, *f.*
Intolerant, *adj. s.* intolérant, *m.*, e, *f.*
Intolerantly, *adv.* intolérament, avec *or* par intolérance
Intomb, &c. *V.* **Entomb,** &c.
Intonate, Intone, *v.a.n.* entonner; chanter
Intonation, Intoning, *s.* intonation, *f.*
Intoxicate, *v.a.* enivrer ('*with,*' de). *To become* or *get —d,* s'enivrer
Intoxicated, *adj.* ('*with,*' de) ivre; enivré
Intoxication, *s.* ivresse, *f.*; enivrement, *m.*
Intractability, *s.* naturel intraitable, *m.*; indocilité, *f.*
Intractable, *adj.* intraitable; indocile; obstiné
Intractableness. *V.* **Intractability**
Intractably, *adv.* d'une manière intraitable; indocilement, avec indocilité
Intrados, *s.* intrados, *m.*
Intramural, *adj.*, **Intra-muros,** *adv.* intramuros
Intransitive, *adj.* intransitif
Intransitively, *adv.* intransitivement
Intransmutability, *s.* intransmuabilité, *f.*
Intransmutable, *adj.* intransmuable
Intransparency, *s.* intransparence, *f.*
Intrench, *v.a.* retrancher; — **on,** *v.n.* empiéter sur, entreprendre sur, envahir
Intrenchment, *s.* retranchement, *m.*
Intrepid, *adj.* intrépide
Intrepidity, *s.* intrépidité, *f.*
Intrepidly, *adv.* intrépidement, avec intrépidité
Intricacy, *s.* embrouillement, *m.*; nature compliquée, *f.*; embarras, *m.*; complication, *f.*; confusion, *f.*; difficulté, *f.*; intrigue, *f.*; détour, *m.*; obscurité, *f.*
Intricate, *adj.* embrouillé; compliqué; obscur
Intricately, *adv.* d'une manière embrouillée *or* compliquée; obscurément
Intricateness. *V.* **Intricacy**
Intrigue, *s.* intrigue, *f.*; — *v.n.* intriguer
Intriguer, *s.* intrigant, *m.*, e, *f.*
Intriguing, *adj.* intrigant; — *part.* intriguant; — *s.* action d'intriguer, *f.*, intrigues, *f.pl.*
Intriguingly, *adv.* par intrigue, au moyen d'intrigues
Intrinsic, -al, *adj.* intrinsèque
Intrinsically, *adv.* intrinsèquement
Introduce, *v.a.* introduire; faire entrer; présenter; faire connaître; (*a person to another*) présenter
Introducer, *s.* introducteur, *m.*, -trice, *f.*
Introduction, *s.* introduction, *f.*; (*of a person to another*) présentation, *f.*; (*by letter*) recommandation *f.*
Introductive, Introductory, *adj.* introductif, introductoire, d'introduction; qui sert d'introduction (à); préliminaire. *To be — of* or *to,* servir d'introduction à
Introit, *s.* introït, *m.*
Intromission, *s.* intromission, *f.*
Intromit, *v.a.* admettre, laisser entrer
Introspect, regarder dans l'intérieur de, examiner l'intérieur de
Introspection, *s.* examen de l'intérieur, *m.*, introspection, *f.*
Introspective, *adj.* introspectif
Introvert, *v.a.* tourner en dedans
Intrude, *v.a.* fourrer, glisser, couler, introduire, présenter, imposer, importuner (...) de; — *v.n.* s'introduire; se présenter; s'imposer (à); se fourrer; être de contrebande *or* de trop; être importun; être indiscret — **on** *or* **upon,** *v.n.* (*a person*) déranger, importuner; (*a person's time,* &c.) abuser de; (*encroach*) empiéter sur
Intruder, *s.* importun, *m.*, e, *f.*; intrus, *m.*, e, *f.*; indiscret, *m.*, -ète, *f.*; usurpateur, *m.*, -trice, *f.*
Intrusion, *s.* importunité, *f.*; intrusion, *f.*; imposition, *f.*; indiscrétion, *f.*; (*encroachment*) empiètement, *m.*, usurpation, *f.*
Intrusive, *adj.* importun, intrus, indiscret. — *rock,* roche d'intrusion, *f.*
Intrusively, *adv.* importunément, avec importunité; indiscrètement, avec indiscrétion
Intrusiveness. *V.* **Intrusion**
Intrust, *v.a.* confier. *To — a person with ...,* confier ... à quelqu'un; charger quelqu'un de ...
Intuition, *s.* intuition, *f.*
Intuitive, *adj.* intuitif, d'intuition, par intuition
Intuitively, *adv.* intuitivement, par intuition
Intumescence, *s.* intumescence, *f.*
Intumescent, *adj.* intumescent
Intussusception, *s.* intussusception, *f.*
Intwine, &c. *V.* **Entwine,** &c.
Inuendo. *V.* **Innuendo**
Inundate, *v.a.* inonder ('*with,*' de)
Inundation, *s.* inondation, *f.*; débordement, *m.*
Inurbanity, *s.* inurbanité, *f.*
Inure, *v.a.* accoutumer (à), habituer (à); (*harden*) endurcir (à), aguerrir (à), rompre (à), faire (à). *To — to war,* aguerrir
Inurement, *s.* habitude, *f.*
Inutility, *s.* inutilité, *f.*
Inutilizable, *adj.* inutilisable
Invade, *v.a.* envahir; attaquer
Invader, *s.* envahisseur, *m.*; agresseur, assaillant, *m.*
Invading, *adj.* envahissant; d'invasion
Invagination, *s.* invagination, *f.*
Invalid, *adj.* infirme; malade; (*things*) de malade; des malades, pour les malades; (*weak*) faible; (*law, mil., nav.*) invalide; — *s.* invalide, *m.f.*; malade, *m.f.*; valétudinaire, *m.f.*; — *v.a.* mettre à la réforme, réformer. — **carriage,** *s.* voiture de malade, *f.*; (*rail.*) coupé-lit, *m.* — **chair,** *s.* chaise de malade, *f.*
Invalidate, *v.a.* infirmer, affaiblir; (*law*) invalider, infirmer
Invalidation, *s.* invalidation, infirmation, *f.*
Invalided, *adj.* réformé, en réforme
Invalidity, Invalidness, *s.* invalidité, *f.*
Invalidly, *adv.* invalidement
Invaluable, *adj.* inestimable, inappréciable
Invaluably, *adv.* inappréciablement
Invaria-bility, bleness. *V.* page 3, § 1
Invariable, *adj.* invariable
Invariably, *adv.* invariablement; constamment; toujours
Invasion, *s.* invasion, *f.*; envahissement, *m.*; (*violation*) atteinte, violation, *f.*; (*encroachment*) empiètement, *m.*
Invasive, *adj.* invasif, d'invasion; (*pers.*) envahissant
Invective, *s.* invective, *f.*; — *adj.* invectif, plein d'invectives, injurieux, satirique
Invectively, *adv.* injurieusement, avec des invectives
Inveigh, *v.n.* invectiver, se déchaîner
Inveigle, *v.a.* séduire, enjôler, capter; attirer
Inveiglement, Inveigling, *s.* séduction, captation, *f.*
Inveigler, *s.* séducteur, *m.*, -trice, *f.*, enjôleur, *m.*, -euse, *f.*
Invent, *v.a.* inventer
Invention, *s.* invention, *f.*
Inventive, *adj.* inventif
Inventiveness, *s.* nature inventive, invention, *f*
Inventor, *s.* inventeur, *m.*
Inventorial, *adj.* d'inventaire
Inventorially, *adv.* en forme d'inventaire
Inventory, *s.* inventaire, *m.*; — *v.a.* inventorier
Inventress, *s.* inventrice, *f.*
Inverse, *adj.* inverse [(*log.*) en raison inverse
Inversely, *adv.* inversement, en sens inverse;
Inversion, *s.* interversion, *f.*, renversement, *m.*; (*gram.*) inversion, *f.*; (*log., math., mus.*) renversement, *m*
Inversive, *adj.* inversif
Invert, *v.a.* renverser, invertir; (*reverse*) intervertir; (*log., math., mus.*) renverser
Invertebrate, *adj. s.* invertébré, *adj. m.*, e, *f.*, invertébré, *s.m.*
Inverted, *adj.* renversé, inverse; (*of order*) interverti
Invertedly, *adv.* dans un ordre inverse; dans un ordre interverti

Invest, *v.a.* vêtir (de), revêtir (de); (*to place in possession*) investir (de); (*money*) placer; (*mil.*) investir
Investigable, *adj.* susceptible d'investigation
Investigate, *v.a.* rechercher; examiner
Investigating, Investigative, *adj.* investigateur; scrutateur
Investigation, *s.* investigation, recherche, *f.*
Investigator, *s.* investigateur, *m.*, -trice, *f.*; scrutateur, *m.*, -trice, *f.*
Investiture, *s.* investiture, *f.*
Investive, *adj.* qui revêt; qui investit
Investment, *s.* action de revêtir, *f.*; (*of power,* &c.) action d'investir, *f.*; (*of money*) placement, *m.*; (*mil.*) investissement, *m.*; (*garment*) [vêtement, *m.*
Investor, *s.* spéculateur, *m.*
Inveteracy, Inveterateness, *s.* état invétéré, *m.*; (*obstinacy*) acharnement, *m.*
Inveterate, *adj.* invétéré; vieux; endurci; (*obstinate*) acharné; (*fam., of smokers,* &c.) enragé. *To become* or *grow* —, s'invétérer
Inveterately, *adv.* d'une manière invétérée; profondément; (*obstinately*) avec acharnement
Invidious, *adj.* odieux; irritant, offensant, blessant, vexatoire, désagréable
Invidiously, *adv.* odieusement; d'une manière irritante *or* &c. (*V.* **Invidious**)
Invidiousness, *s.* nature odieuse, *f.*, odieux, *m.*; nature irritante *or* &c. (*V.* **Invidious**), *f.*
Invigorate, *v.a.* fortifier, donner de la vigueur à
Invigoration, *s.* action de donner de la vigueur, action de fortifier, *f.*; état de vigueur, *m.*; accroissement de force *or* de forces, renforcement, *m.*, invigoration, *f.*
Invinci-bility, bleness. *V.* page 3, § 1
Invincible, *adj.* invincible
Invincibly, *adv.* invinciblement
Inviola-bility, bleness. *V.* page 3, § 1
Inviolable, *adj.* inviolable
Inviolably, *adv.* inviolablement
Inviolate, *adj.* inviolé, intact, pur; inviolable
Invisi-bility, bleness. *V.* page 3, § 1
Invisible, *adj.* invisible
Invisibly, *adv.* invisiblement
Invitation, *s.* invitation, *f.*
Invitatory, *adj.* invitatif, d'invitation; invitatoire; — *s.* (*Cath. lit.*) invitatoire, *m.*
Invite, *v.a.* inviter (à); appeler, attirer; pro- [voquer
Inviter, *s.* personne qui invite, *f.*; hôte, *m.*, hôtesse, *f.*, amphitryon, *m.*
Inviting, *adj.* attrayant; engageant; tentant; appétissant; ragoûtant
Invitingly, *adv.* d'une manière attrayante *or* [engageante
Invitingness, *s.* nature attrayante *or* en- [gageante, *f.*
Invocation, *s.* invocation, *f.*
Invocatory, *adj.* invocatoire
Invoice, *s.* facture, *f.*; — *v.a.* facturer. — **book,** *s.* facturier, livre des factures, *m.* — **clerk,** *s.* facturier, *m.* — **top,** *s. V.* **Bill-head**
Invoke, *v.a.* invoquer; réclamer
Invoker, *s.*, **Invoking,** *adj.* invocateur, *m.*, [-trice, *f.*
Involucel, *s.* involucelle, *m.*
Involucre, *s.* involucre, *m.*
Involuntarily, *adv.* involontairement
Involuntariness, *s.* nature involontaire, *f.*
Involuntary, *adj.* involontaire
Involute, *s.* (*geom.*) développante, *f.*
Involution, *s.* enveloppement, *m.*, involution, *f.*; complication, *f.*; (*math.*) élévation aux puissances, *f.*; (*gram.*) incise, *f.*
Involve, *v.a.* envelopper; renfermer, comprendre, embrasser; impliquer; entraîner; nécessiter; engager; embarrasser; enlacer, entrelacer, entortiller; jeter, précipiter, plonger; (*mingle*) confondre. *To — oneself in,* se jeter dans; s'attirer; (*in money matters*) déranger ses affaires
Involved, *part. adj.* enveloppé, &c. (*V.* **Involve**); (*in debt*) obéré, endetté; (*of estates*) grevé de dettes; (*of circumstances*) de gêne; (*of style*) entortillé
Involvedness, Involvement, *s.* enveloppement, *m.*; involution, *f.*; complication, *f.*; (*of money matters*) embarras, *m.*, gêne, difficulté, *f.*
Invulnera-bility, bleness. *V.* page 3, § 1
Invulnerable, *adj.* invulnérable
Invulnerably, *adv.* invulnérablement
Inwall, *v.a.* entourer de murs
Inward, *adj.* intérieur; interne; intime; — *adv.* à l'intérieur, au dedans, en dedans, intérieurement
Inwardly, *adv.* à l'intérieur, en dedans, in- [térieurement
Inwardness, *s.* intériorité, *f.*
Inwards, *adv. V.* **Inward**
Inweave, *v.a.* enlacer, entrelacer, tresser
Inwrap, *v.a.* envelopper; entortiller; embarrasser; transporter, ravir
Inwreathe, *v.a.* couronner, ceindre
Inwrought, *adj.* tissu; ouvragé; broché; in- [crusté
Iodate, *s.* iodate, *m.*
Iodic, *adj.* iodique
Iodide, *s.* iodure, *m.*
Iodidize, *v.a.* iodurer
Iodine, *s.* iode, *m.*
Iodize, *v.a.* ioder
Iodous, *adj.* iodeux
Ionian, *adj.* ionien
Ionic, *adj.* ionique, ionien
Iota, *s.* iota, *m.*
I O U, *s.* reconnaissance, *f.*
Ipecacuanha, *s.* ipécacuana, *m.*
Ipso facto, *adv.* ipso facto, par le fait
Irasci-bility, bleness. *V.* page 3, § 1
Irascible, *adj.* irascible
Irascibly, *adv.* avec irascibilité
Irate, *adj.* courroucé, furieux
Ire, *s.* courroux, *m.*, colère, *f.*
Ireful, *adj. V.* **Irate**
Irefully, *adv.* avec courroux, avec colère
Iridescence, *s.* iridescence, *f.*
Iridescent, *adj.* iridescent
Iridium, *s.* (*chem.*) iridium, *m.*
Iris, *s.* iris, *m.* — **pea,** pois à cautère, *m.* — **root,** *s.* racine d'iris, *f.*, iris, *m.* *Powdered — root,* poudre d'iris, *f.*
Irisate, *v.a.* iriser; — *v.n.* s'iriser
Irisation, *s.* irisation, *f.*
Irish, *adj.* irlandais, d'Irlande; — *s.* (*people*) (les) Irlandais, *m.pl.*; (*language*) l'irlandais, *m.*, la langue irlandaise, *f.* — **boy,** *s.* (petit) Irlandais, *m.* — **brigade,** *s.* brigade irlandaise, *f.* — **girl,** *s.* (petite *or* jeune) Irlandaise, *f.* — **lady,** *s.* dame irlandaise, *f.* — **linen,** *s.* toile d'Irlande, *f.* — **man,** *s.* Irlandais, *m.* — **moss,** *s.* varech comestible, *m.* — **poplin,** *s.* popeline d'Irlande, *f.* — **woman,** *s.* Irlandaise, *f.*
Irishism, *s.* hibernisme, *m.*
Iritis, *s.* iritis, *f.*
Irk, *v.a.* fâcher, peiner; répugner; (*weary*) ennuyer, fatiguer
Irksome, *adj.* ennuyeux, fatigant, désagréable, fastidieux
Irksomely, *adv.* ennuyeusement, fastidieuse- [ment
Irksomeness, *s.* nature fastidieuse, nature fatigante, *f.*, ennui, *m.*
Iron, *s.* fer, *m.*; (*— work*) ferrement, *m.*, ferrure, *f.*; — *adj.* de fer; en fer; — *v.a.* ferrer, garnir de fer; (*linen*) repasser; (*fetter*) mettre aux fers; charger de chaînes. *Grey* —, fonte grise, *f.* *Old* —, ferraille, *f.* *One must not have too many —s in the fire,* (*Proverb*) il ne faut pas courir deux lièvres à la fois. *Strike while the — is hot,* il faut battre le fer pendant qu'il est chaud. — **age,** *s.* âge de fer, *m.* — **bedstead,** *s.* lit de fer, *m.* — **bridge,** *s.* pont de fer, *m.* — **cased,** *adj.* (*nav.*) cuirassé, blindé. — **casing,** *s.* (*nav.*) blindage, *m.* — **chest,** *s.* coffre-fort, *m.* — **clad,** *adj.* (*nav.*) cuirassé, blindé; *s.* navire *or* bâtiment cuirassé (*or* blindé), *m.* — **coated,** *adj. V.* — **cased.** — **dealer,** *s.* ferronnier, *m.*, -ière, *f.* — **dross,** *s.* scorie de fer, *f.* — **dust, -filings,** *s.* limaille de fer, *f.* — **founder,** *s.* fondeur de fer, *m.* — **foundry,** *s.* fonderie de fer, *f.* — **grey,** *adj.* gris de fer. — **manufacture,** *s.*

fabrication du fer, *f.* — **manufacturer, -master,** *s.* maître de forges, *m.* — **mine,** *s.* mine de fer, *f.* —**monger,** *s.* quincaillier, *m.*; ferronnier, *m.* — **mongery, -ware,** *s.* quincaillerie, *f.*; ferronnerie, *f.*; (*build.*) serrurerie, *f.* — **mould,** *s.* lingotière, *f.*; (*spot*) tache de rouille, *f.* — **ore,** *s.* minerai de fer, *m.* — **plate,** *s.* plaque de fer, *f.* — **plated,** — **plating,** *V.* — **cased,** — **casing.** — **safe,** *s.* *V.* **Safe.** — **shod,** *adj.* ferré. — **side,** *s.* (*nav.*) *V.* — **clad;** (*Engl. hist.*) côte de fer, *f.*; (*middle ages*) bras de fer, *m.* — **store, -trade,** *s.* ferronnerie, *f.* — **ware, -wares,** *s.* *V.* — **mongery.** — **wire,** *s.* fil de fer, *m.* — **wood,** *s.* bois de fer, *m.* — **work,** *s.* ferrure, *f.*; ferrement, *m.* — **worker,** *s.* ouvrier de forges, *m.*; forgeron, *m.* — **works,** *s.pl.* usine à fer, forge, *f.*, forges, *f.pl.* — **wort,** *s.* crapaudine, *f.*

Ironer, *s.* ferreur, *m.*; (*of linen*) repasseuse, *f.*
Iron-ical, -ically. *V.* page 3, § 1
Ironing, *s.* ferrage, *m.*; ferrement, *m.*; (*smoothing*) repassage, *m.*; (*adject.*) à repasser
Irony, *s.* ironie, *f.*
Irradiance, Irradiation, *s.* rayonnement, *m.*, irradiation, *f.*; splendeur, *f.*, éclat, *m.*
Irradiate, *v.a.n.* rayonner sur; éclairer; animer; (*shine*) briller
Irrational, *adj.* irrationnel; irraisonnable; déraisonnable, absurde; (*math.*) irrationnel
Irrationality, *s.* absurdité, *f.*; déraison, *f.*
Irrationally, *adv.* irrationnellement; irraisonnablement; déraisonnablement
Irreclaimable, *adj.* incorrigible, irréformable; indomptable
Irreclaimably, *adv.* incorrigiblement
Irreconcilable, *adj.* irréconciliable; (*things*) inconciliable, incompatible
Irreconcilableness, Irreconcilability, *s.* irréconciliabilité, nature irréconciliable, *f.*; implacabilité, *f.*; (*of things*) incompatibilité, *f.*
Irreconcilably, *adv.* irréconciliablement; inconciliablement [incompatibilité, *f.*
Irreconcilement, *s.* non-réconciliation, *f.*;
Irrecoverable, *adj.* irrecouvrable; irrécupérable; irréparable; irrémédiable; perdu sans ressource [(*loss*) perte sans ressource, *f.*
Irrecoverableness, *s.* nature irréparable, *f.*;
Irrecoverably, *adv.* irréparablement; irrémédiablement; (*beyond recovery*) sans ressource
Irredeemable. *V.* **Unredeemable**
Irreducible, *adj.* irréductible
Irreducibleness, *s.* irréductibilité, *f.* [*f.*
Irrefraga-bility, bleness, *s.* irréfragabilité,
Irrefragable, *adj.* irréfragable
Irrefragably, *adv.* irréfragablement
Irrefutable, *adj.* irréfutable
Irrefutably, *adv.* irréfutablement
Irregular, *adj.* irrégulier; (*disorderly*) déréglé; — *s.* soldat de corps franc, *m.*
Irregularity, *s.* irrégularité, *f.*; (*of conduct*) dérèglement, désordre, *m.*
Irregularly, *adv.* irrégulièrement [rapport
Irrelative, *adj.* irrélatif; sans liaison, sans
Irrelevancy, *s.* inapplicabilité, *f.*
Irrelevant, *adj.* inapplicable (à); sans rapport (avec); étranger (à); déplacé, hors de propos [hors de propos
Irrelevantly, *adv.* sans aucun rapport (avec);
Irreligion, *s.* irréligion, *f.*
Irreligious, *adj.* irréligieux
Irreligiously, *adv.* irréligieusement
Irreligiousness, *s.* irréligiosité, *f.*
Irremediable, *adj.* irrémédiable, sans remède, irréparable; incurable
Irremediableness, *s.* nature irrémédiable, *f.*
Irremediably, *adv.* irrémédiablement, sans remède, irréparablement
Irremissible, *adj.* irrémissible
Irremissibleness, *s.* nature irrémissible, *f.*
Irremissibly, *adv.* irrémissiblement
Irremovability, *s.* inamovibilité, *f.*
Irremovable, *adj.* inamovible; inébranlable
Irremovably, *adv.* à vie
Irrepara-bility, bleness, *s.* irréparabilité, *f.*
Irreparable, *adj.* irréparable
Irreparably, *adv.* *V.* **Irretrievably** [*f.*
Irrepeala-bility, bleness, *s.* irrévocabilité,
Irrepealable, *adj.* irrévocable
Irrepealably, *adv.* irrévocablement
Irreprehensible, *adj.* irrépréhensible
Irreprehensibleness, *s.* irrépréhensibilité, *f.*
Irreprehensibly, *adv.* irrépréhensiblement
Irrepressible, *adj.* irrépressible; (*of laughter*) inextinguible
Irrepressibly, *adv.* irrépressiblement
Irreproachable, *adj.* irréprochable
Irreproachableness, *s.* irréprochabilité, *f.*
Irreproachably, *adv.* irréprochablement, d'une manière irréprochable
Irreproductive, *adj.* irreproductif
Irreproductively, *adv.* irreproductivement
Irreprovable, &c. *V.* **Irreprehensible,** &c.
Irresisti-bility, bleness, *s.* irrésistibilité, *f.*
Irresistible, *adj.* irrésistible
Irresistibly, *adv.* irrésistiblement
Irresoluble, *adj.* irrésoluble
Irresolute, *adj.* irrésolu; incertain
Irresolutely, *adv.* irrésolûment [tion, *f.*
Irresoluteness, Irresolution, *s.* irrésolu-
Irrespective, *adj.* sans égard (à); indépendant (de)
Irrespectively, *adv.* indépendamment
Irrespirability, *s.* irrespirabilité, *f.*
Irrespirable, *adj.* irrespirable
Irresponsibility, *s.* irresponsabilité, *f.*
Irresponsible, *adj.* irresponsable
Irresponsibly, *adv.* irresponsablement
Irretractable, *adj.* irrétractable
Irretrievable, *adj.* irréparable
Irretrievableness, *s.* irréparabilité, *f.*
Irretrievably, *adv.* irréparablement; sans retour; sans ressource [respect, *m.*
Irreverence, *s.* irrévérence, *f.*; manque de
Irreverent, *adj.* irrévérent; irrespectueux
Irreverently, *adv.* irrévéremment, avec irrévérence; irrespectueusement
Irreversible, &c. *V.* **Irrevocable,** &c.
Irrevoca-bility, bleness, *s.* irrévocabilité, *f.*
Irrevocable, *adj.* irrévocable
Irrevocably, *adv.* irrévocablement
Irrigate, *v.a.* irriguer, arroser [rosement, *m.*
Irrigation, *s.* irrigation, *f.*, arrosage, *m.*; ar-
Irrigating, *adj.* irrigatoire
Irrita-bility, bleness. *V.* page 3, § 1
Irritable, *adj.* irritable [*s. m.*
Irritant, *adj.* *s.* irritant, *adj. m.*, e, *f.*, irritant,
Irritate, *v.a.* irriter
Irritation, *s.* irritation, *f.*
Irritative, *adj.* irritatif
Irruption, *s.* irruption, *f.*
Irruptive, *adj.* qui fait irruption
Isabel, Isabelle, *adj.* isabelle; — *s.* couleur isabelle, *f.*, isabelle, *m.*
Isagon, *s.* isogone, *m.*
Isagonal, *adj.* isogone
Ischium, *s.* ischion, *m.*
Ischuretic, *adj.* ischurétique
Ischuria, Ischury, *s.* ischurie, rétention d'urine, *f.* [*m.f.*
Ishmaelite, *s.* **Ishmaelitish,** *adj.* Ismaélite,
Isinglass, *s.* colle de poisson, ichthyocolle, *f.*
Islam, *s.* Islam, *m.*
Islamism, *s.* islamisme, *m.*
Islamite, *s.* islamite, *m.f.*
Islamitic, *adj.* islamite, islamique
Island, *s.* île, *f.*
Islander, *s.* insulaire, *m.f.*
Isle, *s.* île, *f.*
Islet, *s.* îlot, *m.*, petite île, *f.*
Isochron-al, ous, *adj.* isochrone
Isochron-ic, al, -ically, -ism. *V.* p. 3, § 1
Isolate, *v.a.* isoler
Isolation, *s.* isolement, *m.*

Isometric, -al, *adj.* isométrique
Isosceles, *adj.* isoscèle
Isothermal, *adj.* isotherme
Israelite, *s.* Israélite, *m f.*
Israelitic, Israelitish, *adj.* israélite
Issuable, *adj.* émissible
Issue, *s.* (*egress*) sortie, issue, *f.*; (*result*) résultat, *m.*; (*end*) fin, issue, *f.*; (*discharge*) écoulement, épanchement, *m.*; (*despatch*) expédition, *f.*; (*delivery*) délivrance, distribution, *f.*; (*of bank-notes, shares,* &c.) émission, *f.*; (*of orders,* &c.) publication, *f.*; (*print.*) impression, *f.*; (*surg.*) cautère, *m.*; (*offspring*) postérité, *f.*, enfants, *m.pl.*; (*law*) question, *f.*; — *v.n.* sortir (*'out of,' 'from,'* de); (*spring*) jaillir (de); (*emanate*) émaner (de); provenir (de); descendre (de); (*end*) se terminer, finir; (— *forth, mil.*) déboucher; faire une sortie; — *v.a.* expédier, envoyer; délivrer, distribuer; publier; (*orders*) donner; (*bank-notes, shares,* &c.) émettre; (*a mandate or warrant or writ*) lancer. *At* —, en désaccord; en litige; en question, contesté; à débattre; dont il s'agit. *To join* —, (*fig.*) engager la discussion, discuter; différer d'opinion (avec), n'être pas de l'avis (de); (*to fight*) en venir aux mains. —**less,** *adj.* sans postérité, sans enfants. — **pea,** *s.* pois à cautère, *m.* [*m.f.*, personne qui émet, *f.*
Issuer, *s.* émetteur, *m.*, -euse, *f.*, émissionnaire,
Isthmian, *adj.* isthmique, isthmien
Isthmus, *s.* isthme, *m.*
Istrian, *s. adj.* Istrien, *m.*, -ne, *f.*
It, *pron.* (*nominative*) il, *m.*, elle, *f.*; (*obj. of a verb.*) le, *m.*, la, *f.*; (*dative*) lui, *m f.*; (*imp.*) il, *m.*; ce, c', *m.*; (*when used for 'that,' 'that thing,' 'things,'*) cela, *m.*, (*before the verb 'to be,'*) ce, c', cela, *m.*; (*when used for 'the thing,' 'the matter,'*) la chose; la question. *At* —, *by* —, y; en. *For* —, en; y; pour cela. *From* —, en. *Of* —, en. *To* —, y. [*V.* **About, After, Against, Around, Before, Behind, In, Into,** *and other prepositions.*] — *rains,* il pleut, — *is fine,* il fait beau. — *is the* 10*th,* c'est le dix. — *is six o'clock,* il est six heures. — *is you,* c'est vous. — *is they,* ce sont eux. — *is a pleasure,* c'est un plaisir. — *is so,* cela est ainsi. *That is* —, c'est cela. *That is not* —, ce n'est pas cela. *That will do* —, cela fera l'affaire. [*'It' is untranslated in some phrases, as : I have thought — necessary to stay,* j'ai jugé nécessaire de rester; *I have heard — said that . . .,* j'ai entendu dire que . . ., &c.] — *is said,* on dit
Italian, *adj.* italien, d'Italie; — *s.* Italien, *m.*, -ne, *f.*; (*language*) l'italien, *m.*, la langue italienne, *f.* — *boy,* (petit) Italien, *m.* — *girl,* (petite *or* jeune) Italienne, *f.* — *iron,* (*of laundresses*) fer à boudin, *m.* — *lady,* dame italienne, Italienne, *f.* — *master,* maître *or* professeur d'italien, *m.* — *paste,* pâte d'Italie, *f.* — *school,* (*paint.*) école italienne, *f.* — *warehouse,* magasin de pâtes d'Italie, *m.* — *warehouseman,* vermicellier, *m.* — *woman,* Italienne, *f.*
Italianism, *s.* italianisme, *m.*
Italianize, *v.a.* italianiser
Italic, *adj.* italique; — *s.* italique, (*type*) *m.*, (*letter*) *f.*
Italicism, *s.* italicisme, *m.*
Italicize, *v.a.* imprimer (*or* mettre) en italiques; (*underline*) souligner
Itch, *v.n.* démanger, avoir des démangeaisons; — *s.* démangeaison, *f.*; (*med.*) gale, *f.* *My hands or fingers* —, les mains me démangent (*'to,' . . .,* de . . .) j'ai des démangeaisons aux mains
Itching, *s.* démangeaison, *f.*
Itchy, *adj.* galeux [(*main point*) item, *m*
Item, *adv.* item; — *s.* article, *m.*; objet, *m.*;
Iterate, *v.a.* réitérer, répéter
Iteration, *s.* réitération, répétition, *f.*
Iterative, *adj.* répété, itératif
Iteratively, *adv.* itérativement
Itinerant, *adj.* ambulant; ambulatoire; itinérant; — *s.* personne ambulante, personne qui mène une vie nomade, *f.*; (*preacher*) prédicateur itinérant, *m.* [itinéraire, *m.*
Itinerary, *adj.* itinéraire; ambulant; — *s.*
Itinerate, *v.n.* aller de lieu en lieu, voyager, mener une vie nomade
Itinerating, *adj.* ambulant
Its, *pron. poss.* (*before a noun*) son, sa, (*pl.*) ses; (*not before a noun*) le sien, la sienne, (*pl.*) les siens, les siennes
Itself, *pron.* lui-même, *m.*, elle-même, *f.*; soi-même, *m.*; lui, elle; soi; (*in a reflect. verb*) se; (*alone*) seul. *To go of* —, aller tout seul
Ivied, *adj.* couvert de lierre
Ivory, *s.* ivoire, *m.*; — *adj.* d'ivoire; en ivoire; —**ies,** *s. pl.* (*teeth*) ivoire, *m.* *Vegetable* —, ivoire végétal, corozo, *m.* — **black,** *s.* noir d'ivoire, *m.* — **carver,** *s.* sculpteur sur (*or* en) ivoire, *m.* — **nut,** *s.* corozo, *m.* — **shell,** *s.* éburne, *f.* — **turner,** *s.* tourneur en ivoire, *m.* — **work,** *s.* ouvrage en ivoire, *m.* — **worker,** *s.* ivoirier, *m.* — **working, -works,** *s.* ivoirerie, *f.*
Ivy, *s.* lierre, *m.* — **berry,** *s.* grain de lierre, *m.* — **crowned,** *adj.* couronné de lierre. — **mantled,** *adj.* couvert de lierre
Izard, *s.* (*zool.*) isard, izard, *m.*

J

J, *s.* (*letter*) j, *m.*
Jabber, *v.n.a.* jaboter, jacasser; (*to talk indistinctly*) bredouiller; baragouiner; — *s.* *V.* **Jabbering**
Jabberer, *s.* jaboteur, *m.*, -euse, *f.*, jacasseur, *m.*, -euse, *f.*; bredouilleur, *m.*, -euse, *f.*, baragouineur, *m.*, -euse, *f.*
Jabbering, *s.* jabotage, *m.*, jacasserie, *f.*; (*indistinct talk*) bredouillement, *m.*; baragouinage, [baragouin, *m.*
Jabiru, *s.* jabiru, *m.*
Jacamar, *s.* jacamar, *m.*
Jacana, *s.* jacana, jacane, *m.*
Jacconet, *s.* jaconas, *m.*
Jacent, *adj.* gisant, étendu, couché
Jacinth, *s.* jacinthe, *f.*
Jack, *s.* (*for John*) Jean, *m.*; Jeannot, *m.*; (*sailor*) marin, matelot, *m.*; (*a male*) mâle, *m.*; (*fish*) brocheton, filardeau, lanceron, *m.*; (*spit*) tournebroche, *m.*; (*for boots*) tire-bottes, *m.*; (*pitcher*) broc, *m.*; (*of leather*) outre, *f.*; (*machine*) cric, *m.*; (*for lifting a carriage*) chèvre, *f.*; (*of sawyers*) chevalet, *m.*; (*flag*) pavillon, *m.*; (*of harpsichords,* &c.) sautereau, *m.*; (*at bowls*) cochonnet, *m.*; (*of clocks*) jaquemart, *m.*; (*common figure*) bonhomme, *m.*; (*puppet*) godenot, *m.* *Cheap* —, camelot, *m.*; (*shop*) (la) boutique à cinq sous, *f.* — *-in-the-box,* joujou à surprise, *m.*, boîte à surprise, surprise, *f.* — *in office,* bureaucrate, *m.* — *of all trades,* Michel Morin, *m.* — *of all trades and master of none,* Jean fait tout et bon à rien. — *of all work,* maître Jacques, homme à tout faire, factotum, *m.* — *o' lantern,* feu follet, *m.* — *of the clockhouse,* jaquemart, *m.* —*'s-alive,* (*game*) petit bonhomme vit encore, *m.* — **ass,** *s.* âne, baudet, *m.*, bourrique, *f.* — **boot,** *s.* botte à genouillère, grosse botte, *f.* — **daw,** *s.* choucas, *m.*, corneille des clochers, corneille d'église, *f.* *The —daw in peacock's feathers,* le geai paré des plumes du paon. — **Ketch,** *s.* Charlot, Monsieur de Paris, le Faucheur, le bourreau, *m.* — **knife,** *s.* (grand) couteau de poche, couteau-poignard, *m.* — **plane,** *s.* riflard, *m.* — **pudding,** *s* paillasse, *m.*; pierrot, *m.*; paradiste, *m.*; pitre, *m.* — **sauce,** *s.* impertinent, *m.* — **screw,** *s.* vérin, *m.* — **smith, -maker,** *s.* faiseur de tournebroches, *m.* — **snipe,** *s.* *V.* **Juddock.** — **sprat,** *s.* étourdi, écervelé, *m.* — **tar,** *s.* loup de mer,

m. — **towel,** *s.* essuie-mains à rouleau, *m.*, [touaille, *f.*
Jackal, *s.* chacal, *m.*
Jackanapes, *s.* fat, *m.*
Jacket, *s.* jaquette, *f.*; (*down to the waist only, and round*) veste, *f.*; (*of firemen, jockeys, convicts,* &c.) casaque, *f.*; (*of ladies*) caraco, *m.*; (*morning or dressing* —, *of ladies*) camisole, *f.*; (*of hussars and other cavalry corps, shell* —) dolman, *m.*
Jacobin, Jacobine, *s. adj.* jacobin, *m*, e, *f.*
Jacobinic, -al, *adj.* jacobin
Jacobinism, *s.* jacobinisme, *m.*
Jacobite, *s.* jacobite, *m.*
Jaconet, *s.* jaconas, *m.*
Jacquart loom, *s.* métier à la Jacquart, *m.*
Jacquerie, *s.* jacquerie, *f.*
Jade, *s.* rosse, haridelle, *f.*, carcan, *m.*; (*min.*) jade, *m.*; — *v.a.* surmener, harasser; excéder de fatigue, fatiguer, excéder, éreinter; (*the senses*) énerver, affaiblir, émousser; (*dispirit*) décourager; — *v.n.* se fatiguer, se lasser; se décourager
Jadish, *adj.* de rosse, méchant, mauvais
Jag, *v.a.* ébrécher; denteler; — *s.* brèche, *f.*; [dentelure, *f.*
Jaggedness, *s.* dentelure, *f.*
Jagger, Jagging-iron, *s.* videlle, *f.*
Jaggery, *s.* sucre de palmier, *m.*
Jaggy, *adj.* ébréché; dentelé
Jaguar, *s.* jaguar, *m.*
Jail, *s.* prison, *f.*; — *v.a.* mettre en prison, emprisonner. — **bird,** *s.* prisonnier, *m.*, -ière, *f.*; gibier de potence, *m.* — **book,** *s.* registre *or* livre d'écrou, *m.* — **delivery,** *s.* mise en jugement, *f.* — **fever,** *s.* fièvre des prisons, *f.* — **keeper,** *s. V.* **Jailer**
Jailer, *s.* concierge (de prison), *m.f.*; (*obsolete, and used only in a bad sense now*) geôlier, *m.*, [-ière, *f.*
Jakes, *s. pl.* latrines, *f.pl.*
Jalap, *s.* jalap, *m.*
Jam, *s.* confitures (de ...), *f.pl.*, confiture (de ...), *f.*; — *v.a.* presser, serrer, prendre
Jamaica, *s.* la Jamaïque, *f.* — **pepper,** *s.* poivre de la Jamaïque, *m.*
Jamaican, *s. adj.* Jamaïcain, *m.*, e, *f.*
Jamb, *s.* (*arch.*) jambage, *m.*; (*build.*) montant, *m.*; (*of chimneys*) chambranle, *m.*
Jangle, (*sound*) *V.* **Jingle**; (*quarrel*) *V.* **Wrangle**
Janissary, Janizary, *s.* janissaire, *m.*
January, *s.* janvier, *m.*
Japan, *s.* laque, vernis laque, vernis, *m.*; (*geog.*) le Japon, *m.*; — *v.a.* laquer, vernisser, vernir. — **earth,** *s.* terre du Japon, *f.*, cachou, *m.* — **ink,** *s.* encre du Japon, encre double, *f.* — **ware,** *s.* japon, *m.*
Japanese, *adj.* japonais, du Japon; — *s.* Japonais, *m.*, e, *f.*; (*language*) le japonais, *m.*, la langue japonaise, *f.*
Japanner, *s.* vernisseur, *m.*
Japanning, *s.* vernissure en laque, *f.*
Jar, *v.n.* (*of sound*) être discordant; (*to clash*) s'entre-choquer; choquer, jurer; (*to vibrate*) vibrer; (*to quarrel*) se quereller, se disputer; — *v.a.* faire discorder; choquer; ébranler; (*the nerves*) agacer; — *s.* son discordant, *m.*; contestation, *f.*, débat, *m.*, querelle, *f.*; conflit, *m.*; (*of a door*) entre-bâillement, *m.*; (*of clocks*) vibration, *f.*; (*vessel*) jarre, *f.*; cruche, *f.*; (*for pomade, tobacco,* &c.) pot, *m.*; (*of glass*) bocal, *m.*; (*electr.*) bouteille, *f.* *Electrical* —, bouteille de Leyde, *f.* *On the* —, (*of doors*) *V.* **Ajar.** *To put upon the* —, entre-bâiller, entr'ouvrir, mettre tout contre
Jargon, *s.* jargon, *m.*; — *v.a.n* jargonner
Jargonel, Jargonelle, *s.* jargonelle, *f.*
Jargoon, *s.* jargon, *m.*
Jarring, *adj.* discordant; en contestation, en conflit; — *s. V.* **Jar**
Jarvey, Jarvy, *s.* (*cabby*) automédon, *m.*
Jasmin, Jasmine, *s.* jasmin, *m.*
Jasper, *s.* jaspe, *m.*
Jaundice, *s.* jaunisse, *f.*
Jaundiced, *adj.* atteint de jaunisse; (*fig.*) prévenu
Jaunt, *s.* course, tournée, excursion, promenade, *f.*; partie, *f.*; — *v.n.* se promener, faire une partie
Jauntily, *adv.* avec grâce, gracieusement, légèrement, avec enjouement
Jauntiness, *s.* grâce, légèreté, *f.*, enjouement, *m.*
Jaunting, *s.* excursions, promenades, *f.pl.*; — *adj.* de promenade. — **car,** *s.* char à bancs, *m.*
Jaunty, *adj.* gracieux, léger, enjoué; (*showy*) voyant
Javanese, *s. adj.* Javanais, *m.*, e, *f.*
Javelin, *s.* javeline, *f.*, javelot, *m.*
Jaw, *s.* mâchoire, *f.*; (*mouth*) *V.* **Mouth;** (*talk*) caquet, *m.*; (*scolding*) crierie, criaillerie, *f.*; —**s,** *pl.* mâchoires, *f.pl.*; (*mouth*) *V.* **Mouth;** (*of death*) bras, *m.pl.*; étreintes, *f.pl.*; (*of the grave*) portes, *f.pl.*; — *v.n.* crier, gueuler; bougonner; — *v.a.* crier *or* gueuler après; bougonner. *To hold o.'s* —, se taire. — **bone,** *s.* os maxillaire, *m.*, (*vulgarly*) mâchoire, *f.* — **fallen,** *adj. V.* **Chop-fallen.** [— **tooth,** *s. V.* **Grinder**
Jay, *s.* geai, *m.*
Jealous, *adj.* jaloux
Jealously, *adv.* jalousement, avec *or* par jalousie
Jealousness, Jealousy, *s.* jalousie, *f.*
Jean, *s.* coutil rayé, *m.* *Satin* —, coutil satiné, *m.*
Jeer, *v.a.n.* railler, se railler de, se moquer de; — *s.* raillerie, moquerie, *f.*
Jeerer, *s.*, **Jeering,** *adj.* railleur, *m.*, -euse, *f.*, moqueur, *m.*, -euse, *f.*
Jeering, *s.* raillerie, moquerie, *f.*
Jeeringly, *adv.* railleusement, par raillerie, par moquerie
Jehu, *s.* (*driver*) phaéton, automédon, *m.*
Jejune, *adj.* sec, aride; (*poor*) pauvre, maigre
Jejuneness, *s.* sécheresse, aridité, froideur, *f.*; pauvreté, pénurie, disette, *f.*
Jejunum, *s.* jéjunum, *m.*
Jellied, *adj.* en gelée
Jelly, *s.* (*cook.*) gelée (de ...), *f.*; (*of meat,* &c.) coulis, *m.* — **broth, -soup,** *s.* consommé, *m.* — **fish,** *s.* méduse, *f.* — **mould,** *s.* moule à gelées, *m.*
Jemmy, *s.* (*tool*) monseigneur, *m.*
Jennet, *s.* (*Spanish horse*) genet, *m.*
Jenneting, *s.* passe-pomme, *f.*
Jenny, *s.* jenny, *f.* — **ass,** *s.* ânesse, bourrique, *f.*
Jeopardize, *v a.* mettre en danger, mettre en péril, hasarder, risquer, exposer, compromettre
Jeopardy, *s.* danger, péril, *m.*
Jerboa, *s.* gerboise, *f.*
Jeremiade, *s.* jérémiade, *f.*
Jerk, *v.a.* donner une saccade *or* une secousse à, secouer; (*throw*) jeter, lancer; (*of horses*) saccader; (*meat*) mariner, saler; — *s.* saccade, *f.*; secousse, *f.*
Jerkin, *s.* justaucorps, *m.*
Jersey, *s.* laine fine, *f.*, peigné, *m.*; (*garment*) chemise en tricot, *f.*
Jess, *s.* longe, *f.*, lien, *m.*
Jessamine, *s.* jasmin, *m.*
Jessed, *adj.* longé
Jest, *s.* plaisanterie, *f.*, mot plaisant, mot pour rire, bon mot, *m.*; farce, *f.*; badinage, *m.*; (*laughing stock*) risée, *f.*; jouet, *m.*; — *v.n.* plaisanter, badiner, rire; railler; — *v.a.* plaisanter, railler. *In* —, pour rire, par plaisanterie, en plaisantant. *To be in* —, (*pers.*) rire, plaisanter. *To be full of* —, avoir toujours le mot pour rire. *He cannot take a* —, il n'entend pas la plaisanterie, il n'entend pas raillerie. — **book,** *s.* recueil de bons mots, *m.*
Jester, *s.* plaisant, farceur, *m.*, -euse, *f.*; bouffon, *m.*; (*in a bad sense*) railleur, *m.*, -euse, *f.*, mauvais plaisant, *m.*; (*court-fool*) bouffon, fou, *m.*
Jesting, *s.* plaisanterie, *f.*, badinage, *m.*; raillerie, *f.*; — *adj.* de plaisanterie, pour rire; railleur
Jestingly, *adv.* pour rire, par plaisanterie, en plaisantant
Jesuit, *s.* jésuite, *m.* —*s' bark,* quinquina, *m.*
Jesuitess, *s.* jésuitesse, *f.*
Jesuitic, -al, *adj.* jésuitique, de jésuite, jésuite
Jesuitically, *adv.* jésuitiquement, en jésuite
Jesuitism, *s.* jésuitisme, *m.*
Jet, *s.* (*of gas*) jet, *m.*; (*of water*) jet d'eau, jet, *m.*; (*min.*) jais, *m.* — **black,** *adj.* noir comme du jais

Jetsam, Jettison, *s.* jet à la mer, *m.*
Jetty, *s.* jetée, *f.*; — *adj.* de jetée; (*like jet*) de jais, noir comme du jais. —**head,** *s.* jetée de port, *f.*, môle, musoir, *m.*
Jew, *s.* Juif, Israélite, *m.*; — *v.a.* juifer, judaïser. — **bush,** *s.* ipécacuana bâtard, *m.* —**'s ear,** *s.* pezize oreille de Judas, *f.* —**'s harp,** *s.* guimbarde, *f.*
Jewel, *s.* bijou, *m.*; joyau, *m.*; perle fine, *f.*; (*of watches*) rubis, diamant, *m.*; (*pers.*) bijou, *m.*; —**s,** *pl.* bijoux, *m. pl.*, &c.; pierreries, *f.pl.*; diamants, *m.pl.*; — *v.a.* orner de joyaux *or* de pierreries, parer de bijoux; (*watches*) monter sur rubis. *It is the finest — in his crown,* c'est le plus beau fleuron de sa couronne. — **box, -case,** *s.* écrin, *m.* — **house, -office,** *s.* dépôt des diamants (*or* joyaux) de la couronne, *m.*
Jewelled, *part. adj.* orné de joyaux, &c. (*V.* **Jewel,** *v.a.*); (*of watches*) monté sur rubis.— *in* 3, 4, &c. *holes,* avec 3, 4, &c. rubis
Jeweller, *s.* bijoutier, *m.*, -ière, *f.*, joaillier, *m.*, -ière, *f.* —*'s trade* or *business,* bijouterie, joaillerie, *f.*
Jewellery, Jewelry, *s.* bijouterie, joaillerie, *f.*
Jewess, *s.* Juive, *f.*
Jewish, *adj.* juif, judaïque, israélite
Jewishly, *adv.* en juif, en juive
Jewishness, rit juif, *m.*
Jewry, *s.* juiverie, *f.*
Jezebel, *s.* mégère, *f.*
Jib, *s.* (*nav.*) foc, *m*; —*v.n.* (*of horses*) s'acculer, se défendre. —**boom,** *s.* bâton de foc, *m.*
Jibber, *s.* (*horse, mare*) cheval (*m.*) *or* jument (*f.*) sujet (*or* sujette) à s'acculer
Jibbing, *s.* (*of horses*) acculement, *m.*
Jig, *s.* gigue, *f.*; —*v.n.* danser une gigue
Jigger, *s.* (*insect*) chique, *f.*; (*print.*) visorium, *m.*
Jiggish, *adj.* de gigue
Jill. *V.* **Gill.**
Jilt, *s.* coquette, *f.*; — *v.a.* duper, tromper (en amour) jouer; planter là; — *v.n.* faire la coquette
Jimble. *V.* **Gimbal**
Jingle, *v.n.* tinter; retentir; sonner; résonner; (*clash*) s'entre-choquer; — *v.a.* tinter; faire tinter; faire retentir; faire sonner; faire résonner; — *s.* *V.* **Jingling**
Jingling, *s.* tintement, *m.*; bruit, *m.*; (*clashing*) cliquetis, *m.*; (*little bell*) clochette, *f.*, (*round*) grelot, *m.*; (*in rhymes*) concordance, *f.*
Jingo (By), *int.* sapristi!
Jink, *v.a.* faire sonner; —*v.n.* sonner [ravi
Jinks, *s. pl.* *In high* — très gai, tout joyeux,
Job, *s.* affaire, *f.*; (*work*) ouvrage, travail, *m.*, besogne, *f.*; (*task*) tâche, pièce, *f.*; (*contract*) forfait, *m.*; entreprise, *f.*; marché, *m.*; (*lot*) lot à bon marché, *m.*; solde, *m.*; (*forced work*) corvée, *f.*; (*botching*) raccommodage, *m.*; (*unfair dealing*) intrigue, *f.*; tripotage, *m.*; —**s,** *pl.* affaires, *f.pl.*, &c.; (*print.*) éventuel, bilboquet, *m.*; — *v.n.* travailler à la tâche; (*intrigue*) tripoter; (*in the funds*) agioter, faire l'agiotage; (*let carriages, horses*) louer des voitures, louer des chevaux; — *v.a.* tripoter; (*strike*) frapper; (*carriages,* &c.) louer. *Bad* —, mauvaise *or* vilaine affaire, *f.* *Good* —, bonne affaire, *f.* *It is a bad* —, c'est une mauvaise affaire; c'est malheureux. *It is a good* —, c'est une bonne affaire; c'est bien heureux. *By the* —, à la tâche, aux pièces; (*contract*) à forfait, à l'entreprise. *To give it up as a bad* —, y renoncer; n'y tenir plus; en faire son deuil. — **carriage,** *s.* voiture de louage, *f.*; voiture de remise, *f.*, remise, *m.* — **chase,** *s.* (*print.*) ramette, *f.* — **horse,** *s.* cheval de louage, *m.* — **lot,** *s.* (*com.*) solde, *m.* — **master,** *s.* loueur de voitures *or* de chevaux, louageur, remiseur, *m.* — **post master,** *s.* relayeur, *m.* — **work,** *s.* (*print.*) *V.* **Jobbing**
Jobation, *s.* semonce, *f.* sermon, savon, suif, *m.*
Jobber, *s.* ouvrier à la tâche, *m.*; spéculateur, *m.*; faiseur d'affaires, *m.*; (*in stocks*) agioteur, *m.*; (*intriguer*) tripotier, *m.*; exploiteur, faiseur, *m.*
Jobbernowl, *s.* butor, balourd, *m.*
Jobbery, *s.* tripotage, *m.*
Jobbing, *s.* ouvrage *or* travail à la tâche, *m.*; (*print.*) éventuel, bilboquet, *m.*, ouvrage de ville, *m.*; (*of stocks*) agiotage, *m.*; (*intriguing*) tripotage, *m.*; — *adj.* (*things*) d'occasion. — *workman,* ouvrier qui travaille à la tâche *or* aux pièces, tâcheron, chambrelan, *m.* — *tailor,* tailleur à façon, *m.* — *hand,* (*print.*) homme en conscience, *m.*
Jockey, *s.* jockey, *m.*; (*horse-dealer*) maquignon, *m.*; (*a cheat*) fripon, *m.*; — *v.a.* tromper, duper, friponner. — **cap,** *s.* toque de jockey, *f.* — **club,** *s.* jockey-club, *m.* — **coat,** *s.* casaque de jockey, *f.*
Jockeying, *s.* tromperie, duperie, friponnerie, *f.*
Jockeyship, *s* équitation, *f.*
Jocose, *adj.* plaisant, badin, jovial, comique
Jocosely, *adv.* en plaisantant, en badinant, comiquement
Jocoseness, *s.* humeur plaisante, *f.*
Jocular, *adj.* plaisant, gai
Jocularity, *s.* humeur plaisante, gaieté, *f.*
Jocularly, *adv.* en plaisantant, plaisamment, en riant
Jocund, *adj.* gai, joyeux, enjoué
Jocundly, *adv.* gaiment, joyeusement
Jocundness, *s.* gaieté, *f.*, enjouement, *m.*
Jodeln, *s.* ioulement, *m.*
Jog, *v.a.* pousser, secouer, remuer, agiter; — *v.n.* se mouvoir; (*on, along*) aller *or* marcher *or* avancer tout doucement; — *s.* secousse, *f.* — **trot,** *s.* petit trot, *m.*; *adj.* au petit trot; (*fig.*) qui va son petit bonhomme de chemin; routinier; terre à terre; simple; *adv.* au petit trot, tout doucement
Joggle, *v.a.* *V.* **Jog**; — *v.n.* remuer, vaciller, s'agiter
Join, *v.a.* joindre; unir, réunir; associer; (*roads,* &c.) relier; (*after parting*) rejoindre; (*associate oneself with*) se joindre à; — *v.n.* se joindre (à); se toucher; s'unir; se réunir; s'associer (à). *To — battle,* engager le combat, se livrer bataille, en venir aux mains. *To — hands,* se donner la main. *To — issue, V.* **Issue**
Joiner, *s.* menuisier, *m.* —*'s work,* menuiserie, *f.*
Joinery, *s.* menuiserie, *f.*
Join-hand, *s* coulée, *f.*
Joining, *s.* jonction, *f.*; assemblage, *m.*; union, réunion, *f.*; (*joinery*) menuiserie, *f.*
Joint, *s.* joint, *m.*, jointure, *f.*; articulation, *f.*; (*hinge*) charnière, *f.*; (*knot*) nœud, *m.*; (*of meat*) gros morceau, morceau, *m.*, pièce, *f.*; quartier, m.; — *adj.* réuni; commun; collectif; (*in compounds*) co . . .; — *v.a.* couper dans la jointure; (*unite*) joindre, rapporter. — *debtor,* codébiteur, *m.*, -trice, *f.* — *guardian,* cotuteur, *m.*, -trice, *f.* — *heir, -ess,* cohéritier, *m.*, -ière, *f.* — *sharer,* copartageant, *m.*, e, *f.* *Out of* —, disloqué, démis, luxé; (*fig.*) dérangé. *With — consent,* d'un commun accord. *To put out of* —, démettre, disloquer; (*fig.*) déranger. *To put o.'s arm out of* —, se démettre *or* se disloquer le bras. *To put a person's nose out of* —, supplanter quelqu'un, couper l'herbe sous les pieds à quelqu'un. — **oil,** *s.* synovie, *f.* — **pin,** *s.* goupille, *f.* — **stock,** *adj.* par actions; anonyme
Jointed, *adj.* articulé; (*cut*) coupé par le joint, séparé; (*united*) joint; (*of animals*) jointé. — **handle,** *adj.* brisé
Jointer, Jointing-plane, *s.* varlope, *f.*
Jointly. *V.* **Conjointly**
Jointress, *s.* douairière, *f.*
Jointure, *s.* douaire, *m.*; — *v.a.* assigner un douaire à. *To be —d,* avoir un douaire
Joist, *s.* solive, *f.*, madrier, *m.*; — *v.a.* poser des solives *or* des madriers à
Joke, Joker, Joking &c. *V.* **Jest, Jester, Jesting,** &c.
Jole, *s.* *V.* **Jowl**
Jollification, *s.* jubilation, noce, *f.* *To have a* —, faire la noce, (*with an adj*) faire une noce . . .
Jollily, *adv.* joyeusement, gaiment

Jolliness, Jollity, *s.* joie, gaieté, *f.*
Jolly, *adv.* joyeux, gai, gaillard; réjoui, jovial. — **boat,** *s.* petit canot, *m.*
Jolt, *v.a.n.* cahoter; — *s.* cahot, *m.* — **head,** *s.* [lourdaud, butor, *m.*
Jolting, *s.* cahotage, *m.*
Jonquil, *s.* (*bot.*) jonquille, *f.*; (*colour*) jonquille, *m.*; — *adj.* jonquille, de couleur jonquille. — **colour,** *s.* couleur jonquille, *f.*, jonquille, *m.* — **coloured,** *adj.* de couleur jonquille, couleur jonquille, jonquille
Jorden, *s.* vase de nuit, pot de chambre, dépotoir, Jules, *m.*
Jostle, *v.a.* coudoyer, pousser; heurter; — *v.n.* se coudoyer, se pousser; se heurter; — *s.* *V.* **Jostling** [sade, *f.*; heurt, *m.*
Jostling, *s.* coudoiement, *m.*, poussée, pous-
Jot, *s.* iota, brin, *m.*, idée, *f.*; — *v.a.* noter, prendre note de
Jotting, *s.* note, *f.*; appréciation, *f.*
Journal, *s.* journal, *m.*; (*parl.*) procès-verbal, *m.*; (*of machines*) marche, révolution, *f.*; (*tech.*) tourillon, *m.* *Sea* —, journal nautique, *m.* *Ship's* —, livre de bord, *m.*
Journal-ism, -ist. *V.* p. 3, § 1 [*or* des journaux
Journalistic, *adj.* journaliste, de journal, de
Journalize, *v.a.* insérer dans un journal; (*com.*) porter au journal; — *v.n.* journaliser
Journey, *s.* voyage, *m.*; marche, *f.*; route, *f.*; (*distance*) trajet, *m.*; parcours, *m.*; — *v.n.* voyager; être en route (pour), aller (à), se rendre (à). *By slow —s*, à petites journées. *On a* —, en voyage. *On the* —, en route. *A pleasant — to you!* bon voyage! — **man,** *s.* garçon, *m.*; (*workman*) ouvrier, journalier, *m.* — **work,** *s.* ouvrage à la journée, *m.*; journée, [*f.*
Journeyer, *s.* voyageur, *m.*, -euse, *f.*
Journeying, *s.* voyage, *m.*
Joust, *s.* joute, *f.*; — *v.n.* jouter
Jouster, *s.* jouteur, *m.* [ma foi!
Jove (By), *int.* sacrebleu! mâtin! parbleu!
Jovial, *adj.* jovial, joyeux, gai
Joviality, Jovialness, *s.* jovialité, humeur joviale *or* joyeuse, joie, gaieté, *f.* [ment
Jovially, *adv.* jovialement, joyeusement, gai-
Jowl, *s.* (*of fish*) hure, *f.*; (*of birds*) jabot, *m.* *V.* **Cheek**
Joy, *s.* joie, *f.* *To give* or *wish* —, féliciter. *To leap for* —, tressaillir *or* sauter de joie. —**ful,** *adj.* joyeux; réjouissant; (*happy*) heureux. —**fully,** *adv.* joyeusement. —**fulness,** *s.* joie, *f.* —**less,** *adj.* sans joie, triste. —**lessly,** *adv.* sans joie, tristement. —**lessness,** *s.* [tristesse, *f.*
Joyous, *adj.* joyeux
Joyously, *adv.* joyeusement
Joyousness, *s.* joie, *f.*
Jubilant, *adj.* jubilant, qui jubile, triomphant. *To be* —, être jubilant, jubiler
Jubilation, *s.* jubilation, *f.*; triomphe, *m.*; réjouissances, *f.pl.*
Jubilee, *s.* jubilé, *m.*; réjouissance, allégresse, *f.*
Judæan, *adj.* de Judée
Judaic, -al, *adj.* judaïque
Judaically, *adv.* judaïquement
Judaism *s.* judaïsme, *m.*
Judaize, *v.n.a.* judaïser
Judas-tree, s. arbre de Judée, gaînier, *m.*
Juddock, Judcock, *s.* bécassin, bécasson, *m.*
Judean, *adj.* de Judée
Judge, *v.a.n.* juger; décider; — *s.* juge, *m.*; arbitre, *m.*; (*of painting, &c.*) connaisseur (en), *m.*; (*of wines and good living*) gourmet, *m.* —*'s notes*, notes de l'audience, *f.pl.* —*ing from* or *by*, à en juger par. *To — for oneself*, juger par soi-même. *To be a* —, s'y connaître. *To be a — of*, se connaître à *or* en, être connaisseur en. *To be a good — of*, se connaître bien à *or* en, être très connaisseur en
Judgeship, *s.* fonctions de juge, *f.pl.*; dignité de juge, *f.*; judicature, *f.*
Judgment, *s.* jugement, *m.*; sentence, *f.*; (*opinion*) avis, sens, *m.*, opinion, *f.* *To give — against*, condamner. — **day,** *s.* jour du jugement, *m.* — **hall,** *s.* salle de justice, *f.* — **seat,** *s.* tribunal, *m.*
Judicative, *adj.* judiciaire [justice, *f.*
Judicature, *s.* justice, *f.*; (*court*) cour de
Judicial, *adj.* judiciaire; juridique. — *separation*, séparation de corps et de biens, séparation judiciaire, *f.*
Judicially, *adv.* judiciairement; juridiquement. — *separated*, séparé de corps et de biens, séparé judiciairement
Judiciary, *adj.* judiciaire
Judicious, *adj.* judicieux, sage, prudent
Judiciously, *adv.* judicieusement, sagement
Judiciousness, *s.* nature judicieuse, sagesse, *f.*
Jug, *s.* cruche, *f.*; cruchon, *m.*; broc, *m.*; pot, *m.*; (*water* —) pot à l'eau, *m.* —**ful,** *s.* potée, *f.*
Jugged, *adj.* — *hare*, *V.* **Hare**
Juggle, *v.n.* jongler, faire des tours de passe-passe, faire des tours de gobelets, escamoter; (*fig.*) user de fourberie; — *v.a.* jouer, tromper, duper; — *s.* jonglerie, *f.*, tour de passe-passe, tour de gobelets, escamotage, *m.*; (*fig.*) jonglerie, tromperie, *f.*, tour de passe-passe, *m.* — **away,** *v.a.* escamoter
Juggler, -ess, *s.* jongleur, *m.*, -euse, *f.*, escamoteur, *m.*, -euse, *f.*, bateleur, *m.*, -euse, *f.*
Jugglery, *s.* *V.* **Juggle,** *s.*
Juggling, *adj.* qui fait des tours de passe-passe, qui escamote; (*fig.*) trompeur, fourbe; — *s.* *V.* **Juggle,** *s.*
Jugglingly, *adv.* par jonglerie, en jongleur
Jugular, *adj.* *s.* jugulaire, *adj. m.f.*, *s.f.*
Juice, *s.* jus, *m.*; (*sap*) suc, *m.*; (*of animals*) suc, *m.* *Gastric* —, suc gastrique, *m.* *The — of the grape*, le jus du raisin, *m.*; (*jest. for 'wine'*) le jus de la treille, *m.* — **less,** *adj.* sans jus; sans suc; sec
Juiciness, *s.* abondance de jus *or* de suc, *f.*
Juicy, *adj.* juteux, plein de jus; succulent, plein de suc [**tree,** *s.* jujubier, *m.*
Jujube, *s.* jujube, (*fruit*) *f.*, (*extract*) *m.* —
Julep, *s.* julep, *m.*
Julian, *adj.* julien
Julienne, *s.* julienne, *f.*
Julus, *s.* iule, *m.*
July, *s.* juillet, *m.*
Jumart, *s.* jumart, *m.*
Jumble, *v.a.* mêler ensemble, mêler confusément, confondre, brouiller; — *s.* mélange confus, *m.*, confusion, *f.*, pêle-mêle, fouillis, *m.*; —**s,** *s.pl.* petits tours, *m.pl.*
Jump, *v.a.n.* sauter; (*rush on*) se précipiter, se jeter; (*agree*) s'accorder; se rencontrer; — *s.* saut, *m.* — **about,** *v.n.* se remuer, s'agiter, se démener. — **at,** *v.a.* sauter à *or* après; se jeter sur; saisir avec empressement; accepter bien vite; en venir bien vite à
Jumper, *s.* sauteur, *m.*, -euse, *f.*
Jumping, *adj.* sauteur. — **hare,** *s.* gerboise, *f.* — **mouse,** *s.* gerbille, *f.*
Junction, *s.* jonction, *f.*; (*place*) point de jonction, *m.*; (*of roads*) croisement, *m.*; carrefour, *m.*; (*rail.*) embranchement, *m.*
Juncture, *s.* conjoncture, *f.*; moment, *m.*; (*joint*) jointure, articulation, *f.*
June, *s.* juin, *m.* [mégapode, *m.*
Jungle, *s.* jungle, *f.*, fourré, *m.* — **fowl,** *s.*
Jungly, *adj.* plein de jungles *or* de fourrés
Junior, *adj.* *s.* jeune; cadet, *m.*, -ette, *f.*; nouveau; (*son*) fils, *m.*; (*of classes*) bas, inférieur; (*under . . ., assistant*) second; *V.* **Clerk**
Juniority, *s.* infériorité d'âge, *f.*
Juniper, *s.* genièvre, *m.* — **berry,** *s.* baie de genièvre, *f.*, genièvre, *m.* — **tree,** *s.* genévrier, *m.*
Junk, *s.* jonque, *f.*; (*old cable*) bout de cable, *m.*
Junket, *s.* partie fine, *f.*, petit régal, *m.*; — *v.n.* faire une partie fine, être en partie fine; se régaler, faire bombance
Junketing, *adj.* de *or* en partie fine, de régal; — *s.* partie fine, *f.*, petit régal, *m.*, bombance, *f.* — **party,** *s.* personnes en partie fine, *f.pl.*

Junta, Junto, *s.* junte, *f.*; (*fig.*, cabale, faction, ligue, *f.*
Jupiter, *s.* (*myth.*, *astr.*) Jupiter, *m.*
Jupiterian, *adj.* jupitérien
Jurassic, *adj.* jurassique
Juratory, *adj.* juratoire
Jure (De), *adv.* de droit
Juridical, *adj.* juridique
Juridically, *adv.* juridiquement
Jurisconsult, *s.* jurisconsulte, *m*
Jurisdiction, *s.* juridiction, *f.*; compétence, *f.*
Jurisdictional, *adj.* juridictionnel
Jurisprudence, *s.* jurisprudence, *f.*
Jurist, *s.* juriste, *m.*; jurisconsulte, *m.*
Juror, *s.* juré, membre du jury, *m.* *Common* or *petty* —, membre d'un jury de jugement. *m* *Grand* —, membre d'un jury d'accusation, *m.*
Jury, *s.* jury, *m.* *Common* or *petty* —, jury de jugement, *m.* *Grand* —, (*in England*) grand jury, jury d'accusation, *m.*, (*in France*) chambre des mises en accusation, *f.* *Gentlemen of the* —! messieurs les jurés! — **box,** *s.* banc du jury, *m.* — **man,** *s.* juré, membre du jury, *m.* — **mast,** *s.* mât de fortune, *m.*
Just, *adj.* juste; équitable; exact; fidèle; — *adv.* juste, justement, tout juste; précisément; immédiatement; (*only*) seulement; (*quite*) tout; (*fam.*) un peu. — *tell me*, dites-moi un peu. — *as*, tout comme. — *as good*, — *as well*, &c., tout aussi bon, tout aussi bien, &c. — *at present*, en ce moment, pour le moment. — *by*, tout près. — *now*, tout à l'heure, à l'instant; en ce moment, pour le moment. — *out!* — *published!* (*of books*) vient de paraître. — *so*, précisément. — *then*, dans le (*or* ce) moment. — *yet*, tout de suite; pour le moment. *To have* or *be* — (*followed by a past part. in English*), venir de (*followed by an inf. in French*). *To have* or *be but* —, ne faire que de. *I have — met him*, je viens de le rencontrer. *He is — gone out*, il vient de sortir. *We had — dined*, nous venions de dîner. *I have — returned*, je reviens à l'instant, j'arrive. *I had but — got up*, je ne faisais que de me lever. *He is but — gone out*, il ne fait que de sortir
Justice, *s.* justice, *f.*; (*judge*) juge, conseiller, *m.*; (*magistrate*) juge de paix, *m.* *Chief* —, président, *m.* *Lord chief* —, grand juge, premier président, *m.* — *of the peace*, juge de paix, *m.* *To do* —, faire justice; rendre justice; faire droit; faire honneur
Justiceship. *V.* **Judgeship**
Justicia, *s.* (*bot.*) justicie, justiciée, *f.*
Justiciar, -y, *s.* justicier, *m.*; premier président, *m.*
Justifiable, *adj.* justifiable
Justifiableness, *s.* nature justifiable, *f.*
Justifiably, *adv.* justifiablement
Justification, *s.* justification, *f.*; défense, *f.*
Justificative, Justificatory, *adj.* justificatif
Justifier, *s.* justificateur, *m.*, -trice, *f.*, défenseur, *m.*
Justify, *v.a.* justifier; (*to, in*) donner le droit (de), mettre en droit (de), permettre (de), autoriser (à). *To be —ied* (*to, in*) avoir le droit (de), être en droit (de), être autorisé (à), être fondé (à), avoir un motif (pour); devoir. *To think* or *feel oneself —ied* (*to, in*), croire devoir. *I should not be —ied in doing so*, je ne le dois pas
Justifying, *adj.* justifiant, justificateur
Justle, &c. *V.* **Jostle,** &c.
Justly, *adv.* justement, avec justice, à bon droit, à juste titre; avec raison; précisément; exactement; avec justesse
Justness, *s.* justesse, *f.*; exactitude, *f.*; justice, *f.*
Jut, *v n.* (— **out**) être en saillie, faire saillie; avancer, s'avancer, projeter, sortir de l'alignement; bomber; — *s.* saillie, *f.*
Jute, *s.* jute, *m.* — **spinner,** *s.* filateur de jute, *m.*
Jutting, *adj.* en saillie
Juvenile, *adj.* (*young*) juvénile; jeune; (*of youth*) de jeunesse, de la jeunesse; (*of children*) d'enfants. — **ball,** *s.* bal d'enfants, *m.* — **offender,** *s.* jeune détenu, *m.* — **party,** *s.* soirée d'enfants, *f.* — **warehouse,** *s.* magasin de confection pour enfants, *m.*
Juvenilely, *adv.* juvénilement
Juvenility, *s.* juvénilité, jeunesse, *f.*
Juxtapose, Juxtaposit, *v.a.* juxtaposer
Juxtaposition, *s.* juxtaposition, *f.* *In* —, vis-à-vis; en regard

K

K, *s.* (*letter*) k, *m.*
Kabyle, *s. adj.* Kabyle, *m.f.*
Kaffir, Kafir, *s. adj* Cafre, *m.f.*
Kaftan. *V.* **Caftan**
Kakerlac, *s.* cancrelas, cancrelat, *m.*
Kakodyle, *s.* kakodyle, *m.*
Kale, Kail, *s.* chou, *m.*
Kaleidoscope, *s.* kaléidoscope, *m.*
Kalends, Kalendar, Kalender. *V.* **Calends, Calendar, Calender**
Kali, *s.* kali, *m.*
Kalif, Kaliph. *V.* **Caliph**
Kalmia, *s.* kalmie, *f.*
Kalmuck, *s.* Calmouk, *m.*
Kalpack, *s.* kalpack, *m.*
Kangaroo, *s.* kanguroo, kangourou, *m.*
Kaolin, *s.* kaolin, *m.*
Kedge, — anchor, *s.* ancre de touée, ancre à jet, *f.*
Keel, *s.* (*nav.*) quille, carène, *f.*; (*bot.*) carène, *f.* — **haul,** *v.a.* donner la cale à. — **hauling,** *s.* cale, *f.*
Keelage, *s.* droit de mouillage, *m.*
Keeling, *s.* (*fish*) cabillaud, *m.*
Keelson, *s.* contre-quille, *f.*
Keen, *adj.* affilé, aceré, tranchant; aigu; perçant, pénétrant, vif; subtil, fin; mordant, piquant, âpre, aigre, amer, sévère, sanglant; poignant; ardent; (*of appetite*) grand, vif; (*deep*) approfondi. — **sighted,** *adj.* clairvoyant
Keenly, *adv.* vivement; subtilement, finement, avec finesse; ardemment; rudement; d'une manière mordante
Keenness, *s.* vivacité, *f.*; (*of mind*, &c.) subtilité, finesse *f.*; (*eagerness*) ardeur, âpreté, *f.*; (*bitterness*) amertume, aigreur, *f.*; rigueur, sévérité, *f.*; (*depth*) profondeur, *f.*; (*of tools*) finesse, *f.*
Keep, *v.a.* tenir; garder; maintenir; (*com.*) tenir; (*not to part with, to remain in, to take care of*) garder; (*detain*) retenir; (*have in custody, retain*) conserver, garder; (*have, dogs, horses, carriage, servants*, &c.) avoir; (*a school, inn*, &c.) tenir; (*feed, support*) entretenir; nourrir; faire vivre; (*a woman*) entretenir; (*keep in a state*) entretenir, tenir; (*observe*) observer, suivre; ne pas manquer à; remplir, accomplir; célébrer, observer; (*save from danger*) préserver; protéger; (*prevent*) empêcher; (*keep off*) détourner, éloigner; (*conceal*) cacher (à); (*deprive*) priver (de); (*continue*) poursuivre, continuer; (*be always*) être toujours (à), ne faire que; (*not leave off*) ne (pas) cesser (de), ne faire que. *He —s telling me*, il est toujours à me dire, il ne cesse *or* ne cesse pas de me dire, il me dit toujours, il ne fait que me dire. *To — walking*, marcher *or* aller toujours, continuer de marcher, continuer, ne pas s'arrêter. — **away,** tenir éloigné; éloigner, repousser. — **back,** retenir; garder; retarder; (*prevent*) empêcher (de); (*conceal*) cacher (à). — **by,** garder, tenir en réserve. — **down,** maintenir bas; tenir baissé, ne pas lever; contenir, modérer; réprimer; (*subject, subdue*) tenir dans l'abaissement; tenir dans le respect; tenir en bride, dompter, maîtriser, assujettir. — **in,** tenir enfermé; garder; retenir, modérer, contenir; (*conceal*)

cacher; (*fire, light*) entretenir; (*at school*) mettre en retenue, consigner. — **off,** tenir éloigné; éloigner; (*prevent*) empêcher; (*repel*) repousser, détourner; (*save*) préserver. — **on,** continuer; ne (pas) cesser; (*o.'s hat,* &c.) garder. — **out,** tenir dehors, faire rester dehors; empêcher d'entrer (dans), ne pas laisser entrer (dans), ne pas admettre (dans); empêcher d'être admis (dans); exclure (de); empêcher de se mettre (dans); garantir (de), préserver (de); détourner (de); (*discard*) éloigner; (*deprive*) priver (de). — **to,** (*closed*) tenir fermé. — **under,** *V.* — **down.** — **up,** tenir en haut, tenir levé; maintenir, soutenir; (*fire, light, establishment,* &c.) entretenir; (*mil.*) maintenir; (*preserve*) conserver; garder; (*continue*) continuer; prolonger; (*from going to bed*) faire veiller; (*from falling asleep*) tenir éveillé, empêcher de dormir. — **it up,** (*of parties,* &c.) rester; s'amuser, s'en donner; aller toujours

Keep, *v.n.* se tenir; se maintenir; (*stay*) rester, demeurer; (*go*) aller toujours, aller; (*continue,* &c.) *V.* **Keep,** *v.a.*; (*of eatables*) se garder, se conserver; (*stick to*) s'en tenir (à); rester fidèle (à); (*from*) s'empêcher (de); se garder (de); s'abstenir (de); se tenir à distance (de). — **away,** se tenir éloigné; se tenir à l'écart; s'absenter. — **back,** se tenir en arrière; rester en arrière; se tenir à l'écart; (*refrain*) se retenir. — **down,** rester en bas; (*refrain*) se contenir; se tenir dans le respect; se tenir dans l'abaissement; (*of prices*) se maintenir bas; se maintenir à bas prix. — **in,** rester dedans; se tenir enfermé; rester chez soi; garder la maison; ne pas sortir; (*refrain*) se contenir, se retenir; (*conceal*) se cacher. — **in with,** conserver l'amitié de, rester bien avec; (*the shore,* &c.) ne pas s'éloigner de. — **off,** s'éloigner; se tenir éloigné, se tenir à distance, se tenir à l'écart; (*refrain from*) s'empêcher (de); s'abstenir (de); (*guard off*) se préserver (de); (*o.'s hat,* &c.) ne pas mettre; (*nav., mil.*) tenir le large (*int.* au large!). — **on,** avancer, aller en avant, aller *or* marcher toujours, poursuivre son chemin; (*fig.*) continuer, aller son train; ne pas s'arrêter, ne pas se lasser. — **on with,** continuer. — **out,** se tenir dehors, rester dehors, ne pas entrer; (*keep off*) se tenir éloigné, s'éloigner, se tenir à distance *or* à l'écart; (*guard*) se garantir (de). — **to,** s'attacher à; s'en tenir à; rester fidèle à; observer; (*o.'s word*) tenir; (*keep shut*) se tenir fermé. — **under,** se tenir dessous; (*refrain*) se contenir; se maîtriser. — **up,** se tenir levé; rester levé; se soutenir; se maintenir; s'entretenir; se conserver; continuer; ne (pas) cesser; se prolonger; (*sit up at night*) veiller, ne pas se coucher; (*o.'s spirits*) ne pas se laisser abattre. — **up with,** aller aussi vite que, ne pas se laisser dépasser par; (*be equal*) aller de pair avec, marcher de front avec; (*follow*) suivre

Keep, *s.* état, *m.*, condition, *f.*; (*care*) garde, *f.*; (*food*) entretien, *m.*, nourriture, *f.*; (*of castles*) donjon, *m.*; (*for game*) *V.* **Preserve**

Keeper, *s.* personne qui tient *or* qui garde ..., *f.*; garde, *m.*; gardien, *m.*; surveillant, *m.*; (*of a prison*) gardien, *m.*; (*game* —) garde-chasse, *m.*; (*of museums, libraries,* &c.) conservateur, *m.*; (*of com. books*) teneur, *m.*; (*ring*) jonc, anneau, *m.* — *of the seals,* garde des sceaux, *m.*

Keeping, *s.* garde, *f.*; surveillance, *f.*; conservation, *f.*; (*food*) nourriture, *f.*, entretien, *m.*; (*conformity*) accord, *m.*, harmonie, *f.*; (*paint.*) harmonie, *f.* *In — with,* en harmonie avec, d'accord avec; (*fam.*) à l'avenant de

Keepsake, *s.* souvenir, *m.*; (*book*) album, [keepsake, *m.*

Keg, *s.* caque, *f.*; baril, *m.*

Kelp, *s.* soude de varech, *f.*

Kelson, *V.* **Keelson**

Ken, *s.* vue, *f.*; portée de la vue, *f.*; (*fig.*) portée, *f.*

Kennel, *s.* (*a dog's house*) niche, cabane, *f.*; (*for hounds*) chenil, *m.*; (*of foxes*) terrier, *m.*; (*of wild beasts*) trou, *m.*; (*gutter*) ruisseau, *m.*; (*puddle*) mare, *f.*; (*pack of hounds*) meute, *f.*; — *v.n.* (*of dogs*) se coucher, se loger; (*of foxes*) se terrer; — *v.a.* mettre *or* tenir dans un [chenil

Kentledge, *s.* quintelage, *m.*

Kepi, *s.* képi, *m.*

Kept, *adj.* entretenu

Kerb, *s.* (*arch.*) cintre, *m.*; (*of pavements*) bordure de trottoir, *f.*, parement, *m.*; (*of wells*) margelle, *f.*; — *v.a.* (*pavements*) border; (*wells*) entourer d'une margelle. — **stone,** *s.* bordure de trottoir, *f.*, parement, *m.*; (*of a well*) margelle, *f.* [*wrapper*) fanchon, marmotte, *f.*

Kerchief, *s.* mouchoir, fichu, *m.*; (*as a head-*

Kermes, *s.* kermès, *m.*; (*feast*) kermesse, *f.*

Kern, *v.n.* se former en grain

Kernel, *s.* (*of nuts,* &c.) amande, *f.*; (*stone of a fruit*) noyau, *m.*; (*of apples, pears,* &c.) pépin, *m.*; (*seed*) graine, *f.*, grain, *m.*; (*of fir-cones*) pignon, *m.*; (*of meat*) noix, *f.*; (*med.*) glande, *f.*; (*nucleus*) noyau, *m.*; — *v.n.* se former en grain. — **fruit,** *s.* fruit à pépins, *m.*

Kernelly, *adj.* de grains *or* &c. (*V.* **Kernel**); plein de grains *or* &c.; semblable à des grains *or* &c.; (*med.*) glanduleux

Kersey, *s.* gros drap, *m.*

Kerseymere, *s.* casimir, *m.*

Kestrel, *s.* crécerelle, *f.*, émouchet, *m.*

Ketch, *s.* (*nav.*) quaiche, *f.*

Ketchup, *s.* *V.* **Catchup**

Kettle, *s.* (*large, to heat water*) chaudière, *f.*; (*to boil things*) chaudron, *m.*; (*small, for tea,* &c.) bouilloire, *f.* *The — boils,* l'eau bout. *A pretty — of fish,* une jolie (*or* une belle) affaire, *f.* — **drum,** *s.* timbale, *f.* — **drummer,** *s.* timbalier, *m.*

Key, *s.* clé, clef, *f.*; (*fig., of books,* &c.) clé, clef, *f.*; (*of books containing errors to be corrected by the student, translation, to arithmetic,* &c.) corrigé, *m.*; (*of an enigma*) mot, *m.*; (*of a piano or organ*) touche, *f.*; (*mus.*) clé, clef, *f.*; (*arch.*) clé de voûte, *f.*; (*tone*) ton, *m.*; (*of mind*) situation d'esprit, *f.*; (*tech.*) clé, clef, *f.*; (*pin*) clavette, *f.*; (*rail.*) coin, *m.*; (*rock, shoal, rocky islet*) caie, caye, *f.*; — *adj.* de clé, &c.; (*with a key*) à clé, &c.; (*with keys*) à clés, &c.; — *v.a.* fixer; (*to pin*) claveter; (*rail.*) coincer. — **bit,** *s.* panneton, *m.* — **board,** *s.* clavier, *m.* — **chain,** *s.* châtelaine, *f.* — **hole,** *s.* trou de la serrure, *m.* — **note,** *s.* tonique, *f.* — **ring,** *s.* anneau à clés, porte-clés, clavier, *m.* — **stone,** *s.* clé de voûte, *f.*

Keyed, *adj.* à clés, à clefs; (*of a piano,* &c.) à touches; (*with pins*) à clavettes

Keying, *s.* (*rail.*) coinçage, *m.*

Khan, *s.* kan, khan, *m.*

Khanate, *s.* kanat, khanat, *m.*

Khedive, *s.* khédive, *m.*

Khuskhus. *V.* **Kuskus**

Kibble, *s.* (*mining*) cuffat, cuveau, *m.*

Kibe, *s.* gerçure, mule, *f.*

Kick, *v.a.* donner un coup (*or* des coups) de pied à; (*stamp*) frapper du pied; (*push away*) pousser du pied; — *v.n.* donner des coups de pied; (*of beasts*) ruer; (*resist*) regimber, se gendarmer ('*at,*' contre); (*of fire-arms*) repousser, reculer; — *s.* coup de pied, *m.*; (*from a beast*) ruade, *f.*; (*of fire-arms*) recul, *m.* — **about,** *v.a.* ballotter à coups de pied; *v.n.* gigotter. — **down,** *v.a.* renverser d'un coup de pied. — *down stairs,* faire dégringoler l'escalier à coups de pied. — **out,** *v.a.* chasser à coups de pied. — **shaw,** *s.* colifichet, *m.* — **up,** *v.a.* faire; *s.* grabuge, tapage, *m.*

Kicker, *s.* personne qui donne des coups de pied, *f.*; (*of horses, mares*) rueur, *m.*, -euse, *f.*

Kicking, *s.* coups de pied, *m.pl.*; (*of beasts*) ruades, *f.pl.*; (*fig.*) coups, *m.pl.* — **longe, -strap,** *s.* plate-longe, *f.*

Kid, *s.* chevreau, *m.*, -elle, *f.*, cabri, *m.*; (*leather*) chevreau, *m.*; (*child*) bambin, marmot, môme, *m.*; — *v.n.* chevroter, chevreter, biqueter — **gloves,** *s.pl.* gants de chevreau, *m.pl.*

Kidnap, *v.a.* enlever

Kidnapper, *s.* enleveur, *m.*

Kidnapping, *s.* enlèvement, *m.*

Kidney, *s.* (*anat.*) rein, *m.*; (*meat*) rognon, *m.*; (*fig.*) espèce, trempe, *f.*, acabit, *m.* — **bean,** *s. V.* **Bean.** — **potato,** *s.* pomme de terre de Hollande, *f.*, (*red*) vitelotte, *f.* — **shaped,** [*adj.* réniforme

Kilderkin, *s.* demi-baril, *m.*

Kill, *v.a.* tuer, faire mourir; (*butch.*) abattre; (*time*) tuer; (*destroy*) détruire [-ère, *f.*

Killer, *s.* tueur, *m.*, -euse, *f.*; meurtrier, *m.*,

Killing, *s.* tuerie, *f.*, carnage, *m.*; meurtre, *m.*; (*butch.*) abattage, *m.*; — *adj.* tuant; mortel; assommant; écrasant; assassin

Killingly, *adv.* d'une manière tuante *or* &c. (*V.* **Killing,** *adj.*) [étuver

Kiln, *s.* four, *m.* — **dry,** *v.a.* sécher au four;

Kilogramme, *s.* kilogramme, *m.*

Kilolitre, *s.* kilolitre, *m.*

Kilometre, *s.* kilomètre, *m.*

Kilometric, -al, *adj.* kilométrique

Kilometrically, *adv.* kilométriquement

Kilt, *s.* jupe (de montagnard écossais), *f.*

Kimbo, *adj.* crochu, courbé; plié. *With his arms a* —, les poings sur les hanches

Kin, *s.* parenté, *f.*; (*pers.*) parent, *m.*, e, *f.*; allié, *m.*, e, *f.*; (*class*) famille, *f.*; nature, *f.* *The next of* —, le plus proche parent, *m.*, la plus proche parente, *f.*

Kind, *s.* genre, *m.*, espèce, sorte, *f.*; (*individuals of o.'s kind*) pareils, semblables, *m.pl.*; (*produce*) nature, *f.* . . . *of the* —, . . . de la sorte. *Nothing of the* —, rien de la sorte. *To pay in* —, payer en nature

Kind, *adj.* ('*to*,' pour) bon; aimable; obligeant; complaisant; bienfaisant; bienveillant; (*of compliments*) affectueux. *To be so — as to*, être assez bon pour, avoir la bonté de. *It is — of you*, *V.* **Of**

Kindle, *v.a.* allumer; (*fig.*) enflammer, embraser; (*revive*) réveiller; — *v.n.* s'allumer; (*fig.*) s'enflammer, s'embraser; (*revive*) se réveiller [*f.*; bonté, *f.*; douceur, *f.*

Kindliness, *s.* bienfaisance, *f.*; bienveillance,

Kindly, *adj.* bienfaisant; bienveillant; bon; doux; favorable; — *adv.* avec bienfaisance; avec bienveillance; avec bonté; obligeamment; complaisamment; volontiers; avec douceur; favorablement. *To* — (*do one a service*, &c.), avoir la bonté de . . . (&c.). *To take* —, prendre en bonne part, bien prendre; (*of*) savoir bon gré (à). *To take — to*, affectionner, aimer bien, s'adonner volontiers à, ne pas se priver de. *Thank you* —, merci bien

Kindness, *s.* bonté, bienveillance, *f.*; obligeance, *f.*; complaisance, *f.*; amabilité, *f.*; faveur, *f.*; service, *m.*, amitié, *f.*; bienfait, *m.* *To do a* —, rendre service, faire une amitié. *To have the — to*, avoir la bonté de, être assez bon pour. *A — is never thrown away*, un bienfait n'est jamais perdu

Kindred, *s.* parenté, *f.*; parents, *m.pl.*; affinité, *f.*, rapport, *m.*; — *adj.* de la même famille, du même ordre, de la même nature, du même genre; analogue; sympathique

Kine, *old pl. of* **Cow**

King, *s.* roi, *m.*; (*draughts*) dame, *f.*; — *v.a.* (*draughts*) damer. —*at-arms*, roi d'armes, *m.* — **Charles,** *s.* (*spaniel*) King-Charles, *m.*, babichon, *m.*, -ne, *f.* — **crab,** *s.* limule, *m.* — **craft,** *s.* politique, *f.*, art de régner, *m.* —**cup,** *s.* bouton d'or, *m.* —**dom,** *s.* royaume, *m.*; région, *f.*; empire, *m.*; (*nat. hist.*) règne, *m.* *United* —, royaume uni. *Animal, vegetable, mineral* —, règne animal, végétal, minéral. — **fish,** *s. V.* **Opah.** —**fisher,** *s.* martin-pêcheur, *m.* —**less,** *adj.* sans roi. —**let,** *s.* roitelet, *m.* **like, -ly,** *adj.* royal; *adv.* royalement, en roi. — **post,** *s.* (*build.*) poinçon, *m.* —**'s evil,** *s.* écrouelles, *f.pl.* —**'s scholar,** *s.* boursier, *m.*, -ière, *f.* —**ship,** *s.* royauté, *f.* —**wood,** *s.* bois de violette, *m.*

Kink, *s.* coque, *f.*; — *v.n.* prendre des coques

Kinkajou, *s.* kinkajou, *m.*

Kino, *s.* kino, *m.*

Kinsfolk, *s.* parents, *m.pl.*; parenté, *f.*

Kinship, *s.* parenté, *f.* [frère, *m.*

Kinsman, *s.* parent, *m.*; (*of the same sort*)

Kinswoman, *s.* parente, *f.*; (*of the same sort*)

Kiosk, *s.* kiosque, *m.* [sœur, *f.*

Kipper, *v.a.* saler et fumer; — *s.* poisson salé

Kirb. *V.* **Kerb** [et fumé, *m.*

Kirk, *s.* (*in Scotland*) église, *f.* [*m.*

Kirschwasser, Kirschenwasser, *s.* kirsch,

Kirtle, *s.* manteau, *m.*; (*petticoat*) jupon, *m.*

Kiss, *s.* baiser, *m.*; (*sweetmeat*) papillote, *f.*; (*at billiards*) contre-coup, contre, *m.*; — *v.a.* (*a person on the face*) embrasser; donner un baiser (*or* des baisers) à; caresser; (*things, a person's hands or feet*) baiser. *To — each other*, s'embrasser. *To — a person's hand*, baiser la main à quelqu'un. *To — o.'s (own) hand to a person*, envoyer un baiser (*or* des baisers) à quelqu'un

Kisser, *s.* embrasseur, *m.*, -euse, *f.*; baiseur, *m.*, -euse, *f.*

Kissing, *s.* embrassade, *f.*, embrassement, *m.*, baisers, *m.pl.*; (*of the Pope's toes*) baisement, *m.* — *of hands*, baisemain, *m.* — **crust,** *s.* biseau, *m.*, baisure, *f.*

Kit, *s.* petit (*or* jeune) chat, *m.*, petite (*or* jeune) chatte, *f.*; (*fiddle*) pochette, *f.*; (*tub*) seau, *m.*; (*for butter*) tinette, *f.*; (*of soldiers*) petit équipement, sac, *m.*; (*fam.*) hardes, *f.pl.*; (*of shoemakers*) saint-Crépin, *m.*

Kitchen, *s.* cuisine, *f.*; (*an utensil*) cuisinière, *f.*; — *adj.* de cuisine. — **boy,** *s.* marmiton, *m.* — **dresser,** *s.* table de cuisine, *f.* — **fat,** *s. V.* — **stuff.** — **garden,** *s.* jardin potager, potager, *m.* — **jack,** *s.* tournebroche, *m.* — **maid,** *s.* fille de cuisine, *f.* — **range,** fourneau de cuisine, *m.* — **stuff,** *s.* graisses de cuisine, *f.pl.* — **table,** *s.* table de cuisine, *f.* — **utensils,** *s.pl.* ustensiles de cuisine, *m.pl.*; batterie de cuisine, *f.* — **wench,** *s.* laveuse de vaisselle, *f.* — **work,** *s.* cuisine, *f.*

Kitchener, *s.* fourneau de cuisine, *m.*

Kite, *s.* (*bird*) milan, *m.*; (*toy*) cerf-volant, *m.*; (*pers.*) vautour, *m.* *To fly a* —, enlever un cerf-volant [amis, *m.pl.*

Kith, *s.* connaissance, *f.* — *and kin*, parents et

Kitten, *s.* petit (*or* jeune) chat, *m.*, petite (*or* jeune) chatte, *f.*; — *v.n.* mettre bas, chatter. *With* —, (*of she-cats*) pleine

Kittiwake, *s.* mouette rieuse, *f.*

Klepht, *s.* clephte, *m.*

Klephtic, *adj.* clephtique

Kleptomania. *V.* **Cleptomania**

Klick. *V.* **Click**

Knab. *V.* **Nab**

Knack, *s.* colifichet, *m.*, bagatelle, babiole, *f.*; (*dexterity*) adresse, *f.*, talent, chic, truc, *m.*; (*habit*) habitude, *f.*; mauvaise habitude, *f.*, tic, *m.*

Knacker, *s.* abatteur de chevaux, équarrisseur, *m.* —*'s yard*, abattoir de chevaux, chantier d'équarrissage, *m.*, écorcherie, *f.*

Knag, *s.* (*of a tree*) nœud, *m.*; (*peg*) cheville, *f.*

Knaggy, *adj.* noueux; (*crabbed*) hargneux

Knapsack, *s.* sac, havresac, *m.*; (*mil.*) sac, *m.*

Knapweed, *s.* jacée, *f.* [valet, *m.*

Knave, *s.* fripon, coquin, fourbe, *m.*; (*at cards*)

Knavery, *s.* friponnerie, coquinerie, fourberie, *f.*; (*trick*) malice, *f.*; tour, *m.*

Knavish, *adj.* de fripon, de coquin, malhonnête; (*mischievous*) malicieux, malin, espiègle. — *fellow*, fourbe, coquin, *m.* — *trick*, tour de coquin, *m.*, friponnerie, *f.*

Knavishly, *adv.* en fripon, en coquin; (*mischievously*) malicieusement

Knavishness, *s.* friponnerie, fourberie, *f.*; [malice, espièglerie, *f.*

Knead, *v.a.* pétrir

Kneader, *s.* pétrisseur, *m.*, -euse, *f.*; (*machine*) pétrin mécanique, *m.*
Kneading, *s.* pétrissage, *m.* — **machine, -mill,** *s.* pétrin mécanique, *m.* — **trough,** *s.* pétrin, *m.*, huche, *f.*
Knee, *s.* genou, *m.*; (*of machines*) coude, *m.*; (*nav.*) courbe, *f.*; (*a square*) équerre, *f.* *Broken — or —s*, (*of horses*) couronnement, *m.* *On o's —s*, sur ses genoux, sur les genoux; (*kneeling*) à genoux. *Down on your —s!* à genoux! *To bring on o.'s —s*, faire mettre à genoux; amener à demander pardon, faire demander pardon. — **boot,** *s.* botte à genouillère, *f.* — **breeches,** *s.pl.* culotte courte, *f.* —**cap,** *s.* genouillère, *f.*; (*anat.*) rotule, *f.* —**deep,** *adj. adv.* jusqu'aux genoux; à hauteur du genou. — **guard,** *s.* genouillère, *f.* — **high,** *adj. adv.* à hauteur du genou. — **holly,** *s.* brusc, *m.* — **joint,** *s.* articulation du genou, *f.* — **jointed,** *adj.* géniculé. — **pad, -piece,** *s.* genouillère, *f.* — **pan,** *s.* rotule, *f.* — **roll,** *s.* (*of a saddle*) avance, *f.* — **string,** *s.* attache, *f.*, cordon de culotte, *m.* — **trousers,** *s.pl.* culotte courte, *f.*
Kneed, *adj.* (*in compounds*) à genoux . . ., qui a les (*or* des) genoux . . .; (*of things*) coudé; (*bot.*) géniculé. *In- —*, *adj. s.* cagneux, *m.*, -euse, *f.*
Kneel, — down, *v.n.* s'agenouiller, se mettre [à genoux
Kneeling, *s.* agenouillement, *m.*; génuflexion, *f.*; — *part. adj.* (*action*) s'agenouillant; (*state*) agenouillé, à genoux. — **stool,** *s.* agenouil-[loir, *m.*
Knell, *s.* glas, *m.*
Knickerbockers, *s.pl.* culotte bretonne, cu-[lotte, *f.*
Knick-knack. *V.* **Nicknack**
Knife, *s.* couteau, *m.*; (*mach.*) coupoir, *m.*; (*chopper*) couperet, *m.*; (*surg.*) bistouri, *m.*; (*for pens*) canif, *m.*; (*dagger*) poignard, *m.* — *and fork*, couvert, *m.* — *War to the —*, guerre à mort *or* à outrance, guerre d'extermination, *f.* — **basket,** *s.* panier à couteaux, *m.* — **board,** *s.* planche à couteaux, *f.*; (*of a bus*) impériale, *f.* — **box,** *s.* boîte à couteaux, *m.* — **case,** *s.* (*sheath*) étui (*m.*) *or* gaîne (*f.*) de couteau; (*box*) boîte à couteaux, *f.* — **cleaner, -cleaning machine,** *s.* poli-couteaux, *m.* — **grinder,** *s.* repasseur de couteaux, rémouleur, *m.* — **rest,** *s.* porte-couteau, *m.* — **sharpener,** *s.* fusil, affiloir, *m.* — **tray,** *s.* *V.* — **basket**
Knight, *s.* chevalier, *m.*; (*chess*) cavalier, *m.*; — *v.a.* faire *or* créer chevalier; (*in France*) décorer. — *of the post*, chevalier d'industrie, *m.* — *of the rueful countenance*, chevalier de la triste figure, *m.* — **errant,** *s.* chevalier errant, *m.* (*V.* **Errantry**). — **head,** *s.* (*nav.*) apôtre, *m.* —**hood,** *s.* chevalerie, *f.* — **liness,** *s.* devoirs d'un chevalier, *m.pl.*; caractère chevaleresque, *m.* —**ly,** *adj.* de chevalier; de la chevalerie; *adv.* en chevalier. — **marshal,** *s.* maréchal du palais, *m.*
Knit, *v.a.n.* (*stockings*, &c.) tricoter; (*weave*) tresser; (*tie*) attacher, lier, nouer; unir; joindre; (*the brow*) froncer
Knitter, *s.* tricoteur, *m.*, -euse, *f.*
Knitting, *s.* tricotage, *m.*; (*fig.*) union, *f.* — **needle,** *s.* aiguille à tricoter, *f.*
Knittle, *s.* cordon, *m.*; (*nav.*) raban, *m.*
Knob, *s.* bosse, *f.*; (*of doors*) bouton, *m.*; (*of wood*) nœud, *m.* — **stick,** *s.* (*pers.*) antigréviste, *m.* [**Knotted, Knottiness, Knotty**
Knobbed, Knobbiness, Knobby. *V.*
Knock, *v.a.n.* frapper; heurter; cogner; — *s.* coup, *m.*; (*with a knocker*) coup de marteau, *m.*; (*way of knocking*) manière de frapper, *f.* *To — oneself*, se heurter, se cogner. *To give a —*, frapper, frapper un coup. *To hear a —*, entendre frapper. *There is a — at the door*, on frappe à la porte. — **about,** *v.a.* maltraiter, rudoyer; *v.n.* frapper de tous côtés; (*ramble*) aller de par le monde, (*fam.*) rouler sa bosse. — **away,** *v.n.* (*keep knocking*) frapper à coups redoublés. — **down,** *v.a.* renverser, terrasser, abattre, assommer; (*at auctions*) adjuger. — **in,** *v.a.* enfoncer; cogner. — **kneed,** *adj.* cagneux, jarreté. — **off,** *v.a.* faire sauter; faire tomber; finir, achever, expédier, faire, abattre (de la besogne), débiter (de l'ouvrage); (*of price*) rabattre. — **out,** *v.a.* faire sortir; faire tomber; (*the brain*) faire sauter. — **over,** *v.a.* faire tomber. — **under,** *v.n.* se rendre, se soumettre, céder. — **up,** *v.a.* (*weary*) éreinter, briser, rompre; (*awake*) réveiller, faire lever [(*of doors*) marteau, *m.*
Knocker, *s.* (*pers.*) personne qui frappe, *f.*;
Knocking, *s.* coups, *m.pl.*; coups de marteau, *m.pl.*
Knoll, *s.* tertre, monticule, *m.*, butte, *f.*; (*ringing*) tintement, son, *m.*; glas, *m.*; — *v.a.n.* tinter, sonner
Knot, *s.* nœud, *m.*; (*bond*) lien, *m.*; (*porter's —*) crochet, *m.*; (*group*, &c.) groupe, *m.*; troupe, *f.*; bande, *f.*; (*of gardens*) compartiment, *m.*; (*defect in glass*) boudine, *f.*, bouillon, *m.*; (*difficulty*) difficulté, *f.*, embarras, *m.*; (*nav.*) nœud, *m.*; (*bird*) maubèche, *f.*; — *v.a.* nouer, lier; (*entangle*) embrouiller, embarrasser; — *v.n.* faire des nœuds; (*bot.*) se nouer. *To run* or *make ten —s an hour*, filer dix nœuds à l'heure. *To tie* or *untie a —*, faire *or* défaire un nœud. — **berry,** *s.* *V.* **Cloudberry.** — **grass,** *s.* renouée, *f.* —**less,** *adj.* sans nœuds
Knotted, *adj.* noueux; (*of gardens*) à compartiments. — *stitch*, point de chaînette, *m.*
Knottiness, *s.* nature noueuse, nodosité, *f.*; (*fig.*) embrouillement, *m.*, difficulté, *f.*
Knotty, *adj.* noueux; (*rugged*) raboteux, rude; (*difficult*) difficile, embrouillé, épineux
Knout, *s.* knout, *m.*
Know, *v.a.n.* (*to be acquainted with through the senses: to have experienced, viz. seen, heard, smelt, tasted or felt before*) connaître; (*to be aware or conscious of, to have learnt by the application of the mind, by heart*, &c.) savoir; (*to be well aware*) savoir bien; (*recognize*) reconnaître ('*by*,' à); (*distinguish*) distinguer; (*see*) voir. *To — oneself*, se connaître. "— *thyself!*" "connais-toi toi-même." *To be known to*, être connu de. *Not that I — of*, pas que je sache. *I —!* connu! j'en réponds! *I don't —*, (*am not aware*) je ne sais pas; (*am not quite sure*) je ne sais pas trop. *To — better than to*, être trop prudent *or* trop raisonnable pour, n'avoir garde de, n'être pas si sot que de. *I — better!* je sais à quoi m'en tenir, je sais ce qui en est, je sais le contraire; (je ne suis) pas si bête! je connais ça! *I thought you would have known better*, je vous croyais plus de finesse *or* plus de raison. *You ought to have known better*, vous n'auriez pas dû vous y laisser prendre. *How do I —?* est-ce que je sais? *How do I — that . . .?* qu'est-ce qui me dit que . . .? — **again,** *v.a.* reconnaître, remettre. — **nothing,** *adj. s.* ignare [savoir
Knowable, *adj.* connaissable; qu'on peut
Knowing, *adj.* instruit, savant; éclairé; intelligent; (*cunning*) fin, rusé; déluré; — *s.* savoir, *m.*, science, *f.* *A — customer*, un rusé compère, *m.* [avec finesse; d'un air malin
Knowingly, *adv.* sciemment; (*cunningly*)
Knowledge, *s.* savoir, *m.*, science, *f.*; connaissance, *f.*; (*acquirements*) instruction, *f.*, connaissances, *f.pl.*; lumières, *f.pl.* *To my —*, à ma connaissance; que je sache. *Without my —*, à mon insu [de); &c. (*V.* **Know**)
Known, *part. adj.* connu ('*to*,' de); su ('*to*,'
Knubs, *s.pl.* coconille, *f.*, strasses, *f.pl.*
Knuckle, *s.* (*of the fingers*) jointure, articulation (des doigts), *f.*; (*finger*) doigt, *m.*; (*of veal*) jarret, *m.*; (*meat of a leg of mutton*) souris, *f.*; (*of hinges*) charnière, *f.*; — *v.n.* (— **down**) *See below.* — *of ham*, demi-jambon, *m.* *To rap a person's —s, to give a person a rap over the —s*, donner sur les doigts à quelqu'un. — **bone,** *s.* (*of a leg of mutton*) manche

(de gigot), *m.* — **bones,** *s. pl.* (*game*) osselets, *m.pl.* — **down,** *v.n.* se rendre, mettre (*or* coucher) les pouces. — **duster,** *s.* coup de poing, *m.* — **joint,** *s.* joint articulé, *m.*
Knuckled, *adj.* articulé
Kola, *s.* kola, cola, *m.*
Kohl-rabi, *s.* chou-rave, *m.*
Kopec, &c. *V.* **Copec,** &c.
Koran, *s.* Coran. Alcoran, *m.*
Kris, *s. V.* **Creese**
Krum-horn, *s* cromorne, *m.*
Kuskus, *s.* couscous, couscoussou, *m.*
Kyanite, *s.* cyanite, *f.*
Kyanize, *v.a.* kyaniser
Kymric. *V.* **Cymric**
Kyrie, *s.* kyrié, *m.*

L

L, *s.* (*letter*) l, *f.*; (*pound*) livre sterling, livre, *f.*
La, *int.* là! tenez! voyez donc! — *s.* (*mus.*) la, *m.*
Label, *s.* étiquette, *f.*; écriteau, *m.*; (*her.*) lambel, *m.*; (*bot.*) labelle, *m.*; — *v.a.* étiqueter
Labial, *adj. s.* labial, *adj. m.*, e, *f.*, labiale, *s.f.*
Labiate, Labiated, *adj.* labié
Laboratory, *s.* laboratoire, *m.*
Laborious, *adj.* laborieux; (*difficult*) pénible
Laboriously, *adv.* laborieusement; péniblement [difficulté, *f.*
Laboriousness, *s.* laboriosité, *f.*; labeur, *m.*;
Labour, *s.* travail, *m.*; peine, *f.*; labeur, *m.*; (*manual*) main-d'œuvre, *f.*, travail, *m.*; (*piece of work*) ouvrage, *m.*; œuvre, *f.*; (*childbirth*) travail d'enfant, *m.*; — *v.a.n.* travailler; (*strive*) s'efforcer (de), s'attacher (à), s'appliquer (à), tâcher (de); (— **under**) être tourmenté *or* travaillé (par), souffrir (de); éprouver; (*struggle*) lutter (contre); (*of error*) être dans (l'erreur). *Division of* —, division du travail, *f.* *Hard* —, (*punishment*) travail dans l'intérieur de la prison, *m.*; emprisonnement pénal, *m.*, réclusion, *f.* *Manual* —, travail manuel, travail *or* ouvrage de manœuvre, *m*; main-d'œuvre, *f.* *To have o.'s — for o.'s pains,* avoir l'aller pour le venir, perdre sa peine, en être pour sa peine *or* pour ses frais. *The —s of Hercules,* les travaux d'Hercule. *The mountain in* —, la montagne qui accouche
Labourer, *s.* ouvrier, *m.*, -ière, *f.*; homme de peine, *m.*; (*by the day*) journalier, *m.*, -ière, *f.*; (*build.*, &c.) manœuvre, *m.*; (*road* —) cantonnier, *m.*; (*dock* —) déchargeur, *m.*; (*fig.*) travailleur, *m.*, -euse, *f.*
Labouring, *adj.* qui travaille; ouvrier. — **class,** *s.* classe ouvrière, *f.* — **man,** *s. V.* **Labourer**
Laburnum, *s.* faux-ébénier, aubour, *m.*
Labyrinth, *s.* labyrinthe, dédale, *m.*
Labyrinthian, Labyrinthic, *adj.* labyrinthique [—, gomme laque, *f.*
Lac, *s.* laque, *f.*; (*of rupees*) lack, lac, *m.* *Gum*
Lace, *s.* dentelle, *f.*; (*vellum* —) guipure, *f.*; (*of boots, stays,* &c.) lacet, *m.*; (*tape*) cordon, ruban, *m.*; (*of gold,* &c.) galon, passement, *m.*; — *v.a.* (*fasten*) lacer; (*trim*) garnir de dentelle; (*with gold,* &c.) galonner, passementer; (*fig.*) broder; (*thrash*) étriller, rosser. — **-bark tree,** *s.* bois dentelle, laget, *m.* — **boot,** *s.* brodequin, *m.* — **cap,** *s.* bonnet de dentelle, *m.* — **frame, -machine,** *s.* métier à dentelle, *m.* — **hole,** *s.* œillet, *m.* — **maker,** *s.* fabricant de dentelle, *m.*; dentellière, *f.*; passementier, *m.*, -ière, *f.* — **man,** *s.* marchand de dentelles, *m.*; passementier, *m.* — **paper,** *s.* papier-dentelle, *m.* — **trade,** *s.* commerce de dentelle, *m.*; passementerie, *f.* — **woman,** *s.* marchande de dentelle, *f.*; dentellière, *f.*; passementière, *f.* — **work,** *s.* dentelle, *f.*; passementerie, *f.*

Laced, *part. adj.* lacé, &c. (*V.* **Lace,** *v.a.*); (*with lace*) à dentelle, &c.; (*of coffee*) à l'eau-de-vie. — *paper,* papier-dentelle, *m.*
Lacedæmonian, *s. adj.* Lacédémonien, *m.*, [-ne, *f.*
Lacer, *s.* laceur, *m.*, -euse, *f.*
Lacerable, *adj.* lacérable [**Lacerated**
Lacerate, *v.a.* déchirer, lacérer; — *adj. V.*
Lacerated, *part. adj.* déchiré, lacéré. — *wound,* plaie par arrachement, déchirure, *f.*
Laceration, *s.* déchirement, *m.*, déchirure, lacération, *f.*
Laches, *s.* négligence, *f.*; retard, retardement, *m.*
Lachryma-christi, *s.* lacryma-christi, *m.*
Lachrymal, *adj.* lacrymal
Lachrymary, *adj.* lacrymatoire
Lachrymatory, *s.* lacrymatoire, *m.*
Lachrymose, *adj.* larmoyant [terie, *f.*
Lacing, *s.* lacement, *m.*; (*articles*) passemen-
Lack, *v.a.* manquer de, n'avoir pas, être dénué de, avoir besoin de; — *v.n.* manquer; être dans le besoin; — *s. V.* **Want;** (*of rupees*) *V.* **Lac.** — **brain,** *s.* écervelé, *m.*, e, *f.*, tête sans cervelle, *f.* — **land,** *adj.* sans terre
Lackadaisical, *adj.* minaudier; sentimental;
Lack-a-day, *int.* hélas! [langoureux
Lacker. *V.* **Lacquer** [faire le laquais; suivre
Lackey, *s.* laquais, valet de pied, *m.*; — *v.n.*
Laconian, *s. adj.* Laconien, *m.*, -ne, *f.*
Lacon-ic, al, -ically, -ism. *V.* page 3, 1
Lacquer, *s.* laque, *m.*; — *v.a.* laquer, vernisser de laque. — **work,** *s.* laque, *m.*
Lacquerer, *s.* vernisseur en laque, *m.*
Lacquering, *s.* vernissure en laque, *f.*
Lacrymal, &c. *V.* **Lachrymal,** &c.
Lactary, *adj.* lactaire
Lactate, *s.* lactate, *m.*
Lactation, *s.* lactation, *f.*
Lacteal, Lacteous, *adj.* lacté; — *s.* vaisseau lacté, *m.*, veine lactée, *f.*
Lactescence, *s.* lactescence, *f.*
Lactescent, *adj.* lactescent
Lactic, *adj.* lactique
Lactiferous, *adj.* lactifère
Lactometer, *s.* lactomètre, *m.*
Lacustral, Lacustrine, *adj.* lacustre
Lad, *s.* jeune garçon, garçon, jeune homme, *m.*; (*in addressing*) ami, garçon, enfant, brave, *m.*
Ladder, *s.* échelle, *f.*; (*stairs*) escalier, *m.* — **rope,** *s.* tire-veille, *f.*
Lade, *v.a.* charger ('*with*,' de); — *v.n.* faire un chargement; être en charge. — **out,** *v.a.* [vider, écoper
Lading, *s.* chargement, *m.*
Ladle, *s.* cuiller à potage *or* à soupe, grande cuiller, louche, poche, *f.*; cuiller, *f.*; — *v.a.* (— **out**) servir. —**ful,** *s.* cuillerée, *f.*
Lady, *s.* dame, *f.*; (*title*) lady (*English*), *f.*; (*woman*) femme, *f.*; (*well-bred woman*) femme comme il faut, femme bien élevée, *f.* *Young* —, jeune dame, *f.*; (*unmarried*) demoiselle, jeune personne, *f.*; (*in addressing*) mademoiselle! *Ladies!* mesdames! *Young ladies!* mesdemoiselles! *My* —, madame la comtesse *or* la marquise *or*, &c., madame. *That* —, *that young* —, cette dame, cette demoiselle. *This* (or *the*) —, *this* (or *the*) *young* —, (*here present*) madame, mademoiselle. *These* or *those* —*s, young* —*s,* ces dames, ces demoiselles. *A —'s watch,* une montre de femme *or* de dame. *She is a* —, c'est une femme comme il faut. *She is a perfect* —, c'est une femme très comme il faut. ('*Lady,' followed by another noun of which it serves to indicate the gender, is generally rendered in French by one word, with its feminine ending; as,* — *friend,* amie, — *passenger,* voyageuse, — *reader,* lectrice, — *rider,* cavalière. — *superintendent,* directrice; &c.) — **bird, -cow, -fly,** *s.* bête à Dieu, bête à bon Dieu, coccinelle, *f.* —**'s companion,** (or *companion to a* —), *s.* dame (*or* demoiselle) de compagnie, *f.* —**day,** *s.* fête de l'Annonciation, *f.* (le) vingt-cinq mars, *m.* —**'s finger,** *s.* biscuit à la cuiller, *m.* — **killer,** *s.* homme

à bonnes fortunes, lovelace, *m.* — **killing,** *s.* bonne fortune, *f.*, bonnes fortunes, *f.pl.* — **like,** *adj.* de dame; délicat; élégant; distingué; (*pers.*) bien élevé, comme il faut, de bon ton, de bonne société, de manières distinguées, bien; (*in contempt*) efféminé. —**love,** *s.* amante, bien-aimée, (la) dame de ses (*or* mes, &c.) pensées, *f.* —**'s maid,** *s.* femme de chambre, *f.* —**ies' man,** *s.* (la) coqueluche des femmes, *f.* —**'s mantle,** *s.* (*bot.*) alchimille, *f.* —**ship,** *s.* *Your —ship,* madame (*or* madame la comtesse, &c.) vous. *Her —ship,* (madame) la comtesse *or* &c. —**'s slipper,** *s.* (*bot.*) cypripède, *m.*

Lag, *v.n.* rester en arrière; traîner; lambiner

Laggard, Lagger, *s.* traînard, traîneur, *m.*, [lambin, *m.*, e, *f.*

Lagomys, *s.* lagomys, *m.*

Lagoon, Lagune, *s.* lagune, *f.*

Laic, -al, *adj.* laïque

Laid, *part. adj.* posé, &c. (*V.* **Lay,** *v.a.*); (*paper manu.*) vergé (*blue* —, vergé bleu); (*of cables*) commis. — **up,** *part. adj.* mis de côté, &c. (*V.* **Lay up**); (*in bed*) alité, au lit; (*with*) retenu au lit *or* chez soi (par), ma ade (de) (*To be — up,* être alité *or* &c.; garder la chambre); (*of ships*) désarmé

Lair, *s.* repaire, *m.*; antre, *m.*; (*hunt.*) fort, *m.*, reposée, *f.*; (*grass-land*) prairie, *f.*, pré, *m.*

Laird, *s.* (*Scotch*) seigneur, propriétaire, laird, *m.*

Laity, *s.* laïques, *m.pl.*

Lake, *s.* lac, *m.*; (*colour*) laque, *f.* —**coloured,** *adj.* laqueux. — **School,** *s.* (*Engl. liter.*) [lakistes, *m.pl.*

Lakelet, *s.* laquet, petit lac, *m.*

Lallation, *s* lallation, *f.*

Lama, *s.* lama, *m.*

Lamantin, *s.* lamantin, *m.*

Lamb, *s.* agneau, *m.*, (*ewe* —) agnelle, *f.*; — *v.n.* agneler. *With* —, (*of ewes*) pleine. *God tempers the wind to the shorn* —, à brebis tondue Dieu mesure le vent. — **chop,** *s.* côtelette d'agneau, *f.* —**kin,** *s.* petit agneau, agnelet, *m.* —**like,** *adj.* d'agneau; doux comme un agneau. —**'s fry,** *s.* issues d'agneau, *f.pl.* —**skin,** *s.* peau d'agneau, *f.* —**'s lettuce,** *s.* mâche, doucette, *f.* —**'s wool,** *s.* laine [d'agneau, *f.*

Lambent, *adj.* léger, qui effleure

Lambing, *s.* agnellement, agnelage, *m.*

Lame, *adj.* estropié; (*in one leg*) boiteux; (*fig.*) imparfait, défectueux; mauvais; (*of stories*) borgne; (*of language*) qui cloche; — *v.a.* estropier. *A — story,* un conte borgne, *m.* *To walk* or *go* —, boiter, clocher

Lamellar, *adj.* lamellaire

Lamellate, Lamellated, *adj.* lamellé

Lamellose, *adj.* lamelleux

Lamely, *adv.* en boitant, en clochant; (*fig.*) imparfaitement, mal [imperfection, faiblesse, *f.*

Lameness, *s.* boitement, clochement, *m.*; (*fig.*)

Lament, *v.n.* se lamenter, s'affliger, gémir, pleurer; — *v.a.* regretter, déplorer, pleurer; — *s.* lamentation, plainte, *f.*; complainte, *f.*

Lamentable, *adj.* lamentable; déplorable; pitoyable, misérable

Lamentably, *adv.* lamentablement; déplorablement; pitoyablement, misérablement

Lamentation, *s.* lamentation, *f.*

Lamenting, *s.* lamentations, plaintes, *f.pl.*

Lamia, *s.* lamie, *f.*

Lamina, *s.* lame, *f.*; (*bot.*) limbe, *m.*

Laminability, *s.* laminabilité, *f.*

Laminable, *adj.* laminable

Laminar, -y, *adj.* laminaire

Laminaria, *s.* laminaire, *f.*

Laminate, *v.a.* laminer

Laminating, *s.* laminage, *m.*

Laminitis, *s.* avalure, *f.*

Laminose, Laminous, *adj.* lamineux

Lamish, *adj.* légèrement boiteux

Lammas, *s.* jour de Saint-Pierre-ès-Liens, pre- [mier août, *m.*

Lämmergeier, *s.* gypaète, *m.*

Lamp, *s.* lampe, *f.*; (*of carriages, boats*) lanterne, *f.*; (*bull's-eye* —) fanal, *m.*; (*of streets*) candélabre, *m.*; (*for illuminations*) verre, lampion, *m.*; (*of locomotives*) fanal, *m.*; (*poet.*) lumière, *f.*, flambeau, *m.*; —**s,** *pl.* lampes, &c.; (*theat.*) rampe, *f.* *Argand* —, lampe d'Argand, *f.*, quinquet, *m.* *Carcel* —, lampe Carcel, carcel, *f.* *To smell of the* —, sentir l'huile. — **black,** *s.* noir de fumée, *m.*; *adj.* de noir de fumée. — **chimney,** *s.* verre de lampe, *m.* — **cotton,** *s.* mèche (*f.*, *or* mèches, *f.pl.*) de lampe (*or* de lampes). — **globe,** *s.* globe de lampe, *m.* — **keeper,** *s.* lampiste. *m.* — **light,** *s.* lumière de lampe *or* &c., *f.* — **lighter,** *s.* allumeur, *m.*; lampiste, *m.* — **maker,** *s.* lampiste, *m.* — **making,** *s.* lampisterie, *f.* — **mat,** *s.* dessous de lampe, *m.* — **oil,** *s.* huile à brûler, *f.* —**post,** *s.* candélabre, *m.*; lampadaire, *m.* — **room,** *s.* lampisterie, *f.* — **rug,** *s.* *V.* — **mat.** — **shade,** *s.* abat-jour, *m.* — **shell,** *s.* térébratule, *f.* — **stand,** *s.* pied de lampe, *m.* — **wick,** *s.* mèche de lampe, *f.*

Lampas, Lampass, *s.* lampas, *m.*, fève, *f.*

Lampern, *s.* lamproie de rivière, *f.*

Lampic, *adj.* lampique

Lampoon, *s.* libelle, *m.*, satire, *f.*; — *v.a.* écrire un libelle *or* une satire contre

Lampooner, *s.* libelliste, satiriste, *m.* [*m.*

Lamprel, *s.* petite lamproie de rivière, *f.*, sucet,

Lamprey, *s.* lamproie, *f.* — **net,** *s.* lam- [presse, *f.*

Lanate, Lanated, *adj.* laineux

Lancasterian, *adj.* lancastérien

Lancastrian, *adj.* lancastrien, de Lancastre; — *s.* Lancastrien, *m.*, -ne, *f.*

Lance, *s.* lance, *f.*; — *v.a.* percer d'un coup de lance, percer; (*surg.*) donner un coup de lancette à, percer *or* ouvrir (avec la lancette). — **bucket,** *s.* porte-lance, *m.* — **corporal,** *s.* (*of infantry*) élève-caporal, caporal postiche, *m.*; (*of cavalry*) sous-brigadier, *m.* — **head,** *s.* pointe de lance, *f.* — **rest,** *s.* arrêt de lance, *m.* — **shaped,** *adj.* lancéolé, lancéolaire. — — **wood,** *s.* bois d'arc, *m.*

Lanceolar, *adj.* lancéolaire

Lanceolate, Lanceolated, *adj.* lancéolé

Lancer, *s.* lancier, *m.*

Lancet, *s.* lancette, *f.*; (*dentist's*) déchaussoir, *m.*; — *adject.* (*arch.*) ogival, ogive, en ogive, en lancette. — **case,** *s.* (*surg.*) lancetier, *m.* — **window,** *s.* fenêtre en ogive *or* en lancette, *f.*

Lanch, &c. *V.* **Launch,** &c.

Lancinate, *v.n.* lanciner

Lancing, *s.* coup de lancette, *m.*

Land, *s.* terre, *f.*; domaine, *m.*; (*country*) pays, *m.*; contrée, *f.*; (*real estate*) bien-fonds, *m.*, terre, *f.*; — *adj.* de terre; (*by land*) par terre; (*of property*) foncier; — *v.a.n.* débarquer; aborder; atterrer, atterrir. *To make* —, or *the* —, atterrer, atterrir. — **agent,** *s.* agent d'affaires, *m.* — **breeze,** *s.* brise de terre, *f.* — **carriage,** *s.* transport par terre, roulage, *m.* — **chain,** *s.* (*civ. engin.*) chaîne d'arpenteur, *f.*; (*math.*) chaîne, *f.* — **crab,** *s.* crabe de terre, gécarcin, *m.* — **fall,** *s.* atterrage, *m.* — **fight,** *s.* combat sur terre, *m.* — **flood,** *s.* inondation, *f.*, débordement, *m.* — **force,** *s.* armée de terre, *f.*, troupes de terre, *f.pl.* —**grave,** *s.* landgrave, *m.* — **graviate,** *s.* landgraviat, *m.* —**gravine,** *s.* landgravine, *f.* —**holder,** *s.* propriétaire foncier, *m.* —**ing,** *s.* *See below.* — **jobber,** *s.* spéculateur sur les biens-fonds *or* sur les terrains, *m.* —**lady,** *s.* (*owner*) propriétaire, *f.*; (*of hotels and inns*) maîtresse d'un hôtel *or* d'une auberge, hôtelière, aubergiste, hôtesse, *f.*; (*of a house, abusively in the sense of 'tenant having lodgers'*) propriétaire, *f.*; principale locataire, *f.* —**locked,** *adj.* entouré par des terres, situé au milieu des terres. — **lord,** *s.* (*owner*) propriétaire, *m.*; (*of hotels and inns*) maître d'un hôtel *or* d'une auberge, hôtelier, aubergiste, hôte, *m.*; (*of a house, abusively in the sense of 'tenant having lodgers'*) propriétaire, *m.*; principal locataire, *m.* — **lubber,** *s.* marin d'eau douce. *m.* — **man,** *s.*

homme de terre, *m.*; soldat de l'armée de terre, *m.*; compatriote, *m.*; (*nav.*) marin d'eau douce, *m.* —**mark,** *s.* limite, borne, *f.*; point de reconnaissance, *m.*; (*fig.*) guide, fanal, *m.*; (*nav.*) amer, *m.* — **measure,** *s.* mesure agraire, *f.* — **measuring,** *s.* *V.* — **surveying.** — **office,** *s.* bureau de cadastre, *m.* — **owner,** *s.* propriétaire foncier, *m.* — — **presser,** rouleau plombeur, *m.* —**rail,** *s.* (*bird*) râle de genêts, *m.* —**reeve,** sous-intendant, *m.* — **roller,** *s.* rouleau plombeur, *m.* —**scape,** *s.* paysage, *m.*; (*prospect*) point de vue, coup d'œil, *m.* —**scape gardener,** *s.* architecte-paysagiste, dessinateur *or* architecte de jardins, jardiniste, *m.* —**scape gardening,** *s.* architecture paysagiste, *f.*, dessin de jardins, *m.* —**scape painter** *or* **paintress,** *s.* peintre de paysage, *m.f.*, paysagiste, *m.f.* — **scape painting,** *s.* peinture de paysage, *f.*, le paysage, *m.* — **service,** *s.* service militaire, *m.* —**slip, -slide,** *s.* éboulement de terre, *m.* —**sman,** *s.* *V.* — **man.** — **sturm,** *s.* landsturm, *m.* — **surveying,** *s.* arpentage, *m.*; lever des plans, *m.* — **surveyor,** *s.* arpenteur, *m.* — **tax,** *s.* impôt foncier, *m.*, contribution foncière, *f.* — **trade** *or* **travelling,** *s.* commerce *or* voyage par terre, *m.* — **waiter,** *s.* douanier de la côte, douanier, *m.* — **ward,** *adv.* du côté de la terre, vers la terre. — **wehr,** *s.* landwehr, *f.* — **wind,** *s.* vent de terre, *m.*

Landau, *s.* landau, *m.*

Landed, *adj.* foncier, de bien-fonds, territorial. — *property* or *estate*, bien-fonds, *m.*, propriété foncière, *f.*

Landing, *s.* débarquement, *m.*; (*of staircases*) palier, carré, *m.*; perron, *m.*; (*of quays*, &c.) débarcadère, *m.* — **net,** *s.* épuisette, *f.* — **place,** *s.* débarcadère, *m.*; (*of stairs*) palier, carré, *m.*; perron, *m.* — **stage,** *s.* débarcadère *or* embarcadère flottant, *m.* — **step,** *s.* marche-palier, *f.* — **waiter,** *s.* *V.* **Landwaiter**

Lane, *s.* ruelle, *f.*, sentier, *m.*; allée, *f.*; (*in towns*) ruelle, *f.*, passage, *m.*, rue, *f.*

Langrage, Langrel, *s.* mitraille, *f.*

Language, *s.* langage, *m.*; expression, *f.*; style, *m.*; (*speech*) parole, *f.*; (*vernacular tongue*) langue, *f.*; idiome, *m.* *Bad* or *ill* —, mauvais style, *m.*; (*abuse*) grossièreté, *f.*; grossièretés, *f.pl.*, gros mots, *m.pl.*

Languedocian, *s.adj.* Languedocien, *m.*, -ne, *f.*

Languid, *adj.* languissant; faible

Languidly, *adv.* languissamment, avec langueur; faiblement

Languidness, *s.* langueur, *f.*; faiblesse, *f.*

Languish, *v.n.* languir; — *s.* langueur, *f.*

Languishing, *adj.* languissant; langoureux

Languishingly, *adv.* languissamment; langoureusement

Languor, *s.* langueur, *f.*

Laniard, *s.* (*nav.*) garant, *m.*; (*of buoys*) corde, *f.*; (*of shrouds, stays*) ride, *f.*; (*of stoppers*) aiguillette, *f.*; (*artil.*) tire-feu, *m.*

Laniferous, *adj.* lanifère

Lanigerous, *adj.* lanigère

Lank, *adj.* (*loose*) flasque, mou; (*thin*) maigre, mince, fluet; (*flat*) plat; (*languid*) languissant; (*bot.*) effilé, élancé. — *fellow*, grand sec, grand flandrin, *m.*

Lankly, *adv.* mollement; maigrement

Lankness, *s.* (*laxity*) mollesse, *f.*; (*leanness*) maigreur, *f.*

Lanky, *adj.* *V.* **Lank**

Lanner, *s.* lanier, *m.*

Lanneret, *s.* laneret, *m.*

Lansquenet, *s.* lansquenet, *m.*

Lantana, *s.* lantanier, *m.*

Lantern, Lanthorn, *s.* lanterne, *f.*; (*nav.*) fanal, phare, *m.* — **fly,** *s.* fulgore, porte-lanterne, *m.* *Chinese* — *fly*, porte-chandelle, *m.* — **jawed,** *adj.* qui a les joues creuses, aux joues creuses. — **jaws,** *s. pl.* joues creuses, *f.pl.* — **light,** *s.* lanterne, *f.* — **maker,** *s.* lanternier, *m.* — **tower,** *s.* lanterne, *f.* — **wheel,** *s.* lanterne, *f.*

Lanuginous, *adj.* lanugineux

Lanyard. *V.* **Laniard**

Lap, *s.* (*of coats*) pan, *m.*; (*knees*) genoux, *m.*; (*bosom*) giron, sein, *m.*; (*of the ear*) lobe, *m.*; (*tech.*) recouvrement, *m.*; — *v.a.n.* (*fold*) plier; envelopper; rouler; (*lick*) laper; (*cover*) retomber. *In the* — *of*, sur les genoux de; (*fig.*) dans le sein *or* &c. de. — **dog,** *s.* chien de salon, chien d'appartement, petit chien, *m.*; levrette, *f.* — **eared,** *adj.* *V.* **Lop-eared.** —**ful (A),** *s.* plein son tablier. — **over,** *v.n.* retomber, recouvrir. — **sided,** *adj.* bordier. — **stone,** *s.* pierre à battre. — **up,** *v.a.* laper, avaler. — **wing,** *s.* vanneau, pivite, *m.* — **work,** *s.* ouvrage à clin, *m.*

Lapel, *s.* revers, *m.*

Lapidary, *s.* lapidaire, *m.*; joaillier, *m.*, -ière, *f.*; — *adj.* de lapidaire; lapidaire

Lapidate, *v.a.* lapider

Lapidation, *s.* lapidation, *f.*

Lapidescence, *s.* lapidescence, *f.*

Lapidescent, *adj.* lapidescent

Lapidific, *adj.* lapidifique

Lapidification, *s.* lapidification, *f.*

Lapidify, *v.a.* lapidifier; — *v.n.* se lapidifier

Lapis lazuli, *s.* lapis-lazuli, *m.*

Lapithæ, *s pl.* les Lapithes, *m.pl.*

Laplander, *s.*, **Laplandish,** *adj.* Lapon, *m.*, e, *f.*

Lappet, *s.* (*of head-dresses*) barbe, *f.*; (*of coats*) pan, *m.*; (*lapel*) revers, *m.*

Lapping, *s.* (*licking*) lapement, *m.*; (*tech.*) recouvrement, *m.*; rebord, *m.*; — *adj.* (*tech.*) à recouvrement. — **over,** *s.* recouvrement, *m.*

Lapse, *s.* (*of streams*) chute, *f.*, cours, *m.*; (*course*) cours, *m.*, marche, *f.*; (*of time*) laps, laps de temps, *m.*; (*error*) faute, erreur, méprise, *f.*; (*slip*) faux pas, écart, *m.*; oubli, *m.*; (*of livings*) dévolu, *m.*; (*theol.*) chute, *f.*; — *v.n.* (*fall*) tomber; (*fail*) faillir, faire un faux pas, commettre une faute *or* une erreur; (*of time*) s'écouler, passer; (*sink*) déchoir; (*pass out of date*) périmer, se périmer; (*of legacies*) être caduc; (*can. law*) tomber en dévolu par péremption

Lapsed, *part. adj.* tombé, périmé, &c. (*V.* **Lapse,** *v.n.*); (*omitted*) omis; échappé; (*of legacies*) caduc; (*can. law*) laps, dévolu par péremption

Larboard, *s.* bâbord, *m.*

Larceny, *s.* vol, *m.*; larcin, *m.*; filouterie, *f.* *Petty* —, vol simple

Larch, — **tree,** *s.* mélèze, *m.*

Lard, *s.* saindoux, *m.*; (*pharm.*) axonge, *f.*; — *v.a.* ('*with*,' de) larder, piquer; (*fig.*) larder, assaisonner

Lardaceous, *adj.* lardacé

Larder, *s.* garde-manger, *m.*, office, *f.*

Larding, *s.* action de larder, *f.* — **needle, -pin,** *s.* lardoire, *f.*

Lardite, *s.* lardite, *f.*

Lardoon, *s.* lardon, *m.*

Lares, *s. pl.* lares, *m.pl.*

Large, *adj.* (*big*) gros; (*tall, high, long*) grand; (*extensive*) grand; fort; large; vaste; étendu; considérable; (*main*) principal; (*numerous*) nombreux; (*nav.*) largue. *At* —, amplement, au long; en liberté; en général. *To grow* —, grandir, grossir. — **hand, -text,** *s.* (*writ.*) grosse, *f.* — **sized,** *adj.* grand; grand modèle; de grande taille

Largely, *adv.* grandement, avec étendue; largement; amplement; au long; abondamment; libéralement, avec libéralité

Largeness, *s.* (*bulk*) grosseur, *f.*; (*greatness*) grandeur, *f.*; (*wideness*) largeur, *f.*; (*extent*) étendue, *f.*; (*liberality*) libéralité, *f.*

Larger, *adj. comp.* plus gros, plus grand, &c. (*V.* **Large**). *To grow* —, grandir, grossir. *To make* —, agrandir; grossir

Largess, *s.* largesse, libéralité, *f.*

Lark, *s.* (*bird*) alouette, *f.*; (*cook.*) mauviette, *f.*; (*sport*) farce, *f.*; escapade, *f.* *To have a* —, *To* — (*v.n.*), faire une farce *or* une escapade; rigoler. — **spur,** *s.* pied-d'alouette, *m.*

Larker, *s.* oiseleur (d'alouettes), *m.*

Larva, Larve, *s.* larve, *f.* [laryngien
Laryngeal, Laryngean, *adj.* laryngé,
Laryngitis, *s.* laryngite, *f.*
Laryngoscope, *s.* laryngoscope, *m.*
Laryngo-scopic, al, -scopy, -tomy, &c.
Larynx, *s.* larynx, *m.* [*V.* page 3, § 1
Lascar, *s.* lascar, *m.*
Lascivious, *adj.* lascif
Lasciviously, *adv.* lascivement
Lasciviousness, *s.* lasciveté, *f.*
Lash, *s.* (*thong*) lanière, *f.*; (*point of a whip*) mèche, *f.*; (*stroke*) coup de fouet, *m.*; coup d'étrivières, *m.*; (*lashing*) (le) fouet, *m.*, (les) étrivières, *f.pl.*; (*for dogs*) laisse, *f.*; (*sarcasm*) trait, coup de langue, coup de patte, *m.*; (*of the eye*) cil, *m.*; — *v.a.n.* fouetter; cingler; (*against*) battre; (*censure*) critiquer, abîmer, flageller; (*fasten*) attacher; (*nav.*) amarrer
Lasher, *s.* fouetteur, *m.*, -euse, *f.* [amarrage, *m.*
Lashing, *s.* flagellation, *f.*; —**s,** *pl.* (*nav.*)
Lass, Lassie, *s.* jeune fille, fille, fillette, *f.*
Lassitude, *s.* lassitude, *f.* [prendre au lasso
Lasso, *s.* lasso, *m.*; — *v.n a.* chasser au lasso;
Lassoing, *s.* chasse au lasso, *f.*
Last, *adj.* dernier; — *adv.* dernièrement; en dernier lieu; enfin; à la fin; après tout; (*last time*) la dernière fois; pour la dernière fois; (*of place*) le dernier, au dernier rang, en dernière ligne; — *s.* dernier, *m.*, -ière, *f.*; (*end*) fin, *f.*; bout, *m.*; (*of shoemakers*) forme, *f.*; (*load*) charge, *f.*; (*measure*) mesure, *f.*; — *v.n.* durer; (*keep*) se conserver; (— **out**) surpasser en durée; (*tide over*) passer. — *but one*, avant-dernier. — *but two, three,* &c., dernier moins deux, trois, &c. *At —,* enfin; à la fin. *To the —,* jusqu'à la fin, jusqu'au bout, jusqu'au dernier moment. — *Monday*, lundi dernier. — *week*, la semaine dernière. *The — week*, la dernière semaine. — *time, the — time*, la dernière fois. *The — judgment*, le jugement dernier. *I have not seen him for these — ten years*, je ne l'ai pas vu depuis dix ans, *or* il y a dix ans que je ne l'ai vu. *Dinner has been waiting for these — two hours*, le dîner attend depuis deux heures, *or* il y a deux heures que le dîner attend. *When I saw him —*, la dernière fois que je l'ai vu. *When did you see him — ?* combien de temps y a-t-il que vous ne l'avez vu? *To breathe o.'s —*, *V.* **Breathe.** — *come best served*, aux derniers les bons. — **maker,** *s.* formier, *m.*
Lastage, *s.* lestage, lest, *m.*; chargement, fret, *m.*
Lasting, *adj.* durable; permanent; (*colour*) solide; — *s.* (*stuff*) lasting, *m.*
Lastingly, *adv.* durablement, permanemment, d'une manière durable *or* permanente, perpétuellement
Lastingness, *s.* durabilité, *f.*; durée, *f.*
Lastly, *adv.* en dernier lieu, finalement, enfin
Latakia, *s.* latakia, *m.*
Latania, *s.* latanier, *m.*
Latch, *s.* loquet, *m.*; — *v.a.* fermer au loquet, fermer. *On the —*, fermé au loquet. — **key,** *s.* clé de loquet, *f.*; (*one of several*) passe-par-
Latchet, *s.* cordon (de soulier), *m.* [tout, *m.*
Late, *adj. adv.* tard; (*behind a fixed time*) en retard; (*tardy*) tardif; (*hort.*) tardif; d'arrière-saison; (*far advanced*) avancé; (*remote*) reculé; (*last*) dernier; récent; (*former*) ancien; ex- , . .; (*of the dead*) feu; (*no longer in a situation*) ex- . . .; (*lately*) récemment, dernièrement. *The — king*, le feu roi, feu le roi. *My — uncle*, feu mon oncle. *The — queen*, la feue reine, feu la reine. *A — minister*, un ex-ministre. *Of —*, dernièrement, depuis peu, depuis quelque temps, dans ces derniers temps. *Of — years*, depuis quelques années. — *of London*, dernièrement domicilié à Londres. *Till —*, tard; jusqu'à (*or*, *after a neg.*, avant) une heure avancée, jusqu'à (*or* avant) un âge avancé. *To be —*, arriver *or* venir tard; (*home*) rentrer tard; (*behind o.'s or its time*) être en retard; (*of time itself, imp.*) être tard. *To be getting* or *growing —, to get* or *grow —*, (*of time*) se faire tard. *To make —*, retarder, mettre en retard. *To keep — hours*, *V.* **Hour.** *Better — than never*, mieux vaut tard que jamais
Lateen, *adj.* — *sail*, voile latine, *f.* — *yard*, vergue latine, antenne, *f.*
Lately, *adv.* dernièrement, récemment, fraîchement, depuis peu. *Till* or *until —*, jusqu'à ces derniers temps, jusqu'à une époque récente; (*after a neg.*) ne . . . que depuis quelque temps
Lateness, *s.* retard, *m*; (*of days, nights*) heure avancée, *f.*; (*of life, seasons*) époque avancée, *f.*; (*of fruits*, &c.) tardiveté, tardivité, *f.*; (*recency*) nature récente, *f.*; (*remoteness*) époque reculée, *f.* — *of the hour*, heure avancée, *f.*
Latent, *adj.* caché; secret; (*phys.*) latent
Latently, *adv.* secrètement; (*phys.*) latemment, d'une manière latente
Later, *adj. adv. comp.* plus tard, &c. (*V.* **Late**); postérieur (à), ultérieur (à), subséquent
Lateral, *adj.* latéral, de côté
Laterally, *adv.* latéralement, de côté
Lateran, *s.* Latran, *m.*
Latest, *adj. adv. super.* plus récent, dernier; (*remotest*) plus reculé; &c. (*V.* **Late**). *At the —, at —*, au plus tard. — *news* or *intelligence*, dernières nouvelles, *f.pl.*
Lath, *s.* latte, *f.*; planchette, *f.*; — *v.a.* latter. — **render,** *s.* fendeur de lattes, *m.* — **work,**
Lathe, *s.* tour, *m.* [*s.* lattis, lattage *m.*
Lather, *v.n.* mousser; — *v.a.* savonner; — *s.* mousse, *f.*; (*of perspiration*) écume, *f.*
Lathing, *s.* lattage, *m.* [flasque
Lathy, *adj.* comme une latte; sec, décharné;
Latin, *adj.* latin, *m.*, e, *f.*; — *s.* le latin, *m.*, la langue latine, *f.* *Low —*, la basse latinité, *f.*
Latin-ism, -ist. *V.* page 3, § 1
Latinity, *s.* latinité, *f.*
Latinization, *s.* latinisation, *f.*
Latinize, *v a.n.* latiniser
Latinizer, *s.* latiniseur, *m.*
Latish, *adj.* un peu tard *or* &c. (*V.* **Late**)
Latitude, *s.* latitude, étendue, *f.*; (*astr., geog.*) latitude, *f.*; (*nav.*) parage, *m.*
Latitudinarian, *adj. s.* latitudinaire
Latitudinarianism, *s.* latitudinarisme, *m.*
Latrines, *s.pl.* latrines, *f.pl.*
Latten, *s.* ferblanc, *m.*; (*brass*) laiton, cuivre jaune, *m.*; cuivre laminé, *m.*
Latter, *adj.* dernier. *The —*, celui-ci, celle-ci, ceux-ci, celles-ci. *The — . . .*, ce dernier . . ., cette dernière . . ., ces derniers . . ., ces dernières . . .; ce *or* cet . . ., cette . . ., ces . . . — *end* or *part*, fin, *f.* —**day saint,** *s.* mormon, *m.* —**math,** *s.* regain, *m.*
Latterly, *adv.* dernièrement, récemment, depuis peu, dans ces derniers temps; dans les derniers temps; vers la fin
Lattice, *s.* treillis, *m.* treillage, *m.*; (*of wire*) grillage, *m.*; — *adj.* de treillis, de treillage; de grillage; (*furnished with*) à treillis, à treillage; à grillage; — *v.a.* treillisser. garnir d'un treillis; former en treillis; grillager. — **maker,** *s.* treillageur, *m.* — **window,** *s.* fenêtre treillissée, *f.* — **work,** *s.* treillage, treillis, *m.*; (*of wire*) grillage, *m.*
Laud, *s.* louange, *f.*; (—**s,** *pl., prayers*) laudes, *f.pl.*; — *v.a.* *V.* **Praise,** *v.a.*
Laudable, *adj.* louable
Laudableness, Laudability, *s.* nature louable, *f.*, caractère louable, mérite, *m.*
Laudably, *adv.* louablement, d'une manière
Laudanum, *s.* laudanum, *m.* [louable
Laudation, *s.* *V.* **Praise,** *s.*
Laudative, Laudatory, *adj.* laudatif, louangeur; — *s.* éloge, panégyrique, *m.*
Laudator, Lauder. *V.* **Praiser**
Laugh, *v.n.* rire (de); (*deride, ridicule*) se moquer (de), se rire (de), rire (de); (*smile*) sourire; — *s.* rire, *m.*; éclat de rire, *m.*; hilarité, *f.*;

(*mockery*) risée, *f.* *To — the wrong side of o.'s mouth*, rire jaune. *To burst out —ing*, éclater de rire, partir d'un éclat de rire. *To force a —*, s'efforcer de rire, rire du bout des dents *or* du bout des lèvres. *To raise a —*, faire rire. *To set up a —*, se mettre à rire. *There is nothing to — at*, il n'y a pas de quoi rire. *Let them — that win*, rira bien qui rira le dernier. (*A —*), [*in reports of speeches*, &c.] (On rit), (Rires dans l'auditoire), (Rires)
Laughable, *adj.* risible
Laughableness, *s.* risibilité, *f.*
Laughably, *adv.* risiblement
Laugher, *s.* rieur, *m.*, -euse, *f.*
Laughing, *part. adj.* riant; rieur; enjoué; (*to be laughed at*) risible; — *s.* rire, *m.*, rires, *m.pl.* — **gas,** *s.* gaz hilarant, *m.* — **matter,** *s.* chose risible, *f.*; objet de risée, *m.* —**stock,** *s.* risée, *f.*, jouet, plastron, *m.*
Laughingly, *adv.* en riant
Laughter, *s. V.* **Laugh**
Launce, *s.* équille, *f.*, lançon, *m.*
Launch, *v.a.* lancer, mettre à l'eau; (*fig.*) lancer; — *v.n.* se lancer; se jeter; — *s.* lancement, *m.*, mise à l'eau, *f.*; (*boat*) chaloupe, *f.* — **out,** *v.n.* se lancer (dans); se jeter (dans); s'étendre (sur)
Launching, *s.* lancement, lançage, *m.*, mise à l'eau, *f.* — **ways,** *s.pl. V.* **Bilge-ways**
Launderer, *s.* blanchisseur, *m.*; buandier, *m.*
Laundress, *s.* blanchisseuse, *f.*; laveuse, *f.*; buandière, *f.*; (*in chambers*) femme de ménage, *f.*
Laundry, *s.* blanchisserie, *f.*; blanchissage, *m.*; buanderie, *f.*; lavoir, *m.* — **cart,** *s.* voiture de blanchisseur, *f.* — **company,** *s.* compagnie de blanchissage, *f.* — **man,** *s. V.* **Launderer.** — **works,** *s.pl.* blanchisserie, *f.*
Laureate, *adj.* (*things*) couronné de lauriers; (*pers.*) lauréat; — *s.* lauréat, *m.*; — *v.a.* couronner
Laureated, *adj. V.* **Laurelled**
Laurel, *s.* laurier, *m.*; — *adj.* de laurier. — **bay, -cherry,** *s.* laurier-cerise, *m.* — **grove, -plantation,** *s.* laurière, *f.* — **water,** *s.* eau de laurier-cerise, *f.* — **wreath,** *s.* couronne de laurier, *f.*
Laurelled, *adj.* couronné de laurier, lauré
Laurestine. *V.* **Laurustine**
Laurine, *s.* laurine, *f.*
Laurustine, Laurustinus, *s.* laurier-tin, *m.*
Lava, *s.* lave, *f.*
Lavabo, *s.* lavabo, *m.*
Lavatera, *s.* (*bot.*) lavatère, *f.*
Lavaterian, *adj.* lavatérien
Lavatic, *adj.* lavique
Lavation, *s.* lavage, *m.*, (*fam.*) lavation, *f.*
Lavatory, *s.* lavoir *m.*; (*in schools*) salle de toilette, *f.*
Lave, *v.a.* laver, baigner; — *v.n.* se laver, se baigner
Lavender, *s.* lavande, *f.* *To bring up in —*, élever dans du coton. — **water,** *s.* eau de lavande, *f.*
Laver, *s.* bassin (*m.*) *or* cuve (*f.*) d'airain; (*bot.*) ulve, laitue de mer, *f.*; varech comestible, *m.*
Lavic, *adj* lavique
Lavish, *adj.* prodigue; excessif; — *v.a.* prodiguer. — **away,** *v.a.* prodiguer; dissiper
Lavisher, *s.* prodigueur, *m.*, -euse, *f.*
Lavishly. *V.* **Prodigally**
Lavishment, Lavishness, *s.* prodigalité, *f.*
Law, *s.* loi, *f.*; (*jurisprudence*) droit, *m.*; (*bar*) barreau, *m.*; (*chicanery*) la chicane, *f.*, les procès, *m.pl.* *Civil —*, droit civil, *m.*; droit romain, *m.* *Criminal —*, droit criminel, *m.* *Martial —*, loi martiale, *f.*, lois militaires, *f.pl.*; code militaire, *m.* — *of nations*, droit international, (*old*) droit des gens, *m.* *Court of —*, cour de justice, *f.* *Courts of —*, (*building*) palais de justice, *m.* *Going to —*, les procès, *m.pl.* *In —*, de droit; en droit; (*of relations*) beau-, *m.*, belle-, *f.* *To be —*, avoir force de loi; faire loi. *To be at —*, être en procès. *To give — to*, faire la loi à, donner des lois à. *To go to —*, avoir recours à la justice, recourir en justice, plaider. *To go to — with one, to sue one at —*, citer quelqu'un en justice, poursuivre quelqu'un, faire *or* intenter un procès à quelqu'un. *To study —*, étudier le droit; (*of a regular course*) faire son droit. *To take the — into o.'s own hands*, se faire justice à soi-même. — **abiding,** *adj.* qui observe la loi. — **book,** *s.* livre de droit, *m.* — **breaker,** *s.* transgresseur de la loi, *m.* — **courts,** *s.pl.* cours de justice, *f.pl.*; (*building*) palais de justice, *m.* — **day,** *s.* jour de palais, *m.* — **expenses, -costs,** *s.pl.* frais de procédure, *m.pl.* —**ful,** *adj.* légal; légitime; (*allowable*) permis, loisible. —**fully,** *adv.* légalement; légitimement. —**fulness,** *s.* légalité, *f.*; légitimité, *f.* —**giver,** *s. V.* — **maker.** —**less,** *adj.* sans loi; illégal; (*uncontrolled*) sans frein, effréné, déréglé. —**lessly,** *adv.* sans loi; illégalement. —**lessness,** *s.* illégalité, *f.*; licence, *f.*, désordre, *m.* — **maker,** *s.* législateur, *m.*, -trice, *f.* — **making, -giving,** *adj.* (*pers.*) législateur; (*things*) législatif. — **merchant,** *s.* droit commercial, *m.* — **officer,** *s.* officier civil, officier de justice, *m.* — **report,** *s.* bulletin judiciaire, *m.*, gazette des tribunaux, *f.* — **school,** *s.* école de droit, *m.* — **stationer,** *s.* expéditionnaire, *m.* — **student,** *s.* étudiant en droit, *m.* —**suit,** *s.* procès, *m.* — **term,** *s.* (*word*) terme de droit *or* de pratique *or* de palais, *m.*; (*time*) session, *f.* — **writer,** *s. V.* — **stationer**
Lawn, *s.* pelouse, *f.*, gazon, boulingrin, tapis vert, *m.*; (*linen*) linon, *m.*; (*of bishops*) robe, *f.*; *adj.* de pelouse, de gazon, &c.; de linon. — **mower,** — **mowing-machine,** *s.* tondeuse de gazon, *f.* —**sleeve,** *s.* manche de linon, *f.*
Lawyer, *s* homme de loi, *m.*; légiste, jurisconsulte, juriste, *m.*; (*solicitor*) avoué, *m.*; (*pleader*) avocat, *m.*
Lawyerly, *adj.* judiciaire
Lax, *adj.* (*not tight*) lâche, relâché; (*flabby*) flasque, mou; (*in morals*, &c.) relâché
Laxation, *s.* relâchement, *m.*
Laxative, *adj. s.* laxatif, *adj.m.*, -ive, *f.*, laxatif, *s.m.*
Laxativeness, *s.* propriété laxative, *f.*
Laxity, *s.* laxité, *f.*; relâchement, *m.*; (*flabbiness*) flaccidité, *f.*; (*want of exactness*) manque d'exactitude *or* de précision, *m.*
Laxly, *adv.* lâchement; flasquement, mollement; négligemment; sans précision
Laxness. *V.* **Laxity**
Lay, *v.a.n.* mettre, poser, placer; ranger; appliquer; (*lay down*) déposer; (*lay flat, lay along, the corn or &c.*) coucher; (*beat down, the dust or &c.*) abattre; (*calm, the wind or &c.*) apaiser, calmer; (*rest*) reposer; (*bury*) déposer; (*spread, stretch*) étendre; (*exhibit*) exposer, soumettre; (*impute*) imputer (à) attribuer (à), mettre sur le compte (de); (*impose*) imposer ('*upon*,' à); (*a tax*) mettre; (*scheme*) former, tramer, concerter; (*a wager*) faire; (*to wager*) parier, gager; (*a snare*, &c.) tendre, dresser; (*dishes on table*) servir; (*tech., build.*) poser; (*paint*) peindre; (*eggs*) pondre; (*strike*) frapper; — *s.* (*song*) chant, *m.*; (*poem*) lai, *m.*; — *adj.* laïque, lai. — **about** *one*, frapper de tous côtés, frapper de droite et de gauche. — **apart,** mettre à part *or* de côté. — **aside,** mettre de côté *or* à part; garder; écarter; abandonner, quitter, renoncer à; abdiquer; (*send away*) renvoyer. — **away,** ôter; quitter. — **brother,** *s.* frère lai, frère convers, convers, *m.* — **by,** mettre de côté, garder. — **clerk,** *s.* répondant, *m.*; chantre, *m.* — **day,** *s.* (*com. nav.*) jour de planche, jour de starie, *m.* — **down,** déposer; poser; mettre bas; coucher; reposer; établir; renoncer à; quitter; donner; exposer, expliquer; tracer; (*a book, shut it*) fermer. — **figure,** *s.* (*paint.*) mannequin, *m.*, maquette, *f.* — **in,** présenter; amasser; (*a stock*) faire (une *or* sa provision). —**man,** *s.* laïque, *m.*; (*of cathedrals*) chantre, *m.*; (*paint., old*) *V.* — **figure.** — **off,** ôter. —

on, étendre; appliquer; poser; imputer (à), mettre sur le compte (de); imposer; (*strike*) frapper fort. — *it* **on,** (*beat*) étriller; (*lie*) broder, exagérer; (*in price*) surfaire, saler. — **open,** ouvrir; découvrir, mettre à découvert, mettre à nu; faire voir; exposer. — **out,** arranger, disposer; (*a table, a plan*) dresser; (*ground*) tracer, disposer, distribuer; (*a corpse*) ensevelir; (*display*) déployer; (*spend*) dépenser; employer; (*invest*) placer. — **over,** étendre; (*cover*) couvrir; enduire; (*inlay*) incruster. — **sister,** *s.* sœur laie, sœur converse, converse, *f.* — **stall,** *s.* tas de fumier, *m.*; dépôt d'immondices, *m.* — **to,** imputer *or* &c. à; (*nav.*) mettre en panne. — **together,** rassembler, réunir. — **up,** mettre de côté; (*keep*) garder; (*to store*) amasser; économiser; (*a ship*) désarmer; (*in bed*) retenir au lit, tenir renfermé. *To be laid up*, (*in bed*) *V.* **Laid**

Layer, *s.* (*bed, stratum*) couche, *f.*, lit, *m.*; (*of plants*) marcotte, *f.*, (*of vine*) provin, *m.*; (*hen*) pondeuse, *f.*; (*pers.*) poseur, *m.*, -euse, *f.*; — *v.a.* marcotter; (*vine*) provigner

Layering, *s.* marcottage, *m.*

Laying, *s.* (— **on, down**) mise, *f.*; (*of birds*) ponte, *f.*; (*hort.*) *V.* **Layering**; (*tech.*) pose, *f.*, posage, *m.*; — **time,** *s.* saison de la ponte, ponte, *f.*

Lazar-house, Lazaret, Lazaretto, *s.* [lazaret, *m.*

Laze, *v.n.* paresser, fainéanter

Lazily, *adv.* dans la paresse; avec paresse, nonchalamment; (*slowly*) lentement

Laziness, *s.* paresse, fainéantise, *f.*

Lazuli, *s.* lazuli, *m.*

Lazulite, *s.* lazulite, *f.*

Lazy, *adj.* paresseux, fainéant; (*things*) indolent; de paresse. —*bones*, (*s.*) fainéant, *m.*, e, *f.*, cagnard, *m.*, e, *f.* — *fellow* or *man* or *boy*, — *thing* or *woman* or *girl*, *V.* **Idle**

Lazzarone, *s.* lazzarone, *m.* (*pl.* lazzaroni)

Lb., (*abbrev.*) *V.* **Pound**

Lea, *s.* pré, *m.*, prairie, *f.*; plaine, *f.*; (*skein*) [échevette, *f.*

Leach, *s.* cendre de lessive, *f.*; — *v.a.* lessiver. — **tub,** *s.* cuve à lessive, *f.*, cuvier, *m.*

Lead, *s.* (*min.*) plomb, *m.*; (*for pencils*) mine de plomb, *f.*; (*print.*) interligne, *f.*; (*nav.*) sonde, *f.* —**s,** *s.pl.* (*roof*) toiture en plomb, *f.*, plombs, *m.pl.*, toit, *m.*; — *adj.* de plomb; — *v a.* plomber; (*print.*) interligner. *To heave the* —, sonder, jeter la sonde. — **colic,** *s.* colique de plomb, colique saturnine, *f.* — **coloured,** *adj.* couleur de plomb, plombé. — **glance,** *s.* galéne, *f.* — **line,** *s.* ligne de sonde, *f.* — — **manufactory, -manufacture,** *s.* plomberie, *f.* — **mine,** *s.* mine de plomb, *f.* — **pencil,** *s.* crayon de mine de plomb, *m.* — **ore,** *s.* minerai (*m.*) *or* mine (*f.*) de plomb. — **shot,** *s.* plomb de chasse, *m.* —**sman,** *s.* (*nav.*) sondeur, *m.* — **wire,** *s.* plomb filé, *m.* — **work,** *s.* plombage, *m.* — **works,** *s.pl.* plomberie, *f.* — **wort,** *s.* dentelaire, *f.*

Lead, *s.* (*guidance*) conduite, direction, *f.*; (*precedence*) pas, *m.*, préséance, *f.*; première place, *f.*; (*influence*) influence, *f.*; (*at play*) début, *m.*; (*at cards*) main, *f.*; (*billiards*) acquit, *m.*; — *v.a.n* conduire, mener; guider, diriger; dominer; commander; marcher le premier; (*spend*) mener; (*induce*) porter (à), faire; (*entice*) induire (à), entraîner (à), pousser (à); (*at play*) débuter; (*at cards*) avoir la main, jouer le premier. *To have the* —, (*at play*) jouer le premier; (*at cards*) avoir la main. *To take the* —, marcher en avant; se mettre à la tête; occuper la première place; être à la tête; dominer, primer; présider. *To — one to believe*, porter quelqu'un à croire, faire croire à quelqu'un. — **along,** conduire, mener. — **astray,** égarer; détourner (de). — **away,** emmener; entraîner. — **back,** reconduire, remener. — **off,** détourner; (*take away*) emmener; (*v.n.*) marcher en tête, se mettre à la tête. — **on,** conduire; (*drag*) entraîner; (*v.n.*) marcher en tête. — **out,** conduire dehors; conduire. — **out** *of the* **way,** égarer. — **to,** (*to cause*) être cause de, causer, occasionner, donner lieu à, motiver. — *the* **way,** marcher en tête *or* en avant, marcher le premier, ouvrir la marche; montrer *or* frayer le chemin; entraîner; amener

Leaden, *adj.* de plomb; couleur de plomb, [plombé; (*heavy*) lourd

Leader, *s.* conducteur, *m.*, -trice, *f.*, guide, *m.*; chef, *m.*; coryphée, *m.*; commandant, *m.*; (*of a party*) chef de parti, *m.*; (*of a faction*) meneur, *m.*; (*going first*) premier, *m.*; (*of newspapers*) article principal, article de fond, *m*; (*barrister*) avocat principal, *m.*; (*mus.*) premier violon, *m.*; (*of carriage horses*) cheval de volée, *m.*; (*of cart or waggon horses*) cheval de devant, *m.*; (*leash*) laisse, *f.*

Leadership, *s.* direction, *f.*; conduite, *f.*

Leading, *s.* (*plumbing*) plombage, *m.*

Leading, *s.* (*guidance*) conduite, direction, *f.*; — *adj.* (*chief*) principal, premier; (*great*) grand. — **article,** *s.* article principal, article de fond, *m.* — **man,** *s.* homme le plus important, *m.*; chef, *m.*; notabilité, *f.* — **note,** *s.* note sensible, sensible, *f.* — **strings,** *s. pl.* lisière, *f.*, lisières, *f.pl.* — **wind,** *s.* (*nav.*) [vent arrière, *m.*

Leady, *adj.* *V.* **Leaden**

Leaf, *s.* feuille, *f.*; (*of books*) feuillet, *m.*; (*of doors*) battant, *m.*; (*flap of a table*) pan, *m.*; (*insertion in telescope-tables*) allonge, rallonge, *f.*; — *v.n.a.* feuiller. *To turn down the* —, faire une corne au feuillet *or* à la page. *To turn over the leaves of a book*, feuilleter un livre. *To turn over a new* —, (*fig.*) changer de gamme, changer de conduite. — **bud,** *s.* bourgeon, bouton, *m.*; (*of grafting*) écusson, *m.* — **gold,** *s.* or en feuilles, *m.* — **insect,** *s.* phyllie, *f.* —**less,** *adj.* sans feuilles; effeuillé. —**lessness,** *s.* effeuillement, *m.* —**let,** *s.* petite feuille, *f.*; (*bot.*) foliole, *f.* — **stalk,** *s.* pétiole, *m.* — **tobacco,** *s.* tabac en feuilles, *m.* — **turner,** *s.* tourne-feuilles, tourne- [feuillets, *m.*

Leafage, *s.* feuillage, *m.*

Leafy, *adj.* feuillu; touffu; ombragé; (*bot.*) feuillé

League, *s.* ligue, *f.*; (*distance*) lieue, *f.*; — *v.a.* liguer, coaliser; — *v.n.* se liguer, se coaliser

Leaguer, *s.* confédéré, *m.*; (*hist.*) ligueur, *m.*

Leak, *s.* (*of liquids*) fuite, *f.*; (*of ships*) voie d'eau, *f.*; (*of canals*, &c.) perte d'eau, *f.*; — *v.n.* fuir, couler; (*nav.*) faire eau

Leakage, *s.* (*of liquids*) fuite, perte, *f.*; (*quantity lost*) coulage, *m.*; (*nav.*) voies d'eau, *f.pl.*

Leaky, *adj.* qui fuit, qui coule; (*nav.*) qui fait eau

Lean, *v.n.* pencher; (*of attitude*) se pencher; (*rest*) s'appuyer; — *v.a.* faire pencher, pencher; (*rest*) appuyer; — *adj.* maigre; (*poor*) pauvre, chétif, misérable; — *s.* maigre, *m.* *Growing* —, amaigrissement, *m.* *To get* or *grow* —, maigrir. *To make* —, amaigrir. — **to,** *s.* *V.* **Penthouse**

Leaning, *s.* action de pencher, *f.*, penchement, *m.*; action de s'appuyer, *f.*; (*fig.*) penchant, *m.*; tendance, *f.*; partialité, *f.* — *part.* (*active sense*) appuyant; (*neuter sense*) s'ap- [puyant; appuyé

Leanly, *adv.* maigrement

Leanness, *s.* maigreur, *f.*; amaigrissement, *m.*

Leap, *v.a.n.* sauter; (*clear*) franchir; (*rush*) s'élancer, se précipiter; (*of male animals*) saillir, monter; — *s.* saut, *m.*; bond, *m.*; (*of male animals*) saut, *m.*, monte, *f.* — **frog,** *s.* saute-mouton, *m.* — **off,** *v.n.* sauter. — **year,** *s.* année bissextile, *f.*

Leaper, *s.* sauteur, *m.*, -euse, *f.*

Leaping, *adj.* sauteur; — *s.* saut, *m.*, sauts, *m.pl.*

Leapingly, *adv.* en sautant, par sauts

Learn, *v.a.n.* apprendre; s'instruire

Learnable, *adj.* apprenable

Learned, *adj.* savant; instruit, érudit, lettré, docte; (*of professions*) libéral

Learnedly, *adv.* savamment

Learner, *s.* personne qui apprend, *f.*; écolier, *m.*, -ière, *f.*, élève, *m.f.*; apprenti, *m.*, e, *f.*

Learning, *s.* science, *f*, savoir, *m.*, instruction, érudition, *f.*; acquisition, *f.*; (*literature*) lettres, belles-lettres, *f.pl.*

Lease, *s.* bail, *m.*; — *v.a.* donner *or* louer à bail; — *v.n.* glaner. *To take a new* (or *a fresh*) — *of life,* faire corps neuf, renouveler son bail de vie. —**hold,** *s.* tenure par bail, *f.*; *adj.* à bail; par bail. —**holder,** *s.* locataire à bail, *m.f.*

Leaser, *s.* glaneur, *m.*, -euse, *f.*

Leash, *s.* laisse, *f.*; — *v.a.* attacher; mener à la laisse; tenir en laisse

Least, *adj.* moindre, plus petit; — *adv.* moins; le moins; — *s.* moins, *m.* *At* —, (*minimum*) au moins; (*restriction*) du moins; au moins. *At the* —, *at the very* —, tout au moins, pour le moins. *In the* —, le moins du monde. *Not in the* —, nullement, pas (*or* point) du tout, pas le moins du monde. *To say the* — *of it,* pour ne pas dire plus, au moins, au bas mot. — *said, soonest mended,* trop gratter cuit, trop parler nuit

Leather, *s.* cuir, *m.*; peau, *f.*; (*of spurs*) monture, *f.*; — *adj.* de (*or* en) cuir; de (*or* en) peau; — *v.a.* (*put leather*) garnir de cuir; (*beat*) étriller, rosser, donner les étrivières à. *Upper* —, (*of boots*) empeigne, *f.* *There is nothing like* —, (*jest.*) prenez mon ours. — **breeches,** *s. pl.* culotte de peau, *f.* — **bottle,** *s.* outre, bouteille de cuir, *f.* — **cloth,** *s.* tissu de cuir, *m.* — **cutter,** *s.* coupeur de cuir, *m.* — **dresser,** *s.* mégissier, *m.* — **dressing,** *s.* mégisserie, *f.* — **market,** *s.* halle aux cuirs, *f.* — **seller,** *s.* marchand (*m.*, e, *f.*) de cuirs, peaussier, *m.* — **trade,** *s.* commerce de cuirs, *m.* — **wood,** *s.* bois de cuir, *m.*

Leathering, *s.* (*blows*) râclée, *f.*

Leathern, *adj.* *V.* **Leather,** *adj.*

Leathery, *adj.* comme le cuir; (*tough*) coriace

Leave, *s.* permission ('*to*,' de), *f.*; liberté, *f.*; (— *of absence*) congé, *m.*; (*ticket*) permis, *m.*; exeat, *m.*; (*farewell*) congé, adieu, *m.*; — *v.a.n.* quitter; laisser; abandonner; (*not to take away, not to go to*) laisser; (*trust*) s'en remettre (à), s'en rapporter (à); (*depart*) partir. *On* —, *on* — *of absence,* en congé. *To give* —, donner la permission (à ... de ...), permettre (à ... de ...). *To take* —, prendre congé (de); faire ses adieux (à), dire adieu (à); s'en aller. *To take French* —, partir sans prendre congé; décamper *or* filer sans rien dire; s'absenter sans permission; prendre la permission sous son bonnet. *To* — *the house* or *the room,* sortir. *To* — *one to himself,* laisser quelqu'un de côté *or* dans son coin; livrer quelqu'un à lui-même. *To be left* ..., *V.* **Left.** — *it to me!* laissez-moi faire! — **about,** laisser traîner. — **alone,** *V.* **Let.** — **off,** quitter; laisser de côté; laisser là; cesser, discontinuer, s'arrêter; renoncer à; (*stop*) en rester. — **out,** laisser dehors; omettre, passer; supprimer. — **taking,** *s.* adieux, *m.pl.* — *it* **to,** s'en rapporter à; laisser faire

Leaved, *adj.* feuillé; (*in compounds*) à feuilles ..., à ... feuilles; (*of doors*) à ... battants; &c. (*V.* **Leaf**). *Double* — *door,* porte à deux battants, *f.*

Leaven, *s* levain, *m.*; — *v.a.* faire lever; (*taint*) [gâter, corrompre, infecter

Leavened, *adj.* où il y a du levain; (*fig.*) infecté. — *bread,* pain au levain, *m.*

Leavings, *s. pl.* restes, *m.pl.*

Lecher, *s.* débauché, libertin, *m.*

Lecherous, *adj.* lascif, lubrique

Lecherously, *adv.* lascivement, lubriquement

Lecherousness, Lechery, *s.* lasciveté, [lubricité, *f.*

Lectern, *s.* lutrin, *m.*

Lection, *s.* leçon, *f.*

Lectionary, *s.* lectionnaire, épistolier, *m.*

Lecture, *s.* ('*on*,' de, sur) leçon, *f.*; ('*on*,' sur) conférence, *f.*, ('*on*,' de) séance, *f.*; ('*on*,' sur) discours, *m.*; (*sermon*) sermon, prêche, prône, *m.*; (*reprimand*) semonce, *f.*; —*s, course of* —*s,* cours, *m.* ('*on*,' de); — *v.n.a.* faire une leçon (de, sur); faire une conférence (sur); donner une séance (de); prononcer un discours (sur); faire un cours (de); (*reprimand*) donner une semonce à, sermonner. *To deliver* or *give a* —, *V. To* —, *v.n.a.* — **hall, -room,** *s.* salle de cours, *f.*; salle des conférences, *f.*; (*of hospitals*) amphithéâtre, *m.*

Lecturer, *s.* professeur, maître de conférences, *m.*; conférencier, *m.*, -ière, *f.*; démonstrateur, *m.*; orateur, *m.*; (*at church*) prédicateur, *m.*

Lectureship, *s.* professorat, *m.*; chaire, *f.*

Lecturn, *s.* *V.* **Lectern**

Led, *part.* conduit, mené, &c. (*V.* **Lead,** *v.a.n.*); — *adj.* (*of horses*) de conduite, de main

Ledge, *s.* rebord, bord, *m.*; (*layer*) couche, *f.*; (*of rocks*) chaîne, *f.*; (*a rock*) récif, *m.*; (*arch.*) saillie, *f.*; (*of a wall-map,* &c.) gorge, *f.*

Ledger, *s.* grand livre, *m.* — **line,** *s.* *V.* **Leger-line**

Lee, *s.* (*dregs*) lie, *f.*; (*nav.*) côté opposé au vent, côté de dessous le vent, *m.*; — **s,** *s. pl.* lie, *f.*; — *adj.* sous le vent. — **board,** *s.* semelle, dérive, *f.* — **gage,** *s.* dessous du vent, *m.* — **sheet,** *s.* écoute sous le vent, *f.* — **shore,** *s.* terre sous le vent, *f.* — **side,** *s.* côté sous le vent, *m.* —**ward,** *adj. adv.* sous le vent. — **way,** *s.* dérive, *f.*

Leech, *s.* sangsue, *f.* — **culture,** *s.* hirudiniculture, hirudiculture, *f.* — **fisher, -gatherer,** *s.* pêcheur de sangsues, *m.* — **fishing, -gathering,** *s.* pêche de sangsues, *f.* — **grower,** *s.* hirudiniculteur, hirudiculteur, *m.*

Leek, *s.* poireau, *m.* [— **net,** *s.* pêchette, *f.*

Leer, *v.n.a.* regarder du coin de l'œil, faire de l'œil (à); lorgner; — *s.* œillade, *f.*; regard du coin de l'œil, regard de côté, *m.*

Leering, *s.* œillades, *f.pl.*; regards du coin de l'œil, regards de côté, *m.pl.* [avec une œillade

Leeringly, *adv.* en regardant du coin de l'œil,

Leet, *s.* cour de centurie, *f.*

Left, *part.* laissé, &c. (*V.* **Leave,** *v.a.n.*); — *adj.* gauche; (*remaining*) qui reste, de reste (*to be* —, rester); — *s.* gauche, *f.* *At the* —, *on the* —, *to the* —, à gauche. *Over the* —, (*fam.*) par-dessus l'épaule. — *face!* (*mil.*) à gauche! — *about face!* — *about!* (*mil.*) demi-tour à gauche! *To be* — *without* ..., rester *or* être sans ... *I have six of them* —, il m'en reste six, j'en ai encore six. *What is* — (*anyone*)? que reste-t-il (à quelqu'un)? *I have nothing* —, il ne me reste rien. *I have* — *nothing,* je n'ai rien laissé. *There is some wine* —, il reste du vin, il y a encore du vin. *There is not one drop* —, il ne reste pas une goutte, il n'y a plus une seule goutte. — **hand,** *s.* main gauche, *f.*; (*side*) gauche, *f.*; *adj.* de gauche. — **handed,** *adj.* gaucher; (*of marriages*) de la main gauche. — **luggage office,** *s.* bureau des bagages en dépôt, dépôt de bagages, *m*, consigne, *f.* — **off,** *adj.* de rebut, abandonné

Leg, *s.* (*pers.*) jambe, *f.*; (*of animals, except those with a hoof*) patte, *f.*; (*of animals with a hoof*) jambe, *f.*; (*of a fowl*) cuisse, *f.*; (*of mutton or lamb*) gigot, *m.*; (*of beef*) trumeau, jarret, *m.*; (*of boots*) tige, *f.*; (*of tables, chairs*) pied, *m.*; (*of compasses*) branche, *f.* — *of lamb,* gigot d'agneau, *m.* — *of mutton,* gigot de mouton, gigot, *m.* — *-of-mutton sleeve,* manche à gigot, *f.* *To be on o.'s last* —*s,* tirer à sa fin; n'avoir plus que le souffle, ne battre plus que d'une aile; être aux abois. *To stand on o.'s own* —*s,* être indépendant. — **guard,** *s.* jambière, *f.* — **rest,** *s.* appui pour la jambe, *m.*

Legacy, *s.* legs, *m.* *To leave a* — *to,* faire un legs à. — **duty,** *s.* droit de succession, *m.* — **hunter,** *s.* coureur de legs, *m.*

Legal, *adj.* (*conformable to the law*) légal; (*connected with law*) de loi; de droit; (*pertaining to courts of justice*) juridique, judiciaire; (*of a lawyer*) d'un homme de loi; d'un avocat. *To take* — *advice,* consulter un avocat

Legality, *s.* légalité, *f.*
Legalizable, *adj.* légalisable
Legalization, *s.* légalisation, *f.*
Legalize, *v.a.* légaliser ; régulariser ; autoriser
Legally, *adv.* légalement ; judiciairement, [juridiquement
Legate, *s.* légat, *m.*
Legatee, *s.* légataire, *m.f.*
Legateship, *s.* légation, *f.*
Legation, *s.* légation, *f.*
Lega-tor, trix, *s.* légateur, *m.*, -trice, *f.*
Legend, *s.* légende, *f.*
Legendary, *adj. s.* légendaire, *adj. m.f., s.m.*
Legerdemain, *s.* tour de main *or* de passe-passe *or* d'escamoteur, escamotage, *m.*
Leger-line, *s.* (*mus.*) fausse ligne, ligne postiche, *f.*
Legged, *adj.* (*in compounds*) à jambes ..., à ... jambes ; à pattes ..., à ... pattes ; à pieds ..., à ... pieds
Legging, *s.* jambière, molletière, grande guêtre, longue guêtre, guêtre de chasse, *f.*
Leghorn, *s.* (*straw*) paille d'Italie, *f.*
Legibility, Legibleness, *s.* lisibilité, *f.*
Legible, *adj.* lisible
Legibly, *adv.* lisiblement
Legion, *s.* légion, *f.*
Legionary, *adj. s.* légionnaire, *adj. m.f., s.m.*
Legislate, *v.n.* faire des lois, légiférer
Legislation, *s.* législation, *f.*
Legislative, *adj.* législatif, de législation
Legisla-tor, tress, trix, *s.* législateur, *m.*, [-trice, *f.*
Legislature, *s.* législature, *f.*
Legist, *s.* légiste, *m.*
Legitimacy, *s.* légitimité, *f.* ; justesse, *f.*
Legitimate, *adj.* légitime ; juste, exact, naturel ; — *v.a.* légitimer
Legitimately, *adv.* légitimement
Legitimation, *s.* légitimation *f.*
Legitimist, *s.* légitimiste, *m.f.*
Legitimize, *v.a.* légitimer
Legume, Legumen, *s.* légume, *m.*
Legumine, *s.* légumine, *f.*
Leguminous, *adj.* légumineux
Leisure, *s.* loisir, *m.* ; liberté d'esprit, *f.* ; commodité, convenance, *f.* ; — *adj.* de loisir, de liberté, libre. — *time,* loisir, *m.* *At* —, à loisir. *At o.'s* —, à sa convenance. *To be at* —, être de loisir, être libre
Leisurely, *adj.* (*things*) fait à loisir ; (*pers.*) qui a du loisir ; — *adv.* à loisir
Leman, *s. V.* **Lover**
Lemanic, *adj.* lémanique
Lemma, *s.* lemme, *m.*
Lemming, *s.* lemming, *m.*
Lemnian, *adj.* lemnien, de Lemnos ; — *s.* Lemnien, *m.*, -ne, *f.*
Lemon, *s.* citron, *m.* ; — *adj.* de citron. *Salt of —s,* sel d'oseille, *m.* — **colour,** *s.* couleur de citron, *f.*, citron, *m.* — **coloured,** *adj.* citron. — **flavoured,** *adj.* citronné. — **grass,** *s.* schénanthe, jonc odorant, *m.* — **grove,** *s.* citronnaie, *f.* — **juice,** *s.* jus de citron, *m.* — **peel,** *s.* écorce de citron, *f.* *Candied — peel,* citronnat, *m.* — **plant, -scented verbena,** *s.* verveine citronnelle, *f.* — **tree,** *s.* citronnier, *m.*
Lemonade, *s.* limonade, *f.* *Dealer in* —, [limonadier, *m.*, -ière, *f.*
Lemur, *s.* lémur, *m.*
Lend, *v.a.*, — **out,** prêter ; (*to let*) louer
Lendable, *adj.* prêtable
Lender, *s.* prêteur, *m.*, -euse, *f.* ; (*letter*) loueur, [*m.*, -euse, *f.*
Lending, *s.* prêt, *m.* ; (*letting*) location, *f.* — **library,** *s.* location de livres, *f.*, cabinet *or* abonnement de lecture, *m.*
Length, *s.* longueur, *f.* ; étendue, *f.*, espace, *m.* ; degré, point, *m.* ; durée, *f.* ; extrémité, *f.* ; pièce, *f.* *Ten yards in* —, dix mètres de longueur. *Full-* —, (*portraits*) en pied. *Half-* —, (*portraits*) en buste. *Short* —, (*of stuffs*) coupon, *m.* *At* —, enfin ; à la fin ; (*in full*) au long ; (*in the long run*) à la longue. *At full* —, tout au long ; (*of writing*) en toutes lettres ; (*pers.*) tout de son long ; (*of portraits*) en pied. *At great* —, fort au long, longuement. *To great —s,* fort loin. *To the — of,* jusqu'à ; jusqu'au bout de. *To such* —, (*so far*) si loin. *To go the — or the whole — of,* aller jusqu'à ; aller jusqu'au bout de. *To go that* —, aller jusque-là. *To be ten yards in* —, avoir dix mètres de long (*or* de longueur). — **ways, -wise,** *adv.* en long, de long, en longueur
Lengthen, *v.a.* allonger ; étendre ; prolonger ; — *v.n.* s'allonger ; s'étendre ; se prolonger ; (*of days*) croître, rallonger
Lengthening, *s.* allongement, *m.* ; extension, *f.* ; prolongement, *m.*, prolongation, *f.* ; (*piecing*) rallongement, *m.*
Lengthily, *adv.* longuement
Lengthiness, *s.* longueur, prolixité, *f.*
Lengthy, *adj.* long, prolongé, prolixe, détaillé, ennuyeux
Lenienc-e, y, *s.* douceur, *f.* ; indulgence, *f.*
Lenient, *adj.* adoucissant ; doux ; de douceur ; indulgent ; (*med.*) lénitif, calmant ; — *s.* (*med.*) lénitif, calmant, *m.*
Leniently, *adv.* avec douceur ; avec indulgence
Lenitive, *adj. s V.* **Lenient**
Lenity, *s. V.* **Leniency**
Lens, *s.* lentille, *f.*, verre lenticulaire, *m.* *Burning —es,* verre ardent, *m.* — **shaped,** *adj.* lenticulaire
Lent, *s.* carême, *m.* *To keep* —, faire carême
Lenten, *adj.* de carême
Lenticular, Lentiform, *adj.* lenticulaire, [lentiforme
Lentiginous, *adj.* (*med.*) lentigineux
Lentigo, *s.* (*med.*) lentigo, *m.*
Lentil, *s.* lentille, *f.*
Lentisk, *s.* lentisque, *m.*
Leo, *s.* (*astr.*) le Lion, *m.*
Leonine, *adj.* de lion ; léonin
Leopard, *s.* léopard, *m.*
Leper, *s.* lépreux, *m.*, -euse, *f.* — **asylum, -hospital, -house,** *s.* léproserie, *f.*
Lepidopter, Lepidopteran, *s.* lépidoptère, *m.*
Lepidopteral, Lepidopterous, *adj.* lépidoptère [doptère
Leporine, *adj.* de lièvre
Lepra, Leprosy, lèpre, *f.*
Leprous, *adj.* lépreux, ladre
Lernean, *adj.* de Lerne
Lesion, *s.* lésion, *f.*
Less, *adj.* moindre, plus petit, moins grand ; inférieur ; — *adv.* moins ; (*before a noun*) moins de ; (*in compounds*) sans ... [*lifeless,* sans vie ; &c.] ; — *s.* moins, *m.* ; moindre, *m.* *No* —, pas moins ; rien moins. *None the* —, n'en ... pas moins. *The* —, *all the* —, *so much the* —, d'autant moins (que). *The* — (*repeated, or opposed to* '*the more*'), moins — *and* —, de moins en moins. *To get* or *grow* or *make* —, diminuer, amoindrir, rapetisser. *A man* —, un homme de moins
Lessee, *s.* locataire, *m.f.* ; preneur, *m.*, -euse, *f.*
Lessen, *v.a.n.* amoindrir ; diminuer ; (*shorten*) rapetisser ; (*degrade*) rabaisser, ravaler
Lesser, *adj.* moindre, plus petit, moins grand, moins important ; inférieur ; (*astr., geog., bot., zool.*) petit ; (*of Asia*) mineure
Lesson, *s.* leçon, *f.* *To be a — to,* être une leçon pour, servir de leçon à. *To say o.'s —s,* réciter ses leçons. *To teach a* —, donner une leçon à. *To teach anyone his* —, faire sa leçon à quelqu'un, endoctriner quelqu'un
Lessor, *s.* bailleur, *m.*, -eresse, *f.*
Lest, *conj.* de peur que, de crainte que (*with the subj. and* ne *before it*) ; (*after* '*to fear*') que (*with ditto*)
Let, *v.a.* (*allow*) laisser, permettre, souffrir ; (*cause to ..*) faire ; (*rent, hire*) louer ; (*initiate*) initier (à), mettre (dans) ; — *v.n.* se louer ; — *s. V.* **Hindrance.** *Without — or hindrance,* sans entrave, sans le moindre obstacle, en toute liberté. *To — be,* laisser, laisser là ; laisser tranquille ; ne pas toucher à. *To — drop, to — fall,* laisser tomber ; (*words*) pro-

noncer, dire, proférer; (*observations*) faire; (*opinions*) émettre; (*exclamations*) laisser échapper; (*an affair*) ne pas donner suite à; (*geom.*) abaisser. *To — go*, laisser aller; laisser partir; lâcher; relâcher; (*fig.*) affranchir; (*nav.*) larguer. *To — have*, donner; (*of bargains*) laisser; céder. *To — have back*, V. **Have.** *To — oneself be* (*dazzled*, or *&c.*), V. **Suffer.** *To — one know*, faire savoir à quelqu'un. *To — see*, (*not oppose*) laisser voir; (*show*) faire voir. *To —! to be —!* à louer! *To be — with immediate possession*, à louer présentement. *— it be so! — it be!* soit! *— us see*, voyons. *— me see*, (*together with you*) voyons. *— him come*, qu'il vienne. *— them go away*, qu'ils s'en aillent, qu'ils partent. *— no one go out*, que personne ne sorte. *Don't — him go out*, ne le laissez pas sortir. *Don't — me disturb you*, que je ne vous dérange pas. — **alone,** laisser seul; (*not to interfere*) laisser; laisser tranquille; ne pas toucher à; (*let go on*) laisser faire; (*exclusive of*) non compris, sans parler de, sans compter. — **down,** laisser descendre; faire descendre; descendre; (*lower*) baisser; abaisser; abattre. — **for** (*a price*), louer; *v.n.* se louer. — **in,** (*not oppose*) laisser entrer; (*introduce*) faire entrer, admettre, introduire; ouvrir la porte à; laisser *or* faire pénétrer; (*water*) prendre (l'eau); (*insert*) insérer; (*of arts*) encastrer, enchâsser; (*nav.*) entrer, (*a reef*) prendre. — **into,** laisser entrer dans; faire entrer dans, admettre *or* introduire dans; (*a secret*, &c.) initier à, mettre dans; faire connaître, communiquer. — **off,** laisser partir; laisser échapper; lâcher; (*forgive*) faire grâce à, pardonner à; tenir quitte (de); (*firearms*) tirer, décharger; (*fireworks*) tirer; (*arrows*) décocher; (*darts*) lancer. — **off ... for,** faire grâce à ... de, tenir ... quitte de. *To be —* **off with,** en être quitte pour. — **out,** laisser sortir; laisser échapper; lâcher; relâcher; (*extend*) élargir, rélargir; (*on hire*) louer; (*fire, light*) laisser éteindre; (*nav.*) (*a reef*) larguer

Lethargic, *adj.* léthargique

Lethargy, *s.* léthargie, *f.*

Lethe, *s.* (*myth.*) Léthé, *m.*; (*fig.*) oubli, *m.*

Lethean, *adj.* du Léthé; de l'oubli

Letter, *s.* lettre, *f.*; (*in a candle*) champignon, *m.*; (*pers.*) loueur, *m.*, -euse, *f.*; (*print. type*) caractère, *m.*, caractères, *m.pl.*; —**s,** *pl.* lettres, *f.pl.*; littérature, *f.*; alphabet, *m.*; — *v.a.* (*of book-bindings*) imprimer. — **balance,** *s.* pèse-lettres, *m.* — **book,** *s.* livre de copies de lettres, copie-lettres, *m.* — **box,** *s.* boîte aux lettres, *f.* — **carrier,** *s.* facteur de la poste, facteur, *m.* — **case,** *s.* porte-lettres, *m.*; (*print.*) casse, *f.* — **clip,** *s.* serre-papiers, serre-notes, *m.* — **cutter,** *s.* graveur en lettres, *m.* — **founder, -founding,** &c., *V.* **Type-founder,** &c. — **paper,** *s.* grand papier à lettres, *m.* — **press,** *s.* impression typographique, *f.*; caractères d'imprimerie, *m.pl.* — **press printer,** *s.* typographe, *m.* — **press printing,** typographie, *f.* — **rack,** *s.* semainier, *m.* — **scales, -weigher,** *s.* pèse-lettres, *m.* — **wood,** *s.* bois de lettres, *m.* — **wood tree,** *s.* piratinier, *m.* — **writer,** *s.* (*pers.*) épistolaire, *m.*, épistolier, *m.*, -ière, *f.*; (*by profession*) écrivain public, *m.*; (*book*) recueil de lettres, épistolaire, *m.*; (*machine*) polygraphe, *m.*

Lettered, *adj.* (*pers.*) lettré; (*things*) littéraire; (*of books bound*) avec couverture imprimée; (*of the binding itself*) imprimé

Lettering, *s.* lettres, *f.pl.*; (*title*) titre, *m.*

Lettern, *s. V.* **Lectern**

Letting, — out, *s.* (*on hire*) louage, *m*; location, *f.*

Lettuce, *s.* laitue, *f.* — **opium,** *s.* lactucarium, *m.*, thridace, *f.*

Leucorrhœa, *s.* leucorrhée, *f.*, fleurs blanches, *f.pl.*

Levant, *s.* Levant, *m.*: — *v.n.* filer, décamper, lever le pied, décaniller. — **nut,** *s.* coque du Levant, *f.*

Levantine, *s. adj.* Levantin, *m.*, e, *f.*; (*silk stuff*) levantine, *f.*

Levator, *s. V.* **Elevator;** — *s. adj.* (*anat.*) releveur, *m.*

Levee, *s.* (*of sovereigns*) lever, *m.*; réception, *f.*; [(*a bank*) levée, levée de terre, *f.*

Level, *adj. adv.* (*even*) uni; (*even with*) de niveau; au niveau; horizontal; (*equal*) égal; — *s.* niveau, *m.*; (*plane*) surface plane, surface unie, *f.*; (*country*) pays plat, *m.*; (*mining*) galerie, *f.*, canal *or* conduit d'écoulement, *m.*; (*of a canal*) bief, *m.*; (*— run, rail.*) palier, *m.*; (*fig.*) visée, *f.*; — *v.a.* niveler, mettre de niveau; aplanir; égaliser; affleurer; (*to aim*) pointer, ajuster, diriger présenter; (*a blow*) porter, asséner, allonger; (*to adapt, suit*) mettre au niveau (de). — *with, on* or *upon a — with*, de niveau avec, au niveau de; à fleur de; (*fig.*) à la portée de. — *with the ground*, à fleur de terre, à rase terre. *To — to* or *with the ground*, raser. *To make —*, aplanir; (*with*) mettre de niveau (avec). *To put out of —*, déniveler. *Putting out of —*, dénivellement, *m.* — **crossing,** *s.* passage au niveau, *m.* — **indicator,** *s.* nivelette, *f.*

Leveller, *s.* niveleur, *m.*, -euse, *f.*; (*hist., polit.*) niveleur, égalitaire, *m.*

Levelling, *s.* nivellement, *m.*; aplanissement, *m.*; régalage, *m.*; affleurage, affleurement, *m.*; (*artil.*) pointage, *m.*; — *adj.* niveleur; égalitaire. — **pole** *or* **staff,** *s.* mire pour nivellement, *f.*

Levelness, *s.* niveau, *m.*; (*fig.*) égalité, *f.*

Lever, *s.* levier, *m.*; (*of a breech-loader*) clé, *f.*; (*door or window fastening*) bascule, *f.* *Bent —*, levier coudé, *m.* — **escapement,** *s.* échappement à ancre, *m.* — **handle,** *s.* maneton, *m.* — **rod,** *s.* tige à levier, *f.* — **valve,** *s.* soupape à levier, *f.* — **watch,** *s.* montre à échappement à ancre, montre à ancre, *f.*

Leverage, *s.* puissance d'un levier, *f.*; moment, *m.*; force, *f.*; engin, *m.*

Leveret, *s.* levraut, *m.*; — *v.n.* levretter

Leviathan, *s.* léviathan, *m.*

Levigate, *v.a.* léviger, porphyriser, pulvériser

Levigation, *s.* lévigation, porphyrisation, pulvérisation, *f.*

Levite, *s.* Lévite, *m.*

Levitical, *adj.* lévitique, des Lévites

Levitically, *adv.* en Lévite

Leviticus, *s.* Lévitique, *m.*

Levity, *s.* légèreté, *f.*

Levy, *v.a.* lever; (*a fine*) imposer; — *s.* levée, *f.*

Lewd, *adj.* impudique, débauché, dissolu, licencieux, lubrique, lascif, polisson

Lewdly, *adv.* impudiquement, lubriquement, lascivement, d'une manière dissolue, dans la débauche

Lewdness, *s.* impudicité, luxure, débauche, lubricité, lasciveté, *f.*

Lexicographer, *s.* lexicographe, *m.*

Lexico-graphic, al, -graphy, -logy, &c. *V.* page 3, § 1

Lexicon, *s.* lexique, dictionnaire, *m.*

Ley. *V.* **Lea**

Leyden jar *or* **phial,** *s.* bouteille de Leyde, *f.*

Liability, *s.* responsabilité, *f.*; susceptibilité, *f.*; tendance, *f.*; danger, *m.*; (*to a penalty*, &c.) passibilité, *f.*; —**ies,** *pl.* engagements, *m.pl.*, obligations, *f.pl.*; (*com.*) passif, *m.* *With limited —*, (*com.*) en commandite, à responsabilité limitée

Liable, *adj.* responsable (de); sujet (à), exposé (à); (*to a penalty*, &c.) passible (de)

Liana, *s.* liane, *f.*

Liar, *s.* menteur, *m.*, -euse, *f.*

Lias, *s.* lias, liais, *m.*

Libation, *s.* libation, *f.*

Libel, *s.* libelle, *m.*; diffamation, *f.*; — *v.a.* diffamer. *Action for —*, plainte en diffamation, *f.*

Libeller, *s.* libelliste, *m.*; (*law*) diffamateur, *m.*, -trice, *f.*

Libellous, *adj.* diffamatoire, diffamant

Liberal, *adj.* libéral; généreux; prodigue;

large; abondant, copieux, ample; honnête; honorable; libre, ouvert, franc. — *arts*, arts libéraux, *m.pl.* — *education*, éducation libé-

Liberalism, *s.* libéralisme, *m.* [rale, *f.*

Liberality, *s.* libéralité, *f.*; générosité, *f.*; candeur, sincérité, franchise, *f.*

Liberalize, *v.a.* libéraliser

Liberally, *adv.* libéralement; généreusement; largement; (*freely*) librement

Liberate, *v.a.* affranchir (de); (*prisoners*) mettre en liberté, élargir; (*to free*) délivrer (de); dégager (de); (*law*) libérer

Liberation, *s.* délivrance, *f.*; (*of slaves*) affranchissement, *m.*; (*of prisoners*) élargissement, *m*, mise en liberté, *f.*

Liberator, *s.* libérateur, *m.*, -trice, *f.*

Liberticidal, *adj.* liberticide

Liberticide, *s.* liberticide, (*pers.*) *m.f.*, (*act*) *m.*

Libertine, *s. adj.* libertin, *m.*, e, *f.*

Libertinism, *s.* libertinage, *m.*

Liberty, *s.* liberté, *f.*; permission, *f.*; privilége, *m.*; territoire, *m.* *At* —, en liberté, libre; (*fig.*)

Libidinous, *adj.* libidineux, lascif [libre (de)

Libidinously, *adv.* lascivement

Libidinousness, *s.* libidinosité, lasciveté, *f.*

Libra, *s.* la Balance, *f.*

Librarian, *s.* bibliothécaire, *m.*; (*bookseller*) libraire, *m.f.* *Assistant* —, sous-bibliothécaire, *m.*

Librarianship, *s.* place de bibliothécaire, *f.*

Library, *s.* bibliothèque, *f.*; (*circulating*) cabinet de lecture, abonnement de lecture, *m.*; (*bookseller's shop*) librairie, *f.*

Librate, *v.a.* balancer; — *v.n.* se balancer

Libration, *s.* libration, *f.*, balancement, équi-

Libratory, *adj.* en équilibre [libre, *m.*

Librettist, *s.* librettiste, *m.f.*

Libretto, *s.* livret, libretto, *m.*

Licence, *s.* permission, autorisation, liberté, *f.*; (*excess*) licence, *f.*; (*certificate*) licence, *f.*; (*of tradesmen*) patente, *f.*; (*of printers*, &c.) brevet, *m.*; (*of marriage*) dispense de bans, *f.*; (*for shooting*) port d'armes, permis de chasse, *m.*; — *v.a.* autoriser; (*com.*) patenter; (*printers*) breveter; (*theatres*) privilégier

Licensable, *adj.* patentable

License. *V.* **Licence** [*f.*; privilégié, *m.*, e, *f.*

Licensee, *s.* patenté, *m.*, e, *f.*; breveté, *m.*, e,

Licenser, *s.* agent pour les autorisations, *m.*; (*of the press*) censeur, *m.*

Licentiate, *s.* licencié, *m.*

Licentious, *adj.* licencieux

Licentiously, *adv.* licencieusement

Licentiousness, *s.* licence, *f.*; dérèglement, *m.*;

Lichen, *s.* lichen, *m.* [libertinage, *m.*

Lick, *v.a.* lécher; laper; (*beat*) rosser, rouler. — **spittle,** *s.* chien couchant, *m.* — **up,** *v.a.*

Licker, *s.* lécheur, *m.*, -euse, *f.* [dévorer, laper

Lickerish, *adj.* friand; (*eager*) avide; ardent

Lickerishly, *adv.* avec friandise; (*eagerly*) avidement, avec avidité; ardemment, avec

Lickerishness, *s.* friandise, *f.* [ardeur

Licking, *s.* rossée, roulée, râclée, volée, *f.*

Licorice. *V.* **Liquorice**

Lictor, *s.* licteur, *m.*

Lid, *s.* couvercle, *m.*; (*of the eye*) paupière, *f.*; (*horol.*) recouvrement, *m.*; (*nat.hist.*) opercule, *m.*

Lie, *s.* mensonge, *m.*; (*contradiction*) démenti, *m.* *White* —, petit mensonge, mensonge innocent *or* officieux, *m.* *To give the* — *to*, donner un démenti à, démentir

Lie, *v.n.* (*speak false*) mentir

Lie, *v.n.* être couché, être étendu; se coucher, coucher; être situé, être, se trouver; (*remain*) rester, demeurer, se tenir; (*be laid*) être déposé; (*rest in o.'s grave, rest*) reposer; (*lean*) s'appuyer; (*consist*) consister; (*be comprised*) être renfermé; (*be imputed*) être imputé (à), retomber (sur); (*depend*) dépendre (de); (*belong*) appartenir (à); (*be an obligation*) incomber (à); (*of ships*) être à l'ancre, être mouillé; (*at law*) se soutenir. *To let* —, laisser. *Here* —*s!* ici repose! ici gît! ci-gît! — **about.** être dispersé çà et là; traîner. — **along,** être le long de *or* &c. (*V.* **Along**); (*nav.*) donner de la bande, être à la bande. — **by,** (*things*) être tenu en réserve; (*pers.*) se tenir en réserve; (*to rest*) se reposer. — **down,** être couché; se coucher, coucher; (*to rest*) se reposer; (*in the grave*) descendre; (*of collars*, &c.) être rabattu. — *down!* (*to a dog*) couchez! couchez là! — **idle,** (*mach.*, *com.*) chômer; (*of money*) dormir. — **in,** (*pers.*) être en couche *or* en couches, faire ses couches; (*of*) accoucher (de). — **open,** être ouvert; être exposé; (*nav.*) être à découvert. — **out,** découcher, coucher dehors. — **over,** être en suspens; être différé; (*nav.*) *V.* — **along.** — **to,** (*nav.*) être en panne. — **under,** se trouver (*or* être) sous *or* dans; être sujet *or* exposé à; subir

Lief, *adv.* *V.* **Lieve**

Liege, *adj.* lige; — *s.* (*feud.*) vassal lige, *m.*; (*a lord*) suzerain, *m.*, e, *f.*; souverain, *m.*, e, *f.* — **man,** *s.* homme lige, vassal, *m.*

Lien, *s.* droit de saisie, *m.*; (*pledge*) gage, nan-

Lienteric, *adj.* lientérique [tissement, *m.*

Lientery, *s.* lienterie, *f.*

Lieu. *In* — *of*, au lieu de, à la place de, en place de. *To stand in* — *of*, tenir lieu de

Lieutenancy, *s.* lieutenance, *f.*; grade de lieutenant, *m.*; (*body*) corps de lieutenants, *m.*; (*governorship*) fonctions de gouverneur, *f.pl.*

Lieutenant, *s.* lieutenant, *m.*; (*governor*) gouverneur, *m.* *First* —, lieutenant en premier, *m.* *Second* —, sous-lieutenant, lieutenant en second, *m.* — *general*, lieutenant général, *m.*; (*mil.*) général de division, *m.*

Lieutenantship. *V.* **Lieutenancy**

Lieve, *adv.* volontiers. *I had just as* —, j'aime autant, j'aimerais autant

Life, *s.* vie, *f.*; existence, *f.*; (*time*) vivant, *m.*; (*period*) âge, *m.*; (*rank in society*) monde, *m.*; (*animation*) vie, *f.*, mouvement, *m.*, vivacité, *f.*; activité, *f.*; (*soul*) âme, *f.*; (*blood*) sang, *m.*; (*a living being*) être animé, *m.*; (*resemblance*) naturel, *m.*, nature, *f.*; (*nav.*, *fire*, &c.) sauvetage, *m.*; — *adj.* de vie, de la vie, &c.; (*for the preservation of life*) de sauvetage; (*of annuities*, &c.) viager. *Advanced* —, (un) âge avancé, *m.* *High* —, vie du grand monde, *f.*; grand monde, *m.*, haute société, *f.* *Humble* or *low* —, vie de la basse classe, *f.*; basse classe, classe pauvre, *f.* *Manner* or *mode* or *way* or *course of* —, manière de vivre, *f.*, genre *or* train de vie, *m.* *As large as* —, de grandeur naturelle. *For* —, à vie, pour la vie; (*of pensions*) viager; (*of punishment*) à perpétuité. *From the* —, *to the* —, d'après nature, au naturel; vivant; exactement; à s'y méprendre. *In my* —, de ma vie. *In his* —*time*, de son vivant. *In the vigour of* — dans la force de l'âge. *Late in* —, dans un âge avancé. 50 *lives have been lost*, 50 personnes ont péri. *To come to* —, naître, venir au monde. *To come to* — *again*, ressusciter, renaître. *To fly for o.'s* —, chercher son salut dans la fuite. *To have nine lives*, avoir la vie dure. *I lay my* — *upon it*, j'en donnerais ma tête à couper, j'en mettrais ma main au feu. — **annuity,** *s.* rente viagère, *f.* — **annuitant,** *s.* rentier viager, *m.*, rentière viagère, *f.* — **assurance,** *V.* — **insurance.** — **belt,** *s.* ceinture de sauvetage, *f.* — **blood,** *s.* le plus pur de son sang, *m.*; (*sinews*) nerf, *m.*, âme, *f.* — **boat,** *s.* canot de sauvetage, *m.* — **boat institution,** *s.* société de sauvetage des naufragés, *f.* — **boat system,** *s.* système de sauvetage, *m.* — **brigade,** *s.* brigade de sauvetage, *f.* — **buoy,** *s.* bouée de sauvetage, *f.*, salvanos, *m.* — **drag,** *s.* gaffe de sauvetage, *f.* — **estate,** *s.* propriété à vie, *f.*; viager, *m.*; usufruit, *m.* — **guard,** *s.* garde du corps (*body*) *f.*, (*man*) *m.*; (*rail.*) chasse-pierres, *m.* — **guardsman,** *s.* garde du corps, *m.* — **insurance,** *s.* *V.* **Insurance.** — **insurance company** *or* **office,** *s.* compagnie (*f.*) *or* bureau (*m.*) d'assurance sur la vie. —**interest,** *s. V.* —**estate.** —**less,** *adj.* sans vie, inanimé, mort; (*fig.*) sans force, sans vigueur, sans âme. —**lessly,** *adv.* sans vie; (*fig.*) sans force, sans vigueur, sans âme. —**lessness,** *s.* manque de vie, manque de vigueur, *m.* —**like,** *adj.* comme un être vivant, vivant, animé; naturel; d'après nature. —**line,** *s.* (*rail.*) garde-corps, garde-fous, *m.*; (*nav.*) amarre de sauvetage, *f.* —**long,** *adj.* de toute la vie. —**mortar,** *s.* porte-amarre, *m.* —**office,** *s.* bureau d'assurance sur la vie, *m.* —**policy,** *s.* police d'assurance sur la vie, *f.* —**preserver,** *s.* appareil de sauvetage, *m.*; (*weapon*) assommoir, casse-tête, *m.* —**preserving, -saving,** *s.* (*from wreck, drowning, fire,* &c.) sauvetage, *m.*; *adj.* de sauvetage. —**rent,** *s.* usufruit, *m.* —**renter,** *s.* usufruitier, *m.*, -ière, *f.* —**rocket,** *s.* fusée porte-amarre, *f.* —**size,** *s.* grandeur naturelle, *f.*; *adj.* de grandeur naturelle. —**time,** *s.* vie, *f.*, vivant, *m.* *In o.'s —time,* pendant sa vie, de son vivant

Lift, *v.a.* (— **up**) lever, soulever, hausser; (*in rank, fortune,* &c., *o.'s voice or eyes*) élever; (*in spirit*) relever; (*with pride*) enorgueillir; (*rob*) piller, voler; — *s.* effort, *m.*; (*load*) charge, *f.*, poids, *m.*; (*help*) coup de main, *m.*; (*machine*) cric, treuil, guindal, guindeau, *m.*; (*in a warehouse*) élévatoire, *m.*; (*for raising pers.*) ascenseur, *m.*; (*of flags*) guindant, *m.*; (*of pumps*) tige, *f.*; (*nav.*) balancine, *f.*; (*of locks*) chute, *f.* — *and force pump,* pompe aspirante et foulante, *f.* *To give a —,* (*help*) donner un coup de main; (*in travelling*) faire monter avec soi, épargner une partie de la route; (*raise*) soulever, hausser

Lifting, *s.* élevation, *f.*; (*robbery*) enlèvement (de ...), vol (de ...), *m.* —**jack,** *s.* cric à soulever les fardeaux, cric, *m.*; chèvre, *f.* —**pump,** *s.* pompe élévatoire, *f.*; pompe aspirante, *f.*

Ligament, *s.* lien, *m.*; (*anat.*) ligament, *m.*

Ligature, *s.* lien, *m.*; (*surg.*) ligature, *f.*; (*mus.*) liaison, *f.*

Light, *s.* lumière, *f.*; (*day*) jour, *m.*; (*glimmer*) lueur, clarté, *f.*; (*lighting*) éclairage, *m.*; (*candle*) bougie, *f.*, (*of tallow*) chandelle, *f.*; (*for the night in a bedroom*) veilleuse, *f.*; (*for churches*) cierge, *m.*; (*signal or watch —*) fanal, *m.*; (*torch*) flambeau, *m.*; (*fire*) feu, *m.*; (*fusee, match,* &c.) allumette, *f.*; (*point of view*) point de vue, *m.*; (*paint.*) jour, clair, *m.*, lumière, *f.*; (*arch.*) jour, *m.*; fenêtre, *f.*; (*nav.*) feu, *m.*; —**s,** *s.pl.* (*lungs*) mou, *m.*, poumons, *m.pl.* *Blue, red —,* lumière bleue, rouge, *f.*; (*Bengal —*) feu de Bengale, *m.* *To be —,* faire jour; faire clair. *To bring to —,* mettre au jour; exposer au grand jour; découvrir; faire connaître. *To come to —,* venir au jour; se faire jour, se manifester, se découvrir, se produire; paraître. *To give — to,* éclairer. *To give a —,* (*for cigar,* &c.) donner du feu. *To oblige with a —,* (*for cigar,* &c.) avoir l'obligeance de donner du feu à. *To show a —,* éclairer. *To stand* (or *be*) *in ...'s —,* cacher le jour à ...; (*fig.*) faire tort à ..., nuire à ... *To stand in o.'s own —,* se mettre contre le jour; (*fig.*) se faire tort, se nuire. *He has fuel and — found for him,* on lui fournit le chauffage et l'éclairage. —**ball,** *s.* balle à éclairer, *f.* —**bearer,** *s.* porte-flambeau, *m.* —**house,** *s.* phare, *m.* —**house keeper,** *s.* gardien de phare, *m.* —**less,** *adj.* sans lumière; sans clarté, sombre, obscur. —**port,** *s.* (*nav.*) hublot, *m.* —**room,** *s.* (*nav.*) soute vitrée, *f.* —**ship, -vessel,** *s. V.* **Beacon-ship**

Light, *adj.* léger; agile, leste; gai; facile; frivole; (*of weight*) faible; faux; (*bright, pale*) clair; (*fair*) blond; (*of rooms,* &c., *well lit*) bien éclairé; (*of infantry, cavalry, artillery*) léger; (*nav.*) lége; (*adverb.*) *V.* **Lightly.** — *of belief,* crédule. *To make — of,* traiter légèrement, faire peu de cas de, mépriser, dédaigner: plaisanter de; se faire un jeu de. —**armed,** *adj* armé à la légère. —**brained,** *adj.* étourdi, écervelé. —**fingered,** *adj.* aux doigts légers, qui a la main légère; (..., *with a noun, cheat*) filou, *s.m.* —**foot, -footed,** *adj.* agile, au pied léger. —**hair,** *s.* cheveux blonds, *m.pl.* —**haired,** *adj.* blond. —**headed,** *adj.* étourdi; (*delirious*) en délire. —**headedness,** *s.* étourderie, *f.*; (*delirium*) délire, *m.* —**hearted,** *adj.* gai, enjoué. —**minded,** *adj.* léger

Light, *v.a.*, — **up,** (*set fire, kindle*) allumer; (*give light*) éclairer; illuminer; — *v.n.* s'allumer; (*fig.*) s'enflammer; s'animer; briller; (*fall on*) tomber (sur), rencontrer (...); (*of birds*) s'abattre; (*alight*) descendre

Lighten, *v.a.* éclairer; (*alleviate*) alléger, soulager; (*cheer*) égayer, réjouir; — *v.n.* faire des éclairs, éclairer; (*shine*) briller, étinceler

Lighter, *s.* (*pers.*) allumeur, *m.*, -euse, *f.*; (*thing*) allumeuse, *f.*; allumette, *f.*; (*a boat*) allége, gabare, *f.* —**man,** *s.* gabarier, *m.*

Lighterage, *s.* gabarage, *m.*, frais d'allége, *m.pl.*

Lighting, *s.* éclairage ('*with gas,*' &c., au gaz, &c.), *m.*; illumination, *f.*

Lightly, *adv.* légèrement; à la légère; agilement, lestement; facilement, aisément; gaiment; (*little*) peu

Lightness, *s.* légèreté, *f.*; agilité *f.*

Lightning, *s.* (*flash*) éclair, *m.*, éclairs, *m.pl.*; (*fluid*) foudre, *f.* *A flash of —,* un éclair. *Struck by —,* frappé de la foudre. —**conductor, -rod,** *s.* paratonnerre, *m.*

Lightsome, *adj.* clair, éclairé; gai

Lightsomeness, *s.* clarté, *f.*; gaieté, *f.*

Lign-aloe, Lign-aloes, *s.* bois d'aloès, *m.*

Ligneous, *adj.* ligneux

Lignite, *s.* lignite, *m.*

Lignum-vitæ, *s.* bois de gaiac, bois saint, *m.*

Like, *adj.* pareil (à), semblable (à); analogue (à); (*of likeness*) ressemblant; (*equal*) égal, tel; (*probable*) vraisemblable, probable; (*fit for*) à même (de), fait (pour); (*geom.*) homologue; — *adv.* comme, de même que, tel que; en; vraisemblablement, probablement; — *s.* pareil, *m.*, -le, *f.*, semblable, *m.f.*; même chose, chose semblable, *f.* — *as,* tel que. — *as if,* comme si. *And the —, and such —,* et autres choses semblables. *To be* or *look —,* ressembler (à), avoir l'air (de). *To be — each other,* se ressembler. *To be as — as two peas,* se ressembler comme deux gouttes d'eau. *I have one — it,* j'en ai un pareil. *To do the —,* en faire autant. *To give — for —,* rendre la pareille. *To have — to,* faillir. — *father — son,* tel père tel fils. — *master — man,* tel maître tel valet

Like, *v.a.n.* aimer (à); (*approve*) trouver à son goût; trouver bien; trouver bon; trouver beau; plaire; se plaire à (*or* dans *or* &c.); (*of plants*) se plaire dans (*or* à); (*wish*) vouloir; plaire; faire plaisir; vouloir bien; désirer; (*be glad*) être bien aise. *I — to read,* j'aime à lire. *I — coffee,* j'aime le café. *I — French better than German,* j'aime mieux le français que l'allemand. *To — best,* aimer mieux préférer. *How do you — your coffee?* comment trouvez-vous votre café? *I do not — it,* je ne le trouve pas bon. *Thanks for your present, I — it very much,* merci de votre présent, il me plaît beaucoup. *I — that,* j'aime cela; cela me plaît; cela me fait plaisir. *Don't go there, you know he does not — it,* n'y allez pas, vous savez qu'il n'aime pas cela (*or,* que cela ne lui plaît pas, *or,* que cela lui déplaît). *Henry —s his school,* Henri se plaît à sa pension. *As you —,* comme il vous plaît, comme vous voulez, comme bon vous semble; (*future*) comme il vous plaira, comme vous voudrez, comme bon vous semblera. *If you —,* si vous voulez; si cela vous plaît. *When you —,* quand vous voudrez. *I should — to know, to see,* &c., je voudrais bien (*or* je serais bien aise de) savoir, voir, &c. — *I should — to be there,* je voudrais être là. *I should — to have been there,* j'aurais voulu être là

Likelihood, Likeliness, *s.* probabilité, apparence, vraisemblance, *f.* *In all —,* en toute probabilité ; selon toute apparence

Likely, *adj.* probable ; vraisemblable ; (*capable*) dans le cas (de); propre (à), de nature (à), fait (pour); (*liable*) exposé (à) ; (*pleasing*) agréable, avenant ; — *adv.* probablement, vraisemblablement. *I am — to go out,* il est probable que je sortirai. *He seemed — to be victorious, to succeed,* &c., il semblait devoir être vainqueur, devoir réussir, &c.

Liken, *v.a.* comparer (à) ; faire ressembler (à)

Likeness, *s.* ressemblance, *f.*; air, *m.*; portrait, *m.* *To be a good —,* être ressemblant

Likening, *s.* comparaison, *f.*

Likewise, *adv.* pareillement, également, de même, aussi

Liking, *s.* goût, *m.*, inclination, *f.*, gré, *m.*; (*friendship*) amitié, *f.* *To have a — for,* avoir du goût pour. *To take a — to,* prendre goût à ; (*pers.*) prendre en amitié

Lilac, *s. adj.* lilas, *s.m.*, *adj. m.f.*

Liliaceous, *adj.* liliacé

Lilied, *adj.* orné de lis

Lilliput, *s.* Lilliput, *m.*

Lilliputian, *s.* Lilliputien, *m.*, -ne, *f.*

Lily, *s.* lis, *m.* *— of the valley,* muguet, *m.*

Limb, *s.* membre, *m.*; (*border*) bord, *m.*; (*of trees*) branche, *f.*; (*astr., math., bot.,* &c.) limbe, *m.* *— of the law,* robin, *m.* **—less,** *adj.* sans membres

Limbed, *adj.* membré. *Large* or *strong —,* membru

Limber, *adj.* souple, flexible ; (*fig.*) frêle, fragile ; facile ; — *s.* (*artil.*) avant-train, caisson, *m.*; — *v.a.* (— **up**) attacher (une pièce) à son avant-train, mettre l'avant-train. — **hole,** *s.* (*nav.*) anguiller, *m.* — **ness,** *s.* souplesse, flexibilité, *f.*; (*fig.*) faiblesse, fragilité, *f.*; facilité, *f.*

Limbo, Limbus, s. limbes, *m.pl.*; (*fig.*) prison, *f.*; (*bot.*) limbe, *m.*

Lime, *s.* chaux, *f.*; (*for birds*) glu, *f.*; (*lemon*) lime, *f*, citron, *m.*; (*lemon-tree*) limettier, citronnier, *m.*; (*linden*) tilleul, *m.*; — *v.a.* (*manure*) chauler ; (*smear*) gluer, engluer ; (*birds*) prendre au gluau ; (*fig.*) prendre au piége ; (*entangle*) embarrasser, engager. — **burner,** *s.* chaufournier, *m.* — **juice,** *s.* jus de citron, *m.* — **kiln,** *s.* four à chaux, *m.* — **pit, -quarry,** *s.* carrière de pierre à chaux, carrière de chaux, *f.* —**stone,** *s.* pierre calcaire, pierre à chaux, *f.* — **tree,** *s.* (*lemon*) limettier, *m.*; (*linden*) tilleul, *m.* — **twig,** *s.* gluau, *m.* —**twigged,** *adj.* glué. — **wash,** *s.* lait *or* blanc de chaux, *m.*; échaudage, *m.*; *v.a.* blanchir à la chaux, échauder. —**washing,** *s.* blanchissage à la chaux, échaudage, *m.* — **water,** *s.* eau de chaux, *f.*, lait de chaux, *m.* —**white,** *s.* blanc *or* lait de chaux, *m.*

Limit, *s.* limite, borne, *f.*; — *v.a.* limiter; borner; restreindre. —**less,** *adj.* *V.* **Boundless**

Limitation, *s* limitation, restriction, réserve, *f.*; (*law*) prescription, *f.*

Limited, *part. adj.* limité, borné, restreint ; (*of companies*) à responsabilité limitée, en commandite

Limn, *v.a.* enluminer ; peindre

Limner, *s.* enlumineur, *m.*, -euse, *f.*; peintre, *m.*

Limning, *s.* enluminure, *f.*; peinture, *f.*

Limp, *adj.* mou, flasque ; souple ; — *v.n.* clocher, boiter, clopiner ; — *s.* clochement, boitement, *m.* —**away, off,** *v.n.* s'en aller en clochant *or* &c.

Limper, *s.* boiteux, *m.*, -euse, *f.*

Limpet, *s.* lépas, *m.*, patelle, *f.*

Limpid, *adj.* limpide

Limpidity, Limpidness, *s.* limpidité, *f.*

Limping, *s.* *V.* **Limp,** *s.*

Limpingly, *adv.* en clochant

Limy, *adj.* calcaire ; (*viscous*) gluant, visqueux

Linchpin, *s.* clavette, esse, *f.*

Linden, — tree, *s.* tilleul, *m.*

Line, *s.* ligne, *f.*; file, *f.*; (*series*) suite, *f.*; (*of poetry*) vers, *m.*; (*short letter*) mot, *m.*, ligne, *f.*; (*dash*) trait, *m.*; (*string*) cordeau, *m.*, corde, ligne, *f.*; (*for angling*) ligne, *f.*; (*nav., tech.*) ligne, *f.*; amarre, *f.*; (*mil.*) ligne, *f.*; (*for sounding*) sonde, ligne de sonde, *f.*; (*limit*) limite, *f.*; (*straight line*) alignement, *m.*; (*outline*) contour, *m.*; (*sketch*) esquisse, *f.*; (*of conduct*) genre, *m.*; (*of business*) partie, spécialité, *f.*; profession, *f.*, métier, *m.*; (*fig.*) ressort, *m.*; (*equator*) ligne, *f.*, équateur, *m.*; (*rail.*) ligne, voie, *f.*; (*of steamers*) service, *m.*; —**s,** *pl.* lignes, &c.; (*black lines, for guiding the hand when writing*) transparent, guide-âne, *m.*; — *v.a.* (*clothes,* &c.) doubler ; garnir ; (*edge*) border ; (*mas.*) revêtir ; (*mining*) cuveler ; (*of animals*) couvrir, saillir. — *of business,* partie, spécialité, *f.*; profession, *f.*, métier, *m.* — *of packets,* service de paquebots, *m.*, messageries maritimes, messageries, *f.pl.* *Ship of the —,* vaisseau de ligne, *m.* *Single —,* (*rail.*) voie simple, *f.* *Troops* or *infantry of the —,* troupes (*f.pl.*) *or* infanterie (*f.*) de ligne. *In a —* en ligne ; aligné. *To draw a —,* tirer une ligne ; tracer une ligne de démarcation. *To drop* or *write* or *send a —,* (*message*) écrire un mot. *To run off* or &c. *the —,* V. **Rail.** *That is out of my —,* cela n'est pas de mon ressort. — **engraving,** *s.* gravure au trait, *f.* —**-of-battle ship,** *s.* vaisseau de ligne, *m.* — **steamship, -steamer, -ship,** *s.* *V.* **Liner**

Lineage, *s.* race, famille, *f.*

Lineal, *adj.* linéaire ; linéal ; (*pers.*) en ligne directe, direct

Lineally, *adv.* linéalement, en droite ligne, en ligne directe

Lineament, *s.* linéament, trait, *m.*

Linear, *adj.* linéaire

Linen, *s.* toile, toile de lin, *f.*; (*made up*) linge, *m.*; — *adj.* de *or* en toile, de lin ; (*made up*) de linge. *Clean —,* linge blanc. *Dirty —,* linge sale. — **cloth,** *s.* toile de lin, *f.* —**draper,** *s.* marchand de nouveautés, *m.*; (*for linen*) marchand de toiles, *m.* —**drapery,** *s.* (*business*) nouveauté, *f.*, (*for linen*) toilerie, *f.*; (*goods*) nouveautés, *f.pl.*, (*linen*) toilerie, *f.* — **goods,** *s.pl.* toilerie, *f.*; lingerie, *f.* — **press,** *s.* armoire à linge, *f.* — **prover,** *s.* compte-fils, *m.* — **room,** *s.* lingerie, *f.* — **trade,** *s.* commerce de toiles, *m*, lingerie, *f.* — **warehouse,** *s.* magasin (*m.*) *or* spécialité (*f.*) de blanc, lingerie, *f.* — **yarn,** *s.* fil de lin, *m.*

Liner, *s.* (*packet-ship*) paquebot, *m.*; (*man-of-war*) vaisseau de ligne, *m.*; — **s,** *pl.* (*line of packets*) messageries maritimes, messageries, *f.pl.*

Ling, *s.* (*fish*) lingue, *f.*

Linger, *v.n.* tarder, lambiner ; traîner ; languir ; hésiter ; (*in suspense*) demeurer

Lingerer, *s.* traînard, lambin, *m.*; (*languishing*) personne qui languit, *f.*

Lingering, *adj* qui tarde ; lent ; prolongé ; languissant ; hésitant ; — *s.* lenteur, *f.*; hésitation, *f.*; langueur, *f.*

Lingeringly, *adv.* lentement, avec lenteur ; languissamment, avec langueur ; avec hésitation

Lingo, *s.* jargon, langage, *m.*

Lingual, *adj. s.* lingual, *adj. m*, e, *f.*, linguale, *s.f.*

Linguiform, *adj.* linguiforme

Linguist, *s.* linguiste, *m.f.*

Linguistic, -al, *adj* linguistique ; —**s,** *s.pl.* linguistique, *f.*

Liniment, *s.* liniment, *m.*

Lining, *s.* (*of clothes,* &c.) doublure, *f.*; garniture, *f.*; (*of hats*) coiffe, *f.*; (*inner side*) paroi, *f.*; (*mas.*) revêtement, *m.*; (*mining*) cuvelage, cuvellement, *m.*; (*fig.*) intérieur, *m.* *Glazed —,* lustrine, *f.*

Link, *s.* (*of a chain*) chaînon, anneau, *m.*; attache, *f.*; (*chain itself*) chaîne, *f.*; (*fig.*) lien, *m.*; enchaînement, *m.*; (*torch*) torche, *f.*, flambeau, *m.*; (*moor*) bruyère, *f.*; — *v.a.* lier, attacher, enchaîner ; joindre, unir ; — *v.n.* s'enchaîner. —**boy, -man,** *s.* porte-flambeau, *m.*

Linking, *s.* enchaînement, *m.*

Linnæan, Linnean, *adj.* linnéen (*m.*, -ne, *f.*)

Linnet, *s.* linotte, *f.*

Linoleum, *s.* linoléum, *m.*
Linseed, *s.* graine de lin, *f.* — **cake,** *s.* tourteau de lin, *m.* — **meal,** (**-poultice**) *s.* farine (*f.*, cataplasme, *m.*) de graine de lin. —**oil,** *s.* huile de lin, *f.*
Linsey, —**woolsey,** *s.* tartanelle, *f.*; — *adj.* de tartanelle; (*fig.*) bas, vil, grossier
Linstock, *s.* (*old artil.*) bâton à mèche, porte-mèche, *m.* [lasse, *f.*
Lint, *s.* peluche de lin, charpie, *f.*; (*flax*) fi-
Lintel, *s.* linteau, *m.*
Lion, *s.* lion, *m.*; (*fig.*) célébrité, *f.*, personnage remarquable, objet de curiosité, *m.*, curiosité, *f.* *Young* —, —*'s cub* or *whelp*, lionceau, *m.* — **hearted,** *adj.* qui a un cœur de lion. *Richard the — hearted*, Richard Cœur de Lion. — **hunting,** *s.* chasse au lion, *f.* — **killer,** *s.* tueur de lions, *m.* —**like,** *adj.* semblable à un lion, de lion [quable, célébrité, *f.*
Lioness, *s.* lionne, *f.*; (*fig.*) femme remar-
Lionet, *s.* lionceau, *m.*
Lionize, *v.n.* aller voir les curiosités
Lip, *s.* lèvre, *f.*; (*edge*) bord, *m.*; (*of a beast*) babine, *f.*; (*bot.*) lèvre, *f.* *To open o.'s —s*, desserrer les dents. —**less,** *adj.* sans lèvres. — **salve,** *s.* pommade pour les lèvres, *f.*
Lipped, *adj.* (*in compounds*) aux lèvres ..., qui a des lèvres ...; (*bot.*) labié
Lippitude, *s.* lippitude, *f.*
Liquate, *v.a.* liquater, faire ressuer
Liquation, *s.* liquation, *f.*, ressuage, *m.*
Liquefaction, *s.* liquéfaction, *f.*
Liquefiable, *adj.* liquéfiable
Liquefy, *v.a.* liquéfier; — *v.n.* se liquéfier
Liquescence, *s.* fusibilité, *f.*
Liquescent, *adj.* fusible [*V.* **Liquor**
Liqueur, *s.* liqueur, *f.* —**bottle, -case,** &c.,
Liquid, *adj.* liquide; (*soft*) doux; (*gram.*) liquide; (*of letter* l) mouillé; — *s.* liquide, *m.*; (*gram.*) liquide, *f.*
Liquidambar, *s.* liquidambar, *m.*
Liquidate, *v.a.* liquider; (*a debt*) acquitter, solder, payer [quittement, solde, paiement, *m.*
Liquidation, *s.* liquidation, *f.*; (*of a debt*) ac-
Liquidator, *s.* liquidateur, *m.*
Liquidity, Liquidness, *s.* liquidité, *f.*
Liquor, *s.* liqueur, *f.*; (*drinking*) boisson; (*fam.*) rogomme, *m.* *To be in* — or *the worse for* —, être ivre. — **bottle,** *s.* (*small*) carafon, flacon, *m.* — **case,** *s.* cave à liqueurs, *f.* — **frame,** *s.* porte-liqueurs, *m.* — **glass,** *s.* verre à liqueur, *m.*
Liquorice, *s.* réglisse (*plant*) *f.*, (*extract*) *m.* *Spanish* —, —*juice*, jus de réglisse, *m.* *Stick of* —, bâton de réglisse, *m.*; réglisse en bâton, *m.*
Lisp, *v.a.n.* zézayer; (*fig.*) bégayer; — *s.* zézayement, *m.*; (*fig.*) bégayement, *m.*
Lisper, *s.* personne qui zézaye, *f.* [*s.* *V.* **Lisp,** *s.*
Lisping, *adj.* qui zézaye; (*fig.*) qui bégaye; —
Lispingly, *adv.* en zézayant; (*fig.*) en bégayant
Lissom, Lissome, *adj.* souple, pliant, flexible; léger, agile, actif
Lissomness, Lissomeness, *s.* souplesse, flexibilité, *f.*; légèreté, agilité, activité, *f.*
List, *s.* liste, *f.*; (*memorandum*) note, *f.*; (*roll*) rôle, contrôle, *m.*; (*of cloth*) lisière, *f.*; (*arena*) lice, arène, *f.*; (*end*) terme, but, *m.*; (*limit*) bord, *m.*, limite, *f.*; (*arch.*) listel, filet, *m.*; (*mil.*) états, contrôles, *m.pl.*; cadres, *m.pl.*; (*nav.*) faux-côté, *m.*; — *v.a.* (*register*) enregistrer; (*mil.*) enrôler; (*enclose*) disposer en arène; (*with cloth*) garnir de lisière; — *v.n.* (*mil.*) s'engager, s'enrôler; (*fig.*) débuter; (*desire*) avoir envie (de), vouloir, désirer. — *of wines* (*in an eating house*) carte des vins, *f.* *To enter the* —*s*, entrer en lice; (*fig.*) se mettre sur les rangs. —**less,** *adj.* inattentif; nonchalant, insouciant. —**lessly,** *adv.* inattentivement; nonchalamment, avec insouciance. —**lessness,** *s.* inattention, *f.*; nonchalance, insouciance, *f.* — **shoe, -slipper,** *s.* chausson de lisière, chausson, *m.*

Listen, *v.n.* écouter. — **to,** écouter
Listener, *s.* auditeur, *m.*; (*in a bad sense*)
Litany, *s.* litanie, *f.* [écouteur, *m.*, -euse, *f.*
Literal, *adj.* littéral
Literality, *s.* littéralité, *f.* [au pied de la lettre
Literally, *adv.* littéralement; (*fig.*) à la lettre,
Literalness, *s.* littéralité, *f.*
Literarily, *adv.* littérairement
Literary, *adj.* littéraire; (*pers.*) lettré. — *character*, — *man*, *s.* homme de lettres, littérateur, *m.* — *woman*, femme lettrée, littératrice, *f.*
Literate, *s.* (*pl.* **Literates** *or* **Literati**) lettré, littérateur, savant, *m.*; — *adj.* lettré, savant
Literature, *s.* littérature, *f.*
Litharge, *s.* litharge, *f.*
Lithe, Lithesome, *adj.* *V.* **Lissome**
Litheness, Lithesomeness, *s.* *V.* **Lis-**
Lithic, *adj.* lithique [**someness**
Lithofracteur, *s.* lithofracteur, *m.*
Lithograph, *v.a.* lithographier; — *s.* litho-
Lithographer, *s.* lithographe, *m.* [graphie, *f.*
Lithographic, -al, *adj.* lithographique; lithographié; (*pers.*) lithographe. — *printer* or &c., imprimeur *or* &c. lithographe, *m.* — *printing*, lithographie, *f.*
Lithograph-ically, -y. *V.* page 3, § 1
Lithophane, *s.* lithophanie, *f.*
Lithotom-ic, -ist. *V.* page 3, § 1
Lithotomy, *s.* lithotomie, *f.* — **knife,** *s.* lithotome, *m.*
Lithotrite, *s.* brise-pierre, lithotriteur, *m.*
Lithotrity, *s.* lithotritie, *f.*
Lithuanian, *s.* *adj.* Lithuanien, *m.*, -ne, *f.*
Litigant, *adj.* plaidant, contestant; — *s.*
Litigate, *v.a.n.* plaider [plaideur, *m.*, -euse, *f.*
Litigation, *s.* litige, *m.*; procès, *m.*, *m.pl.*
Litigious, *adj.* litigieux, contentieux; processif
Litigiously, *adv.* d'une manière litigieuse
Litigiousness, *s.* nature *or* humeur litigieuse (*or* contentieuse), *f.*, esprit litigieux (*or* contentieux), *m.* [de tournesol, papier réactif, *m.*
Litmus, *s.* tournesol, *m.* — **paper,** *s.* papier
Litotes, *s.* litote, *f.*
Litre, *s.* litre, *m.*
Litter, *s.* litière, *f.*; (*disorder*) fouillis, désordre, *m.*; (*brood*) portée, *f.*; — *v.a.* faire la litière à; garnir de litière; mettre en désordre; (*scatter*) éparpiller, jeter çà et là; (*fill, cover*) remplir, couvrir, encombrer; (*bring forth*) mettre bas; — *v.n.* coucher, se coucher, faire sa litière (de)
Littered, *adj.* désordonné, de désordre; en désordre; — *part. adj.* éparpillé, &c. (*V.* **Litter,** *v.a.n.*)
Little, *adj.* (*small, short*) petit; (*slight*) faible; (*scanty*) exigu, minime; — *adv.* (*not much*) peu; guère, ne ... guère; (*before a noun*) peu de; guère de, ne ... guère de; — *s.* (*small amount or quantity*) peu, *m.*; peu de chose, *m.*; (*before a noun*) peu de. *A* —, un peu. *Not a* —, pas peu, pas mal. — *and* —, — *by* —, *by* — *and* —, peu à peu, petit à petit. *But* —, ne ... guère. *Ever so* —, tant soit peu *Be it ever so* —, si peu que ce soit. *However* —, pour peu que. — **go,** *s.* (*exam.*) examen préliminaire *or* préparatoire, *m.*, (*fam.*) colle, *f.* — **one,** *s.* enfant, petit enfant, *m.*; (*of animals*) petit, *m.*
Littleness, *s.* petitesse, *f.*
Littoral, *adj.* littoral
Liturg-ic, al, -ist, -y. *V.* page 3, § 1
Live, *v.n.* vivre ('*on*,' '*upon*,' '*by*,' de); se nourrir (de); (*reside*) demeurer; habiter; (*fig.*) respirer; — *v.a.* mener; — *adj.* vivant; en vie; (*of coal, not extinct*) ardent; (*of colours*) vif. — **away,** *v.n.* faire bonne chère; mener joyeuse vie. — **down,** *v.a.* survivre à. — **out,** *v.a.* passer. *To — up to o.'s income*, dépenser tout son revenu. *To — well* or *high*, faire bonne chère, se nourrir bien. *To — happily* or *unhappily*, (*of husband and wife*) faire bon *or* mauvais ménage. *To have enough to — on*, avoir de quoi vivre. *Long — ...!*

vive ...! (*pl.*) vivent ...! — **oak,** *s.* chêne vert, *m.*

Lived, *adj.* de vie. *Long* —, d'une longue vie, qui vit longtemps. *Short* —, d'une courte vie, qui vit peu de temps; de peu de durée; passager

Livelihood, *s.* vie, existence, *f.*; (*means of living*) gagne-pain, *m.* *To get* or &c. *a* —, *V.*

Livelily, *adv.* vivement; gaiment [**Living**

Liveliness, *s.* vivacité, *f.*; gaieté, *f.*

Livelong, *adj.* de toute la vie; long; durable, sans fin, éternel. *The — day,* toute la journée, toute la sainte journée

Lively, *adj.* vif, animé; gai, enjoué; (*of place*) vivant, gai, riant; (*witty*) spirituel; — *adv. V.* **Livelily.** *As* — (or *gay*) *as a lark, V.* **Gay**

Liver, *s.* foie, *m.*; (*pers.*) celui qui vit ..., *m.* *Good* —, (*vers.*) épicurien, *m.*; gourmet, *m.*; gourmand, *m.*; gastronome, *m.* — **complaint,** *s.* maladie de foie, *f.* — **sick,** *s.* envie, *f.* — **stone,** *s.* hépatite, *f.* — **wort,** *s.* hépatique, *f.*

Livered, *adj.* (*in compounds*) qui a le foie ...

Liveried, *adj.* en livrée; à livrée; galonné

Livery, *s.* (*dress*) livrée, *f.*; (*of horses*) pension, *f.*; (*in London*) corps municipal, *m.*; (*law*) mise en possession, *f.* *Full* —, grande livrée, *f.* *Undress* —, petite livrée, *f.* — **coach,** *s.* voiture de remise, *f.* — **man,** *s.* homme qui porte la livrée, *m.*; (*freeman in London*) membre du corps municipal, *m.* — **servant,** *s.* domestique en (*or* à) livrée, *m.* — **servants,** *s. pl.* livrée, *f.* — **stable,** *s.* écurie de chevaux de louage, *f.*; (*for keeping*) pension pour les chevaux, *f.* — **stable keeper,** *s.* loueur de chevaux, louageur, *m.*; (*feeder*) personne qui prend les chevaux en pension, *f.*

Livid, *adj.* livide

Lividity, Lividness, *s.* lividité, *f.*

Living, *adj.* vivant; en vie; (*of water,* &c.) vif; (*quickening*) vivifiant; — *s.* vie, subsistance, existence, *f.*; (*maintenance*) nourriture, *f.*, entretien, *m.*; (*fare*) chère, cuisine, *f.*; (*of clergymen*) cure, *f.*, bénéfice, *m.* — *force,* force vive, *f.* — *language,* langue vivante, *f.* — *or dead,* mort ou vif. *For a* —, pour vivre, pour gagner sa vie. *While* —, de son vivant. *To make* or *earn* or *get a* —, gagner sa vie, gagner de quoi vivre. *To work for o.'s* —, travailler pour vivre *or* pour gagner sa vie

Livonian, *s. adj.* Livonien, *m.*, -ne, *f.*

Livre, *s.* livre, *f.*

Lixiviate, *v.a.* lessiver

Lixiviation, *s.* lessive, *f.*; (*chem.*) lixiviation, *f.*

Lixivium, *s.* lessive, *f.*; (*chem.*) lixivium, *m.*

Lizard, *s.* lézard, *m.*

Llama. *V.* **Lama**

Llanero, *s.* llanéro, *m.*

Llano, *s.* llano, *m.*

Lloyd, *s.* Lloyd, *m.*

Lo, *int.*, — **and behold,** regardez! voyez! voici! voilà! voilà que

Loach, *s.* loche, dormille, *f.*, cobite, *m.*

Load, *s.* charge, *f.*; (*burden*) fardeau, *m.*; (*weight*) poids, *m.*; (*quantity*) tas, *m.*, quantité, *f.*; — *v.a.* charger ('*with,*' de); (*bestow*) combler (de); (*in a bad sense*) accabler (de); (*a stick,* &c.) plomber; (*dice*) piper, charger. — **line, -water-line, -water-mark,** *s.* (*nav.*) ligne de charge, *f.* — **star,** *s.* étoile, *f.*, phare, *m.* — **stone,** *s.* aimant, *m.*, pierre aimantée, *f.*

Loader, *s.* chargeur, *m.*

Loading, *s.* charge, *f.*; (*nav.*) chargement, *m.*

Loaf, *s.* pain, *m.*; — *v.n.* fainéanter, vagabonder, flâner, gouêper, gouaper. — *of bread,* pain, *m.* — *of sugar, sugar* —, pain de sucre, *m.* — **sugar,** *s.* sucre en pain, sucre blanc, sucre raffiné, *m.*

Loafer, *s.* fainéant, cagnard, vagabond, flâneur, gouêpeur, gouapeur, *m.*; bricoleur, bricolier, *m.* [flânerie, *f.*

Loafing, *s.* fainéantise, *f.*, vagabondage, *m.*,

Loam, *s.* terre glaise, glaise, *f.*; — *v.a.* glaiser

Loamy, *adj.* glaiseux [— **pit,** *s.* glaisière, *f.*

Loan, *s.* (*lending*) prêt, *m.*; (*borrowing*) emprunt, *m.*; — *v.a.* prêter. — **bank,** *s.* caisse de prêts sur nantissement, *f.*, mont-de-piété, *m.* — **fund,** *s.* caisse d'emprunt, *f.* — **office,** *s.* maison de prêt, *f.* — **society,** *s.* société de prêts, *f.*

Loath, *adj.* qui a de la répugnance (à), qui n'a pas envie (de); (*sorry*) fâché (de). *To be — to,* avoir de la répugnance à

Loathe, *v.a.* haïr, détester, abhorrer, avoir en horreur; avoir du dégoût pour

Loathing, *s.* horreur, *f.*; dégoût, *m.*; aversion répugnance, *f.* [avec répugnance

Loathingly, Loathly, *adv.* avec horreur;

Loathness, *s.* répugnance, *f.* [dégoûtant

Loathsome, *adj.* horrible, détestable, odieux;

Loathsomely, *adv.* avec dégoût; d'une manière dégoûtante

Loathsomeness, *s.* dégoût, *m.*; répugnance, *f.*

Lob, *s.* rustre, lourdaud, *m.* — **worm,** *s.* laiche, aiche, *m.*

Lobby, *s.* couloir, *m.*; (*closet*) cabinet, *m.*; (*anteroom*) antichambre, *f.*; (*waiting-room*) salle d'attente, *f.*; (*entrance hall*) vestibule, *m.*

Lobe, *s.* lobe, *m.*

Lobed, *adj.* lobé

Lobelia, *s.* lobélie, *f.*

Lobster, *s.* homard, *m.*, écrevisse de mer, *f.* — **salad,** *s.* salade de homard, *f.* — **sauce,** *s.* sauce au homard, *f.*

Lobule, Lobulus, *s.* lobule, *m.*

Local, *adj.* local; topographique

Locality, *s.* localité, *f.*; présence, *f.*

Localization, *s.* localisation, *f.*

Localize, *v.a.* localiser

Locally, *adv.* localement

Locate, *v.a.* placer; établir; fixer; loger [logé

Located, *part. adj.* placé; établi; fixé; situé;

Location, *s.* emplacement, *m.*; placement, *m.*; établissement, *m.*; situation, *f.*; habitation, *f.*, domicile, *m.*; (*law*) location, *f.*

Loch, *s.* lac, *m.*; (*old pharm.*) looch, *m.*

Lock, *s.* serrure, *f.*; (*of fire-arms*) pièces, *f.pl.*, ressort, *m.*; (*gun itself*) fusil, *m.*; (*of canals*) écluse, *f.*; (*of hair*) boucle, mèche, *f.*, (*pl.*) cheveux, *m.pl.*; (*of hay*) botte, *f.*; (*of wool*) flocon, *m.*; (*embrace*) étreinte, *f.*; (*stoppage*) obstruction, *f.*, embarras, *m.*, bagarre, *f.*; — *v.a.n.* fermer à clé; fermer; (*shut up*) enfermer; renfermer; (*embrace*) serrer; (*of wheels,* &c.) accrocher, (*with the drag*) enrayer; (*print.*) serrer; (*canals,* &c.) écluser. *Under — and key,* sous clé; (*pers.*) sous les verrous. — **chain,** *s.* enrayure, *f.* — **gate,** *s.* porte d'écluse, *f.* — **hospital,** *s.* hôpital des vénériens, syphilicome, *m.* — **in,** *v.a.* enfermer. — **jaw,** *s.* trisme, *m.* — **keeper, -man,** *s.* garde-éclusier, éclusier, *m.*, -ière, *f.* — **less,** *adj.* sans serrure. — **maker,** *s.* serrurier mécanicien, *m.* — **out,** *s.* (*of factories,* &c.) fermeture des ateliers *or* des usines (*or* de l'usine), *f.* — (*one*) **out,** *v.a.* fermer la porte à (quelqu'un); (*workmen*) renvoyer; *v.n.* fermer les (*or* ses) ateliers. — **plate,** *s.* platine, *f.* — **sill,** *s.* heurtoir, *m.* — **smith,** *s.* serrurier, *m.* — **stitch,** *s.* point de navette, *m.*, piqûre arrêtée, *f.* — **stitch sewing-machine,** *s.* machine à coudre à point de navette, machine à coudre à navette, *f.* — **up,** *v.a.* enfermer, mettre sous clé, serrer; (*imprison*) coffrer, emballer; (*print.*) serrer; (*v.n., mil., in marching*) emboîter le pas; *s.* (*police cell*) violon, *m.* *In the — up,* au violon

Lockage, *s.* écluses, *f.pl.*; (*quantity of water*) éclusée, chute d'écluse, *f.*; (*duty*) péage d'écluse, *m.*

Locker, *s.* coffre, tiroir, *m.*, armoire, baraque, *f.*

Locket, *s.* médaillon, *m.*

Locomotion, *s.* locomotion, *f.*

Locomotive, *adj. s.* locomotif, *adj. m.*, -ive, *f.*; de locomotion; locomotive, *s.f.* — *engine,* machine locomotive, *f.*

Locomotiveness, Locomotivity, *s.* locomotivité, *f.*
Locust, *s.* sauterelle, *f.*; (*bot.*) *V.* **Carob**
Locution, *s.* locution, *f.*
Lode, *s.* filon, *m.*
Lodesman, *s.* lamaneur, *m.*
Lodesmanage, *s.* lamanage, *m.*
Lodgeable, *adj.* logeable
Lodge, *v.a.* placer, mettre; déposer; enfoncer; planter; fixer; (*corn*) coucher, verser; (*to harbour*) loger; abriter; (*money*) déposer, verser; (*a complaint*) déposer, porter; (*an appeal*) interjeter; — *v.n.* se loger; loger; se fixer; s'arrêter; (*of corn*) se coucher; — *s.* (*of porters*, &c.) loge, *f.*; (*habitation*) demeure, *f.*; (*of animals*) tanière, *f.*; (*shooting or hunting* —) *V.* **Shooting** *and* **Hunting**
Lodger, *s.* locataire, *m.f.*
Lodging, *s.* logement, logis, *m.*; chambre, *f.*; appartement, *m.*; garni, *m.*; (*of an appeal*) interjection, *f.* *Furnished* —, *Private* —*s*, chambre garnie, *f.*, appartement meublé, *m.*; (*house*) maison meublée *or* garnie, *f.* *A night's* —, le logement pour la nuit. *At o.'s* —*s*, chez soi. *To be in* —*s* or *in private* —*s*, être en garni. *To let* —*s*, louer en garni. — **house,** *s.* hôtel meublé, *m.*; (*for working-men, model — house*) cité ouvrière, *f.* —**house keeper,** *s.* maître (*m.*) *or* maîtresse (*f.*) d'hôtel meublé, maître *or* maîtresse de garni, propriétaire (*m.f.*) d'hôtel garni, loueur (*m.*) *or* loueuse (*f.*) en garni; (*for working-men*) logeur, *m.*, -euse, *f.*
Lodgment, *s.* logement, *m.*; (*of money*) dépôt, *m.*
Loft, *s.* grenier, *m.*; soupente, *f.*; galerie, tribune, *f.*; (*story*) étage, *m.*
Loftily, *adv.* haut; avec sublimité, pompeusement; (*proudly*) fièrement, avec hauteur
Loftiness, *s.* hauteur, élévation, *f.*; sublimité, *f.*; pompe, *f.*; (*pride*) fierté, hauteur, *f.*
Lofty, *adj.* haut, élevé; sublime; pompeux; (*proud*) fier, altier
Log, *s.* bûche, *f.*; bloc, *m.*; (*build.*) poutre, solive, *f.*, soliveau, *m.*; (*nav.*) loch, *m.* *To heave the* —, jeter le loch. —**board,** *s.* table de loch, *f.* —**book,** *s.* casernet, journal de navigation, *m.* — **cabin, -house, -hut,** *s.* hutte de bois, *f.* — **line,** *s.* ligne de loch, *f.* — **man,** *s.* porteur de bois, *m.*; (*cutter*) bûcheron, *m.* — **ship,** *s.* bateau de loch, *m.* —**wood,** *s.* bois de Campêche, campêche, *m.*
Logarithm, *s.* logarithme, *m.*
Logarithmic, *adj.* logarithmique [engagé
Logged, *adj.* (*nav.*) engagé à moitié dans l'eau,
Loggerhead, *s.* bûche, bête, *f.*, sot, *m.*, sotte, *f.*, lourdaud, *m.*, e, *f.* *At* —*s*, aux prises; en désaccord, en guerre. *To fall* or *go* or *come to* —*s*, en venir aux mains; se quereller. — **turtle,** *s.* caouane, *f.*
Loggerheaded, *adj.* lourd, stupide
Logic, *s.* logique, *f.*
Log-ical, -ically. *V.* page 3, § 1
Logicalness, *s.* logique, *f.*
Logician, *s.* logicien, *m.*, -ne, *f.*
Logistic, *adj.* logistique; —**s,** *s.pl.* logistique, *f.*
Logogram, *s.* logogramme, *m.*
Logo-graphy, -machy, &c. *V.* page 3, § 1
Logogriph, *s.* logogriphe, *m.*
Loin, *s.* (*of veal*) longe, *f.*; (*of mutton*) filet, *m.*; —**s,** *pl.* (*anat.*) reins, lombes, *m.pl.* — **chop,** *s.* côtelette de filet, *f.* — **strap,** *s.* surdos, *m.*
Loiter, *v.n.* tarder, lambiner; s'arrêter; flâner, s'amuser; rôder [-euse, *f.*
Loiterer, *s.* traînard, *m.*, e, *f.*; flâneur, *m.*,
Loll, *v.n.* s'étendre, s'étaler, se prélasser; se coucher; (*lean*) s'appuyer; se pencher; (*of the tongue*) pendre; — *v.a.* tirer
Lollard, *s.* Lollard, *m.*
Lolling, *part. adj.* étendu, étalé, couché, penché; (*of the tongue*) pendant
Lollipop, *s.* bonbon, *m.*, dragée, *f.*
Lombard, Lombardian, Lombardic, *s. adj.* Lombard, *m.*, e, *f.*
Lombardo-Venetian, *adj.* lombard-vénitien
Londoner, *s.* habitant (*m.*, e, *f.*) de Londres, Londonien, *m.*, -ne, *f.*
Londonish, *adj.* londonien
Lone, *adj.* *V.* **Lonely**
Loneliness, *s.* solitude, *f.*; isolement, *m.*; (*love of* —) amour de la solitude, *m.*
Lonely, *adj.* solitaire; désert; isolé; délaissé; qui a le goût de la solitude
Loneness, *s.* *V.* **Loneliness** [**Loneliness**
Lonesome, Lonesomeness. *V.* **Lonely,**
Long, *adj.* long; (*great*) grand; (*drawn to a length, in shape*) allongé; (*protracted*) prolongé; (*measure*) de longueur; — *adv. See below.* *A — time*, longtemps (*adv.*). *Ten yards* —, dix mètres de long, long de dix mètres. *To be six yards — by four yards broad*, avoir six mètres de long (*or* de longueur) sur quatre mètres de large (*or* de largeur). *To know the — and the short of it*, en connaître le fort et le faible, en savoir les brèves et les longues. *That is the — and the short of it*, voilà ni plus ni moins l'affaire. — **boat,** *s.* (*nav.*) chaloupe, *f.* —**dated,** *adj.* à longue date, à longue échéance. — **ears,** *s.pl.* longues oreilles, *f.pl.*; (*ass*) l'animal aux longues oreilles, l'âne, *m.* — **head,** *s.* tête carrée, *f.* —**headed,** *adj.* à tête carrée. — **holidays,** *s.pl.* grandes vacances, *f.pl.* —**legs,** *s.* (*insect.*) *V.* **Daddy.** —**lived,** *adj.* qui vit longtemps; qui dure longtemps, de longue durée; qui dure depuis longtemps. —**ness,** *s.* longueur, *f.* —**pated,** *adj.* rusé, malin. — **robe,** *s.* robe, *f.* —**rope,** *s.* *V.* **Rope.** — **sighted,** *adj.* *V.* **Far-sighted.** —**suffering,** *s.* longanimité, patience, *f.*; *adj.* plein de longanimité, endurant, patient. —**vacation,** *s.* grandes vacances, *f.pl.* —**winded,** *adj.* *V.* **Winded.** —**wise, -ways,** *adv.* de long, en long
Long, *adv.* longtemps; (*during*) durant, pendant; le long de; (*long since, long before*) depuis longtemps; (*before an adj.*) fort. *All his — long*, pendant toute sa vie, toute sa vie durant. *All night* —, toute la nuit. *As — as*, aussi longtemps que, tant que (*followed by the verb in the future, in French, if the English present means the future*). *As — ago as* 1870 *or* &c., déjà en 1870 *or* &c. *Before* —, *ere* —, avant peu, dans peu, sous peu, bientôt. *How* — ? combien de temps? combien? depuis combien de temps? depuis quand? *How — is it since ...?* combien y a-t-il que ...? *How — have you been in England?* combien y a-t-il que vous êtes en Angleterre? depuis combien de temps *or* depuis quand êtes-vous en Angleterre? *How — were you in England?* combien de temps avez-vous été en Angleterre? *How — you have been!* comme vous avez été longtemps! *Have you been here — ?* y a-t-il longtems que vous êtes ici? *Not — before* or *after*, peu de temps avant *or* après. *Not to be* —, (*be quick*) ne pas tarder, ne pas être longtemps. *So — as*, aussi longtemps que, tant que; (*since*) du moment que. —**lived,** &c., *See above*
Long, *v.n.* tarder (*imp.*); brûler d'envie, mourir d'envie, brûler; (*for*) soupirer (après), désirer ardemment *or* vivement. *I — to see him*, il me tarde de le voir, je brûle *or* meurs d'envie de [le voir
Longanimity, *s.* longanimité, *f.*
Longe, *s.* (*rid.*) longe *f.*; — *v.a.* mettre à la longe. — **whip,** *s.* chambrière, *f.*
Longer, *adj.* plus long; — *adv.* plus longtemps. *He sees no* —, il ne voit plus. *How much* —, combien de temps encore. *Some time* —, quelque temps encore. *Three hours* —, encore trois heures; trois heures de plus
Longer, *s.* personne qui désire ardemment, personne qui soupire (après), *f.*
Longeval, *adj.* qui vit longtemps
Longevity, *s.* longévité, *f.*
Longimetry, *s.* longimétrie, *f.*
Longing, *s.* envie, *f.*, désir ardent, *m.*; — *adj.*

d'envie, ardent; (*pers.*) qui a des envies, qui désire ardemment. —**whip,** *s. V.* **Longe-whip**

Longingly, *adv.* avec ardeur, impatiemment

Longish, *adj.* un peu long, assez long, longuet

Longitude, *s.* longitude, *f.*

Longitudinal, *adj.* longitudinal; en long

Longitudinally, *adv.* en long, longitudinalement

Loo, *s.* (*at cards*) mouche, *f.* — **table,** *s.* table de salon *or* de milieu, *f.*, guéridon, *m.*

Loobily, *adj.* niais, nigaud; — *adv.* niaisement

Looby, *s.* niais, *m.*, e, *f.*, nigaud, *m.*, e, *f.*, lourdaud, *m.*, e, *f.*

Loof. *V.* **Luff**

Look, *v.n.a.* regarder; considérer, réfléchir; (*look like*) avoir l'air; avoir un aspect; (*seem*) paraître, sembler; (*show oneself*) se montrer; (*be*) être ... à voir; faire un effet ...; (*watch*) veiller (à *or* sur); avoir soin (de); (*face*) avoir vue (sur), donner (sur); (*to the north, south, &c.*) être exposé (au nord, au midi, &c.); — *s.* regard, *m.*; (*glance*) coup d'œil, *m.*; (*air*) air, *m.*, mine, *f.*; apparence, *f.*; aspect, *m.* — *here!* vois! voyez! écoute! écoutez! tiens! tenez! *To — to see if*, regarder si. *To — ill*, (*pers.*) avoir mauvaise mine; avoir l'air malade; (*things*) avoir une mauvaise apparence; faire (un) mauvais effet; faire mal. *To — well*, (*pers.*) avoir bonne mine; avoir l'air bien portant; (*things*) avoir une belle apparence; avoir bon air; faire (un) bon effet; faire bien; aller bien; promettre. *How he —s*, quel air il a; de qui (*or* de quoi) il a l'air. *How does it —?* quel effet cela fait-il? de quoi cela a-t-il l'air? *How did he — when you told him that?* (*of the expression of countenance*) quelle mine (*or* quelle figure) a-t-il faite quand vous lui avez dit cela? *By the — of him*, à le voir. *By the — of it*, à ce qu'il paraît. *To give a —*, jeter un regard *or* un coup d'œil, regarder. *To give a good —*, regarder bien. *To take* or *have a — at*, regarder. *To take a last — at*, jeter un dernier regard sur. — **about,** regarder autour de soi; (*watch*) prendre garde (à), avoir l'œil ouvert (sur); (*know where one is*) s'orienter; (*make haste*) se dépêcher. — **about for,** chercher autour de soi, chercher. — **after,** regarder à; (*watch*) veiller à, avoir soin de, soigner; surveiller; garder; (*seek*) chercher. — **at,** regarder; examiner; considérer; (*a clock or watch to know the time*) regarder à; (*fig.*) envisager, considérer; (*see*) voir. — **away,** détourner les yeux, détourner ses regards. — **back,** regarder en arrière; (*fig.*) se reporter (à); faire un retour (sur). — **down,** regarder en bas, regarder par terre, regarder; baisser les yeux; (*fig.*) abaisser ses regards; (*com.*) être en baisse. — **down upon,** regarder du haut en bas; dominer; (*despise*) mépriser. — **for,** (*seek*) chercher; chercher des yeux; rechercher; (*expect*) attendre; s'attendre (à); (*hope*) espérer. — **forward,** regarder devant soi; (*expect*) attendre, s'attendre (à); se promettre, espérer. — **in,** regarder; entrer; passer (chez); aller; venir; *s.* petite visite, *f.*, petit bonjour, *m.* *To give a — in*, faire une petite visite à, aller *or* venir *or* entrer dire un petit bonjour à, passer chez. — **into,** examiner; (*to face*) avoir vue sur, donner sur. — **on,** regarder, considérer; (*watch over*) surveiller. *To be —ing on*, être spectateur. — **out,** regarder; (*seek*) chercher; (*discover*) découvrir, trouver; (*choose*) choisir; (*watch*) être sur ses gardes; (*beware*) prendre garde; (*mind*) faire attention; (*int.*) gare! garde à vous! prenez garde! (*to face*) avoir vue (sur), donner (sur); (*mil.*) être en sentinelle *or* en observation; *s.* vue, *f.*; (*watch*) guet, *m.*; vigilance, *f.*; surveillance, *f.*; observation, *f.*; (*place*) lieu d'observation, *m.*; belvédère, *m.*, lanterne, *f.*; (*view, prospect*) vue, perspective, *f.*; (*nav.*) découverte, vigie, *f.* (*— out ship*, bâtiment d'observation, *m.*); (*business*) affaire, *f.* *To be on the — out*, veiller, être sur ses gardes, avoir l'œil au guet. *To keep a good — out*, faire bonne garde, avoir l'œil au guet. *To keep a sharp* (*a proper*) *— out*, veiller activement (convenablement). *That is his* (*your*, &c.) *— out*, c'est son (votre, &c.) affaire. — **out for,** tâcher de trouver, chercher à trouver, chercher; (*expect*) s'attendre à; attendre; (*beware*) prendre garde à; — *out for your ...!* gare le *or* la *or* les ...! — **over,** regarder par-dessus; examiner, parcourir, jeter les yeux sur; (*a house*) visiter; (*a lesson, &c.*) repasser; (*watch over*) surveiller; (*forgive*) fermer les yeux sur, pardonner. — **round for,** chercher des yeux. — **through,** regarder à travers; (*understand*) voir clair à; (*examine*) parcourir. — **to,** regarder; considérer; (*watch*) veiller à; veiller sur; (*resort to*) avoir recours à; s'adresser à; (*expect*) mettre son espoir en; (*nurse*) soigner. —**up,** lever les yeux; relever la tête; (*com.*) être en hausse; (*fig.*) aller mieux; (*collect*) chercher; (*call upon*) aller *or* venir voir, passer chez. — **up to,** regarder, considérer; respecter; mettre son espoir en; s'adresser à; (*expect*) s'attendre à. — **upon,** *V.* — **on**

Looked-for, *adj.* attendu. *Not —*, inattendu; inespéré

Looker-on, *s.* spectateur, *m.*, -trice, *f.*, regardant, *m.*, e, *f.*, curieux, *m.*

Looking, *adj.* (*in compounds*) à ... mine, à l'air ..., qui a l'air ..., d'un aspect ... *Dirty —*, sale. *Fine* or *good —*, beau. *Horrid —*, horrible à voir, qui a un air affreux. *Ill —*, à (*or* de) mauvaise mine; laid, vilain. — **glass,** *s.* miroir, *m.*, glace, *f.*; (*bot.*) *V.* **Venus.** — **glass maker,** *s.* miroitier, *m.*, -ière, *f.* — **glass making, -manufactory, -trade, -business,** *s.* miroiterie, *f.*

Loom, *s.* métier à tisser, métier, *m.*; — *v.n.* paraître sur l'horizon, paraître, s'élever, se dessiner (dans le lointain)

Looming, *s.* mirage, *m.*

Loon, *s.* coquin, *m.*, e, *f.*, drôle, *m.*, drôlesse, *f.*, vaurien, chenapan, *m.*; (*bird*) plongeon glacial, grand plongeon, imbrim, *m.*

Loop, *s.* repli, *m.*; (*for fastening*) bride, *f.*, brandebourg, *m.*; (*hole*) trou, *m.*, ouverture, *f.*; (*fort.*) meurtrière, *f.*; (*of churches*) rayère, *f.*; (*of iron-works*) loupe, *f.*; (*tech.*) tenon, *m.* — **hole,** *s.* trou, *m.*, ouverture, *f.*; (*fort.*) meurtrière, *f.*; (*of churches*) rayère, *f.*; (*shift*) fauxfuyant, *m.*, échappatoire, *f.*; défaite, *f.*; — *v.a.* percer de meurtrières. — **holed,** *part. adj.* percé de meurtrières, crénelé; plein de trous, plein d'ouvertures, troué. —**up,** *v.a.* retrousser

Looper, *s.* (*zool.*) arpenteuse, *f.*, géomètre, *m.*

Loose, *v.a.* (*untie*) délier, détacher; défaire; (*relax*) desserrer, lâcher, relâcher; (*free*) dégager; (*nav.*) larguer; — *adj.* détaché, délié; défait; (*escaped*) échappé; (*unchained*) déchaîné; (*free*) libre; (*not tight*) lâche; large, ample; (*slack*) lâche, mou, mort; (*shaking*) qui branle; (*scattered*) épars; (*fig.*) vague; diffus, décousu, sans liaison; (*in morals*) relâché, libre, licencieux, dissolu; (*med.*) relâché; — *s.* liberté, *f.* — *in* (*o.'s pocket*, &c.), à même (sa poche, &c.) — *cash* or *coin* or *money*, monnaie, *f.* — *fish*, personne d'une réputation équivoque, *f.* *To break —*, *V.* **Break.** *To come —*, se détacher, se défaire. *To get —*, se détacher, se délier; se défaire; se desserrer; se relâcher; se lâcher; (*escape*) s'échapper; (*shake*) branler; (*get rid of*) se débarrasser. *To give a — to*, donner cours à; s'abandonner à, se livrer à. *To let —*, lâcher; (*set free*) donner la liberté à; (*fig.*) donner (un) libre cours à; (*in a bad sense*) déchaîner. *To set* or *turn —*, délier, &c. (*See above, To* **Loose** *v.a.*). — **strife,** *s.* (*bot.*) lysimaque, lysimachie, chasse-bosses, *f.*

Loosely, *adv.* lâchement; (*carelessly*) négligemment, nonchalamment; (*freely*) librement; (*feebly*) mollement, sans énergie; (*vaguely*)

vaguement; d'une manière décousue, sans liaison, sans suite; sans ordre; (*dissolutely*) librement, licencieusement

Loosen, *v.a.* (*shake*) ébranler; (*untie*, &c.) *V.* **Loose,** *v.a.*; — *v.n. V. To get loose*

Looseness, *s.* relâchement, *m.*; (*fulness*) ampleur, *f.*; (*desultoriness*) nature décousue, *f.*, état décousu, *m.*; caractère vague, *m.*; (*in morals*) licence, *f.*; (*of a ground, texture*) légèreté, *f.*; (*tech.*) jeu, *m.* [relâchement, *m.*

Loosening, *s.* desserrage, *m.*; desserre, *f.*;

Loot, *v.a.* piller; — *s.* pillage, *m.*

Looter, *s.* pillard, pilleur, *m.*

Looting, *s.* pillage, *m.*

Lop, *v.a.* élaguer, émonder, ébrancher; — *s.* émondes, *f.pl.*, élagage, *m.* — **eared,** *adj.* à oreilles pendantes; (*of horses*) oreillard

Lopper, *s.* élagueur, *m.*, -euse, *f*

Lopping, *s.* élagage, *m.*; (*collectively*) élagage, *m.*, émondes, *f.pl.*, ramassis, *m.*

Loquacious, *adj.* loquace

Loquaciously, *adv.* loquacement

Loquaciousness, Loquacity, *s.* loquacité, *f.*

Lord, *s.* maître, *m.*; (*spouse*) mari, époux, *m.*; (*title*) seigneur (*old French*), lord (*English*), *m.*; (*peer*) pair, *m.*; (*nobleman*) noble, *m.*; (*God*) Seigneur, *m.*; — *v.n.* (— *it over*) dominer; (*in a bad sense*) faire le maître (avec); tyranniser. *My* —, (*to princes, archbishops and bishops only, in France*) monseigneur; (*to noblemen*) monsieur le duc *or* le comte *or* &c., monsieur; vous; (*to an Englishman*) milord. *My* —*s*, (*old French*) messeigneurs; (*to Englishmen*) milords. *House of* —*s*, (*in England*) chambre des lords, *f.*; (*formerly in France*) chambre des pairs, *f.* *The year of our* —, l'année de Notre-Seigneur, *f.*, l'an de grâce, *m.* *O* —! Seigneur! mon Dieu! — *mayor*, (*in England*) lord maire, maire de Londres, *m.* — *lieutenant* (*of Ireland*), vice-roi (d'Irlande), *m.* —*'s prayer*, oraison dominicale, *f.*, pater, *m.* —*'s supper*, cène, *f.* — **like,** *adj.* en seigneur; (*in a bad sense*) en grand seigneur. —**liness,** *s.* dignité, *f.*; (*pride*) fierté, hauteur, morgue, *f.* —**ling,** *s.* gentillâtre, *m.*; petit seigneur, *m.* —**ly,** *adj.* seigneurial; de seigneur; noble; magnifique; (*proud*) altier, fier, hautain; *adv.* en seigneur; (*proudly*) avec fierté, superbement. —**ship,** *s.* (*title*) seigneurie, *f.*; (*power*) pouvoir, empire, *m.* *His* — *ship*, Sa Seigneurie; (*of French noblemen*) monsieur le duc *or* le comte *or* &c.; (*of bishops*) Sa Grandeur; monseigneur. *Your* —*ship*, Votre Seigneurie; monseigneur; (*of French noblemen*) monsieur le duc *or* le comte *or* &c.; (*of bishops*) Votre Grandeur; monseigneur [doctrine, *f.*

Lore, *s.* science, *f.*, savoir, *m.*, instruction, *f.*;

Lorette, *s.* lorette, *f.*

Loricate, *v.a.* enduire, couvrir

Lorimer, Loriner, *s.* lormier, *m.* —*'s article or trade or work*, lormerie, *f.*

Loriot, *s.* loriot, *m.*

Lorrain, Lorrainer, *s.* Lorrain, *m.*, e, *f.*

Losable, *adj.* perdable

Lose, *v.a.n.* perdre ('*by*,' à; '*by it*,' y); (*of clocks, watches*) retarder; retarder de (...); (*to make one lose ..., to cost*) faire perdre; coûter. *To* — *oneself*, — *o.'s way*, s'égarer, se perdre. (*V.* **Lost**)

Loser, *s.* perdeur, *m.*, -euse, *f.*; (*at play, lotteries*) perdant, *m.*, e, *f.* *To be a* —, être en perte, perdre ('*by*,' ..., à ...; '*by it*,' y). *I am a* — *by it*, j'y perds

Losing, *adj.* de perte, à perte; (*at play, lotteries*) perdant (*V.* **Game**); —**s,** *s.pl.* pertes, *f.pl.*, perte, *f. sing.*

Loss, *s.* perte, *f.*; (*gradual*) déperdition, *f.*; (*of voice*) extinction, *f.* — *of life*, mort, *f.*, décès, *m.*; perte de la vie, *f.* *At a* —, à perte. *To be at a* — (*to*), être en peine (de), être embarrassé (pour *or* de); ne pouvoir pas; ne savoir; (*for*) être embarrassé de trouver

Lost, *part. adj.* perdu, &c. (*V.* **Lose,** *v.a.n.*); déchu; (*stray*) égaré; (*sunk*) abîmé; absorbé. *To be* —, (*perish*) périr. *To be* — *to*, être perdu pour; (*to have lost*) avoir perdu. *To be* — *upon* (*a person*), être perdu auprès de. —, *a dog or* &c. ..., (*on bills*) il a été perdu un chien *or* &c. ...

Lot, *s.* sort, lot, *m.*; part, quote-part, *f.*; quantité, *f.*; tas, *m.*; masse, *f.*; (*of sales*) lot, *m.*; (*com.*) partie, *f.*; — *v.a.* assigner; (*com.*) lotir. *Bad* —, tas de vauriens, *m.*, maudite engeance, *f.* *All the* — *of you*, tous tant que vous êtes. *By* —, *by drawing* —*s*, au sort; par voie de tirage. *To cast or draw* —*s*, tirer au sort. *To cast in o.'s* — *with*, partager le sort de. *To cut* —*s*, tirer à la courte paille. *To fall to o.'s* —, *V.* **Share** [bier, *m.*

Lote, — **tree,** *s.* micocoulier, fabreguier, juju-

Loth, Lothe, &c. *V.* **Loath, Loathe,** &c.

Lothario, *s.* Lothaire, *m.*; (*lady-killer*) love-

Lotion, *s.* lotion, *f.*; — *v.a.* lotionner [lace, *m.*

Loto, *s.* (*game*) loto, *m.*

Lotos, Lotus, *s.* lotus, lotier, *m.* — **eater,** *s.*, — **eating,** *adj.* lotophage, *s.m.*, *adj. m.f.*

Lottery, *s.* loterie, *f.* — **ticket,** *s.* billet de

Lotting, *s.* lotissement, lotissage, *m.* [loterie, *m.*

Loud, *adj.* haut, fort; (*of cries*, &c.) grand; (*noisy*) bruyant; retentissant; éclatant; tapageur; — *adv. V.* **Loudly.** *In a* — *voice*, à haute voix

Loudly, *adv.* haut, tout haut, à haute voix; fort; hautement; à grand bruit; à grands cris; d'une manière éclatante

Loudness, *s.* (*of sound*) force, *f.*; (*noise*) bruit, grand bruit, *m.*; retentissement, *m.*; éclat, [*m.*; tapage, *m.*

Lough, *s.* lac, *m.*

Louis, — **d'or,** *s.* (*old Fr. coin*) louis, louis d'or, *m.*

Lounge, *v.n.* flâner; rôder; (*loll*) se coucher, s'étaler, s'étendre, se prélasser; — *s. V.* **Lounging;** (*couch*) chaise longue, *f.*

Lounger, *s.* flâneur, *m.*, -euse, *f.*, badaud, *m.*, e, *f.*, désœuvré, *m.*, e, *f.*

Lounging, *s.* flânerie, *f.*; oisiveté, *f.*; promenade, *f.*; — *adj.* flâneur; nonchalant. — **chair,** *s.* chaise longue, *f.*

Loungingly, *adv.* en flâneur; nonchalamment

Loup. *V.* **Loop**

Louse, *s.* pou, *m.*; — *v.a.* pouiller, épouiller, ôter les poux à. — **wort,** *s.* pédiculaire, *f.*

Lousily, *adv.* en pouilleux

Lousiness, *s.* pouillerie, *f.*

Lousy, *adj.* pouilleux

Lout, *s.* rustre, *m.f.*, rustaud, *m.*, e, *f.*; lourdaud, *m.*, e, *f.* *Lazy* —, fainéant, *m.*, e, *f.*

Loutish, *adj.* rustre, rustaud

Loutishly, *adv.* en rustre [**board**

Louvre, *s.* Louvre, *m.*; (*lufferboard*) *V.* **Luffer-**

Lovable, *adj.* aimable; chérissable

Lovage, *s.* livèche, *f.*

Love, *v.a.* aimer; affectionner; chérir; — *s.* amour, *m.*; affection, *f.*; sympathie, *f.*; (*friendship*) amitié, *f.*; (*pers.*) amour, *m.*, ami, *m.*, e, *f.*; (*object of love, of delight*) amours, *f.pl.*; (*Cupid*) l'Amour, *m.* *To be in* —, être amoureux *or* épris (de), être amouraché (de). *To fall in* —, devenir *or* tomber amoureux (de), s'éprendre (de), s'amouracher (de). *To give o.'s* — *to*, faire ses amitiés à. *Give my best* — *to*, (*fam.*) embrasse bien pour moi. *To make* —, faire l'amour; faire la cour (à). *To play for* —, jouer pour le plaisir *or* pour l'honneur. *For* — *or money*, (*anyhow*) pour tout l'or du monde. — *me* — *my dog*, qui m'aime aime mon chien. — **affair,** *s.* affaire d'amour, amourette, *f.* — **apple,** *s.* pomme d'amour, tomate, *f.* — **bird,** *s.* psittacule, *m.*, perruche, *f.* — **charm,** *s.* philtre, *m.* — **feast,** *s.* agape, *f.* — **grass,** *s.* éragrostide, *f.* — **knot,** *s.* lacs d'amour, nœud, *m.* —**less,** *adj.* sans amour; insensible. — **letter,** *s.* billet doux, poulet, *m.* — **-lies-bleeding,** *s.* amarante à fleurs en queue, *f.*

— **lily,** *adv.* aimablement; délicieusement. —**liness,** *s.* amabilité, *f.*; beauté, *f.*; charme, *m.*, charmes, *m.pl.* — **lorn,** *adj.* abandonné. —**ly,** *adj.* aimable; beau; charmant, ravissant, délicieux; *adv.* aimablement; délicieusement. — **making,** *s.* cour, *f.*, assiduités, *f.pl.* — **match,** *s.* mariage d'inclination, *m.* —**potion,** *s.* philtre, *m.* — **sick,** *adj.* malade d'amour, qui languit d'amour; qui exprime l'amour, plaintif. — **sickness,** *s.* langueur amoureuse, *f.* —**song,** *s.* chanson d'amour, romance, chansonnette, *f.* — **suit,** *s.* cour, *f.*, assiduités, *f.pl.* — **tale, -story,** *s.* histoire galante, *f.*, roman, *m.*, historiette, *f.* — **trick,** *s.* amourette, *f.*

Lover, *s.* celui qui aime, adorateur, prétendant, *m.*, amante, *f.*; (*fam.*) amoureux, *m.*, -euse, *f.*; (*poet.*) amant, *m.*, e, *f.*; (*intended*) prétendu, *m.*, e, *f.*; (*fancier*) amateur, *m.*; (*friend*) ami, *m.*, e, *f.*

Loving, *adj.* aimant, affectueux, tendre, affectionné; (*things*) d'amour, de l'amour; d'amitié, de l'amitié. — **cup,** *s.* coupe de l'amitié, *f.*

Lovingly, *adv.* affectueusement, tendrement, avec amour, avec amitié

Lovingness, *s.* affection, tendresse, *f.*

Low, *adj.* bas; peu élevé; inférieur; (*humble*) petit, humble; (*mean*) bas, vil; (*vulgar*) commun, vulgaire, trivial; canaille; (*deep*) profond; (*weak*) faible; (*dejected*) abattu; (*of hats*) bas de forme, petit; (*of dresses*) décolleté; (*of bows*) profond; (*of public gatherings*) mal composé; (*of diet*) peu substantiel, débilitant; pauvre; (*of fevers*) lent; (*of sounds*) grave, bas; (— *priced*) à bas prix; — *adv.* bas; à voix basse; (— *down*) bas; en bas; (*deeply*) profondément; (*of bowing*) profondément; (*com.*) à bas prix; — *v.n.* mugir, beugler. — *body,* (*of a dress*) corsage décolleté; (*under*) chemisette, *f.* *In a — voice,* à voix basse. *To bring —,* abattre; humilier; réduire; affaiblir. *To get* or *run —,* baisser. *To lay —,* abattre, faire tomber, descendre, coucher par terre; ensevelir. *To lie —,* être enseveli, reposer. — **born, -bred,** *adj.* de basse naissance, de basse extraction, vulgaire; mal élevé. — **built,** *adj.* (*nav.*) de bas bord. — **Church,** *s.* basse Église; *adj.* de la basse Église, *f.* — **Countries (The),** *s. pl.* les Pays-Bas, *m.pl.* — **crowned,** *adj.* (*of hats*) bas de forme, petit. — **fed,** *adj.* mal nourri. — **land,** *s.* terrain bas, *m.*; plaine, basse terre, *f.*; (— **lands,** *pl.* terrains bas, &c.; *Netherlands,* Pays-Bas, *m.pl.*). —**lander,** *s.* habitant (*m.*, e, *f.*) des basses terres *or* des plaines. — **mass,** *s.* *V.* **Mass.** — **minded,** *adj.*, — **mindedness,** *s.* *V.* **Base-minded,** &c. — **pressure,** *s.* basse pression, *f.*; *adj.* à basse pression. — **priced,** *adj.* à bas prix, à bon marché. — **relief,** *s.* bas-relief, *m.* — **spirited,** *adj.* abattu, triste; (*cowardly*) lâche, sans cœur, pusillanime. — **spiritedness,** *s.* manque de cœur, *m.*, pusillanimité, *f.*; (*depression*) abattement, *m.* — **Sunday,** *s.* Quasimodo, *f.* — **water,** *s.* *V.* **Water.** — **water mark,** *s.* niveau des basses eaux, étiage, *m.*

Lower, *adj.* plus bas; moins élevé; inférieur; bas; de *or* du dessous, du bas, d'en bas; (*of Houses of Parliam., geog.*) bas; (*geog.*) inférieur; —, — **down,** *adv.* plus bas; — *v.a.n.* baisser; abaisser; descendre; diminuer; humilier, (*debase*) avilir, ravaler; (*make fall*) faire baisser, faire descendre; (*nav.*) amener; (*of the sky*) s'obscurcir; s'assombrir; (*of clouds*) s'amonceler; (*threaten*) menacer. *To — oneself,* s'abaisser, se dégrader, s'avilir, se ravaler; s'humilier. — **Canada,** *s.* le Bas-Canada, *m.* — **case,** *s.* (*print.*) bas-de-casse, *m.* — **Egypt,** *s.* la Basse-Égypte, *f.* — **Empire,** *s.* Bas-Empire, *m.* — **House,** (*of parliam.*) Chambre basse, *f.* — **lip,** *s.* lèvre inférieure, *f.* — **mast,** *s.* bas mât, *m.* — **most,** *adj.* (le) plus bas, inférieur, dernier; (le) plus profond. — **part,** *s.* bas, *m.*; dessous, *m.* — **regions,** *s. pl.* régions infernales, *f.pl.*, enfer, *m.* — **Rhine,** *s.* Bas-Rhin, *m.* — **Seine,** *s.* Seine inférieure, *f.* — **side,** *s.* *V.* — **part.** — **tenor,** *s.* basse-contre, *f.* — **town,** *s.* basse ville, *f.* — **yard,** *s.* (*nav.*) basse vergue, *f.*

Lowering, *s.* abaissement, *m.*, diminution, *f.*; descente, *f.*; — *adj.* sombre; menaçant

Loweringly, *adv.* d'une manière (*or* d'un air) sombre, d'un air menaçant; tristement

Lowest, *adj.* (le) plus bas, dernier

Lowing, *s.* mugissement, beuglement, *m.*

Lowliness, *s.* humilité, *f.*

Lowly, *adj.* humble; — *adv.* humblement

Lowness, *s.* bassesse, *f.*; petitesse, *f.*; humilité, *f.*; (*weakness*) faiblesse, *f.*; (*dejection*) abattement, *m.*; (*shallowness*) peu de profondeur, *m.*; (*of places*) situation basse, *f.*; (*of sound*) gravité, *f.*; (*of prices, funds*) dépréciation, *f.*; (*vulgarity*) vulgarité, *f.*

Loxodrom-ic, -ism, -y. *V.* page 3, § 1

Loyal, *adj.* fidèle

Loyal-ism, -ist. *V.* page 3. § 1

Loyally, *adv.* fidèlement

Loyalty, *s.* attachement au souverain *or* au chef de l'État, *m*, fidélité, *f.*

Lozenge, *s.* losange, *m.*, (*her.*) *f*; (*cake*) pastille, *f.*; tablette, *f.*; — *v.a.* losanger. — **shaped,** *adj.* en losange, losangique

Lozenged, Lozengy, *adj.* losangé

Lubber, *s.* lourdaud, *m.*, e, *f.*, mastoc, *m.*; (*nav.*) marin d'eau douce, *m.*

Lubberly, *adj.* lourd, gauche, mastoc; — *adv.* en lourdaud, gauchement

Lubricant, *s.* lubrifiant, *m.*

Lubricate, *v.a.* lubrifier; adoucir

Lubrication, *s.* lubrification, *f.*

Lubricator, *s.* lubrifiant, *m.*

Lubricity, *s.* nature glissante, *f.*; inconstance, *f.*; (*lewdness*) lubricité, *f.*

Luce, *s.* lis, *m.*; (*fish*) brochet, *m.*

Lucent, *adj.* luisant, resplendissant

Lucern, Lucerne, *s.* luzerne, *f.* — **field,** *s.* champ de luzerne, *m.*, luzernière, *f.* — **grass,** *s.* luzerne, *f.*

Lucid, *adj.* lumineux; limpide, transparent; [(*fig.*) lucide

Lucidity, *s.* transparence, limpidité, *f.*; (*fig.*) lucidité, *f.*

Lucidly, *adv.* lucidement, clairement

Lucifer, *s.* (*myth., astr.*) Lucifer, *m.*; (— *match*) allumette chimique, *f.*

Luciferian, *adj.* luciférien

Luciferous, *adj.* lucifère

Luck, *s.* chance, *f.*, hasard, *m.*, fortune, *f.*; (*happiness*) bonheur, *m.*, bonne fortune, bonne chance, chance, *f.* *Good —,* bonheur, *m.*, bonne fortune, bonne chance, *f.* *Good — to you!* bonne chance! *Ill* or *bad —,* malheur, *m.*, mauvaise fortune, mauvaise chance, *f.*, guignon, *m.* *To bring good* or *ill —,* porter bonheur *or* malheur

Luckily, *adv.* heureusement, par bonheur

Luckiness, *s.* bonheur, *m.*

Luckless, Lucklessly. *V.* **Unlucky** *and* [**Unluckily**

Lucky, *adj.* heureux; propice, favorable. *To be —,* être heureux, avoir du bonheur *or* de la [chance

Lucrative, *adj.* lucratif

Lucratively, *adv.* lucrativement

Lucre, *s.* lucre, *m.*

Lucubrate, *v.a.n.* élucubrer

Lucubration, *s.* élucubration, *f.*

Lucubrator, *s.* élucubrateur, *m.*

Lucubratory, *adj.* élucubratif

Ludicrous, *adj.* plaisant, comique, risible, [burlesque

Ludicrously, *adv.* plaisamment, comiquement, burlesquement

Ludicrousness, *s.* plaisant, burlesque, *m.*, [nature comique, *f.*

Luff, *s.* lof, *m.*, aulofée, *f.*; — *v.n.* venir au lof, lofer

Lufferboard, Lufferboarding, *s.* abat-vent, clin, *m.*; persienne fixe, *f.*; (*of steeples*) abat-son, *m.*

Lug, *v.a.* tirer, traîner. — **about,** *v.a.* traîner, trimbaler. — **away, off,** *v.a.* entraîner, enlever. — **in,** *v.a.* faire entrer de force, faire entrer, introduire. — **out,** *v.a.* faire sortir de force; tirer, sortir. — **sail,** *s.* voile de fortune, *f.* — **worm,** *s.* laiche, aiche, *m.*

Luggage, *s.* bagages, *m.pl.*, bagage, *m.*, effets, *m.pl.*; (*goods*) marchandises, *f.pl.* — **office,** *s.* bureau des bagages, *m.* — **room,** *s.* salle des bagages, *f.*; (*left luggage, cloak-room*) *V.* **Cloak-room.** — **ticket,** *s.* bulletin de bagages, *m.* — **train,** *s. V.* **Train.** — **van,** *s.* fourgon (*m.*) *or* voiture (*f.*) de (*or* des) bagages

Lugger, *s.* lougre, chasse-marée, *m.*

Lugubrious, *adj.* lugubre

Lugubriously, *adv.* lugubrement

Lukewarm, *adj.* tiède. *To become* or *get* —, s'attiédir. *To make* —, attiédir

Lukewarmly, *adv.* tièdement, avec tiédeur

Lukewarmness, *s.* tiédeur, *f.*; attiédissement, *m.*

Lull, *v.a.* bercer; endormir; calmer, apaiser; (*a pain*) assoupir; (*to*) inviter (à); — *v.n.* se calmer, s'apaiser; — *s.* moment de calme, calme, intervalle de beau temps, intervalle, *m.*; (*of water*, &c.) murmure, *m.*; (*nav.*) accalmie, embellie, *f.* *To — with hopes*, bercer d'espérances. *To — asleep*, endormir. *To — to sleep*, inviter au sommeil, endormir

Lullaby, *s.* berceuse, chanson de nourrice, *f.*, chant, *m.*

Lumachel, Lumachella, *s.* lumachelle, *f.*

Lumbago, *s.* lumbago, *m.*

Lumbar, *adj.* lombaire

Lumber, *s.* vieilleries, *f.pl.*; meubles inutiles, *m.pl.*; (*fig.*) rebut, *m.*; fatras, *m.*; (*timber*) bois de charpente, *m.*; — *v.a.* entasser; embarrasser; — *v.n.* se mouvoir pesamment, se traîner lourdement. — **man,** *s.* coupeur, bûcheron, défricheur, *m.* — **place,** *s.* lieu de décharge, *m.* — **room,** *s.* chambre de débarras, *f.*, pièce (*f.*) *or* cabinet (*m.*) de décharge, grenier, *m.*

Lumberer, *s.* coupeur, bûcheron, défricheur, *m.*

Lumbering, *adj.* lourd, pesant; — *s.* marche pesante, *f.*

Luminary, *s.* corps lumineux, *m.*; (*fig.*) lumière, *f.*, flambeau, *m.*; (*theol., poet.*) luminaire, *m.*

Luminosity, *s.* luminosité, *f.*

Luminous, *adj.* lumineux

Luminously, *adv.* lumineusement

Luminousness, *s.* luminosité, *f.*

Lump, *s.* masse, *f.*; morceau, *m.*; paquet, *m.*; — *v.a.* mettre en masse *or* en bloc, réunir; prendre en bloc; comprendre. *By the* —, *In a* or *the* —, en bloc. *In one* —, en tas. — **fish, -sucker,** *s.* lompe, cycloptère, *m.* — **sugar,** *s.* sucre en pain, sucre blanc, *m.* — *of sugar*, morceau de sucre, *m.*

Lumper, *s.* débardeur, déchargeur, gabarier, *m.*

Lumping, Lumpish, *adj.* gros, lourd, pesant; (*coarse*) grossier, massif

Lumpishly, *adv.* lourdement, pesamment; (*coarsely*) grossièrement

Lumpishness, *s.* lourdeur, pesanteur, *f.*; (*coarseness*) grossièreté, *f.*

Lumpy, *adj.* en petits morceaux, par petites masses

Lunacy, *s.* folie, démence, aliénation mentale, *f.*

Lunar, Lunary, *adj.* lunaire; en forme de lune; — *s.* lunaire, *f.* — **caustic,** *s.* pierre infernale, *f.*

Lunarian, *s.* sélénien, *m.*, -ne, *f.*

Lunatic, *adj.* d'aliéné, d'aliénés, de fou, de fous; (*pers.*) aliéné, fou; — *s.* aliéné, *m.*, e, *f.*, fou, *m.*, folle, *f.* — *asylum*, maison (*f.*, *or* hospice, *m.*) d'aliénés

Lunation, *s.* lunaison, *f.*

Lunch, Luncheon, *s.* déjeuner, *m.*; second déjeuner, *m.*; — *v.n.* déjeuner ('*on*,' de, avec); faire son second déjeuner. — **biscuit,** *s.* brèchetelle, *f.* — **rooms,** *s. pl.* café, *m.*; restaurant, *m.* — **time, -hour,** *s.* heure du (second) déjeuner, *f.*

Lunette, *s.* lunette, *f.*

Lung, *s.* poumon, *m.* — **wort,** *s.* pulmonaire, *f.*

Lunge, *s.* (*fenc.*) botte, *f.*; — *v.n.* se fendre; caver. *To give* or *make a* —, porter *or* pousser une botte; se fendre; caver

Lunged, *adj.* à poumons

Luniform, *adj.* luniforme; en lune

Lunisolar, *adj.* luni-solaire

Lupin, *s.* lupin, *m.*

Lupine, *s.* (*bot.*) lupin, *m.*; — *adj.* (*wolfish*) de loup

Lupuline, *s.* (*chem., principle*) lupuline, *f.*; (*bot., powder*) lupulin, *m.*; (*bot., plant*) lupuline, *f.*

Lupus, *s.* (*med.*) lupus, *m.*

Lurch, *s.* embarras, *m.*

Lurcher, *s.* chien qui guette le gibier, lévrier, *m.*

Lure, *s.* leurre, *m.*, amorce, *f.*, appât, attrait, *m.*; — *v.a.* leurrer, amorcer, attirer

Lurid, *adj.* luride; blafard; fauve; (*dismal*) sombre, triste, lugubre, sinistre

Lurk, *v.n.* être aux aguets, être en embuscade; se cacher; (*things*) couver

Lurker, *s.* personne aux aguets *or* en embuscade, personne qui se cache, *f.*

Lurking, *adj.* d'embuscade; (*fig.*) qui se cache, caché, secret; (*nav.*) à fleur d'eau; — *s.* aguets, *m.pl.*, embuscade, *f.* — **hole,** *s.* trou, *m*, cachette, *f.* — **place,** *s.* embuscade, *f.*; cachette, *f.*; (*a den*) repaire, *m.*

Luscious, *adj.* mielleux; doucereux; succulent; délicieux; (*of wine*) liquoreux

Lusciously, *adv.* avec douceur; délicieusement

Lusciousness, *s.* douceur excessive, fadeur, *f.*; (*of wine*) liqueur, *f.*

Lust, *s.* (*desire*) convoitise, *f.*; (*concupiscence*) luxure, *f.*; — *v.n.* — **after,** convoiter, désirer avec passion. —**ful,** *adj.* convoiteux; (*lewd*) luxurieux, lascif. —**fully,** *adv.* avec convoitise; (*lewdly*) luxurieusement, lascivement. —**fulness,** *s. V.* **Lust.** —**ily,** *adv.* vigoureusement, fort et ferme; (*stoutly*) avec embonpoint. *To cry out —ily*, jeter de grands cris. —**iness,** *s.* vigueur, *f.*; (*stoutness*) embonpoint, *m.* —**ing,** *s. V.* **Lust.** —**y,** *adj.* vigoureux, fort, robuste; gros, corpulent; copieux

Lustral, *adj.* lustral

Lustrate, *v.a.* purifier

Lustration, *s.* lustration, *f.*; (*fig.*) purification, *f.*

Lustre, *s.* (*splendour*) lustre, éclat, *m.*, splendeur, *f.*; (*gloss*) lustre, *m.*; (*candlestick*) lustre, *m.*; (*space of five years*) lustre, *m.* — **maker,** *s.* lustrier, *m.*

Lustring, *s.* (*stuff*) lustrine, *f.*

Lustrum, *s.* lustre, *m.*

Lusty, *adj.* *See under* **Lust**

Lutation, *s.* lutation, *f.*

Lute, *s.* (*mus.*) luth, *m.*; (*chem.*) lut, *m.*; — *v.a.* (*chem.*) luter. — **maker,** *s.* luthier, *m.*

Lutestring, *s.* (*stuff*) lustrine, *f.*

Lutheran, *s. adj.* luthérien, *m.*, -ne, *f.*

Lutheranism, *s.* luthéranisme, *m.*

Luting, *s.* (*chem.*) lut, *m.*

Lutist, *s.* joueur de luth, *m.*

Luxate, *v.a.* luxer

Luxation, *s.* luxation, *f.*

Luxemburger, *s.* Luxembourgeois, *m.*, e, *f.*

Luxurianc-e, y, *s.* luxuriance, exubérance, *f.*

Luxuriant, *adj.* luxuriant, exubérant

Luxuriantly, *adv.* avec luxuriance, avec exubérance, avec fertilité

Luxuriate, *v.n.* croître abondamment, croître avec exubérance, exubérer; (*live*) vivre dans l'abondance; (*enjoy*) nager (dans); (*delight*) se livrer avec délices (à), s'abandonner (à); se plaire (dans, en)

Luxurious, *adj.* luxueux; somptueux; (*pers.*) adonné au luxe; efféminé, mou; (*lewd*) luxurieux, voluptueux

Luxuriously, *adv.* luxueusement, avec luxe; somptueusement; voluptueusement; agréablement

Luxuriousness, *s.* luxe, *m.*, somptuosité, *f.*; volupté, *f.*

Luxury, *s.* luxe, *m.*; somptuosité, *f.*; régal,

m.; jouissance, volupté, *f.*; objet de luxe, *m.*
Lyceum, *s.* lycée, *m.* [de Lydie
Lydian, *s.* Lydien, *m.*, -ne, *f.*; — *adj.* lydien,
Lye, — **washing,** *s.* lessive, *f.*
Lying, *part. adj.* (*recumbent,* &c.) couché, étendu, &c. (*V.* **Lie,** *v.n., Second Entry*); situé, placé; (*false,deceptive*) (*pers.*) menteur; (*things*) mensonger; — *s.* mensonge, *m.* — **along,** *adj.* (*nav.*) à la bande. — **in,** *adj.* en couche, en couches; *s.* couches, *f.pl.* — *in hospital,* hôpital de la Maternité, *m.* — *in institution,* maison d'accouchement, *f.* —**ly,** *adv.* avec mensonge. — **to,** *adj.* (*nav.*) en panne
Lyme-grass, *s.* élyme, *m.*
Lymph, *s.* lymphe, *f.*; (*vaccine* —) vaccin, *m.*
Lymphatic, *adj.* lymphatique; — *s.* vaisseau lymphatique, *m.*
Lynch, *s.* Lynch, *m.*; — *v.a.* lyncher, exécuter sommairement. — **law,** *s.* loi de Lynch, *f.*
Lyncher, *s.* lyncheur, *m.*
Lynx, *s.* lynx, loup-cervier, *m.* *Female* —, loup-cerve, *f.* — **eyed,** *adj.* aux yeux de lynx
Lyre, *s.* lyre, *f.* — **bird, -pheasant, -tail,** *s.*
Lyric, -al, *adj.* lyrique [ménure, *m.*
Lyric, *s.*, **Lyrics,** *s. pl.* lyrique, *m.*
Lyricism, *s.* lyrisme, lyrique, *m.*
Lyriform, *adj.* lyriforme
Lyrist, *s.* joueur de lyre, *m.*

M

M, *s.* (*letter*) m, *f.*
Mab, *s.* Mab, la reine des fées, *f.*
Macacus, *s.* macaque, *m.*
Macadam, *s.* macadam, *m.*
Macadamization, *s.* macadamisage, *m.*
Macadamize, *v.a.* macadamiser [cadam, *m.*
Macadamizing, *s.* macadamisage, *m.*; ma-
Macaroni, *s.* macaroni, *m.*
Macaronic, *s.* macaronée, *f.*
Macaron-ic (*adj.*), **-ism, -ist.** *V.* page 3, § 1
Macaroon, *s.* macaron, *m.*
Macaw, *s.* ara, *m.* — **tree,** *s.* palmier-éventail, *m.*
Mace, *s.* masse, *f.*; (*weapon*) masse d'armes, *f.*; (*spice*) macis, *m.*; (*seed-coat*) arille, *f.* — **bearer,** *s.* massier, *m.*
Macedonian, *s. adj.* Macédonien, *m.*, -ne, *f.*
Macer, *s.* massier, *m.*
Macerate, *v.a.n.* macérer
Maceration, *s.* macération, *f.*
Machiavelian, *adj.* machiavélique; — *s.* machiavéliste, *m.f.*
Machiavelism, *s.* machiavélisme, *m.*
Machicolation, *s.* mâchicoulis, *m.*
Machinate, *v.a.* machiner, tramer
Machination, *s.* machination, *f.*
Machinator, *s.* machinateur, *m.*, -trice, *f.*
Machine, *s.* machine, *f.*; mécanique, *f.*; instrument, *m.*; (*bathing-cart*) voiture, *f.*; — *adj.* de machine; (*by machinery*) à la mécanique. — **builder,** &c. *V.* **Engine.** — **factory,** *s.* atelier de construction pour les machines, *m.* — **folded,** *adj.* plié à la mécanique. — **made,** *adj.* fait à la mécanique, à la mécanique, mécanique. — **maker,** *s.* constructeur de machines, *m.* — **minder,** *s.* surveillant de machine, *m.*; (*print.*) conducteur de machine (à imprimer), *m.*
Machinery, *s.* mécanisme, *m.*; appareil, *m.*, appareils, *m.pl.*; (*machines*) machinerie, *f.*, machines, *f.pl.*; mécanique, *f.*; (*theat.*) machine, *f.*; (*of poems*) merveilleux, *m.* *Made by* —, fait à la mécanique
Machin-ism, -ist. *V.* page 3, § 1
Mackerel, *s.* maquereau, *m.* — **boat,** *s.* maquilleur, *m.* — **pike,** *s.* scombrésoce, *m.*
Macintosh, Mackintosh, *s.* mackintosh, *m.*
Macula, *s.* tache, *f.*; (*astr.*) macule, *f.*
Maculate, *v.a.* tacher; (*print.*) maculer
Maculation, *s.* maculation, *f.*
Mad, *adj.* fou; aliéné; insensé; furieux; (*fam., off hinges*) hors de soi; (*of hydrophobia*) enragé. *To be — after,* être fou de, avoir la rage de. *To drive* or *make* or *turn* —, rendre fou. *To go* or *run* —, devenir fou; (*of hydrophobia*) devenir enragé. — **apple,** *s.* aubergine, *f.* — **bull,** *s.* taureau furieux, *m.* — **cap,** *s. adj.* fou, *m.*, folle, *f.*, écervelé, *m.*, e, *f.* — **doctor,** *s.* médecin de fous, *m.* — **dog,** *s.* chien enragé, *m.* — **house,** *s.* maison de fous *or* d'aliénés, *f.* — **like,** *adj.* comme un fou *or* &c. — **man,** *s.* fou, insensé, *m.* — **woman,**
Madam, *s.* madame, *f.* [*s.* folle, insensée, *f.*
Madden, *v.a.* rendre fou; affoler; (*vex*) faire enrager; — *v.n.* devenir fou, tomber en démence
Maddening, *adj.* qui rend fou, à rendre fou; (*fam.*) enrageant, démontant; (*fig.*) furieux; (*horrid*) affreux
Madder, *s.* (*bot., dyeing*) garance, *f.*; (*colour*) garance, *m.*; — *v.a.* garancer. — **coloured, -dyed,** *adj.* garance. — **dyer,** *s.* garanceur, *m.* — **dyeing,** *s.* garançage, *m.* — **field, -plantation, -works,** *s.* garancière, *f.* — **roots,** *s. pl.* alizari, *m.*
Maddering, *s.* garançage, *m.*
Made, *part. adj.* fait, &c. (*V.* **Make,** *v.a.*); rendu; forcé (de); (*ready* —) *See Letter* **R;** (*of dishes, of earth*) *V.* **Dish** *and* **Earth;** (*pers.*) qui a fait sa fortune, riche; (*in compounds*) fait à *or* en ..., de façon ...; de construction ... — **up,** (*V. To* **Make up**); artificiel, faux; (*story*) fait à plaisir, inventé, controuvé; (*of o.'s face*) maquillé, peint; (*of clothing,* &c.) confectionné [madère, *m.*
Madeira, *s.* Madère, *f.*; (*wine*) vin de Madère,
Madly, *adv.* follement, en fou; furieusement
Madness, *s.* folie, démence, *f.*; fureur, *f.*; rage, *f.*; (*hydrophobia*) rage, *f.* *To drive to* —,
Madonna, *s.* madone, *f.* [rendre fou
Madrepore, *s.* madrépore, *m.*
Madrigal, *s.* madrigal, *m.*
Madrigal-ic, -ist. *V.* page 3, § 1
Mag, *s.* margot, caquet-bon-bec, *f.*
Magazine, *s.* magasin, *m.*; (*periodical*) publication (*f.*) *or* recueil (*m.*) périodique, revue, *f.*, magasin, *m.*; (*nav.*) soute aux poudres, *f.*
Magdalen asylum *or* **hospital,** *s.* madelonnettes, filles repenties, *f.pl.*
Magenta, *adj. s.* magenta, *adj. m.f., s.m.*
Maggot, *s.* asticot, ver, *m.*; larve, *f.*; (*whim*) lubie, *f.*, caprice, *m.*
Maggoty, *adj.* véreux, plein de vers *or* de mites; (*whimsical*) capricieux, bizarre
Magi, *s. pl.* mages, *m.pl.*
Magian, *s.* mage, *m.*; — *adj.* des mages
Magianism, *s.* magisme, *m.*
Magic, -al, *adj.* magique; — *s.* magie, *f.*; enchantement, *m.*
Magically, *adv.* par magie, par enchantement
Magician, *s.* magicien, *m.*, -ne, *f.*
Magisterial, *adj.* de maître; de magistrat; (*haughty*) magistral [ment
Magisterially, *adv.* en maître, magistrale-
Magisterialness, *s.* air *or* ton de maître, *m.*; (*haughtiness*) air magistral, *m.*
Magistracy, *s.* magistrature, *f.*
Magistral, *adj.* *V.* **Magisterial;** (*pharm., engin., fort.*) magistral; — *s.* (*metal.*) magistral, *m.*; (*engin., fort.*) magistrale, *f.*
Magistrate, *s.* magistrat, *m.*; juge de paix, *m.*; tribunal de police, *m.*, police, *f.*; (*crim. law*) juge d'instruction, *m.*
Magna Charta, *s.* la Grande Charte, *f.*
Magnanimity, *s.* magnanimité, *f.*
Magnanimous, *adj.* magnanime
Magnanimously, *adv.* magnanimement, avec magnanimité
Magnate, *s.* magnat, *m.*; (*fig.*) grand personnage, grand, homme influent, *m.*, puissance,

f.; (*fam.*) gros bonnet, matador, *m.* *Commercial* —, gros commerçant, *m.*
Magnesia, *s.* magnésie, *f.*
Magnesian, *adj.* magnésien
Magnesiated, *adj.* magnésié
Magnesic, *adj.* magnésique
Magnesium, *s.* magnésium, *m.* — **light,** *s.* lumière magnésique, *f.* [*v.a.* aimanter
Magnet, *s.* aimant, *m.*, pierre d'aimant, *f.*; —
Magnetic, -al, *adj.* magnétique; aimanté; (*fig.*) attractif. — *needle*, aiguille aimantée, *f.*
Magnetically, *adv.* magnétiquement
Magneticalness, *s.* propriété magnétique, *f.*
Magnetics, *s.pl.* science du magnétisme, *f.*
Magnetism, *s.* magnétisme, *m.*
Magnetization, *s.* aimantation, *f.*; (*pers.*) magnétisation, *f.* [— *v.n.* s'aimanter
Magnetize, *v.a.* aimanter; (*pers.*) magnétiser;
Magnetizer, *s.* magnétiseur, *m.*, -euse, *f.*
Magnetising, *adj.* magnétiseur; — *s.* *V.* **Magnetization**
Magneto-electric, *adj.* magnéto-électrique
Magneto-electricity, *s.* magnéto-électricité, *f.*
Magnetograph, *s.* magnétographe, *m*,
Magnetometer, *s.* magnétomètre, *m.*
Magnificence, *s.* magnificence, *f.*
Magnificent, *adj.* magnifique
Magnificently, *adv.* magnifiquement
Magnified, *part.adj.* grossi, &c. (*V.* **Magnify**); à vue de loupe
Magnifier, *s.* grossisseur, *m.*, chose qui grossit *or* augmente, *f.*; appareil propre à augmenter (le son, la lumière, &c.), *m.*; (*lens*) verre grossissant, *m.*, loupe, *f.*; (*pers.*) personne qui exalte *or* exagère, *f.*
Magnify, *v.a.* grossir; grandir; augmenter; exagérer; (*extol*) exalter, louer, glorifier
Magnifying glass, *s.* verre grossissant, *m.*,
Magniloquence, *s.* emphase *f.* [loupe, *f.*
Magniloquent, *adj.* emphatique, pompeux
Magniloquently, *adv.* avec emphase, pompeusement [dimension, *f.*; importance, *f.*
Magnitude, *s.* grandeur, *f.*; grosseur, *f.*;
Magnolia, *s.* magnolia, magnolier, *m.*
Magpie, *s.* pie, *f.*
Magyar, *s. adj.* Magyar, *m.*, e, *f.*
Mahee, *s.* tacahout, *m.* [acajou
Mahogany, *s.* acajou, *m.*; — *adj.* d'acajou, en
Mahomedan, Mahommedan, Mahometan, *s. adj.* mahométan, *m.*, e, *f.*
Mahomedanism, Mahommedanism, Mahometanism, *s.* mahométisme, *m.*
Mahratta, *s. adj.* Mahratte, *m.f.*
Maid, *s.* fille, jeune fille, demoiselle, vierge, *f.*; (—*servant*, *servant*—) domestique, bonne, servante, *f.* — *of all work*, *V.* **General servant.** — *of honour*, demoiselle d'honneur, *f.* *The — of Orleans*, la pucelle d'Orléans, *f.* *An old* —, une vieille fille, *f.* *To remain an old* —, rester fille, (*fam.*) coiffer sainte Catherine
Maiden, *s.* fille, jeune fille, vierge, *f.*; (*gallows*) guillotine, *f.*; — *adj.* virginal, de jeune fille; (*fresh, new*) vierge, neuf; (*of names*) de demoiselle. —*hair*, (*bot.*) capillaire, *m.* — *lady*, demoiselle, *f.* — *speech*, premier discours, début, *m.*
Maidenhood, *s.* virginité, *f.*; (*fig.*) pureté, *f.*
Maidenliness, *s.* pudeur de jeune fille, modestie, *f.*
Maidenly, *adj.* virginal, de jeune fille, modeste; doux; délicat; — *adv.* en jeune fille
Maigre, *s.* (*fish*) maigre, *m.*
Mail, *s.* (*coat*) maille, cotte de mailles, *f.*; (*post*) malle, *f.*; dépêche, *f.*; poste, *f.*; courrier, *m.*; — *v.a.* couvrir de mailles; couvrir, cuirasser; (*post*) expédier. — **bag,** *s.* sac à dépêches, *m.*; dépêches, *f.pl.*, malle, *f.* — **boat,** *s.* paquebot-poste, *m.* — **carriage,** *s.* (*rail.*) wagon-poste, fourgon des dépêches, *m.* — **cart,** *s.* tilbury des dépêches, *m.* — **cart driver,** — **driver,** *s.* courrier convoyeur, courrier, *m.* — **coach,** *s.* malle-poste, *f.* — **guard,** *s.* chef de brigade (de la poste), *m.*; (*of the Ocean mail*) courrier de la malle, *m.* — **packet,** *s.* paquebot-poste, *m.* — **steamer,** *s.* vapeur-poste, *m.* — **train,** *s.* *V.* **Train**
Mailed, *adj.* à mailles [*f.*; (*injury*) blessure, *f.*
Maim, *v.a.* estropier, mutiler; — *s.* mutilation,
Main, *adj.* principal, premier, capital, grand; important, essentiel; général; (*powerful*) puissant; (*nav.*) grand; — *s.* force, vigueur, *f.*; (*bulk*) gros, fort, principal, *m.*, masse, plupart, *f.*; (*sea*) océan, *m.*; (*land*) continent, *m.*, terre ferme, *f.*; (*pipe*) grand tuyau *or* conduit, tuyau *or* conduit principal, *m.* *In the* —, en général; en somme; au fond. — **beam,** *s.* maîtresse poutre, *f.* — **body,** *s.* gros, corps de bataille, *m.* — **deck,** *s.* premier pont, *m.* — **guard,** *s.* (*mil.*) grand'garde, *f.* —**land,** *s.* terre ferme, *f.* — **line,** (*rail.*) voie principale, *f.* —**mast,** *s.* grand mât, *m.* —**sail,** *s.* grande voile, *f.* — **sewer,** *s.* égout principal, égout collecteur, collecteur, *m.* — **shaft,** *s.* arbre moteur, *m.* —**sheets,** *s.pl.* écoutes de la grande voile, *f.pl.* —**shrouds,** *s.pl.* grands haubans, *m.pl.* — **spring,** *s.* grand ressort, *m.*; (*fig.*) cheville ouvrière, *f.*; mobile, *m.* —**stay,** *s.* principal soutien *or* support, *m.*; (*nav.*) grand étai, *m.* —**top,** *s.* grande hune, *f.* —**top-mast,** *s.* grand mât de hune, *m.* —**top-gallant-mast,** *s.* mât de grand perroquet, *m.* —**top-sail,** *s.* voile de grand hunier, *f.* —**top-yard,** *s.* vergue de grand hunier, *f.* —**top-gallant-yard,** *s.* vergue de grand perroquet, *f.* — **yard,** *s.* grande vergue, *f.*
Mainly, *adv.* principalement, surtout; beaucoup, grandement, puissamment
Maintain, *v.a.n.* maintenir; soutenir; conserver; (*feed*) entretenir; nourrir; faire vivre
Maintainable, *adj.* soutenable; tenable
Maintainer, *s.* soutien, appui, *m.*; (*fig.*) défenseur, *m.*
Maintenance, *s.* maintien, *m.*; conservation, *f.*; (*protection*) soutien, *m.*; (*food, &c.*) entretien, *m.*; subsistance, *f.*; moyen d'existence, *m.*; (*law*) pension alimentaire, *f.* *Separate* —, séparation de biens, *f.*
Maize, *s.* maïs, blé de Turquie, *m.* — **beer,** *s.* chica, *m.* — **hasty-pudding,** *s.* gaude, *f.*
Majestic, -al, *adj.* majestueux [majesté
Majestically, *adv.* majestueusement, avec
Majesticalness, *s.* air majestueux, *m.*
Majesty, *s.* majesté, *f.* *His* or *Her* —, sa
Majolica, *s.* majolica, majolique, *f.* [Majesté
Major, *adj.* majeur; (*mil.*) major; — *s.* majeur, *m.*, e, *f.*; (*logic*) majeure, *f.*; (*of infantry*) chef de bataillon, commandant, *m.*; (*of cavalry*) chef d'escadron, commandant, *m.* — **domo,** *s.* majordome, *m.* —**domoship,** *s.* majordomat, *m.* —**general,** *s.* général de division, *m.*
Majorat, *s.* majorat, *m.*
Majoration, *s.* majoration, *f.*
Majority, *s.* majorité, *f.*; (*of infantry*) grade de chef de bataillon, *m.*; (*of cavalry*) grade de chef d'escadron, *m.*
Make, *v.a.* faire; former; créer; composer; produire; (*render*) rendre; (*put*) mettre; (*compel*) forcer (à), faire; (*gain*) gagner, amasser, faire; (*enrich*) faire la fortune de; (*of*) comprendre; (*think*) penser (de); (*reach*) atteindre, gagner; (*a pen*) tailler; (*enemies to oneself*) se faire; (*friends*) *V.* **Friend;** (*com.*) confectionner, fabriquer, manufacturer, faire; — *v.n.* (*for*) aller (à), se rendre (à), se diriger (vers), s'avancer (vers), courir (vers, sur); se sauver (à, dans); contribuer (à); tendre (à); prouver; agir; (*appear*) faire semblant (de), avoir l'air (de); — *s.* façon, forme, *f.*; figure, *f.*; structure, *f.*; nature, *f.*; construction, *f.*; fabrique, fabrication, *f.* *To — believe*, faire croire. *To — known*, faire connaître; faire savoir. *To — oneself heard, understood, known*, &c., se faire entendre, comprendre, connaître, &c. *To — little of*, faire

peu de cas de; tirer peu de parti de; (*pers.*) mal accueillir. *To — much* (or *a great deal*) *of*, faire grand cas de; donner *or* attacher de l'importance à; tirer bon parti de; faire valoir; (*pers.*) traiter avec égard, bien accueillir; (*children*) choyer, dorloter, câliner. *To — the most of*, tirer le plus grand parti possible de; employer bien; (*save*) économiser; (*show off*) faire valoir; (*value*) faire le plus grand cas de; (*enjoy*) jouir le plus possible de. *To — nothing of*, ne tirer aucun parti de; ne faire aucun cas de; ne rien comprendre à. *I can — nothing of it*, je n'y comprends rien. *I don't know what to — of it*, je n'y comprends rien, je ne sais à quoi m'en tenir. *To — one of us, of you, of them*, être des nôtres, des vôtres, des leurs. — **again,** refaire. — **against,** prouver contre. — **at,** courir *or* s'élancer *or* se jeter sur. — **away,** s'éloigner. — **away with,** se défaire (de); (*kill*) tuer; (*destroy*) détruire; (*spend*) dissiper; gaspiller; dilapider; (*misappropriate*) détourner. — **away with oneself,** se suicider, se donner la mort, se détruire, mettre fin à ses jours. — **believe,** *s* feinte, couleur, *f.*; *adj.* feint. — **off,** s'enfuir, décamper, filer. — **out,** comprendre; expliquer; déchiffrer; prouver, établir; fournir; composer, rédiger; (*accounts*) faire, dresser, établir; (*succeed, manage*) réussir (à), venir à bout (de), parvenir (à). *I can't — it out*, je n'y comprends rien. *How do you — it out?* (*of accounts*) comment faites-vous votre compte? — **over,** transférer, céder. — **peace,** *s.* pacificateur, *m.*, -trice, *f.* — **shift,** *s.* pis aller, à-peu-près, expédient, *m.* — **up,** faire; compléter; conclure; réparer; combler; tenir compte de, compenser, suppléer à; accommoder; arranger; préparer; former, façonner; composer; amasser, rassembler; (*accounts*) régler, établir, balancer; (*clothes*, &c.) confectionner; (*type*) mettre en pages; (*paint o.'s face*) se grimer, se maquiller, se peindre; (*advance*) s'avancer; *s.* (*of actors*) grimage, *m.*, manière de se grimer, *f.* — **it up,** se réconcilier, se raccommoder. — **up for,** suppléer à; tenir lieu de; compenser; dédommager de; rattraper. — **up to,** s'approcher de; s'avancer vers; (*fig.*) faire des avances à. — **weight,** *s.* supplément, complément de poids, *m.*; (*fig.*) remplissage, *m.*

Maker, *s.* créateur, *m.*; auteur, *m.*; (*fam.*) faiseur, *m.*, -euse, *f.*; (*manufacturer*) fabricant (de ...), *m.*, e, *f.*; (*of clothing*) confectionneur (de ...), *m.*, -euse, *f.*; (*worker*) ouvrier ('*of*,' en), *m.*, -ière, *f.* — **up,** *s.* (*print.*) metteur en pages, *m.*

Making, *s.* façon, *f.*; forme, *f.*; construction, *f.*; structure, *f.*; (*doing*) fait, *m.*; (*com.*) fabrication (de ..., du ..., de la ..., des ...), *f.*; (*of clothing, and preparations*) confection, *f.*; (*creation*) création, *f.*; (*prosperity*) fortune, *f.* — **up,** *s.* *V.* **Make-up,** *s.*; (*of clothes and preparations*) confection, *f.*; (*print.*) mise en pages, *f.*

Malacca, *s.* (*— cane*) jonc, *m.*

Malachite, *s.* malachite, *f.*

Maladministration, *s.* maladministration, mauvaise administration, mauvaise gestion, *f.*

Maladroit, *adj.* maladroit

Maladroitly, *adv.* maladroitement

Maladroitness, *s.* maladresse, *f.*

Malady, *s.* maladie, *f.*

Malaga, *s.* vin de Malaga, malaga, *m.*

Malaguetta pepper, *s.* malaguette, maniguette, *f.*

Malanders, *s.pl.* malandre, *f.*

Malapert, *adj.* impertinent, insolent, malappris

Malaperty, *adv.* impertinemment, insolemment

Malapertness, *s.* impertinence, insolence, *f.*

Malapropos, *adv.* mal à propos

Malar, *adj.* malaire

Malaria, *s.* malaria, *f.*, air infect, air malfaisant, *m.*, miasmes, *m.pl.*, moufette, *f.*

Malarious, *adj.* miasmatique

Malate, *s.* malate, *m.*

Malay, *s. adj.* **Malayan,** *adj.* malais, *m.*, e, *f.*

Malcontent, *adj. s.* mécontent

Male, *s.* mâle, *m.*; — *adj.* mâle; (*things*) masculin; (*bot.*) mâle. ("*Male," together with the noun following it, are often rendered in French by one word, with its masculine ending; as,* — **cousin,** cousin, — **friend,** ami, — **prisoner,** prisonnier, prévenu, détenu, accusé, — **relation,** parent; &c. (*V.* **He**)

Malediction, *s.* malédiction, *f.*

Malefactor, *s.* malfaiteur, *m.*, -trice, *f.*

Maleficence, *s* malfaisance, *f.*

Maleficent, *adj.* malfaisant

Malevolence, *s.* malveillance, *f.*

Malevolent, *adj.* malveillant

Malevolently, *adv.* avec malveillance, malignement

Malfeasance, *s.* malfaisance, *f.*; méfait, *m.*

Malformation, *s.* malformation, mauvaise conformation, conformation vicieuse, *f.*, vice de conformation, *m.*

Malformed, *adj.* mal conformé, mal constitué

Malic, *adj.* malique

Malice, *s.* malice, méchanceté, malveillance, *f.* — *aforethought*, — *prepense*, (*law*) préméditation, *f.* *To bear* —, vouloir du mal (à), en vouloir (à); garder rancune (à)

Malicious, *adj.* malveillant, malicieux, méchant

Maliciously, *adv.* avec malveillance, malicieusement, méchamment

Maliciousness, *s.* *V.* **Malice**

Malign, *v.a.* maltraiter; envier; nuire à; diffamer, noircir; — *adj.* *V.* **Malignant**

Malignancy. *V.* **Malignity**

Malignant, *adj.* malin, méchant; malfaisant; nuisible; (*med.*) malin

Malignantly, *adv.* malignement, méchamment

Maligner, *s.* personne méchante, *f.*; diffamateur, *m.*, -trice, *f.*

Malignity, *s.* malignité, *f.*; méchanceté, malveillance, *f.*

Malignly. *V.* **Malignantly**

Malinger, *v.n.* faire le malade, flâner, carotter

Malingerer, *s.* flâneur, carotteur, *m.*

Malingering, *s.* maladie feinte, flânerie, *f.*

Malison, *s.* malédiction, *f.*

Malkin, *s.* écouvillon, *m.*; (*pers.*) *V.* **Dowdy**

Mall, *s.* mail, *m.*; — *v.a.* frapper, battre, &c. (*V.* **Maul**)

Mallard, *s.* malart, *m.*

Mallea-bility, bleness, *s.* malléabilité, *f.*

Malleable, *adj.* malléable

Malleate, *v.a.* malléer, marteler

Malleation, *s.* malléation, *f.*

Mallet, *s.* maillet, *m.*; (*for playing*) mail, *m.*

Mallow, *s.*, **Mallows,** *s.pl.* mauve, *f.*

Malmsey, *s.* malvoisie, *m.*

Malpractice, *s.* méfait, *m.*; déportements, *m.pl.*; malversation, *f.*; incurie, *f.*, mauvais traitement, *m.*

Malt, *s.* drèche, *f.*, malt, *m.*; — *v.a* malter. — **distillery,** *s.* brasserie, *f.* — **drink,** *s.* bière, *f.* — **house,** *s.* germoir, *m.*, malterie, *f.* — **ing,** *s.* maltage, *m.* — **kiln,** *s.* touraille, *f.* — **liquor,** *s.* bière, *f.* — **man,** — **ster,** *s.* malteur, *m.* — **refuse,** — **waste,** *s.* marc de drèche, *m.*

Maltese, *s.* Maltais, *m.*, e, *f.*; — *adj.* maltais, de Malte. — *cross*, croix de Malte, *f.* — *dog*, — chien de Malte, *m.*

Malthusian, *s.adj.* malthusien. *m.*, -ne, *f.*

Malthusianism, *s.* malthusianisme, *m.*

Maltreat, *v.a.* maltraiter, malmener

Maltreatment, *s.* mauvais traitement, *m.*

Malurus, *s.* mérion, *m.*

Malvaceous, *adj.* malvacé

Malversation, *s.* malversation, *f.*

Mamelon, *s.* mamelon, *m.*

Mameluke, *s.* mameluk, mamelouk, *m.*

Mamma, *s.* (*mother*) maman, mère, *f.*; (*breast*) mamelle, *f.*; téton. *m.*

Mammal, *s.* mammifère, *m.*

Mammalia, *s.pl.* mammifères, *m.pl.*

Mammalian, *adj.* mammifère

Mammalog-ic, al, -ist, -y. *V.* page 3, § 1

Mammary, *adj.* mammaire
Mammifer, *s.* **Mammiferous,** *adj.* mammifère, *s.m., adj. m.f.*
Mammiform, *adj.* mammiforme
Mammillary, *adj.* mamillaire
Mammillated, *adj.* mamillé, mamelonné
Mammon, *s.* Mammon, *m.* [monstre
Mammoth, *s.* mammouth, *m.*; — *adj.* géant,
Man, *s.* homme, *m.*; (*exclam.*) brave, *m.*; (*person*) personne, *f.*; (*servant*) domestique, valet, *m.*; (*workman*) ouvrier, *m.*; (*in a public establishment, com., assistant, porter,* &c.) employé, *m.*; garçon, *m.*; (*husband*) mari, *m.*; (*in compounds*) mâle, *m.*; natif de ..., *m.*; (*dealer*) marchand de ..., *m.*; (*chess*) pièce, *f.*; (*draughts*) pion, *m.*; (*ship*) bâtiment, vaisseau, *m.*; — *v.a.* (*a town*) mettre une garnison dans, garnir de troupes, garnir; (*a gun*) servir; (*a rampart,* &c.) garder, défendre, occuper; (*nav.*) armer, équiper; monter, mettre du monde à; (*a prize*) amariner; (*fig.*) fortifier. **Men,** *s.pl.* hommes, *m.pl.*, &c.; (*people*) gens, *m.pl.*; (*soldiers*) soldats, *m.pl.*, troupes, *f.pl.*, armée, *f.*, hommes, *m.pl.*, (*after a number*) hommes, *m.pl.* [*"Man," together with the noun following it, are sometimes rendered in French by one word, with its masculine ending; as* " — *cook,*" cuisinier, &c.] *My —! —!* mon garçon! mon brave! vous! *No* —, aucun homme, nul homme, personne, *m.* *Old —, Young —,* &c., *V.* **Old, Young,** &c. — *and wife,* mari et femme. — *of business, V.* **Business-man.** — *of pleasure,* viveur, *m.* — *of straw,* homme de paille, *m.* — *of war,* vaisseau (*or* bâtiment) de guerre, *m.* — *of the world,* homme qui connaît le monde, homme du monde, *m.* *All to a* —, tous sans exception, tous jusqu'au dernier. — **eater,** *s.* anthropophage, cannibale, *m.* —**hater,** *s.* misanthrope, *m.* —**hole,** *s.* (*of sewers*) regard, *m.*, cuvette, *f.*; (*steam-eng.*) trou d'homme, *m.* — **rope,** *s.* (*nav.*) tire-veille, *f.* —**servant,** *s. V.* **Servant.** —**slayer, -killer,** *s.* tueur d'hommes, homicide, meurtrier, *m.* —**trap,** *s.* piége, *m.*, chausse-trappe, *f.* [*For other compounds, See below*]
Manacle, *v.a.* emmenotter, menotter, mettre les menottes à; (*fig.*) garrotter, enchaîner; — *s.* menotte, *f.*
Manage, *v.a.* conduire, diriger, gouverner, mener; arranger; administrer, gérer; (*to work*) exploiter; (*machines*) manœuvrer; (*prepare, contrive*) ménager; (*carry out, get over*) venir à bout de, parvenir à; (*handle*) manier; (*animals*) dompter, dresser, manier; (*set about*) faire, (*it*) s'y prendre; (*com.*) gérer; — *v.n.* s'arranger (pour), faire en sorte (que); faire; agir; s'y prendre; manœuvrer; (*succeed*) venir à bout (de), parvenir (à); (*know how to*) savoir, trouver moyen (de); (*get off*) s'en tirer
Manageable, *adj.* traitable, docile, gouvernable; maniable, facile à manier; flexible; praticable, faisable
Manageableness, *s.* docilité, *f.*; flexibilité, *f.*
Management, *s.* conduite, direction, administration, *f.*, maniement, *m.*; économie, *f.*, savoir-faire, arrangement, *m.*, combinaison, *f.*, esprit d'ordre, ordre, *m.*; (*working*) exploitation, *f.*; prudence, adresse, *f.*; conduite habile, *f.*; manœuvre, *f.*; artifice, *m.*; (*com., admin.*) gérance, gestion, *f.* *Domestic* —, économie domestique, *f.*
Manager, *s.* directeur, *m.*; chef, *m.*; régisseur, *m.*; administrateur, *m.*; (*economist*) ménager, *m.*, -ère, femme de ménage, *f.*; (*theat.*) régisseur, *m.*; (*com.*) gérant, *m.*; (*manu.,* &c.) chef d'exploitation, *m.* *General* —, directeur général, chef d'exploitation, *m.*
Manageress, *s.* directrice, *f.*; (*com.*) gérante, *f.*
Managing, *adj.* qui dirige, qui conduit, qui gouverne; directeur; (*com., admin.*) gérant; — *s. V.* **Management.** — *clerk, V.* **Clerk.** —*man,* gérant, chef, *m.*
Manakin, *s.* manakin, *m.*
Manatee, *s.* manate, lamentin, *m.*
Manchineel, *s.* (— tree) mancenillier, *m.*; (*fruit*) mancenille, *f.*
Manciple, *s.* régisseur, *m.*; intendant, *m.*; économe, *m.*; pourvoyeur, *m.*
Mandamus, *s.* mandement, *m.*
Mandarin, *s. adj.* mandarin, *s.m.*, mandarin, *adj. m.*, e, *f.* — **orange,** *s.* orange mandarine, mandarine, *f.* — **orange-tree,** *s.* mandarinier, *m.*
Mandarin-ic, -ism. *V.* page 3, § 1
Mandarinship, *s.* mandarinat, *m.*
Mandatary, *s.* mandataire, *m.f.* [mandat, *m.*
Mandate, *s.* mandement, *m.*; ordre, *m.*; (*law*)
Mandatory, *adj.* mandatif; — *s.* mandataire, *m.f.*
Mandible, *s.* mandibule, *f.*
Mandibular, *adj.* mandibulaire
Mandibulate, *adj. s.* mandibulé
Mandolin, Mandoline, *s.* mandoline, *f.*
Mandore, *s.* mandore, *f.*
Mandragora, Mandrake, *s.* mandragore, *f.*
Mandrel, *s.* mandrin, *m.*
Mandrill, *s.* mandrill, *m.*
Mane, *s.* crinière, *f.* — **sheet,** *s.* crinière, *f.*
Maned, *adj.* à crinière ...
Manege, *s.* manége, *m.*
Manes, *s.pl.* mânes, *m.pl.*
Manful, *adj. V.* **Manly**
Manfully, *adv.* en homme, courageusement, hardiment; honorablement, noblement
Manfulness, *s. V.* **Manliness**
Mangabey, *s.* mangabey, *m.*
Manganate, *s.* manganate, *m.*
Manganese, *s.* manganèse, *m.*
Mange, *s.* gale, *f.*
Mangel-wurzel, *s. V.* **Mangold**
Manger, *s.* mangeoire, *f.*; (*for cattle*) crèche, *f.*
Manginess, *s.* état galeux, *m.*
Mangle, *v.a.* déchirer; mutiler; (*linen*) calandrer; — *s.* calandre, *f.*; (*bot.*) manglier, *m.*
Mangler, *s.* calandreur, *m.*, -euse, *f.*
Mangling, *s.* mutilation, *f.*; (*of linen*) calandrage, *m.*
Mango, *s.* mangue, *m.* — **fish,** *s.* polynème, *m.* — **ginger,** *s.* curcuma du Bengale, *m.* — **tree,** *s.* manguier, *m.* [betterave, *f.*
Mangold, — wurzel, *s.* betterave champêtre,
Mangosteen, *s.* (*tree*) mangostan, mangoustan, *m.*; (*fruit*) mangouste, *f.*
Mangouste, *s.* mangouste, *f.*
Mangrove, *s.* manglier, *m.*
Mangy, *adj.* galeux
Manhater; Manhole. *V.* **Man**
Manhood, *s.* virilité, *f.*; âge viril, *m.*; nature humaine, humanité, *f.*; homme, *m.* — **suffrage,** *s.* suffrage universel, *m.*
Mania, *s.* folie, rage ('*for,*' de), *f.*; (*whim*) manie, *f.*; monomanie, *f.*
Maniac, -al, *adj. s.* fou, *m.*, folle, *f.*, furieux, *m.*, -euse, *f.*, maniaque, *m.f.* [chéen, *m.*, -ne, *f.*
Manichean, *adj. s.*, **Manichee,** *s.* mani-
Manicheism, *s.* manichéisme, *m.*
Manifest, *v.a.* manifester, montrer, témoigner; — *adj.* manifeste, clair, évident; — *s.* manifeste, *m.*
Manifestation, *s.* manifestation, *f.*
Manifestly, *adv.* manifestement
Manifestness, *s.* évidence, *f.*
Manifesto, *s.* manifeste, *m.*
Manifold, *adj.* nombreux; divers; de plusieurs sortes; multiplié; multiple. — *writer,* polygraphe, *m.*
Manifoldly, *adv.* diversement
Maniform, *adj.* maniforme
Manikin, *s.* (*pers.*) nabot, petit homme, bout d'homme, homuncule, *m.*; (*things*) mannequin, *m.*
Manilla, *s.* (*geog.*) Manille, *f.*; (*a cigar*) manille, cigare de Manille, *m.* — **hemp,** *s.* chanvre de Manille, abaca, *m.*
Manillese, *s. adj.* Manillais, *m.*, e, *f.*
Manioc, *s.* manioc, *m.*
Maniple, *s.* manipule, *m.*
Manipulate, *v.a.n.* manipuler

Manipulation, *s.* manipulation, *f.*
Manipulator, *s.* manipulateur, *m.*
Mankind, *s.* le genre humain, *m.*, l'espèce humaine, l'humanité, *f.*, les hommes, *m.pl.*
Manlike, *adj.* d'homme, mâle; (*in contempt*) hommasse
Manliness, *s.* air mâle, *m.*; caractère viril, *m.*; courage, *m.*; bravoure, *f.*; force, énergie, *f.*; dignité, noblesse, *f.*
Manly, *adj.* mâle, viril, d'homme; courageux, brave, hardi; fort, vigoureux, énergique; digne, noble, honorable; — *adv. V.* **Manfully**
Manna, *s.* manne, *f.* — **ash, -tree,** *s.* orne, *m.* — **croup, -groats,** *s.* semoule, *f.* — **grass,** *s.* glycérie, *f.*
Manner, *s.* manière, façon, *f.*, air, genre, *m.*; allures, *f.pl.*; procédés, *m.pl.*; sorte, espèce, *f.*; habitude, coutume, *f.*, usage, *m.*; (*condition*) naturel, *m.*, humeur, *f.*; **—s,** *pl.* manières, *f.pl.*, &c.; mœurs, *f.pl.*; politesse, *f.*, savoir-vivre, *m.* *—s and customs,* us et coutumes, mœurs. *After the — of,* à la manière de, à la façon de; selon l'habitude de, selon l'usage de. *After this —,* de cette manière, de cette façon, ainsi. *Good —s,* bonnes manières, *f.pl.*; bon ton, *m.* *In a —, in some —,* en quelque sorte, pour ainsi dire. *In a ... manner,* d'une manière ... *In like —,* de la même manière, de même. *In this —,* de cette manière, ainsi. *In the same — as,* de même que, ainsi que, comme. *No — of,* aucune espèce de. *To have no —s,* être grossier, ne savoir pas vivre. *To learn* or *teach —s,* apprendre la politesse, apprendre à vivre. *The — in which,* la manière dont. *The — and the matter,* la forme et le fond. **—s piece** *or* **bit,** *s.* (*at table*) morceau honteux, *m.*
Mannered, *adj.* (*in compounds*) aux manières ...; (*of habits*) aux mœurs ...
Mannerism, *s.* maniérisme, *m.*
Mannerist, *s.* maniériste, *m.f.*
Mannerliness, *s.* politesse, civilité, urbanité, *f.*
Mannerly, *adj.* poli; — *adv.* poliment
Manning, *s.* armement, équipement, *m.*, [monture, *f.*
Mannish, *adj.* hommasse
Mannite, *s.* mannite, *f.*
Manœuvre, *s.* manœuvre, *f.*; — *v.n.* manœuvrer; — *v.a.* faire manœuvrer; manœuvrer
Manœuvrer, *s.* manœuvrier, *m.*, -ière, *f.*
Manœuvring, *s.* manœuvres, *f.pl.*
Manometer, *s.* manomètre, *m.*
Manor, *s.* manoir, *m.*; château, *m.*; seigneurie, *f.* *Lord of a* (or *the*) —, seigneur foncier, châtelain, *m.* — **house, -seat,** *s.* maison seigneuriale, *f.*, château *or* manoir seigneurial, château, manoir, *m.*
Manorial, *adj.* seigneurial
Manoscope, *s.* manoscope, *m.*
Mansard-roof, *s.* toit en mansarde, comble brisé *or* coupé, *m.*
Manse, *s.* presbytère, *m.*; (*farm*) ferme, *f.*
Mansion, *s.* (*in towns*) hôtel, *m.*; (*country-seat*) château, *m.*; (*residence*) demeure, *f.*, séjour, *m.* — **house,** *s.* mairie, *f.*; (*in Paris*) préfecture de la Seine, *f.*, hôtel de ville, *m.*
Manslaughter, *s.* homicide, meurtre, *m.*; (*law*) homicide involontaire, *m.*
Manslayer. *V.* **Man**
Mansuetude, *s.* mansuétude, *f.*
Mantel, *s. V.* **Mantle**
Mantilla, *s.* mantille, *f.*
Mantis, *s.* mante, *f.*
Mantle, *s.* manteau, *m.*, mante, *f.*, mantelet, *m.*; (*of shells, and arch.*) manteau, *m.*; (*fig.*) manteau, voile, *m.*; — *v.a.* couvrir, voiler, déguiser; — *v.n.* (*spread*) s'étendre; (*open*) s'offrir (à); (*of wine*) écumer; (*of blood*) monter à la figure. — **clock,** *s.* pendule de cheminée, *f.* — **maker,** *s.* couturière, *f.* — **piece, -shelf,** *s.* cheminée, *f.*; dessus de (*or* de la) cheminée, *m.*; manteau de (*or* de la) cheminée, *m.*
Mantled, *adj.* mantelé
Mantlet, *s.* mantelet, *m.*
Mantling, *s.* mantelure, *f.*; (*her.*) lambrequin, *m.*
Mantua, *s.* (*obsolete*) *V.* **Mantle**
Manual, *adj.* manuel, de la main; — *s.* manuel, *m.* — *exercise,* (*mil.*) maniement des [armes, *m.*
Manually, *adv.* manuellement
Manufactory, *s.* manufacture, fabrique, usine, *f.*; ateliers, *m.pl.*
Manufactural, *adj.* manufacturier
Manufacturally, *adv.* manufacturièrement
Manufacture, *s.* manufacture, fabrication, fabrique, *f.*; produit fabriqué, article, objet, *m.*; tissu, *m.*; — *v.a.* manufacturer, fabriquer; (*work*) travailler
Manufacturer, *s.* manufacturier, *m.*, -ière, *f.*; fabricant, *m.*, e, *f.* (de ...); industriel, *m.* *—s' price,* prix de fabrique, *m.*
Manufacturing, *adj.* manufacturier, industriel; mécanicien. — *chemist, V.* **Chemist.** — *locksmith,* serrurier mécanicien, *m.* *For — purposes,* pour l'industrie
Manumission, *s.* manumission, *f.*, affran-[chissement, *m.*
Manumit, *v.a.* affranchir
Manure, *s.* engrais, *m.*; — *v.a.* engraisser; fumer; fertiliser [scrit, *adj. m.*, e, *f.*
Manuscript, *s. adj.* manuscrit, *s.m.*, manu-
Many, *adj.* beaucoup (de); bien (des); un grand nombre (de, d'entre); nombreux; (*various*) divers; (*many people*) beaucoup de personnes, bien des gens; — *s.* multitude, foule, *f.*, grand nombre, *m.*; (*in contempt*) peuple, *m.* — *a,* plus d'un, maint. — *persons,* beaucoup de personnes, bien des personnes. — *a time,* plus d'une fois, mainte fois, souvent. — *and — a,* maint et maint. *A good —,* bon nombre (de). *A great —, very —,* un grand nombre (de), beaucoup (de), bien (des). *As —,* autant; (*before a noun*) autant de. *As — as,* autant que, tant que; (*before a numeral*) jusqu'à, (*neg.*) même. *As — again,* deux fois autant, le double; encore autant. *How —?* combien? (*before a noun*) combien de ...? (*how many people*) combien de personnes? *So —,* tant (de), un si grand nombre (de); autant (de). *So — as,* tant que; autant que; (*even*) même. *Too —,* trop; (*before a noun*) trop de. *The —, s.* la multitude, *f.* — **coloured,** *adj.* de diverses couleurs, multicolore. — **cornered,** *adj.* multangulaire, multangulé, polygone. — **flowered,** *adj.* qui a beaucoup de fleurs, multiflore. — **headed,** *adj.* aux têtes nombreuses. — **legged,** *adj.* multipède, polypode. — **peopled,** *adj.* fort peuplé. — **plies,** *s.* feuillet, *m.* — **shaped,** *adj.* multiforme. — **sided,** *adj.* qui a un grand nombre de côtés, multilatère; complexe, compliqué, multiple
Manzanilla, *s.* manzanilla, *m.*
Maori, *s.* Maori, *m.*
Map, *s.* carte (géographique), *f.*; (*of a town*) plan, *m.*; — *v.a.* dessiner *or* tracer sur une carte, faire une carte (*or* un plan) de. — *of the world,* mappemonde, *f.* — *with names,* carte écrite, *f.* — **maker,** *s.* cartographe, *m.* — **seller,** *s.* marchand de cartes géographiques, *m.*
Maple, — tree, *s.* érable, *m.* *Sugar —,* érable à sucre, érable du Canada, *m.* — **sugar,** *s.* sucre d'érable, *m.*
Mapping, *s.* cartographie, *f.*
Mar, *v.a.* gâter; (*happiness*) détruire; (*joy*) troubler; (*to deform*) défigurer. — **joy,** *s.* rabat-joie, trouble-fête, *m.f.* — **plot,** *s.* brouillon, *m.*, -ne, *f.* [bout, *m.*
Marabou, Marabout, Marabut, *s.* mara-
Maraschino, *s.* marasquin, *m.*
Maraud, *v.n.* marauder
Marauder, *s.* maraudeur, *m.*
Marauding, *s.* maraudage, *m.*, maraude, *f.*
Marble, *s.* marbre, *m.*; (*for playing*) bille, *f.*; — *adj.* de marbre; (*veined*) marbré; — *v.a.* marbrer. — **cutter,** *s.* marbrier, *m.* —

cutting, *s.* marbrerie, *f.* — **grainer,** *s.* peintre marbrier, marbrier, *m.* — **graining,** *s.* marbrure, *f.* — **mason,** *s.* marbrier, *m.* — **merchant,** *s.* marbrier, *m.* — **mill,** *s.* marbrerie, *f.* — **polisher,** *s.* marbrier, *m.* — **quarry,** *s.* carrière de marbre, marbrière, *f.* — **top,** *s.* dessus de marbre, *m.*; *adj.* à dessus de marbre. — **work,** *s.* ouvrage en marbre, *m.*; marbrerie, *f.*; — **worker,** *s.* marbrier, *m.* — **working, -works, -yard,** *s.* marbrerie, *f.*

Marbler, *s.* marbreur, *m.*

Marbling, *s*, marbrure, *f.*

Marc, *s.* marc, *m.*

March, *v.n.* marcher; être en marche; avancer; — *v.a.* faire marcher, faire avancer, diriger; mener; — *s.* (*walking, walk*) marche, *f.*; (*progress*) marche, *f.*, progrès, *m.*; (*step, pace*) pas, *m.*; (*geog., mil.*) marche, *f.*; (*month*) mars, *m.* *To steal a — upon*, gagner une marche sur, dérober une marche à. — **back,** *v.n.* (*come back*) revenir; (*go back*) retourner; *v.a.* faire revenir; faire retourner. — **-brewed beer,** *s.* bière de mars, *f.* — **in,** *v.n.* entrer; *v.a.* faire entrer. — **off,** *v.n.* s'en aller, partir; plier bagage; se mettre en marche; *v.a.* faire décamper; faire marcher. — **on,** *v.n.* marcher; avancer. — **out,** *v.n.* sortir; *v.a.* faire sortir. — **past,** *v.n.* (*mil.*) défiler; (...) défiler devant (...); *s.* (*mil.*) défilé, *m.* — **route,** *s.* feuille de route, *f.*

Marching, *s.* marche, *f.*; — *adj.* marchant, en marche; de marche. — **past,** *s.* (*mil.*) défilé, *m.* — **regiment,** *s.* régiment de marche, *m.*

Marchioness, *s.* marquise, *f.*

Marchpane, *s.* massepain, *m.*

Mare, *s.* jument, cavale, *f.* — **pony,** *s.* ponette, *f.* —**'s-nest,** *s.* merle blanc, *m.* —**'s-tail,** *s.* (*cloud*) cirrus, *m.*, queue-de chat, *f.*; (*bot.*) hippuride, *f.*

Margin, *s.* bord, *m.*; (*of books, paper*) marge, *f.*; — *v.a.* border; (*of books, paper*) marginer. *In the* —, en marge

Marginal, *adj.* marginal; en marge

Marginally, *adv.* en marge, à la marge

Margrave, *s.* margrave, *m.*

Margravial, *adj.* margravial

Margraviate, *s.* margraviat, *m.*

Margravine, *s.* margravine, margrave, *f.*

Mariet, *s.* mariette, *f.*

Marigold, *s.* souci, *m.* *African* —, œillet d'Inde, *m.*, rose d'Inde, *f.*

Marine, *adj.* marin, de *or* de la mer; naval; de marine; maritime; (*pers.*) de marine; — *s.* marine, *f.*; (*pers.*) soldat de la marine, *m.*; —**s,** *s. pl.* soldats (*m.pl.*) *or* troupes (*f.pl.*) de la marine, infanterie (*f.*) de marine. — **insurance,** *s.* assurance maritime, *f.* — **painter** *or* **paintress,** *s.* peintre de marine, *m.* — **stores,** *s. pl.* bric-à-brac, *m.*, friperie, *f.* — **store dealer,** — **clothier,** *s.* marchand (*m.*, e, *f.*) de bric-à-brac; fripier, *m.*, -ière, *f.*

Mariner, *s.* marin, *m.* —*'s card*, rose des vents, *f.* —*'s compass* or *needle*, boussole, *f.*

Mariolatry, *s.* mariolâtrie, *f.*

Marionette, *s.* marionnette, *f.*

Marital, *adj.* marital

Maritally, *adv.* maritalement

Maritime, *adj.* maritime

Marjoram, *s.* origan, *m.* *Sweet* —, marjolaine, *f.*

Mark, *s.* marque, *f.*; signe, *m.*; (*aim*) but, blanc, *m.*, cible, *f.*; (*at school*) point, *m.*, note, *f.*; (*signature*) marque, croix, *f.*; (*fig.*) but, *m.*; réalité, vérité, *f.*; chose même, *f.*; (*hint*) avertissement, *m.*; (*weight*) marc, *m.*; (*of grapes, &c.*) marc, *m.*; (*of waters*) ligne, *f.*; (*nav.*) amer, *m.*, reconnaissance, *f.*; — *v.a.n.* marquer; (*notice*) remarquer, faire attention à. *To come up to the* —, atteindre à la hauteur voulue. *To be hardly up to the* —, laisser à désirer. — *me!* — *my words!* faites bien attention à ce que je vous dis, écoutez-moi bien, prenez-y garde. — **for,** *v.a.* (*deem*) juger. — **out,** *v.a.* marquer; tracer; désigner. — **point,** *s.* point de repère, *m.*

Marked, *part. adj.* marqué, &c. (*V.* **Mark,** *v.a.n.*); (*of accent*, &c.) prononcé

Marker, *s.* marqueur, *m.*, -euse, *f.*; (*mark*) marque, *f.*; (*counter*) jeton, *m.*; (*of books*) signet, *m.*

Market, *s.* marché, *m.*, halle, *f.*; (*Exchange*) place, *f.*; (*price*) cours, prix, *m.*; (*sale*) débit, débouché, *m.*; — *v.n.* (*buy*) acheter au marché, faire son marché, faire ses provisions; (*sell*) vendre au marché. *In the* —, au marché; à la halle; (*com.*) sur la place. — **day,** *s.* jour de marché, *m.* — **garden,** *s.* marais, jardin maraîcher, jardin légumier, légumier, *m.* — **gardener,** *s.* maraîcher, *m.*, -ère, *f.*, jardinier-maraîcher, *m.*, jardinière-maraîchère, *f.*, légumiste, *m.f.* — **gardening,** *s.* culture maraîchère, *f.* — **house,** *s.* marché, *m.*, halle, *f.* — **keeper, -man, -officer,** *s.* hallier, *m.* — **place,** *s.* place du marché, *f.*, marché, *m.*, place publique, *f.* — **porter,** *s.* fort de la halle, *m.* — **price,** *s.* prix courant, cours, *m.* — **town,** *s.* ville à marché, *f.*, bourg, *m.*; (*small*) bourgade, *f.* — **woman,** *s.* femme (*or* dame) de la halle, *f.*

Marketable, *adj.* marchand, de vente

Marketing, *s.* marché, *m.*

Marking, *s.* marquage, *m.* — **ink,** *s.* encre à marquer, *f.* — **iron,** *s.* fer à marquer, *m.* — **nut,** *s.* anacarde, noix de marais, *f.*

Marksman, *s.* (*good* —) bon tireur, *m.* *Bad* —, mauvais tireur, *m.* — **ship,** *s.* adresse *or* habileté au tir, *f.*

Marl, *s.* marne, *f.*; — *v.a.* marner; (*nav.*) merliner. — **digger,** *s.* marneron, *m.* — **manurer,** *s.* marneur, *m.* — **pit,** *s.* marnière, *f.*

Marline, *s.* merlin, *m.* — **spike,** *s.* épissoir, *m.*

Marling, *s.* marnage, *m.*

Marly, *adj.* marneux

Marmalade, *s.* marmelade (de ...), *f.* — **box,** *s.* (*bot.*) marmolier, *m.*

Marmorean, *adj.* marmoréen, de marbre

Marmose, *s.* marmose, *m.*

Marmoset, *s.* ouistiti, *m.*

Marmot, *s.* marmotte, *f.*

Maronite, *s. adj.* Maronite, *m.f.*

Maroon, *adj.* marron; — *s.* marron, *m.*; (*pers.*) marron, *m.*, -ne, *f*

Marque, *s.* marque, *f.*

Marquee, *s.* marquise, tente, *f.*

Marquess, *s.* marquis, *m.*

Marquetry, *s.* marqueterie, *f.*

Marquis, *s.* marquis, *m.*

Marquisate, *s.* marquisat, *m.*

Marrer, *s.* personne (*f.*) qui gâte *or* &c. (*V.* **Mar,** *v.a.*)

Marriage, *s.* mariage, *m.*; (*poet.*) hymen, hyménée, *m.*; (*wedding*) noces, *f.pl.*, noce, *f.*, mariage, *m.* — **articles,** *s. pl.* contrat de mariage, *m.* — **bed,** *s.* lit nuptial, *m.* — **certificate,** *s.* acte de mariage, *m.* — **favours,** *s.pl.* livrée de la noce, *f.* — **licence,** *s.* dispense de bans, *f.* — **portion,** *s.* dot, *f.* — **settlement,** *s.* contrat de mariage, *m.*; douaire, *m.* — **song,** *s.* *V.* **Wedding.** — **tie,** *s.* lien conjugal, *m.* — **treaty,** *s.* contrat de mariage, *m.*

Marriageable, *adj.* mariable, nubile

Married, *adj.* (*pers.*) marié; (*things*) conjugal. — *couple*, mari et femme, *m.pl.*, ménage, *m.*, époux, *m.pl.* *New* or *newly* — *couple*, nouveaux mariés, *m.pl.* — *life* or *state*, mariage, état conjugal, *m.*

Marrier, *s.* épouseur, *m.*, -euse, *f.*

Marron. *V.* **Maroon**

Marrow, *s.* moelle, *f.* — **bone,** *s.* os à moelle, *m.* *On* or *upon o.'s* — *bones*, à genoux. — *bone stage*, plancher des vaches, *m.* — **fat, -pea,** *s.* pois carré, *m.* —**less,** *adj.* sans moelle. — **spoon,** *s.* tire-moelle, *m.*

Marrowy, *adj.* moelleux

Marry, *v.a.* (*take*) épouser, se marier avec; (*give or unite*) marier: — *v.n.* se marier. —

again, se remarier. — *below o.'s station*, se mésallier. — *each other*, s'épouser, se marier
Mars, *s.* (*myth.*, *astr.*) Mars, *m.*
Marsala, *s.* marsala, *m.*
Marseillaise, — **hymn**, *s.* marseillaise, *f.*
Marseillese, *s. adj.* Marseillais, *m.*, e, *f.*
Marsh, *s.* marais, *m.* — **cinquefoil**, *s.* comaret, *m.* — **fever**, *s.* fièvre de marais, fièvre paludéenne, *f.* — **gas**, *s. V.* **Firedamp.** — **harrier**, *s.* harpaye, *m.* — **hen**, *s.* poule d'eau, *f.* — **land**, *s.* pays marécageux, *m.* — **mallow**, **-s**, *s.* guimauve, *f.* — **marigold**, *s.* populage, *m.* — **rosemary**, *s.* statice, *f.* — **snail**, *s.* paludine, *f.* — **tortoise**, *s.* émyde, *f.* — **trefoil**, *s.* minyanthe, *m.*
Marshal, *s.* maréchal, *m.*; (*nav.*) prévôt, *m.*; — *v.a.* ranger, mettre en ordre. —*'s wife*, maréchale, *f.* — **sea**, *s.* maréchaussée, *f.* — **ship**, *s.* maréchalat, grade de maréchal, *m.*
Marshy, *adj.* marécageux; (*produced in marshes*) de marais [marsupial, *s.m.*
Marsupial, *adj. s.* marsupial, *adj. m.*, e, *f.*,
Mart, *s.* marché, *m.*; entrepôt, *m.*; magasin, *m.*; (*of auctions*) salles de vente, *f.pl.*; (*outlet*) débouché, *m.* [martello, *m.*
Martello tower, *s.* tour à la martello, *f.*,
Marten, *s.* (*quadruped*) martre, *f.*; fouine, *f.*
Martial, *adj.* martial; (*pers.*) guerrier, belliqueux; militaire; (*of war*) de guerre; (*suited to battle*) de bataille. — *law*, code militaire, *m.*; loi militaire, *f.*; gouvernement militaire, *m.*; état de siége, *m.*; lois de la guerre, *f.pl.* — *array*, ordre de bataille, *m.*
Martially, *adv.* martialement
Martialness, *s.* martialité, *f.* [**Marten**
Martin, *s.* (*bird*) martinet, *m.*; (*quadruped*) *V.*
Martinet, *s.* (*pers.*) officier sévère, rigoriste, ratapoil, *m.*; (*bird*) *V.* **Martin**; (*nav.*) *V.*
Martingale, *s.* martingale, *f.* [**Martnet**
Martinmas, *s.* la Saint-Martin, *f.*
Martlet, *s.* (*bird*) martinet, *m.*, merlette, *f.*
Martnet, *s.* (*nav.*) martinet, *m.*
Martyr, *s.* martyr, *m.*, e, *f.*; — *v.a.* martyriser
Martyrdom, *s.* martyre, *m.*
Martyrize, *v.a.* martyriser
Martyrolog-ic, al, -ist. *V.* page 3, § 1
Martyrology, *s.* martyrologe, *m.*
Marvel, *s.* merveille, *f.*; — *v.n.* s'étonner, s'émerveiller ('*at*,' '*to*,' de). — *of Peru*, belle-
Marvellous, *adj.* merveilleux [de-nuit, *f.*
Marvellously, *adv.* merveilleusement, à merveille
Marvellousness, *s.* merveilleux, *m.*
Masculine, *adj.* masculin; mâle; d'homme; (*in a bad sense*) hommasse; (*gram.*) masculin; — *s.* masculin, *m.* *In the — gender*, au masculin
Masculinely, *adv.* masculinement [linité, *f.*
Masculineness, **Masculinity** *s.* mascu-
Mash, *s.* mélange, *m.*; pâte, *f.*; (*fam.*) tripotage, *m.*; (*for horses*, &c.) mâche, *f.*; (*cook.*) purée, *f.*; — *v.a.* mêler, mélanger; (*bruise*) écraser, broyer; (*brew.*) brasser. — **tub**, **-tun**, **-vat**, *s.* brassin, *m.*
Mashed, *part. adj.* mêlé, &c. (*V.* **Mash**, *v.a.*); (*cook.*) en purée. — *potatoes*, *turnips*, &c., purée de pommes de terre, de navets, &c., *f.*
Mashing, *s.* (*bruising*) écrasage, *m.*; (*brew.*) brassage, *m.*; mélange, *m.* — **tub**, *s. V.* **Mash-tub**
Mask, *s.* masque, *m.*; (*a woman's*) loup, *m.*; (*arch.*) mascaron, *m.*; (*masquerade*) mascarade, *f.*; — *v.a.* masquer; (*fig.*) masquer, cacher, couvrir, déguiser; — *v.n.* se masquer
Masker, *s.* masque, *m.*
Mason, *s.* maçon, *m.*; (*free* —) franc-maçon, maçon, *m.*; — *adj.* (*zool.*) maçon (*m.*, -ne, *f.*);
Masonic, *adj.* maçonnique [— *v.a.* maçonner
Masonry, *s.* maçonnerie, *f.*; maçonnage, *m.*; (*occupation*) état de maçon, *m.*; (*free* —) franc-maçonnerie, maçonnerie, *f.*
Masque, *s.* masque, *m.*
Masquerade, *s.* mascarade, *f.*; — *v.n.* se masquer; faire une mascarade
Masquerader, *s.* masque, *m.*
Mass, *s.* masse, *f.*; (*heap*) amas, monceau, *m.*; (*of smoke, revolving*) tourbillon, *m.*; (*Cath. rel.*) messe, *f.*; — *v.a.* masser; — *v.n.* se masser. *High* or *grand* —, grand'messe, *f.* *Low* —, messe basse, petite messe, *f.* — **book**, *s.* livre de messe, missel, *m.* — **meeting**, *s.* réunion *or* assemblée en masse, *f.*; (*Engl. and Amer. polit.*) meeting en masse, *m.*
Massacre, *s.* massacre, *m.*; — *v.a.* massacrer
Massicot, *s.* massicot, *m.*
Massiness. *V.* **Massiveness**
Massing, *s.* massement, *m.*
Massive, *adj.* massif; solide
Massively, *adv.* massivement; en masse
Massiveness, *s.* massiveté, nature massive,
Massy, *adj. V.* **Massive** [*f.*; solidité, *f.*
Mast, *s.* mât, *m.*; (*bot.*) fruit, *m.*; (*of oak*) gland, *m.*; (*of beech*) faîne, *f.*; (*nut*) noisette, *f.*; (*chestnut*) châtaigne, *f.*; — *v.a.* mâter. — **head**, *s.* tête de mât, *f.* —**less**, *adj.* sans mât. — **maker**, *s.* mâteur, *m.* — **shed**, **-store**, **-yard**, *s.* mâture, *f.* [mât, à ... mâts
Masted, *part. adj.* mâté; (*in compounds*) à ...
Master, *s.* maître, *m.*; directeur, *m.*; chef, *m.*; intendant, *m.*; propriétaire, *m.*; professeur, *m.*; (*head of a college*) principal; proviseur, *m.*; (*of workmen*) patron, bourgeois, *m.*; (*title of boys*) monsieur, *m.*; (*nav.*) maître d'équipage, *m.*; patron, *m.*; (*of a merchant-ship*) capitaine marchand, capitaine, patron, *m.*; (*in compounds, nav.*: *Two* —, deux-mâts, *m.*, *Three* —, trois-mâts, *m.*); — *adj.* principal, premier, grand; dominant; de maître; — *v.a.* maîtriser; dompter; soumettre; vaincre, surmonter; (*manage*) venir à bout de; (*learn*) vaincre les difficultés de, se rendre maître de, se rendre familier, acquérir. —*s and men*, patrons et ouvriers. *Committee of —s and men*, conseil de prud'hommes. *Grand* —, — *general*, grand maître, *m.* — *-at-arms*, capitaine d'armes, *m.* — *of arts*, licencié ès-lettres, *m.* — *of the horse*, grand écuyer, *m.* — *of the hounds*, grand veneur, *m.* — *of the Mint*, directeur de la Monnaie, *m.* — *of the rolls*, garde des archives, *m.* —*'s degree*, licence, *f.* — or *my* — *is not at home*, (*servant speaking*) Monsieur n'y est pas. *To be — of*, être maître de; (*know*) posséder; entendre. *To be — of oneself*, être maître de soi, se posséder. *To be o.'s own* —, être son maître, s'appartenir, ne dépendre que de soi, être libre. *To make oneself — of*, se rendre maître de, s'emparer de; se rendre familier, acquérir. — **hand**, *s.* main de maître, *f.* — **key**, *s.* passe-partout, *m.* — **mariner**, *s.* capitaine au long cours, *m.* — **mind**, *s.* esprit supérieur, aigle, *m.*; (la) plus forte tête, *f.*, (l') aigle, *m.* —**piece**, chef-d'œuvre, *m.* — **string**, *s.* corde principale, *f.* —**stroke**, **-touch**, *s.* coup de maître, *m.* —**work**, *s.* ouvrage de maître, *m.* — **wort**, *s.* impératoire, *f.*
Masterdom, *s.* domination, *f.*, empire, *m.*
Masterless, *adj.* sans maître [habileté, *f.*
Masterliness, *s.* talent de maître, *m.*, grande
Masterly, *adj.* de maître; de main de maître; supérieur; parfait; impérieux; — *adv.* en maître, habilement
Mastership, *s. V.* **Mastery**; direction, *f.*; (*in contempt*) seigneurie, *f.*; (*in colleges*) chaire, *f.*; (*in schools*) place de maître, *f.*; (*head* —) *V.* **Head**
Mastery, *s.* pouvoir, *m.*; autorité, *f.*; commandement, *m.*; domination, *f.*, empire, *m.*; supériorité, prééminence, *f.*; avantage, *m.*; possession, *f.*; grande habileté, *f.*; connaissance approfondie, connaissance, *f.* *To contend* or *struggle for the — with*, le disputer à. *To get the — over*, l'emporter sur
Mastic, *s.* mastic, *m.*; (*bot.*) lentisque, *m.* — **tree**, *s.* lentisque, *m.*

Masticate, *v.a.* mâcher
Mastication, *s.* mastication, *f.*
Masticatory, *adj.* masticatoire; — *s.* mâchicatoire, *m.*; (*med.*) masticatoire, *m.*
Mastich. *V.* **Mastic**
Masticot. *V.* **Massicot**
Mastiff, *s.* mâtin, dogue, *m.* [*s.* mâture, *f.*
Masting, *s.* mâtage, *m.*; mâture, *f.* — **house,**
Mastodon, *s.* mastodonte, *m.*
Mat, *s.* paillasson, *m.*; natte, *f.*; (*of india-rubber*, &c.) essuie-pieds, *m.*; (*under dishes*) rond de table, *m.*; (*of lamps*) dessous (de lampe), *m.*; — *v.a.* couvrir de paillassons *or* de nattes; (*twist*) natter; (*press*) aplatir; (*stick*) coller ensemble, coller. *To become matted,* s'aplatir; se coller ensemble, se coller. — **grass,** *s.* nard, *m.* — **maker,** *s.* nattier, *m.*, -ière, *f.* — **weed,** *s.* spart, sparte, *m.* — **work,** *s.* nattes, *f.pl.*
Matachin, *s.* matassin, *m.*
Matador, Matadore, *s.* matador, *m.*
Match, *s.* (*for lighting*) allumette, *f.*; (*artil.*) mèche, *f.*; (*marriage*) mariage, *m.*, alliance, *f.*; (*person to be married*) parti, *m.*; (*equal*) égal, pareil, *m.*; partie égale, *f.*; (*suit*) assortiment, *m.*; (*companion-piece*) pendant, *m.*; (*contest*) lutte, *f.*, concours, *m.*; (*wager*) pari, *m.*; (*game*) partie, *f.*; (*race*) course, *f.*; (*wrestling*) lutte, *f.*, (*on the water*) joute, *f.*; (*fight*) combat, *m.*; (*with swords*, &c.) assaut, *m.*; — *v.a.* (*equal*) égaler; (*oppose*) tenir tête à; faire face à; lutter contre; se mesurer avec; (*suit*) assortir, appareiller; apparier; (*proportion*) proportionner; (*dispose*) disposer, régler; (*marry*) marier, allier; (*animals*) accoupler, apparier; (*purify*) mécher, soufrer; — *v.n.* s'assortir, aller ensemble; s'accorder; convenir; être assorti, être pareil; (*marry*) se marier, s'allier; (*of animals*) s'accoupler, s'apparier. *Good* —, riche parti, riche mariage, *m.* *Quick* —, (*artil.*) étoupille, mèche d'étoupille, *f.* *Slow* —, mèche à canon, mèche incendiaire, corde à feu, traînée de poudre, *f.* *With ... to* —, ... pareil; ... pendant. *To be a — for,* être de la force de, être de force à lutter avec; pouvoir résister à; ne pas convenir à. *To be more than a — for,* être plus fort que; être trop fort pour. *To be a bad* or *a good* —, aller mal *or* bien ensemble. *To find* or *meet o.'s* —, trouver son égal; trouver son maître; trouver à qui parler. *He has not his* —, il n'a pas son pareil. — **box, -holder,** *s.* porte allumettes, *m.* —**less,** *adj.* sans pareil, sans égal, unique, incomparable. —**lessly,** *adv.* incomparablement. —**lessness,** *s.* incomparabilité, *f.* —**lock,** *s.* mousquet, *m.* — **maker,** *s.* fabricant (*m.*, e, *f.*) d'allumettes, allumettier, *m.*, -ière, *f.*; (*of marriage*) marieur, *m.*, -euse, *f.*, faiseur (*m.*, -euse, *f.*) de mariages; (*agent*) courtier, (*m.*, -ière, *f.*) de mariages. —**wood,** *s.* amadou, *m.*
Mate, *s.* camarade, *m.f.*, compagnon, *m.*, compagne, *f.*; (*assistant*) aide ..., *m.f.*; (*nav.*) aide, second, *m.*; (*chess*) mat, *m.*; — *v.a.* *V.* **Match,** *v.a.*; (*at chess*) faire mat, mater. *Second* —, lieutenant, *m.* —**less,** *adj.* sans camarade, sans compagnon, sans compagne, seul
Maté, *s.* maté, *m.*
Matelote, *s.* matelote, *f.*
Materia medica, *s.* matière médicale, *f.*
Material, *adj.* matériel; important, essentiel; sérieux; — *s.* matière, *f.*; (*stuff for clothing*) étoffe, *f.*; tissu, *m.*; (*stock, stores*) matériel, *m.*; —**s,** *s.pl.* matières, *f.pl.*, &c.; (*for building, for a work*) matériaux, *m.pl.*; (*photog.*, &c.) fournitures, *f.pl.*
Materialism, *s.* matérialisme, *m.*
Materialist, *s.*, **Materialistic,** *adj.* matérialiste, *m.f.*
Materiality, Materialness, *s.* matérialité, *f.*; importance, *f.*
Materialize, *v.a.* matérialiser
Materially, *adv.* matériellemment; essentiellement; sérieusement
Maternal, *adj.* maternel. — *grandfather,* aïeul maternel, *m.* — *grandmother,* aïeule maternelle, *f.*
Maternally, *adv.* maternellement
Maternity, *s.* maternité, *f.*
Math, *s.* récolte, *f.*
Mathematical, *adj.* mathématique; de mathématiques. — *instrument, master,* instrument, professeur de mathématiques
Mathematically, *adv.* mathématiquement
Mathematician, *s.* mathématicien, *m.*, -ne, *f.*
Mathematics, *s.pl.* mathématiques, *f.pl.*
Matico, *s.* matico, *m.*
Matin, *adj.* du matin; matinal; (*Cath. rel.*) des matines; — *s.* matin, jour, *m.*; —**s,** *s.pl.* (*Cath. rel.*) matines, *f.pl.*
Matrass, *s.* (*chem.*) matras, *m.*
Matricaria, *s.* matricaire, *f.*
Matricidal, *adj.* matricide, parricide
Matricide, *s.* matricide, parricide, (*pers.*) *m.f.*, (*murder*) *m.*
Matrice, *s.* matrice, *f.*
Matricula, *s.* matricule, *f.*
Matricular, *adj.* matriculaire
Matriculate, *v.a.* immatriculer; — *v.n.* (*of a student*) prendre ses inscriptions; — *s.* matriculaire, *m.*; — *adj.* immatriculé
Matriculation, *s.* immatriculation, matricule, *f.*; (*of a student*) inscription, *f.* *Certificate of* —, matricule, *f.* — **book,** *s.* matricule, *f.*, registre matricule, *m.*
Matrimonial, *adj.* conjugal, de (*or* du) mariage; (*law*) matrimonial
Matrimonially, *adv.* conjugalement; matrimonialement; maritalement
Matrimony, *s.* mariage, *m.*; (*poet.*) hymen, hyménée, *m.*
Matrix, *s.* matrice, *f.*
Matron, *s.* dame, femme, *f.*; mère de famille, *f.*; matrone, *f.* —**like,** *adj.* *V.* **Matronal**
Matronal, *adj.* de dame; de mère de famille; de matrone, matronal; respectable; grave, sérieux
Matronly, *adj.* d'un certain âge, d'un âge mûr; respectable; grave, sérieux
Matter, *s.* matière, *f.*; affaire, chose, *f.*; question, *f.*; cas, *m.*; sujet, point, *m.*, matière, *f.*; objet, *m.*; importance, *f.*; distance, *f.*; espace de temps, *m.*; (*of a tumour*, &c.) pus, *m.* — *of taste*, &c., affaire de goût, &c. *A small* —, une bagatelle, *f.*, un rien, *m.* *For the — of that, for that* —, si ce n'est que cela, qu'à cela ne tienne; ce n'est pas l'embarras; quant à cela, pour ce qui est de ça; à cela près. *In — of, in —s of,* en matière de, en fait de. *No — !* n'importe! *No great* —, peu de chose, pas grand'chose. *That* (or *it*) *is* or *makes no* —, il n'importe, cela ne fait rien. *There is something the* —, il y a quelque chose. *What is the — ?* qu'est-ce qu'il y a? qu'y a-t-il? de quoi s'agit-il? *What is the — with you ?* qu'est-ce que vous avez? qu'avez-vous? qu'est-ce qui vous prend? *What is the — with him ?* qu'est-ce qu'il a? qu'a-t-il? qu'est-ce qui lui prend? *Nothing is the — with me, there is nothing the — with me,* je n'ai rien. *As if nothing at all was the* —, comme si de rien n'était. — **of fact,** *s.* fait, *m.*; *adj.* positif, pratique
Matter, *v.n.* (*imp.*) importer; faire. *It —s little,* il importe peu, peu importe ('*whether,*' que, *with the subj.*). *It —s much,* il importe beaucoup. *It —s not, it* or *that does not* —, n'importe, il n'importe; cela ne fait rien. *What —s it ?* qu'importe? *What —s it to him ?* que lui importe? qu'est-ce que cela lui fait?
Matterless, *adj.* sans matière
Mattery, *adj.* purulent
Matting, *s.* paillasson, *m.*; (*rush* —) natte, *f.*
Mattock, *s.* pioche, *f.*
Mattrass, Mattress, *s.* matelas, *m.*; (*under* —), sommier, *m.* — **maker,** *s.* matelassier, *m.*, -ière, *f.*
Maturation, *s.* maturation, *f.*
Maturative, *adj.* *s.* maturatif, *adj.* *m.*, -ive, *f.*, maturatif, *s.m.*
Mature, *adj.* mûr; mûri; — *v.a.n.* mûrir; (*of bills*, &c.) arriver *or* venir à échéance, échoir

Matured, *adj.* mûri, mûr; (*of wine*) mûr, fait,
Maturely, *adv.* mûrement [en boite
Matureness, Maturity, *s.* maturité, *f.*; (*of bills,* &c.) échéance, *f.*
Matutinal, *adj.* matutinal, matinal, du matin
Maudlin, *adj.* gris, en train, ému; pleureur, larmoyant; céladonique; affecté, exagéré; stupide; — *s.* sensiblerie d'ivrogne, *f.*; céladonisme, *m.*; (*bot.*) mille-feuilles, achillée, *f.*
Maugre, *prep.* malgré, en dépit de
Maukin. *V.* **Malkin**
Maul, *v.a.* battre, meurtrir; (*fig.*) tirailler, tracasser. — **stick,** *s.* appui-main, *m.*
Maunder, *v.n.* gronder, murmurer
Maundy-Thursday, *s.* jeudi saint, *m.*
Mausoleum, *s.* mausolée, *m.*
Mauve, *adj. s.* mauve, *adj.m.f., s.m.* — **colour,** *s.* mauve, *m.* — **coloured,** *adj.* mauve
Mavis, *s.* grive ordinaire, grive chanteuse, *f.*
Maw, *s.* panse, *f.*; (*of birds*) jabot, *m.*; (*—worm*) *See below.* —**seed,** *s.* graine de pavot, *f.* — **worm,** *s.* ver intestinal, *m.*; ver rongeur, *m.*; (*pers.*) cafard, cagot, tartufe, *m.*
Mawkish, *adj.* fade, insipide; dégoûtant. — **ly,** *adv.* fadement; dégoûtamment. —**ness,** *s.* fadeur, insipidité, *f.*; dégoût, *m.*
Maxillar, -y, *adj.* maxillaire
Maxim, *s.* maxime, *f.*
Maxima, *s.pl.* maxima, *m.pl.* [mum, maximer
Maximize, *v.a.* porter *or* mettre au maxi-
Maximum, *s* maximum, *m.* — **thermometer,** *s.* thermomètre à maximum, *m.*
May, *v. auxil.* pouvoir. *I* —, (*present tense*) je peux *or* je puis; (*future*) je pourrai. — *I?* (*present tense*) puis-je? (*future*) pourrai-je? *I* — *go,* je peux (*or* puis) aller; il se peut que j'aille. *It* — *rain,* il peut pleuvoir; il se peut qu'il pleuve. — *I go out?* puis-je sortir? voulez-vous me permettre de sortir? — *I see her again!* puissé-je la revoir! —*you be happy!* puissiez-vous être heureux! — *she live long!* puisse-t-elle vivre longtemps! — *I die if ...,* que je meure si ... *You* — *have seen,* vous avez pu (*or* aurez pu, *according to the tense meant by the English phrase*) voir. *You* — *not have seen,* vous avez pu ne pas voir. *One* (or *I, thou,* &c.) — *as well ...,* (*it will be the same to ...*) autant vaut ..., autant ... *It* or *that* — *be, it* — *be so,* cela se peut, c'est possible. *It* — *be that ...,* il se peut que ..., il peut se faire que ... *That I* —, (*subj.*) que je puisse. (*As the sign of the subj. of another verb, it is not expressed separately in French.*) *That I* — *receive,* (*subj. of "may"*) que je puisse recevoir; (*subj. of "receive"*) que je reçoive. — **be,** *adv.* peut-être
May, *s.* (*month*) mai, *m.*; (*bot.*) aubépine, *f.*; — *v.n.* cueillir de l'aubépine. —**beetle,** *s.* méloé, *m.* — **bloom, -blossom,** *s.* aubépine, *f.* — — **bug,** *s.* hanneton, *m.* — **bush,** *s.* aubépine, *f.* —**day,** *s.* (le) premier mai, *m.* — **fair,** *s.* foire de mai, *f.* —**flower,** *s.* aubépine, *f.* — **fly,** *s.* éphémere, *m.f.* — **game,** *s.* divertissement du premier mai, *m.* —**lily,** *s.* muguet, *m.* —**pole,** *s.* mai, *m.* — **queen, -lady,** *s.* reine du premier mai, *f.* —**weed,** *s.* marute, *f.*
Mayonnaise, *s.* mayonnaise, *f.*
Mayor, *s.* maire, *m.* —*'s house,* mairie, *f.*
Mayoralty, *s.* mairie, *f.*
Mayoress, *s.* femme du maire, *f.*
Mazagan, *s.* (— *bean*) gourgane, *f.*
Mazarine, *s.* bleu foncé, *m.*
Maze, *s.* labyrinthe, dédale, *m.*; perplexité, *f.*, embarras, *m.*; — *v.a. V.* **Amaze** *and* **Bewilder**
Mazurka, *s.* mazourka, mazurka, masurka, *f.*
Mazy, *adj.* de labyrinthe, sinueux; (*intricate*) embrouillé, compliqué, confus, embarrassé
M.D. (*abbrev.*) D.M. (docteur-médecin), docteur
Me, *pron.* me; moi [en médecine
Mead, *s.* (*liquor*) hydromel, *m.*; (*meadow*) *V.* **Meadow**
Meadow, *s.* prairie, *f.*, pré. *m.* —**grass,** *s.* paturin, *m.* — **green,** *adj. s.* vert pré, *m.* — **ground,** *s.* terrain en prairies, *m.* —**lark,** *s.* étourneau d'Amérique, *m.* — **mouse,** *s.* campagnol, *m.* — **rue,** *s.* pigamon, *m.* — **saffron,** *s.* colchique, *m.* —**sweet,** *s.* ormiere, [spirée ulmaire, *f.*
Meadowy, *adj.* prairial
Meagre, *adj.* maigre; pauvre
Meagrely, *adv.* maigrement; pauvrement
Meagreness, *s.* maigreur, *f.*; (*poorness*) pauvreté, *f.*
Meal, *s.* repas, *m.*; (*flour*) farine, *f.*; gruau, *m.* — **house,** *s.* meunerie, *f.* — **man,** *s.* farinier, marchand de farine, *m.* —**time,** *s.* heure du (*or* des) repas, *f.* — **tub,** *s.* huche, farinière, *f.* —**worm,** *s.* ver blanc de la farine, meunier, ténébrion, *m.*
Mealiness, *s.* nature farineuse, *f.*; (*of fruits*) nature cotonneuse, *f.*; (*softness*) douceur, *f.*
Mealy, *adj.* farineux; (*of fruits*) cotonneux; (*fig.*) poudreux; (*soft*) doucereux. —**mouthed,** *adj.* doucereux, qui a la langue doucereuse, qui a des paroles mielleuses. —**mouthedness,** *s.* langue doucereuse, *f.*
Mean, *adj.* (*low*) bas; (*despicable*) vil, abject, méprisable; (*poor*) pauvre, chétif, médiocre; (*niggardly*) mesquin, sordide; (*small*) petit; faible; (*middle*) moyen. —*time,* —*while, in the —time* or *while, adv.* dans l'intervalle, pendant ce temps-là, en attendant; d'ici là; cependant; sur ces entrefaites. —**spirited,** *adj.* bas; méprisable; mesquin; ladre. —**spiritedness,** *s.* bassesse, *f.*; mesquinerie, *f.*; ladrerie, *f.*
Mean, *s.* milieu, moyen terme, *m.*; médiocrité, *f.*; (*math.*) moyenne, *f.*; —**s,** *pl.* moyen, *m.*, voie, manière, *f.*; moyens, *m.pl.*, voies, *f.pl.*; cause, *f.*, instrument, *m.*; organe, *m.*; remède, *m.*, remèdes, *m.pl.*; (*pecuniary*) moyens, *m.pl.*, fortune, *f.*; ressources, *f.pl.* *Just* or *golden* —, juste milieu, *m.* *By fair —s,* par des moyens légitimes, par des voies honnêtes; par les voies de douceur, par la douceur. *By foul — s,* par des moyens peu légitimes, par des voies injustes; par les voies de rigueur, par la rigueur. *By —s of,* au moyen de; moyennant. *By all —s, by any — s,* certainement; mais oui; (*anyhow*) à toute force, à quelque prix que ce soit; de toute nécessité; par tous les moyens; absolument; avant tout. *By no —s,* nullement, aucunement, pas du tout, en aucune manière. *By some —s or other,* d'une manière ou d'autre. *By this —s, by that —s,* par ce moyen, par là
Mean, *v.a.n.* (*intend*) se proposer; avoir l'intention (de); entendre; vouloir; (*do on purpose*) faire exprès; (*signify*) signifier, vouloir dire; (— *to say*) vouloir dire; (— *to speak of*) vouloir parler de; (*think*) penser; (*for*) destiner (à). *Does he — it?* est-il sérieux? *What does he — by that?* qu'entend-il par là? *What do you —?* que voulez-vous dire? *What does this word —?* que veut dire *or* que signifie ce mot? *To — well,* avoir de bonnes intentions
Meander, *s.* détour, *m.*, sinuosité, *f.*, méandre, *m.*; labyrinthe, dédale, *m.*; — *v.n.* serpenter, aller en serpentant [tueux
Meandering, *adj.* qui serpente, sinueux, tor-
Meandrian, *adj.* méandrique
Meaning, *s.* pensée, idée, *f.*; sens, *m.*, signification, *f.*; intention, *f.*, dessein, *m.* *Double* —, sens double, double sens, *m.*; (*ambiguity*) double entente, *f.* *To be without —, to be —less,* être dénué de sens, ne signifier rien. *To know the — of anything,* savoir ce que quelque chose signifie *or* veut dire. *What is the — of that?* qu'est-ce que cela signifie? —**less,** *adj.* dénué de sens, vide de sens
Meaning, *adj.* (*pers.*) à intentions, intentionné; (*things*) significatif. *Ill* —, à mauvaises intentions, mal intentionné. *Well* —, à bonnes intentions, bien intentionné
Meanly, *adv.* bassement; vilement; médiocrement; (*poorly*) pauvrement, chétivement,

(*stingily*) mesquinement, sordidement; (*unfavourably*) défavorablement, peu avantageusement. *To think — of*, avoir une triste opinion de, faire peu de cas de

Meanness, *s.* bassesse, *f.*; caractère vil, *m.*; médiocrité, *f.*; (*poorness*) pauvreté, *f.*; (*stinginess*) mesquinerie, vilenie, avarice, lésinerie, pingrerie, *f.* [qui a la rougeole; (*of pigs*) ladre

Measled, Measly, *adj.* atteint de rougeole,

Measles, *s.pl.* rougeole, *f.*; (*of pigs*) ladrerie, *f.*

Measurable, *adj.* mesurable; (*moderate*) modéré, mesuré; modique [surabilité, *f.*

Measurableness, *s.* nature mesurable, men-

Measurably, *adv.* modérément, avec mesure

Measure, *s.* mesure, *f.*; capacité, *f.*; nombre, *m.*; proportion, *f.*; (*of the mind*) portée, *f.*; (*of parts*) division, partie aliquote, *f.*; (*mus., vers.*) mesure, *f.*; — *v.a.n.* mesurer; proportionner; (*land*) arpenter; (*a person for clothes*) prendre mesure à; (*be*) avoir, mesurer ('*in*,' de). *Beyond —, beyond all —, out of all —*, outre mesure; sans mesure. *Coal —s*, formation houillère, *f.* *In a great —*, en grande partie. *In a —, in some —*, en partie; jusqu'à un certain point; en quelque sorte. *To have hard —*, être maltraité. *To have ... made to —*, faire faire ... sur mesure. *To have no —s to keep with*, n'avoir aucun ménagement à garder avec. *To take —s*, prendre des mesures. *To take legal —s*, avoir recours aux voies légales. **—less,** *adj.* immense, infini, illimité

Measured, *adj.* mesuré; (*equal*) égal, uniforme

Measurement, *s.* mesurage, *m.*; (*of land*) arpentage, *m.*; (*measure*) mesure, *f.* [teur, *m.*

Measurer, *s.* mesureur, *m.*; (*of land*) arpen-

Measuring, *s.* mesurage, *m.*; (*of land*) arpentage, *m.*

Meat, *s.* (*flesh*) viande, *f.*; chair, *f.*; (*food*) aliment, *m.*, nourriture, *f.* *Dead —*, viande, *f.* — **ball,** *s.* boulette de viande, *f.* — **breakfast,** *s.* déjeuner à la fourchette, *m.* — **cover,** *s.* couvre-plat, *m.*, cloche, *f.* — **dresser,** *s.* (*butch.*) dépeceur, *m.* — **fly,** *s.* mouche à viande, *f.* — **hastener,** *s.* rôtissoire, *f.* — **hook,** *s.* allonge, patte, *f.* — **market,** *s.* marché à la viande, *m.* — **offering,** *s.* sacrifice sanglant, *m.* — **safe,** *s.* garde-manger, *m.* — **salesman,** *s.* boucher (aux halles), *m.* — **screen,** *s.* cuisinière, rôtissoire, *f.* — **soup,** *s.* potage gras, *m.*,

Meaty, *adj.* charnu [soupe grasse, *f.*

Mechanic, -al, *adj.* mécanique; (*involuntary*) machinal; (*pers.*) de la classe ouvrière; — *s.* mécanicien, *m.*; artisan, *m.*; **—s,** *s.pl.* (*pers.*) mécaniciens, *m.pl.*; artisans, *m.pl.*; (*thing*) mécanique, *f.* (*V.* **Dentist, Dentistry,** *and* **Engineer**) [*out intelligence*) machinalement

Mechanically, *adv.* mécaniquement; (*with-*

Mechanicalness, *s.* nature mécanique, *f.*; nature machinale, *f.*

Mechanician, *s.* mécanicien, *m.*

Mechanism, *s.* mécanisme, *m.*

Mechanist, *s.* mécanicien, *m.*

Mechlin, — lace, *s.* malines, *f.*

Mecklenburger, *s.* Mecklembourgeois, *m.*, e, *f.*

Medal, *s.* médaille, *f.*

Medalet, *s.* médaille, *f.*

Medallic, *adj.* de médaille, des médailles

Medallion, *s.* médaillon, *m.*

Medallist, *s.* médailliste, *m.*; (*rewarded*) médaillé, *m.*; décoré, *m.*

Meddle, *v.n.* se mêler (de); s'immiscer (dans); s'ingérer (dans, de); intervenir (dans); s'occuper (de); se mêler des affaires (de); toucher (à)

Meddler, *s.* touche-à-tout, *m.f.*; tatillon, *m.*, -ne, *f.*; importun, *m.*, e, *f.*; intrigant, *m.*, e, *f.*

Meddlesome, *adj.* *V.* **Meddling**

Meddling, *adj.* indiscret; impertinent; importun; intrigant; qui se mêle de tout; qui touche à tout; — *s.* *V.* **Intermeddling**

Mediæval, *adj.* du moyen âge

Mediævalism, *s.* médiévisme, moyen-âgisme, *m.*

Mediævalist, *s.* médiéviste, moyen-âgiste, *m.*

Medial, *adj.s.* médial, *adj.m.*, e, *f.*, médiale, *s.f.*

Medially, *adv.* médialement

Mediate, *adj.* médiat; intermédiaire; interposé; — *v.n.* s'interposer, s'entremettre

Mediately, *adv.* médiatement

Mediation, *s.* médiation, *f.*; entremise, *f.*; intermédiaire, *m.*; intercession, *f.*

Mediatization, *s.* médiatisation, *f.*

Mediatize, *v.a.* médiatiser

Mediator, *s.* médiateur, *m.* [teur, médiateur

Mediatorial, Mediatory, *adj.* de média-

Mediatress, Mediatrix, *s.* médiatrice, *f.*

Medic, *s.* luzerne, *f.*

Medicable, *adj.* guérissable, curable; salutaire

Medical, *adj.* médical; de médecine; de médecin; (*fit for healing*) médicinal. — *question*, question médicale. — *school*, — *book*, école, livre de médecine. — *profession*, profession de médecin, médecine, *f.*; médecins, *m.pl.* — *science* or *art*, science (*f.*) médicale, art (*m.*) médical, médecine, *f.* — *student*, étudiant en médecine. — *man*, — *adviser*, — *attendant*, médecin, *m.* — *officer*, médecin, *m.*; officier de santé, *m.* — *practitioner*, médecin praticien, praticien, médecin exerçant, médecin traitant, *m.* — *friend*, ami médecin. *Our — friend*, notre ami le médecin. — *body* or *staff*, corps de (*or* des) médecins, corps médical, *m.* — *advice* or *attendance*, consultations, *f.pl.*; visites d'un (*or* du *or* de) médecin, *f.pl.*; soins d'un (*or* du) médecin, *m.pl.* [*To take — advice*, consulter un médecin]. — *jurisprudence*, médecine légale

Medically, *adv.* médicalement, au point de vue médical, sous le rapport médical; en médecine; en médecin; médicinalement, comme une médecine

Medicament, *s.* médicament, *m.*

Medicamental, *adj.* médicamentaire

Medicamentally, *adv.* en médicament, comme médicament

Medicaster, *s.* médicastre, *m.*

Medicate, *v.a.* médicamenter; imprégner *or* mêler de drogues; (*wine*) droguer, frelater

Medicated, *part. adj.* médicamenté, &c. (*V.* **Medicate**); médicamenteux; médicinal. — *paper*, papier médicamenté, *m.* — *candle*, bougie médicinale, *f.*

Medication, *s.* médication, *f.*

Medicinable, *adj.* *V.* **Medicable**

Medicinal, *adj.* médicinal

Medicinally, *adv.* médicinalement

Medicine, *s.* médecine, *f.*; médicament, *m.*; remède ('*for*,' contre), *m.* — **chest,** *s.* phar-

Medick, *s.* luzerne, *f.* [macie, *f.*, droguier, *m.*

Mediocre, *adj.* médiocre

Mediocrity, *s.* médiocrité, *f.*

Meditate, *v.n.* méditer; avoir l'intention (de), se proposer (de); — *v.a.* méditer; projeter

Meditation, *s.* méditation, *f.*

Meditative, *adj.* méditatif; de méditation

Meditatively, *adv.* méditativement

Meditativeness, *s.* nature méditative, *f.*

Mediterranean, *adj.* méditerrané; — *s.* Méditerranée, *f.* — *Sea*, Mer Méditerranée, Méditerranée, *f.*

Medium, *s.* milieu, *m*; terme moyen, moyen terme, *m.*; (*expedient*) moyen, *m.*; accommodement, *m.*; (*agency*) intermédiaire, *m.*; entremise, voie, *f.*; organe, *m.*; agent, *m.*; (*math.*) moyenne, *f.*; (*phys.*) milieu, *m.*; (*in spiritualism*) médium, milieu, *m.*; — *adj.* moyen. *Circulating —, — of circulation*, (*polit. economy*) agent de circulation, agent monétaire, *m.* *Just —*, juste milieu, *m.*

Medlar, *s.* nèfle, *f.* — **tree,** *s.* néflier, *m.*

Medley, *s.* mélange, *m.*; — *adj.* mêlé, confus

Medulla, *s.* moelle, *f.* — *oblongata*, moelle

Medullar, -y, *adj.* médullaire [allongée, *f.*

Medusa, *s.* méduse, *f.*
Meed, *s.* recompense, *f.*, prix, *m.*; (*gift*) don, présent, *m.*; (*share*) part, *f.*; (*praise*) louange, *f.*
Meek, *adj.* doux; paisible; humble, soumis
Meekly, *adv.* avec douceur; humblement, avec humilité
Meekness, *s.* douceur, *f.*; humilité, *f.*
Meerschaum, *s.* écume de mer, *f.*
Meet, *adj.* propre (à); à propos, convenable; — *s.* rendez-vous (de chasse), *m.*, assemblée, *f.*; — *v.a.* (*pers.*) rencontrer; (*make an appointment*) trouver, rejoindre, retrouver; (*in society*) voir, se trouver avec; (*things*) rencontrer, trouver; (*receive*) recevoir; trouver; (*to experience*) éprouver, essuyer; (*success*) obtenir, avoir; (*assemble*) assembler, rassembler, réunir; (*to face*) affronter; aborder; (*expenses*, &c.) faire face à; (*com.*) faire honneur à; (*obviate*) obvier à; (*trains, said of omnibuses*) desservir; (*a train, catch it, said of pers.*) *V.* **Catch**; (*answer*) répondre à; (*anticipate*) prévenir, aller au-devant de; (*foresee and provide for or against*) prévoir; (*satisfy*) satisfaire; (*fulfil*) remplir; (*accommodate*) arranger, s'arranger avec; (*fight*) se battre avec, combattre; — *v.n.* se rencontrer; se voir; se trouver ensemble, se trouver; se rejoindre, se retrouver; s'assembler, se réunir; (*end*) aboutir; (*of extremes*) se toucher. *To — with*, rencontrer; trouver; tomber sur; recevoir; (*experience*) éprouver, essuyer; (*success*) obtenir, avoir; (*see*) voir; (*happen, imp.*) arriver. *To go* or *come to —*, aller *or* venir au-devant de *or* à la rencontre de (... *to — me*, ... au-devant de moi *or* à ma rencontre; ... *to — him*, &c., ... au-devant de lui, &c., *or* à sa rencontre, &c.). *To — one half-way*, faire la moitié du chemin; partager le différend. *To — death*, affronter la mort. *To — o.'s death*, trouver la mort, mourir, être tué. *He has met with an accident*, il lui est arrivé un accident. *When shall we — again?* quand nous reverrons-nous?
Meeting, *s.* rencontre, *f.*; entrevue, *f.*; conférence, *f.*; assemblée, *f.*; réunion, *f.*; congrès, *m.*; séance, *f.*; duel, *m.*; (*public — in England*) meeting, *m.*; (*races*) courses, *f.pl*; (*competitive*) concours, *m.*; (*of rivers*) confluent, *m.*; (*of roads*) jonction, *f.*; (*of dissenters*) office, service, *m.*; (*gram.*) concours, *m.*, rencontre, *f.* *Right of —*, droit de réunion, *m.* — **house,** *s.* maison de réunion, *f.*; (*of dissenters*) temple, *m.*, chapelle, *f.*; congrégation, *f.*
Meetly, *adv.* convenablement, à propos; comme il faut
Meetness, *s.* convenance, *f.*; propriété, *f.*
Megalosaurus, *s.* mégalosaure, *m.*
Megatherium, *s.* mégathérium, *m.*
Megrims. *V.* **Staggers**
Melancholily, *adv.* mélancoliquement; (*sadly*) tristement [colique; (*sad*) triste
Melancholy, *s.* mélancolie, *f.*; — *adj.* mélan-
Melasses, *s.pl.* mélasse, *f.*
Melilot, *s.* mélilot, *m.*
Meliorate, &c. *V.* **Ameliorate, &c.**
Melliferous, *adj.* mellifère
Mellification, *s.* mellification, *f.*
Mellifluence, *s.* douceur, *f.*
Mellifluent, Mellifluous, *adj.* melliflu, doux, suave, plein de douceur
Mellow, *adj.* (*of fruit*) blet; (*ripe*) mûr; (*tender*) tendre, mou; (*to the ear*) mélodieux, doux; (*to the taste, touch, or sight*) moelleux; (*in liquor*) en train, gai, gris; (*of land*) meuble; — *v.a.* mûrir, faire mûrir; (*fruit*) blettir, rendre blet; (*soften*) amollir; (*fig.*) adoucir; (*of taste or touch*) rendre moelleux; (*of land*) ameublir; — *v.n.* s'amollir; s'adoucir; (*ripen*) mûrir; (*of fruit*) blettir, devenir blet
Mellowing, *s.* amollissement, *m.*; adoucissement, *m.*; (*of fruit*) blettissement, *m.*; (*agr.*) ameublissement, *m.*
Mellowness, *s.* (*ripeness*) maturité, *f.*; (*of fruit*) blettissure, *f.*; (*softness*) mollesse, *f.*; douceur, *f.*; (*of sound*) mélodie, *f.*; (*of taste, touch, or sight*) moelleux, *m.*
Mellowy, *adj.* *V.* **Mellow,** *adj.*
Melod-ic, -ically, -ist. *V.* page 3, § 1
Melodious, *adj.* mélodieux
Melodiously, *adv.* mélodieusement [lodie, *f.*
Melodiousness, *s.* nature mélodieuse, mé-
Melodize, *v.a.* rendre mélodieux
Melodrama, *s.* mélodrame, *m.*
Melodramatic, *adj.* mélodramatique [ment
Melodramatically, *adv.* mélodramatique-
Melodramatist, *s.* mélodramaturge, *m.*
Melody, *s.* mélodie, *f.*
Melomania, *s.* mélomanie, *f.*
Melomaniac, *s. adj.* mélomane, *m.f.*
Melon, *s.* melon, *m.* — **bed, -ground, -pit,** *s.* couche de melons, melonnière, *f.* — **shaped,** *adj.* meloné. — **thistle,** *s.* mélocacte, *m.*
Melt, *v.a.n.* fondre; (*soften*) attendrir; (*get softened*) s'attendrir; (*into tears*) fondre (en larmes); — *s.* *V.* **Milt.** — **away,** *v.a.* fondre; *v.n.* fondre, se fondre; (*fig.*) disparaître
Melter, *s.* fondeur, *m.*
Melting, *adj.* fondant; (*affecting*) touchant; (*of the weather*) étouffant; — *s.* fonte, fusion, *f.* — **house,** *s.* fonderie, *f.* — **pot,** *s.* creuset, *m.* — **steel,** *s.* acier de fusion, *m.*
Melwel, *s.* merluche, *f.* [parlement, député, *m.*
Member, *s.* membre, *m.*; (*M.P.*) membre du
Membered, *adj.* qui a des membres ...; membré. *Large* or *strong —*, membru
Membership, *s.* qualité de membre, *f.*; sociétariat, *m.*; association, communauté, *f.*
Membranaceous, *adj.* membranacé
Membrane, *s.* membrane, *f.*
Membraneous, *adj.* membrané, membraneux
Membraniform, *adj.* membraniforme
Membranous, *adj.* membraneux
Membranule, *s.* membranule, *f.*
Memento, *s.* mémento, *m.*; souvenir, *m.*
Memoir, *s.* mémoire, *m.*
Memoirist, *s.* mémorialiste, *m.f.*
Memorable, *adj.* mémorable
Memorably, *adv.* mémorablement, d'une manière mémorable
Memorandum, *s.* note, *f.*, mémoire, *m.* *To make a — of*, prendre note de, noter. — **book,** *s.* agenda, *m.*; carnet, *m.*
Memorial, *s.* souvenir, *m.*; monument commémoratif, monument, *m.*; (*report*) mémoire, *m.*; exposé, *m.*; (*written note*) note, *f.*; (*petition*) requête, pétition, *f.*; — *adj.* commémoratif, mémoratif [naire, *m.f.*
Memorialist, *s.* mémorialiste, *m.f.*; pétition-
Memorialize. *V.* **Petition,** *v.a.*
Memory, *s.* mémoire, *f.*; (*remembrance*) souvenir, *m.* *Within the — of man*, de mémoire [d'homme
Men, *s.pl.* *V.* **Man**
Menace. *V.* **Threat** *and* **Threaten**
Menagerie, Menagery, *s.* ménagerie, *f.*
Mend, *v.a.* (*clothes, common utensils*) raccommoder; (*various senses*) arranger; réparer; corriger, réformer; améliorer; rétablir; rectifier; (*a pen*) retailler; tailler; (*the pace*) hâter; — *v.n.* se corriger; s'améliorer; (*in sickness*) se rétablir; (*of the weather*) se remettre au beau, se remettre
Mendable, *adj.* raccommodable; réparable; améliorable; corrigible
Mendacious, *adj.* mensonger
Mendaciously, *adv.* mensongèrement
Mendacity, *s.* mensonge, *m.*
Mender, *s.* raccommodeur, *m.*, -euse, *f.*; réparateur, *m.*, -trice, *f.*; améliorateur, *m.*, -trice, *f.*; correcteur, *m.*, -trice, *f.*
Mendicancy, *s.* mendicité, *f.*
Mendicant, *adj.* mendiant; de mendicité, de mendiant; — *s.* mendiant, *m.*, e, *f.*; (*monk*) frère mendiant, *m.*
Mendicity, *s.* mendicité, *f.*

Mending, *s.* raccommodage, *m.*; réparation, *f.* *Past* —, sans remède ; irréparable ; incorrigible
Menial, *adj.* domestique; subalterne; servile, bas ; — *s.* domestique, *m.f.* ; valet, laquais, *m.*
Menilite, *s.* ménilite, *f.*
Meninges, *s.pl.* méninges, *f.pl.*
Meningitis, *s.* méningite, *f.*
Menses, *s.pl.* *V.* **Catamenia**
Menstrual, *adj.* menstruel
Menstruated, *adj. f.* menstruée, réglée
Menstruation, *s.* menstruation, *f.*
Mensura-bility, bleness. *V.* page 3, § 1
Mensurable, *adj* mensurable [suration, *f.*
Mensuration, *s.* mesurage, *m.*; (*math.*) men-
Mental, *adj.* mental ; moral
Mentally, *adv.* mentalement ; moralement
Mention, *s.* mention, *f.*; rapport, *m.* *To make* — *of*, *V.* *To* **Mention,** *v.a.*
Mention, *v.a.* mentionner, faire mention de, parler de, dire ; rapporter ; indiquer ; (*in reports*, &c.) constater ; (— *the name of*) nommer; (*an instance*) citer. *Not to* —, (*putting aside*) sans parler de ; sans compter. *Don't* — *it !* (*in reply to* merci !) ce n'est rien *or* n'en parlez pas (, monsieur, &c.) ; (*in reply to* pardon !) du tout (, monsieur, &c.) !
Mentor, *s.* mentor, guide, *m.*
Mephistopheletic, Mephistophelic, *adj.* méphistophélétique
Mephitic, *adj.* méphitique
Mephitism, *s.* méphitisme, *m.*
Mercantile, *adj.* mercantile, de commerce; commerçant ; marchand. — *establishment*, maison de commerce, *f.* — *law*, droit commercial, code de commerce, *m.* — *community*, classe commerçante, *f.*, commerce, *m.* — *navy*, marine marchande, *f.* — *steamer*, bateau à vapeur marchand, *m.*
Mercantilism, *s.* mercantilisme, *m.*
Mercator's chart *or* **projection,** *s.* carte réduite, *f.*
Mercenarily, *adv.* mercenairement
Mercenariness, *s.* mercenarité, vénalité, *f.*
Mercenary, *adj.* mercenaire, vénal ; — *s.* mercenaire, *m.f.*
Mercer, *s.* mercier, *m.*, -ière, *f.*
Mercery, *s.* mercerie, *f.*
Merchandise, *s.* marchandise, *f.* ; — *v.n.* commercer, faire le commerce, faire le négoce
Merchant, *s.* négociant (en ...), *m.*, e, *f.*; (*retailer*) marchand (de ...), *m.*, e, *f.* ; commerçant, *m.*, e, *f.* ; — *adj.* commercial, du commerce ; marchand. *The* — *of Venice*, le marchand de Venise. —**like,** *adj.* en (*or* de) négociant ; en (*or* de) marchand ; en (*or* de) commerçant, commercial. —**man, -ship,** *s.* navire *or* bâtiment marchand, navire de commerce, *m.* — **seaman,** *s.* marin de la marine marchande, *m.* — **service,** *s.* marine marchande, *f.* — **tailor,** *s.* marchand tailleur, *m.*
Merchantable, *adj.* marchand
Merciful, *adj.* ('*to*,' pour) miséricordieux, clément ; compatissant ; indulgent. —**ly,** *adv.* miséricordieusement, avec clémence ; avec compassion, avec pitié ; avec indulgence. —**ness,** *s.* miséricorde, clémence, *f.* ; compassion, pitié, *f.* ; indulgence, *f.*
Merciless, &c. *V.* **Unmerciful,** &c.
Mercurial, *adj.* (*chem.*) mercuriel, de (*or* du) mercure ; (*myth.*) de Mercure ; (*fig.*) vif, actif, allègre, ardent ; — *s.* mercurial, *m.*
Mercuriale, *s.* (*Fr. hist.*) mercuriale, *f.*
Mercurialism, *s.* mercurialisme, *m.*
Mercurialize, *v.a.* mercurialiser
Mercuric, *adj.* mercurique
Mercurification, *s.* mercurification, *f.*
Mercurous, *adj.* mercureux
Mercury, *s.* mercure, *m.* ; (*sprightliness*) vivacité, activité, ardeur, *f.* ; (*astr.*, *myth.*) Mercure, *m.*; (*bot.*) mercuriale, *f.*
Mercy, *s.* miséricorde, clémence, *f.* ; compassion, pitié, *f.* ; indulgence, *f.* ; pardon, *m.*, grâce, *f.* ; bienfait, *m.* ; discrétion, merci, *f.* *Sister of* —, sœur de charité, *f.* *At* or *to the* — *of*, à la merci de, à la discrétion de. *At the* — *of the wind*, au gré du vent. *With a recommendation to* —, (*law*) avec des circonstances atténuantes. *To have* — *on*, avoir pitié de. — **seat,** *s.* propitiatoire, *m.*
Mere, *adj.* simple, pur, seul, unique ; vrai ; rien que, pas autre chose que, ne ... que ; — *s.* mare, *f.*, étang, lac, *m.* ; (*boundary*) borne, limite, *f.*
Merely, *adv.* simplement, purement, seulement, uniquement ; rien que, pas autre chose que, ne ... que [cherché, emprunté, faux
Meretricious, *adj.* de courtisane ; (*fig.*) re-
Merganser, *s.* harle, *m.*
Merge, *v.a.* fondre ; plonger ; consumer, perdre, laisser s'éteindre ; — *v.n.* se fondre ; se consumer, se perdre, s'éteindre
Meridian, *s.* méridien, *m.* ; (*noon*) midi, *m.* ; (*of glory*, &c.) apogée, *m.* ; — *adj.* (*astr.*, *geog.*) méridien ; (*of noon*) de midi ; (*of glory*, &c.) à son apogée, à l'apogée
Meridional, *adj.* méridional
Meridionality, *s.* exposition au midi, *f.*
Meridionally, *adv.* au midi, vers le sud
Meringue, *s.* meringue, *f.* [mérine, *f.*
Merino, *s.* mérinos, *m.* — **breed,** *s.* race
Merit, *v.a.* mériter ; — *s.* mérite, *m.*; qualité, *f.*
Meritorious, *adj.* méritoire ; (*pers.*) méritant
Meritoriously, *adv.* méritoirement, d'une manière méritoire
Meritoriousness, *s.* mérite, *m.*
Merlin, *s.* émerillon, *m.*
Merlon, *s.* merlon, *m.*
Mermaid, *s.* sirène, *f.*
Merman, *s.* triton, *m.* [— *s.* Mérovingien, *m.*
Merovingian, *adj.* mérovingien (*m.*, -ne, *f.*) ;
Merrily, *adv.* gaiment, joyeusement
Merriment, *s.* gaieté, joie, *f.* ; réjouissance, *f.* ; divertissement, *m.* ; plaisanterie, *f.*
Merriness, *s.* gaieté, joie, *f.*
Merry, *adj.* gai, joyeux ; jovial ; plaisant ; — *s.* merise, *f.* *As* — *as a lark* (or *as a grig*), gai comme un pinson. *To make* — *with*, se réjouir de ; se divertir de, s'égayer de ; (*joke*) plaisanter sur. *The more the merrier*, plus on est de fous plus on rit. — **andrew,** *s.* paillasse, bouffon, *m.* ; paradiste, pitre, *m.* — **-go-round,** *s.* manége, *m.* ; jeu de bagues, *m.* — **making,** *s.* réjouissances, *f.pl.*, divertissement, *m.*, fête, *f.* ; *adj.* joyeux, de fête. — **thought,** *s.* lunette, fourchette, *f.*
Mesdames, *s.pl.* mesdames, *f.pl.*; les dames *f.pl.*
Meseems. *V.* **Methinks** [mésentérie, *f.*
Mesenteric, *adj.* mésentérique. — *disease*,
Mesenteritis, *s.* mésentérite, *f.*
Mesentery, *s* mésentère, *m.*
Mesh, *s.* maille, *f.* ; (*of a screw*) pas, *m.* ; (*for netting*) moule, *m.* ; — *v.a.* prendre au filet. — **work,** *s.* *V.* **Net-work**
Meshy, *adj.* maillé, réticulé, en réseau
Meslin, *s.* mixture, *f.* ; méteil, *m.* ; passe-
Mesmeree, *s.* magnétisé, *m.*, e, *f.* [méteil, *m.*
Mesmeric, *adj.* mesmérique, mesmérien ; magnétique [(animal), *m.*
Mesmerism, *s.* mesmérisme, magnétisme
Mesmerist, *s.* mesmériste, *m.f.*, magnétiseur, *m.*, -euse, *f.*
Mesmerization, *s.* magnétisation, *f.*
Mesmerize, *v.a.* magnétiser
Mesmerizer, *s.* magnétiseur, *m.*, -euse, *f.*
Mesne, *adj.* moyen
Mess, *s.* (*dish*) mets, plat, *m.* ; (*slop*) gâchis, margouillis, *m.* ; saleté, *f.* ; (*failure*) cacade, *f.*, fiasco, *m.* ; (*scrape*) pétrin, *m.* ; affaire, *f.* ; (*mil.*, *nav.*) (*bowl*) gamelle, *f.* ; (*of mil. officers*) mess, pension, table, *f.* ; ordinaire, *m.* ; (*of nav. officers*) table, *f.* ; — *v.n.* manger ; (*mil.*, *nav.*) manger ensemble ; (*dabble*) faire du gâchis ; — *v.a.* gâcher, salir, gâter, abîmer. —

of pottage, (*of Esau's swap*) plat de lentilles, *m.* *To get into a* —, (*fig.*) *V.* **Scrape.** *To make a* —, faire du gâchis; (*do o.'s needs*) faire. *To make a — of*, (*bungle*) gâcher, gâter; (*confuse*) embrouiller, barbouiller; (— *of it*) se blouser, patauger, gâter tout; faire fiasco; finir mal. — **man,** *s.* cuisinier, *m.* — **mate,** *s.* camarade de table, *m.* — **room,** *s.* chambre d'ordinaire, *f.* — **tin,** *s.* gamelle, *f.*

Message, *s.* message, *m.*; commission, *f.*; (*telegraphic*) dépêche, *f.*

Messenger, *s.* messager, *m.*, -ère, *f.*; courrier, *m.*; commissionnaire, *m.*; (*fig.*) avant-coureur, *m.*, avant-courrière, *f.*; (*bit of paper on a kite-string*) courrier, postillon, *m.*

Messenian, *s. adj.* Messénien, *m.*, -ne, *f.*

Messiah, *s.* Messie, *m.* —**ship,** *s.* messianité, *f.*

Messian-ic, -ism. *V.* page 3, § 1 [*m.pl.*

Messieurs, Messrs., *s.pl.* Messieurs, MM.,

Messuage, *s.* maison et dépendances, *f.pl.*,

Mestiza, *s.* métisse, *f.* [maison, habitation, *f.*

Mestizo, Mestino, *s.* métis, *m.*

Metacarpal, *adj.* métacarpien

Metacarpus, *s.* métacarpe, *m.*

Metage, *s.* mesurage, *m.*

Metal, *s.* métal, *m.*; (*rail.*) rail, *m.*; (*ballast*) empierrement, cailloutis, *m.*; — *v.a.* (*roads*) ferrer, empierrer, caillouter. — **dealer,** *s.* ferretier, ferrailleur, *m.* — **engraver (-engraving),** *s.* graveur (*m.*, gravure, *f.*) sur métaux. — **refiner,** *s.* affineur de métaux, *m.* — **turner** *or* **worker,** *s.* tourneur *or* ouvrier en métaux, *m.* [raire, *m.*

Metallic, *adj.* métallique. — *currency*, numé-

Metalliferous, *adj.* métallifère

Metalline, *adj.* métallin

Metalling, *s.* empierrement, *m.*

Metallist, *s.* ouvrier en métaux, *m.*

Metallization, *s.* métallisation, *f.*

Metallize, *v.a.* métalliser

Metallographer, *s.* métallographe, *m.*

Metallograph-ic, -y. *V.* page 3, § 1

Metalloid, *adj.s.* métalloïde, *adj.m.f.*, *s.m.*

Metallurg-ic, al, -ist, -y. *V.* page 3, § 1

Metamorph-ic, -ism, -ist, -osic. *V.* page

Metamorphose, *v.a.* métamorphoser [3, § 1

Metamorphosis, *s.* métamorphose, *f.*

Metaphor, *s.* métaphore, *f.*

Metaphor-ic, al, -ically, -ist; Metaphys-ical, -ically. *V.* page 3, § 1

Metaphysician, *s.* métaphysicien, *m.*, -ne, *f.*

Metaphysics, *s.pl.* métaphysique, *f.*

Metatarsal, *adj.* métatarsien

Metatarsus, *s.* métatarse, *m.*

Mete, *v.a.* (— **out**) mesurer; — *s.* mesure, *f.*

Metempsychosis, *s.* métempsycose, *f.*

Metempsychosist, *s.* métempsycosiste, *m.f.*

Meteor, *s.* météore, *m.*

Meteorism, *s.* météorisme, *m.*

Meteorite, *s.* météorite, *f.m.*

Meteorographer, *s.* météorographe, *m.*

Meteoro-graphic, al, -graphy, -logic, al, ally, -logist, -logy. *V.* page 3, § 1

Meteorolite, *s.* météorolithe, *m.*

Meter, *s.* mesureur, *m.*; (*of gas*, &c.) comp-

Metheglin, *s.* hydromel, *m.* [teur, *m.*

Methinks, *v.imp.* il me semble (que); (*of what precedes*) ce me semble, il me semble

Method, *s.* méthode, *f.*; (*way*) manière, *f.*; moyen, *m.*; (*order*) ordre, *m.*

Method-ic, al, -ically, -ism, -ist. *V* p.3, § 1

Methodize, *v.a.* méthodiser; arranger avec méthode; mettre de l'ordre dans; régler

Methought, *v. imp.* il me semblait, il me

Methyl, *s.* méthyle, *m.* [sembla

Methylamine, *s.* méthylamine, *f.*

Methylate, *v.a.* méthyler

Methyle, *s.* méthyle, *m.*

Methylene, *s.* méthylène, *m.*

Methylic, *adj.* méthylique [par métonymie

Metonymic, -al, *adj.* métonymique, employé

Metonymically, *adv.* par métonymie

Metonymy, *s.* métonymie, *f.*

Metre, *s.* (*poet.*) mesure, *f.*, mètre, *m.*; vers, *m.*; (*French yard*) mètre, *m.*

Metric, -al, *adj.* métrique

Metrically, *adv.* d'après le système métrique; (*vers.*) d'une manière métrique, en vers

Metro-graphic, -graphy, -logic, al, -logist, -logy. *V.* page 3, § 1

Metromania, *s.* métromanie, *f.*

Metromaniac, *s.adj.* métromane, *m.f.*

Metronome, *s.* métronome, *m.* [tropole, *f.*

Metropolis, *s.* capitale, *f.*; (*eccl.*, *antiq.*) mé-

Metropolitan, *adj.* de la capitale; (*eccl.*) métropolitain; — *s.* métropolitain, *m.*

Metropolite, *s.* métropolite, *m.*

Mettle, *s.* fougue, ardeur, vivacité, *f.*, feu, *m.*; (*pers.*) courage, cœur, *m.* *To put on o.'s* —, mettre sur le point d'honneur, piquer d'honneur

Mettled, *adj.* fougueux, vif, ardent; (*pers.*) courageux, plein de cœur

Mettlesome, *adj.* fougueux, ardent

Mettlesomely, *adv.* avec feu, avec ardeur

Mettlesomeness, *s.* *V.* **Mettle**

Mew, *s.* (*gull*) mouette, *f.*; (*cage*) mue, *f.*; (*fig.*) prison, *f.*; (*of cats*) miaulement, *m.*; —**s,** *s.pl.* (*stables*) écuries, *f.pl.*; — *v.a.* enfermer; — *v.n.* (*of cats*) miauler

Mewing, *s.* miaulement, *m.*

Mewl, *v.n.* vagir

Mewling, *s.* vagissement, *m.*

Mexican, *s.* Mexicain, *m.*, e, *f.*; —*adj.* mexicain, du Mexique [bois, *m.*

Mezereon, *s.* mézéréon, bois gentil, garou des

Mezzanine, — **floor,** *s.* mezzanine, *f.*, entre-

Mezzo.relievo, *s.* demi-relief, *m.* [sol, *m.*

Mezzotint, Mezzotinto, *s.* mezzotinto, *m.*, manière noire, gravure à la manière noire, *f.* *In* —, en mezzotinto, à la manière noire

Miasm, Miasma, *s.* miasme

Miasmatic, -al, *adj.* miasmatique

Mica, *s.* mica, *m.* — **schist, -slate,** *s.* mica-

Micaceous, *adj.* micacé [schiste, *m.*

Michaelmas, — **day,** *s.* la Saint-Michel, *f.*

Mickle, *adj.* grand; — *adv.* beaucoup. *Many a* (or *Every*) *little makes a* —, les petits ruisseaux font les grandes rivières

Microcosm, *s.* microcosme, *m.*

Micro-cosmic, -logic, &c. *V.* page 3, § 1

Micrometer, *s.* micromètre, *m.*

Microscope, *s.* microscope, *m.* [page 3, § 1

Microscop-ic, al, -ically, -ist, -y. *V.*

Miction *s.* miction, *f.*

Micturition, *s.* micturition, *f.*

Mid, *adj.* du milieu; moyen; (*in compounds*) mi-... — **course,** *s.* moitié du chemin, *f.*; moitié de la course, *f.* —**day,** *s.* midi, *m.*; *adj.* de midi. —**heaven,** *s.* milieu du ciel, *m.* —**leg,** *s.* mi-jambe, *f.* —**lent,** *s.* la mi-carême, *f.* —**land,** *adj.* de l'intérieur, intérieur, méditerrané; central. —**most,** *adj.* du milieu, du centre, central. —**night,** *s.* minuit, *m.*; *adj.* de minuit; de nuit, nocturne. —**rib,** *s.* (*bot.*) nervure médiane, *f.* —**riff,** *s.* diaphragme, *m.* —**ship,** *s.* milieu du vaisseau, *m.* —*ship beam*, maître bau, *m.* —*ship frame*, maître couple, *m.* (—*ships*) *adv.* *V.* **Amidships.**) —**shipman,** *s.* aspirant *or* élève de marine (de première classe), *m.* *Passed —shipman*, enseigne de vaisseau, *m.* —**stream,** *s.* milieu du courant, *m.* —**summer,** *s.* milieu *or* cœur de l'été, *m.*; (*astr.*) solstice d'été, *m.*; (—*summer day*) la Saint-Jean, *f.* —**way,** *s.* milieu du chemin, *m.*; (*fig.*) milieu, *m*; *adj. adv.* à moitié chemin, à mi-chemin; (*up*) à mi-côte. —**wife,** *s.* sage-femme, accoucheuse, *f.* *Man —wife*, accoucheur, *m.* —**wife,** *v.n.* faire l'office de sage-femme. —**wifery,** *s.* obstétrique, *f*, art des accouchements, *m.*; accouchement, *m.*; assistance de sage-femme *or* d'accoucheuse, *f.* —**winter,** *s.* milieu *or* cœur de l'hiver, *m.*; (*astr.*) solstice d'hiver, *m.* *In —winter*, au cœur de l'hiver

Midden, *s.* fumier, *m.*
Middle, *adj.* du milieu; central, du centre; (*fig.*) moyen; intermédiaire, (*half*) demi; — *s.* milieu, *m.*; centre, *m.*; (*waist*) ceinture, *f.*; (*mus.*) médium, *m.* *In the — of*, au milieu de; au centre de. *In the — of it* or *of them* (*things*), au milieu. *Of — size*, (*pers.*) de taille moyenne. *Up to o.'s —*, jusqu'à la ceinture. —**age,** *s.* âge moyen, moyen âge, *m.* —**aged,** *adj.* de moyen âge, entre deux âges. —**ages,** *s.pl.* (*hist.*) moyen âge, *m.* —**course,** *s.* milieu, *m.* —**finger,** *s.* doigt du milieu, médius, *m.* —**man,** *s.* intermédiaire, *m.*; agent, *m.*; (*mil.*) homme du centre, *m.* —**most,** *adj.* le plus au milieu. —**sized,** *adj.* de moyenne grosseur *or* grandeur, de taille moyenne, moyen
Middling, *adj.* moyen; (*moderate*) médiocre; (*tolerable*) passable; (*of the health*) passablement bien, assez bien, tout doucement, comme ci comme ça; (*com.*) bon ordinaire, demi-fin, entre-fin
Middlingly, *adv.* moyennement; (*moderately*) médiocrement; (*tolerably*) passablement, assez
Middy, *s.* (*jest.*) *V.* **Midshipman** [bien
Midge, *s.* cousin, moucheron, *m.*
Midst, *s.* milieu, *m.*; fort, cœur, *m.*; — *adv.* au milieu. *In the — of*, au milieu *or* &c. de; dans le sein de. *In the — of it* or *of them* (*things*),
Mien, *s* mine, *f.*, air, *m.* [au milieu
Miff, *s.* brouille, fâcherie, *f.*; boutade, *f.*; accès de mauvaise humeur, *m.*
Miffed, *adj.* brouillé, fâché; blessé
Might. *I —*, (*was allowed to, was likely to*, &c.) je pouvais, (*should be allowed to, should likely or possibly*, &c.) je pourrais. *I — go*, je pouvais (*or* pourrais) aller; il se pourrait que j'allasse. *It — rain*, il pourrait pleuvoir, il se pourrait qu'il plût. *It* or *that — be, it — be so*, cela se pourrait. *It — be that ...*, il se pourrait que ..., il pourrait se faire que ... *You — see*, vous pouviez (*or* pourriez) voir. *You — have seen*, vous aviez pu (*or* auriez pu, *according to the tense meant by the English context*) voir. *You — not have seen*, vous aviez (*or* auriez) pu ne pas voir. *You — have been ten years old*, vous pouviez avoir dix ans. *It — have been ten o'clock*, il pouvait être dix heures. *That I —*, (*subj.*) que je pusse. (*As the sign of the subj. of another verb, it is not expressed separately in French.*) *That I — receive*, (*pret. subj. of "may"*) que je pusse recevoir; (*pret. subj. of "receive"*) que je reçusse. *One* (or *I, thou*, &c.) *— as well ...*, (*it would be the same to ...*) autant vaudrait ..., autant ...
Might, *s.* force, *f.*; puissance, *f.*, pouvoir, *m.* *— against right*, la force contre le droit, le droit du plus fort. *With — and main*, de toutes ses forces; à corps perdu, éperdument
Mightily, *adv.* fortement, vigoureusement; (*powerfully*) puissamment; (*greatly*) grandement, considérablement, extrêmement, infiniment, bien [*f.*; (*greatness*) grandeur, *f.*
Mightiness, *s.* force, *f.*; (*power*) puissance,
Mighty, *adj.* fort, vigoureux; (*powerful*) puissant; (*great*) grand; — *adv.* très, bien, fort, ex-
Mignonette, *s.* réséda, *m.* [trêmement
Migrate, *v.n.* émigrer; passer
Migration, *s.* migration, *f.*
Migratory, *adj.* (*pers.*) émigrant, migrateur, nomade; (*of animals*) voyageur, migrateur, mi-
Mikado, *s.* mikado, *m.* [gratoire, de passage
Milanese, *s. adj.* Milanais, *m.*, e, *f.*
Milch, *adj.* à lait, laitière
Mild, *adj.* doux; mitigé; peu rigoureux; (*weak*) faible; (*of drink*) léger. *To get* or *grow —*, s'adoucir. —**spirited,** -**tempered,** *adj.* d'un caractère doux [(*weaker*) plus faible
Milder, *adj.* plus doux; moins rigoureux;
Mildew, *s.* (*on plants*) rouille, *f.*; (*on cloth, paper*) tache d'humidité, piqûre, *f.*; — *v.a.* frapper de rouille; (*spoil*) tacher, gâter par l'humidité, piquer

Mildly, *adv.* doucement, avec douceur; mo-
Mildness, *s.* douceur, *f.* [dérément
Mile, *s.* mille, *m.* [5 —*s*, 8 kilomètres.] —**man,** *s.* cantonnier, *m.* —**post,** *s.* borne *or* colonne milliaire, *f.* —**stone,** *s.* pierre milliaire, *f.* [mille, *m.*
Mileage, *s.* prix par mille, *m.*; péage par
Milfoil, *s.* mille-feuilles, *f.*
Miliaria, *s.* fièvre miliaire, suette miliaire, *f.*
Miliary, *adj. s.* miliaire; (*relating to miles*) *V.* **Milliary.** *— fever*, fièvre miliaire, suette
Militant, *adj.* militant [miliaire, miliaire, *f.*
Militarily, *adv.* militairement
Militarism, *s.* militarisme, *m.*
Militarize, *v.a.* militariser
Military, *adj.* militaire; — *s.* militaires, soldats, *m.pl.*, troupes, *f.pl.*, troupe, armée, force armée, *f.* *— academy*, école militaire, *f.* *— examination*, examen *or* concours d'admission aux écoles militaires, *m.* *— man*, militaire, *m.* *— train*, V. **Train**
Militate, *v.n.* militer, combattre
Militia, *s.* garde nationale, *f.*; milice, *f.* — —**man,** *s.* garde nationale, *m.*; soldat de la milice, milicien, *m.*
Milk, *s.* lait, *m.*; *adj.* de lait; laiteux; à *or* au lait; — *v.a.* traire; (*in horse-racing slang*) faire parier sous main contre. *Condensed —*, lait concentré, *m.* —**and water,** *s.* lait coupé, *m.*; *adj.* de lait coupé; (*fig.*) fade; doux; d'eau sucrée; mou, indécis. —**can,** *s.* pot à (*or* au) lait, *m.* —**cart,** *s.* voiture de laitier, *f.* —**coffee,** *s.* café au lait, *m.* —**diet,** *s.* laitage, *m.*, diète lactée, *f.* —**fever,** *s.* fièvre laiteuse, fièvre de lait *f.* —**food,** *s.* laitage, *m.* —**maid,** *s.* laitière, *f.* —**man,** *s.* laitier, *m.* —**pail,** *s.* seau à lait, *m.* —**pan,** *s.* terrine *or* jatte à lait, *f.* —**porridge,** -**pottage,** *s.* soupe au lait, *f.* —**pot,** *s.* *V.* —**can.** —**receiver,** *s.* garde-sein, *m.* —**shop,** *s.* crèmerie, laiterie, *f.* —**sop,** *s.* poule mouillée, *f.* —**soup,** *s.* soupe au lait, *f.* —**sugar,** *s.* sucre de lait, *m.*, lactine, lactose, *f.* —**thistle,** *s.* chardon lacté, *m.* —**tooth,** dent de lait, *f.* —**trade,** *s.* laiterie, *f.* —**tree,** *s.* arbre à lait, *m.* —**walk,** *s.* clientèle de laitier, *f.* —**weed,** -**wort,** *s.* herbe au lait, *f.* —**white,** *adj.* blanc comme du lait. —**woman,** *s.* laitière, *f.*
Milker, *s.* personne qui trait, *f.*, trayeur, *m.*, -euse, *f.*; vacher, *m.*, -ère, *f.*; (*animal yielding milk*) laitière, *f.* [ceur, *f.*
Milkiness, *s.* nature laiteuse *f.*; (*fig.*) dou-
Milky, *adj.* laiteux; (*of milk*) de lait; (*yielding milk*) à lait; (*mild, soft*) doux; (*jewel.*) pâteux; (*astr.*) lacté. —**way,** *s.* voie lactée, galaxie, *f.*
Mill, *s.* moulin, *m.*; (*manufactory, works*) *V.* **Manufactory;** (*of fabrics*) fabrique, filature, *f.*; (*of coins*) moulinet; (*fight*) brossée, frottée, peignée, *f.*; — *v.a.* moudre; (*chocolate*) faire mousser; (*coin*) cordonner, créneler, machiner; (*cloth*, &c.) fouler; (*to beat*) moudre de coups, rouer de coups, rosser. —**board,** *s.* carton de pâte, *m.* —**board maker,** *s.* cartonnier, *m.* —**clack,** *s.* claquet de moulin, *m.* —**course,** *s.* biez, canal de moulin, *m.* —**dam,** *s.* écluse de moulin, *f.* —**dust,** *s.* folle farine, *f.* —**handle,** *s.* queue de moulin, *f.* —**hopper,** *s.* trémie, *f.* —**horse,** *s.* cheval de moulin, *m.* —**man,** *s.* (*of silk-trade*) organsineur, *m.* —**owner,** *s.* propriétaire de moulin, *m.*; (*manu.*) chef de fabrique, manufacturier, usinier, *m.* —**pond,** -**race,** *s.* biez, *m.* —**rind,** *s.* fer de moulin, *m.* —**stone,** *s.* meule de moulin, *f.*; (*min.*) pierre meulière, *f.* —**stone grit,** *s.* grès à meule, *m.*, pierre meulière, *f.* —**stone quarry,** *s.* meulière, *f.* —**wheel,** *s* roue de moulin, *f.* —**wright,** *s.* constructeur de moulins, *m.*; (*tech.*) ajusteur, *m.*
Milled, *part. adj.* moulu, &c. (*V.* **Mill,** *v.a.*); *— edge*, cordon, *m.* (*V.* **Double**)
Millefoil. *V.* **Milfoil**
Millenarian, *adj. s.* *V.* **Millenary**

Millenarianism, Millenarism, Millennianism, *s.* millénarisme, *m.*
Millenary, *adj.s.* millénaire, *adj.m.f., s.m.*
Millennial, *adj.* du millénaire
Millennialist, *s.* milléniste, *m.*
Millennium, *s.* millénium, *m.*; (*chron.*) millénaire, *m.*
Milleped, *s.* mille-pattes, mille-pieds, myriapode, *m.*
Millepore, *s.* millépore, *m.*
Miller, *s.* meunier, *m.*, -ière, *f.* —*'s wife,* meunière, *f.* —*'s dog,* (*fish*) milandre, *m.* —*'s thumb,* (*fish*) chabot, meunier, *m.*
Millesimal, *adj.* de millième
Millet, *s.* millet, *m.* — **grass,** *s.* millet, *m.* — **seed,** *s.* graine de millet, *f.*, millet, *m.*
Milliare, *s.* milliare, *m.*
Milliary, *adj.s.* milliaire, *adj.m.f., s.m.*
Milligramme, *s.* milligramme, *m.*
Millilitre, *s.* millilitre, *m.*
Millime, *s.* millime, *m.*
Millimetre, *s.m.* millimètre, *m.*
Milliner, *s.* modiste, *f.*, marchande de modes, *f.* *Man* —, modiste, *m.*, marchand de modes, *m.*
Millinery, *s.* modes, *f.pl.*
Milling, *s.* (*of cloth,* &c.) foulage, *m.*; (*coin.*) cordonnage, crénelage, machinage, *m.*; (*fighting*) *V.* **Mill,** *s.*
Million, *s.* million, *m.* *The* —, la multitude, *f.*, les masses, *f.pl.*, le peuple, *m.*, la masse du peuple, *f.* *Thousand —s,* billion, *m.*; (*fin.*) milliard, *m.* *Worth —s,* (*pers.*) millionnaire, riche à millions
Millionaire, *s.adj.* millionnaire, *m.f.*
Millionary, *adj.* de *or* par millions
Millionth, *adj.s.* millionième, *adj.m.f., s.m.*
Milliped. *V.* **Milleped**
Millistere, *s.* millistère, *m.*
Milt, *s.* rate, *f.*; (*of fish*) laitance, laite, *f.*; — *v.a.* féconder. — **wort,** *s.* doradille, *f.*
Milter, *s.* poisson laité, *m.*
Miltonian, *adj.* miltonien
Mime, *s.* mime, *m.*; (*pers.*) mime, *m.f.*; — *v.a.n.* mimer
Mimetic, *adj.* d'imitation
Mimic, *adj.* mimique; imitatif; (*pers.*) imitateur; — *s.* mime, *m.f.*; imitateur, *m.*, -trice, *f.*; — *v.a.* imiter, contrefaire. — **art,** *s.* mimique, *f.* — **beetle,** *s.* hister, *m.*
Mimical, *adj.* *V.* **Mimic**
Mimicker, *s.* contrefaiseur, *m.*, -euse, *f.*
Mimicology, *s.* mimicologie, *f.*
Mimicry, *s.* mimique, *f.*; bouffonnerie, *f.*; imitation, *f.*
Mimodrama, *s.* mimodrame, *m.*
Mimographer, *s.* mimographe, mimique, *m.*
Mimograph-ic, al, -ism, -y. *V.* page 3, § 1
Mimolog-ic, al, -ism, -y. *V.* page 3, § 1
Mimologist, *s.* mimologue, *m.*
Mimoplastic, *adj.* mimoplastique
Mimosa, *s.* mimosa, *m.*, mimeuse, *f.*
Mimulus, *s.* mimule, *m.*
Mina bird, *s.* mino, *m.*
Minaret, *s.* minaret, *m.*
Minatory, *adj.* menaçant
Mince, *v.a.* hacher menu, hacher; émincer; (*fig.*) atténuer, pallier; mâcher; (*words*) manger; — *v.n.* minauder; marcher avec affectation. *Not to — matters,* ne pas y aller par quatre chemins, ne pas mâcher ce qu'on pense, ne pas le mâcher, trancher le mot, parler franchement, ne rien cacher. —**meat,** *s.* émincé, hachis, *m.* —**pie,** *s.* pâté d'émincé, *m.*
Mincer, *s.* (*instr.*) hachoir, *m.*
Mincing, *adj.* minaudier, affecté. — **knife,** *s.* hachoir, *m.* — **machine,** *s.* machine à hacher, *f.*, hachoir, *m.*
Mincingly, *adv.* menu; (*fig.*) avec minauderie, avec affectation
Mind, *s.* esprit, *m.*; intelligence, tête, *f.*; (*soul*) âme, *f.*; (*heart*) cœur, *m.*; (*liking, inclination, desire*) goût, désir, *m.*, envie, *f.*; idée, *f.*; intention, *f.*; (*memory*) mémoire, *f.*; (*opinion*) opinion, *f.*, sentiment, avis, *m.* *Men's —s,* les esprits. *Right* —, esprit droit. *In my* —, dans mon esprit; (*opinion*) à mon avis. *In o.'s right* —, dans son bon sens. *Of one* —, d'accord, unanime, du même sentiment. *Of sound* —, sain d'esprit. *Of unsound* —, qui n'est pas sain d'esprit. *Time out of* —, de temps immémorial. *To alter* or *change o.'s* —, changer d'avis *or* d'idée; se raviser. *To bear* or *keep in* —, se souvenir de, se rappeler, ne pas oublier, penser à. *To be of the same* —, être d'accord, être du même sentiment. *To be easy, uneasy in o.'s* —, avoir, n'avoir pas l'esprit tranquille. *To be out of o.'s* —, *Not to be right in o.'s* —, (*be mad*) avoir perdu la raison *or* la tête. *To bring* or *call to* —, rappeler, rappeler le souvenir de; (*remember*) se rappeler. *To give o.'s — to,* s'adonner à. *To go out of o.'s* —, (*go mad*) perdre la raison *or* la tête. *That went out of my* —, cela m'est sorti de la tête. *To have a — to,* avoir envie de. *To have o.'s — clear about,* avoir le cœur net de. *To know o.'s own* —, savoir ce qu'on veut. *To make up o.'s* —, se décider; prendre son parti; se résigner. *To put one in — of a thing,* faire penser quelqu'un à une chose, rappeler une chose à quelqu'un. *To set o.'s — upon,* se mettre dans l'esprit, se mettre en tête. *To speak* or *tell o.'s* —, dire sa pensée *or* sa façon de penser, dire ce que l'on pense
Mind, *v.a.* faire attention à; s'occuper de; penser à, songer à; ne pas oublier (de); (*meddle with*) se mêler de; (*beware*) prendre garde à, (*before a verb*) prendre garde de; (*listen to*) écouter; (*take into account*) tenir compte de; (*care*) s'inquiéter de; (*have a care*) avoir soin de; (*watch*) veiller sur, surveiller; garder; (*stick at*) regarder à; (*fear*) craindre, avoir peur de. *I don't — !* cela m'est égal; je veux bien. *If you don't* —, si cela vous est égal; si vous le voulez bien; si vous n'y prenez garde. *Never — !* n'importe! peu importe! c'est égal! ne vous inquiétez pas; n'ayez pas peur; (*to a child hurt*) ce n'est rien; (*to a servant after ringing the bell,* &c.) j'ai ce que je voulais. *Never — ...,* ne vous inquiétez pas de ..., ne faites pas attention à ..., &c. — *you tell him so,* n'oubliez pas de le lui dire. — *you don't fall,* prenez garde de tomber
Minded, *adj.* disposé, porté, enclin; intentionné; à esprit ..., d'un esprit ...; (*of opinion*) d'un avis ...
Mindedness, *s.* disposition, inclination, *f.*
Mindful, *adj.* attentif (à), soigneux (de); (*bearing in mind*) qui se souvient (de)
Mindfully, *adv.* attentivement, soigneusement, avec soin
Mindfulness, *s.* attention, *f.*; soin, *m.*; souvenir, *m.*
Mindless, *adj.* inattentif (à), insouciant (de); (*forgetful*) oublieux (de)
Mine, *pron. poss.* le mien, la mienne, les miens, les miennes; mes; (*pron. pers.*) à moi, de moi. *This drawing is* —, (*belongs to me*) ce dessin est à moi; (*comes from me; I am the author of it*) ce dessin est de moi. *A friend of* —, un de mes amis, *m.*, une de mes amies, *f.* *An old aunt of* —, une vieille tante à moi. *That is no fault of* —, ce n'est pas ma faute
Mine, *s.* mine, *f.*; — *v.a.n.* miner; saper
Miner, *s.* mineur, *m.*
Mineral, *adj.s.* minéral, *adj.m.*, e, *f.*, minéral, *s.m.*
Mineralization, *s.* minéralisation, *f.*
Mineralize, *v.a.n.* minéraliser
Mineralog-ic, al, -ically, -ist, -y. *V.* page 3 § 1
Minever, *s.* petit-gris, *m.*
Mingle, *v.a.* mélanger; mêler; entremêler; confondre; — *v.n.* se mélanger; se mêler; s'entremêler; se confondre
Mingling, *s.* mélange, *m.*
Miniature, *s.* miniature, *f.*; — *adj.* en miniature. — **painter** *or* **paintress,** *s.* peintre en miniature, *m.f.*, miniaturiste, *m.f.* — **painting,** *s.* miniature, *f.*
Miniaturist, *s.* miniaturiste, *m f.*
Minikin, *adj.s.* mignon, petit; (— *pin*) camion, *m.*

Minim, *s.* nain, *m.*, e, *f.*; (*monk*) minime, *m.*; (*mus.*) blanche, *f.*; (*drop*) goutte, *f.* **— rest,** *s.* (*mus.*) demi-pause, *f.*
Minima, *s.pl.* minima, *m.pl.*
Minimess, *s.* (*nun*) minimesse, *f.*
Minimize, *v.a.* réduire *or* mettre au minimum
Minimum, *s.* minimum, *m.* **— thermometer,** *s.* thermomètre à minimum, *m.*
Mining, *adj.* minier; de *or* des mines; de mineur; — *s.* exploitation des mines, *f.*; travail dans les mines, *m.*
Minion, *s.* mignon, favori, *m.*; (*print. type*) mignonne, *f.* **—like, —ly,** *adv.* mignardement
Minister, *s.* ministre, *m.*; — *v.a.n.* donner, fournir, procurer; administrer; servir; (*do duty*) desservir; officier; (*relieve*) assister, secourir; (*provide*) pourvoir (à); (*contribute*) contribuer (à); (*take care of*) soigner
Ministerial, *adj.* ministériel; de ministre; des ministres; du gouvernement; (*eccl.*) d'ecclésiastique
Ministerialism, *s.* ministérialisme, *m.*
Ministerialist, *s.* ministériel, *m.*
Ministerially, *adv.* ministériellement
Ministration, *s.* ministère, *m.*; entremise, *f.*; office, service, *m.*; fonctions, *f.pl.*
Ministry, *s.* ministère, *m.*
Minium, *s.* minium, *m.*
Miniver. *V.* **Minever**
Mink, *s.* vison, *m.*
Minnikin. *V.* **Minikin**
Minnow, *s.* véron, *m.*
Minor, *adj.* moindre, minime, petit; léger; accessoire; secondaire; (*geog.*, *mus.*, *log.*, *of rel. orders*) mineur; — *s.* (*pers.*) mineur, *m.*, e, *f.*; (*log.*) mineure, *f.* *In a — key*, en mineur
Minorite, *s.* mineur, *m.*, e, *f.*
Minority, *s.* minorité, *f.*
Minotaur, *s.* Minotaure, *m.*
Minster, *s.* cathédrale, *f.*; monastère, *m.*
Minstrel, *s.* ménestrel, *m.*; musicien, *m.*, -ne, *f.*; (*jest.*) ménétrier, *m.* [ménestrel, *m.*
Minstrelsy, *s.* musique, *f.*, chant, *m.*; art du
Mint, *s.* monnaie, *f.*; hôtel de la monnaie, *m.*; (*fig.*) fabrique, *f.*; mine, *f.*, trésor, *m.*; (*bot.*) menthe, *f.*; — *v.a.* monnayer, frapper; (*fig.*) inventer, forger, fabriquer, controuver. **— man,** *s.* monnayeur, *m.* **— sauce,** *s.* sauce à la menthe, *f.*
Mintage, *s.* objet monnayé, *m.*; droit de monnayage, *m.*; (*fig.*) empreinte, *f.*
Minter, *s.* monnayeur, *m.*; (*fig.*) forgeur, fabricateur, inventeur, *m.* [invention, *f.*
Minting, *s.* monnayage, *m.*; (*fig.*) fabrication,
Minuet, *s.* menuet, *m.*
Minus, *adv.* moins; (*without*) sans; (*losing*) en perte de; — *s.* moins, *m.*
Minute, *adj.* menu; très petit; (*exact*) minutieux; — *s.* minute, *f.*; instant, *m.*; note, *f.*; **—s,** *pl.* minutes, &c.; (*of proceedings*) procès-verbal, *m.*; — *v.a.* minuter; prendre note de. *Many —s*, longtemps. *This —*, (*directly*) à l'instant. *This very —*, à l'instant même. *I am expecting him every —*, je l'attends d'un moment (*or* d'un instant) à l'autre. *To make a — of it*, en prendre note. **— book,** *s.* agenda, *m.*; carnet, *m.*; registre des procès-verbaux, *m.*; (*admin.*) journal (*or* registre) de correspondance et d'actes, *m.*; (*law*) plumitif, *m.* **— glass,** *s.* sablier d'une minute, *m.* **— gun,** *s.* (*nav.*) canon d'alarme, *m.* **— hand,** *s.* (*of dials*) aiguille des minutes, grande aiguille, *f.* **— watch,** *s.* montre à minutes, *f.*
Minutely, *adv.* menu; exactement, minutieusement, en détail; (*every minute*) à chaque minute, toutes les minutes; — *adj.* de chaque minute, de toutes les minutes
Minuteness, *s.* petitesse, *f.*; exiguïté, *f.*; minutie, *f.*; détails minutieux, *m.pl.*
Minutia, *s.*, **Minutiæ,** *s.pl.* minutie, *f.*, minuties, *f.pl.* [(*zool.*) *V.* **Mink**
Minx, *s.* coquine, friponne, *f.*; péronelle, *f.*;
Miny, *adj.* riche en mines; souterrain
Mirabelle, *s.* mirabelle, *f.*
Miracle, *s.* miracle, *m.* **— monger,** *s.* faiseur de miracles, *m.*
Miraculous, *adj.* miraculeux
Miraculously, *adv.* miraculeusement, d'une manière miraculeuse, par miracle
Miraculousness, *s.* nature miraculeuse, *f.*, caractère miraculeux, miraculeux, *m.*
Mirage, *s.* mirage, *m.*
Mire, *s.* boue, fange, bourbe, *f.*; (*place*) bourbier, *m.*; (*ant*) fourmi, *f.*; — *v.a.* embourber, enfoncer dans la fange; salir de boue, crotter; — *v.n.* s'embourber, s'enfoncer dans la fange, tomber dans un bourbier
Miriness, *s.* état boueux, état fangeux, *m.*
Mirky, &c. *V.* **Murky,** &c.
Mirror, *s.* miroir, *m.*, glace, *f.*; — *v.a.* miroiter, réfléchir. **— business, -making, -manufactory, -trade,** *s.* miroiterie, *f.* **— maker,** *s.* miroitier, *m.*, -ière, *f.*
Mirth, *s.* joie bruyante, joie, gaieté, *f.*; allégresse, *f.*; hilarité, *f.*, rire, *m.* **—ful,** *adj.* joyeux, gai **—fully,** *adv.* joyeusement, avec allégresse. **—less,** *adj.* triste, sans joie, sans
Miry, *adj.* boueux, fangeux, bourbeux [gaieté
Mis, (*in compounds*) mé-, més-, mal, à tort, à faux; mauvais, faux [ronée, *f.*
Misacceptation, *s.* acception fausse *or* er-
Misadventure, *s.* mésaventure, *f.*; désagrément, *m.*
Misadvise, *v.a.* conseiller mal, mal conseiller
Misadvised, *part. adj.* mal conseillé; (*things*) mal vu; imprudent, irréfléchi
Misallegation, *s.* fausse allégation, *f.*
Misallege, *v.a.* alléguer à tort
Misalliance, *s.* mésalliance, *f.*
Misally, *v.a.* mésallier [thrope, *m.*
Misanthrope, Misanthropist, *s.* misan-
Misanthropic, -al, *adj.* (*things*) misanthropique; (*pers.*) misanthrope
Misanthrop-ically, -y. *V.* page 3, § 1
Misapplication, *s.* fausse (*or* mauvaise) application, *f.*; mauvais emploi, abus, *m.*
Misapply, *v.a.* appliquer mal à propos; mal appliquer; mal employer; détourner
Misappreciate, *v.a.* mal apprécier
Misapprehend, *v.a.* se méprendre sur, comprendre mal, entendre mal [tendu, *m.*
Misapprehension, *s.* méprise, *f.*, malen-
Misappropriate, *v.a.* détourner, distraire
Misappropriation, *s.* détournement (de fonds), mauvais emploi, *m.*
Misarrange, *v.a.* arranger mal, mal arranger
Misarrangement, *s.* mauvais arrangement, *m.*
Misbecome, *v.a.* convenir mal à [venant
Misbecoming, *adj.* peu convenable; incon-
Misbecomingness, *s.* inconvenance, *f.*
Misbegot, Misbegotten, *adj.* illégitime
Misbehave, — oneself, *v.n.r.* se conduire mal, se comporter mal, avoir une mauvaise conduite [duite, *f.*
Misbehaviour, *s.* mauvaise conduite, incon-
Misbelief, *s.* fausse croyance, incrédulité, *f.*
Misbeliever, *s.* mécréant, infidèle, incrédule, *m.*
Misbelieving, *adj.* mécréant, infidèle, incrédule [culer; se tromper, s'abuser
Miscalculate, *v.a.n.* calculer mal, mal cal-
Miscalculation, *s.* faux (*or* mauvais) calcul, *m.*; erreur de calcul *or* de compte, erreur, *f.*; mécompte, *m.*
Miscall, *v.a.* nommer improprement
Miscarriage, *s.* insuccès, *m.*; affaire manquée, *f.*, coup manqué, *m.*; échec, *m.*; chute, *f.*; accident, *m.*; faute, *f.*; (*med.*) fausse couche, *f.*; avortement, *m.*
Miscarry, *v.n.* (*fail*) échouer, manquer, avorter, ne pas réussir; (*be lost*) faire fausse route, s'égarer, ne pas arriver à destination, ne pas parvenir; (*med.*) faire une fausse couche; avorter
Miscarrying, *s.* *V.* **Miscarriage**

Miscellanarian, *adj.* de mélanges; — *s.* auteur de mélanges, *m.*
Miscellaneous, *adj.* mêlé, varié; divers; général; de toute espèce; de mélanges; d'articles divers; (*in accounts, statistics*) divers. — *news,* faits divers, *m.pl.* — *works,* mélanges, *m.pl.* [riété, *f.*
Miscellaneousness, *s.* mélange, *m.*, va-
Miscellanist, *s.* auteur de mélanges, *m.*
Miscellany, *s.* mélange, *m.*; (*books*) mélanges, *m.pl.*
Mischance, *s.* mauvaise chance, *f.*; malheur, *m.*, infortune, *f.*; mésaventure, *f.*, accident, *m.*
Mischarge, *v.a.* porter à tort au compte de; — *s.* somme portée à tort au compte de
Mischief, *s.* mal, *m.*; tort, dommage, *m.*; dégât, *m.*; (*wickedness*) méchanceté, *f.*; malice, *f.* *For —, out of —,* par méchanceté, par malice. *To make — between,* brouiller. — **maker,** *s.* brouillon, brandon de discorde, *m.* — **making,** *adj.* malfaisant, qui sème la discorde
Mischievous, *adj.* méchant, malicieux; malfaisant; (*things*) nuisible, pernicieux, méchant, mauvais
Mischievously, *adv.* méchamment, malicieusement, mal; (*with injury*) nuisiblement, pernicieusement
Mischievousness, *s.* malice, méchanceté, *f.*; mal, *m.*; malfaisance, *f.*, caractère malfaisant, *m.*, nature nuisible, *f.*
Mischoose, *v.a.* mal choisir
Miscibility, *s.* miscibilité, *f.*
Miscible, *adj.* miscible [**Misquote**
Miscitation, Miscite. *V.* **Misquotation,**
Miscomputation, Miscompute. *V.* **Miscalculation, Miscalculate**
Misconceive, *v.a.n.* concevoir mal, juger mal
Misconception, *s.* idée fausse, *f.*; malentendu, *m.*
Misconduct, *v.a.* conduire mal; mal diriger, mal gérer; — *s.* mauvaise conduite, inconduite, *f.*; (*of business*) mauvaise gestion, *f.* *To — oneself,* se conduire mal
Misconjecture, *s.* fausse conjecture, *f.*; — *v.a.n.* mal conjecturer, conjecturer à tort
Misconstruction, *s.* fausse (*or* mauvaise) interprétation, mésinterprétation, *f.*; contresens, *m.*
Misconstrue, *v.a.* interpréter mal, mésinterpréter; interpréter en mauvaise part; traduire mal; dénaturer [mal, *f.*; faux interprète, *m.*
Misconstruer, *s.* personne qui interprète
Miscopy, *v.a.* mal copier, copier incorrecte-
Miscounsel, *v.a.* *V.* **Misadvise** [ment
Miscount, *v.a.n.* compter mal, mal compter; — *s.* erreur de calcul, *f.*
Miscreant, *s.* mécréant, *m.*; (*wretch*) misérable, vaurien, gredin, *m.*; — *adj.* vil, infâme
Misdate, *v.a.* dater mal, mal dater; — *s.* fausse date, *f.*
Misdeal, *s.* maldonne, *f.*; — *v.a.n.* maldonner
Misdeed, *s.* méfait, *m.* [se comporter mal
Misdemean oneself, *v.r.* se conduire mal,
Misdemeanant, *s.* délinquant, *m.*, e, *f.*
Misdemeanour, *s.* mauvaise conduite, inconvenance, *f.*; offense, faute, *f.*; (*law*) délit, *m.*
Misdirect, *v.a.* diriger (*or* &c., *V.* **Direct**) mal; (*letters, &c.*) mettre mal l'adresse [adresse, *f.*
Misdirection, *s.* fausse direction, *f.*; fausse
Misdo, *v.a.n.* faire mal
Misdoer, *s,* malfaiteur, *m.*, -trice, *f.*
Misdoing, *s.* faute, offense, *f.*; méfait, *m.*
Misemploy, *v.a.* employer mal, mal employer
Misemployment, *s.* mauvais emploi, mauvais usage, *m.* [faux; (*com.*) contre-poser
Misenter, *v.a.* inscrire inexactement (*or* à
Misentry, *s.* inscription fausse *or* inexacte, *f.*; (*com.*) contre-position, *f.* [avare; sordide
Miser, *s.* avare, *m.f.* — **like,** *adj.* d'avare,
Miserable, *adj.* misérable; malheureux; (*in a wasted condition*) délabré; (*horrid*) horrible, affreux; (*paltry*) pitoyable, méchant; (*shabby*) mesquin. *To make anyone's life —,* rendre la vie dure à quelqu'un
Miserably, *adv.* misérablement; malheureusement; horriblement; affreusement; pitoyablement; mesquinement
Miserableness, *s.* condition misérable, *f.*, état misérable, *m.*; (*wasted condition*) délabrement, *m.* [miséricorde, *f.*
Miserere, *s.* (*Cath. lit.*) miséréré, *m.*; (*arch.*)
Miserly, *adj.* d'avare, avare; sordide
Misery, *s.* misère, *f.*; tourment, supplice, *m.*; (*suffering, sufferings*) souffrance, *f.*, souffrances, *f.pl.* *To put one out of his —,* mettre fin aux souffrances de quelqu'un [mal
Misestimate, *v.a.* estimer à tort; apprécier
Misfashion, *v.a.* former mal, mal former, façonner mal, mal façonner [action, *f.*
Misfeasance, *s.* dommage, tort, *m.*, mauvaise
Misfit, *s.* vêtement manqué, pour-compte, loup, *m.*; (*boots*) chaussure manquée, *f.*
Misform, *v.a.* *V.* **Misshape**
Misfortune, *s.* malheur, *m.*; calamité, *f.*; infortune, *f.* —*s never come single,* un malheur n'arrive jamais seul
Misgive, *v.a.* faire craindre à; faire pressentir; inspirer des doutes *or* de la méfiance à; manquer à [doute, *m.*; méfiance, *f.*; soupçon, *m.*
Misgiving, *s.* crainte, *f.*; pressentiment, *m.*;
Misgovern, *v.a.* gouverner mal; mal administrer; (*of business*) mal gérer
Misgovernment, *s.* mauvais gouvernement, *m.*; mauvaise administration, *f.*; (*of business*) mauvaise gestion, *f.*
Misguidance, *s.* fausse direction, *f.*
Misguide, *v.a.* diriger mal, guider mal; égarer; fourvoyer; (*to blind*) aveugler
Misguided, *part. adj.* mal dirigé, mal guidé; mal inspiré; (*astray*) égaré; fourvoyé; abusé; (*blinded*) aveuglé, aveugle
Mishap, *s.* malheur, *m.*, mésaventure, *f.*; accident, contre-temps, désagrément, *m.*
Mishmash, *s.* mélange, galimatias, salmigondis, fatras, *m.*, galimafrée, *f.*, pot-pourri, mêli-mêlo, *m.*
Misinform, *v.a.* informer mal, instruire mal; mal renseigner, donner de faux renseignements à [information inexacte, *f.*
Misinformation, *s.* faux renseignement, *m.*,
Misinstruct, *v.a.* instruire mal, enseigner mal
Misinstruction, *s.* mauvaise *or* fausse instruction, *f.* [*information*) faux renseignement, *m.*
Misintelligence, *s.* mésintelligence, *f.*; (*mis-*
Misinterpret, Misinterpretation. *V.* **Misconstrue, Misconstruction**
Misjoin, *v.a.* joindre mal; joindre à tort
Misjudge, *v.a.* juger mal, mal juger, méjuger; — *v.n.* méjuger (de), se tromper (sur)
Misjudgment, *s.* jugement erroné, *m.*, fausse idée, *f.*; jugement inique, *m.* [égarer
Mislay, *v.a.* placer mal, mal placer; (*lose*)
Mislead, *v.a.* égarer, fourvoyer, faire tromper, induire en erreur; (*seduce*) tromper, séduire
Misletoe. *V.* **Mistletoe**
Mismanage, *v.a.* conduire mal, diriger mal, administrer mal; gérer mal; gaspiller; — *v.n.* s'y prendre mal
Mismanagement, *s.* mauvaise conduite, mauvaise direction, mauvaise administration, *f.*; mauvais arrangement, *m.*; (*of business*) mauvaise gestion, *f.*
Mismanager, -ess, *s.* mauvais administrateur, *m.*, mauvaise administratrice, *f.*; mauvais gérant, *m.*, mauvaise gérante, *f.*; personne qui conduit mal *or* dirige mal, *f.*; mauvaise femme de ménage, *f.*; brouillon, *m.*, -ne, *f.*
Mismatch, *v.a.* assortir mal, mal assortir, appareiller mal; mésallier
Mismeasure, *v.a.* mesurer mal [nommer
Misname, *v.a.* nommer improprement, mal
Misnomer, *s.* nom *or* titre mal approprié, *m.*, fausse appellation, appellation impropre, *f.*; erreur de nom, *f.*, faux nom, *m.*

Misogamist, *s.* misogame, *m.f.*
Misogamy, *s.* misogamie, *f.*
Misogynist, *s.* misogyne, *m.*
Misogyny, *s.* misogynie, *f.*
Mispersuasion, *s.* fausse persuasion, fausse opinion, *f.*
Misplace, *v.a.* placer mal, mal placer ; déplacer
Mispoint, *v.a.* ponctuer mal
Mispointing, *s.* mauvaise ponctuation, *f.*
Misprint, *v.a.* imprimer incorrectement; — *s.* faute d'impression, erreur typographique, *f.*
Misprision, *s.* erreur, méprise, inadvertance, négligence, *f.*
Mispronounce, *v.a.n.* prononcer mal
Mispronunciation, *s.* mauvaise prononciation, *f.*
Misproportion, *v.a.* proportionner mal
Misquotation, *s.* fausse citation, citation inexacte, *f.*
Misquote, *v.a.* citer mal, citer à faux, citer inexactement
Misreckon, *v.a.n.*, **Misreckoning,** *s.* *V.* **Miscalculate** and **Miscalculation**
Misreport, *v.a.* rapporter inexactement; — *s.* rapport inexact, faux rapport, *m.*
Misrepresent, *v.a.* représenter mal, représenter sous un faux jour, dénaturer, altérer, fausser; calomnier; travestir
Misrepresentation, *s.* compte-rendu inexact, faux rapport, faux exposé, *m.*; déguisement, *m.*
Misrule, *s.* désordre, *m.*, confusion, *f.*, tumulte, *m.*; mauvaise administration, *f.*, mauvais gouvernement, gouvernement tyrannique, *m.*, tyrannie, *f.*
Miss, *s.* (*pers.*) mademoiselle, *f.*; demoiselle, *f.*; (*fail to hit*) manque de touche, *m.*; coup perdu, *m.*; (*loss*) perte, *f.*; (*want*) manque, *m.*; (*error, mistake*) erreur, faute, méprise, *f.*; pas de clerc, *m.*; (*failure*) affaire manquée, *f.*, coup manqué, *m.* *Yes, —*, oui, mademoiselle. *A little —*, une petite demoiselle. *— Smith*, mademoiselle Smith. *The —es Smith*, Mesdemoiselles Smith, les demoiselles Smith. *The two —es Smith*, les deux demoiselles Smith
Miss, *v.a.n.* manquer; s'apercevoir de (*or* remarquer) l'absence de; s'apercevoir que (...) manque, ne pas voir, ne plus voir; regretter l'absence de; regretter; (*not to find*) ne pas trouver, ne plus trouver; (*be in want of*) avoir besoin de; (*mistake*) se tromper de; (*lose*) perdre; (*leave out*) passer, omettre; (*do without*) se passer de; (*billiards*) manquer de touche. *I —ed my aim*, je manquai mon but. *I — a book*, il me manque un livre. *I — her*, je m'aperçois de son absence; je regrette son absence; je la regrette; elle me manque. *I — that*, cela me fait défaut. *To be —ing*, manquer; être absent; faire défaut; avoir disparu. **— cue,** *s.* (*at billiards*) fausse queue, *f.* **— fire,** *s.* raté, *m.* **— out,** *v.a.* passer, omettre
Missal, *s.* missel, *m.*
Missaying, *s.* expression impropre, *f.*
Missel. **— bird, -thrush,** *s.* draine, lutrone, *f.*
Misshape, *v.a.* former mal; (*deform*) défigurer, rendre difforme
Misshaped, Misshapen, *adj.* difforme, contrefait
Missile, *adj.* de jet, de trait, projectile; — *s.* projectile, *m.*
Missing, *part. adj.* manquant, égaré, perdu, &c. (*V.* **Miss,** *v.a.n.*); qui manque; de moins; absent; disparu. *Killed, wounded, or —*, tués, blessés, ou disparus. *To be —*, *V.* **Miss,** *v.a.n.*
Mission, *s.* mission, *f.*
Missionary, *s.* missionnaire, *m.*; — *adj.* de mission; des missions; de missionnaire
Missive, *s.adj.* missive, *f.*
Misspell, *v.a.* épeler mal; (*of writing*) écrire mal, mal écrire, écrire incorrectement
Misspelling, *s.* orthographe vicieuse, *f.*; faute d'orthographe, *f.*
Misspend, *v.a.* dissiper, gaspiller, dépenser follement, dépenser mal à propos, prodiguer; employer mal, mal employer
Misstate, *v.a.* rapporter inexactement *or* incorrectement, exposer inexactement, rendre un compte inexact de
Misstatement, *s.* rapport inexact *or* incorrect, exposé inexact, *m.*
Mist, *s.* brouillard, *m.*, brume, *f.*; (*drizzle*) bruine, *f.*; (*fig.*) nuage, *m.*
Mistakable, *adj.* susceptible d'être mal compris, qui prête à l'erreur
Mistake, *v.a.n.* se méprendre (à, sur); se tromper (de, sur); (*for* ...) prendre (pour ...). *To — o.'s* ..., se tromper de ... *To be —n*, se tromper, se méprendre, être dans l'erreur. *To be much —n*, se tromper fort. *If I — not*, si je ne me trompe
Mistake, *s.* (*taking one for another*) méprise, *f.*; (*wrong notion, error*) erreur, *f.*; (*failing*) faute, *f.* *By —* (*inadvertence*), par mégarde. *To lie under a —*, être dans l'erreur. *And no —!* j'en réponds! à coup sûr!
Mistaken, *adj.* (*pers.*) dans l'erreur; aveugle; (*things*) erroné, faux; aveugle; mal entendu
Mistakenly, Mistakingly, *adv.* par erreur, par méprise; faussement
Mistaught, *adj.* mal élevé
Misteach, *v.a.* mal enseigner, mal instruire
Mister, *s.* *V.* **Mr.**; — *v.a.* appeler "Monsieur"
Misterm, *v.a.* nommer improprement
Mistime, *v.a.* faire à contre-temps
Mistimed, *adj.* inopportun; déplacé
Mistiness, *s.* état brumeux, *m.*; brouillard, *m.*; (*fig.*) obscurité, *f.*
Mistitle, *v.a.* donner un faux titre à
Mistle. **— bird, -thrush,** *s.* draine, lutrone, *f.*
Mistletoe, *s.* gui, *m.* **— thrush,** *s.* draine, lutrone, *f.*
Mistral, *s.* mistral, *m.*
Mistranslate, *v.a.* traduire mal, mal traduire
Mistranslation, *s.* mauvaise traduction, traduction inexacte, *f.*; contre-sens, *m.*
Mistress, *s.* maîtresse, *f.*; (*directress*) directrice, *f.*; (*governess*) institutrice, *f.*; (*intended*) prétendue, future, *f.*; (*title*) Madame, *f.* *My —, or — is not at home,* (*servant speaking*) Madame n'y est pas
Mistrust, *v.a.* se méfier de; se défier de; soupçonner; — *s.* méfiance, *f.*; défiance, *f.*; soupçon, *m.* **—ful,** *adj.* méfiant; défiant; soupçonneux. **—fully, —ingly,** *adv.* avec méfiance; avec défiance. **—less,** *adj.* sans méfiance; sans défiance; confiant
Mistune, *v.a.* accorder mal; désaccorder
Misty, *adj.* brumeux; (*of light*, &c.) vaporeux; (*fig.*) obscur
Misunderstand, *v.a.* comprendre mal, mal comprendre, entendre mal; se méprendre sur le sens de
Misunderstanding, *s.* conception erronée, *f.*; (*mistake*) malentendu, *m.*; (*disagreement*) mésintelligence, *f.*
Misusage, *s.* mauvais usage, mauvais emploi, *m.*; abus, *m.*; mauvais traitements, *m.pl.*; (*misapplication*) application fausse *or* erronée, *f.*
Misuse, *v.a.* abuser de, mésuser de; (*ill-treat*) maltraiter; — *s.* *V.* **Misusage**
Mite, *s.* (*insect*) mite, *f.*; (*a trifle*) rien, iota, centime, *m.*; légère offrande, *f.*; obole, *f.*; ('*widow's*') denier, *m.*
Mitigable, *adj.* qui peut s'adoucir, susceptible d'adoucissement
Mitigant, *adj.* adoucissant; qui apaise, qui calme, qui mitige; qui tempère
Mitigate, *v.a.* adoucir, calmer, apaiser; mitiger; tempérer, modérer; atténuer
Mitigation, *s.* adoucissement, *m.*; mitigation, *f.*; soulagement, *m.*; atténuation, *f.*
Mitigative, Mitigatory, *adj.* mitigatif; adoucissant; qui apaise, qui calme, qui mitige; qui tempère
Mitral, *adj.* mitral
Mitre, *s.* mitre, *f.*; (*build.*) onglet, *m.*; — *v.a.* orner d'une mitre; (*build.*) assembler à onglet. **— bearer,** *s.* porte-mitre, *m.*
Mitred, *adj.* mitré; (*build.*) à *or* en onglet
Mitriform, *adj.* mitriforme
Mitt, *s.* miton, *m.*, mitaine, *f.*

Mitten, *s.* mitaine, *f.*
Mittimus, *s.* (*civ. law*) ordre de renvoi de pièces, *m.*; (*crim. law*) mandat de dépôt, *m.*
Mity, *adj.* qui a des mites, plein de mites
Mix, *v.a.* mêler ('*with*,' avec; *fig.* de, à), mélanger; (*a salad*) retourner; (*pharm.*) mixtionner; — *v.n.* se mêler, se mélanger; fréquenter [mélangé; mixte; (*chem.*) composé
Mixed, *adj.* mêlé ('*with*,' avec; *fig.* de, à);
Mixture, *s.* mélange, *m.*; (*pharm.*) mixtion, *f.*, (*compound, specific*) mixture, *f.*
Mizen, Mizzen, *s.* artimon, *m.* — **mast,** *s.* mât d'artimon, *m.* — **stay,** *s.* étai d'artimon, *m.* — **top,** *s* hune d'artimon, *f.* — **yard,** *s.* vergue d'artimon, *f.*
Mizzle, *v.n.* brouillasser, bruiner; — *s.* brouillard, *m.*, bruine, *f.*
Mnemonic, -al, *adj.* mnémonique
Mnemonically, *adv.* mnémoniquement
Mnemonics, *s.pl.* mnémonique, *f.* [*m.*, -ne, *f.*
Mnemotechnician, *s.* mnémotechnicien,
Mnemotechny, *s.* mnémotechnie, *f.*
Moabite, *s.adj.* Moabite, *m.f.*
Moan, *v.n.* gémir, se lamenter; geindre; — *v.a.* pleurer, déplorer, gémir sur, se lamenter sur; — *s.* gémissement, *m.*, lamentation, plainte, *f.* —**ful,** *adj.* plaintif, lamentable; (*gloomy*) lugubre, triste. —**fully,** *adv.* plaintivement, lamentablement; (*gloomily*) lugubrement, tristement
Moaning, *s. V.* **Moan,** *s.*
Moat, *s.* fossé, *m.*; — *v.a.* entourer (*or* environner) d'un fossé *or* de fossés
Mob, *s.* (*crowd*) foule, cohue, *f*; rassemblement, attroupement, *m.*; (*rabble*) populace, canaille, *f.*, bas peuple, *m.*; — *v.a.* houspiller. — **cap,** *s.* simple bonnet, *m.*, cornette, *f.* — **rule,** *s.* ochlocratie, voyoucratie, *f.*
Mobile, *adj.* mobile
Mobility, *s.* mobilité, *f.*; agilité, activité, *f.*; (*fickleness*) légèreté, inconstance, *f.*; (*mob*) populace, canaille, *f.*, bas peuple, *m.*
Mobilizable, *adj.* mobilisable
Mobilization, *s.* mobilisation, *f.*
Mobilize, *v.a.* mobiliser
Mobocracy, *s.* voyoucratie, *f.*
Mocassin, Moccasin, Moccassin, *s.* (*shoe*) mocassin, *m.*; (*snake*) trigonocéphale, *m.*
Mocha, *s.* (*coffee*) moka, *m.* — **stone,** *s.* agate mousseuse, *f.*
Mock, *v.a.n.* se moquer de, se jouer de, se rire de, railler; (*deceive*) tromper, frustrer; — *s. V.* **Mockery;** — *adj.* dérisoire; burlesque; (*false*) faux; contrefait; imitation de; simulé; pour rire. — **doctor (The),** *s.* (*of Molière*) le médecin malgré lui, *m.* — **fight,** *s. V.* **Sham.** — **heroic,** *adj.* héroi-comique. — **lead,** *s.* blende, *f.* — **moon,** *s.* parasélène, *f.* — **orange,** *s.* seringa, seringat, *m.* — **privet,** *s.* phillyrée, *f.* — **sun,** *s.* parhélie, *m.* — **turtle,** *s. V.* **Turtle**
Mocker, *s.* moqueur, *m.*, -euse, *f.*, railleur, *m.*, -euse, *f.*; trompeur, *m.*, -euse, *f.*, imposteur, *m.*
Mockery, *s.* moquerie, raillerie, *f.*; dérision, *f.*; risée, *f.*; (*sport*) jouet, jeu, *m.*; (*false show*) illusion, *f.*
Mocking, *s. V.* **Mockery;** — *adj.* moqueur. — **bird,** *s.* oiseau moqueur, *m.* — **stock,** *s.* risée, *f.*, jouet, *m.*
Mockingly, *adv.* en se moquant, par dérision
Mocmain, *s.* soie végétale, *f.*
Modal, *adj.* modal
Modality, *s.* modalité, *f.*
Mode, *s.* mode, manière, façon, *f.*; genre, *m.*; (*form*) mode, *m.*, forme, *f.*; (*degree*) degré, *m.*; (*gram., mus.,* &c.) mode, *m.*
Model, *s.* modèle, *m.*; — *adj.* modèle; — *v.a.* modeler; former, faire, façonner, dessiner, tracer
Modeller, *s.* dessinateur, *m.*; (*arts*) modeleur, *m.*
Modelling, *s.* (*act*) modelage, *m.*; (*result*) modelé, *m.*; (*art*) plastique, *f.*
Modenese, *s.adj.* Modénais, *m.*, e, *f.*, Modénois, *m.*, e, *f.*
Moderate, *v.a.* modérer, tempérer; adoucir; — *v.n.* se modérer; — *adj.* modéré; (*in value*) modique; (*middling*) ordinaire; passable; médiocre; raisonnable
Moderately, *adv.* modérément; modiquement; passablement; médiocrement; raisonnablement
Moderateness, *s.* modicité, *f.*; médiocrité, *f.*; (*state*) état modéré, état moyen, *m.*
Moderation, *s.* modération, *f.* *In* —, modérément, raisonnablement, avec mesure
Moderating, *adj.* modérateur; — *s.* modération, *f.*
Moderator, *s.* modérateur, *m.*; (*of assemblies*) président, *m.*; (*univers.*) examinateur, *m.* — **lamp,** *s.* lampe à modérateur, lampe modérateur, *f.* [*f.pl.*; présidence, *f.*
Moderatorship, *s.* fonctions de modérateur,
Moderatrix, *s.* modératrice, *f.*
Modern, *adj.s.* moderne, *adj.m.f.*, *s.m.*
Modern-ism, -ist. *V.* page 3, § 1
Modernization, *s.* modernisation, *f.*
Modernize, *v.a.* moderniser, rendre moderne, rajeunir; (*arch.*) moderner
Modernly, *adv.* modernement
Modernness, *s.* modernité, *f.*
Modest, *adj.* modeste
Modestly, *adv.* modestement, avec modestie
Modesty, *s.* modestie, *f.*
Modicum, *s.* petite portion, petite *or* faible quantité, *f.*, peu, *m.*, pitance, *f.*
Modifiability, *s.* modifiabilité, *f.*
Modifiable, *adj.* modifiable
Modification, *s.* modification, *f.*
Modificative, *s.* modificatif, *m.*
Modificatory, *adj.* modificatif
Modifier, *s.* modificateur, *m.*, -trice, *f.*
Modify, *v.a.* modifier; — *v.n.* faire des modifications
Modifying, *adj.* modificateur
Modillion, *s.* modillon
Modish, *adj.* à la mode, de mode
Modishly, *adv.* à la mode
Modishness, *s.* asservissement à la mode, *m.*
Modular, *adj.* modulaire
Modulate, *v.a.* moduler
Modulation, *s.* modulation, mélodie, *f.*
Modulator, *s.* modulateur, *m.*, -trice, *f.*
Module, Modulus, *s.* module, *m.*
Mogul, *s.* mogol, *m.*
Mohair, *s.* poil de chèvre, *m.*; (*cloth*) mohair, *m.*
Mohammedan, &c. *V.* **Mahomedan,** &c.
Mohican, *s.* Mohican, *m.*
Moiety, *s.* moitié, *f.*
Moil, *v.n.* fatiguer, s'échiner
Moire, *s.* moire, *f.*
Moist, *adj.* moite, humide
Moisten, *v.a.* humecter, rendre humide
Moistness, Moisture, *s.* moiteur, humidité, *f.*
Mokassin. *V.* **Mocassin**
Moke, *s.* (*donkey*) âne, *m.*, bourrique, *f.*, grison, *m.*
Molar, *adj.* molaire
Molasses, *s.pl.* mélasse, *f.*
Moldavian, *s.adj.* Moldave, *m.f.* [*m.f.*
Moldo-Wallachian, *s.adj.* Moldo-Valaque,
Mole, *s.* (*of harbours*) môle, *m.*, jetée, *f.*; (*of works*) digue, pile, *f.*; (*spot*) tache de naissance, *f.*, grain de beauté, signe, *m.*, (*med.*) môle, *f.*; (*animal*) taupe, *f.*; — *v.a.* étaupiner. — **bat, -but,** *s.* môle, *f.* — **catcher,** *s.* taupier, *m.* — **cricket,** *s.* taupe-grillon, taupette, courtilière, *f.* — **hill,** *s.* taupinière, *f.* — **rat,** *s.* spalax, rat-taupe, *m.* — **skin,** *s.* moleskin, moleskine, *f.* — **track,** *s.* traînée de taupe, *f.* — **trap,** *s.* taupière, *f.*
Molecular, *adj.* moléculaire
Molecule, *s.* molécule, *f.*
Molest, *v.a.* molester, tourmenter, inquiéter
Molestation, *s.* molestation, contrariété, vexation, importunité, *f.*; embarras, encombre, *m.*

Molin-ism, -ist. *V.* page 3, § 1
Mollification, *s.* mollification, *f.*, amollissement, *m.*; adoucissement, *m.*
Mollify, *v.a.* mollifier, amollir; (*assuage*) adoucir; (*calm*) apaiser, calmer
Mollusc, *s.* mollusque, *m.* [couche, *m.*
Molly-coddle, *s.* fouille-au-pot, chauffe-la-
Molten, *adj.* fondu, de fonte. — *calf*, veau
Molybdenum, *s.* molybdène, *m.* [d'or, *m.*
Moment, *s.* moment, *m.*; instant, *m.*; importance, *f.*; (*mech.*) moment, *m.* *At every* —, à tout moment, à chaque instant. *At the present* —, en ce moment, à l'heure qu'il est, à présent, maintenant, actuellement. *Every* —, à tout moment, d'un moment à l'autre, à chaque instant. *In a* —, (*presently*) dans un moment; (*in no time*) en un instant, à l'instant, aussitôt, en un clin d'œil. *The* — (*that*), (*as soon as*) aussitôt que, dès que. *This* —, (*directly, just now*) à l'instant. *This very* —, à l'instant même
Momentarily, *adv.* momentanément; à tout moment, à chaque instant
Momentary, *adj.* momentané; de tous les instants, continuel; imminent
Momently, *adv.* momentanément; à tout moment, d'un moment à l'autre, à chaque instant; dans un moment
Momentous, *adj.* important, de la dernière importance; difficile, critique [comble, *m.*
Momentum, *s.* (*mech.*) moment, *m.*; (*height*)
Monachal, *adj.* monacal
Monachally, *adv.* monacalement
Monachism, *s.* monachisme, *m.*
Monad, *s.* monade, *f.*
Monad-ic, al, -ism, -ist. *V.* page 3, § 1
Monarch, *s.* monarque, *m.* [*V.* page 3, § 1
Monarch-ic, al, -ically, -ism, -ist, -y.
Monarchistic, *adj.* monarchiste
Monarchize, *v.a.n.* monarchiser
Monastery, *s.* monastère, *m.*
Monastic,-al, *adj.* monastique; — *s.* moine, *m.*
Monastically, *adv.* en moine
Monasticism, *s.* monasticité, vie monastique, *f.*
Monday, *s.* lundi, *m.* *To keep Saint-* —, faire
Monetary, *adj.* monétaire [le lundi
Monetization, *s.* monétisation, *f.*
Monetize, *v.a.* monétiser
Money, *s.* argent, *m.*; (*coin*) monnaie, *f.*; pièces, *f.pl.*; (*price*) prix, *m.*; (*sum*) somme, *f.*; —**s**, *pl.* propriété, *f.*; fonds, *m.pl.*; deniers, *m.pl.* *Even* —, somme ronde, *f.*, compte rond, *m.* *Hard* —, espèces, *f.pl.*, numéraire, *m.* *Public* —, deniers publics, *m.pl.* *Made of* —, (*pers.*) cousu d'or. *Ready* —, — *down*, argent comptant. *To be worth* —, avoir du prix, avoir de la valeur, valoir de l'argent; (*pers.*) avoir du bien, avoir de la fortune, être riche. *To make* —, faire de l'argent. — **agent,** *s.* banquier, *m.* — **article,** *s.* (*of newspapers*) bulletin financier, *m.* — **bag,** *s.* sac à argent, *m.*, sacoche, *f.* — **bill,** *s.* loi de finances, *f.* — **box,** *s.* tirelire, *f.*; caisse, *f.*; cassette, *f.* — **broker -changer, -dealer,** *s.* changeur, *m.*, -euse, *f.* (de monnaies). — **grubber,** *s.* grippe-sou, *m.* — **grubbing,** *adj.* accumulateur, parcimonieux, avare; *s.* gains sordides, *m.pl.* — **jobber,** *s.* agioteur, *m.* — **lender,** *s.* prêteur d'argent, *m.*; (*com.*) bailleur de fonds, *m.* —**less,** *adj.* sans argent, sans le sou, pauvre. — **making,** *adj.* qui fait de l'argent; *s.* action de faire de l'argent, *f.*, gain, *m.* — **market** *s.* Bourse, *f.* — **market intelligence,** *s.* (*of newspapers*) bulletin financier, *m.* — **matter,** *s.* affaire d'argent, *f.* — **order,** *s.* mandat, *m.* — **pot,** *s.* tirelire, *f.* — **taker,** *s.* (*theat.*) buraliste, *m.f.* — **till,** *s.* caisse de comptoir, *f.* — **wort,** *s.* herbe aux écus, nummulaire, monnayère, lysimaque, lysimachie, *f.* [(*things*) en argent
Moneyed, *adj.* (*pers.*) riche, qui a de l'argent;
Monger, *s.* (*in compounds*) marchand (de ...), *m.*, e, *f.*; débitant (de ...), *m.*, e, *f.*

Mongol, Mongolian, *s.adj.* Mongol, *m.*, e, *f.*
Mongoose. *V.* **Mangouste**
Mongrel, *adj.* métis, bâtard; (*fig.*) mélangé; bâtard; — *s.* métis, *m.*, -se, *f.*
Monied. *V.* **Moneyed**
Monition, *s.* admonition, *f.*, avertissement, avis, conseil, *m.*; indication, *f.*, indice, *m.*; (*eccl.*) monition, *f.*
Monitor, *s.* moniteur, *m.*; (*zool., nav.*) monitor, *m.*
Monitorial, Monitory, *adj.* d'admonition, d'avertissement; (*of monitors*) de moniteur; (*of schools*) par des moniteurs, au moyen de moniteurs; (*eccl.*) monitorial, monitoire; — *s.*
Monitress, *s.* monitrice, *f.* [monitoire, *m.*
Monk, *s.* moine, religieux, *m.* — **bat,** *s.* (*zool.*) myoptère, mulot volant, *m.* — **fish,** *s.* ange de mer, *m.* —**'s hood,** *s.* (*bot.*) aconit, *m.*
Monkery, *s.* moinerie, *f.*
Monkey, *s.* singe, *m.*, (*she* —) guenon, *f.*; (*tech., rammer*) mouton, *m.* *She* —, guenon, *f.* — **flower,** *s.* mimule, *m.* — **trick,** *s.* singerie, *f.*
Monkhood, *s.* moinerie, *f.*
Monkish, *adj.* de moine, monacal
Monkishness, *s.* moinerie, *f.*
Monochord, *s.* monocorde, *m.*
Monochrom-atic, -y. *V.* page 3, § 1
Monocle, *s.* monocle, *m.* [cotylédonée, *f.*
Monocotyledon, *s.* monocotylédone, mono-
Monocotyledonous, *adj.* monocotylédoné, monocotylédone
Monocular, *adj.* monoculaire
Monocule, Monoculus, *s.* monocle, *m.*
Monodist, *s.* auteur d'une monodie, *m.*
Monody, *s.* monodie, *f.*
Monogam-ic, al, -y. *V.* page 3, § 1
Monogamist, *s.*, **Monogamous,** *adj.* monogame, *m.f.*
Monogram, *s.* monogramme, *m.*
Monogramm-atic, -ic, -ist. *V.* page 3, § 1
Monograph, Monographer, *s.* monographe, *m.*
Monograph-ic, al, -y. *V.* page 3, § 1
Monolith, *s.* monolithe, *m.*
Monolithal, Monolithic, *adj.* monolithe
Monolog-ic, al, -ist, -y. *V.* page 3, § 1
Monologue, *s.* monologue, *m.*
Monomania, *s.* monomanie, *f.* [mane, *m.f.*
Monomaniac, *s.adj.* monomaniaque, mono-
Monomial, *s.adj.* monôme, *s.m.*, *adj.m.f.*
Monopetalous, *adj.* monopétale, monopétalé
Monopolist, *s.* monopoleur, *m.*, monopolisateur, *m.*, -trice, *f.*; accapareur, *m.*, -euse, *f.*
Monopolization, *s.* monopolisation, *f.*
Monopolize, *v.a.* monopoliser; accaparer
Monopolizer, *s.* *V.* **Monopolist**
Monopolizing, *s.* monopolisation, *f.*; — *adj.* monopolisateur
Monopoly, *s.* monopole, *m.*; accaparement, *m.*
Monosepalous, *adj.* monosépale [syllabique
Monosyllabic, -al, *adj.* monosyllabe, mono-
Monosyllable, *s.* monosyllabe, *m.*
Monotheism, *s.* monothéisme, *m.*
Monotheist, *s.* monothéiste, *m.f.*
Monotheistic, -al, *adj.* monothéiste
Monotonous, *adj.* monotone
Monotonously, *adv.* avec monotonie, d'une manière monotone
Monotony, *s.* monotonie, *f.*
Monsoon, *s.* mousson, *f.*
Monster, *s.* monstre, *m.*; — *adj.* monstre
Monstrance, *s.* ostensoir, *m.*
Monstrosity, *s.* monstruosité, *f.*
Monstrous, *adj.* monstrueux; horrible; énorme; prodigieux
Monstrously, *adv.* monstrueusement; horriblement; énormément; prodigieusement; furieusement
Monstrousness, *s.* monstruosité, *f.*
Montenegrin, *s.adj.* Monténégrin, *m.*, e, *f.*
Month, *s.* mois, *m.* *Twelve* —*s*, un an, *m.*, une année, *f.* *What is the day of the* —? quelle date aujourd'hui?

Monthly, *adj.* de tous les mois; mensuel; (*by the month*) au mois; — *adv.* tous les mois; mensuellement; par mois. — *nurse,* garde d'accouchée, *f.* — *rose,* rose des quatre saisons, rose du Bengale, *f.* [tombe, *f.*
Monument, *s.* monument, *m.*; tombeau, *m.*,
Monumental, *adj.* monumental; de monument; du tombeau, de la tombe
Monumentally, *adv.* comme monument
Mood, *s.* disposition, humeur, *f.*; caractère, *m.*; (*gram., log., mus.*) mode, *m.*
Moodiness, *s.* humeur, mauvaise humeur, *f.*; (*sadness*) tristesse, *f.* [triste, pensif
Moody, *adj.* de mauvaise humeur; (*sad*)
Moon, *s.* lune, *f.*; — *v.n.* flâner, muser, musarder. *Full* —, pleine lune. *New* —, nouvelle lune. *By the light of the* —, au clair (*or* à la clarté) de la lune. — **beam,** *s.* rayon de lune, rayon lunaire, *m.* — **blindness,** *s.* cécité lunatique, *f.* — **calf,** *s.* monstre, *m*; (*a dolt*) idiot, imbécile, *m.* — **eye,** *s.* œil lunatique, *m.* — **eyed,** *adj.* lunatique; (*purblind*) aveugle. — **fish,** *s.* poisson-lune, *m.* —**less,** *adj.* sans lune, obscur. — **light,** *s.* clair de lune, *m.*; *adj.* de *or* au clair de lune; éclairé par la lune. — **shaped,** *adj.* en forme de lune, luniforme. — **sheered,** *adj.* (*nav.*) enhuché. — **shine,** *s.* clair de lune, *m.*; (*fig.*) illusion, *f.*; faux brillant, *m.*; calembredaines, *f.pl.* — **shine, -shiny,** *adj. V.* — **light.** — **stone,** *s.* adulaire, *f.* — **struck,** *adj.* lunatique. — **wort,** *s.* lunaire, *f.*
Mooned, *adj.* luné; de croissant
Moony, *adj.* de la lune; de croissant
Moor, *s.* lande, bruyère, *f.*; friche, *f.*; (*marsh*) marais, *m.*; (*pers.*) More, Maure, *m.*; — *v.a.* amarrer; — *v.n.* s'amarrer. — **berry,** *s.* airelle, *f.* — **buzzard,** *s.* harpaye, *m.* — **cock, -fowl, -game,** *s.* coq de bruyère, *m.* — **hen,** *s.* poule d'eau, *f.* — **land,** *s.* lande, bruyère, *f.*; pays marécageux, *m.*; *adj.* de landes, de bruyères; de pays marécageux. — **shooting,** *s.* chasse dans les landes, *f.*; chasse au marais *f.*
Mooress, *s.* Moresque, Mauresque, *f.*
Mooring, *s.* amarre, *f.*; (*nav.*) amarrage, *m.*
Moorish, *adj.* more, maure, moresque, mau-
Moory, *adj.* marécageux [resque
Moose, — **deer,** *s.* élan, *m.*
Moot, *v.a.* discuter; (*start*) soulever; — *adj.* discutable, disputable, contestable, sujet à contestation, indécis, incertain, douteux
Mooting, *s.* discussion, *f.*
Mop, *s.* balai à laver, balai de chiffons, *m.*; (*nav.*) faubert, *m.*; (*head of hair*) tignasse, crinière, hure, *f.*; — *v.a.* laver avec un balai, laver, nettoyer; (*nav.*) fauberter; (*fig.*) éponger. — **board,** *s.* (*of a wall*) *V.* **Skirting**
Mope, *v.n.* se séquestrer; être rêveur, être triste, rêver; s'ennuyer; être hébété; — *v.a.* rendre triste, plonger dans la mélancolie, abattre; ennuyer; hébéter, rendre stupide; — *s.* reclus, *m.*, e, *f.*; personne mélancolique, *f.*; personne qui s'ennuie, *f.*; personne hébétée, bûche, *f.*, crétin, *m.*
Moping, *adj.* triste, mélancolique; — *s.* profonde mélancolie, *f.*; ennui profond, *m.*
Mopish, *adj.* mélancolique, triste, abattu; ennuyé; hébété
Mopishly, *adv.* tristement, dans l'abattement
Mopishness, *s.* stupidité, *f.*, hébétement, *m.*; (*dejection*) tristesse, mélancolie, *f.*, abattement, *m.*; ennui, air d'ennui, *m.*
Moppet, Mopsey, Mopsy, *s.* poupée, marionnette, *f.*; (*darling*) pouponne, petite, *f.*; (*slattern*) sagouine, souillon, *f.*
Moraine, *s.* moraine, *f.*
Moral, *adj.* moral; de morale; — *s.* morale, *f.*; (*mind*) moral, *m.*; —**s,** *pl.* mœurs, *f.pl.*; moralité, *f.*; (*ethics*) morale, *f.* — *philosopher,* philosophe, moraliste, *m.* — *writer,* moraliste, *m.f.*
Moralist, *s.* moraliste, *m.f.*
Morality, *s.* morale, *f.*; moralité, *f.*
Moralization, *s.* moralisation, *f.*; (*of fables,*
Moralize, *v.n.a.* moraliser [&c.) morale, *f.*
Moralizer, *s.* moraliseur, moraliste, *m.*, moralisateur, *m.*, -trice, *f.* [sation, *f.*
Moralizing, *adj.* moralisateur; — *s.* morali-
Morally, *adv.* moralement, dans un sens moral
Morass, *s.* marécage, marais, *m.*
Morassy, *adj.* marécageux
Moravian, *s. adj.* Morave, *m.f.*
Morbid, *adj* morbide; maladif
Morbidezza, *s.* morbidesse, *f.*
Morbidly, *adv.* morbidement; maladivement
Morbidness, Morbidity, *s.* morbidité, maladiveté, *f.*, état morbide, état morbifique, état
Morbific, *adj.* morbifique [maladif, *m.*
Mordacious, *adj.* mordant, piquant
Mordaciously, *adv.* d'une manière mordante
Mordacity, *s.* mordacité, *f.* [*or* piquante
Mordant, *adj.* (*keen*) mordant; (*pungent*) cuisant, poignant; — *s.* mordant, *m.*; — *v.a.* mor-
Mordanting, *s.* mordançage, *m.* [dancer
Mordella, *s.* mordelle, *f.*
Mordicant, *adj.* mordicant
Mordication, *s.* mordication, *f.*
More, *adv.* plus, davantage, autrement; (*before a noun*) plus de, (*again*) encore du *or* de la *or* des; — *adj.* plus grand; supérieur; plus nombreux; (*other*) autre; autres; d'autres; (*more than one, several*) plusieurs; — *s.* plus, *m.* — *A little* —, un peu plus, encore un peu. *Nay* —, bien plus, il y a plus. *Never* —, jamais plus, plus jamais; plus. *No* —, *Not any* —, pas davantage; plus; plus de ...; (*no longer*) ne ... plus. *Once* —, encore une fois. *One* —, encore un, un de plus. *Some* —, davantage, encore; encore quelques-uns. *The* —, *all the* —, *so much the* —, d'autant plus (que); d'autant mieux (que); (n'en ...) que plus (...); à plus forte raison. *The* —, (*repeated, or opposed to 'the less'*), plus. — *and* —, de plus en plus. — *or less,* plus ou moins. *A man* —, un homme de plus; encore un homme. *No* — *lessons!* plus de leçons! *Give me some* — (*of it, of them*), donnez m'en encore, donnez m'en davantage. *Give me some* — *apples,* donnez-moi encore des pommes. *Will you have any* or *some* — (*of it, of them*)? en voulez-vous encore? *To be no* [—, n'être plus
Moreen, *s.* damas de laine, *m.*
Morel, *s.* morille, *f.*
Morella, Morello, *s.* (— *cherry*) amarelle, cerise amarelle, griotte, *f.*; (— *tree*) griottier, *m.*
Moreover, *adv.* de plus, en outre, d'ailleurs, encore; il y a plus
Moresque, *adj. s.* moresque, *adj.m.f.*, *s.f.*
Morgana, Morgane, *s.* Morgane, *f.*
Morganat-ic, -ically. *V.* page 3, § 1
Moribund, *s. adj.* moribond, *m.*, e, *f.*
Morine, *s.* morine, *f.*
Morion, *s.* morion, *m.*
Morling, *s.* laine morte, *f.*
Mormon, *s.* (*bird*) mormon, macareux, *m.*; — *s. adj.* (*pers.*) Mormon, *m.*; -ne, *f.*
Mormonism, *s.* mormonisme
Mormonite, *s. adj.* Mormon, *m.*, -ne, *f.*
Morning, Morn, *s.* matin, *m.*; (*whole morning, in regard to work, occupation, or weather*) matinée, *f.*; (*poet.*) aurore, *f.*; — *adj.* du matin; (*poet.*) matinier. *In the* —, (*morning time*) le matin; (*in the course of the morning*) dans la matinée; (*of the hour*) du matin. *This* —, ce matin. *The next* or *following* —, le lendemain matin. *The* — *after* ..., le lendemain matin de ... *The* — *after to-morrow,* après-demain matin. *The* — *before,* la veille au matin (de ...). *The* — *before yesterday,* avant-hier matin. *Good* —, bonjour; je vous salue; je vous salue bien; j'ai l'honneur de vous saluer. — **concert,** *s.* matinée musicale, *f.* — **dew,** *s.* rosée du matin, *f.* — **dress,** *s.* déshabillé du matin, *m.* — **gown,** *s.* robe de chambre, *f.* — **gun,**

s. coup de canon de diane, *m.* — **paper,** *s.* journal du matin, *m.* — **performance, -recital,** *s.* matinée, *f.* — **star,** *s.* étoile du matin, *f.* — **wrapper,** *s.* *V.* — **dress**

Moroc, *s.* indicateur, *m.*

Moroccan, *s. adj.* Marocain, *m.*, e, *f*

Morocco, *s.* maroquin, *m.* — **dresser,** *s.* maroquinier, *m.* — **leather,** *s.* maroquin, *m.* — **leather manufactory** *or* **trade** *or* **factory** *or* **articles,** *s.* maroquinerie, *f.* — **paper,** *s.* [papier maroquin, *m.*

Morose, *adj.* morose

Morosely, *adv.* d'une manière morose, d'un air morose, avec humeur

Moroseness, *s.* morosité, *f.*

Morphew, *s.* dartre farineuse, *f.*

Morphia, Morphine, *s.* morphine, *f.*

Morpholog-ic, al, -ically, -ist, -y. *V.* page 3, § 1

Morrice, Morris, — dance, *s.* moresque, [danse moresque, *f.*

Morrow, *s.* demain, *m.*; lendemain, *m.* *On the* —, le lendemain. *V.* **To-morrow**

Morse, *s.* morse, *m.*

Morsel, *s.* morceau, *m.*

Mortal, *adj.* mortel; sujet à la mort; de la mort; fatal; humain, des mortels; (*of combats*) à outrance, à mort; (*in the world*) au monde; — *s.* mortel, *m.*, -le, *f.*; être humain, *m.*, homme, *m.*, femme, *f.* *A mere* —, un simple mortel. *Every — thing,* tout au monde; n'importe quoi, quoi que ce soit; tout ce qui, tout ce que

Mortality, *s.* mortalité, *f.*; mort, *f.*; humanité, nature humaine, *f.* [*highest degree*) à la mort

Mortally, *adv.* mortellement; à mort; (*to the*

Mortar, *s.* mortier, *m.*; (*for salt*) égrugeoir, *m.*; (*artil.*) mortier, *m.* — **vessel,** *s.* bombarde, *f.* [théquer

Mortgage, *s.* hypothèque, *f.*; — *v.a.* hypo-

Mortgageable, *adj.* hypothécable [caire

Morgagee, *s.* créancier (*m.*, -ière, *f.*) hypothé-

Mortgager, Mortgagor, *s.* débiteur sur hypothèque, *m.* [mortifère

Mortiferous, *adj.* mortel, funeste; (*med.*)

Mortification, *s.* mortification, *f.*; (*med.*) mortification, gangrène, *f.*

Mortify, *v.a.* mortifier; (*med.*) gangrener; — *v.n.* se mortifier; (*med.*) se gangrener

Mortifyingly, *adv.* d'une manière mortifiante

Mortise, *s.* mortaise, *f.*; — *v.a.* mortaiser, emmortaiser. — **chisel,** *s.* ébauchoir, *m.* — **gauge,** *s.* équilboquet, *m.* — **lock,** *s.* serrure encastrée, *f.* [*s.* mortaiseuse, *f.*

Mortising, *s.* mortaisage, *m.* — **machine,**

Mortling, *s.* laine morte, *f.*

Mortmain, *s.* mainmorte, *f.*

Mortuary, *adj.* mortuaire; — *s.* droit mortuaire, *m.*; (*burial-place*) cimetière, *m.*; (*dead-house*) morgue, *f.*

Mosaic, *adj.* mosaïque, de Moïse; (*arts*) en mosaïque; — *s.* mosaïque, *f.* *The — law,* la loi de Moïse, *f.* — **gold,** *s.* or moulu, *m.*; (*bronze powder*) or musif, *m.* — **painting,** *s.* peinture en mosaïque, *f.* — **work,** *s.* ouvrage en mosaïque, *m*, mosaïque, *f.*

Mosaism, *s.* mosaïsme, *m.*

Mosaist, *s.* mosaïste, *m.*

Moschatel, *s.* moscatelle, moscatelline, *f.*

Moslem, *s.* moslem, m.

Mosque, *s.* mosquée, *f.*

Mosquito, *s.* moustique, *m.*; (*geog.*) Mosquito, *m.* — **net,** *s.* moustiquaire, *f.*; cousinière, *f.*

Moss, *s.* (*bot.*) mousse, *f.*; (*marsh*) marais; — *v.a.* couvrir de mousse. — **agate,** *s.* agate mousseuse, *f.* —**clad, -grown,** *adj.* moussu, couvert *or* tapissé de mousse. — **herbarium,** *s.* moussier, *m.* — **land,** *s.* terrain tourbeux, *m.* — **rose,** *s.* rose mousseuse, *f.* — **trooper,** *s.* maraudeur, bandit, *m.*

Mossiness, *s.* état moussu, *m*

Mossy, *adj* moussu, couvert de mousse

Most, *adj.* le plus; (*most part*) la plupart (de, d'entre); (*greatest*) plus grand; — *adv. s.* le plus; plus; (*extremely, highly*) très, fort, bien, extrêmement, excessivement; des plus, on ne peut plus, on ne peut pas plus, tout ce qu'il y a de plus; — *s.* le plus grand nombre, *m.*, la plupart, *f.* *At* —, *at the* —, au plus, tout au plus. — *of all,* principalement. *To make the — of, V.* **Make**

Mostly, *adv.* principalement; pour la plupart; en grande partie; le plus souvent, la plupart [du temps

Mote, *s.* atome, *m.*; fétu, *m.*, paille, *f.*

Motet, *s.* motet, *m.*

Moth, *s.* teigne, *f.*; gerce, *f.*; mite, *f.*; ver, *m.*; (*butterfly*) papillon, *m.*; papillon de nuit, *m.*, phalène, *f.*; (*fig.*) ver rongeur, *m.* *Plumed* —, fissipenne, ptérophore, *m.* — **eaten,** *adj.* mité, mangé aux vers, rongé des vers

Mother, *s.* mère, *f.*; (*old woman*) bonne femme, bonne vieille, mère, *f.*; (*of liquids*) moisissure, *f.*; moisi, *m.*, mère, *f.*; — *adj.* mère; maternel; naturel; national; — *v.a.* servir de mère à, adopter; — *v.n.* (*of liquids*) se moisir, moisir. — **in-law,** *s.* belle-mère, *f.* — **church,** *s.* église métropolitaine, *f.*; (*Church of Rome*) mère des fidèles, *f.* — **clove,** *s.* *V.* **Clove.** — **country,** *s.* mère patrie, *f.*; métropole, *f.* —**Goose's tales,** *s.pl.* les contes de ma mère l'Oie, *m.pl.* —**hood,** *s.* maternité, *f.* —**less,** *adj.* sans mère, orphelin. —**like,** *adj.* *V.* —**ly.** —**liness,** *s.* tendresse maternelle, *f.* —**ly,** *adj.* maternel; de mère; *adv.* maternellement; en mère. — **of pearl,** *s* *V.* **Pearl.** — **of vinegar,** *s.* mère de vinaigre, *f.* — **spot,** —**'s mark,** *s.* *V.* **Nævus.** — **tongue,** *s.* propre langue, langue maternelle, *f.* — **water, -liquor,** *s.* eau mère, *f.* — **wit,** *s.* esprit naturel, *m.* — **wort,** *s.* agripaume, *f.*, léonure, *m.* —**y,** *adj.* (*of liquids*) moisi

Mothy, *adj.* plein de teignes *or* de gerces, plein [de vers, miteux

Motility, *s.* motilité, *f.*

Motion, *s.* mouvement, *m.*; signe, *m.*; (*proposal*) proposition, motion, *f.*; (*med.*) selle, *f.*; déjection, *f.*; — *v.n.* faire signe. —**less,** *adj.* immobile, sans mouvement

Motive, *s.* motif, *m.*; — *adj.* moteur; (*fig.*) qui fait agir, déterminant. — *power,* force motrice, [*f.*; moteur, *m.*

Motivity, *s.* motricité, *f.*

Motley, *adj.* bigarré; (*of wood, porcelain*) madré; (*of soap*) marbré; (*of iron, horses, dogs*) truité; (*mixed*) mêlé, mélangé, varié; (*odd*) [bizarre

Motor, *s.* moteur, *m.*

Motory, *adj.* moteur

Mottle, *v.a.* madrer; moirer; (*soap*) marbrer

Mottled, *adj.* *V.* **Motley**

Motto, *s.* devise, *f.* — *of a device,* âme, (*f.*) *or* mot (*m.*) d'une devise

Mouflon, *s.* mouflon, *m.*

Mould, *s.* moule, *m.*, forme, *f.*; calibre, *m.*, trempe, *f.*; (*earth*) terreau, *m.*, terre, *f.*; (*mustiness*) moisi, *m.*, moisissure, *f.*; (— *candle*) chandelle moulée, *f.*; — *v.a.* mouler, former; (*knead*) pétrir; (*agr., hort., to earth up*) butter, chausser; — *v.n.* se moisir, moisir. — **board,** *s.* (*of a plough*) oreille, *f.*, oreillon, versoir, m. — **candle,** *s.* chandelle moulée, *f.* — **maker,** *s.* moulier, *m.*, mouliste, *m.f.* [moulable

Mouldable, *adj.* susceptible d'être moulé,

Moulder, *s.* mouleur, *m.*; — *v.n.* se réduire en poussière, tomber en poussière; (*fig.*) diminuer, dépérir, fondre; — *v.a.* réduire en poussière

Mouldiness, *s.* moisissure, *f.*, moisi, *m.*

Moulding, *s.* (*act*) moulage, *m.*, (*result*) moulure, *f.*; (*agr., hort., earthing up*) buttage, *m.* — **maker,** *s.* moulurier, *m.* — **plane,** *s.* doucine, *f.* — **plough,** *s.* buttoir, *m.*

Mouldy, *adj.* moisi. *To get* or *grow* or *become* —, se moisir, moisir. *To smell* —, sentir le [moisi

Moulinet, *s.* moulinet, *m.*

Moult, *v.n.* muer

Moulting, *s,* mue, *f.*

Mound, *s.* monticule, *m.*, butte, *f.*, tertre, remblai, *m.*; rempart, *m.*, digue, levée, *f.*; (*her.*) monde, *m.*; — *v.a.* fortifier par un rempart *or* par une digue *or* par une levée

Mount, *s.* mont, *m.*, montagne, *f.*; monticule, tertre, *m.*; (*mounting*) monture, *f.*; (*frame*) encadrement, *m.*; — *v.n.* monter; (*a horse*) monter à cheval, monter; (*rise*) s'élever; — *v.a.* faire monter, monter, élever; (*ascend*) monter sur *or* à; (*a horse* or &c., *a cannon, jewels*, &c., *tech., mil.*) monter. — *Vesuvius*, le Mont Vésuve. *The — of Olives*, le Mont (*or* la Montagne des Oliviers. *To — o.'s horse*, monter à cheval. *To — the throne*, monter sur le trône

Mountain, *s.* montagne, *f.*; (*heap*) monceau, *m.*; (*wine*) malaga, *m.*; — *adj.* de montagne, de la montagne, des montagnes; montagnard; (*of scenery*) montagneux; (*fig.*) vaste, immense. *Waves — high*, des vagues hautes comme des montagnes. *To make —s of mole-hills*, faire d'une mouche un éléphant. — **ash,** *s.* sorbier des oiseaux, avrelon, *m.* — **flax,** *s.* amiante, *m.* – **green,** *s.adj.* vert de montagne, *m.* — **range,** *s.* chaîne de montagnes, *f.* — **soap,** *s.* savon de montagne, *m.* — **spinach,** *s.* arroche des jardins, follette, belle-dame, bonne-dame, *f.*

Mountaineer, *s.* montagnard, *m.*, e, *f.*

Mountainous, *adj.* montagneux, de montagnes, montueux; (*huge*) énorme

Mountainousness, *s.* situation élevée, nature montagneuse, *f.* [(*fig.*) charlatan, *m.*

Mountebank, *s.* saltimbanque, bateleur, *m.*;

Mounted, *part. adj.* monté; armé (de); portant; (*on horseback*) à cheval

Mounter, *s.* monteur, *m.*, -euse, *f.*

Mounting, *s.* (*going up, ascent*) montée, *f.*; (*act of setting, framing*, &c.) montage, *m.*, (*result of ditto, piece in which a gem or &c. is set*) monture, *f.*; (*equipment*) équipement, *m.*

Mourn, *v.n.* pleurer, se lamenter; s'affliger; (*wear mourning*) porter le deuil; — *v.a.* pleurer, lamenter, déplorer. *To — for*, pleurer

Mourner, *s.* affligé, *m.*, e, *f.*, malheureux, *m.*, -euse, *f.*; (*of funeral*) personne qui suit le convoi, *f.*, (*hired*) pleureur, *m.*, -euse, *f.* *To be a —*, (*at a funeral*) suivre le convoi. *To be chief —*, conduire le deuil

Mournful, *adj.* lugubre, triste; déplorable, lamentable; (*afflicted*) affligé. —**ly,** *adv.* lugubrement, tristement; déplorablement; avec affliction. —**ness,** *s.* affliction, douleur, tristesse, *f.*, deuil, *m.*; air chagrin, *m.*

Mourning, *s.* deuil, *m.*; affliction, *f.*; lamentation, *f.*; — *adj.* de deuil. *To be in —, to wear —*, être en deuil ('*for*,' de). *To go into —*, prendre le deuil. *To go out of —*, quitter le deuil. — **coach,** *s.* voiture de deuil, *f.* — **hatband,** *s.* crêpe, *m.* — **suit,** *s.* habit de deuil, *m.* — **warehouse,** *s.* magasin de deuil, *m.*

Mouse, *s.* souris, *f.*; rat, *m.*; — *v.n.* prendre des souris. — **bird,** *s.* coliou, *m.* — **buttock,** *s.* (*of beef*) gîte, *m.* — **colour,** *s.*, — **coloured,** *adj.* gris souris, souris, *m.*; (*of horses*) poil de souris. — **ear,** *s.* (*bot.*) oreille de souris, piloselle, *f.* — **hole,** *s.* trou de souris, *m.* — **hunt,** *s.* chasse aux souris, *f.* — **hunter,** *s.* *V.* **Mouser.** — **piece,** *s.* (*of beef*) gîte, *m.* — **tail,** *s.* queue de souris, *f.*; (*bot.*) queue de souris, queue de rat, ratoncule, *f.*, myosurus, *m.* — **trap,** *s.* souricière, *f.*

Mouser, *s.* preneur (*m.*, -euse, *f.*) de souris. *He is a good —*, il est bon pour les souris

Moustache, *s.* moustache, *f.*

Moustached, *adj.* à moustaches, moustachu

Mouth, *s.* (*pers.*) bouche, *f.*; (*of carnivorous beasts, fish, reptiles*) gueule, *f.*; (*of herbivorous animals*, &c.) bouche, *f.*; (*of birds*) bec, *m.*; (*teeth*) dents, *f.pl.*; (*voice*) voix, *f.*; (*speaker*) orateur, organe, *m.*; (*opening*) ouverture, *f.*; orifice, *m.*; (*of pitchers, jugs*) gueule, *f.*; (*of bottles*) trou, goulot, *m.*; (*of a cave*, &c.) entrée, *f.*; (*of harbours*) entrée, *f.*, (*if narrow*) goulet, *m.*; (*of rivers, of a wind instr.*) embouchure, *f.*; (*of a cannon*) bouche, gueule, *f.*; (*of a hand-gun*) bouche, *f.*; (*of a pistol*) gueule, *f.*; (*ugly face*) grimace, *f.*; — *v.n.a.* crier, beugler, déclamer; insulter, injurier, outrager; (*chew*) mâcher; (*eat*) manger; (*devour*) dévorer; (*seize*) happer, saisir avec les dents. *To be in everybody's —*, être dans toutes les bouches. *To have in o.'s —*, (*words*) avoir sur le bout de la langue, avoir sur le bord des lèvres. *To make —s*, faire des grimaces. *To stop anyone's —*, fermer la bouche à quelqu'un, faire taire quelqu'un. — **friend,** *s.* soi-disant ami, *m.* —**ful,** *s.* bouchée, *f.* *At a —*, d'une seule bouchée. — **glue,** *s.* colle à bouche, *f.* — **less,** *adj.* sans bouche; silencieux. — **organ,** *s.* flûte de Pan, *f.* – **piece,** *s.* (*of instruments, and tech.*) embouchure, *f.*, (*reed of a clarinet or* &c.) anche, *f.*; (*of a bridle-bit*) embouchure, *f.*, canon, *m.*; (*of a tobacco-pipe*) bout, bouquin, *m.*; (*speaker*) organe, *m.*, interprète, *m.f.*, orateur, *m.*

Mouthed, *adj.* qui a une bouche; (*in compounds*) à la bouche ..., qui a la bouche ... *Broken —*, *V.* **Broken.** *Foul —*, mal embouché. *Full —*, qui a la voix forte. *Hard —, Tender —*, *V.* **Hard** *and* **Tender.** *Hundred —*, aux cent bouches. *Wide —*, qui a la bouche (*or* &c.) large

Mouthing, *s.* criaillerie, déclamation, *f.*

Movable, *adj.* mobile; (*of steam-engines*) loco, mobile; (*law*) meuble, mobilier; —**s,** *s.pl.* meubles, biens meubles, biens *or* effets mobiliers, *m.pl.* — *feast*, fête mobile, *f.*

Movableness, *s.* mobilité, *f.*

Movably, *adv.* d'une manière mobile

Move, *v.a.* remuer; (*set going*) mouvoir, mettre en mouvement; faire aller; (*shake*) ébranler; agiter; (*furniture*) déménager; (*goods*) transporter; (*troops*) faire marcher, faire avancer, porter (sur), diriger (sur); (*at chess*, &c.) jouer; bouger; (*one step or several*) faire; (*affect*) toucher, émouvoir; exciter (à), porter (à); soulever; (*propose*) proposer; (*produce*) produire; (*law*) demander; — *v.n.* se mouvoir; se mettre en mouvement; (*walk*) marcher, avancer, aller; (*get on*) aller; (*stir*) remuer, se remuer; bouger; s'agiter, s'ébranler; se déplacer; (*backward, aside*) se reculer; (*turn*) tourner; (*live*) vivre; (*change residence*) déménager; se transporter; (*at chess*, &c.) jouer; (*propose*) faire une motion, faire une proposition; (*law*) demander; — *s.* mouvement, *m.*; (*good or bad*, &c.) coup, trait, *m.*; manœuvre, *f.*; (*at chess*, &c.) coup, *m.*, (*turn*) tour, *m.*, (*regular motion*) marche, *f.* *It is my — (turn)*, c'est à moi à jouer. *To — in high* (or &c.) *society*, vivre dans le grand (*or* &c.) monde, fréquenter le grand (*or* &c.) monde. — **about,** aller çà et là, aller et venir, se promener; circuler; (*stir much*) se secouer, se donner du mouvement; (*change places*) se déplacer. — **away,** *v.a.* éloigner, ôter; *v.n.* s'éloigner; s'écarter. — **back,** reculer. — **down,** descendre. — **in,** entrer; (*of furniture*) emménager. — **off,** *v.a.* ôter, enlever; *v.n.* s'en aller; s'éloigner; décamper, filer. — **on,** s'avancer, avancer; marcher; circuler; passer. — **out,** sortir; déloger, déguerpir; (*of furniture*) déménager. — **up,** monter; avancer, s'avancer. — **round,** tourner; (*pers.*) se tourner; se retourner [citation, *f.*

Movement, *s.* mouvement, *m.*; agitation, ex-

Mover, *s.* moteur, *m.*, -trice, *f.*; mobile, *m.*; (*proposer*) celui qui propose, auteur d'une motion *or* d'une proposition, *m.* *First* or *prime —*, (*mech.*) principe moteur, moteur, *m.*, force motrice, *f.*; (*fig.*) premier mobile, *m.*

Moving, *adj.* mouvant; mobile; touchant, émouvant; persuasif; (*giving motion*) moteur; — *s.* mouvement, *m.*; déplacement, *m.*; déménagement, *m.* — *power*, force motrice, *f.*

Movingly, *adv.* d'une manière touchante

Mow, *s.* fauchée, *f.*; (*heap*) tas en grenier, **tas,**

m., gerbière, *f.*; (*part of a barn*) grenier, gerbier, *m.*; — *v.a.n.* faucher; (*a lawn*) tondre; (*lay in a heap*) mettre en tas. — **burn,** *v.n.* (*agr.*) s'échauffer. — **down,** faucher; (*fig.*) moissonner; abattre

Mower, *s.* faucheur, *m.*; (*machine*) faucheuse, *f.*; (*for lawns*) tondeuse, *f.*

Mowing, *s.* fauchage, *m.*; (*produce*) fauche, *f.* — **machine,** *s.* faucheuse, *f.*; (*for lawns*) tondeuse, *f.* — **time,** *s.* fauchaison, *f.*

Moxa, *s.* moxa, *m.*

Mr., Monsieur, M., Mr.; (*before certain titles*) Monsieur le ... — *mayor,* — *president* or *chairman,* &c., Monsieur le maire, Monsieur le [président, &c.

Mrs., Madame, Mme.

Much, *adv. adj. s.* beaucoup; bien; (*strongly*) fortement; vivement; (*before a noun*) beaucoup de, bien du, bien de la, bien des; (*very*) très, fort; (*nearly,* — *about*) à peu près; (*by far*) de beaucoup. *As* —, autant; (*before a noun*) autant de. *As — as,* autant que, tant que; jusqu'à; (*even*) même; (*as if*) comme pour. *As — again, as — more,* deux fois autant, le double; encore autant. *By* —, (*by far*) de beaucoup. *Foras*—, *V.* **For,** *conj.* *How*—? combien? (*before a noun*) combien de ...? *Not* —, pas beaucoup. *Not* —, *nothing* —, pas grand'chose; peu de chose. *So* —, tant; autant; (*before a noun*) tant de; autant de; (*before a past part.*) si, tellement; (*much*) beaucoup, bien; (*very*) très, bien. *So — as,* autant que; assez pour; (*even*) même. *So — for ...!* *thus — for ...!* voilà pour ...! *So — so that* (or *as*), au point que (*or* de), à tel point que, si bien que. *So very* —, tant et tant, &c. (*V.* **Very**); *This* —, *V.* **This.** *Thus* —, autant. *Too* —, trop; de trop; par trop; (*before a noun*) trop de. *Very* —, beaucoup, bien; très; grandement, très fort; excessivement; infiniment. *To be — the same,* être à peu près la même [chose (*or* de même)

Mucilage, *s.* mucilage, *m.*

Mucilaginous, *adj.* mucilagineux

Mucilaginousness, *s.* état mucilagineux, *m.*

Muck, *s.* fumier, *m.*; (*mean object*) boue, fange, *f.*; — *v.a.* fumer. *To run a* —, *V.* **Amuck.** — **worm,** *s.* ver de fumier, *m.*; (*miser*) ladre, *m.*

Muckiness, *s.* saleté, malpropreté, *f.*

Mucky, *adj.* sale, malpropre

Mucosity, Mucousness, *s.* mucosité, *f.*

Mucous, *adj.* muqueux

Mucus, *s.* mucosité, *f.*, mucus, *m.*

Mucusine, *s.* mucosine, *f.*

Mud, *s.* boue, *f.*; fange, *f.*; (*deposit by rivers,* &c.) limon, *m.*; (*in ponds,* &c.) vase, *f.*; (*slough*) bourbier, *m.*; (*earth*) terre, *f.*; (*build.*) bousillage, *m.* — **cart,** *s.* tombereau, *m.* — **fish,** *s.* pélamide, amie, *f.* — **guard,** *s.* paracrotte, garde-crotte, *m.* — **lark,** *s.* ravageur, tafouilleux, *m.* — **lighter,** *s.* marie-salope, *f.* — **sill,** *s.* plate-forme, *f.* — **wall,** *s.* mur de terre, mur de bousillage, torchis, bousillage, *m.* — **wort,** *s.* limoselle, *f.*

Mudar, *s.* mudar, *m.*

Muddily, *adv.* salement

Muddiness, *s.* état boueux, état bourbeux, état fangeux, *m.*; état trouble, *m.*

Muddle, *v.a.* troubler; (*stupefy*) hébéter; (*intoxicate*) griser; — *v.n.* barboter, patauger, faire du gâchis; — *s.* embrouillamini, désordre, *m.*; gâchis, *m.* *All in a* —, tout brouillé. — **headed,** *adj. V.* **Muddy-headed**

Muddled, *part. adj.* troublé; trouble; hébété; (*in liquor*) en train, gris

Muddy, *adj.* boueux, bourbeux; fangeux; limoneux; vaseux; (*of clothes,* &c.) couvert de boue, crotté; (*of wine,* &c.) trouble; (*jewel.*) nuageux; (*of colour*) couleur de boue. — **brained, -headed,** *adj.* à cervelle de boue, bouché [cornichon, melon, *m.*, huître, *f.*

Muff, *s.* manchon, *m.*; (*pers.*) serin, jobard,

Muffin, *s.* muffin (*English cake*), *m.*

Muffle, *v.a.* envelopper; (*in jest*) emmitoufler; (*blindfold*) bander; (*a drum*) voiler, couvrir de crêpe, encrêper; (*a bell*) assourdir, couvrir de crêpe, encrêper; (*oars*) assourdir; (*fig.*) couvrir, étouffer; — *s.* (*chem.*) moufle, *f.*; (*boxing-glove*) gant bourré, *m.*

Muffler, *s.* capuchon, *m.*; (*for the face*) cache-nez, *m.*; (*for the hand*) moufle, *f.*

Mufflon, *s.* mouflon, *m.*

Mufti, *s.* mufti, muphti, *m.*

Mug, *s.* gobelet, *m.*, timbale, *f.*; tasse, *f.*; pot, *m.*; (*mouth*) gueule, *f.* —**wort,** *s.* armoise, *f.*

Muggy, *adj.* humide; (*of weather*) mou, lourd

Mulatta, *s.* mulâtresse, *f.*

Mulatto, *s. adj.* mulâtre, *s.m.*, *adj.m.f.*

Mulattress, *s.* mulâtresse, *f.*

Mulberry, *s.* mûre, *f.* — **grove,** *s.* mûreraie, *f.* — **shaped,** *adj.* mûriforme. — **tree,** *s.* mûrier, *m.* [enchausser, pailler, réchauffer

Mulch, *s.* paillis, fumier, réchaud, *m.*; — *v.a.*

Mulching, *s.* enchaussement, paillement, paillage, réchauffement, *m.*

Mulct, *s.* amende, *f.*; — *v.a.* mettre à l'amende, punir d'une amende, condamner *or* forcer à payer, taxer; punir; priver (de)

Mule, *s.* mulet, *m.*, (*she* —) mule, *f.*; — *adj.* de mulet; à mulet; mulassier; muletier. *He* —, mulet, *m.* *She* —, mule, *f.* — **breeding,** *s.* mulasserie, *f.*; *adj.* mulassier. — **breeding mare,** *s.* jument mulassière, mulassière, *f.* — **driver,** *s.* muletier, *m.*, -ière, *f.* — **jenny,** *s.* mule-jenny, *f.*, banc à broches, *m.* — **litter,** *s.* cacolet, *m.* — **species,** *s.* espèce mulas-[sière, *f.*

Muleteer, *s.* muletier, *m.*, -ière, *f.*

Mulish, *adj.* de mulet; comme un mulet; mulassier; obstiné, entêté, têtu

Mulishly, *adv.* obstinément

Mulishness, *s.* obstination, *f.*, entêtement, *m.*

Mull, *v.a.* faire chauffer; brûler; — *s.* (*blunder*) brioche, boulette, *f.*, four, *m.* *To make a — of,* gâcher. — **muslin,** *s.* mallemolle, *f.*

Mulled, *adj.* chaud et épicé, brûlé, chaud

Mullein, *s.* molène, *f.*, bouillon-blanc, *m.*

Muller, *s.* (*for grinding*) molette, *f.*

Mullet, *s.* (*fish*) mulet, muge, *m.*; (*her.*) molette, *f.* *Grey* —, surmulet, *m.* *Red* —, rouget, *m.*

Mulligrubs, *s.pl.* colique, *f.* [meneaux

Mullion, *s.* meneau, *m.*; — *v.a.* former en

Multangular, *adj.* multangulaire, multangulé

Multicoloured, *adj.* multicolore

Multifarious, *adj.* varié, divers; multiplié

Multifariously, *adv.* avec variété, diversement

Multifariousness, *s.* variété, diversité, *f.*

Multiflorous, *adj.* multiflore

Multiform, *adj.* multiforme

Multiformity, *s.* multiformité, *f.*

Multilateral, *adj.* multilatère

Multilocular, *adj.* multiloculaire

Multiparous, *adj.* multipare

Multiped, *adj. s.* multipède, *adj.m.f.*, *s.m.*

Multiple, *adj. s.* multiple, *adj.m.f.*, *s.m.* [pliable

Multipliable, Multiplicable, *adj.* multi-

Multiplicand, *s.* multiplicande, *m.*

Multiplicate, *adj.* multiple

Multiplication, *s.* multiplication, *f.* *Compound* —, multiplication complexe, *f.* — **table,** *s.* table de multiplication, table de Pythagore, *f.*

Multiplicative, *adj.* multiplicatif

Multiplicator, *s.* multiplicateur, *m.*

Multiplicity, *s.* multiplicité, *f.* [plieur, *m.*

Multiplier, *s.* multiplicateur, *m.*; (*pers*) multi-

Multiply, *v.a.* multiplier; — *v.n.* (*of plants, abstract things*) se multiplier; (*of animals*) multiplier

Multiplying, *s.* multiplication, *f.*; — *adj.* multipliant; multiplicateur. - **glass,** *s.* verre à facettes, verre multipliant, multipliant, *m.*

Multisonous, *adj.* qui rend plusieurs sons

Multitubular boiler, *s.* chaudière à bouil-[leurs, *f.*

Multitude, *s.* multitude, *f.*

Multitudinous, *adj.* nombreux, en grand nombre

Multivalve, *adj. s.* multivalve, *adj.m.f.*, *s.m.*

Multure, *s.* (*grinding*) mouture, *f.*; (*grist*) grain *or* blé à moudre, *m.*; (*grain ground*) grain *or* blé moulu, *m.*; (*due*) moulage, *m.*

Mum, *s.* bière de froment, *f.*; — *adj.* silencieux, muet; — *int.* chut! motus!

Mumble, *v.n.a.* marmotter; (*chew*) mâchonner

Mumbler, *s.* grogneur, *m.*, -euse, *f.*, marmotteur, *m.*, -euse, *f.*; mâchonneur, *m.*, -euse, *f.*

Mumbling, *s.* marmottement, marmottage, *m.*; mâchonnement; — *adj.* marmotteur; mâchonneur [en mâchonnant

Mumblingly, *adv.* en marmottant; (*chewing*)

Mumm, *v.a.* masquer; — *v.n.* se masquer, se déguiser

Mummer, *s.* masque, *m.*, personne masquée, *f.*

Mummery, *s.* mascarade, *f.*; momerie, *f.*

Mummification, *s.* momification, *f.*

Mummify, *v.a.* momifier

Mummy, *s.* momie, *f.*; (*anything pounded*) poudre, pâte, *f.* *To beat to a* —, battre comme plâtre, piler, rouer de coups

Mump, *v.a.n.* (*nibble*) grignoter; (*talk*) marmotter, mâchonner; (*beg*) mendier; (*cheat*) duper; (*be sullen or sulky*) se refrogner, bouder; (*sham*) faire des momeries [-euse, *f.*

Mumper, *s.* mendiant, *m.*, e, *f.*, gueux, *m.*,

Mumping, *s.* ruses de mendiant, *f.pl.*; momeries, grimaces, *f.pl.* [sombre, triste, abattu

Mumpish, *adj.* refrogné, boudeur, maussade;

Mumpishly, *adv.* en boudant, maussadement; sombrement, tristement

Mumpishness, *s.* refrognement, *m.*, bouderie, maussaderie, mauvaise humeur, *f.*; tristesse, *f.*, abattement, *m.* [lons, *m.pl.*

Mumps, *s.pl.* *V.* **Mumpishness;** (*med.*) oreil-

Munch, *v.a.n.* mâcher, manger à grosses

Muncher, *s.* mâcheur, *m.*, -euse, *f.* [bouchées

Munching, *s.* action de manger à grosses bouchées, *f.* [(*theol.*) mondain

Mundane, *adj.* du monde, de ce monde;

Mundanely, *adv.* mondainement

Mundanity, *s.* mondanité, *f.*

Mundanize, *v.a.* mondaniser [toyage, *m.*

Mundification, *s.* mondification, *f.*, net-

Mundificative, *adj.* mondificatif, détersif

Mundify, *v.a.* mondifier, nettoyer, déterger

Mungo, *s.* (*shoddy*) mungo, effilochage, effiloché, *m.*; (*bot.*) (*snake-root*) mungos, *m.*, (*pulse*) mungo, *m.*

Municipal, *adj.* municipal; (*of law*) civil

Municipality, *s.* municipalité, *f.*

Municipalize, *v.a.* municipaliser

Municipally, *adv.* municipalement

Municipium, *s.* municipe, *m.*

Munificence, *s.* munificence, *f.*

Munificent, *adj.* plein de munificence, libéral

Munificently, *adv.* avec munificence, libéralement

Muniment, *s.* titre, *m.*, charte, *f.*, archives, *f.pl.*; document, *m.*; (*obsolete senses*) fortification, *f.*, rempart, *m.*; moyen de défense, *m.*; défense, *f.* — **house, -room,** *s.* chartier, chartrier, *m.*; archives, *f.pl.*

Munition. *V.* **Ammunition**

Muræna, *s.* murène, *f.*

Mural, *adj.* mural; de mur; perpendiculaire. — *circle*, cercle mural, *m.* — *crown*, couronne murale, *f.*

Murder, *v.a.* assassiner, tuer; (*a work*) massacrer, estropier; (*destroy*) détruire; (*languages*) écorcher; (*names*) estropier; — *s.* assassinat, meurtre, homicide, *m*; — *int.* à l'assassin! *Wilful* —, assassinat, *m.*; homicide volontaire, *m.* *To call out* —, crier à l'assassin; (*fig.*) crier au meurtre. — *will out*, la vérité se sait toujours. *Killing no* —, tant de tués que de blessés, il n'y a personne de mort

Murderer, *s.* assassin, meurtrier, *m.*

Murderess, *s.* meurtrière, *f.* [guinaire

Murderous, *adj.* homicide; meurtrier; san-

Murderously, *adv.* meurtrièrement, par le meurtre, par l'assassinat

Mure, *v.a.* *V.* **Immure**

Murex, *s.* murex, *m.*

Muriate, *s.* chlorhydrate, *m.*

Muriatic, *adj.* chlorhydrique

Murine, *adj.* de souris, des souris

Murk, *s.* *V.* **Murkiness;** (*residuum*) marc, *m.*

Murkiness, *s.* obscurité, *f.*, ténèbres, *f.pl.*

Murky, *adj.* obscur, sombre, noir, ténébreux

Murmur, *v.a.n.* murmurer; — *s.* murmure, *m.*

Murmurer, *s.* murmurateur, *m.*, -trice, *f.*

Murmuring, *adj.* murmurant, qui murmure, murmurateur; — *s.* murmure, *m.*, murmures, *m.pl.* [murmures

Murmuringly, *adv.* en murmurant, par des

Murrain, *s.* épizootie, *f.*

Murre, *s.* pingouin, *m.* [rhin, *s.m.*

Murrhine, *adj s.* murrhin, *adj.m.*, e, *f.*, mur-

Murry, *s.* (*fish*) murène, flûte, *f.*

Muscadel, *s.* (*pear*) muscadelle, *f.*; (*other pear, grape, wine*) *V.* **Muscatel** [lantes, *f.pl.*

Muscæ volitantes, *s pl.* (*med.*) mouches vo-

Muscat, Muscatel, *s. adj.* muscat, *m.*

Muscivorous, *adj.* muscivore

Muscle, *s.* muscle, *m.*; (*bad spelling for* "*mussel*") *V.* **Mussel;** — *v.a.* muscler

Muscovado, *s.* moscouade, *f.*

Muscovite, *s. adj.* Moscovite, *m.f.*

Muscular, *adj.* (*force*, &c.) musculaire; (*limb, pers.*, &c.) musculeux [losité, *f.*

Muscularity, Musculosity, *s.* muscu-

Musculous, *adj.* musculeux

Muse, *s.* muse, *f.*; (*thought*) rêverie, méditation, *f.*; — *v.n.* méditer, réfléchir; (*be absent*) rêver, être rêveur

Muser, *s.* rêveur, *m.*, -euse, *f.*

Museum, *s.* musée, *m.*

Mush, *s.* gaude, *f.*

Mushroom, *s.* champignon, *m.*; champignon comestible, *m.*; (*upstart*) parvenu, *m.*, e, *f.* — **bed, -ground, -pit, -house,** *s.* champignonnière, *f.* — **grower,** *s.* champignoniste, *m.f.* — **sauce,** *s.* sauce aux champignons, *f.*

Music, *s.* musique, *f.*; harmonie, *f.* *Rough* —, musique enragée, *f.*, charivari, *m.* *To set to* —, mettre en musique. — **band,** *s.* *V.* **Band.** — **book,** *s.* livre *or* cahier de musique, *m.* — **composer,** *s.* compositeur (de musique), *m.* — **copier, -copyist,** *s.* copiste de musique, *m.f.*, noteur, *m.* — **desk,** *s.* pupitre à musique, *m.* — **engraver,** *s.* graveur de musique, *m.* — **hall,** salle de concerts, *f.*; café chantant, café-concert, *m.* — **mad,** *adj.* mélomane. — **master,** *s.* maître de musique, *m.* — **mistress,** *s.* maîtresse de musique, *f.* — **paper,** *s.* papier de musique, *m.* — **paper ruler,** *s.* régleur de papier de musique, *m.* — **pen,** *s.* griffe, *f.* — **printer,** *s.* imprimeur de musique, m. — **publisher,** *s.* éditeur de musique, *m.* — **room,** *s.* salle de musique, *f.*; (*for concerts*) *V.* — **hall.** — **seller,** *s.* marchand (*m.*, e, *f.*) de musique. — **shop,** *s.* magasin de musique, *m.* — **smith,** mécanicien pour pianos, *m.* — **stand,** *s.* *V.* — **desk.** — **stool,** *s.* tabouret de piano, *m.* — **warehouse,** *s.* magasin de musique, *m.*

Musical, *adj.* musical; à *or* de musique; harmonieux, mélodieux; (*pers.*) musicien. *The* — *art*, l'art musical, *m.*, la musique, *f.* — *festival*, fête musicale, *f.* — *box*, boîte à musique, *f.* — *instrument*, instrument de musique, *m.* — *instrument maker*, facteur d'instruments de musique, *m.* — *sounds*, des sons harmonieux, *m.pl.* — *glasses*, harmonica, *m.* *To have a* — *ear*, avoir de l'oreille pour la musique, avoir de l'oreille (*a very* — *ear*, beaucoup d'oreille)

Musically, *adv.* musicalement; en musique; harmonieusement, mélodieusement

Musicalness, *s.* nature harmonieuse *or* mélodieuse, harmonie, mélodie, *f.*

Musician, *s.* musicien, *m.*, -ne, *f.* *Noisy* or *rough* —, musicien enragé, *m.*, charivariste,*m.f.*
Musicograph, Musicographer, *s.* musicographe, *m.*
Musing, *s.* méditation, rêverie, *f.*
Musk, *s.* musc, *m.*; — *adj.* de musc; (*in compounds*) musqué; — *v.a.* musquer. — **apple,** *s.* pomme musquée, *f.* — **cat,** *s.* chat musqué, *m.* — **deer,** *s.* chevrotain porte-musc, porte-musc, musc, *m.* — **duck,** *s.* canard musqué, *m.* — **melon,** *s.* melon musqué, *m.* — **ox,** *s.* bœuf musqué, ovibos, *m.* — **pear,** *s.* poire musquée, *f.* — **rat,** *s.* rat musqué, *m.* — **rose,** *s.* rose muscade, *f.* — **rose tree,** *s.* rosier musqué, *m.* — **seed,** *s.* ambrette, *f.*
Musket, *s.* (*matchlock*) mousquet, *m.*; (*flint-gun or percussion-gun*) fusil de munition, fusil, *m.* — **ball, -bullet,** *s.* balle de fusil, *f.* — **barrel,** *s.* canon de fusil, *m.* — **proof,** *adj.* à l'épreuve des balles. — **shot,** *s.* coup de fusil, *m.*; (*ball*) balle de fusil, *f.*; (*distance*) portée de fusil, *f.* — **stock,** *s.* crosse de fusil, *f.*
Musketeer, *s.* mousquetaire, *m.*
Musketoon, *s.* mousqueton, *m.*
Musketry, *s.* fusillade, *f.*; mousqueterie, *f.*; (*muskets*) fusils, *m.pl.* *Discharge* or *fire* or *volley of* —, décharge de mousqueterie, fusillade, *f.* *School of* —, école de tir, *f.* — **instructor,** *s.* instructeur, *m.* — **practice,** *s.* exercice du fusil, *m.*; exercice à feu, *m.*
Muskiness, *s.* odeur de musc, *f.*
Muskito. *V.* **Mosquito**
Musky, *adj.* musqué; de musc
Muslin, *s.* mousseline, *f.*; — *adj.* de mousseline. — **de laine,** *s.* mousseline de laine, *f.* — **manufacturer,** *s.* mousselinier, *m.* — **printer,** *s.* imprimeur de mousseline, *f.* — **warehouseman,-weaver,** *s.* mousselinier, *m.*
Muslinet, *s.* mousselinette, *f.*
Musmon, *s.* mouflon, *m.*
Musquash, *s.* ondatra, rat musqué, *m.*
Musquito. *V.* **Mosquito**
Musrole, *s.* muserolle, *f.*
Mussel, *s.* moule, *f.* — **bed, -farm, -fishery,** *s.* moulière, *f.*, bouchot, *m.* — **plum,** *s.* quetsche, *f.* — **plum tree,** *s.* quetschier, *m.* — **scalp,** *s.* *V.* — **bed**
Mussulman, *s.* musulman, *m.*, e, *f.*
Mussulmanic, *adj.* musulman
Mussulmanism, *s.* musulmanisme, *m.*
Must, *v.n.* (*implying necessity, obligation, duty,* &c.) falloir (*imp.*), devoir; (*implying a supposition, an inference*) devoir. *I — answer,* il faut que je réponde. — *he not write?* ne faut-il pas qu'il écrive? *My son — go to Paris,* il faut que mon fils aille à Paris. *My son — be in Paris by this time,* mon fils doit être maintenant à Paris. *We — be just,* nous devons être justes *or* il faut être juste. *What — I do when I get there?* que faudra-t-il que je fasse quand je serai là? *I saw clearly that I — yield,* je vis bien qu'il fallait céder. *It* or *that — be done,* il faut que cela ce fasse. *It* or *that — not be done,* cela ne doit pas se faire. *It — be so,* (*should be done*) il le faut; (*cannot but be the case*) cela doit être ainsi. *You — know,* vous devez savoir; (*shall*) vous saurez. *You — have made a mistake,* il faut que vous ayez fait une erreur. *You — have seen,* vous avez dû voir. *The pain which he — have felt,* la douleur qu'il dut (*or* qu'il a dû, *or* qu'il avait dû, *or* qu'il aura dû, *according to the tense meant by the English phrase*) éprouver. (*Implying want.*) *I — have a new hat,* il me faut un chapeau neuf. *She — have a book,* il lui faut un livre
Must, *v.a.* (*make mouldy*) moisir; — *v.n.* (*grow mouldy*) se moisir, moisir
Must, *s.* moût, *m.*
Mustache, Mustachio, &c. *V.* **Moustache,** &c.
Mustard, *s.* moutarde, *f.* — **maker, -pot,** *s.* moutardier, *m.* — **seed,** *s.* graine de moutarde, *f.*
Mustee, *s.* octavon, *m.*, -ne, *f.*

Musteline, *adj.* de belette
Muster, *v.a.* faire l'appel de; passer en revue; (*gather*) rassembler, réunir; ramasser, recueillir; — *v.n.* s'assembler, se réunir; s'attrouper; (*amount*) être; être au nombre de, compter, s'élever à, se monter à; — *s.* appel, *m.*; revue, *f.*; (*gathering*) rassemblement, *m.*, réunion, *f.*; foule, *f.*; (*of birds*) troupe, bande, *f.*; (*register*) états, contrôles, *m.pl.* *To pass* —, passer à l'appel; être porté sur les contrôles; être passé en revue; (*fig.*) passer; être approuvé, être admis, être toléré. — **master,** *s.* officier d'appel, *m.* — **roll,** *s.* rôle, contrôle, *m.* *To call over the — roll,* faire l'appel
Mustiness, *s.* moisi, *m.*; relent, renfermé, *m.*
Musty, *adj.* moisi; (*sour*) aigre; (*of smell*) qui sent le relent *or* le renfermé. — *smell,* odeur de relent, *f.* *To smell* —, sentir le relent *or* le renfermé
Mutability, Mutableness, *s.* mutabilité, *f.*; inconstance, instabilité, variabilité, *f.*
Mutable, *adj.* muable; inconstant, variable
Mutably, *adv.* muablement; inconstamment, variablement
Mutage, *s.* mutage, *m.*
Mutation, *s.* mutation, *f.*, changement, *m.*
Mute, *adj.* muet; silencieux; (*gram.*) muet; — *s.* muet, *m.*, -te, *f.*; (*of the seraglio*) muet, *m.*; (*of a funeral*) personne placée à la porte d'une maison mortuaire, *f.*; (*gram.*) lettre muette, *f.*; (*mus.*) sourdine, *f.*
Mutely, *adv.* en muet; en silence, silencieusement
Muteness, *s.* mutisme, *m.*; silence, *m.*
Mutilate, *v.a.* mutiler; estropier; tronquer
Mutilating, *adj.* mutilateur
Mutilation, *s.* mutilation, *f.*
Mutilator, *s.* mutilateur, *m.*, -trice, *f.*
Mutineer, *s.* mutin, *m.*, e, *f.*, rebelle, *m.f.*
Mutinous, *adj.* mutin, mutiné; séditieux, rebelle
Mutinously, *adv.* en mutin; séditieusement
Mutinousness, *s.* mutinerie, *f.*
Mutiny, *s.* mutinerie, *f.*; sédition, rébellion, *f.*; — *v.n.* se mutiner; s'insurger, se révolter
Mutism, *s.* mutisme, *m.*
Mutter, *v.n.a.* murmurer, marmotter, gronder, grommeler; prononcer, proférer, dire; — *s.* murmure, *m.*
Mutterer, *s.* murmurateur, *m.*, -trice, *f.*, marmotteur, *m.*, -euse, *f.*
Muttering, *adj.* murmurant, qui murmure, murmurateur, marmotteur; — *s.* murmure, *m.*, murmures, *m.pl.*, marmottage, marmottement, *m.*
Mutteringly, *adv.* en murmurant, en marmottant
Mutton, *s.* mouton, *m.*; — *adj.* de mouton. — **broth,** *s.* bouillon de mouton, *m.* — **chop, -cutlet,** *s.* côtelette de mouton, *f.*
Mutual, *adj.* mutuel, réciproque; (*bad English for 'common,' as in " our — friend"*) commun
Mutual-ism, -ist. *V.* page 3, § 1
Mutuality, *s.* mutualité, réciprocité, *f.*
Mutually, *adv.* mutuellement, réciproquement
Muzzle, *s.* museau, *m.*; (*for the mouth*) muselière, *f.*; (*of bellows*) canon, bec, tuyau, *m.*; (*of pipes*) bout, *m.*; (*of a cannon*) bouche, gueule, *f.*; (*of a pistol*) gueule, *f.*, bout, *m.*; (*of a rifle or gun*) bouche, *f.*, bout, *m.*; — *v.n.* approcher son museau, flairer; — *v.a.* museler. — **loader,** *s.* arme (*f.*) à feu (fusil *or* &c.) se chargeant par la bouche *or* par la gueule. — **loading,** *adj.* se chargeant *or* qui se charge par la bouche *or* par la gueule. — **ring,** *s.* (*artil.*) ceinture de la bouche, *f.* — **stopper,** *s.* (*mil.*) bouchon de fusil *or* de carabine, *m.*
Muzzy, *adj.* distrait, préoccupé; troublé, trouble, confus; hébété; à moitié ivre
My, *pron. poss.* mon, ma, mes
Mygale, *s.* mygale, *f.*
Myiology, Myo-graphy, -logic, al, -logist, -logy, &c. *V.* page 3, § 1
Myope, *s.* myope, *m.f.*
Myopia, *s.* myopie, *f.*
Myopic, *adj.* myope

Myopy, *s.* myopie, *f.*
Myosotis, *s.* myosotis, *m.*
Myriad, *s.* myriade, *f.*
Myriagramme, *s.* myriagramme, *m.*
Myrialitre, *s.* myrialitre, *m.*
Myriametre, *s.* myriamètre, *m.*
Myriapod, *s.* myriapode, *m.*
Myriare, *s.* myriare, *m.*
Myrmidon, *s.* myrmidon, *m.* [myrobolan, *m.*
Myrobalan, Myrobolan, *s.* myrobalan,
Myrrh, *s.* myrrhe, *f.*
Myrrhed, *adj.* myrrhé
Myrtle, *s.* myrte, *m.* — **berry,** *s.* baie de myrte, *f.* — **tree,** *s.* myrte, *m.* [*verb*) me
Myself, *pron.* moi-même; moi; (*in a reflect.*
Mystagog-ic, al, -y. *V.* page 3, § 1
Mystagogue, *s.* mystagogue, *m.*
Mysterious, *adj.* mystérieux
Mysteriously, *adv.* mystérieusement
Mysteriousness, *s.* nature mystérieuse, *f.*, caractère mystérieux, mystère, *m.*
Mystery, *s.* mystère, m.
Myst-ic, al, -ically, -ism. *V.* page 3, § 1
Mysticalness, *s.* mysticité, *f.*
Mystification, *s.* mystification, *f.*; embarras, *m.*, confusion, perplexité, *f.*; obscurité, *f.*
Mystificator, Mystifier, *s.* mystificateur, *m.*, -trice, *f.*
Mystify, *v.a.* mystifier; embarrasser, dérouter; (*things*) envelopper de mystère; embrouiller, compliquer; obscurcir
Mystifying, *adj.* mystificateur; — *s.* *V.* [**Mystification**
Myth, *s.* mythe, *m.*
Myth-ic, al, -ically, -ography. *V.* p. 3, § 1
Mythicism, *s.* mythisme, *m.*
Mytholog-ic, al, -ically, -ist, -y. *V.* p. 3, § 1
Mythologize, *v.a.n.* mythologiser

N

N, *s.* (*letter*) n, *f.* [pincer
Nab, *v.a.* empoigner, happer, saisir; attraper,
Nabob, *s.* nabab, *m.* — **ship,** *s.* nababie, *f.*
Nacarat, *s.adj.* nacarat, *m.*
Nacre, *s.* nacre, *f.*; — *v.a.* nacrer
Nacred, Nacreous, *adj.* nacré
Nadir, *s.* nadir, *m.*
Nadiral, *adj.* nadiral
Nævus, *s.* nævus, nævus maternel, *m.*, tache de naissance, couenne, envie, *f.*
Nag, *s.* petit cheval, bidet, *m.*, (*jest.*) bique, *f.*
Naia, *s.* naia, *m.*
Naiad, *s.* naïade, *f.*
Nail, *s.* clou, *m.*; (*of persons, animals*) ongle, *m.*; (*screw*) vis, *f.*; — *v.a.* (— **down,** — **up**) clouer; attacher; (*a cannon*) enclouer; (*trees*) palisser; (*a door,* &c.) condamner; (*adorn*) clouter, garnir de clous; (*of bargains*) prendre au mot. *To hit the* — (or *the right* —) *on the head,* frapper juste, mettre le doigt dessus. *One — drives out another,* un clou chasse l'autre. — **box,** *s.* cloutière, *f.* — **brush,** *s.* brosse à ongles, *f.* — **file,** *s.* lime à ongles, *f.* — **head,** *s.* tête de clou, *f.* — **maker,** *s.* cloutier, *m.*, -ière, *f.* — **making, -manufactory, -manufacture,** *s.* clouterie, *f.* — **nippers, -scissors,** *s.pl.* ciseaux à ongles, *m.pl.* — **seller,** *s.* cloutier, *m.*, -ière, *f.* — **trade,** *s.* clouterie, *f.* — **work,** *s.* clouage, *m.* — **works,** *s.pl.* (*place*) clouterie, *f.*
Nailed, *part. adj.* (*fastened,* &c.) cloué, &c. (*V.* **Nail,** *v.a.*); (*furnished with nails*) à clous
Nailer, *s.* cloutier, *m.*, -ière, *f.*
Nailery, *s.* clouterie, *f.*
Nailing, *s.* clouage, clouement, *m.*
Nainsook, *s.* nansouck, nansouk, *m.*
Naive, *adj.* naïf
Naively, *adv.* naïvement
Naïveté, *s.* naïveté, *f.*

Naja, *s.* naja, *m.*
Naked, *adj.* nu; à nu; à découvert; dégarni sans défense, sans armes; découvert; ouvert; évident; simple, pur
Nakedly, *adv.* à nu; nûment; à découvert; sans défense; ouvertement; évidemment; simplement, purement
Nakedness, *s.* nudité, *f.*; état sans défense, manque de moyens de défense, *m.*; évidence, *f.*; simplicité, *f.* [mignard, minaudier
Namby-pamby, *adj.* prétentieux, affecté,
Name, *s.* nom, *m.*; renommée, réputation, *f.*; — *v.a.* nommer; (*call*) nommer, appeler; intituler; (*point out*) désigner, mentionner; indiquer; fixer; dire; parler de. *Assumed* —, pseudonyme, nom d'emprunt, nom de guerre, *m.* *Christian* —, nom de baptême, prénom, *m.* *Family* —, nom de famille. *Maiden* —, nom de demoiselle. *Another — for,* synonyme de. *By* —, de nom; nommé. *By the — of,* sous le nom de; du nom de. *By o's* —, par son nom; sous son nom. *By that* —, sous ce nom-là. *In* —, de nom. *In my* —, en mon nom; de ma part. *In the — of,* au nom de; sous le nom de; de la part de. *The mere — of it,* (*very little*) une idée, un soupçon. *To call* (*a person*) —*s,* dire des injures *or* des sottises à, injurier. *To mention a person's* —, nommer quelqu'un; se servir du nom de quelqu'un. *I mention no —s,* je ne nomme personne. *What is your —?* comment vous appelez-vous? *What is that gentleman's —?* comment s'appelle ce monsieur? *My — is F ...,* je m'appelle F ... — **day,** *s.* fête, *f.* —**less,** *adj.* sans nom, anonyme; (*unknown*) inconnu, obscur; (*inexpressible*) inexprimable, ineffable, indicible. ... *that shall be — less,* ... dont on taira le nom, ... que je ne nommerai pas. —**ly,** *adv.* savoir, nommément, particulièrement; c'est-à-dire. — **plate,** *s.* plaque pour le nom, *f.*; (*manu.*) plaque portant le nom du constructeur, *f.* — **sake,** *s.* homonyme, *m.* [*or* qui désigne, *f.*
Namer, *s.* personne qui nomme *or* qui appelle
Nandu, *s.* nandou, nandu, *m.*
Nankeen, Nankin, *s.* nankin, *m.*
Nankinet, *s.* nanquinette, *f.*
Nap, *s.* (*sleep*) somme, *m.*; (*of cloth, hats*) poil, *m.*; (*of plants*) duvet, *m.*; — *v.n.* faire un somme, sommeiller. *Afternoon's* —, sieste, *f.* *Noon's* —, méridienne, *f.* *To catch —ping,* surprendre, prendre au dépourvu, prendre à l'improviste; prendre en défaut. —**less,** *adj.* sans poil, ras; (*worn out*) pelé, râpé, usé
Nape, *s.* nuque, *f.*
Naphtha, *s.* naphte, *m.*
Naphthaline, *s.* naphtaline, *f.*
Naphtheine, *s.* naphtéine, *f.*
Napiform, *adj.* napiforme
Napkin, *s.* serviette de table, serviette, *f.*; (*baby's wrapper*) couche, *f.* — **ring,** *s.* rond de serviette, *m.*
Napoleon, *s.* (*Fr. coin*) napoléon, *m.*
Napoleonic, *adj.* napoléonien
Napoleonism, *s.* napoléonisme, *m.*
Napoleonist, *s.adj.* napoléoniste, *m.f.*, napoléonien, *m.*, -ne, *f.*
Napoleonistic, *adj.* napoléonien
Napped, *adj.* à poil
Narcissus, *s.* narcisse, *m.*
Narcosis, *s.* narcotisme, *m.*
Narcotic, *adj.s.* narcotique, *adj.m.f.*, *s.m.*
Narcotine, *s.* narcotine, *f.*
Narcotism, *s.* narcotisme, *m.*
Narcotize, *v.a.* narcotiser
Nard, *s.* nard, *m.* [narguilé, *m.*
Narghile, Nargile, Nargileh, *s.* narghilé,
Narrate, *v.a.* narrer, raconter, conter
Narration, *s.* narration, *f.*, récit, *m.*
Narrative, *adj.* narratif; — *s.* *V.* **Narration**
Narratively, *adv.* en récit, en forme de narration [*m.*, -euse, *f.*
Narrator, *s.* narrateur, *m.*, -trice, *f.*, conteur,

Narratory, *adj.* narratif
Narrow, *adj.* étroit ; limité, resserré, restreint, gêné ; exact, soigneux, scrupuleux, attentif ; rigoureux ; (*of the mind*) étroit, borné, rétréci ; (*small*) petit ; exigu ; (*sparing*) mesquin ; (*near*) de près ; — *s.* (*of water*) détroit, *m.* ; (*of mountains*) défilé, *m.* ; — *v.a.* rétrécir ; limiter, resserrer, restreindre ; — *v.n.* se rétrécir, &c. — **brimmed,** *adj.* à petits bords
Narrowing, *s.* rétrécissement, *m.*
Narrowly, *adv.* étroitement, à l'étroit ; (*fig.*) d'une manière bornée *or* rétrécie ; (*accurately*) exactement, soigneusement, scrupuleusement, attentivement ; (*sparingly*) mesquinement ; (*nearly*) de près ; de peu. *To — escape, to have a narrow escape, V.* **Escape.** *He — escaped being killed,* il a manqué être tué, peu s'en est fallu qu'il ne fût tué
Narrowness, *s.* étroitesse, *f.*, manque de largeur, *m.* ; manque d'étendue, *m.* ; (*of mind*) petitesse, *f.* ; (*of fortune,* &c.) exiguïté, modicité, petitesse, *f.* ; (*illiberality*) mesquinerie, *f.*
Narwhal, *s.* narval, *m.* [*f.* ; (*med.*) errhin, *m.*
Nasal, *adj.* nasal ; — *s.* nasale, lettre nasale,
Nasalis, *s.* (*zool.*) nasique, *f.*
Nasality, *s.* nasalité, *f.*
Nasalization, *s.* nasalisation, *f.*
Nasalize, *v.a.* nasaliser
Nasally, *adv.* nasalement
Nascent, *adj.* naissant
Nastily, *adv.* salement ; grossièrement ; vilainement ; désagréablement
Nastiness, *s.* saleté, *f.* ; grossièreté, *f.*
Nasturtion, Nasturtium, *s.* capucine, *f.* *Pickled —,* câpre capucine, *f.*
Nasty, *adj.* sale ; dégoûtant ; grossier ; vilain ; mauvais, désagréable. — **smelling,** *adj.* qui sent mauvais, d'une odeur désagréable
Natal, *adj.* natal, de naissance
Natality, *s.* natalité, *f.*
Natant, *adj.* nageant
Natatores, *s.pl.* oiseaux nageurs, *m.pl.*
Natatorial, Natatory, *adj.* natatoire ; (*that swims*) nageant
Nation, *s.* nation, *f.* ; peuple, *m.*
National, *adj.* national ; (*pers.*) national ; de son pays. — *debt,* dette publique, *f.* — *calamity,* calamité publique, *f.* — *school,* école d'enseignement mutuel, *f.*
Nationalism, *s.* nationalisme, *m.*
Nationalists, *s.pl.* nationaux, *m.pl.*
Nationality, *s.* nationalité, *f.*
Nationalization, *s.* nationalisation, *f.*
Nationalize, *v.a.* nationaliser
Nationally, *adv.* nationalement
Native, *adj.* naturel, natif ; (*pers.*) né (en, à), (*admin.*) natif ; (*of a place*) natal ; (*of language*) propre, maternel ; (*of people*) indigène ; (*of productions, animals,* &c.) indigène, originaire (de) ; du pays ; (*min.*) natif ; (*ingenuous*) naïf. — *country* or *land,* patrie, *f.*, pays natal, *m.*, terre natale, *f.* — *oyster,* huître parquée, *f.* — *subjects,* (*polit.*) nationaux, *m.pl.* — *tongue* or *language,* propre langue, langue maternelle, *f.* *I am (a) — of England (, of London),* je suis né (née, *f.*) en Angleterre (, à Londres), je suis Anglais (*m.*, e, *f.*) de naissance. *The coco-tree is (a) — of India,* le cocotier est originaire de l'Inde
Native, *s.* homme né (, *m. or* personne née, *f.*) dans le pays, natif, *m.*, -ive, *f.*, habitant, *m.*, e, *f.*, citoyen, *m.* ; (*of savage tribes,* &c.) naturel, *m.* ; indigène, *m.* ; (*oyster*) huître parquée, *f.* ; —**s,** *pl.* gens du pays, natifs, habitants, *m.pl.* ; naturels, *m.pl.* ; (*polit.*) nationaux, *m.pl.*
Natively, *adv.* nativement
Nativism, *s.* nativisme, *m.*
Nativity, *s.* naissance, *f.* ; (*place*) lieu de naissance, *m.* ; (*origin*) origine, *f.* ; (*theol.*) nativité, *f.* *To cast the — of,* tirer l'horoscope de
Natron, *s.* natron, natrum, *m.*
Natty, *adj.* propret, pimpant, gentil
Natural, *adj.* naturel ; naïf, simple ; réel ; (*mus.*) bécarre ; (*paint.*) au naturel ; — *s.* imbécile, idiot, *m.* ; (*mus.*) bécarre, *m.*
Natural-ism, -ist. *V.* page 3, § 1
Naturalization, *s.* naturalisation, *f.*
Naturalize, *v.a.* naturaliser
Naturally, *adv.* naturellement ; au naturel
Naturalness, *s.* naturalité, *f.* ; naturel, *m.* ; (*simplicity*) naïveté, *f.*
Nature, *s.* nature, *f.* ; (*temper*) naturel, *m.* *Good- —,* bon naturel, *m.* ; (*kindness*) bonté, *f.*, bonhomie, *f.* *Ill- —,* mauvais naturel, *m.* ; (*wickedness*) méchanceté, *f.* *From —,* (*arts*) d'après nature. *Of a — to,* de nature à
Natured, *adj.* de nature ... ; d'un ... naturel, d'un naturel ... *Good- —,* d'un bon naturel, bon. *Ill- —,* d'un mauvais naturel, méchant
Naturedly, *adv.* *Good- —,* avec bonté ; avec bonhomie ; sans se fâcher. *Ill- —,* avec *or* par malice, avec *or* par méchanceté, méchamment
Naught, *s.* rien, *m.* ; néant, *m.* ; (*arith.*) zéro, *m.* ; — *adv.* nullement, aucunement, en aucune façon. *To come to —,* échouer, ne pas réussir. *To set at —,*mettre au (*or* à) néant, mépriser, ne compter pour rien, ne tenir aucun compte de, ne faire aucun cas de ; braver, défier
Naughtily, *adv.* avec *or* par méchanceté, méchamment, vilainement, mal
Naughtiness, *s.* méchanceté, *f.*
Naughty, *adj.* méchant, vilain. — *boy,* — *girl,* vilain, *m.*, e, *f.* — *dog !* méchante bête !
Nausea, *s.* nausée, *f.* [— *trick,* méchanceté, *f.*
Nauseate, *v.n.a.* avoir des nausées ; (*fig.*) avoir du dégoût (pour) ; dégoûter [dégoûtant
Nauseating, Nauseous, *adj.* nauséabond,
Nauseously. *V.* **Disgustingly**
Nauseousness, *s.* nature nauséabonde, *f.* ; (*fig.*) dégoût, *m.*
Nautic, -al, *adj.* nautique ; naval ; maritime ; marin ; de marine. — *almanac,* almanach nautique, *m.*, connaissance des temps, *f.* — *instrument,* instrument de marine, *m.* — *man,*
Nautically, *adv.* nautiquement [marin, *m.*
Nautilus, *s.* nautile, *m.*
Naval, *adv.* naval ; maritime ; (*of the service*) de la marine ; (*of officers, expressions*) de marine. — *architecture,* architecture navale, construction de vaisseaux, *f.* — *architect,* constructeur de vaisseaux, *m.* — *examination,* concours d'admission à l'école de marine, *m.* — *power,* puissance maritime, *f.* — *school,* — *cadet, V.* **School** *and* **Cadet**
Nave, *s.* (*of churches*) nef, *f.* ; (*of wheels*) moyeu, *m.* — **box,** *s.* moyeu, *m.*
Navel, *s.* nombril, *m.* ; (*fig.*) centre, cœur, *m.* — **gall,** *s.* mal de rognons, *m.* — **string,** *s.* cordon ombilical, *m.* — **wort,** *s.* cotylédon,
Navew, *s.* navette, *f.* [cotylet, cotylier, *m.*
Navicula, *s.* navicule, *f.*
Navicular, *adj.* naviculaire
Naviform, *adj.* naviforme [bilité, *f.*
Navigability, Navigableness, *s.* naviga-
Navigable, *adj.* navigable
Navigate, *v.n.* naviguer ; — *v.a.* naviguer sur, naviguer ; (*to steer*) gouverner [navigation, *f.*
Navigating, *adj.* navigant ; navigateur ; — *s.*
Navigation, *s.* navigation, *f.* — **laws,** *s.pl.* législation sur la marine marchande, *f.*
Navigator, *s.* navigateur, *m.* ; (*workman*) *V.*
Navvy, *s.* terrassier, excavateur, *m.* [**Navvy**
Navy, *s.* marine, *f.* — **agency,** *s.* agence maritime, *f.* — **agent,** *s.* agent maritime, *m.* — **board,** *s.* conseil de la marine, *m.* — **clothier, -contractor,** *s.* entrepreneur de marine, *m.* — **list,** *s.* annuaire de la marine, *m.* — **office,** *s.* bureaux de la marine, *m.pl.* — **officer,** *s.* officier de marine, *m.* — **yard,** *s.* arsenal de marine, *m.*
Nay, *adv. int.* non ; non pas ; même, bien plus, qui plus est, il y a plus ; eh bien ! eh mais ! erreur ! bah ! — *s. V.* **No,** *s.*

Nazarean, Nazarene, Nazarite, *s.* Nazaréen, *m.*, -ne, *f.*
Neap, *adj.* bas, mort, de morte eau. — *tide,* morte marée, morte eau, *f.*, eaux mortes, *f.pl.*
Neapolitan, *s.adj.* Napolitain, *m.*, e, *f.*
Near, *adj.* près, près de; voisin, prochain, proche, rapproché; (*of relations*) proche; (*fig.*) intime, cher; exact, fidèle; (*parsimonious*) regardant, mesquin, serré; (*short*) court; (*left*) gauche, de gauche; —*prep. adv.* près, près de; de près; (*almost*) presque, près de; (*about*) *V.* **Nearly;** — *v.a.* approcher de, s'approcher de. — *it, them* (*things*), auprès. — *and dear to* ..., qui touche de près ... *To be — and dear to* ..., toucher de près ... *To bring —* or *—er,* approcher (de). *To come* or *go* or *get —* or *—er,* approcher (de); s'approcher (de); &c. (*V.* **Come** —). *Not to be — so* ..., &c., *V.* **Nearly.** *That would go — to ruin me,* cela me ruinerait presque. *This apple is — ripe,* cette pomme est presque mûre. *This apple is not — ripe,* cette pomme est loin d'être mûre, cette pomme n'est pas mûre à beaucoup près, il s'en faut que cette pomme soit mûre. *It is — ten o'clock,* il est près de dix heures. — **sighted,** *adj. V.* **Short-sighted**
Nearly, *adv.* de près; (*about*) à peu près, environ; presque, près de; (*parsimoniously*) mesquinement. *Not to be — so* ..., n'être pas à beaucoup près aussi ... *He was — killed,* peu s'en est fallu qu'il ne fût tué, il a failli (*or* manqué) être tué. *This apple is — ripe,* &c., *V.* **Near**
Nearness, *s.* proximité, *f.*; (*of relations*) proche parenté, *f.*; (*parsimony*) mesquinerie, parcimonie, *f.* — *of relationship,* proche parenté, *f.*
Neat, *adj.* propre; (*fair, clear*) net; (*tidy*) rangé; soigné; joli; (*pure, unmingled*) pur; (*clever*) adroit; (*pretty*) joli, gentil; (*of compliments*) joli, bien tourné; (*com.*) net; — *adv.* (*of drinking*) sec; — *s.* (*— cattle*) gros bétail, *m.* — **herd,** *s.* bouvier, vacher, pâtre, *m.* —**'s foot,** *s.* pied de bœuf, *m.* —**'s leather,** *s.* cuir de vache, *m.* —**'s tongue,** *s.* langue de bœuf, *f.*
Neatly, *adv.* proprement; purement; adroitement
Neatness, *s.* propreté, *f.*; pureté, *f.*
Neb, *s.* bec, *m.*
Nebula, *s.* nébuleuse, *f.*
Nebulosity, *s.* nébulosité, *f.*
Nebulous, *adj.* nébuleux, nuageux
Nebuly, *adj.* nébulé
Necessaries, *s.pl.* nécessaire, *m.*, objets de nécessité, *m.pl.*, nécessités (de la vie), *f.pl.*; (*privy*) lieux d'aisances, lieux, *m.pl.*, commodités, *f.pl.*
Necessarily, *adv.* nécessairement
Necessariness, *s.* nécessité, *f.*
Necessary, *adj.* nécessaire; (*not free*) obligé, forcé; — *s.* chose nécessaire, *f.*; (*closet*) lieux d'aisances, lieux, *m.pl.*, commodités, *f.pl.* *To be —*, être nécessaire; falloir. *Longer, more than —*, plus longtemps, plus qu'il ne faut
Necessitate, *v.a.* nécessiter; obliger, contraindre
Necessitous, *adj.* (*pers.*) nécessiteux, dans la nécessité, besoigneux, indigent; (*things*) de nécessité, de dénûment
Necessitousness, *s.* nécessité, *f.*, dénûment, *m.*
Necessity, *s.* nécessité, *f.*; (*want*) besoin, *m.*, nécessité, *f.* *Of —*, nécessairement. *— is the mother of invention,* la nécessité est la mère de l'industrie. *To make a virtue of —*, faire de nécessité vertu
Neck, *s.* cou, *m.*; (*of bottles,* &c.) cou, goulot, *m.*; (*of mountains*) col, *m.*; (*of land*) langue, *f.*; (*of mutton, veal*) collet, *m.*; (*of beef*) collier, *m.*, (*of violins,* &c.) manche, *m.*; (*of a chimney*) tuyau, *m.*; (*anat., of the bladder*) col, *m.* *Best end of the —*, (*of mutton*) carré, *m.* *By a —*, (*in horse racing*) d'une encolure, d'une tête. — *and crop, V.* **Outright,** *adv.* — *or nothing,* tout ou rien. — **band,** *s.* rabat, *m.* — **chain,** *s.* chaîne de cou, *f.* —**chop,** *s.* côtelette (de mouton) ordinaire, *f.* — **cloth,** *s.* cravate, *f.* — **handkerchief,** — **kerchief,** *s.* (*of women*) fichu, *m.*; (*of men*) cravate, *f.*; (*mil.*) col, *m.* —**lace,** —**let,** *s.* collier, *m.*; chaîne de cou, *f.* — **piece,** *s.* gorgerin, *m.* —**tie,** *s.* cravate, *f.*
Necked, *adj.* (*in compounds*) au cou ..., qui a le cou ...
Necrologic, -al, *adj.* nécrologique
Necrologist, *s.* nécrologue, *m.*
Necrology, *s.* nécrologie, *f.*
Necromancer, *s.* nécromancien, *m.*, -ne, *f.*
Necromancy, *s.* nécromancie, *f.*
Necromantic, *adj.* nécromantique
Necrophagan, *s.*, **Necrophagous,** *adj.* nécrophage, *s.m.*, *adj.m.f.*
Necropolis, *s.* nécropole, *f.*
Necrose, *v.a.* nécroser
Necrosis, *s.* nécrose, *f.*
Nectar, *s.* nectar, *m.*
Nectarean, Nectared, Nectareous, *adj.* nectaréen, nectaré, de nectar
Nectarine, *s.* (*clingstone —*) brugnon, *m.*; (*freestone —*) pêche lisse, *f.*
Nectary, *s.* nectaire, *m.*
Née, *part. adj. f.* (*Fr.*) née
Need, *s.* besoin, *m.*, nécessité, *f.* *If — be,* s'il le faut, s'il est nécessaire, au besoin. *In case of —*, en cas de besoin, au besoin. *To be* or *stand in — of, to have — of,* avoir besoin de
Need, *v.a.* avoir besoin de; (*require*) exiger, demander; — *v.n.* avoir besoin (de, *with the inf.*; que, *with the subj.*); être nécessaire (de, que), devoir, falloir; être obligé (de); avoir (à). *You — not laugh,* il n'y a pas là de quoi rire
Needed, Needful, *adj.* nécessaire
Needful, *s.* *The —*, le nécessaire, *m.*; ce qu'il faut, *m.*; (*money*) le *or* du quibus, *m.*
Needfully, *adv.* nécessairement
Needily, *adv.* dans le besoin
Neediness, *s.* besoin, *m.*, nécessité, *f.*; indigence, *f.*
Needle, *s.* aiguille, *f.*; (*mariner's compass*) boussole, *f.* — **case,** *s.* étui à aiguilles, étui, *m.* —**fish,** *s.* aiguillat, *m.* —**ful,** *s.* aiguillée, *f.* — **gun,** *s.* fusil à aiguille, *m.* — **holder,** *s.* porte-aiguilles, *m.* — **maker,** *s.* aiguillier, *m.*, -ière, *f.* —**shaped,** *adj.* en forme d'aiguille, en aiguille, aiguillé, acéreux. — **woman,** *s.* couturière, lingère, *f.* —**work,** *s.* ouvrage à l'aiguille, *m.*; (*plain*) couture, *f.*; (*fancy*) tapisserie, *f.* [*also,* broderie, tricotage, &c.] *To do —work,* travailler à l'aiguille
Needless, *adj.* inutile. —**ly,** *adv.* inutilement, sans nécessité. —**ness,** *s.* inutilité, *f.*
Needs, *adv.* nécessairement, de toute nécessité; inévitablement; absolument
Needy, *adj.* nécessiteux, besoigneux, indigent
Nefarious, *adj.* abominable, exécrable
Nefariously, *adv.* abominablement, exécrablement
Negation, *s.* négation, *f.*
Negative, *adj.* négatif; — *s.* négative, *f.*; (*gram.*) négation, *f.*; (*in photography*) épreuve négative, négative, *f.*, (*plate*) cliché, *m.*; — *v.a.* décider négativement; (*a proposition,* &c.) rejeter. *In the —*, négativement
Negatively, *adv.* négativement
Neglect, *v.a.* négliger; dédaigner; abandonner; — *s. V.* **Negligence**
Neglectful, -ly. *V.* **Negligent, -ly**
Negligee, *s.* négligé, *m.*
Negligence, *s.* négligence, *f.*; abandon, *m.*; inattention, *f.*; (*carelessness*) nonchalance, *f.*; (*omission, forgetfulness*) oubli, *m.*
Negligent, *adj.* négligent; (*of*) qui néglige; (*careless*) nonchalant. *To be — of,* négliger
Negligently, *adv.* négligemment; nonchalamment
Negociable, &c. *V.* **Negotiable,** &c.
Negotiability, *s.* négociabilité, *f.*
Negotiable, *adj.* négociable
Negotiate, *v.a.n.* négocier

Negotiation, *s.* négociation, *f.*
Negotia-tor, trix, *s.* négociateur, *m.*, -trice, *f.*
Negress, *s.* négresse, *f.*
Negro, *s.* nègre, *m.*; — *adj.* nègre, de nègre; noir. — **boy,** *s.* négrillon, *m.* — **girl,** *s.* négrillonne, *f.* — **jail,** *s.* nègrerie, *f.* — **woman,** *s.* négresse, *f.* — **yard,** *s.* nègrerie, *f.*
Negus, *s.* négus, vin chaud, *m.*
Neigh, *v.n.* hennir; — *s.* hennissement, *m.*
Neighbour, *s.* voisin, *m.*, e, *f.*; (*fellow-creature*) prochain, *m.*; — *v.a.* avoisiner, être voisin de. *To — it,* voisiner
Neighbourhood, *s.* voisinage, *m.*; environs, alentours, *m.pl.*; (*part of a town*) quartier, *m.*; (*part of a country*) localité, *f.*, pays, *m.*
Neighbouring, *adj.* voisin, avoisinant, du voisinage; des environs
Neighbourliness, *s.* qualité de bon voisin, conduite d'un bon voisin, *f.* [en bon voisin
Neighbourly, *adj. adv.* de *or* en voisin, de *or*
Neighing, *s.* hennissement, *m.*
Neither, *pron.* ni l'un (l'une, *f.*) ni l'autre; aucun (e, *f.*); — *conj.* ni; ne ... pas non plus. — *you nor he shall have it,* ni vous ni lui ne l'aurez
Nem. con., (*Latin*) nemine contradicente, sans opposition, à l'unanimité, unanimement
Nemean, *adj.* Néméen
Neo, (*in compounds*) néo- ...
Neographer, *s.* néographe, *m.* [*V.* page 3, § 1
Neolog-ic, al, -ism, -y, &c., néologique, &c.
Neologist, *s.* néologue, néologiste, *m.f.*
Neophyte, *s. adj.* néophyte, *m.f.*
Neorama, *s.* néorama, *m.*
Nepaulese, *s. adj.* Népalais, *m.*, e, *f.*
Nephew, *s.* neveu, *m.*
Nephrite, *s.* néphrite, *f.*
Nephritic, *adj. s.* néphritique
Nephritis, *s.* néphrite, *f.*
Ne plus ultra, *s.* (*Latin*) nec plus ultra, *m.*
Nepot-ic, -ism, -ist, népotique, &c. (*V.* p. 3, § 1)
Neptunian, *s. adj.* neptunien, *m.*, -ne, *f.*
Neptun-ism, -ist. *V.* page 3, § 1
Nereid, *s.* néréide, *f.*
Neroli, *s.* néroli, *m.*
Neronian, *adj.* néronien
Nervation, *s.* nervation, *f.*
Nerve, *s.* nerf, *m*; courage, sang-froid, *m.*; (*arch., bot.*) nervure, *f.*; — *v.a.* donner du nerf *or* de la vigueur à, fortifier. —**less,** *adj.* énervé, sans vigueur, sans force [nervé
Nerved, *part. adj.* fortifié; vigoureux; (*bot.*)
Nervine, *adj.* nerval; nervin; — *s.* nervin, *m.*
Nervosity, *s.* nervosité, *f.*
Nervous, *adj.* nerveux; vigoureux, fort; timide; impressionnable; intimidé, effrayé, troublé; inquiet; (*bot.*) nerval. — *fit,* attaque de nerfs, *f.* — *system,* système nerveux, *m.*
Nervously, *adv.* nerveusement; vigoureusement, avec vigueur
Nervousness, *s.* nervosité, *f.*; (*med.*) état nerveux, nervosisme, *m.*; (*fam.*) agacement des nerfs, *m.*, irritation nerveuse, *f.*; (*fig.*) nerf, *m.*, vigueur, force, *f.*; timidité, *f.*; trouble, *m.*; inquiétude, *f.*
Nervure, *s.* nervure, *f.*
Nescience, *s.* ignorance, *f.*
Nest, *s.* nid, *m.*; (*brood*) nichée, *f.*; (*fig.*) repaire, *m.*; — *v.n.* *V.* **Nestle.** — *of drawers,* casier, *m.* — **building,** *adj.* nicheur, nidulant; *s.* construction d'un nid (*or* de nids), nidification, *f.* — **egg,** *s.* nichet, *m.*
Nestle, *v.n.* nicher; (*harbour*) se nicher, se loger, s'établir; — *v.a.* nicher, loger; (*cherish*) chérir, choyer. — **in,** *v.a.* cacher, enfermer
Nestling, *s.* (*young bird*) petit oiseau au nid, *m.*; (*smallest bird*) culot, *m.*; — *adj.* encore au nid
Net, *s.* filet, *m.*; réseau, rets, *m.*; (*for dress*) tulle, *m.*; (*knitting*) tricot, *m.*; — *adj.* (*com.*) net; (*pure*) pur; — *v.a.* filer; (*catch*) prendre au filet; (*com.*) (*produce*) produire *or* donner un bénéfice net de, rapporter net; (*gain*) gagner net; — *v.n.* faire du filet. — **cost,** *s.* prix de revient, *m.* — **maker,** *s.* faiseur (*m.*, -euse, *f.*) de filets; (*of fabrics*) tulliste, *m.f.* — **making,** *s.* fabrication de filets, *f.*; (*of fabrics*) tullerie, *f.* —**work,** *s.* réseau, *m.*; filet, *m.*; [(*knitting*) tricot, *m.*
Nether, *adj.* *V.* **Lower**
Netherlander, *s.*, **Netherlandish,** *adj.* [Néerlandais, *m.*, e, *f.*
Nett, *adj.* *V.* **Net**
Netting, *s.* *V.* **Net,** *s.* — **mesh,** *s.* moule, *m.* — **needle,** *s.* navette, *f.* — **rule,** *s.* moule, *m.* — **silk,** *s.* cordonnet, *m.*
Nettle, *s.* ortie, *f.*; — *v.a.* ortier; (*fig.*, '*at*,' de) piquer, blesser, irriter, fâcher, vexer, provoquer, aigrir. — **creeper,** *s.* fauvette babillarde, *f.* — **rash,** *s.* urticaire, *f.* — **tree,** *s.* micocoulier, fabreguier, *m.* — **tribe,** *s.* urticées, *f.pl.*
Nettler, *s.* provocateur, *m.*, -trice, *f.*
Neural axis, névraxe, *m.*
Neuralgia, Neuralgy, *s.* névralgie, *f.*
Neuralgic, *adj.* névralgique
Neurine, *s.* névrine, *f.*
Neuritis, *s.* névrite, *f.*
Neuro, (*in compounds*) névro ...
Neurographer, *s.* névrographe, *m.*
Neurography, *s.* névrographie, *f.*
Neurologic,-al, *adj.* névrologique
Neurologist, *s.* névrologue, *m.*
Neurology, *s.* névrologie, *f.*
Neuropathic, *adj.* névropathique
Neuropathy, *s.* névropathie, *f.*
Neuropteral, Neuropterous, *adj.* névroptère
Neuropteran, *s.* névroptère, *m.*
Neurosis, *s.* névrose, *f.*
Neurotic. *V.* **Nervine**
Neurotomy, *s.* névrotomie, *f.*
Neustrian, *s. adj.* Neustrien, *m.*, -ne, *f.*
Neuter, *adj. s.* neutre, *adj.m.f.*, *s.m.*
Neutral, *adj.* neutre; indifférent; — *s.* neutre, *m.*
Neutrality, *s.* neutralité, *f.*; indifférence, *f.*
Neutralization, *s.* neutralisation, *f.*
Neutralize, *v.a.* neutraliser
Neutrally, *adv.* neutralement
Neuvaine, *s.* (*Cath rel.*) neuvaine, *f.*
Never, *adv.* jamais; pas; nullement, aucunement; (*with a verb*) ne ... jamais; ne ... pas; ne ... nullement, ne ... aucunement; ne ... rien; quelque ... que ce soit; (*indeed!*) allons donc! bah! *Were it — so pleasant,* quelque agréable que ce soit. —**ceasing,** *adj.* continuel, incessant. —**ending,** *adj.* *V.* **Ending.** —**failing,** *adj.* infaillible. — **-to-be-forgotten,** *adj.* à jamais mémorable
Nevertheless, *adv.* néanmoins, cependant, toutefois; n'en ... pas moins
New, *adj.* (*fresh from the maker, not used or little used yet, in prime condition, untried, unexplored,* &c.) neuf; (*different, additional, novel, of a later season*) nouveau; (*recent*) récent; frais; (*bread*) tendre, frais; (*milk*) du jour; (*in compounds*) nouvellement, nouveau, de nouveau, re- ... *A — book,* (*not used*) un livre neuf; (*newly out*) un livre nouveau; (*a different one*) un nouveau livre. *As good as —,* ayant peu servi, presque neuf. *To repair equal to —, to make as good as —,* remettre à neuf. — **baked,** *adj.* nouvellement cuit, frais, tendre. — **born,** *adj.* nouveau-né (nouveau-née, *f.*, nouveau-nés, *m.pl.*, nouveau-nées, *f.pl.*). — **comer,** *s.* nouveau-venu, *m.*, nouvelle-venue, *f.*, nouveaux-venus, *m.pl.*, nouvelles-venues, *f.pl.* — **dress,** *v.a.* habiller à neuf. — **Englander,** *s.* habitant (*m.*, e, *f.*) de la Nouvelle-Angleterre. — **fangled,** *adj.* de nouvelle invention, d'un nouveau genre. — **fangledness,** — **fangleness,** *s.* nouvelle invention, nouveauté, *f.* — **fashioned,** *adj.* de nouvelle mode. — **foot,** *v.a.* rempiéter. —**foundland,** *s.* (*geog.*) Terre-Neuve, *f.*; (*dog*) terre-neuve, *m.*, chien de Terre-Neuve, *m.*; *adj.* terre-neuvier, terre-neuvien. —*foundland fisher,* terre-neuvier, *m.* — **front,** *v.a.* (*boots*)

remonter. — **gild,** *v.a.* redorer. — **laid,** *adj.* (*egg*) frais. — **line,** *v.a.* redoubler. — **seat,** *v.a.* remettre un fond à. — **silver,** *v.a.* réargenter. — **sole,** *v.a.* ressemeler. — **soling,** *s.* ressemelage, *m.* — **stock,** *v.a.* remonter. — *year,* &c. *V.* **Year.** — **Yorker,** *s.* New-Yorkais, *m.*, e, *f.* — **Zealander,** *s.* Nouveau-Zélandais, *m.*

Newal, Newel, *s.* noyau d'escalier, noyau, *m.*

Newgate. — **bird,** *s.* gibier de potence, *m.* — **calendar,** *s.* recueil de causes célèbres, *m.*

Newish, *adj.* assez neuf; assez nouveau; assez frais; assez récent

Newly, *adv.* nouvellement; récemment; fraîchement; (*again*) de nouveau, re- ...

Newness, *s.* nouveauté, *f.*

News, *s.* nouvelle, *f.*, nouvelles, *f.pl.* *Piece of* —, nouvelle, *f.* *No —s, good —s,* point de nouvelles, bonnes nouvelles. — **agent,** *s.* commissionnaire pour les journaux, *m.* — **boy, -man,** *s.* marchand de journaux, *m.* — **letter,** *s.* nouvelles à la main, *f.pl.* — **machine,** *s.* machine à journaux, *f.* — **monger,** *s.* débitant (*m.*, e, *f.*) de nouvelles, nouvelliste, *m.f.* — **office,** *s.* *V.* — **shop.** — **paper,** *s.* journal, *m.* —**paper agent, boy,** &c., *V.* — **agent,** &c. —**paper compositor,** —**paper writer,** *s.* journaliste, *m.* — **room,** *s.* cabinet de lecture, *m.* — **shop,** *s.* boutique de marchand de journaux, *f.* — **vendor** *or* **vender,** *s.* marchand (*m.*, e, *f.*) de journaux. — **writer,** *s.* journaliste, *m.*

Newt, *s.* salamandre aquatique, *f.*, triton, *m.*

Newter, *s.* castorin, *m.*

Newtonian, *s.adj.* Newtonien, *m.*, -ne, *f.*

Newtonianism, *s.* newtonianisme, *m.*

Next, *adj.* (*of place*) voisin; d'à-côté; (*of place and order*) suivant; (*of time to come, coming*) prochain; (*having followed a time now past*) suivant, d'après; (*of degree, rank*) plus proche; (*first*) premier; (*dearest*) plus cher. — *but one,* second, deuxième. — *but two,* &c., troisième, &c. — *Monday,* lundi prochain. *The — Monday,* le lundi suivant *or* d'après. — *week,* la semaine prochaine. *The — week,* la semaine suivante *or* d'après. *The — page,* la page suivante. — *time,* la prochaine fois. *My — visit will be* ..., ma prochaine visite sera ... *The — world,* l'autre monde. *The — thing to be done,* la première chose à faire ensuite. *What was the — thing he did?* qu'a-t-il fait (*or* que fit-il) ensuite?

Next, *adv.* après; ensuite; immédiatement. — *to,* (*close by*) auprès de, près de, à côté de; tout contre; (*on*) sur; (*after*) après; (*almost*) presque, à peu près. — *to it, them* (*things*), auprès, à côté; tout contre; dessus; après, ensuite. *What — ?* après? ensuite? et ensuite?

Nib, *s.* (*of birds, pens*) bec, *m.*; (*end*) pointe, *f.*, bout, *m.*; (*of cocoa,* &c.) morceau, *m.*; — *v.a.* couper le bec *or* la pointe *or* le bout de

Nibbed, *adj.* à bec ...; à pointe ...

Nibble, *v.a.n.* grignoter, ronger; mordiller; (*grass, leaves*) brouter; (*of birds*) becqueter; (*of fishes*) mordre à l'hameçon, mordre; (*cavil*) épiloguer (sur); — *s.* coup de dent, *m.*; (*the rat, in fables*) Ronge-maille, *m.* *Squire —,* maître Ronge-maille, *m.*

Nibbler, *s.* grignoteur, *m.*, -euse, *f.*, rongeur, *m.*, -euse, *f.*; (*caviller*) épilogueur, *m.*, -euse, *f.*

Nice, *adj.* bon; délicat; agréable; (*comfortable*) bon; (*fine*) beau, joli, gentil; fin; (*tidy*) propre, soigné; (*amiable*) aimable, gentil, charmant; (*exact*) exact, scrupuleux, soigneux; rigoureux; juste; (*keen*) subtil; (*refined*) recherché; (*sensitive*) sensible, chatouilleux; (*particular*) difficile, exigeant; (*punctilious*) pointilleux. — *and* ..., (*very* ...) bien ... — **looking,** *adj.* beau, joli, gentil. — **smelling,** *adj.* qui sent bon, d'une odeur agréable

Nicely, *adv.* bien; délicatement; gentiment; exactement, scrupuleusement, soigneusement; rigoureusement; justement; subtilement; sensiblement; (*of dressing*) d'une manière recherchée

Nicene, *adj.* de Nicée. — *creed,* symbole de [Nicée, *m.*

Niceness, Nicety, *s.* goût agréable, *m.*; amabilité, gentillesse, *f.*; finesse, délicatesse, *f.*; exactitude, précision, *f.*; justesse, *f.*; subtilité, *f.*; sensibilité, *f.*; (*care*) soin, *m.*; (*in dress*) recherche, *f.*; raffinement, *m.* **Niceties,** *pl.* (*dainties*) friandises, *f.pl.* *To a —,* à point; parfaitement; exactement

Niche, *s.* niche, *f.*

Nick, *s.* (*of time*) moment précis, *m.*; (*notch*) coche, encoche, entaille, *f.*; (*at play*) point gagnant, *m.*; — *v.a.* (*hit*) rencontrer juste; (*notch*) faire une coche *or* une encoche *or* une entaille dans, cocher, encocher; (*a ticket*) contrôler; (*a horse's tail*) niqueter, anglaiser. *In the — of time,* à point nommé, tout à point; à propos. — **nack,** *s.* bibelot, brimborion, colifichet, *m.*, babiole, *f.* — **name,** *s.* sobriquet, *m.*; *v.a.* donner un sobriquet à, baptiser, [appeler

Nickar-tree, *s.* guilandine, *f.*

Nickel, *s.* nickel, *m.* — **silver,** *s.* maillechort, alfénide, *m.*

Nicking, *s.* (*of a horse's tail*) niquetage, *m.*

Nicotiana, *s.* nicotiane, *f.*

Nicotic, *adj.* nicotique

Nicotine, *s.* nicotine, *f.*

Nicotize, *v.a.* nicotiser

Nictitating, *adj.* nictitant

Nidification, *s.* nidification, *f.*

Nidorous, *adj.* nidoreux

Niece, *s.* nièce, *f.*

Niello, *s.* nielle, *m.* — **cutting, -work,** *s.* niellure, *f.*, nielle, *m.* — **worker,** *s.*, — **working,** *adj.* nielleur, *m.* [gardly

Niggard, *s.* avare, ladre, *m.*; — *adj.* *V.* **Niggardly**

Niggardliness, *s.* avarice, ladrerie, vilenie, *f.*; mesquinerie, *f.*

Niggardly, *adj.* avare, ladre; mesquin, chiche; — *adv.* en avare, mesquinement

Nigger, *s.* nègre, *m.*, négresse, *f.*, moricaud, *m.*, e, *f.*; (*insect*) fausse-chenille, *f.*

Nigh. *V.* **Near.** *Well —,* à peu près, presque

Night, *s.* nuit, *f.*; (*evening*) soir, *m.*; (*in compounds*) de nuit, nocturne; (*theat.*) représentation, *f.* ... *a —,* (*so much a —*) ... par soirée. *At —,* la nuit, pendant la nuit, dans la nuit; le soir; (*of the hour*) du soir. *Over —,* dans la soirée; la veille au soir; (*yesterday*) hier soir. *Dark —,* nuit noire, nuit close. *Good —!* bonsoir! bonne nuit! *Last —,* cette nuit, la nuit dernière; hier soir, hier au soir. *The —* (*evening*) *after* or *before* ..., &c., *V.* **Evening.** *The — before last,* avant-hier soir. *To- —,* ce soir; cette nuit. *To be —,* faire nuit. *To turn — into day,* faire du jour la nuit. — **bird,** *s.* oiseau de nuit, oiseau nocturne, *m.* — **blindness,** *s.* (*med.*) héméralopie, *f.* — **boat,** *s.* bateau de nuit, *m.* — **born,** *adj.* né des ténèbres. — **cap,** *s.* bonnet de nuit, serre-tête, *m.*; verre de grog, grog, *m.* — **cart,** *s.* voiture de vidange, *f.* — **dew,** *s.* serein, *m.*, rosée du soir, *f.* — **dress,** *s.* chemise de nuit, *f.* — **fall,** *s.* tombée de la nuit, *f.*; nuit, *f.* — **fire,** *s.* feu de nuit, *m.*; (*ignis fatuus*) feu follet, *m.* — **gear,** *s.* toilette de nuit, *f.* — **gown,** *s.* chemise de nuit, *f.* — **ingale,** *s.* rossignol, *m.* — **jar,** *s.* engoulevent, *m.* — **lamp, -light,** *s.* veilleuse, *f.* — **long,** *adj.* de toute la (*or* une) nuit. — **ly,** *adj.* de nuit, nocturne; *adv.* de nuit, la nuit, pendant la nuit; (*every night*) toutes les nuits; tous les soirs. — **mail,** *s.* malle de nuit, *f.* — **man,** *s.* vidangeur, *m.* — **manure,** *s.* engrais humain, *m.*, gadoue, *f.* — **mare,** *s.* cauchemar, *m.* — **piece,** *s.* (*paint.*) effet de nuit, *m.* — **post,** *s.* poste de nuit, *f.* — **shade,** *s.* morelle, *f.* — **shirt,** *s.* chemise de nuit, *f.* — **soil,** *s.* vidanges, *f.pl.*; (*as manure*)

V. — **manure.** —**'s rest,** s. nuit, *f.* *To have a good —'s rest,* passer une bonne nuit, bien reposer. — **thoughts,** s. *pl.* *Young's — Thoughts,* les Nuits d'Young. *f.pl.* — **time,** s. nuit, *f.* — **train,** s. train de nuit, *m.* — **walk,** s. promenade nocturne, *f.* — **walker,** s. coureur de nuit, *m.*; somnambule, *m.f.* — **walking,** *adj.* qui rôde *or* court la nuit; somnambule; s. somnambulisme, *m.* — **watch,** s. garde de nuit, *f.*; veille de nuit, *f.*; sentinelle, *f.* — **watchman,** s. gardien *or* garde de nuit, veilleur de nuit, veilleur, *m.* — **work,** s. travail de nuit, ouvrage de nuit, *m.*

Nigrescent, *adj.* nigrescent

Nihil-ism, -ist. *V.* page 3, § 1

Nil, s. rien, néant, *m.*; (*com.*) nul

Nill, *v.a.n.* ne pas vouloir, refuser. *Will or —,* bon gré mal gré, de gré ou de force

Nilometer, s. nilomètre, *m.*

Nilotic, *adj.* nilotique, du Nil

Nimble, *adj.* agile, leste, dispos, léger, vif; (*of the tongue*) délié, bien pendu, bien affilé. — **footed,** *adj.* au pied léger; leste. — **witted,** *adj.* à l'esprit vif [cité, *f.*

Nimbleness, s. agilité, *f.*; légèreté, *f.*; viva-

Nimbly, *adv.* agilement, lestement, légèrement, vivement

Nimbus, s. (*halo*) nimbe, *m.*; (*cloud*) nimbus, *m.*

Nincompoop, s. nicodème, nigaud, *m.*

Nine, *adj. s.* neuf (*adj.m.f.*, *s.m.*); (*elliptically*) (*of the clock*) neuf heures, *f.pl.*, (*of o.'s age*) neuf ans, *m.pl.* *Dressed up* (or *out*) *to the —s,* tiré à quatre épingles. —**fold,** *adj. adv.* nonuple, neuf fois autant, neuf fois. — **holes,** *s.pl.* balle au pot, *f.*; (*at marbles*) bloquette, *f.* — **pins,** *s.pl.* quilles, *f.pl.*

Nineteen, *adj.* dix-neuf

Nineteenth, *adj. s.* dix-neuvième; (*of the month*) dix-neuf. *The —,* (*of sovereigns*) dix-neuf

Ninetieth, *adj.* quatre-vingt-dixième

Ninety, *adj.* quatre-vingt-dix. — *one,* quatre-vingt-onze. — *two,* &c., quatre-vingt-douze, &c. — *first,* quatre-vingt-onzième. — *second,* &c., quatre-vingt-douzième, &c.

Ninevite, *adj.* ninivite

Ninny, Ninnyhammer, s. nigaud, *m.*, e, *f.*, benêt, niais, *m.*, e, *f.*

Ninth, *adj.* neuvième; — s. neuvième, (*part*) *m.*, (*pers.*) *m.f.*, (*mus.*) *f.*; (*of the month*) neuf, *m.* *The —,* (*of sovereigns*) neuf

Ninthly, *adv.* neuvièmement

Niobic, *adj.* niobique

Niobium, s. niobium, *m.*

Nip, *v.a.* (— **off**) (*pinch*) pincer; (*cut*) couper; (*bite*) mordre; (*blast*) flétrir, brûler; (*destroy*) détruire; (*vex*) piquer; — s. (*of the nails*) coup d'ongle, *m.*; (*of the teeth*) coup de dent, *m.*; (*of liquor*) coup, *m.*, goutte, *f.*; (*blast*) flétrissure, *f.*; (*taunt*) sarcasme, trait piquant, coup de

Nipper, s. pince, *f.* [patte, lardon, *m.*

Nippingly, *adv.* d'une manière sarcastique *or* piquante

Nipple, s. bout de sein, mamelon, *m.*; (*of fire-arms*) cheminée, *f.* — **lump,** s. (*of fire-arms*) mamelon, *m.* — **shield,** s. bout de sein, *m.* — **wort,** s. lampsane, *f.* — **wrench,** s. (*of*

Nit, s. lente, *f.* [*fire-arms*) clé à cheminée, *f.*

Nitrate, s. nitrate, azotate, *m.*

Nitrated, *adj.* nitraté

Nitre, s. nitre, salpêtre, *m.* — **bed, -vein,** s. nitrière, *f.* — **works,** *s.pl.* nitrière, sal-

Nitred, *adj.* nitré [pêtrière, *f.*

Nitriary, s. nitrière, salpêtrière, *f.*

Nitric, *adj.* nitrique, azotique

Nitride, s. nitrure, *m.*

Nitrification, s. nitrification, *f.*

Nitrify, *v.a.* nitrifier; — *v.n.* se nitrifier

Nitrite, s. nitrite, azotite, *m.*

Nitro, (*in compounds*) nitro ...

Nitrobenzole, s. nitrobenzine, *f.*

Nitrogen, s. nitrogène, azote, *m.*

Nitrogenize, *v.a.* nitrogéner, azoter

Nitrogenous, *adj.* nitrogène

Nitroglycerine, s. nitroglycérine, *f.*

Nitrous, Nitry, *adj.* nitreux, azoteux

Nitty, *adj.* plein de lentes

Nival, Niveous, *adj.* nivéal, neigeux, de neige

No, *adv.* non; pas; — *adj.* aucun, nul; pas, point; pas un; pas moyen de; pas à; — s. non, *m.*; (*vote*) voix contre, voix contraire, *f.*; boule noire, *f.*; (*abbrev. of 'number'*) N° (numéro), *m.* — **one,** *V. Nobody.* —**where,** *See below.* *He has — friends,* il n'a pas *or* point d'amis. *That is — bad day's work,* ce n'est pas une mauvaise journée. *There is — avoiding it,* il n'y a pas moyen de l'éviter, il est impossible de l'éviter. *There is — hesitating,* il n'y a pas à hésiter

Nob, s. caboche, *f.*; (*pers.*) gros bonnet, aristo,

Nobility, s. noblesse, *f.* [*m.* *V.* **Knob**

Noble, *adj.* noble; grand, illustre; beau, superbe, magnifique; excellent; généreux; (*of metals*) précieux; — s. noble, *m.*; gentilhomme, *m.* — **man,** s. noble, *m.*; gentilhomme, *m.* — **woman,** s. femme noble, *f.*

Nobleness, s. noblesse, *f.*; grandeur, élévation, *f.*; beauté, magnificence, *f.*

Nobly, *adv.* noblement; magnifiquement; (*of birth*) de condition noble, de famille noble

Nobody, s. personne, *m.* *To be —,* n'être rien; être un pleutre *or* un zéro *or* un homme sans conséquence. *I see —,* je ne vois personne. — *sees me,* personne ne me voit

Noctambulism, s. noctambulisme, *m.*

Noctule, s. (— *bat*) noctule, *f.*

Nocturn, s. (*Cath. rel.*) nocturne, nocturnal, *m.*

Nocturnal, *adj. s.* nocturne, *adj.m.f.*, *s.m.*

Nocturnally, *adv.* nocturnement

Nocturne, s. (*mus.*) nocturne, *m.*

Nod, *v.n.* faire un signe de tête; (*salute*) saluer; s'incliner; (*from drowsiness*) dodeliner; (*be drowsy*) s'assoupir; sommeiller; (*things*) se balancer; — *v.a.* incliner; balancer; (*express*) exprimer par une inclination de tête; — s. signe de tête, signe, *m.*; (*bow*) inclination de tête, *f.*, salut, *m.*; (*command*) ordre, *m.*, disposition, *f.*; (*of things*) balancement, *m.*

Nodal, *adj.* nodal

Noddle, s. caboche, boule, coloquinte, *f.*

Noddy, s. (*pers.*) niais, *m.*, e, *f.*, sot, *m.*, -te, *f.*;

Node, s. nœud, *m.* [(*bird*) noddi, oiseau fou, *m.*

Nodose, Nodous, *adj.* noueux

Nodosity, s. nodosité, *f.*

Nodular, Nodulous, *adj.* noduleux

Nodule, s. nodule, *m.*

Noggin, s. petit pot, *m.*; godet, *m.*

Noise, s. bruit, *m.*; (*bustle*) fracas, *m.*; (*uproar*) tapage, vacarme, *m.*; éclat, *m.*; retentissement, *m.*; (*in o.'s ears*) tintement, bourdonnement, *m.*; — *v.a.* (— *abroad*) répandre, divulguer, ébruiter. *To hold o.'s —,* se taire. *It is —d abroad,* le bruit court. *To make a —,* faire du bruit (*with an adj.*, un bruit ...). —**less,** *adj.* sans bruit; silencieux, tranquille, calme. — **lessly,** *adv.* sans bruit, silencieusement, en silence, tranquillement. — **lessness,** s. silence, *m.*, tranquillité, *f.*, calme, *m.*

Noisily, *adv.* bruyamment

Noisiness, s. bruit, *m.*; turbulence, *f.*

Noisome, *adj.* nuisible, malfaisant; insalubre, malsain; dégoûtant, désagréable, infect

Noisomely, *adv.* nuisiblement; dégoûtamment

Noisomeness, s. nature nuisible, *f.*; nature dégoûtante, *f.*; dégoût, *m.*; infection, *f.*

Noisy, *adj.* bruyant; tumultueux; éclatant; (*pers.*) turbulent, tapageur; (*gaudy*) tapageur

Nolens volens, *adv.* bon gré mal gré, de gré ou de force

Noli me tangere, s. noli me tangere, *m.*

Nomad, *adj. s.*, **Nomadic,** *adj.* nomade, [*adj.m.f.*, *s.m.*

Nomarch, s. nomarque, *m.*

Nomarchy, s. nomarchie, *f.* [donyme, *m.*

Nom de plume, s. nom de guerre, pseu-

Nomencla-tor, tress, s. nomenclateur, *m.*, [-trice, *f.*

Nomenclature, s. nomenclature, *f.*

Nominal, *adj.* nominal; de nom
Nominally, *adv.* nominalement, de nom
Nominal-ism, -ist. *V.* page 3, § 1
Nominate, *v.a.* nommer; désigner; (*at elections*, &c.) présenter, proposer
Nomination, *s.* nomination, *f.*; présentation, *f.*
Nominative, *s.* (*— case*) nominatif, *m.* *In the —*, au nominatif
Nominatively, *adv.* nominativement
Nominator, *s.* nominateur, *m.*, -trice, *f.*
Nominee, *s.* nominataire, *m.f.*, celui qui est nommé, *m.*, personne dénommée, *f.*; candidat, *m.*, e, *f.*; créature, *f.*
Non, *adv.* (*in compounds*) non, défaut, manque, *m.*, in . . ., im . . . **—ability,** *s.* incapacité, inhabileté, *f.* **—acceptance,** *s.* non-acceptation, inacceptation, *f.*, refus, *m.* **—acquaintance,** *s.* défaut *or* manque de connaissance, *m.*, ignorance, *f.* **—acquiescence,** *s.* *V.* **—compliance.** **—activity,** *s.* non-activité, *f.* **—admittance,** *s.* refus d'admettre, *m.* **—age,** *s.* minorité, *f.* **—aged,** *adj.* mineur. **—appearance,** *s.* absence, *f.*; (*civ. law*) défaut de comparution, défaut, *m.*; (*crim. law*) contumace, *f.* **—appointment,** *s.* défaut de nomination, *m.* **—arrival,** *s.* inexactitude, *f.*; retard, *m.*; absence, *f.* **—attendance,** *s.* absence, *f.*; défaut d'assiduité, *m.*; manque de service, *m.* **—combatant,** *s.* non-combattant, *m.* **—commissioned,** *adj.* sans brevet. *—commissioned officer, s.* sous-officier, *m.* **—communion,** *s.* défaut de communion, *m.* **—compliance,** *s.* non-acquiescement, refus, *m.* **—complying,** *adj.* qui refuse d'acquiescer, qui ne se conforme pas. **— compos, — compos mentis,** *adj.* atteint d'aliénation mentale. **—condensing,** *adj.* sans condenseur. *— condensing engine*, machine à vapeur à haute pression, *f.* **—conducting,** *adj.*, **—conductor,** *s.* non-conducteur, *m.*, -trice, *f.* **—conforming,** *adj.*, **— conformist,** *s.* non-conformiste, *m.f.* **—conformity,** *s.* défaut de conformité, *m.*; (*eccl.*) non-conformité, *f.* **—contagious,** *adj.* non contagieux. **—contagiousness,** *s.* nature non contagieuse, *f.* **—content,** *s.* voix contre, *f.*, votant contre, *m.* **—delivery,** *s.* manque de livraison, *m.* **—descript,** *adj.* non décrit; indéfinissible; déclassé; inclassable; innommé, sans nom; *s.* chose sans nom, chose indéfinissable, chose extraordinaire, *f.*, objet sans nom *or* &c., *m.*, animal déclassé *or* inclassable, *m.*, plante déclassée *or* inclassable, *f.*, (*pers.*) original, *m.*, e, *f.* **—effective,** *s.* non-activité; *adj.* en non-activité. **— ego,** *s.* non-moi, *m.* **—electric,** *adj.* non-électrique; *s.* substance non-électrique, *f.* **—entity,** *s.* *V.* **—existence.** **—essential,** *s.* chose non-essentielle, *f.* **— execution,** *s.* non-exécution, inexécution, *f.* **—existence,** *s.* non-existence, *f.*, non-être, néant, *m.*; chose qui n'existe pas, *f.* **—existing,** *adj.* non-existant, qui n'existe pas. **— exportation,** *s.* non-exportation, *f.* **—feasance,** *s.* omission, négligence, *f.* **—fulfilment,** *s.* non-exécution, inexécution, *f.*, manque d'accomplissement, *m.*; engagement non rempli, *m.* **—importation,** *s.* non-importation, *f.* **—inflammable,** *adj.* non-inflammable; incombustible. **—interference,** *s.* laisser-faire, laissez-faire, *m.* **—intervention,** *s.* non-intervention, *f.* **—juring,** *adj.* qui refuse de prêter serment de fidélité. **— juror,** *s.* personne qui refuse de prêter serment de fidélité, *f.* **—manufacturing,** *adj.* non manufacturier. **—member,** *s.* celui qui n'est pas membre, *m.* **—metallic,** *adj.* non métallique. **—natural,** *s.* (*med.*) cause qui n'est pas naturelle, *f.* **—obedience,** *s.* non-obéissance, désobéissance, *f.* **—observance,** *s.* inobservation, *f.* **—pareil,** *adj.* nonpareil, sans égal; *s.* nonpareille, *f.* **—payment,** *s.* non-payement, *m.* **—performance,** *s.* inexécution, *f.* **—plus,** *s.* embarras, *m.*; *v.a.* embarrasser, dérouter. *At or to a —plus*, au pied du mur. **—presentation,** *s.* défaut de présentation, *m.* **—production,** *s.* non-production, *f.* **—professional,** *adj.* *s.* qui n'appartient pas à une profession; qui n'est pas fait par des hommes de l'art; profane. **—proficiency,** *s.* faiblesse, *f.*, peu de progrès, *m.* **—proficient,** *adj.* faible; arriéré. **—resemblance,** *s.* défaut de ressemblance, *m.*, dissemblance, *f.* **— residence,** *s.* non-résidence, *f.* **—resident,** *adj.* *s.* non-résident; externe; (*of land-owners*) forain. **—resistance,** *s.* non-résistance, obéissance passive, *f.* **—resistant,** *adj.* qui ne résiste pas. **—sense,** *s.* absurdité, sottise, bêtise, *f.*, non-sens, *m.*; galimatias, *m.*; (*trifles*) baliverne, fadaise, niaiserie, *f.*; (*int.*) allons donc! laissez donc! bah! *Soft —sense*, fleurette, *f.* *To talk —sense*, dire des sottises, déraisonner; dire des balivernes, faire des contes. *To talk soft —sense*, conter fleurette. **—sensical,** *adj.* vide de sens, qui n'a pas le sens commun, absurde, bête. *—sensical stuff*, sottises, bêtises, *f.pl.* **—sensically,** *adv.* contre le bon sens, sottement, bêtement. **—sensicalness,** *s.* absurdité, sottise, bêtise, *f.* **— solution,** *s.* non-solution, *f.* **—submission,** *s.* insoumission, *f.* **—such,** *V.* **Nonesuch.** **—suit,** *s.* désistement, *m.*; débouté, *m.*; *v.a.* débouter, mettre *or* renvoyer hors de cour. **— transferable,** *adj.* personnel. **—usance,** *s.* non-usage, *m.* **—use,** *s.* non-jouissance, *f.* **— user,** *s.* non-usage, *m.*; non-exercice de fonctions, *m.*
Nonagenarian, *s. adj* nonagénaire, *m.f.*
Nonagesimal, *adj.* nonagésime, nonagésimal
Nonagon. *V.* **Enneagon**
Nonce, *s.* *For the —*, pour cette fois, pour le moment, quant à présent, pour le quart d'heure; pour cette fois-ci; en passant; pour la circonstance; de circonstance; à cet effet
None, *adj. pron.* aucun, nul, pas un; pas; (*preceded by a verb*) en . . . pas [*I have —*, je n'en ai pas]; (*nobody*) personne, *m.*; *— s.* none, *f.* **—such,** *s.* sans pareil, *m.*; (*jest.*) phénix, merle blanc, *m.*; (*apple*) nonpareille, *f.*
Nonius, *s.* nonius, *m.*
Nonuple, *adj. s.* nonuple, *adj.m.f.*, *s.m.*; *— v.a.n.* nonupler
Noodle, *s.* nigaud, *m.*, e, *f.*, niais, *m.*, e, *f.*, benêt, *m.* **—dom,** *s.* nigauderie, *f.*
Nook, *s.* coin, recoin, réduit, *m.*; enfoncement, *m.* *—s and corners*, coins et recoins, *m.pl.*
Noon, *s.* midi, *m.*; *— adj.* de midi. **—day, -tide,** *s.* midi, *m.*; *adj.* de midi. *At —day*, en plein midi. *At the — of night*, à minuit
Noose, *s.* nœud coulant, *m.*; (*a snare*) lacet, lacs, filet, piége, *m.*; *— v.a.* attacher par un nœud coulant; (*ensnare*) prendre au piége, attraper
Nopal, *s.* nopal, *m.* **— plantation, Nopalry,** *s.* nopalerie, nopalière, *f.*
Nor, *conj.* ni; ni . . . ne; et . . . ne . . . pas; ne . . . pas non plus. *— is this all*, et ce n'est pas tout. *— do I, — shall I, — did I*, &c., ni moi non plus. *Neither . . . —*, *V.* **Neither**
Noria, *s.* noria, *f.*
Noric, *adj.* Norique
Norium, *s.* norium, *m.*
Normal, *adj.* normal
Normality, Normalness, *s.* normalité, *f.*
Normally, *adv.* normalement
Norman, *s.* Normand, *m.*, e, *f.*; *— adj.* normand, de Normandie, des Normands. *—conquest*, conquête des Normands, *f.*
Normanism, *s.* normandisme, normanisme, *m.*
Norse, *s.* Norse, *m.*
North, *s.* nord, *m.*; septentrion, *m.*; *— adj.* du nord, de nord, nord, septentrional; (*of the pole*) nord; *— adv.* au nord. **— German,** *adj.* de l'Allemagne du nord. **— star,** *s.* étoile polaire, étoile du nord, *f.* **—ward, -s,** *adj. adv.* vers le nord. **—western,** *adj.* du nord-ouest

Northerly, *adj.* du (*or* de) nord, nord; septentrional; — *adv.* vers le nord, au nord

Northern, *adj.* du nord, de nord, nord, vers le nord; boréal. — **light,** *s.* aurore boréale, lumière polaire, *f.* —**most,** *adj.* (le) plus au nord, à l'extrême nord. — **railway,** *s.* chemin de fer du nord, *m.*

Northerner, *s. adj.* septentrional, *m.*, e, *f.*; (*American polit.*) nordiste, *m.f.*

Norwegian, *s.* Norvégien, *m.*, -ne, *f.*; — *adj.* norvégien, de Norvége

Nose, *s.* nez, *m.*; (*of certain animals*) museau, *m.*; (*of bellows*) canon, tuyau, *m.*; (*end*) bout, *m.*; (*tech.*) bec, *m.* *Bleeding at the nose*, saignement de nez, *m.* *To lead by the* –, mener par le bout du nez. *To poke* or *thrust o.'s — in*, fourrer le nez dans, se mêler de. *To speak through o.'s* –, parler du nez. *To turn up o.'s* —, faire la petite bouche; (*at*) faire fi (de). *To wipe the — of*, moucher. (*V.* **Blow,** *v.a.*) *My — bleeds*, je saigne du nez. —**bag,** *s.* (*for horses*) musette, *f.*, sachet, *m.* —**band,** *s.* muserolle, *f.* —**cap,** *s.* (*of a rifle*, &c.) bouchon, *m.* —**gay,** *s.* bouquet, *m.* —**less,** *adj.* sans nez. —**pipe,** *s.* (*of a hose branch*) orifice, *m.*

Nosed, *adj* qui a le nez ..., au nez ...; (*fig.*) qui a le nez fin, au nez fin

Noso-graphic, -graphy, -logical, -logist, -logy. *V.* page 3, § 1

Nostalgia, *s.* nostalgie, *f.*

Nostalgic, *adj. s.* nostalgique

Nostoc, *s.* nostoc, nostoch, *m.*

Nostril, *s.* narine, *f.*; (*of horses, dogs*, &c.) naseau, *m.* [poudre de perlimpinpin, *f.*

Nostrum, *s.* remède secret, *m.*; panacée, *f.*;

Not, *adv.* ne ... pas, ne ... point; non; pas; non pas. *I know* —, *I do* — (or *don't*) *know*, je ne sais pas. *I believe* (or *think* or *hope*) —, je crois (*or* pense, j'espère) que non, je ne le crois (*or* pense, ... l'espère) pas. *It may* or *might* —, il se peut *or* se pourrait que non. *Good or* —, bon ou non. — *here*, pas ici. — *but*, — *that*, non que, non pas que; ce n'est pas que. — *but that*, ce n'est pas que ... ne. — *I* or *he* or *she*, &c.! oh que non! il n'y a pas de danger! je ne suis (*or* il n'est, &c.) pas si bête. '*Is it* —?' '*Does it* —?' '*Do they* —?' '*Are you* —?' '*Will you* —?' '*Shall we* —?' '*Would he* —?' '*Would it* —?' '*Was she* —?' &c., &c. (*at the end of a sentence*) n'est-ce pas? (*if expressing surprise*) vraiment?

Notability, *s.* notabilité, *f.*

Notable, *adj.* notable, remarquable; (*distinguished*) insigne, grand; (*fam.*) laborieux, actif, économe, entendu, habile; — *s.* notable, *m.*

Notableness, *s.* nature remarquable, *f.*; singularité, *f.*; (*fam.*) activité, *f.*, travail, soin, *m.*, économie, habileté, *f.*

Notably, *adv.* notablement, remarquablement; (*specially*) notamment; (*fam.*) laborieusement, activement, avec économie, soigneusement, habilement

Notalgia, Notalgy, *s.* notalgie, *f.*

Notarial, *adj.* (*pertaining to a notary*) notarial, de notaire; (*done or taken by a notary*) notarié, par-devant notaire

Notary, *s.* notaire, *m.* —*'s business*, notariat, *m.*

Notation, *s.* notation, *f.* (*arith.*) numération écrite, *f.*; (*alg.*) notation, *f.*

Notch, *s.* coche, encoche, entaille, *f.*; (*of edge-tools*) brèche, dent, *f.*; (*of machines*) cran, *m.*; — *v.a.* faire une coche *or* une encoche *or* une entaille à, cocher, encocher, entailler; denteler; (*edge-tools*) ébrécher. — **board,** *s.* limon, *m.* — **weed,** *s.* arroche, *f.*

Note, *s.* note, *f.*; marque, *f.*, signe, *m.*; distinction, *f.*; réputation, *f.*; remarque, *f.*; (*letter*) billet, *m.*, lettre, *f.*; (*com., bank.*) billet, *m.*; (*sound*) son, accent, accord, *m.*; (*mus., dipl.*) note, *f.*; (*mus.*) ton, *m.*; (*gram.*) point, *m.*; — *v.a.* (— **down**) noter, prendre note de; signaler; observer, remarquer; (*mus.*) noter. — *of hand*, billet à ordre, billet, *m.* — **book,** *s.* cahier de notes, *m.*; calepin, *m.*; (*com.*) carnet, agenda, *m.* — **paper,** *s.* papier à lettres, *m.* —**worthy,** *adj.* digne de remarque

Noted, *part.adj.* noté; remarquable, illustre, éminent, distingué; insigne; renommé, célèbre, fameux, bien connu

Nothing, *s.* rien, *m.*; néant, *m.*; (*math.*) zéro, *m.*; (*before an adj. or a part.*) rien de; (*adverb., in no way*) nullement, aucunement, en aucune manière. *A mere* –, une pure bagatelle, un rien. — *but*, rien que; pas autre chose que; que. — *else*, pas autre chose, rien autre, (ne ...) que cela. — *new*, — *done*, rien de nouveau, rien de fait. — *like it*, rien comme cela; rien de semblable (*or* de pareil); rien qui en approche. *Next to* —, presque rien, si peu que rien. *To* —, (*entirely*) entièrement, complètement. *To come to* —, (*things*) n'aboutir à rien, se réduire à rien; (*pers.*) tomber dans la misère. *To do — but*, ne faire que. *To go for* —, (*things*) compter pour rien. *He does — but talk*, il ne fait que causer. *That* (or *it*) *is — to me*, cela ne me regarde pas; cela ne me fait rien, cela m'est égal. *He knows* —, il ne sait rien. — *affects him*, rien ne le touche. *There is — to laugh at, to boast of*, &c., il n'y a pas de quoi rire, se vanter, &c.

Nothingness, *s.* néant, *m.*; rien, *m.*

Notice, *s.* connaissance, *f.*; observation, *f.*; attention, *f.*; (*regard*) égard, *m.*; (*advice*) avis, *m.*; avertissement, *m.*; information, *f.*; (*stuck up*) avis, *m.*; (*of writings*) notice, *f.*; (*of apartments*, &c.) congé, *m.*; (*law*) notification, *f.*; sommation, *f.* — *to quit*, congé, *m.* *At* or *without a moment's* —, sur-le-champ, immédiatement. *At the shortest* —, dans le plus court délai. *Under o.'s* —, à sa connaissance. *Until further* —, jusqu'à avis contraire. *To bring into* or *introduce to* —, faire connaître, produire. *To bring under the — of*, porter à la connaissance de. *To give* —, donner avis, prévenir, avertir, avertir (...) d'avance, faire savoir. *To give — to quit*, donner congé. *To take — of*, (*same as To* **Notice,** *v.a., See below*). *Take* — (*that* ...!) vous êtes prévenu (que ...!) avis! avis au public! le public est prévenu (que ...!). *To rise to* —, se faire connaître. *He is beneath your* —, il ne mérite pas que vous fassiez attention à lui *or* que vous vous occupiez de lui *or* que vous lui répondiez

Notice, *v.a.* prendre connaissance de; (*observe*, &c.) remarquer, observer; s'apercevoir de, faire attention à, prendre garde à; prendre note de (*or* que); (*to mention*) faire remarquer, faire observer, mentionner; (*to show regard*) avoir des attentions *or* des égards pour; (*to meddle with*) s'occuper de, s'inquiéter de

Noticeable, *adj.* perceptible, visible, sensible; remarquable, saillant

Noticeably, *adv.* perceptiblement, visiblement, sensiblement; remarquablement

Notification, *s.* notification, *f.*; avis, avertissement, *m.* [annoncer

Notify, *v.a.* notifier; faire savoir; déclarer;

Notion, *s.* notion, idée, *f.*; opinion, *f.*; prétention, *f.*; intention, *f.*, dessein, *m.*, envie, *f.* *To my* —, à mon idée; suivant moi

Notional, *adj.* idéal, imaginaire, chimérique; (*pers.*) à lubies, fantasque [imagination

Notionally, *adv.* idéalement, en idée, en

Notionist, *s.* songe-creux, *m.*

Notoriety, *s.* notoriété, *f.*

Notorious, *adj.* notoire, public; (*in a bad sense*) insigne, fameux [manière notoire

Notoriously, *adv.* notoirement, d'une

Notoriousness, *s.* notoriété, *f.*

Notwithstanding, *prep.* malgré; — *adv.* néanmoins, malgré cela, quand même; — [*conj.* (*although*) quoique

Nougat, *s.* nougat, *m.*

Nought. *V.* **Naught**

Nouilles, *s.pl.* nouilles, *f.pl.*

Noun, *s.* nom, *m.* [(*foment*) fomenter
Nourish, *v.a.* nourrir; (*support*) entretenir;
Nourishable, *adj.* nourrissable
Nourishing, *adj.* nourrissant [nutritive, *f.*
Nourishment, *s.* nourriture, *f.*; propriété
Nous, *s.* verve, *f.*; talent, chic, *m.*
Nova-Scotian, *s. adj.* Nouvel-Écossais, *m.* (Nouveaux-Écossais, *m. pl.*), Nouvelle-Écos-
Novation, *s.* (*law*) novation, *f.* [saise, *f.*
Nova-tor, tress, *s.* novateur, *m.*, -trice, *f.*, innovateur, *m.*, -trice, *f.*
Novel, *adj.* nouveau; neuf; étrange; — *s.* roman, *m.*; (*very short*) nouvelle, *f.*; (*Rom. law*) novelle, *f.* — **writer,** *s.* romancier, *m.*, -ière, *f.*
Novelist, *s.* romancier, *m.*, -ière, *f.*
Novelize, *v.a.* romanciser
Novelty, *s.* nouveauté, *f.*
November, *s.* novembre, *m.*
Novenary, *adj.* novénaire
Novennial, *adj.* qui a lieu tous les neuf ans, de neuf en neuf ans; qui dure neuf ans
Novercal, *adj.* de belle-mère; (*in a bad sense*)
Novice, *s.* novice, *m.f.* [de marâtre
Novitiate, *s.* noviciat, *m.*
Now, *adv.* maintenant, à présent, actuellement, en ce moment; donc; (*sometimes*) tantôt; (*then*) alors; (*too*) aussi; (*now that*) maintenant que; — *conj.* or; — *adj.* présent, actuel; — *s.* présent, *m.*, moment présent, *m.* — *Barabbas was a robber*, Or Barabbas était un brigand. *Before —, ere —*, auparavant, déjà. *But —*, (*not long since*) naguère. *Good —!* à la bonne heure! *Not —*, (*not any more*) ne ... plus. —, — *then*, maintenant; or; (*exclam.*) voyons! voyons donc! ah çà! enfin! allons! allons donc! tenez! tiens! eh bien! mais! (*look out!*) gare! attention! — *and then, every — and then*, de temps en temps, de temps à autre; (*of place*) de distance en distance, çà et là. — ..., *then* ... (or — ..., — ...), tantôt ..., tantôt [maintenant
Nowadays, *adv.* de nos jours, aujourd'hui,
Noway, Noways. *V.* **Nowise**
Nowhere, *adv.* nulle part. — *at all*, nulle part. — *else*, *V.* **Else.** *To be —*, n'y être plus; (*beaten*) être aplati [aucune façon
Nowise, *adv.* nullement, aucunement, en
Noxious, *adj.* nuisible, pernicieux, malfaisant
Noxiously, *adv.* nuisiblement, pernicieusement
Noxiousness, *s.* nocuité, nature nuisible *or*
Noyade, *s.* noyade, *f.* [pernicieuse, *f.*
Noyau, *s.* eau *or* crème de noyau, *f.*, noyau, *m.*
Nozzle, *s.* nez, *m.*; (*of things*) bec, bout, *m.*; (*tube*) tuyau, *m.*
Nubian, *s.adj.* Nubien, *m.*, -ne, *f.*
Nubile, *adj.* nubile
Nubility, *s.* nubilité, *f.*
Nuciform, *adj.* nuciforme
Nucivorous, *adj.* nucivore
Nucleal, *adj.* nucléal
Nuclear, *adj.* nucléaire
Nucleate, -d, *adj.* nucléé
Nucleus, *s.* noyau, *m.*
Nudation, dépouillement, *m.*
Nude, *adj.* nu; (*law*) nul; — *s.* nu, *m.*
Nudge, *s.* coup de coude, *m.*; — *v.a.* donner un coup de coude à, pousser du coude
Nudity, *s.* nudité, *f.*; (*arts*) nudité, *f.*; nu, *m.*
Nugatory, *adj.* futile, frivole; inefficace, de
Nugget, *s.* pépite, *f.* [nul effet, nul
Nuisance, *s.* incommodité, *f.*; plaie, peste, *f.*; embarras, *m.*; désagrément, *m.*; ennui, *m.*, scie, corvée, *f.*; tourment, cauchemar, *m.*; (*aversion, pers.*) bête noire, *f.*; (*law*) dommage, *m.*; abus, *m.*; établissement insalubre, *m.*; (*dirt*) immondices, ordures, *f.pl.* *Inspector of —s*, inspecteur de salubrité, *m.* *Commit no —*, défense (*or* il est défendu) de déposer ici aucune ordure; défense d'uriner
Null, *adj.* nul. — *and void*, nul et de nul effet, nul et comme non avenu
Nullification, *s.* annulement, *m.*; (*American polit.*) nullification, *f.*
Nullifier, *s.* (*American polit.*) nullificateur, *m.*
Nullify, *v.a.* annuler, rendre nul, casser; (*American polit.*) nullifier
Nullity, *s.* nullité, *f.*
Numantine, *s.adj.* Numantin, *m.*, e, *f.*
Numb, *adj.* engourdi; transi; — *v.a.* engourdir; transir. — **fish,** *s.* torpille, *f.*
Number, *s.* (*arith.*) nombre (*pl.* nombres), *m.*; (*quantity, singular or plural*, —, —**s**) nombre, *m.*; (*sign of distinction among many*) numéro, *m.*; (*of books: part*) livraison, *f.*; (*gram.*) nombre, *m.*; (*rhet.*) harmonie, *f.*, nombre, *m.*; (*poet.*) vers, *m.*, *m.pl.*; (—**s,** *of the Pentateuch*) Nombres, *m.pl.*; (—**s,** *elliptical for —s of people*) nombre de gens, une foule de personnes; — *v.a.* compter, supputer, nombrer; dénombrer; (*to reckon among*) mettre au nombre ('*with*,' de), compter ('*with*,' parmi, au nombre de); (*to mark*) numéroter; — *v.n.* (*to amount*) se monter à. —*s of, a — of*, nombre de, un grand nombre de, une foule de. *In great —s*, en grand nombre. *Ten in —*, au nombre de dix. *The advantage of —s*, l'avantage du nombre. — 25 *St. James's street*, rue St.-Jacques numéro (N°) 25. —**less,** *adj.* innombrable, sans nombre [(*marker*) numéroteur, *m.*
Numberer, *s.* calculateur, *m.*, -trice, *f.*;
Numbering, *s.* calcul, *m.*, supputation, *f.*; (*marking*) numérotage, *m.*
Numbness, *s.* engourdissement, *m.*
Numerable, *adj.* nombrable
Numeral, *adj.* numéral; numérique; numératif; — *s.* lettre numérale, *f.*, signe numéral, *m.*; chiffre, *m.*; (*gram.*) numératif, *m.*
Numerally, *adv.* numériquement
Numerary, *adj.* numéraire
Numerate, *v.a.* nombrer
Numeration, *s.* numération, *f.*
Numerator, *s.* (*arith.*) numérateur, *m.*; (*pers.*) calculateur, *m.*
Numeric, -al, *adj.* numérique
Numerically, *adv.* numériquement
Numerous, *adj.* nombreux
Numerously, *adv.* nombreusement, en grand nombre, en nombre
Numerousness, *s.* nombre, grand nombre, *m.*, multitude, *f.*; (*rhet.*) harmonie, *f.*
Numidian, *s.adj.* Numide, *m.f.* — *crane*, demoiselle de Numidie, demoiselle, *f.*
Numismatic, -al, *adj.* numismatique; —**s,** *s.pl.* numismatique, *f.* [*m.f.*
Numismatist, *s.* numismatiste, numismate,
Numismatographer, *s.* numismatographe, *m.* [**ical,** &c. *V.* page 3, § 1
Numismato-graphy, ic, ical, -logy, ic,
Nummulite, *s.* nummulite, *f.*
Numskull, *s.* benêt, *m.*, bûche, *f.*
Nun, *s.* religieuse, *f.*, (*jest.*) nonne, nonnette, *f.* *White —*, (*bird*) nonnette blanche, piette, *f.*
Nunciature, *s.* nonciature, *f.*
Nuncio, *s.* nonce, *m.* [nuncupatif
Nuncupative, *adj.* nominal, de nom; (*law*)
Nunnery, *s.* couvent de femmes, couvent de religieuses, *m.* [—**s,** *s.pl.* noces, *f.pl.*
Nuptial, *adj.* nuptial, de noces; conjugal;
Nuraghe, *s.* nurage, nuraghe, *m.*
Nurse, *s.* (*wet*) nourrice, *f.*; (*maid*) bonne (d'enfant), *f.*; (*for the sick*) garde-malade, garde, *f.*; (*in hospitals*) infirmière, *f.*; — *v a.* (— **up**) nourrir, allaiter; (*bring up*) élever; (*keep up*) entretenir; (*attend*) garder, soigner; (*coddle*) dorloter, choyer; (*cherish*) chérir; (*encourage*) encourager, fomenter; (*spare*) ménager; (*supply*) alimenter; (*of omnibuses*, &c.) brûler. *At —*, en nourrice. *To put out to —*, mettre en nourrice. — **bed,** *s.* lit de veille, *m.* — **child,** *s.* nourrisson, *m.*, -ne, *f.* — **girl,** *s.* petite bonne d'enfant, *f.* — **maid,** *s.* bonne d'enfant, *f.* — **pond,** *s.* alevinier, vivier, *m.*
Nursery, *s.* chambre des enfants, *f.*; (*public,*

for the infants of working mothers) crèche, garderie, *f.*; (*for plants, and fig.*) pépinière, *f.*; (*of silkworms*) magnanerie, *f.* — **garden, -ground,** *s.* jardin-pépinière, *m.* — **governess,** *s.* gouvernante pour le premier âge, *f.* — **maid,** *s.* bonne d'enfant, *f.* — **man,** *s.* pépiniériste, *m.* — **rhymes, tales,** *s.pl.* chansons (*f.pl.*), contes (*m.pl.*) de nourrices

Nursling, *s.* nourrisson, *m.*, -ne, *f.*; (*fig.*) favori, *m.*, -te, *f.*, mignon, *m.*, -ne, *f.*

Nursy, *s.* nounou, *f.*

Nurture, *s.* nourriture, *f.*, aliments, *m.pl.*; éducation, *f.*; — *v.a.* nourrir; (*educate*) élever. — **up,** *v.a.* élever

Nut, *s.* noix, *f.*; (*hazel-nut*) noisette, *f.*; (*walnut*) noix, *f.*; (*of violins,* &c.) sillet, *m.*; (*of screws*) écrou, *m.*; (*mach.*) cheville, *f.*; — *v.n.* cueillir des noisettes. — **bolt,** *s.* boulon à écrou, *m.* — **breaker,** *s.* *V.* — **hatch.** — **brown,** *adj.* noisette; (*of hair*) châtain. — **cracker,** *s.* (*bird*) casse-noix, *m.* — **cracker,** *s.*, — **crackers,** — **cracks,** *s.pl.* (*instr.*) casse-noisettes, casse-noix, *m.* — **gall,** *s.* noix de galle, *f.* — **hatch,** *s.* (*bird*) casse-noisettes, *m.*, sittelle, *f.* — **iron,** *s.* ferraille, *f.* — **like,** *adj.* nuciforme. — **meg,** *s.* muscade, noix muscade, *f.* — **meg tree,** *s.* muscadier, *m.* — **pecker,** *s.* *V.* — **hatch.** — **shaped,** *adj.* nuciforme. — **shell,** *s.* coquille de noix, *f.* *The question lies in a — shell,* la question peut se résumer en un mot. — **tree,** *s.* noisetier, *m.*

Nutation, *s.* nutation, *f.*

Nutria, *s.* castorin, *m.* [riture, *f.*, aliment, *m.*

Nutrient, *adj.* *V.* **Nutritious;** — *s.* nour-

Nutriment, *s.* nourriture, *f.*, aliment, *m.*

Nutrimental, *adj.* *V.* **Nutritious**

Nutrition, *s.* nutrition, *f.*; (*food*) nourriture, *f.*; aliment, *m.*

Nutritious, Nutritive, *adj.* nourrissant, nutritif; nourricier; succulent; (*med.*) ali-

Nutritiveness, *s.* nutritivité, *f.* [menteux

Nutting, *s.* cueillette des noisettes, *f.* *To go —,* aller cueillir des noisettes, aller faire la cueillette (des noisettes) [noisette

Nutty, *adj.* de noisette; qui a un goût de

Nux vomica, *s.* noix vomique, *f.* — **tree,** *s.* vomiquier, *m.*

Nyctalopia, Nyctalopy, *s.* nyctalopie, *f.*

Nyctalopic, *adj.* nyctalopique

Nyctalops, *s.* nyctalope, *m.f.*

Nyl-ghau, *s.* nilgaut, *m.*

Nymph, Nympha, *s.* nymphe, *f.*

Nymphean, Nymphish, *adj.* nymphéen

Nymphlike, Nymphly, *adj.* comme une nymphe

O

O, *s.* (*letter*) o, *m.*

O, *int.* ô! oh!

Oaf, *s.* imbécile, idiot, benêt, *m.*

Oafish, *adj.* stupide, imbécile

Oafishness, *s.* stupidité, *f.*

Oak, *s.* (*bot.*) chêne, *m.*; (*wood*) chêne, bois de chêne, *m.*; — *adj.* de chêne; en chêne. *Carved —,* chêne sculpté. — **apple,** *s.* pomme de chêne, *f.* — **bark,** *s.* écorce de chêne, *f.*; (*with tanners*) tan, *m.* — **grove, -plantation,** *s.* chênaie, *f.* — **leaf,** *s.* feuille de chêne, *f.* — **ling,** *s.* chêneau, chêneteau, *m.* — **timber,** *s.* bois de chêne, *m.* — **tree,** *s.* chêne, *m* — **wood,** *s.* (*material*) bois de chêne, *m.*; (*plantation*) bois de chênes, *m.*

Oaken, *adj.* de chêne

Oakum, *s.* étoupe, *f.* *To pick —,* faire de l'étoupe. — **picker,** *s.* étoupier, *m.*, -ière, *f.*

Oaky, *adj* de chêne, dur comme du chêne

Oar, *s.* rame, *f.*, aviron, *m.*; — *v.a.* conduire à la rame; — *v.n.* ramer. *To back the —s,* scier. *To pull the —s,* ramer, nager. — **maker,** *s.* avironnier, *m.* — **making, -shed, -shop, -trade,** *s.* avironnerie, *f.*

Oared, *adj.* ramé; à ... rames, à ... avirons

Oarsman, *s.* rameur, *m.* —**ship,** *s.* art de ramer, talent de rameur, *m.*

Oary, *adj.* ramé, en forme de rame

Oases, *s.pl.* oasis, *f.pl.*

Oasian, *s.* *adj.* oasien, *m.*, -ne, *f.*

Oasis, *s.* oasis, *f.*

Oat, Oats, *s.* avoine, *f.* *Wild —s,* folle avoine, *f.*, avèneron, *m.* *To sow o.'s wild —s,* jeter sa gourme. — **bin,** *s.* coffre à l'avoine, *m.* — **cake,** *s.* gâteau d'avoine, *m.* — **chaff,** *s.* paille d'avoine, *f.*, balles d'avoine, *f.pl.* — **field,** *s.* champ d'avoine, *m.*, avoinerie, aveinerie, aveinière, *f.* — **grass,** *s.* avoine élevée, *f.*, fromental, *m.* — **meal,** *s.* farine

Oaten, *adj.* d'avoine [d'avoine, *f.*, gruau, *m.*

Oath, *s.* serment, *m.*; (*blasphemous*) jurement, juron, *m.* *To take an —,* prêter serment. *To take o.'s — of it,* en lever la main. *To put one on his —,* faire prêter serment à quelqu'un. *To swear an —,* faire un serment

Oats. *V.* **Oat**

Obbligato, *adj.* obligé

Obduracy, *s.* endurcissement, *m.* [opiniâtre

Obdurate, *adj.* endurci; inflexible; obstiné,

Obdurately, *adv.* avec endurcissement; inflexiblement; obstinément

Obedience, *s.* obéissance, *f.*; soumission, *f.*; (*theol.*) obédience, *f.*

Obedienciary, *s.* obédiencier, *m.*

Obedient, *adj.* obéissant; soumis

Obediential, *adj.* d'obéissance; de soumission; respectueux; (*theol.*) obédienciel

Obediently, *adv.* avec obéissance, obéissamment; avec soumission. *Yours —,* votre serviteur, votre tout dévoué serviteur, votre tout dévoué [inclination, *f.*

Obeisance, *s.* révérence, *f.*; (*bow*) salut, *m.*,

Obeliscal, *adj.* obéliscal, en forme d'obélisque, en obélisque

Obelisk, *s.* obélisque, *m.*; (*print.*) croix, *f.*

Obese, *adj.* obèse

Obesity, *s.* obésité, *f.* [être obéi

Obey, *v.a.* obéir à; — *v.n.* obéir. *To be —ed,*

Obfuscate, *v.a.* offusquer, obscurcir

Obfuscation, *s.* offuscation, *f.*, obscurcisse-

Obit, *s.* obit, *m.* [ment, *m.*

Obituary, *s.* obituaire, *m.*; nécrologe, *m.*; nécrologie, *f.*; — *adj.* obituaire, nécrologique. — *notice,* notice nécrologique, *f.*

Object, *s.* objet, *m.*; (*end*) but, *m.*; considération, *f.*; (*fright*) horreur, *f.*; (*gram.*) régime, complément, *m.*; — *v.a.* objecter (à), opposer (à); reprocher (à); — *v.n.* s'opposer (à); trouver à dire *or* à redire (à); refuser (de), se refuser (à); (...) répugner (à). *That is an —,* (*of consequence*) c'est important. *I — to that man,* cet homme me répugne. — **glass,** *s.* objectif, *m.* — **less,** *adj.* sans objet, sans but

Objection, *s.* objection, *f.*; difficulté, *f.*, inconvénient, empêchement, *m.*; reproche, *m.* *To have an — to,* s'opposer à; avoir de la répugnance pour. *I have no — (to it),* je ne m'y oppose pas, je le veux bien; cela m'est égal; je n'ai rien à dire à (*or* centre) cela. *I have not the slightest —,* je ne demande pas mieux

Objectionable, *adj.* inadmissible; répréhensible; répugnant; désagréable

Objectionableness, *s.* nature inadmissible *or* &c. (*V.* **Objectionable**), *f.*

Objective, *adj.* objectif; — *s.m.* objectif, *m.*; (*aim*) but, *m.*; (*gram.*) régime direct, *m.* — *case,* régime direct, *m.*

Objectively, *adv.* objectivement

Objectiveness, Objectivity, *s.* objectivité, *f.*

Objector, *s.* personne qui fait une objection *or* des objections, *f.*

Objurgation, *s.* objurgation, *f.*

Objurgatory, *adj.* objurgatoire

Oblate, *adj.* aplati; — *s.* (*Cath. rel.*) oblat, *m.*
Oblateness, *s.* aplatissement, *m.*
Oblation, *s.* oblation. offrande, *f.*
Obligation, *s.* obligation, *f.* *To lie under an — to,* (*to do a thing*) être dans l'obligation de, être tenu de; (*to a person*) avoir obligation *or* une obligation *or* de l'obligation à. *To lay one under —,* obliger quelqu'un
Obligato, *adj.* obligé
Obligatorily, *adv.* obligatoirement
Obligatory, *adj.* obligatoire
Oblige, *v.a.* obliger (à); (*do a service*) obliger (de); faire plaisir à; être utile à. *To — with,* (*give*) avoir l'obligeance de donner (à)
Obliged, *part. adj.* (*indebted, in duty bound*) obligé ('*to,*' à; '*for,*' de; '*for it,*' en); (*compelled*) obligé ('*to,*' de)
Obligee, *s.* obligataire, obligationnaire, *m.f.*
Obliger, *s.* personne qui oblige, *f.*
Obliging, *adj.* obligeant, complaisant, serviable
Obligingly, *adv.* obligeamment, complaisamment, serviablement [serviabilité, *f.*
Obligingness, *s.* obligeance, complaisance,
Obligor, *s.* obligé, *m.*, e, *f.*
Obliquation, *s.* obliquité, *f.* [(*gram.*) oblique
Oblique, *adj.* oblique; indirect, détourné;
Obliquely, *adv.* obliquement; indirectement
Obliqueness, Obliquity, *s.* obliquité, *f.*; irrégularité, *f.* [biffer; (*admin., post.*) oblitérer
Obliterate, *v.a.* oblitérer; effacer; (*cancel*)
Obliteration, *s.* oblitération, *f.*; effaçure, rature, *f.*; (*admin., post.*) oblitération, *f.*
Oblivion, *s.* oubli, *m.*; (*polit.*) amnistie, *f.* *To bury in —, to consign to —,* ensevelir dans l'oubli [oublieux, sujet à oublier
Oblivious, *adj.* d'oubli, de l'oubli; (*forgetful*)
Oblong, *adj.* oblong; — *s.* figure *or* forme oblongue, *f.*
Oblongly, *adv.* d'une forme oblongue
Oblongness, *s.* forme oblongue, *f.*
Obloquy, *s.* blâme, reproche, *m.*; (*odium*) honte, *f.*, déshonneur, *m.*
Obnoxious, *adj.* sujet (à), exposé (à); soumis (à); blâmable, répréhensible; odieux (à); désagréable (à); (*hurtful*) nuisible, dangereux
Obnoxiously, *adv.* dans un état de sujétion *or* d'assujettissement; d'une manière répréhensible; odieusement; d'une manière désagréable
Obnoxiousness, *s.* sujétion, *f.*, assujettissement, *m.*; odieux, *m.*; nature désagréable, *f.*
Oboe, &c. *V.* **Hautboy,** &c.
Obole, Obolus, *s.* obole, *f.*
Obreption, *s.* obreption, *f.*
Obreptitious, *adj.* obreptice
Obreptitiously, *adv.* obrepticement
Obscene, *adj.* obscène; sale, dégoûtant
Obscenely, *adv.* d'une manière obscène, avec obscénité; salement, dégoûtamment
Obsceneness, Obscenity, *s.* obscénité, *f.*
Obscurant, *s.* obscurant, *m.*
Obscurant-ism, -ist. *V.* page 3, § 1
Obscuration, *s.* obscurcissement, *m.*; (*astr.*) obscuration, *f.*
Obscure, *adj.* obscur; ténébreux; (*living in darkness*) des ténèbres; — *v.a.* obscurcir; éclipser, offusquer; (*hide*) cacher
Obscurely, *adv.* obscurément; dans l'obscurité; indirectement, à demi-mot
Obscureness, Obscurity, *s.* obscurité, *f.*
Obsecration, *s.* obsécration, *f.*
Obsequies, *s.pl.* obsèques, *f.pl.*
Obsequious, *adj.* soumis, obéissant; officieux; (*servile*) obséquieux
Obsequiously, *adv.* avec soumission, avec obéissance; officieusement; (*servilely*) obséquieusement
Obsequiousness, *s.* soumission, obéissance, *f.*; officieuseté, *f.*; (*servility*) obséquiosité, basse complaisance, *f.*
Observable, *adj.* observable, appréciable, sensible; remarquable, digne d'attention
Observably, *adv.* d'une manière appréciable *or* remarquable
Observance, *s.* observation, *f.*, accomplissement, *m.*; (*theol.*) observance, pratique, *f.*; (*respect*) égards, *m.pl.*, attentions, *f.pl.*
Observant, *adj.* observateur; attentif; exact. — *Franciscan,* observantin, *m.*
Observantist, *s.* observantin, *m.*
Observation, *s.* observation, *f.*; remarque, *f.*; attention, *f.* [*s.* (*rail.*) vigie vitrée, *f.*
Observatory, *s.* observatoire, *m.* — **window,**
Observe, *v.a.* observer, remarquer; faire observer, faire remarquer
Observer, *s.* observateur, *m.*, -trice, *f.*
Observing, *adj.* observateur; attentif
Observingly, *adv.* attentivement
Obsession, *s.* obsession, *f.*
Obsidian, *s.* obsidiane, obsidienne, *f.*
Obsidional, *adj.* obsidional
Obsolescence, *s.* vieillissement, *m.*
Obsolescent, *adj.* vieillissant, qui vieillit; (*of laws*) qui tombe en désuétude
Obsolete, *adj.* vieux, suranné, hors d'usage; (*of words*) vieilli, inusité, archaïque; (*of laws*) tombé en désuétude; (*nat. hist.*) obsolète. *To become* (or *grow* or *get*) —, vieillir; tomber en désuétude [*or* en désuétude, *m.*, vétusté, *f.*
Obsoleteness, *s.* état de ce qui est suranné
Obstacle, *s.* obstacle, *m.*
Obstetric, -al, *adj.* obstétrique, obstétrical; — **s,** *s.pl.* obstétrique, *f.*
Obstetrician, *s.* accoucheur, *m.*, -euse, *f.*
Obstinacy, *s.* obstination, opiniâtreté, *f.*; acharnement, *m.*; (*stubbornness*) entêtement, *m.*
Obstinate, *adj.* obstiné, opiniâtre; acharné; rebelle; (*stubborn*) entêté
Obstinately, *adv.* obstinément; opiniâtrément; avec acharnement; (*stubbornly*) avec
Obstreperous. *V.* **Noisy** [entêtement
Obstruct, *v.a.* encombrer, obstruer; boucher; barrer; fermer; (*fig.*) mettre obstacle à, arrêter, empêcher; retarder; intercepter; interrompre; (*med.*) obstruer. *To become —ed,* s'encombrer, s'obstruer; se boucher, &c.
Obstruction, *s.* encombrement, embarras, empêchement, obstacle, *m.*; (*med.*) obstruction, *f.* *To cause an —,* (*in the streets*) gêner la circulation
Obstructive, Obstruent, *adj.* qui obstrue, qui bouche; (*hindering*) embarrassant; (*med.*) obstructif
Obtain, *v.a.* obtenir ('*for,*' pour); acquérir; procurer (*for others,* '*for,*' à); se procurer (*for oneself*); (*gain*) gagner, remporter; (*find*) pouvoir trouver; (*bring*) valoir; (*attain*) atteindre; (*hold*) occuper, tenir; *v.n.* s'accréditer, s'établir; avoir cours; exister, subsister, se maintenir, se conserver; prévaloir, régner
Obtainable, *adj.* qu'on peut obtenir, à obtenir; accessible (à)
Obtainer, *s.* obtenteur, *m.*, personne qui obtient *or* qui procure, *f.*
Obtaining, Obtainment, *s.* obtention, action d'obtenir *or* de procurer, *f.*
Obtrude, Obtrusion, Obtrusive, &c. *V.* **Intrude,** &c. [tir, adoucir; (*quell*) assoupir
Obtund, *v.a.* (*blunt*) émousser; (*deaden*) amor-
Obturating, *adj.* obturateur
Obturation, *s.* obturation, *f.*
Obturator, *s.* obturateur, *m.* [sangle
Obtusangular, *adj.* obtusangulaire, obtu-
Obtuse, *adj.* obtus; (*blunt*) émoussé; (*of sound*) sourd [stupidement; (*of sound*) sourdement
Obtusely, *adv.* sans pointe; (*fig.*) obtusement,
Obtuseness, Obtusion, *s.* forme obtuse, *f.*; (*bluntness*) état émoussé, *m.*; (*fig.*) obtusion, *f.*; stupidité, *f.*; (*of sound*) nature sourde, *f.*
Obumbrate, *v.a.* obombrer
Obumbration, *s.* obombration, *f.*
Obverse, *s.* obvers, obverse, *m.*; (*print.*) recto, *m.*
Obvert, *v.a.* tourner
Obviate, *v.a.* obvier à, prévenir

Obvious, *adj.* évident, clair, sensible, qui saute aux yeux [siblement
Obviously, *adv.* évidemment, clairement, sen-
Obviousness, *s.* évidence, clarté, *f.*
Oca, *s.* oca, *m.*
Occasion, *s.* occasion, *f.*; circonstance, *f.*; (*need*) besoin, *m.*, nécessité, *f.*; (*cause*) sujet, motif, *m.*, cause, *f.*, lieu, *m.*, raison, *f.*; — *v.a.* occasionner, causer, être cause de, produire; (*influence*) déterminer. *For the* —, pour la circonstance. *On* or *upon this* or *that* —, dans (*or* en *or* à) cette occasion, dans cette circonstance. *On another* —, une autre fois. *On* or *upon* — or *the* —, au besoin· dans l'occasion. *On the* — *of,* à l'occasion de. *To have* — *for,* avoir besoin de. *To take* —, profiter (de). *There is no* — *for it,* il n'en est pas besoin; cela n'est pas nécessaire
Occasional, *adj.* (*causing*) occasionnel; (*occurring at times*) par occasion; de temps en temps; accidentel, casuel, fortuit; intermittent; (*for the occasion*) de circonstance. — *chair,* chaise de fantaisie, *f.* — *table,* petite table, table de canapé, table de fantaisie, *f.*
Occasionally, *adv.* occasionnellement; par occasion, dans l'occasion, quand l'occasion s'en présente; (*sometimes*) quelquefois, parfois, de temps en temps; par hasard
Occasioner, *s.* auteur, *m.*, cause, *f.*
Occident, *s.* occident, *m.*
Occidental, *adj.* occidental
Occipital, *adj.* occipital
Occiput, *s.* occiput, *m.*
Occlusion, *s.* occlusion, *f.*
Occult, *adj.* occulte; — *v.a.* occulter
Occultation, *s.* occultation, *f.*
Occultly, *adv.* occultement
Occultness, *s.* nature occulte, *f.*; secret, *m.*
Occupancy, *s.* occupation, *f.*
Occupant. *V.* **Occupier**
Occupation, *s.* occupation, *f.*; travail, *m.*; emploi, *m*; (*profession*) état, métier, *m.*; (*tenure*) possession, *f.*; (*mil.*) occupation, *f.*
Occupier, *s.* occupateur, *m.*, -trice, *f.*; occupant, *m.*, e, *f.*; possesseur, *m.*; (*of houses*) habitant, *m.*, e, *f.*; (*tenant*) locataire, *m.f.* *First* —, premier occupant, *m.*
Occupy, *v.a.* occuper; employer; (*of houses*) habiter. *To* — *oneself in* or *with,* s'occuper à *or* de
Occur, *v.n.* venir à l'esprit *or* à l'idée; venir; se présenter, s'offrir; se rencontrer, se trouver; (*happen*) arriver. *It —s to me that* ..., j'ai dans l'idée que ... *It did not — to me that* ..., il ne m'est pas venu à l'idée que ..., l'idée ne m'est pas venue que ... *The case —ring,* le cas échéant. — **again,** arriver encore, se renouveler (*won't — again,* n'arrivera plus)
Occurrence, *s.* occurrence, *f.*; circonstance, *f.*; événement, *m.*; accident, *m.*; rencontre, *f.*; fait, *m.* *To be of common* or *frequent* —, arriver souvent, avoir lieu souvent. — **book,** *s.* (*police*) livre de consignation, *m.*
Occurrent, *adj.* occurrent
Ocean, *s.* océan, *m.*; (*fig.*) immensité, *f.*, abîme, *m.*; — *adj.* de l'océan. — **Sea,** *s.* mer océane, *f.* — **ship, -steamer,** *s.* long-courrier, *m.*
Oceanian, *s. adj.* Océanien, *m.*, -ne, *f.*
Oceanic, *adj.* océanique
Ocellated, *adj.* ocellé
Ocellation, *s.* ocellation, *f.*
Ocellus, *s.* ocelle, *m.*
Ocelot, *s.* ocelot, *m.*
Ochlocracy, *s.* ochlocratie, *f.*
Ochlocrat-ic, al, -ically. *V.* page 3, § 1
Ochraceous, *adj.* ocracé, ochracé
Ochre, *s.* ocre, *f.* — **pit,** *s.* mine d'ocre, *f.*
Ochreous, Ochry, *adj.* ocreux
O'clock. *V.* **Clock**
Octagon, *s.* octogone, *m.*
Octagonal, *adj.* octogonal, octogone
Octahedral, *adj.* octaèdre
Octahedron, *s.* octaèdre, *m.*
Octangular, *adj.* octogonal, octogone
Octant, *s.* octant, *m.*
Octave, *s.* octave, *f.* — **cask,** (*of French wine generally, and beer*) *s.* quartaut, *m.*; (*of Champagne wine*) caque, *f.* — **flute,** *s.* octavin, *m.*
Octavo, *s. adj.* in-octavo, *m.* *In* —, in-octavo
Octennial, *adj.* qui a lieu tous les huit ans, de huit en huit ans; qui dure huit ans
Octennially, *adv.* tous les huit ans
October, *s.* octobre, *m.*
Octogenarian, *s. adj.* octogénaire, *m.f.*
Octopod, Octopus, *s.* octopode, *m.*; poulpe, [*m.*, pieuvre, *f.*
Octoroon, *s.* octavon, *m.*, -ne, *f.*
Octroi, *s.* octroi, *m.* [octupler
Octuple, *adj. s.* octuple, *adj.m.f, s.m.*; — *v.a.n.*
Ocular, *adj.* oculaire
Ocularist, *s.* ocularisté, *m.* [yeux
Ocularly, *adv.* oculairement; de ses propres
Oculate, Oculated, *adj.* oculé
Oculiform, *adj.* oculiforme
Oculist, *s.* oculiste, *m.*
Odalisk, Odalisque, *s.* odalisque, *f.*
Odd, *adj.* (*not even*) impair; (*some*) quelques; (*remaining*) de reste; d'appoint; (*one of a set*) dépareillé; (*one of a pair*) déparié; (*small*) petit; (*strange*) singulier, étrange; bizarre; (*not regular*) irrégulier; particulier; en dehors; extraordinaire; (*of time*) perdu, de loisir. — *end,* reste, *m.*; bribe, *f.* — *fish,* *s.* drôle de corps, *m.* — *money,* appoint, *m.*, passe, *f.* — *number,* nombre impair, *m.* — *or even,* pair ou non. *Twenty* — *pounds,* vingt et quelques livres. *Thirteen francs* —, treize francs et quelque chose. *Sixteen hundred and — years after the deluge,* environ seize cents ans après le déluge. *An — volume,* un volume dépareillé, *m.* *An — glove,* un gant déparié, *m.*
Oddity, *s.* singularité, *f.*; bizarrerie, *f.*; excentricité, *f.*; (*whim*) fantaisie, *f.*; (*pers.*) original, *m.*, e, *f.* [zarrement
Oddly, *adv* singulièrement, étrangement; bi-
Oddness, *s.* singularité, étrangeté, *f.*; bizarrerie, *f.*
Odds, *s.pl.* inégalité, disparité, *f.*; avantage, *m.*, supériorité, *f.*, dessus, *m.*; probabilité, *f.*, chances, *f.pl.*; (*stake*) enjeu, *m.*; (*difference*) différence, *f.*; (*quarrel*) différend, *m.*, dispute, querelle, *f.* — *and ends,* petits bouts, pièces et morceaux, fragments, *m.pl.*, bribes, *f.pl.* *To be at* —, être en querelle, être en contestation. *To lay* —, parier. *To set at* —, brouiller, mettre la désunion entre. *The — are that* ..., il y a à parier que ... *It makes no* —, cela ne fait pas de différence, c'est la même chose, cela ne fait rien. *What — is that to him?* qu'est-ce que [cela lui fait?
Ode, *s.* ode, *f.*
Odelet, *s.* odelette, *f.*
Odeon, *s.* odéon, *m.*
Odious, *adj* odieux; détestable
Odiously, *adv.* odieusement
Odiousness, *s.* odieux, *m.*
Odium, *s.* odieux, *m.*; haine, *f.*; fiel, *m.* — *theologicum,* haine théologique, haine de prêtre, *f.* *To cast — upon,* rendre odieux
Odometer. *V.* **Hodometer**
Odontalgia, Odontalgy, *s.* odontalgie, *f.*
Odontalgic, *adj. s.* odontalgique, *adj.m.f., s.m.*
Odontography, &c. *V.* page 3, § 1
Odoration, *s.* odoration, *f.* [odorant, odorable
Odoriferous, Odorous, *adj.* odoriférant,
Odoriferousness, Odorousness, *s.* odorabilité, *f.*; parfum, *m.* [(*of wine*) bouquet, *m.*
Odour, *s.* odeur, *f.*; parfum, *m.*; senteur, *f.*;
Odyssey, *s.* Odyssée, *f.*
Œ. [*For words not found under* **Œ**, *V.* **E**]
Œcumenic, -al, *adj.* œcuménique
Œcumenically, *adv.* œcuméniquement
Œcumenicity, *s.* œcuménicité, *f.*
Œdema, *s.* œdème, *m.* [s'œdématier
Œdematize, *v.a.* œdématier. *To become —d,*
Œdematous, *adj.* œdémateux

Œnanthic, *adj.* œnanthique
Œnolog-ic, al, -y. *V.* page 3, § 1
Œnologist, *s.* œnologue, œnologiste, *m.*
Œnometer, *s.* œnomètre, *m.*
Œnometric, -al, *adj.* œnométrique
Œnometry, *s.* œnométrie, *f.*
Œnophilic, *adj.*, **Œnophilist,** *s.* œnophile, [*m.f.*
Œsophagean, *adj.* œsophagien
Œsophagus, *s.* œsophage, *m.*
Of, *prep.* de; (*in*) en; (*among*) parmi, entre; (*among and above, before 'all'*) entre; (*of among*) d'entre; (*over*) sur. *On the third — March,* le trois mars. *It is very kind — you* (*to* ...), c'est bien aimable à vous (de ...), c'est bien bon de votre part (de ...). *It was well said — you,* c'était bien dit à vous. *V.* **Bad,** *adj.*, *and* **Wrong,** *adj.*
Off, *prep.* (*from on*) de dessus; (*out of*) hors de; (*on, from*) de; (*nav.*) à la hauteur de, devant, en vue de. *Take that — the table,* ôtez cela de dessus la table. *— hinges,* hors des gonds. *To dine — a pie,* dîner d'un pâté. *A piece — the ribs,* un morceau des côtes, *m.*, une entre-côtes, *f.* **-hand,** *adj.* dégagé, libre, cavalier, sans gêne, sans cérémonie; aisé; nonchalant; improvisé, impromptu, fait sur le moment; *adv.* librement, cavalièrement; haut la main; (*at once*) d'un coup; tout de suite; (*fluently*) couramment; sans préparation, d'abondance; sans peine; (*of writing*) à main levée. **—handed,** *adj.* grossier, sans façon, sans gêne. **—handedness,** *s.* grossièreté, *f.*, sans-façon, sans-gêne, *m.*
Off, *adv. adj.* (*of place*) loin, de distance; d'ici; de là; (*aside*) à l'écart; éloigné; (*farthest*) éloigné; (*denoting separation*) séparé; enlevé, ôté; détaché; (*from on it*) de dessus; (*denoting cessation*) manqué, rompu; (*void*) nul; (*shut*) fermé; (*against*) contre; (*right-hand*) droit, de droite; (*nav.*) au large. *A mile —,* à un mille de distance *or* d'ici (*or, 'from there,'* de là). *— and on,* de temps à autre, de temps en temps; par intervalles; par boutades; à bâtons rompus; (*nav.*) bord à terre bord au large. *— with!* (*things*) ôtez! enlevez! à bas! (*pers.*) emmenez! *— with you! be —!* allez-vous-en! allez vous promener *or* vous coucher! *To be —,* (*pers.*) s'en aller, partir, se sauver, s'enfuir; aller; (*things*) être manqué, être rompu. *To be badly —* or *ill —,* être mal dans ses affaires, être dans la gêne *or* dans l'embarras; être malade; être malheureux; être mal; être maltraité; (*for*) être mal monté (en) *or* pourvu (de), avoir grand besoin (de). *To be well —,* être bien dans ses affaires, être dans l'aisance, être à son aise, être riche; être heureux; être bien; (*for*) être bien monté (en) *or* pourvu (de). **— side,** *s.* côté droit, *m.*; (*rid.*) hors main, hors montoir, *m.*
Offal, *s.* entrailles, *f.pl.*, peau (*f.*) et tripes (*f.pl.*); carcasse, *f.*; (*butch.*) abats, *m.pl.*, issues, *f.pl.*; (*of a table*) restes, *m.pl.*, desserte, *f.*; (*coarse meat*) carne, *f.*; (*carrion*) charogne, *f.*; (*rubbish*) rebut, *m.*
Offence, *s.* offense, *f.*; outrage, *m.*; affront, *m.*; déplaisir, *m.*; injure, *f.*; infraction, atteinte, *f.*; (*law*) infraction de la loi, atteinte, *f.*; (*law*) contravention, *f.*; (*law*) délit, *m.*; (*law*) crime, *m.*; (*theol.*) scandale, *m.*; (*sin*) péché, *m.* *Fresh —,* (*law*) récidive, *f.* *Indictable —,* fait qualifié crime ou délit, *m.* *To give —,* offenser, blesser; froisser; faire ombrage (à); déplaire (à). *To take —,* s'offenser (de), se fâcher (de). **—less,** *adj.* inoffensif; innocent
Offend, *v.a.* offenser, blesser, froisser, choquer; fâcher; déplaire à; (*transgress*) violer, transgresser, enfreindre; *— v.n.* offenser, déplaire; commettre une infraction; (*to sin*) pécher, faillir
Offender, *s.* offenseur, *m.*; (*culprit*) coupable, *m.f.*, criminel, *m.*, -le, *f.*, malfaiteur, *m.*, -trice, *f.*; (*sinner*) pécheur, *m.*, pécheresse, *f.*; (*law*) délinquant, *m.*, e, *f.*; (*law*) contrevenant, *m.*, e, *f.*, (*law*) criminel, *m.*, -le, *f.* *Old —,* (*law*) récidiviste, *m.f.* *To be an old —,* (*fam.*) être coutumier du fait
Offending, *s.* action d'offenser *or* &c. (*V.* **Offend,** *v.a.n.*), *f.*; violation, transgression, infraction, *f.*; péché, *m.*; faute, *f.*
Offense, *s. V.* **Offence**
Offensive, *adj.* offensant, blessant, choquant, injurieux; désagréable; (*aggressive*) offensif; *— s.* offensive, *f.*
Offensively, *adv.* d'une manière offensante *or* blessante; désagréablement; (*in attacking*) offensivement
Offensiveness, *s.* nature offensante *or* blessante, *f.*; nature désagréable, *f.*
Offer, *v.a.* offrir (à); présenter (à); proposer (à); (**— up**) offrir, sacrifier; *— v.n.* s'offrir (à), se présenter (à); offrir (de); essayer (de), vouloir; *— s.* offre, *f.*; (*attempt*) tentative, *f.*, essai, *m.* *To — violence, an insult,* faire violence, une insulte. *Not to — to speak,* ne pas ouvrir la bouche
Offerable, *adj.* offrable, présentable, que l'on peut offrir, qui peut s'offrir
Offerer, *s.* offreur, *m.*, personne qui fait une offre, *f.*; personne qui fait une offrande, *f.*; (*in worship*) sacrificateur, *m.* [sacrifice, *m.*
Offering, *s.* offrande, *f.*; présent, *m.*; (*theol.*)
Offertory, *s.* (*Cath. lit.*) offertoire, *m.*, offerte, *f.*; (*Protestant lit.*) lecture pendant la quête, *f.*; (*collection*) quête, *f.*
Office, *s.* charge, *f.*, emploi, *m.*; fonction, *f.*, fonctions, *f.pl.*, office, *m.*; (*duty*) devoir, *m.*; (*power*) place, *f.*, pouvoir, *m.*; (*turn*) service, office, *m.*; (*room*) bureau, cabinet, *m*; agence, *f.*; (*of lawyers*) étude, *f.*; (*counting-house*) comptoir, *m.*; (*ministry*) ministère, *m.*; (*prayers*) office, *m.*; — *s* (*pl.*), *domestic* or *servants' —s,* offices, *f.pl.*, communs, *m.pl.*, dépendances, *f.pl.* *In —,* en place; au pouvoir. **— bell,** *s.* (*call-bell*) timbre (de table), *m.* **— copy,** *s.* ampliation, *f.* **— holder,** *s.* homme en place, *m.* **— hours,** *s.pl.* heures de bureau, *f.pl.* **— keeper,** *s.* buraliste, *m.f.* **— lead,** *s.* presse-papiers, *m.* **— requisites,** *s.pl.*, **— stationery,** *s.* fournitures de bureau, *f.pl.*
Officer, *s.* (*mil.*, *nav.*, &c.) officier, *m.*; (*public*) fonctionnaire, *m.*; (*dignitary*) dignitaire, *m.*; (*of police, justice*) agent, *m.*; (*sheriff's or summoning —*) huissier, *m.*; (*clerk*) commis, employé, préposé, *m.*; *— v.a.* pourvoir d'officiers, donner pour officier *or* pour officiers à. *To be —ed with,* avoir pour officier *or* pour officiers. *To be —ed by,* être commandé par
Official, *adj.* officiel; d'office; public; *— s.* employé, *m.*; fonctionnaire, *m.*; (*eccl.*) official, *m.*; **—s,** *s.pl.* employés, *m.pl.*; administration, *f.* *— assignee,* syndic, *m.* *— envelope,* enveloppe administrative, *f.* *— paper,* papier ministre, *m.*; (*newspaper*) journal officiel, *m.* *— seal,* sceau réglementaire, *m.*
Officially, *adv.* officiellement
Officialty, *s.* officialité, *f.*
Officiant, *s.* officiant, *m.*, e, *f.*
Officiate, *v.n.* exercer, exercer ses fonctions; (*do the duty of*) remplir les fonctions (de); (*of clergymen*) officier
Officinal, *adj.* officinal
Officio (Ex), *adv.* d'office
Officious, *adj.* officieux
Officiously, *adv.* officieusement
Officiousness, *s.* officieuseté, officiosité, *f.*, empressement, *m.*; impertinence, *f.*
Offing, *s.* large, *m.* *In the —,* au large
Offscouring, *s.* rebut, *m.*
Offscum, *s.* écume, *f.*, rebut, *m.*
Offset, *s.* (*hort.*) œilleton, *m.*; (*build.*) retraite, *f.*, retrait, *m.*; (*geom.*) ordonnée, *f.*; (*in accounts*) compensation, *f.*; *— v.a.* compenser. *V.* **Set-off**
Offshoot, *s.* rejeton, *m.*; œilleton, *m.*
Offskip, *s.* (*paint.*) lointain, *m.*

Offspring, *s.* enfant, *m.*, descendants, *m.pl.*, postérité, race, *f.*; famille, *f.*; (*of animals*) petits, *m.pl.*; (*fam.*) progéniture, *f.*; (*fig.*) fruit, produit, *m.*
Offuscate. *V.* **Obfuscate**
Offward, *adv.* vers le large, vers la mer
Oft, Often, Oftentimes, *adv.* souvent, fréquemment. *As — as,* aussi souvent que. *How —?* combien de fois? *How — do you go there?* y allez-vous souvent? *How — in a week do you go there?* combien de fois y allez-vous par semaine? *Not —,* pas souvent, rarement. *It is not — that ...,* il n'arrive pas souvent que ... (*with the subj.*). *So —,* si souvent, tant de fois. — **repeated, -told,** *adj.* souvent répété; (*trite*) rebattu
Ogee, *s.* cymaise, *f.*; ogive, *f.*
Ogival, *adj.* ogival
Ogive, *s.* ogive, *f.*; — *adj.* en ogive
Ogle, *v.a.* lorgner; reluquer; faire de l'œil à; — *s.* œillade, *f.*
Ogler, *s.* lorgneur, *m.*, -euse, *f.*
Ogling, *s.* lorgnerie, lorgnade, *f.*, œillades, *f.pl.*
Ogre, *s.* ogre, *m.*
Ogress, *s.* ogresse, *f.*
Oh, *int.* ah! oh! ô! tiens! — *me!* malheureux que je suis!
Oidium, *s.* oïdium, *m.*
Oil, *s.* huile, *f.*; (*of turpentine,* &c.) essence, *f.*; — *v.a.* huiler; (*the tongue*) délier. *In —,* (*paint.*) à l'huile. — **baize,** *s.* toile cirée, *f.* — **beetle,** *s.* méloé, *m.* — **cake,** *s.* tourteau, *m.* — **cake breaker,** *s.* concasseur à tourteaux, brise-tourteaux, *m.* — **can,** *s.* huilière, burette, *f.*; (*large*) bidon, *m.*, tourie, *f.* — **case, -cloth,** *s.* toile cirée, *f.* — **colour,** *s.* couleur à l'huile, *f.* — **cruet,** *s.* burette à l'huile, *f.* — **cup,** *s.* godet à huile, *m.* — **gas,** *s.* gaz tiré de l'huile, *m.* — **maker,** *s.* huilier, *m.* — **man,** *s.* marchand d'huile, *m.* — **mill,** *s.* huilerie, *f.* — **nut,** *s.* noix de ben, *f.*; ricin, *m.* — **painting,** *s.* peinture à l'huile, *f.* — **plant,** *s.* plante oléagineuse, *f.* — **poppy,** *s.* œillette, *f.* — **press,** *s.* pressoir à huile, *m.* — **pressing,** *s.* expression de l'huile, *f.* — **refiner,** *s.* épurateur d'huiles, *m.* — **refinery,** *s.* usine à épurer les huiles, *f.* — **refining,** *s.* épuration des huiles, *f.* — **seed,** *s.* graine oléagineuse, *f.* — **seed cake,** *s. V.* — **cake.** — **shop,** *s.* magasin d'huile, *m.*, huilerie, *f.* — **silk,** *s.* taffetas gommé, *m.* — **skin,** *s.* toile vernie, *f.* — **stone,** *s.* pierre à l'huile, affiloire, *f.* — **trade,** *s.* commerce des huiles, *m.* — **tree,** *s.* ricin, *m.* — **well,** *s.* source de pétrole, *f.* — **works,** *s.pl.* huilerie, *f.*
Oiled, *part. adj.* huilé. *Well —,* (*of the tongue*) bien pendue, bien affilée. — **silk,** *s.* taffetas gommé, *m.* — **skin,** *s.* toile vernie, *f.*
Oilery, *s.* huilerie, *f.*; huiles, *f.pl.*
Oiliness, *s.* nature huileuse, *f.*; onctuosité, *f.*
Oiling, *s.* huilage, huilement, *m.*
Oily, *adj.* huileux; oléagineux; onctueux. — **grain,** *s.* sésame, *m.*
Ointment, *s.* onguent, *m.*, pommade, *f.*
Old, *adj.* vieux, vieil; âgé; ancien; antique. — *age,* vieillesse, *f.* — *man,* vieillard, homme vieux, vieil homme, *m.*; (*jest.*) vieux, *m.*; (*goodman, husband*) homme, *m.*; (*a plant*) citronnelle, *f.* — *people,* vieillards, *m.pl.*, vieilles gens, *f.pl.* — *woman,* vieille femme, (*jest.*) vieille, *f.* — *Tom,* le père Tom. — *enough* (*to*), assez âgé (pour), d'âge (à), en âge (de). *Of —,* autrefois, jadis. *Ten years —,* âgé de dix ans. *At ten years —,* à l'âge de dix ans. *To be ten years —,* avoir dix ans, être âgé de dix ans. *To be an — man,* être âgé, être vieux, être un vieillard. *To be an — woman,* être âgée, être vieille. *To grow* or *get —, V.* **Grow.** *How — are you?* quel âge avez-vous? *I am ten years —,* j'ai dix ans. *How — should you take him to be?* quel âge lui donneriez-vous? — **established,** *adj.* établi (*or* fondé) depuis longtemps, ancien. — **fashioned,** *adj.* à l'ancienne mode, antique, ancien; du vieux temps; passé de mode, démodé; suranné; (*in contempt*) rococo
Olden, *adj.* vieux, ancien
Oldish, *adj.* un peu vieux, assez âgé, d'un certain âge, vieillot
Oldness, *s.* vieillesse, *f.*; ancienneté, *f.*; antiquité, *f.*; (*deterioration*) vétusté, *f.*
Oleaginous, *adj.* oléagineux
Oleaginousness, *s.* nature oléagineuse, *f.*
Oleander, *s.* oléandre, laurier-rose, *m.*
Oleaster, *s.* olivier de Bohême, olivier sauvage, chalef, *m.*
Oleate, *s.* oléate, *m.*
Olefiant, *adj.* oléfiant
Oleic, *adj.* oléique
Oleiferous, *adj.* oléifère
Oleine, *s.* oléine, *f.*
Oleography, &c., oléographie, &c. (*V.* p.3, § 1)
Oleometer, *s.* oléomètre, *m.*
Oleraceous, *adj.* oléracé, potager
Olfaction, *s.* olfaction, *f.* [odorat, *m.*
Olfactory, *adj.* olfactif; — *s.* nerf olfactif, *m.*
Olibanum, *s.* oliban, *m.*
Oligarch, *s.* oligarque, *m.*
Oligarch-ic, al, -ically, -ist, -y. *V.* p.3, § 1
Olio, *s.* (*cook*) oille, *f.*; (*fig.*) pot-pourri, *m.*, macédoine, *f.*, salmigondis, *m.*
Olivary, *adj.* olivaire
Olivaster, *adj.* olivâtre
Olive, *s.* olive, *f.*; (*tree*) olivier, *m.*; (*colour*) olive, *m.*; — *adj.* d'olive, d'olives; d'olivier; (*of colour*) de couleur olive, olive, olivâtre. *Garden of —s,* Jardin des Oliviers, *m.* — **branch,** *s.* branche (*f.*) *or* rameau (*m.*) d'olivier; (*children*) enfants, *m.pl.* — **bead, -button,** *s.* olive, *f.* — **colour,** *s.* couleur olive, *f.*, olive, *m.* — **coloured,** *adj.* de couleur olive, couleur olive, olive, olivâtre. — **complexion,** *s.* teint olivâtre, *m.* — **crop,** *s.* olivaison, *f.* — **garden, -grove,** *s.* olivaie, olivette, *f.* — **green,** *adj.* *s.* vert olive, *m.* — **harvest,** *s.* olivaison, *f.* — **moulding,** *s.* olive, *f.* — **oil,** *s.* huile d'olive *or* d'olives, *f.* — **oil mill** *or* **works,** *s.* oliverie, *f.* — **orchard, -plantation,** *s.* olivaie, olivette, *f.* — **season,** *s.* olivaison, *f.* — **shaped,** *adj.* oliviforme, olivaire. — **tree,** *s.* olivier, *m.* — **wood,** *s.* bois d'olivier, olivier, *m.* — **yard,** *s.* olivaie, olivette, *f.*
Olived, *adj.* garni d'oliviers; orné de branches d'olivier
Olivine, *s.* olivine, *f.*
Olla-podrida, *s.* olla-podrida, *f.*, pot-pourri, *m.*
Ollite, *s.* pierre ollaire, *f.*
Olograph, &c. *V.* **Holograph,** &c.
Olympiad, *s.* olympiade, *f.*
Olympian, *adj.* olympien
Olympic, *adj.* olympique; — *s.* (*Pindar's*) Olympique, *f.*; —**s,** *s.pl.* jeux Olympiques, *m.pl.*; (*Pindar's*) Olympiques, *f.pl.*
Olynthiac, *s.* Olynthienne, *f.*
Olynthian, *adj.* olynthien
Ombre, *s.* hombre, *m.*
Ombrometer, *s.* ombromètre, *m.*
Omega, *s.* oméga, *m.*
Omelet, *s.* omelette, *f.* *A two-egg —,* une omelette de deux œufs
Omen, *s.* augure, présage, pronostic, *m.*
Omened, *adj.* d'augure, de présage (*V.* **Ill**)
Omental, *adj.* épiploïque
Omentitis, *s.* omentite, *f.*
Omentum, *s.* épiploon, *m.*
Ominous, *adj.* de mauvais augure, sinistre; (*of looks,* &c.) menaçant
Ominously, *adv.* de mauvais augure
Ominousness, *s.* nature sinistre, *f.*
Omissible, *adj.* qui peut être omis
Omission, *s.* omission, *f.*; (*forgetfulness*) oubli, *m.* *Sin of —,* péché d'omission, *m.*
Omissive, *adj.* qui omet; (*forgetful*) oublieux
Omit, *v.a.* omettre; (*neglect*) négliger; (*forget*) oublier
Omnibus, *s.* omnibus, *m.* — **boat,** *s.* bateau à vapeur omnibus, *m.* — **conductor, -cad,**

s. conducteur d'omnibus, *m.* — **driver,** *s.* cocher d'omnibus, *m.* — **train,** *s.* train-omnibus, *m.*

Omnicoloured, *adj.* omnicolore

Omnifarious, *adj.* de toute sorte, de toute espèce, varié

Omnipotence, *s.* omnipotence, toute-puissance, *f.*

Omnipotent, *adj. s.* omnipotent, tout-puissant

Omnipresence, *s.* omniprésence, *f.*

Omnipresent, *adj.* omniprésent, présent partout

Omniscience, *s.* omniscience, *f.*

Omniscient, *adj.* omniscient

Omnium, *s.* omnium, *m.* — **gatherum,** *s.* capharnaüm, *m.*

Omnivorous, *adj.* omnivore

Omoplate, *s.* omoplate, *f.*

Omphalotomy, *s.* omphalotomie, *f.*

On, *prep.* sur; (*adverb., in opposition*) dessus; (*at, to, about*) à; (*of, from, towards*) de; (*in, into, while*) en; dans; (*after*) après; (*according to*) d'après; (*against*) contre; (*of weather*) par; — *it, them* (*things*), dessus; y; d'après, en conséquence. [*Untranslated before the word 'day,' or before the names of the days of the week, or before the numbers of the days of a month.*] — *the table*, sur la table (*V.* **Under**). —*the right* or *left hand*, à droite, à gauche. — *my entrance, departure, arrival*, or *return*, à mon entrée, départ, arrivée, *or* retour. *A ring — o.'s finger*, une bague au doigt. *my side*, de mon côté. — *the part of*, de la part de. — *entering*, en entrant. — *examination*, après examen. — *the day of* ..., le jour de ... — *Tuesday*, mardi; (*regularly*) le mardi. — *Tuesdays*, les mardis. — *the first of May*, le premier mai. — *a fine day*, par un beau jour

On, *adv.* dessus; (*forward*) en avant; devant soi; avant; toujours; (*in the year*, &c.) avancé; (*taking place*) qui a lieu; (*of clothes*) sur soi; (*of head-gear*) sur la tête; (*of boots*, &c.) aux pieds; *V. To* **Have on,** *To* **Put on,** *To* **Keep on,** *and To* **Try on;** — *adject.* (*open*) ouvert. *Far — in the night*, bien avant dans la nuit. *Read* —, lisez toujours, continuez de lire, continuez. *Walk* —, marchez toujours, allez toujours. —*!* en avant! — *with it!* continuez! *He entered with his hat* —, il entra le chapeau sur la tête. *With o.'s shoes or boots* —, chaussé; botté. *With o.'s gloves* —, ganté. *And so* —, *V.* **So.** —**looker,** *s. V.* **Looker-on**

Onager, *s.* onagre, *m.*

Once, *adv.* une fois; (*only* —) une seule fois; (*formerly*) autrefois, anciennement, jadis; (*when once*) une fois que. — *before*, une première fois. —*for all*, une fois pour toutes, une bonne fois. — *in a way*, une fois par hasard, de temps à autre. — *too often*, une fois de trop. *At* —, (*immediately*) tout de suite, à l'instant, sur-le-champ; sans délai, sans tarder; (*at a time*) à la fois; d'un coup; (*at the same time*) à la fois, en même temps, tous ensemble; (*suddenly*) tout d'un coup, tout à coup. *All at* —, tout d'un coup, tout à coup. *For* —, une fois, une seule fois, une fois du moins; pour cette fois; une fois pour toutes. *This* —, pour cette fois-ci, pour cette fois. *When* —, une fois que, quand une fois, lorsqu'une fois; du moment que

One, *adj. pron.* un, *m.*, une, *f.*; (*only* —, *even* —) un seul, *m.*, une seule, *f.*; (*only*) seul (e, *f.*), unique; (*the same*) le même, *m.*, la même, *f.*; (*elliptically*) (*of the clock*) une heure, *f.*, (*of o.'s age*) un an, *m.*; (*man, people, they, we*) on; (*somebody*) quelqu'un, *m.*; (*a person*) une personne, *f.*; (*a man*) un homme, *m.*; (*a woman*) une femme, *f.*; (*the* —) celui, *m.*, celle, *f.*; (*one of those*) de ceux, *m.pl.*, de celles, *f.pl.*; (*after 'a' or any numeral*) en. [*Often untranslated.*] *Any* —, *See Letter* **A.** *At* —, uni; d'accord (*To set at* —, unir, réunir; mettre d'accord). *No* —, *Some* —, *See Letters* **N** *and* **S.** — *and all*, tous sans exception, tous tant que nous sommes (*or* vous êtes *or* &c.). — *another*, *V.* **Each other.** — *with another*, (*on an average*) l'un (*m.*, l'une, *f.*) dans l'autre, l'un (*or* l'une) portant l'autre. *With — another*, l'un (*or* l'une) avec l'autre; (*of more than two*) les uns (*m.pl.*, les unes, *f.pl.*) avec les autres. *That is all* —, c'est la même chose, cela revient au même, c'est tout un. *It is all — to me*, cela m'est égal, cela m'est indifférent, c'est la même chose pour moi. *That* —, celui-là, *m.*, celle-là, *f.* *This* —, celui-ci, *m.*, celle-ci, *f.* *The* —, *V.* **That.** — *Smith*, un nommé Smith, (*in contempt*) un certain Smith. — *may say*, on peut dire. *He is not — who thinks* ..., il n'est pas de ceux qui pensent ... *A bad thing and a good* —, *and two good* —*s*, une mauvaise chose et une bonne, et deux bonnes. *I have a good* —, j'en ai un bon (*m.*, une bonne, *f.*). *I have two good* —*s*, j'en ai deux bons (*or* bonnes). *I have good* —*s*, j'en ai de bons (*or* bonnes). *Good* —*s are rare*, les bons (*or* bonnes) sont rares. *I have* —, j'en ai un (*or* une). *Only* —, un seul, une seule; ne ... qu'un (*or* qu'une). *I have only* (or *but*) —, je n'en ai qu'un (or qu'une). *The only* —, le seul, la seule. *The black* —, le noir, la noire. *The small* or *little* —*s*, les petits, les petites. *The best* —, le meilleur, la meilleure. *It makes — shudder*, cela fait frémir. — *hundred and ten*, cent-dix. *Number* —, numéro un; (*o.'s own self*) mon (*or* ton *or* son *or* &c.) individu, *m.*, ma (*or* ta *or* sa *or* &c.) petite personne, *f.* *I for* — ..., pour ma part je ...; moi du moins je ... *It is — thing*, c'est quelque chose; voilà ce qu'il y a de bon. *It is — thing to propose, another to execute*, autre chose est de proposer, et autre chose d'exécuter. *To talk about — thing and another*, causer de choses et d'autres. —**armed,** *adj. s.* manchot, *m.*, e, *f.* — **berry,** *s.* parisette, *f.* —**eyed,** *adj. V.* **Eyed.** —**footed,** *adj.* à un pied, qui n'a qu'un pied. —**handed,** *adj. s.* manchot, *m.*, e, *f.* *A* —**horse** *carriage* (, *chaise*), &c., une voiture (, chaise), &c. à un cheval, *f.* —**'s,** —**self,** *pron. See below.* —**sided,** *adj.* qui n'a qu'un côté; partial; exclusif; injuste. —**sidedness,** *s.* partialité, *f.*; exclusivisme, *m.*

Oneness, *s.* unité, *f.*

Onerous, *adj.* onéreux

Onerously, *adv.* onéreusement

Onerousness, *s.* poids, *m.*, charge, *f.*

One's, *pron.* son, *m.*, sa, *f.*, ses, *pl.*

Oneself, *pron.* soi-même; soi; (*in a reflect. verb*) se

Onion, *s.* ognon, *m.* — **bed,** *s.* ognonière, ognonnière, *f.* —**peel,** *s.* pelure d'ognon, *f.* — **sauce,** *s.* purée d'ognons, sauce Robert, sauce soubise, soubise, *f.* —**seed,** *s.* ognonette, ognonnette, *f.*; — **stew,** *s.* ognonade, ognonnade, *f.*

Only, *adj.* seul; unique; (*of a child, son or daughter*) unique; — *adv.* seulement; rien que; uniquement; (*except*) excepté, sauf; si ce n'est; (*not farther back than*) pas plus loin que, pas plus tard que; encore. *His* or *her — hope*, son seul espoir, son unique espoir. *His* or *her — son*, son fils unique. *His* or *her — daughter*, sa fille unique. — *that!* rien que cela! — *think!* songez un peu! — *see!* voyez un peu! — *yesterday*, pas plus loin (*or* pas plus tard) qu'hier; hier encore. *If* —, pour peu que; si ... encore; (*were it* —) ne fût-ce que. *Not* —, non seulement; ne ... pas seulement. *To* — (*and a verb*), (*no more than, never except*) ne ... que, (*do nothing but*) ne faire que ... *I will give you — four pounds* (£4), je ne vous donnerai que cent francs. *He is — ten years old*, il n'a que dix ans. *He eats — when he is hungry*, il ne mange que quand il a faim. *It — irritates him*, cela ne fait que l'irriter. *It — increased his fury*, cela ne fit qu'augmenter sa fureur

Onomatope, Onomatopœia, Onomatopy, *s.* onomatopée *f.*

Onset, Onslaught, *s.* attaque, charge, *f.*, assaut, *m.*; choc, *m.*; commencement, début, *m.* *At the first* —, d'emblée

Ontolog-ic, al, -ically, -ist, -y. *V.* p. 3. § 1
Onus. — *probandi*, *V.* **Burden** *of proof*
Onward, *adj.* en avant; avancé; progressif; envahissant; —, **—s,** *adv.* en avant; plus loin; progressivement. *To come* or *go* —, [avancer, s'avancer
Onyx, *s.* onyx, *m.*
Oolite, *s.* oolithe, *m.*
Oolitic, *adj.* oolithique
Oolog-ic, al, -ist, -y. V. page 3, § 1
Ooze, *v.n.* (— **out**) suinter; filtrer; découler, s'écouler; s'échapper; (*fig.*) glisse, s'échapper; (*become known*) transpirer, s'ébruiter; — *s.* vase, *f.*, limon, *m.*; (*flow, spring*) suintement, *m.*; (*tan-liquor*) jusée, *f.* — **weed,** *s.* plante limoneuse, plante aquatile, *f.*
Oozing, *s.* (— **out**) suintement, *m.*; filtration, *f.*; (*disclosure*) ébruitement, *m.*
Oozy, *adj.* vaseux, limoneux
Opacity, *s.* opacité, *f.*; (*fig.*) obscurité, *f.*
Opah, *s.* lampris, poisson-lune, *m.*
Opal, *s.* opale, *f.*
Opalescence, *s.* opalescence, *f.*
Opalescent, *adj.* opalescent
Opaline, *adj.* opalin, d'opale
Opaque, *adj.* opaque; (*fig.*) obscur
Opaqueness, *s.* *V.* **Opacity**
Open, *v.a.* ouvrir; (*partly*) entr'ouvrir; (*uncover*) découvrir; (*lay open*) exposer; expliquer; révéler; (*unfold*) déplier; (*unseal*) décacheter, ouvrir; (*undo*) défaire; (*uncork*) déboucher; (*cut roads, streets, doors and windows in a wall*) percer; (*split*) fendre; (*the skin*) entamer; (*an abscess, a vein,* &c.) ouvrir; (*begin*) ouvrir, commencer; (*o.'s legs*) écarter (les jambes); — *v.n.* s'ouvrir; (*partly*) s'entr'ouvrir; (*to the view*) se découvrir; (*of flowers*) s'épanouir, s'ouvrir; (*begin*) ouvrir, s'ouvrir, commencer; (*on, into, of gates and doors*) donner (sur), ouvrir (sur); (*to fire*) tirer (sur); (*to bark, hunt.*) aboyer
Open, *adj.* ouvert; (*uncovered,* &c.) découvert; à découvert; exposé; manifeste, clair; déclaré; public; libre, accessible; permis; (*of weather*) doux; (*middle* or *midst, full, of the sea, of a champaign country, of day,* &c.) plein; (*of the air*) plein, grand; (*of a question*) indécis, non résolu, à décider; (*in open-work*) à jour; à claire-voie; (*of boats,* &c.) non ponté; — *s.* (*open air*) plein air, grand air, *m.*; (*mil.*) pleine campagne, rase campagne, *f.* — *to*, disposé à écouter; prêt à accepter; en position d'accepter. *The — air*, le grand air, *m.* *In the — air, in the —*, en plein air, au grand air. *In the — field, in the —*, en pleine (*or* en rase) campagne. *To break —, cut —, get —, lay —, lie —,* &c., *V.* **Break, Cut,** &c. — **account,** *s.* compte ouvert, *m.* — **air exercise,** *s.* exercice en plein air, exercice au grand air, *m.* — **carriage,** *s.* voiture découverte, *f.* — **eyed,** *adj.* qui a les yeux ouverts, vigilant. — **handed,** *adj.* libéral, généreux. — **handedness,** *s.* libéralité, générosité, *f.* — **hearted,** *adj.* franc, sincère. — **heartedly,** *adv.* à cœur ouvert, franchement, sincèrement. — **heartedness,** *s.* franchise, sincérité, *f.* — **mouthed,** *adj.* qui a la bouche ouverte, la bouche ouverte, bouche béante; (*clamorous*) criard, bruyant. — **work,** *s.* ouvrage à jour, *m.*; ouvrage à claire-voie, *m.*; *adj.* à jour; à claire-voie
Opener, *s.* ouvreur, *m.*, -euse, *f.*
Opening, *s.* ouverture, *f.*; (*split*) fente, *f.*; (*in clouds, fog*) éclaircie, *f.*; (*fig.*) ouverture, *f.*; commencement, début, *m.*; introduction, *f.*; chance, occasion, perspective, *f.*; (*com.*) débouché, *m.*; — *adj.* (*med.*) apéritif
Openly, *adv.* ouvertement; publiquement; (*plainly*) franchement, sans détour, à découvert; (*clearly*) clairement, évidemment
Openness, *s.* franchise, sincérité, *f.*; (*unreservedness*) abandon, *m.*; (*clearness*) clarté, évidence, *f.*; (*of the weather*) douceur, température douce, *f.*

Opera, *s.* opéra, *m.* — **book,** *s.* livret, libretto, *m.* — **cloak,** *s.* sortie de bal, *f.* — **dancer,** *s.* danseuse d'opéra, *f.* — **glass,** *s.* lorgnette (de théâtre), *f.*; (*double*) jumelle *f.* — **hat,** *s.* claque, *m.* — **house,** *s.* opéra, théâtre lyrique, *m.* — **mantle,** *s.* sortie de bal, *f.* — **night,** *s.* jour d'opéra, *m.* — **tie,** *s.* col américain, *m.* — **writer,** *s.* auteur d'opéras, *m.*, librettiste, *m.f.*, parolier, *m.*, -ière, *f.*
Operable, *adj.* opérable
Operate, *v.n.a.* opérer; agir; produire son effet; spéculer. — *for a rise, for a fall,* (*on 'Change*) jouer à la hausse, à la baisse
Operatic, -al, *adj.* d'opéra; lyrique. — *drama*, drame lyrique, *m.*
Operating, *adj.* qui opère; opératif, opératoire. — **room** *or* **theatre,** *s.* (*of hospitals*) amphithéâtre, *m.* — **surgeon,** *s.* médecin opérant, opérateur, *m.*
Operation, *s.* opération, *f.*; action, *f.*; activité, *f.*; effet, *m.*; (*surg.*) opération, *f.* *To perform an — upon*, opérer
Operative, *adj.* opératif; opératoire; actif; efficace; (*of workmen*) ouvrier, des ouvriers, des artisans; — *s.* artisan, ouvrier, *m.* — *arts*, arts manuels, *m.pl.* — *surgery*, médecine opératoire, *f.*
Operator, *s.* opérateur, *m.*, -trice, *f.*; agent, *m.*; spéculateur, *m.* — *for a rise, for a fall,* (*on 'Change*) joueur à la hausse, à la baisse, *m.*, haussier, baissier, *m.*
Opercular, *adj.* operculaire
Operculate, -d, *adj.* operculé
Operculum, *s.* opercule, *m.*
Operetta, *s.* opérette, *f.*
Ophicleid, Ophicleide, *s.* ophicléide, *m.*
Ophio-graphy, -logy, &c. *V.* page 3, § 1
Ophthalmia, *s.* ophthalmie, *f.* [p. 3, § 1
Ophthalm-ic, -ography, -ology, -y. *V.*
Ophthalmoscope, *s.* ophthalmoscope, *m.*
Ophthalmoscop-ic, -y, &c. *V.* page 3, § 1
Opiate, *s.* opiacé, *m.*; — *adj.* narcotique, [soporifique
Opine, *v.n.* opiner
Opiniative, &c. *V.* **Opinionative,** &c.
Opinion, *s.* opinion, *f.*; sentiment, avis, *m.*; consultation, *f.* *In the — of*, selon l'opinion de. *In my —*, à mon avis, suivant moi, selon moi. *To be of —*, être d'avis
Opinionated, Opinionative, *adj.* opiniâtre, obstiné, entêté; (*conceited*) suffisant
Opinionately, Opinionatively, *adv.* opiniâtrément, obstinément; (*conceitedly*) avec suffisance
Opinionativeness, *s.* opiniâtreté, obstination, *f.*, entêtement, *m.*; (*conceitedness*) suffisance, *f.*
Opinioned, *adj.* plein de soi même, suffisant
Opinionist, *s.* obstiné, *m.*, e, *f.*, entêté, *m.*, e, *f.*; (*conceited*) suffisant, *m.*, e, *f.*
Opium, *s.* opium, *m.* — **eater,** *s.* preneur (*m.*, -euse, *f.*) *or* mangeur (*m.*, -euse, *f.*) d'opium, opiophage, *m.f.* — **eating,** *s.* opiophagie, *f.* — **poppy,** *s.* pavot somnifère, *m.*
Opobalsam, *s.* opobalsamum, *m.*
Opodeldoc, *s.* opodeldoch, *m.* [opoponax, *m.*
Opopanax, Opoponax, *s.* opopanax,
Opossum, *s.* opossum, *m.*, sarigue, *m.f.*
Oppian, *adj.* — *law*, loi oppienne, *f.*
Oppidan, *s.* (*at Eton*) externe, *m.*
Opponent, *adj.* opposé, contraire; — *s.* antagoniste, adversaire, *m.f.*, concurrent, *m.*, e, *f.*, rival, *m.*, e, *f.*; opposant, *m.*, e, *f.*
Opportune, *adj.* opportun, à propos, convenable
Opportunely, *adv.* à propos, en temps opportun, opportunément
Opportuneness, *s.* opportunité, *f.*, à-propos, *m.*
Opportunity, *s.* occasion, *f.* — *makes the thief*, l'occasion fait le larron
Opposable, *adj.* opposable
Oppose, *v.a.* opposer (à); (*resist*) s'opposer à, combattre, résister à; (*hinder*) arrêter, empêcher; (*compete with*) *V.* **Compete**

Opposed, *adj.* opposé, contraire (à); contre ...
Opposer, *s. V.* **Opponent**
Opposite, *adj. prep. adv.* opposé ; en face (de), vis-à-vis (de) ; en regard (de) ; contraire (à) ; — *s.* opposé, *m.*; (*opponent*) *V.* **Opponent.** — *to* (*facing*) *it, them* (*things*), en face, vis-à-vis
Oppositely, *adv.* en face, vis-à-vis ; (*adversely*) en sens contraire, de côtés opposés
Oppositeness, *s.* situation opposée, *f.*; (*fig.*) état opposé, état contraire, *m.*
Opposition, *s.* opposition, *f.*; obstacle, empêchement, *m.*; résistance, *f.*; répugnance, *f*; (*competition*) concurrence, *f.*; (*opposite situation*) situation opposée, *f.*
Oppositionist, *s.* membre de l'opposition, *m.*; opposant, *m.*, e, *f.*; frondeur, *m*, - euse *f.*
Oppress, *v.a.* oppresser ; (*tyrannize over*) opprimer ; (*crush, overwhelm*) écraser ; accabler ; (*med.*) oppresser
Oppression, *s.* oppression, *f.*; (*calamity*) accablement, *m* ; (*depression*) abattement, accablement, *m.*
Oppressive, *adj.* oppressif ; accablant
Oppressively, *adv.* oppressivement ; avec accablement, d'une manière accablante
Oppressiveness, *s.* nature oppressive, *f.*, caractère oppressif, *m.*; nature accablante, *f.*
Oppressor, *s.* oppresseur, *m.*
Opprobrious, *adj.* infamant ; injurieux, outrageant ; couvert d'opprobre
Opprobriously, *adv.* d'une manière outrageante ; avec opprobre
Opprobriousness, *s.* nature infamante, infamie, *f.*; nature outrageante, *f.*
Opprobrium, *s.* opprobre, *m.* [résister à
Oppugn, *v.a.* s'opposer à, combattre, attaquer ;
Oppugnancy,Oppugnation, *s.* opposition, résistance, *f.*
Oppugner, *s.* antagoniste, adversaire, *m.f.*
Optative, *s. adj.* optatif, *m.* *In the* —, *in the* — *mood*, à l'optatif, au mode optatif
Optic, Optical, *adj.* optique ; d'optique. — *nerve*, nerf optique, *m.* — *instrument*, instrument d'optique, *m.* — *illusion* or *delusion* or *deception*, illusion d'optique, *f.*
Optically, *adv.* optiquement
Optician, *s.* opticien, *m.*
Optics, *s.pl.* optique, *f.*
Optim-ism, -ist. *V.* page 3, § 1
Option, *s.* option, *f.*, choix, *m.*, alternative, faculté, *f.*; (*on 'Change*) différence (de report), *f.*
Optional, *adj.* facultatif, laissé au choix ; [loisible
Optionally, *adv.* facultativement
Optometer, *s.* optomètre, *m.*
Opulence, *s.* opulence, *f.*
Opulent, *adj.* opulent
Opulently, *adv.* opulemment, avec opulence
Opuscule, *s.* opuscule, *m.*
Or, *conj.* ou ; (*negat.*) ni ; — *s.* (*her.*) or, *m.* — *else*, ou bien, autrement, ou
Orach, Orache, *s.* arroche, follette, *f.*
Oracle, *s.* oracle, *m.*
Oracular, Oraculous, *adj.* qui rend des oracles ; d'oracle ; prophétique ; ambigu, obscur, énigmatique [oracle, en oracle
Oracularly, Oraculously, *adv.* comme un
Oraculousness, *s.* don des oracles, *m.*; ton d'oracle, *m.*; autorité d'oracle, *f.*
Oral, *adj.* oral
Orally, *adv.* oralement [outang, *m.*
Orang, *s.* orang, *m.* — **outang,** *s.* orang-
Orange, *s.* orange, *f.*; (*tree*) oranger, *m.*; (*colour*) orange, *m.*, orangé, *m.*; — *adj.* d'orange ; couleur d'orange, couleur orange, orange, orangé. *Seville* —, bigarade, *f.*; (*tree*) bigaradier, *m.* — **berry,** *s.* orangette, *f.*, petit grain, *m.* — **blossom, -bud,** *s. V.* — **flower** — **chips,** *s.pl.* orangeat, *m.* — **colour,** *s.* couleur d'orange, couleur orange, *f.*, orange, *m.*, orangé, *m.* — **coloured,** *adj.* orange, orangé. — **dye,** *s.* teinture orange, *f.* — **flower,** *s.* fleur d'oranger, fleur d'orange, *f.* — **flower water,** *s.* eau de fleurs d'oranger, eau de fleur d'orange, *f.* — **girl,** *s. V.* — **woman.** — **grove,** *s.* orangerie, *f.* — **grower,** *s.* orangiste, *m. f.* — **house,** *s.* orangerie, *f.* — **man,** *s.* marchand d'oranges, oranger, *m.*; (*polit.*) Orangiste, *m.* — **marmalade,** *s.* marmelade d'oranges, *f.* — **milked agaric,** *s.* oronge, *f.* — **peel,** *s.* écorce d'orange, *f.* *Candied* — *peel*, orangeat, *m.* — **root,** *s.* hydraste, *m.* — **salad,** *s.* salade d'oranges, *f.* — **tree,** *s.* oranger, *m.* — **woman,** *s.* marchande d'oranges, orangère, *f.*
Orangeade, *s.* orangeade, *f.*
Orangery, *s.* orangerie, *f.*
Orang-ism, -ist. *V.* page 3, § 1
Oration, *s.* discours, *m.*, harangue, oraison, *f.*
Orator, *s.* orateur, *m.*
Oratorial, Oratorical, *adj.* oratoire
Oratorially, Oratorically, *adv.* oratoire-[ment
Oratorian, *s. adj.* oratorien, *m.*
Oratorio, *s.* (*mus.*) oratorio, *m.*
Oratorium, *s.* oratoire, *m.*
Oratory, *s.* art oratoire, *m.*; éloquence, *f.*; [(*chapel*) oratoire, *m.*
Oratress, *s.* oratrice, *f.*
Orb, *s.* globe, *m.*; sphère, *f.*, orbe, *m.*; période, *f.*; — *v.a.* arrondir ; couvrir. — **fish,** *s.* orbe, *m.*
Orbed, *adj.* sphérique, rond, circulaire. *Full* [—, (*of the moon*) pleine
Orbic, *adj. V.* **Orbed**
Orbicular, *adj.* orbiculaire ; sphérique, rond, circulaire [ment
Orbicularly, *adv.* orbiculairement ; sphérique-
Orbicularness, *s.* sphéricité, *f.*
Orbiculate, -d, *adj.* orbiculé
Orbit, *s.* orbite, *f.m.*
Orbital, *adj.* orbitaire
Orc, *s.* orque, *f.*, épaulard, *m.*
Orchal. *V.* **Orchil**
Orchanet, *s.* orcanète, orcanette, *f.*
Orchard, *s.* verger, *m.* — **grass,** *s.* dactyle, *m.* — **house,** *s.* forcerie, *f.*
Orcharding, *s.* fructiculture, *f.*
Orchardist, *s.* fructiculteur, *m.*
Orchel, Orchella. *V.* **Orchil**
Orchestra, Orchestre, *s.* orchestre, *m.* — **stall,** *s.* stalle (*f.*) *or* fauteuil (*m.*) d'orchestre
Orchestral, *adj.* orchestral, de l'orchestre, d'orchestre
Orchestration, *s.* orchestration, *f.*
Orchestrino, *s.* orchestrino, *m.*
Orchestrion, *s.* orchestrion, *m.*
Orchid, *s.* orchide, *f.*, orchis, *m.* — **house,** *s.* serre à orchides, *f.*
Orchil, Orchilla, *s.* roccelle, orseille, *f.*
Orchis. *V.* **Orchid**
Orchitis, *s.* orchite, *f.*
Ordain, *v.a.* ordonner, commander, prescrire ; établir, instituer ; destiner ; (*eccl.*) ordonner
Ordainable, *adj.* que l'on peut ordonner
Ordainer, *s.* ordonnateur, *m.*, -trice, *f.*; instituteur, *m.*, -trice, *f.*; (*eccl.*) ordinant, *m.*
Ordaining, *adj.* ordonnateur ; (*eccl.*) ordinant ; — *s.* action d'ordonner, &c. (*V.* **Ordain**) *f.*; établissement, *m.*, institution, *f.*; (*eccl.*) ordi-[nation, *f.*
Ordeal, *s.* épreuve, *f.*
Order, *s.* ordre, *m.*; (*rule*) règle, *f.*, règlement, *m.*; (*rank*) rang, *m.*; classe, *f.*; (*duty*) devoir, *m.*; (*condition*) état, *m.*; (*decree*) ordonnance, *f.*; arrêté, *m.*; (*manner*) manière, coutume, *f.*; (*badge*) décoration, *f.*; (*ticket*) billet de faveur, billet, *m.*; permission, *f.*; (*for bread or &c. to the poor*) bon, *m.*; (*for money*) mandat, *m.*; (*com.*) commande, demande, *f.*, (*in writing*) bon, *m.*; —**s,** *pl.* ordres, *m.pl.*, &c.; (*eccl.*) ordres, *m.pl.* — ! à l'ordre ! *In* —, (*things*) en ordre ; en état ; en règle ; (*alphabetical, chronological*, &c.) par ordre. *In* —*s*, dans les ordres. *In* — *to*, afin de ; pour. *In* — *that*, afin que, pour que. *Of a high* —, d'un ordre élevé. *Of the highest* —, du premier ordre. *To* —, de commande ; sur commande ; (*of bills*) à ordre. *Until* (or *till*) *further* — (or —*s*), jusqu'à nouvel ordre. *To keep* —, maintenir l'ordre. *To keep in* —, tenir dans l'ordre ;

tenir dans le devoir; (*children*) tenir. *To put in* —, mettre en ordre. *To put out of* — (*things*) mettre en désordre, déranger, détraquer; (*pers.*) incommoder, rendre malade. *Out of* —, en désordre, dérangé, détraqué; irrégulier; (*pers.*) indisposé, malade. — **book,** *s.* (*com.*) livre de commandes, *m.*; (*mil.*) livre d'ordres, *m.*

Order, *v.a.* ordonner; donner l'ordre à; commander; demander; charger; régler, disposer; conduire, diriger; (*engage*) retenir; (*com.*) commander, demander, (*to be made*) faire faire; — *v.n.* ordonner; (*to decree*) arrêter. *To — a person* (*to* . . .), ordonner (*or* donner l'ordre) à quelqu'un (de . . .). *To be —ed,* (*pers.*) recevoir *or* avoir reçu des ordres, avoir ordre (de), recevoir *or* avoir reçu l'ordre (de). *To — a coat, a dress,* faire faire un habit, une robe. *They —ed him to put her in prison,* ils lui ordonnèrent de la mettre en prison. *They —ed him to be put in prison,* ils ordonnèrent qu'on le mît en prison, ils le firent mettre en prison. *The troops are —ed for India,* les troupes ont ordre de partir pour les Indes. *The dinner is —ed,* le dîner est commandé. *I am going to — a coat, a dress,* je vais me faire faire un habit, une robe. — **about,** donner des ordres à, faire aller de côté et d'autre. — **along,** faire avancer; ordonner (à . . .) de poursuivre sa route. — **away, off,** ordonner (à . . .) de s'en aller. — **in, out,** &c., ordonner (à . . .) d'entrer, de sortir, &c.

Orderer, *s.* ordonnateur, *m.*, -trice, *f.*

Ordering, *s.* ordre, arrangement, *m.*, ordonnance, disposition, *f.* [sordonné

Orderless, *adj.* sans ordre, en désordre, dé-

Orderliness, *s.* ordre, *m.*, régularité, *f.*, bon ordre, *m.*; esprit d'ordre, *m.*, méthode, *f.*; tranquillité, *f.*; bonne conduite, *f.*

Orderly, *adj.* d'ordre; régulier, méthodique; réglé, en bon ordre; (*pers.*) rangé, tranquille; (*mil.*) d'ordonnance; (*on duty*) de planton; — *adv.* en ordre; avec ordre; méthodiquement; régulièrement; — *s.* ordonnance, *f.*; (*street-sweeper*) balayeur de rues, *m.* — **book,** *s.* (*mil.*) livre d'ordres, *m.* — **officer,** *s.* (*mil.*) officier d'ordonnance, *m.* — **room,** *s.* (*mil.*) salle du rapport, *f.*; (*among the marines*) aubette, *f.*

Ordinal, *adj.* ordinal; — *s.* nombre ordinal, *m.*; (*eccl.*) ordinal, *m.* [glement, *m.*

Ordinance, *s.* ordonnance, *f.*; décret, *m.*; rè-

Ordinand, *s.* ordinand, *m.*

Ordinant, *s.* ordinant, *m.*

Ordinarily, *adv.* ordinairement, d'ordinaire

Ordinary, *adj.* ordinaire; — *s.* ordinaire, *m.*; (*of hotels*) table d'hôte, *f.*; (*eccl.*) ordinaire, *m.*; (*jail-chaplain*) aumônier, *m.*; (*her.*) pièce, *f.*; (*book*) dictionnaire héraldique, *m.* *In* —, ordinaire [donnée, *f.*

Ordinate, *adj.* régulier; — *s.* (*geom.*) or-

Ordinately, *adv.* régulièrement

Ordination, *s.* ordination, *f.*

Ordnance, *s.* artillerie, *f.* *Piece of* —, pièce d'artillerie, bouche à feu, *f.* — **map,** *s.* carte départementale, *f.* — **office,** *s.* bureau de l'artillerie, *m.* — **survey,** *s.* (*V.* **Survey**); (*maps*) cartes du dépôt de la guerre, *f.pl.* — **surveyor,** *s.* ingénieur-topographe, *m.* — **yard,** *s.* polygone, *m.*

Ordonnance, *s.* ordonnance, *f.*

Ordure, *s.* ordure, *f.*

Ore, *s.* minerai, *m.*, mine, *f.*; métal, *m.*

Oread, *s.* oréade, *f.*

Oreide, *s.* oréide, *m.*

Oremus, *s.* orémus, *m.* [&c. (*V.* page 3, § 1)

Oreography, Oreology, &c., oréographie,

Organ, *s.* organe, *m.*; (*mus. instr.*) orgue, *m.* — **blower,** *s.* souffleur d'orgues, *m.* — **builder,** *s.* organier, facteur d'orgues, *m.* — **case,** *s.* buffet d'orgue, *m.* — **grinder,** *s.* joueur d'orgue, *m.* — **loft,** *s.* tribune d'orgues, *f.* — **pipe,** *s.* tuyau d'orgue, *m.* — **player,** *s.* joueur d'orgue, *m.* — **point,** *s.* point d'orgue, *m.* — **stop,** *s.* jeu d'orgues, *m.* — **tuner,** *s.* accordeur d'orgues, *m.*

Organdi, — **muslin,** *s.* organdi, *m.*

Organ-ic, al, -ically, -ism, -ist. *V.* p. 3, § 1

Organizable, *adj.* organisable

Organization, *s.* organisation, *f.*

Organize, *v.a.* organiser. *To become* (or *get*) —*d,* s'organiser

Organizer, *s.* organisateur, *m.*, -trice, *f.*

Organizing, *adj.* organisateur; — *s.* organi-

Organography, &c. *V.* page 3, § 1 [sation, *f.*

Organzine, *s.* organsin, *m.*; — *v.a.* organsiner

Organzining, *s.* organsinage, *m.*

Orgasm, *s.* orgasme, *m.*

Orgeat, *s.* orgeat, *m.*

Orgy, *s.* orgie, *f.*

Oriel, — **window,** *s.* fenêtre en saillie, *f.*

Orient, *adj.* (*rising*) levant, naissant; (*eastern*) oriental, d'orient; (*bright*) brillant, éclatant, étincelant; — *s.* orient, *m.* [*m.*, e, *f.*

Oriental, *adj.* oriental, d'Orient; — *s.* Oriental,

Oriental-ism, -ist. *V.* page 3, § 1

Orientalize, *v.a.* orientaliser. *To become —d,*

Orientate, *v.a.* orienter [s'orientaliser

Orientation, *s* orientation, *f.*, orientement, *m.*

Orifice, *s.* orifice, trou, *m.*, ouverture, *f.*

Oriflamme, *s.* oriflamme, *f.*

Oriform, *adj.* oriforme [nance, *f.*

Origin, *s.* origine, *f.*; (*produce,* &c.) prove-

Original, *adj.* original; (*primitive*) primitif, originel; (*theol.*) originel; — *s.* original, *m.*; (*origin*) origine, *f.*, principe, *m.*

Originality, *s.* originalité, *f.*

Originally, *adv.* originairement, primitivement, dans l'origine, dans le principe; (*by the first author*) originalement; (*theol.*) originelle-

Originary, *adj.* originaire [ment

Originate, *v.a.* produire, faire naître, donner naissance à, créer; concevoir, inventer; — *v.n.* tirer son origine (de), prendre sa source (dans), provenir (de), venir (de); commencer; naître, prendre naissance

Origination, *s.* génération, production, création, *f.*; origine, *f.*, principe, *m.*, cause, *f.*

Originator, *s.* cause première, *f.*; auteur, *m.*

Orillon, *s.* orillon, *m.*

Oriole, *s.* loriot, *m.* (*V.* **Golden**)

Orion, *s.* Orion, *m.*

Orison, *s.* oraison, prière, *f.*

Ork. *V.* **Orc**

Orle, *s.* orle, *m.*

Orleanism, *s.* Orléanisme, *m.*

Orleanist, *s. adj.* Orléaniste, *m.f.*

Orleans. — **cloth,** *s.* orléans, *m.* — **plum,** *s.* prune de Monsieur, *f.*

Orlop, — **deck,** *s.* faux pont, *m.*

Ormolu, Or-moulu, *s.* or moulu, *m.*; imitation d'or moulu, *f.*; — *adj.* en or moulu; en imitation d'or moulu

Ornament, *s.* ornement, *m.*; décoration, *f.*; parure, *f.*; — *v.a.* ('*with,*' de) orner, décorer, parer; (*arts*) ornementer

Ornamental, *adj.* ornemental, d'ornement; artificiel; agréable; d'agrément — **painter,** *s.* peintre décorateur, décorateur, *m.* — **printing,** *s.* décor, *m.* (*Sheet of*) — **water,** *s.* pièce d'eau, *f.* [comme (or pour) ornement

Ornamentally, *adv.* de manière à orner,

Ornamentation, *s.* ornementation, décoration, *f.*, embellissement, ornement, *m.*

Ornamenter, Ornamentist, *s.* orne-

Ornate, *adj.* orné, paré [mentiste. *m.f.*

Ornately, *adv.* avec ornement

Ornateness, *s.* élégance, *f.*

Ornitholog-ic, al, -ist, -y. *V.* page 3, § 1

Ornithorhynchus, *s.* ornithorhynque, *m.*

Orobanche, *s.* orobanche, *f.*

Orobus, *s.* orobe, *f.*

Oro-gnosy, -graphy, -logy, &c. *V.* p. 3, § 1

Orphan, *s. adj.* orphelin, *m.*, e, *f.* — **asylum,**

s. orphelinat, m. — **boy,** s. orphelin, m. — **child,** s. orphelin, m., e, f. — **girl,** s. orpheline, f. [phelinat, m.
Orphanage, s. orphelinage, m.; (*asylum*) or-
Orphaned, *adj.* orphelin
Orphean, *adj.* d'Orphée
Orpheon, s. orphéon, m.
Orpheonic, *adj.* orphéonique
Orpheonist, s. orphéoniste, m.f.
Orphic, *adj.* orphique
Orpiment, s. orpiment, orpin, m.
Orpin, Orpine, s. orpin, m.
Orrach. *V.* **Orach**
Orrery, s. planétaire, m.
Orris. *V.* **Iris;** (*lace*) galon, m.
Orsedew, Orsedue, Orsidue, s. oripeau, clinquant, m.
Ort, s., **Orts,** s.pl. rebut, m., épluchures, f.pl.
Orthodox, *adj.* s. orthodoxe
Orthodoxly, *adv.* orthodoxement
Ortho-doxy, -dromy, &c. *V.* page 3, § 1
Orthographer, s. orthographiste, m.f.
Orthograph-ic, al, -ically. *V.* page 3, § 1
Orthography, s. orthographe, f.; (*arch., fort., geom.*) orthographie, f. [*V.* page 3, § 1
Orthoped-ic, al, -ist, -y, orthopédique, &c.
Orthopraxy, s. *V.* page 3, § 1
Ortolan, s. ortolan, m.
Ortyx, s. (*bird*) colin, m.
Orval, s. orvale, f. [hésiter
Oscillate, v.n. osciller; (*hesitate*) balancer,
Oscillation, Oscillancy, s. oscillation, f.
Oscillatory, *adj.* oscillatoire
Osculating, *adj.* osculateur
Osculation, s. osculation, f. [paix, f.
Osculatory, *adj.* osculateur; — s. (*Cath. rel.*)
Osier, s. osier, m.; — *adj.* d'osier; en osier. — **ground, -holt, -plot,** s. champ d'osier, m.,
Osiery, s. oseraie, f. [oseraie, f.
Osmanli, s. Osmanli, m.
Osmazome, s. osmazôme, m.
Osmium, s. osmium, m.
Osmund, s. osmonde, f.
Ospray, Osprey, s. orfraie, f.
Osselet, s. osselet, m.
Osseous, *adj.* osseux
Ossian-ic, -ism. *V.* page 3, § 1
Ossicle, s. ossicule, osselet, m.
Ossiculated, *adj.* ossiculé
Ossiferous, *adj.* ossifère
Ossific, *adj.* ossifique
Ossification, s. ossification, f.
Ossify, v.a. ossifier; — v.n. s'ossifier
Ossuary, s. ossuaire, charnier, m.
Ostensi-bility, bleness. *V.* page 3, § 1
Ostensible, *adj.* ostensible; (*of partners*)
Ostensibly, *adv.* ostensiblement [gérant
Ostentation, s. ostentation, f., faste, m., vanité, f., étalage, m. [fastueux
Ostentatious, *adj.* plein d'ostentation, vain,
Ostentatiously, *adv.* avec *or* par ostentation, avec faste, fastueusement, avec *or* par vanité, avec étalage
Ostentatiousness. *V.* **Ostentation**
Osteocolla, s. ostéocolle, f.
Osteo-graphy, -logy, &c., ostéographie, ostéologie, &c. (*V.* page 3, § 1)
Ostler, s. garçon *or* valet d'écurie, palefrenier, m.
Ostracean, s. ostracé, m.
Ostraceous, *adj.* ostracé
Ostracism, s. ostracisme, m.
Ostracize, v.a. ostraciser
Ostreicultural, *adj.* ostréicole, ostréicultural
Ostreiculture, s. ostréiculture, f.
Ostrich, s. autruche, f. — **feather,** s. plume d'autruche, f.
Ostrogoth, s. Ostrogoth, m., e, f.
Otacoustic, *adj.* otacoustique; —**s,** s.pl. ota-
Otary, s. otarie, f. [coustique, f.
Other, *adj. pron.* autre. —*s*, — *people*, — *folks*, (*generally*) les autres; d'autres; autrui; (*particularly*) les autres personnes. *Some* ... *or* — quelque ... *Of all —s*, entre tous. *The property of —s*, le bien d'autrui. —**wise,** *adv.* autrement; sans cela, sans quoi; (*besides*)
Otoscope, s. otoscope, m. [d'ailleurs
Ottar. *V.* **Otto**
Otter, s. loutre, f.; (*caterpillar*) louvette f. — **hunter,** s. loutreur, loutrier, m.
Otto, s. (— *of roses*) essence de roses, f.
Ottoman, s. *adj.* (*pers.*) Ottoman, m., e, f.; (*sofa*) ottomane, f. *Box* —, banc à coffre, m. *Centre* —, *V.* **Centre.** *Fender* —, garde-feu m. — **seat,** s. pouf, m.
Oubliettes, s.pl. oubliettes, f.pl.
Ought, *pron. s. V.* **Aught**
Ought, v. *def.* devoir; falloir. *It — to be so*, cela doit être ainsi. *It is as it — to be*, c'est comme il faut, c'est bien. *You — to see*, (*must*) vous devez voir; (*should*) vous devriez voir; il faudrait voir; il faut voir. *You — to have seen*, vous auriez dû voir; il aurait fallu voir;
Ouistiti, s. ouistiti, m. [il fallait voir
Ounce, s. (*animal, Engl. and old Fr. weight*) once, f.; (*Fr. modern weight*) 30 grammes
Our, *pron. poss.* notre, m.f. *sing.*, nos, *pl.* — **self,** *sing.*, —**selves,** *pl.*, *pron. pers.* nous-même, *sing.*, nous-mêmes, *pl.*; nous; (*in a re-*
Ourang-outang. *V.* **Orang** [*flect. verb*) nous
Ourari, s. ourari, curare, m.
Ours, *pron. poss.* le nôtre, la nôtre, les nôtres; nos; (*pron. pers.*) à nous, de nous (*V. for examples,* **Mine, His, Hers, Yours**) [d'eau, m.
Ousel, s. merle, m. *Water* —, cincle, merle
Oust, v.a. déloger, débusquer, dégommer; expulser, chasser; (*law*) déposséder, évincer
Ouster, s. dépossession, éviction. f.
Out, *adv. adj.* s. dehors; hors; en dehors; (*gone*) sorti; (*taken off*) ôté, enlevé; (*pulled out*) arraché; (*unharnessed*) dételé; (*let out*) lâché; (*adject., out-door*) externe; (*way out*) sortie, s.f.; (*omission in print.*) bourdon, s.m.; (*end*) fin, s.f.; (*loud*) haut, tout haut; à haute voix; distinctement; (*openly*) ouvertement; (*found out*) découvert, connu; (*published*) publié, paru; (*empty*) vide; (*expired*) expiré; échu; (*fulfilled*) accompli; (*finished*) fini, épuisé; (*past*) passé; (*worn out*) usé; (*to the end*) jusqu'au bout, jusqu'à la fin; (*wholly*) complètement, entièrement, en entier; (*of fashion*) passé de mode; (*confused*) brouillé, embarrassé; (*in error*) dans l'erreur, en défaut; (*let*) loué; (*invested*) placé; (*not in power*) non au pouvoir, ne ... plus au pouvoir, non en fonctions, ne ... plus en fonctions; (*of fire, light*) éteint; (*of clothes*) troué, percé; (*of troops*) sur pied; (*at sea*) en mer; (*of sails*) dehors, déployé, orienté. — *and* —, (*adject.*) complet, entier; extrême; franc, vrai, fieffé; renforcé; (*adverb.*) complètement, entièrement; extrêmement. — *of*, hors de; (*down from*) à bas de; (*from*) de; (*above*) au-dessus de; (*beyond*) outre, au-delà de; (*by, through*) par; (*in*) dans; à même; (*of numbers*) de; sur; (*with*) avec; (*without any*) sans; (*at the end of*) à bout de; (*opposed to*) contraire à. — *of doors*, — *-door*, *V.* **Door.** — *of hand*, &c., *V.* **Hand,** &c. — *of number*, innombrable, sans nombre. — *of ammunition*, à bout de munitions. — *of sight*, hors de vue; à perte de vue; éloigné, absent; caché. — *of mind*, oublié; (*of time*) immémorial. — *of sight — of mind*, (*Proverb*) loin des yeux loin du cœur. — *of the window*, par la fenêtre. — *of charity*, par charité. *To drink — of a glass*, — *of a bottle*, boire dans un verre, à même une bouteille. — *of ten*, de dix. *Six — of ten*, six sur dix. — *of whom*, dont. — *of which*, d'où; dont. — *of measure*, outre mesure. — *of place*, sans place; (*fig.*) déplacé. *To be — of*, être hors de; être sorti de; n'être pas *or* n'être plus en (*or* dans le *or* la *or* les); (*without any left*) n'avoir plus de, manquer de, être à bout de, être sans. *To be — with*, être brouillé

avec. *To be —, quite —, far —,* (*not to have hit it*) être dans l'erreur, se tromper, n'y être pas, n'y être pas du tout, en être bien loin. *The sun is —,* le soleil luit, il fait du soleil. *You are — in your reckoning,* vous vous êtes trompé dans votre calcul, vous êtes loin de compte

Out, *int.* dehors! hors d'ici! fi! fi donc!—*upon ...!* fi de ...! — *with it!* achevez! finissez! accouchez! dites ce que c'est! voyons! faites voir! montrez-le! — *with him!* mettez-le à la porte! faites-le sortir! — *with you!* sortez! hors d'ici! à la porte! — *with the laughers!* à la porte les rieurs!

Out, *v.n.* se faire jour; sortir; se manifester; se découvrir, se savoir; — *v.a. V.* **Oust**

Outact, *v.a.* faire au-delà de, dépasser, excéder; outrer; surpasser

Outbalance, *v.a.* l'emporter sur, surpasser

Outbid, *v.a.n.* enchérir, surenchérir

Outbidder, *s.* surenchérisseur, *m.*

Outblaze, *v.a.* éclipser [l'étranger

Outbound, *adj.* (*nav.*) en destination pour

Outbrave, *v.a.* braver, défier

Outbrazen, *v.a.* surpasser en effronterie; soutenir avec impudence; déconcerter à force d'impudence

Outbreak, *s.* explosion, *f.*; éruption, *f.*; éclat, *m.*; débordement, *m.*; déchaînement, *m.*; insurrection, *f.*, soulèvement, *m.*; rupture, *f.*; commencement, *m.*; (*of epidemics*) invasion, *f.*; (*epidemic itself*) épidémie, *f.*; (*murrain*) épizootie, *f.*; (*fire*) incendie, *m.*

Outbuilding, *s. V.* **Outhouse**

Outburst, *s. V.* **Burst,** *s.*

Outcast, *adj.* rejeté; banni, exilé, proscrit; chassé, expulsé; sans asile; maudit; — *s.* banni, exilé, *m.*, e, *f.*, proscrit, *m.*; paria, *m.*; (*refuse*) rebut, *m.* [quence, *f.*

Outcome, *s.* issue, *f.*; résultat, *m.*; consé-

Outcrop, *s.* affleurement, *m.*; — *v.n. V.* **Crop**

Outcry, *s.* cri, *m.*, clameur, *f.*; tollé, *m.* [**out**

Outdare, *v.a.* braver, affronter

Outdated, *adj.* vieilli, suranné, passé, tombé en désuétude; périmé

Outdazzle, *v.a.* éclipser, effacer

Outdo, *v.a.* surpasser; renchérir sur; l'emporter sur; devancer; (*fam.*) damer le pion à;

Outdrink, *v.a.* boire plus que [(*balk*) jouer

Outer, *adj.* extérieur, du dehors; externe; (*upper, over*) de dessus; — *s. V.* **Ouster.** — **most,** *adj.* (le) plus en dehors, (le) plus extérieur, (le) plus avancé

Outface, *v.a.* faire baisser les yeux à, dévisager, déconcerter, intimider; affronter, braver, défier [chure, *f.*

Outfall, *s.* chute d'eau, *f.*; (*engin*) embou-

Outfit, *s.* trousseau, *m.*; équipement, *m.*; — *v.a. V.* **Fit out.** — **allowance,** *s.* frais d'équipement, *m.pl.* [confectionneur, *m.*

Outfitter, *s.* fabricant d'équipements, *m.*;

Outfitting, *s.* équipement, *m.*; confection, *f.*; — *adj.* d'équipement, d'équipements; de con-

Outflank, *v.a.* déborder [fection

Outflanking, *s.* débordement, *m.*

Outflow, *v.n.* s'écouler, découler, provenir, venir; — *s. V.* **Efflux**

Outfly, *v.a.* dépasser, devancer

Outgeneral, *v.a.* surpasser en tactique; (*fig.*) surpasser, l'emporter sur, (*fam.*) damer le pion à

Outgo, *v.a.* dépasser, devancer, laisser en arrière; surpasser, l'emporter sur, circonvenir; — *s.* dépense, *f.* [*or* locataire, *m.*

Outgoer, *s.* sortant, *m.*; ancien propriétaire

Outgoing, *adj.* sortant, qui sort; (*former*) ancien; (*laid out*) qui sort, déboursé, dépensé; — *s.* sortie, *f.*; —**s,** *s.pl.* déboursés, frais, *m.pl.*, dépenses, *f.pl.*

Outgrow, *v.a.* dépasser; devenir trop grand pour; se corriger (*or* se défaire) de ... en grandissant [excessive, *f.*; résultat, *m.*

Outgrowth, *s.* excroissance, *f.*; croissance

Outguard, *s.* garde avancée, *f.*

Outherod, *v.a.* surpasser en cruauté; (*fig.*) surpasser; dépasser. *To — Herod,* renchérir sur (*or* surpasser) Hérode en cruauté; (*fig.*) dépasser le but; dépasser tout

Outhouse, *s.* bâtiment extérieur, *m.*; dépendance, *f.*; pavillon isolé, *m.*; hangar, *m.*; appentis, *m.*; —**s,** *pl.* (*domestic offices*) communs, *m.pl.*, offices, dépendances, *f.pl.* [*f.*; tour, *m.*

Outing, *s.* sortie, *f.*; excursion, *f.*; promenade,

Outlandish, *adj.* étranger; rustique, grossier; bizarre

Outlandishness, *s.* caractère étranger, *m.*; rusticité, grossièreté, *f.*; bizarrerie, *f.*

Outlast, *v.a.* durer plus longtemps que, surpasser en durée; (*outlive*) survivre à

Outlaugh, *v.a.* rire plus que, rire plus haut *or* plus fort que; déconcerter par des moqueries

Outlaw, *s.* proscrit, *m.*; (*law*) personne mise hors la loi, *f.*; (*civ. law*) défaillant, *m.*, e, *f.*; — *v.a.* proscrire, bannir; (*law*) mettre hors la loi

Outlawry, *s.* proscription, *f.*; (*law*) mise hors la loi, *f.*; (*civ. law*) défaut, *m.*

Outlay, *s.* déboursés, *m.pl*; dépense, *f.*

Outlet, *s.* issue, *f.*; sortie, *f.*; (*com.*) débouché, *m.*

Outline, *s.* contour, *m.*; (*sketch*) esquisse, ébauche, *f.*; (*of schemes*) aperçu, *m.*; — *adj.* au trait; — *v.a.* contourner, dessiner le contour de; (*to sketch*) esquisser, ébaucher. *Map in —,* — **map,** *s.* carte muette, *f.*

Outlive, *v.a.* survivre à; (*live beyond*) passer

Outliver, *s.* survivant, *m.*, e, *f.*

Outlook, *s. V.* **Look-out,** *s.*; — *v.a. V.* **Outface**

Outlustre, *v.a. V.* **Outshine**

Outlying, *adj.* extérieur; (*distant*) éloigné; isolé; (*mil.*) avancé; (*nav.*) au large; (*of bills, &c.*) à percevoir

Outmanœuvre, *v.a.* surpasser en manœuvre

Outmarch, *v.a.* devancer, dépasser, laisser en arrière

Outmeasure, *v.a.* surpasser en étendue

Outmost. *V.* **Outermost**

Outness, *s.* extériorité, *f.*

Outnumber, *v.a.* surpasser en nombre, être supérieur en nombre à, être plus nombreux que, accabler *or* écraser par le nombre

Outpace, *v.a. V.* **Outmarch**

Outparish, *s.* paroisse extérieure, *f.*

Outpart, *s.* partie extérieure *or* éloignée, *f.*

Outpass, *v.a.* dépasser

Outporch, *s.* portique extérieur, *m.*; parvis, *m.*

Outport, *s.* port éloigné, *m.*

Outpost, *s.* avant-poste, *m.*

Outpour, *v.a.* épancher, verser à flots

Outpouring, *s.* épanchement, *m.*, effusion, *f.*

Output, *s.* production, *f.*

Outrage, *v.a.* outrager, faire outrage à; — *s.* outrage, *m.*; violence, *f.*; (*law*) atteinte, *f.*

Outrageous, *adj.* outrageant, outrageux; scandaleux; énorme, atroce; violent, furieux; turbulent, tumultueux; (*exaggerated*) outré, exagéré, excessif; exorbitant; (*wretched*) abominable

Outrageously, *adv.* outrageusement; scandaleusement; énormément; atrocement; abominablement; affreusement; violemment, furieusement; excessivement, avec excès, à outrance; exorbitamment

Outrageousness, *s.* nature outrageante, *f.*; scandale, *m.*; énormité, atrocité, *f.*; violence, fureur, *f.*; turbulence, *f.*; excessiveté, *f.*; exorbitance, *f.*; abomination, *f.*

Outreach, *v.a.* dépasser

Outreckon, *v.a.* dépasser dans ses calculs

Outride, *v.a.* devancer, dépasser

Outrider, *s.* piqueur, *m.*

Outrigger, *s.* (*nav.*) aiguille de carène, *f.*; arc-boutant de hune, *m.*; (*of a boat*) balancier, *m.*; (*boat itself*) outrigger, *m.*; (*post-chaise extra horse*) bricolier, *m.*

Outright, *adv.* sur-le-champ; sur le coup; tout à fait, entièrement, complètement, fort

et ferme; tout droit, net, carrément. *To laugh* —, partir d'un grand éclat de rire
Outroot, *v.a.* déraciner [passer
Outrun, Outsail, *v.a.* gagner de vitesse; dé-
Outset, *s.* début, commencement, *m.*
Outshine, *v.a.* surpasser en éclat, éclipser, effacer; surpasser [delà de, dépasser
Outshoot, *v.a.* tirer plus loin que; aller au-
Outside, *s.* dehors, extérieur, *m.*; (*of coaches*) impériale, *f.*; (*of omnibuses*) impériale, *f.*, dessus, *m.*; (*of cabs*) dessus, *m.*; (*of roast meat*) rissolé, *m.*; (*utmost*) (le) plus, (le) maximum, *m.*; —**s**, *pl.* (*paper*) papier cassé, *m.*; — *adj.* extérieur; du (*or* de) dehors; de l'extérieur; de l'impériale, d'impériale; — *adv.* en dehors, dehors, à l'extérieur; sur l'impériale, sur le dessus; — *prep.* à l'extérieur de, en dehors de. — *the door*, à la porte. *At the* —, tout au plus. *On the* —, en dehors. *To ride* —, aller sur l'impériale *or* (*on the box*) sur le siége du cocher. — **passenger,** *s.* voyageur (*m.*, -euse, *f.*) d'impériale. — **shutter,** *s.* contrevent, *m.*
Outsider, *s.* étranger, *m.*, -ère, *f.*; (*jest.*) profane, *m.f.*; (*on 'Change*) coulissier, *m.*; —**s**, *pl.* (*in a general sense*) public, *m.* *There is an — here*, il y a ici quelqu'un qui n'est pas des nôtres
Outsit, *v.a.* rester assis plus longtemps que
Outskirt, *s.* bord, *m.*; (*of woods, &c.*) lisière, *f.*; (*of towns*) faubourg, *m.*
Outsleep. *V.* **Oversleep** [tinct, net, articulé
Outspoken, *adj.* franc; clair, explicite; dis-
Outspokenness, *s.* franchise, *f.*; clarté, *f.*; netteté, *f.*
Outspread, *v.a.* étendre, déployer; répandre
Outstand. *V.* **Stand out**
Outstanding, *adj.* saillant, en saillie, qui avance; (*old*) vieux; (*unpaid*) non payé, à percevoir; (*com.*) courant
Outstare, *v.a.* faire baisser les yeux à, décontenancer, dévisager
Outstep, *v.a.* dépasser, excéder
Outstreet, *s.* rue écartée, *f.*
Outstretch, *v.a.* étendre [surpasser
Outstrip, *v.a.* gagner de vitesse, devancer;
Outswear, *v.a.* jurer plus que
Outtalk, *v.a.* parler plus que, avoir plus de langue que, surpasser en babil; accabler de paroles
Outthrow, *s.* (*mining, geol.*) faille, *f.*, rejet, *m.*
Outvie, *v.a.* l'emporter sur, surpasser
Outvote, *v.a.* obtenir la majorité sur
Outwalk, *v.a.* marcher plus vite que, devancer, dépasser
Outwall, *s.* avant-mur, mur extérieur, *m.*
Outward, *adj.* extérieur; externe; (*upper, over*) de dessus; (*nav.*) d'aller; — *adv.* à l'extérieur, au dehors, en dehors, extérieurement; (*nav.*) pour l'étranger. *Bound* —, — **bound,** *adj.* (*nav.*) en destination pour l'étranger, en cours de voyage. — **room,** *s.*, — **rooms,** *s.pl.* antichambre, *f.* — **voyage** *or* **passage,** *s.* (*nav.*) voyage d'aller, aller, *m.* [térieurement; en apparence
Outwardly, *adv.* à l'extérieur, en dehors, ex-
Outwardness, *s.* extériorité, *f.*
Outwards, *adv.* *V.* **Outward**
Outwear, *v.a.* durer plus longtemps que
Outweed, *v.a.* arracher, extirper
Outweep, *v.a.* pleurer plus que
Outweigh, *v.a.* peser plus que; (*fig.*) avoir plus de poids (*or* de prix *or* d'importance) que, l'emporter sur, surpasser
Outwit, *v.a.* surpasser en finesse, en revendre à, jouer, duper, attraper, mettre dedans
Outwork, *s.* ouvrage avancé, ouvrage extérieur, *m.*; — *v.a.* surpasser dans ses œuvres,
Ouzel. *V.* **Ousel** [surpasser
Oval, *adj.* *s.* ovale, *adj.m.f.*, *s.m.*
Ovalbumen, *s.* blanc d'œuf, *m.*
Ovalness, *s.* ovalité, *f.*
Ovarial, Ovarian, *adj.* ovarien
Ovar-ic, al, -ism, -ist. *V.* page 3, § 1
Ovariotom-ic, al, -y. *V.* page 3, § 1
Ovarious, *adj.* d'œufs
Ovaritis, *s.* ovarite, *f.*
Ovarium, Ovary, *s.* ovaire, *m.*
Ovate, Ovated, *adj.* ové
Ovation, *s.* ovation, *f.*
Oven, *s.* four, *m.* —**baked,** *adj.* cuit au four. — **bird,** *s.* fournier, *m.* — **builder,** *s.* constructeur de fours, *m.* — **cakes,** *s.pl.* fours, petits fours, *m.pl.* — **fork, -rake,** *s.* fourgon, râble, *m.* —**ful,** *s.* fournée, *f.* — **man, -woman,** *s.* fournier, *m.*, -ière, *f.* — **peel,** *s.* pelle de four, *f.*
Over, *prep.* (*at a distance up, on high; on the surface, on, upon*) sur; (*from one side down to the other; covering all*) par-dessus; (*at top of*) au-dessus de; (*more than*) au-dessus de; plus de; (*in addition to*) par-dessus; en sus de; (*on the other side*) de l'autre côté de; (*beyond*) au-delà de; (*through*) par, dans; d'un bout à l'autre de; (*to the close of*) jusqu'à la fin de; (*during*) pendant, durant; (*covered with*) couvert de; — *adv. adj.* dessus; par-dessus; au-dessus; de l'autre côté; au-delà; (*more*) davantage; (*extra*) en sus; (*of surplus*) de reste; (*covered*) couvert (de); (*at an end*) *V.* **End** (*At an*); (*wide*) de large; (*entirely*) tout, entièrement; (*too, too much*) trop, par trop; à l'excès; plus qu'il ne faut; (*too great*) trop grand; excessif; (*turn over!*) tournez; (*book-keep.*) à reporter. — **it,** *them* (*things*), dessus; par-dessus; au-dessus; de l'autre côté; au-delà; en sus; de reste; (*more*) davantage. — *and above*, par-dessus, en sus de ...; (*adverb.*) par-dessus; en sus, en outre. *All* —, par *or* dans tout (*m.*, or toute, *f.*) ...; (*gone, done*) passé, fini, terminé, fait; (*covered*) tout couvert (de); (*everywhere*) partout; d'un bout à l'autre; (*from head to foot*) des pieds à la tête; (*of trembling*) de tout son corps, de tous ses membres; (*entirely*) entièrement, en entier; tout à fait; dans toute la force du terme. *All the world* —, par toute la terre, dans le monde entier. *It is all* —, tout est fini, c'en est fait. *It is all — with*, c'en est fait de. *Red all* —, tout rouge. — *and* —, sans cesse, bien souvent, mille fois; tant et plus; dans tous les sens. — *again*, de nouveau, encore une fois. — *and — again*, mille et mille fois. — *against*, *V.* **Against.** — *or under*, plus ou moins
Overabound, &c. *V.* **Superabound,** &c.
Overact, *v.a.n.* exagérer, outrer, charger
Overagitate, *v.a.* agiter trop; discuter trop
Overall, *s.* (*coat*) *V.* **Overcoat;** (*shoe*) *V.* **Overshoe;** —**s**, *pl.* (*pair of trousers*) pantalon de dessus, *m.*; (*of workmen*) cotte, parisienne, *f.*; (*of cavalrymen*) charivari, *m.*
Overanxiety, *s.* trop grande inquiétude *or* &c. (*V.* **Anxiety**), inquiétude (*or* &c.) excessive, *f.*
Overanxious, *adj.* trop inquiet *or* &c. (*V.* **Anxious**), inquiet (*or* &c.) à l'excès
Overarch, *v.a.* voûter
Overassess, *v.a.* surtaxer
Overassessment, *s.* surtaux, *m.* [timider
Overawe, *v.a.* imposer à, tenir en respect; in-
Overbaked, *part. adj.* trop cuit
Overbalance, *v.a.* excéder; (*fig.*) surpasser, l'emporter sur; — *s.* excédant, surplus, *m.*; (*fig.*) prépondérance, *f.* *To — oneself*, faire la bascule
Overbalancing, *s.* prépondérance, *f.*
Overbear, *v.a.* subjuguer, vaincre, soumettre; (*fig.*) surmonter, maîtriser; surpasser, l'emporter sur; (*overwhelm*) accabler, écraser, opprimer [périeux, arrogant, hautain
Overbearing, *adj.* accablant, écrasant; im-
Overbearingly, *adv.* d'une manière accablante; impérieusement, arrogamment, hautainement
Overbearingness, *s.* *V.* **Imperiousness**

Overbend, *v.a.* plier *or* courber *or* tendre trop (*or* à l'excès) [pour (*or* de)

Overbid, *v.a.* enchérir sur; (*things*) offrir trop

Overblow, *v.n.* souffler avec trop de violence, surventer; passer, cesser; — *v.a.* chasser, dissiper [*water*) à l'eau; (*in the sea*) à la mer

Overboard, *adv.* par-dessus le bord; (*in the*

Overboil, *v.a.* faire trop bouillir; — *v.n.* bouillir trop longtemps

Overboiled, *adj.* trop bouilli

Overbuilt, *adj.* couvert *or* chargé de bâtiments (*or* de constructions). *That place is* —, on a trop bâti dans cet endroit [cabler

Overburden, *v.a.* ('*with,*' de) surcharger; ac-

Overburn, *v.a.n.* brûler trop [officieux

Overbusy, *adj.* trop affairé, trop occupé; trop

Overbuy, *v.a.* acheter trop; acheter trop cher

Overcareful, *adj.* soigneux *or* &c. (*V.* **Careful**) à l'excès

Overcast, *v.a.* obscurcir; (*of price*) évaluer trop haut; (*need.*) surjeter, faire un surjet à; — *part. adj.* obscurci; (*of weather*) couvert; (*need.*) surjeté

Overcasting, *s.* (*need.*) surjet, *m.*

Overcaution, *s.* prudence excessive, *f.*

Overcautious, *adj.* par trop prudent, trop circonspect [spection

Overcautiously, *adv.* avec trop de circon-

Overcharge, *v.a.n.* surcharger, accabler ('*with,*' de); (*fire-arms*) charger trop; (*exaggerate*) charger; (*in price*) prendre trop cher, surfaire; rançonner; (*of taxes*) surtaxer; — *s.* surcharge, charge excessive, *f.*; (*in price*) prix exorbitant, *m.*; item de trop, *m.*; (*of taxes*) surtaxe, *f.*; surtaux, *m.* [scurcir

Overcloud, *v.a.* couvrir de nuages; (*fig.*) ob-

Overcloy, *v.a.* gorger

Overcoat, *s. V.* **Coat** (*Great*)

Overcold, *adj.* trop froid, excessivement froid

Overcolour, *v.a.* colorer trop; (*fig.*) charger, exagérer, outrer

Overcome, *v.a.* vaincre, dompter, subjuguer, soumettre; (*fig.*) surmonter, vaincre; (*overwhelm*) accabler ('*with,*' de); — *v.n.* l'emporter, avoir le dessus, vaincre

Overcomer, *s.* vainqueur, *m.*

Overconfidence, *s.* trop grande confiance, confiance excessive, *f.*, excès de confiance, *m.*

Overconfident, *adj.* trop plein de confiance

Overconfidently, *adv.* avec trop de confiance; trop hardiment

Overcredulous, *adj.* trop crédule

Overcrowd, *v.a.* encombrer à l'excès

Overcrowding, *s.* encombrement excessif, *m.*

Overcurious, *adj.* trop curieux *or* &c. (*V.* **Curious**)

Overdiligent, *adj.* trop diligent, actif à l'excès

Overdo, *v.a.* faire trop; (*exaggerate*) exagérer, outrer, excéder, pousser trop loin; surcharger, charger; harasser, fatiguer; (*in cooking*) faire trop cuire; — *v.n.* en faire trop

Overdone, *part. adj.* exagéré, &c. (*V.* **Overdo**); (*cook.*) trop cuit

Overdose, *s.* trop forte dose, *f.*

Overdraw, *v.a.n.* tirer trop; charger; excéder ('*by,*' de). — *o.'s account,* excéder son crédit, dépasser son actif. —*n account,* compte découvert, *m.* [avec excès

Overdress, *v.a.* habiller trop; (*adorn*) parer

Overdrink, *v.n.* boire avec excès, boire trop

Overdrive, *v.a.* faire aller trop vite; (*carry too far*) pousser trop loin; (*animals*) surmener

Overdry, *v.a.* sécher trop; — *adj.* trop sec

Overdue, *adj.* en retard; périmé

Overeager, *adj.* trop ardent, trop empressé *or* &c. (*V.* **Eager**)

Overeagerly, *adv.* trop ardemment, avec trop d'ardeur, avec trop d'empressement, &c. (*V.* **Eagerly**)

Overeagerness, *s.* excès d'ardeur, excès d'empressement *or* &c. (*V.* **Eagerness**), *m.*

Overeat, *v.n.* manger avec excès, manger trop

Overelegant, *adj.* trop élégant

Overestimate, *v.a. V.* **Overrate**; — *s.* surestimation, surévaluation, *f.*

Overexcite, *v.a.* surexciter

Overexcitement, *s.* surexcitation, *f.*

Overextension, *s.* surextension, *f.*

Overfall, *s.* chute d'eau, cataracte, *f.*

Overfatigue, *s.* fatigue excessive, *f.*, excès de fatigue, *m.*; — *v.a.* fatiguer trop, excéder de fatigue

Overfeed, *v.a.* nourrir trop; gorger; rassasier

Overfill, *v.a.* remplir trop; (*fig.*) surcharger

Overflow, *v.n.* déborder; (*abound*) surabonder, regorger ('*with,*' de); (*expand*) s'épancher; — *v.a.* inonder; (*to fill too much*) faire déborder; — *s.* débordement, *m.*, inondation, *f.*; surabondance, *f.*, excès *m.*; trop-plein, *m.* — **pipe,** *s.* tuyau de trop-plein, *m.*

Overflowing, *adj.* qui déborde, trop plein; surabondant, exubérant; — *s.* débordement, *m.*; surabondance, exubérance, *f.*; trop-plein, *m.*; (*effusion*) épanchement, *m.*, effusion, *f.* *Filled* or *full to* —, tout plein, comble [ment

Overflowingly, *adv.* à l'excès, surabondam-

Overfond, *adj.* qui aime trop, trop passionné (pour), fou (de); trop tendre; trop ardent

Overfondly, *adv.* trop passionnément; trop tendrement; trop ardemment

Overfondness, *s.* trop grande passion, *f.*, attachement trop fort, *m.*; tendresse excessive, *f.*

Overforward, *adj.* trop empressé, trop pressé, trop ardent; trop présomptueux; (*hort.*) trop hâtif

Overforwardness, *s.* empressement excessif, trop grand empressement, *m.*, ardeur excessive, trop grande ardeur, *f.*; présomption excessive, trop grande assurance, *f.*; (*hort.*) hâtiveté ex- [cessive, *f.*

Overfraught, *adj.* surchargé

Overfree, *adj.* trop libre; trop libéral, prodigue [ralement; prodiguement

Overfreely, *adv.* trop librement; trop libé-

Overfreight, *v.a.* surcharger; — *s.* surcharge, *f.*

Overfruitful, *adj.* trop fertile, trop fécond

Overfull, *adj.* trop plein, comble

Overgild, *v.a.* dorer à l'excès

Overgo, *v.a.* franchir; surpasser

Overgreat, *adj.* trop grand, excessif

Overgreedy, *adj.* trop avide

Overgrow, *v.n.* (*things*) croître trop, surcroître; (*pers.*) grandir trop; — *v.a.* couvrir, recouvrir, tapisser ('*with,*' de); dépasser en croissant, s'élever au-dessus de; (*pers.*) grandir plus que, grandir trop pour

Overgrown, *part. adj.* ('*with,*' de) couvert, recouvert, plein; immense; énorme; trop développé, trop grand

Overgrowth, *s.* croissance excessive, surcroissance, *f.*; trop grande augmentation, *f.*, accroissement excessif, accroissement démesuré, *m.*

Overhang, *v.a.* être suspendu sur, pencher sur, planer sur; surplomber; (*threaten*) menacer; — *v.n.* pencher; avancer, surplomber

Overhanging, *adj.* suspendu (sur); qui penche; en saillie, en surplomb; perpendiculaire [trop

Overharden, *v.a.* durcir trop; (*fig.*) endurcir

Overhaste, *s.* trop grande précipitation, *f.*

Overhastily, *adv.* trop précipitamment, avec trop de précipitation, trop à la hâte; (*passionately*) trop vivement, avec emportement

Overhastiness, *s.* trop grande précipitation, trop grande hâte, *f.*; (*passion*) vivacité excessive, *f.*, emportement, *m.* [trop vif, emporté

Overhasty, *adj.* trop précipité; (*passionate*)

Overhaul, *v.a.* (*unfold*) étendre; (*loosen*) larguer; (*a rope*) affaler, larguer; (*overtake*) gagner, atteindre; (*examine*) examiner, inspecter, visiter; (*accounts, &c.*) revoir, revenir sur

Overhead, *adv.* au-dessus de la tête, au-dessus,

en l'air, en haut; au ciel; (*immerged*) par-dessus la tête

Overhear, *v.a.* entendre par hasard, entendre sans le vouloir, saisir, surprendre

Overheat, *v.a.* chauffer à l'excès, échauffer trop; (*fig.*) échauffer; (*tech.*) surchauffer. *To — oneself, to become* or *get —ed,* s'échauffer

Overheating, *s.* échauffement, *m.*; (*tech.*) [surchauffage, *m.*

Overhigh, *adj.* trop haut

Overhonest, *adj.* trop honnête

Overhours. *V.* **After-hours**

Overinsurance, *s.* assurance pour une valeur exagérée, *f.* [en trop grand nombre

Overissue, *s.* surémission, *f.*; — *v.a.* émettre

Overjealous, *adj.* trop jaloux

Overjoy, *v.a.* ('*at*,' '*to*,' de) transporter de joie, ravir; — *s.* transport de joie, ravissement, [*m.*

Overkind, *adj.* trop bon

Overkindness, *s.* bonté excessive, *f.*

Overlabour, *v.a.* (*pers.*) faire travailler à l'excès, harasser de travail; (*things*) travailler trop, élaborer à l'excès

Overlade, *v.a.* surcharger ('*with*,' de)

Overland, *adj.* par voie de terre. — **journey,** *s.* voyage par voie de terre, *m.* — **mail,** *s.* dépêches par voie de terre, *f.pl.* *By — mail,* par voie de terre. — **route,** *s.* voie de terre, *f.*

Overlap, *v.a.* recouvrir; dépasser; enchevaucher; — *v.n.* se recouvrir; chevaucher; — *s.* *V.* **Overlapping**

Overlapping, *s.* recouvrement, *m.*; chevauchement, *m.*, chevauchure, *f.*

Overlarge, *adj.* trop grand; trop gros; trop considérable; trop étendu [cessive, *f.*

Overlargeness, *s.* grandeur *or* grosseur ex-

Overlay, *v.a.* couvrir; (*smother*) étouffer; (*cloud*) obscurcir; (*overwhelm*) accabler, surcharger ('*with*,' de)

Overlaying, *s.* couverture, *f.*

Overleap, *v.a.* sauter par-dessus, franchir

Overlearned, *adj.* trop savant

Overlearnedness, *s.* trop de savoir, *m.*

Overliberal, *adj.* trop libéral, trop généreux

Overlie, *v.a.* couvrir, recouvrir

Overlight, *s.* trop de lumière, *m.*, lumière trop forte *or* trop vive, *f.*; — *adj.* trop léger; trop clair

Overlighted, *part. adj.* trop éclairé

Overlive. *V.* **Outlive**

Overload, *v.a.* surcharger ('*with*,' de)

Overlong, *adj.* trop long; — *adv.* trop longtemps

Overlook, *v.a.* avoir vue sur; dominer, commander; examiner; (*watch*) surveiller, avoir l'œil sur, inspecter; (*review*) revoir, retoucher; (*excuse*) passer sur, passer, pardonner, fermer les yeux sur; (*not to notice*) laisser échapper, laisser passer, ne pas voir, ne pas remarquer, ne pas faire attention à; perdre de vue; (*neglect*) négliger, laisser de côté; (*disdain*) dédaigner, mépriser

Overlooker, *s.* inspecteur, *m.*; surveillant, *m.*; (*of factories*) contre-maître, *m.*

Overlooking, *s.* surveillance, *f.*

Overlying, *part. adj.* qui couvre, qui recouvre; [superposé

Overman, *s.* contre-maître, *m.*

Overmasted, *adj.* trop mâté

Overmaster, *v.a.* maîtriser

Overmatch, *v.a.* être trop fort pour; surpasser; (*conquer*) vaincre, maîtriser; (*oppress*) accabler; — *s.* trop forte partie, *f.*; force supérieure, *f.*; (*conqueror*) vainqueur, *m.*

Overmeasure, *v.a.* mesurer trop largement; estimer trop, priser trop, avoir une trop haute idée de; — *s.* trop bonne mesure, bonne mesure (en sus), *f.*, surplus, *m.*

Overmodest, *adj.* trop modeste

Overmuch, *adv.* trop, par trop, excessivement; — *adj.* excessif, trop grand; — *s.* excès, *m.* [cherché

Overneat, *adj.* excessivement propre; re-

Overnice, *adj.* trop délicat; trop difficile

Overnight, *s.* (la) soirée, *f.*; — *adv.* *V.* **Night** (*Over*) [pressé, importun

Overofficious, *adj.* trop officieux, trop em-

Overpaid, *adj.* trop payé, payé trop cher

Overpaint, *v.a.* peindre de trop vives couleurs; surcharger de couleur

Overpass, *v.a.* passer sur, franchir, traverser; (*not to notice*) laisser passer, ne pas faire attention à, ne pas remarquer; (*omit*) omettre, passer; (*exclude*) ne pas comprendre, exclure

Overpast, *adj.* passé [trop cher

Overpay, *v.a.* surpayer, payer trop; payer

Overpayment, *s.* surpaye, *f.*

Overpeopled, *adj.* trop peuplé [trop-plein, *m.*

Overplus, *s.* surplus, excédant, *m.*; excès, *m.*;

Overpoise, *v.a.* *V.* **Outweigh**; — *s.* poids plus fort, poids qui l'emporte, *m.*; (*fig.*) plus qu'un contre-poids; (*fig.*) prépondérance, *f.*

Overpolish, *v.a.* polir à l'excès

Overponderous, *adj.* trop pesant

Overpopulated, Overpopulous, *adj.* trop peuplé, trop populeux

Overpower, *v.a.* être trop fort pour, être plus fort que; (*crush*) accabler, écraser; (*get over*) vaincre, subjuguer, surmonter; (*overwhelm*) accabler ('*with*,' de; '*by*,' par); (*with fatigue*) excéder, accabler; (*dazzle*) éblouir; (*astound*) étonner [cablante, excessivement

Overpoweringly, *adv.* d'une manière ac-

Overpraise, *v.a.* louer à l'excès [excessif, *m.*

Overpraising, *s.* louange excessive, *f.*, éloge

Overpress, *v.a.* presser vivement; (*crush*) accabler, écraser

Overprize, *v.a.* estimer trop haut, priser trop, faire un trop grand cas de

Overproduction, *s.* production excessive, *f.*

Overprompt, *adj.* trop prompt, trop vif

Overpromptness, *s.* promptitude excessive, *f.*, trop grand empressement, *m.*

Overproud, *adj.* trop fier

Overrate, *v.a.* surévaluer, surestimer, estimer trop haut, estimer trop; faire trop de cas de; exagérer; s'exagérer; présumer de, présumer trop de; (*of taxes*) surtaxer

Overreach, *v.a.* dépasser; (*deceive*) tromper, duper, jouer, attraper, mettre dedans; — *v.n.* (*of horses*) (*rid.*) forger, se friser, (*vet.*) se nerférer, se nerférir; — *s.* (*vet.*) nerf-férure, *f.* — *oneself,* se faire tort à soi-même, se trahir soi-même, (*fam.*) se mettre dedans

Overreacher, *s.* trompeur, *m.*, -euse, *f.*

Overreaching, *s.* tromperie, *f.*; — *adj.* trompeur

Overread, *v.a.* lire en entier, parcourir. — *oneself,* se rendre malade à force de lire

Overready, *adj.* trop prompt, trop empressé

Overrent, *v.a.* louer trop cher [richesses

Overrich, *adj.* énormément riche, gorgé de

Override, *v.a.* (*ride over*) parcourir à cheval, parcourir; (*ride too much*) surmener; (*be superior to*) primer; (*supersede*) *V.* **Supersede.** *Might —s right,* la force prime le droit

Overrigged, *adj.* qui a de trop gros agrès

Overrigid, *adj.* trop rigide, trop sévère

Overripe, *adj.* trop mûr

Overripen, *v.a.n.* mûrir trop

Overroast, *v.a.* rôtir trop; griller trop

Overrule, *v.a.* gouverner, diriger, régir; dominer, maîtriser; être plus fort que, l'emporter sur; (*law*) rejeter

Overrun, *v.a.* couvrir (de); inonder (de); envahir; infester (de); (*tread down*) fouler; (*run faster*) aller plus vite que, devancer; (*print.*) remanier; — *v.n.* déborder; regorger

Overrunner, *s.* envahisseur, ravageur, *m.*

Overrunning, *s.* envahissement, *m.*, invasion, *f.*; ravages, *m.pl.*, dévastation, *f.*; inondation, *f.*; (*print.*) remaniement, *m.*

Oversaturate, *v.a.* saturer à l'excès

Overscrupulous, *adj.* trop scrupuleux; méticuleux

Oversea, *adj.* d'outre-mer [ticuleux

Overseason, *v.a.* assaisonner *or* &c. (*V.* **Season,** *v.a.*) trop

Oversee, *v.a.* (*to watch, superintend*) surveiller, avoir l'œil sur; (*to fail to see*) laisser passer, laisser échapper, ne pas voir, ne pas remarquer, ne pas faire attention à
Overseer, *s.* surveillant, *m.*; inspecteur, *m.*; (*of the poor*) administrateur (de la taxe des pauvres), *m.*; (*of factories*) contre-maître, *m.*; (*print.*) prote, *m.* *Assistant* —, (*of the poor*) sous-percepteur de la taxe des pauvres, *m.*
Oversell, *v.a.* vendre trop; vendre trop cher
Overset, *v.a.* renverser; bouleverser; (*a carriage*) faire verser, verser; (*a boat*) faire chavirer, chavirer; — *v.n.* se renverser; (*of carriages*) verser; (*of boats*) chavirer
Overshade, Overshadow, *v.a.* ombrager; (*protect*) protéger; (*eclipse*) éclipser; (*darken*) obscurcir [caoutchouc, *m.*
Overshoe, *s.* claque, galoche, *f.*, socque,
Overshoot, *v.a.* porter au-delà de; dépasser; (*pass swiftly*) passer rapidement; — *v.n.* porter trop loin, dépasser le but
Overshot wheel, *s.* roue en dessus, roue mue en dessus, roue à augets, *f.*
Oversight, *s.* oubli, *m.*, inadvertance, négligence, méprise, erreur, *f.*; (*superintendence*) surveillance, inspection, *f.*
Overskip, *v.a.* sauter par-dessus, franchir; (*omit*) sauter, passer
Oversleep, *v.a.* dormir plus longtemps que, dormir au-delà de, laisser passer. *To — oneself,* dormir trop longtemps, s'éveiller *or* se réveiller trop tard (*or* après l'heure), rester endormi, s'oublier
Overslip, *v.a.* glisser sur, omettre, négliger, passer, laisser passer, laisser échapper
Oversoon, *adv.* trop tôt [éreinté, rendu
Overspent, *adj.* épuisé, excédé, exténué,
Overspot, *v.a.* couvrir de taches [pandre sur
Overspread, *v.a.* couvrir ('*with,*' de), se ré-
Overstate, *v.a.* exagérer [céder, dépasser
Overstep, *v.a.* franchir, passer; (*exceed*) ex-
Overstock, Overstore, *v.a.* encombrer ('*with,*' de), approvisionner à l'excès
Overstory, *s.* *V.* **Clerestory**
Overstrain, *v.n.* faire de trop grands efforts; — *v.a.* outrer; forcer. — *oneself,* se donner un effort [damment
Oversupply, *v.a.* approvisionner surabon-
Overswell, *v.a.* déborder; inonder
Overt, *adj.* ouvert; découvert; évident, manifeste, patent; public; (*law*) préparatoire. — *act,* commencement d'exécution, *m.*
Overtake, *v.a.* atteindre; rejoindre; rattraper; (*surprise*) surprendre; gagner
Overtask, *v.a.* imposer une tâche trop forte à, surcharger de travail; abuser de, excéder; (*a horse,* &c.) surmener
Overtax, *v.a.* surtaxer; surcharger d'impôts; (*overwork*) surmener; (*abuse*) abuser de, ex-
Overtaxation, *s.* surtaxe, *f.* [céder
Overtedious, *adj.* trop ennuyeux, ennuyeux à l'excès
Overthrow, *v.a.* renverser; détruire, ruiner; (*defeat*) défaire, vaincre, mettre en déroute; — *s.* renversement, *m.*; destruction, ruine, *f.*; (*defeat*) défaite, déroute, *f.*
Overthrower, *s.* renverseur, *m.*, -euse, *f.*
Overtime, *s.* temps en sus, *m.*, heures de travail en sus (de la journée ordinaire), heures supplémentaires, *f.pl.*; (*com. nav.*) retardement, *m.*; — *adv.* après les heures (de travail), passé l'heure
Overtire, *v.a.* excéder de fatigue
Overtly, *adv.* ouvertement, manifestement
Overtop, *v.a.* s'élever au-dessus de, dépasser; surpasser; effacer, éclipser
Overtower, *v.a.* dominer [de marchandises
Overtrade, *v.n.* spéculer à l'excès, s'encombrer
Overtrading, *s.* spéculation excessive, *f.*, encombrement de marchandises, *m.*
Overtrust, *v.a.* se fier trop à
Overture, *s.* ouverture, *f.*
Overturn, *v.a.n.* *V.* **Overset;** — *s.* renversement, *m.*; bouleversement, *m.*; (*of a carriage*)
Overturnable, *adj.* renversable [versade, *f.*
Overturner, *s.* renverseur, *m.*, -euse, *f.*
Overturning, *s.* renversement, *m.*; bouleversement, *m.*; (*of a carriage*) versade, *f.*
Overvaluation, *s.* surévaluation, surestimation, *f.*
Overvalue, *v.a.* surévaluer, évaluer trop haut, surestimer; (*fig.*) estimer trop haut, estimer trop, priser trop, faire trop de cas de, avoir une trop haute opinion de, exagérer; — *s.*
Overweak, *adj.* trop faible [survaleur, *f.*
Overweary, *v.a.* *V.* **Overfatigue**
Overween, *v.n.* s'en faire accroire, être présomptueux; se faire illusion, se flatter à tort; (*to* ...) présumer (de ...), oser (...)
Overweening, *adj.* présomptueux, outrecuidant; — *s.* présomption, outrecuidance, *f.*
Overweeningly, *adv.* présomptueusement, avec outrecuidance
Overweigh. *V.* **Outweigh**
Overweight, *s.* supériorité de poids, prépondérance, *f.*; (*surplus*) excédant de poids, excédant, surpoids, *m.*
Overwhelm, *v.a.* accabler (de), écraser; (*with good things*) combler (de) [cablante
Overwhelmingly, *adv.* d'une manière ac-
Overwise, *adj.* par trop sage
Overwork, *s.* travail excessif, excès de travail *m.*; (*extra*) travail en sus, surplus de travail ouvrage de surcroît, *m.*; — *v.a.* excéder de travail, fatiguer; (*a horse,* &c.) surmener, forcer; (*things*) travailler trop; (*overload*) surcharger. *To — oneself,* travailler trop, s'excéder de travail, se fatiguer
Overworn, *adj.* usé; fané; accablé de fatigue
Overzeal, *s.* zèle excessif, trop de zèle, *m.*
Overzealous, *adj.* trop zélé, trop ardent
Oviduct, *s.* oviducte, *m.*
Oviferous, *adj.* ovifère
Oviform, *adj.* oviforme
Ovine, *adj.* ovine, *f.*; de *or* de la brebis, de *or* du mouton. — *species* or *race,* espèce *or* race
Oviparous, *adj.* ovipare [ovine, *f.*
Ovipositor, *s.* pondoir, *m.*
Ov-ism, -ist. *V.* page 3, § 1
Ovivorous, *adj.* ovivore
Ovoid, *adj. s.* ovoïde, *adj. m.f., s.m.*
Ovoidal, *adj.* ovoïdal
Ovolo, *s.* ove, *m.*
Ovolog-ic, al, -ist, -y. *V.* page 3, §
Ovoviviparous, *adj.* ovovivipare
Ovular, Ovulary, *adj.* ovulaire
Ovule, Ovulum, *s.* ovule, *m.*
Owe, *v.a.* devoir. *You must — it to me,* vous me devrez cela
Owing, *part. adj.* dû (à); à cause (de); par suite de; grâce (à); l'effet (de; qui tient (à)
Owl, *s.* hibou, *m.* — **light,** *s.* faible lueur, *f.*; (*twilight*) crépuscule, *m.*, brune, tombée de la nuit, *f.* *To be — light,* faire brun. —**like,**
Owlet, *s.* hulotte, *f.* [*adj.* comme un hibou
Owlish, *adj.* de hibou
Own, *adj.* propre; — *v.a.* (*possess*) avoir, posséder, être propriétaire de; (*acknowledge*) reconnaître; (*confess*) avouer, confesser, reconnaître, convenir de; (*claim*) s'attribuer, réclamer. *O.'s —,* son propre, son (sa, ses); (*when not used before a noun*) le sien; à soi; sien; (*coming from*) de soi; sien; (*relations*) les siens. *A house of his —, of her —,* une maison à lui, à elle. *At* or *in his — house,* chez lui. *A trick of his —,* un tour de sa façon. *To give* or *pay anyone his —,* (*jest.*) donner son fait à quelqu'un, rendre la pareille à quelqu'un. *To hold o.'s —,* tenir sa place; maintenir son rang; se soutenir, se maintenir; tenir bon; résister (à), tenir tête (à). *To tell anyone his —,* dire à quelqu'un son fait
Owner, *s.* propriétaire, *m.f.*; possesseur, *m.*; maître, *m.*, -esse, *f.*; (*of ships*) armateur, *m.*

Ownership, *s.* propriété, *f.*
Ox, *s.* bœuf, *m.* — **bane,** *s.* mort aux bœufs, *f.* — **calf,** *s.* veau mâle, *m.* — **driver,** *s.* bouvier, *m.*, -ière, *f.* — **eye,** *s.* œil de bœuf, *m.* — **eyed,** *adj.* aux yeux de bœuf. — **fly,** *s.* taon, *m.* — **gall,** *s.* fiel de bœuf, *m.* — **gang,** *s.* charruage, *m.* — **goad,** *s.* aiguillon (de bouvier), *m.* — **hide,** *s.* peau de bœuf, *f.* —**like,** *adj.* comme un bœuf. — **lip,** *s.* primevère élevée, *f.* — **pecker,** *s.* pique-bœufs, *m.* — **stall,** *s.* étable à bœufs, *f.* — **tail,** *s.* queue de bœuf, *f.* — **tail soup,** *s.* potage à la queue de bœuf, *m.* — **tongue,** *s.* [langue de bœuf, *f.*
Oxalate, *s.* oxalate, *m.*
Oxalic, *adj.* oxalique
Oxalis, *s.* oxalide, *f.*
Oxidability, *s.* oxydabilité, *f.*
Oxidable, *adj.* oxydable
Oxidate, *v.a.* oxyder; — *v.n.* s'oxyder
Oxidation, Oxidization, *s.* oxydation, *f.*
Oxidizable, Oxidize. *V.* **Oxidable, Oxi-** [**date**
Oxidulated, *adj.* oxydulé
Oxonian, *s.* étudiant de l'université d'Oxford, *m.*; (*shoe*) napolitain, *m.*
Oxyde, &c. *V.* **Oxide,** &c.
Oxygen, *s.* oxygène, *m.*
Oxygenable, Oxygenizable, *adj.* oxygé- [**nable**
Oxygenate, Oxygenize, *v.a.* oxygéner; — *v.n.* s'oxygéner
Oxygenation, Oxygenization, *s.* oxygé- [nation, *f.*
Oxygenous, *adj.* d'oxygène
Oxymel, *s.* oxymel, *m.*
Oxysalt, *s.* oxysel, *m.*
Oyster, *s.* huître, *f.* — **bed,** *s.* banc d'huîtres, *m.*, huîtrière, *f.* — **brood,** *s.* *V.* — **spat.** — **catcher,** *s.* (*bird*) huîtrier, *m.* — **culture,** *s.* ostréiculture, *f.* — **dredger,** *s.* pêcheur d'huîtres, *m.* — **farmer,** *s.* *V.* — **grower.** — **fisher,** *s.* pêcheur d'huîtres, *m.* — **fishery,** *s.* pêche des huîtres, *f.*; (*bed*) *V.* — **bed.** — **fork,** *s.* fourchette à huîtres, *f.* — **green,** *s.* laitue de mer, *f.* — **grower,** *s.* ostréiculteur, *m.* — **knife,** *s.* ouvre-huîtres, *m.* — **man,** *s.* marchand d'huîtres, écailler, *m.* — **opener,** *s.* écailler, *m.*, -ère, *f.*; (*instr.*) ouvre-huîtres, *m.* — **patty,** *s.* petit pâté d'huîtres, *m.* — **pie,** *s.* pâté d'huîtres, *m.* — **plant,** *s.* salsifis, *m.* — **sauce,** *s.* sauce aux huîtres, *f.* — **scalp,** *s.* *V.* — **bed.** — **shell,** *s.* écaille (*or* coquille) d'huître, *f.* — **spat,** *s.* frai d'huîtres, naissain, *m.* — **wife, -woman,** *s.* écaillère, marchande d'huîtres, *f.*
Oz., (*abbrev.*) *V.* **Ounce**
Ozæna, Ozena, *s.* ozène, *m.*
Ozonation. *V.* **Ozonization**
Ozone, *s.* ozone, *m.*
Ozoniferous, *adj.* ozonifère
Ozonization, *s.* ozonisation, *f.*
Ozonize, *v.a.* ozoniser, ozoner
Ozonometer, *s.* ozonomètre, *m.*
Ozonometric, -al, *adj.* ozonométrique
Ozonometry, *s.* ozonométrie, *f.*

P

P, *s.* (*letter*) p, *m.* *To mind o.'s —'s and Q's,* mettre les points sur les i, observer les longues et les brèves; être *or* se mettre sur son bien-dire; être attentif, être sur ses gardes. — **jacket,** *s.* *V.* **Pea**
Pabular, *adj.* alimentaire
Pabulous, *adj.* alimenteux
Pabulum, *s.* aliment, *m.*, nourriture, *f.*
Pace, *s.* (*step, gait, pace*) pas, *m.*; (*of a horse*) pas, *m.*, allure, *f.*; (*mil.*) pas, *m.*; (*rate*) train, *m.*; — *v.n.* aller au pas; aller, marcher; — *v.a.* mesurer; (*to walk*) arpenter; (*to follow*) suivre; (*to direct*) faire aller, faire marcher. *At a foot* (or *foot's*) —, *V.* **Foot.** *At a good* —, d'un bon pas, bon train. *At a great* —, à grands pas, grand train. *At a slow* —, à pas lents; au petit pas. *To keep — with,* suivre; (*fig.*) marcher de pair avec. *To mend* or *hurry o.'s* —, hâter le pas. *To — up and down,* se promener à grands pas dans
Paced, *adj.* qui a le pas ..., à pas ...; (*trained*) dressé, exercé. *Easy* —, (*of horses,* &c.) aisé et doux au montoir. *Slow* —, qui a le pas lent, [à pas lent
Pacer, *s.* cheval qui va le pas, *m.*
Pacha, &c. *V.* **Pasha,** &c.
Pachyderm, *s.* pachyderme, *m.*
Pachyderm-al, atous, *adj.* pachyderme
Pacifiable, *adj.* pacifiable
Pacific, *adj.* pacifique; calme, paisible; (*geog.*) pacifique; — *s.* (*geog.*) Pacifique, *m.*
Pacifically, *adv.* pacifiquement
Pacification, *s.* pacification, *f.*
Pacifica-tor, tress, *s.* pacificateur, *m.*, -trice, *f.*
Pacificatory, *adj.* pacificateur
Pacifier, *s.* pacificateur, *m.*, -trice, *f.*
Pacify, *v.a.* pacifier; calmer, apaiser
Pack, *s.* paquet, *m.*, balle, *f.*, ballot, *m.*; (*load*) fardeau, *m.*, charge, *f.*; (*heap*) tas, *m.*, masse, *f.*; (*of people*) bande, *f.*, tas, *m.*; (*of cards*) jeu, *m.*; (*of dogs*) meute, *f.* — *of hounds,* meute de chiens, meute, *f.* — **cloth,** *s.* *V.* **Packing-cloth.** — **horse,** *s.* cheval de bât *or* de charge, *m.* — **ice,** *s.* embâcle, *m.* — **man,** *s.* porte-balle, *m.* — **needle,** *s.* *V.* **Packing-needle.** — **saddle,** *s.* bât, *m.* — **saddle maker,** *s.* bâtier, *m.* — **staff,** *s.* bâton pour porter un paquet, *m.* — **thread,** *s.* ficelle, *f.*
Pack, *v.a.* emballer; empaqueter; (*in a case*) encaisser; (*in a cask*) embariller, mettre en baril; (*fish*) paquer, encaquer; (*pers.*) entasser; (*a jury,* &c.) choisir subrepticement; ramasser; (*cards*) préparer; — *v.n.* s'emballer; s'empaqueter; (*to close*) se fermer; (*pers.*) emballer, faire son paquet (*or* ses paquets), faire sa malle (*or* ses malles); (*run off*) plier bagage, décamper. — **off,** *v.a.* emballer; (*despatch*) expédier, se débarrasser de; *v.n.* plier bagage, décamper. — **up,** *v.a.* emballer; empaqueter; encaisser; expédier; *v.n.* emballer, faire sa malle *or* ses malles, faire son paquet *or* ses paquets. *To send —ing,* envoyer promener, envoyer paître. *A —ed assembly,* un ramassis de gens corrompus, *m.*
Package, *s.* emballage, *m.*; (*bundle*) paquet, *m.*, (*com., rail.*) colis, *m.*
Packer, *s.* emballeur, *m.*, -euse, *f.*; (*of fish*) paqueur, encaqueur, *m.*, -euse, *f.*
Packet, *s.* paquet, *m.*; (*boat*) paquebot, *m.* — **boat, -ship,** *s.* paquebot, *m.*
Packfong, *s.* packfong, métal blanc, mail- [lechort, *m.*
Packing, *s.* emballage, *m.*; empaquetage, *m.*; (*of fish*) paquage, encaquement, *m.* — **case** *or* **box,** *s.* caisse d'emballage, *f.* — **case maker,** *s.* layetier, *m.* — **cloth,** *s.* toile d'emballage, serpillière, *f.* — **needle,** *s.* aiguille à emballer, aiguille d'emballage, *f.* — **press,** *s.* presse à empiler, *f.* — **stick,** *s.* [garrot, *m.*
Pact, *s.* pacte, *m.*
Pad, *s.* (*horse*) cheval (aisé et doux au montoir), *m.*; (*robber*) voleur de grand chemin, *m.*; (*cushion*) coussinet, *m.*; bourrelet, *m.*; matelas, *m.*; (*of rags, and stamp inking-* —) tampon, *m.*; (*for writing*) sous-main, *m.*; (*for fencing*) plastron, *m.*; (*saddle*) sellette, *f.*; (*of neck-handkerchiefs*) col, *m.*; (*basket*) panier, *m.*, bourriche, *f.*; — *v.a.* rembourrer; matelasser; (*garments*) ouater; (*in calico-printing*) plaquer; — *v.n.* voyager doucement. *To — the hoof,* aller à pied, marcher
Padding, *s.* (*material*) bourre, *f.*; (*for garments*) ouate, *f.*; (*liter.*) remplissage, *m.*, bourre, *f.*; (*act of padding*) rembourrage, *m.*, (*of garments*) ouatage, *m.*, (*in calico-printing*) placage, *m.* — **machine,** *s.* machine à plaquer, *f.*
Paddle, *v.n.* pagayer, ramer; (*to dabble*) patrouiller, barboter, patauger; (*to finger*)

jouer; — *v.a.* pagayer; — *s.* pagaie, *f.*; (*of wheels*) palette, aube, *f.*; —**s**, *pl.* (*wheels*) roues, *f.pl.*; — *adj.* à aubes; à roues. — **board,** *s.* palette, *f.* — **box,** *s.* tambour, *m.* — **ship,** *s.* vapeur à roues, *m.* — **wheel,** *s.* roue à aubes, *f.*; *adj.* à aubes; à roues [*m.*, -euse, *f.*

Paddler, *s.* pagayeur, *m.*; (*dabbler*) barboteur,

Paddock, *s.* enclos, pâturage, herbage, pré, *m.*; (*of a race-ground*) promenoir, *m.*; (*a toad*) gros crapaud, *m.*

Paddy, *s.* Irlandais, *m.*; (*rice*) riz non mondé, riz, *m.* — **field,** *s.* rizière, *f.*

Padella, *s.* lampion, *m.*

Padishah, *s.* padichah, *m.* [fermer au cadenas

Padlock, *s.* cadenas, *m.*; — *v.a.* cadenasser;

Paduan, *s. adj.* Padouan, *m.*, e, *f.*

Pæan, *s.* hymne, *m.*

Pæon, *s.* péon, *m.*

Pæony, *s.* pivoine, *f.*

Pagan, *s. adj.* païen, *m.*, -ne, *f.*

Paganism, *s.* paganisme, *m.*

Paganize, *v.a.n.* paganiser

Page, *s.* (*boy*) page, *m.*; (*in livery*) groom, *m.*; petit domestique, *m.*; (*of a book*) page, *f.*; — *v.a.* paginer

Pageant, *s.* spectacle, *m.*, pompe, *f.*, — *adj.* d'apparat, pompeux, fastueux

Pageantry, *s.* pompe, *f.*, apparat, faste, *m.*

Paginal, *adj.* composé de pages; des pages

Pagination, *s.* pagination, *f.*

Paging, *s.* pagination, *f.*; (*print.*) numérotage, *m.* — **machine,** *s.* machine à numéroter, *f.*, numéroteur mécanique, *m.*

Pagod, Pagoda, *s.* pagode, *f.* — **sleeve,** *s.* manche pagode, *f.*

Paid, *part. adj.* payé, &c. (*V.* **Pay,** *v.a.*); (*of bills*) acquitté; (*to be written on a receipt before o.'s signature*) pour acquit, acquitté; (*of letters, &c.*) affranchi; (*on a parcel*) port payé. —, — **up,** payé; (*of capital, fin.*) versé; (*of shares, fin.*) libéré. *Fully* — *up,* entièrement libéré. 25 *francs* — *up,* libéré de 25 francs

Pail, *s.* seau, *m.* —**ful,** *s.* seau, seau plein,

Paillasse, *s.* paillasse, *f.* [plein un seau, *m.*

Pain, *s.* (*bodily*) douleur, *f.*, mal, *m.*; (*mental*) peine, *f.*; (*penalty*) peine, *f.*; —**s**, *pl.* peine, *f.*, travail, *m.*, fatigue, *f.*; (*care*) soins, *m.pl.*; — *v.a.* faire mal à, causer de la douleur à; (*afflict*) peiner, faire de la peine à, affliger. *In* —, souffrant. *In great* —, très souffrant. *On* or *under* — *of,* sous peine de. *To be at the* (or *some*) —*s*, prendre la peine (de); faire des frais (pour). *To be in* —, être souffrant, souffrir. *To be in great* —, être très souffrant, souffrir beaucoup. *To have o.'s labour for o.'s* —*s*, en être pour sa peine. *To give* — *to,* (*bodily*) faire du mal à, faire mal à, causer de la douleur à; (*mentally*) faire de la peine à, affliger. *To suffer* —, souffrir. *To take* —*s*, prendre *or* se donner de la peine; (*with* ...) soigner (...). —**ful,** *adj.* douloureux; (*distressing*) pénible, douloureux; (*toilsome*) pénible, laborieux. — **fully,** *adv.* douloureusement; (*with affliction*) péniblement, douloureusement; (*with toil*) péniblement, laborieusement. —**fulness,** *s.* douleur, *f.*; (*affliction*) peine, douleur, *f.*; (*toil*) peine, *f.*, labeur, travail, *m.*, fatigue, *f.* —**less,** *adj.*, —**lessly,** *adv.* sans douleur; sans peine. —**lessness,** *s.* absence de douleur, *f.* —**s-taker,** *s.* travailleur, *m.*, -euse, *f.* —**s-taking,** *adj.* laborieux; *s.* peine, *f.*, labeur, travail, *m.*; (*care*) soin, *m.*

Paint, *v.a.n.* peindre; (*o.'s face*) se farder; se grimer, se maquiller; — *s.* couleur, *f.*; peinture, *f.*; enduit, *m.*; (*for the face*) fard, rouge, *m.* *To* — *black, red,* &c., peindre en noir, en rouge, &c. — **box,** *s.* boîte de *or* à couleurs, *f.* — **brush,** *s.* pinceau, *m.*

Painted, *part. adj.* peint, &c. (*V.* **Paint,** *v.a.*); (*of glass*) peint; de couleur

Painter, *s.* peintre, *m.*; (*nav.*) câbleau, *m.* —**s'** *colic,* colique des peintres, *f.* —*s' cream,* pommade à retoucher, *f.* — **stainer,** *s.* peintre de blason, *m.* [*m.*, peinture, *f.*

Painting, *s.* peinture, *f.*; (*picture*) tableau,

Paintress, *s.* peintre, peintresse, *f.*

Pair, *s.* (*things*) paire, *f.*; (*pers.*) couple, *m.*; (*live animals*) paire, *f.*, (*male and female*) paire, *f.*, couple, *m.*; (*brace, of game, poultry, fish, &c., for the table*) couple, *f.*; — *v.a.* accoupler; (*fig.*) assortir, apparier, appareiller; (*pers.*) unir; (*of colours*) marier; — *v.n.* (*of birds*) s'accoupler, s'apparier; (*suit*) s'assortir, se convenir; (— **off**) (*parliam.*) s'abstenir *or* s'absenter simultanément, s'abstenir par compensation de votes contraires. *Carriage* (*chaise,* &c.) *and* —, voiture (chaise, &c.) à deux chevaux, *f.* — **royal,** *s.* (*at cards*) brelan, *m.*

Pairing, *s.* accouplement, *m.*; appariement, *m.* — **off,** *s.* (*parliam.*) abstention *or* absence simultanée, absence convenue d'un membre ministériel et d'un membre de l'opposition, *f.* — **time,** *s.* saison de l'accouplement, *f.*

Pal, *s.* compère, *m.*, acolyte, *m.f.*, complice, *m.f.*, (*slang*) franc, *m.*

Palace, *s.* palais, *m.*; (*bishop's*) évêché, *m.*; (*archbishop's*) archevêché, *m.*

Paladin, *s.* paladin, *m.*

Palæo ..., *V.* **Paleo ...**

Palanquin, *s.* palanquin, *m.*

Palatable, *adj.* agréable au goût; agréable; bon

Palatableness, *s.* goût agréable, *m.*

Palatably, *adv.* agréablement

Palatal, *adj.s.* palatal, *adj.m.*, e, *f.*, palatale, *s.f.*

Palate, *s.* palais, *m.*; (*taste*) goût, *m.* *Hard* —, voûte du palais, *f.* *Soft* —, voile du palais, *m.*

Palatial, *adj.* du palais

Palatinate, *s.* palatinat, *m.* *Lower* —, Bas palatinat. *Upper* —, Haut palatinat

Palatine, *adj.s.* palatin, *adj.m.*, e, *f.*, palatin, *s.m.*

Palaver, *s.* palabre, *f.*, verbiage, *m.*, discours frivoles, *m.pl.*, sornettes, *f.pl.*; (*flattery*) flagornerie, *f.*; — *v.n.* parler pour ne rien dire, faire des phrases; verbiager; radoter; déclamer; (*flatter*) flagorner; — *v.a.* flagorner

Palaverer, *s.* (*twaddler*) *V.* **Twaddler;** (*flatterer*) flagorneur, *m.*, -euse, *f.*

Pale, *adj.* pâle; (*weak*) faible, lâche; (*of red wine*) paillet, clairet; (*of beer*) blanc; — *s.* pieu, palis, *m.*; (*enclosure*) enceinte, sphère, *f.*; (*bounds*) limites, *f.pl.*; (*of the Church*) giron, sein, *m.*; (*torture, her.*) pal, *m.*; — *v.a.* palissader, clore, entourer de palis; (*encompass*) embrasser; contenir; (*make pale*) faire pâlir; pâlir; ternir; effacer, éclipser; — *v.n.* pâlir; se ternir; s'effacer, s'éclipser. — *as a sheet,* blanc comme un linge. — *as death,* — *as ashes,* pâle comme la mort, d'une pâleur mortelle. *To grow* or *turn* or *make* —, pâlir ('*with,*' de). — **eyed,** *adj.* aux yeux ternes. — **faced,** *adj.* au teint pâle

Palely, *adv.* avec pâleur

Paleness, *s.* pâleur, *f.*

Paleographer, *s.* paléographe, *m.*

Pale-ographic, al, -ography, -ology, -ontography, -ontology, &c., paléographique, &c. (*V.* page 3, § 1)

Paleontologist, *s.* paléontologue, *m.*

Paleosaurus, *s.* paléosaure, *m.*

Paleotherium, *s.* paléothérium, *m.*

Paletot, *s.* paletot, *m.*

Palette, *s.* palette, *f.* — **knife,** *s.* couteau à palette, *m.*, amassette, *f.*

Palfrey, *s.* palefroi, *m.*

Palfreyed, *adj.* monté sur un palefroi

Pâli, *adj. s.* pâli, *adj. m.*, e, *f.*, pâli, *s.m.*

Palification, *s.* palification, *f.*

Palify, *v.a.* palifier

Palikare, Palikary, *s.* palikare, *m.*

Palimpsest, *s.* palimpseste, *m.*

Paling, *s.* palis, *m.*, palissade, *f.*; (*enclosing*) palissadement, *m.*

Palingenes-ia, is, y, *s.* palingénésie, *f.*

Palinode, Palinody, *s.* palinodie, *f.*

Palisade, *s.* palissade, *f.*; — *v.a.* palissader
Palisading, *s.* palissadement, *m.*
Palish, *adj.* un peu pâle, pâlot
Pall, *s.* manteau, *m.*; (*eccl.*) pallium, *m.*; (*chalice-covering*) pale, palle, *f.*; (*of funerals*) poêle, drap mortuaire, *m*; (*of a ratchet wheel*) palette, *f.*; (*her.*) pallium, pairle, *m.*; — *v.a.* couvrir d'un manteau; couvrir, recouvrir, envelopper; (*make vapid*) éventer; (*fig.*) affadir, rendre fade *or* insipide; (*the taste*) blaser; (*to blunt*) émousser; (*deaden*) amortir; (*depress*) abattre, décourager, refroidir; éteindre; (*satiate, cloy*) rassasier; (*weaken, impair*) affaiblir, altérer; — *v.n.* s'éventer; (*fig.*) s'affadir, devenir fade *or* insipide; (*weaken*) s'affaiblir, diminuer, baisser. *To hold* or *bear the* —, tenir *or* porter les coins (*or* les cordons) du poêle (*or* du drap mortuaire). — **bearer, -holder,** *s.* personne qui porte un des coins du poêle, *f.* — **mall,** *s.* mail, *m.*
Palladium, *s.* palladium, *m.*
Pallas, *s.* Pallas, *f.*
Pallet, *s.* palette, *f.*; (*a bed*) grabat, lit de veille, *m.*
Palliass, Palliasse, *s.* paillasse, *f.*
Palliate, *v.a.* pallier
Palliating, *adj.* palliatif
Palliation, *s.* palliation, *f.*
Palliative, *adj. s.* palliatif, *adj.m.*, -ive, *f.*, palliatif, *s.m.*
Palliator, *s.* palliateur, *m.*, -trice, *f.*
Palliatory, *adj.* palliateur, palliatif
Pallid, *adj.* pâle; blême
Pallidity, Pallidness, *s.* pâleur, *f*
Pallium, *s.* pallium, *m.*
Pallor, *s.* pâleur, *f.*
Palm, *s.* (*of the hand*) paume, *f.*; (*of a glove*) empaumure, *f.*; (*hand*) main, *f.*; (*sailmaker's*) paumelle, *f.*; (*of an anchor*) patte, *f.*; (*meas.*) palme, *m.f.*; (*tree*) palmier, *m.*; (*branch*) palme, *f.*; (*victory*) palme, victoire, *f.*, triomphe, *m.*; — *adj.* (*of the tree*) de palmier; palmiste; — *v.a.* (*conceal*) cacher dans la paume de la main, escamoter; (*to handle*) manier; (*impose*) imposer, glisser, couler; faire passer (pour); (*attribute*) attribuer. — **bird,** *s.* palmiste, *m.* — **branch,** *s.* palme, *f.* — **cabbage,** *s.* chou-palmiste, *m.* — **cat,** *s.* genette, *f.* — **honey,** *s.* miel de palme, *m.* — **house,** *s.* palmerie, serre à palmiers, *f.* — **leaf,** *s.* feuille de palmier, *f.*; (*ornament*) palmette, *f.* — **oil,** *s.* huile de palme, *f.*, pumicin, *m.* — **plantation,** *s.* palmerie, *f.* — **sap,** *s.* palmite, *m.* — **sugar,** *s.* sucre de palme, *m.* — **Sunday,** *s.* dimanche des Rameaux, *m.* — **tree,** *s.* palmier, *m.* — — **wax,** *s.* cire de palme, *f.* — **wine,** *s.* vin de palme, *m.*
Palma-christi, *s.* palma-christi, ricin, *m.*
Palmar, *adj.* palmaire
Palmary, *adj.* principal; fameux, célèbre
Palmate, Palmated, *adj.* palmé
Palmature, *s.* palmature, *f.*
Palmed, *adj.* palmé [— **worm,** *s.* chenille, *f.*
Palmer, *s.* (*pers.*) pèlerin, *m.*; (*thing*) férule, *f.*
Palmetto, *s.* palmette, *f.*; palmiste, *m.*
Palmiped, *adj. s.* palmipède, *adj.m.f.*, *s.m.*
Palmister, *s.* chiromancien, *m.*, -ne, *f.*
Palmistry, *s.* chiromancie, *f.*; (*jest.*) escamotage, *m*
Palmitic, *adj.* palmitique
Palmitine, *s.* palmitine, *f.*
Palmy, *adj.* chargé de palmes; (*fig.*) victorieux, triomphant, glorieux; (*prosperous*) heureux; (*happy*) heureux, beau; joyeux
Palp, *s.* palpe, *m.*
Palpa-bility, bleness. *V.* page 3, § 1
Palpable, *adj.* palpable; visible; évident; manifeste
Palpably, *adv.* palpablement, d'une manière palpable, visiblement, évidemment
Palpation, *s.* palpation, *f.*, palper, *m.*
Palpitate, *v.n.* palpiter
Palpitation, *s.* palpitation, *f.*
Palsgrave, *s.* comte palatin, *m.*
Palsgravine, *s.* comtesse palatine, *f.*
Palsical, *adj.* paralytique; paralysé
Palsy, *s.* paralysie, *f.*; — *v.a.* paralyser
Palter, *v.n.* tergiverser, biaiser; (*trifle*) jouer, plaisanter
Palterer, *s.* tergiversateur, *m.*, -trice, *f.*, biaiseur, *m.*, -euse, *f.*
Paltering, *s.* tergiversation, *f.*, biaisement, *m.*
Paltrily, *adv.* mesquinement
Paltriness, *s.* petitesse, mesquinerie, *f.*
Paltry, *adj.* méchant, misérable, mesquin, chétif, pauvre
Paludal, Paludine, *adj.* paludéen
Paly, *adj.* (*her.*) palé
Pampa, *s.* pampa, *f.* —**s grass,** *s.* gynérion, *m.* —**s hare,** *s.* pampa, *m.*
Pampean, *adj.* pampéen
Pamper, *v.a.* gorger, rassasier; (*indulge*) choyer; dorloter; caresser, flatter
Pampered, *part. adj.* gorgé, &c. (*V.* **Pamper**); bien nourri; riche, abondant. — *menial*, valet fainéant, *m.*
Pamphlet, *s.* brochure, *f.*; (*violent*) pamphlet, *m.*
Pamphleteer, *s.* auteur de brochures, *m.*; (*violent*) pamphlétaire, *m.*
Pamphleteering, *adj.* qui écrit des brochures *or* des pamphlets; — *s.* publication de brochures *or* de pamphlets, *f.*
Pan, *s.* chaudière, *f.*; (*frying* —) poêle, *f.*; (*sauce* or *stew* —) casserole, *f.*; poêlon, *m.*; bassine, *f.*; (*earthen*) terrine, *f.*; jatte, *f.*; (*pharm.*, &c.) bassine, *f.*; (*tech.*, &c.) bassine, *f.*; bassin, *m.*; cuvette, *f.*; (*of flint-locks*) bassinet, *m.*; (*subsoil*) tuf, *m.*; (*myth.*) Pan, *m.* *V.* **Baking, Coal, Dripping, Frying, Preserving, Warming,** &c. —**cake,** *s.* crêpe, *f.* —**ful,** *s.* poêlée, *f.* —**'s-pipes,** *s.pl.* flûte de Pan, *f.*
Panacea, *s.* panacée, *f.*
Panache, *s.* panache, *m.*
Panada, *s.* panade, *f.*
Panakin, *s.* réchaud, vase, dessus de veilleuse, *f.*
Panama. — **grass,** *s.*, — **hat,** *s.* panama, *m.*
Panary, *adj.* panaire
Pancake, *s.* crêpe, *f.*
Pancarte, Pancharta, *s.* pancarte, *f.*
Pancreas, *s.* pancréas, *m.*
Pancreatic, *adj.* pancréatique
Panda, *s.* panda, *m.*
Pandean, *adj.* de Pan. — **pipes,** *s.pl.* flûte de Pan, *f.*
Pandect, *s.* traité complet, *m.*; —**s,** *pl.* (*law*) Pandectes, *f.pl.*
Pandemonium, *s.* Pandémonium, *m.*
Pander, *s.* complaisant, *m*; — *v.n.* se prêter (à), favoriser; (*to a person*) se faire complaisant (de)
Panderism, *s.* métier de complaisant *or* d'entremetteur, *m.*
Panderly, *adj.* complaisant
Pandit, *s.* pandit, *m.*
Pandour, *s.* pandour, *m.*
Pane, *s.* panneau, compartiment, *m.*; carreau, *m.*; (*of glass*) vitre, *f.*, (*square*) carreau, *m.*; (*of a hammer*) panne, *f.* — *of glass*, — *of window*, vitre, *f.*, carreau de vitre, *m.* — *of painted glass*, — *of painted window*, vitre de couleur, *f.* —**less,** *adj.* sans vitres
Panegyric, -al, *adj. s.* panégyrique, *adj.m.f.*, *s.m.*
Panegyrist, *s.* panégyriste, *m.*
Panegyrize, *v.a.* faire le panégyrique de, louer, élogier; — *v.n.* faire un panégyrique
Panel, *s.* (*arch.*, *carp.*) panneau, *m.*; (*law*) liste, *f.*, tableau, *m.*; jury, *m.*; (*pannel*) *V.* **Pannel**; — *v.a.* diviser par panneaux, faire à panneaux or à compartiments; (*wainscot*) lambrisser. — **door,** *s.* porte à placard, *f.* — **plank,** *s.* feuillet, *m.*
Panelled, *adj.* à panneaux
Panelling, *s.* panneaux, lambris, *m.pl.*, boiserie, *f.*; lambrissage, *m.*
Panful, *s.* poêlée, *f.*
Pang, *s.* angoisse, douleur, *f.*, tourment, *m.*; serrement de cœur, *m.*; saisissement, *m.*; — *v.a.* tourmenter, faire souffrir
Pangermanism, *s.* pangermanisme, *m.*
Pangolin, *s.* pangolin, *m.*
Panhellen-ic, -ism, panhellénique, &c. (*V.* page 3, § 1)
Panic, *adj.* panique; — *s.* panique, terreur panique, *f.*; frayeur subite, *f.*; (*bot.*) panic,

panis, *m.* — **grass,** *s.* panic, panis, *m.* — **struck, -stricken,** *adj.* saisi d'une terreur panique *or* d'une frayeur subite
Panicle, Panicule, *s.* panicule, *f.*
Panicled, Paniculate, -d, *adj.* paniculé
Panifiable, *adj.* panifiable
Panification, *s.* panification, *f.*
Panify, *v.a.n.* panifier
Pannade, *s.* courbette, *f.*
Pannage, *s.* panage, *m.*
Pannel, *s.* (*rough saddle*) bât, *m.*; (*part of a saddle*) panneau, *m.*; (*falc.*) mullette, *f.*; (*panel*) *V.* **Panel**
Pannier, *s.* panier, *m.*; hotte, *f.*; cacolet, *m.*
Pannikin. *V.* **Panakin**
Pannonian, *s. adj.* Pannonien, *m*, -ne, *f.*
Panoply, *s.* panoplie, armure, *f.*
Panoptical, *adj.* panoptique
Panopticon, *s.* panoptique, *m.*
Panorama, *s.* panorama, *m.* [rama
Panoramic, -al, *adj.* panoramique, de pano-
Panslavism, *s.* panslavisme, *m.*
Pansteorama, *s.* panstéorama, *m.*
Pansy, *s.* pensée, *f.*
Pant, *v.n.* haleter; palpiter, battre; (*to long for*) soupirer (après). *To — for breath,* haleter
Pantagraph. *V.* **Pantograph**
Pantalets, Pantalettes, *s.pl. V.* **Trousers**
Pantaloon, *s.* pantalon, *m.*; (*tight* —) pantalon collant, *m.*; (*pers.*) Pantalon, *m.*; **—s,** *pl.* pantalon. *m.*; (*tight* —) pantalon collant, *m.*; (*more than one pair*) pantalons, *m.pl.*; pantalons collants, *m.pl.* *A pair of —s,* un pantalon, *m.*; (*tight* —) un pantalon collant, *m.*
Pantaloonery, *s.* pantalonnade, *f.*
Pantechnicon, *s.* garde-meubles, *m.*
Panthe-ism, -ist, &c., panthéisme, &c. (*V.* page 3, § 1)
Pantheon, *s.* Panthéon, *m.*
Panther, *s.* panthère, *f.*
Pantherine, *adj.* panthérin
Pantile, *s.* tuile faîtière, faîtière, *f.*
Panting, *part. adj.* haletant, &c. (*V.* **Pant,** *v.n.*); — *s.* palpitation, *f.*, battement de cœur, *m.*; respiration difficile, *f.*; ardent désir, *m.*
Pantingly, *adv.* en haletant; en palpitant
Pantler, *s.* panetier, *m.*
Pantograph, *s.* pantographe, singe, *m.*
Pantograph-ic, al, -ically, -y. *V.* p. 3, § 1
Pantometer, *s.* pantomètre, *m.*
Pantomime, *s.* pantomime, (*thing*) *f.*, (*pers.*) *m.f.*; — *adj.* pantomime
Pantomim-ic, al, -ically. *V.* page 3, § 1
Pantomimist, *s.* pantomime, *m.f.*
Panton, — shoe, *s.* fer à pantoufle, *m.*
Pantoscope, *s.* pantoscope, *m.*
Pantoscopic, *adj.* pantoscopique
Pantry, *s.* office, *f.*, garde-manger, *m.*
Pants, *s.pl. V.* **Trousers** [*fruit*) pulpe, *f.*
Pap, *s.* mamelon, *m.*; (*food*) bouillie, *f.*; (*of*
Papa, *s.* papa, père, *m.*; (*a bird*) pape, *m.*
Papacy, *s.* papauté, *f.*
Papal, *adj.* papal, du pape. *The — States,* les États du pape (*or* de l'Église), *m.pl.*
Papaveraceæ, *s.pl.* papavéracées, *f.pl.* [véracé
Papaveraceous, Papaverous, *adj.* papa-
Papaverine, *s.* papavérine, *f.*
Papaw, *s.* papaye, *f.* — **tree,** *s.* papayer, *m.*
Paper, *s.* papier, *m.*; document, *m.*; mémoire, *m.*; bulletin, *m.*; liste, *f.*; écrit, *m.*; discours écrit, *m.*; essai, *m.*; (*sheet of* —) feuille de papier, *f.*; (*bill, of lodgings to let,* &c.) écriteau, *m.*; (*leaflet*) imprimé, *m.*; (*written task, in schools*) copie, *f.*; (*of exam.*) composition, *f.*; (*in newspapers,* &c.) article, *m.*; (*newspaper*) journal, *m.*; (*com.*) papier, *m.*, valeurs, *f.pl.*, billets, *m.pl.*; (*packet*) paquet, *m.*; (*screw*) cornet, *m.*; (*curl —, and cook.*) papillote, *f.*; — *adj.* (*of paper*) de papier; (*for paper*) à papier; (*thin*) mince; — *v.a.* couvrir *or* recouvrir de papier; envelopper de papier; (*a room*) tapisser *or* tendre (de papier peint), décorer de papier; (*write*) coucher par écrit. *Public —s,* papiers publics, journaux, *m.pl.* — **balance,** *s.* pèse-papier, *m.* — **cap,** *s.* (*for wrapping*) cornet de papier, cornet, *m.* — **case,** *s.* papeterie, *f.*; buvard, *m.* — **clip,** *s. V.* — **holder.** — **cone,** *s. V.* — **cap.** — **credit,** *s. V.* — **money.** — **cup,** *s. V.* — **cap.** — **currency,** *s. V.* — **money.** — **cutter, -cutting machine,** *s.* coupe-papier, *m.* — **folder,** *s.* plioir, *m.* — **hanger,** *s.* colleur, de papier, colleur, *m.*; décorateur, *m.* — **hanging,** *s.* papier peint, papier de tenture, *m.* — **holder,** *s.* serre-papiers, serre-notes, *m.* — **kite,** *s.* cerf-volant, *m.* — **knife,** *s.* couteau à papier, coupe-papier, *m.* — **maker, -manufacturer,** *s.* fabricant de papier, *m.* — **making, -manufacture,** *s.* fabrication du papier, papeterie, *f.* — **manufactory,** *s.* fabrique de papier, papeterie, *f.* — **mill,** *s.* moulin à papier, *m.*, papeterie, *f.* — **money,** *s.* papier-monnaie, *m.* — **mulberry,** *s.* broussonétie, *f.*, mûrier à papier, *m.* — **nautilus,** *s.* nautile papyracé, argonaute, *m.* — **ruler,** *s.* régleur (de papier), *m.* — **stainer,** *s.* fabricant de papiers peints, *m.*; dominotier, *m.* — **staining,** *s.* fabrication de papiers peints, *f.*; dominoterie, *f.* — **trade,** *s.* papeterie, *f.* — **war,** *s.* guerre de plume, polémique, *f.* — **warehouse,** *s.* magasin de papier, *m.*, papeterie, *f.* — **weigher,** *s.* pèse-papier, *m.* — **weight,** *s.* presse-papiers, *m.* — **window,** *s.* châssis de papier, *m.*
Papered, *part. adj.* tapissé *or* décoré de papier, &c. (*V.* **Paper,** *v.a.*); de papier
Papess, *s.* papesse, *f.*
Papier mâché, *s.* papier mâché, *m.*
Papilionaceous, *adj.* papilionacé
Papilla, *s.* papille, *f.*
Pap-ism, -ist, -istic. *V.* page 3, § 1
Papistry, *s.* papisme, *m.* [culent
Pappy, *adj.* comme de la bouillie; mou; suc-
Papuan, *s. adj.* Papou, *m.*, e, *f.*
Papyraceous, *adj.* papyracé
Papyrus, *s.* papyrus, *m.*
Par, *s.* pair, *m.*; (*fish*) *V.* **Parr.** *Above —,* au-dessus du pair. *At —,* au pair. *Below —,* au-dessous du pair; (*fig.*) au-dessous du médiocre. *On a —,* de pair (avec), sur un pied d'égalité (avec), égal (à), au niveau (de)
Parable, *s.* parabole, *f.*
Parabola, *s.* parabole, *f.*
Parabol-ic, al, -ically. *V.* page 3, § 1
Paraboloid, *s.* paraboloïde, *m.*
Paracentesis, *s.* paracentèse, *f.*
Para-centric, -chronism. *V.* page 3, § 1
Parachute, *s.* parachute, *m.*
Paraclete, *s.* paraclet, *m.*
Parade, *s.* parade, *f.*; (— *ground*) place d'armes, place, *f.*; (*public walk*) promenade, *f.*; avenue, *f.*; terrasse, *f.*; esplanade, *f.*; cours, *m.*; boulevard, *m.*; — *v.a.* faire faire la parade à; promener; (*boast*) faire parade de; — *v.n.* parader. *On —,* (*mil.*) à la parade. *To make a — of,* faire parade de
Paradigm, *s.* paradigme, *m.*
Paradise, *s.* paradis, *m.* *Bird of —,* oiseau de paradis, *m.* *Grain of —,* graine de paradis, *f.*
Paradisiacal, Paradisian, *adj.* paradisiaque
Paradox, *s.* paradoxe, *m.*
Paradoxical, *adj.* paradoxal
Paradoxically, *adv.* paradoxalement
Paradoxicalness, *s.* nature paradoxale, *f.*
Paraffin, Paraffine, *s.* paraffine, *f.*
Paragon, *s.* modèle parfait, *m.*
Paragrandine, *s.* paragrêle, *m.*
Paragraph, *s.* paragraphe, *m.*; (*in a newspaper*) entre-filets, article, *m.*; (*break in a line*) alinéa, *m.* [composé d'alinéas
Paragraphic, -al, *adj.* divisé en paragraphes;
Paragraphically, *adv.* par paragraphes; par
Paragraphist, *s.* faiseur d'alinéas, *m.* [alinéas
Para grass, *s.* piassava, *m.*
Paraguayan, *adj. s.* paraguayen, paraguéen
Paralipomena, *s.pl.* Paralipomènes, *m.pl.*

Parallactic, -al, *adj.* parallactique
Parallax, *s.* parallaxe, *f.*
Parallel, *adj.* ('*to*' *or* '*with*,' à) parallèle; (*similar*) pareil, semblable; (*adverb.*) parallèlement (à); — *s.* ligne parallèle, parallèle, *f.*; (*geom.*, *fort.*) parallèle, *f.*; (*astr.*, *geog.*) parallèle, *m.*; (*comparison*) parallèle, *m.*; comparaison, *f.*; (*conformity*) conformité, *f.*; ressemblance, *f.*; (*equal*) égal, *m.*; (*example*) exemple, *m.*; — *v.a.* mettre en parallèle, comparer (à); (*to place parallelly*) placer parallèlement; (*to level, equal*) mettre sur la même ligne; (*correspond*) correspondre à; (*to be equal*) être pareil à. — **ruler,** *s.* parallélographe, parallèle, *m.*
Parallelepiped, *s.* parallélépipède, parallélipipède, *m.*
Parallelism, *s.* parallélisme, *m.*; comparaison, *f.*; ressemblance, *f.*; conformité, *f.*; correspondance, *f.*
Parallelistic, *adj.* parallélique
Parallelly, *adv.* parallèlement
Parallelogram, *s.* parallélogramme, *m.*
Parallelopiped. *V.* **Parallelepiped**
Paralogism, &c. *V.* page 3, § 1
Paralysis, *s.* paralysie, *f.*
Paralytic, *adj.* paralytique; de paralysie; — *s.* paralytique, *m.f.* — *stroke,* attaque de paralysie, *f.* *To be affected by a — stroke,* être frappé de paralysie, avoir une attaque de paralysie
Paralyze, *v.a.* paralyser
Paramount, *adj.* (*things*) souverain, suprême; (*to*) supérieur (à); (*pers.*) principal, en chef; (*feud.*) dominant, suzerain. *Lord* —, seigneur dominant *or* suzerain, *m.*
Paramour, *s.* amant, *m.*, maîtresse, *f.*
Parapet, *s.* parapet, *m.* — **wall,** *s.* parapet, *m.*
Paraph, *s.* parafe, *m.*; — *v.a.* parafer
Paraphernal, *adj.* paraphernal
Paraphernalia, *s. pl.* biens paraphernaux, paraphernaux, *m. pl.*; (*trappings*) attirail, équipement, équipage, *m.*; (*finery*) atours, affiquets, chiffons, falbalas, *m.pl.*
Paraphernality, *s.* paraphernalité, *f.*
Paraphrase, *s.* paraphrase, *f.*; — *v.a.n.* paraphraser
Paraphraser, *s.* paraphraseur, *m.*, -euse, *f.*
Paraphrast, *s.* paraphraste, *m.*
Paraphrast-ic, al, -ically. *V.* page 3, § 1
Paraplegia, *s.* paraplégie, *f.*
Paraselene, *s.* parasélène, *f.*
Parasite, *s.* parasite, *m.f.*; (*bot.*) plante parasite, *f.*
Parasitic, -al, *adj.* parasitique, de parasite, parasite; (*plant, insect*) parasite
Parasit-ically, -ism. *V.* page 3, § 1
Parasiticalness, *s.* parasitisme, *m.*
Parasol, *s.* parasol, *m.*; (*of ladies*) ombrelle, *f.* *Jointed-handle* —, marquise, *f.*
Parboil, *v.a.* faire bouillir à demi, faire cuire à demi
Parboiled, *adj.* à demi bouilli, à demi cuit
Parbuckle, *s.* trévire, *f.*; — *v.a.* trévirer
Parcæ, *s. pl.* Parques, *f.pl.*
Parcel, *s.* (*bundle*) paquet, *m.*; (*of corn cut down*) javelle, *f.*; (*set*) tas. *m.*; (*piece*) parcelle, pièce, *f.*; partie, *f.*; — *v.a.* (— **out**) partager, diviser; distribuer; parceller; (*land*) morceler. *By —s,* par parcelles, par parties. *A — of nonsense, of people,* un tas de sottises, de gens. *In my next* —, (*com.*) dans mon prochain envoi. *To be part and — of,* faire partie intégrante de. **—s delivery,** *s.* factage, *m.* **—s delivery company,** *s.* compagnie de factage, *f.* **—s office,** *s.* bureau de factage *or* de messagerie, *m.*
Parcelling, — out, *s.* division, distribution, *f.*, partage, *m.*; parcellement, *m.*; (*of land*) morcellement, *m.*
Parcenary, *s.* propriété indivise, *f.* *In* —, par indivis
Parcener, *s.* propriétaire indivis, *m.*
Parch, *v.a.* brûler, griller, rôtir; (*to dry*) dessécher; — *v.n.* se brûler, être grillé, se rôtir; (*to become dry*) se dessécher
Parchedness, *s.* état brûlé, *m.*; (*dryness*) aridité, sécheresse, *f.*
Parching, *adj.* brûlant
Parchment, *s.* parchemin, *m.* — **factory,** *s.* parcheminerie, *f.* — **like,** *adj.* parcheminé. — **maker,** *s.* parcheminier, *m.* — **making,** *s.* parcheminerie, *f.* — **paper,** *s.* papier parchemin, *m.* — **trade,** *s.*, — **works,** *s. pl.* parcheminerie, *f.*
Pardon, *v.a.n.* *V.* **Forgive;** (*law*) gracier; — *s.* pardon, *m.*; (*law*) grâce, remise, *f.* — *me!* pardonnez-moi! pardon! *I beg your* —, je vous demande pardon; pardon!
Pardonable, *adj.* pardonnable, excusable; (*law*) graciable
Pardonableness, *s.* nature pardonnable, *f.*
Pardonably, *adv.* d'une manière pardonnable
Pardoner, Pardoning. *V.* **Forgiver, Forgiving**
Pare, *v.a.* rogner; (*fruit, cheese,* &c.) peler; (*turf, cloth,* &c.) tondre; (*quills,* &c.) ébarber; (*o.'s nails*) se rogner (les ongles); (*a horse's hoof*) parer. — *and burn,* (*peat lands,* &c.) écobuer. — **away, off,** couper, enlever, ôter
Paregoric, *adj. s.* parégorique, *adj.m.f.*, *s.m.*
Parella, *s.* parelle, *f.*
Parenchyma, *s.* parenchyme, *m.*
Parenchymatous, *adj.* parenchymateux
Parent, *s.* père, *m.*, mère, *f.*; (*cause*) cause, source, *f.*; **—s,** *pl.* parents, *m.pl.*; — *adj.* mère, principal. — **bank,** *s.* banque mère, *f.* — **country** *or* **state,** *s.V.* **Mother-country.** **—less,** *adj.* sans père, sans mère, sans parents
Parentage, *s.* parentage, *m.*, extraction, naissance, famille, *f.*
Parental, *adj.* des parents; de père, paternel; de mère, maternel
Parenthesis, *s.* parenthèse, *f.* *By way of* —, par parenthèse. *In a* —, entre parenthèses
Parenthetic, -al, *adj.* par parenthèse, entre parenthèses
Parenthetically, *adv.* par parenthèse
Parer, *s.* rogneur, *m.*, -euse, *f.*; (*of fruit*) peleur, *m.*, -euse, *f.*; (*tool*) rognoir, ébarboir, paroir, *m.*; (*vet.*) boutoir, paroir, *m.*
Parget, *s.* (*mas.*) pigeonnage, *m.*; — *v.a.* pigeonner
Pargeting, *s.* pigeonnage, *m.*
Parhelion, *s.* parhélie, *m.*
Paria, Pariah, *s.* paria, *m.* — **dog,** *s. V.* **Cur**
Parian, *adj.* parien, de Paros; — *s.* biscuit, *m.*
Parietal, *adj.* de mur; (*anat.*) pariétal
Parietary, *s.* pariétaire, *f.*
Paring, *s.* (*refuse*) rognures, *f.pl.*; (*of fruit, cheese,* &c.) pelures, *f.pl.*; (*of vegetables,* &c.) épluchures, *f.pl.*; (*act*) rognage, rognement, *m.*; épluchage, épluchement, *m.* — *and burning,* (*of peat-lands,* &c.) écobuage, *m.* — **chisel,** *s.* (*carp.*) bédane, bec-d'âne, *m.* — **knife,** *s.* tranchet, éplucheir, *m.* — **plough, -spade,** *s. V.* **Breast-plough**
Paris, *s.*, *Herb* —, parisette, *f.*
Parish, *s.* (*civil*) commune, *f.*, (*in England*) paroisse, *f.*; (*eccl.*) paroisse, *f.*; — *adj.* (*civil*) communal; de (*or* de la) commune; (*eccl.*) paroissial; de (*or* de la) paroisse; (*of roads*) communal, vicinal; (*of schools, rates*) communal. *To be brought* (or *to come*) *upon* (or *on*) *the* —, tomber à la charge de la commune (*in England,* ... de la paroisse). — **church,** *s.* paroisse, église paroissiale, *f.* — **clerk,** *s.* clerc de (*or* de la) paroisse, clerc de l'œuvre, *m.* — **poor,** *s.pl.* pauvres de la paroisse, *m.pl.* — **road,** *s.* chemin communal *or* vicinal, *m.* — **school,** *s.* école communale, *f.*
Parishioner, *s.* (*civil*) habitant (*m.*, e, *f.*) de la commune; (*eccl.*) paroissien, *m.*, -ne, *f.*
Parisian, *s.* Parisien, *m.*, -ne, *f.*; — *adj.* parisien, de Paris. — *woman* or *lady* or *girl,* Parisienne, *f.*
Paritor, *s.* appariteur, huissier, *m.*
Parity, *s.* parité, *f.*, rapport, *m.*
Park, *s.* parc, *m.*; — *adj.* de *or* du parc; (*of carriages*) de promenade; — *v.a.* parquer. *A — of artillery,* un parc d'artillerie. *Greenwich* —, le parc de Greenwich. — **keeper,** *s.* gardien de parc, *m.*
Parker, *s.* gardien de parc, *m.*; garde-chasse, *m.*

Parlance, *s.* conversation, *f.*; langage, *m.*
Parley, *v.n.* s'entretenir, converser; conférer; être en pourparler; discuter, raisonner; (*mil.*) parlementer; — *s.* pourparler, *m.*, conférence, *f.* *To beat* or *sound a* —, demander à parlementer, battre la chamade
Parliament, *s.* parlement, *m.*; (*in Republican France*) (l') Assemblée législative, *f.*; (*in Imperial do.*) (le) Corps législatif et (le) Sénat, *m.*, (*in Royal do.*) (la) Chambre des députés et (la) Chambre des pairs, (les) Chambres, *f.pl.*; (*of England, and in Fr. hist. till* 1790) parlement, *m.*; (*gingerbread*) pain d'épice, *m.* *Act of* —, acte du Parlement, *m.*, loi, *f.* *The Houses of* —, le palais du Parlement, *m.*, les Chambres, *f.pl.* [*s.m.*, *adj.m.f.*
Parliamentarian, *s. adj.* parlementaire,
Parliamentarianism, *s.* parlementarisme, *m.*
Parliamentarily, *adv.* parlementairement
Parliamentarism, *s.* parlementarisme, *m.*
Parliamentary, *adj.* parlementaire; du parlement; de la tribune. *V.* **Train**
Parlour, *s.* petit salon, *m.*; (*of a public-house,* &c.) salon, *m.*; salle commune, salle, *f.*; (*of convents, schools,* &c.) parloir, *m.* — **boarder,** *s.* pensionnaire (*or* élève) en chambre, *m.f.*
Parmelia, *s.* parmélie, *f.*
Parmesan, *s.* Parmesan, *m.*, e, *f.*; — *adj.* parmesan, de Parme. — **cheese,** *s.* parmesan, *m.*
Parnassia, *s.* parnassie, *f.*
Parnassian, *s.* Parnassien, *m.*, -ne, *f.*; — *adj.* parnassien, du Parnasse
Parnassius, *s.* parnassien, *m.*
Parochial, *adj.* *V.* **Parish,** *adj.* [par paroisse
Parochially, *adv.* (*civil*) par commune; (*eccl.*)
Parod-ic, al, -ist. *V.* page 3, § 1
Parody, *s.* parodie, *f.*; — *v.a.* parodier
Parole, *s.* parole, *f.*; — *adj.* (*law*) oral, verbal. *On* —, sur parole
Paroled, *adj.* sur parole; prisonnier sur parole
Paronomasia, *s.* paronomase, *f.*
Paronym, *s.* paronyme, *m.*
Paronym-ic, al, -y. *V.* page 3, § 1
Paronymous, *adj.* paronyme
Paroquet, *s.* perruche, *f.*
Parotid, *adj. s.* parotide, *f.*
Paroxysm, *s.* paroxysme, *m.*
Paroxysmal, *adj.* paroxyntique
Parquet, *s.* parquet, *m.*
Parquetage, *s.* parquetage, *m.*
Parquetry, *s.* parqueterie, *f.*
Parr, *s.* (*young salmon*) digitale, *f.*
Parricidal, *adj.* parricide
Parricide, *s.* parricide, (*pers.*) *m.f.*, (*murder*) *m.*
Parroquet. *V.* **Paroquet**
Parrot, *s.* (*bird*) perroquet, *m.*, (*female* —, *hen* —) perruche, *f.*; (*pers.*) perroquet, *m.* — **fish,** *s.* scare, poisson-perroquet, *m.*
Parry, *v.a.n.* parer; (*avoid*) éviter, éluder; (*fenc.*) parer; — *s.* parade, *f.* — *and thrust,* (*v.n.*) riposter; (*s.*) riposte, *f.*
Parrying, *s.* (*fenc.*) parade, *f.*
Parse, *v.a.* analyser
Parsee, *s. adj.* Parsi, *m.*, e, *f.*, Parse, *m.f.*
Parsimonious, *adj.* parcimonieux; économe
Parsimoniously, *adv.* parcimonieusement
Parsimoniousness, Parsimony, *s.* parcimonie, *f.*
Parsing, *s.* analyse, *f.*
Parsley, *s.* persil, *m.*
Parsnep, Parsnip, *s.* panais, *m.*
Parson, *s.* prêtre, ecclésiastique, *m.*; (*of a parochial church*) curé, *m.* —**'s nose,** *s.* (*of a fowl*) sot-l'y-laisse, *m.*
Parsonage. *V.* **Vicarage**
Parsonic, *adj.* de prêtre, d'ecclésiastique, ecclésiastique; de curé
Part, *s.* partie, *f.*; (*share*) part, *f.*; portion, *f.*; (*side, party*) parti, *m.*; (*place*) endroit, *m.*; localité, *f.*; point, *m.*; (*of towns*) quartier, *m.*; (*character*) rôle, *m.*; personnage, *m.*; (*duty*) devoir, *m.*; (*book-selling*) livraison, *f.*; (*butch.*) morceau, *m.*; (*mus.*) partie, *f.*; —**s,** *pl.* parties, *f.pl.*, &c.; (*qualities*) moyens, talents, *m.pl.*; (*regions*) contrées, *f.pl.*, pays, *m.pl.*; — *adv.* en partie, partie; — *v.a.* partager, diviser; (*of people*) séparer; (*nav.*, *of cables*) casser, rompre; — *v.n.* se séparer ('*from,*' '*with,*' de), se quitter, quitter; partir, s'en aller; (*let go*) se dessaisir (de); (*get rid of*) se défaire (de), abandonner, céder; (*nav.*) aller en dérive, démarrer; (*of cables*) se casser, se rompre. *For my* —, pour ma part; pour mon compte, pour moi, quant à moi. *For the most* —, pour la plupart; la plupart du temps. *From all* —*s*, de tous côtés. *In* —, en partie. *In a great* —, en grande partie. *In good* —, en bonne part, bien. *In ill* —, en mauvaise part, mal. *In* —*s*, (*of books*) par livraisons; en livraisons. *In the early* (or *latter*) — *of*, (*of a week, month,* &c.) dans les premiers (*or* derniers) jours de. *On my, his* or &c. —, de ma part, de sa part, &c.; de mon côté, de son côté, &c. *The greatest* —, *the most* —, la plus grande partie, la plupart. *Three* —*s*, (*three fourths, adject.*) aux trois quarts ... *To be* or *form a* — *of*, faire partie de. *To* — *from* (or *with*) *one*, se séparer de quelqu'un. *To* — *with*, (*get rid of*) se défaire de; abandonner, céder. *To perform* or *play* or *act a* —, jouer *or* remplir un rôle. *To take anyone's* —, prendre le parti *or* la défense de quelqu'un, prendre parti pour quelqu'un. *To take a* — *in*, prendre part à; partager. — **music,** *s.* morceau (*m.*, *or* morceaux, *m.pl.*) d'ensemble. — **owner,** *s.* copropriétaire, *m.f.*
Partake, *v.a.n.* partager, prendre part (à); participer (à), avoir part (à); (*to have the same qualities*) participer (de), tenir de la nature (de), tenir (de); (*eat of, a dish*) manger (de); (*have, a meal*) faire; (*take, some food or refreshment*) prendre. *To* — *of breakfast* or *lunch,* &c., déjeuner, &c.
Partaker, *s.* participant, *m.*; e, *f.* *To be a* — *of*, participer à, avoir *or* prendre part à; partager
Parte (Ex), *adj. adv.* d'une seule partie, de l'une des parties, d'un seul côté
Parterre, *s.* parterre, *m.*
Parthian, *s. adj.* Parthe, *m.f.*
Parthenon, *s.* Parthénon, *m.*
Parthenope, *s.* Parthénope, *f.*
Partial, *adj.* partial; (*fond of*) qui aime; (*in part*) partiel; particulier. *To be* — *to*, aimer, être amateur de, affectionner; avoir un faible pour. *To be very* — *to*, aimer beaucoup, être grand amateur de, &c.
Partiality, *s.* partialité, *f.*; préférence, prédilection, *f.*; affection, *f.*; faible, *m.*, faiblesse, *f.*
Partially, *adv.* partialement, avec partialité; (*in part*) partiellement, en partie
Partible, *adj.* partible, divisible
Partibus (In), in partibus
Participant, *adj.* participant (à), qui prend part (à), qui partage; — *s.* participant, *m.*, e, *f.*
Participate, *v.a.n.* *V.* **Partake** [part, *f.*
Participation, *s.* participation, *f.*; (*division*)
Participative, *adj.* participatif
Participatively, *adv.* participativement
Participial, *adj.* participial
Participially, *adv.* participialement
Participle, *s.* participe, *m.*
Particle, *s.* particule, *f.*; (*very small portion*) parcelle, *f.*; molécule, *f.*
Particular, *adj.* particulier; spécial; singulier; remarquable; à part; certain; tel; exact, précis, difficile, exigeant; recherché; pointilleux, scrupuleux, minutieux; détaillé, circonstancié; intime; — *s.* détail, *m.*, particularité, *f.*; point, *m.* *In* —, particulièrement, en particulier; spécialement. *To be* — *about it*, y regarder de près; y tenir. *I am not* — *to a franc*, je ne regarde pas à un franc. *Further* —*s*, plus amples détails. *For further* —*s apply to* ..., pour tous les renseignements s'adresser chez ... (*or* à ...)
Particular-ism, -ist. *V.* page 3, § 1

Particularity, *s.* particularité, *f.*; détail, *m.*
Particularization, *s.* particularisation, *f.*
Particularize, *v.a.* particulariser; spécifier; — *v.n.* entrer dans des détails
Particularly, *adv.* particulièrement; principalement, surtout; individuellement
Parting, *s.* séparation, *f.*; départ, *m.*; adieu, *m.*; (*of the hair*) raie, *f.*; — *adj.* d'adieu, de séparation; (*declining*) qui finit. — **cup, -glass,** *s.* vin *or* coup de l'étrier, *m.*
Partisan, *s.* partisan, *m.*; homme de parti, *m.*; (*halberd*) pertuisane, *f.* — **corps,** *s.* corps de partisans, *m.* — **warfare,** *s.* guerre de partisans, *f.*
Partisanship, *s.* esprit de parti, *m.*
Partition, *s.* partage, *m.*, répartition, *f.*; séparation, division, *f.*; morcellement, *m.*; (*of rooms*) cloison, *f.*; (*mus.*) partition, *f.*; — *v.a.* partager, diviser; morceler; (*rooms*) cloisonner, séparer par une cloison, séparer. — **wall,** *s.* mur de refend, *m.*; (*of a staircase*) échiffe, échiffre, *m.* [titif, *s.m.*
Partitive, *adj. s.* partitif, *adj.m.*, -ive, *f.*, par-
Partitively, *adv.* comme partitif
Partly, *adv.* en partie, partie. — *well and — ill*, *V.* **Well,** *adv.*
Partner, *s.* (*com.*) associé, *m.*, e, *f.*; sociétaire, *m.f.*; (*in dancing*) cavalier, *m.*, dame, *f.*, danseur, *m.*, -euse, *f.*, partenaire, *m.f.*; (*at play*) partenaire, *m.f.*; (*companion*) compagnon, *m.*, compagne, *f.*
Partnership, *s.* (*com.*) association, société, *f.*; (*law*) société, *f.*; (*arith.*) règle de société, *f.* *Dissolution of* —, dissolution de société, *f.* *To enter into — with*, s'associer avec
Partridge, *s.* perdrix, *f.* *Young* —, — **poult,** *s.* perdreau, *m.* — **shooting,** *s.* chasse aux perdrix, *f.*
Parturient, *adj.* prête à enfanter, qui accouche
Parturition, *s.* parturition, *f.*; enfantement, *m.*
Party, *s.* parti, *m.*; (*person contending at law, or contracting*, &c.) partie, *f.*; (*person concerned in*) partie intéressée, *f.*, intéressé, *m.*, e, *f.*; (*an accomplice*) complice (de), *m.f.*; (*an individual*) personne, *f.*, individu, *m.*; (*company*) réunion, société, *f.*; groupe, *m.*; troupe, *f.*; (*for certain expeditions*, &c.) caravane, *f.*; (*retinue*) suite, *f.*, cortége, *m.*; (*in the evening*) soirée, *f.*; (*excursion*) partie (de ...), *f.*; (*mil.*) détachement, parti, *m.*, troupe, *f.*; colonne, *f.* *Attacking* —, (*mil.*) colonne *or* troupe d'attaque, *f.* *Dancing* —, *Dinner* —, *Evening* —, *Fatigue* —, &c., *V.* **Dancing,** &c., &c. *Flying* —, (*mil.*) détachement de tirailleurs, *m.* *Foraging* —, (*mil.*) détachement (*m.*) *or* troupe (*f.*) de fourrageurs. *Hunting* —, partie de chasse, *f.* *Leader* or *head of a* —, chef de parti, *m.* *Pleasure* —, partie de plaisir, *f.* *Storming* —, (*mil.*) colonne d'assaut, *f.* *Working* —, détachement de travailleurs, *m.*, travailleurs, *m.pl.* *To be a — to*, prendre part à; concourir à; s'associer à; être complice de, tremper dans. *To give a* —, donner une soirée. *To go on a ...* —, faire une partie de ... *To go* (or *go out*) *to a* —, aller à une soirée, aller en soirée. —**coloured,** *adj.* bigarré. — **entitled,** *s.* (*law*) ayant-droit, *m.* — **man,** *s.* homme de parti, factieux, *m.* — **spirit,** *s.* esprit de parti, *m.* — **wall,** *s.* mur mitoyen, *m.*
Parvenu, *s.* parvenu, *m.*
Parvis, Parvise, *s.* parvis, *m.*
Paschal, *adj.* pascal, de Pâques
Pasha, *s.* pacha, *m.*
Pashalic, *s.* pachalik, *m.*
Pasigraph-ic, al, -y. *V.* page 3, § 1
Pasque-flower, *s.* pulsatille, *f.*
Pasquin, *s.* pasquin, *m.*; — *v.a.n.* pasquiniser
Pasquinade, *s.* pasquinade, *f.*; — *v.a.n.* pasquiniser
Pass, *v.n.* passer; (*of time*) passer, se passer, s'écouler; (*occur*) se passer; (*be at an end*) passer, finir; — *v.a.* passer; (*send*) passer, faire passer; (*for*) faire passer (pour); (*transfer*) transférer; (*a sentence*, &c., *utter*) prononcer; (*a judgment*) porter; (*remarks, compliments*, &c.) faire; (*a trick, a jest*) faire; (*a resolution*, &c.) adopter; (*a law*, &c.) faire, porter, rendre, édicter; (*omit*) passer, oublier; (*forgive*) pardonner; (*end*) finir, mettre un terme à; (*o.'s word*) engager; (*through the hands of*) passer par les mains de; (*pass close to*) passer à côté de *or* auprès de, passer devant; se croiser avec, croiser; (*go beyond*) dépasser; passer; (*surpass*) surpasser, passer; (*swallow*) avaler; (*approve*) approuver; — *s.* passage, défilé, *m.*; (*state*) état, état de choses, *m.*, situation, *f.*; point, *m.*; passe, *f.*; (*licence, ticket*) passe, *f.*; laisser-passer, *m.*; permis de circulation, permis, *m.*; permission, *f.*; exeat, *m.*; billet gratuit, *m.*; carte d'entrée *or* d'admission (gratuite), entrée, carte, *f.*; passeport, *m.*; (*of mesmerists*) passe, *f.*; (*fenc.*) passe, botte, *f.* *To bring to* —, effectuer, accomplir, amener; faire (que, *with subj*). *To be brought to* —, s'accomplir, arriver, avoir lieu. *To come to* —, arriver. *To — each other*, se croiser. — **along,** *v.n.* passer. — **away,** *v.n.* passer; (*of time*) passer, se passer, s'écouler; (*disappear*) disparaître, s'évanouir; (*die*) mourir; *v.a.* passer; (*to waste*) dissiper. — **book,** *s.* (*bank*) carnet de position (de compte), *m.*; (*com.*) livre de compte particulier, *m.*; — **by,** *v.n.* passer à côté de, passer devant; passer par là *or* par ici, passer; *v.a.* passer à côté de, passer auprès de; (*omit*) omettre, négliger; passer; (*forgive*) pardonner, oublier; (*in silence*) passer (sous silence). — **check,** *s.* contre-marque, *f.* — **key,** *s.* passe partout, *m.* —**less,** *adj.* sans passage. — **off,** *v.n.* passer; se passer; se dissiper; (*for, as*) passer (pour); se donner (pour); *v.a.* faire passer (pour); donner (pour). *To — oneself off for*, se faire passer pour, se donner pour. — **on,** *v.n.* passer; passer son chemin, continuer sa route; passer outre; (*occur*) se passer. — **out,** *v.n.* sortir. — **over,** *v.n.* passer; (*to cross*) franchir; *v.a.* (*to cross*) passer, franchir; (*overlook*) ne pas faire attention à; glisser sur, ne pas parler de; (*omit*) omettre, passer; (*forgive*) pardonner. — **parole,** *s.* passe-parole, *m.* —**port,** *s.* passeport, *m.*; (*fig.*) passe-partout, *m.* — **round,** *v.n.* circuler; *v.a.* faire circuler. — **word,** *s.* mot de passe, *m.*; mot d'ordre, *m.*
Passable, *adj.* (*tolerable*) passable, tolérable; (*of roads*, &c.) praticable; (*of rivers*, &c.) navigable; (*penetrable*) pénétrable, perméable; (*of coin*) ayant cours, qui a cours
Passably, *adv.* passablement
Passade, *s.* passade, *f.*
Passage, *s.* (*passing over*) passage, *m.*; (*crossing by sea*) traversée, *f.*; (*of a house*) corridor, couloir, *m.*; (*hall*) vestibule, *m.*; (*road*) chemin, accès, *m.*; (*entrance*) entrée, *f.*; (*rid., mus., of a book*) passage, *m.*; (*fight*) pas d'armes, *m.*; assaut, *m.*; — *v.a.n.* (*rid.*) passager. — *-at-arms*, — *of arms*, pas d'armes, *m.* *Bird of* —, oiseau de passage, *m.* — **boat,** *s.* bateau de passage, bac, *m.* — **money,** *s.* prix du passage *or* de la traversée, *m.*
Passant, *adj.* (*her.*) passant
Passenger, *s.* (*on a road*) passant, *m.*, e, *f.*; (*by sea*) passager, *m.*, -ère, *f.*; (*by rail, omnibus, or coach*) voyageur, *m.*, -euse, *f.* — **boat,** *s.* bateau de voyageurs, *m.* — **carriage,** *s.* voiture de voyageurs, *f.* — **pigeon,** *s.* pigeon de passage, *m.* — **traffic,** *s.* (*rail.*) transport *or* mouvement des voyageurs, *m.* — **train,** *s.* *V.* **Train**
Passe-partout, *s.* passe-partout, *m.*
Passer, — by, *s.* passant, *m.*, e, *f.*
Passerine, — bird, *s.* passereau, *m.*
Passi-bility, bleness. *V.* page 3, § 1
Passible, *adj.* passible
Passing, *s.* passage, *m.*; (*of a bill in parliam.*, &c.) adoption, *f.*; (*of a contract*, &c.) passation, *f.*; (*of a sentence*) prononcé, *m.*; — *adj.* passager, fugitif; (*present*) actuel; du jour; (*surpassing*) éminent, supérieur; rare; (*adverb.*)

extrêmement, excessivement, éminemment, fort. — **bell,** *s.* glas, *m.* — **note,** *s.* (*mus.*) note de passage, *f.*

Passion, *s.* passion, *f.*; ardeur, *f.*; (*anger*) colère, *f.*, (*theol.*) Passion, *f.* *In a* —, en colère. *To fall* or *fly* or *get into a* —, se mettre en colère, s'emporter. — **cross,** *s.* croix de la passion, *f.* — **flower,** *s.* grenadille, fleur de la passion, passiflore, *f.* —**less,** *adj.* exempt de passion; d'un caractère calme. — **week,** *s.* semaine sainte, semaine de la Passion, *f.*

Passionary, *s.* passionnaire, *m.*

Passionate, *adj.* (*pers.*) emporté, colère, irascible, vif; (*things*) passionné, ardent, vif

Passionately, *adv.* passionnément, à la passion, à la folie; (*angrily*) avec colère, avec emportement [irascible, *m.*

Passionateness, *s.* vivacité, *f.*, caractère

Passionist, *s. adj.* passioniste, *m.*

Passive, *adj.s.* passif, *adj.m.*, -ive, *f.*, passif, *s.m.* *In the — voice*, à la voix passive, au passif

Passively, *adv.* passivement [sivité, *f.*

Passiveness, Passivity, *s.* passiveté, pas-

Passover, *s.* Pâque, *f.*

Passport, &c. *See under* **Pass**

Past, *adj.* passé; dernier; — *s.* passé, *m.*; — *prep.* au-delà de; (*near*) à côté de, près de; (*in front of*) devant; (*above*) au-dessus de; (*without*) sans; hors de; (*of age*) plus de, passé; (*of time*) passé, après, et; (*no longer able*) devenu incapable de; — *adv.* au-delà; à côté, près; devant; (*previously*) auparavant, avant. *For some time* —, depuis quelque temps. *In the* —, dans le passé; (*gram.*) au passé. — *doubt*, hors de doute. —*remedy*, sans remède. —*cure*, *V.* **Cure.** — *bearing*, — *age*, hors d'âge. — *childbearing*, hors d'âge d'avoir des enfants. *He is — sixty*, il a plus de soixante ans, il a soixante ans passés. *It is — ten*, il est dix heures passées. *It is ten minutes — two*, il est deux heures dix minutes (*or* deux heures dix). *Half- — six* (or &c.), six heures (*or* &c.) et demie. *It is half* —, il est la demie. *A quarter — one* (or &c.), une heure (*or* &c.) un quart. *It is a quarter* —, il est le quart

Paste, *s.* pâte, *f.*; (*for gluing*) colle de farine, colle, *f.*; (*jewel.*) stras, strass, *m.*; — *v.a.* coller; (— *up*) afficher. — **board,** *s.* carton, *m.*; (*for rolling dough on*) planche (à pâte), *f.*; *adj.* de carton. — **board box,** *s.* boîte de carton, *f.*, carton, *m.* — **board maker,** *s.* cartonnier, *m.* — **board manufactory,** *s.* cartonnerie, *f.* — **brush,** *s.* (*cook.*) doroir, *m.* — **cutter,** *s.* coupe-pâte, *m.* — **pin,** *s.* rouleau, *m.* — **up,** *v.a.* afficher; poser

Pastel, *s.* (*bot.*) pastel, *m.*, guède, *f.*; (*draw.*) pastel, *m.*

Pastern, *s.* pâturon, *m.* — **joint,** *s.* boulet, *m.*

Pasticcio, *s.* pastiche, *m.*

Pastil, Pastile, Pastille, *s.* pastille, *f.*

Pastime, *s.* passe-temps, *m.*, récréation, distraction, *f.*, amusement, *m.*

Pastor, *s.* pasteur, *m.*; (*a bird*) martin, *m.* — **like,** *adj.* *V.* **Pastorly** [pastorale, *s.f.*

Pastoral, *adj.* *s.* pastoral, *adj.* *m.*, e, *f.*,

Pastorally, *adv.* pastoralement

Pastorate, *s.* pastorat, *m.*

Pastorly, *adj.* pastoral, de pasteur

Pastorship, *s.* pastorat, *m.*

Pastry, *s.* pâtisserie, *f.* — **cook,** *s.* pâtissier, *m.*, -ière, *f.* — **table, -board,** *s.* pâtissoire, *f.*

Pasturable, *adj.* pâturable

Pasturage, *s.* pâturage, *m.*

Pasture, *s.* pâture, *f.*; pâturage, *m.*; — *v.a.* faire paître; nourrir; (*eat*) paître, pâturer; — *v.n.* paître, pâturer. — **ground, -land,** *s.* pâturage, *m.* —**less,** *adj.* sans pâture; sans

Pasturer, *s.* pâtureur, *m.* [pâturage

Pasty, *adj.* pâteux; — *s.* pâté, *m.*

Pat, *adj. adv.* à propos, tout juste (pour); — *s.* tape, *f.*; (*mould for butter*) moule (à beurre), *m.*; — *v.a.* taper; caresser. — *of butter*, beurre, pain de beurre, rond de beurre, *m.*, coquille de beurre, *f.*

Patagonian, *s. adj.* Patagon, *m.*, e, *f.*

Patavinity, *s.* patavinité, *f.*

Patch, *s.* pièce, *f.*, morceau, *m.*; plaque, *f.*; (*of flowers, plants*) touffe, *f.*; (*of land*) morceau, coin, *m.*; (*on the face*) mouche, *f.*; (*of inlaid work*) pièce de rapport, *f.*; — *v.a.* mettre une pièce *or* des pièces à, rapiécer, rapièceter; rapetasser, raccommoder, rafistoler; (*the face*) mettre des mouches à. — **up,** *v.a.* plâtrer; bâcler. — **work,** *s.* rapiéçage, rapiècetage, *m.*; replâtrage, *m.*; pièces cousues (*f.pl.*) *or* morceaux cousus (*m.pl.*) ensemble; assemblage de pièces et de morceaux, *m.*; ouvrage de morceaux de différentes couleurs, *m.*; habit d'arlequin, *m.*; mosaïque, *f.*; (*medley*) mélange, *m.*

Patcher, *s.* rapiéceur, *m.*, -euse, *f.*; rapetasseur, *m.*, -euse, *f.*, raccommodeur, *m.*, -euse, *f.*

Patching, *s.* rapiéçage, rapiècetage, *m.*; rapetassage, *m.*; replâtrage, *m.*

Patchouli, Patchouly, *s.* patchouli, *m.*

Patchy, *adj.* *V.* **Botchy**

Pate, *s.* caboche, boule, tête, *f.*

Pated, *adj.* (*in compounds*) à tête . . ., à caboche . . .

Patella, *s.* (*anat.*) rotule, *f.*

Paten, *s.* patène, *f.*

Patent, *adj.* patent; (*of inventions*) breveté; — *s.* lettres patentes, *f.pl.*; privilége, *m.*; (*of inventions*) brevet, *m.*; — *v.a.* accorder par lettres patentes; (*of inventions*) breveter. — *for invention*, brevet d'invention, *m.* — *of nobility*, lettres de noblesse, *f.pl.* *Letters* —, lettres patentes, *f.pl.*; brevet, *m.* *To take out a* —, prendre un brevet. — **agent,** *s.* agent pour les brevets d'invention, *m.* — **fuel,** *s.* briquette, *f.*, briquettes, *f.pl.* — **leather,** *s.* cuir verni, *m.*; *adj.* verni. — **office,** *s.* bureau de brevets, bureau pour les brevets d'invention, *m.* — **right,** *s.* privilége du brevet, *m.* — **rolls,** *s. pl.* registre des brevets, *m.*

Patentable, *adj.* brevetable

Patentee, *s.* concessionnaire, *m.f.*; (*of inventions*) breveté, *m.*, e, *f.*

Patently, *adv.* patemment

Patera, *s.* patère, *f.*

Paternal, *adj.* paternel. — *grandfather*, aïeul paternel, *m.* — *grandmother*, aïeule paternelle, *f.*

Paternally, *adv.* paternellement

Paternity, *s.* paternité, *f.* [patenôtre, *f.*

Paternoster, *s.* pater, pater noster, *m.*,

Path, *s.* sentier, *m.*; chemin, *m.*; (*in gardens*) allée, *f.*; (*roadside*) *V.* — **way;** (*fig.*) voie, *f.*, chemin, *m.*; (*astr.*) cours, *m.*, route, *f.* —**less,** *adj.* sans sentier, sans chemin frayé; non frayé, qui n'est pas frayé. — **way,** *s.* sentier, *m.*; (*roadside*) bas-côté, accotement, *m.*; (*in towns*) trottoir, *m.*

Pathetic, -al, *adj. s.* pathétique, *adj. m.f.*, *s.m.*

Pathetically, *adv.* pathétiquement

Patheticalness, *s.* pathétique, *m.*

Patholog-ic, al, -ically, -ist, -y. *V.* p. 3, § 1

Pathos, *s.* pathétique, *m.*

Patibulary, *adj.* patibulaire

Patience, *s.* patience, *f.*; (*bot.*) patience, *f.* *To be out of* —, être à bout de patience. *To get out of* —, perdre patience, s'impatienter. *To have* —, avoir patience, avoir de la patience; prendre patience, patienter. *To put out of* —, faire perdre patience à, impatienter. *I am out of — with it*, cela a mis ma patience à bout

Patient, *adj.* patient; — *s.* (*under medical care*) malade, *m.f.*; (*under a surgical operation*) patient, *m.*, e, *f.*

Patiently, *adv.* patiemment, avec patience

Patina, *s.* patine, *f.*

Patly, *adv.* à propos, à point

Patness, *s.* à-propos, *m.*, justesse, *f.*

Patois, *s.* patois, *m.*

Patriarch, *s.* patriarche, *m.*

Patriarchal, *adj.* patriarcal
Patriarchally, *adv.* patriarcalement
Patriarchate, Patriarchship, *s.* patriarcat, *m.*
Patriarch-ism, -y. *V.* page 3, § 1
Patrician, *s. adj.* patricien, *m.*, -ne, *f.*
Patriciate, *s.* patriciat, *m.*
Patrimonial, *adj.* patrimonial
Patrimonially, *adv.* patrimonialement
Patrimony, *s.* patrimoine, *m.*
Patriot, *s.* patriote, *m.f.*; — *adj. V.* **Patriotic**
Patriotic, *adj.* (*things*) patriotique; (*pers.*) patriote
Patriot-ically, -ism. *V.* page 3, § 1
Patrol, *s.* patrouille, *f.*; — *v.n.* faire patrouille, faire la patrouille; — *v.a.* faire patrouille dans; parcourir
Patron, *s.* patron, *m.*; protecteur, *m.* — **saint,** *s.* patron, *m.*, patronne, *f.*, saint patron, *m.*, sainte patronne, *f.*
Patronage, *s.* patronage, *m.*; protection, *f.*
Patronal, *adj.* patronal
Patronate, *s.* patronat, *m.*
Patroness, *s.* patronne, *f.*; protectrice, *f.*; (*of charities, societies,* &c.) patronnesse, dame patronnesse, *f.*
Patronize, *v.a.* patronner; protéger; favoriser; défendre, soutenir
Patronizer, *s.*, **Patronizing,** *adj.* protecteur, *m.*, -trice, *f.*
Patronship, *s.* patronat, *m.*
Patronymic, *adj.* patronymique; — *s.* nom patronymique, *m.*
Patten, *s.* socque, *m.*; (*out of use in France*) patin, *m.*; (*arch.*) soubassement, *m.* — **shoe,** *s.* (*of horses*) fer à patin, patin, *m.*
Patter, *v.n.* battre, frapper, fouetter; grésiller; (*talk*) caqueter; — *s. V.* **Pattering**
Pattering, *s.* petit bruit, *m.*; grésillement, *m.*; (*talk*) caquet, *m.*; volubilité, *f.*
Pattern, *s.* modèle, *m.*; patron, *m.*; (*sample*) échantillon, *m.*; (*design*) dessin, *m.*; (*example*) exemple, *m.*; — *v.a.* patronner. *To have ... made to* —, faire faire ... sur échantillon. — **book** *or* **card,** *s.* livre (*m.*) *or* carte (*f.*) d'échantillons. — **drawer,** *s.* dessinateur, *m.*, -trice, *f.*
Patty, *s.* petit pâté, *m.* — **pan,** *s.* moule à pâtés, *m.*
Paucity, *s.* paucité, *f.*, petit nombre, *m.*, petite quantité, *f.*; manque, *m.*, disette (de), *f.*
Pauline, *adj.* paulinien
Paullinia, *s.* paullinia, *m.*
Paulownia, *s.* paulownia, *m.*
Paunch, *s.* panse, *f.*; ventre, *m.*; — *v.a.* éventrer
Pauper, *s.* pauvre, *m.*, -sse, *f.*, indigent, *m.*, -e, *f.*; mendiant, *m.*, e, *f.*
Pauperism, *s.* paupérisme, *m.*
Pauperize, *v.a.* réduire à la mendicité
Pause, *s.* pause, *f.*; intervalle, *m.*; (*in a colloquy*) moment de silence, silence, *m.*; (*vers.*) repos, *m.*; (*gram.*) pause, *f.*; (*print.*) tiret, *m.*; (*mus.*) point d'orgue, *m.*; — *v.n.* faire une pause; s'arrêter; réfléchir
Pave, *v.a.* paver ('*with,*' de); (*fig.*) frayer, préparer
Pavement, *s.* pavage, pavement, *m.*; pavé, *m.*; (*of tiles*) carreau, *m.*; (*of flags*) dalles, *f.pl.*; (*side path*) trottoir, *m.*
Paver, Pavier, *s.* paveur, *m.*
Pavilion, *s.* pavillon, *m.*; (*tent*) tente, *f.*; — *v.a.* pourvoir *or* couvrir de tentes; (*shelter*) abriter sous une tente
Paving, *s. V.* **Pavement;** (*act of paving*) pavage, *m.* — **beetle,** *s. V.* — **rammer.** — **brick,** *s.* chantignole, *f.*, carreau, matton, *m.* — **rammer,** *s.* demoiselle, hie, *f.* — **stone,** *s.* pavé, *m.*; (*flag*) dalle, cadette, *f.* — **tile,** *s.* carreau, *m.*
Pavior, Paviour, *s.* paveur, *m.*
Pavonia, *s.* (*bot., zool.*) pavonie, *f.*
Pavonine, *adj.* pavonien
Paw, *s.* patte, *f.*; — *v.a.* frapper du pied; (*to scratch*) griffer, donner des coups de griffe à; (*handle roughly*) patiner, manier rudement; (*to fawn*) caresser, flatter; — *v.n.* piaffer. *To — the ground,* piaffer
Pawed, *adj.* à pattes
Pawn, *s.* gage, *m.*; (*at chess*) pion, *m.*; — *v.a.* mettre en gage, engager; mettre au mont-de-piété. *In* —, en gage, engagé. *To put in* —, mettre en gage, engager. *To take out of* —, dégager. —**broker,** *s.* prêteur sur gages, *m.*; commissionnaire au (*or* du) mont-de-piété, *m.* *At* or *to the —broker's,* au mont-de-piété. — **broker's shop,** *s. V.* — **shop.** —**broking,** *s.* commerce de prêteur sur gages, prêt sur gages, *m.* — **shop,** *s.* maison de prêt, *f.*; mont-de-piété, *m.*; succursale du mont-de piété, *f.* — **ticket,** *s.* reconnaissance du mont de-piété, *f.*
Pawnee, *s.* prêteur (*m.*, -euse, *f.*) sur gage (*or* sur gages)
Pawner, *s.* emprunteur (*m.*, -euse, *f.*) sur gage (*or* sur gages)
Pax, *s.* paix, *f.*, instrument de paix, *m.*
Pay, *v.a.* payer; s'acquitter de, acquitter; (*visits, respects, homage*) rendre, faire; (*compliments*) faire; (*regard*) avoir, montrer; (*attention*) faire; (*to beat*) battre, taper, rosser; (*remunerate*) rétribuer; (*com.*) payer; verser, (*com., bring in*) rapporter; rapporter un bénéfice à; (*to smear, nav.*) brayer, courayer, goudronner. *To — for.* payer; (*suffer*) payer cher, expier. *To — a person,* payer quelqu'un. *To — a person for a thing,* payer quelque chose à quelqu'un. *To — attention,* faire attention (à); avoir des attentions (pour), &c. *V.* **Attention.** *To — o.'s addresses, to — court* (or *o.'s court*), faire la cour (à). *It does not* —, cela ne rapporte rien. *It does not — to do so,* on n'a aucun bénéfice (*or* aucun avantage *or* aucun intérêt) à faire cela. *That does not — me,* cela ne me rapporte rien, cela ne me rapporte aucun bénéfice, je n'y gagne rien; cela ne fait pas mon compte *or* mon affaire, je ne trouve pas mon compte à cela, je n'y trouve pas mon compte. — **away,** payer; (*a cable*) filer. — **back,** rendre. — **down,** payer argent comptant, payer. — **in,** verser. — **off,** payer, acquitter; rembourser, désintéresser; (*dismiss*) renvoyer, congédier, donner son compte à; (*retaliate*) rendre la pareille à, donner son compte *or* son fait à; (*retort on*) rembarrer. — **out,** payer; (*retaliate*) *V.* — **off;** (*a cable*) filer. — **up,** payer; (*shares,* &c.) libérer
Pay, *s.* paye, *f.*; (*mil., nav.*) solde, *f.*; paye, *f.*; (*of servants*) gages, *m.pl.*; (*of workmen*) salaire, *m.*; (*salary*) appointements, *m.pl.*; (*reward*) salaire, *m.*; (*profit*) rapport, produit, bénéfice, *m.* *Extra* —, supplément de solde, *m.*, haute solde, haute paye, paye en sus, paye supplémentaire, surpaye, *f.* *Full* —, paye entière, solde d'activité, *f.* *Half* —, demi-solde, *f.*; *adj.* en demi-solde. *To be on half* —, être à la demi-solde, être à la suite. *To be in the — of,* être à la solde (*or* aux gages) de. *To put on half* —, mettre à la demi-solde, mettre à la suite. *He is a bad* —, c'est une mauvaise paye. — **bill,** *s.* état de solde, *m.* — **day,** *s.* jour de paye, *m.* — **master,** *s.* payeur, *m.*; (*admin., mil.*) trésorier, *m.*; (*nav.*) *V.* **Purser.** —**mistress,** *s.* payeuse, *f.* — **office,** *s.* caisse, *f.*
Payable, *adj.* payable; à payer; qui peut être payé. — *to,* (*com.*) à l'ordre de. — *to bearer,* au porteur. — *to order,* à ordre
Payee, *s.* porteur, *m.*
Payer, *s.* payeur, *m.*, -euse, *f.*; payant, *m.*, e, *f.*
Payment, *s.* payement, paiement, *m.*; (*fin.*) versement, *m.* *Heavy* —, fort payement. — *in full of all demands,* solde de compte, *m.* *In part* —, à-compte. *A sum in part* —, un à-compte, un acompte, *m.*
Pea, *s.* pois, *m.*; (*bird*) paon, *m.* —**beetle, -chafer,** *s.* cusson, *m.* — **chick,** *s.* paonneau, *m.* — **coat,** *s.* vareuse, *f.* — **cock,** *s.* paon, *m.* *The daw in —cock's feathers,* le geai paré des plumes du paon. —**cock butterfly,** *s.* paon de jour, *m.* —**cock fish,** *s.* paon bleu, paon de mer, *m.* —**cock moth,** *s.* paon de nuit, grand paon, *m.* — **cod,** *s. V.* — **pod.**

— **crab,** *s.* pinnothère, *m.* — **fowl,** *s.* paon, *m.* — **green,** *s. adj.* vert pois, *m.* — **hen,** *s.* paonne, *f.* — **jacket,** *s.* vareuse, *f.* — **nut,** *s.* arachide, *f.* — **pod, -shell,** *s.* cosse de pois, *f.* — **shooter,** *s.* tube, *m.*, sarbacane, *f.* — **soup,** *s.* purée de pois, *f.* — **stick,** *s.* rame, *f.* — **stone,** *s.* pisolithe, *m.*

Peace, *s.* paix, *f.*; tranquillité, *f.*; (*law*) ordre public, *m.* *At* —, en paix. *To hold o.'s* —, se taire. *To keep the* —, ne pas troubler l'ordre public; s'abstenir de voies de fait (envers). — **breaker,** *s.* perturbateur, *m.* —**less,** *adj.* sans paix, sans tranquillité, sans repos. — — **loving,** *adj.* qui aime la paix. — **maker,** *s.* pacificateur, *m.*, -trice, *f.*, conciliateur, *m.*, -trice, *f.* — **making,** *s.* pacification, *f.*; — *adj.* pacificateur. — **offering,** *s.* sacrifice de propitiation, sacrifice, *m.* — **officer,** *s.* officier de paix, *m.* [fique; tranquille; calme

Peaceable, Peaceful, *adj.* paisible; paci-

Peaceableness, Peacefulness, *s.* tranquillité, *f.*, calme, *m.*; humeur pacifique, caractère paisible, *m.*; état de paix, *m.*

Peaceably, Peacefully, *adv.* paisiblement; pacifiquement; tranquillement; avec calme

Peach, *s.* (*fruit*) pêche, *f.*; (*tree*) pêcher, *m.* — **blossom,** *s.* fleur de pêcher, *f.* — **colour,** *s.*, — **coloured,** *adj.* couleur de fleur de pêcher. — **house,** *s.* serre à pêchers, *f.* — **orchard,** *s.* pêcheraie, *f.* — **stone,** *s.* noyau de pêche, *m.* — **tree,** *s.* pêcher, *m.*

Peak, *s.* (*geog.*) pic, *m.*; (*of mountains*) cime, *f.*, sommet, piton, *m.*; (*point*) pointe, *f.*; (*of caps*) visière, *f.*; — *v.n.* avoir l'air malade *or* chétif, avoir mauvaise mine; languir

Peaked, *adj.* pointu; (*of caps*) à visière

Peaking, *adj.* maladif, chétif, languissant

Peal, *s.* (*noise*) bruit, *m.*; retentissement, *m.*; (*of bells*) carillon, *m.*, volée, *f.*; (*of thunder*) coup, éclat, *m.*; (*of cannon*) salve, *f.*, coup, grondement, *m.*; (*of an organ*) ronflement, *m.*; (*of applause*) salve, *f.*; (*of laughter*) éclat, *m.*; — *v.n.* retentir, résonner; (*of thunder, cannons*) gronder; — *v.a.* faire retentir, faire résonner; (*bells*) carillonner; (*to stun*) étourdir. *To ring a* —, carillonner. *To ring in* —, sonner en branle *or* en volée

Pean, *s.* hymne, *m.*; (*her.*) panne, *f.*

Pear, *s.* poire, *f.* — **main,** *s. See below.* — **shaped,** *adj.* en forme de poire, piriforme. — **tree,** *s.* poirier, *m.*

Pearl, *s.* perle, *f.*; (*print. type*) perle, *f.*; (*med.*) taie, perle, *f.*; (*her.*) argent, *m.*; — *adj.* de perle, de perles; perlier; — *v.a.n.* perler. *Mother of* —, nacre, nacre de perles, *f.* *Mother of — manufacturer* or *worker*, nacrier, *m.*, -ière, *f.* — **ash,** *s.* perlasse, cendre gravelée, *f.* — **diver,** *s.* pêcheur de perles, *m.* — **eyed,** *adj.* qui a une taie sur l'œil. — **fishery,** *s.* pêche des perles, *f.* — **grass,** *s.* sagine, *f.* — **oyster,** *s.* huître perlière, *f.* — **powder,** *s.* blanc de perle, blanc de fard, *m.* — **shell,** *s.* huître perlière, *f.*; nacre de perle, *f.* — **white,** *s.* *V.* — **powder.** — **wort,** *s.* V. — **grass**

Pearled, *adj.* orné de perles; perlé

Pearly, *adj.* de perle, perlé

Pearmain, *s.* pomme-poire, *f.*

Peasant, *s.* paysan, *m.*, -ne, *f.*; — *adj.* *V.* — **like.** — **boy,** *s.* petit paysan, *m.* — **girl,** *s.* petite paysanne, *f.* —**like, -ly,** *adj.* de paysan, campagnard, rustique. —**ry,** *s.* paysannerie, *f.*, paysans, *m.pl.*

Peat, *s.* tourbe, *f.*; (*piece for fuel*) motte à brûler, motte, *f.* — **bog, -fen,** *s.* tourbière, *f.* — **carrier, -owner, -worker,** *s.* tourbier, *m.* — **moss,** *s.* tourbe, *f.*; tourbière, *f.*, dépôt

Peaty, *adj.* tourbeux [tourbeux, *m.*

Pebble, *s.* caillou, *m.* — **jeweller,** *s.* bijoutier en pierres dures, *m.* — **jewellery,** *s.* bijouterie de pierres dures, *f.* — **stone,** *s.* caillou, *m.* — **work,** *s.* cailloutage, *m.*

Pebbled, Pebbly, *adj.* caillouteux

Peccability, *s.* peccabilité, *f.*

Peccable, *adj.* peccable

Peccadillo, *s.* peccadille, *f.* [vice, *m.*

Peccancy, *s.* nature peccante, *f.*; défaut,

Peccant, *adj.* (*pers.*) coupable de péché, pécheur; (*things*) défectueux, qui pèche; (*med.*)

Peccary, *s.* pécari, *m.* [peccant

Peccavi, *s.* peccavi, *m.*

Peck, *s.* (*of oats*) picotin, *m.*; (*fig.*) grande quantité, foule, *f.*; (*blow*) coup de bec, *m.*; — *v.a.* becqueter; donner des coups de bec à; picoter, percer. — **up,** *v.a.* ramasser avec le bec; (*fig.*) ramasser

Pecker, *s.* (*bird*) pivert, *m.*

Pecking, *s.* coups de bec, *m.pl.*

Peckish, *adj.* en appétit

Pecten, *s.* (*mollusc*) peigne, *m.*

Pectic, *adj.* pectique

Pectinal, Pectinate, *adj.* pectiné, en peigne

Pectine, *s.* pectine, *f.* [toral, *s.m.*

Pectoral, *adj. s.* pectoral, *adj.m.*, e, *f.*, pec-

Pectorally, *adv.* pectoralement

Pectoriloquy, *s.* pectoriloquie, *f.* [péculat

Peculate, *v.n.* être (*or* se rendre) coupable de

Peculation, *s.* péculat, *m.*

Peculator, *s.* péculateur, concussionnaire, *m.*

Peculiar, *adj.* particulier; propre; à soi; spécial; singulier; bizarre; original; — *s.* propriété particulière, *f.*; particularité, *f.*; chapelle privilégiée, *f.* [*f.*; originalité, *f.*

Peculiarity, *s.* particularité, *f.*; singularité,

Peculiarize, *v.a.* particulariser; approprier

Peculiarly, *adv.* particulièrement; spécialement; singulièrement

Peculium, *s.* pécule, *m.*

Pecuniarily, *adv.* pécuniairement

Pecuniary, *adj.* pécuniaire

Pecunious, *adj.* pécunieux

Pedagog-ic, al, -ically, -ism, -y, pédagogique, &c. (*V.* page 3, § 1)

Pedagogue, *s.* pédagogue, *m.*

Pedal, *adj.* de *or* du pied; — *s.* pédale, *f.* — **clavier,** *s.* clavier de pédales, *m.* — **board,** *s.* marche (de pédale), *f.* — **harmony,** *s.* point d'orgue, *m.* — **note,** *s.* pédale, note soutenue, *f.* — **organ,** *s.* orgue à pédales, *m.* — **point,** *s.* point d'orgue, *m.* — **stop,** *s.* pédale *f.*

Pedant, *s.* pédant, *m.*, e, *f.* [dantesque

Pedantic-al, *adj.* (*pers.*) pédant; (*things*) pé-

Pedantically, *adv.* pédantesquement

Pedantism, *s.* pédantisme, *m.*

Pedantize, *v.n.* pédantiser, pédanter

Pedantry, *s.* pédanterie, *f.*, pédantisme, *m.*

Peddle, *v.n.* niaiser, s'occuper de bagatelles, s'amuser, chipoter; tatillonner; — *v.n.a.* — **about,** (*to hawk*) colporter

Peddler, *s.* chipotier, *m.*, -ière, *f.*; tatillon, *m.*, -ne, *f.*; (*hawker*) *V.* **Pedlar**

Peddling, *adj.* petit, futile, de peu de valeur; — *s.* colportage, *m.*

Pedestal, *s.* piédestal, *m.*; (*mach.*) palier, *m.* *Bed-room* —, table de nuit, *f.* — *toilet-table* or *dressing-table* or *washstand*, toilette-commode, commode-toilette *f.*

Pedestrian, *adj.* à pied, pédestre; — *s.* piéton, *m.*, -ne, *f.*; (*walker*) marcheur, *m.*, -euse, *f.*; (*runner*) coureur, *m.*, -euse, *f.*

Pedestrianism, *s.* pédestrianisme, *m.*, course (*f.*, *or* courses, *f.pl.*) à pied

Pedicel, *s.* pédicelle, *m.*

Pedicellate, *adj.* pédicellé

Pedicle, *s.* pédicule, *m.*

Pedicular, *adj.* pédiculaire

Pedicularis, *s.* pédiculaire, *f.*

Pediculate, *adj.* pédiculé

Pediform, *adj.* pédiforme

Pedigree, *s.* généalogie, *f.*; (*in turf-slang*) pedigree, *m.*; — *adject.* généalogique

Pediment, *s.* fronton, *m.* [*m.*, colporteuse *f.*

Pedlar, Pedler, -ess, *s.* colporteur, camelot,

Pedlary, Pedlery, *s.* colportage, *m.*; marchandise de colportage, *f.*

Pedobaptism, *s.* baptême des enfants, *m.*
Pedobaptist, *s.* partisan du baptême des enfants, *m.* [pas, *m.*
Pedometer, *s.* pédomètre, hodomètre, compte-
Pedometrical, *adj.* pédométrique
Peduncle, *s.* pédoncule, *m.*
Peduncular, *adj.* pédonculaire
Pedunculate, -d, *adj.* pédonculé [faire pipi
Pee, *s.* pipi, *m.*; — *v.n.* faire pipi. *To go* —,
Peel, *v.a.* peler; — *v.n.* se peler; s'écailler; — *s.* pelure, *f.*; (*of oranges, lemons*) écorce, *f.*; (*shovel*) pelle de four, *f.*, pelleron, *m.*; (*print.*) étendoir, *m.* — **off,** *v.a.* écorcher; enlever, emporter; *v.n.* se peler; s'écailler; s'enlever
Peeler, *s.* (*policeman*) agent de police ar-
Peeling, *s. V.* **Peel,** *s.* [gousin, *m.*
Peep, *v.n.* (*to look*) regarder; voir; (*of the day*) poindre, paraître; (*of the sun, moon,* &c., *show through*) percer; se montrer, paraître; poindre; (*of flowers*) éclore; — *s.* (*a look*) coup d'œil, *m.*; (*appearance*) première apparition, *f.*; (*of the day*) point, *m.*, pointe, *f.*, aube, *f.* *To give* or *have* or *take a — at,* donner un coup d'œil à, regarder, voir. — **hole,** *s.* judas, *m.* —**show,** *s.* optique, *f.*
Peeper, *s.* curieux, *m.*, -euse, *f.*; espion, *m.*; (*chick*) poussin, *m.*; —**s,** *pl.* (*eyes*) quinquets, lampions, ardents, *m.pl.*
Peeping-hole, *s.* judas, *m.*
Peer, *s.* pair, égal, *m.*; compagnon, *m.*, compagne, *f.*; (*nobleman*) pair, *m.*; — *v.n. V.* **Peep.** —**less,** —**lessly,** —**lessness,** *V.* **Matchless,** &c.
Peerage, *s.* pairie, *f.*; (*lords*) pairs, *m.pl.* *Life* —, pairie à vie, *f.* — **book,** *s.* nobiliaire, *m.*
Peeress, *s.* pairesse, femme de pair, *f.*
Peevish, *adj* maussade, chagrin; bourru, hargneux, acariâtre. —**ly,** *adv.* avec mauvaise humeur, maussadement, d'une manière bourrue. —**ness,** *s.* humeur chagrine *or* acariâtre, mauvaise humeur, maussaderie,
Peewit. *V.* **Lapwing** [humeur bourrue, *f.*
Peg, *s.* cheville, *f.*; (*of casks*) fausset, *m.*; (*for hanging clothes,* &c.) portemanteau, *m.*, patère, *f.*, champignon, *m.*; (*forked, and used to fasten linen* or *prints to a rope*) épingle (de bois), *f.*, fichoir, *m.*; (*of ladders,* &c.) ranche, *f.*; (*of violins,* &c.) sillet, *m.*; (*degree*) cran, degré, *m*; — *v.a.* cheviller; marquer. *Row of coat-* —*s,* portemanteau, *m.* *To come down a* —, baisser d'un cran. *To rise a — higher,* monter *or* hausser d'un cran. *Not to stir a* —, ne pas bouger d'une semelle. *I took him down a* —, je lui ai rabattu le caquet. *To keep —ging away at it,* piocher toujours. — **ladder,** *s.* échelier, échellier, rancher, *m.* — **top,** *s.*
Pegasean, *adj.* pégasien [toupie, *f.*
Pegasus, *s.* (*myth., astr., zool.*) Pégase, *m.*
Pegging, *s.* chevillage, *m.*
Peggy, *s.* (*tooth*) quenotte, *f.*
Pekan, *s.* pékan, *m.*
Pekin, *s.* pékin, *m.*
Pekoe, *s.* (*tea*) péko, pékoe, *m.*
Pelagian, Pelagic, *adj.* pélagien, pélagique
Pelargonic, *adj.* pélargonique
Pelargonium, *s.* pélargonium, *m.*
Pelerine, *s.* pèlerine, *f.*
Pelf, *s.* biens, *m.pl.*, richesses, *f.pl.*, argent, *m.*; gain, lucre, *m.*; amour des richesses, *m.*
Pelican, *s.* (*zool., chem., surg.*) pélican, *m.*
Pelisse, *s.* pelisse, *f.*
Pellagra, *s.* pellagre, *f.*
Pellagrous, *adj.* pellagreux
Pellet, *s.* boulette, *f.*; (*shot*) balle, *f.*, (*small*) [grain de plomb, *m.*
Pellicle, *s.* pellicule, *f.*
Pellicular, *adj.* pelliculaire
Pellitory, *s.* pariétaire, *f.*
Pell-mell, *adv.* pêle-mêle
Pellucid, *adj.* transparent, pellucide
Pellucidity, Pellucidness, *s.* transparence, pellucidité, *f.*
Peloponnesian, *adj.* du Péloponèse

Pelt, *s. V.* **Fell,** *s.*; (*iron binding*) ferrure, *f.*; — *v.a.* assaillir *or* poursuivre à coups de (pierres, *or* boules de neige, *or* &c.); (*throw*) jeter, lancer; (*beat*) battre; (*bind with iron*) ferrer. — **wool,** *s.* pelade, *f.*
Pelting, *adj.* furieux; (*of rain*) battant; — *s.* attaque, *f.*, assaut, *m*; (*iron binding*) ferrure, *f.*
Peltry, *s.* peausserie, *f.*; pelleterie, *f.*
Pelvic, *adj.* pelvien
Pelvis, *s.* bassin, *m.*
Pemmican, *s.* pemmican, *m.*
Pen, *s.* plume, *f.*; (*for cattle*) parc, *m.*; (*coop*) poulailler, *m.*; — *v.a.* écrire, mettre par écrit; (*compose*) rédiger, écrire; (*shut*) enfermer; (*cattle*) parquer. *With the* —, à la plume. — *and ink,* une plume et de l'encre. — *and ink drawing* (or *sketch*), dessin à la plume. — **box, -case,** *s.* porte-plumes, *m.* — **cutter,** *s.* taille-plumes, *m.* —**ful,** *s.* plumée, *f.* — **holder,** *s.* porte-plume. *m.* — **knife,** *s.* canif, *m.* — **making machine,** *s.* taille-plumes, *m.* — **man,** *s.* calligraphe, *m.*; (*author*) écrivain, auteur, *m.* *To be a good* —, avoir une bonne (*or* belle) écriture. —**manship,** *s.* écriture, *f.*; calligraphie, *f.* — **rack,** *s* porte-plumes, *m.* — **stock,** *s.* vanne, *f.* — **wiper,** *s.* essuie-plume, *m.*
Penal, *adj.* pénal; punissable, passible d'une peine; (*law*) prévu par la loi pénale. — *servitude,* travaux forcés, *m.pl.*; réclusion, *f.* [*Seven years'* — *servitude,* sept ans de travaux forcés [*or* &c.]
Penality, *s.* pénalité, *f.*
Penally, *adv.* pénalement
Penalty, *s.* peine, pénalité, *f.*; (*fine*) amende, *f.*
Penance, *s.* pénitence, *f.*
Penates, *s.pl.* pénates, *m.pl.*
Pence, *pl.* of **Penny,** *which See*; (*contribution*) denier, *m.* *St. Peter's* —, le denier de St-Pierre, *m.*
Pencil, *s.* crayon, *m.*; (*brush*) pinceau, *m.*; (*opt.*) faisceau, *m.*; — *v.a.* (*paint*) peindre; (*draw*) dessiner au crayon, dessiner; (*write*) écrire au crayon. *In* —, au crayon. — **case,** *s.* porte-crayons, *m.* — **cloth,** *s.* torche-pinceau, *m.* — **holder,** *s.* porte-crayon, *m.* — **lead,** *s.* mine de plomb pour porte-crayons, *f.* — **mark,** *s.* marque au crayon, *f.* — — **pointer,** *s.* taille-crayons, *m.* — **rag,** *s.* *V.* — **cloth.** — **sketch,** *s.* dessin au crayon, *m.*
Pendant, *s.* pendant, *m.*; pendeloque, *f.*; (*of a watch-chain*) breloque, *f.*; (*arch.*) cul-de-lampe, *m.*; (*nav.*) flamme, *f.*, pennon, *m.*, (*broad* —) guidon, *m.*, (*small* —) banderole, *f.*
Pendency, *s.* (*law*) litispendance, *f.*
Pendent, *adj.* pendant; (*hanging*) suspendu; (*jutting*) saillant, en saillie
Pendentive, *s.* pendentif, *m.*
Pending, *adj. prep.* pendant
Pendular, *adj.* pendulaire [incertitude, *f.*
Pendulosity, *s.* suspension, *f.*; suspens, *m.*;
Pendulous, *adj.* pendant; suspendu; oscillant, balancé; (*irresolute*) en suspens, irrésolu, indécis, incertain
Pendulousness, *s. V.* **Pendulosity**
Pendulum, *s.* pendule, *m.*; (*horol.*) pendule, balancier, *m.*: — *adj.* (*of a pendulum*) de pendule, (*with ditto*) à pendule. — **clock,** *s.* pendule, *f.*; horloge à pendule, *f.* — **rod,** *s.* verge de pendule. *f.*
Penelope, *s.* (*zool.*) pénélope, *f.*
Penetrability, *s.* pénétrabilité, *f.*
Penetrable, *adj.* pénétrable
Penetrate, *v.a.n.* pénétrer
Penetratingly, *adv.* pénétramment
Penetration, *s.* pénétration, *f.*
Penetrative, *adj.* pénétratif
Penetratively, *adv.* pénétrativement
Penetrativeness, *s.* pénétration, *f.*
Penguin, *s.* pingouin, *m.*
Peninsula, *s.* péninsule, presqu'île, *f.*
Peninsular, *adj.* péninsulaire; de la Pénin

sule. *The — war*, la guerre de la Péninsule, la guerre d'Espagne, *f.*

Penitenc-e, y, *s.* pénitence, *f.*, repentir, *m.*

Penitent, *adj. s.* pénitent, *m.*, e, *f.*

Penitential, *adj. s.* pénitentiel, *adj. m.*, -le, *f.*, pénitentiel, *s.m.* — *psalms*, psaumes pénitentiaux, *m.pl.*

Penitentiary, *adj.* pénitentiaire; — *s.* (*pers.*) pénitencier, *m.*; (*thing*) maison pénitentiaire, *f.*; pénitencier, *m.*; colonie pénitentiaire, *f.*; maison centrale, *f.*; (*court of Rome*) pénitencerie, *f.*

Penitently, *adv.* avec pénitence, avec repentir

Pennant, *s.* (*nav.*) *V.* **Pendant**

Pennate, -d, *adj.* ailé; (*bot.*) penné

Pennatula, *s.* pennatule, *f.*

Penned, *adj.* à plumes ...

Penner, *s.* rédacteur, *m.*, -trice, *f.*, auteur, [écrivain, *m.*

Penniform, *adj.* penniforme

Penniless, *adj.* sans le sou, sans argent; pauvre [nine, *f.*

Pennine, *s.* pennine, *f.*; — *adj.* (*geog.*) Pen-

Penning, *s.* écriture, *f.*; (*composing*) rédaction, *f.*; (*of cattle*) parcage, *m.*

Pennon, *s.* (*nav.*) *V.* **Pendant**

Pennsylvanian, *s.adj.* Pensylvanien.*m.*,-ne, *f.*

Penny, *s.* (*Engl. coin*) penny, *m.*, (*Fr. equivalent*) dix centimes, deux sous, *m.pl.*; (*admin.*) décime, *m.*; — *adj.* (d'un penny); de dix centimes, de deux sous. *Five pence, V.* **Five.** *Ten pence*, 1 franc, *m.* *Not to have* or *be worth a* —, (*pers.*) n'avoir pas le sou. *To turn an honest* —, faire un profit légitime; gagner honnêtement sa vie. — **-a-liner,** *s.* correspondant *or* rédacteur (de journal) à dix centimes la ligne, *m.* — **loaf,** *s.* pain de dix centimes, *m.* — **royal,** *s.* pouliot, *m.* — **stamp,** *s.* timbre de dix centimes, *m.* — **weight,** *s.* (*coin.*) denier de poids, *m.* — **winkle,** *s.* *V.* **Periwinkle.** — **wise,** *adj.* liardeur, ménager de bouts de chandelles, *m.*; — *wise and pound-foolish*, économe dans les petites choses et prodigue dans les grandes. — **wort,** *s.* hydrocotyle, *f.* — **worth,** *s.* pour deux sous, pour dix centimes; (*bargain*) marché, *m.*, (*fam.*) pour son argent. *Two — worth*, pour vingt centimes

Pensile, *adj.* pendant; suspendu

Pensileness, *s.* suspension, *f.*

Pension, *s.* pension, *f.*; rente, *f.*; (*of officers*, &c.) retraite, *f.*; — *v.a.* pensionner. — **off,** mettre à la retraite, retraiter

Pensionary, *adj.* pensionné; qui consiste en une pension; — *s.* pensionnaire, *m.f.*

Pensioner, *s.* pensionnaire, *m.f.*; rentier, *m.*, -ière, *f.*; (*of soldiers, sailors*) invalide, *m.* *Out* —, invalide externe, externe, *m.* [triste, morne

Pensive, *adj.* pensif, rêveur, préoccupé; (*sad*)

Pensively, *adv.* pensivement, tristement, d'un air pensif *or* &c. (*V.* **Pensive**)

Pensiveness, *s.* air pensif, air rêveur, *m.*; (*sadness*) air triste, *m.*, tristesse, *f.*

Pentachord, *s. adj.* pentacorde, *s.m.*, *adj. m.f.*

Pentagon, *s.* pentagone, *m.*

Pentagonal, *adj.* pentagonal, pentagone

Pentahedral, *adj.* pentaèdre

Pentahedron, *s.* pentaèdre, *m.*

Pentameter, *s.* pentamètre, *m.* [tamètre

Pentameter, Pentametric, -al, *adj.* pen-

Pentateuch, *s.* Pentateuque, *m.*

Pentecost, *s.* Pentecôte, *f.*

Pentecostal, *adj.* pentécostaire, de la Pentecôte

Penthouse, Pentice, *s.* auvent, abat-vent, appentis, *m.*

Penult, Penultima, *s.*, **Penultimate,** *adj. s.*, pénultième, *s.f.*, *adj. m.f.*

Penumbra, *s.* pénombre, *f.*

Penurious, *adj.* avare, mesquin, ladre, sordide; stérile; pauvre

Penuriously, *adv.* mesquinement, avec ladrerie, en lésinant; avec pénurie

Penuriousness, Penury, *s.* pénurie, disette, *f.*; pauvreté extrême, misère, *f.*, parcimonie, mesquinerie, ladrerie, *f.*

Peon, Peony. *V.* **Pæon, Pæony**

People, *s.* (*nation*) peuple, *m.*; nation, *f.*; (*individuals : anywhere*) gens, *m.f.pl.*; (*considered together, within certain limits*) monde, *m.*; (*if a number is mentioned, persons*) personnes, *f.pl.*; (*inhabitants*) habitants, *m.pl.*; population, *f.*; (*men*) hommes, *m.pl.*; (*subjects*) peuple, *m.*; (*common folks, lower class*) peuple, *m.*; (*they, one*) on; — *v.a.* peupler ('*with*,' de). — *say*, on dit. *Little* —, les petites personnes, *f.pl.*, les enfants, *m.f.pl.*; (*fig.*) les petites gens, *f.pl.* *Great* —, les grandes personnes, *f.pl.*; (*fig.*) les grands personnages, les grands, *m.pl.* *Learned* —, les gens instruits, *m.pl.*, les personnes instruites, *f.pl.* *Common* —, *other* —, *young* —, &c., *V.* **Common, Other, Young,** &c. *The French* —, *the English* —, les Francais, les Anglais, *m.pl.* (*nation*) le peuple français, le peuple anglais, *m.* *They are French* —, ce sont des Français; ils sont Français. *There were a great many — at church*, il y avait beaucoup de monde à l'église

Peplus, *s.* péplum, péplus, *m.*

Pepper, *s.* poivre, *m.*; — *v.a.* poivrer; (*with shot, blows*, &c.) cribler. — **box,** *s.* poivrier, *m.*, poivrière, *f.* — **brand,** *s.* (*agr.*, *bot.*) *V.* **Bunt.** — **caster,** *s.* *V.* — **box.** — **corn,** *s.* grain de poivre, *m.*; (*fig.*) bagatelle, *f.*; (*agr.*) nielle, *f.* — **mint,** *s.* menthe poivrée, menthe, *f.* —*mint drops* or *lozenges*, pastilles de menthe, *f.pl.* —*mint water*, eau de menthe, *f.* — **grass,** *s.* *V.* **Dittander.** — **plant,** *s.* poivrier, *m.*; tasmannie, *f.* — **plantation,** *s.* poivrière, *f.* — **sauce,** *s.* poivrade, *f.* — **tree,** *s.* poivrier, *m.* — **wort,** *s.* *V.* **Dittander**

Peppery, *adj.* poivré, de poivre; (*fig.*, *pers.*) vif, irascible, irritable; pétulant; (*fig.*, *things*) [vif, vert, fort; chaud

Pepsine, *s.* pepsine, *f.*

Per, *prep.* par; (*pers.*) par l'entremise de, par; (*according to*) suivant; (*in accounts, bills*) le, *m.*, la, *f.*, les, *pl.* — *annum*, par an. — *diem*, par jour. — *cent*, pour cent. — *hundred*, le cent. *As* —, (*com.*) suivant [hasard, peut-être

Peradventure, *adv.* par aventure, par

Perambulate, *v.a.* parcourir; visiter; in- [specter

Perambulating, *adj.* ambulant

Perambulation, *s.* tournée, *f.*, voyage, *m.*; visite, *f.*; inspection, *f.*

Perambulator, *s.* hodomètre, compte-pas, *m.*; (*carriage*) voiture d'enfant, *f.*

Perceivable, *adj.* perceptible; sensible; visible

Perceivably, *adv.* perceptiblement; sensiblement; visiblement

Perceive, *v.a.* (*see, with the eye or mind*) apercevoir; découvrir; (*find out, notice, by the mind only*) s'apercevoir de; découvrir; remarquer; (*philos.*) percevoir; — *v.n.* s'apercevoir ('*that*,' que)

Percentage, *s.* tant pour cent, pour-cent, pourcentage, tantième, *m.*; droit de ... (tant) pour cent, *m.*; intérêt (de tant pour cent), *m.*; taux, *m.*; commission, *f.*; remise, *f*; escompte, *m.*; profit, *m.*; proportion, *f.*

Perceptibility, *s.* perceptibilité, *f.*

Percepti-ble, -bly. *V.* **Perceiva-ble, -bly**

Perception, *s.* perception, *f.*; sensibilité, *f.*; découverte, *f.*; observation, *f.*

Perceptive, *adj.* perceptif

Perch, *s.* (*pole*) perche, *f.*; (*bird's*) perchoir, *m.*; (*of a carriage*) flèche, *f.*; (*fish*) perche, *f.*; (*measure*) perche, *f.*; — *v.a.* percher; — *v.n.* percher, se percher. *To — oneself*, se percher. *To get one off his* —, *V.* **Oust**

Perchance, *adv.* par hasard; peut-être

Percher, *s.* percheur, *m.*

Perching, *adj.* percheur

Perchlorate, *s.* perchlorate, *m.*

Perchloric, *adj.* perchlorique

Perchloride, *s.* perchlorure, *m.* [tion

Percipient, *adj.* intelligent, doué de percep-

Percolate, *v.a.n.* filtrer; passer
Percolation, *s.* filtration, *f.*
Percolator, *s.* filtre, *m.*
Percuss, *v.a.n.* percuter
Percussing, *adj.* *V.* **Percussive**
Percussion, *s.* percussion, *f.*; — *adj.* à percussion, percutant, percuteur. — **cap,** *s.* capsule, *f.* — **gun,** *s.* fusil à percussion, fusil à piston, *m.* [cussion
Percussive, *adj.* percutant, percuteur, à per-
Percutient, *adj.* *V.* **Percussive;** — *s.* per-
Perdefume, *s.* fumivore, *m.* [cuteur, *m.*
Perdition, *s.* ruine, destruction, *f.*; (*theol.*) perdition, *f.* [biter l'étranger
Peregrinate, *v.n.* voyager, pérégriner; ha-
Peregrination, *s.* voyage, *m.*, pérégrination, *f.*; séjour à l'étranger, *m.*
Peregrinator, *s.* voyageur, pérégrinateur, *m.*
Peremptorily, *adv.* péremptoirement; absolument
Peremptoriness, *s.* nature péremptoire, *f.*; (*pers.*) manière tranchante, *f.*, ton tranchant *or* absolu *or* dogmatique, *m.*
Peremptory, *adj.* péremptoire; (*pers.*) tranchant, absolu, dogmatique; (*law*) péremptoire; (*law*) de rigueur
Perennial, *adj.* pérenne, qui dure toute l'année; perpétuel, continuel; (*of fevers*) continu; (*of plants,* &c.) vivace, pérenne; — *s.* plante vivace, *f.* [lement, incessamment
Perennially, *adv.* perpétuellement, continuel-
Perennity, *s.* pérennité, *f.*; perpétuité, *f.*
Perfect, *adj.* parfait; achevé; fini; accompli; excellent; (*real*) vrai; (*of insects*) parfait; (*bot.*) complet; (*gram., mus.*) parfait; — *s.* (*gram.*) parfait, *m.*; — *v.a.* rendre parfait; achever; compléter; accomplir; (*improve*) perfectionner. — *tense,* parfait, *m.*
Perfecter, *s.* personne *or* chose qui rend parfait *or* &c. (*V.* **Perfect,** *v.a.*), *f.*
Perfectibility, *s.* perfectibilité, *f.*
Perfectible, *adj.* perfectible
Perfectibly, *adv.* perfectiblement
Perfecting, *s.* achèvement, *m.*; accomplissement, *m.*; (*improving*) perfectionnement, *m.*
Perfection, *s.* perfection, *f.*; excellence, *f.* *To* —, dans la perfection, en perfection, parfaitement
Perfection-ism, -ist. *V.* page 3, § 1
Perfectly, *adv.* parfaitement
Perfectness, *s.* *V.* **Perfection**
Perfidious, *adj.* perfide
Perfidiously, *adv.* perfidement
Perfidiousness, Perfidy, *s.* perfidie, *f.*
Perforate, *v.a.* perforer, percer
Perforating, *adj.* perforant, perforateur
Perforation, *s.* perforation, *f.*, percement, *m.*; (*hole*) trou, *m.*
Perforative, *adj.* perforatif
Perforator, *s.* perforateur, *m.*
Perforce, *adv.* par force, de force, forcément
Perform, *v.a.n.* faire; exécuter; accomplir; effectuer; exercer; (*fulfil*) remplir, s'acquitter de; (*theat., mus.*) jouer
Performable, *adj.* exécutable, faisable, praticable; (*theat., mus.*) jouable
Performance, *s.* exécution, *f.*, accomplissement, *m.*; exercice, *m.*; action, *f.*, acte, *m.*; (*work*) œuvre, *f.*, ouvrage, *m.*; (*mus.*) exécution, *f.*; (*theat.*) représentation, *f.*; (*of acrobats, horse-riders,* &c.) exercice, *m.*; (*way of acting*) jeu, *m.* *No* —*!* (*theat.*) relâche!
Performer, *s.* auteur, *m.*; (*mus.*) musicien, *m.*, -ne, *f.*; exécutant, *m.*, e, *f.*; (*theat.*) acteur, *m.*, actrice, *f.*, artiste, *m.f.*
Perfume, *v.a.* ('*with,*' de) parfumer; embaumer; — *s.* parfum, *m.*
Perfumer, *s.* parfumeur, *m.*, -euse, *f.*
Perfumery, *s.* parfumerie, *f.*
Perfuming, *s.* action de parfumer, *f.*; — *adj.* qui parfume. — **pan,** *s.* cassolette, *f.*, parfumoir, *m.*

Perfunctorily, *adv.* légèrement, négligemment, par manière d'acquit, pour la forme
Perfunctoriness, *s.* légèreté, négligence, exécution par manière d'acquit, *f.*
Perfunctory, *adj.* léger, négligent; fait par manière d'acquit, fait pour la forme, fait négligemment
Perhaps, *adv.* peut-être. — *so,* peut-être que oui, peut-être bien. — *not,* peut-être que non. — *you have,* vous avez peut-être, peut-être que
Peri, *s.* péri, *m.f.* [vous avez
Perianth, *s.* périanthe, *m.*
Pericardiac, Pericardial, *adj.* péricardique
Pericarditis, *s.* péricardite, *f.*
Pericardium, *s.* péricarde, *m.*
Pericarp, *s.* péricarpe, *m.*
Pericranium, *s.* péricrâne, *m.*
Perigee, *s* périgée, *m.*
Perihelion, *s.* périhélie, *m.*
Peril, *s.* péril, danger, *m.*; — *v.a.* *V.* **Imperil.** *At the* — *of,* au péril de. *At o.'s* —, à ses risques et périls
Perilous, *adj.* périlleux, dangereux [ment
Perilously, *adv.* périlleusement, dangereuse-
Perilousness, *s.* nature périlleuse, *f.*, péril,
Perimeter, *s.* périmètre, *m.* [danger, *m.*
Period, *s.* période, *f.*; (*duration*) espace *or* laps (de temps), *m.*; délai, *m.*; durée, *f.*, temps, *m.*; (*limit*) limite, *f.*, terme, *m.*; (*epoch*) époque, *f.*; (*degree*) période, *m.*, degré, *m.*; (*astr., chron., gram., med.*) période, *f.*; (*full stop*) point, *m.* *At a later* —, plus tard
Periodic, *adj.* périodique
Periodical, *adj.* périodique; — *s.* périodique, *m.*, ouvrage *or* recueil périodique, *m.*, publication périodique, *f.*
Periodicalist, *s.* périodiste, *m.*
Periodically, *adv.* périodiquement [dicité, *f.*
Periodicalness, Periodicity, *s.* pério-
Periodide, *s.* periodure, *m.*
Periosteum, *s.* périoste, *m.*
Periostitis, *s.* périostite, périostéite, *f.*
Peripatetic, *s. adj.* péripatéticien, *m.*, -ne, *f.*
Peripatetically, *adv.* péripatétiquement
Peripateticism, *s.* péripatétisme, *m.*
Peripheric, -al, *adj.* périphérique
Periphery, *s.* périphérie, *f.*
Periphrase, Periphrasis, *s.* périphrase, *f.*; — *v.n.a.* périphraser [rect; verbeux
Periphrastic, -al, *adj.* périphrastique; indi-
Periphrastically, *adv.* périphrastiquement; indirectement; verbeusement
Peripneumonia, *s.* péripneumonie, *f.*
Peripneumonic, *adj.* péripneumonique
Perish, *v.n.* périr ('*with,*' de); dépérir
Perishable, *adj.* périssable; éphémère; (*of goods*) qui ne se garde pas; sujet à s'avarier
Perishableness, *s.* nature périssable *or* éphémère, *f.* [éphémère
Perishably, *adv.* d'une manière périssable *or*
Perishing, *adj.* qui périt; éphémère; (*killing*)
Peristaltic, *adj.* péristaltique [tuant
Peristyle, *s.* péristyle, *m.*
Peritoneal, *adj.* péritonéal
Peritoneum, *s.* péritoine, *m.*
Peritonitis, *s.* péritonite, *f.*
Periwig, *s.* perruque, *f.*
Periwinkle, *s.* (*shell fish*) vigneau, vignot, bigorneau, *m.*; (*bot.*) pervenche, *f.*
Perjure, *v.a.* parjurer
Perjured, Perjurious, *adj.* parjure
Perjurer, *s.* parjure, *m.f.*; (*law*) faux témoin, *m.*
Perjury, *s.* parjure, *m.*; (*law*) faux témoignage, *m.*
Perk, (— **up**), *v.n.* se rengorger, porter le nez au vent; minauder; — *v.a.* attifer, parer, orner; — *adj.* pétulant; fier; pimpant, coquet; éveillé, vif
Perkin, *s.* petit cidre, *m.* [quet; éveillé, vif
Perky, *adj.* *V.* **Perk** [*tions*) inamovibilité, *f.*
Permanenc-e, y, *s.* permanence, *f.*; (*of situa-*
Permanent, *adj.* permanent; en permanence; (*of situations*) à vie; inamovible; sûr. *The* — *way,* (*rail.*) la voie, *f.*

Permanently, *adv.* d'une manière permanent, permanemment; en permanence
Permanganate, *s.* permanganate, *m.*
Permeability, *s.* perméabilité, *f.*
Permeable, *adj.* perméable
Permeate, *v.a.* pénétrer
Permeation, *s.* pénétration, *f.* [permis
Permissible, *adj.* qui peut se permettre,
Permission, *s.* permission, *f.*; (*admin.*) permis, *m.*, permission, *f.*
Permissive, *adj.* permissif; permis, toléré; tolérant; (*optional*) facultatif
Permissively, *adv.* avec permission, par tolérance, sans empêchement; (*optionally*) facultativement
Permit, *v.a.* permettre (*for constructions, V.* **Allow**); — *s.* permis, *m.*; laisser-passer, *m.*; passavant, *m.*; congé, *m.*; acquit-à-caution, *m.*
Permittee, *s.* permissionnaire, *m.f.*
Permuta-bility, bleness. *V.* page 3, § 1
Permutable, *adj.* permutable [échange, *m.*
Permutation, *s.* permutation, *f.*; (*com.*)
Permute, *v.a.* permuter; — *v.n.* se permuter
Permuter, *s.* permuteur, permutant, *m.*
Pern, Pernis, *s.* (*bird*) bondrée, *f.*
Perna, *s.* (*mollusc*) perne, *f.*
Pernicious, *adj.* pernicieux
Perniciously, *adv.* pernicieusement
Perniciousness, *s.* nature pernicieuse, *f.*
Perorate, *v.n.* pérorer
Peroration, *s.* péroraison, *f.*
Peroxidate, Peroxidize, *v.a.* peroxyder
Peroxide, *s.* peroxyde, *m.*
Perpend, *v.a.* peser, examiner
Perpendicle, *s.* perpendicule, *m.* [*adj.m.f.*, *s.f.*
Perpendicular, *adj. s.* perpendiculaire,
Perpendicularity, *s.* perpendicularité, *f.*
Perpendicularly, *adv.* perpendiculairement
Perpetrate, *v.a.* commettre; exécuter; (*law*) commettre, perpétrer
Perpetration, *s.* action de commettre, commission, *f.*; exécution, *f.*; (*law*) perpétration, *f.*; (*deed*) forfait, crime, *m.*
Perpetrator, *s. V.* **Committer**
Perpetual, *adj.* perpétuel; continuel; constant. — *screw*, vis sans fin, *f.*
Perpetually, *adv.* perpétuellement; continuellement; constamment
Perpetualty, *s.* perpétualité, *f.*
Perpetuate, *v.a.* perpétuer
Perpetuation, *s.* perpétuation, *f.*
Perpetuity, *s.* perpétuité, *f.* [embarrasser
Perplex, *v.a.* embrouiller, brouiller; (*puzzle*)
Perplexedly, *adv.* d'une manière embrouillée, confusément; avec embarras, avec perplexité
Perplexedness, Perplexity, *s.* perplexité, *f.*, embarras, *m.*; embrouillement, *m.*
Perquisites, *s.pl.* revenants-bons, émoluments, *m.pl.*; casuel, *m.*; (*of servants*) petits profits, profits, *m.pl.*; (*from jobbery*) (le) tour du bâton, *m.*; (*gratuities, tips*) gratifications, *f.pl.*, pourboires, *m.pl.*
Perquisition, *s.* perquisition, recherche, *f.*
Perquisitor, *s.* perquisiteur, *m.*
Perron, *s.* perron, *m.*
Perry, *s.* poiré, *m.*
Persecute, *v.a.* persécuter
Persecuting, *adj.* persécuteur
Persecution, *s.* persécution, *f.*
Persecu-tor, trix, *s.* persécuteur, *m.* -trice, *f.*
Perseverance, *s.* persévérance, *f.* [**sist**)
Persevere, *v.n.* persévérer ('*in* ...,' *V.* **Per-**
Perseveringly, *adv.* avec persévérance, persévéramment
Persian, *s. adj.* Persan, *m.*, e, *f.*; (*of antiquity*) Perse, *m.f.*; (*of or from Persia*) de Perse; (*arch.*) persique; (*the — language*) le persan, *m.*, la langue persane, *f.* — *Gulf*, golfe Persique, *m.* — *lilac*, lilas de Perse, *m.*
Persic, *adj.* persique
Persicaria, *s.* persicaire, *f.*
Persicot, *s.* persicot, *m.*
Persist, *v.n.* persister ('*in a thing*,' dans une chose; '*in doing a thing*,' à faire une chose; ['*in it*,' y)
Persistenc-e, y, *s.* persistance, *f.*
Persistent, Persisting, *adj.* persistant
Person, *s.* personne, *f.*; personnage, *m.*; extérieur, *m.*, dehors, *m.pl.*, physique, *m.*; (*stature*) taille, *f.*; —**s**, *pl.* personnes, *f.pl.*, gens, *m.f.pl.*; monde, *m.*; (*they, one*) on, quelqu'un, *m.* *A French* —, un Français, *m.*, une Française, *f.*
Personable, *adj.* beau, gracieux, de bonne mine
Personage, *s.* personnage, *m.*
Personal, *adj.* personnel; (*of property*) mobilier, meuble. — *action*, (*law*) action personnelle, action mobilière, *f.* — *share*, (*com.*, *fin.*) action nominative, *f.* — *tax*, contribution personnelle, *f.*
Personalism, *s.* personnalisme, *m.*
Personality, *s.* personnalité, *f.*
Personalization, *s.* personnalisation, *f.*
Personalize, *v.a.* personnaliser
Personally, *adv.* personnellement; en personne; soi-même [*m.pl.*
Personalty, *s.* biens mobiliers, biens meubles,
Personate, *v.a.* représenter; imiter, contrefaire; feindre, jouer; — *adj.* (*bot.*) personnée, *f.*
Personation, *s. V.* **Impersonation**
Personator, *s.* personne qui passe pour une autre, *f.*; acteur, *m.*, actrice, *f.*
Personification, *s.* personnification, *f.*
Personifier, *s.* personnificateur, *m.*, -trice, *f.*
Personify, *v.a.* personnifier
Perspective, *adj.* perspectif; optique; — *s* perspective, *f.*; (*glass*) verre optique, *m.*, lunette, *f.*
Perspectively, *adv.* selon les règles de la perspective; au moyen d'un verre optique
Perspicacious, *adj.* perspicace, pénétrant
Perspicacity, *s.* perspicacité, pénétration, *f.*
Perspicuity, *s.* perspicuité, clarté, netteté, *f.*
Perspicuous, *adj.* clair, net
Perspicuously, *adv.* clairement, nettement
Perspicuousness. *V.* **Perspicuity**
Perspirability, *s.* transpirabilité, *f.*
Perspirable, *adj.* transpirable
Perspiration, *s.* transpiration, sueur, *f.* *Profuse* —, sueur abondante. *To be in a profuse* —, être tout en sueur *or* tout en nage *or*
Perspire, *v.n.* transpirer, suer [tout en eau
Persuadable, *adj.* persuasible
Persuade, *v.a.* persuader ('*to*,' '*of*,' de); (*induce*) décider ('*to*,' à). — **from,** dissuader de
Persuader, *s.* persuadeur, *m.*
Persuasible, *adj.* persuasible
Persuasion, *s.* persuasion, *f.*; opinion, croyance, foi, *f.*; religion, *f.*, culte, *m.*
Persuasive, *adj.* persuasif
Persuasively, *adv.* d'une manière persuasive
Persuasiveness, *s.* talent de persuader, *m.*, force persuasive, *f.*
Persulphide, *s.* persulfure, *m.*
Pert, *adj.* vif, éveillé, sémillant; pétulant; leste, inconvenant, impertinent, insolent
Pertain, *v.n.* appartenir; avoir rapport, se
Pertinacious, *adj.* opiniâtre [rapporter
Pertinaciously, *adv.* opiniâtrément
Pertinaciousness, Pertinacity, *s.* opiniâtreté, pertinacité, *f.* [*f.*, à-propos, *m.*
Pertinenc-e, y, *s.* pertinence, convenance,
Pertinent, *adj.* pertinent; convenable, à propos
Pertinently, *adv.* pertinemment, convenablement, à propos
Pertly, *adv.* avec vivacité, avec pétulance; impertinemment, avec impertinence, insolemment [nence, insolence, *f.*
Pertness, *s.* vivacité, pétulance, *f.*; imperti-
Perturbation, *s.* perturbation, *f.*; désordre, bouleversement, *m.*; (*of the mind*) trouble, *m.*,
Peruke. *V.* **Wig** [agitation, *f.*
Perusal, *s.* lecture, *f.*; examen, *m.*
Peruse, *v.a.* lire, parcourir; examiner, étudier
Peruser, *s.* lecteur, *m.*, -trice, *f.*; observateur, *m.*, -trice, *f.*

Peruvian, *s.* Péruvien, *m.*, -ne, *f.*; — *adj.* péruvien, du Pérou. — *balsam*, baume du Pérou, *m.* — *bark*, quinquina, *m.*
Pervade, *v.a.* pénétrer, pénétrer dans, passer à travers; se répandre dans; être répandu dans; régner dans; remplir; (*seize*) s'emparer [de
Pervasion, *s.* pénétration, *f.*
Perverse, *adj.* pervers; méchant; mauvais; intraitable [sité; méchamment
Perversely, *adv.* perversement, avec perver-
Perverseness, Perversity, *s.* perversité, *f.*; méchanceté, *f.*
Perversion, *s.* perversion, *f.*
Perversive, *adj.* propre à pervertir
Pervert, *v.a.* pervertir; — *s.* pervers, *m.*, e, *f.*
Perverter, *s.* pervertisseur, *m.*, -euse, *f.*, corrupteur, *m.*, -trice, *f.*
Pervertible, *adj.* pervertissable [accessible
Pervious, *adj.* pénétrable; perméable; (*fig.*)
Perviousness, *s.* pénétrabilité, *f.*; perméabi-
Pesade, *s.* pesade, *f.* [lité, *f.*
Pessary, *s.* pessaire, *m.*
Pessim-ism, -ist. *V.* page 3, § 1
Pest, *s.* peste, *f.*; fléau, *m.* — **house,** *s.* hôpital de pestiférés, *m.*; lazaret, *m.*
Pester, *v.a.* tourmenter, importuner, ennuyer
Pestiferous, *adj.* pestilentiel; pernicieux, malfaisant [tion, *f.*; poison, *m.*
Pestilence, *s.* peste, *f.*; épidémie, *f.*; corrup-
Pestilent, Pestilential, *adj.* pestilentiel; (*fig.*) contagieux; pernicieux, malfaisant
Pestilently, *adv.* pernicieusement, d'une manière funeste
Pestle, *s.* pilon, *m.*; — *v.a.* piler
Pet, *s.* boutade, *f.*, dépit, accès d'humeur, *m.*; (*a fondling*) chéri, *m.*, e, *f.*; favori, *m.*, -te, *f.*; enfant gâté, *m.*, enfant gâtée, *f.*; — *adj.* favori; — *v.a.* dorloter, câliner, choyer; caresser; (— *too much, spoil*) gâter. — *name*, petit nom d'amitié, *m.* *In a* —, dans un accès de mauvaise humeur; de dépit. *To be in a* —, être de mauvaise humeur, être fâché. *To be a great* —, être très aimé. *To take* —, se dépiter, se gendarmer
Petal, *s.* pétale, *m.*
Petaled, Petalous, *adj.* pétalé; à pétales
Petalism, *s.* pétalisme, *m.*
Petard, *s.* pétard, *m.*
Petardier, *s.* pétardier, *m.*
Petchary, *s.* (*bird*) tyran, tyranneau, *m.*
Petechiæ, *s.pl.* pétéchies, *f.pl.*
Petechial, *adj.* pétéchial
Peter-pence, *s.pl.* *V.* **Pence**
Petiolar, *adj.* pétiolaire
Petiolate, Petioled, *adj.* pétiolé
Petiole, *s.* pétiole, *m.*
Petitio principii, *s.* pétition de principe, *f.*
Petition, *s.* pétition, *f.*; demande, *f.*; (*entreaty*) prière, supplication, supplique, *f.*; (*law*) requête, *f.*; — *v.a.n.* présenter une pétition à, pétitionner; (*supplicate*) supplier; demander; (*law*) présenter une requête à. — *of rights*, pétition des droits, *f.* — **paper,** *s.* papier-ministre, papier-tellière, *m.*
Petitionary, *adj.* de pétition; de supplication; suppliant
Petitioner, *s.* pétitionnaire, *m.f.*; suppliant, *m.*, e, *f.*; (*law*) demandeur, *m.*, -eresse, *f.*; requérant, *m.*, e, *f.*
Petitioning, *s.* pétitionnement, *m.*; pétitions, *f.pl.*; droit de pétition, *m.* *Right of* —, droit
Petitory, *adj.* pétitoire [de pétition, *m.*
Petong. *V.* **Packfong**
Petrary, *s.* pierrière, *f.* [tempête, *m.*
Petrel, *s.* pétrel, *m.* *Storm* or *stormy* —, pétrel
Petrifaction, Petrification, *s.* pétrification, *f.*
Petrifactive, Petrific, *adj.* pétrifiant
Petrify, *v.a.* pétrifier; — *v.n.* se pétrifier
Petroleum, *s.* pétrole, *m.* — **oil,** *s.* huile de pétrole, *f.* — **works,** *s.pl.* pétrolerie, *f.*
Petroliferous, *adj.* pétrolifère
Petroline, *s.* pétroline, *f.*
Petrology, &c. pétrologie, &c. (*V.* page 3, § 1)
Petrosilex, *s.* pétrosilex, *m.*
Petrous, *adj.* pierreux
Pettichaps, *s.* *V.* **Pettychaps**
Petticoat, *s.* jupon, *m.*; jupe, *f.*; (*jest.*) cotillon, *m.*; —**s,** *pl.* (*of children*) jaquette, *f.* — **body,** *s.* corsage de dessous, *m.* — **government,** *s.* régime du cotillon, *m.* — **lane,** *s.* friperie, *f.*
Petticoating, *s.* étoffe pour jupons, *f.*
Pettifog, *v.n.* avocasser
Pettifogger, *s.* petit avoué, *m.*; petit avocat, avocassier, chicaneur, m.
Pettifoggery, *s.* avocasserie, chicane, *f.*
Pettifogging, *adj.* avocassier, chicanier, chicaneur; — *s.* avocasserie, chicane, *f.*
Pettiness, *s.* petitesse, *f.*
Pettish, *adj.* sujet à des accès d'humeur, irritable, maussade, bourru [de *or* par dépit
Pettishly, *adv.* avec humeur, d'un air bourru;
Pettishness, *s.* humeur chagrine, mauvaise humeur, *f.*, air bourru, *m.*
Pettitoes, *s.pl.* pieds de cochon de lait, *m.pl.*; (*of children*) petons, *m.pl.*; (*of grown up people, in contempt or jest.*) pieds, *m.pl.*, pattes, *f.pl.*
Petto (In), *adv.* in petto, en secret. *To keep in* —, réserver in petto
Petty, *adj.* petit; menu; bas; inférieur, subalterne; (*poor*) chétif, pauvre. — **chaps,** *s.* (*bird*) fauvette des jardins, *f.*, becfigue, *m.* — **charges,** *s pl.* (*com.*) menus frais, *m.pl.*
Petulanc-e, y, *s.* pétulance, *f.*; impertinence, *f.*
Petulant, *adj.* pétulant; impertinent
Petulantly, *adv.* pétulamment, avec pétulance; impertinemment, avec impertinence
Petunia, *s.* pétunia, *m.*
Petunse, *s.* pétunsé, *m.*
Pew, *s.* banc d'église, banc, *m.* — **opener,** *s.* gardien (*m.*, -ne, *f.*) des bancs (à l'église)
Pewet, Pewit, *s.* *V.* **Lapwing**
Pewter, *s.* étain, *m.*; vaisselle d'étain, *f.*; pot d'étain, *m.*; — *adj.* d'étain. — **articles,** *s.pl.* *V.* — **ware.** — **pot,** *s.* pot d'étain, *m.* — **ware** *or* **wares,** *s.* poterie d'étain, vaisselle
Pewterer, *s.* potier d'étain, *m.* [d'étain, *f.*
Phaeton, *s.* victoria, *f.*; phaéton, *m.* *Cab* —, milord, *m.* *Mail* —, phaéton, *m.* *Park* —, *Victoria* —, victoria, *f.*
Phalanger, Phalangist, *s.* phalanger, *m.*
Phalanx, *s.* phalange, *f.*
Phantascope, *s.* fantasmascope, *m.*
Phantasm, Phantasma, *s.* fantôme, *m.*; (*med.*) fantasme, *m.*
Phantasmagoria, *s.* fantasmagorie, *f.*
Phantasmagoric, *adj.* fantasmagorique
Phantasmagorically, *adv.* fantasmagoriquement [tasmatique
Phantasmal, Phantasmatical, *adj.* fan-
Phantasy, &c. *V.* **Fantasy,** &c.
Phantom, *s.* fantôme, *m.*
Pharisaic, -al, *adj.* pharisaïque
Pharisaically, *adv.* pharisaïquement
Pharisaism, *s.* pharisaïsme, *m.*
Pharisee, *s.* pharisien, *m.*, -ne, *f.*
Pharmaceut-ic, al, -ically. *V.* page 3, § 1
Pharmaceutics, *s.pl.* pharmaceutique, *f.*
Pharmaceutist, Pharmacist, *s.* pharmacien, *m.*
Pharmacolog-ic, al, -ist, -y. *V.* p. 3, § 1
Pharmacopœia, *s.* pharmacopée, *f.*, codex, *m.*
Pharmacopolist, *s.* pharmacopole, *m.*
Pharmacy, *s.* pharmacie, *f.*
Pharo, *s.* (*game*) pharaon, *m.*
Pharos, *s.* phare, *m.* [pharyngien
Pharyngeal, Pharyngean, *adj.* pharyngé,
Pharyngitis, *s.* pharyngite, *f.*
Pharyngoscope, *s.* pharyngoscope, *m.*
Pharyngo-scopic, al, -scopy, -tomy,
Pharynx, *s.* pharynx, *m.* [&c. *V.* page 3, § 1
Phase, *s.* phase, *f.*; face, *f.*; aspect, *m.*
Phasel, *s.* faséole, *f.*
Phasis, *s.* *V.* **Phase**

Pheasant, *s.* faisan, *m.* *Young* —, faisandeau, *m.* — **breeder,** *s.* faisandier, *m.*, -ière, *f.* — **shell,** *s.* phasianelle, *f.* — **shooting,** *s.* chasse au faisan, *f.*
Pheasantry, *s.* faisanderie, *f.*
Pheese, *v.a.* peigner, étriller
Phenic, *adj.* phénique
Phenix, *s.* phénix, *m.*
Phenol, *s.* phénol, *m.*
Phenomenal, *adj.* phénoménal
Phenomenology, *s.* phénoménologie, *f.*
Phenomenon, *s.* phénomène, *m.*
Phenyl, *s.* phényle, *m.*
Phial, *s.* fiole, *f.*; flacon, *m*; (*jar*) bouteille, *f.*; (*ampulla*) ampoule, *f.*
Philander, *v.n.* faire l'amour; faire la cour
Philanthropic, -al, *adj.* (*things*) philanthropique; (*pers.*) philanthrope
Philanthrop-ically, -ism, -y. *V.* p 3, § 1
Philanthropist, *s.* philanthrope, *m.f.*
Philharmonic, *adj.* philharmonique
Philhellene, Philhellenist, *s.* philhellène, *m.f.*
Philhellenic, *adj.* philhellène
Philhellenism, *s.* philhellénisme, *m.*
Philibeg, *s. V.* **Kilt**
Philippic, *s.* philippique, *f.*
Philippize, *v.n.* invectiver
Philistine, *s.* Philistin, *m.*
Philogynist, *s.* philogyne, *m.*
Philogyny, *s.* philogynie, *f.*
Philolog-ic, al, -ically, -y. *V.* page 3, § 1
Philologist, Philologer, *s.* philologue, *m.*
Philomath-ic, al, -y. *V.* page 3, § 1
Philoprogenitiveness, *s.* philogéniture, *f.*
Philosopher, *s.* philosophe, *m.*; savant, *m.*; (*moral* —) moraliste, *m.*; (*natural* —) physicien, *m.* —**'s-stone,** *s.* pierre philosophale, *f.*
Philosophic, -al, *adj.* philosophique; (*pers.*) philosophe; (*of physics*) de physique. — *instrument,* instrument de physique, *m.*
Philosoph-ically, -ism, -ist. *V.* p. 3, § 1
Philosophize, *v.n.* philosopher
Philosophy, *s.* philosophie, *f.*; (*moral* —) philosophie morale, morale, *f.*; (*natural* —) physique, *f.*
Philotechnic, *adj.* philotechnique
Philter, *s.* philtre, *m.*
Phiz, *s.* face, trogne, binette, frimousse, balle, touche, *f.*
Phlebitis, *s.* phlébite, *f.*
Phlebo-tomist, -tomy, &c. phlébotomiste, &c. (*V.* page 3, § 1)
Phlebotomize, *v.a.* phlébotomiser
Phlegm, *s.* flegme, *m.*, mucosité, *f.*, glaire, *m.*, pituite, *f.*; (*fig*) flegme, sang-froid, *m.*
Phlegmasia, Phlegmasy, *s.* flegmasie, *f.*
Phlegmatic, *adj.* flegmatique
Phlegmatically, *adv.* flegmatiquement, avec flegme
Phlegmon, *s.* flegmon, *m.*
Phlegmonous, *adj.* flegmoneux
Phlox, *s.* phlox, *m.*
Phocæan, Phocean, *s.adj.* Phocéen, *m.*, -ne, *f.*
Pholas, *s.* pholade, *f.*
Phœnician, *s. adj.* Phénicien, *m.*, -ne, *f.*
Phœnix. *V.* **Phenix**
Phonet-ic, al, -ically, -ism, phonétique, &c. (*V.* page 3, § 1)
Phonetics, *s.pl.* phonétique, *f.*
Phonic, *adj.* phonique; —**s,** *s.pl.* phonique, *f.*
Phonograph, Phonographer, *s.* phonographe, *m.*
Phono-graphy, -logy, &c. *V.* page 3, § 1
Phonometer, *s.* phonomètre, *m.*
Phormium, *s.* phormion, phormium, *m.*
Phosphate, *s.* phosphate, *m.*
Phosphated, *adj.* phosphaté
Phosphatic, *adj.* phosphatique
Phosphide, *s.* phosphure, *m.*
Phosphite, *s.* phosphite, *m.*
Phosphor. *V.* **Phosphorus**
Phosphorate, *v.a.* phosphorer
Phosphoresce, *v.n.* être phosphorescent
Phosphorescence, *s.* phosphorescence, *f.*
Phosphorescent, *adj.* phosphorescent
Phosphoric, *adj.* phosphorique
Phosphorism, *s.* phosphorisme, *m.*
Phosphorite, *s.* phosphorite, *f.*
Phosphorization, *s.* phosphorisation, *f.*
Phosphorize, *v.a.* phosphoriser
Phosphorous, *adj.* phosphoreux
Phosphorus, *s.* phosphore, *m.* — **box,** *s.* briquet phosphorique, *m.* — **match,** *s.* allumette phosphorique, *f.* — **paste,** *s.* pâte phosphorée, *f.*
Phosphuret, *s. V.* **Phosphide**
Phosphureted, Phosphuretted, *adj.* phosphuré
Photo- ..., (*in compounds*) photo ...
Photogen, *s.* photogène, *m.*
Photogen-ic, -y, &c. photogénique, &c. (*V.* page 3, § 1)
Photograph, *v.a.* photographier; — *s.* photographie, *f.* *To have* or *get o.'s — taken,* se faire photographier
Photographer, *s.* photographe, *m.*
Photographic, *adj.* photographique, de photographie; (*pers.*) photographe. — *artist, colourist* (or *tinter*), *painter, printer* &c., artiste, retoucheur, peintre, imprimeur, &c., photographe, *m.* — *printing,* imprimerie photographique, *f.* — *studio,* atelier photographique, atelier de photographie, *m.*, photographie, *f.*
Photograph-ically, -y. *V.* page 3, § 1
Photolithography, Photology, &c. *V.* page 3, § 1
Photometer, *s.* photomètre, *m.*
Photometric, -al, *adj.* photométrique
Photometry, *s.* photométrie, *f.*
Photophobia, *s.* photophobie, *f.*
Photoscope, *s.* photoscope, *m.*
Photoscopic, *adj.* photoscopique
Photosculptural, *adj.* photosculptural
Photosculpture, *s.* photosculpture, *f.*
Photosphere, *s.* photosphère, *f.*
Phrase, *s.* phrase, locution, *f.*; (*mus.*) phrase, *f.*; — *v.a n.* phraser; nommer, appeler, désigner; exprimer; (*mus.*) phraser. — **book,** *s.* phrasaire, *m.*
Phraseologic, -al, *adj.* phraséologique
Phraseology, *s.* phraséologie, *f.*
Phrenic, *adj.* phrénique
Phrenitis, *s.* phrénite, *f.*
Phrenolog-ic, al, -ically, -y, phrénologique, &c. (*V.* page 3, § 1)
Phrenologist, *s.* phrénologiste, phrénologue, *m.*
Phrygian, *s.* Phrygien, *m.*, -ne, *f.*; — *adj.* phrygien, de Phrygie
Phthiriasis, *s.* phthiriase, *f.*, phthiriasis, *m.*
Phthisical, *adj. s.* phthisique
Phthisis, *s.* phthisie, *f.*
Phylactery, *s.* phylactère, prophylactère, *m.*
Physic, *s.* médecine, *f.*; médicament, *m.*; —**s,** *pl.* physique, *f.*; — *v.a. V.* **Doctor,** *v.a.* — **nut,** *s.* médicinier, *m*
Physical, *adj.* physique. — **science,** *s.* (la) physique, *f.*
Physically, *adv.* physiquement
Physician, *s.* médecin consultant, médecin, *m.*
Physicist, *s.* physicien, *m.*
Physiognomic, -al, *adj.* physiognomonique; —**s,** *s.pl.* physiognomonie, *f.*
Physiognomist, *s.* physionomiste, *m.f.*
Physiognomy, *s.* physionomie, *f.*; (*art*) physiognomonie, *f.*
Physiographer, *s.* physiographe, *m.*
Physiograph-ic, al, -y. *V.* page 3, § 1
Physiolog-ic, al, -ically, -ist, -y. *V.* p. 3, § 1
Phytographer, *s.* phytographe, *m.*
Phyto-graphy, -logy, -tomy, &c. *V.* p. 3, § 1
Phytolite, *s.* phytolithe, *m.*
Phytophagous, *adj.* phytophage
Pia-mater, *s.* pie-mère, *f.*
Pianette, Pianino, *s.* pianino, *m.*
Pianissimo, *adv.* pianissimo
Pianist, *s.* pianiste, *m.f.*
Piano, Pianoforte, *s.* piano, *m.* *Cottage —, upright —,* piano droit. *Grand —,* piano à queue. *Semi-cottage —, piccolo —,* petit piano droit. *Semi-grand —,* petit piano à queue. *To play on* or *upon the —, to play the —,* jouer du

piano. — **maker,** s. facteur de pianos, m. — **tuner,** s. accordeur de pianos, m.
Piassaba, Piassava, s. piassava, m.
Piaster, Piastre, s piastre, f.
Piazza, s. (*in Italy*) place, f.; (*in England*) [arcade, galerie, f., passage, m.
Pic. V. **Pick**
Pica, s. (*med.*) pica, m.; (*print. type*) cicéro, m. *Small* —, philosophie, f.
Picador, s. picador, m.
Picamar, Picamare, s. picamare, f.
Picard, s. adj. Picard, m., e, f.
Picaroon, s. pirate, forban, écumeur de mer, m.
Piccolo, s. (*flute*) piccolo, octavin, m. — [piano, s. V. **Piano**
Picea, s. picéa, m.
Pick, v.a. (*gather*) cueillir; (*cull*) choisir; trier; (— *dirt out of*) éplucher; (*collect*) ramasser; (*take from*) ôter, enlever; (*peck*) becqueter; (*nibble*) grignoter; (*a bone*) ronger; (*o.'s teeth, ears, nails*) curer; (*o.'s nose*) nettoyer; (*a lock*) crocheter; (*a pocket*) vider; prendre dans; (*a fowl*) plumer; (*oakum*) décorder, détordre; (*seek, a quarrel* or &c.) chercher; — v.n. grignoter, pignocher, chipoter, chicoter, manger du bout des dents; — s. (*tool*) pic, m.; (*choice*) choix, m.; élite, f. — **aback,** — **apack,** — **back,** adj. adv. sur le dos. — **axe,** s. pioche, f.; pic, m. — **lock,** s. crochet, rossignol, m; (*pers.*) crocheteur (m., -euse, f.) de serrures. — **lock key,** s. crochet de serrurier, m. — **off,** v.a. cueillir; enlever, ôter; (*cull*) choisir. — **out,** v.a (*pull off*) arracher; enlever; (*clean*) éplucher; (*select*) choisir. - **pocket,** — **purse,** s. filou, m.; voleur (m., -euse, f.) à la tire, tireur, m., -euse, f., voleur, m., -euse, f. — **up,** v.a. ramasser; relever; raccrocher; recueillir; attraper; prendre; (*glean*) glaner; (*a living*) gagner péniblement (sa vie). — **up again,** v.n. reprendre, se refaire
Pickable, adj. (*of locks*) crochetable
Picked, adj. (*sharp*) pointu; (*select*) choisi, de choix, (*mil.*) d'élite
Picker, s. (*gatherer*) cueilleur, m., -euse, f.; éplucheur, m., -euse, f.; (*of quarreis*) chercheur (m., -euse, f.) de querelles; (*of locks*) crocheteur, m., -euse, f.; (*a pickaxe*) pioche, f.; pic, m.; (*instr. for horses' hoofs*) cure-pieds, m.; (*mil.*) épinglette, f.
Pickerel, s. brocheton, filardeau, lanceron, m.
Picket, s. piquet, m.; — v.a. fortifier par des piquets; entourer de piquets; (*fasten*) attacher à un piquet; (*mil.*) former en piquet. — **line,** s. corde à piquet, f.
Picking, s. (*gathering*) cueillage, m., cueillette, cueille, f.; (*selection*) épluchement, épluchage, m.; choix, m.; triage, m.; (*of oakum*) décordage, détordage, m.; —**s,** pl. épluchures, f.pl., petits morceaux, m.pl.; profits, m.pl. — *pockets*, filouterie, f., vol à la tire, m.
Pickle, s. saumure, marinade, f.; (*thing preserved*) conserve au vinaigre, f.; (*from India*) achars, m.pl.; (*state*) état, m., condition, f.; affaire, f.; embarras, pétrin, m.; — v.a. mariner; conserver (*or* confire) dans du vinaigre, conserver (*or* confire) au vinaigre, conserver; (*to salt*) saler; (*pers.*) saucer. — **dish,** s. ravier, m. — **herring,** s. paillasse, bouffon, m.
Pickled, adj. mariné; conservé (*or* confit) au vinaigre, au vinaigre; (*salted*) salé; (*pers.*) achevé, fieffé [*a* —, faire un pique-nique
Picnic, s. pique-nique, m. *To get up* or *go for*
Picotee, s. œillet tiqueté, œillet jaspé, m.
Picquet. V. **Picket**
Picrate, s. picrate, m.
Picric, adj. picrique
Pict, s. Picte, m. [ture; illustré, pittoresque
Pictorial, adj. de peintre; de *or* de la pein-
Pictorially, adv. en peintre; par des peintures; pittoresquement
Picture, s. tableau, m., peinture, f.; (*engraving*) gravure, f., (*fam.*) image, f.; (*likeness*) portrait, m.; — v.a. peindre; dépeindre; représenter. *Dark side of the* —, revers de la médaille, m. *To* — *to oneself*, se figurer, se représenter. — **book,** s. livre d'images, m. — **card,** s. (*court-card*) figure, f. — **cleaning,** s. nettoyage de tableaux, m. — **dealer,** s. marchand de tableaux, m. — **frame,** s. encadrement, cadre, m. — **gallery, -room,** s. galerie de peintures *or* de tableaux, f. — **restorer,** s, restaurateur de tableaux, m.
Picturesque, adj s. pittoresque, adj. m.f., s.m.
Picturesquely, adv. pittoresquement, d'une manière pittoresque
Picturesqueness, s. pittoresque, m.
Piculet, s. picumne, m.
Piddle, v.n. grignoter, pignocher, chipoter, chicoter, manger du bout des dents; s'amuser à des bagatelles, s'occuper de futilités, perdre son temps à des niaiseries, niaiser, tatillonner; uriner; pissoter; (*of children*) faire pipi. — **-a-bed,** s. pissenlit, m.
Piddler, s. chipotier, m., -ière, f.
Piddling, adj. chipotier; futile, frivole
Piddock, s. pholade, f.
Pie, s. (*of meat*) pâté, m.; (*of fruit*) tourte, f.; (*print.*) pâté, m., pâte, f.; (*mag*) pie, f. *To eat humble* —, filer doux; s'humilier; céder, mettre les pouces. *To have a finger in the* —, avoir part au gâteau; y être pour quelque chose; avoir mis la main à la pâte. — **bald,** adj. pie; s. cheval pie, m., jument pie, f. — **crust,** s. croûte de pâté, f. — **dish,** s. tourtière, f. — **man,** s. marchand de pâtés, m.
Piece, s. morceau, m.; bout, m.; fragment, m.; (*of water, land, coin, artil., theat.*) pièce, f.; (*stuff of determined length and width*) pièce, f.; (*of arts, liter.*) morceau, m.; (*an act*) acte, trait, exemple, m.; (*paint.*) tableau, m.; (*handgun*) fusil, m.; — v.a. rapiécer, mettre une pièce *or* des pièces à. *A* — *of business*, une affaire, f.; (*work*) une besogne, f. *A* — *of fun*, une farce, f. *A* — *of impertinence*, une impertinence, f. *A* — *of poetry*, un morceau de poésie, une pièce de vers. *A* — *of wit*, un trait d'esprit. *A* — *of work, of news*, &c., V. **Work, News,** &c. *Broken* —, fragment, m.; tronçon, m.; (*of crockery*, &c.) tesson, m. *A* —, (*each*) V. **Apiece.** *A five franc* —, une pièce de cinq francs. *Five francs a* —, cinq francs pièce *or* la pièce *or* &c. [V. **Apiece**]; (*pers.*) cinq francs par personne *or* &c. *Of a* —, *all of a* —, d'un seul morceau, d'une seule pièce, tout d'une pièce; (*with*) de la même espèce (que); à l'avenant (de). - *by* —, pièce à pièce. *By the* —, à la pièce; (*of work*) à la tâche, aux pièces. *To break, dash, knock, pull to* —*s*, mettre en pièces. *To come* or *fall to* —*s*, se démonter; se défaire; tomber en morceaux *or* en pièces; s'écrouler. *To cut, tear to* —*s*, V. **Cut** *and* **Tear.** *To take to* —*s*, v.a. démonter; (*a garment*) découdre; v.n. se démonter; se joindre. — **broker,** s. marchand de coupons et morceaux de drap, m. — **goods,** s. pl. marchandises (f.pl.) *or* articles (m.pl.) à la pièce. —**less,** adj. entier. — **meal,** adv. adj. par (*or* en) morceaux, par (*or* en) pièces; pièce à pièce; par parties; en détail; peu à peu; séparé; détaché. — **out,** v.a. allonger, mettre une pièce à; augmenter. — **up,** v.a. (*fig.*) plâtrer. — **work,** s. ouvrage (*or* travail) à la tâche *or* aux pièces *To do* — *work*, travailler à la tâche *or* aux pièces. — **worker,** s. ouvrier (m., -ière, f.) à la tâche *or* aux pièces, tâcheron, m.
Piecer, s. ravaudeur, m., -euse, f.
Pied, adj. bigarré, bariolé; (*of horses*) pie
Piedness, s. bigarrure, f.
Piedmontese, s. Piémontais, m., e, f.; — adj. piémontais, du Piémont
Piedouche, s. piédouche, m.
Pier, s. (*of bridges*) pile, f.; (*of harbours*, &c., *on the seaside*) jetée, f.; (*wharf*) embarcadère, débarcadère, m.; (*arch.*) trumeau, entre-deux (de croisées), m.; (*of churches*) pilier, m. — **due,**

s. droit de jetée, *m.* — **glass,** *s.* trumeau, *m.* — **head,** *s.* bout de la jetée, *m.*; musoir, *m.* — **piece** (*of furniture*), *s.* meuble d'entre-deux, entre-deux, *m.* — **table,** *s.* console, *f.*
Pierage, *s.* droit de jetée, *m.*
Pierce, *v.a.n.* percer; pénétrer; (*affect*) toucher, émouvoir. — **through,** *v.a.* transpercer. — **through and through,** *v.a.* percer de part en part, percer d'outre en outre
Pierceable, *adj.* pénétrable
Piercer, *s.* perceur, *m.*, -euse, *f.*; (*tool*) perçoir, *m.*
Piercingly, *adv.* d'une manière perçante *or* pénétrante
Piercingness, *s.* nature perçante, *f.*; pénétration, *f.*
Pietism, *s.* piétisme, *m.*
Pietist, *s.*, **Pietistic, -al,** *adj.* piétiste, *m.f.*
Piety, *s.* piété, *f.*
Piezometer, *s.* piézomètre, *m.*
Pig, *s.* cochon, porc, pourceau, *m.*; (*of metal*) saumon, *m.*; — *v.a.* mettre bas; — *v.n.* (*of sows*) cochonner; (*pers.*) vivre comme des pourceaux. — **driver,** *s.* porcher, *m.*, -ère, *f.* —**eyed,** *adj.* qui a des yeux de cochon. —**headed,** *adj.* à grosse tête; (*obstinate*) entêté, obstiné, têtu; stupide. —**headedly,** *adv.* avec entêtement, obstinément, opiniâtrément. —**headedness,** *s.* entêtement, *m.*, obstination, opiniâtreté, *f.* — **iron,** *s.* fonte en saumon, gueuse, *f.* — **lead,** *s.* plomb en saumon, *m.* — **nut,** *s.* terre-noix, *f.* — **salesman,** *s.* charcutier forain, gargot, *m.* —**sty,** *s.* *V.* **Piggery.** — **tail,** *s.* queue, *f.*; (*of tobacco*) carotte, andouille, *f.* —**tub,** *s.* baquet aux restes, baquet des cochons, *m.*
Pigeon, *s.* pigeon, *m.*; (*pers.*) pigeon, *m.*, dupe, *f.*; — *v.a.* pigeonner, tromper, duper. *Young* —, pigeonneau, *m.* — **breasted, -chested,** *adj.* (*pers.*) bossu par-devant. — **dung,** *s.* fiente de pigeon, *f.*; (*agr.*) colombine, *f.* — —**hearted,** *adj.* timide. —**hole,** *s.* boulin, *m.*; (*of desks,* &c.) case, *f.*; (*print.*) colombier, *m.* — **holes,** *s.pl.* (*set of — holes*) casier, *m.*; (*game*) trou-madame, *m.* — **house,** *s.* pigeonnier, colombier, *m.* — **livered,** *adj.* doux, sans fiel. — **pie,** *s.* pâté (*m.*, *or* tourte, *f.*) de pigeonneaux. —**toed,** *adj.* qui marche les pieds en dedans
Piggery, *s.* étable à porcs *or* à cochons, *f.*, toit à porcs, *m.*, porcherie, *f.*
Piggin, *s.* grande cuiller de bois, *f.*
Piggish, *adj.* de cochon; sale
Piggishly, *adv.* salement
Piggishness, *s.* saleté, *f.*
Pigmean. *V.* **Pygmean**
Pigment, *s.* couleur, *f.*; (*anat.*) pigment, *m.*
Pigmental, Pigmentary, *adj.* pigmentaire
Pigmentation, *s.* pigmentation, *f.*
Pigmy. *V.* **Pygmy**
Pignorative, *adj.* pignoratif
Pika, *s.* pika, *m.*
Pike, *s.* (*weapon*) pique, *f.*; (*tool*) pic, *m.*; pointe, *f.*; (*fish*) brochet, *m.* *Young* —, brocheton, *m.* — **man,** *s.* piquier, *m.* — **perch,** *s.* sandre, *m.* —**staff,** *s.* bois de pique, *m.*; (*stick*) bâton ferré, *m.* *It is as plain as a —staff,* cela saute aux yeux
Piked, *adj.* pointu, en pointe
Pilaff. *V.* **Pilau**
Pilaster, *s.* pilastre, *m.*
Pilau, Pilaw, *s.* pilau, *m.*
Pilch, *s.* (*saddle*) panneau, *m.*; (*garment*) houppelande, pelisse fourrée, *f.*
Pilchard, *s.* pilchard, célan, *m.*
Pile, *s.* pile, *f.*; tas, *m.*; monceau, amas, *m.*; (*of firewood*) bûcher, *m.*; (*of arms*) faisceau, *m.*; (*of pieces of money rolled up in paper*) rouleau, *m.*; (*of shot*) pile, *f.*; (*phys.*) pile, *f.*; (*on coins*) pile, *f.*; (*building*) construction, *f.*, bâtiment, édifice, *m.*; (*of churches*) basilique, *f.*; (*a stake*) pieu, *m.*; (*for building*) pilot, pilotis, *m.*; (*nap*) poil, *m.*; —**s,** *pl.* piles, *f.pl.*, &c.; (*med.*) hémorroïdes, hémorrhoïdes, *f.pl.* (*blind —s,* hémorroïdes sèches); — *v.a.n.* empiler, mettre en pile; entasser; (*mil.*) mettre (*or* ranger) en faisceau (*or* en faisceaux), former les faisceaux; (*to drive piles, to support with piles*) piloter. — *of building,* construction, *f.*, édifice, *m.* *To drive a* —, enfoncer un pieu *or* un pilot *or* un pilotis. — **bridge,** *s.* pont sur pilotis, *m.* — **driver, -engine,** *s.* sonnette, *f.* — **driving,** *s.* enfoncement des pieux, *m.*; pilotage, *m.* — **driving engine,** *s.* sonnette, *f.* — **plank,** *s.* palplanche, *f.* — **work,** *s.* pilotage, *m.*, pilotis, *m.pl.* — **worm,** *s.* taret, *m.* **wort,** *s.* hémorroïdale, ficaire, *f.*
Pilfer, *v.a.n.* dérober, soustraire, chiper; grappiller; butiner
Pilferer, *s.* fripon, *m.*, -ne, *f.*, chipeur, *m.*, -euse, *f.*
Pilfering, *s.* soustraction, *f.*, larcin, *m.*
Pilgarlic, *s.* pauvre diable, *m.*
Pilgrim, *s.* pèlerin, *m.*, e, *f.*
Pilgrimage, *s.* pèlerinage, *m.*
Piling, *s.* empilement, *m.*; entassement, *m.*; (*of buildings*) pilotage, *m.*, pilotis, *m.pl.*
Pill, *s.* pilule, *f.*; — *v.a.* administrer des pilules à. — **beetle,** *s.* cloporte, *m.* — **box,** *s.* boîte à pilules, *f.* — **machine,** *s.* pilulier, *m.* — **mass,** *s.* mass pilulaire, *f.* — **shaped,** *adj.* pilulaire. —**wort,** *s.* pilulaire, *f.*
Pillage, *s.* pillage, *m.*; — *v.a.* piller
Pillager, *s.*, **Pillaging,** *adj.* pillard, *m.*, e, *f.*
Pillar, *s.* pilier, *m.*, colonne, *f.*; borne, *f.*; (*bearer*) support, soutien, pilier, *m.*; (— *of salt*) statue (de sel), *f.* *Hercules'* —*s,* les Colonnes d'Hercule. *Pompey's* —, la colonne de Pompée. *To send from — to post,* renvoyer de Caïphe à Pilate. — **letter-box, -box,** *s.* borne-boîte, *f.*
Pillared, *adj.* à piliers, à colonnes; (*like pillars*) en pilier, en colonne
Pillau, Pillaw. *V.* **Pilau**
Pillion, *s.* (*saddle*) selle de femme, *f.*; (*saddle-pad*) coussinet, *m.*
Pillory, *s.* pilori, *m.*; carcan, *m.*; — *v.a.* pilorier, mettre au pilori
Pillow, *s.* oreiller, *m.*; (*poet.*) couche, *f.*; (*for making lace,* &c.) coussin, tambour, *m.*; (*of machines*) coussinet, coussin, *m.*; — *v.a.* poser, reposer, appuyer; (*to support*) soutenir. — **case, -slip,** *s.* taie d'oreiller *f.* — **lace,** *s.* dentelle au tambour *or* au fuseau, *f.*
Pilose, *adj.* pileux, poilu, velu
Pilot, *s.* pilote, *m.*; — *v.a.* piloter. — **balloon,** *s.* ballon d'essai, *m.* — **boat,** *s.* bateau-pilote, *m.* — **coat,** *s.* paletot-pilote, *m.*; (*nav.*) vareuse, *f.* — **engine,** *s.* (*rail.*) machine de réserve *or* de recours, *f.*, remorqueur, *m.*, remorqueuse, *f.*, machine-pilote, *f.* — **fish,** *s.* pilote, fanfre, *m.*
Pilotage, Piloting, *s.* pilotage, *m.*
Pilous. *V.* **Pilose**
Pimenta, Pimento, *s.* piment, *m.*
Pimp, *s.* entremetteur, *m.*, -euse, *f.*, complaisant, *m.*, e, *f.*
Pimpernel, Pimpinella, *s.* mouron, *m.*; pimprenelle, *f.*
Pimping, *adj.* de peu de valeur, petit, chétif; (*pers.*) complaisant
Pimple, *s.* bouton, bourgeon, *m.*, pustule, *f.*
Pimpled, *adj.* bourgeonné, pustuleux, boutonné, plein de boutons
Pin, *s.* épingle, *f.*; (*peg*) cheville, *f.*; (*for curtains,* &c.) patère, *f.*; (*of watches,* &c.) goupille, *f.*; (*of wheels*) clavette, esse, *f.*; (*of hinges*) fiche, *f.*; (*of key-locks*) broche, *f.*; (*of pulleys*) essieu, *m.*; (*to play with*) quille, *f.*; (*a trifle*) rien, *m.*, bagatelle, *f.*, (le) moins du monde, *m.*; — *v.a.* attacher avec une épingle *or* avec des épingles, épingler; (*with a peg,* &c.) cheviller; goupiller; (*fig.*) clouer, attacher; (*enclose*) fermer. *To be on —s and needles,* être sur les épines *or* sur les charbons. — **basket,** *s.* dernier enfant, Benjamin, *m.* — **case,** *s.* étui à épingles, étui, *m.* — **cushion,** *s.* pelote à épingles, pelote, *f.* — **down,** *v.a.* (*fig.*) clouer, lier; fixer. — **dust,** *s.* limaille d'épingles, *f.* — **hole,** *s.* trou d'épingle, *m.* — **maker,** *s.* épinglier, *m.*, -ière, *f.*, fabricant (*m.*, e, *f.*) d'épingles. — **manufactory,** *s.* épinglerie, *f.* — **money,** *s.* ar-

gent pour ses menus plaisirs, *m.*; épingles, *f.pl.* —**tail**, *s. See below.* — **up**, *v.a.* (*loop up*) trousser
Pinafore, *s.* blouse, *f.*; (*apron*) tablier, *m.*
Pinaster, *s.* pinastre, *m.*
Pincers, *s pl.* pinces, *f.pl.*; tenailles, *f.pl.*
Pinch, *v.a.n.* pincer; serrer; presser; (*spare*) épargner sur, refuser à, priver; (*straiten*) gêner; (*live close*) se priver du nécessaire, se gêner; (*to bear hard upon*) être pressant; — *s.* pinçon, *m.*; (*fig.*) difficulté, *f.*, embarras, besoin, *m.*, extrémité, *f.*; (*pang*) angoisse, *f.*; (*quantity*) pincée, *f.*; (*of snuff*) prise, pincée, *f.* *At* or *on a* —, au besoin; à l'extrémité. *To — oneself*, se refuser le nécessaire, se priver du nécessaire. *To give him a* —, (*nip*) le pincer; lui faire un pinçon. *To know where the shoe —es*, savoir où est le mal *or* où le bât blesse. — **off,** *v.a.* arracher, emporter, enlever. — **penny,** *s.* grippe-sou, *m.*, pingre, *m.*, pingresse, *f.*
Pinchbeck, *s.* peinchebec, pinchebeck, chrysocale, *m.*
Pincher, *s.* pinceur, *m.*, -euse, *f.*; —**s**, *pl.* *V.* [**Pincers**
Pinching, *adj.* qui pince; pressant; (*of cold*) piquant; — *s.* pincement, *m.*
Pindaric, *adj.* pindarique; — *s.* ode pindarique, *f.*
Pindar-ism, -ist. *V.* page 3, § 1
Pine, *s.* pin, *m.*; sapin, *m.*; (— *apple*) ananas, *m.*; — *v.n.* (— *away*) languir, dépérir; (*to groan*) gémir; (*to long for*) soupirer (après), languir (après); — *v.a.* faire languir, faire dépérir; (*moan*) pleurer, regretter. —**apple,** *s.* ananas, *m.* —**apple strawberry,** *s.* fraise ananas, *f.*, ananas, *m.* — **cone, -nut,** *s.* pomme de pin, *f.* — **grove,** *s.* *V.* — **plantation.** — **plant,** *s.* ananas, *m.* — **plantation,** *s.* pinière, pinaie, pineraie, pinède, *f.* — **seed,** *s.* pigne, *f.*, pignon, *m.* — **stove,** *s.* serre à ananas, *f.* — **strawberry,** *s.* fraise ananas, *f.*, ananas, *m.* — **tree,** *s.* pin, *m.* — **wood,** *s.* bois de pin, bois de sapin, *m.*
Pineal, *adj.* pinéal
Pinery, *s.* champ d'ananas, *m.*; (*hot-house*) [serre à ananas, *f.*
Pinetum, *s.* *V.* **Pine-plantation**
Pinguid, *adj.* gras
Pinic, *adj.* pinique
Piniferous, *adj.* pinifère
Pining, *adj.* languissant; de langueur; — *s.* langueur, *f.*; dépérissement, *m.*; ardent désir, *m.*
Pinion, *s.* aileron, *m.*; bout d'aile, *m.*; (*wheel*) pignon, *m.*; (*for the arms*) liens, *m.pl.*; — *v.a.* lier les ailes à; (*to cut*) couper le bout de l'aile à; (*pers.*, — *down* or *up*) garrotter, lier, attacher; (*fig.*) enchaîner
Pinioning, *s.* (*of criminals*) saisissement, *m.*
Pink, *adj.* rose; — *s.* (*colour*) rose, *m.*; (*flower*) œillet, *m.*; (*fig.*) fleur, fine fleur, perle, crème, *f.*, modèle, *m.*; (*fish*) véron, *m.*; (*salmon*) saumoneau, *m.*; (*ship*) pinque, *f.*; — *v.a.* faire des œillets à; (*cut*) découper, travailler à jour; (*pierce*) percer; — *v.n.* clignoter. — **eye,** *s.* petit œil, *m.* —**eyed,** *adj.* qui a de petits yeux
Pinker, *s.* découpeur, *m.*, -euse, *f.*
Pinkish, *adj.* rosâtre
Pinna, *s.* pinne marine, *f.*
Pinnace, *s.* pinasse, *f.*, grand canot, *m.*
Pinnacle, *s.* pinacle, *m.*; (*fig.*) faîte, sommet, [pinacle, *m.*
Pinnate, -d, *adj.* pinné
Pinnock, *s.* mésange, *f.*
Pinnule, *s.* pinnule, *f.*
Pint, *s.* (*Engl. meas.*) pinte, *f.*; (*old Fr. meas.*) demi-pinte, chopine, *f.* (*equivalent modern Fr. meas.*) demi-litre, *m.*; (*of beer*) canette, *f.*; (*of wine, in small eating-houses*) chopine, *f.* — **bottle,** *s.* demi-bouteille, *f.* **Half** —, *s.* (*Engl. meas.*) demi-pinte, *f.* (*Fr. meas.*) quart de litre, *m.*; (*of beer*) bock, *m.*, chope, *f.*; (*of wine, in eating-houses*) carafon, *m.* **Quarter of a** —, *s.* (*of wine or spirits, in public-houses*) canon, *m.* (*pop.*)
Pintado, *s.* pintade, *f.* — **chick,** *s.* pintadeau, *m.*
Pintail, — **duck,** *s.* pilet, canard à longue queue, *m.*
Pintle, *s.* cheville, clavette, *f.*; (*nav.*) aiguillot, *m.*
Pinule, *s.* pinnule, *f.*
Piny, *adj.* couvert de pins; pinifère
Pioneer, *s.* pionnier, *m.*; — *v.n.* pionner
Pioneering, *s.* pionnage, *m.*
Pious, *adj.* pieux
Piously, *adv.* pieusement, avec piété
Pip, *s.* (*of birds*) pépie, *f.*; (*on cards, on dominoes*) point, *m.*; (*of fruit*) pépin, *m.*; — *v.n.* (*of birds*) pépier, crier; (*of chicks*) piper
Pipa, *s.* pipa, *m.*
Pipe, *s.* (*tube*) tuyau, conduit, *m.*; (*for smoking*) pipe, *f.*; (*flute*) chalumeau, pipeau, *m.*, flûte, *f.*; (*of organs*) tuyau, *m.*; (*of syringes, enemas*) canule, *f.*; (*of keys*) canon, *m.*; (*of the voice*) organe, *m.*; (*voice itself*) voix, *f.*, son de voix, *m.*; (*meas.*) pipe, *f.*; pièce (anglaise), *f.*; (*of the old muzzle-loading muskets*) porte-baguette, *m.*; (*nav.*) sifflet, *m.*; — *v.n.a.* jouer du chalumeau *or* de la flûte *or* du flageolet; jouer de ...; jouer ... (sur); (*whistle*) siffler; (*call*) appeler d'un coup de sifflet, appeler; (*of birds*) siffler; (*of things*) crier, siffler. — *of peace*, calumet de (*or* de la) paix, *m.* *Short* —, (*cutty*) brûle-gueule, *m.* — **case,** *s.* porte-pipe, étui à pipe, *m.* — **clay,** *s.* terre à (*or* de) pipe, *f.* — **fish,** *s.* syngnathe, *m.* — **laying,** *s.* pose de tuyaux, *f.* — **light,** *s.* *V.* **Spill.** — **mouth,** *s.* fistulaire, *m.* — **smoker,** *s.* fumeur (*m.*, -euse, *f.*) de pipes. — **stem,** *s.* tuyau de pipe, *m.*
Piped, *adj.* à tuyau; tubulé, en forme de tube. — *key*, clé forée, *f.*
Piper, *s.* joueur de flûte, *m.*, (*jest.*) flûteur, *m.*; (*in general*) joueur, *m.*; (*fish*) lyre, *f.* *To pay the* —, (*fig.*) payer les violons
Pipette, *s.* pipette, *f.*
Piping, *adj.* qui joue du chalumeau *or* &c., qui siffle, &c. (*V.* **Pipe,** *v.n a.*); (*of the voice*) flûté; (*weak*, &c.) faible, languissant; maladif; (*hot*) brûlant; — *s.* (*need.*) passe-poil, *m.*; (*hort.*) bouture, *f.* — **hot,** tout chaud, tout [bouillant
Pipistrelle, — **bat,** *s.* pipistrelle, *f.*
Pipit, *s.* pipit, *m.*
Pipkin, *s.* poêlon, coquemar, boulier, *m.*
Pippin, *s.* reinette, pomme de reinette, *f.* *Normandy* —*s*, pommes tapées, *f.pl.*
Piquancy, *s.* goût piquant, *m.*; (*fig.*) piquant, *m.*
Piquant, *adj.* piquant [piquamment
Piquantly, *adv.* d'une manière piquante,
Pique, *s.* pique, brouille, brouillerie, *f.*; (*of honour*) point, *m.*; — *v.a.* piquer ('*on*,' de). *To take a* —, se piquer. *To — oneself on*, se [piquer de, se glorifier de
Piqué, *s.* piqué, *m.*
Piquet. *V.* **Picket**
Piquette, *s.* piquette, *f.* [façon, *f.*
Piracy, *s.* piraterie, *f.*; (*in literature*) contre-
Pirate, *s.* pirate, *m.*; (*in literature*) contrefacteur, *m.*; — *v.n.* pirater; — *v.a.* contrefaire, piller
Pirated, *part. adj.* contrefait, de contrefaçon
Piratical, *adj.*, **Piratically,** *adv.* piratique, de pirate; en pirate; (*of books*) de contrefaçon
Pirogue, *s.* pirogue, *f.*
Pirouette, *s.* pirouette, *f.*; — *v.n.* pirouetter
Pirouetting, *s.* pirouettement, *m.*
Pisan, *s.* Pisan, *m.*, e, *f.*; — *adj.* pisan, de Pise
Piscatorial, Piscatory, *adj.* piscatorial, de la pêche, de pêche
Pisces, *s.pl.* les Poissons, *m.pl.* [de pisciculture
Piscicultural, *adj.* piscicultural, piscicole,
Pisciculture, *s.* pisciculture, *f.*
Pisciculturist, *s.* pisciculteur, *m.*
Pisciform, *adj.* pisciforme
Piscina, Piscinary, *s.* piscine, *f.*
Piscine, *adj.* de poisson, des poissons
Piscivorous, *adj.* piscivore
Pisé, *s.* pisé, *m.*
Pish, *int.* bah! — *v.n.* faire bah, faire nargue (de)
Pisiform, *adj.* pisiforme
Pismire, *s.* fourmi, *f.*

Pisolite, *s.* pisolithe, *m.*
Pisolitic, *adj.* pisolithique
Piss, *v.a.n.* pisser; — *s.* pisse, *f.*; (*of animals*) pissat, *m.* —**abed,** *s.* (*pers., plant*) pissenlit, *m.* — **burnt,** *adj.* taché d'urine
Pissasphalt, -um, *s.* pissasphalte, *m.*
Pissasphaltic, *adj.* pissasphaltique
Pissing, *s.* pissement, *m.*
Pist, Piste, *s.* piste, *f.*
Pistachio, *s.* pistache, *f.* — **nut,** *s.* pistache, *f.* — **tree,** *s.* pistachier, *m.*
Pistil, *s.* pistil, *m.*
Pistillar, *adj.* pistillaire [tillifère
Pistillate, Pistilliferous, *adj.* pistillé, pis-
Pistol, *s.* pistolet, *m.*; — *v.a.* (*old, jest.*) pistoler. — **ball,** *s.* balle de pistolet, *f.* — **butt,** *s.* crosse de pistolet, *f.* — **case,** *s.* fourreau de pistolet, *m.*; boîte à pistolet, *f.* — **gallery,** *s.* tir au pistolet, *m.* — **proof,** *adj.* à l'épreuve du pistolet. — **shot,** *s* coup de pistolet, *m.*; (*distance*) portée de pistolet, *f.*
Pistole, *s.* pistole, *f.*
Pistolet, *s.* petit pistolet, *m.*
Piston, *s.* piston, *m.* — **rod,** *s.* tige de piston, *f.* — **stroke,** *s.* coup de piston, *m.*
Pit, *s.* fosse, *f.*; (*abyss*) abîme, *m.*; (*cavity*) creux, *m.*, cavité, *f.*; (*of the stomach*) creux, *m.*; (*of the arm*) aisselle, *f.*; (*of theatres*) parterre, *m.*; (*for cock-fighting*) arène, *f.*; (*quarry*) carrière, *f.*; (*shaft*) puits, *m.*; (*mark*) marque, empreinte, *f.*; — *v.a.* creuser; marquer; opposer (à), mettre aux prises (avec). — **box,** *s.* (*theat.*) baignoire, *f.* — **coal,** *s.* charbon de terre, *m.*, houille, *f.* — **door,** *s.* (*theat.*) entrée du parterre, *f.* — **fall,** *s.* trappe, *f.*, piége, *m.* —**ful,** *s.* (*theat.*) parterre, *m.* — **man,** *s.* mineur, *m.* — **sand,** *s.* sable de carrière, *m.* — **saw,** *s.* scie de scieur de long, *f.* — **tier,** *s.* (*theat.*) pourtour, *m.* — **tier box,** *s.* (*theat.*) baignoire, *f.*
Pitapat, *adv.* en palpitant, en battant; — *s.* palpitation, *f.*, battement, *m.* *To go* —, palpiter, battre
Pitch, *s.* (*resin*) poix, *f.*; (*degree*) point, degré, *m.*; (*height*) hauteur, élévation, *f.*; faîte, *m.*; (*slope*) pente, *f.*, penchant, *m.*; (*of the voice*) étendue, *f.*; portée, *f.*; (*mus.*) diapason, ton, *m.*; (*size*) taille, stature, *f.*; — *v.a.* (*smear*) poisser, enduire de poix; (*darken*) noircir, obscurcir; (*throw*) jeter; plonger; (*strike in*) planter, fixer; (*a camp*) asseoir; (*a tent*) dresser; (*a net*) tendre; (*mus.*) donner le diapason à; — *v.n.* se jeter; (*fall*) tomber; (*of birds*) s'abattre; (*of carriages*) plonger; (*of ships*) tanguer, plonger; (*fix o.'s choice*) jeter son dévolu (sur), choisir, faire choix (de), s'arrêter (à). — *and tar*, goudron, *m.* — *and toss*, pile ou face. *Dark as* —, *V.* — **dark.** *The highest* or *utmost* —, le comble, le faîte. — **coal,** *s.* jais, *m.* — **dark,** *adj.* noir comme un four, noir comme dans un four; (*of night*) nuit noire. — **farthing,** *s.* fossette, *f.* — **fork,** *s.* fourche, *f.* — **pine,** *s.* pin à trochets, picéa, *m.*, pesse, *f.*, sapin rouge, *m.* — **pipe,** *s.* (*mus.*) sifflet-diapason, *m.*
Pitched, *adj.* (*of battles*) rangé; (*sloping*) en pente; à pente ...; — *part. adj.* *V.* **Pitch,** *v.a.n.*
Pitcher, *s.* cruche, *f.* *The — goes so often to the well that it comes home broken at last*, tant va la cruche à l'eau qu'à la fin elle se casse. — **plant,** *s.* népenthe, *m.*, bandure, *f.*
Pitchiness, *s.* noirceur, obscurité, *f.*
Pitching, *s.* (*of carriages, engines,* &c.) plongement, *m.*; (*nav.*) tangage, *m.*; — *adj.* incliné, en pente [sombre, obscur, ténébreux
Pitchy, *adj.* de poix; poissé; (*dark*) noir,
Piteous, *adj.* piteux, pitoyable; (*contemptible*) pitoyable; (*compassionate*) compatissant
Piteously, *adv.* piteusement; pitoyablement; (*kindly*) avec pitié, avec compassion [pitié, *f.*
Piteousness, *s.* tristesse, *f.*; (*compassion*)

Pith, *s.* moelle, *f.*; sève, *f.*; force, vigueur, énergie, *f.*; quintessence, *f.*; substance, *f.*; essentiel, *m.*; importance, *f.* —**ily,** *adv.* fortement, vigoureusement, énergiquement, avec force, avec vigueur, avec énergie. —**iness,** *s.* force, vigueur, énergie, *f.* —**less,** *adj.* sans moelle; sans sève; sans force, sans vigueur, sans énergie. —**y,** *adj.* moelleux; plein de sève; fort, vigoureux, énergique
Pitiable, *adj.* (*pers.*) digne de pitié; (*things*) pitoyable, à faire pitié
Pitiableness, *s.* état pitoyable, *m.*
Pitiful, Pitifully. *V.* **Piteous, Piteously**
Pitifulness, *s.* pitié, compassion, *f.*; (*wretchedness*) état pitoyable, *m.*
Pitiless, *adj.* impitoyable, cruel; barbare; (*things*) qui n'excite pas de pitié. —**ly,** *adv.* impitoyablement, sans pitié. —**ness,** *s.* nature impitoyable, *f.*
Pittacal, *s.* pittacale, *m.* [quantité, *f.*
Pittance, *s.* pitance, *f.*; petite portion *or*
Pitted, *part. adj.* creusé, &c. (*V.* **Pit,** *v.a.*); (*with the small pox*) grêlé, gravé, marqué
Pituitary, *adj.* pituitaire [(' *with*,' de)
Pituite, *s.* pituite, *f.*
Pituitous, *adj.* pituiteux
Pity, *s.* pitié, compassion, *f.*; (*matter for regret*) dommage, *m.*; — *v.a.* plaindre; avoir pitie de. *It is a* —, c'est dommage. *It is a great* —, c'est bien dommage. *The more is the* —, c'est d'autant plus dommage; tant pis. *What a* —! quel dommage! *To have* or *take* — *on*, avoir pitié de. *He is to be pitied*, il est à plaindre
Pityriasis, *s.* pityriasis, *m.*
Pivot, *s.* pivot, *m.*; — *v.n.* pivoter; — *v.a.* faire
Pix. *V.* **Pyx** [pivoter
Placa-bility, bleness. *V.* page 3, § 1
Placable, *adj.* placable, facile à apaiser
Placard, *s.* placard, *m.*; affiche, *f.*; — *v.a.* placarder (' *with*,' de); afficher
Place, *s.* (*particular spot, seat, situation,* &c.) place, *f.*, (*wider*) endroit, *m.*, (*wider still, and in a vague sense*) lieu, *m.*, localité, *f.*; (*site*) emplacement, *m.*; (*square or row of houses or* &c. *in a town; and mil.*) place, *f.*; (*house*) maison, *f.*; local, *m.*; établissement, *m.*; (*estate*) propriété, terre, *f.*; (*country seat*) château, *m.*; (*residence*) logis, *m.*, demeure, résidence, *f.*; (*city, town*) ville, *f.*; (*county, province*) pays, *m.*; (*employment*) emploi, *m.*, place, *f.*; (*rank*) rang, *m.*, position, *f.*; (*at school*) place, *f.*; (*precedence*) préséance, *f.*, pas, *m.*; — *v.a.* placer; mettre; (*carry*) porter. *At* or *to my, his, your,* &c. —, (*dwelling*) chez moi, chez lui, chez vous, &c. *In* —, (*in office*) en place. *In my, your,* &c. —, à ma place, à votre place, &c. *In* (*the*) — *of*, à la place de; en place de; au lieu de; en remplacement de. *In high* —*s*, (*fig.*) en haut lieu. *In the first* —, d'abord, en premier lieu; premièrement. *In the next* —, ensuite, puis, en second lieu. *Out of* —, *V.* **Out.** *Time and* —, temps et lieu. *To give* —, faire place (à); (*precedence*) céder le pas (à). *To take* —, avoir lieu, arriver, se passer; (*pers.*) prendre le pas (sur). — **holder, -man,** *s.* homme en place, employé du gouvernement, *m.* —**less,** *adj.* sans place
Placeable, *adj.* plaçable
Placenta, *s.* placenta, *m.*
Placental, Placentary, *adj.* placentaire
Placer, *s.* placeur, *m.*, -euse, *f.*; (*of seats*) placier, *m.*, -ière, *f.*; (*of gold-diggings*) placer, *m.*
Placid, *adj.* placide, tranquille, paisible, doux; calme, serein
Placidity, Placidness, *s.* placidité, tranquillité, douceur, *f.*; calme, *m.*, sérénité, *f.*
Placidly, *adv.* placidement tranquillement, paisiblement, doucement, avec calme
Placket, — hole, *s.* fente de jupon *or* de jupe,
Plagal, *adj.* plagal [*f.*; (*pocket*) poche, *f.*
Plagiarism, *s.* plagiat, *m.*; contrefaçon, *f.*
Plagiarist, *s.* plagiaire, *m.*; contrefacteur, *m.*

Plagiarize, *v.a.* s'approprier par plagiat, contrefaire, piller; — *v.n.* commettre un plagiat *or* des plagiats; faire la contrefaçon
Plagiary, *adj.* plagiaire; — *s.* plagiaire, *m.*; contrefacteur, *m.*
Plague, *s.* peste, *f.*; (*torment*) fléau, *m.*; plaie, *f.*; tourment, *m.*; (*worrier*) tourment, *m.*; — *v.a.* infecter de la peste; tourmenter, harceler, importuner, faire souffrir, taonner, tanner, assommer, être un fléau *or* un tourment pour. —*s of Egypt*, plaies d'Égypte, *f.pl.* *To — to death*, assommer. — *on* . . . ! peste de . . . !
Plaguily, *adv.* furieusement, horriblement
Plaguy, *adj.* maudit, affreux
Plaice, *s.* plie, *f.*, carrelet, *m.*
Plaid, *s.* (*garment*) plaid, *m.*; (*stuff*) tartan, cachemire d'Écosse, *m.*
Plain, *adj.* (*smooth*) uni, égal; (*flat*) plat; (*geom.*) *V.* **Plane**; (*not ornamented with designs or carvings,* &c.; *of one colour*) uni; (*simple*) simple; (*common*) ordinaire; (*sincere*) franc, sincère; (*mere,bare*) simple; (*evident*) évident, clair; bon, intelligible; (*ugly*) laid; commun; (*of the hair*) en bandeaux; (*without sauce,* &c.) au naturel; — *adverb.V.***Plainly**; —*s.*plaine,*f.* *The — truth,* la pure vérité. *In — English*, en bon anglais. — **chant,** *s. V.* — **song.** — **clothes,** *s.pl. V.* **Clothes.** — **cooking,** *s.* cuisine bourgeoise, *f.* — **dealer,** *s.* homme franc et loyal, *m.*, femme franche et loyale, *f.*, personne de bonne foi, *f.* — **dealing,** *adj.* franc, honnête, loyal; *s.* franchise, bonne foi, droiture, *f.* — **dress,** *s. V.* **Clothes** (*Plain*). — **needlework, -sewing,** *s.* couture, *f.* — **song,** *s.* plain-chant, *m.* — **speaking,** *s.* franchise, *f.*; clarté, *f.* — **spoken,** *adj.* franc; clair, explicite. — **work,** *s.* (*need.*) couture, *f.*
Plainly, *adv* simplement; sans façon; franchement, sincèrement, sans déguisement, nettement; clairement; distinctement; évidemment; (*without sauce,* &c.) au naturel
Plainness, *s.* égalité, *f.*; simplicité, *f.*; franchise, sincérité, *f.*; netteté, *f.*; évidence, clarté, *f.*; (*ugliness*) laideur, *f.*, air commun, *m.*
Plaint, *s.* plainte, *f.* — **less,** *adj.* qui ne se plaint pas; résigné
Plaintiff, *s.* (*civ. law*) demandeur, *m.*, -eresse, *f.*; plaignant, *m.*, e, *f.*; (*crim. law*) partie civile, *f.*
Plaintive, *adj.* plaintif
Plaintively, *adv.* plaintivement, d'un ton plaintif, d'une voix plaintive
Plaintiveness, *s.* ton plaintif, *m.*; tristesse, *f.*
Plaister. *V.* **Plaster**
Plait, *s.* pli, *m.*; (*of hair,* &c.) tresse, natte, *f.*; — *v.a.* plisser; (*the hair,* &c.) tresser, natter
Plaited, *adj.* plissé; à plis . . .; (*of the hair,* &c.) tressé, natté; à tresses . . ., à nattes . . .
Plaiter, *s.* tresseur, *m.*, -euse, *f.*
Plaiting, *s.* plissement, plissage, *m.*; plissure, *f.*; (*of hair,* &c.) tressage, *m.*
Plan, *s.* plan, *m.*; système, *m.*; (*project*) plan, dessein, projet, *m.*; (*means*) moyen, *m.*; (*course*) parti, *m.*; — *v.a.* faire *or* tracer le plan de; tracer, dessiner; (*to scheme*) projeter; préparer; arranger. —**less,** *adj.* sans plan
Planchet, *s.* (*coin., obsolete*) *V.* **Blank,** *s.*
Plane, *adj.* plan (*m.*, e, *f.*); — *s.* plan, *m.*, surface plane, *f.*; (*persp., math.*) plan, *m.*; (*a tool*) rabot, *m.*; (*a tree*) platane, *m.*; — *v.a.* (— *down*) aplanir; égaliser; (*join., carp.*) raboter; (*coop.,* &c.) planer; (*print.*) taquer. — *surface*, surface plane, *f.* — *trigonometry*, trigonométrie rectiligne, *f.* — **table,** *s.* planchette, *f.* — **tree,** *s.* platane, *m.*
Planer, *s.* (*pers.*) raboteur, *m.*; planeur, *m.*; (*machine*) *V.* **Planing-machine**; (*print.*) taquoir, *m.*
Planet, *s.* planète, *f.* — **struck,** *adj.* atteint par l'influence d'un astre
Planetarium, *s.* planétaire, *m.*
Planetary, *adj.* planétaire
Planetoid, *s.* astéroïde, *m.*
Planimeter, *s.* planimètre, *m.*
Planimetric, -al, *adj.* planimétrique
Planimetry, *s.* planimétrie, *f.*
Planing, *s.* rabotage, *m.* — **machine, -mill,** *s.* raboteur (*m.*) *or* raboteuse (*f.*) mécanique
Planish, *v.a.* planer
Planisher, *s.* planeur, *m.*
Planisphere, *s.* planisphère, *m.*
Planispheric, *adj.* planisphérique
Plank, *s.* planche, *f.*; madrier, *m.*; **ais,** *m.*; (*nav.*) bordage, *m.*; — *v.a.* planchéier, plancheyer; (*nav.*) border. — **sheer,** *s.* (*nav.*) plat-bord, *m.*
Planking, *s.* planchéiage, plancheyage, *m.*; [(*nav.*) bordage, *m.*
Planner, *s.* auteur d'un plan *or* d'un projet, *m.*, projeteur, *m.*, -euse, *f.*
Planning, *s.* tracé d'un plan, *m.*; (*fig.*) invention, conception, *f.*
Plant, *s.* plante, *f.*; pied, *m.*; (*young plant to set*) plant, *m.*; (*com.*) matériel, équipage, outillage, *m.*; — *v.a.n.* planter; (*sow*) semer; (*settle*) établir, fonder; (*fix*) poser, placer, fixer; (*a cannon*) braquer, pointer. — **louse,** *s.* puceron, *m.* — **out,** *v.a.* repiquer
Plantain, *s.* (*grass*) plantain, *m.*; (— *tree*) plantanier, bananier, *m.* — **eater,** *s.* musophage, *m.*
Plantation, *s.* plantation, *f.*; (*fig.*) colonie, *f.*; établissement, *m.*; fondation, *f.*; introduction, *f.*
Planter, *s.* planteur, colon, *m.*; (*fig.*) fondateur, *m.*; propagateur, *m.*
Plantership, *s.* état de planteur *or* de colon, *m.*; direction d'une plantation, *f.*
Plantigrade, *adj.s.* plantigrade, *adj.m.f.*, *s.m.*
Planting, *s.* plantage, *m.*, plantation, *f.*; (*fig.*) fondation, *f.*; établissement, *m.* — **out,** *s.* repiquage, *m.* — **tool,** *s.* plantoir, *m.*
Plantule, *s.* plantule, *f.*
Plash, *s.* flaque, *f.*; (*splash; splashing; of waves*) *V.* **Splash,** *s.*; — *v.n.* patauger, barboter; (*splash*) éclabousser; (*of waves*) clapoter; — *v.a.* entrelacer
Plashy, *adj.* boueux, bourbeux, gâcheux
Plaster, *s.* plâtre, *m.*; (*pharm.*) emplâtre, *m.*; — *v.a.* plâtrer; (*med.*) mettre un emplâtre sur. — *of Paris*, gypse, *m.* — **kiln,** *s.* four à plâtre, *m.* — **quarry,** *s.* carrière de plâtre, plâtrière, *f.* — **stone,** *s.* gypse, *m.* — **work,** *s.* plâtrage, *m.*
Plasterer, *s.* plâtrier, *m.*; (*in figures*) mouleur, *m.*
Plastering, *s.* plâtrage, *m.*
Plastery, *adj.* plâtreux
Plastic, *adj.* plastique
Plasticity, *s.* plasticité, *f.*
Plastron, *s.* plastron, *m.*
Plat, *s.* tresse, natte, *f.*; (*field*) morceau de terre, champ, *m.*; — *v.a.* tresser, natter
Platane, *s.* platane, *m.*
Platband, *s.* plate-bande, *f.*
Plate, *s.* (*piece of metal*) plaque, lame, *f.*; (*tech.*) platine, *f.*; (*silver for table*) vaisselle plate, argenterie, *f.*; (*a dish*) assiette, *f.*, (—*ful*) assiettée, *f.*; (*for collections*) plat, bassin, *m.*; (*for engraving*) planche, *f.*; (*print.*) cliché, *m.*; (*in photography*) verre, *m.*, glace, *f.*, (*with the negative*) cliché, *m.*; (*of a railway*) rails, *m.pl.*; (*dial*) cadran, *m.*; (*prize*) prix en vaisselle plate, prix, *m.*, (*in French turf-slang*) plate, *m.*; — *v.a.* plaquer; (*adorn with plates*) orner de plaques; (*to silver*) argenter, plaquer; (*a looking-glass*) étamer; (*ships*) cuirasser, blinder; (*beat flat*) mettre en lames, laminer. *A clean* —, une assiette blanche. *Gold* —, vaisselle d'or. *Piece of* —, pièce d'argenterie, *f.* *Silver* —, argenterie, vaisselle d'argent. — **basket,** *s.* panier à l'argenterie, *m.* —**ful,** *s.* assiettée, *f.* — **glass,** *s.* glace, *f.*; *adj.* de glace. — **iron,** *s.* feuillard de fer, *m.* — **layer,** *s.* (*rail.*) poseur de voie, poseur, *m.*; cantonnier, *m.* — **mark,** *s.* contrôle, *m.* — **paper,** *s.* papier à estampes, *m.* — **powder,** *s.* blanc d'Espagne, *m.*; rouge, *m.* — **rack,** *s.* porte-assiettes, *m.*; égouttoir, *m.* — **shelf,** *s.* planche aux assiettes, *f.* — **stand,** *s.* porte-assiettes, *m.* — **warmer,** *s.* chauffe-assiettes, *m.*

Plateau, *s.* plateau, *m.*
Plated, *adj.* plaqué. — *metal,* — *articles,* — *goods,* — *ware,* plaqué, *m.* — *manufacture,* fabrique de plaqué, *f.*
Platen, *s.* platine, *f.*
Plater, *s.* plaqueur, *m.*
Platform, *s.* plate-forme, *f.*; estrade, *f.*; tribune, *f.*; (*rail.*) quai, *m.*; (*sketch*) plan horizontal, *m.*, ichnographie, *f.*; (*American polit.*) programme politique, *m.*
Platina, *s.* (*obsolete*) *V.* **Platinum**
Plating, *s.* placage, *m.*; (*of looking-glasses*) étamage, *m.*; (*of ships*) blindage, *m.*
Platinic, *adj.* platinique
Platiniferous, *adj.* platinifère
Platinous, *adj.* platineux
Platinum, *s.* platine, *m.*
Platitude, *s.* platitude, *f.*
Platon-ic, al, -ically, -ism. *V.* page 3, § 1
Platonist, Platonician, *s.* platonicien, *m.*, -ne, *f.*
Platonize, *v.n.a.* platoniser
Platoon, *s.* peloton, *m.* — **exercise,** *s.* école de peloton, *f.*
Platted, *adj.* tressé, natté; à tresses ..., à nattes ...
Platter, *s.* plat, *m.*; (*mil., nav.*) gamelle, *f.*; (*pers.*) tresseur, *m.*, -euse, *f.*
Platting, *s.* (*action*) tressage, *m.*; (*plat, plats*) tresse, *f.*, tresses, *f.pl.*
Plaudit, *s.* applaudissement, *m.*
Plausi-bility, bleness. *V.* page 3, § 1
Plausible, *adj.* plausible; (*pers.*) qui donne des raisons plausibles, qui a la langue dorée
Plausibly, *adv.* plausiblement
Play, *v.n.* jouer; (*laugh at, mock*) se jouer (de); (*wave*) flotter, onduler; (*on any musical instrument*) jouer (de); (*glisten*) chatoyer, briller, étinceler; (*run in a race*) courir. — *fair,* jouer beau jeu. — *false,* tricher; tromper, user d'artifice. — *first,* jouer le premier, débuter; (*at cards*) avoir la main. — *high,* jouer gros jeu. — *low,* jouer petit jeu. — *at sight, V.* **Read.** — *sure,* jouer à coup sûr. — **at ...,** jouer à ...; jouer au ... *or* à la ... *or* aux ... — **on the,** (*mus.*) jouer du *or* de la *or* des. — **to** (*a person*), faire de la musique à. — **with,** jouer avec; (*mock*) se jouer de
Play, *v.a.* jouer; (*a musical instrument*) jouer de; (*music*) faire (de la musique); (*a tune*) jouer, exécuter; (*a game at* ... or *of* ...) faire (une partie de ...); (*abusively, for* — '*at*') jouer au *or* à la *or* aux; (*pranks, tricks*) *V.* **Prank** *and* **Trick;** (*antics*) faire; (*pretend to be, act like*) faire; (*make, do*) faire; (*machines,* &c., *ply*) faire jouer; (*the cannon*) faire jouer, tirer. — *cards,* jouer aux cartes. — *the violin, the piano, the harp,* &c., jouer du violon, du piano, de la harpe, &c. — **away,** perdre au jeu. — **off,** mettre en jeu, employer, déployer; (*a person*) exposer à la risée; (*against*) opposer (à); (*tricks*) jouer, faire. — **... to,** jouer *or* &c. ... à
Play, *s.* jeu, *m.*; récréation, *f.*, amusement, *m.*; (*sport* badinage, *m.*; (*scope*) essor, *m.*, carrière, *f.*; (*drama*) pièce de théâtre, pièce, *f.*; (*theatre*) spectacle, théâtre, *m.*; (*mus.*) exécution, *f.*, jeu, *m.* — *of colours,* chatoiement, *m.* *A book of the* —, un livret, *m.*, la pièce, *f.* *By fair* —, de bon jeu. *Fair* —, beau jeu; (*honesty*) justice, *f.*; loyauté, bonne foi, *f.*; (*adject., adverb.*) juste, loyal, de bonne guerre. *False* —, *foul* —, mauvais jeu, *m.*; (*dishonesty*) déloyauté, mauvaise foi, *f.*; mauvais tour, mauvais procédé, *m.*, tromperie, perfidie, *f.* *Full of* —, folâtre, badin, qui aime à jouer *or* à badiner, très joueur. *Rough* —, *V.* **Horse-play.** *In* —, pour badiner, pour rire. *To be at* —, jouer, être en récréation. *To bring* or *call into* — (or *into action*) *V.* **Action.** *To give fair* — *to,* donner beau jeu à; (*deal fairly*) jouer franc jeu avec, jouer cartes sur table avec. *To give full* — *to,* donner un libre essor à. — **bill,** *s.* (*on walls,* &c.) affiche de théâtre, *f.*, (*flying*) programme de spectacle, *m.* — **book,** *s.* recueil de pièces de théâtre, *m.*; (*theat.*) livret, *m.* — **day,** *s.* jour de congé, *m.* — **debt,** *s.* dette de jeu, *f.* — **fellow,** *s.* camarade de jeu, camarade, *m.f.* —**ful,** *adj.* qui aime à jouer, joueur; enjoué; folâtre, badin, gai. —**fully,** *adv.* avec enjouement, d'une manière enjouée *or* folâtre, en badinant, en folâtrant, gaiment. —**fulness,** *s.* enjouement, *m.*; gaieté, *f.*; badinage, *m.* —**goer,** *s.* personne qui fréquente les spectacles, *f.*, habitué, (*m.*, e, *f.*) de spectacle. —**going,** *adj.* qui va au spectacle, qui fréquente les spectacles. — **ground,** *s.* cour (de récréation), *f.* — **hours,** *s.pl.* récréation, *f.* —**house,** *s.* salle de spectacle, *f.*, théâtre, *m.* —**mate,** *s.* *V.* —**fellow.** — **night,** *s.* jour de spectacle, *m.* —**room,** *s.* salle de récréation, *f.* —**thing,** *s.* jouet, *m.*, (*fam.*) joujou, *m.*; (*fig.*) jouet, *m.* — **time,** *s.* récréation, *f.* —**wright,** *s.* faiseur (*m.*, -euse, *f.*) de pièces de théâtre. — **writer,** *s.* auteur dramatique, *m.*
Playable, *adj.* jouable
Player, *s.* joueur, *m.*, -euse, *f.*; musicien, *m.*, -ne, *f.*, artiste, *m.f.*, exécutant, *m*, e, *f.*; (*theat.*) acteur, *m.*, -trice, *f.* — *on the* ..., joueur (*m.*, -euse, *f.*) de ...
Playing, *s.* jeu, *m.* — **card,** *s.* carte à jouer, *f.*
Plea, *s.* procès, *m.*, cause, *f.*; défense, excuse, allégation, justification, *f.*; prétexte, *m.*; (*law*) exception, *f.* *Common* —*s,* (*Engl. law*) plaids communs, *m.pl.*
Plead, *v.n.* plaider; se défendre; alléguer, donner pour excuse; (*in favour*) militer; (*law*) se déclarer; se reconnaître, s'avouer; — *v.a.* plaider; défendre; (*argue*) invoquer; (*allege*) alléguer; s'excuser sur; (*support*) soutenir; (*law*) opposer. *To* — *guilty,* se reconnaître *or* s'avouer *or* se déclarer coupable, avouer l'accusation. *To* — *not guilty,* se déclarer innocent
Pleadable, *adj.* plaidable; invocable; allégable
Pleader, *s.* avocat, *m.*; défenseur, *m*; (*fig.*) partisan, *m.* *Special* —, avocat consultant, *m.*
Pleading, *s.* plaidoirie, *f.*; —**s,** *pl.* débats, *m.pl.*
Pleasant, *adj.* agréable (à); aimable (pour), charmant (pour); gracieux; doux; riant; gai, enjoué; (*good*) bon; (*ludicrous*) plaisant, singulier. — **smelling,** *adj.* qui sent bon, d'une odeur agréable
Pleasantly, *adv.* agréablement; d'une manière aimable *or* charmante, gracieusement; gaiment; (*ludicrously*) plaisamment, ridiculement
Pleasantness, *s.* agrément, charme, *m.*; aménité, *f.*; gaieté, *f.*; plaisant, *m.*
Pleasantry, *s.* plaisanterie, *f.*
Please, *v.a.* plaire à, faire plaisir à; charmer; contenter, satisfaire; — *v.n.* plaire; vouloir; trouver bon; daigner. *I* —, (*am agreeable*) je plais (à); (*choose*) il me plaît (de). *To be* —*d to,* se faire un plaisir de; être heureux de; se plaire à; se flatter que; (*be willing*) vouloir bien, avoir la bonté de; daigner. *To be* —*d with, V.* **Pleased.** *To* — *oneself,* se plaire; se contenter; faire comme on veut; (*to select*) choisir, faire son choix. —, s'il vous plaît; veuillez; pardon! — *God,* s'il plaît à Dieu. *As* or *when you* —, comme *or* quand vous voulez *or* (*future*) voudrez, comme *or* quand il vous plaît *or* (*future*) plaira. *If you* —, s'il vous plaît; si cela vous fait plaisir *or* vous est agréable *or* vous plaît. *If I* —, si cela me plaît; s'il me plaît (de ...). *May it* —, plaise à. *You are* —*d to say so,* cela vous plaît à dire
Pleased, *part. adj.* (*with pers. or things*) content (de); charmé (de); (*with things only*) satisfait (de); heureux (de). *To be* — *to,* &c., *V.* **Please.** *Ill* —, *Well* —, *V.* **Ill** *and* **Well.** — *as Punch,* dans la joie de son âme, aux anges
Pleasing, -ly, -ness. *V.* **Pleasant, -ly, -ness**
Pleasurable, *adj.* agréable, charmant, délicieux
Pleasurableness, *s.* agrément, charme, *m.*

Pleasurably, *adv.* agréablement, avec plaisir
Pleasure, *s.* plaisir, *m.*; agrément, *m.*; satisfaction, *f.*; charme, *m.*; (*will*) volonté, *f.*, gré, *m.*; — *adj.* d'agrément; de plaisir; — *v.a.* faire plaisir à, plaire à. *At* —, à plaisir, à volonté. *At his* —, à son gré, à sa volonté; comme *or* quand bon lui semble. *Do your* —, suivez votre goût, faites à votre gré. *What is your* — *?* que voulez-vous ? que désirez-vous ? qu'y a-t-il pour votre service ? *To give* or *afford anyone* —, faire plaisir à quelqu'un. *To take o.'s* —, s'amuser. *To take a* — *in*, se faire un plaisir de, prendre plaisir à, se plaire à. *Mr. A. requests the* — *of Mr. B.'s company to dinner on Monday*, M. A. prie M. B. de lui faire le plaisir de venir dîner avec lui lundi. — **boat,** *s.* bateau *or* canot de plaisance, bateau *or* canot de promenade, *m.* — **farm,** *s.* ferme d'agrément, *f.* — **garden, -ground,** *s.* jardin d'agrément, jardin anglais, *m.*; parc, *m.* — **house,** *s.* maison de plaisance, *f.* — **navigation,** *s.* navigation de plaisance, *f* — **party,** *s.* partie de plaisir, *f.* — **seeking,** *adj.* qui cherche le plaisir, ami du plaisir. — **trip,** *s.* voyage d'agrément, *m.*; partie de plaisir, *f.* — **van,** *s.* char à bancs, *m.* — **yacht,** *s.* yacht de plaisance, *m.*
Plebeian, *adj. s.* plébéien, *m.*, -ne, *f.*; roturier, [*m.*, -ière, *f.*
Plebeianism, *s.* plébéianisme, *m.*
Plebiscitary, *adj.* plébiscitaire
Plebiscite, Plebiscitum, *s.* plébiscite, *m.*
Pledge, *s.* gage, *m.*; (*surety*) garantie, *f.*, garant, *m.*; (*law*) nantissement, *m.*; (*bail*) caution, *f.*; (*mil.*) otage, *m.*; (*promise*) promesse, *f.*; assurance, *f.*; (*teetotal*) vœu de tempérance, *m.*; (*of polit. principles*) profession de foi, *f.*; (*a health*) toast, *m.*, santé, *f.*; — *v.a.* engager, mettre en gage; (*fig.*) engager (à); (*answer for*) garantir; (*in drinking*) faire raison à. *To* — *oneself*, s'engager (à), se faire fort (de); garantir (que), répondre (que). *To put in* —, mettre en gage, engager. *Unredeemed* —*s*, effets non dégagés (du mont-de-piété), *m.pl.*
Pledgee, *s.* créancier nanti d'un gage, *m.*
Pledger, *s.* personne qui met en gage, *f.*, débiteur (*m.*, -trice, *f.*) sur gage; garant, *m.*, e, *f.*; (*in drinking*) personne qui fait raison à un toast, *f.*
Pledget, *s.* bourdonnet, plumasseau, tampon, *m.*
Pleiads, Pleiades, *s.pl.* Pléiades, *f.pl.*
Plenarily, *adv.* pleinement, entièrement, [complètement
Plenariness, *s.* plénitude, *f.*
Plenary, *adj.* plein, entier, complet; (*of indulgences*) plénière
Plenipotentiary, *s adj.* plénipotentiaire, *m.*
Plenitude, *s.* plénitude, *f.*
Plenteous, Plentiful, *adj.* abondant
Plenteously, Plentifully, *adv.* abondamment, en abondance [dance, *f.*
Plenteousness, Plentifulness, *s.* abon-
Plenty, *s.* abondance, *f.*; (*adject.*) abondant, en abondance; (*adverb.*) beaucoup, en abondance, abondamment; bien assez, plus qu'il n'en faut; (*quite*) bien. *There is* — *of it*, il y en a une grande quantité *or* un grand nombre, il y en a à foison *or* en masse, il n'en manque pas; il y en a bien assez, &c. *There is* — *of time*, nous avons plus de temps qu'il ne nous en faut, nous avons tout le temps
Plenum, *s.* plein, *m.*
Pleonasm, *s.* pléonasme, *m.*
Pleonastic, -al, *adj.* pléonastique
Pleonastically, *adv.* par pléonasme, d'une manière pléonastique
Plesiosaur, Plesiosaurus, *s.* plésiosaure, *m.*
Plethora, *s.* pléthore, *f.*
Plethoric, *adj. s.* pléthorique
Pleura, *s.* plèvre, *f.*
Pleural, *adj.* pleural
Pleurisy, *s.* pleurésie, *f.*
Pleuritic, *adj.* pleurétique
Pleurodynia, *s.* pleurodynie, *f.*
Pleuro-pneumonia, *s.* pleuropneumonie, *f.*
Plexiform, *adj.* plexiforme
Plexigraph, *s.* plessigraphe, *m.*
Pleximeter, *s.* plessimètre, *m.*
Pleximetric, -al, *adj.* plessimétrique
Pleximetry, *s.* plessimétrie, *f.*
Plexus, *s.* plexus, *m.*
Pliability, Pliableness. *V.* **Pliancy**
Pliable, Pliant, *adj.* pliable, pliant; flexible, souple
Pliancy, Pliantness, *s.* flexibilité, souplesse, *f.*
Plica, — **Polonica,** *s.* plique, *f.*
Plicature, *s.* plicature, *f.*
Plier. *V.* **Plyer**
Plight, *v.a.* engager; — *s.* état, *m.*, situation, condition, *f.*; (*pledge*) gage, *m.*
Plighter, *s.* personne *or* chose qui engage, *f.*
Plinth, *s.* plinthe, *f.*
Plod, *v.n* travailler assidûment; (*study*) piocher, pâlir (sur); (*walk*) marcher avec peine *or* péniblement, marcher laborieusement
Plodder, *s.* travailleur assidu, piocheur, *m.*
Plodding, *adj.* laborieux; — *s.* travail assidu, *m.*
Ploddingly, *adv.* assidûment, péniblement, laborieusement
Plot, *s.* morceau de terre, champ, *m.*; plantation, *f.*; (*surveying*) plan de terrain, plan, *m.*; (*conspiracy*) complot, *m.*, trame, *f.*; (*stratagem*) ruse, *f.*, stratagème, *m.*; (*knot, of novels or plays*) intrigue, *f.*; — *v.a.n.* (*land-surveying*) rapporter, faire *or* lever le plan de; lever (un plan); (*fig.*) (*pers.*) comploter; conspirer; tramer, machiner; (*of things*) se tramer. *To form* or *lay a* —, tramer *or* faire un complot
Plotter, *s.* comploteur, *m.*, -euse, *f.*, conspirateur, *m.*, -trice, *f.*, machinateur, *m.*, -trice, *f.*; (*schemer*) *V.* **Schemer**
Plotting, *s.* action de comploter, *f.*; complots, *m.pl.*, machinations, *f.pl.*; (*land-surveying*) rapportage, lever (*or* levé) des plans, *m.* — **scale,** *s.* échelle à rapporter, *f.*
Plotus, *s.* (*bird*) anhinga, *m.*
Plough, *s.* charrue, *f.*; (*carp.*) bouvet à rapprofondir; — *adj.* de charrue; — *v.n.* labourer; — *v.a.* labourer; (*fig.*) fendre, sillonner; (*carp.*) creuser. — **boy,** *s.* garçon (*or* valet) de charrue, *m.* — **gang, -gate,** *s.* charruage, *m.* — **handle,** *s.* mancheron, *m.* — **horse,** *s.* cheval de labour *or* de charrue, *m.* — **land,** *s.* terre labourable, terre de labour, *f.* — **man,** *s.* laboureur, *m.*; (*a rustic*) paysan, *m.* — **Monday,** *s.* premier lundi après l'Épiphanie, *m.* — **ox,** *s.* bœuf de labour, *m.* — **share,** *s.* soc de charrue, *m.* — **staff,** *s.* curoir, *m.* — **tail,** *s.* manche de charrue, *m.* — **up,** *v.a.* déterrer, découvrir en labourant. — **wright,** *s.* *V.* **Wheelwright**
Plougher, *s.* laboureur, cultivateur, *m.*
Ploughing, *s.* labourage, *m.* — **match,** *s.* concours de charrues, *m.*
Plover, *s.* pluvier, *m.*
Pluck, *v.a.* tirer; (*pull off*) arracher, enlever; (*fowls*) plumer; (*flowers*) cueillir; (*of exam.*) refuser; — *s.* action de tirer, action d'arracher, *f.*; (*an animal's heart, liver, and lights*) fressure, *f.*; (*fig.*) courage, cœur, *m.*, (*fam.*) toupet, *m.* *To be* —*ed*, (*at an exam.*) être refusé, (*after a stage, in certain schools*, &c.) être *or* sortir fruit sec. *To* — **up** (*courage*), reprendre courage
Pluckily, *adv.* courageusement, bravement
Plucky, *adj.* courageux, brave
Plug, *s.* tampon, *m.*; bouchon, *m.*; (*peg*) cheville, *f.*; (*of a pump*) piston, *m.*; (*of water-pipes*) robinet, *m.*; crapaudine, *f.*; (*valve*) soupape, *f.*; (*of a tobacco-pipe*) culot, *m.*; (*surg.*) tampon, *m.*; — *v.a.* tamponner; boucher; (*with a peg*) cheviller; (*with a plugger*) fouler. — **hole,** *s.* (*of water-pipes*) bouche d'eau, *f.*
Plugger, *s.* (*dentist's instr.*) fouloir, plomboir, *m.*
Plum, *s.* prune, *f.*; (*dried*) pruneau, *m.*; (*raisin*) raisin sec, *m.* *Dried* or *French* —*s*, pruneaux,

m.pl. — **cake,** *s.* baba, *m.* — **orchard,** *s.* prunelaie, *f.* — **pie,** *s.* tourte aux prunes, *f.* — **pudding,** *s.* plum-pudding, *m.* — **pudding stone,** *s.* conglomérat, *m.* — **stone,** *s.* noyau de prune, *m.* — **tart,** *s.* tarte aux prunes, *f.* — **tree,** *s.* prunier, *m.*

Plumage, *s.* plumage, *m.*

Plumassier, *s.* plumassier, *m.*, -ière, *f.*

Plumb, *s.* plomb, *m.*; — *adj. adv.* à plomb; — *v.a.* plomber; mettre à plomb. — **level,** *s.* niveau à perpendicule, niveau, *m.* — **line,** *s.* fil à plomb, *m.*; (*nav.*) ligne de sonde, *f.* — **rule,** *s.* chas, chat, *m.*

Plumbago, *s.* plombagine, *f.*

Plumbate, *s.* plombate, *m.* [berie, *f.*

Plumber, *s.* plombier, *m.* —*'s work,* plom-

Plumbery, *s.* plomberie, *f.*

Plumbic, *adj.* plombique

Plumbiferous, *adj.* plombifère

Plumbing, *s.* plombage, *m.*

Plume, *s.* plume, *f.*; (*as ornament*) plume, *f.*, plumet, panache, *m.*; (*mil.*) plumet, *m.*; (*mil., horsehair — of a helmet*) crinière, *f.*; (*honour*) palme, *f.*, honneur, *m.*; (*bot.*) plumule, *f.*; — *v.a.* plumer; (*clean*) nettoyer; (*adorn with*) orner d'une plume *or* d'un panache, empanacher. *To — oneself,* (*pers.*) se piquer (de) se targuer (de), se glorifier de, faire parade (de); (*of birds*) se nettoyer, nettoyer ses plumes. — **alum,** *s.* alun de plume, *m.* — **bird,** *s.* épimaque, *m.* —**less,** *adj.* sans plumes; sans panache; (*fig.*) sans gloire

Plumigerous, *adj.* plumigère

Plumiped, *adj. s.* plumipède, *adj.m.f.*, *s.m.*

Plummet, *s.* plomb, *m.*; (*weight*) contre-poids, *m.* —**line,** *s.* fil à plomb, *m.*

Plumose, Plumous, *adj.* plumeux

Plump, *adj.* dodu, potelé, gras, gros, gros et gras, rondelet; (*blunt*) brusque, cru; — *adv.* tout d'un coup, droit; lourdement; — *v.n.* tomber à plomb, tomber lourdement; (*swell*) s'enfler; (*at elections*) donner un double vote (à); — *v.a.* laisser tomber lourdement

Plumper, *s.* bourde, *f.*, conte, *m.*; (*of elections*) double vote, *m.*

Plumply, *adv.* nettement, rondement

Plumpness, *s.* embonpoint, *m.*; rondeur, *f.*; (*bluntness*) brusquerie, *f.*

Plumularia, *s.* plumulaire, *f.*

Plumule, *s.* plumule, *f.*

Plumy, *adj.* couvert de plumes, emplumé; orné d'un panache, empanaché

Plunder, *v.a.* piller; voler; dépouiller; — *s.* pillage, *m.*; (*booty*) butin, *m.* [-euse, *f.*

Plunderer, *s.* pillard, *m.*, e, *f.*; voleur, *m.*,

Plunge, *v.a.* plonger; précipiter; — *v.n.* plonger, se plonger; se précipiter, se jeter, s'élancer; — *s.* plongement, plongeon, *m.*; élan, *m.*; (*step*) pas, *m.*; (*difficulty*) embarras, *m.*;

Plungeon, *s.* plongeon, *m.* [abîme, *m.*

Plunger, *s.* plongeur, *m.*

Plunging, *s.* *V.* **Plunge,** *s.*

Pluperfect, *s.* plus-que-parfait, *m.*

Plural, *adj.* composé; (*gram.*) pluriel; — *s.* pluriel, *m.* *In the — number, in the —,* au plu-

Pluralism, *s.* cumul, *m.* [riel

Pluralist, *s.* ecclésiastique qui a plus d'un bénéfice, cumulard, *m.* [&c.) cumul, *m.*

Plurality, *s.* pluralité, *f.*; (— *of emoluments,*

Pluralization, *s.* pluralisation, *f.*

Pluralize, *v.a.* pluraliser

Plurally, *adv.* en pluralité; (*gram.*) au pluriel

Plus, *adv.* plus

Plush, *s.* peluche, *f.*; panne, *f.* — **breeches,** *s.pl.* culotte (*if more than one pair,* culottes, *f.pl.*) de panne, *f.*

Plushy, *adj.* peluché, pelucheux

Plutocracy, *s.* plutocratie, *f.*

Plutocratic, *adj.* plutocratique

Plutonian, *s.adj.* plutonien, *m.*, -ne, *f.*

Pluton-ic, -ism, -ist. *V.* page 3, § 1

Pluvial, *adj. s.* pluvial *adj.m.*, e, *f.*, pluvial, *s.m.*

Pluviameter, Pluviometer, *s.* pluviomètre, *m.*

Pluvious, *adj.* pluvieux

Ply, *v.a.n.* s'appliquer à, s'attacher à; appliquer, exercer, employer; travailler avec; (*to handle*) manier; (*set going*) faire jouer; (*urge*) presser, supplier, solliciter; (*canvass*) offrir ses services; (*encumber*) accabler (de); importuner (de); bourrer (de); servir à; verser à; (*work*) travailler rudement; (*be busy*) s'occuper; (*between two points*) aller; faire le parcours *or* le trajet; faire le service; desservir la ligne (de ... à ...), desservir; (*go in haste*) aller à la hâte, se rendre à la hâte; (*nav.*) bouliner, louvoyer; — *s.* pli, *m.* *To — an oar,* manier la rame, ramer, ramer avec force. — **for,** tâcher d'obtenir, chercher; demander

Plyer, *s.* personne qui travaille *or* &c. (*V.* **Ply**); —**s,** *pl.* (*balance*) bascule, *f.*; (*pincers*) pinces, tenailles, *f.pl.* [(*in time-tables*) soir

P.M. de l'après-midi; (*evening or night*) du soir;

Pneumatic, -al, *adj.* pneumatique; —**s,** *s.pl.* pneumatique, *f.* — *trough,* cuve pneumato-chimique, *f.*

Pneumatology, &c. *V.* page 3, § 1

Pneumonia, *s.* pneumonie, *f.*

Pneumonic, *adj. s.* pneumonique

Poach, *v.a.n.* (*eggs*) pocher; (*upon*) voler, piller; (*game*) braconner; (*of animals*) chasser, aller à

Poachard, *s.* milouin, *m.* [la chasse

Poacher, *s.* braconnier, *m.*

Poachiness, *s.* humidité, *f.*

Poaching, *s.* braconnage, *m.*

Poachy, *adj.* humide, mou

Pochard, *s.* milouin, *m.*

Pock, *s.* grain de petite vérole, *m.* — **mark, -hole,** *s.* marque de petite vérole, *f.* — **marked, -pitted,** *adj.* marqué de la petite vérole, grêlé

Pocket, *s.* poche, *f.*; (*billiards*) blouse, *f.*; (*of hops, wool*) petit sac, demi-sac, *m.*; — *adj.* de poche; — *v.a.* empocher; mettre en poche; (*conceal*) cacher dans sa poche; (*steal*) dérober, soustraire; (*an insult*) avaler, digérer; (*at billiards*) blouser, bloquer, faire. *To be in —,* gagner ('*by,*' à). *To be out of —,* être en perte (de), perdre ('*by,*' à). *To pick —s,* filouter. *I am* 20 *shillings out of —,* je suis en perte de 25 francs. *I am* 20 *shillings out of — by that speculation, by it,* je perds 25 francs à cette spéculation, j'y perds 25 francs. *To pay out of one's own —,* payer de sa poche. —**book,** *s.* portefeuille, *m.*; carnet, *m.* — **dictionary,** *s.* dictionnaire de poche, *m.* —**ful,** *s.* poche pleine, *f.* — **flap,** *s.* patte de poche, *f.* — **glass,** *s.* miroir de poche, *m.* —**handkerchief,** *s.* mouchoir de poche, *m.* — **hole,** *s.* ouverture de poche, *f.* — **knife,** *s.* couteau de poche, *m.* — **money,** *s.* argent de poche, *m.*, menus plaisirs, *m.pl.*, cassette, *f.*; (*weekly*) semaine, *f.* —**picking,** *s.* filouterie, *f.*, vol à la tire, *m.* — **pistol,** *s.* pistolet de poche, *m.* — **volume,** *s.* volume portatif, *m.*

Pococurante, *s.* pococurante, *m.*

Pococurantism, *s.* pococurantisme, *m.*

Pod, *s.* cosse, *f.*; gousse, *f.*; — *v.n.* produire des

Podagra, *s.* podagre, *f.* [cosses

Podagric, -al, *adj.* podagrique; (*pers.*) podagre

Podded, Poddy, *adj.* cossu; (*in compounds*) à cosse, à cosses; à gousse, à gousses

Podesta, *s.* podestat, *m.*

Podgy, *adj.* *V.* **Squabby**

Podology, &c. *V.* page 3, § 1

Poem, *s.* poème, *m.*; poésie, *f.*, vers, *m.pl.*

Poesy, *s.* poésie, *f.*

Poet, *s.* poète, *m.* *Minor —,* poète de second ordre, *m.* —**like,** *adj.* de poète; (*adverb.*) en

Poetaster, *s.* poétriau, poètereau, *m.* [poète

Poetess, *s.* femme poète, *f.*, poète, *m.*

Poetic, -al, *adj.* poétique

Poetically, *adv.* poétiquement

Poetics, *s.pl.* poétique, *f.*

Poetize, *v.n.a.* poétiser

Poetry, *s.* poésie, *f.* *Minor* —, poésie légère, *f.*
Pogge, *s.* (*fish*) aspidophore, *m.*
Pogonias, *s.* (*bird, fish*) pogonias, *m.*
Poh. *V.* **Pooh.** [sel, *m.*; (*of grief*) violence, *f.*
Poignancy, *s.* piquant, *m.*; (*of wit*) pointe, *f.*,
Poignant, *adv.* piquant, mordant; (*of grief*) poignant, cuisant
Poignantly, *adv.* d'une manière piquante; d'une manière poignante *or* cuisante
Point, *s.* point, *m.*; (*sharp end*) pointe, *f.*; (*tagged point*) aiguillette, *f.*; (*of wit*) pointe, *f.*; piquant, *m.*; (*wit itself*) esprit, sel, *m.*; (*of land*) pointe, *f.*; (*gram.*, *geom.*, *mus.*, *cards*, &c.) point, *m.*; (*sculptor's tool*) pointe, *f.*, poinçon, ébauchoir, *m.*; (*engr.*) pointe, *f.*, poinçon, *m.*; (*print.*) pointure, *f.*; (*rail.*) aiguille, *f.*; (*nav.*) (*of compass*) aire de vent, *f.*, quart de vent, *m.*; (*of sails*) garcette de ris, *f.*; (*question*) question, *f.*; affaire, *f.*; essentiel, *m.*; (*assertion*) dire, *m.*; (*aim*) but, *m.*; (*feature*) trait, *m.*; qualité, *f.*; (*side*) côté, *m.*; (*lace*) point, *m.*; — *v.a.* (*sharpen*) affiler, aiguiser, affûter, donner une pointe à, rendre pointu; (*cut*) tailler en pointe, tailler; (*with stops*) pointer, ponctuer; (*show*) indiquer, montrer; (*direct*) diriger; adresser; (*cannon, a telescope, books*, &c.) pointer; (*gram.*) ponctuer; (*nav.*) pointer, compasser; (*sails*) garnir de garcettes de ris; (*needles*, &c.) empointer, affiner; (*sculp.*) mettre aux points (*or* au point), ébaucher; (*print.*) pointer; (*mas.*) jointoyer, gobeter; (*rail.*) aiguiller; — *v.n.* se tourner; (*of dogs*) arrêter; (*of abscesses*) aboutir; (*rail.*) aiguiller; (*mas.*) jointoyer, gobeter. — *of the compass*, (*nav.*) aire de vent, *f.*, quart de vent, *m.* — *of distance*, (*pers.*) point de vue, *m.* — *of sight*, point de vue, *m.*; (*of fire-arms*) point de mire, *m.* — *of view*, point de vue, *m.* *Chief* or *main* —, point capital, essentiel, *m.* *Decimal* —, virgule décimale, *f.* *At the* — *of death*, *V.* *On the* — *of death* [*below*]. *At all* —*s*, (*armed*) de toutes pièces. *In all* —*s*, *in every* —, de tous points, en tout point. *In* —, en question; 'ad hoc'; à propos. *In* — *of*, en fait de, en matière de. *In* — *of fact*, dans *or* par le fait, au fait; en effet. *On the* — *of*, sur le point de, au moment de. *On the* — *of death*, près de mourir, à l'article de la mort, à la mort, à l'agonie. *To the* —, (*in* —) à propos. *To come* (or *speak*) *to the* —, venir *or* arriver au fait. *To gain* (or *carry*) *o.'s* —, atteindre son but, arriver (*or* en venir) à ses fins. *To have come to the* —, y être. *To make a* — (*of*), *to make it a* — (*to*), se faire une loi *or* une règle (de); se faire un devoir (de); s'arranger (pour); avoir soin de; prendre à tâche (de); affecter (de). *To maintain* or *press o.'s* —, maintenir son dire. *To press the* —, insister. *To stretch a* —, forcer ses moyens. — **at,** *v.a.* montrer du doigt; (*in contempt*) montrer au doigt. — **blank,** *adv.* (*artil.*) de but en blanc; (*of small arms, close*) à bout portant; (*fig.*) à brûle-pourpoint; (*directly*) directement; droit au but; (*positively*) positivement, net; (*inconsiderately*) de but en blanc; *adj.* (*fig.*) à brûle-pourpoint; direct; positif, net, formel. — **lace,** *s.* point, *m.* —**less,** *adj.* sans pointe; (*fig.*) fade, plat. — **out,** *v.a.* *V.* — **to.** —**sman,** *s.* (*rail.*) aiguilleur, *m.* —**to,** *v.a.* indiquer, désigner, montrer, signaler. faire remarquer
Pointed, *adj.* pointu, à pointe, acéré; (*fig.*) piquant, mordant, acéré; épigrammatique; direct; personnel; évident; (*arch.*) ogival, en ogive
Pointedly, *adv.* d'une manière piquante; positivement, expressément; directement
Pointedness, *s.* forme pointue, *f.*; pointe, épigramme, *f.*
Pointer, *s.* index, *m.*; (*of a dial, rail.*) aiguille, *f.*; (*engr.*) poinçon, *m.*; (*dog*) chien d'arrêt, *m.*
Pointing, *s.* (*artil.*, *nav.*) pointage, *m.*; (*gram.*) ponctuation, *f.*; (*of books*) pointage, *m.*; (*sculpt.*) ébauchage, *m.*; (*of needles*, &c.) empointage, affinage, *m.*; (*mas.*) jointoiement, gobetage, gobetis, *m.*
Poise, *s.* poids, *m.*; importance, *f.*; équilibre, *m.*, pondération, *f.*; contre-poids, *m.*; — *v.a.* peser; balancer; équilibrer, tenir *or* maintenir en équilibre, pondérer [en équilibre; juste
Poised, *part. adj.* pesé, &c. (*V.* **Poise,** *v.a.*);
Poiser, *s.* *V.* **Balancer**
Poison, *s.* poison, *m.*; — *v.a.* empoisonner. —*ed wound*, plaie envenimée, *f.*; plaie empoisonnée, *f.* — **fang,** *s.* crochet venimeux, *m.*, dent venimeuse, *f.* — **gland,** *s.* glande venimeuse, *f.* — **nut,** *s.* noix vomique, *f.* — **tree,** *s.* toxicodendron, *m.*
Poisoner, *s.* empoisonneur, *m.*, -euse, *f.*
Poisoning, *s.* empoisonnement, *m.*
Poisonous, *adj.* (*general sense*) toxique; (*particularly of animals*) venimeux; (*particularly of plants, of animals eaten, of inorganic substances*) vénéneux; (*poisoned*) empoisonné; (*fig.*) empoisonné; venimeux; funeste
Poisonously, *adv.* en empoisonnant
Poisonousness, *s.* (*general sense*) toxicité, *f.*; (*particularly of animals*) venimosité, *f.*; (*particularly of plants, of animals eaten, of inorganic substances*) vénénosité, *f.*; (*fig.*) poison, venin, *m.*
Poke, *s.* poche, *f.*; (*stroke*) coup, *m.*; (*cuff*) coup de poing; — *v.a.* (*thrust*) pousser; fourrer, mettre; (*feel*) chercher à tâtons; (*the fire*) attiser, remuer, fourgonner; (*to cuff*) donner un coup de poing à; pousser; (*of horned cattle*) donner des coups de corne à, corner; — *v.n.* (*fumble*) fouiller, farfouiller; (*feel*) tâtonner; se fourrer; (*of horned cattle*) donner des coups de corne. *To buy a pig in a* —, acheter chat en poche. — **net,** *s.* *V.* **Stake-net**
Poker, *s.* tisonnier, fourgon, *m.* [taudis, *m.*
Poking, *adj.* servile; obscur; sale. — *hole*,
Polacca, Polacre, *s.* polaque, polacre, *f.*
Polander, *s.* Polonais, *m.*, e, *f.*
Polar, *adj.* polaire
Polarimeter, *s.* polarimètre, *m.*
Polarimetric, -al, &c. polarimétrique, &c. (*V.* page 3, § 1)
Polariscope, *s.* polariscope, *m.*
Polarity, *s.* polarité, *f.*
Polarization, *s.* polarisation, *f.*
Polarize, *v.a.* polariser
Polarizing, *adj.* polarisateur
Pole, *s.* (*geog.*, *astr.*, *geom.*, *phys.*) pôle, *m.*; (*staff*) perche, *f.*; mât, *m.*; bâton, *m.*; (*top of a mast*) flèche, *f.*; (*for hops*) perche, *f.*, échalas, *m.*; (*for curtains*, &c.) bâton, *m.*; (*of carriages*) timon, *m.*; (*of stables*) barre, *f.*; (*of rope-dancers*) balancier, *m.*; (*meas.*) perche, *f.*; (*pers.*) Polonais, *m.*, e, *f.*; — *v.a.* (*hort.*) ramer. *Under bare* —*s*, (*nav.*) à sec de voiles, à mâts et à cordes. — **axe,** *s.* hache d'armes, *f.*; (*halberd*) hallebarde, *f.*; (*of butchers*) merlin, assommoir, *m.* — **cat,** *s.* putois, *m.* — **chain,** *s.* (*of a carriage*) chaînette, *f.* — **crab,** *s.* (*of a carriage*) crapaud de timon, *m.* — **piece,** *s.* (*of a carriage*) chaînette (en cuir), *f.* — **ring,** *s.* porte-barres, *m.* — **screen,** *s.* écran à pied, *m.* — **star,** *s.* étoile polaire, *f.*
Polemic, -al, *adj.* polémique
Polemic, Polemist, *s.* polémiste, *m.*
Polemics, *s.pl.* polémique, *f.*
Polemoscope, *s.* polémoscope, *m.*
Polenta, *s.* polenta, *f.*
Police, *s.* police, *f.*; (*rural, armed, mounted*) gendarmerie, *f.* —! à la garde! *County* —, gendarmerie. *Mounted* —, gendarmerie à cheval. — **cell,** *s.* violon, *m.* — **court,** *s.* tribunal de police, *m.* — **man,** *s.* agent de police, sergent de ville, *m.*; (*rural, armed, mounted*) gendarme, *m.* — **office,** *s.* bureau de police, *m.*; mairie, *f.* — **officer,** *s.* *V.* — **man.** — **regulation,** *s.* règlement de police, *m.* — **sergeant,** *s.* brigadier de police, brigadier de sergents de ville, *m.*; (*rural*)

brigadier de gendarmerie, *m.* — **sheet,** *s. V.* **Charge-sheet.** — **spy,** *s.* espion de police, *m.*; (*in contempt*) mouchard, *m.* — **station,** *s.* bureau du commissaire de police, commissariat de police, *m.*; poste de police, poste, *m.* — **superintendent,** *s.* commissaire de police, *m.* — **van,** *s.* voiture cellulaire, *f.*

Policy, *s.* politique, *f.*; vues, *f.pl.*; système, plan, *m.*; utilité, *f.*; prudence, *f.*; (*of insurance*) police, *f.* — **holder,** *s.* assuré, *m.*, e, *f.*

Polish, *adj.* (*geog.*) polonais, de Pologne; — *s.* (*language*) le polonais, *m.*, la langue polonaise, *f.*

Polish, *v.a.* polir; (*furniture, to French-polish*) vernir (des meubles), vernir à l'esprit de vin; (*boots*) cirer; (*refine*) polir, policer, civiliser, (*fam.*) façonner, dégourdir; — *v.n.* se polir; (*pers.*) se dégourdir

Polish, *s.* (*material*) enduit, vernis, *m.*; (*gloss*) poli, luisant, *m.*; (*pers.*) vernis, *m.*; élégance, politesse, *f.* *French* —, vernis à l'alcool, vernis à l'esprit de vin, vernis, *m.*

Polishable, *adj.* polissable

Polished, *part. adj.* poli, &c. (*V.* **Polish,** *v.a.n.*); (*pers.*) policé; de bon ton; (*of manners*) poli, distingué

Polisher, *s.* polisseur, *m.*, -euse, *f.*; (*a tool*) polissoir, *m.* *French* —, vernisseur (en meubles), *m.*

Polishing, *s.* poli, *m.*; (*act of* —) polissage, *m.*; (*of furniture, French* —) vernissage (de meubles), vernissage à l'esprit de vin, *m.*; (*of boots*) cirage, *m.*; (*refining*) policement, *m.* — **rush,** *s.* prêle d'hiver, asprêle, *f.*

Polite, *adj.* poli; élégant; complaisant; attentif; (*to ladies*) galant. — *literature* or *letters* or *learning*, belles-lettres, *f.pl.* — *thing*, politesse, *f.*

Politely, *adv.* poliment; (*to ladies*) galamment

Politeness, *s.* politesse, *f.*; (*to ladies*) galanterie, *f.*

Politic, -al, *adj.* politique

Politically, Politicly, *adv.* politiquement

Politicaster, *s.* politiqueur, *m.*

Politician, *s.* politique, *m.*

Politics, *s.pl.* politique, *f.*

Polity, *s.* gouvernement, *m.*, forme de gouvernement, *f.*, constitution, *f.*, régime politique, *m.*; police, *f.*

Polk, *v.n.* polker, danser la polka

Polka, *s.* polka, *f.*

Polker, *s.* polkeur, *m.*, -euse, *f.*

Poll, *s.* (*back part of the head*) occiput, *m.*; (*head*) tête, *f.*; (*of horses*) nuque, *f.*; (*register, &c.*) liste, *f.*; liste électorale, *f.*; inscription des votes, *f.*; élection, *f.*; (*place*) lieu de l'élection, *m.*; (*of English elections*) poll, *m.*; (*voting*) vote, *m.*; (*votes*) voix, *f.pl.*, suffrages, *m.pl.*; (*parrot*) perroquet, *m.*; Jacquot, *m.*; — *v.a.n.* (*trees*) étêter; (*shear*) tondre; (*to vote*) voter, donner sa voix, se faire inscrire; (*electors*) inscrire; (*of votes*) (*to give*) donner, (*to obtain*) obtenir. *To demand a* —, demander le scrutin. — **evil,** *s.* (*vet.*) taupe, *f.* — **parrot,** *s.* perroquet, *m.* — **tax,** *s.* capitation, *f.*

Pollack, *s.* pollack, merlan jaune, *m.*

Pollan, *s.* lavaret, *m.*

Pollard, *s.* (*flour and bran*) issues, *f.pl.*, repasse, *f.*; (*tree*) têtard, *m.*; (*fish*) meunier, chabot, *m.*; — *v.a.* étêter

Polled, *part. adj.* étêté, &c. (*V.* **Poll,** *v.a.n.*); (*of cattle*) sans cornes

Pollen, *s.* (*bran*) petit son, *m.*; (*bot.*) pollen, *m.*

Polling, *s.* vote, *m.*, élection, *f.*; (*of trees*) étêtement, *m.* — **booth, -place,** *s.* section de vote, *f.*; lieu de l'élection, *m.*

Pollute, *v.a.* polluer; profaner; (*tarnish*) souiller ('*with*,' de), flétrir; (*corrupt*) corrompre

Pollutedness, *s. V.* **Pollution**

Polluter, *s.* profanateur, *m.*, -trice, *f.*; corrupteur, *m.*, -trice, *f.*

Pollution, *s.* pollution, *f.*; profanation, *f.*; souillure, *f.*

Polonaise, *s.* polonaise, *f.*

Polonese, *s.* (*language*) le polonais, *m.*

Polonism, *s.* polonisme, *m.*

Poltroon, Poltroonery. *V.* **Coward, Cowardice**

Poly, (*in compounds*) poly ...

Polyandria, Polyandry, *s.* polyandrie, *f.*

Polyandrian, Polyandrous, *adj.* polyandre

Polychrom-atic, -y. *V.* page 3, § 1

Polychrome, *adj. s.* polychrome, *adj.m.f., s.m.*

Polygam-ic, al, -y. *V.* page 3, § 1

Polygamist, *s.*, **Polygamous,** *adj.* polygame, *m.f.* [*s.m.f.*, (*Bible*) *s.f.*

Polyglot, *adj. s.* polyglotte, *adj. m.f.*, (*pers.*)

Polygon, *s.* polygone, *m.*

Polygonal, *adj.* polygonal, polygone

Polygraph, *s.* polygraphe, *m.*

Polygraph-ic, al, -y. *V.* page 3, § 1

Polyhedral, *adj.* polyèdre

Polyhedron, *s.* polyèdre, *m.*

Polygynia, Polygyny, *s.* polygynie, *f.*

Polygynian, Polygynous, *adj.* polygyne

Polymath-ic, al, -y. *V.* page 3, § 1

Polymathist, *s.* polymathe, *m.*

Polymorph-ism, -y, &c. *V.* page 3, § 1

Polynesian, *s. adj.* Polynésien, *m.*, -ne, *f.*

Polynomial, *s. adj.* polynôme, *s.m.*, *adj. m.f.*

Polyorama, *s.* polyorama, *m.*

Polype, *s.* polype, *m.*

Polypetalous, *adj.* polypétale, polypétalé

Polyphon-ic, -y, &c. *V.* page 3, § 1

Polypous, *adj.* polypeux

Polypus, *s.* polype, *m.*

Polyscope, *s.* polyscope, *m.*

Polyscopic, *adj.* polyscopique

Polysepalous, *adj.* polysépale

Polystyle, *s. adj.* polystyle, *s.m.*, *adj. m.f.*

Polysyllabic, *adj.* polysyllabe, polysyllabique

Polysyllable, *s.* polysyllabe, *m.*

Polytechnic, *adj.* polytechnique

Polytechnician, *s.* polytechnicien, *m.*

Polytheism, *s.* polythéisme, *m.*

Polytheist, *s.* polythéiste, *m.f.*

Polytheistic, -al, *adj.* polythéiste

Pomace, *s.* pommage, *m.*; marc de pommes, *m.*

Pomade, Pomatum, *s.* pommade, *f.*; — *v.a.* pommader. — **jar,** *s.* pot à pommade, *m.*

Pomegranate, *s.* grenade, *f.* — **grove, -plantation,** *s.* grenadière, *f.* — **tree,** *s.* grenadier, *m.*

Pomelo, *s.* pamplemousse, *f.*

Pomeranian, *s. adj.* Poméranien, *m.*, -ne, *f.*

Pomiculture, *s.* pomiculture, *f.*

Pomiculturist, *s.* pomiculteur, *m.*

Pomiferous, *adj.* pomifère

Pomiform, *adj.* pomiforme

Pommel, *s.* pommette, *f.*; (*of beds, canes*) pomme, *f.*; (*of swords, saddles*) pommeau, *m.*; — *v.a.* rosser, frotter

Pomolog-ic, al, -y. *V.* page 3, § 1

Pomologist, *s.* pomologue, *m.*

Pomona, *s.* (*bot.*) pomone, *f.*; (*myth., astr.*) Pomone, *f.*

Pomp, *s.* pompe, *f.*, éclat, *m.*

Pompeian, *s. adj.* Pompéien, *m.*, -ne, *f.*

Pompelmoose, *s.* pamplemousse, *f.*

Pompion, *s. V.* **Pumpkin**

Pomposity, *s.* pompe, *f.*, éclat, *m.*; ostentation, *f.*; (*of language*) emphase, *f.*

Pompous, *adj.* pompeux

Pompously, *adv.* pompeusement; avec ostentation

Pompousness, *s. V.* **Pomposity**

Pond, *s.* (*for fish*) étang, *m.*; (*small*) vivier, *m.*; (*pool*) mare, *f.*; (*for cattle*) abreuvoir, *m.* — **snail,** *s.* limnée, *f.* — **weed,** *s.* potamot, *m.*

Ponder, *v.n.* réfléchir, méditer; — *v.a.* peser, considérer, réfléchir à

Pondera-bility, bleness, *s.* pondérabilité, *f.*

Ponderable, *adj.* pondérable

Ponderal, *adj.* pondéral

Ponderation, *s.* pondération, *f.*

Ponderer, *s.* personne qui pèse *or* qui considère *or* qui réfléchit, *f.*

Ponderingly, *adv.* avec réflexion

Ponderosity, *s.* poids, *m.*, pesanteur, *f.*

Ponderous, *adj.* pesant, lourd; important

Ponderously, *adv.* pesamment

Ponderousness, *s.* poids, *m.*, pesanteur, *f.*
Pongo, *s.* pongo, *m.*
Poniard, *s.* poignard, *m.*; — *v.a.* poignarder
Pontage, *s.* pontonage, *m.*
Pontic, *adj.* pontique
Pontiff, *s.* pontife, *m.*
Pontifical, *adj.* pontifical; — *s.* (*book*) pontifical, *m.*; —**s,** *s.pl.* habits pontificaux, *m.pl.*
Pontifically, *adv.* pontificalement; en pontife
Pontificate, *s.* pontificat, *m.*
Pontine, *adj.* pontin
Pontonier, *s.* pontonnier, pontonier, *m.*
Pontoon, *s.* ponton, *m.* — **bridge,** *s.* pont de pontons, pont de bateaux, *m.*, pontons, *m.pl.* — **train,** *s.* équipage de pont, *m.*
Pony, *s.* poney, ponet, *m.*, (*mare* —) ponette, *f.* — **chaise,** *s.* chaise à poney, *f.*
Poodle, *s.* caniche, *m.* — **dog,** *s.* chien caniche, caniche, *m.*
Pooh, *int.* bah! allons donc!
Pooh-pooh, *v.a.* traiter légèrement; mépriser, faire fi de, narguer, se moquer de
Pool, *s.* mare, *f.*; étang, *m.*; (*play*) poule, *f.*
Poop, *s.* dunette, poupe, *f.*
Poor, *adj.* pauvre; malheureux; indigent; (*wretched*) pauvre, chétif, pitoyable, misérable; (*bad*) mauvais, triste; (*barren*) pauvre, maigre; (*lean*) maigre. — *man,* (*not rich*) homme pauvre, pauvre, *m.*; (*term of pity*) pauvre homme, *m.* — *woman* (*not rich*) femme pauvre, pauvresse, *f.*; (*term of pity*) pauvre femme, *f.* — *people,* pauvres gens, pauvres, *m.pl.* — *people ashamed to beg,* pauvres honteux, *m.pl.* *My* — *boy,* mon pauvre garçon. *The* —, les pauvres, les indigents, *s.m.pl.* *To grow* (or *get* or *become*) —, *V.* **Grow.** *As* — *as a church mouse,* gueux comme un rat d'église. — **box,** *s.* tronc pour les pauvres, *m.* — **house,** *s.* asile des indigents, dépôt de mendicité, *m.* — **law,** *s.* loi sur l'assistance publique (*or* sur le paupérisme), *f.*; assistance publique, *f.* — **law board** *or* **commissioners,** *s.* conseil (*or* bureau) de l'assistance publique, *m.* — *law commissioner,* membre du conseil de l'assistance publique, *m.* — **rate,** *s.* contribution à la taxe des pauvres, *f.*; taxe des pauvres, *f.* — **rates,** *s.pl.* taxe des pauvres, *f.* — **spirited,** *adj.* pusillanime. — **spiritedness,** *s.* pusillanimité, *f.*
Poorly, *adv.* pauvrement; (*badly*) mal; (*very little*) très peu; (*adject.*) indisposé, souffrant
Poorness, *s.* pauvreté, *f.*; indigence, *f.*; stérilité, *f.*; bassesse, *f.*; mauvaise qualité, *f.*
Pop, *s.* petit bruit vif et aigu, petit coup, *m.*; — *v.n.* survenir; (*go off*) partir; sauter; (*shoot at*) tirer (sur); — *v.a.* mettre précipitamment *or* bien vite; fourrer; passer; lâcher; — *int.* crac! — *goes . . . !* voilà . . . qui part! *To* — *the question,* offrir d'épouser, se présenter pour le bon motif, lancer *or* lâcher sa déclaration. — **down,** *v.n.* descendre subitement. — **gun,** *s.* canonnière, *f.* — **in,** *v.n.* entrer subitement; entrer pour un moment. — **off,** *v.a.* lancer; *v.n.* (*depart*) filer; (*die*) claquer. — **out,** *v.n.* sortir subitement, s'esquiver; *v.a.* (*thrust out*) passer; (*a word*) lâcher. — **shop,** *s.* mont-de-piété, (le) clou, *m.* — (*v.n.*) **upon,** tomber (comme une bombe) sur
Pope, *s.* pape, *m.*; (*of the Greek Church*) pope, *m.*; (*a fish*) gremille, perche goujonnière, *f.* — **Joan,** *s.* la papesse Jeanne, *f.*; (*game*) le nain jaune, *m.* —**'s eye,** *s.* (*of meat*) noix, *f.* —**'s head,** *s.* (*brush*) tête-de-loup, *f.*
Popedom, *s.* papauté, *f.*; (*territory*) les États du pape (*or* de l'Église), *m.pl.*
Popery, *s.* papisme, *m.*
Popinjay, *s.* papegai, *m.*; (*woodpecker*) pivert, *m.*; (*fop*) fat, petit-maître, *m.*
Popish, *adj.* (*pers.*) papiste; (*things*) de papiste
Popishly, *adv.* en papiste
Poplar, *s.* peuplier, *m.* — **grove, -plantation,** *s.* peupleraie, *f.*
Poplin, *s.* popeline, *f.*
Poppy, *s.* pavot, *m.*; (*arch.*) poupée, *f.* *Red* —, coquelicot, *m.* — **colour,** *s*, — **coloured,** *adj.* ponceau, *m.* — **flower,** *s.* fleur de pavot, *f.* — **head,** *s.* tête de pavot, *f.*; (*arch.*) poupée, *f.* — **oil,** *s.* huile de pavot, huile d'œillette, *f.*
Populace, *s* populace, *f.*
Popular, *adj.* populaire; aimé; en vogue; [couru
Popularity, *s.* popularité, *f.*
Popularization, *s.* popularisation, *f.*
Popularize, *v.a.* populariser; vulgariser
Popularly, *adv.* populairement
Populate, *v.a.* peupler; — *v.n.* se peupler
Population, *s.* population, *f.*
Populous, *adj.* populeux
Populously, *adv.* d'une manière populeuse
Populousness, *s.* populosité, *f.*; nombreuse population, *f.*
Porcelain, *s.* porcelaine, *f.* — **clay,** &c. *V.* **China-clay,** &c. — **painter** *or* **paintress,** *s.* peintre sur porcelaine, *m.f.*, peintresse, *f.* — **painting,** *s.* peinture sur porcelaine, *f.* — **shell,** *s.* porcelaine, *f.*
Porcelaneous, *adj.* porcelanique
Porch, *s.* porche, *m.*; (*anc. philos.*) Portique, *m.*
Porcine, *adj.* porcine, *f*; de *or* du porc. — *species* or *race,* espèce *or* race porcine, *f.*
Porcupine, *s.* porc-épic, *m.*
Pore, *s.* pore, *m.*; — *v.n.* avoir les yeux fixés (sur); regarder attentivement. *To* — *over* (*a book*), avoir les yeux collés sur, dévorer
Pork, *s.* porc, cochon, *m.* — **butcher,** *s.* charcutier, *m.*, -ière, *f.* — **butchery,** *s.* charcuterie, *f.* — **cheese,** *s.* fromage de cochon, *m.* — **chop,** *s.* côtelette de porc, *f.* — **man,** *s.* *V.* **Pig-salesman.** — **pie,** *s.* pâté de porc, *m.* — **sausage,** *s.* saucisson, *m.*; saucisse, *f.*
Porker, *s.* porc, cochon, *m.*
Porosity, Porousness, *s.* porosité, *f.*
Porous, *adj.* poreux
Porphyraceous, *adj.* porphyré
Porphyrite, *s.* porphyrite, *f.*
Porphyritic, *adj.* porphyritique, porphyrique
Porphyry, *s.* porphyre, *m.*
Porpoise, *s.* marsouin, *m.*
Porraceous, *adj* porracé
Porridge, *s.* pâtée, bouillie, *f.*; soupe, *f.* — **pot,** *s.* marmite, *f.*
Porriginous, *adj.* porrigineux
Porrigo, *s.* porrigo, *m.*
Porringer, *s.* écuelle, *f.* —**ful,** *s.* écuellée, *f.*
Port, *s.* port, *m.*; (*of a ship*) sabord, *m.*, (*larboard*) bâbord, *m.*; (*of a steam-engine*) lumière, *f.*; (*mien*) port, maintien, air, *m.*; (*of the voice*) conduite, *f.*; (*gate*) porte, *f.*; (*wine*) vin d'Oporto, porto, *m.*; — *v.a.* (*carry*) porter. — ! bâbord! — *the helm!* bâbord la barre! *Hard a* — ! bâbord tout! — *a little!* bâbord un peu! *To put into* —, relâcher. — **admiral,** *s.* amiral commandant dans un port, *m.* — **charges,** *s.pl.* frais de port, *m.pl.* — **dues,** *V.* **Harbour.** — **fire,** — **folio,** &c., *See below.* — **hole,** *s.* sabord, *m.* — **last,** *s.* plat-bord, *m.* — **lid,** *s.* mantelet de sabord, *m.* — **town,** *s.* ville maritime, *f.*, port de mer, *m.* — **wine,** *s.* vin d'Oporto, porto, *m.*
Portability. *V.* **Portableness**
Portable, *adj.* portatif; (*of steam-engines and of machines generally*) locomobile; transportable [transportable, *f.*
Portableness, *s.* nature portative, *f.*; nature
Portage, *s.* portage, *m.*; port, *m.*
Portal, *s.* portail, *m.*; porte, *f.*; — *adj.* portal. — *vein,* veine porte, *f.*
Port-crayon, *s.* porte-crayon, *m.*
Portcullis, *s.* herse, *f.*
Portcullised, *adj.* à herse
Porte, *s.* (*in Turkey*) Porte, *f.* *The Sublime* —, [la Sublime Porte
Porte-monnaie, *s.* portemonnaie, *m.*
Portend, *v.a.* présager, augurer
Portent, *s.* présage sinistre, mauvais augure, *m.*
Portentous, *adj.* de mauvais présage, de

mauvais augure; sinistre; effroyable; monstrueux, prodigieux
Portentously, *adv.* sinistrement; effroyablement; monstrueusement, prodigieusement
Porter, *s.* (*door-keeper*) concierge, portier, *m.*; (*carrier*) portefaix, crocheteur, *m.*; porteur, *m.*, -euse, *f.*; (*licensed, in a town*) commissionnaire, *m.*; (*market-porter, heaver*) porteur (de ...), *m.*, -euse, *f.*; (*rail.*) facteur de chemin de fer, facteur, *m.*; (*com.*) garçon de magasin, garçon, *m.*; garçon (*or* homme) de peine, *m.*; (*admin.*) garçon de bureau, *m.*; (*beer*) porter, *m.*, bière brune, *f.* —*'s knot*, crochet de portefaix, *m.* [chetage, *m.*
Porterage, *s.* factage, *m.*; portage, *m.*; cro-
Portfire, — stick, *s.* lance à feu, *f.*
Portfolio, *s.* portefeuille, *m.*
Portico, *s.* portique, *m.*
Portion, *s.* portion, part, *f.*; partie, *f.*; (*in marriage*) dot, *f.*; — *v.a.* partager, distribuer, répartir; (*in marriage*) doter. *Disposable* —, (*law*) quotité disponible, *f.* —**less,** *adj.* sans dot. — **out,** *v.a.* distribuer, répartir
Portioner, *s.* distributeur, *m.*, -trice, *f.*, répartiteur, *m.* [distribution, répartition, *f.*
Portioning, Portionment, *s* partage, *m.*,
Portliness, *s.* port majestueux, port noble, noble maintien, *m.*, prestance, *f.*; corpulence, *f.*
Portly, *adj.* d'un port majestueux, d'un port *or* d'un maintien noble; gros, corpulent
Portmanteau, *s.* portemanteau, *m.*, valise, *f.*
Portmonnaie, *s.* portemonnaie, *m.*
Portrait, *s.* portrait, *m.* — **painter** *or* **paintress,** *s.* peintre de portraits, *m.f.*, portraitiste, *m.f.* — **painting,** *s.* peinture de portraits, *f.*, le portrait, *m.* [peinture, *f.*
Portraiture, *s.* portrait, *m.*; (*fig.*) tableau, *m.*,
Portray, *v.a.* peindre; représenter; décrire
Portrayer, *s.* peintre, *m.f.*
Portress, *s.* concierge, portière, *f.*
Portuguese, *s.* Portugais, *m.*, e, *f.*; (*language*) le portugais, *m.*, la langue portugaise, *f.*; — *adj.* portugais, de Portugal. — *wine*, vin de Portugal, *m.*
Pose, *v.a.* embarrasser, confondre, mettre au pied du mur, mettre à quia, fermer la bouche à, coller; questionner, poser des questions captieuses à, tâcher d'embarrasser par des questions; (*at dominoes*) poser; — *v.n.* (*paint., sculp., photography*, &c., *and dominoes*) poser; — *s.* pose, *f.*
Poser, *s.* personne qui embarrasse, *f.*; examinateur, *m.*, -trice, *f.*; question embarrassante, *f.*
Position, *s.* position, situation, *f.*; situation, *f.*, état, *m.*; disposition, *f.*; principe posé, *m.*, assertion, *f.*; idée, *f.*; (*gram., mil.*) position, *f.*; (*nav.*) point, emplacement, *m.*; (*arith.*) fausse position, *f.* *In a — to*, en position de, en état de
Positive, *adj.* positif; réel; absolu; certain, sûr et certain; précis, exprès; (*decisive*) tranchant; (*obstinate*) opiniâtre, obstiné, entêté, entier; (*gram., phys.*, &c.) positif; — *s.* positif, *m.*
Positively, *adv.* positivement; absolument; certainement, sûrement, assurément; précisément; affirmativement; (*decisively*) d'une manière tranchante; (*obstinately*) opiniâtrément
Positiveness, *s.* positiveté, positivité, *f.*; réalité, *f.*; certitude, *f.*; précision, *f.*; ton décisif, *m.*, manière tranchante, *f.*; opiniâtreté, obstination, *f.*, entêtement, *m.*
Positiv-ism, -ist. *V.* page 3, § 1
Posse (— *comitatus*), *s.* force publique, *f.*; (*crowd*) foule, cohue, *f.*
Possess, *v.a.* posséder; (*enjoy*) jouir de; (*give possession*) rendre maître de; (*occupy*) occuper; (*seize*) s'emparer de *To — oneself of*, s'emparer de, se saisir de, prendre possession de. *To — with*, remplir de. *To be —ed of*, posséder; être possesseur de, être en possession de; être muni *or* pourvu de; être saisi *or* nanti de; être doué de. *To be —ed with the devil*, être possédé du démon
Possession, *s.* possession, *f.*
Possessional, *adj.* possessionnel
Possessive, *adj. s.* possessif, *adj.m.*, -ive, *f.*, possessif, *s.m.* [teur, *m.*
Possessor, *s.* possesseur. *m.*; (*of bills*) por
Possessorily, *adv.* possessoirement [sède
Possessory, *adj.* possessoire; (*pers.*) qui pos-
Posset, *s.* posset, *m.* [(*means*) moyen, *m*
Possibility, *s.* possibilité, *f.*; possible, *m.*;
Possible, *adj.* possible
Possibly, *adv.* d'une façon possible, possiblement; par possibilité; bien; en quelque manière, le moins du monde; absolument; (*perhaps*) peut-être
Post, *s.* (*of letters and travelling*) poste, *f*; (*station, situation*, &c.) poste, *m.*; (*piece of timber*) poteau, *m.*; (*pillar*) pilier, *m.*; (*mile —, limit, boundary*) borne, *f.*; (*of beds*) colonne, *f.*; (*of doors*) montant, *m.*; dormant, *m.*; (*paper of a certain size, in stationery*) écu, *m.*, coquille, *f.*; (*mil.*) poste, *m.*; (*nav.*) étambot, *m.*; — *adj.* de (*or* de la) poste; postal; — *adv.* en poste; — *v.n.* voyager en poste; courir la poste; (*to*) aller *or* se rendre en poste (à); — *v.a.* (*a letter*, &c.) mettre *or* jeter *or* déposer à la poste; (*to*) envoyer (à); (— **up,** *book-keep.*) porter au grand livre; (*to place*) poster; (*a sentry*) poser; (— **up,** *bills*, &c.) placer, mettre, poser, coller; afficher; (*stigmatize*) afficher. *By* —, par la poste. *By return of* —, poste pour poste. *To put into the* —, mettre à la poste. *To ride* —, aller en poste, courir la poste. —**boy,** *s.* postillon, *m.*; (*mail*) courrier, *m.* — **captain, -commander,** *s.* capitaine de vaisseau, *m.* — **card,** *s.* carte postale, *f.* — **chaise,** *s.* chaise de poste, *f.* — **day,** *s.* jour de courrier, *m.* — **free,** *adj. adv.* *V.* **Prepaid.** — **haste,** *s.* train de poste, *m.*; *adv.* en toute hâte, à toute bride, (un) train de poste. — **horse,** *s.* cheval de poste, *m.* — **house,** *s.* poste aux chevaux, *f.* —**man,** *s.* facteur, facteur de la poste, *m.* — **mark,** *s.* timbre de la poste, timbre, *m.*; *v.a.* timbrer. —**master,** *s.* maître de poste, *m.*; directeur des postes (*or* d'un bureau de poste), *m.* —*master general*, directeur général des postes, *m.* — **note,** *s.* mandat de la banque, *m.* — **office,** *s.* bureau de poste, *m.*, poste aux lettres, poste, *f.*; (*department*) administration des postes, poste, *f.*; (*in addressing letters*) poste restante; *adj.* de la poste, postal. *General — office*, grande poste, *f*, hôtel des postes, *m.*; administration générale des postes, *f.* — *office directory*, almanach des adresses, annuaire du commerce *or* &c., *m.* — *office order*, mandat sur la poste, *m.* —**paid,** *adj. adv.* *V.* **Prepaid.** — **paper,** *s.* (*note-paper, letter-paper*) papier à lettres, *m.*; (*in stationery*) écu, *m.*, coquille, *f.* —**road,** *s.* route postale, route de poste, *f.* — **stage,** *s.* relais de poste, *m.* — **time,** *s.* heure du courrier, *f.* — **town,** *s.* ville à bureau de poste, *f.*; (*for horses*) ville avec une poste aux chevaux, *f.*
Postage, *s.* port de lettre, port, *m*; (*prepaid*) affranchissement, *m.*; (*admin.*) taxe, *f.* *Extra or additional* —, supplément de port, *m.*; (*admin.*) surtaxe, *f.* *To pay the — of*, affranchir, payer le port de. — **scales,** *s.pl.* pèse-lettres, *m.* — **stamp,** *s.* timbre-poste, timbre, *m.*
Postal, *adj.* postal
Postally, *adv.* postalement
Postcommunion, *s.* postcommunion, *f.*
Postdate, *s.* postdate, *f.*; — *v.a.* postdater, reculer la date de
Postdiluvian, *adj.* postdiluvien
Poster, *s.* (*bill*) placard, *m.*, affiche, *f.*; (*pers.*) colleur (d'affiches), afficheur, *m.* — **bearer,** *s.* porte-affiches, homme-affiche, *m.*
Poste restante, *s.* poste restante, *f.*
Posterior, *adj.* postérieur; —**s,** *s.pl.* postérieur, derrière, *m.*
Posteriori (A), *adv.* à postériori

Posteriority, *s.* postériorité, *f.*
Posteriorly, *adv.* postérieurement
Posterity, *s.* postérité, *f.* *The latest —,* la postérité la plus reculée
Postern, *s.* poterne, *f.*
Postface, *s.* postface, *f.*
Postfix, *s.* postfixe, *m.*
Posthumous, *adj.* posthume
Posthumously, *adv.* après la mort, après décès
Postil, *s.* postille, *f.*; — *v.a.* annoter, commenter
Postilion, *s.* postillon, *m.*
Posting, *s.* voyage en poste, *m.*; (*hiring, letting*) louage de chevaux de poste, *m.*; (*of bills, &c.*) collage (d'affiches, &c.), affichage, *m.*; (*book-keep.*) inscription au grand livre, *f.*; (*of sentinels, &c.*) pose, *f.* — **bill,** *s.* affiche, *f.* — **house, -station,** *s.* poste aux chevaux, *f.*
Postique, *s.* application, applique, *f.*
Postliminiar, Postliminious, *adj.* ultérieur, subséquent; (*law*) postliminaire
Postliminy, *s.* postliminie, *f.*
Postmeridian, *adj.* de l'après-midi
Post-mortem, *adv.* après la mort, après décès. — *examination,* autopsie, *f.* — *rigidity,* rigidité cadavérique, *f.*
Postnatal, *adj.* postérieur à la naissance
Postnuptial, *adj.* postnuptial
Post-obit. — **bond,** *s.* contrat exécutoire après décès, *m.*, obligation payable à la mort d'un tiers, *f.*
Postpone, *v.a.* (*to put off*) remettre, différer, ajourner; (*to delay*) retarder; (*to subordinate*) placer (après), faire passer (après), mettre au-dessous (de), subordonner (à), sacrifier (à)
Postponement, *s.* ajournement, *m.*, remise, *f.*; délai, *m.*
Postprandial, *adj.* *V.* **After-dinner,** *adj.*
Postscript, *s.* post-scriptum, *m.*; apostille, *f.*
Postulant, *s.* postulant, *m.*, e, *f.*
Postulate, *s.* postulat, *m.*; — *v.a.* postuler; (*assume*) s'arroger; (*suppose*) supposer
Postulation, *s.* supplication, *f.*; supposition, *f.*; (*suit*) cause, *f.*; (*can. law*) postulation, *f.*
Postulatory, *adj.* supposé, sans preuves
Postulatum, *s.* postulatum, postulat, *m.*
Posture, *s.* posture, *f.*; pose, *f.*; attitude, *f.*; position, situation, *f.*, état, *m.*; disposition, *f.*
Posy, *s.* (*of rings*) devise, *f.*; (*of flowers*) bouquet, *m.*
Pot, *s.* pot, *m.*; (*cook.*) pot, *m.*, marmite, *f.*; (*for preserved meat*) pot, *m.*, terrine, *f.*; (*for jam, &c.*) pot, *m.*; (*melting —*) creuset, *m.*; (*quart*) litre, *m.*; (*paper*) pot, *m.*; — *v.a.* empoter, mettre en pot *or* en terrine; conserver en pot; (*hort.*) empoter. *To go to —,* s'en aller au diable, se ruiner, se perdre, se couler, s'enfoncer, faire fiasco. *To keep the — boiling,* faire aller le pot-au-feu. — **barley,** *s.* *V.* **Barley.** — **bellied,** *adj.* ventru, pansu. — **belly,** *s.* gros ventre, *m.*, bedaine, *f.*; (*pers.*) ventru, *m.* — **boy,** *s.* garçon de cabaret, *m.* — **companion,** *s.* camarade de bouteille, *m.*; pilier de cabaret, ami de la bouteille, *m.* — **ful,** *s.* potée, *f.*; marmite, *f.* — **hanger,** *s.* crémaillère, *f.* — **herb,** *s.* herbe (*or* plante) potagère, *f.* — **hook,** *s.* crémaillère, *f.*; (*a scrawl*) griffonnage, *m.* — **house,** *s.* cabaret, bouchon, *m.*, taverne, *f.*, caboulot, *m.* — **lid,** *s.* couvercle, *m.* — **luck,** *s.* fortune du pot, *f.* *To take — luck,* courir la fortune du pot. — **man,** (*servant*) *s.* garçon de cabaret, *m.*; (*drinker*) pilier de cabaret, ami de la bouteille, biberon, *m.* — **metal,** *s.* potin, *m.* — **uaper,** *s.* papier pot, *m.* —**sherd,** *s.* tesson, *m.* — **stone,** *s.* pierre ollaire, *f.* — **valiant,** *adj.* brave le verre en main, brave après avoir bu
Potable, *adj.* potable; — *s.* liquide potable, *m.*
Potableness, *s* potabilité, *f.*
Potage, *s.* potage, *m.*
Potash, Potass, *s.* potasse, *f.*
Potassium, *s* potassium, *m.* [bauche, orgie, *f.*
Potation, *s.* boisson, *f.*; libations, *f.pl.*, dé-
Potato, *s.* pomme de terre, *f.* *New —es,* pommes de terre nouvelles. — **digger,** *s.* (*machine*) arracheur de pommes de terre, *m.* — **disease,** *s.* maladie des pommes de terre, *f.* — **eater,** *s.* mangeur (*m.*, -euse, *f.*) de pommes de terre. — **flour,** *s.* fécule de pomme de terre, *f.* — **rot,** *s.* *V.* — **disease.** — **salesman,** *s.* marchand de pommes de terre, *m.* — **spirit,** *s.* huile de pomme de terre, *f.* — **stalk,** *s.* pied de pomme de terre, *m.* — **stone,** *s.* géode, *f.*
Potence, *s.* potence, *f.*
Potency, *s.* force, vigueur, *f.*; (*fig.*) puissance, *f.*, pouvoir, *m.*; efficacité, *f.* [(*her.*) potencé
Potent, *adj.* fort; (*fig.*) puissant, efficace;
Potentate, *s.* potentat, *m.*
Potential, *adj.* *s.* potentiel; virtuel; (*gram., and of cauteries*) potentiel
Potentiality, *s.* potentialité, *f.*; virtualité, *f.*
Potentially, *adv.* potentiellement; virtuelle-
Potentilla, *s.* potentille, *f.* [ment
Potently, *adv.* puissamment; efficacement
Pother, *s.* bruit, vacarme, tintamarre, *m.*; confusion, *f.*; tourment, ennui, *m.*; — *v.a.* ennuyer, tracasser, tourmenter; — *v.n.* se tré-
Potion, *s.* potion, *f.* [mousser
Potoroo, *s.* potoroo, potorou, *m.*
Pottage, *s.* potage, *m.*
Potted, *adj.* en pot, en terrine; conservé de ...
Potter, *s.* potier, *m.*; — *v.n.* *V.* **Piddle;** (*meddle*) se mêler (de), s'amuser (à). —*'s clay,* —*'s earth,* terre à potier, *f.* —*'s ware,* poterie,
Pottery, *s.* poterie, *f.* [*f.*
Potting, *s.* empotage, *m.*, mise en pot *or* en pots, mise en terrine, *f.*
Pottle, *s.* (*basket*) panier, *m.*
Potto, *s.* potos, potot, *m.*
Pouch, *s.* poche, *f.*; sac, *m*; bourse, *f.*; (*of monkeys*) abajoue, *f.*; (*of birds*) poche, *f.*; (*of sportsmen*) gibecière, *f.*; carnassière, *f.*; (*mil.*) giberne, *f.*; — *v.a.* empocher, mettre en poche; prendre; (*of birds*) avaler. — **belt,** *s.* (*mil.*)
Poudrette, *s.* poudrette, *f.* [porte-giberne, *m.*
Poulp, Poulpe, *s.* poulpe, *m.*
Poult, *s.* jeune volaille, *f.*, jeune oiseau, *m.*
Poulterer, *s.* marchand (*m.*, e, *f*) de volailles
Poultice, *s.* cataplasme, *m*; — *v.a* mettre *or* appliquer un cataplasme à; entretenir de cataplasmes. *Mustard —,* sinapisme, *m.*
Poulticing, *s.* application de cataplasmes, *f.*, cataplasmes, *m.pl.*
Poultry, *s.* volaille, *f.*; oiseaux de basse-cour, *m.pl.* — **house,** *s.* poulailler, *m.* — **man,** *s.* basse-courier, *m.* — **market,** *s.* marché à la volaille, *m.* — **salesman,** *s.* marchand de volailles, poulailler, *m.* — **show,** *s.* exposition de volailles, *f.* — **woman,** *s.* basse-courière, *f.* — **yard,** *s.* basse-cour, *f.*
Pounce, *s.* serre, griffe, *f.*; (*for paper*) sandaraque, *f.*; (*for drawing*) ponce, *f.*; — *v.n.* fondre (sur); — *v.a.* poudrer; (*draw.*) poncer; (*of birds of prey*) fondre sur; saisir avec ses serres; enlever, lier, empiéter. — **bag,** *s.* poncette, *f.* — **box,** *s.* poudrier, *m.*
Pouncing, *s.* ponçage, *m.* — **paper,** *s.* poncis, poncif, *m.*
Pound, *s.* (*weight*) demi-kilogramme, *m.*; livre, *f.*; (*coin*) livre sterling, livre [25 francs], *f.*; (*enclosure*) fourrière, *f.*; — *v.a.* (*pulverize*) piler, broyer, concasser; (*salt, &c.*) égruger; (*strike*) frapper, battre; (*beasts*) *V.* **Impound;** — *v.n.* frapper à coups redoublés, frapper. *So many shillings in the —, so much in the —,* au centime le franc. — **cake,** *s.* baba, *m.* — **foolish,** *adj.* *V.* **Penny-wise** [*weight*) pondage, *m.*
Poundage, *s.* (*of money*) commission, *f.*; (*of*
Pounder, *s.* pilon, *m.*; (*in compounds*) de ... livres. *Twelve —,* (*gun*) canon de douze (livres de balle), *m.*
Pounding, *s.* broiement, pilage, *m.*
Pour, *v.a.* verser; répandre; (*send forth*) lancer, lâcher, envoyer; — *v.n.* (*flow*) couler; (*of rain*)

pleuvoir à verse; (*to rush*) fondre (sur). *To — with rain*, pleuvoir à verse. **— down,** (*flow*) couler; (*of rain*) tomber à verse; (*to rush*) fondre (sur); tomber, pleuvoir, descendre; (*send forth*) lancer. **— forth,** verser; répandre. **— in,** verser; lancer; entrer partout; arriver en foule. **— out,** verser; répandre; décharger; lâcher, envoyer

Pouring, *adj.* torrentiel

Pourtray. *V.* **Portray**

Pout, *v.n* bouder, faire la moue, faire la mine; (*jut*) saillir; — *s.* bouderie, moue, *f.*; (*fish*) tacaud, *m.*; (*bird*) francolin, *m.*

Pouter, *s.* boudeur, *m.*, -euse, *f.*; (*zool.*) pigeon à grosse gorge, *m.*

Pouting, *adj.* boudeur; (*jutting*) saillant; — *s.* bouderie, *f.*; (*face*) moue, *f.* — *lips*, grosses lèvres, *f.pl.* [en faisant la moue

Poutingly, *adv.* en boudant, d'un air boudeur,

Poverty, *s.* pauvreté, *f.*; indigence, *f.*; misère, *f.* **— struck,** *adj.* dans la misère

Powan, *s.* lavaret, *m.*

Powder, *s.* poudre, *f.*; — *v.a.* pulvériser, réduire en poudre, piler; (*hair*) poudrer; (*sprinkle*) saupoudrer (de); saler; (*fig.*) parsemer (de); —*v.n.* se réduire en poudre; tomber en poussière. *It is not worth — and shot*, le jeu ne vaut pas la chandelle. **— box,** *s.* boîte à poudre, *f.* **— cart,** *s.* caisson, *m.* **— chest,** *s.* caisse d'artifice, *f.*, caisson à poudre, *m.* **— factory,** *s.* *V.* **— manufactory.** **— flask, -horn,** *s.* poire à poudre, *f.* **— magazine,** *s.* magasin à poudre, *m.*, poudrière, *f.*; (*nav.*) soute aux poudres, *f.* **— manufactory, -mill,** *s.* poudrerie, poudrière, *f.* **— monkey,** *s.* gargoussier, pourvoyeur, goujat (de vaisseau), *m.* **— pan,** *s.* bassinet, *m.* **— puff,** *s.* houppe à poudrer, *f.* **— room,** *s.* (*nav.*) soute aux poudres, *f.* **— works,** *s.pl.* poudrière, *f.*

Powdered, *adj.* pulvérisé, en poudre, réduit en poudre; (*of hair*) poudré; (*sprinkled*) saupoudré; salé; (*her.*) semé. — *sugar*, sucre en poudre, sucre pilé, *m.* — *butter*, beurre demi-sel, *m.*

Powdering, *s.* pulvérisation, *f.*; (*of hair*) action de poudrer, *f.*; (*sprinkling*) saupoudration, *f.*; salaison, *f.* **— tub,** *s.* saloir, *m.*

Powdery, *adj.* poudreux; (*like powder*) comme de la poudre; friable

Power, *s.* (*might, inherent and extensive*) puissance, *f.*; (*effective strength*) force, *f.*; (*capacity, ability*) pouvoir, *m.*; faculté, *f.*; (*acquired authority, command, influence*) pouvoir, *m.*; empire, *m.*, autorité, *f.*; (*discretion*) pouvoir, *m.*; (*means*) moyens, *m.pl.*; forces, *f.pl.*; talent, *m.*; (*nation, mighty being*) puissance, *f.*; (*math.*) puissance, *f.*; (*of machines*) force, puissance, *f.*; — *adj.* mécanique. — *of the keys*, (*theol.*) puissance des clés, *f.* —*s that be*, autorités constituées, *f.pl.* *Full —s*, plein pouvoir, *m.* *In —*, (*in office*) au pouvoir. *In my —*, en mon pouvoir. *Of* 80 *horse- —*, de la force de 80 chevaux. *It is out of my — to* ..., je n'ai pas le pouvoir de ... **—ful,** *adj.* puissant; fort; efficace; actif, agissant; (*deep*) profond. **—fully,** *adv.* puissamment; fortement; efficacement; activement. **—fulness,** *s.* puissance, force, *f.*; efficacité, *f.* **— less,** *adj.* impuissant; faible; inefficace. **—lessness,** *s.* impuissance, *f.*; faiblesse, *f.*; inefficacité, *f.* **— loom,** *s.* métier mécanique, métier à tisser, *m.* *By — loom*, à la mécanique. **— press,** *s.* presse mécanique, *f.*

Pox, *s.* vérole, *f.* *Small —*, petite vérole, *f.*

Poy, *s.* contre-poids, balancier, *m.*

Practicability, Practicableness, *s.* praticabilité, *f.*

Practicable, *adj.* praticable, faisable, exécutable [praticablement

Practicably, *adv.* d'une manière praticable,

Practical, *adj.* pratique. **— joke,** *s.* tour, mauvais tour, *m.*, farce, mauvaise farce, mauvaise plaisanterie, *f.*

Practically, *adv.* pratiquement; dans la pratique, en pratique; réellement, en effet

Practicalness, *s.* nature pratique, *f.*

Practice, *s.* pratique, *f.*; usage, *m.*, habitude, coutume, *f.*; coutumes, *f.pl.*; règle, *f.*; système, *m.*; méthode, *f.*, moyen, *m.*; exercice, *m.*; (*shooting, firing*) tir, *m.*; (*connection of professional men*) clientèle, *f.*; (*proceeding*) procédé, *m.*; (*of law-courts*) procédure, *f.*; pratique, *f.*; (*artifice*) menée, intrigue, pratique, *f.*; (*arith.*) méthode des parties aliquotes, *f.*; — *v.a.n.* *V.* **Practise.** *In —*, (*of professional men*) en exercice. *To be or get out of —*, se perdre la main. *To make a — of*, se faire une habitude (*or* une règle) de. **— firing,** *s.* exercice à feu, *m.* **— ground,** *s.* tir, *m.*

Practise, *v.a.* pratiquer; (*a profession*) exercer; pratiquer; (*to commit*) exercer; (*study*) étudier; s'exercer à; — *v.n.* pratiquer; (*of professions*) exercer; (*to study*) étudier; s'exercer; (*use artifices*) employer des menées, intriguer; — *s.* *V.* **Practice.** *To — what one (oneself) preaches*, prêcher d'exemple. **— upon,** (*deceive*) tromper, en imposer à; jouer; entortiller; exploiter; spéculer sur; abuser de

Practised, *adj.* exercé; expérimenté; versé; habile, émérite; — *part.* pratiqué, &c. (*V.* **Practise,** *v.a.*); en usage

Practiser, *s.* personne qui pratique, *f.*; (*not an amateur*) professeur, *m.*; (*in a bad sense*) personne qui emploie des menées, *f.*

Practising, *adj.* praticien; (*of physicians*) praticien, exerçant, traitant; (*of lawyers*) exerçant, en exercice

Practitioner, *s.* praticien, *m.*

Prad, *s.* bidet, poulet d'Inde, *m.*

Præfect, Prætor, &c. *V.* **Prefect, Pretor,** &c.

Prætexta, *s.* prétexte, robe prétexte, *f*

Pragmatic, -al, *adj.* pragmatique; importun. — *sanction*, pragmatique sanction, pragmatique, *f.* [importunité

Pragmatically, *adv.* pragmatiquement; avec

Pragmaticalness, *s.* nature pragmatique, *f.*; importunité, *f.*

Prairie, *s.* prairie, *f.* **— dog,** *s.* spermophile, souslic, *m.* **— hen,** *s.* tétras Cupidon, *m.*

Praisable, *adj.* louable, digne d'éloge

Praisably, *adv.* louablement, d'une manière louable

Praise, *v.a.* louer; vanter; prôner; faire l'éloge de; glorifier, chanter *or* célébrer les louanges de; — *s.* louange, *f.*, éloge, *m.*; gloire, *f.* *In — of*, à la louange de. *To speak in — of*, faire l'éloge de. **—less,** *adj.* sans louange. **— worthily,** *adv.* louablement, d'une manière louable. **—worthiness,** *s.* nature louable, *f.*, mérite, *m.* **—worthy,** *adj.* louable, digne d'éloges

Praiser, *s.* louangeur, *m.*, -euse, *f.*, laudateur, *m.*, -trice, *f.*, prôneur, *m.*, -euse, *f.*; approbateur, *m.*, -trice, *f.*; panégyriste, *m.*

Prance, *v.n.* bondir; piaffer; (*pers.*) se pavaner

Prancer, *s.* piaffeur, *m.*, -euse, *f.*

Prancing, *s.* piaffement, *m.*; (*fig.*) piaffe, *f.*

Prank, *s.* escapade, folie, fredaine, *f.*; (*trick*) tour, *m.*, farce, malice, *f.*; — *v.a.* attifer, ajuster, orner. *To play a —*, faire un tour *or* une farce *or* une malice

Prate, &c. *V.* **Prattle,** &c.

Praticulture, *s.* praticulture, *f.*

Praticulturist, *s.* praticulteur, *m.*

Pratingly, *adv.* en babillard, en jasant

Pratique, *s.* pratique, *f.*

Prattle, *v.n.* (*pers.*) babiller, jaser, bavarder, caqueter; (*things*) murmurer, gazouiller; — *s.* (*pers.*) babil, caquet, bavardage, *m.*; (*of things*) murmure, gazouillement, *m.*

Prattler, *s.* babillard, *m.*, e, *f.*, jaseur, *m.*, -euse, *f.*, bavard, *m.*, e, *f.*

Prawn, *s.* grande crevette, *f.*, palémon, bouquet, *m.* —**net,** *s. V.* **Shrimp-net**

Praxis, *s.* pratique, *f.*, exercice, *m.*; exemple, *m.*

Pray, *v.a.n.* prier (de); (*law*) demander. *I — you!* —! je vous prie! je vous en prie! de grâce! je vous le demande; dites-moi. — *tell me*, dites-moi, je vous prie. —**for,** prier pour; (*ask*) demander. —**to** *God*, prier Dieu

Prayer, *s.* prière, *f.*; (*law*) demande, *f.* *To say —s*, faire la prière. —**book,** *s.* livre de prières, *m.* —**desk,** *s.* prie-Dieu, *m.* —**ful,** *adj.* porté à la prière. —**fully,** *adv.* à force de prières. —**less,** *adj.* qui ne fait pas de prières. —**lessness,** *s.* oubli de la prière, *m.*

Prayingly, *adv.* en priant, par la prière

Preach, *v.a n.* prêcher. —**down,** prêcher contre; dénigrer. —**up,** prêcher, vanter, prôner [prêcheur, *m.*, -euse, *f.*

Preacher, *s.* prédicateur, *m.*; (*in contempt*)

Preaching, *s.* prédication, *f.*; sermons, *m.pl.*

Preachment, *s.* prêche, sermon, *m.*

Preadamic, *adj.* préadamite

Preadamism, *s.* préadamisme, *m.*

Preadamite, *s.* préadamite, *m.*

Preadamitic, *adj.* préadamite [térieure, *f.*

Preadministration, *s.* administration an-

Preadmonish, *v.a.* prévenir, avertir d'avance

Preadmonition, *s.* avertissement préalable, *m.*

Preamble, *s.* préambule, *m.*; — *v.a.* dire en forme de préambule

Preambulary, *adj.* préambulaire

Preaudience, *s.* préséance (d'avocat) aux

Prebend, *s.* prébende, *f.* [audiences, *f.*

Prebendal, *adj.* prébendé, de prébende

Prebendary, *s.* prébendier, *m.*

Prebendaryship, *s.* prébende, *f.*

Precarious, *adj.* précaire, incertain

Precariously, *adv.* précairement

Precariousness, *s.* précarité, nature précaire, *f.*, état précaire, *m.*, incertitude, *f.*

Precative, Precatory, *adj.* précatif

Precaution, *s.* précaution, *f.*; — *v a.* précautionner [précaution, précautionnel

Precautional, Precautionary, *adj.* de

Precede, *v.a.* précéder; (*to be superior*) avoir le pas *or* la préséance sur; (*a thing by another*) faire précéder (... par ...)

Precedenc-e, y, *s.* précédence, *f.*; (*of rank*, &c.) préséance, *f.*, pas, *m.*; premier rang, *m.*; priorité, *f.*; supériorité, *f.* [précédent, *s.m.*

Precedent, *adj. s.* précédent, *adj. m.*, e, *f.*,

Precedented, *adj.* dont on a vu un exemple; autorisé par un précédent

Precedently, *adv.* précédemment

Preceding, *adj.* précédent

Preceltic, *adj.* préceltique

Precentor, *s.* maître de chapelle, *m.*; chantre, *m.*

Precentorship, *s.* maîtrise, *f.*; chantrerie, *f.*

Precentory, *s.* maîtrise, maison du maître de chapelle, maison du chantre, *f.*

Precept, *s.* précepte, *m.*

Preceptor, *s.* précepteur, *m.*

Preceptorial, *adj.* préceptoral, de précepteur

Preceptorship, *s.* préceptorat, *m.*

Preceptory, *s.* préceptorerie, *f.*

Preceptress, *s.* institutrice, *f.*

Precession, *s.* précession, *f.*

Precincts, *s.pl.* enceinte, *f.*; limites, bornes, *f.pl.*

Precious, *adj.* précieux; (*great, fam.*) fameux, fier; fichu; (*adverb.*) *V.* **Preciously**

Preciously, *adv.* précieusement; (*very*) bien, joliment, richement, fameusement, fièrement, furieusement, diablement

Preciousness, *s.* prix, *m.*, valeur, *f.*

Precipe, *s.* sommation, *f.*

Precipice, *s.* précipice, *m.*

Precipitable, *adj.* précipitable

Precipitanc-e, y, *s.* précipitation, *f.*; empressement, *m.* [— *s.* précipitant, *m.*

Precipitant, *adj.* qui se précipite; précipité;

Precipitantly, *adv. V.* **Precipitately**

Precipitate, *v.a.n,* précipiter; — *adj.* qui se précipite; précipité; (*hasty*) précipité; — *s.* précipité, *m.* [précipitation

Precipitately, *adv.* précipitamment, avec

Precipitation, *s.* précipitation, *f.*

Precipitous, *adj.* précipiteux, précipité; rapide; escarpé; (*hasty*) précipité

Precipitously, *adv.* en précipice; (*hastily*) précipitamment

Precipitousness, *s.* précipitation, *f.*; (*steepness*) escarpement, *m.*

Precis, *s.* précis, *m.*

Precise, *adj.* précis, exact; juste; scrupuleux; strict; pointilleux, vétilleux; cérémonieux, affecté; recherché

Precisely, *adv.* précisément, exactement; au juste; scrupuleusement; (*of the hour*) précis, *adj.* *Three o'clock* —, trois heures précises

Preciseness, *s.* précision, exactitude, *f.*; scrupule, *m.*; formalité, cérémonie, affectation, *f.*

Precision, *s.* précision, *f.* [prévenir; écarter

Preclude, *v.a.* exclure; (*prevent*) empêcher;

Preclusion, *s.* exclusion, *f.*; empêchement, *m.*

Preclusive, *adj.* qui exclut; (*preventive*) qui empêche, qui prévient, qui écarte

Preclusively, *adv.* avec exclusion

Precocious, *adj.* précoce

Precociously, *adv.* précocement

Precociousness, Precocity, *s* précocité, *f.*

Precognition, *s.* préconnaissance, *f.*; (*law*) enquête préliminaire, *f.*

Preconceit, *s. V.* **Preconception**

Preconceive, *v.a.* concevoir d'avance, préconcevoir; préjuger

Preconception, *s.* préconception, *f.*; opinion préconçue, *f.*, préjugé, *m.*, prévention, *f.*

Preconceptive, *adj.* préconceptif

Preconcert, *v.a.* concerter d'avance

Preconization, *s.* préconisation, *f.*

Preconize, *v.a.* préconiser

Precordial, *adj.* précordial

Precursor, *s.* précurseur, avant-coureur, *m.*

Precursory, *adj.* précurseur

Predaceous, qui vit de proie *or* de butin

Predatory, *adj.* déprédateur; de proie, rapace; (*things*) de rapine, de vol, de pillage

Predecease, *v.a.* mourir avant; — *v.n.* prédécéder, mourir avant; — *s.* prédécès, *m.*

Predecessor, *s.* prédécesseur, *m.*; devancier, *m.*

Predesign, *v.a.* projeter *or* &c. (*V.* **Design,** *v.a.*) d'avance

Predestinarian, *s.adj.* prédestinatien, *m.*, -ne, *f.*

Predestinarianism, *s.* prédestinatianisme, *m.*

Predestinate, *v.a. V.* **Predestine;** — *s. adj.* prédestiné, *m.*, e, *f.*

Predestination, *s.* prédestination, *f.*

Predestinator, *s.* prédestinateur, *m.*

Predestine, *v.a.* prédestiner, destiner d'avance

Predeterminate, *adj.* prédéterminé

Predetermination, *s.* détermination prise d'avance, *f.*; (*theol.*) prédétermination, *f.*

Predetermine, *v.a.* déterminer *or* arrêter d'avance; (*theol.*) prédéterminer

Predial, *adj.* en biens-fonds, en terres; attaché à la glèbe; provenant de la terre; de serf, de *or* des serfs

Predicability, *s.* nature prédicable, *f.*

Predicable, *adj.* prédicable; — *s.* universel, *m.* (*pl.* universaux)

Predicament, *s.* catégorie, *f.*; ordre, *m.*; position, *f.*; état, *m.*, passe, *f.*; cas, *m.*; (*log.*) prédicament, *m.* [dicat, *m.*

Predicate, *v.a.n.* affirmer; — *s.* attribut, pré-

Predication, *s.* affirmation, *f.* [affirmatif

Predicative, Predicatory, *adj.* prédicatif;

Predict, *v.a.* prédire

Predicter, *s.* prédiseur, *m.*, -euse, *f.*, prophète, *m.*, prophétesse, *f.*

Prediction, *s.* prédiction, *f.*

Predictive, *adj.* qui prédit, prophétique

Predictively, *adv.* prophétiquement

Predilection, *s.* prédilection, *f.*

Predispose, *v.a.* prédisposer

Predisposition, *s.* prédisposition, *f.*
Predominanc-e, y, *s.* prédominance, *f.*
Predominant, *adj.* prédominant [dominante
Predominantly, *adv.* d'une manière pré-
Predominate, *v.n.* prédominer; prévaloir; l'emporter; régner
Predomination, *s.* prédomination, *f.*
Preelect, *v.a.* élire d'avance
Preelection, *s.* élection antérieure, *f.*
Preeminence, *s.* prééminence, *f.*; supériorité, *f.*
Preeminent, *adj.* prééminent; supérieur; extraordinaire, remarquable
Preeminently, *adv.* supérieurement; souverainement; extraordinairement; par excellence; entre tous
Preempt, *v.a.* préempter
Preemption, *s.* préemption, *f.*
Preengage, *v.a.* engager d'avance
Preengagement, *s.* engagement antérieur, *m.*
Preestablish, *v.a.* préétablir [rieur, *m.*
Preestablishment, *s.* établissement anté-
Preexamination, *s.* examen préalable, *m.*
Preexamine, *v.a.* examiner préalablement
Preexist, *v.n.* préexister
Preexistence, *s.* préexistence, *f.*
Preexistent, *adj.* préexistant
Preface, *s.* préface, *f.*; — *v.a.* faire une préface à; faire précéder ('*with*,' '*by*,' de); commencer; — *v.n.* dire en forme de préface, commencer par dire
Prefatorial, Prefatory, *adj.* qui sert de préface, préliminaire, introductif
Prefatorily, *adv.* par forme de préface
Prefect, *s.* préfet, *m.*
Prefectoral, Prefectorial, *adj.* préfectoral
Prefectship, Prefecture, *s.* préfecture, *f.*
Prefer, *v.a.* préférer, aimer mieux; (*promote*) avancer, élever; (*offer*) présenter; (*a complaint, a charge, an indictment*) déposer *or* porter (une plainte), intenter *or* former (une accusation). — *red stock*, actions privilégiées, *f.pl.*
Preferable, *adj.* préférable
Preferableness, *s.* avantage, *m.* [rence
Preferably, *adv.* préférablement, de préfé-
Preference, *s.* préférence, *f.* *In* —, de préférence. — **share,** *s.* action privilégiée, *f.*; obligation, *f.* — **shareholder,** *s.* actionnaire privilégié, *m.*, actionnaire privilégiée, *f.*, porteur (*m.*, -euse, *f.*) d'actions privilégiées *or* d'obligations, obligataire, *m.f.* [ference
Preferential, *adj.* — **share,** &c. *V.* **Pre-**
Preferment, *s.* avancement, *m.*, promotion, élévation, *f.*; place éminente, *f.*, hautes fonc-
Prefigure, *v.a.* préfigurer [tions, *f.pl.*
Prefix, *v.a.* préfixer; mettre en tête ('*to*,' de); — *s.* préfixe, *m.* [dité, fertilité, *f.*
Pregnancy, *s.* grossesse, *f.*; (*fertility*) fécon-
Pregnant, *adj.* enceinte, grosse; (*fruitful*) fécond (en), fertile (en), gros (de), plein (de)
Pregnantly, *adv.* avec fertilité
Prehensible, *adj.* préhensible
Prehensile, *adj.* préhensile, préhenseur. — *tail*, queue prenante, *f.*
Prehension, *s.* préhension, *f.*
Prehistoric, *adj.* préhistorique
Prehnite, *s.* prehnite, *f.*
Prejudge, Prejudicate, *v.a.* préjuger
Prejudgment, Prejudication, *s.* préjugement, *m.*
Prejudice, *s.* préjugé, *m.*, prévention, *f.*; (*injury*) préjudice, tort, dommage, *m.*; — *v.a.* prévenir; (*injure*) préjudicier à, porter préjudice à, nuire à, faire tort à; juger trop sévèrement
Prejudiced, *adj.* prévenu, à préjugés
Prejudicial, -ly. *V.* **Detrimental, -ly**
Prejudicialness, *s.* nature préjudiciable, .
Prelacy, *s.* prélature, *f.*; épiscopat, *m.*
Prelate, *s.* prélat, *m.*
Prelateship, *s.* prélature, *f.*
Prelatic, -al, *adj.* de prélat
Prelatically, *adv.* en prélat
Prelatism, *s.* épiscopat, *m.*
Prelection, *s.* leçon, *f.*
Prelector, *s.* professeur, *m.*
Preliminarily, *adv.* préliminairement
Preliminary, *adj.s.* préliminaire, *adj.m.f.*, *s.m.*
Prelude, *v.a.n.* préluder (à); — *s.* prélude, *m.*
Prelusive, Prelusory, *adj.* préparatoire, préliminaire [turer
Premature, *adj.* prématuré; — *v.a.* préma-
Prematurely, *adv.* prématurément; avant le temps [turité, *f.*
Prematureness, Prematurity, *s.* préma-
Premeditate, *v.a.* préméditer
Premeditatedly, *adv.* avec préméditation
Premeditation, *s.* préméditation, *f.*
Premier, *adj.* premier; — *s.* premier ministre, *m.*; (*in France*) président du conseil des ministres, *m.*
Premiership, *s.* dignité, (*f.*) *or* fonctions (*f.pl.*) de premier ministre; (*in France*) présidence du conseil des ministres, *f.*
Premise, *v.a.n.* exposer d'avance; dire d'abord, commencer par dire, annoncer; commencer
Premises, *s.pl.* lieux, *m.pl.*; local, *m.*; propriété, terre, *f.*, bien-fonds, *m.*; (*log.*, *wrong spelling for* "*premisses*") prémisses, *f.pl.* *Large* —, local vaste. — *for sale*, propriété à vendre. *On the* —, sur les lieux; sur place; dans l'éta-
Premiss, *s.* (*log.*) prémisse, *f.* [blissement
Premium, *s* prime, *f.*; (*bonus*) pot-de-vin, *m.*; (*prize, reward*) prix, *m.*, récompense, *f.* *High* —, forte prime. *At a* —, à prime; en prime
Premolar, *s.* fausse molaire, petite molaire, *f.*
Premonish, *v.a.* prévenir, avertir d'avance
Premonition, *s.* avertissement préalable, *m*
Premonitory, *adj.* qui avertit d'avance, avertisseur; d'avertissement; (*med.*) prémonitoire, précurseur. — *diarrhœa*, diarrhée prémonitoire, *f.* — *symptom*, symptôme précurseur, prodrome, *m.* [prémontré, *m.*
Premonstrant, Premonstratensian, *s.*
Premotion, *s.* prémotion, *f.*
Prenomen, *s.* prénom, *m.*
Prenominate, *v.a..* prénommer
Prenomination, *s.* privilége d'être nommé le premier, *m.*
Prenotion, *s.* prénotion, notion antérieure, *f.*
Prentice. *V.* **Apprentice**
Preobtain, *v.a.* obtenir d'avance
Preoccupancy, *s.* occupation antérieure, *f.*; droit d'occupation, *m.*
Preoccupation, *s.* occupation antérieure, *f.*; (*of the mind*) préoccupation, prévention, *f.*
Preoccupy, *v.a.* occuper antérieurement; (*prepossess*) préoccuper
Preordain, *v.a.* préordonner, ordonner *or* disposer *or* arranger d'avance
Preordinate, *v.a.* préordonner
Preordination, *s.* préordination, *f.*
Preorganization, *s.* préorganisation, *f.*
Preorganize, *v.a.* préorganiser
Prepaid, *adj.* affranchi, franc de port; — *adverb.* franco. *All letters to be* —, (*at the end of advertisements*) affranchir
Preparable, *adj.* préparable
Preparation, *s.* (*making fit for a state or purpose, thing prepared*) préparation, *f.*; (*making ready for an occasion*) préparatifs, apprêts, *m.pl.*, dispositions, *f.pl.*; (*making fit for a certain use*) apprêt, *m.*; (*condition*) état, *m.*
Preparative, *adj.* préparatoire; — *s.* préparatif, *m.*; préparatoire, *m.*
Preparatively, *adv.* d'une manière préparatoire; préalablement
Preparator, *s.* préparateur, *m.*
Preparatory, *adj.* préparatoire; — *adverb.* comme préparation; préalablement; (*to* ...); avant (...) avant de (..., *before the inf.*)
Prepare, *v.a.* préparer; apprêter; disposer; (*provide*) se pourvoir de; (*of fabrics, &c., and food*) apprêter; — *v.n.* se préparer (à); s'apprêter (à); se disposer (à)

Prepared, *part. adj.* préparé; apprêté; disposé; en position (de); (*ready*) prêt

Preparedly, *adv.* par la préparation, par des mesures préparatoires

Preparedness, *s.* état de préparation, *m.*

Preparer, *s.* préparateur, *m.*, -trice, *f.*; (*dresser*) apprêteur, *m.*, -euse, *f.* [franchir

Prepay, *v.a.* payer d'avance; (*letters,* &c.) af-

Prepayment, *s.* payment fait d'avance, *m.*; (*of letters,* &c.) affranchissement, *m.*

Prepense, *adj.* prémédité

Preponderanc-e, y, *s.* prépondérance, *f.*; (*of weight*) supériorité de poids, *f.*, excès de poids, *m.* [qui surpasse par le poids

Preponderant, *adj.* prépondérant; (*of weight*)

Preponderate, *v.a.* avoir la prépondérance sur, l'emporter sur; (*in weight*) surpasser en poids, peser plus que; — *v.n.* avoir la prépondérance, l'emporter; (*of weight*) avoir le plus de poids, peser le plus

Preponderating, *adj.* prépondérant

Preposition, *s.* préposition, *f.*

Prepositional, Prepositive, *adj.* prépositif

Prepositively, *adv.* prépositivement

Prepositor, *s.* moniteur, *m.*

Prepossess, *v.a.* prévenir; préoccuper; gagner

Prepossessing, *adj.* prévenant, engageant

Prepossession, *s.* prévention, *f.*, préjugé, *m.*

Preposterous, *adj.* absurde; le monde ren-

Preposterously, *adv.* absurdement [versé

Preposterousness, *s.* absurdité, *f.*

Prepotenc-e, y, *s.* prépotence, *f.*

Prepuce, *s.* prépuce, *m.*

Preputial, *adj.* préputial

Prerogative, *s.* prérogative, *f.*

Presage, *s.* présage, *m.*; — *v.a.n.* présager

Presanctified, *adj* présanctifié

Presbyopia, Presbyopy, *s.* presbyopie, *f.*

Presbyopic, *adj.* presbyte

Presbyte, *s.* presbyte, *m.f.*

Presbyter, *s.* (*an elder*) ancien, presbytre, *m.*; (*priest*) prêtre, *m.*; (*presbyterian*) presbytérien,

Presbyterate, *s.* presbytériat, *m.* [*m.*, -ne, *f.*

Presbyterian, *adj. s.* presbytérien, *m.*, -ne, *f.*

Presbyterianism, *s.* presbytérianisme, *m.*

Presbytership, *s.* presbytériat, *m.*

Presbytery, *s.* presbytère, *m.*

Presbytia, *s.* presbytie, *f.*

Presbyt-ic, al, -ism. *V.* page 3, § 1

Prescience, *s.* prescience, *f.*

Prescient, *adj.* prescient, doué de prescience

Prescribe, *v.a.n.* prescrire, ordonner; (*med.*) ordonner; faire une ordonnance; (*give law*) faire la loi; (*law*) prescrire [ordonne, *f.*

Prescriber, *s.* personne qui prescrit *or* qui

Prescript, *s.* précepte, *m.*, règle, ordonnance, *f.*

Prescriptible, *adj.* prescriptible

Prescription, *s.* prescription, ordonnance, *f.*, précepte, *m.*; (*med.*) ordonnance, *f.*; (*law*) prescription, *f.* [cription

Prescriptive, *adj.* établi *or* acquis par pres-

Presence, *s.* présence, *f.*; air, port, maintien, *m.*, mine, prestance, représentation, *f.*; assemblée, réunion, société, *f.* — *of mind,* présence d'esprit, *f.* *In the — of,* en présence de. *In such a —,* devant une telle réunion *or* assemblée. *Saving your —,* sauf votre respect. — **chamber, -room,** *s.* salle de réception, salle d'audience, salle du trône, *f.*

Present, *adj.* présent; actuel; courant; attentif; (*gram.*) présent. — *tense,* présent, *m.* *In the — tense,* au présent. *To be — at,* être présent à, assister à

Present, *s.* (*time*) présent, *m.*; (*gram.*) présent, *m.*; (*gift*) présent, cadeau, don, *m.*; (*letter*) présente lettre, présente, *f.*; **—s,** *pl.* (*letters,* &c.) présentes, *f.pl.* *At —,* à présent, maintenant, actuellement, aujourd'hui. *For the —,* quant à présent, pour le présent; pour le moment, (*fam.*) pour le quart-d'heure. *In the —,* (*gram.*) au présent

Present, *v.a.* présenter (à); offrir (à); faire présent de, faire cadeau de; (*a living*) présenter, nommer à; (*to introduce*) présenter. *To — anyone with a thing,* faire présent (*or* cadeau *or* don) de (*or* offrir) quelque chose à quelqu'un. *To — at,* (*take aim*) coucher en joue, viser. *— !* (*mil.*) en joue !

Presentable, *adj.* présentable

Presentation, *s.* présentation, *f.*; (*display*) représentation, *f.* *On —,* à présentation. — **copy,** *s.* exemplaire dont on a fait hommage, exemplaire donné *m.*

Presentee, *s.* collataire, nominataire, *m.*

Presenter, *s.* présenteur, *m.*, -euse, *f.*; (*eccl.*) présentateur, *m.*, -trice, *f.*, collateur, nomina-

Presentiment, *s.* pressentiment, *m.* [teur, *m.*

Presently, *adv.* tout à l'heure; bientôt; peu de temps après

Presentment, *s.* présentation, *f.*; représentation, *f.*; apparence, *f.*; (*com.*) présentation, *f.*; (*law*) dénonciation spontanée, *f.*; requête, *f.* *On —,* à présentation

Preservable, *adj.* qui peut se conserver

Preservation, *s.* conservation, *f.*; salut, *m.*; (*from*) protection (contre), préservation (de), *f.* — *of life from shipwreck* or *drowning* or *fire* or &c., sauvetage, *m.* *Instinct of —,* instinct de conservation, *m.*

Preservative, *adj.* préservatif; préservateur; — *s.* préservatif, *m.*

Preserve, *v.a.* (*from*) préserver (de); garantir (de); (*keep*) conserver; garder; (*in sugar,* &c.) confire; — *s.* conserve (alimentaire), *f.*; (*fruit, in sugar*) conserves, *f.pl.*, fruits confits, *m.pl.*; (*jam*) confitures, *f.pl.*, confiture, *f.*; (*for game*) chasse réservée, chasse, réserve, *f.*; parc, *m.* —*d articles of food,* —*d provisions,* conserves alimentaires, *f.pl.*

Preserver, *s.* conservateur, *m.*, -trice, *f.*; (*benefactor*) sauveur, *m.*; bienfaiteur, *m.*, -trice, *f.*; (*of fruit*) confiseur, *m.*; (*thing*) préservateur, *m.*; (*weapon*) porte-respect, *m.*, &c. (*V.* **Life** —); **—s,** *pl.* (*spectacles*) conserves (pour les yeux), *f.pl.*

Preserving, *s.* *V.* **Preservation;** — *adj.* qui conserve *or* &c. (*V.* **Preserve,** *v.a.*); à conserver; à confire. — **pan,** *s.* bassine, *f.*

Preside, *v.n.* présider (à)

Presidency, *s.* présidence, *f.* [dente, *f.*

President, *s.* président, *m.*, (*lady* —) prési-

Presidentess, *s.* présidente, *f.*

Presidential, *adj.* présidentiel

Presidentship, *s.* présidence, *f.* [garnison

Presidial, Presidiary, *adj.* de garnison; à

Presiding, *part. adj.* présidant. —*judge,* président, *m.*

Press, *v.a.* presser; serrer; (*squeeze out*) pressurer; (*urge*) pousser (à); (*compel*) forcer (à, de); (*impose*) imposer (à); (*inculcate*) faire sentir (à), faire voir (à); (*insist upon*) insister sur; (*for public service, mil., nav.*) *V.* **Impress;** (*paper, cloth*) satiner, mettre en presse; (*land*) plomber; — *v.n.* se presser; se serrer; pousser; (*run*) accourir, se précipiter; (*encroach*) empiéter, envahir. *To be —ed for time,* être pressé. — **down,** *v.a.* presser, fouler; appuyer sur. — **forward,** *v.a.* pousser; faire avancer; *v.n.* se porter en avant; s'empresser; (*go fast*) presser *or* hâter le pas, se presser, se hâter. — **on,** *v.n.* se dépêcher. — **out,** *v.a.* exprimer; (*fruit*) pressurer

Press, *s.* (*machine*) presse, *f.*; (*print.*) presse, *f.*; (*for fruit*) pressoir, *m.*; (*for garments*) armoire, *f.*; (*crowd*) foule, presse, *f.*; (*urgency*) urgence, presse, *f.*; (*nav., of sails*) force, *f.*; (*for sailors*) presse, *f.* *Error of the —,* faute d'impression, erreur typographique, *f.* *For — ! — !* (*order for —, ready for —*) (*print.*) bon à tirer. *In the —,* sous presse. *In time, too late for —,* à temps, trop tard pour l'impression. *Liberty* or *freedom of the —,* liberté de la presse, *f.* *The newspaper —,* le journalisme, *m.*, la presse, *f.* *To correct for the —,* corriger les épreuves.

To go to —, (pers.) mettre sous presse; (things) être mis sous presse. To send to —, mettre sous presse. — **bed,** s. lit à or en armoire, lit-armoire, m. — **error,** s. faute d'impression, erreur typographique, f. —**ful,** s. pressée, f. —**gang,** s. presse, f., presseurs, m.pl. — **house,** s. pressoir, m. — **maker,** s. fabricant de presses, m. —**man,** s. pressureur, m.; (of fabrics) presseur, m.; (print.) pressier, m.; (writer) journaliste, m.; (of a press-gang) presseur, m. — **money,** s. gratification (à un homme enrôlé par la presse), f. — **proof, -revise,** s. (print.) tierce, f. —**room,** s. (print.) salle des presses, f. — **work,** s. ouvrage fait à la presse, m.; (print.) tirage, m.

Presser, s. pressureur, m.; (of fabrics) presseur, m.

Pressing, adj. pressant, urgent; qui presse; pressé; — s. pressement, m.; pression, f.; pressée, f.; (of fruit) pressurage, m.; (of fabrics) pressage, m.; (of paper) satinage, m.; (solicitation) instance, f.; (impressment) V. **Impressment.** To require —, (pers.) se faire prier, se faire tirer l'oreille (pour). — **iron,** s. carreau, m. — **mill,** s. pressoir, m.

Pressingly, adv. pressamment, d'une manière pressante; vivement; instamment, avec instance

Pression, s. pression, f.

Pressure, s. pression, f.; calamité, affliction, f.; poids, m., oppression, f.; force, f.; presse, urgence, f.; (of fruit) pressurage, m.; (of the air) pression, f. — **engine,** s. presseur, m. — **gauge,** s. manomètre, m. — **screw,** s. vis de pression, f.

Prestation, s. prestation, f.

Prestidigitation, s. prestidigitation, f.

Prestidigitator, s. prestidigitateur, m.

Prestige, s. prestige, m.

Prestissimo, adv. (mus.) prestissimo

Presto, adv. preste, prestement; (mus.) presto

Presumable, adj. présumable

Presumably, adv. probablement, d'une manière présumable

Presume, v.a.n. présumer; prétendre; (upon) présumer trop (de), avoir trop bonne opinion (de), compter trop (sur); (dare) se permettre (de), prendre la liberté (de), s'aviser (de), oser hardiment

Presumer, s. présomptueux, m., -euse, f.

Presuming, adj. présomptueux

Presumingly, adv. présomptueusement;

Presumption, s. présomption, f.

Presumptive, adj. présumé; (too confident) présomptueux; (of heirs) présomptif; (of arrests) préventif; (of evidence) V. **Circumstantial**

Presumptively, adv. présomptivement, par présomption; (of arrests) préventivement

Presumptuous, adj. présomptueux

Presumptuously, adv. présomptueusement

Presumptuousness, s. présomption, f.

Presupposal, s. présupposition, f.

Presuppose, v.a. présupposer

Presupposition, s. présupposition, f.

Pretence, s. prétexte, m.; (feint) feinte, défaite, f. Under —, sous prétexte. Under false —s, par moyens frauduleux. To make — to, faire semblant de

Pretend, v.a. prétexter; (feign) feindre, affecter, faire; (claim) prétendre; — v.n. prétendre (à), avoir des prétentions (à); (feign) feindre (de), faire semblant (de), faire (le, la, les). To — ignorance, prétexter l'ignorance; faire l'ignorant. To — to be ill, feindre d'être malade, faire semblant d'être malade, faire le malade [(feigned) feint, faux

Pretended, adj. prétendu, soi-disant, supposé;

Pretendedly, adv. par prétexte, faussement

Pretendence, s. prétendance, f.

Pretender, s. prétendant, m., e, f.; (feigner) personne qui feint or qui prétend, f., tartufe [(de), m.f.

Pretendership, s. prétendance, f.

Pretendingly, adv. avec prétention, f.

Pretentious, adj. prétentieux; ambitieux

Pretentiously, adv. prétentieusement; ambitieusement

Pretentiousness, s. air prétentieux, m., prétention, f.

Preterit, Preterite, s. prétérit, m. In the —, au prétérit

Preterition, s. prétérition, f.

Pretermission, s. omission, f.

Pretermit, v.a. omettre, passer, &c. (V. **Disregard,** v.a.)

Preternatural, adj. contre nature, surnaturel, irrégulier, insolite, extraordinaire

Preternaturally, adv. contre nature, surnaturellement, irrégulièrement, extraordinairement

Preternaturalness, Preternaturality, s. état contre nature, état surnaturel, m., surnaturalité, f.

Pretext, s. prétexte, m.

Pretor, s. préteur, m.

Pretorial, adj. de préteur [prétorien, s.m.

Pretorian, adj. s. prétorien, adj.m., -ne, f.,

Pretorium, s. prétoire, m.

Pretorship, s. préture, f.

Prettily, adv. joliment; gentiment; avec grâce

Prettiness, s. beauté, élégance, f.; gentillesse, f.; grâce, f.; agrément, m.

Pretty, adj. joli; gentil; élégant; gracieux; — adv. passablement, assez; (nearly) presque, à peu près; (prettily) V. **Prettily.** — good, assez bon. — much, — near, à peu près, presque; assez. — well, assez bien; assez

Prevail, v.n. prévaloir; (extend over) régner, dominer; être répandu; (have influence) avoir de l'influence; (persuade) décider (à), persuader (de). To — on any one to do a thing, décider quelqu'un à (or persuader quelqu'un de) faire une chose. To be —ed (on, upon), se laisser entraîner (à) or persuader (de), consentir (à)

Prevailing, adj. V. **Prevalent**

Prevalenc-e, y, s. prévalence, f.; ascendant, empire, m., influence, f.; règne, m.; efficacité, f.; généralité, f.; durée, f.; existence, f.

Prevalent, adj. dominant, régnant; général; efficace, puissant; victorieux

Prevalently, adv. efficacement, puissamment, fortement

Prevaricate, v.n. prévariquer; (shuffle) tergiverser

Prevaricating, adj. prévaricateur; (shuffling) tergiversateur [tergiversation, f.

Prevarication, s. prévarication, f.; (shuffling)

Prevaricator, s. prévaricateur, m., -trice, f.; (shuffler) tergiversateur, m., -trice, f.

Prevent, v.a. prévenir; (hinder) empêcher (de)

Preventable, adj. empêchable, évitable

Preventer, s. personne or chose qui empêche, f.

Preventible, adj. empêchable, évitable

Preventingly, adv. de manière à empêcher

Prevention, s. empêchement, m.; obstacle, m.

Preventive, adj. préventif; propre à prévenir or à empêcher; — s. préservatif ('of,' contre), m.

Preventively, adv. préventivement

Previous, adj. antérieur, précédent, préalable. — to, avant

Previously, adv. antérieurement, précédemment; préalablement, auparavant, d'avance. — to, avant; (before an inf.) avant de

Previousness, s. antériorité, priorité, f.

Prevision, s. prévision, f.

Prey, s. proie, f.; — v.n. (on, upon) dévorer; piller, ravager; voler, victimer; (waste) miner, consumer, ronger; (worry) tourmenter, obséder. To be a — to, être en proie à; être la proie de. To fall a — to, devenir la proie de

Preyer, s. spoliateur, m., -trice, f.

Price, s. prix, m.; (fin.) cote, f.; — v.a. tarifer; coter; marquer; (to prize) V. **Prize,** v.a. All at one —, all one — au choix. At reduced —s. under —, au rabais. At greatly reduced —s, au grand rabais. Is that the lowest —? est-ce là le dernier (or le plus juste) prix? To rise or fall in —, hausser (or augmenter) or baisser de prix. To set a — on, mettre un prix à; (pers.) mettre à prix. —**less,** adj. sans prix; inappréciable; inestimable; impayable. — **list,**

s. liste des prix, *f.*, tarif, *m.*; (*of quotations on 'Change*) cotes, *f.pl.*

Prick, *v.a.* piquer; (*fix*) enfoncer; (*o.'s ears*) dresser; (*mark*) marquer; (*excite, spur*) aiguillonner, exciter, pousser, éperonner; (*with remorse*) causer des remords à, tourmenter; (*mus.*) noter; (*nav.*) pointer (la carte, les voiles), compasser (la carte); — *s.* piqûre, *f.*; (*pointed thing*) piquant, *m.*; pointe, *f.*; (*pain*) douleur poignante, *f.*, remords, *m.pl.*; (*mark*) but, blanc, *m.*, cible, *f.*; (*of a hare*) trace, *f.* — **off,** *v.a.* marquer, piquer. — **on,** *v.a.n.* piquer, exciter, aiguillonner; (*rush on*) s'élancer au galop. — **song,** *s.* air noté, *m.* — **up,** *v.a.* dresser. — **wood,** *s.* fusain, *m.*

Pricker, *s.* pointe, *f.*; piquant, *m.*; (*mil.*)

Pricket, *s.* daguet, broquart, *m.* [épinglette, *f.*

Pricking, *s.* piqûre, *f.*; picotement, *m.*; (*nav.*) pointage, *m.* [**back,** *s.* (*fish*) épinoche, *f.*

Prickle, *s.* piquant, *m.*; aiguillon, *m.* —

Prickliness, *s.* abondance de piquants *or* d'aiguillons, *f.*

Prickly, *adj.* plein de piquants, aiguillonné, épineux — **broom,** *s.* genêt épineux, *m.* — **pear,** *s.* raquette, *f.*, opuntia, *m.*

Pride, *s* orgueil, *m.*, fierté, *f.*; (*pomp*) faste, *m.*, pompe, *f.*; (*fish*) lamprillon, lamproyon, *m.*; — *v.n.r.* (*oneself on*) se glorifier (de), se faire gloire (de), s'enorgueillir (de), être fier (de); se piquer (de). *To take — in*, être fier **de,** tirer vanité de. —**less,** *adj.* sans orgueil

Prie-Dieu, *s.* prie-Dieu, *m.*

Prier, *s.* curieux, *m.*, -euse, *f.*; espion, *m.*

Priest, *s.* prêtre, *m.* — **ridden,** *adj.* gouverné par les prêtres

Priestcraft, *s.* intrigues de prêtres, *f.pl.*

Priestess, *s* prêtresse, *f.*

Priesthood, *s.* prêtrise, *f.*, sacerdoce, *m.*; clergé, *m.*; (*in contempt*) prêtraille, *f.*

Priestlike, *adj.* de prêtre; sacerdotal

Priestliness, *s.* air de prêtre, *m.*

Priestling, *s.* prestolet. *m.*

Priestly, *adj.* *V.* **Priestlike**

Prig, *v.a.* chiper, escamoter, filouter; — *s.* freluquet, fat, *m.*; (*thief*) filou, *m.*

Prigging, *s.* escamotage, *m.*, filouterie, *f.*

Priggish, *adj.* suffisant, vaniteux; pédant

Priggishly, *adv.* avec suffisance, vaniteusement [fectation, *f.*

Priggishness, *s.* suffisance, vanité, *f.*; af-

Prim, *adj.* affecté, précieux, collet monté; tiré à quatre épingles; — *v.a.* parer avec

Prima, *s.* (*print.*) réclame, *f.* [affectation

Primacy, *s.* primatie, *f.*; (*supremacy*) primauté, *f.*

Prima donna, *s.* prima donna, *f.* (*pl.* prime

Primâ facie, *adj. adv.* de prime abord [donne)

Primage, *s.* primage, *m.*

Primal, *adj.* premier; primitif

Primarily, *adv.* primitivement, dans le principe

Primary, *adj.* primitif; principal, premier; (*preparatory*) primaire; élémentaire; — *s.* principal, essentiel, *m.*; (*feather*) rémige extérieure, *f.*

Primate, *s.* primat, *m.*

Primateship, *s.* primatie, *f.*

Primatial, Primatical, *adj.* primatial

Prime, *adj.* premier; principal; meilleur, de première qualité, excellent; (*blooming*) florissant; — *s.* (*dawn*) aube, aurore, *f.*, point du jour, *m.*; (*beginning*) commencement, *m.*, naissance, origine, *f.*; (*spring*) printemps, *m.*; (*of life*, &c.) fleur, fraîcheur, beauté, *f.*; force, *f.*; première jeunesse, *f.*; (*best*) élite, *f.*, choix, meilleur, *m.*; (*perfection*) comble de la perfection, *m.*; (*of fire-arms*) amorce, *f.*; (*prayers*) prime, *f.*; — *v.a.* (*fire-arms*) amorcer; (*a ship*) abreuver; (*a fire-ship*) amorcer; (*paint.*) imprimer, préparer. — *minister*, premier ministre, *m.* — *number*, (*arith.*) nombre premier, nombre simple, *m.* (*In the*) — *of life*, — *of o.'s age*, (à la) fleur de l'âge, *f.*

Primely, *adv.* primitivement; parfaitement

Primer, *s.* (*Cath. rel.*) heures canoniales, *f.pl.*; (*prayer-book*) livre d'heures, *m.*, heures, *f.pl.*; (*first book*) premier livre de l'enfance, livre élémentaire, *m.*; grammaire élémentaire, *f.*; abécédaire, syllabaire, *m.*; (*print.*) romain, *m.*; (*artil.*) *V.* **Priming-wire.** *Great* —, (*print.*) gros romain. *Long* —, petit romain, *m.*

Primeval, *adj.* primitif; premier; primordial

Priming, *s.* (*of fire-arms*) (*powder*, &c.) amorce, *f.*, (*action*) amorçage, *m.*; (*paint.*) empreinte, impression, *f.*; (*steam-eng.*) premier jet d'eau et de vapeur mélangées, *m.*, ébullitions, *f.pl.* — **horn,** *s.* corne d'amorce, *f.*, pulvérin, *m.* — **iron,** *s.* *V.* — **wire.** — **pan,** *s.* bassinet, *m.* — **powder,** *s.* pulvérin, *m.* — **wire,** *s.* épinglette, *f.*, dégorgeoir, *m.*

Primitive, *adj. s.* primitif, *adj. m.*, -ive, *f.*, primitif, *s.m.* — *number*, (*arith.*) nombre premier, *m.*

Primitively, *adv.* primitivement

Primitiveness, *s.* primitivité, *f.*; antiquité, *f.*

Primness, *s.* affectation, afféterie, *f.*

Primogeniture, *s* primogéniture, *f.*

Primogenitureship, *s.* droit de primogéniture, droit d'aînesse, *m.*

Primordial, *adj.* primordial

Primordiality, *s.* primordialité, *f.*

Primordially, *adv.* primordialement

Primrose, *s.* primevère, *f.*

Prince, *s.* prince, *m.* —**dom,** *s.* principat, *m.*, principauté, *f.* — **let,** *s.* principicule, princillon, principion, *m.* — **like,** *adj.* *V.* —**ly.** —**liness,** *s.* caractère (*or* air) de prince, *m.*; magnificence, *f.* —**ling,** *s.* *V.* —**let.** —**ly,** *adj.* de prince; de princesse; digne d'un prince; princier; royal, magnifique, superbe; *adv.* en prince; en princesse

Princess, *s.* princesse, *f.*

Principal, *adj.* principal; premier; en chef; (*of staircases*) grand; (*of courts*) d'honneur; — *s.* chef, *m.*; (*of colleges*) principal, *m.*; proviseur, *m.*; directeur, *m.*; (*lady* —) directrice, *f.*; (*partner*) associé principal, *m.*; (*law*) mandant, *m.*; (*not an accomplice*) exécuteur, *m.*, -trice, *f.*; (*in a duel*) combattant, *m.*; (*of money*) capital, principal, *m.*; (*main point*) principal, *m.*

Principality, *s.* principauté, *f.*

Principally, *adv.* principalement; surtout

Principalship, *s.* *V.* **Head-mastership**

Principle, *s.* principe, *m.* *On* —, par principe; en principe. *Of no* —, *void of* —, *without* —, sans principes. *To be a man of* —, avoir des principes

Principled, *adj.* qui a des principes. *High* —, qui a des principes élevés, qui a des sentiments nobles. *Ill* —, qui a de mauvais principes. *Well* —, qui a de bons principes

Print, *v.a.* imprimer; (*to mark*) faire une empreinte sur, laisser une trace sur; — *s.* empreinte, marque, trace, *f.*; (*of books*) impression, *f.*; (*stamp*) moule, *m.*; (*type*) caractère d'imprimerie, caractère, *m.*; (*printed sheet*) imprimé, *m.*; (*printed matter*) imprimé, *m.*; publication, *f.*; (*newspaper*) feuille, *f.*, journal, *m.*; (*cut*) estampe, gravure, *f.*; (*photographic*, &c.) épreuve, *f.*; (*printed cotton*) indienne, *f.* *In* —, imprimé. *Out of* —, épuisé. *To appear in* —, (*pers.*) se faire imprimer; se faire auteur. **colourer,** *s.* coloriste, *m.f.* — **dress,** *s.* robe d'indienne, *f.* —**less,** *adj.* qui ne laisse aucune trace. — **off,** *v.a.* tirer. — **seller,** *s.* marchand (*m.*, e, *f.*) d'estampes *or* de gravures. — **shop,** *s.* magasin d'estampes *or* de gravures, *m.* — **works,** *s.pl.* imprimerie d'étoffes, *f.*

Printed, *part. adj.* imprimé. — *by*, imprimé par; (*on books*) imprimerie (*or* typographie) de. — *for*, imprimé pour; (*on books*) librairie de, chez. — **calico, -cotton,** *s.* toile peinte, *f.*; indienne, *f.*; rouennerie, *f.* — **paper,** *s.* imprimé, *m.*

Printer, *s.* imprimeur, *m.* —*'s ink*, encre d'imprimerie, *f.* —*'s reader*, correcteur d'imprimerie, *m.*

Printing, *s.* impression, *f.*; (*art*) imprimerie,

f. — **house,** *s.* imprimerie, *f.* — **ink,** *s.* encre d'imprimerie, *f.* — **letter,** *s.* caractère d'imprimerie, *m.* — **machine,** *s.* machine à imprimer, imprimeuse, *f.* — **materials,** *s.pl.* matériel d'imprimerie, *m.* — **off,** *s.* tirage, *m.* — **office,** *s.* imprimerie, *f.* — **paper,** *s.* papier d'impression, papier à imprimer, *m.* — **press,** *s.* presse d'imprimerie, presse à imprimer, *f.* — **type,** *s.* caractère (*m.*) *or* caractères (*m.pl.*) d'imprimerie, caractères typographiques

Prior, *adj.* antérieur; (*adverb.*) antérieurement (à), (*before an inf.*) avant (de); — *s.* [prieur, *m.*

Priorate, *s.* priorat, prieuré, *m.*

Prioress, *s.* prieure, *f.*

Priori (A), *adv.* à priori

Priorial, *adj.* prieural

Priority, *s.* priorité, *f.*

Priorship, *s.* prieuré, priorat, *m.*

Priory, *s.* prieuré, *m.*

Prise, *s.* levier, *m.*; — *v.a.* — **open,** ouvrir *or* forcer (à l'aide d'un levier). — **up,** soulever, [lever, élever

Prism, *s.* prisme, *m.*

Prismatic, -al, *adj.* prismatique

Prismatically, *adv.* en forme de prisme

Prismatization, *s.* prismatisation, *f.*

Prismatized, *adj.* prismatisé

Prismoid, *s.* prismoïde, *m.*

Prismoidal, *adj.* prismoïde

Prismy, *adj.* prismé

Prison, *s.* prison, *f.* — **base,** *s.*, — **bars,** *s.pl.* barres, *f.pl.* — **bird,** *s. V.* **Jail-bird.** — **discipline,** *s.* régime des prisons, régime pénitentiaire, *m.* — **house,** *s.* prison, *f.* — **ship,** *s.* vaisseau-prison, *m.* — **van,** *s.* voiture cellulaire, *f.* — **yard,** *s.* préau (de prison), *m.*

Prisoner, *s.* prisonnier, *m.*, -ière, *f.*; détenu, *m.*, e, *f.*; (*law*) prévenu, *m.*, e, *f.*, accusé, *m.*, e, *f.*; (*after trial*) condamné, *m.*, e, *f.*; (*mil.*) prisonnier, *m.* —*'s evidence, witness for the —,* témoin à décharge, *m.* —*s' base,* barres, *f.pl.* — *at the bar,* prévenu, *m.*, e, *f.*, accusé, *m.*, e, *f.* — *of war,* prisonnier de guerre. *To take —,* faire prisonnier [jeunesse

Pristine, *adj.* primitif, premier, ancien; de

Prithee, *int.* de grâce! je t'en prie!

Privacy, *s.* secret, *m.*; retraite, solitude, *f.*; intérieur, *m.*; intimité, *f.* *In —,* en son particulier; dans son intérieur

Private, *adj.* particulier; personnel; intime; confidentiel; domestique; (*not public*) privé; (*secret*) secret; (*retired*) retiré; (*common*) simple; (*of dress or clothes*) civil, bourgeois, &c. (*V.* **Clothes**); (*of schools and teachers*) libre; (*of staircases, doors*) dérobé; (*of sales*) à l'amiable; (*on a letter,* &c.) personnelle; confidentielle; (*law*) à huis clos; — *s.* simple soldat, soldat, *m.* — *asylum* or *hospital,* maison de santé, *f.* — *bill,* (*Engl. parliam.*) bill d'intérêt local, *m.* — *carriage,* voiture particulière, voiture bourgeoise, voiture de maître, *f.* — *education,* éducation particulière, *f.*; enseignement libre, *m.* — *gentleman,* — *individual,* — *man,* simple particulier, particulier, *m.*; rentier, *m.* — *family,* famille bourgeoise, *f.* — *hotel,* maison meublée, *f.* — *lessons,* leçons particulières, *f.pl.*; répétitions, *f.pl.* — *life,* vie privée, *f.*; vie domestique, *f.* — *pupil,* élève particulier, *m.* — *room,* (*for business or consultations*) cabinet, *m.*; (*in eating-houses,* &c.) salon *or* cabinet de société, salon particulier, *m.*, (*small*) cabinet particulier, *m.* — *school,* école libre, *f.*; pension, *f.*, pensionnat, *m.*; institution, *f.* — *soldier,* simple soldat, *m.* — *student,* personne qui étudie sans maître, *f.* — *teacher,* professeur libre, *m.* — *teaching,* — *tuition,* enseignement libre, *m.*, éducation particulière, *f.*; leçons en ville, *f.pl.*; répétitions, *f.pl.* — *tutor,* précepteur, *m.*; répétiteur, *m.* *In —,* en particulier; dans le particulier; dans son intérieur; en secret; retiré; en bourgeois; (*law*) à huis clos

Privateer, *s.* corsaire, *m.*; — *v.n.* faire la course, aller en course. —**sman,** *s.* corsaire, *m.*

Privateering, *s.* course, *f.*

Privately, *adv.* en particulier; secrètement, en secret; (*amicably*) de gré à gré, à l'amiable; (*of living,* &c.) en rentier, en bourgeois; (*law*) [à huis clos

Privateness, *s. V.* **Privacy**

Privation, *s.* privation, perte, *f.*

Privative, *adj.* qui prive; négatif; (*gram.*) privatif; — *s.* négation, *f.*; (*gram.*) privatif, *m.*

Privatively, *adv.* négativement; (*gram.*) privativement

Privet, *s.* troène, *m.*

Privilege, *s.* privilége, *m.*; — *v.a.* privilégier

Privileged, *adj.* privilégié; confidentiel

Privily, *adv.* secrètement, en secret

Privity, *s.* connaissance, *f.*; assentiment, *m.*

Privy, *adj.* privé; secret, caché; retiré, dérobé; (*acquainted*) instruit (de), initié (à); — *s.* lieux, lieux d'aisances, *m.pl.*, commodités, latrines, *f.pl.* — *chamber,* chambre du conseil privé, *f.* — *council,* conseil privé, *m.* — *councillor,* conseiller privé, membre du conseil privé, *m.* — *purse,* cassette, *f.* [*Keeper of the — purse,* trésorier de la maison du roi *or* de la reine *or* &c.]. — *seal,* petit sceau, *m.*

Prize, *s.* (*capture*) prise, *f.*; capture, *f.*; proie, *f.*, butin, *m.*; (*reward*) prix, *m.*; (*premium*) prime, *f.*; (*of lotteries*) lot, *m.*; (*windfall*) aubaine, trouvaille, *f.*; (*lever*) levier, *m.*; (*nav.*) prise, *f.*, bâtiment pris, *m.*; — *adj.* qui a remporté le (*or* un) prix, primé, médaillé; (*liter.*) couronné; — *v.a.* priser; évaluer; estimer; apprécier; faire cas de; (*with a lever*) *V.* **Prise.** *To carry* or *take* or *win a —,* remporter un prix. *To be a lawful —,* être de bonne prise. — **court,** *s.* conseil des prises, *m.* — **essay,** *s.* essai (*or* ouvrage) couronné *or* qui a remporté le prix, *m.* — **exhibitor,** *s* médaillé, *m.*, e, *f.* — **fight,** *s.* combat de boxeurs, *m.* — **fighter,** *s.* boxeur, *m.* — **fighting,** *s.* (la) boxe, *f.*; combat de boxeurs, *m.* — **firing,** *s.* concours de tir, *m.* — **holder, -man,** *s. V.* — **taker.** — **master,** *s.* commandant d'une prise, *m.* — **match,** *s.* concours, *m.* — **medal,** *s.* médaille d'honneur, *f.* — **money,** *s.* part (*f.*) *or* parts (*f.pl.*) de prise. — **ox** (*The*), *s.* (le) bœuf gras, *m.* — **ring,** *s.* association des boxeurs, *f.*; réunion de boxeurs, *f.*; boxeurs, *m.pl.* — **shooting,** *s.* concours de tir, *m.* — **show,** *s.* concours, *m.* — **taker,** *s.* remporteur (*m.*, -euse, *f.*) de prix, lauréat, *m.*; médaillé, *m.*, e, *f.*

Pro, *prep.* pour; — *s.* pour, *m.* — *and con,* pour et contre; le pour et le contre, *m.*

Proa, *s.* pro, *m.*

Probabil-ism, -ist. *V.* page 3, § 1

Probability, *s.* probabilité, *f.*

Probable, *adj.* probable

Probably, *adv.* probablement

Probang, *s.* sonde œsophagienne, *f.*

Probate, *s.* vérification d'un testament *or* des testaments, vérification, *f.* — **office,** *s.* bureau de vérification, *m.*

Probation, *s.* épreuve, *f.*; essai, *m.*; examen, *m.*; stage, *m.*; (*rel. orders*) noviciat, *m.*, probation, *f.* *On —,* à l'essai [probatoire

Probationary, Probatory, *adj.* d'épreuve,

Probationer, *s.* candidat, *m.*, e, *f.*; aspirant, *m.*, e, *f.*; stagiaire, *m.*; novice, *m.f.*

Probationership, *s.* noviciat, *m.*

Probe, *s.* sonde, *f.*, stylet, *m.*; — *v.a.* sonder

Probity, *s.* probité, *f.*

Problem, *s.* problème, *m.*

Problematic, -al, *adj.* problématique

Problematically, *adv.* problématiquement

Proboscidate, *adj.* proboscidé

Proboscidian, *adj.* *s.* proboscidien, *adj. m.*, -ne, *f.*, proboscidien, *s.m.*

Proboscis, *s.* trompe, proboscide, *f.* — **monkey,** *s.* nasique, *f.*

Procedure, *s.* procédé, *m.*; (*law*) procédure, *f.*

Proceed, *v.n.* procéder; (*come from*) provenir

(de); venir (de); partir (de); naître (de); procéder (de); (*follow out*) poursuivre, continuer; passer; (*advance*) marcher, avancer, aller; faire des progrès; aller plus loin; (*to go*) se rendre, aller; (*to act*) agir, procéder; (*to manage*) s'y prendre; (*to ..., and a verb*) se mettre (à); ... ensuite; se disposer (à); aller (pour); (*come to blows*) en venir (aux coups *or* aux mains); (*to extremities, excesses*) se porter (à des extrémités, à des excès); (*law*) procéder. — **against,** poursuivre, exercer des poursuites contre, procéder contre. — **with,** poursuivre, continuer; (*to act towards*) agir envers, en user avec

Proceeding, *s.* procédé, *m.*, manière d'agir, *f.*; acte, *m.*; mesure, *f.*; événement, fait, *m.*; —**s,** *pl.* procédés, *m.pl.*, &c.; démarches, mesures, *f.pl.*, moyens, *m.pl.*; (*of assemblies*) actes, *m.pl.*; (*law*) procédure, *f.*; poursuites, *f.pl.* *To take —s against,* exercer des poursuites contre, poursuivre

Proceeds, *s. pl.* produit, *m.*; rapport, *m.*; revenu, *m.*; bénéfice, *m.*

Process, *s.* cours, progrès, *m.*, marche, *f.*; (*of time*) suite, *f.*; (*in arts and sciences*) procédé, *m.*; opération, *f.*; travail, *m.*; (*anat.*) apophyse, *f.*; (*nat. hist.*) appendice, *m.*; (*law*) procès, *m.*; (*writ*) exploit judiciaire, exploit, *m.*; assignation, *f.* *In — of,* en cours de, en train de. *In — of time,* avec le temps. — **server,** *s.* huissier, *m.*

Procession, *s.* cortége, *m.*; marche, *f.*; (*funeral*) cortége, convoi, *m.*; (*rel.*) procession, *f.*; (*ramble*) promenade, *f.*; marche, *f.*; procession, *f.* *To walk in —,* défiler. — **caterpillar,** chenille processionnaire, *f.*

Processional, *adj.* processionnel; — *s.* processionnal, processionnel, *m.*

Processionally, *adv.* processionnellement

Processionist, *s.* processioniste, *m.f.*; promeneur, *m.*, -euse, *f.*

Procidence, *s.* procidence, *f.*

Proclaim, *v.a.* proclamer; publier; annoncer; déclarer; (*outlaw*) mettre hors la loi

Proclaimer, *s.* proclamateur, *m.*, -trice, *f.*

Proclamation, *s.* proclamation, *f.*; publication, *f.*; déclaration, *f.*; (*decree*) édit, *m.*, ordonnance, *f.* [disposition, facilité, *f.*

Proclivity, *s.* inclination, *f.*, penchant, *m.*;

Proconsul, *s.* proconsul, *m.*

Proconsular, -y, *adj.* proconsulaire

Proconsulate, Proconsulship, *s.* proconsulat, *m.* [temporiser

Procrastinate, *v.a.n.* différer, remettre,

Procrastination, *s.* délai, *m.*, temporisation, *f.*; lenteur, *f.* [sateur, *m.*, -trice, *f.*

Procrastinator, *s.* temporiseur, *m.*, tempori-

Procrastinatory, *adj.* temporiseur, tempori-

Procreate, *v.a.* procréer; produire [sateur

Procreating, *adj.* procréateur; productif

Procreation, *s.* procréation, production, *f.*

Procreative, *adj.* procréateur; productif

Procreativeness, *s.* faculté de procréer, *f.*

Procreator, *s.* père, *m.*

Procrustean, *adj.* de Procruste, de Procuste

Proctor, *s.* avoué, *m.*; (*univers.*) censeur, *m.*

Proctorship, *s.* (*univers.*) fonctions de censeur, *f.pl.*

Procumbent, *adj.* procombant, couché

Procurable, *adj.* facile à procurer *or* à se procurer, procurable, gagnable

Procuracy, *s.* procuratie, *f.*

Procuration, *s.* procuration, *f.*

Procurator, *s.* procureur, *m.*; agent, *m.*; (*of Genoa and Venice*) procurateur, *m.*

Procuratorial, *adj.* procuratorial

Procure, *v.a.* procurer, obtenir, faire avoir; (*to oneself*) se procurer; (*to cause*) causer, occasionner; — *v.n.* procurer

Procurement, *s.* obtention, *f.*; entremise, *f.*

Procurer, *s.* entremetteur, *m.*; source, *f.*

Procuress, *s.* entremetteuse, *f.*

Prod, *v.a.* piquer, percer; enfoncer; (*fig.*) éperonner, aiguillonner [fant prodigue, *m.*

Prodigal, *adj. s.* prodigue. *The — son,* l'en-

Prodigality, *s.* prodigalité, *f.*

Prodigally, *adv.* avec prodigalité, prodiguement, prodigalement

Prodigious, *adj.* prodigieux

Prodigiously, *adv.* prodigieusement

Prodigiousness, *s.* nature prodigieuse, *f.*;

Prodigy, *s.* prodige, *m.* [énormité, *f.*

Produce, *v.n.* produire; montrer; exhiber; (*geom.*) prolonger; — *s.* produit, *m.*; (*provisions*) denrées, *f.pl.*

Producer, *s.* producteur, *m.*, -trice, *f.*

Producible, *adj.* productible

Producibleness, *s.* productibilité, *f.*

Product, *s.* produit, *m.*; effet, résultat, *m.*

Production, *s.* production, *f.*; produit, *m.*

Productive, *adj.* productif. *To be — of,* pro-

Productively, *adv.* productivement [duire

Productiveness, *s.* productivité, nature productive, *f.*

Proem, *s.* proême, *m.*, préface, introduction, *f.*

Proemial, *adj.* préliminaire

Profanation, *s.* profanation, *f.*

Profane, *adj.* profane; — *v.a.* profaner

Profanely, *adv.* profanement

Profaneness, *s.* impiété, *f.*

Profaner, *s.* profanateur, *m.*, -trice, *f.*

Profanity, *s.* impiété, *f.*

Profess, *v.a.* professer, faire profession de; exercer; déclarer; dire; (*boast of*) se piquer de, avoir la prétention de. *To — oneself,* se déclarer, se dire [fession; (*of monks*) profès

Professed, *adj.* déclaré; ostensible; de pro-

Professedly, *adv.* ouvertement; ostensiblement; de profession; de son propre aveu

Profession, *s.* (*declaration*) profession, déclaration, *f.*; (*calling*) profession, *f.*; état, métier, *m.*; carrière, *f.*; (*people*) hommes de l'art, gens du métier, *m.pl.* *Military —,* métier des armes. *By —,* de profession; de son état

Professional, *adj.* professionnel; de sa profession; de la profession, du métier; de profession; de la médecine, de la chirurgie; de médecin, de chirurgien; — *s.* homme du métier, *m.*; homme de l'art, *m.*; (*not an amateur*) professeur, *m.* — *man,* homme de profession libérale, *m.*; homme de l'art, *m.*; homme du métier, *m.* — *dealings,* relations d'affaires, *f.pl.*

Professionally, *adv.* professionnellement; de (*or* par) profession, par état; dans l'exercice de sa profession

Professo (Ex), *adv.* ex professo

Professor, *s.* professeur, *m.*; (*of religion*) personne qui professe, *f.*

Professorial, *adj.* professoral, de professeur

Professoriat, Professorship, *s.* professorat, *m.*; chaire, *f.* [sition, *f.*

Proffer, *v.a.* offrir, proposer; — *s.* offre, propo-

Profferer, *s.* personne qui offre *or* qui propose, *f.* [*f.*; talent, *m.*

Proficienc-e, y, *s.* progrès, *m.*, *m.pl.*, force,

Proficient, *adj.* avancé, fort; versé, expert, habile [profil

Profile, *s.* profil, *m.*; — *v.a.* profiler. *In —,* de

Profit, *s.* profit, avantage, *m.*, utilité, *f.*; (*revenue*) rapport, produit, revenu, *m.*; (*com.*) bénéfice, profit, *m.* — *and loss,* (*book-keep.*) profits et pertes. *On half- —s,* de moitié dans les bénéfices, de compte à demi

Profit, *v.a.* profiter à, être utile à, faire du bien à, avancer; (*improve*) améliorer, perfectionner; — *v.n.* profiter, faire des progrès; servir. *To be —ed by,* gagner à; profiter de. *To — by,* profiter de. *What will it — you to ...?* à quoi vous servira de ...? [lucratif

Profitable, *adj.* profitable; utile; avantageux;

Profitableness, *s.* utilité, *f.*, avantage, profit, *m.*

Profitably, *adv.* profitablement, utilement, avantageusement; lucrativement

Profitless, *adj.* sans profit, inutile
Profligacy, *s.* dérèglement, libertinage, *m.*, licence, *f.*; atrocité, scélératesse, *f.*
Profligate, *adj.* dissolu, débauché, déréglé, libertin; prodigue; atroce, scélérat; — *s.* libertin, *m.*, e, *f.*; scélérat, *m.*, e, *f.*
Profligately, *adv.* sans mœurs; sans honte; dans le dérèglement, dans le libertinage; avec scélératesse
Profound, *adj.* profond; — *s.* abîme, gouffre, *m.*
Profoundly, *adv.* profondément
Profoundness, Profundity, *s.* profondeur, *f.*
Profuse, *adj.* prodigue; (*things*) extravagant; excessif; abondant, profus
Profusely, *adv.* prodiguement, prodigalement, avec prodigalité; profusément, avec profusion; excessivement; abondamment
Profuseness, Profusion, *s.* profusion, *f.*; prodigalité, *f.*; abondance, *f.*
Prog, *s.* nourriture, *f.*, vivres, *m.pl.*
Progenitor, *s.* aïeul, ancêtre, premier père, *m.*
Progeny, *s. V.* **Offspring**
Prognosis, *s.* prognostic, *m.*, prognose, *f.*
Prognostic, *adj.* pronostique, prognostique; — *s.* pronostic, *m.*
Prognosticate, *v.a.* pronostiquer, présager
Prognostication, *s.* pronostication, *f.*; pronostic, présage, *m.*
Prognosticator, *s.* pronostiqueur, *m.*, -euse, *f.*, pronosticateur, *m.*, -trice, *f.*
Programme, *s.* programme, *m.*
Progress, *s.* progrès, *m.*, *m.pl.*; marche, course, *f.*, cours, *m.*; (*journey*) voyage, *m.*; — *v.n.* s'avancer; continuer; faire des progrès, progresser, avancer. *To make* —, faire des progrès (*pl.*). *To report* —, faire un exposé de l'état de la question; (*fam.*) faire son rapport
Progression, *s.* progression, *f.*
Progressionist, *s. adj.* progressiste, *m.f.*
Progress-ism, ist. *V.* page 3, § 1
Progressive, *adj.* progressif
Progressively, *adv.* progressivement
Progressiveness, *s.* marche progressive, *f.*
Prohibit, *v.a.* défendre, interdire; (*law, cust.*) prohiber
Prohibiter, *s.* prohibeur, *m.*, -euse, *f.*
Prohibition, *s.* défense, interdiction, *f.*; (*law, cust.*) prohibition, *f.*
Prohibitionist, *s.* prohibitioniste, *m.f.*
Prohibitive, *adj. V.* **Prohibitory**
Prohibitively, *adv.* prohibitivement
Prohibitory, *adj.* de défense, d'interdiction, qui défend, qui interdit; (*cust.*) prohibitif
Project, *v.a.n.* projeter; (*jut out*) faire saillie, avancer; se projeter; — *s.* projet, dessein, *m.*
Projectile, *adj. s.* projectile, *adj.m.f.*, *s.m.*
Projecting, *adj.* saillant, en saillie
Projection, *s.* projection, *f.*; (*jutting*) saillie, *f.*
Projector. *V.* **Schemer**
Prolapsus, *s.* (*surg., med.*) prolapsus, renversement, *m.*; chute, *f.*; (*hernia*) hernie, descente, *f.* —*ani*, chute de l'anus, *f.* — *uteri*, prolapsus de la matrice, abaissement de la matrice, *m.*, descente de matrice, *f.*
Prolegomena, *s.pl.* prolégomènes, *m.pl.*
Proletarian, *adj. s.* prolétaire, *m.f.*
Proletarianism, Proletariat, *s.* prolétariat, *m.*
Proletary, *s.* prolétaire, *m.f.*
Prolific, *adj.* fécond, fertile; (*med., bot.*) prolifique
Prolifically, *adv.* avec fécondité, d'une manière prolifique
Prolificness, *s.* fécondité, fertilité, *f.*
Prolix, *adj.* prolixe
Prolixity, Prolixness, *s.* prolixité, *f.*
Prolixly, *adv.* prolixement
Prolocutor, *s.* orateur, *m.*; président, *m.*
Prolocutorship, *s.* présidence, *f.*
Prologue, *s.* prologue, *m.*; — *v.a.* introduire par un prologue, faire précéder d'un prologue
Prolong, *v.a.* prolonger; (*to delay*) différer, retarder
Prolongation, *s.* (*of extent*) prolongement, *m.*; (*of duration*) prolongation, *f.*
Prolonge, *s.* prolonge, *f.*
Prolonger, *s.* personne *or* chose qui prolonge, *f.*
Promenade, *s.* promenade, *f.*; — *v.n.* se promener
Promenader, *s.* promeneur, *m.*, -euse, *f.*
Promethean, *adj.* de Prométhée
Prominenc-e, y, *s.* proéminence, *f.*; saillie, *f.*; (*conspicuousness*) distinction, *f.*
Prominent, *adj.* proéminent; (*jutting out*) saillant, en saillie, qui fait saillie; (*eminent*) éminent, distingué; (*conspicuous*) prononcé, marqué, marquant, remarquable; frappant; en évidence, en vue. — *eyes*, yeux à fleur de tête. — *features*, traits saillants *or* prononcés. *In a* (or *occupying a*) — *position*, en évidence, en vue
Prominently, *adv.* d'une manière proéminente; en saillie; (*eminently*) éminemment, d'une manière éminente; (*strikingly*) d'une manière frappante *or* prononcée; (*conspicuously*) en évidence, en vue
Promiscuity. *V.* **Promiscuousness**
Promiscuous, *adj.* mêlé; confus, sans ordre, sans méthode; général
Promiscuously, *adv.* sans distinction, indistinctement; en commun; ensemble; confusément, sans ordre, pêle-mêle
Promiscuousness, *s.* mélange confus, *m.*, promiscuité, *f.*
Promise, *s.* promesse, *f.*; (*hopes*) espérances, *f.pl.*, espérance, *f.*; avenir, *m.*; — *v.a.n.* promettre. *Of* —, qui donne des espérances; qui a de l'avenir. *Breach of* —, violation de promesse, *f.* *Land of* —, terre promise, terre de promission, *f.* *To break o.'s* —, manquer à sa promesse. *To keep o.'s* —, tenir sa promesse
Promiser, *s.* prometteur, *m.*, -euse, *f.*
Promising, *adj.* qui promet; de grande espérance; plein d'avenir; qui a des moyens, intelligent
Promisor, *s.* promettant, *m.*
Promissorily, *adv.* par forme de promesse
Promissory, *adj.* qui contient une promesse. — *note*, promesse, *f.*; (*com.*) billet à ordre, billet, *m.*, obligation, *f.*
Promontory, *s.* promontoire, *m.*
Promote, *v.a.* encourager, favoriser; servir; (*raise*) avancer, promouvoir; élever; (*bring on*) provoquer. *To be* —*d*, obtenir de l'avancement; (*of rank*) être promu
Promoter, *s.* promoteur, *m.*, -trice, *f.*; (*speculating schemer*) faiseur (*or* lanceur) d'affaires, *m.*
Promoting, Promotive, *adj.* promoteur
Promotion, *s* promotion, *f.*; avancement, *m.*; élévation, *f.*; encouragement, *m.*
Prompt, *adj.* prompt; empressé; (*of money*) comptant; — *v.a.* porter (à), pousser (à), exciter (à); suggérer, dicter, inspirer (à); (*a speaker*) souffler. — **book,** *s.* exemplaire du souffleur, *m.*
Prompter, *s.* souffleur, *m.* —*'s book*, exemplaire du souffleur, *m.*
Prompting, *s.* suggestion, *f.*; instigation, *f.*
Promptitude, Promptness, *s.* promptitude, *f.*; empressement, *m.*
Promptly, *adv.* promptement; avec empressement
Promptuary, *s.* promptuaire, *m.*
Promulgate, *v.a.* promulguer; publier
Promulgation, *s.* promulgation, *f.*; publication, *f.*
Promulgator, *s.* promulgateur, *m.*
Pronation, *s* pronation, *f.*
Pronator, *s. adj.* pronateur, *s.m.*, *adj.m.*
Prone, *adj.* (*disposed*) enclin (à), porté (à), disposé (à); (*sloping*) penché, incliné, en pente; (*bending*) courbé; (*lying down*) couché la face contre terre, couché
Proneness, *s.* (*disposition*) penchant, *m.*, inclination, disposition, *f.*; (*slope*) pente, inclinaison, *f.*; (*bending*) position courbée *or* renversée, *f.*
Prong, *s.* dent, *f.*, fourchon, *m.* *A three — fork*, une fourche (*or* une fourchette) à trois dents
Pronged, *adj.* à dents, à fourchons
Pronominal, *adj.* pronominal

Pronominally, *adv.* pronominalement

Pronoun, *s.* pronom, *m.*

Pronounce, *v.a.* prononcer; déclarer; dire

Pronounceable, *adj.* prononçable

Pronouncer, *s.* prononceur, *m.*

Pronouncing, *s.* prononcement, *m.*; prononciation, *f.*; — *adj.* de prononciation; donnant (*or* qui donne) la prononciation

Pronunciamento, Pronunciamiento, *s.* pronunciamento, *m.* [débit, *m.*

Pronunciation, *s.* prononciation, *f.*; (*delivery*)

Proof, *s.* preuve, *f.*; (*trial*) épreuve, *f.*; essai, *m.*; (*print.*, *engr.*, *photography*) épreuve, *f.*; (*alg.*, *arith.*, *dist.*) preuve, *f.*; (*of a debt or claim, in bankruptcy*) affirmation (de créance, en matière de faillite), *f.*; — *adj.* à l'épreuve (du, de la, des). *Bullet-* —, *fire-* —, &c., *V.* **Bullet, Fire,** &c. *In* —, *as a* —, pour preuve. *Over* or *above* —, (*spirit*) au-dessus de preuve. *Under* —, au-dessous de preuve. *To be* — *against*, être à l'épreuve de. —**less,** *adj.*, —**lessly,** *adv.* sans preuve, sans preuves. — **sample,** *s.* preuve, *f.* — **sheet,** *s.* épreuve, *f.* — **spirit,** *s.* esprit de preuve, *m.* — **stick,** *s.* sonde, *f.*

Prop, *v.a.* appuyer; soutenir; étayer; (*vines, trees*) échalasser; mettre un tuteur à; (*carp.*) étayer, étançonner; (*nav.*) accorer; — *s.* étai, support, *m.*; (*fig.*) appui, soutien, *m.*; (*for vines, hops*, &c.) échalas, *m.*; (*for trees*) tuteur, *m.*; (*carp.*) étai, étançon, *m.*; (*nav.*) accore, *m.*

Propagable, *adj.* susceptible de propagation

Propaganda, *s.* propagande, *f.*

Propagand-ism, -ist. *V.* page 3, § 1

Propagate, *v.a.* propager; (*increase*) étendre, accroître, augmenter; (*a report, news*, &c.) répandre; — *v.n.* se propager

Propagation, *s.* propagation, *f.*

Propagator, *s.* propagateur, *m.*, -trice, *f.*

Propel, *v.a.* propulser, pousser en avant, mettre en mouvement, faire mouvoir; (*throw*) lancer

Propeller, *s.* propulseur, *m.*; moteur, *m.*, -trice, *f.*; (*screw* —) propulseur à hélice, *m.*, hélice propulsive, *f.*; (*steamer*) vapeur à hélice, *m.*

Propelling, *adj.* propulsif, moteur. — *pencil*, crayon porte-mine, porte-mine, *m.* — *power*, force propulsive, force motrice, *f.*

Propense, *adj.* porté, enclin, disposé

Propension, Propensity, *s.* propension, *f.*, penchant, *m.*, inclination, disposition, tendance, *f.*, goût, *m.*

Proper, *adj.* propre; particulier; naturel; juste; exact; mérité; (*fit, becoming*) convenable, à propos; bon; bien; (*gram.*) propre. — *name*, nom propre, *m.* — *sense*, sens propre, *m.* *In a* — *sense*, au propre. *To the* — *party*, à qui de droit. *To think* —, juger convenable *or* à propos. *This is the* — *way to do it*, voici comment il faut s'y prendre

Properly, *adv.* proprement; particulièrement; convenablement, à propos; comme il faut, bien; naturellement; exactement; (*by rights*) pour bien faire; à la rigueur. — *called*, — *so called*, proprement dit. — *speaking*, à proprement parler. *More* — *speaking*, pour mieux dire. *To do a thing* —, faire une chose comme il faut *or* proprement

Property, *s.* propriété, *f.*; bien, *m.*, biens, *m.pl.*; fortune, *f.*; (*peculiar quality*) propriété, qualité, *f.*; (*theat.*) accessoire, *m.* *Man of* —, propriétaire, homme riche, homme qui a de la fortune, *m.* *This house is my* —, cette maison m'appartient. *To become public* —, (*of books*) tomber dans le domaine public. — **man,** *s.* (*theat.*) fournisseur (de théâtre *or* d'accessoires), *m.* — **tax,** *s.* impôt foncier, *m.*

Prophecy, *s.* prophétie, *f.*; prédiction, *f.*

Prophesier, *s.* prophète, *m.*, prophétesse, *f.*

Prophesy, *v.a.n.* prophétiser; prédire

Prophesying, *s.* prophétie, *f.* [de malheur

Prophet, *s.* prophète, *m.* — *of evil*, prophète

Prophetess, *s.* prophétesse, *f.*

Prophetic,-al, *adj.* prophétique

Prophetically, *adv.* prophétiquement [*s.m.*

Prophylactic, *adj.* *s.* prophylactique, *adj.m.f.*,

Prophylaxis, *s.* prophylaxie, prophylactique, *f.*

Propinquity, *s.* proximité, *f.*; (*kindred*) parenté, *f.*

Propitiable, *adj.* qu'on peut rendre propice

Propitiate, *v.a.* propitier, rendre propice, rendre favorable, apaiser [pitiateur

Propitiating, *s.* propitiation, *f.*; — *adj.* pro-

Propitiation, *s.* propitiation, *f.*

Propitiator, *s.* propitiateur, *m.*, -trice, *f.*

Propitiatory, *adj.* *s.* propitiatoire, *adj.m.f.*,*s.m.*

Propitious, *adj.* propice, favorable [ment

Propitiously, *adv.* propicement, favorable-

Propitiousness, *s.* nature propice *or* favorable, *f.*; disposition propice *or* favorable, *f.*

Propolis, *s.* propolis, *f.*

Proportion, *s.* proportion, *f.*; partie, quantité, *f.*; — *v.a.* proportionner. *In* — *to*, en *or* à proportion de; proportionné à. *In* — *as*, à mesure que [*adv.*, en *or* à proportion (de)

Proportionable, *adj.*, **Proportionably,**

Proportional, *adj.* en *or* à proportion; (*math.*) proportionnel; — *s.* proportionnelle, *f.* — *compass*, compas de réduction, *m.*

Proportionality, *s.* proportionnalité, *f.*

Proportionally, *adv.* proportionnellement, en *or* à proportion [proportionner

Proportionate, *adj.* proportionné; — *v.a.*

Proportionately, *adv.* proportionnément, proportionnellement, en *or* à proportion

Proportionateness, *s.* proportion, *f.*; (*math.*) proportionnalité, *f.*

Proportionless, *adj.* sans proportion

Proportionment, *s.* proportionnement, *m.*

Proposable, *adj.* proposable

Proposal, *s.* proposition, *f.*; offre, *f.*; —**s,** *pl.* propositions, offres, *f.pl.*; (*com.*) prospectus, *m.*

Propose, *v.a.* proposer; offrir; (*a toast*) porter; — *v.n.* se proposer. *To* — (*v.n.*) *to*, offrir d'épouser, demander en mariage. *To* — *to oneself*, se proposer

Proposer, *s.* proposeur, *m.*, -euse, *f.*, proposant, *m.*, e, *f.*, auteur d'une proposition, *m.*

Proposition, *s.* proposition, *f.*

Propound, *v.a.* proposer; exposer; avancer; mettre en avant; soumettre; (*a will*) soumettre à la vérification

Propounder. *V.* **Proposer**

Propping, *s.* appui, soutien, *m.*; (*carp.*) étayement, *m.*; (*hort.*) échalassement, *m.*

Proprietary, *adj.* de propriété; en propriétaire; par actions; — *s.* actionnaires, *m.pl.* — *school*, école par actions, *f.*

Proprie-tor, tress, *s.* propriétaire, *m.f.*; maître, *m.*, -esse, *f.*

Proprietorial, *adj.* *V.* **Proprietary**

Proprietorially, *adv.* propriétairement

Proprietorship, *s.* propriété, *f.*

Proprietory. *V.* **Proprietary**

Propriety, *s.* décence, bienséance, *f.*, convenances, *f.pl.*; (*correctness*) propriété, *f.*

Propulsion, *s.* propulsion, *f.*

Propulsive, *adj.* propulsif

Pro rata, *adv.* à proportion, au prorata

Prorogation, *s.* prorogation, *f.*

Prorogative, *adj.* prorogatif

Prorogue, *v.a.* proroger [saisme, *m.*

Prosaic, -al, *adj.* prosaïque. — *form*, pro-

Prosaically, *adv.* prosaïquement

Prosaicalness, Prosaicism, Prosaism, [*s.* prosaïsme, *m.*

Prosaist, *s.* prosateur, *m.*

Prosaize, *v.a.n.* prosaïser [cénium, *m.*

Proscenium, *s.* avant-scène, *f.*; (*anc.*) pros-

Proscribe, *v.a.* proscrire

Proscriber, *s.* proscripteur, *m.*

Proscript, *s.* proscrit, *m.*

Proscription, *s.* proscription, *f.*

Proscriptive, *adj.* de proscription

Prose, *s.* prose, *f.*; — *v.a.n.* proser, écrire en

prose; (*fig.*) faire un récit fastidieux de. — **book,** *s.* prosier, *m.* —**writer,** *s.* prosateur, *m.*
Prosector, *s.* prosecteur, *m.*
Prosecutable, *adj.* poursuivable
Prosecute, *v.a.* poursuivre
Prosecution, *s.* poursuite, *f.*; (*crim. law*) accusation, *f.*; poursuites, *f.pl.* *For the* —, (*of witnesses*) à charge
Prosecutor, *s.* poursuivant, *m.*; plaignant, *m.* *Public* —, ministère public, *m.*
Prosecutrix, *s.* poursuivante, *f.*; plaignante, *f.*
Proselyte, *s.* prosélyte, *m.f.*
Proselytism, *s.* prosélytisme, *m.*
Proselytize, *v.a.n.* convertir; faire des prosélytes [eux, *m.*
Proser, *s.* prosateur, *m.*; (*fig.*) conteur ennuy-
Prosiness, *s.* prosaïsme, terre à terre, *m.*; verbosité, *f.*
Prosod-ic, al, -ically, -ist, -y. *V.* p. 3, § 1
Prosopopœia, *s.* prosopopée, *f.*
Prospect, *s.* vue, perspective, *f.*, coup d'œil, point de vue, *m.*; (*expectation*) avenir, *m.*, espérance, *f.*; perspective, *f.* [d'approche
Prospective, *adj.* en perspective; (*of glasses*)
Prospectively, *adv.* en perspective, pour l'avenir [pailleur, *m.*
Prospector, *s.* explorateur, *m.*; (*for gold*) or-
Prospectus, *s.* prospectus, *m.*
Prosper, *v.n.* prospérer; réussir; être florissant; — *v.a.* faire prospérer, faire réussir, [favoriser
Prosperity, *s.* prospérité, *f.*
Prosperous, *adj.* florissant, heureux, prospère; favorable [ment, avec prospérité
Prosperously, *adv.* heureusement, prospère-
Prosperousness, *s.* prospérité, *f.*, bonheur, succès, *m.*
Prostate, *s. adj.*, — **gland,** prostate, *f.*
Prostatic, *adj.* prostatique
Prostitute, *v.a.* prostituer; — *adj.* prostitué; — *s.* prostituée, *f.*
Prostitution, *s.* prostitution, *f.* [-trice, *f.*
Prostitu-tor, tress, *s.* prostituteur, *m.*,
Prostrate, *adj.* prosterné; couché; (*fig.*) abattu; (*med.*) prostré; — *v.a.* (*lay flat*) coucher; (*throw down*) abattre, renverser; (*to ruin*) ruiner, détruire; (*in humility or adoration*) prosterner. *To — oneself —, to fall —,* se prosterner
Prostration, *s.* prostration, *f.*, prosternation, *f.*, prosternement, *m.*; (*dejection*) abattement, *m.*; (*med.*) prostration, *f.*; (*throwing down*) renversement, *m.*; destruction, ruine, *f.*; (*of trade*) [stagnation, *f.*
Prostyle, *s. adj.* prostyle, *m.*
Prosy, *adj.* prosaïque, terre à terre; verbeux, lourd, ennuyeux
Prosyllog-ism, -istic. *V.* page 3, § 1
Protagonist, *s.* protagoniste, *m.*
Protean, *adj.* protéen, de Protée
Protect, *v.a.* protéger ('*from,*' contre; '*with,*' de); défendre (de); garantir (de); (*shelter*) abriter (contre), mettre à l'abri (de); (*interests, &c.*) sauvegarder
Protection, *s.* protection ('*from,*' contre), *f.*; défense, *f.*; garantie, *f.*; sauvegarde, *f.*; abri, *m.*; (*from arrest*) privilége contre les arrestations, *m.* — *of life from fire,* or *shipwreck,* or &c., sauvetage, *m.*
Protection-ism, -ist. *V.* page 3, § 1
Protective, *adj.* protecteur, qui protége. *To be — of,* protéger [gardien, *m.*
Protector, *s.* protecteur, *m.*; défenseur, *m.*;
Protectoral, Protectorial, *adj.* protectoral
Protectorate, Protectorship, *s.* protectorat, *m.*
Protectress, *s.* protectrice, *f.*; gardienne, *f.*
Protégé, e, *s.* protégé, *m.*, e, *f.*
Proteiform, *adj.* protéiforme
Proteine, *s.* protéine, *f.*
Protest, *v.n.* protester; — *v.a.* protester; (*call as witness*) prendre à témoin, attester; (*a bill*) protester, faire protester; — *s.* protestation, *f.*; (*of bills*) protêt, *m.* — *for non-acceptance,* protêt faute d'acceptation. — *for non-payment,* protêt faute de payement. *Under* —, protesté
Protestant, *adj. s.* protestant, *m.*, e, *f.*
Protestantism, *s.* protestantisme, *m.*
Protestation, *s.* protestation, *f.*
Protester, *s.* personne qui proteste, *f.*; (*com.*) créancier qui fait faire un protêt, *m.*
Proteus, *s.* (*zool.*) protée, *m.*
Prothesis, *s.* prothèse, *f.*
Prothetic, *adj.* prothétique
Prothonotary, Protonotary, *s.* protonotaire, *m.* [*s.* protonotariat, *m.*
Prothonotaryship, Protonotaryship,
Protocol, *s.* protocole, *m.*
Protogene, *s.* protogyne, *m.*
Protomartyr, *s.* protomartyr, premier [martyr, *m.*
Protoplasm, *s.* protoplasma. *m.*
Protoplasmic, *adj.* protoplasmique
Protoplast, *s.* protoplaste, *m.*
Protoplastic, *adj.* protoplaste
Prototype, *s.* prototype, *m.*
Prototypic, -al, *adj.* prototypique
Protoxide, *s.* protoxyde, *m.*
Protract, *v.a.* prolonger; (*to delay*) différer, ajourner, remettre, retarder; (*lengthen in time*) traîner en longueur
Protraction, *s.* prolongation, *f.*
Protractive, *adj.* qui prolonge; (*of time*) qui traîne en longueur
Protractor, *s.* rapporteur, *m.*
Protrude, *v.a.* pousser en avant; pousser dehors; chasser; faire passer; — *v.n.* s'avancer; se projeter; passer; sortir
Protrusion, *s.* protrusion, *f.*
Protrusive, *adj.* qui pousse en avant, qui pousse dehors; qui chasse
Protuberance, *s.* protubérance, bosse, *f.*; proéminence, saillie, *f.*
Protuberant, *adj.* protubérant; proéminent, saillant, en saillie; (*swollen*) enflé
Protuberate, *v.n.* faire saillie, être en saillie, saillir, ressortir, s'avancer; (*swell*) s'enfler
Proud, *adj.* fier; orgueilleux; glorieux; hautain, superbe; grand, noble, magnifique; (*med.*) fongueux, baveux; (*of animals*) en chaleur. — *branch,* (*hort.*) branche gourmande, *f.* — *flesh,* bourgeons charnus, *m.pl.*, chairs baveuses, *f.pl.* *As — as Lucifer,* fier comme Artaban *or* comme un paon
Proudish, *adj.* un peu fier, fiérot
Proudly, *adv.* fièrement, orgueilleusement
Provable, *adj.* prouvable
Prove, *v.a.* prouver; démontrer; (*show*) montrer; (*a will*) vérifier, homologuer; (*a debt*) affirmer (une créance); (*try*) éprouver; (*arith.*) faire la preuve de; — *v.n.* se montrer; (*be found to be*) se trouver, se trouver être; (*be*) être; (*turn out*) tourner; (*become*) devenir
Provençal, *s. adj.* Provençal, *m.*, e, *f.*
Provender, *s.* fourrage, *m.*; nourriture, *f.*; provisions de bouche, *f.pl.*, vivres, *m.pl.*
Prover, *s.* personne *or* chose qui prouve *or* qui éprouve, *f.*; (*instr.*) éprouvette, *f.*
Proverb, *s.* proverbe, *m.*
Proverbial, *adj.* proverbial [verbes, *f.*
Proverbialist, *s.* personne qui parle par pro-
Proverbialize, *v.a.* proverbialiser; — *v.n.* parler par proverbes
Proverbially, *adv.* proverbialement
Provide, *v.a.n.* (*with*) pourvoir (de); se pourvoir (de); (*for a thing*) pourvoir (à); (*for a pers.*) pourvoir ...; pourvoir aux besoins *or* à l'entretien de ..., nourrir ...; mettre ... à l'abri du besoin; faire un sort à ...; faire une pension à ...; (*against*) se pourvoir (contre), se prémunir (contre); prendre des mesures (contre); parer (à); obvier (à); (*foresee, &c.*) prévoir; préparer; stipuler, porter ('*that,*' que). *To — for oneself,* se suffire. *To be —d for,* être pourvu; avoir son avenir assuré
Provided, *conj.* pourvu que. — *that,* pourvu que

Providence, *s.* prévoyance, prudence, *f.*; économie, *f.*; (*theol.*) Providence, *f.*
Provident, *adj.* pourvoyant, prévoyant, prudent. — *society,* société de secours mutuels, société de prévoyance, *f.*
Providential, *adj.* providentiel
Providentially, *adv.* providentiellement
Providently, *adv.* avec prévoyance, prudemment
Provider, *s.* pourvoyeur, *m.*, -euse, *f.*
Province, *s.* province, *f.*; (*business*) département, domaine, ressort, *m.*, compétence, *f.*; (*task*) emploi, *m.*, affaire, *f.* *It is not in* or *within* (or *It is out of*) *my* — (*to*), il n'est pas de ma compétence (de)
Provincial, *adj.* provincial, de province; — *s.* provincial, *m.*, e, *f.*; (*of convents*) provincial, *m.*
Provincialism, *s.* provincialisme, *m.*
Provincialship, *s.* provincialat, *m.*
Proving, *s.* épreuve, *f.*; vérification, *f.*
Provision, *s.* provision, *f.*; précaution, mesure, *f.*; stipulation, disposition, *f.*; —**s,** *pl.* provisions, *f.pl.*, &c.; (*victuals*) vivres, *m.pl.*; denrées, *f.pl.*; comestibles, *m.pl.*; — *v.a.* approvisionner de vivres, avitailler. *To make — for,* prendre des mesures pour. *To make a — for,* (*things*) pourvoir à; (*pers.*) pourvoir aux besoins *or* à l'entretien de; mettre à l'abri du besoin; faire une pension **à**; assurer l'avenir de, faire un sort *or* un avenir **à.** — **dealer,** *s.* marchand (*m.*, e, *f.*) de comestibles. — **warehouse,** *s.* magasin de comestibles, *m.*
Provisional, *adj.* provisoire; (*law*) provisionnel
Provisionally, *adv.* provisoirement; (*law*) provisionnellement, par provision
Proviso, *s.* clause, condition, *f.* *With a — that,* à *or* sous condition que
Provisorily, *adv.* provisoirement; (*law*) conditionnellement
Provisory, *adj.* provisoire; (*law*) conditionnel
Provocation, *s.* provocation, *f.*
Provocative, *adj.* provocatif; provocateur; provocant; — *s.* chose qui provoque, *f.*; aiguillon, stimulant, *m.*
Provoke, *v.a.* provoquer; vexer, contrarier, ennuyer, agacer, irriter, fâcher, vexer, impatienter; exciter; (*challenge*) défier
Provoker, *s.* provocateur, *m.*, -trice, *f.*
Provoking, *part.* provoquant, &c. (*V.* **Provoke**); — *adj.* provocant, provocateur; (*vexatious*) contrariant, ennuyeux, fâcheux, agaçant, vexant, impatientant
Provokingly, *adv.* d'une manière offensante; (*vexatiously*) d'une manière provocante; d'une manière contrariante *or* fâcheuse *or* agaçante *or* impatientante
Provost, *s.* prévôt, *m.*; (*univers.*) recteur, président, *m.*; (*in Scotland*) maire, *m.* — *marshal,* (*mil.*) grand prévôt, *m.*; (*nav.*) commissaire rapporteur, *m.*
Provostal, *adj.* prévôtal
Provostship, *s.* prévôté, *f.*; (*univers.*) rectorat, *m.*, présidence, *f.*; (*in Scotland*) mairie, *f.*
Prow, *s.* proue, *f.*
Prowess, *s.* bravoure, valeur, *f.*; (*in jest*) prouesse, *f.*
Prowl, *v.n.* rôder
Prowler, *s.* rôdeur, *m.*, -euse, *f.*
Proximate, *adj.* proche, prochain; immédiat
Proximately, *adv.* immédiatement
Proximity, *s.* proximité, *f.*
Proximo, *adv.* du mois prochain
Proxy, *s.* procuration, *f.*; (*pers.*) fondé de pouvoir (*or* de pouvoirs), *m.*, délégué, *m.*, e, *f.*, mandataire, *m.f.* *By —,* par procuration
Proxyship, *s.* qualité de mandataire *or* de fondé de pouvoir, *f.*
Prude, *s.* prude, *f.*
Prudence, *s.* prudence, sagesse, *f.*
Prudent, *adj.* prudent, sage. — *marriage* or *match,* mariage de convenance *or* de raison, *m.*
Prudential, *adj.* de prudence, dicté *or* commandé par la prudence; —**s,** *s. pl.* maximes de prudence, *f.pl.*
Prudentially, Prudently, *adv.* prudemment, sagement
Prudery, *s.* pruderie, *f.*
Prudish, *adj.* prude; de prude
Prudishly, *adv.* en prude, avec pruderie
Prune, *v.a.* (*trees*) élaguer, tailler, émonder; (*to cut*) couper, rogner; (*to trim*) parer, ajuster, arranger; — *s.* pruneau, *m.*, prune sèche, *f.*; (*plum, not dried*) prune, *f.* — **sauce,** *s.* compote de pruneaux, *f.*
Prunella, Prunello, *s.* prunelle, *f.* — **salt,** *s.* sel de prunelle, *m.*
Pruner, *s.* élagueur, *m.*, -euse, *f.*
Pruning, *s.* élagage, émondage, *m.*; (*of fruit-trees*) taille, *f.*; (*collectively*) élagage, *m.*, émondes, *f.pl.* — **bill, -hook,** *s.* serpe, *f.*; croissant, *m.* — **knife,** *s.* serpette, *f.* — **shears, -scissors,** *s.pl.* sécateur, *m.*
Prurienc-e, y, *s.* démangeaison, *f.*; (*desire*) désir violent, désir immodéré, *m.*, démangeaison, *f.*; (*med.*) prurit, *m.*
Prurient, *adj.* qui démange; qui brûle de désir; obscène
Pruriginous, *adj.* prurigineux
Prurigo, *s.* prurigo, *m.*
Pruritus, *s.* prurit, *m.*
Prussian, *s.* Prussien, *m.*, -ne, *f.*; — *adj.* prussien, de Prusse. — *blue,* bleu de Prusse, *m.* — *carp,* gibèle, *f.*
Prussianize, *v.a.* prussianiser
Prussiate, *s.* prussiate, *m.*
Prussic, *adj.* prussique
Prussophobia, *s.* prussophobie, *f.*
Prussophobiac, *s.* prussophobe, *m.f.*
Prussophobic, *adj.* (*thing*) prussophobique; (*pers.*) prussophobe
Prussophobist, *s.* prussophobe, *m.f.*
Pry, *v.n.* scruter; fureter, fouiller; chercher à pénétrer *or* à voir; (*meddle*) se mêler (de), (*fam.*) fourrer son nez (dans); — *s.* regard scrutateur, regard indiscret, *m.*; (*pers.*) curieux indiscret, *m.* *He is a perfect Paul —,* c'est un curieux indiscret
Prying, *adj.* curieux; indiscret; — *s.* regards curieux, *m.pl.*; curiosité, *f.*; indiscrétion, *f.*
Pryingly, *adv.* curieusement; indiscrètement
Prytanæum, Prytaneum, *s.* prytanée, *m.*
Prythee. *V.* **Prithee**
Psalm, *s.* psaume, *m.* — **book,** *s.* livre de psaumes, psautier, *m.* — **singing,** *s.* psalmodie, *f.*
Psalmist, *s.* psalmiste, *m.*; (*singer*) chantre, *m.*
Psalm-istic, -odic, -odist, -ody, -ograpy. *V.* page 3, § 1
Psalmodize, *v.n.* psalmodier
Psalter, *s.* psautier, *m.*
Psaltery, *s.* psaltérion, *m.*
Pseudo, *adj.* pseudo, faux
Pseudonym, *s.* pseudonyme, *m.*
Pseudonymous, *adj. s.* pseudonyme, *adj. m.f., s.m.* [sous un pseudonyme
Pseudonymously, *adv.* pseudonymement,
Pseudonymousness, *s.* caractère pseudonyme, *m.*, pseudonymie, *f.*, pseudonyme, *m.*
Pseudoscope, *s.* pseudoscope, *m.*
Pshaw, *int.* bah!
Psora, *s.* psora, *m.*, psore, *f.*
Psoriasis, *s.* psoriasis, *m.*
Psoric, *adj.* psorique
Psycholog-ic, al, -ically, -ist, -y. *V.* p. 3, § 1
Ptarmic, *adj. s.* ptarmique, *adj. m.f., s.m.*
Ptarmica, *s.* ptarmique, *f.*
Ptarmigan, *s.* ptarmigan, *m.*
Ptisan, *s.* tisane, *f.*
P.T.O., (*abbrev. of 'Please turn over'*) T. S.V.P. [(Tournez s'il vous plaît)
Ptolemaic, *adj.* ptoléméen, de Ptolémée
Ptyalism, *s.* ptyalisme, *m.*
Puberty, *s.* puberté, *f.*
Pubescence, *s.* (*pers.*) âge de puberté, *m.*; [(*bot.*) pubescence, *f.*
Pubescent, *adj.* (*pers.*) pubère; (*bot.*) pubescent
Pubic, *adj.* pubien. — *artery,* artère obturatrice, *f.* — *bone,* os pubis, *m.*
Pubis, *s.* pubis, *m.* *Os —,* os pubis, *m.*
Public, *adj. s.* public, *adj. m.*, publique, *f.*, public, *s.m.* — **accounts,** *s.pl.* budget, *m.* — **bill,** *s.* (*Engl. parliam.*) bill d'intérêt public, *m.* — **house,** *s.* cabaret, *m.*; auberge, *f.*; estaminet, *m.* — **line,** *s.* commerce de cabaretier,

m. — **school,** *s. V.* **School.** — **servant,** *s.* serviteur de l'État, *m.* — **speaking,** *s.* discours en public, *m.*; art oratoire, *m.* — **spirit,** *s.* esprit public, *m.* — **spirited,** *adj.* animé de l'amour du bien public. — **spiritedness,** *s.* amour du bien public, *m.*
Publican, *s.* cabaretier, *m.*; aubergiste, *m.*; (*hist.*) publicain, *m.*
Publication, *s.* publication, *f.*
Publicist, *s.* publiciste, *m.*
Publicity, *s.* publicité, *f.*
Publicly, *adv.* publiquement; en public
Publicness, *s.* publicité, *f.*
Publish, *v.a.* publier. —*ed by,* publié par; (*on books*) librairie de, chez. *Just —ed! V.* **Just**
Publisher, *s.* publieur, *m*, publicateur, *m.*, -trice, *f.*; (*of books,* &c.) éditeur, *m.*; (*bookseller and* —) libraire-éditeur, *m.*
Publishing, *s.* publication, *f.* — **trade, -warehouse,** *s.* librairie, *f.*
Puce, *adj. s.* puce, *adj. m.f., s.m.* — **colour,** *s.* puce, *m.* — **coloured,** *adj.* puce
Puceron, *s.* puceron, *m.*
Puck, *s.* lutin, esprit follet, *m.*
Pucker, *v.a.* rider; (*clothes,* &c.) plisser, froncer; faire goder; — *v.n.* grimacer, goder; — *s.* ride, *f.*; (*of clothes,* &c.) fronce, *f.*, (*collection of ditto*) froncis, *m*; (*crease*) mauvais pli, *m.*, poche, *f.*, godet, *m.*, godure, *f.*
Puckering, *s.* froncement, froncis, *m.*; (*creases*) mauvais plis, *m.pl.*
Puddening, *s.* (*nav.*) boudinure, *f.*, bourrelet, *m.*
Pudding, *s.* pudding, *m.*; (*of rice, sago, semolina,* &c.) gâteau, *m.*; (*sausage*) boudin, *m.*; saucisse, *f. Black* —, boudin, *m.* — **sleeve,** *s.* grande manche, *f.* — **stone,** *s.* poudingue, *m.*
Puddle, *s.* mare, flaque d'eau, *f.*; gâchis, *m.*; (*mortar*) corroi, *m.*; — *v.a.* troubler, rendre trouble; remplir de boue; (*mortar*) corroyer; (*metal*) puddler
Puddler, *s.* (*metal.*) puddleur, *m.*
Puddling, *s.* corroyage, *m.*; (*metal.*) puddlage, *m.*
Puddly, *adj.* bourbeux, trouble
Pudenda, *s. pl.* parties honteuses, parties naturelles, parties, *f.pl.*
Pudgy, *adj. V.* **Squabby**
Pudicity, *s.* pudicité, *f.*
Puerile, *adj.* puéril
Puerilely, *adv.* puérilement
Puerility, *s.* puérilité, *f.*
Puerperal, *adj.* puerpéral
Puff, *s.* (*of wind*) bouffée, *f.*; (*from the mouth*) souffle, *m.*; (*of smoke, of air*) bouffée, *f.*; (*for hair*) houppe (à poudrer), *f.*; (*of a dress*) bouillon, *m.*; (*of a sleeve*) bouffant, *m.*; (*vain boast*) pouf, *m.*; réclame, *f.*; (*pastry*) soufflé, *m.*; (*bot.*) lycoperdon, *m.*, vesse-de-loup, *f.*; (*of steam*) échappement de la vapeur, *m.*; — *v.a.n.* (*blow*) souffler; (*pant*) haleter; (*smoke*) fumer; lancer des bouffées (de tabac); (*swell out*) bouffer; (*swell*) bouffir, enfler, gonfler, boursouffler; (*boast*) faire mousser; faire de la réclame; faire l'article; pouffer; (*boast oneself*) se faire mousser; (*at an auction*) allumer, pousser, biller. *To — and blow, V.* **Huff** (— *and puff*). — **adder,** *s.* vipère clotho, *f.* — **ball,** *s.* lycoperdon, *m.*, vesse-de-loup, *f. Giant — ball,* lycoperdon géant, bovista, boviste, *m.* — **bird,** *s.* tamatia, *m.* — **paste,** *s.* pâte feuilletée, *f.*, feuilleté, feuilletage, *m.* — **pie,** *s.* vol-au-vent, *m.* — **up,** *v.a.* enfler, bouffir. *To be —ed up with,* être bouffi *or* gonflé de [(*of dress*) bouffant
Puffed, *part. adj.* soufflé, &c. (*V.* **Puff,** *v.a.n.*);
Puffer, *s.* personne qui souffle, *f.*; (*boaster*) pouffiste, *m.f.*, faiseur (*m.*, -euse, *f.*) de réclames; charlatan, *m.*; (*at auctions*) allumeur, *m.*
Puffery, *s.* poufferie, *f.*, pouf, *m.*; réclame, *f.*; charlatanerie, *f.*, charlatanisme, *m.*
Puffin, *s.* macareux, mormon, *m.* — **petrel,** *s.* puffin, *m.* [(*surg.*) empâtement, *m.*
Puffiness, *s.* enflure, *f.*; boursoufflure, *f.*;
Puffing, *s.* pouf, *m.*; — *adj.* pouffiste; qui sait faire l'article. — *advertisement,* réclame, *f.*
Puffingly, *adv.* haletant; (*swelling*) avec enflure; (*boasting*) par des poufs, par le pouf, par le charlatanisme [boursoufflé
Puffy, *adj.* enflé, gonflé, bouffi; (*of style*)
Pug, *s.* (*dog*) carlin, doguin, *m.*; bichon, *m.*, -ne, *f.*; (*monkey*) singe, *m.*; Jacquot, Fagotin, *m.*; — *v.a.* broyer. — **dog,** *s. V.* **Pug.** — **faced,** *adj.* chafouin. — **mill,** *s.* broyeur, *m.* — **nose,** *s.* nez épaté, nez camus, *m.* —
Pugh, *int.* fi! pouah! [**nosed,** *adj.* camus
Pugilism, *s.* pugilat, *m.*
Pugilist, *s.* pugiliste, boxeur, *m.*
Pugilistic, *adj.* pugilistique, de pugilat
Pugnacious, *adj.* querelleur, batailleur, guerroyant [faisant mine de se battre
Pugnaciously, *adv.* d'un air batailleur, en
Pugnaciousness, Pugnacity, *s.* humeur querelleuse *or* batailleuse *or* guerroyante, pugnacité, *f.*
Puisne, *adj.* inférieur, subalterne. — *judge* or *justice,* (*law*) conseiller, *m.*; assesseur, *m.*
Puissance, *s.* puissance, force, *f.*
Puissant, *adj.* puissant
Puke, *v.n.* vomir; — *s.* vomissement, *m.*; vomitif, émétique, *m.*
Pule, *v.n.* piauler, piailler; (*weep*) pleurnicher; (*whine*) gémir, geindre
Puling, *s.* cri, *m.*; (*whining*) gémissement, *m.*
Pulingly, *adv.* en piaulant; en pleurnichant; en gémissant
Pull, *v.a.n.* tirer; (*tear*) arracher; déchirer; (*gather*) cueillir, récolter; (*the trigger*) presser (la détente); (*ring a bell*) sonner; agiter; (*nav.*) ramer, nager; voguer; — *s.* secousse, *f.*; coup, *m.*; effort, *m.*; assaut, *m.*; action de tirer, *f.*; (*help*) coup de main, *m.*; (*of the collar, and fig.*) coup de collier, *m.*; (*work*) besogne, tâche, *f.*; (*struggle*) lutte, *f.*; (*at an oar*) coup de rame, *m.*; (*print.*) impression, *f.*; (*expense*) dépense, charge, *f.*; (*burden*) charge ('*upon,*' pour); (*advantage*) avantage, *m.*; (*bell-rope*) cordon, *m.* — **asunder,** *v.a.* déchirer en deux. — **away,** *v.a.* arracher. — **back,** *v.a.* tirer en arrière; reculer, faire reculer; (*stop*) arrêter; *s. V.* **Drawback.** — **down,** *v.a.* faire descendre; (*to lower*) baisser; (*sink*) enfoncer; (*demolish*) démolir, abattre, renverser; (*weaken*) abattre; (*humble*) rabattre, abaisser. — **in,** *v.a.* tirer dedans, tirer, faire entrer; (*horses*) retenir; (*to shelter*) serrer, rentrer. — **off,** *v.a.* arracher; (*boots,* &c.) tirer; ôter; (*print.*) tirer. — **on,** *v.a.* (*boots,* &c.) mettre. — **open,** *v.a.* ouvrir. — **out,** *v.a.* tirer dehors, tirer, arracher, enlever, ôter; faire sortir, sortir; (*hair, teeth*) arracher. — **through,** *v.n.* réussir. — **together,** *v.n.* s'accorder, s'entendre. — **up,** *v.a.* lever; (*nav.*) hisser; (*root out, pluck*) déraciner, arracher; extirper; (*stimulate*) stimuler; remonter; (*scold*) saucer, sabouler; (*bring before a court*) traduire, citer; accuser; *v.a.n.* (*stop, arrest*) arrêter [meur, *m.*
Puller, *s.* tireur, arracheur, *m.*; (*in a boat*) ra-
Pullet, *s.* poulette, *f. Fat* —, poularde, *f.*
Pulley, *s.* poulie, *f.* — **maker,** *s.* poulieur, *m.*
Pulmonary, *adj. s.* pulmonaire, *adj. m.f.*, (*bot.*) *s.f.*, (*zool.*) *s.m.*
Pulmonic, *adj. s.* pulmonique
Pulp, *s.* pulpe, *f.*; (*of bones*) moelle, *f.*; (*of paper*) pâte, *f.*; — *v.a.* pulper, réduire en pâte; (*deprive of its integument*) décortiquer
Pulper, *s.* (*machine*) décortiqueur, *m.*, décortiqueuse, *f.*
Pulpiness, *s.* nature pulpeuse, nature molle, *f.*
Pulpit, *s.* (*for ecclesiastics*) chaire, *f.*; (*for orators*) tribune, *f.*; (*of auctioneers*) tribune aux enchères, *f.*, bureau, *m.* — **cloth,** *s.* tapis de chaire, *m.* — **eloquence, -oratory,** *s.* éloquence de la chaire, *f.*
Pulpous, Pulpy, *adj.* pulpeux; mou

Pulpousness. *V.* **Pulpiness**
Pulsate, *v.n.* battre
Pulsatile, *adj.* de percussion; (*med.*) pulsatile
Pulsation, *s.* pulsation, *f.*
Pulsative, Pulsatory, *adj.* pulsatif, pulsateur
Pulse, *s.* pouls, *m.*; (*phys.*) pulsation, *f.*; (*bot.*) plante légumineuse, *f.*; légume, *m.*; — *v.n.* battre. *To feel anyone's* —, tâter le pouls à quelqu'un; (*fig.*) sonder quelqu'un. —**less,** *adj.* sans pouls
Pulverizable, *adj.* pulvérisable
Pulverization, *s.* pulvérisation, *f.*
Pulverize, *v.a.* pulvériser [*m.*, -trice, *f.*
Pulverizer, *s.* pulvériseur, *m.*, pulvérisateur,
Pulverulence, *s.* pulvérulence, *f.*
Pulverulent, *adj.* pulvérulent; (*of animals*)
Puma, *s.* puma, *m.* [pulvérateur
Pumice, *s.* ponce, *f.*; — *v.a.* poncer — **stone,** *s.* pierre ponce, *f.*
Pumiceous, *adj.* ponceux
Pumiciform, *adj.* pumiciforme
Pumicing, *s.* ponçage, *m.*
Pummel. *V.* **Pommel**
Pump, *s.* pompe, *f.*; (*shoe*) escarpin, *m.*; — *adj.* de pompe; — *v.a.n.* pomper; (*question*) sonder, tirer les vers du nez à; (*things*) tirer; (*med.*) doucher. *Forcing* or *force* —, pompe foulante. — *ship!* (*nav.*) à la pompe! — **business,** *s.* pomperie, *f.* — **gauge,** *s.* sonde de pompe, *f.* — **hose,** *s.* manche de pompe, *f.* — **maker,** *s.* pompier, *m.* — **making,** *s.* pomperie, *f.* — **room,** *s.* buvette, *f.* — **trade,** *s.* pomperie, *f.* — **water,** *s.* eau de pompe, *f.* — **well,** *s.* (*nav.*) archipompe, *f.*
Pumper, *s.* personne qui pompe, *f.*, pompier, *m.*
Pumpernickel, *s.* pain de seigle, pain noir, *m.*
Pumping, *s.* pompement, *m.*; (*in mines*) épuisement, *m.* — **engine,** *s.* machine d'épuisement, *f.* [*m.*, citrouille, *f.*
Pumpkin, Pumpion, *s.* courge, *f.*, potiron,
Pun, *s.* calembour, jeu de mots, *m.*; — *v.n.* faire des calembours, jouer sur les mots; jouer (sur)
Punch, *s.* (*tool*) emporte-pièce, *m.*; poinçon, *m.*; (*dentist's*) repoussoir, *m.*; (*blow*) coup de poing, *m.*; (*drink*) punch, *m.*; (*horse*) cheval ramassé, *m.*; (*pers.*) personne trapue, *f.*, courtaud, *m.*, e, *f.*; (*in shows*) polichinelle, *m.*; (*newspaper*) Punch, *m.*, (*in France*) le Charivari, *m.*; — *v.a.* percer; découper; poinçonner; (*strike*) gourmer, donner un coup (*or* des coups) de poing à; (*anyone's eye*) pocher. — *and Judy*, —*'s show*, le théâtre de Guignol, *m.* — **out,** *v.a.* enlever par l'emporte-pièce; repousser
Puncheon, *s.* poinçon, *m.*; (*measure*) pièce (anglaise), *f.* [(*tool*) *V.* **Punch**
Puncher, *s.* (*pers.*) poinçonneur, *m.*, -euse, *f.*;
Punchinello, *s.* polichinelle, *m.*
Punching-machine, *s.* machine à poinçonner, poinçonneuse, *f.*
Punchy, *adj.* trapu, ramassé
Punctilio, *s.* détail minutieux, *m.*, pointillerie, vétille, *f.*; formalité, cérémonie, étiquette, *f.* *To stand upon* —*s*, être méticuleusement cérémonieux; mettre les points sur les i; s'amuser à des vétilles
Punctilious, *adj.* pointilleux; minutieux; exact; cérémonieux; tenant à l'étiquette
Punctiliously, *adv.* minutieusement
Punctiliousness, *s.* exactitude scrupuleuse, *f.*; attention minutieuse, *f.*; soins minutieux,
Punction, *s.* ponction, *f.* [*m.pl.*
Punctual, *adj.* ponctuel, exact
Punctuality, Punctualness, *s.* ponctualité, exactitude, *f.*
Punctually, *adv.* ponctuellement, exactement
Punctuate, *v.a.* ponctuer
Punctuation, *s.* ponctuation, *f.*
Puncture, *s.* piqûre, *f.*; (*surg.*) ponction, *f.*; — *v.a.* piquer; (*surg.*) ponctionner
Punctured, *part. adj.* piqué; (*surg.*) ponctionné. — *wound*, plaie par instrument
Pundit, *s.* pandit, *m.* [piquant, piqûre, *f.*
Pungency, *s.* nature piquante, *f.*; âcreté, acrimonie, *f.*; (*of sarcasm*, &c.) piquant, mordant, *m.* [(*of grief*, &c.) poignant, cuisant
Pungent, *adj.* piquant; âcre, acrimonieux;
Pungently, *adv.* d'une manière piquante, piquamment; vivement
Punic, *adj.* punique [tiveté, *f.*
Puniness, *s.* petitesse, nature chétive, ché-
Punish, *v.a.* ('*for*,' de) punir, châtier; corriger; (*injure*) maltraiter
Punishable, *adj.* punissable; passible ('*by*,' de)
Punishableness, *s.* nature punissable, *f.*
Punisher, *s.* personne qui punit *or* qui châtie, *f.*, punisseur, châtieur, correcteur, *m.*, -trice, *f.*
Punishment, *s.* punition, *f.*; châtiment, *m.*; peine, *f.*; (*capital*) supplice, *m.* — *of death*, *capital* —, peine de mort, peine capitale, *f.*
Punk, *s.* agaric, amadou, *m.*; (*pers.*) prostituée, catin, *f.* [pantène, pantenne, *f.*
Punnet, *s.* panier rond, panier, maniveau, *m.*;
Punning, *s.* calembours, jeux de mots, *m.pl.*; — *adj.* calembourique
Punster, *s.* calembouriste, *m.f.*
Punt, *s.* (*boat*) bateau plat, bachot, ras de carène, *m.*; (*hollow part under a bottle*) cul, *m.*; — *v.n.* conduire un bachot; (*at play*) ponter. — **gun,** *s.* canardière, *f.*
Punter, Punto, *s.* (*at play*) ponte, *m.*
Puny, *adj.* petit, chétif, faible
Pup, *s.* petit (*or* jeune) chien, *m.*, petite (*or* jeune) chienne, *f.* (—**s,** *pl.* petits, *m.pl.*); (*pers.*) roquet, freluquet, fat, *m.*; drôle, *m.*; — *v.n.* mettre bas, chienner. *With* —, (*of bitches*)
Pupa, Pupe, *s.* chrysalide, *f.* [pleine
Pupil, *s.* (*of the eye*) pupille, prunelle, *f.*; (*scholar*) élève, *m.f.*; (*a ward*) pupille, *m.f.* — **teacher,** *s.* élève-maître, *m.*, élève-maîtresse, *f.*
Pupilage, *s.* éducation, *f.*; (*nonage*) pupillarité, minorité, *f.* [norité, *f.*
Pupilarity, Pupillarity, *s.* pupillarité, mi-
Pupilary, Pupillary, *adj.* pupillaire
Puppet, *s.* marionnette, *f.*; poupée, *f.* — **man, -master, -player,** *s.* joueur de marionnettes, *m.*; (*fig.*) personne qui tire la ficelle, *f.* — **show,** *s.* spectacle de marionnettes, *m.*, marionnettes, *f.pl.*
Puppy, *s.* & *v.n.* *V.* **Pup**
Puppyism, *s.* fatuité, impertinence, *f.*
Pur, *v.n.* faire ronron, ronronner, filer, faire le rouet; — *s.* ronron, *m.* [presque aveugle
Purblind, *adj.* myope; qui ne voit pas clair,
Purblindness, *s.* myopie, vue basse, *f.*
Purchasable, *adj.* achetable, qu'on peut acheter, qui peut s'acheter
Purchase, *v.a.* acheter ('*of*,' à); (*estates*, &c.) acquérir. — **for** (*a price*), acheter
Purchase, *s.* achat, *m.*; acquisition, emplette, *f.*; (*mech.*, *power*) force mécanique, *f.*; abattage, *m.*; (*hold*) prise, *f.*; (*mil.*) achat des grades militaires, *m.* *To make* —*s*, (*shopping*) faire des emplettes. — **deed,** *s.* contrat d'acquisition, *m.* — **money,** *s.* prix d'achat, *m.* — **system,** *s.* achat des grades militaires, *m.*
Purchaser, *s.* acheteur, *m.*, -euse, *f.*; chaland, *m.*, e, *f.*; (*of estates*, &c.) acquéreur, *m.*,
Pure, *adj.* pur [-euse, *f.*
Purée, *s.* purée, *f.*
Purely, *adv.* purement
Pureness, *s.* pureté, *f.*
Purgation, *s.* purgation, *f.* [gatif, *s.m.*
Purgative, *adj.* *s.* purgatif, *adj.m.*, -ive, *f.*, pur-
Purgatorial, *adj.* du purgatoire
Purgatory, *s.* purgatoire, *m.*; — *adj.* purificateur, purificatif; expiatoire
Purge, *v.a.* purger; (*cleanse*) nettoyer; purifier; (*liquids*) clarifier; (*law*) purger; — *v.n.* se purger; — *s.* purgation, *f.* [(*V.* **Purge,** *v.a.*), *f.*
Purger, *s.* personne *or* chose qui purge *or* &c.
Purging, *s.* purgation, *f.*; (*diarrhœa*) diarrhée, *f.*
Purification, *s.* purification, *f.*; épuration, *f.*

Purificative, *adj.* purificatif, qui purifie
Purificator. *V.* **Purifier** [ficatif, qui purifie
Purificatory, *s.* purificatoire, *m.*; — *adj.* puri-
Purifier, *s.* (*pers.*) purificateur, *m.*, -trice, *f.*; épurateur, *m.*, -trice, *f.*; (*thing*) chose qui purifie, *f.*; appareil pour purifier *or* pour l'épuration, *m.*; filtre, *m.*; (*med.*) dépuratif, *m.*
Purify, *v.a.* purifier; épurer; — *v.n.* se purifier;
Purim, *s.* purim, *m.* [s'épurer
Pur-ism, -ist. *V.* page 3, § 1
Puritan, *s. adj.* puritain, *m.*, e, *f.*
Puritanic, -al, *adj.* puritain, de puritain
Puritanically, *adv.* en puritain
Puritanism, *s.* puritanisme, *m.*
Purity, *s.* pureté, *f.*
Purl, *s.* bordure en broderie, *f.*; (*of lace*) engrêlure, *f.*; (*noise*) murmure, gazouillement, *m.*; (*a drink*) mélange de bière, de genièvre, de sucre et de gingembre, *m.*; — *v.a.* orner de broderie; (*lace*) engrêler; — *v.n.* murmurer, gazouiller. *V. Supplt.* [voisinage, *m.*; limites, *f.pl.*
Purlieu, *s.* alentours, environs, confins, *m.pl.*,
Purlin, *s.* panne, ventrière, *f.*
Purling, *adj.* murmurant, qui murmure; — *s.* murmure, gazouillement, *m.*
Purloin, &c. *V.* **Pilfer,** &c.
Purple, *s.* pourpre, (*colouring matter, textile fabric, dignity*) *f.*, (*colour*) *m.*; —**s,** *pl.* (*med.*) pourpre, *m.*; (*agr.*) *V.* **Ear-cockles**; — *adj.* de pourpre, pourpre, pourpré; (*med.*) pourpré; — *v.a.* teindre en pourpre; (*fig.*) empourprer; rougir. *Tyrian* —, pourpre de Tyr, *f.* — *of Cassius,* pourpre de Cassius, *m.* — **bronze,** *s.* purpurine, *f.* — **emperor,** *s.* (*butterfly*) grand Mars, *m.* — **fish,** *s.* pourpre, *m.* — **heart, -wood,** *s.* bois violet, bois d'amarante, *m.*
Purplish, *adj.* purpurin
Purport, *s.* but, objet, *m.*; (*sense*) sens, contenu, *m.*, teneur, *f.*; (*import*) portée, valeur, force, *f.*; — *v.a.n.* signifier, vouloir dire, donner à entendre; montrer (par le sens), faire voir, indiquer; tendre à montrer; sembler, être censé; prétendre, avoir la prétention (de); tendre (à), avoir pour but (de)
Purpose, *s.* but, *m.*; fin, *f.*; intention, vue, *f.*, projet, dessein, *m.*; effet, *m.*; utilité, *f.*; usage, *m.*; intérêt, *m.*; (*want*) besoin, *m.*; — *v.a.* se proposer (de), avoir dessein (de); se décider (à). *For the — of,* dans le but de. *On* or *of* —, exprès, à dessein; (*for*) exprès (pour). *On* or *of set* —, de propos délibéré. *To good* —, avantageusement, utilement; avec fruit; fort bien. *To little* —, *to no* —, en vain, inutilement, en pure perte. *To some* —, utile; utilement; bien. *To the* —, à propos; dans un but utile (*Much to the* —, fort à propos). *To what* —? à quoi bon? à quoi sert? *It is nothing to the* —, cela ne signifie rien, cela ne fait rien à l'affaire. *To answer a* —, *V.* **Answer.** —**less,** *adj.* sans but, sans intention
Purposed, *adj.* proposé, projeté
Purposely, *adv.* à dessein, exprès, de propos délibéré; (*for*) exprès (pour)
Purpura, *s.* (*med., zool.*) purpura, pourpre, *m.*
Purpure, *s.* pourpre, *m.*
Purpuric, *adj.* purpurique
Purpurine, *s.* (*chem.*) purpurine, *f.*
Purr, *v.n.* faire ronron, ronronner, filer, faire le rouet; — *s.* ronron, *m.*; (*bird*) *V.* **Purre**
Purre, *s.* (*bird*) brunette, *f.*, bécasseau variable, *m.*
Purring, *s.* (*of the cat*) ronron, *m.*; — *adj.* qui fait ronron, qui ronronne, qui file. — *tremor,* (*med.*) frémissement cataire, *m.*
Purse, *s.* (*bag*) bourse, *f.*; (*the new sort*) portemonnaie, *m.*; — *v.a.* embourser; (*fig.*) plisser, froncer. *Long* —, *heavy* —, *well lined* —, bourse bien garnie. — **bearer,** *s.* celui qui porte la bourse *or* qui tient les cordons de la bourse, *m.* — **maker,** *s.* boursier, *m.*, -ière, *f.* — **net,** *s.* filet en bourse, *m.*; (*fish.*) boursal, ableret, boulier, *m.*, manche, poche, pochette, *f.* — **pride,** *s.* orgueil des richesses, *m.* — **proud,** *adj.* fier de ses richesses *or* de son argent. — **string,** *s.* cordon de (*or* de la) bourse, *m.*
Purser, *s.* (*old nav.*) commissaire, *m.* [saire, *m.*
Pursership, *s.* (*old nav.*) emploi de commis-
Pursiness, *s.* enflure, bouffissure, boursouflure, *f.*; (*shortness of breath*) courte haleine, *f.*
Purslain, Purslane, *s.* pourpier, *m.*
Pursuable, *adj.* poursuivable
Pursuance, *s.* suite, conséquence, *f.* *In — of,* en conséquence de, par suite de, suivant, conformément à
Pursuant, *adj.* en conséquence (de), par suite (de); conforme (à); (*adverb.*) conformément (à)
Pursuantly, *adv.* conformément (à)
Pursue, *v.a.n.* poursuivre; suivre; (*seek*) chercher; (*persecute*) persécuter [vant, *m.*, e, *f.*
Pursuer, *s.* personne qui pursuit, *f.*, poursui-
Pursuit, *s.* poursuite, *f.*; recherche, *f.*; occupations, *f.pl.*, travaux, *m.pl.*, carrière, *f.* *In — of,* à la poursuite de; à la recherche de [*m.*
Pursuivant, *s.* (*-at-arms*) poursuivant (d'armes),
Pursy, *adj.* bouffi; (*short-breathed*) poussif
Purulenc-e, y, *s.* purulence, *f.*
Purulent, *adj.* purulent
Purvey, *v.a.* faire provision de; pourvoir; fournir; procurer; — *v.n.* faire ses provisions; se pourvoir; pourvoir (à)
Purveyance, *s.* approvisionnement, *m.*; provisions, *f.pl.*
Purveyor, *s.* pourvoyeur, *m.*, -euse, *f.*, fournisseur ('*to,*' de), *m.*
Purview, *s.* limites, *f.pl.*; (*law*) dispositif, texte, *m.*
Pus, *s.* pus, *m.*
Puseyism, *s.* puséisme, *m.*
Puseyite, *s.* puséiste, *m.f.*
Push, *v.a.n.* pousser; (*urge, hurry*) presser; (*make an effort*) faire un effort; — *s.* coup, *m.*; impulsion, *f.*; poussade, poussée, bousculade, *f.*; attaque, *f.*, assaut, *m.*; effort, *m.*; moment critique, *m.*, extrémité, conjoncture, *f.*; presse, *f.* *At* or *on a* —, dans un cas pressant; au moment critique. *At one* —, d'un seul coup. *To give a* —, pousser. *To have plenty of* —, (*pers.*) être fort entreprenant, aller de l'avant. *To be —ed for,* être pressé de. — **against,** pousser contre; heurter; bousculer. — **away,** — **back,** repousser. — **down,** faire tomber; renverser; faire descendre. — **forward,** avancer; faire avancer; pousser. — **in,** faire entrer. — **on,** pousser; activer; hâter; faire avancer; pousser en avant. — **open,** ouvrir, pousser. — **out,** chasser, mettre dehors. — **pin,** *s.* poussette, *f.* — **to,** fermer, pousser. — **up,** pousser; faire monter; lever; élever
Pusher, *s.* pousseur, *m.*, -euse, *f.*
Pushing, *adj.* entreprenant; hardi; vigoureux; — *s.* poussade, poussée, *f.*; impulsion, *f.*, effort, *m.*; caractère entreprenant, esprit d'entreprise, *m.*, hardiesse, *f.*, toupet, *m.*; vigueur, *f.*
Pushingly, *adv.* d'une manière entreprenante, hardiment; vigoureusement
Pusillanimity, *s.* pusillanimité, *f.*
Pusillanimous, *adj.* pusillanime
Pusillanimously, *adv.* pusillanimement
Puss, Pussy, *s.* (*cat*) minet, *m.*, -te, *f.*; mimi, *m.f.*; (*hare*) lièvre, *m.* — *in boots,* le chat botté, *m.* *To play at — in the corner,* jouer aux quatre coins
Pustular, Pustulous, *adj.* pustuleux
Pustulation, *s.* pustulation, *f.*
Pustule, *s.* pustule, *f.*
Put, *v.a.n.* mettre; (*to place*) placer; (*to lay*) poser; (*to apply, and various other senses*) appliquer; supposer; proposer; soumettre; donner; attribuer (à), imputer (à), mettre sur le compte (de); réduire (à); obliger, contraindre (à); engager (à); présenter; offrir; employer (à); (*ask*) demander; (*a question*) faire; poser; adresser; (*of plants*) pousser, germer; (*nav.*) se mettre; — *s.* extrémité, nécessité, *f.*; (*attempt*) tentative, *f.* *If I may — it so,* si je puis m'exprimer ainsi, pour ainsi dire. — **about,**

faire passer, faire circuler; (*distu. o*, &c.) gêner, déranger; embarrasser. — **again,** remettre; (*repeat*) répéter. — **aside,** mettre de côté; écarter. — **away,** ôter; (*place in safety*) garder, serrer; (*send away*) renvoyer; (*banish*) bannir. — **back,** remettre; reculer; retarder; (*nav.*) rentrer au port; retourner; revenir. — **by,** détourner; éloigner, écarter, évincer; ôter; (*save*) mettre de côté; garder; (*place in safety*) serrer; ranger. — **down,** poser *or* mettre par terre; déposer; poser; supprimer; réprimer; vaincre; humilier, rabattre; (*the blind*, &c.) baisser; (*to answer*) relancer; interloquer; remettre à sa place; réfuter; (*write down*) mettre par écrit, écrire, inscrire; (*to the account of*) mettre au compte (de); (*to consider, to style*) considérer (comme); qualifier (de), traiter (de); (*arith.*) poser. — **forth,** mettre en avant; avancer; sortir; proposer; publier; (*spread*) étendre; allonger; (*display*) déployer; (*leaves*, &c.) pousser. — **forward,** mettre en avant; avancer; proposer; pousser; (*hasten*) hâter, presser. *To — oneself forward*, se mettre en avant; se pousser, se produire. — **in,** mettre (dans, en, &c.); mettre dedans; insérer; introduire; placer; présenter; (*bail*) fournir; (*to harness*) atteler; (*com.*) passer, céder; (*nav.*) entrer au port; relâcher; (*for*) se présenter comme candidat, se mettre sur les rangs (pour); (*at play*) mettre au jeu. — — **into,** (*nav.*) entrer dans le port de. — **off,** ôter; quitter; (*postpone*) remettre; (*discard*) renvoyer; mettre de côté; (*pass*) faire passer; (*nav.*) prendre le large; *s.* retard, délai, *m.*, remise, lenteur, *f.*; excuse, *f.*, faux-fuyant, *m.*, échappatoire, défaite, lanternerie, blague, *f.* — **on,** mettre; prendre; se revêtir de; imposer (à); attribuer (à), imputer (à); (*add*) ajouter; (*a kettle*, or &c., *on the fire*) mettre sur le feu; (*dishes, on table*) servir; (*airs*, &c.) prendre; se donner; affecter; feindre; emprunter; (*a clock, a watch*) avancer; (*the break, rail.*) serrer; (*the screw, the steam*, &c.) *V.* **Screw, Steam,** &c.; *s.* duperie, *f.*; feinte, *f.*; colle, *f.*; excuse, défaite, *f.* — **out,** mettre dehors; (*of*) mettre hors (de); sortir; chasser; faire sortir; (*o.'s tongue*) tirer, montrer, faire voir; (*unharness*) dételer; (*a fire, light*) éteindre; (*eyes*) crever; (*blot out*) effacer; (*money*) placer; (*a book*) publier; (*disconcert*, &c.) déconcerter, embarrasser, troubler; embrouiller; dérouter, faire tromper; faire oublier; démonter; vexer, tracasser, chagriner; (*inconvenience*) déranger; (*as plants*) pousser; (*extend*) étendre, avancer; (*unfold*) déployer; (*to service, to nurse, to grass*) mettre. — **over,** mettre sur; mettre dessus; (*postpone*) remettre. — **to,** (*horses*) atteler; (*add*) ajouter, joindre; (*shut*) fermer; (*to death, to flight, to the test*, &c.) *V.* **Death, Flight, Test,** &c. — **to it,** embarrasser; mettre aux abois; obliger, contraindre; (*tease*) pousser à bout. — **together,** mettre ensemble; rassembler; réunir; (*of machines*) monter. — **under,** mettre *or* placer *or* &c. sous; soumettre à. — **up,** mettre; fixer; (*curtains, bells*) poser; (*raise*) lever; élever; (*put back*) remettre; (*pack up*) emballer, empaqueter, serrer; (*save*) mettre de côté; (*a prayer*, &c.) adresser, faire, offrir; (*a petition*) présenter, adresser; (*a motion*) proposer; (*an umbrella*) ouvrir; (*a sword*) remettre dans le fourreau; (*for sale*) mettre en vente; (*at auctions*) mettre aux enchères, mettre à prix, mettre; offrir; (*as candidate*) se présenter comme candidat, se mettre sur les rangs (pour); (*lodge*) loger, descendre. — **up to,** instruire, apprendre, mettre au fait *or* au courant de; (*incite*) pousser (à); (*nav.*) se mettre. — **up with,** supporter, souffrir, endurer; se soumettre à, se résigner à; s'accommoder de, s'arranger de, se contenter de. — **upon,** tromper; abuser de; exploiter; opprimer; maltraiter; (*incite*) pousser (à). — *oneself upon*, se mettre sur, &c.; en appeler à

Putative, *adj.* supposé, censé, réputé, prétendu; (*of fathers*) putatif

Putatively, *adv.* putativement, censément

Putlog, — hole, *s.* boulin, *m.*

Putrefaction, *s.* putréfaction, *f.*

Putrefactive, *adj.* putréfactif; putréfiant;

Putrefiable, *adj.* putrescible [de putréfaction

Putrefy, *v.a.* putréfier; — *v.n.* se putréfier

Putrescence, *s.* putrescence, *f.*

Putrescent, *adj.* putrescent

Putrescibility, *s.* putrescibilité, *f.*

Putrescible, *adj.* putrescible

Putrid, *adj.* putride; (*of water*) croupi

Putridity, Putridness, *s.* putridité, *f.*

Putter, *s.* metteur, *m.*, -euse, *f.* — **off,** *s.* temporisateur, *m.*, -trice, *f.*, temporiseur, lanternier, *m.* — **on,** *s.* instigateur, *m.*, -trice, *f.*

Putting, *s.* action de mettre *or* de placer *or* de poser, mise, pose, *f.* — **asunder,** *s.* écartement, *m.*, séparation, *f.* — **back,** *s.* reculement, *m.*; remise, *f.*; (*nav.*) retour, *m.* — **net,** *s.* (*fish.*) bouteux, *m.* — **off,** *s.* délai, *m.*, remise, *f.* — **up,** *s.* candidature, *f.*; (*mach.*) installation, *f.*

Putty, *s.* mastic, *m.*; (*of tin*) potée, *f.*; — *v.a.* mastiquer. — *of tin*, — *powder*, potée d'étain, *f.*

Puzzle, *v.a.* embarrasser, intriguer; (*fam.*) coller; (*the brain*) *V.* **Brain;** (*disconcert*) déconcerter, démonter; — *s.* embarras, *m.*, difficulté, *f.*; énigme, *f.*; (*play*) jeu de patience, casse-tête, *m.* *To be* (*much*) —*d how to* ..., être (fort) en peine de savoir comment ..., être (fort) embarrassé de ...

Puzzler, *s.* *V.* **Poser**

Pyæmia, *s.* pyohémie, *f.* [très petit

Pygmean, *adj.* pygméen, de pygmée, de nain,

Pygmy, *s.* pygmée, *m.*; — *adj.* *V.* **Pygmean**

Pyloric, *adj.* pylorique

Pylorus, *s.* pylore, *m.*

Pyohæmia, *s.* pyohémie, *f.*

Pyracanth, *s.* pyracanthe, *f.*, buisson ardent, *m.*

Pyramid, *s.* pyramide, *f.*

Pyramidal, Pyramidical, *adj.* pyramidal

Pyramidally, Pyramidically, *adv.* pyramidalement, en pyramide

Pyre, *s.* bûcher, *m.* [midalement, en pyramide

Pyrenean, *adj.* pyrénéen, des Pyrénées. — *Mountains*, *s.pl.* Monts Pyrénées, *m.pl.*, Pyrénées, *f.pl.*

Pyretic, *adj.* pyrétique [nées, *f.pl.*

Pyriform, *adj.* piriforme, pyriforme

Pyrite, Pyrites, *s.* pyrite, *f.*

Pyroligneous, *adj.* pyroligneux

Pyrolignite, *s.* pyrolignite, *m.*

Pyrometer, *s.* pyromètre, *m.*

Pyrope, *s.* pyrope, *m.*

Pyrophorus, *s.* pyrophore, *m.*

Pyrosis, *s.* pyrose, *f.*, pyrosis, *m.*

Pyrotechnic, -al, *adj.* pyrotechnique; **—s,** *s.pl.* pyrotechnie, *f.*

Pyrotechnist, *s.* pyrotechniste, artificier, *m.*

Pyrotechny, *s.* pyrotechnie, *f.*

Pyrotic, *adj.* pyrotique

Pyroxylic, *adj.* pyroxylique

Pyrrhic, *adj.* pyrrhique; — *s.* pyrrhique, (*vers.*) *m.*, (*dance*) *f.*

Pyrrhonic, *adj.* pyrrhonien

Pyrrhonism, *s.* pyrrhonisme, *m.*

Pyrrhonist, *s.* pyrrhonien, *m.*, -ne, *f.*

Pythagorean, *adj. s.*, **Pythagoric, -al,** *adj.* pythagoricien, *m.*, -ne, *adj. s. m.f.*, pythagorique, *adj. m.f.* — *diet*, régime (*m.*) *or* diète (*f.*) pythagorique

Pythagor-ism, -ist. *V.* page 3, § 1

Pythian, *adj.* pythien, pythique

Python, *s.* python, *m.*

Pythoness, *s.* pythonisse, *f.*

Pyx, *s.* (*coin.*) boîte de monnaies à essayer, *f.*; (*Cath. rel.*) ciboire, saint ciboire, *m.* *Trial of the* —, essai des monnaies, *m.* — **cover,** *s.* (*Cath. rel.*) custode, *m.* — **jury,** *s.* jury pour l'essai des monnaies, *m.*

Q

Q, *s.* (*letter*) q, *m.*

Quack, *v.n.* crier comme le canard, nasiller; (*in music*) canarder, faire un canard (*or* des canards), faire un couac (*or* des couacs); (*to boast*) se vanter, faire le charlatan, faire de la charlatanerie; — *s.* (*noise of a duck,* &c.) couac, *m.*; (*false note*) canard, couac, *m.*; (*pers.*) charlatan, *m.*; empirique, *m.*; — *adj.* de charlatan; d'empirique; faux. — **doctor,** *s.* charlatan, marchand d'orviétan, *m.* — **medicine,** *s.* orviétan, *m.*, drogues de charlatan, *f.pl.*

Quackery, *s.* charlatanisme, *m.*, charlatanerie, *f.*; empirisme, *m.* [d'empirique; faux

Quackish, *adj.* de charlatan, charlatanesque;

Quadragenarian, *s. adj.* quadragénaire, *m.f.*

Quadragesima, *s.* Quadragésime, *f.*

Quadragesimal, *adj.* quadragésimal

Quadrangle, *s.* quadrangle, *m.*; carré, *m.*; place, cour, *f.*

Quadrangular, *adj.* quadrangulaire

Quadrangularly, *adv.* quadrangulairement

Quadrant, *s.* quart de cercle, *m.*

Quadrat, *s.* cadrat, *m.* *M* —, cadratin, *m.* *N* —, demi-cadratin, *m.*

Quadrate, *adj. s.* carré, *adj.m.*, e, *f.*, carré, *s.m.*

Quadratic, *adj.* quadratique

Quadratrix, *s.* quadratrice, *f.*

Quadrature, *s.* quadrature, *f.*

Quadrennial, Quadriennial, *adj.* quatriennal [tous les quatre ans

Quadrennially, Quadriennially, *adv.*

Quadrilateral, *adj.* quadrilatère, quadrilatéral; — *s.* quadrilatère, *m.*

Quadrille, *s.* quadrille, *m.* [quadrisyllabique

Quadrisyllabic, -al, *adj.* quadrisyllabe,

Quadrisyllable, *s.* quadrisyllabe, *m.*

Quadroon, *s.* quarteron, *m.*, -ne, *f.* [mane, *m.*

Quadruman, Quadrumane, *s.* quadru-

Quadrumanous, *adj.* quadrumane

Quadruped, *s. adj.* quadrupède, *adj. m.f.*, *s.m.*

Quadruple, *adj. s.* quadruple, *adj. m.f.*, *s.m.*; — *v.a.n.* quadrupler [quadrupler

Quadruplicate, *adj.* quadruplé; — *v.a.*

Quadruplication, *s.* quadruplication, *f.*

Quadruply, *adv.* quadruplement

Quære, Quæstor, &c. *V.* **Query, Questor,** &c.

Quaff, *v.a.n.* boire à grands coups *or* à longs traits, lamper. — **off,** sabler, avaler, flûter

Quaffer, *s.* buveur, grand buveur, *m.*

Quag, *s.* fondrière, *f.*

Quagga, *s.* couagga, *m.*

Quaggy, *adj.* marécageux

Quagmire, *s.* fondrière, *f.*

Quail, *s.* caille, *f.*; — *v.n.* perdre courage, faiblir; fléchir; trembler; reculer; se troubler. — **call, -pipe,** *s.* cailler, courcaillet, appeau, *m.* — **net,** *s.* cailler, *m.* [original

Quaint, *adj.* affecté, prétentieux; singulier,

Quaintly, *adv.* d'une manière affectée; d'une manière originale, bizarrement; adroitement

Quaintness, *s.* singularité, bizarrerie, originalité, *f.*

Quake, *v.n.* trembler; — *s.* tremblement, *m.* — **grass,** *s.* brize, amourette, *f.*

Quaker, *s.* trembleur, *m.*, -euse, *f.*; (*eccl.*) quaker, *m.* — **bird,** *s.* albatros brun, *m.*

Quakeress, *s.* quakeresse, *f.*

Quakerism, *s.* quakerisme, *m.* [quakers

Quakerly, Quakerish, *adj.* de quaker; des

Quaking-grass, *s.* brize, amourette, *f.*

Quakingly, *adv.* en tremblant

Qualifiable, *adj.* qualifiable

Qualification, *s.* qualité, *f.*; qualité requise, *f.*; talent, *m.*; capacité, *f.*; titre, *m.*; préparation, *f.*; modification, restriction, *f.*; réserve, *f.*; (*designation*) qualification, désignation, *f.*; (*electoral*) cens, *m.*; (*in horse-racing*) qualification, *f.*

Qualificative, *adj. s.* qualificatif, *adj. m.*, -ive, *f.*, qualificatif, *s.m.*

Qualificator, *s.* qualificateur, *m.*

Qualified, *part. adj.* capable (de), propre (à), apte (à), en état (de), qui a les qualités requises (pour); préparé (à); fait (pour); autorisé; admissible; modifié, restreint; tempéré; conditionnel; (*of electors*) censitaire; (*law*) apte (à), qui a qualité (pour); (*designated, and in horse-racing*) qualifié

Qualify, *v.a.* rendre capable (de) *or* propre (à), mettre en état (de); préparer (à); autoriser (à); modifier, restreindre; tempérer, modérer, calmer; (*as*) qualifier (de); (*law*) donner le droit (de); (*in horse-racing*) qualifier; — *v.n.* [se préparer (à)

Qualifying, *adj.* qualificatif

Qualitative, *adj.* qualitatif

Quality, *s.* qualité, *f.*

Qualm, *s.* nausée, envie de vomir, *f.*, mal de cœur, soulèvement de cœur, *m.*; (*of conscience*) scrupule, *m.*; remords, *m.*

Qualmish, *adj.* qui a des nausées, qui a envie de vomir, qui a mal au cœur

Qualmishness, *s.* nausée, envie de vomir, *f.*, soulèvement de cœur, *m.*

Quamash, *s.* camassie, *f.*

Quamoclit, *s.* quamoclit, *m.* [impasse, *f.*

Quandary, *s.* incertitude, *f.*; embarras, *m.*;

Quantitative, *adj.* quantitatif [quantité

Quantity, *s.* quantité, *f.* *In —ties,* en grande

Quantum, *s.* quantum, *m.*; quantité, *f.*, montant, total, *m.* — *sufficit,* — *suff.*, (*med.*) quantité suffisante [en quarantaine

Quarantine, *s.* quarantaine, *f.*; — *v.a.* mettre

Quarrel, *v.n.* se quereller; chercher querelle (à); se brouiller; (*find fault*) trouver à redire (à); réprimander, blâmer; — *s.* querelle, dispute, *f.*; brouille, *f.*; (*glazier's diamond*) diamant de vitrier, diamant de nature, diamant, *m.*; (*pane of glass, square tile,* or &c., *arrow*) carreau, *m.* *Groundless* or *trumpery* —, — *for nothing,* querelle d'Allemand. *To pick a — with, to want to — with,* chercher querelle à

Quarreller, *s.* querelleur, *m.*, -euse, *f.*

Quarrelling, *s.* querelle, dispute, *f.*; dé-

Quarrelsome, *adj.* querelleur [saccord, *m.*

Quarrelsomely, *adv.* en querellant

Quarrelsomeness, *s.* humeur querelleuse, *f.*

Quarrier, *s.* carrier, *m.*

Quarry, *s.* carrière, *f.*; (*hunt.*) curée, *f.*; (*prey*) proie, *f.*; (*pane, square, arrow*) carreau, *m.*; — *v.a.* extraire de la carrière, extraire, tirer. — **man,** *s.* carrier, *m.*

Quarrying, *s.* extraction (de la carrière), *f.* — **bed,** *s.* lit de carrière, *m.*

Quart, *s.* (*cards*) quatrième, *f.*; (*measure*) litre, *m.* — **bottle,** *s.* bouteille d'un litre, *f.*

Quartan, *adj.* quarte, (*f.*); — *s.* fièvre quarte, *f.* — *ague,* fièvre quarte, *f.*

Quartation, *s.* quartation, *f.*

Quarte, *s.* (*fenc.*) quarte, *f.*

Quarter, *s.* quart, *m.*; (*in weight*) quart de quintal, *m.* [*French equivalent,* 12·70 kilos]; (*in dry measure*) quart de tonne, *m.*; (*of a year*) trimestre, *m.*; (*side*) côté, *m.*; point, *m.*; partie, *f.*; (*place*) lieu, endroit, *m.*; (*of a town, of meat, shoes, moon, mil., her.*) quartier, *m.*; (*of a walnut*) quartier, *m.*, cuisse, *f.*; (*of an annuity,* &c.) quartier, *m.*; (*of rent*) terme, *m.*; (*nav.*) parage, *m.*; (*of a ship*) arrière, *m.*, hanche, *f.*; **—s,** *pl.* (*dwelling*) logement, *m.*, demeure, *f.*; (*premises*) local, *m.*; (*place*) lieu, endroit, *m.*; (*mil.*) quartiers, *m.pl.*; quartier, *m.*; — *v.a.* partager en quarts; diviser en quatre parties; (*tear in pieces*) écarteler; (*mil.*) loger, mettre; (*her.*) écarteler; — *v.n.* être en quartier, loger, être. *Four —s of the world,* quatre parties du monde. *From all —s,* de tous côtés, de toutes parts. — *of an hour,* quart d'heure, *m.* — *of* *a hundred*, quarteron, *m.* — *of a year*, trois mois, *m.pl.*, trimestre, *m.* —*'s rent*, terme, *m.* *Fore —s*, avant-main, train de devant, avant-train, *m.* *Head —s*, *V.* **Head.** *Hind —s*, arrière-main, train de derrière, arrière-train, *m.* *At free —s*, à discrétion. *In high —s*, en haut lieu. *In* or *to the proper* —, à qui de droit. *To come to close —s*, en venir aux prises *or* aux mains. *To crave* —, demander quartier, demander grâce. *To give* —, faire *or* donner quartier. *To give no* —, ne pas faire de quartier. *To — in barracks, to be —ed in barracks*, caserner. — **cask,** *s.* (*of French wine*) demi-pièce, feuillette, *f.* — **clock,** *s.* pendule (*or* horloge) sonnant les quarts, *f.* — **day,** *s.* terme, *m.* — **deck,** *s.* gaillard d'arrière, *m.* — **gallery,** *s.* (*nav.*) bouteilles, *f.pl.* — **master,** *s.* (*nav.*) quartier-maître, *m.*; (*cavalry*) maréchal des logis, *m.*; (*infantry*) fourrier, sergent-fourrier, *m.* —**master general,** *s.* chef d'état-major général, *m.* — **round,** *s.* quart de rond, *m.* — **sessions,** *s.pl.* assises trimestrielles, *f.pl.* — **staff,** *s.* bâton à deux bouts, *m.*

Quartering, *s.* division par quarts, *f.*; (*mil.*) logement, quartier, *m.*; (*punishment*) écartellement, *m.*; (*her.*) écartelure, *f.*, écartellement, *m.* — *in barracks* casernement, *m.*

Quarterly, *adj.* trimestriel; (*by the quarter*) au trimestre; — *s.* trimestriel, *m.*; — *adv.* par trimestre, trimestriellement, tous les trimestres, tous les trois mois

Quartern, *s.* (*of flour*) kilo et demi, *m.*; (*gill*) canon, *m.* (*pop.*). — **loaf,** *s.* pain de deux kilogrammes, pain de quatre livres, *m.*

Quartet, Quartette, Quartetto, quatuor, quartette, *m.*

Quartile, *adj.s.* quartil, *adj.m.*, e, *f.*, quartil, *s.m.*

Quarto, *s. adj.* in-quarto, *s.m.*, *adj.m.f.*

Quartz, *s.* quartz, *m.*; roche, *f.* — **rock,** *s.* quartz en roche, *m.*, quartzite, *f.*

Quartziferous, *adj.* quartzifère

Quartzite, *s.* quartzite, *f.*

Quartzose, Quartzous, Quartzy, *adj.* [quartzeux

Quash, *v.a.* briser, écraser; (*subdue*) subjuguer, dompter, vaincre; (*repress*) étouffer, réprimer, apaiser; (*law*) casser, annuler, infirmer; — *s.* (*bot.*) *V.* **Pumpkin**

Quasi, *adv.* (*in compounds*) quasi

Quasimodo, *s.* Quasimodo, *f.* — *Sunday*, dimanche de la Quasimodo, *m.*

Quass, *s.* kwas, quass, *m.*

Quassia, *s.* (*bot.*) quassier, *m.*; (*pharm.*) quassia, *m.*

Quaternary, *adj.* quaternaire; — *s.* quaterne, *m.*

Quaternion, *s.* nombre (*m.*) *or* série (*f.*) de quatre, quaterne, *m.*

Quatrefoil, *s.* quatre-feuilles, *f.*

Quatrefoiled, *adj.* quadrilobé

Quatuor. *V.* **Quartet**

Quatrain, *s.* quatrain, *m.*

Quaver, *v.n.* faire trembler sa voix; trembler; (*mus.*) triller; — *s.* tremblement de voix, *m.*; (*mus.*) croche, *f.*; (*shake in music*) trille, *m.* — **rest,** *s.* demi-soupir, *m.*

Quavering, *s.* tremblement de voix, *m.*; (*mus.*) trille, *m.*; — *adj.* tremblant; vibrant. — *motion*, vibration, *f.*

Quay, *s.* quai, *m.*; — *v.a.* border de quais

Quayage, *s.* quayage, *m.*

Quean, *s.* coquine, gueuse, catin, *f.*

Queasiness, *s.* dégoût, *m.*, nausée, envie de vomir, *f.*

Queasy, *adj.* qui a mal au cœur, qui a des nausées, qui a envie de vomir; nauséabond, dégoûtant; trop délicat, trop difficile

Queen, *s.* reine, *f.*; (*at cards*) dame, *f.*; (*at chess*) reine, dame, *f.*; — *v.n.* (— *it*) faire la reine; trôner. — **apple,** *s.* reinette, *f.* — **bee,** *s.* reine *or* mère abeille, *f.* —**like, -ly,** *adj.* de reine, comme une reine. — **mother,** *s.* reine mère, *f.* —**'s scholar,** *s.* boursier, *m.*, -ière, *f.*

Queer, *adj.* étrange, bizarre, singulier, original; drôle; (*ill*) tout chose. — *customer*, (*fig.*) drôle de paroissien, *m.* —*fish*, (*fig.*) drôle de corps, *m.* *I feel rather* —, je me sens tout chose *or* tout je ne sais comment [casse

Queerish, *adj.* un peu drôle, assez drôle, cocasse

Queerly, *adv.* bizarrement, singulièrement; drôlement

Queerness, *s.* bizarrerie, singularité, *f.*

Quell, *v.a.* réprimer, étouffer; dompter; apaiser

Queller, *s.* personne qui réprime *or* qui étouffe, *f.*, dompteur, *m.*

Quench, *v.a.* éteindre; apaiser; amortir. *To — o.'s thirst*, étancher sa soif, se désaltérer

Quenchable, *adj.* extinguible; apaisable

Quencher, *s.* personne *or* chose qui éteint *or* &c. (*V.* **Quench**), *f.*

Quenchless, *adj.* inextinguible; inapaisable; implacable

Quercitron, *s.* quercitron, *m.*

Querist, *s.* interrogateur, *m.*, -trice, *f.*; questionneur, *m.*, -euse, *f.*

Querulous, *adj.* plaintif; maussade

Querulously, *adv.* plaintivement; maussadement

Querulousness, *s.* habitude de se plaindre, *f.*; maussaderie, *f.*

Query, *s.* question, demande, *f.*; point d'interrogation, *m.*; ? — *v.a.* questionner; demander; douter de; douter ('*that*,' que); mettre en doute *or* en question; marquer d'un point d'interrogation

Quest, *s.* *In — of*, à la recherche de; en quête de; pour chercher. *In — of him* (or *her*), *of them, of us* or &c., à sa, à leur, à notre *or* &c., recherche

Question, *s.* question, *f.*; demande, *f.*; interrogation, *f.*; (*in political assemblies*) interpellation, *f.*; (*torture*) question, torture, *f.*; (*doubt*) doute, *m.*; (*matter*) affaire, *f.*; (*dispute*) discussion, *f.*; (*math.*) question, *f.*, problème, *m.*; — *v.a.n.* questionner, interroger; mettre en doute *or* en question, douter de; se demander (si), douter (que); mettre un point d'interrogation à. *Begging the* —, *V.* **Begging.** *Beyond* —, *beyond all* —, *out of* —, *past* —, hors de doute. *Without* —, sans aucun doute, sans contredit. *To ask* (*a person*) *a* —, faire une question (à quelqu'un). *To beg the* —, supposer ce qui est en question, tourner dans un cercle vicieux, faire une pétition de principe. *To bring into* —, mettre en question. *To call in* —, mettre en question, mettre *or* révoquer en doute. *To make a — of*, douter de, révoquer en doute. *To put a* —, faire *or* poser *or* adresser une question; (*in political assemblies*) faire une interpellation. *To put to* —, mettre en question. *To put to the* —, mettre à la question *or* à la torture. *That is out of the* —, c'est une autre affaire; il ne faut pas y songer; c'est impossible; cela est hors de cause *or* hors de doute

Questionable, *adj.* contestable, douteux; suspect, équivoque

Questionableness, *s.* contestabilité, nature contestable, nature douteuse, *f.*; nature suspecte *or* équivoque, *f.*

Questionably, *adv.* contestablement

Questioner, *s.* questionneur, *m.*, -euse, *f.*, interrogateur, *m.*, -trice, *f.*

Questioning, *s.* questions, *f.pl.*; interrogation, *f.*

Questionist. *V.* **Questioner**

Questionless, *adj.* hors de doute, certain, incontestable

Questor, *s.* questeur, *m.*

Questorship, *s.* questure, *f.*

Quib, *s.* sarcasme, lardon, *m.*

Quibble, *s.* chicane de mots, argutie, *f.*; faux-fuyant, *m.*; (*pun*) jeu de mots, calembour, *m.*; — *v.n.* ergoter, jouer *or* chicaner sur les mots; (*to pun*) faire des calembours

Quibbler, *s.* ergoteur, *m.*, -euse, *f.*; calembouriste, *m.f.*

Quibbling, *s.* arguties, chicanes de mots, *f.pl.*; calembours, *m.pl.*

Quick, *adj.* vif; ardent; prompt, rapide; leste, agile, actif; diligent; pressé, précipité; pénétrant; intelligent; (*of the pulse, breathing*) fréquent; (*living*) vivant; vif; (*of pace or step*) rapide; (*of the ear*) *V.* **Ear;** — *adv.* vite, promptement, lestement; — *s.* vif, *m.*; (*thorn*) plante vive, *f.*; (*living men*) vivants, *m.pl.* — *or dead*, mort ou vif. *The — and the dead*, les vivants et les morts. — *pace* or *step* or *time* or *march*, (*mil.*) pas accéléré, pas de charge, *m.* *At a — pace* or *step*, d'un pas rapide; (*mil.*) au pas accéléré, au pas de charge. *To the —*, au vif; dans le vif. *To be —*, (*go fast*) aller vite; (*make haste*) se dépêcher [*Be —!* dépêchez-vous!] — **born,** *adj.* né vivant. — **eared,** *adj. V.* **Eared.** — **flesh,** *s.* chair vive, *f.* — **grass,** *s.* agrostide, *f.* — **hatch,** *s.* glouton, *m.* — **lime,** *s.* chaux vive, *f.* — **match,** *s. V.* **Match.** —**sand,** *s.* sable mouvant, *m.* —**set,** *s.* plante vive, *f.* —**set hedge,** *s.* haie vive, *f.* — **sighted,** *adj.* aux yeux perçants, qui a la vue perçante, pénétrant, clairvoyant. — **silver,** *s.* vif-argent, mercure, *m.*; *v.a.* étamer. —**silvering,** *s.* tain, *m.*; (*action*) étamage, *m.* — **sticks.** *In — sticks*, en deux temps deux mouvements; en un clin d'œil. — **tempered,** *adj.* emporté; vif. —**witted,** *adj.* à l'esprit vif

Quicken, *v.a.* vivifier, animer; (*hasten*) hâter, accélérer; activer; (*rouse*) exciter; réveiller; — *v.n.* s'animer. — **tree,** *s.* sorbier des oiseaux, *m.*

Quickener, *s.* principe vivifiant, *m.*; chose [qui accélère, *f.*

Quickens, *s.* chiendent, *m.*

Quickly, *adv.* vite, promptement; rapidement; vivement; (*soon*) bientôt

Quickness, *s.* vitesse, *f.*; promptitude, *f.*; rapidité, célérité, *f.*; vivacité, *f.*; activité, *f.*; pénétration, *f.*; intelligence, *f.*; (*of the pulse*, [*breathing*) fréquence, *f.*

Quid, *s.* chique, *f.*

Quiddity, *s.* chicane, subtilité, *f.*; (*philos.*) quiddité, *f.*

Quidnunc, *s.* chercheur *or* colporteur de nouvelles, *m.*, commère, *f.*, olibrius, *m.*; politique au petit pied, *m.* [quiproquo, *m.*

Quid pro quo, *s.* équivalent, *m.*; (*mistake*)

Quiescence, *s.* repos, *m.*; quiétude, tranquillité, *f.*; (*gram.*) quiescence, *f.*

Quiescent, *adj.* en repos; calme, tranquille, paisible; (*gram.*) quiescent

Quiet, *adj.* tranquille; paisible; calme; serein; (*soft, gentle*) doux; (*unostentatious*) modeste, sans éclat; — *s.* repos, *m.*, tranquillité, paix, *f.*; calme, *m.*; sérénité, *f.*; silence, *m.*; — *v.a.* tranquilliser; calmer, apaiser; (*make silent*) faire taire. *To be —*, être tranquille *or* &c.; rester tranquille; (*be silent*) se taire, garder le silence. *To keep —*, tenir tranquille; (*to be —*) se tenir tranquille. *To make — or be —*, tranquilliser; apaiser; (*make still*) faire rester tranquille; (*make silent*) faire taire. *Be* or *keep —!* restez tranquille; taisez-vous! silence! *Let me be —!* laissez-moi tranquille! *On the —*, tranquillement, sans bruit, en silence; en secret, en cachette

Quieter, *s.* personne *or* chose qui tranquillise *or* qui calme, *f.*

Quietism, *s.* quiétisme, *m.*

Quietist, *s.*, **Quietistic,** *adj.* quiétiste, *m.f.*

Quietly, *adv.* tranquillement; paisiblement; avec calme; en silence, sans bruit; doucement, tout doucement [*m.*; repos, *m.*

Quietness, *s.* tranquillité, *f.*; paix, *f.*; calme,

Quietude, *s.* quiétude, *f.*

Quietus, *s.* coup mortel, coup de grâce, *m.*; repos, *m.*, mort, *f.*; calmant, *m.*; satisfaction, *f.*; (*acquittance*) quitus, *m.* *To give a* (or ... *one his*) —, faire taire, river (à quelqu'un) son clou; donner le coup de grâce à; (*pop.*) mettre à l'ombre, faire passer le goût du pain à

Quill, *s.* plume, *f.*; plume d'oie, *f.*; (*of porcupines*) piquant, *m.*; — *v.a.* rucher; (*to plait*) plisser; (*mus.*) emplumer. — **driver,** *s.* gratte-papier, plumitif, *m.* — **driving,** *s.* métier de gratte-papier, *m.* — **pen,** *s.* plume d'oie, *f.* — **pen maker,** *s.* taille-plumes, *m.*

Quilling, *s.* ruche, *f.*; (*plaiting*) plissement, *m.*

Quilt, *s.* courte-pointe, *f.*; couvre-pieds, *m.*; — *v.a.* piquer

Quilting, *s.* piqué, *m.*

Quinary, *adj.* quinaire

Quince, *s.* coing, *m.* — **jelly (-marmalade),** *s.* gelée (marmelade) de coings, *f.* — **tree,** *s.* cognassier, *m.*

Quincuncial, *adj.* quinconcial

Quincunx, *s.* quinconce, *m.*

Quindecagon, *s.* quindécagone, *m.*

Quindecagonal, *adj.* quindécagone

Quinic, *adj.* quinique

Quinine, *s.* quinine, *f.* — **wine,** *s.* vin de quinquina, *m.*

Quininism, *s.* maladie quinique, *f.*

Quinquagenarian, *s.adj.* quinquagénaire, *m.f.*

Quinquagesima, *s.* Quinquagésime, *f.*

Quinquennial, *adj.* quinquennal

Quinquina, *s.* quinquina, *m.*

Quinsy, *s.* esquinancie, *f.*

Quint, Quinte, *s.* quinte, *f.* [tane, *f.*

Quintan, *adj.* quintane (*f.*); — *s.* fièvre quin-

Quintessence, *s.* quintessence, *f.*

Quintessential, *adj.* quintessenciel

Quintet, Quintette, Quintetto, *s.* quintette, quintetto, *m.*

Quintroon, *s.* quinteron, *m.*, -ne, *f.*

Quintuple, *adj. s.* quintuple, *adj. m.f.*, *s.m.*; — *v.a.n.* quintupler

Quip, *v.a.n.* railler; — *s.* sarcasme, lardon, *m.*

Qui pro quo. *V.* **Quid pro quo**

Quire, *s.* main, *f.*; (*old spelling*) *V.* **Choir.** *In* [—*s*, en feuilles

Quirinal, *s.* Quirinal, *m.*

Quirk, *s.* subtilité, *f.*; pointe, *f.*; (*of a glove*) carabin, *m.*; (*arch.*) angle (de moulure), *m.*

Quit, *v.a.* quitter; sortir de; acquitter; tenir quitte; — *adj.* quitte; —**s,** *adv.* quitte, quitte à quitte. *To — oneself*, s'acquitter (de). *To get — of*, s'acquitter de; se débarrasser de. *To — cost*, payer les frais. *To — scores*, être quitte à quitte. *We'll cry —s*, nous voilà quittes. — **claim,** *s.* remise, *f.* — **rent,** *s.* redevance, *f.*

Quitch, — **grass,** *s.* chiendent, *m.*

Quite, *adv.* tout à fait, entièrement, complètement, tout (toute, *f.*, *before a consonant*), bien, parfaitement; (*very, much*) tout (toute, *f.*, *before a consonant*); très, bien. — *another* ..., un tout autre ..., *m.*, une tout autre ..., *f.* — *as well*, tout aussi bien. — *as much*, tout autant. *Not — so much*, pas tout à fait autant. — *differently*, tout autrement. — *enough*, bien assez; tout ce qu'il faut. — *good enough*, bien assez bon. — *ready*, tout prêt, *m.*, toute prête, *f.*, tout prêts, *m.pl.*, toutes prêtes, *f.pl.* — *right*, parfaitement juste; très bien; très exact; (*of watches, clocks*) bien à l'heure; (*pers.*, '*to be*,' avoir) bien raison, parfaitement raison. *He is — young*, il est tout jeune. *She is — young*, elle est toute jeune. *To be — sure*, être très sûr, être bien sûr. *He is — dead*, il est bien mort. *I have — done*, j'ai tout à fait [fini

Quittance, *s. V.* **Acquittance**

Quitter, *s.* personne qui quitte, *f.*

Quittor, *s.* (*vet.*) solbature, *f.* — **bone,** *s.* (*vet.*) javart, *m.*

Quiver, *s.* carquois, *m.*; (*quivering*) *V.* **Quivering;** — *v.n.* trembler, frissonner; (*of flesh*) [palpiter

Quivered, *adj.* armé d'un carquois

Quivering, *s.* tremblement, *m.*; frissonnement, frisson, *m.*

Quiveringly, *adv.* en tremblant, en frissonnant

Quixotic, *adj.* Don-Quichottique, de Don Quichotte

Quixotically, *adv.* en Don Quichotte

Quixotism, *s.* Don-Quichottisme, *m.*

Quiz, *s.* (*pers.*) railleur, *m.*, -euse, *f.*, persifleur, *m.*, -euse, *f.*; (*wag*) loustic, *m.*; (*hoax*) *V.* **Hoax;** (*puzzle*) énigme, *f.*; (*old fellow*) *V.* **Guy;** — *v.a.n.* lorgner; (*joke*) railler, persifler, berner; (*puzzle*) embarrasser

Quizzer, *s.* (*pers.*) *V.* **Quiz**
Quizzical, *adj.* railleur, comique
Quizzing, *s.* lorgnerie, *f.*; (*joke*) raillerie, *f.*, persiflage, *m.* — **glass,** *s.* lorgnon, *m.*
Quod, *s.* bloc, violon, *m.*, prison, *f.*; — *v.a.* mettre au bloc *or* au violon, bloquer, coffrer, emballer
Quoin, *s.* (*tech.*, &c.) *V.* **Coin;** (*nav.*) cale, *f.*
Quoit, *s.* palet, *m.*; (*antiq.*) disque, *m.* *To play at —s*, jouer au palet
Quondam, *adj.* ancien, ci-devant
Quorum, *s.* nombre suffisant, *m.*
Quota, *s* quote-part, quotité, *f.*, contingent, *m.*
Quotation, *s.* citation, *f.*; (*com.*) cote, *f.*; (*of stock-exchange*) cours, *m.*
Quote, *v.a.* citer; (*com.*) coter
Quoter, *s.* citateur, *m.*, -trice, *f.*
Quoth, *v.* *V.* **Say**
Quotidian, *adj.* quotidien; — *s.* fièvre quotidienne, *f.*
Quotient, *s.* quotient, *m.*

R

R, *s.* (*letter*) r, *f.*
R.A., membre de l'académie royale de peinture, *m.*
Rabbet, *s.* feuillure, *f.*; (*nav.*) râblure, *f.*; — *v.a.* faire une feuillure à; lingueter; chanfreiner. — **plane,** *s.* guillaume, *m.*
Rabbi, Rabbin, *s.* rabbin, *m.* *Chief* or *head —*, grand rabbin. —**ship,** *s.* rabbinat, *m.*
Rabbin-ic, al, -ism, -ist. *V.* page 3, § 1
Rabbit, *s.* lapin, *m.*, e, *f.*; — *adj.* de lapin. *Young —*, lapereau, *m.* — **burrow, -hole,** *s.* terrier de lapin, terrier, clapier, *m.*, rabouillère, *f.* — **fish,** *s.* chimère, *f.*, régalec, *m.* — **hutch,** *s.* clapier, *m.* — **skin,** *s.* peau de lapin, *f.* — **skin man,** *s.* marchand de peaux de lapins, *m.* — **warren,** *s.* garenne à lapins, garenne, *f.*
Rabbitry, *s.* clapier, *m.*, clapiers, *m.pl.*
Rabble, *s.* canaille, populace, *f.*; (*crowd*) cohue, *f.* — **rout,** *s.* assemblée tumultueuse, *f.*
Rabelaisian, *adj.* rabelaisien
Rabid, *adj.* (*of animals*) (*fierce*) féroce, (*mad*) enragé; (*pers.*, *bulls*) furieux; (*of hunger, appetite*) dévorant
Rabidly, *adv.* rageusement, furieusement. *To be — hungry*, avoir une faim dévorante
Rabidness, *s.* rage, *f.*; (*fig.*) fureur, *f.*
Rabies, *s.* rage, *f.*
Raccoon, *s.* raton, *m.*
Race, *s.* (*lineage, breed*) race, *f.*; (*running, match*) course, *f.*; (*prize*) prix de course, *m.*; (*career*) carrière, *f.*; (*of tide*) ras de marée, *m.*; (*of wine*) *V.* **Raciness;** — *v.n.* courir; faire une course. *Boat —*, course de bateaux *or* de canots. *Flat —*, course plate. *Foot —*, course à pied. *Horse —*, course de chevaux. *Hurdle —*, course de haies. *Short —*, course de petite distance. *To run a —*, faire une course; (*fig.*) poursuivre *or* suivre *or* fournir une carrière. *To win the —*, remporter le prix. — **calendar,** *s.* *V.* **Racing.** — **course, -ground,** *s.* champ (*or* terrain) de courses, *m.*; piste, *f.*; hippodrome, *m.*; carrière, *f.* — **cup,** *s.* *V.* **Racing.** — **horse,** *s.* cheval de course, *m.* — **stand,** *s.* tribunes, *f.pl.*
Racer, *s.* coureur, *m.*; cheval de course, *m.*
Rachis, *s.* (*anat.*, *bot.*) rachis, *m.*
Rachitic, *adj.* rachitique
Rachitis, *s.* rachitis, rachitisme, *m.*
Raciness, *s.* goût de terroir, *m.*; sève, vinosité, *f.*; (*fig.*) caractère particulier, *m.*; verve, *f.*; piquant, *m.*
Racing, *adj.* de course, de courses; hippique; rapide; — *s.* courses, *f.pl.*, course, *f.* *Horse —*, courses (*or* course) de chevaux; turf, *m.* *Boat —*, &c., *V.* **Race.** — **calendar,** *s.* Journal des courses, &. — **cup, -plate,** *s.* prix de course, *m.* — **stand,** &c., *V.* **Race.** — **stud,** *s.* chevaux de course, *m pl.*
Rack, *s.* (*punishment*) roue, question, *f.*; torture, *f.*; (*for stretching*) chevalet, *m.*; (*of stables, and for tools, arms*, &c.) râtelier, *m.*; (*toothed —*) crémaillère, *f.*; (*of watches, clocks*) rochet, *m.*; (*plank*) planche, *f.*; (*of a cart*) échelette, *f.*; ridelle, *f.*; (*in compounds generally*) porte-..., *m.*; (*mist*) brume, vapeur, *f.*, léger nuage, *m.*; (*liquor*) *V.* **Arrack;** — *v.a.* mettre à la question; (*fig.*) mettre à la torture, torturer; pressurer, opprimer; (*the brain*) *V.* **Brain;** (*liquors, — off*) soutirer; — *v.n.* commettre des exactions. — *and pinion*, engrenage à crémaillère. *To be, to put on the —*, être, mettre à la torture. — **ladder,** *s.* *V.* **Peg-ladder.** — **rent,** *s.* maximum de loyer, *m.*; loyer excessif, *m.* — **rented,** *adj.* qui paye le maximum du loyer
Racket, *s.* raquette, *f.*; (*game*) paume, *f.*; (*noise*) tintamarre, tapage, bruit, *m.*; —**s,** *pl.* (*game*) paume, *f.*; — *v.n.* faire du tapage; (*revel*) faire la vie, s'amuser; courir. — **court, -ground,** *s.* jeu de paume, *m.* — **maker,** *s.* raquetier, *m.*
Racketing, Rackety, *adj.* bruyant, tapageur; (*revelling*) désordonné, qui fait la vie, qui s'amuse; coureur. — *noise*, tapage, *m.*
Racking, *s.* supplice de la roue, *m.*; (*fig.*) torture, *f.*; (*of wine*, &c.) soutirage, *m.*; — *adj.* de la roue; (*fig.*) de torture; (*of pain*) atroce; (*drifting*) qui fuit. — **pace,** *s.* traquenard, *m.*
Racoon, *s.* raton, *m.*
Racoonda, *s.* raconde, *f.*, castorin, *m.*
Racquet. *V.* **Racket**
Racy, *adj.* (*of wine*) qui a un goût de terroir; qui a de la sève, vineux; (*fig.*) piquant
Raddle, *s.* *V.* **Reddle;** — *v.a.* tresser, entrelacer. — **hedge,** *s.* clayon, *m.*
Radial, *adj.* radial
Radianc-e, y, *s.* éclat, lustre, *m.*, splendeur, *f.*, rayonnement, *m.*
Radiant, *adj.* rayonnant ('*with*,' de); radieux; (*bot.*, *her.*) radié
Radiantly, *adv.* en rayonnant, avec éclat, d'une manière radieuse, splendidement
Radiate, *v.n.* rayonner; — *v.a.* émettre; — *adj.* *s.* radié, *adj. m.*, e, *f.*, radié, *s.m.*
Radiation, *s.* rayonnement, *m.*, radiation, *f.*
Radical, *adj.s.* radical, *adj.m.*, e, *f.*, radical, *s.m.*
Radicalism, *s.* radicalisme, *m.*
Radically, *adv.* radicalement
Radication, *s.* radication, *f.*
Radicle, Radicule, *s.* radicule, *f.*
Radish, *s.* radis, *m.*; rave, *f.* *Long —*, rave, . — **bed,** *s.* ravière, *f.* — **dish,** *s.* ravier, *m.*
Radius, *s.* rayon, *m.*; (*anat.*) radius, *m.* — *vector*, rayon vecteur, *m.*
Radix, *s.* racine, *f.*
Raff, *s.* galopin, voyou, *m.*, canaille, *f.*
Raffle, *s.* loterie, *f.*; — *v.n.* faire une loterie. *To — for, to put up to —*, mettre en loterie. — **net,** *s.* râfle, *f.*
Rafflesia, *s.* rafflésie, *f.*
Raffling, *s.* mise en loterie, *f.*
Raft, *s.* radeau, *m.*; train de bois, *m.*; — *v.a.* flotter
Rafter, *s.* chevron, *m.*, poutre, *f.*; — *v.a.* chevronner
Raftered, *part. adj.* chevronné, à chevrons, soutenu par des chevrons *or* des poutres
Rafting, *s.* flottage, *m.*
Raftsman, *s.* flotteur, *m.*
Rag, *s.* chiffon, *m.*; morceau de linge, linge, *m.*; (*duster*) torchon, *m.*; (*of garments*) haillon, *m.*, guenille, *f.*, lambeau, *m.*, loque, *f.* *In —s*, en haillons, en guenilles, déguenillé, en loques. *Boiled* or *done to —s*, (*cook.*) pourri de cuisson, en charpie, en compote. *To tear to —s*, mettre en lambeaux. — **doll,** *s.* poupée de chiffons, *f.* — **fair,** *s.* friperie, *f.* — **collector, -dealer, -gatherer, -man, -merchant, -picker, -woman,** *s.* chiffonnier, *m.*, -ière, *f.* — **stone,** *s.* moellon, *m.*; pierre fusilière, *f.*; pierre à aiguiser, *f.* — **trade, -business,** *s.* chiffonnerie, *f.*, commerce de chiffons, *m.* —

-weed, -wort, *s.* jacobée, *f.*, séneçon, *m.* — **wheel,** *s.* hérisson, *m.* [polisson, *m.*

Ragamuffin, *s.* va-nu-pieds, gueux, goujat,

Rage, *s.* fureur, rage, *f.*; violence, force, *f.*; (*mania*) manie, *f.*; — *v.n.* (*pers.*) être furieux, être en fureur, enrager, jeter feu et flamme; faire rage; (*of the sea*) être en fureur, se courroucer; (*of the winds, storms*) se déchaîner, être déchaîné; faire rage; (*of famine*) sévir; (*of epidemics*) sévir, faire (*or* exercer) des ravages; (*of fire*) faire des ravages, faire rage, (*till* ...) durer avec violence; (*of fights*) faire fureur, faire rage. *To be in a* —, être furieux, être en fureur, être en colère. *To put in a* —, mettre en fureur *or* en colère, faire enrager. *To be the* — or *all the* — or *quite the* —, faire fureur, faire rage. —**ful,** *adj.* furibond

Ragged, *adj.* déchiré, en lambeaux, délabré; (*pers.*) en haillons, en guenilles, déguenillé; (*jagged*) ébréché; (*uneven*) inégal. — **school,** *s.* école de charité, *f.* [haillons, en guenilles

Raggedly, *adv.* en lambeaux; (*pers.*) en

Raggedness, *s.* délabrement, déguenillement, *m.*, lambeaux, haillons, *m.pl.*, guenilles, *f.pl.*; (*roughness*) inégalité, *f.*

Raging, *adj.* furieux, en fureur; en courroux; déchaîné; violent, impétueux; acharné; terrible; destructeur; — *s.* fureur, rage, *f.*; violence, *f.* [rageusement, avec rage

Ragingly, *adv.* furieusement, avec fureur,

Ragout, *s.* ragoût, *m.*

Raid, *s.* incursion, *f.*; invasion, *f.*; razzia, *f.*

Raider, *s.* maraudeur, *m.*

Rail, *s.* barre, *f.*; barreau, *m.*; (*railing*) grille, *f.*; (*baluster*) rampe, balustrade, *f.*; (*of a cart*) ridelle, *f.*; (*of a chair*) panneau, barreau, *m.*; (*fence*) barrière, *f.*; (*of bridges*) parapet, garde-fou, *m.*; (*nav.*) lisse, *f.*; (*of railway*) rail, *m.*; (*railway itself*) chemin de fer, *m.*; (*bird*) râle, *m.*; — *v.a.* griller, fermer d'une grille; — *v.n.* — **at,** injurier; médire de. — **in, off,** *v.a.* entourer; griller. — **fence,** *s.* barrière, *f.* — **road,** —**way,** *s. See below. Line of* —, ligne ferrée, voie ferrée, ligne, voie, *f. To run* or *come* or *go off the —s, to throw off the —s,* dérailler. *Running* or *throwing off the —s,* déraillement, *m.*

Railer, *s.* personne qui injurie, *f.*, frondeur, *m.*, -euse, *f.*; médisant, *m.*, e, *f.*

Railing, *adj.* injurieux; — *s.* grille, *f.*; rampe, balustrade, *f.*; palissade, *f.*; (*of bridges*) garde-fou, parapet, *m.*; (*abuse*) injures, *f.pl.*

Railingly, *adv.* injurieusement

Raillery, *s.* raillerie, *f.*

Railroad. *V.* **Railway**

Railway, *s.* chemin de fer, *m.*; — *adj.* de *or* du chemin de fer, de *or* des chemins de fer. — **carriage, -car,** *s.* voiture, (*f.*) *or* wagon (*m.*) de chemin de fer. — **carrier,** *s.* correspondant de chemin de fer, *m.* — **clock,** *s.* horloge du chemin de fer, *f.* — **company,** *s.* compagnie de (*or* du) chemin de fer, *f.* — **contractor,** *s.* entrepreneur de chemins de fer, *m.* — **debenture,** *s.* obligation de chemin de fer, *f.* — **guard,** *s.* chef de train, conducteur de train, *m.* — **guide,** *s.* indicateur des chemins de fer, *m.* — **insurance,** *s.* assurance contre les accidents en chemin de fer, *f.* — **market,** *s.* cours des actions de chemins de fer, *m.* — **passenger,** *s.* voyageur (*m.*, -euse, *f.*) en chemin de fer. — **plant,** *s.* matériel de chemin de fer, *m.* — **porter,** *s.* facteur de chemin de fer, *m.* — **rug,** *s. V.* — **wrapper.** — **share,** *s.* action de chemin de fer, *f.* — **share market,** *s. V.* — **market.** — **signal,** *s.* signal de chemin de fer, *m.* — **speed,** *s.* (la) rapidité de la vapeur, *f.* — **station,** *s.* station *or* gare de (*or* du) chemin de fer, *f.* — **stock,** *s.* actions de chemin de fer, *f.pl.* — **terminus,** *s.* gare de (*or* du) chemin de fer, *f.* — **ticket,** *s.* billet de chemin de fer, *m.* — **train,** *s.* train de chemin de fer, *m.* — **wrapper,** *s.* couverture de voyage, *f.*

Raiment, *s.* vêtement, habillement, *m.*

Rain, *v.n.* pleuvoir; — *v.a.* faire pleuvoir, verser, répandre; — *s.* pluie, *f. Fine* —, pluie fine. *Heavy* —, grosse *or* forte pluie. *In the* —, à la pluie. *To* — *fast* or *hard,* pleuvoir à verse, pleuvoir fort. *To* — *cats and dogs,* pleuvoir (*or* tomber) des hallebardes. *It* —*s* (or *is* —*ing*) *in here,* il pleut ici, la pluie entre ici. — **bow,** *s.* arc-en-ciel, *m.* — **cloud,** *s.* nuage de pluie, nimbus, *m.* — **drop,** *s* goutte de pluie, *f.* — **fall,** *s.* quantité de pluie. *Heavy* — *fall,* pluie abondante, *f.* — **gauge,** *s.* pluviomètre, *m.* — **water,** *s.* eau de pluie, *f.*

Raininess, *s.* nature pluvieuse, *f.*, état pluvieux, *m.*, disposition à la pluie, *f.*

Rainy, *adj.* pluvieux, de pluie. *It looks* —, le temps est à la pluie. *To lay by something for a* — *day,* garder une poire pour la soif

Raise, *v.a.* (*o.'s hand, head, a blind, a veil, a blister, a siege, a blockade, troops, taxes,* &c.) lever; (*dough, dust*) faire lever; (*lift, as a weight, waves, dust,* &c., *a tempest, a question, stir up, make*) soulever; (*to dignities, build, rear, elevate, a pretension, the voice*) élever; (*pick up*) relever; (*a difficulty, a doubt, a scruple*) élever, faire naître; (*hopes, suspicions*) donner, faire naître; (*a statue,* &c., *erect*) élever, ériger; (*found*) fonder; (*bring, carry, take*) porter; (*make higher*) hausser; (*make rise*) faire hausser; (*increase*) augmenter; porter (à); (*excite*) exciter; provoquer; (*produce*) produire, faire naître; (*a quarrel*) susciter; (*grow, cultivate*) faire venir, cultiver, élever; (*money*) trouver, se procurer, obtenir; recueillir, réunir; fournir; (*a fund*) former; (*a loan*) faire, contracter; (*the wind*) *V.* **Wind;** (*a cry*) pousser, jeter; (*a rumour*) faire courir; (*o.'s courage or spirits*) ranimer, relever (son courage); (*strengthen*) fortifier; (*ghosts*) évoquer; (*the dead*) ressusciter; (*o.'s hat*) ôter (son chapeau); (*a mast,* &c.) guinder

Raised, *part. adj.* levé, &c. (*V.* **Raise**); (*embossed, of maps,* &c.) en relief

Raiser, *s.* personne *or* chose qui lève *or* &c. (*V.* **Raise**), *f.*; fondateur, *m.*, -trice, *f.*; (*breeder*) éleveur, *m.*; (*agr., hort.*) cultivateur, *m.*, -trice, *f.*; (*of a stair*) contre-marche, *f.*

Raisin, *s.* raisin sec, *m.*

Raising, *s.* (*of a siege, a blockade, troops, taxes*) levée, *f.*; (*other senses: V.* **Raise**) soulèvement, *m.*; élévation, *f.*; augmentation, *f.*, accroissement, *m.*; excitation, *f.*; production, *f.*; culture, *f.*; (*breeding*) élevage, *m.*, élève, *f.*; (*of ghosts*) évocation, *f.*; (*of the dead*) ressuscitation, *f.*, ressuscitement, *m.*; (*of ores,* &c.) extraction, *f.*; exploitation, *f.*

Raja, Rajah, *s.* raja, rajah, *m.*

Rake, *s.* râteau, *m.*; (*for ovens*) fourgon, *m.*; (*nav.*) (*of mast*) inclinaison, *f.*, (*of stem*) élancement, *m.*, (*of stern-post*) quête, *f.*; (*pers.*) libertin, *m.*, e, *f.*, débauché, *m.*, e, *f.*, roué, *m.*, e, *f.*; — *v.a.n.* (*agr.*) râteler; (*hort.*) râteler, ratisser; (*collect*) ramasser, rassembler; (*search*) fouiller dans; fouiller; (*stir*) remuer; (*cover up*) couvrir; (*with guns*) enfiler, prendre d'enfilade; (*to scrape*) gratter; (*be rakish*) libertiner. —**ful,** *s.* râtelée, *f.* — **off,** *v.a.* enlever au râteau. — **out,** *v.a.* (*stir*) remuer; (*put out*) éteindre. — **up,** *v.a.* (*to rake*) *V.* —; (*bring to light, revive*) exhumer; raviver, réveiller [fureteur, *m.*, -euse, *f.*

Raker, *s.* râteleur, *m.*, -euse, *f.*; (*searcher*)

Raking, *s.* (*agr.*) râtelage, *m.*; (*hort.*) râtelage, ratissage, *m.*; (*fig.*) ramassis, *m.*; (*course of life*) libertinage, *m.*; (*with guns*) prise d'enfilade, *f.* — **fire,** *s.* feu d'enfilade, *m.* — **out,** *s.* (*of the fires*) extinction, *f.* [*ships*) élancé

Rakish, *adj.* libertin, débauché, dissolu; (*of*

Rakishly, *adv.* en libertin, dissolument

Rakishness, *s.* libertinage, *m.*, débauche, *f.*

Rallier, *s.* railleur, *m.*, -euse, *f.*

Rally, *v.a.* rallier; rassembler, réunir; (*recover*) reprendre; (*joke*) railler; — *v.n.* se rallier; se rassembler, se réunir; (*regain strength*) se remettre; (*joke*) railler; — *s. V.* **Rallying**

Rallying, *s.* ralliement, *m.*; (*improvement*) amélioration, *f.*, mieux, *m.*; (*joking*) raillerie, *f.*; — *adj.* de ralliement; (*jocular*) railleur. — *point, sign, word* or &c., point, signe, mot *or* &c. de ralliement, *m.*

Ram, *s.* (*zool.*, *astr.*, *engine*) bélier, *m.*; (*for piles*) mouton, *m.*; (*of paviers*) demoiselle, hie, *f.*; (*beak of an ironclad ship*) éperon, *m.*; (*ship itself*) vaisseau éperonné, *m.*; — *adj.* de bélier, &c.; (*stinking*) puant; (*nav.*) éperonné; — *v.a.* enfoncer; battre; (*fire-arms*) bourrer; (*of paviers*) battre à la hie, hier; (*build.*) damer. *Hydraulic* —, bélier hydraulique. — **frigate,** *s.* frégate éperonnée, *f.* — **lamb,** *s.* agneau, *m.*

Ramadan, *s.* ramazan, ramadan, *m.*

Ramakin, *s.* ramequin, *m.*

Ramazan. *V.* **Ramadan**

Ramble, *s.* excursion, course, promenade, *f.*, tour, *m.*; (*fig.*) divagation, *f.*; — *v.n.* errer, rôder; aller çà et là, battre la campagne; courir; se promener; (*fig.*) divaguer. — **over,** parcourir

Rambler, *s.* rôdeur, *m.*, -euse, *f.*; vagabond, *m.*, e, *f.*; (*fig.*) divagateur, *m.*, -trice, *f.*

Rambling, *adj.* vagabond; errant; hors de la question; divagateur, divagant, plein de divagations; extravagant; détaché; — *s.* excursion, *f.* (-s, *pl.*), course, *f.* (-s, *pl.*), promenade, *f.* (-s, *pl.*), tour, *m.* (-s, *pl.*); vagabondage, *m.*; (*fig.*) divagation, *f.* (-s, *pl.*) [divaguant

Ramblingly, *adv.* en rôdant; en courant; en

Ramekin, Ramequin, *s.* ramequin, *m.*

Ramification, *s.* ramification, *f.*

Ramify, *v.a.* ramifier — *v.n.* se ramifier

Rammekin, *s.* ramequin, *m.*

Rammer, *s.* baguette, *f.*; (*for cannon*) refouloir, *m.*; (*of paviers*) demoiselle, hie, *f.*; (*for piles*) mouton, *m.* [odeur forte

Rammish, *adj.* qui sent le bouc, qui a une

Rammishness, *s.* odeur de bouc, odeur

Rammy, *adj. V.* **Rammish** [forte, *f.*

Ramose, Ramous, *adj.* rameux, branchu

Ramp, *v.n.* sauter, bondir; (*creep*) grimper; — *s.* rampe, *f.*; (*leap*) saut, bond, *m.*; —**s,** *pl.* (*bot.*) ail sauvage, *m.*

Rampancy, *s.* surabondance, *f.*, excès, *m.*; empire, *m.*, influence, *f.*, pouvoir, *m.*

Rampant, *adj.* surabondant, commun, répandu; dominant; effréné, exalté; (*her.*) ram-

Rampart, *s.* rempart, *m.* [pant

Rampion, *s.* raiponce, *f.*

Ramrod, *s.* baguette, *f.*; (*for cannon*) refouloir, *m.*

Ramshackle, *adj.* délabré, décrépit, qui tombe en ruines *or* en loques

Ramskin, *s.* ramequin, *m.*

Ramsons, *s.pl.* ail sauvage, *m.*

Rancid, *adj.* rance. *To become* or *get* —, rancir

Rancidity, Rancidness, *s.* rancidité, rancissure, *f.*

Rancorous, *adj.* rancunier; haineux

Rancorously, *adv.* avec *or* par rancune

Rancour, *s.* rancune, *f.*

Random, *s.* hasard, *m.*; — *adj.* au hasard, fait *or* dit (*or* donné *or* &c.) au hasard. *At* —, au hasard; à l'aventure; à l'abandon; (*in speaking*) à tort et à travers. — **shot,** *s.* coup perdu, *m.*; (*bullet*) balle perdue, *f.*

Range, *v.a.* ranger; arranger; aligner; (*go over*) parcourir; franchir; (*print.*) aligner; (*sift*) bluter; — *v.n.* être rangé, se ranger; être aligné, s'aligner; s'étendre, aller; varier; errer, courir, rôder; (*print.*) être aligné, s'aligner; (*nav.*) ranger la côte; — *s.* rangée, *f.*, rang, *m.*; ligne, *f.*; classe, *f.*, ordre, *m.*; espace, *m.*, étendue, distance, *f.*, champ, *m.*; excursion, course, *f.*; (*fig.*) essor, *m.*; carrière, *f.*; (*reach*) portée, *f.*; (*of kitchen*) fourneau, *m.*; (*sieve*) blutoir, *m.*; (*of a ladder*) échelon, *m.*; (*of mountains*) chaîne, *f.*; (*reach of fire-arms*) portée, *f.*, (*firing-ground*) tir, *m.* *Within* —, à portée. — **about,** *v.n.* aller çà et là. — **over,** *v.a.* parcourir; courir

Ranger, *s.* conservateur, garde forestier, *m.*; (*soldier*) chasseur, *m.*; (*a dog*) chien courant, *m.*

Rangership, *s.* charge de conservateur, *f.*

Ranging, *s.* rangement, *m.*; arrangement, *m.*; alignement, *m.*; classement, *m.*; vagabondage, *m.*, vie errante, *f.*; excursion, course, *f.*

Ranine, *adj.* ranin

Rank, *s.* rang, *m.*; ordre, *m.*; mérite, *m.*; distinction, *f.*; (*of soldiers*) rang, *m.*; (*standing of officers in the army or navy*) grade, *m.*; (*high* —) haut rang, *m.*, (*mil.*, *nav.*) grade supérieur, *m.*; (*of cabs*) place, station, *f.*; —**s,** *pl.* rangs, *m.pl.*; grades, *m.pl.*; (*privates*) simples soldats, *m.pl.*; — *v.a.* ranger; placer; classer; — *v.n.* se ranger; être rangé *or* placé *or* classé; (*take rank*) avoir *or* prendre rang; avoir *or* occuper un rang; — *adj.* fort, vigoureux; luxuriant, plantureux, fertile, fécond, abondant; (*thick*) épais; (*rancid*) rance, fort; (*excessive*) grand, violent, excessif; (*coarse*) grossier; (*downright*) vrai. — *and file*, soldats, hommes, *m.pl.* [200 — *and file*, 200 hommes]. *From the* —*s*, (*of rising*) des derniers rangs. *To leave* or *quit the* —*s*, sortir des rangs; se débander. *To reduce to the* —*s*, casser. *To rise from the* —*s*, sortir des derniers rangs [*An officer risen from the* —*s*, un officier de fortune]. *To* — *high as*, occuper un rang élevé parmi. *To* — *with*, avoir le rang de

Rankle, *v.n.* s'envenimer, s'enflammer. *Jealousy* —*s in his breast*, la jalousie lui ronge le cœur

Rankly, *adv.* fortement, grandement; abondamment, plantureusement; (*coarsely*) grossièrement

Rankness, *s.* force, vigueur, surabondance, exubérance, luxuriance, abondance, *f.*; (*rancidness*) rancidité, *f.*, goût, fort, *m.*; (*smell*) odeur forte, *f.*; (*excess*) excès, *m.*, extravagance, *f.* [tribution; (*search*) fouiller dans

Ransack, *v.a.* saccager, piller; mettre à con-

Ransacking, *s.* saccagement, sac, pillage, *m.*; (*search*) perquisition, *f.*, recherches, *f.pl.*

Ransom, *s.* rançon, *f.*; délivrance, *f.*; — *v.a.* racheter; (*a merchant ship*) rançonner. — **less,** *adj.* sans rançon

Ransomer, *s.* personne qui rachète, *f.*

Ransoming, *s.* rachat, *m.*; délivrance, *f.*

Rant, *s.* déclamation, *f.*, clabaudage, *m.*, déblatération, *f.*, phrases, *f.pl.*, galimatias, *m.*; — *v.n.* déclamer avec extravagance, extravaguer; tempêter; clabauder, déblatérer; parler pour ne rien dire, faire des phrases [mène, *m.f.*

Ranter, *s.* déclamateur, *m.*, -trice, *f.*; énergu-

Ranting, *adj.* extravagant; enragé; d'énergumène; — *s. V.* **Rant,** *s.*

Rantipole, *adj.* extravagant, écervelé, timbré

Ranula, *s.* ranule, *f.*

Ranunculus, *s.* renoncule, *f.*

Rap, *v.a.n.* frapper; ravir; — *s.* (*with a knocker*) *V.* **Knock,** *s.*; (*blow*) coup, *m.*; (*slap*) tape, *f.*, tapin, *m.*; (*money, fig.*) centime, *m.* *Not to be worth a* —, (*pers.*) n'avoir pas un centime; (*things*) ne valoir pas les quatre fers d'un chien, ne valoir pas le diable. *To* — *and rend*, empoigner, saisir, faire main basse sur. *I don't care a* —, je m'en soucie comme de cela, je m'en moque. — **out,** *v.a.* laisser échapper, [lâcher

Rapacious, *adj.* rapace

Rapaciously, *adv.* rapacement, avec rapacité

Rapaciousness, Rapacity, *s.* rapacité, *f.*

Rape, *s.* enlèvement, rapt, *m.*; (*law*) viol, *m.*; (*bot.*) navette, *f.*; colza, *m.*; (*of grapes*) râpe, *f.*; marc, *m.* *The* — *of the Sabines* (or *of the Sabine women*), l'enlèvement des Sabines. — **seed,** *s.* graine de navette, navette, *f.*; colza, *m.* — **seed oil,** — **oil,** *s.* huile de navette, *f.*;

huile de colza, *f.* — **wine,** *s.* râpé, *m.*, piquette, *f.*
Raphaelesque, *adj.* raphaélesque
Rapid, *adj.* rapide ; (*of consumption*) galopante ; — *s.* rapide, *m.*
Rapidity, Rapidness, *s.* rapidité, *f.*
Rapidly, *adv.* rapidement
Rapier, *s.* rapière, *f.*
Rapine, *s.* rapine, *f.*
Rappee, *s.* tabac râpé, *m.*
Rapper, *s.* frappeur, *m.*, -euse, *f.* ; (*on a door*) marteau, *m.*
Rapping, *adj.* qui frappe, frappeur. — **spirit,** *s.* esprit frappeur, *m.*
Rapscallion. *V.* **Rascallion**
Rapt, *adj.* ravi, transporté, extasié, en extase
Raptorial, Raptorious, *adj.* rapace ; de proie
Rapture, *s.* transport, *m.* ; extase, *f.*, ravissement, *m.*; enthousiasme, *m* ; ivresse, *f.* *In —s,* en extase, dans le ravissement
Raptured, *adj.* *V.* **Rapt**
Rapturous, *adj.* ravissant ; enivrant ; enthousiaste, frénétique ; (*pers.*) ravi
Rapturously, *adv.* avec transport, avec enthousiasme, avec frénésie, à outrance
Rare, *adj.* rare ; extraordinaire ; (*thin*) clairsemé ; peu nombreux ; (*nearly raw*) incuit, peu cuit, saignant ; (*exquisite*) exquis, excellent ; impayable ; (*great*) fameux, furieux, fier
Rareeshow, *s.* curiosité, *f.*; spectacle ambulant, *m.*
Rarefaction, *s.* raréfaction, *f.*
Rarefiable, *adj.* raréfiable
Rarefy, *v.a.* raréfier ; — *v.n.* se raréfier
Rarely, *adv.* rarement ; (*greatly*) parfaitement, fameusement, furieusement, bien
Rareness, Rarity, *s.* rareté, *f.*; (*phys.*) raréfaction, *f.*
Rascal, *s.* coquin, *m.*, e, *f.*, gredin, *m.*, e, *f.*, fripon, *m.*, -ne, *f.*
Rascality, *s.* coquinerie, gredinerie, friponnerie, *f.*; (*populace*) canaille, *f.*
Rascallion, *s.* drôle, polisson, *m.*
Rascally, *adj.* de coquin, coquin de . . ., misérable
Rase, *v.a.* raser ; démolir ; extirper, déraciner ; (*graze*) raser, friser, effleurer ; (*erase*) rayer, biffer, effacer
Rash, *adj.* téméraire ; inconsidéré, irréfléchi ; imprudent ; emporté ; — *s.* éruption, *f.* ; — *v.a.* couper en morceaux, tailler en pièces
Rasher, *s.* tranche, *f.*
Rashly, *adv.* témérairement ; inconsidérément, sans réflexion ; imprudemment
Rashness, *s.* témérité, *f.*; imprudence, *f.*; précipitation, *f.*
Rasp, *s.* râpe, *f.* ; (*surg.*) rugine, *f.* ; — *v.a.* râper ; (*bread*) chapeler ; (*surg.*) ruginer. — **like,** *adj.* râpeux
Raspberry, *s.* framboise, *f.* — **bush,** *s.* framboisier, *m.* — **jam,** *s.* confitures de framboises, *f.pl.* — **vinegar,** *s.* vinaigre à la framboise, vinaigre framboisé, *m.*
Rasper, *s.* râpeur, *m.*, -euse, *f.*; (*rasp*) râpe, *f.*
Rasping, *s.* râpage, *m.* ; —**s,** *pl.* râpure, *f.*; (*of bread*) chapelure, *f.* — **mill,** *s.* moulin à râper, *m.*
Rat, *s.* rat, *m.*; (*pers.*) (*turncoat*) transfuge, *m.*, (*underworker*) gâte-métier, *m.* ; — *v.n.* (*change sides*) tourner casaque ; (*underwork*) gâter le métier. (*V.* **Smell.**) *Brown* or *Norway* —, surmulot, *m.* — **catcher,** *s.* preneur de rats, ratier, *m.* —**s'-bane,** *s.* mort aux rats, *f.* — **trap,** *s.* ratière, *f.*
Ratable, *adj.* évaluable ; imposable, sujet aux impôts
Ratably, *adv.* proportionnellement, en proportion
Ratafia, *s.* ratafia, *m.*
Ratan. *V.* **Rattan**
Ratanhia, Ratanhy, Ratany, *s.* ratanhia, *m.*
Ratch, *s.* (*horol.*) rochet, *m.*
Ratchet, *s.* (*horol.*) guide chaîne, *m.* ; (*tech.*) dent d'engrenage, *f.* ; (*of locks*) rochet, *m.* — **brace,** *s.* cliquet à percer, *m.* — **engine,** *s.* machine à tailler les dents d'engrenage, *f.* — **wheel,** *s.* (*horol.*) roue à rochet, *f.* ; (*tech.*) roue d'engrenage, *f.*
Rate, *s.* proportion, *f.* ; taux, *m.*; prix, *m.*; rang, ordre, *m.*; classe, *f.*; nombre, *m.*; mesure, *f.*; (*speed*) vitesse, *f.*; (*tax*) impôt, *m.*, contribution, taxe, *f.*; (*of interest and discount, of wages*) taux, *m.*; (*of exchange*) cours, *m.*; (*of ships*) rang, *m.*, classe, *f.*; — *v.a.* évaluer ; tarifer ; coter ; estimer ; apprécier ; (*tax*) taxer ; (*assess*) coter ; (*ships,* &c.) classer ; (*chide*) gronder, tancer, secouer ; — *v.n.* être classé, compter. *First-* —, de premier ordre *or* rang, de première classe, de première qualité, excellent, parfait, admirable, éminent, supérieur ; (*adverb.*) parfaitement, admirablement, à merveille. *Second-* —, de second ordre *or* rang, de seconde classe *or* qualité, inférieur. *At any* —, quoi qu'il en soit ; de toute manière, de toute façon ; (*at all events*) en tout cas ; (*at any cost*) à tout prix. *At a cheap* —, à bon compte. *At the* — *of,* à raison de ; sur le pied de ; (*of speed*) à la vitesse de. *At a great* —, grand train, bon train, rondement, vite ; grandement. *At a tremendous* —, d'un train formidable ; ventre à terre. *At this* —, *at that* —, à (*or* de) ce train, à (*or* de) ce train-là ; de cette façon ; sur ce pied-là ; à ce compte là ; à ce taux-là. — **payer,** *s.* contribuable, *m.f.*
Rateable. *V.* **Ratable**
Ratel, *s.* ratel, *m.*
Rathe, *s.* (*of a cart*) échelette, ridelle, *f.*, cornes, *f.pl.*
Rather, *adv* (*slightly, somewhat*) un peu ; (*tolerably*) assez ; (*in preference*) plutôt ; (*better*) mieux. *Or* —, ou plutôt ; ou pour mieux dire. *The* — *because* (or *that*) d'autant plus que. *To have* or *choose* —, aimer mieux, préférer. *I had* or *would* —, j'aime mieux ; j'aimerais mieux. *I* — *think,* ('*that*' . . ., que . . .), je suis porté à croire, je suis d'avis, j'ai idée, je soupçonne, il me semble
Ratification, *s.* ratification, *f.*
Ratifier, *s.* personne qui ratifie, *f.*
Ratify, *v.a.* ratifier
Ratifying, *adj.* ratificatif
Rating, *s.* évaluation, *f.*; tarification, *f.*; classement, *m.*; taxation, *f.*; taxe, *f.*, impôt, *m.*; (*assessment*) répartition de l'impôt, *f.*; (*proportion of tax*) cote, quotité, *f.*; (*chiding*) semonce, *f.*, savon, *m.*
Ratio, *s.* proportion, raison, *f.*, rapport, *m.*
Ratiocinate, *v.n.* ratiociner, raisonner
Ratiocination, *s.* ratiocination, *f.*, raisonnement, *m.* ; logique, *f.*
Ration, *s.* ration, *f.* ; — *v.a.* rationner
Rational, *adj.* rationnel ; raisonnable ; raisonné
Rationale, *s.* analyse raisonnée, *f.*
Rational-ism, -ist. *V.* page 3, § 1
Rationalistic, *adj.* rationaliste
Rationality, *s.* raisonnement, *m.*; justesse, *f.*; (*philos.*) rationalité, *f.*
Rationalize, *v.a* rationaliser
Rationally, *adv.* rationnellement ; raisonnablement
Ratline, Ratling, *s.* (*nav.*) enfléchure, *f.*
Rattan, *s.* rotin, *m.*
Rattany, *s.* ratanhia, *m.*
Ratteen, *s.* ratine, *f.*
Ratten, *v.a.* empêcher de travailler, intimider
Ratting, *s.* apostasie, *f.* ; (*underworking*) action de gâter le métier
Rattle, *v.n.* faire du bruit ; résonner, retentir ; crier ; grincer ; (*beat, patter*) battre ; grésiller ; (*in the throat*) râler ; (*scold*) gronder ; — *v.a.* faire résonner, faire retentir ; faire sonner ; (*chains*) secouer ; — *s.* (*noise*) bruit, *m.*; (*of metal*) cliquetis, *m.* ; (*empty talk*) bavardage, *m.*; (*chiding*) réprimande, *f.*; (*instrument*) crécelle, *f.*; (*toy*) hochet, *m.* ; (*little bell*) grelot, *m.*; (*of a rattle-snake*) grelot, *m.*; (*in the throat*) râle, *m.*; —**s,** *s.pl.* râle, *m.*; (*croup*) croup, *m.* — **along,** *v.n.* rouler. — **away,** — **off,** *v.n.* dégoiser, aller toujours. — **brained, -headed,** *adj.* étourdi. — **into,** *v.n.* entrer bruyamment dans. —**snake,** *s.* serpent à sonnettes, *m.* — **traps,** *s.pl.* bagages, *m.pl.*, bataclan, *m.*
Rattling, *s.* bruit, *m.* ; — *adj.* bruyant ; (*slang*) huppé, de premier numéro

Raucity, *s.* raucité, *f.*
Ravage, *v.a.* ravager; — *s.* ravage, *m.*
Ravager, *s.* ravageur, destructeur, *m.*, dévastateur, *m.*, -trice, *f.*
Rave, *v.n.* avoir le délire, être en délire, délirer; (*fig.*) extravaguer, déraisonner, battre la campagne; radoter; (*at*) s'emporter *or* être furieux (contre); (*upon*) être fou (de), raffoler (de); (*lament*) se désespérer, se désoler; — *s.* *V.* **Rathe**
Ravel, *v.a.* embrouiller; — *v.n.* s'embrouiller, s'embarrasser, s'enchevêtrer. — **out,** *v.a.* débrouiller, démêler; (*a tissue*) effiler, effiloquer; [*v.n.* s'effiler
Ravelin, *s.* ravelin, *m.*
Ravelling, *s.*, **Ravellings,** *s.pl.* (*of a tissue*) effilure, *f*
Raven, *s.* corbeau, *m.*; — *adj.* de corbeau; (*black*) noir; — *v.a.* dévorer. — **black,** *s. adj.* noir de corbeau, *m.*
Raveners, *s.pl.* (*zool.*) rapaces, ravisseurs, *m.pl.*
Ravenous, *adj.* vorace; (*fig., of hunger, appetite*) dévorant
Ravenously, *adv.* avec voracité. *To be — hungry,* avoir une faim dévorante
Ravenousness, *s.* voracité, *f.*
Ravine, *s.* ravin, *m.*; ravine, *f.*
Raving, *adj.* en délire, délirant; furieux, frénétique; — *s.* délire, *m.*; frénésie, *f.*; radotage, *m.*, radoterie, *f.*; divagation, *f.* — *mad,* fou à lier, fou furieux
Ravingly, *adv.* avec frénésie, furieusement
Ravinous, *adj.* ravineux
Ravish, *v.a.* ravir; (*law*) enlever; violer
Ravishable, *adj.* ravissable
Ravisher, *s.* ravisseur, *m.*
Ravishing, *adj.* ravissant; ravisseur; — *s.* *V.* **Ravishment** [à ravir
Ravishingly, *adv.* d'une manière ravissante,
Ravishment, *s.* ravissement, *m.*; (*law*) enlèvement, *m.*; viol, *m.*
Raw, *adj.* (*not cooked*) cru; (*unripe*) vert; (*unskilled*) novice, ignorant, inexpérimenté; (*sore*) écorché; ulcéré; (*of products*) brut; (*of temperature*) froid et humide; (*of liquors*) pur; (*of silk, thread*) grége, écru; — *s.* vif, *m.* —**boned,** *adj.* maigre, décharné, qui n'a que la peau et les os. — **flesh,** *s.* chair vive, *f.* — **hand,** *s.* novice, *m.f.* — **head,** *s.* loup-garou, *m.* — **hide,** *s.* cuir vert, cuir brut, *m.* — **materials,** *s.pl.* matières premières, matières brutes, *f.pl.* [vellement; sans provision
Rawly, *adv.* crûment; sans expérience; nou-
Rawness, *s.* crudité; inexpérience, *f.* (*of weather*) froid humide, *m.*
Ray, *s.* rayon, *m.*; (*fish*) raie, *f.*; — *v.a.* lancer, darder. — **grass,** *s.* ivraie vivace, *f.*, ray-grass, *m.* —**less,** *adj.* sans rayons; sans [éclat, obscur
Rayah, *s.* raïa, raya, rayah, *m.*
Raze, *v.a.* *V.* **Rase**
Razee, *s.* vaisseau rasé, *m.*; — *v.a.* raser
Razor, *s.* rasoir, *m.*; (*boar's tusk*) défense, *f.* — **back,** *s.* (*zool.*) jubarte, *f.* — **bill,** *s.* pingouin commun, *m.* — **cloth,** *s.* linge à barbe, *m.* — **fish,** *s.* rason, rasoir, coryphène, *m.*; (*shell-fish*) *V.* — **shell.** — **hone,** *s.* pierre à rasoir, *f.* — **shell,** *s.* solen, manche de couteau, *m.* — **strop,** *s.* cuir à rasoir, *m.*
Razzia, *s.* razzia, *f.* [nouveau (*after the verb*)
Re ..., (*before a verb*) re ..., ré ..., r ...; de
Reabsorb, *v.a.* réabsorber; (*med.*) résorber
Reabsorption, *s.* réabsorption, *f.*; (*med.*) résorption [site, *f.*; retour, *m.*
Reaccess, *s.* nouvel accès, *m.*; nouvelle vi-
Reach, *v.a.* (*to touch*) atteindre, toucher; (*to hand*) passer, donner; (*arrive at*) arriver à; gagner; (*come to hand*) parvenir à; (*have access*) parvenir jusqu'à; (*stretch*) étendre; (*extend*) s'étendre à; — *v.n.* s'étendre; pénétrer; (*carry*) porter; (*V.* **Retch.**) — *s.* (*distance*) portée, *f.*; (*extent,* &c.) étendue, *f.*; capacité, *f.*; pouvoir, *m.*; (*of a canal*) bief, biez, *m.* *Beyond —, out of —,* hors de (*or* de la) portée; (*escaped*) hors d'atteinte. *Within —,* à (*or* à la) portée. — **after,** *v.a.* s'efforcer d'atteindre
Reachable, &c. *V.* **Attainable,** &c.
React, *v.n.* réagir; résister; — *v.a.* rejouer
Reacting, *adj.* réactif; — *s.* *V.* **Reaction**
Reaction, *s.* réaction, *f.*; résistance, *f.*
Reactionary, *adj.*, **Reactionist,** *s.* réactionnaire, *m.f.*
Read, *v.a.n.* lire; déclamer; (*music*) lire; (*translate*) traduire, expliquer; (*study*) étudier; (*for*) se préparer (à); (*fathom*) pénétrer, démêler, lire dans; (*a lecture, reprimand*) faire; (*a lesson*) donner; (*be read*) se lire; être lisible; supporter la lecture. — or *play at sight,* (*music*) déchiffrer; (*books, V.* **Sight**). *To — to a person,* faire la lecture à quelqu'un. *This sentence does not —,* cette phrase ne fait aucun sens; dans cette période le sens n'est pas achevé *or* reste suspendu. *This does not — well,* cela ne fait pas bien. *How does it —?* quel effet cela fait-il? *I have — of a man who ...,* j'ai lu quelque part l'histoire d'un homme qui ...; ... *which we — of, ...* dont on parle *or* dont on fait mention dans les livres. — **again, over again,** relire; retraduire; étudier de nouveau; &c. — **over,** parcourir. — **over and over,** lire et relire
Read, *part. adj.* lu, &c. (*V.* **Read,** *v.a.n.*). *Well —, deeply —,* (*pers.*) instruit, savant, érudit, lettré, qui a beaucoup lu. *To be well — in,* connaître bien, être versé dans
Readable, *adj.* lisible; qui se lit
Readableness, *s.* lisibilité, *f.*
Readably, *adv.* lisiblement
Reader, *s.* lecteur, *m.*, -trice, *f.*; (*fond of reading*) liseur, *m.*, -euse, *f.*; (*in church*) clerc, *m.*; (*univers.*) professeur, *m.*; (*print.*) correcteur, lecteur, *m.*; (*reading-book*) livre de lecture, *m.*; (*reading-machine*) liseuse, *f.* *Kind* or *courteous* or *friendly* or *gentle —,* ami lecteur. *He is a great —,* c'est un grand liseur, il est grand liseur, il lit beaucoup
Readership, *s.* (*eccl.*) emploi de clerc qui lit les prières, *m.*; (*univers.*) chaire *f.*; (*print.*) emploi de correcteur, *m.*
Readily, *adv.* immédiatement, tout de suite; (*gladly*) volontiers, avec plaisir, avec joie, de bon cœur, de bonne grâce, avec empressement, sans hésiter; (*easily*) aisément, sans peine
Readiness, *s.* promptitude, *f.*; (*willingness*) empressement, *m.*; (*ease*) facilité, *f.*; (*of wit*) présence d'esprit, *f.*; (*in reply*) talent de repartie, *m.* *In —,* prêt, tout prêt
Reading, *s.* lecture, *f.*; (*of professors*) leçon, *f.*; (*translation*) traduction, explication, *f.*; (*study*) étude, *f.*; (*print.*) lecture, correction, *f.*; (*in politics*) discussion, lecture, *f.*; (*variation in a text*) leçon, *f.*; variante, *f.*; (*of the barometer,* &c.) variation, *f.*; indication, *f.* — **book,** *s.* livre de lecture, *m.* — **boy,** *s.* (*print.*) apprenti lecteur, *m.* — **cover,** *s.* grébiche, *f.* — **desk,** *s.* pupitre, &c. (*V.* **Desk**). — **hook,** *s.* liseuse, *f.* — **man,** *s.* travailleur, piocheur, *m.* — **portfolio,** *s.* grébiche, *f.* — **room,** *s.* (*of public libraries, clubs,* &c.) salle de lecture, *f.*; salon de lecture, *m.*; (*news-rooms*) cabinet de lecture, *m.* — **stand,** *s.* pupitre, *m.*
Readjourn, *v.a.* réajourner
Readjournment, *s.* réajournement, *m.*
Readjust, *v.a.* rajuster
Readjuster, *s.* rajusteur, *m.*
Readjustment, *s.* rajustement, *m.*
Readmission, Readmittance, *s.* réad- [mission, *f.*
Readmit, *v.a.* réadmettre
Readopt, *v.a.* réadopter
Readoption, *s.* réadoption, *f.*
Ready, *adj.* prêt (à); prompt (à); empressé (à); disposé (à), porté (à); de bonne volonté; (*clever*) qui a de la facilité; (*near*) près (de); (*easy*) facile; (*of money*) comptant; (*just published, on sale*) qui vient de paraître, publié, en vente; — *adv.* tout. —! (*int.*) (*mil.*) apprêtez

vos armes! *Making* —, préparation, *f.*; (*print.*, &c.) mise en train, *f.* *To get* or *make* —, (*v.a.*) préparer; apprêter; tenir prêt; (*print.*, &c.) mettre en train; (*v.n.*, *to get* or *make oneself* —) se préparer; s'apprêter; se tenir prêt. *Now* —, (*new book*) vient de paraître, en vente. — **armed,** *adj.* tout armé. —**formed,** *adj.* tout formé (*m.sing.*, toute formée, *f.sing.*, tout formés, *m.pl.*, toutes formées, *f.pl.*). —**made,** *adj.* confectionné, tout fait (*m.sing.*, toute faite, *f.sing.*, tout faits, *m.pl.*, toutes faites, *f.pl.*). —**made clothes shop,** *s.* maison de confection, *f.* —**made clothier,** *s.* confectionneur, marchand tailleur, *m.* —**made dresses,** *s.pl.* confections, *f.pl.* —**money,** *s.* argent comptant, *m.* — **reckoner,** *s.* [barême, *m.*

Reaffirm, *v.a.* réaffirmer

Reagent, *s.* réactif, *m.*

Real, *adj.* réel; vrai, véritable; effectif; (*of property*) immobilier, immeuble; — *s.* (*coin*) réal, *m.* — *action,* (*law*) action réelle, *f.* — *presence,* (*theol.*) présence réelle, *f.*

Realgar, *s.* réalgar, sulfure rouge d'arsenic, *m.*

Realism, *s.* réalisme, *m.*

Realist, *s.*, **Realistic,** *adj.* réaliste, *m.f.*

Reality, *s.* réalité, *f.*, réel, *m.* *In* —, en réalité, réellement

Realizable, *adj.* réalisable [bilisation, *f.*

Realization, *s.* réalisation, *f.*; (*law*) immo-

Realize, *v.a.* réaliser; effectuer; (*law*) immobiliser; (*understand,* &c.) comprendre, bien comprendre, bien sentir, se faire une idée juste de; calculer, se rendre compte de; mesurer; apprécier; concevoir; se figurer, se représenter; se faire; (*obtain*) obtenir; (*derive*) tirer, recueillir

Realizer, *s.* réalisateur, *m.*, -trice, *f.* [**zation**

Realizing, *adj.* réalisateur; — *s.* *V.* **Reali-**

Really, *adv.* réellement; en réalité, en effet, effectivement; vraiment, véritablement, en vérité; ma foi; (*candidly*) franchement

Realm, *s.* royaume, *m.*; domaine, *m.*; région, *f.*

Realty, *s.* (*law*) nature immobilière, *f.*; (*estate*) immeuble, bien immeuble, *m.*; immeubles, [biens immeubles, *m.pl.*

Ream, *s.* rame, *f.*

Reanimate, *v.a.* ranimer

Reanimation, *s.* action de ranimer, *f.*

Reap, *v.a.n.* moissonner; (*fig.*) recueillir, retirer. *To — the harvest,* faire la moisson

Reaper, *s.* moissonneur, *m.*, -euse, *f.*; (*machine*) moissonneuse, *f.*

Reaping, *s.* moisson, *f.*, moissonnage, *m.* — **hook,** *s.* faucille, *f.* — **machine,** *s.* moissonneuse, *f.* — **time,** *s.* temps de la moisson, *m.*, [moisson, *f.*

Reappear, *v.n.* reparaître

Reappearance, *s.* réapparition, *f.*; (*return of an actor to a theatre, reentering*) rentrée, *f.*; (*law*) comparution nouvelle, *f.*

Reappease, *v.a.* rapaiser

Reappeasement, *s.* rapaisement, *m.*

Reappoint, *v.a.* renommer; réélire

Reappointment, *s.* nouvelle nomination, *f.*; réélection, *f.*

Rear, *s.* dernier rang, *m.*, queue, *f.*; (*back*) arrière, derrière, dos, *m.*; (*mil.*) arrière-garde, *f.*; derrières, *m.pl.*; — *adj.* dernier; (*nearly raw*) *V.* **Rare**; (*in compounds*) arrière- ...; — *v.a.* élever; — *v.n.* se cabrer. *At* or *in the* —, derrière; par derrière. *At* or *in the* — *of,* derrière. *To bring up the* —, fermer la marche; (*mil.*) former l'arrière-garde; être en serre-file. *To attack in* —, attaquer en queue. — **admiral,** *s.* contre-amiral, *m.* — **guard,** *s.* arrière-garde, *f.* — **rank,** *s.* dernier rang, arrière-rang, serre-file, *m.* — **up,** *v.a.* élever; *v.n.* se cabrer

Rearer, Rearing. *V.* **Breeder, Breeding**

Rearm, *v.a.* réarmer

Rearmament, *s.* réarmement, *m.*

Reascend, *v.a.n.* remonter [montée, *f.*

Reascent, *s.* nouvelle ascension, nouvelle

Reason, *s.* raison, *f.*; — *v.a.n.* raisonner. *By — of,* en raison de; pour cause de. *The — for which, the — why, the — that,* la raison par *or* pour laquelle. *For that very — that ..,* par cela même que ..., précisément parce que ... *To bring to* —, mettre à la raison. *To have, to give — to,* avoir, donner lieu de. *There is every — to,* il y a tout lieu de. *To listen to* —, entendre raison. *That stands to* —, cela tombe sous le sens, cela est évident, cela va sans dire; cela est parfaitement raisonnable, c'est trop juste. *It stands to — that ...,* la raison (*or* le bon sens) dit que ..., il est évident que ..., il va sans dire que ... —**less,** *adj.* sans raison [modique

Reasonable, *adj.* raisonnable; (*tolerable*)

Reasonableness, *s.* raison, *f.*; justesse, *f.*; modération, *f.*

Reasonably, *adv.* raisonnablement

Reasoner, *s.* logicien, dialecticien, *m.*

Reasoning, *s.* raisonnement, *m.*

Reassemble, *v.a.* assembler de nouveau, rassembler; — *v.n.* s'assembler de nouveau, se rassembler

Reassert, *v.a.* affirmer *or* &c. (*V.* **Assert**) de nouveau [**Assess**) de nouveau

Reassess, *v.a.* réimposer, imposer *or* &c. (*V.*

Reassessment, *s.* réimposition, *f.*

Reassign, *v.a.* réassigner

Reassignment, *s.* réassignation, *f.*

Reassume, &c. *V.* **Resume,** &c.

Reassurance, *s.* rassurance, *f.*; (*reinsurance*) réassurance, *f.*

Reassure, *v.a.* rassurer; (*reinsure*) réassurer

Reassurer, *s.* réassureur, *m.*

Reattach, *v.a.* rattacher

Reattachment, *s.* nouvel attachement, *m.*

Reattempt, *v.a.* tenter *or* &c. (*V.* **Attempt**) de nouveau [tion, *f.*

Rebaptism, Rebaptization, *s.* rebaptisa-

Rebaptize, *v.a.* rebaptiser

Rebaptizer, *s.* rebaptisant, rebaptisateur, *m.*

Rebate, *v.a.* émousser; diminuer, adoucir; — *s.* diminution, *f.*, rabais, *m.*, réduction, *f.*; (*com.*) réfaction, *f.*; (*arith.*) règle d'escompte, *f.*; (*rabbet*) *V.* **Rabbet**

Rebatement, *s.* *V.* **Rebate**; (*her.*) brisure, *f.*

Rebec, *s.* rebec, *m.* [*v.n.* se révolter

Rebel, *s. adj.* rebelle, *m.f.*, révolté, *m.*, e, *f.*; —

Rebellion, *s.* rébellion, révolte, *f.*

Rebellious, *adj.* rebelle, révolté

Rebelliously, *adv.* en rebelle

Rebelliousness, *s.* caractère de rébellion, *m.*; nature rebelle, *f.*

Reblossom, *v.n.* refleurir

Reboil, *v.n.* rebouillir

Rebound, *v.n.* rebondir; rejaillir; (*resound*) retentir; — *s.* rebond, *m.*; rebondissement, *m.*; rejaillissement, *m.*; contre-coup, *m.*

Rebounding, *s.* *V.* **Rebound**

Rebreathe, *v.a.* respirer de nouveau

Rebuff, *s.* rebuffade, *f.*; rebut, *m.*; refus, échec, *m.*; — *v.a.* repousser; rebuter

Rebuild, *v.a.* rebâtir, reconstruire

Rebuilding, *s.* reconstruction, *f.*

Rebukable, *adj.* répréhensible, blâmable

Rebuke, *v.a.* réprimander, reprendre; — *s.* réprimande, *f.*; (*rebuff*) rebuffade, *f.*

Rebuker, *s.* personne qui réprimande, *f.*, censeur, *m.*

Rebukingly, *adv.* avec une réprimande

Rebus, *s.* rébus, *m.*; (*her.*) armes parlantes, *f.pl.*

Rebut, *v.a.* repousser; — *v.n.* riposter; (*law*) dupliquer, faire une duplique

Rebutter, *s.* (*law*) duplique, *f.* *To put in a* —, faire une duplique, dupliquer

Recalcitrant, *adj.* récalcitrant

Recalcitrate, *v.n.* récalcitrer

Recall, *v.a.* rappeler; rétracter, retirer; révoquer; (*remember*) se rappeler; — *s.* rappel, *m.*; rétractation, *f.*; révocation, *f.*

Recallable, *adj.* rappelable; révocable

Recant, *v.a.* rétracter; abjurer; — *v.n.* se rétracter, se dédire; abjurer; (*in contempt*) chanter la palinodie

Recantation, *s.* rétractation, *f.*; abjuration, *f.*; (*in contempt*) palinodie, *f.*

Recanter, *s.* personne qui se rétracte *or* se dédit *or* abjure, *f.*; (*in contempt*) personne qui chante la palinodie, *f.*

Recapitulate, *v.a.* récapituler

Recapitulation, *s.* récapitulation, *f.*

Recapitulatory, *adj.* récapitulatif

Recaption, *s.* reprise, *f.*

Recaptor, *s.* repreneur, *m.*, -euse, *f.*

Recapture, *s.* reprise, recousse, *f.*; — *v.a.* reprendre

Recapturing, *adj.* repreneur; — *s.* reprise, *f.*

Recarry, *v.a.* reporter, rapporter

Recast, *v.a.* refondre; recompter, calculer *or* additionner *or* &c. (*V.* **Cast**) de nouveau

Recede, *v.n.* reculer, se retirer, s'éloigner (de); se désister (de); se rétracter (de); décliner; — *v.a.* recéder

Receding, *adj.* qui se retire, qui s'éloigne, qui fuit; — *s.* éloignement, *m.*; rétractation, *f.*; désistement, *m.*

Receipt, *s.* (*of a letter,* &c.) réception, *f.*; reçu, *m.*; (*recipe*) recette, *f.*; (*of money,* &c.) reçu, *m.*, quittance, *f.*; acquit, *m.*; (*money received*) recette, *f.*; (*of papers*) récépissé, *m.*; — *v.a.* donner un reçu pour; (*com.*) acquitter. — *in full,* quittance pour solde de compte. *On — of,* au reçu de; (*stamps, P.O. order,* &c.) contre envoi de (timbres-poste, &c.). *To acknowledge the — of,* accuser réception de. *To be in — of,* avoir reçu. *To put a — to,* acquitter. — **book,** *s.* livre de quittances, livre de mémoires acquittés, *m.*; (*household*) livre de ménage, *m.*; (*of receipts*) livre de recettes, *m.* — **stamp,** *s.* papier timbré pour quittance, *m.*

Receivable, *adj.* recevable, admissible, valable; (*com.*) à recevoir

Receivableness, Receivability, *s.* recevabilité, admissibilité, validité, *f.*

Receive, *v.a.* recevoir; (*conceal*) recéler. *To — stolen goods,* recéler des objets volés

Received, *part. adj.* reçu, &c.; (*to be written on a receipt before o.'s signature*) pour acquit

Receiver, *s.* receveur, *m.*, -euse, *f.*, recevant, *m.*, e, *f.*; (*of*) personne qui reçoit ..., *f.*; (*sharer*) dispensataire, distributaire, *m.f.*; (*com.*) réceptionnaire, *m.f.*; (*of letters, parcels*) destinataire, *m.f.*; (*admin.*) receveur, percepteur, *m.*; (*of stolen goods*) recéleur, *m.*, -euse, *f.*; (*a vessel*) récipient, *m.* — *of stolen goods,* recéleur, *m.*, -euse, *f.*

Receivership, *s.* emploi (*m.*) *or* charge (*f.*) de receveur, recette, *f.*

Receiving, *s.* réception, *f.*; (*of stolen goods*) recel, recèlement, *m.* — **house, -office,** *s.* (*for goods*) bureau de messagerie, *m.*; (*for parcels delivery*) bureau de factage, *m.*; (*post.*) boîte de quartier, petite poste, *f.*, petit bureau de poste, *m.*; (*of the Royal Humane Society*) maison de secours pour les noyés, *f.* — **ship,** *s.* vaisseau-cayenne, *m.*

Recency, *s.* récence, nouveauté, date récente, *f.*

Recension, *s.* recension, *f.*; énumération, *f.*

Recensionist, *s.* recenseur, *m.*

Recent, *adj.* récent, nouveau

Recently, *adv.* récemment, nouvellement. *Until —,* jusque dans ces derniers temps

Recentness, *s. V.* **Recency**

Receptacle, *s.* réceptacle, *m.*; (*retreat*) retraite, *f.*, asile, refuge, *m.*; (*anat.*) réservoir, *m.*

Receptacular, *adj.* réceptaculaire

Reception, *s.* réception, *f.*; admission, *f.*; (*welcome*) accueil, *m.*

Receptive, *adj.* capable de recevoir

Receptivity, *s.* réceptivité, *f.*

Recess, *s.* retraite, *f.*; (*in a wall*) renfoncement, enfoncement, *m.*; niche, *f.*; (*for a bed*) alcôve, *f.*; (*secret*) secret, mystère, *m.*; (*of the heart*) repli, *m.*; (*vacation*) vacances *f.pl.*; (*hist., dipl.*) recez, recès, *m.*

Recession, *s.* récession, retraite, *f.*; (*from a claim*) désistement, *m.*; (*giving back*) restitution, *f.*

Rechabite, *s.* réchabite, *m.*

Recharge, *v.a.n.* recharger

Recheat, *s.* rappel, requêté, *m.*; — *v.n.* sonner le rappel *or* le requêté

Recipe, *s.* recette, *f.*, récipé, *m.*; (*med.*) ordonnance, *f.*

Recipient, *s.* (*pers.*) recevant, *m.*, e, *f.*, (*of*) personne (*f.*) *or* celui (*m.*, celle, *f.*) qui reçoit ...; &c. (*V.* **Receiver**); (*of a diploma,* &c.) impétrant, *m.*, e, *f.*; (*things*) réceptacle, *m.*, (*of*) chose qui reçoit ..., *f.*, ce qui reçoit ..., *m.*; (*chem., tech.*) récipient, *m.*

Reciprocal, *adj. s.* réciproque, *adj. m.f.*, *s.f.*

Reciprocally, *adv.* réciproquement

Reciprocalness, *s.* réciprocité, *f.*

Reciprocate, *v.a.* échanger; rendre; répondre à; éprouver de son côté *or* pour sa part

Reciprocating, *adj.* alternatif, de va et-vient

Reciprocation, Reciprocity, *s.* réciprocité, *f.*; échange, *m.*; retour, *m.*; (*mech.*) révolution, *f.*, tour de roue, *m.*

Recision, *s.* rescision, *f.*

Recital, *s.* récitation, répétition, *f.*; (*tale*) récit, *m.*, narration, *f.*; (*entertainment*) séance (musicale, *or* de déclamation, &c.), *f.*; (*law*) exposé, *m.*

Recitation, *s.* récitation, *f.*

Recitative, *s.* récitatif, *m.*

Recitatively, *adv.* en récitatif

Recite, *v.a.n.* réciter, répéter; (*relate*) raconter; exposer

Reciter, *s.* récitateur, *m.*, -trice, *f.*, réciteur, *m.*, -euse, *f.*

Reck, *v.n.a.* se soucier (de); s'inquiéter (de); (*imp.*) importer. *What —s it?* qu'importe? *It —s me not,* peu m'importe. *Little he'll —,* peu lui importe. **—less,** *adj.* insouciant; nonchalant; imprévoyant; imprudent; téméraire; insensé. **—lessly,** *adv.* avec insouciance; avec nonchalance; avec imprévoyance; imprudemment; témérairement; furieusement. **—lessness,** *s.* insouciance, *f.*; nonchalance, *f.*; imprévoyance, *f.*; imprudence, *f.*; témérité, *f.*

Reckon, *v.a.n.* compter ('*on,*' '*upon,*' sur); évaluer; estimer, juger, considérer comme, regarder comme. *—ing from to-day,* à compter d'aujourd'hui; dès aujourd'hui. — **again,** recompter. — **off,** décompter, défalquer. — **up,** additionner

Reckoner, *s.* calculateur, *m.*, -trice, *f.*, compteur, *m.*, -euse, *f.*, chiffreur, *m.*, -euse, *f.* (*V.* **Ready**)

Reckoning, *s.* compte, calcul, *m.*; (*nav.*) estime, *f.*; (*at an inn*) compte, écot, *m.*; (*at an eating-house*) addition, *f.* *Short —s make long friends,* les bons comptes font les bons amis. — **off,** *s.* décompte, *m.*, défalcation, *f.* — **up,** *s.* addition, *f.*

Reclaim, *v.a.* réformer, corriger, ramener au bien, ramener dans la bonne voie; (*criminals*) moraliser; (*from*) faire revenir (de); tirer (de); (*waste lands*) défricher, cultiver; bâtir sur; (*to claim, claim back*) réclamer, redemander

Reclaimable, *adj.* (*pers.*) réformable, ramenable, corrigible; (*of waste lands*) défrichable, cultivable; (*claimable*) réclamable

Reclaimant, *s. V.* **Claimant**

Reclaimer, *s.* réformateur, *m.*, -trice, *f.*; (*of waste lands*) défricheur, *m.*

Reclaiming, Reclamation, *s.* réforme, *f.*; (*of criminals*) moralisation, *f.*; (*of waste lands*) défrichement, *m.*, culture, *f.*; (*claim*) *V.* **Claim,** *s.*

Reclassing, *s.* reclassement, *m.*

Reclination, *s.* position inclinée, *f.*; (*dialling, surg.*) réclinaison, *f.*

Reclinant, *adj.* réclinant

Reclinate, *adj.* récliné

Recline, *v.n.* s'incliner, se pencher; s'appuyer; se coucher; se reposer; (*dialling*) récliner;

— *v.a.* incliner, pencher; appuyer; coucher; reposer; (*dialling*) récliner

Reclining, *adj.* incliné, penché; appuyé; couché; — *s.* position inclinée, *f.* — **chair,** *s.* fauteuil à la Voltaire, *m.*

Reclose, *v.a.* refermer; — *v.n.* se refermer

Recluse, *adj.* reclus; de reclus; (*sequestered*) séparé, éloigné; — *s.* reclus, *m.*, e, *f.*

Reclusely, *adv.* en reclus

Recluseness, Reclusion, *s.* réclusion, *f.*

Recognition, *s.* reconnaissance, *f.*

Recognitory, *adj.* récognitif

Recognizable, *adj.* reconnaissable

Recognizance, *s.* reconnaissance, *f.*; (*law*) obligation, *f.* *To enter into —s,* s'engager à comparaître; souscrire une obligation en due forme

Recognize, *v.a.* reconnaître. *He is not to be —d,* il n'est pas reconnaissable, il est méconnaissable

Recoil, *v.n.* reculer (*from,* devant; *with,* de); (*upon*) retomber (sur), retourner (sur); — *s.* recul, *m.*; (*fig.*) répugnance, aversion, horreur, *f.* — **escapement,** *s.* échappement à recul, *m.*

Recoiling, *s.* *V.* **Recoil,** *s.*

Recoin, *v.a.* refondre, refrapper

Recoinage, *s.* (*of money*) refonte (de monnaie, des monnaies), *f.*; (*new coin*) monnaie de refonte, nouvelle monnaie, *f.*

Recollect, *v.a.* *V.* **Remember.** — *oneself,* se recueillir; se remettre

Recollection, *s.* souvenir, *m.*

Recombination, *s.* combinaison nouvelle, *f.*

Recombine, *v.a.* recombiner

Recomfort, *v.a.* reconsoler, consoler de nouveau; (*give strength*) reconforter, fortifier

Recommence, *v.a.n.* recommencer

Recommencement, *s.* recommencement, *m.*

Recommend, *v.a.* recommander; (*in o.'s favour*) pour, *prep.* *He has nothing else to — him,* il n'a que cela pour lui

Recommendable, *adj.* recommandable

Recommendableness, *s.* nature recommandable, *f.*, mérite, *m.*

Recommendably, *adv.* recommandablement

Recommendation, *s.* recommandation, *f.*; (*on a petition*) apostille, *f.*

Recommendatory, *adj.* de recommandation

Recommender, *s.* recommandeur, *m.*, -euse, *f.*

Recommit, *v.a.* renvoyer en prison; renvoyer à une commission

Recommitment, Recommittal, *s.* nouvelle incarcération, *f.*; renvoi à une commission, *m.*

Recompense, *v.a.* récompenser; (*indemnify*) dédommager, indemniser; (*compensate*) compenser; réparer; — *s.* récompense, *f.*; dédommagement, *m.*, indemnité, *f.*; compensation, *f.*; réparation, *f.*; retour, équivalent, *m.*

Recompenser, *s.* récompenseur, *m.*

Recomposable, *adj.* recomposable

Recompose, *v.a.* recomposer; tranquilliser, calmer

Recomposition, *s.* recomposition, *f.*

Reconcilable, *adj.* (*pers.*) réconciliable; (*things*) conciliable, compatible

Reconcilableness, *s.* (*pers.*) possibilité d'être réconcilié, *f.*; (*things*) possibilité de conciliation, compatibilité, *f.*

Reconcile, *v.a.* réconcilier; accorder, mettre d'accord; (*accustom*) accoutumer, habituer; (*things*) concilier; arranger. *To — oneself to, to become* or *get* or *be —d to* (*things*), s'accoutumer à, s'habituer à, se faire à; se résigner à

Reconcilement, *s.* *V.* **Reconciliation**

Reconciler, *s.* réconciliateur, *m.*, -trice, *f.*; conciliateur, *m.*, -trice, *f.*

Reconciliation, *s.* réconciliation, *f.*, raccommodement, *m.*; (*things*) conciliation, *f.*; expiation, *f.*

Reconciliatory, *adj.*(*pers.*) réconciliatoire, réconciliateur; (*things*) conciliatoire, conciliateur

Recondite, *adj.* secret, caché; abstrus; profond; mystérieux

Reconduct, *v.a.* reconduire

Reconfirm, *v.a.* reconfirmer

Reconfirmation, *s.* reconfirmation, *f.*

Reconnaissance, *s.* reconnaissance, *f.*

Reconnoitre, *v.a.* reconnaître; — *v.n.* faire une reconnaissance. *To go and —,* pousser une reconnaissance sur *or* jusqu'à. *To go —ing,* aller en reconnaissance, faire une reconnaissance

Reconnoitring, *s.* reconnaissance, *f.*; — *adj.* de reconnaissance. — **party,** *s.* détachement envoyé en reconnaissance, *m.*

Reconquer, *v.a.* reconquérir; (*fig.*) recouvrer

Reconsider, *v.a.* reconsidérer; revenir sur

Reconsideration, *s.* reconsidération, *f.*

Reconsolidate, *v.a.* reconsolider

Reconsolidation, *s.* reconsolidation, *f.*

Reconstitute, *v.a.* reconstituer

Reconstitution, *s.* reconstitution, *f.*

Reconstruct, *v.a.* reconstruire

Reconstruction, *s.* reconstruction, *f.*

Reconvert, *v.a.* reconvertir

Reconvey, *v.a.* reporter, ramener; (*law*) rétrocéder

Reconveyance, *s.* nouveau transport, *m.*; (*law*) rétrocession, *f.*

Recopy, *v.a.* recopier

Record, *v.a.* enregistrer; inscrire, consigner; graver, imprimer; mentionner, rapporter; indiquer; célébrer; — *s.* registre, *m.*; mention, trace, *f.*, signe, *m.*, marque, *f.*, souvenir, *m.*; **—s,** *pl.* registres, *m.pl.*, &c.; annales, *f.pl.*, fastes, *m.pl.*; archives, *f.pl.*; notes, *f.pl.*, mémoires, *m.pl.* *Keeper of the —s,* archiviste, *m.*; greffier, *m.* *On* or *upon —,* enregistré; inscrit; dans les annales de l'histoire, rapporté dans l'histoire. *It is on — that ...,* il est fait mention dans l'histoire que ... — **office,** *s.* archives, *f.pl.*; greffe, *m.*

Recorder, *s.* archiviste, *m.*; greffier, *m.*; historiographe, historien, *m.*; juge, *m.*

Recordership, *s.* charge d'archiviste *or* de greffier, *f.*; fonctions de juge, *f.pl.*

Recorrect, *v.a.* recorriger

Recount, *v.a.* raconter, rapporter; (*count again*) recompter

Recoup, *v.a.* indemniser, dédommager (de); compenser; recouvrer, rattraper; reprendre; (*o.'s expenses*) rentrer dans (ses fonds). — *oneself,* (*by*) se rattraper (sur), se retirer (sur)

Recoupment, *s.* indemnité, *f.*; reprise, *f.*

Recourse, *s.* recours, *m.* *To have — to,* avoir recours à, recourir à

Recover, *v.a.* (*to get again*) recouvrer; retrouver; regagner; rattraper; ravoir; (*health*) recouvrer; (*pers.*) rétablir, guérir; faire revenir; remettre; (*repair*) réparer; (*retake*) reprendre; reconquérir; (*obtain*) obtenir; (*com., fin.*) recouvrer; (*cover anew*) recouvrir; — *v.n.* (*from illness*) se rétablir, se remettre, guérir; relever; revenir; (*from surprise, fright,* &c.) revenir; se remettre; (*from misfortune, losses*) se relever; (*law*) avoir gain de cause. *To — oneself,* revenir à soi; (*from illness*) se remettre, se rétablir

Recoverable, *adj.* recouvrable, retrouvable; réparable; (*of money,* &c.) recouvrable; (*pers.*) guérissable

Recovery, *s.* recouvrement, *m.*; reprise, *f.*; (*of health*) rétablissement, recouvrement, *m.*, guérison, *f.*; (*law*) obtention, *f.*; (*of debts,* &c.) recouvrement, *m.* *Past —,* désespéré, incurable; sans remède; sans ressource

Recreant, *adj. s.* lâche, *m.f.*, poltron, *m.*, -ne, *f.*; infidèle, *m.f.*; apostat, *m.*

Recreate, *v.a.* (*create again*) recréer; (*divert*) récréer, distraire, divertir

Recreation, *s.* (*new creation*) nouvelle création, *f.*; (*diversion*) récréation, distraction, *f.*, divertissement, *m.*

Recreative, *adj.* récréatif, divertissant, amusant

Recreatively, *adv.* récréativement

Recreativeness, *s.* nature récréative, *f.*

Recriminate, *v.n.* récriminer

Recrimination, *s.* récrimination, *f.*

Recriminating, Recriminative, *adj.* récriminateur

Recriminator, *s.* récriminateur, *m.*, -trice, *f.*

Recriminatory, *adj.* récriminatoire

Recross, *v.a.* retraverser ; repasser

Recrudescenc-e, y, *s.* recrudescence, *f.*

Recrudescent, *adj.* recrudescent

Recruit, *v.a.* réparer, rétablir, refaire ; (*troops,* &c.) recruter ; — *v.n., v.r.* (— *oneself*) se rétablir, se remettre, se refaire, se retremper, reprendre ; (*of troops,* &c.) se recruter ; — *s.* recrue, *f.* ; (*young soldier*) conscrit, *m.* ; (*fig.*) renfort, *m.*

Recruiter, *s.*, **Recruiting,** *adj.* recruteur, *m.*

Recruiting, Recruitment, *s.* recrutement, *m.*

Rectal, *adj.* rectal

Rectangle, *s.* rectangle, *m.*

Rectangled, Rectangular, *adj.* rectangle, rectangulaire ; à angle droit

Rectangularity, *s.* rectangularité, *f.*

Rectangularly, *adv.* à angles droits

Rectifiable, *adj.* rectifiable

Rectification, *s.* rectification, *f.*

Rectificatory, *adj.* rectificatif

Rectifier, *s.* rectificateur, *m.*, -trice, *f.*

Rectify, *v.a.* rectifier ; redresser ; corriger

Rectilineal, Rectilinear, *adj.* rectiligne

Rectitude, *s.* (*intellectual*) rectitude, *f.* ; (*moral*) droiture, *f.* [*Protestants*) ministre, pasteur, *m.*

Rector, *s.* recteur, *m.* ; (*eccl.*) curé, *m.* ; (*among*

Rectoral, Rectorial, *adj.* rectoral ; (*eccl.*) curial, de *or* du curé, de la cure [(*eccl.*) cure, *f.*

Rectorate, Rectorship, *s.* rectorat, *m.* ;

Rectory. *V.* **Vicarage**

Rectum, *s.* rectum, *m.*

Recumbenc-e, y, *s.* position d'une personne couchée, *f.* ; repos, *m.* [appuyé ; (*bot.*) couché

Recumbent, *adj.* couché, étendu ; (*leaning*)

Recuperation, *s.* récupération, *f.*

Recur, *v.n.* revenir à l'esprit; revenir, reparaître, se représenter ; se reproduire, arriver ; (*pers.*) avoir recours (à), recourir (à)

Recurrence, *s.* retour, *m.* ; renouvellement, *m.* ; recours, *m.* *To be of frequent* —, revenir fréquemment [périodique

Recurrent, Recurring, *adj.* qui revient,

Recurvate, Recurve, *v.a.* recourber; —, —**d,** *adj.* recourbé

Recusancy, *s.* non-conformité, *f.*

Recusant, *s. adj.* non-conformiste, *m.f.*

Red, *adj.* rouge ; (*of the hair*) roux ; (*of the face, nose*) rouge ; enluminé ; (*rosy*) vermeil ; (*of herrings*) saur ; — *s.* rouge, *m.* ; (*of the hair*) roux, *m.* — **berried,** *adj.* à baies rouges. —**breast,** *s.* rouge-gorge, *m.* — **chalk,** *s.* craie rouge, *f.* ; (*min.*) sanguine, *f.* ; (*carp.*) rubrique, *f.* — **coat,** *s.* troupier, *m.* ; tourlourou, pioupiou, *m.* — **face,** *s.* visage enluminé, *m.* — **gum,** *s.* strophule, *m.* —**haired,** *adj.* roux. —**heat,** *s.* rouge, *m.* *At a — heat,* chauffé au rouge. — **hot,** *adj.* rouge, tout rouge, chauffé au rouge, tout chaud ; (*of fire, coals*) ardent. — **lead,** *s.* minium, *m.* —**legged,** *adj.* (*of partridges,* &c.) rouge. —**letter day,** *s.* jour de fête, jour férié, *m.* —**pole,** *s.* sizerin, *m.*, linotte cabaret, *f.* — **River,** *s.* (la) Rivière Rouge, *f.* — **root,** *s.* céanothe, *m.* — **Sea,** *s.* (la) Mer Rouge, *f.* —**shank,** *s.* (*bird*) chevalier, *m.*, gambette, *f.* —**snow,** *s.* terre rouge de la neige, neige rouge, *f.* —**start, -tail,** *s.* rouge-queue, *m.* —**tape,** *s.* ruban (de fil) rouge, *m.* ; (*fig.*) routine administrative, routine, *f.* ; réglementation, *f.* ; bureaucratie, *f.* ; *adj.* routinier ; bureaucratique. —**tapism,** *s.* bureaucratie, *f.* ; formalités surannées, *f.pl.*, formalisme, *m.*, routine, *f.* — **tapist,** *s.* bureaucrate, plumitif, *m.* ; routinier, *m.* — **wing,** *s.* mauvis, *m.*

Redan, *s.* redan, *m.* — **line,** *s.* ligne à redans, *f.*

Redden, *v.a.n.* rougir

Reddish, *adj.* rougeâtre

Reddishness, *s.* couleur *or* teinte rougeâtre, *f.*

Reddle, *s.* craie rouge, rubrique, *f.* ; (*min.*) ocre rouge, *f.*

Redeem, *v.a.* racheter ; délivrer, libérer ; compenser ; (*out of pawn*) dégager, retirer ; (*o.'s word,* &c.) dégager ; (*a promise,* &c.) s'acquitter de, acquitter, remplir, accomplir ; (*time, a fault*) réparer ; (*com., fin.*) rembourser, racheter ; amortir [boursable, rachetable

Redeemable, *adj.* rachetable ; (*com., fin.*) rem-

Redeemableness, *s.* nature rachetable *or* remboursable, *f.* ; faculté de rachat, *f.*

Redeemer, *s.* racheteur, *m.*, -euse, *f.* ; libérateur, *m.*, -trice, *f.* ; (*theol.*) Rédempteur, *m.*

Redeeming, *adj.* qui rachète, réparateur, rédempteur ; — *s.* rachat, *m.* ; délivrance, *f.* ; libération, *f.* ; dégagement, *m.* ; compensation, *f.* ; réparation, *f.* ; (*com., fin.*) remboursement, rachat, *m.*; amortissement, *m.* *A— quality,* une qualité qui rachète des défauts [nouveau

Redeliver *v.a.* restituer, rendre ; délivrer de

Redelivery, *s.* restitution, *f.* ; nouvelle délivrance, *f.* [de restitution, *f.*

Redemand, *v.a.* redemander ; — *s.* demande

Redemandable, *adj.* redemandable

Redemise, *v.a.* rétrocéder ; — *s.* rétrocession, *f.*

Redemption, *s.* rachat. *m.* ; délivrance, *f.* ; (*theol.*) rédemption, *f.* ; (*com., fin.*) remboursement, rachat, *m.* ; amortissement, *m.* ; (*law*) réméré, rachat, *m.*

Redemptive, Redemptory, *adj.* rédempteur

Redescend, *v.n.a.* redescendre

Redintegrate, *v.a.* réintégrer, rétablir

Redintegration, *s.* réintégration, *f.*, rétablissement, *m.* [compte, *m.*

Rediscount, *v.a.* réescompter; — *s.* rées-

Redissolve, *v.a.* redissoudre

Redistil, *v.a.* redistiller

Redistillation, *s.* redistillation, *f.*

Redistribute, *v.a.* redistribuer

Redistribution, *s.* redistribution, *f.*

Redness, *s.* rougeur, *f.*, rouge, *m.*, couleur rouge, *f.*; (*carrotiness*) rousseur, couleur rousse, *f.* *To heat to* —, chauffer au rouge

Redolenc-e, y, *s.* parfum, *m.*, odeur agréable, odeur, senteur, *f.*

Redolent, *adj.* odoriférant, odorant, parfumé ; qui exhale une odeur *or* un parfum (de), qui

Redouble, *v.a.n.* redoubler [sent (le, la, les)

Redoubling, *s.* redoublement, *m.*

Redoubt, *s.* redoute, *f.* ; fort, *m.* ; fortification, *f.* *Castle* —, château fort, *m.* *Field* —, fortification de campagne, *f.* [redouté

Redoubtable, Redoubted, *adj.* redoutable,

Redound, *v.n.* rejaillir (sur) ; revenir (à) ; contribuer (à), tendre (à)

Redout, *s.* *V.* **Redoubt**

Redowa, *s.* rédowa, *f.*

Redraft, *s.* (*com.*) retraite, *f.*

Redress, *v.a.* redresser, rectifier ; réparer ; réformer, corriger ; (*pers.*) faire *or* rendre justice à ; (*relieve*) soulager, secourir ; — *s.* réparation, satisfaction, *f.* ; justice, *f.* ; réformation, *f.* ; soulagement, secours, *m.* ; remède, *m.* —**less,** *adj.* irréparable, sans remède

Redresser, *s.* redresseur, *m.*, -euse, *f.*

Redressible, *adj.* réparable

Reduce, *v.a.* réduire ; convertir ; (*bring, put*) mettre ; (*impoverish*) appauvrir ; (*in flesh*) maigrir ; (*degrade*) dégrader ; (— *to the ranks*) casser. *To — to practice,* mettre en pratique. *To — to rule,* soumettre à des règles fixes. *To be in —d circumstances,* être tombé dans la gêne. —**d** *scale,* échelle réduite, *f.*

Reducer, *s.* réducteur, *m.*

Reducible, *adj.* réductible

Reducibleness, *s.* réductibilité, *f.*

Reduct, *s.* réduit, *m.*

Reduction, *s.* réduction, *f.* ; baisse, *f.*

Reductive, *adj.* réductif

Reductively, *adv.* réductivement

Reduit, *s.* réduit, *m.*

Redundanc-e, y, *s.* surabondance, *f.*; (*of style*) redondance, *f.*

Redundant, *adj.* surabondant; (*of style*) redondant [*style*) redondamment

Redundantly, *adv.* surabondamment; (*of*

Reduplicable, *adj.* réduplicable

Reduplicate, *v.a.* redoubler; — *adj.* rédupliqué, redoublé, double [ment, *m.*

Reduplication, *s.* réduplication, *f.*, redouble-

Reduplicative, *adj. s.* réduplicatif, *adj.m.*, -ive, *f.*, réduplicatif, *s.m.*

Reduplicatively, *adv.* réduplicativement

Reecho, *v.a.* répéter; redire; — *v.n.* retentir, résonner; — *s.* écho répété, retentissement, *m.*

Reed, *s.* roseau, *m.*; canne, *f.*; (*pipe*) chalumeau, *m.*; (*mouth-piece*) anche, *f.*; (*arrow*) flèche, *f.*; (*of weavers*) peigne, *m.*; (*anat.*) caillette, *f.*; — *v.a.* canneler. — **bed,** *s. V.* — **marsh.** — **bird,** *s. V.* **Rice-bird.** — **bunting,** *s.* bruant de roseau, *m.* — **cane,** *s.* roseau, *m.* — **field,** *s. V.* — **marsh.** — **grass,** *s.* rubanier, *m.* — **less,** *adj.* sans roseaux. — **mace,** *s.* typha, *m.*, massette, *f.* — **marsh,** *s.* roselière, *f.*, marais roselier, *m.* — **pipe,** *s.* chalumeau, *m.*; (*of an organ*) tuyau à anche, *m.* — **sparrow,** *s. V.* — **bunting.** — **stop, -work,** *s.* (*of an organ*) jeu à anches, *m.* — **warbler,** *s.* rousserolle, salicaire, *f.*

Reeded, *adj.* couvert *or* plein de roseaux; (*channelled*) cannelé; (*mus.*) à anche

Reedification, *s.* réédification, *f.*

Reedify, *v.a.* réédifier, rebâtir

Reeding, *s.* cannelure, *f.*

Reedit, *v.a.* rééditer

Reedy, *adj.* couvert *or* plein de roseaux

Reef, *s.* (*rock*) récif, *m.*; écueil, *m.*; (*of coral*) banc, *m.*; (*of sails*) ris, *m.*; — *v.a.* (*nav.*) prendre un ris (*or* des ris) à, riser, carguer. *To let out a* —, larguer un ris. *To take in a* —, prendre un ris. — **band,** *s.* bande de ris, *f.* — **knot,** *s.* nœud plat, *m.* — **line, -point,** *s.* garcette de ris, *f.* — **tackle,** *s.* palan de ris, *m.*

Reek, *v.n.* fumer; s'exhaler; — *s.* fumée, *f.*; vapeur, exhalaison, *f.* —*ing*, fumant. —*ing with*, tout fumant de. —*ing hot*, tout chaud et [tout fumant

Reeky, *adj.* enfumé, noirci

Reel, *s.* (*turning frame*) dévidoir, *m.*; (*roller*) bobine, *f.*; (*fish.*) moulinet, *m.*; (*of ropemakers*) touret, *m.*; (*nav.*) tour, *m.*; (*dance*) branle, *m.*; — *v.a.* (— **off**) dévider; — *v.n.* tourner; (*stagger*) chanceler, tituber, aller en zigzag, faire des zigzags. *Scotch* —, branle écossais, *m.*, [écossaise, *f.*

Reelect, *v.a.* réélire

Reelection, *s.* réélection, *f.*

Reeligibility, *s.* rééligibilité, *f.*

Reeligible, *adj.* rééligible

Reembarcation, *s.* rembarquement, *m.*

Reembark, *v.a.* rembarquer; — *v.n.* se rembarquer

Reembarkation, Reembarking, Reembarkment, *s.* rembarquement, *m.*

Reembodiment, *s.* réincorporation, *f.*

Reembody, *v.a.* réincorporer

Reemigrate, *v.n.* réémigrer

Reemigration, *s.* réémigration, *f.*

Reemission, *s.* réémission, *f.*

Reemit, *v.a.* réémettre

Reemploy, *v.a.* remployer

Reemployment, *s.* remploi, *m.*

Reenact, *v.a.* ordonner *or* passer de nouveau; remettre en vigueur [blissement, *m.*

Reenactment, *s.* remise en vigueur, *f.*, réta-

Reenforce. *V.* **Reinforce**

Reengage, Reenlist, *v.a.* rengager, réengager; — *v.n.* se rengager, se réengager

Reengagement, Reenlistment, *s.* rengagement, nouvel engagement, *m.*

Reenter, *v.a.* rentrer dans *or* à; — *v.n.* rentrer

Reentering, *part.adj.* rentrant; — *s.* rentrée, *f.*

Reentrance, *s.* rentrée, *f.*

Reequip, *v.a.* réquiper

Reestablish, *v.a.* rétablir; restaurer; réintégrer [teur, *m.*, -trice, *f.*

Reestablisher, *s.* rétablisseur, *m.*; restaura-

Reestablishment, *s.* rétablissement, *m.*; restauration, *f.*; réintégration, *f.*

Reeve, *s.* (*under-steward*) *V.* **Bailiff;** (*bird*) combattant, *m.* — **out,** *v.a.* éfaufiler

Reexamination, *s.* nouvel examen, *m.*; (*of a prisoner*) nouvel interrogatoire, *m.*

Reexamine, *v.a.* réexaminer, examiner de nouveau; revoir; (*a prisoner*) interroger de nouveau [rechange, *m.*

Reexchange, *s.* nouvel échange, *m.*; (*of bills*)

Reexhibit, *v.a.* réexposer [tion, *f.*

Reexport, *v.a.* réexporter; — *s.* réexporta-

Reexportation, *s.* réexportation, *f.*

Reexpose, *v.a.* réexposer

Refection, *s.* réfection, *f.*, repas, *m.*, collation, *f.*

Refective, *adj. s.* restaurant, *adj.m.*, e, *f.*, res-

Refectory, *s.* réfectoire, *m.* [taurant, *s.m.*

Refer, *v.a.* référer (à), renvoyer (à); soumettre (à); remettre à la décision (de); (*attribute*) rapporter (à); (*pers.*) adresser (à); renvoyer (à), envoyer (à); — *v.n.* (*have relation*) se rapporter (à), avoir rapport (à); (*allude*) faire allusion (à); vouloir parler (de), vouloir dire (...); (*rely on*) s'en rapporter (à), s'en remettre (à); (*report to*) en référer (à); (*appeal*) en appeler (à); (*cite*, &c.) citer, donner pour garant, offrir le témoignage (de), renvoyer au témoignage (de); (*consult*) consulter; avoir recours (à); (*apply*) s'adresser (à); (*make use of the name of*) se recommander (de), se réclamer (de)

Referable, *adj.* référable, rapportable; attribuable [*m.*, e, *f.*

Referee, *s.* arbitre, *m.f.*; (*reference*) répondant,

Reference, *s.* (*direction*) renvoi, *m.*; (*relation*) rapport, *m.*; allusion, *f.*; (*information*) renseignement, *m.*; recommandation, *f.*; témoignage, *m.*; garantie, *f.*; (*com.*) référence, *f.*; (*pers.*) répondant, *m.*, e, *f.*; (*print.*) renvoi, *m.*, lettrine, *f.*; (*law*) renvoi, *m.* *Book* or *work of* —, ouvrage de référence, livre *or* ouvrage à consulter, *m.* *List of* —*s*, (*on maps*, &c.) légende, *f.* *For* —, à consulter. *In* — *to*, (*things*) quant à, à l'égard de, par rapport à, relativement à; (*pers.*) en s'en référant à. *To have* — *to*, se rapporter à, avoir rapport à; faire allusion à. *To make* — *to*, parler de; citer; faire allusion à. — **number,** *s.* (*com.*, *of articles*) référence, *f.*

Referendary, *s.* référendaire, *m.*

Referendaryship, *s.* référendariat, *m.*

Referrible, *adj. V.* **Referable**

Refinage, *s. V.* **Refining**

Refine, *v.a.* (*liquids*) épurer, clarifier; (*metals*) affiner; (*sugar*, &c.) raffiner; (*fig.*) polir; purifier, épurer; — *v.n.* s'épurer; se raffiner; se purifier; se perfectionner; (*subtilize*) raffiner, subtiliser; chicaner, ergoter; (*outdo*) renchérir (sur), enchérir (sur), raffiner (sur)

Refined, *part. adj.* épuré, &c. (*V.* **Refine**); fin; cultivé; poli; pur; délicat; élégant; subtil; affecté, recherché

Refinedly, *adv.* avec raffinement

Refinedness, *s. V.* **Refinement**

Refinement, *s.* (*of liquids*) épuration, *f.*; (*of metals*) affinage, *m.*; (*of sugar*, &c.) raffinage, *m.*; (*fig.*) pureté, *f.*; politesse, *f.*; poli, vernis, *m.*; élégance, *f.*; affectation, recherche, *f.*; raffinement, *m.*; subtilité, *f.*

Refiner, *s.* (*of liquids*) épurateur, *m.*, -trice, *f.*; (*of metals*) affineur, *m.*; (*of sugar*, &c.) raffineur, *m.*, -euse, *f.*; (*fig.*) purificateur, *m.*, -trice, *f.*, épurateur, *m.*, -trice, *f.*; perfectionneur, *m.*; raffineur, *m.*, -euse, *f.*, subtiliseur, *m.*, -euse, *f.*; puriste, *m.f.*

Refinery, *s.* (*of liquids*) usine à épurer, *f.*; (*of metals*) affinerie, *f.*; (*of sugar*, &c.) raffinerie, *f.*

Refining, *s.* (*of liquids*) épuration, *f.*; (*of metals*) affinage, *m.*; (*of sugar*, &c.) raffinage, *m.*; (*fig.*) épuration, *f.*; affectation, *f.*; subtilisation, *f.*

Refit, Refitting. *V.* **Repair, Repairing**
Reflect, *v.a.* réfléchir; refléter; (*fig.*) faire rejaillir (sur); rapporter, procurer, valoir (à); (*honour or credit on*) faire (honneur à); — *v.n.* se réfléchir, réfléchir; (*fig.*) réfléchir, rejaillir, retomber (sur); (*discredit*) faire tort (à); (*think*) réfléchir (à, sur); songer (à, que); (*blame*) [blâmer, critiquer
Reflected, *adj.* réfléchi
Reflecting, *adj.* (*surface*) réfléchissant; réflecteur; (*mind,* &c.) réfléchi; méditatif
Reflectingly, *adv.* avec réflexion; avec blâme
Reflection, *s* (*of light,* &c.) réflexion, *f.*; (*flash*) reflet, *m.*; (*thought*) réflexion, *f.*; (*censure*) blâme, *m.*. critique, *f.*; reproche, *m.* *On* or *upon* —, en y réfléchissant, réflexion faite, décidément
Reflective, *adj. V* **Reflecting;** (*verb*) réfléchi
Reflector, *s.* (*pers.*) réfléchisseur, *m*, -euse, *f.*; (*thing*) réflecteur, *m.*
Reflex, *adj.* réfléchi; (*phys., physiology*) réflexe; (*bot.*) réfléchi; (*paint.*) reflété; — *s.* [reflet, *m.*
Reflexibility, *s.* réflexibilité, *f.*
Reflexible, *adj.* réflexible
Reflexion. *V.* **Reflection**
Reflexive, *adj.* réflexif; (*gram.*) réfléchi
Reflexively, *adv.* réflexivement
Reflorescence, *s.* refleurissement, *m.*
Reflourish, *v.n.* refleurir
Reflow, *v.n.* refluer, retourner en arrière
Reflower, *v.n.* refleurir
Refluenc-e, y, *s.* reflux, *m.*
Refluent, *adj.* qui reflue
Reflux, *s.* reflux, *m.*; nouvelle fluctuation, *f.*
Reform, *v.a.* réformer; (*criminals*) moraliser; (*form again*) reformer; — *v.n.* se réformer, se corriger; (*form again*) se reformer; — *s.* réforme, *f.*; — *adj.* de réforme; réformiste
Reformable, *adj.* réformable
Reformation, *s.* réformation, réforme, *f.*; (*of criminals*) moralisation, *f.*; (*new formation*) nouvelle formation, *f.*
Reformatory, *adj.* réformatoire; de correction, correctionnel. — *institution, V.* **Reformatory,** *s.*
Reformatory, *s.* (— *school*) maison de jeunes détenus, maison de correction, maison d'éducation correctionnelle, *f.* [formiste, *m.f.*
Reformer, *s.* réformateur, *m.*, -trice, *f.*; ré-
Reformist, *s.* réformiste, *m.f.*; (*of monks, nuns*) réformé, *m.*, e, *f.*
Refortification, *s.* nouvelle fortification, *f.*
Refortify, *v.a.* refortifier [refonder
Refound, *v.a.* (*recast*) refondre; (*reestablish*)
Refounder, *s.* (*recaster*) refondeur, *m.*
Refounding, *s.* (*recasting*) refonte, *f.*
Refract, *v.a.* réfracter
Refracting, *adj.* à réfraction; réfringent. — *telescope,* réfracteur, *m.*
Refraction, *s.* réfraction, *f.*
Refractive, *adj.* réfractif
Refractor, *s.* réfracteur, *m.* [ment
Refractorily, *adv.* opiniâtrément; indocile-
Refractoriness, *s.* opiniâtreté, *f.*; indocilité, insoumission, *f.*
Refractory, *adj.* opiniâtre; réfractaire, récalcitrant, indocile, insoumis, mutin, intraitable; (*of horses*) rétif; (*of metals*) réfractaire
Refrain, *v.n.* (*before a verb*) se retenir (de), s'empêcher (de); se garder (de); (*before a noun*) retenir; (*abstain, do without, before either a verb or a noun*) s'abstenir (de). *To — from tears,* retenir ses larmes
Refrain, *s.* (*burden of a song,* &c.) refrain, *m.*
Refrangibility, *s.* réfrangibilité, *f.*
Refrangible, *adj.* réfrangible
Refresh, *v a* rafraîchir; (*strengthen*) redonner des forces à, refaire; (*rest*) délasser, reposer; (*relieve*) soulager; (*cheer*) récréer; (*a cask of wine*) corriger, raccommoder, repasser; ouiller
Refresher, *s.* personne *or* chose qui rafraîchit *or* qui délasse, *f.*; (*fee*) supplément d'honoraires, *m.*; (*in a bad sense*) pot-de-vin, *m.*
Refreshing, *adj.* rafraîchissant; réparateur; qui repose, délassant; calmant; récréatif
Refreshingly, *adv.* d'une manière rafraîchissante *or* &c. (*V.* **Refreshing**)
Refreshment, *s.* rafraîchissement, *m.*; (*rest, relaxation*) repos, délassement, *m.*; récréation, *f.* — **booth, -marquee, -stand,** *s.* buvette, *f.* — **room,** *s.* buffet, *m.*; café, *m.*; restaurant, *m.*
Refrigerant, *adj. s.* réfrigérant, *adj. m.*, e, *f.*, réfrigérant, *s.m.*
Refrigerate, *v.a.* réfrigérer; refroidir
Refrigeration, *s.* réfrigération, *f.*; refroidissement, *m.* [-ive, *f.*, réfrigératif, *s.m.*
Refrigerative, *adj. s.* réfrigératif, *adj. m.*,
Refrigerator, Refrigeratory, *s.* appareil réfrigérant, *m.*; glacière, *f.*, rafraîchissoir, *m.*; (*chem.*) réfrigérant, *m.*
Refringenc-e, y, *s.* réfringence, *f.*
Refringent, *adj. s.* réfringent, *adj. m.*, e, *f.*, réfringent, *s.m.*
Refuge, *s.* refuge ('*from,*' contre), *m.*; asile, *m.* *To take —, to fly for —,* se réfugier
Refugee, *s.* réfugié, *m*, e, *f.*
Refulgenc-e, y, *s.* éclat, *m.*, splendeur, *f.*
Refulgent, *adj.* éclatant, brillant, resplendis-
Refulgently, *adv.* avec éclat [sant
Refund, *v.a.* rembourser; rendre, restituer
Refurnish, *v.a.* remeubler
Refusable, *adj.* refusable
Refusal, *s.* refus, *m.*; (*option*) choix, choix de refuser *or* d'accepter, *m.*; première offre, *f.*
Refuse, *v.a.n.* refuser; — *s.* rebut, *m.*; — *adj.* de rebut. *It is not to be —d,* cela n'est pas de refus [personne qui refuse, *f.*
Refuser, *s.* refuseur, *m.*, -euse, *f.*, refusant, *m.*, e, *f.*,
Refutable, *adj.* réfutable
Refutation, *s* réfutation, *f.*
Refute, *v.a.* réfuter
Refuter, *s.* réfutateur, *m.*, -trice, *f.*
Regain, *v.a.* regagner; recouvrer; reprendre; rattraper; reconquérir. *Paradise —d,* (*of Milton*) le Paradis reconquis
Regal, *adj.* royal
Regale, *v.a.* régaler; charmer, réjouir; — *v.n.* se régaler; — *s. V.* **Regalement**
Regalement, *s.* régal, festin, banquet, *m.*
Regalia, *s.* (*cigar*) régalia, londrès, *m.*; — *s. pl.* insignes de la royauté, *m.pl.*; joyaux (*or* diamants) de la couronne, *m.pl.*; (*garments*) habits de cérémonie, *m.pl.*, (*of freemasons*) décors, *m.pl.*; (*law*) droits régaliens, *m.pl.*
Regally, *adv.* royalement
Regard, *v.a.* regarder; considérer; avoir égard à; prendre garde à; faire attention à; estimer, faire cas de; avoir rapport à; (*theol.*) observer, garder. *As —s,* quant à, pour ce qui est de
Regard, *s.* égard, *m.*; considération, *f.*, respect, *m.*, estime, *f.*; attention, *f.*; intérêt, *m.*; (*relation*) rapport, *m.*; —**s**, *pl.* amitiés, *f.pl.* *My kind —s to,* mes sincères amitiés à. *With — to,* à l'égard de, quant à. *To give* or *send o.'s —s to,* faire ses amitiés à
Regardant, *adj.* (*her.*) regardant
Regardful, *adj.* attentif (à); plein d'égards (pour); qui songe (à), qui s'inquiète (de)
Regardfully, *adv.* avec égard, respectueusement; attentivement, avec soin
Regarding, *prep. V.* **Concerning**
Regardless, *adj.* indifférent (à), insouciant (de), sans égard (pour, à), sans se soucier (de), sans regarder (à) [insouciance
Regardlessly, *adv.* avec indifférence, avec
Regardlessness, *s.* indifférence, insou-
Regatta, *s.* régate, *f.* [ciance, *f.*
Regelation, *s.* regel, *m.*, regélation, *f.*
Regency, *s.* régence, *f.*
Regeneracy, *s.* régénération, *f.*
Regenerate, *v.a.* régénérer; — *adj.* régénéré
Regenerating, *adj.* régénérateur
Regeneration, *s.* régénération, *f.*
Regenerative, *adj.* régénératif

Regenerator, *s.* régénérateur, *m.*, -trice, *f.*
Regent, *s. adj.* régent, *m.*, e, *f.*
Regicidal, *adj.* régicide
Regicide, *s. adj.* régicide (*pers.*) *m.f.*, (*murder*) [*m.*, (*adj.*) *m.f.*
Regild, *v.a.* redorer
Regimen, *s.* régime, *m.*
Regiment, *s.* régiment, *m.*
Regimental, *adj.* régimentaire, de (*or* du) régiment; (*of schools*) régimentaire; (*of clothes*) d'ordonnance, d'uniforme; **—s,** *s.pl.* uniforme, *m.*; habit d'ordonnance, *m.* — **officer,** *s.* officier de compagnie *or* de corps, *m.*
Regimentally, *adv.* régimentairement
Region, *s.* région, *f.*
Register, *s.* registre, *m.*; (*of voters*) liste électorale, *f.*; (*nav.*) acte de nationalité, *m.*; casernet, *m.*; (*tonnage*) jauge officielle, *f.*; (*of furnaces*, &c.) registre, *m.*; plaque, *f.*; (*tech.*) registre, *m.*; — *v.a.* enregistrer; inscrire; enrôler; (*luggage*) enregistrer, inscrire; (*designs, patterns, inventions, to prevent imitation*) déposer; (*a letter*) charger; recommander. *—ed share*, action nominative, *f.* — **office,** *s.* bureau d'enregistrement, *m.*; (*for inquiries*) bureau de renseignements, *m.*; (*for servants*) bureau de placement, *m.* — **thermometer,** *s.* thermomètre à registre, *m.*
Registrar, *s.* secrétaire, *m.*; (*law*) greffier, *m.*; (*univers.*) archiviste, *m.*; (*of births, deaths, and marriages*) officier de l'état civil, *m.* *—'s office*, (*of births, deaths, and marriages*) bureaux de l'état civil, *m.pl.*, mairie, *f.*
Registrarship, *s.* place, (*f.*) de secrétaire *or* de &c., *V.* **Registrar**
Registration, *s.* enregistrement, *m.*; (*of designs, patterns, inventions*) dépôt, *m.*; (*of letters*) chargement, *m.*
Registry, *s.* secrétariat, *m.*; (*law*) greffe, *m.*; (*registration*) *V.* **Registration.** — **book,** *s.* matricule, *f.* — **office,** *s. V.* **Register**
Reglet, *s.* (*arch.*) réglet, *m.*; (*print.*) réglette, *f.*
Regnant, *adj.* régnant
Regorge, *v.a.n.* regorger, revomir, vomir; (*swallow back*) ravaler
Regraft, *v.a.* regreffer, réenter
Regrate, *v.a.* revendre, regratter; (*engross*) accaparer; (*mas.*) regratter
Regrater, *s.* revendeur, *m.*, -euse, *f.*, regrattier, *m.*, -ière, *f.*; (*engrosser*) accapareur, *m.*, -euse, *f.*
Regrating, *s.* revendage, *m.*, revente, regratterie, *f.*; (*engrossing*) accaparement, *m.*; (*mas.*) regrattage, *m.*
Regress, *s.* retour, *m.*; (*can. law*) regrès, *m.*
Regression, *s.* retour, *m.*; (*rhet.*) régression, *f.*
Regressive, *adj.* régressif
Regressively, *adv.* régressivement
Regret, *v.a.* regretter; se repentir de; — *s.* regret, *m.* *With —*, avec regret; (*reluctantly*) à regret, à contre-cœur. *It is to be —ted that ...*, il est à regretter que ..., il est regrettable [que ...
Regretful, *adj.* plein de regrets
Regretfully, *adv.* avec des regrets
Regrettable, *adj.* regrettable, à regretter
Regrettably, *adv.* regrettablement
Regretter, *s.* regretteur, *m.*
Regular, *adj.* régulier; (*steady*) réglé; (*in due form*) en règle; dans les règles; (*usual*) ordinaire; (*true, downright*) vrai; franc; positif; (*of rhymes*) plat, suivi; — *s.* régulier, *m.*; **—s,** *s.pl.* réguliers, *m.pl.*; troupes régulières, *f.pl.* *— price*, prix fait, *m.*
Regularity, *s.* régularité, *f.*
Regularization, *s.* régularisation, *f.*
Regularize, *v.a.* régulariser
Regularly, *adv.* régulièrement; dans les règles; en règle; (*thoroughly*) complètement; (*truly*) vraiment; positivement, bien
Regulate, *v.a.n.* régler; réglementer; diriger
Regulating, *adj.* régulateur
Regulation, *s.* règlement, *m.*; (*mech.*) régulation, *f.*; *—adject.* réglementaire; d'ordonnance
Regulator, *s.* régulateur, *m.*, -trice, *f.*; (*of machines*) régulateur, *m.*
Regurgitate, *v.a.* régurgiter
Regurgitation, *s.* régurgitation, *f.*
Rehabilitate, *v.a.* réhabiliter
Rehabilitation, *s.* réhabilitation, *f.*
Rehear, *v.a.* entendre de nouveau
Rehearing, *s.* nouvelle audition, *f.*
Rehearsal, *s.* récitation, *f.*; (*narration*) récit, *m.*, narration, *f.*; (*mus., theat.*) répétition, *f.*
Rehearse, *v.a.* réciter; (*relate*) raconter; (*mus., theat.*) répéter
Reign, *v.n.* régner; (*prevail*) dominer; — *s.* règne, *m.*; (*authority*) souveraineté, *f.*
Reimbursable, *adj.* remboursable
Reimburse, *v.a.* rembourser
Reimbursement, *s.* remboursement, *m.*
Reimport, *v.a.* réimporter; — *s.* réimportation, *f.*
Reimportation, *s.* réimportation, *f.*
Reimpose, *v.a.* réimposer
Reimposition, *s.* réimposition, *f.*
Reimprison, *v.a.* remprisonner
Reimprisonment, *s.* remprisonnement, *m.*
Rein, *s.* rène, *f.*; **—s,** *pl.* rênes, *f.pl.*; (*anat., build.*) reins, *m.pl.*; — *v.a.* conduire à la bride; (*to bridle*) rêner, brider; (*to control*) contenir, gouverner. *To give the — to*, lâcher la bride à. *To keep a tight — over*, tenir la bride courte (*or* serrée) à; avoir la haute main sur. — **back,** *v.n.* reculer; *v.a.* faire reculer. — **in,** retenir; maintenir. **—less,** *adj.* sans rênes; (*fig.*) sans frein, effréné. — **up,** relever; (*control*) contenir, gouverner
Reincorporate, *v.a.* réincorporer
Reincorporation, *s.* réincorporation, *f.*
Reindeer, *s.* renne, *m.* — **moss,** *s.* lichen des rennes, *m.*
Reinforce, *v.a.* renforcer; fortifier
Reinforcement, *s.* renforcement, *m.*; (*body of men*) renfort, *m.*; (*fig.*) secours, appui, *m.*
Reingratiate, *v.a.* faire rentrer en grâce, remetter en faveur. *To — oneself, to be —d*, rentrer en grâce
Reinhabit, *v.a.* réhabiter
Reinscribe, *v.a.* réinscrire
Reinsert, *v.a.* réinsérer
Reinsertion, *s.* réinsertion, *f.*
Reinstall, *v.a.* réinstaller; rétablir
Reinstallation, Reinstalment, *s.* réinstallation, *f.*; rétablissement, *m.*
Reinstate, *v.a.* rétablir; réintégrer
Reinstatement, *s.* rétablissement, *m.*; réintégration, *f.*
Reinsurance, *s.* réassurance, *f.*
Reinsure, *v.a.* réassurer
Reinsurer, *s.* réassureur, *m.*
Reintegrate, &c. *V.* **Redintegrate, &c.**
Reinter, *v.a.* réenterrer
Reinterment, *s.* réenterrement, *m.*
Reinterrogate, *v.a.* réinterroger, interroger de nouveau
Reintroduce, *v.a.* réintroduire
Reinvest, *v.a.* revêtir; investir de nouveau; (*money*) replacer [(*of money*) replacement, *m.*
Reinvestment, *s.* nouvel investissement, *m.*;
Reinvigorate, *v.a.* ranimer
Reinvitation, *s.* réinvitation, *f.*
Reinvite, *v.a.* réinviter
Reis, *s.* reis, *m.* — *-effendi*, reis-effendi, *m.*
Reissue, *v.a.* réémettre; redistribuer; réimprimer; republier, rééditer; — *s.* réémission, *f.*; redistribution, *f.*; réimpression, *f.*; republication, réédition, nouvelle édition, *f.*
Reiterate, *v.a.* réitérer
Reiteration, *s.* réitération, *f.*
Reiterative, *adj.* réitératif
Reiteratively, *adv.* réitérativement
Reject, *v.a.* rejeter
Rejection, *s.* rejet, *m.*; réjection, *f.*
Rejoice, *v.a.* réjouir; — *v.n.* se réjouir (de)
Rejoicing, *s.* réjouissance, *f.*; joie, *f.*
Rejoicingly, *adv.* joyeusement, avec joie
Rejoin, *v.a.n.* rejoindre; (*reply*) répliquer, repartir, répondre; (*law*) répliquer [plique, *f.*
Rejoinder, *s.* réplique, repartie, *f.*; (*law*) ré-

Rejudge, *v.a.* rejuger
Rejuvenate, *v.a.* rajeunir
Rejuvenescenc-e, y, *s.* rajeunissement, *m.*
Rejuvenize, *v.a.* rajeunir
Rekindle, *v.a.* rallumer
Relapse, *v.n.* retomber; — *s.* rechute, *f.*
Relapsed, *adj.* relaps
Relapser, *s.* relaps, *m.*, e, *f.*
Relate, *v.a.n.* raconter, rapporter, conter; (*have reference*) se rapporter, avoir rapport (à)
Related, *adj.* qui a rapport (à); (*allied: to a person*) parent (de), (*to a family*) allié (à). *Closely* or *nearly* —, proche parent, allié de près. *Distantly* —, parent éloigné, allié de loin
Relater, *s.* narrateur, *m.*, -trice, *f.*, conteur, *m.*, -euse, *f.*
Relating, *adj.* relatif (à), qui a rapport (à)
Relation, *s.* relation, *f.*; récit, *m.*; (*connection*) rapport, *m.*; (*kin*) parent, *m.*, e, *f.*; —**s,** *pl.* (*intercourse*) relations, *f.pl.*, rapports, *m.pl.* *Distant* —*s*, parents éloignés. *Near* —*s*, proches parents. *In* — *to*, *V.* **Reference**
Relationship, *s.* parenté, *f.*
Relative, *adj.* relatif; — *s.* (*kin*) *V.* **Relation;** (*gram.*) relatif, pronom relatif, *m.*; (*log.*) terme [relatif, *m.*
Relatively, *adv.* relativement
Relativeness, Relativity, *s.* relativité, *f.*
Relax, *v.a.* relâcher; (*relieve*) délasser, reposer; — *v.n.* se relâcher; se détendre; (*rest*) se délasser, se reposer; (*get mild*) s'adoucir
Relaxation, *s.* relâchement, *m.*; (*rest*) repos, relâche, délassement, *m.* [énervant; mou
Relaxing, *adj.* qui relâche, relâchant, laxatif;
Relay, *s.* relais, *m.*; — *v.a.* reposer, replacer
Release, *v.a.* (*from confinement*) relâcher, élargir, libérer; (*free from*) délivrer (de); (*from obligation*) décharger (de), dégager (de), délier (de), tenir quitte (de); (*let go*) lâcher; (*relinquish*) abandonner; (*a debt*, &c.) remettre, faire remise de; — *s.* (*from confinement*) élargissement, *m.*; (*fig.*) délivrance, *f.*; (*from pain*) soulagement, *m.*; (*from obligation*) dégagement, *m.*, libération, *f.*; (*rest*) relâche, *m.*; (*law*) abandon, renoncement, *m.*, cession, *f.*; (*of a debt*, &c.) décharge, remise, *f.* —*d convict* or *transport*, forçat libéré, *m.*
Releaser, *s.* libérateur, *m.*, -trice, *f.*
Relegate, *v.a.* reléguer
Relegation, *s.* relégation, *f.*
Relent, *v.n.* s'adoucir, s'attendrir; (*yield*) fléchir, céder; (*abate*) se ralentir; (*repent*) se repentir. —**less,** *adj.* inflexible; impitoyable, inexorable. —**lessly,** *adv.* inflexiblement; impitoyablement, inexorablement. —**lessness,** *s.* inflexibilité, *f.*; rigueur, dureté, *f.*
Relenting, *s.* radoucissement, attendrissement, *m.*; (*abatement*) ralentissement, *m.*; (*repentance*) repentir, *m.*
Relessee, *s.* abandonnataire, renonciataire, *m.f.*
Relessor, *s.* renonciateur, *m.*, -trice, *f.*
Relevanc-e, y, *s.* rapport, *m.*, relation, convenance, *f.*; applicabilité, *f.*; à-propos, *m.*
Relevant, *adj.* qui a rapport (à); applicable (à); à propos (de) [*f.*; véracité, *f.*; exactitude, *f.*
Reliability, *s.* crédibilité, *f.*; foi, *f.*; certitude,
Reliable, *adj.* sur lequel on peut compter, auquel on peut se fier; digne de confiance, digne de foi, croyable; de confiance; sûr, assuré, certain, positif; exact; solide; bien fondé
Reliableness, *s.* *V.* **Reliability**
Reliably, *adv.* d'une manière digne de foi, d'une manière croyable; sûrement, assurément, certainement, positivement; exactement
Reliance, *s.* confiance, *f.* *To place* — *on*, mettre sa confiance dans (*or* en), se fier à
Relic, *s.* reste, *m.*; (*of saints*) relique, *f.*
Relict, *s.* veuve, *f.*
Relief, *s.* soulagement, adoucissement, *m.*; secours, *m.*; assistance, *f.*; subvention, *f.*; (*remedy at law*) recours, *m.*; (*redress*) réparation, *f.*; justice, *f.*; (*sculp., paint.*) relief, *m.*; (*of sentries*) pose, *f.* *Demi* —, *Full* —, *High* —, *Low* —, *V.* **Demi, Full, High,** *and* **Low.** *In* —, en relief. *In-door* —, secours (*m.pl.*) dans les maisons de charité. *Out-door* —, secours (*m.pl.*) à domicile. *To bring out in strong* —, faire vivement (*or* vigoureusement) ressortir. *To stand out in* —, ressortir. — **ticket,** *s.* bon de secours, *m.* [en), *f.*
Relier, *s.* personne qui a confiance (dans *or*
Relievable, *adj.* secourable
Relieve, *v.a.* soulager, adoucir, alléger; secourir; aider; délivrer (de); faire justice à; (*set off*) relever, mettre en relief; (*a guard*) relever
Reliever, *s.* personne (*f.*) *or* chose, (*f.*) qui soulage *or* adoucit *or* &c. (*V.* **Relieve**)
Relieving, *s.* soulagement, adoucissement, *m.*; secours, *m.*, assistance, aide, *f.*; subvention, *f.*; (*of a guard*) relèvement, *m.*; — *adj.* qui soulage; qui donne du secours. — **officer,** *s.* commissaire des pauvres, *m.* — **tackle,** *s.* (*nav.*) attrape, *f.*, attrapes, *f.pl.*
Relievo, *s.* relief, *m.*
Relight, *v.a.* éclairer de nouveau; rallumer
Religion, *s.* religion, *f.*
Religionism, *s.* bigoterie, *f.*; fanatisme, *m.*
Religionist, *s.* bigot, *m.*, e, *f.*; fanatique, *m.f.*
Religiosity, *s.* religiosité, *f.*
Religious, *adj.* religieux; de religion; de piété. — *book*, livre de piété *or* de dévotion, *m.*
Religiously, *adv.* religieusement; pieusement, avec piété
Religiousness, *s.* religiosité, *f.* [noncer à
Relinquish, *v.a.* abandonner, quitter; re-
Relinquisher, *s.* personne qui abandonne, *f.*; personne qui renonce (à), *f.* [tion, *f.*
Relinquishment, *s.* abandon, *m.*; renoncia-
Reliquary, *s.* reliquaire, *m.*, châsse, *f.*
Relish, *v.a.* donner du goût à, relever; (*like*) goûter; savourer; (*of eating*) trouver bon, aimer; manger de bon appétit; — *v.n.* avoir bon goût; (*fig.*) plaire (à); (*of*) sentir (le, la, les); — *s.* goût, *m.*; saveur, *f.*; plaisir, *m.*; charme, *m.*; piquant, *m.*; (*dainty*) friandise, *f.*; (*seasoning*) assaisonnement, *m.*; (*cook.*) appétit, *m.*; béatille, *f.*; (*small quantity*) idée, *f.* *With a* —, de bon appétit
Relishable, Relishing, *adj.* ragoûtant, appétissant, savoureux, agréable
Reload, *v.a.* recharger
Reluctance, *s.* répugnance, *f.*
Reluctant, *adj.* (*pers.*) qui a de la répugnance (à), peu disposé (à), peu empressé (à), hésitant; (*things*) forcé; embarrassé. *To be or feel* —, répugner (à), avoir *or* éprouver de la répugnance (à). *To be very* —, avoir beaucoup de répugnance (à). *I am* or *feel* —, je répugne (à), il me répugne (de), j'ai *or* j'éprouve de la répugnance (à) [cœur, à regret
Reluctantly, *adv.* avec répugnance, à contre-
Relume, *v.a.* rallumer
Rely, *v.n.* compter (sur), se reposer (sur); se fonder (sur); se fier (à). *V.* **Depend**
Remain, *v.n.* rester; demeurer; séjourner; (*be*) être. *It only* —*s for me to* . . ., il ne me reste plus qu'à . . . *That* —*s to be proved*, cela n'est pas prouvé. *That* —*s to be seen*, c'est ce que nous verrons. *It* —*s to be seen whether* . . ., reste à savoir si . . . *I* — *respectfully, A.B.*, je suis avec respect, A.B. 2 *from* 6, *there* — 4, de 6 ôtez 2, reste 4 [sibilité, *f.*
Remainder, *s.* reste, restant, *m.*; (*law*) rever-
Remaining, *part. adj.* restant, qui reste, de reste (*to be* —, rester). *There is* or *are* . . . —, il reste . . .
Remains, *s.pl.* restes, *m.pl.*; reste, *m.sing.*; vestiges, *m.pl.*, traces, *f.pl.*; ruines, *f.pl.*; débris, *m.pl.*; (*of bodies*) cendre, *f.*, cendres, *f.pl.*, restes, *m.pl.*, dépouille mortelle, *f.*
Remake, *v.a.* refaire
Reman, *v.a.* remettre du monde à, réarmer; (*fig.*) raffermir, armer d'un nouveau courage

Remand, *v.a.* rappeler, faire revenir; contremander; (*com.*) décommander; (*law*) renvoyer à une autre audience, renvoyer. *To — for a week*, renvoyer à huitaine
Remanet, *s.* (*law*) cause remise, *f.*
Remark, *v.a.* remarquer, observer; (*point out*) faire remarquer, faire observer; — *s.* remarque, observation, *f.*
Remarkable, *adj.* remarquable
Remarkableness, *s.* nature remarquable, *f.*, caractère remarquable, *m.*, singularité, *f.*
Remarkably, *adv.* remarquablement
Remarker, *s.* observateur, *m.*, -trice, *f.*
Remarriage, *s.* remariage, *m.*
Remarry, *v.a.* (*give*) remarier; (*take*) répouser; — *v.n.* se remarier
Remblai, *s.* remblai, *m.*
Remediable, *adj.* remédiable; réparable
Remediably, *adv.* remédiablement; réparablement [cursoire
Remedial, *adj.* réparateur; curatif; (*law*) ré-
Remedially, *adv.* d'une manière réparatrice; curativement; (*law*) récursoirement
Remedi-less, -lessly, -lessness. *V.* **Irremedia-ble, -bly, -bleness**
Remedy, *s.* remède, *m.*; (*in law*) recours, *m.*; — *v.a.* remédier à
Remedying, *s.* remédiement, *m.*
Remelt, *v.a.* refondre
Remember, *v.a.* se rappeler, se souvenir de, ne pas oublier; (*recognize*) reconnaître; (*of compliments*) rappeler au souvenir (de). — *me to your sister*, rappelez-moi au souvenir de votre sœur. — *me kindly to* &c., rappelez-moi au bon souvenir de &c. — *me at home*, mes compliments chez vous. *If I — aright* or *right* or *rightly*, si je m'en souviens bien, si j'ai bonne mémoire
Remembrance, *s.* souvenir, *m.*; mémoire, *f.* *My kind — to*, bien des choses de ma part à; mes amitiés à
Remembrancer, *s.* moniteur, *m.*; souvenir, *m.*; aide-mémoire, *m.*; mémento, *m.*; mémorial, *m.*; (*officer*) secrétaire-archiviste, *m.*
Rememorate, *v.a.* remémorer
Rememoration, *s.* remémoration, *f.*
Rememorative, *adj.* remémoratif
Remigrate, &c. *V.* **Reemigrate,** &c.
Remind, *v.n.* faire penser (à), faire souvenir (de), rappeler; (*look like*) faire l'effet (de), représenter
Reminder, *s.* souvenir, *m.*; aide-mémoire, *m.*; mémento, *m.*; mémorial, *m.*; (*advice*) avis, *m.*; (*pers.*) personne qui fait souvenir, *f.*
Reminiscence, *s.* réminiscence, *f.*
Remiss, *adj.* négligent, nonchalant; mou
Remissibility, *s.* rémissibilité, *f.*
Remissible, *adj.* rémissible, pardonnable
Remission, *s.* rémission, *f.*; (*pardon*) pardon, *m.*, remise, grâce, *f.*; (*of sins*) rémission, *f.*; (*abatement*) relâchement, *m.*; adoucissement, *m.*
Remissly, *adv.* négligemment
Remissness, *s.* relâchement, *m.*; négligence, nonchalance, *f.*
Remit, *v.a.* se relâcher de; apaiser, adoucir, calmer; (*forgive*) remettre, pardonner; (*fines*, &c.) remettre; faire remise de; (*send on*) envoyer, faire remettre, faire une remise de; — *v.n.* se relâcher; s'apaiser, diminuer, se calmer
Remittance, *s.* remise, *f.*, envoi de fonds, [envoi, *m.*
Remittent, *adj.* rémittent
Remitter, *s.* personne qui pardonne, *f.*; (*com.*) remetteur, *m.*, -euse, *f.*
Remnant, *s.* reste, *m.*, restes, *m.pl.*; débris, *m.pl.*; (*of stuffs*) coupon, *m.*; bout, *m.*; — *adj.* restant, qui reste [manier
Remodel, *v.a.* remodeler; (*fig.*) refondre; re-
Remodelling, *s.* remodelage, *m.*; (*fig.*) refonte, *f.*; remaniement, *m.*
Remonstrance, *s.* remontrance, *f.*; (*Cath. rel.*) ostensoir, *m.*
Remonstrant, *s. adj.* remontrant, *m.*, e, *f.*

Remonstrate, *v.a.n.* remontrer; faire des remontrances (à); se plaindre
Remonstrator, *s.* remontreur, *m.*
Remontoir, *s.* remontoir, *m.*
Remora, *s.* rémora, *m.*
Remorse, *s.* remords, *m.* **—ful,** *adj.* dévoré de remords. **—less,** *adj.* sans remords; sans pitié, impitoyable. **—lessly,** *adv.* sans remords; sans pitié, impitoyablement. **—lessness,** *s.* cruauté, dureté, *f.*
Remote, Remotely. *V.* **Distant, Distantly**
Remoteness, *s.* éloignement, *m.*, distance, *f.*; époque reculée, *f.*; degré de parenté éloignée, *m.*; faible degré, *m.*; (*slightness*) faiblesse, *f.*
Remoulade, *s.* rémoulade, *f.*
Remould, *v.a.* remouler; (*fig.*) refondre
Remount, *v.a.n.* remonter; — *s.* remonte, *f.*
Remounting, *s.* remonte, *f.*
Removability, *s.* amovibilité, *f.*
Removable, *adj.* (*pers.*) amovible; (*things*) transportable
Removal, *s.* déplacement, changement de place, *m.*; éloignement, *m.*; départ, *m.*; changement de domicile, *m.*; (*of furniture from a place*) déménagement, *m.*, (*of furniture to a place*) emménagement, *m.*; (*taking away*) enlèvement, *m.*; transport, *m.*; translation, *f.*; abolition, suppression, *f.*; extirpation, *f.*; (*dismission*) destitution, *f.*, renvoi, *m.*; (*of a pain*) soulagement, *m.*; (*of bandages*) levée, *f.*; (*cure*) guérison, cure, *f.*
Remove, *v.a.* déplacer; (*discard, place at a distance*) éloigner; écarter; (*withdraw*) retirer; (*take away*) ôter, enlever; effacer; faire disparaître; abolir, supprimer, détruire, faire cesser; extirper; chasser; (*a difficulty*, &c.) lever; (*bandages*) lever; (*furniture from a place*) déménager, (*furniture to a place*) emménager; (*carry*) transporter; transférer; (*law*) porter; (*dismiss*) destituer, renvoyer; — *v.n.* se déplacer; s'éloigner; (*change o.'s residence*) déménager; se transporter; (*go from*) aller (de); (*go to*) aller (à), aller demeurer (à); — *s.* degré, *m.*; distance, *f.*; départ, *m.*; (*of dinners*) relevé, *m.*; (*at play*) coup, *m.*; (*of furniture*, &c.) *V.* **Removal.** *Far —d from*, très loin de, bien éloigné de. *Three —s are as bad as a fire*, trois déménagements valent un incendie
Remover, *s.* personne (*f.*) *or* chose (*f.*) qui déplace *or* enlève *or* &c. (*V.* **Remove,** *v.a.*)
Remunerable, *adj.* rémunérable
Remunerate, *v.a.* rémunérer, rétribuer
Remunerating, *adj.* rémunérant, rémunérateur; lucratif
Remuneration, *s.* rémunération, rétribution, *f.*
Remunerative, *adj.* rémunératif, rémunérateur; lucratif. — *justice*, justice distributive, *f.*
Remunerator, *s.* rémunérateur, *m.*, -trice, *f.*
Remuneratory, *adj.* rémunératoire
Renaissance, *s.* renaissance, *f.*
Renal, *adj.* rénal, des reins. — *colic*, colique
Rename, *v.a.* renommer [néphrétique, *f.*
Renard. *V.* **Reynard**
Renascenc-e, y, *s.* renaissance, *f.*
Renascent, *adj.* renaissant
Renavigable, *adj.* renavigable
Renavigate, *v.n.a.* renaviguer
Rencounter, *v.a.* rencontrer; — *v.n.* se rencontrer; (*to fight*) en venir aux mains, se battre, combattre; — *s.* rencontre, *f.*; choc, *m.*
Rend, *v.a.* déchirer; (*split*) fendre; — *v.n.* se déchirer; se fendre. *To — the air with acclamations*, faire retentir l'air de ses acclamations
Render, *v.a.* rendre; (*mas.*) enduire, cueillir; — *v.n.* (*mas.*) enduire, faire une cueillie; — *s.* déchireur, *m.*, -euse, *f.*; (*splitter*) fendeur, *m.*, [-euse, *f.*
Renderable, *adj.* rendable
Renderer, *s.* rendeur, *m.*, -euse, *f.*
Rendering, *s.* traduction, *f.*; (*mas.*) enduit, *m.*, cueillie, *f.*

Rendez-vous, *s.* rendez-vous, *m.*; — *v.a.* donner rendez-vous à; réunir, rassembler; — *v.n.* se donner rendez-vous; se réunir, se rassembler
Renegade, *s.* renégat, *m.*, e, *f.*; déserteur, *m.*; vagabond, *m.* *To turn — from,* renier
Renegation, *s.* renégation, *f.*, reniement, *m.*
Renerve, *v.a.* redonner de la vigueur à
Renew, *v.a.* renouveler
Renewable, *adj.* renouvelable
Renewal, *s.* renouvellement, *m.*; rénovation, *f.*
Renewed, *adj.* renouvelé; redoublé; nouveau
Renewer, *s.* renouveleur, *m.*, -euse, *f.*; rénovateur, *m.*, -trice, *f.* [ment, *m.*
Renewing, *adj.* rénovateur; — *s.* renouvelle-
Reniform, *adj.* réniforme
Renitenc-e, y, *s.* rénitence, *f.*
Renitent, *adj.* rénitent [(*apple*) *V.* **Pippin**
Rennet, *s.* présure, *f.*; (*anat.*) caillette, *f.*;
Renounce, *v.a.* renoncer à; (*deny*) renoncer, nier, désavouer; — *v.n.* renoncer; — *s.* renonce, *f.* [ment, *m.*
Renouncement, *s.* renonciation, *f.*, renonce-
Renouncer, *s.* renégat, *m.*, e, *f.*
Renovate, *v.a.* renouveler; rajeunir
Renovation, *s.* rénovation, *f.*; renouvellement, *m.*; rajeunissement, *m.*
Renovating, *adj.* rénovateur
Renovator, *s.* rénovateur, *m.*, -trice, *f.*
Renown, *s.* renom, *m.*, renommée, réputation, *f.* —**less,** *adj.* sans renom, sans gloire
Renowned, *adj.* renommé
Rent, *s.* (*laceration*) déchirure, *f.*; déchirement, *m.*; (*fissure*) fente, *f.*; (*fig.*) schisme, *m.*; rupture, *f.*; (*revenue*) rente, redevance, *f.*; (*of houses*) loyer, *m.*; (*of lands*) fermage, *m.*; —**s,** *pl.* (*block of buildings*) cité, *f.*; — *v.a.* (*let out*) donner à loyer *or* à ferme, louer; (*take*) prendre à loyer *or* à ferme, louer; — *v.n.* se louer. — **free,** *adj.* exempt de loyer, sans payer de loyer. — **roll,** *s.* état de revenus, *m.*
Rentable, *adj.* affermable, qui peut être loué
Rental, *s.* revenu, *m.*; prix de location, *m.*; loyer, *m.*; (*list,* or *rent-roll*) état de loyers *or* de fermages *or* de revenus, *m.*
Renter, *s.* locataire, *m.f.*; fermier, *m.*, -ière, *f.*
Renting, *s.* affermage, louage, *m.*, location, *f.*
Renunciation, *s.* renonciation, *f.*, renonce-
Reobtain, *v.a.* réobtenir [ment, *m.*
Reoccupation, *s.* réoccupation, *f.*
Reoccupy, *v.a.* réoccuper
Reopen, *v.a.* rouvrir; — *v.n.* se rouvrir; (*begin again*) rouvrir; (*of schools, courts,* &c.) rentrer
Reopening, *s.* réouverture, *f.*; (*of schools, courts,* &c.) rentrée, *f.*
Reordain, *v.a.* réordonner
Reordination, *s.* réordination, *f.*
Reorganization, *s.* réorganisation, *f.*
Reorganize, *v.a.* réorganiser
Reorganizer, *s.* réorganisateur, *m.*, -trice, *f.*
Reorganizing, *adj.* réorganisateur; — *s.* réorganisation, *f.*
Rep, *s.* reps, *m.*; — *adj.* de reps
Repack, *v.a.* rempaqueter, repaqueter, réemballer, remballer; rencaisser
Repacking, *s.* rempaquetage, repaquetage, réemballage, remballage, *m.*; rencaissage,
Repaint, *v.a.* repeindre [rencaissement, *m.*
Repair, *v.a.n.* réparer; (*health,* &c.) rétablir; (*clothes, common utensils*) raccommoder; (*a ship*) radouber; (*to go*) se rendre, aller; — *s.* réparation, *f.*; entretien, *m.*; (*of clothes, common utensils*) raccommodage, *m.*; (*of a ship*) radoub, *m.* *In —,* en état. *In thorough —,* en bon état. *Out of —,* en mauvais état. *Under —, undergoing —s,* en réparation. *To keep in —,* entretenir
Repairer, *s.* réparateur, *m.*, -trice, *f.*; raccommodeur, *m.*, -euse, *f.*; (*tech.*) répareur, *m.*
Repairing, *s.* *V.* **Repair,** *s.* — **dock,** *s.* bassin de radoub, *m.*
Reparable, *adj.* réparable
Reparably, *adv.* réparablement
Reparation, *s.* réparation, satisfaction, *f.*; (*restoration*) rétablissement, *m.*
Reparative, *adj.* réparatoire
Repartee, *s.* repartie, riposte, *f.*; — *v.n.* re- [partir, riposter
Repass, *v.a.n.* repasser
Repassage, Repassing, *s.* repassage, *m.*
Repast, *s.* repas, *m.*
Repatriate, *v.a.* rapatrier
Repatriation, *s.* rapatriement, *m.*
Repave, *v.a.* repaver
Repaving, *s.* repavage, *m.*
Repay, *v.a.* rembourser; récompenser, payer (de); rendre, payer de retour. *To — perusal, inspection,* &c., valoir la peine (*or* mériter) d'être lu, examiné, &c.
Repayable, *adj.* remboursable, payable
Repayment, *s.* remboursement, *m.* *In —,* en retour
Repeal, *v.a.* rapporter, révoquer, abroger; abolir; — *s.* révocation, abrogation, *f.*; abolition, *f.* — *of the Union,* rappel de l'union, rappel, *m.*
Repealable, *adj.* révocable
Repealer, *s.* personne qui révoque *or* qui abroge *or* qui abolit, *f.*; (*Engl. polit.*) partisan du rappel de l'union, *m.*
Repeat, *v.a.* répéter; réitérer; (*by heart*) réciter; — *s.* répétition, *f.*; (*mus.*) reprise, *f.*
Repeated, *adj.* répété; réitéré; redoublé
Repeatedly, *adv.* plus d'une fois, plusieurs fois, bien des fois, souvent; à plusieurs reprises; à chaque instant
Repeater, *s.* personne qui répète, *f.*; rediseur, *m.*, -euse, *f.*; (*repeating watch*) montre à répétition, *f.*; (*repeating ship*) répétiteur, *m.*
Repeating, *adj.* qui répète. — *circle,* cercle répétiteur, *m.* — *s ring,* (*horol.*) ressort de répétition, *m.* — *ship,* répétiteur, *m.* — *watch,* montre à répétition, *f.* — *works,* (*horol.*) répétition, *f.* [percuter
Repel, *v.a.* repousser; combattre; (*med.*) ré-
Repellenc-e, y, *s.* force répulsive, *f.*
Repellent, *adj. s.* répulsif, *adj. m.*, -ive, *f.*; (*med.*) répercussif, *adj m.*, -ive, *f.*, répercussif, *s.m.*; (*med.*) révulsif, *adj.m.*, -ive, *f.*, révulsif, *s.m.* [*f.*; (*tool*) repoussoir, *m.*
Repeller, *s.* personne *or* chose qui repousse,
Repelling, *adj.* *V.* **Repellent**
Repent, *v.n.a.* se repentir de
Repentance, *s.* repentir, *m.*
Repentant, *adj.* repentant; (*things*) de repentir; — *s.* repenti, *m.*, e, *f.*, pénitent, *m.*, e, *f.*
Repenter, *s.* *V.* **Repentant**
Repentingly, *adv.* avec repentir
Repeople, *v.a.* repeupler
Repeopling, *s.* repeuplement, *m.*
Repercuss, *v.a.* répercuter
Repercussion, *s.* répercussion, *f.*
Repercussive, *adj.* répercussif, répercutant; — *s.* répercussif, *m.*
Repertory, *s.* répertoire, *m.*
Reperusal, *s.* relecture, *f.*
Reperuse, *v.a.* relire
Repetition, *s.* répétition, *f.*; (*by heart*) récitation, *f.*; (*mus.*) répétition, *f.*; (*mus.*) reprise, *f.*; (*mus.*) rentrée, *f.*
Repine, *v.n.* s'affliger (de), se chagriner (de), gémir (de *or* sur); (*complain*) se plaindre (de), murmurer (contre) [*m.*, -trice, *f.*
Repiner, *s.* mécontent, *m.*, e, *f.*, murmurateur,
Repining, *s.* plainte, *f.*; regret, *m.*; murmure, *m.*; mécontentement, *m.*; — *adj.* disposé à s'affliger; disposé à murmurer; mécontent
Repiningly, *adv.* en murmurant, en se plaignant [(*by a substitute*) remplacer
Replace, *v.a.* (*put back*) replacer, remettre;
Replaceable, *adj.* replaçable; (*by a substitute*) remplaçable
Replacement, *s.* (*putting back*) replacement, *m.*; (*substitution*) remplacement, *m.*; (*surg.*) [réduction, *f.*
Replait, *v.a.* replisser; replier
Replant, *v.a.* replanter; (*woods*) reboiser

Replantable, *adj.* replantable

Replantation, Replanting, *s.* replantation, *f.*, replantement, *m.*; (*of woods*) reboisement, *m.*

Replate, *v.a.* replaquer

Replating, *s.* replacage

Replead, *v.a.* replaider

Repleader, *s.* nouveaux débats, *m.pl.*

Replenish, *v.a.* remplir (‘*with*,’ de); — *v n.*

Replete, *adj.* rempli (de), plein (de) [se remplir

Repletion, *s.* plénitude, *f.*; (*med.*) réplétion, *f.*

Repletive, *adj.* réplétif

Repletively, *adv.* réplétivement

Replevin, *s.* main-levée, *f.*

Replica, *s.* (*paint.*, &c.) répétition, *f.*, double, *m.*

Replicate, *adj.* (*bot.*) replicatif; — *s.* (*mus.*) ré-

Replication, *s.* réplique, *f.* [plique, *f.*

Replier, *s.* personne qui réplique, *f.*

Replunge, *v a.* replonger

Reply, *v.a.n.* répliquer, répondre, repartir; — *s.* réplique, réponse, *f.*

Repolish, *v.a.* repolir

Repolishing, *s.* repolissage, *m.*

Repopulation, *s.* repopulation, *f.*

Report, *v.a.* (*tell*) rapporter, raconter, dire; (*give an account*) faire un rapport sur; rendre compte de; constater; — *v.n.* faire un rapport; — *s.* (*rumour*) bruit, rapport, *m.*; (*news*) nouvelle, *f.*; (*statement*) rapport, *m.*; exposé, *m.*; (*relation*) récit, *m.*; (*of societies, meetings*, &c.) compte-rendu, *m.*; (*repute*) réputation, *f.*; (*of fire-arms*) détonation, *f.*, coup, *m.* *Official —*, rapport officiel, *m.*; (*law*) procès-verbal, *m.* *By mere —*, par ouï-dire. *Of good —*, considéré. *It is —ed, there is a — abroad*, on dit, le bruit court. *To — oneself*, se présenter, faire sa déclaration, faire viser ses papiers

Reporter, *s.* rapporteur, *m.*; (*of newspapers*) correspondant, rédacteur, reporter, *m.*; (*short-hand writer*) sténographe, *m.* *—s' gallery*, tribune des journalistes, *f.*

Reporting, *s.* comptes-rendus (de journaux), *m.pl.*, correspondance, *f.*; (*short-hand*) sténographie, *f.*

Repose, *v.a.n.* reposer; se reposer; (*to trust*) se fier (à), s'en remettre (à); (*confidence*) mettre; — *s.* repos, *m.* *To — confidence in*, mettre sa confiance dans *or* en, avoir confiance dans,

Reposedness, *s.* repos, *m.* [croire à

Reposit, *v.a.* déposer

Repository, *s.* dépôt (de ...), *m.*; magasin (de ...), *m.*; (*book*) répertoire, *m.*; (*for horses*) écuries, *f.pl.*

Repossess, *v.a.* reposséder, rentrer en possession de. *To — oneself of*, rentrer (*or* se remettre) en possession de [possession, *f.*

Repossession, *s.* repossession, rentrée en

Repot, *v.a.* rempoter

Repoussé, — work, *s.* repoussé, *m.* [blâmer

Reprehend, *v.a.* reprendre, réprimander;

Reprehender, *s.* répréhenseur, censeur, *m.*

Reprehensible, *adj.* répréhensible

Reprehensibleness, *s.* répréhensibilité, *f.*

Reprehensibly, *adv.* répréhensiblement

Reprehension, *s.* répréhension, *f.* [de blâme

Reprehensive, *adj.* répréhensif, de reproche,

Reprehensively, *adv.* répréhensivement

Represent, *v.a.* représenter

Representable, *adj.* représentable

Representation, *s.* représentation, *f.*

Representative, *adj.* représentatif; qui représente; — *s.* représentant, *m.*; député, *m.*; (*thing*) représentation, *f.*

Representatively, *adv.* représentativement

Representativeness, *s.* qualité représentative, *f.* [représentant, *m.*

Representer, *s.* personne qui représente, *f.*;

Repress, *v.a.* réprimer

Represser, *s.* réprimeur, *m.*

Repressibility, *s.* répressibilité, *f.*

Repressible, *adj.* répressible, réprimable

Repression, *s.* répression, *f.*

Repressive, *adj.* répressif

Repressively, *adv.* répressivement

Reprieve, *v.a.* (*law*) accorder un sursis à; (*fig.*) donner du répit à; — *s.* (*law*) sursis, *m.*; (*fig.*) répit, *m.*; délai, *m.* [mande, *f.*

Reprimand, *v.a.* réprimander; — *s.* répri-

Reprint, *v.a.* réimprimer; — *s.* réimpression, *f.*

Reprinting, *s.* réimpression, *f.*

Reprisal, *s.* représaille, *f.*; (*law*) reprise, *f.* *To make —s*, user de représailles

Reprise, *s.* (*nav.*) reprise, *f.*

Reproach, *s.* reproche, *m.*; blâme, *m.*; (*shame*) honte, *f.*; — *v.a.* faire *or* adresser des reproches à; (*with* or *for*) reprocher; blâmer, accuser, réprimander. *To — ... (a person) with a thing, with having done ...*, reprocher à ... (quelqu'un) quelque chose, d'avoir fait ... *To be —ed with*, recevoir des reproches de. *I am —ed with having said*, on me reproche d'avoir dit. *He is a — to*, il est la honte de. **—ful,** *adj.* plein de reproches; de reproche; injurieux, outrageant, offensant; (*shameful*) honteux, infâme. **—fully,** *adv.* avec reproche, d'un air *or* d'un ton de reproche; injurieusement; (*shamefully*) honteusement, avec honte. **—fulness,** *s.* air *or* ton de reproche, *m.* **—less,** *adj.* sans reproche, irréprochable

Reproachable, *adj.* reprochable

Reproachableness, *s.* nature reprochable, *f.*

Reproachably, *adv.* reprochablement

Reproacher, *s.* reprocheur, *m.*, -euse, *f.*

Reprobate, *adj. s.* réprouvé, *m.*, e, *f.*; — *v.a.* réprouver

Reprobateness, *s.* état de réprobation, *m.*

Reprobater, *s.* réprobateur, *m.*, -trice, *f.*

Reprobating, *adj.* réprobateur; — *s.* répro-

Reprobation, *s.* réprobation, *f.* [bation, *f.*

Reprobative, *adj.* réprobatif

Reprobatively, *adv.* réprobativement

Reprobatory, *adj.* réprobateur

Reproduce, *v.a.* reproduire

Reproducer, *s.* reproducteur, *m.*, -trice, *f.*

Reproducible, *adj.* reproductible

Reproducibleness, *s.* reproductibilité, *f.*

Reproducing, *adj.* reproducteur; — *s.* repro-

Reproduction, *s.* reproduction, *f.* [duction, *f.*

Reproductive, *adj.* reproductif; reproducteur

Reproductively, *adv.* reproductivement

Reproductiveness, *s.* reproductivité, *f.*

Reproof, *s.* reproche, *m.*; réprimande, *f.*; blâme, *m.*

Reprovable, *adj.* répréhensible, blâmable

Reprovably, *adv.* répréhensiblement

Reprove, *v.a.* reprendre, réprimander; blâmer

Reprover, *s.* répréhenseur, censeur, *m.*

Reprov-ing, -ingly. *V.* **Reprehens-ive,**

Reps, *s.* reps, *m.*; — *adj.* de reps [**-ively**

Reptation, *s.* reptation, *f.*

Reptatory, *adj.* reptatoire; rampant

Reptile, *adj.* reptile; (*low*) rampant, bas, vil;

Republic, *s.* république, *f.* [— *s.* reptile, *m.*

Republican, *adj. s.* républicain, *m.*, e, *f.*

Republicanism, *s.* républicanisme, *m.*

Republicanist, *s.* républicaniste, *m.f.*

Republicanize, *v.a.* républicaniser

Republicanly, *adv.* républicainement

Republication, *s.* réimpression, réédition, nouvelle édition, *f.*; (*law*) renouvellement, *m.*

Republish, *v.a.* republier; rééditer; (*law*) re-

Repudiable, *adj.* répudiable [nouveler

Repudiate, *v.a.* répudier

Repudiation, *s.* répudiation, *f.*

Repugnanc-e, y, *s.* répugnance, *f.*; contrariété, *f.*; opposition, résistance, *f.*

Repugnant, *adj.* répugnant, qui répugne (à), contraire (à), incompatible (avec)

Repugnantly, *adv.* avec répugnance

Repulse, *s.* rebuffade, *f.*; rebut, *m.*; refus, échec, *m.*; — *v.a.* repousser; renvoyer; rebuter; refuser [seur, *m.*, -euse, *f.*

Repulser, *s.* personne qui repousse, *f.*, repous-

Repulsion, *s.* répulsion, *f.*; action de rebuter, *f.*

Repulsive, *adj.* repoussant ; rebutant ; (*phys.*) répulsif
Repulsiveness, *s.* force répulsive, *f.* ; nature repoussante, *f.* ; caractère rebutant, *m.*
Repulsory, *adj. V.* **Repulsive**
Repump, *v.a.* repomper
Repumping, *s.* repompement, *m.*
Repurchase, *v.a.* racheter ; — *s.* rachat, *m.*
Reputable, *adj.* honorable ; considéré
Reputableness, *s.* honorabilité, *f.*
Reputably, *adv.* honorablement, avec honneur
Reputation, *s.* réputation, *f.*
Repute, *v.a.* réputer ; — *s.* réputation, *f.*, renom, *m.*, renommée, *f.* *To bring into* —, mettre en réputation *or* en vogue, faire la réputation de [— *father*, père putatif
Reputed, *adj.* réputé, censé ; qui passe pour.
Reputedly, *adv.* censément ; d'après l'opinion commune ; (*of fathers*) putativement
Request, *s.* demande, prière, *f.* ; instance, *f.* ; (*law*) requête, *f.* ; (*vogue*) vogue, réputation, *f.* *In* —, en vogue ; à la mode ; (*com.*) demandé, recherché ; (*pers.*) recherché, répandu. *In great* —, très demandé, très recherché ; très répandu
Request, *v.a.* demander ; solliciter ; prier ; inviter. *To — a thing*, demander *or* solliciter une chose. *To — a person* (*to* ...), demander à une personne *or* prier une personne (de ...) ; inviter une personne (à ...)
Requester, *s.* demandeur, *m.*, -euse, *f.*, solliciteur, *m.*, -euse, *f.*
Requicken, *v.a.* ranimer, raviver [quiem, *f.*
Requiem, *s.* requiem, *m.* ; (*mass*) messe de re-
Requirable, *adj.* demandable
Require, *v.a.* demander, réclamer ; vouloir ; (*as a right*) requérir, exiger ; (*have occasion for, want*) avoir besoin de ; (*must have*) falloir (*imp.*). *You have brought your umbrella, but I hope you won't — it*, vous avez apporté votre parapluie, mais j'espère que vous n'en aurez pas besoin. *The candle —s snuffing*, la chandelle a besoin d'être mouchée. *She —s a book*, il lui faut un livre. *Two are —d*, il en faut deux
Required, *adj.* requis, voulu ; nécessaire
Requirement, *s.* besoin, *m.* ; exigence, nécessité, *f.* ; condition *or* qualité requise, *f.*
Requirer, *s.* personne qui requiert *or* qui demande *or* qui exige, *f.*
Requisite, *adj.* requis, voulu ; nécessaire, indispensable ; — *s.* condition requise, *f.* ; chose nécessaire, chose indispensable, *f.* ; article, *m.*
Requisitely, *adv.* nécessairement
Requisiteness, *s.* nécessité, *f.*
Requisition, *s.* réquisition, *f.* ; demande, réclamation, *f.* ; convocation, invitation, *f.* ; — *v.a.* mettre en réquisition
Requisitionist, *s.* signataire (d'une convocation *or* invitation), *m.f.*, convocateur, *m.*, -trice, *f.*
Requisitorial, *adj.* réquisitorial
Requisitory, *s.* réquisitoire, *m.*
Requital, *s.* retour, *m.* ; récompense, *f.* ; revanche, *f.*
Requite, *v.a.* récompenser, reconnaître, payer (de) ; (*return*) rendre ; rendre la pareille
Requiter, *s.* personne qui récompense *or* qui
Reredos, *s.* retable, arrière-dos, *m.* [rend, *f.*
Resaddle, *v.a.* resseller
Resale, *s.* revente, *f.*
Rescind, *v.a.* annuler ; révoquer ; rapporter ; abroger ; abolir ; (*law*) rescinder, casser, annuler
Rescindable, *adj.* rescindable, annulable
Rescission, *s.* annulation, *f.* ; révocation, *f.* ; abrogation, *f.* ; (*law*) rescision, annulation, *f.*
Rescissory, *adj.* rescisoire
Rescript, *s.* rescrit, *m.*
Rescue, *v.a.* délivrer (de), sauver (de), tirer (de), arracher (à) ; secourir ; reprendre (à, sur) ; ressaisir ; — *s.* délivrance, *f.* ; secours, *m.* ; sauvetage, *m.*
Rescuer, *s.* libérateur, *m.*, -trice, *f.* ; secoureur, *m.*, -euse, *f.* ; sauveteur, *m.*
Research, *s.* recherche, *f.* ; — *v.a.* rechercher
Reseat, *v.a.* rasseoir ; remettre, replacer ; rétablir ; réélire ; (*chairs*, &c.) remettre un fond à
Resect, *v.a.* réséquer
Resection, *s.* résection, *f.*
Reseda, *s.* réséda, *m.*
Reseize, *v.a.* ressaisir [qui ressaisit, *f.*
Reseizer, *s.* personne qui saisit de nouveau *or*
Reseizure, *s.* nouvelle saisie, *f.*
Resell, *v.a.* revendre, vendre de nouveau
Resemblance, *s.* ressemblance, *f.* ; rapport, *m.* ; image, *f.* [*other*, se ressembler
Resemble, *v.a.* ressembler à. *To — each*
Resent, *v.a.* se ressentir de ; se venger de ; prendre en mauvaise part ; se souvenir de, conserver le souvenir de
Resentful, *adj.* plein de ressentiment, rancunier, vindicatif
Resentingly, *adv.* avec ressentiment
Resentment, *s.* ressentiment, *m.*
Reservation, *s.* réserve, *f.* ; restriction, *f.* ; (*thought*) arrière-pensée, *f.* ; (*law*) réservation, réserve, *f.* *Mental* —, restriction mentale, [arrière-pensée, *f.*
Reservatory, *s.* dépôt, *m.*
Reserve, *v.a.* réserver ; se réserver ; — *s.* réserve, *f.* ; restriction, *f.* ; (*prudence*) réserve, retenue, discrétion, *f.* ; (*law*) réservation, réserve, *f.* ; (*mil.*) réserve, *f.* ; — *adj.* de réserve. *To — oneself*, se réserver. — **fund,** *s.* fonds de prévoyance, *m.*
Reserved, *adj.* réservé. — *price*, mise à prix, *f.*
Reservedly, *adv.* réservément, avec réserve
Reservedness, *s.* réserve, retenue, discrétion, *f.*
Reservoir, *s.* réservoir, *m.* ; bassin, *m.*
Reset, *v.a.* reposer, replacer, remettre ; fixer *or* indiquer de nouveau ; &c. *V.* **Set ;** (*print.*) recomposer
Resetting, *s.* (*print.*) recomposition, *f.*
Reship, *v.a.* rembarquer
Reshipment, *s.* rembarquement, *m.*
Reside, *v.n.* résider ; demeurer
Residence, *s.* résidence, *f.* ; demeure, *f.* ; (*law*) domicile, *m.* ; (*stay*) séjour, *m.*, résidence, *f.* ; (*lodging*) logement, *m.* *Board and* —, la table et le logement
Resident, *adj.* résidant ; (*living in the house where employed*) interne ; — *s.* habitant, *m.*, e, *f.* ; résident, *m.*, e, *f.* ; (*of schools*) maître interne, *m.*, institutrice interne, *f.*
Residential, *adj.* de résidence
Residentiary, *adj.* en résidence ; résidant ; — *s.* ecclésiastique obligé à résidence, *m.*
Residual, *adj.* résiduel
Residuary, *adj.* résiduel ; (*of legacies and legatees*) à titre universel
Residue, *s.* reste, restant, résidu, *m.* ; (*of a debt or account*) reliquat, *m.* ; (*law*) résidu, reste, *m.*
Residuum, *s.* marc, *m.* ; (*chem., law*) résidu, *m.*
Resign, *v.a.* résigner ; (*an office*) donner sa démission de, se démettre de ; (*yield*) céder, abandonner, renoncer à ; (*submit*) soumettre ; (*sign again*) resigner, signer de nouveau ; — *v.n.* démissionner, donner sa démission ; (*eccl.*) résigner. *To — oneself*, se résigner, se soumettre
Resignable, *adj.* résignable [mettre
Resignation, *s.* résignation, *f.* ; (*from an office*) démission, *f.* ; (*cession*) abandon, *m.*, renonciation, *f.* ; (*submission*) soumission, *f.* *To send in* or *tender o.'s* —, donner sa démission
Resigned, *adj.* résigné ; (*from an office*) démissionnaire
Resignedly, *adv.* avec résignation
Resignee, *s.* résignataire, *m.f.*
Resigner, *s.* démissionnaire, *m.f.* ; (*eccl.*) résignant, *m.*, e, *f.* ; (*law*) résignateur, *m.*, -trice, *f.*
Resilienc-e, y, *s.* rebondissement, *m.*
Resilient, *adj.* rebondissant
Resilver, *v.a.* réargenter
Resilvering, *s.* réargenture, *f.* [colophane, *f.*
Resin, *s.* résine, *f.* ; (*colophony, for violins*, &c.)
Resiniferous, *adj.* résinifère
Resinous, *adj.* résineux

Resinously, *adv.* résineusement
Resinousness, *s.* nature résineuse, *f.*
Resipiscence, *s.* résipiscence, *f.*
Resist, *v.a.* résister à; se raidir contre; s'opposer à; se refuser à; — *v.n.* résister
Resistance, *s.* résistance, *f.*; (*law*) rébellion, *f.*
Resistant, *adj.* résistant; — *s. V.* **Resister**
Resister, *s.* personne qui résiste, *f.*
Resistibility, Resistibleness, *s.* résisti-
Resistible, *adj.* résistible [bilité, *f.*
Resistibly, *adv.* résistiblement
Resistless, &c *V.* **Irresistible,** &c.
Resoluble, &c. *V.* **Resolvable,** &c.
Resolute, *adj.* résolu
Resolutely, *adv.* résolûment
Resoluteness, Resolution, *s.* résolution, *f.*; fermeté, *f.*; décision, *f.* — *of forces,* décomposition des forces, *f.* [solubilité, *f.*
Resolvability, Resolvableness, *s.* ré-
Resolvable, *adj.* résoluble
Resolve, *s.* résolution, *f.*; — *v.a.* résoudre; décider, arrêter; (*med., math.*) résoudre; — *v n.* résoudre; décider (de); se résoudre (à), se décider (à); (*into*) se résoudre (en); se réduire (à), revenir (à). *To fully* —, se promettre bien (de). *To — itself into* (*a committee,* &c.), se constituer *or* se former (en comité, &c.)
Resolvent, *adj. s.* résolutif, *adj. m.*, -ive, *f.*, résolutif, *s.m.*, résolvant, *adj. m.*, e, *f.*, résolvant, *s.m.* [ment, *m.*
Resonance, *s.* résonnance, *f.*; retentisse-
Resonant, *adj* résonnant; retentissant
Resort, *v.n.* avoir recours (à), recourir (à); (*to go*) se rendre, aller; fréquenter, hanter; (*law*) retourner; — *s.* recours, *m.*; ressource, *f.*; (*gathering*) concours, *m.*, affluence, *f.*; réunion, assemblée, *f.*; fréquentation, *f.*; (*place*) rendez-vous, *m.*; (*law*) ressort, *m.* *Place of* —, lieu *or* endroit fréquenté, *m.* *In the last* —, en dernier ressort
Resound, *v.n.* résonner, retentir ('*with,*' de); — *v a.* faire résonner, faire retentir; répéter; célébrer
Resounding, *s.* résonnement, *m.*; retentissement, *m.*; — *adj.* retentissant
Resource, *s* ressource, *f* *Beyond* —, sans ressource. —**less,** *adj.* dénué de ressources, sans ressource
Resow, *v.a.*(*land*) réensemencer; (*seed*) ressemer
Resowing, *s.* (*of land*) réensemencement, *m.*
Respect, *v.a.* respecter; (*esteem*) considérer; (*concern*) concerner, regarder, avoir égard à; — *s.* respect, *m.*; considération, estime, *f.*; (*relation*) rapport, égard, *m.*; —**s,** *pl.* devoirs, hommages, respects, *m pl.* — *of persons,* (*preference*) acception (de personnes), *f.* *As —s,* à l'égard de, quant à. *In — of,* sous le rapport de. *In all —s, in every* —, sous tous les rapports, à tous égards. *In no* —, sous aucun rapport. *In other —s,* d'ailleurs, sous d'autres rapports. *In some* —, en quelque sorte. *In some —s,* sous quelques rapports, à quelques égards. *In this* (or *that*) —, sous ce rapport, à cet égard, en cela. *Out of — to,* par égard pour, par considération pour. *With — to,* sous le rapport de, à l'égard de, quant à. *To have — of persons, to — persons,* faire acception de personnes
Respectability, *s.* respectabilité, *f.*; honorabilité, *f.*; considération, *f.*, crédit, *m.*; décence, *f* *Of* —, respectable; honorable
Respectable, *adj.* respectable; honorable; considéré; honnête; très bien; comme il faut; décent, convenable; passable; (*of public gatherings*) bien composé
Respectableness. *V.* **Respectability**
Respectably, *adv.* respectablement; honorablement; honnêtement; très bien; comme il faut; décemment, convenablement; passablement
Respected, *part. adj.* respecté; considéré; respectable, vénérable, digne
Respecter, *s.* personne qui respecte, *f.* *To be a — of persons,* faire acception de personnes
Respectful, *adj.* respectueux [respect
Respectfully, *adv.* respectueusement, avec
Respectfulness, *s.* nature respectueuse, *f.*
Respecting, *prep.* par rapport à, à l'égard de, quant à; au sujet de; sur le compte de
Respective, *adj* respectif; relatif [ment
Respectively, *adv.* respectivement; relative-
Respectless, *adj.* sans respect; sans égards; sans rapport
Respira-bility, bleness. *V.* page 3, § 1
Respirable, *adj.* respirable
Respiration, *s.* respiration, *f.*
Respirator, *s.* respirateur, *m.*
Respiratory, *adj.* respiratoire
Respire, *v.n.a.* respirer
Respite, *s.* répit, relâche, *m.*; (*law*) sursis, *m.*; — *v.a.* donner du répit à; (*defer*) suspendre, remettre, différer; (*law*) surseoir, surseoir à; accorder un sursis à
Resplendenc-e, y, *s.* resplendissement, *m.*; éclat, *m.*, splendeur, *f.*
Resplendent, *adj.* resplendissant ('*with,*' de)
Resplendently, *adv.* avec éclat, avec splen-
Respond, *v.n.* répondre (à) [deur
Respondent, *s.* répondant, *m.*, e, *f.*; (*law*) défendeur, *m.*, -eresse, *f.*
Respondentia, *s.pl.* prêt sur faculté, *m.*
Response, *s.* réponse, *f.*; écho, *m.*; (*lit.*) répons, *m.*
Responsibility, *s.* responsabilité, *f.* *On his own* —, sous sa propre responsabilité; de son
Responsible, *adj.* responsable [chef
Responsive, *adj.* responsif
Responsory, *adj.* responsif; — *s.* répons, *m.*
Rest, *v.n.* se reposer; (*lie dead, sleep*) reposer; dormir; (*lean, be supported*) s'appuyer; (*lay oneself down, go to sleep*) se coucher; (*remain, be*) se tenir, être; (*stop*) s'arrêter; (*trust*) se fier (à), se confier (à); s'en rapporter (à); se fonder (sur); (*bear on*) porter, reposer; (*be dependent on*) dépendre (de); (*lie as an obligation*) incomber (à); — *v.a.* reposer; faire reposer; (*lean*) appuyer; poser; fonder; — *s.* repos, *m.*; (*sleep*) sommeil, *m.*; (*support*) appui, support, *m.*; (*mus.*) silence, *m.*; (*poet.*) césure, *f.*; (*for a knife*) porte-couteau, *m.*; (*for a telescope*) affût, *m.*; (*for a rifle*) chevalet, support, *m.*; (*for an arquebuse*) fourchette, *f.*; (*for a lance*) arrêt, *m.*; (*remains*) reste, restant, *m.*; (les) autres, *m.f.pl.* *Among the* —, entre autres. *At* —, en repos, tranquille. *To go* or *retire to* —, se retirer; aller se coucher. *To set at* —, tranquilliser, calmer; (*fig.*) décider, résoudre, éclaircir, régler, vider, mettre fin à, en finir avec. *It —s with him to say ...,* il lui appartient de dire ... —**harrow,** *s.* bugrane, *f.*, arrête-bœuf, *m.* —**less,** &c., *See below*
Restaurant, *s.* restaurant, *m.*
Restiff, -ness. *V.* **Restive, -ness**
Resting, *part.* se reposant, &c. (*V.* **Rest,** *v.n.a.*); (*leaning: active sense*) appuyant; (*leaning: neut. sense*) s'appuyant; appuyé; posé; (*laying oneself down*) se couchant; (*lying down*) couché; — *s.* repos, *m.* —**place,** *s.* lieu de repos, *m.*; abri, *m.*; gîte, *m.*; coucher, *m.* *Last — place,* dernière demeure, *f.*; dernier sommeil, *m.* —**point,** *s.* point de repos, *m.*
Restitute, *v.a.* restituer
Restitution, *s.* restitution, *f.*
Restitutor, *s.* restituteur, *m.*
Restitutory, *adj.* restitutoire
Restive, *adj.* rétif; opiniâtre, obstiné, entêté
Restiveness, *s.* rétiveté, retivité, *f.*; opiniâtreté, obstination, *f.*, entêtement, *m.*
Restless, *adj.* sans repos; (*anxious*) inquiet; agité; (*turbulent*) remuant, turbulent. — *night,* nuit agitée, mauvaise nuit, *f.*
Restlessly, *adv.* sans repos; d'une manière agitée; avec inquiétude; avec turbulence, turbulemment

Restlessness, *s.* inquiétude, *f.*; agitation, *f.*; caractère remuant, *m.*, turbulence, *f.*; (*sleeplessness*) insomnie, *f.*
Restock, *v.a.* pourvoir *or* &c. (*V.* **Stock,** *v.a.*) de nouveau; (*a shop*) remonter, rassortir; (*a park with deer*, &c.) repeupler; (*a pond*) rempoissonner, repeupler; (*a farm*) remeubler, remonter; (*a fire-arm*) remonter
Restocking, *s.* nouvel approvisionnement, *m.*; remontage, *m.*; rassortiment, *m.*; (*with fish*) rempoissonnement, *m.* [rétabli; restituable
Restorable, *adj.* restaurable; qui peut être
Restoration, *s.* (*of a building, dynasty, picture*, &c.) restauration, *f.*; (*reestablishment*) rétablissement, *m.*; rénovation, *f.*; (*giving back*) restitution, *f.*
Restorative, *adj.* restaurant, restauratif; réparateur; (*strengthening*) fortifiant; — *s.* restauratif, restaurant, *m.*
Restore, *v.a.* (*a dynasty, building, picture*, &c.) restaurer; (*health*, &c.) rétablir; remettre; faire revenir; (*confidence*, &c.) ramener; (*a text*, &c.) rétablir; (*to replace*) remettre; (*to mend*) raccommoder; (*wine*) corriger, raccommoder, repasser; (*give back*) rendre; (*things stolen*) restituer
Restorer, *s.* restaurateur, *m.*, -trice, *f.*; rétablisseur, *m.*; régénérateur, *m.*, -trice, *f.*; réparateur, *m.*, -trice, *f.*; rénovateur, *m.*, -trice, *f.*; restituteur, *m.* [**Restoration**
Restoring, *adj.* *V.* **Restorative;** — *s.* *V.*
Restrain, *v.a.* retenir, contenir; réprimer; (*limit*) restreindre; (*hinder*) arrêter; gêner; (*prevent*) empêcher
Restrainable, *adj.* qui peut être retenu *or* contenu *or* réprimé *or* restreint [avec retenue
Restrainedly, *adv.* d'une manière restreinte;
Restrainer, *s.* personne *or* chose qui retient *or* contient *or* réprime *or* restreint, *f.*
Restraining, *adj.* qui retient; restrictif
Restraint, *s.* contrainte, *f.*; gêne, *f.*; restriction, *f.*; (*hindrance*) empêchement, *m.*, entrave,
Restrict, *v.a.* restreindre [*f.*; (*curb*) frein, *m.*
Restriction, *s.* restriction, *f.*
Restrictive, *adj.* restrictif
Restrictively, *adv.* avec restriction
Restringenc-e, y, *s.* restringence, *f.*
Restringent, *adj.* *s.* restringent, *adj.m.*, e, *f.*, restringent, *s.m.* [—, finalement
Result, *v.n.* résulter; — *s.* résultat, *m.* *In the*
Resultant, *s.* résultante, *f.* [peut reprendre
Resumable, *adj.* qui peut être repris, qu'on
Resume, *v.a.* reprendre; continuer, poursuivre
Resummon, *v.a.* réassigner
Resummons, *s.* réassignation, *f.*
Resumption, *s.* reprise, *f.*; continuation, *f.*
Resumptive, *adj.* *s.* résomptif, *adj.m.*, -ive, *f.*, résomptif, *s.m.*
Resurrection, *s.* résurrection, *f.* — **man,** *s.* résurrectioniste, déterreur, *m.* — **pie,** *s.* pâté de restes de viande, *m.* [reur, *m.*
Resurrectionist, *s.* résurrectioniste, déter-
Resurrective, *adj.* résurrectif
Resurvey, *v.a.* revoir; (*land*) réarpenter; — *s.* révision, *f.*; (*of land*) réarpentage, *m.*
Resuscitate, *v.a.n.* *V.* **Revive**
Resuscitation, *s.* rappel à la vie, *m.*; retour à la vie, *m.*; (*chem.*) renouvellement, *m.*
Ret, *v.a.* rouir
Re-table, *s.* retable, *m.*
Retail, *v.a.* détailler, vendre en détail, débiter; (*tell*) débiter; colporter; — *s.* détail, *m.*, vente en détail, *f.*, commerce de détail, *m.*; — *adj.* en détail; de détail. *By* —, en détail. — **dealer,** *s.* marchand (*m.*, e, *f.*) en détail, détaillant, *m.*, e, *f.* — **price,** *s.* prix de détail, *m.* — **trade,** *s.* commerce de détail, *m.*
Retailer, *s.* détaillant, *m.*, e, *f.*, marchand (*m.*, e, *f.*) en détail, débitant, *m.*, e, *f.*; (*teller*) débiteur, *m.*, -euse, *f.*; colporteur, *m.*, -euse, *f.*
Retain, *v.a.* retenir; garder; conserver; engager; prendre à son service

Retainer, *s.* adhérent, partisan, *m.*; dépendant, *m.*; vassal, *m.*; (*attendant*) personne de la suite, *f.*; (*hanger-on*) familier, *m.*; (*one who retains*) personne qui retient *or* qui garde *or* qui conserve, *f.*; (*fee*) honoraires (donnés d'avance), *m.pl.*; —**s,** *pl.* adhérents, &c., *m.pl.*; (*attendants*) suite, *f.*, personnes de la suite, *f.pl.*, gens, *m.pl.*
Retaining, *adj.* qui retient, qui garde; qui engage; (*of bandages*) contentif. — **fee,** *s.* honoraires (donnés d'avance), *m.pl.* — **wall,** *s.* mur de soutènement, *m.*
Retake, *v.a.* reprendre
Retaking, *s.* reprise, *f.*
Retaliate, *v.a.* user de représailles pour, rendre la pareille de, rendre; — *v.n.* user de représailles ('*upon,*' envers), rendre la pareille ('*upon,*' à)
Retaliation, *s.* représailles, *f.pl.*, revanche, *f.*; talion, *m.*, peine du talion, *f.* *Law of* —, loi *or* peine du talion, *f.* *By way of* —, par représailles, en revanche
Retaliatory, *adj.* de représailles
Retard, *v.a.* retarder [&c.) retardation, *f.*
Retardation, *s.* retardement, *m.*; (*mech., phys.*,
Retardative, *adj.* retardatif
Retarder, *s.* personne qui retarde, *f.*; (*things*) cause de retard, *f.*
Retarding, *adj.* retardateur; — *s.* retard, *m.*
Retardment, *s.* retardement, retard, *m.*
Retch, *v.n.* faire (*or* avoir) des haut-le-corps; — *s.* haut-le-corps, *m.*
Retching, *s.* haut-le-corps, *m.*, vomiturition, *f.*, efforts nauséeux, *m.pl.*
Retell, *v.a.* redire, répéter [(*med.*) rétention, *f.*
Retention, *s.* conservation, *f.*; mémoire, *f.*;
Retentive, *adj.* qui retient; qui conserve; (*of the memory*) fidèle, sûr; (*med.*) rétentif; (*of bandages*) contentif
Retentiveness, *s.* pouvoir de retenir, *m.*; ténacité; (*of the memory*) fidélité, sûreté, *f.*; (*med.*) rétentivité, *f.*
Retiarius, *s.* rétiaire, *m.*
Retiary, *s.* aranéide, araignée fileuse, fileuse, tendeuse, *f.*; — *adj.* fileuse (*f.*)
Reticenc-e, y, *s.* réticence, *f.*
Reticent, *adj.* réservé, taciturne
Reticle, *s.* (*small net*) réticule, petit filet, *m.*; (*bag*, &c.) *V.* **Reticule**
Reticular, *adj.* réticulaire
Reticulate, -d, *adj.* réticulé
Reticulation, *s.* disposition rétiforme, *f.*
Reticule, *s.* (*bag*) sac, ridicule, *m.*; (*of telescopes*, &c.) réticule, *m.*
Reticulum, *s.* réticule, *m.*
Retiform, *adj.* rétiforme
Retina, *s.* rétine, *f.*
Retinal, *adj.* rétinien
Retinite, Retinitis, *s.* rétinite, *f.*
Retinue, *s.* suite, *f.*; cortége, *m.*
Retire, *v.a.* retirer; — *v.n.* se retirer, s'en aller; alier
Retired, *adj.* retiré; (*superannuated*) en retraite, retraité; (*former, old*) ancien; (*hidden*) secret, caché; (*of places*) retiré, écarté, solitaire. — *list*, (*mil.*) contrôle des officiers en retraite, *m.*; (*civil*) contrôle des personnes admises à la retraite, *m.* *On the* — *list*, en retraite, retraité. *To put on the* — *list*, mettre à la retraite, retraiter
Retiredly, *adv.* dans la retraite
Retiredness. *V.* **Retirement** [ment, *m.*
Retirement, *s.* retraite, *f.*; solitude, *f.*, isole-
Retiring, *adj.* qui se retire; (*leaving office or* &c.) sortant; (*of pensions*, &c.) de retraite; (*reserved*) réservé, modeste; — *s.* *V.* **Retirement.** — *allowance* or *pension*, pension de retraite, *f.* — *fund*, caisse de retraite, *f.*
Retorsion, *s.* rétorsion, *f.*
Retort, *s.* réplique, *f.*; riposte, *f.*; repartie, *f.*; (*chem. and gas*) cornue, *f.*; — *v.a.* renvoyer; (*an argument*, &c.) rétorquer; (*reply*) répliquer;

— *v.n.* riposter, répliquer. — **on, upon,** rembarrer
Retortable, *adj.* rétorquable
Retorter, *s.* personne qui rétorque *or* qui réplique, *f.*
Retorting, *s.* renvoi, *m.*; (*of an argument*) rétorsion, *f.*
Retortion, *s.* rétorsion, *f.*
Retortive, *adj.* rétorsif
Retouch, *v.a.* retoucher; — *s.* retouche, *f.*
Retoucher, *s.* retoucheur, *m.*, -euse, *f.*
Retouching, *s.* retouchage, *m.*
Retrace, *v.a.* revenir sur, reprendre; (*investigate*) remonter à, rechercher; (*a line,* &c.) retracer. *To — o.'s steps,* revenir (*or* retourner) sur ses pas
Retract, *v.a.* rétracter; (*withdraw*) retirer; — *v.n.* se rétracter, se dédire
Retractation, *s.* rétractation, *f.*
Retractibility, Retractility, *s.* rétractibilité, rétractilité, *f.*
Retractible, Retractile, *adj.* rétractible, rétractile
Retraction, *s.* rétractation, *f.*; (*shrinking*) rétraction, *f.*; (*withdrawal*) abandon, *m.*; désistement, *m.*
Retractive, *adj.* rétractif
Retractor, *s.* rétracteur, *m.*
Retranscribe, *v.a.* retranscrire
Retranslate, *v.a.* retraduire
Retranslation, *s.* retraduction, *f.*
Retraxit, *s.* désistement, *m.*
Retreat, *s.* retraite, *f.*; — *v.n.* se retirer; (*mil.*) battre en retraite, (*to, into,* &c.) se retirer (à, dans, &c.) [en retraite, en retraite
Retreating, *adj.* qui se retire; (*mil.*) qui bat
Retrench, *v.a.* retrancher; — *v.n.* se retrancher
Retrenchment, *s.* retranchement, *m.*; (*of expenses*) économie, *f.*, économies, *f.pl.*
Retribute, *v.a.* rétribuer
Retribu-ter, tress, *s.* rétributeur, *m.*, -trice, *f.*
Retribution, *s.* récompense, *f.*; rétribution, *f.*; châtiment, *m.*; représailles, *f.pl.*
Retributive, Retributory, *adj.* qui rétribue; distributif
Retrievable, *adj.* recouvrable; réparable; qui peut être rétabli, qui peut se rétablir
Retrievably, *adv.* réparablement
Retrieve, *v.a.* rétablir; réparer; retrouver, recouvrer; (*reclaim*) faire revenir (de), tirer (de); (*com.*) récupérer
Retriever, *s.* chien retrouveur et rapporteur, *m.*
Retroact, *v.n.* rétroagir
Retroaction, *s.* rétroaction, *f.*
Retroactive, *adj.* rétroactif. — *effect,* effet rétroactif, *m.*; rétroactivité, *f.*
Retroactively, *adv.* rétroactivement
Retrocede, *v.a.* rétrocéder; — *v.n.* reculer, rétrograder [sif. — *gout,* goutte remontée, *f.*
Retrocedent, Retroceding, *adj.* rétrocessif
Retrocession, *s.* rétrocession, *f.*
Retrogradation, *s.* rétrogradation, *f.*
Retrograde, *adj.* rétrograde; — *v.n.* rétrograder
Retrogradingly, *adv.* en rétrogradant
Retrogression, *s.* rétrogression, rétrogradation, *f.*
Retrogressive, *adj.* rétrogressif
Retrogressively, *adv.* rétrogressivement
Retrospect, Retrospection, *s.* revue rétrospective, revue, *f.*, examen rétrospectif, examen, regard jeté en arrière, coup d'œil, *m.*
Retrospective, *adj.* rétrospectif; rétroactif
Retrospectively, *adv.* rétrospectivement; rétroactivement
Retroversion, *s.* rétroversion, *f.*; renversement, *m.*
Retrovert, *v.a.* renverser
Retting, *s.* rouissage, *m.*
Return, *v.n.* (*go back*) retourner; (*come back*) revenir; (*inside, in-doors*) rentrer; (*answer*) répondre, répliquer; — *v.a.* rendre; restituer; (*send back*) renvoyer; transmettre; (*requite*) reconnaître; rendre; (*thanks, an answer*) rendre, faire; (*a verdict*) rendre; (*put back*) remettre; (*give an account*) rapporter, rendre compte de; (*produce*) rapporter; (*elect*) élire, nommer; — *s.* retour, *m.*; rentrée, *f.*; (*giving back*) restitution, *f.*; (*sending back*) renvoi, *m.*; (*profit*) profit, gain, avantage, *m.*; (*of money*) remise, rentrée, *f.*; (*answer*) réponse, *f*; (*requital*) retour, *m.*, récompense, *f.*; (*account*) rapport, compte-rendu, *m.*; état, *m.*; relevé, *m.*; chiffres, *m.pl.*; résultat, *m.*; liste, *f.*; statistique, *f.*; (*balance-sheet*) bilan, *m.*; (*com.*) montant des opérations, *m.*, affaires, *f.pl.*; (*arch.*) retour, *m.*; (*election*) élection, *f.*; (*mil.*) liste, *f.*, état, *m.*; — *adj.* de retour, &c.; (*of carriages and horses*) de renvoi. — ! (*at a rail. ticket office*) aller et retour ! *But to —,* (*after a digression*) Mais revenons. *In — for,* en retour de. *To make some — for,* reconnaître, payer de retour. *Small profits and quick —s,* de petits bénéfices et de promptes ventes. — **journey, -voyage,** *s.* (*rail., nav.*) retour, *m.* — **match,** *s.* revanche, *f.* — **shock,** *s.* (*phys.*) choc en retour, *m.* — **ticket,** *s. V.* **Ticket**
Returnable, *adj.* restituable; éligible; (*com.*) en commission; (*law*) de renvoi
Returned, *part. adj.* retourné, revenu, rentré, rendu, &c. (*V.* **Return,** *v.n.a.*). *To be* or *have —,* (*be back*) être de retour. — **convict** *or* **transport,** *s.* forçat libéré, repris de justice, *m.*
Returning, *adj.* qui retourne, qui revient, &c. (*V.* **Return,** *v.a.n.*); — *s. V.* **Return,** *s.* — **officer,** *s.* (*of votes*) scrutateur, *m.*
Reunion, *s.* réunion, *f.*
Reunite, *v.a.* réunir; — *v.n.* se réunir
Revaccinate, *v.a.* revacciner
Revaccination, *s.* revaccination, *f.*
Revalenta Arabica, *s.* revalescière, *f.*
Reveal, *v.a.* révéler
Revealer, *s.* révélateur, *m.*, -trice, *f.*
Reveille, *s.* réveil, *m.*, diane, *f.*
Revel, *v.n.* se réjouir; (*feast*) faire bombance, faire ripaille, ripailler, riboter; (*to delight*) se plaire; (*give oneself up*) se livrer (à), s'abandonner (à); — *s.* réjouissances, *f.pl.*, fête, *f.*; festin, *m.*; débauche, bombance, ripaille, orgie, *f.*
Revelation, *s.* révélation, *f.*; (*in the Bible*) Apocalypse, *f.* *Book of —s,* Apocalypse, *f.*
Reveller, *s.* joyeux convive, *m.*; viveur, *m.*, -euse, *f.*, noceur, *m.*, -euse, *f.*, bacchante, *f.*, celui (*m.*) *or* celle (*f.*) qui fait la vie
Revelling, *s.* réjouissances, fêtes, *f.pl.*; festin, *m.*, festins, *m.pl.*, orgie, *f.*, orgies, *f.pl.*
Revelly, *s. V.* **Reveille**
Revelry, *s. V.* **Revelling**
Revendicate, *v.a.* revendiquer
Revendication, *s.* revendication, *f.*
Revenge, *v.a.* venger; se venger de; — *s.* vengeance, *f.*; (*in a mild sense*) revanche, *f.* —**ful,** *adj.* vindicatif; (*avenging*) vengeur. —**fully,** *adv.* vindicativement, par vengeance. —**fulness,** *s.* caractère vindicatif, *m.*; esprit de vengeance, *m.* —**less,** *adj.* sans vengeance
Revenger, *s.* vengeur, *m.*, -eresse, *f.*
Revengingly, *adv. V.* **Revengefully**
Revenue, *s.* revenu, *m.*; (*treasury*) fisc, trésor, *m.* — **board,** *s.* administration des revenus publics, *f.* — **cutter,** *s.* (*nav.*) patache, *f.*
Reverberant, *adj.* qui renvoie, qui réfléchit; réverbérant
Reverberate, *v.a.* réverbérer; réfléchir; (*sound*) renvoyer, répercuter
Reverberating, *adj. V.* **Reverberatory**
Reverberation, *s.* réverbération, *f.*; réflexion, *f.*; (*of sound*) répercussion, *f.*
Reverberatory, *adj.* à réverbère; — *s.* fourneau à réverbère, *m.*
Revere, *v.a.* révérer, respecter
Reverence, *s.* révérence, *f.*; — *v.a.* révérer, respecter
Reverencer, *s.* personne qui révère *or* qui respecte, *f.*
Reverend, *adj.* *s.* vénérable, respectable; (*of the clergy: Catholic*) abbé, (*Protestant*) pasteur, (*monk, English clergyman*) révérend. *The — Mr. P.,* Monsieur l'abbé P.; Monsieur le pasteur P.; le Révérend Père P.; (*Engl.*) le Révérend Mr. P. *The — gentleman,* l'abbé; le pasteur; le révérend père; le révérend. — *Sir,*

monsieur l'abbé; monsieur le pasteur; (*to a monk*) mon révérend
Reverent, *adj.* révérencieux
Reverential, *adj.* révérencieux, très respectueux. —*fear*, crainte révérencielle, *f.*
Reverentially, Reverently, *adv.* révérencieusement, révéremment, avec vénération
Reverer, *s. V.* **Reverencer**
Reverie, *s.* rêverie, *f.*
Reversal, *s.* cassation, annulation, *f.*; révocation, *f.*; réhabilitation, *f.*
Reverse, *v.a.* renverser; casser, annuler, infirmer; révoquer; détruire; — *s.* vicissitude, *f.*, changement, *m.*; (*misfortune*) revers, *m.*; (*contrary*) inverse, opposé, contraire, *m.*; (*of a medal*) revers, *m.*; (*print.*) verso, *m.* *The very —, quite the —*, tout l'opposé, tout le contraire. *To — the engine*, renverser la marche de la machine, changer la marche, renverser la vapeur, faire machine arrière
Reversedly, Reversely, *adv.* en sens inverse
Reversible, *adj.* reversible; renversable; (*of stuffs and clothes*) à envers reversible, à deux endroits, sans envers; (*fig.*) révocable; (*law*) annulable
Reversing, *adj.* qui renverse; — *s.* action de renverser, *f.*, renversement, *m.*; (*law, fig.*) *V.* **Reversal.** — **gear,** *s.* leviers de renversement, *m.pl.* — **handle,** *s.* manette de renversement, *f.* — **lever,** *s.* levier de renversement, *m.*
Reversion, *s.* reversion, *f.*, retour, *m.*; survivance, *f.*; succession, *f.*
Reversionary, *adj.* reversible; de survivance
Reversioner, *s.* survivancier, *m.*
Revert, *v.n.* revenir ('*to*,' sur); (*law*) retourner ('*to*,' à), faire retour ('*to*,' à)
Revertible, *adj.* reversible
Revet, *v.a.* revêtir
Revetement, Revetment, *s.* revêtement, *m.*
Revictual, *v.a.* ravitailler; — *v.n.* se ravitailler
Revictualling, *s.* ravitaillement, *m.*
Review, *v.a.* revoir, réviser; (*a book*) rendre compte de, faire la critique de, analyser; (*mil.*) passer en revue; — *s.* revue, révision, *f.*; examen, *m.*; (*of a book*) compte-rendu, *m.*, critique, analyse, *f.*; article, *m.*; (*of theat. performances*, &c.) revue, critique, *f.*; (*periodical*) revue, *f.*; (*law*) révision, *f.*; (*mil.*) revue, *f.* *To take a — of*, faire la revue de, passer en revue
Reviewer, *s.* réviseur, *m.*; (*of books*) critique, *m.*; (*of a Review*) rédacteur (d'une revue), *m.* *Edinburgh —*, rédacteur de la Revue d'Édimbourg
Revile, *v.a.* injurier, insulter, outrager
Reviler, *s.* personne qui injurie *or* qui insulte *or* qui outrage, *f.*
Reviling, *s.* injures, *f.pl.*
Revilingly, *adv.* injurieusement, outrageusement
Revisal, *s.* révision, *f.*; vérification, *f.*; (*print.*) relute, *f.*
Revise, *v.a.* revoir; réviser; vérifier; — *s.* (*print.*) épreuve de révision, seconde épreuve, *f.* *Second —*, troisième épreuve. *Third —*, quatrième épreuve
Reviser, *s.* réviseur, *m.*; vérificateur, *m.*
Revising, *adj.* qui revoit *or* qui révise *or* qui vérifie; — *s. V.* **Revisal.** — **barrister,** *s.* vérificateur des listes électorales, *m.*
Revision, *s.* révision, *f.*; vérification, *f.*
Revisional, Revisionary, *adj.* de révision
Revisit, *v.a.* revisiter, visiter de nouveau; revoir
Revival, *s.* (*to life*) retour à la vie, *m.*; (*of strength*) rétablissement, *m.*; (*of letters, arts*, &c.) renaissance, *f.*; (*renewal*) renouvellement, *m.*; (*of religion*) réveil religieux, réveil, revival, *m.*; (*theat.*) reprise, *f.*
Revive, *v.a.* faire revivre, ressusciter, rappeler à la vie; (*rouse*) ranimer; réveiller; raviver; (*of learning*) faire renaître; (*put in use*) remettre en vigueur, rétablir, renouveler; (*the soul, and chem.*) revivifier; — *v.n.* revivre, renaître, ressusciter; (*recover*) se ranimer; se rétablir; reprendre; se raviver; (*of learning*) renaître; (*chem.*) se revivifier
Reviver, *s.* restaurateur, *m.*, -trice, *f.*, personne *or* chose qui ranime, *f.*
Revivification, *s.* revivification, *f.*
Revivify, *v.a.* revivifier
Reviviscenc-e, y, *s.* reviviscence, *f.*
Reviviscent, *adj.* reviviscent
Reviviscible, *adj.* reviviscible
Revivor, *s.* reprise de procès, *f.* *Bill of —*, demande en reprise de procès, *f.*
Revoca-bility, bleness, *s.* révocabilité, *f.*
Revocable, *adj.* révocable
Revocation, *s.* révocation, *f.*
Revoke, *v.a.* révoquer; — *v.n.* renoncer; — *s.* renonce, *f.*
Revolt, *v.a.* révolter; — *v.n.* se révolter, se soulever, s'insurger; — *s.* révolte, *f.* *To cause to —*, révolter, soulever
Revolter, *s.* révolté, *m.*, e, *f.*, rebelle, *m.f.*
Revoltingly, *adv.* d'une manière révoltante
Revolution, *s.* révolution, *f.*; (*turn*) révolution, *f.*, tour, *m.*
Revolutionarily, *adv.* révolutionnairement
Revolutionary, *adj.* révolutionnaire
Revolutionism, *s* révolutionisme, *m.*
Revolutionist, *s.* révolutionnaire, révolutioniste, *m.f.*
Revolutionistic, *adj.* révolutioniste
Revolutionize, *v.a.* révolutionner
Revolve, *v.a.n.* tourner; (*meditate*) rouler, méditer; (*return*) retourner, revenir; (*astr.*) tourner, faire sa révolution
Revolver, *s.* révolver, *m.*
Revolving, *adj.* tournant; (*fig.*) qui retourne, qui revient; périodique; (*astr.*) qui tourne. — *pistol*, pistolet tournant, révolver, *m.*
Revomit, *v.a.* revomir
Revulsion, *s.* révulsion, *f.*
Revulsive, *adj. s.* révulsif, *adj. m.*, -ive, *f.*, révulsif, *s.m.*
Reward, *v.a.* récompenser ('*for*,' de); — *s.* récompense, *f.*
Rewardable, *adj.* digne de récompense, récompensable
Rewarder, *s.* rémunérateur, *m.*, -trice, *f.*, récompenseur, *m.*
Rewarding, *adj.* rémunérateur, récompenseur; — *s.* action de récompenser, *f.*
Rewrite, *v.a.* récrire
Rex, *s.* roi, *m.*
Reynard, *s.* maître Renard, *m.*; renard, *m.*
Rhamadan, *s.* ramazan, ramadan, *m.*
Rhabdo-logy, -mancy, &c. *V.* page 3, § 1
Rhapsodic, -al, *adj.* rhapsodique, rapsodique
Rhapsodist, *s.* rhapsode, rapsode, *m.*; (*in contempt*) rhapsodiste, rapsodiste, *m.*
Rhapsodize, *v.a.n.* rhapsoder, rapsoder
Rhapsody, *s.* rhapsodie, rapsodie, *f.*
Rhatany. *V.* **Rattany**
Rhenish, *adj.* du Rhin; (*geog.*) rhénan
Rhetoric, *s.* rhétorique, *f.*; (*fig.*) éloquence, *f.*
Rhetorical, *adj.* de (*or* de la) rhétorique; (*in contempt*) de rhéteur
Rhetorically, *adv.* suivant les règles de la rhétorique
Rhetorician, *s.* rhétoricien, *m.*, -ne, *f.*; rhéteur, *m.*
Rhetorize, *v.n.* faire de la rhétorique
Rheum, *s.* catarrhe, *m.*; flux muqueux, *m.*, mucosité, *f.*; pituite, *f.*
Rheumatic, *adj.* rhûmatismal, rhumatique. — *disease*, affection rhumatismale, *f.* — *fever*, rhumatisme aigu, *m.* — *gout*, rhumatisme goutteux, *m.*
Rheumatically, *adv.* rhumatismalement
Rheumatism, *s.* rhumatisme, *m.*
Rhino, *s.* quibus, *m.*
Rhinoceros, *s.* rhinocéros, *m.*
Rhodian, *s.* Rhodien, *m.*, -ne, *f.*; — *adj.* rhodien, de Rhodes
Rhodium, *s.* rhodium, *m.*
Rhododendron, *s.* rhododendron, *m.*
Rhodomontade, *s.* (*bad spelling*) *V.* **Rodomontade**
Rhomb, *s.* rhombe, *m.*; (*nav.*) *V.* **Rhumb**
Rhombic, *adj.* rhombique

Rhombiform, *adj.* rhombiforme
Rhombohedral, *adj.* rhomboèdre
Rhombohedron, *s.* rhomboèdre, *m.*
Rhomboid, *s. adj.* rhomboïde, *s.m., adj. m.f.*
Rhomboidal, *adj.* rhomboïdal
Rhoncus, *s.* rhonchus, rhoncus, râle, *m.*
Rhubarb, *s.* rhubarbe, *f.*
Rhumb, *s.* rumb, *m.* — **line,** *s.* rumb de [vent, *m.*
Rhyme, *s.* rime, *f.*; (*verse*) vers, *m.pl.*; (*not blank verse*) vers rimés, *m.pl.*; — *v.a.n.* rimer; (*in contempt*) rimailler. *In* —, rimé. *To put in* —, mettre en rimes, rimer. —**less,** *adj.* sans rimes, non rimé
Rhymer, Rhymist, *s.* versificateur, *m.*, -trice, *f.*; (*in contempt*) rimeur, *m.*, -euse, *f.*
Rhymster, *s.* rimailleur, *m.*, -euse, *f.*
Rhythm, Rhythmus, *s.* rhythme, *m.*
Rhythmic, -al, *adj.* rhythmique
Rhythmics, *s.pl.* rhythmique, *f.*
Rial, *s.* réal, *m.*
Rib, *s.* côte, *f.*; (*of an umbrella*) branche, *f.*; (*build.*) ferme, *f.*; (*wife*) moitié, épouse, femelle, *f.*; — *v.a.* garnir de côtes. *Short* —*s*, fausses côtes, *f.pl.* — **grass,** *s.* plantain lancéolé, *m.* — **wall,** *s.* compartiment, *m.*
Ribald, *adj.* vil, bas; obscène, licencieux, graveleux; — *s.* débauché, *m.*, e, *f.*, libertin, *m.*, e, *f.*, ribaud, *m.*, e, *f.*
Ribaldry, *s.* obscénité, ribauderie, *f.*, langage obscène, *m.*, gravelure, *f.*
Riband, *s.* *V.* **Ribbon;** (*nav.*) lisse, *f.*
Ribbed, *adj.* à côtes
Ribbon, *s.* ruban, *m.*; (*of knighthood*) cordon, ruban, *m.*; (*fig.*) lambeau, *m.*; — *v.a.* garnir de rubans, rubaner; (*bedizen*) enrubaner. — **fish,** *s.* ténioïde, *m.* — **macaroni,** *s.* lasagne, lazagne, *f.* — **manufacture, -trade,** *s.* rubanerie, *f.* — **weaver, -manufacturer,** *s.* rubanier, *m.* — **weaving,** *s.* rubanerie, *f.* — **wire,** *s.* cannetille, *f.*
Rice, *s.* riz, *m.*; — *adj.* de riz. *Ground* —, riz moulu, *m.*, farine de riz, *f.* *Whole* —, riz en grains, *m.* — **bird, -bunting,** *s.* bruantin, mangeur de riz, *m.*, passerine, *f.* — **cake,** *s.* gâteau de riz, *m.* — **field, -ground, -plantation,** *s.* rizière, *f.* — **flour,** *s.* farine de riz, *f.* — **milk,** *s.* riz au lait, *m.* — **paper,** *s.* papier de riz, papier de Chine, *m.* — **plantation,** *s.* rizière, *f.* — **powder,** *s.* poudre de riz, *f.* — **pudding,** *s.* gâteau de riz, *m.* — **soup,** *s.* riz au gras, *m.* — **straw,** *s.* paille de riz, *f.* — **swamp,** *s.* rizière, *f.* — **water,** *s.* eau de riz, *f.*
Rich, *adj.* riche; fécond, fertile; abondant; précieux; magnifique, superbe, beau; fameux; impayable; (*of eatables*) succulent; corsé; exquis; savoureux; (*high seasoned*) relevé, de haut goût; (*of wine*) qui a du corps, corsé, vineux; velouté; (*of furniture*) riche, bien meublant; — *s.pl.* riches, *m.pl.* *To grow* or *get* or *become* —, devenir riche, s'enrichir. *To be a* — *man*, être riche, avoir de la fortune
Riches, *s.pl.* richesses, *f.pl.*, richesse, *f.*
Richly, *adv.* richement; abondamment, amplement, largement; magnifiquement; bien
Richness, *s.* richesse, *f.*; fertilité, fécondité, *f.*; magnificence, beauté, *f.*; (*price*) prix, *m.*; (*of eatables*) succulence, nature succulente, *f.*; haut goût, *m.*; (*of wine*) vinosité, sève, *f.*
Ricinus, *s.* ricin, *m.*
Rick, *s.* meule, *f.*; — *v.a.* *V.* **Stack,** *v.a.* — **cloth,** *s.* bâche de meule, bâche, *f.* — **stand,** *s.* *V.* **Stack-stand**
Rickets, *s.pl.* rachitis, rachitisme, *m.* *To have the* —, être rachitique, (*fam.*) être noué
Rickety, *adj.* rachitique, (*fam.*) noué; (*of mind*) faible, un peu dérangé; (*of furniture*) boiteux
Ricochet, *s.* ricochet, *m.*; — *v.n.* ricocher, faire un ricochet *or* des richochets, tirer à ricochets; — *v.a.* faire ricocher. — **battery,** *s.* batterie à ricochets, *f.* — **firing,** *s.* tir (*or* feu) à ricochets, *m.*

Rid, *v.a.* délivrer; débarrasser. *To get* — *of*, se débarrasser de, se défaire de
Riddance, *s.* délivrance, *f.*; débarras, *m.* *A good* — ! bon débarras!
Riddle, *s.* énigme, *m.*; (*sieve*) crible, *m.*; — *v.a.* [cribler
Ride, *v.n.a.* (*on a horse*) monter à cheval; monter; être *or* aller *or* venir *or* se promener à cheval; aller, courir; passer; (*on an ass*) monter *or* être *or* &c. à âne; (*on any other animal*) monter *or* être *or* voyager *or* &c. (sur ...); (*on a stick*) monter *or* être à cheval (sur un bâton); (*upon, on*) être monté (sur); (*in a carriage*) *V.* **Drive;** (*in a rail. train*, &c.) être *or* aller *or* venir en chemin de fer, &c.; aller, voyager, faire route; (*on the water*) voguer, flotter; être porté (sur); (*on the winds*, &c.) être porté (sur); (*move*) se mouvoir; (*go*) aller; (*nav.*, — *at anchor*) être à l'ancre, être mouillé; (*print.*) chevaucher; (*a distance*) faire ... à cheval; (*a horse*, &c.) monter; (*persons, fig.*) mener, conduire, gouverner; — *s.* promenade (*or* distance) à cheval *or* en voiture, promenade, *f.*; voyage, *m.*; course, *f.*; trajet, *m*; parcours, *m.*; (*place*) promenade, allée, *f.* *Shall you* — *to-day?* monterez-vous à cheval aujourd'hui? *Shall we walk or* —? irons-nous à pied ou à cheval? *I rode a part of the way*, j'ai fait une partie du chemin à cheval (*or* en voiture *or* en chemin de fer, &c.). *Some were riding*, quelques-uns étaient à cheval. *To* — *hard*, aller vite; fatiguer; (*nav.*) fatiguer beaucoup. *To* — *well*, monter bien, monter bien à cheval. *To* — *on the top* or *outside*, aller sur l'impériale. *To* — *with o.'s back to the engine*, tourner le dos *or* avoir le dos tourné à la locomotive, aller à reculons. *Good to* — *or drive, for riding or driving*, (*horse*) à deux fins. *He gave me a* —, il m'a fait monter avec lui; il m'a fait faire une promenade, il m'a promené. — **about,** se promener (*or* faire une promenade) à cheval (*or* en voiture). — **away,** partir; s'en aller; se sauver. — **back,** s'en retourner. — **backwards,** aller à reculons. — **behind,** être *or* aller à cheval derrière; (*on the same beast*) monter en croupe. — **off,** *V.* — **away.** — **on,** (*go along*) poursuivre son chemin. — **out,** sortir, aller se promener; (*of a ship*) tenir bon sur les ancres. — **over,** parcourir; (*a person*, &c.) passer sur. — **up,** arriver, venir, s'avancer
Rideau, *s.* rideau, *m.* [cer
Rider, *s.* cavalier, *m.*, -ière, *f.*; écuyer, *m.*, -ère, *f.*; (*professional*) écuyer, *m.*, -ère, *f.*; (*in a carriage*) personne en voiture, *f.*; (*horse-breaker*) écuyer, *m.*; (*at horse-races*) jockey, *m.*; (*of deeds*, &c.) annexe, *f.*; renvoi, *m.*; codicille, *m.*; (*com.*) allonge, *f.* *Gentleman* —, écuyer amateur
Ridge, *s.* sommet, *m.*, cime, *f.*; (*eminence*) élévation, hauteur, *f.*; tertre, *m.*; butte, *f.*; (*of edifices*) faîte, *m.*; (*of mountains*) chaîne, *f.*; (*mountain-top*) crête, *f.*; (*agr.*) billon, *m.*, butte, *f.*; (*nav.*) récif, banc de rochers, *m.*; — *v.a.* sillonner; (*agr.*) billonner, butter. — **lead, -piece,** *s.* faîtage, *m.* — **plough,** *s.* buttoir, *m.* — **tile,** *s.* faîtière, *f.* — **tiles,** *s.pl.* faîtières, *f.pl.*, faîtage, *m.* — **tree,** *s.* faitage, *m.*
Ridger, *s.* (*agr.*) buttoir, *m.*
Ridging, *s.* sillonnage, *m.*; (*agr.*) billonnage, buttage, *m.* — **plough,** *s.* buttoir, *m.*
Ridicule, *s.* ridicule, *m.*; — *v.a.* tourner en ridicule, ridiculiser. *To bring into* —, rendre [ridicule
Ridiculous, *adj.* ridicule
Ridiculously, *adv.* ridiculement
Ridiculousness, *s.* ridiculité, *f.*, ridicule, *m.*
Riding, *adj.* à cheval; monté; d'équitation; de voyage; (*nav.*, — *at anchor*) à l'ancre; — *s.* action de monter (*or* d'aller) à cheval, *f.*; exercice à cheval, *m.*; promenade à cheval, *f.*; (*horsemanship*) équitation, *f.*; manége, *m.*; (*in a carriage*) promenade en voiture, *f.*; (*ride*) *V.* **Ride,** *s.*; (*district*) arrondissement, *m.* *To like* —, aimer à monter (*or* à aller) à cheval *or* &c.

(*V.* **Ride,** *v.n.a.*). — **boot,** *s.* botte à l'écuyère, *f.* — **coat,** *s.* redingote (de voyage), *f.* — **habit,** *s.* amazone, *f.m.*, habit d'amazone, *m.* — **hood,** *s.* capote, *f.*, chaperon, *m.* *Little red — hood,* le petit chaperon rouge. — **horse,** *s.* cheval de selle, *m.* — **house,** *s.* manége, *m.* — **master,** maître d'équitation, *m.* — **school,** *s.* manége, *m.*, école d'équitation, *f.* — **whip,** [*s.* cravache, *f.*

Ridotto, *s.* redoute, *f.*

Rife, *adj.* qui règne; qui court; abondant; répandu, commun; général; accrédité; (*full*) plein (de). *To be* —, régner; courir; être abondant *or* &c. [généralement

Rifely, *adv.* abondamment; communément;

Rifeness, *s.* abondance, grande quantité, *f.*

Riffraff, *s.* rebut, *m.*, ordures, *f.pl.*; (*mob*) canaille, racaille, lie du peuple, *f.*

Rifle, *v.a.* dévaliser, voler, piller; (*empty*) vider; (*a gun*) rayer; — *s.* carabine, *f.*; fusil, *m.*; —**s,** *pl.* (*rifle-corps*) *V.* — **corps.** — **ball,** *s.* balle de carabine, *f.* — **barrelled,** *adj.* à canon rayé, rayé. — **bird,** *s.* ptiloride, *m.* — **brigade,** *s.* *V.* — **corps.** — **bullet,** *s.* *V.* — **ball.** — **butt,** *s.* butte de tir, *f.*; (*butt-end*) crosse de carabine, *f.* — **corps,** *s.* corps des carabiniers, *m.*, carabiniers, *m.pl.*; (*skirmishers*) corps de tirailleurs, *m.*, tirailleurs, *m.pl.*; (*French corps*) corps des chasseurs, *m.*, chasseurs, *m.pl.* — **gallery,** *s.* tir à la carabine, *m.* —**man,** *s.* (*general sense*) carabinier, *m.*; (*skirmisher*) tirailleur, *m.*; (*French corps*) chasseur, *m.* — **match,** *s.* concours à la carabine, *m.* — **pit,** *s.* caponnière, *f.* — **practice,** *s.* tir à la carabine, *m.* — **range,** *s.* tir à la carabine, *m.*; (*distance*) portée de carabine, *f.* — **shooting,** *s.* *V.* — **practice.** — **shot,** *s.* coup de carabine, *m.*; (*ball, distance*) *V.* — **ball** *and* — **range.** — **sword,** *s.* sabre-baïonnette, *m.*

Rifler, *s.* pillard, *m.*, e, *f.*; (*of guns*) rayeur, *m.*

Rifling, *s.* pillage, *m.*; (*of guns*) (*action*) rayage, *m.*, (*grooves*) rayure, *f.*

Rift, *s.* fente, *f.*; trouée, *f.*; (*in a cloud,* &c.) éclaircie, *f.*; (*ford*) gué, *m.*; — *v.a.* fendre; — *v.n.* se fendre

Rig, *s.* affublement, accoutrement, harnachement, *m.*; farce, *f.*, tour, *m.*; (*nav.*) gréement, *m.*; — *v.a.* (— *out*) équiper, accoutrer, harnacher, attifer; (*a ship*) gréer. *To — the market,* faire hausser les prix

Rigadoon, *s.* rigodon, *m.*

Rigged, *part. adj.* équipé, &c. (*V.* **Rig,** *v.a.*); (*nav.*) gréé; (*referring to the sails*) voilé

Rigger, *s.* gréeur, *m.*; (*of a wheel*) tambour, *m.*

Rigging, *s.* (*of a ship*) gréement, *m.*, agrès, *m.pl.*; manœuvres, *f.pl.*; (*of dress*) accoutrement, attifement, *m.* *Running* —, manœuvres courantes. *Standing* —, manœuvres dormantes

Right, *adj.* (*straight*) droit; (*direct*) direct, en ligne droite, en droite ligne; (*not the left*) droit; (*fit, proper*) convenable, propre, bon, bien, comme il faut; (*wanted*) . . . qu'il faut, qu'il fallait; (*just, honest*) juste, honnête; (*correct*) juste, exact; correct; (*regular*) régulier, en règle; (*true*) vrai, véritable, bon, légitime; (*com.*) régulier. *All* —, très bien; (*regular*) en règle; (*quite ready*) tout prêt; *int.* c'est bien! tout va bien! (*good!*) à la bonne heure! (*done!*) ça y est! (*of motion*) marchez! allez! partez! en route! en avant! *The — book* or &c., le livre *or* &c. qu'il faut *or* qu'il fallait. *The — one,* celui (*m.*) *or* celle, (*f.*) qu'il faut *or* qu'il fallait. *The — way* or *road,* le bon chemin, le bonne voie; le chemin, la route. *The — train,* &c., le train, &c. *To be* —, être juste *or* &c.; aller bien; (*pers.*) avoir raison (de); (*of clocks, watches*) aller bien; être à l'heure. *To come* or *get* —, s'arranger; se rarranger; se remettre; se rétablir. *To set* or *make* —, arranger, mettre en bon ordre, régulariser, mettre en règle; corriger, redresser, rectifier, remettre; rétablir; (*cure*) guérir; (*clocks, watches*) mettre à l'heure, régler. *Is it* —? est-ce bien? *That is* — or *all* —, c'est bien, c'est très bien; (*good!*) à la bonne heure! (*done!*) ça y est! — **angle,** *s.* angle droit, *m.* — **angled,** *adj.* rectangulaire, rectangle. —**ful,** &c., *See below.* — **hand,** *s.* main droite, *f.*; (*side*) droite, *f.*; *adj.* droit, de droite. —**handed,** *adj.* droitier. — **hand side,** *s.* droite, *f.* côté droit, *m.* —**minded,** *adj.* qui a l'esprit juste *or* droit. — **mindedness,** *s.* justesse d'esprit, droiture, *f.* — **whale,** *s.* baleine franche, rétoile, *f.*

Right, *adv.* droit; directement; juste, justement; (*properly*) bien; comme il faut; (*quite*) tout à fait; entièrement, tout; (*with titles*) très; — *int.* bien! bon! — *away,* — *off,* — *on,* tout droit. — *honourable,* très honorable. — *reverend,* très révérend. — *and left,* à droite et à gauche. — *at the top,* tout en haut. — *or wrong,* à tort ou à raison. — *face!* (*mil.*) à droite! — *about face!* — *about!* (*mil.*) demi-tour à droite! — **thinking,** *adj.* bien pensant

Right, *s.* (*justice*) droit, *m.*, justice, raison, *f.*; (*claim, o.'s due*) droit, *m.*; (*what is right, good*) bien, *m.*; (*right side*) droite, *f.*, côté droit, *m.* — *and wrong,* le bien et le mal, le juste et l'injuste. *By* —, de droit. *By —s,* pour bien faire; à la rigueur. *In o.'s own* —, de son chef; en propre. *In — of,* du chef de. *On the —, to the* —, à droite. *To be in the* —, avoir raison; être dans son droit. *To have a — to,* (*full right*) avoir le droit de; (*a claim to, reason to expect*) avoir droit (*or* des droits) à. *To set* or *put to —s, V. To set* — (*adj.*); (*pers.*) mettre à la raison

Right, *v.a.* rendre *or* faire justice à, faire droit à; (*things*) redresser; rectifier; corriger; arranger, remettre; (*the helm*) dresser

Righteous, *adj.* juste, droit; saint. —**ly,** *adv.* justement. —**ness,** *s.* droiture, justice, *f.*

Righter, *s.* redresseur, *m.*, -euse, *f.*

Rightful, *adj.* légitime; véritable. —**fully,** *adv.* légitimement, justement, à juste titre; véritablement. —**fulness,** *s.* légitimité, *f*

Rightly, *adv.* comme il faut, bien; (*justly*) à juste titre. — *or wrongly,* à tort ou à raison

Rightness, *s.* rectitude, *f.*; (*justice*) droiture, équité, *f.*; (*propriety*) convenance, *f.*

Rigid, *adj.* rigide; (*stiff*) raide

Rigidity, *s.* rigidité, *f.*; (*stiffness*) raideur, *f.*

Rigidly, *adv.* rigidement; (*stiffly*) avec raideur

Rigidness. *V.* **Rigidity**

Rigmarole, *s.* amphigouri, galimatias, *m.*

Rigor, *s.* *V.* **Rigour;** (*med.*) rigidité, *f.*; (*shivering*) frisson, *m.* — *mortis,* rigidité cadavérique, *f.*

Rigor-ism, -ist. *V.* page 3, § 1

Rigorous, *adj.* rigoureux; de rigueur

Rigorously, *adv.* rigoureusement; à la rigueur

Rigorousness, Rigour, *s.* rigueur *f.*

Rile, *v.a.* (*stir*) remuer, agiter, troubler; (*vex*) faire enrager, vexer, embêter

Rill, *s.* ruisseau, *m.*

Rim, *s.* bord, rebord, *m.*; (*of wheels*) jante, *f.*

Rime, *s.* givre, *m.*; — *v.n.* geler blanc

Rimple. *V.* **Wrinkle** *and* **Ripple**

Rimy, *adj.* couvert de givre

Rind, *s.* écorce, peau, pelure, *f.*; (*of cheese*) croûte, pelure, *f.*; (*of bacon*) couenne, *f.*; — *v.a.* écorcer

Rinderpest, *s.* *V.* **Cattle-plague**

Ring, *s.* (*for fingers*) bague, *f.*, anneau, *m.*; (*for curtains, keys,* &c.) anneau, *m.*; (*circle*) cercle, rond, *m.*; (*for napkins*) rond, *m.*; (*enclosure*) enceinte, *f.*; (*ground for fighting*) arène, *f.*, terrain, *m.*; (*for riding*) piste, *f.*; (*boxers*) boxeurs, pugilistes, *m.pl.*, canaille, *f.*; (*boxing*) boxe, *f.*; (*sound*) son, bruit, *m.*; (*of bells*) sonnerie, *f.*; (*of house-bells*) coup de sonnette, *m.*; (*tinkling*) tintement, *m.*; retentissement, *m.*; (*way of ringing*) manière de sonner, *f.*, (*in the grain of trees*) couche, *f.*; (*of bottles*) collier, *m.*; (*of wheels*) jante, *f.*; (*on a coin*) cordon, filet, *m.*; (*to a handle*) virole, *f.*; (*med., of a sore*) cerne, *m.*; (*astr., nav.*) anneau, *m.*; (*of an anchor*) organeau, *m.*; — *v.n.* sonner; (*to toll, to tinkle; also of the ears*) tinter; (*resound: 'with,'* de) résonner, retentir; — *v.a.* sonner; faire sonner; (*surround, encircle*) entourer; (*put rings to*) mettre un anneau *or* des anneaux à; (*a hog in the nose*) anneler, boucler, ferrer (un porc); (*a mare*) boucler (une cavale, une jument); (*a bull*) boucler (un taureau); (*cut round the bark of a tree*) baguer (un arbre, une branche). *To give a* —, sonner, sonner un coup. *To hear a* —, entendre sonner. *To — a coin*, faire sonner une pièce. *To — the bees*, carillonner les abeilles. *To — for the waiter* or &c., sonner le garçon *or* &c. *The bells are —ing*, on sonne les cloches. *There is a — at the door*, on sonne à la porte. *—ed snake*, couleuvre à collier, *f.* — **away,** *v.n.* carillonner. — **bolt,** *s.* (*nav.*) piton, *m.* — **bone,** *s.* forme, *f.* — **box,** *s.* baguier, *m.* — **dove,** *s.* pigeon ramier, ramier, *m.* — **finger,** *s.* doigt annulaire, *m.* — **leader,** *s.* chef (d'une faction), meneur, *m.* —**let,** *s.* petit anneau, *m.*; cercle, *m.*; (*of hair*) boucle, *f.*, tire-bouchon, *m.*, anglaise, *f.* — **ousel, -ouzel,** *s* merle à plastron *or* à collier, *m.* — **screw,** *s.* piton, *m.* — **shaped,** *adj.* annulaire. — **streaked,** *adj.* annelé. — **tail,** *s.* (*bird*) busard bleu, *m.* — **worm,** *s.* impétigo, *m.*, teigne, dartre, *f.*

Ringer, *s.* anneleur, *m*; (*of bells*) sonneur, *m.*

Ringing, *s.* action de sonner, *f.*; (*sound*) son, *m.*; sonnerie, *f.*; (*tolling, tinkling; noise in the ears*) tintement, *m.*; (*resounding*) retentissement, *m.*; (*of a tree*) baguage, *m.* — *of bells*, son de cloches, *m.* (*of small bells*, bruit de sonnettes, *m.*), sonnerie, *f.* — *in the ears*, tintement d'oreilles. — **shears,** *s.pl.* (*hort.*) coupe-sève, *m.* — **sound,** *s.* tintement, son [argentin, son clair

Rinse, *v.a.* rincer

Rinser, *s.* rinceur, *m.*, -euse, *f.*

Rinsing, *s.* rinçage, rincement, *m.*; (*slops*) rinçure, *f.*; —**s,** *pl.* rinçure, *f.*, rinçures, *f.pl.*

Riot, *s.* tumulte, vacarme, *m.*; excès, *m.*; festins, *m. pl.*; débauche, *f.*; désordre, *m.*, dissipation, *f.*; ripaille, *f.*, orgies, *f.pl.*; (*law*) attroupement, *m.*; (*polit., sedition*) émeute, *f.*; —*v.n.* faire du tumulte *or* du vacarme; (*revolt*) faire une émeute, se mutiner; (*revel*) se livrer à la débauche, faire des excès, ripailler, riboter; se réjouir, se divertir; (*fly out*) s'emporter, se déchaîner. *To run* —, faire des excès; s'indiscipliner; faire les cent coups; se dévergonder; s'emporter, se déchaîner, ne plus connaître de frein. — **act,** *s.* loi contre les attroupements, *f.* *To read the — act*, faire une sommation; faire les trois sommations

Rioter, *s.* émeutier, séditieux, mutin, *m.*; débauché, *m.*; (*noisy person*) tapageur, *m.*, -euse, *f.*

Rioting, *s.* *V.* **Riot,** *s.*

Riotous, *adj.* tumultueux; séditieux; déréglé, désordonné; intempérant, débauché

Riotously, *adv.* tumultueusement; séditieusement; avec dérèglement, dans la dissipation, dans les orgies, licencieusement; avec intempérance

Riotousness, *s.* nature tumultueuse, *f.*; nature séditieuse, *f.*; dérèglement, désordre, *m.*; intempérance, débauche, *f.*

Rip, *v.a.* fendre, déchirer, ouvrir; (*take away*) arracher; (*need.*) découdre; — *s.* fente, déchirure, ouverture, *f.*; (*fellow*) garnement, mauvais garnement, mauvais sujet, vaurien, polisson, *m.*, canaille, *f.*; (*woman*) rosse, *f.* — **off,** *v.a.* arracher; enlever. — **open,** *v.a.* ouvrir; (*man or beast*) éventrer. — **up,** *v.a.* fendre, ouvrir; (*man or beast*) éventrer; (*fig.*) fouiller, sonder, pénétrer; exhumer, découvrir; remettre sur le tapis

Riparian, *adj.* riverain

Ripe, *adj.* mûr; (*consummate*) consommé, accompli, parfait; — *v.a.n.* mûrir

Ripely, *adv.* mûrement; à temps, à propos

Ripeness, *s.* maturité, *f.*

Ripening, *s.* maturation, *f.* [-euse, *f.*

Ripper, *s.* fendeur, *m.*, -euse, *f.*; déchireur, *m.*,

Ripping, *s.* fendage, *m.*; déchirage, déchirement, *m.*; ouverture, *f.*; (*fig.*) action de fouiller, *f.* [— *s.* ride, *f.*

Ripple, *v.a.* rider; — *v.n.* se rider; clapoter;

Rippling, *s.* action de rider, *f.*; rides, *f.pl.*; clapotage, clapotis, *m.*; murmure, *m.*; (*nav.*) remous de courant, *m.*

Ripuarian, *s. adj.* Ripuaire, *s.m.*, *adj. m.f.*

Rise, *v.n.* (*get up*) se lever; (*get up again*) se relever; (*heave, swell*) se soulever; (*revolt*) se soulever; (*aloft, mount up*) s'élever, monter; (*increase*) s'accroître, s'augmenter; grossir; (*improve*) gagner; (*originate, proceed*) naître (de), venir (de), provenir (de); sortir (de); (*appear*) se présenter, s'offrir; (*of rivers*) prendre sa source; (*ferment*) lever; (*of prices, stocks*) hausser, augmenter, monter, s'élever; (*in price*) renchérir; (*in honours*) s'élever, monter; (*of the dead*) ressusciter; renaître; (*of assemblies*) se séparer; (*of law-courts*) se lever. — **again,** se relever; (*of the dead*) ressusciter; renaître. — **up,** se lever; s'élever; se soulever. *To — up in arms*, se révolter, s'insurger, prendre les armes

Rise, *s.* lever, *m.*; (*ascent*) montée, *f.*; (*rising ground*) hauteur, éminence, élévation, *f.*; butte, *f.*; (*preferment, eminence, greatness*) avancement, *m.*, élévation, *f.*; grandeur, *f.*; (*origin*) naissance, *f.*; source, *f.*; origine, *f.*; commencement, *m.*; (*beginning of a stream*) source, *f.*; (*increase*) accroissement, *m.*; (*of the waters of rivers*, &c.) crue, *f.*; (*of prices*) hausse, *f.*; augmentation, *f.*; (*phys., of vapours, of water in pumps, of the mercury*, &c.) ascension, *f.*; (*of stairs*) *V.* **Riser.** *The — and fall of the stocks*, la hausse et la baisse des fonds. *The — and fall of empires*, la grandeur et la décadence des empires. *The — and fall of the mercury*, l'ascension et la descente du mercure. *On the* —, (*of prices*) en hausse; à la hausse. *To give — to*, faire naître, donner naissance à; provoquer; donner lieu à

Riser, *s.* (*pers.*) personne qui se lève, *f.*; (*upright piece in a stair*) contre-marche, *f.* *Early* —, personne matinale, personne qui se lève de bon matin (*or* de bonne heure), *f.* *Late* —, personne qui se lève tard, *f.*, dormeur, *m.*, -euse, *f.*

Risi-bility, bleness. *V.* page 3, § 1

Risible, *adj.* risible

Risibly, *adv.* risiblement

Rising, *adj.* levant; (*of tide*) montant; (*growing*) naissant; (*promising*) d'avenir, qui a de l'avenir; (*improving*) qui gagne. — **ground,** *V.* **Rise,** *s.*

Rising, *s.* (*of the sun*, &c., *getting out of bed*) lever, *m.*; (*heaving, swelling*) soulèvement, *m.*; (*revolt*) soulèvement, *m.*, insurrection, *f.*; (*of the dead*) résurrection, *f.*; renaissance, *f.*; (*of assemblies*) levée, clôture, *f.*; (*ascent; rising ground; increase;* &c.) *V.* **Rise,** *s.* — *and falling*, *V.* **Rise and fall.** — *of the stomach*, soulèvement du cœur, *m.*, nausée, *f.* *I like early* —, j'aime à me lever de bonne heure, je suis matinal

Risk, *s.* risque, *m.*; — *v.a.* risquer. *At the — of*, au risque de; au péril de. *At o.'s* —, à ses [risques et périls

Rissole, *s.* rissole, *f.*

Rite, *s.* rite, *m.*; cérémonie, *f.*

Ritornelle, Ritornello, *s.* ritournelle, *f.*

Ritual, *adj s.* rituel, *adj.m.*, -le, *f.*, rituel, *s.m.*

Ritual-ism, -ist. *V.* page 3, § 1

Ritualistic, *adj.* ritualiste

Ritually, *adv.* selon le rite *or* les rites

Rival, *adj. s.* rival, *m.*, e, *f.*; — *v.a.* *V.* **Emulate**

Rivality, Rivalry, Rivalship, *s.* rivalité, *f.*

Rive, *v.a.* fendre; —*v.n.* se fendre; —*s. V.* **Rift**

River, *s.* rivière, *f.*, (*running into the sea*) fleuve, *m.*; — *adj.* de (*or* de la) rivière; fluvial. *The Blue —,* le Fleuve Bleu, *m.* — **crab,** *s.* thelphuse, *f.* — **dragon,** *s.* crocodile, *m.* — **god,** *s.* fleuve, *m.* — **horse,** *s.* hippopotame, *m.* — **keeper,** *s.* garde-pêche, *m.* — **limpet,** *s.* limnée, *f.* — **side,** *s.* bord de l'eau, *m.*; *adj.* du (*or* au) bord de l'eau; (*geog., and of estates*) riverain. *By* or *on the —side,* au bord de l'eau. — **snail,** [s. paludine, *f.*

Riverain, *adj.* riverain

Rivet, *v.a.* river; (*boots, shoes*) clouer, cheviller; (*fig.*) river; clouer; fixer; affermir; consolider; —*s.* rivet, *m.*; rivure, *f.*; (*for china*) at- [tache *f.*

Rivetter, *s.* riveur, *m.*

Rivetting, *s.* rivement, *m.* — **hammer,** *s.* rivoir, chasse-rivets, *m.* — **machine,** *s.* ma- [chine à river, *f.*

Rivulet, *s.* ruisseau, *m.*

Rixdollar, *s.* rixdale, risdale, *f.*

R.N., (*Royal Navy*) de la marine royale. *Lieutenant ..., R.N., ...,* lieutenant de vaisseau

Roach, *s.* gardon, *m.*

Road, *s.* route, *f.*; chemin, *m.*; voie, *f.*; (*of streets*) chaussée, *f.*, pavé, *m.*; (*street itself*) rue, *f.*; (*nav.*) rade, *f.* —*s and bridges,* (*admin.*) ponts et chaussées. *On the —,* sur la route; en route, en chemin. *On the — to,* sur le chemin de, sur la route de; en route pour. — **book,** *s.* itinéraire, *m.* — **engine, -locomotive,** *s.* locomotive routière, *f.* — **labourer,** *s.* cantonnier, *m.* — **maker,** *s.* constructeur de routes, *m.* — **making,** *s.* construction de routes, *f.* — **metal,** *s.* empierrement, cailloutis, *m.* — **scraper,** *s.* râcloir, *m.*; éboueur, *m.*; (*pers.*) boueur, *m.* — **scrapings,** *s.pl.* boue des rues, *f.*, immondices, *f.pl.* —**side,** *s.* bord de la route, *m.*; bas-côté, *m. By* or *on the —side,* au bord de la route. —**sman,** *s.* cantonnier, *m.* —**stead,** *s.* rade, *f. In the —stead,* en rade. — **steamer,** *s.* locomotive routière, *f.* —**ster,** *s.* (*horse*) cheval de poste, *m.*; cheval de fatigue, bouleux, bidet, *m.*; (*ship*) navire (*or* vaisseau) en rade, *m.* —**way,** *s.* chaussée, *f.*, pavé, *m.*; voie, *f.*

Roader, *s.* (*ship*) *V.* **Roadster**

Roam, &c. *V.* **Ramble,** &c.

Roan, *adj.* (*of horses,* &c.) rouan; — *s.* (*colour*) rouan, *m.*; (*horse*) cheval rouan, *m.*; (*leather*) basane maroquinée, basane marorée, peau maroquinée, *f.*, maroquin, *m.* — **tree,** *s. V.* **Rowan-tree**

Roar, *v.n.a.* (*of wild beasts*) rugir; (*fig.*) rugir; (*like a bull, the sea,* &c.) mugir; (*of elephants*) barrir; (*of horses*) corner; (*of cannons, thunder*) gronder; ronfler; (*of fire*) ronfler; (*cry out*) vociférer, beugler, crier, brailler; (*weep*) pleurer comme un veau; —*s.* (*of wild beasts*) rugissement, *m.*; (*of anger*) rugissement, *m.*; (*of bulls, the sea,* &c.) mugissement, *m.*; (*of horses*) cornage, *m.*; (*of cannons, thunder*) grondement, *m.*; ronflement, *m.*; (*cry*) clameur, vocifération, *f.*; (*noise*) bruit, fracas, *m.*; (*of laughter*) éclat, éclat de rire, *m. To — with laughter,* rire aux éclats. *To set* or *keep in a —,* faire rire aux éclats. — **out,** *v.n.a.* vociférer, beugler, crier

Roarer, *s.* animal qui rugit *or* qui mugit, *m.*; (*horse, mare*) cheval cornard, cheval corneur, corneur, *m.*, jument cornarde, jument corneuse, corneuse, *f.*; (*pers.*) braillard, *m.*, e, *f.*

Roaring, *s. V.* **Roar,** *s.*; — *part. adj.* rugissant; mugissant; qui gronde; ronflant, &c. (*V.* **Roar,** *v.n.a.*); (*of horses*) cornard, corneur; (*noisy*) bruyant; (*great*) étourdissant; ébouriffant. *To drive a — trade,* faire énormément d'affaires, faire des affaires d'or

Roaringly, *adv.* en rugissant; en mugissant; en grondant; en ronflant; avec bruit, avec fracas; aux éclats

Roast, *v.a.n.* rôtir; faire rôtir, faire cuire, cuire; (*coffee*) brûler, torréfier; (*fig.*) griller, rôtir, brûler; (*to jeer*) railler; (*metal.*) griller; — *adj.* rôti; — *s.* rôti, *m. To rule the —,* avoir la haute main, faire la pluie et le beau temps, gouverner. — **beef,** *s. V.* **Beef.** — **dish, -meat,** *s.* rôti, *m.*

Roaster, *s.* rôtissoire, *f.*; (*for coffee*) brûloir, *m.*

Roasting, *s.* rôtissage, *m.*; cuisson, *f.*; (*of coffee*) torréfaction, *f.*; (*metal.*) grillage, *m.*; (*bantering*) raillerie, *f.*, railleries, *f.pl.* — **jack,** *s.* tournebroche, *m.*

Rob, *v.a.* voler, dérober; piller; (*deprive*) priver (de), dépouiller (de), frustrer (de). *To — a person,* voler *or* piller quelqu'un. *To — an orchard,* &c., piller un verger, &c. *To — a person of a thing,* voler *or* dérober un objet à quelqu'un; priver *or* dépouiller *or* frustrer quelqu'un d'une chose. *They have —bed me of everything,* on m'a tout pris. *To — Peter to pay Paul,* faire un trou pour en boucher en autre

Robber, *s.* voleur, *m.*, -euse, *f.*; brigand, *m.*

Robbery, Robbing, *s.* vol à main armée, vol, *m.*; brigandage, *m.* — *with violence,* vol à main armée, *m.*

Robe, *s.* robe, *f.*; —**s,** *pl.* robes, *f.pl.*; vêtements, ornements, *m.pl.*, (*of sovereigns*) garde-robe, *f.*; — *v.a.* revêtir d'une robe; revêtir de ses vêtements; (*with*) revêtir (de)

Robin, *s.* rouge-gorge, *m.* — **goodfellow,** *s.* lutin domestique, *m.* — **red-breast,** *s* rouge- [gorge, *m.*

Robing-room, *s.* vestiaire, *m.*

Robinia, *s.* robinier, *m.*

Robust, *adj.* robuste, vigoureux; rude

Robustly, *adv.* robustement, vigoureusement

Robustness, *s.* robustesse, vigueur, force, *f.*

Roc, *s.* rock, roc, *m.*

Rocambole, *s.* rocambole, *f.*

Rochet, *s.* rochet, *m.*

Rock, *s.* rocher, roc, *m.*; roche, *f.*; (*geol., min.*) roche, *f.*; (*nav.*) récif, *m.*; (*distaff*) quenouille, *f.*; (*bird*) rock, roc, *m.*; (*sweetmeat*) caramel, sucre d'orge, *m.*; — *v.a.* (*a child, and fig.*) bercer; (*the cradle*) remuer, balancer; (*swing*) balancer; (*shake*) ébranler; — *v.n.* se balancer; faire la bascule; (*quake*) trembler, s'ébranler. *Hidden* or *lurking —,* récif, *m.* — **alum,** *s.* alun de roche, *m.* — **badger,** *s.* daman, *m.* — **bound,** *adj.* retenu par les récifs. — **crystal,** cristal de roche, *m.* — **dove,** *s.* biset, *m.*, rocheraie, *f.* — **fish,** *s.* labre, *m.* —**less,** *adj.* sans rochers. —**ling,** *s. See below.* — **oil,** *s.* pétrole, *m.*, huile de pierre, *f.* — **pigeon,** *s. V.* — **dove.** — **rose,** *s.* ciste, *m.* — **salt,** *s.* sel gemme, *m.* — **shell,** *s.* murex, *m.* — **snake,** *s.* bongare, *m.* — **soap,** *s.* savon de montagne, savon naturel, *m.* — **staff,** *s.* (*of a forge*) branloire, courbotte, *f.*, fléau, *m.* — **work,** *s.* rocaille, *f.*; rocher artificiel, *m.*; cailloutage, *m.* **work maker,** *s.* rocailleur, *m.*

Rocker, *s.* bascule, *f.*; (*in the body of a carriage*) brancard, *m.*; (*pers.*) berceuse, *f.*

Rockery, *s.* rocher artificiel, *m.*

Rocket, *s.* (*firework, mil.*) fusée, *f.*; (*bot.*) julienne, roquette, *f.* — **apparatus,** *s.* (*nav.*) porte-amarre, *m.*, fusée porte-amarre, *f.* — **gunner,** *s.* (*mil.*) fuséen, *m.* — **stick,** *s.* baguette de fusée, *f.*

Rocketer, *s.* fuséen, *m.*

Rockiness, *s.* nature rocailleuse, abondance [de rochers, *f.*

Rocking, *s.* (*of a child, and fig.*) bercement, *m.*; (*swinging*) balancement, *m.*; (*quaking, shaking*) tremblement, ébranlement, *m.* — **chair,** *s.* chaise à bascule, *f.* — **horse,** *s.* cheval à bascule, *m.* — **stone,** *s.* rocher branlant, *m.*

Rockling, *s.* (*fish*) motelle, *f.*

Rocky, *adj.* rocailleux, plein de rochers; (*of rock*) de roc, de roche; (*geol.*) rocheux. *The — Mountains,* les Montagnes rocheuses, *f.pl.*

Rococo, *s. adj.* rococo, *s.m., adj.m.f.*

Rod, *s.* baguette, *f.*; verge, *f.*; (*bundle of birch-twigs, punishment*) verges, *f.pl.*; (*sway*) sceptre, *m.*; (*for fishing*) canne, *f.*; (*of curtains,* &c.) tringle, *f.*; (*of pumps, pistons,* &c.) tige, *f.*; (*mach.*) bielle, *f.*; (*eccentric*) tirant, *m.*; (*glass —, chem.*) agitateur, *m.*, baguette, *f.*; (*meas.*) 5

mètres, *m.pl.*; (*square meas.*) 25,29 **centiares**, *m.pl.* *Bundle of —s*, (*fasces*) faisceau, *m.* — *and line*, ligne, *f.* *With the* (or *a*) - - *and line*, à la ligne. *Spare the — and spoil the child*, (*Proverb*) qui aime bien châtie bien. *To have a — in pickle for*, la garder bonne à. — **fisher,** *s.* pêcheur à la ligne, *m.* — **fishing,** *s.* pêche [à la ligne, *f.*
Rodent, *adj. s.* rongeur, *m.*
Rodomont, *s.* rodomont, *m.*
Rodomontade, *s.* rodomontade, *f.*; — *v.n.* faire le rodomont, faire des rodomontades
Roe, *s.* (*deer*) chevreuil, *m.*, chevrette, *f.*; biche, *f.* *Hard* —, (*of fish*) œufs, *m.pl.* *Soft* —, laitance, laite, *f.* — **buck,** *s.* chevreuil, *m.* — **deer,** *s.* chevreuil, *m.*, chevrette, *f.*; biche, *f.* — **stone,** *s.* oolithe, *m.*
Roed, *adj.* plein. *Hard* —, œuvé. *Soft* —, laité
Rogation, *s.* rogation, *f.*; (*Cath. lit.*) Rogations, *f.pl.* — **week, -days,** *s.* semaine des Rogations, *f.*, Rogations, *f.pl.*
Rogue, *s.* coquin, *m.*, e, *f.*, fripon, *m.*, -ne, *f.*; fourbe, *m.f.*; (*wag*) espiègle, *m.f.*; (*law*) vagabond, *m.*
Roguery, *s.* friponnerie, coquinerie, fourberie, *f.*; (*malice*) espièglerie, malice, *f.*; (*law*) vagabondage, *m.* [*gish*) espiègle, malin
Roguish, *adj.* de coquin, coquin, fripon; (*wag-*
Roguishly, *adv.* en coquin, en fripon; (*waggishly*) en espiègle, avec espièglerie
Roguishness, *s.* coquinerie, friponnerie, *f.*; (*waggishness*) espièglerie, malice, *f.* [fanfaron
Roister, *v.n.* faire du tapage; (*boast*) faire le
Roisterer, *s.* tapageur, *m.*; (*boaster*) fanfaron, *m.*
Roistering, *adj.* tapageur, bruyant; (*boasting*) fanfaron; — *s.* tapage, *m.*; (*boasting*) fanfaronnade, *f.*
Roll, *v.a.* rouler; (*metal*) laminer; (*a field, walk*, &c.) rouler, cylindrer. — *v.n.* rouler; se rouler; (*turn*) tourner; revenir; (*mil.*) faire un roulement de tambour. — **back,** *v.n.* revenir; retourner; reculer. — **down,** *v.a.n.* rouler en bas. — **round,** *v.a.* peloter; rouler en boule; *v.n.* se peloter; se rouler en boule. — **up,** *v.a.* rouler en haut; rouler; enrouler. — *oneself* **up,** s'enrouler; (*cuddle*) se ramasser, se pelotonner, se blottir
Roll, *s.* rouleau, *m.*; (*rolling*) roulement, *m.*; roulade, *f.*; (*of drum*) roulement, *m.*; (*of musketry*) feu roulant, *m.*; (*of the sea*) roulis, coup de roulis, *m.*; (*of butter*) motte, *f.*; (*loaf*) petit pain, *m.*; —**s,** *pl.*, —, *sing.* (*list*) rôle, *m.*, liste, *f.*, tableau, *m.*; (*mil., and of certain societies*) contrôles, *m.pl.*, contrôle, *m.*; (*nav.*) rôle, *m.*; (*records*) archives, *f.pl.*; annales, *f.pl.*; (*of attorneys*) tableau, *m.*; (*succession*) suite, succession, *f.*; (*of metals*) laminoir, *m.*; (*of tobacco*) rouleau, *m.*, carotte, andouille, *f.*; (*cook.*) cannelon, *m.* *To call the* —, faire l'appel. *To strike off the —s*, rayer du rôle *or* du contrôle *or* du tableau. — **call,** *s.* appel, *m.* — **collar waistcoat,** *s.* gilet à châle, *m.* — **muster,** *s.* contrôle, *m.* —**s court,** *s.* cour des rôles, *f.*
Roller, *s.* rouleau, *m.*; cylindre, *m.*; (*caster*) roulette, *f.*; (*surg., print., hort., agr.*) rouleau, *m.*; (*bird*) rollier, *m.*; (*pers.*) rouleur, *m.*, (*of tobacco*) rôleur, *m.* — **blind,** *s.* store, *m.* — **towel,** *s.* *V.* **Jack-towel** [rigoler
Rollic, *v.n.* aller joyeusement, faire du tapage;
Rollicking, *adj.* joyeux; tapageur, bruyant; rigoleur; déréglé
Rolling, *part. adj.* roulant, qui roule; — *s.* roulement, *m.*; (*of metals*) laminage, *m.*; (*nav.*) roulis, *m.* *A — stone gathers no moss*, pierre qui roule n'amasse pas de mousse. — **hitch,** *s.* nœud de fouet, *m.* — **machine, -mill,** *s.* laminoir, *m.* — **pin,** *s.* rouleau, *m.* — **press,** *s.* presse à cylindre, *f.* — **stock,** *s.* (*rail.*) matériel roulant, *m.* — **tackle,** *s.* (*nav.*) palan [de roulis, *m.*
Rollster. *V.* **Roster**
Romaic, *adj. s.* romaïque, *adj.m.f.*, *s.m.*
Roman, *adj.* romain, de Rome; (*print.*) romain; (*of the nose*) aquilin; — *s.* Romain, *m.*, e, *f.*; (*print.*) romain, *m.* — **candle,** *s.* chandelle romaine, *f.* — **cement,** *s.* ciment romain, *m.* —**like,** *adj.* à la romaine. — **school,** *s.* (*paint.*) école romaine, *f.*
Romance, *s.* roman de chevalerie, *m.*; roman, *m.*; (*mus.*) romance, *f.*; — *adj.* roman; — *v.a.* romancer, romanciser, romantiser; — *v.n.* faire un roman *or* des romans; broder. — **writer,** *s.* romancier, *m.*, -ière, *f.*
Romancer, *s.* (*writer*) romancier, *m.*, -ière, *f.*; (*in contempt*) faiseur (*m.*, -euse, *f.*) de contes; brodeur, *m.*, -euse, *f.*
Romancing, *adj.* de roman; — *s.* romans, *m.pl.*
Romancist. *V.* **Romancer** [roman
Romanesque, *adj.* (*arts.*) romanesque; (*liter.*)
Romanic, *adj.* roman
Roman-ism, -ist. *V.* page 3, § 1
Romanize, *v.a.n.* romaniser
Romantic, *adj.* romanesque, de roman; (*of scenery, style*) romantique
Romantically, *adv.* romanesquement; (*of scenery, style*) romantiquement
Romanticism, *s.* (*system, school*) romantisme, *m.*; (*style*) romantique, *m.*
Romanticist, *s.* romantique, *m.*
Romanticnesss, *s.* nature romanesque, *f.*; (*of scenery, style*) nature romantique, *f.*
Romish, *adj.* romain
Romp, *s.* (*girl*) garçonnière, gamine, *f.*; (*play*) jeu grossier, divertissement bruyant, tapage, *m.*; — *v.n.* jouer rudement, jouer bruyamment, jouer, faire du tapage, sauter, danser, folâtrer; gaminer [bruyants, *m.pl.*, tapage, *m.*
Romping, *s.* jeux grossiers, divertissements
Rompish, *adj.* qui joue rudement, rude; joueur, folâtre
Rompishness, *s.* goût des jeux grossiers, *m.*; nature *or* humeur joueuse, folâtrerie, *f.*
Rondeau, Rondo, *s.* rondeau, *m.*
Rood, *s.* (*square meas.*) 10 ares, *m.pl.*, quart d'arpent, *m.*; (*cross*) crucifix, *m.*, croix, *f.* — **loft, -screen,** *s.* jubé, *m.*
Roof, *s.* toit, *m.*; (*vault*) voûte, *f.*; (*of omnibuses, railway carriages, and coaches*) impériale, *f.*, dessus, *m.*; (*of cabs*, &c.) dessus, *m.*; (*of the mouth*) palais, *m.*; — *v.a.* couvrir d'un toit, couvrir; (*to shelter*) abriter. —**less,** *adj.* sans toit, sans couverture, découvert; (*fig.*) sans toit, sans abri, sans asile. — **timber,** *s.* faîtage, *m.* — **work,** *s.* toiture, *f.*
Roofer, *s.* couvreur, *m.*
Roofing, *s.* toiture, *f.*
Roofy, *adj.* couvert d'un toit, couvert
Rook, *s.* freux, *m.*, grolle, corneille chauve, corneille, *f.*; (*at chess*) tour, *f.*; (*a cheat*) tricheur, *m.*
Rookery, *s.* lieu habité par des freux *or* des corneilles, *m.*, colonie de corneilles, *f.*; (*fig.*) bas quartier, *m.*; repaire de voleurs, *m.*; lupanar, *m.* [neilles
Rooky, *adj.* habité par des freux *or* des cor-
Room, *s.* (*any part of a house*) pièce, *f.*; (*one for public use*) salle, *f.*; (*one for private use, bed-room, chamber*) chambre, *f.*; (*small*) cabinet, *m.*; (*in barracks*) chambrée, *f.*; (*nav.*) chambre, *f.*, logement, *m.*; (*nav.*) (*for stores*) soute, *f.*; (*workroom, workshop*) atelier, *m.*; —**s,** *pl.* (*suite*) appartement, *m.*; (*space*) place, *f.*; espace, *m.*; intervalle, *m.*; (*fig.*) latitude, marge, *f.*; (*stead*) place, *f.*, lieu, *m.*; (*reason*) lieu, sujet, *m.*, matière, *f.*, motif, *m.*; (*possibility*) possibilité, *f.*; — *v.n.* loger. *In — of*, au lieu de, à la place de. *To make* —, ('*for*,' à) faire de la place; faire place [pièces
Roomed, *adj.* (*of houses, in compounds*) de ...
Roomer, *s.* (*ship*) vaisseau spacieux, *m.*
Roomful, *s.* chambre pleine, chambrée, *f.*
Roomily, *adv.* spacieusement
Roominess, *s.* vaste étendue, grandeur, *f.*
Roomless, *adj.* étroit, petit, restreint
Roomy, *adj.* vaste, spacieux, grand
Roost, *s.* juchoir, perchoir, *m.*; poulailler, *m.*; — *v.n.* jucher, se jucher, percher. *To be at*

—, être juché. *To go to* —, se jucher, se percher; (*fam.*) aller se coucher. *To rule the* —, *V.* **Roast.** — **ladder,** *s. V.* **Peg-ladder**
Roosting, *s.* action de jucher, *f.* — **place,** *s.* juchoir, *m.*
Root, *s.* racine, *f.*; fondement, *m.*, fondation, *f.*; source, *f.*; (*gram.*) radical, *m.*, racine, *f.*; (*math.*) racine, *f.*; (*mus.*) base, *f.*; — *v.n.* prendre racine, s'enraciner; (*as swine*) fouiller; — *v.a.* enraciner. — **crop,** *s.*, — **crops,** *s.pl.* racinage, *m.* — **cutter,** *s.* coupe-racines, *m.* — **fed,** *adj.* nourri de racines. —**less,** *adj.* sans racines. — **let,** *s.* radicule, *f.* — **out,** *v.a.* déraciner, extirper; (*ferret out*) découvrir, trouver. — **pulper,** *s.* décortiqueur à racines, *m.* — **stalk, -stock,** *s.* rhizome, *m.*, souche, *f.* — **up,** *v.a. V.* — **out.** — **washer** *s.* laveur de racines, lave-racines, *m.*
Rooted, *part. adj.* enraciné; invétéré
Rootedly, *adv.* profondément
Rootedness, *s.* enracinement, *m.*
Rooter, *s.* (*out*) exterminateur, *m.*, -trice, *f.*; (*discoverer*) personne qui découvre, *f.*
Rooting, *s.* enracinement, *m.*; (*out, up*) déracinement, *m.*
Rooty, *adj.* plein de racines
Rope, *s.* corde, *f.*; cordage, *m.*; (*of house-bells*) cordon, *m.*; (*of onions*) glane, *f.*; (*row, string*) rang, fil, *m.*; (*nav.*) cordage, *m.*, manœuvre, *f.*; (*room*) latitude, *f.*; ses coudées franches *f.pl.*; — *v.n.* filer. *Long* —, (*for skipping*) grande corde. *Running* —, manœuvre courante. *Slack* —, corde lâche, voltige, *f.* *Tight* —, corde raide, corde tendue. *To be on* (or *upon*) *the high* —, être monté sur ses grands chevaux. *To give* — *to*, lâcher la courroie (*or* la bride) à. — **band,** *s.* (*nav.*) raban, *m.* — **dancer,** *s.* danseur (*m.*, -euse, *f*) de corde, acrobate (*m.f.*). — **house,** *s.* corderie, *f.* — **ladder,** *s.* échelle de corde, *f.* — **maker,** *s.* cordier, *m.* — **making, -manufacture,** *s.* corderie, *f.* — **roll,** *s.* tambour, *m.* — **trade, -walk,** *s.* corderie, *f.* — **walker,** *s.* funambule, acrobate, *m.f.* — **yard,** *s.* corderie, *f.* — **yarn,** *s.* fil de caret, *m.*
Roper, *s.* cordier
Ropery, *s.* corderie, *f.*
Ropiness, *s.* viscosité, *f.*; (*of wine*) graisse, *f.*
Ropy, *adj.* filant, visqueux; (*of wine, brandy, beer*) gras
Roquelaure, *s.* roquelaure, *f.*
Rorqual, *s.* rorqual, *m.*
Rosaceæ, *s. pl.* rosacées, *f.pl.*
Rosaceous, *adj.* rosacé
Rosarium, *s.* roseraie, *f.*
Rosary, *s.* (*of roses*) roseraie, *f.*; (*beads*) rosaire, *m.*
Rose, *s.* rose, *f.*; (*of ribbons*) rosette, *f.*; (*arch.*) rosace, *f.*; (*of a water-pot*) pomme, *f.*; (*of pipes, pumps,* &c.) crépine, *f.*; — *v.a.* roser. *Bed of* —*s*, lit de roses, *m.*; (*hort.*) massif de rosiers, *m.*; corbeille de roses, roseraie, *f.* *Under the* —, sous la cheminée, sous le manteau de la cheminée, sous le manteau, en secret. — **acacia,** *s.* acacia rose, *m.* — **apple,** *s.* pomme de rose, *f.* — **bay,** *s.* laurier-rose, *m.* — **bed,** *s.* roseraie, *f.* — **beetle,** *s.* cétoine dorée, *f.*, hanneton vert, *m.* — **bud,** *s.* bouton de rose, *m.* — **bug,** *s. V.* — **beetle.** — **bush,** *s.* rosier, *m.* — **campion,** *s.* agrostemme, coquelourde, *f.* — **chafer,** *s. V.* — **beetle.** — **cheeked,** *adj.* aux joues rosées. — **colour,** *s.* rose, *m.* — **coloured,** *adj.* couleur de rose, rose, rosé. — **diamond,** *s.* rose, *f.* — **engine,** *s.* guilloche, *f.* — **fly,** *s. V.* — **beetle.** — **gall,** *s.* bédegar, *m.* — **garden,** *s.* roseraie, *f.* — **grower,** *s.* rosiériste, *m.f.* — **laurel,** *s.* laurier-rose, *m.* — **leaf,** *s.* feuille de rose, *f.* — **lipped,** *adj.* aux lèvres rosées. — **mallow,** *s.* rose trémière, *f.* —**mary,** *s.* romarin, *m.* — **rash,** *s.* roséole, *f.* — **show,** *s.* exposition de roses, *f.* — **tree,** *s.* rosier, *m.* — **tribe,** *s.* rosacées, *f.pl.* — **water,** *s.* eau de rose, *f.*; *adj.* d'eau de rose; à l'eau de rose. — **window,** *s.* rosace, rose, *f.* — **wood,** *s.* palissandre, *m.*; *adj.* de (*or* en) palissandre. — **work,** *s.* rosace, *f*, rosaces, *f.pl.*
Roseate, *adj.* orné de roses; (*of colour*) rosé, de rose, couleur de rose; vermeil
Roseola, *s.* roséole, *f.*
Rosery, *s.* roseraie, *f.*
Rosette, *s.* rosette, *f.*; (*ear-knot*) *V.* **Ear-knot**
Rosetum, *s.* roseraie, *f.*
Rosicrucian, *s.* rose-croix, *m.*; — *adj.* des (*or* de) rose-croix
Rosin, *s. V.* **Resin;** — *v.a.* frotter de résine *or* de colophane, résiner
Rosiness, *s.* couleur rose, *f.*; rose, *m.*; vermillon, *m.*
Rosing, *s.* rosage, *m.*
Rosland, *s.* bruyère, *f.*, terrain marécageux, *m.*
Roster, *s.* règlement, *m.*; rôle, *m.*, liste, *f.*, cadres, *m.pl.*
Rostral, *adj.* rostral
Rostrum, *s.* (*platform*) rostre, *m.*, tribune aux harangues, tribune, *f.*; (*of ships*) éperon, bec, *m.*; (*nat. hist.*) rostre, *m.*
Rosy, *adj. V.* **Roseate;** (*child*) aux joues vermeilles. — **cheeked, -lipped,** &c., *V.* **Rose** — **cross,** *s.* rose-croix, *f.* — **drop,** *s.* goutte rose, couperose, dartre pustuleuse, *f.* — **fingered,** *adj.* aux doigts de rose
Rot, *v.a.* pourrir; (*bones, teeth*) carier; — *v.n.* pourrir, se pourrir; (*of the bones, teeth*) se carier; — *s.* pourriture, *f.*; (*vet.*) tac, *m.*; clavelée, *f.*, claveau, *m.* — **gut,** *s.* tord-boyaux, *m.*
Rota, *s.* (*at Rome*) rote, *f.* *On the* —, (*law*) de tournée; en tournée
Rotacism, *s.* rotacisme, grasseyement, *m.*
Rotang. *V.* **Rottang**
Rotary, *adj. V.* **Rotatory**
Rotate, Rotated, *adj.* rotacé
Rotating, *adj.* à rotation, tournant
Rotation, *s.* rotation, *f.*; roulement, *m.*; succession, *f.* — *of crops*, assolement, *m.* *By* or *in* —, à tour de rôle
Rotative, *adj.* rotatif; à rotation
Rotator, *s.* rotateur, muscle rotateur, *m.*
Rotatoria, *s.pl.* rotateurs, rotatoires, *m.pl.*
Rotatory, *adj.* à rotation, tournant; de rotation, rotatoire; alternatif, successif; (*anat.*) rotateur; — *s.* rotateur, rotatoire, *m.*
Rotche, *s.* mergule, *m.*
Rote, *s.* routine, *f.*; (*anc. mus. instr.*) rote, *f.*; — *v.n.* rouler, alterner. *By* —, par routine; par cœur
Rotifer, *s.* rotifère, rotateur, *m.*
Rotiform, *adj.* rotiforme
Rottang, *s.* rotang, rotin, *m.*
Rotted, *adj.* (*vet.*) clavelé
Rotten, *part. adj.* pourri; (*of bones*) carié; (*of teeth*) gâté, carié; (*insolvent, suspicious, bad: fig.*) véreux. *To get* —, pourrir, se pourrir; (*of bones, teeth*) se carier. — **stone,** *s.* terre pourrie, *f.*, tripoli, *m.*
Rottenness, *s.* pourriture, *f.*; (*of bones, teeth*) carie, *f.*
Rotting, *part. adj.* qui pourrit, en putréfaction; — *s.* putréfaction, *f.*
Rotund, *adj.* rond, arrondi
Rotunda, *s.* rotonde, *f.*
Rotundifolious, *adj.* rotundifolié
Rotundity, Rotundness, *s.* rondeur, *f.*; (*pers.*) rotondité, *f.*
Roturier, *s. adj.* roturier, *m.*, -ière, *f.*
Rouble, *s.* rouble, *m.*
Rouche, *s.* ruche, *f.*
Roucou, *s.* roucou, *m.*
Roué, e, *s.m.f.* roué, *m.*, e, *f.*
Rouge, *s.* rouge, fard, *m.*; — *v.a.* farder, maquiller, mettre du rouge à; — *v.n.* se farder, se maquiller, se mettre du rouge. — **et noir,** *s.* trente et quarante, *m.*
Rough, *adj.* rude; dur; (*to the taste*) âpre; (*rugged*) raboteux; (*stern*) rude, sévère; (*coarse*) grossier; gros; (*in manner*) brusque; brutal; (*not polished*) brut; (*of glass*) dépoli; (*ruffled, of the hair*) ébouriffé; (*not exact*) approximatif; (*stormy*) orageux; (*of the sea*) grosse (*f.*), houleuse (*f.*), agitée (*f.*); (*adverb.*) *V.* **Roughly;** — *s.* voyou, polisson, *m.*; boxeur, *m.*; —**s,** *s.pl.* voyous, &c.; canaille, racaille, *f.*; rouges,

m.pl.; — *v.a.* endurer; (*a horse*) rompre; (*rough-shoe*) ferrer à glace; (*glass*, &c.) dépolir. *V.* **Roughen.** *In the* —, brut; en gros; (*roughed out*) ébauché. *To — it*, lutter contre l'adversité *or* contre les difficultés, manger de la vache enragée; gagner sa vie. — **cast,** *v.a.* ébaucher; (*a wall*) crépir; *s.* ébauche, *f.*; (*of walls*) crépi, *m.* — **casting,** *s.* ébauchage, *m.*; (*of a wall*) crépissage, crépissement, *m.*, crépissure, *f.* — **coat,** — **coating,** (*of a wall*) *V.* — **cast,** &c. — **down,** *v.a.* dégrossir; (*metals, glass*) adoucir. — **draught,** *s.* (*writing*) brouillon, *m.*; (*drawing*) esquisse, ébauche, *f.* — **draw,** *v.a.* (*write*) brouillonner; (*sketch*) esquisser, ébaucher. — **drawing,** *s. V.* — **draught.** — **footed,** *adj.* pattu. — **haired,** *adj.* (*animals*) au poil rude; (*pers.*) ébouriffé. — **hew,** *v.a.* dégrossir; (*fig.*) ébaucher. — **hewn,** *adj.* dégrossi; ébauché; (*pers.*) rude, grossier. — **legged,** *adj.* pattu. — **model,** *v.a.* ébaucher. — **out,** *v.a.* ébaucher. — **rider,** *s.* dresseur de chevaux, casse-cou, *m.* — **shod,** *adj.* grossièrement ferré; (*for ice*) ferré à glace; (*pers.*) grossièrement chaussé. *To ride — shod over*, brusquer. — **shoe,** *v.a.* ferrer grossièrement; (*for ice*) ferrer à glace. — **sketch,** *s.* ébauche, esquisse, *f.*, croquis, *m.*; *v.a.* ébaucher, esquisser. — **wall,** *v.a.n.* limousiner, hourder. — **waller,** *s.* limousineur, *m.* — **walling,** *s.* limousinage, hourdage, *m.* — **work,** *s.* grosse besogne, *f.*; *v.a.* travailler (*or* faire) grossièrement. — **wrought,** *part. adj.* travaillé (*or* fait) grossièrement

Roughen, *v.a.* rendre rude; — *v.n.* devenir rude. — **down,** *v.a.* dégrossir

Roughening, Roughing, *s.* action de rendre rude, *f.*; action d'endurer, *f.*, &c. (*V.* **Roughen** *and* **Rough,** *v.a.*). — **down,** *s.* dégrossissage, *m.*; (*of metals*) adoucissage, *m.*; (*of glass*) adouci, *m.*

Roughly, *adv.* rudement; durement; brusquement; brutalement; âprement; grossièrement; approximativement, par aperçu; à peu près

Roughness, *s.* aspérité, *f.*; (*of temper*) rudesse, *f.*; âpreté, *f.*; (*coarseness*) grossièreté, *f.*; (*of manner*) brusquerie, *f.*; sans-façon, *m.*; (*of a road*) état raboteux, mauvais état, *m.*; (*to the taste*) âpreté, *f.*; (*to the ear*) dureté, rudesse, *f.*; (*of sea, wind*) agitation, *f.*; violence, *f.*

Roulade, *s.* roulade, *f.*

Rouleau, *s.* rouleau, *m.*

Roulette, *s.* roulette, *f.*

Rouman, Roumanian, *s. adj.* Rouman, *m.*, e, *f.*, Roumain, *m.*, e, *f.*

Roumelian, *s. adj.* Roumélien, *m.*, -ne, *f.*, [Rouméliste, *m.f.*

Rounce, *s.* manivelle, *f.*

Round, *adj.* rond; arrondi; (*open, fair*) franc; (*of style*) facile, coulant; (*positive*) positif, absolu, net; (*of price, sum*) bon, joli, grand. — *numbers*, nombre rond, *m.*, chiffres ronds, *m.pl.*, compte rond, *m.* *To become* or *get* or *grow* —, s'arrondir. *To make* —, arrondir. — **backed,** *adj.* voûté. **hand,** *s.* (*writ.*) ronde, *f.* — **head,** *s.* (*Engl. hist.*) tête ronde, *f.*, puritain, *m.* — **headed,** *adj.* à tête ronde; au sommet rond. — **leaved,** *adj.* à feuilles rondes, rotundifolié. — **robin,** *s.* pétition (*or* pièce) revêtue de signatures en cercle, *f.* — **shot,** *s. V.* **Shot.** — **shouldered,** *adj.* voûté. — **shoulders,** *s.pl.* dos voûté, *m.* — **towel,** *s. V.* **Jack-towel**

Round, *s.* rond, *m.*; cercle, *m.*; (*turning*) tour, *m.*; (*circuit, walk*) tournée, *f.*; (*inspection*) ronde, tournée, *f.*; (*course*) cours, *m.*; (*beat*) *V.* **Beat;** (*of applause*) salve, *f.*; (*of ladders*) échelon, *m.*; (*buttock of an ox*) cimier, gîte, *m.*; (*piece of beef cut off ditto*) rouelle, *f.*; (*fenc.*) assaut, *m.*; (*in a fight*) attaque, *f.*, assaut, *m.*; reprise, *f.*; (*at play*) tour, *m.*; (*dance*) ronde, *f.*; (*draw., paint.*) bosse, *f.*; (*sculp.*) ronde bosse, *f.*; (*mus.*) ronde, *f.*; (*mach.*) rondelle, *f.*; (*mil., of police, watchmen*) ronde, *f.*; (*of musketry*) décharge, *f.*; coup, *m.*; (*of cannon*) volée, salve, décharge, *f.*; coup, *m.*; (*cartridge*) cartouche, *f.* — *of ammunition*, cartouche, *f.* — *of toast*, rôtie, *f.* *From the* —, (*draw., paint.*) d'après la bosse. *In a* —, en rond. *In the* —, (*sculp.*) en ronde bosse. *On the* —, en tournée; (*mil.*, &c.) en ronde. *Silver side of the* —, (*of beef*) gîte à la noix, *m.* *To fire a* —, *V.* **Volley.** *To go the* — (or —*s*), faire le tour; circuler, courir; faire la tournée; faire la ronde. — **house,** *s.* corps de garde, *m.*; violon, *m.*; (*nav.*) chambre du conseil, *f.* — **man,** *s.* homme de tournée, *m.* — **way,** *s.* chemin de ronde, *m.*

Round, *prep. V.* **Around,** *prep.*; — *adv.* (*circularly*) en rond; en tournant; (*about*, &c.) *V.* **Around,** *adv.* *All* —, — *about*, (*prep.*) tout autour de (...); (*adv.*) tout autour; (*by turns*) à la ronde. — **about,** *adj. & s.* [*See below*]. *All the year* —, pendant toute l'année, toute l'année. *To walk* or *come* or *go* or *get* —, (*a place*) aller autour de (...); faire le tour de (...); (*a thing*) tourner autour de (...); (*adv.*) aller autour; faire le tour; faire un détour; tourner autour; (*fig.*) circuler. *To come* —, (*various other senses*) *V.* **Come.** *To go* or *get* —, (*veer, revolve*) tourner; se tourner *To get* —, (*recover*) se rétablir, se remettre; (*surround*) entourer; (*wheedle*) circonvenir; entortiller. *To go — to*, visiter, aller voir. *To go all* —, (*another way*) se détourner

Round, *v.a.* arrondir; (*surround*) entourer; environner; (*go round*) faire le tour de, contourner; tourner; (*a cape*) arrondir; (*an island*) contourner, arrondir; (*complete*) compléter, achever, terminer; — *v.n.* s'arrondir. — **off,** *v.a.* arrondir; finir; *v.n.* s'arrondir; finir, s'achever, se terminer

Roundabout, *adj.* détourné; indirect; vague; — *s.* manége, *m.*; jeu de bagues, *m.*

Roundel, Roundelay, *s.* (*mus.*) ronde, *f.*; (*poet.*) rondeau, *m.*

Rounders, *s.pl.* (*game*) balle au camp, *f.*

Roundish, *adj.* rondelet; arrondi

Roundishness, *s.* forme arrondie, *f.*

Roundly, *adv.* rondement

Roundness, *s.* rondeur, *f.*

Roup, *s.* (*disease in birds*) pépie, *f.*

Rouse, *v.a.* réveiller, éveiller; exciter, animer; agiter, soulever; (*the fire*) activer; (*game*) *V.* **Start.** *To — the sleeping lion*, (*fig.*) éveiller le chat qui dort

Rousing, *part. adj.* qui réveille *or* &c. (*V.* **Rouse**); (*of fire*) grand, bon

Rousselet, *s.* rousselet, *m.*

Roussette, *s.* roussette, *f.*

Rout, *s.* réunion, assemblée, *f.*, (*old*) raout, *m.*; réception, soirée, *f.*; (*crowd*) cohue, foule, multitude, *f.*; (*mil.*) déroute, *f.*; — *v.a.* mettre en déroute; — *v.a.n.* (*to search*) fouiller. *To put to the* —, mettre en déroute. *To be completely* —*ed*, être en pleine déroute. — **out,** *v.a.* découvrir, déterrer; (*turn out*) faire déguerpir

Route, *s.* route, *f.*; voie, *f.*; itinéraire, *m.*; (*document ordering to move, mil.*) feuille de [route, *f.*

Routine, *s.* routine, *f.*

Roux, *s.* (*cook.*) roux, *m.* [staphylin, *m.*

Rove, *s. & v.n. V.* **Ramble.** — **beetle,** *s.*

Rover, *s.* coureur, *m.*, -euse, *f.*; rôdeur, *m.*, -euse, *f.*, vagabond, *m.*, e, *f.*; pirate, écumeur de mer, *m.* [**Rambling,** *s.*

Roving, *adj.* vagabond; errant; — *s. V.*

Rovingly, *adv. V.* **Ramblingly**

Row, *s.* rang, *m.*; rangée, *f.*; ligne, file, *f.*; bordure, *f.*; (*street*) rue, ruelle, *f.*; (*arith.*) colonne, *f.*; (*tumult*) tapage, vacarme, *m.*; querelle, *f.*; scène, *f.*; (*in a boat*) promenade à la rame, *f.*; — *v.n.* ramer, nager, voguer; — *v.a.* (*a boat*) faire aller; conduire; (*a pers.*) conduire *or* mener *or* transporter à la rame;

promener en bateau. *In a —*, en rang, en ligne. *In —s*, par rangs; (*hort.*) en rayons. *In two* or &c. *—s*, sur deux *or* &c. rangs. *To get into a —*, se faire une mauvaise affaire. *To make* or *kick up a —*, faire du tapage *or* du bruit *or* du train, (*with an adj.*) faire un tapage *or* &c. ... — **boat,** *s.* bateau à rames, *m.* — **lock,** *s.* toletière, *f.*

Rowan-tree, *s.* sorbier des oiseaux, *m.*

Rowdiness. *V.* **Rowdyism**

Rowdy, *s.* voyou, *m.*; tapageur, *m.*; émeutier, *m.*; gredin, bandit, *m.*; — *adj. V.* **Rowdyish**

Rowdyish, *adj.* canaille, voyou; turbulent, tapageur [turbulence, *f.*; gredinerie, *f.*

Rowdyism, *s.* polissonnerie, *f.*; tapage, *m.*,

Rowel, *s.* (*of spurs*) molette, *f.*; (*of bits*) bossette, *f.*; (*vet.*) séton, *m.*, ortie, rouelle, *f.*

Rower, *s.* rameur, nageur, canotier, *m.*

Rowing, *adj.* qui va à la rame; — *s.* action de ramer, *f.*; promenade à la rame, *f.*; (*nav.*) nage, *f.* *To like* (or *be fond of*) —, aimer à ramer. — **boat,** *s.* bateau à rames, *m.* — **club,** *s.* société des régates, *f.* — **match,** *s.* course à la rame *or* à l'aviron, *f.*

Rowland, *s.* Roland, *m.* *A — for an Oliver*, un prêté rendu; à bon chat bon rat. *To give a — for an Oliver*, rendre pois pour fève, rendre la pareille

Royal, *adj.* royal; de roi; du roi; (*of paper*) raisin; — *s.* (*of a stag's head*) branche (de bois de cerf), *f.*; (*paper*) raisin, *m.*; (*artil.*) petit mortier, *m.*; (*nav.*) cacatois, *m.* — *blue*, bleu de roi. — *navy*, marine de l'État, marine militaire, marine royale, *f.*

Royal-ism, -ist. *V.* page 3, § 1

Royalize, *v.a.* royaliser

Royally, *adv.* royalement

Royalty, *s.* royauté, *f.*; (*payment*) redevance, *f.*

Rub, *v.a.n.* frotter; (*med.*) frictionner. — **along,** aller son petit bonhomme de chemin. — **down,** frotter; polir; (*a horse*) bouchonner. — **off,** enlever en frottant, enlever; effacer; (*neut.*) s'enlever, s'effacer, (*fig.*) s'user. — **out,** enlever; effacer; (*neut.*) s'effacer. — **on,** — **through,** faire son chemin, se tirer d'affaire, s'en tirer. — **up,** frotter; polir; (*the rust*) dérouiller; (*to brush*) donner un coup de brosse à; (*with a cloth*) donner un coup de torchon à; (*fig.*) retoucher; rafraîchir; (*rouse*) réveiller, éveiller, exciter; (*o.'s knowledge*) se remettre à *or* au; (*neut.*) se polir, se dérouiller

Rub, *s.* frottement, *m.*; (*with a brush*) coup de brosse, *m.*; (*with a cloth*) coup de torchon, *m.*; (*of ground*, &c.) aspérité, inégalité, *f.*; (*difficulty*) difficulté, *f.*; hic, *m.*; (*sarcasm*) coup de patte, coup de langue, *m.*; (*whist*, &c.) *V.* **Rubber.** *There's the —!* voilà le hic! — **down,** *s.* (*to a horse*) coup de bouchon, *m.*

Rubasse, *s.* rubace, rubasse, *f.*

Rubber, *s.* frotteur, *m.*; (*professional, medical*) frictionneur, *m.*, -euse, *f.*; (*things*) frottoir, *m.*; (*paint.*) torche-pinceau, *m.*; (*stone*) pierre à aiguiser, *f.*; (*at play*) partie liée, *f.*; (*third deciding game*) belle, *f.*; (*whist*) partie de whist, *f.*, rob, robre, rubber, *m.*; (*India —*) *V.* **India-rubber**

Rubbing, *s.* frottement, *m.*; frottage, *m.*; (*med.*) friction, *f.*, frictions, *f.pl.*; (*pattern rubbed*) impression, *f.* *Professional —*, frictionnement, *m.*

Rubbish, *s.* décombres, débris, *m.pl*; gravats, gravois, *m.pl.*; déblais, *m.pl.*; (*dirt*) ordures, immondices, *f.pl.*; (*trash*) rebut, *m.*, drogue, *f.*; vieillerie, *f.*; (*nonsense*) fadaises, *f.pl.*, bêtise, *f.*; fatras, *m.* *Old —*, vieillerie, *f.*, vieilleries, *f.pl.* — **basket,** *s.* panier aux ordures, *m.* — **cart,** *s.* tombereau, *m.* — **carter,** *s.* gravatier, *m.*

Rubbishing, Rubbishy, *adj.* de rebut; sans valeur, mauvais, méchant, de la drogue

Rubble (— stone), *s.* pierre brute, *f.*, moellon brut, *m.*, blocaille, *f.*, blocage, *m.*; (*build.*) remplage, *m.* — **drain,** *s.* pierrée, *f.* — **work,** *s.* maçonnerie de moellons bruts *or* de blocaille, *f.*, blocage, *m.* [rubéfiant, *s.m.*

Rubefacient, *adj. s.* rubéfiant, *adj. m.*, e, *f.*,

Rubefaction, *s.* rubéfaction, *f.*

Rubescent, *adj.* rubescent

Rubican, *adj. s.* rubican, *m.*

Rubicund, *adj.* rubicond

Rubicundity, *s.* rubicondité, *f.*

Rubidium, *s.* rubidium, *m.*

Rubied, *adj.* rouge, de rubis

Rubification, *s.* rubéfaction, *f.*

Rubify, *v.a.* rubéfier; — *v.n.* se rubéfier

Rubiginous, *adj.* rubigineux

Ruble, *s.* rouble, *m.*

Rubric, *s.* rubrique, *f.* [des rubriques; rouge

Rubrical, *adj.* des rubriques; contenu dans

Rubricate, *v.a.* marquer de rouge

Rubrician, Rubricist, *s.* rubricaire, *m.*

Ruby, *s.* rubis, *m.*; (*colour*) incarnat, *m.*, couleur rouge, *f.*; (*print. type*) parisienne, sédanoise, *f.*; — *adj.* de rubis, rouge, vermeil. — *lips*, lèvres vermeilles, lèvres de corail, *f.pl.* — *tailed fly*, guêpe dorée, chryside, *f.*

Ruche, *s.* ruche, *f.* [— *v.a.* plisser

Ruck, *s.* pli, *m.*; sillon, *m.*; (*heap*) *V.* **Ruckle;**

Ruckle, *s.* tas, amas, monceau, *m.*

Rudd, *s.* (*fish*) rouget, *m.*

Rudder, *s.* gouvernail, *m.* [cheur, *f.*

Ruddiness, *s.* rougeur, *f.*; incarnat, *m.*; fraî-

Ruddle, *s. V.* **Reddle;** — *v.a.* marquer de rouge; (*theat.*) grimer, maquiller; — *v.n.* se grimer, se maquiller [teint frais, *m.*

Ruddy, *adj.* rouge; vermeil. — *complexion*,

Rude, *adj.* rude; grossier; (*untaught*) grossier, rude; (*uncivil*) impoli, malhonnête, impertinent, insolent, grossier; (*rough*) dur, sévère, rude; (*strong*) violent; vigoureux

Rudely, *adv.* rudement; grossièrement; (*uncivilly*) impoliment, insolemment, grossièrement; (*roughly*) durement, sévèrement; violemment; vigoureusement

Rudeness, *s.* rudesse, *f.*; grossièreté, *f.*; (*incivility*) impolitesse, malhonnêteté, impertinence, insolence, grossièreté, *f.*; (*roughness*) dureté, sévérité, *f.*; violence, *f.*; vigueur, *f.*

Rudenture, *s.* rudenture, *f.*

Rudiment, *s.* rudiment, *m.*; élément, *m.*

Rudiment-al, ary, *adj.* rudimentaire; élémentaire

Rue, *v.a.* se repentir de, regretter; — *s.* (*bot.*) rue, *f.* —**ful,** *adj.* triste. —**fully,** *adv.* tristement. —**fulness,** *s.* tristesse, *f.*

Ruellia, *s.* ruellie, *f.*

Ruff, *s.* (*collar*) fraise, *f.*; (*bird*) combattant, paon de mer, *m.*; (*fish*) *V.* **Ruffe;** (*mil.*) *V.* **Ruffle**

Ruffe, *s.* (*fish*) gremille, perche goujonnière, *f.*

Ruffian, *s.* brigand, bandit, *m.*; scélérat, *m.*; chenapan, gredin, *m.*; brutal, *m.*; — *adj.*, — **like,** *adj. V.* **Ruffianly** [*f.*; brutalité, *f.*

Ruffianism, *s.* brigandage, *m.*; scélératesse,

Ruffianly, *adj.* de brigand, de bandit; brutal

Ruffle, *v.a.* (*plait*) froncer, plisser; (*wrinkle, ripple*) rider; (*rumple*) chiffonner, froisser; (*the feelings*) froisser; (*disorder*) déranger; (*the hair*) rebrousser; ébouriffer; (*agitate*) troubler, agiter; irriter; (*put ruffles*) mettre des manchettes à; — *s.* (*of a dress*) manchette, *f.*; (*disturbance*) trouble, *m.*, agitation, *f.*; (*wrinkle, ripple*) ride, *f.*; (*mil.*) roulement (de tambour), coup de baguette, appel, ra, *m.*

Ruffling, *s.* (*plaiting*) froncement, plissement, *m.*; (*wrinkling, rippling*) action de rider, *f.*; rides, *f.pl.*; (*rumpling*) chiffonnage, froissement, *m.*; (*of the feelings*) froissement, *m.*; (*disturbance*) trouble, *m.*, agitation, émotion, *f.*

Rufus, *adj.* roux. *William —*, Guillaume le Roux, *m.*

Rug, *s.* tapis, *m.*; (*centre —*) carpette, *f.*; (*for beds*) tapis (*m.*) *or* descente (*f.*) de lit; (*covering*) couverture, *f.* — **work,** *s.* tapisserie, *f.*

Rugged, *adj.* raboteux ; rude ; âpre ; (*of the hair*) hérissé ; (*of temper*) refrogné, rechigné
Ruggedly, *adv.* rudement ; âprement
Ruggedness, *s.* aspérité, *f.* ; nature raboteuse, *f.* ; (*of temper, manners*) rudesse, *f.* ; âpreté, *f.*
Rugine, *s.* rugine, *f.*
Rugose, Rugous, *adj.* rugueux
Rugosity, *s.* rugosité, *f.*
Ruin, *v.a.* ruiner ; perdre ; — *v.n.* tomber en ruine ; (*pers.*) se ruiner, être ruiné ; — *s.* ruine, *f.* ; perte, *f.* *To go to* —, tomber en ruine, dépérir
Ruination, *s.* ruine, perte, *f.*
Ruiner, *s.* destructeur, *m.*, -trice, *f.* ; fléau, *m.*
Ruinous, *adj.* ruineux ; en ruine, en ruines
Ruinously, *adv.* ruineusement
Ruinousness, *s.* état de ruine, *m.* ; nature ruineuse, *f.*
Rule, *v.a.* gouverner, régir ; (*to conduct*) régler, conduire, diriger ; (*to decide*) décider, déterminer, régler ; (*to draw lines*) régler ; — *v.n.* gouverner ; (*over*) régner (sur) ; (*to decide*) décider ; — *s.* règle, *f.* ; règlement, *m.* ; empire, gouvernement, *m.*, autorité, domination, *f.* ; (*law*) décision, ordonnance, *f.* ; (*print.*) filet, tiret, *m.* ; (*instr.*) règle, *f.* ; (*yard*) mètre, *m.* — *of company*, (*arith.*) règle de société. — *of three*, (*arith.*) règle de trois. *As a* —, en général, règle générale, en thèse générale. *To live by* —, vivre de régime. *To make it a* — (*to*), se faire une règle (de). *I make it a* — *to* ..., je me suis fait une règle de ...
Ruler, *s.* (*polit.*) gouvernant, *m.* ; (*supreme master*) dominateur, *m.*, -trice, *f.*, maître, *m.*, -esse, *f.* ; souverain, *m.*, e, *f.* ; arbitre, *m.f.* ; (*one who draws lines, paper* —, &c.) régleur, *m.*, -euse, *f.* ; (*instr.*) règle, *f.* ; (*machine*) régloir, *m.*
Ruling, *adj.* régnant ; dominant ; — *s.* décision, *f.* ; (*tech.*) réglure, *f.* — **machine,** *s.* machine à régler, *f.*, régloir, *m.*
Rum, *s.* rhum, rum, *m.* ; (*unsalable book*) rossignol, *m.* ; — *adj.* drôle, cocasse. *A — fellow, a — one*, un drôle de corps, un original, *m.*, une originale, *f.* — **punch,** *s.* punch au rhum, *m.*
Rumble, *v.n.* gronder ; murmurer ; — *s.* train de derrière, *m.* ; (*seat*) siége de derrière, *m.* ; (*noise*) *V.* **Rumbling,** *s.*
Rumbling, *adj.* sourd ; — *s.* bruit sourd, grondement, roulement, *m.* ; bruit, *m.*
Ruminant, *adj. s.* ruminant, *adj.m.*, e, *f.*, ruminant, *s.m.*
Ruminate, *v.n.a.* ruminer
Rumination, *s.* rumination, *f.*
Rummage, *s.* remue-ménage, remuement, *m.* ; fouille, *f.* ; — *v.a.* fouiller, farfouiller, bouleverser ; (*wine being fined*) daudiner, dodiner
Rummager, *s.* farfouilleur, *m.*, -euse, *f.*
Rummaging, *s. V.* **Rummage,** *s.* — **stick,** *s.* (*for fining wine*) daudine, dodine, *f.*
Rummer, *s.* grand verre à patte, gobelet, *m.*
Rumour, *s.* rumeur, *f.* ; bruit, *m.* ; — *v.a.* faire courir (le bruit), prétendre ; ébruiter. *There is a —, it is —ed*, le bruit court
Rump, *s.* croupe, *f.* ; croupion, *m.* ; (*of fowls*) croupion, *m.* ; (*butch.*) culotte, cuisse, *f.* ; (*pers.*) croupion, postérieur, *m.* — **parliament,** *s.* (*Engl. hist.*) parlement croupion, *m.* — **steak,** *s.* (*cook.*) bifteck chateaubriand, chateaubriand, *m.* ; (*butch.*) rumpsteak, *m.* ; filet, *m.*
Rumple, *v.a.* chiffonner, friper, froisser ; — *s.* pli, *m.*, froissure, *f.*
Rumpus, *s.* chamaillis, *m.* ; bagarre, *f.* ; grabuge, *m.*
Run, *v.n.* courir ; (*to the place we are at in body or mind*) accourir ; (*rush*) se précipiter, se jeter ; (*fall*) tomber ; (*knock*) heurter, se heurter, se cogner ; (*flee*) fuir, s'enfuir, se sauver ; se réfugier ; (*go, get on, move*) aller ; marcher ; (*pass*) passer ; (*enter*) entrer, pénétrer ; (*roll*) rouler ; (*turn*) tourner ; (*of discourse*) rouler (sur) ; (*extend*) s'étendre ; (*glide*) glisser ; (*rise*) monter, s'élever ; (*incline*) porter ; (*become*) devenir ; commencer à être ; (*turn into*) se changer (en) ; (*to be*) être ; (*flow*) couler ; (*drop, drip*) dégoutter ; suinter ; (*melt, fuse*) fondre. couler ; (*of the eyes*) pleurer ; (*of the nose*) couler ; (*of time*) passer, s'écouler ; (*of liquids, candles*) couler ; (*of casks, jugs, &c., to leak*) fuir ; (*of ink through paper*) pénétrer ; (*of wounds*) suppurer ; (*of coaches, trains, packets, &c.*) faire le service, faire le parcours, faire le trajet (entre ... et ; *or* de ... à), desservir, desservir la ligne (de ... à ...) ; (*of writings*) être conçu ; s'exprimer ; (*of colours*) se fondre ; (*of stars*) filer ; (*of prices, figures*) aller, monter ; (*of bills*) courir ; (*ropes, knots, ship's speed, nav.*) filer ; (*... miles an hour*) faire (... milles à l'heure) ; — *v.a.* pousser ; enfoncer ; forcer, introduire ; fourrer ; précipiter, lancer, jeter, mettre ; passer ; (*knock*) cogner ; (*incur*) courir ; (*pursue*) poursuivre ; (*chase*) chasser ; (*cattle, &c., in order to make their flesh tender*) vener ; (*horses, dogs*) faire courir ; (*a coach, &c., drive, conduct*) faire marcher ; conduire ; (*trains*) faire circuler ; (*a race*) *V.* **Race ;** (*rigs*) faire ; (*melt, cast*) fondre, couler ; (*liquids*) répandre ; (*pour*) couler ; (*roll*) rouler ; (*o.'s eye*) jeter (un coup d'œil) ; (*a line*) tirer ; (*smuggle*) passer ; (*a* (*blockade*) forcer ; (*a coast*) suivre ; (*to change*) changer, convertir ; — *s.* course, *f.* ; promenade, *f.*, tour, *m.* ; poursuite, *f.* ; attaque, *f.* ; (*hunt*) chasse, *f.* ; (*course*) cours, *m.* ; courant, *m.* ; (*succession*) suite, *f.* ; (*generality*) commun, ordinaire, *m.* ; plupart, *f.* ; (*of lodes*) gisement, *m.* ; (*of luck*) veine, *f.* ; (*success*) succès, *m.* ; vogue, *f.* ; (*duration*) durée, *f.* ; (*on a bank*) irruption, *f.* ; (*clamour*) cri, *m.*, clameur, opposition, *f.* ; (*... hours' —, by rail*, &c.) trajet (de ... heures), m. ; parcours, *m.* ; (*crossing*) traversée, *f.* ; (*navvy's*) relai, *m.* ; (*free access*) libre accès, *m.* ; (*of millstones*) paire, *f.* ; (*nav.*) route, *f.* ; voyage, *m.* ; — *part. adj.* couru, &c. ; (*melted*) fondu ; (*contraband*) de contrebande ; [*Per foot* —, le pied courant]. *Long* —, longue course *or* &c. ; (*fig.*) issue, fin, *f.* *In the long* —, à la longue, avec le temps ; en dernier résultat, en fin de compte, à la fin. *To — bills*, prendre à crédit, faire des dettes. *To — horses*, faire courir des chevaux, faire courir. *To be hard* —, être poursuivi *or* serré de près, être pressé vivement, être aux abois. *To have* or *take a* —, *to go for a* —, faire une course ; faire une promenade ; trotter. *To have a great* —, être très couru. *To have had o.'s* —, avoir eu son temps. *It —s in the blood*, c'est dans le sang. *It keeps —ning in his head*, cela lui trotte dans la tête. — **about,** courir çà et là, courir partout, courir ; (*of a child*) courir, trotter, marcher. — **across,** traverser en courant, traverser. — **after,** courir après ; poursuivre ; (*fig.*) chercher ; rechercher. — **against,** heurter *or* donner contre ; attaquer. — **aground,** — **ashore,** *V.* **Aground.** — **at,** courir sur, se jeter sur, se précipiter sur, se ruer sur, fondre sur ; attaquer. — **away,** s'enfuir, se sauver ; s'éloigner ; s'en aller ; (*of* (*time*) passer, s'écouler ; (*of liquids*) s'écouler ; (*of horses*) s'emporter. — **away with,** emporter ; (*a woman, a child, &c.*) enlever ; (*imagine*) s'imaginer. — **back,** retourner (en courant) ; (*come back*) revenir (en courant) ; (*go backwards*) reculer ; (*reascend*) remonter. — **down,** descendre en courant, descendre, courir ; (*from the capital*) aller ; venir ; (*of liquids*) découler, couler, (*in drops*) dégoutter, (*in streams*) ruisseler ; (*hunt*) poursuivre ; forcer ; mettre aux abois ; (*crush*) écraser, abattre ; (*debase*) avilir ; décrier ; (*silence*) réduire au silence ; (*a ship*) couler bas. *My watch is — down*, ma montre n'est pas montée. — **for,** courir chercher ; (*a prize or plate, in a race*) courir. *To — for o.'s life*, chercher son salut dans la fuite. — **high,** monter *or* s'élever haut, s'élever ; s'échauffer ; être *or* devenir violent ; être en fureur ; être au comble ; être acharné ; être agité. *Words ran high between them*, ils en sont venus (*or* ils en vinrent) aux gros mots. — **in,** entrer en courant, entrer,

courir; (*v.a.*) rentrer; enfoncer. — **in again,** rentrer. — **in close,** (*nav.*) serrer *or* ranger la côte. — **into,** (— *oneself into*) se jeter *or* se lancer *or* se précipiter *or* se mettre dans; tomber dans; (*debt*) *V.* **Debt;** (*go inside*) courir dans (*or* à); (*sharp point,* &c.) enfoncer; (*of ships, running foul*) aborder; enfoncer; (*of ships, into port*) entrer au port de . . ., faire route à . . . *The express has — into the up mail,* l'express a fait collision avec le train-poste d'aller. — **low,** baisser; diminuer d'intensité. — **off,** s'enfuir, se sauver; s'échapper; s'en aller; (*of liquids*) couler, s'écouler. *To — off the line* or *the rails, V.* **Rail.** — **on,** courir en avant; courir; aller; continuer, poursuivre; (*keep talking*) dégoiser, ne pas déparler; (*roll*) rouler sur; (*strike*) donner sur; (*print.*) suivre, faire suivre. — **out,** sortir en courant, sortir, courir; (*into*) se lancer *or* se jeter (dans); (*flow*) s'écouler; (*of the tide*) descendre; (*leak*) couler, fuir; (*exhaust*) s'épuiser; (*expire*) expirer, finir, se terminer; (*be wasted*) se dissiper; (*extend, enlarge*) s'étendre; s'allonger. — **out of,** être à sec de, n'avoir plus de; épuiser; arriver au bout de; (*squander*) gaspiller, dissiper, manger. — **over,** passer sur; (*a pers.*) passer sur le corps à, écraser; (*to*) passer (à); courir (à); aller *or* venir (à); (*of fluids*) déborder; (*a distance, and fig. read cursorily*) parcourir; (*seize*) s'emparer de. — **through,** courir à travers; passer par, passer au travers de, traverser; enfiler; parcourir; (*go direct, rail.*) aller directement (à); (*with a weapon*) percer, transpercer; (*squander*) gaspiller, dissiper, manger. *He ran him through the body,* (*with a sword*) il lui passa son épée au travers du corps, il le perça d'un coup d'épée. — **up,** accourir; (*ascend*) monter; remonter; (*go*) aller; (*come*) venir; (*of accounts*) s'élever (à), monter (à); (*v.a.*) élever; (*an account*) faire monter. *To — up bills,* faire des dettes. — **upon,** courir sur; (*roll*) rouler sur; (*strike*) donner sur

Runagate. *V.* **Renegade**

Runaway, *s.* fugitif, *m.*, -ive, *f.*; fuyard, *m.*, e, *f.*; déserteur, *m.*; échappé, *m.*, e, *f.*; — *adj.* fugitif; échappé. — *slave,* esclave (*m.f.*) fugitif (*m.*, -ive, *f.*) — *horse,* cheval échappé, *m.* — *marriage* or *match,* mariage d'enlèvement, *m.*

Runcinate, *adj.* ronciné, runciné

Rundle, *s.* (*of a ladder*) échelon, *m.*; (*mech.*) cylindre, treuil, *m.*

Rundlet, *s.* barillet, *m.*

Runer, *s.* poète runique, *m.*

Runes, *s.pl.* runes, *f.pl.*

Rung, *s.* (*of a ladder*) échelon, *m.*; (*of a chair,* &c.) barreau, *m.*; bâton, *m.*

Runic, *adj.* runique

Runlet, *s.* ruisseau, *m.*; (*rundlet*) barillet, *m.*

Runnel, *s.* ruisseau, *m.*

Runner, *s.* coureur, *m.*, -euse, *f.*; (*a ring*) coulant, anneau mobile, *m.*; (*a sprig*) rejeton, *m.*, trainasse, *f.*; (*of strawberries*) filet, coulant, *m.*; (*kind of bean*) haricot grimpant, *m.*; (*upper millstone*) courante, surmeule, *f.*; (*nav.*) itague, *f.*

Runnet. *V.* **Rennet**

Running, *adj.* courant; (*of horses*) de course; (*consecutive*) de suite, consécutif; (*of water*) courant, vif; (*of wounds*) en suppuration; (*of knots*) coulant; (*of accounts*) courant; (*of bills*) à échoir; (*of firing*) roulant; (*print., nav.*) courant; — *s.* course, *f.*; (*flowing*) écoulement, *m.*; (*of wounds*) suppuration, *f.*; (*of the pen*) courant (de la plume), *m.*; (*of needlework*) point devant, *m.*; (*of trains, steamers,* &c.) service, *m.* — *day,* (*com. nav.*) jour de planche, *m.* — *fight,* (*mil.*) escarmouche de route, *f.*; (*nav.*) combat en chasse, *m.* — *hand,* — *heats,* &c., *V.* **Hand, Heat,** &c. — **across,** *s.* traversée, *f.* — **aground** *or* **ashore,** *s.* (*by accident*) échouement, *m.*; (*voluntarily*) échouage, *m.* — **away,** *s.* fuite, *f.*; désertion, *f.*; (*with a woman, a child,* &c.) enlèvement, *m.* — **back,** *s.* retour, *m.*; (*going backwards*) reculement, *m.* — **foul,** *s.* (*nav.*) abordage, *m.* — **off,** *s.* fuite, *f.*; (*escape*) évasion, *f.*; (*of liquids*) écoulement, *m.* — *off the line* or *the rails, V.* **Rail**

Runologist, *s.* runologue, *m.*

Runt, *s.* animal rabougri, *m.*; pigeon mondain, *m.*; (*pers.*) avorton, *m.*, nabot, *m.*, e, *f.*, ora-poussin, *m.*, e, *f.*

Rupee, *s.* roupie, *f.*

Rupert's (*or* **Prince Rupert's**) **drop,** *s.* *V.* **Glass-drop**

Rupia, *s.* rupia, *m.*

Rupicola, *s.* rupicole, *m.*

Rupture, *s.* rupture, *f.*; (*hernia*) hernie, *f.*; — *v.a.n.* rompre; se rompre. *To be —d,* (*pers.*) avoir une hernie. — **wort,** *s.* herniaire, herniole, *f.*

Rupturing, *s.* rupture, *f.*

Rural, *adj.* rural, champêtre, des champs; agreste, rustique; agricole, d'agriculture. — — *postman,* facteur rural, piéton, *m.*

Ruralist, *s.* habitant (*m.*, e, *f.*) de la campagne

Rurality, *s.* ruralité, *f.*

Ruralize. *V.* **Rusticate**

Rurally, *adv.* ruralement, d'une manière champêtre

Ruralness, *s.* ruralité, *f.*

Ruse, *s.* ruse, *f.*

Rush, *s.* (*bot.*) jonc, *m.*; (*trifle*) fétu, rien, *m.*; (*crowd*) foule, *f.*; (*violent motion*) élan, *m.*; choc, *m.*; mouvement précipité, *m.*; impétuosité, *f.*; violence, *f.*; — *v.n.* se précipiter, s'élancer, se lancer, se jeter, se ruer, ('*upon,*' sur), fondre (sur); (*of the wind, in chimneys,* &c.) s'engouffrer. *I would not give a — for it,* je n'en donnerais pas un centime. *It is not worth a —,* cela ne vaut pas un centime. *A — was made to the door,* on se précipita vers la porte. *There was a — to . . .,* on se précipita pour . . . *There is a — after it,* (*fig.*) on se l'arrache. — **basket,** *s.* panier de jonc, *m.* — **broom,** *s.* genêt *or* jonc d'Espagne, joncier, *m.* — **candle,** *s.* chandelle de veille, veilleuse, *f.* — **light,** *s.* veilleuse, *f.* —**like,** *adj.* comme un jonc; (*weak*) faible; fragile; (*shaped*) jonciforme. — **mat, -matting,** *s.* natte de jonc, natte, *f.* — **nut,** *s.* souchet comestible, *m.* — —**shaped,** *adj.* jonciforme.

Rushiness, *s.* abondance de joncs, *f.*

Rushing, *s.* élan, *m.*; précipitation, *f.*; impétuosité, *f.*; violence, *f.*

Rushingly, *adv.* avec précipitation, précipitamment; avec impétuosité, impétueusement; avec violence, violemment

Rushy, *adj.* (*full of*) plein de joncs; (*made of*) de *or* en jonc, de *or* en joncs, fait de jonc

Rusk, *s.* biscotte, *f.*

Russet, *adj.* roussâtre, roux; (*coarse*) grossier, rustique; — *s.* (*colour*) roux, *m.*; (*apple*) reinette grise, *f.*; (*pear*) rousselet, *m.*

Russeting, *s.* (*apple, pear*) *V.* **Russet**

Russety, *adj.* roussâtre, roux

Russia leather, *s.* cuir de Russie, *m.*

Russian, *s.* Russe, *m.f.*; (*language*) le russe, *m.*, la langue russe, *f.*; — *adj.* russe, de Russie

Russo-, (*in compounds*) Russo- . . .

Russophobia, *s.* russophobie, *f.*

Russophobiac, *s.* russophobe, *m.f.*

Russophobic, *adj.* (*thing*) russophobique; (*pers.*) russophobe

Russophobist, *s.* russophobe, *m.f.*

Rust, *s.* rouille, *f.*; — *v.a.* rouiller; — *v.n.* se rouiller. *Black —,* charbon, *m.*, nielle, *f.* *Brown —,* carie, cloque, *f.* *To rub* or *get the — off,* dérouiller

Rustic, *adj.* rustique; — *s.* rustre, paysan, campagnard, *m.*; rustaud, *m.* — *work,* (*arch.*) ouvrage rustique, *m.*

Rustically, *adv.* rustiquement

Rusticalness, *s.* rusticité, *f.*

Rusticate, *v.a.* reléguer à la campagne; (*accustom*) habituer à la campagne *or* à la vie des champs; (*of colleges*) renvoyer *or* expulser temporairement; (*build.*) rustiquer; — *v.n.* habiter la campagne. *To — oneself,* se retirer à la campagne, aller en villégiature. *To be —ing,* être en villégiature. *To go and —, to go*

—*ing*, aller en villégiature. —*d work*, (*arch.*) ouvrage rustique, *m.*

Rusticating, Rustication, *s.* villégiature, *f.*; (*of colleges*) renvoi (*m.*) *or* expulsion (*f.*) temporaire; (*build.*) rusticage, *m.*

Rusticity, *s.* rusticité, *f.*

Rustily, *adv.* à l'état de rouille

Rustiness, *s.* rouillement, enrouillement, *m.*, rouillure, rouille, *f.*; (*mustiness*) moisissure, *f.*; rancidité, rancissure, *f.*

Rusting, *s.* rouillement, enrouillement, *m.*

Rustle, *v.n.* bruire, frémir; (*of dresses*, &c.) faire froufrou; — *s.* *V.* **Rustling.** *To — against* ..., frôler ...

Rustling, *s.* bruissement, frémissement, *m.*; (*of dresses*, &c.) frôlement, froufrou, flouflou, *m.*

Rusty, *adj.* rouillé; (*worn out*) usé, délabré, vieux; (*of colour*) roux; (*of voice*) rauque, de rogomme; (*musty*) moisi; rance; (*surly*) maussade, chagrin, bourru. *To become* or *get* or *grow* or *turn* —, se rouiller; s'user; vieillir; roussir; devenir rauque; moisir, se moisir; rancir, se rancir; (*surly*) devenir maussade; renâcler; montrer les dents

Rut, *s.* (*of a wheel*) ornière, *f.*; (*of animals*) rut, *m.*; (*of the sea*) choc, *m.*; — *v.a.* couper d'ornières; — *v.n.* être en rut

Rutaceæ, *s.pl.* rutacées, *f.pl.*

Ruthenium, *s.* ruthénium, *m.*

Ruthful, *adj.* compatissant

Ruthless, &c. *V.* **Pitiless,** &c.

Rutilant, *adj.* rutilant

Rutilate, *v.n.* rutiler

Rutile, *s.* rutile, *m.*

Rutilite, *s.* rutilite, *f.*

Rutting, *s.* rut, *m.* — **season,** *s.* rut, *m.*

Rutty, *adj.* coupé d'ornières

Ryder, *s.* *V.* **Rider;** (*Dutch coin*) ryder, *m.*

Rye, *s.* seigle, *m.* — **bread,** *s.* pain de seigle, *m.* — **grass,** *s.* fromental, *m.*; ivraie vivace, *f.*

Ryot, *s.* ryott, *m.*

S

S, *s.* (*letter*) s, *f.* — **hole,** *s.* (*of violins*, &c.) esse, *f.*

'S, (*possessive case*) de ...; (*that of* ...) celui de ..., *m.*, celle de ..., *f.*; (*those of* ...) ceux de ..., *m.pl.*, celles de ..., *f.pl.*; (*belonging to* ..., *after the verb* '*to Be*') à ...; (*the house or shop of* ...) chez ... *John's book*, le livre de Jean. *Take my book and give me John's*, prenez mon livre et donnez-moi celui de Jean. *That book is John's*, ce livre-là est à Jean. *I am going to your sister's, to the baker's*, je vais chez votre sœur, chez le boulanger. *I was at your sister's, at the baker's*, j'étais chez votre sœur, chez le boulanger. *I come from your sister's, from the baker's*, je viens de chez votre sœur, de chez le boulanger

Sabadilla, *s.* cévadille, *f.*

Sabadilline, *s.* sabadilline, *f.*

Sabæan, *s. adj.* sabéen, *m.*, -ne, *f.*

Sabæanism, Sabæism, Sabaism, *s.* sabéisme, *m.*

Sabbat, *s.* sabbat, *m.*

Sabbatarian, *s. adj.* sabbataire, *m.f.*; rigide observateur du dimanche, *m.*; (*in contempt*) dimanchier, *m.*, -ière, *f.*

Sabbath, *s.* (*of the Jews*) sabbat, *m.*; (*Sunday*) dimanche, *m.*; (*rest*) repos, *m.* *Observance of the* —, repos du dimanche, *m.* — **day,** *s.* jour du sabbat, sabbat, *m.*; (*Sunday*) dimanche, *m.* — **breaker,** *s.* violateur (*m.*, -trice, *f.*) du sabbat *or* du dimanche. — **breaking,** *s.* violation du sabbat *or* du dimanche, *f.* —**less,** *adj.* sans sabbat; sans repos

Sabbatia, *s.* sabbatie, *f.*

Sabbatic, -al, *adj.* sabbatique; du sabbat. — *year*, année sabbatique

Sabbatism, *s.* repos, *m.*, abstention du travail, observation du dimanche, *f.*

Sabean, Sabian. *V.* **Sabæan**

Sabeism, Sabianism. *V.* **Sabæanism**

Sabine, *s.* (*bot.*) *V.* **Savin;** — *s. adj.* (*antiq.*) Sabin, *m.*, e, *f.* — *woman*, Sabine, *f.*

Sable, *s.* (*animal, its fur*) zibeline, martre zibeline, *f.*; (*her.*) sable, *m.*; (*mourning*) vêtement *or* habit de deuil, *m*; — *adj.* de zibeline; (*her.*) de sable; (*black*) noir; (*of mourning*) de deuil. — **mouse,** *s.* lemming, *m.*

Sabot, *s.* sabot, *m.*

Sabre, *s.* sabre, *m.*; — *v.a.* sabrer. — **bayonet,** *s.* sabre-baionnette, *m.* — **cut,** *s.* coup de sabre, *m.* — **fish,** *s.* trichiure, *m.* — **poniard,** *s.* sabre-poignard, *m.* — **tache,** — **tasche,** *s.* sabretache, *f.*

Sac, *s.* sac, *m.*, bourse, *f.*

Saccade, *s.* saccade, *f.*

Saccharate, *s.* saccharate, *m.*

Saccharic, *adj.* saccharique

Sacchariferous, *adj.* saccharifère

Saccharification, *s.* saccharification, *f.*

Saccharify, *v.a.* saccharifier; — *v.n.* se saccharifier

Saccharine, *adj.* saccharin

Saccharometer, *s.* saccharimètre, *m.*

Sacerdotal, *adj.* sacerdotal

Sacerdotalism, *s.* sacerdotalisme, *m.*

Sachel, *s.* *V.* **Satchel**

Sachet, *s.* sachet, *m.*

Sack, *s.* sac, *m.*; (*wine*) vin d'Espagne, *m.*; vin de liqueur, *m.*; — *v.a.* ensacher, mettre en sac; (*pillage*) saccager, mettre à sac; (*dismiss*) congédier, renvoyer. *Jumping in —s*, course en sac, *f.* *To give* ... *the* —, donner le sac à ..., donner à ... son compte, congédier ..., renvoyer ... — **but,** *s.* saquebute, *f.* — **cloth,** *s.* toile à sacs, *f.*; (*theol.*) sac, *m.* — **clothed,** *adj.* couvert d'un sac. — **cloth maker,** *s.* toilier, *m.* — **coat,** *s.* paletot-sac, *m.* —**ful,** *s.* *V.* **Bagful**

Sackage, *s.* saccagement, *m.*

Sacker, *s.* saccageur, *m.*

Sacking, *s.* (*pillage*) sac, saccagement, *m.*; (*coarse cloth*) toile à sacs, *f.*; (*of a bed*) sangle, *f.* *With — bottom*, à fond de sangle

Sacral, *adj.* (*anat.*) sacré

Sacrament, *s.* sacrement, *m.*; communion, *f.* *To receive* or *take the* —, communier. *To receive the last* —, être administré

Sacramental, *adj.* sacramentel

Sacramentally, *adv.* sacramentellement

Sacramentarian, Sacramentary, *s. adj.* sacramentaire, *s.m.*, *adj. m.f.*

Sacrarium, Sacrary, *s.* sacraire, *m.*

Sacred, *adj.* sacré (*generally after the noun, in French*); saint; (*to*) consacré (à). — *history*, histoire sacrée, histoire sainte, *f.* — *music*, musique sacrée, *f.* *The — heart* (*of Jesus*), le sacré cœur (de Jésus), *m.* *The — college*, le sacré collége, *m.*

Sacredly, *adv.* saintement; religieusement

Sacredness, *s.* caractère sacré, *m.*, sainteté, *f.*

Sacrificable, *adj.* sacrifiable

Sacrificatory, *adj.* sacrificatoire

Sacrifice, *v.a.n.* sacrifier; — *s.* sacrifice ('*to*,' à), *m.*; victime ('*to*,' de), *f.* *To fall a — to*, être victime de. *Alarming* —, (*tradesman's puff*) vente forcée pour cause de liquidation, *f.*

Sacrificer, *s.* sacrificateur, *m.*, -trice, *f.* — **ship,** *s.* sacrificature, *f.*

Sacrificial, *adj.* des sacrifices

Sacrificing, *adj* sacrificateur; — *s.* action de sacrifier, *f.*

Sacrilege, *s.* sacrilége, *m.*

Sacrilegious, *adj.* sacrilége

Sacrilegiously, *adv.* sacrilégement

Sacrilegiousness, *s.* nature sacrilége, *f.*

Sacrilegist, *s.* sacrilége, *m.f.*

Sacrist, Sacristan, *s.* sacristain, *m.*

Sacristy, *s.* sacristie, *f.*

Sacro- (*in compounds, anat.*) sacro- ...

Sacrum, *s.* (*anat.*) sacrum, *m.* *Os* —, os sacrum, sacrum, *m.*

Sad, *adj.* triste; pitoyable; déplorable; (*of a loss*) cruel. — *yellow*, triste sire, *m.*
Sadden, *v.a.* attrister; — *v.n.* s'attrister
Saddle, *s.* selle, *f.*; (*of mutton*, &c.) selle, *f.*; — *v.a.* seller; (*with a pack-saddle*) bâter; (*burden*) charger, accabler; (*clog*) empêtrer, embarrasser; (*implicate*) mettre sur le dos. *Lady's* —, *side* —, selle de dame *or* de femme. — *or harness*, (*horse*) à deux fins. — *of mutton*, selle de mouton. — **back,** *s.* dos ensellé, *m.*; (*tech.*) dos d'âne, *m.* — **backed,** *adj.* ensellé; (*tech.*) à *or* en dos d'âne. — **bag,** *s.* sacoche, *f.* — **bow,** *s.* arçon, *m.* — **cloth,** *s.* housse, *f.* — **gall,** *s.* écorchure, *f.* — **horse,** *s.* cheval de selle, *m.* — **maker,** *s.* sellier, *m.*; bourrelier, *m.* — **my nag,** *s.* (*game*) cheval fondu, *m.* — **room,** *s.* sellerie, *f.* — **tree,** *s.* pontet, *m.*
Saddler, *s.* sellier, *m.*
Saddlery, *s.* sellerie, *f.*; bourrellerie, *f.*
Saddling, *s.* sellage, *m.*
Sadducean, *adj.* saducéen
Sadducee, *s.* saducéen, *m.*, -ne, *f.*
Sadduceeism, Sadduceism, Sadducism, *s.* saducéisme, *m.*
Sadly, *adv.* tristement; d'une manière pitoyable *or* déplorable, pitoyablement, déplorablement; bien mal, mal; cruellement; (*much*) grandement, beaucoup, bien; très
Sadness, *s.* tristesse, *f.*
Safe, *adj.* (*without hurt*) sain et sauf; sans accident; (*not dangerous*) sans danger; sûr; (*affording safety, trusty, certain*) sûr; (*in safety, secure, sheltered*) en sûreté (contre), à l'abri (de); (*untouched*) intact; (*consistent with safety*) prudent; (*of distance*) sûr, convenable, respectueux; — *s.* (*for meat*, &c.) garde-manger, *m.*; (*iron* —, *for money*, &c.) caisse de sûreté, *f.*, coffre-fort, *m.* — *and sound*, sain et sauf. *It is not — to* ..., il y a du danger à ..., il n'est pas prudent de ... — **conduct,** *s.* sauf-conduit, *m.*; escorte, *f.* — **guard,** *s.* sauvegarde, protection, *f.*; (*rail.*) chasse-pierres, *m.*; *v.a.* sauvegarder, protéger. — **keeping,** *s.* bonne garde, *f.*; sûreté, *f.*
Safely, *adv.* sain et sauf; sans accident; (*in a safe place*) en sûreté, en lieu sûr; (*surely*) sûrement; (*without danger or fear*) sans danger; en toute sûreté; en toute sécurité, sans crainte
Safety, *s.* sûreté, *f.*; (*preservation*) salut, *m.*; — *adj.* de sûreté *Committee of public* —, comité de salut public, *m.* — **belt, — buoy,** *V.* **Life-belt,** &c. — **cock,** *s.* robinet de sûreté, *m.* — **fuse,** *s.* mèche anglaise à mines, *f.* — **lamp,** *s.* lampe de sûreté, *f.* — **valve,** *s.* soupape de sûreté, *f.* [franum, *m.*
Safflower, *s.* (*bot.*) carthame, *m.*; (*chem.*) sa-
Saffron, *s.* safran, *m.*; — *adj.* safrané, de safran, couleur de safran; — *v.a.* safraner. — **flower,** *s.* crocus, *m.* — **grower,** *s.* safranier, *m.* — **plantation,** *s.* safranière, *f.* — **seed,** *s.* graine de perroquet, *f.*
Saffrony, *adj* safrané
Sag, *v.n.* pencher, incliner, plier, ployer, se courber, pendre; dépasser; (*sink*) s'affaisser; (*stagger*) chanceler; (*nav.*) tomber; — *v.a.* faire pencher, pencher, incliner, plier, ployer, courber; (*sink*) affaisser [ligent
Sagacious, *adj.* sagace, pénétrant, fin, intel-
Sagaciously, *adv.* avec sagacité, sagacement
Sagaciousness, Sagacity, *s.* sagacité, *f.*
Sage, *s.* sage, *m.*; (*herb.*) sauge, *f.*; — *adj.* sage; prudent. — **cheese,** *s.* fromage persillé, *m.* — **tea,** *s.* eau de sauge, *f.*
Sagely, *adv.* sagement; prudemment
Sageness, *s.* sagesse, *f.*; prudence, *f.*
Sagger, *s.* casette, cazette, *f.*
Sagging, *s.* courbure, *f.*; affaissement, *m.*
Sagittal, *adj.* sagittal
Sagittarius, Sagittary, *s.* le Sagittaire, *m.*
Sagittate, *adj.* sagitté
Sago, *s.* sagou, *m.* — **palm, -tree,** *s.* sagoutier, palmier-sagou, *m.* — **soup,** *s.* potage au sagou, *m.*
Sagouin, *s.* sagouin, *m.*, e, *f.* [sauge
Sagy, *adj.* plein de sauge; qui a un goût de
Saic, *s.* saïque, *f.*
Said, *adj.* dit; susdit
Sail, *s.* voile, *f.*; (*collectively*) voilure, *f.*, voiles, *f.pl.*; (*ship*) vaisseau, *m.*; (*excursion*) promenade à la voile, *f.*; (*of windmills*) aile, *f.*; toile, *f.* *Under* —, à la voile, sous voiles. *To crowd* or *press* —, faire force de voiles. *To set* —, mettre à la voile, appareiller. *To shorten* —, diminuer de voiles. *To strike* —, amener les voiles; saluer des voiles; baisser pavillon. — **cloth,** *s.* toile à voiles, *f.* — **fish,** *s.* pèlerin, *m.* — — **loft,** *s.* voilerie, *f.* — **maker,** *s.* voilier, *m.* — **making,** *s.* voilerie, *f.* — **room,** *s.* soute aux voiles, *f.*
Sail, *v.n.* (*move on*) faire voile, naviguer, marcher, aller; faire route; (*depart*) mettre à la voile, appareiller, partir; (*swim*) voguer, flotter, nager; (*fly*) voler; (*hover*) planer; (*run*) courir; aller; (*cross*) faire la traversée (de ... à...); (... *knots*) filer (... nœuds); (*for amusement*) se promener en bateau, faire une promenade sur l'eau; — *v.a.* manœuvrer; naviguer sur; voguer dans. *To be on the point of —ing*, être en partance. — **about,** croiser; se promener. — **down,** (*a river*) descendre. — **up,** (*a river*) [remonter
Sailable, *adj.* navigable
Sailer, *s.* voilier, *m.* *Fast* or *fine* or *good* —, bon voilier. *Heavy* —, mauvais voilier. *Prime* —, grand *or* fin voilier. *She is a good* —, il est bon voilier, c'est un bon voilier
Sailing, *s.* navigation, *f.*; (*setting sail*) appareillage, *m.*; (*departure*) départ, *m.*, partance, *f.*; (*speed*, &c.) marche, *f.*; (*crossing*) traversée, *f.*; (*excursion*) promenade à la voile, *f.*; (*flight*) vol, *m.*; —**s,** *pl.* bâtiments en partance, *m.pl.*; départs, *m.pl.*; — *adj.* à voiles; (*of speed*) d'une marche ... *Fast* —, d'une marche rapide. — **boat,** *s.* bateau à voiles, *m.* — **club,** *s.* société des régates, *f.* — **match,** *s.* course à la voile, *f.* — **order,** *s.* ordre de marche, *m.* — **packet,** *s.* paquebot à voiles, *m.* — **vessel,** *s.* navire à voiles, *m.*
Sailor, *s.* marin, *m.*; (*common* —) matelot, *m.* —*s' home*, asile des matelots, *m.*
Sainfoin, *s.* sainfoin, *m.*
Saint, *s. adj.* saint, *m.*, e, *f.*; (*in contempt*) béat, *m.*, e, *f.*; — *v.a.* canoniser. —*'s bell*, cloche de l'élévation, *f.* —*'s day*, fête, *f.* (*V.* **All**). — **Andrew's cross,** *s.* croix de Saint-André, *f.* — **John's wort,** *s.* herbe de la Saint-Jean, *f.* — **Paul's,** *s.* Saint-Paul, *m.* — **Simonian,** *s. adj.* saint-simonien, *m.*, -ne, *f.* — **Simonianism,** *s.* saint-simonisme, *m.* — **Vitus's dance,** *s.* (la) danse de saint-Guy, *f.*
Sainted, *adj.* saint; sacré; canonisé
Saintfoin, *s.* sainfoin, *m.*
Saintlike, *adj.* (*pers.*) saint; (*things*) de saint
Saintliness, *s.* sainteté, *f.* [**Saintlike**
Saintly, *adv.* saintement, en saint; — *adj.* *V.*
Saintship, *s.* sainteté, *f.*
Sajou, *s.* sajou, sapajou, *m.*
Sake, *s.* *For the — of* ..., *for* ...*'s* —, pour l'amour de, pour, à cause de; par égard pour; par; (*in order to, for*) pour; (*in order to have*) pour avoir. *For my* —, pour l'amour de moi, pour moi, à cause de moi, par égard pour moi. *For argument's* —, pour les besoins de la cause; pour un instant. *For charity's* —, pour l'amour de Dieu. *For conscience* —, pour l'acquit de sa conscience. *For form's* —, pour la forme. *For God's* —, pour l'amour de Dieu; pour Dieu; je vous en supplie. *For goodness* or *mercy's* —, par grâce; de grâce. *For o.'s own* —, pour soi-même, pour soi. *For pity's* —, par pitié
Saker, *s.* sacre, *m.*
Sakeret, *s.* sacret, *m.*
Saki, *s* saki, *m.*
Sal, *s.* (*salt*) sel, *m.*; (*tree, wood*) sal, *m.* — **am-**

moniac, sel ammoniac, *m.* — *volatile*, sel volatil, *m.* [bonne vente
Salable, *adj.* vendable; facile à vendre, de
Salableness, *s.* facilité de vente, *f.*
Salably, *adv.* d'une manière vendable
Salacious, *adj.* lascif, lubrique
Salaciously, *adv.* lascivement, lubriquement
Salaciousness, Salacity, *s.* lasciveté, lubricité, *f.*
Salad, *s.* salade, *f.* — **basket,** *s.* panier à salade, *m.* — **bowl, -dish,** *s.* saladier, *m.* — **mixture,** *s.* assaisonnement pour salades, *m.* — **oil,** *s.* huile à manger, *f.* — **spoon,** *s.* cuiller à salade, *f.*
Salading, *s.* salade, *f.*
Salamander, *s.* salamandre, *f.*; (*cook.*) fer à gratiner, *m.*; four de campagne, *m.*
Salamandrine, *adj.* de salamandre
Salary, *s.* appointements, *m.pl.*, traitement, *m.*; honoraires, *m.pl.*; (*of ambassadors, high functionaries*) traitement, *m.*; (*fig.*) salaire, *m.*; — *v.a.* salarier; appointer
Sale, *s.* vente, *f.*; débit, *m.*; (*putting up for sale*) mise en vente, *f.* *For* —, à vendre; en vente. *For private* —, à vendre à l'amiable. *On* —, en vente. *On* — *or return*, en dépôt, à condition. *To offer* (or *put up*) *for* —, mettre en vente. *To meet with a ready* —, être de bonne vente, se vendre bien. — **bill,** *s.* affiche de vente, *f.* *Bill of* —, lettre de vente, *f.* — **goods,** *s.pl.* marchandises de pacotille, *f.pl.* — **room,** *s.* salle de vente, *f.* —**s-book,** *s.* livre de vente, *m.* —**sman,** *s.* (*dealer*) marchand (de ...), *m.*; (*seller*) vendeur, *m.*; (*agent*) facteur (de la halle), courtier (de commerce), *m.* —**swoman,** *s.* (*dealer*) marchande (de ...), *f.*; (*seller*) vendeuse, *f.*
Saleable, &c. *V.* **Salable,** &c.
Salentine, *s. adj.* Salentin, *m.*, e, *f.*
Salep, *s.* salep, *m.*
Saliant, *adj.* *V.* **Salient**
Salic, *adj.* salique
Salicaria, *s.* salicaire, *f.*
Salicine, *s.* salicine, *f.*
Salient, *adj.* qui saute; bondissant; (*projecting, prominent, conspicuous, math., fort., her.*) saillant; — *s.* (*fort.*) saillant, *m.*
Saliferous, *adj.* salifère
Salifiable, *adj.* salifiable
Salification, *s.* salification, *f.*
Salify, *v.a.* salifier
Salina, *s.* salin, *m.*; saline, *f.*
Saline, *adj.* salin; — *s.* source salée, *f.*; salin, *m.*; saline, *f.*
Salinometer, *s.* salinomètre, *m.*
Saliva, *s.* salive, *f.*
Salivant, *adj. s.* salivant, *adj.m.*, e, *f.*, salivant, *s.m.*
Salivary, *adj.* salivaire
Salivate, *v.a.* faire saliver; — *v.n.* saliver
Salivation, *s.* salivation, *f.* *To be under* —, saliver
Salivous, *adj.* saliveux
Sallenders, *s.pl.* (*vet.*) solandre, *f.*
Sallow, *adj.* jaunâtre, jaune; pâle, blême, blafard; — *s.* *V.* **Willow.** — **thorn,** *s.* argousier, *m.*, hippophaé, *f.*
Sallowness, *s.* teinte jaunâtre, *f.*; (*complexion*) teint jaunâtre, teint blême, *m.*, pâleur, *f.*
Sally, *s.* saillie, *f.*, trait d'esprit, *m.*; folie, boutade, *f.*; écart, *m.*; excursion, *f.*; (*mil.*) sortie, *f.*; — *v.n.* (— **forth,** — **out**) faire une sortie, sortir. — **lunn,** *s.* madeleine, brioche, *f.* — **port,** *s.* porte de sortie, *f.*; (*nav.*) sabord de fuite, *m.*
Salmagundi, *s.* *V.* **Hotch-potch**
Salmi, Salmis, *s.* salmis, *m.*
Salmon, *s.* saumon, *m.* *Young* —, saumoneau, *m.* — **fishery,** *s.* pêche du saumon, *f.*; saumonerie, *f.* — **kettle,** *s.* saumonière, *f.* — **peal, -pink,** *s.* saumoneau, *m.* — **trout,** *s.* truite saumonée, *f.*
Salmonet, *s.* saumoneau, *m.*
Salmonidæ, *s.pl.* salmones, *m.pl.*
Saloon, *s.* salon, *m.*; (*of a vessel*) grand salon, *m.*, premières, *f.pl.*; (*theat.*) foyer (du public), *m.* — **passenger,** *s.* voyageur (*m.*, -euse, *f.*) de premières
Salsafy, Salsify, *s.* salsifis, *m.*
Salt, *s.* sel, *m.*; (*seaman*) marin, loup de mer, *m.*; —**s,** *pl.* sels, *m.pl.*; sel de ..., *m.*; — *adj.* de sel; à sel; (*containing salt*) salé; — *v.a.* saler. *Bitter* —*s*, *Epsom* —*s*, sel anglais, sel d'Epsom, *m.* *To* — *it on* or *upon*, saler; rançonner. *He is not worth his* —, il ne vaut pas le pain qu'il mange. — **beef,** *s.* bœuf salé, *m.* — **box,** *s.* boîte au sel, salière, *f.* — **cat,** *s.* salignon, *m.* — **cellar,** *s.* salière, *f.* — **duty,** *s.* *V.* — **tax.** — **fish,** *s.* poisson salé, *m.*, salaison, *f.*; (*cod*) morue salée, *f.* — **garden,** *s.* salin, *m.*, saline, *f.* — **holder,** *s.* salière, *f.* — **lake,** *s.* lac salé, *m.* — **maker,** *s.* saunier, *m.* — **making,** *s.* saunaison, *f.* — **marsh, -meadow,** *s.* marais salant, *m.*, paludière, *f.*; pré salé, *m.* — **marsh worker,** *s.* paludier, *m.* — **meat,** *s.* viande salée, salaison, *f.* — **mine,** *s.* saline, mine de sel, *f.* — **pan,** *s.* salin, *m.* — **pit,** *s.* saline, *f.*, parc, *m.* — **pork,** *s.* porc salé, salé, *m.* — **provisions,** *s.pl.* viandes salées, salaisons, *f.pl.* — **rock,** *s.* rocher de sel, *m.* — **selling,** *s.* saunage, *m.* — **spoon,** *s.* pelle à sel, *f.* — **spring,** *s.* source salée, *f.* — **tax,** *s.* impôt sur le sel, *m.*, (*old*) gabelle, *f.* — **trade,** *s.* saunage, commerce de sel, *m.* — **water,** *s.* eau salée, eau de mer, *f.* — **water fish,** *s.* poisson de mer, *m.* — **works,** *s.pl.* salin, *m.*, saline, saunerie, *f.* — **wort,** *s.* soude, *f.*; salicorne, *f.*
Saltation, *s.* saut, *m.*; palpitation, *f.*, battement, *m.*
Saltatorial, *adj.* du saut
Salter, *s.* saleur, *m.*, -euse, *f.*; (*salt-seller*) saunier, marchand de sel, *m.*
Saltern, *s.* saline, *f.*, salin, *m.*
Saltier. *V.* **Saltire**
Saltigrade, *adj.s.* saltigrade, *adj.m.f.*, *s.m.*
Salting, *s.* salaison, *f.*, salage, *m.* — **tub,** *s.* saloir, *m.*
Saltire, *s.* sautoir, *m.* — **ways, -wise,** *adv.* en sautoir
Saltish, *adj.* un peu salé; saumâtre
Saltishness, *s.* goût salin, *m.*; goût saumâtre, *m.*
Saltless, *adj.* sans sel; fade
Saltness, *s.* salure, *f.*
Saltpetre, *s.* salpêtre, *m.* — **bed,** *s.* nitrière, *f.* — **maker,** *s.* salpêtrier, *m.* — **making,** *s.* salpêtrage, *m.* — **works,** *s.pl.* salpêtrière, *f.*
Saltpetrous, *adj.* salpêtreux
Salty, *adj.* salé
Salubrious, *adj.* salubre
Salubriously, *adv.* salubrement
Salubrity, *s.* salubrité, *f.*
Salutarily, *adv.* salutairement
Salutariness, *s.* nature salutaire, *f.*
Salutary, *adj.* salutaire
Salutation, *s.* salut, *m.*, salutation, *f.*
Salute, *v.a.* saluer; (*to kiss*) embrasser; (*to welcome*) accueillir; — *s.* salut, *m.*; salutation, *f.*; (*kiss*) baiser, *m.*; (*artil.*) salve, *f.*; (*mil., nav.*) salut, *m.* *A* — *of* 101 *guns*, une salve de cent-un coups. *To beat a* —, battre aux champs. *To fire a* —, tirer une salve; (*nav.*) saluer. *To return a* —, rendre un salut
Saluter, *s.* personne qui salue, *f.*
Salvage, *s.* (*due*) droit de sauvetage, *m.*; (*act*) sauvetage, *m.*; (*goods*) objets sauvés, *m.pl.* — **money,** *s.* prime de sauvetage, *f.*
Salvation, *s.* salut, *m.*
Salve, *s.* onguent, *m.*, pommade, *f.*; emplâtre, *m.*; (*fig.*) remède, *m.*; baume, *m.*; — *v.a.* (*to save*) sauver; (*from shipwreck, fire,* &c.) sauveter; (*fig.*) remédier à; secourir; sauver. — **over,** *v.a.* adoucir; faire peu de cas de
Salver, *s.* (*waiter*) plateau, *m.*; (*saucer*) soucoupe, *f.*
Salvo, *s.* réserve, restriction, exception, *f.*; subterfuge, *m.*, échappatoire, *f.*; (*artil.*) salve, *f.*
Salvor, *s.* sauveteur, *m.*
Samaritan, *s. adj.* Samaritain, *m.*, e, *f.*
Sambo (*m.*), **Samba** (*f.*), *s.* griffe, *m.f.*; (*jest.*) moricaud, *m.*, e, *f.*
Same, *adj.* même; (*substant.*) même chose, *f.*

The —, (*the above-mentioned*) ledit, *m.*, ladite, *f.*, lesdits, *m.pl.*, lesdites, *f.pl.*; (*the same thing*) la même chose; (*in the same manner*) de même. *All* or *just the* –, tout de même. *One and the* –, un seul et même. *To do, to say the* —, en faire, en dire autant (*or* faire, dire de même). *It is the* — *to me*, cela m'est égal. *It is all the* —, cela ne fait rien; cela m'est égal. *It is the* — *as saying*, cela revient à dire

Sameness, *s.* identité, *f.*; ressemblance, *f.*; uniformité, *f.*; monotonie, *f.*

Samian, *s. adj.* Samien, *m.*, -ne, *f.*

Samlet, *s.* saumoneau, *m.*

Samnites, *s.pl.* Samnites, *m.pl.*

Samoyeds, Samoyedes, *s.pl.* les Samoyèdes, *m.pl.*

Samp, *s.* gaude, *f.*

Samphire, *s.* passe-pierre, crête-marine, *f.*

Sample, *s.* échantillon, *m.*; — *v.a.* échantillonner. *By* — *post*, comme échantillon. — **bottle,** *s.* bouteille d'échantillon, *f.*

Sampler, *s.* modèle, patron, *m.*; canevas (pour marquer), marquoir, *m.*; (*pers.*) échantillonneur, *m.*, -euse, *f.*

Sampling, *s.* échantillonnage, *m.*

Samson's post, *s.* (*nav.*) épontille des écoutilles, *f.*

Sanability, Sanableness, *s.* curabilité, *f.*

Sanable, *adj.* guérissable

Sanative, *adj.* *V.* **Sanatory**

Sanativeness, *s.* vertu curative, *f.*

Sanatorium, *s.* maison de santé, *f.*; infirmerie, *f.*

Sanatory, *adj.* curatif; sanitaire

Sanctification, *s.* sanctification, *f.*

Sanctified, *adj.* sanctifié; (*in contempt*) béat

Sanctifier, *s.* sanctificateur, *m.*, -trice, *f.*

Sanctify, *v.a.* sanctifier

Sanctifying, *adj.* sanctifiant, sanctificateur; — *s.* sanctification, *f.*

Sanctimonious, *adj.* saint, dévot; (*in contempt*) béat, hypocrite

Sanctimoniously, *adv.* saintement, dévotement; (*in contempt*) d'un air béat, hypocritement

Sanctimoniousness, Sanctimony, *s.* sainteté, dévotion, *f.*; air de sainteté, *m.*

Sanction, *s.* sanction, *f.*; autorité, *f.*; — *v.a.* sanctionner; approuver

Sanctity, *s.* sainteté, *f.*

Sanctuary, *s.* sanctuaire, *m.*; asile, refuge, *m.*

Sanctum, *s.* sanctuaire, *m.*; retraite, *f.*; cabinet particulier, cabinet, *m.* — *sanctorum*, le saint des saints, *m.*

Sanctus, *s.* sanctus, *m.*

Sand, *s.* sable, *m.*, (*fine*) sablon, *m.*; — *v.a.* sabler. *Small* or *fine* —, sablon, sable fin, *m.* — **bag,** *s.* (*for doors, windows*) bourrelet, *m.*; (*mil.*) sac de *or* à terre, *m.* — **bank,** *s.* banc de sable, *m.* *To run on a* — *bank*, s'ensabler. — **bath,** *s.* bain de sable, *m.* — **bed,** *s.* lit de sable, *m.* — **blind,** *adj.* qui a la vue trouble. — **box,** *s.* poudrier, *m.* — **box tree,** *s.* sablier, *m.* — **coloured,** *adj.* couleur de sable. — **crack,** *s.* (*vet.*) solbature, *f.* — **drift,** *s.* amas de sable, *m.* — **eel,** *s.* équille, *f.*, lançon, *m.* — **flea,** *s.* talitre, *m.* — **flood,** *s.* mer de sable, *f.* — **glass,** *s.* sablier, *m.* — **grouse,** *s.* ganga, *m.* — **hill,** *s.* dune, *f.* — **hopper,** *s.* talitre, *m.* — **launce,** *s.* *V.* — **eel.** — **man,** *s.* sablier, sablonnier, *m.* — **mole,** *s* *V.* **Mole-rat.** — **paper,** *s.* papier de sable, papier sablé, papier de verre, *m.* — **pipe,** *s.* puits naturel, *m* — **piper,** *s.* bécasseau, chevalier, *m.* — **pit,** *s.* sablière, sablonnière, *f.* — **ray,** *s.* *V.* **Homelin.** – **reed,** *s.* roseau des sables, *m.* — **smelt,** *s.* athérine, *f.* — **stone,** *s.* grès, *m.* — **stone grit,** *s.* grès siliceux, *m.* — **stone quarry,** *s.* grésière, *f.* — **worm,** *s.* arénicole, *m.* — **wort,** *s.* sabline, *f.*

Sandal, *s.* sandale, *f.*; (*wood*) santal, sandal, *m.* — **wood,** *s.* bois de santal, santal, *m.*

Sandarach, *s.* sandaraque, *f.*

Sanded, *adj.* sablé; (*sandy*) sablonneux

Sanderling, *s.* sanderling, *m.*

Sandiness, *s.* nature sablonneuse, *f.*; (*colour*) couleur rousse, *f.*

Sandiver, *s.* suint de verre, sel de verre, fiel de verre, *m.*

Sandwich, *s.* sandwich, *m.* — **man,** *s* (*jest.*) *V.* **Board-man**

Sandy, *adj.* sablonneux; sableux; de sable; (*of colour*) d'un blond ardent, roux; (*of flour*) sableux. — **coloured,** *adj.* d'un blond ardent, roux. — **haired,** *adj.* roux

Sane, *adj.* sain, sain d'esprit. — *man*, homme d'un jugement sain, *m.*; bon esprit, *m.*

Saneness, *s.* sanité, sainеté, *f.*

Sangaree, *s.* sang-gris, *m.*

Sang-froid, *s.* sang-froid, *m.*

Sangraal, Sangreal, *s.* Saint Graal, *m.*

Sanguiferous, *adj.* sanguifère

Sanguification, *s.* sanguification, *f.*

Sanguify, *v.a.* sanguifier; — *v.n.* se sanguifier

Sanguinaria, *s.* sanguinaire, *f.*

Sanguinarily, *adv.* sanguinairement

Sanguinariness, *s.* nature sanguinaire, *f.*

Sanguinary, *adj.* sanguinaire

Sanguine, *adj.* sanguin; ardent, vif; confiant, plein de confiance. *I am not very* — *as to* ..., je n'ai pas grande confiance en ...

Sanguinely, *adv.* ardemment, vivement; avec confiance

Sanguineness, *s.* nature sanguine, *f.*; couleur de sang, *f.*; ardeur, vivacité, *f.*; confiance, *f.*; vive attente, *f.*; grand espoir, *m.*

Sanguineous, *adj.* sanguin

Sanguinolent, *adj.* sanguinolent

Sanhedrim, *s.* sanhédrin, *m.*

Sanies, *s.* sanie, *f.*

Sanious, *adj.* sanieux

Sanitarian, Sanitarist, *s.* hygiéniste, *m.*

Sanitarium. *V.* **Sanatorium**

Sanitary, *adj.* sanitaire; hygiénique; de salubrité. — *inspector*, inspecteur de salubrité, *m.*

Sanity, *s.* sanité, *f.*, état sain, jugement sain, *m.*

Sanscrit, Sanskrit, *s. adj.* sanscrit, *s.m.*, sanscrit, *adj.m.*, e, *f.*

Sanscrit-ic, -ism, -ist. *V.* page 3, § 1

Santon, *s.* santon, *m.*

Santonine, *s.* santonine, *f.*

Sap, *s.* sève, *f.*; (*mil.*) sape, *f.*; — *v.a.n.* saper. — **colour,** *s.* couleur végétale, *f.* — **green,** *s.* vert de vessie, *m.* —**less,** *adj.* sans sève; (*dry*) sec, desséché. — **wood,** *s.* aubier, *m.*

Sapajou, *s.* sapajou, *m.*

Sapan, *s.* sapan, bois de sapan, *m.* — **tree,** *s.* sapan, *m.* — **wood,** *s.* bois de sapan, *m.*

Saphena, *s.* saphène, *f.*

Sapid, *adj.* sapide

Sapidity, Sapidness, *s.* sapidité, *f.*

Sapience, *s.* sagesse, *f.*

Sapient, *adj.* sage

Sapling, *s.* plant, plantard, plançon, *m.*

Sapodilla, *s.* sapotille, *f.* — **tree,** *s.* sapotillier, sapotier, *m.*

Saponaceous, *adj.* saponacé

Saponic, *adj.* saponique

Saponifiable, *adj.* saponifiable

Saponification, *s.* saponification, *f.*

Saponify, *v.a.* saponifier; — *v.n.* se saponifier

Saponine, *s.* saponine, *f.*

Saponite, *s.* saponite, *f.*

Saponule, *s.* savonule, saponule, *m.*

Sapor, *s.* saveur, *f.*

Saporific, *adj.* saporifique

Sapper, *s.* sapeur, *m.* —*s and miners*, corps du génie, *m.*, troupes (*f.pl.*) *or* soldats (*m.pl.*) du génie

Sapphic, *adj. s.* saphique, *adj. m.f.*, *s.m.*

Sapphire, *s.* saphir, *m.*

Sapphirine, *adj.* saphirin

Sappiness, *s.* abondance de sève, *f.*

Sapping, *s.* sapement, *m.*, sape, *f.*

Sappy, *adj.* séveux; de sève; plein de sève

Saraband, *s.* sarabande, *f.*

Saracen, *s. adj.* Sarrasin, *m.*, e, *f.*

Saracenic, -al, *adj.* sarrasin, sarracénique
Sarcasm, *s.* sarcasme, *m.*
Sarcastic, -al, *adj.* sarcastique
Sarcastically, *adv.* d'une manière sarcastique
Sarcenet, *s.* florence, *m.*
Sarcocele, *s.* sarcocèle, *f.*
Sarcocol, Sarcocolla, *s.* sarcocolle, *f.* — **tree,** *s.* sarcocollier, *m.*
Sarcolog-ic, al, -y. *V.* page 3, § 1
Sarcoma, *s.* sarcome, *m.*
Sarcomatous, *adj.* sarcomateux
Sarcophagus, *s.* sarcophage, *m.*; (*cellaret*) cave à vin, *f.*
Sardanapal-ic, -ism. *V.* page 5, § 1
Sardine, *s.* sardine, *f.* — **boat, -net,** *s.* [sardinier, *m.*
Sardinian, *s. adj.* Sarde, *m.f.*
Sardonic, Sardonian, *adj.* sardonique, [sardonien
Sardonyx, *s.* sardoine, *f.*
Sargasso Sea, *s.* Mer des Sargasses, *f.*
Sarigue, *s.* sarigue, *m.f.*
Sarmatian, *s. adj.* Sarmate, *m.f.*
Sarplier, *s.* serpillière, *f.*
Sarracenia, *s.* sarracénie, *f.*
Sarsaparilla, *s.* salsepareille, *f.*
Sartorius, *s.* couturier, *m.*
Sash, *s.* ceinture, *f.*; (*mark of distinction*) écharpe, *f.*; (*frame*) châssis, *m.*; — *v.a.* parer d'une ceinture; garnir de châssis. — **door,** *s.* porte vitrée, *f.* — **frame,** *s.* châssis dormant, *m.* — **window,** *s.* fenêtre à coulisse *or* à guillotine, *f.* — **work,** *s.* châssis, *m.*
Sassafras, *s.* sassafras, *m.*
Satanic, -al, *adj.* satanique
Satanically, *adv.* d'une manière satanique
Satchel, *s.* sachet, petit sac, *m.*; (*of lawyers*) sac, *m.*; (*of children*) cartable, *m.*, gibecière, *f.*, sac, carton, *m.* [insatiable
Sate, *v.a.* rassasier ('*with,*' de). —**less,** *adj.*
Satellite, *s.* satellite, *m.*
Satiate, *v.a.* rassasier ('*with,*' de); — *adj.* [rassasié
Satiety, *s.* satiété, *f.*
Satin, *s.* satin, *m.*; — *adj.* de satin; satiné; — *v.a.* satiner. — **bird,** *s.* piroll, pirolle, *m.* — **stitch,** *s.* plumetis, *m.* — **wood,** *s.* citronnier, bois de citron, espénille, *m.*
Satinet, *s.* satinet, *m.*, satinade, *f.*
Satining, *s.* satinage, *m.*
Satiny, *adj.* satiné
Satire, *s.* satire, *f.*
Satir-ic, al, -ically. *V.* page 3, § 1
Satiricalness, *s.* nature satirique, *f.*
Satirist, *s.* satirique, *m.*, satiriste, *m.f.*
Satirize, *v.a.* satiriser
Satisfaction, *s.* satisfaction, *f.*; contentement, *m.*; réparation, *f.*; (*of a debt*) acquittement, *m.* [sante; suffisamment
Satisfactorily, *adv.* d'une manière satisfai-
Satisfactoriness, *s.* nature satisfaisante, *f.*
Satisfactory, *adj.* satisfaisant
Satisfied, *part. adj.* (*with things*) satisfait (de), (*with pers., or things*) content (de); (*convinced*) convaincu (de), certain (de), sûr (de); (*settled*) fixé; &c. (*V.* **Satisfy**)
Satisfy, *v.a.n.* satisfaire; satisfaire à; contenter; (*with food*) rassasier; (*o.'s passions*) contenter, assouvir; (*persuade*) convaincre, persuader; (*assure*) assurer; (*settle*) fixer; (*a debt*) acquitter
Satisfyingly, *adv.* d'une manière satisfaisante
Satrap, *s.* satrape, *m.*
Satrapal, *adj.* satrapique
Satrapy, *s.* satrapie, *f.*
Satteen, *s.* satinade, *f.*
Saturability, *s.* saturabilité, *f.*
Saturable, *adj.* saturable [rant, *s.m.*
Saturant, *adj. s.* saturant, *adj. m.*, e, *f.*, satu-
Saturate, *v.a.* saturer ('*with,*' de)
Saturator, *s.* saturateur, *m.*
Saturday, *s.* samedi, *m.*
Saturnalia, *s.pl.* saturnales, *f.pl.*
Saturnalian, *adj.* des saturnales
Saturnian, *adj.* saturnien
Saturnine, *adj.* sombre, taciturne, mélancolique; (*chem., med.*) saturnin
Saturnite, *s.* saturnite, *f.*
Satyr, *s.* satyre, *m.*
Satyre, *s.* satyre, *f.*
Satyriasis, *s.* satyriasis, *m.*
Satyric, *adj.* satyrique
Satyrion, Satyrium, *s.* satyrion, *m.*
Sauce, *s.* sauce, *f.*; purée (de ...), *f.*; (*of stewed fruit*) compote (de ...), *f.*; (*fig.*) impertinence, insolence, *f.*; — *v.a.* assaisonner; (*the taste*) flatter; (*be saucy to*) dire des impertinences à. — **boat,** *s.* (petite) saucière, *f.* — **box,** *s.* impertinent, *m.*, e, *f.*, insolent, *m.*, e, *f.* — **ladle,** *s.* cuiller à sauce, *f.* — **pan,** *s.* casserole, *f.*; poêlon, *m.*; bassine, *f.*; marmite, *f.* — **panful,** *s.* casserolée, *f.*; poêlonnée, *f.* — **tureen,** *s.* saucière, *f.*
Saucer, *s.* soucoupe, *f.*; (*of a capstan*) saucier, *m.*, écuelle, *f.*, chaudron, *m.* —**ful,** *s.* soucoupe pleine, *f.*
Saucily, *adv.* insolemment, impertinemment
Sauciness, *s.* impertinence, impudence, insolence, *f.* [cisson, *m.*
Saucisse, Saucisson, *s.* saucisse, *f.*, sau-
Saucy, *adj.* impertinent, impudent, insolent. — *fellow* or *thing,* impudent, *m.*, e, *f.*, insolent, [*m.*, e, *f.*
Sauerkraut, *s.* *V.* **Sourkrout**
Saunter, *v.n.* flâner; — **away,** *v.a.* dissiper, [perdre
Saunterer, *s.* flâneur, *m.*, -euse, *f.*
Sauntering, *s.* flânerie, *f.*
Saurian, *adj. s.* saurien, *adj. m.*, -ne, *f.*, sau- [rien, *s.m.*
Saury pike, *s.* scombrésoce, *m.*
Sausage, *s.* (*small*) saucisse, *f.*; (*large, and highly seasoned*) saucisson, *m.* — **cake,** *s.* *V.* — **meat cake.** — **finger,** *s.* (*jest.*) boudin, *m.* — **making machine,** *s.* hachoir à saucisses, *m.* — **meat,** *s.* chair à saucisse, *f.* — **meat cake,** *s.* pain de porc frais, *m.*, attignole, *f.* — **roll,** *s.* pantin, *m.*
Savage, *adj.* sauvage; féroce; brutal; furieux; — *s.* sauvage, *m.f.* *A — animal* (*dog,* &c.), un animal (chien, &c.) féroce
Savagely, *adv.* d'une manière féroce *or* barbare; en sauvage; cruellement; furieusement; brutalement [fureur, *f.*; brutalité, *f.*
Savageness, *s.* sauvagerie, *f.*; férocité, *f.*;
Savagery, *s.* férocité, barbarie, cruauté, *f.*
Savanna, Savannah, *s.* savane, *f.*
Savant, *s.* savant, *m.*
Save, *v.a.* (*rescue, preserve*) sauver; préserver; (*spare, as trouble* &c.) épargner, éviter; (*keep from wear and tear, use sparingly*) ménager, (*till* ...) garder (jusqu'à ...); (*lay by, put by*) mettre de côté, garder; réserver; (*lay up, prevent waste*) économiser, épargner; (*gain, as time* &c.) gagner; (*not to miss*) ne pas manquer, ne pas perdre, profiter de; (*help, as appearances*) sauver; (*avoid*) éviter; (*prevent*) prévenir; — *v.n.* économiser, faire des économies; — *prep.* sauf, hors, excepté; si ce n'est; (ne ...) que. *God* — ..., Dieu sauve ...! Dieu protège ...! vive ...! (*pl.*) vivent ...! *God — the king, the queen!* Dieu sauve le roi, la reine! vive le roi, la reine! — **all,** *s.* brûle-tout, binet, *m.* — **up,** *v.a.* épargner; [garder
Saveloy, *s.* cervelas, *m.*
Saver, *s.* sauveur, *m.*, libérateur, *m.*, -trice, *f.*; (*economist*) économe, *m.f.*, ménager, *m.*, -ère, *f.*
Savin, Savine, *s.* sabine, *f.*, savinier, *m.*
Saving, *adv.* sauveur; (*sparing*) économe, ménager; (*things*) économique; de réserve; (*of the soul*) salutaire; — *s.* épargne, économie, réserve, *f.*; (*rescue from wreck, drowning, fire,* &c.) sauvetage, *m.*; (*of the soul,* &c.) salut, *m.*; — *prep.* *V.* **Save,** *prep.* — *of life,* — *of property,* (*from wreck, drowning, fire,* &c.) sauvetage, *m.* —**s-bank,** *s.* caisse d'épargne, *f.*
Savingly, *adv.* économiquement, avec économie; (*of the soul*) pour le salut
Savingness, *s.* économie, *f.*; épargne, *f.*
Saviour, *s.* Sauveur, *m.*

Savonette, *s.* savonnette, *f.*
Savory, *s.* (*bot.*) sarriette, *f.*
Savour, *s.* saveur, *f.*; goût, *m.*; odeur, *f.*, parfum, *m.*; — *v.n.a.* avoir le goût (de); savourer; (*smell*) sentir; (*of*) sentir (le, la, les). **—less,** *adj.* sans saveur, fade, insipide; sans odeur
Savourily, *adv.* savoureusement, avec plaisir
Savouriness, *s.* saveur, *f.*; bon goût, *m.*; odeur agréable, *f.*
Savoury, *adj.* savoureux; exquis, délicieux; ragoûtant; (*of smell*) suave, doux, agréable; (*of herbs*) *V.* **Sweet.** — *tongue*, langue fourrée, *f.*
Savoy, *s.* la Savoie, *f.*; (— *cabbage*) chou de Milan, *m.*, chou frisé, *m.* **— cake, -biscuit,** *s.* gâteau de Savoie, *m.*
Savoyard, *s. adj.* Savoisien, *m*, -ne, *f.*; (*chimney-sweeper*, &c., *or in contempt*) Savoyard, *m.*, e, *f.*
Saw, *s.* scie, *f.*; (*book-bind.*) grecque, *f.*; (*a saying*) dicton, adage, proverbe, *m.*; — *v.a.* scier; — *v.n.* scier; (*things*) se scier. *Circular* —, scie circulaire, *f.* **— bench,** *s.* scierie, *f.* **— bones,** *s.* (*pers.*) carabin, *m.* **—dust,** *s.* sciure de bois, *f.*; sciure, *f.* **— file,** *s.* lime à scie, *f.*, tiers-point, *m.* **— fish,** *s.* scie, *f.* **— fly,** *s.* porte-scie, *m.* **— frame,** *s.* scie à découper, *f.* **— mill,** *s.* machine à scier, *f.*; scierie, *f.* **— pad,** *s.* porte-scie, *m.* **— pit,** *s.* fosse de scieur de long, *f.* **— wort,** *s.* sarrette, *f.* **— yard,** [*s.* scierie, *f.*
Sawable, *adj.* sciable
Sawder (Soft). *V.* **Soft**
Sawing, *s.* sciage, *m.* **— machine,** *s.* machine à scier, scierie, *f.* **— works,** *s.pl.* scierie, *f.*
Sawn, *adj.* scié; de sciage
Sawyer, *s.* scieur, *m.*; scieur de long, *m.*
Saxatile, *adj.* saxatile
Saxhorn, *s.* saxhorn, *m.*
Saxicolous, *adj.* saxicole
Saxifrage, *s.* saxifrage, *f.*
Saxifragous, *adj.* saxifrage
Saxon, *s.* Saxon, *m.*, -ne, *f.*; (*language*) le saxon, *m.*, la langue saxonne, *f.*; — *adj.* saxon, de [Saxe
Saxonic, *adj.* saxonique
Saxophone, *s.* saxophone, *m.*
Saxtuba, *s.* saxtuba, *m.*
Say, *v.a.* dire; répéter, réciter; (*o.'s prayers*) faire, (*to* ...) dire; (*know*) savoir; (*mark*) marquer, indiquer; — *v.n.* dire; — *s.* mot à dire, mot, *m.*; dire, *m.* *To have o.'s* —, dire son mot. *I* —! dites donc! écoutez! (*of wonder*, &c.) sapristi! diable! voyons! par exemple! *That is to* —, c'est-à-dire. *That is —ing a good deal*, c'est beaucoup dire. *It is said that* ..., *they* — *that* ..., on dit que ... *Be it said*, soit dit. *I must* — (*I confess*) *that* ..., j'avoue que ...; franchement ... *Don't — another word*, pas un mot de plus. *To — nothing of*, (*passing over*) sans parler de. *Let us — no more about it*, n'en parlons plus. *It is hard to* —, on ne sait (pas). *You don't — so!* pas possible! ah bah! vraiment! — 5 *francs*, disons 5 francs. *To be said*, (*being said*) se dire; *as*, *That is said every day*, cela se dit tous les jours. **— again,** redire, répéter. **— over and over again,** dire [et redire
Sayer, *s.* diseur, *m.*, -euse, *f.*
Sayette, *s.* sayette, *f.*
Saying, *s.* mot, *m.*, parole, *f.*; (*statement*) dire, *m.*; (*proverb*) dicton, adage, proverbe, *m.*; maxime, sentence, *f.* *As the — is*, comme dit le proverbe, comme on dit
Sbirro, *s.* sbire, *m.*
Scab, *s.* croûte, *f.*; (*vet.*) gale, rogne, *f.*
Scabbard, *s.* fourreau, *m.*
Scabbed, *adj.* galeux; vil [sesse, *f.*
Scabbiness, *s.* état galeux, *m.*; vilenie, bas-
Scabby, *adj.* galeux
Scabellum, *s.* scabellon, escabeion, escablon, *m.*
Scabious, *adj.* scabieux; — *s.* scabieuse, *f.*
Scad, *s.* saurel, caranx, *m.*
Scaffold, *s.* échafaud, *m.*; — *v.a.* échafauder. **— pole,** *s.* écoperche, *f.*
Scaffolding, *s.* échafaudage, *m.*
Scagliola, *s.* scagliola, *f.*
Scalable, *adj.* qu'on peut escalader
Scald, *v.a.* échauder; blanchir; (*burn*) brûler, échauder; (*boil*) faire bouillir; — *s.* brûlure, échaudure, *f.*; (*a poet*) scalde, *m.* **— head,** *s.* achores, *m.pl.*, teigne, *f.* [scalde, *m.*
Scalder, *s.* échaudeur, *m.*, -euse, *f.*; (*a poet*)
Scalding, *s.* échaudage, *m.*; (*burning*) brûlure, *f.*; — *adj.* bouillant, brûlant. **— hot,** *adj.* tout bouillant, brûlant. **— house, -tub,** *s.* échaudoir, *m.*
Scale, *s.* (*geog.*, *math.*, *geom.*, &c., *measure of prices*, &c.) échelle, *f.*; (*mus.*) gamme, *f.*; échelle, *f.*; (*list of prices*) tarif, *m.*; (*of fish, metals*, &c.) écaille, *f.*; (*of a balance*) plateau, bassin, *m.*; (*balance itself*, —, *sing.*) **—s,** *pl.*, *pair of —s*, balance, *f.*; (*sediment*) tartre, *m.*; (*insect*) gallinsecte, *m.*; (*mil.*) contre-épaulette, *f.*; — *v.a.* écailler; (*a boiler, the teeth*) enlever le tartre de, nettoyer; (*climb*) escalader; (*a gun*) flamber; — *v.n.* s'écailler. *On a large* —, sur une grande échelle; sur un grand pied; en grand. *On a small* —, sur une petite échelle; en petit. *Drawn to a — of ... to the foot*, dressé à l'échelle de ... millimètres par mètre. **— board,** *s.* placage, *m.* **— insect,** *s.* gallinsecte, *m.* **— less,** *adj.* sans écailles. **— maker,** *s.* balancier, fabricant de balances, *m.*
Scaled, *adj.* écailleux, écaillé, à écailles
Scalene, *adj.* scalène; — *s.* triangle scalène, *m.*
Scaliness, *s.* nature écailleuse, *f.*; (*meanness*) mesquinerie, *f.*
Scaling, *s.* écaillage, *m.*; (*climbing*) escalade, *f.*; (*of a boiler, of the teeth*) nettoyage, *m.*; (*of a gun*) flambage, *m.* **— instrument,** *s.* (*dentist's*) rugine, *f.* **— ladder,** *s.* échelle d'escalade, échelle de siége, *f.*
Scallion, *s.* ciboule, *f.*
Scallop, *s.* pétoncle, *f.*, peigne, *m.*, coquille de Saint-Jacques, *f.*, pèlerin Saint-Jacques, *m.*; coquille, *f.*; (*indentation*) feston, *m.*; (*for furniture, arch.*) lambrequin, feston, *m.*; — *v.a.* festonner; (*cook.*) arranger *or* accommoder en coquille
Scalloped, *adj.* festonné; (*cook.*) en coquille
Scalp, *s.* (*skull*) os frontal, *m.*; crâne, *m.*; (*skin*) cuir chevelu, *m.*; (*cut off by savages*) chevelure, *f.*, scalpe, *m.*; (*of false hair*) toupet, *m.*; (*fig.*) sommet, front, *m.*; (*surg. instr.*) rugine, *f.*; (*bed of oysters or mussels*) banc *or* parc (d'huîtres *or* de moules), *m.*, huîtrière, moulière, *f.* — *v.a.* scalper. *A hairless* —, un crâne chauve, (*jest.*) [un genou, *m.*
Scalpel, *s.* scalpel, *m.*
Scalper, *s.* (*pers.*) scalpeur, *m.*; (*surg. instr.*) rugine, *f.*
Scalping, *s.* scalpement, *m.* **— iron,** *s.* rugine, *f.* **— knife,** *s.* couteau à scalper, couteau de scalpe, *m.* [minable
Scaly, *adj.* écailleux, écaillé; (*mean*) mesquin,
Scammony, *s.* scammonée, *f.*
Scamp *s.* chenapan, vaurien, polisson, mauvais garnement, *m.* *Young* —, (*in joke*) petit polisson, *m.*
Scamper, *v.n.* (**— away, off**) décamper, se sauver, détaler, s'enfuir, s'esquiver, filer, jouer des jambes *or* des talons, prendre ses jambes à son cou; — *s.* fuite, *f.*
Scan, *v.a.* scruter, éplucher; examiner; mesurer; calculer; (*verses*) scander
Scandal, *s.* scandale, *m.*; (*shame*) honte, *f.*, opprobre, *m.*; reproche, *m.*; (*slander*) médisance, *f.*; calomnie, *f.*; — *v.a.* *V.* **Scandalize.** *To raise* —, faire *or* donner du scandale. **— monger,** *s.* médisant, *m.*, e, *f.*, mauvaise langue, *f.* [*der*) médire de, calomnier
Scandalize, *v.a.* scandaliser ('*at*,' de); (*slan-*
Scandalous, *adj.* scandaleux; honteux; infâme; calomnieux, diffamatoire
Scandalously, *adv.* scandaleusement; honteusement; calomnieusement [infamie, *f.*
Scandalousness, *s.* nature scandaleuse, *f.*;

Scandent, *adj.* (*bot.*) grimpant
Scandinavian, *s. adj.* Scandinave, *m.f.*
Scanning, *s.* examen minutieux, *m.*; calcul, *m.*; (*of verses*) scansion, *f.*
Scansion, *s.* scansion, *f.*
Scant, *adj. V.* **Scanty;** (*of the wind, nav.*) qui refuse, échars; — *v.a.* restreindre, rétrécir, resserrer; — *v.n.* (*of the wind, nav.*) refuser, écharser
Scantily, *adv.* étroitement, à l'étroit; modiquement; mesquinement; chichement; (ne ...) guère; à peine; faiblement
Scantiness, *s.* étroitesse, *f.*; modicité, exiguité, *f.*; mesquinerie, *f.*; (*scarcity*) rareté, disette, *f.*; insuffisance, *f.*
Scantle, *v.a.* couper en morceaux, morceler, [diviser
Scantling, *s.* petite quantité, *f.*; un peu, *m.*; fragment, *m.*; (*carp.*) volige, *f.*; (*cask-stand*) chantier, porte-fût, *m.*; (*nav.*) échantillon, *m.*
Scantly, Scantness. *V.* **Scantily, Scantiness**
Scanty, *adj.* limité; (*narrow*) étroit, étriqué; (*small*) modique, faible, exigu; (*poor*) mesquin, chétif, mince, maigre; (*scarce*) rare, peu abondant; peu nombreux; insuffisant; (*sparing*) chiche, économe, ménager
Scape, *s. V.* **Escape;** (*bot.*) scape, *m.*, hampe, *f.* —**goat,** *s.* bouc émissaire, *m.* —**grace,** *s.* mauvais garnement, vaurien, chenapan, *m.*
Scapple, *v.a.* smiller. — **axe,** *s.* smille, *f.*
Scapula, *s.* omoplate, *f.*
Scapular, Scapulary, *adj. s.* scapulaire, *adj.m.f.*; (*of monks,* &c.) scapulaire, *s.m.*; (*feather, anat.*) scapulaire, *s.f.*
Scar, *s.* cicatrice, *f.*; balafre, *f.*; (*rock*) rocher, *m.*; (*fish*) scare, *m.*; — *v.a.* cicatriser; balafrer
Scarab, Scarabæus, Scarabee, *s* scarabée, *m.*
Scaramouch, *s.* scaramouche, *m.*
Scarce, *adj.* rare; — *adv. V.* **Scarcely.** *To make oneself* —, filer, décamper
Scarcely, *adv.* à peine; (ne ...) presque pas, guère, pas trop; (ne ...) presque. — *any,* (ne ...) presque pas (de). — *anybody* or *anyone,* (ne ...) presque personne. — *anything,* (ne ...) presque rien. — *anyone* or *anything but,* (ne ...) guère que. — *any more, any left, any now,* (ne ...) presque plus. — *anywhere,* (ne ...) presque nulle part. — *ever,* (ne ...) presque jamais
Scarceness, Scarcity, *s.* rareté, *f.*; disette, *f.*
Scare, *v.a.* effrayer, faire peur à, effaroucher; effarer. — **crow,** *s.* épouvantail, *m.*
Scarf, *s.* (*for men*) cravate longue, cravate, *f.*, (*for women*) châtelaine, *f.*; (*worn over the shoulders*) écharpe, *f.*; (*carp.*) assemblage, *m.*; — *v.a.* nouer en écharpe; (*carp.*) assembler. — **pin,** *s.* épingle (de cravate), *f.* — **skin,** *s.* épiderme, *m.*
Scarfed, *adj.* paré d'une écharpe; (*carp.*) assemblé
Scarfing, *s.* (*carp.*) assemblage, *m.*
Scarification, *s.* scarification, *f.*
Scarificator, Scarifier, *s.* scarificateur, *m.*
Scarify, *v.a.* scarifier
Scarifying, *adj.* scarificateur; — *s.* scarification, *f.*
Scarlatina, *s.* fièvre scarlatine, scarlatine, *f.*
Scarlet, *adj.* écarlate; — *s.* écarlate, *f.* — **fever,** *s.* fièvre scarlatine, *f.* — **runner,** *s.* haricot d'Espagne, *m.*
Scarp, *s.* escarpe, *f.*; — *v.a.* escarper
Scatch, — **mouth,** *s.* escache, *f.*
Scath, Scathe, *v.a.* endommager, frapper; nuire à; — *s.* dommage, tort, mal, *m.*; coup, *m.* —**ful,** *adj. V.* **Scathing.** —**less,** *adj. V.* **Unhurt**
Scathing, *adj.* dommageable, nuisible; qui porte coup; écrasant
Scathingly, *adv.* dommageablement, nuisiblement; d'une manière écrasante
Scatter, *v.a.* disperser; dissiper; éparpiller; répandre; semer; (*of fire-arms*) écarter; — *v.n.* se disperser; se dissiper; s'éparpiller; se répandre; s'écarter

Scattered, *part. adj.* dispersé, dissipé; (*spread over*) éparpillé, épars; clair-semé
Scatteringly, *adv.* çà et là
Scavenge, *v.a.* ébouer, nettoyer, balayer
Scavenger, *s.* boueur, balayeur, *m.* — **beetle,** *s.* bousier, *m.*
Scavenging, *s.* ébouage, nettoyage, balayage, *m.*
Scear. *V.* **Sear**
Scene, *s.* scène, *f.*; (*scenery*) décoration, *f.*, décor, *m.*; (*of great events*) théâtre, *m.* *Behind the —s,* derrière le rideau, par derrière; dans la coulisse; à la cantonade. *To get up a — with,* faire une scène à. *The — is laid* or *lies ...,* la scène se passe *or* est ... — **painter,** *s.* peintre en décors, décorateur, *m.* — **painting,** *s.* peinture de décors, scénographie, *f.* — **shifter,** *s.* machiniste, *m.* — **shifting,** *s.* changement de décorations, *m.*
Scenery, *s.* scène, vue, *f.*, point de vue, coup d'œil, *m.*, perspective, *f.*; (*landscape*) paysage, site, *m.*; (*theat.*) décors, *m.pl.*; mise en scène, *f.*
Scenic, -al, *adj.* scénique, de (*or* de la) scène, dramatique, théâtral. — *artist,* peintre en décors, décorateur, *m.* — *effect,* mise en scène, *f.*
Scenographic, &c., scénographique, &c. (*V.* page 3, § 1)
Scent, *s.* odeur, *f.*; parfum, *m.*; (*power of smell in animals*) odorat, flair, *m.*, (*in dogs*) nez, *m.*; (*track of animals*) piste, voie, trace, *f.*, assentement, *m.*; — *v.a.* parfumer ('*with,*' de); (*of animals*) flairer, sentir; — *v.n.* suivre à la piste, assentir. *To be off the* —, être en défaut. *To find the — again,* relever le défaut, reprendre. *To put on the wrong* —, mettre en défaut, donner le change à, fourvoyer. *To throw* or *put off the* —, dépister, mettre en défaut. — **bag,** *s.* sachet, *m.* — **bottle,** *s.* flacon d'odeur, *m.* — **box,** *s.* cassolette, *f.* —**less,** *adj.* inodore, sans odeur; (*of animals*) qui n'a pas d'odorat, qui n'a pas de nez
Scented, *adj.* parfumé (de ...); odorant; qui a une odeur ..., qui sent (le ..., la ..., les ...)
Scept-ic, al, -ically, -icism. *V.* page 3, § 1
Sceptre, *s.* sceptre, *m.*
Sceptred, *adj.* qui porte un sceptre
Schedule, *s.* inventaire, *m.*; liste, *f.*; bordereau, *m.*; cahier, *m.*; (*of deeds, agreements,* &c.) annexe, *f.*; (*balance-sheet*) bilan, *m.*; — *v.a.* inscrire, enregistrer; inventorier. *To file* or *give in o.'s* —, déposer son bilan
Scheik, *s.* cheik, cheick, *m.*
Scheme, *s.* plan, *m.*; projet, *m.*; système, *m.*; (*for a new rail. line,* &c.) étude, *f.*; — *v.n.* former un projet; faire des projets; intriguer; ruser; — *v.a. V.* **Plan,** *v.a.*
Schemer, *s.* projeteur, *m.*, -euse, *f.*, faiseur (*m.*, -euse, *f.*) de projets, homme (*m.*, femme, *f.*) à projets; auteur d'un projet, *m.*; inventeur, auteur, *m.*; rêveur, *m.*, -euse, *f.*; (*intriguer*) intrigant, *m.*, e, *f.*; (*jobber*) exploiteur, *m.*, -euse, *f.*
Scheming, *adj.* à projets; rusé, intrigant
Scherif, *s.* chérif, *m.*
Schiedam, *s.* genièvre de Hollande, *m.*
Schirrhus, Schirrus, &c. *V.* **Scirrhus,** &c.
Sch-ism, -ismatic, al, -ismatically. *V.* page 3, § 1
Schismatize, *v.n.* faire schisme
Schist, *s.* schiste, *m.*
Schistous, *adj* schisteux
Scholar, *s.* écolier, *m.*, -ière, *f.*, élève, *m.f.*; (*man of letters*) homme de lettres, homme lettré, lettré, *m.*; savant, érudit, homme instruit, *m.*; (*on a foundation*) boursier, *m.*, -ière, *f.* *Arabic* —, arabisant, *m.* *Classical* —, humaniste, *m.* *Chinese* —, sinologue, *m.* *Greek* —, helléniste, *m.* *Hebrew* —, hébraïsant, *m.* *Latin* —, latiniste, *m.* *Oriental* —, orientaliste, *m.* *Sanscrit* —, sanscritisant, indianiste, *m.* *To be a good French* —, savoir bien le français, posséder à fond le français
Scholarlike, Scholarly, *adj.* d'élève; (*of learned men*) de savant; (*learned*) savant,

lettré, instruit; (*adverb.*) en élève; en savant
Scholarship, *s.* éducation classique, *f.*; (*learning*) savoir, *m.*, instruction, érudition, *f.*; (*foundation*) bourse, *f.*
Scholastic, -al, *adj.* scolastique, scolaire, des écoles; — *s.* scolastique, *m.*
Scholastically, *adv.* scolastiquement
Scholasticism, *s.* scolastique, *f.*
Scholiast, *s.* scoliaste, *m.* [*metry*) *m.*
Scholium, *s.* scolie, (*in philology*) *f.*, (*in geo-*
School, *s.* école, *f.*; (*government middle-school, grammar school*) collége, *m.*; (*government high school, for science or art*) école, *f.*; conservatoire, *m.*; (*national, government or private lower school*) école primaire, école, *f.*; (*private boarding-school*) pension, *f.*, pensionnat, *m.*, maison d'éducation, *f.*; institution, *f.*; (*med., vet., law, mil., nav., paint., science, theol., philos., sect*) école, *f.*; (*lesson*) classe, *f.*; — *adj.* de l'école, des écoles, du collége, des colléges, &c., scolastique, scolaire; — *v.a.* instruire; réprimander. — *of arms,* salle d'armes, *f.* *Boarding* —, pension, *f.*, pensionnat, internat, *m.*; institution, *f.* *Charity* —, école gratuite. *Commercial* —, école de commerce. *Day* —, externat, *m.* *Evening* —, école du soir, *f.*; classe du soir, *f.* *Free* —, *V.* **Free.** *Infant* —, salle d'asile, école maternelle, *f.* *Law* —, *Medical* —, *V.* **Law,** &c. *Military* —, école militaire, *f.* *National* —, *V.* **National.** *Naval* —, école de marine, école navale, *f.* *Normal* —, école normale, *f.* *Parish* —, *V.* **Parish.** *Private* —, *V.* **Private.** *Public* —, école publique, *f.*; collége, lycée, *m.* *Ragged* —, *V.* **Ragged.** *Sunday* —, école du dimanche, *f.* *Young gentlemen's* —, pension *or* institution de jeunes gens, *f.* *Young ladies'* —, pension de demoiselles, institution de jeunes demoiselles, *f.* *At* —, *to* —, à l'école; en pension; (*to o.'s* —) à la pension. *In* —, en classe. *Of the old* —, (*old sort*) de la vieille roche. *The* — *for scandal,* l'école de la médisance. — **agent,** *s.* agent scolastique, *m.* — **apparatus,** *s.* matériel d'école, *m.* — **assistant,** *s.* sous-maître, maître d'étude, *m.*, sous-maîtresse, *f.* — **book,** *s.* livre de classe, livre classique, *m.* — **boy,** *s.* écolier, pensionnaire, collégien, *m.*; élève, *m.* — **days,** *s.pl.* temps des classes, *m.*, études, classes, *f.pl.* — **fellow,** *s* camarade de collége *or* de pension *or* d'école, camarade, condisciple, *m.*; (*of girls*) camarade de pension, camarade, *f.* — **frigate,** *s.* vaisseau-école, *m.* — **girl,** *s.* écolière, pensionnaire, *f*; élève, *f.* — **hours,** *s.pl.* heures de classe, *f.pl.*, classe, *f.* — **house,** *s.* maison d'école, école, *f.* — **man,** *s.* scolastique, *m.*; savant, *m.* — **master,** *s.* maître de pension, *m.*; chef d'institution, instituteur, *m.*; (*of a parish*) maître d'école, instituteur primaire, *m.* — **mistress,** *s.* maîtresse de pension, institutrice, *f.*; (*of a parish*) maîtresse d'école, *f.* — **room,** *s.* classe, *f.*; salle d'étude, étude, *f.* — **ship,** *s* vaisseau-école, *m.* — **time,** *s.* classe, *f.*, temps de la classe, *m.*
Schooling, *s.* enseignement, *m.*; (*price*) pension, *f.*; (*reproof*) réprimande, *f.*
Schooner, *s.* schooner, *m*, goëlette, *f.*
Schorl, *s.* schorl, *m.* [schotisch, *f.*
Schottische, Schottish, *s.* schottish,
Sciagraph-ic, al, -ically, -y. *V.* p. 3, § 1
Sciatic, -al, *adj.* sciatique
Sciatica, *s.* sciatique, *f.*
Science, *s.* science, *f.*
Scientific, *adj.* scientifique; (*pers.*) savant. — *chemist,* chimiste, *m.* — *corps,* (*mil.*) armes savantes, armes spéciales, *f.pl.* — *man,* savant, homme de science, *m.*
Scientifically, *adv.* scientifiquement
Scimitar, *s.* cimeterre, *m.*
Scink, *s.* scinque, *m.*
Scintillant, *adj.* scintillant
Scintillate, *v.n.* scintiller
Scintillation, *s.* scintillation, *f.*
Sciograph-ic, al, -ically, -y. *V.* p. 3, § 1
Sciolism, *s.* connaissances superficielles, *f.pl.*,
Sciolist, *s.* demi-savant, *m.* [demi-savoir, *m.*
Sciolous, *adj.* qui sait superficiellement,
Scion, *s.* scion, *m.* [superficiel
Scioptic, *adj.* scioptique
Scirrhosis, *s.* scirrhose, *f.*
Scirrhosity, *s.* squirrhosité, squirrosité, *f.*
Scirrhous, *adj.* squirrheux, squirreux
Scirrhus, *s.* squirrhe, squirre, *m.*
Scissars. *V.* **Scissors**
Scissible, Scissile, *adj.* scissile
Scission, *s.* scission, division, *f.*
Scissors, *s.pl.* ciseaux, *m.pl.* — **bill,** *s.* bec-en-ciseaux, fauchet, *m.* — **case,** *s.* étui à
Scissure, *s.* scissure, fente, *f.* [ciseaux, *m.*
Sclavonian, &c. *V.* **Slavonian,** &c.
Sclerotic, -al, *adj.* sclérotical. — *membrane* or *coat* or *tunic,* sclérotique, *f.*
Sclerotic, -a, *s.* sclérotique, *f.* [scories. *f.pl.*
Scobs, *s.pl.* râpure, *f.*, râpures, *f.pl.*; scorie, *f.*,
Scoff, *v.n.* se moquer (de), tourner (...) en dérision, railler; — *s.* moquerie, raillerie *f.*
Scoffer, *s.* moqueur, *m.*, -euse, *f.*, railleur, *m.*, -euse, *f.* [*adj.* moqueur
Scoffing, *s.* moquerie, raillerie, dérision, *f.*; —
Scoffingly, *adv.* par moquerie; en dérision
Scold, *v.a.n.* gronder; — *s.* (*scolding*) gronderie, *f.*; (*woman*) grondeuse, mégère, *f.*
Scolder, *s.* grondeur, *m.*, -euse, *f.*
Scolding, *adj.* grondeur; — *s.* gronderie, *f.* *To give* (...) *a* —, gronder (...), laver la tête à
Scoldingly, *adv.* en grondant [(...)
Scollop. *V.* **Scallop** [pendre, *f.*
Scolopendra, Scolopendrium, *s.* scolo-
Sconce, *s.* (*socket*) bobèche, *f.*; (*bracket*) bras de lumière, bras, *m.*; bras de piano, bras, *m.*; (*hanging support*) lampadaire, *m.*; (*head*) caboche, boule, balle, coloquinte, *f.*
Scoop, *s.* grande cuiller, *f.*; (*for cheese*) couteau, *m.*; (*shovel*) pelle à main, pelle, *f.*; (*surg.*) curette, *f.*; (*nav.*) écope, *f.*; — *v.a.* vider; (*hollow out*) creuser; (*nav.*) écoper. — **out,** (*remove*) enlever; (*gouge an eye*) arracher; (*empty*) vider; (*nav.*) écoper
Scope, *s.* (*room*) espace, *m.*, place, *f.*; étendue, *f.*; (*fig.*) carrière, *f.*; essor, cours, *m.*; liberté, *f.*; (*aim, drift*) but, objet, *m.*; (*import, reach*) portée, *f.* *Within the* — *of,* à portée de; dans le cadre de. *To give* — or *free* —, donner l'essor (à), donner libre carrière *or* libre essor (à). *To have free* or *full* —, avoir libre carrière; (*fam.*) avoir les coudées franches, avoir carte blanche
Scorbutic, -al, *adj.* scorbutique
Scorbutically, *adv.* par le scorbut
Scorch, *v.a.n.* brûler, griller
Score, *s.* (*notch*) entaille, coche, *f.*; (*twenty*) vingtaine, *f.*; (*a line*) ligne, *f.*; trait, *m.*; (*mark*) marque, *f.*; (*reckoning*) compte, écot, *m.*; (*of debt*) article de compte, *m.*; (*in games, contests*) point, *m.*; nombre de points, *m.*; (*reason, account*) raison, *f.*, motif, *m.*, cause, *f.*, compte, *m.*; (*mus.*) partition, *f.* *Four* —, *V.* **Four.** *Six* —, cent-vingt. *Three* —, soixante, *m.*, soixantaine, *f.* *On, upon the* — *of,* en considération de, à cause de; au sujet de, sur; sur le compte de. *On, upon that* (or *this*) —, par ce motif, par cette raison; sur ce chapitre, à cet égard. *On, upon a new* —, de nouveau, sur nouveaux frais
Score, *v.a.* (*notch*) entailler; (*mark*) marquer; tracer; (*of accounts*) porter en compte, compter; (*mus.*) orchestrer. — **out,** marquer, tracer; (*rub out*) effacer. — **up,** marquer; comp-
Scorer, *s.* marqueur, *m.*, -euse, *f.* [ter
Scoria, *s.* scorie, *f.*
Scoriaceous, *adj.* scoriacé
Scorification, *s.* scorification, *f.*
Scorifier, *s.* scorificatoire, *m.*; four, *m.*

Scorify, *v.a.* scorifier
Scoring, *s.* orchestration, *f.*
Scorn, *v.a.n.* mépriser, dédaigner ('*to*,' de); railler; — *s.* mépris, dédain, *m.*; raillerie, dérision, *f.* *To laugh to* —, couvrir de mépris, mépriser, se moquer de. **—ful,** *adj.* dédaigneux, méprisant; railleur. **—fully,** *adv.* dédaigneusement, avec dédain, avec mépris, méprisamment. **—fulness,** *s.* nature méprisante *or* dédaigneuse, *f.*
Scorner, *s.* contempteur, *m.*, -trice, *f.*; railleur, *m.*, -euse, *f.*
Scorning, *s.* mépris, dédain, *m.*
Scorpio, *s.* le Scorpion, *m.*
Scorpion, *s.* scorpion, *m.* **— fish,** *s.* scorpène, *f.* **— fly,** *s.* mouche-scorpion, panorpide, *f.* **— grass,** *s.* scorpione, herbe aux scorpions, *f.* **— oil,** *s.* huile de scorpion, scorpiojelle, *f.* **— shell,** *s.* ptérocère, *m.* **—'s tail, — wort,** *s.* [*V.* **— grass**
Scorzonera, *s.* scorsonère, *f.*
Scot, *s.* écot, *m.*; quote-part, *f.*; (*tax*) contribution, *f.*, impôt, *m.*; (*Scotch*) Écossais, *m.*, e, *f.*, (*formerly*) Scot, *m.* — *and lot*, contributions communales, *f.pl.* *To pay — and lot*, payer sa quote-part des contributions communales, payer sa part d'impôt. **— free,** *adj.* franc, exempt de payement, sans rien payer, sans frais; (*law*) exempt de contribution; (*unhurt*) sain et sauf. **—sman,** *s.* Écossais, *m.*
Scotch, *adj.* écossais, d'Écosse; — *s.* (*cut*) taillade, *f.*; (*of a wheel*) enrayure, *f.*; arrêt, *m.*; (*people*) (les) Écossais, *m.pl.*; (*language*) l'écossais, *m.*, la langue écossaise, *f.*; — *v.a.* (*a wheel*) enrayer; arrêter; (*wedge*) caler; (*cut*) taillader; entamer; (*eels*) harponner. *Broad* —, patois écossais, *m.* **— barley,** *s.* *V.* **Barley.** **— bonnet,** *s.* bonnet écossais, béret, *m.* **— boy,** *s.* (petit) Écossais, *m.* **— collop,** *s.* escalope, *f.* **— fir,** *s.* *V.* **Fir.** **— girl,** *s.* (petite *or* jeune) Écossaise, *f.* **— hoppers,** *s.pl.* marelle, *f.* **— kale,** *s.* chou frisé, *m.* **— lady,** *s.* dame écossaise, Écossaise, *f.* **—man,** *s.* Écossais, *m.* **— mist,** *s.* bruine, *f.* **— woman,** *s.* Écossaise, *f.*
Scoter, *s.* macreuse, *f.*
Scotodinia, Scotomy, *s.* scotodinie, scotomie, *f.*
Scotticism, *s.* scoticisme, *m.*
Scottish, *adj.* écossais, d'Écosse
Scoundrel, *s.* drôle, *m.*, -sse, *f.*, gredin, *m.*, e, *f.*, misérable, *m.f.*, coquin, *m.*, e, *f.*, gueux, *m.*, -euse, *f.*
Scoundrelism, *s.* gredinerie, coquinerie, *f.*
Scour, *v.a.n.* écurer, récurer; nettoyer; (*clothes*) dégraisser, décrasser, détacher; (*the country*, &c.) battre, parcourir; (*graze*) raser; (*the sea*) écumer; (*run*) courir; (*med.*) évacuer; avoir le dévoiement; — *s.* (*vet.*) diarrhée, *f.*; dyssenterie, *f.* **— about,** rôder. **— away,** se sauver, s'enfuir
Scourer, *s.* écureur, *m.*, -euse, *f.*, récureur, *m.*, -euse, *f.*; nettoyeur, *m.*, -euse, *f.*; (*of clothes*) dégraisseur, *m.*, -euse, *f.*, détacheur, *m.*, -euse, *f.*; (*runner*) coureur, *m.*; (*purgative*) violent purgatif, *m.*
Scourge, *s.* fouet, *m.*; (*affliction*) fléau, *m.*; — *v.a.* flageller, fouetter; (*chastise*) châtier; affliger
Scourger, *s.* flagellateur, *m.*, -trice, *f.*; (*fig.*) châtieur, *m.*; (*rel. order*) flagellant, *m.* [teur
Scourging, *s.* flagellation, *f.*; — *adj.* flagella-
Scouring, *s.* écurage, récurage, *m.*; nettoyage, *m.*; (*of clothes*) dégraissage, détachage, *m.*; (*med.*) purgation, *f.*; (*looseness*) dévoiement, *m.*, diarrhée, *f.*; **—s,** *pl.* lavure, *f.*; (*fig.*) rebut, *m.* **— brick,** *s.* brique anglaise, *f.* **— drops,** *s.pl.* essence à dégraisser, *f.* **— paper,** *s.* papier à récurer, *m.* **— tub,** *s.* auge, *f.*
Scout, *s.* (*mil.*) éclaireur, coureur, *m.*; (*nav.*) éclaireur, *m.*, vedette, *f.*; (*servant*) garçon, *m.*; — *v.n.* aller en éclaireur; (*nav.*) aller à la découverte; — *v.a.* traiter avec dédain; se moquer de; repousser avec indignation *or* avec mépris
Scouting-party, *s.* parti d'éclaireurs, *m.*
Scovel, *s.* écouvillon (de four), *m.*
Scowl, *v.n.* se refrogner, froncer le sourcil; menacer; — *s.* air refrogné, air maussade, *m.*; aspect sombre *or* menaçant, *m.*
Scowling, *adj.* refrogné, maussade; menaçant
Scowlingly, *adv.* d'un air refrogné *or* maussade; d'un air sombre *or* menaçant
Scrag, *s.* corps décharné, squelette, *m.*; (*butch.*) bout saigneux, *m.* **— end,** *s.* bout saigneux, *m.*
Scragged. *V.* **Scraggy**
Scraggily, *adv.* avec rudesse; (*with leanness*) avec maigreur
Scragginess, *s.* rudesse, inégalité, *f.*; état rocailleux, *m.*; anfractuosité, *f.*; (*leanness*) maigreur, *f.*, état décharné, *m.*
Scraggy, *adj.* rude, raboteux; rocailleux; anfractueux; abrupt; (*lean*) décharné, maigre
Scramble, *v.n.* se traîner; (*up*) grimper (à quatre pattes); (*try to catch*) tâcher d'attraper, se disputer; — *s.* dispute, lutte, *f.*; mêlée, *f.*; (*in a bad sense*) curée, *f.*; (*play*) gouille, gribouillette, *f.* *To throw for a* —, jeter à la gouille *or* à la gribouillette. *They will — for it.* *There will be a — for it*, on se l'arrachera, on se battra pour l'avoir. **— over, up,** grimper (à quatre pattes)
Scrambler, *s.* grimpeur, *m.*, -euse, *f.*; (*fig.*) aspirant, prétendant, *m.*
Scrambling, *s.* *V.* **Scramble,** *s.*
Scramblingly, *adv.* en se traînant; (*up*) en grimpant; (*contending*) en se disputant, en se battant
Scranch. *V.* **Scraunch**
Scrap, *s.* morceau, bout, fragment, *m.*, bribe, *f.*; morceau détaché, *m.*; extrait, *m.*; (*of paper*) bout, chiffon, *m.*; **—s,** *pl.* restes, *m.pl.*, bribes, *f.pl.* **— book,** *s.* album, *m.* **— iron,** *s.* ferraille, *f.*, riblons, *m.pl.* **— iron dealer,** *s.* ferrailleur, *m.* **— metal,** *s.* vieux métaux, *m.pl.*, mitraille, *f.*
Scrape, *v.a.n.* gratter; râcler; (*clean*) ratisser; (*the mud or dirt off*) décrotter; (*gather*) ramasser; (*on a fiddle*) râcler; (*with the foot*) traîner le pied. *To bow and* —, faire des courbettes. **— along,** *v.n.* boulotter. **— off,** *v.a.* gratter; râcler; enlever. *To — the mud or dirt off*, décrotter. **— penny,** *s.* grippe-sou, *m.* **— together, — up,** *v.a.* ramasser
Scrape, *s.* embarras, *m.*, difficulté, *f.*; mauvaise affaire, *f.* *To get into a* —, se mettre dans l'embarras *or* dans le pétrin; se faire une mauvaise affaire; donner dans un guêpier. *To get out of a* —, se tirer d'affaire
Scraper, *s.* grattoir, *m.*; râcloir, *m.*; (*agr.*) ratissoire, *f.*; (*for the feet*) décrottoir, *m.*; (*for the streets*) râcloir, *m.*; éboueur, *m.*; boueur, *m.*; (*for horses*) couteau de chaleur, *m.*; (*for tools*, &c.) curette, *f.*; (*miser*) grippe-sou, *m.*; (*fiddler*) râcleur, *m.*
Scraping, *s.* grattage, grattement, *m.*; (*of ivory*, &c.) râclure, *f.*; (*agr.*) ratissage, *m.*; (*of vegetables*) ratissure, *f.*; (*rubbing*) frottement, *m.*; (*music*) musique de râcleurs, *f.*; **—s,** *pl.* gratture, râclure, ratissure, *f.*; (*things collected*) ramassis, *m.*; (*of money*) épargnes faites sou à sou, *f.pl.*; petits profits, *m.pl.*; boursicaut, *m.*; (*of the roads*) immondices, *f.pl.* *Bowing and* —, courbettes, *f.pl.*
Scratch, *v.a.n.* gratter; (*dig*) creuser; (*wound slightly: with the nails, a pin*, &c.) égratigner, (*with claws*) égratigner, griffer; (*mark a smooth surface*) rayer; — *s.* égratignure, *f.*; coup de griffe, *m.*; (*on a smooth surface*) rayure, raie, *f.*; **—es,** *s.pl.* égratignures, &c.; (*vet.*) crevasses, *f.pl.*, mal d'âne, *m.* *Old* —, le diable, *m.* *To come up to the* —, se prendre aux cheveux; (*to pay*) financer. *To — o.'s head*, se gratter la tête. **— brush,** *s.* brosse forte, *f.*; (*tech.*) gratte-bosse, *m.* **— out,** *v.a.* gratter; effacer; raturer, rayer; (*pull out*) arracher. **— up,** *v.a.* gratter. **— weed,** *s.* grateron, *m.*, râpette, *f.*
Scratcher, *s.* gratteur, *m.*, -euse, *f.*; égratigneur, *m.*, -euse, *f.*; (*things*) grattoir, *m.*
Scratching, *s.* grattage, grattement, *m.*; égratignure, *f.*; **—s,** *pl.* gratture, *f.*, grattures, *f.pl.*; égratignures, *f.pl.*

Scraunch, *v.a.* croquer; — *v.n.* croquer; craquer
Scrawl, *v.n.a.* griffonner; barbouiller; tracer; — *s.* griffonnage, *m.*, pattes de mouches, *f.pl.*
Scrawler, *s.* griffonneur, *m*, -euse, *f.*
Scray, *s.* hirondelle de mer, *f.*
Screak, Scream, (— **out**) *v.n.* crier; jeter *or* pousser un cri (*or* des cris); — *s.* cri, *m.*
Screamer, *s.* crieur, *m.*, -euse, *f.*; (*bird*) kamichi, *m.*, palamédée, *f.*
Screaming, *s.* cris, *m.pl.*
Screech. *V.* **Scream.** — **owl,** *s.* effraie, *f.*
Screen, *s.* écran, *m.*; (*folding*) paravent, *m.*; (*out of doors*) abri, *m.*; (*fig.*) abri, *m.*; défense, *f.*; rideau, *m.*; voile, *m.*; (*arch.*) grille, *f.*; boiserie, *f.*; (*of an altar*) retable, arrière-dos, *m.*; (*hort.*) brise-vent, *m.*; (*sieve*) claie, *f.*, crible, *m.*; — *v.a.* abriter (contre), protéger (contre), mettre à couvert *or* à l'abri (de); pallier, excuser; (*from a punishment*) soustraire (à); (*sift*) passer à la claie *or* au crible, cribler. — **stick,** *s.* manche d'écran, *m.* — **wall,** *s.* avant-mur, *m.*
Screenings, *s.pl.* criblure, *f.*, criblures, *f.pl*
Screw, *s.* vis, *f.*; (*hollow screw*) écrou, *m.*; (*mech.*) vis, *f.*; (*nav.*) hélice, *f.*; (*steamer*) vapeur à hélice, *m.*; (*of paper*) cornet, *m.*; (*pers.*) grippe-sou, pingre, juif, *m.*, arabe, *m.f.*; (*jade*) rosse, *f.*; — *adj.* à vis; (*nav.*) à hélice. *Box —, female —, hollow —,* écrou, *m.* *Male —,* vis, *f.* *A — loose,* (*fig.*) quelque fer qui loche, quelque chose qui va mal (*or* qui cloche). *To put the — on ...,* serrer les pouces *or* le bouton à ... — **bolt,** *s.* boulon à vis, *m.* — **crane,** *s.* vérin, *m.* — **driver,** *s.* tournevis, *m.* — **handle,** *s.* poignée à vis, *f.* — **head,** *s.* tête de vis, *f.* — **jack,** *s.* cric, *m.* — **nail,** *s.* clou à vis, *m.*, vis, *f.* — **nut,** *s.* écrou, *m.* — **pine,** *s.* pandanus, baquois, vaquois, *m.* — **plate,** *s.* filière, *f.* — **press,** *s.* presse à vis, *f.* — **propeller,** *s.* *V.* **Propeller.** — **shank,** *s.* tige de vis, *f.* — **shell,** *s.* turbo, sabot, *m.* — **ship,** *s.* vaisseau *or* bâtiment à hélice, *m.* — **steamer,** *s.* vapeur à hélice, *m.* — **stud,** *s.* *V.* — **nail.** — **thread, -worm,** *s.* filet de vis, *m.* — **wheel,** *s.* roue-vis, *f.* — **wrench,** *s.* clé anglaise, *f.*
Screw, *v.a.* visser; (*press*) serrer, presser; (*fig.*) pressurer, opprimer, écraser; (*distort*) déformer; — *v.n.* se visser. — **down,** visser; (*fig.*) pressurer, opprimer; (*of profits*) rogner les ongles à. — **in,** visser; serrer; introduire, faire entrer. — **out,** faire sortir; (*fig.*) extorquer, arracher ('*of*,' à). — **up,** visser; (*shut*) fermer; (*an instr.*) monter; (*fig.*) élever; forcer, outrer. — *up o.'s face,* faire une grimace. — *up o.'s lips,* pincer les lèvres. — *up o.'s courage,* affermir son courage; prendre son courage à deux mains, se monter
Screwed, *part. adj.* vissé, &c. (*V.* **Screw,** *v.a.*); (*having a screw*) à vis; (*tipsy*) gris, pochard, pompette
Scribble, *v.a.n.* griffonner; barbouiller; (*in bad style*) écrivasser, écrivailler; — *s.* griffonnage, *m.*; barbouillage, *m.*; (*bad style*) écrivasserie, écrivaillerie, *f.*
Scribbler, *s.* griffonneur, *m.*, -euse, *f.*, barbouilleur, *m.*, -euse, *f.*, gratte-papier, *m.*; (*petty author*) écrivassier, *m.*, -ière, *f.*, écrivailleur, *m.*, -euse, *f.*, gratte-papier, *m.*
Scribbling, *s.* *V.* **Scribble,** *s.*; — *adj.* griffonneur, barbouilleur; (*of style*) écrivassier, écrivailleur
Scribe, *s.* scribe, *m.*; écrivain, *m.*; — *v.a.* [(*tech.*) étriquer
Scrimmage, *s.* prise de bec, querelle, rixe, *f.*, grabuge, *m.*, lutte, bagarre, *f.*
Scrimp, *adj.* court; serré; étriqué
Scrip, *s.* (*bag*) gibecière, *f.*; (*of paper*) chiffon, *m.*; (*fin.*) inscription, *f.*, titres, *m.pl.*, valeurs, *f.pl.*
Script, *s.* (*print.*) anglaise, américaine, *f.*, [caractère d'écriture, *m.*
Scriptor, *s.* scripteur, *m.*
Scriptural, *adj.* scriptural, scripturaire, biblique
Scripture, *s.* Écriture, Écriture sainte, *f.* *Holy —,* Écriture sainte. — **history,** *s.* histoire sainte, histoire sacrée, *f.*
Scrivener, *s.* agent d'affaires, *m.*; agent de change, *m.*; notaire, *m.*
Scrofula, *s.* scrofule, *f.*, scrofules, humeurs froides, *f.pl.*
Scrofulous, *adj.* scrofuleux
Scrofulousness, *s.* nature scrofuleuse, *f.*
Scroll, *s.* rouleau, *m.*; rôle, *m.*; (*flourish*) enjolivement, *m.*; (*arch.*) enroulement, *m.*
Scrotal, *adj.* scrotal
Scrotocele, *s.* scrotocèle, *f.*
Scrotum, *s.* scrotum, *m.*
Scrub, *v.a.* frotter, nettoyer, écurer, récurer; laver; — *v.n.* s'éreinter; droguer; — *adj.* *V.* **Scrubby**; — *s.* (*pers.*) homme de peine, *m.*, femme de peine, *f.*; (*wretch*) pauvre diable, *m.*; (*thing*) drogue, *f.*; (*old brush*) vieille brosse usée, *f.*; (*scrubbing*) *V.* **Scrubbing.** *To keep —bing away,* frotter sans cesse
Scrubbed, *adj.* *V.* **Scrubby**
Scrubber, *s.* frotteur, *m.*, -euse, *f.*
Scrubbing, *s.* frottage, nettoyage, écurage, récurage, *m.*; lavage, *m.* *To give a good —,* frotter ferme; bien laver. — **brush,** *s.* brosse à récurer, *f.*
Scrubby, *adj.* pauvre, chétif, méchant, mesquin; (*stunted*) rabougri
Scrunch. *V.* **Scraunch**
Scruple, *s.* scrupule, *m.*; — *v.n.* se faire scrupule (de); hésiter (à)
Scrupler, *s.* scrupuleux, *m.*, -euse, *f.*
Scrupulosity, *s.* scrupulosité, humeur scrupuleuse, *f.*, esprit scrupuleux, *m.*; nature scrupuleuse, *f.*; scrupules, *m.pl.*; scrupule, *m.*; doute, *m.*, hésitation, *f.*
Scrupulous, *adj.* scrupuleux
Scrupulously, *adv.* scrupuleusement
Scrupulousness. *V.* **Scrupulosity**
Scrutineer, *s.* scrutateur, *m.*, -trice, *f.*
Scrutinize, *v.a.* scruter, sonder; examiner, rechercher
Scrutinizer, *s.* scrutateur, *m.*, -trice, *f.*
Scrutinizing, *adj.* scrutateur; inquisiteur
Scrutiny, *s.* examen rigoureux, *m.*, recherche minutieuse, enquête sévère, *f.*; (*of votes*) dépouillement du scrutin *m.*
Scrutoire, *s.* *V.* **Escritoire**
Scud, *v.n.* s'enfuir, se sauver; courir; (*nav.*) faire vent arrière, courir, cingler; — *s.* fuite précipitée, course rapide, *f.*; (*cloud*) léger nuage, *m.*; (*shower*) ondée, *f.* *To — under bare poles,* courir à sec
Scuffle, *s.* lutte, rixe, querelle, bagarre, *f.*; — *v.n.* lutter, se battre; se quereller
Sculk, *v.n.* se tenir caché, se cacher; rôder. — **away,** caponner; s'esquiver, aller se cacher. — **in,** entrer furtivement *or* à la dérobée. — **out,** sortir à la dérobée
Sculker, *s.* poltron, capon, *m.*
Scull, *s.* petit bateau, batelet, canot, *m.*, nacelle, *f.*; (*stern oar*) godille, *f.*; —**s,** *pl.* avirons à couple, *m.pl.*; — *v.n.* godiller, manœuvrer à la godille
Sculler, *s.* godilleur, *m.*
Scullery, *s.* lavoir, *m.* — **maid,** *s.* laveuse de vaisselle, *f.*
Scullion, *s.* marmiton, *m.*; (*girl*) laveuse de vaisselle, *f.*
Sculpin, *s.* callionyme lyre, doucet, *m.*
Sculp-tor, tress, *s.* sculpteur, *m.*, -trice, *f.*
Sculptural, *adj.* sculptural, de sculpture
Sculpturally, *adv.* sculpturalement
Sculpture, *s.* sculpture, *f.*; — *v.a.* sculpter
Sculpturing, *s.* sculptage, *m.*
Scum, *s.* écume, *f.*; (*of metals*) crasse, scorie, *f.*; (*fig.*) lie, *f.*, rebut, *m.*; — *v.a.* écumer. *The lowest —,* la lie; l'écume. — *of the earth,* excrément de la terre, *m.*
Scummer, *s.* (*pers.*) écumeur, *m.*, -euse, *f.*; [(*thing*) écumoire, *f.*
Scumming, *s.* écumage, *m.*; (*scum*) écume, *f.*
Scummy, *adj.* écumeux
Scupper, *s.* dalot, *m.* — **hole,** *s.* dalot, *m.* — **hose,** *s.* mauge, maugère, *f.*

Scurf, *s.* (*on the head*) crasse, crasse qui forme croûte, *f.*; teigne, *f.*; (*on the skin, a surface*) [croûte, *f.*
Scurfiness, *s.* encroûtement, *m.*
Scurfy, *adj.* crasseux; teigneux; couvert de croûte [sière, *f.*
Scurrility, *s.* grossièreté, *f.*; raillerie gros-
Scurrilous, *adj.* grossier, bas, trivial, insultant
Scurrilously, *adv.* grossièrement
Scurrilousness. *V.* **Scurrility** [ment
Scurvily, *adv.* vilement, bassement, indigne-
Scurviness, *s.* (*scurfiness*) encroûtement, *m.*; (*vileness*) caractère vil, *m.*, bassesse, nature misérable, *f.*; (*stinginess*) ladrerie, *f.*
Scurvy, *s.* scorbut, *m.*; — *adj.* (*scurfy*) *V.* **Scurfy;** (*med.*) atteint du scorbut; (*vile*) vil, méprisable, misérable, vilain; (*stingy*) ladre. — **grass,** *s.* cochléaria, *m.* [mâche, *f.*
Scutch, *v.a.* teiller, broyer; — *s.* broyoire,
Scutcheon. *V.* **Escutcheon**
Scutcher, *s.* broyoire, mâche, *f.*; (*pers.*) teilleur, *m.*, -euse, *f.*, broyeur, *m.*, -euse, *f.*
Scutching, *s.* teillage, broyage, *m.* — **mill,** *s.* teilleuse, broyeuse, *f.*
Scutiform, *adj.* scutiforme
Scuttle, *s.* panier, seau, *m.*, boîte, *f.*; (*nav.*) écoutillon, *m.*; — *v.a.* (*nav.*) saborder; — *v.n.* courir, galoper. — **away,** *v.n.* s'enfuir, se sauver, décamper, détaler. —**ful,** *s.* panier plein, seau plein, *m.*
Scuttling, *s.* (*nav.*) sabordement, *m.*
Scytale, *s.* (*snake*) scytale, *m.*
Scythe, *s.* faux, *f.* — **man,** *s.* faucheur, *m.*
Scythed, *adj.* armé de faux
Scythian, *s.* Scythe, *m.f.*; — *adj.* scythe, des
Scythic, *adj.* scythique [Scythes
Sea, *s.* mer, *f.*; (*quantity*) multitude, infinité, *f.*, déluge, *m.*; (*of blood,* &c.) mer, *f.*; (*in compounds, adject.*) de mer; marin; maritime; naval; (*by sea*) par mer; (*a surge, billow*) lame, *f.*; coup de mer, *m.* *Deep* —, pleine mer, haute mer. *Half —s over,* à demi ivre, entre deux vins. *Heavy* —, *high* —, mer houleuse; (*wave*) gros coup de mer, *m.* *High —s,* océan, *m.*, pleine mer, *f.* *Main* —, pleine mer, haute mer. *Narrow* —, détroit, *m.* *Open* —, pleine mer. *Rough* —, grosse mer, mer houleuse. *At* —, en mer, sur mer; (*fig., all at* —) embarrassé, dérouté, perdu, confondu, dans l'erreur. *Beyond* —, outre-mer, d'outre-mer. *By — and land,* par mer et par terre. *On the high —s,* en pleine mer, sur l'océan. *To go to* —, prendre (*again,* reprendre) la mer; s'embarquer; (*as a profession*) se faire marin. *To head the* —, franchir la lame. *To put to* —, mettre en mer, mettre à la mer. *To stand out to* —, gagner le large, se tenir au large. — **acorn,** *s.* gland de mer, balane, *m.* — **adder,** *s.* épinoche, *f.* — **air,** *s.* air de la mer, *m.* — **anemone,** *s.* actinie, anémone de mer, *f.* — **bank,** *s.* (*shore*) côte (de la mer), *f.*; (*defence*) digue, *f.* — **bar,** *s.* hirondelle de mer, *f.* — **bath,** *s.* bain de mer, *m.* — **bathed,** *adj.* baigné par la mer. — **bathing,** *s.* bains de mer, *m.pl.* — **bear,** *s.* (*seal*) ours marin, phoque ourson, *m.*; (*white bear*) ours blanc, *m.* — **biscuit,** *s.* biscuit de mer, *m.* — **board,** *s.* bord de la mer, *m.*; littoral, *m.* — **boat,** *s.* navire, *m.* — **born,** *adj.* né de la mer; né sur mer. — **borne,** *adj.* porté par la mer; (*of coals,* &c.) transporté par mer. — **bound,** *adj.* borné *or* limité par la mer. — **boy,** *s.* novice, *m.*; mousse, *m.* — **bream,** *s.* brème de mer, *f.*, canthère, *m.* — **breeze,** *s.* brise de mer, brise du large, *f.*; (*insect*) taon marin, *m.* — **brief,** *s.* passeport (de navire), *m.* — **built,** *adj.* construit pour la mer. — **calf,** *s.* veau marin, *m.* — **captain,** *s.* *V.* **Captain** (— *of a ship*); (*as opposed to coasting*) capitaine au long cours, *m.* — **card,** *s.* rose des vents, *f.*; compas de mer, *m.* — **cat,** *s.* (*weever*) vive, *f.*, dragon de mer, *m.*; (*wolf-fish*) *V.* **Cat-fish.** — **chart,** *s.* carte marine, *f.* — **coal,** *s.* charbon transporté par mer, *m.*; (*old sense*) charbon de terre, *m.*, houille, *f.* — **coast,** *s.* côte (de la mer), *f.*; littoral, *m.* — **compass,** *s.* boussole, *f.*, compas de mer, *m.* — **cook,** *s.* coq, *m.* — **cow,** *s.* (*manatee*) lamantin, manate, *m.*, vache marine, *f.*; (*walrus*) morse, *m.*, vache marine, *f.* — **cucumber,** *s.* holothurie, *f.* — **devil,** *s.* *V.* **Fishing-frog.** — **dog,** *s.* (*dogfish*) chien de mer, *m.*; (*seal*) veau marin, *m.* — **dragon,** *s.* dragon de mer, *m.*, vive, *f.* — **duck,** *s.* macreuse, *f.* — **eagle,** *s.* aigle de mer, aigle pêcheur, haliète, pygargue, *m.*, orfraie, *f.* — **ear,** — **ear shell,** *s.* haliotide, *f.* — **eel,** *s.* anguille de mer, *f.*, congre, *m.*, murène, *f.* — **egg,** *s.* oursin, *m.* — **elephant,** *s.* éléphant marin, *m.* — **fan,** *s.* panache de mer, *m.* — **farer,** *s.* homme de mer, marin, *m.* — **faring,** *adj.* marin; (*things*) de marin. — **faring man,** *s.* marin, *m.* — **fencibles,** *s.pl.* garde-côtes, *m.* — **fennel,** *s.* *V.* **Samphire.** — **fight,** *s.* combat naval, *m.* — **fish,** *s.* poisson de mer, *m.* — **fog,** *s.* brume, *f.* — **fowl,** *s.* oiseau de mer, *m.* — **gate,** *s.* entre-deux de lames, *m.* — **gauge,** *s.* tirant d'eau, *m.* — **girdles,** *s.pl.* laminaire, *f.* — **girt,** *adj.* entouré par la mer. — **god,** *s.* dieu marin, *m.* — **goddess,** *s.* déesse marine, néréide, *f.* — **going,** *adj.* allant en mer; de mer; de long cours. — **grape,** *s.* uvette, éphèdre, *f.* — **grass,** *s.* herbe marine, *f.* — **green,** *s. adj.* vert de mer, vert d'eau, *m.*; (*bot.*) saxifrage, *f.* — **gull,** *s.* mouette, *f.* — **hare,** *s.* aplysie, *f.* — **hedgehog,** *s.* oursin, *m.* — **hen,** *s.* guillemot, *m.* — **hog,** *s.* marsouin, *m.* — **holly,** *s.* panicaut maritime, *m.* — **horse,** *s.* cheval marin, *m.*, (*walrus*) morse, *m.*, (*fish*) hippocampe, *m.* — **jellies,** *s.pl.* méduses, *f.pl.* — **kale,** *s.* chou marin, chou de mer, crambe, *m.* — **lavender,** *s.* statice, *f.* — **legs,** *s.pl* (le) pied marin, *m.* — **lemon,** *s.* doris, *f.* — **letter,** *s.* passeport (de navire), *m.* — **life,** *s.* vie maritime, *f.* — **like,** *adj.* semblable à la mer. — **lion,** *s.* lion marin, phoque à crinière, *m.* — **loach,** *s.* motelle, *f.* — **louse,** *s.* calige, argule, *m.* — **man,** *s.* marin, homme de mer, *m.*; matelot, *m.* —**manlike,** *adj. adv.* de marin; en marin. —**manship,** *s.* habileté à manœuvrer (un navire), habile manœuvre, *f.*; navigation, *f.*, art nautique, *m.*; matelotage, *m.* *Good —manship,* habile manœuvre, *f.* *Bad —manship,* mauvaise manœuvre, *f.* — **mark,** *s.* amer, *m.*, reconnaissance, *f.* — **mew,** *s.* mouette, *f.* — **monster,** *s.* monstre marin, *m.* — **mouse,** *s.* aphrodite, *f.* — **nettle,** *s.* ortie de mer, *f.* — **nymph,** *s.* néréide, *f.* — **onion,** *s.* scille marine, *f.* — **ooze,** *s.* vase, *f.* — **otter,** *s.* loutre marine, *f.* — **pen,** *s.* pennatule, *f.* — **perch,** *s.* bar, bars, *m.*; serran, *m.* — **pheasant,** *s.* faisan de mer, pilet, *m.* — **pie,** *s.* (*bird*) pie de mer, *f.* — **piece,** *s.* marine, *f.* — **pike,** *s.* orphie, aiguille de mer, *f.*, brochet de mer, *m.*, loubine, *f.* — **pink,** *s.* armérie, *f.* — **plant,** *s.* plante marine, *f.* — **pool,** *s.* lac d'eau salée, *m.* — **port,** *s.* port de mer, *m.* —**port town,** *s.* ville maritime, *f.*, port de mer, *m.* — **risk,** *s.* périls de la mer, *m.pl.* — **robber,** *s.* pirate, corsaire, *m.* — **room,** *s.* eau à courir, *f.*, le large, *m.* — **route,** *s.* voie de mer, *f.* — **rover,** *s.* pirate, forban, écumeur de mer, *m.* — **salt,** *s.* sel marin, *m.* — **sand,** *s.* sable de (*or* de la) mer, *m.* — **scorpion,** *s.* cotte scorpion, *m.* — **serpent,** *s.* serpent marin *or* de mer, *m.* — **service,** *s.* service de la marine, *m.* — **shell,** *s.* coquille de mer, *f.*, coquillage, *m.* — **shore,** *s.* rivage de la mer, *m.*, côte, *f.*; littoral, *m.* — **sick,** *adj* qui a le mal de mer, pris du mal de mer. *To be — sick,* avoir le mal de mer. — **sickness,** *s.* mal de mer, *m.* — **side,** *s.* bord de la mer, *m.* —**side grape,** *s.* raisinier, *m.* — **slug,** *s.* holothurie, *f.* — **snail,** *s.* porce-

laine, *f.* — **snipe,** *s.* *V.* **Trumpet-fish.** — **spider,** *s.* araignée de mer, *f.*, maia, *m.* — **surgeon,** *s.* chirurgien de vaisseau, *m.* — **swallow,** *s.* hirondelle de mer, *f.* — **term,** *s.* terme de marine, *m.* — **tossed,** *adj.* ballotté par les flots. — **trade,** *s.* commerce par mer, *m.* — **travelling,** *s.* voyages par (*or* sur) mer, *m.pl.* — **trout,** *s.* truite saumonée, *f.* — **trumpet,** *s.* ecklonie, trompette marine, *f.* — **unicorn,** *s.* narval, *m.* — **urchin,** *s.* oursin, hérisson de mer, *m.* — **voyage,** *s.* voyage par (*or* sur) mer, *m.* — **wall,** *s.* digue, *f.*, endiguement, *m.* — **walled,** *adj.* entouré par la mer. — **war,** *s.* guerre maritime, *f.* — **ward,** *adj.* dirigé vers la mer; *adv.* vers la mer, du côté de la mer. — **ware,** *s.* balayures de mer, choses de la mer, épaves, *f.pl.*; varech, *m.* — **water,** *s.* eau de mer, eau salée, *f.* — **water fish,** *s.* *V.* — **fish.** — **wave,** *s.* vague de la mer, *f.* — **weed,** *s.* herbe *or* plante marine, *f.*; algue, *f*, varech, *m.* — **wind,** *s.* vent de mer, *m.* — **wolf,** *s.* loup marin, loup de mer, *m.* — **worm,** *s.* ver de mer, *m.* — **worthiness,** *s.* navigabilité, *f.* — **worthy,** *adj.* navigable, en état de tenir la mer. — **wrack,** *s.* varech, *m.*

Seal, *s.* sceau, *m.*; (*private*) cachet, *m.*; (*cust.*) plomb, *m.*; (*law*) scellé, *m.*, scellés, *m.pl.*; (*animal*) phoque, veau marin, *m.*; — (— **up**), *v.a.* sceller; (*letters, parcels, bottles*) cacheter; (*cust.*) plomber; (*law*) mettre le scellé *or* les scellés sur, sceller; (*imprint*) imprimer, graver; (*ratify*) ratifier; (*close*) fermer, clore. *Great* —, grand sceau. *Privy* —, petit sceau. *Solomon's* —, (*bot.*) sceau de Salomon, grenouillet, *m.* *Their fate* (or *their doom*) *is —ed*, leur sort est décidé, leur perte est arrêtée *or* assurée *or* certaine. — **engraver,** *s.* graveur en creux, graveur sur pierres fines, *m.* — **engraving,** *s.* gravure en creux, gravure sur pierres fines, *f.* — **fishery,** *s.* pêche du phoque, *f.* — **oil,** *s.* huile de phoque, *f.* — **ring,** *s.* chevalière, *f.* — **skin,** *s.* peau de veau marin, *f.* — **skin cap,** *s.* casquette en veau marin, *f.*

Sealer, *s.* cacheteur, *m.*, -euse, *f.*; (*official*) scelleur, *m.*, -euse, *f.*; (*of weights and measures*) étalonneur, *m.*; (*fisherman*) pêcheur de phoques, *m.*

Sealing, *s.* scellement, *m.*; (*of letters, parcels, bottles*) action de cacheter, *f.*; (*cust.*) plombage, *m.*; (*fishing*) pêche du phoque, *f.* — **wax,** *s.* cire à cacheter, *f.*

Seam, *s.* couture, *f.*; (*scar*) cicatrice, *f.*; (*of the skull*) suture, *f.*; (*geol.*) couche, veine, *f.*; (*of metals*) soudure, *f.*; (*of masts*) joint, *m.*; — *v.a.* coudre; faire une couture à; (*scar*) couturer, cicatriser. *To rip up the —s of*, découdre. — **less,** *adj.* sans couture; (*of metals*) sans soudure. — **rent,** *s.* décousure, *f.* —**ster,** *s.* couturier, *m.* —**stress,** s. couturière, lingère, *f.* —**y,** *adj.* plein de coutures, à couture; (*of sides*) de l'envers

Sear, *v.a.* brûler; cautériser; (*a horse*) donner *or* mettre le feu à; (*wither*) faner, flétrir, dessécher; (*harden*) endurcir; — *adj.* brûlé; (*withered*) fané, flétri, desséché, séché, sec; (*dead*) mort; — *s.* (*of a firelock*) gâchette, *f.*

Searce. *V.* **Searse**

Search, *v.a.n.* chercher; rechercher; examiner; visiter; (*a person*) fouiller; (*a wound*) sonder; (*cust.*) visiter; (*law*) faire une perquisition dans. — **after,** chercher, rechercher. — **for,** chercher. — **into,** approfondir. — **out,** découvrir, trouver

Search, *s.* recherche, *f.*; (*cust.*) visite, *f.*; (*law*) perquisition, visite, descente, *f.* *In — of*, *V.* **Quest** (*In — of*). *Right of* —, droit de visite, *m.* *To make a — for*, chercher. —**less,** *adj.* impénétrable, inscrutable. — **warrant,** *s.* mandat de perquisition, *m.*

Searcher, *s.* personne qui cherche *or* qui recherche, *f.*, chercheur, *m.*, -euse, *f.*; fouilleur, *m.*, -euse, *f.*; investigateur, *m.*, -trice, *f.*; (*of hearts*) scrutateur, *m.*, -trice, *f.*; (*cust.*, &c.) visiteur, *m.*, (*female* —) visiteuse, *f.*; (*tasting instr.*) sonde, *f.*; (*artil.*) chat, *m.*

Searching, *adj.* pénétrant; scrutateur; pressant; minutieux; — *s.* visite, *f.*, examen, *m.*, recherche, *f.*

Searchingly, *adv.* d'une manière pénétrante *or* pressante; d'un regard scrutateur; minutieusement [fond, *m.*

Searchingness, *s.* subtilité, *f.*; examen pro-

Searedness, *s.* sécheresse, *f.*; (*fig.*) endurcissement, *m.*, insensibilité, *f.*

Searse, *s.* sas, tamis, *m.*; — *v.a.* sasser, tamiser

Season, *s.* saison, *f.*; temps, *m.*; moment, *m.*; époque, *f.*; — *v.a.* assaisonner; imprégner; tempérer; acclimater; accoutumer, faire, endurcir, aguerrir; (*wood*) préparer, sécher; (*dry*) sécher; (*a cask*, &c.) (*with water*) abreuver, combuger, (*with wine*) aviner; — *v.n.* s'acclimater; (*of wood*) se sécher. *In* —, de saison; à temps, au bon moment; à propos. *Out of* —, hors de saison; hors de propos, mal à propos. — **ticket,** *s.* *V.* **Ticket**

Seasonable, *adj.* de saison; à propos, opportun, convenable

Seasonableness, *s.* opportunité, *f.*, à-propos, *m.*

Seasonably, *adv.* de saison, à propos, en temps opportun [**son,** *v.a.*); (*dry*) sec

Seasoned, *part. adj.* assaisonné, &c. (*V.* **Sea-**

Seasoner, *s.* (*pers.*) assaisonneur, *m.*, -euse, *f.*; (*things*) assaisonnement, *m.* [séchage, *m.*

Seasoning, *s.* assaisonnement, *m.*; (*of wood*)

Seat, *s.* siége, *m.*; place, *f.*; situation, *f.*, emplacement, lieu, *m.*; (*of war*, &c.) théâtre, *m.*; (*abode*) séjour, *m.*, demeure, *f.*; (*of a hare*) gîte, *m.*; (*country house*) château, *m.*, maison de campagne, *f.*; (*in church*) banc, *m.*, place, *f.*; (*in tiers*) gradin, *m.*; (*of chairs, trousers*) fond, *m.*; (*of windows*) avance, saillie, banquette, *f.*; (*of saddles*) siége, *m.*; (*riding*) assiette, *f.*; — *v.a.* asseoir; faire asseoir; placer, mettre; établir; fixer; implanter; (*hold*) contenir; (*chairs*, &c.) mettre un fond à. *To keep o.'s* —, garder sa place; rester assis. *To take a* —, (*a chair*) s'asseoir prendre un siége. *To take o.'s* —, *to — oneself*, prendre sa place; s'asseoir; s'établir, se fixer

Seated, *part. adj.* assis; placé, &c. (*V.* **Seat,** *v.a.*); (*with seats*) à ... places. *Double* —, à deux places. *To be* —, être assis *or* &c. *Be* — ! asseyez-vous!

Seating, *s.* fond, *m.*

Sebaceous, *adj.* sébacé

Secant, *adj. s.* sécant, *adj.m.*, e, *f.*, sécante, *s.f.*

Secede, *v.n.* se séparer; faire scission; se retirer

Seceder, *s.*, **Seceding,** *adj.* scissionnaire, *m.f.*; dissident, *m.*, e, *f.*; (*in the American war*) sécessioniste, *m.f.* [cession, *f.*; retraite, *f.*

Secession, *s.* séparation, *f.*; scission, *f.*; sé-

Secessionist, *s. adj.* sécessioniste, *m.f.*

Seclude, *v.a.* séparer, éloigner; retirer; exclure; (*shut up*) renfermer, reclure

Secluded, *part. adj.* retiré; reclus

Seclusion, *s.* retraite, *f.*; exclusion, *f.*; réclusion, *f.*; solitude, *f.*

Seclusive, *adj.* qui tient dans la retraite

Second, *adj.* second; deuxième; (*after* 20, 30, &c.) deuxième; (*of the month*) deux; (*fig.*) inférieur; (*of cousins*) issu de germain, au deuxième degré; (*mil., nav.*) en second, sous; — *s.* second, appui, *m.*; (*of duels*) témoin, second, *m.*; (*part of a minute, and mus.*) seconde, *f.*; —**s,** *s.pl.* seconde qualité, *f.*; (*of meal*) farine de seconde qualité, *f.*; recoupe, *f.*; — *v.a.* seconder, appuyer. *The* —, (*of sovereigns*) deux. *My — best hat*, or &c., mon numéro 2. *To be — to none*, ne le céder à personne. — **captain,** *s.* capitaine en second, *m.* — **class** *carriage, ticket*, &c., voiture billet, &c. de seconde (*or* deuxième) classe. — **engineer,** *s.* (*nav.*) quartier-maître mécanicien, *m.* — **fiddle,** *V.* **Fiddle.** — **floor,** *s.* second (*or* deuxième) étage, second, deuxième, *m.* — **hand,** *adj. adv.* de seconde main; (*things not new*) d'occasion; *s.* (*of a dial plate*) aiguille des secondes, *f.* *At* —*hand,* (*by hearsay*) de seconde main. —*hand bookseller,* marchand (*m.*, e, *f.*) de livres d'occasion, libraire d'occasion, bouquiniste, *m.f.* — **lieutenant,** *s.* lieutenant en second, *m.* — **mate,** *s.* (*nav.*) lieutenant, *m.* — **rate,** *V.* **Rate.** —**sight,** *s.* seconde vue, *f.* — **sighted,** *adj.* doué de seconde vue. —**thought,** *V.* **Thought**

Secondarily, *adv.* secondairement

Secondary, *adj.* secondaire; (*subordinate*) subordonné, subalterne; — *s.* délégué, *m.*; subalterne, *m.* — *cause,* cause seconde, *f.* — *colour,* couleur composée, *f.* [appuie, *f.*

Seconder, *s.* personne qui seconde *or* qui

Secondly, *adv.* secondement, deuxièmement, en second lieu [retraite, *f.*

Secrecy, *s.* secret, *m.*; discrétion, *f.*; solitude,

Secret, *adj.* secret; retiré; discret; — *s.* secret, *m.* *In* —, en secret; sous le secret. *To keep* —, tenir secret. *To keep a* —, garder un secret. — **drawer,** *s.* tiroir à secret, secret, *m.* — **lock,** *s.* serrure à secret, *f.* — **service,** *s.* service secret, *m.* — **service fund** *or* **money,** *s.* fonds secrets, *m.pl.* — **spring,** *s.* secret, *m.* — **spring lock,** *s.* *V.* —**lock**

Secretary, *s.* secrétaire, *m.*; (*minister*) ministre, *m.*; (*bird, piece of furniture*) secrétaire, *m.* —*'s office,* secrétariat, *m.* — *of state,* secrétaire d'état. — **bird,** *s.* secrétaire, *m.*

Secretaryship, *s.* secrétariat, *m.*; (*ministry*) ministère, *m.*

Secrete, *v.a.* sécréter; (*to hide*) cacher

Secreting, *adj.* sécréteur

Secretion, *s.* sécrétion, *f.*

Secretly, *adv.* secrètement, en secret

Secretness, *s.* nature secrète, *f.*; discrétion, *f.*

Secretory, *adj.* sécrétoire, sécréteur

Sect, *s.* secte, *f.*

Sectarian, *s. adj.* sectaire, *m.f.*

Sectarianism, *s.* esprit de secte, *m.*

Sectary, *s.* sectaire, *m.f.*

Sectile, *adj.* sectile

Section, *s.* (*division*) section, *f.*; (*part*) partie, *f.*; (*draw., arch., geol.*) coupe, *f.*; profil, *m.*; (*book-bind.*) cahier, *m.* — *from A to B,* coupe suivant A B. *Longitudinal* —, profil en long

Sectional, *adj.* sectionnel; en coupe

Sector, *s.* secteur, *m.*; compas de proportion, *m.*

Secular, *adj.* séculier; temporel; (*of music*) profane; (*of years*) séculaire; — *s.* séculier, laïque, *m.*; chantre laïque, *m.*

Secularism, Secularity, *s.* sécularité, *f.*

Secularization, *s.* sécularisation, *f.*

Secularize, *v.a.* séculariser [culairement

Secularly, *adv.* séculièrement; (*of years*) sé-

Secundine, *s.* (*bot.*) secondine, *f.*; —, —**s,** *pl.* (*in obstetrics*) délivre, *m.*, secondines, *f.pl.*

Secure, *adj.* (*safe*) en sûreté (contre), à l'abri (de); (*confident*) dans la sécurité; (*sure*) sûr, assuré; — *v.a.* mettre en sûreté, protéger ('*from,*' contre); mettre à l'abri (de); (*make certain*) assurer, (*to oneself*) s'assurer; (*seize*) s'assurer de, se saisir de, s'emparer de, mettre la main sur; (*imprison*) mettre en lieu de sûreté; (*engage*) retenir; (*payments, creditors,* &c.) garantir; (*make fast*) consolider, affermir; fixer; attacher; barrer; fermer; (*procure*) valoir ('*for,*' à)

Securely, *adv.* en sûreté; sans danger; (*in confidence*) dans la sécurité; sans crainte; (*surely*) sûrement; bien; (*strongly*) fortement,

Secureness, *s.* sécurité, *f.* [solidement; bien

Securer, *s.* (*pers.*) protecteur, *m.*, -trice, *f.*, défenseur, *m.*; (*things*) protection, défense, *f.*

Security, *s.* sûreté, *f.*; assurance, certitude, *f.*; (*pledge*) garantie, *f.*, nantissement, *m.*, caution, *f.*, cautionnement, *m.*; (*confidence*) sécurité, *f.*; —**ies,** *pl.* (*fin.*) effets, titres, *m.pl.*, valeurs, *f.pl.* *To give* —, fournir caution, fournir un cautionnement; donner des garanties

Sedan, — **chair,** *s.* chaise à porteurs, *f.*

Sedate, *adj.* posé, calme; rassis

Sedately, *adv.* posément, avec calme

Sedateness, *s.* calme, *m.*; manière posée, *f.*

Sedative, *adj. s.* calmant, *adj.m.*, e, *f.*, sédatif, *adj.m.*, -ive, *f.*, calmant, *s.m.*, sédatif, *s.m.*

Sedentarily, *adv.* sédentairement

Sedentariness, *s.* sédentarité, *f.*, état sédentaire, *m.*; vie sédentaire, *f.*

Sedentary, *adj.* sédentaire; inactif, inerte

Sederunt, *s.* séance, *f.*

Sedge, *s.* laiche, *f.*; jonc, *m.* — **bird,** **-warbler,** *s.* rousserolle, salicaire, *f.*

Sedged, *adj.* de laiche; de joncs

Sedgy, *adj.* plein de laiche *or* de joncs

Sedilium, *s.* (*pl.* **Sedilia**) siége, *m.*

Sediment, *s.* sédiment, dépôt, résidu, *m.*

Sedimentary, *adj.* sédimentaire

Sedimentation, *s.* sédimentation, *f.*

Sedition, *s.* sédition, *f.*

Seditionary, Seditionist, *s.* séditieux, *m.*,

Seditious, *adj.* séditieux [-euse, *f.*

Seditiously, *adv.* séditieusement

Seditiousness, *s.* caractère séditieux, *m.*; esprit séditieux, *m.*; excitation à la sédition, *f.*

Sedlitz, *s.* Sedlitz, *m.* — **powders,** *s.pl.* poudres gazeuses, *f.pl.* — **water,** *s.* eau de

Seduce, *v.a.* séduire [Sedlitz, *f.*

Seducer, *s.* séducteur, *m.*, -trice, *f.*

Seducible, *adj.* qui peut être séduit, corruptible

Seduction, *s.* séduction, *f.*

Seductive, *adj.* séducteur, séduisant

Sedulous, &c. *V.* **Assiduous,** &c.

See, *s.* siége, *m.*

See, *v.a.n.* voir; (*understand*) comprendre; (*attend*) conduire; reconduire; accompagner; (*take care*) avoir soin (de), veiller (à); (*consider*) penser (à); aviser (à). *Fit to be seen,* présentable. *To* — *to a thing,* s'occuper d'une chose. *To* — *that* ..., veiller à ce que ... *I will* — *about it,* j'y penserai, je verrai. *I will* — *to it,* je m'en occuperai, j'y veillerai. *I* — *your brother coming,* je vois venir votre frère, je vois votre frère qui vient. — **again,** revoir. — **into,** pénétrer, voir le fond de. — **off,** voir partir; conduire. — **out,** voir la fin de, rester jusqu'au bout de; (*a person*) reconduire. — **over,** visiter, voir. — **through,** deviner, pénétrer, voir, comprendre

Seed, *s.* semence, *f.*; (*of vegetables*) graine, *f.*; (*corn*) grain, *m.*; (*for sowing*) semailles, *f.pl.*; (*of silkworms*) œufs, *m.pl.*, graine, *f.*; (*offspring*) race, *f.*; — *adj.* (*produced from seed*) de semence; — *v.n.* monter en graine; grener; (*shed seed*) s'égrener; — *v.a.* semer. *To run to* —, monter en graine. *To sow the* — *of,* semer. — **bearing,** *adj.* qui porte des semences *or* des graines, séminifère. — **bed,** *s.* semis, *m.* — **cake,** *s.* gâteau anisé, *m.*; (*of oil-seed*) tourteau, *m.* — **coat,** *s.* épisperme, *m.*; arille, *m.* — **cod,** *s.* semoir, *m.* — **garden,** *s.* semis, *m.* — **leaf,** *s.* feuille séminale, *f.* —**ling,** *s.* semis, *m.*; (*tree*) sauvageon, *m.* —*ling carrots,* semis de carottes, *m.* — **lip, -lop,** *s.* semoir, *m.* — **merchant,** *s.* marchand grainier, grainier, grainetier, *m.* — **oil,** *s.* huile de graines, *f.* — **pearl,** *s.* semence de perles, *f.* — **plot,** *s.* semis, *m.* —**sman,** —**swoman,** *s.* grainier, *m.*, -ière, *f.*, grainetier, *m.*, -ière, *f.* — **time,** *s.* semailles, *f.pl.*, semaison, *f.* — **trade,** *s.* graineterie, *f.* — **vessel,** *s.* péricarpe, *m.*

Seeding, *s.* grenaison, *f.*; (*sowing*) semaison, *f.*

Seedy, *adj.* grenu; (*of clothes*) râpé, usé; (*exhausted*) éreinté; défait; abattu; fatigué; (*unwell*) mal à son aise; (*penniless*) dans la dé-

Seeing, *s.* vue, *f.*; vision, *f.* [bine, panné

Seeing, — **that,** *conj.* vu que, puisque

Seek, *v.a.n.,* — **after, for, out,** chercher; tâcher de trouver; poursuivre; rechercher; (*ask*) demander (' *of*,' '*from*,' à). *To — the life of*, en vouloir à la vie de
Seeker, *s.* chercheur, *m.*, -euse, *f.*
Seeking, *s.* recherche, *f.*; poursuite, *f.*
Seel, *v.n.* rouler fort; — *s.* fort roulis, *m.*
Seeling, *s.* fort roulis, *m.*
Seem, *v.n.* sembler, paraître; avoir l'air (de); (*feign*) faire semblant (de), feindre (de). *It —s, it would —, so it —s,* (*as it seems*) à ce qu'il paraît
Seeming, *adj.* apparent; (*sham*) feint, faux; — *s.* apparence, *f.*, dehors, *m.*; semblant, *m.*
Seemingly, *adv.* en apparence
Seemingness, *s.* apparence spécieuse, *f.*
Seemliness, *s.* bienséance, convenance, *f.*; grâce, *f.* [avec bienséance, convenablement
Seemly, *adj.* bienséant, convenable; — *adv.*
Seer, *s.* *V.* **Beholder;** (*prophet*) prophète, voyant, *m.*, prophétesse, voyante, *f.*
See-saw, *s.* bascule, *f.*; (*mech.*) va-et-vient, *m.*; (*play*) balançoire, bascule, *f.*; — *v.n.* faire la bascule, basculer. — **motion,** *s.* mouvement
Seethe, *v.a.n.* *V.* **Boil** [de va-et-vient, *m.*
Seether, *s.* marmite, *f.*
Seething, *adj* bouillant; (*mass*) grouillant
Segar. *V.* **Cigar**
Seggar. *V.* **Sagger** [partie, portion, *f.*
Segment, *s.* (*geom.*) segment, *m.*; (*part*)
Segmental, *adj.* segmentaire
Segregate, *v.a.* séparer, isoler, séquestrer
Segregation, *s.* ségrégation, séparation, *f.*, isolement, *m.*, séquestration, *f.*, séquestre, *m.*
Segregative, *adj.* ségrégatif
Segregatively, *adv.* ségrégativement
Seignior, *s.* seigneur, *m.* *Grand —,* grand seigneur, *m.*
Seigniorage, *s.* seigneuriage, *m.*
Seigniorial, *adj.* seigneurial
Seigniory, *s.* seigneurie, *f.*; (*feud.*) suzerai-
Seidlitz. *V.* **Sedlitz** [neté, *f.*
Seikh. *V.* **Sikh**
Seine, — **net,** *s.* seine, *f.*
Seir-fish, *s.* tassart, *m.*
Seismograph, &c. *V.* **Sismograph,** &c.
Seizable, *adj.* saisissable
Seize, *v.a.n.*, — **on, upon,** saisir; se saisir de, s'emparer de, prendre; arrêter; (*law*) saisir; (*nav.*) aiguilleter; amarrer; (*a rope*) frapper, brider. *To — again,* ressaisir; reprendre
Seized, *part.* saisi, &c. (*V.* **Seize**); (*with illness*) saisi (de), atteint (de), attaqué (de)
Seizer, *s.* personne qui saisit, *f.*; (*law*) saisis-
Seizin, *s.* saisine, *f.* [sant, *m.*, e, *f.*
Seizing, *s.* action de saisir, *f.*; (*nav.*) aiguilletage, *m.*; amarrage, *m.*
Seizure, *s.* prise, *f.*; capture, *f.*; arrestation, *f.*; prise de possession, *f.*; confiscation, *f.*; possession, *f.*; (*law*) saisie, *f.*; (*med.*) attaque, *f.*, accès, *m.*
Seldom, *adv.* rarement; — *adj.* rare
Select, *v.a.* choisir; — *adj.* choisi, de choix; d'élite; (*of public gatherings*) bien composé. *The — few,* le petit nombre des élus, *m.*; l'élite de la société, l'élite, *f.*
Selectedly, *adv.* avec choix
Selection, *s.* choix, *m.*; recueil, *m.* *Choice —,* excellent choix, *m.*; (*liter.*) recueil choisi, *m.*
Selective, *adj.* sélectif
Selectively, *adv.* sélectivement
Selectness, *s.* choix, *m.*
Selector, *s.* personne qui choisit, *f.*; (*compiler*) auteur d'un recueil, *m.*
Selenic, *adj.* sélénique
Selenious, *adj.* sélénieux
Selenite, *s.* sélénite, (*min.*) *f.*, (*chem.*) *m.*
Selenitic, -al, *adj.* séléniteux
Selenium, *s.* sélénium, *m.*
Selenographer, *s.* sélénographe, *m.*
Selenographic, -al, *adj.* sélénographique
Selenography, *s.* sélénographie, *f.*

Self, *pron.* *s.* même; soi-même, soi, se; personne, *f.* *My own —, thy own —,* &c., moi-même, toi-même, &c. (*V.* **Myself, Thyself,** &c.). — **abased,** *adj.* humilié. — **abasement,** *s.* humiliation volontaire, *f.* — **abasing,** *adj.* qui s'humilie. — **accusing,** *adj.* qui s'accuse soi-même. — **acting,** *adj.* (*mech.*) automoteur, automobile, automatique. — *acting lathe,* tour à chariot, *m.* — **admiration,** *s.* admiration de soi-même, *f.* — **approbation,** *s.* approbation de soi-même, *f.* — **colour,** *s.* couleur naturelle, *f.* — **command,** *s.* empire sur soi-même, *m.*; sang-froid, *m.* *To have — command,* avoir de l'empire sur soi-même, être maître de soi. — **conceit,** *s.* *V.* **Conceit.** — **confidence,** *s.* assurance, *f.* — **confident,** *adj.* plein de confiance en soi-même, sûr de soi. — **consciousness,** *s.* sentiment intérieur, *m.* — **contradiction,** *s.* contradiction avec soi-même, *f.* — **contradictory,** *adj.* qui se contredit, contradictoire. — **control,** *s.* *V.* — **command.** — **convicted,** *adj.* convaincu par soi-même. — **deceit, -deception,** *s.* illusion, *f.* — **defence,** *s.* défense personnelle, *f.*; légitime défense, *f.* *In — defence,* pour se défendre. — **delusion,** *s.* illusion, *f.* — **denial,** *s.* abnégation (de soi-même), *f.*, désintéressement, dévouement, *m.* — **denying,** *adj.* qui fait abnégation de soi-même, désintéressé, dévoué; d'abnégation, de dévouement. — *denying ordinance,* (*Engl. hist.*) ordonnance de renoncement à soi-même, *f.* — **dependent, -depending,** *adj.* indépendant. — **destroyed,** *adj.* détruit de ses propres mains, suicidé. — **destroyer,** *s.* suicide, *m.f.* — **destroying,** *adj.* suicide. — **destruction,** *s.* suicide, *m.* — **devotion,** *s.* *V.* — **denial.** — **educated,** *adj.* qui a fait son éducation lui-même *or* sans maîtres, qui s'est instruit seul. — **education,** *s.* éducation de soi-même *or* sans maîtres, instruction acquise par soi-même, *f.* — **esteem,** *s.* estime de soi-même, *f.* — **evident,** *adj.* évident de soi, de toute évidence, qui tombe sous le sens, qui parle de soi-même, (*fam.*) clair comme le jour. — **examination,** *s.* examen de soi-même, examen de conscience, *m.* — **existence,** existence indépendante, *f.* — **existent,** *adj.* qui existe par soi-même. — **governed,** *adj.* (*polit.*) gouverné par soi-même; autonome. — **government,** *s.* (*polit.*) gouvernement du pays par lui-même, *m.*; autonomie, *f.* — **heal,** *s.* (*bot.*) brunelle, *f.* — **improvement,** *s.* culture de soi-même, *f.*; instruction sans maîtres, *f.* — **indulgence,** *s.* indulgence pour soi-même, *f.* — **interest,** *s.* intérêt personnel, *m.*; égoïsme, *m.* — **interested,** *adj.* intéressé, personnel, égoïste. — **knowledge,** *s.* connaissance de soi-même, *f.* — **love,** *s.* égoïsme, *m.*; amour-propre, *m.* — **made,** *adj.* *He is a —made man,* il s'est fait ce qu'il est, il est fils de ses œuvres, il est l'artisan de sa fortune. — **moving,** *adj.* *V.* — **acting.** — **murder,** &c., *V.* — **destruction,** &c. — **opinionated, -opinioned,** *adj.* *See Letter* **O.** — **possession,** *s.* empire sur soi-même, *m.*; calme, sang-froid, *m.*; aplomb, *m.* — **praise,** *s.* éloge de soi-même, *m.* — **preservation,** *s.* conservation de soi-même, *f.* — **registering,** *adj.* (*thermometer*) à maxima et à minima. — **regulating,** *adj.* *V.* — **acting.** — **reliance,** *s.* confiance en soi-même, *f.*; indépendance, *f.* — **repugnant,** *adj.* *V.* — **contradictory.** — **respect,** *s.* estime de soi-même, *f.*, amour-propre, *m.* — **restraint,** *s.* retenue, *f.* — **sacrifice,** *s.* sacrifice de soi-même, *m.* — **same,** *adj.* *The — same,* absolument le (*or* la) même. — **satisfied,** *adj.* content de soi. — **seeking,** *adj.* égoïste. — **styled,** *adj.* soi-disant, prétendu. — **sufficiency,** *s.* suffisance, *f.* — **sufficient,** *adj.* suffisant. — **supported,** *adj.* indépendant. — **supporting,** *adj.* qui se suffit à soi-même; qui paye (*or* fait) ses frais. — **taught,** *adj.* qui s'est instruit seul, instruit par soi-même. — **will,** *s.* obstination, opiniâtreté, *f.* — **willed,** *adj.* obstiné entêté, volontaire

Selfish, *adj.* égoïste, intéressé [par égoïsme

Selfishly, *adv.* égoïstement, avec égoïsme,

Selfishness, *s.* égoïsme, *m.*; intérêt, *m.*

Sell, *v.a.* vendre; — *v.n.* (*pers.*) vendre; (*things*) se vendre; — *s.* duperie, attrape, *f.* *To be sold,* être vendu; (*duped*) être attrapé, être joué, être mis dedans, être volé; (*for sale*) à vendre. — **for** (*a price*), *v.a.* vendre; *v.n.* se vendre. — **off,** *v.a.* liquider, solder; *v.n.* (*com.*) se liquider; (*things*) s'écouler. — **out,** vendre; (*mil.*) vendre son grade. *To be sold out,* (*pers.*) être à court

Sellanders. *V.* **Sallenders**

Seller, *s.* vendeur, *m.*, -euse, *f.* (de ...); marchand, *m.*, e, *f.* (de ...)

Selling, *s.* *V.* **Sale;** (*in compounds*) commerce (de ...), *m.* — **off,** *s.* liquidation, *f.*; vente au rabais, *f.* — **out,** *s.* vente totale, *f.*; (*mil.*) vente de son grade, *f.* — **price,** *s.* prix de vente, *m.*

Seltzer-water, *s.* eau de Seltz (*or* Selz), *f.* *A bottle of —,* une bouteille d'eau de Seltz, *f.*; (*in coffee-houses and eating-houses*) un siphon, *m.*

Seltzogene, *s.* seltzogène, selzogène, *m.*

Selvage, Selvedge, *s.* lisière, *f.*

Selvaged, Selvedged, *adj.* à lisière

Semaphore, *s.* sémaphore, *m.*

Semaphor-ic, al, -ically, -ist, sémaphorique, &c. (*V.* page 3, § 1)

Semblance, *s.* semblant, *m.*, apparence, *f.*; (*likeness*) ressemblance, image, *f.*

Semecarpus, *s.* sémécarpe, *m.*

Semen-contra, *s.* semen-contra, *m.*

Semi, *adj.* semi; demi; à demi, à moitié. — **annual,** *adj* semestriel. —**barbarian,** *s. adj.*, —**barbarous,** *adj.* semi-barbare, *m.f.* — **breve,** *s.* ronde, *f.* —**breve rest,** *s.* pause, *f.* —**circle,** *s.* demi-cercle, *m.* —**circular,** *adj.* demi-circulaire, en demi-cercle; demi-cylindrique. —*circular arch,* voûte en plein cintre, *f.* —**colon,** *s.* point et virgule, *m.* —**-demisemiquaver,** *s.* quadruple croche, *f.* —**detached,** *adj.* (*house*) (maison) contiguë à une autre; (*of two similar houses*) (maisons) jumelles. —**diameter,** *s.* demi-diamètre, *m.* —**lunar,** *adj.* semi-lunaire. —**official,** *adj.* semi-officiel, officieux. —**officially,** *adv.* semi-officiellement, officieusement. —**ped,** *s.* demi-pied, *m.* —**pedal,** *adj.* d'un demi-pied. — **quaver,** *s.* double croche, *f.* —**quaver rest,** *s.* quart de soupir, *m.* —**savage,** *s.* personne à demi sauvage, *f.* —**spheric, -al,** *adj.* hémisphérique. —**tone,** *s.* demi-ton, *m.* — **tonic,** *adj.* de demi-ton. —**vowel,** *s.* semi-voyelle, *f.*

Seminal, *adj.* séminal

Seminarist, *s.* séminariste, *m.*

Seminary, *s.* *V.* **School;** (*clerical*) séminaire, *m.*; (*fig.*) pépinière, *f.*

Semination, *s.* sémination, *f.*; (*fig.*) propagation, *f.*

Seminiferous, *adj.* séminifère

Semolina, *s.* semoule, *f.* — **pudding,** *s.* gâteau de semoule, *m.*

Sempiternal, *adj.* sempiternel, éternel

Sempiternally, *adv.* sempiternellement, éternellement

Sempiternity, *s.* sempiternité, éternité, *f.*

Sempster, Sempstress. *V.* **Seamster, Seamstress**

Senary, *adj.* senaire

Senate, *s.* sénat, *m.* —**house,** *s.* sénat, *m.*

Senator, *s.* sénateur, *m.*; (*in the Bible*) ancien, membre du conseil, *m* —**ship,** *s.* sénatorerie, *f.*

Senatorial, Senatorian, *adj.* sénatorial, sénatorien; du sénat

Senatorially, *adv.* en sénateur

Senatus-consultum, *s.* sénatus-consulte, *m.*

Send, *v.a.n.* envoyer; expédier, faire partir; (*grant*) accorder, donner; (*com.*) expédier. — **away,** renvoyer; éloigner; faire partir. — **back,** renvoyer. — **down,** faire descendre; envoyer. — **for,** envoyer chercher, faire venir, faire demander, faire appeler. — **forth,** envoyer; (*produce*) produire; (*throw*) jeter; lancer; pousser; (*exhale*) exhaler, répandre; (*publish*) publier. — **forward,** envoyer; expédier. — **in,** envoyer; (*introduce*) introduire, faire entrer; (*deliver*) livrer; déposer; (*serve up*) servir; (*announce*) annoncer. — **off,** *V.* — **away;** (*com.*) expédier. — **on,** envoyer; expédier. —**out,** faire sortir; renvoyer, chasser; émettre, exhaler, répandre; (*on an errand*) envoyer en course; (*to*) envoyer (à, en) *or* expédier (à, en). — **up,** faire monter; envoyer; envoyer dans les airs; lancer en l'air; (*serve up*) servir

Sender, *s.* envoyeur, *m.*, -euse, *f.*; (*com.*) expéditeur, *m.*, -trice, *f.*; (*post.*) envoyeur, *m.*, -euse, *f.*, expéditeur, *m.*, -trice, *f.*

Sending, *s.* envoi, *m.*; (*com.*) expédition, *f.*

Senega, *s.* sénéga, *m.*

Senescence, *s.* vieillissement, déclin, *m.*

Senescent, *adj.* vieillissant, qui vieillit

Seneschal, *s.* sénéchal, *m.* *High —,* grand sénéchal. —*'s court* or *jurisdiction,* sénéchaussée, *f.*

Sengreen, *s.* joubarbe, *f.*

Senile, *adj.* sénile, de vieillard

Senilely, *adv.* sénilement, en vieillard

Senility, *s.* sénilité, *f.*

Senior, *adj. s.* (*in age*) aîné, *m.*, e, *f.*; (*in time*) plus ancien; ancien, *m.*, -ne, *f.*; doyen, *m.*; (*father*) père, *m.*; (*of classes*) élevé, supérieur; (*chief*) premier; (*of partners*) principal; (*of assemblies*) doyen, *m.* [— *by age,* doyen d'âge]. — *officer,* (*mil.*) supérieur, *m.* *She is my — by* 10 *years,* elle est mon aînée de dix ans

Seniority, *s.* séniorat, *m.*, supériorité d'âge, *f.*, âge, *m.*; doyenneté, *f.*; (*in office*) ancienneté, *f.*

Senna, *s.* séné, *m.*

Sennight, *s.* *V.* **Week**

Sensation, *s.* sensation, *f.*; — *adj.* à sensation, à effet, qui fait (*or* qui a fait) sensation, qui vise à l'effet; frappant, saisissant; célèbre. *To create* or *make a —,* faire sensation (*with an adj.*, une ... sensation ...)

Sensational, *adj.* *V.* **Sensation,** *adj.*

Sensationally, *adv.* de manière à faire sensation; pour l'effet

Sense, *s.* sens, *m.*; (*perception*) sentiment, *m.*; (*wits, intellect*) esprit, *m.*, raison, *f.*, bon sens, *m.*; intelligence, *f.*; jugement, *m.*; discernement, *m.*; (*meaning*) signification, *f.*, sens, *m.*; (*good or bad acceptation*) part, *f.*; (*opinion*) opinion, *f.*, avis, *m.*; (*notion*) idée, *f.*; (*sensation*) sensation, *f.*; sensibilité, *f.* *Common —,* *V.* **Common.** *Good —,* bon sens. *Plain good —,* gros bon sens. *Man of —,* homme de sens, homme sensé, *m.* *The five —s,* les cinq sens. *In a good —,* en bonne part. *In a bad —,* en mauvaise part. *In the full — of the word,* dans toute l'acception du mot, dans toute la force du terme. *There is no — in that,* cela n'a pas de sens, cela ne fait aucun sens, cela ne signifie rien; cela n'a pas le sens commun. *To be in o.'s —s* (or *right —s*), être dans son bon sens. *To be out of o.'s —s* (or *right —s*), être hors de son bon sens. *To bring to o.'s —s,* ramener *or* mettre à la raison. *To come to o.'s —s, to recover o.'s —s,* reprendre ses sens, reprendre connaissance, revenir à soi; (*fig.*) revenir à la raison. *To drive* (...) *out of his —s,* faire perdre la tête (à). *To have a — of,* avoir le sentiment de; (*appreciate*) sentir. *To have a lively — of,* avoir un vif sentiment de; sentir vivement. *To lose o.'s —s,* perdre la raison; perdre la tête; (*become unconscious*) perdre connaissance. *To retain o.'s —s,* *V.* **Conscious** (*To be*). *To take the — of,* consulter, prendre l'avis de. *To talk —,* dire des choses

sensées; parler raison. **—less,** *adj.* (*of*) insensible (à); (*unconscious*) sans connaissance; (*foolish*) insensé, vide de sens, déraisonnable, absurde. *To become* or *lie —less, V.* **Unconscious.** *To knock —less,* étourdir. **—lessly,** *adv.* déraisonnablement, sottement, d'une manière insensée. **—lessness,** *s.* absurdité, sottise, déraison, *f.*
Sensibility, *s.* sensibilité, *f.*; sentiment, *m.*
Sensible, *adj.* sensible (à); qui a le sentiment (de); (*wise*) sensé, raisonnable, sage; (*conscious*) en pleine connaissance; (*mus.*) sensible. *To be — of,* être sensible à, sentir; avoir le sentiment de
Sensibleness, *s.* sensibilité, *f.*; perception, *f.*; (*judgment*) bon sens, esprit, *m.*, raison, sagesse, *f.*
Sensibly, *adv.* sensiblement; vivement; (*wisely*) sensément, raisonnablement, sagement. *To talk —,* parler sensément, parler raison, dire des choses sensées
Sensitive, *adj.* sensitif; sensible; impressionnable; (*touchy*) susceptible; ombrageux. **— plant,** *s.* sensitive, *f.*
Sensitively, *adv.* sensiblement
Sensitiveness, *s.* sensibilité, *f.*; (*of temper*) [susceptibilité, *f.*
Sensorial, *adj.* sensorial
Sensorium, *s.* sensorium, *m.*; organe des sens, *m.*
Sensory, *adj.* sensoriel; — *s. V.* **Sensorium**
Sensual, *adj.* sensuel; des sens
Sensualism, *s.* sensualisme, *m.* [sualiste, *m.*
Sensualist, *s.* sensuel, *m.*, -le, *f.*; (*philos.*) sen-
Sensualistic, *adj.* sensualiste
Sensuality, *s.* sensualité, *f.*
Sensualization, *s.* sensualisation, *f.*
Sensualize, *v.a.* sensualiser, rendre sensuel
Sensually, *adv.* sensuellement
Sentence, *s.* (*judgment*) sentence, *f.*, jugement, arrêt, *m.*, condamnation, *f.*; (*maxim*) sentence, maxime, *f.*; (*gram.*) phrase, *f.*; — *v.a.* condamner, prononcer un jugement contre. *Under — of death,* condamné à mort. *To pass —,* prononcer un jugement; passer condamnation
Sententious, *adj.* sentencieux; laconique
Sententiously, *adv.* sentencieusement; laconiquement [laconisme, *m.*
Sententiousness, *s.* nature sentencieuse, *f.*;
Sentient, *adj.* sentant, sensitif, sensible
Sentiment, *s.* sentiment, avis, *m.*, opinion, *f.*; (*idea*) pensée, *f.*; (*feeling*) sentiment, *m.*
Sentimental, *adj.* sentimental
Sentimentalism. *V.* **Sentimentality**
Sentimentalist, *s.* sentimentaliste, *m.f.*
Sentimentality, *s.* sentimentalité, *f.*, sentimentalisme, *m.*, sensiblerie, *f.*, céladonisme, *m.*
Sentimentalize, *v.n.* faire du sentiment
Sentimentally, *adv.* sentimentalement
Sentinel, Sentry, *s.* (*pers.*) factionnaire, *m.*, sentinelle, *f.*; (*guard*) faction, sentinelle, *f.* *To stand* or *keep —, to be on —,* faire sentinelle, faire faction, être en sentinelle, être en fac-[tion. **— box,** *s.* guérite, *f.*
Sepal, *s.* sepale, *m.*
Separa-bility, bleness, *s.* séparabilité, *f.*
Separable, *adj.* séparable
Separably, *adv.* séparablement
Separate, *v.a.* séparer; diviser; désunir; — *v.n.* se séparer; se diviser; se désunir; — *adj.* séparé; distinct, à part; particulier, personnel, dotal. **— *estate,*** biens dotaux, *m.pl.*, dot, *f.*
Separately, *adv.* séparément; à part
Separateness, *s.* séparation, *f.*, état à part, *m.*
Separation, *s.* séparation, *f.*
Separatism, *s.* séparatisme, *m.*
Separatist, *s. adj.* séparatiste, *m.f.*
Separatistic, *adj.* séparatiste
Separative, *adj.* séparatif
Separa-tor, tress, *s.* séparateur, *m.*, -trice, *f.*
Separatory, *adj.* séparatoire
Sepawn, *s.* gaude, *f.*
Sepia, *s.* sépia, *f.*
Sepon, *s.* gaude, *f.*
Sepoy, *s.* cipaye, *m.*
Seps, *s.* seps, *m.*
Septangular, *adj.* à sept angles
September, *s.* septembre, *m.*
Septemvir, *s.* septemvir, *m.*
Septemviral, *adj.* septemviral
Septemvirate, *s.* septemvirat, *m.*
Septenary, *adj. s.* septénaire, *adj.m.f., s.m.*
Septennate, *s.* septennat, *m.*
Septennial, *adj.* septennal
Septennially, *adv.* tous les sept ans
Septentrional, *adj.* septentrional
Septet, Septette, *s.* septuor, *m.*
Septic, *adj. s.* septique, *adj.m.f., s.m.*
Septicity, *s.* septicité, *f.*
Septuagenarian, *s. adj.* septuagénaire, *m.f.*
Septuagesima, *s.* Septuagésime, *f.*
Septuagint, *s.* version des Septante, *f.*
Septum, *s.* septum, *m.*
Septuor. *V.* **Septet** [*v.a.n.* septupler
Septuple, *adj. s.* septuple, *adj.m.f., s.m.*; —
Sepulchral, *adj.* sépulcral. — *mound,* tumu-
Sepulchre, *s.* sépulcre, *m.* [lus, *m.*
Sepulture, *s.* sépulture, *f.*
Sequel, *s.* suite, *f.*
Sequence, *s.* suite, succession, série, *f.*
Sequent, *adj.* suivant; qui est la suite *or* la conséquence (de)
Sequester, *v.a.* séquestrer; — *s.* séquestre, *m.*
Sequestered, *adj.* retiré; écarté; (*law*) en séquestre
Sequestrable, *adj.* sujet à séquestre
Sequestrate, *v.a.* séquestrer
Sequestration, *s.* séquestre, *m.*, séquestration, *f.*; (*retirement*) isolement, *m.*, retraite, *f.*
Sequestrator, *s.* séquestre, *m.*, séquestrateur, *m.*
Sequin, *s.* sequin, *m.*
Seraglio, *s.* sérail, *m.*
Seraph, *s.* séraphin, *m.*
Seraphic, *adj.* séraphique
Seraphim, *s.pl.* séraphins, *m.pl.*
Seraphina, Seraphine, *s.* séraphine, *f.*
Seraskier, *s.* séraskier, sérasquier, *m.*
Seraskierat, *s.* séraskiérat, sérasquiérat, *m.*
Serb, Serbian, *s. adj.* Serbe, *m.f.*
Sere, *adj. V.* **Sear,** *adj.* [sérénade à, sérénader
Serenade, *s.* sérénade, *f.*; — *v.a.* donner une
Serenader, *s.* donneur de sérénades, *m.*
Serene, *adj.* serein; (*of titles*) sérénissime. *All — !* tout va bien! parfait! *Most —,* séré-
Serenely, *adv.* avec sérénité [nissime
Sereneness, Serenity, *s.* sérénité, *f.*
Serf, *s.* serf, *m.*, serve, *f.* **—dom,** *s.* servage, *m.*
Serge, *s.* serge, *f.* **— maker,** *s.* sergier, *m.* **— manufactory, -trade,** *s.* sergerie, *f.*
Sergeant, *s.* (*of infantry*) sergent, *m.*; (*of cavalry*) maréchal des logis, *m.*; (*of police*) brigadier, *m.* **—-at-arms,** *s.* sergent d'armes, *m.*; huissier, *m.* **— instructor,** *s.* (*mil.*) sergent-instructeur, instructeur, *m.* **—major,** *s.* (*of infantry*) sergent-major, *m.*; (*of cavalry*) maréchal des logis chef, *m.*
Sergeantcy, *s.* (*of infantry*) grade de sergent, *m.*; (*of cavalry*) grade de maréchal des logis, *m.*; (*of police*) grade de brigadier, *m.*
Sergeantship, Sergeanty, *s.* sergenterie, *f.*
Serial, *adj.* sérial, sériaire; (*of liter. works*) paraissant par série *or* par livraisons, paraissant périodiquement; — *s. V.* **Periodical,** *s.*
Serially, *adv.* par série
Seriate, *v.a.* sérier; — *adj.* sérié
Seriated, *part. adj.* sérié
Seriatim, *adv.* régulièrement, par ordre
Seriation, *s.* sériation, *f.*
Sericeous, *adj.* soyeux
Sericicultural, *adj.* séricicole
Sericiculture, *s.* sériciculture, *f.*
Sericiculturist, *s.* sériciculteur, *m.*
Sericultural, &c. *V.* **Sericicultural,** &c.
Series, *s.* série, suite, *f.*
Serio-comic, *adj.* héroï-comique
Serious, *adj.* sérieux; grave

Seriously, *adv.* sérieusement; gravement
Seriousness, *s.* sérieux, *m.*; gravité, *f.*
Serjeant, *s.* huissier, *m*, (*obsolete*) sergent, *m.*; (— *-at-law*) avocat (de premier rang), *m.*; (*mil.*, *of police*, — *-at-arms*) *V.* **Sergeant**
Serjeantcy, Serjeantship, *s.* fonctions d'huissier, *f.pl.*; (*law*) grade d'avocat (de premier rang), *m.*
Sermon, *s.* sermon, *m.*
Sermonize, *v.a.* sermonner
Sermonizer, *s.* sermonneur, *m.*, -euse, *f.*
Sermountain, *s.* sermontain, *m.*
Seron, Seroon. *V.* **Ceroon**
Serosity, *s.* sérosité, *f.*
Serous, *adj.* séreux
Serpent, *s.* serpent, *m.*; (*squib*) serpenteau, *m.* **—eater,** *s.* messager, secrétaire, *m.*
Serpentaria, *s.* serpentaire, *f.*
Serpentarius, *s.* serpentaire, *m.*
Serpentiform, *adj.* serpentiforme
Serpentine, *adj.* serpentin, de serpent, en serpent; (*twisted*) qui serpente, tortueux; (*of marble*) serpentin; — *s.* serpentin, *m.*; (*min.*, *bot.*) serpentine, *f.* — **marble, -stone,** *s.* serpentine, *f.*
Serpula, *s* serpule, *f.*
Serrate, Serrated, *adj.* serraté, dentelé, en scie; (*of machines*) à engrenage; (*of mats*, &c.) à surface raboteuse
Serried, *adj.* serré, compacte
Serum, *s.* sérum, *m.*
Servable, *adj.* servable
Serval, *s.* serval, *m.*
Servant, *s.* serviteur, *m.*, servante, *f.*; (*domestic*) domestique, *m.f.*, bonne, *f.*, servante, *f.*; (*of public companies*, &c.) employé, *m.*, e, *f.*; garçon, *m.*, fille, femme, *f.*; (*soldier waiting on a military officer*) brosseur, *m.* *Man* —, domestique, domestique mâle, *m.* *Woman* —, domestique, domestique femme, bonne, servante, *f.* — *of all work*, *V.* **General —.** — **boy,** *s.* (petit) domestique, *m.* — **girl,** *s.* (petite) domestique *or* bonne *or* servante, *f.* — **maid,** *s.* domestique, domestique femme, bonne, servante, *f.* — **man,** *s.* domestique, domestique mâle, *m.*
Serve, *v.a.n.* servir; (*a purpose*) remplir, servir à; (*satisfy*) satisfaire, contenter, suffire à; (*treat*) traiter, agir envers, agir à l'égard de, en agir avec, en user avec; (*a trick*) jouer; *comply with*) s'accommoder à, se conformer à; (*obey*) obéir à, être esclave de; (*a church*) desservir; (*o.'s time, an apprenticeship, a campaign*, &c.) faire; (*a rope*) fourrer; (*artil.*) exécuter (un canon), desservir (une batterie); (*law*) signifier ('*upon*,' à); (*suffice*) suffire; (*be favourable*) être favorable; (*mil.*) servir, être au service. *To — as, to — for*, servir de. *To be —d right*, n'avoir que ce qu'on mérite. *He —d you right*, il vous a traité comme vous le méritiez. *It —s* or *—d him* (*her, you*, &c.) *right*, il (elle, &c.) n'a que ce qu'il (elle, &c.) mérite, il (elle, &c.) ne l'a pas volé, c'est bien fait. — **out,** finir; distribuer; (*pay off*) rendre la pareille à, arranger. *I will — you out*, je vous revaudrai cela; vous me le payerez. —**up,** servir
Server, *s.* (*basket*) vannette, *f.*
Servian, *s. adj.* Servien, *m.*, -ne, *f.*, Serbe, *m.f.*
Service, *s.* service, *m.*; (*in church*) office, service, *m.*; (*respect*) hommage, devoir, *m.*; (*bidding*) ordres, *m.pl.*; (*obedience*) obéissance, *f.*; (*use*) utilité, *f.*, avantage, *m.*; secours, *m.*; (*good*) bien, *m.*; (*law*) signification, *f.*; (*mil.*) service, *m.*; armée, *f.*; (*nav.*) service, *m.*; marine, *f.*; (*of a rope*) fourrure, *f.* *At* —, *In* —, en service, en condition. *In active* —, en activité. *In the* —, au service; à l'armée; dans la marine. *In the — of*, au service de. *Of* —, utile (à). *On* —, de service. *Out of* —, hors de service, sans place. *To do a* —, rendre service. *To enter the* —, entrer au service. *To enter into —, to go to* —, (*of domestics*) entrer en condition, se mettre en service. — **berry,** *s.* sorbe, corme, *f.* — **book,** *s.* rituel, *m.* — **pipe,** *s.* tuyau de service, *m.* — **tree,** *s.* sorbier, cormier, *m.*
Serviceable, *adj.* utile (à); avantageux (à); servable; de bon service; (*obliging*) serviable
Serviceableness, *s.* utilité, *f.*; avantage, *m.*; (*obligingness*) serviabilité, *f.*
Serviceably, *adv.* utilement; avantageusement; (*obligingly*) serviablement
Servile, *adj.* servile; (*in subjection*) asservi, esclave
Servilely, *adv.* servilement, avec servilité
Servileness, Servility, *s.* servilité, bassesse, *f.*; (*slavery*) servitude, *f.*
Serving, *adj.* qui sert, qui est en service; servant. — **maid,** — **man,** *V.* **Servant**
Servitor, *s.* serviteur, *m.*; (*univers.*) étudiant servant, *m.*
Servitorship, *s.* place d'étudiant servant, *f.*
Servitude, *s.* servitude, *f.* (*V.* **Penal**)
Sesame, Sesamum, *s.* sésame, *m.* *Open, Sesame!* Sésame, ouvre-toi!
Seseli, *s.* séséli, *m.*
Sessile, *adj.* sessile
Session, *s.* session, *f.*; (*sitting*) séance, *f.*; **—s,** [*pl.* assises, *f.pl.*
Sesterce, *s.* sesterce, *m.*
Sestet, Sestuor. *V.* **Sextet**
Set, *v.a.* mettre; poser; placer; planter; fixer; ajuster; indiquer; déterminer; régler; établir; présenter, offrir, donner; (*a watch*, &c.) régler ('*by*,' sur), mettre à l'heure; (*a task, lesson*) donner, marquer, imposer; (*a price*) mettre; (*an example*) donner; (*of dogs*) arrêter; (*gems*, &c.) monter; (*razors, knives*, &c.) affiler, repasser; (*a tool*) affûter; (*to music*) mettre (en); (*snares*) tendre, dresser; (*birds*) faire couver; (*a seal, signature*) apposer; (*a limb*) remettre, remboiter; (*print.*) composer; (*mas.*) (*to lay*) poser, (*to plaster*) berteller; (*nav.*) relever. *To — in motion*, mettre en mouvement. — *oneself* **about or to,** se mettre à; (*apply*) s'appliquer à; (*undertake*) entreprendre. — **abroad,** divulguer, publier; répandre, propager. — **again,** remettre. — **against,** mettre contre, mettre près de; opposer à; indisposer *or* exciter contre. *To — oneself against*, s'opposer à; combattre, attaquer. — **agoing,** *V.* — **going.** — **apart,** mettre à part *or* de côté; (*keep*) réserver; destiner; affecter (à). — **aside,** mettre *or* laisser de côté; (*discard*) écarter; (*reject*) rejeter; (*not to mention or include*) ne pas parler de; faire abstraction de; (*annul*) annuler, casser. — **at,** exciter après, agacer contre. — **by,** mettre de côté; (*discard*) écarter; (*reject*) rejeter; (*regard*) considérer, estimer; (*a watch*, &c.) *See above*. *To — a watch by the right time*, mettre une montre à l'heure. — **down,** mettre par *or* à terre, déposer; (*from a carriage*) descendre; (*lower*) baisser; (*write down*) mettre par écrit, inscrire; mettre; porter; prendre note de, noter; (*relate*) citer, mentionner, rapporter; (*establish*) établir, fixer, arrêter, déterminer; (*give a clincher*) *V.* **Clincher;** (*as* or *for*) considérer (comme), estimer; appeler. — **forth,** faire paraître, faire voir, déployer, montrer; rehausser, relever, faire ressortir; orner; exposer; publier. — **forward,** avancer; faire avancer; pousser, favoriser; animer, encourager. — **going,** faire aller, faire marcher, faire jouer, mettre en train *or* en action, mettre en mouvement *or* en branle, donner le branle à. — **in,** planter; fixer; établir; mettre en train. — **off,** (*start*) faire partir; (*adorn*) orner, parer, embellir; (*show off*) rehausser, relever, mettre en relief, faire ressortir; dessiner; (*against*) comparer (à, avec), mettre en comparaison (avec); compenser (par). — **on,** employer (à), occuper (à), mettre (à); pousser (à), porter (à), exciter (à). — **open,** ouvrir. — **out,** assigner, fixer; marquer, tracer; (*adorn*) orner, parer; (*show off*) *V.* — **off;** (*spread*) étaler; mettre. — **over,** établir sur; préposer à. — **together,** mettre ensemble; comparer. — **up,** (*erect*) dresser,

ériger, élever; planter; placer, mettre; (*establish*) établir, monter, fonder; (*a person*) relever, mettre sur ses pieds; (*exalt*) exalter, élever; (*expose to view*) exposer, mettre en évidence; (*an opinion*, &c.) avancer, mettre en avant; (*cries*) pousser, jeter; (*at auctions*) mettre à prix, mettre; (*print.*) composer; (*a carriage*) se donner. *To — up its back*, (*of a cat*) faire le gros dos. *To — up in business*, établir dans le commerce, établir. *To — up business for oneself*, s'établir pour (*or* à) son compte. — **up for,** ériger en

Set, *v.n.* (*of the sun*, &c.) se coucher; (*fig.*) s'éteindre; (*be fixed*) se fixer; (*on a journey*) se mettre; (*congeal*, &c.) se figer, se coaguler, se prendre, prendre; (*of plants*) prendre racine, prendre; (*of fruit on the tree*) se nouer; (*hunt.*) chasser au chien d'arrêt; (*of a dog*) arrêter; (*mas.*) berteller. — **about,** se mettre à; faire; commencer; (*apply oneself*) s'appliquer à; (*undertake*) entreprendre. — **about** *it*, (*to fall to*) s'y mettre; (*to proceed*) s'y prendre. — **against,** s'opposer à; combattre, attaquer. — **forth,** — **forward,** se mettre en marche, partir; s'avancer; (*begin*) commencer, débuter. — **in,** commencer; se déclarer, se manifester, avoir lieu; (*of the weather*) se mettre à; commencer; (*of a gale*) s'élever; (*be felt*) se faire sentir. *It has — in for rain*, le temps est à la pluie. *The fine weather is —ting in*, le temps se met au beau. — **off,** partir, se mettre en route; marquer. — **on,** déterminer, décider; commencer, s'y mettre; attaquer; s'attacher à; s'acharner à. — **out,** partir; (*begin*) commencer; débuter. — **to,** se mettre à; s'appliquer à; (*to work*) *V.* **Work,** *s.* — **up,** s'établir. — **up for ...,** s'ériger en ..., se poser en ..., faire le *or* la *or* les ...; avoir des prétentions (à), prétendre (à). *To — up in business*, se mettre dans le commerce, s'établir. *To — up for oneself*, s'établir pour (*or* à) son compte; agir pour soi. — **upon,** *V.* — **on**

Set, *part. adj.* mis, posé, placé, &c. (*V.* **Set,** *v.a. & v.n.*); fixé; fixe; réglé; régulier; suivi, soutenu; établi, prescrit; formel; étudié; apprêté; préparé; d'apparat; conformé, fait, constitué, bâti, pris; ferme, résolu, délibéré; (*of phrases*) d'usage, toute faite, fixe; (*of price*) fixe; (*of battles*) rangé; (*of fruit on the tree*) noué

Set, *s.* assortiment, *m.*; collection, *f.*; série, *f.*; réunion, *f.*; (*of buttons, ribbons*, &c.) garniture, *f.*; (*of plate, china*) service, *m.*; (*of diamonds*, &c.) parure, *f.*; (*row*) rang, *m.*, rangée, *f.*; (*body of pers.*) société, *f.*, corps, *m.*, réunion, *f.*, assemblage, *m.*, classe, *f.*, (*in contempt*) tas, *m.*, bande, troupe, clique, coterie, *f.*; (*young plant*) plant, *m.*; (*at play*) partie, *f.*; (*of horses*) attelage, *m.*; (*of harness*) paire, *f.*; (*of whippletrees*) volée, *f.*; (*of chess, oars, sails*, &c.) jeu, *m.*; (*of the sun*, &c.) coucher, *m.*; (*against*) opposition (à), *f.*; attaque (contre), *f.*; combat, assaut (contre, avec), *m.* — *of furniture*, ameublement, *m.* — *of teeth*, denture, *f.*, (*jest.*) râtelier, *m.*; (*artificial*) dentier, *m.* *To make a — against*, attaquer; combattre. *To make a dead — against*, attaquer vivement; rompre en visière à. — **down,** *s.* *V.* **Clincher.** — **off,** *s.* ornement, embellissement, *m.*; relief, *m.*; compensation, *f.*; contre-partie, *f.*; contre-poids, *m.*; déduction, *f.*; (*law*) reconvention, *f.*; (*paint.*) repoussoir, *m.*; (*build.*) retraite, *f.* — **out,** *s.* étalage, appareil, attirail, *m.*; affaire, *f.*; commencement, début, *m.*; (*row*) vie, *f.*; (*dinner*) festin, *m.* — **to,** *s.* assaut, *m.*; peignée, brossée, *f.*; (*of words*) dispute, prise de bec, *f.* [séton, *f.*

Seton, *s.* séton, *m.* — **needle,** *s.* aiguille à

Settee, *s.* causeuse, *f.*, tête-à-tête, *m.*

Setter, *s.* (*dog*) chien couchant, *m.*; (*pers.*) (*fig.*) embaucheur, *m.*, (*tech.*) poseur, *m.*, -euse, *f.*, monteur, *m.*, -euse, *f.*, (*of music*) compositeur, *m.*; (*thing for lifting a carriage*) chèvre, *f.* — **on,** *s.* instigateur, *m.*, -trice, *f.*, fauteur, *m.*, -trice, *f.*

Setting, *adj.* (*sun, dog*) couchant; — *s.* mise, *f.*; pose, *f.*; placement, *m.*; établissement, *m.*; fixation, *f.*; emploi, *m.*; (*of the sun*, &c.) coucher, *m.*; (*of gems*, &c.) *V.* **Mounting;** (*of razors, knives*, &c.) repassage, *m.*; (*of tools*) affûtage, *m.*; (*of music*) mise (en musique), *f.*; (*of seals, signatures*) apposition, *f.*; (*of streams*) cours, *m.*; (*getting hard*) figement, *m.*, coagulation, prise, *f.*; (*of limbs*) remboîtement, *m.*; (*build.*) pose, *f.*, (*plastering*) bertellage, *m.*; (*print.*) composition, *f.*; (*hunt.*) chasse au chien couchant, *f.*; (*nav.*) (*of the wind, of a current*) direction, *f.*, (*of the compass*) relèvement, *m.* — **dog,** *s.* chien couchant, *m.* — **free,** *s.* *V.* **Liberation.** — **in,** *s.* commencement, *m.* — **off,** *s.* départ, *m.* — **on,** *s* instigation, *f.* — **out,** *s.* départ, *m.*; (*beginning*) début, commencement, *m.* — **rule,** *s.* (*print.*) filet à composer, *m.* — **stick,** *s.* (*print.*) composteur, *m.* — **sun,** *s.* soleil couchant, *m.* — **up,** *s.* établissement, *m.*; (*print.*) composition, *f.*

Settle, *s.* banc à dossier, banc à dos, banc, *m.*; — *v.a.* fixer; établir; régler; déterminer; décider; arrêter; conclure; arranger; organiser; apaiser; calmer; tranquilliser; (*marry*) établir, marier; (*property*, '*on*') assurer (à); (*an annuity, a portion*, '*on*,' à) constituer, assigner; (*accounts*) régler, arrêter; (*pay*) payer; (*a question*) résoudre; trancher; (*liquids*) faire déposer; (*colonize*) coloniser; (*a clergyman*) installer; (*build.*) tasser, faire tasser; (*slang for* '*kill*,') escoffier, occire; — *v.n.* se fixer; s'établir; se décider; s'arranger; s'organiser; devenir réglé; reposer; s'apaiser; se calmer; se tranquilliser; (*get married*) se marier, faire une fin; se mettre en ménage; (*sit*) s'asseoir; (*of birds*) se poser; (*of the weather*) se remettre au beau, se remettre, se rassurer; (*of liquids*) déposer, se rasseoir; (*com.*) régler; s'arranger; (*build.*) tasser, se tasser. — **down,** *v.n.* se fixer, s'établir, &c. (*V.* —, *v.n.*). — **down to,** s'appliquer à. — **into,** (*become*) devenir, se faire; finir par former

Settled, *part. adj.* fixé, établi, &c. (*V.* **Settle**); fixe; permanent; calme, tranquille; beau. — *price*, prix fait, *m.*

Settledness, *s.* stabilité, *f.*; permanence, *f.*

Settlement, *s.* établissement, *m.*; fixation, *f.*, règlement, *m.*; décision, *f.*; (*of a question*) solution, *f.*; (*of annuities*) constitution, *f.*; (*annuity*) rente, pension, *f.*; (*jointure*) douaire, *m.*; (*of marriage*) contrat, *m.*; (*adjustment*) arrangement, *m.*; (*of accounts*) règlement, *m.*; liquidation, *f.*; (*colony*) colonie, *f.*; (*colonization*) colonisation, *f.*; (*of a clergyman*) installation *f.*; (*of liquids*) dépôt, sédiment, résidu, *m.*; (*build.*) tassement, *m.*; (*legal residence*) domicile légal, *m.* *Act of* —, (*Engl. hist.*) Acte de succession, *m.* *Deed of* —, contrat de [constitution, *m.*

Settler, *s.* colon, *m.*

Settling, *s.* *V.* **Settlement.** — **day,** *s.* (*com.*) jour de liquidation, *m.*

Seven, *adj. s.* sept (*adj. m.f.*, *s.m.*); (*elliptically*) (*of the clock*) sept heures, *f.pl.*, (*of o.'s age*) sept ans, *m.pl.* — **fold,** *adj. adv.* septuple, sept fois autant, sept fois. — **hilled,** *adj.* aux sept collines. — **score,** *adj.* cent-quarante

Seventeen, *adj.* dix-sept

Seventeenth, *adj. s.* dix-septième; (*of the month*) dix-sept. *The* —, (*of sovereigns*) dix-sept

Seventh, *adj.* septième; — *s.* septième, (*part*) *m.*, (*pers.*) *m.f.*, (*mus.*) *f.*; (*of the month*) sept, *m.* *The* —, (*of sovereigns*) sept

Seventhly, *adv.* septièmement

Seventieth, *adj.* soixante-dixième

Seventy, *adj.* soixante-dix. — *one*, soixante-et-onze. — *two*, &c., soixante-douze, &c. — *first*, soixante-et-onzième. — *second*, &c., soixante-douzième, &c. *The* —, (*of the Septuagint*) les Septante, *m.pl.*

Sever, *v.a.* séparer; diviser; désunir; démembrer; (*cut*) couper; trancher; (*law*) disjoindre; — *v.n.* se séparer, être séparé
Several, *adj.* plusieurs; divers; différent; particulier; séparé, distinct, à part; respectif
Severally, *adv.* séparément; individuellement; en particulier; distinctement; à part; respectivement [tion, *f.*
Severance, *s.* séparation, désunion, disjonc-
Severe, *adj.* sévère; rigoureux, rude; violent, grand; grave, sérieux; vif, aigu; cruel, atroce; (*of a cold*) fort, gros. *A — winter,* un hiver rigoureux *or* rude
Severely, *adv.* sévèrement; rigoureusement, rudement; violemment; gravement, sérieusement; vivement; cruellement
Severeness, Severity, *s.* sévérité, *f.*; rigueur, *f.*; violence, *f.*; gravité, *f.*
Sew, *v.a.n.* (**— on, up**) coudre; (*books*) brocher
Sewage, *s.* immondices des égouts, eaux d'égouts, *f.pl.*; curures, *f.pl.*, gadoue, *f.*; égouts, *m.pl.*
Sewer, *s.* (*with a needle*) couseur, *m.*, -euse, *f.*, couturier, *m.*, -ière, *f.*; (*of books*) brocheur, *m.*, -euse, *f.*; (*a drain*) égout, *m.* **— man,** *s.* [égoutier, *m.*
Sewerage. *V.* **Sewage**
Sewing, *s.* couture, *f.*; — *adj.* à coudre. **— cotton,** *s.* coton à coudre, fil d'Écosse, *m.* **— machine,** *s.* machine à coudre, couseuse (mécanique), *f.* **— needle,** *s.* aiguille à coudre, *f.* **— press,** *s.* (*book-bind.*) cousoir, *m.* **— silk,** *s.* soie à coudre, *f.*
Sex, *s.* sexe, *m.* *The fair —,* les dames, les femmes, *f.pl.*, (*jest.*) le beau sexe, *m.* *The female —,* le sexe féminin. *The male —,* le sexe masculin
Sexagenarian, *s. adj.* sexagénaire, *m.f.*
Sexagesima, *s.* Sexagésime, *f.*
Sexagesimal, *adj.* sexagésimal
Sexangular, *adj.* à six angles
Sexennial, *adj.* sexennal
Sexennially, *adv.* tous les six ans
Sextant, *s.* sextant, *m.*
Sextet, Sextette, *s.* (*mus.*) sextuor, *m.*
Sextile, *adj. s.* sextil, *adj. m.*, e, *f.*, sextil, *s.m.*
Sexton, *s.* sacristain, *m.*; (*grave-digger*) fossoyeur, *m.* **— beetle,** *s.* nécrophore, fossoyeur, *m.* **—ship,** *s.* charge de sacristain *or* de fossoyeur, *f.* [*v.a.n.* sextupler
Sextuple, *adj. s.* sextuple, *adj. m.f.*, *s.m.*; —
Sexual, *adj.* sexuel
Sexuality, *s.* sexualité, *f.*, sexualisme, *m.*
Sgraffito, — work, *s.* sgraffite, *m.*
Shabbily, *adv.* mesquinement. **—** *dressed,* mal mis, mal vêtu, pauvrement vêtu, à l'air râpé [pauvreté, *f.*
Shabbiness, *s.* mesquinerie, *f.*; (*poorness*)
Shabby, *adj.* mesquin, petit; méprisable; (*of clothes, threadbare*) vieux, usé, râpé, (*of hats*) vieux, usé, pelé; (*ill-clad*) mal vêtu. **— genteel,** *adj.* à demi râpé. **— looking,** *adj.* de mauvaise apparence; (*ill-clad*) à l'air râpé
Shabrack, Shabracque, *s.* schabraque, chabraque, *f.*
Shackle, *v.a.* enchaîner; (*to tie*) lier, garrotter; (*fig.*) entraver; **—s,** *s.pl.* chaînes, *f.pl.*, fers, liens, *m.pl.*; (*fig.*) entraves, *f.pl.*
Shad, *s.* alose, *f.*
Shaddock, *s.* pamplemousse, (*tree*) *m.*, (*fruit*) *f.*
Shade, *s.* ombre, *f.*; ombrage, *m.*; (*ghost*) ombre, *f.*; (*draw., engr., paint.*) ombre, *f.*, (*of colours*) nuance, *f.*; (*degree, quantity*) idée, *f.*; (*to protect the eye*) garde-vue, abat-jour, *m.*; (*of caps*) visière, *f.*, garde-vue, *m.*; (*of lamps,* &c.) abat-jour, *m.*; (*of clocks,* &c.) cylindre, verre, globe, *m.*; (*hort.*) contre-sol, *m.*; **—s,** *pl.* ombres, &c.; (*for wine*) caveaux, *m.pl.*; (*of an hotel,* &c.) estaminet, *m.*; — *v.a.* ombrager; couvrir de son ombre; mettre à l'ombre; (*shelter, screen, protect*) abriter, mettre à l'abri, couvrir, protéger; (*hide*) cacher, masquer, obscurcir; (*draw., engr.*) ombrer; (*paint.*) ombrer, (*with gradations of colour*) nuancer. *In* or *under the —,* à l'ombre. *To throw into the —,* faire ombre à; éclipser. **—less,** *adj.* sans ombre
Shaded, *adj.* ombré; (*of place*) à l'ombre, ombragé ('*by,*' de); — *part.* *V.* **Shade,** *v.a.*
Shadiness, *s.* ombrage, *m.*; ombre, *f.*
Shading, *s.* ombrage, *m.*; action d'ombrer, *f.*
Shadow, *s.* ombre, *f.*; — *v.a.* *V.* **Shade,** *v.a.*; (**— forth, out**) figurer, représenter. **—less,** *adj.* sans ombre; (*of lamps*) sinombre
Shadowy, *adj.* ombragé; sombre, obscur, ténébreux; figuré; chimérique; faible
Shady, *adj.* ombragé, ombreux; à l'ombre; de l'ombre; (*dark*) sombre, obscur; (*thick*) épais; (*cool*) frais
Shaft, *s.* (*arrow*) flèche, *f.*; dard, trait, *m.*; (*fig.*) trait, *m.*; (*of pillars*) fût, *m.*; (*chimney-stack*) souche, *f.*; (*of carriages*) brancard, *m.*; (*of carts*) brancard, limon, *m.*; (*of quills*) tuyau, *m.*; (*of lances*) bois, *m.*; (*of weapons*) manche, *m.*; (*of machines*) arbre, *m.*; (*of mines*) puits, *m.*; bure, *f.* **— horse,** *s.* cheval de brancard, *m.*; (*of carts*) limonier, *m.*
Shafted, *adj.* à manche
Shag, *s.* (*cloth*) peluche, panne, *f.*; (*hair*) poil rude, *m.*; (*tobacco*) caporal, *m.*; (*bird*) nigaud, *m.*
Shagged. *V.* **Shaggy**
Shaggedness, Shagginess, *s.* rudesse de poil, *f.*; état poilu *or* hérissé, *m.*
Shaggy, *adj.* peluché, pelucheux; (*hairy*) poilu, velu, à poil long et rude; (*rough*) hérissé; (*rugged*) raboteux, inégal
Shagreen, *s.* chagrin, *m.*, peau de chagrin, *f.*; — *adj.* de chagrin, de peau de chagrin; — *v.a.* chagriner. **— maker,** *s.* chagrinier, *m.*
Shah, *s.* schah, *m.*
Shake, *v.a.* (*agitate*) secouer; agiter; (*to make totter or tremble or waver*) ébranler; (*move*) remuer; (*frighten*) effrayer; (*affect*) émouvoir, agiter; (*weaken*) affaiblir; (*rouse*) réveiller, faire sortir, tirer (de); (*throw down*) renverser, faire tomber; (*o.'s head*) secouer (la tête); (*anyone's hand*) serrer (la main à ...); (*o.'s fist, a weapon or &c. at anyone*) menacer (quelqu'un) de ...; (*wood*) fendiller, gercer; (*mus.*) triller; — *v.n.* remuer, branler; s'ébranler; trembler ('*with,*' de); (*totter*) chanceler; (*be weak*) être faible, être affaibli; (*rail.*) ballotter; (*mus.*) triller; — *s.* secousse, *f.*; tremblement, *m.*; agitation, *f.*; (*of the hand*) poignée (de main), *f.*; (*in wood*) fente, gerçure, *f.*; (*mus.*) trille, *m.* *No great —s,* pas grand' chose. *To — hands with,* serrer la main à, donner une poignée de main à. *To — hands (together),* se donner une *or* la poignée de main, se donner la main. *To — o.'s fist at,* montrer le poing à, menacer du poing. *To — o.'s sides with laughter* (*or with laughing*), se tenir les côtes de rire. **— down,** faire tomber. **— off,** faire tomber; (*agitate*) secouer; (*get rid of*) se débarrasser de, se défaire de; (*free oneself*) s'affranchir de; (*the yoke*) secouer (le joug). **— out,** faire sortir; secouer. **— up,** remuer, agiter, secouer
Shaker, *s.* secoueur, *m.*, -euse, *f.*; (*quaker*) trembleur, *m.*, -euse, *f.* [shakespearien
Shakespearean, Shakespearian, *adj.*
Shaking, *part. adj.* secouant, &c. (*V.* **Shake,** *v.a.n.*); tremblant; chancelant; effrayé; ému; affaibli, faible; — *s.* secousse, *f.*; ébranlement, *m.*; tremblement, *m.*; (*rail.*) ballottement, *m.*; (*of hands*) serrement, *m.* *To give a —,* secouer. **— piece,** *s.* (*of oxen*) fanon, *m.*
Shako, *s.* shako, *m.* [spearean
Shakspearean, Shakspearian, *V.* **Shake-**
Shaky, *adj.* peu solide, branlant, qui branle; tremblant; chancelant; mal assuré; infirme, cassé, tombé; (*of wood*) plein de gerçures, fendillé, éclaté
Shale, *s.* schiste, *m.* **— oil,** *s.* huile de schiste, *f.*
Shall, *v. auxil.* *I — go,* j'irai. *— I go?* irai-je? dois-je aller? faut-il aller? faut-il que j'aille?

voulez-vous que j'aille ? *You — do it,* je veux que vous le fassiez, vous le ferez. *I — go* (*immediately*), je vais aller

Shalloon, *s.* escot, *m.*

Shallop, *s.* chaloupe, barque, *f.*

Shallot, *s.* échalote, *f.* — **sauce,** *s.* sauce aux échalotes, *f.*

Shallow, *adj.* peu profond, bas; (*of plates,* &c.) plat; (*fig.*) léger, superficiel; frivole, futile; (*—brained*) borné, superficiel; — *s.* bas-fond, *m.*; (*dangerous for ships*) haut-fond, *m.*; écueil, *m.* — *dish,* assiette plate, *f.* —**ly,** *adv.* de peu de profondeur; (*fig.*) superficiellement; sottement. —**ness,** *s* peu de profondeur, *m.*; (*of intellect*) manque de profondeur, *m.*, nature superficielle, *f.*, esprit borné *or* superficiel, *m.*

Shaly, *adj.* schisteux

Sham, *s.* feinte, *f.*; prétexte, *m.*; imposture, *f.*; hypocrisie, *f.*; (*fam.*) frime, couleur, craque, bourde, colle, *f.*, calembredaines, *f.pl.*; — *adj.* simulé, feint, faux; pour rire; (*bad*) mauvais; — *v.a.* simuler, feindre; jouer, faire (le, la, les); (*make believe*) faire accroire; — *v.n.* feindre, user de feinte. *To — Abraham,* faire l'innocent; faire le malade. *To — blindness,* contrefaire l'aveugle. — **fight,** *s.* combat simulé, simulacre (de combat), *m.*, (la) petite guerre, *f.*

Shamanism, *s.* schamanisme, *m.*

Shamanist, *s.* schamaniste, *m.*

Shamble, *v.n.* marcher lourdement *or* gauchement; — *s.* *V.* **Shambling,** *s.*; —**s,** *s.pl.* boucherie, *f.*; (*slaughter-house*) abattoir, *m.*

Shambling, *adj.* lourd, traînant; — *s.* démarche lourde *or* gauche, *f.*; pas lourd, *m.*

Shame, *s.* honte, *f.*; pudeur, *f.*; — *v.a.* faire honte à. *For —,* de honte; par pudeur; (*exclam.*) fi donc! quelle honte! c'est honteux! quelle horreur! c'est indigne! *To cry for —,* pleurer de honte. *To cry —,* crier au scandale *or* à l'infamie. *To put to —,* faire honte à. *The more — for him,* c'est d'autant plus honteux pour lui. —**faced.** *V.* **Bashful.** —**ful,** *adj.* honteux. —**fully,** *adv.* honteusement. —**fulness,** *s.* honte, ignominie, *f.* —**less,** *adj.* éhonté, effronté; impudent. —**lessly,** *adv.* effrontément, impudemment. —**lessness,** *s.* effronterie, impudence, *f.*

Shammer, *s.* simulateur, *m.*, -trice, *f.*, trompeur, *m.*, -euse, *f.*, imposteur, *m.*

Shammy, Shamoy, *s.* chamois, *m.*; — *v.a.* chamoiser. — **dress,** *v.a.* chamoiser. — **dresser,** *s.* chamoiseur, *m.* — **dressing, -factory,** *s.* chamoiserie, *f.* [nettoyer (la tête)

Shampoo, *v.a.* masser; frictionner; (*the head*)

Shampooer, *s.* masseur, *m*, -euse, *f.*

Shampooing, *s.* massage, *m.*; frictionnement, *m.*, frictions, *f.pl.*; (*of the head*) nettoyage de

Shamrock, *s.* trèfle, *m.* [tête, *m.*

Shan, Shanny, *s.* baveuse, *f.*

Shandredhan, Shandrydan, *s.* guimbarde, *f.*, chariot, *m.*

Shank, *s.* jambe, *f.*; (*jest.*) gigue, quille, *f.*; (*bone*) os de la jambe, *m.*; (*shaft*) tige, branche, *f.*; (*of anchors*) verge, *f.*; (*of a tobacco-pipe*) tuyau, *m.*; (*of buttons*) queue, *f.*; (*of keys, nails*) tige, *f.*; (*of horses*) canon, *m.*; (*of a column*) fût, *m.* — **painter,** *s.* serre-bosse, *m.*

Shanked, *adj.* à jambes ...; à tige ..., &c. (*V.* **Shank**)

Shanty, *s.* hutte, baraque, *f.*; appentis, *m.*

Shape, *v.a.* former; façonner; (*govern*) régler ('*by,*' '*on,*' sur); diriger; (*nav.*) commander, donner; — *s.* forme, figure, *f.*; (*pers.*) taille, tournure, *f.*; (*fashion*) façon, *f.*; coupe, *f.*; (*of a bonnet*) forme, *f.*; (*idea*) idée, *f.*, modèle, *m.* *In the — of a,* sous la forme de; (*shaped like*) en forme de, en. *To get out of —,* se déformer, se gauchir, s'avachir. *To put out of —,* déformer, gauchir. —**less,** *adj.* sans forme; informe. —**lessness,** *s.* défaut de forme, *m.*; informité, *f.* —**liness,** *s* belle forme, *f.*; symétrie, *f.* —**ly,** *adj.* bien fait

Shaped, *part. adj.* fait; formé, &c. *V.* **Shape,** *v.a.*; (*in compounds*) en forme de ..., en ... *To be ill —,* être mal bâti *or* mal fait, avoir une mauvaise tournure. *To be well —,* être bien fait, avoir une belle tournure

Shaping-machine, *s.* machine à dresser, *f.*; [contoureuse, *f.*

Shapska, *s.* schapzka, *m.*

Shard, *s.* tesson, *m.*; (*bot.*) carde, *f.* — **borne beetle,** *s.* bousier, *m.*

Share, *s.* part, *f.*; portion, *f.*; (*com.*) action, *f.*; (*interest*) intérêt, *m.*; (*quota*) contingent, *m.*; (*of ploughs*) soc, *m.*; — *v.a.* partager; diviser; distribuer; — *v.n.* partager; participer (à); prendre part (à). *In half —s,* de compte à demi. *To fall to o.'s —,* tomber *or* échoir en partage (à), échoir (à), devenir le partage (de), revenir (à); être donné (à); (*happen*) arriver (à). *To go —s,* partager. — **bone,** *s.* os pubis, *m.* — **broker,** *s.* agent de change, *m.* — **holder,** *s.* actionnaire, *m.f.* — **list,** *s.* cours de la Bourse, *m.* [e, *f.*; distributaire, *m.f.*

Sharer, *s.* partageant, *m.*, e, *f.*; participant, *m.*,

Sharing, *s.* partage, *m.*; participation, *f.*

Shark, *s.* requin, *m.*; (*pers.*) escroc, *m.*; — *v.n.* [escroquer

Sharker, *s.* escroc, *m.*

Sharking, *s.* escroquerie, *f.*; — *adj.* d'escroc

Sharp, *adj.* (*general sense, edged*) tranchant; (*particular sense, sharp-edged*) qui coupe bien, affilé; (*pointed*) aigu, pointu; (*subtle*) fin, subtil; (*cunning*) fin, rusé, pénétrant; roué; (*clever*) intelligent; habile; éveillé; dégourdi; (*brisk*) vif; (*acute*) vif, violent, fort; (*of sight, hearing*) perçant, pénétrant; (*clear, distinct*) net; (*acid*) acide; (*in taste*) aigre, piquant, âpre; (*harsh, biting*) dur, piquant, mordant, amer; (*of cold, wind,* &c.) vif, piquant, pénétrant; (*of angles, corners*) saillant; (*of features*) saillant, anguleux; accentué; dur; (*of sound*) aigu, perçant; (*mus.*) dièse; (*of appetite*) dévorant, fort, violent; (*of fights*) rude; (*of the tongue*) bien affilé. *A — instrument,* un instrument tranchant. *A — knife,* un couteau qui coupe bien. *This knife is not —,* ce couteau ne coupe pas. *As — as a needle,* fin comme l'ambre. — **dealer,** *s.* fin matois, *m.*, fine matoise, *f.* —**edged,** *adj.* qui coupe bien, affilé; (*build.*) à vive arête. — **practice,** *s.* rouerie, *f.*; filouterie, *f.* — **practitioner,** *s.* roué, *m.*; habile, *m.*; filou, *m.* — **sauce,** *s.* sauce piquante, *f.* — **set,** *adj.* aux expédients; (*hungry*) affamé; (*eager*) avide. — **shooter,** *s.* tirailleur, *m.* — **sighted,** *adj.* *V.* **Quick-sighted**

Sharp, *adv.* *V.* **Sharply;** (*of the hour*) précise (*adj.f.*). *One o'clock —,* une heure précise. *Two, three,* &c. *o'clock —,* deux, trois, &c. heures précises. *To look —,* faire attention; être vigilant; (*make haste*) se dépêcher. *To look — after,* surveiller activement *or* soigneusement, avoir l'œil sur. *Look —!* attention! dépêchez-vous! vivement!

Sharp, *s.* son aigu, *m*; (*mus.*) dièse, *m.*; (*pers.*) matois, malin, *m.*; habile, exploiteur, *m.* *The —s and the flats,* les exploiteurs et les exploités [*v.n.* filouter

Sharp, *v.a.* (*V.* **Sharpen**); (*mus.*) diéser; —

Sharpen, *v.a.* affiler; (*whet, improve*) aiguiser; (*cut*) tailler en pointe; (*excite*) exciter; (— **up**) aiguiser; (*a pers.*) dégourdir

Sharpener, *s.* (*pers. or thing*) affileur, aiguiseur, *m.*; (*thing*) affiloir, *m.*

Sharpening, *s.* affilage, *m.*; aiguisage, aiguisement, *m.* [trie, *m.*

Sharper, *s.* escroc, filou, chevalier d'indus-

Sharping, *s.* escroquerie, filouterie, *f.*

Sharply, *adv* d'une manière perçante; rudement, sévèrement; violemment, fortement; fort, ferme; vivement; activement; brusquement; (*distinctly*) nettement; (*wittily*) spirituellement

Sharpness, *s.* tranchant, *m*; pointe, *f.*; acidité, *f.*; vivacité, *f.*; pénétration, *f.*; subtilité, finesse, *f.*; intelligence, habileté, *f.*; rigueur, inclémence, *f.*; violence, force, *f.*; (*of language*) piquant, *m.*, aigreur, amertume, *f.*; rudesse, âpreté, *f.*; (*of the voice, and of sounds generally*) son aigu, *m.*; éclat, *m.*; acuité, *f.*; (*clearness*) netteté, *f.*

Shatter, *v.a.* briser, fracasser, mettre en pièces; (*impair*) délabrer; déranger; (*rend*) déchirer; — *v.n.* se briser. — **brained,** *adj.* timbré; (*giddy*) étourdi, écervelé

Shatters, *s.pl.* morceaux, éclats, *m.pl.*, pièces, [*f.pl.*

Shattery, *adj.* fragile, cassant

Shave, *v.a.* raser; (*beasts, turf*) tondre; (*cheat*) écorcher, plumer; (*plane*) planer; (*paper*) rogner; — *v.n.* se raser, se faire la barbe; (*in bargains*) rogner; (*charge low*) mettre au plus bas prix; — *s.* action de raser *or* de se raser, *f.*, rasement, *m.*; (*tech.*) plane, *f.* *To have a* —, se raser. — **grass,** *s.* prêle, *f.*

Shaveling, *s.* tonsuré, prêtre, moine, *m.*

Shaver, *s.* raseur, *m.*; barbier, *m.*; (*close* —) usurier, pingre, *m.*; (*cheat*) fripon, voleur, *m.*; (*cunning fellow*) malin, *m.*; (*chap*) gaillard, *m.* *A deep old* —, un fin matois, *m.*

Shaving, *s.* action de raser *or* de se raser, *f.*, rasement, *m.*; (*of wood*) copeau, *m.*; (*of paper, &c.*) rognure, *f.* *To leave off* —, ne plus se raser, laisser pousser sa barbe. *It is very close* —, c'est bien juste; (*of charges*) c'est au plus bas prix, il y a fort peu de bénéfice. — **box,** *s.* boîte à savonnette, *f.* — **brush,** *s.* pinceau à barbe, blaireau, *m.* — **cloth,** *s.* linge à barbe, *m.* — **day,** *s.* jour de barbe, *m.* — **dish, -basin,** *s.* plat à barbe, *m.* — **soap,** *s.* [savon à barbe, *m.*

Shawl, *s.* châle, *m.*

She, *pron. adj.* elle, *f.*; (*the one, anyone, before 'who,' 'whom,' 'that,' or 'whose'*) celle, *f.*; (*before the verb* être *followed by* une *and a noun*) ce, c'; (*of some animals*) femelle; (*of women*) *V.* **Female;** (*of a ship*) il (*masc.*), ce, c' (*followed by* un, *masc., for* 'a'); — *s.* (*of animals*) femelle, *f.*; (*woman, in contempt*) femme, femelle, *f.* — *speaks*, elle parle. — *who speaks*, celle qui parle. — *will be* or — *is a handsome woman*, ce sera *or* c'est une belle femme. — *ass*, ânesse, *f.* — *bear*, ourse, *f.* — *cat*, chatte, *f.* — *devil*, diablesse, *f.* — *elephant*, éléphant femelle, *m.f.*, éléphante, *f.* [un éléphant femelle, une éléphante; l'éléphant femelle a été prise, &c.]. — *fox*, renarde, *f.* — *goat*, chèvre, *f.* — *mouse*, souris femelle, *f.* — *wolf*, louve, *f.* [**tree,** *s.* bassie butyracée, *f.*

Shea. — **butter,** *s.* beurre de Galam, *m.* —

Sheaf, *s.* (*of corn*) gerbe, *f.*, (*loose, not bound up*) javelle, *f.*; (*of arrows*) faisceau, *m.*; — *v.a.* engerber, gerber, mettre en gerbe; (*in loose sheaves, not bound up*) javeler. — **binder,** *s.* botteleur, lieur, *m.* — **delivery apparatus,** *s.* appareil javeleur, *m.* — **delivery reaper,** *s.* (*machine*) moissonneuse avec appareil jave- [leur, *f.*

Sheafing, *s.* engerbage, gerbage, *m.*

Sheafy, *adj.* de gerbes; comme des gerbes

Shear, *v.a.* tondre; couper; (*fig.*) dépouiller, priver; —**s,** *s.pl.* ciseaux, *m.pl.*; (*tech.*) cisailles, forces, *f.pl.* — **grass,** *s.* prêle, *f.* — **man,** *s.* tondeur. *m.* — **steel,** *s.* acier corroyé, *m.* — **water,** *s.* puffin, *m.* [tondeuse, *f.*

Shearer, *s.* tondeur, *m.*, -euse, *f.*; (*machine*)

Shearing, *s.* tonte, *f.*; (*manu.*) tondage, *m.*; —**s,** *pl.* tonture, *f.* — **machine,** *s.* tondeuse (mécanique), *f.* — **time,** *s.* tonte, *f.*

Shearling, *s.* mouton d'une tonte, *m.*

Sheat-fish, *s.* glanis, saluth, *m.*

Sheath, *s.* étui, *m.*; gaîne, *f.*; (*scabbard*) fourreau, *m.*; (*bot., anat.*) gaîne, *f.*; (*of insects*) élytre, étui, *m.* — **bill,** *s.* bec-en-fourreau, *m.* —**less,** *adj.* sans étui; sans gaîne; sans fourreau; (*drawn*) hors du fourreau, nu. — **maker,** *s.* gaînier, *m.* — **making, -trade,** *s.* gaînerie, *f.* — **winged,** *adj.* à élytre, à étui

Sheath, Sheathe, *v.a.* rengaîner; remettre dans le fourreau; (*cover*) recouvrir; (*a ship*) [doubler

Sheathing, *s.* doublage, *m.*

Sheave, *s.* (*tech.*) rouleau, *m.*, poulie, *f.*; (*nav.*) rouet, *m.*; —**s,** *pl. of* **Sheaf** *&* *of* **Sheave**

Shed, *v.a.* verser; répandre; (*of animals*) jeter, quitter; (*of plants*) se dépouiller de, perdre; — *s.* appentis, hangar, *m.*, remise, *f.*; (*for cattle*) étable, *f.*; (*hovel*) hutte, *f.*; (*build.*) chantier, *m.*

Shedder, *s.* personne qui verse *or* qui répand, *f.*

Shedding, *s.* (*of blood*) effusion, *f.*; (*loss*) perte, *f.* [*f.*; — *adj.* *V.* **Sheeny**

Sheen, *s.* lustre, éclat, brillant, *m.*, splendeur,

Sheeny, *adj.* luisant, éclatant, brillant, étincelant, éblouissant

Sheep, *s.* mouton, *m.*; brebis, *f.*; (*leather*) basane, *f.*, mouton, *m.*; (*theol.*) brebis, *f.*; (*a fool*) mouton, sot, *m.* *Lost* or *stray* —, (*fig.*) brebis égarée. — **bell,** *s.* bélière, *f.* — **cot, -cote,** *s.* parc à moutons, *m.*, bergerie, *f.* — **dog,** *s.* chien de berger, *m.* — **farmer,** *s.* éleveur de moutons, *m.* — **fold,** *s.* bergerie, *f.*, parc à moutons, bercail, *m.* — **hook,** *s.* houlette, *f.* — **leather,** *s.* basane, *f.*, mouton, *m.* — **like,** *adj.* de mouton; moutonnier. — **louse,** *s.* mélophage, *m.* — **master,** *s.* *V.* — **farmer.** — **pen,** *s.* parc à moutons, *m.* — **run,** *s.* *V.* — **walk.** —**'s-eye,** *s.* œil de mouton, *m.*; (*fig.*) œillade, *f.*, les yeux doux, *m.pl.* *To cast* —*'s eyes at* or *on*, faire les yeux doux à, lancer des œillades à. — **shank,** *s.* (*nav.*) jambe de chien, *f.* —**'s head,** *s.* tête de mouton, *f.*; (*fish*) sarge, sargue, *m.* — **shearer,** *s.* tondeur de moutons, *m.* — **shearing,** *s.* tonte des moutons, *f.* — **skin,** *s.* peau de mouton, *f.*; (*leather*) basane, *f.* — **station,** *s.* *V.* — **walk.** — **stealer,** *s.* voleur (*m.*, -euse, *f.*) de moutons. — **stealing,** *s.* vol de moutons, *m.* — **tick,** *s.* mélophage, *m.* — **walk, -yard,** *s* pâturage de moutons, *m.*

Sheepish, *adj.* penaud; niais [niaisement

Sheepishly, *adv.* d'un air penaud, en penaud;

Sheepishness, *s.* bêtise, niaiserie, *f.*

Sheer, *adj.* pur; — *adv.* tout d'un coup, tout, net; — *v.n.* faire des embardées; — *s.* (*nav.*) tonture, *f.*; relèvement, *m.*; —**s,** *s.pl.* (*nav.*) bigue, *f.* — **hook,** *s.* grappin, corbeau, croc, *m.* — **hulk,** *s.* machine à mâter, *f.* — **off,** *v.n.* s'enfuir, filer; s'esquiver. — **sail,** *s.* arceau, *m.*

Sheet, *s.* (*of a bed*) drap, *m.*; (*of paper*) feuille, *f.*; (*of metal*) feuille, *f.*; lame, *f.*; (*fig.*) rideau, *m.*; (*of water, ice*) nappe, *f.*; (*nav.*) écoute, *f.*; — *v.a.* garnir de draps; (*to cover*) couvrir; (*build.*) blinder. *White* (*pale*) *as a* —, blanc comme un linge. *Three —s in the wind*, lancé, pompette, gris, pris de vin. — **anchor,** *s.* maîtresse ancre, grande ancre, *f.*; (*fig.*) ancre de salut, planche de salut, *f.* — **cable,** *s.* maître câble, grand câble, *m.* — **copper,** *s.* cuivre en feuilles, *m.* — **glass,** *s.* verre à vitres, *m.* — **iron,** *s.* tôle, *f.* — **lead,** *s.* plomb en feuilles, *m.* — **lightning,** *s.* éclair en nappe, *m.* — **tin,** *s.* ferblanc, *m.*

Sheeting, *s.* toile pour draps de lit, *f.*; grosse toile, *f.*; (*build.*) blindage, *m.* — **pile,** *s.* palplanche, *f.*

Sheik, Sheikh, *s.* cheik, cheick, *m.*

Shekel, *s.* sicle, *m.*

Sheldrake. *V.* **Shieldrake**

Shelf, *s.* planche, *f.*; (*of a book-case*) rayon, *m.*, tablette, *f.*; (*ledge*) bord, *m.*; (*at sea*) écueil, récif, *m.* *On the* —, (*fig.*) mis de côté, sous la remise. *To put on the* —, (*fig.*) mettre de côté, mettre sous la remise, mettre au rancart *or* [aux oubliettes

Shelfy, *adj.* plein d'écueils

Shell, *s.* (*of fruit*) coque, coquille, *f.*; (*of eggs, nuts*) coquille, *f.*; (*of seeds*) cosse, écale, *f.*; (*of shell-fish*) coquille, écaille, *f.*; coquillage, *m.*; (*of oysters, tortoises, turtles, lobsters, &c.*) écaille, *f.*; (*of snails*) coquille, *f.*; (*of serpents*) écaille, *f.*; (*of trees, plants*) écorce, *f.*; (*outside*) écorce, *f.*, extérieur, *m.*; (*build., arch.*) carcasse, charpente, *f.*; (*of a drum*) caisse, *f.*; (*of a pulley*) corps, *m.*; (*of a cartridge*) enveloppe, douille, *f.*; (*on a coat*) brandebourg, *m.*; (*a coffin*) cercueil de bois, *m.*; (*artil.*) obus, *m.*, bombe, *f.*; (*of iron ships*) coque, *f.*; (*mus.*) lyre, *f.*, luth, *m.*; — *v.a.* (*fruit*) écaler, ôter la coquille de; (*seeds*) écosser, égrener; (*peas, beans*) écosser; (*shrimps*) éplucher; (*fire upon*) lancer *or* diriger des obus sur, bombarder; — *v.n.* s'écailler; (*of fruit*) s'écaler; (*of seeds*) s'égrener. *In the* —, (*of eggs, cook.*) à la coque. — **board,** *s. V.* **Rathe.** — **drake,** *s. V.* **Shieldrake.** — **fish,** *s.* mollusque, coquillage, *m.*, (*as opposed to other fish*) homards, crevettes, huîtres, moules, &c. — **foundry,** *s.* bomberie, *f.* — **jacket,** *s.* dolman, *m.* — **lac,** *s. V.* **Shellac.** — **marl,** *s.* falun, *m.* — **marl pit,** *s.* falunière, *f.* — **off,** *v.n. V.* —, *v.n.* — **out,** *v.n.* s'exécuter, &c. (*V.* **Fork out**). — **proof,** *adj.* à l'épreuve des obus *or* des bombes. — **sand,** *s.* crag, *m.* — **work,** *s.* ouvrage en coquillage, coquillage, *m.*

Shellac, *s.* laque plate, laque en feuilles, laque en écailles, *f.*

Sheller, *s.* (*machine*) égrenoir, *m.*

Shelling, *s.* égrenage, *m.*; (*firing*) bombardement, *m.*

Shelly, *adj.* abondant en coquillages; (*made of shell*) de coquille, de coquillage

Shelter, *s.* abri, couvert, *m.*; asile, refuge, gîte, *m.*; protection, défense, *f.*; — *v.a.* abriter, mettre à l'abri; donner un asile à; protéger, défendre; (*hide*) cacher, voiler, déguiser. *Under* —, à l'abri (de), à couvert (de). *To get under* —, *to take* —, *to* — *oneself*, s'abriter, se mettre à l'abri; se réfugier. — **less,** *adj. V.* **Houseless**

Sheltered, *adj.* abrité, à l'abri

Shelterer, *s.* protecteur, *m.*, -trice, *f.*

Shelve, *v.n.* aller *or* être en pente, incliner; — *v.a.* mettre sur une planche *or* sur un rayon; (*a room*) rayonner; (*fig.*) mettre de côté, se débarrasser de; — *s.* pente, inclinaison, *f.*

Shelving, *adj.* incliné, en pente; — *s.* pente, inclinaison, *f.*; (*of a cart*) *V.* **Rathe**

Shelvy, *adj. V.* **Shelfy** *&* **Shelving**

Shemite, *s.* Sémite, *m.*

Shemitic, *adj.* sémitique

Shemitism, *s.* sémitisme, *m.*

Shepherd, *s.* berger, *m.*; (*fig.*) pasteur, *m.* — **boy,** *s.* jeune berger, *m.* —**ess,** — **girl,** *s.* jeune bergère, *f.* —**ly,** *adj.* pastoral, champêtre. —**'s dog,** *s.* chien de berger, *m.* — **spider,** *s.* faucheux, *m.*

Sherbet, *s.* sorbet, *m.*

Sherd. *V.* **Shard**

Sherif, *s.* (*Arab chief*) chérif, *m.*

Sheriff, *s.* préfet, *m.*; (*in England*) shérif, shériff, *m.* —*'s officer*, huissier, *m.*; garde du commerce, *m.* —**ship,** *s. V.* **Shrievalty**

Sherry, *s.* vin de Xérès, xérès, *m.* — **cobbler,** *s.* punch américain à la glace, *m.*

Shew. *V.* **Show**

Shibboleth, *s.* schibboleth, *m.*

Shield, *s.* bouclier, *m.*; (*in the middle ages*) écu, *m.*; (*protection*) égide, *f.*, bouclier, *m.*, défense, protection, *f.*; défenseur, protecteur, *m.*; (*of Minerva, &c.*) égide, *f.*; (*her.*) écu, écusson, *m.*; (*hort.*) écusson, *m.*; — *v.a.* couvrir, protéger, défendre (contre); (*ward off*) garantir (de). —**bearer,** *s.* écuyer, *m.* — **fern,** *s.* aspidie, *f.*

Shieldrake, *s.* tadorne, *m.*

Shift, *v.n.a.* changer; changer de place; changer de vêtements *or* de linge, changer; (*rail.*) changer de voiture; changer de voie; transborder; (*turn*) tourner; (*fig.*) trouver des expédients; se tirer d'affaire; s'arranger; (*play loose*) biaiser, ruser, finasser; (*transfer*) transférer, transporter, faire passer; changer; (*mus.*) démancher. *To* — *for oneself*, s'arranger. — **about,** changer. — **off,** détourner, tourner; éviter; échapper à; se débarrasser de; s'affranchir de; secouer

Shift, *s.* chemise (de femme), *f.*; expédient, moyen, *m.*, ressource, *f.*; (*subterfuge*) fauxfuyant, *m.*, défaite, *m.*, détour, biais, *m.*; (*change*) changement, *m.*; (*gang, tech.*) pose, *f.*; (*mus.*) démanché, *m.* *To make* — *to*, trouver moyen de, s'arranger pour; avoir de la peine à. *To make-— with*, s'accommoder de, s'arranger de. *To make* — *without*, se passer de. *To use* —*s*, user de biais. —**less,** *adj.* stupide; sans ressources; sans énergie. —**lessness,** *s.* manque d'énergie *or* de ressources, *m.*

Shifter, *s.* homme plein d'artifices, *m.*; biaiseur, *m.*, -euse, *f.*; (*scene*—) machiniste, *m.*

Shifting, *adj.* changeant; (*of ground*) mouvant; (*pers.*) chicaneur; (*cunning*) retors; — *s.* changement, *m.*; changement de place, &c. (*V.* **Shift,** *v.n.a.*); transbordement, *m.*; transport, *m.*; subterfuge, détour, biais, *m.*; (*mus.*) démanchement, *m.*

Shiftingly, *adv.* en changeant; (*deceitfully*) par des détours

Shillelagh, Shillelah, *s.* gourdin, assommoir, casse-tête, *m.*

Shilling, *s.* (*Engl. coin*) shilling, *m.*, (*equivalent in Fr. money*) 1 franc 25 centimes. *Four* —*s in the pound*, (*in bankruptcy*) vingt pour cent

Shilly-shally, *v.n.* lanterner, barguigner; — *s.* lanternerie, *f.*, barguignage, *m.*; — *adj.* irrésolu, indécis

Shilly-shallying, *s. adj. V.* **Shilly-shally**

Shimmer, *v.n.* briller, reluire, rayonner

Shin, (— **bone**) *s.* os de la jambe, tibia, *m.*; (*of beef*) jarret, *m.*

Shindy, *s.* (*quarrel*) chamaillis, *m.*; grabuge, *m.*; (*noise, row*) tapage, train, bousin, boucan, *m.* *To kick up a* —, *V.* **Row**

Shine, *v.n.* luire; reluire; briller; paraître; (*pers.*) briller; — *s.* éclat, *m.*; clarté, *f.* — **forth,** éclater. *The sun* —*s*, le soleil luit, (*fam.*) il fait du soleil. *The moon* —*s*, il fait clair de lune. *To take the* — *out of*, éclipser; remettre à sa place

Shiness. *V.* **Shyness**

Shingle, *s.* (*pebble*) galet, *m.*; caillou, *m*; (*board*) bardeau, *m.*; aisseau, *m.*, aissante, *f.*; —**s,** *pl.* (*med.*) zona, *m.*

Shingly, *adj.* de galets; abondant en galets, couvert de galets

Shininess, *s. V.* **Shining,** *s.*

Shining, *s.* brillant, *m.*; éclat, *m.*, splendeur, *f.*; lueur, *f.*; — *adj. V.* **Shiny**

Shiny, *adj.* luisant; reluisant; brillant; éclatant

Ship, *s.* (*chiefly for war*) vaisseau, (*chiefly for trade*) navire, (*general term*) bâtiment, *m.*; (*boat*) bateau, *m.*; — *v.a.* embarquer; (*the oars*) armer, border; (*the helm*) monter; (*a sea*) recevoir *or* embarquer (un coup de mer); — *v.n.* s'embarquer. — *of the line, line-of-battle* —, *line* —, *V.* **Line.** — *of war*, vaisseau de guerre. *Hundred gun* —, vaisseau de cent canons. *His* or *Her Majesty's* —, vaisseau de la marine royale. *To take* —, s'embarquer. — **biscuit,** *s.* biscuit de mer, *m.* — **board, (On),** *adv.* à bord. —**'s boat,** *s.* grand canot, *m.*, chaloupe, *f.* — **boy,** *s.* mousse, *m.* — **broker,** *s.* courtier *or* agent maritime, courtier de navires, *m.* — **builder,** *s.* constructeur de vaisseaux *or* de navires, *m.* — **building,** *s.* construction de vaisseaux *or* de navires, architecture navale, *f.* — **carpenter,** *s.* charpentier de navires, *m.* —**'s carpenter,** *s.* (*nav.*) maître charpentier, *m.* — **chandler,** *s.* approvisionneur de navires, *m.* —**ful,** *s. V.* — **load.** — **insurance,** *s. V.* **Insurance.** —**less,** *adj.* sans vaisseau, sans navire. — **load,** *s.* chargement, *m.*, cargaison, *f.* — **master,** *s.* patron de vaisseau, *m.* —**mate,** *s.* camarade de vaisseau, *m.* — —**money,** *s.* taxe des vaisseaux, *f.* — **off,** *v.a.* embarquer. — **owner,** *s.* armateur, *m.* —**'s papers,** *s.pl.* papiers de bord, *m.pl.* —**shape,** *adj.* bien arrangé; (*of sails*) bien orienté; *adv.* bien, proprement, comme il faut. —**wreck,** *s.* naufrage, *m.*; *v.a.n. V.* **Wreck.** — **worm,** *s.* taret, *m.* —**wright,** *s. V.* — **builder.** — **yard,** *s.* chantier de construction navale, *m.*

Shipment, *s.* chargement, embarquement, *m.*, mise à bord, expédition, *f.*
Shipper, *s.* expéditeur, *m.*
Shipping, *s.* vaisseaux, *m.pl.*; (*navy*) marine, *f.*; (*loading*) chargement, embarquement, *m.*; — *adj.* maritime, naval. *To take* –, s'embarquer. — **agent,** *s.* commissionnaire-expéditeur, *m.* — **intelligence,** *s.* événements de mer, *m.pl.* — **interest,** *s.* intérêt maritime, *m.*
Shire, *s. V.* **County**
Shirk, *v.n.* finasser; — *v.a.* éluder, éviter, se soustraire à; se dispenser de, manquer à. *To — it,* (*back out*) reculer
Shirt, *s.* chemise (d'homme), *f.*; — *adj.* de chemise. *Clean* —, chemise blanche. *To sell the — off o.'s back,* vendre jusqu'à sa chemise. — **button,** *s.* bouton de chemise, *m.* — **collar,** *s.* col de chemise, faux-col, *m.* — **front,** *s.* devant de chemise, *m.*; (*dicky*) chemisette, *f.* — **ing,** *s.* étoffe pour chemises, *f.* —**less,** *adj.* sans chemise. —**maker,** *s.* chemisier, *m.*, -ière, *f.* — **making,** *s.* chemiserie, *f.* — **sleeve,** *s.* manche de chemise, *f.* *In o.'s — sleeves,* en manches de chemise
Shist, &c. *V.* **Schist,** &c.
Shit, *v.n.a.* chier; — *s.* merde, *f.*
Shive, *s.* morceau, fragment, *m.*
Shiver, *v.a.* briser; fracasser; (*a lance*) rompre; (*sever*) démembrer; — *v.n.* se briser, se fracasser; se rompre; (*tremble*) frissonner, grelotter, trembler; (*of sails*) fasier; — *s.* éclat, fragment, morceau, *m.*; (*severance*) démembrement, *m.*; (*trembling*) frissonnement, frisson, tremblement, *m.* *To break to —s,* briser en éclats. *To have the —s,* avoir le frisson
Shivering, *s.* brisement, *m.*; (*severance*) démembrement, *m.*; (*trembling*) frissonnement, *m.*; frisson, *m.*
Shiveringly, *adv.* en frissonnant, en grelottant, en tremblant
Shivery, *adj.* cassant; friable
Shoal, *s.* foule, multitude, *f.*; (*of fish*) banc, *m.*; (*of rivers*) barre, *f.*; (*nav.*) haut-fond, écueil, *m.*; — *adj.* bas, peu profond; — *v.n.* s'attrouper; affluer; (*of fish*) se réunir en bancs; (*of water*) diminuer, baisser. *In —s,* en troupes; en foule
Shoaliness, *s.* manque de profondeur, *m.*; abondance de hauts-fonds *or* d'écueils, *f.*
Shoaly, *adj.* plein de hauts-fonds *or* d'écueils
Shock, *s.* choc, *m.*; (*fig.*) coup, *m.*; saisissement, *m.*; (*of corn*) moyette, *f.*, meulon, *m.*; (*of electricity*) secousse, commotion, *f.*; (*of earthquakes*) secousse, *f.*; (*hair on the head*) tignasse, crinière, hure, *f.*; — *v.a.* choquer; révolter, scandaliser; heurter; offenser; saisir, secouer; (*agr.*) mettre en moyettes, ameulonner. — **dog,** *s.* chien à poil long et hérissé, *m.* — **head,** *s.* tignasse, crinière, hure, *f.* — **headed,** *adj.* à tous crins
Shocking, *adj.* choquant, blessant, offensant; révoltant; horrible, affreux; abominable, détestable; repoussant. *Oh! — !* fi, l'horreur!
Shockingly, *adv.* horriblement, affreusement
Shockingness, *s.* horreur, nature affreuse, *f.*
Shod, *part.* ferré, &c. (*V.* **Shoe,** *v.a.*); (*pers.*) chaussé
Shoddy, *s.* effilochage, effiloché, *m.*; — *adj.* d'effilochage; (*trumpery*) de camelote, de pacotille; (*upstart*) parvenu. — **manufacturer,** *s.* effilocheur (de laines), *m.* — **mill,** *s.* (*machine*) effilocheuse, *f.*; (*factory*) fabrique d'effilochage, *f.* — **trade,** *s.* effilochage (de laines), *m.*
Shoe, *s.* soulier, *m.*; (*of animals*) fer, *m.*; (*of carriages, piles,* &c.) sabot, *m.*; (*of anchors*) semelle, savate, *f.*; (*tech.*) sabot, *m.*; coussinet, *m.*; — *v.a.* (*horses,* &c.) ferrer; (*pers.*) chausser; (*tech.*) saboter; (*a wheel*) embattre, ferrer; (*an anchor*) brider. *Wooden* —, sabot, *m.* *To stand* or *be in anyone's —s,* être à la place de quelqu'un. *To step into anyone's —s,* prendre la place de quelqu'un. *To walk in anyone's —s,* courir *or* aller sur les brisées (*or* sur le marché) de quelqu'un. — **black, -boy,** *s.* décrotteur, *m.* — **horn,** *s.* chausse-pied, *m.*, corne, *f.* — **leather,** *s.* cuir de bottes, *m.* —**less,** *adj.* sans souliers. — **maker,** *s.* cordonnier, *m.*, -ière, *f.* — **making, -manufactory,** *s.* cordonnerie, *f.* — **mart,** *V.* — **shop.** — **room,** *s.* cordonnerie, *f.* — **shop,** *s.* magasin de chaussures, *m.*, cordonnerie, *f.* —**string, -tie,** *s.* cordon de soulier, *m.* — **trade,** *s.* cordonnerie, *f.*
Shoeing, *s.* ferrage, *m.*; (*shoes*) ferrure, *f.* — **forge,** *s.* forge maréchale, *f.* — **hammer,** *s.* brochoir, *m.* — **smith,** *s.* maréchal ferrant, maréchal, *m.*
Shoot, *v.a.* (*fire-arms*) tirer; (*an arrow*) lancer, décocher; (*hit*) atteindre, frapper ('*in*,' à); (*with an arrow*) percer (d'une flèche); (*with fire-arms*) tirer un coup de feu (*or* de fusil, &c.) à, tirer sur, faire feu sur; (*kill*) tuer d'un coup de feu, tuer; (*particularly with a gun or pistol*) tuer d'un coup de fusil *or* de pistolet; (*a succession of pers. or animals with a gun or pistol*) tuer à coups de fusil *or* de pistolet; (*execute militarily*) fusiller; (*go out shooting*) chasser; (*dart*) lancer, darder; (*push forth*) pousser; (*out of a sack,* &c.) décharger, verser, déposer; (*carp.*) ajuster. *To — oneself,* se tirer un coup de pistolet *or* de fusil. *To — dead* (*with a* ...), étendre mort (d'un coup de ...), tuer raide, tuer sur le coup. *He was shot in the arm,* il reçut un coup de feu au bras; il fut atteint *or* frappé au bras. *He was shot through the arm,* il eut le bras traversé par une balle. — **forth,** pousser; (*dart*) lancer, darder. — **off,** (*fire-arms*) tirer, décharger; (*carry off*) emporter; (*artil.*) faire jouer, tirer. — **out,** *V.* — **forth.** — **through,** traverser, percer de part en part, percer d'outre en outre
Shoot, *v.n.* tirer; (— *out: of plants*) pousser, croître; (*to form*) se former; se développer; (*rush*) s'élancer, se précipiter, courir; (*jut*) s'avancer, faire saillie, saillir; (*penetrate*) traverser, percer, pénétrer; (*of pain*) élancer, avoir des élancements à; (*pass swiftly*) passer rapidement; (*of stars, ships*) filer; (*of ballast*) rouler; (*as a sportsman*) chasser. *To — with ball,* tirer à balle. *To go out —ing,* aller à la chasse. *My finger —s,* le doigt m'élance, j'ai des élancements au doigt. — **ahead,** courir *or* se précipiter en avant; passer (comme un trait). — **ahead of,** devancer, dépasser. — **at,** tirer à *or* sur; tirer un coup de feu *or* de fusil *or* de pistolet *or* &c. à; (*game*) tirer sur, tirer. — **forth,** s'élancer; (*of light,* &c.) jaillir; (*of plants*) pousser. — **out,** s'élancer, sortir; (*jut*) s'avancer, se projeter, faire saillie, saillir; (*of plants*) pousser. — **up,** (*grow up*) croître, grandir, pousser; (*become*) devenir; (*dart*) s'élancer; monter; (*of water,* &c.) jaillir
Shoot, *s.* rejeton, jet, *m.*; germe, *m.*; (*of streams*) remous, *m.*; rapide, *m.*; (*spout*) gouttière, *f.*; (*of an arch*) poussée, *f.*
Shooter, *s.* tireur, *m.*; (*of bows*) archer, *m.*; (*sportsman*) chasseur, *m.*; (*print.*) décognoir, *m.*
Shooting, *s.* (*of fire-arms*) tir, *m.*, décharge, *f.*; (*of arrows*) décochement, *m.*; (*of rubbish,* &c.) décharge, *f.*; dépôt, *m.*; (*of pain*) élancement, *m.*; (*slaughter*) tuerie, *f.*; (*execution*) exécution, *f.*; (*sporting*) chasse à *or* au tir, chasse au fusil, chasse, *f.*; (*of plants*) pousse, *f.*; — *adj.* de tir, de chasse; (*of pain*) lancinant; (*of stars*) filant; (*jutting*) saillant. — **boot,** *s.* botte de chasse, *f.* — **box,** *s. V.* — **lodge.** — **coat,** *s.* habit de chasse, *m.* — **gallery, -ground,** *s.* tir, *m.* — **jacket,** *s.* veste de chasse, *f.* — **licence,** *s.* port d'armes, permis de chasse, *m.* — **lodge,** *s.* rendez-vous de chasse, pavillon de chasse, *m.* — **match,** *s.* concours de tir, *m.* — **pain,** *s.* élancement, *m.*, douleur lancinante, *f.* — **pouch,** *s.* gibe-

cière, *f.* — **powder,** *s.* poudre de chasse, poudre à tirer, *f.* — **practice,** *s.* exercice à feu, *m.* — **season,** *s.* saison de la chasse, *f.* — **star,** *s.* étoile filante, *f.* — **stick,** *s.* (*print.*) décognoir, *m.* — **trunk,** *s.* sarbacane, *f.*

Shop, *s.* boutique (de ...), *f.*; (*large*) magasin (de ...), *m.*; (*workshop*) atelier, *m.*; (*build.*) chantier, *m.*; — *v.n.* faire des emplettes. *To go —ping,* aller faire des emplettes. *To be fond of —ping,* aimer à courir les magasins. — **board,** *s.* établi, *m.* — **book,** *s.* livre de comptes, *m.* — **boy,** *s.* garçon de boutique *or* de magasin, *m.* — **front,** *s.* devanture de boutique, *f.* — **girl,** *s.* fille de boutique, demoiselle de magasin, *f.* — **keeper,** *s.* marchand, *m.*, e, *f.*; (*small*) boutiquier, *m.*, -ière, *f.* *Old — keeper,* garde boutique, garde-magasin, rossignol, *m.* — **keeping,** *adj.* boutiquier; de *or* des boutiquiers. — **lifter,** *s.* auteur d'un vol dans un magasin *or* de vols de magasin, *m.*, voleur (*m.*, -euse, *f.*) à la carre *or* à la détourne, détourneur, *m.*, -euse, *f.* — **lifting,** *s.* vol commis dans un magasin, vol à la carre *or* à la détourne, *m.* —**like,** *adj.* de marchand; vulgaire, commun. — **man,** *s.* garçon de boutique, commis de magasin, commis, *m.* — **walker,** *s.* inspecteur, *m.* — **window,** *s.* étalage de boutique *or* de magasin, *m.* — **woman,** *s.* fille de boutique, dame de magasin, *f.*

Shopper, *s.* faiseur (*m.*, -euse, *f.*) d'emplettes, coureur (*m.*, -euse, *f.*) de magasins

Shopping, *s.* emplettes, *f.pl.*

Shorage, *s.* droit de rivage, *m.*

Shore, *s.* côte, *f.*, rivage, bord, *m.*; littoral, *m.*; (*prop*) étai, étançon, *m.*; (*nav.*) accore, accotoir, *m.*; — *v.a.* (— **up**) étayer, étançonner; (*nav.*) accorer. *On —,* V. **Ashore.** *To come on —,* débarquer. *To go on —,* aborder, aller à terre *or* à bord. —**less,** *adj.* sans rivage, sans côte

Shoreling, Shorling, *s.* laine de toison, *f.*

Shorn, *part.* tondu, &c. (*V.* **Shear**); (*fig.*) dépouillé, privé. — *of hope,* sans espoir

Short, *adj.* court; petit; exigu, maigre; réduit, diminué; insuffisant; incomplet; défectueux; (*curt, concise*) bref, succinct; (*of short duration*) de courte durée; (*pers.*) petit; (*of*) au-dessous (de), inférieur (à), moins (que), (*near*) près (de), (*next to*) après, (*in want of*) à court (de); (*deprived*) privé (de); (*narrow*) borné, étroit; (*abrupt*) brusque; bref; (*gram., mus.*) bref; (*of commercial measures and weights*) faux; (*crisp, brittle*, cassant; (*of earth*) friable; (*of pastry*) brisé, croquant; (*of metals*) cassant, sec; (*of the sea*) clapoteux; — *adv.* court, tout court; peu; trop peu; en moins; — *s.* court, *m.*; (*gram.*) brève, *f.*; —**s,** *s.pl.* (*coarse flour, bran*) remoulage, *m.*; (*breeches*) culotte courte, *f.* *A pair of —s,* une culotte courte. *In —,* bref, enfin, en un mot. *To be or come* or *fall — of,* être au-dessous de, être loin de; ne pas atteindre; ne pas répondre à; (*want: of things*) s'en falloir de (*imp.*), (*of persons*) être à court de, manquer de. *To cut —,* couper court (à); abréger; retrancher, réduire, rogner; (*pers.*) couper la parole à, interrompre. *To fall* or *come —,* manquer; être insuffisant. *To fall — of, V. To be — of. To stop —,* s'arrêter tout court; (*fig.*) rester court. *To stop — of,* manquer de. *To take up —,* rembarrer, reprendre vertement *To turn —,* tourner court *or* tout court; (*round*) se retourner brusquement. *To become* or *get —er,* se raccourcir, raccourcir. *To take a drop of something —,* (*pop.*) prendre un petit verre de schnick. *It falls very — of it.* il s'en faut de beaucoup. *It does not fall very — of it,* il ne s'en faut guère. — **coming,** *s. V.* **Deficiency.** — **dated,** *adj.* à courte date, à courte échéance. — **grained,** *adj.* (*of metals*) sec. — **hand,** *s.* sténographie, *f.* *To take* or *write down in — hand,* sténographier. — **hand writer,** *s.* sténographe, *m.* — **hand writing,** *s.* écriture sténographique, *f.* — **horn,** *adj.* à cornes courtes. — **lived,** *adj.* d'une courte vie, qui vit peu de temps; (*fig.*) de courte durée; passager; éphémère. —**ly,** *adv.* (*within a short space*) en peu de temps; (*hence, thence*) dans peu de temps, bientôt, sous peu, prochainement; (*briefly*) brièvement. —**ness,** *s.* peu de longueur, *m.*; peu, *m.*; courte durée, *f.*; brièveté, *f.*; imperfection, faiblesse, *f.*; (*smallness*) petitesse, *f.*; (*want*) défaut, manque, *m.*; (*gram., mus.*) brièveté, *f.* —*ness of breath, V.* **Breath.** —*ness of memory,* (la) mémoire courte, *f.* —*ness of sight,* vue basse, vue courte, myopie, *f.* — **sighted,** *adj.* myope, qui a la vue basse *or* courte; (*fig.*) peu clairvoyant; peu éclairé; peu prévoyant; peu intelligent. — **sightedness,** *s.* myopie, *f.*; (*fig.*) manque de clairvoyance *or* de prévoyance *or* d'intelligence, peu de clairvoyance *or* de prévoyance *or* d'intelligence, *m.* — **stuff,** *s.* (*spirit*) schnick, *m.* — **winded,** *adj.* *V.* **Winded**

Shorten, *v.a.* raccourcir; rapetisser; abréger; diminuer; (*contract*) resserrer; (*deprive*) priver (de); (*o.'s days or life*) abréger; — *v.n.* se raccourcir; se resserrer; se rapetisser, rapetisser; diminuer; (*of days*) décroître, diminuer, raccourcir [qui diminue, *f.*

Shortener, *s.* personne *or* chose qui abrége *or*

Shortening, *s.* raccourcissement, *m.*; rapetissement, *m.*; diminution, *f.*; (*contraction*) resserrement, *m.*

Shot, *s.* (*discharge of fire-arms*) coup de feu, *m.*; (*if the fire-arm is mentioned*) coup (de ...), *m.*; (*of a bow*) trait, *m.*; (*cannon-ball*) boulet, *m.*; boulets, *m.pl.*; (*bullet*) balle, *f.*; balles, *f.pl.*; (*for sporting*) plomb, plomb de chasse, *m.*; (*for a fishing-line*) grain de plomb, plomb, *m.*; (*artil. load*) charge, *f.*; (*reach*) portée, *f.*; (*marksman*) tireur, *m.*; (*reckoning*) écot, *m.*; — *part. V.* **Shoot;** — *adj* (*of colours*) gorge-de-pigeon, chatoyant, changeant; (*of velvet*) glacé; — *v.a.* (*bottles*) laver avec du plomb; (*artil.*) charger à boulet. *Round —,* boulet (de canon), *m.*; boulets, *m.pl.* *At a —,* d'un seul coup. *Like a —,* (*fast*) comme un trait. *Within ... —,* à portée de ... *Without firing a —,* sans brûler une amorce. *To fire a —,* tirer un coup de feu *or* un coup. — **belt,** *s.* ceinture de chasse, *f.* — **free,** *adj. V.* **Scot-free.** — **locker,** *s.* parc à boulets, *m.* — **plug,** *s.* (*nav.*) tape de combat, *f.* — **pouch,** *s.* sac à plomb, *m.* — **proof,** *adj.* à l'épreuve du boulet *or* des balles. — **tower,** *s.* tour à plomb de chasse, *f.*

Shotten, *adj.* (*of herrings*) gai; (*dried*) saur

Should, (*as the sign of the conditional, is not expressed separately in French*) *I — go,* j'irais; (*neither is it so, as the sign of the subjunctive*) *That I — go,* que j'aille (*present tense*), que j'allasse (*pret.*). *— I see him, if I — see him,* si je le voyais. *As I was walking ..., whom — I see but my friend Smith?* comme je me promenais ..., qu'est ce que je vois? mon ami Smith! (*When* should *stands for* ought to, *V.* **Ought**)

Shoulder, *s.* épaule, *f.*; (*mach.*) épaulement, *m.*; (*tech.*) languette, *f.*; (*of knife,* &c.) embase, mitre, *f.*; (*hort.*) fente, *f.*; — *v.a.* prendre *or* charger sur ses épaules, mettre sur l'épaule, porter sur les épaules; donner un coup d'épaule à, pousser avec violence; (*mil.*) (*arms*) porter. *Across the —s, over the —,* (*slung*) en bandoulière; en sautoir. *Over the left —,* (*fam.*) par-dessus l'épaule. *To give the cold — to,* battre froid à. *To lay o.'s — to the wheel,* pousser à la roue; se mettre à l'œuvre. — **band,** *s. V.* — **strap.** — **belt,** *s.* baudrier, *m.*; bandoulière, *f.* — **blade,** *s.* omoplate, *f.* — **high,** *adv.* sur les épaules. —

joint, s. moignon de l'épaule, m. — **knot,** s. aiguillette, f. — **of mutton,** s. épaule de mouton, f. — *-of-mutton sail,* voile aurique, f. — **piece,** s. épaulette, f. — **plate,** s. épaulière, f. — **scale,** s. (*mil.*) contre-épaulette, f. — **strap,** s. bretelle, f.; (*of porters*) bricole, f.; (*of linen*) épaulette, f.; (*surg.*) scapulaire, m.

Shouldered, *adj.* à épaules

Shout, *v.a.n.* crier, vociférer, pousser des cris; — s. cri, m., acclamation, f.; (*of laughter*) éclat, m. —*s of applause,* acclamations, f.pl.

Shouter, s. acclamateur, m., -trice, f.

Shouting, s. acclamation, f., acclamations, f.pl.; cris, m.pl.

Shove, *v.a.* pousser; (*put*) fourrer; — *v.n.* pousser; avancer; (*from the shore*) s'éloigner; — s. coup, m.; poussée, f. *To give a —,* pousser. — **away,** *v.a.* repousser, éloigner; *v.n.* pousser toujours; (*push off*) s'éloigner. — **back,** *v.a.* faire reculer, repousser. — **down,** *v.a.* pousser en bas, faire tomber, renverser. — **forward,** *v.a.* faire avancer. — **from,** *v.a.* repousser de, éloigner de. — **off,** *v.a.* repousser; (*a boat*) lancer, pousser à l'eau; *v.n.* pousser en avant; (*go away*) s'éloigner; (*nav.*) pousser au large. — **on,** *v.a.* fourrer. — **out,** *v.a.* pousser dehors, faire sortir, chasser

Shovel, s. pelle, f.; (*of bricklayers*) gâche, f.; — *v.a.* pelleter, peller; (*gather*) amasser; ramasser. — **away,** *v.a.* déblayer. —**ful,** s. pelletée, f. — **handle,** s. manche de pelle, m. — **hat,** s. tricorne, m. — **out,** *v.a.* jeter dehors avec la pelle; vider par pelletées. — **up,** *v.a.* ramasser

Shoveller, s. (*pers.*) pelleteur, m.; (*bird*) souchet, m., rhynchée, f., rouge, m.

Shovelling, s. pelletage, pellage, m.

Show, *v.a.* montrer, faire voir; témoigner; prouver; constater; indiquer; faire connaître; exposer; conduire; — *v.n.* se montrer; paraître, se voir; se dessiner; (*seem*) avoir l'air de. *To — a person how to do a thing,* montrer à quelqu'un à faire (*or* comment il faut faire) quelque chose. — **forth,** manifester; exposer. — (*one*) **in,** faire entrer, introduire. — **off,** faire valoir; étaler, faire parade de; (*embellish*) rehausser, relever, mettre en relief, faire ressortir; dessiner; (*v.n.*) ressortir; se dessiner; (*pers.*) (*— oneself off*) se donner du relief, se faire remarquer, briller, paraître; se pavaner, se donner des airs, poser. — (*one*) **out,** reconduire; (*get rid of*) éconduire. — **over,** faire visiter. — (*one*) **up,** faire monter; (*expose*) démasquer; pilorier

Show, s. apparence, f.; semblant, m.; spectacle, m.; (*display*) étalage, m.; parade, ostentation, f.; pompe, f., apparat, m.; représentation, f.; (*sight*) vue, f., coup d'œil, m.; (*exhibition*) exposition (de ...), f.; théâtre, spectacle, m.; (*of shops*) étalage, m., montre, f. — *of hands,* vote à main levée, m. *For —,* pour la montre. *To make a —,* briller, paraître, faire figure; (*of*) faire parade (de); étaler; afficher; (*pretend*) faire semblant (de), faire mine (de), feindre (de); faire profession (de). — **bill,** s. *V.* — **card.** — **board,** s. enseigne, f. — **box,** s. optique, f. — **bread,** s. pain de proposition, m. — **card,** s. affiche de montre, pancarte, f. — **case, -glass,** s. montre, vitrine, f. — **man,** s. saltimbanque, m.; directeur de spectacle forain, impresario, m.; montreur de curiosités, montreur, m.; explicateur, m. — **room,** s. salle (f.) *or* salon (m.) d'exposition, salon de montre, magasin, m. — **window,** s. montre, f., étalage, m.

Showable, *adj.* montrable

Shower, s. (*pers.*) montreur, m., -euse, f.; (*of rain*) (*slight*) ondée, f., (*heavy*) averse, f., (*in the spring*) giboulée, f.; (*fig.*) pluie, grêle, f.; (*of arrows*) grêle, nuée, f.; (*of shower-baths*) ondée, f. *Heavy —,* forte averse. — **bath,** s. douche, f. —**less,** *adj.* sans ondée, sans averse, sans pluie

Shower, — down, *v.a.* faire pleuvoir, verser, répandre; (*to water*) arroser, inonder; — *v.n.* pleuvoir, tomber

Showeriness, s. état pluvieux, m.

Showery, *adj.* pluvieux

Showily, *adv.* brillamment; d'une manière voyante; pompeusement

Showiness, s. faste, m., ostentation, f., étalage, m.; éclat, m.; couleur voyante, f.; couleurs voyantes, f.pl.

Showing, s. aveu, m., représentation, f.; démonstration, f.; exposition, f. *By* or *on o.'s own —,* de son propre aveu. *By* or *on the adversary's own —,* de l'aveu même de l'adversaire

Showy, *adj.* brillant, éclatant; tapageur; voyant; pompeux, fastueux

Shrapnel,— shell, s. shrapnel, obus à balles, m.

Shred, *v.a.* couper par bandes, couper en morceaux; (*cut small*) hacher; — s. bande, f., lambeau, morceau, m.; chiquet, m.; (*fig.*) fragment, lambeau, bout, m.

Shrew, s. (*woman*) mégère, pie-grièche, f.; (*zool.*) musaraigne, f. *The Taming of the —,* la mégère mise à la raison. — **mole,** s. scalope, m. — **mouse,** s. musaraigne, f.

Shrewd, *adj.* pénétrant, fin, rusé, malin, adroit

Shrewdly, *adv.* finement, adroitement, avec sagacité, avec ruse. *To — suspect,* soupçonner fort

Shrewdness, s. pénétration, sagacité, finesse, adresse, ruse, f.

Shrewish, *adj.* acariâtre, grondeur

Shrewishly, *adv.* avec humeur

Shrewishness, s. humeur acariâtre, f.

Shriek. *V.* **Scream**

Shrievalty, s. charge (f.) *or* fonctions (f.pl.) juridiction (f.) de shériff

Shrift, s. confession, f. —**less,** *adj.* sans confession

Shrike, s. pie-grièche, f.

Shrill, *adj.* aigu, perçant

Shrillness, s. son aigu, m.; éclat, m.

Shrilly, *adv.* d'un son aigu, d'une voix perçante

Shrimp, s. crevette, salicoque, f.; (*pers.*) nabot, m., e, f., avorton, criquet, m. — **net,** s. crevettière, f., avano, haveneau, lunet, bouteux, bouqueton, m., treille, grenadière, f. — **sauce,** s. sauce aux crevettes, f.

Shrimper, s. pêcheur de crevettes, m.

Shrine, s. châsse, f., reliquaire, m.; (*altar, fig.*) autel, m.; sanctuaire, temple, m.; — *v.a.* *V.* **Enshrine**

Shrink, *v.n.* se rétrécir, rétrécir, se retirer, se resserrer; se rapetisser; (*fig.*) diminuer; (*wrinkle*) se rider, se ratatiner; (*recoil*) reculer (devant), fuir (devant); trembler (devant); avoir horreur (de); — *v.a.* rétrécir; contracter; diminuer. — **away,** se rétrécir, se retirer, se resserrer; se dérober; disparaître; se dissiper; s'évanouir. — **back,** reculer. — **in,** se retirer; (*pers.*) rentrer en soi. — **up,** se rétrécir, se retirer; se ratatiner, se recoquiller, se recroqueviller, (*v.a.*) recoquiller

Shrinkage, Shrinking, s. rétrécissement, m.; contraction, f.; recoquillement, m.; (*of metals, earth*) retrait, m.; (*fright*) saisissement, m.

Shrive, *v.a.* confesser; donner l'absolution à

Shrivel (up), *v.a.* rider; faire ratatiner; racornir; recoquiller, recroqueviller; — *v.n.* se rider; se ratatiner; se racornir; se recoquiller, se recroqueviller

Shroud, s. (*shelter*) abri, couvert, m.; (*winding-sheet*) linceul, suaire, drap mortuaire, m.; (*nav.*) hauban, m.; — *v.a.* (*to shelter*) abriter, mettre à l'abri, mettre à couvert; (*to cover*) couvrir, envelopper; (*bury*) ensevelir; (*hide*) cacher, dérober; — *v.n.* s'abriter, se mettre à l'abri *or* à couvert. —**less,** *adj.* sans linceul

Shroudy, *adj.* qui abrite, qui couvre

Shrove. — **tide,** s. les jours gras, m.pl., le carnaval, m. — **Tuesday,** s. mardi gras, m.

Shrub, s. arbuste, arbrisseau, m.; (*drink*) shrub,

m.; — *v.a.* arracher les arbustes de, déplanter. —**less,** *adj.* sans arbustes, sans arbrisseaux

Shrubbery, *s.* plantation d'arbustes, *f.*, buissonnier, bosquet, *m.*; (*shrubs*) arbustes, arbrisseaux, *m.pl.*

Shrubby, *adj.* d'arbuste, d'arbrisseau; plein (*or* couvert) d'arbustes *or* d'arbrisseaux, touffu; ressemblant à un arbuste *or* à un arbrisseau

Shrug, *v.a.* hausser *or* lever (les épaules); — *s.* haussement d'épaules, *m.*

Shudder, *v.n.* ('*with*,' de) frissonner, frémir; — *s.* frissonnement, frémissement, *m.*

Shuffle, *v.a.n.* mêler, mettre en désordre; (*throw*) fourrer; (*cards*) mêler, battre, faire; (*dominoes*) remuer, mêler, brouiller; (*cheat*) tromper; (*change position*) changer de position; (*evade, shift*) biaiser, tergiverser, équivoquer; ruser; (*get out of*) se tirer d'affaire, s'arranger; (*of the feet*) traîner les pieds *or* les jambes; — *s.* mélange, *m.*, confusion, *f.*; (*evasion*) faux-fuyant, *m.*, échappatoire, *f.*, subterfuge, *m.*, défaite, *f.*; équivoque, *f.*; (*trick*) tour, artifice, *m.* — **along,** *v.n.* traîner la patte *or* la savate. — **away,** *v.a.* escamoter. — **in,** *v.a.* introduire adroitement. — **off,** *v.a.* rejeter; se débarrasser de; éluder; (*a person*) se débarrasser de, planter là, éconduire; *v.n.* reculer honteusement. — **up,** *v.a.* faire à la hâte, bâcler

Shuffler, *s.* biaiseur, *m.*, -euse, *f.*, fourbe, *m.f.*, chicaneur, *m.*, -euse, *f.*; (*of cards*) personne qui mêle *or* qui fait les cartes, *f.*

Shuffling, *adj.* évasif; (*of gait*) traînant; (*pers.*) chicaneur; — *s.* confusion, *f.*; (*of cards*) battement (des cartes), *m.*; (*evading, shifting*) détour, *m.*, détours, *m.pl.*, subterfuge, *m.* (-s, *pl.*), défaite, *f.* (-s, *pl.*), équivocation, ruse, *f.* (-s, *pl.*); chicane, *f.*; (*gait*) marche traînante, *f.*

Shufflingly, *adv.* d'une manière évasive; en biaisant; (*of the gait*) d'un pas traînant

Shumac. *V.* **Sumach**

Shun, *v.a.* éviter, fuir. —**less,** *adj.* inévitable

Shunt, *s.* (*rail.*) *V.* **Siding**; — *v.a.* changer de voie, garer; — *v.n.* changer de voie, se garer

Shunting, *s.* garage, *m.*; voie de garage *or* d'évitement, *f.*

Shut, *v.a.* fermer; (*enclose*) enfermer; (*from*) exclure; (*to*) défendre, interdire; — *v.n.* fermer; se fermer. — **again,** refermer. — **down,** fermer. — **in,** enfermer. — **off,** intercepter; (*steam,* &c.) couper. — **out,** fermer la porte à; interdire l'entrée à; empêcher d'entrer; exclure; intercepter; séparer; éloigner; (*prohibit*) défendre, interdire. — **up,** fermer; enfermer; (*imprison*) mettre en prison; (*to silence*) fermer la bouche à, faire taire; désarçonner, interloquer, coller; (*leave off*) finir, cesser; (*hold o.'s tongue or o.'s noise*) se taire, taire son bec. — *up!* assez comme ça! finissez! arrêtez! taisez-vous!

Shutter, *s.* (*inside*) volet, *m.*; (*outside*) contrevent, *m.*; (*louvred, Venetian*) persienne, *f.*; (*of a shop*) volet, *m.*; —**s,** *pl.* volets, *m.pl.*, &c.; (*of a shop*) volets, *m.pl.*, fermeture, *f.* *To put up the —s,* mettre les volets

Shutting, — **up,** *s.* fermeture, *f.*

Shuttle, *s.* navette, *f.*; — *adj.* à navette. — **cock,** *s.* volant, *m.* — **pike,** *s.* broche, *f.*

Shy, *adj.* timide, sauvage; honteux; réservé; prudent, circonspect; soupçonneux; (*of horses*) ombrageux; (*of animals*) farouche. *To be — of,* se défier de; craindre de; hésiter à

Shy, *v.n.* avoir peur (de), se jeter de côté, faire un écart; être ombrageux; — *v.a.* jeter, lancer, flanquer

Shyly, *adv.* timidement; avec réserve; avec circonspection, avec prudence; (*of horses*) ombrageusement

Shyness, *s.* timidité, sauvagerie, *f.*; fausse honte, réserve, retenue, *f.*; (*of horses*) nature ombrageuse, *f.*

Siamese, *s. adj.* Siamois, *m.*, e, *f.*

Siberian, *s.* Sibérien, *m.*, -ne, *f.*; — *adj.* sibérien, de Sibérie

Sibilance, *s.* sibilance, *f.*

Sibilant, *adj.* sifflant, sibilant; — *s.* lettre sifflante, sifflante, *f.*

Sibilation, *s.* sifflement, *m.*, sibilation, *f.*

Sibyl, *s.* sibylle, *f.*

Sibylline, *adj.* sibyllin

Siccative, *adj. s.* siccatif, *adj. m.*, -ive, *f.*; siccatif, *s.m.*

Sicilian, *s.* Sicilien, *m.*, -ne, *f.*; — *adj.* sicilien, de Sicile. *The — Vespers,* les Vêpres siciliennes, *f.pl.*

Sick, *adj.* malade; (*inclined to vomit*) qui a mal au cœur; (*weary*) dégoûté (de), las (de), fatigué (de); — *s.pl.* (*The —*) (les) malades, *m.pl.* *To be —,* avoir mal au cœur; vomir; être malade; être dégoûté *or* las *or* fatigué (de). *To be — at heart,* avoir la mort dans l'âme, être navré *or* &c. (*V.* **Heart-sick**). *To feel —,* se sentir mal au cœur, avoir des envies de vomir. *To make —,* écœurer, faire mal au cœur à, soulever le cœur à; faire vomir. — **bay,** *s. V.* — **berth.** — **bed,** *s.* lit de douleur, *m.* — **berth,** *s.* (*nav.*) poste des malades, *m.* — **boy,** *s.* malade, *m.* — **brained,** *adj.* qui a le cerveau malade. — **fund,** *s.* caisse de secours mutuels, caisse de malades, *f.* — **girl,** *s.* malade, *f.* — **headache,** *s.* (la) migraine, *f.* — **house,** *s.* infirmerie, *f.* — **list,** *s.* rôle des malades, *m.* — **man,** *s.* malade, *m.* — **nurse,** *s.* garde-malade, *f.* — **room, -ward,** *s.* chambre de malade, *f.*; chambre (*or* salle) des malades, *f.*; infirmerie, *f.* — **woman,** *s.* malade, *f.*

Sicken, *v.a.* rendre malade; (*heave the stomach*) soulever (le cœur); soulever le cœur à, écœurer (*a person*); (*disgust*) dégoûter; — *v.n.* tomber malade; (*of the stomach*) se soulever; (*to be weary*) se dégoûter (de), être dégoûté (de); (*languish*) languir. *I —ed at the sight of ...,* le cœur me souleva à la vue de ..., la vue de ... me souleva le cœur

Sickish, *adj.* (*pers.*) un peu malade; ayant un peu mal au cœur; (*things*) fade, nauséabond

Sickishness, *s.* (*pers.*) état maladif, *m.*; disposition à éprouver des nausées, *f.*; (*things*) fadeur, nature nauséabonde, *f.*

Sickle, *s.* faucille, *f.*

Sickled, *adj.* pourvu d'une faucille

Sickliness, *s.* (*pers.*) maladiveté, *f.*, état maladif, défaut de santé, *m.*; (*things*) insalubrité, *f.*; (*nauseousness*) fadeur, nature nauséabonde, *f.*

Sickly, *adj.* (*pers.*) maladif, malingre; languissant, faible; (*plants*) délicat, étiolé, chétif; (*things*) malsain, insalubre; (*nauseous*) fade, nauséabond, écœurant

Sickness, *s.* maladie, *f.*; (*— of stomach*) mal au cœur, *m.*; (*sea —*) mal (de mer), *m.* *Bed of —,* lit de douleur, *m.*

Side, *s.* côté, *m.*; flanc, *m.*; bord, *m.*; (*slope*) pente, *f.*, penchant, *m.*; (*party*) parti, *m.*; (*in boys' matches*) camp, *m.*; (*of a book-cover,* &c., *flat —*) plat, *m.*; (*inner —, of a vase, tube,* &c.) paroi, *f.*; (*masonry*) paroi, *f.*; — *adj.* de côté, latéral; indirect, oblique; — *v.n.* (*with*) se mettre (*or* se ranger) du côté *or* du parti (de), prendre parti (pour), se mettre du même côté (que); donner raison (à). *By my —,* à côté de moi, près de moi. *By the — of,* à côté de, près de; (*of roads, rivers*) sur le bord de, au bord de. *From — to —,* d'un côté (*or* d'un bout) à l'autre. *On all —s,* de tous côtés; de toutes parts. *On both —s,* des deux côtés; de part et d'autre. *On each —,* de chaque côté, des deux côtés; de part et d'autre. *On every —,* de tous les côtés, de tous côtés; de toutes parts. *On my —,* de mon côté; (*in my favour*) pour moi. *On neither —,* d'aucun côté, ni d'un côté ni de l'autre; d'aucune part, ni d'une part ni de l'autre. *On one —,* d'un côté; d'une part. *On the other —,* de l'autre côté; au-delà; de l'autre part, d'autre part. *On the* —, du côté ('*of*,' de); (*laid down*) sur le côté, couché. *On that* —, de ce côté-là, de ce côté; au-delà. *On this* —, de ce côté-ci, de ce côté; en deçà. *On the right* —, du côté droit; à droite; (*fig.*) du bon côté; (*of stuffs*) à l'endroit. *Wrong* —, mauvais côté, *m.*; (*of stuffs*) envers, *m.* *The wrong — out* or *outwards*, à l'envers. *The wrong — up*, sens dessus dessous. *This — up*, (*on cases*, &c.) dessus. — *by* —, côte à côte, à côté l'un de l'autre. *To take anyone's* —, prendre le parti de quelqu'un, se ranger du côté de quelqu'un. — **alley,** *s.* contre-allée, *f.* — **arm,** *s.* arme blanche, *f.* —**board,** *s.* buffet, *m.* — **box,** *s.* (*theat.*) loge de côté, *f.* — **comb,** *s.* peigne à papillotes, *m.* — **dish,** *s.* (*of first course*) entrée, *f.*; (*small*) hors-d'œuvre, *m.*; (*of second course*) entremets, *m.*; (*ware*) *V.* **Corner-dish.** — **door,** *s* porte latérale, *f.* — **face,** **-front,** *s.* profil, *m.* —**faced,** *adj.* de profil. —**long,** *adj.* oblique; de côté; *adv.* obliquement; latéralement, de côté. — **look,** *s.* regard oblique, *m.* *To cast a — look upon*, regarder du coin de l'œil, lorgner. — **note,** *s.* (*print.*) addition marginale, manchette, *f.* — **path,** *s. V.* —**way.** — **pocket,** *s.* poche de côté, *f.* — **rail,** *s.* contre-rail, *m.* —**saddle,** *s. V.* **Saddle.** —**saddle flower,** *s.* sarracénie, *f.* — **scene,** *s.* coulisse, *f.* — **table,** *s. V.* **Table.** — **view,** *s.* vue de côté, vue de profil, *f.* — **walk,** *s.* contre-allée, *f.* —**way,** *s.* bas-côté, accotement, *m.* -**ways, -wise,** *adv.* de côté; obliquement: de champ; de travers. — **wind,** *s.* (*nav.*) demi-vent, *m.*

Sided, *adj.* (*in compounds*) à ... côté, à ... côtés; à ... face, à ... faces. *Two* —, à deux côtés; à deux faces [sidéral; (*starry*) étoilé

Sideral, Sidereal, *adj.* des astres; (*astr.*)

Siding, *s.* (*rail.*) gare d'évitement, voie de garage, voie de service, *f.*; (*in a railway of a single line of rail*) croisière, *f.*; (*of canals*) gare, *f.*

Sidle, *v.n.* marcher (*or* aller) de côté; (*lie on the side*) être sur le côté

Siege, *s.* siége, *m.*; — *adj.* de siége. *In a state of* —, en état de siége. *To lay — to*, faire le siége de, assiéger. — **artillery,** *s.* artillerie de siége, *f.* — **gun,** *s.* pièce de siége, *f.* — **train,** *s.* équipage de siége, *m.* — **works,** *s.pl.* travaux de siége, *m.pl.* [Sienne, *f.*

Sienna, *s.* (*geog.*) Sienne, *f.*; (— *earth*) terre de

Siesta, *s.* sieste, *f.* *To take o.'s* —, faire sa sieste [**maker,** *s.* criblier, tamisier, *m.*

Sieve, *s.* crible, *m.*; tamis, *m.*; filtre, *m.*; —

Sift, *v.a.* cribler; tamiser; séparer; (*fig.*) éplucher; examiner; sonder; (*find out*) découvrir

Sifter, *s.* (*sieve*) *V.* **Sieve;** (*for cinders*) tamiseur, *m.*; (*for sugar*) cuiller, *f.*; (*pers.*) cribleur, *m.*, -euse, *f.*, tamiseur, *m.*, -euse, *f.*

Sifting, *s.* criblage, *m.*; tamisage, *m.*; (*fig.*) examen, *m.*; —**s,** *pl.* criblure, *f.*; criblures, *f.pl.*; — *adj.* minutieux [soupir, *m.*

Sigh, *v.n.* soupirer ('*for*,' '*after*,' après); — s.

Sigher, *s.* soupireur, *m.*, -euse, *f.*; (*lover*) soupirant, *m.*

Sighing, *s*; soupirement, *m.*; soupirs, *m.pl.*

Sight, *s.* vue, *f.*; spectacle, *m.*; scène, *f.*; curiosité, *f.*; caricature, *f.*; degré, *m.*; quantité, *f.*; (*looks*) yeux, regards, *m.pl.*; (*of math. instr.*) lumière, *f.*; (*of fire arms, front* or *fore* —) mire, *f.*; guidon, *m.*; (*tech.*) alidade, *f.*; — *v.a.* apercevoir. *At* —. (*com.*) à vue. *At* —, *at first* —, à (la) première vue, au premier coup d'œil; (*of reading*, &c.) à livre ouvert; (*mus.*) *V.* **Read;** *v.a.n.* *At the — of*, à la vue de. *By* —, de vue. *Far* or *long* —, presbytie, vue longue, *f.* *In* —, *within* —, en vue; à portée de la vue. *In the — of*, (*fig.*) aux yeux de. *Out of* —, *V.* **Out.** *Short* or *near* —, myopie, vue basse, vue courte, *f.* *Two days* or *months after* —, à deux jours *or* mois de vue. *To come in* —, paraître. *To gain* or *get* or *have* or *catch* (*a*) — *of*, voir, apercevoir. *To keep in* —, ne pas perdre de vue; (*not to go away*) ne pas s'éloigner. *To keep from* (or *out of*) —, se tenir éloigné *or* caché; (*fig.*) s'effacer. *To lose — of*, perdre de vue. *To see a* —, voir un spectacle, assister à un spectacle, jouir d'une vue (...). *To take* —, (*artil.*) viser, pointer. *To take a — of*, jeter un coup d'œil sur. *To take a — at anyone*, faire un pied-de-nez à quelqu'un. *To vanish out of* —, disparaître. *I hate* (or *cannot bear*) *the — of him* or *her*, je ne peux pas le *or* la voir (*or*, le *or* la sentir), c'est ma bête noire. — **seeing,** *s.* *To be fond of — seeing*, aimer à voir les curiosités. — **seer,** *s.* curieux, *m.*, -euse, *f.*; badaud, *m.*, e, *f.* [**Short, Far, Quick,** &c.)

Sighted, *adj.* qui à la vue ..., à vue ... (*V.*

Sightedness, *s.* (*in compounds*) vue, *f.*; (*V.* **Short, Far,** &c.)

Sightless, *adj.* aveugle, privé de la vue. —**ness,** *s,* privation de la vue, cécité, *f.*

Sightliness, *s.* beauté, *f.*, charme, *m.*

Sightly, *adj.* qui plaît à l'œil, beau, charmant; (*conspicuous*) apparent, en vue, visible

Sightsman, *s.* déchiffreur, *m.*

Sign, *s.* signe, *m.*; (*of a house*) enseigne, *f.*; — *v.a.* signer; (*show*) montrer; — *v.n.* signer; (*make signs or a sign*) faire signe. — *of the times*, signe du temps *or* des temps, *m.* — **board,** *s.* enseigne, *f.*; (*with a notice or directions*) écriteau, *m.*; volet, *m.* — **manual,** *s.* seing, *m.*, signature, *f.* — **painter,** *s.* peintre d'attributs, peintre d'enseignes, *m.* — **painting,** *s.* peinture d'attributs, peinture d'enseignes, *f.* — **post,** *s.* poteau d'enseigne, *m.*; (*of roads*) poteau-guide, poteau indicateur, *m.*; (*fig.*) fanal, *m.*

Signal, *s.* signal, *m.*; (*whistle for a train to start*) coup de sifflet, *m.*; — *v.a.* signaler; — *adj.* signalé, insigne. — **ball,** *s.* (*nav.*) bombe de signaux, *f.* — **fire,** *s.* feu, *m.* — **gun,** *s.* coup de canon de signal, *m.* — **light,** *s.* fanal, *m.*; feu, *m.* — **man, -woman,** *s.* signaliste, *m.f.*, guetteur, *m.*, -euse, *f.* — **word,** *s.* signal, *m.*

Signalist, *s.* signaliste, *m.f.*

Signalize, *v.a.* signaler

Signally, *adv.* d'une manière signalée

Signatary, Signatory, *s.adj.* signataire, *m.f.*

Signature, *s.* signature, *f.*; (*stamp*) cachet, *m.*, empreinte, marque, *f.*

Signer, *s.* signataire, *m.f.*

Signet, *s.* sceau, *m.*; (*in England*) cachet, *m.* *Writer* (or *clerk*) *to the* —, (*in Scotland*) avoué, *m.*; notaire, *m.* — **ring,** *s.* bague à cachet, *f.*, anneau avec cachet, *m.*, chevalière, *f.*

Significanc-e, y, *s.* signification, *f.*, sens, *m.*; force, énergie, *f.*; importance, portée, *f.*

Significant, *adj.* significatif, signifiant; expressif, énergique; important

Significantly, *adv.* significativement

Signification, *s.* signification, *f.*

Significative, *adj.* significatif

Significatively, *adv.* significativement

Signify, *v.a.n.* (*to mean*) signifier, vouloir dire; (*make known*) faire connaître, signifier, notifier, communiquer; faire signe, montrer; (*matter*) [*V.* **Matter,** *v.n.*

Signing, *s.* signature, *f.*

Signior. *V.* **Seignior**

Sikh, *s.* Seikh, Syke, Sykh, *m.*

Silence, *s.* silence, *m.*; — *v.a.* imposer silence à, faire taire, réduire au silence; (*stop*) arrêter, faire cesser; (*artil.*) éteindre le feu de. *In* —, en silence. *To keep* —, garder le silence, faire silence. *To pass by* or *over in* —, passer sous silence. — *gives* (or *is*) *consent*, qui ne dit mot [consent

Silene, *s.* silène, *f.*

Silent, *adj.* silencieux; taciturne; muet; calme, tranquille; (*gram.*) muet; (*of imprisonment*) cellulaire. *William the* —, Guillaume le taciturne. *To be* or *remain* —, faire silence, garder le silence, se taire. — **system,** *s.* régime *or* système cellulaire, *m.*

Silently, *adv.* en silence, silencieusement, sans bruit; (*without mention*) sous silence

Silesian, *s.* Silésien, *m.*, -ne, *f.*; — *adj.* silésien, de Silésie
Silex, *s.* silex, *m.*
Silhouette, *s.* silhouette, *f.*
Silica, *s.* silice, *f.*
Silicate, *s.* silicate, *m.*
Silicic, *adj.* silicique
Silicious, *adj.* siliceux
Silicium, Silicon, *s.* silicium, *m.*
Silk, *s.* soie, *f.*; (*thread*) fil de soie, *m.*, soie à coudre, *f.*; **—s,** *pl.* soieries, *f.pl.*; — *adj.* de soie; en soie; (*of thread*) de fil de soie; (*pertaining to the silk-trade or to silk-growing*) soyer, séricicole. — **breeder,** *s.* éducateur de vers à soie, magnanier, sériciculteur, *m.* — **breeding,** *s.* éducation des vers à soie, sériciculture, *f.* — **business,** *s.* (*trade*) soierie, *f.*; (*house*) maison de soieries, *f.* — **cotton,** *s.* soie végétale, *f.* — **cotton tree,** *s.* fromager, gossampin, *m.*, sterculie, *f.*, sterculier, *m.* — **culture,** *s.* sériciculture, *f.* — **dress,** *s.* robe de soie, *f.* — **goods, -stuffs,** *s.pl.* soieries, *f.pl.* — **gown,** *s.* robe de soie, *f.* — **grower,** *s.* *V.* — **breeder.** — **growing,** *s.* sériciculture, industrie séricicole, *f.*; *adj.* séricicole. — **handkerchief,** *s.* mouchoir de foulard, foulard, *m.* — **husbandry,** *s.* *V.* — **growing.** — **manufactory, -mill,** *s.* fabrique de soie, *f.* — **manufacture,** *s.* fabrication de la soie, *f.* — **mercer,** *s.* marchand de soieries, *m.* — **merchant,** *s.* négociant en soieries, *m.* — **producer,** *s.*, — **producing,** *s. adj.*, *V.* — **breeder** & — **growing.** — **spinner,** *s.* filateur de soie, *m.* — **spinning,** *s.* filature de soie, *f.* — **throwing,** *s.* organsinage, *m.* — **throwster,** *s.* organsineur, *m.* — **trade,** *s.* soierie, *f.* — **weaver,** *s.* tisserand en soie, *m.*, (*at Lyons*) canut, *m.* —**worm,** *s.* ver à soie, *m.* —**worm gut,** *s.* boyau de ver à soie, crin marin, *m.*, racine, *f.* —**worm nursery,** *s.* magnanerie, *f.* —**worm rot,** *s.* muscardine, *f.*
Silken, *adj.* de soie: (*soft*) soyeux, doux, moelleux; délicat; (*pliant*) souple
Silkiness, *s.* nature soyeuse, *f.*; douceur, *f.*
Silky, *adj.* *V.* **Silken**
Sill, *s.* (*of doors*) seuil, *m.*; (*of windows*) appui, *m.*; (*of locks*) heurtoir, *m.*; (*young herring*) harenguet, *m.*
Sillily, *adv.* sottement, bêtement, niaisement
Silliness, *s.* niaiserie, sottise, bêtise, *f.*
Silly, *adj.* niais, sot, bête; naïf; simple; bouché; — *s.* godiche, *m.f.*, bêta, *m.*, -sse *f.* *To be* —, (*play the fool*) faire la bête. — **Billy,** *s.* nicodème, *m.* — **fellow,** *s.* sot, *m.* — **girl,** *s.* sotte, *m.* — **thing,** *s.* sottise, *f.*; (*girl*) sotte, *f.*
Silt, *s.* vase, *f.*, limon, *m.*; — *v.a.* (— **up**) envaser, atterrir; — *v.n.* s'envaser
Silting, *s.* envasement, atterrissement, *m.*
Silty, *adj.* vaseux, limoneux
Silure. *V.* **Silurus**
Silurian, *adj.* silurien
Silurus, *s.* silure, *m.* *Sly* —, glanis, *m.*
Silvan, &c. *V.* **Sylvan,** &c.
Silver, *s.* argent, *m.*; (*silver change*) argent blanc, *m.*, monnaie d'argent, *f.*; (*plate*) argenterie, *f.*; — *adj.* d'argent; en argent; (*of colour*) argenté; (*of sound*) argentin; — *v.a.* argenter; (*looking-glasses*) étamer. — **age,** *s.* âge d'argent, *m.* — **change, -coin,** *s.* argent blanc, *m.*, monnaie d'argent, *f.* — **fir,** *s.* sapin argenté, sapin blanc, *m.* — **fish,** *s.* argentine, *f.* — **gilt,** *s.* vermeil, argent doré, *m.* — **glance,** *s.* argent rouge, *m.* —**grey,** *adj. s.* gris argenté, *m.* — **haired,** *adj.* aux cheveux argentés, aux cheveux blancs. — **headed,** *adj.* à pomme d'argent. — **hilted,** *adj.* à poignée d'argent, à garde d'argent. — **lace,** *s.* galon, (*m.*) *or* broderie (*f.*) d'argent. —**laced,** *adj.* bordé d'un galon d'argent; brodé d'argent. — **leaf,** *s.* feuille d'argent, *f.*; argent en feuilles, *m.* —**mounted,** *adj.* monté en argent. — **paper,** *s.* *V.* **Tissue-paper.** —**smith,** *s.* orfèvre, *m.* —*smith's art, trade, work,* orfèvrerie, *f.* — **spoon,** *s.* cuiller d'argent, *f.* *To be born with a — spoon in o.'s mouth,* être né coiffé (*m.*, née coiffée, *f.*). — **tongue,** *s.* langue dorée, *f.* — **tongued,** *adj.* à la langue dorée. — **wedding,** *s.* noces d'argent, *f.pl.* — **weed,** *s.* argentine, *f.* — **work, -working,** *s.* orfèvrerie, *f.*
Silverer, *s.* argenteur, *m.*; (*of looking-glasses*) étameur, *m.*
Silvering, *s.* argenture, *f.*; (*of looking-glasses*) étamage, *m.* — **foil,** *s.* tain, *m.*
Silverly, *adv.* comme l'argent
Silvery, *adj.* *V.* **Silver,** *adj.*
Simar, Simare, Simarre, *s.* simarre, *f.*
Similar, *adj.* semblable, pareil, similaire; (*geom.*) semblable
Similarity, *s.* ressemblance, similitude, similarité, *f.*
Similarly, *adv.* pareillement, de la même manière
Simile, *s.* similitude, *f.*; comparaison, *f.*
Similitude, *s.* similitude, *f.*; (*rhet.*) similitude, comparaison, *f.*
Similor, *s.* similor, *m.*
Simious, *adj.* simien
Simmer, *v.n.* bouillir à petits bouillons, bouilloter, mijoter; frémir, commencer à bouillir; mitonner; — *v.a.* mijoter; mitonner
Simmering, *s.* mijotement, mitonnage, *m.*; frémissement, *m.*
Simon, *s.* — *pure, Simple* —, véritable niais, nicodème, *m.* *The real — pure,* (*pers.*) l'homme même, l'homme en personne, *m.*; (*thing*) la chose même, *f.*
Simoniac, *s.* simoniaque, *m.*
Simoniacal, *adj.* simoniaque
Simoniacally, *adv.* avec simonie
Simony, *s.* simonie, *f.*
Simoom, *s.* simoun, *m.*
Simper, *v.n.* sourire, minauder; (*sillily*) sourire niaisement; — *s.* sourire, *m.*, minauderie, *f.*; (*silly*) sourire niais, *m.*
Simperer, *s.* minaudier, *m.*, -ière, *f.*, grimacier, *m.*, -ière, *f.*
Simpering, *adj.* minaudier, grimacier; — *s.* minauderie, *f.*, minauderies, *f.pl.*, grimacerie, *f.*, grimaceries, *f.pl.*
Simperingly, *adv.* en minaudant; en souriant niaisement
Simple, *adj.* simple; (*of contracts*) non scellé; — *s.* simple, *m.* — **minded,** *adj.* simple, naïf. — **mindedness,** *s.* simplicité, ingénuité, *f.*
Simpleness, *s.* simplicité, *f.*
Simpleton, *s.* nigaud, *m.*, e, *f.*, niais, *m.*, e, *f.*, jobard, gobe-mouches, *m.*
Simplicity, *s.* simplicité, *f.*; état simple, *m.*
Simplifiable, *adj.* simplifiable
Simplification, *s.* simplification, *f.*
Simplifier, *s.* simplificateur, *m.*
Simplify, *v.a.* simplifier. *To become —ied,* se simplifier
Simplifying, *adj.* simplificateur; — *s.* simplification, *f.*
Simply, *adv.* simplement; nettement; tout bonnement
Simulate, *v.a.* simuler, feindre, contrefaire
Simulation, *s.* simulation, feinte, *f.*
Simulator, *s.* simulateur, *m.*, -trice, *f.*
Simultaneity, *s.* simultanéité, *f.*
Simultaneous, *adj.* simultané
Simultaneously, *adv.* simultanément
Simultaneousness, *s.* simultanéité, *f.*
Sin, *s.* péché, *m.*; — *v.n.* pécher. — **ful, —less,** &c., *See below* — **offering,** *s.* sacrifice expiatoire, *m.*
Sinapism, *s.* sinapisme, *m.*
Since, *prep.* depuis. *Ever* —, depuis. — *my arrival,* depuis mon arrivée
Since, *adv.* depuis; (*ago*) *V.* **Ago.** *Ever* —, depuis, depuis ce temps-là. *A year* —, il y a un an. *I have not seen him* —, je ne l'ai pas vu depuis. *Long —, a long time* —, depuis longtemps; il y a longtemps. *Not long* —, depuis peu, il n'y a pas longtemps
Since, *conj.* (*of time*) depuis que; que; (*inasmuch as*) puisque. *Ever* —, depuis que. — *he wishes it,* puisqu'il le veut. — *I saw him,* depuis que je l'ai vu. *It is not long* — . . ., il n'y a pas longtemps que . . . *It is a long time — I saw him,* il y a longtemps que je ne l'ai vu. *Is*

it long — you saw him? y a-t-il longtemps que [vous ne l'avez vu?
Sincere, *adj.* sincère
Sincerely, *adv.* sincèrement. *V.* **Yours**
Sincereness, Sincerity, *s.* sincérité, *f.*
Sincipital, *adj.* sincipital
Sinciput, *s.* sinciput, *m.*
Sine, *s.* (*math.*) sinus, *m.*
Sinecure, *s.* sinécure, *f.*
Sinecurism, *s.* sinécurisme, *m.*
Sinecurist, *s.* sinécuriste, *m.*
Sine die, (*Latin*) *adv.* indéfiniment; — *adject.* [indefini
Sinew, *s.* nerf, *m.*; (*anat.*) tendon, *m.*; **—s,** *pl.* nerfs, &c.; (*fig.*) nerf, *m.*, force, *f.* *The —s of war,* le nerf de la guerre. *The —s of government,* la force du gouvernement. **—less,** *adj.* sans nerf, sans vigueur, faible. — **shrunk,** [*adj.* efflanqué
Sinewed, *adj. V.* **Sinewy**
Sinewiness, *s.* vigueur, force, *f.*, nerf, *m.*
Sinewy, *adj.* nerveux, vigoureux
Sinful, *adj.* (*pers.*) pécheur; coupable; (*things*) de pécheur, de pécheurs; de péché; méchant; coupable; criminel. **—ly,** *adv.* coupablement, d'une manière coupable; criminellement. — **ness,** *s.* méchanceté, *f.*; iniquité, *f.*; corruption, *f.*; culpabilité, *f.*
Sing, *v.a.n.* chanter; (*of the cat*) faire ronron; (*of the ears*) tinter. *To — to a person,* chanter quelque chose *or* une chanson (*or* une romance) à quelqu'un. *To — a person to sleep,* endormir quelqu'un en chantant. *To — small,* déchanter; filer doux. — **out,** *v.n.* (*fam.*) crier. — **song,** *s.* chant monotone, *m.*; psalmodie, *f.*
Singe, *v.a.* flamber; (*o's clothes,* &c.) roussir; (*tech.*) griller; (*a horse*) donner le feu à
Singeing, *s.* flambage, *m.*; (*tech.*) grillage, *m.*
Singer, *s.* chanteur, *m.*, -euse, *f.*; (*professional*) chanteur, *m.*, cantatrice, *f.*; (*of churches*) chantre, *m.*; (*bird*) oiseau chanteur, *m.*
Singing, *s.* chant, *m.*; (*of the cat*) ronron, *m.*; (*tingling*) tintement, bourdonnement, *m.*; — *adj.* chantant, qui chante; (*of birds*) chanteur. — **bird,** *s.* oiseau chanteur, *m.* — **book,** *s.* cahier de chant, *m.* — **boy,** *s.* enfant de chœur, *m.* — **class,** *s.* classe de chant, *f.* — **man,** *s.* chantre, *m.* — **master,** *s.* maître *or* professeur de chant, *m.* — **mistress,** *s.* maîtresse de chant, *f.* — **school,** *s.* école de chant, *f.*; (*for choristers*) maîtrise, *f.* — **woman,** *s.* chanteuse, *f.*
Singingly, *adv.* en chantant
Single, *adj.* simple; (*alone, only, solitary*) seul, unique; (*particular*) particulier; individuel; (*unmarried*) non marié, dans le célibat, célibataire; (*of combat*) singulier; (*of watches*) à simple boîte; (*theol.*) simple, pur; — *v.a.* (— **out**) choisir; distinguer; remarquer; séparer. *I am —,* je suis garçon. — **armed,** *adj.* manchot. **—barrelled,** *adj.* à un coup, simple. — **cased,** *adj.* (*watch*) à simple boîte. **—flowered,** *adj.* à fleurs simples. — **gentleman,** *s.* célibataire, garçon, *m.* — **handed,** *adj.* manchot, à une main; (*unhelped*) seul, tout seul, sans aide, sans secours. — **hearted,** *adj.* sincère. **—heartedness,** *s.* sincérité, *f.* **—journey,** *s.* (*rail.*) aller, *m.* — **lady,** *s.* demoiselle, fille, *f.* *She is a — lady,* elle n'est pas mariée. — **life,** *s.* célibat, *m.* — **line,** *s. V.* — **railway.** — **man,** *s.* célibataire, garçon, *m.* — **minded,** *adj.* simple, naïf. — **people,** *s.pl.* célibataires, *m.pl.* — **railway,** *s.* chemin de fer à une seule voie, *m.* — **state,** *s.* célibat, *m.* — **stick,** *s.* jeu de canne *or* de bâton, *m.*, canne, *f.*, bâton, *m.* — **ticket,** *s. V.* **Ticket.** — **woman,** *s.* demoiselle, fille, *f.*
Singleness, *s.* unité, *f.*; sincérité, simplicité, *f.*
Singly, *adv.* simplement; (*only*) seulement, uniquement; (*separately*) séparément, individuellement; (*by oneself*) seul, à part; (*sincerely*) sincèrement
Singular, *adj.* singulier; (*alone*) seul; (*simple*) simple; (*gram.*) singulier, du singulier; — *s.* singulier, *m.* *In the — number, in the —,* au [singulier
Singularity, *s.* singularité, *f.*
Singularize, *v.a.* singulariser [singulier
Singularly, *adv.* singulièrement; (*gram.*) au
Sinister, *adj.* sinistre; pervers, méchant, inique; (*her.*) sénestre, gauche
Sinisterly, Sinistrously, *adv.* sinistrement, d'une manière sinistre
Sink, *v.n.* s'enfoncer; enfoncer; aller au fond; entrer, pénétrer; plonger; descendre; (*fall, fail*) tomber, baisser; (*pers.*) se laisser tomber; tomber; (*lose height*) s'abaisser, descendre; (*decline, decay*) décliner; périr; (*be weighed down*) s'affaisser; (*be overwhelmed*) succomber; (*be dejected*) être abattu; (*be reduced to*) dégénérer (en); (*of ships*) couler bas, couler à fond, sombrer; (*of buildings*) se tasser. *He is —ing fast,* (*dying*) il baisse rapidement. — **away,** tomber. — **back,** retomber. — **down,** s'enfoncer, aller au fond; s'engloutir; (*fall prostrate*) s'affaisser; (*to lower*) s'abaisser; (*of the sun,* &c.) descendre, se coucher; (*pers.*) se laisser tomber; tomber. — **under,** succomber à
Sink, *v.a.* enfoncer; faire aller au fond; plonger; précipiter (dans), faire tomber (dans); (*lower*) faire baisser; diminuer; (*degrade*) abaisser; (*depress*) abattre, accabler; faire succomber; (*waste*) dissiper; (*lose*) perdre; (*reduce to*) faire dégénérer (en); (*not to mention*) ne pas parler de; (*dig*) creuser; (*a well or shaft*) creuser, foncer, forer; (*engr.*) graver en creux; (*money*) placer à fonds perdu; (*an annuity,* &c.) amortir; (*a ship*) couler bas, couler à fond. — *ing the offal,* (*meat*) abats non compris
Sink, *s.* évier, *m.*; (*in roads*) égout, *m.*; (*nav.*) sentine, *f.*; (*of iniquity,* &c.) cloaque, *m.* — **hole,** *s.* trou d'évier, *m.* — **stone,** *s.* évier, *m.*, pierre d'évier, *f.*
Sinker, *s.* (*pers.*) fonceur, *m.*; (*weight*) poids, *m. V.* **Die,** *s.*, **Well,** *s.*, &c.
Sinking, *s.* (*under a weight*) affaissement, *m.*; (*of buildings*) tassement, *m.*; (*med.*) affaissement, *m.*; défaillance, *f.*; (*of a well or shaft*) forage, foncement, *m.*; (*of money*) placement à fonds perdu, *m.*; (*of an annuity,* &c.) amortissement, *m.* — **fund,** *s.* (*capital*) fonds d'amortissement, *m.*; (*office*) caisse d'amortissement, *f.*
Sinless, *adj.* exempt de péché; pur; innocent. **—ly,** *adv.* sans péché; purement; innocemment. **—ness,** *s.* pureté, innocence, *f.*
Sinner, *s.* pécheur, *m.*, pécheresse, *f.*
Sinolog-ic, al, -y. *V.* page 3, § 1
Sinologist, Sinologue, *s.* sinologue, *m.*
Sinuosity, *s.* sinuosité, *f.*
Sinuous, *adj.* sinueux [*surg.*) sinus, *m.*
Sinus, *s.* cavité, *f.*; (*geog.*) baie, *f.*; (*anat.,*
Sip, *v.a.n.* boire à petites gorgées *or* à petits traits, buvoter, siroter; — *s.* petit coup, *m.*, gorgée, *f.* [baromètre à siphon, *m.*
Siphon, *s.* siphon, *m.* — **barometer,** *s.*
Sipper, *s.* siroteur, *m.*, -euse, *f.*
Sippet, *s.* croûton, *m.*; mouillette, *f.*
Sir, *s.* monsieur, *m.* (**-s,** *pl.* messieurs); (*of a knight*) le chevalier ..., *m.*; sir ... (*English title*), *m.*; (*to sovereigns*) sire, *m.* *My good —,* mon cher monsieur; (*of begging*) mon bon monsieur. *Did you call, —?* (*servant speaking*) Monsieur a-t-il appelé? [sire, *m.*
Sire, *s.* (*father*) *V.* **Father;** (*to sovereigns*)
Siren, *s.* sirène, *f.*; — *adj.* de sirène
Sirius, *s.* Sirius, *m.*
Sirloin, *s.* aloyau, *m.*
Sirocco, *s.* siroco, *m.*
Sirrah, *s.* coquin, *m.*, e, *f.*, fripon, *m.*, -ne, *f.*
Sirup, &c. *V.* **Syrup,** &c.
Siskin, *s.* tarin, *m.*
Sismograph, *s.* sismographe, *m.*
Sissy, *s.* sœurette, *f.*
Sister, *s.* sœur, *f.*; (*adject.*) de même espèce, de même nature. *Fatal —s,* Parques, *f.pl.*

The — island or *country*, l'Irlande, *f.* —**hood,** *s.* communauté de sœurs, *f.*, sœurs, *f.pl.* — **in-law,** *s.* belle-sœur, *f.* —**ly,** *adj.* de sœur, d'une sœur, sororal; *adv.* en sœur, comme une sœur

Sit, *v.n.* (*seat oneself*) s'asseoir; (*be seated*) être assis; se tenir assis, rester assis; (*to be*) être; (*stay, remain*) rester, demeurer, se tenir; (*on a horse*) se tenir; (*of assemblies*) tenir séance, siéger, se réunir; être assemblé; (*of members of an assembly*) siéger; (*in judgment*) juger; (*for o.'s portrait*) poser; (*bear on*) peser (sur); (*on the face*) être empreint; (*of birds: brood*) couver, (*not to be on the wing*) être au repos; être perché; se percher; se poser, poser; (*fit, become*) aller (à); (*place oneself at table*) se mettre, se placer. *To — in judgment on,* juger. — **close,** (*to make room*) se serrer; être serré. — **down,** s'asseoir; (*down again*) se rasseoir; (*to breakfast, to dinner, to table*) se mettre (à table); (*begin a siege*) mettre le siége (devant). — **for,** (*o.'s likeness*) poser pour (son portrait); (*in parliament*) représenter. — **on,** s'asseoir *or* &c. sur; (*eggs*) couver; (*of coroners,* &c.) faire une enquête sur. — **up,** (*straight*) se tenir droit; (*rise*) se lever sur son séant; (*watch*) veiller; passer la nuit. — **up for,** attendre. — **up with,** (*an invalid*) garder, veiller. — **upright,** se tenir droit; se mettre sur son séant

Sit-at-home, *adj.* sédentaire; casanier

Site, *s.* situation, assiette, *f.*; (*spot*) emplacement, *m.*; (*of landscapes*) site, *m.*

Sitfast, *s.* (*vet.*) cor, durillon, *m.*

Sitter, *s.* personne sédentaire, *f.*; (*paint.,* &c.) poseur, *m.*, -euse, *f.*, modèle, *m.*; (*hen*) couveuse, *f.* — **up,** *s.* veilleur, *m.*, -euse, *f.*; garde, *m.f.*

Sitting, *adj.* assis; (*not on the wing*) au repos, au posé; perché; (*brooding*) couveuse; (*bot.*) sessile; — *s.* posture, *f.*; session, *f.*; audience, *f.*; (*for o.'s portrait*) séance, *f.*; pose, *f.*; (*time of —*) séance, *f.*; (*brooding*) couvaison, incubation, *f.*; (*church-seat*) banc, *m.*, place, *f.* *In a — posture,* sur son séant. — **room,** *s.* salon, *m.*; (*space*) place pour s'asseoir, *f.* — **up,** *s.* veille, veillée, *f.*

Situate, Situated, *adj.* situé; (*pers.*) placé; dans une position. *Awkwardly —d,* (*circumstanced*) dans une position embarrassante. *This is how I am —d,* voici comme je suis placé; voici ma position

Situation, *s.* situation, *f.*; (*state*) état, *m.*, position, *f.*; (*office*) place, *f.*, emploi, *m.*; (*theat.*) situation, *f.* *To hold a —,* occuper un emploi. *To be in a —,* être dans une situation *or* position (...); (*office*) être en place; avoir une place (...); (*to* ...) être en position (de ...). *To be out of a —,* être sans place

Sitz-bath, *s.* bain de siége, *m.*

Six, *adj. s.* six (*adj. m.f., s.m.*); (*elliptically*) (*of the clock*) six heures, *f.pl.*, (*of o.'s age*) six ans, *m.pl.* *Carriage and —,* voiture à six chevaux, *f.* *At —es and sevens,* à l'abandon, à la débandade; sens dessus dessous. *It is — of one and half-a-dozen of the other,* c'est bonnet blanc et blanc bonnet. —**fold,** *adj. adv.* sextuple, six fois autant, six fois. — **foot way,** — **foot,** — **feet,** *s.* (*rail.*) entre-voies, *f.* — **foot,** *adj.* de six pieds. — **pence,** *s.pl.* soixante centimes, *m.pl.* — **penny,** *adj.* de soixante centimes. — **score,** *adj.* cent vingt

Sixteen, *adj.* seize; — *s.* (*print.*) in-seize, *m.* — **mo,** *s. adj.* in-seize, *s.m., adj. m.f.*

Sixteenth, *adj. s.* seizième; (*of the month*) seize. *The —,* (*of sovereigns*) seize

Sixth, *adj.* sixième; — *s.* sixième, (*part*) *m.*, (*pers.*) *m.f.*; (*mus.*) sixte, *f.*; (*of the month*) six, *m.* *The —,* (*of sovereigns*) six

Sixthly, *adv.* sixièmement

Sixtieth, *adj.* soixantième

Sixty, *adj. s.* soixante, *adj. m.f., s.m.*

Sizable, *adj.* de grosseur considérable; (*of suitable size*) de grosseur convenable

Sizar, *s.* (*univers.*) étudiant servant, *m.*

Size, *s.* grandeur, *f.*; (*bulk*) grosseur, dimension, *f.*, volume, *m.*; (*thickness*) épaisseur, *f.*; (*pers.*) taille, *f.*; (*of a book, of an envelope*) format, *m.*; (*of guns and shot*) calibre, *m.*; (*measure*) mesure, *f.*; (*com.*) numéro, *m.*; (*shoemaker's, for shoes or boots*) compas, *m.*, (*of shoes or boots*) pointure, *f.*; (*of gloves*) numéro, *m.*; (*of apertures*) surface, *f.*; (*glue*) colle, *f.*; encollage, *m.*; — *v.a.* coller; encoller. — **stick,** *s.* compas, *m.*

Sized, *adj.* (*in compounds*) d'une grandeur ...; d'une grosseur ..., d'une dimension ...; de taille ..., d'une taille ...; — *part.* collé

Sizer. *V.* **Sizar**

Sizing, *s.* collage, *m.*; encollage, *m.*

Sizy, *adj.* glutineux, gluant, visqueux

Skald, *s.* scalde, *m.*

Skate, *s.* patin, *m.*; (*fish*) raie, *f.*; — *v.n.* patiner. — **maker,** *s.* patinier, *m.*

Skater, *s.* patineur, *m.*, -euse, *f.*

Skating, *s.* patinage, *m.* *To like —,* aimer à patiner. — **club,** *s.* cercle *or* club des patineurs, *m.*

Skedaddle, *v.n.* *V.* **Scamper**

Skeet, *s.* écope, *f.*

Skein, *s.* écheveau, *m.*

Skeletal, *adj* squelettique

Skeletology, *s.* squelettologie, *f.*

Skeleton, *s.* squelette, *m.*; (*fig.*) charpente, carcasse, *f.*; (*arts*) carcasse, monture, *f.*; (*liter.*) canevas, *m.*; (*mil.*) cadre, *m.*; (*open work*) ouvrage à jour, *m.*; — *adj.* (*open-work*) à jour. — **key,** *s.* crochet, rossignol, passe-partout, *m.* — **map,** *s.* carte muette, *f.*

Sketch, *s.* esquisse, *f.*; ébauche, *f.*; croquis, *m.*; plan, *m.*; (*fig.*) aperçu, *m.*; (*liter.*) esquisse ('*of,*' de), *f.*; étude ('*of,*' sur), *f.*; — *v.a.* esquisser, ébaucher; faire un croquis de; tracer le plan de. — **book,** *s.* album, *m.*

Sketcher, *s.* dessinateur, *m.*, -trice, *f.*

Sketching, *s.* dessin, *m.*

Sketchy, *adj.* poché; (*fig.*) descriptif; léger

Skew, *adj.* oblique, de biais, biais; — *adv.* en biais, obliquement; en arc de cercle. — **arch,** *s.* voûte en biais, *f.* — **back,** *s.* redan, *m.* — **bald,** *adj.* pie. — **bridge,** *s.* pont oblique, pont biais, *m.*

Skewer, *s.* brochette, *f.*; — *v.a.* brocheter, attacher avec des brochettes

Skid, *s.* sabot, frein, *m.*, enrayure, *f.*; (*nav. const.*) défense, *f.*; — *v.a* enrayer. — **chain,** *s.* chaîne à enrayer, enrayure, *f.*

Skiff, *s.* esquif, *m.*

Skilful, *adj.* habile; adroit; entendu; expérimenté; compétent; (*in*) versé (dans). — **ly,** *adv.* habilement; adroitement. —**ness,** *s.* *V.* **Skill**

Skill, *s.* habileté, adresse, *f.*; art, *m.*; talent, *m.*; savoir-faire, *m.*

Skilled, *adj.* *V.* **Skilful**

Skillet, *s.* coquemar, *m.*; bassine, *f.*

Skilley, Skilly, *s.* bouillie, *f.*

Skim, *v.a.* écumer; (*milk*) écrémer; (*pass near*) effleurer, raser; — *v.n.* passer légèrement (sur); (*run*) courir, voler. — **milk,** *s.* lait écrémé, *m.* — **off,** *v.a.* écumer; (*milk*) écrémer. — **over,** *v.a.* effleurer, raser

Skimmer, *s.* écumoire, *f.*; (*for milk*) écrémoire, *f.*; (*bird*) rhynchops, bec-en-ciseaux, coupeur d'eau, *m.* — **coulter,** *s.* rasette, *f.*

Skimming, *s.* (*of milk*) écrémage, *m.*; —**s,** *pl.* écume, *f.* — **dish,** *s.* (*for milk*) écrémoire, *f.*

Skin, *s.* peau, *f.*; (*hide*) cuir, *m.*; (*of parchment*) feuille, *f.*; (*fig.*) écorce, *f.*; — *v.a.* écorcher; (*potatoes,* &c.) peler, éplucher; (*cover*) couvrir de peau; — *v.n.* se couvrir de peau. *Next to o.'s —,* sur la peau. *Outer —,* épiderme, *m.* (*V.* **Wet**). *To have a fair —,* avoir la peau blanche. *To be nothing but — and bone,* n'avoir que la peau et les os. *To — a flint*, tondre sur un œuf. *To come off with a whole —*, s'être tiré d'affaire. *To sleep in a whole —*, dormir sur les deux oreilles. — **deep,** *adj.* peu profond; superficiel. — **disease,** *s.* maladie de la peau, *f.* — **flint,** *s.* fesse-mathieu, pingre, grippe-sou, *m.* —**less,** *adj.* sans peau; qui a la peau très mince; (*of peas*) mange-tout. — **over,** *v.a.* couvrir superficiellement; *v.n.* se couvrir de peau. — **wool,** *s.* pelade, *f.*

Skink, *s.* (*zool.*) scinque, *m.*

Skinned, *adj.* (*in compounds*) qui a la peau ..., à peau ...

Skinner, *s.* écorcheur,*m.*; (*dealer*) peaussier,*m.*

Skinniness, *s.* décharnement,*m.*, maigreur,*f.*

Skinny, *adj.* de peau; (*thin*) décharné, maigre

Skip, *v.n.a.* sauter; bondir; (*omit*) passer, sauter; — *s.* saut; bond, *m.* *To — with a rope,* sauter à la corde. — **jack,** *s.* (*upstart*) parvenu, *m.*; (*an insect*) taupin, *m.* — **kennel,** *s.* saute ruisseau, *m.* — **over,** *v.a.* sauter par-dessus; sauter; passer

Skipper, *s.* sauteur, *m.*, -euse, *f.*; (*of a ship*) patron, *m.*; (*fish*) scombrésoce, *m.*; (*maggot*) ver de fromage, *m.*

Skipping, *s.* action de sauter, *f.* — **rope,** *s.* corde à sauter, *f.* [bonds

Skippingly, *adv.* en sautant, par sauts, par

Skirmish, *s.* escarmouche, *f.*; — *v.n.* escar-

Skirmisher, *s.* tirailleur, *m.* [moucher

Skirmishing, *s.* escarmouches, *f.pl.*

Skirret, *s.* chervis, *m.*, berle, ache d'eau, *f.*

Skirt, *s.* (*of garments generally*) pan, *m.*; (*of a frock-coat*) jupe, *f.*, pan, *m.*; (*of a dress-coat*) basque, *f.*, pan, *m.*; (*of a gown*) jupe, *f.*; (*edge*) bord, *m.*; (*of forests*) bord, *m.*, lisière, *f.*; (*of a town*) extrémité, *f.*; faubourg, *m.*; (*of the wall of a room*) *V.* **Skirting;** (*anat.*) diaphragme, *m.*; — *v.a.* border; garnir; (*go alongside*) longer; — *v.n.* être sur les bords

Skirting, *s.* bordure, *f.*; garniture, *f.*; (*of the wall of a room, — board*) lambris d'appui, bandeau, *m.*, plinthe, *f.*; (*materials for skirts*) étoffe pour jupes (*or* pour robes), *f.*

Skit, *s.* raillerie, moquerie, *f.*

Skittish, *adj.* volage, capricieux, folâtre, léger; (*of horses*) ombrageux. —**ly,** *adv.* capricieusement, d'une manière folâtre, légèrement. —**ness,** *s.* caractère folâtre, *m.*, légèreté, *f.*; (*of horses*) *V.* **Shyness**

Skittle, *s* quille, *f.* — **alley, -ground,** *s.* jeu de quilles, quillier, *m.*

Skua, — **gull,** *s.* labbe, stercoraire, *m.*

Skulk, Skulker, &c. *V.* **Sculk,** &c.

Skull, *s.* crâne, *m.* — **cap,** *s.* calotte, *f.*

Skunk, *s.* chinche, *m.*, moufette, *f.*, putois d'Amérique,*m.*; (*pers.*) puant, *m.*, e, *f.*, cochon, *m.*, -ne, *f.* *Mean —*, ladre, *m.*; chafouin, *m.*

Sky, *s.* ciel, *m.* **Skies,** *pl.* (*clouds*) nues, *f.pl.* — **blue, -colour,** *s.* azur, bleu de ciel, *m.* — **coloured,** *adj.* azuré. — **lark,** *s.* alouette des champs, *f.* — **light,** *s.* abat-jour, *m.*; lucarne, *f.*; (*nav.*) claire-voie, *f.* — **rocket,** *s.* fusée volante, *f.* — **sail, -scraper,** *s.* papillon, *m.*, grecque, *f.*

Skyey, *adj.* du ciel, éthéré

Slab, *s.* plaque, *f.*; table, dalle, *f.*; (*print.*) marbre, *m.* [— *s.* bave, *f.*

Slabber, *v.n.* baver; — *v.a.* couvrir de bave;

Slabberer, *s.* baveux, *m.*, -euse, *f.*; idiot, *m.*,

Slabbering, *adj.* baveux [e, *f.*

Slabby, *adj.* baveux; gluant,visqueux; humide

Slack, *adj.* (*not tight*) lâche; (*weak*) faible, mou; (*slow*) lent, nonchalant; (*com.*) faible, mort; — *s.* (*of a rope*) mou, *m.*; (*coal*) menu charbon, *m.*, braise, *f.*; — *v.a.* *V.* **Slacken;** (*lime*) éteindre. *To grow —*, *V.* **Slacken.** *Trade is —*, les affaires ne vont pas

Slacken, *v.n.* se relâcher, se détendre; (*be remiss*) faiblir, mollir; (*abate*) se ralentir; diminuer; tomber, baisser; — *v.a.* (*loose*) relâcher, détendre; (*relax*) se relâcher de; (*mitigate*) adoucir, calmer; (*abate*) ralentir; diminuer; modérer; (*fire*) amortir

Slackening, *s.* relâchement, *m.*; ralentissement, *m.*; diminution, *f.*

Slacking, *s.* (*of lime*) extinction, *f.*

Slackly, *adv.* mollement; nonchalamment, négligemment

Slackness, *s.* relâchement, *m.*; (*weakness*) mollesse, *f.*; (*negligence*) nonchalance, négligence, *f.*; (*slowness*) lenteur, *f.*

Slade, *s.* (*of ploughs*) sabot, *m.*

Slag, *s.* scorie, *f.*; laitier, *m.*

Slain, *part. adj.* (*killed*) tué; (*dead*) mort

Slake, *v.a.* *V.* **Quench;** (*lime*) éteindre. — **less,** *adj.* inextinguible

Slaking, *s.* extinction, *f.*; apaisement, *m.*; (*of lime*) extinction, *f.* [chelem, *v.n.*

Slam. *V.* **Bang;** (*at whist*) chelem, *s.m.*; faire

Slander, *s.* médisance, *f.*; calomnie, *f.*; (*law*) diffamation, *f.*; — *v.a.* médire de; calomnier; (*law*) diffamer

Slanderer, *s.* médisant, *m.*, e, *f.*; calomniateur, -trice, *f.*; détracteur, *m.*, -trice, *f.*; (*law*) diffamateur, *m.*, -trice, *f.*

Slanderous, *adj.* médisant; (*things*) calomnieux, calomniateur; (*law*) diffamatoire, diffa-

Slanderously, *adv.* calomnieusement [mant

Slanderousness, *s.* caractère calomnieux,*m.*

Slang, *s.* langage trivial, argot, *m.*; langue verte, *f.*; — *adj.* trivial, d'argot

Slangy, *adj.* trivial, d'argot

Slant, *v.n.* être en pente *or* de biais; — *v.a.* incliner,mettre en pente; — *adj.s.V.* **Slanting**

Slanting, *adj.* oblique, de biais, en biais; incliné; en pente; (*fort.*) en écharpe; — *s.* biais, *m.*, direction oblique, *f.*; pente, *f.*; talus, *m.* [pente

Slantingly, *adv.* obliquement, en biais; en

Slap, *v.a.* taper, claquer, frapper. *To — ...'s face,* souffleter ..., (*fam.*) claquer ..., calotter ..., gifler ..., donner sur les oreilles à ...

Slap, *s.* tape, claque, *f.*, coup, *m.* — *in the face,* soufflet, *m.*, (*fam.*) claque, calotte, gifle, *f.*

Slap, *adv.* droit, tout droit, raide, (*fam.*) raide comme balle; en plein; (*headlong*) la tête la première; — *int.* crac! patatras! vlan! pan!

Slapdash, *adv.* vite, tout d'un coup, d'emblée; raide comme balle; (*hurriedly*) bredi-breda; (*at random*) au hasard, à tort et à travers, brelique-breloque, comme une corneille qui abat des noix

Slapping, *adj.* fameux, bon; rapide

Slap-up, *adj.* soigné, fameux

Slash, *v.a.n.* taillader; balafrer; sabrer; massacrer; (*lash*) *V.* **Lash;** — *s.* taillade, *f.*; (*on the face*) balafre, *f.*; (*of old costumes*) crevé, *m*

Slashed, *part. adj.* tailladé, &c. (*V.* **Slash,** *v.a.n.*); (*of old costumes*) crevé, à crevés

Slashing, *adj.* (*fig.*) piquant, mordant, (*fam.*) bien tapé; (*withering*) sanglant; (*first-rate*)

Slat, *s.* planchette, *f.* [fameux; huppé

Slatch, *s.* (*of fair weather*) embellie, *f.*

Slate, *s.* ardoise, *f.*; — *v.a.* ardoiser, couvrir d'ardoise, couvrir en ardoise. — **axe, -hammer,** *s.* assette, *f.* — **clay,** *s.* argile schisteuse, *f.*, schiste, *m.* — **colour, -coloured,** *adj.* ardoisé. — **knife,** *s.* couperet à ardoise,*m.* — **pencil,** *s.* crayon d'ardoise, *m.* — **quarrier,** *s.* ardoisier, *m.* — **quarry,** *s.* ardoisière, *f.* — **worker,** *s.* ardoisier, *m.*

Slater, *s.* couvreur en ardoise, *m.*; (*insect*) porcellion, *m.*

Slating, *s.* couverture *or* toiture en ardoise, *f.*

Slattern, *s.*, **Slatternly,** *adj. adv.* *V.* **Sloven, Slovenly**

Slatting, *s.* planchettes, *f.pl.* [ardoisé

Slaty, *adj.* ardoiseux; ardoisier; (*of colour*)

Slaughter, *s.* carnage, massacre, *m.*, tuerie, boucherie, *f.*; (*of beasts*) abattage, *m.*; — *v.a.* massacrer, égorger; tuer; (*butch.*) abattre. — **house,** *s.* abattoir, *m.* — **man,** *s.* *V.* **Slaughterer**

Slaughterer, *s.* abatteur, assommeur, équarrisseur, *m.*
Slaughterous, *adj.* meurtrier, destructif
Slaughterously, *adv.* meurtrièrement, destructivement
Slave, *s.* esclave, *m.f.*; — *s. adj.* (*of Slavonia*) Slave, *m.f.*; — *v.n.* travailler comme un esclave. *A — to*, esclave de. — **born,** *adj.* né dans l'esclavage. **dealer,** *s.* marchand d'esclaves, marchand négrier, négrier, *m.* — **holder,** *s.* propriétaire d'esclaves, *m.f.* — **like,** *adj.* d'esclave, comme un esclave. — **merchant,** *s.* marchand d'esclaves, *m.* — **owner,** *s. V.* — **holder.** — **ship,** *s.* bâtiment *or* vaisseau négrier, négrier, *m.* — **State,** *s.* État à esclaves, *m.* — **trade,** *s.* traite des nègres *or* des noirs, traite, *f.*
Slaver, *v.n.a. V.* **Slabber;** — *s. V.* **Slave-ship** *&* **Slabber**
Slaverer, *s. V.* **Slabberer**
Slavery, *s* esclavage, *m.*
Slavic, *adj.* slavique, slavon, slave
Slavish, *adj.* d'esclave; asservissant, assujettissant; servile, bas
Slavishly, *adv.* en esclave; servilement
Slavishness, *s.* servilité, *f.*
Slavon, Slavonic, *adj.* slavon, slave; — *s.* (*language*) le slave, *m.*, la langue slave, *f.*
Slavonian, *s. adj.* Slave, *m.f.*
Slay, *v.a.* tuer
Slayer, *s.* tueur (de ...), *m.*; meurtrier, *m.*
Slaying, *s.* destruction, *f.*; massacre, *m.*
Sledge, *s.* traîneau, *m*; (*on mountains*) ramasse, *f.*; (*hurdle*) tombereau, *m.*, charrette, *f.* — **driver,** *s.* conducteur de traîneau, traîneur, *m.*; ramasseur, *m.* — **hammer,** *s.* marteau de forge, marteau, *m.*
Sleek, *adj.* lisse; poli; (*of the skin*) luisant; (*fat*) gras; (*of horses*) d'un beau poil; (*mealy-mouthed*) doucereux; — *v.a.* lisser; lustrer, rendre luisant. —**ly,** *adv.* d'une manière lisse. —**ness,** *s.* surface lisse, *f.*
Sleep, *v.n.* dormir; (*spend the night*) coucher; — *s.* sommeil, *m.*; (*duration of sleep*) somme, *m.* *Want of* —, insomnie, *f.* *To go to* —, s'endormir. *To go to — again*, se rendormir. *To have* —, dormir. *To have a ... —*, avoir un sommeil ... *To have a — (nap)*, faire un somme. *To have a good* —, dormir bien; faire un bon somme. *To have a little* (or *short*) —, dormir un peu; faire un petit somme. *To have a long* —, dormir longtemps; faire un long somme. *To have no* —, ne pas dormir. *To send to* —, envoyer se coucher; (*make one sleep*) endormir, faire dormir. *To start out of o.'s* —, se réveiller en sursaut. *To startle (one) out of his* —, réveiller (quelqu'un) en sursaut. *To — like a top*, dormir comme un sabot; *like a dormouse*, comme un loir *or* comme une marmotte; *like a log*, comme une souche. *I got an hour's* —, j'ai dormi une heure. *He is gone to* —, il s'est endormi. *He walks in his* —, il est somnambule. — **away,** *v.a.* faire passer en dormant. — **off,** *v.a.* faire passer en dormant; (*wine*, &c.) cuver (son vin, &c.). — **out,** *v.n.* découcher. — **waker,** *s.* magnétisé, *m.*, e, *f.* — **waking,** *s.* magnétisation, *f.* — **walker,** *s.* somnambule, *m.f.* — **walking,** *s.* somnambulisme, *m.*; *adj.* (*pers.*) somnambule; (*things*) somnambulique
Sleeper, *s.* dormeur, *m.*, -euse, *f.*; (*carp.*) traverse, *f.*, sleeper, *m.*, (*longitudinal*) longuerine, *f.*; (*ear-ring*) dormeuse, *f.* *To be a sound* —, avoir le sommeil dur
Sleepily, *adv.* en dormant; d'un air endormi; (*heavily*) lourdement
Sleepiness, *s.* envie de dormir, *f.*, assoupissement, *m.*; (*heaviness*) pesanteur, *f.*; (*of fruit*) blettissure, *f.*
Sleeping, *adj.* endormi, dormant; de sommeil; (*of partners*) commanditaire; — *s.* sommeil, *m.* — **berth,** *s.* lit, *m.*; couchette, *f.* — **carriage, -compartment,** *s.* dormeuse, *f.*; (*rail.*) coupé-lit, *m.* — **partner,** *s.* associé (*m.*, e, *f.*) commanditaire, commanditaire, *m.f.* — **place,** *s.* endroit pour dormir, *m*; abri, gîte, coucher, *m.* — **potion** *or* **draught,** *s.* potion calmante, *f.* — **room,** *s.* chambre à coucher, *f.*; dortoir, *m.*
Sleepless, *adj.* sans sommeil; (*pers.*) éveillé; (*fig*) sans repos [(*fig*) sans repos
Sleeplessly, *adv.* sans sommeil, sans dormir;
Sleeplessness, *s.* insomnie, *f.* *Fit of* —, insomnie, *f.*
Sleepy, *adj.* qui a sommeil, qui a envie de dormir; (*asleep*) endormi; (*things*) soporifique, somnifère; (*heavy*) lourd; (*of fruit*) blet. *To be* or *feel* or *get* —, avoir sommeil, avoir envie de dormir
Sleet, *v.n.* grésiller; — *s.* grésil, *m.*
Sleety, *adj.* de grésil
Sleeve, *s.* manche, *f.*; — *v.a.* mettre des manches à. *To laugh in o.'s* —, rire sous cape, rire dans sa barbe. — **board,** *s.* passe-carreau, *m.* — **button,** *s.* bouton de manche, *m.* — **fish,** *s.* calmar, encornet, *m.* —**less,** *adj.* sans manche, sans manches; (*fig.*) absurde, futile, sans rime ni raison. — **link, -stud,** *s.* bouton de manchette, *m.*
Sleeved, *adj.* à manches
Sleigh, *s. V.* **Sledge**
Sleighing, *s* transport par traîneau, *m.*
Sleight, *s.* tour d'adresse, *m.* — *of hand*, — *of hand trick*, prestidigitation, *f.*, escamotage, tour de passe-passe, *m.*; (*adject.*) de prestidigitation. — *of hand man*, prestidigitateur, *m.*
Slender, *adj.* (*thin*) mince, grêle; (*in waist*) svelte, élancé; (*feeble*) léger, faible; (*sparingly supplied*) pauvre, maigre
Slenderly, *adv.* légèrement; (*insufficiently*) pauvrement, médiocrement
Slenderness, *s.* finesse, petitesse, *f.*; légèreté, *f.*; pauvreté, médiocrité, *f.*; (*of waist*) sveltesse, *f.*
Slew, *v.a.n. V.* **Slue;** — *pret. of* **Slay,** *which see*
Slice, *v.a.* couper par tranches; (*of fowls*) couper par aiguillettes; (*to cut, divide*) couper, partager; — *s.* tranche, *f.*; (*of fowls*) aiguillette, *f.*; (*kitchen-utensil*) écumoire, *f.*; (*for fish*) truelle, *f.*; (*spatula*) spatule, *f.*; (*print.*) palette, *f.*; (*furrow-slice in ploughing*) bande (de terre), *f.* — *of bread, of meat*, tranche de pain, de viande. — *of bread and butter*, tartine de beurre, beurrée, *f.* — *of bread and jam*, tartine de confitures, *f.* — *of toast*, rôtie, *f.*
Slide, *v.a n.* glisser; (*into*) tomber; (*draw out*) tirer; (*introduce*) introduire; couler; (*of wheels*) patiner; — *s.* (*of ice*) glissoire, glissade, *f.*; (*sliding, slip*) glissade, *f.*; (*of earth, rock*) éboulement, *m.*; (*of a steam-engine*) tiroir, *m*; (*tech.*) coulisse, *f.*; curseur, *m.*; (*of umbrellas, parasols*) coulant, *m.*; (*of magic lanterns*) verre, *m.*; (*of stereoscopes*) vue, *f.*; (*of wheels*) patin, *m.*; (*vehicle*) chariot, *m.*; (*for casks*) poulain, *m.*; (*of wind-instr.*, &c.) pompe, *f.*; (*in dancing*) coulé, *m.* — **bars,** *s.pl.* glissoires, *f.pl.* — **box,** *s.* boîte de tiroir, *f.* — **rail,** *s.* languette, *f.* — — **rest,** *s.* support à coulisse *or* à chariot, *m.* — **rod,** *s.* tige de tiroir, *f.* — **rule,** *s.* règle à calcul, règle mobile, *f.* — **valve,** *s.* tiroir, *m.*
Slider, *s.* (*pers.*) glisseur, *m.*, -euse, *f.*; (*thing*) glissoir, *m.*; curseur, *m.*; coulisse, *f.*
Sliding, *adj.* à coulisse, à coulisses; glissant; coulant; mobile; — *s.* glissement, *m.* — **door,** *s.* porte à coulisse, *f.* — **frame table,** *s.* table à coulisses, *f.* — **gauge,** *s.* vernier, nonius, *m.* — **knot,** *s.* nœud coulant, *m.* — **rule,** *s. V.* **Slide-rule.** — **scale,** *s.* échelle mobile, *f.*
Slight, *adj.* léger; (*thin*) mince; (*weak*) faible; (*small*) petit, peu considérable; (*of little consequence*) peu important, insignifiant. —**er,** *comp.*, —**est,** *super.*, plus léger *or* &c.; moindre; moins important
Slight, *s.* dédain, mépris, *m.*, marque de mépris, *f.*, manque d'égards, manque de respect, *m.*

Slight, *v.a.* (*pers.*) manquer à; (*things*) faire peu de cas de; dédaigner, mépriser; négliger
Slighter, *s.* personne qui fait peu de cas (de), personne qui dédaigne *or* qui méprise, *f.*, contempteur, *m.*, -trice, *f.*; — *comp. of* **Slight,** *adj.*, *which see*
Slightest, *super. V.* **Slight,** *adj.*
Slightingly, *adv.* avec dédain, avec mépris
Slightly, *adv.* légèrement; faiblement; peu solidement; (*a little*) un peu; (*little*) peu
Slightness, *s.* légèreté, *f.*; faiblesse, *f.*
Slily, *adv.* finement; sournoisement; (*in secret*) *V.* **Sly** (*On the*) [faible, léger
Slim, *adj.* élancé, svelte, mince; grêle; (*weak*)
Slime, *s.* (*spittle*) bave, *f.*; (*mud*) vase, *f.*, limon, *m.*
Sliminess, *s.* viscosité, *f.*; nature limoneuse, *f.*
Slimness, *s.* sveltesse, minceur, *f.*; (*weakness*) faiblesse, légèreté, *f.* [limoneux
Slimy, *adj.* visqueux, gluant; (*muddy*) vaseux,
Sliness, *s.* ruse, *f.*; finesse, matoiserie, *f.*; sournoiserie, *f.*
Sling, *s.* (*for throwing stones*) fronde, *f.*; (*bandage*) écharpe, *f.*; (*for horses*) sangle, *f.*; (*of hand-guns, muskets,* &c.) bretelle, *f.*; (*nav.*) élingue, *f.* *To carry* or *wear* or *have o.'s arm in a* —, porter *or* avoir le bras en écharpe. — **cart, -waggon,** *s.* camion, *m.* — **shot,** *s.* frondée, *f.*
Sling, *v a.* lancer avec une fronde; jeter, lancer; suspendre; (*nav.*) élinguer. *To — over the shoulder,* mettre (*or* porter) en bandoulière *or* en sautoir. *Slung over the shoulder,* en bandoulière, en sautoir
Slinger, *s.* frondeur, *m.*
Slink, *v.n.* se dérober, s'échapper, s'esquiver; se cacher, se tenir caché; — *v.a.* mettre bas avant terme, avorter de. — **away,** s'échapper, s'esquiver. — **in,** entrer furtivement. — **off, out,** *V.* — **away**
Slip, *v.n.* glisser; (*run*) couler; (*creep into*) se glisser; (*escape*) échapper, s'échapper, s'esquiver; (*to err*) faillir, faire une faute, faire un faux pas; (*of the tongue*) tourner, fourcher; (*of wheels*) patiner; (*suffer abortion*) avorter. — **away,** s'échapper, s'esquiver; (*of time*) passer, s'écouler, fuir. — **down,** tomber. — **in,** se glisser (dans), entrer (dans); entrer furtivement. — **off,** glisser, couler, tomber (de), s'échapper, s'esquiver; s'en aller. — **out,** s'échapper, s'esquiver; sortir. — **over,** glisser sur; passer sur
Slip, *v.a.* glisser, couler; filer; (*lose*) laisser échapper; (*let loose*) lâcher; (*tear off*) arracher; (*disengage oneself*) se dégager de, se débarrasser de; (*a cable,* &c.) filer; (*her young*) mettre bas avant terme, avorter de. — **in,** glisser, couler, introduire. — **off,** se dégager de; (*tear off*) arracher; (*clothes*) ôter. — **on,** passer, mettre, (*fam.*) fourrer. — **out,** (*let fall*) lâcher
Slip, *s.* glissade, *f.*; (*of earth*) éboulement, *m.*; (*error*) erreur, inadvertance, *f.*; faute, *f.*; faux pas, *m.*; oubli, *m.*; (*narrow piece*) bande, *f.*; morceau, *m.*; (*of bacon*) barde, *f.*; (*of turf*) parterre *or* cordon de gazon, tapis vert, *m.*, coulée, *f.*; (*petticoat*) jupon de dessus, *m.*; (*over a table-cloth*) napperon, *m.*; (*of thyme,* &c.) brin, *m.*; (*stalk*) bouture, *f.*; (*of dogs*) laisse, *f.*; (*print.*) placard, *m.*; (*book-bind.*) nerf, *m.*; (*of writing*) exemple, modèle, *m.*; (*for ships*) cale, *f.*; (*of machines*) éclisse, *f.*; —**s,** *pl.* (*theat.*) troisièmes loges de côté, *f.pl.*, (*if there is a fourth tier, as in some large houses*) quatrièmes loges de côté, *f.pl.* — *of the pen,* erreur de plume, faute d'inattention, *f.*, 'lapsus calami,' *m.* — *of the tongue,* 'lapsus linguæ,' *m.*, (*fam.*) bévue, *f.* *To give* (...) *the* —, fausser compagnie à (...), planter là (...); faire faux bond à (...). *To make a* —, glisser; (*fig.*) commettre une erreur; faire un faux pas *or* une faute. *He has made a — of the tongue,* la langue lui a tourné *or* fourché. *There is many a — between the cup and the lip,* de la main à la bouche se perd souvent la soupe. — **board,** *s.* coulisse, *f.* — **carriage,** *s.* wagon laissé en route par un train qui continue à marcher à toute vitesse, *m.* — **door,** *s.* guichet, *m.*; porte bâtarde, *f.* — **knot,** *s.* nœud coulant, *m.* — **shod,** *adj.* en pantoufles, en savates; chaussé en pantoufle *or* en savate; mal chaussé; (*fig.*) négligé; débraillé; sans gêne. — **shoe,** *s.* pantoufle, *f.*; soulier en pantoufle, *m.*
Slipper, *s.* pantoufle, *f.*; (*of the pope*) mule, *f.*; (*skid*) sabot, *m.*; (*bed-pan*) bourdalou, *m.* *Hunt the* —, (*game*) la savate, *f.* —**bath,** *s.* demi-bain, *m.* — **pan,** *s.* bourdalou, *m.*
Slippered, *adj.* en pantoufles [glissante
Slipperily, *adv.* en glissant, d'une manière
Slipperiness, *s.* nature glissante, *f.*, état glissant, *m.*; incertitude, *f.*; (*of the tongue*) volubilité, *f.*
Slippery, *adj.* glissant; difficile à tenir; peu sûr; incertain; dangereux; changeant; inconstant; (*delicate*) scabreux. *To be — (on the roads),* faire glissant. — *customer,* rusé compère, *m.* — *tricks,* tours de souplesse, *m.pl.*
Slipping, *s.* glissement, *m.*
Slipslop, *s.* ripopée, lavasse, *f.*, margouillis, *m.*; — *adj.* faible, mou, lâche; décousu, irrégulier, désordonné
Slit, *v.a.* fendre; — *v.n.* se fendre; — *s.* fente, *f.*; (*hort.*) enture, *f.* — **iron,** *s.* fer fendu, fen-
Slitter, *s.* fendeur, *m.*, -euse, *f.* [ton, *m.*
Slitting, *s.* fendage, *m.*; (*of iron*) fenderie, *f.* — **mill,** *s.* fenderie, *f.*
Sliver, *s.* (*tech.*) ruban, *m.*
Slobber, &c. *V.* **Slabber,** &c.
Sloe, *s.* prunelle, *f.* — **tree, -thorn,** *s.* prunellier, *m.*, épine noire, *f.* — **wine,** *s.* prunelet, *m.*, piquette, *f.*
Sloke, *s.* (*bot.*) *V.* **Laver**
Sloop, *s.* sloop, *m.*; corvette, *f.*; chaloupe, *f.* — *of war,* sloop de guerre, *m.*, corvette, *f.*
Slop, *v.a.* (*drink*) boire salement; (*let fall*) laisser tomber, verser, répandre; (*soil*) salir, faire du gâchis sur; — *s.* gâchis, margouillis, *m.*; (*mean liquor*) ripopée, lavasse, *f.*; (*garment*) blouse, *f.*, bourgeron, *m.*; (*policeman*) *V.* **Bobby;** —**s,** *pl.* rinçure, *f.*, rinçures, *f.pl.*; eau sale, *f.*; eaux ménagères, *f.pl.*; (*washy drink*) lavasse, *f.*; (*clothes*) habits tout faits, *m.pl.*, confection, *f.*, (*of sailors*) hardes (de matelots), *f.pl.*; — *adj.* de pacotille. — **basin,** *s.* rince-tasse, *m.* — **goods,** *s.pl.* vêtements de pacotille, *m.pl.*; confections, *f.pl.* — **made,** *adj.* de pacotille. — **man,** *s.* *V.* —**seller.** — **pail,** *s.* seau de toilette, *m.* — **room,** *s.* (*nav.*) soute aux hardes, *f.* — **seller,** *s.* confectionneur, *m.* — **shop,** *s.* magasin de confection, *m.* — **work,** *s.* confection, *f.*
Slope, *s.* biais, *m.*; échancrure, *f.*; (*declivity*) pente, inclinaison, rampe, côte, *f.*, talus, *m.*; — *v.a.* couper *or* tailler en (*or* de) biais; échancrer; (*of the ground*) former en talus, taluter; (*incline*) pencher, incliner; — *v.n.* aller en pente; pencher; biaiser
Sloping, *adj.* de biais; échancré; (*inclined*) en pente; en talus; — *s.* *V.* **Slope,** *s.*
Slopingly, *adv.* en biais; (*inclined*) en pente; en talus
Sloppiness, *s.* état bourbeux *or* gâcheux, *m.*
Sloppy, *adj.* gâcheux; (*muddy*) bourbeux
Slot, *s.* (*hunt.*) trace, *f.*, abattures, foulées, foulures, *f.pl.*; — *v.a.* dépister
Sloth, *s.* paresse, oisiveté, fainéantise, *f.*; indolence, *f.*; lenteur, *f.*; (*an animal*) paresseux, *m.* [**Laziness**
Slothful, -ly, -ness. *V.* **Lazy, Lazily,**
Slouch, *s.* (*pers.*) gros lourdaud, gros manant, *m.*; (*manner or gait*) attitude gauche, démarche lourde, *f.*; (*of the head*) inclinaison, *f.*; — *v.a.* rabattre, rabaisser; — *v.n.* se dandiner lourdement, traîner en marchant, marcher des

épaules, marcher comme un paysan, bouliner. *—ed hat*, chapeau à bords pendants *or* rabattus, claque-oreilles, *m.* *To walk with a —, to — along*, se dandiner, &c. (*as above*)

Slouching, *adj.* incliné ; rabattu, rabaissé. *— gait*, démarche lourde, *f.*

Slough, *s.* (*of mud*) bourbier, *m.*, fondrière, *f.*, (*fig.*) abîme, *m.* ; (*of serpents*) dépouille, *f.* ; (*med.*) eschare, *f.* ; — *v.n.* s'escharifier

Sloughy, *adj.* bourbeux

Sloven, *s.* homme (*m.*) *or* femme (*f.*) malpropre *or* sale, sagouin, *m.*, e, *f.*, souillon, *f.*, salop, *m.*, e, *f.*, salaud, *m.*, e, *f.*, saligaud, *m.*, e, *f.*

Slovenliness, *s.* malpropreté, saleté, *f.* ; négligence, *f.*

Slovenly, *adj.* malpropre, sale ; négligent ; — *adv.* malproprement, salement ; négligemment

Slow, *adj.* lent ; tardif ; (*stupid*) lourd, pesant ; paresseux, indolent ; (*tedious*) ennuyeux, monotone ; (*of clocks, watches*) en retard ; (*of railway-trains*) de petite vitesse ; (*adverb.*) lentement. *To be* — or *too —, to go too —*, (*of clocks*, &c.) retarder (de . . .) ; être en retard. *To grow* (or *get* or *become*) —, se ralentir. *He was not — to . . .* (or *in . . . ing . . .*), il ne tarda pas à . . . *— and sure*, qui va piano va sano. — **back,** *s.* lambin, *m.*, e, *f.* — **coach,** *s.* *V.* **Coach.** — **going,** *adj.* qui va lentement. —**ly,** *adv.* lentement ; doucement ; tardivement. — **match,** *s.* *V.* **Match.** — **ness,** *s.* lenteur, *f.* ; nature tardive, *f.* ; paresse, indolence, *f.* ; (*dulness*) lourdeur, pesanteur d'esprit, *f.* ; (*of clocks, watches*) retard, *m.* — **paced,** *adj.* qui va lentement. — **worm,** *s.* [orvet, envoye, aveugle, *m.*

Sludge, *s.* *V.* **Slush**

Slue (— round), *v.a.* faire pivoter, faire tourner ; — *v.n.* pivoter, tourner

Slug, *s.* fainéant, *m.*, e, *f.*, lambin, *m.*, e, *f.* ; (*a snail*) limace, *f.* ; (*— shot*) lingot, *m.*

Sluggard, *s.* paresseux, *m.*, -euse, *f.*, fainéant, *m.*, e, *f.* ; dormeur, *m.*, -euse, *f.* ; — *adj.* *V.* **Sluggish**

Sluggish, *adj.* paresseux, fainéant ; lourd, indolent, apathique ; nonchalant

Sluggishly, *adv.* avec paresse ; avec indolence, avec apathie, lourdement ; nonchalamment

Sluggishness, *s.* paresse, *f.* ; indolence, *f.* ; apathie, *f.* ; lenteur, *f.* ; nonchalance, *f.*

Sluice, *s.* écluse, *f.* ; (*of ponds*) bonde, *f.* ; (*stream*) courant, *m.* ; (*opening*) issue, *f.* ; — *v.a.* débonder, lâcher par une écluse ; inonder ; (*fig.*) répandre à flots ; inonder ; — *v.n.* couler à flots. — **gate,** *s.* vanne, *f.* ; écluse, *f.*

Sluicy, *adj.* à flots, torrentiel

Slumber, *v.n.* sommeiller ; dormir ; — *s.* assoupissement, *m.* ; repos, *m.* ; sommeil, *m.*

Slumberer, *s.* personne qui sommeille, *f.* ; dormeur, *m.*, -euse, *f.* [endormi

Slumbering, *s.* sommeil, *m.* ; — *adj.* assoupi,

Slums, *s.pl.* bas quartiers, *m.pl.*

Slur, *v.a.* (*over*) passer légèrement *or* rapidement sur, glisser sur ; faire bon marché de ; ignorer ; (*conceal*) cacher, masquer ; (*sully*) tacher, salir ; gâcher ; (*mus.*) couler, lier ; — *s.* tache, *f.* ; atteinte, *f.* ; blâme, *m.* ; (*trick*) tour, *m.* ; (*mus.*) liaison, *f.*, coulé, *m.* ; port de voix, *m.* *To cast* or *throw a — upon*, déverser le blâme sur, blâmer ; salir, diffamer, dénigrer

Slurring, *s.* liaison, *f.*

Slush, *s.* gâchis, *m.*, boue, fange, bourbe, *f.*

Slut, *s.* salope, salaude, saligaude, souillon, sagouine, *f.* ; coquine, guenipe, coureuse, *f.*

Sluttery, *s.* saleté, *f.*

Sluttish, *adj.* (*pers.*) salaud, sale ; (*things*) de souillon, sale. —**ly,** *adv.* salement. —**ness,** *s.* saleté, *f.*

Sly, *adj.* sournois, en dessous ; (*cunning*) rusé, fin, malin. *On the —*, en cachette ; à la sourdine ; à la dérobée, furtivement. — **boots,** *s.* sournois, *m.* ; fin matois, finaud, *m.* — **puss,** *s.* sournoise, *f.*

Slyly, Slyness. *V.* **Slily, Sliness**

Smack, *v.n.* (*of lips, whips*) claquer ; (*have a taste*) sentir (le, la, les), avoir un goût (de) ; — *v.a.* faire claquer ; (*strike*) *V.* **Slap ;** — *s.* (*kiss*) gros baiser, *m.* ; (*of the lips*) claquement, bruit, *m.* ; (*of whips*) claquement, clic-clac, *m.* ; (*slap*) claque, tape, *f.* ; (*taste*) goût, *m.*, saveur, *f.* ; (*tincture*) teinture, teinte, *f.* ; (*small quantity*) légère quantité, *f.*, soupçon, *m.*, idée, *f.* ; (*boat*) semaque, *m.* ; — *adv. int.* *V.* **Slap.** *Fishing —*, semaque, *m.* *To — o.'s lips*, (*after eating or drinking something good*) se lécher les [lèvres

Smacker, *s.* (*on the face*) gifle, *f.*

Smacking, *adj.* bruyant, retentissant ; qui [claque

Smala, *s.* smala, *f.*

Small, *adj.* petit ; (*in small pieces or parts, composed of small individuals*) menu ; (*slender*) fin, délié ; (*of writing, printing type*) fin ; (*petty*) mince ; chétif ; minime ; exigu ; (*unimportant*) faible, léger ; insignifiant ; peu considérable ; (*not numerous*) peu nombreux ; (*moderate*) modique ; (*narrow*) étroit ; — *s.* partie mince, *f.* ; petit bout, *m.* ; (*— bits*) menu, *m.* ; (*of the leg*) bas, *m.* ; (*of anchors*) tige, *f.* ; —**s,** *s.pl.* culotte, culotte courte, *f.* — *arms*, (*mil.*) menues armes, armes portatives, *f.pl.* — *beer*, petite bière, *f.* — *card*, (*play*) basse carte, *f.* — *cattle*, menu (*or* petit) bétail, *m.* — *clothes*, *V.* **Clothes.** — *coal*, menu charbon, *m.* — *fry*, *V.* **Fry.** — *hand*, (*writ.*) écriture fine, *f.* — *intestine*, intestins grêles, *m.pl.* — *pox*, *V.* **Pox.** — *shot*, menu plomb, *m.* — *sized*, petit. — *talk*, *V.* **Talk.** — *wares*, *V.* **Ware.** — *of the back*, chute des reins, *f.*, défaut des côtes, *m.* *To cut —*, couper en petits morceaux, hacher menu

Smallage, *s.* ache, *f.* [un peu fin

Smallish, *adj.* un peu petit ; un peu menu ;

Smallness, *s.* petitesse, *f.* ; petite étendue, *f.* ; peu de volume, *m.* ; (*thinness*) finesse, *f.* ; exiguïté, *f.* ; (*weakness*) faiblesse, *f.* ; (*of importance*) peu d'importance, *m.* ; (*of number*) petit nombre, *m.* ; (*moderateness*) modicité, *f.* ; (*gentleness, softness*) douceur, *f.*

Smally, *adv.* petitement, peu, légèrement

Smalt, *s.* smalt, bleu d'azur, *m.*

Smart, *v.n.* cuire ; souffrir cruellement ; (*to bear a penalty*) porter la peine (de) ; — *s.* cuisson, douleur cuisante, douleur aiguë, *f.* ; (*of mind*) chagrin dévorant, *m.* ; — *adj.* (*of pain*) cuisant, aigu ; (*caustic*) mordant, piquant ; (*vigorous*) vif, rude, vigoureux ; vert ; (*brisk*) fringant ; (*good*) bon, fameux ; (*witty*) fin, spirituel ; (*spruce*) beau, élégant ; pimpant ; (*quick*, &c.) actif ; éveillé ; intelligent ; habile. *My hand —s*, la main me cuit. *He shall — for it*, il lui en cuira. *You may — for it*, il pourra vous en cuire. *To make one — for a thing*, faire payer cher une chose à quelqu'un. *To — under the lash*, (*fig.*) sentir l'aiguillon (de). — **money,** *s.* rachat, dégagement, *m.* — **ticket,** *s.* certificat de blessure, *m.* — **weed,** *s.* persicaire, *f.* [rendre pimpant

Smarten, *v.a.* requinquer, attifer, faire beau,

Smarting, *adj.* cuisant, douloureux, poignant ; — *s.* cuisson, douleur cuisante, *f.*

Smartly, *adv.* douloureusement ; (*sharply*) d'une manière mordante ; (*vigorously*) vivement, vigoureusement ; vertement ; (*wittily*) finement, spirituellement ; (*showily*) brillamment ; avec élégance

Smartness, *s.* vivacité, *f.* ; force, *f.* ; finesse, *f.* ; élégance, *f.* ; éclat, *m.* ; intelligence, habileté, *f.*

Smash, *v.a.* briser ; (*crush*) écraser ; — *s.* fracas, *m.* ; (*bankruptcy*, &c.) déconfiture, *f.* *To go to —*, se briser ; (*be a bankrupt*) faire faillite. *Gone to —*, brisé *or* mis en morceaux (*or* en mille miettes) ; ruiné

Smasher, *s.* (*coiner*) faux monnayeur, *m.* ; (*utterer*) émissionnaire, *m.f.*

Smatter, *v.n.* parler en ignorant ; n'avoir

qu'une connaissance superficielle *or* qu'une légère teinture (de) ; — *s. V.* **Smattering**

Smatterer, *s.* homme superficiel, demi-savant, *m.*

Smattering, *s.* teinture, *f.*

Smear, *v.a.* ('*with,*' de) enduire, couvrir ; (*in a bad sense*) barbouiller ; souiller

Smell, *v.a.n.* sentir ; (*suspect*) flairer, se douter de ; (*of animals*) sentir, flairer ; (*of*) sentir (le, la, les) ; (*be smelt*) se sentir ; avoir de l'odeur ; — *s.* (*sense*) odorat, *m.* ; (*odour*) odeur, *f.* ; (*perfume*) parfum, *m.*, senteur, bonne odeur, *f.* *To — bad* or *badly* or *nasty*, sentir mauvais. *To — nice* or *nicely* or *sweet*, sentir bon. *To — close,* (*of rooms*) sentir le renfermé *To — a rat,* se douter de (*or* flairer) quelque chose, soupçonner anguille sous roche, se méfier. — **out,** *v.a.* découvrir

Smeller, *s.* personne qui sent, *f.*, flaireur, *m.*, -euse, *f.* ; (*nose*) nez, *m.* ; (*blow*) coup de poing sur le nez, *m.*

Smelling, *adj.* qui sent ; — *s.* odorat, *m.* — **bottle,** *s.* flacon d'odeur, *m.* — **salts,** *s.pl.* sel de vinaigre, *m.*, sels à respirer, sels, *m.pl.*

Smelt, *s.* éperlan, *m.* ; — *v.a.* fondre

Smelter, *s.* fondeur, *m.*

Smeltery, *s.* fonderie, forge, *f.* [fonderie, *f.*

Smelting, *s.* fonte, fusion, *f.* — **house,** *s.*

Smew, *s.* piette, nonnette blanche, *f.*

Smile, *v.n.* sourire ('*on,*' '*upon,*' à ; '*at,*' *pers.*, à, *things*, de) ; — *s.* sourire, *m.*

Smiler, *s.* sourieur, *m.*, -euse, *f.*

Smiling, *adj.* (*pers.*) souriant ; (*things*) riant

Smilingly, *adv.* en souriant ; d'un air riant

Smilingness, *s.* air souriant, *m.*

Smirch. *V.* **Begrime**

Smirk. *V.* **Simper**

Smite, *v.a.* frapper ; (*kill*) tuer ; (*destroy*) détruire ; (*punish*) châtier, frapper, punir ; (*with love*) enflammer, captiver ; — *v.n.* se heurter, se choquer, se frapper

Smith, *s.* forgeron, *m.* ; (*in compounds*) ouvrier, artisan, *m.* (*V.* **Black, White, Shoeing, Gold, Silver, Lock, Gun, Coach,** &c.). —*'s coal,* houille de forge, *f.* —*'s shop,* forge, *f.* — **craft,** *s.* art du forgeron, métier de forgeron, *m.*

Smithery, *s.* forge, *f.* ; (*work*) ouvrage de forgeron, *m.* [forgeron, *m.*

Smithing, *s.* forgeage, forgement, *m.* ; art du

Smithy, *s.* forge, *f.*

Smitten, *part. adj.* frappé, &c. (*V.* **Smite**) ; (*with love*) épris (de), amoureux (de)

Smock, — **frock,** *s.* blouse, *f.*, sarrau, *m.*, souquenille, *f.*

Smokable, *adj.* fumable

Smoke, *s.* fumée, *f.* ; vapeur, exhalaison, *f.* ; — *v.n.a.* fumer ; (*annoy, injure, cover with —*) enfumer. *To end in —,* s'en aller en fumée. — **box,** *s.* boîte à fumée, *f.* — **consumer,** *s.* fumivore, *m.* — **consuming,** *adj.* fumivore. — **consuming apparatus,** *s.* fumivore, *m.* — **disperser,** *s.* girouette à fumée, *f.* — **doctor,** *s.* fumiste, *m.* — **dry,** *v.a.* fumer, boucaner. — **hole,** *s.* (*of volcanoes*) fumerolle, *f.* — **jack,** *s.* (*of chimneys*) moulinet à vent, *m.* ; (*for roasting*) tournebroche à courant d'air, *m.* —**less,** *adj.* sans fumée. — **out,** *v.a.* enfumer ; (*a cigar or pipe*) fumer jusqu'au bout. — **preventer,** *s.* fumifuge, *m.* — **preventing,** *adj.* fumifuge. — **sail,** *s.* masque, *m.* — **tree,** *s.* fustet, *m.*

Smoker, *s.* fumeur, *m.*, -euse, *f.*

Smokiness, *s.* état enfumé, *m.*

Smoking, *adj.* fumant ; qui fume ; — *s.* action de fumer, (*fam.*) fumerie, *f.* ; habitude de fumer, *f.* ; usage du tabac à fumer, *m.* *To like —, to be fond of —,* aimer à fumer. *No — allowed, — strictly prohibited,* il est défendu de fumer, défense de fumer. — **cap,** *s.* bonnet grec, *m.*, calotte grecque, calotte, *f.* — **carriage,** *s.* voiture pour les fumeurs, *f.*, wagon des fumeurs, *m.* — **chair,** *s.* fumeuse, *f.* — **compartment,** *s.* compartiment des fumeurs, *m.* — **divan,** *s.* salon-fumoir, fumoir, *m.* — **pipe,** *s.* pipe à fumer, *f.* — **room,** *s.* fumoir, salon-fumoir, *m* ; estaminet, *m.* ; (*in a bad sense*) tabagie, *f.*

Smoky, *adj.* qui fume ; fumeux ; (*smoke-like*) de fumée ; (*full of smoke, begrimed*) enfumé ; (*fig.*) sombre, noir

Smolt, *s.* saumoneau, *m.*

Smooth, *adj.* (*level*) uni ; (*polished*) poli ; (*soft*) doux ; (*glossy*) lisse ; (*of the sea*) calme ; (*of speech*) facile ; — *adv. V.* **Smoothly.** — **bore,** *adj.* (*of guns and pistols*) à canon lisse ; (*of cannon*) à âme lisse, lisse. — **spoken, -talking, -tongued,** *adj.* au doux parler ; (*soapy*) doucereux, mielleux, à langue dorée

Smooth, *v.a.* unir ; polir ; (*the hair,* &c.) lisser ; (*soften*) adoucir ; (*calm*) apaiser, calmer ; (*flatter*) flatter, cajoler ; caresser ; (*difficulties, wood*) aplanir ; (*the brow*) dérider

Smoothing, *s.* aplanissement, *m.* ; adoucissement, *m.* ; (*tech*) adoucissage, *m.* ; (*of glass*) adouci, *m.* — **iron,** *s.* fer à repasser, *m.* ; (*tailor's goose*) carreau, *m.* — **plane,** *s.* petit rabot, *m.*

Smoothly, *adv.* uniment ; d'une manière égale ; (*gently, softly*) doucement ; (*easily*) aisément, facilement, sans difficulté ; bien

Smoothness, *s.* égalité, *f.* ; (*softness*) douceur, *f.* ; (*polish*) poli, *m.* ; (*of the sea*) calme, *m.*

Smother, *v.a.n.* suffoquer, étouffer ; asphyxier ; (*fig.*) étouffer, éteindre ; (*smoulder*) *V.* **Smoulder** ; — *s.* atmosphère suffocante, *f.* ; fumée épaisse, *f.* ; (*dust*) nuée de poussière, *f.* *To make a —,* (*dust*) faire de la poussière. *What a — there is !* on étouffe !

Smothering, *s.* suffocation, *f.*, étouffement, *m.* ; asphyxie, *f.* ; — *adj.* suffocant, étouffant ; — *part.* suffoquant, étouffant

Smoulder, *v.n.* couver, couver sous la cendre ; brûler lentement *or* sourdement, fumer sans flamber, charbonner [**Smoulder**)

Smouldering, *part. adj.* qui couve *or* &c. (*V.*

Smudge, *v.a.* salir, noircir ; barbouiller ; — *s.* saleté, noircissure, tache de noir, *f.*, noir, *m.* ; barbouillage, *m.*

Smudgy, *adj.* noir de suie, noir, sale

Smug, *adj.* pimpant, propret, coquet

Smuggle, *v.n.* faire la contrebande ; — *v.a.* passer en contrebande *or* en fraude ; faire la contrebande de. — **in,** introduire *or* faire entrer en contrebande, passer en contrebande, introduire par fraude ; (*fig.*) introduire clandestinement, faire entrer

Smuggled, *adj.* de contrebande

Smuggler, *s.* contrebandier, *m.*

Smuggling, *s.* contrebande, *f.*

Smugly, *adv.* d'un air pimpant, gentiment, coquettement ; avec recherche, d'une manière recherchée [propreté, *f.* ; recherche, *f.*

Smugness, *s.* air pimpant, air coquet, *m.*,

Smut, *s.* (*spot*) noir, *m.*, tache, *f.* ; (*fig.*) saleté, *f.* ; (*in corn*) charbon, *m.*, nielle, *f.* ; — *v.a.* salir, noircir ; (*corn*) nieller. — **ball,** *s.* carie, cloque, *f.*, noir, *m.*, pourriture, *f.*

Smutch. *V.* **Smudge**

Smuttily, *adv.* salement [leté, *f.*

Smuttiness, *s.* noirceur, *f.* ; (*of language*) sa-

Smutty, *adj.* noirci ; (*of corn*) niellé ; (*fig.*) obscène, sale, graveleux, grivois

Snack, *s.* portion, part, *f.* ; (*hasty repast*) morceau, morceau sur le pouce, *m.* *To go —s with,* être de moitié avec. *To take a —,* manger un morceau

Snaffle, — **bridle,** *s.* bridon, filet, *m.*

Snag, *s.* nœud, *m.*, bosse, *f.* ; branche, *f.* ; (*tooth*) croc, *m.* ; (*in rivers*) arbre submergé, *m.*

Snagged, Snaggy, *adj.* noueux

Snail, *s.* limaçon, colimaçon, *m.* ; escargot, *m.*, (*pers.*) lambin, *m.*, e, *f.*, tortue, *f.* *Edible —,* escargot comestible, escargot, *m.*, vigneronne, *f.* —**like,** *adj.* de limaçon ; (*slow*) lent, de tortue ; *adv.* en limaçon ; (*slowly*) lentement, comme une tortue. — **pace, —'s pace,** *s.* pas de tortue, m. — **paced,** *adj.* lent, qui va à pas de tortue

Snake, *s.* serpent, *m.*; (*common snake*) couleuvre, *f.* *A — in the grass,* quelque anguille sous roche. — **bird,** *s.* anhinga, *m.* — **charmer,** *s.* charmeur (*m.*, -euse, *f.*) de serpents. — **fly,** *s.* raphidie, *f.* — **root,** *s.* sénéga, *m.*, serpentaire, *f.* — **weed,** *s.* bistorte, *f.* — **wood,** *s.* bois de couleuvre, *m.*

Snakish, Snaky, *adj.* de serpent; à serpents; tortueux, sinueux; (*sly*) rusé

Snap, *v.a.n.* (*break*) casser net, casser, rompre, éclater; (*the fingers,* &c.: *v.a.*) faire claquer, (*v.n.*) claquer; (*bite*) mordre; (*catch*) happer, attraper, se saisir de; (*scold*) bourrer. *To — o's fingers at,* narguer, se moquer de, se ficher de. — **at,** tâcher de happer *or* de mordre, vouloir happer *or* mordre; se jeter sur. — **off,** — **up,** casser; (*catch*) happer, attraper, se saisir de; (*scold*) brusquer, bourrer; rembarrer

Snap, *s.* (*breaking*) cassure, rupture, *f.*; éclat, *m.*; (*bite*) coup de dent, *m.*; (*effort*) effort, *m.*; (*noise*) bruit sec, *m.*; (*of fingers,* &c.) claquement, *m.*; (*cake*) croquet, craquelin, *m.*; (*insect*) taupin, *m.*; (*glutton*) glouton, *m.*, -ne, *f.*; (*fastening*) agrafe, *f.*; (*clasp*) fermoir, *m.*; —**s,** *pl.* cassures, &c.; (*snappers*) cliquettes, *f.pl.* *To give a —,* se casser, éclater; (*try to bite*) tâcher de mordre. *To make a — at,* tâcher de mordre, donner un coup de dent à, tâcher de happer *I don't care a — of my finger for him,* je m'en soucie comme de ça (*suiting the action to the word*)

Snap-bug, *s.* taupin, *m.*

Snapdragon, *s.* (*bot.*) muflier, *m.*, gueule-de-loup, *f.*

Snappers, *s pl.* cliquettes, *f.pl.*

Snappish, *adj.* hargneux; (*things*) aigre

Snappishly, *adv.* d'une manière hargneuse; aigrement

Snappishness, *s.* humeur hargneuse, *f.*; aigreur, *f.*

Snare, *s.* piége, *m.*; — *v.a.* *V.* **Ensnare**

Snarl, *v.n.* gronder, grogner, montrer les dents

Snarler, *s.* grogneur, *m.*, -euse, *f.*, grognon, *m.f.*; bourru, *m.*, e, *f.*

Snarling, *adj.* hargneux

Snatch, *v.a.* saisir; (*wrest*) arracher (à, de); (*steal*) dérober (à). — **away, off,** arracher; emporter; enlever. — **up,** saisir, ramasser; — *v.n.* — **at,** se jeter sur, tâcher de saisir *or* d'attraper; (*cling*) se raccrocher à

Snatch, *s.* prise, *f.*; effort pour saisir, *m.*; (*fit*) accès, moment, *m.*; (*bit*) morceau, *m.* *By —es,* par boutades, à bâtons rompus. — **block,** *s.* poulie coupée, *f.*

Snatcher, *s.* personne qui saisit, *f.*; personne qui arrache, *f.*

Snatchingly, *adv.* vivement, brusquement, avidement; par boutades, par accès

Sneak, *v.n.* se glisser; (*crouch, truckle*) ramper; rapporter, cafarder, caponner; — *s.* homme rampant, pied plat, *m.*, hypocrite, *m.f.*; rapporteur, *m.*, -euse, *f.*, cafard, capon, *m.* — **away, off,** s'échapper furtivement, s'échapper; caponner

Sneakiness. *V.* **Sneakingness**

Sneaking, *adj.* sournois, hypocrite, cafard; rapporteur; de cafard, de capon; bas, vil, rampant, servile; lâche; (*niggardly*) avare, sordide

Sneakingly, *adv.* surnoisement; furtivement, à la dérobée; en cafard, en capon; bassement, servilement; sordidement

Sneakingness, *s.* sournoiserie, *f.*; bassesse, servilité, *f.*; lâcheté, *f.*; caractère sordide, *m.*

Sneer, *v.n.* ricaner ('*at,*' de); (*jeer*) railler, se moquer (de); — *s.* ricanement, *m.*, ricanerie, *f.*, rire moqueur, *m.*; air de mépris, *m.*; sarcasme, *m.*, raillerie, moquerie, *f.*

Sneerer, *s.* ricaneur, *m.*, -euse, *f.*; railleur, *m.*, -euse, *f.*

Sneering, *adj.* ricaneur; railleur, moqueur, ironique; — *s.* *V.* **Sneer,** *s.*

Sneeringly, *adv.* en ricanant; avec un rire moqueur, d'un ton *or* d'un air moqueur, railleusement

Sneeze, *v.n.* éternuer; (*vet.*) s'ébrouer; — *s.* éternuement, *m.* *That is not to be —d at,* cela n'est pas à dédaigner, cela n'est pas de refus. — **wort,** *s.* éternue, ptarmique, *f.*

Sneezer, *s.* éternueur, *m.*, -euse, *f.*

Sneezing, *s.* éternuement, *m.*; (*vet.*) ébrouement, *m.*

Sniff, *v.n.a.* renifler ('*at,*' sur); — *s.* reniflement, *m.*

Sniffer, *s.* renifleur, *m*, -euse, *f.*

Sniffing, *s.* reniflement, *m.*, reniflerie, *f.*

Snigger, *v.n.* ricaner, rire tout bas, rire sous cape, rire en dessous

Sniggering, *s.* ricanement, *m.*

Sniggle, *v.n.* pêcher des anguilles; — *v.a.* prendre au piége

Sniggling, *s.* pêche aux anguilles, *f.*

Snip, (— **off, up**) *v.a.* couper; — *s.* coup de ciseaux, *m.*; (*bit*) morceau, bout, *m.*; (*share*) part, portion, *f.*

Snipe, *s.* bécassine, *f.* — **fish,** *s.* *V.* **Trumpet-fish**

Snippet, *s.* tantinet, petit morceau, *m.*

Snivel, *s.* roupie, *f.*; — *v.n.* avoir la roupie au nez; (*whine*) pleurnicher

Sniveller, *s.* pleurnicheur, *m.*, -euse, *f.*

Snivelling, *s.* pleurnicherie, *f.*; — *adj.* roupieux; (*whining*) pleurnicheur

Snivelly, *adj.* *V.* **Snivelling**

Snob, *s.* (*upstart*) parvenu, *m.*; (*fop, pedant*) fat, faraud, *m.*; cuistre, *m.*; (*attitudinarian*) poseur, *m.*; (*mean fellow*) goujat, *m.*

Snobbish, *adj.* commun, vulgaire, de mauvaise compagnie, de mauvais ton, de bas étage; sot

Snobbishness, *s.* vulgarité, *f.*; sottise, *f.*

Snooze, *v.n.* roupiller, pioncer; — *s.* somme, *m.* *To have* or *take a —,* faire un somme

Snoozer, *s.* roupilleur, *m.*, -euse, *f.*

Snore, Snort, *v.n.* ronfler; — *s.* ronflement, *m.*

Snorer, Snorter, *s.* ronfleur, *m.*, -euse, *f.*

Snoring, Snorting, *s.* ronflement, *m.*

Snot, *s.* morve, *f.*; — *v.a.* moucher

Snottiness, *s.* état morveux, *m.*

Snotty, *adj.* morveux. —**nosed,** *adj.* morveux

Snout, *s.* museau, *m.*; (*of swine*) groin, *m.*; (*of wild boars*) boutoir, *m.*; (*nozzle*) *V.* **Nozzle.** — **beetle,** *s.* charançon, *m.* [à bec

Snouted, *adj.* à museau; (*nozzled*) à bout,

Snow, *s.* neige, *f.*; (*nav.*) senau, *m.*; — *v.n.* neiger. —**ball,** *s.* boule de neige, *f.*; *v.a.* poursuivre à coups de boules de neige. —**ball tree,** *s.* obier, *m.* — **berry,** *s.* symphorine, *f.* — **bird,** *s.* (*finch*) nivereau, *m.*, niverolle, *f.*; (*bunting*) bruant de neige, *m.* — **bunting,** *s.* bruant de neige, *m.* —**capped, -covered, -crowned,** *adj.* couvert *or* couronné de neige, neigeux. — **drift,** *s.* monceau *or* amas de neige, *m.* — **drop,** *s.* perce-neige, nivéole, *f.* — **drop tree,** *s.* halésie, *f.* — **finch,** *s.* nivereau, *m.*, niverolle, *f.* — **flake,** *s.* flocon de neige, *m.*; (*bot.*) perce-neige, nivéole, *f.* — **fleck,** *s.* bruant de neige, *m.* — **flower,** *s.* arbre de neige, chionanthe, *m.* —**less,** *adj.* sans neige. —**like,** *adj.* de neige, comme la neige. —**line,** *s.* limite des neiges, *f.* — **plough,** *s.* chasse-neige, *m.* — **shoe, -skate,** *s.* raquette, *f.*, patin, *m.* — **slip,** *s.* avalanche, *f.* — **storm,** *s.* tempête de neige, *f.*, orage de neige, *m.* — **track,** *s.* trace de neige, *f.* —**white,** *adj.* blanc comme la neige, de neige

Snowed up, *adj.* pris *or* arrêté par (*or* retenu dans) les neiges

Snowy, *adj.* neigeux; de neige; blanc comme la neige; pur, sans tache. — **owl,** *s.* harfang, *m.*

Snub, *v.a.* gourmander, réprimander, reprendre; relancer; — *s.* leçon, *f.*, coup de patte, camouflet, *m.* — **nose,** *s.* nez camus, *m.* — **nosed,** *adj.*, *With a — nose,* *V.* **Flat-nosed**

Snuff, *s.* tabac à priser, tabac, *m.*; (*of a candle*) lumignon, *m.*; (*bit snuffed off*) mouchure, *f.*; — *v.a.n.* (— **in, up**) aspirer; renifler; (*to smell*) flairer, sentir; (*a candle*) moucher. — **out,** *v.a.* éteindre; (*fig.*) exterminer. *Pinch of —,* prise de tabac, *f.* *To take —,* priser, prendre du tabac. *To be up to —,* avoir le fil; **ne pas**

se moucher du pied. *To put up to* —, dégourdir. — **box,** *s.* tabatière, *f.* — **colour,** *s.*, — **coloured,** *adj.* marron, *m.* — **taker,** *s.* priseur, *m.*, -euse, *f.* — **taking,** *s. adj.* priseur; *s.* usage du tabac à priser, *m.*; action *or* habitude de priser, *f.*

Snuffers, *s.pl.* mouchettes, *f.pl.* — **stand, -tray,** *s.* porte-mouchettes, *m.*

Snuffle, *v.n.* souffler; nasiller, parler du nez

Snuffler, *s.* nasilleur, *m.*, -euse, *f.*, nasillard, *m.*, e, *f.*

Snuffles, *s.pl.* enchifrènement, *m.*

Snuffling, *s.* nasillement, *m.*; — *adj.* nasillard

Snuffy, *adj.* barbouillé *or* plein de tabac

Snug, *adj.* (*close*) serré; (*quiet*) tranquille; retiré; (*neat*) gentil; (*comfortable*) *V.* **Comfortable**

Snuggle, *v.n.* *V.* **Cuddle**

Snugly, *adv.* commodément, à son aise

Snugness, *s.* commodité, *f.*, confortable, *m.*

So, *adv.* (*then, thus*) ainsi; (*in like manner*) ainsi, de cette manière; comme cela, comme ça; de même; aussi; (*this is the way to do it*) comme ça! c'est cela! (*therefore*) donc, aussi; (*to such a degree*) si, tellement, tant; aussi; (*very*) très, bien; (*about*) environ, à peu près; (*used for an adj.* or *a verb*) le; en; que oui; (*that*) cela; (*provided that*) pourvu que; (*that is or was what*) c'est ce que; (*exclam.*) eh bien! soit! *Be it* —! soit! — *be it!* ainsi soit-il! (*fam.*) soit! — *it is*, il en est ainsi, c'est ainsi, c'est comme cela; c'est juste, c'est vrai; c'est cela; en effet; justement. *I think* —, *V.* **Think.** *I believe* —, je le crois, je crois que oui. *I fear* —, *I am afraid* —, je le crains, j'en ai peur. *I hope* —, je l'espère. *I did not say* —, je n'ai pas dit cela. — *I say*, c'est ce que je dis. — *I thought*, c'est ce que je pensais. — *I did*, c'est ce que j'ai fait. *If* —, s'il en est ainsi, si c'est ainsi. *Nearly* —, à peu près. *Not* —, *it is not* —, il n'en est pas ainsi, ce n'est pas ainsi. *Why* —? pourquoi cela? pourquoi? — *do I* or *can I* or *shall I* or &c., moi aussi. — *good an opportunity*, une si bonne occasion. — *proud a man*, un homme si fier. — *true it is*, tant il est vrai. — *so*, passablement, doucement, comme ça. — *and* —, de telle ou telle manière; (*this and that*) telle et telle chose, (*fam.*) ça et ça; (*pers.*) un tel, *m.*, une telle, *f.* — *as to*, de manière à; (*in order to*) afin de. — ... *as to*, assez ... pour. — *that*, de sorte que, de manière que; tellement que; si bien que; (*provided that*) pourvu que. — *then*, ainsi donc. *And — forth, and — on*, et ainsi de suite; et le reste

Soak, *v.a.n.* tremper; faire tremper; imbiber; pénétrer. — **in,** boire; pénétrer

Soaker, *s.* (*drinker*) buveur, *m.*, -euse, *f.*, biberon, *m.*, -ne, *f.*, ivrogne, *m.*, -esse, *f.*, sac à vin, *m.*; (*shower*) averse, *f.* [ivrognerie, *f.*

Soaking, *s.* trempée, *f.*; (*drinking*) boisson,

Soap, *s.* savon, *m.*; — *v.a.* savonner; (*fig.*) flagorner. — **ball,** *s.* savonnette, *f.* — **berry,** *s.* savonnier, *m.* — **boiler,** *s.* savonnier, *m.* — **bubble,** *s.* bulle de savon, *f.* — **dish,** *s.* *V.* — **tray.** — **factory,** *s.* savonnerie, *f.* — **maker, -manufacturer,** *s.* savonnier, fabricant de savon, *m.* — **making, -manufactory,** *s.* savonnerie, *f.* — **paste,** *s.* pâte de savon, ressence, *f.* — **plaster,** *s.* sparadrap, *m.* — **stone,** *s.* pierre de savon, *f.*, saponite, *m.*, stéatite, *f.*, pierre de lard, *f.* — **suds,** *s.pl.* eau de savon, *f.* — **trade,** *s.* savonnerie, *f.* — **tray,** *s.* boîte à savon, *f.* — **tree,** *s.* savonnier, *m.* — **works,** *s.pl.* savonnerie, *f.* — **wort,** *s.* saponaire, savonnière, *f.*

Soapery, *s.* savonnerie, *f.*

Soaping, *s.* savonnage, *m.* [doucereux

Soapy, *adj.* savonneux; savonné; (*fig.*)

Soar, *v.n.* prendre l'essor; s'élever; (*over, above*) planer (sur)

Soaring, *adj.* qui plane; transcendant; ardent; — *s.* essor, *m.*; élan, *m.*

Soaringly, *adv.* en prenant l'essor; avec élan; d'une manière transcendante; ardemment

Sob, *v.n.* sangloter; — *s.* sanglot, *m.*

Sobbing, *s.* sanglots, *m.pl.*

Sober, *adj.* sobre; tempérant; modéré; sensé, raisonnable; de sang-froid, calme; grave, sérieux; posé; (*not drunk*) pas ivre, à jeun; — *v.a.* (— **down**) désenivrer, dégriser; (*fig.*) rendre raisonnable, calmer; refroidir; désillusionner; *v.n.* se désenivrer, se dégriser, &c. *To get* or *grow* —, se désenivrer, se dégriser; ne plus s'enivrer. *To sleep oneself* —, se désenivrer *or* se dégriser en dormant, cuver son vin. *To appeal from Philip drunk to Philip* —, en appeler de Philippe ivre à Philippe à jeun. — **minded,** *adj.* raisonnable, calme; sage; sérieux. — **mindedness,** *s.* modération, *f.*; sagesse, *f.*

Soberly, *adv.* sobrement; modérément; sensément, raisonnablement; de sang-froid, froidement, avec calme; gravement, sérieusement

Soberness, Sobriety, *s.* sobriété, tempérance, *f.*; modération, *f.*; bon sens, *m.*, raison, *f.*; sang-froid, calme, *m.*; gravité, *f.*, sérieux, *m.*; réserve, *f.*

Sobriquet, *s.* sobriquet, *m.*

Sociability, Sociableness, *s.* sociabilité, *f.*

Sociable, *adj.* sociable; — *s.* (*carriage*) sociable, *m.*

Sociably, *adv.* sociablement, d'une manière sociable

Social, *adj.* social; sociable

Social-ism, -ist. *V.* page 3, § 1

Socialistic, *adj.* socialiste

Sociality, Socialness, *s.* socialité, *f.*; sociabilité, *f.* [socialiser

Socialize, *v.a.* socialiser. *To become* —*d*, se

Socially, *adv.* socialement; (*sociably*) *V.* **Sociably**

Society, *s.* société, *f.*; (*people generally*) monde, *m.* *London* —, le monde de Londres. *To go into* —, aller dans le monde

Socinian, *s. adj.* socinien, *m.*, -ne, *f.*

Socinianism, *s.* socinianisme, *m.*

Sociolog-ic, al, -y. *V.* page 3, § 1

Sock, *s.* (*half-hose*) chaussette, *f.*; (*inner sole*) semelle, *f.*; (*of ancient actors*) socque, *m.*; (*fig.*) comédie, *f.* —**less,** *adj.* sans chaussettes

Socket, *s.* emboîture, *f.*; (*of bayonets and tools*) douille, *f.*; (*of furniture*, &c.) sabot, *m.*; (*for candles*) bobèche, *f.*; (*of lamps*) bec, *m.*; (*hollow*) cavité, *f.*; (*of eyes*) orbite, *f.m.*; (*of teeth*) alvéole, *f.* *Reducing* —, (*gas pipe*) manchon à réduction, *m.*

Socle, *s.* socle, *m.*

Socotrine, *adj.* socotrin, succotrin

Socratic, -al, *adj.* socratique

Sod, *s.* gazon, *m.*; motte de gazon, *f.*; — *v.a.* gazonner. — **burning,** *s.* écobuage, *m.* — **cutter,** *s.* *V.* **Turf-knife**

Soda, *s.* soude, *f.* — **factory, -works,** *s.* soudière, *f.* — **water,** *s.* eau de Seltz (artificielle), *f.*

Sodden, *v.a.* imprégner d'eau, imprégner, tremper, alourdir; — *part. adj.* imprégné d'eau, imprégné, trempé, alourdi; lourd; pâteux, mollasse, mat; (*of bread*) gras-cuit; (*part of 'To Seethe'*) bouilli

Sodding, *s.* gazonnement, *m.*

Soddy, *adj.* gazonneux, couvert de gazon

Sodic, *adj.* sodique

Sodium, *s.* sodium, *m.*

Sodomite, *s.* sodomite, *m.*

Sodomitical, *adj.* sodomitique

Sodomy, *s.* sodomie, *f.* [**However**

Soever, *conj.* ... que ce soit. *How* ... — *V.*

Sofa, *s.* canapé, *m.*; sofa, *m.* — **bedstead,** *s.* lit-canapé, canapé-lit, *m.*

Soffit, *s.* soffite, *m.*

Sofi, *s.* sofi, sophi, *m.*

Soft, *adj.* (*yielding, not hard in substance*) mou, (*before a vowel or* h *mute*) mol; tendre; (*of eggs*) mollet, à la coque; (*of bread, beds*, &c.) mollet; (*not rough, and fig. not hard or harsh or strong, gentle, sweet*) doux; tendre; délicat;

efféminé; faible; facile; coulant; calme; (*stone, wood*) tendre; (*iron*) doux; (*sex*) aimable; (*silly*) simple, sot; (*gram.*) doux. — **grass,** *s.* (*bot.*) houque, *f.* — **sawder,** *s.* eau bénite de cour, râpe douce, blague, *f.*; monnaie de singe, *f.*; *v.a.* payer en monnaie de singe; blaguer; flagorner. — **soap,** *s.* savon à dégraisser, savon noir, savon vert, *m.*; (*fig.*) *V.* — **sawder.** — **solder,** *s.* soudure tendre, *f.* — **spoken,** *adj. V.* **Smooth-spoken**

Soften, *v.a.* amollir, ramollir; (*make less harsh or glaring*) adoucir; (*appease*) apaiser, radoucir, fléchir; (*move*) attendrir; (*weaken*) affaiblir, amollir; (*gram.*) radoucir; (*paint.*) adoucir, fondre; (*iron*) adoucir; (*steel*) détremper; — *v.n.* s'amollir, se ramollir; s'adoucir; s'apaiser, se calmer, se radoucir, s'affaiblir; (*of the heart*) s'attendrir; se fondre

Softener, *s.* personne *or* chose qui amollit *or* qui adoucit, *f.*; (*brush in paint.*) blaireau, *m.*

Softening, *s.* amollissement, *m.*; (*to the touch, of colours,* &c.) adoucissement, *m.*; (*weakening*) affaiblissement, *m.*; (*of feeling*) attendrissement, *m.*; (*med.*) ramollissement, *m.*

Softish, *adj.* un peu mou, mollet; un peu doux, doucereux; (*silly*) un peu simple

Softly, *adv.* mollement; (*without noise, gently*) doucement; délicatement; tendrement

Softness, *s.* mollesse, *f.*; (*to the touch, gentleness*) douceur, *f.*; délicatesse, *f.*; (*of feeling*) tendresse, *f.*

So-ho, Soho, *int.* holà! ho! tout beau!

Soil, *v.a.* tacher; salir; souiller; profaner; (*agr.*) fumer, engraisser; — *s.* (*earth*) sol, *m.*, terre, *f.*; terrain, *m.*; terroir, *m.*; (*geol.*) terrain, *m.*; (*manure*) fumier, engrais, *m.*; (*stain*) tache, *f.*; souillure, *f.*; (*hunt.*) souille, *f.*

Sojourn, *v.n.* séjourner; — *s.* séjour, *m.*

Sojourner, *s.* étranger de passage, *m.*

Sojourning, Sojournment, *s.* séjournement, séjour, *m.*

Sol, *s.* (*mus.*) sol, *m.*; (*the sun*) soleil, *m.*

Solace, *v.a.* consoler ('*with,*' de; par); (*to calm*) soulager, adoucir; (*cheer*) égayer, réjouir; — *s.* consolation, *f.*; (*relief*) soulagement, adoucissement, *m.*

Solacement, *s. V.* **Solace** [solandre, *f.*

Solanders, *s.pl.*, (*vet.*), **Solandra,** *s.* (*bot.*)

Solar, *adj.* solaire; du soleil. — *plexus,* plexus solaire, *m.*

Solarization, *s.* solarisation, *f.*

Solarize, *v.a.* solariser

Sold, *part. V.* **Sell**

Solder, *v.a.* souder; (*fig.*) souder, unir, joindre; — *s.* soudure, *f.*

Solderer, *s.* soudeur, *m.*, -euse, *f.*

Soldering, *s.* soudure, *f.*; (*action*) soudage, *m.* — **iron,** *s.* soudoir, fer à souder, *m.*

Soldier, *s.* soldat, *m.*; militaire, *m.* *A great* —, un grand capitaine, *m.* *To play at* —*s,* jouer aux soldats. — **beetle,** *s.* téléphore, *m.* —**like,** —**ly,** *adj.* de soldat; militaire; martial. —**ship,** *s.* état *or* service militaire, *m.*; qualités militaires, *f.pl.*; talents militaires, *m.pl.*; bravoure, *f.*, courage, *m.* —**y,** *s.* soldats, militaires, *m.pl.*; troupes, *f.pl.*, troupe, *f.*; (*in contempt*) soldatesque, *f.*

Sole, *s.* (*of the foot*) plante, *f.*; (*of shoes*) semelle, *f.*; (*fish*) sole, *f.*; (*of horses,* &c.) sole, *f.*; (*tech.*) châssis, *m.*; — *v.a.* ressemeler; — *adj.* seul, unique; (*of legatees*) universel

Solecism, *s.* solécisme, *m.*

Solecize, *v.n.* soléciser

Soled, *adj.* à semelles . . .

Solely, *adv.* seulement, uniquement

Solemn, *adj.* solennel; grave, sérieux

Solemnity, *s.* solennité, *f.*; gravité, *f.*; air *or* ton solennel, *m.* [bration, *f.*

Solemnization, *s.* solennisation, *f.*; célé-

Solemnize, *v.a.* solenniser; célébrer

Solemnly, *adv.* solennellement; gravement

Solen, *s.* solen, *m.*

Solfa, *v.a.n.* solfier; —*s.* gamme, *f.*

Solfaing, *s.* solfiation, *f.*

Solfatara, *s.* solfatare, soufrière, *f.*

Solfeggio, *s.* solfége, *m.*

Solicit, *v.a.* solliciter; inviter

Solicitation, *s.* sollicitation, *f.*; instance, *f.*; (*law*) excitation, *f.*

Solicitor, *s.* solliciteur, *m.*; (*lawyer*) avoué, notaire, *m.*; (*as a pleader, in county-courts,* &c.) avocat, *m.*; (*to a public establishment, company,* &c., *admin.*) chef du contentieux, *m.* — **general,** *s.* avocat général, *m*

Solicitous, *adj. V.* **Anxious**

Solicitress, *s.* solliciteuse, *f.*

Solicitude, *s.* sollicitude, *f.*

Solid, *adj.* solide; (*not hollow*) massif; plein; (*measure*) de capacité; (*pers.*) solide, sérieux, posé; — *s.* solide, *m.*; (*tech.*) plein, *m.* — *rock,* roc vif, *m.* *Of* — *mahogany,* en acajou massif

Solidarily, *adv.* solidairement

Solidarity, *s.* solidarité, *f.*

Solidary, *adj.* solidaire

Solidification, *s.* solidification, *f.*

Solidify, *v.a.* solidifier; — *v.n.* se solidifier

Solid-ism, -ist, -ity, -ness. *V.* page 3, § 1

Solidly, *adv.* solidement [monologue

Soliloquize, *v.n.* faire un soliloque *or* un

Soliloquy, *s.* soliloque, monologue, *m.*

Soling, *s.* ressemelage, *m.* [*adj.m.f.*, *s.m.*

Soliped, *adj. s.*, **Solipedous,** *adj.* solipède,

Solist, Soloist, *s.* (*mus.*) soliste, *m.f.*

Solitaire, *s.* solitaire, *m.*

Solitarily, *adv.* solitairement [isolement, *m.*

Solitariness, *s.* solitude, *f.*; retraite, *f.*;

Solitary, *adj.* solitaire; retiré; isolé; désert; (*single*) seul; unique; (*of confinement*) cellulaire; — *s.* solitaire, *m.f.* — *flower,* solitaire, *f.*

Solitude, *s.* solitude, *f.*

Solmization, *s.* solmisation, *f.*

Solo, *s.* solo, *m.*

Soloist. *V.* **Solist**

Solstice, *s.* solstice, *m.*

Solstitial, *adj.* solsticial

Solubility, *s.* solubilité, *f.*

Soluble, *adj.* soluble

Solution, *s.* solution, *f.* [tif, *s.m.*

Solutive, *adj. s.* solutif, *adj.m.*, -ive, *f.*, solu-

Solvability, Solvableness, *s.* solubilité, *f.*; (*solvency*) solvabilité, *f.*

Solvable, *adj.* soluble, résoluble; (*that can be*

Solve, *v.a.* résoudre [*paid*) qui peut être payé

Solvency, *s.* solvabilité, *f.*

Solvent, *adj.* dissolvant; (*able to pay*) solvable; (*sufficient to pay*) suffisant pour payer; — *s.* dissolvant, *m.*

Somat-ic, -ology, &c. *V.* page 3 § 1

Sombre, *adj.* sombre

Some, *adj. art. adv.* (*some or other, a small amount of, a short . . ., a few*) quelque; quelques, *pl.*; (*an indefinite quantity or number*) du, *m.*, de la, *f.*, des, *pl.*; (*certain*) certain; (*of it, of them*) en; (*about*) environ, à peu près, quelque; — *pron.* quelques-uns, *m.pl.*, quelques-unes, *f.pl.*, les uns, *m.pl.*, les unes, *f.pl.*; (*a little*) un peu de, une partie. — *books,* des livres; certains livres; (*a few*) quelques livres. — *of my books,* quelques-uns de mes livres. — *of them,* quelques-uns d'entre eux. — *bread,* du pain. — *water,* de l'eau. *I have* —, j'en ai. — *ten years ago,* il y a environ dix ans, il y a quelque dix ans, il y a une dizaine d'années. — *people say,* certaines gens disent, il y a des gens qui disent. — *persons who were there say,* des personnes qui y étaient disent. — *say,* quelques-uns disent. — *say yes, others say no,* les uns disent oui, les autres disent non. *I have* — *of them,* j'en ai une partie, j'en ai quelques-uns. — *of his property,* une partie de son bien. — **one,** *See below*

Somebody, *s.* quelqu'un, *m.*; on; (*person of consideration*) quelque chose, quelqu'un, un personnage, *m.* — *or other,* quelqu'un. *He*

thinks he is —, il se croit quelque chose (*or* quelqu'un *or* un personnage)
Somehow, *adv.* (— *or other*) d'une manière ou d'une autre, de manière ou d'autre, de façon ou d'autre; tant bien que mal; (*I can't tell how*) je ne sais comment
Someone. *V.* **Somebody**
Somersault, Somerset, *s.* culbute, *f.*; (le) saut périlleux, *m.* *To turn a* —, faire une culbute; faire le saut périlleux
Something, *s.* quelque chose, *m.*; (*before an adj. or part. or certain adverbs*) quelque chose de ..., *m.*; (*part*) une partie (de), *f.*; (*adverb.*) quelque peu, un peu, tant soit peu. *A* —, je ne sais quoi. — *good*, — *broken*, — *more*, quelque chose de bon, quelque chose de cassé, quelque chose de plus. — *or other*, je ne sais quoi. *To be — between ... and*, tenir le milieu entre ... et. *There is — in that*, cela mérite considération; c'est une idée; c'est une raison; c'est assez juste; ça n'est pas bête, ça! *There is — to laugh at, to boast of*, &c., il y a de quoi rire, se vanter, &c. *He is — of a judge*, il est quelque peu connaisseur
Sometime, *adv.* un jour. — *ago*, il y a quelque temps. — *or other*, quelque jour
Sometimes, *adv.* quelquefois; parfois; (*when repeated*) tantôt. — *one and — another*, tantôt l'un, tantôt l'autre
Somewhat, *s.* quelque chose, *m.*; (*adverb.*) quelque peu, un peu, tant soit peu, assez
Somewhere, *adv.* quelque part. — *else*, *V.* **Else** [(*things*) somnambulique
Somnambulic, *adj.* (*pers.*) somnambule;
Somnambulism, *s.* somnambulisme, *m.*
Somnambulist, *s.* somnambule, *m.f.*
Somnambulistic, *adj.* *V.* **Somnambulic**
Somniferous, *adj.* somnifère
Somniloquist, *s.*, **Somniloquous,** *adj.* somniloque, *m.f.*
Somniloquy, *s.* somniloquie, *f.*
Somnolenc-e, y, *s.* somnolence, *f.*; assoupissement, *m.* [au sommeil
Somnolent, *adj.* somnolent; assoupi, enclin
Son, *s.* fils, *m.*; (*boy*) garçon, *m.*; (*child, native*) enfant, *m.*; (*fig.*) descendant, *m.* —**-in-law,** *s.* gendre, *m.* —**less,** *adj.* sans fils. —**ship,** *s.* filiation, *f.*; qualité de fils, *f.*
Sonant, *adj.* sonnant; sonore
Sonata, *s.* sonate, *f.*
Sonatina, *s.* sonatine, *f.*
Song, *s.* chanson, *f.*; (*of birds*, &c.) chant, *m.*; (*mus.*) romance, *f.*; (*poetry*) poème, *m.*, poésie, *f.*; (*sacred*) cantique, chant, *m.*; (*nav.*) voix, *f.* — *of Solomon*, Cantique des Cantiques, *m.* *For an old* —, *for a* —, *for a mere* —, (*for a trifle*) pour rien, pour un morceau de pain. *No* —, *no supper*, nul bien sans peine. —**bird,** *s.* oiseau chanteur, *m.* — **book,** *s.* chansonnier, *m.* —**less,** *adj.* sans voix, muet. — **thrush,** *s.* *V.* **Mavis.** — **writer,** *s.* chansonnier, *m.*, [-ière, *f.*
Songster, *s.* chantre, *m.*
Songstress, *s.* chanteuse, *f.*; (*of birds*) chantre, *m.*
Soniferous, *adj.* sonnant; sonore; résonnant
Soniped, *adj. s.*, **Sonipedous,** *adj.* sonipède, *adj.m.f.*, *s.m.* [sonnets, *m.*
Sonnet, *s.* sonnet, *m.* — **writer,** *s.* auteur de
Sonneteer, *s.* auteur de sonnets, *m.*; (*in contempt*) poétereau, poétriau, *m.*
Sonometer, *s.* sonomètre, *m.* [page 3, § 1)
Sonometr-ic, al, -y, sonométrique, &c. (*V*
Sonority. *V.* **Sonorousness**
Sonorous, *adj.* sonore [sonore
Sonorously, *adv.* sonorement, d'une manière
Sonorousness, *s.* sonorité, nature sonore, *f.*; son éclatant, *m.*
Soon, *adv.* bientôt; tôt; prochainement; (*early*) de bonne heure, tôt; (*willingly*) volontiers, aisément. — *after*, bientôt après. *As — as*, aussitôt que, dès que; (*as much as*) autant que. *How* —? quand? *So* —, si tôt ('*as*,' que); (*as soon*) aussitôt ('*as*,' que). *Too* —, trop tôt. *Too — by an hour*, trop tôt d'une heure. *Very* —, bientôt, très prochainement, dans (*or* en) très peu de temps; de très bonne heure. *I had* (or *would*) *just as — go there as stay here*, j'aimerais (*or* j'aime) autant (*or* tout autant) y aller que de rester ici
Sooner, *adv.* (*earlier*) plus tôt; (*rather*) plutôt. — *or later*, tôt ou tard. *No* —, (... ne ...) pas plus tôt, à peine (...). *I had* or *would* —, *V.* **Rather.** *No — had he spoken* (*than* ...), il n'eut pas plus tôt parlé (que ...), à peine eut-il parlé (que ...), il avait à peine parlé (que ...). *No — said than done*, aussitôt dit, aussitôt fait
Soonest, *adv.* le plus tôt. *At* —, au plus tôt
Soot, *s.* suie, *f.*; — *v.a.* couvrir de suie. — **bag,** *s.* sac à suie, *m.* — **wart,** *s.* cancer des ramoneurs, *m.*
Sooth, *s.* vérité, *f.*; présage, *m.* *In* —, en vérité
Soothe, *v.a.* adoucir, calmer, apaiser; flatter, caresser; charmer, plaire à, satisfaire
Soother, *s.* personne qui apaise *or* calme *or* adoucit, *f.*; chose qui apaise *or* calme *or* adoucit, *f.*, calmant, adoucissant, *m.*; flatteur, *m.*, -euse, *f.* [tendre; consolant
Soothing, *adj.* adoucissant, calmant; doux;
Soothingly, *adv.* doucement; d'un ton consolant
Soothsay, *v.n.* prophétiser, prédire l'avenir
Soothsayer, *s.* devin, *m.*, devineresse, *f.*
Soothsaying, *s.* divination, *f.*; prédiction, *f.*
Sootiness, *s.* fuliginosité, *f.*
Sooty, *adj.* de suie; plein *or* couvert de suie; fuligineux; noir. — *tern*, *V.* **Egg-bird**
Sop, *s.* morceau trempé, *m.*; boulette, gobe, *f.*; (*fig.*) os à ronger, *m.*; —**s,** *pl.* (*bread and milk*) panade au lait, *f.*; — *v.a.* tremper, saucer
Sophi, *s.* sophi, sofi, *m.*
Sophism, *s.* sophisme, *m.*
Sophist, Sophister, *s.* sophiste, *m.*
Sophistic, -al, *adj.* (*things*) sophistique; (*pers.*) sophiste
Sophistically, *adv.* sophistiquement
Sophisticate, *v.a.* sophistiquer, falsifier, frelater, travailler [tion, *f.*, frelatage, *m.*
Sophistication, *s.* sophistication, falsifica-
Sophisticator, *s.* sophistiqueur, falsificateur, frelateur, *m.*
Sophistry, *s.* sophisterie, sophistiquerie, *f.*; sophismes, *m.pl.*; (*art*) sophistique, *f.*
Soporative, *adj. s.* soporatif, *adj.m.*, -ive, *f.*,
Soporiferous, *adj.* soporifère [soporatif, *s.m.*
Soporiferousness, *s.* nature soporifère, *f.*
Soporific, *adj. s.* soporifique, *adj.m.f.*, *s.m.*
Soporous, *adj.* soporeux
Soppy, *adj.* trempé
Sopranist, *s.* sopraniste, soprano, *m.f.*
Soprano, *s.* soprano, (*voice*) *m.*, (*pers.*) *m.f.*
Sorb, *s.* sorbe, corme, *f.*; (*tree*) *V.* **Service-tree.** — **apple,** *s.* sorbe, corme, *f.*
Sorbon-ical, -ist. *V.* page 3, § 1
Sorcerer, *s.* sorcier, magicien, *m.*
Sorceress, *s.* sorcière, magicienne, *f.* [lége, *m.*
Sorcery, *s.* sorcellerie, *f.*; magie, *f.*; sorti-
Sordes, *s.pl.* (*med.*) saburre, *f.*
Sordet, *s.* (*mus.*) sourdine, *f.*
Sordid, *adj.* sordide; avare; misérable; vil, bas, méprisable; (*dirty*) sale
Sordidly, *adv.* sordidement
Sordidness, *s.* sordidité, *f.*; avarice, *f.*; bassesse, *f*; (*dirtiness*) saleté, *f.*
Sordine, *s.* sourdine, *f.*
Sore, *s.* plaie, *f.*; ulcère, *m.*; mal, *m.*; (*fig.*) mal, *m.*, douleur, *f.*; — *adj.* (*tender*) douloureux, sensible; endolori; (*affected with inflammation*) malade; (*touchy*) susceptible, sensible; (*vexed*) fâché, affligé, tourmenté, vexé; (*afflictive*) douloureux; triste; (*severe*) cruel, rude, violent, grand; (*adverb.*) *V.* **Sorely.** — *throat*, mal de gorge, *m.* *To have a — throat*, avoir mal à la gorge; (*with an adjective*) avoir un mal de gorge. — *ears*, mal aux oreilles. — *eyes*, mal

aux yeux. — *fingers*, mal aux doigts. *A — finger, a — leg*, mal au doigt, mal à la jambe

Sorely, *adv.* douloureusement; (*fig.*) sévèrement; grièvement, gravement; cruellement; vivement, fortement; violemment; rudement; grandement [*m.*; sensation pénible, *f.*

Soreness, *s.* sensibilité, *f.*; douleur, *f.*; mal,

Sorgho, — grass, *s.* sorgho, *m.*

Sorites, *s.* sorite, *m.*

Sororicidal, *adj.* sororicide [*der*), *m.*

Sororicide, *s.* sororicide, (*pers.*) *m.f.*, (*mur-*

Sorrel, *adj.* alezan saure; — *s.* (*bot.*) oseille, *f.*; (*colour*) couleur alezan saure, *f.* *Salt of* —, sel d'oseille, *m.*

Sorrily, *adv.* tristement, chétivement, pauvrement, misérablement, pitoyablement

Sorriness, *s.* triste état, *m.*; nature chétive, *f.*; mesquinerie, *f.*

Sorrow, *s.* chagrin, *m.*, affliction, *f.*; douleur, peine, *f.*; tristesse, *f.*; déplaisir, *m.*; déboire, *m.*; — *v.n.* s'affliger, être affligé, s'attrister. *To o.'s* —, à son grand chagrin. —**ful,** *adj.* (*pers.*) chagrin, affligé; (*sad*) triste, mélancolique; (*things*) affligeant; triste. —**fully,** *adv.* avec chagrin, avec affliction, avec douleur, tristement. —**fulness,** *s.* *V.* **Sorrow.** —**ing,** *s.* chagrin, *m.*, affliction, *f.*; *adj.* affligé, chagrin. —**less,** *adj.* sans chagrin

Sorry, *adj.* fâché ('*for' a thing*, de, '*for' a person*, pour; '*to*,' de; '*that*,' que), contrarié, affligé, peiné (de); (*sad*) triste, mélancolique; (*bad, poor*) triste, pauvre, pitoyable, méchant, mauvais; maigre. *A — jester*, un mauvais plaisant, *m.* *A — poet*, un méchant poète, *m.* *A — meal*, un maigre repas, *m.* *To be very* or *extremely* —, être très fâché *or* très contrarié (de, que), être désolé (de, que). *I am —, extremely — for it*, j'en suis fâché, désolé. *I am — to say*, je regrette d'avoir à dire ('*that*' ..., que ...); à mon grand regret, malheureusement

Sort, *s.* sorte, *f.*, genre, *m.*, espèce, *f.*; nature, *f.*; manière, façon, *f.*; condition, classe, *f.*; —**s,** *pl.* (*print.*) assortiment, *m.* *A decent — of*, un très bon (*m.*), une très bonne (*f.*) *Queer* or *strange — of*, drôle de ..., ... bizarre, ... étrange. ... singulier. *Right* —, bonne sorte. *I did say something of the* —, j'ai dit quelque chose comme cela. *Nothing of the* —, rien de semblable; rien de tout cela; il n'en est rien. *I shall do nothing of the* —, je n'en ferai rien. *To be out of —s*, n'être pas dans son assiette, être détraqué, être mal en train; (*out of temper*) être de mauvaise humeur. *To put out of —s*, détraquer; mettre de mauvaise humeur

Sort, *v.a.* classer; (*separate*) séparer; trier; (*match*) assortir; (*conjoin*) réunir; (*letters, rags*, &c.) trier

Sorter, *s.* trieur, *m.*, -euse, *f.*

Sortie, *s.* sortie, *f.*

Sorting, *s.* (*separating, choosing*) triage, *m.*; (*matching*) assortiment, *m.*

Sot, *s.* sot, *m.*, -te, *f.*, imbécile, *m.f.*; (*drunkard*) ivrogne, *m.*, ivrognesse, *f.*; — *v.a.* *V.* **Besot.** *A drunken* —, un ivrogne, *m.*, une ivrognesse, *f.*

Sottish, *adj.* sot, imbécile; abruti par l'ivrognerie, abruti

Sottishly, *adv.* sottement; en ivrogne

Sottishness, *s.* sottise, bêtise, *f.*; (*from drunkenness*) abrutissement, *m.*

Sou, *s.* sou, *m.*

Souchong, *s. adj.* souchong, *m.*

Soufflé, *adj. s.* soufflé, *adj. m.*, e, *f.*, soufflé, *s.m.*

Sought, *part. adj* cherché, &c. (*V.* **Seek**); recherché. — **after,** recherché

Soul, *s.* âme, *f.*; (*a person*) créature, *f.*, être, *m.*; (*man*) homme, *m.*; (*woman*) femme, *f.*; (*life*) vie, *f.* *Good* —, bonne âme, &c. *Poor* —, pauvre créature, pauvre homme, pauvre femme. *A town of five thousand —s*, une ville de cinq mille âmes. *The life and — of*, (*a company*, &c.) l'âme de; (*exhilarating companion*) le boute-en-train de. *There was not a* —, il n'y avait pas une âme (*fam.*, pas un chat). *With all my* —, de toute mon âme. — **felt,** *adj.* intime. —**less,** *adj.* sans âme. — **sick,** *adj.* malade au moral. — **stirring,** *adj.* qui émeut *or* remue l'âme

Souled, *adj.* qui a l'âme ..., à l'âme ...

Sound, *adj.* sain; en bon état; pur, vrai; légitime; valide; (*of mind*) sain; (*good, strong, of blows, scolding*, &c.) bon, fort, vigoureux; solide; (*of sleep*) profond; (*of health*) bon, parfait; (*well founded*) bien fondé; — *adv.* *V.* **Soundly.** — *doctrines*, doctrines saines. — *principles*, bons principes. *To be of a — mind*, être sain d'esprit; avoir sa raison. *To give a — flogging* or *whipping*, fouetter (*or* donner le fouet) d'importance

Sound, *s.* son, *m.*; (*noise*) bruit, *m.*; (*strait*) détroit, *m.*, (*proper name*) Sund, *m.*; (*surg. instr.*) sonde, *f.*; (*of fish*) vessie natatoire, *f.*; (*cook.*) noue, *f.*, noves, *f pl.* *For the sake of* —, par euphonie. — **board,** — **post,** *V.* **Sounding.** — **bow,** *s.* (*of a bell*) panse, pause, faussure, *f.* — **hole,** *s.* (*of violins*, &c.) esse, *f.* —**less,** *adj.* sans son, sans bruit; (*fathomless*) insondable

Sound, *v.a.n.* (*of instruments, metals, the retreat*, &c.) sonner; (*letters*) faire sonner, prononcer; (*v.n.*) sonner; (*be pronounced*) se prononcer; (*resound*) faire sonner, faire résonner, faire retentir; faire entendre; (*v.n.*) résonner, retentir ('*with*,' de); (*be heard*) se faire entendre; (— *like*) avoir le son (de); (*fig.*) avoir l'air (de); ressembler (à); paraître, faire un effet (...); (*proclaim*) publier, proclamer; faire retentir; (*try, fathom, probe*) sonder. *To — a trumpet*, sonner de la trompette. *To — to horse*, sonner le boute-selle. *To — well*, sonner bien; sembler bon; faire bon effet, faire bien

Soundable, *adj.* sondable

Sounding, *adj.* sonore, retentissant; ronflant; (*in compounds*) à son ...; — *s.* action de sonner, *f.*; sonnerie, *f.*; (*noise*) résonnement, retentissement, *m.*; (*trying*) sondage, *m.*; —**s,** *pl.* (*nav.*) sondes, *f.pl.* *To strike —s*, avoir fond. *To take s*, sonder. — **board,** *s.* table d'harmonie, *f.*; (*of organs*) sommier, *m.*; (*of pulpits*, &c.) abat-voix, *m.* — **lead,** *s.* sonde, *f.*, plomb de sonde, *m.* — **line,** *s.* sonde, ligne de sonde, *f.* — **machine,** *s.* appareil de sondage, *m.* — **post,** *s.* âme, *f.*

Soundly, *adv.* sainement; solidement; vigoureusement, fort et ferme; (*of sleep*) profondément, d'un profond sommeil; (*well*) bien, comme il faut, d'importance

Soundness, *s.* sanité, *f.*, état sain, bon état, *m.*; (*health*) santé, *f.*; (*strength*) vigueur, force, *f.*; (*firmness*) solidité, *f.*; (*rectitude*) rectitude, justesse, droiture, *f.*; vérité, *f.*; pureté, *f.*

Soup, *s.* potage, *m.*, soupe, *f.*; (*broth*) bouillon, *m.*; (*mash*) purée, *f.* — **kitchen,** *s.* (*for the poor*) fourneau économique, *m.* — **ladle,** *s.* cuiller à potage *or* à soupe, louche, poche, *f.* — **plate,** *s.* assiette à potage *or* à soupe, assiette creuse, *f.* — **ticket,** *s.* bon de soupe, *m.* — **tureen,** *s.* soupière, *f.*

Sour, *adj.* aigre, sur, acide; tourné; (*unripe*) vert; (*fig.*) aigre; âpre; morose; — *v.a.* aigrir; surir; (*to trouble*) détruire, gâter; (*chem.*) acidifier; — *v.n.* s'aigrir, aigrir; surir; (*turn into*) dégénérer (en). *To make* —, aigrir, surir. *To turn* —, s'aigrir, aigrir; surir. *The grapes are* —, (*Proverb.*) ils sont trop verts. — **crout,** — **krout,** *s.* *See below.* — **sop,** *s.* (*fruit*) corossol, *m.*; (*tree*) corossolier, *m.*

Source, *s.* source, *f.*

Sourdine, *s.* sourdine, *f.*

Souring, *s.* aigrissement, *m.*

Sourish, *adj.* aigrelet, suret; âpre

Sourkrout, Sourcrout, *s.* choucroute, *f.*

Sourly, *adv.* avec aigreur; aigrement

Sourness, *s.* aigreur, *f.*; acidité, *f.*

Souse, *s.* marinade, *f.*; — *v.a.* mariner, saumurer; (*plunge*) plonger; (*wet*) tremper, mouiller, saucer; — *adv.* tout à coup. *To go — into,* tomber la tête la première dans

Souslik, *s.* souslic, souslik, *m.*

South, *s.* sud, *m.*; midi, *m.*; — *adj.* du sud, de sud, sud; vers le sud; du midi, méridional; austral; (*of the pole*) sud; — *adv.* au sud; au midi. *Sea Company,* Compagnie de la Mer du Sud, *f.* — **down** (*sheep* or *mutton*), *s.* présalé, *m.* — **eastern,** *adj.* du sud-est. — **German,** *adj.* de l'Allemagne du sud. — **ward, -s,** *adj. adv.* vers le sud. — **western,** *adj.* du sud-ouest

Southerly, *adj.* du (*or* de) sud, sud; méridional, du midi; — *adv.* vers le sud, au sud

Southern, *adj.* *V.* **South,** *adj.* —**most,** *adj.* (le) plus au sud, à l'extrême sud. — **wood,** *s.* citronnelle, *f.*

Southerner, *s. adj.* méridional, *m.*, e, *f.*; (*American polit.*) sudiste, *m.f.*

Southing, *adj.* qui se dirige vers le sud *or* le midi; — *s.* (*astr.*) passage au méridien, *m.*; (*nav.*) route au sud, *f.*

Souvenir, *s.* souvenir, *m.*

Sovereign, *s. adj.* souverain, *m.*, e, *f.*; (*Engl. coin*) souverain, *m.*, (*equivalent in Fr. money*) 25 francs. *Half-a-* —, (*Engl.*) demi-souverain, *m.*, (*Fr.*) 12 francs 50 centimes

Sovereignly, *adv.* souverainement

Sovereignty, *s.* souveraineté, *f.*

Sow, *s.* truie, *f.*; (*iron*) gueuse, *f.*; (*lead*) saumon *m.* *Wild* —, laie, *f.* — **bread,** *s.* (*bot.*) cyclame, cyclamen, pain de pourceau, *m.* — **thistle,** *s.* (*bot.*) laiteron, *m.*

Sow, *v.a.n.* semer; (*a land*) semer, ensemencer; (*spread*) semer, parsemer; répandre; (*discord,* &c.) semer (*V.* **Whirlwind**)

Sower, *s.* semeur, *m.*, -euse, *f.*

Sowing, *s.* semaille, *f.*, semis, ensemencement, *m.*; (*fig.*) propagation, *f.* — **machine,** *s.* semoir, *m.* — **seed,** *s.* semailles, *f.pl.* — **time,** *s.* semaison, *f.*, semailles, *f.pl.*

Soy, *s.* soui, soy, *m.*

Spa, *s.* (*geog.*) Spa, *f.*; (*any spring*) source d'eau minérale, *f.* — **water,** *s.* eau de Spa, *f.*; eau minérale, *f.*

Space, *s.* espace, *m.*; étendue, *f.*; intervalle, *m.*; (*geom.*) surface, *f.*; (*mus.*) interligne, *m.*, espace, *m.*; (*print.*) espace, *f.*; — *v.a.* (— **out**) espacer. *Our limited* —, (*writing*) le peu d'espace dont nous disposons, notre cadre restreint. — **between,** *s.* entre-deux, *m.*; intervalle, *m.* — **line,** *s.* (*print.*) interligne, *f.*

Spacing, *s.* espacement, *m.*

Spacious, *adj.* spacieux; vaste

Spaciously, *adv.* spacieusement

Spaciousness, *s.* spaciosité, grandeur, grande étendue, vaste étendue, *f.*

Spade, *s.* (*for digging*) bêche, *f.*; (*shovel*) pelle, *f.*; (—**s,** *pl., at cards*) pique, *m.*; — *v.a.* bêcher. *To call a — a* —, appeler un chat un chat. — **ful,** *s.* bêchée, *f.*; pelletée, *f.* — **husbandry,** *s.* petite culture, *f.*

Spadiceous, *adj.* (*bot.*) spadicé

Spadille, *s.* spadille, *f.*

Spadix, *s.* spadice, *m.*

Spahee, Spahi, *s.* spahi, *m.*

Spalt, *s.* spalt, *m.*

Span, *s.* (*of the hand*) empan, *m.*; longueur de la main, main, *f.*; (*of wings*) envergure, *f.*; (*of horses, oxen*) paire, couple, *f.*; (*arch.*) ouverture, *f.*; (*duration*) durée, *f.*; (*moment*) moment, instant, *m.*; — *v.a.* mesurer par empan; mesurer, entourer, embrasser; (*cross*) traverser; (*nav.*) brider; — *v.n.* s'assortir. — **counter, -farthing, -feather,** *s.* fossette, *f.* — **long,** *adj.* de la longueur de la main. — **new,** *adj.* tout neuf, tout battant neuf, tout flambant neuf. — **worm,** *s.* arpenteuse, *f.*

Spandrel, *s.* (*of a vault*) naissance, *f.*; (*of a bridge*) tympan, *m.*

Spangle, *s.* paillette, *f.*; — *v.a.* ('*with,*' de) pailleter; (*fig.*) émailler; (*to star*) étoiler

Spaniard, *s.* Espagnol, *m.*, e, *f.*

Spaniel, *s.* épagneul, *m.*, e, *f.*

Spanish, *adj.* espagnol, d'Espagne; — *s.* (*language*) l'espagnol, *m.*, la langue espagnole, *f.* — **broom,** *s.* genêt d'Espagne, spartier, *m.* — **fly,** *s.* cantharide, *f.* — **forge,** *s.* forge catalane, *f.* — **grass,** *s.* sparte, spart, *m.* — **juice,** *s.* *V.* **Liquorice.** — **school,** *s.* (*paint.*) école espagnole, *f.* — **white,** *s.* blanc d'Espagne, *m.* — **wine,** *s.* vin d'Espagne, *m.* — **wool,** *s.* laine d'Espagne, *f.*

Spanker, *s.* gros gaillard, *m.*; (*nav.*) brigantine, *f.*

Spanking, *adj.* vigoureux, de première force; gros [*monkey* —, clé anglaise

Spanner, *s.* (*tech.*) clé, clef, *f.* *Shifting* or

Spar, *s.* espar, *m.*, pièce de bois, *f.*, mâtereau, *m.*; (*min.*) spath, *m.*; — *v.n.* se quereller; se battre, boxer; s'essayer au combat, s'escrimer. — **deck,** *s.* (*of merchantmen*) pont, *m.*; (*of frigates,* &c.) faux-pont, *m.* — **hawk,** *s.* *V.* **Sparrow-hawk**

Sparagus. *V.* **Asparagus**

Spare, *v.a.* épargner, ménager; économiser; (*do without*) se passer de; disposer de; (*forbear*) se dispenser de; (*yield, give*) céder; accorder; donner; laisser; (*remit*) remettre, faire grâce de; (*use tenderly*) épargner; (*not to impose, not to take away*) épargner (à), faire grâce de (à); (*a trouble*) épargner (à); (*save oneself trouble*) s'épargner, s'éviter; (*to preserve*) conserver; (*to find, as time,* &c.) trouver; (*to lose, as time*) perdre; — *v.n.* épargner, faire des économies; être économe. *To — oneself,* s'épargner; se ménager; (*dispense with*) se dispenser de. *Enough and to* —, plus qu'il n'en faut, de reste. *To have* (*some, any*) *to* —, en avoir de reste *or* de trop, en avoir à revendre. *Have you any money to — ?* avez-vous de l'argent de reste *or* de trop? *I have not* 5 *minutes to* —, je n'ai pas 5 minutes à moi *or* à perdre. *I can't — time,* je n'ai pas le temps. *To — his life,* lui épargner la vie, lui faire grâce de la vie. *If his life is —d a few years longer,* s'il lui est donné de vivre encore quelques années

Spare, *adj.* frugal, sobre; (*pers.*) économe; (*thin*) maigre; sec; (*not wanted*) de reste, de trop, de réserve; (*of time*) libre, de loisir; (*for replacing*) de rechange. — *hours,* heures libres, heures de loisir, *f.pl.* — *moments,* moments de loisir, moments perdus, *m.pl.* — *diet,* maigre chère, *f.* *Of — habit,* maigre et sec. — *money,* argent mignon, *m.* — *room or bed,* chambre (*f.*) *or* lit (*m.*) d'ami (*or* à donner). — *time,* loisir, *m.*; temps disponible, *m.*; un moment à moi (*or* à lui *or* &c.), *m.* — **rib,** *s.* côte de [porc, *f.*

Sparely, *V.* **Sparingly**

Spareness, *s.* maigreur, *f.*

Sparing, *adj.* frugal; sobre; économe, ménager; parcimonieux, chiche, avare; modéré; faible, léger; pauvre; peu abondant

Sparingly, *adv.* frugalement; sobrement; économiquement; chichement, maigrement, mesquinement; modérément; faiblement, légèrement, peu; (*seldom*) rarement, peu souvent

Sparingness, *s.* frugalité, *f.*; sobriété, *f.*; économie, *f.*; parcimonie, *f.*; modération, *f.*; peu, *m.*

Spark, *s.* étincelle, *f.*; bluette, *f.*; (*fig.*) étincelle, *f.*; éclair, *m.*; lueur, *f.*; (*fop*) petit-maître, mirliflore, élégant, gandin, *m.* *Wild* —, étourdi, écervelé, *m.* [gant pimpant

Sparkful, Sparkish, *adj.* vif, fringant; élé-

Sparkle, *s.* étincelle, *f.*; — *v.n.* étinceler; (*of wine,* &c.) mousser; pétiller

Sparkler, *s.* personne qui brille, *f.*; (*thing*) chose qui étincelle, *f.*; (*insect*) cicindèle, *f.*

Sparklet, *s.* étincelette, petite étincelle, *f.*

Sparkling, *adj.* étincelant; (*of wine,* &c.)

mousseux; — *s.* étincellement, *m.*; pétillement, *m.*; (*fig.*) éclat, *m.*

Sparklingly, *adv.* d'une manière étincelante; en pétillant; avec éclat

Sparklingness, *s. V.* **Sparkling,** *s.*

Sparling, *s. V.* **Smelt**

Sparring, *s.* querelle, dispute, *f.*; combat, *m.*, boxe, *f.*; prélude de combat, *m.*

Sparrow, *s.* moineau, passereau, *m.* —**grass,** *s. V.* **Asparagus.** —**hawk,** *s.* épervier, émouchet, *m.* — **wort,** *s.* passerine, *f.*

Sparry, *adj.* spathique

Sparse, *adj.* épars, éparpillé, clair-semé; peu nombreux, rare

Sparsely, *adv.* çà et là, de loin en loin, à de rares intervalles; en petit nombre, peu

Sparseness, *s.* petit nombre, peu, *m.*, rareté, *f.*

Spartan, *s. adj.* Spartiate, *m.f.*

Spasm, *s.* spasme, *m.*

Spasm-odic, al, -odically, -ology. *V.* page 3, § 1

Spat, *s.* (*blow*) tape, taloche, *f.*; (*of shell-fish*) frai, naissain, *m.*

Spathe, *s.* spathe, *f.*

Spathed, *adj.* spathé

Spathic, *adj.* spathique

Spatter. *V.* **Bespatter**

Spatterdashes, *s.pl.* jambières, *f.pl.*; (*formerly*) houseaux, *m.pl.*

Spatula, *s.* spatule, *f.*

Spatulate, *adj.* spatulé

Spavin, *s.* éparvin, *m.*

Spavined, *adj.* atteint d'éparvins

Spawl, *v.n.* cracher

Spawling, *s.* crachement, *m.*

Spawn, *s.* (*of fishes, frogs,* &c.) frai, *m.*; (*fig.*) fruit, produit, *m.*; (*pers.*) engeance, race, *f.*; — *v.n.* (*of fishes, frogs,* &c.) frayer; (*fig.*) provenir, naître; — *v.a.* (*of fishes, frogs,* &c.) engendrer; (*fig.*) produire, engendrer

Spawner, *s.* poisson femelle, *m.*

Spawning, *s.* frai, *m.* — **place,** *s.* frayère, *f.*, frayoir, *m.* — **season, -time,** *s.* fraieson, fraie, *f.*, temps du frai, *m.*

Spay, *v.a.* couper, châtrer

Speak, *v.n.a.* parler; (*say*) dire; (*pronounce*) prononcer; (*express*) exprimer; (*a ship*) héler. *To — of* (...) *as a* ..., qualifier (...) de ...; traiter (...) de ... *To — ill of,* dire du mal de, médire de. *To — well* or *highly of,* dire du bien de, parler avantageusement de. *To — well for,* faire honneur à, être à l'honneur de. *To — loud,* parler haut. *So to* —, pour ainsi dire. — **down,** parler contrer, dénigrer, décrier. — **out,** parler tout haut; parler distinctement; parler hardiment *or* librement; se prononcer; s'expliquer; parler ouvertement *or* franchement, dire le fond de sa pensée, dire tout haut sa pensée. — **up,** parler haut; parler en faveur de, louer. — **up for,** parler hautement pour

Speakable, *adj.* exprimable; que l'on peut dire

Speaker, *s.* orateur, *m.*; (*talker*) parleur, *m.*, -euse, *f.*; (*teller*) diseur, *m.*, -euse, *f.*; (*in a dialogue*) interlocuteur, *m.*, -trice, *f.*; (*in parliam.*) président, *m.* *The last* —, l'honorable préopinant, *m.*

Speakership, *s.* présidence, *f.*

Speaking, *s.* parole, *f.*, discours, *m.*; parler, langage, *m.* — **pipe,** *s.* tuyau *or* cordon acoustique, porte-voix, *m.* — **trumpet,** *s.* porte-voix, *m.*; cornet acoustique, *m.* — **tube,** *s. V.* — **pipe**

Spear, *s.* lance, *f.*; (*for fishing*) harpon, *m.*; (*for eels*) trident, *m.*; (*gig*) foëne, *f.*; (*for hunting*) épieu, *m.*; (*of a pump*) tige, *f.*; (*of plants*) *V.* **Spire;** — *v.a.* percer d'un coup de lance *or* d'un coup d'épieu; harponner; (*with a gig*) prendre à la foëne; — *v.n. V.* **Spire.** — **foot,** *s.* pied droit de derrière, *m.* — **grass,** *s.* chiendent, *m.* — **head,** *s.* pointe de lance, *f.* — **man,** *s.* lancier, *m.* — **mint,** *s.* menthe verte, *f.* — **staff,** *s.* hampe de lance, *f.* — **wort,** *s.* flammette, flammule, douve, *f.*, basinet, *m.*

Spec, *s.* (*vulgar*) *V.* **Speculation**

Special, *adj.* spécial; particulier; exprès; grand; extraordinaire. — *department* or *line* or *branch* or *trade,* — *study,* spécialité, *f.* — *expense,* (*fin.*) spécialité, *f.* (*V.* **Pleader**)

Specialist, *s. adj.* spécialiste, *m.*

Speciality, *s.* spécialité, *f.*

Specialization, *s.* spécialisation, *f.*

Specialize, *v.a.* spécialiser

Specially, *adv.* spécialement; particulièrement; principalement, surtout

Specialness, *s.* caractère spécial *or* particulier, *m.*, nature spéciale *or* particulière, *f.*, spécialité, *f.*

Specialty, *s.* spécialité, *f.*; cas spécial, *m.*; (*contract*) contrat sous seing privé, *m.*

Specie, *s.* numéraire, *m.*, espèces, *f.pl.*

Species, *s.* espèce, *f.*

Specific,-al, *adj.* spécifique; spécial; particulier; (*med., phys.*) spécifique; — *s.* spécifique, *m.* — *gravity,* pesanteur spécifique, *f.* — *legacy,* legs particulier, *m.*

Specifically, *adv.* spécifiquement

Specificalness, *s.* spécificité, *f.*

Specification, *s.* spécification, *f.*; chose spécifiée, *f.*; (*of patents*) description, *f.*; (*of contracts,* &c.) devis, *m.*; mémoire descriptif, *m.*; (—**s,** *pl.*) cahier des charges, *m.*

Specificative, *adj.* spécificatif

Specify, *v.a.* spécifier; déterminer; (*of time*) fixer d'avance

Specimen, *s.* modèle, *m.*; (*sample*) échantillon, spécimen, *m.* — **page,** *s.* page spécimen, *f.*

Specious, *adj.* spécieux; agréable à l'œil

Speciously, *adv.* spécieusement

Speciousness, *s.* spéciosité, nature spécieuse, *f.*

Speck, *s.* tache, *f.*; marque, *f.*; point, *m.*; (*med.*) taie, *f.*; (*of whales,* &c.) *V.* **Blubber;** — *v.a.* tacher

Speckle, *s.* tache, *f.*; (*of animals*) tacheture, moucheture, grivelure, *f.*; — *v.a.* tacheter, marqueter, moucheter

Speckled, *part. adj.* tacheté, marqueté, moucheté, (*like a tiger*) tigré, (*like a thrush*) grivelé, (*like a trout*) truité. — *iron,* fer truité, *m.*

Speckledness, *s.* tacheture, moucheture, grivelure, *f.*

Spectacle, *s.* spectacle, *m.*; —**s,** *pl.* (*glasses*) lunettes, *f.pl.* — **case,** *s.* étui à lunettes, *m.* — **maker,** *s.* lunettier, *m.* — **making, -trade, -business,** *s.* lunetterie, *f.* — **snake,** *s.* serpent à lunettes, *m.*

Spectacled, *adj.* lunetté, à lunettes

Spectacular, *adj.* de spectacle, théâtral

Specta-tor, tress, *s.* spectateur, *m.*, -trice, *f.*; assistant, *m.*, e, *f.*; curieux, *m.*, -euse, *f.*

Spectral, *adj.* spectral

Spectre, *s.* spectre, *m.*; fantôme, *m.*; revenant, *m.*

Spectro-logy, -scopy, &c. *V.* page 3, § 1

Spectrometer, &c. *V. French-English part*

Spectrum, *s.* spectre solaire, spectre, *m.* — **analysis,** *s.* analyse spectrale, *f.*

Specular, *adj.* spéculaire

Speculate, *v.n.* spéculer, méditer; conjecturer; prévoir; (*rely*) compter (sur); (*com., 'Change, and fig.*) spéculer; (*for a rise, a fall*) *V.* **Operate**

Speculation, *s.* spéculation, *f.*; méditation, *f.*; contemplation, *f.*; réflexion, pensée, *f.*; conjecture, *f.* *On* —, comme spéculation

Speculative, *adj.* speculatif; (*com., pers.*) spéculateur

Speculatively, *adv.* spéculativement

Speculativeness, *s.* nature spéculative, *f.*, caractère spéculatif, *m.*

Speculator, *s.* spéculateur, *m.*, -trice, *f.*; observateur, *m.*, -trice, *f.*; (*for a rise, for a fall, on 'Change*) *V.* **Operator**

Speculum, *s.* miroir (optique), miroir de métal, miroir métallique, *m.*; (*surg.*) spéculum, *m.* — **metal,** *s.* métal de miroir, *m.*

Speech, *s.* parole, *f.*; langage, *m.*; (*tongue*) langue, *f.*, idiome, *m.*; (*address*) discours, *m.*; harangue, *f.*; (*talk*) discours, langage, *m.*; (*few words*) propos, *m.*, paroles, *f.pl.*; (*of barristers*)

plaidoyer, *m.*; (*gram.*) discours, *m.* — *of the crown*, discours du trône, *m.* *Figure of* —, figure de rhétorique, *f.* *Part of* —, (*gram.*) partie du discours, *f.* *To be slow of* —, parler lentement. —**less,** *adj.* privé de la parole; muet; sans voix; interdit. —**lessness,** *s.* privation de la parole, *f.*, mutisme, *m.* — **maker,** *s.* péroreur, *m.*, -euse, *f.*
Speechifier, *s.* péroreur, *m.*, -euse, *f.*, faiseur (*m.*, -euse, *f.*) de beaux discours
Speechify, *v.n.* pérorer
Speechifying, *s.* beaux discours, *m.pl.* *To be fond of* —, aimer à pérorer
Speed, *v.n.* se hâter, se dépêcher, se presser; (*run*) courir; (*succeed*) réussir; (*to fare*) aller; — *v.a.* hâter, presser; aider, assister; protéger; favoriser; faire réussir; — *s.* vitesse, célérité, rapidité, vélocité, *f.*; (*haste*) hâte, diligence, promptitude, *f.*; (*success*) succès, *m.* *God's* —, *good* —, bonne chance, *f.*, succès, *m.* *At full* —, *full* —, en toute hâte, au plus vite; (*pers. running*) à toutes jambes; (*of birds' flying*) à tire-d'aile; (*of horses and their riders*) à toute bride, à bride abattue, à franc étrier, ventre à terre, à fond de train; (*of carriages*) à toute vitesse, à fond de train; (*of railway trains, steamers*) à toute vitesse, à toute vapeur; (*of sailing vessels*) à toutes voiles. *With all possible* —, en toute hâte, au plus vite. —**well,** *s.* véronique, *f.*
Speedily, *adv.* vite, avec célérité, avec diligence, promptement, rapidement, en toute hâte [hâte, diligence, *f.*
Speediness, *s.* célérité, vitesse, promptitude,
Speedy, *adj.* prompt, expéditif; rapide, vite
Speiss, *s.* speiss, *m.*
Spell, *s.* charme, *m.*; sort, *m.*; prestige, *m.*; (*time*) temps, intervalle, *m.*; (*turn*) tour, *m.*, volée, *f.*; — *v.a.n.* épeler; (*write*) écrire; orthographier; (*read*) lire; (*enchant*) enchanter, charmer; (*nav.*, &c.) relever. *To break a* —, rompre un charme. *To cast a* —, jeter un sort, ensorceler. *To have a* — *at*, prendre son tour à (*or* de). *To learn to* —, apprendre à mettre l'orthographe. *Spelt in full*, en toutes lettres. *At a* —, *V.* **Stretch** (*At a* —). —**bound,** *adj.* retenu par un charme, sous l'influence d'un charme, charmé, sous le charme, fasciné
Speller, *s.* personne qui épelle, *f.*; orthographiste, *m.f.*
Spellican, *s.* onchet, *m.*
Spelling, *s.* épellation, *f.*; orthographe, *f.*; (*turn*) tour de rôle, *m.* —**book,** *s.* abécédaire, syllabaire, livre de lecture, *m.*
Spelt, *s.* (*bot.*) épeautre, *m.f.*, blé rouge, *m.*; [(*min.*) *V.* **Spalt**
Spelter, *s.* zinc, *m.*
Spencer, *s.* spencer, *m.*
Spend, *v.a.n.* dépenser; (*time*) passer; (*waste*) perdre; dissiper; (*devote*) consacrer, employer; (*exhaust*) épuiser; (*to be lost*) se perdre, se consumer; (*be used*) s'employer; (*flow*) couler. —**thrift,** *s.* dépensier, *m.*, -ière, *f.*, dissipateur, *m.*, -trice, *f.*, prodigue, *m.f.*
Spender, *s.* personne qui dépense, *f.*; (*spendthrift*) *V.* **Spendthrift**
Spending, *s.* action de dépenser, *f.*; dépense, *f.*
Spent, *part. adj.* dépensé; passé, &c. (*V.* **Spend**); (*of shot*) mort, amorti; (*of masts*, &c.) cassé
Sperm, Spermaceti, *s.* sperme, *m.*; (*of whales*) sperme de baleine, spermaceti, blanc de baleine, *m.* — **candle,** *s.* bougie diaphane, bougie de blanc de baleine, *f.* — **oil,** *s.* huile de baleine, *f.* — **ointment,** *s.* onguent de spermaceti, *m.* — **whale,** *s.* cachalot, *m.*
Spermatic,-al, *adj.* spermatique. — *cord*, cordon spermatique, *m.*
Spermato-graphy, -logy. *V.* page 3, § 1
Spew, *v.a.n.* vomir, dégobiller
Spewing, *s.* vomissement, dégobillage, *m.*
Sphenoid, *adj.* sphénoïde; — *s.* sphénoïde, *m.* — *bone*, os sphénoïde, sphénoïde, *m.*
Sphenoidal, *adj.* sphénoïdal
Sphere, *s.* sphère, *f.* *Limited* —, cadre limité, *m.*
Spheric,-al, *adj.* sphérique; —**s,** *s.pl.* sphériques, *m.pl.*
Spherically, *adv.* sphériquement
Sphericalness, Sphericity, *s.* sphéricité, *f.*
Spherograph, *s.* sphérographe, *m.*
Spheroid, *s.* sphéroïde, *m.*
Spheroidal, *adj.* sphéroïdal
Spheroidic,-al, *adj.* sphéroïdique
Sphincter, — **muscle,** *s.* sphincter, *m.*
Sphinx, *s.* sphinx, *m.*
Sphygmograph, *s.* sphymographe, *m.*
Sphygmometer, *s.* sphygmomètre, *m.*
Sphygmoscope, *s.* sphygmoscope, *m.*
Spica, — **bandage,** *s.* spica, *m.*
Spicate, Spicated, *adj.* épié
Spice, *s.* épice, *f.*; (*small quantity*) teinte, teinture, idée, *f.*, grain, *m.*; — *v.a.* épicer [ment
Spicily, *adv.* fameusement, fièrement, crânement
Spick and span, *adj.* brillant; (— *new*) tout neuf, tout battant neuf, tout flambant neuf
Spicy, *adj.* épicé; d'épices; fertile en épices; aromatique, parfumé, embaumé; (*showy*) pimpant; (*pungent*) piquant; (*capital*) fameux, impayable; huppé; chic
Spider, *s.* araignée, *f.* — **catcher,** *s.* (*bird*) tichodrome échellette, grimpereau de murailles, *m.* — **crab,** *s.* maïa, *m.* — **fly,** *s.* ornithomyze, *m.* —**like,** *adj.* d'araignée, comme une araignée. — **monkey,** *s.* atèle, *m.* —**'s web,** — **work,** *s.* toile d'araignée, *f.* — **wort,** [*s.* commeline, *f.*
Spier, *s.* épieur, *m.*, -euse, *f.*
Spigelia, *s.* spigélie, *f.*
Spigot, *s.* fausset, *m.*
Spike, *s.* pointe, *f.*; (*nail*) clou, *m.*; broche, *f.*; (*of wood*) cheville, *f.*; (*of grain*, &c.) épi, *m.*; (*a plant*) aspic, *m.*; — *v.a.* clouer; (*a cannon*) enclouer; (*a gate*, &c.) hérisser. — **lavender,** *s.* aspic, *m.* —**let,** *s.* épillet, spicule, *m.* — **nail,** *s.* clou barbelé, *m.*, cheville barbelée, *f.* —**nard,** *s.* nard indien, spicanard, *m.*
Spiky, *adj.* à pointe aiguë
Spilikin. *V.* **Spellican**
Spill, *v.a.* verser, répandre; renverser; (*destroy, lose*) détruire; perdre; (*a sail*) carguer; — *s.* (*peg, pin*) cheville, *f.*; (*spigot*) fausset, *m.*; (*for lighting*) allumette (*of paper*, de papier; *of chip*, en copeau), *f.*; (*fam., upset*) bouleversement, *m.*, culbute, *f.* — **cup,** *s.* porte-allumettes, *m.*
Spiller, *s.* personne qui verse *or* qui répand, *f.*
Spillikin. *V.* **Spellican**
Spin, *v.a.n.* filer; (*unroll*) dérouler; (*protract*) prolonger, allonger, traîner en longueur; (*a top*, &c.) faire tourner, faire aller; (*turn*) tourner; (*hay*) tordre. — **out,** allonger; prolonger, traîner en longueur; délayer. — **round,** tourner; retourner. — **round and round,** tourner et retourner
Spina bifida, *s.* spina-bifida, *m.*
Spinach, Spinage, *s.* (*bot.*) épinard, *m.*; (*cook.*) épinards, *m.pl.*
Spinal, *adj.* spinal. — *column*, colonne vertébrale, *f.* — *complaints*, maladies de la moelle épinière, *f.pl.* — *cord* or *marrow*, moelle épinière, *f.* — *curvature*, déviation de la colonne vertébrale, *f.*
Spina ventosa, *s.* spina-ventosa, *m.*
Spindle, *s.* fuseau, *m.*; broche, *f.*; pivot, *m.*; (*of compasses*) aiguille, *f.*; (*of machines*) essieu, axe, *m.* —**ful,** *s.* fusée, *f.* — **legs, -shanks,** *s.pl.* jambes de fuseau, *f.pl.* — **legged, -shanked,** *adj.* à jambes de fuseau. — **shaped,** *adj.* fusiforme. — **tree,** *s.* fusain, *m.*
Spine, *s.* épine dorsale, épine du dos, colonne vertébrale, *f.*; (*bot.*) épine, *f.* *Curvature of the* —, déviation de la colonne vertébrale, *f.*
Spinel, Spinelle, *s.* spinelle, *f.*
Spinet, *s.* épinette, *f.*; (*spinny*) *V.* **Spinny**
Spiniferous, *adj.* spinifère
Spiniform, *adj.* spiniforme
Spininess, *s.* nature épineuse, *f.*

Spinnable, *adj.* filable
Spinnaret. *V.* **Spinneret**
Spinner, *s.* fileur, *m.*, -euse, *f.*; (*mill-owner*) filateur, *m.*; (*spider*) araignée, *f.*; (*spinneret*) filière, *f.* [*f.*; (*of caterpillars*, &c.) filière, *f.*
Spinneret, *s.* (*of spiders*) filière, mammule,
Spinney. *V.* **Spinny**
Spinning, *s.* filature, *f.*, filage, *m.* — **factory,** *s.* filature, *f.* — **frame,** *s.* métier à filer, *m.* — **jenny,** *s.* métier à filer, *m.*, jenny, *f.* — **machine,** *s.* machine à filer, *f.* — **mill,** *s.* filature, *f.* — **top,** *s.* toupie, *f.*; sabot, *m.* — **wheel,** *s.* rouet à filer, *m.*
Spinny, *s.* épinaie, *f.*
Spinosity, *s.* nature épineuse, *f.*; (*difficulty*)
Spinous, *adj.* épineux [matière épineuse, *f.*
Spinozism, *s.* spinosisme, *m.*
Spinozist, *s.* spinosiste, *m.f.*
Spinster, *s.* fileuse, *f.*; (*not married*) demoi-
Spinule, *s.* spinule, *f.* [selle, *f.*
Spiny, *adj.* épineux
Spiracle, *s.* pore, *m.*
Spiræa, *s.* spirée, *f.*
Spiral, *adj.* spiral (*m.*, e, *f.*); (*of staircases*) tournant, à vis, en hélice, en limaçon; — *s.* spirale, *s.f.*
Spirally, *adv.* spiralement, en spirale
Spire, *s.* spirale, *f.*; (*tip*) pointe, *f.*; (*of steeples*) flèche, aiguille, *f.*; (*of plants*) germe, *m.*; (*of grass*) brin, *m.*; — *v.n.* s'élever en flèche; (*of*
Spired, *adj* à flèche [*plants*) germer
Spirit, *s.* esprit, *m.*; âme, *f.*; fantôme, *m.*; génie, *m.*; caractère, *m*, nature, disposition, *f.*; courage, cœur, *m.*; fermeté, *f.*; ardeur, *f.*, feu, *m.*; vigueur, *f.*; élan, *m.*; gaieté, *f.*; vivacité, *f.*; animation, vie, *f.*, mouvement, entrain, *m.*, verve, *f.*; essence, *f.*; (*liquor*) spiritueux, *m.*, liqueur spiritueuse, liqueur, *f.*; (*of wine*, &c.) esprit, *m.*; esprit-de-vin, *m.*; alcool, *m.*; (*of potatoes*, &c.) eau-de-vie, *f.*; (*of turpentine*, &c., *essential oil*) essence, *f.*; —**s,** *pl.* (*life, senses*, &c.) esprits, *m.pl.*; (*animation, cheerfulness*, &c.) gaieté, *f.*, entrain, *m.*, vivacité, *f.*; moral, *m.*; (*courage*) courage, *m.*; (*liquors*) spiritueux, &c. *Depressed —s, depression of —s*, abattement, *m.* *Evil —*, esprit malin, malin esprit, esprit malfaisant, *m.*; mauvais génie, *m.* *Good —s*, gaieté, *f.*, entrain, *m.* *High —*, fierté, *f.*; cœur, courage, *m.* *High —s*, gaieté, *f.*, entrain, *m.* *Low —s, lowness of —s*, abattement, *m.* *To be in —s* or *in good —s* or *in high —s*, être gai, être de bonne humeur, être en train; être en verve; être tout joyeux. *To be in low —s*, être abattu, être triste. *To keep up o.'s —s*, ne pas perdre courage, ne pas se décourager, ne pas se laisser abattre. *To put in —s* or *in good —s*, mettre en train, mettre de bonne humeur, égayer. *To recover o.'s —s*, reprendre courage. — **dealer,** *s.* liquoriste, *m.f.* — **lamp,** *s.* lampe à esprit-de-vin, *f.* — **level,** *s.* niveau à bulle d'air, *m.* — **rapper, -medium,** *s.* médium, *m.* — **rapping,** *s.* spiritisme, *m.* — **room,** *s.* (*nav.*) cale au vin, *f.* — **stirring,** *adj.* émouvant. — **store,** *s.* magasin d'eaux-de-vie, magasin de liqueurs, *m.*; chai, *m.* — **trade,** *s.* commerce des spiritueux, *m.* — **varnish,** *s.* vernis à l'esprit-de-vin, *m.*
Spirit, *v.a.* animer, encourager; exciter; transporter. — **away,** enlever; entraîner; faire disparaître, éloigner, écarter; supprimer; escamoter; séduire. — **up,** exciter; pousser
Spirited, *adj.* vif, animé; ardent, plein d'ardeur, plein de feu, plein de verve, fougueux; plein de courage *or* de cœur; vigoureux, plein de vigueur, plein d'énergie, fort; plein de vivacité; (*bold*) hardi; (*of horses*) fougueux, ardent; (*in compounds*) à esprit ... (*V.* **Bold, High, Low,** &c.)
Spiritedly, *adv.* ardemment, avec ardeur, avec feu; avec courage; vigoureusement, vivement; (*of writing or speaking*) avec feu, chaleureusement, avec verve
Spiritedness, *s.* ardeur, *f.*, feu, *m.*; courage, cœur, *m.*; vigueur, *f.*; (*of speech*, &c.) verve, *f.*; (*of horses*) fougue, ardeur, *f.* (*V.* **High,** **Low,** &c.)
Spiritism, *s.* spiritisme, *m.*
Spiritist, *s. adj.* spiritiste, *m.f.*; spirite, *m.f.*
Spiritless, *adj.* sans âme, sans vie; sans courage, sans cœur; sans ardeur; sans vigueur, énervé, mou; (*cast down*) abattu; (*of speech*, &c.) sans verve
Spiritlessly, *adv.* sans cœur, sans courage, lâchement; sans vigueur, sans énergie
Spiritlessness, *s.* manque de courage *or* de cœur, *m.*; manque d'ardeur *or* de vigueur, *m.*; (*of speech*, &c.) manque de verve, *m.*
Spiritual, *adj. s.* spirituel, *adj. m.*, -le, *f.*, spirituel, *s.m.* [spiritualisme, *m.*
Spiritualism, *s.* spiritisme, *m.*; (*philos.*)
Spiritualist, *s. adj.*, **Spiritualistic,** *adj.* spiritiste, *m.f.*; (*philos.*) spiritualiste, *m.f.*
Spirituality, *s.* spiritualité, *f.*; spirituel, *m.*
Spiritualization, *s.* spiritualisation, *f.*
Spiritualize, *v.a.* spiritualiser
Spiritually, *adv.* spirituellement
Spiritualness, *s.* spiritualité, *f.*
Spirituous, *adj.* spiritueux
Spirituousness, *s.* propriété spiritueuse, *f.*
Spirling. *V.* **Smelt**
Spirometer, *s.* spiromètre, *m.*
Spirt, *v.n.* jaillir; (*of pens*) cracher; — *v.a.* faire jaillir; — *s.* jaillissement, *m.*; (*fig.*) effort, *m.*; boutade, *f.*
Spirting, *s.* *V.* **Spirt,** *s.*
Spiry, *adj* spiral; pyramidal
Spit, *s.* broche, *f.*; — *v.a.n.* embrocher, mettre à la broche; (*pierce*) embrocher; (*from the mouth*) cracher; (*of cats*) félir. *To put upon the —*, mettre à la broche. — **out,** *v.a.* cracher. — **rack,** *s.* hâtier, *m.*
Spitchcock, *v.a.* griller
Spite, *s.* dépit, *m.*; (*hatred*) haine, rancune, *f.*; — *v.a.* avoir du dépit contre, avoir une dent contre, en vouloir à; (*vex*) dépiter; contrarier; blesser; tourmenter; outrager. *In —* (*to*), de *or* par dépit (pour). *In — of*, *— of*, en dépit de, malgré. *Out of —*, par dépit; par rancune. *To have a — against*, avoir du dépit contre, avoir une dent contre, en vouloir à, garder rancune à. —**ful,** *adj.* rancunier, plein de rancune, haineux; vindicatif; plein de dépit; (*cat*) méchant. —**fully,** *adv.* avec *or* par dépit; avec *or* par rancune, par haine; par méchanceté. —**fulness,** *s.* rancune, *f.*; méchanceté, *f.* [daguet, *m.*
Spitter, *s.* cracheur, *m.*, -euse, *f.*; (*young deer*)
Spitting, *s.* crachement, *m* — **box,** *s.*
Spittle, *s.* salive, *f.*, crachat, *m.* [crachoir, *m.*
Spittoon, *s.* crachoir, *m.*
Splash, *v.a.* éclabousser; faire jaillir; — *v.n.* éclabousser; jaillir; (*of sea-waves*) clapoter; (*fall with noise*) tomber avec bruit (*or* avec fracas); — *s.* éclaboussure, *f.*; gâchis, *m.*; (*act of splashing*) éclaboussement, *m.*; (*of sea-waves*) clapotage, clapotement, *m.*; (*fall, noise*) chute d'un corps dans l'eau, *f.*; bruit d'un corps (tombant dans ...), bruit, *m.* — **board, -wing,** *s.* garde-crotte, paracrotte, *m.*
Splasher, *s.* (*of a carriage*) garde-crotte, paracrotte, *m.*
Splashing, *s.* (*act*) éclaboussement, *m.*; (*result*) éclaboussure, *f.*; &c. (*V.* **Splash,** *s.*)
Splashy, *adj.* gâcheux; bourbeux
Splat, *s.* (*of a chair*) panneau, barreau, *m.*
Splay, *v.a.* épauler; (*display*) déployer, étendre; (*arch.*) ébraser, évaser; — *v.n.* se déployer, s'étendre. — *s.* (*arch.*) ébrasement, évasement, *m.* — **foot,** *s.* pied plat, *m.* — **footed,** *adj.* au pied plat
Spleen, *s.* rate, *f.*; (*anger, spite*) bile, mauvaise humeur, *f.*, fiel, *m.*; (*low spirits*) mélancolie, hypocondrie, maladie noire, humeur noire, *f.*,

papillons noirs, *m.pl.*, spleen, *m.*; — *v.a.* dérater, érater. —**less,** *adj.* dératé; (*fig.*) doux. — **wort,** *s.* doradille, *f.*, cétérac, *m.*
Spleened, *adj.* dératé
Splenalgia, Splenalgy, *s.* splénalgie, *f.*
Splendid, *adj.* splendide; somptueux; magnifique; grand; (*illustrious*) brillant, éclatant
Splendidly, *adv.* splendidement; somptueusement; magnifiquement; brillamment, avec éclat [eclat, *m.*
Splendour, *s.* splendeur, magnificence, *f.*,
Splenetic, *adj. s.* splénétique, atrabilaire, hypocondriaque, *m.f.*
Splenic, *adj.* splénique
Splenitis, *s.* splénite, *f.*
Splent, *s.* (*vet.*) suros, *m.*
Splice, *v.a.* attacher; (*nav.*) épisser; — *s.* nœud, *m.*; (*nav.*) épissure, *f.* *To get —d,* (*jest.*) se marier
Splint, *s.* éclat de bois, *m.*, écharde, *f.*; éclat, *m.*; (*of bones*) esquille, *f.*; (*surg.*) éclisse, attelle, *f.*; (*vet.*) suros, *m.*
Splinter, *s.* *V.* **Splint;** — *v.a.* briser, faire éclater, fendre; (*surg.*) éclisser, mettre une attelle à; — *v.n.* se briser, éclater, voler en éclats. — **bar,** *s.* volée, *f.* [esquilles
Splintery, *adj.* écailleux; en éclats; en
Split, *v.a* fendre; diviser, partager; (*a vote*) partager; (*cloth, linen,* &c.) déchirer; (*peas*) casser; — *v.n.* se fendre; se diviser; (*on a rock*) se briser, échouer; (*with laughter*) éclater (de); (*to quarrel*) se diviser; — *s.* fente, *f.*; (*fig.*) scission, division, *f.*, différend, *m.* *To — the difference,* *V.* **Difference.** *To — a hair,* fendre *or* couper *or* partager un cheveu en quatre. *To — hairs,* chercher du poil aux œufs, épiloguer. *To — o.'s sides* (or *to —*) *with laughter* (or *with laughing*), crever de rire, se tordre de rire. *To — words,* jouer *or* chicaner sur les mots. — **asunder,** *v.a.* fendre en deux; *v.n.* se fendre en deux. — **on** *or* **upon,** (*betray*) dénoncer, moutonner, coquer, manger. — **open,** *v.a.* ouvrir, fendre. — **peas,** *s.pl.* pois cassés, *m.pl.* — **ring,** *s.* anneau brisé, *m.*
Splitter, *s.* fendeur, *m.*, -euse, *f.* (*V.* **Hair**)
Splitting, *s.* fendage, *m.* (*V.* **Hair**); — *adj.* *A — headache,* un mal de tête fou, *m.* — **mill,** *s.* fenderie, *f.*
Splutter, *s.* tapage, vacarme, *m.*; — *v.n.* bredouiller; (*scatter*) s'éparpiller
Spluttering, *s.* bredouillement, *m.*
Spoil, *v.a.* corrompre; (*mar*) gâter; abîmer; (*scribble over, blot*) barbouiller; (*a person*) gâter; (*fail in*) manquer; mal réussir; (*ruin*) ruiner, détruire; (*strip*) dépouiller; (*plunder*) ravager, piller, dévaster; (*seize*) se saisir de, s'emparer de; — *v.n.* se corrompre; se gâter, s'abîmer; — *s.* pillage, *m.*; (*booty*) dépouilles, *f.pl.*, butin, *m.*; (*of animals*) dépouille, *f.*; (*ruin*) perte, ruine, *f.*; (*earthwork*) déblai, *m.* *—ed* or *—t child,* enfant gâté, *m.* — **bank,** *s.* remblai, *m.*
Spoiler, *s.* spoliateur, *m.*, -trice, *f.*; corrupteur, *m.*, -trice, *f.*; destructeur, *m.*, -trice, *f.*; (*who mars*) personne qui gâte, *f.*, (*thing*) chose qui gâte, *f.* [vastation, *f.*; détérioration, *f.*
Spoiling, *s.* spoliation, *f.*; pillage, *m.*; dé-
Spoke, *s.* rayon, rais, *m.* *To put a — in the wheel,* mettre des bâtons dans les roues. — **brush,** *s.* passe-partout, *m.* — **shave,** *s.* plane, *f.*
Spoken, *part.* parlé, &c. (*V.* **Speak**); (*in compounds, pers.*) au parler ... (*V.* **French**)
Spokesman, *s.* orateur, *m.*, personne qui porte la parole, *f.*; organe, *m.*
Spoliate, *v.a.* dépouiller, spolier; — *v.n.* exercer des spoliations
Spoliation, *s.* spoliation, *f.*
Spoliative, *adj.* spoliatif
Spoliator, *s.* spoliateur, *m.*
Spondaic, *adj.* spondaïque
Spondee, *s.* spondée, *m.*

Sponge, *s.* éponge, *f.*; (*artil.*) écouvillon, *m.*; (*in bread-making*) masse de pâte, *f.*; — *v.a.n.* éponger; (*cloth*) décatir; (*artil.*) écouvillonner; (*hang on*) vivre aux dépens de; quêter *or* attraper un dîner, piquer l'assiette. — **bag,** *s.* sac à éponge, *m.* — **bath,** *s.* bain anglais, *m.*; hydrothérapie, *f.* — **cake,** *s.* biscuit léger, biscuit de caisse, biscuit de Savoie, biscuit de Reims, *m.* — **crab,** *s.* dromie, *f.* — **man,** *s.* épongier, *m.* — **out,** *v.a.* effacer. — **rod,** *s.* (*artil.*) écouvillon, *m.* — **up,** *v.a.* éponger
Sponger, *s.* parasite, pique-assiette, *m.f.*; (*of cloth*) décatisseur, *m.*
Spongiform, *adj.* spongiforme
Spongilla, *s.* spongille, *f.* [gieuse, *f.*
Sponginess, *s.* spongiosité, nature spon-
Sponging, *s.* action d'éponger, *f.*, épongement, *m.*; (*of cloth*) décatissage, *m.*; (*hanging on*) écornifierie, *f.* — **bath,** *s.* *V.* **Sponge-bath.** — **house,** *s.* prison pour dettes, *f.*
Spongy, *adj.* spongieux
Sponsor, *s.* garant, répondant, *m.*; (*at a christening*) parrain, *m.*, marraine, *f.*
Spontaneity, *s.* spontanéité, *f.*
Spontaneous, *adj.* spontané
Spontaneously, *adv.* spontanément
Spontaneousness, *s.* spontanéité, *f.*
Spontoon, *s.* esponton, *m.*
Spool, *s.* bobine, *f.*, espoulin, *m.*; — *v.a.* bobiner, espouliner, spouliner
Spoon, *s.* cuiller, cuillère, *f.*; (*for salt* or *ice*) pelle, *f.* — *and fork* (*to match*), couvert, *m.* (*V.* **Silver**). —**bill,** *s.* spatule, palette, *f.*, bec-en-cuiller, *m.* —**drift,** *s.* éclaboussure, *f.* —**ful,** *s.* cuillerée, *f.* — **maker,** *s.* cuilleriste, *m.* — **meat,** *s.* aliments liquides, *m.pl.*, soupe, *f.*, potage, *m.*, laitage, *m.*
Spooniness, *s.* niaiserie, nigauderie, bêtise, *f.*
Spoony, Spooney, *adj. s.* niais, nigaud, bête, imbécile; amoureux, langoureux
Sporad-ic, al, -ically. *V.* page 3, § 1
Sporadicalness, Sporadicity, *s.* sporadicité, *f.*
Spore, *s.* spore, *f.* [dicité, *f.*
Sport, *s.* jeu, amusement, divertissement, passe-temps, *m.*; plaisir, *m.*; (*plaything*) jouet, *m.*; (*jesting*) raillerie, moquerie, plaisanterie, *f.*; (*exercise*) exercice, *m.*; (*hunting, fishing, racing,* &c.) sport, *m.* *Good —,* (*of game*) bonne chasse, *f.*; (*of fish*) bonne prise, *f.* *In —,* par plaisanterie, pour rire, en badinant. *To make — of,* s'amuser de; se jouer de; se rire de; se moquer de
Sport, *v n.* jouer, s'amuser, se divertir, badiner; (*frolic*) folâtrer, s'ébattre; (*with*) se jouer (de); (*fly*) flotter; — *v.a.* faire parade de, montrer; (*wear*) porter. —**less,** *adj.* triste
Sportful, &c. *V.* **Sportive**
Sporting, *s.* (la) chasse, *f.*, (le) sport, *m.*; — *adj.* de chasse; de sport. — **character,** *s.* amateur de sport, sportsman, *m.* — **dog, gun,** &c., chien, fusil, &c. de chasse. — **gunpowder, -powder,** *s.* poudre de chasse, *f.* — **man,** *s.* *V.* **Sportsman**
Sportive, *adj.* enjoué, gai, joyeux; folâtre; plaisant, amusant. —**ly,** *adv.* avec enjouement, en plaisantant, en badinant, gaîment. —**ness,** *s.* enjouement, *m.*, gaieté, folâtrerie, *f.*, badinage, *m.*
Sportsman, *s.* chasseur, *m.*; (*of fishing*) pêcheur, *m.*; (*of races*) amateur de sport, sportsman, sportman, *m.*
Spot, *s.* (*stain*) tache, *f.*; (*mark*) tacheture, moucheture, marque, *f.*; (*place*) *V.* **Place;** point, *m.*; place, *f.*; (*of ground, of earth*) morceau, coin, *m.*; (*astr.*) tache, *f.*; — *v.a* (*stain*) tacher; (*blemish*) souiller, entacher (de); (*speckle*) tacheter, moucheter, marquer, tigrer; (*slang*) reconnaître. *On the —,* sur la place, sur place; sur les lieux; (*immediately*) sur-le-champ. *Dead on the —,* raide mort. *Killed on the —,* tué sur le coup. —**less,** *adj.* sans tache; pur; irréprochable. —**lessness,** *s.* pureté, *f.*

Spottedness, *s.* tachetures, mouchetures, *f.pl.*
Spotty, *adj.* taché, couvert de taches; (*speckled*) tacheté, moucheté
Spousal. *V.* **Wedding**
Spouse, *s.* époux, *m.*, épouse, *f.*; mari, *m.*, femme, *f.* **—less,** *adj.* sans époux, sans épouse; veuf (*m.*, veuve, *f.*)
Spout, *s.* (*pipe*) tuyau, *m.*; (*of houses*) gouttière, *f.*; (*of utensils*) bec, goulot, *m.*; (*of mills*) auget, *m.*; (*mach.*) tuyau, *m.*; lance, *f.*; (*jet*) jet, *m.*; (*of water*) jet d'eau, *m.*; (*a phenomenon*) trombe, *f.*; — *v.n.* jaillir, rejaillir; (*to speechify*) déclamer, pérorer; — *v.a.* lancer, jeter; déclamer. *To put up the* —, (*pawn*) mettre au clou. **— fish,** *s.* souffleur, *m.* **— hole,** *s.* (*nat. hist.*) évent, *m.*
Spouter, *s.* déclamateur, *m.*, -trice, *f.*, péroreur, *m.*, -euse, *f.*
Spouting, *s.* jaillissement, *m.*; déclamation, *f.*
Sprain, *v.a.* se fouler, se donner une entorse à; (*fig.*) forcer, fouler, donner une entorse à; — *s.* foulure, entorse, *f.* *To — o.'s foot,* se fouler le pied, se donner une entorse au pied
Sprained, *part. adj.* foulé; (*fig.*) forcé
Sprat, *s.* sprat, esprot, melet, *m.*, melette, *f.*, harenguet, *m.* *To give* (or *throw*) *a — to catch a herring* (or *a whale*), donner un œuf pour avoir un bœuf
Sprawl, *v.n.* s'étaler, s'étendre, s'épater; se débattre. *To lie —ing on,* être étalé sur, être couché tout de son long sur; (*in a bad sense*) se vautrer. *To send* (...) *—ing,* étendre (...) tout de son long par terre
Spray, *s.* (*of water*) pulvérin, *m.*, poussière d'eau, poussière, *f.*, brouillard, *m.*; (*on the sea*) embrun, *m.*, poussière de mer, *f.*; (*twigs*) ramilles, brindilles, *f.pl.*
Spread, *v.a.* étendre; (*display*) étendre, déployer; (*scatter, publish*) répandre; semer; propager; (*emit*) répandre, exhaler; (*cover*) couvrir; (*a net*) tendre; (*a table*) servir; couvrir (de); (*the cloth*) mettre; (*sails*) tendre, déployer; (*a tent*) dresser; — *v.n.* s'étendre; se déployer; (*to be propagated*) se répandre, se propager; — *s.* étendue, expansion, *f.*; (*interval*) espacement, *m.*; (*fig.*) développement, *m.*; propagation, *f.*; progrès, *m.*; (*a feast*) régal, festin, repas, *m.* **— abroad,** *v.a.* répandre, divulguer; *v.n.* se répandre. **— eagle,** *s.* aigle aux ailes éployées, *m.*; (*her.*) aigle éployée, *f.* **— out,** étendre; déployer; étaler
Spreader, *s.* personne qui répand, *f.*; propagateur, *m.*, -trice, *f.*, divulgateur, *m.*, -trice, *f.*; auteur, *m.*; (*of news*) semeur, -euse, *f.*, débiteur, *m.*, -euse, *f.*, colporteur, *m.*, -euse, *f.*
Spreading, *adj.* étendu; qui s'étend; qui se répand; — *s.* extension, *f.*; (*fig.*) *V.* **Spread,** *s.*
Spree, *s.* bamboche, bosse, bombance, *f.*; — *v.n.* rigoler. *To have a —, to be out on the —,* faire bombance; faire une noce; être en goguette
Sprig, *s.* brin, *m.*, brindille, branche, *f.*; (*nail*) pointe, *f.*; (*pin*) cheville, *f.*; (*lad*) jeune garçon, jeune homme, *m.* *A — of nobility,* un fils de famille, *m.*
Spright, *s.* *V.* **Sprite**
Sprightliness, *s.* vivacité, *f.*, feu, *m.*; gaieté, *f.*, enjouement, *m.*
Sprightly, *adj.* vif, éveillé; gai, enjoué; égrillard
Spring, *v.a.n.* (*grow*) pousser, croître; (*of water*) jaillir, rejaillir; (*leap*) s'élancer, bondir, sauter; (*proceed from*) provenir (de); venir (de); (*issue*) sortir (de); (*descend from*) descendre (de); (*arise*) naître, surgir; (*of the day*) poindre, paraître; (*set going, let off*) faire jouer; (*a rattle*) agiter, faire jouer, sonner; (*a mine*) faire sauter, faire jouer; (*a leak*) faire; (*game*) (*v.a.*) faire lever, (*v.n.*) se lever, partir; (*warp*) (*v.n.*) se déjeter, (*v.a.*) faire déjeter; (*of a mast or yard*) (*v.n.*) consentir, (*v.a.*) faire consentir. **— back,** reculer; faire ressort. **— up,** pousser; (*fig.*) s'élever, grandir; (*of water*) jaillir; (*arise*) naître, surgir
Spring, *s.* (*season*) printemps, *m.*; (*a leap*) élan, saut, bond, *m.*; (*elastic body*) ressort, *m.*; (*of seats, braces, boots*) élastique, *m.*; (*of doors, casements*) bascule, *f.*; (*elasticity*) élasticité, *f.*; (*fountain*) source, *f.*; fontaine, *f.*; (*origin*) source, origine, *f.*; cause, *f.*; (*rise*) naissance, *f.*; (*of an arch*) naissance (de voûte), *f.*; (*nav.*) fente, *f.*; — *adj.* de *or* du printemps, printanier; (*having a spring*) à ressort; à élastiques; élastique; (*of carriages*) suspendu; (*piston*) métallique. *Boiling* —, source d'eau bouillante, *f.* *Hot* —, source d'eau chaude, *f.* *In the* —, (*season*) au printemps. *With —s,* à ressorts; à élastiques; (*of carriages*) suspendu. *Without —s,* (*of carriages*) non suspendu. *To give* or *take a* —, faire un bond, s'élancer; prendre son élan. **— balance,** *s.* balance à ressort, *f.* **— bar,** *s.* (*of a saddle*) porte-étrivière, *m.* **— beetle,** *s.* taupin, *m.* **— blind,** *s.* store, *m.* **— board,** *s.* tremplin, *m.* **— box,** *s.* (*horol.*) barillet, *m.* **— carriage,** *s.* voiture suspendue, *f.* **— day,** *s.* jour de printemps, *m.* **— gun,** *s.* piége à fusil, *m.* **— halt,** *s.* éparvin sec, *m.* **— head,** *s.* source, *f.* **— herring,** *s.* gasparot, gasperau, *m.* **—less,** *adj.* (*of carriages*) non suspendu. **— lock,** *s.* houssette, *f.*; bec-de-cane, *m.* **— mattress,** *s.* sommier élastique, *m.* **— roller blind,** *s.* store, *m.* **— soup,** *s.* potage printanier, printanier, *m.*, printanière, *f.* **— tail,** *s.* podure, *m.* **— tide,** *s.* grande marée, *f.*, eaux vives, *f.pl.*, maline, *f.* **— time,** *s.* printemps, *m.* **— water,** *s.* eau de source, eau de fontaine, *f.* **— water cress** *or* **cresses,** *s.* cresson de fontaine, *m.* **— weather,** *s.* temps de printemps, *m.* **— wheat,** *s.* blé de mars, *m.*
Springe, *s.* lacet, filet, *m.*; — *v.a.* prendre au lacet
Springer, *s.* (*kind of dog*) petit épagneul, *m.*
Springiness, *s.* élasticité, *f.*; (*of land*) abondance de sources, *f.*
Springing, *s.* (*growth*) croissance, crue, *f.*; (*descent*) descendance, *f.*; (*rise*) naissance, *f.*; (*of an arch*) naissance (de voûte), *f.*; (*spirting*) jaillissement, *m.*; (*leaping*) saut, élan, *m.*; (*springiness*) élasticité, *f.* **— board,** *s.* tremplin, *m.*
Springy, *adj.* élastique; (*of land*) plein de sources
Sprinkle, *v.a.* (*scatter*) répandre; (*with liquids*) arroser; asperger; humecter; (*with holy water*) asperger; (*with salt, &c.*) saupoudrer; (*fig.*) parsemer (de); — *s.* quantité répandue, *f.*
Sprinkler, *s.* aspersoir, *m.*; goupillon, *m.*
Sprinkling, *s.* arrosement, arrosage, *m.*; (*of salt, &c.*) saupoudration, *f.*; (*of holy water*) aspersion, *f.*; (*rain*) pluie fine, *f.*, quelques gouttes d'eau, *f.pl.*; (*fig.*) petite quantité, *f.*; petit nombre, *m.*; (*smattering*) teinture, *f.*
Sprit, *s.* (*nav.*) livarde, *f.*; — *v.a.* livarder. **— sail,** *s.* civadière, *f.*
Sprite, *s.* esprit, fantôme, follet, lutin, *m.*
Sprocket, — wheel, *s.* hérisson, *m.*
Sprout, *v.n.* germer, pousser; (*bud*) bourgeonner; — *s.* jet, rejeton, *m.*; pousse, *f.*; germe, *m.*; (*cabbage*) jeune chou, chou, *m.* (*V.* **Brussels**)
Sprouting, *adj.* qui germe, qui pousse; — *s.* germination, *f.*
Spruce, *adj.* paré, orné, bien mis, pimpant, tiré à quatre épingles; — *v.n.* se parer, se faire beau, se bichonner, se requinquer; — *v.a.* afistoler, bichonner, requinquer; — *s.* sapin, *m.* **— beer,** *s.* pruce, sapinette, *f.*
Sprucely, Spruceness *or* **Sprucery.** *V.* **Smugly, Smugness**
Sprung, *part. adj.* poussé, &c. (*V.* **Spring,** [*v.a.n.*); (*issued*) issu
Spry, *adj.* vif, actif; agile; prompt; vigoureux
Spud, *s.* petit couteau, *m.*; (*agr.*) béquille, *f.*; sarcloir, *m.*; — *v.a.* béquiller
Spume, &c. *V.* **Foam,** &c.
Spunge, &c. *V.* **Sponge,** &c.
Spunk, *s.* amadou, *m.*; (*fig.*) vivacité, activité, *f.*; feu, *m.*, fougue, *f.*; (*spirit*) cœur, courage, *m.*; (*bot.*) bolet, *m.*
Spur, *s.* éperon, *m.*; (*of birds*) ergot, *m.*; (*in-*

citement) aiguillon, stimulant, *m.*; excitation, *f.*, feu, *m.*; (*bot.*) éperon, *m.*; (*of rye,* &c.) ergot, *m.*; (*buttress*) arc-boutant, *m.*; (*fort.*) éperon, *m.*; — *v.a.* (*prick*) donner de l'éperon à; éperonner; (*incite*) aiguillonner, stimuler, exciter, animer; (*put spurs on*) armer d'éperons, éperonner; — *v.n.* jouer des éperons, se hâter, se presser. *On* or *upon the — of,* sous le feu de, dans l'excitation de; sous l'impulsion de. *On* or *upon the — of the moment,* dans le premier moment, dans l'ardeur du moment, sous l'impulsion du moment. *To give a — to,* aiguillonner; éperonner. *To set —s to,* donner de l'éperon à, éperonner. — **gall,** *s.* blessure d'éperon, *f.* — **gear,** *s.* hérisson, *m.* — **leather,** *s.* monture d'éperon, éperonnière, *f.* — **maker,** *s.* éperonnier, *m.* — **on,** (*v.a.*) pousser, aiguillonner, exciter, stimuler, animer; (*v.n.*) se presser, se hâter. — **post, -stone,** *s.* chasse-roues, borne, *f.* — **strap,** *s. V.* — **leather.** — **wheel,** *s.* hérisson, *m.*

Spurge, *s.* euphorbe, *f.* — **laurel,** *s.* lauréole, *f.*

Spurious, *adj.* faux; (*adulterated*) falsifié, sophistiqué; (*of writings*) apocryphe; (*of* (*books*) contrefait, de contrefaçon; (*of birth*) illégitime; (*med., bot.*) faux

Spuriously, *adv.* faussement; illégitimement; (*of books*) par (*or* en) contrefaçon

Spuriousness, *s.* falsification, sophistication, *f.*; (*fig.*) fausseté, *f.*; (*of books,* &c.) nature (*f.*) *or* caractère (*m.*) apocryphe; (*of birth*) illégitimité, *f.*

Spurling. *V.* **Smelt**

Spurn, *v.a.* pousser du pied; (*scorn*) repousser; dédaigner; traiter avec mépris; rebuter; (*drive away*) chasser; — *s.* coup de pied, *m.*; (*scorn*) mépris, dédain, rebut, *m.*

Spurner, *s.* (*scorner*) contempteur, *m.*, -trice, *f.*

Spurred, *adj.* éperonné; (*of rye*) ergoté

Spurrey, Spurry, *s.* spergule, *f.*

Spurrier, *s.* éperonnier, *m.*

Spurt. *V.* **Spirt**

Sputation, *s.* sputation, *f.*

Sputter, *v.n.* cracher en parlant, bredouiller; (*of pens*) cracher; — *s. V.* **Sputtering.** *To* — **out,** cracher

Sputterer, *s.* bredouilleur, *m.*, -euse, *f.*

Sputtering, *s.* bredouillement, *m.*; (*noise*) vacarme, tintamarre, *m.*; (*of pens*) crachement, *m.*

Sputum, *s.* crachat, *m.*

Spy, *s.* espion, *m.*, -ne, *f.*; — *v.a.n.* épier, espionner; (— *out, see*) *V.* **Espy.** — **boat,** *s.* aviso, *m.* — **glass,** *s.* longue-vue, lunette d'approche, lorgnette, *f.* — **into,** *v.a.* examiner de près, chercher à pénétrer, scruter. — **system,** *s.* espionnage, *m.*

Spying, *s.* espionnage, *m.* — **glass,** *s. V.* **Spy-glass**

Squab, *s.* matelas, coussin, coussinet, *m.*; — *adj. V.* **Squabby**; (*of birds*) sans plumes; — *adv.* lourdement. — **chick,** *s.* poussin, *m.*

Squabble, *v.n.* se chamailler; — *s.* querelle, *f.*; bagarre, *f.*; chamaillis, *m.*

Squabbler, *s.* querelleur, *m.*, -euse, *f.*

Squabbling, *s. V.* **Squabble,** *s.*

Squabby, *adj.* gros, gras, dodu, potelé, ragot, boulot

Squad, *s.* (*mil.*) escouade, *f.*; (*in a bad sense*) clique, *f.* *Awkward* —, recrues, *f.pl.*, conscrits, Jean-Jeans, *m.pl.* — **drill,** *s.* école de peloton, *f.*

Squadron, *s.* (*mil.*) escadron, *m.*; (*nav.*) escadre, *f.*; division, *f.*

Squalid, *adj.* malpropre, sale

Squalidness, *s.* malpropreté, saleté, *f.*

Squall, *v.n.* crier, brailler; — *s.* cri, *m.*; (*of wind*) rafale, bourrasque, *f.*; grain, *m.*

Squaller, *s.* criard, *m.*, e, *f.*, brailleur, *m.*, -euse, *f.*

Squalling, *s.* criaillerie, *f.*; — *adj.* criard, braillard

Squally, *adj.* orageux, venteux, à rafales

Squalor. *V.* **Squalidness**

Squamous, *adj.* squameux, squammeux

Squander, *v.a.* dissiper, gaspiller, prodiguer, manger, dilapider; — *s. V.* **Squandering**

Squanderer, *s.* dissipateur, *m.*, -trice, *f.*, gaspilleur, *m.*, -euse, *f.*; gâcheur, *m.*, -euse, *f.*; prodigue, *m.f.*

Squandering, *s.* dissipation, *f.*, gaspillage, *m.*

Square, *adj.* carré; (*honest,* &c.) juste, équitable, honnête; conforme; exact; en règle; (*of accounts*) balancé, égalisé; (*of measure*) de superficie; (*adverb.*) carrément, en carré; — *s.* carré, *m.*; (*place*) place, *f.*; square, *m.*; (*parade*) place d'armes, *f.*; (*rule*) équerre, *f.*; (*of chess-boards, draught-boards, registers*) case, *f.*; (*of stuffs, of brick, tile, glass*) carreau, *m.*; (*geom., arith.*) carré, *m.*; — *v.a.* carrer; (*timbers*) équarrir; (*fig.*) mesurer; régler; adapter, ajuster, proportionner; (*accounts*) balancer, égaliser; (*arith.*) carrer; (*nav.*) brasser carré; — *v.n.* cadrer; s'accorder. — *brick* or *tile,* — *pane,* &c., carreau, *m.* — *pane of glass,* — *of glass,* carreau de vitre, *m.* — *root,* racine carrée, *f.* — *measure,* mesure de superficie, *f.* — *rule,* équerre, *f.* *To make* —, balancer; égaliser; arranger. — **up,** *v.n.* régler ses comptes

Squarely, *adv.* carrément; (*honestly*) justement, honnêtement

Squareness, *s.* forme carrée, *f.*; équarrissage, *m.*

Squaring, *s.* équarrissage, équarrissement, *m.* — *of the circle,* quadrature du cercle, *f.*

Squarish, *adj.* à peu près carré

Squash, *v.a.* écraser; — *s.* chose molle, *f.*; quelque chose qu'on écrase, *m.*; (*fall*) chute lourde, *f.*; (*crushing*) écrasement, *m.*; (*boys' play*) presse, *f.*; (*bot.*) *V.* **Pumpkin**

Squasher, *s.* écraseur. *m.*

Squashing, *s.* écrasement, écrasage, *m.*

Squashy, *adj.* mou, mollasse, qui s'écrase

Squat, *v.n.* (— **down**) s'accroupir; se blottir, se tapir; — *adj.* accroupi; blotti, tapi; (*short and thick*) trapu, ramassé. *To lie* or *sit* —, s'accroupir; se blottir, se tapir

Squatter, *s.* colon (qui n'a pas acheté la terre), squatter, *m.*

Squeak, *s.* cri aigu, cri, *m.*; — *v.n.* crier (comme un porc)

Squeaker, *s.*, **Squeaking,** *adj.* criard, *m.*, e, *f.*

Squeal, *s.* cri, *m.*; — *v.n.* crier (comme un rat)

Squeamish, *adj.* délicat; dégoûté; (*over nice*) trop difficile; qui fait le dégoûté (*or* la dégoûtée, *f.*); bégueule (*f.*). —**ly,** *adv.* trop délicatement; avec dégoût. —**ness,** *s.* délicatesse, *f.*; goût difficile, *m.*; bégueulerie, *f.*

Squeeze, *v.a.* presser, serrer; — *s.* étreinte, *f.*; compression, *f.*; (*of hands*) serrement, *m.* — **into,** *v.a.* comprimer dans; faire entrer de force dans. — **out,** *v.a.* exprimer; tirer, extorquer, faire cracher (à)

Squeezing, *s. V.* **Squeeze**; (*that which is squeezed out*) pressurage, *m.*

Squelch, *v.a.* écraser, aplatir

Squib, *s.* serpenteau, *m.*; pétard, *m.*; (*fig.*) satire, *f.*; pasquinade, *f.*; pamphlet, *m.*

Squid, *s.* calmar, encornet, *m.*

Squill, *s.* (*bot.*) scille, *f.*; (*zool.*) squille, *f.*

Squilla, *s.* (*zool.*) squille, *f.*

Squint, *adj.* louche; — *s.* regard louche, *m.*; — *v.n.* loucher. — **at,** *v.n.* regarder en louchant; regarder de travers. — **eyed,** *adj.* louche

Squinter, *s.* loucheur, *m.*, -euse, *f.*

Squinting, *s.* louchement, *m.*, loucherie, *f.*; (*med.*) strabisme, *m.*; — *adj.* loucheur, louche

Squintingly, *adv.* en louchant; de travers

Squire, *s.* écuyer, *m.*; (*gentleman*) propriétaire, *m.*; (*to a lady*) cavalier, *m.*; (*in fables*) sire, maître; — *v.a.* servir d'écuyer à; (*to a lady*) servir de cavalier à, escorter

Squireen, *s.* hobereau, gentillâtre, *m.*

Squirm, *v.n.* se tortiller

Squirrel, *s.* écureuil, *m.* — **monkey,** *s.* sagouin, *m.*

Squirt, *v.a.* seringuer; faire jaillir; lancer; — *v.n.* jaillir; — *s.* seringue, *f.*; (*of water*) jet d'eau, *m.* —*ing cucumber,* ecbalium, *m.*

Squitch. *V.* **Quitch**

Stab, *v.a.* percer, frapper; (*kill*) poignarder,

donner un coup de couteau à ; (*fig.*) porter un coup mortel à, frapper mortellement ; — *s.* coup, *m.* ; coup de poignard *or* de couteau *or* &c., *m.*
Stabat mater, *s.* stabat mater, stabat, *m.*
Stability, *s.* stabilité, *f.*; constance, *f.* ; fermeté, *f.*; solidité, *f.* ; (*of a horse*) fond, *m.*
Stable, *adj.* stable ; fixe ; constant ; ferme ; solide. — *equilibrium,* équilibre stable, *m.*
Stable, *s.* écurie, *f.* ; (*for oxen, cows*) étable, *f.* — **boy,** *s.* garçon d'écurie, palefrenier, *m.* ; (*in contempt*) valet d'écurie, *m.* — **coat,** *s.* casaque, souquenille, *f.* — **dung,** *s.* fumier, *m.* — **man,** *s. V.* — **boy.** — **yard,** *s.* basse-cour, *f.*
Stable, *v.a* (*oxen, cows*) établer ; (*horses*) loger
Stableness. *V.* **Stability**
Stabling, *s.* stabulation, *f.*; (*stables : for horses*) écuries, *f.pl.*, (*for oxen, cows*) étables, *f.pl.*
Stably, *adv.* stablement
Stabulation, *s.* stabulation, *f.*
Stachys, *s.* stachyde, *f.*
Stack, *s.* (*agr.*) meule, *f.* ; (*of wood, bottles*) pile, *f.* ; (*of bricks,* &c.) tas, *m.* ; (*of chimneys*) souche, *f.*, corps, *m.* ; (*of arms*) faisceau, *m.* ; (*of houses*) *V.* **Block ;** — *v.a.* empiler ; entasser ; (*agr.*) emmeuler. — **cloth,** *s. V.* **Rick.** — **frame, -stand,** *s.* tréteau *or* support de meule, *m.* — **yard,** *s.* cour de ferme, *f.*
Stacking, *s.* empilage, empilement, *m.* ; entassement, *m.* ; (*agr.*) emmeulage, *m.*
Staddle, *s.* baliveau, *m.*
Stade, Stadium, *s.* stade, *m.*
Stadtholder, *s.* stathouder, *m.*
Stadtholderate, *s.* stathoudérat, *m.*
Stadtholderian, *adj.* stathoudérien
Staff, *s.* bâton, *m.*; (*cudgel*) gourdin, *m.* ; (*of pilgrims*) bourdon, *m.* ; (*crosier*) crosse, *f.* ; (*badge of office*) bâton de commandement, *m.* ; (*support*) appui, soutien, *m.* ; (*of a chair*) bâton, barreau, *m.* ; (*pole*) mât, *m.* ; (*mus.*) portée, *f.* ; (*pers.*) personnel, *m.* ; corps, *m.* ; (*editorial*) rédaction, *f.* ; (*mil.*) état-major, *m.*; (*nav.*) mâtereau, bâton, *m.* *The — of life,* le soutien de la vie. — **office,** *s.* état-major, *m.* — **officer,** *s.* officier d'état-major, *m.*
Stag, *s.* cerf, *m.*; (*outsider on 'Change*) coulissier, *m.* ; (*jobber*) agioteur, loup, *m.* — **beetle,** *s.* cerf-volant, lucane, *m.* — **evil,** *s.* (*vet.*) mal de cerf, tétanos, *m.* —**hound,** *s.* limier, *m.* — **hunt,** *s.* chasse au cerf, *f.*
Stage, *s.* (*platform*) estrade, *f.*; (*scaffolding*) échafaudage, échafaud, *m.* ; (*of theatres*) scène, *f.*; (*theatre, drama*) théâtre, *m.* ; (*mountebank's*) tréteaux, *m.pl.* ; (*relay*) relais, *m.* ; (*vehicle*) diligence, *f.* ; voiture publique, *f.* ; (*degree, step*) phase, *f.* ; période, *m.* ; degré, *m.* ; (*med.*) période, *f.*, stade, *m.* ; (*med.*) degré, *m.* ; (*process*) procédé, *m.*; (*of a press*) établi, *m.* ; (*nav.*) plancher, *m.* *Front of the —,* avant-scène, *f.* *By short —s,* à petites journées. *In the last — of consumption,* au dernier degré de la phthisie. — **box,** *s.* loge d'avant-scène, *f.* — **carpenter,** *s.* machiniste, *m.* — **carriage,** *s.* voiture publique, *f.* — **coach,** *s.* diligence, voiture publique, *f.* — **door,** *s.* entrée de la scène, entrée des artistes, *f.* — **effect,** *s.* mise en scène, *f.* ; coup de théâtre, *m.* ; tableau, *m.* — **lights,** *s.pl.* rampe, *f.* — **manager,** *s.* régisseur-metteur en scène, régisseur de la scène, *m.* — **plate,** *s.* (*of a microscope*) platine, *f.* — **play,** *s.* pièce de théâtre, *f.* — **player,** *s.* comédien, *m.*, -ne, *f.*, acteur, *m.*, actrice, *f.* — **waggon,** *s.* patache, *f.* — **wait,** *s.* avertisseur, *m.*
Stager, *s.* routier, *m.*
Stagger, *v.n.* chanceler, vaciller ; hésiter ; — *v.a.* faire chanceler ; (*fig.*) ébranler ; étonner
Staggering, *s.* chancellement, *m.*; hésitation, *f.* ; ébranlement, *m.* ; étonnement, *m.* ; — *adj.* chancelant, vacillant ; hésitant, incertain ; étonnant. *A — blow,* (*fig.*) un coup foudroyant
Staggeringly, *adv.* en chancelant ; avec hésitation
Staggers, *s.pl.* (*vet.*) vertigo, *m.*
Stagnancy, *s.* stagnation, *f.*
Stagnant, *adj.* stagnant, dormant ; croupissant ; (*dull*) dans un état de stagnation ; inactif ; mort
Stagnate, *v.n.* être stagnant, stagner, croupir ; (*of business,* &c.) être dans un état de stagnation ; être mort
Stagnation, *s.* stagnation, *f.*
Staid, *adj.* grave, posé, sérieux. —**ly,** *adv.* gravement, posément, sérieusement. —**ness,** *s.* gravité, *f.*, sérieux, *m.*
Stain, *v.a.* tacher, salir ('*with,*' de) ; (*disgrace*) souiller, entacher ; (*dye*) teindre ; (*wood,* &c.) mettre en couleur ; peindre ; imprimer ; — *s.* tache, *f.* ; (*blemish*) souillure, *f.* ; (*disgrace*) opprobre, *m.*, honte, *f.* ; (*colour*) couleur, teinte, *f.* —**less,** *adj.* sans tache, pur
Stained, *part. adj.* taché, &c. (*V.* **Stain,** *v.a.*) ; (*of glass*) de couleur ; (*of paper*) peint, de couleur
Stainer, *s.* teinturier, *m.*
Staining, *s.* teinture, *f.*; (*of wood*) coloration, *f.*
Stair, *s.* marche, *f.*, degré, *m.*; —**s,** *pl.*, escalier, *m.*, escaliers, *m.pl.* *Pair of —s,* escalier, *m.* *One pair of —s,* au premier. *Two pair of —s,* au second. *Above —s,* dans le salon, au salon. *Below —s,* dans (*or* à) la cuisine, à l'office. *Down —s,* en bas. *Up —s,* en haut. *To come* or *go down —s,* descendre, descendre l'escalier. *To come or go up —s,* monter, monter l'escalier. *To fall down —s,* rouler en bas des escaliers. — **carpet,** *s.* tapis d'escalier, chemin, *m.* — **case,** *s,* escalier, *m.* — **head,** *s.* haut de l'escalier, *m.* ; carré, palier, *m.* — **rod,** *s.* tringle de tapis d'escalier, *f.*
Staith, *s.* pont volant d'un quai aux vaisseaux, *m.*
Stake, *s.* (*post*) pieu, *m.* ; poteau, *m.* ; piquet, *m.* ; jalon, *m.* ; (*martyr's*) poteau, *m.*; (*funeral pile*) bûcher, *m.* ; (*at play*) enjeu, *m.*, mise, *f.*; (*prize*) prix, *m.* ; —**s,** *pl.* pieux, &c. ; (*in horse-racing*) enjeux, *m.pl.*, mises, *f.pl.* ; prix, *m.* *Our honour is at —,* il y va *or* il s'agit de notre honneur ; notre honneur est en jeu. *Life was at —,* il y allait *or* il s'agissait de la vie. *There were several interests at —,* il y avait plusieurs intérêts en jeu. — **holder,** *s.* dépositaire des mises, *m.f.* — **net,** *s.* avaloir, duit, guideau, congrier, congre, *m.*, tournée, *f.*
Stake, *v.a.* garnir de pieux ; soutenir avec des pieux ; marquer avec des poteaux ; (*at play*) mettre au jeu ; (*bet*) jouer, parier ; (*risk*) risquer, hasarder, exposer. — **out,** jalonner
Stalactite, *s.* stalactite, *f.*
Stalagmite, *s.* stalagmite, *f.*
Stalder, *s.* chantier, porte-fût, *m.* ; — *v.a.* mettre sur le chantier
Stale, *adj.* vieux ; (*trite*) suranné, usé ; (*of bread*) rassis ; (*of liquors*) éventé, plat ; — *s.* urine, *f.*, pissat, *m.* ; — *v.n.* uriner
Stalemate, *s.* pat, *m.* ; — *v.a.* faire pat
Staleness, *s.* vieillesse, *f.* ; (*triteness*) état suranné, *m.* ; banalité, *f.* ; (*of bread*) état rassis, *m.* ; (*of liquors*) évent, *m.*
Stalish, *adj.* un peu vieux *or* &c. (*V.* **Stale,** *adj.*)
Stalk, *s.* tige, *f.*; (*of plants*) tige, *f.* ; (*a shoot*) pied, *m.* ; (*of flowers and fruits*) pédoncule, *m.*, queue, *f.* ; (*of a leaf*) pétiole, *m.*, queue, *f.* ; (*of a cabbage*) trognon, *m.* ; (*of a bunch*) rafle, *f.*; (*of quills*) tuyau, *m.* ; (*of chimneys*) tuyau, *m.*, souche, *f.* ; (*walk*) démarche fière, *f.* ; — *v.n.* marcher fièrement, marcher à pas comptés, se carrer, se pavaner, se prélasser ; marcher ; (*hunt.*) se mettre à l'affût. —**less,** *adj.* sans tige *or* &c.
Stalked, *adj.* à tige
Stalker, *s.* personne à la démarche fière, *f.* ; (*hunt.*) chasseur à l'affût, *m.*
Stalking, *s.* (*hunt.*) chasse à l'affût, *f.* — **horse,** *s.* tonnelle, *f.*, cheval d'abri, *m.*, vache artificielle, *f.* ; (*fig.*) masque, prétexte, *m.*
Stalky, *adj.* comme une tige
Stall, *s.* (*of stables*) stalle, place, *f.* ; (*stable*) étable, *f.*; (*for sale of goods*) étalage, *m.* ; échoppe,

f.; boutique, *f.*; (*of butchers*) étal, *m.*; (*of churches, theatres*) stalle, *f.*; — *v.a.* établer. — **fed,** *adj.* nourri au fourrage. — **feeding,** *s.* nourrissage au fourrage, *m.*, pouture, *f.* — **food,** *s.* pouture, *f.* — **holder,** *s.* étalagiste, *m.f.*, échoppier, *m.*, -ière, *f.* — **keeper,** *s. V.* — **holder;** (*theat.*) placeur (*m.*, -euse, *f.*) de [stalles

Stallage, *s.* étalage, *m.*

Stalled, *adj.* (*in compounds*) à . . . stalle. *Two-* — *stable*, écurie à deux stalles

Stallion, *s.* étalon, *m.*

Stalwart, *adj.* robuste, vigoureux ; intrépide

Stamen, Stamina, *s.* base, *f.*; (*strength*) nerf, *m.*, force, vigueur, *f.*; (*bot.*) étamine, *f.*

Stamened, *adj.* étaminé, à étamines

Stamina. *V.* **Stamen**

Staminal, *adj.* staminal

Staminar, *adj.* staminaire

Staminate, *adj.* staminé

Staminiferous, *adj.* staminifère

Stammer, *v.a.n.* bégayer, balbutier

Stammerer, *s.* bègue, *m.f.*; (*fig.*) bredouilleur, *m.*, -euse, *f.*

Stammering, *s.* bégayement, bégaiement, *m.*; (*fig.*) bredouillement, *m.*; — *adj.* bègue; — *adv.* en bégayant; en balbutiant

Stammeringly, *adv. V.* **Stammering,** *adv.*

Stamp, *v.a.n.* (*with the foot*) frapper du pied; piétiner; trépigner; (*mark*) marquer, poinçonner; (*impress*) empreindre, imprimer; marquer; (*to complete*) mettre le sceau à; (*letters, papers,* &c.) timbrer; (*prepay letters,* &c.) affranchir, mettre un timbre à; (*to hall-mark gold, silver, to mark arms*) contrôler; (*goods*) estampiller; (*tickets,* &c.) poinçonner; (*weights and measures*) étalonner; (*cust.*) plomber; (*coin*) frapper; estamper; (*to pound*) piler, broyer; (*ore*) bocarder. *That —s him,* cela montre ce qu'il est. — **out,** (*cut out*) couper; (*fire*) éteindre; (*fig.*) étouffer, éteindre, écraser, détruire

Stamp, *s.* (*of the foot*) coup de pied, *m.*; piétinement, *m.*; trépignement, *m.*; (*instrument*) coin, poinçon, *m.*; (*for pounding*) pilon, *m.*; (*seal*) cachet, *m.*; (*impression*) empreinte, marque, *f.*; (*fig.*) sceau, cachet, *m.*; marque, empreinte, *f.*; (*on paper, admin., post.*) timbre, *m.*; (*postage-stamp*) timbre-poste, timbre, *m.*; (*stamped paper*) papier timbré, *m.*; (*hall-mark on gold, silver, mark on arms*) contrôle, *m.*; (*on goods*) estampille, *f.*; (*character*) caractère, genre, *m.*, espèce, *f.*, ordre, *m.*; (*pers.*) trempe, *f.*, calibre, *m.*; —**s,** *pl.* (*for ore*) bocard, *m.* *On a —,* sur papier timbré. *On receipt of —s,* contre envoi de timbres-poste. — **act,** *s.* loi sur le timbre, *f.* — **duty,** *s.* droit de timbre, *m.* — **head,** *s.* (*metal.*) pilon, *m.* — **office,** *s.* bureau de timbre, *m.*

Stampede, *s.* sauve qui peut, *m.*, débandade, *f.*; — *v.a.* effaroucher, mettre en fuite

Stamper, *s.* poinçon, *m.*; estampoir, *m.*; (*for pounding*) pilon, *m.*; (*for crushing ores*) bocard, *m.*; (*pers.*) poinçonneur, *m.*, -euse, *f.*, (*of letters,* &c.) timbreur, *m.*, (*government — on gold, silver, arms*) contrôleur, *m.*, (*of coin*) estampeur, *m.*

Stamping, *s.* (*with the feet*) coups de pied, *m.*; piétinement, *m.*; trépignement, *m.*; (*tech., V.* **Stamp,** *v.a.*) action de marquer, marque, *f.*; poinçonnage, poinçonnement, *m.*; timbrage, *m.*; affranchissement, *m.*; contrôlage, contrôlement, *m.*; estampillage, *m*; estampage, *m.*; étalonnage, étalonnement, *m.*; plombage, *m.*; pilage, broyage, broiement, *m.*; bocardage, *m.*; (*cutting out*) découpage, *m.* — **machine,** *s.* machine à poinçonner, poinçonneuse, *f.* — **mill,** *s.* moulin à pilons, *m.*; (*for crushing ores*) bocard, *m.* — **press,** *s.* presse à percussion, *f.*

Stanch, *adj.* solide, fort; ferme, inébranlable; vrai, zélé; (*hunt.*) sûr; — *v.a.* étancher, arrêter; (*to dress*) panser; — *v.n.* s'arrêter. — **less,** *adj.* impossible à étancher; insatiable. —**ness,** *s.* solidité, force, *f.*; fermeté, *f.*; [zèle, *m.*

Stanching, *s.* étanchement, *m.*

Stanchion, *s.* étançon, *m.*; (*nav.*) épontille, *f.*, étancon, *m.*

Stand, *v.n.* se tenir; (— *up*) se tenir debout; être debout; (*keep —ing*) rester debout; (— *unsupported*) se soutenir; (*be, be placed*) être; se trouver; être situé; (*stay, remain*) rester, demeurer, se tenir; stationner; (*place oneself*) se placer, se mettre; (*stop, delay*) s'arrêter; arrêter; (*last*) durer; subsister; (*resist*) résister (à), faire face (à); (*remain in force*) tenir, se maintenir; (*hold on: also of colours and bargains*) tenir; (*persist*) persister, persévérer; (*adhere*) adhérer (à); (*offer oneself*) se présenter; (*of the hair*) se dresser; (*of cabs, carriages*) stationner; (*of liquids*) reposer; (*soak in a liquid*) s'infuser, infuser; macérer; (*at cards*) s'y tenir; (*mil.*) faire halte; (*nav.*) porter; faire route, faire voile. — *!* halte! halte-là! — *and deliver!* la bourse ou la vie! *As it —s, as it stood, V.* **As** (— *it is*). *As the case —, as matters* (or *things* or *affairs*) —, dans l'état actuel des choses, au point où en sont les choses. *How do we —?* où en sommes-nous? (*at school*) quelles sont nos places? ... *how the case* (or *matter*) *—s, ... how matters —,* ... l'état des choses, ... ce qui en est. *To — looking,* rester à regarder. — **against,** être contre; tenir contre; résister à; faire face à; s'opposer à; combattre. — **aside,** se ranger; (*aloof*) se tenir à l'écart. — **away,** s'éloigner. — **back,** se tenir en arrière; (*move back*) reculer, se reculer; *int.* arrière! — **by,** être présent; être auprès, être tout près; (*defend*) défendre, soutenir, appuyer; (*abide*) s'en tenir à (— *by it,* s'y tenir); (*nav.*) se tenir prêt, être prêt. *To — by oneself,* être seul; se tenir à l'écart. — **close** *together,* serrez-vous un peu! — **down,** descendre. — **fair,** *V.* **Fair.** — **fast, firm,** tenir ferme *or* bon. — **for,** représenter; (*mean*) signifier, vouloir dire; (*an office,* &c.) être candidat pour, se mettre sur les rangs pour, se présenter pour; (*declare for*) se déclarer pour, être pour; défendre; (*nav.*) se diriger vers. — **forth, forward,** s'avancer, avancer; se présenter, s'offrir. — **from,** s'éloigner de. — **good,** *V.* **Hold good.** — **high** *as a,* être estimé comme. — **idle,** (*mach., com.*) chômer. — **in,** rentrer; (*cost*) coûter, revenir à; (*for*) se diriger (vers). — **off,** se tenir éloigné; se tenir à l'écart; (*nav.*) porter au large; (*a place at sea*) être à la hauteur de ...; (*mil.*) passer au large; *int.* au large! — **on,** (*nav.*) suivre la même route; (— *upon*) *V.* — **upon.** — **out,** (*project*) être en saillie, faire saillie, avancer; (*show off*) ressortir; se dessiner; (*resist*) résister (à), tenir bon (contre), faire tête (à); soutenir; (*move out*) s'ôter; se retirer; (*nav.*) porter au large, se tenir au large. — **over,** attendre; être ajourné, être remis. — **to,** soutenir; (*keep to*) s'en tenir à (— *to it,* s'y tenir); tenir à; (*nav.*) se diriger vers, faire route vers. — **together,** se tenir ensemble; (*agree*) s'accorder. — **up,** se tenir debout; (*upright*) se tenir droit; (*to rise*) se lever; (*of hair*) se dresser. — **up for,** se lever pour; (*defend*) tenir pour, défendre, soutenir, prendre le parti de. — **upon,** se tenir sur, être sur; s'appuyer sur, reposer sur; se baser sur; (*to pride in*) se prévaloir de; (*to value*) faire cas de; tenir à; (*to insist*) insister sur; (*ceremony*) faire (des cérémonies *or* des façons); (*trifles*) tenir à, s'arrêter à (des riens *or* des vétilles). — **upright,** se tenir droit; se tenir debout; se dresser. — **with,** s'accorder avec, être conforme à

Stand, *v.a.* (*bear*) supporter, souffrir, endurer; (*undergo*) subir, essuyer; (*defend*) défendre, maintenir; (*withstand*) soutenir; résister à; (*allow*) permettre, souffrir; (*have, as a chance,* &c.) avoir; (*run, as a risk*) courir; (*to place*) poser, mettre; (*treat, pay for*) payer. *To — treat,* régaler. *What a smoke! how can you —*

it? quelle fumée! comment pouvez-vous y tenir?

Stand, *s.* position, *f.*; place, *f.*; (*halt*) halte, pause, *f.*, arrêt, *m.*; (*of cabs*) station, place, *f.*; (*pedestal*) pied, dessous, *m.*; piédestal, *m.*; (*prop*) support, *m.*; (*for clocks, busts, vases*) socle, *m.*; (*for a parrot*) bâton, perchoir, *m.*; (*for a telescope*) affût, *m.*; (*of milliners*) champignon, *m.*; (*in compounds*) porte- . . ., *m.* (*V.* **Cask, Flower, Hat, Snuffers, Umbrella,** &c.); (*desk*) pupitre, *m.*; (*round table*) guéridon, *m.*; (*platform*) estrade, *f.*; tribune, *f.*; (*booth*) baraque, *f.*; gradins, *m.pl.*; (*race-stand*) tribunes, *f.pl.*; (*stall*) étalage, *m.*, boutique, *f.*; (*fig.*) résistance, *f.*; soulèvement, *m.*, levée, *f.*; difficulté, *f.*, embarras, *m.* — *of arms*, armement (d'un soldat), *m.* — *of colours*, (*mil.*) drapeaux, *m.pl.* *The grand —*, (*at races*) les tribunes, *f.pl.* *At a —*, (*fig.*) arrêté; (*of trade*) mort; (*in trouble*) dans l'embarras; (*at a loss*) au pied du mur. *To be brought to a —, to come to a —*, demeurer court; s'arrêter; être arrêté; (*stand idle*) chômer. *To make a —*, faire halte, faire une pause, s'arrêter; (*rise against*) se lever, se soulever (contre); (*resist*) opposer de la résistance (à), résister (à). *To make a good —*, bien résister, tenir bon, tenir ferme. *To put to a —*, embarrasser, mettre au pied du mur. *To take o.'s —*, prendre position; se placer; (*fig.*, '*upon*,' à) se tenir. — **point,** *s.* position, *f.*; principe, *m.*; point de vue, *m.* — **post,** *s.* poteau d'arrosement, *m.* — **still,** *s.* arrêt, *m.*; suspension, *f.*; impossibilité d'avancer, *f.*; inaction, *f.* *At a — still*, arrêté; suspendu; inactif. *To come to a — still*, s'arrêter; ne pouvoir plus avancer; ne savoir que faire; (*of trade*) être mort. — **up,** *adj.* (*of collars*, &c.) montant; droit; (*of fights*) en règle

Standard, *s.* (*ensign*) étendard, drapeau, *m.*; (*nav.*) pavillon, *m.*; (*best*) modèle, type, *m.*; (*of prices*) régulateur, *m.*; (*of weight, measure*) étalon, type, *m.*; (*of gold, silver*) titre, *m.*; (*fig.*) mesure, *f.*; degré, *m.*; (*height*) taille, *f.*; (*tech.*) support mobile, *m.*; (*of church-candles*) souche, *f.*; (*of trees*) arbre en plein vent, *m.*; (*bot.*) étendard, *m.*; — *adj.* type; (*of books, authors*) classique; (*of gold, silver*) au titre; (*of weight, measure*) type; légal; (*of prices, levers*, &c.) régulateur; (*of trees*) en plein vent; (*fig.*) régulateur. — **bearer,** *s.* porte-étendard, porte-drapeau, *m.* — **peach,** *s.* pêche de vigne, *f.*

Standing, *adj.* debout; sur pied; placé; fixe; permanent; constant; invariable; perpétuel; éternel; ordinaire, établi, de tous les jours, de fondation; (*of water*) dormant, stagnant; (*of colours*) solide, bon teint; (*of rigging*) dormant; (*having a foot, tech.*) à pied; — *s.* durée, date, *f.*; exercice, *m.*; service, *m.*; place, *f.*; rang, *m.*, position, *f.*; (*posture*) pose, *f.*; (*booth, stall*, &c.) *V.* **Stand.** *Of long —*, de longue date, d'ancienne date, de vieille date. — **army,** *s.* armée permanente, *f.* — (or *growing*) **corn** *or* **crops,** *V.* **Growing.** — **form** *or* **forme,** *s.* (*print.*) conservation, *f.* — **orders,** *s.pl.* (*mil.*) ordre permanent, *m.*; (*parl.*) règlement, *m.* — **out,** *s.* résistance, *f.* — **part,** *s.* dormant, *m.* — **room,** *s.* place pour se tenir debout, *f.* — **stone,** *s.* pierre levée, *f.*, pelvan, *m.* — **vice,** *s.* (*tech.*) étau à pied, *m.*

Stannary, *s.* mine d'étain, *f.*; — *adj.* des mines d'étain

Stannate, *s.* stannate, *m.*

Stannic, *adj.* stannique

Stanniferous, *adj.* stannifère

Stannous, *adj.* stanneux

Staphylinus, *s.* staphylin, *m.*

Staphyloma, *s.* staphylôme, *m.*

Stanza, *s.* stance, strophe, *f.*, couplet, *m.*

Staple, *s.* entrepôt, *m.*; (*production*) produit principal, *m.*, denrée principale, *f.*; (*fig.*) objet (*or* sujet) principal, fond, *m.*; (*of land*) qualité, *f.*; (*of wool*, &c.) brin, *m.*; (*of cotton*, &c.) soie, *f.*; (*of locks*) gâche, *f.*; — *adj.* établi, fixe; principal

Stapled, *adj.* (*in compounds*) à brin . . .; à . . . soie

Star, *s.* étoile, *f.*; astre, *m.*; (*fig.*) étoile, *f.*; (*pers.*) astre, *m.*, célébrité, *f.*; (*performer*) étoile, célébrité, *f.*, grand artiste, *m.*, grande artiste, *f.*; (*badge*) croix, plaque, décoration, *f.*, crachat, *m.*; (*print.*) étoile, *f.*, astérisque, *m.*; — *v.a.* étoiler; (*stud*) parsemer; — *v.n.* briller comme une étoile; (— *it*) jouer brillamment, brûler les planches; jouer. — *of Bethlehem*, ornithogale, *m.* *Three —s*, (*print.*) trois étoiles. *The seven —s*, (*astr.*) la Pléiade, *f.*, les Pléiades, *f.pl.* — **chamber,** *s.* chambre étoilée, *f.* — **fish,** *s.* étoile de mer, astérie, *f.* — **fort,** *s.* fort à étoile, *m.* — **gazer,** *s.* astrologue, *m.*; astronome, *m.*; (*fish*) uranoscope, *m.* — **gazing,** *s.* astrologie, *f.*; astronomie, *f.* — **jelly,** *s.* nostoc, *m.* — **less,** *adj.* sans étoiles. — **light,** *s.* lumière *or* clarté des étoiles, *f.*; *adj.* étoilé. —**like,** *V.* **Starry.** —**lit,** *adj.* étoilé, éclairé par les étoiles. — **lizard,** *s.* stellion, *m.* —**nose,** *s.* (*zool.*) condylure, *m.* — **room,** *s.* (*theat.*) loge (d'acteur *or* d'actrice *or* d'artiste), *f.* — **shoot, -shot,** *s.* nostoc, *m.* — **stone,** *s.* astérie, *f.* — **thistle,** *s.* chausse-trappe, *f.* — — **wheel,** *s.* étoile, *f.* — **wort,** *s.* aster, *m.*

Starboard, *s.* tribord, *m.*; — *adj.* de tribord; — *adv.* tribord. *Hard a —*, tout à tribord

Starch, *s.* amidon, *m.*; (*diluted for stiffening linen*, &c.) empois, *m.*; (*fig.*) raideur, *f.*; — *v.a.* amidonner; (*stiffen, as linen, and fig.*) empeser. — **maker, -manufacturer,** *s.* amidonnier, *m.*, -ière, *f.* — **making, -manufacture, -works,** *s.* amidonnerie, *f.*

Starchedness, *s.* raideur, *f.*

Starcher, *s.* empeseur, *m.*, -euse, *f.*

Starchy, *adj.* empesé; (*chem.*) amilacé

Stare, *v.n.* regarder fixement; (*from astonishment*) ouvrir de grands yeux; (*stand out*) avancer, s'avancer; (*of hair*) se hérisser; — *s.* regard fixe, *m.*; yeux effarés, *m.pl.*; (— *of astonishment or amazement*) regard ébahi, *m.* — **at,** regarder fixement, fixer; regarder; (*in amazement*) ouvrir de grands yeux à. — *in the face*, crever les yeux à; (*pers.*) regarder en face. — *right in the face*, (*pers.*) regarder dans le blanc des yeux, dévisager. — *out of countenance*, faire baisser les yeux à, faire perdre contenance à, dévisager. *Ruin —s us in the face!* la ruine est là!

Staring, *adj.* qui regarde fixement; (*things*) éclatant, voyant; (*of hair*) hérissé. *A — coat*, le poil hérissé, *m.*

Staringly, *adv.* fixement

Stark, *adv.* tout à fait, tout, entièrement, complètement; — *adj.* vrai, franc, pur; (*strong*) fort; (*stiff*) raide. — *mad*, — *staring mad*, tout à fait fou, fou à lier. — *naked*, tout nu, entièrement nu, nu comme un ver, nu comme la main

Starling, *s.* sansonnet, étourneau, *m.*; (*of a bridge*) (*upper —*) avant-bec, brise-glace, *m.*, (*lower —*) arrière-bec, *m.*; —**s,** *pl.* (*of a bridge*) fraisement, *m.*, fraise, *f.*

Starred, *adj.* étoilé; parsemé d'étoiles; parsemé (de . . .); (*in compounds*) né sous une étoile . . .

Starry, *adj.* étoilé; des étoiles; (*bright*) étincelant, brillant, rayonnant

Start, *v.n.* (*thrill*) tressaillir ('*with*,' de; '*at*,' à); (*set out*) partir; (*rise*) se lever; (*leap*) sauter, bondir, s'élancer; (*deviate*) s'écarter (de), s'éloigner (de); (*begin*) commencer, débuter. — **aside,** se jeter de côté, faire un écart. — **back,** se jeter en arrière, reculer. — **off,** partir. — **out,** sortir précipitamment (*V.* **Sleep**). — **up,** se lever précipitamment; s'élever tout à coup; (*appear suddenly*) apparaître, surgir, naître; (— *out of o.'s sleep*) se réveiller en sursaut

Start, *v.a.* alarmer; (*startle*) faire tressaillir;

(*send off*) faire partir; (*produce*) produire. mettre en avant; faire naître; inventer, découvrir; (*a question*) soulever, mettre sur le tapis; (*a difficulty, a quarrel*) soulever; (*a doubt*) élever; (*an opinion*) émettre, avancer; (*game*) lancer, faire lever, faire partir, débûcher; (*a pers.*) lancer dans le monde; (*mach.*) mettre en marche; (*a cask*) défoncer

Start, *s.* (*thrill*) tressaillement, *m.*; (*spring*) saut, bond, *m.*; (*from*) écart, *m.*; (*sally*) élan, *m.*; (*first motion*) premier pas, *m.*; (*beginning*) commencement, début, *m.*; (*departure*) départ, *m.*; (*way in advance*) avance ('*of*,' sur), *f.* *False* —, faux départ *By —s*, par sauts; (*fig.*) par boutades; à bâtons rompus. *To get the — of*, devancer, prendre les devants sur. *To have the — of*, avoir l'avance (*or* de l'avance) sur. *To wake with a* —, se réveiller en sursaut

Starter, *s.* inventeur, auteur, *m.*; celui qui soulève une question, *m.*; (*in races*) starter, celui qui donne le signal du départ, *m.*; (*rail.*) sous-chef de gare, *m.*

Starting, *s.* (*thrilling*) tressaillement, *m.*; (*departure*) départ, *m.*; (*beginning*) commencement, début, *m.*; (*of machines*) mise en marche, mise en train, *f.* — **point,** *s.* point de départ, *m.* — **post,** *s.* poteau de départ, *m.*, barrière, *f.* [tades, à bâtons rompus

Startingly, *adv.* par élans; (*fig.*) par bou-

Startle, *v.a.* faire tressaillir; faire frémir; épouvanter; effraver; alarmer; frapper; saisir; étonner; (*from sleep*) réveiller (*V.* **Sleep**); — *v.n.* tressaillir; frémir; s'effrayer; s'alarmer; — *s.* tressaillement, *m.*; frémissement, *m.*; saisissement, *m.*; effroi, *m.*; alarme, *f.*

Startling, *adj.* éclatant; foudroyant; renversant; étourdissant; saisissant; frappant

Starvation, *s.* inanition, faim, *f.*; famine, *f.*; besoin, dénûment, *m.*

Starve, *v.a.* (*with hunger, — out, — to death*) faire mourir de faim, affamer; (*subdue*) réduire par la faim *or* par la famine; (*with cold*) faire mourir de froid; (*fig.*) réduire; — *v.n.* (*with hunger*) mourir de faim *or* d'inanition; (*with cold*) mourir de froid; (*fig.*) languir. *To be —d*, (*with hunger*) mourir de faim; (*with cold*) mourir de froid

Starveling, *s. adj.* affamé, *m.*, e, *f.*, famélique, *m.f.*; (*fam.*) meurt-de-faim, *m.f.*

Starving, *adj.* mourant de faim, qui meurt de faim, affamé

State, *s.* état, *m.*; condition, *f.*; situation, *f.*; disposition, *f.*; ordre, *m.*, classe, *f.*; rang, *m.*; pompe, *f.*, apparat, *m.*; dignité, grandeur, *f.*; (*government*) état, État, *m.*; — *adj.* d'état; d'apparat; de gala; de cour; d'honneur; officiel. *—s general*, états généraux, *m.pl.* — *of life*, existence, *f.* *Bed of* —, lit de parade, *m.* *Chair of* —, fauteuil d'apparat, trône, *m.* *Robes of* —, costume d'apparat, *m.* *In* —, en grande cérémonie, en grand apparat; en grand cortége. *In a — of*, en état de; dans un état de; dans. *Lying in* —, exposition, *f.* *To lie in* —, être exposé sur un lit de parade. — **affairs,** *s.pl.* affaires d'état, *f.pl.* — **ball,** *s.* bal de la cour, grand bal officiel, *m.* — **bed,** *s.* lit de parade, *m.* — **cabin,** *s.* grand salon, *m.* — **carriage,** *s.* voiture de gala, voiture de cérémonie officielle, voiture d'apparat, *f.* — **court,** *s.* cour d'honneur, *f.* —**craft,** *s.* politique, *f.* — **dinner,** *s.* dîner de gala, grand dîner officiel, dîner d'apparat, *m.* — **house,** *s.* salle des États, *f.* — **paper,** *s.* papier d'état, document officiel, *m.* — **performance,** *s.* représentation de gala, *f.* — **prison,** *s.* prison d'état, *m.* — **prisoner,** *s.* prisonnier d'état, détenu politique, *m.* — **robes,** *s.pl.* costume d'apparat, *m.* — **room,** *s.* salle de réception, *f.* —**sman,** &c. *See below.* — **trials,** *s.pl.* procès politiques, *m.pl.*

State, *v.a.* exposer, dire; avancer, prétendre, affirmer; assurer; déclarer; constater; poser; annoncer, faire connaître; (*of witnesses in court*) déposer (de, que); (*of writings*) porter (que); (*relate*) rapporter; (*set*) fixer, arrêter, régler; (*math.*) poser

Stated, *part.* exposé, &c. (*V.* **State,** *v.a.*); — *adj.* fixe; établi; réglé; déterminé; certain

Statedly, *adv.* régulièrement

Stateliness, *s.* grandeur, *f.*; dignité, *f.*; apparat, *m.*; pompe, *f.*; ostentation, *f.*

Stately, *adj.* imposant, majestueux; magnifique; princier; noble, plein de dignité; pompeux; fastueux; — *adv.* majestueusement

Statement, *s.* exposé, énoncé, compte-rendu, compte, *m.*; récit, *m.*; rapport, *m.*; exposition, *f.*; déclaration, *f.*; assertion, *f.*, dire, *m.*; affirmation, *f.*; (*of a witness in court*) déposition, déclaration, *f.*; (*of accounts*) relevé (de compte), *m.*, situation, *f.* *According to the — of . . .*, à ce que dit . . ., au dire de . . .

Statesman, *s.* homme d'état, *m.* —**like,** *adj.* d'homme d'état. —**ship,** *s.* politique, science du gouvernement, *f.*

Stat-ic, al, -ically. *V.* page 3, § 1

Statice, *s.* (*bot.*) statice, *f.*

Statics, *s.pl.* statique, *f.*

Station, *s.* station, *f.*; poste, *m.*; place, *f.*; position, condition, *f.*, rang, *m.*; (*com.*) dépôt, *m.*; (*of public vehicles, of missionaries, church,* &c., *Cath.rel., build., astr., math., surveying, telegraphs, and nav.*) station, *f.*; (*rail.*) station, *f.*; (*terminus, and also goods* —) gare, *f.*; (*mil., police*) poste, *m.*; (*of a fire-brigade*) caserne (de sapeurs-pompiers), *f.*; — *v.a.* placer; (*mil.*) poster; (*a sentry*) poser. — *in life*, position sociale, *f.* *Principal* —, (*of fire-brigade*) état-major (des sapeurs-pompiers), *m.* *To take o.'s* —, se placer; se poster. — **clerk,** *s.* chef de station, *m.* — **house,** *s.* (*military*) poste, *m.*; (*police*) *V.* **Police-station.** — **master, -superintendent,** *s.* (*com.*) chef de dépôt, *m.*; (*rail.*) chef de gare, chef de station, *m.*

Stational, *adj.* de station; de poste. — *church*, église stationnale, *f.*

Stationary, *adj.* (*at a stand*) stationnaire; (*of engines,* &c.) fixe, à demeure

Stationer, *s.* papetier, *m.*; (*wholesale*) marchand de papier, *m.* —**s' hall,** *s.* dépôt de la librairie, *m.* *Entered at —s' hall*, déposé

Stationery, *s.* papeterie, *f.*; (*office* —) fournitures de bureau, *f.pl.*; — *adj.* de papeterie; de papetier. — **binding,** *s.* confection de registres, *f.* — **box, -case,** *s.* papeterie, *f.*

Statism, *s.* politique, *f.*

Statist, *s.* homme d'état, politique, *m.*; publiciste, *m.*; statisticien, *m.*

Statist-ic, al, -ically. *V.* page 3, § 1

Statistician, *s.* statisticien, *m.*, -ne, *f.*

Statistics, *s.pl.* statistique, *f.*

Statuary, *s.* (*art*) statuaire, *f.*, sculpture, *f.*; (*pers.*) statuaire, *m.*; — *adj.* statuaire (*m.f.*)

Statu quo, *s.* statu quo, *m.*

Statue, *s.* statue, *f.*

Statuette, *s.* statuette, *f.*

Stature, *s.* stature, taille, *f.*

Status, *s.* position, *f.*, rang, *m.*; état, *m.*; condition, *f.* — **quo,** *s.* statu quo, *m.*

Statutable, *adj.* prévu par la loi [*or* à la loi

Statutably, *adv.* conformément aux statuts

Statute, *s.* statut, *m.*; loi, *f.* — **book,** *s.* bulletin des lois, *m.* — **fair,** *s.* fête de campagne, *f.* — **labour,** *s.* corvée, *f.* — **law,** *s.* droit écrit, *m.* — **work,** *s.* corvée, *f.*

Statutorily, *adv.* statutairement

Statutory, *adj.* établi par des statuts, statutaire; établi par la loi; (*of offences*) prévu par [la loi

Staunch. *V.* **Stanch**

Stave, *s.* (*of casks*) douve, *f.*; (*of psalms*) verset, *m.*; (*mus.*) portée, *f.*; — *v.a.* (— *in*) briser, crever, enfoncer; (*a cask*) défoncer. — **off,** repousser, éloigner, écarter; empêcher; (*defer*) différer, retarder

Staves, *s.pl.* (*pl. of* **Stave** & *of* **Staff**)

Stavesacre, *s.* staphisaigre, *f.*

Stay, *v.n.* rester; demeurer; séjourner; continuer; (*wait*) attendre; (*stop*) s'arrêter; (*rest*) s'appuyer; — *v.a.* arrêter, retenir; modérer, réprimer, contenir; retarder; (*hinder*) empêcher (de), détourner (de); (*prop up*) étayer. *To — o.'s stomach,* apaiser la grosse faim. — **-at-home,** *adj. s.* casanier, *m.*, -ière, *f.* — **away,** s'absenter, s'éloigner. — **for,** attendre. — **in,** rester chez soi, rester à la maison, ne pas sortir; garder la chambre; (*as school-punishment*) rester en retenue, être en retenue; être consigné. — **up,** veiller

Stay, *s.* séjour, *m.*; visite, *f.*; (*fixed state*) stabilité, fixité, *f.*; (*a prop*) étai, appui, soutien, *m.*; (*a brace*) bride, *f.*; (*nav.*) étai, *m.*; —**s,** *pl.* (*a female's*) corset, *m.*, (*more than one pair*) corsets, *m.pl.* *A pair of —s,* un corset. *Back —,* (*nav.*) galhauban, *m.* — **lace,** *s.* lacet, *m.* — **maker,** *s.* corsetier, *m.*, -ière, *f.* — **sail,** *s.* voile d'étai, *f.*; foc, *m.* — **supporter,** *s.* étançon, *m.*

Stead, *s.* lieu, *m.*, place, *f.*; utilité, *f.*, profit, avantage, *m.*; — *v.a.* tenir lieu de, remplacer; être utile à, servir; aider. *To stand* (...) *in —,* être utile *or* avantageux (à ...), rendre service (à ...), servir (...). *In my —,* à ma place. *To stand in — of,* tenir lieu de. *To stand* (...) *in good —,* être très utile (à ...), être d'un grand secours (à ...)

Steadfast, *adj.* solide; ferme; fixe; stable; constant; résolu. —**ly,** *adv.* fermement; avec constance. —**ness,** *s.* stabilité, *f.*; solidité, *f.*; fermeté, *f.*; constance, *f.*

Steadily, *adv.* fermement, avec fermeté; avec constance; avec persévérance; régulièrement; sans s'arrêter; toujours; (*of conduct*) d'une manière rangée; sagement

Steadiness, *s.* fermeté, *f.*; constance, *f.*; (*pers.*) conduite rangée, sagesse, régularité, *f.*

Steady, *adj.* ferme; solide; fixe; sûr; assuré; constant; continu; régulier; (*fastened*) assujetti; (*of the wind*) fait, étale; (*pers.*) rangé, tranquille, sage; assidu; — *v.a.* affermir; assurer; (*fasten*) assujettir; —*! int.* restez tranquille! doucement! (*mil.*) fixe! (*nav.: of hoisting,* &c.) doucement! (*of steering*) comme ça! — *hand,* main sûre, *f.* *To keep —,* maintenir; (*fasten*) assujettir; (*not to move*) ne pas bouger, rester tranquille [(*beef —*) bifteck, *m.*

Steak, *s.* tranche, *f.*; (*broiled*) grillade *f.*;

Steal, *v.a.n.* voler, dérober ('*from,*' '*out of,*': *pers.,* à; *things,* dans); (*fig.*) dérober (à); (*gain, win*) gagner, séduire; (*a march*) dérober (à), gagner (sur); (*slip*) se glisser; s'insinuer, s'introduire. — **away, off,** se dérober, s'esquiver. — **down,** descendre furtivement *or* à la dérobée; (*o.'s cheek*) couler furtivement (le long de). — **in,** entrer furtivement *or* à la dérobée; se glisser dans. — **on,** avancer insensiblement; se glisser; gagner. — **out,** sortir furtivement *or* à la dérobée. — **up,** monter furtivement *or* à la dérobée. — **upon,** surprendre

Stealer, *s.* voleur, *m.*, -euse, *f.* (de ...)

Stealing, *s.* vol, *m.* [tivement

Stealth, *s.* vol, *m.* *By —,* à la dérobée, furtivement

Stealthily, *adv.* à la dérobée, furtivement

Stealthy, *adj.* furtif, dérobé

Steam, *s.* vapeur, *f.* *By —,* à la vapeur. *With the — on,* en vapeur. *With all the — on,* en pleine vapeur. *The — is up,* on est en pleine vapeur. *To put on the —, to get up the —,* chauffer, mettre en vapeur; (*fig.*) se mettre en train; se presser. — *boat* (*-boiler, -coal, -packet, -plough, -vessel,* &c.), bateau (*m.*, chaudière, *f.*, charbon, *m.*, paquebot, *m.*, charrue, *f.*, bâtiment *or* navire, *m.*, &c.) à vapeur. — *engine,* machine à vapeur, *f.*; (*pump for extinguishing fires,* &c.) pompe à vapeur, *f.* — *gauge,* manomètre, *m.* — *locomotion,* — *navigation,* — *cultivation,* locomotion, navigation, culture à la vapeur, *f.* — *power,* force de la vapeur, *f.* (*By — power,* à la vapeur). — *roller,* rouleau compresseur à vapeur, *m.* — *tight,* imperméable à la vapeur

Steam, *v.n.* jeter de la vapeur; (*smoke*) fumer; (*navigate*) naviguer *or* aller à la vapeur; (*to*) se diriger (vers); (*into*) entrer (dans); (*out of*) sortir (de); — *v.a.* passer à la vapeur; (*cook.*) cuire à la vapeur. — **away,** s'évaporer; (*move away*) s'éloigner. — **back,** (*go back*) retourner; (*come back*) revenir. — **down,** descendre. — **in,** entrer. — **off,** s'éloigner. — **out,** sortir (de). — **up,** jeter *or* lancer de la vapeur; (*go or come up*) remonter

Steamer, *s.* machine à vapeur, *f.*; (*boat, ship*) bateau à vapeur, vapeur, steamer, *m.*; (*cook.*) appareil de cuisson à la vapeur, *m.*, marmite à vapeur, *f.*

Steaming, *part.* *V.* **Steam,** *v.a.n.*; — *adj.* qui s'évapore; fumant; — *s.* (*cook.*) cuisson à la vapeur, *f.* — **apparatus,** *s.* appareil de cuisson à la vapeur, *m.*

Stearaffine, *s.* stéaraffine, *f.*

Stearate, *s.* stéarate, *m.*

Stearic, *adj.* stéarique

Stearine, *s.* stéarine, *f.*

Steatite, *s.* stéatite, *f.*

Steed, *s.* coursier, *m.*

Steel, *s.* acier, *m.*; (*weapon*) fer, *m.*, épée, lame, *f.*; (*to strike a light with*) briquet, *m.*; (*for sharpening knives*) fusil, *m.*; (*pharm., fig.*) fer, *m.*; — *adj.* d'acier; (*fig.*) de fer, dur; (*pharm.*) ferrugineux, chalybé; — *v.a.* acérer; (*sharpen*) aiguiser; (*harden*) endurcir; (*fortify*) armer. — **engraver (-engraving),** *s.* graveur (*m.*, gravure, *f.*) sur acier. — **pen,** *s.* plume de fer, plume d'acier, plume métallique, *f.* — **pills,** *s.pl.* pilules ferrugineuses, *f.pl.* — **toys,** *s.pl.* bijouterie d'acier, *f.* — **wine,** *s.* vin chalybé, vin ferrugineux, *m.* — **wire,** *s.* fil d'acier, *m.* — **works,** *s.pl.* aciérie, *f.* — **yard,** *s.* romaine, *f.*; peson, *m.*

Steeliness, *s.* dureté de l'acier, *f.*; (*fig.*) dureté, insensibilité, *f.*

Steely, *adj.* d'acier; (*fig.*) de fer, dur; opiniâtre; (*of iron, iron ore*) acérain

Steep, *adj.* escarpé, raide, rude; (*of staircases,* &c.) raide; (*nav.*) à pic; — *s.* escarpement, *m.*; précipice, *m.*; — *v.a.* tremper; infuser; plonger; (*fill with*) abreuver (de)

Steeple, *s.* clocher, *m.* — **chase,** *s.* steeple-chase, *m.*, course au clocher, *f.*

Steepled, *adj.* à clocher

Steepness, *s.* raideur, *f.*, escarpement, *m.*

Steer, *s.* jeune bœuf, bouvillon, *m.*; — *v.a.n.* gouverner; (*a course*) diriger, conduire; suivre; (*fig.*) se diriger, se gouverner; manœuvrer

Steerage, *s.* timonerie, *f.*; (*fig.*) direction, *f.*, gouvernement, *m.* — **passenger,** *s.* passager (*m.*, -ère, *f.*) d'entrepont *or* de troisième classe. — **way,** *s.* sillage, *m.*

Steering, *s.* gouvernement, *m.*, gouverne, *f.* — **wheel,** *s.* roue de (*or* du) gouvernail, *f.*

Steersman, *s.* timonier, *m.*

Steganograph, -y, &c. *V.* *French-English part, and page* 3, § 1

Stellar, Stellary, *adj.* stellaire

Stellate, Stellated, *adj.* étoilé; (*bot.*) radié

Stelliform, *adj.* stelliforme

Stellio, Stellion, *s.* stellion, *m.*

Stem, *s.* tige, *f.*; (*of a family*) souche, *f.*, tronc, *m.*; (*race*) rejeton, *m.*, branche, *f.*; (*of plants*) tige, *f.*; (*of flowers and fruits*) pédoncule, *m.*, queue, *f.*; (*of a leaf*) pétiole, *m.*, queue, *f.*; (*of tobacco-leaves*) côte, *f.*; (*of a bunch*) râfle, *f.*; (*of a quill, of a tobacco-pipe*) tuyau, *m.*; (*of mus. notes*) queue, *f.*; (*of a ship*) avant, *m.*, proue, étrave, *f.*; — *v.a.* aller contre; lutter contre; résister à; s'opposer à; arrêter; refouler; vaincre; (*tobacco*) écôter. *From — to stern,* de l'avant à l'arrière. —**less,** *adj.* sans tige *or* &c.

Stemson, *s.* (*nav.*) marsouin d'avant, m.
Stench, *s.* puanteur, mauvaise odeur, infection, *f.* — **trap,** *s.* valve contre les émanations, *f.*
Stencil, *s.* patron, *m.*; — *v.a.* peindre *or* imprimer *or* marquer au patron, patronner; égratigner. — **plate,** *s.* patron, *m.*
Stenciller, *s.* égratigneur, *m.*, -euse, *f.*
Stenograph, *v.a.* sténographier
Stenographer, *s.* sténographe, *m.*
Stenographic, -al, *adj.* (*things*) sténographique; (*pers.*) sténographe
Stenographically, *adv.* sténographiquement
Stenography, *s.* sténographie, *f.*
Stentor, *s.* Stentor, *m.*; (*zool.*) *V.* **Howler**
Stentorian, *adj.* de Stentor
Step, *v.n.* (*move*) faire un pas; (*go, walk*) marcher, aller; passer; se mettre; (*come*) venir; (*into a carriage*) monter; (*out of a carriage*) descendre; — *v.a.* (*measure*) arpenter. — **after,** courir après; suivre; rappeler. — **aside,** se ranger; s'écarter. — **back,** reculer; (*return*) rebrousser chemin, revenir sur ses pas. — **backward,** reculer. — **down,** descendre; (*to*) aller (à), venir (à). — **forth, forward,** s'avancer. — **in,** entrer; (*into a carriage*) monter; (*come*) venir; (*interfere*) intervenir. — **into,** entrer dans; (*a carriage*) monter dans; (*come*) venir dans; (*interfere*) intervenir dans. — **on, upon,** marcher sur, fouler. — **out,** sortir; (*from a carriage*) descendre; (*walk fast*) allonger le pas. — **over,** traverser, franchir; (*stride across*) enjamber. — **round,** faire le tour (de). — **up,** monter; (*come near*) s'approcher, s'avancer; (*go*) aller (*come*) venir
Step, *s.* (*pace, footstep*) pas, *m.*; (*stair*) marche, *f.*; degré, gradin, *m.*; (*gait*) démarche, *f.*; (*progression*) progrès, acheminement, pas, *m.*; mouvement, *m.*; (*improvement*) progrès, *m.*; (*measure*) démarche, *f.*; mesure, *f.*; pas, *m.*; manœuvre, *f.*; (*of carriages*) marchepied, *m.*; (*threshold*) pas, seuil, *m.*; (*of ladders*) échelon, *m.*; (*of machines*) piédestal, *m.*; (*of a mast*) emplanture, *f.*; —**s,** *pl.* pas, *m.pl.*, &c.; (*of beds*) escabeau, *m.*; (*ladder*) échelle, *f.*; (*flight of stone —s*) escalier de pierre, *m.*; (*of gardens*) perron, *m.*; (*of a carriage*) marchepied, *m.* *A good —,* un bon bout de chemin, loin. *A — in the right direction,* une bonne démarche. *Pair of —s,* échelle double, *f.* — *by —,* pas à pas. *By his —,* à son pas. *By —s,* successivement. *To keep —,* être au pas. *To keep — with, V.* **Pace.** *To take a —,* faire un pas; (*fig.*) faire une démarche; prendre un parti. *To take —s,* faire des démarches; prendre des mesures. *To tread in anyone's —s,* aller *or* courir sur les brisées (*or* sur le marché) de quelqu'un. — **aunt,** *s.* belle-tante, *f.* — **board,** *s.* (*rail.*) banquette, *f.* — **brother,** *s.* beau-frère, *m.* — **child,** *s.* beau-fils, *m.*, belle-fille, *f.* — **daughter,** *s.* belle-fille, *f.* — **father,** *s.* beau-père, *m.* — **mother,** *s.* belle-mère, *f.*; (*in a bad sense*) marâtre, *f.* — **sister,** *s.* belle-sœur, *f.* — **son,** *s.* beau-fils, *m.* — **uncle,** *s.* [bel-oncle, *m.*
Steppe, *s.* steppe, *m.f.*
Stepper, *s.* cheval qui a de l'action, *m.* *High —,* steppeur, *m.*
Stepping-stone, *s.* marchepied, *m.*; préparation, introduction, *f.*
Stercoraceous, *adj.* stercoraire
Stercoral, *adj.* stercoral
Stercorary, *adj.* stercoraire
Stercoration, *s.* stercoration, *f.*
Stere, *s.* stère, *m.* [&c. (*V.* page 3, § 1)
Stereo, (*in compounds*) stéréo ... —**graphy,**
Stereoscope, *s.* stéréoscope, *m.*
Stereoscopic, *adj.*, &c. stéréoscopique, &c. (*V.* page 3, § 1)
Stereotype, *s.* cliché, *m.*; (*art*) clichage, *m.*; — *adj.* stéréotype, stéréotypé, cliché; — *v.a.* stéréotyper, clicher. — **founder,** *s.* stéréotypeur, clicheur, *m.* — **foundry,** *s.* stéréotypie, clicherie, *f.* — **plate,** *s.* cliché, *m.* — **printing,** *s.* stéréotypie, *f.* — **printing-office,** *s.* stéréotypie, *f.*
Stereotyper, *s.* stéréotypeur, clicheur, *m.*
Stereotypic, *adj.* stéréotypique
Stereotyping, *s.* (*act*) stéréotypage, clichage, *m.*; (*art*) stéréotypie, clicherie, *f.*, clichage, *m.*
Stereotypographer, *s.* stéréotypeur, *m.*
Stereotypography, Stereotypy, *s.* stéréotypie, *f.*
Sterile, Sterility. *V* **Barren, Barrenness**
Sterilization, *s.* stérilisation, *f.*
Sterilize, *v.a.* stériliser
Sterlet, *s.* sterlet, *m.* [solide
Sterling, *adj.* sterling; (*fig.*) vrai, pur, réel,
Stern, *adj.* sévère; austère; rigide; (*harsh*) dur, rude; (*cross*) rébarbatif; — *s.* (*nav.*) arrière, *m.*, poupe, *f.* — **cable,** *s.* croupière, *f.* — **chaser,** *s.* canon de retraite, *m.* — **fast,** *s.* croupière, *f.* — **frame,** *s.* arcasse, *f.* —**most,** *adj. See below.* — **port,** *s.* sabord de retraite, *m.* — **post,** *s.* étambot, *m.* — **sheets,** *s.pl.* arrière, *m.* — **way,** *s.* culée, *f.*
Sternal, *adj.* sternal
Sterned, *adj.* à poupe ...
Sternly, *adv.* sévèrement; rigidement; durement, rudement; d'une manière rébarbative
Sternmost, *adj.* le plus en arrière, en serre-file. —**ship,** *s.* serre-file, *m.*
Sternness, *s.* sévérité, *f.*; dureté, *f.*
Sternum, *s.* sternum, *m.* [ment, *m.*
Sternutation, *s.* sternutation, *f.*, éternuement
Sternutative, *adj.* sternutatif
Sternutatory, Sternutory, *adj.* *s.* sternutatoire, *adj. m.f.*, *s.m.*
Stertorous, *adj.* stertoreux
Stet, (*print.*) bon
Stethometer, *s.* stéthomètre, *m.*
Stethoscope, *s.* stéthoscope, *m.*
Stethoscopic, -al, *adj.* stéthoscopique
Stethoscopically, *adv.* stéthoscopiquement
Stethoscopy, *s.* stéthoscopie, *f.*
Stevedore, *s.* arrimeur, *m.*
Stew, *v.a.* mettre en ragoût; (*fruit*) mettre en compote; (*cook.*) étuver, cuire à l'étuvée; — *v.n.* cuire à l'étuvée; (*pers.*) étouffer, cuire dans sa peau, cuire dans son jus. — **down,** *v.a.* réduire
Stew, *s.* (*cook.*) ragoût, *m.*, étuvée, *f.*; (*of hare*) civet, *m.*; (*of rabbit*) gibelotte, *f.*; (*of fish*) matelote, *f.*; (*of fruit*) compote, *f.*; (*funk*) venette, *f.*, trac, *m.*, suée, *f.*; (*place*) étuve, *f.*; (*pond*) vivier, *m.*; (*bad house*) maison publique, *f.*, maison, (*f.*) *or* lieu (*m.*) de prostitution. *Irish —,* haricot de mouton, *m.* *To be in a —,* être sur les charbons; avoir la venette, avoir le trac. — **pan,** *s.* casserole, *f.*; poêlon, *m.*; bassine, *f.*
Steward, *s.* maître d'hôtel, *m.*; (*manager*) régisseur, intendant, *m.*; (*of assemblies*) commissaire, *m.*; (*of colleges*) économe, *m.*; (*theol.*) dispensateur, *m.*; (*nav.*) commis aux vivres, *m.* —**'s mate,** (*nav.*) distributeur des vivres, cambusier, *m.* —**'s room,** *s.* office, *f.*; (*nav.*) cambuse, *f.*
Stewardship, *s.* emploi de maître d'hôtel, *m.*; emploi de régisseur, *m.*, charge d'intendant. intendance, *f.*; commissariat, *m.*; économat, *m.*; administration, *f.*
Stewed, *adj.* en ragoût, à l'étuvée; (*of hare*) en civet; (*of rabbit*) en gibelotte; (*of fish*) en matelote; (*of fruit*) en compote. — *mutton* or &c., ragoût de mouton *or* &c., *m.* — *hare, V.* **Hare.** — *rabbit,* gibelotte de lapin, gibelotte, *f.* — *eels* or &c., matelote d'anguilles *or* &c., *f.* — *pears* or &c, compote de poires *or* &c., *f.*
Stewing, *s.* étuvée, *f.*; cuisson à l'étuvée, *f.* — **pear,** *s.* poire à cuire, *f.*
Stibial, *adj.* stibial
Stibiated, *adj.* stibié
Stick, *s.* (*rough, as a blindman's —,* &c.) bâton, *m.*; (*light walking —*) canne, *f.*; (*rod, switch,*

wand, small —, a drummer's —, &c.) baguette, *f.*; (*of a small bundle of firewood*) cotret, *m.*; (*of trees*) branche, *f.*; (*timber*) tronc, *m.*; mât, *m.*; (*for vines,* &c.) échalas, *m.*; (*for peas, beans,* &c.) rame, *f.*; (*handle*) manche, *m.*; (*of violins*) archet, *m.*; (*of sealing-wax, chocolate,* &c.) bâton, *m.*; **—s,** *pl.* (*firewood*) du bois, *m.* *Blow with a —,* coup de bâton, *m.*; coup de canne, *m.* *Loaded —,* canne plombée. (*V.* **Cut.**) **—lac,** *s.* laque en bâtons, *f.* **— peas,** *s.pl.* pois ramés, *m.pl.*

Stick, *v.a.* (*pierce*) percer; piquer; (*thrust in*) enfoncer, ficher, planter; mettre; (*to gum, to glue*) coller; (*fix*) fixer; attacher; (*peas, beans,* &c.) ramer; (*kill*) saigner, tuer; (*cook.*) piquer, larder. **— on,** coller; fixer; attacher. **— *it* on,** (*overcharge*) surfaire, saler. **— out,** faire ressortir. **— up,** coller; (*to placard*) afficher; (*put upright*) dresser, mettre droit, mettre

Stick, *v.n.* s'attacher (à), se coller (à), tenir (à), adhérer (à); (*get entangled*) rester pris; être engagé, être pris; s'enfoncer; (*remain*) rester; (*stop*) s'arrêter; (*at*) hésiter (devant), reculer (devant), s'arrêter (devant, à), regarder (à). *Stuck in the mud,* embourbé; (*of a ship*) envasé. *I am stuck fast!* me voilà empêtré! *To —* (or *hold*) *fast, V.* **Fast.** **— by,** s'attacher à, soutenir. **— on,** se coller, tenir, adhérer, s'attacher. **— out,** ressortir, avancer, se projeter; sortir; (*not to yield*) tenir bon *or* ferme. **— to,** s'attacher *or* &c. à; ne pas quitter; s'appliquer à; rester à *or* dans; persévérer *or* persister dans; ne pas démordre de; (*abide by*) s'en tenir à; (*keep true to*) rester *or* être fidèle à. **— up,** rester droit; se dresser, se redresser; être debout; être planté. **— up for,** tenir pour, prendre fait et cause pour, prendre le parti de

Sticker, *s. V.* **Clincher;** (*in America*) garde-boutique, garde-magasin, rossignol, *m.*

Stickiness, *s.* viscosité, *f.*; ténacité, *f.*

Sticking, *s.* (*of peas,* &c.) ramage, *m.* **— place,** *s.* point d'arrêt, *m.*, dernière limite, *f.* **—plaster,** *s.* emplâtre adhésif, sparadrap, *m.*; (*court —*) taffetas d'Angleterre, *m.*

Stickle, *v.n.* disputer; batailler; insister

Stickleback, *s.* (*fish*) épinoche, *f.*

Stickler, *s* partisan, champion, *m.* *To be a great — for,* tenir beaucoup à

Stick-up, *adj.* droit, montant

Sticky, *adj.* collant, gluant, visqueux, tenace

Stiff, *adj.* raide; inflexible; (*starched*) empesé; (*not natural*) gêné, contraint, affecté, guindé, empesé; (*obstinate*) opiniâtre, obstiné, dur; (*of pastes, liquids,* &c.) dur, ferme; (*strong*) fort; (*hard*) dur; rude; (*of soil*) tenace; (*excessive, fam.*) salé; (*nav., of wind*) carabiné; (*of ships*) dur. *As — as a poker,* raide comme un bâton. *To become* or *grow —,* raidir, se raidir. **—neck,** *s.* (*med.*) (le) torticolis, *m.* **—necked,** *adj.* au cou raide; (*med.*) qui a le torticolis; (*fig.*) opiniâtre, obstiné

Stiffen, *v.a.* raidir; (*make torpid*) engourdir; (*fig.*) endurcir; (*paste*) durcir, rendre ferme; (*sauces,* &c.) lier; — *v.n.* raidir, se raidir; (*fig.*) s'endurcir; (*of paste*) durcir, devenir ferme, s'affermir; (*of sauces,* &c.) se lier

Stiffener, *s.* raidisseur, *m.*; (*of boots, shoes*) sous-contrefort, *m.*; cambrillon, *m.*; (*of a cravat*) col, *m.* [tien, *m.*

Stiffening, *s.* raidissement, *m.*; (*support*) soutien, *m.*

Stiffly, *adv.* avec raideur; avec opiniâtreté, opiniâtrément, obstinément; inflexiblement; (*strongly*) fortement

Stiffness, *s.* raideur, *f.*; inflexibilité, *f.*; (*torpidness*) engourdissement, *m.*; (*constraint*) gêne, contrainte, *f.*; (*obstinacy*) opiniâtreté, *f.*; (*thickness*) consistance, *f.*; (*unnaturalness*) air guindé, *m.*; style guindé, *m.*

Stifle, *v.a.* étouffer; — *s.,* **— joint,** *s.* grasset, *m.*

Stifling, *adj.* étouffant; — *s.* étouffement, *m.*; suffocation, *f.* *It is — hot!* on étouffe!

Stigma, *s.* stigmate, *m.*; (*stain*) flétrissure, *f.*

Stigmatize, *v.a.* stigmatiser, flétrir [tache, *f.*

Stile, *s.* (*of dials*) style, *m.*, aiguille, *f.*; (*of hedges*) barrière, *f.*, échalis, échalier, *m.*

Stiletto, *s.* poinçon, *m.*; (*weapon*) stylet, *m.*

Still, *v.a.* calmer, apaiser; tranquilliser; (*silence*) faire taire; (*distil*) distiller

Still, *adj.* calme, tranquille; paisible; silencieux; taciturne; en repos; fixe; immobile; (*of wine*) non mousseux. *To sit —,* rester tranquille; ne pas bouger; rester en place; ne pas se déranger. *To stand —,* se tenir *or* rester tranquille; ne pas bouger; rester en place *or* en plant; stationner; (*stop*) s'arrêter; être arrêté. *— water,* eau stagnante, *f.* *— waters run deep,* il n'y a pire eau que l'eau qui dort. **—born,** *adj.* mort-né. **— life,** *s.* (*paint.*) nature morte, *f.*

Still, *s.* alambic, *m.*; (*stillness*) calme, silence, *m.* **— burn,** *v.a.* brûler (par distillation). **— house,** *s.* distillerie, *f.* **— room,** *s.* (*for distilling*) distillerie, *f.*; (*for keeping liquors,* &c.) cellier, *m.* **— room maid,** *s.* cellerière, *f.*

Still, *adv.* encore, toujours; (*nevertheless*) cependant, néanmoins, toutefois, malgré cela; toujours est-il que. *— less,* encore moins; à plus forte raison. *— more,* encore plus; à plus forte raison

Stillion, *s.* chantier, porte-fût, *m.*

Stillness, *s.* calme, *m.*, tranquillité, *f.*; silence, *m.*; taciturnité, *f.*; repos, *m.*; immobilité, *f.*

Stilt, *s.* échasse, *f.* **— bird,** *s.* échasse, *f.*

Stilted, *adj.* guindé, collet monté, compassé, tiré par les cheveux [raideur, affectation, *f.*

Stiltedness, *s.* air *or* ton *or* style guindé, *m.*, raideur, affectation, *f.*

Stimulant, *adj. s.* stimulant, *adj.m.*, e, *f.*, stimulant, *s.m.* [guillonner

Stimulate, *v.a.* stimuler, exciter, piquer, aiguillonner

Stimulation, *s.* stimulation, *f.*

Stimulative, *adj.* stimulant, stimulateur; — *s.* stimulant, *m.* [-trice, *f.*

Stimula-tor, tress, *s.* stimulateur, *m.*, -trice, *f.*

Stimulus, *s.* stimulant, aiguillon, *m.*; (*med.*) stimulus, *m.*; (*bot.*) aiguillon, *m.*

Sting, *v.a.n.* piquer; (*afflict*) percer, navrer; déchirer. *Stung to the quick,* piqué au vif. *Stung with remorse,* bourrelé de remords

Sting, *s.* aiguillon, dard, *m.*; (*wound*) piqûre, *f.*; (*fig.*) aiguillon, *m.*; (*of conscience*) remords, *m.*; (*of an epigram*) pointe, *f.* **— bull, -fish,** *s.* vive, *f.* **—less,** *adj.* sans aiguillon, sans dard; sans pointe. **— ray,** *s.* pastenague, altavelle, *f.* [*face*) gifle, *f.*

Stinger, *s.* chose qui pique, *f.*; (*slap on the face*) gifle, *f.*

Stingily, *adv.* sordidement, mesquinement, chichement [pingrerie, lésinerie, *f.*

Stinginess, *s.* avarice, mesquinerie, ladrerie, pingrerie, lésinerie, *f.*

Stinging, *s.* piqûre, *f.*; — *adj.* piquant [pingre

Stingy, *adj.* avare, mesquin, chiche, ladre, pingre

Stink, *v.n.* puer, empester; (*of*) puer (le, la, les); — *v.a.* empuantir; — *s.* puanteur, mauvaise odeur, infection, *f.* **— pot,** *s.* composition puante, *f.*; (*artil.*) boulet asphyxiant, *m.* **— stone,** *s.* pierre puante, *f.* **— trap,** *s.* valve contre les émanations, *f.* **— weed,** *s.* ansérine vermifuge, *f.* [(*zool.*) mydas, télagon, *m.*

Stinkard, *s.* puant, *m.*; (*fig.*) goujat, *m.*; (*zool.*) mydas, télagon, *m.*

Stinker, *s.* chose puante, *f.*

Stinking, *adj.* puant; — *s.* puanteur, *f.*

Stinkingly, *adv.* puamment, avec puanteur

Stint, *v.a.* limiter, borner, restreindre; (*in food*) compter *or* reprocher les morceaux à; (*stop*) arrêter; (*retrench*) rogner; — *s.* limite, borne, *f.*; restriction, *f.*; part, portion, *f.*; (*bird*) petite maubèche, *f.* *Without —,* à son gré; sans restrictions; sans bornes; à discrétion. *To — oneself,* se priver

Stipe, *s.* stipe, *m.* [— *oneself,* se priver

Stipel, *s.* stipelle, *f.*

Stipend, *s.* salaire, *m.*; (*of clergymen,* &c.) traitement, *m.*, appointements, *m.pl.*; — *v.a.* salarier, gager, appointer; (*in a bad sense*) stipendier, soudoyer

Stipendiary, *adj. s.* salarié, appointé; (*in a bad sense*) stipendiaire, stipendié, à gages. — *magistrate*, juge, *m.* [tillé, *m.*
Stipple, *v.a.* pointiller, pointer; — *s.* poin-
Stippling, *s.* (*act*) pointillage, *m.*; (*result*) pointillé, *m.*
Stipulate, *v.n.a.* stipuler ('*that*,' que); convenir (de); stipuler. — **for,** stipuler
Stipulation, *s.* convention, *f.*, contrat, *m.*; (*law*) stipulation, *f.*
Stipulator, *s.* partie contractante, *f.*
Stipule, *s.* stipule, *f.*
Stir, *v.a.* remuer; agiter; (*the fire*) remuer, attiser, fourgonner; (*incite*) exciter (à), pousser (à), porter (à); (*excite*) émouvoir, exciter, irriter; — *v.n.* remuer; (*about*) se remuer, s'agiter, se donner du mouvement; (*from*) bouger (de). *To be —ring*, (*pers.*) être debout; se lever; (*things*) exister. *There is no air —ring*, il ne fait pas d'air. — **out,** sortir. — **up,** remuer; exciter, émouvoir; réveiller, animer; (*the fire*) remuer, attiser, fourgonner
Stir, *s.* remuement, remue-ménage, tumulte, bruit, *m.*; agitation, *f.*, mouvement, *m.*; mêlée, *f.*; (*disturbance*) trouble, *m.*
Stirabout, *s.* bouillie (de farine d'avoine), *f.*
Stirrer, *s.* instigateur, *m.*, -trice, *f.*; boute-en-train, *m.*
Stirring, *adj.* actif, agissant; remuant; éclatant; (*of scenes*, &c.) émouvant, qui émeut ...; — *s.* agitation, *f.*
Stirrup, *s.* étrier, *m.*; (*shoemaker's* —) tire-pied, *m.* — **bandage,** *s.* (*surg.*) étrier, *m.* — **bar,** *s.* porte-étrivière, *m.* — **cup,** *s.* vin *or* coup de l'étrier, *m.* — **leather,** *s.* étrivière, *f.* — **oil,** *s.* huile de cotret, *f.* — **strap,** *s.* étrivière, *f.*
Stitch, *v.a.* coudre; piquer; (*books*) brocher; — *s.* point, *m.*; piqûre, *f.*; (*of knitting*) maille, *f.*; (*pain*, — *in o.'s side*) point de côté, point, *m.* — *in the side*, point de côté, *m.* — **up,** *v.a.* mettre un point à. *A — in time saves nine*, un point à temps en épargne cent. — **wort,** *s.* stellaire, *f.* [brocheur, *m.*, -euse, *f.*
Stitcher, *s.* arrière-pointeuse, *f.*; (*of books*)
Stitching, *s.* arrière-point, *m.*; (*of books*) bro-
Stiver, *s.* (*fig.*) centime, *m.* [chage, *m.*
Stoat, *s.* belette, *f.*; (*ermine*) hermine d'été, *f.*, roselet, *m.*
Stock, *s.* (*of a tree*) tronc, *m.*; (*race*) souche, race, *f.*, tronc, *m.*, famille, *f.*; (*store*) fonds, *m.*, provision, *f.*; (*handle*) manche, *m.*; (*of fire-arms*) monture, *f.*, bois, fût, *m.*; (*of a pump*) corps, *m.*; (*of wood, stone*) bloc, *m.*; (*log*) bûche, *f.*; (*stupid person*) bûche, bête, *f.*; (*bot.*) matthiole, giroflée, *f.*; (*for grafting on*) sujet, *m.*, ente, *f.*; (*wild* —) sauvageon, *m.*; (*capital*) fonds, capitaux, *m.pl.*; (*shares*) actions, *f.pl.*; (*goods on hand*) marchandises en magasin, *f.pl.*; assortiment, *m.*; (*book-keep.*) capital, *m.*; (*of manufactures*, &c., *dead — of a farm*) matériel, *m.*; (*cattle, live* —) bétail, *m.*, bestiaux, *m.pl.*; (— *of plays or pieces, theat., mus.*) répertoire, *m.*; (*cravat*) col, *m.*; (*at cards*) talon, *m.*; (*cook.*) consommé, *m.*; (*tech.*) fût, *m.*; (*for ship-building*) chantier, *m.*, cale de construction, *f.*; (*of an anchor*) jas, *m.*, cape, *f.*; (*print.*) fonte, *f.*; —**s,** *pl.* troncs, &c.; (*surg.*) bottines, *f.pl.*; (*at the exchange*) fonds, fonds publics, *m.pl.*, rentes, *f.pl.*; effets, effets publics, *m.pl.*; (*punishment*) bloc, *m.* — *-in-trade*, fonds de commerce, *m.* — *of plays*, répertoire, *m.* — *on hand*, marchandises en magasin, *f.pl.* *Dead* —, (*agr.*) mobilier mort, matériel, *m.*; (*com.*) fonds de magasin, fonds de boutique, *m.* *Rolling* —, *Surplus* —, *Working* —, *V.* **Rolling,** &c. *Live* —, mobilier vif, bétail, *m.*, bestiaux, *m.pl.* *Virginian* —, (*bot.*) mahonille, *f.* *Wild* —, (*hort.*) sauvageon, *m.* *In* —, en magasin. *In the —s*, (*punishment*) au pilori. *On the —s*, sur le chantier; (*fig.*) sur le métier; (*of a project., bill in parliam.*, &c.) à l'étude. *To lay in or take in a* —, faire une provision (de). *To take* —, faire l'inventaire (de). *To take in* —, recevoir des marchandises. — **account,** *s.* compte de capital, *m.* — **book,** *s.* magasinier, *m.* — **broker,** *s.* agent de change, *m.* — **dove,** *s.* colombin, petit ramier, *m.* — **exchange,** *s.* Bourse, *f.* — **exchange committee,** *s.* chambre syndicale (*f.*) *or* syndicat (*m.*) des agents de change, *m.* — **fish,** *s.* stockfisch, *m.* — **holder,** *s.* rentier, *m.*, -ière, *f.*; (*shareholder*) actionnaire, *m.f.*; (*fin.*) détenteur de fonds publics, *m.* — **jobber,** *s.* agioteur, *m.* — **jobbing,** *s.* agiotage, *m.* — **piece, -play,** *s.* (*theat., mus.*) pièce de répertoire, *f.* — **still,** *adj.* immobile comme un terme, immobile. — **taking,** *s.* inventaire, *m.*
Stock, *v.a.* pourvoir (de), fournir (de), monter (en), approvisionner (de); (*the mind*) meubler; (*a shop*) monter, assortir; (*a park with deer*, &c.) peupler; (*a pond*) empoissonner; (*a farm*) meubler, monter, pourvoir de bétail; (*put by*) amasser, mettre de côté; (*cards*) rassembler
Stockade, *s.* palissade, *f.*; (*of rivers, canals*, &c.) estacade, *f.*; — *v.a.* palissader; (*rivers, canals*, &c.) estacader
Stocking, *s.* bas, *m.* — **frame,** *s.* métier à bas, *m.* — **maker,** *s.* fabricant de bas, *m.* — **mender,** *s.* ravaudeur, *m.*, -euse, *f.* — **net,** *s.* tricot, *m.* — **stitch,** *s.* tricot au crochet, *m.* — **trade,** *s.* bonneterie, *f.* — **weaver,** *s.*
Stocky, *adj.* trapu [tisserand en bas, *m.*
Stoic, *s.* stoïcien, *m.*, -ne, *f.*
Stoic, Stoical, *adj.* stoïcien; (*things*) stoïque
Stoically, *adv.* stoïquement
Stoicalness, Stoicism, *s.* stoïcisme, *m.*
Stoke, *v.a.* remuer, attiser, toucher; chauffer. — **hole,** *s.* embrasure, *f.*
Stoker, *s.* chauffeur, *m.*
Stoking, *s.* chauffage, *m.*
Stole, *s.* garde-robe, *f.*; (*Cath. rel.*) étole, *f.*; (*Rom. hist.*) stole, *f.* *Groom of the* —, premier gentilhomme de la chambre, *m.*
Stolen, *part. adj.* volé, &c. (*V.* **Steal**); clan-
Stolid, *adj.* stupide, lourd [destin
Stolidity, *s.* stupidité, *f.*
Stollage. *V.* **Stalder**
Stoma, *s.* stomate, *m.*
Stomacace, *s.* stomacace, *f.*
Stomach, *s.* estomac, *m.*; (*of feeling sick*) cœur, *m.*; (*fig.*) appétit, *m.*; envie, *f.*; goût, *m.*; — *v.a.* se fâcher de; (*to bear*) supporter, souffrir, endurer, digérer, avaler. *On* or *with an empty* —, l'estomac vide; à jeun. *To turn anyone's* —, soulever le cœur à quelqu'un. — **ache,** *s.* mal d'estomac, *m.* *To have the* (or *a*) — *ache*, avoir mal à l'estomac. — **pump,** *s.* pompe stomacale, pompe œsophagienne, *f.*
Stomachal, *adj.* stomacal [fâché
Stomached, *adj.* irrité, courroucé, en colère,
Stomacher, *s.* corsage lacé, *m.*
Stomachic, *adj. s.* stomachique, *adj. m.f.*, *s.m.*; (*abusively for* '*stomachal*') stomacal
Stomata, *s.pl.* (*pl. of* **Stoma**) stomates, *m.pl.*
Stomate, *s.* stomate, *m.*
Stomatoscope, *s.* stomatoscope, *m.*
Stone, *s.* pierre, *f.*; (*flint*) caillou, *m.*; (*ware*) grès, *m.*; (*boundary*) borne, *f.*; (*of mills*) meule, *f.*; (*fig., med.*) pierre, *f.*; (*of fruit*) noyau, *m.*; (*of grapes*) pépin, *m.*; (*weight*) 6 kilos; (*anat.*) testicule, *m.*; — *adj.* de *or* en pierre; (—*ware*) de *or* en grès; — *v.a.* jeter des pierres à, assaillir *or* poursuivre à coups de pierres; lapider; (*fruit*) vider; (*walls*, &c.) maçonner; (*roads*) empierrer, caillouter, ferrer *To leave no — unturned*, mettre tout en œuvre *or* en usage, remuer ciel et terre. *Not to leave a — standing*, ne pas laisser pierre sur pierre. *Within a —'s throw*, à la portée d'une pierre; à deux pas. — **blind,** *adj.* complètement aveugle. — **blue,** *s.* bleu, *m.* — **borer,** *s.* lithophage, *m.* — **bottle,** *s.* bouteille de grès, *f.*; cruchon, *m.* — **bow,** *s.* arbalète à

jalet, *f.* — **break,** *s.* saxifrage, *f.* — **bridge,** *s.* pont de pierre, *m.* — **chat,** *s.* traquet rubicole, *m.* — **coal,** *s.* anthracite, *m.* — **colour,** *s.* couleur de pierre, *f.* — **crop,** *s.* orpin, *m.* — **cutter,** *s.* tailleur de pierre (*or* de pierres), *m.* — **cutting,** *s.* taille de la pierre, *f.* — **dead,** *adj.* raide mort. — **deaf,** *adj.* complètement sourd. — **fly,** *s.* perle, *f.* — **fruit,** *s.* fruit à noyau, *m.* — **grig,** *s.* lamprillon, lamproyon, *m.* — **hearted,** *adj.* qui a un cœur de roche, insensible. — **horse,** *s.* cheval entier, *m.* — **jar,** *s.* jarre *or* pot *or* &c. (*V.* **Jar**) de grès. — **lily,** *s.* encrinite, *m.* — **mason,** *s.* maçon, *m.* — **pine,** *s.* pinier, *m.* — **pit,** *s.* carrière de pierre, *f.* — **post,** *s.* borne, *f.* — **potter,** *s.* potier de grès, *m.* — **quarry,** *s.* *V.* — **pit.** — **turner,** *s.* tourneur en pierre, *m.* — **waggon,** *s.* fardier, *m.* — **wall,** *s.* mur de pierre, *m.* — **ware,** *s.* grès, *m.*, poterie de grès, *f.* — **work,** *s.* maçonnerie, *f.*, ouvrage en maçonnerie, *m.* — **yard,** *s.* chantier de pierre, *m.*

Stoniness, *s.* nature pierreuse, *f.*; (*fig.*) [dureté, insensibilité, *f.*

Stoning, *s.* lapidation, *f.*; (*engin.*) chaussée, *f.*; (*of fruit*) vidage, *m.*; (*of roads*) empierrement, cailloutis, *m.*; cailloutage, *m.*

Stony, *adj.* de pierre; (*full of stones*) pierreux; (*hard*) de pierre, de roche, dur, insensible; (*of Arabia*) Pétrée. — **hearted,** *adj.* *V.* **Stone-** [**hearted**

Stook, *s.* & *v.a.* (*agr.*) *V.* **Shock**

Stool, *s.* tabouret, escabeau, *m.*; (*med.*) selle, *f.*; (*hort.*) pied mère, *m.*, plante mère, *f.* — *of repentance,* sellette, *f.* *Close —, night —,* chaise percée, *f.* — **ball,** *s.* (*game*) balle en rond, *f.*

Stoop, *v.n.* se pencher, se baisser; (*in walking*) se tenir courbé, (*from age*) se voûter; (*yield*) s'humilier, s'incliner (devant), le céder (à); (*to submit*) se soumettre (à); (*to descend*) s'abaisser (à), s'avilir; (*of birds of prey*) fondre (sur); (*to perch*) se poser, s'abattre (sur); — *v.a.* pencher; baisser; (*carry off*) enlever; — *s.* action de fondre (sur), *f.*; coup, *m.*; inclination, *f.*; (*humiliation*) abaissement, *m.*; (*pitcher*) cruche, *f.*; (*aspersorium*) bénitier, *m.* *To make a — at,* fondre sur. *She —s to conquer,* elle s'abaisse pour vaincre. — **down,** *v.n.* se baisser. — **forward,** *v.n.* se pencher en [avant

Stooping, *adj.* courbé

Stoopingly, *adv.* en se baissant; en se tenant courbé; en baissant la tête

Stop, *v.a.* arrêter; (*prevent*) empêcher; (*hinder*) entraver, gêner; (*intercept,* &c.) intercepter; supprimer; faire cesser; interrompre; (*close*) boucher, fermer; (*the breath*) couper (la respiration); (*a tooth*) plomber, (*with gold*) aurifier; (*wages,* &c.) retenir; (*payment*) cesser, suspendre; (*steamers*) stopper; (*gram.*) ponctuer; — *v.n.* s'arrêter; arrêter; (*stay*) rester; demeurer; (*leave off*) cesser (de); (*wait*) attendre; (*of payments*) cesser (ses payements); (*of steamers*) stopper. *To — there,* (*leave off*) en rester là. — *!* arrêtez-vous! arrêtez! attendez! (*nav.*) stop! — **for,** attendre. — **up,** boucher, fermer; obstruer, engorger; (*a door, window,* &c.) condamner; (*roads*) fermer; (*streets*) encombrer; barrer. — **up with,** (*a pers. ill,* &c.) veiller

Stop, *s.* pause, halte, *f.*; interruption, *f.*; retard, *m.*; (*hindrance*) empêchement, obstacle, *m.*; (*on a payment*) opposition, *f.*; (*of machines, trains, nav.*) arrêt, *m.*; (*tech., nav.*) heurtoir, *m.*; stoppeur, *m.*; (*of clocks*) détente, *f.*; (*mus.*) touche, *f.*; (*of flutes*) trou, *m.*; (*of organs*) jeu, *m.*; (*tail-piece of a violin* or &c.) queue, *f.*, cordier, *m.*; (*gram.*) point, *m.* *To make a —,* faire halte, s'arrêter. *To put a — to,* mettre fin à, mettre un terme à; arrêter; empêcher; s'opposer à. — **chain,** *s.* chaînette d'arrêt, *f.* — **cock,** *s.* robinet d'arrêt, obturateur, *m.* — **gap,** *s.* bouche-trou, *m.* — **plank,** *s.* poutrelle, *f.* — **valve,** *s.* soupape d'arrêt, *f.* — **watch,** *s.* montre à arrêt, *f.*

Stoppage, *s.* (*closing*) fermeture, *f.*; (*rest*) repos, arrêt, temps d'arrêt, *m.*, pause, halte, *f.*; interruption, *f.*; cessation, *f.*; (*of a train*) arrêt, *m.*; (*of labours*) chômage, *m.*; (*obstacle*) obstruction, *f.*; embarras, *m.*; (*stand-still*) stationnement, *m.*; (*place*) station, *f.*; (*on a salary, on wages, or pay*) retenue, *f.*; opposition, *f.*; (*of payments*) cessation, suspension, *f.*; (*of a tooth*) plombage, *m.*, (*with gold*) aurifiage, *m.*

Stopper, *s.* bouchon, *m.*; (*of rags*) tampon, *m.*; (*of a cornopean*) piston, *m.*; (*tech., nav.*) stoppeur, *m.*; — *v.a.* boucher

Stopping, *s.* *V.* **Stoppage.** — **up,** *s.* fermeture, *f.*; (*at night*) veillée, *f.*

Stopple, *s.* bouchon, *m.*

Storage, *s.* emmagasinage, magasinage, *m.*

Storax, *s.* storax, *m.*

Store, *s.* abondance, *f.*; provision, *f.*; approvisionnement, *m.*; (*fig.*) fonds, *m.*; (*hoard*) amas, *m.*; (*warehouse*) magasin, dépôt, *m.*; —**s,** *pl.* magasins, *m.pl.*; magasin, *m.*; dépôts, *m.pl.*; dépôt, *m.*; (*supplies*) matériel, *m.*; (*food*) vivres, *m.pl.* — *is no sore,* abondance de biens ne nuit pas. *In —,* en réserve. *To keep* or *lay in —,* réserver, garder *or* tenir en réserve, mettre en réserve. *To lay in a — of,* faire une provision de. *To set — by* (or *on*), attacher du prix à, faire cas de. — **house,** *s.* magasin, dépôt, *m.*; entrepôt, *m.*; (*for grain*) grenier, *m.* — **keeper,** *s.* garde-magasin, magasinier, *m.*; (*admin.*) chef du matériel, *m.*; (*nav.*) cambusier, *m.*; (*dealer*) marchand, *m.*, -e, *f.* — **room,** *s.* magasin, dépôt, *m.*; grenier, *m.*; (*nav.*) soute, *f.*; cambuse, *f.* — **ship,** *s.* vaisseau d'approvisionnement, transport, *m.*, gabare, *f.* — **waggon,** *s.* chariot à munitions, fourgon, *m.*

Store, *v.a.* ('*with,*' de) pourvoir, munir, fournir; (*stock*) approvisionner; (*to warehouse*) emmagasiner; (*lay by*) mettre en réserve; (*the mind*) meubler; enrichir. — **up,** amasser, accumuler

Storer, *s.* personne qui accumule, *f.*

Storey, *s.* (*floor*) *V.* **Story**

Storied, *adj.* historié; chargé *or* gravé d'inscriptions; ornementé; (*of houses*) à ... étage, à ... étages. *A two- — house,* une maison à deux étages, *f.*

Stork, *s.* cigogne, *f.* —*'s-bill.* (*bot.*) bec-de- [grue, *m.*

Storm, *s.* orage, *m.*, tempête, *f.*; (*at sea*) tempête, *f.*; (*mil.*) assaut, *m.*; — *v.a.* donner *or* livrer l'assaut à, attaquer; — *v.n.* (*imp.*) faire de l'orage; (*pers.*) tempêter, s'emporter. — *of hail,* grêle, *f.* — *of rain,* orage, *m.* — *of wind,* vent de tempête, *m.*, tempête, *f.* — *in a teacup* (or *teapot* or *slop-basin*), tempête dans un verre d'eau. *To blow a —,* faire une tempête. *To carry* or *take by —,* prendre *or* emporter d'assaut. — **bell,** *s.* tocsin, *m.* — **cloud,** *s.* nuage d'orage, *m.* — **jib,** *s.* trinquette, *f.*, tourmentin, *m.* — **sail, -stay-sail,** *s.* taille-vent, *m.*

Stormily, *adv.* orageusement, tempêtueuse- [ment

Storminess, *s.* état orageux, *m.*

Storming, *s.* (*mil.*) assaut, *m.*, prise d'assaut, *f.*; (*fig.*) violence, rage, *f.*; — *adj.* d'assaut

Stormy, *adj.* orageux; tempêtueux. *The weather is —,* le temps est à l'orage

Storthing, *s.* storthing, *m.*

Story, *s.* histoire, *f.*; (*tale*) conte, *m.*; (*falsehood*) mensonge, *m.*; (*floor*) étage, *m.* *On the first —, On the same —,* *V.* **Floor.** *To tell a —,* raconter une histoire, faire un conte; (*a fib*) faire un conte. *As the — goes,* dit-on, à ce qu'on dit, à ce qu'on prétend, comme dit la chanson. *There is a — (of, that),* on raconte (que). *The best of the — is,* le plus beau de l'histoire est. — **book,** *s.* livre de contes, *m.* — **teller,** *s.* conteur, *m.*, -euse, *f.*; (*liar*) menteur, *m.*, -euse, *f.*

Stound, *s.* (*Scotch*) élancement, *m.*, douleur [lancinante, *f.*

Stoup, *s. V.* **Stoop**
Stout, *adj.* fort, vigoureux, robuste; brave, vaillant, courageux, intrépide ; résolu, ferme, décidé ; (*fat*) gros, fort, corpulent, puissant; (*of things*) fort, solide ; — *s.* stout, *m.*, bière forte, bière brune, *f.* *To be getting —, to grow —*, prendre de l'embonpoint, engraisser. — **built,** *adj.* gros. — **hearted,** *adj.* brave, courageux, intrépide
Stoutly, *adv.* vigoureusement, fortement; bravement; résolûment ; ferme ; fort et ferme
Stoutness, *s.* vigueur, *f.* ; corpulence, *f.*, embonpoint, *m.*; courage, *m.*, bravoure, *f.*; fermeté, résolution, *f.*
Stove, *s.* (*fire-place*) cheminée à l'anglaise, grille, *f.* ; (*iron box*) poêle, *m.* ; calorifère, *m.*; (*for cooking, washing*) fourneau, *m.*; (*hot-house*) serre, serre chaude, *f.* ; (*tech.*) étuve, *f.* ; — *v.a.* étuver. — **room,** *s.* étuve, *f.*
Stow, *v.a.* (— **away**) arranger; mettre ; (*lay up*) serrer ; entasser ; (*nav.*) arrimer ; (*an anchor*) brider
Stowage, *s.* emmagasinage, *m.* ; place, *f.*; (*nav.*) [arrimage, *m.*
Stower, *s.* arrimeur, *m.*
Strabism, Strabismus, *s.* strabisme, *m.*
Strabotom-ist, -y. *V.* page 3, § 1
Straddle, *v.n.* écarter les jambes ; se tenir les jambes écartées ; (*walk*) marcher les jambes écartées ; — *v.a.* enfourcher, se mettre (*or* être) à califourchon sur
Straggle, *v.n.* errer, rôder ; s'écarter (de), se détacher (de), s'éloigner (de) ; être écarté *or* dispersé *or* éparpillé *or* éloigné ; (*mil.*) traîner
Straggler, *s.* rôdeur, *m.*, -euse, *f.*, vagabond, *m.*, e, *f.* ; retardataire, *m.f.* ; (*mil.*) traînard, *m.*
Straggling, *adj.* écarté, éloigné ; (*stray*) égaré ; (*scattered*) éparpillé, épars ; (*irregular*) irrégulier
Stragglingly, *adv* en traînard ; en rôdant, à l'aventure ; (*sparsely*) çà et là, de loin en loin
Straight, *adj.* droit. *As — as an arrow* (or *as a line*), droit comme un i. *To make* or *set —*, dresser, redresser, rendre droit ; (*fig.*) arranger. *To make — again*, redresser. — **edge,** *s.* règle à araser, *f.*
Straight, *adv.* droit, tout droit ; directement ; (*at once*) immédiatement, tout de suite. *— on, — ahead, — forward*, tout droit, droit devant soi. *To keep — on*, aller tout droit
Straighten, *v.a.* redresser, rendre droit ; (*arts*) [dresser
Straightforward, *adj.* droit ; franc, loyal, honnête. **—ly,** *adv.* avec droiture ; avec franchise ; (*fam.*) carrément. **—ness,** *s.* droiture, *f.* ; franchise, loyauté, honnêteté, *f.*
Straightly, *adv.* droit
Straightness, *s.* rectitude, *f.*; ligne directe, *f.*
Straightway, *adv. V.* **Straight**
Strain, *v.a.n.* tendre ; forcer ; outrer ; serrer, presser ; (*the eyes*) fatiguer ; (*the voice*) forcer ; (*filter*) passer, filtrer ; (*sprain*) se fouler, se donner une entorse à ; (*endeavour*) s'efforcer (de), faire de violents efforts (pour). *To — oneself*, se forcer; se donner un effort. *To — a point*, faire un extra ; (*relax a rule for once*) faire une exception ; fermer les yeux. *To — every nerve*, faire tous ses efforts, se mettre en quatre, faire feu des quatre pieds, faire les cent coups, suer sang et eau. — **at,** faire des efforts pour avaler ; (*reject*) rejeter ; repousser. — **out,** exprimer, extraire
Strain, *s.* effort, *m.* ; tension, *f.* ; fatigue, *f.* ; (*sprain*) effort, *m.* ; entorse, *f.* ; foulure, *f.* ; (*style*) style, *m.*, manière, *f.*; (*flight*) élan, essor, *m.* ; (*song, note*) chant, *m.*, accords, accents, *m.pl.* ; (*sound*) son, *m.* ; (*tone*) ton, *m.*
Strainer, *s.* passoire, *f.* ; filtre, *m.*
Straining, *s.* tension, *f.* ; effort, *m.* ; exagération, violence, *f.* ; (*spraining*) foulure, *f.* ; (*filtration*) filtrage, *m.*
Strait, *adj.* étroit ; difficile, gêné, embarrassé ; (*tight*) serré. — *jacket* or *waistcoat*, camisole de force, *f.* — **laced,** *adj.* lacé étroitement ; (*fig.*) raide, collet monté ; rigide, prude, bégueule
Strait, *s.*, **Straits,** *s.pl.* (*at sea*) détroit, *m.* ; (*on land*) défilé, *m.* ; gorge, *f.* ; (*distress*) gêne, difficulté, *f.*, embarras, *m.* *In a —, in great —s*, dans la gêne, dans l'embarras, gêné, embarrassé. *To be driven, to put to —s*, être, mettre dans la gêne (*or* dans l'embarras)
Straiten, *v.a.* (*narrow*) rétrécir ; (*contract*) resserrer, restreindre ; (*tighten*) tendre ; (*distress*) gêner, embarrasser. *—ed circumstances*, gêne pécuniaire, *f.* *In —ed circumstances*, gêné dans ses affaires, gêné, dans la gêne
Straitly, *adv.* étroitement
Straitness, *s.* étroitesse, *f.* ; (*distress*) gêne, *f.*, embarras, *m.* ; (*want*) besoin, *m.*
Strake, *s. V.* **Streak**
Stramonine, *s.* stramonine, *f.*
Stramonium, Stramony, *s.* stramonium, *m.*, stramoine, *f.*
Strand, *s.* rivage, *m.*, plage, grève, *f.* ; (*of ropes, &c.*) cordon, *m.* ; toron, *m.* ; — *v.a.n.* échouer
Stranding, *s.* échouement, *m.*
Strange, *adj.* étrange ; singulier ; bizarre ; extraordinaire ; (*foreign, new, unknown*) étranger; inconnu. — *to say !* chose étrange !
Strangely, *adv.* étrangement ; singulièrement
Strangeness, *s.* étrangeté, *f.* ; singularité, *f.* ; bizarrerie, *f.* ; (*novelty*) nouveauté, *f.*
Stranger, *s.* étranger, *m.*, -ère, *f.* ; inconnu, *m.*, e, *f.* ; spectateur, *m.*, -trice, *f.* *To become* or *get quite a —*, devenir bien rare. *To make a — of*, traiter en étranger. *To make oneself a —*, agir en étranger ; devenir rare. *He is quite a — to me*, je ne le connais pas du tout, je ne le connais ni d'Ève ni d'Adam
Strangle, *v.a.* étrangler
Strangler, *s.* étrangleur, *m.*, -euse, *f.*
Strangles, *s.pl.* gourme, *f.*, étranguillon, *m.*
Strangling, *s.* étranglement, *m.* ; strangula-[tion, *f.*
Strangulated, *adj.* étranglé
Strangulation, *s. V.* **Strangling**
Strangury, *s.* strangurie, *f.*
Strap, *s.* courroie, *f.* ; (*of iron*) bande, *f.*, lien, *m.* ; (*shoulder —*) bretelle, bricole, *f.* ; (*of trousers*) sous-pied, *m.* ; (*of boots*) tirant, *m.* ; (*of a carriage window*) bricole, *f.* ; (*of stirrups*) étrivière, *f.*; (*for razors*) *V.* **Strop ;** (*nav.*) estrope, *f.* ; — *v.a.* attacher, lier ; (*beat*) donner les étrivières à ; (*a razor, and nav.*) *V.* **Strop.** — **oil,** *s.* huile de cotret, *f.* — **wort,** *s.* corrigiole, *f.*
Strappado, *s*, estrapade, *f.* ; — *v.a.* estrapader
Strapper, *s.* grand gaillard, *m.*
Strapping, *s.* bande, bandelette, *f.* ; — *adj.* grand, bien bâti, bien découplé. *A good —*, des étrivières
Strasburger, *s.* Strasbourgeois, *m.*, e, *f.*
Strass, *s.* strass, stras, *m.*
Stratagem, *s.* stratagème, *m.*
Stratagemical, *adj.* stratagématique
Strategic, -al, *adj.* stratégique
Strategically, *adv.* stratégiquement
Strategist, *s.* stratégiste, *m.*
Strategy, *s.* stratégie, *f.*
Stratification, *s.* stratification, *f.*
Stratify, *v.a.* stratifier
Stratigraph-ic, al, -ically, -y. *V.* p. 3, § 1
Stratocracy, *s.* stratocratie, *f.*
Stratocrat-ic, al, -ically, -ism. *V.* p. 3, § 1
Stratum, *s.* couche, strate, *f.*
Stratus, *s.* stratus, *m.*
Straw, *s.* paille, *f.* ; (*trifle*) fétu, zeste, *m.* ; [*V.* **Rap**] ; — *adj.* de paille. *In the —*, (*animals*) sur la litière ; (*pers.*) en couches. — **bed,** *s.* lit de paille, *m.* ; paillasse, *f.* — **berry,** *s. See below.* — **bonnet,** *s.* chapeau de paille, *m.* — **bottomed,** *adj.* à fond de paille. — **built,** *adj.* fait de paille. — **colour,** *s.* couleur de paille, *f.* — **coloured,** *adj.* de couleur de paille, jaune paille, paille. — **cutter,** — **cutting machine,** *s.* hache-paille, *m.* — **hat,** *s.*

chapeau de paille, *m.* —**loft,** *s.* pailler, grenier à fourrages, *m.* —**mat,** *s.* paillasson, *m.* —**mattress,** *s.* paillasse, *f.* —**paper,** *s.* papier de paille, *m.* —**rick,** *s.* pailler, *m.*

Strawberry, *s.* fraise, *f.* —**bed,** *s.* fraisière, *f.* —**plant,** *s.* fraisier, *m.* —**tree,** *s.* arbousier, *m.* [paille

Strawy, *adj.* de paille; (*like straw*) comme la

Stray, *v.n.* errer; (*lose o.'s way*) s'égarer; (*deviate*) s'écarter (de), s'éloigner (de); — *adj.* égaré; (*law*) épave; (*fig.*) accidentel; exceptionnel; (*of* (*thoughts*) détaché; — *s.* bête épave, *f.*

Streak, *s.* raie, bande, *f.*; ligne, *f.*; sillon, *m.*; traînée, *f.*: filet, *m.*; (*variegation*) bigarrure, panachure, *f.*; (*nav.*) virure, *f.*; — *v.a.* rayer; sillonner; (*variegate*) bigarrer, barioler, panacher

Streaked, Streaky, *adj.* rayé; (*variegated*) bigarré, bariolé, panaché, vergeté; (*of tissues*) vergé; (*of meat*) entrelardé

Stream, *s.* courant, *m.*; (*running water in general*) cours d'eau, *m.*; (*rivulet*) ruisseau, *m.*; (*river*) rivière, *f.*; fleuve, *m.*; (*of mountains*) torrent, *m.*; (*of life,* &c.) cours, *m.*; (*of light,* &c.) jet, flot, torrent, *m.*; (*of words*) flux, *m.*; — *v.n.* couler; ruisseler; (*of light,* &c.) jaillir; rayonner; (*to wave*) flotter; — *v.a.* rayer ('*with,*' de). —**anchor,** *s.* ancre de touée, *f.* —**cable,** *s.* câble de touée, *m.* —**tin,** *s.* étain d'alluvion, *m.* [(*nav.*) banderole, *f.*

Streamer, *s.* (*flag*) drapeau, *m.*, bannière, *f.*;

Streamlet, *s.* filet d'eau, *m.*; (*rivulet*) petit ruisseau, *m.*

Streamy, *adj.* ruisselant; (*of light,* &c.) jaillissant; (*full of streams*) sillonné de ruisseaux

Street, *s.* rue, *f.*; (*mil.*) haie, *f.* *To turn into the* —, mettre sur le pavé. —**band,** *s.* musiciens des rues, musiciens ambulants, *m.pl.* —**boy,** *s.* gamin, voyou de la rue, *m.* —**cab,** *s.* voiture de place, *f.* —**door,** *s.* porte de la rue, porte d'entrée, *f.* —**lamp,** *s.* candélabre, *m.* —**messenger,** *s.* commissionnaire, *m.* —**organ,** *s.* orgue portatif, orgue de Barbarie, *m.* —**performer,** *s.* musicien ambulant, *m.*; (*tumbler,* &c.) saltimbanque, *m.* —**robbery,** *s.* vol sur la voie publique, *m.* —**sweeper,** *s.* balayeur de rues, *m.* —**sweeping machine,** *s.* balayeuse, *f.* —**walker,** *s.* fille publique, coureuse, gourgandine, *f.*

Strength, *s.* force, *f.*; (*of the whole frame*) forces, *f.pl.*; force, *f.*; (*of materials*) solidité, *f.*; résistance, *f.*; effort, *m.* *By main* or *sheer* —, *by — of arms*, de vive force, de haute lutte, à force de bras. *On the — of*, sur la foi de, sur. *With all o.'s* —, de toutes ses forces. *To gather* —, se rétablir, reprendre des forces, recouvrer ses forces. —**less,** *adj.* sans force, faible [mir; encourager

Strengthen, *v.a.* fortifier; renforcer; affer-

Strengthener, *s.* fortifiant, *m.*

Strenuous, *adj.* ardent, zélé; courageux; énergique, vigoureux, ferme; vif; constant

Strenuously, *adv.* ardemment, avec zèle; courageusement; énergiquement, vigoureusement; vivement; ferme; fort et ferme

Strenuousness, *s.* ardeur, *f.*, zèle, *m.*; vigueur, *f.*

Stress, *s.* force, importance, *f.*; (*of the weather*) violence, *f.*; (*mechanics*) effort, *m.*; fatigue, *f.*; (*gram.*) accent, *m.* *To lay — on*, appuyer sur, insister sur, attacher de l'importance à. *By — of weather*, par le gros temps par la tempête, par les vents. *We have been driven by — of weather into* . . ., les vents nous ont contraints (la violence de la tempête nous a obligés) de relâcher dans . . .

Stretch, *v.a.* (*extend*) étendre; (*display*) déployer; (*make tense*) tendre; (*widen*) élargir; (*exaggerate*) exagérer, forcer, outrer; (*take the numbness off*) dégourdir; — *v.n.* s'étendre; (*spread*) se déployer; (*become tense*) se tendre; (*of shoes, gloves,* &c.) prêter, s'élargir; (*exaggerate*) exagérer, embellir, hâbler. *To — oneself,* se détirer, s'étirer; (*lie down*) s'étendre; se jeter. —**forth,** —**out,** *v.a.* étendre; (*display*) déployer; (*the hand,* &c.) tendre; (*present*) tendre, allonger, avancer; (*prolong*) prolonger

Stretch, *s.* extension, *f.*; tension, *f.*; (*widening*) élargissement, *m.*; (*exaggeration*) exagération, *f.*; abus, *m.*; (*strength*) force, vigueur, *f.*; (*strain*) effort, *m.*; (*fig.*) portée, étendue, *f.*; (*direction*) direction, *f.*; (*nav.*) bordée, *f.* *At a* —, tout d'un trait, tout d'une haleine, tout d'une tirade. *On the* —, tendu. *To put upon the* —, mettre à la torture

Stretcher, *s.* (*hand-barrow*) brancard, *m.*, civière, *f.*; (*for gloves*) baguette, *f.*; (*for boots*) forme brisée, *f.*; (*of umbrellas, parasols*) fourchette, *f.*; (*of boats*) traversin, marchepied, *m.*; (*mas.*) carreau, *m.*; (*of spinners*) étendeuse, *f.*; (*fig.*) blague, *f.*

Stretching, *s.* tension, *f.*; (*widening*) élargissement, *m.*; (*of metals*) étirage, *m.*; (*of silks,* &c.) tordage, *m.*

Strew, *v.a.* (*scatter over*) répandre, semer; (*cover with*) joncher (de), parsemer (de), couvrir (de); (*scatter about*) disperser

Stria, *s.* (*pl.* **Striæ**) strie, *f.*

Striate, Striated, *adj.* strié

Striation, *s.* striation, *f.*

Striature, *s.* striure, *f.*

Stricken, *part.* frappé, &c. (*V.* **Strike**). — *in years*, avancé en âge, chargé d'années

Strickle, *s.* râcloire, radoire, *f.*

Strict, *adj.* strict; exact; rigide, rigoureux, sévère; exprès, formel

Strictly, *adv.* strictement; exactement; rigoureusement; sévèrement; expressément, formellement. — *speaking*, rigoureusement parlant, à parler rigoureusement, à la rigueur; à vrai dire

Strictness, *s.* exactitude, *f.*; rigueur, sévérité, *f.*

Stricture, *s.* critique, remarque, observation, *f.*; (*med.*) stricture, *f.*, rétrécissement, étranglement, *m.*

Stride, *s.* enjambée, *f.*; pas, *m.*; — *v.a.n.* enjamber. *With giant —s*, à pas de géant. *To make rapid —s*, avancer à grands pas. —**along,** marcher à grands pas, enjamber. — [**over,** enjamber

Strident, *adj.* strident

Strife, *s.* lutte, *f.*; contestation, *f.*, différend, *m.*; guerre, *f.*

Strike, *v.a.* frapper; (*a blow*) frapper, (*deal a blow to anyone*) porter, asséner, donner; (*reach*) atteindre; (*impress*) frapper, saisir; (*occur to*) *V.* **Occur**; (*produce*) faire, produire; (*a bargain*) faire, conclure; (*a balance*) établir; (*an average*) prendre, établir; (*a steel, iron,* &c.) battre; (*of clocks*) sonner; (*a mus. instr.*) jouer de; (*throw, spread*) jeter; répandre; (*erase*) rayer (de); (*a measure*) râcler, raser; (*root*) prendre; (*coin*) frapper; (*nav.: o.'s colours or flag, a sail*) amener (son pavillon, une voile); (*a mast*) abaisser; (*ground*) toucher; (*mil: a tent*) détendre *or* plier (une tente); (*the tents*) lever (le camp). — *all of a heap*, atterrer, abasourdir. — *blind*, rendre aveugle, frapper de cécité. — *dead*, frapper de mort. — *dumb*, rendre muet, frapper de mutisme, priver de la parole; (*fig.*) réduire au silence, interdire. — *fire*, faire du feu, faire feu; étinceler; (*with steel and flint*) battre le briquet. — *a light*, allumer une allumette; (*with steel and flint*) battre le briquet. — *o.'s head against*, se cogner la tête contre. — *root*, prendre racine. — *with horror,* &c., frapper *or* saisir d'horreur, &c. — *work*, faire grève, se mettre en grève. *It —s me*, il me semble; j'ai idée. *It did not — me that* . . ., l'idée ne m'est pas venue que . . . *Without striking a blow*, sans coup férir. —**asunder,** fendre; séparer, diviser. —**down,** abattre, renverser, faire tomber. —**in,** enfoncer. —**off,** effacer, rayer; retrancher; (*cut down*) couper, trancher, enlever, séparer; (*throw down*) abattre; (*print.*) tirer. — **out,** faire jaillir; effacer, rayer, biffer; supprimer; retrancher; former, créer, inventer, imaginer; (*a new path*) frayer. — **through,** traverser. — **up,** (*mus.*) jouer, commencer à jouer; (*a song*) entonner; (*the drums*) battre, commencer à battre; (*an acquaintance*) faire; (*a bargain*) conclure

Strike, *v.n.* frapper; (*dash against*) heurter, frapper, donner (contre *or* sur); (*at*) porter un coup (à); s'attaquer (à); attenter (à); (*penetrate*) pénétrer, entrer; s'engager; (*break out*) jaillir; (*appear*) percer (à travers), éclater (dans); (*of clocks,* &c.) sonner; (*of drums*) battre; (*of workmen*) faire grève, se mettre en grève; (*of plants*) prendre racine, pousser; (*of ships*) toucher, échouer; (*of flags*) amener, baisser pavillon. *It has struck ten,* dix heures sont sonnées. —! (*nav.*) amène! bas le pavillon! — *while the iron is hot,* (*Proverb*) il faut battre le fer pendant qu'il est chaud. — **against,** heurter *or* &c. contre; heurter. — **in,** (*enter*) entrer tout à coup; (*of eruptions,* &c.) rentrer. — **in with,** se conformer à; (*join with*) se joindre à, s'unir à. — **out,** s'étendre au loin; se jeter (dans); se lancer. — **up,** (*mus.*) commencer à jouer; (*of voices*) commencer à chanter

Strike, *s.* (*of measure*) râcloire, radoire, *f.*; (*of workmen*) grève, *f.* *On* —, en grève

Strike, *adj.* (*of measures*) ras, râcle

Striker, *s.* frappeur, *m.*, -euse, *f.*; (*hammer*) marteau, *m.*

Striking, *adj.* frappant; remarquable, marquant; imposant; surprenant; (*of colours*) tranchant; (*of clocks*) sonnant; — *s.* frappement, *m.*; (*of metals*) battage, *m.*; (*of clocks*) sonnerie, *f.*; (*strokes*) coups, *m.pl.*; (*sound*) son, *m.* — **clock,** *s.* horloge (*or* pendule) sonnante (*or* à sonnerie), *f.* — **off** *or* **out,** *s.* radiation, *f.* — **part, -train,** *s.* (*of a clock*) sonnerie, *f.* [remarquablement

Strikingly, *adv.* d'une manière frappante;

Strikingness, *s.* nature frappante *or* remarquable, *f.*; exactitude frappante, *f.*

String, *s.* corde, ficelle, *f.*; (*of shoes, aprons, purse,* &c.) cordon, *m.*; (*of bonnets, caps*) bride, *f.*; (*thread*) fil, *m.*; (*row, line, series*) file, *f.*; suite, *f.*: série, *f.*; enchaînement, *m.*; kyrielle, ribambelle, *f.*; tirade, *f.*; (*of onions, beads*) chapelet, *m.*; (*of mus. instr., of a bow*) corde, *f.*; (*for spinning tops*) fouet, *m.*; (*of plants, and fig. of the heart*) fibre, *f.*; (*of meat*) filandres, *f.pl.*; — *v.a.* munir *or* garnir de cordes; garnir de ficelle; (*beads,* &c.) enfiler; (*make tense*) tendre, bander; (*strengthen*) fortifier; (*put in tune*) accorder; (*plants*) effiler. — **board,** *s.* limon (d'escalier), *m.* — **course,** *s.* cordon, *m.* — **halt,** *s.* éparvin sec, *m.* — **instrument,** *s.* instrument à cordes, *m.* —**less,** *adj.* sans cordes. — **reel, -roller,** *s.* ficellier, *m.* — **up,** *v.a.* (*hang*) pendre

Stringed, *adj.* à cordes. — *instrument,* instrument à cordes, *m.* *Four* —, à quatre

Stringency, *s.* rigueur, sévérité, *f.* [cordes

Stringent, *adj.* strict, rigoureux, sévère

Stringently, *adv.* strictement, rigoureusement, sévèrement

Stringy, *adj.* fibreux; filandreux

Strip, *v.a.* dépouiller (de); (*take off*) ôter, enlever; (*undress*) déshabiller; (*hemp, flax*) tiller; (*a ship*) dégréer; — *v.n.* se déshabiller; — *s.* bande, *f.*; ruban, *m.*; (*of land*) morceau, coin, *m.* — **off,** dépouiller; ôter, enlever; (*peel*) peler; (*trees*) écorcer

Stripe, *s.* raie, *f.*; (*strip*) bande, *f.*; (*mil.*) chevron, galon, *m.*; (*lash*) coup, coup de fouet, *m.*; (*weal*) marque, vergeture, *f.*; — *v.a.* rayer. *With —s, striped.* (*of stuffs*) à raies

Stripling, *s.* tout jeune homme, jeune garçon, *m.*; (*in contempt*) blanc-bec, gamin, *m.* *He is a mere* —, il est encore tout jeune, il n'est pas encore formé, ce n'est qu'un enfant (*or* qu'un gamin)

Strive, *v.n.* tâcher (de), s'efforcer (de); faire des efforts (pour), se donner du mal (pour); (*struggle*) lutter (contre); se débattre (contre); (*vie*) le disputer (à). *To — hard to,* faire tous ses efforts pour . . . [lutte, *f.*

Striving, *s.* effort, *m.*, efforts, *m.pl.*; (*contest*)

Strivingly, *adv.* avec effort; à l'envi

Stroke, *s.* coup, *m.*; (*touch*) touche, *f.*; (*dash*) trait, *m.*; (*of a pen*) coup *or* trait de plume, *m.*; (*of a drawing-pencil*) coup de crayon, *m.*; (*of a brush*) coup de pinceau, *m.*; (*effort*) effort, *m.*; (*in swimming*) brasse, brassée, *f.*; (*of a piston*) coup, *m.*; (*of an oar*) coup d'aviron, *m.*; (*of paralysis, apoplexy*) attaque, *f.*; — *v.a.* caresser. *Little —s fell great oaks,* petit à petit l'oiseau fait son nid. *Up* —, (*writ.*) délié, *m.*; (*mach.*) mouvement ascensionnel, *m.* *Down* —, (*writ.*) plein, *m.*; (*mach.*) mouvement descendant, *m.* *Thin* or *fine* or *hair* —, (*writ.*) délié, *m.* *Thick* —, (*writ.*) plein, *m.* *Straight* —, (*writ.*) bâton, *m.* *At a* —, d'un coup; d'un trait. *Upon* or *on the — of four,* sur le coup de quatre heures. *It is upon the — of four,* il est près de quatre heures. *The clock is upon the — of four,* l'horloge (*or* la pendule) va sonner quatre heures. *To have a great — of,* avoir beaucoup de. *To keep* —, aller en mesure; ramer *or* nager ensemble. *To pull a long* —, nager de long. *To pull the — oar,* donner la nage. 10 *feet* —, course (*f.*) *or* jeu (*m.*) de 10 pieds. — **engraving,** *s.* gravure au burin, *f.* — **oarsman, —sman,** *s.* brigadier, *m.*

Stroking, *s.* caresse, *f.*, caresses, *f.pl.*

Stroll, *v.n.* (— **about**) errer; aller çà et là; se promener à l'aventure; courir le pays; rôder; (*idle in the streets*) flâner; — *s.* promenade, *f.*, tour, *m.*; flânerie, *f.* *To take a* —, faire un tour; flâner

Stroller, *s.* coureur, *m.*; flâneur, *m.*, -euse, *f.*; vagabond, *m.*, e, *f.*; comédien ambulant, *m.*, comédienne ambulante, *f.*

Strolling player *or* **musician,** *s.* comédien *or* musicien ambulant, *m.*

Strombus, *s.* strombe, *m.*

Strong, *adj.* fort; solide; vigoureux; énergique; ferme; ardent; vif; violent; puissant; (*great*) grand; — *adv.* *V.* **Strongly;** (*in great numbers*) en grand nombre 5000 —. (*mil.*) fort (*m.*, e, *f.*) de 5,000 hommes; au nombre de 5000 hommes. *To muster* —, s'assembler *or* &c. (*V.* **Muster**) en grand nombre. —**backed,** *adj.* qui a les reins forts. — **box,** *s.* coffre-fort, *m.* —**hold,** *s.* forte prise, *f.*; grande place, *f.*; (*fortress*) place forte, forteresse, *f.*; fort, *m.* — **minded,** *adj.* à esprit fort, qui a l'esprit solide. — **set,** *adj.* solidement bâti. — **smelling,** *adj.* d'une odeur forte, qui sent fort

Strongly, *adv.* fortement; fort; solidement; vigoureusement; énergiquement; violemment; fermement; vivement; particulièrement; (*numerously*) en grand nombre

Strongylus, *s.* strongle, *m.*

Strontia, Strontian, *s.* strontiane, *f.*

Strontium, *s.* strontium, *m.*

Strop, *s.* cuir à repasser, cuir à rasoir, *m.*; (*nav.*) estrope, *f.*; — *v.a.* repasser (sur le cuir); (*nav.*) estroper

Strophe, *s.* strophe, stance, *f.*

Strophule, Strophulus, *s.* strophule, *m.*

Structural, *adj.* de structure

Structure, *s.* structure, *f.*; construction, *f.*, édifice, *m.*; (*anat.*) tissu, *m.*

Struggle, *v.n* faire de grands efforts (pour), s'efforcer (de); (*contend*) lutter ('*with,*' contre; '*to,*' pour); (*move*) se débattre, se démener, s'agiter; — *s.* grand effort, effort, *m.*; (*contest*) lutte, *f.*, combat, *m.*

Struggler, *s.* personne qui fait de grands

efforts, *f.*; (*contending*) personne qui lutte, *f.*, [lutteur, *m.*
Struggling, *s.* *V.* **Struggle,** *s.*
Strum. *V.* **Thrum**
Struma, *s.* (*bot.*) renflement, goître, *m.*; (*med.*) scrofule, *f.*, scrofules, *f.pl.*
Strumous, *adj.* (*med.*) scrofuleux
Strumpet, *s.* prostituée, *f.*
Strut, *v.n.* se pavaner, se carrer; — *s.* démarche fière *or* affectée, *f.*; pas mesuré, *m.*; (*carp.*) potelet, étai, support, *m.*
Struthious, *adj.* du genre de l'autruche
Strychnia, Strychnine, *s.* strychnine, *f.*
Strychnos, *s.* strychnos, *m.*
Stub, *s.* souche, *f.*, chicot, tronçon, *m.*; — *v.a.* déraciner, arracher, extirper. — **nail,** *s.* clou à caboche, clou sans tête, *m.*
Stubble, *s.* chaume, *m*, éteule, *f.* — **field, -ground,** *s.* chaume, *m.* — **rick, -stack,** *s.* meulon, *m.*
Stubbled, Stubbly, *adj.* plein de chaume
Stubborn, *adj* opiniâtre, obstiné, entêté, têtu; volontaire; inflexible; (*of horses*) rétif. *Facts are — things*, rien de si brutal qu'un fait. — **ly,** *adv.* opiniâtrément, obstinément. —**ness,** *s.* opiniâtreté, obstination, *f.*, entêtement, *m.*; inflexibilité, *f.*
Stubby, *adj.* plein de chicots; (*pers.*) trapu, ramassé; (*of beard*) hérissé; buissonneux
Stucco, *s.* stuc, *m.*; (*work*) ouvrage en stuc, *m.*; — *v.a.* revêtir de stuc. — **plasterer,** *s.* stucateur, *m.*
Stuccoer, *s.* stucateur, *m.*
Stuck, *part. of* **Stick,** *v.a.n., which see.* — **over with,** garni de. — **up,** *adj.* prétentieux; (*conceited*) suffisant
Stud, *s.* (*nail*) clou, *m.*; (*of shirts*) bouton (de chemise), *m.*; (*of horses*) chevaux, *m.pl.*; écurie, *f.*, écuries, *f.pl.*; (*breeding-* —) haras, *m.*; (*of a bridle*) bossette, *f.*; (*build.*) montant, *m.*; — *v.a.* (*with nails*) clouter, garnir de clous; (*adorn*) garnir (de), orner (de); (*strew*) parsemer (de), semer (de). — **book,** *s.* registre des chevaux, stud-book, *m.* — **groom,** *s.* palefrenier, *m.*; (*riding*) piqueur, *m.* — **horse,** *s.* étalon de haras, *m.*
Studding-sail, *s.* bonnette, *f.*
Student, *s.* personne qui étudie (le, la, les ...), *f.*; étudiant, *m.*; élève, *m.f.*; (*of law, medicine,* &c.) étudiant (en ...), *m.*
Studied, *adj.* étudié; savant; (*affected*) recherché, apprêté; (*premeditated*) prémédité; calculé
Studio, *s.* atelier, *m.*
Studious, *adj.* studieux; attentif (à); empressé (de). —**ly,** *adv.* studieusement; attentivement; avec soin; avec empressement; avec affectation. —**ness,** *s.* application, *f.*
Study, *s.* étude, *f.*; attention, application, *f.*, soin, *m.*; méditation, *f.*; rêverie, *f.*; (*room*) cabinet, *m.*; (*of schools*) salle d'étude, étude, *f.*; — *v.n.a.* étudier; travailler; faire son étude de; (*go through o.'s course of studies*) faire ses études; (*for*) se préparer (à); (*to endeavour, to aim at*) s'appliquer (à), s'étudier (à), s'attacher (à), chercher (à), viser (à); (*reflect on*) réfléchir à, méditer sur, considérer; (*have regard for*) avoir égard à, avoir des égards pour. *To — hard*, travailler ferme, piocher. *To — economy*, viser à l'économie, chercher l'économie. *To — o.'s comfort*, rechercher *or* chercher ses aises. *To make it o.'s — to*, s'étudier à, s'attacher à, s'appliquer à, chercher à, prendre à tâche de. — **table,** *s.* table de travail, *f.*
Stuff, *s.* (*cloth*) étoffe, *f.*; tissu, *m.*; (*texture of wool thinner and slighter than cloth*) stoff, *m.*; (*matter*) matière, chose, *f.*; (*materials*) matériaux, *m.pl.*; (*fig. of pers.*) bois, *m.*; (*rubbish*) drogue, *f.*; (*nonsense*) fatras, *m.*, bêtise, *f.*; (*nav.*) suif, courai, *m.* — *!* bah! quelle bêtise! allons donc! laissez donc! laissez-moi donc tranquille! *All — !* balivernes que tout cela! *Bad* or *poor* —, drogue, *f.* *Beastly* or *filthy* or *nasty* —, saleté, cochonnerie, *f.* *Old* —, vieillerie, *f.* *Silly* —, sottises, *f.pl.* *Wretched* —, saleté, drogue. *This wine is excellent* —, ce vin est excellent. *The — that cardinals are made of*, le bois dont on fait les cardinaux
Stuff, *v.a.* (*fill*) remplir (de), garnir (de); (*seats,* &c.) rembourrer (de); (*with eating*) bourrer (de), gorger (de); (*obstruct*) boucher; (*fowls, meat*) farcir; (*dead animals*) empailler; — *v.n.* se bourrer. — **out,** rembourrer. — **up,** boucher, encombrer; prendre
Stuffer, *s.* empailleur, *m.*, -euse, *f.*
Stuffing, *s.* (*materials*) bourre, *f.*, (*cook.*) farce, *f.*; (*act of stuffing*) rembourrage, rembourrement, *m.*, (*cook.*) farcissure, *f.*; (*preserving dead animals*) empaillage, *m.*; (*creature comforts*) boustifaille, mangeaille, *f.* — **box,** *s.* (*tech.*) presse-étoupe, *m.*
Stultify, *v.a.* hébéter, abrutir; (*things*) neutraliser; rendre nul, annuler; infirmer; (*belie*) démentir
Stum, *s.* râpé, *m.*; — *v.a.* passer sur le râpé; (*with brimstone*) soufrer, mécher, muter
Stumble, *v.n.* trébucher, faire un faux pas; broncher; (*err*) faillir; — *v.a.* faire trébucher; embarrasser; — *s.* faux pas, *m.* — **on, upon,** rencontrer, tomber sur
Stumbling, *s.* bronchement, trébuchement, faux pas, *m.* —**block, -stone,** *s.* pierre d'achoppement, *f.*; écueil, *m.*
Stump, *s.* tronçon, *m.*; (*of limbs*) moignon, *m.*; (*of teeth*) chicot, *m.*; (*of trees*) tronçon, chicot, *m.*; (*of cabbages,* &c.) trognon, *m.*; (*of pens, cigars,* &c.) bout, *m.*; (*drawing*) estompe, *f.*; (*at cricket*) bâton des barres, *m.*; (*leg*) gigue, quille, *f.*; (*platform*) estrade, *f.*; (*hustings*) *V.* **Hustings;** — *v.a.* (*draw*) estomper; (*canvass*) haranguer; (*puzzle*) embarrasser, coller. *To stir o.'s —s*, se démener, se dépêcher, se remuer, se donner du mouvement. — **bedstead,** *s.* lit à un seul dossier, *m.* — **orator,** *s.* orateur de carrefours, déclamateur, péroreur, *m.* — **out,** *v.a.* (*fig.*) mettre à sec. — **speech,** *s.* harangue populaire, *f.* — **up,** *v.a.n.* cracher, abouler, financer
Stumping, *s.* (*draw.*) estompage, *m.*
Stumpy, *adj.* plein de tronçons; (*pers.*) trapu
Stun, *v.a.* étourdir; abasourdir; ébouriffer
Stunner, *s.* merveille, *f.*
Stunning, *adj.* étourdissant; ébouriffant; fameux
Stunt, *v.a.* empêcher de croître, rabougrir; atrophier, faire avorter
Stunted, *adj.* rabougri; atrophié; chétif; (*in mind*) borné, bouché
Stuntedness, *s.* rabougrissement, *m.*; atrophie, *f.*; chétiveté, *f.*
Stupefacient, *s.* stupéfiant, *m.*
Stupefaction, *s.* stupéfaction, *f.*
Stupefactive, *adj.* *s.* stupéfactif, *adj.m.*, -ive, *f.*, stupéfactif, *s.m.*, stupéfiant, *adj.m.*, e, *f.*, stupéfiant, *s.m.*
Stupefier, *s.* stupéfiant, *m.*
Stupefy, *v.a.* hébéter, abrutir; (*benumb*) stupéfier, engourdir
Stupendous, *adj.* prodigieux, étonnant, foudroyant. —**ly,** *adv.* prodigieusement, étonnamment. —**ness,** *s.* nature prodigieuse, *f.*
Stupid, *adj.* stupide, bête; engourdi, lourd
Stupidity, Stupidness, *s.* stupidité, bêtise, *f.*
Stupidly, *adv.* stupidement, bêtement
Stupify, &c. *V.* **Stupefy,** &c.
Stupor, *s.* stupeur, *f.*
Sturdied, *adj.* atteint du tournis
Sturdily, *adv.* hardiment; résolûment; fortement, vigoureusement; brutalement, brusquement
Sturdiness, *s.* hardiesse, *f.*; résolution, *f.*; force, vigueur, *f.*; brutalité, brusquerie, *f.*
Sturdy, *adj.* hardi; résolu; fort, vigoureux, valide; brutal, brusque; — *s.* (*vet.*) tournis, tournoiement, *m.*
Sturgeon, *s.* esturgeon, *m.*
Stutter, &c. *V.* **Stammer,** &c.
Sty, *s.* (*pig* —) *V.* **Piggery;** (*on the eye*) *V.* **Stye;** — *v.a.* établer

Stye, *s.* compère-loriot, orgelet, *m.*
Stygian, *adj.* stygien, stygial, du Styx
Style, *s.* style, *m.*; (*manner*) manière, *f.*, genre, style, goût, *m.*; ton, *m.*; (*superior*) cachet, style, *m.*; (*beauty*) élégance, grâce, coquetterie, *f.*; (*in the fine arts*) style, *m.*; (*fam.*) chic, *m.*; (*title*) titre, *m.*; nom, *m.*; (*of a commercial firm*) raison, raison sociale, *f.*; (*bot., of writing, chron., and of dials*) style, *m.*; (*surg.*) stylet, *m.* *In* —, comme il faut; (*fine*) magnifique, superbe. *In fine* —, de la belle manière; brillamment; magnifiquement; (*of thrashing, &c.*) d'importance. *In good* —, dans le bon genre; de bon goût; de bon ton. *That's the* —, c'est cela! bravissimo! allez! *The* — *of the firm*, la raison sociale de la maison. *To live in great or in first-rate* —, avoir un grand train de maison, mener grand train. *The* — *in which he lives*, la manière dont il vit, son genre de vie, le train qu'il mène
Style, *v.a.* appeler; donner le titre de, qualifier de. *To* — *oneself*, s'appeler, se faire appeler, se donner le titre de, se dire
Stylish, *adj.* dans le style; comme il faut; brillant, beau; élégant, de bon ton; pimpant; coquet; (*tiptop*) huppé. **—ly,** *adv.* élégamment; grandement. **—ness,** *s.* élégance, grâce, coquetterie, *f.*
Styptic, -al, *adj. s.* styptique, *adj.m.f., s.m.*
Stypticity, *s.* stypticité, *f.*
Styrian, *s. adj.* Styrien, *m.*, -ne, *f.* [Souabe
Suabian, *s.* Souabe, *m.f.*; — *adj.* souabe, de
Suable, *adj.* poursuivable
Suave, *adj.* suave
Suavity, *s.* suavité, *f.*
Sub, (*in compounds*) sous- . . .; sub . . .
Subacetate, *s.* sous-acétate, *m.*
Subacid, *adj.* acidule; — *s.* substance acidule, *f.*
Subacrid, *adj.* légèrement âcre
Subacute, *adj.* subaigu
Subaerial, *adj.* subaérien
Subagent, *s.* sous-agent, *m.*
Subalmoner, *s.* sous-aumônier, *m.*
Subalpine, *adj.* subalpin
Subaltern, *s. adj.* subalterne, *m.f.* [terniser
Subalternate, Subalternize, *v.a.* subal-
Subalternately, *adv.* subalternement
Subalternation, Subalternization, *s.* subalternisation, subalternité, *f.*
Subapennine, *adj.* subapennin
Subaquatic, *adj.* subaquatique
Subaxillary, *adj.* sous-axillaire
Subbrigadier, *s.* sous-lieutenant, *m.*
Subcarbonate, *s.* sous-carbonate, *m.*
Subcelestial, *adj.* terrestre
Subchanter, *s.* sous-chantre, *m.*
Subcommission, *s.* sous-commission, *f.*
Subcommittee, *s.* sous-comité, *m.*; sous-commission, *f.*
Subcontract, *v.n.* sous-traiter; — *s.* sous-traité, *m.* [traitant, *m.*
Subcontractor, *s.* sous-entrepreneur, sous-
Subcostal, *adj.* sous-costal
Subcutaneous, *adj.* sous-cutané
Subdeacon, *s.* sous-diacre, *m.*
Subdeaconry, *s.* sous-diaconat, *m.*
Subdean, *s.* sous-doyen, *m.*
Subdeanery, *s.* sous-doyenné, *m.*
Subdecuple, *adj.* sous-décuple
Subdelegate, *s.* sous-délégué, *m.*, e, *f.*, subdélégué, *m.*, e, *f.*; — *v.a.* sous-déléguer, subdéléguer
Subdelegation, *s.* sous-délégation, subdélégation, *f.* [(-trice, *f.*)
Subdirector (-tress), *s.* sous-directeur, *m.*
Subdistrict, *s.* (*of country*) canton, *m.*; (*of town*) quartier, *m.*
Subdivide, *v.a.* subdiviser; — *v.n.* se subdiviser
Subdivision, *s.* subdivision, *f.*
Subdivisional, *adj.* subdivisionnaire
Subdominant, *s.* (*mus.*) sous-dominante, *f.*
Subduable, *adj.* domptable

Subdual, *s.* assujettissement, asservissement, *m.*, réduction, soumission, *f.* [enlever
Subduce, Subduct, *v.a.* retirer, soustraire,
Subduction, *s.* soustraction, *f.*, enlèvement, *m.*
Subdue, *v.a.* (*conquer*) subjuguer, soumettre, vaincre, réduire, assujettir, dompter, triompher de; (*tame, break*) maîtriser, dompter; (*of diseases*) vaincre, abattre; (*repress*) réprimer; (*the light*) adoucir; (*stop*) arrêter. *—d light*, demi-jour, *m.* *In a —d voice*, d'une voix étouffée. *In a —d tone*, d'un ton bas; d'un ton soumis
Subduer, *s.* vainqueur, *m.*; dompteur, *m.*
Subduple, *adj.* sous-double
Subduplicate, *adj.* sous-doublé
Sub-editor, *s.* rédacteur gérant, gérant, secrétaire de la rédaction, *m.* [gérant
Sub-editorial, *adj.* de (*or* du) rédacteur-
Sub-editorship, *s.* gérance, *f.*
Sub-editress, *s.* gérante, *f.*
Suberous, *adj.* subéreux
Subfossil, *adj.* subfossile
Subgeneric, *adj.* sous-générique
Subgenus, *s.* sous-genre, *m.*
Subgovernor, *s.* sous-gouverneur, *m.*
Subhead, *s.* (*print.*) sous-titre, *m.*
Subinflammation, *s.* subinflammation, *f.*
Subinspector (-tress), *s.* sous-inspecteur, *m.* (-trice, *f.*)
Subjacent, *adj.* sous-jacent, subjacent
Subject, *v.a.* assujettir (à), soumettre (à); exposer (à); — *adj.* assujetti (à), soumis (à); (*liable*) sujet (à); exposé (à); — *s.* sujet, *m.*; (*pers., polit.*) sujet, *m.*, sujette, *f.*; (*an individual, fam.*) sujet, individu, *m.*, personne, *f.*; (*gram., anat.*) sujet, *m.*; (*mus.*) motif, *m.* — *to*, (*adverb.*) à *or* sous la condition de; sauf; sauf à recourir à. — **matter,** *s.* sujet, *m.*, matière, *f.*
Subjection, *s.* sujétion, *f.*, assujettissement, *m.*; soumission, *f.*; dépendance, *f.* *To bring under* —, assujettir, soumettre
Subjective, *adj. s.* subjectif, *adj. m.*, -ive, *f.*, subjectif, *s.m.*
Subjectively, *adv.* subjectivement
Subjectiveness, Subjectivity, *s.* subjectivité, *f.*
Subjectiv-ism, -ist. *V.* page 3, § 1
Subjoin, *v.a.* ajouter (à), joindre (à)
Subjoined, *adj.* ci-joint; (*opposite*) ci-contre
Subjugate, *v.a.* subjuguer, soumettre, dompter, réduire, assujettir, asservir
Subjugation, *s.* subjugation, soumission, *f.*, assujettissement, *m.*
Subjugator, *s.* subjugueur, vainqueur, *m.*
Subjunction, *s.* adjonction, *f.*
Subjunctive, *s. adj.* subjonctif, *m.* — *mood*, subjonctif, *m.* *In the* —, au subjonctif
Sub-kingdom, *s.* (*nat. hist.*) sous-règne, *m.*
Sublet, Subletting. *V.* **Underlet, Underletting**
Sublibrarian, *s.* sous-bibliothécaire, *m.*
Sublieutenancy, *s.* sous-lieutenance, *f.*
Sublieutenant, *s.* sous-lieutenant, *m.*
Sublimable, *adj.* sublimable
Sublimate, *v.a.* élever; (*chem.*) sublimer; — *s.* sublimé, *m.*; — *adj.* sublimé (*m.*, e, *f.*)
Sublimation, *s.* sublimation, *f.*
Sublimatory, *s. adj.* sublimatoire, *m.*
Sublime, *adj.* sublime; (*high*) élevé; — *s.* sublime, *m.*; — *v.a.* *V.* **Sublimate**
Sublimely, *adv.* sublimement, d'une manière sublime, avec sublimité
Sublimeness, *s.* sublimité, *f.*, sublime, *m.*
Subliming, *s.* sublimation, *f.* — **pot,** *s.* sublimatoire, *m.* [élévation, grandeur, *f.*
Sublimity, *s.* sublimité, *f.*, sublime, *m.*;
Sublimize, *v.a.* sublimiser
Sublingual, *adj.* sublingual
Sublunar, Sublunary, *adj.* sublunaire
Submanag-er, eress, *s.* sous-directeur, *m.*, sous-directrice, *f.*

Submarine, *adj.* sous-marin
Submaxillary, *adj.* sous-maxillaire
Submerge, *v.a.* submerger ; — *v.n.* plonger
Submergence, *s.* submergement, *m.*
Submergible, *adj.* submersible
Submersion, *s.* submersion, *f.*
Submission, *s.* soumission, *f.* ; résignation, *f.* ; déférence, *f.*
Submissive, *adj.* soumis (à) ; humble ; résigné (à). **—ly,** *adv.* avec soumission ; humblement ; avec déférence, respectueusement. **—ness,** *s.* soumission, *f.* ; humilité, *f.* ; déférence, *f.*
Submit, *v.a.* soumettre (à) ; — *v.n.* se soumettre (à) ; se résigner (à) ; souffrir (. . .) ; (*to an operation*) subir (. . .). *To — oneself,* se soumettre (à)
Submultiple, *s.adj.* sous-multiple, *s.m., adj.m.f.*
Subnormal, *s.* sous-normale, *f.*
Sub-officer, *s.* sous-officier, *m.*
Subordinacy, *s.* subordination, soumission, dépendance, *f.*
Subordinary, *s.* (*her.*) meuble, *m.*
Subordinate, *adj. s.* subordonné, subalterne, inférieur ; sous- . . . ; (*gram.*) incident ; — *v.a.* subordonner (à), soumettre (à). — *ordinary,* (*her.*) meuble, *m.*
Subordinately, *adv.* subordonnément, subalternement, en sous-ordre
Subordinateness, Subordination, *s.* subordination, *f.* ; soumission, *f.* ; dépendance, *f.* ; rang inférieur, *m.*
Suborn, *v.a.* suborner
Subornation, *s.* subornation, *f.*
Suborner, *s.* suborneur, *m.*, -euse, *f.*
Suboxide, *s.* sous-oxyde, *m.*
Subphosphate, *s.* sous-phosphate, *m.*
Subpœna, *s.* assignation, citation, *f.* ; — *v.a.* assigner, citer
Sub-prefect, *s.* sous-préfet, *m.*
Sub-prefectoral, Sub-prefectorial, *adj.* sous-préfectoral
Sub-prefecture, *s.* sous-préfecture, *f.*
Subprior, *s.* sous-prieur, *m.*
Subrector, *s.* sous-recteur, *m.*
Subreption, &c. *V.* **Surreption**
Subrogation, *s.* subrogation, *f.*
Subrogatory, *adj.* subrogatoire
Subsalt, *s.* sous-sel, *m.*
Subscribe, *v.a.n.* (*sign, take shares, agree, on a list*) souscrire (' *to,*' à ; ' *towards* ' or ' *for,*' pour) ; (*engage for a series, as to take in papers, — to baths, theatres,* &c.) s'abonner (à) [*to — for anyone,* abonner quelqu'un] ; être abonné (à). *To — oneself,* se dire
Subscriber, *s.* (*on a list,* &c.) souscripteur, *m.* ; (*for a series, as to a paper, season-tickets,* &c.) abonné, *m.*, e, *f.*
Subscript, *adj.* (*Gr. gram.*) souscrit
Subscription, *s.* (*on a list,* &c.) souscription, *f.* ; (*for a series, as to a paper, season-tickets,* &c.) abonnement, *m.* *To discontinue* or *withdraw o.'s —,* se désabonner. — **library,** *s.* abonnement de lecture, cabinet de lecture, *m.*
Subsequenc-e, y, *s.* subséquence, postériorité, *f.*
Subsequent, *adj.* subséquent ; postérieur, [ultérieur
Subsequently, *adv.* ensuite, après, par la suite, plus tard, subséquemment, postérieurement, ultérieurement. — *to . . .,* après . . .
Subserve, *v.a.* servir ; aider à ; contribuer à ; favoriser ; servir d'instrument à
Subservienc-e, y, *s.* dépendance, *f.* ; subordination, *f.* ; obéissance, *f.* ; concours, *m.* ; utilité, *f.*
Subservient, *adj.* subordonné (à), inférieur (à) ; secondaire ; accessoire ; utile (à). *To make — to,* faire servir à
Subserviently, *adv.* subordonnément ; en sous-ordre ; utilement ; conformément (à)
Subside, *v.n.* tomber au fond ; tomber ; diminuer, baisser ; s'abaisser ; se calmer, s'apaiser ; (*sink*) s'affaisser ; (*build.*) tasser, se tasser ; (*into*) descendre (dans) ; se changer (en) ; devenir (. . .)
Subsidence, Subsidency, Subsiding, *s.* affaissement, *m.*, considence, *f.* ; (*build.*) tassement, *m.*
Subsidiarily, *adv.* subsidiairement
Subsidiary, *adj.* subsidiaire, auxiliaire ; — *s.* auxiliaire, *m.*
Subsidize, *v.a.* donner des subsides à ; subventionner
Subsidy, *s.* subside, *m.* ; subvention, *f.*
Subsist, *v.n.* subsister (' *on,*' de) ; exister ; — *v.a.* faire subsister, entretenir, nourrir
Subsistenc-e, y, *s.* subsistance, *f.* ; (*keeping*) entretien, *m.* ; (*being*) existence, *f.*
Subsistent, *adj.* subsistant ; inhérent (à)
Subsoil, *s.* (*geol., agr.*) sous-sol, *m.* ; (*law*) tréfonds, *m.* ; — *adj.* du sous-sol. — **plough, Subsoiler,** *s.* charrue défonceuse, charrue fouilleuse, défonceuse, fouilleuse, *f.*, coutrier, *m.* — **ploughing,** *s.* défoncement, *m.*
Subspecies, *s.* sous-espèce, *f.*
Substance, *s.* substance, *f.* ; fond, *m.* ; matière, *f.* ; réalité, *f.* ; corps, *m.* ; résumé, *m.* ; (*wealth*) biens, *m.pl.*, fortune, *f.*, avoir, *m.*
Substantial, *adj.* substantiel ; essentiel ; matériel ; sensible ; réel, vrai ; solide, fort ; fondé ; sérieux ; riche, cossu ; — *s.* partie essentielle, *f.*
Substantiality, *s.* existence réelle, *f.* ; existence matérielle, *f.* ; matérialité, *f.* ; solidité, *f.*
Substantialize, *v.a.* substantialiser
Substantially, *adv.* substantiellement ; en substance ; essentiellement ; matériellement ; sensiblement ; réellement ; solidement, fortement ; (*comfortably*) dans l'aisance
Substantialness, *s.* solidité, force, *f.* ; réalité, *f.*
Substantiate, *v.a.* établir ; confirmer ; appuyer ; prouver
Substantival, *adj.* substantif
Substantivally, *adv.* substantivement
Substantive, *adj. s.* substantif, *m.*
Substantively, *adv.* en substance ; (*gram.*) substantivement
Substitute, *v.a.* substituer (' *for,*' à) ; — *s.* remplaçant, *m.*, e, *f.*, substitut, suppléant, *m.*, e, *f.* ; délégué, *m.*, e, *f.* ; mandataire, *m.f.* ; (*of professors*) professeur suppléant, suppléant, agrégé, *m.* ; (*theat.*) doublure, *f.* double, *m.* ; (*mil.*) remplaçant, *m.* ; (*things*) chose qui remplace, *f.* *As a — for,* pour remplacer. *To be a — for,* remplacer, servir pour remplacer
Substitution, *s.* substitution, *f.*
Substitutive, *adj.* substitutif
Substratum, *s.* couche inférieure, souscouche, *f.* ; (*agr.*) sous-sol, *m.*
Substruction, Substructure, *s.* substruction, substructure, *f.*, sous-œuvre, *m.*, fondation, *f.*
Subsulphate, *s.* sous-sulfate, *m.*
Subsulphide, *s.* sous-sulfure, *m.*
Subtangent, *s.* sous-tangente, *f.*
Subtenant, *s. V.* **Undertenant**
Subtend, *v.a.* sous-tendre
Subtense, *s.* sous-tendante, *f.*
Subterfuge, *s.* subterfuge, faux-fuyant, détour, *m.*, échappatoire, *f.*
Subterranean, Subterraneous, *adj.* souterrain. — **place** *or* **passage,** *s.* souterrain, *m.*
Subterraneously, *adv.* souterrainement
Subtile, *adj.* subtil ; (*fine*) fin, délié ; (*sly*) adroit, fin ; (*piercing*) aigu, perçant
Subtilely, *adv.* subtilement
Subtileness, Subtility, *s.* subtilité, *f.*
Subtilization, *s.* subtilisation, *f.*
Subtilize, *v.a.n.* subtiliser
Subtilizer, *s.* subtiliseur, *m.*, -euse, *f.*
Subtilizing, *s.* subtilisation, *f.*
Subtle, *adj.* subtil ; (*sly*) fin, rusé
Subtleness, Subtlety, *s.* subtilité, *f.* ; (*sliness*) finesse, ruse, *f.*

Subtly, *adv.* subtilement; (*slily*) finement, avec finesse, avec ruse

Subtract, *v.a.* soustraire; retrancher; défalquer; déduire; ôter

Subtraction, *s.* soustraction, *f.*; retranchement, *m.*; défalcation, *f.*; déduction, *f.*; (*arith.*) soustraction, *f.*

Subtractive, *adj.* soustractif

Subtrahend, *s.* nombre à soustraire, nombre à retrancher, *m.*

Subtutor, *s.* sous-gouverneur, sous-précepteur, *m.*

Suburb, *s.* faubourg, *m.*; **—s,** *pl.* faubourgs, *m.pl.*; banlieue, *f.*

Suburban, *adj.* de faubourg; des faubourgs, de la banlieue; faubourien; (*admin.*) suburbain; — *s.* habitant (*m.*, e, *f.*) des faubourgs, faubourien, *m.*, -ne, *f.*

Subvariety, *s.* sous-variété, *f.*

Subvention, *s.* subvention, *f.*; — *v.a.* subventionner

Subvention-al, ary, *adj.* subventionnel

Subversion, *s.* subversion, *f.*, renversement, *m.*

Subversive, *adj.* subversif

Subvert, *v.a.* subvertir, renverser, bouleverser

Subverter, *s.* subvertisseur, *m.*; destructeur, *m.*, -trice, *f.*

Subway, *s.* galerie souterraine, *f.*, souterrain, *m.*

Subworker, *s.* auxiliaire, aide, *m.f.*

Succedaneous, *adj.* qui remplace (...), qui peut être substitué (à); (*med.*) succédané

Succedaneum, *s.* chose qui remplace, *f.*; (*med.*, &c.) succédané, *m.*

Succeed, *v.a.n.* (*take the place of*) succéder (à); (*supersede*) remplacer; (*follow*) suivre; (*inherit*) hériter (de); (*be successful*) réussir (*'in,' before a noun,* dans, en; *before a present part.*, à, *with the inf. in French*); (*manage to*) parvenir *or* réussir (*'in doing'* ..., à faire ...). *To — each other,* se succéder

Succeeding, *adj.* (*following*) suivant; (*in order*) successif; (*future*) futur, à venir

Succentor, *s.* sous-chantre, *m.*; basse, *f.*

Success, *s.* (*of pers.*) succès, *m.*; (*of things*) succès, *m.*, réussite, *f.*; (*luck*) bonne chance, *f.* *Great —,* grand succès. *I wish you —,* je vous souhaite de réussir; (*fam.*) bonne chance! **—ful,** *adj.* heureux, couronné de succès, qui réussit; fructueux; victorieux; (*satisfactorily performed or done or made*) réussi (*very —ful,* bien réussi; *more —ful, most —ful,* mieux réussi). *To be —ful,* être heureux *or* &c.; réussir, avoir du succès. *To be —ful in doing* ..., réussir (*or* parvenir) à faire ... **—fully,** *adv.* heureusement, avec succès; victorieusement. **—fulness,** *s.* (*pers.*) succès, *m.*; (*things*) succès, *m.*, réussite, *f.* **—less,** *adj.*, **—lessly,** *adv.* sans succès. **—lessness,** insuccès, *m.*

Succession, *s.* (*series*) succession, suite, *f.*; (*in the place of another*) succession, *f.*; (*inheritance*) succession, *f.*; héritage, *m.*; (*right of ditto*) droit de succession, *m.*; (*accession to the throne*) avénement, *m.*; (*lineage*) postérité, *f.*, descendants, *m.pl.*; (*mus.*) succession, *f.* *— of crops,* assolement, *m.* *In —,* successivement, de suite; tour à tour. **— Act,** *s.* Acte de succession, *m.* **— duty,** *s.* droit de succession, *m.* **— war,** *s.* guerre de succession, *f.*

Successive, *adj.* successif; consécutif

Successively, *adv.* successivement

Successiveness, *s.* successivité, *f.*

Successor, *s.* successeur, *m.*

Succinct, *adj.* succinct

Succinctly, *adv.* succinctement, avec concision

Succinctness, *s.* concision, brièveté, *f.*

Succinic, *adj.* succinique

Succory, *s.* chicorée, *f.*

Succour, *s.* secours, *m.*; — *v.a.* secourir. **—less,** *adj.* sans secours, privé de secours

Succourer, *s.* secoureur, *m.*, -euse, *f.*

Succuba, Succubus, *s.* succube, *m.*

Succulenc-e, y, *s.* succulence, *f.*

Succulent, *adj.* succulent

Succulently, *adv.* succulemment

Succumb, *v.n.* succomber (*'under': a weight,* sous; *fig.*, à); céder (*'to,'* à); se soumettre (*'to,'* à)

Succussion, *s.* succussion, *f.*

Such, *adj.* tel; pareil; semblable; (*these, those*) ces; (*adverb.: thus*) tel, ainsi, (*so*) si, tellement, tant; aussi. *— is* ..., tel (*m.*, telle, *f.*) est ... *— are,* tels (telles, *f.*) sont ... *— a one,* un tel, *m.*, une telle, *f.*; (*similar*) un pareil, *m.*, une pareille, *f.* *I have — a one,* j'en ai un pareil *or* un semblable. *— a one as,* tel que. *— and —,* tel ou tel. *— a man,* un tel homme. *— a man as this,* un homme tel que celui-ci. *— a studious man,* un homme si studieux. *— cruelty,* une telle cruauté, une pareille cruauté, une semblable cruauté. *On — occasions,* dans ces occasions, dans ces circonstances. *— as,* tel que; comme; (*those who* or *whom* or *which*) ceux (*m.*, celles, *f.*) qui (*nom.*) *or* que (*acc.*); (*who* or *which*) qui; (*whom* or *which*) que; (*of a nature to*) qui est de nature à (*with the inf.*); (*the like of whom* or *which*) comme ... en. *Take — as are within your reach,* prenez ceux qui sont à votre portée. *A smile — as would gladden* ..., un sourire qui réjouirait ... *A smile — as I have never seen,* un sourire comme je n'en ai jamais vu. *Offer me — things as I can accept,* offrez-moi des choses que je puisse accepter. *No — thing,* rien de semblable, rien de la sorte; point. *It is no — thing,* il n'en est rien; point. *There is no — thing as* ..., il n'y a pas de ...; (*no possibility*) il n'y a pas moyen de ... *There is no — thing as that,* il n'y en a pas; cela n'existe pas. *Did anybody ever see — a thing?* vit-on jamais rien de pareil?

Suck, *v.a.n.* sucer; (*at the breast*) téter; (*inhale*) aspirer, pomper; (*as pumps*) aspirer; (*absorb*) absorber, pomper, boire. *It is teaching o.'s grandmother how to — eggs,* (*Proverb*) c'est Gros-Jean qui en remontre à son curé. **— down,** sucer; (*ingulf*) attirer, engloutir, entraîner. **— in,** sucer; aspirer; humer; (*believe*) gober. **— out, up,** sucer; pomper; absorber

Suck, *s.* sucement, *m.*; aspiration, *f.*; (*milk*) lait, *m.*; (*sugar-stick*) sucre d'orge, *m.* *To give — to,* donner à téter à, donner le sein à, allaiter

Sucker, *s.* suceur, *m.*, -euse, *f.*; (*of insects*) suçoir, *m.*; (*of plants*) drageon, surgeon, œilleton, *m.*; (*of a pump*) piston, *m.*; (*fish*) *V.* **Sucking-fish**

Sucking, *s.* sucement, *m.*, succion, *f.*; aspiration, *f.*; absorption, *f.*; — *adj.* suçant, qui suce; qui tette, de lait; (*tech.*) aspirant, d'aspiration. **— bottle,** *s.* *V.* **Feeding-bottle.** **— calf,** *s.* veau de lait, *m.* **— fish,** *s.* suceur, sucet, rémora, lompe, *m.* **— infant, -child,** *s.* enfant à la mamelle, *m.* **— pig,** *s.* cochon de lait, *m.* **— pipe, — pump,** *s.* *V.* **Suction**

Suckle, *v.a.* allaiter, nourrir; donner le sein à

Suckling, *s.* enfant à la mamelle, *m.*; (*nursling*) nourrisson, *m.*, -ne, *f.*; (*animal*) animal qui tette encore, *m.*; (*act of —*) allaitement, *m.*

Suction, *s.* sucement, *m.*, succion, *f.*; aspiration, *f.*; absorption, *f.*; (*in compounds*) d'aspiration, aspirant. **— pipe,** *s.* tuyau d'aspiration, tuyau aspirant, *m.* **— pump,** *s.* pompe aspirante, *f.*

Suctorial, *adj.* suceur

Suctorian, *s.* suceur, *m.*

Sudamina, *s.pl.* sudamina, *m.pl.*, suette miliaire, *f.*

Sudation, *s.* sudation, *f.*

Sudatory, *adj. s.* sudatoire, *adj m.f.*, *s.m.*

Sudden, *adj.* subit, soudain; inopiné; imprévu. *— death,* mort subite, *f.* *All of a —, on a —,* *V.* **Suddenly**

Suddenly, *adv.* subitement, soudainement, tout à coup; tout d'un coup

Suddenness, *s.* soudaineté, *f.*

Sudoriferous, *adj.* sudorifère

Sudorific, *adj. s.* sudorifique, *adj.m.f.*, *s.m.*

Suds, *s.pl.* eau de savon, *f.* *In the —,* (*fig.*) dans le pétrin

Sue, *v.a.n.* poursuivre en justice, poursuivre

[See over

('*for*,' pour); solliciter ('*for*,' ...), demander ('*for*,' ...); implorer ('*for*,' ...). *To — for damages*, poursuivre en dommages et intérêts

Suet, *s.* graisse de rognons, graisse, *f.*; (*candle-stuff*) suif, *m.*

Suety, *adj.* de graisse, gras

Suevi, *s.pl.* Suèves, *m pl.*

Suffer, *v.a.n.* souffrir ('*by*,' '*with*,' '*from*,' de); supporter, endurer; (*undergo*) subir; (*a loss*, &c.) éprouver; (*to lose*) perdre ('*by*,' à); (*allow*) permettre (de, que), laisser. *To — oneself to be* (*dazzled, beaten*, &c.) se laisser (éblouir, battre, &c.). *He will — for it*, il en portera la peine; (*fam.*) il ne le portera pas en paradis, il s'en mordra les pouces. *— me to tell you*, permettez-moi de vous dire, permettez (*or* souffrez) que je vous dise, laissez-moi vous dire. *He was —ed to remain*, on lui permit de rester. *He was —ed to go*, on le laissa aller

Sufferable, *adj.* supportable

Sufferably, *adv.* supportablement

Sufferance, *s.* tolérance, *f.* *On —*, par tolérance

Sufferer, *s.* personne qui souffre, *f.*; victime ('*by*,' de), *f.*; patient, *m.*, e, *f.*; (*of illness*) malade, *m.f.*; (*from fire*) victime (d'un incendie), *f.*, incendié, *m.*, e, *f.* *To be a —*, souffrir ('*by*' de); (*lose*) perdre ('*by*,' à; '*by it*,' y) [... *a great* or *heavy* —, ... beaucoup]

Suffering, *s.* souffrance, *f.*; — *adj.* souffrant

Sufferingly, *adv.* avec douleur, en souffrant; péniblement

Suffice, *v.a.* suffire à; satisfaire; — *v.n.* suffire ('*for*,' à; '*to*,' à, de). *— it to say* (*that* ...), qu'il suffise de dire (que ...); suffit (que ...). *— it* (*that* ...), suffit (que ...)

Sufficiency, *s.* suffisance, *f.*; (*of fortune*) aisance, *f.*; (*capacity*) capacité, compétence, aptitude, *f.* *A —*, suffisamment, assez; de l'aisance, le nécessaire, de quoi vivre

Sufficient, *adj.* suffisant; (*adverb.*) assez. *To be —*, suffire ('*for*,' à; '*to*, à, de). *That is —*, cela suffit, c'est assez. *— for the day is the evil thereof*, à chaque jour suffit sa peine

Sufficiently, *adv.* suffisamment, assez

Suffix, *s.* suffixe, *m.*

Suffocate, *v.a.* suffoquer, étouffer; asphyxier

Suffocating, *adj.* suffocant, étouffant; — *part.* suffoquant, étouffant

Suffocatingly, *adv.* d'une manière suffocante *or* étouffante, à suffoquer, à étouffer

Suffocation, *s.* suffocation, *f.*, étouffement, *m.*; asphyxie, *f.*

Suffocative, *adj.* suffocant, étouffant

Suffragan, *adj. s.* suffragant, *adj m.*, e, *f.*, suffragant, *s.m.*

Suffrage, *s.* suffrage, *m.*

Suffrutex, *s.* sous-arbrisseau, *m.*

Suffuse, *v.a.* répandre; couvrir (de); remplir (de)

Suffusion, *s.* suffusion, *f.*; épanchement, *m.*; (*fig.*) voile, *m.*

Sugar, *s.* sucre, *m.*; —*v.a.* sucrer; (*fig.*) adoucir. *Brown* or *moist* or *raw* —, cassonade, *f.*, sucre brut, *m.* *— of lead*, sucre de plomb, acétate de plomb, *m.* *— and water*, eau sucrée, *f.* *To sweeten with —*, sucrer. — **baker,** *s.* raffineur de sucre, *m.* — **bakery,** *s.* raffinerie de sucre, *f.* — **baking,** *s.* raffinage de sucre, *m.* — **basin,** *s.* sucrier, *m.* — **candy,** *s.* sucre candi, *m.* — **cane,** *s.* canne à sucre, *f.* — **crusher,** *s.* pilon à sucre, *m.* — **grass,** *s.* houque saccharine, plante à sucre, *f.* — **house,** *s.* sucrerie, *f.* — **loaf,** *s.* pain de sucre, *m.*; *adj.* en pain de sucre. — **maker,** *s.* sucrier, *m.* — **manufacture,** *s.* fabrication de sucre, *f.* — **maple,** *s.* *V.* **Maple.** — **mill,** *s.* moulin à cannes à sucre, *m.*, sucrerie, *f.* — **nippers,** *s.pl.* casse-sucre, *m.* — **plantation,** *s.* plantation de cannes à sucre, *f.* — **planter,** *s.* planteur de cannes à sucre, *m.* — **plum,** *s.* dragée, *f.* — **rasp,** *s.* râpe à sucre, *f.* — **refiner,** *s.* raffineur de sucre, *m.* — **refinery,** *s.* raffinerie de sucre, sucrerie, *f.* — **refining,** *s.* raffinage de sucre, *m.* — **sifter,** *s.* cuiller à sucre, *f.* — **tongs,** *s.pl.* pince à sucre, *f.* — **trade,** *s.* commerce des sucres, *m.*, sucrerie *f.* — **works,** *s.pl.* sucrerie, *f.*

Sugariness, *s.* nature sucrée, *f.*; goût sucré, *m.*

Sugary, *adj.* sucré

Suggest, *v.a.* suggérer; inspirer; faire naître, donner; faire penser à; donner à entendre; conseiller; proposer. *To — itself*, se présenter

Suggester, *s.* suggesteur, *m.*

Suggestion, *s.* suggestion, *f.*; idée, *f.*; avis, *m.*; proposition, *f.*

Suggestive, *adj.* suggestif; (*of* ...) qui suggère (...), qui fait penser (à ...)

Suicidal, *adj.* de suicide, suicide

Suicidally, *adv.* par le suicide

Suicide, *s.* (*self-murderer, self-murderess*) suicide, *m.f.*, suicidé, *m.*, e, *f.*; (*self-murder*) suicide, *m.* *To commit —*, se suicider, se donner la mort

Suit, *s.* collection, *f.*; (*set*) assortiment, *m.*; (*of clothes*) habillement complet, habillement, *m.*; (*at cards*) couleur, *f.*; (*request*) demande, requête, instance, pétition, *f.*; (*courtship*) cour, recherche en mariage, *f.*; (*law*) procès, *m.*, action, *f.*; (*suite*) *V.* **Suite;** — *v.a.* adapter (à), approprier (à); assortir; convenir à, aller à; faire *or* être l'affaire de; contenter, satisfaire, plaire à; arranger, accommoder; pourvoir; — *v.n.* s'accorder (avec), cadrer (avec), convenir. *— at law*, (*s.*) action, poursuite, *f.*, procès, *m.* *— of armour*, armure complète, *f.* *— of clothes*, habillement complet, habillement, *m.* *New —*, habillement neuf, *m.* *To follow —*, (*at cards*) donner de la couleur *or* de la carte

Suitability, *s.* *V.* **Suitableness**

Suitable, *adj.* approprié (à); convenable (à); conforme (à); proportionné (à); qui correspond (à); qui convient (à); suffisant; commode

Suitableness, *s.* convenance, *f.*; conformité, *f.*; rapport, *m.*

Suitably, *adv.* convenablement; conformément

Suite, *s.* suite, *f.*; (*— of furniture*), ameublement complet, ameublement, meuble, *m.* *— of rooms, — of apartments*, appartement, *m.* *A — of bedroom furniture*, un ameublement de chambre. *V.* **Drawing-room**

Suitor, *s.* (*law*) plaideur, *m.*; (*applicant*) postulant, *m.*; (*lover*) prétendant, *m.* *—s' fund*, caisse des dépôts et consignations, *f.*

Suliot, *s. adj.* Souliote, *m.f.*

Sulk, *v.n.* bouder, faire la mine; **—s,** *s.pl.* mauvaise humeur, *f.* *In the —s*, de mauvaise humeur

Sulker, *s.* boudeur, *m.*, -euse, *f.*

Sulkily, *adv.* en boudant, maussadement, d'un air maussade

Sulkiness, Sulking, *s.* bouderie, maussaderie, *f.*

Sulky, *adj.* boudeur, maussade; — *s.* (*carriage*) désobligeante, *f.*

Sullen, *adj.* maussade; sombre, triste, chagrin; rechigné, refrogné; obstiné

Sullenly, *adv.* maussadement; tristement; d'un air refrogné; obstinément; à contre-cœur

Sullenness, *s.* maussaderie, *f.*; air sombre, *m.*; mauvaise humeur, *f.*; obstination, *f.*

Sully, *v.a.* ('*with*,' de) souiller, tacher, ternir; — *v.n.* se ternir; — *s.* souillure, tache, *f.*

Sulphate, *s.* sulfate, *m.*; — *v.a.* sulfater

Sulphatic, *adj.* sulfatique; sulfaté

Sulphatization, *s.* sulfatisation, *f.*

Sulphide, *s.* sulfure, *m.*

Sulphite, *s.* sulfite, *m.*

Sulpho ..., (*in compounds, chem.*) sulfo ...

Sulphur, *s.* soufre, *m.*; — *v.a.* soufrer. — **mine,** *s.* soufrière, *f.* — **wort,** *s.* paucédane, *m.*

Sulphurate, *v.a.* sulfurer

Sulphuration, *s.* sulfuration, *f.*

Sulphureous, *adj.* sulfureux

Sulphureousness, *s.* nature sulfureuse, *f.*

Sulphurer, *s.* soufreur, *m.*

Sulphuret, *s.* *V.* **Sulphide**

Sulphureted, Sulphuretted, *adj.* sulfuré

Sulphuric, *adj.* sulfurique

Sulphu[illegible], *s.* soufrage, *m.*; — *adj.* à soufrer. —**apparatus,** *s.* machine à soufrer, *f.* — **stove,** *s.* soufroir, *m.*
Sulphurization, *s.* sulfuration, *f.*
Sulphurize, *v.a.* sulfurer, soufrer
Sulphurizing, *s.* soufrage, *m.*
Sulphurous, Sulphury, *adj.* sulfureux
Sulphydric, *adj.* sulphydrique
Sultan, *s.* sultan, *m.*
Sultana, Sultaness, *s.* sultane, *f.*; (— **bird**) poule sultane, *f*
Sultanate, Sultanship, *s.* sultanat, *m.*
Sultanic, *adj.* du sultan
Sultriness, *s.* chaleur étouffante, *f.*
Sultry, *adj.* etouffant, suffocant; brûlant; d'une chaleur excessive *or* étouffante. *To be — or very — (weather),* faire une chaleur étouffante
Sum, *s.* somme, *f.*; (*abstract*) résumé, sommaire, *m.*; (*height*) comble, sommet, *m.*; (*arith.*) règle, *f.*, calcul, *m.* — *total,* total, *m.*, somme totale, *f.* *A stated* —, une somme de. *To do* or *work a* —, faire un calcul. *To set a* —, poser une règle. —**less,** *adj.* incalculable; innombrable
Sum, *v.a.* — **up,** additionner; résumer, récapituler; (*summarize*) *V.* **Summarize**
Sumac, Sumach, *s.* sumac, *m.* — **tree,** *s.* [sumac, *m.*
Sumbul, *s.* sumbul, *m.*
Summarily, *adv.* sommairement; sur-le-champ, tout de suite; sans aucune explication; sans enquête; rondement
Summarize, *v.a.* exposer *or* donner sommairement; résumer
Summary, *adj.* sommaire; expéditif, prompt, immédiat [cis, *m.*
Summary, *s.* sommaire, abrégé, résumé, pré-
Summer, *s.* été, *m.*; — *adj.* d'été; estival; — *v.n.* passer *or* rester l'été, estiver. *In* —, en été. *In the —, in the — time,* dans l'été, en été. — **fallow,** *s.* jachère d'été, *f.*; *v.a.* labourer pendant l'été. — **holidays,** *s.pl.* vacances d'été, grandes vacances, *f.pl.* — **house,** *s.* pavillon, kiosque, *m.*; habitation d'été, *f.* — **season,** *s.* saison d'été, *f.*; (*nat. hist.*) estivation, *f.*
Summersault, Summerset. *V.* **Somerset**
Summing-up, *s.* addition, *f.*; (*recapitulation*) [résumé, *m.*
Summit, *s.* sommet, *m.*; faîte, *m.*
Summon, *v.a.* convoquer (à); assembler; faire venir; (*call upon, bid*) sommer (de); inviter (à), appeler (à); exhorter (à); adjurer (de); (*call*) appeler; (— *to appear*) citer (à); (*require*) réclamer; (*law*) assigner, citer. — **away,** ordonner de s'eloigner; rappeler; appeler. — **up,** exciter, animer; rassembler; rappeler
Summoner, *s.* personne qui convoque *or* qui somme *or* qui cite, *f.*, sommateur, *m.*, convocateur, *m.*, -trice, *f.*; (*law*) huissier, *m.*
Summoning officer, *s.* huissier, *m.*
Summons, *s.* (*call*) appel, *m.*; invitation, *f.*; convocation, *f.*; (— *to surrender,* &c.) sommation, *f.*; (*law*) assignation, citation, *f.*; (*crim. law*) mandat de comparution, *m.*; sommation, *f.* *To grant* or *issue a* —, lancer une assignation *or* une citation; lancer un mandat de comparution. *To take out a* —, se faire délivrer une assignation *or* &c.
Sump, *s.* (*mining*) puisard, *m.* [somme, *m.*
Sumpter-horse, *s.* sommier, cheval de
Sumptuary, *adj.* somptuaire
Sumptuous, *adj.* somptueux
Sumptuously, *adv.* somptueusement
Sumptuousness, *s.* somptuosité, *f.*
Sun, *s.* soleil, *m.*; — *v.a.* exposer au soleil, ensoleiller; chauffer au soleil; insoler. *In the* —, dans le soleil; (*sunshine*) au soleil. *The — shines,* le soleil luit, il fait du soleil. — **beam,** *s.* rayon de soleil, rayon solaire, *m.* — **bird,** *s.* soui-manga, *m.* — **blind,** *s.* abat-jour, *m.* — **bright,** *adj.* radieux, *m.* —**burn,** *s.* hâle, *m.* — **burnt,** *adj.* brûlé par le soleil; (*of the complexion*) hâlé, basané. — **clad,** *adj.* radieux. — **dew,** *s.* drosère, *f.* — **dial,** *s.* cadran solaire, *m.* — **dried,** *adj.* séché au soleil. — **fish,** *s.* poisson-soleil, poisson-lune, *m.* — **flower,** *s.* soleil, tournesol, hélianthe, *m.* —**less,** *adj.* sans soleil. — **light,** *s.* lumière du soleil, *f.* — **like,** *adj.* semblable au soleil. —**lit,** *adj.* éclairé par le soleil. — **proof,** *adj.* impénétrable aux rayons du soleil. — **rise, -rising,** *s.* lever du soleil, soleil levant, *m.* — **set, -setting,** *s.* coucher du soleil, soleil couchant, *m.* — **shade,** *s.* abat-jour, *m.*; (*of a telescope*) recouvrement, cache-lumière, *m.*; (*parasol*) en-tout-cas, en-cas, *m.* — **shine,** *s.* clarté du soleil, *f.*, soleil, *m.*; (*fig.*) éclat, *m.*; bonheur, *m.* *In the —shine,* au soleil. *In the bright —shine, in broad* or *full —shine,* en plein soleil. — **shiny,** *adj.* de soleil. — **stone,** *s.* adulaire, *f.* — **stroke,** *s.* coup de soleil, *m.* — **worship,** *s.* culte (*m.*) *or* adoration (*f.*) du soleil. — **worshipper,** *s.* adorateur (*m.*, -trice, *f.*) du soleil
Sunday, *s.* dimanche, *m.*; — *adj.* du dimanche. *On —, On —s, V.* **On.** *When two —s come together,* la semaine des quatre jeudis. — **clothes,** *s.pl.* habits des dimanches. *To put o.'s — clothes on,* s'endimancher. — **letter,** *s.* lettre dominicale, *f.* (*V.* **School**)
Sunder, *v.a.* séparer, diviser; (*cut*) couper; (*break*) rompre. *In* —, en deux
Sundries, *s.pl.* diverses choses, *f.pl.*; (*expenses*) frais divers, faux frais, *m.pl.*; (*com.*) divers, *m.pl.*; articles divers, *m.pl.*; fournitures, *f.pl.*
Sundry, *adj.* divers
Sunk, Sunken, *part. adj.* enfoncé; affaissé; &c. (*V.* **Sink,** *v.a.n.*); (*hollow*) creux; (*of eyes, cheeks*) creux, cave; (*emaciated*) amaigri; (*overwhelmed*) accablé (de)
Sunna, Sunnah, *s.* sonna, *f.*
Sunnite, *s.* sonniste, sonnite, *m.*
Sunny, *adj.* de *or* du soleil; brillant; vermeil; exposé au soleil; ensoleillé; (*fig.*) heureux, riant. *It is* —, il fait du soleil
Sup, *v.a.* (— **up**) humer, avaler; (*to sip*) *V.* **Sip;** — *v.n.* souper ('*on,*' de, avec); — *s. V.* **Sip**
Superable, *adj.* surmontable
Superableness, *s.* nature surmontable, *f.*
Superably, *adv.* de manière à être surmonté
Superabound, *v.n.* surabonder ('*with,*' de)
Superabundance, *s.* surabondance, *f.*
Superabundant, *adj.* surabondant
Superabundantly, *adv.* surabondamment
Superadd, *v.a.* surajouter, ajouter, joindre
Superaddition, *s.* suraddition, *f.*, surcroît, *m.*, addition, *f.*
Superannuate, *v.a.* (*disqualify*) rendre suranné; (*impair*) affaiblir par l'âge; (*pension off*) mettre à la retraite, retraiter
Superannuated, *part. adj.* suranné; hors d'âge; (*on pension*) retraité, en retraite
Superannuation, *s.* mise à la retraite, *f.*; pension de retraite, *f.* — **fund,** *s.* caisse de [retraite, *f.*
Superb, *adj.* superbe
Superbly, *adv.* superbement
Supercargo, *s.* subrécargue, *m.*
Superciliary, *adj.* sourcilier
Supercilious, *adj.* sourcilleux, hautain, arrogant, impérieux, fier. —**ly,** *adv.* sourcilleusement, avec hauteur, avec dédain, arrogamment, avec arrogance, impérieusement, fièrement. —**ness,** *s.* hauteur, *f.*, dédain, *m.*, arrogance, fierté, *f.* [éminence, *f.*
Supereminenc-e, y, *s.* supériorité, pré-
Supereminent, *adj.* prééminent, suréminent
Supereminently, *adv.* supérieurement; par excellence
Supererogate, *v.n.* faire plus qu'on n'est obligé, faire plus que son devoir, faire plus qu'on n'a promis
Supererogation, *s.* surérogation, *f.*
Supererogatorily, *adv.* surérogatoirement

Supererogatory, *adj.* surérogatoire
Superexcellent, *adj.* surfin ; parfait
Superfetation, *s.* superfétation, *f.*
Superfetative, *adj.* superfétatif [superficie
Superficial, *adj.* superficiel ; (*measure*) de
Superficiality, *s. V.* **Superficialness**
Superficially, *adv.* superficiellement
Superficialness, *s.* superficialité, *f.*, peu de profondeur, *m.*; légèreté, *f.*
Superficiary, *adj.* superficiaire
Superficies, *s.* superficie, *f.*
Superfine, *adj.* surfin, superfin
Superfineness, *s.* qualité surfine, *f.*, surfin, *m.*
Superfluity, *s.* superfluité, *f.*; superflu, *m.*
Superfluous, *adj.* superflu
Superfluously, *adv.* avec superfluité, d'une manière superflue ; inutilement
Superfluousness, *s. V.* **Superfluity**
Superfœtation, *s.* superfétation, *f.*
Superheat, *v.a.* surchauffer
Superheating, *s.* surchauffage, *m.*
Superhuman, *adj.* surhumain
Superimpose, *v.a.* surimposer
Superimposition, *s.* surimposition, *f.*
Superincumbent, *adj.* surincombant, superposé, supérieur
Superinduce, *v.a.* introduire, ajouter
Superinduction, *s.* introduction, addition, *f.*, surcroît, *m.*
Superintend, *v.a.* surveiller; diriger
Superintendence, *s.* surveillance, surintendance, inspection, *f.* ; direction, *f.*
Superintendent, *s.* surveillant, *m.*, e, *f.*, surintendant, *m.*, e, *f.*, inspecteur, *m.*, -trice, *f.* ; chef, *m.*, directeur, *m*, -trice, *f.* ; (*of railways*) chef de gare, *m.* ; (*of police*) commissaire (de police), *m.*; (*eccl.*) supérieur, *m.*
Superior, *adj. s.* supérieur, *m.*, e, *f.*
Superioress, *s.* supérieure, *f.*
Superiority, *s.* supériorité, *f.*
Superiorly, *adv.* supérieurement
Superiorship, *s.* supériorat, gardiennat, *m.*
Superjacent, *adj.* sus-jacent
Superlative, *adj.* suprême; supérieur; extrême ; (*gram.*) superlatif ; — *s.* superlatif, *m.* — *degree,* superlatif, *m.* *In the — (degree),* au superlatif
Superlatively, *adv.* au suprême degré, au superlatif, extrêmement, (*fam.*) superlativement ; (*gram.*) au superlatif
Superlativeness, *s.* suprême degré, *m.*
Superlunar, -y, *adj.* surlunaire
Supermundane, *adj.* supramondain
Supernal, *adj.* supérieur ; céleste
Supernally, *adv.* par en haut, d'en haut
Supernatant, *adj.* qui surnage, surnageant
Supernatation, *s.* action de surnager, *f.*
Supernatural, *adj.* surnaturel
Supernatural-ism, -ist. *V.* page 3, § 1
Supernaturally, *adv.* surnaturellement
Supernaturalness, *s.* caractère *or* état surnaturel, *m.*, surnaturalité, *f.*
Supernumerary, *adj.* surnuméraire ; (*things*) supplémentaire ; extraordinaire ; — *s.* surnuméraire, *m.* ; (*theat.*) (*substitute*) doublure, *f.*, (*performer not speaking*) figurant, *m.*, e, *f.*, comparse, *m.f.* — *tooth,* surdent, *f.*
Superoxidate, *v.a.* suroxyder ; — *v.n.* se suroxyder
Superoxidation, *s.* suroxydation, *f.*
Superoxide, *s.* suroxyde, *m.* [se suroxygéner
Superoxygenate, *v.a.* suroxygéner ; — *v.n.*
Superoxygenation, *s.* suroxygénation, *f.*
Superphosphate, *s.* hyperphosphate, *m.*
Superpose, *v.a.* superposer
Superposition, *s.* superposition, *f.*
Superroyal, *adj. s.* jésus, *adj.m.*, *s.m.*
Supersalt, *s.* sursel, *m.*
Supersaturate, *v.a.* sursaturer
Supersaturation, *s.* sursaturation, *f.*
Superscribe, *v.a.* mettre l'adresse à, adresser; mettre une inscription à
Superscription, *s.* suscription, adresse, *f.*; inscription, *f.*; (*of coins*) légende, *f.*
Supersede, *v.a.* rendre nul, annuler; remplacer; supplanter; suspendre; faire abandonner, faire supprimer; (*of dress*) démoder; (*law*) surseoir à ; rejeter, annuler. — *d,* (*done away with*) supprimé; (*of dress*) démodé
Supersession, *s.* substitution, *f.*; remplacement, *m.*; suspension, *f.*; abandon, *m.*; sup-
Superstition, *s.* superstition, *f.* [pression, *f.*
Superstitious, *adj.* superstitieux. —**ly,** *adv.* superstitieusement. —**ness,** *s.* superstitiosité, *f.*
[superposée, *f.*
Superstratum, *s.* couche supérieure, couche
Superstruction, Superstructure, *s.* superstruction, superstructure, *f.* ; édifice, *m.*
Supertonic, *adj. s.* sustonique, *adj.m.f.*, *s.f.*
Supervene, *v.n.* survenir
Supervenient, *adj.* survenant, qui survient, qui arrive ; supplémentaire [venance, *f.*
Supervention, *s.* survenue, *f.*; (*law*) sur-
Supervise, *v.a.* surveiller, inspecter ; contrôler ; (*books,* &c.) réviser
Supervision, *s.* surveillance, inspection, *f.* contrôle, *m.* ; (*of books*) révision, *f.* ; (*of police*) surveillance, *f.*
Supervisor, *s.* surveillant, inspecteur, *m.*; contrôleur, *m.* ; (*of books,* &c.) réviseur, *m.*
Supination, *s.* supination, *f.*
Supinator, *adj. s.* supinateur, *adj.m.*, *s.m.*
Supine, *adj.* couché sur le dos ; incliné ; penché ; (*indolent*) nonchalant, insouciant, négligeant, indolent ; — *s.* supin, *m.*
Supinely, *adv.* sur le dos; (*fig.*) nonchalamment, négligemment, avec indolence
Supineness, *s.* supination, *f.* ; (*fig.*) nonchalance, négligence, indolence, *f.*
Supper, *s.* souper, *m.* *To eat —,* souper. —**eater,** *s.* soupeur, *m*, -euse, *f.* — **hour, -time,** *s.* heure du souper, *f.* —**less,** *adj.* sans souper. — **table,** *s.* table servie pour le
Supplant, *v.a.* supplanter [souper, *f.*; table, *f.*
Supplantation, Supplanting, *s.* supplantation, *f.*, supplantement, *m.*
Supplanter, *s.* supplantateur, *m.*, -trice, *f.*
Supple, *adj.* souple ; — *v.a.* assouplir. — **jack,** *s.* liane, *f.* [pléer ; compléter
Supplement, *s.* supplément, *m.* ; — *v.a.* sup-
Supplemental, Supplementary, *adj.*
Suppleness, *s.* souplesse, *f.* [supplémentaire
Suppletory, *adj.* supplétif, supplétoire
Suppliant, Supplicant, *adj. s.* suppliant, *m.*, e, *f.*; pétitionnaire, *m.f.*; (*law*) requérant,
Suppliantly. *V.* **Supplicatingly** [*m.*, e, *f.*
Supplicate, *v.a.n.* supplier
Supplicatingly, *adv.* en suppliant, d'un air *or* d'un ton suppliant
Supplication, *s.* supplication, *f.*; supplique, *f.*
Supplicatory, *adj.* suppliant
Supplier, *s.* fournisseur, *m.*
Supply, *v.a.* pourvoir ('*with,*' de), fournir (... à ; '*with,*' de); approvisionner ('*with,*' de); (*afford, as means,* &c.) procurer, offrir, fournir ; (*wants*) pourvoir à, subvenir à ; satisfaire ; (*serve instead of*) suppléer à, remplacer ; (*complete*) suppléer ; (*fill*) remplir ; (*com.*) être fournisseur de. *To — one with a thing,* pourvoir quelqu'un d'une chose, fournir une chose à quelqu'un *or* fournir quelqu'un d'une chose. *To — the place of,* remplacer. *The tradespeople who — us,* nos fournisseurs
Supply, *s.* fourniture, *f.*, approvisionnement, *m.*; provision, *f.*; (*help*) secours, renfort, *m.*; (*parliam*, —, *sing.*, —**ies,** *pl.*) budget des dépenses, *m.*, dépenses, *f.pl.*; (*politic. econ.*) offre, *f.* *The demand and —,* l'offre et la demande. *To stop the —ies,* (*fam.*) couper les vivres ; (*parliam.*) refuser des fonds [ment, *m.*
Supplying, *s.* fourniture, *f.*, approvisionne-
Support, *v.a.* (*bear*) supporter ; soutenir ; (*suffer*) supporter ; souffrir ; (*keep up*) entretenir, soutenir ; défrayer ; (*feed*) entretenir, nourrir,

faire vivre; (*help, stand by*) appuyer, soutenir, épauler; (*as an electoral body*) porter; (*attend*) assister. — *!* (*mil.*) arme au bras! *To — oneself*, se soutenir; (*keep oneself*) s'entretenir, se suffire à soi-même
Support, *s.* support, soutien, appui, *m.*; (*countenance*) appui, suffrage, *m.*; (*maintenance*) entretien, *m.*, nourriture, *f.*; (*upholding*) maintien, *m.* *In — of*, à l'appui de; (*for the benefit of*) au bénéfice de, au profit de. **—less,** *adj.* sans soutien, sans appui
Supportable, *adj.* supportable, tolérable; (*maintainable*) soutenable
Supportableness, *s.* nature supportable, *f.*
Supportably, *adv.* supportablement
Supporter, *s.* soutien, appui, *m.*; défenseur, *m.*; adhérent, partisan, *m.*; (*attendant*) personne qui assiste, *f.*; (*surg.*) supporteur, bandage contentif, *m.*; (*her.*) support, *m.*
Supposable, *adj.* supposable
Suppose, *v.a.* supposer; (*conjecture*) présumer, supposer; (*fancy*) s'imaginer; (*think*) penser, croire. — (*let us —, — now*), supposons, supposé (que), en supposant; (*what if*) si (*to be followed, in French, by the Imperfect of the Indicative*; *as, —we go*, si nous allions; — *he should come*, s'il venait)
Supposed, *part. adj.* supposé; prétendu; (*reputed*) censé; (*of fathers*) putatif
Supposer, *s.* supposeur, *m.*
Supposing, *prep.* en supposant (que); supposons *or* supposé (que)
Supposition, *s.* supposition, *f.*; hypothèse, *f.*
Suppositional, *adj.* hypothétique
Supposititious, *adj.* supposé
Supposititiously, *adv.* par une supposition
Supposititiousness, *s.* nature supposée, [supposition, *f.*
Suppositive, *adj.* suppositif
Suppositively, *adv.* par supposition, par hypothèse
Suppository, — tube, *s.* suppositoire, *m.*
Suppress, *v.a.* supprimer; (*crush*) réprimer; (*forbear*) retenir; (*keep secret, stifle, check*) étouffer; (*stop*) arrêter
Suppressed, *part. adj.* supprimé, &c. (*V.* **Suppress,** *v.a.*); (*med.*) rentré
Suppressible, *adj.* supprimable; répressible
Suppression, *s.* suppression, *f.*; (*crushing*) répression, *f.* [pressif
Suppressive, *adj.* suppressif; (*subduing*) ré-
Suppressor, *s.* personne qui supprime *or* qui réprime *or* qui étouffe, *f.*
Suppurate, *v.n.* suppurer
Suppuration, *s.* suppuration, *f.*
Suppurative, *adj. s.* suppuratif, *adj.m.*, -ive, *f.*, suppuratif, *s.m.*
Supracostal, *adj.* surcostal
Supramaxillary, *adj.* sus-maxillaire
Supramundane, *adj.* supramondain
Supranasal, *adj.* sus-nasal
Supranatural-ism, -ist. *V.* page 3, § 1
Suprarenal, *adj.* surrénal
Suprascapular, *adj.* sus-scapulaire
Supraspinal, *adj.* surépineux
Supremacy, *s.* suprématie, *f.*
Supreme, *adj.* suprême; souverain
Supremely, *adv.* suprêmement, au suprême de-[gré; souverainement
Sura, Surah, *s.* surate, *f.*
Sural, *adj.* sural
Surbase, *s.* corniche (de lambris d'appui), *f.*
Surbased, *adj.* à corniche; (*of vaults*) sur-[baissé
Surbasement, *s.* surbaissement, *m.*
Surbasic, *adj.* surbasique
Surbate, *v.a.* meurtrir, blesser; excéder de [fatigue, harasser
Surbated, *adj.* solbatu
Surcharge, *v.a.* surcharger, charger trop; (*of money*) surfaire, faire trop payer; (*admin.*) surtaxer; — *s.* surcharge, trop forte charge, *f.*; (*of money*) demande exorbitante, *f.*; (*admin.*) sur-[taxe, *f.*
Surcingle, *s.* surfaix, *m.*
Surcoat, *s.* surcot, *m.*
Surd, *adj.* (*math.*) irrationnel; — *s.* nombre ir-[rationnel, *m.*
Sure, *adj.* sûr; certain; assuré; — *adv. V.* **Surely.** — *enough!* à coup sûr! *To be —!* assurément, certainement, sans doute, mais oui, parbleu, sur ma parole, ma foi, c'est vrai, allez, donc, quoi; au fait; par exemple! *To be — to*, ne pas manquer (de); ne pouvoir pas manquer (de). *To be — not to*, se garder de; être sûr de ne pas; ne pouvoir pas. *To make —*, assurer. *To make — (of, that)*, s'assurer (de, que); (*believe, rely upon*) se croire sûr (de); croire bien (que); être persuadé (de, que); compter (sur, que). *I am —!* ma foi! assurément, très certainement, certainement, certes, vraiment. *I am — I don't know*, ma foi je n'en sais rien, je n'en sais ma foi rien, je n'en sais vraiment rien. **—footed,** *adj.* qui a le pied sûr
Surely, *adv.* sûrement; assurément, à coup sûr, certainement, en vérité, vraiment; (*safely*) en sûreté. — *he does not mean to deceive me?* est-ce que par hasard il voudrait me tromper?
Sureness, *s.* sûreté, *f.*
Surety, *s.* sûreté, *f.*; certitude, *f.*; (*of payment*) garantie, *f.*; (*bail*) caution, *f.*, garant, répondant, *m.* *Of a —*, pour sûr
Surf, *s.* ressac, *m.*; houle, *f.*
Surface, *s.* surface, *f.* **— grub,** *s.* triphène, *m.* **— table,** *s.* (*engin.*) écharpe, *f.* **— well,** *s.* puits pleureur, *m.*
Surfeit, *v.a.* rassasier (de); (*fig.*) blaser (sur), dégoûter (de); — *v.n.* être rassasié (de); se gorger (de); — *s.* réplétion, *f.*, rassasiement, dégoût, *m.*, satiété, *f.*; excès, *m.*; indigestion, *f.* *To have a — of, to be —ed with*, être rassasié [*or* gorgé de
Surfeiter, *s.* glouton, *m.*, -ne, *f.*
Surfeiting, *s.* excès, *m.*, gloutonnerie, *f.*
Surfy, *adj.* agité, houleux, écumant
Surge, *s.* vague, lame, houle, *f.*; — *v.n.* s'élever, s'enfler; — *v.a.* larguer. **— less,** *adj.* calme
Surgeon, *s.* chirurgien, *m.*; médecin-chirurgien, médecin, *m.*; officier de santé, *m.* *Army —*, chirurgien militaire, *m.* **— dentist,** *s.* chirurgien-dentiste, *m.* **— general,** *s.* chirurgien en chef, *m.* **— major,** *s.* chirurgien-major, *m.*
Surgeoncy, Surgeonship, *s.* poste de chi-[rurgien, *m.*; officiat, *m.*
Surgery, *s.* (*art*) chirurgie, *f.*; (*place*) pharmacie, *f.*
Surgical, *adj.* chirurgical, chirurgique, de chirurgie. — *instrument*, instrument de chirurgie, *m.*
Surgico-, (*in compounds*) chirurgico- . . .
Surgy, *adj.* agité, houleux
Surlily, *adv.* d'un air rechigné; d'une ma-[nière hargneuse
Surliness, *s.* morosité, *f.*; caractère *or* naturel bourru *or* hargneux, *m.*
Surly, *adj.* morose, maussade, bourru, hargneux; (*of dogs*) hargneux
Surmise, *v.a.* soupçonner; conjecturer; — *s.* soupçon, *m.*; conjecture, *f.*
Surmount, *v.a.* surmonter
Surmountable, *adj.* surmontable
Surmullet, *s.* surmulet, *m.*
Surmulot, *s.* surmulot, *m.*
Surname, *s.* surnom, *m.*; nom de famille, nom, *m.*; — *v.a.* surnommer. *O.'s christian and —*, ses nom et prénoms
Surpass, *v.a.* surpasser
Surpassable, *adj.* surpassable
Surpassing, *adj.* éminent; rare
Surpassingly, *adv.* éminemment
Surplice, *s.* surplis, *m.* **— fees,** *s.pl.* droits de surplis, *m.pl.*, casuel, *m.*
Surpliced, *adj.* à surplis
Surplus, *s.* surplus, excédant, *m.*; — *adj.* de surplus. **— stock,** *s.* solde, *m.*
Surplusage, *s.* surplus, excédant, *m.*; (*law*) superfluité, *f.*; (*liter.*) remplissage, *m.*
Surprise, *v.a.* surprendre ('*at*,' de); — *s.* surprise, *f.* *To take by —*, surprendre
Surpriser, *s.* surpreneur, *m.*
Surprising, *adj.* surprenant, étonnant

Surprisingly, *adv.* étonnamment, d'une manière surprenante

Surrebut, *v.n.* (*law*) faire une triplique, tripliquer

Surrebutter, *s.* (*law*) triplique, *f.* *To put in a* —, faire une triplique, tripliquer

Surrejoin, *v.n.* (*law*) faire une duplique, dupliquer

Surrejoinder, *s.* (*law*) duplique, *f.* *To put in a* —, faire une duplique, dupliquer

Surrenal, *adj.* surrénal

Surrender, *v.a.* rendre, livrer; (*yield*) abandonner, céder; (*resign*) renoncer à; (*law*) rendre; — *v.n.* (— **oneself,** *v.r.*) se rendre; (*law*) se constituer prisonnier; (*of a bankrupt*) se mettre à la disposition de ses créanciers; — *s.* (*mil.*) reddition, *f.*; (*resignation*) abandon, *m.*, renonciation, *f.*; (*law*) cession, reddition, *f.*; (*international law*) extradition, *f.* — *of property*, cession de biens, *f.* *To — oneself a prisoner*, se rendre prisonnier; (*law*) se constituer prisonnier; (*of a bankrupt*) se mettre à la disposition de ses créanciers

Surrenderer, *s.* redditionnaire, *m.f.*

Surreption, *s.* subreption, *f.*

Surreptitious, *adj.* subreptice; clandestin; frauduleux

Surreptitiously, *adv.* subrepticement; clandestinement, à la dérobée; frauduleusement

Surrogate, *v.a.* substituer; (*law*) subroger; — *s.* délégué, *m.*; (*eccl.*) délégué de l'évêque, *m.*

Surround, *v.a.* ('*with,*' de) entourer, environner

Surrounding, *adj.* environnant; voisin; —**s,** *s.pl.* alentours, entours, *m.pl.*, entourage, *m.*

Surtax, *s.* surtaxe, *f.*; — *v.a.* surtaxer

Surtout, *s.* surtout, pardessus, *m.*

Surveillance, *s.* surveillance, *f.*

Surveillant, *s.* surveillant, *m.*, e, *f.*

Survey, *v.a.* considérer, regarder, jeter un coup d'œil sur; inspecter; examiner; (*to value*) expertiser; (*to measure land*) arpenter; lever le plan de (*v.n.* lever un plan *or* des plans)

Survey, *s.* vue, *f.*, coup d'œil, *m.*; inspection, *f.*; examen, *m.*; (*valuation*) expertise, *f.*; (*of land*) arpentage, *m.*; (*engin.*) lever (*or* levé) des plans, *m.*; plan, *m.*; (*official — of landed property*) cadastre, *m.* *To make* or *take a — of*, *V.* *To* **Survey,** *v.a.*

Surveying, *s.* arpentage, *m.*; (*engin.*) lever (*or* levé) des plans, *m.* — **wheel,** *s.* pédomètre, hodomètre, compte-pas, *m.*

Surveyor, *s.* (*of land*) arpenteur, *m.*; géomètre, *m.*; (*ordnance* —) ingénieur du cadastre, *m.*; (*of buildings*, &c.) inspecteur, *m.*; intendant, *m.*; surintendant, *m.*; (*valuer*) expert, *m.*; (*of taxes*) contrôleur, *m.*

Surveyorship, *s.* place (*f.*) *or* emploi (*m.*) d'inspecteur, inspection, *f.*; place de contrôleur (des contributions directes), *f.*

Survival, *s.* survie, *f.*

Survive, *v.a.* survivre à; (*live beyond*) passer; [— *v.n.* survivre

Survivor, *s.* survivant, *m.*, e, *f.*

Survivorship, *s.* survivance, *f.*

Suscepti-bility, bleness, *s.* susceptibilité, *f.*; sensibilité, *f.*

Susceptible, *adj.* susceptible (de); sensible

Suscitate, *v.a.* susciter

Suscitation, *s.* suscitation, *f.*, suscitement, *m.*

Suslik. *V.* **Souslik**

Suspect, *v.a.n.* soupçonner ('*that*' ..., que); (*doubt*) suspecter, douter de, se défier de; (*apprehend*) se douter de, (— '*that*' ... se douter que ...)

Suspectable, *adj.* soupçonnable

Suspected, *adj.* suspect

Suspectedly, *adv.* de manière à exciter le soupçon

Suspectedness, *s.* nature suspecte, *f.*

Suspecter, *s.* soupçonneur, *m.*, -euse, *f.*, personne qui soupçonne, *f.*

Suspend, *v.a.* suspendre; (*a priest*, &c.) suspendre, interdire; — *v.n.* (*com.*) suspendre ses payements

Suspender, *s.* personne qui suspend, *f.*; [(*strap*) bretelle, *f.*

Suspense, *s.* incertitude, indécision, *f.*, doute, *m.*; suspension, cessation, *f.*; (*law*) suspension, *f.*; — *adj.* suspendu; en suspens; dans l'incertitude. *In* —, en suspens

Suspensible, *adj.* qui peut être suspendu

Suspension, *s.* suspension, *f.*; (*can. law*) suspense, interdiction, *f.*; (*com.*) suspension de payements, *f.* — **bridge,** *s.* pont suspendu, *m.* — **chains,** *s.pl.* chaînes de suspension, *f.pl.* — **pier,** *s.* jetée suspendue, *f.*

Suspensor, *s.* suspensoir, *m.*

Suspensory, *adj.* suspenseur; — *s.* suspensoir, *m.* — **bandage,** *s.* suspensoir, *m.*

Suspicion, *s.* soupçon, *m.*; (*law*) suspicion, *f.* *Imprisonment on* —, mise en prévention, prévention, *f.*, emprisonnement préventif, *m.*, détention préventive, *f.* *Taken up on* —, mis en prévention, détenu préventivement

Suspicious, *adj.* (*distrustful*) soupçonneux; (*doubtful, queer*) suspect (à), louche, équivoque

Suspiciously, *adv.* (*distrustfully*) soupçonneusement, avec soupçon; (*doubtfully, queerly*) d'une manière suspecte

Suspiciousness, *s.* (*distrust*) nature soupçonneuse, *f.*, caractère soupçonneux, *m.*, méfiance, *f.*; (*doubtfulness, queerness*) nature suspecte, *f.*

Suspiral, *s.* soupirail, *m.*

Suspirious, *adj.* suspirieux

Sustain, *v.a.* soutenir; (*feed*) entretenir, nourrir; (*endure*) souffrir, endurer; (*undergo*) éprouver, essuyer, subir

Sustainable, *adj.* soutenable

Sustainer, *s.* soutien, appui, *m.*

Sustenance, *s.* subsistance, *f.*, entretien, *m.*, nourriture, *f.*, aliments, *m.pl.*; (*support*) soutien, *m.*

Sustentation, *s.* sustentation, *f.*

Sutler, *s.* vivandier, *m.*, -ière, *f.*, cantinier, *m.*, -ière, *f.*

Sutling-booth, *s.* buvette, cantine, *f.*

Suttee, *s.* suttee, suttie, *f.*

Sutural, *adj.* sutural

Suture, *s.* suture, *f.*; — *v.a.* suturer

Suzerain, *s.* suzerain, *m.*

Suzerainty, *s.* suzeraineté, *f.*

Swab, *s.* balai à laver, torchon, *m.*; (*nav.*) faubert, *m.*; (*for guns*) écouvillon, *m.*; — *v.a.* laver; (*nav.*) fauberter; (*guns*) écouvillonner

Swabber, *s.* (*nav.*) fauberteur, *m.*

Swabian. *V.* **Suabian**

Swaddle. *V.* **Swathe**

Swaddling, *s.* emmaillottement, *m.* — **clothes,** *s.pl.* maillot, *m.*, langes, *m.pl.*

Swag, *v.n.* s'affaisser; — *s.* affaissement, *m.*; (*slang*) ravage, *m.* — **bellied,** *adj.* ventru, pansu

Swagger, *v.n.* faire le fanfaron *or* le rodomont, faire le crâne; faire du tapage; — *s.* *V.* **Swaggering**

Swaggerer, Swaggering fellow, *s.* fanfaron, matamore, rodomont, crâne, *m.*

Swaggering, *s.* fanfaronnade, rodomontade, crânerie, *f.*; bruit, tapage, *m.*; — *adj.* fanfaron, crâne; tapageur

Swaggy, *adj.* pendant

Swain, *s.* jeune homme, *m.*; jeune paysan, *m.*; (*shepherd*) berger, *m.*; (*lover*) amant, berger, *m.*

Swallow, *v.a.* (— **down, up**) avaler; (*ingulf*) engloutir; (*absorb*) absorber, consumer; (*believe*) gober; — *s.* (*bird*) hirondelle, *f.*; (*throat*) gosier, *m.*; avaloire, *f.*; (*voracity*) voracité, *f.*; (*what is swallowed at once*) gorgée, *f.* *To — the wrong way*, avaler de travers. — **fish,** *s.* hirondelle de mer, *f.* — **stone,** *s.* pierre d'hirondelle, *f.* — **tail,** *s.* (*dovetail*) queue d'aronde, *f.*; (*of coats*) queue de morue, *f.* — **tail, -tailed,** *adj.* (*dovetailed*) en queue d'aronde; (*of coats*) à queue de morue. — **wort,** *s.* asclépiade, *f.*, dompte-venin, *m.*

Swallower, *s.* avaleur, *m.*, -euse, *f.*

Swallowing, *s.* avalement, *m.*; engloutissement, *m.*; absorption, *f.*

Swamp, *s.* marais, marécage, *m.*

Swamp, *v.a.* enfoncer dans un marais; plonger;

submerger; couler; inonder; absorber; perdre; (*ruin*) couler. — **oak,** *s.* filao, *m.*

Swampy, *adj.* marécageux

Swan, *s.* cygne, *m.* *The song of the dying* —, le chant du cygne, *m.* —**like,** *adj.* de cygne, semblable au cygne. —**'s-down,** *s.* duvet de cygne, *m.*; (*cloth*) drap de vigogne, *m.*, vigogne, *f.* — **shot,** *s.* plomb à cygne, *m.* — **skin,** *s.* molleton, *m.* [troc, *m.*; — *adv.* vite

Swap, *v.a.* échanger, troquer; — *s.* échange,

Sward, *s.* gazon, *m.*, pelouse, *f.*; (*of bacon*) couenne, *f.*; — *v.a.* couvrir de gazon. — **cutter,** *s.* *V.* **Lawn-mower**

Swardy, *adj.* couvert de gazon

Swarm, *s.* (*of bees*) essaim, *m.*; (*crowd*) multitude, nuée, *f.*, essaim, *m.*; (*of ants, and fig.*) fourmilière, *f.*; — *v.n.* essaimer (de); (*with*) fourmiller (de); (*to crowd*) accourir en foule

Swarming, *s.* essaimage, essaimement, *m.*

Swarthiness, *s.* couleur basanée, *f.*, teint

Swarthy, *adj.* basané, hâlé [basané, *m.*

Swash, *v.n.* (*of liquids*) clapoter; (*to bluster*) *V.* **Swagger**; — *s.* clapotage, clapotement, clapotis, *m.*; (*bluster*) *V.* **Swaggering.** — **buckler,** *s.* *V.* **Swaggerer**

Swath, Swathe, *s.* maillot, lange, *m.*; (*of grass,* &c.) andain, *m.*; fauchée, *f.*; — *v.a.* em-

Swathing, *s.* *V.* **Swaddling** [maillotter

Sway, *v.a.* (*to cause to lean*) faire pencher; (*to move to and fro*) balancer; faire aller; ballotter; (*to rule*) gouverner, régir, dominer; (*to direct*) diriger, conduire; (*to influence*) influencer, influer sur; (*from*) détourner (de); (*wield*) manier, porter; — *v.n.* (*to lean*) pencher, incliner; (*to move to and fro*) se balancer; aller et venir; (*to have influence*) influer (sur), avoir de l'influence (sur); (*to rule*) gouverner, régner, dominer; commander; — *s.* pouvoir, *m.*, autorité, puissance, *f.*, gouvernement, *m.*, domination, *f.*; sceptre, *m.*; empire, *m.*, influence, *f.*; force, *f.*; prépondérance, *f.*; balancement, *m.*; secousse, *f.*; chance, *f.*, sort, *m.*; masse, *f.*; (*of weapons*) course, *f.* *To bear* —, dominer, régner, porter le sceptre. — **up,** *v.a.* (*nav.*) guinder; (*a yard*) hisser

Swaying, *s.* (*vet.*) effort, *m.*

Swear, *v.a.n.* jurer ('*to*,' de); (*blaspheme*) jurer; (*of cats*) jurer; (*a solemn oath*) prêter (serment); (*a blasphemous oath*) faire *or* proférer (un jurement); (*make oath*) prêter serment; (*give evidence*) déposer; (*a person*) faire prêter serment à; (— *in*) assermenter; (*declare*) déclarer sous serment. *To be sworn* or *sworn in*, prêter serment. *To — false* or *falsely*, faire un faux serment, se parjurer; (*law*) porter faux témoignage. *To — by all that is good* or *sacred, to — by all the powers*, jurer ses grands dieux. *To — like a trooper*, jurer comme un charretier. *To curse and* —, jurer et sacrer. *To be always cursing and —ing*, ne parler que par F. et par B. — **at,** jurer après; injurier en paroles

Swearer, *s.* jureur, *m.*, -euse, *f.*, blasphémateur, *m.*, -trice, *f.*

Swearing, *s.* serments, *m.pl.*; (*act of — officials,* &c.) prestation de serment, *f.*; (*blasphemy*) jurements, jurons, *m.pl.* *False* —, *V.* **False.** *Profane* —, jurements, jurons, *m.pl.* — **in,** *s.* assermentation, *f.*

Sweat, *v.n.* suer; — *v.a.* faire suer; — *s.* sueur, *f.*; (*toil*) fatigue, *f.*, sueurs, *f.pl.* *All in a* —, tout en sueur. *By the — of o.'s brow*, à la sueur de son front

Sweating, *s.* *V.* **Sweat,** *s.*; — *adj.* en sueur, tout en sueur. — **bath,** *s.* bain de vapeur, *m.* — **house,** *s.* étuve, *f.* — **room,** *s.* étuve, *f.*; (*for things generally*) séchoir, *m.*; (*for tobacco*) suerie, *f.* — **sickness,** *s.* suette, *f.*

Sweaty, *adj.* en sueur, couvert de sueur

Swede, *s.* Suédois, *m.*, e, *f.*; (*turnip*) navet de Suède, rutabaga, *m.*

Swedish, *adj.* suédois, de Suède; — *s.* (*language*) le suédois, *m.*, la langue suédoise, *f.* — *turnip*, navet de Suède, rutabaga, *m.*

Sweep, *v.a.n.* balayer; (*chimneys*) ramoner; *run, glide over*) glisser sur; raser; passer; *look at*) parcourir des yeux; parcourir; (*drive away*) chasser; (*carry away*) enlever, emporter; razzier; (*bend*) cambrer; (*a lyre,* &c.) frapper; (*an anchor, a river*) draguer; (*extend*) s'étendre; (*move to and fro*) se balancer, osciller, aller et venir. *The train swept thundering past*, le train passa comme la foudre. — **along,** balayer; (*display*) étaler. — **away, off,** balayer; (*carry off*) enlever, emporter; râfler; razzier. — **round,** se tourner rapidement; (*go round*) faire le tour; décrire une courbe. — **up,** balayer

Sweep, *s.* balayage, *m.*; (*of chimneys*) ramonage, *m.*; (*pers.*) ramoneur, *m.*; (*stroke with a broom*) coup de balai, *m.*; (*stroke*) coup, *m.*; (*in swimming*) brassée, *f.*; (*carrying off*) râfle, *f.*; razzia, *f.*; (*course*) cours, *m*, course, *f.*; passage, *m.*; (*motion to and fro*) balancement, *m.*, oscillation, *f.*, mouvement de va-et-vient, va-et-vient, *m.*; (*extent*) étendue, *f.*; champ, *m.*; (*reach*) portée, *f.*; (*turning*) courbe, *f.*; (*in the arts*) cambrure, *f.*; (*metal.*) fourneau de coupelle, *m.*; (*of a wind-mill*) aile, *f.*; (*nav.*) aviron de galère, *m.* *At one* —, tout d'un coup, tout d'un trait; d'un coup de filet. *To make a clean* —, (*over*) passer par-dessus; balayer d'un bout à l'autre; (*carry off*) faire râfle; (*do away with*) faire table rase. — **net,** *s.* épervier, *m.*, râfle, *f.* —**'s machine,** *s.* hérisson, ramon, *m.* — **stake, -stakes,** *s.* (*sum*) enjeu, *m.*; (*race*) course par enjeux, poule, *f.*, sweepstakes, *m.*

Sweeper, *s.* balayeur, *m.*, -euse, *f.*; (*machine*) balayeuse mécanique, balayeuse, *f.*; (*of chimneys*) ramoneur, *m.*

Sweeping, *s.* balayage, *m.*; (*of chimneys*) ramonage, *m.*; —**s,** *pl.* balayures, *f.pl.*; (*fig.*) ramassis, *m.*; — *adj.* rapide; impétueux, violent; irrésistible; vigoureux; hardi; destructeur; absolu; entier; complet; général; aveugle; qui n'épargne personne. — **machine,** *s.* balayeuse mécanique, balayeuse, *f.*

Sweepingly, *adv.* rapidement; violemment; vigoureusement, sans ménagement; en masse, sans distinction; aveuglément

Sweepy, *adj.* rapide; ondulé

Sweet, *adj.* doux; suave; odorant, aromatique, fin; bon; mélodieux; (*to the taste*) succulent; délicieux; bon; (*upon*) tendre (pour); doux; (*sugary, sugared*) sucré; (*of wine*) liquoreux, de liqueur, sucré; (*pretty*) beau; joli; (*pleasant*) doux, agréable, charmant, délicieux; (*gentle*) doux, aimable; (*fresh*) frais; — *s.* plaisir, *m.*, douceur, *f.*; (*sweetmeat*) sucrerie, *f.*, bonbon, *m.* — ! (*to birds*) petit! *Between — and sour*, aigre-doux. — **bag,** *s.* sachet, *m.* — **bay,** *s.* laurier-sauce, *m.* — **bread,** *s.* (*calf's*) ris de veau, ris, *m.*; (*sheep's*) collier (de mouton), *m.*; (*bullock's*) fagoue, *f.*; (*anat.*) pancréas, *m.* — **briar, -brier,** *s.* *V.* **Briar.** — **broom,** *s.* bruyère, *f.* — **cicely,** *s.* *V.* **Cicely.** — **creature,** *s.* charmante créature, *f.*; cher trésor, *m.* — **flag,** *s.* jonc odorant, *m.* — **heart,** *s.* amoureux, *m.*, -euse, *f.*, bon ami, *m.*, bonne amie, *f.* — **herbs,** *s.pl.* fines herbes, herbes aromatiques, *f.pl.* — **meat,** *s.* sucrerie, *f.*, bonbon, *m.* — **oil,** *s.* huile d'olive, *f.* — **pea,** *s.* pois de senteur, *m.* — **pod,** *s.* caroube, *f.* — **potato,** *s.* patate, *f.* — **rush,** *s.* jonc odorant, *m.* — **scented, -smelling,** *adj.* odorant, odoriférant; embaumé. — **sop,** *s.* (*bot.*) pommier canelle, *m.* — **things,** *s.pl.* douceurs, *f.pl.* — **tongued,** *adj.* doucereux, mielleux. — **toothed,** *adj.* qui aime les friandises, friand. — **water grape,** *s.* chasselas, *m.* — **william,** *s.* œillet de poète, *m.*

Sweeten, *v.a.* adoucir; purifier, désinfecter;

embaumer, parfumer; (*refresh*) rafraîchir, rendre frais; (*with sugar*, &c.) sucrer; (*chem., pharm.*, &c.) édulcorer; — *v.n.* devenir doux, [s'adoucir
Sweetener, *s.* adoucissant, *m.*
Sweetening, *s.* adoucissement, *m.*; désinfection, *f.*; (*chem., pharm.*, &c.) édulcoration, *f.*
Sweetish, *adj.* assez doux; douceâtre. —**ness,** *s.* goût douceâtre, *m.*
Sweetly, *adv.* doucement, avec douceur; suavement; agréablement; mélodieusement
Sweetness, *s.* douceur, *f.*; suavité, *f.*, parfum, *m.*; fraîcheur, *f.*; mélodie, *f.*; agrément, charme, attrait, *m.*
Swell, *v.n.* enfler, s'enfler, se gonfler; (*puff*) bouffer; (*increase*) grossir, croître, augmenter; (*rise*) s'élever; se soulever; (*with pride*) bouffir (de); (*become worse*) s'aggraver; (*into*) devenir (...); — *v.a.* enfler, gonfler (de); grossir, grandir, augmenter; aggraver; élever; soulever; bouffir; (*of stuffs*) faire bouffer; (*into*) convertir (en). *A swelled* or *swollen face*, (*fam.*) une fluxion. — **out,** enfler, &c. (*as above*); (*to bulge*) bomber. — **up,** enfler, &c. (*as above*)
Swell, *s.* bombement, *m.*; (*rise*) élévation, *f.*; (*of the sea*) houle, *f.*; (*of sound*) renflement, *m.*; (*of organs*) pédale d'expression, *f.*; (*pers.*) gandin, *m.*, élégant, *m.*, e, *f.*, fashionable, *m.f.*; (*in a bad sense*) faraud, *m.*, e, *f.*; (*nob*) *V.* **Nob;** — *adj.* à la mode; (*crack*) *V.* **Crack,** *adj.* — **mob,** *s.* (la) haute pègre, *f.* *One of the — mob, A —* **mobsman,** *s.* un voleur de la haute pègre, un franc bourgeois, un chevalier d'industrie, *m.* — **organ,** *s.* orgue expressif, *m.*
Swelling, *s.* gonflement, *m.*; enflure, *f.*; (*bump*) bosse, *f.*; (*jutting out*) bombement, *m.*; (*increase*) augmentation, *f.*; (*of rivers*) crue, *f.*; (*of waves*) soulèvement, *m.*; (*of anger, grief*, &c.) transport, mouvement, *m.*; (*of pride*) bouffissure, *f.*; (*arch.*) galbe, *m.*; — *part. adj.* qui enfle *or* &c. (*V.* **Swell,** *v.n.a.*); grossissant, croissant; (*bombastic*) enflé, ampoulé
Swellish, *adj.* à la mode, élégant, coquet; recherché, affecté, prétentieux
Swelter, *v.n.* étouffer de chaleur, étouffer; — *v.a.* accabler de chaleur, accabler. *It is —ing hot*, on étouffe, il fait une chaleur étouffante
Swerve, *v.n.* s'écarter (de), dévier (de), se détourner (de); obliquer; (*of horses*) faire un [écart
Swerving, *s.* déviation, *f.*
Swift, *adj.* rapide, prompt; (*of animals*) agile, vite, léger à la course, léger; (*nav.*) rapide, bon marcheur; — *s.* (*bird*) martinet, *m.*; (*of a wind-mill*) aile, *f.* — **footed,** *adj.* léger à la course, léger, aux pieds légers. — **sailing,** *adj.* rapide, bon marcheur. — **winged,** *adj.* à l'aile rapide
Swiftly, *adv.* rapidement; promptement; vite
Swiftness, *s.* rapidité, *f.*; promptitude, *f.*; vitesse, *f.*
Swig, *v.n.* boire à longs traits *or* à grands coups; — *v.a.* humer; — *s.* long trait, grand coup, *m.* — **at,** humer
Swill, *v.a.n.* (— **down, off, out**) avaler, boire à grands coups, boire avidement, pomper, sabler, siffler; (*to wash*) laver; arroser; (*intoxicate*) griser, enivrer; (*get drunk*) se griser, s'enivrer; — *s.* grand coup, coup, trait, *m.*; excès de boisson, *m.*; (*wash*) lavure, *f.* *To have a —*, boire un coup. — **tub,** *s.* *V.* **Pig-** [**tub**
Swiller, *s.* grand buveur, ivrogne, *m.*
Swillings, *s.pl.* lavure (de vaisselle), *f.*
Swim, *v.n.a.* nager; (*float*) surnager, flotter; (*be overflowed*) être inondé ('*with*,' de); (*be dizzy*) tourner; (— *across*) passer (...) *or* traverser (...) à la nage; (*inundate*) inonder ('*with*,' de), faire flotter; (*to follow*) suivre; — *s.* *V.* **Swimming;** (*air-bladder*) vessie natatoire, *f.* *My head is —ming*, la tête me tourne
Swimmer, *s.* nageur, *m.*, -euse, *f.*; (*bird*) palmipède, *m.*
Swimming, *s.* (*art*) natation, *f.*; (*act*) nage, *f.*; (*dizziness*) vertige, *m.* *By —*, en nageant; à la nage. *I like —*, j'aime à nager. *To learn —*, apprendre à nager. *To have a — in o.'s head*, avoir des vertiges. — **bath,** *s.* bain de natation, *m.* — **belt,** *s.* ceinture de natation, *f.* — **bladder,** *s.* vessie natatoire, *f.* — **jacket,** *s.* scaphandre, *m.* — **match,** *s.* course (*f.*) *or* pari (*m.*) à la nage. — **school,** *s.* école de natation, *f.*
Swimmingly, *adv.* aisément; le mieux du monde; à merveille; comme sur des roulettes; (*rapidly*) rondement; (*successfully*) d'emblée
Swindle, *v.a.* escroquer; — *s.* escroquerie, *f.* *To — a person out of a thing*, escroquer quelque chose à quelqu'un
Swindler, *s.* escroc, chevalier d'industrie, *m.*
Swindling, *s.* escroquerie, *f.*
Swine, *s.* pourceau, cochon, porc, *m.* — **herd,** *s.* porcher, *m.*, -ère, *f.* — **pox,** *s.* varicelle pustuleuse globuleuse, *f.*
Swing, *v.n.* osciller; se balancer; aller de droite et de gauche; battre; faire la bascule; (*in walking*) se dandiner; (*vibrate*) vibrer; (*hang loose*) pendiller, pendre; (*suffer hanging*) danser en l'air, être basculé; (*nav.*) éviter (à); — *v.a.* balancer; agiter; brandir; faire aller; (*hang*) pendre. — **about,** *v.n.* tourner; tournoyer; *v.a.* agiter. — **round,** *v.n.a.* tourner; pivoter; faire pivoter
Swing, *s.* oscillation, *f.*, va-et-vient, *m.*; balancement, *m.*; vibration, *f.*; (*in walking*) dandinement, *m.*; (*of bells*) branle, *m.*; (*see-saw*) escarpolette, balançoire, *f.*; bascule, *f.*; (*influence*) influence, action, force, *f.*; (*free scope*) essor, *m.*, carrière, *f.*, libre cours, *m.*; (*tendency*) penchant, *m.*; (*sweep*) ligne parcourue, courbe décrite, *f.* *Full —*, (*fig.*) essor, libre cours, *m.*; pleine activité, *f.* — **bar,** *s.* palonnier, *m.* — **bed,** *s.* hamac, *m.* — **boat,** *s.* bateau-balançoire, *m.*, balançoire, *f.* — **bridge,** *s.* pont tournant, *m.* — **cot,** *s.* berceau, *m.* — **door,** *s.* porte battante, *f.* — **gate,** *s.* porte *or* barrière à bascule, bascule, *f.*, tape-cul, *m.* — **glass, -looking-glass,** *s.* miroir à bascule, *m.* — **plough,** *s.* charrue sans avant-train, *f.*, araire, *m.f.*, sochet, *m.* — **tree,** *s.* palonnier, *m.*
Swinging, *s.* *V.* **Swing,** *s.*; (*nav.*) évitage, *m.*; — *adj.* énorme; fort. — **room,** *s.* (*nav.*) évi- [tée, *f.*
Swingingly, *adv.* énormément
Swingletree, *s.* palonnier, *m.*
Swinish, *adj.* de cochon, de pourceau; malpropre, sale; grossier; bestial; vil
Swinishly, *adv.* malproprement, salement; grossièrement
Swipes, *s.pl.* mauvaise petite bière, *f.*; abon- [dance, *f.*; piquette, *f.*
Swish, *v.a.* remuer, agiter
Swiss, *s.* Suisse, *m.*, Suissesse, *f.*; — *adj.* [suisse, de Suisse
Switch, *s.* badine, baguette, houssine, *f.*; (*of railways*) aiguille, *f.*; — *v.a.* houssiner, cingler, sangler. — **man,** *s.* aiguilleur, *m.* — **tail,** *s.* queue en balai, queue à tous crins, *f.*
Switcher, *s.* aiguilleur, *m.*
Swivel, *s.* tourniquet, *m.*; (*mil., and of a watch-chain*) porte-mousqueton, *m.*; (*artil.*) canon à pivot, pierrier, *m.* — **bridge,** *s.* pont tournant, *m.* — **gun,** *s.* pierrier, *m.*
Swoon, *v.n.* (— **away**) s'évanouir, se trouver mal, tomber en défaillance; — *s.* évanouissement, *m.*, défaillance, faiblesse, syncope, *f.*
Swooning, *s.* *V.* **Swoon,** *s.*
Swoop, (*of birds of prey*) *V.* **Stoop.** *At a* or *one —, at one fell —*, d'un coup, d'un seul coup. *To come down with a — upon*, fondre sur
Swop. *V.* **Swap**
Sword, *s.* (*thin and straight, to thrust*) épée, *f.*; (*broad —, to cut*) sabre, *m.*; (*harlequin's*) batte, *f.*; (*poet.*) fer, *m.*; (*fig.*) glaive, *m.*; (*in Scripture*) destruction, *f.* *At the point of the —*, à la pointe de l'épée. — *in hand*, l'épée à la main. *To cross* or *join —s*, croiser l'épée. *To fight with —s*, se battre à l'épée. *To put to the —*, passer au fil de l'épée. *To put to (or to*

waste or *lay waste with*) *fire and* —, mettre à feu et à sang. — **bayonet,** *s.* sabre-baïonnette, *m.* — **bearer,** *s.* porte-épée, *m.* — **belt,** *s.* ceinturon, *m.* — **blade,** *s.* lame d'épée, *f.*; lame de sabre, *f.* — **cane,** *s.* canne à épée, *f.* — **cut,** *s.* coup de sabre, *m.* — **cutler,** *s.* fourbisseur, *m.*; armurier, *m.* — **fight,** *s.* combat à l'épée, *m.* — **fish,** *s.* espadon, *m.* — **grass,** *s.* morgeline, *f.* — **hanger,** *s.* porte-épée, *m.* — **knot,** *s.* dragonne, *f.* — **law,** *s.* droit du plus fort, *m.* —**less,** *adj.* sans épée. —**sman,** *s.* tireur d'armes, *m.*, lame, *f.*; sabreur, *m.* —**smanship,** *s.* escrime, *f.*; force à tirer des armes, *f.* — **stick,** *s.* canne à épée, *f.* — **thrust,** *s.* coup d'épée, *m.*

Sworn, *adj.* (*of enemies,* &c.) juré, acharné; (*of friends,* &c.) intime, dévoué, à la vie et à la mort; (*admin.,* — *in, of interpreters, brokers,* &c.) juré, assermenté; — *part. V.* **Swear.** — *to,* (*bound*) obligé par serment à

Sybarite, *s.* Sybarite, *m.* [(*pers.*) sybarite

Sybaritic, -al, *adj.* sybaritique, de Sybarite;

Sybaritism, *s.* sybaritisme, *m.*

Sycamore, — **tree,** *s.* sycomore, *m.*

Sycophancy, *s. V.* **Sycophantism**

Sycophant, *s.* sycophante, *m.*; (*flatterer*) adulateur, *m.*, -trice, *f.*, flagorneur, *m.*, -euse, *f.*; — *v.a.n.* flagorner, aduler

Sycophantic, -al, *adj.* de sycophante; (*flattering*) adulateur, flagorneur; (*parasitical*) parasite [*tery*) adulation, flagornerie, *f.*

Sycophantism, *s.* sycophantisme, *m.*; (*flat-*

Sycophantize, *v.a.n.* flagorner, aduler

Syllab-ic, al, -ically, -ism. *V.* page 3, § 1

Syllabicate, Syllabify, *v.a.* syllaber, syllabiser [bation, syllabisation, *f.*

Syllabication, Syllabification, *s.* sylla-

Syllable, *s.* syllabe, *f.* [sumé, abrégé, *m.*

Syllabus, *s.* programme, *m.*; sommaire, ré-

Syllepsis, *s.* syllepse, *f.*

Syllept-ic, al, -ically. *V.* page 3, § 1 [3, § 1

Syllog-ism, -istic, al, -istically. *V.* page

Syllogization, *s.* syllogisation, *f.*

Syllogize, *v.n.* syllogiser

Sylph, Sylphid, *s.* sylphe, *m.*, sylphide, *f.*

Sylvæ, *s.pl.* (*Rom. liter.*) sylves, *f.pl.*

Sylvan, *adj.* sylvain, sylvatique, sylvestre, des bois, des forêts; champêtre; — *s.* sylvain, *m.*

Sylvatic, *adj.* sylvatique

Sylvestrian, *adj.* sylvestre

Sylvia, *s.* sylvie, *f.*

Sylvicultural, *adj.* sylvicultural, sylvicole

Sylviculture, *s.* sylviculture, *f.*

Sylviculturist, *s.* sylviculteur, *m.*

Symbol, *s.* symbole, *m.* [*V.* page 3, § 1

Symbol-ic, al, -ically, -ism, -ology, &c.

Symbolization, *s.* symbolisation, *f.*

Symbolize, *v.a.n.* symboliser

Symmetrical, *adj.* symétrique

Symmetrically, *adv.* symétriquement

Symmetrize, *v.n.a.* symétriser [triser

Symmetry, *s.* symétrie, *f.* *To be in* —, symé-

Sympathetic, -al, *adj.* sympathique

Sympathetically, *adv.* sympathiquement, avec (*or* par) sympathie [compatir (à)

Sympathize, *v.n.* sympathiser (avec); (*pity*)

Sympathizer, *s.* personne *or* âme sympathique, *f.*; partisan, adhérent, *m.*

Sympathy, *s.* sympathie, *f.*

Symphon-ic, -ically. *V.* page 3, § 1

Symphonious, *adj.* symphonique, harmo-

Symphonist, *s.* symphoniste, *m.* [nieux

Symphony, *s.* symphonie, *f.*; harmonie, *f.*

Symphysis, *s.* symphyse, *f.*

Sympiezometer, *s.* sympiézomètre, *m.*

Symposium, *s.* banquet, *m.*

Symptom, *s.* symptôme, *m.*

Symptomatic, -al, *adj.* qui est un symptôme; (*med.*) symptomatique

Symptomatically, *adv.* par des symptômes; d'après les symptômes

Symptomatology, *s.* symptomatologie, *f.*

Synæresis, *s.* synérèse, *f.*

Synagogical, *adj.* de la synagogue

Synagogue, *s.* synagogue, *f.*

Synallagmatic, *adj.* synallagmatique

Synchron-al, ous, *adj.* synchrone

Synchron-ic, al, -ically, -ism, -ology. *V.* page 3, § 1

Synchronize, *v.n.a.* synchroniser

Syncopal, *adj.* syncopal

Syncopate, *v.a.* syncoper

Syncopation, *s.* syncope, *f.*

Syncope, *s.* syncope, *f.*

Syncretism, *s.* syncrétisme, *m.*

Syndic, *s.* syndic, *m.*

Syndical, *adj.* syndical

Syndicate, *s.* syndicat, *m.*; — *v.a.* syndiquer

Synecdoche, *s.* synecdoche, synecdoque, *f.*

Syneresis, *s.* synérèse, *f.*

Synneurosis, *s.* synnévrose, *f.*

Synod, *s.* synode, *m.*; (*astr.*) conjonction, *f.*

Synodal, Synodic, -al, *adj.* synodal; synodique; (*astr.*) synodique [ment

Synodically, *adv.* synodalement, synodique-

Synonym, *s.* synonyme, *m.*

Synonym-ic, al, -ist. *V.* page 3, § 1

Synonymize, *v.a.* exprimer par un synonyme *or* par des synonymes, synonymiser, rendre, traduire [*to synonymy*) synonymique

Synonymous, *adj.* synonyme; (*pertaining*

Synonymously, *adv.* synonymiquement

Synonymousness, *s.* synonymie, *f.*

Synonymy, *s.* synonymie, *f.*

Synopsis, *s.* synopsis, *f.*, tableau synoptique, *m.*

Synopt-ic, al, -ically. *V.* page 3, § 1

Synovia, *s.* synovie, *f.*

Synovial, *adj.* synovial. — *fluid,* synovie, *f.*

Syntact-ic, al, -ically. *V.* page 3, § 1

Syntax, *s.* syntaxe, *f.*

Synthesis, *s.* synthèse, *f.*

Synthet-ic, al, -ically, synthétique, -ment

Syphilis, *s.* syphilis, *f.*

Syphil-ism, -itic, -ology, &c. *V.* p. 3, § 1

Syphilization, *s.* syphilisation, *f.*

Syphilize, *v.a.* syphiliser

Syphiloid, *adj.* syphiloïde

Syphon, Syren. *V.* **Siphon, Siren**

Syracusan, *s. adj.* Syracusain, *m.*, e, *f.*

Syriac, *adj. s.* syriaque, *adj. m.f., s.m.*

Syrian, *s.* Syrien, *m.*, -ne, *f.*; — *adj.* syrien, de Syrie, de la Syrie

Syringa, *s.* seringa, seringat, *m.*

Syringe, *s.* seringue; — *v.a.* seringuer

Syringing, *s.* seringage, seringuement, *m.*

Syrinx, *s.* syringe, flûte de Pan, *f.*

Syrup, *s.* sirop, *m.*

Syruped, *adj.* au sirop

Syrupy, *adj.* sirupeux

System, *s.* système, *m.*; régime, *m.*; économie, constitution, *f.*, organisme, *m.*; corps, *m*; (*lines of rail.*) réseau, *m.* — **maker,** *s.* faiseur (*m.*, -euse, *f.*) de systèmes. — **monger,** *s.* systématiste, *m.f.* [*tory,* &c.) raisonné

Systematic, -al, *adj.* systématique; (*of his-*

Systematically, *adv.* systématiquement

Systemat-ism, -ist, -ology, &c., systématisme, &c. (*V.* page 3, § 1)

Systematization, *s.* systématisation, *f.*

Systematize, *v.a.* systématiser

Systematizer, *s.* systématiseur, *m.*

Systole, *s.* systole, *f.*

Systolic, *adj.* systolique

Sythe. *V.* **Scythe**

Syzygy, *s.* syzygie, *f.*

T

T, *s.* (*letter*) t, T, *m.* — **bandage,** — **iron,** — **square,** *s.* T, té, *m.* *To a* —, parfaitement

Tab, *s.* patte, *f.*
Tabard, *s.* (*of heralds*) tabard, *m.*, cotte d'armes, *f.*
Tabaret, *s.* satin rayé, *m.*
Tabby, *adj.* tavelé, tacheté, moucheté, tigré; — *s.* tabis, *m.*; — *v.a.* tabiser
Tabernacle, *s.* tabernacle, *m.*; sanctuaire, *m.*; — *v.n.* habiter, séjourner, demeurer
Tabernacular, *adj.* (*latticed*) treillissé
Tabes, *s.* tabes, *m.*, consomption, *f.*, marasme, *m.* — *mesenterica,* carreau, *m.*
Tabid, *adj.* tabide. **—ness,** *s.* dépérissement, *m.*, consomption, *f.*
Tabific, -al, *adj.* tabifique [blature, *f.*
Tablature, *s.* peinture, fresque, *f.*; (*mus.*) ta-
Table, *s.* table, *f.*; (*drawing-room centre* —) guéridon, *m.*; (*board, synopsis*) tableau, *m.*, table, *f.*; (*index, and anat.*) table, *f.*; (*tablet*) tablette, *f.*; (*parliam.*) bureau, *m.*; — *adj.* de table. *Pembroke* —, table à volets. *Raised* —, (*sculp.*) abaque, *m.* *Side* —, *V.* **Occasional** —. *Sutherland* —, table-portefeuille. *To bring* or *put upon* —, servir. *To clear the* —, (*after a meal*) desservir. *To keep a good* —, tenir bonne table. *To lay the* —, mettre le couvert. *To lay on the* —, (*parliam.*) déposer sur le bureau. *To lie on the* —, (*parliam.*) être déposé sur le bureau. *To rise from* —, se lever de table, sortir de table, quitter la table. *To sit at* —, manger à table; être *or* rester à table, s'attabler, être attablé. *To sit down to* —, se mettre à table. *To turn the* —*s,* tourner *or* retourner la médaille; intervertir les rôles. [*The* —*s are turned,* les affaires ont changé de face.] *To turn the tables upon* or *against,* renvoyer la balle à; se retourner contre. — **apple,** *s.* pomme à couteau, *f.* — **beer,** *s.* bière ordinaire, petite bière, *f.* — **bell,** *s.* timbre de table, *m.* — **book,** *s.* tablettes, *f.pl.* — **cloth,** *s.* (*of linen, for meals*) nappe, *f.*; (*not of linen*) *V.* — **cover.** — **companion,** *s.* ami de table, *m.* — **cover,** *s.* tapis de table, *m.*, couverture de table, *f.*, dessus de table, *m.* — **d'hôte,** *s.* table d'hôte, *f.* — **fork,** *s.* fourchette de table, *f.* — **friend,** *s.* ami de table, *m.* —**ful,** *s.* tablée, *f.* — **knife,** *s.* couteau de table, *m.* — **land,** *s.* plateau, *m.* — **length,** *s.* tablée, *f.* — **linen,** *s.* linge de table, *m.* — **mat,** *s.* garde-nappe, *m.* — **money,** *s.* indemnité pour frais de table, *f.* — **oil,** *s.* huile à manger, *f.* — **spoon,** *s.* cuiller de table, cuiller à bouche, cuiller, *f.* — **spoon and fork** (*to match*), couvert de table, *m.* — **spoonful,** *s.* cuillerée à bouche, grande cuillerée, *f.* — **talk,** *s.* propos de table, *m.* — **turning,** *s.* les tables tournantes, *f.pl.* — **wine,** *s.* vin ordinaire, *m.*
Tableaux vivants, *s.pl.* tableaux vivants, *m.pl.*
Tablet, *s.* tablette, *f.*; (*plate*) plaque, *f.*; (*of soap*) pain, *m.* [*nav.*) assemblage, *m.*
Tabling, *s.* classification, *f.*; (*of timbers, and*
Taboo, *s.* tabou, *m.*; (*fig.*) interdiction, *f.*; (*pers.*) interdit, *m.*, e, *f.*; — *v.a.* tabouer; (*fig.*)
Tabooing, *s.* interdiction, *f.* [interdire
Tabor, Tabour, *s.* tambourin, *m.*; — *v.n.* tambouriner
Taborer, Tabourer, *s.* tambourin, *m.*
Tabouret, *s.* petit tambourin, *m.*; (*stool*) tabouret, *m.*
Tabular, *adj.* tabulaire, en forme de table; arrangé en tableau (*or* tableaux)
Tabulate, *v.a.* disposer en forme de table (*or* tables); arranger en tableau (*or* tableaux); (*level*) aplanir; (*register*) enregistrer
Tabulated, *adj.* plan, plat, uni; (*of diamonds*)
Tacahout, *s.* tacahout, *m.* [en table
Tace, *s.* T, té, *m.*
Tacet, *s.* (*mus.*) tacet, *m.*
Tachometer, *s.* tachymètre, *m.*
Tacit, *adj.* tacite, implicite
Tacitly, *adv.* tacitement, implicitement
Taciturn, *adj.* taciturne
Taciturnity, *s.* taciturnité, *f.*
Taciturnly, *adv.* taciturnement
Tack, *v.a.* (— **on**) lier, attacher, joindre; accoupler; ajouter; (*stitch*) faufiler, bâtir; (*nail*) clouer; — *v.n.* (— **about**) virer de bord; louvoyer
Tack, *s.* addition, *f.*, supplément, *m.*; (*nail*) pointe, broquette, *f.*; (*of ships*) bordée, *f.*, bord, *m.*; (*of sails*) amure, *f.*; (*of flags*) œillet, *m.*; (*of sheets*) point. *m.*; (*agr.*) nourriture, *f.* *Main* —, amure de la grande voile, *f.* *To make* or *run a* —, faire *or* courir une bordée. *To be on the* ... —, courir la bordée de ... *To be on the right* —, être en bonne voie. *To be on the starboard* —, avoir les amures à tribord. *To haul aboard the* —, amurer. *To hold* or *bear* —, durer, tenir ferme. *To stand on the same* —, courir le même bord
Tacking, *s.* accouplement, *m.*; addition, *f.*; (*need.*) faufilure, *f.*, bâti, *m.*; (*nav.*) virement, *m.*
Tackle, *s.* (*pulley*) poulie, *f.*; (*utensils*) ustensiles, engins, *m.pl.*, attirail, *m.*; (*weapons*) armes, *f.pl.*; (*mach.*) moufle, *m.*; (*of ships*) palan, *m.*; cordages, *m.pl.*; — *v.a.* attacher; (*seize*) saisir, prendre. — **block,** *s.* (*mach.*) moufle, *m.*; (*nav.*) poulie de palan, *f.* — **fall,** *s.* garant, *m.*
Tact, *s.* tact, *m.* —**less,** *adj.* sans tact
Tactic, -al, *adj.* tactique, de la tactique
Tactically, *adv.* par la tactique
Tactician, *s.* tacticien, *m.*
Tactics, *s.pl.* tactique, *f.*
Tactile, Tactual, *adj.* tactile
Tactility, *s.* tactilité, *f.*
Taction, *s.* taction, *f.*; (*geom.*) tangence, *f.*
Tadorna, *s.* tadorne, *m.*
Tadpole, *s.* têtard, *m.*
Tænia, *s.* ténia, ver solitaire, *m.*
Taffeta, Taffety, *s.* taffetas, *m.*
Taffrail, *s.* couronnement, *m.*
Tafia, *s.* tafia, *m.*
Tag, *s.* ferret, afféron, bout ferré, *m.*; (*ornament*) aiguillette, *f.*; (*yearling*) *V.* **Teg;** — *v.a.* ferrer; (*join*) joindre (à); (*fasten*) attacher. — **end,** *s.* queue, *f.*, bout, *m.* — **rag,** *s.* racaille, *f.* — *rag and bobtail,* quatre pelés et un tondu
Tahitian, *s. adj.* Taïtien, *m.*, -ne, *f.*
Tail, *s.* queue, *f.*; (*end*) bout, *m.*; fin, *f.*; (*of a coat,* &c.) pan, *m.*; (*of ploughs*) manche, *m.*, mancherons, *m.pl.*; (*of carts*) derrière, *m.* *In* —, (*law*) par substitution. *To turn* —, tourner les talons, prendre la fuite, décamper, décaniller. — **board,** *s.* (*of vans,* &c.) layon, ayon, *m.* — **coat,** *s.* *V.* **Dress-coat.** — **feather,** *s.* plume de la queue, rectrice, *f.* — **iron,** *s.* (*vet.*) brûle-queue, *m.* —**less,** *adj.* sans queue. — **piece,** *s.* queue, *f.*; (*of a violin,* &c.) queue, *f.*, cordier, *m.*; (*print.*) fleuron, cul-de-lampe, *m.* — **rope,** *s.* corde de remorque, *f.* — **water,** *s.* queue d'eau, *f.*
Tailed, *adj.* à queue. *Long* —, à longue queue. *Three* — *pasha,* pacha à trois queues, *m.*
Tailing, *s.* (*mas.*) corbeau, *m.*, queue, *f.*; (*of grain*) grenaille, *f.*
Tailor, *s.* tailleur, *m.*; — *v.n.* exercer l'état de tailleur. — **bird,** *s.* orthotome, *m.*
Tailoress, *s.* tailleuse, *f.*
Tailoring, *s.* état *or* métier de tailleur, *m.*; (*work*) ouvrage de tailleur, *m.*
Taint, *v.a.* corrompre; gâter; infecter; souiller, ternir; — *v.n.* se corrompre; se gâter; — *s.* corruption, infection, *f.*; souillure, *f.*; (*blemish*) tache *f.*; (*tincture*) teinte, *f.* —*ed meat,* viande gâtée, *f.* —**less,** *adj.* sans tache, pur. —**lessly,** *adv.* sans tache
Take, *v.a.* prendre; (*bring with oneself, and without carrying*) conduire, mener; (*by carrying*) porter; (*away*) emmener; emporter; enlever; ôter; (*someone's life*) ôter (la vie à); (*a prize*) remporter; (*a walk, run, ride, drive, round, trip or journey, ramble, jump or leap, nap, the pledge, an inventory, a prisoner,* to

make) faire; (*o.'s meals*) prendre *or* faire (ses repas); (*a meal, two, three or &c. meals, o.'s two, three or &c. meals*) faire; (*exercise*) prendre (de l'exercice); (*some trouble*) prendre, se donner; (*breath*) *V.* **Breath;** (*fill, occupy: of time*) prendre; (*devote, be employed, be on the road: of time*) mettre; (*catch, ensnare*) attraper, prendre; surprendre; (*arrest*) arrêter; (*seize*) saisir; (*an opportunity*) saisir, profiter de; (*draw*) tirer (de); (*captivate*) captiver, séduire, fasciner; (*choose*) choisir, adopter, prendre; (*hire*) louer; (*engage, bespeak*) retenir; arrêter; (*periodicals*) être abonné à, recevoir; (*understand*) comprendre, concevoir; (*suppose*) supposer, présumer, croire, imaginer; (*accept*) accepter, recevoir; (*a bet*) tenir; (*admit*) admettre; (*revenge,* &c.) tirer (de); (*inscribe*) inscrire; (*a likeness*) saisir, reproduire; (*a portrait*) faire; (*farewell*) *V.* **Bid;** (*the chair, as president*) ouvrir (la séance); occuper (le fauteuil),être président,présider; (*endure*) essuyer, subir; recevoir; (*consequences,*&c.)subir; (*deduct*) ôter; retrancher; (*deduce*) déduire, conclure; (*esteem, consider*) considérer (comme), regarder (comme); (*one's eyes from or off ...*) détourner (les yeux de ...); (*require*) prendre, demander, exiger,(*imp.*) falloir. *To — to be,*(*believe*) croire; (*mistake for*) prendre pour; (*of a person's years of age*) donner. *I should — him to be thirty* [*years old*], je lui donnerais trente ans. *I should have —n him to be older* [*than that*], je l'aurais cru plus âgé, je lui aurais donné plus que cela. *To — it ill, To be —n ill, V.* **Ill.** *To — care, pleasure, o.'s chance, an oath, o.'s word,* &c., *V.* **Care, Pleasure, Chance, Oath, Word,** &c. *How long does it — to go ...?* combien faut-il de temps pour aller ...? — **again,** reprendre; (*lead*) reconduire. — **along** *with one*, prendre avec soi; emporter. — **aside,** prendre à part, prendre en particulier. — **asunder,** défaire, démonter. — **away,** (*without carrying*) emmener; (*by carrying, and fig.*) emporter; enlever, ôter; (*steal*) dérober; soustraire; (*withdraw*) retirer; (*except*) excepter, faire abstraction de; (*from ..., diminish*) diminuer (...); (*a person from his occupation*) déranger (de ses occupations, de ses affaires); (*clear the table*) desservir, desservir la table. *To — away the things,* (*from table*) desservir, desservir la table. *To — away anyone's life*, ôter la vie à quelqu'un. — **away again,** (*without carrying*) remmener; (*by carrying*) remporter; enlever *or* ôter de nouveau, reprendre. — **back,** reprendre; (*carry again*) reporter; (*carry away*) remporter; (*lead*) reconduire. — **down,** descendre; détacher, décrocher, dépendre; (*off*) ôter, enlever; (*lead down*) faire descendre, emmener; (*take to pieces, as a bed,* &c.) démonter; (*demolish*) abattre, démolir; (*humble*) humilier, abaisser; (*supplant*) prendre la place de; (*swallow*) avaler, prendre; (*write*) prendre par écrit, prendre note de, écrire; inscrire. — **for,** prendre pour; (*consider*) regarder comme; (*a walk, a ride, a drive,* &c.) mener faire (une promenade; mener promener). — **from,** prendre de, accepter de; (*deprive of*) prendre à, enlever à, ôter à, dérober à; (*subtract*) soustraire de, retrancher de; (*detract*) enlever à, diminuer de. — **in,** entrer, faire entrer; rentrer, faire rentrer; (*receive*) recevoir, admettre, prendre; introduire; (*lodge*) loger; (*enclose*) enclore; (*comprise*) comprendre, embrasser; (*contain*) contenir; (*contract*) resserrer, contracter, rétrécir; (*provisions*) faire sa provision de; (*periodicals*) être abonné à, recevoir; (*work generally*) prendre (de l'ouvrage) chez soi; (*sewing, washing,* &c.) faire; travailler à; (*swallow*) avaler; (*cheat*) tromper, duper, voler, prendre, mettre dedans; (*need.*) remplier, rentrer; (*sails, nav.*) serrer. — **off,** ôter; enlever; retirer; détacher; (*the mask, the seals*) lever; (*carry*) emporter; (*lead*) emmener; (*unharness*) dételer; (*cut*) couper, trancher; (*swallow*) avaler; (*diminish*) diminuer, affaiblir; (*abate, knock off*) rabattre; (*destroy*) détruire; (*suppress*) supprimer; (*draw away*) détourner; éloigner; (*buy*) acheter; (*copy*) copier; (*imitate*) imiter; (*mimic*) contrefaire; (*make fun of*) caricaturer,faire la charge de. (*V.* **Hand**). *To — oneself off,* décamper, filer, se sauver, s'esquiver, s'en aller, partir; sortir. — *that off the table,* ôtez cela de dessus la table. *To — off o.'s eyes from,* ôter les yeux de dessus, quitter des yeux; détourner les yeux de. — **on,** (*new hands*) engager; arrêter; (*carry*) porter; (*lead, conduct*) mener; conduire. — **out,** faire sortir, sortir; (*unharness*) dételer; (*remove, as stains,* &c.) enlever, ôter; (*extract*) arracher; tirer; (*produce, withdraw*) tirer; (*redeem from pawn*) dégager, retirer; (*take*) prendre. *To — it out in,* se payer en. — **over,** passer, faire traverser; mener (à, en), emmener (à, en). — **up,** prendre; (*pick up*) ramasser, relever; recueillir; (*lift*) soulever, lever; (*carry up*) monter; (*conduct up*) faire monter; (*remove*) enlever; (*buy*) acheter; (*arrest*) arrêter; (*begin*) commencer; (*continue*) reprendre, continuer, poursuivre; (*accept*) accepter; (*admit*) admettre; (*adopt*) adopter; (*reprimand*) réprimander, tancer; relancer; (*contradict*) relever, reprendre; (*fill, employ*) occuper, remplir, prendre; (*comprise*) comprendre, embrasser; (*see to, attend to*) s'occuper de; (*make it o.'s business*) s'emparer de; (*undertake*) se charger de, entreprendre; (*a quarrel*) épouser; (*o.'s quarters* or *residence*) établir (sa demeure), élire (domicile); (*o.'s cross*) porter (sa croix); (*collect*) rassembler, recueillir; (*a stitch*) rabattre; (*surg.*) lier; (*pay*) payer, acquitter. — **upon** *oneself*, prendre sur soi, se charger de. *To be —n* **with,** être pris de; (*fond of*) être épris *or* fou de; être charmé de; être entiché de

Take, *v.n.* (*succeed*) réussir, prendre; (*please*) plaire, prendre. — **after,** ressembler à, tenir de; (*imitate*) imiter. — **off,** s'enlever. — **on,** s'affliger, se tourmenter; enrager, s'emporter. — **to,** (*get fond of*) prendre en affection *or* en amitié, s'attacher à; (*things*) prendre goût à; mordre à; (*apply oneself*) s'appliquer à; se mettre à; (*addict oneself*) s'adonner à, se livrer à; (*go towards*) se diriger vers; (*have recourse*) avoir recours à; se réfugier dans *or* sur *or* vers, se retirer dans; (*adopt*) adopter, embrasser, choisir; se mettre dans. *To — to the business,* faire (*or* reprendre) la succession. — **up** *with*, se contenter de; s'associer à, être le compagnon de. — **with,** plaire à

Take, *s.* prise, *f.*; (*of fish*) pêche, quantité, *f.* — **in,** *s.* duperie, *f.*; tour, *m.*, attrape, *f.*; (*pers.*) trompeur, *m.*, -euse, *f.* — **off,** *s.* caricature, charge, *f.*; (*set off*) *V.* **Set off**

Taker, *s.* preneur, *m.*, -euse, *f.*

Taking, *adj.* attrayant; séduisant; (*infectious*) contagieux; — *s.* prise, *f.*; (*fishing*) pêche, *f.*; (*apprehension*) arrestation, *f.*; (*stealing*) soustraction, *f.*; (*distress of mind*) trouble, *m.*, agitation, *f.*; embarras, *m.*; — **s,** *pl.* recettes, *f.pl.*

Takingly, *adv.* d'une manière attrayante

Takingness, *s.* charme, attrait, *m.*

Talapoin, *s.* talapoin, *m.*

Talbot, *s.* chien courant, *m.*

Talc, *s.* talc, *m.* — **slate,** *s.* talc feuilleté, *m.*

Talcky, *adj.* talcaire, talcique

Talcose, Talcous, *adj.* talqueux

Tale, *s.* (*fable*) conte, *m.*, historiette, nouvelle, *f.*; (*narrative*) histoire, *f.*; (*disclosure*) rapport, *m.*; (*number*) nombre, chiffre, *m.*; (*reckoning*) compte, *m.* — *of a tub, idle —, V.* **Idle.** *To tell —s,* mentir; rapporter. — **bearer,** *s.* rapporteur, *m.*, -euse, *f.*, mauvaise langue, *f.*

— **bearing,** *s.* rapport, bavardage, cancan, *m.*; *adj.* rapporteur, qui rapporte. — **teller,** *s.* [conteur, *m.*, -euse, *f.*
Talent, *s.* talent, *m.*
Talented, *adj.* de talent, habile, savant,
Tales, *s.pl.* (*law*) jurés supplémentaires, *m.pl.*
Talipat, Talipot, — palm *or* **tree,** *s.* talipot, [*m.*
Talisman, *s.* talisman, *m.*
Talismanic, *adj.* talismanique
Talk, *v.n.* parler (' *of*,' ' *about*,' ' *over*,' de), causer, converser; (*prate*) jaser, bavarder; — *v.a.* (*pers.*) parler à; (*things*) dire; — *s.* conversation, causerie, *f.*, entretien, *m.*; paroles, *f.pl.*; propos, *m.*, *m.pl.*; sujet de conversation, *m.*; (*prate*) bavardage, *m.*; (*rumour*) bruit, *m.*, rumeur, *f.* *Small* —, banalités, *f.pl.*, lieux communs, discours frivoles, propos insignifiants, *m.pl.*, sornettes, *f.pl.*, conversation sur la pluie et le beau temps, *f.* *To — small*, dire des banalités *or* des sornettes, causer de la pluie et du beau temps; (*fig.*) se faire petit, s'effacer. *To — anyone into*, persuader quelqu'un de. *There is a — of*, il est question de, on parle de; (*it is rumoured*) le bruit court (que). *To be full of* —, aimer beaucoup à causer, être bavard. —*ing of*, (*as connected with*) à propos de. *He is all* —, ce n'est qu'un bavard. *What are you —ing about?* de quoi parlez-vous? (*just consider*) y pensez-vous? vous n'y pensez pas. — **at,** *v.a.* haranguer. — **away,** *v.n.* parler toujours, parler. — **book,** *s.* livre de conver- [sation, *m.*
Talkative, *adj.* causeur; bavard
Talkativeness, *s.* loquacité, *f.*, bavardage, *m.*
Talker, *s.* parleur, *m.*, -euse, *f.*, causeur, *m.*, -euse, *f.*; (*chatterer*) bavard, *m.*, e, *f.*; diseur, *m.*, -euse, *f.* (de ...); (*boaster*) vantard, *m.*, e, *f.*, fanfaron, *m.*
Talking, *adj.* causeur; (*in a bad sense*) bavard; — *s.* bavardage, *m.*; conversation, causerie, *f.*; (*noise*) bruit de conversation, *m.*
Tall, *adj.* haut, grand; (*pers.*) grand; (*hat*) haut de forme, grand; (*glass*) long; (*peas, beans*) à rames. *A — man*, un homme grand, *m.* —**ness,** [*s.* grandeur, grande taille, *f.*
Tallage, *s.* taille, *f.*
Tallow, *s.* suif, *m.*; — *v.a.* suifer. — **candle,** *s.* chandelle de suif, chandelle, *f.* — **chandler,** *s.* fabricant *or* marchand de chandelles, *m.* — **chandlery,** *s.* chandellerie, *f.* — **trade,** *s.* commerce des suifs, *m.* — **tree,** *s.* arbre à [suif, *m.*
Tallowy, *adj.* suifeux, de suif
Tally, *v.a.n.* marquer sur une taille; (*fit*) adapter; (*with*) s'accorder (avec); correspondre (à); cadrer (avec); — *s.* (*stick*) taille, *f.*; (*label*) étiquette, *f.*, porte-numéro, *m.*; (*fellow*) pendant, *m.*; (*com.*) tempérament, *m.* — **ho,** *int.* taïaut! — **man,** *s.* marchand qui vend à tempérament, *m.* — **trade, -system,** *s.* commerce à tempé- [rament, *m.*
Talmud, *s.* Talmud, *m.*
Talmud-ic, al, -ist. *V.* page 3, § 1
Talmudistic, *adj.* talmudiste
Talon, *s.* (*of birds*) serre, *f.*; (*arch.*, *fin.*) talon, *m.*
Tamable, *adj.* apprivoisable, privable; (*to be subdued*) domptable. —**ness,** *s.* nature apprivoisable *or* domptable, *f.*
Tamarin, *s.* tamarin, *m.*
Tamarind, *s.* tamarin, *m.* — **tree,** *s.* tama- [rinier, *m.*
Tamarisk, *s.* tamarisc, tamaris, *m.*
Tambour, *s.* tambour de basque, *m.*; (*arts, fort.*) tambour, *m.*; — *v.a.* broder au tambour. — **frame,** *s.* tambour, métier à broder, *m.* — **work,** *s.* broderie au tambour, *f.*
Tambourine, *s.* tambour de basque, *m.*
Tame, *adj.* (*tamed*) apprivoisé, privé; (*not shy, gentle*) peu farouche; (*born not wild*) domestique; (*pers.*) soumis, docile; paisible; (*things*) doux; (*poor*) plat, pâle, faible, peu fort; — *v.a.* apprivoiser; (*subdue*) dompter. *To grow* —, [s'apprivoiser
Tameless, *adj.* *V.* **Untamable**
Tamely, *adv.* sans résistance; tranquillement; avec soumission; (*cowardly*) lâchement, timidement, sans cœur; servilement; (*poorly*) faiblement
Tameness, *s.* apprivoisement, *m.*; domesticité, *f.*; soumission, *f.*; servilité, *f.*; (*feebleness*) faiblesse, *f.*; mollesse, *f.*
Tamer, *s.* apprivoiseur, *m.*, -euse, *f.*; (*subduer*) [dompteur, *m.*
Tamil, *s. adj.* Tamoul, *m.*, e, *f.*; (*language*) le tamoul, *m.*, la langue tamoule, *f.*
Tamine, Taminy, Tammin, *s.* étamine, *f.*; [tamise, *f.*
Taming, *s.* apprivoisement, *m.*; domestication, *f.*; (*subduing*) domptement, *m.* (*V.* **Shrew**)
Tammy, *s.* (*stuff*) étamine, *f.*; tamise *f.*; (*sieve, strainer*) étamine, *f.*, tamis, filtre, *m.*
Tam o'Shanter cap, *s.* béret, *m.*
Tamp, *v.a.* tamponner; (*mil.*) bourrer
Tamper, *v.n.* employer de petits moyens (pour), jouer (avec), tâtonner; (*meddle*) se mêler (de); toucher (à); déranger; fausser; falsifier; prendre des libertés (avec); s'attaquer (à), se frotter (à); tremper (dans); (*try to bribe*) chercher à corrompre, pratiquer, travailler, suborner; transiger (avec)
Tamping, *s.* (*act*) bourrage, *m.*; (*material*) bourre, *f.* — **bar,** *s.* bourroir, *m.*
Tampion, *s.* tape, *f.*
Tam-tam, *s.* tam-tam, *m.*
Tamul. *V.* **Tamil**
Tan, *v.a.* tanner; (*the complexion*) hâler, basaner, bronzer; — *s.* tan, *m.* — **ball,** *s.* motte à brûler, motte, *f.* — **bed, -stove,** *s.* *V.* **Bark-stove.** — **colour,** *s.* tanné, *m.* — **coloured,** *adj.* tanné. — **house,** *s.* tannerie, *f.* — **liquor,** *s.* jusée, *f.* — **pit, -vat,** *s.* fosse à tan, *f.* — **waste,** *s.* tannée, *f.* — **works, -yard,** *s.* [tannerie, *f.*
Tanager, *s.* tangara, *m.*
Tandem, *s.* attelage en flèche, tandem, *m.*; — *adj. adv.* en flèche
Tang, *s.* (*taste*) *V.* **Twang;** (*sea-weed*) *V.* **Tangle;** (*tech.*) queue, *f.*
Tangency, *s.* tangence, *f.*
Tangent, *adj.* *s.* tangent, *adj. m.*, e, *f.*, tangente, *s.f.* *To go* or *fly off at a* —, s'échapper [par la tangente
Tangential, *adj.* tangentiel
Tanghin, *s.* tanghin, *m.*
Tangi-bility, bleness, *s.* *V.* p. 3, § 1
Tangible, *adj.* tangible; palpable, sensible, [réel
Tangibly, *adv.* tangiblement; palpablement
Tangle, *v.a.* *V.* **Entangle;** — *s.* embarras, *m.*, confusion, *f.*, embrouillement, enchevêtrement, *m.*; nœud, *m.*, tresse, *f.*; (*brake*) fourré, *m.*; (*sea-weed*) laminaire, *f.*
Tank, *s.* réservoir, *m.*; citerne, *f.*; (*of pumps*) bâche, *f.*; (*basin*) cuvette, *f.*
Tankard, *s.* pot, *m.*; (*old*) hanap, *m.*
Tannate, *s.* tannate, *m.*
Tanner, *s.* tanneur, *m.* —*'s bark*, tan, *m.*
Tannery, *s.* tannerie, *f.*
Tannic, *adj.* tannique
Tannin, *s.* tannin, *m.*
Tanning, *s.* tannage, *m.* — **infusion,** *s.* [jusée, *f.*
Tanrec, *s.* tanrec, tenrec, *m.*
Tansy, *s.* tanaisie, *f.*
Tantalism, Tantalization, *s.* supplice de Tantale, *m.*, tentation, *f.*
Tantalize, *v.a.* tantaliser, tenter
Tantalizing, *adj.* tantalisant, bien tentant
Tantalum, *s.* tantale, *m.*
Tantalus, *s.* (*myth.*) Tantale, *m.*; (*bird*) tantale, *m.* —*'s cup*, vase de Tantale, *m.*
Tantamount, *adj.* équivalent (à), égal (à). *To be — to*, équivaloir à, revenir à. *This is — to saying ...*, cela revient à dire ...
Tantivy, *adv.* à fond de train, à bride abattue
Tantrum, *s.* mauvaise humeur, *f.*, mouvement d'humeur, *m.* *To put oneself in a* —, prendre la mouche
Tap, *v.a.n.* (*strike*) taper, frapper; (*a cask*) mettre en perce; (*draw*) tirer; (*a screw-nut*) tarauder; (*trees*) inciser, gemmer; (*surg.*) ponctionner, faire la ponction à; — *s.* (*blow*) tape, *f.*, coup, *m.*; (*pipe for drawing liquids*) robinet, *m.*; (*of casks*) cannelle, *f.*, robinet, *m.*; (*of taverns*) comptoir, *m.*; (*instr.*) taraud, *m.* *On* —, en perce. *A fresh* —, un nouveau baril en perce. — **borer,** *s.* taraud, *m.* — **maker,** *s.* robinetier, *m.* — **making,** *s.* robineterie, *f.* — **net,** *s.* cabas,

m. — **room,** s. (*of a public-house*) petite salle, f.; (*attached to an hotel*) buvette, f., estaminet, m.; (*pot-house*) cabaret, m.; (*low smoking-place*) tabagie, f. — **root,** s. racine pivotante, f., pivot, m. — **rooted,** adj. à racine pivotante; pivotant. —**tub,** s. baquet à cœur, m., couloire, f.
Tape, s. ruban (de fil *or* de coton), m.; (*fig.*) routine administrative, f. —**line, -measure,** s. mètre en ruban, m. —**worm,** s. ver solitaire, m.
Taper, s. bougie, f.; (*for churches*) cierge, m.; (*rolled* —) bougie filée, f., rat de cave, m.; (*fig.*) flambeau, m.; — v.n. se terminer en pointe; s'effiler; — v.a. effiler; — adj. V. **Tapering.** — **stand,** s. bougeoir, chandelier, m.
Tapering, adj. terminé en pointe, pointu; [effilé; conique
Taperingly, adv. en pointe
Tapestry, s. tapisserie, f.; — v.a. tapisser. — **carpet,** s. tapis bouclé, m. — **maker, -weaver, -worker,** s. tapissier, m., -ière, f.
Tapioca, s. tapioca, m. — **soup,** s. potage [au tapioca, m.
Tapir, s. tapir, m.
Tapis, s. tapis, m.
Tapping, s. (*of casks*) mise en perce, f.; (*of trees*) incision, f., gemmage, m.; (*boring*) taraudage, m.; (*surg.*) ponction, f.
Tapster, s. garçon de cabaret, cabaretier, m.
Tar, s. goudron, m.; (*sailor*) marin, loup de mer, m.; — v.a. goudronner. — **barrel,** s. baril de (*or* à) goudron, m.; (*nav.*) gonne, f. — **maker,** s. goudronnier, m. — **paper,** s. papier goudronné, m. — **pit,** s. puits à goudron, m. — **water,** s. eau de goudron, eau goudronnée, f. — **works, -factory,** s. goudronnerie, f.
Tarantella, s. tarentelle, f. [rentin, de Tarente
Tarantine, s. Tarentin, m., e, f.; — adj. ta-
Tarantism, Tarantismus, s. tarentisme, m.
Tarantula, s. tarentule, f.
Taraxacine, s. taraxacine, f.
Taraxacum, s. taraxacum, pissenlit, m.
Tarboosh, Tarbouch, s. tarbouch, m.
Tardigrade, adj. s. tardigrade, adj.m.f., s.m.
Tardily, adv. lentement, avec lenteur; (*late*) tardivement
Tardiness, s. lenteur, f.; (*lateness*) tardiveté, tardivité, f., retard, m.; (*reluctance*) répugnance, f.
Tardy, adj. (*slow*) lent; paresseux; nonchalant; (*late*) tardif; (*backward*) en retard; (*reluctant*) qui a de la répugnance, mal disposé
Tare, s. (*weed*) ivraie, f.; (*bot.*) ers, m.; (*vetch*) vesce, f.; (*com.*) tare, f.; —**s,** pl. (*weed*) ivraie, f.; (*bot.*) vesces, f.pl.; — v.a. (*com.*) tarer
Tarentella, &c. V. **Tarantella,** &c.
Target, s. (*to fire at*) cible, f., but, m.; (*shield*) targe, f.; (*of lamb*) quartier de devant moins l'épaule, m. — **practice,** s. tir à la cible, m.
Tariff, s. tarif, m.; —v.a. tarifer
Tariffable, adj. tarifiable
Tariffing, s. tarification, f.
Tarin, s. tarin, m.
Tarlatan, s. tarlatane, f.
Tarn, s. (*lake*) lac, m., mare, f.; (*marsh*) marais, m.
Tarnish, v.a. ternir; — v.n. se ternir
Tarpaulin, s. toile goudronnée, f., prélart, m.
Tarpeian, adj. Tarpéien. *The — rock,* la roche [Tarpéienne, f.
Tarragon, s. estragon, m.
Tarrier, s. personne qui diffère, f., temporiseur, m.
Tarring, s. goudronnage, m. —**loft,** s. (*nav.*) gou- [dronnerie, f.
Tarrock, s. mouette tridactyle, f.
Tarry, v.n. rester; s'arrêter; (*wait*) attendre; (*delay*) tarder, différer; (*stay behind*) rester en arrière; — adj. goudronneux, de goudron. — **for,** (*wait for*) attendre
Tarrying, s. retard, m.; séjour, m.
Tarsal, adj. tarsien
Tarse, Tarsus, s. tarse, m.
Tarsier, s. tarsier, m.
Tart, adj. aigre, âcre; acide; (*fig.*) aigre, piquant, mordant; — s. tarte, tourte, f. — **dish, -pan,** s. tourtière, f.
Tartan, s. tartan, m.; (*vessel*) tartane, f.
Tartar, s. (*chem., of the teeth*) tartre, m.; (*pers.*) Tartare, m.; (*fig.*) bourru, Turc, m.; — adj. de tartre; (*geog.*) tartare, de Tartarie. *To catch a* —, trouver à qui parler, trouver son maître, trouver plus méchant que soi
Tartarean, adj. (*geog.*) de Tartarie; (*myth.*) du Tartare [tartreux
Tartareous, adj. (*myth.*) du Tartare; (*chem.*)
Tartaric, adj. tartrique
Tartarize, v.a. tartariser
Tartarous, adj. tartreux
Tartish, adj. aigrelet
Tartlet, s. tartelette, tourtelette, f.
Tartly, adv. vertement; avec aigreur
Tartness, s. aigreur, f.
Tartrate, s. tartrate, m.
Tartufe, Tartuffe, s. tartufe, m. [hypocrite
Tartufish, Tartuffish, adj. de tartufe,
Tartufism, Tartuffism, s. hypocrisie, f.
Task, s. tâche, f.; travail, ouvrage, m., besogne, f.; emploi, m.; (*lesson*) devoir, m.; (*punishment*) pensum, m.; — v.a. donner *or* imposer une tâche à; exercer; éprouver, mettre à l'épreuve; exiger, réclamer; (*require to do*) charger (de); (*be a burden*) être à charge à; (*accuse*) accuser ('*with,*' de); (*reproach*) reprocher à (quelqu'un) ('*with,*' de). *To take to* —, prendre à partie; entreprendre; réprimander, gronder, sermonner. — **master,** s. maître, m.; tâcheron, m. — **work,** s. ouvrage (*or* travail) à la tâche, m.; tâche, f. — **worker,** s. ouvrier (m., -ière, f.) à la tâche
Tasmanian, s. adj. Tasmanien, m., -ne, f.
Tasmannia, s. (*bot.*) tasmannie, f.
Tassel, s. gland, m., (*large*) houppe, f.; (*of a cap*) gland, m., flamme, f.; (*of a book*) signet, m.; (*of a flag*) cravate, f.; (*arch.*) tasseau, m.
Tasselled, adj. à glands, à gland, orné de glands (*or* d'un gland)
Tastable, adj. qu'on peut goûter; savoureux
Taste, v.a.n. goûter; goûter de; (*to test, as wines,* &c.) déguster; (*to perceive*) sentir, s'apercevoir de; (*to experience*) éprouver; (*to have a taste*) avoir du goût; (*to have a particular taste*) avoir un goût (...); — s. goût, m.; (*specimen*) échantillon, spécimen, m.; (*a little*) idée, f., soupçon, m. *A wee* —, une idée, un petit peu. *Everyone to his* —, (à) chacun son goût. *To o.'s* (or *his*) —, à son goût. *To — of, to have a — of,* avoir un goût de, sentir le (la, les); (*pers.*) goûter de, goûter; éprouver. *To — good* or *nice,* avoir un bon goût. *To — bad* or *nasty,* avoir un mauvais goût. —**ful,** adj. agréable au goût, savoureux; de bon goût. —**fully,** adv. avec goût. — **fulness,** s. bon goût, m. —**less,** adj. sans goût; fade, insipide. —**lessly,** adv. sans goût; fadement, insipidement. —**lessness,** s. manque de goût, m.; fadeur, insipidité, f.
Tasted, adj. (*in compounds*) qui a un goût, d'un goût. *Bad* —, d'un mauvais goût. *Good* —, d'un bon goût
Taster, s. (*pers.*) dégustateur, m.; (*instr.*) sonde, f.; (*for liquids*) pipette, f. [gustation, f.
Tasting, s. gustation, f.; (*of beverages*) dé-
Tasty, adj. de bon goût; savoureux
Tat, v.n. faire de la frivolité
Ta-ta, int. adieu!
Tatou, s. (*quadruped*) V. **Armadillo**
Tatted, adj. en frivolité
Tatter, s. haillon, lambeau, m., guenille, f.; — v.a. déguenniller; mettre en lambeaux, déchirer, délabrer
Tatterdemalion, s. déguenillé, va-nu-pieds, gueux, m., déguenillée, gueuse, f.
Tattered, adj. (*pers.*) déguenillé; (*of garments*) en lambeaux, en haillons, en loques, tout déchiré, délabré [frivolité
Tatting, s. frivolité, f. *To do* —, faire de la
Tattle, v.n. babiller, bavarder, jaser; cancaner; —s. babil, bavardage, caquet, m.; cancans, m.pl.
Tattler, s. babillard, m., e, f., bavard, m., e, f., cancanier, m., -ière, f.
Tattling, s. bavardage, m.; — adj. bavard

Tattoo, *s.*(*mil.*) retraite, *f.*; (*on the body*) tatouage, *m.*; — *v.a.* tatouer; — *v.n.* (*beat the devil's* —) tambouriner (avec les doigts)
Tattooing, *s.* tatouage, *m.*
Taught, *part. of* **Teach;** (*nav.*) *V.* **Taut**
Taunt, *v.a.* réprimander, tancer; faire des reproches à, reprocher à; insulter, injurier; railler, se moquer de; critiquer; — *s.* réprimande, *f.*; reproche, *m.*; insulte, *f.*; raillerie, *f.*
Tauntingly, *adv.* avec reproche; injurieusement
Taurine, *s.* taurine, *f.*; — *adj.* de taureau
Taurus, *s.* le Taureau, *m.* [*To haul* —, raidir
Taut, *adj.*(*nav.*) raide, tendu; (*of sails*) enflé, plein.
Tautolog-ic, al, -y. *V.* page 3, § 1
Tautologize, *v.n.* se répéter
Tavern, *s.* (*inn*) auberge, *f.*, hôtel, *m.*; restaurant, *m.*; (*dram-shop*) cabaret, *m.*, taverne, *f.* — **haunter,** *s.* pilier de cabaret, *m.* — **keeper,** *s.* aubergiste, *m.*; cabaretier, *m.*
Taw, *v.a.* mégisser; — *s.* calot, *m.*, grosse bille, *f.*
Tawdrily, *adv.* avec un faux éclat; d'une manière voyante; sans goût [mauvais goût, *m.*
Tawdriness, *s.* clinquant, faux brillant, *m.*;
Tawdry, *adj.* de clinquant; (*showy*) voyant, éclatant; de mauvais goût; prétentieux
Tawer, *s.* mégissier, *m.*
Tawing, *s.* mégisserie, *f.* [*animals*) fauve
Tawny, *adj.* tanné, basané, bronzé; (*of*
Tax, *s.* impôt, *m.*; contribution, *f.*; taxe, *f.*; imposition, *f.*; — *v.a.* imposer, taxer; (*fix, require, employ*) taxer; mettre à contribution; (*charge*) accuser (de), taxer (de); blâmer; (*law*) taxer. *Assessed* or *direct —es*, contributions directes, *f.pl.* — **collector, -gatherer,** *s.* percepteur des contributions, percepteur, *m.* — **free,** *adj.* exempt d'impôts. — **payer,** *s.* contribuable, *m.f.* — **paying,** *adj.* imposé
Taxa-bility, bleness, *s.* *V.* page 3, § 1
Taxable, *adj.* imposable, taxable
Taxation, *s.* taxation, taxe, *f.*, impôt, *m.*
Taxer, *s.* taxeur, *m.*; (*law, admin.*) taxateur, *m.*
Taxiderm-ic, al, -ist, -y. *V.* page 3, § 1
Taxing-master, *s.* taxateur, *m.*
Tazza, *s.* coupe, *f.*
Tea, *s.* thé, *m.*; (*of meat*) bouillon, *m.*; (*of plants*) eau, infusion, tisane, *f.* *To come to* —, venir prendre le thé. — **board,** *s.* cabaret à thé, plateau, *m.* — **broker,** *s.* courtier en thés, *m.* — **caddy,** *s.* boîte à thé, *f.* — **cake,** *s.* gâteau à thé, *m.* — **canister,** *s.* boîte à thé, *f.* — **chest,** *s.* caisse à thé, *f.* — **cloth,** *s.* torchon, *m.* — **cup,** *s.* tasse à thé, *f.* *A* — **cupful,** plein une tasse à thé; une demi-tasse, *f.* — **dealer,** *s.* marchand de thé, *m.* — **drinker,** *s.* buveur (*m.*, -euse, *f.*) de thé. — **drinking,** *adj.* qui boit du thé; *s.* usage du thé, *m.*; thé, *m.* — **dust,** *s.* poussière de thé, *f.* — **equipage,** *s.* *V.* — **board.** — **garden,** *s.* guinguette, *f.* — **grower,** *s.* cultivateur de thé, *m.* — **kettle,** *s.* bouilloire, *f.* — **leaves,** *s.pl.* feuilles de thé, *f.pl.* — **man,** *s.* *V.* — **dealer.** — **meeting,** *s.* thé, *m.* — **merchant,** *s.* négociant en thés, *m.* — **party,** *s.* thé, *m.* — **plant,** *s.* *V.* — **tree.** — **pot,** *s.* théière, *f.* *A* — *potful*, plein une théière, une théière pleine. — **rose, -scented rose,** *s.* rose-thé, *m.* — **service, -set,** *s.* service à thé, *m.* — **spoon,** *s.* cuiller à café, petite cuiller, *f.* — **spoonful,** *s.* cuillerée à café, petite cuillerée, *f.* — **strainer,** *s.* passe-thé, *m.* — **table,** *s.* table à thé, *f.* *Set of* — **things,** *s.* service à thé, *m.*; thé, *m.* *To clear* or *take away the — things*, desservir. — **time,** heure du thé, *f.* — **trade,** *s.* commerce des thés, *m.* — **tray,** *s.* plateau à thé, *m.* — **tree,** *s.* thé, arbre à thé, *m.* — **urn,** *s.* fontaine à thé, *f.*
Teach, *v.a.* enseigner; (*a lesson*) donner; faire; (*manual labour*) montrer; — *v.n.* enseigner, donner des leçons [*s.* docilité, *f.*
Teachable, *adj.* enseignable; docile. —**ness,**
Teacher, *s.* instituteur, *m.*, -trice, *f.*; précepteur, *m.*; maître, *m.*, -sse, *f.*; professeur, *m.*; instructeur, *m.*; (*eccl.*) évangéliste, *m.*; prédicateur, *m.*
Teaching, *s.* enseignement, *m.*; instruction, *f.*
Teak, — wood, *s.* teck, tek, bois de teck, *m.*
Teal, *s.* sarcelle, *f.* [(d'attelage), *m.*
Team, *s.* attelage, *m.* —**ster,** *s.* conducteur
Tear, *s.* (*pronounced* '*teer*') larme, *f.*; —**s,** *pl.* larmes, *f.pl.*, pleurs, *m.pl.*; (*pronounced* '*tare*') *See below.* *In* —*s*, en larmes, en pleurs. *With —s in o.'s eyes*, les larmes aux yeux. — **drop,** *s.* larme, *f.* —**ful,** *adj.* rempli de larmes; tout en larmes, en pleurs, pleurant, éploré. —**fully,** *adv.* les larmes aux yeux. —**less,** *adj.* sans larmes, sec; insensible. — **pit,** *s.* (*of the deer*) larmier, *m.*, larmière, *f.* — **shaped,** *adj.* larmeux; (*bot.*) larmaire. —**y,** *adj.* larmeux
Tear, *s.* (*rent*) déchirure, *f.*; (*wear*) usure, *f.*
Tear, *v.a.* déchirer; (*pull*) arracher (à). *To — to pieces*, mettre (*or* déchirer) en pièces *or* en morceaux; (*fig.*) déchirer; abîmer. — **asunder,** déchirer en deux, déchirer. — **away, down, off, out,** arracher. — **up,** mettre en pièces *or* en morceaux; déchirer; arracher; démolir; (*a railway*) enlever les rails de, détruire
Tear, *v.n.* se déchirer; s'agiter; se démener. — **along** (*the road*), filer, galoper, aller ventre à terre, brûler le pavé. — **away,** partir au grand galop, partir ventre à terre, partir comme un trait. — **down,** descendre précipitamment; se précipiter avec fureur; (*a staircase*) descendre quatre à quatre. — **in,** entrer précipitamment. — **into,** se précipiter dans. — **off,** *V.* — **away.** — **up,** monter précipitamment; (*a staircase*) monter quatre à quatre
Tearer, *s.* déchireur, *m.*, -euse, *f.*
Tearing, *s.* déchirement, *m.*; (*pulling*) arrachement, *m.*
Tease, *v.a.* taquiner, agacer, tourmenter; (*animals*) agacer; (*cloth*) lainer; — *s.* taquin, *m.*, e, *f.*, tourment, *m.*
Teasel, *s.* cardère, *f.*; (*fuller's* —) cardère à foulon, *f.*, chardon à foulon, *m.*; — *v.a.* lainer, chardonner
Teaseler, *s.* laineur, *m.*, -euse, *f.*
Teaseling, *s.* lainage, *m.*
Teaser, *s.* (*pers.*) taquin, *m.*, e, *f.*; (*stallion*) boute-en-train, *m.* [trariant, vexant
Teasing, *s.* taquinerie, *f.*; — *adj.* taquin; con-
Teasle, Teazel, Teazle, &c. *V.* **Teasel,** &c.
Teat, *s.* bout de sein, mamelon, tétin, *m.*; (*of animals*) tette, *f.*
Techily, *adv.* maussadement
Techiness, *s.* maussaderie, humeur bourrue, *f.*
Technical, *adj.* technique. — *education*, enseignement professionnel, *m.* — *school*, école professionnelle, *f.*
Technicality, *s.* technicité, *f.*, caractère technique, *m.*; technique, *m.*; terme technique, *m.*; formalité, *f.*; —**ies,** *pl.* termes techniques, *m.pl.*; jargon, *m.*; technique, *m.*; formalités, *f.pl.*
Technically, *adv.* techniquement
Technicalness, *s.* technicité, *f.*
Technics, *s.pl.* technique, *f.*
Techno-graphical, -graphy, -logical, -logist, -logy, &c. *V.* page 3, § 1
Techy, *adj.* maussade, hargneux, bourru
Ted, *v.a.* (*agr.*) étendre, faner
Te Deum, *s.* Te Deum, *m.* [(*slow*) lent, long
Tedious, *adj.* ennuyeux, fastidieux, fatigant;
Tediously, *adv.* ennuyeusement, fastidieusement [*ness*) lenteur, longueur, *f.*
Tediousness, Tedium, *s.* ennui, *m.*; (*slow-*
Teel, *s.* sésame d'Orient, sésame de l'Inde, *m.*, jugeoline, *f.* — **oil,** *s.* huile de sésame, *f.* — **seed,** *s.* graine de sésame, *f.*
Teem, *v.a.n.* (*bring forth*) enfanter; produire; (*be prolific*) être fécond (en); (*be full*) surabonder (de, en); être plein (de); fourmiller (de); regorger (de) [(en); (*full of*) plein (de)
Teeming, *adj.* surabondant; fécond, fertile
Teens, *s. pl.* âge de treize ans à dix-neuf ans, *m.* *To be in o.'s* —, avoir de treize

ans à dix-neuf ans; (*still be in o.'s* —) n'avoir pas vingt ans; être dans son printemps
Teeth, *s.pl.* dents, *f.pl.*; — *v.n.* (*be —ing*) faire ses dents. — **range,** *s.* denture, *f.*
Teething, *s.* dentition, *f.* [rant, abstème
Teetotal, *adj.* de tempérance; (*pers.*) tempé-
Teetotalism, *s.* abstinence de liqueurs alcooliques, *f.*
Teetotaller, *s.* membre d'une société de tempérance, buveur d'eau, *m.*; (*jest.*) grenouillard, *m.*
Teetotum, *s.* tonton, *m.* [laine agneline, *f.*
Teg, *s.* (*yearling*) antenois, *m.*, e, *f.* —**wool,** *s.*
Tegument, *s.* tégument, *m.*
Tegumentary, *adj.* tégumentaire
Teil, — **tree,** *s.* tilleul, *m.*
Telamones, *s.pl.* télamons, *m.pl.*
Teledu, *s.* mydas, télagon, *m.*
Telegram, *s.* télégramme, *m.*
Telegraph, *s.* télégraphe, *m.*; (*at horse-races*) tableau, *m.*; — *v.a.* télégraphier. — **clerk,** *s.* stationnaire, *m.* — **company,** *s.* compagnie de télégraphe, *f.* — **office, -station,** *s.* bureau de télégraphe, *m.* — **post,** *s.* poteau télégraphique, *m.* — **wire,** *s.* fil télégraphique, *m.*
Telegraphic, -al, *adj.* télégraphique
Telegraphically, *adv.* télégraphiquement
Telegraphist, *s.* télégraphiste, *m.*
Telegraphy, *s.* télégraphie, *f.*
Telemeter, *s.* télémètre, *m.* [(*V.* page 3, § 1)
Telemetry, Teleology, &c., télémétrie, &c.
Telescope, *s.* télescope, *m.*; (*fam.*) lunette d'approche, longue-vue, *f.* — **table,** *s.* table à rallonges, *f.*
Telescopic, -al, *adj.* télescopique
Telescopically, *adv.* télescopiquement
Tell, *v.a.n.* dire; (*express*) exprimer; (*relate*) raconter; (*mention*) citer, rapporter; (*inform*) apprendre, informer (de); indiquer; (*show*) montrer; indiquer; (*prove*) prouver; (*warn*) avertir, prévenir; (*report, denounce*) redire, répéter, rapporter; (*disclose*) révéler; (*betray*) trahir; (*reckon*) compter; (*confess*) avouer; (*publish*) proclamer, publier; annoncer; (*explain*) expliquer; (*discover*) découvrir, trouver; (*distinguish*) distinguer; discerner; voir; (*judge*) juger ('*by*,' par); (*know*) savoir; (*take effect, hit*) porter; porter coup; (*be felt*) se faire sentir; (*act*) agir; influer; (*be seen*) se voir, s'apercevoir, être visible *or* perceptible; (*be*) être. *To — a thing*, dire *or* &c. une chose. *To — a person*, dire *or* &c. à une personne. *To — it*, le dire *or* &c. *To — him*, lui dire *or* &c. *To — well* or *badly*, produire un bon *or* un mauvais effet, faire bien *or* mal. *I have been told*, on m'a dit, j'ai entendu dire. *I can — you!* je vous en réponds! allez! *I cannot* —, je ne sais pas; je ne saurais vous dire. — *that to others! don't — me!* à d'autres! allons donc! laissez donc! — **of,** parler de, dire, raconter; indiquer; dénoncer. — **off,** énumérer; compter; désigner; détacher; envoyer; diviser (en); distinguer (en); discerner. — **on,** *V.* — **upon.** — **up,** monter. — **upon,** agir sur; influer sur; modifier; affecter
Teller, *s.* conteur, *m.*, -euse, *f.* (de ...); diseur, *m.*, -euse, *f.* (de ...); (*one who reckons*) personne qui compte, *f.*; (*of votes*) dépouilleur, scrutateur, *m.*; (*accountant*) agent comptable, *m.*; (*thing*) compteur, *m.*
Telling, *adj.* qui porte; expressif, énergique; frappant; mordant; puissant; efficace; qui produit son effet; à effet; —**s,** *s.pl.* secret, *m.*
Tell-tale, *s.* (*pers.*) rapporteur, *m.*, -euse, *f.*; (*instr.*) compteur, *m.*; (*nav.*) axiomètre, *m.*; — [*adj.* rapporteur
Tellurium, *s.* tellure, *m.*
Temerity, *s.* témérité, *f.*
Temper, *v.a.* (*moderate*) tempérer; adoucir; (*mix*) mêler; mélanger; combiner; (*proportion*) proportionner, mesurer, ménager; (*fit*) approprier, accommoder; adapter, ajuster; (*metals*) tremper; (*colours, lime*) délayer, détremper; — *s.* (*disposition*) caractère, naturel, *m.*; (*humour*) humeur, *f.*; (*of the body*) constitution, *f.*, tempérament, *m.*; (*mixture*) mélange, *m.*, combinaison, *f.*; (*coolness*) calme, sang-froid, *m.*; (*ill humour*) mauvaise humeur, humeur, irritation, colère, *f.*; (*of metals, and fig. by comparison*) trempe, *f.* *Out of* —, de mauvaise humeur, en colère; hors de soi. *To keep o.'s* —, se posséder, se maîtriser, être maître de soi, ne pas se fâcher, ne pas s'emporter, garder son sang-froid. *To lose o.'s —, to get out of* —, s'emporter, se fâcher, se mettre en colère, ne pas être maître de soi, ne pas se posséder; perdre patience. *To show* —, montrer de l'humeur
Tempera, *s.* (*paint.*) détrempe, *f.*
Temperament, *s.* tempérament, *m.*
Temperance, *s.* tempérance, sobriété, *f.*; modération, *f.*; patience, *f.* — **society,** *s.* société de tempérance, *f.*
Temperate, *adj.* tempérant, sobre; modéré; calme; patient; (*of climates*) tempéré. — *heat, zone*, chaleur, zone tempérée, *f.*
Temperately, *adv.* avec tempérance, avec sobriété; modérément; avec calme, de sang-froid
Temperateness, *s.* modération, *f.*; (*mildness*) douceur, *f.*; (*coolness*) calme, sang-froid, *m.*
Temperature, *s.* température, *f.*
Tempered, *part.* tempéré, &c. (*V.* **Temper,** *v.a.*); — *adj.* (*in compounds*) d'humeur ..., d'un caractère ... *Good* —, d'un bon caractère, aimable; bon, doux, pas méchant; (*of animals*) doux; facile; pas méchant. *Ill* or *bad* —, (*pers.*) d'un mauvais caractère, maussade; (*pers. and animals*) méchant, hargneux. *To be good* or *ill* —, avoir un bon *or* un mauvais caractère, avoir le caractère bien *or* mal fait, être bon *or* méchant *or* &c.
Tempering, *s.* (*of metals*) trempe, *f.*
Tempest, *s.* tempête, *f.*; orage, *m.* *A — in a teacup* (or *teapot* or *slop-basin*) une tempête dans un verre d'eau. — **tossed,** *adj.* ballotté par la tempête
Tempestuous, *adj.* tempêtueux, orageux
Tempestuously, *adv.* tempêtueusement, orageusement [*or* orageuse, *f.*
Tempestuousness, *s.* nature tempêtueuse
Templar, *s.* templier, *m.*; (*student*) étudiant en droit, *m.* *Knight* —, templier, chevalier du Temple, *m.* [**bone,** *s.* os temporal, *m.*
Temple, *s.* temple, *m.*; (*anat.*) tempe, *f.* —
Temporal, *adj.* temporel; (*anat.*) temporal; — *s.* temporel, *m.*
Temporality, *s.* temporalité, *f.*; bien temporel, *m.*; —**ies,** *pl.* temporel, *m.*
Temporally, *adv.* temporellement
Temporalty. *V.* **Temporality**
Temporarily, *adv.* temporairement; momentanément; provisoirement [soire, *m.*
Temporariness, *s.* état temporaire, provi-
Temporary, *adj.* temporaire; provisoire
Tempore (Pro), *adject.* (*now*) actuel; (*then*) d'alors; (*provisional*) provisoire
Temporization, *s.* temporisation, *f.*
Temporize, *v.n.* temporiser; (*comply*) s'accommoder (à); transiger (avec)
Temporizer, *s.* temporiseur, *m.*, temporisateur, *m.*, -trice, *f.*; (*who complies*) personne qui s'accommode (à), *f.*
Temporizing, *adj.* temporisateur; (*complying*) accommodant; — *s.* temporisation, *f.*
Temporizingly, *adv.* en temporisant
Tempt, *v.a.* tenter ('*to*,' de); (*urge*) pousser ('*to*,' à); (*draw*) entraîner (à)
Temptable, *adj.* sujet à la tentation
Temptation, *s.* tentation, *f.* *To lead into* —, induire en tentation
Tempter, *s.* tentateur, *m.*
Tempting, *adj.* tentant; séduisant; attrayant; (*morsel*, &c.) appétissant; ragoûtant
Temptingly, *adv.* d'une manière tentante

Temptress, *s.* tentatrice, *f.*
Ten, *adj.* dix; (*elliptically*) (*of the clock*) dix heures, *f.pl.*, (*of o.'s age*) dix ans, *m pl.*; — *s.* dix, *m.*; (*round number*) dizaine, *f.* **—fold,** *adj. adv.* décuple, dix fois autant, dix fois. *To increase —fold,* décupler
Tenable, *adj.* (*mil.*) tenable; (*fig.*) soutenable
Tenacious, *adj.* tenace; (*of*) fortement attaché (à). *To be very — of,* tenir fortement à. *To be — of life,* avoir la vie dure
Tenaciously, *adv.* tenacement, avec ténacité; obstinément, opiniâtrément
Tenaciousness, Tenacity, *s.* ténacité, *f.*; obstination, opiniâtreté, *f.*
Tenaculum, *s.* ténaculum, *m.*
Tenaille, *s.* tenaille, *f.*
Tenancy, *s.* location, *f.*; bail, *m.*; jouissance, possession, *f.*; (*feud.*) tenance, *f.* *Joint —,* colocation, *f.*; copropriété, *f.* *In joint —,* par indivis
Tenant, *s.* locataire, *m.f.*; (*one who underlets*) principal locataire, *m.*, principale locataire, *f.*; (*dweller*) habitant, *m.*, e, *f.*; hôte, *m.*; (*of farms*) fermier, *m.*, -ière, *f.*; (*feud.*) tenancier, *m.*, -ière, *f.*; — *v.a.* louer; occuper; habiter. *Joint —,* colocataire, *m.f.*; copropriétaire, *m.f.* **— farmer,** *s.* fermier (*or* cultivateur) à bail, *m.* **—less,** *adj.* inhabité. **— right,** *s.* droit de tenancier, *m.*
Tenantable, *adj.* habitable, logeable; (*of repairs, risks,* &c.) locatif
Tenantry, *s.* locataires, *m.pl.*; (*of farms*) fermiers, *m.pl.*; (*feud.*) tenanciers, *m.pl.*
Tench, *s.* tanche, *f.*
Tend, *v.a.* garder, veiller sur; veiller; avoir soin de, soigner; — *v.n.* tendre (à); contribuer (à); aboutir (à); se diriger (vers), aller, venir
Tendency, *s.* tendance, *f.*; penchant, *m.*; disposition, *f.*; but, *m.*
Tender, *s.* offre, *f.*; (*of contracts*) soumission, *f.*; (*of railways*) tender, *m.*; (*nav.*) bâtiment de servitude, *m.*, allége, *f.* *Contract for the lowest —,* rabais, *m.* *Legal —,* monnaie légale, *f.*
Tender, *v.a.* offrir; présenter; proposer; (*of oaths*) faire prêter, déférer; — *v.n.* soumissionner. *To — for,* soumissionner
Tender, *adj.* tendre; délicat; (*sensitive*) sensible (à); (*of subjects*) scabreux. *To be — of,* être soigneux *or* soucieux *or* jaloux de; se faire scrupule de, craindre de. **— hearted,** *adj.* sensible, compatissant. **— heartedly,** *adv.* avec sensibilité. **— heartedness,** *s.* sensibilité, *f.* **— mouthed,** *adj.* qui a la bouche tendre
Tenderer, *s.* (*admin.*) soumissionnaire, *m.f.* *Lowest —,* moins enchérisseur, *m.*
Tenderly, *adv.* tendrement; délicatement
Tenderness, *s.* tendresse, *f.*; sensibilité, *f.*; délicatesse, *f.*; douceur, *f.*; indulgence, *f.*, égards, *m.pl.*; sollicitude, *f.*; bonté, bienveillance, *f.*; soin, ménagement, *m.*; scrupule, *m.*; (*of eatables*) tendreté, *f.*
Tendinous, *adj.* tendineux
Tendon, *s.* tendon, *m.*
Tendril, *s.* vrille, *f.*
Tenement, *s.* habitation, maison, *f.*; local, *m.*
Tenesmus, *s.* ténesme, *m.*
Tenet, *s.* dogme, principe, *m.*, doctrine, *f.*
Tenfold. *V.* **Ten**
Tennis, *s.* paume, *f.*; jeu de paume, *m.* **— ball,** *s.* balle du jeu de paume, *f.* **— court,** *s.* jeu de paume, *m.*
Tenon, *s.* tenon, *m.*; — *v.a.* tenonner
Tenor, *s.* (*mus.*) ténor, *m.*; (*instr.*) alto, *m.*; (*old spelling of* "*tenour*") *V.* **Tenour.** **— violin,** *s.* alto, *m.*
Tenour, *s.* ton, style, *m.*; caractère, *m.*; tendance, *f.*; portée, *f.*; sens, esprit, *m.*; cours, *m.*; (*law*) teneur, *f.*
Tenotomy, *s.* ténotomie, *f.* **— knife,** *s.* [ténotome, *m.*
Tenrec, *s.* tenrec, tanrec, *m.*

Tense, *adj.* tendu, raide; — *s.* temps, *m.*
Tension, *s.* tension, *f.*
Tensor, *s. adj.* tenseur, *s.m.*, *adj.m.*
Tent, *s.* tente, *f.*; pavillon, *m.*; (*surg.*) tente (de charpie), mèche, *f.*; (*wine*) malaga, *m.*; — *v.a.* tenter; (*surg.*) sonder; — *v.n.* camper; habiter sous des tentes. **— bedstead,** *s.* lit d'ange, *m.* **— cloth,** *s.* coutil, *m.* **—less,** *adj.* sans tente, sans tentes. **— maker,** *s.* fabricant de tentes, *m.* **— wine,** *s.* vin de [Malaga, *m.*
Tentacle, *s.* tentacule, *m.*
Tentacular, *adj.* tentaculaire
Tentaculated, *adj.* tentaculé
Tentative, *adj.* tentatif, d'essai, pour essayer, [expérimental
Tentatively, *adv.* expérimentalement
Tented, *adj.* couvert de tentes; (*pers.*) campé, habitant sous des tentes
Tenter, *s.* crochet, *m.*; courroi, *m.*; étendoir, *m.*; séchoir, *m*; — *v.a.* ramer; courroyer; étendre. **— frame,** *s.* rame, *f.* **— hook,** *s.* clou à crochet, *m.* *To be on — hooks,* être sur les charbons, être sur les (*or* des) épines, être dans des transes [étendage, *m.*
Tentering, *s.* ramage, *m.*; courroyage, *m.*;
Tenth, *adj.* dixième; — *s.* dixième, (*part*) *m.*, (*pers.*) *m.f.*, (*mus.*) *f.*; (*of the month*) dix, *m.* *The —,* (*of sovereigns*) dix
Tenthly, *adv.* dixièmement
Tenuirostral, *adj.* ténuirostre
Tenuirostre, *s.* ténuirostre, *m.*
Tenuity, *s.* ténuité, *f.*
Tenuous, *adj.* ténu
Tenuously, *adv.* ténument
Tenure, *s.* possession, jouissance, occupation, *f.*; (*duration*) durée, *f.*; (*right*) droit, *m.*; (*state*) état, *m.*; (*feud.*) tenure, *f.* *During his — of office,* pendant son administration
Tepefaction, *s.* attiédissement, *m.*
Tepefy, *v.a.* attiédir; — *v.n.* tiédir
Tepid, *adj.* tiède, tépide
Tepidity, Tepidness, *s.* tiédeur, tépidité, *f.*
Tepor, *s.* chaleur douce, *f.*; tiédeur, *f.*
Teratology, &c., tératologie, &c. (*V.* p. 3, § 1)
Terce. *V.* **Tierce**
Tercentenary, *adj.* de trois siècles; — *s.* trois-centième anniversaire, *m.*
Terebinth, *s.* térébinthe, *m.*
Terebinthine, *adj.* de térébenthine
Terebration, *s.* térébration, *f.*
Teredo, *s.* taret, *m.* [ness) inconstance, *f.*
Tergiversation, *s.* tergiversation, *f.*; (*fickle-*
Tergiversator, *s.* tergiversateur, *m.*
Term, *s.* terme, *m.*; (*limit*) limite, *f.*; (*duration*) durée, *f.*; temps, *m.*; (*condition*) condition, *f.*; (*charge*) prix, *m.*; (*law*) session, *f.*; (*univers.*) session, partie de l'année scolaire, *f.*; (*half-year*) semestre, *m.*; inscription, *f.*; (*quarter day*) terme, *m.*; (*catamenia*) règles, époques, *f.pl.*, mois, *m.pl.*; — *v.a.* appeler, nommer; dire. *Hilary —,* session du mois de janvier. *Trinity —,* session après la Trinité. *In plain —s,* en termes précis; en propres termes. *On those —s,* à ces conditions; à ce prix. *On moderate —s,* à prix modéré. *On intimate —s,* sur le pied d'intimité. *On good —s* (*with*), en bons termes (avec), dans de bons termes (avec), bien (avec); en bonne intelligence (avec). *On bad —s* (*with*), en mauvais termes (avec), dans de mauvais termes (avec), mal (avec); en mauvaise intelligence (avec). *To be on good* or *bad —s with …,* être dans de bons *or* de mauvais termes *or* &c. avec … *We are not on good —s,* nous sommes mal ensemble. *On what —s are you with …?* comment êtes-vous avec …? *To live on good* or *bad —s with …,* vivre en bonne *or* mauvaise intelligence avec … *To bring to —s,* amener à un arrangement, faire capituler. *To come to —s,* s'arranger, prendre des arrangements, s'accommoder, tomber d'accord; (*submit*) céder, se rendre, mettre les pouces. *To keep —s with,* garder des mesures avec, ménager.

To keep a —, (*univers.*) prendre une inscription. *To keep —s at an inn of court,* faire son stage. *To reduce to the lowest —s,* (*math.*) réduire à la plus simple expression. *What are your —s?* quelles sont vos conditions? quel est votre prix? —**less,** *adj.* illimité, infini
Termagancy, *s.* turbulence, disposition acariâtre, *f.* [acariâtre, méchant
Termagant, *s.* mégère, *f.*; — *adj.* turbulent,
Terminable, *adj.* qu'on peut terminer, terminable; qu'on peut limiter, qui peut être limité, limitable. — *annuity,* annuité amortissable *or* rachetable, annuité, *f.*
Terminal, *adj.* extrême; (*nat. hist.*) terminal; — *s.* terminal, *m.*
Terminate, *v.a.* terminer; (*put an end to*) finir, mettre un terme à; achever; — *v.n.* se terminer; (*fig.*) aboutir (à); finir (par); (*cease*) cesser, s'arrêter
Termination, *s.* fin, *f.*; conclusion, *f.*; résultat, *m.*; limitation, *f.*; limite, *f.*, limites, *f.pl.*; extrémité, *f.*, bout, *m.*; (*last purpose*) but final, *m.*; (*gram.*) terminaison, *f.*
Terminational, *adj.* terminationnel; final
Terminative, *adj.* terminatif
Termin-ism, -ist, -ology, &c. *V.* p. 3, § 1
Terminus, *s.* gare, *f.*
Termite, *s.* termite, *m.*, fourmi blanche, *f.*
Tern, *s.* (*bird*) sterne, *m.*
Ternary, *adj.* ternaire; — *s.* terne, *m.*
Ternate, *adj.* terné [Terpsichore
Terpsichorean, *adj.* terpsichoréen, de
Terra, *s.* terre, *f.* — **cotta,** *s.* terre cuite, *f.* — **di Sienna,** *s,* terre de Sienne, *f.* — **firma,** *s.* terre ferme, *f.*, continent, *m.* — **Japonica,** *s.* terre du Japon, *f.*, cachou, *m.*
Terrace, *s.* terrasse, *f.*; — *v.a.* terrasser, former en terrasse *or* en terrasses
Terraced, *part.* terrassé; — *adj.* à terrasse
Terraqueous, *adj.* terraqué
Terrene, *adj.* terrestre
Terre-plein, *s.* terre-plein, terre-plain, *m.*
Terrestrial, *adj.* terrestre
Terrestrially, *adv.* terrestrement
Terrestrialness, *s.* terrestréité, *f.*
Terrible, *adj.* terrible [*f.*; horreur, *f.*
Terribleness, *s.* nature terrible, terribilité,
Terribly, *adv.* terriblement
Terrier, *s.* terrier, *m.*
Terrific, *adj.* terrible, épouvantable [blement
Terrifically, *adv.* terriblement, épouvanta-
Terrify, *v.a.* terrifier, épouvanter
Territorial, *adj.* territorial
Territorially, *adv.* territorialement
Territory, *s.* territoire, *m.*; (*state*) état, *m.*, (*states*) états, *m.pl.*
Terror, *s.* terreur, *f.*; effroi, *m.* *The reign of* —, la terreur, *f.*, le règne de la terreur, *m.*
Terror-ism, -ist. *V.* page 3, § 1
Terrorize, *v.a.n.* terroriser
Terry, *adj.* (*of fabrics*) épinglé
Terse, *adj.* net, pur, élégant, bien tourné. —**ly,** *adv.* nettement, purement, élégamment. —**ness,** *s.* netteté, pureté, élégance, *f.*; verve, *f.*
Tertian, *adj.* (*med.*) tierce, *f.*; — *s.* fièvre tierce, *f.* — *fever,* fièvre tierce, *f.*
Tertiary, *adj.* tertiaire
Tesselate, *v.a.* tesseller, marqueter
Tesselated, *adj.* tessellé, marqueté; en mosaïque. — *pavement,* mosaïque, *f.*
Tesselation, *s.* mosaïque, *f.*
Tessera, *s.* tesselle, *f.*
Test, *s.* (*trial*) essai, *m.*, épreuve, *f.*; (*proof*) preuve, *f.*; (*standard*) pierre de touche, *f.*; critérium, *m.*; (*characteristic*) caractère distinctif, *m.*; (*distinction*) distinction, différence, *f.*; (*chem.*) réactif, *m.*; (*metal.*) têt, test, *m.*; (*Engl. hist.*) test, *m.*; — *v.a.* essayer, éprouver, faire l'essai de, mettre à l'épreuve; (*metal.*) coupeller. *To put to the* —, mettre à l'épreuve. *To stand the* —, subir l'épreuve. — **object,** *s.* test-objet, *m.* — **paper,** *s.* papier réactif, *m.* — **tube,** *s.* éprouvette, *f.*
Testable, *adj.* qui peut être légué
Testacean, *s.* testacé, *m.*
Testaceous, *adj.* testacé
Testament, *s.* (*law, rel.*) testament, *m.* *New* —, nouveau Testament. *Old* —, ancien Testament
Testamentary, *adj.* testamentaire
Testate, *adj. s.* testat, *adj. m.*, *s.m.*
Testa-tor, trix, *s.* testateur, *m.*, -trice, *f.*
Tester, *s.* (*of a bed*) ciel de lit, *m.*; (*canopy*) baldaquin, *m.* — **bedstead,** *s.* lit à balda-
Testicle, *s.* testicule, *m.* [quin, *m.*
Testicular, *adj.* testiculaire
Testification, *s.* témoignage, *m.*, attestation, *f.*
Testificator, Testifier, *s.* témoin, *m.*
Testify, *v.n.a.* certifier, attester; témoigner; témoigner de; rendre témoignage de; (*law*) déposer de
Testily, *adv.* maussadement, avec humeur
Testimonial, *s.* certificat, *m.*; attestation, *f.*; témoignage, *m.*; témoignage de reconnaissance, témoignage d'estime, témoignage de bon souvenir, souvenir, *m.*; — *adj.* testimonial
Testimonially, *adv.* testimonialement
Testimony, *s.* témoignage, *m.*; attestation, *f.*; (*proof*) preuve, *f.* *In — whereof,* en foi de quoi. *To bear* —, rendre témoignage, attester
Testiness, *s.* maussaderie, humeur, colère, pétulance, *f.*
Testing, *s.* essai, *m.*, épreuve, *f.* [susceptible
Testy, *adj.* maussade, bourru, irritable, vif,
Tetanic, *adj. s.* tétanique, *adj. m.f.*, *s.m.*
Tetanus, *s.* tétanos, *m.*
Tête-à-tête, *s. adv. adj.* tête-à-tête (*s.m.*)
Tête-de-pont, *s.* tête-de-pont, *f.*
Tether, *s.* attache, longe, *f.*; — *v.a.* attacher, mettre à l'attache. *At the end of o.'s* —, (*fig.*) au bout de son rouleau
Tetrachord, *adj. s.* tétracorde, *adj. m.f.*, *s.m.*
Tetragon, *s.* tétragone, *m.*
Tetragonal, *adj.* tétragonal, tétragone
Tetrahedral, *adj.* tétraèdre
Tetrahedron, *s.* tétraèdre, *m.*
Tetrameter, *s. adj.* tétramètre, *m.*
Tetrapetalous, *adj.* tétrapétale
Tetrarch, *s.* tétrarque, *m.*
Tetrarchate, *s.* tétrarchat, *m.*
Tetrarchy, *s.* tétrarchie, *f.*
Tetter, *s.* dartre, *f.*
Teuton, *s.* Teuton, *m.*, -ne, *f.*
Teutonic, *adj.* teutonique, teuton
Text, *s.* texte, *m.* — *hand, large* —, écriture en gros, *f.* — **book,** *s.* livre de classe, *m.*; manuel, guide, *m.*
Textile, *adj. s.* textile, *adj. m f.*, *s.m.* — *fabric,*
Textility, *s.* textilité, *f.* [tissu, *m.*
Textual, *adj.* textuel
Textually, *s.* textuellement
Texture, *s.* tissage, *m.*; (*of cloth,* &c.) tissu, *m.*; (*fig.*) texture, contexture, *f.*
Thaler, *s.* thaler, *m.*
Thallium, *s.* thallium, *m.*
Thallus, *s.* thalle, *m.*
Thames, *s.* Tamise, *f.* *The —, the river* —, la Tamise. *He will never set the — on fire,* il n'a pas inventé la poudre
Than, *adv.* que; (*before a numeral*) de; (*followed by a verb not in the inf.*) que … ne, *as: He is richer — he thinks,* il est plus riche qu'il ne pense. — *that …, V.* **That,** *conj.*
Thank, *v.a.* remercier ('*for*' *a thing,* de; '*for*' *a person,* pour). — *you!* merci! *No, — you!* merci! — *God!* Dieu merci! (*owing to*) grâce à Dieu! *I will — you for …,* auriez-vous la bonté de me donner …? (*of helping at table*) je vous demanderai … *I will — you to …,* je vous serai obligé de … *To — oneself,* s'en prendre à soi-même ('*for,*' de; '*that,*' si). *You may — yourself for it,* prenez-vous-en à vous-même

Thank, *s.* remercîment, *m.* **—ful,** *adj.* reconnaissant (*'for,'* de); (*happy*) heureux (de). *I am —ful to say!* Dieu merci! **—fully,** *adv.* avec reconnaissance. **—fulness,** *s.* reconnaissance, gratitude, *f.* **—less,** *adj.* ingrat. **—lessness,** *s.* ingratitude, *f.* **— offering,** *s.* action de grâces, *f.*

Thanks, *s.pl.* remercîments, *m.pl.* (*'for' a thing,* pour, de; *'for' a person,* pour); (*owing to*) grâce (à). *— !* merci! *Best —,* vifs remercîments. *Many —,* bien des remercîments, mille remercîments. *To give* or *return— to,* remercier, faire des remercîments à; (*to God, to Heaven*) rendre grâce (*or* grâces) à, remercier. *Give* or *return him my best —,* remerciez-le bien de ma part. **—giving,** *s.* action de grâces, *f.*

Thapsia, *s.* thapsie, *f.*

That, *pron. dem.* (*before a noun*) ce cet, *m.*, cette, *f.*; (*if speaking pointedly or in contradistinction*) ce ... -là, cet ... -là, cette ... -là (*with the noun between in French*); (*the one, followed by 'which,' 'who,' 'whom,' 'whose,' 'where,' 'of'*) celui, *m.*, celle, *f.*; (*that one, the one there*) celui-là, *m.*, celle-là, *f.*; (*that thing, those things*) cela, ça, *m.*; (*that thing, those things, before a verb*) cela, ça, ce, c', *m.*; (*it, so*) le, l', *m.*; (*that point; there*) là. *— which,* (*what*) ce qui (*nom.*), ce que (*obj.*) *or* ce qu'. *About —,* là-dessus. *By —,* par là. *For all —,* malgré cela; malgré tout; néanmoins; tout de même. *From —,* de cela; en. *In —,* en cela; là-dedans; y. *Of —,* de cela; en. *On —,* là-dessus. *To —,* à cela; y. *Under —,* là-dessous. *Upon —,* là-dessus. *With —,* avec cela; (*thereupon*) là-dessus. *We have not come to — yet,* nous n'en sommes pas encore là. *— is,* cela est, c'est; (*there is*) voilà; (*that is to say*) c'est-à-dire. *— is true,* cela est vrai, c'est vrai. *— is what I fear,* c'est là (*or* c'est *or* voilà) ce que je crains. *Is — your book?* est-ce là votre livre? *— is all, V.* **All,** *adj.* *— you are! — he does! — I will! — it is! — it does! — it will!* &c., &c., pour ça oui! bien sûr! ça c'est certain! je vous en réponds! je vous le jure! *— you are not!* &c., &c., &c., pour ça non! bien sûr! ça c'est certain! je vous en réponds! je vous le jure! *You have not seen him: — I have,* vous ne l'avez pas vu: si fait. *— much,* cela

That, *pron. relat. V.* **Who, Whom,** *and* **Which**

That, *conj.* que; (*in order that*) afin que, pour que; de sorte que, de manière que. [*Untranslated sometimes.*] *To see — a thing be done,* voir (*or* veiller) à ce qu'une chose se fasse. *Nothing is so disagreeable as — you should do that,* rien n'est si désagréable que de vous voir faire cela. *Nothing is more evident than — whatever lives must die,* rien n'est plus évident que tout ce qui vit doit mourir. *It is better that he should come to our house than — we should go to his,* il vaut mieux qu'il vienne chez nous que si nous allions chez lui. *It is better that he should ask for nothing than — he should be refused,* il vaut mieux qu'il ne demande rien que de se voir refuser. *I had much rather that he should not try than — he should fail,* j'aimerais beaucoup mieux qu'il n'essayât pas que de le voir échouer. *Had you rather Cæsar were living, and die all slaves, than — Cæsar were dead, to live all freemen?* aimeriez-vous mieux voir César vivant et mourir tous esclaves, que de voir César mort et de vivre tous libres?

Thatch, *s.* chaume, *m.*; *— v.a.* couvrir de (*or* en) chaume. *—ed house,* chaumière, *f.*

Thatcher, *s.* chaumier, couvreur en chaume, *m.*

Thaumatrope, *s.* thaumatrope, *m.*

Thaumaturg-ic, al, -y. *V.* page 3, § 1

Thaumaturg-ist, us, *s.* thaumaturge, *m.*

Thaw, *v.n.* dégeler; (*fig.*) fondre; *— v.a.* dégeler; (*fig.*) fondre; attendrir; *— s.* dégel, *m.*

The, *art.* le, l', *m.*, la, l', *f.*, les, *m.f. pl.*; (*this, that*) ce *or* cet, *m.*, cette, *f.*, ces, *m.f.pl.* [*At* or *to —, of* or *from —, See all grammars.*] *Book — first,* livre premier. *Charles — Twelfth,* Charles douze. *— richer people are, — more covetous they are,* plus on est riche, plus on est avare

Theatine, *s.* théatin, *m.*, e, *f.*

Theatre, *s.* théâtre, *m.* *Minor —,* petit théâtre. **— goer,** &c. *V.* **Play**

Theatrical, *adj.* théâtral, de théâtre, du théâtre, des théâtres; scénique; **—s,** *pl.* spectacle, *m.*, représentation, *f.* *Private* or *amateur —,* comédie de société *or* d'amateurs, comédie bourgoise, comédie de salon, *f.* **— piece,** *s.* pièce de théâtre, *f.*

Theatrically, *adv.* théâtralement

Theave, *s.* antenoise, *f.*

Thebaid, *s.* Thébaide, *f.*

Thebaine, *s.* (*chem.*) thébaïne, *f.*

Theban, *s. adj.* Thébain, *m.*, e, *f.*

Thee, *pron. pers.* toi, te

Theft, *s.* vol, larcin, *m.*

Theine, *s.* théine, *f.*

Their, *pron. poss.* leur, *m.f. sing.*, leurs, *pl.*; en

Theirs, *pron. poss.* le leur, la leur, les leurs; leurs; (*pron. pers.*) à eux, à elles; d'eux, d'elles (*V. for examples,* **Mine, His, Hers, Yours**)

Theism, *s.* théisme, *m.*

Theist, *s.* théiste, *m.f.*

Theistic, -al, *adj.* théiste

Them, *pers. pron.* eux, *m.*, elles, *f.*; (*obj. of a verb.*) les; (*to them*) leur; (*demonstrative*) ceux, *m.*, celles, *f.* *At —, by —, for —,* (*of things*) y; en. *From —, of —,* (*of things*) en. *To —,* (*of things*) y. [*V.* **About, After, Against, Around, Before, Behind, In, Into,** *and other prepositions.*] **—selves,** *pron. pers.* eux-mêmes, elles-mêmes; eux, elles; soi-meme; soi; (*in a reflect. verb.*) se

Theme, *s.* thème, *m.*; sujet, *m.*; texte, *m.*; narration, *f.*; discours, *m.*; amplification, *f.*

Then, *adv.* (*at that time, in that case*) alors; (*after that, next*) ensuite, puis; (*therefore*) donc, par conséquent; (*adject.*) d'alors; du moment. *By —,* alors, déjà. *Since —, ever since —,* depuis ce temps-là, depuis, depuis lors. *What — ?* et ensuite? et puis? et après? après? eh bien! (*V.* **There**)

Thence, *adv.* de là, en; pour cette raison; depuis ce temps, depuis lors, dès lors (*From —, same meaning*). **—forth, -forward,** *adv.* depuis ce temps, depuis lors, dès lors, désormais; de là

Theobroma, *s.* théobrome, *m.*

Theobromine, *s.* théobromine, *f.*

Theocracy, *s.* théocratie, *f.*

Theocratic, -al, *adj.* théocratique

Theocratically, *adv.* théocratiquement

Theodicea, Theodicy, *s.* théodicée, *f.*

Theodolite, *s.* théodolite, *m.*

Theodosian, *adj.* théodosien

Theogon-y, &c., théogonie, &c. (*V.* page 3, § 1)

Theologian, *s.* théologien, *m.*

Theological, *adj.* théologique. *The three — virtues,* les trois vertus théologales, *f.pl.*

Theologically, *adv.* théologiquement

Theologism, *s.* théologisme, *m.*

Theologize, *v.n.a.* théologiser

Theology, *s.* théologie, *f.*

Theorbo, *s.* téorbe, théorbe, *m.*

Theorem, *s.* théorème, *m.*

Theoretic, -al, *adj.* théorique; spéculatif; (*pers.*) théoricien

Theoretically, *adv.* théoriquement, en théorie

Theorist, *s.* théoricien, *m.*, -ne, *f.*

Theorize, *v.n.* théoriser

Theorizer, *s.* théoriseur, *m.*, -euse, *f.*

Theory, *s.* théorie, *f.*

Theosoph-ic, al, -ism, -y, théosophique, &c. (*V.* page 3, § 1)

Theosophist, *s.* théosophe, *m.*

Therapeutic, -al, *adj.* thérapeutique (*m.f.*); **—s,** *s.pl.* thérapeutique, *f.*

Therapeutist, *s.* thérapeutiste, *m.*

There, *adv.* (*place not mentioned before*) là; y (*place mentioned before*) y; (*emphatically*) là; (*over there*) là-bas; (*whom* or *which you see*

there) que voilà; (*on that point*) en cela; quant à cela; (*exclam.*) là! voilà! (*in imp. verbs*) il. *About* —, *V.* **About.** *Down* —, *V.* **Down.** *In* —, là-dedans; (*in it, in them*) y. *On* —, là-dessus. *Out* —, là-dehors. *Over* —, là-bas. *Under* —, là-dessous. *Up* —, là-haut; (*upon*) là-dessus. — *he* or *she is* (or *goes*), le *or* la voilà. — *it is*, le (*or* la) voilà; (*that is it*) c'est cela; voilà ce que c'est; voilà la chose; (*exactly*) précisément! justement! — *they are* (or *go*), les voilà. — *is* or *are*, *V.* **Be.** — *remains* or *remain*, il reste. — *and back*, aller et retour. *To go* — *and back*, aller et revenir, aller et venir. — *and then, then and* —, en temps et lieu; séance tenante, pendant qu'on y est, sur place, sur-le-champ, sans désemparer. — *now!* là! — *I have him*, c'est par là que je le tiens

Thereabout, Thereabouts, *adv.* par là, près de là; (*nearly*) environ, à peu près

Thereafter, *adv.* après cela; (*according to that*) d'après cela; (*accordingly*) en conséquence, conformément

Thereat, *adv.* à cela, à ce sujet, y; (*of place*) par là, là, y [manière, ainsi; par conséquent

Thereby, *adv.* par là, par ce moyen, de cette

Therefore, *adv.* c'est pourquoi; donc, aussi, par conséquent; en conséquence

Therefrom, *adv.* de là; de cela, en

Therein, *adv.* là-dedans, là, y; (*fig.*) là-dedans, en cela, y [dont

Thereof, *adv.* de cela, en; d'eux, d'entre eux;

Thereon, *adv.* là-dessus, à ce sujet; en; y

Thereto, Thereunto, *adv.* à cela, à quoi, y

Thereupon, *adv.* là-dessus

Therewith, *adv.* avec cela; avec; en; y

Therewithal, *adv.* en outre, de plus; avec cela; en même temps

Theriac, Theriaca, *s.* thériaque, *f.*; — *adj.*

Theriacal, *adj.* thériacal [thériacal

Thermæ, *s.pl.* thermes, *m.pl.*

Thermal, *adj.* thermal. — *baths*, thermes, *m.pl.*

Thermo, (*in compounds*) thermo ...

Thermometer, *s.* thermomètre, *m.*

Thermometric, -al, *adj.* thermométrique

Thermometrically, *adv.* thermométriquement [mopathe, *m.*

Thermopath, Thermopathist, *s.* ther-

Thermopath-ic, al, -ically, -y. *V.* p. 3, § 1

Thermoscope, *s.* thermoscope, *m.*

Thermoscop-ic, al, -y. *V.* page **3**, § **1**

Thermostat, *s.* thermostat, *m.*

Thermotic, -al, *adj.* thermotique (*m.f.*); **—s,** *s.pl.* thermotique, *f.*

Thesaurus, *s.* trésor, *m.*

These, *pl. of* **This** (*V.* **This**), *pron. dem.* ces, *m.f.*; ces ... -ci, *m.f.*; ceux-ci, *m.*, celles-ci, *f.* *Are not — your gloves?* est-ce que ce ne sont pas là vos gants? — *are yours*, voici les vôtres. *I have been waiting* — or — *last two hours, I have not seen him for* — or — *last two hours*, &c., &c., *V.* **Last**

Thesis, *s.* thèse, *f.*; (*mus.*) frappé, *m.*

Thespian, *adj.* tragique, de la tragédie

Thessalian, *s. adj.* Thessalien, *m.*, -ne, *f.*

Thessalonian, *s.adj.* Thessalonicien, *m.*, -ne, *f.*

Theurg-ic, al, -ist, -y, théurgique, &c. (*V.*

Thew, *s.* nerf, muscle, *m.* [page 3, § 1

Thewy, *adj.* nerveux, musculeux

They, *pron.* ils, *m.*, elles, *f.*; (*when neither directly connected with nor placed immediately before a following verb*) eux, *m.*, elles, *f.*; (*those, before 'who,' 'whom,' 'that,' or 'whose'*) ceux, *m.*, celles, *f.*; (*people, anyone*) on (*with the verb in the sing.*); (*before the verb* être *followed by a noun*) ce, c'. — *say*, ils *or* elles disent. *You and* —, vous et eux *or* elles. *It is — who say*, ce sont eux *or* elles qui disent. — *who say*, ceux *or* celles qui disent. — *say so*, on le dit. — *are* or — *were poor people*, ce sont *or* c'étaient de pauvres gens

Thick, *adj.* épais; (*muddy*) trouble; (*large*) gros; (*of bar iron*, &c.) fort, solide; (*close*) serré, dru; (*intimate*) intime, lié; (*frequent*) fréquent, nombreux; (*of the voice*) embarrassé; (*of pronunciation*) gras; (*of hearing*) dur; (*stupid*) grossier, stupide; (*adv.*) épais; rapidement, à coups pressés; tout près les uns des autres, en troupe, en foule; dru; grossièrement; (*deeply*) profondément; (*in thickness*) d'épaisseur. *To become* or *grow* or *get* —, s'épaissir, épaissir, devenir épais; (*muddy*) devenir trouble, se troubler. *To make* —, épaissir; (*muddle*) troubler. *To speak* —, grasseyer, parler gras. — **coming,** *adj.* nombreux. — **faced,** *adj.* (*print.*) gras. — **head,** *s.* *V.* — **skull.** — **headed,** *adj.* épais, lourd. — **knee,** *s.* (*bird*) œdicnème, *m.* — **lipped,** *adj.* lippu, aux grosses lèvres. — **necked,** *adj.* au gros cou. — **set,** *adj.* épais, serré; dru; touffu; (*pers.*) trapu. — **skinned,** *adj.* à peau épaisse; (*fig., jest.*) peu impressionnable, coriace, dur à cuire. — **skull,** *s.* lourdaud, *m.*, e, *f.*, balourd, *m.*, e, *f.*, tête dure, *f.* — **skulled,** *adj.* *V.* — **headed.** — **soled,** *adj.* à semelles épaisses *or* fortes. — **sown,** *adj.* semé dru, serré, épais

Thick, *s.* épaisseur, *f.*; partie épaisse, *f.*; (*middle*) fort, *m.*; (*fight*) mêlée, *f.* — *of the leg*, gras de la jambe, *m.* *In the — of*, au plus fort de. *Through — and thin*, à travers tous les obstacles; en dépit de tout; envers et contre tous

Thicken, *v.a.* épaissir; (*make close*) serrer, resserrer; (*increase*) grossir, augmenter, multiplier; (*a sauce*, &c.) lier; — *v.n.* s'épaissir, épaissir; se serrer, se resserrer; se grossir, augmenter, se multiplier; (*be crowded*) se presser; (*get dark*) s'obscurcir; (*become animated*) s'animer; (*of sauces*, &c.) se lier

Thickening, *s.* épaississement, *m.*; (*cook.*) liaison, *f.*

Thicket, *s.* fourré, hallier, taillis, *m.*; (*cluster*) massif, *m.*, touffe d'arbres, *f.*; (*of bushes*) buisson, *m.*; (*grove*) bosquet, *m.* [*adj.*)

Thickish, *adj.* un peu épais *or* &c. (*V.* **Thick,**

Thickly, *adv.* *V.* **Thick,** *adv.*, *and* **Densely**

Thickness, *s.* épaisseur, *f.*; (*of liquids*) consistance, *f.*; (*of wine*) état trouble, *m.*; (*of hearing*) dureté, *f.*; (*of pronunciation*) grasseyement, *m.*

Thief, *s.* voleur, *m.*, -euse, *f.*, larron (*obsolete*), *m.*; (*of candles*, &c.) voleur, champignon, *m.* *Thieves'* or *Marseilles vinegar*, vinaigre des quatre voleurs, *m.* *Thieves!* aux voleurs! *Stop —!* au voleur! arrêtez! *Set a — to catch a* —, à corsaire corsaire et demi. — **catcher,** *s.* agent de police, *m.* — **proof,** *adj.* à l'épreuve des voleurs

Thieve, *v.n.* voler, dérober

Thievery, Thieving, *s.* vol, *m.* [de voleur

Thievish, *adj.* voleur, adonné au vol; (*things*)

Thievishly, *adv.* en voleur; par le vol

Thievishness, *s.* penchant au vol, *m.*

Thigh, *s.* cuisse, *f.*; (*of a horse*) jambe, *f.* — **bone,** *s.* os de la cuisse, fémur, *m.*

Thill, *s.* limon, brancard, *m.* — **horse, thiller,** *s.* limonier, cheval de brancard, *m.*

Thimble, *s.* dé, dé à coudre, *m.*; (*nav.*) cosse, *f.* *A* —**ful,** *s.* plein un dé; (*fig.*) un doigt, *m.* — **rig,** *s.* tour de gobelet, *m.*; *v.n.* jouer des gobelets. — **rigger,** *s.* joueur (*m.*, -euse, *f.*) de gobelets. — **rigging,** *s.* tours de gobelets, *m.pl.*, jeu des gobelets, *m.*

Thin, *adj.* mince; (*slender*) mince; élancé; délié; (*small*) petit; (*not close*) clair; (*of liquids*) clair; (*light*) léger; (*rare*) rare, subtil; (*lean*) maigre; (*thin-sown, scattered*) clair-semé; (*in small number*) peu nombreux; (*of the voice*) faible, grêle; (*adv.*) *V.* **Thinly;** — *v.a.* amincir; éclaircir; dégarnir; réduire; atténuer; raréfier; faire maigrir, maigrir, amaigrir. *To become* (or *get* or *grow*) —, s'amincir; s'éclaircir; (*pers., animals*) maigrir. *To make* —, *V.* *To*

Thin, *v.a.* — **bodied,** *adj.* maigre; au corsage fluet; (*wine*) léger. —**skinned,** *adj.* à peau fine; (*fig.*) susceptible; pointilleux. — **soled,** *adj.* à semelles minces

Thine, *pron. poss.* le tien, la tienne, les tiens, les tiennes; tes; à toi; de toi

Thing, *s.* chose, *f.*; objet, *m.*; affaire, *f.*; action, *f.*; machine, *f.*; créature, *f.*, être, *m.*; (*man*) homme, *m.*; (*woman*) femme, *f.*; (*girl*) fille, *f.*; (*little one*) petit, *m.*, e, *f.*; (*animal*) bête, *f.*; —**s,** *pl.* choses, les choses, &c.; affaires, *f.pl.*, effets, *m.pl.*; (*clothes*) habits, *m.pl.*; (*everything*) tout, *m.* *Good* —, bonne chose, *f.*; bonne affaire, *f.*; bien, *m.* *It is a* (*very*) *good — that* ..., c'est un (grand) bien que ...; il est (très *or* fort) heureux que ... *Old* —, (*woman*) vieille, *f.* *Poor* — *!* pauvre créature *or* &c.! *Poor little* — *!* pauvre petit (*m.*)! pauvre petite (*f.*)! *Above all —s,* surtout; par-dessus tout; avant tout. *Another* —, *Any* —, *Such* —, &c., *V.* **Another, Any, Such,** &c. *One* —, une chose, &c. (*for idiomatic phrases, V.* **One**). *For one* —, d'abord. *That is the* —, c'est cela; c'est ce qu'il faut. *That is the very* — *!* c'est cela même! voilà l'affaire! *Not to be quite the* —, n'être pas tout à fait cela; n'être pas précisément ce qu'il faut. —**umbob,** —**ummy,** *s.* chose, *f.*, machin, *m.*

Think, *v.a.n.* penser; (*to have a thought of*) penser ('*of*' *or* '*on*' *or* '*about*,' à; '*of it*' *or* '*on it*' *or* '*about it*,' y); (*to have an opinion of*) penser ('*of*,' de; '*of it*,' en); (*reflect*) songer ('*of*,' à; '*that*,' que), réfléchir (à); (*believe*) croire (que); (*deem*) juger, trouver; (*be of opinion*) être d'avis; (*imagine*) s'imaginer, s'aviser (de); (*suspect*) se douter (de, que); (*intend*) compter; (*hope*) espérer; (*esteem*) croire, estimer, juger; considérer comme, regarder comme, compter pour; (*remember*) se souvenir (de), se rappeler. *I was —ing of him,* je pensais à lui. *I told him what I thought of him,* je lui ai dit ce que je pensais de lui. *I — of it,* j'y pense. *What do you — of it?* qu'en pensez-vous? *I — it very beautiful,* je le trouve très beau. *I can't — of it* (*remember it*), je ne peux pas m'en souvenir, je ne peux pas me le rappeler. *To — twice before* ..., y regarder à deux fois avant de ... *To — fit* or *good,* juger convenable (de), juger à propos (de), trouver bon (de, que). *To — ill* or *well of,* avoir mauvaise *or* bonne opinion de. *To — much* or *highly of,* avoir une haute opinion (*or* une haute idée) de, faire beaucoup de cas de, faire grand cas de; (*to esteem a great matter*) faire difficulté de, regarder comme grand' chose de. *To — little of,* avoir une mince opinion de, faire peu de cas de. *I little thought that* ..., je ne me doutais guère que ... *To — nothing of,* compter pour rien. *I should — so,* je le pense; je crois bien! *I — so,* je le pense, je pense que oui. *I don't — so,* je ne le pense (*or* crois) pas, je ne pense (*or* crois) pas, je pense (*or* crois) que non; je ne suis pas de cet avis; je ne trouve pas. *I will — it over,* j'y réfléchirai. *He thought he would try,* &c. *V.* **Would.** *And to — that* ... *!* et dire que ...!

Thinker, *s.* penseur, *m.*, -euse, *f.*

Thinking, *adj.* pensant, qui pense; intelligent; réfléchi; raisonnable; sérieux; — *s.* pensée, réflexion, méditation, *f.*; jugement, *m.*; opinion, *f.*, avis, *m.* *Way of* —, façon de penser, opinion, *f.* *To my* —, à mon avis, selon moi

Thinly, *adv.* maigrement; faiblement; (*lightly*) légèrement; (*sparsely*) clair; de loin en loin; (*few*) peu; en petit nombre, peu nombreux; par un petit nombre; par une population peu nombreuse. — *sown,* clairsemé. *It was — attended,* l'assistance était peu nombreuse

Thinness, *s.* minceur, *f.*, peu d'épaisseur, *m.*; ténuité, *f.*; finesse, *f.*; fluidité, *f.*; (*leanness*) maigreur, *f.*; (*paucity*) rareté, *f.*, petit nombre, *m.*

Thinnish, *adj.* un peu mince *or* &c. (*V.* **Thin,** [*adj.*); (*lean*) maigrelet

Third, *adj.* troisième; (*intervening*) tiers (tierce, *f.*); — *s.* (*part of a whole*) tiers, *m.*; (*sixtieth part of a second, and mus.*) tierce, *f.*; (*in order*) troisième, *m.f.*; (*day of a month*) trois, *m.*; — **s,** *s.pl.* (*of meal*) farine de troisième qualité, *f.*; recoupette, *f.* *The* —, (*of sovereigns*) trois. — **estate,** *s.* (*hist.*) tiers état, *m.* — **floor,** *s.* troisième étage, troisième, *m.* *A* — **party** *or* **person,** *s.* tierce personne, *f.*, tiers, *m.*

Thirdly, *adv.* troisièmement

Thirst, *s.* ('*of*,' '*for*,' '*after*,' de) soif, *f.*; — *v.n.* avoir soif (de), être altéré (de)

Thirstiness, *s.* soif, *f.*

Thirsting, *part. adj.* altéré (de)

Thirsty, *adj.* altéré, qui a soif; (*of land*) aride, desséché. *To be* or *feel* —, avoir soif, être altéré. *To make* —, altérer

Thirteen, *adj.* treize

Thirteenth, *adj. s.* treizième; (*of the month*) treize. *The* —, (*of sovereigns*) treize [trente

Thirtieth, *adj. s.* trentième; (*of the month*)

Thirty, *adj.* trente. —*first,* trente et unième; (*of the month*) trente et un

This, *pron. dem.* (*before a noun*) ce. cet, *m.*, cette, *f.*; (*if speaking pointedly or in contradistinction*) ce ... -ci, cet ... -ci, cette ... -ci (*with the noun between in French*); (*this one, the one here*) celui-ci, *m.*, celle-ci, *f.*; (*this thing, these things*) ceci, *m.*; cela, ça, *m.*; (*this thing, these things, before a verb*) cela, ça, ce, c', *m.*; (*this place, here*) ici; (*this moment*) ce moment, cet instant, maintenant, à présent, ici; (*it, so*) le, l', *m.* — *is,* (*this place is*) c'est ici; (*look! listen! here is*) voici. — *is one which,* en voici un qui. — *was,* (*it was*) c'était. — *or that,* (*such*) tel ou tel. *Is not — your hat?* n'est-ce pas là votre chapeau? — *much,* ceci. — *much is certain, that* ..., *V.* **Certain.** *About* —, *for all* —, *from* —, *by* —, *in* —, *of* —, *on* —, *to* —, *under* —, *upon* —, *with* —, &c. *V.* **That.** *Before* —, *long before* — (*time*), *V.* **Time.** *By* — (*time*), *V.* **By.** *I have been waiting* — or — *last hour,* j'attends depuis une heure, il y a une heure que j'attends (*V.* **Last**). — *is true;* — *is what I fear;* *we have not come to — yet;* *V.* **That**

Thistle, *s.* chardon, *m.* — **down,** *s.* duvet du chardon, *m.* — **plantation,** *s.* chardonnière, *f.*

Thistly, *adj.* plein *or* couvert de chardons

Thither, *adv.* là, y. —**to,** *adv.* jusque-là. —**ward, -wards,** *adv.* de ce côté-là, vers ce [lieu, par là

Thlaspi, *s.* thlaspi, *m.*

Thole, — **pin,** *s.* (*nav.*) tolet, *m.*

Thong, *s.* courroie, sangle, lanière, *f.*

Thoracic, *adj.* thoracique

Thorax, *s.* thorax, *m.*

Thorn, *s.* épine, *f.*; (*prickle*) piquant, *m.*; (*hawthorn*) aubépine, *f.*; (*remorse*) remords, aiguillon, *m.* *A — in ...'s side,* une épine au pied de ... *A — in the flesh,* l'aiguillon de la chair, *m.* *To be on —s,* être sur les (*or* des) épines, être sur les charbons. *To take a — out of ...'s side,* tirer une épine du pied à ... — **apple,** *s.* (*plant*) datura, *m.*, stramonium, *m.*, stramoine, *f.*; (*fruit*) pomme épineuse, *f.* — **back,** *s.* raie bouclée, *f.* — **bush,** *s.* buisson épineux, *m.* — **hedge,** *s.* haie vive, *f.* — **less,** *adj.* sans épine, sans épines

Thorny, *adj.* épineux; piquant; (*difficult*) pénible, difficile

Thorough, *adj.* entier, complet, parfait; (*accomplished*) accompli, achevé; (*true*) franc, vrai; (*adverb.*) *V.* **Thoroughly.** — **base,** *s.* *V.* **Base.** — **bred,** *adj.* pur sang, de pur sang; (*pers.*) vrai; accompli; consommé; parfait; franc; *s.* cheval (*m.*) *or* jument (*f.*) de pur sang. —**fare,** *s.* *See below.* —**going,** *adj.* prêt à tout; résolu; entreprenant; consommé, achevé. —**paced,** *adj.* vif d'allures;

(*fig.*) achevé, accompli, consommé, parfait, franc

Thoroughfare, *s.* lieu de passage, passage, *m.*; voie de communication, *f.*; (*street*) rue passante, *f.*; rue fréquentée [*great* —, rue très fréquentée], rue commerçante, *f.* *Street without a* —, impasse, *f.* *There is no* —, il n'y a pas d'issue. *No* — *!* on ne passe pas; rue barrée; la circulation est interdite

Thoroughly, *adv.* bien; entièrement, complètement, tout à fait; à fond; parfaitement; soigneusement

Thoroughness, *s.* état parfait *or* complet, *m.*

Those, *pl. of* **That** (*V.* **That**), *pron. dem.* ces, *m.f.*; ces . . . -là, *m.f.*; ceux, *m.*, celles, *f.*; ceux-là, *m.*, celles-là, *f.* — *are*, ce sont, ce sont là; voilà

Thou, *pron. pers.* tu, toi [*same difference between* tu *and* toi *as between* je *and* moi *for* **"I,"** *which see*]; — *v.a.* tutoyer

Thouer, *s.* tutoyeur, *m.*, -euse, *f.*

Though, *conj.* quoique, bien que (*to be followed by the verb in the subjunctive mood*); (*yet*) pourtant, cependant; malgré cela; tout de même; (*but*) mais; (*even if*) quand, quand même, (*to be followed by the verb in the Conditional mood*); (*really*) vraiment, bien. *As* —, comme si; que. *Even* —, *V.* **Even.** *What* —, *V.* **What**

Thought, *s.* pensée, *f.*; idée, *f.*; opinion, *f.*; réflexion, *f.*; méditation, *f.*; rêverie, *f.*; (*care*) souci, *m.*, inquiétude, *f.*; (*wit*) esprit, *m.*, intelligence, *f.*; (*small quantity, small degree*) idée, *f.*, peu, *m.* *Second* —, seconde pensée, *f.*; changement d'avis, ravisement, *m.* *On second* —*s*, réflexion faite, tout bien considéré, décidément. *To collect o.'s* —*s*, se recueillir. *To get away* or *escape from o.'s* —*s*, s'étourdir. *To give* — or *a* — *to*, penser à, songer à, réfléchir à. *To have some* —*s of*, penser à. *To speak o.'s* —*s*, dire sa pensée. *To take* — *of* or *for*, penser à, songer à; s'inquiéter de, se préoccuper de

Thoughtful, *adj.* pensif, rêveur; méditatif; attentif; prévenant; soigneux; soucieux; réfléchi; (*uneasy*) inquiet; (*provident*) prévoyant. **—ly,** *adv.* pensivement; d'un air rêveur; avec réflexion; avec attention; avec prévenance; avec sollicitude; avec inquiétude; (*providently*) avec prévoyance. **—ness,** *s.* rêverie, *f.*; recueillement, *m.*; méditation, *f.*; attention, *f.*; soins, *m.pl.*; prévenance, *f.*; sollicitude, *f.*; anxiété, inquiétude, *f.*; (*forethought*) prévoyance, *f.*

Thoughtless, *adj.* étourdi, léger; (*careless*) insouciant; négligent; inattentif; (*inconsiderate*) irréfléchi; (*stupid*) sot. **—ly,** *adv.* étourdiment, inconsidérément, légèrement; sans y penser; avec insouciance; (*stupidly*) sottement. **—ness,** *s.* étourderie, légèreté, *f.*; insouciance, *f.*; inattention, *f.*; négligence, *f.*; irréflexion, *f.*; inadvertance, *f.*; indiscrétion, *f.*; inconséquence, *f.*

Thouing, *s.* tutoiement, *m.*

Thousand, *adj.* mille; (*in dates*) mil; — *s.* mille, *m.*; millier, *m.* *It is a* — *to one*, il y a mille à parier contre un. —*s of*, des milliers de. *By* —, par milliers. *One* — *and one, one* — *and two*, &c., mille-un, mille-deux, &c. *In the year one* — *eight hundred and seventy-five*, en l'an mil huit cent soixante quinze

Thousandth, *adj. s.* millième, *adj.m.f.*, *s.m.*

Thracian, *s. adj.* Thrace, *m.f.*

Thraldom, *s.* esclavage, *m.*, servitude, *f.*; (*feud.*) servage, *m.*

Thrall, *s.* esclave, *m.f.*; (*feud.*) serf, *m.*, serve, *f.*

Thrash, *v.a.n.* (*corn*, &c.) battre; (*a person*) battre, rosser, rouler, étriller, donner une raclée à

Thrasher, *s.* (*man*) batteur, *m.*; (*machine*) batteuse, *f.*

Thrashing, *s.* battage, *m.*; (*drubbing*) rossée, roulée, raclée, volée, *f.* **— floor,** *s.* aire, *f.* **— machine,** *s.* machine à battre, batteuse à blé, batteuse, *f.*

Thread, *s.* fil, *m.*; (*of plants*) filament, *m.*, fibre, *f.*; (*of flowers, of screws*) filet, *m.*; (*on plate*, &c.) filet, *m.*; — *adj.* de (or en) fil; — *v.a.* enfiler; (*pass through*) traverser, passer. *Shoemaker's* —, ligneul, *m.* —*ing the tailor's* —, (*game*) passe-passe, *m.* *To* — *o.'s way through*, passer par; se faufiler dans (*or* à travers). **—bare,** *adj.* râpé, usé jusqu'à la corde; (*fig.*) rebattu; usé; trivial. **—bareness,** *s.* état râpé, *m.*; (*fig.*) trivialité, *f.* **—like,** *adj.* (*med.*, &c.) filiforme. **— needle, -the needle,** *s.* (*game*) passe-passe, *m.* **— pattern,** *adj.* à filets. — *pattern spoon and fork* (*to match*), couvert à filets, *m.* **— shaped,** *adj.* (*bot.*, &c.) filiforme. **—worm,** *s.* filaire, *m* f., dragonneau, *m.* [fils

Thready, *adj.* filamenteux, fibreux, plein de

Threat, *s.* menace, *f.*

Threaten, *v.a.* menacer (*'with,' 'to,'* de). *It* —*s to rain*, le temps menace, le temps est à la pluie [sonne qui menace, *f.*

Threatener, *s.* menaceur, *m.*, -euse, *f.*, per-

Threatening, *adj.* menaçant; — *s.* menace, *f.*, menaces, *f.pl.*

Threateningly, *adv.* avec menace; d'une manière menaçante, d'un air de menace

Three, *adj. s.* trois (*adj.m.f.*, *s.m.*); (*elliptically*) (*of the clock*) trois heures, *f.pl.*, (*of o.'s age*) trois ans, *m.pl.*; (*in compounds*) à trois . . ., tri . . . **— angled,** *adj.* triangulaire. **—cornered,** *adj.* à trois coins; triangulaire; (*hat*, à trois cornes. *A* —*cornered hat*, un tricorne, *m.* **— decker,** *s.* *V.* **Decker.** **—edged,** *adj.* triangulaire. **—fold,** *adj. adv.* triple, trois fois autant, trois fois. **— footed,** *adj.* à trois pieds. **— headed,** *adj.* à trois têtes. **— leaved,** *adj.* à trois feuilles. **—masted,** *adj.* à trois mâts. **— master,** *s.* (*nav.*) trois-mâts, *m.* **— pence,** *s.pl.* trente centimes, *m.pl.* **—penny,** *adj.* de trente centimes; (*mean*) de rien, commun. **— score,** *adj.* soixante. —*score and ten*, soixante- [dix

Thresh. *V.* **Thrash**

Threshold, *s.* seuil, pas, *m.*; (*fig.*) entrée, porte, *f.*, portes, *f.pl.*; début, commence- [ment, *m.*

Thrice, *adv.* trois fois

Thrift, *s.* économie, épargne, *f.*; frugalité, *f.*; profit, gain, *m.*; prospérité, *f.*; (*plant*) ar- [mérie, *f.*

Thriftily, *adv.* économiquement

Thriftiness, *s.* économie, épargne, *f.*

Thriftless, *adj.* prodigue, dépensier. **—ly,** *adv.* prodiguement; sans profit, sans avantage. **—ness,** *s.* prodigalité, *f.*; manque de frugalité, *f.*

Thrifty, *adj.* économe; ménager; frugal

Thrill, (*'with,'* de; *'at,'* à) *v.a.* percer; pénétrer; saisir; faire tressaillir; faire frémir; — *v.n.* tressaillir, frémir; — *s.* tressaillement, *m.*; saisissement, *m.*; frémissement, *m.*

Thrilling, *adj.* saisissant; pénétrant; perçant

Thrips, *s.* thrips, *m.*

Thrive, *v.n.* prospérer, réussir; (*pers.*) faire ses affaires, faire son chemin, faire fortune, s'enrichir; (*grow*) croître, grandir, se développer, venir bien, profiter, réussir; (*delight*) se plaire (*'in,'* dans, à) [richit, *f.*

Thriver, *s.* personne qui prospère *or* qui s'en-

Thriving, *adj.* florissant; (*pers.*) dont les affaires marchent bien, qui prospère, qui réussit, qui s'enrichit; (*of plants*) qui vient bien, qui profite, vigoureux; — *s.* *V.* **Thrivingness**

Thrivingly, *adv.* d'une manière florissante, avec succès, heureusement

Thrivingness, *s.* prospérité, *f.*; état florissant, *m.*; succès, *m.*, réussite, *f.*; (*growth*) accroissement, *m.*

Throat, *s.* gorge, *f.*; (*the swallow itself*) gosier, *m.*; (*of a chimney*) gorge, *f.*; (*of bottles*, &c.) entrée, *f.* *To cut o.'s* —, se couper la gorge. **— band,** *s.* sous-gorge, *f.* **— wort,** *s.* gantelée, *f.*

Throated, *adj.* (*in compounds*) à gorge ...

Throb, *v.n.* battre; palpiter; (*of pain*) *V.* **Shoot;** — *s. V.* **Throbbing,** *s.*

Throbbing, *s.* battement, *m.*; palpitation, *f.*; pulsation, *f.*; agitation, *f.*; oscillation, *f.*; (*of pain*) élancement, *m.*; — *adj.* palpitant; de palpitation; agité; oscillant, oscillatoire; (*of pain*) lancinant [agonie, *f.*

Throe, *s.* douleur, *f.*; (*anguish*) angoisse, *f.*;

Throne, *s.* trône, *m.*; — *v.a. V.* **Enthrone;** — *v.n.* trôner. —**less,** *adj.* sans trône. — **room,** *s.* salle du trône, *f.*

Throng. *V.* **Crowd**

Throstle, *s.* (*bird*) *V.* **Mavis**

Throttle, *s.* trachée-artère, *f.*; larynx, *m.*; — *v.a.* étrangler; étouffer, suffoquer. — **valve,** *s.* soupape à gorge, *f.*; registre de vapeur, *m.*

Through, *prep.* à travers; au travers de; par; (*from end to end*) d'un bout à l'autre de; (*in the middle, in*) dans; en; (*between*) entre; (*by means of*) au moyen de; par; par l'entremise de; à cause de; par la faute de; par le mérite de; (*from, out of*) par; (*in consequence of*) par suite de; — *adv.* (*from side to side*) à travers; au travers; de part en part; (*from end to end*) d'un bout à l'autre; jusqu'au bout; jusqu'à la fin; (*completely*) complètement, entièrement; (*without stopping*) directement, droit; — *adject.* (*of trains, tickets*) direct. — *it, them* (*things*), à travers; au travers. — *and* —, de part en part; d'un bout à l'autre. — **passenger,** *s.* voyageur (*m.*, -euse, *f.*) par voie directe

Throughout, *prep.* d'un bout à l'autre de, dans tout, par tout; (*during*) pendant tout; — *adv.* d'un bout à l'autre; (*everywhere*) partout; (*entirely*) entièrement, en entier

Throw, *v.a.* jeter; lancer; précipiter; (*plunge*) plonger; (*put*) mettre; (*overturn*) renverser; (*a rider*) démonter, désarçonner; (*cast off*) jeter, se dépouiller de; abandonner (à); (*at play*) jeter; (*at dice*) amener; (*silk*) tordre, mouliner, organsiner. *To — oneself on,* (*fig.*) s'abandonner à. — **aside,** jeter *or* mettre de côté. — **away,** jeter; rejeter; (*spend*) dissiper, gaspiller; perdre; prodiguer; jeter par la fenêtre. — **back,** jeter en arrière; renverser; rejeter; renvoyer; retarder. — **by,** jeter *or* mettre de côté. — **down,** jeter en bas; (*overthrow*) renverser; abattre; (*on the ground*) jeter à terre, terrasser; jeter; (*the gauntlet*) jeter (le gant); (*cause to fall*) faire tomber; (*destroy*) détruire; (*humble*) abaisser, humilier. *To — oneself down,* se jeter; se jeter *or* se coucher par terre — **in,** jeter dedans; (*give over*) donner par-dessus le marché. — **off,** chasser, se défaire de; rejeter; ôter; (*the mask*) lever, jeter; (*quit*) quitter; renoncer à; (*shake off*) secouer; (*hunt.*) lancer. — *off the line* or *the rails, V.* **Rail.** — **on,** mettre. — **open,** ouvrir subitement *or* vivement; ouvrir. — **out,** jeter dehors; chasser, expulser; exclure; rejeter; (*distance*) devancer, dépasser; (*lead astray*) dérouter; (*send*) lancer; (*utter*) mettre en avant, émettre; (*hint*) donner à entendre; (*spread*) répandre; (*a bill*) rejeter. — **out of** (*a window,* &c.) jeter par (*V.* **Window**); (*employment,* &c.), priver de (*V.* **Work,** *s.*). — **up,** jeter; jeter en l'air; vomir, rendre; rejeter; renoncer à; (*resign*) se démettre de; (*a window*) ouvrir toute grande; (*earthworks,* &c.) élever, construire, faire

Throw, *s.* jet, *m.*; (*stroke*) coup, *m.*; (*— of the die*) coup de dé (*or* de dés), *m.*; (*effort*) élan, *m.* — **off,** *s.* départ, *m.*

Thrower, *s.* personne qui jette *or* qui lance *or* &c. (*V.* **Throw,** *v.a.*), *f.*; tourneur, *m.*; (*of silk*) *V.* **Throwster**

Throwing, *s.* jet, *m.*; lancement, *m.*; (*of silk*) tordage, moulinage, organsinage, *m.* — *off the line* or *the rails, V.* **Rail.** — **mill,** *s.* moulin à organsiner, *m.* — **wheel,** *s.* tour, *m.*

Throwster, *s.* tordeur, *m.*, -euse, *f.*, moulineur, *m.*, -euse, *f.*, organsineur, *m.*

Thrum, *v.n.* jouailler, jouasser, jouer mal, tapoter; (*on the violin*) râcler; — *v.a.* (*an air,* &c.) écorcher

Thrummer, *s.* (*on the piano*) tapoteur, *m.*, -euse, *f.*; (*on the violin*) râcleur, *m.*

Thrush, *s.* (*bird*) grive, *f.*; (*med.*) aphthes, *m.pl.*, muguet, *m.*; (*vet.*) teigne, *f.*

Thrust, *v.a.* pousser; (*away*) repousser; (*throw*) jeter; (*put*) fourrer; (*beyond, through, out of*) passer; sortir; (*press*) presser, serrer; (*compel*) forcer (à); (*obtrude*) imposer (à), faire accepter (à), forcer (. . .) de prendre; — *v.n.* se jeter; se fourrer; (*intrude*) se mêler (de, à, dans), s'ingérer (de, dans); (*fencing*) porter une botte *or* un coup ('*at*,' à); — *s.* coup, *m.*; poussée, *f.*; attaque, *f.*, assaut, *m.*; (*fencing*) botte, *f.*; coup d'épée, coup, *m.*; (*build.*) poussée, *f.* *To make a —,* (*fenc.*) porter une botte *or* un coup (à). — **away,** — **back,** repousser; écarter. — **down,** pousser en bas; précipiter, jeter en bas. — **in,** faire entrer, introduire; (*plunge, stick*) enfoncer; (*put*) fourrer. — **on,** pousser en avant; (*excite*) pousser. — **out,** jeter dehors; mettre dehors, sortir; repousser. — **through,** passer à travers; (*pierce*) transpercer [sourd, coup, *m.*

Thud, *s.* bruit sourd, son mat, *m.*; (*blow*) coup

Thug, *s.* étrangleur, thug, *m.*

Thuja, *s.* thuia, thuya, *m.*

Thumb, *s.* pouce, *m.* *Right —,* pouce de la main droite. *Left —,* pouce de la main gauche. *Tom —,* Tom Pouce, *m.*; (*in the tale*) le petit Poucet, *m.* *Under o.'s —,* (*fig.*) sous sa domination, sous son autorité, en son pouvoir. *To bite o.'s* (or *the*) *— at,* faire un pied-de-nez à; faire la nique à. — **mark,** *s.* marque de pouce, *f.*; *v.a.* marquer (*or* salir) avec le pouce. — **nail,** *s.* ongle du pouce, *m.* — **piece,** *s.* poucette, *f.*; (*of a latch*) poucier, *m.*; (*snack*) morceau sur le pouce, *m.* — **screw,** (*tech.*) vis de pression, *f.*; (*for prisoners, and old instr. of torture*) poucettes, *f.pl.* — **stall,** *s.* poucier, *m.*

Thumb, *v.a.* manier gauchement; (*turn over the leaves*) feuilleter; (*soil*) salir avec le pouce, fatiguer. *Well —ed,* fatigué

Thumbikin, Thumbkin, *s.* poucettes, *f.pl.*

Thump, *s.* grand coup, *m.*; coup de poing, *m.*; torgniole, taloche, *f.*, horion, *m.*; — *v.a.n.* frapper, cogner; frapper du poing; battre

Thumping, *adj.* (*large*) gros; (*heavy*) lourd

Thunder, *v.a.n.* tonner; (*a threat*) fulminer; — *s.* (*noise, and fig.*) tonnerre, *m.*; (*lightning, and fig.*) foudre, *f.* — **bolt,** *s.* foudre, *f.*; (*myth., paint., sculp., her., pers.*) foudre, *m.* — **along,** *v.n.* se précipiter *or* s'avancer comme la foudre; galoper avec grand bruit (*or* grand fracas). — **clap,** *s.* coup de tonnerre, *m.* — **cloud,** *s.* nuage orageux, nuage chargé d'électricité, *m.* — **forth,** *v.a.n.* fulminer. — **shower,** *s.* pluie d'orage, *f.* — **stone,** *s.* pierre de foudre, *f.*, aérolithe, *m.*; (*geol.*) bélemnite, *f.* — **storm,** *s.* orage (accompagné de tonnerre), *m.* — **strike,** *v.a.* foudroyer. — **stroke,** *s.* coup de foudre, *m.*

Thunderer, *s.* *The —,* celui qui lance la foudre, *m.*; Jupiter Tonnant, *m*; le "Times," *m.*

Thundering, *s.* tonnerre, *m.*; (*fam.*) grand bruit, *m.*; grands coups, *m.pl.*; — *part. adj.* de tonnerre; tonnant; foudroyant; (*fam.*) énorme, terrible, furieux. — *voice,* voix de tonnerre, voix tonnante, *f.* — *speech,* discours foudroyant. — *fool,* furieux imbécile, *m.* *To come* or *sweep — past,* passer comme la foudre

Thunderingly, *adv.* avec un bruit de tonnerre; d'une manière foudroyante

Thunderous, *adj.* *V.* **Thundering** *and* **Thundery** [*is*) —, le temps est à l'orage

Thundery, *adj.* orageux. *It is* (*or the weather*

Thurible, *s.* encensoir, *m.*

Thurifer, *s.* thuriféraire, *m.*
Thuriferous, *adj.* thurifère
Thurification, *s.* encensement, *m.* [&c.
Thursday, *s.* jeudi, *m.* *Holy* —, &c., *V.* **Holy,**
Thus, *adv.* ainsi; (*so much*) si, tant. — *much,* autant; autant que cela; c'est assez. — *far* [or *so far,* *V.* **Far** (*so*)
Thuya. *V.* **Thuja**
Thwack, *v.a.* frapper; battre; rosser; — *s.* grand coup, coup, *m.*
Thwacking, *s.* râclée, roulée, *f.*
Thwart, *v.a.* traverser; contrarier, contrecarrer; — *adj.* en travers, transversal; **—s,** *s.pl.* bancs (de rameurs), *m.pl.*
Thwarter, *s.* (*vet.*) tremblée, *f.*
Thwartingly, *adv.* d'une manière contrariante
Thwartness, *s.* esprit de contradiction *or* d'opposition, *m.*
Thy, *pron. poss.* ton, *m.*, ta, *f.*, tes, *m.f.pl.*
Thyme, *s.* thym. *m.* *Wild* —, serpolet, *m.*
Thymy, *adj.* de thym; qui abonde en thym; qui a l'odeur du thym; odoriférant
Thyroid, *adj.* thyroïde, thyréoïde
Thyrsus, *s.* thyrse, *m.*
Thyself, *pron.* toi-même; toi; (*in a reflect. verb*) te; toi
Tiara, *s.* tiare, *f.*
Tibia, *s.* tibia, os de la jambe, *m.*
Tic, *s.* tic, *m.* — *douloureux,* tic douloureux, *m.*
Tick, *v.n.* battre, faire tic-tac; (*buy*) prendre à crédit *or* à l'œil; (*sell*) faire crédit, se fier; — *v.a.* (*mark*) marquer, pointer (— **off,** effacer); — *s.* (*cloth*) coutil, *m.*, toile à matelas, *f.*; (*insect*) tique, mite, *f.*; (*credit*) crédit, *m.*; (*noise*) tic-tac, *m.* *On* —, à crédit, à l'œil. *To buy on* —, *to go on* — *for,* acheter *or* prendre à crédit (*or* à l'œil). — **tack,** *s* tic-tac, *m.*
Ticker, *s.* (*watch*) tocante, toquante, *f.*
Ticket, *s.* (*rail. fare, theat., public gatherings, lottery,* &c.) billet, *m.*; (*of luggage, of insurance, of voting,* &c.) bulletin, *m.*; (*of omnibuses*) carton, numéro, *m.*; (*number*) numéro, *m.*; (*pawn* —) reconnaissance, *f.*; (*of a subscription series*) cachet, *m.*; (*order for goods, provisions*) bon, *m.*; (*mark, label*) étiquette, *f.*; (*badge*) plaque, *f.*; — *v.a.* étiqueter, numéroter. *Annual* —, carte (*f.*) *or* billet (*m.*) d'abonnement à l'année, abonnement (*m.*) à l'année. *Return* —, billet d'aller et retour, billet de retour. *Season* —, carte d'abonnement, *f.*, billet d'abonnement, abonnement, *m.* *Single* —, billet simple, billet d'aller. *Through* —, billet direct. — **collector, -examiner,** *s.* contrôleur, *m.* — **office,** *s.* bureau des billets, *m.* — **-of-leave,** *s.* libération, *f.* — **-of-leave-man,** *s.* forçat libéré, *m.* — **porter,** *s.* commissionnaire médaillé, *m.*; (*rail.*) facteur, *m.*
Ticking, *s.* (*noise*) tic-tac, battement, *m.*; (*cloth*) coutil, *m.*, toile à matelas, *f.*
Tickle, *v.a.n.* chatouiller
Tickling, *s.* chatouillement, *m.*
Ticklish, *adj.* chatouilleux; susceptible; (*fig.*) difficile, délicat, scabreux; (*shaky*) chancelant, mal assuré. **—ly,** *adv.* d'une manière délicate. **—ness,** *s.* nature chatouilleuse, *f.*; susceptibilité, *f.*; (*fig.*) difficulté, nature scabreuse, *f.*
Tidal, *adj.* de marée; de la marée; à marée. — *harbour,* port à marée, havre, *m.* (*V.* **Train**)
Tidbit. *V.* **Titbit**
Tide, *s.* marée, *f.*; (*stream*) courant, *m*; (*course*) cours, *m.*, marche, *f.*; (*violence*) force, *f.*; (*height*) fort, *m.*; (*time*) époque, *f.*, temps, *m.*, saison, *f.* *Half* —, mi-marée, *f.*, mi-flot, *m.* *High* —, haute marée, *f.* *Low* —, basse marée, marée basse, *f.* (*At low* —, à marée basse). *Rising* —, marée montante, *f.* *To go with the* —, suivre le courant. — **dock,** *s.* avant-port, *m.* — **gate,** *s.* écluse, *f.*; (— *way*) *V.* —**way.** — **gauge,** *s.* échelle de marée, *f.* — **harbour,** *s.* port à marée, havre, *m.* —**less,** *adj.* sans marée. — **mill,** *s.* moulin à marée, *m.* — **table,** *s.* table des marées, *f.*; (*in harbours*) établissement des marées, *m.* — **waiter,** *s.* douanier, *m.* — **wave,** *s.* rapport, *m.* — **way,** *s.* ras de marée, lit de marée, *m.*
Tide, *v.a.* entraîner *or* pousser par la marée; entraîner par le courant; — *v.n.* aller avec la marée. — **over,** passer par-dessus; passer, attraper le bout de; surmonter, venir à bout de, se tirer de. *To* — (*a person*) *over* . . ., faire passer *or* faire traverser . . . (à quelqu'un). *To* — *it* **up** *or* **down,** monter *or* descendre à la faveur de la marée
Tidily, *adv.* proprement; en bon ordre; convenablement; passablement; raisonnablement; adroitement, habilement, bien
Tidiness, *s.* propreté, *f.*; bonne tenue, *f.*, bon ordre, *m.*
Tidings, *s.pl.* nouvelle, *f.*, nouvelles, *f.pl.*
Tidy, *adj.* propre; en ordre, rangé, soigné, bien arrangé, bien tenu; soigneux; gentil; convenable; passable, assez bon, honnête, raisonnable; adroit, habile; — *v.a.* approprier; arranger, mettre en ordre. *To* — *oneself up,* faire un bout de toilette
Tie, *v.a.* lier, attacher; (*by a knot*) nouer; (*a knot*) serrer, faire; (*oblige*) lier, astreindre (à), obliger (à); (*surg., mus.*) lier; — *v.n.* se lier, s'attacher; — *s.* lien, *m.*; attache, *f.*; liaison, *f.*; (*of shoes*) cordon, *m.*; (*for the neck*) cravate, *f.*; (*knot*) nœud, *m.*; (*bond*) engagement, assujettissement, *m.*; (*of hair*) nœud, *m.*; (*mus.*) barre de jonction, *f.*; (*in games*) partie égale, *f.* —*d for time,* pris par l'heure, pressé. — **beam,** *s.* entrait, tirant, *m.* — **down,** *v.a.* lier, assujettir; (*oblige*) astreindre; (*fig.*) lier les mains à. — **in,** *v.a.* attacher; serrer. — **piece,** *s.* entretoise, *f.* — **up,** *v.a.* attacher, lier; nouer; (*turn up*) retrousser; (*animals*) mettre à l'attache. — **wig,** *s.* perruque à nœuds, *f.*
Tier, *s.* rangée, *f.*, rang, *m.*; étage, *m.*; (*of guns*) batterie, *f.* — *of boxes,* (*theat.*) rang de loges, *m.*; loges, *f.pl.* —*s of benches,* gradins, *m.pl.* *First, second,* &c. — *of boxes,* (*theat.*) premières, deuxièmes, &c. loges, *f.pl.*
Tierce, *s.* (*cards, fenc., mus., Cath. rel., her.*) tierce, *f.*; (*meas.*) tierçon, *m.* — **point,** *s.* [(*arch.*) tiers-point, *m.*
Tiercet, *s.* tercet, *m.*
Tiff, *s.* (*drink*) petit coup, coup, *m.*, goutte, *f.*; (*anger*) boutade, *f.*; dépit, *m.*; (*bickering*) pique, bisbille, *f.*; — *v.n.* se piquer, se fâcher, bisquer; se quereller, se chamailler. *To get into a* —, prendre la mouche
Tiffany, *s.* gaze de soie, *f.*
Tiffin, *s.* *V.* **Lunch**
Tiger, *s.* tigre, *m.*; (*servant*) tigre, groom, *m.* — **beetle,** *s.* cicindèle, *f.* — **cat,** *s.* chat-tigre, *m.* — **flower,** *s.* tigridie, *f.* — **moth,** [*s.* arctie, *f.*
Tigerish, *adj.* de tigre
Tight, *adj.* serré; (*stretched*) tendu, raide; (*narrow*) étroit, juste; (*of trousers*) collant; (*shut*) bien fermé, hermétiquement fermé; (*strong*) fort; (*dear*) cher; (*niggardly*) parcimonieux, serré; (*well clothed*) propre; (*drunk*) pochard, gris; (*slightly intoxicated*) lancé, en train, gai; (*impervious*) imperméable (au . . ., à la . . ., aux . . .); impénétrable (au . . ., à la . . ., aux . . .); (*nav.*) étanche; — *adv.* *V.* **Tightly;** —**s,** *s.pl.* pantalon collant, *m.*; collants, *m.pl.*; culotte, *f.*; (*of dancers,* &c.) maillot, *m.* *To get* —, (*pers.*) se pocharder, se griser. *To hold* —, tenir bien [serrer; (*fig.*) resserrer
Tighten, *v.a.* (*stretch*) tendre, raidir; (*straiten*)
Tightly, *adv.* serré; (*closely*) étroitement; (*strongly*) fortement, fort, ferme, bien; (*severely*) sévèrement, ferme; (*neatly*) proprement
Tightness, *s.* tension, raideur, *f.*; étroitesse, *f.*; parcimonie, *f.*; propreté, *f.*; imperméabilité, *f.*; (*in the chest*) oppression, *f.*; (*dearness*) cherté, *f.*; (*intoxication*) pocharderie, *f.*; [gaieté, *f.*
Tigress, *s.* tigresse, *f.*
Tigrine, *adj.* de tigre
Til, Tilseed. *V.* **Teel**
Tilbury, *s.* tilbury, *m.*
Tile, *s.* tuile, *f.*; (*flooring* —) carreau, *m.*; (*hat*)

couvre-chef, *m.*; — *adj.* de tuile, de tuiles; — *v.a.* couvrir de (*or* en) tuiles; couvrir, recouvrir. — **coloured,** *adj.* briqueté. — **field, -kiln,** *s.* tuilerie, *f.* — **maker,** *s.* tuilier, *m.* — **making, -work, -works, Tilery,** *s.* tuilerie, *f.* — **shard,** *s.* tuileau, *m.*

Tiler, *s.* couvreur en tuiles, *m.*

Tiling, *s.* (*action*) recouvrement en tuiles, *m.*; (*roof*) toiture en tuiles, *f.*; (*tiles*) tuiles, *f.pl.*

Till, *s.* caisse, *f.*, tiroir, *m.*; — *v.a.* labourer, cultiver; — *prep. conj. V.* **Until**

Tillable, *adj.* labourable

Tillage, *s.* labourage, *m.*, culture, *f.*

Tiller, *s.* laboureur, cultivateur, *m.*; (*shoot*) rejeton, *m.*; (*nav.*) barre, *f.*

Tilling, *s.* labourage, *m.*

Tilt, *s.* tente, *f.*; (*of carriages*) bâche, banne, *f.*; (*agr.*) auvent, *m.*; (*of a sword*, &c.) coup, *m.*; (*combat*) joute, *f.*, tournoi, carrousel, *m.*; (*incline*) pente, inclinaison, *f.*; — *v.a.n.* couvrir d'une tente; (*carriages*) bâcher, banner; (*casks*) pencher, incliner; (*thrust*) pousser, pointer, diriger; (*empty*) vider, décharger; (*fight*) jouter, ferrailler; (*at*) fondre (sur), s'élancer (sur); (*float*) flotter, se balancer; (*lean*) pencher. *Full* —, *V.* **Full.** — **boat,** *s.* bateau *or* canot couvert, *m.* — **cart,** *s.* charrette couverte, *f.* — **hammer,** *s.* marteau à bascule, martinet de forge, *m.* — **yard,** *s.* champ clos, *m.*

Tilter, *s.* jouteur, champion, *m.*

Tilted, *adj.* (*of carriages*) à bâche, couvert

Tilth, *s.* labour, *m.*, culture, *f.*

Tilting, *s.* (*fight*) joute, *f.*

Timbal, Timbale, *s.* timbale, *f.*

Timber, *s.* bois de construction *or* de charpente, bois, *m.*; —**s,** *pl.* charpente, *f.*; (*nav.*) couples, *m.pl.*; — *v.a.* boiser. — **head,** *s.* (*nav.*) bitton, *m.* — **merchant,** *s.* marchand de bois de construction (*or* de charpente), *m.* — **tree,** *s.* arbre de haute futaie, *m.* — **waggon,** *s.* fardier, *m.* — **work,** *s.* charpente, *f.* — **yard,** *s.* chantier de bois, *m.*

Timbering, *s.* boisage, *m.*

Timbre, *s.* timbre, *m.*

Timbrel, *s.* tambourin, *m.*

Time, *s.* (*in general*) temps, *m.*; (*particular instant*) moment, *m.*; (*particular period*) époque, *f.*; (*day*) jour, *m.*; (*days of old, our days*) temps, *m.*; (*age, — of life*) âge, *m.*; (*age, in history*) siècle, *m.*; (*of the clock*) heure, *f.*; (*with regard to repetition*) fois, *f.*; (*periodical part of the year*) saison, *f.*; (*length of time, term, run, course*) temps, *m.*; (*childbirth*) terme, *m.*; (*mus.*) mesure, *f.*; (*in drilling*) cadence, *f.*; (*pace*) pas, *m.*; (*myth.*) Temps, *m.*; — *v.a.* accommoder au temps; faire à propos; (*regulate*) régler ('*by*,' sur); fixer l'heure de; calculer; organiser; arranger; mesurer; (*mus.*, &c.) cadencer. — *flies*, le temps fuit. *This is not the — for doing it*, ce n'est pas là le moment de le faire. *What — is it?* quelle heure est-il? *Three —s a day*, trois fois par jour. *Last* —, la dernière fois. *Next* —, la prochaine fois. *The first* —, la première fois. *Another* —, une autre fois. *At another* —, dans un autre moment; à une autre époque; tantôt. *Old —s*, (les) anciens temps, (le) vieux temps, (le) passé. — *of life*, terme de la vie, *m.*; (*age*) âge, *m.* — *of* (*the*) *day*, heure, *f.*; civilités ordinaires, *f.pl.* *Common* or *simple* —, (*mus.*) mesure à deux temps, *f.* *Triple* —, (*mus.*) mesure à trois temps, *f.* *Quadruple* or *compound* —, (*mus.*) mesure à quatre temps, *f.* *A long* —, *a length of* —, *a considerable* —, longtemps. *A long* — (*past*), *for a long* —, depuis longtemps; pendant longtemps. *A short* or *little* —, quelque temps, peu de temps; un peu. *After a* —, quelque temps après; (*hence*) dans quelque temps. *After o.'s* or *its* or *the* —, en retard; (*of childbirth*) après terme. *Against* —, dans un temps donné; (*mus.*) à contre-mesure. *At a* —, à la fois. *At a — when*, dans un temps où; dans un moment où. *At all —s*, toujours; de tout temps. *At any* —, en tout temps; n'importe quand; un jour ou l'autre; à tout moment; (*hour of day*) à toute heure *or* à n'importe quelle heure (du jour); (*some* —) quelquefois. *At different —s*, à diverses reprises. *At no* —, dans (*or* en) aucun temps, à aucune époque, jamais. *At one* —, un instant; (*formerly*) autrefois; (*repeated*) tantôt (..., tantôt). *At one — ..., at another*, tantôt ..., tantôt. *At one — or other*, un jour ou l'autre. *At other —s*, d'autres fois. *At that* —, (*then*) à cette époque alors. *At the* —, à cette époque, alors; dans le temps; dans le moment, au moment (*or* à l'instant) même, immédiatement. *At the present* —, à présent, maintenant, actuellement, aujourd'hui, à l'heure qu'il est. *At the proper* —, à propos, à point, quand il le faut. *At the same* —, en même temps; (*on another hand*) d'un autre côté, d'autre part; en revanche. *At —s*, parfois, quelquefois, de temps à autre, de temps en temps; par moments. *Before o.'s* or *its* or *the* —, en avance; (*of childbirth*) avant terme. *Before this* —, déjà. *Behind o.'s* or *its* or *the* —, *Behind* —, en retard; arriéré. *By* —, (*of cabs*) à l'heure. *By this* or *that* —, *by the — that*, *V.* **By.** *Every* —, chaque fois, toutes les fois (que). *For a* or *some* —, pour quelque temps; (*during*) pendant quelque temps; (*since*) depuis quelque temps. *For some — to come*, *V.* **Come.** *For the* —, pour le moment. *For the — being*, (*now*) actuel; (*then*) d'alors. *From that* —, depuis ce temps. *From this* —, dès à présent, désormais, dorénavant. *From — to* —, de temps en temps, de temps à autre. *In* —, avec le temps; (*soon enough*) à temps; en son temps; (*by the clock*) à l'heure. *In due* —, *V.* **Due.** *In good* —, à temps; (*opportunely*) à propos; (*early*) de bonne heure. *In a day's* —, dans un jour, dans l'espace d'un jour; en un jour. *In my* —, de mon temps. *In the day* —, dans le jour, de jour, le jour. *In no* —, en aucun temps; (*quickly*) en un clin d'œil, en moins de rien. *In old —s, in —s of old, in —s past*, anciennement, autrefois, jadis. *In — to come*, à l'avenir. *In proper* —, en temps convenable. *In proper — and place*, en temps et lieu. *In quick* —, promptement; (*mil.*) au pas accéléré. *In a short* —, *V.* **Shortly.** *It is — to ...*, il est temps de ...; (*by the clock*) il est l'heure de ... *Long before this* —, depuis longtemps; il y a longtemps. *Once upon a* —, autrefois, une fois. *Once upon a — there was*, il y avait une fois. *Out of* —, prématurément, hors de saison; (*mus.*) hors de mesure, à contre-mesure. *Some* —, quelque temps; quelque jour, un jour. *Some — or other*, un jour ou l'autre. *Some — this morning, this evening, today*, dans la matinée, dans la soirée, dans la journée. *There is no — for*, il ne s'agit pas de. *This is not the — for*, ce n'est pas le moment de. *This — last year*, il y a un an, l'année dernière à pareille époque. *This — twelve months*, (*future*) dans un an; (*past*) il y a un an. *Till the end of* —, jusqu'à la fin des siècles. *Within a given* —, dans un temps donné. *To beat* —, battre la mesure. *To be in* —, arriver à temps (*or* à l'heure), ne pas être en retard. *To have* — (*enough*) *to*, avoir le temps de. [*To have — to write*, avoir le temps d'écrire; *To have — to lose*, avoir du temps à perdre; *I haven't* —, je n'ai pas le temps.] *To have a fine* (or *nice*) — *of it*, être heureux; s'amuser, s'en donner. *To have a hard* (or *unpleasant* or *sorry*) — *of it*, mener une vie dure, être malheureux; en voir de dures (*or* de grises); (*for a moment*) passer un mauvais quart d'heure. [*These are hard —s*, les temps sont durs.] *To have had o.'s* —, avoir fait son temps. *To keep* —, être exact; (*of watches*, &c.) être à l'heure, aller bien; (*mus.*) aller en mesure. *To keep its* or *o.'s* —, arriver à l'heure, être exact. *To take o.'s* — prendre son temps.

— **bargain,** *s.* marché à terme, *m.* — **bill, -book,** *s.* indicateur, livret, *m.* —**honoured,** *adj.* honoré depuis longtemps, depuis longtemps en honneur; vénéré; séculaire. — **keeper,** *s.* garde-temps, chronomètre, *m.*; montre marine, *f.*; (*pers.*) contrôleur, *m.* *To be a good — keeper,* (*watch*) être toujours à l'heure. —**piece,** *s.* horloge, *f.*; pendule, *f.*; montre, *f.*; réveille-matin, *m.* — **server,** *s.* complaisant, *m.*; girouette, *f.* — **serving,** *adj.* servile, complaisant; changeant; *s.* servilité, lâche complaisance, *f.*; unique souci du présent, *m.*; girouetterie, *f.* — **sheet,** *s.* feuille de présence, *f.* —**table,** *s.* tableau des heures, tableau des heures de départ et d'arrivée, *m.*; (*mus.*) division du temps, *f.* — **worn,** *adj.* usé par le temps

Timed, *part.* (*V.* **Time,** *v.a.*); — *adj.* *Ill- —,* *V.* **Unseasonable.** *Well —,* opportun, à propos; réglé

Timeliness, *s.* opportunité, *f.*, à-propos, *m.*

Timely, *adj.* opportun, à propos; de bonne heure; — *adv.* à propos, en temps opportun; [de bonne heure

Timid, *adj.* timide; timoré

Timidity, *s.* timidité, *f.*

Timidly, *adv.* timidement

Timing, *s.* règlement des heures, horaire, *m.*

Timorous, &c. *V.* **Timid,** &c.

Timothy grass, *s.* fléole, *f.*

Tin, *s.* (*metal*) étain, *m.*; (*sheet —*) ferblanc, *m.*; (*utensil*) ustensile en ferblanc, *m.*; (*mould*) moule en ferblanc, *m.*; (*mil.*) bidon, *m.*; (*cash*) quibus, *m.*, pécune, *f.*; — *adj.* d'étain, en étain; de (*or* en) ferblanc; — *v.a.* étamer. — **foil,** *s.* feuille d'étain, *f.*; (*of looking-glasses*) tain, *m.*; (— *plate*) ferblanc, *m.* — **glass,** *s.* bismuth, étain de glace, *m.* — **kettle,** *s.* bouilloire de (*or* en) ferblanc, *f.*; (*bad piano*) chaudron, *m.* — **leaf,** *s.* *V.* — **foil.** — **man,** *s.* ferblantier, *m.* — **mine,** *s.* mine d'étain, *f.* — **plate,** *s.* ferblanc, *m.* — **plates,** *s.pl.* plaques (*or* feuilles) de ferblanc, *f.pl.* — **plate worker, -smith,** *s.* ferblantier, *m.* — **tack,** *s.* broquette étamée, *f.* — **wares,** *s.pl.* ferblanterie, *f.* —**works,** *s.pl.* usine d'étain, *f.*

Tinctorial, *adj.* tinctorial

Tincture, *s.* teinte, *f.*; (*notion*) teinture, *f.*; (*taste*) léger goût, *m.*; (*pharm., chem.*) teinture, *f.*; (*her.*) émail, *m.*; — *v.a.* teindre (de), colorer (de); teinter (de); (*imbue*) empreindre (de), imprégner (de)

Tinctured, *part. adj.* teint, &c. (*V.* **Tincture,** *v.a.*); (*her.*) émaillé. *He is — with,* il a une teinture de [briquet, *m.*

Tinder, *s.* amadou, *m.*; mèche, *f.* — **box,** *s.*

Tine, *s.* fer, *m.*, pointe, *f.*; (*of forks*) dent, *f.*, fourchon, *m.*; (*of harrows*) dent, *f.*

Tinea, *s.* teigne, *f.*

Tinge. *V.* **Tincture**

Tingle, *v.n.* tinter, vibrer; (*of the ears*) tinter; (*of the hands, feet*) fourmiller, picoter, démanger, brûler, cuire; (*of pain*) répondre, se faire sentir; (*to thrill*) tressaillir (de), frémir (de). *My ears —,* les oreilles me tintent

Tingling, *s.* tintement, *m.*; (*of the hands, feet*) fourmillement, picotement, *m.*, démangeaison, chaleur, *f.*; (*thrilling*) tressaillement, frémissement, *m.*

Tinker, *s.* chaudronnier (ambulant), *m.*; rétameur, étameur, *m.*; — *v.a.* raccommoder, rhabiller; rétamer

Tinkering, *s.* métier de chaudronnier, *m.*; raccommodage, rhabillage, *m.*; rétamage, *m.*

Tinkle, *v.n.* tinter; — *v.a.* faire tinter; — *s.* *V.* **Tinkling** [tement, *m.*, (*fam.*) drelin, *m.*

Tinkling, *adj.* retentissant, sonore; — *s.* tin-

Tinman, *s.* ferblantier, *m.*

Tinner, *s.* ouvrier de mine d'étain, *m.*; (*tinman*) ferblantier, *m.*; étameur, *m.*

Tinning, *s.* étamage, *m.*

Tinny, *adj.* d'étain, comme de l'étain; qui abonde en étain, stannifère

Tinsel, *s.* clinquant, *m.*; oripeau, *m*; faux éclat, faux brillant, *m.*; — *adj.* de clinquant; faux; (*showy*) voyant; — *v.a.* clinquanter, charger de clinquant; (*fig.*) brillanter, orner d'un faux éclat

Tint, *s.* teinte, couleur, nuance, *f.*; — *v.a.* teinter, nuancer; (*mechanical &c. drawing*) laver; (*to shade in pencil*) ombrer; (*photographs*) retoucher [toucheur, *m.*, -euse, *f.*

Tinter, *s.* coloriste, *m.f.*; (*of photographs*) re-

Tinting, *s.* (*of mechanical &c. drawing*) lavis, *m.*; (*of photographs*) retouchage, *m.*

Tiny, *adj.* petit, tout petit; mignon. *A — bit,* un tantinet, un tout petit peu

Tip, *s.* (*of the ear, nose, tongue, finger, umbrellas, tobacco-pipes,* &c.) bout, *m.*; (*of the foot, point*) pointe, *f.*; (*of a hat*) calotte, carre, *f.*; (*fee*) gratification, *f.*, pot-de-vin, *m.* *From — to —,* (*of wings*) d'envergure

Tip, *v.a.* embouter, garnir le bout de; (*with iron*) ferrer; (*strike*) frapper légèrement; toucher légèrement, effleurer; (*a waggon,* &c.) décharger; (*to fee*) donner une gratification (*or* un pot-de-vin) à, graisser la patte à; (*give*) donner. — **off,** verser; culbuter, faire tomber. — **over, up,** faire faire la bascule à, basculer, culbuter, renverser, faire tomber

Tip, *v.n.* tomber. — **off,** faire la culbute; (*die*) sauter *or* passer le pas, claquer. — **over, up,** faire la bascule, basculer, culbuter, se renverser, verser; (*of boats*) chavirer; (*pay money*) [financer

Tipcat, *s.* bâtonnet, *m.*

Tippet, *s.* pèlerine, *f.*; (*fur —*) palatine, *f.*

Tipple, *s.* boisson, *f.*; goutte, petite goutte, *f.*; — *v.n.* gobeloter, godailler, flûter, boire, boire sec, boire la goutte, lever le coude; se griser; [(*to tip*) *V.* **Tip**

Tippled, *adj.* ivre, gris

Tippler, *s.* buveur, *m.*, -euse, *f.*, biberon, *m.*, -ne, *f.*, gobeloteur, *m.*, -euse *f.*, ivrogne, *m.*, ivrognesse, *f.*

Tippling, *s.* gobeloterie, ivrognerie, *f.*

Tipsily, *adv.* en ivrogne

Tipsiness, *s.* ivresse, *f.*; ivrognerie, *f.*

Tipstaff, *s.* (*pers.*) huissier, *m.*; (*staff*) verge, *f.*

Tipsy, *adj.* *V.* **Drunk**

Tiptoe, *s.* pointe du pied, *f.* *To stand on —,* se tenir (*or* se dresser *or* s'élever *or* se hausser) sur la pointe du pied; (*fam.*) être dans l'attente; avoir l'oreille au guet

Tiptop, *s.* sommet, faîte, comble, *m.*; — *adj.* excellent; parfait; suprême; huppé; de première volée; de première force; de premier ordre [jures), bordée, sortie, *f.*

Tirade, *s.* tirade, *f.*; (*of abuse*) tirade (d'in-

Tire, *s.* (*attire*) atours, *m.pl.* parure, *f.*; (*of wheels*) bande, *f.*; — *v.a.* (*to attire*) parer, orner; habiller; (*wheels*) embattre, ferrer. — **woman,** *s.* dame d'atours, *f.*; (*theat.*) coiffeuse, *f.*

Tire, *v.a.* ('*of,*' '*with,*' de) (*weary*) fatiguer; lasser; (*bore*) ennuyer (*harass*) *V.* **Harass;** — *v.n.* se fatiguer, se lasser. — **out,** harasser, excéder; éreinter; lasser; (*anyone's patience*) mettre à bout; (*bore*) assommer. *To be —d of,* être fatigué *or* las de. *To get* (or *grow*) *—d,* se fatiguer (de), se lasser (de); s'ennuyer (de)

Tiresome, *adj.* fatigant; (*tedious*) ennuyeux, fastidieux. —**ly,** *adv.* d'une manière fatigante; ennuyeusement, fastidieusement. —**ness,** *s.* nature fatigante, *f.*; fatigue, *f.*; (*tediousness*) ennui, *m.*

Tiring, *s.* toilette, *f.*; (*of wheels*) embattage, *m.* —**room,** *s.* (*theat.*) *V.* **Star-room**

Tiro. *V.* **Tyro**

Tisan, Tisane, *s.* tisane, *f.*

Tissue, *s.* tissu, *m.*; — *v.a.* tisser, brocher, broder; entrelacer, entremêler. — **paper,** *s.* papier de soie, papier joseph, *m.*

Tit, *s.* mignon, petit, mimi, bibi, *m.*; (*pony*) poney, *m.*; (*nag*) bidet, *m.*, bique, *f.*; (*tomtit*) mésange, *f.* — *for tat,* donnant donnant; un prêté rendu; à bon chat bon rat. *To give — for tat,* rendre pois pour fève, rendre la pareille

Titan, *s.* (*myth.*) Titan, *m.*; — *adj.* titanesque, titanique
Titanian, *adj.* titanesque, titanique
Titanic, *adj.* (*myth., fig.*) titanesque, titanique; (*chem.*) titanique
Titanite, *s.* titanite, *m.*
Titanium, *s.* (*chem.*) titane, titanium, *m.*
Titbit, *s.* morceau friand, bon morceau, *m.*, friandise, *f.*; (*fam.*) bonne bouche, *f.*
Tithable, *adj.* dîmable, décimable
Tithe, *s.* dixième, *m.*, dixième partie, *f.*; (*tax*) dîme, *f.*; — *v.a.n.* dîmer. — **collector, -gatherer,** *s.* dîmeur, *m.* — **free,** *adj.* exempt de la dîme. — **owner,** *s.* décimateur, *m.* — **paying,** *adj.* assujetti à la dîme
Tithing, *s.* (*tithe*) dîme, *f.*; (*levying*) dîmée, *f.*; (*Engl. hist.*) dizaine, *f.* — **man,** *s.* dizenier, *m.*
Titillate, *v.a.* titiller, chatouiller
Titillation, *s.* titillation, *f.*, chatouillement, *m.*
Titivate, *v.a.* *V.* **Tidy** *oneself*
Titlark, *s.* alouette des prés, farlouse, *f.*
Title, *s.* titre, *m.*; (*name*) nom, *m.*; — *v.a.* titrer; (*to name*) intituler, nommer, appeler. *Half* or *bastard* —, (*print.*) faux titre, *m.* — **deed,** *s.* titre de propriété, titre, acte, document, *m.* — **page,** *s.* page du titre, *f.*, titre, *m.*
Titmouse, *s.* mésange, *f.*
Titrate, *v.a.* (*chem.*) titrer
Titration, *s.* (*chem.*) titrage, *m.*
Titter. *V.* **Giggle**
Tittle, *s.* point, *m.*; iota, *m.*; ombre, *f.* *To a* —, en tout point. — **tattle,** *s.* bavardage, *m.*; cancans, *m.pl.*; *v.n.* bavarder, causer, jaser
Titubate, *v.n.* tituber
Titubation, *s.* titubation, *f.*
Titular, Titulary, *adj. s.* titulaire, *m.f.*
Titularly, *adj.* de titre; — *adv.* par le titre; en vertu d'un titre
To, (*particle used before an infinitive*) à; de; (*for the purpose of, in order to, so as to*) pour; afin de. (*Sometimes untranslated.*) *To be ready — go,* être prêt à partir. *To refuse — go,* refuser de partir. *I have time — lose,* j'ai du temps à perdre. *I have time — rest,* j'ai le temps de me reposer. *I have written — tell him,* je lui ai écrit pour lui dire. *I have come — see you,* je viens vous voir
To, *prep.* à; (*before names of countries and following a verb of motion*) en; (*into*) en; dans; (*denoting a series*) en; (*towards: of behaviour, with regard to*) envers; (*towards: of direction*) vers; à; (*turned to*) tourné à, tourné vers; (*before, in presence of*) devant; (*as far as, up to, down to, till*) jusqu'à, jusque; (*of*) de; (*with, at or to the dwelling or shop or &c. of*) chez; (*near*) auprès de; (*for*) pour; (*concerning, upon*) sur; (*in comparison with*) en comparaison de, auprès de; (*within*) à ... près; (*against*) contre; (*of the hour*) moins. — ...'*s*, chez. *To speak* —, parler à. *To go — Paris,* aller à Paris. *To go — France,* aller en France. [*A few exceptions, as:* Aller au Canada, au Brésil, aux Indes *or* dans les Indes, &c.] *To go — jail,* aller en prison. *To fall — dust,* tomber en poussière. *To put — flight,* mettre en fuite. *To retreat — a citadel,* se retirer dans une citadelle. *From house — house,* de maison en maison. *From one house — another,* d'une maison à l'autre. *The road* or *the way — Paris,* la route *or* le chemin de Paris. *The road from London — Paris,* la route de Londres à Paris. *A way — Paris,* un chemin pour aller à Paris. *The shortest way — Paris,* le plus court chemin pour aller à Paris. *The way — my room,* le chemin pour aller à ma chambre. *Successor — his father,* successeur de son père. *Apprentice — a joiner,* apprenti chez un menuisier. *To go — the butcher's,* aller chez le boucher. — *a day,* (*within*) à un jour près; (*exactly*) jour pour jour. (*It is*) *ten — one* (*that* ...), (il y a) dix (à parier) contre un (que ...). *Quarter — one,* une heure moins un (*or* le) quart. *It is ten minutes — six,* il est six heures moins dix minutes (*or* six heures moins dix). — *and fro, V.* **Fro**
Toad, *s.* crapaud, *m.* — **eater,** *s.* flagorneur, *m.*, -euse, *f.*, chien couchant, plat valet, *m.*, parasite, *m.f.* — **eating,** *s.* flagornerie, servilité, *f.* — **fish,** *s.* *V.* **Fishing-frog.** — **flax,** *s.* linaire, *f.* — **stone,** *s.* crapaudine, *f.* — **stool,** *s.* champignon vénéneux, *m.*
Toadish, *adj.* de crapaud
Toady, *s.* *V.* **Toad-eater;** — *v.a.n.* flagorner
Toadyism, *s.* flagornerie, servilité, *f.*
Toast, *v.a.* griller, rôtir, faire griller, faire rôtir; (*drink to*) porter un toast *or* des toasts à, toaster; — *v.n.* porter un toast *or* des toasts, toaster; — *s.* (du) pain grillé, *m.*, (une, la) rôtie, *f.*, (des, les) rôties, *f pl.*; (*drinking*) toast, *m.* — **and butter,** *s.* *V.* **Buttered** — (*Letter* **B**). — **and water,** *s.* eau panée, *f.* — **and** *or* **in wine,** *s.* rôtie au vin, *f.* — **master,** *s.* directeur des toasts, *m.* — **rack, -stand,** *s.* porte-rôties, *m.* — **water,** *s.* eau panée, *f.* [(*drinker*) toasteur, *m.*
Toaster, *s.* (*utensil*) gril, *m.*; grille-pain, *m.*;
Toasting, *s.* grillage, rôtissage, *m.*; (*drinking*) usage de porter des toasts, *m.*; action de porter un toast *or* des toasts, *f.*; toasts, *m pl.* — **fork,** *s.* grappin à rôtir, *m.*, fourchette à rôties, *f.*
Tobacco, *s.* tabac, *m.*; (*smoking* —) tabac à fumer, *m.* — **box,** *s.* boîte à tabac, *f.* — **jar,** *s.* pot à tabac, *m.* — **juice,** *s.* jus de tabac, *m.* — **manufacturer,** *s.* fabricant de tabacs, *m.* — **manufactory,** *s.* manufacture de tabacs, *f.* — **pipe,** *s.* pipe à tabac, pipe à fumer, pipe, *f.* — **pipe fish,** *s.* fistulaire, *m.* — **pouch,** *s.* blague (à tabac), *f.* — **shop,** *s.* bureau *or* débit de tabac, *m.* — **smoke,** *s.* fumée de tabac, *f.* — **stopper,** *s.* bourre-pipe, fouloir, *m.*
Tobacconist, *s.* marchand (*m.*, e, *f.*) *or* débitant (*m.*, e, *f.*) de tabac. —'*s shop,* bureau *or* [débit de tabac, *m.*
Tocsin, *s.* tocsin, *m.*
To-day, *adv.* aujourd'hui
Toddle, *v.n.* trottiner, trotter; marcher *or* aller à petits pas; marcher en chancelant. chanceler; (*get away*) décamper, filer, s'en aller
Toddy, *s.* toddy, *m.*
To-do, *s.* fanfaronnade, *f.*; (*fuss*) façons, *f.pl.*, embarras, *m. sing.*, *m.pl.*; (*scene, &c.*) scène, *f.*; [éclat, *m.*
Tody, *s.* (*bird*) todier, *m.*
Toe, *s.* doigt du pied, orteil, *m.*; (*of animals*) doigt, *m.*; (*of a horse*) pince, *f.*; (*of a butt-end*) pointe, *f.*; —**s,** *pl.* doigts du pied, orteils, *m.pl.*, &c.; (*tip*) pointe du pied, *f.*; (*feet*) pieds, *m.pl.* *Big* or *great* —, gros orteil, pouce du pied, *m.* *To kiss the Pope's* —, baiser le pied (*or* la mule) du pape. *To tread on* ...'*s* —*s*, marcher sur le pied à (*or* de) ... — **nails,** *s.pl.* ongles du pied (*or* des pieds), *m pl.* *His — nails,* les ongles de ses pieds
Toffee, Toffy, *s.* caramel au beurre, *m.*
Tog, — **up,** *v.a.* attifer; *v.n.* s'attifer; —**s,** *s.pl.* [*V.* **Toggery**
Toga, *s.* toge, *f.*
Togated, Toged, *adj.* revêtu de la toge
Together, *adv.* ensemble; (*at the same time*) en même temps ('*with,*' que); à la fois; (*in concert*) conjointement; (*consecutively*) de suite; (*combined*) réuni (*adj.*); coalisé (*adj.*). — *with,* avec; ainsi que; joint à; en même temps que
Toggel, Toggle, *s.* (*nav.*) cabillot, *m.*
Toggery, *s.* attifement, *m.*, nippes, hardes, frusques, *f.pl.*
Toil, *v.n.* fatiguer, travailler péniblement; — *s.* fatigue, peine, *f.*; travail, labeur, *m.*; (*net, snare*) filet, piége, *m.*, toiles, *f.pl.* *To — and moil,* s'échiner, suer sang et eau
Toiler, *s.* travailleur, *m.*, -euse, *f.*
Toilet, *s.* toilette, *f.*; — *adj.* de toilette. — **cover,** *s.* dessus de toilette, *m.* — **glass,** *s.* miroir de toilette, *m.* — **pail,** *s.* seau de toilette, *m.* — **quilt,** *s.* dessus de toilette en piqué, *m.* — **requisite,** *s.* article de toilette,

m. — **soap,** *s.* savon de toilette, *m.* — **table,** *s.* table de toilette, toilette, *f.* — **vinegar,** *s.* vinaigre de toilette, *m.* [peine, *f.*

Toiling, *s.* travail pénible, labeur, *m.*, fatigue,

Toilsome, *adj.* fatigant, pénible, laborieux. —**ly,** *adv.* péniblement, laborieusement. — **ness,** *s.* nature fatigante *or* pénible, fatigue, peine, difficulté, *f.*, labeur, *m.*

Tokay, *s.* tokai, tokay, *m.*

Token, *s.* signe, *m.*; marque, *f.*; (*of friendship, esteem,* &c.) témoignage, gage, *m.*; (*coin*) jeton, *m.*; (*print.*) demi-rame, *f.*

Tol-de-rol-lol, *int.* tra, deri, dera! tra, la, la, lire, la! — *s.* flonflon, *m.*, turelure, *f.*

Tolerable, *adj.* tolérable; (*middling*) passable

Tolerably, *adv.* tolérablement; (*rather, so so*) passablement; assez

Tolerance, *s.* tolérance, *f.*

Tolerant, *adj.* tolérant

Tolerate, *v.a.* tolérer

Toleration, *s.* tolérance, *f.*

Toll, *s.* (*of roads,* &c.) péage, *m.*; (*duty*) droit, *m.*, taxe, *f.*; (*town due*) octroi, *m.*; (*of bells*) tintement, *m.*; son, *m.*; coup (de cloche), *m.*; — *v.n.a.* (*of bells*) tinter, sonner; (*to levy*) prélever. — **bar,** *s.* barrage, *m.*, barrière de péage, *f.* — **bridge,** *s.* pont ou l'on prélève un péage, *m.* — **collector,** *s.* péager, *m.* — **free,** *adj.* exempt de péage. — **gate,** *s.* barrière de péage, *f.* — **gatherer,** *s.* péager, *m.* — **house,** *s.* bureau de péage, *m.* — **money,** *s.* péage, *m.*

Tolling, *s.* tintement, *m.*; — *adj.* qui tinte

Tolu, — **balsam,** *s.* baume de Tolu, *m.*

Tom, *s.* Tom, Thomas, *m.*; (*cat*) matou, chat, *m.*; (*bell*) bourdon, *m.* — **bell,** *s.* bourdon, *m.* — **boy,** *s.* garçonnière, *f.*, vrai garçon, *m.*, gamine, tapageuse, *f.* — **cat,** *s.* matou, chat, *m.* — **fool,** *s.* dadais, niais, nigaud, *m.*; bouffon, *m.* — **foolery,** *s.* bêtise, sottise, niaiserie, *f.*; bouffonnerie, *f.* — **noddy,** *s.* dadais, nigaud, *m.* — **Thumb,** *s.* *V.* **Thumb.** — **tit,** *s.* mésange, *f.* — **tom,** *s.* *V.* **Tam-tam**

Tomahawk, *s.* tomahawk, casse-tête, *m.*

Tomata, Tomato, *s.* tomate, *f.* — **sauce,** [*s.* sauce tomate, *f.*

Tomb, *s.* *V.* **Grave**

Tombac, *s.* tombac, *m.*

Tombola, *s.* tombola, *f.*

Tome, *s.* tome, volume, *m.*

To-morrow, *adv.* demain. *The day after* —, après-demain. *The day after — in the evening* or *morning,* après-demain soir *or* matin. — *never comes,* la semaine des quatre jeudis

Tompion. *V.* **Tampion**

Ton, *s.* tonneau, *m.*, tonne, *f.*

Tone, *s.* ton, *m.*; (*photog., tech.*) virage, *m.*; — *v.a.* teindre, colorer, teinter; (*photog.*) virer; (*regulate*) donner le ton à, régler. *In a* —, d'un ton. *To speak in a low* —, parler à voix basse, parler bas. — **down,** *v.a.* adoucir. —**less,** *adj.* peu harmonieux. — **syllable,** *s.* syllabe accentuée, *f.*

Toned, *part. adj.* teint, &c. (*V.* **Tone,** *v.a.*); (*in compounds*) à ton ... — *paper,* papier teinté, *m.* *High* —, à ton élevé

Toner, *s.* (*photog.*) vireur, *m.*

Tongs, *s pl.* pincettes, *f.pl.*, pincette, *f.*; pince, *f.*; (*of smiths,* &c.) tenailles, pinces, *f.pl.*

Tongue, *s.* langue, *f.*; (*of buckles*) ardillon, *m.*; (*of bells*) battant, *m.*; (*of land*) langue de terre, *f.*; (*tech., rail.,* &c.) languette, *f.*; — *v.a.* (*tech.*) langueter. *To hold o.'s* —, se taire. — **bone,** *s.* os hyoïde, hyoïde, *m.* —**less,** *adj.* sans langue; muet. — **scraper,** *s.* cure-langue, gratte-langue, *m.* — **shaped,** *adj.* linguiforme. — **tie,** *s.* ankyloglosse, *m.*, soubrelangue, *f.*; *v.a.* nouer la langue à; (*fig.*) lier la langue à, obliger *or* réduire au silence. — **tied,** *adj.* qui a le filet; (*fig.*) obligé *or* réduit au silence; muet

Tongued, *adj.* à langue; (*tech.*) à languette. — *and grooved,* (*of planks*) à rainure et à languette [*m.*; (*mus.*) tonique, *f.*

Tonic, *adj.* tonique (*m.f.*); — *s.* (*med.*) tonique,

Tonicity, *s.* tonicité, *f.*

Tonify, *v.a.* tonifier

To-night, *adv.* *V.* **Night**

Toning, *s.* (*photog.*) virage, *m.* — **solution,** *s.* bain de virage, *m.* [tonka, *m.*

Tonka bean, *s.* fève de tonka, fève tonka, *f.*,

Tonnage, *s.* tonnage, *m.*; droit de tonnage, *m.* *Register* —, jauge officielle, *f.* — **dues,** *s. pl.* droit de tonnage, *m.*

Tonsil, *s.* amygdale, *f.*

Tonsilar, *adj.* tonsillaire

Tonsilitis, *s.* amygdalite, *f.*

Tonsure, *s.* tonsure, *f.*

Tontine, *s.* tontine, *f.*

Tony, *s.* niais, imbécile, *m.*

Too, *adv.* trop; par trop; (*also*) aussi; également; de même; encore; (*moreover*) de plus, en outre; qui plus est; (*what is worse*) qui pis est. — *long a story,* une trop longue histoire. — *hard a task,* une tâche trop difficile. — *much,* &c., *V.* **Much,** &c.

Tool, *s.* outil, *m.*; instrument, *m.*; (*agent, mere* —) instrument, agent, *m.*; âme damnée, *f.* — **box, -chest,** *s.* boîte d'outils, *f.* — **house,** *s.* cabane aux outils, resserre, *f.*

Tooth, *s.* dent, *f.*; (*taste*) goût, palais, *m.*; — *v.a.* denter; (*indent*) denteler; (*machines*) engrener. *First teeth,* dents de lait, *f.pl.* *In* or *to his* (or *my* or &c.) *teeth,* au nez, à la figure; en face. *In spite of o.'s teeth,* malgré quelqu'un. — *and nail,* bec et ongles; (*fig.*) à belles dents; de toutes ses forces; de tout cœur; comme un enragé. *To be at — and nail,* être aux prises. *To cast in the teeth,* reprocher, jeter au nez *or* à la face. *To have a sweet* —, aimer les friandises. *To have a — out,* se faire arracher une dent. *To shed o.'s teeth,* perdre ses dents de lait. — **ache,** *s.* mal de dents, *m.* *To have the — ache,* avoir mal aux dents; (*with an adjective*) avoir un mal de dents. — **brush,** *s.* brosse à dents, *f.* — **drawer,** *s.* arracheur de dents, *m.* — **drawing,** *s.* extraction de dents, *f.* —**less,** *adj.* sans dents; édenté. — **ornament,** *s.* (*arch.*) dent de scie, *f.* — **pick,** *s.* cure-dents, *m.* — **pick case,** — **pick holder,** *s.* porte-cure-dents, *m.* — **powder,** *s.* poudre dentifrice, poudre pour les dents, *f.* — **shell,** *s.* dentale, *m.* —**some,** *adj.* agréable au goût, friand. —**someness,** *s.* goût agréable, *m.* — **wort,** *s.* dentaire, clandestine, *f.* [à dents ..., à ... dents

Toothed, *adj.* denté; dentelé; (*in compounds*)

Toothing, *s.* (*arch.*) arrachement, *m.*

Top, *s.* (*summit*) haut, sommet, *m.*, cime, *f.*; (*of roofs,* &c.) faîte, haut, *m.*; (*end, tip*) bout, *m.*; (*surface*) surface, *f.*; (*upper side*) dessus, *m.*; (*cover*) couvercle, *m.*; (*acme*) comble, faîte, *m.*; (*of the head*) haut, sommet, *m.*; (*head*) tête, *f.*; (*chief*) chef, *m.*; (*of a piano*) table, *f.*; (*of coaches,* &c.) *V.* **Outside**; (*of a wall*) couronnement, *m.*; (*of boots*) revers, *m.*; genouillère, *f.*; (*of a hat, of a man's cap*) calotte, *f.*, fond, *m.*; (*of a billiard cue*) procédé, *m.*; (*of a fishing-rod*) scion, *m.*; (*plaything*) toupie, *f.*, (*moved by a whip*) sabot, *m.*; (*nav.*) hune, *f.*; —**s,** *pl.* (*of turnips,* &c.) fane, *f.*; — *adj.* supérieur, de *or* du dessus, du haut, d'en haut; premier, principal; (*crack*) huppé, de premier ordre; (*with a — of*) à dessus (de ...); — *v.a.* (*cover*) couronner (de), surmonter (de), couvrir (de); (*reach*) atteindre le sommet de; (*rise above*) dépasser; (*surpass*) surpasser; (*trees,* &c., *lop*) étêter; (*climb*) gravir le sommet de; (*nav.*) apiquer; — *v.n.* dominer; prédominer; exceller, primer; monter, s'élever. — *of the tide,* vif de l'eau, *m.* *At the — of the house,* tout au haut de la maison. *From — to bottom,* du haut en bas; (*of destroying*) de fond en comble. *From — to toe,* de la tête aux pieds.

— **boots,** *s.pl.* bottes à revers, *f.pl.* —**ful,** *adj.* tout plein. — **gallant mast,** *s.* mât de perroquet, *m.* — **heavy,** *adj.* trop lourd du haut. — **knot,** *s.* (*of birds*) huppe, aigrette, *f.*; (*of women*) fontange, *f.*; (*rough tuft of hair*) i (de cheveux), *m.*; (*fish*) rhombe, *m.* —**less,** *adj.* d'une hauteur infinie. —**man,** *s.* (*nav.*) gabier, *m.*; (*fig.*) chef, *m.*; coq, *m.* — **mast,** *s.* mât de hune, hunier, mât de perroquet, *m.* —**most,** *adj.* le plus haut, le plus élevé, supérieur. — **over,** *v.n.* verser. — **rope,** *s.* (*nav.*) guinderesse, *f.* — **sail,** *s.* hunier, *m.* — **shaped,** *adj.* en forme de toupie, turbiné. — **shell,** *s.* toupie, *f.*, troque, *m.* — **sides,** *s.pl.* (*nav.*) œuvres mortes, *f.pl.* — **string,** *s.* (*for spinning a* —) fouet de toupie, *m.* — **yard,** *s.* (*nav.*) vergue de [hunier, *f.*

Topaz, *s.* topaze, *f.*

Tope, *v.n.* *V.* **Tipple;** — *s.* (*fish*) milandre, *m.*; (*Buddhistic monument*) tôpe, *m.*

Toper, &c. *V.* **Tippler,** &c.

Tophaceous, *adj.* tophacé

Tophus, *s.* (*med.*) tophus, *m.*

Topiary, *adj.* *s.* topiaire, *adj.* *m.f.*, *s.f.*

Topic, *s.* sujet, *m.*, matière, *f.*; argument, *m.*; (*log., med.*) topique, *m.*

Topic, -al, *adj.* local; (*med.*) topique

Topically, *adv.* localement; (*med.*) comme [topique

Topographer, *s.* topographe, *m.*

Topograph-ic, al, -ically, -y. *V.* p. 3, § 1

Toppin, *s.* (*artil.*) étoupillon, *m.*

Topping, *adj.* *V.* **Tiptop;** — *s.* couronnement, *m.*; (*of trees,* &c., *lopping*) étêtement, *m.* — **lift,** *s.* (*nav.*) balancine de gui, *f.*

Topple, *v.a.n.* — **down,** *v.a.* jeter en bas, faire tomber; *v.n.* tomber, dégringoler; (*of buildings*) s'écrouler. — **over,** *v.a.* culbuter, faire tomber; *v.n.* faire la culbute *or* la bascule, tomber, dégringoler

Topsy-turvy, *adv.* *V.* **Upside down**

Torch, *s.* torche, *f.*, flambeau, *m.* — **bearer,** *s.* porte-flambeau, *m.* — **light,** *s.* lumière de flambeau *or* des flambeaux *or* des torches, *f.*; *adj.* de flambeau; (*by — light*) aux flambeaux. *By — light,* à la lumière des torches *or* des flambeaux, aux flambeaux. — **light procession,** *s.* promenade aux flambeaux, *f.* — **thistle,** *s.* cierge, cierge du Pérou, cactus, *m.*

Tore, *s.* tore, *m.*

Toreador, *s.* toréador, *m.*

Torment, *v.a.* tourmenter; faire souffrir, vexer; — *s.* tourment, *m.*; torture, *f.*, supplice, *m.*; souffrance, *f.*

Tormenter, *s.* bourreau, *m.*; tourment, *m.*

Tormentil, *s.* tormentille, *f.*

Tormentingly, *adv.* d'une manière tour-[mentante

Tornado, *s.* ouragan, tourbillon, tornado, *m.*

Torpedo, *s.* torpille, *f.*

Torpescent, *adj.* qui s'engourdit

Torpid, *adj.* engourdi, dans la torpeur; inerte, apathique; (*heedless*) nonchalant

Torpidity, Torpidness, Torpor, *s.* torpeur, *f.*, engourdissement, *m.*; apathie, *f.*

Torrefaction, *s.* torréfaction, *f.*

Torrefier, *s.* torréfacteur, *m.*

Torrefy, *v.a.* torréfier; griller

Torrent, *s.* torrent, *m.*; — *adj.* (— *like*) torrentueux. *In —s,* par *or* à torrents

Torricellian, *adj.* de Torricelli

Torrid, *adj.* (*parched*) brûlé, desséché; (*hot*) brûlant; (*zone*) torride

Torridity, Torridness, *s.* chaleur brûlante, *f.*

Torsel, *s.* torsade, *f.* [de torsion, *f.*

Torsion, *s.* torsion, *f.* — **balance,** *s.* balance

Torsk, *s.* (*fish*) brosme, *m.*

Torso, *s.* torse, *m.*

Tort, *s.* (*law*) tort, dommage, préjudice, *m.*

Torticollis, *s.* torticolis, *m.*

Tortile, *adj.* tordu, tors; (*nat. hist.*) tortile

Tortious, *adj.* dommageable, préjudiciable; illégal, injuste [galement, injustement, à tort

Tortiously, *adv.* dommageablement; illé-

Tortoise, *s.* tortue, *f.* — **beetle,** *s.* casside, *f.* — **shell,** *s.* écaille, écaille de tortue, *f.*; *adj.* d'écaille, en écaille; (*of cats*) marqué en écaille de tortue

Tortuosity, Tortuousness, *s.* tortuosité, *f.*

Tortuous, Tortuose, *adj.* tortueux

Tortuously, *adv.* tortueusement

Torture, *s.* torture, *f.*; tourment, *m.*; supplice, *m.*; — *v.a.* torturer, mettre à la torture; faire souffrir; tourmenter

Torturer, *s.* bourreau, *m.*

Torturingly, *adv.* en torturant, en tourmentant; de manière à torturer

Torus, *s.* (*arch., bot.*) tore, *m.*

Tory, *s.* *adj.* tory, *m.*; conservateur, *m.*; [doctrinaire, *m.*

Toryism, *s.* torysme, *m.*

Toss, *v.a.* jeter, lancer; (*up*) lancer en l'air; (*cook,* &c.) faire sauter; (*of horned cattle*) lancer en l'air, corner; (*agitate*) agiter; (*about*) ballotter; (*shake, as o.'s head,* &c.) secouer; (*in a blanket*) berner; — *v.n.* se jeter; (*be tossed*) être ballotté; (*move about*) se démener, s'agiter. — **off,** (*throw*) jeter loin; (*despatch*) expédier; (*drink*) sabler, lamper. — **up,** (*throw*) jeter en l'air; (*lift*) relever; (*play*) jouer à pile ou face. *Let us — up for it,* jouons-le à pile ou face

Toss, Tossing, *s.* jet, *m.*; coup, *m.*; (*shaking*) ballottement, *m.*, secousse, *f.*; (*of the head*) mouvement *or* coup de tête, *m.*; (*with horns*) coup (*m.*, coups, *m.pl.*) de corne

Total, *adj.* total; entier, complet; — *s.* total, *m.*, somme, *f.*

Totality, *s.* totalité, *f.*, total, tout, *m.*

Totally, *adv.* totalement, entièrement, complètement

Toto cœlo, *adv.* du tout au tout, entièrement. *To differ —,* être éloignés comme le ciel et la terre, différer du tout au tout [ruine

Totter, *v.n.* chanceler; vaciller; menacer

Tottering, *adj.* chancelant; tremblant; vacillant; mal assuré; — *s.* chancellement, *m.*; vacillation, *f.*

Totteringly, *adv.* d'une manière chancelante

Toucan, *s.* toucan, *m.*

Touch, *v.a.n.* toucher; (*alter, disturb, meddle with, begin to use*) toucher à; (*reach*) toucher à, atteindre; (*each other*) se toucher; (*o.'s hat*) mettre (*or* porter) la main à (son chapeau), toucher (son chapeau), (*to* ...) saluer (... du chapeau); (*corrode or bite* &c. *into*) entamer, attaquer; mordre; (*nav.*) toucher (à), aborder (à). — **me not,** *s.* (*bot., med.*) noli me tangere, *m.* — **off,** ébaucher; retoucher. — **up,** retoucher; (*set off*) rehausser, relever. — **upon, on,** toucher; glisser sur, effleurer

Touch, *s.* (*contact*) attouchement, contact, *m.*; (*feeling*) toucher, tact, *m.*; (*tap*) tape, *f.*, léger coup, *m.*; (*of illness*) légère attaque, *f.*; (*paint.*) touche, *f.*, coup de pinceau, *m.*; (*fenc., billiards,* &c.) touche, *f.*; (*mus.*) toucher, *m.*; (*of metals*) touche, *f.*, essai, *m.*; (*expression, stroke*) trait, *m.*; (*tincture*) teinture, *f.*; (*little*) soupçon, *m.*, idée, *f.*; (*hint*) allusion, *f.* *To give the last* (or *finishing*) *— to,* mettre la dernière main à. — **hole,** *s.* lumière, *f.* — **needle,** *s.* touchau, *m.* — **paper,** *s.* mèche, *f.* — **stone,** *s.* pierre de touche, *f.* — **wood,** *s.* amadou, *m.*

Touchable, *adj.* touchable, tangible, palpable

Touched, *part. adj.* touché, &c. (*V.* **Touch,** *v.a.n.*); affecté; (*of mind*) toqué, timbré, fou

Touchily, *adv.* avec susceptibilité; avec mauvaise humeur

Touchiness, *s.* susceptibilité, *f.*; irritabilité, *f.*

Touching, *adj.* touchant, émouvant; — *s.* touchement, *m.*; toucher, tact, *m.*; — *prep.* au sujet de, sur, touchant

Touchingly, *adv.* d'une manière touchante

Touchy, *adj.* susceptible; chatouilleux; irritable, irascible

Tough, *adj.* dur, raide; résistant; visqueux, gluant; tenace; obstiné, opiniâtre; (*strong*)

fort, vigoureux, robuste, solide ; (*difficult*) rude, difficile ; épineux ; (*of meat*) coriace, dur
Toughen, *v.a.* durcir, raidir ; — *v.n.* s'endurcir, durcir
Toughish, *adj.* un peu dur
Toughly, *adv.* durement ; avec raideur ; avec ténacité, tenacement ; opiniâtrément ; vigoureusement
Toughness, *s.* dureté, raideur, *f.* ; viscosité, *f.* ; ténacité, *f.* ; obstination, opiniâtreté, *f.* ; force, vigueur, solidité, *f.* ; difficulté, *f.* ; (*of meat*) nature coriace, dureté, *f.*
Toupee, Toupet, *s.* toupet, *m.*
Tour, *s.* tour, voyage, *m.*
Touraco, *s.* touraco, *m.*
Tour-ism, -ist. *V.* page 3, § 1
Tourmaline, *s* tourmaline, *f.*
Tournament, *s.* tournoi, *m.*
Tourney, *s.* tournoi, *m.* ; — *v.n.* jouter
Tourniquet, *s.* tourniquet, *m.*
Tout, *v.n.* courir après des pratiques, chercher des pratiques, racoler ; faire l'article ; pousser à la consommation ; — *s.* *V.* **Touter.** — **for,** solliciter, tâcher d'attraper, racoler
Touter, *s.* solliciteur, racoleur, *m.*; placier, *m.*; (*in horse-racing*) espion, *m.*
Touting, *s.* sollicitation, *f.*
Tow, *s.* (*of hemp*) filasse, étoupe, *f.* ; (*of boats*) remorque, *f.* ; touée, *f.* ; — *v.a.* remorquer, haler, touer ; (*rail.*) remorquer. *In* —, à la remorque ; à la touée. — **boat,** *s.* bateau halé, *m.* ; (*tug*) bateau remorqueur, *m.* — **cable,** &c., *V.* **Towing** [(*rail.*) remorquage, *m.*
Towage, *s.* remorquage, halage, touage, *m.* ; (*rail.*) remorquage, *m.*
Toward, Towards, *adv.* (*of place and time*) vers ; (*of behaviour, with regard to*) envers, à l'égard de, pour [— *me* or *you* or &c., envers moi *or* vous *or* &c., à mon *or* votre *or* &c. égard, pour moi *or* vous *or* &c.]
Towel, *s.* serviette de toilette, serviette, *f.* ; essuie-mains, *m.* — **airer, -horse,** *s.* séchoir, porte-serviettes, *m.*
Towelling, *s.* toile pour serviettes (de toilette), *f.*, serviettes (de toilette), *f pl.*
Tower, *s.* tour, *f.* ; — *v.n.* dominer ; s'élever ; monter ; planer. *A — of strength,* une force (*or* une puissance) invincible, *f.*
Towered, *adj.* flanqué de tours ; (*in compounds*) aux tours ... *High* —, aux tours élevées
Towering, *adj.* dominant, élevé ; sublime ; orgueilleux, superbe ; violent, furieux, terrible
Towing, *s.* *V.* **Towage.** — **boat,** *s.* bateau remorqueur, *m.* — **cable, -line, -rope,** *s.* câble de remorque, *m.*, touline, cordelle, *f.* — **engine,** *s.* locomotive remorqueuse, *f.* — **path,** *s.* chemin de halage, *m.* — **vessel,** *s.* vaisseau remorqueur, *m.*
Town, *s.* ville, *f.* ; (*capital*) capitale, *f.* ; (*London*) Londres, *m.* *A man about* —, un viveur. *A woman* or *girl of the* —, une fille publique. *In* —, en ville. *Out of* —, à la campagne. — **adjutant,** *s.* (*mil.*) adjudant de place, *m.* — **clerk,** *s.* secrétaire de la mairie, *m.* — **clerkship,** *s.* secrétariat de la mairie, *m.* — **clock,** *s.* horloge de la ville, *f.* — **council,** *s.* conseil municipal, *m.* — **councillor,** *s.* conseiller municipal, *m.* — **crier,** *s.* crieur public, *m.* — **due,** *s.* droit d'octroi, *m.* — **dues,** *s.pl.* octroi, *m.* — **hall,** *s.* hôtel de ville, *m.* ; mairie, *f.* — **house,** *s.* hôtel de ville, *m.*, maison commune, *f.* ; mairie, *f.* ; (*house in town*) maison en ville, *f.*, hôtel, *m.* —**less,** *adj.* sans villes. — **major,** *s.* (*mil.*) major de place, *m.* — **rate,** *s.* taxe communale, *f.* —**ship,** *s.* commune, *f.* —**sman,** *s.* (*pl.* —**smen** *or* —**speople**) habitant de ville (*or* de la ville), *m.* ; citadin, *m.* ; bourgeois, *m.* ; (*fellow —sman*) concitoyen, *m.* — **surveyor,** *s.* inspecteur des travaux publics, *m.* — **talk,** *s.* propos de ville, *m.* ; sujet de toutes les conversations, *m.* — **traveller,** *s.* (*com.*) placier, *m.*

Toxicolog-ic, al, -ically, -ist, -y. *V.* p. 3, § 1
Toy, *s.* jouet, *m.*, (*fam.*) joujou, *m.* ; (*bauble*) colifichet, *m.* ; babiole, *f.* ; hochet, *m.* ; (*trifle*) niaiserie, *f.* ; (*play*) jeu, *m.* ; — *v.n.* jouer, badiner, folâtrer. — **box,** *s.* boîte à joujoux, *f.* — **dealer,** *s.* marchand (*m.*, e, *f.*) de jouets *or* de joujoux, bimbelotier, *m.*, -ière, *f.* ; tabletier, *m.*, -ière, *f.* — **maker,** *s.* bimbelotier, *m.*, -ière, *f.* ; tabletier, *m.*, -ière, *f.* — **man,** *s.* *V.* — **dealer.** — **shop,** *s.* magasin de jouets *or* de bimbeloterie, *m.*, (*fam.*) boutique de joujoux, *f.* — **trade,** *s.* bimbeloterie, tabletterie, *f.* — **warehouse,** *s.* *V.* — **shop.** — **woman,** *s.* *V.* — **dealer**
Toyer, *s.* joueur, *m.*, -euse, *f.* [folâtrerie, *f.*
Toying, *s.* jeu, *m.*, jeux, *m.pl.*, badinage, *m.*,
Toyish, *adj.* badin, folâtre ; (*trifling*) futile
Toyishness, *s.* humeur badine *or* folâtre, *f.*
Trace, *s.* trace, *f.* ; (*of harness*) trait, *m.* — **bearer,** *s.* porte-traits, *m.* — **bolt,** *s.* atteloire, *f.*
Trace, *v.a.* (*mark, draw*) tracer ; (*draw through transparent paper*) calquer ; (*follow*) suivre la trace de, suivre ; suivre à la piste ; (*investigate*) remonter à l'origine de ; remonter (à) ; faire remonter (à) ; découvrir, trouver. — **back** *or* **up,** remonter à l'origine de ; remonter (à) ; faire remonter (à) ; découvrir ; (*follow*) suivre. — **out,** tracer ; découvrir
Tracer, *s.* (*pers.*) traceur, *m.*, -euse, *f.* ; (*instr.*) traçoir, *m.*
Tracery, *s.* réseau, *m.*
Trachea, *s.* (*anat.*) trachée-artère, trachée, *f.* ; (*of insects, of plants*) trachée, *f.*
Tracheal, *adj.* trachéal
Trachean, *adj.* trachéen
Tracheotomy, *s.* trachéotomie, *f.*
Tracing, *s.* tracement, *m.* ; tracé, *m.* ; cours, *m.* ; (*draw.*) calque, *m.* — **cloth,** *s.* toile à calquer, *f.* — **paper,** *s.* papier à calquer, *m.* — **point,** *s.* traçoir, *m.* ; (*draw.*) calquoir, *m.*
Track, *s.* trace, *f.* ; (*road*) chemin, sentier, *m.* ; (*of roads*) voie, *f.* ; (*of wheels*) ornière, *f.* ; (*of comets*) route, *f.*, cours, *m.* ; (*of mountains*) passe, *f.* ; (*country*) *V.* **Tract ;** (*hunt.*) piste, *f.* ; voie, *f.* ; (*rail.*) voie, *f.* ; (*nav.*) route, *f.* ; sillage, *m.* ; — *v.a.* suivre à la piste ; dépister ; (*nav.*) remorquer, haler. — **boat,** *s.* coche d'eau, *m.* —**less,** *adj.* sans trace ; sans chemin, sans chemins, non frayé, impraticable. — **road,** *s.* chemin de halage, *m.*
Tracking, *s.* poursuite, *f.* ; (*nav.*) *V.* **Towage**
Tract, *s.* étendue, *f.*, espace, *m.* ; contrée, région, *f.* ; district, *m.* ; (*treatise*) petit traité, *m.* ; opuscule, *m.* ; brochure, *f.* ; imprimé, *m.*
Tractable, *adj.* traitable, maniable, doux, docile [douceur, *f.*
Tractableness, Tractability, *s.* docilité,
Tractably, *adv.* d'une manière traitable, docilement
Tractarian, *s.* tractarien, *m.*
Tractarianism, *s.* tractarianisme, *m.*
Tractile, *adj.* ductile
Tractility, *s.* ductilité, *f.*
Traction, *s.* traction, *f.* — **engine,** — **steam-engine,** machine à vapeur locomobile, locomobile, machine de traction, machine tractoire
Tractive, *adj.* tractif ; tractoire [tractoire, *f.*
Tractor, *s.* tracteur, *m.*
Tractory, Tractrix, *s.* tractoire, tractrice, *f.*
Trade, *s.* commerce, *m.* ; négoce, *m.* ; trafic, *m.* ; industrie, *f.* ; affaires, *f.pl.* ; (*calling*) métier, état, *m*, profession, *f.*, emploi, *m.*, occupation, *f.* ; (*guild*) corps de métier, *m.*, corporation, *f.* *By* —, de son métier, de son état. *To drive a good* —, faire de bonnes affaires. *Everyone to his* —, chacun son métier. — **allowance,** *s.* remise, *f.* — **association,** *s.* *V.* — **union.** — **corporation,** *s.* corporation de métier, *f*, corps de métier, *m.* — **mark,** *s.* marque de fabrique, estampille, *f.* — **price,** *s.* prix marchand, *m.* — **sman,** *s.* marchand, commerçant, *m.* ; (*with regard to customers*) fournisseur, *m.* *Brother*

—*sman*, confrère, *m.* —**smen, —speople,** *s.* (*pl. of* —**sman**). —**swoman,** *s.* marchande, commerçante, *f.* — **union,** *s.* association ouvrière, société de compagnonnage, *f.*, compagnonnage, *m.* — **unionism,** *s.* compagnonnage, *m.* — **unionist,** *s.* membre d'une association ouvrière, compagnon, *m.* — **wind,** *s.* vent alizé, *m.*

Trade, *v.n.* commercer, trafiquer, faire le commerce (de); faire des affaires ('*with*,' avec). — **on, upon,** spéculer sur, exploiter

Trader, *s.* commerçant, *m.*, e, *f.*; négociant, *m.*, e, *f.*; (*ship*) *V.* **Merchant-man**

Trading, *adj.* commerçant; commercial, de commerce; marchand; — *s.* commerce, négoce, trafic, *m.* — *town*, ville commerçante. — *vessel*, *V.* **Merchant-man**

Tradition, *s.* tradition, *f.*

Traditional, *adj.* traditionnel

Traditional-ism, -ist. *V.* page 3, § 1

Traditionally, *adv.* traditionnellement

Traditionary, *s. adj.* traditionnaire, *s.m.*, [*adj. m.f.*

Traditive, *adj.* traditif

Traduce, &c. *V.* **Slander,** &c.

Traffic, *s.* trafic, commerce, *m.*; marchandises, *f.pl.*; (*goods — on roads*) transport, roulage, *m.*; (*running to and fro*) circulation, *f.*; (*rail.*) mouvement, *m.*, circulation, *f.*, transport, *m.*; — *v.n.* trafiquer, commercer. *Opened for* —, livré à la circulation. — **manager,** *s.* (*rail.*) chef du mouvement, *m.* — **returns,** *s.pl.* compte des recettes, *m.*

Trafficker, *s.* marchand, *m.*, e, *f.*, commerçant, *m.*, e, *f.*, négociant, *m.*, e, *f.*, traficant, *m.*, e, *f*; (*in a bad sense*) trafiqueur, *m.*, -euse, *f.*

Tragacanth, *s.* (*tree*) tragacanthe, *f.*; (*gum*) *V.* **Gum-dragon**

Tragedian, *s.* tragédien, *m.*, -ne, *f.*; (*author*) auteur tragique, tragique, *m.*

Tragedy, *s.* tragédie, *f.*

Trag-ic, al, -ically. *V.* page 3, § 1

Tragicalness, *s.* caractère tragique, *m.*, nature tragique, *f.*; tragique, *m.*

Tragi-comedy, *s.* tragi-comédie, *f.*

Tragi-comic, al, *adj.* tragi-comique

Tragi-comically, *adv.* d'une manière tragi- [comique

Tragopan, *s.* tragopan, *m.*

Trail, *v.a.n.* (*hunt.*) suivre à la piste; (*draw, drag*) traîner; — *s.* (*track*) piste, trace, voie, *f.*; (*train*) traînée, *f.*; (*of meteors*) queue, *f.* *In the — of*, à la suite de. — **net,** *s. V.* **Drag-net**

Train, *v.a.* traîner; (*teach*, — **up**) former, élever; exercer; instruire, discipliner; dresser; (*accustom*) habituer, accoutumer; (*horses*, &c., *trees*) dresser; (*race-horses, and anyone for a match*) entraîner

Train, *s.* (*retinue*) suite, *f.*, cortége, *m.*; (*course*) cours, *m.*; (*series*) enchaînement, *m.*, suite, série, *f.*; (*file*) file, *f.*; (*rear*) suite, *f.*; (*artifice*) artifice, *m.*, séduction, *f.*; (*of dresses*) traîne, queue, *f.*; (*mantle*) manteau de cour, manteau, *m.*; (*of birds*) queue, *f.*; (*of watches*) marche, *f.*; (*of mach.*) chaîne (de communication), *f.*; (*of boats*) convoi, train, *m.*; (*of powder*) traînée, *f.*; (*artil.*) train, équipage, *m.*; (*of a gun-carriage*) derrière, *m.*; (*rail.*) train, *m.* *Back* —, train de retour. *Down* —, train d'aller; train s'éloignant de Paris. *Excursion* —, train de plaisir. *Express* —, train express, train direct. *Fast* —, train de grande vitesse. *Goods* —, train de marchandises; train de petite vitesse, *m.*, (la) petite vitesse, *f.* *In the — of*, (*after, behind*) à la suite de. *Last* —, dernier train. *Luggage* —, (*see* "*Goods* —," *above*). *Mail* —, train-poste. *Military* —, soldats du train, *m.pl.* *Mixed* —, train mixte. *Next* —, prochain train; train suivant. *Omnibus* —, *Parliamentary* —, train-omnibus. *Passenger* —, train de voyageurs; train de grande vitesse, *m.*, (la) grande vitesse, *f.* *Return* —, train de retour. *Slow* —, train de petite vitesse. *Stopping* —, train-omnibus. *Third-class* —, train de troisième classe; train-omnibus. *Through* —, train direct. *Tidal* —, train de marée. *Up* —, train de retour; train se dirigeant vers Paris. — **band,** *s.* milice bourgeoise, *f.* — **bearer,** *s.* porte-queue, *m.*; (*of cardinals*) caudataire, *m.* — **oil,** *s.* huile de poisson, huile de baleine, *f.* — **starter,** *s.* (*rail.*) sous-chef de gare, *m.*

Trainable, *adj.* enseignable; dressable

Trainer, *s.* (*of pers*) instituteur, *m.*; (*of horses*, &c.) dresseur, *m.*; (*of race-horses, of anyone for a match*) entraîneur, *m.*

Training, *s.* éducation, *f.*; instruction, *f.*; exercice, *m.*; discipline, *f.*; (*of horses*, &c., *of trees*) dressage, *m.*; (*of race-horses, of anyone for a match*) entraînement, *m.* — **collar,** *s.* collier de force, *m.* — **college,** *s.* école normale primaire, *f.* — **ship,** *s.* vaisseau-école, *m*

Traipse, *v.n.* se dandiner

Trait, *s.* trait, *m.*

Traitor, *s.* traître, *m.*; conspirateur, *m.*

Traitorous, -ly. *V.* **Treacherous, -ly**

Traitress, *s.* traîtresse, *f.*; perfide, *f.*

Trajectory, *s. adj.* trajectoire, *f.*

Tram, *s.* chariot à houille, chariot de roulage, *m.*; (*rail.*) rail plat, rail à ornière, *m.* — **plate, -rail,** *s.* rail plat, rail à ornière, *m.* — **road, -way,** *s.* chemin à rails plats, tramway, *m.*; (*in streets*) chemin de fer américain, tramway, *m.*

Trammel, *s.* (*net*) tramail, traîneau, *m.*, râfle, *f.*; (*instr.*) compas à ellipse, *m.*; (*shackle*) entrave, *f.*; — *v.a.* ('*with*,' de) entraver, embarrasser. — **net,** *s.* tramail, traîneau, *m.*, râfle, *f.* [— **wind,** *s.* tramontane, *f.*

Tramontane, *adj. s.* ultramontain, *m.*, e, *f.*

Tramp, *s.* vagabond, *m.*, e, *f.*; rôdeur, *m.*, -euse, *f.*; (*workman*) ouvrier ambulant, *m.*; (*vagrancy*) vagabondage, *m.*; (*tread*) pas, *m.*; (*stamp*) piétinement, *m.*; (*noise of footsteps*) bruit de (*or* des) pas, pas, *m.*; — *v.n.* (*stamp with the foot*) *V.* **Stamp;** (*travel*) marcher, aller à pied; (*stroll*) errer, rôder; — *v.a.* faire à pied; (*stamp with the foot*) *V.* **Stamp.** *To be on the* —, courir le pays

Trample, *v.a.n.* (— **upon**) fouler; marcher sur; fouler aux pieds; piétiner. — *under foot*, — *down*, fouler aux pieds

Trampling, *s.* piétinement, *m.*; bruit de pas, *m.*

Trance, *s.* extase, *f.*; (*med.*) catalepsie, *f.*

Tranced, *adj.* en extase, ravi

Tranquil, *adj.* tranquille

Tranquillity, Tranquilness, *s.* tranquillité, *f.*, calme, *m.*

Tranquillization, *s.* tranquillisation, *f.*

Tranquillize, *v.a.* tranquilliser; calmer; rassurer

Tranquillizer, *s.* tranquilliseur, *m.*

Tranquilly, *adv.* tranquillement, paisiblement

Transact, *v.a.* faire, traiter, être en (affaire *or* affaires)

Transaction, *s.* affaire, *f.*; transaction, opération, *f.*; acte, *m.*; négociation, *f.*; conduite, *f.*; —**s,** *pl.* (*of societies*) mémoires, *m.pl.*; actes, *m.pl.*; comptes-rendus des séances, *m.pl.*; travaux, *m.pl.*

Transactor, *s.* négociateur, *m.*; (*com.*) agent, *m.*

Transalpine, *adj.* transalpin

Transatlantic, *adj.* transatlantique

Transcaucasian, *adj.* transcaucasien

Transcend, *v.a.* dépasser; excéder; (*excel*) surpasser, exceller sur

Transcendenc-e, y, *s.* transcendance, *f.*

Transcendent, *adj.* transcendant

Transcendental, *adj.* transcendantal; (*math., anat.*) transcendant

Transcendentally, *adv.* transcendantalement

Transcendently, *adv.* d'une manière transcendante, éminemment, au suprême degré

Transcontinental, *adj.* transcontinental

Transcribe, *v.a.* transcrire, copier

Transcriber, *s.* transcripteur, copiste, *m.*

Transcript, *s.* transcription, copie, *f.*
Transcription, *s.* transcription, *f.*
Transdanubian, *adj.* transdanubien
Transept, *s.* transept, *m.*
Transfer, *v.a.* transférer ; transporter ; transmettre, céder ; — *s.* transport, *m.*; translation, *f.* ; (*com., law*) transfert, *m.*, transmission, cession, *f.*; (*bank., fin.*) transfert, *m.*; virement, *m.*
Transferability, *s.* transmissibilité, *f.*
Transferable, *adj.* transportable ; transférable ; transmissible, cessible. *Tickets not* —, les billets sont personnels
Transferee, *s.* cessionnaire, *m.f.*; (*of property left in trust*) fidéicommissaire, *m.*
Transference, Transferment, *s.* transfèrement, *m.*
Transferer, *s.* cédant, *m.*, e, *f.*
Transfiguration, *s.* transfiguration, *f.*; transformation, *f.*
Transfigure, *v.a.* transfigurer ; transformer
Transfix, *v.a.* transpercer
Transform, *v.a.* transformer (en) ; — *v.n.* se transformer (en)
Transformation, *s.* transformation, *f.* ; métamorphose, *f.*
Transform-ism, -ist. *V.* page 3, § 1
Transfuse, *v.a.* transfuser
Transfuser, *s.* transfuseur, *m.*
Transfusion, *s.* transfusion, *f.*
Transgangetic, *adj.* transgangétique
Transgress, *v.a.* transgresser, violer, enfreindre, contrevenir à ; (*go beyond*) dépasser ; — *v.n.* transgresser ; (*to sin*) pécher
Transgression, *s.* transgression, violation, *f.* ; (*sin*) péché, *m.*
Transgressive, *adj.* transgressif ; coupable
Transgressor, *s.* violateur, *m.*, -trice, *f.*, transgresseur, *m.*; (*sinner*) pécheur, *m.*, -eresse, *f.*
Tranship, *v.a.* transborder, transférer (à bord de ...)
Transhipment, *s.* transbordement, *m.*, translation (à bord de ...), *f.*
Transient, *adj.* passager, transitoire, fugitif ; éphémère ; momentané ; rapide
Transiently, *adv.* en passant, passagèrement, transitoirement ; momentanément ; rapidement
Transientness, *s.* nature passagère, nature transitoire, *f.* ; brièveté, courte durée, *f.*; rapidité, vitesse, *f.*
Transit, *s.* (*com.*) transit, *m.* ; (*astr.*) passage, *m.* — **circle, -instrument,** *s.* lunette méridienne, *f.* — **duty,** *s.* droit de transit, *m.*
Transition, *s.* transition, *f.*
Transitional, *adj.* de transition
Transitive, *adj.* (*gram.*) transitif, actif
Transitively, *adv.* transitivement, activement
Transitorily, *adv. V.* **Transiently**
Transitoriness, *s. V.* **Transientness**
Transitory, *adj. V.* **Transient**
Transitu (In), *adv.* in transitu
Translatable, *adj.* traduisible
Translate, *v.a.* (*languages*) traduire ; (*a bishop*, &c.) transférer
Translation, *s.* (*of languages*) traduction, *f.*, (*as a school-task*) version, *f.* ; (*of a bishop*, &c.) translation, *f.*
Translat-or, ress, *s.* traducteur, *m.*, -trice, *f.*
Translatory, *adj.* translatif
Transleithan, *adj.* transleithan
Translucency, Translucidity, *s.* translucidité, *f.*
Translucent, Translucid, *adj.* translucide
Transmarine, *adj.* transmarin, d'outre-mer
Transmigrant, *adj. s.* transmigrant, *m.*, e, *f.*
Transmigrate, *v.n.* transmigrer
Transmigration, *s.* transmigration, *f.*
Transmissibility, *s.* transmissibilité, *f.*
Transmissible, *adj.* transmissible
Transmission, *s.* transmission, *f.*
Transmissive, *adj.* transmis, de transmission
Transmit, *v.a.* transmettre
Transmitter, *s.* personne qui transmet, *f.*
Transmontane, *adj.* transmontain
Transmuta-bility, bleness, *s.* transmutabilité, *f.*
Transmutable, *adj.* transmuable
Transmutation, *s.* transmutation, *f.*
Transmute, *v.a.* transmuer
Transmuter, *s.* transmutateur, *m.*
Transoceanic, *adj.* transocéanien, transocéanique
Transom, *s.* traverse, *f.*
Transpacific, *adj.* transpacifique
Transpadane, *adj.* transpadan
Transparenc-e, y, *s.* transparence, *f.* ; (*painting*) transparent, *m.*
Transparent, *adj.* transparent
Transparently, *adv.* avec transparence ; clairement
Transpierce, *v.a.* transpercer, pénétrer
Transpirability, *s.* transpirabilité, *f.*
Transpirable, *adj.* transpirable
Transpiration, *s.* transpiration, *f.*
Transpire, *v.n.* transpirer ; (*happen*) arriver, avoir lieu, se passer ; — *v.a.* suer, exhaler
Transplant, *v.a.* transplanter
Transplantable, *adj.* transplantable
Transplantation, *s.* transplantation, *f.*
Transplanter, *s.* (*pers.*) transplanteur, *m.*; (*machine*) transplantoir, *m.*
Transplanting, *s.* transplantement, *m.* — **apparatus,** *s.* transplantoir, *m.*
Transport, *v.a.* transporter ; (*criminals*) déporter ; (*to delight*) transporter ('*with*,' de) ; — *s.* transport, *m.* ; (*criminal*) déporté, *m.* ; forçat, *m.*; (*ship*) transport, *m.* — **ship, -vessel,** *s.* transport, bâtiment de transport, *m.*
Transportable, *adj.* transportable ; (*crim. law*) punissable de la déportation
Transportation, *s.* transport, *m.* ; transmission, *f.* ; (*of criminals*) déportation, *f.*
Transporter, *s.* transporteur, *m.*
Transporting, *adj.* ravissant
Transposable, *adj.* transposable
Transposal, *s.* transposition, *f.*
Transpose, *v.a.* transposer
Transposer, *s.* transpositeur, *m.*
Transposing, *s.* transposition, *f.*; — *adj* transpositeur
Transposition, *s.* transposition, *f.*
Transpositive, *adj.* transpositif
Transpyrenean, *adj.* transpyrénéen
Transrhenane, *adj.* transrhénan
Transship, -ment. *V.* **Tranship,- ment**
Transubstantiate, *v.a.* transsubstantier
Transubstantiation, *s.* transsubstantiation, *f.*
Transubstantiator, *s.* transsubstantiateur, *m.*
Transudation, *s.* transsudation, *f.*
Transude, *v.n.a.* transsuder
Transversal, *adj. s.* transversal, *adj.m.*, e, *f.*, transversale, *s.f.*
Transversally, *adv.* transversalement, en travers
Transverse, *adj.* transversal ; transverse
Transversely, *adv.* en travers, transversalement
Transylvanian, *s. adj.* Transylvain, *m.*, e, *f.*, Transylvanien, *m.*, -ne, *f.*
Tranter, *s.* chasse-marée, *m.*
Trap, *s.* trappe, *f.* ; (*for men*) chausse-trappe, *f.* ; (*fig.*) piége, *m.*; (*of a pistol*) culotte, *f.* ; (*of drains*) valve, *f.* ; (— *ball*) balle à la volée, *f.*; (*carriage*) petite voiture, *f.*; chaise, *f.*; carriole, *f.*; (*geol., min.*) trapp, *m.* ; —**s,** *pl.* effets, *m.pl.*, affaires, *f.pl.*, bagage, attirail, *m.*; — *v.a.* prendre dans une trappe, attraper ; (*fig.*) prendre au piége, attraper ; (*incline*) faire pencher, basculer ; (— *out*) *See below* ; — *v.n.* faire la bascule, basculer. *A horse and* —, une carriole. *To be up to* ——, (or *to snuff*) *V.* **Snuff.** *To fall into the* —, tomber dans le piége, donner dans le panneau. *To set a* —, tendre un piége. — **ball,** *s.* balle à la volée, *f.* — **bat,** *s.* battoir, *m.* — **door,** *s.* trappe, *f.*; (*over a cellar*) trappon, *m.*; (*theat.*) trappillon, *m.* — **ladder,** *s.* échelle de meunier, *f.* — **net,** *s.* panneau, *m.* — **out,** *v.a.* (*dress out*) harnacher, enharnacher ; (*deck out*) *V.* **Deck,** *v.a.* —**stick,** *s.* marchette, *f.*; (*of carts*) clé (de tombereau *or* de charrette), *f.*; (*bat*) battoir, *m.*

— **tufa, -tuff,** *s.* trapp-tuf, *m.* — **valve,** *s.* valve à bascule, *f.*

Trapan, *s.* piége, panneau, *m.*; — *v.a.* prendre au piége, attraper

Trapeze, *s.* (*gymnastics*) trapèze, *m.*

Trapezian, *adj.* trapézien

Trapezist, *s.* trapéziste, *m.f.*

Trapezium, *s.* (*geom.*) trapézoïde, *m.*; (*anat.*) trapèze, os trapèze, *m.*

Trapezius, *s.* (*anat.*) trapèze, muscle trapèze, *m.*

Trapezoid, *s.* (*geom.*) trapèze, *m.*

Trapezoidal, *adj.* trapéziforme. — *bone,* trapezoïde, os trapézoïde, *m.*

Trappe, *s.* (*rel. order, convent*) Trappe, *f.*

Trapper, *s.* trappeur, *m.*

Trappings, *s.pl.* harnais, harnachement, caparaçon, *m.*; (*of people*) ornements, *m.pl.*, parure, *f.*

Trappist, *s. adj.* trappiste, *s.m.*, *adj.m.f.*

Trappistine, *s.* trappistine, *f.*

Trash, *s.* rebut, *m.*; drogue, camelote, cochonnerie, *f.*; (*of writings*, &c.) fatras, *m.*, fadaises, *f.pl.*; (*of sugar-cane*) bagasse, *f.*; (*pers.*) vaurien, drôle, *m.*

Trashy, *adj.* de rebut, de camelote, mauvais, méchant, vil, sans valeur, qui ne vaut rien

Trass, *s.* trass, *m.*

Traumat-ic, al. -ically, -ism. *V.* p. 3, § 1

Travail, *s.* travail, *m.*; — *v.n.* travailler, fatiguer; (*of childbirth*) être en travail

Trave, *s.* (*for horses*) travail, *m.*; (*build.*) traverse, *f.*

Travel, *v n.* voyager; être en voyage; passer, aller; — *v.a.* — **over,** parcourir, voyager dans; faire (*a stated distance*)

Travel, *s.* voyage (par terre), *m.*; voyages, *m.pl.*

Travellable, *adj.* voyageable

Travelled, *adj.* qui a voyagé, qui voyage beaucoup, voyageur

Traveller, *s.* voyageur, *m.*, -euse, *f.*; (*commercial*) voyageur de commerce, *m.*, (*town* —) placier, *m.* —**'s joy,** *s.* (*bot.*) aubevigne, *f.* —**'s tree,** *s.* ravenala, arbre du voyageur, *m.*

Travelling, *s.* voyages, *m.pl.*; — *adj.* voyageur; (*itinerant*, &c.) ambulant; (*on a journey*) en voyage; (*for a journey, incurred by a journey*) de voyage. *To be fond of* —, aimer à voyager. — **articles** *or* **requisites,** *s.pl.* articles de voyage, *m.pl.* — **bag,** *s.* sac de voyage, sac de nuit, *m.* — **cap,** *s.* casquette de voyage, *f.* — **case,** *s.* nécessaire de voyage, *m.* — **companion,** *s. V.* **Fellow-traveller.** — **crane,** *s.* grue roulante, *f.* — **expenses,** *s.pl.* frais de voyage, *m.pl.* — **post-office,** *s.* bureau ambulant, *m.* — **rug, -wrapper,** *s.* couverture de voyage, *f.*

Traversable, *adj.* niable

Traverse, *s.* traverse, *f.*; (*law*) dénégation, *f.*; (*nav.*) bordée, route oblique, *f.*; — *v.a.* traverser; (*examine*) examiner; (*a cannon*) pointer; (*law*) nier, dénier; — *v.n.* (*turn*) tourner, pivoter; (*nav.*) bordeyer, faire route oblique

Traverser, *s.* partie qui dénie, *f.*

Travertin, Travertine, *s.* travertin, *m.*

Travestier, *s.* travestisseur, *m.*

Travesty, *adj.* travesti; — *s.* travestissement, *m.*; parodie, *f.*; — *v.a.* travestir; parodier

Travis. *V.* **Trave**

Trawl, *s.* (*fish.*) (*line*) cordée, sangle, *f.*, aplet, *m.*; (— **net**) seine, gabare, *f.*, manet, aplet, *m.*; [— *v.n.* seiner

Trawler, *s.* seineur, *m.*

Trawling, *s.* pêche à la seine, *f.*

Tray, *s.* plateau, *m.*; (*trough*) auge, *f.* — **stand,** *s.* porte-plateau, *m.*

Treacherous, *adj.* traître, perfide

Treacherously, *adv.* perfidement, traîtreusement, en traître

Treacherousness, Treachery, *s.* trahison, perfidie, *f.*

Treacle, *s.* mélasse, *f.*; (*pharm.*) thériaque, *f.*; — *v.a.* mélasser. — **mustard,** *s.* (*plant.*) vélar, *m.* — **water,** *s.* eau de thériaque, *f.*

Tread, *v.n.* poser *or* mettre le pied (sur); (*of the foot*) se poser; (*walk*) marcher (sur); (*go*) aller, avancer; (*of birds*) s'accoupler; — *v.a.* marcher sur *or* dans, parcourir; (*press*) fouler aux pieds, fouler; (*a path*) tracer, frayer, battre; (*crush*) écraser; (*of birds*) cocher; — *s.* pas, *m.*; marche, *f.*; (*of horses*) allure, *f.*; (*horizontal part of a step*) giron, *m.*; (*of birds*) fécondation, *f.* *To — on ...'s foot* or *toes, V.* **Toe.** *To — down, — under, — under foot,* fouler aux pieds. *To — in ...'s footsteps,* marcher sur les traces de ... — **mill,** *s.* moulin de discipline, *m.* — **out,** *v.a.* fouler aux pieds, fouler; (*crush*) écraser; (*squeeze*) exprimer; (*corn*) dépiquer

Treader, *s.* personne qui foule *or* qui marche, *f.*

Treading, *s.* foulement, *m.*; pas, *m.*; marche, *f.*; (*of birds*) accouplement, *m.* — **out,** *s.* foulement, *m.*; écrasement, *m.*; (*of corn*) dépiquage, *m.*

Treadle, *s.* marche, pédale, *f.*; (*of a trap*) marchette, *f.*; (*of eggs*) germe, *m.*, chalaze, *f.*

Treason, *s.* trahison, *f.* *High —,* haute trahison, *f.*; lèse-majesté, *f.* *High — against ...,* lèse ..., *f.* (*High — against the nation,* &c., lèse-nation, *f.*, &c.)

Treasonable, *adj.* traître, de trahison; de lèse-majesté; séditieux

Treasonably, *adv.* par trahison, traîtreusement, en traître

Treasure, *s.* trésor, *m.*; trésors, *m.pl.* — **house,** *s.* trésorerie, *f.*, trésor, *m.* — **trove,** *s.* découverte d'un trésor, trouvaille, *f.*, trésor, *m.*

Treasure, — **up,** *v.a.* amasser, accumuler; conserver précieusement

Treasurer, *s.* trésorier, *m.*, -ière, *f.*; (*cashier*) caissier, *m.*, -ière, *f.*; (*bursar*) économe, *m.*

Treasurership, *s.* charge de trésorier, *f.*

Treasuress, *s.* trésorière, *f.*; (*cashier*) caissière, *f.*

Treasury, *s.* trésor, *m.*; trésorerie, *f.*; caisse, *f.*; (*government office*) ministère des finances, *m.* *First lord of the —,* président du conseil des ministres, *m.*

Treat, *s.* régal, *m.*; (*dinner*) festin, banquet, *m.*; (*pleasure*) plaisir, *m.*, fête, *f.*; — *v.a.n.* traiter; (*behave*) traiter, &c. (*V.* **Deal,** *v.n.*); (*regale*) régaler ('*with*,' '*to*,' de); payer à boire; (*discourse*) traiter ('*of*,' de), disserter (sur); (*negotiate*) traiter ('*with*,' avec). *To — a person with* or *to ...,* régaler quelqu'un de ...; (*pay*) payer ... à quelqu'un; (*present with*) faire cadeau de ... à quelqu'un. *To stand —,* régaler; payer à boire, payer une tournée

Treater, *s.* dissertateur, *m.*, -trice, *f.*; négociateur, *m.*, -trice, *f.*; (*at table*) amphitryon, *m.*

Treatise, *s.* traité, *m.*

Treatment, *s.* traitement, *m*; (*behaviour*) traitement, *m.*, manière d'agir, *f.*

Treaty, *s.* traité, *m.*, convention, *f.*; négociation, *f.*; (*bargain*) marché, *m.* *By private —,* (*of sales*) à l'amiable. *In —,* en négociation; en pourparler

Treble, *adj.* triple; (*of sound*) aigu; (*mus.*) de dessus; — *s.* triple, *m.*; (*mus.*) dessus, *m.*; — *v.a.n.* tripler. *Shrill —,* fausset, *m.*, voix de fausset, *f.*; voix de tête, *f.*

Trebleness, *s.* triplicité, *f.*

Trebling, *s.* triplement, *m.*

Trebly, *adv.* triplement, trois fois

Tree, *s.* arbre, *m.*; (*cross*) croix, *f.*; (*of saddles*) pontet, *m.*; (*for boots*) embauchoir, *m.*; — *v.a.* faire grimper sur un arbre; prendre dans l'arbre; — *v.n.* se réfugier sur un arbre; se percher. *To be up a —,* (*fig.*) *V.* **Off** (*To be badly*). — **bug,** *s.* punaise des bois, *f.* — **fern,** *s.* fougère en arbre, *f.* — **frog, -toad,** *s.* rainette, *f.* — **germander,** *s.* germandrée en arbre, *f.* — **ivy,** *s.* lierre grimpant, *m.* — **less,** *adj.* sans arbres. — **like,** *adj.* dendroïde. — **lily,** *s.* vellosie, vellozie, *f.* — **mallow,** *s.* lavatère arborée, *f.* — **nail,** *s.* (*tech.*) cheville, *f.*; (*nav.*) gournable, *m.* — **snake,** *s.* dendrophide, *m.* — **sparrow,** *s.* moineau des bois, friquet, hambouvreux, *m.*

Trefoil, *s.* trèfle, *m.*; — *adj.* tréflé

Trefoiled, *adj.* tréflé

Treillage, *s.* treillage, *m.*
Trellis, *s.* treillis, *m.*; treillage, *m.*; (*of a cage*) barreaux, *m.pl.*; (*blind*) jalousie, *f.*; — *v.a.* treillisser; treillager. — **maker,** *s.* treillageur, *m.*
Tremble, *v.n.* trembler ('*with,*' de); (*of sound*) trembloter; — *s.* tremblement, *m.* *To — in every limb, to — all over,* trembler de tous ses membres *or* de tout son corps
Trembler, *s.* trembleur, *m.*, -euse, *f.*
Trembling, *s.* tremblement, *m.*; (*of sound*) tremblotement, *m.*; — *adj.* tremblant; (*of sound*) tremblotant. — *poplar,* tremble, *m.*
Tremblingly, *adv.* en tremblant; (*of sound*) en tremblotant
Tremendous, *adj.* terrible, effroyable, épouvantable; redoutable, formidable; effrayant
Tremendously, *adv.* terriblement
Tremendousness, *s.* nature terrible *or* formidable *or* effrayante, *f.*
Tremolite, *s.* trémolite, *f.*
Tremolo, *s.* tremolo, *m.*
Tremor, *s.* tremblement, *m.*; tremblotement, *m.*; (*med.*) tremblement, frémissement, *m.*
Tremulous, *adj.* tremblant, frémissant, tremblotant; vacillant; (*of the voice*) chevrotant. — *poplar,* tremble, *m.*
Tremulously, *adv.* en tremblant; en tremblotant; timidement; (*mus.*) en chevrotant
Tremulousness, *s.* tremblement, *m.*; tremblotement, *m.*; vacillation, *f.*; (*of the voice*) chevrotement, *m.*
Trenail, *s. V.* **Tree-nail**
Trench, *v.a.* creuser; (*furrow*) sillonner; (*cut*) couper, trancher; (*fort.*) retrancher; — *v.n.* — **on,** empiéter sur, entreprendre sur, envahir; — *s.* tranchée, *f.*, fossé, *m.*; (*small*) rigole, *f.*; (*fort.*) tranchée, *f.*
Trenchant, *adj.* tranchant
Trencher, *s.* tranchoir, tailloir, *m.*; assiette, *f.*; (*table*) table, *f.* — **friend,** *s.* ami de table, *m.*, parasite, pique-assiette, *m.f.* — **man,** *s.* mangeur, *m.*, (*good — man*) grand *or* fort mangeur, *m.*
Trenching-plough, *s* charrue à effondrer, *f.*
Trend, *v.n.* se diriger; (*extend*) s'étendre; (*bend*) se courber. — **apart,** dévier (de), différer (de)
Trending, *s.* direction, *f.*
Trendle, *s. V.* **Trundle**
Trente. — **et quarante,** *s.* trente et quarante, *m.* — **-et-un,** *s.* trente-et-un, *m.*
Trepan, *s.* trépan, *m.*; — *v.a.* (*surg.*) trépaner; (*fig.*) *V.* **Trapan**
Trepang, *s.* trépang, *m.*, bêche de mer, *f.*
Trepanning, *s.* (*surg.*) trépanation, *f.*, trépan, *m.*
Trephine, *s.* tréphine, *f.*, trépan, *m*; — *v.a.* trépaner
Trephining, *s.* trépanation, *f.*, trépan, *m.*
Trepidation, *s.* trépidation, *f.*, tremblement, *m.*; vibration, *f.*; terreur, *f.*, effroi, *m.*
Trespass, *v.n.* (*intrude*) abuser (de); (*encroach*) empiéter (sur); (*of land*) violer la propriété, s'introduire *or* entrer sans droit; marauder; (*to sin*) pécher. — **against,** offenser; (*infringe*) violer, enfreindre
Trespass, *s.* violation de propriété, *f.*; délit, *m.*; injure, *f.*; (*sin*) offense, *f.*, péché, *m.* *Forgive us our —es as we forgive them that — against us,* pardonnez-nous nos offenses comme nous pardonnons à ceux qui nous ont offensés. — **offering,** *s.* sacrifice expiatoire, *m.*
Trespasser, *s.* délinquant, *m.*, e, *f.*, personne en contravention, *f.*, intrus, *m.*; maraudeur, *m.*; (*sinner*) pécheur, *m.*, pécheresse, *f.*
Tress, *s.* tresse, *f.*; — *v.a.* tresser
Tressed, *adj.* tressé, en tresses
Tressel, Trestle, *s.* tréteau, *m.*; — **s,** *pl.* tréteaux, *m.pl.*; échelle double, *f.* — **bed,** *s.* lit de sangle, *m.* — **bridge,** *s.* pont à chevalets, *m.*
Tret, *s.* réfaction, *f.*
Triad, *s.* triade, *f.*
Trial, *s.* essai, *m.*, épreuve, *f.*; vérification, *f.*; expérience, *f.*; (*suffering*) épreuve, *f.*; (*law*) procès, *m.*; jugement, *m.*; mise en jugement, *f.*; débats, *m.pl.*; cause, *f.* *On —,* à l'essai. *On o.'s —,* en jugement. *To bring to —, to put upon o.'s —,* mettre en jugement, faire le procès à. *To move for a new —,* demander à interjeter appel. *To put to a hard —,* mettre à de rudes épreuves. *To take o.'s —,* passer en jugement, être jugé. — **trip,** *s.* voyage d'essai, *m.*
Triangle, *s.* triangle, *m.*
Triangled, *adj.* triangulé
Triangular, *adj.* triangulaire; (*adverb.*) en triangle. — *compass,* compas à trois branches, *m.*
Triangularity, *s.* triangularité, *f.*
Triangularly, *adv.* triangulairement
Triangulate, *v.a.* trianguler
Triangulation, *s.* triangulation, *f.*
Triarchy, *s.* triarchie, *f.*
Tribe, *s.* tribu, *f.*; peuplade, *f.*; race, *f.*; classe, *f.*
Tribulation, *s.* tribulation. *f.*
Tribunal, *s.* tribunal, *m.*; (*of churches*) tribune, galerie, *f.*
Tribunary, *adj.* tribunitien
Tribunate, *s.* tribunat, *m.*
Tribune, *s.* tribune, *f.*; (*pers.*) tribun, *m.*
Tribuneship, *s.* tribunat, *m.*
Tribunitial, Tribunitian, *adj.* tribunitien
Tributary, *adj. s.* tributaire. — *stream,* tributaire, affluent, *m.*
Tribute, *s.* tribut, *m.* — *money,* *s.* tribut, *m.*
Trice, *s.* instant, clin d'œil, *m.* *In a —,* en un clin d'œil
Tricennial, *adj.* tricennal
Triceps, *adj. s.* triceps. *m.*
Trichiasis, *s.* trichiasis, *m.*
Trichina, *s.* trichine, *f.*
Trichinal, *adj.* trichinal
Trichinated, *adj.* trichiné
Trichiniasis, Trichinosis, *s.* trichinose, *f.*
Trichinous, *adj.* trichineux
Trichiurus, *s.* trichiure, *m.*
Trichord, *adj.* tricorde
Trick, *s.* tour, *m.*; (*dodge*) ruse, *f.*; malice, *f.*; ficelle, *f.*; (*of children*) espièglerie, niche, *f.*; farce, *f.*; (*habit*) habitude, *f.*; tic, *m.*; (*at cards*) levée, *f.*; — *v.a.* duper; tricher; attraper, carotter; (*adorn,* — **out, up**) orner, parer; ajuster; attifer; pomponner; (*draw*) peindre, esquisser. — *of trade,* ruse de métier. *To play a —,* faire un tour *or* une farce; (*to a person*) jouer un tour (à); faire une niche (à)
Trickery, *s.* tromperie, duperie, fourberie, *f.*; tricherie, *f.*
Trickiness, *s.* adresse, *f.*; espièglerie, *f.*; astuce, *f.*; (*cheat*) fourberie, *f.*
Trickish, *adj.* finaud, espiègle, astucieux, trompeur, fourbe; captieux, subtil
Trickishness. *V.* **Trickiness**
Trickle, *v.n.* — **down,** ('*from,*' de) couler, ruisseler, dégoutter. *Tears —d down his* (*or her*) *cheeks,* des larmes coulaient le long de ses joues
Trickling, *s.* écoulement, *m.*; murmure, *m.*
Trickster, *s.* farceur, *m.*, -euse, *f.*; mauvais plaisant, *m.*; (*cheat*) trompeur, *m.*, -euse, *f.*, fourbe, *m.f.*; tricheur, *m.*, -euse, *f.*
Tricksy, *adj.* adroit, habile; (*pretty*) joli; (*lively*) vif
Tricktrack, *s.* trictrac, *m.*
Tricky, *adj* *V.* **Trickish**
Tricolour, *s.* drapeau tricolore, *m.*
Tricoloured, *adj.* tricolore
Tricorn, *adj* tricorne
Tricycle, *s.* tricycle, *m.*
Trident, *s.* trident, *m.*
Tridentate, -d, Tridented, *adj.* tridenté
Tridentine, *adj.* tridentin
Tried, *adj.* éprouvé
Triennial, *adj.* triennal
Trienniality, *s.* triennalité, *f.*
Triennially, *adv.* tous les trois ans
Triennium, *s.* triennat, *m.*
Trier, *s.* expérimentateur, *m.*; essayeur, *m.*; ajusteur, *m.*; examinateur, *m.*; expert, *m.*; (*test*) épreuve, pierre de touche, *f.*
Trifid, *adj.* trifide
Trifle, *s.* bagatelle, *f.*, rien, *m.*; vétille, petite

chose, petite affaire, *f.*; (*small quantity, small degree*) idée, *f.*, soupçon, peu, *m*; (*cake*) charlotte russe, *f.*; — *v.a.n.* s'amuser à des riens, niaiser, baguenauder; (*play*) jouer, folâtrer, badiner. *To give him a* —, lui donner quelque chose pour lui. — **away,** gaspiller, perdre. — **with,** se jouer de, se moquer de; (*play*) jouer avec, plaisanter avec; (*amuse*) amuser

Trifler, *s.* personne légère *or* frivole, *f.*; (*lounger*) lanternier, baguenaudier, *m.*; (*playful person*) badin, *m.*, e, *f.*

Trifling, *adj.* insignifiant; peu important; léger; minime; (*a trifling matter*) peu de chose; (*frivolous*) léger, frivole; (*of debts*) criard; — *s.* frivolité, légèreté, *f.*; (*lounging*) baguenauderie, flânerie, *f.*; (*play*) badinage, *m.*, plaisanterie, *f.*

Triflingly, *adv.* légèrement; en badinant

Triflingness. *V.* **Insignificance**

Trifloral, Triflorous, *adj.* triflore

Trifoliate, -d, *adj.* trifolié

Triforium, *s.* travée, *f.*

Triform, Triformed, *adj.* triforme

Trig, *v.a.* — **open,** arrêter. — **up,** appuyer; [(*wheel*) enrayer

Trigamic, *adj.* trigamique

Trigamist, *s.* trigame, *m.f.*

Trigamous, *adj.* trigame

Trigamy, *s.* trigamie, *f.*

Trigger, *s.* (*of wheels*) enrayure, *f.*; (*of fire-arms*) détente, *f.* — **guard,** *s.* sous-garde, *f.*

Triglyph, *s.* triglyphe, *m.*

Trigonometric, -al, *adj.* trigonométrique

Trigonometrically, *adv.* trigonométrique- [ment

Trigonometry, *s.* trigonométrie, *f.*

Trihedral, *adj.* trièdre

Trihedron, *s.* trièdre, *m.*

Trilateral, *adj.* trilatéral; — *s.* trilatère, *m.*

Trilaterally, *adv.* trilatéralement

Trill, *s.* trille, *m.*; — *v.a.n.* triller

Trillion, *s.* quintillion, *m.*

Trilog-ic, al, -y. *V.* page 3, § 1

Trim, *adj.* propre; gentil; bien tenu; coquet; (*of sails*) bien orienté; — *s.* arrangement, *m.*; parure, *f.*, ornement, *m.*, attirail, *m.*; costume, *m.*; (*state*) état, *m.*; (*of ships*) arrimage, *m.*; (*of sails*) orientement, *m.*; — *v.a.* arranger; ajuster; bichonner; nettoyer; polir; (*adorn*) orner (de), parer (de); (*chastise*) arranger, savonner; (*garments, carriages, dishes,* &c.) garnir (de); (*hair, beard*) couper, tailler, rafraîchir; (*horses*) faire le poil à; (*trees*) émonder; (*timber*) dégauchir, dégrossir; (*lamps*) arranger; (*a boat, the hold of a ship*) arrimer; (*sails*) orienter; — *v.n.* hésiter, balancer, fluctuer; tergiverser, nager entre deux eaux, ménager la chèvre et le chou. *In good* —, en bon état; bien tenu. *Out of* —, dérangé, en [mauvais état

Trimestrial, *adj.* trimestriel

Trimeter, *s. adj.* trimètre, *m.*

Trimly, *adv.* bien, proprement, gentiment

Trimmer, *s.* garnisseur, *m.*, -euse, *f.*; décorateur, *m.*, -trice, *f.*; appareilleur, *m.*, -euse, *f.*; (*time-server*) girouette, *f.*; (*build.*) guigneau, *m.*

Trimming, *s.* arrangement, *m.*; ornement, *m.*; garniture, *f.*; agrément, *m.*; (*goods, trade*) passementerie, *f.*; (*correction*) danse, *f.*; savon, *m.* — **business, -trade,** *s.* passementerie, *f.* — **maker, -seller,** *s.* passementier, *m.* — **warehouse,** *s.* magasin de passementerie, *m.*

Trimness, *s.* propreté, *f.*; bon ordre, *m.*; bonne mine, *f.*; bon état, *m.*; coquetterie, *f.*

Trinal, Trine, *adj.* triple

Trinidadian, *adj.* de la Trinité; — *s.* habitant (*m.*, e, *f.*) de la Trinité

Trinitarian, *s. adj.* trinitaire, *m.f.*

Trinity, *s.* Trinité, *f.* — **Sunday,** *s.* dimanche de la Trinité, *m.*

Trinket, *s.* bijou, *m.*; breloque, *f.*; (*bauble*) colifichet, brimborion, *m.*

Trinomial, *s. adj.* trinôme, *s.m.*, *adj. m.f.*

Trio, *s.* trio, *m.*

Triolet, *s.* triolet, *m.*

Trip, *v.a.* (— **up**) faire tomber, renverser; donner un croc-en-jambe à, renverser d'un croc-en-jambe; supplanter; (*detect*) surprendre; (*deceive*) tromper, jouer; (*an anchor*) faire déraper; — *v.n.* trébucher; broncher; faire un faux pas; (*fall*) tomber; (*err*) se tromper; (*of the tongue*) tourner, fourcher; (*run lightly*) courir; marcher; (*travel*) faire un petit voyage, faire un tour; (*dance*) danser; — *s.* croc-en-jambe, *m.*; (*false step*) faux pas, *m.*; (*mistake*) faute, méprise, boulette, *f.*; (*journey*) petit voyage, tour, *m.*; excursion, *f.*;

Tripartite, *adj.* triparti, tripartite [partie, *f.*

Tripe, *s.* tripes, *f.pl.*; gras-double, *m.* — **de roche,** *s.* (*bot.*) tripe de roche, *f.* — **dresser, man** *or* **woman, -seller,** *s.* tripier, *m.*, -ière, *f.*, marchand (*m.*, e, *f*) d'abats. — **shop, -stall, -market,** *s.* triperie, *f.*

Tripetalous, *adj.* tripétale

Triphthong, *s.* triphthongue, *f.* [tripler

Triple, *adj. s.* triple, *adj. m.f.*, *s.m.*; — *v.a.n.*

Triplet, *s.* trio, *m.*; (*mus.*) triolet, *m.*; (*poet.*) tercet, *m.*; (*backgammon*) triplet, *m.*

Triplicate, *adj.* triple; (*math.*) triplé; — *s.* triple, *m.*; (*copy*) triplicata, *m.*; — *v.a.* tripler

Triplication, *s.* triplication, *f.*, triplement, *m.*

Triplicity, *s.* triplicité, *f.*

Tripling, *s.* triplement, *m.*

Triply, *adv.* triplement, trois fois

Tripod, *s.* trépied, *m.*

Tripoli, *s.* tripoli, *m.* [**Tripolitan**

Tripoline, *adj.* tripoléen; — *adj. s.* (*geog.*) *V.*

Tripolitan, *adj.* tripolitain, de Tripoli; — *s.* Tripolitain, *m.*, e, *f.* [général, *m.*

Tripos, *s.* (*univers.*) grand concours, concours

Tripping, *s.* croc-en-jambe, *m.*; faux pas, *m.*; pas léger, *m.*; danse, *f.*; — *adj.* léger, agile; rapide

Trippingly, *adv.* légèrement, agilement; [rapidement

Trireme, *s.* trirème, *f.*

Trisect, *v.a.* diviser en trois parties, couper [en trois

Trisection, *s.* trissection, *f.*

Trisepalous, *adj.* trisépale

Trismus, *s.* trisme, trismus, *m.*

Trisyllabic, -al, *adj.* trissyllabe, trissylla- [bique

Trisyllable, *s.* trissyllabe, *m.*

Trite, *adj.* trivial, banal, commun, vulgaire, usé, rebattu [ment

Tritely, *adv.* d'une manière banale, triviale-

Triteness, *s.* trivialité, banalité, *f.*

Triton, *s.* triton, *m.*

Tritoxide, *s.* tritoxyde, *m.*

Triturable, *adj.* triturable

Triturate, *v.a.* triturer

Trituration, *s.* trituration, *f.*

Triumph, *s.* triomphe, *m.*; — *v.n.* triompher ('*over*,' de; '*over it*,' '*over them*' [*things*], en)

Triumphal, *adj.* triomphal, de triomphe. — *arch,* arc de triomphe, *m.*

Triumphant, *adj.* triomphant, triomphateur; triomphal; de triomphe

Triumphantly, *adv.* triomphalement; en triomphe; d'un air de triomphe

Triumpher, *s.* triomphateur, *m.*, -trice, *f.*, [vainqueur, *m.*

Triumvir, *s.* triumvir, *m.*

Triumviral, *adj.* triumviral

Triumvirate, *s.* triumvirat, *m.*

Trivet, *s.* trépied, *m.*; (*of kitchen*) triangle, *m.*

Trivial, *adj.* trivial, vulgaire, commun; insignifiant, léger, sans importance

Triviality, Trivialness, *s.* trivialité, *f.*

Trivially, *adv.* trivialement

Trivium, *s.* trivium, *m.*

Troat, *v.n.* réer

Trocar, *s.* trocart, ponctionneur, *m.*

Trochaic, *s. adj.* trochaïque, *m.*

Trochar. *V.* **Trocar**

Troche, *s.* trochisque, *m.*

Trochee, *s.* trochée, *m.*

Trod, Trodden, *part. adj.* foulé, &c. (*V.* **Tread,** *v.a.n.*). *Well —,* bien battu
Troglodyte, *s.* troglodyte, *m.*; **—s,** *pl.* troglodytes, *m.pl.*
Troglodytes, *s.* troglodyte, *m.*
Trojan, *adj.* troyen, de Troie; — *s.* Troyen, *m.*, -ne, *f.*
Troll, *v.a.n.* rouler, tourner; (*fish.*) pêcher à la ligne
Trolling, *s.* pêche au brochet, *f.*
Trollop, *s.* souillon, salope, *f.*
Trolly, *s.* fardier, diable, binard, *m.*
Trombone, *s.* trombone, *m.* — **player,** *s.* tromboniste, trombone, *m.*
Trombonist, *s.* tromboniste, trombone, *m.*
Troop, *s.* troupe, *f.*; (*of cavalry*) compagnie, *f.*, corps, *m.*; — *v.n.* s'attrouper, s'assembler; marcher en corps. *A — of horse,* une compagnie de cavalerie, *f.* — **bird,** *s.* troupiale, *m.* — **horse,** *s.* cheval de troupe, *m.* — **ship,** *s.* transport, *m.*
Trooper, *s.* cavalier, soldat de cavalerie, *m.*
Troopial, *s.* troupiale, *m.*
Trope, *s.* trope, *m.*
Trophied, *adj.* orné de trophées
Trophy, *s.* trophée, *m.*; (*prize*) prix, *m.*
Tropic, *s.* tropique, *m.* — **bird,** *s.* paille-en-queue, oiseau des tropiques, *m.*
Tropical, *adj.* tropical; du tropique; des tropiques; (*of the year*) tropique; (*liter.*) figuré, métaphorique
Tropically, *adv.* figurativement
Trot, *v.n.* trotter; — *s.* trot, *m.* *At a —,* au trot. *At full —,* au grand trot. *At a slow or gentle —,* au petit trot
Troth, *s.* foi, *f.*
Trotter, *s.* trotteur, *m.*, -euse, *f.*; (*slang for 'foot'*) trottin, *m.*, patte, *f.*; (*butch.*) pied de mouton, *m.*
Trotting, *adj.* trotteur; — *s.* trot, *m.* — **match,** *s.* course au trot, *f.*
Troubadour, *s.* troubadour, *m.*
Trouble, *v.a.* ('*with,*' '*about,*' de) troubler; agiter; tourmenter; inquiéter; affliger, chagriner; importuner, déranger; ennuyer; entretenir; occuper; (*give the trouble*) donner la peine (de); embarrasser (de); charger (de); prier (de). *To — oneself,* se déranger; se donner la peine (de); s'occuper (de); s'embarrasser (de); (*be uneasy about*) s'inquiéter (de), se mettre en peine (de). — **feast,** *s.* trouble-fête, *m.f.* — **(...) for,** (*ask*) demander (à ...). *May I — you for ...* (*to pass something*)? auriez-vous la bonté de me passer ...? *May I — you with ...?* auriez-vous la bonté de vous charger de ...? *May I — you to move?* voudriez-vous me permettre de passer?
Trouble, *s.* (*disturbance*) trouble, *m.*; (*affliction*) peine, *f.*, chagrin, *m.*, affliction, *f.*, souci, *m.*; (*annoyance*) ennui, *m.*; (*labour*) peine, *f.*, mal, *m.*; (*inconvenience*) peine, *f.*, dérangement, *m.*; embarras, *m.* *All the — in the world, A world of —,* toutes les peines du monde, un mal de galère; une foule de désagréments. *To be in —,* être dans la peine. *To get into —,* (*hobble*) s'attirer des désagréments, se faire de mauvaises affaires; se mettre dans le pétrin. *To take the —,* prendre *or* se donner la peine (de); se déranger
Troubled, *adj* agité, troublé; de troubles; (*muddy*) trouble
Troubler, *s.* troubleur, *m.*, -euse, *f.*, perturbateur, *m.*, -trice, *f.*
Troublesome, *adj.* ennuyeux, incommode, fatigant; tourmentant; importun; fâcheux; (*burdensome*) à charge (à)
Troublesomely, *adv.* d'une manière ennuyeuse; avec importunité
Troublesomeness, *s.* ennui, embarras, *m.*, gêne, *f.*, désagrément, *m.*; importunité, *f.*
Troublous, *adj.* agité, troublé; orageux; de troubles
Trough, *s.* auge, *f.*, auget, *m.*; baquet, *m.*; cuve, *f.*; (*for kneading*) huche, *f.*, pétrin, *m.*; (*of the sea*) entre-deux, *m.* *Bird's —,* auget, *m.*
Trounce, *v.a.* dénoncer; (*beat*) rosser, étriller; (*whip*) fouetter
Trousering, *s.* étoffe pour pantalons, *f.*
Trousers, *s.pl.* pantalon, *m.*; (*more than one pair*) pantalons, *m.pl.* *A pair of —,* un pantalon, *m.* — **pocket,** *s.* poche de pantalon, *f.* *O.'s — pocket,* la poche de son pantalon. — **strap,** *s.* sous-pied, *m.*
Trousseau, *s.* trousseau, *m.*
Trout, *s.* truite, *f.* — **coloured,** *adj.* truité. — **fishing,** *s.* pêche aux truites, *f.* — **stream,** *s.* vivier à truites, *m.*
Troutling, *s.* truitelle, *f.*, truiton, *m.*
Trouvère, *s.* trouvère, *m.*
Trover, *s.* restitution de chose trouvée, *f.*
Trow, *v.n.* penser, croire, imaginer
Trowel, *s.* truelle, *f.*; (*for gardens*) déplantoir, *m.* —**ful,** *s.* truellée, *f.*
Trowsers. *V.* **Trousers**
Troy, *s.* troy, *m.* — **weight,** *s.* troy, *m.*
Truant, *adj. s.* fainéant, paresseux, flâneur, vagabond; — *v.n.* faire le fainéant, fainéanter, flâner, vagabonder; s'absenter. *To play —,* faire l'école buissonnière
Truantly, *adv.* en fainéant, en paresseux, en flâneur, en vagabond
Truantship, *s.* fainéantise, paresse, flânerie, *f.*, vagabondage, *m.*
Truce, *s.* trêve, *f.* *A — to,* trêve de. —**less,** *adj.* sans trêve
Truck, *v.a.n.* troquer; — *s.* (*barter*) troc, *m.*; (*com.*) payement en marchandises, troc, *m.*; (*carriage*) camion, *m.*; (*hand —*) voiture à bras, *f.*; brouette, *f.*; (*build.*) binard, *m.*; (*wheel*) roue de bois, *f.*; (*artil.*) roue, *f.*; (*rail.*) plate-forme, *f.*; traîneau, *m.*; wagon, *m.*; truc, truck, *m.*; (*nav.*) pomme, *f.* — **system,** *s.* troc, *m.*
Truckage, *s.* troc, trafic, *m.*
Trucker, *s.* troqueur, traficant, *m.*
Truckle, *s.* roulette, *f.*; — *v.n.* se soumettre (à), céder (à); (*crouch,* '*to,*' devant) ramper, s'abaisser, s'humilier; faire le chien couchant *or* le plat valet. — **bed,** *s.* grabat, *m.*, roulette, *f.*
Truckling, *s.* soumission, *f.*; abaissement, *m.*, humiliation, *f.*
Truculenc-e, y, *s.* férocité, brutalité, cruauté, *f.*
Truculent, *adj.* féroce, farouche, brutal, cruel, truculent
Truculently, *adv.* avec férocité, brutalement, cruellement
Trudge, *v.n.* aller à pied, faire route à pied, cheminer; marcher péniblement, aller clopin-clopant, se traîner
True, *adj.* vrai; véritable; sincère, fidèle; honnête, loyal; exact, conforme; juste; direct, droit; — *int.* c'est vrai! c'est juste! *Out of —,* qui porte à faux; gauchi. — **born,** *adj.* vrai, véritable. — **bred,** *adj.* de bonne race, de race; véritable, vrai. — **hearted,** *adj.* sincère. — **heartedness,** *s.* sincérité, *f.* — **love,** *s* bien-aimé, *m.*, e, *f.*; (*bot.*) parisette, *f.* — **love** *or* **lover's knot,** *s.* lacs d'amour, *m.* — **penny,** *s.* honnête garçon, *m.*
Trueness, *s.* vérité, sincérité, franchise, *f.*; fidélité, *f.*; exactitude, *f.*
Truffle, *s.* truffe, *f.*; — *v.a.* truffer. — **bed, -ground,** *s.* truffière, *f.* — **dog -pig,** *s.* truffier, *m.*
Truffled, *adj.* truffé; aux truffes
Truism, *s.* vérité banale, *f.*, truisme, *m.*
Trull, *s.* fille, coureuse, catin, *f.*
Truly, *adv.* vraiment; véritablement; réellement; ma foi; sincèrement; fidèlement; honnêtement, loyalement; exactement. *V.* **Yours**
Trump, *s.* trompe, trompette, *f.*; (*at cards*) atout, *m.*; (*pers.*) brave garçon, brave cœur, bon enfant, *m.*; — *v.a.* (*at cards*) couper; — *v.n.* jouer atout. — **card,** *s.* atout, *m.*; retourne, *f.* — **over,** *v.a.n.* surcouper. — **up,** *v.a.* inventer, controuver, forger
Trumpery, *s.* faux brillant, *m.*; brillantes fanfreluches, *f.pl.*; (*rubbish*) drogue, friperie, camelote, *f.*; (*deception, nonsense*) farce, blague, *f.*; — *adj.* faux; sans valeur; de camelote; mauvais, méchant, pitoyable, mes-

quin, ridicule; insignifiant; inutile. — *thing,* drogue, *f.*; farce, blague, *f.*
Trumpet, *s.* trompette, trompe, *f.*; (*pers.*) trompette, *m.*; (*praiser*) prôneur, *m.*; (*nav.*) porte-voix, *m.*; — *v.a.* trompeter, trompetter, publier à son de trompe; publier; proclamer; — *v.n.* (*of elephants*) barrir. — **blast, -call,** *s.* coup de trompette, *m.* — **fish,** *s.* centrisque bécasse, *m.*, bécasse de mer, *f.* — **flower,** *s.* bignone, *f.* — **major,** *s.* trompette-major, *m.* — **shaped,** *adj.* en trompette; (*bot.*) tubiforme. — **shell,** *s.* trompette, *f.*, buccin, *m.* — **tongued,** *adj.* à langue de trompette, à voix de Stentor. — **tree,** *s.* cécropie, *f.*
Trumpeter, *s.* trompette, *m.*; (*fig.*) trompette, *f.*; (*bird*) oiseau-trompette, agami, *m.*
Truncate, *v.a.* tronquer, mutiler
Truncating, Truncation, *s.* tronquement, *m.*; mutilation, *f.*; (*place*) troncature, *f.*
Truncheon, *s.* bâton, *m.*
Trundle, *v.a.* rouler, faire rouler, faire aller; — *s.* roulette, *f.*; (*low cart*) camion, *m.*; (*of a mill*) lanterne, *f.*
Trunk, *s.* tronc, *m.*; (*box*) malle, *f.*; coffre, *m.*; (*tube*) sarbacane, *f.*; (*of elephants, insects*) trompe, *f.*; (*anat., arch.*) tronc, *m.*; (*sculp., paint.*) torse, *m.* — **fish,** *s.* coffre, *m.* — **light,** *s.* abat-jour, *m.* — **line, -road,** *s.* grande ligne, ligne principale, *f.* — **maker,** [*s.* coffretier, *m.*
Trunnion, *s.* tourillon, *m.*
Truss, *s.* trousse, *f.*; (*of hay, straw*) botte, *f.*; (*package*) balle, *f.*, paquet, *m.*; (*surg.*) bandage herniaire, bandage, brayer, *m.*; (*carp.*) ferme, *f.*; (*of bridges,* &c.) travée, *f.*; (*bot.*) touffe, *f.*; (*nav.*) drosse, *f.*; — *v.a.* empaqueter; (*tie*) lier, attacher; (*hay, straw*) botteler; (*fowls*) trousser. — **maker,** *s.* bandagiste *or* chirurgien herniaire, bandagiste, *m.*
Trussel. *V.* **Trestle**
Trusser, *s.* botteleur, *m.*
Trussing, *s.* (*of hay, straw*) bottelage, *m.*
Trust, *v.a.n.* (*rely on*) se fier à; avoir confiance en; s'en rapporter à; compter sur; (*intrust*) confier (à); (*venture*) aventurer, risquer, hasarder; (*believe*) croire; (*give credit*) faire crédit à ('*for,*' de); (*expect*) espérer, s'attendre (à); se flatter; aimer à croire. *I hope and —,* j'espère bien. *He is not to be —ed,* on ne peut pas se fier *or* s'en rapporter à lui; il est sujet à caution
Trust, *s.* confiance, *f.*; (*hope*) espérance, *f.*; (*deposit*) dépôt, *m.*; (*office*) charge, *f.*; (*charge*) garde, *f.*; mandat, *m.*; (*secret*) confidence, *f.*, secret, *m.*; (*situation*) place de confiance, *f.*; (*turnpike —*) administration (des routes), *f.*; (*com.*) crédit, *m.*; (*law*) fidéicommis, *m.* *On or upon —,* de confiance; sur parole; (*not for cash*) à crédit. *To hold in —,* avoir *or* garder en dépôt; (*law*) tenir par fidéicommis. — **deed,** *s.* acte fiduciaire, *m.* —**ful,** *adj.* *V.* **Trusty.** — **worthy,** *adj.* digne de confiance; digne de foi; (*of news,* &c.) exact
Trusted, *adj.* intime
Trustee, *s.* dépositaire, *m.f.*; commissaire, *m.*; administrateur, *m.*, -trice, *f.*; (*law*) curateur, *m.*, -trice, *f.*; (*of orphans*) tuteur, *m.*, -trice, *f.* *Board of —s,* conseil d'administration, *m.*; conseil de surveillance, *m.* *In the hands of —s,* en régie
Trusteeship, *s.* commissariat, *m.*; administration, *f.*; (*law*) curatelle, *f.*; (*of orphans*) tutelle, *f.*
Truster, *s.* personne qui confie, *f.*; personne qui fait crédit, *f.* [loyalement
Trustily, *adv.* fidèlement; honnêtement,
Trustiness, *s.* fidélité, *f.*; honnêteté, probité,
Trustingly, *adv.* avec confiance [loyauté, *f.*
Trusty, *adj.* fidèle; sûr; honnête, loyal; de confiance
Truth, *s.* vérité, *f.*; vrai, *m.* *In —!* en vérité! vraiment! à vrai dire. *Some —,* du vrai. *To speak* or *tell the —,* dire la vérité; à vrai dire. —**ful,** *adj.* vrai, véridique. —**fully,** *adv.* avec vérité, véridiquement. —**fulness,** *s.* véracité, *f.*; vérité, *f.* —**less,** *adj.* faux; déloyal
Try, *v.a.n.* essayer; tenter, entreprendre; (*test*) éprouver, mettre à l'épreuve; (*experience*) éprouver, faire l'expérience de; (*an experiment*) faire (une expérience); (*sound*) sonder; tâter; (*endeavour*) essayer (de), tâcher (de), s'efforcer (de), chercher (à); (*see*) voir; (*tire*) fatiguer; (*shake*) secouer; (*purify*) purifier; épurer; (*weights, measures*) vérifier, contrôler; (*metals*) essayer; affiner; (*law*) mettre en jugement; juger. — **after, for,** tâcher d'obtenir; concourir pour. — **hard,** s'efforcer (de). — **on,** (*clothes*) essayer. *To — on with,* chercher à mettre dedans. — **sail,** *s.* voile de senau, *f.*
Trying, *adj.* critique, difficile; fatigant; pénible; vexant; (*severe*) dur à passer, dur, rude; rigoureux; cruel. — **plane,** *s.* varlope, *f.*
Trysting. — **day,** *s.* jour d'assemblée, jour de réunion, *m.* — **place,** *s.* rendez-vous, *m.*
Tub, *s.* cuve, *f.*, cuvier, cuveau, *m.*; baquet, *m.*; (*cask*) tonneau, baril, *m.*; (*Diogenes'*) tonneau, *m.*; (*for plants*) caisse, *f.*; (*bad or old ship*) sabot, *m.*, barcasse, *f.*; — *v.a.* encuver; (*hort.*) encaisser; (*mines*) cuveler. —**ful,** *s.* cuvée, *f.*
Tubbing, *s.* encuvage, encuvement, *m.*; (*hort.*) encaissage, *m.*; (*of mines*) cuvelage, cuvellement, *m.*
Tube, *s.* tube, *m.*; tuyau, *m.*; (*of a cannon*) volée, *f.*, (*inner — of ditto*) âme, *f.*; (*for firing cannon*) étoupille (fulminante), *f.*; (*anat., bot.*) conduit, vaisseau, canal, *m.*; — *v.a.* tuber
Tuber, *s.* (*anat.*) tubérosité, *f.*; (*bot.*) tuber-[cule, *m.*
Tubercle, *s.* tubercule, *m.*
Tubercled, *adj.* tuberculé; tuberculeux
Tubercular, *adj.* tuberculeux
Tuberculate, -d, *adj.* tuberculé
Tuberculization, *s.* tuberculisation, *f.*
Tuberculize, *v.a.* tuberculiser
Tuberculous, *adj.* tuberculeux
Tuberose, *s.* tubéreuse, *f.*
Tuberosity, *s.* tubérosité, *f.*
Tuberous, *adj.* tubéreux
Tubiform, *adj.* tubiforme
Tubular, *adj.* tubulaire. — *bridge,* pont tubulaire, pont-tube, *m.*
Tubulate, Tubulated, *adj.* tubulé
Tubule, *s.* tubule, *m.*
Tubulous, *adj.* tubuleux
Tuck, *s.* pli, rempli, *m.*; (*sword*) estoc, *m.*; — *v.a.* relever, retrousser. — **down,** *v.a.* (*swallow*) avaler, gober. — **in,** *v.a.* border, rentrer; (*cover*) envelopper, couvrir; (*swallow*) avaler, gober. — **out,** *s.* bombance, *f.*, régal, gueuleton, *m.* — **up,** *v.a.* relever, retrousser; border; (*fold*) remplier [guimpe, *f.*
Tucker, *s.* collerette, *f.*; chemisette, *f.*;
Tuesday, *s.* mardi, *m.*
Tufa, Tuff, *s.* tuf, tuffeau, *m.*
Tufaceous, *adj.* tufacé, tufier
Tuft, *s.* (*of grass, hair,* &c.) touffe, *f.*; (*of trees, flowers*) bouquet, *m.*; (*of silk, wool,* &c.) houppe, *f.*; (*of birds*) huppe, aigrette, *f.*; (*mil.*) pompon, *m.* — **hunter,** *s.* plat valet (qui se faufile avec les gens huppés), parasite, courtisan, *m.* — **hunting,** *s.* courtisanerie, *f.*, parasitisme, *m.*
Tufted, *adj.* touffu; en touffe; (*of birds*) huppé
Tug, *v.a.n.* tirer, tirailler; (*pluck*) arracher; (*tow*) remorquer; (*struggle*) lutter; (*worry*) houspiller; — *s.* tiraillement, *m.*; effort, *m.*; secousse, *f.*; (*struggle*) lutte, *f.*; (*timber-carriage*) fardier, diable, binard, *m.*; (*boat, rail.*) remorqueur, *m.* *To give a —,* faire un effort, donner un coup de collier; tirer. — **boat,** *s.* bateau remorqueur, *m.*
Tuition, *s.* instruction, *f.*, enseignement, *m.*, éducation, *f.*, leçons, *f.pl.*; direction, *f.*; (*price of schooling*) pension, *f.*, prix de la pension, *m.*

Tulip, *s.* tulipe, *f.* — **tree,** *s.* tulipier, *m.* — **wood,** *s.* bois de rose, *m.*
Tulipist, *s.* tulipier, *m.*
Tulle, *s.* tulle, *m.* — **maker,** *s.* tulliste, *m.f.* — **making,** *s.* tullerie, *f.*
Tumble, *v.n.a.* (*fall*) tomber; (*roll*) rouler, dégringoler, culbuter; (*of things*) tomber, crouler, s'écrouler; (*jump*) sauter; (*throw*) jeter; (*throw oneself*) se jeter; (*turn over*) tourner, retourner; se tourner, se retourner, s'agiter; (*disturb*) bouleverser, bousculer, déranger; (*rumple*) chiffonner. — **down,** tomber par terre, tomber, dégringoler, culbuter; (*things*) tomber, s'écrouler; (*throw down*) renverser; faire dégringoler, faire culbuter
Tumble, *s.* chute, dégringolade, culbute, *f.* *To have* (or *get*) *a* —, faire une chute, tomber, dégringoler, faire la culbute
Tumbledown, *adj.* croulant, délabré, caduc, en ruine, qui menace ruine
Tumble-dung, *s.* (— **beetle**) bousier, *m.*
Tumbler, *s.* sauteur, *m.*, -euse, *f.*; bateleur, saltimbanque, *m.*; (— *pigeon*) pigeon culbutant, culbutant, *m.*; (*dog*) basset, *m.*; (*toy*) culbuteur, ramponeau, sorcier, *m.*; (*glass*) grand verre, verre, *m.*; (*of a lock*) étoquereau, *m.*; (*in fire-arms*) noix, *f.* —**ful,** *s.* grand verre plein, grand verre, *m.*, rasade, *f.*
Tumbrel, Tumbril, *s.* tombereau, *m.*; (*mil.*) caisson, fourgon, *m.*
Tumefaction, *s.* tuméfaction, *f.*
Tumefy, *v.a.* tuméfier, enfler; — *v.n.* se tuméfier, s'enfler
Tumid, *adj.* enflé, gonflé; (*protuberant*) renflé; (*bombastic*) boursouflé, ampoulé. —**ly,** *adv.* avec enflure. —**ity,** —**ness,** *s.* enflure, *f.*, gonflement, *m.*; (*bombast*) boursouflure, emphase, *f.*
Tumour, *s.* tumeur, *f.*
Tump, *s.* motte, butte, *f.*, monticule, *m.*; — *v.a.* butter, chausser
Tumult, *s.* tumulte, *m.*
Tumultuarily, *adv.* tumultuairement
Tumultuary, *adj.* tumultuaire; inquiet, agité
Tumultuous, *adj.* tumultueux; agité; turbulent
Tumultuously, *adv.* tumultueusement, en tumulte
Tumultuousness, *s.* turbulence, *f.*; désordre, *m.*, confusion, *f.*
Tumulus, *s.* tumulus, *m.*
Tun, *s.* tonne, *f.*, tonneau, *m.*; (*meas.*) foudre, *m.*; (*drunkard*) sac à vin, ivrogne, *m.*; — *v.a.* entonner. — **bellied,** *adj.* pansu, ventru
Tunable, *adj.* harmonieux, mélodieux; musical; (*mus.*) accordable
Tunableness, *s.* harmonie, mélodie, *f.*; musique, *f.*; accord, *m.*
Tunably, *adv.* harmonieusement, mélodieusement; (*mus.*) d'accord
Tune, *s.* air, *m.*; son, *m.*; ton, accord, *m.*; harmonie, *f.*; humeur, *f.*; veine, *f.*; — *v.a.* accorder, mettre d'accord; (*sing*) chanter; (*attune*) *V.* **Attune.** *In* —, d'accord. *Out of* —, désaccordé, discord, faux. *To be out of* —, être désaccordé *or* discord, être faux, n'être pas d'accord; (*pers.*) *V.* **Sorts** (*To be out of* —). *To change o.'s* —, (*fig.*) changer de gamme. *To put out of* —, désaccorder, fausser; (*pers.*) *V.* **Sorts.** *To play* or *sing in* —, *out of* —, jouer *or* chanter juste, faux. *To the* — *of*, (*fig.*) au montant de, jusqu'à (*or* pour) la somme de, jusqu'au chiffre de, d'une valeur de; (*at the rate of*) au taux de, à raison de. —**ful,** *adj.* harmonieux, mélodieux. —**less,** *adj.* discordant; (*dumb*) muet
Tuner, *s.* accordeur, *m.*, -euse, *f.*
Tunic, Tunicle, *s.* tunique, *f.*
Tungsten, *s.* tungstène, *m.*
Tuning, *s.* accord, accordage, *m.* —**fork,** *s.* diapason, *m.* —**hammer, -key,** *s.* clé d'accordeur, clé, *f.*, accordoir, *m.*
Tunisian, *s.* Tunisien, *m.*, -ne, *f.*; — *adj.* tunisien, de Tunis
Tunnage. *V.* **Tonnage**
Tunnel, *s.* tunnel, *m.*; (*of mines*) souterrain, *m.*; (*net*) tonnelle, *f.*; (*funnel*) *V.* **Funnel;** — *v.a.* percer. — **net,** *s.* tonnelle, *f.* — **pit, -shaft,** *s.* puits de tunnel *or* de souterrain, *m.*
Tunnelling, *s.* construction de tunnels *or* de souterrains, *f.*; percement, *m.*; tunnels, *m.pl.*; souterrains, *m.pl.*
Tunning, *s.* entonnage, entonnement, *m.*
Tunny, *s.* thon, *m.*
Tup, *s.* bélier, *m.*; — *v.a.* (*cover*) couvrir, flécher; — *v.n.* (*butt*) cosser; (*cover*) lutter
Turanian, *s. adj.* Turanien, *m.*, -ne, *f.*
Turban, *s.* turban, *m.*
Turbaned, *adj.* en turban, enturbané
Turbid, *adj.* trouble, bourbeux. —**ly,** *adv.* dans un état trouble *or* bourbeux. —**ness,** *s.* état trouble, état bourbeux, *m.*
Turbinated, *adj.* turbiné, en cône, en toupie. — *bone*, cornet du nez, cornet, *m.*
Turbine, *s.* turbine, *f.*
Turbit, *s.* pigeon à bec court, *m.*
Turbo, *s.* sabot, *m.*
Turbot, *s.* turbot, *m.* *Young* —, turbotin, *m.* —**kettle,** *s.* turbotière, *f.*
Turbulence, *s.* turbulence, *f.*; trouble, désordre, tumulte, *m.*, agitation, *f.*
Turbulent, *adj.* turbulent; agité, tumultueux
Turbulently, *adv.* turbulemment, avec turbulence, tumultueusement, en tumulte
Turcism, *s.* turcisme, *m.*
Turco, *s.* turco, *m.*; — *adj.* (*in compounds*) turco-...
Turcoman, *s. adj.* Turcoman, *m.*, e, *f.*
Turd, *s.* merde, *f.*; étron, *m.*
Turdus, *s.* (*bird*) turde, *m.*
Tureen, *s.* (*for soup*) soupière, *f.*; (*for sauce*) saucière, *f.*; (*for stew*) plat creux, plat à ragoût, *m.*
Turf, *s.* (*grass*) gazon, *m.*; (*lawn*) pelouse, *f.*; (*fuel*) tourbe, *f.*; (*piece for ditto*) motte à brûler, motte, *f.*; (*race-ground*) hippodrome, turf, *m.*; (*racing*) courses, *f.pl.*, turf, *m.*; — *v.a.* gazonner. *To be on the* —, (*run horses*) faire courir. — **beetle,** *s.* batte, *f.* — **knife, -spade,** *s.* tranche-gazon, coupe-gazon, lève-gazon, *m.*, écobue, écobueuse, *f.* — **less,** *adj.* sans gazon. — **moss, -pit,** *s.* tourbière, *f.*
Turfiness, *s.* abondance de gazon, *f.*; nature du gazon, *f.*; (*of peat*) état tourbeux, *m.*; nature de la tourbe, *f.*
Turfing, *s.* gazonnement, *m.* — **iron, -spade,** [*s. V.* **Turf-knife**
Turfite, *s.* amateur du turf, *m.*, turfiste, *m.f.*; (*blackleg*) escroc, filou, *m.*
Turfy, *adj.* gazonneux; (*turfed over*) gazonné; [(*peaty*) tourbeux
Turgescence, *s.* turgescence, *f.*, gonflement, *m.*, enflure, *f.*; (*bombast*) boursouflure, emphase, *f.*
Turgescent, *adj.* turgescent
Turgid, *adj.* turgide, enflé, gonflé; (*bombastic*) boursouflé, ampoulé. —**ly,** *adv.* avec enflure. —**ity,** —**ness,** *s.* turgidité, enflure, *f.*, gonflement, *m.*; (*bombast*) boursouflure, emphase, *f.*
Turinese, *s. adj.* Turinois, *m.*, e, *f.*
Turk, *s.* Turc, *m.*; (*shrew*) mégère, *f.*; (*beetle*) turc, *m.* *The Grand* —, le Grand-Turc, *m.* —**'s-cap,** *s.* (*bot.*) mélocacte, *m.* —**'s-cap lily,** *s.* (*bot.*) martagon, *m.* —**'s-head,** *s.* (*broom*) tête-de-loup, *f.*; (*bot.*) mélocacte, *m.*
Turkey, *s.* dindon, *m.*, dinde, *f.*; (*cook.*) dinde, *m.*; (*country*) la Turquie, *f.* *Young* —, dindonneau, poulet d'Inde, *m.* — **carpet,** *s.* tapis de Turquie, *m.* — **cock,** *s.* dindon, coq d'Inde, *m.* *As red as a* — *cock*, rouge comme un coq. — **hen,** *s.* dinde, poule d'Inde, *f.* — **merchant,** *s.* négociant faisant le commerce avec la Turquie, *m.* — **poult,** *s.* dindonneau, poulet d'Inde, *m.* — **red,** *s.* rouge d'Andrinople, *m.* —**'s egg,** *s.* œuf de dinde, *m.*
Turkish, *adj.* turc (*m.*, turque, *f.*), de Turquie; — *s.* (*language*) le turc, *m.*, la langue turque, *f.* — *bath*, bain turc, *m.*
Turkism, *s.* turcisme, *m.*
Turko ..., *V.* **Turco ...**
Turmeric, *s.* (*bot.*) curcuma, *m.*; (*dyeing*) terre-mérite, *f.*, safran des Indes, *m.* — **paper,** *s.* papier de curcuma, papier réactif, *m.*

Turmoil, *s.* trouble, tumulte, *m.*; désordre, *m.*; agitation, *f.*; inquiétude, *f.*

Turn, *v.a.* tourner; (*shift sides*) retourner; (*change*) changer; convertir (en); (*translate*) traduire (en); (*put*) mettre; (*earn*) gagner; (*make profitable*) faire profiter; (*transfer*) transférer (à), transmettre (à); (*make turn*) faire tourner; (*the brain*) faire tourner, tourner, troubler, déranger, égarer; (*the stomach*) soulever *or* barbouiller (le cœur); (*sour*) tourner, faire tourner, aigrir; (*change direction*) détourner; (*direct*) diriger *or* tourner (vers); (*revolve*) rouler, agiter; (*blunt*) émousser; (*cause to deviate*) fausser; (*prepare*) préparer; (*a scale*) faire pencher, emporter; (*print.*) bloquer; (*on a lathe*) tourner. *To be —ed thirty,* avoir passé trente ans. — **about,** retourner, tourner. — **aside,** écarter; détourner. — **away,** détourner; chasser, éloigner; (*pers.*) renvoyer; congédier. — **back,** faire retourner; renvoyer; remettre. — **down,** faire descendre; (*a collar,* &c.) rabattre, retourner; (*fold*) plier; (*a scale*) faire pencher, emporter. [*V.* **Bed.**] — **in,** tourner en dedans; remplier, rentrer. — **off,** renvoyer; chasser; (*discharge*) congédier; (*resign*) abandonner; renoncer à; (*from*) détourner (de); (*avoid*) tourner; (*from a pipe*) laisser échapper; fermer le robinet de, fermer; (*to hang, to execute*) exécuter. — **on,** lâcher; ouvrir le robinet de, ouvrir; (*the steam*) faire fonctionner (la vapeur). — **out,** tourner en dehors; (*the inside out*) retourner; (*discharge*) renvoyer; destituer; (*expel*) expulser, chasser; (*out of doors*) mettre à la porte; (*oust*) évincer, déposséder; mettre dehors; (*cattle*) mettre aux champs, mettre au vert; (*hunt*) lancer; (*work*) faire. — **over,** retourner, tourner; renverser; transférer; (*attribute*) renvoyer (à); (*hand over*) livrer; remettre; (*a book*) feuilleter, parcourir, examiner; (*reflect*) réfléchir à, ruminer, rouler (dans son esprit); (*money*) faire profiter; (*nav.*) transborder. — **over and over (again),** tourner et retourner, retourner en tous sens. — **up,** retourner, tourner; relever, lever; (*tuck up*) retrousser; (*start*) faire lever; (*nav.*) faire monter. *—ed up nose,* nez retroussé, *m.*

Turn, *v.n.* tourner; se tourner; se retourner; (*be directed*) se diriger (vers); se porter (sur), se reporter (sur), s'adresser (à); (*pass*) passer (à); (*deviate*) dévier, se détourner (de); (*alter*) se changer (en); (*become*) devenir [*— pale,* devenir pâle, pâlir; *— red,* devenir rouge, rougir; &c.]; (*make oneself*) se faire; (*have recourse*) avoir recours (à), recourir (à), s'adresser (à); (*begin*) se mettre (à); (*change conduct*) se corriger (de), revenir (de); (*keep away*) s'éloigner (de); (*fall upon*) retomber (sur); (*of milk,* &c.) tourner, s'aigrir; (*of tides*) changer. *To — to the right, to the left,* tourner (*or* prendre) à droite, à gauche. — **about,** se tourner, se retourner; tournailler. — **again,** tourner de nouveau, retourner; se retourner; (*become again*) redevenir. — **aside, away,** se tourner; se détourner (de); s'écarter (de); s'éloigner (de); abandonner (...), quitter (...). — **back,** retourner, s'en retourner, rebrousser chemin, revenir sur ses pas. — **down,** se retourner, se renverser; (*of collars,* &c.) se rabattre, se retourner; (*of scales*) trébucher; (*a street*) prendre. — **in,** se tourner en dedans; rentrer; (*go to rest*) se coucher. — **into,** se changer en. — **off,** se détourner; (*things*) tourner. — **on,** tourner sur, rouler sur; dépendre de; (*be given to*) se porter sur, se reporter sur. — **out,** se tourner en dehors; se retourner; (*well or badly*) tourner, finir; (*become*) devenir; se montrer, être; paraître; (*happen*) se trouver; arriver; (*get out*) sortir; (*deviate*) dévier; sortir; (*rise*) se lever; (*to strike work*) faire grève, se mettre en grève. — **over,** se tourner, se retourner; (*be upset*) se renverser; (*of a carriage*) verser; (*tumble*) culbuter; (*change parties*) changer de parti. — **round,** tourner; se tourner; se retourner; (*change*) changer; (*change parties*) tourner casaque. *My head —s round,* la tête me tourne. — **round and round,** tournoyer. — **up,** se relever; se retrousser; (*become*) devenir; (*occur*) survenir, arriver, se présenter; (*to be*) se trouver, être. — **upon,** *V.* — **on**

Turn, *s.* tour, *m.*; (*bend*) détour, tournant, coude, *m.*; (*change*) changement, *m.*; retour, *m.*; (*of mind, style*) tournure, *f.*; (*service*) office, service, *m.*; (*direction*) tournure, *f.*; (*form*) contour, *m.*; (*inclination*) goût, penchant, *m.*; (*purpose*) but, *m.*; (*of a scale*) trébuchement, *m.*; (*mus.*) brisée, *f.*; (*walk*) tour, *m.*; (*official round*) tournée, *f.*; (*of tides*) changement, *m.* *Good —,* bon office, service, *m.* *Ill —,* mauvais office, tour, *m.* *The — of life,* le retour de l'âge. *At every —,* à tout propos, à tout bout de champ, à tout moment, à chaque instant. *By —s, in —,* tour à tour; à tour de rôle. *In o.'s —,* à son tour. *To a —,* à point. *To have a —,* faire un tour. *To have o.'s —,* avoir son tour. *To have several —s at ...,* essayer ... à plusieurs reprises. *To take a —* (*walk, airing*), faire un tour; (*direction, of things*) prendre une tournure. *To take —s,* prendre son tour; procéder à tour de rôle; alterner; se relayer. *To serve a —,* remplir un but; faire l'affaire; être utile au besoin *or* dans l'occasion; (*a trick*) jouer un tour. *It is your —,* c'est votre tour, c'est à votre tour, c'est à vous

Turnbench, *s.* tour à pointes, *m.*

Turncap, *s.* tourne-vent, *m.*

Turncoat, *s.* transfuge, *m.*; renégat, *m.*; (*fam.*) girouette, *f.*

Turncock, *s.* fontainier, *m.*

Turner, *s.* tourneur, *m.*

Turnery, *s.* art du tourneur, *m.*; objets faits au tour, *m.pl.*

Turning, *s.* tour, *m.*; changement, *m.*; déviation, *f.*; mouvement, *m.*; (*bend*) tournant, détour, coude, *m.*; (*street*) rue, *f.*; (*of clothes*) action de retourner, *f.*; (*of milk,* &c.) aigrissement, *m.*; (*tech.: act*) tournement, tournage, *m.*, (*art*) art du tourneur, *m.*, (**—s,** *pl.*, *chips*) tournure, *f.*, tournures, *pl.* — **chisel,** *s.* plane, *f.* — **in,** *s.* (*need.*) rempli, *m.* — **lathe,** *s.* tour, *m.* — **peg, -pin,** *s.* (*of violins,* &c.) sillet, *m.* — **point,** *s.* détour, *m.*; (*fig.*) point décisif, *m.*; moment critique, *m.*

Turnip, *s.* navet, *m.*; (*old-fashioned watch*) ognon, *m.* — **cabbage,** *s.* chou-navet, chou-rave, *m.* — **cutter,** *s.* coupe-racines, *m.* — **field, -ground,** *s.* champ de navets, *m.*, navetière, *f.* — **radish,** *s.* radis, *m.* — **rooted,** *adj.* rond. — **shaped,** *adj.* en forme de navet, napiforme. — **top,** *s.* fane de navet, *f.*

Turnkey, *s.* porte-clés, guichetier, *m.*

Turn-off, *s.* détour, *m*; (*branch*) embranchement, *m.*

Turn-out, *s.* train, équipage, *m.*; gala, *m.*; (*airing*) sortie, promenade, *f.*; (*strike of workmen*) grève, *f.*; (*one on strike*) gréviste, *m.*; (*rail.*) *V.* **Siding**

Turn-over, *s.* *V.* **Overturn;** (*of money*) profit, bénéfice, *m.*; (*pastry*) chausson, *m.*; (*pers.*) apprenti (transféré à un autre maître), *m.*

Turnpike, *s.* barrière de péage, barrière, *f.* — **keeper, -man,** *s.* garde-barrière, péager, *m.* — **road,** *s.* route à barrière *or* à péage, *f.* — **toll,** *s.* droit de péage, *m.* — **trust,** *s.* *V.* **Trust**

Turnplate, *s.* plaque tournante, *f.*

Turnscrew, *s.* tournevis, *m.*

Turnsick, *s.* (*vet.*) tournis, tournoiement, *m.*

Turnsol, Turnsole, *s.* tournesol, *m.*

Turnspit, *s.* tourne-broche, *m.*

Turnstile, *s.* tourniquet, *m.*

Turnstone, *s.* tourne-pierres, *m.*

Turntable, *s.* plaque tournante, *f.*

Turn-up, *adj.* retroussé; (*folding*) pliant; (*fig.*) dédaigneux, impertinent

Turnwrest, Turnwrist, *s.* (— **plough**) tourne-oreille, *m.*, charrue tourne-oreille, *f.*

Turpentine, *s.* térébenthine, *f.* — **tree,** *s.* [térébinthe, *m.*

Turpitude, *s.* turpitude, *f.*

Turquoise, *s.* turquoise, *f.*

Turrel, *s.* tire-fond, *m.*

Turret, *s.* tourelle, *f.* — **clock,** *s.* horloge, *f.* — **shell,** *s.* turritelle, *f.* — **ship,** *s.* navire (*or* vaisseau) à tourelles, *m.*

Turreted, *adj.* garni de tourelles, à tourelles; (*her.*) châtelé; (*shaped*) en forme de tour

Turtle, *s.* (*bird*) tourterelle, *f.*; (*tortoise*) tortue, tortue de mer, *f.* — **dove,** *s.* tourterelle, *f.*, (*young ditto*) tourtereau, *m.* — **shell,** *s.* écaille de tortue, *f.* — **soup,** *s.* potage (*m.*) *or* soupe (*f.*) à la tortue. *Mock — soup,* potage à la tête de veau, *m.*, tête de veau en tortue, *f.*

Tuscan, *s.* Toscan, *m.*, e, *f.*; (*language*) le toscan, *m.*, la langue toscane, *f.*; (*straw*) *V.* **Leghorn;** — *adj.* toscan, de Toscane. — *order,* (*arch.*) ordre toscan, *m.*

Tush, *int.* bah! allons donc! taisez-vous donc; — *s.* (*horse's tooth*) crochet, *m.*, canine, *f.*

Tusk, *s.* croc, *m.*; (*of wild boars, elephants*) défense, *f.*; (*of horses*) *V.* **Tush;** (*a fish*) brosme, *m.* [crocs

Tusked, Tusky, *adj.* muni de défenses *or* de

Tussac grass, *s.* dactyle, *m.*

Tussilage, Tussilago, *s.* tussilage, *m.*

Tussle, *s.* lutte, bataille, bagarre, *f.*

Tut, *s.* globe, *m.*; — *int.* ta! — **work,** *s.* ouvrage à forfait, *m.*, entreprise, *f.*

Tutelage, *s.* tutelle, *f.*; minorité, *f.*

Tutelar, Tutelary, *adj.* tutélaire

Tutenag, *s.* toutenague, tintenague, *f.*

Tutor, *s.* précepteur, *m.*; instituteur, *m.*; maître, *m.* (*French —,* maître *or* professeur de français); (*at college*) répétiteur, préparateur, *m.*; — *v.a.* instruire, enseigner; (*correct*) corriger, reprendre; faire la leçon à; styler; (*to rule*) régenter

Tutorage, *s.* tutelle, *f.*

Tutoress. *V.* **Governess**

Tutoring, *s.* éducation, instruction, *f.*

Tutorship, *s.* préceptorat, *m.*; emploi de précepteur, *m.*; (*of schools*) fonctions de répétiteur, *f.pl.*

Tutress. *V.* **Governess**

Tutrix, *s.* tutrice, *f.*

Tutsan, *s.* millepertuis androsème, *m.*

Tutty, — **powder,** *s.* tutie, *f.*

Tuyere, *s.* tuyère, *f.*

Twaddle. *V.* **Palaver**

Twaddler, *s.* bavard, *m.*, e, *f.*, verbiageur, *m.*, -euse, *f.*, déclamateur, *m.*, -trice, *f.*, péroreur, *m.*, -euse, *f.*, radoteur, *m.*, -euse, *f.*

Twaddling, *s.* *V.* **Palaver,** *s.*

Twaite, — **shad,** *s.* finte, *f.*

Twain, *adj.* deux

Twang, *v.n.* rendre un son aigu, crier; — *v.a.* faire crier, faire sonner; — *s.* son aigu, *m.*; (*nasal —*) nasillement, *m.*; ton *or* accent nasillard, *m.*; (*taste*) mauvais goût, goût, *m.*

Tweak, *v.a.* pincer, serrer; (*pull*) tirer

Tweed, *s.* (*stuff*) tweed, *m.*

Tweezers, *s.pl.* pinces, pincettes, *f.pl.*; (*for hair*) pince-poils, épiloir, *m.*

Twelfth, *adj.* douzième; — *s.* douzième, (*part*) *m.*, (*pers.*) *m.f.*, (*mus.*) *f.*; (*of the month*) douze, *m.* *The —,* (*of sovereigns*) douze. — **cake, -night cake,** *s.* gâteau des Rois, *m.* — **day, -night, -tide,** *s.* jour des Rois, *m.* — *night king* or *queen,* roi (*m.*) *or* reine (*f.*) de la fève. *To celebrate — night,* faire *or* tirer *or* célébrer les Rois

Twelve, *adj. s.* douze (*adj. m.f.*, *s.m.*); (*of the size of books,* 12mo) in-douze (*adj. m.f.*, *s.m.*); (*elliptically, of the clock*) (*noon*) midi, *m.*, (*midnight*) minuit, *m.*; (*of o.'s age*) douze ans, *m.pl.* — *hours,* douze heures, *f.pl.* — *o'clock,* (*noon*) midi, *m.*, (*midnight*) minuit, *m.* —**mo,** *s. adj.* in-douze, *s.m.*, *adj. m.f.* — **month,** *s.* an, *m.*, année, *f.*

Twentieth, *adj. s.* vingtième; (*of the month*) vingt. *The —,* (*of sovereigns*) vingt

Twenty, *adj.* vingt. —*first,* vingt et unième; (*of the month*) vingt et un. —**fold,** *adj. adv.* vingtuple, vingt fois autant, vingt fois. *To increase —fold,* vingtupler

Twibil, *s.* hallebarde, *f.*; (*tech.*) besaiguë, *f.*

Twice, *adv.* deux fois. — *as much,* deux fois autant, le double

Twig, *s.* petite branche, branche, brindille, ramille, *f.*; baguette, *f.* *To hop the —,* (*to die*) passer *or* sauter le pas, claquer. — **rush,** *s.* cladion, *m.*

Twiggy, *adj.* plein de petites branches

Twilight, *s.* crépuscule, *m.*; (*uncertain view*) demi-jour, *m.*; — *adj.* du crépuscule; à la lueur du crépuscule; (*dark*) sombre, obscur

Twill, *v.a.* plisser; (*weave*) croiser; — *s.* étoffe croisée, *f.*, tissu croisé, croisé, *m.*

Twin, *s.* jumeau, *m.*, jumelle, *f.*; (*fig.*) frère, *m.*, sœur, *f.*; (*person resembling another*) Sosie, *m.*; —**s,** *pl.* (*astr.*) Gémeaux, *m.pl.*; — *adj.* jumeau (*m.*, jumelle, *f.*). — **born,** *adj.* jumeau; (*bot.*) double

Twine, *v.a.* enlacer, entortiller; (*twist*) retordre; (*weave*) tisser; (*encircle*) entourer; (*gird*) ceindre; — *v.n.* tourner; (*wind*) serpenter; s'enrouler; (*unite*) s'entrelacer, s'unir; — *s.* entrelacement, entortillement, *m.*; (*arch.*) entrelacs, *m.*; (*string*) ficelle, *f.*

Twinge, *v.a.* causer une douleur aiguë à; tourmenter, torturer; (*pinch*) pincer, serrer; — *v.n.* élancer; — *s.* (*of pain*) tiraillement, élancement, *m.*; tourment, remords, *m.*; (*pinch*) pincement, *m.*

Twinkle, *v.n.* scintiller, étinceler, briller; (*of the eyes*) clignoter; — *s.* *V.* **Twinkling**

Twinkling, *s.* scintillation, *f.*; (*of the eyes*) clin d'œil, *m.*; clignotement, *m.* *In the — of an eye,* en un clin d'œil

Twirl, *v.n.* tourner, tournoyer; (*pers.*) pirouetter; — *v.a.* faire tourner; faire pirouetter; (*a stick,* &c.) faire le moulinet avec, faire aller; — *s.* tournoiement, tour, *m.*, rotation, révolution, *f.*, mouvement circulaire, *m.*; pirouette, *f.*; (*twist*) enroulement, *m.* *To give a —,* faire tourner; faire le moulinet

Twist, *v.a.* tordre, retordre; (*weave*) entrelacer, enlacer; tresser; (*wool, cotton*) filer; (*insert*) entremêler; (*wind*) entortiller; enrouler; nouer; (*encircle*) entourer; (*disfigure*) défigurer, torturer; — *v.n.* s'entrelacer, s'enlacer; s'entremêler; s'entortiller; se tortiller; s'enrouler; se nouer; — *s.* tortis, *m.*; (*string*) cordon, *m.*; (*thread*) cordonnet, fil, *m.*; (*anything twisted*) tortillon, *m.*; torsade, *f.*; (*contortion*) contorsion, *f.*; tortillement, *m.*; enroulement, *m.*; repli, *m.*; natte, *f.*; (*of tobacco*) carotte, *f.*, rouleau, *m.*, andouille, *f.*; (*of a cigar*) bout tourné, bout roulé, *m.*; (*of the thigh*) plat, *m.*; (*cake, loaf*) natte, *f.*; (*arch.*) nervure, *f.*; (*prejudice*) préjugé, *m.*; (*appetite*) appétit, *m.* — *of the fork,* (*jest.*) coup de fourchette, *m.* *To give a —,* tordre

Twisted, *adj.* tordu; (*of thread, arch.*) tors. — *barrel,* canon à ruban, *m.* — *cord* or *fringe,* torsade, *f.*

Twister, *s.* tordeur, *m.*, -euse *f.*; cordier, *m.*, -ière, *f.*; (*machine*) machine à tordre, *f.*

Twisting, *s.* tordage, *m.*; tortillement, *m.*; torsion, *f.*; (*interweaving*) entrelacement, *m.* — **machine,** *s.* machine à tordre, *f.*

Twit, *v.a.* reprocher, jeter au nez; accuser; — *s.* reproche, *m.*

Twitch, *v.a.* tirer; arracher; — *v.n.* se crisper, se contracter; — *s.* *V.* **Twitching;** (*grass*) chiendent, *m.*; (*horse-twitchers*) morailles, *f.pl.*, serre-nez, *m.* — **grass,** *s.* chiendent, *m.*

Twitching, *s.* (*jerk*) secousse, saccade, *f.*; (*contraction*) contraction spasmodique, crispa-

tion, *f.*; (*pain*) tiraillement, pincement, élancement, *m.*; (*of conscience*) remords, *m.*
Twitchers, *s.pl.* (*for horses*) morailles, *f.pl.*,
Twite, *s.* linotte de montagne, *f.* [serre-nez, *m.*
Twitter, *v.n.* frémir; (*of birds*) gazouiller; — *s.* frémissement. *m.*; (*of birds*) gazouillement, *m.*
Two, *adj. s.* deux (*adj.m.f.*, *s.m.*); (*elliptically*) (*of the clock*) deux heures, *f.pl*; (*of o.'s age*) deux ans, *m.pl.*; (*in compounds*) à deux . . ., bi . . . — **cornered,** *adj.* bicorne. *A — cornered hat*, un bicorne, *m.* — **decker,** *s. V.* **Decker.** — **edged,** *adj.* à deux tranchants. —**fold,** *adj.* double; *adv.* doublement, deux fois autant, deux fois. — **footed,** *adj.* à deux pieds. — **handed,** *adj. V.* **Double-handed.** — **headed,** *adj.* à deux têtes. — **horned,** *adj.* bicorne. — **leaved,** *adj.* à deux feuilles; (*of doors*) à deux battants. — **legged,** *adj.* à deux jambes, à deux pieds, bipède. —**masted,** *adj.* à deux mâts. —**master,** *s.* (*nav.*) deux-mâts, *m.* —**pence,** *s.pl.* vingt centimes, *m.pl.* —**penny,** *adj.* de vingt centimes. — **tongued,** *adj. V.* **Double-tongued.** — **valved,** *adj.* [bivalve
Tycoon, *s.* (*of Japan*) taïcoun, *m.*
Tympan, Tympanum, *s.* tympan, *m.*
Type, *s.* type, *m.*; (*print.*) caractère, *m. To be in* —, être composé; être imprimé. *To put* or *set in* —, composer. — **founder,** *s.* fondeur en caractères (d'imprimerie), *m.* — **founding, -foundry,** *s.* fonderie de caractères (d'imprimerie), *f.* — **metal,** *s.* alliage pour les caractères d'imprimerie, *m.*, fonte, *f.*
Typefy, *v.a.* représenter d'une manière typique, symboliser, figurer
Typhic, Typhous, *adj.* typhique
Typhoid, *adj.* typhoïde
Typhoon, *s.* typhon, *m.*
Typhus, *s.* typhus, *m.* —**fever,** . typhus, *m.* — **patient,** *s.* typhique, *m.f.*
Typic, -al, *adj.* typique
Typically, *adv.* d'une manière typique
Typify. *V.* **Typefy**
Typographer, *s.* typographe, *m.*
Typographic, *adj.* typographique; (*pers.*) typographe. — *printer* or *&c.*, imprimeur *or* &c. typographe, *m.*
Typograph-ically, -y. *V.* page 3, § 1
Tyrann-ic, al, -ically. *V.* page 3, § 1
Tyrannicidal, *adj.* tyrannicide [*m.f.*
Tyrannicide, *s.* tyrannicide, (*act*) *m.*, (*pers.*)
Tyrannize, *v.a.n.*, — **over,** tyranniser
Tyranny, *s.* tyrannie, *f.*
Tyrant, *s.* tyran, *m.* — **bird, -shrike,** *s.* tyran, tyranneau, *m.*
Tyre, *s. V.* **Tire**
Tyrian, *s.* Tyrien, *m.*, -ne, *f.*; — *adj.* tyrien, de Tyr [conscrit, *m.*
Tyro, *s.* commençant, novice, *m.*; apprenti, *m.*;
Tyrolese, *s. adj.*, **Tyrolian,** *adj.* Tyrolien, *m.*, -ne, *f.*
Tyrrhenian, *s. adj.* Tyrrhénien, *m.*, -ne, *f.*
Tyrtæan, *adj.* tyrtéen
Tythe, &c. *V.* **Tithe,** &c.
Tzar, &c. *V.* **Czar,** &c.

U

U, *s.* (*letter*) u, *m.*
Ubiquitarian, Ubiquitary, Ubiquist, Ubiquitous, *adj. s.* ubiquitaire, ubiquiste, omniprésent, présent partout, partout à la fois
Ubiquity, *s.* ubiquité, *f.*
Udder, *s.* pis, *m.*, mamelle, *f.*; (*cook.*) tétine, *f.*
Uddered, *adj.* à pis, à mamelles
Udometer, *s.* udomètre, *m.*
Ugh, *int.* pouah!
Uglily, *adv.* laidement, vilainement
Ugliness, *s.* laideur, *f.*
Ugly, *adj.* laid, vilain; mauvais
Uhlan, Ulan, *s.* uhlan, *m.*
Ukase, *s.* ukase, *m.* [aphthe, *m.*
Ulcer, *s.* ulcère, *m.*; (*slight — in the mouth*)
Ulcerate, *v.a.* ulcérer; — *v.n.* s'ulcérer. —*d sorethroat*, mal de gorge avec ulcération, *m.*
Ulceration, *s.* ulcération, *f.*
Ulcerous, *adj.* ulcéreux [d'ulcération, *m.*
Ulcerousness, *s.* nature ulcéreuse, *f.*; état
Ullage, *s.* (*remaining liquor*) vidange, *f.*; (*empty space*) manquant, *m.*; — *v.a.* sonder
Ulna, *s.* cubitus, *m.*
Ulnar, *adj.* ulnaire, cubital
Ulterior, *adj.* ultérieur
Ulteriorly, *adv.* ultérieurement [de compte
Ultimate, *adj.* dernier, final, définitif, en fin
Ultimately, *adv.* finalement, définitivement, en définitive, à la fin, enfin, en résultat
Ultimatum, *s.* ultimatum, *m.*
Ultimo, *adv.* du mois dernier
Ultra, *adj.* extrême; (*in compounds*) ultra- . . .;
Ultraism, *s.* ultraïsme, *m.* [— *s.m.* ultra, *m.*
Ultramarine, *adj.* outremarin, d'outre-mer, outre-mer; — *s.* outremer, *m.*
Ultramontane, *adj. s.* ultramontain
Ultramontanism, *s.* ultramontanisme, *m.*
Ultra-mundane, *adj.* ultra-mondain
Ululate, *v.n.* ululer, hurler [ment, *m.*
Ululation, *s.* ululation, *f.*, ululement, hurlement, *m.*
Ulva, *s.* ulve, *f.*
Umbel, *s.* ombelle, *f.*
Umbellar, Umbellate, -d, *adj.* ombellé
Umbellifer, *s.* ombellifère, *f.*
Umbelliferous, *adj.* ombellifère
Umber, *s.* (*min.*) terre d'ombre, ombre, *f.*; (*fish*) ombre, *m.*; (*bird*) ombrette, *f.*; — *v.a.* ombrer; (*darken*) assombrir
Umbered, *adj.* ombré; (*dark*) sombre, obscur
Umbilical, *adj.* ombilical. — *cord*, cordon [ombilical, *m.*
Umbilicus, *s.* ombilic, *m.*
Umbrage, *s.* ombrage, *m. To give* —, donner de l'ombrage (à), porter *or* faire ombrage (à). *To take* —, prendre ombrage (de)
Umbrageous, *adj.* ombreux; (*shady*) ombragé
Umbrageousness, *s.* ombrage, *m.*, ombre, *f.*
Umbrella, *s.* parapluie, *m.* — **case,** *s.* fourreau de parapluie, *m.* — **maker,** *s.* fabricant de parapluies, *m.* — **stand,** *s.* porte-parapluies, *m.* — **stick,** *s.* manche de parapluie, *m.* — **tree,** *s.* magnolier parasol, *m.*
Umbrina, *s.* ombrine, *f.*
Umbrometer, *s.* ombromètre, *m.*
Umpirage, *s.* arbitrage, *m.*
Umpire, *s.* arbitre, *m.*; juge, *m.*; (*between masters and men*) prud'homme, *m.*
Umpireship, *s.* arbitrage, *m.*
Un- . . ., (*in compounds*) non- . . .; in . . .; im . . .; dé . . .; dés . . .; peu . . .; mal . . .
Unabashed, *adj.* sans honte, non confus
Unabated, *adj.* non diminué, sans diminution; le même, toujours le même; toujours égal; qui ne se ralentit pas; infatigable
Unable, *adj.* incapable (de), hors d'état (de); ne pouvant. *To be — to*, ne pouvoir (pas); n'avoir pas la force de
Unabolished, *adj.* non aboli, en vigueur
Unabridged, *adj.* non abrégé, entier, complet
Unaccented, *adj.* inaccentué, non accentué, sans accent
Unacceptable, *adj.* inacceptable; désagréable
Unacceptableness, *s.* nature inacceptable *or* désagréable, *f.* [table *or* désagréable
Unacceptably, *adv.* d'une manière inaccep-
Unaccepted, *adj.* refusé
Unacclimatizable, *adj.* inacclimatable
Unacclimatized, *adj.* inacclimaté
Unaccommodating, *adj.* peu accommodant
Unaccompanied. *V.* **Unattended**
Unaccomplished, *adj.* inachevé, incomplet; sans talent
Unaccountable, *adj.* inexplicable; inconcevable; étrange, bizarre; inouï; irresponsable

Unaccountableness, *s.* étrangeté, bizarrerie, *f.*; irresponsabilité, *f.*
Unaccountably, *adv.* inexplicablement; inconcevablement; étrangement [voir
Unaccredited, *adj.* non accrédité, sans pou-
Unaccustomed, *adj.* (*pers.*) peu habitué; (*things*) inaccoutumé
Unacknowledged, *adj.* non reconnu; non avoué; (*polit.*) non accrédité; (*of letters*) sans réponse
Unacquainted, *adj.* qui ne connaît pas; qui ignore; non accoutumé (à); étranger (à); peu familier (avec); peu versé (dans). *To be — with*, ignorer, ne pas connaître
Unacquirable, *adj.* inacquérable
Unacquired, *adj.* non acquis, naturel
Unacquitted, *adj.* non acquitté
Unactionable, *adj.* inattaquable
Unadjusted, *adj.* non ajusté; (*law*) en litige
Unadorned, *adj.* sans ornement, simple, naturel
Unadulterated, *adj.* naturel, pur, sans mélange, non falsifié, non frelaté; vrai; candide
Unadvisable, *adj.* peu sage, imprudent; mal vu; peu convenable; inutile; inopportun
Unadvisableness, *s.* imprudence, *f.*; inutilité, *f.*; inopportunité, *f.*
Unadvised, *adj.* irréfléchi; imprudent, inconsidéré; (*of bills*) non avisé [sidérément
Unadvisedly, *adv.* imprudemment, incon-
Unadvisedness, *s.* imprudence, *f.*
Unaffected, *part.* non affecté; inattaqué; — *adj.* naturel, simple, naïf, inaffecté, sans affectation, sans fard; sincère, franc, vrai; aisé; impassible, insensible
Unaffectedly, *adv.* sans affectation, sans prétention, simplement, naturellement; réellement; sincèrement, franchement; impassiblement, insensiblement
Unaffectedness, *s.* inaffectation, *f.*, naturel, *m.*, simplicité, *f.*; sincérité, franchise, *f.*; impassibilité, insensibilité, *f.*
Unaffecting, *adj.* peu touchant
Unaided, *adj.* sans aide, seul, tout seul
Unalienated, *adj.* inaliéné
Unallowable, *adj.* non permis [lange
Unalloyed, *adj.* sans alliage; pur, sans mé-
Unalterable, *adj.* inaltérable, invariable
Unalterableness, *s.* inaltérabilité, *f.*; invariabilité, *f.* [invariablement, immuablement
Unalterably, *adv.* d'une manière inaltérable;
Unaltered. *V.* **Unchanged**
Unambiguous, *adj.* non équivoque, non douteux, sans ambiguïté, clair [ment
Unambiguously, *adv.* sans ambiguïté, claire-
Unambitious, *adj.* sans ambition; sans prétention, simple [prétention, simplement
Unambitiously, *adv.* sans ambition, sans
Unamiable, *adj.* peu aimable
Unanalyzed, *adj.* non analysé
Unanimity, *s.* unanimité, *f.* *With —*, à l'u-
Unanimous, *adj.* unanime [nanimité
Unanimously, *adv.* unanimement, à l'unanimité. *Carried —*, voté à l'unanimité
Unanswerable, *adj.* sans réplique; incontestable; invincible
Unanswerably, *adv.* sans réplique; irréfutablement; incontestablement; invinciblement [plique; incontesté
Unanswered, *adj.* sans réponse; sans ré-
Unappalled, *adj.* sans peur, intrépide
Unapparent, *adj.* inapparent, inapercevable, invisible [sans appel
Unappealable, *adj.*, **Unappealably,** *adv.*
Unappeasable, *adj.* inapaisable, implacable
Unappeased, *adj.* inapaisé
Unapplied, *adj.* inappliqué
Unappreciated, *adj.* inapprécié; incompris
Unapprehended, *adj.* non arrêté; (*not understood*) incompris [peu intelligent
Unapprehensive, *adj.* sans appréhension;
Unapprized, *adj.* ignorant (de)
Unapproachable, *adj.* inaccessible, inabordable
Unapproached, *adj.* dont on n'a point approché, dont on n'approche pas; inaccessible
Unappropriated, *adj.* inapproprié, sans application, sans emploi
Unapproved, *adj.* inapprouvé [inerme
Unarmed, *adj.* sans armes; désarmé; (*bot.*)
Unarmoured, *adj.* (*nav.*) non cuirassé, non
Unarraigned, *adj.* non accusé [blindé
Unarrayed, *adj.* nu; non revêtu; (*not in order*) non rangé
Unartful, *adj.* sans art, sans artifice, inartificieux; naïf [génument
Unartfully, *adv.* sans artifice, naïvement, in-
Unascertainable, *adj* dont on ne peut s'assurer; qu'on ne peut vérifier
Unascertained, *adj.* non déterminé; inconnu
Unasked, *adj.* non demandé; non sollicité; sans être invité; spontané; spontanément
Unaspirated, *adj.* non aspiré
Unaspiring, *adj.* modeste; sans ambition
Unassailable, *adj.* inattaquable; hors d'atteinte [sailli. non attaqué, inattaqué
Unassailed, Unassaulted, *adj.* non as-
Unassignable, *adj.* inassignable
Unassisted. *V.* **Unaided**
Unassisting, *adj.* non secourable
Unassociated, *adj.* non associé
Unassorted, *adj.* inassorti [simple
Unassuming, *adj.* sans prétention, modeste,
Unassured, *adj.* non assuré, inassuré
Unatonable, *adj.* inexpiable
Unatoned, *adj.* non expié, sans expiation
Unattached, *adj.* non attaché (à); indépendant (de), séparé (de), libre; sans affection (pour); (*mil.*, *admin.*) en disponibilité; en non-activité. *To place on the — list*, mettre en disponibilité *or* en non-activité
Unattacked, *adj.* non attaqué, inattaqué
Unattainable, *adj.* impossible à atteindre; inaccessible [teindre, *f.*; inaccessibilité, *f.*
Unattainableness, *s.* impossibilité d'at-
Unattained, *adj.* non atteint, manqué
Unattempted, *adj.* non essayé, non tenté
Unattended, *adj.* non accompagné *or* suivi (de); sans suite, seul; sans soins, négligé; peu suivi, peu couru, sans auditoire
Unattending, *s.* inattentif; distrait, préoccupé [attestation
Unattested, *adj.* non attesté, inattesté, sans
Unattired, *adj.* sans parure, sans ornements
Unattractive, *adj.* peu attrayant
Unau, *s* unau, *m.*
Unauthentic, *adj.* inauthentique, sans authenticité; apocryphe
Unauthenticated, *adj.* non authentiqué, dont l'authenticité n'est pas établie *or* prouvée *or* reconnue; non constaté; (*law*) non légalisé
Unauthorized, *adj.* non autorisé, inautorisé, sans autorisation, sans autorité; illicite, illégal
Unavailable, Unavailing, *adj.* inutile, infructueux, vain; inefficace; (*not valid, not holding good*) non valable [cité, *f.*
Unavailableness, *s.* inutilité, *f.*; ineffica-
Unavenged, *adj.* non vengé, invengé; impuni
Unavoidable, *adj.* inévitable
Unavoidableness, *s.* inévitabilité, *f.*
Unavoidably, *adv.* inévitablement
Unavoided, *adj.* inévité
Unavowable, *adj.* inavouable
Unavowed, *adj.* inavoué
Unaware, *adj.* ignorant; inattentif. *To be — of*, ignorer; n'être pas au courant de
Unawares, *adv.* (*suddenly*) inopinément, à l'improviste; (*unprepared*) au dépourvu; (*by mistake*) par mégarde, par inadvertance; (*unconsciously*) à son insu
Unawed, *adj.* sans crainte; sans être effrayé *or* intimidé; hardi; hardiment
Unbacked, *adj.* non secondé, sans appui

Unbaked, *adj.* non cuit [poids
Unbalanced, *adj.* non balancé ; sans contre-
Unballast, *v.a.* délester
Unballasted, *adj.* délesté ; sans lest
Unbaptized, *adj.* non baptisé, sans baptême
Unbar, *v.a.* débarrer
Unbarricade, *v.a.* débarricader
Unbaste, *v.a.* débâtir
Unbearable, *adj.* insupportable
Unbearably, *adv.* insupportablement
Unbearded, *adj.* imberbe, sans barbe ; (*of wheat*) non barbu, sans barbes
Unbeaten, *adj.* non battu ; non frayé, infrayé, impratiqué
Unbecoming, *adj.* inconvenant, déplacé ; malséant, messéant ; indécent ; (*of clothing*) qui ne va pas (à) [venante ; sans grâce
Unbecomingly, *adv.* d'une manière incon-
Unbecomingness, *s.* inconvenance, *f.*
Unbefitting, *adj.* qui ne convient pas (à) ; qui ne s'accorde pas (avec)
Unbefriended, *adj.* sans amis
Unbegun, *adj.* non commencé
Unbelief, *s.* incroyance, *f.* ; incrédulité, *f.* ; scepticisme, *m.*
Unbeliever, *s.* incrédule, infidèle, *m.f.*, mécréant, *m.*, e, *f.*, sceptique, *m.f.* [fidèle
Unbelieving, *adj.* incroyant, incrédule ; in-
Unbend, *v.a.* détendre, relâcher ; (*rest*) délasser ; (*weaken*) affaiblir, relâcher ; (*a bow*) débander ; (*the brow*) dérider ; (*nav.*) démarrer, détalinguer, (*sails*) désenverguer, déverguer ; — *v.n.* se détendre ; se relâcher ; se dérider. *To — oneself*, se délasser
Unbending, *adj.* inflexible ; raide. **—ly,** *adv.* inflexiblement. **—ness,** *s.* inflexibilité, *f.*
Unbeneficed, *adj.* sans bénéfice
Unbeneficial, *adj.* infructueux, sans profit, sans avantage
Unbenefited, *adj.* sans avantage, sans bénéfice
Unbeseeming, &c. *V.* **Unbecoming,** &c.
Unbesiegeable, *adj.* inassiégeable
Unbewailed, *adj.* non pleuré, non regretté
Unbewitch, *v.a.* désensorceler ; désenchanter
Unbewitching, *s.* désensorcellement, *m.* ; désenchantement, *m.* [jugés ; impartial
Unbiassed, *adj.* sans prévention ; sans pré-
Unbidden, *adj.* sans invitation, sans être invité ; sans ordre ; spontané ; spontanément
Unbigoted, *adj.* exempt de bigoterie
Unbind, *v.a.* délier, détacher ; (*loose*) desserrer ; débander [reproche
Unblamable, *adj.*, **Unblamably,** *adv.* sans
Unbleached, *adj.* écru
Unblemished, *adj* sans tache ; pur
Unblenched, *adj.* sans tache ; pur
Unblenching, *adj.* ferme, intrépide
Unblended, *adj.* pur, sans mélange
Unblessed, Unblest, *adj.* (*not blessed*) non béni ; (*cursed*) maudit ; (*unfortunate*) malheureux, infortuné
Unblighted, *adj.* non broui ; non flétri ; (*fig.*) pur ; frais, dans sa fraîcheur
Unblock, *v.a.* décaler
Unblown, *adj.* non épanoui, en bouton
Unblushing, *adj.* éhonté
Unblushingly, *adv.* sans honte, sans rougir,
Unboiled, *adj.* non bouilli [effrontément
Unbolt, *v.a.* déverrouiller ; ouvrir
Unbolted, *adj.* déverrouillé ; ouvert ; (*of flour*) non bluté
Unbolting, *s.* déverrouillement, *m.*
Unborn, *adj.* pas encore né, encore à naître ; (*things*) à venir, futur. *As innocent as the babe —*, innocent comme l'enfant qui vient de naître
Unborrowed, *adj.* non emprunté ; original ; naturel
Unbosom, *v.a.* confier ; révéler, découvrir ; ouvrir. *To — oneself*, s'ouvrir à, s'épancher dans le sein de
Unbought, *adj.* non acheté ; — *adv.* pour rien
Unbound, *adj.* délié, détaché, dénoué ; (*loose*) desserré ; débandé ; (*free*) libre ; (*of books*) non relié [illimité, infini, immense
Unbounded, *adj.* sans bornes, sans limites,
Unboundedly, *adv.* sans bornes ; infiniment
Unbrace, *v.a.* délier, détacher ; (*relax*) desserrer ; débander ; détendre ; (*weaken*) relâcher, énerver, affaiblir, débiliter ; — *v.n.* se délier, se détacher, &c.
Unbreakable, *adj.* incassable
Unbred, *adj.* mal élevé, grossier
Unbreech, *v.a.* déculotter ; (*fire-arms*) déculasser [*fire-arms*) déculassé
Unbreeched, *adj.* déculotté, sans culotte ; (*of*
Unbrewed, *adj* non brassé ; (*fig.*) pur, naturel, sans mélange
Unbribed, *adj.* non corrompu, non séduit, non acheté ; libre ; — *adv.* sans être acheté
Unbridle, *v.a.* débrider ; (*fig.*) déchaîner
Unbridled, *adj.* débridé, sans bride ; (*fig.*) déchaîné ; effréné, sans frein
Unbroken, *adj.* non rompu, non brisé, non cassé, intact ; respecté, observé, non violé, non enfreint ; non interrompu, continu ; non affaibli ; (*not subdued*) indompté, insoumis ; (*of animals*) non dressé
Unbrotherlike, Unbrotherly, *adj.* indigne d'un frère, infraternel, peu fraternel
Unbuckle, *v.a.* déboucler
Unbuilt, *adj.* à bâtir, à construire
Unbung, *v.a.* débonder, débondonner
Unburden, *v a.* décharger ; (*fig.*) soulager. *To — oneself*, s'ouvrir
Unburied, *adj.* sans sépulture
Unburnt, *adj.* non brûlé, imbrûlé, sans être
Unbury, *v.a.* déterrer [brûlé
Unbusiness-like, *adj.* impropre aux affaires ; irrégulier ; inexact ; peu pratique ; léger,
Unbutton, *v.a.* déboutonner [étourdi
Uncage, *v.a.* lâcher ; délivrer
Uncalcined, *adj.* incalciné
Uncalled, *adj.* sans être appelé. **— for,** sans être demandé ; inutile ; peu convenable ; déplacé ; gratuit ; non mérité, immérité, injuste
Uncancelled, *adj.* non biffé, non barré ; non annulé [sans franchise
Uncandid, *adj.* peu candide, peu sincère,
Uncandidly, *adv.* sans franchise
Uncanny, *adj.* disgracieux ; maladroit ; mal à propos, intempestif, inopportun ; indu ; imprudent ; dangereux ; dur, rude, grand
Uncanonical, *adj.* peu canonique
Uncanonize, *v.a.* décanoniser
Uncap, *v.a.* découvrir ; (*bottles*) décoiffer ; (*fire-arms*) désamorcer ; (*foils, swords*) démou-
Uncapsizable, *adj.* inchavirable [cheter
Uncared for, *adj.* négligé, dans l'abandon, abandonné, dont on ne s'inquiète pas ; dont on ne se soucie pas
Uncarpeted, *adj.* sans tapis
Unceasing, -ly. *V.* **Incessant, -ly**
Uncelebrated, *adj.* incélébré
Unceremonious, *adj.* incérémonieux, sans cérémonie, sans façon ; cavalier, sans gêne. **—ly,** *adv.* sans cérémonie, sans façon ; cavalièrement, sans gêne. **—ness,** *s.* sans-façon, sans-gêne, *m.*
Uncertain, *adj.* incertain ; irrésolu ; peu sûr ; chancelant ; — *s.* incertain, *m.*
Uncertainly, *adv.* d'une manière incertaine
Uncertainty, *s.* incertitude, *f.* ; l'incertain, *m.*
Uncertificated, *adj.* non pourvu d'un certificat, sans certificat ; non diplômé ; non breveté ; (*of bankrupts*) sans concordat
Uncertified, *adj.* non certifié, incertifié
Unchain, *v.a.* déchaîner ; délivrer
Unchaining, *s.* déchaînement, *m.* ; délivrance, *f.*
Unchallenged, *adj.* non relevé, sans être relevé, sans réplique, non contredit ; non provoqué [inaltérable
Unchangeable, *adj.* invariable, immuable ;
Unchangeableness, *s.* immutabilité, invariabilité, *f.* ; inaltérabilité, *f.*

Unchangeably, *adv.* immuablement; invariablement; inaltérablement
Unchanged, *adj.* sans changement; pas changé, inchangé; le même, toujours le même; dans le même état [ne change pas
Unchanging, *adj.* invariable, constant, qui
Unchangingly. *V.* **Unchangeably**
Uncharged, *adj.* non attaqué, inattaqué; (*unloaded*) non chargé. — **for,** *adj.* qu'on ne fait pas payer; exempt de frais, sans frais, gratuit, franco
Uncharitable, *adj.* peu charitable, incharitable
Uncharitableness, *s.* manque de charité, *m.*, incharité, *f.*
Uncharitably, *adv.* sans charité, d'une manière peu charitable, incharitablement
Uncharm, *v.a.* décharmer, désenchanter
Unchaste, *adj.* incontinent, impudique
Unchastely, *adv.* impudiquement
Unchastened, Unchastised, *adj.* inchâtié
Unchastity, *s.* inchasteté, incontinence, impudicité, *f.*
Unchecked, *adj.* sans frein, effréné; non réprimé *or* &c. (*V.* **Check,** *v.a.*)
Uncheerful, *adj.* triste, mélancolique. —**ly,** *adv.* tristement, mélancoliquement. —**ness,** *s.* tristesse, mélancolie, *f.*
Unchewed, *adj.* non mâché, sans être mâché
Unchivalrous, *adj.* peu chevaleresque. —**ly,** *adv.* peu chevaleresquement
Unchristen, *v.a.* débaptiser
Unchristened, *adj.* non baptisé, sans baptême
Unchristian, *adj.* antichrétien, inchrétien, peu chrétien, indigne d'un chrétien; infidèle
Unchristianize, *v.a.* déchristianiser
Unchristianly, *adj.* *V.* **Unchristian;** — *adv.* inchrétiennement, peu chrétiennement
Unchurch, *v.a.* exclure du giron de l'église
Uncial, *adj.* oncial; — *s.* lettre onciale, *f.*
Uncircumcised, *adj.* incirconcis
Uncircumcision, *s.* incirconcision, *f.*
Uncircumscribed, *adj.* incirconscrit
Uncircumspect, *adj.* peu circonspect, imprudent
Uncivil, *adj.* incivil, impoli, grossier
Uncivilizable, *adj.* incivilisable
Uncivilize, *v.a.* déciviliser
Uncivilized, *adj.* non civilisé, barbare, sauvage; (*rude*) grossier
Uncivilly, *adv.* grossièrement, impoliment, avec impolitesse, grossièrement
Unclad, *adj.* sans vêtements, nu
Unclaimed, *adj.* non réclamé; (*of money*) arriéré
Unclarified, *adj.* non clarifié
Unclasp, *v.a.* dégrafer, défaire, ouvrir
Unclass, *v.a.* déclasser
Unclassic, -al, *adj.* peu classique
Unclassically, *adv.* d'une manière peu classique
Unclassifiable, *adj.* inclassable
Unclassified, *adj.* non classé
Unclassing, *s.* déclassement, *m.*
Uncle, *s.* oncle, *m.*; (*pawnbroker*) tante, *f.*
Unclean, *adj.* malpropre, sale; (*Jewish law,* &c.) impur; (*foul*) immonde; (*unchaste*) impudique
Uncleanable, *adj.* innettoyable
Uncleaned, *adj.* non nettoyé *or* &c. (*V.* **Clean,** *v.a.*)
Uncleanliness. *V.* **Uncleanness**
Uncleanly, *adv.* salement; — *adj.* *V.* **Unclean**
Uncleanness, *s.* malpropreté, saleté, *f.*; (*unchastity*) impureté, *f.*
Uncleansable, *adj.* innettoyable
Uncleansed, *adj.* non nettoyé; non purifié
Unclearable, *adj.* (*of land*) indéfrichable
Uncleared, *adj.* (*of land*) indéfriché
Unclench, Unclinch, *v.a.* desserrer, ouvrir
Unclipped, *adj.* non coupé, non taillé; (*of animals*) non tondu; (*of coin*) non rogné
Unclog, *v.a.* ôter les entraves à; (*fig.*) dégager, débarrasser
Uncloister, *v.a.* décloîtrer
Unclose, *v.a.* ouvrir, déclore
Unclosed, *adj.* (*open*) ouvert; (*not fenced*) non clôturé; (*not finished*) inachevé
Unclosing, *s.* ouverture, déclôture, *f.*
Unclothe, *v.a.* dévêtir, déshabiller; (*fig.*) dépouiller, mettre à nu [&c.) dépouillé
Unclothed, *adj.* nu, sans vêtements; (*of trees,*
Unclouded, *adj.* sans nuages, serein, pur
Uncloudedness, *s.* sérénité, pureté, clarté, *f.*
Unclutch, *v.a.* ouvrir, desserrer
Uncock, *v.a.* (*fire-arms*) désarmer
Uncoil, *v.a.* dérouler; (*nav.*) délover
Uncoined, *adj.* non monnayé
Uncollected, *adj.* non rassemblé; dispersé; (*fig.*) non recueilli; (*of money*) non perçu, à percevoir [couvrable
Uncollectible, *adj.* non recouvrable, irre-
Uncolonized, *adj.* non colonisé
Uncoloured, *adj.* non coloré, incoloré; (*colourless*) incolore, sans couleur
Uncombed, *adj.* non peigné; mal peigné, [ébouriffé
Uncombined, *adj.* non combiné
Uncomeatable, *adj.* inaccessible, inabordable
Uncomeliness, *s.* manque de grâce, *m.*; laideur, *f.*; inconvenance, *f.*
Uncomely, *adj.* disgracieux; inconvenant, malséant; laid, vilain; désagréable
Uncomfortable, *adj.* (*pers.*) gêné, mal à son aise; (*things*) gênant, incommode; désagréable; (*sad*) triste, malheureux, mauvais. *To make* —, (*pers.*) gêner; incommoder; contrarier; inquiéter; tracasser; vexer; peiner
Uncomfortableness, *s.* malaise, *m.*, gêne, *f.*; incommodité, *f.*; désagrément, *m.*; ennui, *m.*; inquiétude, *f.*; (*sadness*) tristesse, *f.*
Uncomfortably, *adv.* mal à son aise, mal, dans la gêne; incommodément; désagréablement; avec inquiétude; (*sadly*) tristement
Uncommitted, *adj.* non commis *or* &c. (*V.* **Commit,** *v.a.*)
Uncommon, *adj.* peu commun, rare, extraordinaire; singulier; inouï
Uncommonly, *adv.* rarement, extraordinairement; infiniment. *Not* —, assez souvent. — *good,* excellent; magnifique; (*of jokes*) impayable. — *well,* admirablement, admirablement bien, à merveille
Uncommonness, *s.* rareté, *f.*
Uncommunicable, &c. *V.* **Incommunicable,** &c. [incommuniqué
Uncommunicated, *adj.* non communiqué,
Uncommunicative, *adj.* peu communicatif. —**ness,** *s.* caractère peu communicatif, *m.*
Uncompanionable, *adj.* peu sociable
Uncompared, *adj.* non comparé, incomparé
Uncompassionate, &c. *V.* **Incompassionate,** &c. [taire, spontané
Uncompelled, *adj.* sans contrainte; volon-
Uncompensated, *adj.* sans compensation; sans récompense [plaindre
Uncomplaining, *adj.* sans plainte, sans se
Uncomplaisant, *adj.* sans complaisance, peu complaisant
Uncomplaisantly, *adv.* sans complaisance
Uncompleted, *adj.* inachevé, incomplet
Uncomplying, *adj.* peu complaisant; inflexible; désobéissant; irrémédiable
Uncompounded, *adj.* non composé; simple
Uncompoundedness, *s.* simplicité, *f.*
Uncomprehended, *adj.* incompris [primé
Uncompressed, *adj.* non comprimé, incom-
Uncompromised, *adj.* non compromis
Uncompromising, *adj.* irréconciliable; inflexible; ferme; opiniâtre; intraitable; peu accommodant
Uncompromisingly, *adv.* inflexiblement; fermement; opiniâtrément
Unconcealable. *V.* **Inconcealable**
Unconcealed, *adj.* non caché; ouvert, à découvert
Unconceived, *adj.* inconçu
Unconcern, *s.* insouciance, indifférence, *f.*; sang-froid, *m.*
Unconcerned, *adj.* indifférent (à); insou-

ciant (de); insensible (à); désintéressé (dans), étranger (à) [différemment, avec insouciance
Unconcernedly, *adv.* avec indifférence, in-
Unconciliating, *adj.* inconciliant [inachevé
Unconcluded, *adv.* non conclu, inconclu;
Unconditional, *adj.* inconditionnel, sans conditions; absolu; pur et simple
Unconditionally, *adv.* inconditionnellement, sans conditions; absolument; sans réserve; purement et simplement
Unconfessed, *adj.* non avoué, inavoué; non reconnu; (*of sins*) non confessé, inconfessé
Unconfidence, *s.* inconfiance, *f.*
Unconfident, *adj.* inconfiant
Unconfined, *adj.* libre; illimité
Unconfinedly, *adv.* librement; sans limites
Unconfirmed, *adj.* non confirmé
Unconformable, *adj.* non conforme (à), contraire (à); incompatible (avec)
Unconformably, *adv.* sans conformité; incompatiblement
Unconformity, *s.* non-conformité, inconformité, *f.*; incompatibilité, *f.*
Unconfutable, *adj.* irréfutable
Uncongealed, *adj.* non congelé, incongelé
Uncongenial, *adj.* hétérogène; peu naturel (à), peu conforme (à), peu propre (à)
Unconjugal, *adj.* inconjugal
Unconnected, *adj.* sans liaison, décousu, sans suite; (*with*) sans rapport (avec); séparé (de), détaché (de); isolé (de); étranger (à)
Unconnectedly, *adv.* d'une manière décousue, sans liaison
Unconnectedness, *s.* défaut de liaison, *m.*; décousu, *m.* [able; (*fig.*) insurmontable
Unconquerable, *adj.* invincible. indompt-
Unconquerably, *adv.* invinciblement; insurmontablement
Unconquered, *adj.* non conquis, inconquis; invaincu; indompté, insoumis; (*fig.*) non surmonté
Unconscientious, *adj.* sans conscience, peu consciencieux [orbitant; sans conscience
Unconscionable, *adj.* déraisonnable; ex-
Unconscionableness, *s.* déraison, extravagance, *f.*; exorbitance, *f.*
Unconscionably, *adv.* déraisonnablement; exorbitamment; sans conscience
Unconscious, *adj.* qui n'a pas la conscience (de); inconscient; insensible; (*delirious, senseless*) sans connaissance; (*unaware*) ignorant. *To become* —, (*senseless*) perdre connaissance. *To be* (or *lie*) —, (*senseless*) avoir perdu connaissance, être *or* rester (*or* être étendu) sans connaissance
Unconsciously, *adv.* *V.* **Unknowingly**
Unconsciousness, *s.* ignorance, *f.*; insensibilité, *f.*; perte de connaissance, *f*; (*swoon*) évanouissement, *m*; (*philos.*) inconscience, *f.* *In a state of* —, (*senseless*) sans connaissance
Unconsecrated, *adj.* non consacré; non bénit; (*pers.*) non sacré; (*of saints*) non canonisé [(*law*) non consentant
Unconsenting, *adj.* qui ne consent pas (à);
Unconsidered, *adj.* non considéré; inaperçu
Unconsoled, *adj.* inconsolé
Unconsolidated, *adj.* non consolidé
Unconsonant. *V.* **Inconsonant**
Unconstitutional, *adj.* inconstitutionnel
Unconstitutionality, *s.* inconstitutionnalité, *f.* [nellement
Unconstitutionally, *adv.* inconstitution-
Unconstrainable, *adj.* irréprimable
Unconstrained, *adj.* sans contrainte; libre; spontané, volontaire; (*easy*) aisé, naturel
Unconstrainedly, *adv.* sans contrainte; librement; spontanément
Unconstraint, *s.* liberté, *f.*; aisance, *f.*; abandon, *m.*; laisser-aller, *m.*; naturel, *m.*
Unconsulted, *adj.* non consulté, inconsulté
Unconsumed, *adj.* inconsumé; (*unused*) inconsommé

Uncontaminated, *adj.* sans souillure; pur ('*with*,' '*by*,' de); non corrompu ('*by*,' par)
Uncontested, *adj.* incontesté
Uncontinuous, *adj.* incontinu
Uncontradicted, *adj.* non contredit, non démenti, sans contradiction
Uncontrollable, *adj.* incontrôlable; ingouvernable; indomptable; intraitable; sans frein, effréné; irrésistible; (*of emotions*) qu'on ne peut maîtriser; (*of laughter*) inextinguible. *To become* —, (*of horses*) s'emporter
Uncontrollably, *adv.* d'une manière incontrôlable; indomptablement; irrésistiblement
Uncontrolled, *adj.* incontrôlé, sans contrôle; sans opposition; sans frein, effréné; sans contrainte; libre; irrésistible
Uncontrolledly, *adv.* sans contrôle; sans frein; irrésistiblement [testé, reconnu
Uncontroverted, *adj.* incontroversé, incon-
Unconversable, *adj.* impropre à la conversation; réservé, insociable [versé (dans)
Unconversant, *adj.* peu familier (avec); peu
Unconverted, *adj.* non converti, inconverti; non transformé
Unconvertible, &c. *V.* **Inconvertible,** &c.
Unconvinced, *adj.* non convaincu, inconvaincu
Unconvincing, *adj.* non convaincant
Uncookable, *adj.* incuisable
Uncork, *v.a.* déboucher
Uncorrected, *adj.* non corrigé, incorrigé
Uncorrupted, *adj.* non corrompu, incorrompu; pur; intègre
Uncouple, *v.a.* découpler, détacher; (*mach., tech.*) désengrener
Uncourteous, -ly. *V.* **Discourteous, -ly**
Uncourtliness, *s.* inélégance, *f.*; impolitesse, *f.*; rudesse, *f.*; gaucherie, *f.*; (*in a good sense*) manières simples et dignes, *f.pl.*
Uncourtly, *adj.* inélégant; impoli; rude, rustique, gauche, commun; (*simple-mannered*) étranger au grand monde
Uncouth, *adj.* bizarre, singulier, étrange, baroque, insolite; gauche; grossier, rude; inconnu
Uncouthly, *adv.* bizarrement, étrangement; gauchement; grossièrement; rudement
Uncouthness, *s.* bizarrerie, étrangeté, *f.*; gaucherie, *f.*; grossièreté, *f.*; rudesse, *f.*
Uncover, *v.a.* découvrir; — *v.n.* se découvrir
Uncreatable, *adj.* incréable
Uncreated, *adj.* incréé [dicieux
Uncritical, *adj.* sans discernement, peu ju-
Uncriticizable, *adj.* incritiquable
Uncropped, *adj.* non récolté
Uncrossed, *adj.* intraversé, non traversé
Uncrowned, *adj.* découronné; sans couronne
Uncrystallizable, *adj.* incristallisable
Uncrystallized, *adj.* non cristallisé
Unction, *s.* onction, *f.*; (*balm*) baume, *m.* *Extreme* —, l'extrême-onction, *f.*
Unctuosity, *s.* onctuosité, *f.*
Unctuous, *adj.* onctueux. **—ly,** *adv.* onctueusement. **—ness,** *s.* onctuosité, *f.*
Uncultivable, *adj.* incultivable
Uncultivated, *adj* inculte, sans culture
Uncumbered. *V.* **Unencumbered**
Uncurbed, *adj.* indompté; sans frein, effréné
Uncured, *adj.* non guéri
Uncurl, *v.a.* (*hair*) défriser, déboucler; (*unroll*) dérouler; — *v.n.* se défriser, se déboucler; se dérouler [non frisé, non bouclé, plat
Uncurled, *adj.* défrisé, débouclé; (*not curled*)
Uncurrent, *adj.* incourant
Uncut, *adj.* non coupé; intact; (*not shaped*) non taillé; (*unbegun*) non entamé, entier; (*of books, not machine-cut*) non rogné
Undamaged, *adj.* non endommagé; intact; en bon état; (*nav.*) non avarié [refroidi
Undamped, *adj.* ferme, non découragé, non
Undated, *adj.* non daté, sans date
Undaunted, *adj.* intrépide; inébranlable.

—**ly,** *adv.* intrépidement, sans se laisser abattre. —**ness,** *s.* intrépidité, fermeté, *f.*
Undazzled, *adj.* non ébloui
Undebatable, *adj.* indiscutable [lusionner
Undeceive, *v.a.* détromper, désabuser; désil-
Undecided, *adj.* indécis; incertain; douteux; irrésolu
Undecipherable, *adj.* indéchiffrable
Undecipherably, *adv.* indéchiffrablement
Undeciphered, *adj.* indéchiffré
Undeck, *v.a.* déparer, dépouiller
Undecked, *adj.* sans ornements; déparé, dépouillé; (*nav.*) non ponté
Undeclined, *adj.* invariable
Undecomposed, *adj.* indécomposé
Undefaced, *adj.* non défiguré; non détérioré
Undefended, *adj.* non défendu, indéfendu, sans défense; (*of a prisoner*) sans défenseur, sans avocat; (*of a case*) non contesté
Undefiled, *adj.* pur; sans tache
Undefinable, *adj.* indéfinissable
Undefined, *adj.* indéfini
Undeformed, *adj.* non déformé; non défiguré
Undelivered, *adj.* non délivré; non affranchi; (*not sent in*) non livré
Undeluded, *adj.* désabusé
Undemonstrated, *adj.* indémontré
Undemonstrative, *adj.* peu démonstratif
Undeniable, *adj.* incontestable; irrécusable
Undeniably, *adv.* incontestablement; irrécu-
Undepressed, *adj.* non abattu [sablement
Under, *prep.* sous; dessous; au-dessous de; (*in*) dans, en; (*less than*) moins de, moins que; de moins que; (*in less than*) en moins de; (*for less than*) pour moins de, à moins de, audessous de; (*with the help of*) à l'aide de, avec, à; (*in the midst of*) au milieu de; (*in a bad sense*) sous le coup de. — *it, them,* (*things*) dessous. — *the table,* sous la table. *From — the table,* de dessous la table. *On and — the table,* dessus et dessous la table. — 40, audessous de 40 ans
Under, *adv.* dessous; au-dessous; (*for less*) à moins; (*too little*) trop peu; insuffisamment; mal; (*too low*) trop bas; (*fig.*) soumis, dans un état d'assujettissement *or* d'infériorité; (*insufficient*) insuffisant
Under, *adj.* de dessous; (*of rank*) sous; subalterne; second; aide; (*lower*) inférieur
Under-actor, *s.* (*theat.*) doublure, *f.*
Under-agent, *s.* agent inférieur, sousagent, *m.*
Under-almoner, *s.* sous-aumônier, *m.*
Under-assistant, *s.* sous-aide, *m.f.*
Under-bailiff, *s.* (*law officer*) recors, *m.*
Underbaked, *adj.* pas assez cuit; pas cuit; peu cuit, incuit. *Rather* —, pas trop cuit
Underbearer, *s.* porteur (de mort) *m.*, (*fam.*) croque-mort, *m.*
Underbid, *v.a.* offrir moins que; (*things*) offrir trop peu pour (*or* de); (*undersell*) offrir à plus bas prix
Underbred, *adj.* (*of horses*) demi-sang; (*pers.*) mal élevé, mal appris, vulgaire
Underbridge, *s.* ponceau, *m.*
Underbrush, *s. V.* **Undergrowth**
Under-butler, *s.* aide-sommelier, *m.*
Underbuy, *v.a.* acheter trop peu; acheter à bas prix
Under-captain, *s.* (*of a mine*) contre-maître, *m.*
Under-chanter, *s.* sous-chantre, *m.*
Under-chaplain, *s.* sous-aumônier, souschapelain, *m.*
Undercharge, *v.a.* demander trop peu
Under-clerk, *s.* sous-commis, *m.*; sous-clerc, *m.*
Underclothing, *s.* vêtements de dessous, *m.pl.*; linge, *m.*
Undercoat, *s.* habit de dessous, *m.*
Under-cook, *s.* aide de cuisine, *m.f.*
Undercroft, *s.* voûte souterraine, *f.*; (*of churches*) crypte, *f.*
Undercrust, *s.* croûte de dessous, *f.*
Undercurrent, *s.* courant inférieur, *m.*; courant sous-marin, *m.*
Undercut, *s.* (*of meat*) filet, *m.*
Underdealing, *s.* menée secrète, *f.* [pont, *m.*
Under-deck, *s.* (*nav.*) entrepont, *m.*; faux
Underdone, *part. adj.* (*cook.*) pas assez cuit; pas cuit; peu cuit, incuit, (*bleeding*) saignant. *Rather* —, pas trop cuit [dessécher
Underdrain, *s.* fossé d'écoulement, *m.*; — *v.a.*
Underdress, *s.* vêtement de dessous, *m.*; — *v.a.* habiller trop peu, mal habiller
Underestimate. *V.* **Underrate**
Underfeed, *v.a.* nourrir trop peu, mal nourrir
Underfoot, *adv.* sous les pieds, en bas, par terre, dans la rue; — *adj.* abject
Underfreight, *v.a.* sous-fréter
Under-gardener, *s.* aide-jardinier, *m.*
Undergo, *v.a.* subir, souffrir, endurer, essuyer, éprouver; (*receive*) recevoir; (*bear*) supporter [sous-maîtresse, *f.*
Under-governess, *s.* sous-gouvernante, *f.*;
Under-governor, *s.* sous-gouverneur, *m.*
Undergraduate, *s.* étudiant, élève, *m.*
Underground, *adj.* souterrain (*m.*, e, *f.*); — *s.* souterrain, *m.*; — *adj.* sous terre. — *story,* sous-sol, *m.* [*f.pl.*; sous-bois, *m.*
Undergrowth, *s.* taillis, *m.*; broussailles,
Underhand, *adv.* sous main, clandestinement, en secret, en cachette; sourdement; sournoisement; — *adj. V.* **Underhanded**
Underhanded, *adj.* (*things*) clandestin; secret; caché; sourd; sournois; (*pers.*) caché, en dessous; sournois
Underhire, *v.a.* sous-louer
Under-housemaid, *s.* deuxième bonne, *f.*
Underived, *adj.* non dérivé; indépendant
Under-keeper, *s.* sous-gardien, *m.*
Underlay, *v.a.* soutenir (par), appuyer (sur); poser *or* placer *or* mettre dessous
Underlayer, *s. V.* **Substratum**
Underlease, *s.* sous-bail, *m.*; sous-location, *f.*; sous-ferme, *f.*; — *v.a.* sous-affermer
Underleather, *s.* cuir de dessous, *m.*
Underlessee, *s.* sous-locataire, *m.f.*; (*of a farm*) sous-fermier, *m.*, -ière, *f.*
Underlessor, *s.* sous-bailleur, *m.*, -euse, *f.*
Underlet, *v.a.* sous-louer; (*a farm*) sous-affermer; (*to let below the value*) louer au-dessous de sa valeur, louer à vil prix; (*contracts*) marchander
Underletter, *s.* sous-loueur, *m.*, -euse, *f.*
Underletting, *s.* sous-location, *f.*; (*of contracts*) marchandage, *m.*
Under-librarian, *s.* sous-bibliothécaire, *m.*
Underlie, *v.a.* être sous (...); être au fond de (...); — *v.n.* être dessous; être au fond
Underline, *v.a.* souligner
Underling, *s.* subalterne, *m.*; (*mere tool*) âme damnée, *f.*; instrument, *m.*
Underlip, *s.* lèvre inférieure, *f.* [dessous
Underlying, *part. adj.* qui est sous (...) *or*
Undermasted, *adj.* trop peu mâté
Under-master, *s.* sous-maître, *m.*
Under-mattress, *s.* sommier, *m.*
Undermentioned, *adj.* mentionné ci-dessous, ci-dessous mentionné; ci-dessous
Undermine, *v.a.* miner; (*by water*) affouiller; (*fig.*) détruire [teur, ennemi secret, *m.*
Underminer, *s.* mineur, *m.*; (*fig.*) destruc-
Undermining, *s.* (*foundations by water*) affouillement, *m.* [dernier
Undermost, *adj.* (le) plus bas; inférieur; (le)
Underneath, *adv.* dessous; au-dessous; par dessous; en dessous; là-dessous; — *prep.* sous. *From* — (...), de dessous (...)
Underpaid, *adj.* trop peu payé, pas assez payé, mal payé [incident, *m.*; rôle secondaire, *m.*
Underpart, *s.* dessous, *m.*; accessoire, *m.*;
Underpay, *v.a.* payer trop peu, ne pas payer assez, payer mal [populeux
Underpeopled, *adj.* trop peu peuplé; peu
Underpetticoat, *s.* jupon de dessous, *m.*

Underpin, *v.a.* étayer; (*build.*) reprendre en sous-œuvre

Underpinning, *s.* étayage, étayement, *m.*; (*build.*) reprise en sous-œuvre, *f.*; sous-œuvre, *m.* [crête, *f.*; (*theat.*) sous-intrigue, *f.*

Underplot, *s.* complot secret, *m.*, menée se-

Under-porter, *s.* sous-portier, *m.*

Underpraise, *v.a.* ne pas louer assez

Underpressure, *s.* sous-pression, *f.*

Under-prior, *s.* sous-prieur, *m.*

Underprize. *V.* **Underrate** [sante, *f.*

Underproduction, *s.* production insuffi-

Underprop, *v.a.* soutenir; étayer

Underproportioned, *adj.* sans proportion

Underrate, *v.a.* estimer au-dessous de sa valeur; taxer trop bas; (*fig.*) faire trop peu de cas de, ne pas apprécier suffisamment; déprécier; mépriser; — *s.* bas prix, vil prix, *m.*

Underripe, *adj.* pas assez mûr, vert

Underrun, *v.a.* (*cables*) paumoyer

Under-sacristan, *s.* sous-sacristain, *m.*

Underscore, *v.a.* souligner; faire une marque sous [*of State*, secrétaire général, *m.*

Under-secretary, *s.* sous-secrétaire, *m.* —

Under-secretaryship, *s.* sous-secrétariat, *m.*

Undersell, *v.a.* vendre à plus bas prix (*or* meilleur marché) que; (*sell too cheap*) vendre à trop bas prix; — *v.n.* vendre à trop bas prix, gâter le métier

Underseller, *s.* gâte-métier, *m.*

Underservant, *s.* domestique inférieur, *m.*

Underset, *s.* (*nav.*) courant sous-marin, *m.*

Under-sexton, *s.* sous-sacristain, *m.*

Under-sheriff, *s.* (*in England*) sous-shérif, *m.*; (*in France*) sous-préfet, *m.*

Undershot wheel, *s.* roue en dessous, roue mue en dessous, roue à aubes *or* à palettes

Undershrub, *s.* sous-arbrisseau, *m.*

Underside, *s.* dessous, *m.*

Undersign, *v.a.n.* soussigner

Undersignature, *s.* sous-signature, *f.*

Undersigned, *adj. s.* soussigné, *m.*, e, *f.* *The* —, le soussigné, *m.*, la soussignée, *f.* *I, the* —, je soussigné [moyenne, de petite taille

Undersized, *adj.* au-dessous de la taille

Underskirt, *s.* jupe de dessous, sous-jupe, *f.*

Undersoil, *V.* **Subsoil**

Understand, *v.a.n.* comprendre; (*suppose to mean, agree upon*) entendre; (*know*) s'entendre à *or* en; se connaître à *or* en; connaître; savoir; (*mean without expressing*) sous-entendre; (*learn*) apprendre; entendre dire. *Do you — me?* me comprenez-vous. *I do not — you*, je ne vous comprends pas. *I — it*, (*know all about it*) je m'y connais. *I — nothing at all about it*, je n'y comprends rien; (*no knowledge*) je n'y connais rien, je ne m'y connais pas. *I don't — carving*, je ne m'entends pas à découper, je ne sais pas découper. *Am I to — ...?* dois-je comprendre ...? voulez-vous dire ...? *It is an understood thing that ...*, il est bien entendu que ... *To make oneself understood*, se faire comprendre. *To — each other*, se comprendre; (*be agreed*) s'entendre. *To give to* —, donner à entendre

Understandable, *adj.* intelligible

Understanding, *s.* entendement, *m.*; jugement, *m.*; raison, *f.*; esprit, *m.*; intelligence, *f.*; accord, *m.*, harmonie, *f.*; entente, *f.*; condition, convention, *f.*, arrangement, *m.*; — *adj.* intelligent, entendu. *Good* —, bonne intelligence. *Cordial* —, entente cordiale. *The human* —, l'entendement humain. *There is an — between them*, ils sont d'intelligence. *To come to an — with*, s'entendre avec. *To have an — together*, être d'intelligence

Understandingly, *adv.* en connaissance de cause; avec jugement

Understate, *v.a.* dire moins que, rester au-dessous de; diminuer, atténuer, amoindrir; ne pas exposer suffisamment

Under-steward, *s.* sous-intendant, *m.*

Under-stewardship, *s* sous-intendance, *f.*

Understock, *v.a.* pourvoir *or* &c. (*V.* **Stock,** *v.a.*) insuffisamment

Understrapper. *V.* **Underling**

Understratum. *V.* **Substratum**

Understroke, *v.a.* souligner

Undertakable, *adj.* entreprenable

Undertake, *v.a.n.* entreprendre; se charger de; s'engager (à); se faire fort (de); promettre (de, que); garantir (que), répondre (que); accepter. *To — to say*, gager, parier, garantir, répondre; ne pas craindre d'affirmer, oser affirmer, oser dire

Undertaker, *s.* personne qui entreprend, *f.*; (*of funerals*) entrepreneur des pompes funè-

Undertaking, *s.* entreprise, *f.* [bres, *m.*

Undertax, *v.a.* taxer trop bas [teur, *m.*

Under-teacher, *s.* sous-maître, sous-précep-

Undertenancy, *s.* sous-location, *f.*

Undertenant, *s.* sous-locataire, *m.f.*

Undertone, *s.* ton bas, *m.*, intonation moins élevée, *f.* *In an* —, à demi-voix, à voix basse,

Under-treasurer, *s.* sous-trésorier, *m.* [bas

Under-tutor, *s.* sous-précepteur, *m.*

Undervaluation, *s.* sous-évaluation, *f.*

Undervalue. *V.* **Underrate**

Undervaluer, *s.* dépréciateur, *m.*, -trice, *f.*

Underwaistcoat, *s.* gilet de dessous, *m.*

Underwood. *V.* **Undergrowth**

Underwork, *s.* gros ouvrage, *m.*, grosse besogne, *f.*; — *v.a.* miner, saper; (*neglect*) ne pas assez soigner, ne pas travailler avec assez de soin; (*work cheaper*) travailler à plus bas prix que; — *v.n.* (*work little*) travailler peu; (*work too cheap*) travailler à trop bas prix, (*fam.*) gâter le métier

Underworker, *s.* (*inferior*) ouvrier (*m.*, -ière, *f.*) en sous-ordre; manœuvre, *m.*; (*cheaper*) gâte-métier, *m.* [signer; assurer

Underwrite, *v.a.* écrire au-dessous; souscrire,

Underwriter, *s.* assureur, *m.* [rance, *f.*

Underwriting, *s.* assurance maritime, assu-

Undescribable, &c. *V.* **Indescribable,** &c.

Undescribed, *adj.* non décrit, indécrit

Undescried, *adj.* inaperçu [juste

Undeserved, *adj.* non mérité, immérité, in-

Undeservedly, *adv.* injustement, à tort

Undeservedness, *s.* injustice, *f.*

Undeserving, *adj.* (*pers.*) indigne (de); (*things*) peu méritoire; qui ne mérite pas ... [ment

Undeservingly, *adv.* sans mérite; injuste-

Undesigned, *adj.* involontaire

Undesignedly, *adv.* involontairement

Undesigning, *adj.* sans intention; sans malice, franc, sincère, loyal

Undesirable, *adj.* peu désirable, peu à désirer; (*not suitable*) peu convenable

Undesired, *adj.* non désiré; non sollicité

Undesirous, *adj.* sans désir

Undespairing, *adj.* qui ne désespère pas, soutenu par l'espoir

Undestroyable, *adj.* indestructible

Undestroyed, *adj.* non détruit

Undetected, *adj.* non découvert; secret

Undetermined, *adj.* indéterminé; irrésolu, indécis [**Deter,** *v.a.*)

Undeterred, *part. adj.* non effrayé *or* &c. (*V.*

Undeveloped, *adj.* non développé

Undeviating, *adj.* droit, direct, sans détour; ferme, constant [forme, confus

Undigested, *adj.* indigéré; indigeste; in-

Undignified, *adj.* sans dignité, peu digne; qui manque de noblesse; bas, grossier

Undiminished, *adj.* *V.* **Unabated.** *With — pleasure*, avec un plaisir toujours nouveau

Undimmed, *adj.* non obscurci, pur, brillant

Undine, *s.* ondin, *m.*, e, *f.*; (*astr.*) Undine, *f.*

Undiplomatic, *adj.* peu diplomatique

Undirected, *adj.* sans direction; (*of letters*, &c.) sans adresse

Undiscerned, *adj.* indiscerné, inaperçu, caché

Undiscernible, &c. *V.* **Indiscernible,** &c.

Undiscerning, *adj.* sans discernement
Undisciplined, *adj.* indiscipliné
Undisclosed, *adj.* non découvert, voilé, caché
Undiscountable, *adj.* inescomptable
Undiscoverable, *adj.* impossible à découvrir ; introuvable
Undiscovered, *adj.* non découvert ; inaperçu ; (*unknown*) inconnu ; (*secret*) caché, secret
Undiscussed, *adj.* indiscuté
Undisfigured, *adj.* non défiguré, indéfiguré
Undisguised, *adj.* non déguisé, indéguisé, sans déguisement, sans fard, ouvert, sincère, franc [sans être découragé ; ferme
Undismayed, *adj.* sans peur, sans terreur ;
Undisposed (of), *adj.* dont on n'a pas disposé ; (*unsold*) non vendu, invendu [conteste
Undisputed, *adj.* indisputé, incontesté, sans
Undissembled, *adj.* non dissimulé ; sincère ; déclaré, ouvert
Undissembling, *adj.* sans dissimulation
Undissolvable. *V.* **Indissoluble**
Undissolved, *adj.* non dissous, indissous
Undistilled, *adj.* non distillé
Undistinguishable, *adj.* indistinguible, indistinct, insaisissable, imperceptible ; méconnaissable
Undistinguishably, *adv.* indistinctement
Undistinguished, *adj.* indistingué ; indistinct ; sans distinction
Undistinguishing, *adj.* qui ne distingue pas ; sans discernement
Undisturbed, *adj.* non troublé ; non dérangé ; sans être interrompu ; calme, tranquille, paisible [non diverti
Undiverted, *adj.* non détourné ; (*not amused*)
Undivided, *adj.* non divisé, indivisé, entier, tout entier, sans partage
Undividedly, *adv.* sans partage, entièrement, conjointement, indivisément [paré
Undivorced, *adj.* non divorcé ; (*fig.*) non sé-
Undivulged, *adj.* non divulgué, caché, secret
Undo, *v.a.* défaire ; délier, détacher ; ouvrir ; détruire, annuler ; changer ; ruiner, perdre
Undock, *v.a.* retirer des docks
Undoer, *s.* défaiseur, *m.*, -euse, *f.*
Undone, *part. adj.* défait, &c. (*V.* **Undo**) ; inexécuté, à faire, qui reste à faire ; ruiné, perdu. *To come* —, se défaire ; se délier, se détacher. *To leave* —, négliger de faire, ne pas faire. *What is done cannot be* —, ce qui est fait est fait [certain ; incontestable ; incontesté
Undoubted, *adj.* indubitable, hors de doute,
Undoubtedly, *adv.* indubitablement ; sans doute, sans aucun doute ; incontestablement
Undoubting, *adj.* certain, convaincu
Undreaded, *adj.* non redouté
Undress, *v.a.* déshabiller ; (*disadorn*) déparer ; (*a wound*) lever l'appareil de ; — *v.n.* se déshabiller ; — *s.* déshabillé, *m.* ; négligé, *m.* ; (*mil., nav.*) petite tenue, *f.* — **cap,** *s.* (*mil.*) képi de petite tenue, bonnet de police, *m.* — **uniform,** *s.* petite tenue, *f.*
Undressed, *adj.* déshabillé ; (*in a loose dress*) en déshabillé, en négligé ; (*of food, com.*) non apprêté ; (*of trees*) non taillé ; (*tech.*) non préparé, cru ; (*fig.*) nu
Undried, *adj.* non séché ; vert
Undrinkable, *adj.* imbuvable
Undue, *adj.* non dû ; illégal, irrégulier, injuste ; excessif ; (*undeserved*) non mérité, immérité ; (*improper*) indu ; (*of bills*) non échu. *V.* **Influence** [*v.a.* onduler
Undulate, *v.n.* onduler, ondoyer ; flotter ; —
Undulated, *adj.* ondulé ; (*of ground*) accidenté
Undulating, *adj.* ondoyant, onduleux ; flottant ; (*of ground*) accidenté
Undulatingly, *adv.* d'une manière ondoyante
Undulation, *s.* ondulation, *f.*
Undulatory, *adj.* ondulatoire, d'ondulation
Unduly, *adv.* irrégulièrement ; indûment, mal à propos ; à tort ; à l'excès, trop
Unduteous, Undutiful, *adj.* qui manque à ses devoirs (envers) ; désobéissant ; indocile ; irrespectueux ; mauvais. —**ly,** *adv.* indocilement ; irrespectueusement. —**ness,** *s.* manque de respect, *m.* ; désobéissance, *f.*
Undy, *adj.* ondé
Undyed, *adj.* non teint [immortel
Undying, *adj.* qui ne meurt pas, impérissable,
Unearned, *adj.* non gagné, qu'on n'a pas gagné, non mérité, immérité
Unearth, *v.a.* déterrer
Unearthly, *adj.* qui n'est pas de ce monde ; surhumain ; surnaturel ; infernal, d'enfer ; céleste ; éthéré
Uneasily, *adv.* péniblement, avec peine, difficilement ; mal à son aise ; (*not readily*) avec gêne ; (*in anxiety*) dans l'inquiétude
Uneasiness, *s.* inquiétude, *f.* ; (*uncomfortableness*) gêne, *f.* ; malaise, *m.* ; (*pain*) peine, *f.*, chagrin, *m.* ; (*trouble*) déplaisir, ennui, *m.*
Uneasy, *adj.* inquiet (de, sur) ; préoccupé (de) ; agité ; (*making uncomfortable*) gênant, incommode ; (*constrained*) gêné ; mal à son aise ; (*disagreeable*) désagréable ; pénible. *To make oneself* —, s'inquiéter (de), se mettre en peine (de). *Don't be* — ! soyez tranquille !
Uneatable, *adj.* immangeable
Uneaten, *adj.* non mangé
Unedifying, *adj.* peu édifiant [struction
Uneducated, *adj.* sans éducation, sans in-
Uneffaced, *adj.* ineffacé
Uneffected, *adj.* ineffectué
Unembarrassed, *adj.* non embarrassé ; (*pers.*) à l'aise ; (*free*) libre (de)
Unembellished, *adj.* sans embellissement
Unemployed, *adj.* non employé, inemployé, sans emploi ; inoccupé ; oisif ; sans travail ; inactif
Unenclosed, *adj.* sans clôture, ouvert
Unencumbered, *adj.* non encombré *or* chargé (de) ; non embarrassé (de) ; débarrassé (de), dégagé (de), libre (de) ; libre, à l'aise ; (*of estates*) non grevé ; non hypothéqué
Unending, *adj.* sans fin ; infini
Unendowed, *adj.* non doté, sans dotation ; (*not gifted*) non doué (de) ; dénué (de)
Unendurable, *adj.* insupportable
Unendurably, *adv.* insupportablement
Unenduring, *adj.* pas durable, de courte durée
Unenfranchised, *adj.* non affranchi du cens électoral, privé du droit électoral
Unengaging, *adj.* non attrayant, sans charmes
Un-English, *adj.* pas anglais, rien moins qu'anglais ; indigne d'un Anglais, peu digne d'un Anglais [on n'a pas joui
Unenjoyed, *adj.* dont on ne jouit pas, dont
Unenlightened, *adj.* peu éclairé ; ignorant
Unenslaved, *adj.* inasservi, libre
Unenterprising, *adj.* peu entreprenant
Unentertaining, *adj.* peu amusant, ennuyeux
Unenviable, *adj.* peu digne d'envie, peu dé-
Unenvied, *adj.* peu envié [sirable
Unequal, *adj.* inégal ; disproportionné ; inférieur (à), au-dessous (de) ; insuffisant (pour). — *to the task,* pas à la hauteur de cette (*or* de sa) tâche
Unequalled, *adj.* sans égal, sans pareil, unique
Unequally, *adv.* inégalement
Unequivocal, *adj.* non équivoque ; franc
Unequivocally, *adv.* sans équivoque
Unerring, *adj.* infaillible, sûr
Unerringly, *adv.* infailliblement ; d'une manière sûre ; à coup sûr
Uneven, *adj.* inégal ; (*rugged*) raboteux ; (*of numbers*) impair [impairement
Unevenly, *adv.* inégalement ; (*of numbers*)
Unevenness, *s.* inégalité, *f.*
Uneventful, *adj.* dépourvu d'événements
Unexaggerated, *adj.* non exagéré, nullement exagéré
Unexaminable, *adj.* inexaminable
Unexamined, *adj.* non examiné, sans examen ; non visité ; (*law*) non interrogé

Unexampled. *V.* **Unprecedented**
Unexceptionable, *adj.* irréprochable; irrécusable
Unexceptionableness, *s.* irréprochabilité, nature irréprochable *or* irrécusable, *f.*
Unexceptionably, *adv.* irréprochablement; irrécusablement
Unexecuted, *adj.* inexécuté; ineffectué
Unexemplary, *adj.* peu exemplaire
Unexemplified, *adj.* sans exemple
Unexercised, *adj.* inexercé
Unexhausted, *adj.* inépuisé
Unexpanded, *adj.* non épanoui, inépanoui; non répandu; non dilaté
Unexpected, *adj.* (*pers.*) inattendu; (*things*) inattendu, imprévu, inopiné, subit; (*unhoped for*) inespéré
Unexpectedly, *adv.* inopinément, subitement, à l'improviste [vu, *m.*
Unexpectedness, *s.* soudaineté, *f.*; impré-
Unexpended, *adj.* non dépensé
Unexperienced, *adj.* inexpérimenté; non éprouvé, inéprouvé
Unexpiated, *adj.* inexpié
Unexpired, *adj.* non expiré; (*of bills*) non échu [tion; inéclairci
Unexplained, *adj.* inexpliqué, sans explica-
Unexplored, *adj.* inexploré
Unexposed, *adj.* non exposé; caché, secret
Unexpressed, *adj.* inexprimé; sous-entendu
Unextended, *adj.* inétendu, peu étendu
Unextinct, Unextinguished, *adj.* non
Unextirpated, *adj.* inextirpé [éteint
Unfaded, *adj.* non fané, non flétri, dans toute sa fraîcheur
Unfading, *adj.* qui ne se fane pas, qui ne se flétrit pas; durable; impérissable
Unfailing, *adj.* infaillible, immanquable; (*inexhaustible*) inépuisable, intarissable [blement
Unfailingly, *adv.* infailliblement, immanqua-
Unfailingness, *s.* infaillibilité, *f.*
Unfair, *adj.* injuste; malhonnête, déloyal, de mauvaise foi; (*improper*) inconvenant; (*at play*) (ne ...) pas du jeu. **—ly,** *adv.* injustement; malhonnêtement, déloyalement, avec mauvaise foi. **—ness,** *s.* injustice, *f.*; malhonnêteté, déloyauté, mauvaise foi, *f.*; partialité, *f.*
Unfaithful, &c. *V.* **Faithless,** &c.
Unfallowed, *adj.* non jachéré, non en friche,
Unfalsifiable, infalsifiable [refroissé
Unfaltering, *adj.* assuré, ferme, hardi, décidé, sans hésitation
Unfamiliar, *adj.* peu familier; peu connu
Unfamiliarity, *s.* manque de familiarité, *m.*
Unfashionable, *adj.* (*things*) qui n'est pas de mode; démodé; (*pers.*) qui n'est pas à la mode
Unfashionableness, *s.* inélégance, *f.*
Unfashionably, *adv.* contre la mode, pas à la mode; (*coarsely*) grossièrement [simple
Unfashioned, *adj.* non façonné; informe;
Unfasten, *v.a.* délier, détacher; défaire; (*loose*) desserrer; (*open*) ouvrir
Unfatherly, *adj.* indigne d'un père, peu paternel [impénétrable
Unfathomable, *adj.* insondable; sans fond;
Unfathomableness, *s.* nature insondable, *f.*; impénétrabilité, *f.*
Unfathomably, *adv.* d'une manière insondable; impénétrablement
Unfathomed, *adj.* non sondé; insondable
Unfatigued, *adj.* non fatigué, frais
Unfavourable, *adj.* défavorable, peu favorable; contraire; fâcheux
Unfavourableness, *s.* nature défavorable, *f.*
Unfavourably, *adv.* défavorablement
Unfeared, *adj.* non craint
Unfeasible, *adj.* infaisable, impraticable
Unfeathered, *adj.* sans plumes; (*jest.*) dé-
Unfeatured, *adj.* laid, difforme [plumé
Unfed, *adj.* non nourri, sans nourriture, sans aliments; (*fig.*) non alimenté, non entretenu
Unfeed, *adj.* non rétribué, sans rétribution
Unfeeling, *adj.* insensible; impitoyable; dur; cruel
Unfeelingly, *adv.* avec insensibilité; cruellement, avec cruauté; sans pitié
Unfeelingness, *s.* insensibilité, *f.*; cruauté, *f.*
Unfeigned, *adj.* sincère, vrai
Unfeignedly, *adv.* sincèrement, de bonne foi; réellement; franchement; sans déguisement
Unfeignedness, *s.* sincérité, *f.*; vérité, *f.*
Unfelt, *adj.* non senti, qu'on ne sent pas; qu'on ne ressent pas; (*unknown*) inconnu
Unfence, *v.a.* déclore
Unfenced, *adj.* sans défense; (*of fields*) sans clôture [sans levain
Unfermented, *adj.* non fermenté; (*of bread*)
Unfertile, *adj.* infertile, infécond, stérile
Unfetter, *v.a.* ôter les fers à, délier, déchaîner; (*free*) délivrer (de), affranchir (de)
Unfettered, *adj.* libre; sans entraves
Unfigured, *adj.* sans figures
Unfilial, *adj.* peu filial
Unfilled, *adj.* non rempli; inoccupé; vacant
Unfinished, *adj.* inachevé; imparfait, incomplet
Unfit, *adj.* peu propre (à); impropre (à); qui n'est pas fait (pour) *or* bon (à); incapable (de); hors d'état (de); inopportun, déplacé; — *v.a.* rendre incapable (de); mettre hors d'état (de); rendre impropre (à). — *for human food,* (*admin.*) impropre à la consommation. — *for service,* hors de service; hors d'état de servir; (*mil., nav.*) impropre au service. — *for use,* d'aucun usage
Unfitly, *adv.* mal à propos; à tort; mal
Unfitness, *s.* inaptitude, *f.*; incapacité, *f.*; impropriété, *f.*; inconvenance, *f.*
Unfitting, *adj.* inconvenant
Unfix, *v.a.* détacher, délier; (*mil.*) remettre. *To come —ed,* se détacher. — *bayonets!* remettez la baïonnette!
Unfixed, *adj.* mobile; errant, inconstant; indécis, incertain, irrésolu; (*of ground*) mouvant
Unfixedness, *s.* mobilité, *f.*; inconstance, *f.*; indécision, incertitude, *f.*
Unflag, *v.a.* (*unpave*) dédaller
Unflagging, *adj.* soutenu, toujours égal; infatigable; — *s.* (*unpaving*) dédallage, *m.*
Unfledged, *adj.* sans plumes, frais éclos; (*pers.*) jeune; naïf; inexpérimenté, novice; (*growing*) naissant
Unfleshed, *adj.* (*hunt.*) non acharné; (*raw*) pur de sang [qui ne recule pas
Unflinching, *adj.* ferme, résolu, intrépide,
Unflinchingly, *adv.* résolûment, de pied ferme, sans reculer, sans sourciller
Unfold, *v.a.* déployer; déplier; ouvrir; développer, exposer; dérouler, dévoiler, découvrir, révéler; (*sheep*) déparquer; — *v.n.* se déployer; se déplier; s'ouvrir; se développer; se dérouler, se dévoiler, se découvrir, se révéler
Unfolding, *adj.* (*made to unfold*) pouvant se déplier; — *s.* développement, *m.*; révélation, *f.*; (*of troops*) déploiement, *m.*
Unforbearing, *adj.* intolérant; impatient;
Unforbidden, *adj.* permis [sévère
Unforced, *adj.* libre; naturel; aisé, facile; prompt; spontané
Unfordable, *adj.* inguéable
Unforeseeing, *adj.* qui ne prévoit pas; imprévoyant; imprudent
Unforeseen, *adj.* imprévu; inattendu
Unforfeited, *adj.* non confisqué; non perdu
Unforgiven. *V.* **Unpardoned** [placable
Unforgiving, *adj.* qui ne pardonne pas, im-
Unforgotten, *adj.* non oublié
Unformed, *adj.* informe
Unfortified, *adj.* non fortifié, infortifié, sans défense, ouvert. — *town,* ville ouverte, *f.*
Unfortunate, *adj.* infortuné; malheureux;

fâcheux ; — *s.* infortuné, *m.*, e, *f.*, malheureux, *m.*, -euse, *f.* [malheur
Unfortunately, *adv.* malheureusement ; par
Unfought, *adj.* non combattu ; (*of battles*) non livré ; (*without struggle*) sans combat, sans
Unfound, *adj.* introuvé, non trouvé [lutte
Unfounded, *adj.* dénué de fondement, sans fondement, controuvé, faux ; mal fondé
Unframed, *adj.* non façonné ; (*of pictures, &c.*) non encadré, sans cadre
Unfraternal, *adj.* infraternel
Unfrequenc-e, y. *V.* **Infrequence**
Unfrequent, *adj.* infréquent, rare
Unfrequented, *adj.* infréquenté, peu fréquenté, solitaire, retiré, écarté
Unfrequently, *adv.* infréquemment, peu souvent, rarement. *Not* —, assez souvent
Unfriended, *adj.* sans amis ; sans soutien
Unfriendliness, *s.* manque d'amitié, *m.* disposition peu amicale, *f.*, défaut de bienveillance, *f.* ; froideur, *f.*
Unfriendly, *adj.* peu bienveillant ; peu obligeant ; mal disposé ; (*things*) peu amical ; froid ; hostile, malveillant ; défavorable, contraire,
Unfrock, *v.a.* défroquer [nuisible (à)
Unfrozen, *adj.* non gelé
Unfruitful, *adj.* stérile, infécond, infertile ; (*without effect*) infructueux. **—ly,** *adv.* stérilement, infertilement ; (*without effect*) infructueusement. **—ness,** *s.* stérilité, infécondité,
Unfulfilled, *adj.* non accompli [infertilité, *f.*
Unfunded, *adj.* non consolidé. — *debt,* dette flottante, *f.*
Unfurl, *v.a.* déployer ; (*nav.*) déferler
Unfurnish, *v.a.* dégarnir ; dépouiller ; (*a house or apartment*) démeubler
Unfurnished, *adj.* non garni ; (*stripped*) dégarni (de) ; (*deprived*) dépourvu (de), dénué (de) ; (*of a house or apartment*) (*not furnished*) non meublé, (*stripped of its furniture*) démeublé
Ungainable, *adj.* ingagnable
Ungainful, *adj.* sans profit, ingrat [gingandé
Ungainly, *adj.* maladroit, gauche ; mal bâti, dé-
Ungallant, *adj.* peu galant ; peu courtois
Ungarnished, *adj.* non garni ; sans orne-
Ungarrisoned, *adj.* sans garnison [ments
Ungartered, *adj.* sans jarretières
Ungathered, *adj.* non cueilli ; non recueilli ; pas récolté [rosité ; (*mean*) mesquin
Ungenerous, *adj.* peu généreux, sans géné-
Ungenerously, *adv.* sans générosité ; (*meanly*) mesquinement
Ungenial, *adj.* malsain ; rigoureux, rude ; nuisible ; ennemi ; triste ; (*pers.*) froid
Ungenteel, *adj.* commun, vulgaire ; de mauvais goût ; de mauvais ton ; pas comme il faut ; mal élevé [impoli
Ungentle, *adj.* rude, dur, sévère ; indocile ;
Ungentlemanlike, Ungentlemanly, *adj.* commun, vulgaire, de mauvais ton, de mauvaise compagnie, peu distingué ; (*of behaviour*) indigne d'un homme comme il faut ; indélicat, sans délicatesse ; grossier ; déshonorant
Ungentlemanliness, *s.* vulgarité, *f.* ; impolitesse, *f.* [*f.* ; brusquerie, *f.* ; impolitesse, *f.*
Ungentleness, *s.* rudesse, dureté, sévérité,
Ungently, *adv.* rudement, durement, sévèrement ; impoliment
Ungifted, *adj.* peu doué (de)
Ungild, *v.a.* dédorer
Ungilding, *s.* dédorure, *f.* [non doré
Ungilt, Ungilded, *adj.* dédoré ; (*not gilt*)
Ungird, *v.a.* ôter la ceinture à ; (*untie*) défaire, détacher ; (*horses,* &c.) dessangler
Ungirt, *adj.* sans ceinture ; (*horse,* &c.) dessanglé ; — *v.a.* dessangler
Ungirth, *v.a.* dessangler
Unglazed, *adj.* non vitré ; (*ware*) non verni ; (*paper,* &c.) non glacé ; (*stuff*) non lustré
Unglorified, *adj.* inglorifié
Unglove, *v.a.* déganter
Unglue, *v.a.* décoller
Ungodliness, *s.* impiété, *f.*
Ungodly, *adj.* impie
Ungovernable, *adj.* ingouvernable ; indomptable ; effréné ; violent, emporté ; (*extravagant*) désordonné, déréglé [frein ; désordonnément
Ungovernably, *adv.* indomptablement ; sans
Ungoverned, *adj.* sans gouvernement ; sans lois ; (*unbridled*) effréné ; désordonné, déréglé
Ungraceful, *adj.* sans grâce, disgracieux
Ungracefully, *adv.* sans grâce [gaucherie, *f.*
Ungracefulness, *s.* manque de grâce, *m.*,
Ungracious, *adj.* ingracieux, disgracieux, désagréable ; dur ; (*not favoured*) mal vu
Ungraciously, *adv.* ingracieusement, disgracieusement, d'une manière peu gracieuse ; de mauvaise grâce [rect
Ungrammatical, *adj.* ingrammatical, incor-
Ungrammatically, *adv.* ingrammaticalement, incorrectement [gréable
Ungrateful, *adj.* ingrat ('*to,*' envers) ; désa-
Ungratefully, *adv.* ingratement, avec ingratitude ; désagréablement [désagréable, *f.*
Ungratefulness, *s.* ingratitude, *f.* ; nature
Ungratified, *adj.* non satisfait
Ungrounded, &c. *V.* **Groundless,** &c.
Ungrudged, *adj.* donné de bon cœur
Ungrudging, *adj.* qui donne de bon cœur
Ungrudgingly, *adv.* de bon cœur, volontiers
Ungual, *adj.* unguéal
Unguaranteed, *adj.* non garanti, ingaranti
Unguard, *v.a.* laisser sans protection ; découvrir
Unguarded, *adj* non gardé, sans garde, sans protection, sans défense ; découvert ; (*off o.'s guard*) qui n'est pas sur ses gardes ; inconsidéré, irréfléchi ; d'irréflexion, d'absence, d'oubli ; indiscret ; imprudent ; négligent
Unguardedly, *adv.* étourdiment, sans atten-
Ungueal, *adj.* unguéal [tion
Unguent, *s.* onguent, *m.*
Unguessable, *adj.* indevinable
Unguessed, *adj.* non deviné, indeviné
Unguiculate, -d, *adj.* onguiculé
Unguided, *adj.* sans guide
Unguiferous, *adj.* unguifère
Unguilty, *adj.* innocent
Ungulate, *adj.* ongulé
Ungum, *v.a.* dégommer ; (*silk*) décruser
Unhallow, *v.a.* profaner [profane, impie
Unhallowed, *adj.* non sanctifié ; profané ;
Unhand, *v.a.* lâcher, laisser aller
Unhandily, *adv.* maladroitement, gauchement
Unhandiness, *s.* maladresse, gaucherie, *f.* ; (*of things*) incommodité, *f.*
Unhandsome, *adj.* laid, vilain ; indélicat ; petit, mesquin, peu généreux ; déloyal ; malhonnête. **—ly,** *adv.* indélicatement ; petitement, mesquinement ; mal ; malhonnêtement. **—ness,** *s.* indélicatesse, *f.* ; malhonnêteté, *f.*
Unhandy, *adj.* maladroit, gauche ; (*things*) incommode, gênant [démonter
Unhang, *v.a.* dépendre ; détendre ; descendre ;
Unhappily, *adv.* malheureusement ; par mal-
Unhappiness, *s.* malheur, *m.* [heur
Unhappy, *adj.* malheureux ; infortuné ; funeste [asile
Unharboured, *adj.* sans port ; sans abri, sans
Unharmed. *V.* **Unhurt**
Unharness, *v.a.* déharnacher ; (*take from a vehicle*) dételer ; (*disarm*) désarmer
Unhatched, *adj.* non éclos
Unhealthful. *V.* **Unhealthy**
Unhealthily, *adv.* sans santé ; maladivement ; insalubrement
Unhealthiness, *s.* défaut de santé, *m.* ; maladiveté, *f.* ; (*of places*) insalubrité, *f.* [insalubre
Unhealthy, *adj.* maladif ; (*of places*) malsain,
Unheard, *adj.* sans être entendu, inentendu ; inconnu, ignoré ; (*ungranted*) inexaucé. — *of,* inconnu, ignoré ; (*extraordinary*) inouï
Unheeded, *adj.* inaperçu ; (*disregarded*) méconnu ; (*neglected*) négligé

Unheedful, Unheeding, *adj.* &c. *V.* **Heedless,** &c.
Unhelped, *adj.* sans secours ; sans aide ; (*at table*) pas servi
Unhesitating, *adj.* déterminé, résolu ; ferme ; prompt ; sans hésitation
Unhesitatingly, *adv.* sans hésiter
Unhewn, *adj.* brut, non travaillé ; (*of stones*) non taillé
Unhindered, *adj.* libre, sans obstacle, sans empêchement
Unhinge, *v.a.* dégonder, faire sortir des gonds ; (*fig.*) bouleverser, troubler, déranger, démonter, mettre hors des gonds
Unholiness, *s.* impiété, *f.*
Unholy, *adj.* impie ; profane
Unhonoured, *adj.* sans honneur, inhonoré ; dédaigné, méprisé
Unhook, *v.a.* décrocher ; (*hook and eye*) dégrafer
Unhoop, *v.a.* décercler
Unhoped-for, *adj.* inespéré, inattendu
Unhorse, *v.a.* démonter, désarçonner
Unhouse, *v.a.* déloger ; chasser
Unhurt, *adj.* sans blessure ; sain et sauf ; (*things*) intact
Unichord, *adj.* (*mus.*) unicorde
Unicorn, *s.* licorne, *f.*, unicorne, *m.* — **fish,** *s.* narval, *m.* — **team,** *s.* attelage en arbalète, *m.*
Unicornous, *adj.* unicorne
Unideal, *adj.* réel, positif
Unidiomatic, *adj.* qui n'est pas idiomatique
Unification, *s.* unification, *f.*
Uniflorous, *adj.* uniflore
Unifoliate, *adj.* unifolié
Uniform, *adj. s.* uniforme, *adj.m.f.*, *s.m.* *In full* —, en grand uniforme, en grande tenue
Uniformity, *s.* uniformité, *f.*
Uniformization, *s.* uniformisation, *f.*
Uniformize, *v.a.* uniformiser ; — *v.n.* s'uniformiser
Uniformly, *adv.* uniformément
Unify, *v.a.* unifier ; — *v.n.* s'unifier
Unilateral, *adj.* unilatéral
Unimaginable, *adj.* inimaginable
Unimitated, *adj.* inimité
Unimpairable, *adj.* inaltérable
Unimpaired, *adj.* intact, entier ; non altéré ; non diminué ; non affaibli ; dans toute sa vigueur
Unimpassioned, *adj.* sans passion ; calme
Unimpeachable, *adj.* inattaquable ; irréprochable ; irrécusable ; incontestable ; à toute épreuve
Unimpeached, *adj.* non accusé ; sans reproche ; incontesté
Unimpeded. V. **Unhindered**
Unimportance, *s.* peu d'importance, *m.*, insignifiance, *f.*
Unimportant, *adj.* insignifiant, peu important, sans importance ; léger ; sans prétention
Unimpoverished, *adj.* inappauvri
Unimproved, *adj.* non corrigé ; non amélioré, non perfectionné ; sans progrès, qui n'a rien appris
Uninclosed, Unincumbered, &c. *V.* **Unenclosed, Unencumbered,** &c.
Unindented, *adj.* indenté
Unindustrious, *adj.* inindustrieux ; paresseux
Uninfected, *adj.* non infecté (de)
Uninflammability, *s.* ininflammabilité, *f.*
Uninflammable, *adj.* non inflammable, ininflammable, incombustible
Uninfluenced, *adj.* non influencé (par), libre (de)
Uninfluential, *adj.* sans influence
Uninformed, *adj.* ignorant
Uninhabitable, *adj.* inhabitable
Uninhabited, *adj.* inhabité
Uninitiated, *adj.* non initié
Uninjured. *V.* **Unhurt**
Uninscribed, *adj.* non inscrit ; sans inscription
Uninspired, *adj.* non inspiré, sans inspiration ; (*writer*) profane
Uninstructed, *adj.* sans instruction, ignorant ; (*not directed*) sans instructions
Uninstructive, *adj.* peu instructif
Uninsured, *adj.* non assuré, inassuré
Unintellectual, *adj.* non intellectuel
Unintelligent, *adj.* inintelligent
Unintelligently, *adv.* inintelligemment
Unintelligi-bility, bleness, *s.* inintelligibilité, *f.*
Unintelligible, *adj.* inintelligible
Unintelligibly, *adv.* inintelligiblement
Unintended, Unintentional, *adj.* sans intention, fait (*or* dit *or* &c.) sans intention *or* sans dessein, involontaire
Unintentionally, *adv.* involontairement, sans le vouloir, sans intention
Uninterested, *adj.* désintéressé (dans) ; (*fig.*) indifférent (à), étranger (à)
Uninteresting, *adj.* dénué d'intérêt, sans intérêt, peu intéressant ; plat
Unintermitted, Unintermitting, *adj.* continuel, continu, incessant, sans interruption
Unintermittingly, *adv.* sans cesse, sans interruption
Uninterred, *adj.* sans sépulture
Uninterrupted, *adj.* non interrompu, ininterrompu, sans interruption ; continuel
Uninterruptedly, *adv.* sans interruption
Unintrenched, *adj.* non retranché, sans retranchements
Uninured, *adj.* non endurci ; non aguerri
Uninventive, *adj.* peu inventif
Uninvested, *adj.* non investi ; (*of money*) non placé
Uninvited, *adj.* sans invitation, sans être invité, non invité, inconvié
Uninviting, *adj.* peu attrayant, peu engageant, peu appétissant, peu ragoûtant ; repoussant
Union, *s.* union, *f.* ; (*workhouse*) *V.* **Workhouse ;** (*trade* —) *V.* **Trade ;** (*geog.*) Union, *f.*, États-Unis, *m.pl.* ; (*flag*) pavillon, *m.* — *is strength,* l'union fait la force. — **flag,** — **jack,** *s.* pavillon anglais, yac, yak, *m.* — **goods,** *s.pl.* étoffes mélangées, *f.pl.*
Unionism, *s.* unionisme, *m.*
Unionist, *s. adj.* unioniste, *m.f.* ; (*trade* —) *V.* **Trade**
Uniparous, *adj.* unipare
Unipersonal, *adj.* unipersonnel
Unipersonally, *adv.* unipersonnellement
Unipetalous, *adj.* unipétale, unipétalé
Unique, *adj.* unique
Uniquely, *adv.* uniquement
Uniqueness, *s.* unicité, *f.*
Unison, *s.* unisson, *m.* *In* —, à l'unisson
Unisonance, *s.* unisonnance, *f.*
Unisonant, *adj.* unisonnant
Unit, *s.* unité, *f.*
Unitarian, *s. adj.* unitaire, *m.f.*
Unitarianism, *s.* unitarianisme, unitarisme, *m.*
Unite, *v.a.* unir (' *to* ' or ' *with,*' à, avec) ; joindre (à) ; (*efforts,* &c.) réunir ; joindre ; — *v.n.* s'unir ; se joindre
United, *part. adj.* uni ; joint ; (*efforts,* &c.) réuni. — *Kingdom,* Royaume-Uni, *m.* — *Provinces,* Provinces-Unies, *f.pl.* — *States,* États-Unis, *m.pl.*
Unitedly, *adv.* avec union ; conjointement ; ensemble ; d'accord ; de concert
Unity, *s.* unité, *f.* ; union, concorde, harmonie, *f.*
Univalve, *adj. s.* univalve, *adj. m.f.*, *s.m.*
Univalved, Univalvular, *adj.* univalve
Universal, *adj.* universel, *m.*, universelle, *f.*, universels, *m.pl.*, universelles, *f.pl.* ; — *s.* (*log.*) universel, *m.* (—**s,** *pl.* universaux, *m.pl.*)
Universal-ism, -ist. *V.* page 3, § 1
Universality, Universalness, *s.* universalité, *f.*
Universalize, *v.a.* universaliser
Universally, *adv.* universellement
Universe, *s.* univers, *m.*
University, *s.* université, *f.* ; — *adj.* d'université, de l'université, des universités, universitaire. —**man,** *s.* universitaire, *m.*
Unjust, *adj.* injuste
Unjustifiable, *adj.* injustifiable ; inexcusable
Unjustifiableness, *s.* nature injustifiable *or* inexcusable, *f.*
Unjustifiably, *adv.* injustifiablement ; inexcusablement
Unjustified, *adj.* injustifié, sans justification, sans excuse

Unjustly, *adv.* injustement
Unkempt. *V.* **Uncombed**
Unkennel, *v.a.* lancer; déterrer: (*a stag*) débûcher; (*dogs*) sortir du chenil; (*fig.*) relancer; (*disclose*) découvrir
Unkept, *adj.* non entretenu; non accompli; non gardé, non conservé; non retenu; non observé; non célébré
Unkind, *adj.* peu aimable; désobligeant; (*hard*) dur, méchant (pour)
Unkindly, *adj.* contraire (à), nuisible (à); — *adv.* d'une manière peu aimable; désobligeamment; mal; (*hardly*) durement. *To take a thing* —, prendre une chose en mal
Unkindness, *s.* manque d'amabilité, *m.*; désobligeance, *f.*; malveillance, *f.*; (*harshness*) dureté, méchanceté, *f.*
Unknit, *v.a.* défaire; dénouer; (*the brow*) dé-
Unknot, *v.a.* dénouer [rider (le front)
Unknowable, *adj.* inconnaissable; impénétrable; (*pers.*) méconnaissable
Unknowing, *adj.* ignorant, qui ne sait pas, qui ne connaît pas
Unknowingly, *adv.* à son insu, insciemment, sans le savoir, sans s'en douter, sans s'en apercevoir, sans en avoir conscience; insensiblement; par inadvertance, sans y penser
Unknown, *adj.* inconnu (à); ignoré (de); (*without ...'s knowledge*) à l'insu (de) (— *to me, to him* or *her*, &c., à mon insu, à son insu, &c.); (*unheard of*) inouï
Unlaboured, *adj.* non travaillé; inculte; spontané; naturel; facile, aisé
Unlace, *v.a.* délacer; détacher
Unlade, *v.a.* décharger
Unlading, *s.* déchargement, *m.*
Unladylike, *adj.* commun, peu distingué; (*of behaviour*) peu digne d'une dame, peu comme il faut [pleuré, sans laisser de regrets
Unlamented, *adj.* non regretté, sans être
Unlatch, *v.a.* lever le loquet de, ouvrir
Unlath, *v.a.* délatter
Unlawful, *adj.* illégal; illicite; (*of birth*) illégitime. — *adv.* illégalement; illicitement; illégitimement; (*of children*) d'un commerce illégitime. —**ness,** *s.* illégalité, *f.*; (*of birth*)
Unlearn, *v.a.* désapprendre [illégitimité, *f.*
Unlearnable, *adj.* inapprenable
Unlearned, *adj.* (*pers.*) ignorant, illettré, inérudit; (*things*) non appris, inappris, ignoré
Unlearnedly, *adv.* avec ignorance [azyme
Unleavened, *adj.* sans levain; (*Jew. law*)
Unless, *conj.* à moins que (*with the subj. and* ne); à moins de (*before an inf.*); excepté, si ce n'est, sinon. — *I go there*, à moins que je n'y aille; à moins d'y aller; si je n'y vais pas. — *called*, à moins d'être appelé
Unlettered, *adj.* illettré, ignorant
Unlevel, *v.a.* déniveler [nivelé, inégal
Unlevelled, *adj.* dénivelé; (*not levelled*) non
Unlevelling, *s.* dénivellement, *m.*
Unlicensed, *adj.* non autorisé, sans autorisation; (*of tradesmen*) non patenté, sans patente; (*of brokers and printers*) marron; (*of books*) non déposé; (*of sportsmen*) sans permis
Unlicked, *adj.* mal léché; grossier [allumé
Unlighted, *adj.* non éclairé; (*not kindled*) non
Unlike, *adj.* différent; qui ne ressemble pas à (...); éloigné (de); — *prep.* tout au contraire de, à l'inverse de. *To be not* — ..., ne ressembler pas mal à ..., ressembler assez à ..., être assez semblable à ... *To be* — *each other*, être différents, ne pas se ressembler
Unlikelihood, Unlikeliness, *s.* invraisemblance, improbabilité, *f.*
Unlikely, *adj.* invraisemblable, improbable; peu certain, peu sûr; — *adv.* invraisemblablement. *It is very* — *that* ..., il n'y a pas de probabilité que ... *That is not at all* —, c'est très possible; cela se pourrait bien. *He is not* — *to* ..., il pourrait bien ..., il est capable de ..., il est dans le cas de ...

Unlikeness, *s.* dissemblance, différence, *f.*
Unlimber, *v.a.* détacher *or* dégager (une pièce) de son avant-train
Unlimited, *adj.* illimité, sans bornes; (*undefined*) indéfini, indéterminé. —**ly,** *adv.* sans bornes, sans limites; indéfiniment. —**ness,** *s.* nature illimitée, *f.*; nature indéfinie, *f.*
Unlink, *v.a.* défaire; (*uncoil*) dérouler
Unliquidated, *adj.* non liquidé; non acquitté
Unlistened to, *adj.* inécouté
Unlistening, *adj.* qui n'écoute pas; sourd (à)
Unliterary, *adj.* sans caractère littéraire;
Unliveliness, *s.* lourdeur, *f.* [illettré
Unlively, *adj.* lourd
Unload, *v.a.* décharger [chargé
Unloaded, *adj.* déchargé; (*not charged*) pas
Unloading, *s.* déchargement, *m.*
Unlock, *v.a.* ouvrir
Unlocking, *s.* ouverture, *f.* [espéré
Unlooked-for, *adj.* inattendu, imprévu; in-
Unloose, *v.a.* *V.* **Loose,** *v.a.*
Unloved, *adj.* pas aimé
Unloveliness, *s.* défaut d'amabilité, *m.*; humeur désagréable, *f.*; (*ugliness*) laideur, *f.*
Unlovely, *adj.* peu aimable; désagréable
Unloving, *adj.* peu aimant, peu affectueux; insensible
Unluckily, *adv.* malheureusement; malencontreusement [mauvais présage, *m.*
Unluckiness, *s.* malheur, *m.*, infortune, *f.*;
Unlucky, *adj.* malheureux, infortuné; malencontreux; (*mischievous*) méchant; (*ill-omened*) sinistre, de mauvais présage, de mauvais augure, de malheur. *To be* —, (*in games*, &c.) n'avoir pas de chance, avoir du guignon
Unmake, *v.a.* défaire; détruire; anéantir; ruiner
Unman, *v.a.* dégrader; énerver, efféminer, amollir; (*deject*) abattre, décourager; (*emasculate*) châtrer; (*deprive of men*) dégarnir d'hommes; (*a ship*) désarmer
Unmanageable, *adj.* impossible à conduire *or* à gouverner, ingouvernable; intraitable; indisciplinable; indocile, rebelle; indomptable; (*unwieldy*) pas (*or* peu) maniable. *To become* —, (*of horses*) s'emporter. *That* (*business or &c.*) *is* —, cela n'est pas faisable, c'est impraticable, il est impossible d'en venir à bout
Unmanaged, *adj.* non dressé; indompté; sans éducation [homme
Unmanfully, *adv.* d'une manière indigne d'un
Unmanliness, *s.* conduite indigne d'un homme, *f.*; manque de fermeté, *m.*; lâcheté, *f.*; indignité, *f.*
Unmanly, *adj.* indigne (*or* peu digne) d'un homme; efféminé; lâche; mou; pusillanime
Unmannerliness, *s.* grossièreté, *f.*
Unmannerly, Unmannered, *adj.* *V.* **Ill-mannered**
Unmannerly, *adv.* grossièrement
Unmanufactured, *adj.* non manufacturé, non fabriqué, brut. — *goods*, (les) matières premières, *f.pl.*
Unmanured, *adj.* sans engrais
Unmarked, *adj.* non marqué; (*unseen*) inaperçu, inobservé [dable
Unmarketable, *adj.* non marchand, inven-
Unmarred, *adj.* non gâté; non troublé; pur
Unmarriageable, *adj.* immariable
Unmarried, *adj.* non marié, pas marié, célibataire. — **man,** &c. *V.* **Single**
Unmarry, *v.a.* démarier
Unmask, *v.a.* démasquer; — *v.n.* se démasquer
Unmasked, *adj.* démasqué; sans masque; (*fig.*) sans déguisement
Unmastered, *adj.* indompté; non maîtrisé
Unmatch, *v.a.* désassortir, dépareiller; déparier
Unmatched, *adj.* désassorti, dépareillé; déparié; sans pareil, sans égal, unique, incomparable
Unmeaning, *adj.* sans aucun sens, vide de

sens, qui n'a pas de sens, qui ne signifie rien, insignifiant. —**ly**, *adv.* d'une manière insignifiante. —**ness**, *s.* manque de signification, *m.*, insignifiance, *f.*

Unmeant, *adj.* involontaire

Unmeasured, *adj.* immense; infini; illimité, sans bornes; sans mesure; démesuré

Unmeditated, *adj.* immédité, non médité; non prémédité; improvisé

Unmeet, *adj.* peu convenable; inconvenant

Unmelodious, *adj.* sans mélodie

Unmelodiously, *adv.* d'une manière peu mélodieuse [dri; inflexible, inexorable

Unmelted, *adj.* non fondu; (*pers.*) non atten-

Unmendable, *adj.* irraccommodable

Unmentionable, *adj.* dont on de doit pas parler; innommable; —**s**, *s.pl.* (*trousers*) inexpressible, *m.*

Unmentioned, *adj.* non mentionné, dont on ne parle pas; (*unknown*) ignoré

Unmercenary, *adj.* désintéressé

Unmerchantable. *V.* **Unmarketable**

Unmerciful, *adj.* impitoyable, sans pitié; cruel; sans indulgence; exorbitant. —**ly**, *adv.* impitoyablement, sans pitié; sans indulgence; cruellement. —**ness**, *s.* dureté, *f.*; sévérité, *f.*; cruauté, barbarie, *f.*

Unmerited, *adj.* immérité, non mérité

Unmeritorious, *adj.* imméritoire

Unmethodical, *adj.* imméthodique, sans méthode, confus. —**ly**, *adv.* imméthodiquement, sans méthode, confusément. —**ness**, *s.* défaut (*or* manque) de méthode, *m.*, confusion, *f.*

Unmilitary, *adj.* non militaire

Unminded. *V.* **Unheeded**

Unmindful, *adj.* inattentif (à); (*forgetful*) oublieux (de); (*regardless*) peu soucieux (de), insouciant (de); négligent. —**ly**, *adv.* inattentivement; avec insouciance; négligemment, sans soin. —**ness**, *s.* inattention, *f.*; oubli, *m.*; insouciance, *f.*; négligence, *f.*

Unmingled, *adj.* pur, sans mélange

Unmistakable, *adj.* clair, évident, manifeste, certain, à ne pas s'y méprendre

Unmistakably, *adv.* clairement, évidemment, certainement, à ne pas s'y méprendre

Unmitigable, *adj.* impossible à adoucir, non susceptible d'adoucissement

Unmitigated, *adj.* non mitigé, non adouci; implacable; complet, entier, absolu, positif; (*arrant*) franc; dans toute la force du terme

Unmixed. *V.* **Unmingled**

Unmobilized, *adj.* non mobilisé [tion

Unmodified, *adj.* non modifié, sans modifica-

Unmolested, *adj.* sans être molesté *or* inquiété; sans obstacle, sans empêchement; en paix [gent, sans argent, pauvre

Unmoneyed, Unmonied, *adj.* dénué d'ar-

Unmoor, *v.a.* démarrer

Unmooring, *s.* démarrage, *m.*

Unmortgaged, *adj.* libre d'hypothèque

Unmortified, *adj.* non mortifié, immortifié

Unmotherly, *adj.* indigne d'une mère, peu maternel

Unmounted, *adj.* démonté; (*on foot*) à pied

Unmourned. *V.* **Unlamented**

Unmoved, *adj.* immobile, fixe; sans émotion, impassible, non ému; insensible; ferme, inébranlable; inexorable

Unmuffle, *v.a.* découvrir

Unmusical, *adj.* immusical, peu musical; peu harmonieux; discordant

Unmuzzle, *v.a.* démuseler

Unmuzzled, *adj.* (*freed*) démuselé; (*not having had*) non muselé

Unnail, *v.a.* déclouer

Unnamed, *adj.* innommé; anonyme. . . . . *that shall be* (or *go*) —, . . . dont on taira le nom, . . . que je ne nommerai pas

Unnatural, *adj.* (*things*) contre nature; forcé; factice; (*pers.*) dénaturé. — *mother*, marâtre, *f.*

Unnaturalize, *v.a.* dénaturer

Unnaturalized, *adj.* non naturalisé

Unnaturally, *adv.* contre nature; d'une manière forcée sans naturel; facticement; d'une manière dénaturée. *Not* —, assez naturellement [manque (*or* défaut) de naturel, *m.*

Unnaturalness, *s.* caractère non naturel, *m.*;

Unnavigable, *adj.* innavigable

Unnavigated, *adj.* inconnu à la navigation

Unnecessarily, *adv.* sans nécessité, inutile-

Unnecessariness, *s.* inutilité, *f.* [ment

Unnecessary, *adj.* *V.* **Uncalled-for** [çable

Unnegotiable, *adj.* innégociable, incommer-

Unneighbourly, *adj.* de mauvais voisin, peu obligeant; — *adv.* en mauvais voisin. *In a very* — *way*, en mauvais voisin

Unnerve, *v.a.* énerver; décourager, faire perdre (à . . .) son sang-froid; affaiblir

Unnoticed, *adj.* inaperçu, inobservé; passé sous silence; traité sans égards; négligé; dédaigné; méconnu; sans réponse

Unnumbered, *adj.* non numéroté; (*innumerable*) innombrable, sans nombre

Unobjectionable, *adj.* irréprochable; inattaquable; irrécusable [irrécusablement

Unobjectionably, *adv.* irréprochablement;

Unobliging, *adj.* peu obligeant, peu complaisant, inserviable

Unobliterated, *adj.* ineffacé

Unobserved, *adj.* inaperçu, inobservé

Unobserving, Unobservant, *adj.* peu observateur; inattentif obstacle; libre

Unobstructed, *adj.* non obstrué; (*fig.*) sans

Unobtainable, *adj.* impossible à obtenir

Unobtruding, Unobtrusive, *adj.* discret, réservé, modeste [serve, modestement

Unobtrusively, *adv.* discrètement, avec ré-

Unobtrusiveness, *s.* discrétion, réserve, *f.*

Unoccupied, *adj.* (*idle*) inoccupé, oisif; (*not taken up, vacant; as time, rooms*) libre, disponible; (*untenanted*) inhabité; (*without possessor*) non occupé; (*free*) libre (de), affranchi (de). — *land*, terre en friche, *f.*

Unoffended, *adj.* non offensé, sans s'offenser

Unoffending, *adj.* inoffensif; innocent; (*free from sin*) sans péché

Unoffered, *adj.* non offert

Unofficial, &c. *V.* **Inofficial**, &c.

Unopened, *adj.* fermé; (*of letters*) non décacheté, tout cacheté; non ouvert *or* &c. (*V.* **Open**, *v.a.*) [contesté

Unopposed, *adj.* sans opposition; (*law*) non

Unorganized, *adj.* non organisé; (*nat. hist.*) inorganique

Unornamented, *adj.* sans ornement

Unorthodox, *adj.* hétérodoxe

Unostentatious, *adj.* sans ostentation, simple, modeste; sans éclat. —**ly**, *adv.* sans ostentation. —**ness**, *s.* simplicité, *f.*

Unowned, *adj.* sans possesseur, sans propriétaire; (*not avowed*) non avoué, non reconnu; (*not claimed*) non réclamé

Unpacified, *adj.* non pacifié; (*fig.*) non apaisé, non calmé [queter, défaire

Unpack, *v.a.* déballer; (*undo a parcel*) dépa-

Unpacked, *adj.* déballé; dépaqueté, défait; (*not packed*) non emballé; non empaqueté. *To come* —, se dépaqueter, se défaire

Unpacking, *s.* déballage, *m.*; (*of parcels*) dépaquetage, *m.*

Unpaid, *adj.* non payé, impayé; (*of troops*) sans solde; (*of letters, parcels*) non affranchi. — *for*, non payé [désagréable (à)

Unpalatable, *adj.* désagréable au goût; (*fig.*)

Unparalleled, *adj.* incomparable; sans exemple, sans précédent, sans égal, unique, inouï

Unpardonable, *adj.* impardonnable

Unpardonably, *adv.* impardonnablement

Unpardoned, *adj.* non pardonné, impardonné, sans pardon

Unpardoning. *V.* **Unforgiving**

Unparliamentariness, *s.* nature (*f.*) *or* caractère (*m.*) peu parlementaire

Unparliamentary, *adj.* peu parlementaire
Unpaste, *v.a.* décoller
Unpatented, *adj.* non breveté [triotisme
Unpatriotic, *adj.* peu patriotique, sans pa-
Unpatriotically, *adv.* peu patriotiquement, sans patriotisme
Unpave, *v.a.* dépaver; (*of tiles or bricks*) décarreler; (*of flag-stones*) dédaller
Unpaved, *adj.* dépavé; décarrelé; dédallé; (*not paved*) non pavé; non carrelé; non dallé
Unpaving, *s.* dépavage, *m.*; (*of tiles or bricks*) décarrelage, *m.*; (*of flag-stones*) dédallage, *m.*
Unpensioned, *adj.* sans pension; sans re-
Unpeople, *v.a.* dépeupler [traite
Unperceivable, *adj.* inapercevable
Unperceived, *adj.* inaperçu, sans être aperçu
Unperfected, *adj.* imperfectionné; inachevé, imparfait, incomplet
Unperformed, *adj.* inexécuté; non accompli; ineffectué
Unphilosophic, -al, *adj.* peu philosophique. **—ly,** *adv.* peu philosophiquement. **—ness,** *s.* nature (*f.*) *or* caractère (*m.*) peu philosophique
Unpickable, *adj.* (*of locks*) incrochetable
Unpin, *v.a.* ôter les épingles de; défaire, détacher; (*tech.*) dépingler; décheviller
Unpitied, *adj.* dont on n'a pas pitié, qu'on ne plaint pas, sans être plaint
Unpitying, *adj.* impitoyable, sans pitié
Unplaced, *adj.* non placé, sans place
Unplait, *v.a.* déplisser; détresser, dénatter
Unplanted, *adj.* non planté (' *with*,' de)
Unplat, *v.a.* détresser, dénatter
Unplausible, *adj.* peu plausible
Unplausibly, *adv.* d'une manière peu plausible
Unpleasant, *adj.* désagréable. — *thing,* chose désagréable, *f.*; désagrément, *m.*
Unpleasantly, *adv.* désagréablement
Unpleasantness, *s.* nature désagréable, *f.*; désagrément, *m.*
Unpleasing. *V.* **Unpleasant**
Unpledged, *adj.* non engagé
Unpliant. *V.* **Inflexible**
Unploughable, *adj.* illabourable
Unploughed, *adj.* non labouré, illabouré; (*waste*) inculte
Unplume, *v.a.* déplumer; (*humble*) humilier
Unpoetic, -al, *adj.* prosaïque; antipoétique. **—ly,** *adv.* prosaïquement. **—ness,** *s.* nature prosaïque, *f.*
Unpolished, *adj.* non poli; (*of gold,* &c.) mat; (*of marble*) brut; (*not varnished*) non verni; (*rude*) grossier, impoli; sans éducation; (*of glass*) dépoli; (*of boots*) non ciré
Unpolite, &c. *V.* **Impolite,** &c.
Unpolluted, *adj.* pur; sans tache; non souillé
Unpopular, *adj.* impopulaire
Unpopularity, *s.* impopularité, *f.*
Unpopularly, *adv.* impopulairement
Unportable, *adj.* non portatif
Unportioned, *adj.* sans dot
Unpossessed, *adj.* non possédé. — **of,**
Unpot, *v.a.* dépoter [privé de
Unpractised, *adj.* impratiqué; inexercé; inexpérimenté; novice
Unprecedented, *adj.* sans précédent; sans exemple; sans égal, unique; inouï
Unprejudiced, *adj.* exempt de préjugés, sans préjugés; sans prévention; non prévenu; impartial
Unpremeditated, *adj.* sans préméditation, imprémédité; irréfléchi; improvisé. **—ly,** *adv.* sans préméditation. **—ness,** *s.* impréméditation, *f.*
Unprepared, *adj.* non préparé, impréparé, sans être préparé, sans préparation; loin de s'attendre (à); au dépourvu, à l'improviste. *To be quite* —, (*fam.*) être pris au dépourvu; ne pas s'attendre ('*for*,' à). **—ly,** *adv.* sans préparation. **—ness,** *s.* impréparation, *f.*
Unprepossessed. *V.* **Unprejudiced**
Unprepossessing, *adj.* peu prévenant, peu engageant; disgracieux; désagréable
Unpresuming, Unpresumptuous, Unpretending, *adj.* sans présomption, sans prétention, modeste, simple
Unprincely, *adj.* indigne d'un prince
Unprincipled, *adj.* sans principes; immoral,
Unprintable, *adj.* inimprimable [sans mœurs
Unprinted, *adj.* non imprimé, inimprimé; manuscrit; (*of textile fabrics*) uni; (*of calico*) blanc. — *goods,* du blanc, *m.*
Unproduced, *adj.* improduit
Unproducible, *adj.* improductible
Unproducibleness, *s.* improductibilité, *f.*
Unproducing, *adj.* improducteur
Unproductive, *adj.* improductif; improducteur; qui ne produit pas (...); stérile; peu lucratif. *To be* — *of,* ne pas produire. **—ly,** *adv.* improductivement. **—ness,** *s.* improductivité, *f.*; stérilité, *f.*
Unprofessional, *adj.* non professionnel; étranger à une profession; contraire aux devoirs de sa (*or* ma, &c.) profession
Unprofessionally, *adv.* non professionnellement; contrairement aux devoirs de sa (*or* ma, &c.) profession
Unproficiency, *s.* faiblesse, *f.*; défaut de progrès, *m.* [retard
Unproficient, *adj.* faible; peu avancé, en
Unprofitable, *adj.* improfitable, peu profitable, ingrat; peu lucratif; (*useless*) inutile,
Unprofitableness, *s.* inutilité, *f.* [vain
Unprofitably, *adv.* sans profit; (*uselessly*) inutilement
Unprohibited, *adj.* permis, licite; (*cust.*) non prohibé
Unprolific, *adj.* stérile, infécond, infertile
Unpromising, *adj.* qui promet peu; qui s'annonce mal; de mauvaise apparence; stérile, ingrat
Unpromulgated, *adj.* impromulgué
Unpronounceable, *adj.* imprononçable
Unpronounced, *adj.* non prononcé; inarticulé
Unpropitious, *adj.* peu propice (à), impropice (à), contraire (à), peu favorable (à). **—ly,** *adv.* d'une manière peu propice. **—ness,** *s.* nature peu propice, *f.*
Unproportioned, *adj.* disproportionné
Unprosperous, *adj.* malheureux. **—ly,** *adv.* malheureusement, sans succès. **—ness,** *s.* mauvais succès, insuccès, *m.*
Unprotected, *adj.* non protégé, sans protection, laissé sans protection; sans défense; sans abri; seul
Unprovable, *adj.* non prouvable, improuvable
Unproved, *adj.* non prouvé, sans preuve; (*untested*) non éprouvé, inéprouvé
Unprovided, *adj.* non pourvu; dépourvu; au dépourvu, pris au dépourvu, qui n'est pas préparé; dénué (de ...), sans (...); sans ressources; (*things*) auquel on n'a pas pourvu; non prévu
Unprovoked, *adj.* sans provocation, non provoqué; immérité, injuste; gratuit
Unpublishable, *adj.* impubliable
Unpublished, *adj* non publié, inconnu, secret; (*of books*) inédit, non publié
Unpunctual, *adj.* inexact
Unpunctuality, *s.* inexactitude, *f.*, défaut (*or* manque) de ponctualité, *m.*, irrégularité, *f.*
Unpunctually, *adv.* inexactement, sans ponctualité, irrégulièrement
Unpunished, *adj.* impuni
Unpurchasable, *adj.* qu'on ne peut acheter
Unpurchased, *adj.* non acheté
Unpurified, *adj.* non purifié, impurifié; impur
Unputrefiable, *adj.* imputréfiable
Unputrefied, *adj.* non putréfié, imputréfié
Unqualified, *adj.* incapable (de), pas propre (à), sans talent (pour); inadmissible; non autorisé; sans restriction; sans réserve;

absolu, positif, formel; entier, complet; (*law*) [inhabile (à)

Unqualify, *v.a. V.* **Disqualify**

Unquenchable, *adj.* inextinguible. **—ness,** *s.* inextinguibilité, *f.*

Unquenched, *adj.* non éteint

Unquestionable, *adj.* incontestable

Unquestionably, *adv.* incontestablement, sans contredit

Unquestioned, *adj.* incontesté; incontestable; (*pers.*) sans être interrogé

Unquiet, &c. *V.* **Restless,** &c.

Unransomed, *adj.* non racheté, sans rançon

Unravel, *v.a.* démêler; débrouiller; (*of textile fabrics*) effiler, défaire; (*an intrigue or plot*) dénouer; (*fig.*) démêler, débrouiller, éclaircir; — *v.n.* se démêler, se débrouiller, &c.

Unravelling, *s.* démêlement, débrouillement, *m.*; (*of an intrigue or plot*) dénoûment, *m.*

Unreached, *adj.* non atteint

Unread, *adj.* non lu, sans être lu; sans lecteurs; (*pers.*) illettré, ignorant

Unreadable, *adj.* illisible

Unreadableness, *s.* nature illisible, *f.*

Unreadably, *adv.* illisiblement

Unreadily, *adv.* lentement, sans facilité; sans préparation; (*unwillingly*) à contre-cœur

Unreadiness, *s.* lenteur, *f.*, manque de facilité, *m.*; impréparation, *f.*; (*unwillingness*) manque de bonne volonté, *m.*, répugnance, *f.*

Unready, *adj.* (*slow*) lent; (*not ready*) qui n'est pas prêt (à), impréparé (à), peu préparé (à); (*unwilling*) peu disposé (à), peu empressé (à); (*awkward*) gauche

Unreal, *adj.* irréel, faux, sans réalité, imaginé, imaginaire, fantastique; feint; chimérique, vain; idéal; immatériel; incorporel

Unreality, *s.* non-réalité, fausseté, *f.*; incorporalité, *f.*; chimère, vision, *f.*

Unrealizable, *adj.* irréalisable

Unreaped, *adj.* non moissonné

Unreason, *s.* déraison, *f.*

Unreasonable, *adj.* déraisonnable; extravagant; absurde; injuste; exigeant; exorbitant, immodéré

Unreasonableness, *s.* déraison, *f.*; extravagance, *f.*; absurdité, *f.*; exigence, *f.*

Unreasonably, *adv.* déraisonnablement; sans raison; avec extravagance; à l'excès

Unreasoned, *adj.* non raisonné, irraisonné; déraisonnable

Unreasoning, *adj.* qui ne raisonne pas

Unreceivable, *adj.* irrecevable

Unreclaimed, *adj.* non réformé; non corrigé (de); incorrigible; (*of land*) inculte

Unrecognizable, *adj.* méconnaissable

Unrecognized, *adj.* non reconnu; méconnu; non avoué [sans être recommandé

Unrecommended, *adj.* non recommandé,

Unrecompensed. *V.* **Unrewarded**

Unreconciled, *adj.* irréconcilié

Unrecorded, *adj.* non enregistré; (*forgotten*) oublié [rétabli

Unrecovered, *adj.* non recouvré; (*pers.*) non

Unrectified, *adj.* non rectifié; (*not corrected*) non redressé

Unredeemable, *adj.* irréparable, irrémédiable; (*of funds,* &c.) irrachetable, irremboursable [médiablement

Unredeemably, *adv.* irréparablement, irré-

Unredeemed, *adj.* non racheté, irracheté; (*from pawn*) non dégagé, non retiré (*V.* **Pledge**); (*of funds,* &c.) non racheté, non remboursé; non amorti [non redressé

Unredressed, *adj.* non réformé; (*of wrongs*)

Unreduced, *adj.* non réduit

Unrefined, *adj.* (*of liquids*) non purifié, non épuré; (*of metals*) non affiné; (*of sugar*) non raffiné, brut; (*not polished*) grossier

Unreflecting, *adj.* irréfléchi

Unreformable, *adj.* irréformable

Unreformed, *adj.* non réformé

Unrefreshed, *adj.* non rafraîchi; (*still tired*) toujours fatigué [oublié, méconnu

Unregarded, *adj.* dédaigné, méprisé, négligé,

Unregardful, *adj.* inattentif, négligent. —**ly,** *adv.* inattentivement, négligemment

Unregenerate, *adj.* non régénéré

Unregistered, *adj.* non enregistré; (*of letters,* &c., *by post*) non chargé, non recommandé

Unregulated, *adj.* non réglé [mandé

Unrelatable, *adj.* incontable, irracontable

Unrelated, *adj.* sans rapport (avec), non allié (à); (*of family relations*) sans parenté (avec)

Unrelaxing, *adj.* sans relâche, infatigable

Unrelenting, *adj.* inflexible; inexorable; impitoyable, cruel, implacable; acharné

Unrelentingly, *adv.* inflexiblement; inexorablement; impitoyablement, cruellement, implacablement; avec acharnement

Unreliable, *adj.* sur lequel on ne peut pas compter, auquel on ne peut pas se fier; indigne de confiance *or* de foi, incroyable; incertain; mal fondé

Unreliableness, *s.* incrédibilité, *f.*; incertitude, *f.*; inexactitude, *f.*

Unreliably, *adv.* d'une manière indigne de foi, d'une manière incroyable; incertainement; inexactement

Unrelieved, *adj.* non secouru, sans secours; (*of pain,* &c.) non soulagé, &c. (*V.* **Relieve**)

Unremarkable, *adj.* irremarquable

Unremarked. *V.* **Unnoticed**

Unremedied, *adj* auquel on n'a pas remédié; irrémédiable

Unremembered, *adj.* immémoré, oublié; (*unrecognized*) non reconnu, méconnu

Unremembering, *adj.* oublieux

Unremitting, *adj.* persévérant, infatigable; incessant; constant; soutenu

Unremittingly, *adv.* sans relâche; sans cessé

Unremoved, *adj.* non déplacé, non enlevé, &c. (*V.* **Remove**); (*of furniture*) non déménagé; (*not distant*) non éloigné; non écarté

Unremunerated, *adj.* non rétribué, sans rétribution

Unremunerative, *adj.* qui ne rapporte rien; qui ne donne pas de bénéfice; peu lucratif

Unrepaid, *adj.* non remboursé; non rendu; (*unrewarded*) non récompensé (de); méconnu; (*not reciprocated*) non payé de retour

Unrepaired, *adj.* non réparé, irréparé

Unrepayable, *adj.* irremboursable

Unrepealed, *adj.* non révoqué, irrévoqué, non rapporté, non abrogé

Unrepentant, *adj.* sans repentir; impénitent

Unrepented, *adj.* non expié par le repentir

Unrepenting. *V.* **Unrepentant**

Unrepining, *adj.*, **Unrepiningly,** *adv.* sans se plaindre, sans murmurer

Unrepressed, *adj.* non réprimé

Unreproached, *adj.* sans reproche

Unrequited, *adj.* non récompensé, sans récompense; méconnu; (*not reciprocated*) non payé de retour

Unresented, *adj.* sans ressentiment; enduré, digéré; pardonné; oublié [chise, *f.*

Unreserve, *s.* abandon, *m.*, expansion, fran-

Unreserved, *adj.* sans réserve; franc, ouvert; absolu. — *sale,* liquidation, *f.*

Unreservedly, *adv.* sans réserve; franchement; absolument [franchise, *f.*

Unreservedness, *s.* abandon, *m.*, expansion,

Unresisting, *adj.* sans résistance; (*pers.*) [soumis

Unresistingly, *adv.* sans résistance

Unresolvable, *adj.* insoluble

Unresolved, *adj.* non résolu, sans solution; irrésolu, indécis

Unrespected, *adj.* non respecté

Unrespirable, *adj.* irrespirable

Unrest, *s.* inquiétude, *f.*; (*restless sleep*) sommeil agité, *m.*; (*sleeplessness*) insomnie, *f.*

Unrestored, *adj.* non restitué *or* &c. (*V.* **Restore**)

Unrestrained, *adj.* libre; sans contrainte; sans restriction; (*licentious*) déréglé, effréné, sans frein
Unrestricted, *adj.* sans restriction
Unretracted, *adj.* non rétracté
Unretrieved, *adj.* irréparé
Unrevealed, *adj.* non révélé
Unrevenged, *adj.* non vengé
Unreversed, *adj.* non renversé; non annulé, non révoqué, irrévoqué
Unrevised, *adj.* non revu, non révisé
Unrevoked. *V.* **Unrepealed** [compense
Unrewarded, *adj.* non récompensé, sans ré-
Unriddle, *v.a.* expliquer, résoudre
Unrifled, *adj.* (*smooth-bore*) non rayé, lisse
Unrig, *v.a* déharnacher; (*nav.*) dégréer
Unrighteous, *adj.* injuste, inique, méchant, impie [ment
Unrighteously, *adv.* injustement, inique-
Unrighteousness, *s.* injustice, iniquité, *f.*
Unrip, *v.a. V.* **Rip** [prématuré
Unripe, *adj.* vert, qui n'est pas mûr; (*fig.*)
Unripened, *adj.* qui n'est pas mûr; imparfait
Unripeness, *s.* immaturité, verdeur, *f.*
Unrivalled, *adj.* sans rival; sans pareil, sans égal, unique [cher
Unrivet, *v.a.* dériver; (*unfasten*) défaire, déta-
Unroll, *v.a.* dérouler; (*display*) déployer; — *v.n.* se dérouler; se déployer
Unromantic, *adj.* peu romanesque; (*of places, writers*) peu romantique
Unromantically, *adv.* peu romanesquement; peu romantiquement
Unroof, *v.a.* enlever la toiture de, découvrir
Unroot, *v.a.* déraciner; extirper
Unruffle, *v.n.* se calmer, s'apaiser
Unruffled, *adj.* calme, tranquille; uni, lisse
Unruliness, *s.* dérèglement, *m.*, fougue, *f.*; nature indomptable, *f.*; turbulence, *f.*; insoumission, *f.*
Unruly, *adj.* déréglé; intraitable, indomptable; indisciplinable; fougueux; turbulent; (*stubborn*) mutin, revêche; insoumis
Unrumple, *v.a.* défriper
Unsaddle, *v.a.* (*a horse*) desseller; (*a donkey*) débâter; (*a man*) désarçonner
Unsafe, *adj.* pas sûr, peu sûr; pas en sûreté, en danger, exposé au danger; dangereux, hasardeux, chanceux; incertain; imprudent
Unsafely, *adv.* peu sûrement; sans sûreté; dangereusement; d'une manière hasardeuse
Unsaid, *adj.* non dit; non prononcé; dont on n'a pas parlé. *To leave* —, ne pas dire; taire
Unsalable, *adj.* invendable
Unsalted, *adj.* non salé; sans sel
Unsalutary, *adj.* insalutaire [impie
Unsanctified, *adj.* non sanctifié; profane;
Unsanctioned, *adj.* non sanctionné
Unsated, Unsatiated, *adj.* non rassasié, irrassasié, inassouvi [satisfaisante
Unsatisfactorily, *adv.* d'une manière peu
Unsatisfactoriness, *s.* nature peu satisfaisante, *f.*; insuffisance, *f.* [suffisant
Unsatisfactory, *adj.* peu satisfaisant; in-
Unsatisfied, *adj.* peu satisfait (de), mécontent (de); (*com.*) non soldé, non payé
Unsatisfying, *adj. V.* **Unsatisfactory**
Unsaturated, *adj.* insaturé [ment
Unsavourily, *adv.* sans saveur; désagréable-
Unsavouriness, *s.* insipidité, fadeur, *f.*; (*smell*) mauvaise odeur, *f.*
Unsavoury, *adj.* fade, insipide; désagréable
Unsay, *v.a.* rétracter, se dédire de
Unscanned, *adj.* inconnu, non examiné
Unscared, *adj.* non effrayé; non effarouché
Unscarred, *adj.* sans cicatrices
Unscathed, *adj. V.* **Unhurt**
Unscholarly, *adj.* illettré, ignorant
Unschooled, *adj.* sans éducation, illettré, ignorant; inexpérimenté [à la science
Unscientific, *adj.* peu scientifique, étranger
Unscientifically, *adv.* peu scientifiquement
Unscreened, *adj.* non abrité *or* &c. (*V.* **Screen,** *v.a.*); sans défense; (*of coals,* &c.) non criblé [*To come —ed,* se dévisser
Unscrew, *v.a.* dévisser; — *v.n.* se dévisser.
Unscriptural, *adj.* antibiblique
Unscrupulous, *adj.* peu scrupuleux, indélicat, sans scrupule, dénué de scrupule; sans conscience [conscience
Unscrupulously, *adv.* sans scrupule; sans
Unscrupulousness, *s.* manque de scrupule, *m.*; indélicatesse, *f.*; improbité, *f.*
Unseal, *v.a.* desceller; (*letters,* &c.) décacheter; (*cust.*) déplomber
Unsealed, *part. adj.* (*of letters,* &c.: *opened*) décacheté; (*open*) non cacheté, sans cachet, ouvert [trable
Unsearchable, *adj.* inscrutable; impéné-
Unsearchableness, *s.* inscrutabilité, *f.*; impénétrabilité, *f.* [pénétrablement
Unsearchably, *adv.* inscrutablement; im-
Unseasonable, *adj.* hors de saison, mal à propos; inopportun, intempestif; (*of time*) indu; (*of weather*) peu de saison; (*improper*) déplacé. — *hour,* heure indue, *f.*
Unseasonableness, *s.* inopportunité, *f.*
Unseasonably, *adv.* hors de saison, mal à propos; inopportunément, intempestivement
Unseasoned, *adj.* non assaisonné *or* &c. (*V.* **Season,** *v.a.*)
Unseat, *v.a.* priver (...) de sa place, faire perdre sa place à (...); évincer; supplanter; (*throw down, upset*) renverser
Unseated, *adj.* (*standing*) sans siége, debout
Unseaworthiness, *s.* innavigabilité, *f.*
Unseaworthy, *adj.* innavigable
Unseconded, *adj.* non secondé, mal secondé; non appuyé
Unsecured, *adj.* non garanti; sans garantie; à découvert; mal assuré, inassuré; non protégé *or* &c. (*V.* **Secure,** *v.a.*); (*not shut*) pas [fermé
Unseemliness, *s.* inconvenance, *f.*
Unseemly, *adv.* inconvenant; malséant, messéant; indécent; — *adv.* d'une manière inconvenante *or* indécente
Unseen, *adj.* qui ne se voit pas; invisible; inaperçu; sans être vu; (*by stealth*) à la dérobée [insaisissabilité, *f.*
Unseizable, *adj.* insaisissable. **—ness,** *s.*
Unseized, *adj.* non saisi
Unselfish, *adj.* désintéressé; dévoué. **—ly,** *adv.* avec désintéressement; avec dévouement. **—ness,** *s.* désintéressement, *m.*; dévouement, *m.*; abnégation, *f.*
Unsent, *adj.* non envoyé, sans être envoyé. — **for,** qu'on n'a pas fait appeler; sans être appelé
Unserviceable, *adj.* inutile; de mauvais service; hors de service; bon à rien; (*unobliging*) inserviable
Unserviceableness, *s.* inutilité, *f.*; mauvais état, *m.*; (*unobligingness*) inserviabilité, *f.*
Unserviceably, *adv.* inutilement; (*unobligingly*) inserviablement
Unset, *adj.* non posé *or* &c. (*V.* **Set,** *v.a., v.n., and adj.*); — *v.a.* (*gems,* &c.) démonter, dessertir, désenchâsser
Unsettle, *v.a.* déranger; bouleverser; détraquer; rendre incertain; tenir en suspens; agiter, troubler; ébranler
Unsettled, *adj.* dérangé; agité; troublé; ébranlé; chancelant; incertain; changeant, variable; inconstant; volage; irrégulier; irrésolu, indécis; en suspens; peu ferme, mal établi, mal assis; mal fixé, non fixé, pas encore fixé; comme l'oiseau sur la branche; sans domicile; (*unpaid*) non liquidé, non réglé; (*of liquids*) qui n'a pas déposé
Unsettledness, *s.* instabilité, *f.*; agitation, *f.*, trouble, *m.*; hésitation, irrésolution, indécision, *f.*; incertitude, *f.*; dérangement, *m.*, irrégularité, *f.*; inconstance, variabilité, *f.*
Unsevered, *adj.* non séparé, uni

Unsew, *v.a.* découdre. *To come —ed,* se découdre
Unsewable, *adj.* indécousable
Unsexed, Unsexual, *adj.* insexé
Unshackle, *v.a.* déchaîner ; (*fig.*) délivrer (de), affranchir (de)
Unshackled, *part. adj.* déchaîné ; (*fig.*) délivré (de), affranchi (de) ; libre
Unshaded, *adj.* sans ombrage ; sans ombre ; (*draw., paint.*) non ombré
Unshakable, *adj.* inébranlable
Unshakably, *adv.* inébranlablement
Unshaken, *adj.* non ébranlé, inébranlé ; ferme, inébranlable ; immuable ; à toute épreuve
Unshapen, *adj.* informe ; difforme
Unshared, *adj.* non partagé, impartagé
Unshaved, Unshaven, *adj.* pas rasé, non rasé, sans être rasé
Unsheath, Unsheathe, *v.a.* tirer du fourreau, tirer ; (*nav.*) dédoubler
Unshelled, *adj.* (*of peas,* &c.) non écossé, en cosse ; (*of seeds, grain*) non égrené
Unsheltered, *adj.* pas abrité, non abrité, sans abri ('*from,*' contre) ; exposé ('*from,*' à)
Unship, *v.a.* (*unload*) débarquer ; (*nav.*) désarmer
Unshod, *adj.* déchaussé ; sans chaussure ; (*of horses*) déferré ; non ferré, sans fers
Unshoe, *v.a.* (*a horse*) déferrer
Unshorn, *adj.* non tondu
Unshrinkable, *adj.* irrétrécissable
Unshrinking, *adj.* qui ne recule pas, sans reculer, inébranlable, intrépide
Unsightliness, *s.* laideur, *f.*
Unsightly, *adj.* laid, disgracieux, vilain
Unsilver, *v.a.* désargenter
Unsilvered, *adj.* désargenté ; (*not silvered*) non argenté ; (*of mirrors*) non étamé
Unsilvering, *s.* désargenture, *f.*
Unsinkable, *adj.* insubmersible
Unsisterly, *adj.* indigne (*or* peu digne) d'une sœur
Unsized, *adj.* non collé
Unskid, *v.a.* désenrayer
Unskilful, *adj.* maladroit. **—ly,** *adv.* maladroitement. **—ness,** *s.* maladresse, inhabileté, impéritie, *f.*
Unskilled, *adj.* inexpérimenté, inexpert, inhabile, maladroit
Unslaked, *adj.* non éteint, non étanché. — *lime,* chaux vive
Unsleeping, *adj.* toujours éveillé ; vigilant
Unsmokable, *adj.* infumable
Unsmoked, *adj.* non fumé
Unsocia-bility, bleness, *s.* insociabilité, *f.*
Unsociable, *adj.* insociable ; sauvage ; cassant
Unsociably, *adv.* insociablement
Unsocial, *adj.* insocial ; insociable
Unsoiled, *adj.* sans tache, propre ; (*fig.*) sans souillure, pur ('*by,*' de)
Unsold, *adj.* non vendu, invendu
Unsolder, *v.a.* dessouder
Unsolderable, *adj.* insoudable
Unsoldierlike, Unsoldierly, *adj.* peu digne (*or* indigne) d'un soldat, peu militaire, peu martial
Unsolicited, *adj.* sans sollicitation
Unsolid, *adj.* insolide. **—ly,** *adv.* insolidement
Unsolved, *adj.* non résolu, sans solution
Unsophisticated. *V.* **Unadulterated**
Unsought, *adj.* qu'on n'a pas cherché, sans qu'on le (*or* la *or* les) cherche
Unsound, *adj.* vicieux ; défectueux ; peu solide ; (*sickly*) malsain, maladif ; (*bad*) gâté, mauvais ; (*deceitful*) trompeur ; (*of doctrines*) faux, erroné ; (*of glass*) fêlé ; (*of mind*) dérangé ; (*of sleep*) troublé, agité. *Of — mind,* (*law*) pas sain d'esprit
Unsounded, *adj.* non sondé
Unsoundly, *adv.* défectueusement ; sans solidité ; mal ; sans santé ; faussement
Unsoundness, *s.* imperfection, *f.* ; défauts, vices, *m.pl.* ; mauvais état, *m.* ; manque de force, *m.* ; faiblesse, infirmité, *f.* ; défaut de solidité, *m.* ; fausseté, *f.* ; erreur, *f.* ; état malsain, *m.* ; corruption, *f.*
Unsowed, Unsown, *adj.* non semé ; (*of ground*) non ensemencé
Unsparing, *adj.* libéral, prodigue ; impitoyable, cruel. **—ly,** *adv.* avec profusion ; follement ; sans ménagement ; impitoyablement, sans pitié. **—ness,** *s.* libéralité, prodigalité, *f.* ; nature impitoyable, cruauté, *f.*
Unspeakable, *adj.* inexprimable ; (*rapturous*) ineffable ; (*rapturous, dreadful*) indicible
Unspeakableness, *s.* ineffabilité, *f.*
Unspeakably, *adv.* inexprimablement, d'une manière inexprimable, ineffablement, indiciblement
Unspecified, *adj.* non spécifié
Unspent, *adj.* non dépensé ; (*not exhausted*) non épuisé
Unspit, *v.a.* débrocher
Unspoken, *adj.* non prononcé
Unsportsmanlike, *adj.* indigne d'un chasseur
Unspotted, *adj.* sans tache, pur
Unspottedness, *s.* pureté, *f.*
Unstable, *adj.* instable ; mobile ; inconstant, changeant ; irrésolu, indécis. — *equilibrium,* équilibre instable, *m.*
Unstableness, *s.* défaut de stabilité, *m.*, instabilité, inconstance, *f.* ; irrésolution, *f.*
Unstably, *adv.* instablement ; avec inconstance, inconstamment ; avec irrésolution
Unstained, *adj.* non taché ; pur, sans tache ; (*not dyed*) non teint ; (*of glass*) blanc
Unstamped, *adj.* non timbré ; (*of letters,* &c.) non affranchi, sans timbre ; (*of paper*) libre, non timbré ; (*not printed*) non imprimé
Unstarch, *v.a.* désempeser, évider
Unstarched, *adj.* non empesé, mou
Unstatesmanlike, *adj.* indigne d'un homme d'état
Unsteadfast. *V.* **Unstable**
Unsteadily, *adv.* sans fixité ; légèrement ; irrésolûment ; avec inconstance ; irrégulièrement ; en chancelant
Unsteadiness, *s.* manque de fermeté, *m.* ; légèreté, *f.* ; irrésolution, *f.* ; inconstance, *f.*
Unsteady, *adj.* chancelant, mal assuré, inassuré ; peu sûr ; tremblant ; vacillant ; mobile ; toujours en mouvement ; irrésolu, indécis ; inconstant ; irrégulier ; (*not attentive*) léger : (*of weather*) variable ; (*of furniture*) boiteux
Unstemmed, *adj.* (*of tobacco*) non écôté
Unstinted, *adj.* non restreint ; abondant, copieux ; à discrétion ; illimité, sans bornes
Unstirred, *adj.* non remué, non agité
Unstitch, *v.a.* découdre, défaire
Unstock, *v.a.* (*of animals*) dépeupler ; (*a shop*) désassortir
Unstop, *v.a.* déboucher ; ouvrir ; (*teeth*) déplomber
Unstopped, *adj.* débouché ; (*not hindered*) non arrêté, sans être arrêté
Unstrained, *adj.* aisé, naturel ; non filtré, non passé ; non forcé
Unstrengthened, *adj.* non fortifié, non renforcé
Unstring, *v.a.* détendre, relâcher ; (*untie*) délier, détacher, déficeler, défaire ; (*deprive of strings*) ôter les cordes de ; (*take from a string*) désenfiler
Unstudied, *adj.* inétudié ; naturel, sans étude, sans apprêt
Unstudious, *adj.* instudieux
Unstuffed, *adj.* dégarni, vide ; non rembourré *or* &c. (*V.* **Stuff,** *v.a.*)
Unsubdued, Unsubjected, *adj.* insoumis ; indompté ; inassujetti, inasservi
Unsubmergible. *V.* **Insubmergible**
Unsubmissive, *adj.* insoumis
Unsubmissiveness, *s.* insoumission, *f.*
Unsubstantial, *adj.* insubstantiel, peu substantiel ; peu solide ; sans substance ; sans corps ; immatériel ; sans réalité, imaginaire, chimérique, idéal ; léger ; creux. — *food* or *stuff,* aliment peu substantiel, *m.*, viande creuse, *f.*
Unsuccessful, *adj.* malheureux, sans succès ; infructueux ; vain. *To be —,* ne pas réussir, échouer, n'avoir pas de succès, être malheu-

reux *or* &c. —**ly,** *adv.* sans succès, malheureusement. —**ness,** *s.* insuccès, *m.*
Unsuccoured, *adj.* non secouru, sans secours, sans aide
Unsuitable, *adj.* inconvenable, peu convenable (à), impropre (à), peu propre (à); (*not adapted*) peu approprié (à); (*incongruous*) inconvenant; (*untimely*) inopportun
Unsuitableness, *s.* disconvenance, *f.*; inaptitude, incapacité, *f.*; (*incongruity*) inconvenance, *f.*; (*untimeliness*) inopportunité, *f.*
Unsuitably, *adv.* inconvenablement; improprement; mal; (*incongruously*) avec inconvenance; (*unseasonably*) mal à propos
Unsuited, *adj.* peu adapté *or* approprié (à); peu fait (pour); peu convenable (à); mal as- [sorti
Unsullied. *V.* **Unspotted**
Unsupplied, *adj.* non pourvu (de); dépourvu (de); non approvisionné (de); non satisfait
Unsupported, *adj.* non soutenu, sans soutien, sans support; (*not assisted*) sans appui, (*not fed*) non soutenu, non entretenu, sans moyens d'existence; (*not suffered*) non sup- [porté
Unsuppressed, *adj.* non supprimé
Unsurpassable, *adj.* insurpassable
Unsurpassed, *adj.* non surpassé, transcendant
Unsusceptible. *V.* **Insusceptible**
Unsuspectable, *adj.* insoupçonnable
Unsuspected, *adj.* non suspect; non soupçonné [soupçons, confiant
Unsuspecting, *adj.* peu soupçonneux, sans
Unsuspectingly, *adv.* sans méfiance, sans soupçons [non suspect
Unsuspicious *adj.* confiant; (*not suspected*)
Unsuspiciously, *adv.* sans soupçons
Unsustainable, *adj.* insoutenable; insupportable [supportablement
Unsustainably, *adv.* insoutenablement; in-
Unsustained. *V.* **Unsupported**
Unswathe, *v.a.* démaillotter
Unswayed, *adj.* abandonné; non gouverné, non dirigé; non influencé
Unsweetened, *adj.* non sucré; non édulcoré
Unswept, *adj.* non balayé; (*of chimneys*) non [ramoné
Unsworn, *adj.* inassermenté
Unsymmetrical, *adj.* insymétrique, sans symétrie. —**ly,** *adv.* insymétriquement, sans symétrie. —**ness,** *s.* dissymétrie, *f.*
Unsympathizing, *adj.* peu sympathique, sans sympathie, incompatissant
Unsystematic, -al, *adj.* non systématique. —**ly,** *adv.* sans système [défaire
Untack, *v.a.* délier, détacher; (*need.*) débâtir,
Untainted, *adj.* pur; sans tache; intact; non corrompu; (*of meat,* &c.) non gâté, frais
Untamable, *adj.* indomptable; (*wild*) inapprivoisable. —**ness,** *s.* nature indomptable *or* inapprivoisable, *f.*
Untamably, *adv.* indomptablement
Untamed, *adj.* indompté; (*wild*) inapprivoisé
Untarnished, *adj.* non terni; sans tache
Untasted, *adj.* non goûté; auquel on ne touche pas
Untasteful, &c. *V.* **Tasteless,** &c. [naturel
Untaught, *adj.* ignorant, illettré; (*things*)
Untaxed, *adj.* exempt d'impôts *or* d'impositions, non taxé *or* &c. (*V.* **Tax,** *v.a.*)
Unteach, *v.a.* faire désapprendre
Unteachable, *adj.* incapable, bouché, (*fam.*) indécrottable; indocile. —**ness,** *s.* incapacité, *f.*; indocilité, *f.*
Untearable, *adj.* indéchirable; illacérable
Untempered, *adj.* non tempéré, non adouci; (*of steel*) non trempé; (*not diluted*) non dé- [trempé
Untempted, *adj.* non tenté
Untenable, *adj.* pas tenable, non tenable, intenable; insoutenable
Untenably, *adv.* insoutenablement
Untenantable, *adj.* inhabitable, non logeable
Untenanted, *adj.* sans locataire, inhabité; vide; désert
Untested, *adj.* non éprouvé, inéprouvé

Unthanked, *adj.* sans remerciments; méconnu
Unthankful, *adj.* ingrat ('*to,*' envers). —**ly,** *adv.* ingratement, avec ingratitude. —**ness,** *s.* ingratitude, *f.*
Unthawed, *adj.* non dégelé, encore gelé
Unthinking, *adj.* irréfléchi, inconsidéré, étourdi. —**ly,** *adv.* sans y penser, sans réflexion, inconsidérément, par distraction
Unthought (of), *adj.* auquel on ne pense pas, négligé, oublié; ignoré; (*unexpected*) inattendu, imprévu, inopiné
Unthread, *v.a.* désenfiler; (*to loose*) détacher
Unthreatened, *adj.* non menacé
Unthrifty, &c. *V.* **Thriftless,** &c.
Untidily, *adv.* malproprement; sans soin; sans ordre; en désordre
Untidiness, *s.* malpropreté, *f.*; désordre, *m.*
Untidy, *adj.* malpropre; peu soigneux; désordonné; en désordre, mal tenu; mal arrangé; défait; (*loosely dressed*) débraillé
Untie, *v.a.* délier, détacher; (*a knot*) défaire, dénouer
Until, *prep.* jusqu'à; jusque; en attendant; (*after a neg.*) avant, d'ici à, (ne ...) que. — 6 *o'clock,* jusqu'à six heures. — *to-morrow,* jusqu'à demain. — *now,* – *this day,* jusqu'à présent, jusqu'à ce jour, jusqu'aujourd'hui, jusqu'ici. — *then,* jusqu'alors, jusque-là; en attendant. — *when,* jusqu'à quand. *Not* — *then,* pas avant; (ne ...) qu'alors, alors seulement que. *He did not return* — 6 *o'clock,* il n'est pas revenu avant six heures, il n'est revenu qu'à six heures. *He will not come* — *to-morrow,* il ne viendra pas avant (*or* d'ici à) demain, il ne viendra que demain. *I shall not go* — *after dinner,* je ne sortirai qu'après le dîner. *I shall not go out* — *after you have done,* je ne sortirai qu'après que vous aurez fini. *I shall not come home* — *late this evening,* je ne rentrerai ce soir que très tard
Until, *conj.* jusqu'à ce que, en attendant que, que, (*with the subj. mood*); jusqu'au moment où (*with the indicative mood*); (*to such an extent or degree that*) au point que; au point de (*before an inf.*); (*after a neg.*) avant que (*with the subj.*), avant de (*with the inf.*); (ne ...) que ... ne (*with the subj.*). *He will not come* — *I tell him,* il ne viendra pas avant que je le lui dise. *I will not depart* — *I have seen him,* je ne partirai pas avant de l'avoir vu, je ne partirai qu'après l'avoir vu. *I will not rest* — *I have done it,* je ne me reposerai pas que je ne l'aie fait. *I was restless now,* — *I had accomplished my wish,* dès ce moment je ne goûtai aucun repos que je n'eusse satisfait mon désir
Untillable, *adj.* incultivable, illabourable
Untilled, *adj.* inculte; en friche [tunité, *f.*
Untimeliness, *s.* prématurité, *f.*; inoppor-
Untimely, *adj.* prématuré; avant terme; précoce, hâtif; inopportun, intempestif; — *adv.* prématurément; avant le temps, avant terme; inopportunément, intempestivement, mal à [propos
Untired, *adj.* non fatigué, frais
Untiring, *adj.* infatigable; (*unflagging*) soutenu. —**ly,** *adv.* infatigablement; d'une manière soutenue; sans relâche
Untitled, *adj.* sans titre
Unto, *prep.* *V.* **To**
Untold, *adj.* qu'on ne dit pas; tenu secret; passé sous silence; non compté; innombrable, sans nombre; infini; indéfini; immense, énorme; inexprimable, indicible, inouï
Untouchable, *adj.* intouchable
Untouched, *adj.* intact; (*not hit*) non atteint, non touché; (*not affected*) non ému, peu touché (de), insensible (à). *To leave* (...) —, laisser (...) sans y toucher
Untoward, *adj.* indocile, insoumis, revêche; (*awkward*) maladroit, gauche; (*inconvenient*) malencontreux, fâcheux. —**ly,** *adv.* avec indocilité; maladroitement, gauchement; malencontreusement. —**ness,** *s.* indocilité, *f.*;

maladresse, gaucherie, *f.*; nature malencontreuse *or* fâcheuse, *f.*
Untraced, *adj.* non tracé, intracé ; (*of roads*) non frayé, infrayé ; (*draw.*) non calqué [suivi
Untracked, *adj.* non frayé, non battu ; non
Untractable, &c. *V.* **Intractable,** &c.
Untrained, *adj.* inexercé ; inexpérimenté ; indiscipliné ; (*of animals, trees*) non dressé
Untrammelled, *adj.* sans entraves, sans être entravé, libre
Untransferable, *adj.* intransférable, non transférable ; non transmissible ; (*law*) inaliénable [transmis ; (*law*) non aliéné
Untransferred, *adj.* non transféré ; non
Untranslatable, *adj.* intraduisible. —**ness,** *s.* nature intraduisible, *f.*
Untranslated, *adj.* intraduit, non traduit
Untransmitted, *adj.* non transmis
Untransparent, *adj.* intransparent, non transparent [pas voyagé
Untravelled, *adj.* inexploré ; (*pers.*) qui n'a
Untried, *adj.* inessayé, non essayé *or* &c. (*V* **Try**)
Untrimmed, *adj.* sans ornement ; (*of clothing*) sans garniture ; (*of horses*) auquel on n'a pas fait la toilette ; non arrangé *or* &c. (*V.* **Trim**)
Untrod, Untrodden, *adj.* non foulé ; (*of roads*) non frayé, infrayé, non battu, impratiqué [ble, tranquille ; clair, limpide
Untroubled, *adj.* non troublé ; calme, paisi-
Untrue, *adj.* faux ; inexact ; infidèle. *To be — to,* être infidèle à ; trahir
Untruly, *adv.* faussement ; inexactement ; infidèlement
Untrustiness, *s.* déloyauté, infidélité, perfidie, *f.* [de foi
Untrustworthy, *adj.* indigne de confiance *or*
Untrusty, *adj.* déloyal, infidèle, perfide
Untruth, *s.* mensonge, *m.*; (*want of veracity*) fausseté, *f.* —**ful,** *adj.* (*pers.*) qui ne dit pas la vérité, peu véridique ; peu loyal ; (*of news, &c.*) inexact, faux. —**fulness,** *s.* fausseté, *f.*
Untuck, *v.a.* détrousser ; déplier ; (*a bed*) déborder
Untunable, *adj.* discordant ; (*of instr.*) inaccordable. —**ness,** *s.* discordance, *f.*
Untune, *v.a.* désaccorder ; (*fig.*) déranger,
Unturf, *v.a.* dégazonner [troubler
Unturned, *adj.* non tourné, non retourné, non remué, non renversé (*V.* **Stone**)
Untutored, *adj.* ignorant, sans instruction
Untwine, Untwist, *v.a.* détordre, détortiller
Untwisted, *adj.* détordu, détortillé ; (*not twisted*) non tors ; détors ; plat
Untwisting, *s.* détordage, *m.*
Unurged, *adj.* sans insistance ; sans être excité ; spontané ; spontanément
Unused, *adj.* non employé ; (*of words*) inusité ; (*new*) neuf ; (*not accustomed*) inaccoutumé (à) ; étranger (à)
Unusual, *adj.* rare ; inaccoutumé, extraordinaire ; insolite ; peu habituel, peu commun ; (*of words*) inusité
Unusually, *adv.* rarement ; extraordinairement ; plus que d'habitude
Unusualness, *s.* rareté, étrangeté, *f.*
Unutilized, *adj.* inutilisé
Unutterable, &c. *V.* **Unspeakable,** &c.
Unuttered, *adj.* non proféré, non articulé, inexprimé ; (*not issued*) non émis
Unvaccinated, *adj.* non vacciné
Unvalued, *adj.* non évalué ; (*not prized*) peu estimé, méprisé, dédaigné
Unvanquished, *adj.* invaincu
Unvaried, *adj.* uniforme ; constant ; toujours le même ; invariable
Unvarnished, *adj.* non verni ; naturel, simple
Unvarying, *adj.* *V.* **Unvaried**
Unveil, *v.a.* dévoiler ; découvrir
Unventilated, *adj.* non aéré *or* &c. (*V.* **Ventilate**) ; mal aéré ; sans ventilation
Unversed, *adj.* peu versé (dans)
Unviolated, *adj* non violé ; non enfreint ; respecté ; intact ; pur
Unvisited, *adj.* non visité ; non fréquenté
Unvitiated, *adj.* non gâté, non corrompu ; pur ; (*law, med.*) non vicié
Unwaked, Unwakened, *adj.* non réveillé, endormi
Unwalled, *adj.* sans murs, ouvert
Unwarily, *adv.* sans précaution, inconsidérément, imprudemment [ance, *f.*
Unwariness, *s.* imprudence, *f.*; imprévoy-
Unwarlike, *adj.* peu belliqueux, pacifique
Unwarned, *adj.* non averti (de)
Unwarped, *adj.* non déjeté ; (*fig.*) non faussé
Unwarrantable, *adj.* inexcusable, injustifiable, impardonnable [*or* injustifiable, *f.*
Unwarrantableness, *s.* nature inexcusable
Unwarrantably, *adv.* inexcusablement, injustifiablement, impardonnablement
Unwarranted, *adj.* non autorisé ; incertain ; sans preuve, gratuit ; sans motif, injustifiable ; (*com.*) non garanti, sans garantie
Unwary, *adj.* imprudent ; imprévoyant
Unwashed, *adj.* non lavé ; (*dirty*) sale ; malpropre ; crasseux ; — *s.* crasseux, *m.* *The great —,* la vile multitude, *f.*
Unwasted, *adj.* non perdu ; non consumé
Unwastefully, *adv.* sans perte, avec économie
Unwasting, *adj* inépuisable
Unwatched, *adj.* non surveillé [moiré
Unwatered, *adj.* non arrosé ; (*of stuffs*) non
Unwavering, *adj.* décidé ; ferme ; inébran-
Unweakened, *adj.* non affaibli [lable
Unweaned, *adj.* non sevré
Unwearable, *adj.* pas (*or* non) portable, pas (*or* non) mettable
Unwearied, *adj.* non fatigué ; (*things*) infatigable ; inépuisable ; inouï
Unweariedly, *adv.* sans relâche [fatigable
Unwearying, *adj.* qui ne se lasse jamais, in-
Unweave, *v.a.* détisser ; (*linen*) effiler, défaire ; (*tresses*) détresser ; (*fig.*) démêler
Unwedded, *adj.* non marié
Unwedge, *v.a.* décaler
Unwedging, *s.* décalage, *m.*
Unweighed, *adj.* non pesé, impesé ; (*fig.*) non examiné ; inconsidéré
Unwelcome, *adj.* mal reçu, mal accueilli, mal venu ; désagréable ; fâcheux ; incommode
Unwell, *adj.* indisposé, mal à son aise, mal portant, souffrant
Unwept, *adj.* non pleuré, non regretté, sans être regretté, sans laisser de regrets
Unwholesome, *adj.* malsain, insalubre ; nuisible, pernicieux. —**ly,** *adv.* insalubrement ; nuisiblement, pernicieusement. —**ness,** *s.* insalubrité, *f.*
Unwieldily, *adv.* lourdement, pesamment
Unwieldiness, *s.* lourdeur, pesanteur, *f.*
Unwieldy, *adj.* lourd, pesant ; incommode
Unwilling, *adj.* ne voulant pas, qui ne veut pas (*to be —,* ne vouloir pas) ; peu disposé (à) ; mal disposé ; de mauvaise volonté
Unwillingly, *adv.* à contre-cœur, contre son gré, malgré soi, à regret, avec peine, avec répugnance. *Not —,* assez volontiers, d'assez bon cœur, d'assez bonne grâce, sans trop se faire prier, sans résistance
Unwillingness, *s.* mauvaise volonté, *f.*, mauvais vouloir, *m.*; répugnance, *f.*
Unwind, *v a.* dévider ; détordre ; dérouler ; (*disentangle*) démêler, débrouiller ; — *v.n.* se dérouler [raison, folie, imprudence, *f.*
Unwisdom, *s.* manque de sagesse, *m.*, dé-
Unwise, *adj.* peu sage, peu raisonnable, imprudent, mal avisé
Unwisely, *adv.* pas sagement, peu sagement, follement, imprudemment [haité
Unwished (for), *adj.* non désiré ; non sou-
Unwithered, *adj.* non desséché ; non flétri, non fané, encore dans sa fraîcheur [inaperçu
Unwitnessed, *adj.* sans témoin ; (*not seen*)

Unwittily, *adv.* sans esprit
Unwittingly. *V.* **Unknowingly**
Unwomanly, *adj.* indigne (*or* peu digne) d'une femme ; qui sied peu à une femme
Unwonted, *adj.* rare, extraordinaire ; inaccoutumé. **—ly,** *adv.* rarement. **—ness,** *s.* rareté, *f.*
Unworkable, *adj.* inexploitable ; impraticable
Unworkableness, *s.* inexploitabilité, *f.* ; impraticabilité, *f.*
Unworked, *adj.* inexploité ; impratiqué
Unworldly, *adj.* (*heavenly*) qui n'est pas de ce monde ; (*retired*) étranger au monde
Unworn, *adj.* qui n'a pas été porté ; (*not impaired*) non usé
Unworshipped, *adj.* non adoré
Unworthily, *adv.* indignement ; sans le mériter [mérite, *m.*
Unworthiness, *s.* indignité, *f.* ; défaut de
Unworthy, *adj.* indigne ; peu digne ; sans mérite ; bas, vil, méprisable
Unwounded, *adj.* non blessé ; sans blessure
Unwoven, *adj.* non tissé ; non filé
Unwrap, *v.a.* développer, ouvrir, découvrir
Unwreath, Unwreathe, *v.a.* dérouler, détortiller, défaire
Unwrinkled, *adj.* sans ride, sans rides ; uni
Unwritten, *adj.* non écrit ; blanc, en blanc ; traditionnel, oral, verbal
Unwrought, *adj.* non travaillé ; non ouvré ; brut ; cru ; naturel ; (*of ground*) inculte, en friche
Unyielding, *adj.* rigide ; dur ; inflexible
Unyoke, *v.a.* dételer [été mis sous le joug
Unyoked, *adj.* dételé ; non attelé ; qui n'a pas
Up, *adj.* levé ; élevé ; haut ; (*of the top*) du haut ; (*of trains*) de retour, &c. (*V.* **Train**) ; — *adv.* en haut ; au haut ; (*high*) haut ; (*in the air*) en l'air ; (*standing*) debout, sur pied ; (*risen, out of bed*) levé ; sur pied ; (*gone or come up*) monté ; (*of time*) écoulé, arrivé ; (*over*) fini ; (*closed*) fermé ; (*excited*) excité ; monté ; (*rebelled*) en révolte ; (*com.*) en hausse ; (*of the sun*) levé ; (*of the moon*) levé, sur l'horizon ; (*of the tide*) haut ; (*of prices*) élevé, en hausse ; (*navig.*) en amont ; — *prep.* en haut de ; au haut de ; vers le haut de ; jusqu'au haut de ; jusqu'à ; sur ; en montant, en remontant ; — *s.* haut, *m.* *The —s and downs,* les hauts et les bas, *m.pl.* ; les vicissitudes, *f.pl.* *Well — in,* avancé en, fort en, ferré sur. — *!* debout ! levez-vous ! allons ! en avant ! — *and doing,* occupé, au travail, à l'ouvrage, à la besogne. — *and down,* çà et là ; de long en large ; de côté et d'autre, de tous côtés ; de haut en bas ; partout. — *in arms,* en armes. — *there, V.* **There.** — *to,* jusqu'à ; à la hauteur de ; (*in conformity with*) conformément à, selon, d'après. — *to here,* jusqu'ici. — *to there,* jusque-là. — *with ...!* levez ...! montez ...! — (*the*) *stream,* — *the river,* en amont ; en remontant la rivière, contre le courant. *To be —,* (*effervesce*) mousser. *To be — to,* (*understand*) être au fait de, connaître, savoir ; être à la hauteur de ; (*be doing*) faire ; (*aim at*) vouloir en venir à, vouloir. *It is all — with him,* c'en est fait de lui. — **hill,** *s. adj. adv. See below.* — **line,** *s.* (*rail.*) ligne de [retour, *f.*
Upas, — tree, *s.* upas, *m.*
Upbear, *v.a.* élever, hausser ; supporter, soutenir, porter
Upbraid, *v.a. V.* **Reproach**
Upbraiding, *s.* reproche, *m.* ; réprimande, *f.* ; accusation, *f.* [de reproche
Upbraidingly, *adv.* avec reproche, d'un ton
Upcast, *adj.* jeté en haut, jeté en l'air ; (*raised*) levé
Upheaval, *s.* soulèvement, *m.*
Upheave, *v.a.* soulever, lever
Uphill, *s.* montée, *f.* ; — *adj.* montant ; ardu, difficile, dur, rude, pénible, fatigant ; — *adv.* en montant. — **way,** *s.* côte, *f.*
Uphold, *v.a.* (*lift*) lever, élever ; tenir ; (*support*) soutenir ; maintenir ; (*keep up*) entretenir
Upholder, *s.* soutien, appui, *m.* ; fauteur, partisan, *m.*
Upholding, *s.* soutien, *m.*
Upholsterer, *s.* tapissier, *m.*, -ière, *f.*
Upholstery, *s.* tapisserie, *f.* ; meubles, *m.pl.*
Upland, *s.* pays élevé, *m.* ; terrain élevé, *m.* ; montagne, *f.* ; plateau, *m.* ; — *adj.* élevé, montagneux, escarpé
Uplift, *v.a.* lever ; élever ; lever vers le ciel
Upon, *prep. V.* **On**
Upper, *adj.* supérieur ; haut ; de *or* du dessus, du haut, d'en haut ; (*of Houses of Parliam., geog.*) haut ; —**s,** *s.pl.* (*of boots*) empeignes, *f.pl.* — **boxes,** *s.pl.* (*theat.*) troisièmes loges, *f.pl.* ; loges du cintre, *f.pl.* — **Canada,** *s.* le Haut-Canada, *m.* — **case,** *s.* (*print.*) haut-de-casse, *m.* — **cloth,** *s.* (*for meals*) napperon, *m.* — **deck,** *s.* pont supérieur, *m.* — **Egypt,** *s.* la Haute-Égypte, *f.* — **end,** *s.* haut bout, *m.* — **hand,** *s.* dessus, *m.* — **House,** *s.* (*of parliam.*) Chambre haute, *f.* — **lip,** *s.* lèvre supérieure, *f.* — **most,** *adj.* (le) plus haut, (le) plus élevé, supérieur, premier. *To be — most,* prédominer. — **part,** *s.* haut, *m.* ; dessus, *m.* — **petticoat,** *s.* jupon de dessus, *m.* — **Rhine,** *s.* Haut-Rhin, *m.* — **side,** *s. V.* **part.** — **story,** *s.* étage supérieur, dernier étage, *m.* ; (*head*) tête, caboche, *f.* — **ten,** — **ten thousand,** *s.pl.* (l') aristocratie, *f.*, (les) riches, *m.pl.* — **town,** *s.* haute ville, *f.* — **works,** *s.pl.* (*nav.*) œuvres mortes, *f.pl.* ; (*fig.*) tête, caboche, *f.*
Uppish, *adj.* fier, arrogant
Uppishness, *s.* fierté, arrogance, *f.*
Upraise, *v.a. V.* **Uplift**
Uprear, *v.a.* lever, soulever, dresser
Upright, *adj.* droit, tout droit ; debout ; (*fig.*) honnête, loyal, juste, droit ; — *adv.* droit, tout droit ; debout ; — *s.* ligne perpendiculaire, *f.* ; (*carp.*, &c.) montant, *m.*
Uprightly, *adv.* droit, debout ; (*fig.*) honnêtement, loyalement, droitement, avec droiture [*m.* ; (*honesty*) droiture, loyauté, *f.*
Uprightness, *s.* perpendicularité, *f.*, aplomb,
Uprise, *v.n. V.* **Rise up ;** — *s.* lever, *m.* ; sortie de dîner, *f.*
Uprising, *s. V.* **Uprise**
Uproar, *s.* tumulte, *m.* ; désordre, *m.* ; émeute, *f.* ; vacarme, tapage, *m.*
Uproarious, *adj.* tumultueux, bruyant
Uproariously, *adv.* tumultueusement, bruyamment
Uproariousness, *s. V.* **Tumultuousness**
Uproot, *v.a.* déraciner ; arracher ; extirper
Uprooting, *s.* déracinement, *m.* ; extirpation, *f.*
Upset, *v.a.* renverser ; mettre sens dessus dessous ; retourner ; (*a carriage*) faire verser, verser ; (*a boat*) faire chavirer, chavirer ; (*derange*) déranger ; détraquer ; (*of feelings*) bouleverser ; — *v.n.* se renverser ; (*of carriages*) verser ; (*of boats*) chavirer [*riage*) versade, *f.*
Upsetting, *s.* renversement, *m.* ; (*of a car-*
Upshot, *s.* dénoûment, *m.* ; fin, issue, *f.* ; fin mot, *m.*
Upside, *s.* dessus, *m.* — *down,* sens dessus dessous. *To turn — down,* (*v a.*) mettre sens dessus dessous, bouleverser, renverser ; (*capsize*) chavirer ; (*v.n.*) se renverser sens dessus dessous ; chavirer
Upstart, *s.* parvenu, *m.*, e, *f.* ; — *adj.* qui croît subitement ; (*sudden*) subit ; (*pers.*) parvenu
Upthrow, *s.* (*of strata*) soulèvement, *m.*
Upturn, *v.a.* retourner ; relever
Upward, *adj.* de bas en haut, dirigé en haut ; ascendant ; ascensionnel ; (*of the eyes*) levé. *To show an — tendency,* (*of prices*) être en hausse
Upward, Upwards, *adv.* (*of place*) en haut, en l'air ; en montant ; (*of time*) en remontant ; (*more*) plus, davantage ; au-delà, au-dessus ; (*navig.*) en amont. — *and downward,* en haut et en bas, par haut et par bas
Uralian, *adj.* ouralien
Uranium, *s.* uranium, *m.*
Urano-graphy, -logy, &c. *V.* page 3, § 1

Urate, *s.* urate, *m.*
Urban, *adj.* urbain
Urbane, *adj.* qui a de l'urbanité. plein d'urbanité, poli
Urbanely, *adv.* avec urbanité, poliment
Urbanity, *s.* urbanité, *f.*
Urchin, *s.* gamin, marmot, mioche, môme, bambin, moutard, *m.*; (*zool.*) hérisson. *m.* (*V.* **Sea** —)
Urea, *s.* urée, *f.*
Ureter, *s.* uretère, *m.*
Urethra, *s.* urèthre, *m.*
Urethral, *adj.* uréthral, de l'urèthre
Urethritis, *s.* uréthrite, *f.*
Urge, *v.a.* (— **on**) presser, hâter; (*incite*) pousser (à), exciter (à), porter (à); (*provoke*) provoquer, irriter; (*follow close*) serrer de près; (*solicit*) presser vivement (de), prier instamment (de); exhorter (à); importuner; (*impose*) imposer; (*insist upon*) insister sur, faire valoir; (*allege*) alléguer; (*object*) objecter; (*a reason*, &c.) émettre, avancer
Urgency, *s.* urgence, *f.*; besoin urgent, *m.*; insistance, *f.*; (*solicitation*) instances, *f.pl.*
Urgent, *adj.* urgent; pressant; imminent. *To be — with*, presser
Urgently, *adv.* avec urgence, urgemment; d'une manière pressante; instamment; avec instance; impérieusement
Urging, *adj.* pressant; importun
Uric, *adj.* urique
Urinal, *s.* urinoir, *m.*; vespasienne, *f.*; (*table*) urinal, *m.*
Urinarium, *s.* (*urinal*) urinoir, *m.*; vespasienne, *f.*; (*porter*) ... (*agr.*) purot, *m.*, roussie, *f.*
Urinary, *adj.* urinaire; — *s. V.* **Urinarium.**
Urinate, *v.n.* uriner [— *vessel*, vase de nuit, *m.*
Urination, *s.* urination, *f.*
Urine, *s.* urine, *f.* *Bloody* —, urine sanguinolente, *f.*; hématurie, *f.*
Uriniferous, *adj.* urinifère
Urinous, *adj.* urineux
Urn, *s.* urne, *f.*; vase, *m.*; (*for tea*, &c.) fontaine, *f.*
Ursa, *s.* — *Major*, la grande Ourse, *f.* — *Minor*, la petite Ourse, *f.*
Ursine, *adj.* oursin, d'ours
Urson, *s.* urson, *m.*
Ursuline, *s.* ursuline, *f.*
Urticaria, *s.* urticaire, *f.*
Urtication, *s.* urtication, *f.*
Urus, *s.* urus, ure, *m.*
Us, *pron.* nous; (*slang for* '*me*') me; moi
Usable, *adj.* servable, employable, utile
Usage, *s.* usage, *m.*; traitement, *m.*, traitements, *m.pl.*; procédé, *m.*, procédés, *m.pl.*
Usance, *s.* usance, *f.*
Use, *s.* usage, *m.*; coutume, habitude, *f.*; emploi, *m.*; utilité, *f.*, avantage, profit, *m.*; (*need*) besoin (de), *m.*; (*law*) jouissance, *f.*, usage, *m.*; (*nav. law*) us, *m.* *For the — of*, à l'usage de. *In* —, employé; en usage; usité. *Out of* —, hors d'usage; inusité. *To be of* —, servir (à), être utile (à). *To be of no* —, être inutile (à; *before a verb*, de); ne pas servir; ne servir à rien. *To come into general* —, devenir d'un usage général. *To grow out of* —, passer, vieillir, tomber en désuétude. *To make — of*, faire usage de, se servir de, employer; utiliser. *What is the — of that?* à quoi sert cela? à quoi cela sert-il? *What is the — of crying?* à quoi sert de pleurer *or* que vous pleuriez? — *is second nature*, l'habitude est une seconde nature
Use, *v.a.* (*general sense: reverse of* '*abuse*') user de; (*employ*) se servir de, employer; exercer; (*abstract things as forbearance*, &c.) user de; (*consume*) user, consommer; (*utilize*) utiliser, faire servir; (*finish*) finir, achever; (*accustom*) accoutumer, habituer; (*treat*) traiter, agir envers, agir à l'égard de, en agir avec, en user avec; — *v.n.* (*pers.*) avoir coutume (de); (*things*) être ordinairement. — **up,** user, consommer, employer en entier; (*pers.*) user, épuiser, éreinter; blaser
[*'Used to' and the verb following it are often rendered simply by the Imperfect tense of that second verb: as, I used to see him frequently*, je le voyais souvent; *It used to be so formerly*, c'était comme cela autrefois]
Used, *pret.* (*I* or *&c.* — *to* ...) *See under* **Use,** *v.a.n.*; — *part. adj.* employé, &c. (*V.* **Use,** *v.a.*); (*of words*) usité, en usage. *Not* —, inusité. *Often* or *much* —, très usité. *Very little* —, très peu usité; (*of things, almost new*) ayant peu servi, presque neuf. *To be* —, être usité *or* &c.; être employé *or* &c.; servir (*to be — again*, resservir). *To be — to*, être accoutumé *or* habitué *or* fait à. *To get* (or *become*) — *to*, s'accoutumer à, s'habituer à, se faire à. *To have been* —, (*not to be new, to be second-hand*) avoir servi
Useful, *adj.* utile, avantageux. —**ly,** *adv.* utilement, avantageusement. —**ness,** *s.* utilité, *f.*, avantage, *m.*
Useless, *adj.* inutile. —**ly,** *adv.* inutilement; vainement. —**ness,** *s.* inutilité, *f.*
Usher, *s.* huissier, *m.*; (*of schools*) sous-maître, maître d'étude, maître répétiteur, *m.*, (*in boys' slang*) pion, *m.*; — *v.a.* (— *in*) faire entrer (dans), introduire (dans); annoncer; précéder; être l'avant-courrier de; inaugurer. *To — out*, faire sortir, reconduire
Usnea, *s.* usnée, *f.*
Usquebaugh, *s.* scubac, usquebac, *m.*
Usual, *adj.* usuel; (*customary*) ordinaire, habituel, accoutumé; commun, fréquent; (*in general practice, established or sanctioned by custom*) d'usage; (*of words*) usité. *As* —, comme à l'ordinaire, comme d'habitude; comme toujours. *More* or *less than* —, plus *or* moins qu'à l'ordinaire
Usually, *adv.* ordinairement, habituellement
Usucaption, *s.* usucapion, *f.*
Usufruct, *s.* usufruit, *m.*
Usufructuary, *s.* usufruitier, *m.*, -ière, *f.*; — *adj.* usufructuaire, usufruitier
Usurer, *s.* usurier, *m.*, -ière, *f.*
Usurious, *adj.* (*pers.*) qui fait l'usure; (*things*) usuraire. —**ly,** *adv.* usurairement. —**ness,** *s.* nature usuraire, *f.*
Usurp, *v.a.* usurper
Usurpation, *s.* usurpation, *f.*
Usurpatory, *adj.* usurpatoire
Usurper, *s.* usurpateur, *m.*, -trice, *f.*
Usurping, *adj.* usurpateur; — *s.* usurpation, *f*
Usurpingly, *adv.* par usurpation
Usury, *s.* usure, *f.*
Ut, *s.* (*mus.*) ut, do, *m.*
Utensil, *s.* ustensile, *m.*; instrument, *m.*; vase, *m.* *V.* **Bedroom** *&* **Kitchen**
Uterine, *adj.* utérin
Uterus, *s.* utérus, *m.*
Utilitarian, *s. adj.* utilitaire, *m.f.*
Utilitarianism, *s.* utilitarianisme, utilitarisme, *m.*
Utility, *s.* utilité, *f.*
Utilizable, *adj.* utilisable
Utilization, *s.* utilisation, *f.*
Utilize, *v.a.* utiliser
Utmost, *adj.* dernier, extrême; (le) plus grand, (le) plus haut; — *s.* comble, plus haut degré, dernier degré, *m.*; bout, *m.*; plus, *m.*; (*all one can*) tout son possible, son possible, le plus possible, *m.*; (*com.*) le plus haut prix, *m.* *At the —, at the very* —, tout au plus. *To the* —, à l'extrême, au suprême degré. *To do o.'s* —, faire son possible *or* tout son possible (pour)
Utopia, *s.* utopie, *f.*
Utopian, *adj.* utopique; — *s.* utopiste, *m.f.*
Utopianism, *s.* utopisme, *m.*
Utopist, *s.* utopiste, *m.f.*
Utricule, *s.* utricule, *m.*
Utricular, *adj.* utriculaire, utriculeux
Utriculate, *adj.* utriculé
Utriculous, *adj.* utriculeux
Utter, *adj.* entier, complet, total; extrême; (le) plus grand, (le) plus profond; absolu, positif; (*mere*) vrai; — *v.a.* proférer, prononcer, articuler, dire; (*sounds*) faire entendre; (*cries*, &c.) jeter, pousser; (*divulge*) publier, dire; (*sell*)

vendre, débiter; (*coin*, &c.) mettre en circulation, émettre
Utterable, *adj.* exprimable, prononçable
Utterance, *s.* prononciation, articulation, *f.*; parole, *f.*; élocution, *f.*, débit, *m.*; expression, *f.*, langage, *m.*; émission, *f.*
Utterer, *s.* personne qui profère *or* qui prononce, *f.*; (*of bad money*) émissionnaire, *m.f.*
Uttering, *s.* prononciation, articulation, *f.*; (*of coin*, &c.) émission, *f.*
Utterly, *adv.* entièrement, complètement, totalement, tout à fait; de fond en comble
Uttermost. *V.* **Utmost**
Uvula, *s.* luette, *f.*
Uvular, *adj.* uvulaire
Uxorious, *adj.* esclave de sa femme. **—ly,** *adv.* avec une complaisance excessive pour sa femme. **—ness,** *s.* complaisance excessive pour sa femme, *f.*

V

V, *s.* (*letter*) v, *m.*
Vacancy, *s.* vide, *m.*; lacune, *f.*; (*of offices*) place vacante, *f.*; vacance, *f.*; (*leisure*) loisir, *m.*; repos, *m.*; cessation, interruption, *f.*; (*of thought*) vide de la pensée, *m.*
Vacant, *adj.* (*empty*) vide; (*not occupied*) vacant; (*of time*) libre, de loisir; (*thoughtless*) distrait; (*law*) vacant
Vacate, *v.a.* annuler; quitter, se démettre de, laisser vacant; (*law*) vider; — *v.n.* se retirer
Vacation, *s.* vacances, *f.pl.*
Vaccinal, *adj.* vaccinal
Vaccinate, *v.a.* vacciner
Vaccinating, *adj.* vaccinateur
Vaccination, *s.* vaccination, vaccine, *f.*
Vaccinator, *s.* vaccinateur, *m.*
Vaccine, *adj.* de vache; (*of vaccination*) vaccinal. **— matter, -lymph,** *s.* vaccin, *m.*
Vaccinia, *s.* vaccine, *f.*
Vaccinifer, *s.* vaccinifère, *m.*
Vacciniferous, *adj.* vaccinifère
Vaccinist, *s.* vaccinateur, *m.*
Vacillate, *v.n.* vaciller
Vacillation, *s.* vacillation, *f.*
Vacuity, *s.* vacuité, *f.*; vide, *m.*; néant, *m.*
Vacuous, *adj.* vide [faire le vide
Vacuum, *s.* vide, *m.* (*V.* **Abhor**). *To get a —,*
Vade-mecum, *s.* vade-mecum, *m.*
Vagabond, *s.* vagabond *m.*, e, *f.*; va-nu-pieds, *m.f.*; homme (*pl.* gens) sans aveu, *m.*; mendiant, *m.*; — *adj.* vagabond, errant
Vagabondage, *s.* vagabondage, *m.*
Vagabondize, *v.n.* vagabonder
Vagarious, fantasque, capricieux, original
Vagary, *s.* divagation, *f.*; caprice, *m.*, boutade, [lubie, *f.*
Vagina, *s.* vagin, *m.*
Vaginal, *adj.* vaginal
Vagrancy, *s.* vagabondage. *m.*
Vagrant, *s. adj.* *V.* **Vagabond.** *—'s relief ticket*, bon de secours, *m.*
Vague, *adj.* vague
Vaguely, *adv.* vaguement
Vagueness, *s.* vague, *m.*
Vail, *v.a.* baisser; abaisser; effacer; (*take off*) ôter; — *v.n.* céder (à), s'effacer (devant); s'incliner (devant); **—s,** *s.pl.* profits, *m.pl.*, gratification, *f.*, pourboire, *m.*
Vain, *adj.* vain; vaniteux, glorieux, orgueilleux; (*useless*) vain, inutile; infructueux; (*deceitful*) faux, trompeur. *In —*, en vain, vainement. *As — as a peacock*, glorieux (*or* fier) comme un paon. **— glorious,** *adj.* vaniteux, vain. **— gloriously,** *adv.* vaniteusement. **— glory,** *s.* vaine gloire, gloriole, *f.* **—ly,** *adv.* vainement, en vain, inutilement; (*with vanity*) avec vanité, vaniteusement, orgueilleusement; (*foolishly*) follement. **—ness,** *s.* inutilité, *f.*; vanité, folie, *f.*

Vair, *s.* (*her.*) vair, *m.*
Vairy, *adj.* (*her.*) vairé [nière, *f.*; draperie, *f.*
Valance, *s.* garniture de rideau, pente, canton-
Vale, *s.* vallon, *m.*, vallée, *f.*
Valedictory, *adj.* d'adieu
Valerian, *s.* valériane, *f.*
Valet, *s.* valet de chambre, valet, *m.*
Valetudinarian, *s. adj.* valétudinaire, *m.f.*
Valiant, *adj.* vaillant, brave. **—ly,** *adv.* vaillamment, bravement. **—ness,** *s.* vaillance, valeur, bravoure, *f.*
Valid, *adj.* valide, valable. *To make* or *render —*, rendre valable, valider
Validate, *v.a.* valider
Validation, *s.* validation, *f.*
Validity, Validness, *s.* validité, *f.*
Validly, *adv.* validement, valablement
Valise, *s.* valise, *f.*, portemanteau, *m.*
Vallance, *s.* *V.* **Valance**
Valley, *s.* vallée, *f.*, vallon, *m.*
Vallisneria, *s.* vallisnérie, *f.*
Valonia, *s.* avelanède, *f.*
Valorem (Ad), (*Latin*) ad valorem
Valorous, *adj.* valeureux, vaillant, brave. **—ly,** *adv.* valeureusement, vaillamment, [bravement
Valour, *s.* valeur, bravoure, *f.*
Valse, *s.* valse, *f.*
Valuable, *adj.* de valeur, de prix; précieux; estimable; bon, excellent; **—s,** *s.pl.* objets de valeur *or* de prix, *m.pl.*, valeurs, *f.pl.*
Valuableness, *s* valeur, *f.*, prix, *m.*
Valuation, *s.* évaluation, *f*; estimation, *f.*
Valuator, *s.* estimateur, *m.*
Value, *v.a.* évaluer; estimer, apprécier, faire cas de; tenir à; considérer, respecter; calculer; taxer; — *s.* valeur, *f.*; prix, *m.*; importance, *f.* *For — received*, valeur reçue. *To be of no —*, ne rien valoir. *To set a — on* or *upon*, faire cas de, mettre du prix à, estimer, apprécier. **—less,** *adj.* sans valeur
Valued, *adj.* estimé, apprécié; précieux; [digne
Valuer, *s.* *V.* **Appraiser**
Valvate, *adj.* valvé; valvaire
Valve, *s.* valve, *f.*; (*of machines*) soupape, *f.*; (*of pumps*) clapet, *m.*; (*of stoves*) clé, *f.*; (*of doors*) battant, *m.*; (*anat.*) valvule, *f.*; (*bot.*, *and of shells*) valve, *f.* **— shell,** *s.* valvée, *f.*
Valved, *adj.* à valve, à valves, valvé; valvulé;
Valvular, *adj.* valvulaire [(*mach.*) à soupape
Valvulate, *adj.* valvulé
Valvule, *s.* valvule, *f.*
Vamp, *s.* (*of boots*) empeigne, *f.*, devant, avant-pied, *m.*; — *v.a.* **(— up)** rapiécer; replâtrer; renouveler; (*boots*) remonter
Vampire, *s.* vampire, *m.*
Vampir-ic, al, -ism. *V.* page 3, § 1
Van, *s.* (*mil.*, *nav.*) avant-garde, *f.*; (*for corn*) tarare, *m.*; (*vehicle*) voiture, *f.*; omnibus, *m.*; (*for pleasure-trips*) char à bancs, *m.*; carriole, *f.*; (*for goods*) tapissière, *f.*; fourgon, *m.*; (*on a rail. train*) wagon, *m.*; voiture, *f.*; fourgon, *m.*; (*furniture —*) voiture (de déménagement), *f.* **— courier,** *s.* avant-coureur, précurseur, *m.*; (*mil.*) éclaireur, *m.* **— guard,** *s.* (*mil.*) avant-garde, *f.*; (*guard of a goods —, rail.*) facteur de ville, *m.*
Vandal, *s.* Vandale, *m.*
Vandal-ic, -ism. *V.* page 3, § 1
Vandyke, *v.a.* crêter. **— border,** *s.* crête, *f.*
Vane, *s.* girouette, *f.*; (*of machines*) registre, *m.*; (*of an instr.*) pinnule, *f.*; (*of quills*) barbe, *f.*; (*flag*) guidon, *m.*
Vanilla, Vanille, *s.* vanille, *f.* **— ice,** *s.* glace à la vanille, *f.* **— tree,** *s.* vanillier, *m.*
Vanish, *v.n.* **(-away)** s'évanouir, disparaître; se dissiper; passer; s'en aller
Vanishing, *s.* évanouissement, *m.*, disparition, *f.*; (*pers.*) fuite, *f.* **— point,** *s.* point de fuite, *m.* [vanités, *f.*
Vanity, *s.* vanité, *f.* **— fair,** *s.* la foire aux
Vanquish, *v.a.* vaincre
Vanquishable, *adj.* vincible

Vanquisher, *s.* vainqueur, *m.*
Vantage-ground, *s.* avantage du terrain, *m.*; position supérieure *or* avantageuse, haute position, *f.*; lieu élevé, *m.*, hauteur (-s, *pl.*), éminence (-s, *pl.*), *f.*; avantage, dessus, *m.*, supériorité, *f.*
Vapid, *adj.* insipide, fade, plat; (*of liquors*) éventé, plat [*f.*; (*of liquors*) évent, *m.*
Vapidity, Vapidness, *s.* insipidité, fadeur,
Vaporish. *V.* **Vapourish**
Vaporization, *s.* vaporisation, *f.*
Vaporize, *v.a.* vaporiser; — *v.n.* se vaporiser
Vaporizer, *s.* vaporisateur, *m.*
Vaporous, *adj.* vaporeux; (*windy*) flatueux, venteux; (*vain*) vain, chimérique. **—ness,** *s.* état vaporeux, *m.*
Vapour, *s.* vapeur, *f.*; — *v.a.* exhaler; — *v.n.* s'évaporer; (*boast*) se vanter. — **bath,** *s.* bain de vapeur, *m.*
Vapourer, *s.* vantard, *m.*, e, *f.*
Vapouring, *adj.* vantard, glorieux. **—ly,** *adv.* en se vantant
Vapourish, *adj.* vaporeux
Varec, *s.* varech, varec, *m.*
Variability. *V.* **Variableness**
Variable, *adj.* variable, changeant; inconstant
Variableness, *s.* variabilité, *f.*; inconstance, *f.*
Variably, *adv.* variablement, d'une manière variable *or* changeante
Variance, *s.* variation, *f.*; (*discord*) désaccord, *m.* *At* —, en désaccord, mal ensemble, brouillés, fâchés; mal (avec), brouillé (avec), fâché (avec); (*slightly*) en délicatesse; (*things*) en contradiction. *To set at* —, brouiller
Variation, *s.* variation, *f.*; changement, *m.*; différence, *f.*; déviation, *f.*
Varicella, *s.* varicelle, *f.*
Varicocele, *s.* varicocèle, *f.*
Varicose, Varicous, *adj.* variqueux. — **vein,** *s.* varice, *f.*
Variegate, *v.a.* varier, nuancer
Variegated, *adj.* varié, nuancé, bigarré; (*of flowers*) panaché, jaspé; tiqueté; (*of marble,* &c.) jaspé. — *lamp,* verre de couleur, *m.*
Variegation, *s.* variété de nuances, diversité de couleurs, *f.*; (*of flowers*) panachure, *f.*; tiqueture, *f.*
Variety, *s.* variété, *f.* **Varieties,** *pl.* variétés, *f.pl.*; (*in newspapers*) faits divers, *m.pl.*
Variola, *s.* variole, *f.*
Variolar, *adj.* variolaire
Variolic, *adj.* variolique
Varioloid, *adj.* *s.* varioloïde, *adj. m.f.*, *s.f.*
Variolous, *adj.* varioleux
Variorum. — *edition,* édition variorum, *f.*
Various, *adj.* différent, divers; variable, changeant; (*diversified*) varié
Variously, *adv.* différemment, diversement; [avec variété
Varix, *s.* varice, *f.*
Varlet, *s.* (*hist.*) varlet, *m.*; (*rogue*) drôle, vaurien, coquin, *m.*
Varnish, *s.* vernis, *m.*; — *v.a.* vernir; vernisser; (*fig.*) colorer. — **tree,** *s.* vernis, *m.*
Varnisher, *s.* vernisseur, *m.*
Varnishing, *s.* vernissure, *f.*
Vary, *v.a.* varier; diversifier; — *v.n.* varier; (*deviate*) s'éloigner (de), s'écarter (de); (*disagree*) différer (sur), n'être pas d'accord (sur); (*change*) se succéder, changer. *Not to — a minute, a second,* ne pas varier d'une minute, d'une seconde
Varying, *adj.* changeant, qui change, qui varie, divers
Vascular, *adj.* vasculaire, vasculeux
Vase, *s.* vase, *m.* *Chinese* —, potiche, *m.* — **shaped,** *adj* vasiforme; évasé
Vasiform, *adj.* vasiforme
Vassal, *s.* (*feud.*) vassal, *m.*, e, *f.*; (*dependant*) esclave, *m.f.*, serviteur, *m.*
Vassalage, *s.* (*feud.*) vassalité, *f.*, vasselage, *m.*; (*dependence*) dépendance, sujétion, servitude, *f.*
Vassalry, *s.* vassalité, *f.*
Vast, *adj.* vaste, immense
Vastly, *adv.* immensément, vastement; extrêmement, excessivement
Vastness, *s.* vaste étendue, vastité, *f.*; immensité, *f.*; grandeur, *f.*; importance, *f.*
Vat, *s.* cuve, *f.*, cuvier, *m.* **—ful,** *s.* cuvée, *f.*
Vatican, *s.* Vatican, *m.*
Vaticination, *s.* *V.* **Prophecy**
Vaudeville, *s.* vaudeville, *m.* — **writer,** *s.* vaudevilliste, *m.f.*
Vaudois, *s.* *adj.* Vaudois, *m.*, e, *f.*
Vault, *s.* voûte, *f.*; (*cave*) caveau, *m.*, cave, *f.*; (*for the dead*) caveau, *m.*, sépulture, *f.*; (*leap*) saut, *m.*; voltige, *f.*; — *v.a.* voûter; — *v.n.* sauter; voltiger
Vaulted, *adj.* voûté, en voûte; couvert d'une voûte. — *ceiling* or *roof,* voûte, *f.*
Vaulter, *s.* sauteur, voltigeur, acrobate, *m.*
Vaulting, *s.* construction de voûtes, *f.*; (*vaults*) voûtes, *f.pl.*; (*rid.*) voltige, *f.*
Vaunt, &c. *V.* **Boast,** &c.
Vauxhall, *s.* Vauxhall, *m.*
Veal, *s.* veau, *m.*; — *adj.* de veau. — **broth,** *s.* bouillon de veau, *m.* — **collop,** *s.* escalope de veau, *f.* — **cutlet,** *s.* côtelette de veau, *f.* — **pie,** *s.* pâté de veau, *m.* — **tea,** *s.* bouillon de veau, *m.*, eau de veau, *f.*
Veda, *s.* véda, *m.*
Vedette, *s.* vedette, *f.*
Veer, *v.a.* tourner; changer de direction, changer; (*nav.*) virer, changer de bord
Vegetability, *s.* végétabilité, *f.*
Vegetable, *s.* végétal, *m.*; (*for the table*) légume, *m.*; — *adj.* végétal; (*capable of vegetation*) végétable. — **brimstone, -sulphur,** *s.* soufre végétal, *m.* — **cutter,** *s.* taille-légumes, coupe-légumes, hache-légumes, *m.* — **dish,** *s.* légumier, *m.*, casserole à légumes, *f.* — **garden,** *s.* jardin potager, *m.* — **ivory,** *s.* ivoire végétal, corozo, *m.* — **marrow,** *s.* (*bot.*) courge à la moelle, *f.* — **mould, -soil,** *s.* terre végétale, terre franche, *f.* — **seed,** *s.* graine potagère, *m.* — **silk,** *s.* soie végétale, *f.* — **soup,** *s.* soupe aux herbes, *f.*, soupe (*f.*) *or* potage (*m.*) maigre; julienne, *f.*; printanier, *m.*, printanière, *f.*
Vegetal, *adj.* végétal
Vegetality, *s.* végétalité, *f.*
Vegetarian, *s.* *adj.* légumiste, *m.f.*
Vegetarianism, *s.* légumisme, *m.*
Vegetate, *v.n.* végéter
Vegetation, *s.* végétation, *f.*
Vegetative, *adj.* végétatif, végétateur; végétable. — **ness,** *s.* végétabilité, *f.*
Vehemenc-e, y, *s.* véhémence, violence, force, impétuosité, *f.*; ardeur, *f.*
Vehement, *adj.* véhément, violent, fort, impétueux; ardent
Vehemently, *adv.* avec véhémence, véhémentement, violemment, fortement, impétueusement; ardemment
Vehicle, *s.* voiture, *f.*, véhicule, *m.*; (*fig.*) véhicule, *m.*; (*pharm.*) intermède, véhicule, *m.*; — *v.a.* voiturer, transporter [des voitures
Vehicular, -y, *adj.* véhiculaire; (*of carriages*)
Veil, *s.* voile, *m.*; (*small*) voilette, *f.*; (*fig.*) voile, *m.*; rideau, *m.*; déguisement, *m.*; apparence, *f.*; prétexte, *m.*; — *v.a.* voiler; (*disguise*) déguiser, cacher, dissimuler, masquer, voiler. **—less,** *adj.* sans voile
Vein, *s.* veine, *f.*; (*bot.*) nervure, *f.*; (*min., geol.*) veine, *f.*, filon, *m.*; — *v.a.* veiner. **—less,** *adj.* sans veines; sans nervures. **—let,** *s.* veinule, *f.* — **stone,** *s.* gangue, *f.*
Veined, *adj* veiné; veineux
Veining, *s.* veinage, *m.*
Veinous, *adj.* *V.* **Venous** [flanchet, *m.*
Veiny, *adj.* veiné; veineux. — *piece,* (*of beef*)
Velleity, *s.* velléité, *f.*
Vellum, *s.* vélin, *m.* — **lace,** *s.* guipure, dentelle à cartisane, dentelle de soie, *f.* — **post,** *s.* papier vélin, *m.*
Velocipede, *s.* vélocipède, *m.*

Velocipedist, *s.* vélocipédiste, *m.f.*
Velocity, *s.* vélocité, *f.*; vitesse, rapidité, *f.*
Velvet, *s.* velours, *m.*; (*bot.*) velouté, *m.*; — *adj.* de velours; (*soft*) velouté, doux. —**black,** *s.* noir velouté, *m.* — **down,** *s.* velouté, *m.* — **lace,** *s.* velouté, *m.* —**like,** *adj.* velouté. — **pile,** *s.* moquette, *f.*, velouté, *m.*; *adj.* de *or* en moquette; velouté. — **ribbon,** *s.* velouté, *m.* — **worker,** *s.* veloutier, *m.*
Velveted, *adj.* *V.* **Velvet,** *adj.*
Velveteen, *s.* velours de coton croisé, *m.*, velvetine, *f.*
Velveting, *s.* velouté, *m.*
Velvety, *adj.* velouté
Vena, *s.* veine, *f.* — *cava,* veine cave, *f.* — *portæ,* veine porte, *f.*
Venal, *adj.* vénal
Venality, *s.* vénalité, *f.*
Venally, *adv.* vénalement
Venary, Venatorial, *adj.* de chasse
Venation, *s.* (*bot.*) nervure, *f.*
Vend, *v.a.* vendre; débiter
Vendace, *s.* lavaret, *m.*
Vendee, *s.* acquéreur, *m.*, -euse, *f.*
Vender, *s.* vendeur, *m.*, -euse, *f.*, débitant, *m.*, e, *f.*, marchand, *m.*, e, *f.*; (*law*) vendeur, *m.*, venderesse, *f.*
Vendi-bility, bleness, *s.* *V.* **Salableness**
Vendible, Vendibly. *V.* **Salable, Salably**
Vendor. *V.* **Vender**
Veneer, *v.a.* plaquer ('*with,*' de); — *s.* feuille à plaquer, feuille, plaque, *f.*; (*zool.*) crambe, crambé, *m.*
Veneering, *s.* placage, *m.*
Venerable, *adj.* vénérable [(*f.*) vénérable
Venerableness, *s.* caractère (*m.*) *or* nature
Venerably, *adv.* vénérablement
Venerate, *v.a.* vénérer, révérer
Veneration, *s.* vénération, *f.*
Venerator, *s.* vénérateur, *m.*, -trice, *f.*
Venereal, *adj.* vénérien; (*of illness*) vénérien, syphilitique; (*of medicines*) antivénérien, antisyphilitique; (*aphrodisiac*) aphrodisiaque
Venery, *s.* volupté, sensualité, *f.*; (*hunting*) vénerie, chasse, *f.*
Venesection, *s.* vénésection, *f.*
Venetian, *s.* Vénitien, *m.*, -ne, *f.*; — *adj.* vénitien, de Venise. — **blind,** *s.* jalousie, *f.*; (*of carriages*) vasistas, *m.* — **point,** *s.* point de Venise, *m.* — **school,** *s.* école vénitienne, *f.* — **shutter,** *s.* persienne, *f.*
Vengeance, *s.* vengeance, *f.* *With a* —, à l'excès, à outrance, outre mesure, terriblement, furieusement, vivement, vigoureusement, de toutes ses forces, avec violence; d'importance; fort, ferme; et un peu bien, et bien, et comme il faut; en diable; à mort; et au-delà, et quelque chose de plus; plus qu'il ne faut; plus qu'on n'en veut, à foison, en veux-tu en voilà
Vengeful, *adj.* vindicatif; vengeur
Venial, *adj.* véniel
Veniality, Venialness, *s.* vénialité, *f.*
Venially, *adv.* véniellement
Venison, *s.* venaison, *f.*; chevreuil, *m.*
Venom, *s.* venin, poison, *m.*
Venomous, *adj.* (*of animals*) venimeux; (*of plants, of animals eaten, of inorganic substances*) vénéneux; (*fig.*) venimeux; empoisonné; (*pers.*) méchant. —**ly,** *adv.* d'une manière venimeuse; (*fig.*) méchamment. —**ness,** *s.* (*of animals*) nature venimeuse, venimosité, *f.*, venin, *m.*; (*of plants, of animals eaten, of inorganic substances*) nature vénéneuse, vénénosité, *f.*, venin, *m.*; (*fig.*) venin, poison, *m.*; (*pers.*) méchanceté, *f.*
Venose, Venous, *adj.* (*anat.*) veineux; (*bot.*) veiné
Vent, *s.* ouverture, issue, *f.*, passage, *m.*; (*air*) vent, air, *m.*; (*of feelings*) libre cours, cours, *m.*; (*of guns*) lumière, *f.*; (*of casks*) trou de fausset, *m.*; (*breathing-hole*) soupirail, *m.*; — *v.a.* éventer; donner de l'air à; (*let out*) donner issue *or* passage à, laisser échapper; (*make an opening*) faire une ouverture à, percer; (*fig.*) donner libre cours à; (*spite, &c.*) exhaler, décharger, faire éclater; satisfaire; (*to utter*) articuler; (*divulge*) divulguer, rendre public. *To give — to, V. To* —, *v.a.* *To find* —, trouver issue; être éventé, s'éventer. *To take* —, *V.* **Wind.** — **bit,** *s.* (*artil.*) dégorgeoir, *m.* — **hole,** *s.* soupirail, *m.*; ventouse, *f.*; (*of casks*) trou de fausset, *m.*; (*tech.*) aspirail, *m.*; (*of furnaces*) évent, carnau, *m.* — **peg,** *s.* fausset, *m.*
Ventiduct, *s.* soupirail, *m.*; (*arch.*) ventouse, *f.*
Ventilate, *v.a.* ventiler; (*air*) aérer, donner de l'air à, éventer; (*winnow*) vanner; (*fig.*) publier, faire connaître; discuter; élucider; examiner
Ventilation, *s.* ventilation, *f.*; aération, *f.*; air, *m.*; (*of corn*) vannage, *m.*; (*fig.*) publication, *f.*; examen, *m.*; élucidation, *f.*
Ventilator, *s.* ventilateur, *m.*; ventouse, *f.*
Ventral, *adj.* ventral, ventrier
Ventricle, *s.* ventricule, *m.*
Ventricular, *adj.* ventriculaire
Ventriloquial, *adj.* ventriloque
Ventriloquism, *s.* ventriloquie, *f.*
Ventriloquist, *s.* ventriloque, *m.f.*
Ventriloquize, *v.n.* ventriloquer
Ventriloquous, *adj.* ventriloque
Ventriloquy, *s.* ventriloquie, *f.*
Ventripotent, *adj.* ventripotent
Venture, *v.n.* se hasarder ('*to,*' à), s'aventurer, se risquer; (*presume*) s'aviser (de); (*dare*) oser; ne pas hésiter (à); — *v.a.* risquer, hasarder, aventurer. — **at, on, upon,** (*undertake*) entreprendre, risquer; oser; prendre sur soi de; s'engager dans. *Nothing — nothing have,* qui ne risque rien n'a rien
Venture, *s.* risque, hasard, *m.*, chance, aventure, *f.*; (*com.*) pacotille, *f.* *At a* —, au hasard; à l'aventure
Venturer, *s.* personne aventureuse, *f.*
Venturesome, -ly, -ness. *V.* **Venturous, -ly, -ness**
Venturous, *adj.* aventureux; hasardeux; (*bold*) hardi, entreprenant, intrépide, audacieux; (*rash*) téméraire; (*unsafe*) aventuré, osé. —**ly,** *adv.* aventureusement; (*boldly*) hardiment. —**ness,** *s.* nature aventureuse, *f.*, caractère *or* esprit aventureux, *m.*; (*boldness*) hardiesse, audace, témérité *f.*
Venule, *s.* veinule, *f.*
Venus, *s.* Vénus, *f.* —*'s looking-glass,* (*bot.*) miroir de Vénus, *m.*, mirette, spéculaire, *f.*
Veracious, *adj.* véridique, vrai
Veraciously, *adv.* avec véracité, véridiquement
Veracity, *s.* (*pers.*) véracité, *f.*; (*things*) vérité, sincérité, *f.*
Veranda, Verandah, *s.* véranda, *f.*; marquise, *f.*
Veratria, Veratrine, *s.* vératrine, *f.*
Veratrum, *s.* vératre, *m.*
Verb, *s.* verbe, *m.*
Verbal, *adj.* verbal; littéral
Verbally, *adv.* verbalement; littéralement
Verbatim, *adj.* textuel, mot à mot, mot pour mot; — *adv.* textuellement, mot pour mot, mot à mot; à la lettre
Verbena, *s.* verveine, *f.*
Verbiage, *s.* verbiage, *m.*
Verbose, *adj.* verbeux, diffus
Verbosely, *adv.* verbeusement, diffusément
Verboseness, Verbosity, *s.* verbosité, *f.*
Verdancy, *s.* verdure, *f.*
Verdant, *adj.* verdoyant, vert
Verd-antique, Verde-antique, *s.* vert antique, vert d'Égypte, *m.*
Verderer, *s.* verdier, *m.*
Verdict, *s.* verdict, *m.*; (*fig.*) jugement, *m.*, opinion, *f.* *To bring in* or *give in* or *find a* —, rendre *or* prononcer un verdict
Verdigris, *s.* vert-de-gris, *m.*
Verditer, *s.* vert-de-terre, verdet, *m.*
Verdure, *s.* verdure, *f.*
Verge, *s.* verge, *f.*; (*arch.*) fût, *m.*; (*edge, brink*) bord, *m.*; extrémité, limite, *f.*; (*fig. of time*) veille, *f.*, moment, *m.*; (*of ruin*) penchant, *m.*; (*of forests*) lisière, *f.*; (*of gardens*) bordure, *f.*;

(*law*) ressort, *m.*; — *v.n.* incliner (vers), pencher (vers); (*tend*) tendre (vers), se diriger (vers); approcher (de)
Verger, *s.* bedeau, *m.*; porte-verge, *m.*; huissier à verge, *m.*
Verifiable, *adj.* vérifiable
Verification, *s.* vérification, *f.*
Verificative, *adj.* vérificatif
Verifier, *s.* vérificateur, *m.*, -trice, *f.*
Verify, *v.a.* vérifier
Verily, *adv.* en vérité, vraiment
Verisimilar, *adj.* vraisemblable, probable
Verisimilitude, *s.* vraisemblance, probabilité, apparence de vérité, *f.*
Veritable, *adj.* véritable, vrai
Veritably, *adv.* véritablement, vraiment, en vérité
Verity, *s.* vérité, *f.*; véracité, *f.*
Verjuice, *s.* verjus, *m.*
Vermicelli, *s.* vermicelle, *m.* — **maker,** *s.* vermicellier, *m.* — **soup,** *s.* potage au vermicelle, *m.*
Vermicidal, *adj.*, **Vermicide,** *s. adj.* vermicide, *adj. m.f.*, *s.m.*
Vermicular, *adj.* vermiculaire; (*arch.*, *engr.*) vermiculé
Vermiculate, *v.a.* vermiculer, écheniller; — *adj.* vermiculé
Vermiculation, *s.* vermiculation, *f.*; (*arch.*, &c.) vermiculures, *f.pl.*
Vermicule, *s.* vermisseau, *m.*
Vermiculous, *adj.* vermiculeux
Vermiform, *adj.* vermiforme
Vermifugal, *adj.* vermifuge
Vermifuge, *s.* vermifuge, *m.*
Vermilion, *s.* vermillon, *m.*; — *v.a.* vermillonner
Vermin, *s.* (*insects, and fig.*) vermine, *f.*; (*not insects*) animaux nuisibles, *m.pl.* — **destroyer,** *s.*, — **destroying,** *adj.*, — **killer,** *s.* insecticide, *s.m.*, *adj. m.f.*; mort aux rats, *s.f.*
Vermination, *s.* vermination, *f.*
Verminous, *adj.* vermineux
Vermivorous, *adj.* vermivore
Vermout, *s.* vermout, *m.*
Vernacular, *adj.* vernaculaire; du pays; indigène. — *tongue*, langue du pays, langue nationale, *f.*; (*o.'s own*) propre langue, langue maternelle *or* naturelle, *f.*
Vernal, *adj.* du printemps; printanier; (*young*) jeune; (*of youth*) de la jeunesse. — **grass,** *s.* flouve, *f.*, (*sweet ditto*) flouve odorante, *f.*
Vernier, *s.* vernier, *m.*
Veronese, *s. adj.* Véronais, *m.*, e, *f.*
Veronica, *s.* véronique, *f.*
Verrucose, *adj.* verruqueux
Versatile, *adj.* versatile, changeant, mobile; flexible, souple, propre à différentes choses
Versatility, *s.* versatilité, mobilité, *f.*; flexibilité, souplesse, facilité, *f.*
Verse, *s.* vers, *m.*; (*poetry*) poésie, *f.*, vers, *m.pl.*; (*stanza*) strophe, stance, *f.*, (*of a song*) couplet, *m.*; (*of a chapter*) verset, *m.*
Versed, *adj.* versé
Versicle, *s.* versicule, *m.*; (*lit.*) petit verset, *m.*
Versification, *s.* versification, *f.*
Versifier, *s.* versificateur, *m.*, -trice, *f.*
Versify, *v.n.a.* versifier
Version, *s.* version, *f.*
Verst, *s.* verste, *f.*
Versus, *prep.* contre
Vertebra, *s.* (*pl.* **Vertebræ**) vertèbre, *f.* (*pl.* vertèbres)
Vertebral, *adj.* (*anat.*) vertébral; (*of animals*) vertébré
Vertebrata, *s.pl.* vertébrés, *m.pl.*
Vertebrate, *adj. s.*, **Vertebrated,** *adj.* vertébré, *adj. m.*, e, *f.*, vertébré, *s.m.*
Vertex, *s.* sommet, haut, *m.*; (*astr.*) zénith, *m.*
Vertical, *adj.* vertical. — *circle*, (*astr.*) cercle azimutal, *m.*
Vertically, *adv.* verticalement
Verticalness, Verticality, *s.* verticalité, *f.*
Verticil, *s.* verticille, *m.*
Verticillate, -d, *adj.* verticillé
Verticity, *s.* rotation, révolution, *f.*; (*phys.*) verticité, *f.*
Vertiginous, *adj.* vertigineux. —**ness,** *s.* vertiginosité, *f.*
Vertigo, *s.* vertige, *m.*
Vertu. *V.* **Virtu**
Veruvolver, *s.* cuisinière tourne-broche, *f.*
Vervain, *s.* verveine, *f.*
Very, *adj.* même; (*only*) seul; (*genuine*) franc, vrai. *The — best*, le meilleur de tous; tout ce qu'il y a de mieux. *The — worst*, le pire de tous; tout ce qu'il y a de pire. *The — same*, précisément (*or* absolument) le même. *The — thing*, la chose même. *The — thing! that is the — thing!* c'est cela même! *This — day*, aujourd'hui même, dès aujourd'hui. *This — evening*, ce soir même, dès ce soir, pas plus tard que ce soir. *To the — letter*, au pied de la lettre
Very, *adv.* très, fort, bien; tout; trop, beaucoup; précisément, justement; absolument. *So —*, *So — much*, si; tellement; tant; déjà tant; déjà si. *So — little*, si peu. *So — great*, &c., si grand, &c.
Vesical, *adj.* vésical
Vesicant, *adj. s.* vésicant, *adj. m.*, e, *f.*, vésicant, *s.m.*
Vesication, *s.* vésication, *f.*
Vesicatory, *adj. s.* vésicatoire, *adj. m.f.*, *s.m.*
Vesicle, *s.* vésicule, *f.*
Vesicular, *adj.* vésiculaire
Vesiculous, *adj.* vésiculeux
Vesper, *s.* (*astr.*) Vesper, *m.*, Vénus, *f.*; (*evening*) soir, *m.*; — **s,** *pl.* vêpres, *f.pl.*
Vespertine, *adj.* du soir
Vessel, *s.* vaisseau, vase, *m.*; (*ship*) vaisseau, navire, bâtiment, *m.*; (*anat.*, *bot.*) vaisseau, *m.*
Vest, *s.* veste, *f.*; (*waistcoat*) gilet, *m.*; — *v.a.* ('*with*,' de) revêtir; investir; placer; assigner; déterminer; établir; — *v.n.* être dévolu (à), échoir (à). ... *is —ed in the crown*, ... est assigné à la couronne. *—ed interest*, intérêt direct, intérêt, *m.*
Vesta, — match, *s.* allumette de cire, allumette-bougie, *f.*
Vestal, *s.* vestale, *f.*; — *adj.* de Vesta; de vestale; chaste, pur, virginal; vierge. — *virgin*, vestale, *f.*
Vestiary, *s.* vestiaire, *m.*
Vestibule, *s.* vestibule, *m.*; antichambre, *f.*; (*anat.*) vestibule, *m.*
Vestige, *s.* vestige, *m.*, trace, *f.*
Vesting, *s.* étoffe pour gilets, *f.*
Vestment, *s.* vêtement, habillement, habit, *m.*, habits, *m.pl.*; vêtement *or* ornement d'église, vêtement sacerdotal, *m.*
Vestry, *s.* sacristie, *f.*; (*meeting*) assemblée de la commune, *f.*; assemblée paroissiale, *f.*, comité de la paroisse, *m.*, fabrique, *f.* — **board,** *s.* fabrique, *f.*, conseil de fabrique, *m.* — **clerk,** *s.* secrétaire de la fabrique, *m.* — **man,** *s.* marguillier, *m.* — **pew,** *s.* banc de l'œuvre, *m.* — **meeting,** *s.* assemblée paroissiale, réunion du conseil, *f.* — **room,** *s.* sacristie, *f.*
Vesture, *s.* vêtement, *m.*, vêtements, *m.pl.*
Vesuvian, *adj.* vésuvien, du Vésuve; — *s.* (*min.*, *cigar-light*) vésuvienne, *f.*
Vetch, *s.* vesce, gesse, *f.*
Vetchling, *s.* gessette, *f.*
Veteran, *adj.* vétéran, vieux, ancien, expérimenté, aguerri; de vétéran; de vétérans; — *s.* vétéran, *m.*
Veteranship, *s.* vétérance, *f.*
Veterinarian, *s.* vétérinaire, *m.*
Veterinary, *adj.* vétérinaire. — *surgeon*, vétérinaire, *m.*
Vetiver, *s.* vétiver, *m.*
Veto, *s.* veto, *m.*; — *v.a.* mettre le (*or* son) veto à, s'opposer à
Vex, *v.a.* fâcher, irriter, vexer, contrarier; tourmenter, chagriner; troubler, inquiéter; agiter
Vexation, *s.* contrariété, *f.*; désagrément, *m.*; ennui, *m.*; vexation, *f.*; tracasserie, taquinerie, *f.*; dépit, *m.*; tourment, chagrin, *m.*; trouble, *m.*, agitation, *f.*; déboire, *m.*
Vexatious, *adj.* contrariant, fâcheux, ennuyeux, vexant; vexatoire; irritant; piquant. —**ly,** *adv.* fâcheusement, vexatoirement. —**ness,** *s.* contrariété, *f.*; ennui, *m.*

Vexed, *adj.* (*of questions, subjects*) controversé; rebattu; épineux
Vexer, *s.* personne qui contrarie *or* qui tourmente *or* qui vexe, *f.*, vexateur, *m.*, -trice, *f.*
Vexing, *adj.* contrariant, vexant, ennuyeux
Vexingly, *adv.* d'une manière contrariante *or* [vexante
Viâ, *prep.* par voie de, par, viâ
Viability, *s.* viabilité, *f.*
Viable, *adj.* viable
Viaduct, *s.* viaduc, *m.*
Vial. *V.* **Phial**
Viand, *s.* viande, *f.*, mets, *m.*
Viaticum, *s.* viatique, *m.*
Vibrate, *v.n.* vibrer
Vibration, *s.* vibration, *f.*
Vibratory, *adj.* vibratoire
Viburnum, *s.* viorne, *f.m.*
Vicar, *s.* vicaire; (*of a parish*) curé, *m.*; (*among Protestants*) ministre, pasteur, *m.*
Vicarage, *s.* cure, *f.*; (*house*) presbytère, *m.*, cure, *f.* [cure
Vicarial, *adj.* vicarial; curial, du curé, de la
Vicariate, *s.* vicariat, *m.*; — *adj.* vicarial
Vicarious, *adj.* vicarial; délégué; de substitution; souffert pour un autre (*or* pour d'autres). **—ly,** *adv.* comme délégué; par substitution
Vicarship, *s.* vicariat, *m.*; cure, *f.*
Vice, *s.* vice, *m.*; défaut, *m.*; (*screw*) étau, *m.*; — *adv.* en remplacement de; (*in compounds*) vice- ... *Free from* —, sans défaut. — **admiral,** *s.* vice-amiral, *m.* — **admiralty,** *s.* vice-amirauté, *f.* — **chairman,** &c., *V.* — **president,** &c. — **chamberlain,** *s.* vice-chambellan, *m.* — **chancellor,** *s.* vice-chancelier, *m.* — **consul,** *s.* vice-consul, *m.* — **consular,** *adj.* vice-consulaire. — **consulate, -consulship,** *s.* vice-consulat, *m.* — **gerency,** *s.* vice-gérance, *f.* — **gerent,** *s.* représentant, *m.*, vice-gérant, *m.*, e, *f.* — **king,** *s.* vice-roi, *m.* — **legate,** *s.* vice-légat, *m.* — **legateship,** *s.* vice-légation, *f.* — **prefect,** *s.* vice-préfet, *m.* — **presidency,** *s.* vice-présidence, *f.* — **president, ess,** *s.* vice-président, *m.*, e, *f.* — **presidential,** *adj.* vice-présidentiel. — **principal,** *s.* (*in colleges*) censeur, inspecteur, préfet des études, *m.* — **provost,** *s.* vice-recteur, *m.* — **queen,** *s.* vice-reine, *f.* — **rector,** *s.* vice-recteur, *m.* — **regal,** *adj.* vice-royal, de *or* du vice-roi. — **roy,** *s.* vice-roi, *m.* — **royalty, -royship,** *s.* vice-royauté, *f.* — **versâ,** *adv.* vice versâ, [réciproquement
Vicennial, *adj.* vicennal
Vicesimal, *adj.* vicésimal
Vicinage, *s.* voisinage, *m.* [virons, *m.pl.*
Vicinity, *s.* proximité, *f.*; voisinage, *m.*, en-
Vicious, *adj.* vicieux. **—ly,** *adv.* vicieusement. **—ness,** *s.* nature vicieuse, *f.*; vice, *m.*
Vicissitude, *s.* vicissitude, *f.*
Victim, *s.* victime, *f.* ('*to*,' de)
Victimize, *v.a.* victimer
Victor, *s.* vainqueur, *m.*
Victoria, *s.* (*pers., planet*) Victoria, *f.*; (*plant, phaeton*) victoria, *f.*
Victorine, *s.* palatine, *f.*
Victorious, *adj.* victorieux, vainqueur
Victoriously, *adv.* victorieusement
Victory, *s.* victoire, *f.*
Victual, *v.a.* approvisionner, avitailler; ravitailler; — *v.n.* faire ses vivres
Victualler, *s.* pourvoyeur, *m.* *Licensed* —, marchand de vin traiteur, cabaretier, *m.*; aubergiste, *m.*; maître d'hôtel, *m.*
Victualling, *s.* approvisionnement, *m.*; avitaillement, *m.*; ravitaillement, *m.*; vivres, *m.pl.* — **department,** *s.* administration des vivres, *f.* — **house,** *s.* auberge, *f.* — **office,** *s.* bureau des vivres, *m.*
Victuals, *s.pl.* provisions, *f.pl.*, vivres, *m.pl.*; aliments, *m.pl.*, nourriture, *f.*; (*jest.*) mangeaille, *f.*
Vicugna, Vicuna, Vicunia, *s.* vigogne, *f.*
Videlicet, *adv.* savoir; c'est-à-dire
Vidette. *V.* **Vedette**
Vie, *v.n.* rivaliser (*pers.*, avec; *things*, de), le disputer (*pers.*, à; *things*, en); faire assaut (*things*, de). *To — with each other*, rivaliser (de). *They — in shouting*, ils crient à l'envi *or* à l'envi l'un de l'autre (les uns des autres, *if more than two*), ils crient à qui mieux mieux, c'est à qui criera le plus. *They —d with each other in their attentions to him*, c'était à qui lui montrerait le plus de prévenance
Viennese, *s.* Viennois, *m.*, e, *f.*; — *adj.* viennois, de Vienne
View, *v.a.* regarder, considérer; voir; examiner; envisager; — *s.* vue, *f.*; (*prospect*) vue, *f.*, coup d'œil, point de vue, *m.*; scène, *f.*; tableau, *m.*; (*survey*) examen, aperçu, exposé, *m.*; (*purpose*) intention, *f.*, dessein, but, *m.*; plan, *m.*; (*appearance*) apparence, *f.*, aspect, *m.*; (*opinion*) idée, pensée, opinion, appréciation, vue, manière de voir, *f.* *At a* (or *one*) —, d'un coup d'œil. *On* —, exposé; ouvert au public, exposition publique! *With a — to*, dans le but de, en vue de. *To take a — of*, observer, examiner, regarder; envisager; considérer; voir. *To take a different* —, envisager *or* apprécier différemment. *You take a correct — of the matter*, vous envisagez bien la chose. **—less,** *adj.* invisible, imperceptible
Viewer, *s.* spectateur, *m.*, -trice, *f.*; examinateur, *m.*; inspecteur, *m.*; contrôleur, *m.*; directeur-en-chef, *m.*
Vigil, *s.* veille, *f.*; (*fast*, &c.) vigile, *f.*
Vigilance, *s.* vigilance, *f.*
Vigilant, *adj.* vigilant
Vigilantly, *adv.* avec vigilance, vigilamment
Vignette, *s.* vignette, *f.*
Vignettist, *s.* vignettiste, *m.f.*
Vigonia, *s.* vigogne, *f.*
Vigorous, *adj.* vigoureux, fort
Vigorously, *adv.* vigoureusement, fortement
Vigorousness, Vigour, *s.* vigueur, force, *f.*
Vile, *adj.* vil, bas; abject; (*of no value*) sans valeur
Vilely, *adv.* vilement, bassement; vilainement
Vileness, *s.* bassesse, *f.*; abjection, *f.*, avilissement, *m.* [tion, *f.*
Vilification, *s.* avilissement, *m.*; diffama-
Vilifier, *s.* diffamateur, *m.*, -trice, *f.*
Vilify, *v.a.* avilir, abaisser; (*slander*) vilipender, dénigrer
Villa, *s.* villa, maison de campagne, *f.*
Village, *s.* village, *m.*
Villager, *s.* villageois, *m.*, e, *f.*
Villain, *s.* (*feud.*) vilain, *m.*, e, *f.*; (*a wretch*) misérable, *m.f.*, scélérat, *m.*, e, *f.*, gredin, *m.*, [e, *f.*
Villanage, *s.* vilainage, *m.*
Villanous, *adj.* vil, infâme; scélérat; (*sorry*) vilain, méchant
Villanously, *adv.* vilement, bassement, d'une manière infâme; (*extremely*) horriblement
Villanousness, Villany, *s.* scélératesse, [*f.*; infamie, *f.*
Villenage, *s.* vilainage, *m.*
Villosity, *s.* villosité, *f.*
Villous, *adj.* villeux [vinaigre, *m.*
Vinaigrette, *s.* vinaigrette, *f.*; (*chem.*) sel de
Vindemial, *adj.* vindémial [venger
Vindicate, *v.a.* soutenir, défendre, justifier;
Vindication, *s.* défense, justification, apolo-
Vindicator, *s.* défenseur, *m.* [gie, *f.*
Vindicatory, *adj.* vengeur; justificatif
Vindictive, *adj.* vindicatif; de vengeance. **—ly,** *adv.* vindicativement. **—ness,** *s.* caractère vindicatif, *m.*, nature vindicative, *f.*; esprit de vengeance, *m.*
Vine, *s.* vigne, *f.*; (*bine*) sarment, *m.*; — *adj.* de vigne; de la vigne. — **arbour,** *s.* treille, *f.* — **branch,** *s.* branche de vigne, *f.*, sarment, *m.*; (*poet.*) pampre, *m.* — **cane,** *s.* tige de vigne, *f.*; cep de vigne, *m.* — **disease,** *s.* maladie de la vigne, *f.* — **dresser,** *s.* vigneron, *m.*, -ne, *f.* — **estate,** *s.* vignoble, *m.*;

cru, *m.* — **fretter, -gall, -grub,** *s.* charançon de vigne, rouleur, liset, coupe-bourgeons, *m.*, bêche, *f.* — **grower,** *s.* viticulteur, *m.*; vigneron, *m.*, -ne, *f.* — **growing,** *s.* viticulture, *f.*; *adj.* vignoble, viticole. — **knife,** *s.* serpe, *f.* — **leaf,** *s.* feuille de vigne, *f.* — **mildew,** *s.* oïdium, *m.* — **plant, -stalk, -stock,** *s.* cep de vigne, *m.* — **shoot, -twig,** *s.* sarment, *m.* — **stick, -prop,** *s.* échalas, *m.* — **yard,** *s.* vigne, *f.*, champ de vigne, *m.*; (*large*) vignoble, *m.*; cru, *m.*
Vined, *adj.* à feuille de vigne
Vinegar, *s.* vinaigre, *m.*; — *adj.* de vinaigre; (*for* —) à *or* au vinaigre; (*sour*) aigre, sur. — *of roses,* vinaigre rosat, *m.* — **cruet,** *s.* burette au vinaigre, *f.* — **maker,** *s.* vinaigrier, *m.* — **manufactory, -works,** *s.* vinaigrerie, *f.* — **plant,** *s.* pénicillion, *m.* — **sauce,** *s.* vinaigrette, sauce piquante, *f.* — **trade,** *s.* vinaigrerie, *f.* — **tree,** *s.* vinaigrier, *m.* — **works,** *s.pl.* vinaigrerie, *f.*
Vinery, *s.* serre à vigne, *f.*
Vingt-et-un, *s.* vingt-et-un, *m.*
Vinicultural, *adj.* vinicole
Viniculture, *s.* viniculture, *f.*
Viniculturist, *s.* viniculteur, *m.*
Vinic, *adj.* vinique
Vinification, *s.* vinification, *f.*
Vinnewed, Vinny, *adj.* moisi, chanci
Vinosity, *s.* vinosité, *f.*
Vinous, *adj.* vineux
Vintage, *s.* (*of grapes*) vendange, *f.*; (*of wine*) vinée, *f.*; (*year's growth*) récolte, année, *f.*
Vintager, *s.* vendangeur, *m.*, -euse, *f.*
Vintner, *s.* marchand de vin, cabaretier, *m.*
Viny, *adj.* de vigne; vignoble
Viol, Viola, *s.* viole, *f.*
Violability, *s.* violabilité, *f.*
Violable, *adj.* violable
Violaceous, *adj.* violacé
Violate, *v.a.* violer [viol, *m.*
Violation, *s.* violation, infraction, *f.*; (*rape*)
Violator, *s.* violateur, *m.*, -trice, *f.*, infracteur, *m.*, -trice, *f.*
Violence, *s.* violence, *f.* *To do* or *offer — to,* faire violence à, violenter, user de violence envers
Violent, *adj.* violent; (*of a malady, pain*) fort; aigu; (*of a cold*) fort, gros; (*extreme*) fort. *To die a — death,* mourir de mort violente
Violently, *adv.* violemment, avec violence
Violet, *s.* (*flower*) violette, *f.*; (*colour*) violet, *m.*; — *adj.* violet. — **colour,** *s.* violet, *m.*, couleur violette, *f.* — **coloured,** *adj.* violet
Violin, *s.* violon, *m.* — **case,** *s.* boîte à violon, *f.*
Violinist, *s.* violoniste, *m.f.*, violon, *m.*
Violist, *s.* violiste, *m.*
Violoncellist, *s.* violoncelliste, *m.*
Violoncello, *s.* violoncelle, *m.*, basse, *f.*
Viper, *s.* vipère, *f.* —**'s bugloss,** *s.* vipérine, *f.* —**'s grass,** *s.* scorsonère, *f.*
Viperine, Viperous, *adj.* vipérin, de vipère; venimeux
Virago, *s.* virago, *f.*, dragon, *m.*
Virgilian, *adj.* virgilien
Virgin, *s.* vierge, *f.*; — *adj.* vierge; virginal, de vierge; pur. *The — at the seat,* (*of Raphael*) la Vierge à la chaise. —**'s bower,** *s.* clématite des haies, aubevigne, *f.* —**'s milk,** *s.* lait virginal, *m.* [virginale, *f.*
Virginal, *adj.* virginal, de vierge; —**s,** *s.pl.*
Virginally, *adv.* virginalement
Virginia, *s.* (*tobacco*) tabac de Virginie, *m.*
Virginian, *s.* Virginien, *m.*, -ne, *f.*; — *adj.* virginien, de (la) Virginie. — *creeper,* — *stock,* *V.* **Creeper** *&* **Stock.** — *tobacco,* tabac de Virginie, *m.*
Virginity, *s.* virginité, *f.*
Virgo, *s.* la Vierge, *f.*
Virile, *adj.* viril
Virility, *s.* virilité, *f.*
Virtu, *s.* goût des arts, *m.*; art, *m.* *Articles of* —, objets d'art, *m.pl.*
Virtual, *adj.* virtuel
Virtuality, *s.* virtualité, *f.*
Virtually, *adv.* virtuellement; censément; de fait, par le fait
Virtue, *s.* vertu, *f.* *By* or *in — of,* en vertu de. —**less,** *adj.* sans vertu
Virtuosity, *s.* virtuosité, *f.*
Virtuoso, *s.* virtuose, *m.f.*
Virtuous, *adj.* vertueux
Virtuously, *adv.* vertueusement
Virulenc-e, y, *s.* virulence, *f.*
Virulent, *adj.* virulent
Virulently, *adv.* avec virulence
Virus, *s.* virus, *m.*
Vis, *s.* (*Latin*) force *f.* — *inertiæ,* force d'inertie, *f.* — *major,* force majeure, *f.* — *viva,* force vive, *f.*
Visa, *s.* visa, *m.*; — *v.a.* viser
Visage, *s.* visage, *m.*, figure, *f.*
Visaged, *adj.* à *or* au visage ...
Vis-à-vis, *s.* vis-à-vis, *m.*
Viscera, *s.pl.* viscères, *m.pl.*
Visceral, *adj.* viscéral
Viscid, *adj.* visqueux
Viscidity, Viscosity, *s.* viscosité, *f.*
Viscount, *s.* vicomte, *m.*
Viscountess, *s.* vicomtesse, *f.*
Viscountcy, Viscountship, Viscounty, *s.* vicomté, *m.*
Viscous, *adj.* visqueux. —**ness,** *s.* viscosité, *f.*
Viscus, *s.* viscère, *m.*
Vise, *s.* escalier à vis, *m.*
Visi-bility, bleness, *s.* visibilité, *f.*
Visible, *adj.* visible; évident, clair, manifeste; (*of the horizon*) sensible
Visibly, *adv.* visiblement; (*rapidly*) à vue d'œil
Visigoth, *s.* Visigoth, *m.*, e, *f.*
Visigothic, *adj.* visigothique, visigoth
Vision, *s.* vision, *f.*; (*sight*) vue, *f.*
Visional, *adj.* de vision; de la vue
Visionary, *s. adj.* visionnaire, *m.f.*
Visit, *v.a.* visiter; faire une visite *or* des visites à; se présenter chez; aller voir; (*vent upon*) décharger (sur), se venger de (sur); (*chastise*) châtier, punir; (*inflict*) infliger à (...); (*try*) éprouver ('*with*,' par); — *v.n.* faire des visites; — *s.* visite, *f.*; (*inspection*) tournée, inspection, *f.*; (*stay*) séjour, *m.* *On a —,* en visite (chez)
Visitandine, *s.* Visitandine, *f.*
Visitant, *s.* visitant, *m.*, e, *f.*
Visitation, *s.* visite, *f.*; (*eccl.*) tournée (pastorale), *f.*; (*law*) inspection, *f.*; (*chastisement*) châtiment, *m.*, punition, *f.*; infliction, *f.*; (*trial*) épreuve, affliction, *f.*; (*feast*) visitation, *f.*
Visite, *s.* visite, *f.*
Visiter, *s.* *V.* **Visitor**
Visiting, *part. adj.* en visite; de visite; — *s.* visite, *f.*; visites, *f.pl.* *To go —,* aller faire des visites, aller en visite. — **card,** *s.* carte de visite, *f.*
Visitor, *s.* visiteur, *m.*, -euse, *f.*; inspecteur, *m.*, -trice, *f.*
Visor, *s.* visière, *f.*; masque, *m.*
Visored, *adj.* masqué
Vista, *s.* échappée, *f.*; (*of forests*) percée, éclaircie, *f.*; (*prospect*) perspective, *f.*
Visual, *adj.* visuel
Vital, *adj.* vital; de vie; essentiel, capital; (*of air*) respirable; —**s,** *s.pl.* parties vitales, *f.pl.*; (*fig.*) vie, *f.* — *organ,* partie vitale, *f.*, viscère, *m.*
Vitality, *s.* vitalité, vie, *f.*
Vitally, *adv.* vitalement
Vitiate, *v.a.* vicier; corrompre
Vitiation, *s.* viciation, altération, *f.*; corruption, *f.*
Viticultural, *adj.* viticole
Viticulture, *s.* viticulture, *f.*
Viticulturist, *s.* viticulteur, *m.*
Vitreous, *adj.* vitreux; de verre; (*anat.*, *of humour; phys.*, *of electricity*) vitré
Vitreousness, *s.* vitrosité, *f.*
Vitrifaction, *s.* vitrification, *f.*
Vitrifiability, *s.* vitrifiabilité, *f.*
Vitrifiable, *adj.* vitrifiable
Vitrification, *s.* vitrification, *f.*
Vitrify, *v.a.* vitrifier; — *v.n.* se vitrifier

Vitriol, *s.* vitriol, *m.* — **manufactory,** *s.* vitriolerie, *f.*
Vitriolate, Vitriolize, *v.a.* vitrioler, vitrioliser [tion, *f.*
Vitriolation, Vitriolization, *s.* vitriolisa-
Vitriolic, *adj.* vitriolique
Vitruvian, *adj.* vitruvien. — *scroll,* poste, *f.*
Vituline, *adj.* vitulaire
Vituperate, *v.a.* blâmer, censurer, faire des reproches à ; vilipender
Vituperation, *s.* blâme, reproche, *m.,* reproches, *m.pl.* ; injures, *f.pl.*
Vituperative, *adj.* de blâme, de reproche ; [injurieux
Vitus. *V.* **Saint Vitus**
Vivacious, *adj.* vif, animé
Vivaciously, *adv.* vivement, avec vivacité
Vivaciousness, Vivacity, *s.* vivacité, *f.*
Vivarium, Vivary, *s.* vivier, *m.* ; (*for rabbits,* &c.) garenne, *f.* ; parc, *m.*
Vivâ voce, *adv.* de vive voix ; (*adject.*) oral
Vives, *s.pl.* (*vet.*) avives, *f.pl.*
Vivid, *adj.* vif ; animé ; ardent ; frappant ; tranchant [ment
Vividly, *adv.* vivement ; avec éclat ; ardem-
Vividness, *s.* vivacité, *f.* ; éclat, *m.* ; ardeur, *f.* ; vigueur, *f.*
Vivification, *s.* vivification, *f.*
Vivify, *v.a.* vivifier, animer
Viviparous, *adj.* vivipare
Vivisection, *s.* vivisection, *f.*
Vixen, *s.* renarde, *f.* ; (*pers.*) mégère, *f.*
Viz., savoir, à savoir ; c'est-à-dire
Vizier, Vizir, *s.* vizir, *m.*
Vizieral, Vizierial, Vizirial, *adj.* vizirial
Vizierate, Viziership, Vizirship, *s.* [vizirat, *m.*
Vizor. *V.* **Visor**
Vocable, *s.* mot, vocable, *m.*
Vocabulary, *s.* vocabulaire, *m.*
Vocabulist, *s.* vocabuliste, *m.*
Vocal, *adj.* vocal ; de la voix. — *music,* musique vocale, *f.*
Vocalist, *s.* chanteur, *m.,* cantatrice, *f.*
Vocalization, *s.* vocalisation, *f.*
Vocalize, *v.n.a.* vocaliser
Vocalizer, *s.* vocalisateur, *m.,* -trice, *f.*
Vocally, *adv.* vocalement, par la voix ; verbalement
Vocation, *s.* vocation, *f.* ; (*call*) appel, *m.* ; (*profession*) profession, *f.,* emploi, état, métier, *m.* [vocatif
Vocative, *s.* (— *case*) vocatif, *m.* *In the* —, au
Vociferate, *v.a.n.* vociférer
Vociferation, *s.* vocifération, *f.*
Vociferous, *adj.* qui vocifère ; accompagné de vociférations, bruyant
Vociferously, *adv.* en vociférant, avec des vociférations, bruyamment
Vogue, *s.* vogue, mode, *f.* *In* —, en vogue, à la mode. *To bring into* —, mettre en vogue, mettre à la mode
Voice, *s.* voix, *f.* *At the top of o.'s* —, de toutes ses forces, à tue-tête. *With one* —, d'une seule voix, d'une commune voix, unanimement, à l'unanimité. *Without a dissentient* —, à l'unanimité des voix. *My — fails,* la voix me manque. —**less,** *adj.* muet, sans voix
Voiced, *adj.* à voix . . ., à la voix . . ., qui a la voix . . .
Void, *adj.* vide ; vacant ; (*deprived of*) dépourvu (de), dénué (de) ; (*free from*) exempt (de) ; (*of no effect*) nul ; annulé ; (*of legacies*) caduc ; — *s.* vide, *m.* ; — *v.a.* vider ; évacuer, rendre ; (*vacate ; law*) *V.* **Avoid.** *To make* —, annuler, rendre nul ; violer
Voidable, *adj.* annulable, résoluble
Voidance. *V.* **Avoidance**
Volant, *adj.* volant
Volatile, *adj.* volant ; (*light*) léger ; (*fickle*) volage ; (*thoughtless*) étourdi ; (*chem.*) volatil
Volatileness, Volatility, *s.* légèreté, *f.* ; (*chem.*) volatilité, *f.*
Volatilizable, *adj.* volatilisable
Volatilization, *s.* volatilisation, *f.*
Volatilize, *v.a.* volatiliser ; — *v.n.* se volatiliser
Volcanic, *adj.* volcanique ; volcanisé
Volcanicity, *s.* volcanicité, *f.*
Volcanite, *s.* volcanite, *f.*
Volcanization, *s.* volcanisation, *f.*
Volcanize, *v.a.* volcaniser
Volcano, *s.* volcan, *m.* [vole, *f.*
Vole, *s.* (*zool.*) campagnol, rat, *m.* ; (*at cards*)
Volition, *s.* volition, volonté, *f.*
Volley, *s.* volée, *f.* ; (*firing*) décharge, *f.* ; fusillade, *f.* ; (*of cannon*) volée, *f.* ; (*for a salute*) salve, *f.* ; (*of oaths, abuse,* &c.) grêle, volée, bordée, *f.* *To fire a* —, faire une décharge de mousqueterie *or* d'artillerie, tirer une volée, faire *or* tirer une salve. — **firing,** *s.* feu de peloton, feu de bataillon, feu de régi- [ment, *m.*
Volscian, *s. adj.* Volsque, *m.f.*
Volt, *s.* volte, *f.* ; — *v.n.* volter
Voltaic, *adj.* voltaïque, de Volta
Voltaism, *s.* voltaïsme, *m.*
Voltairian, *s. adj.* voltairien, *m.,* -ne, *f.*
Voltairianism, Voltairism, *s.* voltairianisme, *m.*
Volubility, *s.* volubilité, *f.* ; rotation, *f.*
Voluble, *adj.* volubile ; (*tongue*) délié, bien pendu ; (*speech*) facile, coulant ; (*pers.*) qui parle avec volubilité
Volubly, *adv.* avec volubilité
Volume, *s.* volume, *m.* ; masse, *f.* ; (*of books*) volume, tome, *m.* ; (*of revolving smoke*) tourbillon, *m.* *It speaks —s for,* cela en dit beaucoup pour
Volumetric, *adj.* volumétrique
Voluminous, *adj.* volumineux, gros ; (*of authors*) fécond ; (*rolled*) roulé. —**ly,** *adv.* volumineusement ; en masses ; en tourbillons. —**ness,** *s.* grosseur, longueur, dimension, étendue, *f.*
Voluntarily, *adv.* volontairement ; spontanément [spontanéité, *f.* ; bonne volonté, *f.*
Voluntariness, *s.* nature volontaire, *f.* ;
Voluntary, *adj.* volontaire ; spontané ; (*pers.*) libre ; (*intended*) intentionnel ; — *s.* fantaisie, *f.* ; improvisation, *f.* ; (*mus.*) prélude, *m.*
Volunteer, *s.* volontaire, *m.* ; — *adj.* de volontaire, de *or* des volontaires ; — *v.a.* offrir, donner volontairement ; — *v.n.* s'offrir ; se présenter ; (*be willing*) vouloir bien ; (*mil.*) s'engager comme volontaire
Volunteering, *s.* volontariat, *m.*
Voluptuary, *s.* voluptueux, *m.,* -euse, *f.* ; épicurien, *m.,* -ne, *f.*
Voluptuous, *adj.* voluptueux. —**ly,** *adv.* voluptueusement. —**ness,** *s.* volupté, *f.* ; [voluptuosité, *f.*
Volute, *s.* volute, *f.*
Volution, *s.* spirale, *f.*
Vomer, *s.* vomer, *m.* [**vomica**
Vomic, *adj.* vomique. — **nut,** *s.* *V.* **Nux**
Vomica, *s. adj.* vomique, *f.*
Vomit, *v.a.n.* vomir ; — *s.* (*med.*) vomitif, *m.* ; (*matter thrown up*) vomissement, *m.,* matière vomie, *f.,* matières vomies, matières des vomissements, *f.pl.*
Vomiting, *s.* vomissement, *m.*
Vomitive, *adj.* vomitif
Vomitory, *adj.* vomitif ; — *s.* (*med.*) vomitif, *m.* ; (*anc. arch.*) vomitoire, *m.*
Vomiturition, *s.* vomiturition, *f.*
Voracious, *adj.* vorace ; (*of hunger, appetite*) dévorant ; (*fig.*) avide
Voraciously, *adv.* avec voracité, voracement
Voraciousness, Voracity, *s.* voracité, *f.*
Vortex, *s.* (*pl.* **Vortices**) tourbillon, *m.*
Vortical, *adj.* tourbillonnant, tournant
Votaress, *s.* sectatrice, femme vouée, *f.*
Votary, *s.* sectateur, *m.,* -trice, *f.,* sectaire, *m.f.* ; adorateur, *m.,* -trice, *f.* ; partisan, *m.,* e, *f.,* ami, *m.,* e, *f.* ; admirateur, *m.,* -trice, *f.* ; — *adj.* votif
Vote, *s.* vote, *m.,* voix, *f.* ; — *v.a.n.* voter ; élire ; déclarer. *To come to the* —, aller aux voix

To put (...) *to the* —, mettre (...) aux voix. *To put it* (or *the question*) *to the* —, aller aux voix. *To pass a — of thanks*, voter des remercîments. *To have a* —, voter. — **paper,** *s.* bulletin (de vote), *m.*
Voter, *s.* votant, *m.*, e, *f.*
Voting, *s.* vote, *m.* — **paper,** *s.* bulletin (de vote), *m.*
Votive, *adj.* votif
Voto (Ex), *s.* ex-voto, *m.*
Vouch, *v.a.* attester, prendre à témoin; affirmer, garantir; prouver; — *v.n.* répondre (de)
Vouchee, *s.* personne appelée en garantie, *f.*
Voucher, *s.* (*pers.*) garant, *m.*, e, *f.*; (*things*) garantie, preuve, *f.*, titre, *m.*; pièce justificative, *f.*; (*acknowledgment*) reconnaissance, *f.*; (*law*) demande en garantie, *f.*; (*pers.*) demandeur en garantie, *m.*
Vouchsafe, *v.a.* accorder; — *v.n.* daigner
Vouchsafement, *s.* condescendance, *f.*; don, *m.*, faveur, *f.*, bienfait, *m.*
Voussoir, *s.* voussoir, *m.*
Vow, *s.* vœu, *m.*; — *v.a.* vouer (à); consacrer (à); — *v.n.* faire vœu (de); protester, jurer
Vowel, *s.* voyelle, *f.*
Vowelled, *adj.* formé de voyelles
Voyage, *s.* voyage (par mer), *m.*; traversée, *f.*; — *v.n.a.* *V.* **Travel,** *v.n.a.* *A pleasant — to you!* bon voyage! *On a* —, en voyage
Voyageable, *adj.* voyageable
Voyager, *s.* voyageur, *m.*, -euse, *f.*; passager, *m.*, -ère, *f.*
Vulcanian, *s. adj.* vulcanien, *m.*, -ne, *f.*
Vulcanic, *adj.* vulcanique
Vulcan-ism, -ist. *V.* page 3, § 1
Vulcanite, *s.* vulcanite, *m.*
Vulcanization, *s.* vulcanisation, *f.*
Vulcanize, *v.a.* vulcaniser. —*d indiarubber*, caoutchouc vulcanisé, *m.*
Vulgar, *adj.* vulgaire; commun; ordinaire; trivial; bas; grossier; de mauvais goût; du peuple; (*trite*) banal; — *s.* vulgaire, bas peuple, *m.* — *fractions*, fractions ordinaires, *f.pl.*
Vulgarism, *s.* vulgarisme, *m.*, chose vulgaire, pensée *or* expression vulgaire, *f.*
Vulgarity, *s.* vulgarité, *f.*; grossièreté, *f.*; bassesse, *f.*
Vulgarization, *s.* vulgarisation, *f.*
Vulgarize, *v.a.* vulgariser
Vulgarizer, *s.* vulgarisateur, *m.*, -trice, *f.*
Vulgarizing, *adj.* vulgarisateur; — *s.* vulgarisation, *f.*
Vulgarly, *adv.* vulgairement; grossièrement; communément
Vulgate, *s.* Vulgate, *f.*; — *adj.* vulgate, de la Vulgate
Vulnera-bility, bleness, *s.* vulnérabilité, *f.*
Vulnerable, *adj.* vulnérable
Vulnerably, *adv.* vulnérablement
Vulnerary, *adj. s.* vulnéraire, *adj. m.f.*, (*med.*) *s.m.*, (*bot.*) *s.f.*
Vulpine, *adj.* vulpin, de renard; (*cunning*) rusé
Vulture, *s.* vautour, *m.*
Vulturine, *adj.* de vautour; rapace
Vulva, *s.* vulve, *f.*
Vulvar, *adj.* vulvaire

W

W, *s.* (*letter*) w, *m.*
Wabble, *v.n.* brandiller
Wad, *s.* bourre, *f.*; (*bundle*) paquet, *m.*; — *v.a.* rembourrer, bourrer ('*with*,' de); (*garments*) ouater. — **hook,** *s.* tire-bourre, *m.*
Wadding, *s.* (*material*) bourre, *f.*; (*for garments*) ouate, *f.*; (*act of wadding*) rembourrage, *m.*, (*of garments*) ouatage, *m.*
Waddle, *v.n.* se dandiner; (*fig.*) patauger
Waddling, *s.* dandinement, *m.*
Waddlingly, *adv.* en se dandinant
Wade, *v.n.* marcher (dans l'eau, &c); (*ford*) passer à gué; (*in mud*) patauger, barboter; (*fig.*) se traîner. — **through,** traverser; (*fig.*) examiner en détail; compulser; étudier à fond; (*master*) venir à bout de
Wader, Wading bird, *s.* échassier, *m.*
Wafer, *s.* (*for sealing*) pain à cacheter, *m.*; (*pastry*) oublie, *f.*, plaisir, *m.*; (*host*) hostie, *f.*; — *v.a.* cacheter; coller avec des pains à cacheter
Waffle, *s.* gaufre, *f.* — **iron,** *s.* gaufrier, *m.*
Waft, *v.a.* porter, transporter; soutenir; — *v.n.* flotter; — *s.* souffle, *m.*; corps flottant, *m.*
Wafter, *s.* bateau de transport, *m.*
Wag, *v.a.n.* remuer; agiter; (*o.'s head*) secouer (la tête); — *s.* plaisant, *m.*; loustic, *m.*; farceur, *m.*; (*of children*) espiègle, *m.f.*
Wage, *v.a.* tenter, essayer; (*war*) faire (la guerre à); — *s.* *V.* **Wages,** *below*
Wagel, — gull, *s.* goéland, *m.*
Wager, *s.* pari, *m.*, gageure, *f.*; (*object deposited*) gage, *m.*; — *v.a.* parier, gager. *To lay a* —, faire un pari, parier, gager. — **boat,** *s.* périssoire, *f.*
Wagerer, *s.* parieur, *m.*, -euse, *f.*
Wages, *s.pl.* gages, *m.pl.*; (*of labourers, artisans*) salaire, *m*, paye, *f.*; (*reward*) récompense, *f.*, prix, *m.* *Week's* —, semaine, *f.* — **book,** *s.* livre de paye, *m.*
Waggery, *s.* plaisanterie, *f.*; (*trick*) espièglerie, *f.*
Waggish, *adj.* plaisant, facétieux; espiègle. — **trick,** *s.* plaisanterie, farce, *f.*; espièglerie, *f.*
Waggishly, *adv.* plaisamment; avec espièglerie
Waggishness, *s.* plaisanterie, *f.*; espièglerie, *f.*
Waggle, *v.a.n.* remuer; frétiller
Waggon, *s.* chariot, *m.*; (*com.*) voiture de roulage, *f.*, roulage, *m.*; (*mil.*) caisson, fourgon, *m.*; (*rail.*) wagon, *m.*; — *v.a.* charrier, charroyer, transporter, voiturer. —**ful, -load,** *s.* charretée, *f.* — **master,** *s.* (*mil.*) vaguemestre, *m.* — **office,** *s.* maison *or* entreprise de roulage, *f.* — **office keeper,** *s.* commissionnaire de roulage, *m.* — **train,** *s.* équipages de (*or* du) train, *m.pl.*
Waggonage, Waggoning, *s.* charriage, charroi, transport, *m.*; (*com.*) roulage, *m.*
Waggoner, *s.* roulier, voiturier, charretier, *m.*; (*astr.*) chariot, *m.*
Waggonnette, *s.* wagonnette, *f.*, char à bancs, *m.*
Wagon, &c. *V.* **Waggon,** &c.
Wagtail, *s.* bergeronnette, *f.*, hochequeue, *m.*
Wahabee, Wahabi, Wahabite, *s. adj.* wahabi, wahabite, *s.m.*, *adj.m.f.*
Wahabiism, Wahabitism, *s.* wahabitisme, *m.*
Waif, *s.* épave, *f.* —*s and strays*, épaves, *f.pl.* *The —s of society*, le rebut de la société, *m.*
Wail. *V.* **Moan**
Wain, *s.* chariot, *m.* *Charles's* —, le chariot
Wainage, *s.* charriage, charroi, *m.*, charrettes, *f.pl.*
Wainscot, *s.* lambris, *m.*, boiserie, *f.*; — *v.a.* lambrisser (de), boiser (de)
Wainscoting, *s.* lambrissage, *m.*; boiserie, *f.*
Waist, *s.* ceinture, taille, *f.*; (*nav.*) vibord, entre-deux, *m.* — **band,** *s.* ceinture, *f.* —**coat,** *s.* gilet, *m.* *Roll-collar —coat*, gilet à châle, *m.* —*coat pocket*, poche de gilet, *f.* *O.'s —coat pocket*, la poche de son gilet. —**coating,** *s.* étoffe pour gilets, *f.*
Wait, *v.a.n.* attendre; (*at table*, &c.) servir. *To keep —ing*, faire attendre. *He did not — to be told so twice*, il ne se le fit pas répéter. — **for,** attendre; (*be anxious for or much in want of*) attendre après. — **on, upon,** servir; accompagner; (*call upon*) se rendre (chez, auprès de), se présenter (chez); présenter ses respects (à), rendre ses devoirs (à); (*of business*) vaquer (à)
Wait, *s.* embûche, *f.*, guet-apens, *m.*; (*place*) embuscade, *f.*; —**s,** *pl.* musiciens ambulants de la Noel, musiciens nocturnes, chanteurs de noëls, *m.pl.* *Lying in* —, guet-apens, *m.* *To lay — for*, dresser des embûches à. *To lie in* —, être (*or* se tenir) en embuscade; être aux aguets

Waiter, *s.* garçon, garçon de salle, *m.*; (*tray*) plateau, *m.* —*!* garçon!

Waiting, *s.* attente, *f.*; (*attendance*) service, *m.* *In* —, dans l'attente; (*on duty*) de service. *Gentleman in* —, gentilhomme de service ('*to*,' auprès de), *m.* *Lady in* —, dame d'honneur, *f.* —**maid, -woman,** *s.* femme de chambre, *f.*; (*waitress*) *V.* **Waitress.** —**room,** *s.* salle d'attente, *f.*

Waitress, *s.* fille de salle, fille de service, demoiselle, *f.* —*!* mademoiselle!

Waive, *v.a.* se désister de, renoncer à, abandonner; quitter; ne pas insister sur, passer sur; ne pas parler de; dévier de, s'écarter de; rejeter, écarter, repousser, mettre de côté; éloigner, remettre

Waiver, *s.* renonciation, *f.*; désistement, refus d'accepter, *m.*

Waiwode, &c. *V.* **Waywode,** &c.

Wake, *v.a.n.* (— **up**) *V.* **Awake;** (*watch*) veiller; — *s.* veille, *f.*; (*fair*, &c.) fête de village, fête, *f.*; (*nav.*) sillage, *m.*, eaux, *f.pl.*; (*fig.*) trace, suite, *f.*

Wakeful, *adj.* éveillé; vigilant, attentif. —**ly,** *adv.* avec vigilance, vigilamment. —**ness,** *s.* insomnie, veille, *f.*; vigilance, *f.*

Waken, *v.a.n.* *V.* **Awaken**

Waker, *s.* réveilleur, *m.*, -euse, *f.*; personne qui s'éveille, *f.*; (*watcher*) personne qui veille, *f.*, veilleur, *m.*, -euse, *f.*

Waking, *s.* veille, *f.*; (*awaking*) réveil, *m.*; — *adj.* de veille; éveillé. — *dream*, rêverie, *f.*

Waldenses, *s.pl.* Vaudois, *m.pl.*

Waldensian, *s. adj.* Vaudois, *m.*, e, *f.*

Wale, *s.* (*rib*) côte, *f.*; (*weal*) marque, vergeture, *f.*; (*nav.*) préceinte, *f.*

Walhalla, *s.* walhalla, *m.*

Walk, *v.a.n.* marcher; (*go on foot*) aller à pied; (*come on foot*) venir à pied; (*back*) *V.* — **back;** (*go*) aller; (*come*) venir; (*pass*) passer; (*take a walk*) se promener; (*rove*) errer; (*not to run, in riding*) aller au pas; (*travel over*) parcourir; faire; faire (...) à pied; (*make — on or about*) faire marcher; promener; (*horses*) mettre au pas. *To — the rounds*, (*mil.*) faire la ronde. *To — the streets*, aller *or* se promener par les rues; (*of bad women*) faire le trottoir. —*!* marchez au pas! —**after,** suivre. — **back,** retourner; revenir; retourner *or* s'en retourner *or* revenir à pied. — **by,** passer devant; passer. — **down,** descendre. — **in,** entrer. —**into,** entrer dans; (*fig.*) l'emporter sur; refaire; tancer; relancer; houspiller; faire une sortie à. — **off,** partir, s'en aller, s'éloigner; décamper. — **out,** sortir; (*take a walk*) se promener. — **over,** *v.n.* aller; venir; *v.a.* parcourir *or* traverser (... à pied); (*in riding*) parcourir *or* traverser (...) au pas. — **round,** *V.* **Round.** — **up,** monter; s'avancer (vers), s'approcher (de). — **up and down,** *v.n.* se promener de long en large; *v.a.* parcourir en tous sens

Walk, *s.* marche, *f.*; (*for pleasure*) promenade, *f.*; tour, *m.*; (*place*) promenade, *f.*; promenoir, *m.*; (*for business*) course, *f.*; (*round*) tournée, *f.*; (*beat*) *V.* **Beat;** (*gait*) démarche, *f.*, port, *m.*; (*path*) allée, avenue, *f.*; (*road*) route, voie, *f.*; (*course of life*) voie, ligne, *f.*; (*space*, &c.) espace, champ, *m.*, carrière, *f.*; région, sphère, *f.*; département, domaine, *m.*; rang, *m.*; classe, *f.*; (*of a horse*) pas, *m.*, allure, *f.*; (*pasture*) pâturage, *m.*; (*of a milkman*) clientèle, *f.* *At a* —, au pas. *To go for a* —, aller faire une promenade, aller se promener, se promener. *To go out for a* —, sortir pour se promener, aller faire une promenade. *To take a* —, faire une promenade *or* un tour, se promener. *To take out for a* —, mener promener

Walker, *s.* marcheur, *m.*, -euse, *f.*; (*for pleasure*) promeneur, *m.*, -euse, *f.*; (*pedestrian*) piéton, *m.*, -ne, *f.*

Walking, *s.* marche, *f.*; (*for pleasure*) promenade, *f.*; promenade à pied, *f.*; — *adj.* ambulant; de marche; de promenade; (*of boots*, &c.) de fatigue. *At a — pace*, au pas. *It is bad* —, (*from weather*) il fait mauvais marcher. —**attire,** *s.* toilette de ville, *f.* —**cane,** *s.* canne, *f.* —**coat,** *s.* habit de ville, *m.* —**dress,** *s.* habit *or* costume de ville, *m.*, toilette de ville, *f.*; (*of ladies*) toilette de ville, robe de ville, *f.* —**leaf,** *s.* (*insect*) phyllie, *f.* —**place,** *s.* promenade, *f.*; promenoir, *m.* —**shoes,** *s.pl.* souliers de fatigue, *m.pl.*; souliers de promenade, *m.pl.* —**staff,** *s.* bourdon, bâton, *m.*; canne, *f.* —**stick,** *s.* canne, *f.*; (*insect*) phasma, phasme, *m.* —**suit,** *s.* habit *or* costume de ville, *m.*

Wall, *s.* mur, *m.*, muraille, *f.*; (*fruit* —) espalier, *m.*; (*place of honour*) haut du pavé, *m.*; (*fig.*) rempart, *m.*; (*side, anat.*) paroi, *f.*; — *adj.* de mur, de muraille, mural; — *v.a.* entourer de murs *or* de murailles, murer; (*stop*) murer. *To go to the* —, succomber. —**advertisement, -bill,** *s.* annonce murale, affiche, *f.* —**creeper,** *s.* grimpereau de muraille, *m.*, échelette, *f.* —**cress,** *s.* arabette, *f.* —**eye,** *s.* œil vairon, *m.* —**eyed,** *adj.* vairon. —**flower,** *s.* giroflée jaune, *f.*; (*pers.*) tapisserie, *f.* *To be a — flower*, (*pers.*) faire tapisserie, faire galerie. —**fruit,** *s.* fruit d'espalier, *m.* —**hook,** *s.* gâche, *f.* —**lettuce,** *s.* chondrille, *f.* —**louse,** *s.* cloporte, *m.* —**map,** *s.* carte murale, *f.* —**moss,** *s.* mousse rampante, *f.* —**paper,** *s.* *V.* **Paper-hanging.** —**plant,** *s.* plante murale, *f.* —**plate,** *s.* (*carp.*) sablière, *f.* —**rue,** *s.* sauvevie, *f.* —**sided,** *adj.* à pic. —**tree,** *s.* arbre en espalier, *m.* —**up,** *v.a.* murer, boucher. —**wort,** *s.* hièble, *f.*

Wallachian, *s. adj.* Valaque, *m.f.*

Wallet, *s.* havresac, sac, *m.*; besace, *f.*, bissac, *m.*

Walling, *s.* murs, *m.pl.*, murailles, *f.pl.*; muraillement, *m.*

Walloon, *s. adj.* Wallon, *m.*, -ne, *f.*; (*language*) (le) wallon, *m.*, (la) langue wallonne, *f.*

Wallop, *s.* (*thump*) grand coup, *m.*, torgniole, *f.*, horion, *m.*; — *v.a.* rosser, frotter, cogner, bûcher

Walloping, *s.* (*beating*) rossée, roulée, frottée, *f.*

Wallow, *v.n.* se vautrer, se rouler; nager; croupir

Wallower, *s.* (*mach.*) lanterne, *f.*

Walnut, *s.* (*fruit*) noix, *f.*; (*tree, wood*) noyer, *m.* —**cake,** *s.* (*agr.*) nougat, *m.* —**grove, -plantation,** *s.* noiseraie, *f.* —**husk, -peel,** *s.* brou de noix, *m.* —**oil,** *s.* huile de noix, *f.* —**shell,** *s.* coquille de noix, *f.* —**table,** *s.* table en noyer, *f.* —**tree,** *s.* noyer, *m.* —**wood,** *s.* noyer, *m.*

Walrus, *s.* morse, *m.*

Waltz, *s.* valse, *f.*; — *v.n.a.* valser

Waltzer, *s.* valseur, *m.*, -euse, *f.*

Waltzing, *s.* valse, *f.*

Waly, *adj.* marqué de raies, vergeté

Wamble, *v.n.* se soulever

Wambling, *s.* soulèvement de cœur, *m.*

Wan, *adj.* pâle, blême

Wand, *s.* baguette, *f.*; (*staff*) bâton, *m.*; (*of Mercury*) caducée, *m.*

Wander, *v.n.* errer; (*deviate*) s'écarter (de), dévier (de); (*of the mind*) s'égarer; divaguer; avoir le délire, battre la campagne

Wanderer, *s.* vagabond, *m.*, e, *f.*; voyageur, *m.*, -euse, *f.*; rôdeur, *m.*, -euse, *f.*; fugitif, *m.*, -ive, *f.*

Wandering, *s.* course vagabonde, course errante, course, *f.*; déviation, *f.*; (*of mind*) égarement, écart, *m.*; divagation, *f.*; délire, *m.*; distraction, *f.*; — *adj.* errant; vagabond; divagateur, divagant; en délire; (*absent, of mind*) distrait. *The — Jew*, le Juif errant, *m.*

Wanderingly, *adv.* en errant; en divaguant; d'une manière distraite

Wanderoo, — **monkey,** *s.* ouanderou, *m.*

Wane, *v.n.* (*of the moon*) décroître; (*fig.*) diminuer, baisser, décliner; s'affaiblir; — *s.* (*of the*

moon) décroissement, décours, déclin, m.; (fig.) déclin, m., décadence, f. On the —, sur [son déclin

Wanly, adv. avec pâleur

Wanness, s. pâleur, f.

Wannish, adj. un peu pâle, pâlot

Want, v.a. avoir besoin de; falloir (imp.); (be destitute) manquer de; (miss) manquer (à); (wish) vouloir, désirer; (want to see, ask for) demander; — v.n. manquer; faire défaut. To be —ing in, (fail) manquer à; (be without) manquer de. To be —ed, (things) être nécessaire, falloir (imp.) Do you — him? avez-vous besoin de lui? I — it, (require) j'en ai besoin; il me le faut. I — a book, (require) j'ai besoin d'un livre; il me faut un livre. I have more (of it, of them) than I —, j'en ai plus qu'il ne m'en faut. What I —, (require) ce dont j'ai besoin; ce qu'il me faut. What he —s, (requires) ce dont il a besoin; ce qu'il lui faut. You are —ed, on vous demande; on a besoin de vous. Wanted a coachman, on demande un cocher. What do you —? que voulez-vous? que désirez-vous? What do you — with me (him, &c.)? que me (lui, &c.) voulez-vous? I — you, j'ai besoin de vous. I — you to go, je voudrais que vous allassiez, je désire que vous alliez. The candle —s snuffing, My watch —s cleaning, &c., V. **Require.** A thing much —ed, une chose dont on a grand besoin; (urgent) une chose très pressée. All that which is —ed, tout ce qui est nécessaire, tout ce qu'il faut. A pretext was —ed, il fallait un prétexte. It —s ten minutes to six, il est six heures moins dix minutes. I — only three months of 60, j'ai 60 ans moins trois mois

Want, s. manque, défaut, m.; absence, f.; privation, f.; disette, f.; (need.) besoin, m.; indigence, f. For — of, faute de; à cause du manque de. To be in —, être dans le besoin. To be in — of, avoir besoin de; manquer de

Wantage, s. manquant, m.

Wanting, part.adj. manquant, &c. (V. **Want,** v.a.n.); qui manque; défectueux; absent. — two, moins deux, à l'exception de deux

Wanton, adj. libertin, licencieux, abandonné; flottant; indiscret; léger, inconsidéré; sans motif, fait de gaieté de cœur; gratuit; systématique; extravagant; irrégulier; exubérant; (frolicsome) folâtre, espiègle; — s. libertin, m., e, f.; — v.n. V. **Sport,** v.n.

Wantonly, adv. légèrement, inconsidérément; de gaieté de cœur; à plaisir; gratuitement; licencieusement; (playfully) en folâtrant; capricieusement; (flying) en flottant

Wantonness, s. licence, f., libertinage, m.; cynisme, m.; légèreté, étourderie, irréflexion, f.; folie, f.; gaieté, f., enjouement, m.; abandon, m.; caprice, m.; gratuité, f.

War, s. guerre, f.; — adj. de guerre; — v.n. faire la guerre (à); (struggle) combattre, lutter (avec, contre). Articles of —, code militaire, code maritime, m. At — (with), en guerre (avec). To go to — (with), to make or wage — (on, upon, against), faire la guerre (à). Secretary of state for —, Secretary of or for —, ministre de la guerre, m. — **cry, -whoop,** s. cri de guerre, m. — **department,** s. département or ministère de la guerre, m. — **horse,** s. cheval de bataille, m. — **insurance,** s. prime de guerre, f. — **material,** s. matériel de guerre, m. — **minister,** s. ministre de la guerre, m. — **office,** s. bureaux du ministère de la guerre, bureaux de la guerre, m.pl.; ministère de la guerre, m.; (for ordnance survey, &c.) dépôt de la guerre, m. — **ship,** s. vaisseau de guerre, m. — **song,** s. chant de guerre, m. — **steamer,** s. vaisseau de guerre à vapeur, m. — **stores,** s.pl. matériel de guerre, m. — **tax,** s. impôt de guerre, m.

Warble, v.a.n. gazouiller, chanter; (fig.) murmurer; (pers.) fredonner

Warbler, s. chanteur, m.; (a bird) fauvette, f.

Warbling, s. gazouillement, ramage, chant, m.

Ward, — off, v.a. parer, détourner; repousser; écarter

Ward, s. garde, défense, f.; (an orphan) pupille, m.f.; (of orphans) tutelle, f.; (of towns) quartier, m.; (of a large town) arrondissement, m.; (of hospitals, &c.) salle, f.; (of schools) quartier, m.; (of locks, fenc.) garde, f. — **room,** s. carré des officiers, m., grande chambre, f.

Warden, s. garde, gardien, m.; (officer) gouverneur, m.; (of prisons) directeur, m.; (of a college) principal, m.; directeur, m.; proviseur, m.; (of a convent) supérieur, m., e, f.

Warder, s. gardien, garde, m.; (female —) gardienne, garde, f.

Wardmote, s. conseil d'arrondissement, m.

Wardress, s. gardienne, garde, f.

Wardrobe, s. (piece of furniture) armoire, f.; (room, wearing apparel) garde-robe, f.; (room in schools) lingerie, f., vestiaire, m. — with plate-glass door, armoire à glace, f. — **dealer,** s. marchand (m., e, f.) or revendeur (m., -euse, f.) à la toilette. — **keeper, -woman,** s. (in schools) lingère, f.; (theat.) costumier, m., -ière, f.

Wardship, s. tutelle, f.; minorité, f.

Ware, s. marchandise, denrée, f.; article, m. Small—s, petits objets, m.pl.; petite mercerie, f.

Warehouse, s. magasin, m.; (cust.) entrepôt, m.; — v.a. emmagasiner, magasiner; (cust.) entreposer. — **keeper,** s. garde-magasin, m.; (cust.) entreposeur, m. — **man,** s. (trader) marchand en gros, marchand, magasinier, m.; (servant) magasinier, garde-magasin, garçon de magasin, m. — **rent, -room,** s. magasinage, m.

Warehousing, s. emmagasinage, m.; (time, charge) magasinage, m.; (cust.) entreposage, m., mise en entrepôt, f.

Wareroom, s. magasin, m.

Warfare, s. guerre, f.; combat, m., lutte, f.; vie militaire, f.; art militaire, m.

Warily, adv. prudemment, avec circonspection

Wariness, s. prudence, circonspection, f.

Warlike, adj. guerrier, belliqueux; martial; militaire, de guerre. —**ness,** s. nature belliqueuse, f.

Warm, adj. chaud; ardent, chaleureux; zélé; vif, violent; (difficult) rude, chaud; (wealthy) cossu; (warmly) chaudement. To be —, V. **Be.** To get (or become or grow) —, V. **Grow.** To keep —, (of clothing) tenir chaud à. To keep oneself —, se tenir chaudement. To make —, V. **To Warm,** v.a. — **blooded,** adj. (zool.) à sang chaud. — **headed,** adj. à tête chaude, irritable. — **hearted,** adj. au cœur chaud, au cœur généreux. — **heartedness,** s. chaleur de cœur, bonté généreuse, cordialité, f.

Warm, v.a. chauffer; réchauffer; (pers.) réchauffer; (fig.) échauffer; (with a warming-pan) bassiner; — v.n. chauffer; (fig.) s'échauffer. To — oneself, (near the fire, in the sun, &c.) se chauffer; (by exercise, &c.) se réchauffer. — **again, — over, — up,** réchauffer

Warmer, s. (for a dish) réchaud, m.

Warming, adj. qui chauffe; — s. chauffage, m. — **apparatus,** s. appareil de chauffage, m.; calorifère, m.; réchaud, m. — **pan,** s. bassinoire, f. — **pipe,** s. conduit de chaleur, m.

Warmly, adv. chaudement; (fig.) chaudement, chaleureusement

Warmth, s. chaleur, f.; ardeur, f.; zèle, m.

Warn, v.a. avertir (de); prévenir (de, que), informer (de); (caution) prémunir. — **off,** détourner

Warning, s. avertissement, avis, m.; alarme, f.; (lesson) leçon, f., enseignement, m.; (notice to leave) congé, m.; (of clocks) avant-quart, prodrome, m. — to leave (or quit), congé, m. To give —, donner avis (à), prévenir, avertir, avertir (...) d'avance; (of leaving) donner congé. *To give — to leave* (or *quit*), donner congé. *To receive* or *have — to leave* (or *quit*), recevoir son congé

Warp, *s.* chaîne, *f.*; (*nav.*) touée, *f.*; (*geol.*, *agr.*) dépôts alluviaux, *m.pl.*; — *v.n.* (*of wood*) se déjeter, travailler, jouer, gauchir; (*fig.*) dévier, s'écarter (de); (*to mistake*) se tromper; (*to wave*) tournoyer; (*nav.*) se touer; — *v.a.* (*wood*) faire déjeter, faire travailler, faire jouer, gauchir; (*fig.*) faire dévier (de), détourner (de); pervertir, fausser; influencer; (*of weaving*) ourdir; (*agr.*) colmater; (*nav.*) touer

Warper, *s.* ourdisseur, *m.*, -euse, *f.*

Warping, *s.* (*of wood*) déjettement, gauchissement, *m.*; (*weaving*) ourdissage, *m.*; (*agr.*) colmatage, *m.* — **machine, -mill,** *s.* machine à ourdir, *f.*, ourdissoir, *m.*

Warrant, *v.a.* garantir; autoriser; justifier; attester, assurer; (*answer for*) garantir, répondre de; — *s.* autorisation, *f.*, pouvoir *m.*; garantie, autorité, *f.*; justification, *f.*; ordre, *m.*; (*of public situations*) brevet, *m.*; (*order*) ordre, *m.*; (*com.*) warrant, *m.*; (*for payment*) mandat, *m.*; coupon, *m.*; (*law*, — *of apprehension*) mandat d'amener, mandat d'arrêt, *m.*; mandat (de ...), *m.*; (*of attorney*) procuration, *f.*; (*nav.*) brevet, *m.* — **officer,** *s.* officier breveté, *m.*

Warrantable, *adj.* justifiable; soutenable; légitime; autorisé [légitimité, *f.*

Warrantableness, *s.* nature justifiable, *f.*;

Warrantably, *adv.* justifiablement; légitimement [**rant,** *v.a.*); (*com.*) warranté

Warranted, *part. adj.* garanti, &c. (*V.* **War-**

Warranter. *V.* **Warrantor**

Warranting, *s.* garantie, *f.*, cautionnement, *m.*

Warrantor, *s.* garantisseur, garant, *m.*

Warranty, *s.* garantie, *f.*; autorisation, *f.*, pouvoir, *m.*; (*right*) droit, *m.*

Warren, *s.* garenne, *f.* — **keeper,** *s.* garennier, *m.* — **rabbit,** *s.* lapin de garenne, *m.*

Warrener, *s.* garennier, garde-chasse, *m.*

Warrior, *s.* guerrier, *m.*; militaire, soldat, *m.*

Wart, *s.* verrue, *f.*; poireau, *m.* — **hog,** *s.* phacochère, *m.* — **wort,** réveille-matin, *m.*

Warted, Warty, *adj.* plein de verrues; verruqueux

Wary, *adj.* circonspect, prudent; rusé

Wash, *v.a.n.* laver; (*wet*) arroser, mouiller; (*overflow*) baigner; (*linen*) blanchir; savonner; (*ashore*) rejeter (sur le rivage); (*mechanical* &c. *drawing*) laver; — *v.n.* se laver; (*bathe*) se baigner. *To — o.'s hands,* se laver les mains. — **away,** — **off,** — **out,** — **overboard,** *v.a.* nettoyer; enlever; emporter; (*fig.*) effacer; *v.n.* s'enlever. — **down,** laver; nettoyer; emporter; (*by drinking*) arroser. — **up,** laver; (*cast up*) rejeter. — **for,** blanchir

Wash, *s.* (*of linen*) blanchissage, savonnage, *m.*, lessive, *f.*, lavage, *m.*; (*cosmetic*) cosmétique, *m.*, eau, *f.*; (*for hogs*) lavure, *f.*; (*watery soup or* &c.) lavasse, *f.*; (*marsh*) marécage, *m.*; (*of mechanical* &c. *drawing*) lavis, *m.*; (*med.*) lotion, *f.*; eau (de ...), *f.*; (*of an oar*) plat, *m.* *To send to the —*, envoyer au blanchissage. — **ball,** *s.* savonnette, *f.* — **board,** *s.* (*of a wall*) *V.* **Skirting;** (*of a boat*) falque, fauque, fargue, *f.*; (*for clothes*) *V.* **Washing-board.** — **hand basin,** *s.* cuvette, *f.* — **hand stand,** *V.* —**stand.** —**house,** *s.* lavoir, *m.*; (*for linen*) buanderie, *f.* — **leather,** *s.* peau de chamois, *f.*, chamois, *m.* —**pot,** *s.* cuvette, *f.* —**stand,** *s.* toilette, *f.*; (*small circular*) lavabo, *m.* — **tub,** *s.* cuvier, baquet, *m.*

Washable, *adj.* lavable

Washer, *s.* laveur, *m.*, -euse, *f.*; (*machine*) machine à laver, *f.*; (*ring*) rondelle, *f.* — **man,** *s.* *V.* **Launderer.** — **woman,** *s.* *V.* **Laundress**

Washing, *s.* lavage, *m.*; (*of linen*) blanchissage, *m.*; lessive, *f.*; (*watering*) arrosement, *m.*; (*pers.*) toilette, *f.*, (*fam.*) ablution, lavation, *f.*; (*theol.*) ablution, *f.* — *of feet, of hands,* (*eccl.*) lavement des pieds, des mains, *m.* *To stand —*, (*of stuffs*) se laver. — **bill,** *s.* note de blanchissage, *f.* — **board,** *s.* planche à laver, batte, selle, *f.*, batadoir, *m.* — **house,** *s.* (*metal.*) laverie, *f.* — **machine,** *s.* machine à blanchir, *f.* — **tub,** *s.* cuvier, baquet, *m.*

Washy, *adj.* humide, mouillé; (*weak*) faible; fade. — *stuff,* lavasse, *f.*; (*weak wine-and-water*) abondance, *f.*

Wasp, *s.* guêpe, *f.* — **fly,** *s.* mouche-guêpe, *f.*, asile, asile-frelon, *m.* —**'s nest,** *s.* guêpier, *m.*

Waspish, *adj.* irritable, irascible; maussade. —**ly,** *adv.* avec irritation, avec irascibilité; maussadement. —**ness,** *s.* irritabilité, irascibilité, *f.*; maussaderie, *f.*

Wassail, *s.* (*feast*) fête, partie, bombance, ripaille, *f.*; — *v.n.* festoyer, faire bombance, faire ripaille, ripailler

Waste, *v.a.n.* consumer, user; épuiser; dissiper, gaspiller; gâcher; prodiguer; mal employer; (*impair*) gâter; détériorer; délabrer; (*paper*) barbouiller, brouiller, gâcher, mal employer; (*lay waste*) dévaster, ravager; (*lose*) perdre; (*law*) dégrader; (*be wasted*) s'user, se consumer; s'épuiser; (*decay*) dépérir; diminuer; (*lose flesh*) maigrir. — **away,** *v.a.* user, consumer; épuiser; *v.n.* se consumer, s'user, s'épuiser; se dissiper; se perdre; (*decay*) dépérir

Waste, *adj.* ravagé, dévasté; inculte, en friche; vague; désert; inutile, perdu; (*of no value*) de rebut, sans valeur; — *s.* gaspillage, *m.*; dissipation, *f.*; folle dépense, *f.*; (*loss*) perte, *f.*; (*in goods*) déchet, *m.*; (*injury*) dégât, *m.*; dévastation, *f.*; ravages, *m.pl.*; (*ruin*) ruine, *f.*; (*refuse*) rebut, *m.*; (*country*) désert, *m.*; (*land*) terre inculte, *f.*; friche, *f.*; lande, *f.*; terrain vague, *m.*; (*of water*) trop-plein, *m.*; (*print.*) maculatures, *f.pl.*; (*bookselling*) défet, *m.* *Mere* or *sheer —*, pure perte. *To go* or *run to —*, se dissiper, se perdre, tomber en ruine. *To lay —*, ravager, dévaster. — **basket,** *s.* panier (*m.*) *or* corbeille (*f.*) au papier. — — **book,** *s.* brouillard, *m.*, main courante, *f.* — **gate,** *s.* (*of water-mills*) lancière, *f.* — **land,** *s.* terre inculte, *f.*; terrain vague, *m.* — **paper,** *s.* papier de rebut, papier inutile, *m.*, vieux papiers, *m.pl.*, paperasses, *f.pl.* — **paper basket,** *s.* *V.* — **basket.** — **pipe,** *s.* tuyau de trop-plein, tuyau de dégagement, *m.* — **sheet,** *s.* mauvaise feuille, feuille de rebut, *f.*; (*print*, &c.) maculature, *f.*; défet, *m.* — **steam,** *s.* vapeur déchargée, *f.* — **steam pipe,** *s.* tuyau d'échappement, *m.* — **stuff,** *s.* rebut, *m.* — **tan,** *s.* tannée, *f.*

Wasteful, *adj.* gaspilleur, gâcheur; dissipateur; prodigue; ruineux; destructeur; inutile; désert, solitaire. —**ly,** *adv.* avec prodigalité; (*uselessly*) en pure perte, inutilement. —**ness,** *s.* gaspillage, *m.*; dissipation, *f.*; prodigalité, *f.*

Waster, *s.* dissipateur, *m.*, -trice, *f.*, gaspilleur, *m.*, -euse, *f.*, gâcheur, *m.*, -euse, *f.*, prodigue, *m.f.*; (*of wicks*) champignon, *m.*

Wasting, *adj.* qui consume, qui use; — *s.* dégât, *m.*; perte, *f.*; dissipation, *f.*; gaspillage, *m.*; dévastation, *f.*

Watch, *v.a.* veiller sur; veiller; (*lie in wait for*) épier, guetter; (*observe*) surveiller; suivre des yeux; observer, regarder; — *v.n.* veiller. — **for,** épier, guetter, attendre. — **over,** veiller sur, surveiller. — **with,** veiller auprès de, garder

Watch, *s.* (*time-piece*) montre, *f.*; (*at night*) veille, *f.*; (*guard*) garde, *f.*; surveillance, *f.*; (*attention*) attention, observation, *f.*; vigilance, *f.*; (*watchman*) garde, gardien, *m.*; (*watchmen*) garde, *f.*; (*sentry*) sentinelle, garde, *f.*; (*nav.*) quart, *m.* *To be on* (or *upon*) *the —*, être sur ses gardes; être aux aguets; (*nav.*) faire le quart; (*for* ...) épier (...), guetter (...). *To keep —*, veiller, avoir l'œil au guet. *To keep a* *strict* or *close* or *good* —, faire une surveillance active, faire bonne garde; (*over* ...) surveiller activement (...), surveiller de près (...). — **box,** *s.* guérite, guette, *f.* — **case,** *s.* boîte de montre, *f.* — **case maker,** *s.* penduliste, boîtier, *m.* — **chain,** *s.* chaîne de montre, *f.* — **coat,** *s.* capote, *f.* — **dog,** *s.* chien de garde, mâtin, *m.* — **fire,** *s.* feu de bivouac, *m.* — **glass,** *s.* verre de montre, *m.*; (*nav.*) ampoulette, *f.*, sablier de quart, *m.* — **guard,** *s.* chaîne de montre, chaîne longue, *f.*, sautoir, *m.* — **house,** *s.* corps de garde, *m.* — **jeweller,** *s.* pierriste en horlogerie, *m.f.* — **key,** *s.* clé de montre, *f.* — **light,** *s.* veilleuse, *f.*; (*nav.*) fanal, *m.* — **maker,** *s.* horloger, *m.* —**making,** *s.* horlogerie, *f.* —**man,** *s.* gardien *or* garde de nuit, veilleur, *m.*; (*overseer*) surveillant, *m.*; (*rail.*) garde-ligne, *m.* —*man's box,* guérite, *f.* — **pocket,** *s.* (*fob*) gousset de montre, *m.*; (*for a bed*) porte-montre, *m.* — **spring,** *s.* ressort de montre, *m.* —**stand,** *s.* porte-montre, *m.* — **tower,** *s.* tour d'observation, *f.*; guérite, *f.* — **word,** *s.* mot d'ordre, *m.* — **work,** *s.* mouvement de montre, *m.*

Watcher, *s.* veilleur, *m.*; (*overseer*) surveillant, *m.*; (*observer*) observateur, *m.*; (*of the sick*) garde, *m.f.*; (*nav.*) guetteur, *m.*

Watchful, *adj.* vigilant; attentif; sur ses gardes; en garde ('*against*,' contre); en éveil. *To be — of,* surveiller. —**ly,** *adv.* avec vigilance, vigilamment; attentivement. —**ness,** *s.* vigilance, *f.*; attention, *f.*; surveillance, *f.*; (*want of sleep*) insomnie, *f.*; veilles, *f.pl.*

Watching, *s.* vigilance, *f.*; veille, *f.*, veilles, *f.pl.*; surveillance, observation, *f.*; (*ailment*) insomnie, *f.*

Water, *s.* eau, *f.*; (*rank*) ordre, *m.*; qualité, *f.*; force, *f.*; (*tide*) marée, *f.*; — *adj.* d'eau; à eau; (*engin.*) hydraulique; (*nat. hist.*) aquatique; (*by water*) par eau; — *v.a.* (*to irrigate, sprinkle*) arroser; (*to wet*) mouiller; (*to bathe*) baigner; (*cattle*) abreuver, donner à boire à; (*o.'s wine,* &c.) mettre de l'eau dans; (*stuffs*) moirer; — *v.n.* (*of the eyes*) pleurer; (*nav.*) faire de l'eau. *Fresh* —, *V.* **Fresh.** *High* —, hautes eaux, *f.pl.*; (*nav.*) haute marée, haute mer, *f.* *High — mark, V.* **High.** *Hot* —, *V.* **Hot.** *Low* —, marée basse, basse mer, *f.* *Low — mark, V.* **Low.** *Running* —, eau vive, eau courante. *Salt* —, *V.* **Salt.** *Soft* —, eau douce. *Warm* —, eau chaude. *Under* —, sous l'eau; submergé; inondé. — *on the chest,* (*med.*) hydropisie de poitrine, *f.* — *in the head* or *on the brain,* hydrocéphale, hydrocéphalie, *f.* *To get into hot* —, se mettre dans le pétrin, se faire de mauvaises affaires. *To hold* —, tenir l'eau; (*nav.*) endurer; (*fig.*) être solide. *To let in* —, (*of boots,* &c.) prendre l'eau. *To make* —, faire (*or* lâcher) de l'eau, uriner; (*nav.*) faire eau. *To make o.'s mouth* —, faire venir l'eau à la bouche (à). *To take in* —, faire de l'eau. — **bailiff,** *s.* (*of harbours*) garde-port, *m.*; (*of rivers*) garde-pêche, *m.*; (*of fish-markets*) inspecteur de la halle au poisson, *m.* — **bath,** *s.* (*chem.*) bain-marie, *m.* — **bearer,** *s.* (*astr.*) Verseau, *m.* — **bed,** *s.* matelas à eau, *m.* — **beetle,** *s.* dytique, *m.* — **blowing engine** *or* **machine,** *s.* trompe, trombe, *f.* — **board,** *s.* falque, *f.* — **boatman,** *s.* (*zool.*) notonecte, *m.* — **borne,** *adj.* à flot. — **bottle,** *s.* carafe, *f.* — **brash,** *s.* (*med.*) pyrose, *f.*, pyrosis, *m.*, aigreurs, *f.pl.* — **bug,** *s.* hydrocorise, punaise d'eau, *f.* — **caltrop,** *s.* (*bot.*) tribule aquatique, *m.*, macre, châtaigne d'eau, *f.* — **can,** *s.* broc à eau, *m.* — **carriage,** *s.* transport par eau, *m.* — **carrier,** *s.* porteur d'eau, *m.* — **cart,** *s.* voiture d'arrosement, *f.* — **chestnut,** *s.* marron d'eau, *m.* — **clock,** *s.* clepsydre, *f.* — **closet,** *s.* cabinet d'aisance, *m.*, lieux, *m.pl.*; garde-robe, *f.* — **colour,** *s.*, — **colours,** *s.pl.* aquarelle, *f.* — *colour painter,* peintre à l'aquarelle, *m.*, aquarelliste, *m.f.* — *colour drawing* or *painting, drawing* or *painting in — colours,* peinture à l'aquarelle, aquarelle, *f.* *To draw* or *paint in — colours,* peindre à l'aquarelle. — **colourist,** *s.* aquarelliste, *m.f.* — **company,** *s.* compagnie des eaux, *f.* — **course,** *s.* cours d'eau, *m.*; chute d'eau, *f.*; (*channel*) conduit, *m.* — **crake, -crow,** *s.* cincle, *m.* — **crane,** *s.* château d'eau, *m.* — **cress, -cresses,** *s.* cresson, cresson de fontaine, *m.* — **cress woman,** *s.* cressonnière, *f.* — **cure,** *s.* hydrothérapie, hydropathie, *f.*; *adj.* hydrothérapique, d'hydrothérapie, hydropathique, d'hydropathie; (*pers.*) hydropathe. — **cure doctor,** *s.* médecin hydropathe, hydropathe, *m.* — **dock,** *s.* (*bot.*) oseille aquatique, *f.* — **dog,** *s.* barbet, *m.* — **drinker,** *s.* buveur (*m.*, -euse, *f.*) d'eau. — **dropwort,** *s.* œnanthe, *f.* — **engine,** *s.* machine hydraulique, pompe, *f.* — **fall,** *s.* chute d'eau, cascade, *f.* — **flea,** *s.* daphnie, *f.* — **fowl,** *s.* oiseau aquatique, *m.*; poule d'eau, *f.* — **gate,** *s.* vanne d'écluse, *f.* — **gauge,** *s.* flotteur, *m.* — **gilding,** *s.* dorure au mercure, *f.* — **glass,** *s.* tube d'eau, *m.* — **god,** *s.* dieu des eaux, *m.* — **gruel,** *s.* gruau à l'eau, *m.* — **gruel doctor,** *s.* médecin d'eau douce, *m.* — **hemlock,** *s.* œnanthe safranée, *f.* — **hen,** *s.* poule d'eau, *f.* — **hog,** *s.* cabiai, *m.* — **jug,** *s.* pot-à-l'eau, *m.* —**less,** *adj.* sans eau. — **level,** *s.* niveau d'eau, *m.* — **lily,** *s.* nénuphar, *m.* — **line,** *s.* (*load — line*) ligne d'eau, ligne de flottaison *or* de charge, flottaison, *f.*; (*in paper*) vergeure, *f.* — **logged,** *adj.* engagé à moitié dans l'eau, engagé, rempli d'eau. — **man,** *s.* batelier, marinier, *m.*; (*of public carriages*) épongeur, palefrenier, servant de place, *m.* — **mark,** *s.* niveau des eaux, *m.*; (*of a ship*) *V.* — **line;** (*on paper*) filigrane, *m.*; *v.a.* filigraner. *High, Low — mark, V.* **High** & **Low.** — **melon,** *s.* melon d'eau, *m.*, pastèque, *f.* — **meter,** *s.* compteur à eau, *m.* — **mill,** *s.* moulin à eau, *m.* — **mole,** *s.* ornithorhynque, *m.* — **moss,** *s.* fontinale, *f.* — **nymph,** *s.* naïade, *f.* — **ordeal,** *s.* épreuve de l'eau, *f.* — **organ,** *s.* orgue hydraulique, *m.* — **ousel,** *s. V.* **Ousel.** — **pepper,** *s.* poivre d'eau, *m.* — **pipe,** *s.* conduit (*or* tuyau) d'eau, *m.* — **plantain,** *s.* plantain d'eau, alisme, *m.* — **plug,** *s.* robinet, *m.*; crapaudine, *f.*; bouche d'eau, *f.* — **poise,** *s.* hydromètre, *m.* — **post,** *s.* poteau d'arrosement, *m.*; borne-fontaine, *f.* — **pot,** *s.* pot à eau, *m.*; (*for plants*) arrosoir, *m.* — **power,** *s.* puissance hydraulique, *f.* — **pressure,** *s.* pression de l'eau, *f.* — *pressure engine,* machine à colonne d'eau, *f.* — **proof,** *adj.* imperméable, imperméable à l'eau; *s.* tissu *or* vêtement *or* pardessus imperméable, imperméable, *m.* — **proofer,** *s.* (*thing*) *V.* — **proof,** *s.*; (*maker*) fabricant de tissus imperméables, *m.*; (*workman*) ouvrier en tissus imperméables, *m.* — **purifier,** *s.* appareil de filtrage, *m.* — **rail,** *s.* râle d'eau, *m.* — **ram,** *s.* bélier hydraulique, *m.* — **rat,** *s.* rat d'eau, *m.* — **rate,** *s.* contribution pour l'eau à domicile, *f.* — **raven,** *s.* cormoran, *m.* — **sail,** *s.* bonnette, *f.* — **scorpion,** *s.* népide, *m.*, nèpe, *f.* —**'s edge,** *s.* bord de l'eau, *m.* — **shed,** *s.* versant, *m.* — **shoot,** *s.* gargouille, *f.* — **side,** *s.* bord de l'eau, *m.*; *adj.* au *or* du bord de l'eau; riverain. — **snail,** *s.* (*zool.*) planorbe, *m.*; (*mech.*) vis d'Archimède, *f.* — **soldier,** *s.* (*bot.*) stratiote, *m.* — **spaniel,** *s.* barbet, *m.* — **spout,** *s.* (*pipe*) tuyau, *m.*; (*of houses*) gouttière, gargouille, *f.*; (*jet*) jet d'eau, *m.*; (*a phenomenon*) trombe, *f.* — **station,** *s.* station à prendre de l'eau, *f.* — **supply,** *s.* approvisionnement d'eau, *m.* — **table,** *s.* (*arch.*) empattement, *m.*; larmier, *m.*; (*engin.*) écharpe, *f.* — **tank,** *s.* réservoir d'eau, *m.*, citerne, *f.* — **tight,** *adj.* imperméable à l'eau, imperméable, étanche.

— *tight compartment,* (*nav.*) cloison étanche, *f.* — **tightness,** *s.* imperméabilité à l'eau, *f.* — **violet,** *s.* hottone, hottonie, *f.* — **vole,** *s.* rat d'eau, *m.* — **way,** *s.* voie (*f.*) *or* cours (*m.*) d'eau; (*of a canal*) section, *f.*; (*of a ship*) fourrure de gouttière, *f.*; (*of a bridge*) débouché, *m.* — **wheel,** *s.* roue hydraulique, *f.* — **wing,** *s.* perré, *m.* — **works,** *s.pl.* eaux, *f.pl.*; ouvrages hydrauliques, *m.pl.*; machine hydraulique, *f.*

Waterage, *s.* transport par eau, *m.*; (*money*) prix du transport par eau, *m.*

Waterer, *s.* arroseur, *m.*, -euse, *f.*; (*of stuffs*) moireur, *m.* [(*med.*) sérosité, *f.*

Wateriness, *s.* humidité, *f.*; aquosité, *f.*;

Watering, *s.* (*of plants, land*) arrosage, *m.*; irrigation, *f.*; (*of streets, plants,* &c.) arrosement, *m.*; (*of cattle*) abreuvage, *m.*; (*of stuffs*) moirage, *m.*; moiré, *m.*; (*supply*) approvisionnement d'eau, *m.*; (*nav.*) aiguade, *f.* — **can,** *s.* arrosoir, *m.* — **cart,** *s.* voiture d'arrosement, *f.* — **engine,** *s.* pompe d'irrigation (*or* d'arrosage), *f.*, irrigateur, *m.* — **place,** *s.* (*mineral waters*) ville d'eaux, *f.*; ville de bains, *f.*; eaux, *f.pl.*; (*on the sea*) ville maritime, ville de bains de mer, *f.*; bains de mer, *m.pl.*; (*for cattle*) abreuvoir, *m.*; (*for shipping*) aiguade, *f.* — **pot,** *s.* arrosoir, *m.* — **station,** *s.* *V.* **Water-station.** — **trough,** *s.* auge, *f.* [aqueuse, *f.*

Waterish, *adj.* aqueux. —**ness,** *s.* nature

Watery, *adj.* aqueux; (*wet*) humide; (*marine*) marin, des eaux; (*poet.*) liquide; (*of a grave*) au fond des eaux. *To find a — grave,* être englouti par les flots, être enseveli au fond des eaux

Wattle, *s.* (*hurdle*) claie, *f.*; (*twig*) brindille, *f.*; (*of cocks, turkeys,* &c.) fanon, *m.*, barbe, *f.*, barbillon, *m.*; (*of fishes*) barbe, *f.*, barbillon, *m.*; — *v.a.* entourer de claies; (*bind*) lier; (*twist*) tresser, entrelacer. — **bird,** *s.* glau- [cope, *m.*

Wattling, *s.* natte, tresse, *f.*

Waul. *V.* **Caterwaul**

Wave, *s.* vague, *f.*, flot, *m.*, lame, *f.*; (*fig.*) ondulation, *f.*; (*of ground*) pli (de terrain), *m.*; (*of the hand*) signe (de la main), *m.*; —**s,** *pl.* vagues, &c.; (*poet.*) ondes, *f.pl.*, flots, *m.pl.*; — *v.n.* flotter, ondoyer, onduler; s'agiter; se balancer; (*make a sign*) faire signe (de); — *v.a.* onduler; agiter; faire signe de. (*V.* **Waive**). —**less,** *adj.* calme, uni. —**let,** *s.* petite vague, *f.* [(*print.*) tremblé, *m.*

Waved, *adj.* ondulé; (*of stuffs*) ondé. — *rule,*

Waver, *v.n.* vaciller; flotter; hésiter, balancer; (*totter*) chanceler [*m.*; inconstant, *m.*, e, *f.*

Waverer, *s.* irrésolu, indécis, esprit vacillant,

Wavering, *s.* vacillation, *f.*; hésitation, *f.*; — *adj.* vacillant; indécis, irrésolu, incertain; inconstant. —**ly,** *adv.* avec indécision; avec inconstance. —**ness,** *s.* indécision, *f.*; inconstance, *f.*

Waving, *s.* ondoiement, *m.*, ondulation, *f.*; agitation, *f.*; mouvement, *m.*; balancement, *m.*

Wavy, *adj.* ondoyant, onduleux, ondulé; (*her.*) ondé

Wax, *s.* cire, *f.*; (*of shoemakers*) poix, *f.*; — *adj.* de (*or* en) cire; — *v.a.* cirer; bougier; — *v.n.* *V.* **Grow,** *v.n.* *To get in a —,* (*fam.*) rager. — **candle,** *s.* bougie de cire, *f.*; (*for churches*) cierge, *m.* — **chandler,** *s.* cirier, *m.* — **cloth,** *s.* toile cirée, *f.* — **doll,** *s.* poupée de cire, *f.* — **end,** *s.* ligneul, chégros, *m.* — **flower,** *s.* fleur en cire, *f.* — **light,** *s.* *V.* — **candle.** — **match,** *s.* *V.* **Vesta.** — **moth,** *s.* gallérie, *f.* — **painting,** *s.* encaustique, *f.* — **palm, -shrub,** *s.* cirier, *m.* — **taper,** *s.* bougie filée *or* d'allume, *f.*, rat-de-cave, *m.*; (*for churches*) cierge, *m.* — **tree,** *s.* cirier, *m.* — **wing,** *s.* jaseur, *m.* — **work,** *s.* ouvrage en cire, *m.*; figure de cire, *f.*

Waxed, *adj.* ciré. — *leather,* cuir bouilli, *m.*

Waxen, *adj.* de cire

Waxing, *s.* cirage, *m.*

Waxy, *adj.* cireux

Way, *s.* chemin, *m.*, route, *f.*; voie, *f.*; distance, *f.*; espace, *m.*; passage, *m.*; (*fig., as of the Lord,* &c.) voie, *f.*; (*direction, side*) direction, *f.*; côté, *m.*; sens, *m.*; (*room*) place, *f.*, passage, *m.*, issue, *f.*; (*manner*) manière, façon, *f.*; (*peculiar line or fashion*) genre, *m.*; (*of business*) partie, *f.*; (*means*) moyen, expédient, *m.*; (*views*) desseins, *m.pl.*; (*demeanour*) conduite, *f.*; allure, *f.*; (*custom*) habitude, *f.*; usages, *m.pl.*; (*own will*) idée, guise, *f.*; (*free course*) libre cours, cours, *m.*; (*usual course*) train, *m.*; (*pass*) état, *m.*, passe, *f.*; (*fortune*) fortune, *f.*; (*rail.*) voie, ligne, *f.*; (*nav.*) route, *f.*, chemin, *m.* — **about,** circuit, *m.* — **back,** chemin pour s'en retourner (*or* pour revenir). — **in,** entrée, *f.* — **out,** sortie, *f.* — **through,** passage, *m.* — **to ...,** *V.* **To,** *prep.* —*s and customs,* us et coutumes, mœurs. —*s and means,* (*polit.*) voies et moyens, *m.pl.*; budget, *m.* *A good — off,* assez loin, loin. *A great* or *long — (off),* loin; (*by far*) de beaucoup. *All the —,* tout le chemin, toute la route; (*all along*) tout le long du chemin. *By —,* (*s.*) *V.* **By.** *By — of,* par la voie de; par; en *or* par manière de, en (*or* par) forme de; en guise de; comme. *By the —,* (*on the way*) en chemin, chemin faisant; (*fig.*) en passant; soit dit en passant; par parenthèse; à propos! *Covered* or *covert —,* (*fort.*) chemin couvert, *m.* *Cross —,* *V.* **Cross.** *In this —,* de cette manière. *In o.'s (own) —,* à sa manière, à sa façon, à sa guise; dans son genre. *In a fair —,* en voie (de), en passe (de). *In the —,* (*at hand*) sous la main, à portée, tout près; ici. *In the — of,* sous le rapport de, relativement à; en fait de. *In no —, No —, No —s,* nullement, en aucune façon. *Is this the — (that),* est-ce ainsi que. *On the —,* en chemin; chemin faisant. *On o.'s — to,* en route pour; en allant à; pour aller à. *Out of the —,* hors du chemin; retiré, écarté; à l'écart; éloigné; de côté; caché; absent; peu ordinaire, extraordinaire, peu commun, rare; peu usité, peu connu; insolite; irrégulier, bizarre, étrange; (*int.*) en arrière! rangez-vous! ôtez-vous de là! *Over the —,* vis-à-vis, en face, de l'autre côté. *Right of —,* droit de passage, passage, *m.*, servitude, *f.* *The —,* (*so*) comme cela, ainsi. *The land —,* la voie de terre. *The other —,* l'autre chemin; (*side*) de l'autre côté; (*manner*) de l'autre manière; (*the reverse*) le contraire; en sens (*or* dans le sens) contraire. *The public —,* la voie publique. *The right —,* le bon chemin; (*fig.*) la bonne manière; (*path*) la bonne voie; (*adverb.*) du bon côté; de la bonne manière, bien, comme il faut. *The wrong —,* le mauvais chemin; (*fig.*) la mauvaise manière; (*path*) la mauvaise voie; (*adverb.*) de travers; à rebours; mal. *That —,* (*manner*) de cette manière-là, ainsi; (*side*) de ce côté-là; (*through there, thereby*) par là. *This —,* (*manner*) de cette manière-ci, ainsi; (*side*) de ce côté-ci; (*through here*) par ici. *This — and that,* de côté et d'autre, çà et là. *Under —,* sous voiles, en marche. *Which —,* (*manner*) de quelle manière; comment; (*side*) de quel côté; (*through where*) par où. *To be* or *lie* or *stand on* or *in the —,* être dans le chemin; barrer le passage (à); (*fig.*) gêner, contrarier, embarrasser; faire obstacle (à), s'opposer (à), empêcher; (*be one too many*) être de trop; (*be near*) être sous la main, être (*or* se tenir) à portée, être tout près; être ici. *To be out of the —,* être hors du chemin; être absent, n'être pas là (*or* ici); (*not to inconvenience*) ne pas gêner; (*various senses*) être retiré *or* &c. (*See above, Out of the —*). *To clear the —,* débarrasser le chemin *or* la voie; (*prepare*) préparer la voie; (*move aside*) se ranger; (*make room*) faire place. *To come in the* (or *in o.'s*)

—, se présenter. *To cut* or *beat* or *fight* or *force o.'s* —, se faire jour, se frayer un chemin; (*fig.*) faire son chemin. *To feel o.'s* —, aller (*or* marcher) à tâtons; (*fig.*) sonder le terrain. *To find o.'s* —, trouver son chemin; s'introduire (dans). *To find its* —, se trouver être, se trouver. *To get out of the* —, s'ôter du chemin; se mettre de côté; se ranger; se garer. *Get out of the* —! (*fam.*) ôtez-vous de là! *To get under* —, se mettre en route, faire voile, lever l'ancre. *To give* —, céder (à); fléchir; lâcher pied, reculer, plier; obéir; faire place (à); se laisser aller (à), s'abandonner (à); (*fall*) tomber; (*sink*) s'affaisser; s'enfoncer; (*fail*) manquer; (*break*) se rompre; (*stretch*) prêter; (*relax*) se relâcher. *To go a great* or *a long* —, aller loin; (*with*) faire un grand effet (sur); avoir grande influence (sur); être d'un grand poids (auprès de); (*to*) contribuer beaucoup (à). *To go o.'s* —, passer son chemin. *To go on o.'s own* —, aller son train. *To go out of o.'s* —, sortir de son chemin; s'écarter de la route ordinaire (pour); se déranger. *To go the right* — *to work*, s'y prendre bien, s'y prendre comme il faut. *To have its* —, avoir son cours. *To have o.'s own* —, faire à sa tête *or* à sa volonté, faire ce qu'on veut, faire comme on l'entend, faire ce qui (me, te, lui, &c.) plaît. *To keep out of the* —, se tenir éloigné, se tenir caché, se cacher; s'absenter. *To lead the* —, *To lead out of the* —, *V.* **Lead.** *To lose o.'s* —, *V.* **Lose.** *To make* —, faire du chemin, avancer; (*make room*) faire place ('*for*,' à); se ranger; ouvrir la porte (à). *To make o.'s* —, se frayer un chemin; se diriger (vers); (*fig.*) faire son chemin. *To make o.'s* — *in*, entrer, pénétrer, s'introduire dans; (*the world*) faire son chemin dans (le monde). *To make o.'s* — *out*, sortir de; se tirer de. *To make o.'s* — *through*, se frayer un chemin à travers, se faire jour à travers, pénétrer à travers, percer. *To make o.'s* — *to*, arriver à, parvenir à. *To make o.'s* — *towards*, se diriger vers. *To make o.'s* — *up*, monter; s'élever; se pousser. *To make the best of o.'s* —, *V.* **Best.** *To pay o.'s* — vivre sans faire de dettes, joindre les deux bouts. *To push o.'s* —, se faire *or* se frayer un passage (en poussant); (*fig.*) se pousser. *To put out of the* —, ranger; (*get rid of*) se débarrasser de; (*inconvenience*) déranger. *To stand in the* —, *V. To be in the* — (*above*). *To stand out of the* —, s'ôter du chemin, se garer; se tenir à l'écart, ne pas se montrer. *To stop the* —, barrer le passage. *To work o.'s* — *to*, s'ouvrir un passage vers. — **bill,** *s.* feuille de route, feuille, *f.* —**farer,** *s.* voyageur, *m.*, -euse, *f.*; passant, *m*, e, *f.* —**faring,** *adj.* qui voyage, en voyage; qui passe. — **faring-tree,** *s.* mancienne, *f.* —**lay,** *v.a.* dresser un guet-apens à; (*in a milder sense*) guetter au passage, guetter. —**less,** *adj.* sans direction. — **side,** *s.* bord de (*or* du) chemin, *m.* —**ward,** *adj.* fantasque; capricieux; volontaire, entêté; revêche. —**wardly,** *adv.* fantasquement; capricieusement; avec entêtement, opiniâtrément. —**wardness,** *s.* caprice, *m.*; entêtement, *m.* — **wiser,** *s.* pédomètre, hodomètre, compte-pas, *m.*

Waywode, *s.* vayvode, *m.*

Waywodeship, Waywodate, *s.* vayvodat, *m.*, vayvodie, *f.*

We, *pron.pers.* nous; (*anyone*) on; (*emphatically*) nous autres

Weak, *adj.* faible; débile; infirme. —*part* or *side* côté faible, faible, *m.* *To get* (or *grow* or *become*) —, s'affaiblir

Weaken, *v.a.* affaiblir; débiliter; atténuer; (*the force of a blow*, &c.) amortir

Weakener, *s.* débilitant, *m.*

Weakening, *s.* affaiblissement, *m.*; débilitation, *f.*; atténuation, *f.*

Weakish, *adj.* un peu faible

Weakling, *s.* être faible, *m.*, créature faible, *f.*

Weakly, *adj.* faible, débile; — *adv.* faiblement; débilement

Weakness, *s.* faiblesse, *f.*; débilité, *f.*; (*weak side*) faible, *m.*

Weal, *s.* (*welfare*) bien, *m.*; bien-être, *m.*; bonheur, *m.*; (*mark*) marque, vergeture, *f.*; — *v.a.* marquer, vergeter, sillonner. *The common* —, le bien public

Weald, *s.* bois, *m.*, forêt, *f.*; campagne, *f.*; [district, *m.*]

Wealth, *s.* richesse, opulence, fortune, *f.*; richesses, *f.pl.*, biens, *m.pl.* *The* — *of nations*, la richesse des nations

Wealthily, *adv.* richement

Wealthiness, *s.* richesse, opulence, *f.*

Wealthy, *adj.* riche, opulent

Wealy, *adj.* marqué de raies, vergeté

Wean, *v.a.* sevrer; (*fig.*) priver (de); détacher (de), éloigner (de). *Being —ed*, en sevrage

Weaning, *s.* sevrage, *m.*

Weanling, *s.* enfant *or* animal sevré, *m.*

Weapon, *s.* arme, *f.* —**less,** *adj.* sans armes; désarmé

Wear, *v.a.* user; consumer; (*have on*) porter; avoir; (*put on*) mettre; — *v.n.* s'user; se consumer; passer, se passer, s'écouler. *Fit to* —, portable, mettable. *To* — *badly*, n'être pas d'un bon user. *To* — *well*, être d'un bon user; (*of age*) porter bien son âge, ne pas vieillir, se conserver bien. — **away,** *v.a.* user; consumer; effacer; enlever; (*time*) passer; *v.n.* s'user; se consumer; s'effacer; se passer. — **off,** *v.a.* détruire; effacer; *v.n.* *V.* — **away,** *v.n.* — **on,** *v.n.* s'avancer, s'écouler, passer. — **out,** *v.a.* user; (*exhaust*) excéder, épuiser; harasser; (*o.'s patience*, &c.) lasser; (*time*) passer; *v.n.* s'user; se consumer; se passer, s'écouler

Wear, *s.* user, *m.*; usage, *m.*; (*tear*) usure, *f.*; (*of coin*) frai, *m.*; (*weir*) *V.* **Weir;** (*a net*) *V.* **Weel.** — *and tear*, usure, *f.* *In* —, en usage. *The worse for* —, usé

Wearable, *adj.* portable, mettable

Wearily, *adv.* *V.* **Tiresomely**

Weariness, *s.* fatigue, lassitude, *f.*; (*of mind*) ennui, *m.*; dégoût, *m.*

Wearing, *s.* port, *m.*, action de porter, *f.*; usage, *m.* — **apparel,** *s.* vêtements, habits, *m.pl.*; (*fam.*) hardes, *f.pl.* — **out,** *s.* usure, *f.*; *adj.* lassant, fatigant

Wearisome, -ly, -ness. *V.* **Tiresome,** [-**ly,** -**ness**]

Weary, *v.a.n.* *V.* **Tire;** — *adj.* fatigué; las; (*of mind*) ennuyé; (*tiresome*) fatigant, ennuyeux. — *bed*, lit de douleur, *m.*

Weasand, *s.* trachée-artère, *f.*; (*jest.*) sifflet, *m.*

Weasel, *s.* belette, *f.*

Weather, *s.* temps, *m.*; (*storm*) tempête, *f.*; — *adj.* du vent; au vent; — *v.a.* résister à; (*stone*, &c.) exposer à l'air; (*a cape*, &c.) doubler. *Bad* —, mauvais temps. *Fine* —, beau temps. *Rainy* —, temps pluvieux *or* de pluie. *To be bad* —, faire mauvais temps, faire mauvais. *To be fine* —, faire beau temps, faire beau. *How is the* —? quel temps fait-il? *In warm* —, par un temps chaud; par la chaleur; quand il fait chaud. *In this cold* or &c. —, par le froid *or* &c. qu'il fait. *In very cold* —, quand il fait très froid; dans les grands froids. *In very hot* —, quand il fait très chaud; dans les grandes chaleurs. *In fine* —, quand le temps est beau, quand il fait beau temps. — *permitting*, si le temps le permet. — **beaten,** *adj.* battu par la tempête; (*pers.*) usé par le temps; bronzé. — **board,** *s.* abat-vent, *m.*; auvent, *m.*; larmier, *m.*; (*of boats*) falque, fauque, fargue, *f.* — **boarding,** *s.*, — **boards,** *s.pl.* plancheyage d'abri, *m.*; abat-vent, *m.* — **bound,** *adj.* retenu par le mauvais temps (*or* par les vents contraires). — **cock,** *s.* girouette, *f.* — **driven,** *adj.* poussé *or* chassé *or* emporté par la tempête. — **gage,** *s.* avantage du vent, *m.* — **glass,** *s.* baromètre, *m.*; thermomètre, *m.* — **most,** *adj.* plus au vent. — **moulding,** *s.* larmier, *m.* — **proof,** *adj.* à l'épreuve du temps. — **sheet,** *s.* (*nav.*) écoute du vent, *f.* — **side,** *s.* côté du vent, *m.* — **tide,** *s.* marée contraire au vent, *f.* — **wise,** *adj.* qui prévoit le temps, qui se connaît au temps

Weave, *v.a.n.* tisser; (*the hair,* &c.) tresser; entrelacer; (*intermix*) entremêler (' *with,*' avec)

Weaver, *s.* tisserand, *m.*; tisseur, *m.*; (*insect*) *V.* **Whirligig;** (*spider*) *V.* **Retiary;** (*fish*) *V.* **Weever.** — **bird,** *s.* tisserin, *m.*

Weaveress, *s.* tisseuse, *f.*

Weaving, *s.* tissage, *m.*; (*trade, business*) tisseranderie, *f.* — **factory,** *s.* tisseranderie, *f.*

Weazen, *adj.* mince, maigre, allongé

Web, *s.* tissu, *m.*; (*of spiders*) toile, *f.*; (*on the eye*) taie, *f.*; (*of birds*) palmure, membrane, *f.* *Penelope's* —, la toile de Pénélope, *f.* — **footed,** *adj.* palmipède

Webbed, *adj.* palmé

Wed, *v.a.* épouser; (*unite*) marier (à), unir (à); (*fig.*) unir; attacher; lier; enchaîner; (*become attached to*) s'attacher à; — *v.n.* se marier

Wedded, *adj.* marié; légitime; conjugal; (*fig.*) uni (à); attaché (à); entiché (de)

Wedding, *s.* mariage, *m.*, noces, *f.pl.*, noce, *f.*; — *adj.* de mariage; de noces, de noce; nuptial; conjugal. — **breakfast,** *s.* repas de noce, *m.* — **cake,** *s.* gâteau de noce, *m.* — **card,** *s.* lettre de faire part, *f.* — **day,** *s.* jour de mariage, *m.* *O.'s — day,* le jour de son mariage, *m.* — **dress,** *s.* robe de noce, *f.* — **favours,** *s.pl.* livrée de la noce, *f.*, rubans de la noce, *m.pl.*, faveurs, *f.pl.* — **feast,** *s.* repas de noce, *m.*; noce, *f.* — **outfit,** *s.* trousseau, *m.* — **party,** *s.* gens de la noce, *m.f.pl.*, noce, *f.* — **presents,** *s.pl.* cadeaux de noces, *m.pl.*; corbeille de mariage, *f.* — **ring,** *s.* alliance, *f.*, anneau de mariage, anneau nuptial, *m.* — **song,** *s.* chant nuptial, épithalame, *m.* — **tour,** *s.* voyage de noces, *m.*

Wedge, *s.* coin, *m.*; (*for steadying,* &c.) cale, *f.*; (*of gold,* &c.) lingot, *m.*; (*of soap,* &c.) brique, love, *f.*; — *v.a.* serrer (avec un coin *or* avec des coins), coincer; (*fix*) caler, fixer; (*force*) forcer, ouvrir; (*squeeze*) serrer, presser, prendre; (*pierce*) percer, fendre. *It is the thin end of the* —, c'est un pied de pris. — **in,** *v.a.* faire entrer; intercaler, insérer; (*fix*) caler, fixer; (*squeeze*) serrer, presser, prendre. — **key,** *s.* clé de serrage, *f.* — **shaped,** *adj.* en forme de coin, en coin, cunéiforme. — **up,** *v.a.* caler [calage, *m.*

Wedging, *s.* coinçage, serrage, *m.*; (*fixing*)

Wedlock, *s.* mariage, *m.* *Child born out of* —, enfant né hors mariage, enfant de l'amour, *m.*

Wednesday, *s.* mercredi, *m.*

Wee, *adj.* petit, tout petit, petiot. *Just a* — (or *a — bit*)! un tout petit peu

Weech-elm, *s.* *V.* **Wych-elm**

Weed, *s.* herbe, *f.*; mauvaise herbe, *f.*; (*jest.*) tabac, *m.*; cigare, *m.*; (*crape*) crêpe, *m.*; (*horse*) rosse, *f.*; —**s,** *pl.* (*dress*) habits *or* vêtements de deuil, *m.pl.*, deuil, *m.*; — *v.a.* arracher les mauvaises herbes de, sarcler; (*fig.*) extirper; débarrasser, nettoyer, purger, purifier, épurer. — **ashes,** *s.pl.* védasse, *f.* — **extirpator,** *s.* extirpateur, *m.* — **hook, -grubber,** *s.* sarcloir, *m.* **less,** *adj.* sans mauvaises herbes. — **out,** *v.a.* extirper

Weeder, *s.* sarcleur, *m.*, -euse, *f.*; (*tool*) sarcloir, *m.*; écobue, écobueuse, *f.*; (*fig.*) extirpateur, destructeur, *m.*, -trice, *f.*

Weeding, *s.* sarclage, *m.*; (*fig.*) épuration, *f.* — **fork, -hook, -iron, -tool,** *s.* sarcloir, *m.*

Weedy, *adj.* plein de mauvaises herbes; (*weakly*) chétif

Week, *s.* semaine, *f.* *A* —, une semaine; (*fam., counting the first and last day of the same name*) huit jours, *m.pl.*, une huitaine de jours, une huitaine, *f.* *A — ago,* il y a huit jours. *This day* —, (*to come*) d'aujourd'hui (*or* aujourd'hui) en huit; (*law*) à huitaine; (*past*) il y a aujourd'hui huit jours. *This day last* —, il y a aujourd'hui huit jours. *To-morrow* —, de demain en huit. *Yesterday —, a — ago yesterday,* il y a eu hier huit jours. — **day,** *s.* jour ouvrable, jour de la semaine, *m.* — **days,** *s.pl.* (*of time-tables,* &c.) semaine, *f.*

Weekly, *adj.* hebdomadaire; de chaque semaine; (*by the week*) à la semaine; — *adv.* tous les huit jours, chaque semaine, hebdomadairement; (*per week*) par semaine. — *paper,* journal hebdomadaire, *m.*

Weel, *s.* (*for fish*) nasse, *f.*

Ween, *v.n.* penser, croire, estimer

Weep, *v.a.n.* pleurer. — **for,** (*mourn*) pleurer. *To — for joy,* pleurer de joie

Weeper, *s.* pleureur, *m.*, -euse, *f.*; (*of mourning dresses*) pleureuse, *f.* — **monkey,** *s.* singe pleureur, sapajou, sajou, *m.*

Weeping, *s.* pleurs, *m.pl.*, larmes, *f.pl.*; — *adj.* qui pleure; (*of trees*) pleureur. — **willow,** *s.* saule pleureur, *m.*

Weepingly, *adv.* en pleurant

Weever, *s.* (*fish*) vive, *f.*

Weevil, *s.* charançon, *m.*

Weft, *s.* tissu, *m.*; (*of cloth*) trame, *f.*

Weigh, *v.a.n.* peser; (*consider*) peser, examiner; (*a ship*) soulever; (*anchor*) lever (l'ancre); (*be of importance*) avoir du poids (pour); valoir; — *s.* poids, *m.*; pesée, *f.* *Under —, To get under* — (or *way*), *V.* **Way.** — **bridge,** *s.* pont à bascule, *m.*, bascule, *f.* — **down,** *v.a.* peser plus que; (*press down*) surcharger; affaisser; (*depress*) accabler (' *with,*' de); (*surpass*) l'emporter sur; *v.n.* pencher; faire la bascule; s'affaisser

Weighable, *adj.* pondérable, pesable

Weigher, *s.* peseur, *m.*, -euse, *f.*; ajusteur, *m.*

Weighing, *s.* pesage, *m.*; (*quantity weighed*) pesée, *f.* — **house,** *s.* bureau de pesage, *m.* — **machine,** *s.* bascule, *f.* — **place, -room,** *s.* (*of horse-races*) enceinte du pesage, *f.*

Weight, *s.* poids, *m.*; (*heaviness*) pesanteur, *f.*; — *v.a.* charger; appesantir, alourdir; (*a stick*) plomber. — **less,** *adj.* léger, sans poids. *O.'s — in gold,* son pesant d'or

Weightily, *adv.* pesamment, lourdement; (*fig.*) avec poids; puissamment, fortement

Weightiness, *s.* pesanteur, *f.*; poids, *m.*; (*fig.*) gravité, *f.*; importance, *f.*; puissance, force, *f.*

Weighty, *adj.* pesant, lourd; (*fig.*) grave; important, de poids; puissant, fort

Weir, *s.* barrage, *m.*; déversoir, *m.*; (*fishing* —) nasse, *f.*, duit, *m.*

Weird, *s.* charme, enchantement, *m.*; magie, *f.*; (*pers.*) enchanteur, *m.*, enchanteresse, *f.*; — *adj.* du destin; fantastique; enchanteur; magique; charmant; surnaturel; céleste, éthéré. *The — sisters,* les Parques, *f.pl.*

Welcome, *adj.* bienvenu; (*things*) agréable; acceptable. — ! soyez le bienvenu. *Quite* — ! à votre service! *That is quite* —, cela n'est pas de refus. *You are* —, vous êtes le bienvenu. *You are — to it,* c'est à votre service; jouissez-en *or* usez-en à votre aise. *You are — to do as you please,* vous pouvez faire comme il vous plaira

Welcome, *s.* bienvenue, *f.*; bon accueil, *m.*; accueil, *m.*, réception, *f.* *A hearty* —, un accueil cordial. *To bid anyone* —, souhaiter la bienvenue à quelqu'un. *To give anyone a hearty* —, faire un accueil cordial à quelqu'un, recevoir quelqu'un à bras ouverts

Welcome, *v.a.* souhaiter la bienvenue à; bien accueillir, faire bon accueil à; faire accueil à, accueillir, saluer; fêter

Weld, *v.a.* souder; — *s.* (*bot.*) gaude, *f.*

Welder, *s.* soudeur, *m.*

Welding, *s.* soudage, *m.*; soudure, *f.*

Welfare, *s.* bien-être, bien, bonheur, *m.*, prospérité, *f.*; avantage, intérêt, *m.*

Welkin, *s.* firmament, ciel, *m.*, voûte céleste, voûte éthérée, *f.*

Well, *s.* puits, *m.*; source, fontaine, *f.*; (*of pumps,* &c.) réservoir, *m.*; (*of a ship*) archipompe, *f.*; **—s,** *pl.* eaux (minérales), *f.pl.*; — *v.n.* (— *out*) jaillir, couler. *Blind* or *dry* —, puits perdu. — **boat,** *s.* boutique, *f.*, bouticlar, vivier, *m.*, bascule, *f.* — **drain,** *s.* puits d'écoulement, puisard, *m.*; *v.a.* dessécher. — **head,** *s.* source, *f.* — **hole,** *s.* puits, *m.* — **room,** *s.* buvette, *f.*; (*nav.*) sentine, *f.* — **sinker,** *s.* puisatier, fonceur de puits, *m.* — **sinking,** *s.* foncement de puits, *m.* — **spring,** *s.* source, *f.* — **staircase,** *s.* escalier à vis, *m.* — **water,** *s.* eau de puits, *f.*

Well, *adj.* bien; (*good*) bon; (*in health*) bien portant, en bonne santé; à son aise, bien; (*recovered, cured*) rétabli, guéri, remis; (*happy, lucky*) heureux. *I am very* —, je me porte très bien, je suis très bien portant. *I don't feel* —, je ne me sens pas à mon aise, je ne me sens pas bien. *To get* —, guérir, se guérir, se rétablir. *To be — again,* être guéri, être rétabli, être remis; (*get ditto*) se rétablir, guérir, se guérir. *To be — off, V.* **Off,** *adv.*

Well, *adv.* bien; comme il faut; sans difficulté, facilement; (*correctly*) juste. — *!* bien! eh bien! eh! dame! ma foi! enfin! mais; (*never mind*) c'est égal; (*what next?*) après? — *and good,* à la bonne heure. — *enough,* assez bien, suffisamment bien; assez. *As* —, aussi bien ('*as,*' que); (*also*) aussi. *As — as possible,* aussi bien que possible, le mieux possible; parfaitement; au mieux. *Not* —, *not very* —, (ne ...) pas bien, (ne ...) pas très bien; (*scarcely*) (ne ...) guère, (ne ...) pas trop. *To let* (or *leave*) — *alone,* laisser ce qui est bien. *Let* (or *leave*) — *alone, let — be,* le mieux est l'ennemi du bien. *Partly — and partly ill, as — as one can,* tant bien que mal. *That is all very —, but ...,* tout cela est bel et bon, mais ... — **aday,** *int.* hélas! — **advised,** *adj. V.* **Advised.** —**being,** *s. V.* **Welfare.** — **beloved,** *adj.* bien-aimé. — **born,** *adj.* bien né. — **bred,** *adj.* bien élevé, bien né. — **considered,** *adj.* bien réfléchi. —**disposed,** *adj.* bien disposé; bien intentionné. —**doing,** *adj.* qui va bien; qui fait du bien. — **done,** *adj.* bien fait, &c. (*V.* **Do,** *v.a.*); (*of meat,* &c.) bien cuit; *int. V.* **Done.** — **favoured,** *adj. V.* **Favoured.** — **informed,** *adj.* instruit; (*of facts*) bien informé, bien renseigné. — **intended,** *adj.* fait à bonne intention. — **judged,** *adj.* bien entendu, bien vu. — **known,** *adj.* bien connu. — **mannered,** *adj.* de bonnes manières. — **meaning,** *adj. V.* **Meaning,** *adj.* — **meant,** *adj. V.* — **intended.** — **met,** *int.* heureuse rencontre! bien rencontré! — **off,** *adj. V.* **Off.** — **pleased,** *adj.* très content, très heureux. — **read,** *adj. V.* **Read,** *part. adj.* — **shaped,** *adj. V.* **Shaped.** — **spent,** *adj.* bien employé; vertueux. — **spoken,** *adj.* bien dit; (*pers.*) qui parle bien, beau parleur, dont la conversation est agréable; poli. — **tasted,** *adj.* d'un goût agréable. — **timed,** *adj. V.* **timed.** — **to-do,** *adj.* à son aise, dans l'aisance; aisé; calé. — **wisher,** *s.* ami, *m.*, e, *f.* (de ...), protecteur, *m.*, -trice, *f.* (de ...), personne qui veut du bien (à ...), *f.*

Wellington, — **boot,** *s.* botte, botte ordinaire, *f.*

Wellingtonia, *s.* (*bot.*) wellingtonia, *m.*

Welsh, *adj.* gallois, du pays de Galles; — *s.* (*people*) (les) Gallois, *m.pl.*; (*language*) le gallois, *m.*, la langue galloise, *f.* — **boy,** *s.* (petit) Gallois, *m.* — **flannel,** *s.* flanelle fine, *f.* — **girl,** *s.* (petite *or* jeune) Galloise, *f.* — **lady,** *s.* dame galloise, Galloise, *f.* — **man,** *s.* Gallois, *m.* — **mutton,** *s.* mouton du pays de Galles, *m.* — **onion,** *s.* ciboule, *f.* — **rabbit,** *s.* rôtie au fromage, *f.* — **woman,** *s.* Galloise, *f.*

Welt, *s.* bordure, *f.*; trépointe, *f.*; — *v.a.* border, garnir

Welter, *v.n.* rouler; (*in blood*) nager, être baigné; (*in mud,* &c.) se vautrer

Wen, *s.* loupe, *f.*; (*on the neck*) goître, *m.*

Wench, *s.* donzelle, fillette, jeune fille, petite dame, *f.* *Dirty* —, souillon, *f.*

Wend, *v.a.* poursuivre, aller; — *v.n.* aller. *To — o.'s way,* aller, poursuivre *or* aller son chemin, diriger ses pas

Wennish, Wenny, *adj.* loupeux; goîtreux

Wentletrap, *s.* scalaire, *f.*

Were-wolf, *s.* loup-garou, *m.*

Wesleyan, *s. adj.* wesleyen, *m.*, -ne, *f.*

Wesleyanism, *s.* wesleyanisme, *m.*

West, *s.* ouest, *m.*; occident, couchant, *m.*; — *adj.* de l'ouest, d'ouest, ouest, occidental; (*of Western countries*) occidental, d'occident, de l'occident; — *adv.* à l'ouest, à l'occident. — **Indiaman,** *s.* navire des Indes Occidentales, *m.* —**ward, -s,** *adj. adv.* vers l'ouest, vers l'occident. — **wind,** vent d'ouest, *m.*

Westerly, *adj.* d'ouest, de l'ouest; — *adv.* vers (*or* à) l'ouest, vers (*or* à) l'occident

Western, *adj. V.* **West,** *adj.* — *railway,* chemin de fer de l'ouest, *m.* *Great — railway,* grande ligne de l'ouest, *f.* *The — empire,* l'empire d'Occident, *m.* *The — nations* or *people,* les Occidentaux, *m.pl.*, les nations (*f.pl.*) *or* les peuples, (*m.pl.*) de l'Occident. —**most,** *adj.* (le) plus à l'ouest, à l'extrême ouest

Westphalian, *s.* Westphalien, *m.*, -ne, *f.*; — *adj.* westphalien, de Westphalie. — **ham,** *s.* jambon de Westphalie, *m.*

Wet, *adj.* mouillé; humide; (*of weather*) pluvieux. — *through,* — *to the skin,* trempé, trempé jusqu'aux os. *To be* —, (*to rain*) pleuvoir. — **dock,** *s.* bassin à flot, *m.*, darse, *f.* — **footed, -shod,** *adj.* les pieds mouillés. — **nurse,** *s.* nourrice, *f.* — **weather,** *s.* temps pluvieux, temps de pluie, *m.*, pluie, *f.*

Wet, *s.* humidité, *f.*; (*rain*) pluie, eau, *f.* *Out in the* —, à la pluie

Wet, *v.a.* mouiller; humecter, arroser; (*dip, soak*) tremper. *To — o.'s whistle,* s'humecter le gosier

Wether, *s.* mouton, *m.*

Wetness, *s.* humidité, *f.*

Wetting, *s.* mouillement, mouillage, *m.*; humectation, *f.*; (*dipping, soaking*) trempage, *m.* *To get a* —, se faire tremper (*or* saucer)

Wettish, *adj.* un peu mouillé, un peu humide, moite

Whack, &c. *V.* **Thwack,** &c.

Whale, *s.* baleine, *f.* *Young* —, baleineau, *m.* — **boat,** *s.* baleinière, *f.* — **bone,** *s.* baleine, *f.* — **fishery, -fishing,** *s.* pêche de la baleine, *f.* — **fin,** *s.* fanon de baleine, *m.* — **louse,** *s.* cyame, pou de baleine, *m.* — **man,** *s.* baleinier, *m.* — **oil,** *s.* huile de baleine, *f.* — **tribe,** *s.* cétacés, *m.pl.*

Whaler, *s.* baleinier, *m.*

Whaling, *s.* pêche de la baleine, *f.* — **boat, -ship, -vessel,** *s.* baleinier, *m.*

Whap, *s.* coup, *m.*; — *v.a.* battre, rosser

Whapper, *s.* chose énorme, *f.*; masse, *f.*; (*pers.*) gros gaillard, *m.*; (*lie*) bourde, *f.*, mensonge, *m.* *That is a* —, en voilà une forte *or* une bonne!

Whapping, *adj.* fameux, fier

Wharf, *s.* quai, *m.*; (*for goods*) entrepôt, *m.*; — *v.a.* munir d'un quai

Wharfage, *s.* quayage, *m.*

Wharfing, *s.* quais, *m.pl.*

Wharfinger, *s.* garde-quai, *m.*; (*owner*) propriétaire de quai *or* d'entrepôt, *m.*

What, *pron. rel. adj.* (*what thing*) quoi; (*what thing, inter. before a verb*) qu'est-ce qui (*nom.*), qu'est-ce que *or* que (*obj.*); (*tending to specify a noun following*) quel, *m.*, quelle, *f.*, quels, *m.pl.*, quelles, *f.pl.*; (*that which*) ce qui (*nom.*), ce que (*obj.*); (*that of which, what ... of*) ce dont; (*what it is*) ce que c'est; (*such ... as*) tel ... que; (*how*) comment; (*as*) comme; (*how much*) combien; (*what did you say?*) comment? pardon? (*what is the matter?*) quoi? *With* —, avec quoi. *He said something, but I don't know*

—, il a dit quelque chose, mais je ne sais pas quoi. *I know not* —, je ne sais quoi. *I don't know — to do*, je ne sais pas quoi faire, je ne sais que faire. *By — shall we begin?* par quoi commencerons-nous? *— does he complain of?* de quoi se plaint-il? *— makes you laugh?* qu'est-ce qui vous fait rire? *— are you doing?* qu'est-ce que vous faites? que faites-vous? *— is a bishop?* qu'est-ce qu'un évêque? (*fam.*) qu'est-ce que c'est qu'un évêque? *— is it?* qu'est-ce que c'est? *— is that* (or *this*)? qu'est-ce que c'est que cela? (*which one?*) lequel? *— tissue is this?* qu'est-ce que c'est que ce tissu-là? *You don't know — it is to work at a dictionary*, vous ne savez pas ce que c'est que de travailler à un dictionnaire. *— time is it?* quelle heure est-il? *— weather is it?* quel temps fait-il? *— a quantity!* quelle quantité! *— a pretty book!* quel joli livre! *— a handsome woman Mrs. A. is!* la belle femme que Mme A! *— a brute that man is!* quel animal que cet homme-là! *— are your terms* (*charges*), *— your terms are*, quel est votre prix. *— frightened me so was only a shadow*, ce qui me faisait si peur n'était qu'une ombre. *— I feared has happened*, ce que je craignais est arrivé. *Give me — I want* (*what I am in want of*), donnez-moi ce dont j'ai besoin. *I will tell you* —, je vous dirai ce que c'est; voilà ce que c'est; je vais vous dire! tenez! écoutez-moi bien! *Fix — sum you will*, fixez telle somme que vous voudrez. *— do you call that?* comment appelez-vous cela? *Call it — you will*, appelez-le comme vous voudrez. *— do you sell it for?* combien le vendez-vous? *— for?* pourquoi? (*for what use?*) pour quoi faire? — ... *for?* pourquoi ...? *— of that?* que s'ensuit-il? qu'est-ce à dire? qu'est-ce que cela prouve? eh bien, après? qu'importe? qu'est-ce que cela fait? *— then*, *V.* **Then.** *— do you do that for?* pourquoi faites-vous cela? *— do you take me for?* pour qui me prenez-vous? — ... *to*, à quoi; (*where*) où. *And — not*, et autre chose encore; que sais-je? *I have no doubt but — he will come*, je ne doute pas qu'il ne vienne. *There are few persons but — can* ..., il y a peu de gens qui ne puissent ... *To know — is* —, être fin, en savoir long; avoir vu le loup; savoir ce que valent les choses

What, *adv.* *— by force, — by* ..., tant par force que par ... *— with one thing, — with another*, soit une chose soit une autre. *— with ... and*, tant ... que; d'un côté ..., de l'autre

What, *int.* quoi! comment! *— if*, si, et si (*to be followed by the Imperfect of the Indicative*); (*even though*) quand même (*to be followed by the Conditional mood*). *— though*, qu'importe que (*with the subj.*); quand même (*with the Conditional*). *— if I should go*, si j'allais; quand même j'irais

Whatever, *pron. rel.* (*nom.*) tout ce qui, (*obj.*) tout ce que; quelque ... que; quelconque, quoi que ce soit; quoi que; (*when used adjectively*) quel que, quelle que, quels que, quelles que; (*— be*) quel que soit, quelle que soit, quels que soient, quelles que soient. *— he says is true*, tout ce qu'il dit est vrai. *— you do you will not succeed*, quoi que vous fassiez vous ne réussirez pas. *— talent you may have*, quelque talent que vous ayez. *— be your talent*, quel que soit votre talent. *None* —, aucun, pas un seul. *Nothing* —, rien du tout, absolument rien. *I took no share — in it*, je n'y pris aucune part

Whatnot, *s.* étagère, *f.*

Whatsoever. *V.* **Whatever**

Wheal, *s.* pustule, *f.*, bouton, *m.*; marque, vergeture, *f.* — **worm,** *s.* *V.* **Harvest-bug**

Wheat, *s.* froment, blé, *m.*; *— adj.* de froment, de blé. — **ear,** *s.* épi de blé, *m.*; (*bird*) motteux, cul-blanc, *m.* — **field,** *s.* champ de blé, *m.* — **grass,** *s.* froment rampant, *m.* — **sheaf,** *s.* gerbe de blé, *f.* — **worm,** *s.* *V.* **Harvest-bug**

Wheaten, *adj.* de froment, de blé

Wheedle, *v.a.* cajoler, enjôler

Wheedler, *s.* cajoleur, *m.*, -euse, *f.*, enjôleur, *m.*, -euse, *f.*; câlin, *m.*, e, *f.*

Wheedling, *s.* cajolerie, *f.*, enjôlement, *m.*; câlinerie, *f.*; *— adj.* cajoleur; câlin

Wheel, *s.* roue, *f.*; (*carriage*) voiture, *f.*; (*for spinning*) rouet, *m.*; (*of an umbrella*) noix, *f.*; (*caster*) roulette, *f.*; (*turn*) tour, cercle, *m.*; *— adj.* à roues. *Sun and planet* —, roue excentrique. *— and axle*, treuil, *m.* *— of life*, zoétrope, *m.* *To break upon the* —, rouer. *The man at the* —, (*nav.*) l'homme à la barre. — **animal, -animalcule, -insect,** *s.* rotateur, rotatoire, rotifère, *m.* —**barrow,** *s.* brouette, *f.* —**barrowman,** *s.* brouetteur, brouettier, *m.* — **carriage,** *s.* voiture à roues, *f.* — **horse,** *s.* *V.* **Wheeler.** — **lock,** *s.* mousquet à rouet, *m.*; *adj.* à rouet. — **plough,** *s.* charrue à avant-train, *f.* — **race,** *s.* chemin de roue, *m.* — **rut,** *s.* ornière, *f.* — **setter,** *s.* chèvre, *f.* — **shaped,** *adj.* en forme de roue, rotiforme. — **work,** *s.* rouages, *m.pl.* — **wright,** *s.* charron, *m.*

Wheel, *v.a.* rouler; (*drive*) pousser, conduire; (*with a cart, &c.*) voiturer; mener, conduire, transporter; promener; (*with a barrow*) brouetter, transporter; (*turn*) faire tourner, tourner; *— v.n.* rouler; (*turn*) tourner; (*pers.*) se tourner; (*whirl*) tournoyer. — **about,** tourner; faire une pirouette; (*mil.*) faire volte-face; (*rid.*) caracoler; *v.a.* (*in a perambulator, &c.*) promener

Wheeled, *adj.* à roues. *Four* —, à quatre roues

Wheeler, *s.* (*at the shafts*) cheval de brancard, *m.*; (*at the pole*) timonier, *m.*; (*of carts*) limonier, cheval de brancard, *m.* *Four* —, (*carriage*) voiture à quatre roues, *f.*

Wheeling, *s.* roulage, *m.*; (*mil.*) conversion, *f.*

Wheely, *adj.* rond, circulaire

Wheeze, *v.n.* siffler, souffler, être asthmatique, être poussif

Wheezing, *s.* sifflement de la respiration, râle sibilant, *m.*, respiration bruyante, *f.*; *— adj.* *V.* **Wheezy**

Wheezy, *adj.* asthmatique; poussif; court d'haleine

Whelk, *s.* (*wheal*) *V.* **Wheal;** (*shell-fish*) buccin, *m.*

Whelm, *v.a.* submerger; plonger; couvrir; ensevelir; (*overburden*) accabler (de)

Whelp, *s.* petit, *m.*; (*pup*) jeune chien, *m.*; (*of lions*) lionceau, *m.*; (*of wolves*) louveteau, *m.*; (*of bears*) ourson, *m.*; (*pers.*) gamin, *m.*; *— v.n.* mettre bas

When, *adv.* quand, lorsque; (*inter.*) quand; (*used for* '*and then*') et alors; (*used for* '*a time at which*,' '*an age at which*,' &c.) époque à laquelle, heure à laquelle (*V.* **Time**), âge où, &c.; alors que; (*used for* '*in* or *on* or *at which*') que, où; (*after* '*scarcely*' *or* '*hardly*') que; (*with* '*even*') lors ... que, ... quand; alors ... que; (*since, considering that*) puisque, attendu que. *— he comes*, quand *or* lorsqu'il vient; (*future*) quand *or* lorsqu'il viendra. *— will he come?* quand viendra-t-il? *Come on Monday, — we shall talk about it*, venez lundi, et alors nous en causerons. *At twenty*, —, à vingt ans, âge où. *At 12 o'clock*, —, à midi, heure à laquelle. *The day — I saw him*, le jour où *or* que je le vis. *He was hardly gone*, —, à peine était-il parti, que. *Even* —, lors même que, même quand; alors même que. *Since* —, depuis quand? (*since then*) depuis ce temps-là, depuis. *— necessary*, (*past*) lorsqu'il (*or* lorsque cela) était nécessaire, quand il le fallait, au besoin; (*present*) lorsqu'il (*or* lorsque cela) est nécessaire, quand il le faut, au besoin; (*future*) lorsqu'il (*or* lorsque cela) sera nécessaire, quand il le faudra, au besoin

Whence, *adv.* d'où; de là. —**soever,** *adv.* de quelque côté (*or* endroit *or* part) que

Whenever, Whensoever, *adv.* toutes les fois que ; quand ; à n'importe quel moment que

Where, *adv.* où. — ... *to ?* ou ... ? — ... *from ?* d'où ... ? — *are you going to ?* — *are you off to ?* où allez-vous ? — *do you come from ?* d'où venez-vous ? *Any —, See Letter* **A**

Whereabout, Whereabouts, *adv. s.* où ; (*abode*) demeure, *f.* *To know the — of one,* savoir où quelqu'un est *or* était *or* sera

Whereas, *adv.* tandis que ; au lieu que; (*considering*) attendu que, vu que [quoi, là-dessus

Whereat, *adv.* à quoi; de quoi, dont; sur

Whereby, *adv.* par où; par quoi ; par lequel

Wherefore, *adv.* pourquoi; c'est pourquoi; donc [quel

Wherefrom, *adv.* d'où; dont; de quoi; du-

Wherein, Whereinto, *adv.* où ; dans quoi, en quoi; dans lequel

Whereof, *adv.* dont; de quoi ; duquel

Whereon, Whereupon, *adv.* où; sur quoi, sur lequel; là-dessus

Wheresoever. *V.* **Wherever** [auquel

Whereto, Whereunto, *adv.* où; à quoi;

Wherever, *adv.* partout où, n'importe où

Wherewith, Wherewithal, *adv.* avec quoi; avec lequel; de quoi; dont; pour; — *s.* moyen, *m.*; (*money, fam.*) quibus, *m.* *To find the —,* payer ; fournir les moyens

Wherry, *s.* bateau, bachot, bac, va-et-vient, *m.* — **man,** *s.* batelier, passeur, *m.*

Whet, *v.a.* aiguiser, affiler, repasser; (*fig.*) aiguiser, exciter; irriter; animer; — *s.* aiguisage, aiguisement, repassage, *m.*; (*fig.*) stimulant, excitant, *m.* — **stone,** *s.* pierre à aiguiser, *f.*; (*fig.*) stimulant, aiguillon, *m.*

Whether, *conj.* soit que, que (*with the subj.*); soit; (*if*) si; (*elliptically*) pour *or* de savoir si. *The question —,* la question de savoir si

Whetter, *s.* aiguiseur, *m.*; (*fig.*) stimulant, aiguillon, *m.* [sage, *m.*

Whetting, *s.* aiguisage, aiguisement, repas-

Whey, *s.* petit-lait, *m.*

Which, *pron.rel.adj.* qui (*nom.*), que (*obj.*); (*after a prep.*) lequel, *m.*, laquelle, *f.*, lesquels, *m.pl.*, lesquelles, *f.pl.*; (*used for 'which thing,' after a prep.*) quoi; (*standing for 'a thing which,' or 'a fact which,' or 'a remark which'*) ce qui (*nom.*), ce que (*obj.*); (*standing for 'a thing of which,' 'a fact of which,' or 'a remark of which'*) ce dont; (*which one, out of several*) lequel, *m.*, &c.; (*the one which*) celui (*m.*) *or* celle (*f.*) que; (*used for 'what,' before a noun*) quel, *m.*, quelle, *f.*, quels, *m.pl.*, quelles, *f.pl.* *In —,* dans lequel (*or* laquelle, &c.); où, en quoi. *Of* or *from —,* dont, duquel, *m.*, de laquelle, *f.*, desquels, *m.pl.*, desquelles, *f.pl.*; d'où ; avec lequel, &c. *Of —,* (*whose*) *V.* **Whose.** *That —,* ce qui (*nom.*), ce que (*obj.*). *To —,* auquel, *m.*, à laquelle, *f.*, auxquels, *m.pl.*, auxquelles, *f.pl.*; à quoi; (*where*) où. — *do you like best ?* lequel aimez-vous le mieux ? lequel préférez-vous ? — *is — ?* lequel des deux est le bon (*or* le vrai) ? *To know* or *tell — is —,* les distinguer l'un de l'autre, s'y reconnaître

Whichever, Whichsoever, *pron.* lequel, *m.*, laquelle, *f.*, lesquels, *m.pl.*, lesquelles, *f.pl.*; quelque ... que; (*the one which*) celui (*m.*) *or* celle (*f.*) que

Whiff, *s.* bouffée, *f.*; (*fish*) cardine, calimande, *f.*; — *v.a.* lancer avec une bouffée, lancer en bouffées ; — *v.n.* lancer des bouffées

Whig, *s.* whig, libéral, *m.*; — *adj.* whig, libéral

Whiggism, *s.* whiggisme, *m.*

While, *s.* temps, *m.*; moment, instant, *m.* *A little —, A long* or *great* or *good —, V.* **Time.** *After a —,* quelque temps après. *All the —,* tout le temps. *All this —,* pendant tout ce temps-là. *Between —s,* par intervalles, par moments. *It is not worth —,* cela ne vaut pas la peine. *It is worth your* (or *my* or *&c.*) *—,* cela en vaut la peine ; cela vaut la peine (de)

While, *adv.* pendant que ; tandis que; en même temps que ; (*as long as*) tant que ; (*in, before a present part.*) en, tout en

While, (— away) *v.a.* passer, faire passer; perdre [anciennement

Whilom, Whilome, *adv.* jadis, autrefois,

Whilst, *adv. V.* **While,** *adv.*

Whim, *s.* caprice, *m.*, fantaisie, lubie, *f.*; boutade, *f.*; (*machine*) treuil, cabestan, *m.* *Horse —, — gin,* baritel à chevaux, *m.*

Whimbrel, *s.* courlis, courlieu, *m.*

Whimper. *V.* **Whine** [zarre

Whimsical, *adj.* capricieux, fantasque ; bi-

Whimsicality, *s.* caprice, *m.*; bizarrerie, *f.*

Whimsically, *adv.* capricieusement, fantasquement, par lubies, par boutades; bizarrement [fantasque, *m.*

Whimsicalness, *s.* caractère capricieux *or*

Whin, *s. V.* **Furze.** — **chat,** *s.* tarier, *m.*

Whine, *v.n.* se plaindre; pleurnicher, gémir, geindre ; — *s. V.* **Whining**

Whiner, *s.* pleurnicheur, *m.*, -euse, *f.*

Whining, *adj.* dolent, plaintif, pleurard ; — *s.* plainte, *f.*, plaintes, lamentations, *f.pl.*; pleurnichement, gémissement, *m.*

Whiningly, *adv.* en pleurnichant, en gémissant, d'un ton plaintif

Whinny, *adj. V.* **Furzy ;** — *v.n.* hennir ; — *s.* hennissement, *m.*

Whip, *v.a.n.* fouetter; (*punish*) donner le fouet à, fouetter; flageller; fustiger; (*satirize*) flageller; (*take up*) enlever; (*cream*) fouetter; (*sew*) surjeter, faire un surjet à ; (*run*) courir, se précipiter. — **away, off,** chasser; (*take up*) enlever vivement; expédier promptement; (*depart*) partir. — **down,** descendre promptement. — **in,** *v.a.* faire entrer à coups de fouet, faire entrer vivement; — *v.n.* entrer vivement *or* précipitamment. — **on,** *v.a.* faire marcher; *v.n.* se précipiter en avant. — **out,** *v.a.* chasser; (*draw*) tirer vivement; *v.n.* s'esquiver. — **round,** tourner en un clin d'œil. — **up,** *v.a.* faire monter; (*climb*) grimper; (*snatch*) saisir, enlever vivement; *v.n.* monter vivement

Whip, *s.* fouet, *m.*; (*for riding*) cravache, *f.*; (*driver*) cocher, *m.*; (*need.*) surjet, *m.*; (*nav.*) cartahu, *m.* — *and spur,* bride abattue, ventre à terre. *To be a good* or *bad whip,* (*pers.*) savoir bien *or* mal conduire. — **cord,** *s.* fouet, *m.* — **graft,** *v.a.* greffer en approche. — **grafting,** *s.* greffe en approche, *f.* — **hand,** *s.* avantage, dessus, *m.* — **handle,** *s.* manche de fouet, *m.* — **lash,** *s.* mèche, *f.* — **maker,** *s.* fabricant de fouets, *m.* — **saw,** *s.* passe-partout, *m.* — **staff,** *s.* (*nav.*) manivelle de la barre du gouvernail, *f.* — **stitch,** *v.a.* surjeter, faire un surjet à, coudre en surjet. — **stick, -stock,** *s. V.* — **handle.** — **top,** *s.* sabot, *m.*

Whipper, *s.* fouetteur, *m.*, -euse, *f.* — **in,** piqueur, *m.*; (*polit.*) chef de file, *m.* — **snapper,** *s.* vaurien, gamin, *m.*

Whipping, *s.* (le) fouet, *m.*; flagellation, *f.*; fustigation, *f.*; (*fish.*) pêche à la ligne volante, *f.* — **post,** *s.* poteau des condamnés au fouet, *m.* — **top,** *s.* sabot, *m.*

Whippletree, *s.* palonnier, *m.*

Whipster, *s.* homme alerte, *m.*; (*boy*) gamin, *m.*

Whir, *v.n.* tourner (avec bruit); (*of partridges*) bourrir; — *s. V.* **Whirring**

Whirl, *v.a.* faire tourner; rouler; — *v.n.* tournoyer; tourbillonner; pirouetter; — *s.* tourbillon, *m.*; (*turning*) tournoiement, *m.*; rotation, *f.*; (*toy*) pirouette, *f.*; (*bot.*) *V.* **Whorl.** — **along,** — **past,** *v.n.* passer comme le vent *or* comme la foudre; passer ventre à terre

Whirligig, *s.* pirouette, *f.*; (*insect*) gyrin, tourniquet, *m.*

Whirlpool, *s.* tourbillon (d'eau), *m.*

Whirlwind, *s.* tourbillon (de vent), *m.* *To sow the wind and reap the —,* semer le vent et [recueillir la tempête

Whirr. *V.* **Whir**

Whirring, *s.* bruit (de roue qui tourne, &c.), *m.*; (*of partridges*) bourrissement, *m.*
Whisk, *s.* vergette, époussette, *f.*; petit balai, *m.*; (*cook.*) verge (*f.*) *or* fouet (*m.*) à blancs d'œufs; — *v.a.* vergeter, épousseter; (*sweep*) balayer; (*cook.*) fouetter, battre; (*finings for wine*) fouetter; (*fig.*) fouetter; (*a dog's tail,* &c.) remuer; — *v.n.* passer rapidement, voler. — **away, off,** *v.a.* enlever; *v.n.* filer. —*ed eggs,* œufs à la neige, *m.pl.*
Whisker, *s.* (*pers.*) favori, *m.*; (*of animals*) moustache, *f.* —**less,** *adj.* sans favoris; sans moustaches
Whiskered, *adj.* (*pers.*) à favoris; (*of animals*) à moustaches; (*formed into whiskers*) en favoris
Whiskey. V. **Whisky**
Whisking, *s.* époussetage, *m.*; (*sweeping*) balayage, *m.*; (*cook.*, &c.) fouettement, *m.*
Whisky, *s.* whisky, whiskey, *m.*
Whisper, *v.n.* chuchoter, parler tout bas, parler à voix basse, parler à l'oreille; (*of the wind*) murmurer, soupirer; — *v.a.* dire tout bas, dire à voix basse, dire à l'oreille; chuchoter; couler; souffler; murmurer; (*advise*) conseiller tout bas; (*intrust*) confier; — *s.* chuchotement, *m.*; (*rumour*) bruit qui court, bruit léger, *m.*, rumeur, *f.*; (*fig.*) murmure, *m.* *In a* —, tout bas, à l'oreille
Whisperer, *s.* chuchoteur, *m.*, -euse, *f.*; (*tattler*) bavard, *m.*, e, *f.*; (*backbiter*) médisant, *m.*, e, *f.*
Whispering, *s.* chuchotement, *m.*, chuchoterie, *f.*; bruit léger, *m.*, rumeur, *f.*; murmure, *m.*; (*backbiting*) médisance, *f.* —**dome, -gallery,** *s.* voûte acoustique, *f.*; écho, *m.*
Whisperingly, *adv.* en chuchotant, à voix basse, tout bas
Whist, *s.* whist, *m.*; — *int.* chut! paix!
Whistle, *v.a.n.* siffler; — *s.* sifflet, *m.*; (*sound*) sifflement, *m.*; coup de sifflet, *m.* —**fish,** *s.* motelle, *f.* —**pipe,** *s.* sifflet, *m.* (*V.* **Wet**)
Whistler, *s.* siffleur, *m*, -euse, *f.*
Whistling, *s.* sifflement, *m.*; coup de sifflet, *m.*
Whit, *s.* iota, point, *m.* *Every* —, absolument, de tout point. *Not a* —, pas le moins du monde, pas du tout, nullement. —**monday,** *s.* lundi de la Pentecôte, *m.* —**sunday,** &c., *See below*
White, *adj.* blanc; (*pale*) pâle, blême, blanc; pur, sans tache; — *s.* blanc, *m.*; (*whiteness*) blancheur, *f.*; (*of wood*) aubier, *m.*; —**s,** *s.pl.* (*med.*) fleurs blanches, *f.pl.* *To get* (or *grow* or *become* or *turn*) —, blanchir; (*pale*) pâlir. —**bait,** *s.* able, *m.*, ablette, *f.* —**ear,** *s.* *V.* **Wheat-ear.** —**friar,** *s.* carme, *m.* —**frost,** *s.* gelée blanche, *f.*; (*on the trees*) givre, *m.* *There was a — frost last night,* il a gelé blanc cette nuit. —**heart cherry,** *s.* bigarreau, *m.* —**heart cherry-tree,** *s.* bigarreautier, *m.* —**heat,** *s.* blanc, *m.*, incandescence, *f.* —**hot,** *adj.* chauffé au (*or* à) blanc, incandescent. —**lead,** *s.* céruse, *f.*, blanc de plomb, *m.* —**leather,** *s.* (*gristle*) tirant, *m.* —**lie,** *s.* *V.* **Lie,** *s.* —**lime,** *s.* lait *or* blanc de chaux, *m.*; *v.a.* blanchir à la chaux. —**livered,** *adj.* poltron. —**man,** *s.* blanc, *m.* —**owl,** *s.* effraie, *f.* —**Sea,** *s.* (la) Mer Blanche, *f.* —**smith,** *s.* ferblantier, *m.* —**thorn,** *s.* aubépine, épine blanche, *f.* —**throat,** *s.* (*bird*) grisette, *f.* —**wash,** *s.* lait *or* blanc de chaux, badigeon, *m.*; (*pharm.*) eau blanche, *f.*; cosmétique, *m.*; *v.a.* blanchir; (*with lime*) blanchir à la chaux, badigeonner; (*fig.*) blanchir, disculper; purger de ses dettes. —**washer,** *s.* badigeonneur, *m.* —**washing,** *s.* badigeonnage, *m.* —**woman,** *s.* blanche, *f.*
Whiten, *v.a.n.* blanchir
Whitener, *s.* blanchisseur, *m.*, -euse, *f.*
Whiteness, *s.* blancheur, *f.*; pâleur, *f.*; pureté, *f.*
Whitening, *s.* blanchiment, blanchissage, *m.*; [(*whiting*) blanc d'Espagne, *m.*
Whitey. *V.* **Whity**
Whither, *adv.* *V.* **Where.** —**soever,** *V.* **Wherever**
Whiting, *s.* blanc d'Espagne, *m.*; (*fish*) merlan, *m.* —**pout,** *s.* tacaud, *m.*
Whitish, *adj.* blanchâtre. —**ness,** *s.* couleur *or* teinte blanchâtre, *f.*
Whitlow, *s.* panaris, mal d'aventure, *m.*
Whitsun, *adj.* de la Pentecôte
Whitsunday, *s.* dimanche de la Pentecôte, *m.*
Whitsuntide, *s.* la Pentecôte, *f.*
Whittle, *s.* couteau de poche, *m.*; — *v.a.* couper, déchiqueter
Whity, *adj.* blanchâtre. — *brown,* demi-brun; mi-bis; (*of bread*) bis blanc, jaunet; (*of paper*) bulle [*s.* loup-garou, *m.*
Whiz, *v.n.* siffler; — *s.* sifflement, *m.* —**gig,**
Whizzing, *adj.* sifflant; — *s.* sifflement, *m.*
Who, *pron. rel.* qui; (*what*) quel, *m.*, quelle, *f.*, quels, *m.pl.*, quelles, *f.pl.*
Whoever, *pron. rel.* quiconque, qui que ce soit, quel que soit, qui. — *he may be,* quel qu'il soit. — *you are,* qui que vous soyez
Whole, *adj.* tout; entier; tout entier; total; (*well*) bien portant; (*sound*) sain; (*of coffee, pepper, rice,* &c., *not ground*) en grains. — *meal,* farine entière, *f.* — *morocco,* — *calf,* maroquin plein, veau plein, *m.* *The* — ..., tout le ... (*m.*), toute la ... (*f.*). *The — town,* toute la ville, la ville entière. — *months,* des mois entiers
Whole, *s.* tout, *m.*; totalité, *f.* *The* —, le tout. *The — of,* tout (e, *f.*). *The — of it,* tout, le tout. *The — of that,* tout cela. *The — of us,* nous tous. *In the* —, en général. *In the — or in part,* en totalité ou en partie. *On* or *upon the* —, *as a* —, en somme, somme toute, au total, à tout prendre; (*at bottom*) au fond
Wholeness. *V.* **Entireness**
Wholesale, *s.* gros, *m.*, vente en gros, *f.*, commerce de gros, *m.*; — *adj.* en gros; de gros; (*fig.*) général; en masse. — *and retail,* gros et détail. *By* —, en gros; (*fig.*) en masse. —**dealer,** *s.* marchand (*m.*, e, *f.*) en gros. —**price,** *s.* prix de gros, *m.* —**trade,** *s.* commerce de gros, *m.*
Wholesome, *adj.* sain; salubre; salutaire; moral, pur. —**ly,** *adv.* sainement; salutairement. —**ness,** *s.* sanité, *f.*; salubrité, *f.*; utilité, *f.*; moralité, pureté, *f.*
Wholly, *adv.* entièrement, complètement, tout à fait. — *or partly,* en totalité ou en partie
Whom, *pron. rel.* que; (*after a prep., pers.*) qui; (*after a prep., things or pers.*) lequel, *m.*, laquelle, *f.*, lesquels, *m.pl.*, lesquelles, *f.pl.*; (*what person*) qui. *Of* or *from* —, de qui, dont
Whomsoever. *V.* **Whoever**
Whoop, *v.n.a.* *V.* **Hoot;** — *s.* huée, *f.*; cri, *m.*; (*of war*) cri, *m.*; (*bird*) huppe, *f.* — *and hide,* cache-cache, *m.* [coqueluche, *f.*
Whooping, *s.* *V.* **Hooting.** —**cough,** *s.*
Whop. *V.* **Whap**
Whore, *s.* prostituée, catin, putain, *f.*
Whorl, *s.* (*bot.*) verticille, *m.*
Whortleberry, *s.* airelle, *f.*
Whose, *pron. rel.* (*followed by a noun nom. of the verb*) dont le (la, *f.*, les, *pl.*); (*followed by a noun obj. of the verb*) dont ... le (la, les); (*when there is a prep. between 'whose' and the noun to which it relates*) le (la, les) ... duquel *or* de laquelle *or* desquels *or* desquelles; (*of* or *from what person*) de qui; (*to what person*) à qui. *The pupil — book is on the table,* l'élève dont le livre est sur la table. *The pupil — book I see on the table,* l'élève dont je vois le livre sur la table. *The man to — probity I trust,* l'homme à la probité duquel je me fie. — *son are you?* (*of what person are you the son*) de qui êtes-vous fils? — *drawing is this?* (*from what person,* &c., *who is the author of it?*) de qui est ce dessin? — *hat is this?* (*to what person does this hat belong*) à qui est ce chapeau?

Whosesoever, *pron.* de qui que ce soit
Whosoever. *V.* **Whoever**
Why, *adv.* pourquoi; (*for which*) pour lequel *or* laquelle; (*how*) comment; — *conj. int.* mais; dame; eh bien; comment; c'est que; rien moins que, ni plus ni moins que. — *not?* pourquoi pas? pourquoi non?
Whydaw. — **bird, -finch,** *s.* veuve, *f.*
Wich-elm, *s. V.* **Wych-elm**
Wick, *s.* mèche, *f.* — **holder,** *s.* porte-mèche, lamperon, *m.* —**less,** *adj.* sans mèche
Wicked, *adj.* méchant; pervers; criminel; (*jest.*) méchant; — *s.pl.* méchants, *m.pl.*
Wickedly, *adv.* méchamment; mal
Wickedness, *s.* méchanceté, *f.*; perversité, *f.*
Wicker, *s.* osier, *m.*; — *adj.* d'osier, en osier; clissé; — *v.a.* clisser
Wicket, *s.* guichet, *m.*; (*at cricket*) wicket, guichet, *m.*, barres, *f.pl.* — **work,** *s.* osier, [*m.*; clayonnage, *m.*
Wicky, *adj.* mécheux
Wide, *adj.* large; vaste; grand; étendu; immense; (*distant*) éloigné, loin; — *adv.* loin, au loin; (*fig.*) largement; (*quite*) tout à fait; (*of doors, windows,* &c.) tout grand (toute grande, *f.*, tout grands, *m.pl.*, toutes grandes, *f.pl.*). — *of the mark,* loin du but; loin de la vérité. *Ten yards* —, dix mètres de large, large de dix mètres. *Too — apart,* (*spaced out*) trop espacé. *To open* —, ouvrir tout à fait *or* tout grand; (*o.'s eyes*) écarquiller. — **awake,** *adj.* bien *or* tout éveillé; sur ses gardes; *s.* (*hat*) chapeau marin, feutre (*or* chapeau de feutre) à larges bords, *m.* — **open,** *adj.* tout grand ouvert (toute grande ouverte, *f.*, tout grands ouverts, *m.pl.*, toutes grandes ouvertes, *f.pl.*). — **spread,** *adj.* répandu, général; qui s'étend au loin
Widely, *adv.* (*far*) loin, au loin; (*fig.*) grandement, largement; très, fort, bien, beaucoup
Widen, *v.a.* élargir; (*extend*) étendre, agrandir; — *v.n.* s'élargir; s'étendre, s'agrandir
Wideness. *V.* **Width**
Widening, *s.* élargissement, *m.*; agrandissement, *m.*
Widgeon, *s.* sarcelle, *f.*
Widow, *s.* veuve, *f.*; — *v.a.* rendre veuve *or* veuf; (*deprive*) priver (de); (*survive*) survivre à. — **bird,** *s.* veuve, *f.* — **hunter,** *s.* coureur de veuves, *m.* — **wail,** *s.* camélée, *f.*
Widowed, *adj.* veuf
Widower, *s.* veuf, *m.*
Widowhood, *s.* veuvage, *m.*
Width, *s.* largeur, *f.*; (*extent*) étendue, grandeur, *f.* *To be two yards in* —, avoir deux mètres de largeur *or* de large
Wield, *v.a.* manier; (*carry*) porter
Wieldy, *adj.* maniable
Wife, *s.* femme, *f.*; femme mariée, *f.*; (*law, admin.*) épouse, *f.*; (*jest.*) commère, *f.* *The merry wives of Windsor,* les joyeuses commères de Windsor. *To get a* —, se marier. —**hood,** *s.* état d'une femme mariée, *m.* —**less,** *adj.* sans femme, sans épouse. —**like, -ly,** *adj.* de femme, d'épouse, conjugal. — **ridden,** *adj. V.* **Hen-pecked**
Wifey, Wify, *s.* (ma) petite femme, *f.*
Wig, *s.* perruque, *f.*; — *v.a.* (*fam.*) donner une perruque *or* un savon à, laver la tête à. — **block,** *s.* tête à perruque, *f.* — **maker,** *s.* perruquier, *m.*, -ière, *f.*
Wigeon. *V.* **Widgeon**
Wigging, *s.* (*fam.*) perruque, *f.*, savon, *m.*
Wight, *s.* individu, être, personnage, *m.* *The luckless* —, le malheureux; l'infortuné
Wigwam, *s.* wigwam, *m.*
Wild, *adj.* sauvage; (*of places*) désert, inculte; agreste; (*pers.*) farouche, sauvage; violent; tumultueux, orageux; déréglé, dissolu; extravagant, fou; incohérent; fantasque; (*of the look*) effaré, égaré, hagard; (*of children*) turbulent, dissipé; (*of animals*) sauvage; farouche; (*of plants, fruits*) sauvage; (*of winds*) impétueux; — *s.* désert, *m.*; solitude, *f.* *To grow* —, (*of plants*) être sauvage. *To run* —, errer; (*of children*) vagabonder. *It drives me* —, (*fam.*) j'en perds la tête. *He is — about it,* il est hors de lui. — **beast,** *s.* bête féroce, bête fauve, *f.* — **boar,** — **sow,** *s. V.* **Boar** *and* **Sow.** — **cat, duck, goose,** &c., chat sauvage, canard sauvage, oie sauvage, &c. — **chase,** *s.* folle entreprise, *f.* — **fire,** *s. See below*
Wilderness, *s.* désert, *m.*; solitude, *f.*; multitude, infinité, *f.*
Wildfire, *s.* feu grégeois, *m.*; (*med.*) dartre, *f.*; (*vet.*) érysipèle, *m.* *Like* —, rapidement, comme l'éclair, comme la foudre; en un clin d'œil
Wilding, *s.* sauvageon, *m.*
Wildly, *adv.* à l'état sauvage; sans culture; d'une manière sauvage; d'une manière déréglée; (*heedlessly*) étourdiment; (*of talking*) follement, à tort et à travers; (*of acting*) comme un fou, comme une folle; (*staring*) d'un air effaré
Wildness, *s.* nature sauvage, *f.*, état sauvage, *m.*, sauvagerie, *f.*; nature agreste, *f.*; férocité, brutalité, *f.*; impétuosité, fureur, *f.*; violence, *f.*; désordre, dérèglement, *m.*; (*oddness*) bizarrerie, *f.*; extravagance, folie, *f.*; (*of the look*) égarement, *m.*; (*of children*) turbulence, dissipation, *f.*
Wile, *s.* ruse, *f.*, artifice, *m.*
Wilful, *adj.* (*pers.*) volontaire, entêté, têtu, obstiné; (*of horses*) rétif; (*premeditated*) prémédité, avec préméditation, fait à dessein, volontaire. —**ly,** *adv.* obstinément; (*purposely*) à dessein, de propos délibéré, volontairement; (*law*) avec préméditation. —**ness,** *s.* entêtement, *m.*, obstination, *f.*
Wilily, *adv.* astucieusement
Wiliness, *s.* ruse, astuce, *f.*
Will, *v.a.* vouloir; ordonner, commander; (*bequeath*) léguer; — *v.n. auxil.* vouloir. — *have, won't have, V.* **Have.** (*As a sign of the future of another verb, it is not expressed separately in French, except in the sense of 'immediately'*) *I — go,* je veux aller; (*as a sign of the future*) j'irai, (*immediately*) je vais aller. *Whether he — or no, — or nill,* bon gré mal gré, de gré ou de force. *Do what you* —, quoi que vous fassiez, vous avez beau faire. *Say what you* —, quoi que vous disiez, vous avez beau dire. — **away,** *v.a.* ôter par testament
Will, *s.* volonté, *f.*; vouloir, *m.*; (*choice*) gré, bon plaisir, *m.*; (*desire*) désir, *m.*; (*power*) pouvoir, *m.*; disposition, *f.*; (*divine determination*) décret, *m.*; (*testament*) testament, *m.* — *and pleasure,* volonté, *f.*, bon plaisir, *m.* *At* —, à volonté; à souhait, à son gré; à discrétion. *At o.'s — and pleasure,* à volonté, selon son bon plaisir. *Free* —, *V.* **Free.** *Good* —, bonne volonté, *f.*, bon vouloir, *m.*; bienveillance, *f.*; sympathie, *f.*; (*custom*) clientèle, *f.*; achalandage, *m.* *Ill* —, mauvaise volonté, *f.*, mauvais vouloir, *m.*; malveillance, *f.*; rancune, *f.* *Last — and testament,* dernières volontés, *f.pl.* *With a* —, volontaire; de bon cœur, avec plaisir. *To bear ill* —, vouloir du mal (à), en vouloir (à), garder rancune (à), avoir de la haine (contre). *To have o.'s* —, faire sa volonté, en faire à sa volonté; avoir ce que l'on veut. *What is your* —? que désirez-vous? *Where there is a —, there is a way,* qui veut la fin veut les moyens. — **o' the wisp,** *s.* feu follet, *m.*
Willey. *V.* **Willy**
William, *s.* (*pear*) bon-chrétien, *m.*
Willing, *adj.* de bonne volonté, bien disposé; disposé (à); prêt (à); désireux (de); spontané; volontaire; qui consent, consentant; (*adverb.*) de bon cœur, volontiers. — *or unwilling, — or not,* bon gré mal gré, de gré ou de force. *Able and* —, qui peut et qui veut. *To be able and* —, pouvoir et vouloir. *To be* —, être disposé *or* &c.; vouloir bien; consentir (à). *To be quite* or *most — to,* être tout disposé à, ne demander pas mieux que de. *God* —, Dieu aidant, s'il plaît à Dieu

Willingly, *adv.* volontiers, de bon cœur, volontairement. — *or unwillingly,* bon gré mal gré, de gré ou de force
Willingness, *s.* bonne volonté, *f.*, bon vouloir, *m.* ; disposition, inclination, *f.*, penchant, *m.* ; empressement, *m.*, promptitude, *f.*
Willow, *s.* (*bot.*) saule, *m.*; (*machine*) *V.* **Willy.** — **bed, -ground, -grove, -plantation, -plot,** *s.* saulaie, saussaie, *f.* — **herb,** *s.* herbe de Saint-Antoine, *f.* — **tree,** *s.* saule, *m.*
Willowed, Willowy, *adj.* planté *or* couvert de saules [cheuse, *f.*; — *v.a.* louveter
Willy, *s.* (*machine*) diable, loup, *m.* ; effilo-
Willying, *s.* louvetage, *m.*
Wilton, — carpet, -pile, *s.* moquette, *f.*
Wily, *adj.* rusé, astucieux
Wimble, *s.* vilebrequin, *m.*
Wimple, *s.* guimpe, *f.*, voile, *m.*
Win, *v.a.n.* **(— over)** gagner; (*procure*) acquérir; (*a victory, a prize*) remporter. — **back,** regagner; se racquitter, se rattraper [gimber
Wince, *v.n.* reculer; sourciller; (*kick*) ruer, re-
Wincey, *s.* tartanelle, *f.* [moulinet, *m.*
Winch, *s.* manivelle, *f.* ; treuil, *m.* ; (*fish.*)
Wind, *s.* vent, *m.* ; (*breath*) haleine, respiration, *f.*, souffle, *m.*; (*trifle*) fumée, *f.*; (*med.*) vent, *m.*, (*on the stomach*) flatuosité, *f.* *High* —, grand vent, *m.* *Breath of* —, souffle de vent, *m.* *Between — and water,* à fleur d'eau. *To break* —, lâcher un vent. *To get* or *take* —, s'éventer, s'ébruiter. *To get — of,* avoir vent de, éventer. *To take* or *have the — of,* prendre le dessus sur, s'emparer de. *To raise the* —, se procurer de l'argent, faire ressource, trouver moyen de vivre. *It is an ill — that blows nobody good,* à quelque chose malheur est bon. — **bag,** *s.* ballon, *m.*, vessie, *f.*; (*vain person*) ballon rempli de vent, *m.*; (*lackbrain*) tête vide, *f.* — **blight,** *s.* ventaison, *f.* — **bound,** *adj.* retenu par les vents. — **broken,** *adj.* poussif. — **chest,** *s.* (*of an organ*) porte-vent, *m.* — **dial,** *s.* anémoscope, *m.* — **egg,** *s.* œuf clair, *m.* —**fall,** *s.* fruit abattu par le vent, *m.*; (*fig.*) aubaine, bonne aubaine, bonne fortune, *f.* — **fallen,** *adj.* abattu par le vent. — **flower,** *s.* anémone, *f.* — **gall,** *s.* (*vet.*) molette, *f.* — **gauge,** *s.* anémomètre, *m.* — **hover,** *s. V.* **Kestrel.** — **instrument,** *s.* instrument à vent, *m.* —**lass,** *s. See below.* —**mill,** *s.* moulin à vent, *m.* — **pipe,** *s.* trachée-artère, *f.*; (*fam.*) gosier, sifflet, *m.* — **rose,** *s.* rose des vents, *f.* — **sail,** *s.* (*nav.*) manche à vent, *f.* — **tight,** *adj.* étanche, imperméable à l'air *or* au vent. —**ward,** *s.* côté du vent, *m.*; *adj. adv.* au vent. —*ward Islands,* Iles du Vent, *f.pl.* *To the —ward of,* au vent de
Wind, *v.a.n.* tourner; rouler; (*silk,* &c.) dévider; (*hoist*) guinder, élever; (*wrap up*) envelopper, entortiller; (*introduce*) insinuer; (*change*) changer; (*a horse*) essouffler; (*hunt.*) éventer, halener; (*a horn,* &c.) sonner de, donner de; (*twist*) s'entortiller; (*meander*) serpenter, faire des détours. — **off,** dérouler; (*silk,* &c.) dévider. — **out,** tirer (de). — **up,** rouler, entortiller; (*a watch,* &c.) monter, remonter; (*hoist up*) guinder, élever; (*fig.*) élever; préparer; arranger; régler, conclure; (*com.*) liquider; *s.* dénoûment, *m.*; (*com.*) liquida- [tion, *f.*
Windage, *s.* vent, *m.*
Winded, *adj.* essoufflé; qui a l'haleine ..., à l'haleine ... *Long-* —, qui a l'haleine longue, à longue haleine; (*things*) interminable; (*of speeches*) à perte d'haleine. *Short-* —, qui a l'haleine courte, à courte haleine
Winder, *s.* (*pers.*) dévideur, *m.*, -euse, *f.*; (*instr.*) dévidoir, *m.*; (*bot.*) plante grimpante, *f.*
Windiness, *s.* temps venteux, *m.*; nature venteuse, *f.*; (*puffiness*) enflure, *f.*; (*med.*) flatulence, *f.*
Winding, *adj.* sinueux; tortueux; qui serpente; tournant; (*of staircases*) tournant, en limaçon, à vis, en hélice; — *s.* sinuosité, *f.*; (*of roads*) détour, *m.*; lacet, *m.* — **engine, -machine,** *s.* machine de tour, *f.*, baritel, *m.* — **off,** *s.* dévidage, *m.* — **sheet,** *s.* suaire, linceul, *m.* — **up,** *s.* liquidation, *f.* [tant
Windingly, *adv.* tortueusement, en serpen-
Windlass, *s.* cabestan, treuil, *m.*; guindeau, *m.*
Window, *s.* fenêtre, croisée, *f.*; (*of carriages*) glace, *f.*; (*of shops*) glace, vitrine, *f.*, (*show*) étalage, *m.*, montre, *f.*; (*of churches*) verrière, *f.*, vitrail, *m.*, croisée, fenêtre, *f.*; (*opening*) ouverture, *f.*; (*of heaven*) cataracte (du ciel), *f.*; — *v.a.* garnir de fenêtres. *Glass —s, — s,* vitres, *f.pl.*, carreaux, *m.pl.*, vitrage, *m.*; (*of churches*) vitraux, *m.pl.* *In the* —, en étalage, en montre. *Out of the* —, par la fenêtre; (*of a carriage*) par la portière. *To break the —s,* casser les carreaux *or* les vitres. *To open the* —, ouvrir la fenêtre; (*of a carriage*) baisser la glace. *To shut the* —, fermer la fenêtre; (*of a carriage*) lever la glace. — **blind,** *s. V.* **Blind.** — **curtain,** *s.* rideau de fenêtre, *m.* — **dresser,** *s.* étalagiste, *m.f.* — **duty,** *s. V.* — **tax.** — **frame,** *s.* châssis de fenêtre, *m.* — **glass,** *s.* verre à vitres, *m.* —**less,** *adj.* sans fenêtre, sans fenêtres. — **pad,** *s.* matelas *or* paillasson de fenêtre, *m.* — **pane,** *s.* carreau de vitre, *m.* — **sash,** châssis de fenêtre, *m.* — **seat,** *s. V.* **Seat.** — **shutter,** *s.* volet, contrevent, *m.* — **sill,** *s. V.* **Sill.** — **strap,** *s.* (*of carriages*) bricole, *f.* — **tax,** *s.* impôt des fenêtres, *m.*
Windy, *adj.* venteux, de *or* du vent; (*next the wind*) du vent; (*empty*) vain, vide; (*airy*) aérien. *To be* —, (*of eatables*) être venteux; (*of weather*) faire du vent
Wine, *s.* vin, *m.*; (*fig.*) ivresse, *f.*; — *adj.* de *or* du vin; (*for* —) à vin. *Heavy* —, gros vin. *Light* —, petit vin. — *and water,* eau rougie, *f.*; (*at school*) abondance, *f.* *In* —, (*cook.*) au vin. — **bag,** *s.* outre à vin, *f.* — **bibber,** *s.* buveur, *m.*, -euse, *f.*, biberon, *m.*, -ne, *f.*, sac à vin, *m.* — **bibbing,** *s.* (la) boisson, *f.* — **bin,** *s.* porte-bouteilles, *m.*; cave à vin, *f.* — **bottle,** *s.* bouteille à vin, *f.* (*Bottle of* —, bouteille de vin, *f.*) — **broker,** *s.* courtier en vins, *m.* — **cask,** *s.* fût, *m.* — **cellar,** *s.* cave (à vin), *f.* — **coloured,** *adj.* couleur de vin, vineux. — **cooler,** *s.* rafraîchissoir à vin, *m.*; (*with ice*) seau à frapper, *m.* — **cooper,** *s.* tonnelier, *m.* — **country,** *s.* pays vinicole, *m.* — **dealer, — and spirit dealer,** *s.* marchand de vin, *m.* — **drinking,** *s.* usage du vin, *m.*; boisson, *f.* — **glass,** *s.* verre à vin, *m.* (*Glass of* —, verre de vin, *m.*) — **grower,** *s.* propriétaire de vignobles, *m.* — **growing,** *s.* viniculture, *f.*; *adj.* vinicole. — **harvest,** *s.* récolte de vin, vinée, *f.* — **like,** *adj.* vineux. — **list,** *s.* carte des vins, *f.* — **making,** *s.* fabrication du vin, vinification, *f.* — **market,** *s.* halle aux vins, *f.* — **measure,** *s.* mesure pour les vins *or* pour les liquides, *f.* — **merchant,** *s.* négociant en vins, *m.* — **office,** *s.* magasin de vins, *m.* — **porter,** *s.* encaveur, *m.* — **press,** *s.* pressoir, *m.* — **producing,** *adj.* vinicole. — **sauce,** *s.* sauce au vin, *f.* — **shades,** *s.pl. V.* — **vaults.** — **shop,** *s.* boutique de marchand de vin, *f.*, débit de vin, *m.*; (*drinking shop*) cabaret, *m.* *At the — shop,* chez le marchand de vin; au cabaret. — **shop-keeper,** *s.* marchand de vin, *m.*; cabaretier, *m.* — **stone,** *s.* tartre (du vin), *m.* — **store,** *s.* magasin de vins, *m.*; cellier, *m.*; chai, *m.*; cave, *f.* — **strainer,** *s.* passe-vin, *m.* — **taster,** *s.* dégustateur de vins, gourmet, *m.*; (*cup*) tasse à déguster, *f.*, tâte-vin, *m.* — **vaults,** *s.pl.* caveaux à vin, caveaux, *m.pl.*; cabaret, *m.*
Wing, *s.* aile, *f.*; (*fig. for 'flight'*) vol, *m.*; essor, *m.*; (*theat.*) coulisse, *f.*; (*of ploughs*) versoir, *m.*; — *v.a.* donner des ailes à; élever; (*carry*) porter *or* transporter sur ses ailes; (*traverse*) franchir; (*hit*) atteindre *or* blesser à

l'aile. *On the* —, au vol; volant. *To be on the* —, voler. *To take* —, *to* — *o.'s flight*, s'envoler, prendre son vol; prendre l'essor. — **case,** *s.* élytre, *m.* — **feather,** *s.* plume de l'aile, *f.* — **footed,** *adj.* aux pieds ailés, léger. —**less,** *adj.* sans ailes. —**let,** *s.* ailette, *f.* — **rib,** *s.* (*of beef*) côte d'aloyau, *f.* — **shell,** *s.* pinne marine, *f.*; strombe, *m.*; (*of insects*) élytre, *m.* — **stroke,** *s.* coup d'aile, *m.*

Winged, *adj.* ailé; (*in compounds*) aux ailes . . .; (*flying*) volant; (*swift*) rapide; (*wounded*) blessé à l'aile; (*of furniture*) à plusieurs portes. — *game*, gibier à plumes, *m.*

Wink, *v.n.* cligner l'œil, clignoter; faire signe de l'œil (à), cligner de l'œil; (*connive*) fermer les yeux (sur); (*of light*) vaciller; — *v.a.* cligner; — *s.* clignement d'œil, clignement, clignotement, clin d'œil, *m.*; signe de l'œil, *m.*; œillade, *f.* *To give a* —, faire signe de l'œil. *To have forty* —*s*, faire une sieste. *Not to sleep a* —, ne pas fermer l'œil. *To* — **at,** regarder du coin de l'œil, faire signe de l'œil à, guigner; (*fig.*) permettre; fermer les yeux sur

Winker, *s.* (*of harness*) œillère, *f.*

Winking, *adj.* qui cligne l'œil, clignotant; (*of light*) vacillant, tremblant; — *s.* clignement, clignotement, *m.*; signes de l'œil, *m.pl.*; (*of light*) vacillation, *f.*, tremblement, *m.*; connivence, *f.*

Winkingly, *adv.* en clignant les yeux, en clignotant; (*fig.*) par connivence

Winkle. *V.* **Periwinkle**

Winner, *s.* gagnant, *m.*, e, *f.*; (*at races*) vainqueur, *m.*

Winning, *adj.* gagnant; (*of races*) vainqueur; (*attracting*) attrayant, séduisant, engageant; — *s.* gain, *m.* — **post,** *s.* poteau d'arrivée, but, *m.*

Winnings, *s.pl.* gain, *m.*

Winnow, *v.a.* vanner; éventer; agiter; examiner, éplucher; séparer, trier; (*examine*) éplucher

Winnower, *s.* vanneur, *m.*, -euse, *f.*

Winnowing, *s.* vannage, *m.*; (*fig.*) examen, *m.*; triage, *m.*, épuration, *f.* — **basket,** *s.* van, *m.* — **machine,** *s.* tarare, *m.*

Winsey, *s.* tartanelle, *f.*

Winsome, *adj.* joyeux, gai, riant, agréable, séduisant, charmant. —**ly,** *adv.* joyeusement, gaiment, d'une manière séduisante, avec charme

Winter, *s.* hiver, *m.*; (*print.*) sommier, *m.*; — *adj.* d'hiver; hivernal, hiémal; — *v.n.* hiverner, passer *or* rester l'hiver; — *v.a.* (*feed*) nourrir pendant l'hiver; (*preserve*) conserver dans l'hiver. *In* —, en hiver. *In the* —, *in the* — *time*, dans l'hiver, en hiver. — **barley,** *s.* escourgeon, *m.* — **berry,** *s.* apalanche, *f.* — **cherry,** *s.* coquerelle, *f.*, coqueret, *m.* — **crop,** *s.* hivernage, *m.* — **fallow,** *s.* jachère d'hiver, *f.*; *v.a.* hiverner. — **fallowing,** *s.* hivernage, *m.* — **garden,** *s.* jardin d'hiver, *m.* — **green,** *s.* pirole, *f.*; gaulthérie du Canada, *f.*, palommier, *m.* — **harbour,** *s.* hivernage, *m.* — **pear,** *s.* poire d'hiver, *f.* — **quarters,** *s.pl.* quartiers d'hiver, *m.pl.* — **season,** *s.* saison d'hiver, *f.*; (*nav.*) hivernage, *m.*

Wintering, *s.* hivernage, *m.* — **place,** *s.* hivernage, *m.*

Winterly, Wintry, *adj.* d'hiver; hivernal, hiémal

Winy, *adj.* vineux, de vin

Wipe, *v.a.* essuyer; nettoyer; effacer; purifier; — *s.* essuyage, *m.*; nettoiement, nettoyage, *m.*; coup de torchon *or* d'éponge, *m.*; (*blow*) coup, *m.*, tape, *f.*; (*jeer*) lardon, coup de patte, *m.* *To* — *dry*, essuyer. — **away, off, out,** essuyer, enlever; effacer

Wiper, *s.* (*pers.*) essuyeur, *m.*, -euse, *f.*; (*cloth*) torchon, *m.*; (*jeer*) lardon, coup de patte, *m.*

Wiping, *s.* essuyage, *m.*; nettoiement, nettoyage, *m.*; oblitération, *f.*, oubli, *m.*

Wire, *s.* fil métallique, fil de métal, *m.*; fil (de . . .), *m.*; fil d'archal, *m.*; fil de fer, *m.*; (*of a cage*) barreau, *m.*; (*fig.*) télégraphe électrique, *m.*; — *v.a.* attacher avec un fil métallique, lier; (*grate*) grillager; (*rail*) griller; (*a cap or bonnet*) cannetiller; (*to telegraph*) télégraphier; — *v n.* (— **in**) s'insinuer, s'introduire. *To pull the* —*s*, (*fig.*) tenir les fils (*or* les cordons). — **blind,** *s.* abat-jour en toile métallique, store métallique, *m.* — **bridge,** *s.* pont de fil de fer, *m.* — **cloth,** toile métallique, *f.* — **draw,** *v.a.* tréfiler, tirer en fils, étirer; (*lengthen*) tirer en longueur, allonger, étendre; (*in style*) alambiquer. — **drawer,** *s.* tréfileur, tireur, *m.* — **drawing,** *s.* tréfilerie, filerie, *f.* — **edge,** *s.* morfil, *m.* — **fencing,** *s.* grillage, *m.* — **gauge,** *s.* calibre, *m.* — **gauze,** *s.* gaze métallique, toile métallique, *f.*, tissu métallique, *m.* — **guard,** *s.* grillage, *m.*; (*for the fire*) garde-feu, *m.* — **heel,** *s.* (*vet.*) quarte, *f.*, soyon, *m.*, seime, *f.* — **lattice,** *s.* fer maillé, *m.* — **mark,** *s.* (*in paper*) vergeure, *f.* — **mill,** *s.* filerie, tréfilerie, *f.* — **netting,** *s.* fer maillé, *m.* — **rope,** *s.* cordage métallique, *m.* — **work,** *s.* grillage de fil de fer, grillage métallique, grillage, *m.* — **worker,** *s.* grillageur, *m.* — **works,** *s.pl.* tréfilerie, *f.* — **worm,** *s.* larve du taupin, *f.*

Wiry, *adj.* de fil métallique; (*pers.*) sec et nerveux; (*of the pulse*) vibrant, sec

Wisdom, *s.* sagesse, *f.* — **tooth,** *s.* dent de sagesse, *f.*

Wise, *adj.* sage; prudent; grave; (*well-informed, well-off*) avancé. — *man*, sage, *m.* *The seven* — *men of Greece*, les sept sages de la Grèce. *The* — *men of the East*, les mages. *To be quite as* — *as before*, (*none the better*) être tout aussi avancé qu'avant. *To be none* or *never the* —*r* (*for it*), n'en être pas plus avancé

Wise, *s.* manière, façon, sorte, guise, *f.* *In any* —, de quelque manière que ce soit. *In no* —, nullement, aucunement

Wiseacre, *s.* pédant, sot, imbécile, *m.*

Wisely, *adv.* sagement; prudemment

Wish, *v.a.n.* — **for,** désirer; vouloir; (*of abstract things only, and of future contingencies*) souhaiter. *To* — *for a pair of gloves*, désirer une paire de gants. *To* — *for happiness, riches*, &c., désirer *or* souhaiter le bonheur, les richesses, &c. *I* — *you a pleasant journey*, je vous souhaite un bon voyage. *I* — *to know that*, je désire savoir cela. *I* — *you to know that*, je désire que vous sachiez cela. *I* — *you knew that*, je voudrais que vous sussiez cela. *I would not* — *you to lose*, je ne voudrais pas que vous perdissiez. *I* — *you would tell him*, je voudrais que vous lui dissiez. *I* — *you had not said that*, je voudrais que vous n'eussiez pas dit cela. *I* — *I was asleep*, je voudrais être endormi. *I* — *I could be of use to you*, je voudrais pouvoir vous être utile. *To* — *one good morning, good evening* (or *night*), &c., souhaiter le bonjour *or* le bonsoir *or* &c. à quelqu'un, dire bonjour *or* bonsoir *or* &c. à quelqu'un. *To* — *well* or *harm to*, vouloir du bien *or* du mal à

Wish, *s.* désir, *m.*; (*about future contingencies*) souhait, *m.*; (*solemn*) vœu, *m.* *Good* —*es*, sympathies, *f.pl.* *O.'s best* —*es*, ses compliments; toutes ses sympathies. *At a* —, à souhait. *To have o.'s* —, avoir ce qu'on veut; faire ce qu'on veut. *The* — *is father to the thought*, on croit aisément ce qu'on désire. — **bone,** *s.* lunette, fourchette, *f.* —**ful,** *adj.* désireux (de); avide (de), impatient. —**fully,** *adv.* avidement, ardemment, passionnément. — **maiden,** *s.* walkyrie, valkyrie, *f.* — **wash,** *s.* lavasse, *f.*

Wisher, *s.* personne qui souhaite *or* qui désire, *f.*; (*fam.*) souhaiteur, *m.*, -euse, *f.*

Wishing-bone, *s.* *V.* **Wish-bone**

Wishy-washy, *s.* lavasse, *f.*; — *adj.* faible, clair

Wisp, *s.* bouchon, *m.*, poignée (de paille *or* &c.), *f.*; touffe, *f.*; — *v.a.* bouchonner. *V.* **Will,** *s.*

Wistaria, *s.* wistérie, *f.*

Wistful, *adj.* attentif; pensif; inquiet, anxieux; significatif; ardent, désireux, d'envie; de regret

Wistfully, *adv.* attentivement; fixement; d'un air pensif; avec anxiété; ardemment, avec désir, d'un œil (*or* d'un air) d'envie; avec regret [exemple

Wit. *To* —, *adv.* savoir, c'est-à-dire; par

Wit, *s.* esprit, *m.*; (*pers.*) bel esprit, *m.*, homme d'esprit, *m.*, femme d'esprit, *f.*; —**s,** *pl.* intelligence, *f.*, esprit, jugement, *m.*, raison, *f.*, sens, bon sens, *m.*; (*pers.*) beaux esprits, *m.pl.* —*s jump together*, les beaux esprits se rencontrent. *To be at o.'s —s' end*, être au bout de son rouleau (*or* de son latin), être à bout d'expédients, ne savoir plus quoi faire. *To be out of o.'s —s, to have lost o.'s —s*, avoir perdu l'esprit *or* la raison *or* la tête. *To drive anyone out of his —s*, faire perdre la tête à quelqu'un. *To have o.'s —s about one*, savoir ce qu'on fait, avoir toute sa présence d'esprit, ne pas perdre la carte. *To live by o.'s —s*, vivre d'industrie

Witch, *s.* sorcière, *f.*; — *v.a. V.* **Bewitch.** — **craft,** *s.* sorcellerie, *f.*; (*spell*) sortilége, sort, *m.* — **elm,** *s. V.* **Wych-elm.** — **meal,** *s.* lycopode, soufre végétal, *m.* [charme, *m.*

Witchery, *s.* sorcellerie, *f.*; fascination, *f.*,

With, *prep.* avec; (*by, through*) par, à l'aide de, au moyen de; à; (*of striking*) d'un coup de, à coups de; (*from, of*) de; (*to, at*) à; (*for*) pour; (*in*) en, dans; (*having*) à; (*on*) sur; (*at the house of*) chez; (*among*) chez, parmi; (*of interceding, taking refuge, &c., near*) auprès de; (*in the estimation or eyes of*) auprès de; devant; (*to the care &c. of*) aux soins de, à; entre les mains de; (*at the service of*) à; (*like*) comme; (*as, used after 'the same' ...*) que; (*against*) contre; (*in spite of*) malgré; (*after*) après; (*cook., done in, mixed with*) au, *m.*, à la, *f.*, aux, *pl.* — *it, them* (*things*), avec; en même temps. — *it on*, — *them on*, (*of clothes*) avec. — *his gloves* (*his boots*, &c.) *on*, avec ses gants (ses bottes, &c.). *A house* — (*having*) *two stories*, une maison à (*or* de) deux étages. *A waistcoat* — (*having*) *blue stripes*, un gilet à raies bleues. *The man* — (*having*) *the iron mask*, l'homme au masque de fer. [*In the sense of 'having,' and expressing a way or manner, it is not translated; as, To speak — o.'s hat on o.'s head, — o.'s hands in o.'s pockets*, parler le chapeau sur la tête, les mains dans les poches; *To sleep — o.'s eyes open*, dormir les yeux ouverts; *To be taken — arms in o.'s hands*, être pris les armes à la main; — *tears in his eyes*, les larmes aux yeux; &c.] — *this* or *that*, (*hereupon*) là-dessus, sur ce. *I shall be — you in one moment*, je serai (*or* je suis) à vous dans un moment [du reste

Withal, *adv.* aussi, en même temps, avec cela,

Withdraw, *v.a.* retirer (de); — *v.n.* se retirer

Withdrawal, *s.* (*taking away*) retrait, *m.*; (*going away*) retraite, *f.*

Withdrawing-room, *s.* boudoir, cabinet, *m.*

Withe, *s.* osier, *m.*; hart, *f.*, pleyon, *m.*; — *v.a.* lier, attacher

Wither, *v.n.* se dessécher, se flétrir, se faner; (*fig.*) dépérir, languir; — *v.a.* dessécher, flétrir, faner; — *s. V.* **Withers.** — **band,** *s.* branche d'arçon, *f.* — **wrung,** *adj.* égarrotté, blessé au garrot

Withering, *adj.* qui se flétrit; (*scorching*) brûlant; (*fig.*) foudroyant; écrasant

Withers, *s.pl.* garrot, *m.*

Withhold, *v.a.* retenir; détenir; arrêter; refuser (à); s'abstenir de; (*information*) cacher (à), tenir secret, garder pour soi, ne pas publier, ne pas communiquer (à), ne pas faire connaître (à)

Withholder, *s.* détenteur, *m.* [abstention, *f.*

Withholding, *s.* détention, *f.*; refus, *m.*;

Within, *prep.* dans; en; au dedans de; en deçà de; dans les limites de; (*amidst*) au milieu de; (*of distance*) à ... au plus; à; (*of reach, range, shot*) à; (*within reach of*) à portée de; (*of time*) dans l'espace de; d'ici à; dans un délai de; (*since*) depuis; (*below*) au-dessous de; (*close upon, all but*) à ... près. *To calculate — a week*, calculer à une semaine près. *He paid his debts — four pounds*, il paya ses dettes à cent francs près

Within, *adv.* en dedans, dedans; à l'intérieur; (*fig.*) intérieurement; (*at home*) à la maison, chez soi, y *From* —, de l'intérieur, du dedans. *Is Mr. B. —?* monsieur B. est-il à la maison? monsieur B. est-il chez lui? monsieur B. y est-il? *He is not* —, il est sorti

Without, *prep.* sans; (*of place*) en dehors de, hors de; — *adv.* en dehors, dehors; à l'extérieur; (*fig.*) extérieurement; — *conj.* sans que (*with the subj.*); (*unless*) à moins que (*with* ne *and the subj.*). — *it, them* (*things*), (*wanting*) sans. — ... *or* ..., sans ... ni ... *From* —, de l'extérieur, du dedans. — *my, thy*, &c. (*and a present part.*), sans que je, tu, &c. (*and the subj.*). — *my coming*, (*present or future*) sans que je vienne; (*past*) sans que je vinsse. — *I come*, à moins que je ne vienne

Withstand, *v.a.* résister à, s'opposer à, combattre; (*support*) soutenir, supporter; subir

Withstander, *s.* adversaire, antagoniste, *m.f.*, combattant, *m.*, e, *f.*

Withy, *s.* osier, *m.*; (*twig*) brin d'osier, *m.*; — *adj.* d'osier; flexible, souple. — **bed,** *s.* oseraie, *f.* [esprit, sottement

Witless, *adj.*, sans esprit, sot. —**ly,** *adv.* sans

Witling, *s.* petit esprit, *m.*; (*ironically*) bel esprit, *m.*

Witness, *s.* témoignage, *m.*; (*pers.*) témoin, *m.* — *for the crown*, témoin à charge (*V.* **Defence, Prisoner, & Prosecution**). *In — whereof*, en foi de quoi. *To bear — to*, rendre témoignage de, témoigner de, attester. *To call* or *take to* —, prendre à témoin. *To be called up as a* —, être appelé (*or* cité) comme témoin. — **box,** *s.* (*in England*) place du témoin, *f.*; (*in France*) banc des témoins, *m.* *In the — box*, à la place du témoin; sur le banc des témoins

Witness, *v.a.* (*see*) être témoin de, voir, assister à; voir faire; (*attest*) témoigner de, rendre témoignage de; (*subscribe*) signer à, certifier véritable; — *v.n.* témoigner; déposer

Witted, *adj.* à l'esprit ..., à esprit ... *Quick* or *sharp* —, à l'esprit vif. *Half* —, niais, sot

Witticism, *s.* bon mot, trait *or* jeu d'esprit, *m.*, pointe, *f.*; saillie, *f.*; plaisanterie, *f.*

Wittily, *adv.* spirituellement, avec esprit, [finement

Wittiness, *s.* esprit, *m.*; sel, *m.*

Wittingly, *adv.* sciemment; à dessein

Witty, *adj.* (*clever*) spirituel; (*funny*) plaisant

Witwall, *s.* épeiche, *f.*

Wizard, *s.* sorcier, magicien, *m.*; (*juggler*) escamoteur, prestidigitateur, *m.*; physicien, *m.*; — *adj.* magique, enchanteur

Wizardry, *s.* sorcellerie, magie, *f.*

Wizen, *adj. V.* **Weazen**

Woad, *s.* guède, *f.* *Dyer's* —, guède, *f.*

Woe, *s.* douleur, *f.*; chagrin, *m.*; malheur, *m.*, misère, *f.*; malédiction, *f.* — *to ...!* — *betide ...!* malheur à ...! — **begone,** *adj.* accablé de douleur. —**ful,** *adj.* triste; douloureux; malheureux. —**fully,** *adv.* tristement; douloureusement. —**fulness,** *s. V.* **Woe**

Wold, *s.* (*wood*) bois, *m.*, forêt, *f.*; (*open country*) plaine, campagne, *f.*; (*down*) dune, *f.*

Wolf, *s.* loup, *m.* *She* —, louve, *f.* *Young* —, —*'s cub*, louveteau, *m.* — **dog,** *s.* chien-loup, *m.* — **fish,** *s. V.* **Cat-fish.** — **hole,** *s.* trou-de-loup, *m.* — **hunt, -hunting,** *s.* chasse au loup, louveterie, *f.* — **hunter,** *s.* louvetier, *m.* —**'s-bane,** *s.* aconit, *m.* — **spider,** *s.* tarentule, *f.* [avide

Wolfish, *adj.* de loup; (*fig.*) de loup, rapace,

Wolverene, Wolverine, *s.* (*zool.*) glouton, *m.*

Woman, *s.* femme, *f.*; ...- —, (*dealer*) marchande de .... *f.* — *of pleasure*, viveuse, *f.*

— **hater,** *s.* ennemi des femmes *or* du sexe, misogyne, *m.* — **hood,** *s.* état (*or* âge) de femme, *m.* — **hunter,** *s.* coureur, *m.* — **killer,** *s.* (*fig.*) *V.* **Lady-killer.** — **kind,** *s.* les femmes, *f.pl.*, (*fam.*) le sexe, *m.*

Womanish, *adj.* efféminé, mou. —**ness,** *s.* efféminatiou, mollesse, *f.*

Womanize, *v.a.* efféminer, amollir

Womanliness, *s.* caractère (*m.*) *or* nature (*f.*) de la femme [en femme

Womanly, *adj.* de femme, féminin; — *adv.*

Womb, *s.* matrice, *f.*; (*fig.*) sein, *m.*, entrailles, *f.pl.*, flancs, *m.pl.*

Wombat, *s.* wombat, phascolome, *m.*

Wonder, *v.n.* s'étonner (' *at,*' de; ' *that,*' que); être surpris (de, que); (*doubt*) être curieux de savoir, se demander (' *whether,*' si); — *s.* étonnement, *m.*; admiration, *f.*; (*strange thing*) merveille, *f.*; miracle, *m.*; prodige, *m.* *The seven —s of the world,* les sept merveilles du monde. *The — is that ...,* ce qu'il y a d'étonnant, c'est que ... *The only — is that ...,* la seule chose dont on s'étonne (*or, ... ' to me' ...,* ... dont je m'étonne), c'est que ... *No —!* ce n'est pas étonnant! il ne faut point s'en étonner. —**er,** *s.* admirateur, *m.*, -trice, *f.* — **ful,** *adj.* étonnant, surprenant; merveilleux; inimaginable. *The — lamp,* la lampe merveilleuse, *f.* —**fully,** *adv.* étonnamment; merveilleusement, à merveille. —*fully well,* à merveille. —**fulness,** merveilleux, *m.* — **struck,** *adj.* frappé d'étonnement; émerveillé. — **worker,** *s.* faiseur (*m.*,-euse, *f.*) de prodiges. — **working,** *adj.* qui fait des prodiges

Wondering, *s.* étonnement, *m.*; — *adj.* frappé d'étonnement, dans l'étonnement, étonné, surpris; émerveillé. —**ly,** *adv.* avec étonnement

Wonderment, *s.* *V.* **Wonder**

Wondrous, -ly. *V.* **Wonderful, -ly**

Won't. *V.* **Will not**

Wont, *s.* coutume, habitude, *f.*

Wont, *adj.* *To be —,* *V.* **Use,** *v.n.*

Wonted, *adj.* accoutumé; habituel

Woo, *v.a.* faire la cour à, courtiser; supplier; solliciter, briguer

Wood, *s.* bois, *m.*; (*cask*) pièce, *f.*, fût, *m.*, cercles, *m.pl.*; — *adj.* (*of or from wood, wooden*) de bois; (*made of wood*) en bois; (*of the woods*) des bois. —*s and forests,* (*admin.*) eaux et forêts, *f.pl.* *In the —,* (*of wine,* &c.) en cercles, en fût. — **anemone,** *s.* anémone des bois, *f.* — **ashes,** *s.pl.* cendres de bois, *f.pl.* — **bine,** *s.* chèvrefeuille (des bois), *m.* — **bird,** *s.* oiseau des bois, *m.* — **borer,** *s.* (*insect*) perce-bois, *m.* — **bug,** *s.* punaise des bois, *f.* — **carver,** *s.* sculpteur sur bois, *m.* — **carving,** *s.* sculpture sur bois, *f.* — **charcoal,** *s.* charbon de bois, *m.* — **chat,** *s.* pie-grièche rousse, *f.* — **cock,** *s.* bécasse, *f.*, coq de bruyère, *m.* — **cut,** *s.* gravure sur bois, *f.*; vignette, *f.* — **cut engraver,** *s.* graveur sur bois, *m.* — **cutter,** *s.* bûcheron, *m.*; (*engraver*) graveur sur bois, *m.* — **engraver,** *s.* graveur sur bois, *m.* — **engraving,** *s.* gravure sur bois, *f.* — **fern,** *s.* aspidie, *f.* — **fire,** *s.* feu de bois, *m.* — **flower,** *s.* fleur des bois, *f.* — **fretter,** *s.* (*zool.*) artison, *m.*; vrillette, *f.*; psoque, *m.*; charpentière, *f.* — **hole, -house,** *s.* bûcher, *m.* — **land,** *s.* pays boisé, *m.*; bois, *m.*, forêt, *f.*; *adj.* de *or* des bois, sylvestre, sylvatique. — **lark,** *s.* alouette des bois, *f.* —**less,** *adj.* sans bois; déboisé. — **louse,** *s.* cloporte, *m.* —**man,** *s.* garde forestier, *m.*; (*hunter*) chasseur, *m.*; (*cutter*) bûcheron, *m.* — **merchant,** *s.* marchand de bois, *m.* — **nightshade,** *s.* douce-amère, *f.* — **nymph,** *s.* dryade, *f.* — **owl,** *s.* hulotte, *f.* — **pavement,** *s.* pavage en bois, *m.* — **pecker,** *s.* pic, pivert, *m.* — **pigeon,** *s.* pigeon ramier, ramier, *m.* — **pile, -stack,** *s.* pile de bois, *f.*, bûcher, *m.* — **ranger,** *s.* garde forestier, *m.* — **reeve,** *s.* garde-bois, *m.* — **ruff, -roof,** *s.* aspérule, *f.*, muguet des bois, *m.* — **shed,** *s.* bûcher, *m.* — **sorrel,** *s.* oseille des bois, surelle, *f.* — **spite,** *s.* pivert, *m.* — **steward,** *s.* garde-bois, *m.* — **tar,** *s.* goudron, *m.* — **turner,** *s.* tourneur en bois, *m.* — **vinegar,** *s.* vinaigre de bois, *m.* — **work,** *s.* boisage, *m.*; (*carpenter's work*) charpente, charpenterie, *f.*; (*joiner's work*) menuiserie, *f.* — **yard,** *s.* chantier de bois, *m.*

Wooded, *adj.* boisé

Wooden, *adj.* de bois, en bois

Woody, *adj.* boisé; ligneux. — *nightshade,* douce-amère, *f.*

Wooer, *s.* amoureux, *m.*; prétendant, *m.*

Woof, *s.* *V.* **Weft**

Wooing, *s.* cour, *f.*

Wool, *s.* laine, *f.*; (*hair*) cheveux crépus, *m.pl.*, laine, *f.*; — *adj.* de laine; (*pertaining to the wool-trade*) lainier. — **ball,** *s.* (*vet.*) égagropile, *m.*, gobe, *f.* — **broker,** *s.* courtier en laines, *m.* — **comb,** *s.* carde, *f.* — **comber,** *s.* cardeur de laine, *m.* — **combing,** *s.* cardage de laine, *m.* — **fell,** *s.* peau couverte de sa laine, *f.*, (*of lamb*) agnelin, *m.* — **gathering,** *s.* distraction, *f.*; niaiserie, *f.* — **grower,** *s.* éleveur de bêtes à laine, *m.* — **growing, -husbandry,** *s.* industrie lainière, *f.* — **pack,** *s.* ballot de laine, *m.* — **sack,** *s.* sac de laine, *m.*; siége du lord chancelier à la chambre des lords, *m.*; (*fig.*) dignité de lord chancelier, *f.* — **stapler,** *s.* négociant en laines, *m.* — **trade,** *s.* commerce de laines, *m.* — **tree,** *s.* ériodendron, *m.* — **work,** *s.* tapisserie, *f.* — **worker,** *s.* lainier, *m.*; bourgeteur, *m.*

Woolled, *adj.* à laine. *Long —,* à longue laine. *Short —,* à courte laine

Woollen, *adj.* de laine; (*pertaining to the wool-trade*) lainier; — *s.* étoffe (*f.*) *or* tissu (*m.*) de laine, lainage, *m.* — **cloth,** *s.* drap, *m.* — **draper,** *s.* drapier, marchand de draps, *m.* — **drapery, -goods, -stuffs,** *s.* tissus (*m.pl.*) *or* étoffes (*f.pl.*) de laine, lainages, *m.pl.*, draperie, *f.* — **manufactory, -manufacture,** *s.* draperie, *f.*

Woolliness, *s.* nature laineuse, *f.*

Woolly, *adj.* laineux; (*curly*) crépu, frisé. — **head,** *s.* nègre, *m.*, négresse, *f.*

Woorali, Woorara, Woorari, *s.* curare, *m.*

Wootz, *s.* wootz, *m.*

Word, *s.* (*as a mere sign printed, written, or even pronounced*) mot, *m.*; (*of utterance only*) parole, *f.*; (*form of expression*) terme, *m.*; (*assurance, promise, pledge*) parole, *f.*; (*Scripture*) parole, *f.*; (*theol.*) Verbe, *m.*; —**s,** *pl.* mots, &c.; (*talk*) propos, *m.*, *m.pl.*; (*dispute*) paroles, *f.pl.*, altercation, discussion, *f.*; — *v.a.* exprimer (—*ed thus,* ainsi conçu). *At this —,* à ce mot. *At* (or *with*) *these —s,* à ces mots, à ces paroles. *In a —,* en un mot. *In few —s,* en peu de mots. *In a few —s,* en quelques mots. *In other —s,* en autres termes, en d'autres termes. *In these —s,* en ces termes. *By — of mouth,* verbalement, de vive voix. *Big* or *hard* or *high —s,* gros mots, *m.pl.*, duretés, invectives, *f.pl.*; querelle, dispute, *f.* *Good — for,* mot en faveur de, mot de recommandation. *On* or *upon o.'s —,* (*of affirming*) sur sa parole; (*of believing or trusting*) sur parole. *One's — of honour,* sa parole d'honneur *Vain —s,* paroles en l'air. — *for —,* mot pour mot; mot à mot. *To be as good as o.'s —,* être de parole, tenir parole, faire comme on le dit, n'avoir qu'une parole. *To break* or *forfeit o.'s —,* manquer à sa parole, manquer de parole. *To bring —,* venir informer, venir dire, apporter la nouvelle. *To have a — with,* dire un mot à. *To have —s,* se disputer. *To keep o.'s —,* tenir parole *or* sa parole. *To leave —,* dire; recommander; prévenir. *To send —,* faire savoir, faire dire, envoyer dire. *To speak a —,* dire *or* prononcer un mot. *To speak the —,* (*decide*) trancher le mot. *To write* —, faire savoir, écrire. *Take my — for it,* croyez-m'en, croyez-moi bien. *I can take your* —, je puis vous croire sur parole. *I take you at your* —, je vous prends au mot. *I convict you by your own —s,* je vous prends par vos propres paroles. *He is a man of his* —, il est homme de parole. *He is a man of few —s,* c'est un homme de peu de paroles (*or* de peu de mots), il parle peu. *A — with you, sir,* un mot, monsieur. *A — to the wise is enough,* à bon entendeur demi-mot. — **book,** *s.* vocabulaire, *m.* — **catcher,** *s.* chicaneur, *m.*, -euse, *f.*, épilogueur, *m.*, -euse, *f.*, éplucheur (*m.*, -euse, *f.*) de mots. —**less,** *adj.* sans paroles, silencieux. — **painter,** *s.* narrateur (*m.*, -trice, *f.*) qui excelle dans la description, écrivain pittoresque, *m.* — **painting, -picture,** *s.* vive description, *f.*

Wordily, *adv.* verbeusement, prolixement, diffusément

Wordiness, *s.* verbosité, *f.*; prolixité, *f.*

Wording, *s.* expression, *f.*; style, *m.*; termes, *m.pl.*; (*of a problem*) énoncé, *m.* *With this* —, ainsi conçu; en ces termes

Wordy, *adj.* verbeux, prolixe, diffus

Work, *v.n.* travailler; (*play*) fonctionner, jouer; (*operate*) agir, opérer; (*move*) se mouvoir; s'agiter; aller; marcher; (*enter*) entrer, pénétrer; (*of liquors*) fermenter, travailler; (*of wood*) travailler; (*embroider*) broder; (*nav.*) fatiguer. *To — hard,* travailler dur *or* fort *or* ferme. *To — loose,* se desserrer; branler. *To — well,* travailler *or* &c. bien; (*succeed*) réussir. — **in,** entrer. — **off,** s'en aller; se détacher. — **out,** sortir; se détacher; (*of liquors*) fermenter. — **up,** monter, s'élever. — **upon,** agir sur; influencer; émouvoir, exciter, travailler

Work, *v.a.* travailler; (*employ*) mettre en œuvre; exercer; faire travailler; (*o.'s way*) se faire *or* s'ouvrir (un chemin, un passage); (*to make or do*) faire, opérer, accomplir; exécuter; produire; (*lead*) conduire (à), pousser (à); (*put*) mettre; (*set in motion*) manœuvrer; faire jouer; (*as a speculation*) exploiter; (*to shape*) ouvrer, travailler, façonner; (*to ornament*) façonner; (*embroider*) broder; (*print.*) tirer; (*nav.*) manœuvrer. *To — o.'s passage* (*at sea*), payer son passage en travaillant, s'engager (sur un navire) pour le prix de son passage. *To — to death,* tuer de travail; (*horses*) surmener, crever. *To be —ed by hand or by steam,* fonctionner à la main ou à la vapeur. — **down,** réduire. — **in,** faire entrer; insinuer. — **off,** user; (*finish*) achever; (*print.*) tirer. — **out,** faire; effectuer, accomplir; exécuter; achever, finir, venir à bout de; (*solve*) résoudre; (*exhaust*) épuiser; (*pay*) payer en travail. — **up,** travailler; employer; exciter; exalter; (*mix*) mélanger

Work, *s.* (*pains, labour, toil*) travail, *m.*; (*thing done or to be done, duty,* &c.) ouvrage, *m.*; travail, *m.*; besogne, *f.*; service, *m.*; tâche, *f.*; fonctions, *f.pl.*; (*as opposed to* '*materials*') main-d'œuvre, *f.*; façon, *f.*; (*literary or artistic production*) œuvre, *f.*, ouvrage, *m.*; (*written —, at school*) devoir, *m.*; devoirs, *m pl.*; (*business, affair, matter*) affaire, *f.*; (*effect*) effet, *m.*; action, opération, *f.*; activité, *f.*; (*embroidery*) broderie, *f.*; —**s,** *pl.* travaux, *m.pl.*, ouvrages, *m.pl.*, &c.; (*manufactory*) usine, fabrique, manufacture, *f.*; ateliers, *m.pl.*; (*wheels,* &c.) rouages, *m.pl.*, mécanisme, *m.*; (*of clocks, watches*) mouvement, *m.*; (*public works*) travaux publics, *m.pl.*; (*fort.*) travaux, ouvrages, *m.pl.*; (*of an author, collectively, and as opposed to* '*faith,*' &c., *and nav.*) œuvres, *f.pl.*; — *adj.* de travail; à ouvrage. *Byron's* (*complete*) —*s,* (les) œuvres (complètes) de Byron. *Byron's last — or —s,* le dernier ouvrage *or* les derniers ouvrages de Byron. — *of art,* œuvre (*f.*) *or* ouvrage (*m.*) d'art; objet d'art, *m.* — *of time,* œuvre (*f.*) *or* ouvrage (*m.*) du temps; (*requiring time*) ouvrage de longue haleine, *m.* *Hard* or *rough* —, travail pénible, rude travail, *m.*, rude besogne, *f.* *Hot* —, chaude *or* rude affaire, rude besogne, *f.* *Open* —, *Out* —, *s. V. Letter* **O.** *Out of* —, sans ouvrage. *Plain* —, *V.* **Plain.** *Piece of* —, ouvrage, travail, *m.*; (*in contempt*) belle besogne, *f.* *Public —s,* travaux publics, *m.pl.* *Warm* —, *V. Hot* — (*above*). *To be at* —, être au travail *or* à l'ouvrage *or* à l'œuvre; travailler; (*mach.*) fonctionner. *To be out of* —, être sans ouvrage, chômer. *To cut out — for,* tailler de la besogne à. *To go to* —, aller travailler; (*set to* —) se mettre au travail *or* à l'ouvrage *or* à l'œuvre; s'y mettre; (*proceed*) s'y prendre; (*deal*) y aller. *To make short — of it,* n'en faire ni une ni deux; avoir bientôt fait. *To set to* —, (*v.n.*) se mettre au travail *or* à l'ouvrage *or* à l'œuvre; s'y mettre; (*proceed*) s'y prendre; (*deal*) y aller; (*v.a.*) mettre au travail; (*mach.*) mettre en marche; faire aller. *To throw out of* —, priver d'ouvrage *or* de travail, faire chômer. — **bag,** *s.* sac à ouvrage, *m.* — **basket,** *s.* corbeille à ouvrage, *f.* — **bench,** *s.* établi, *m.* — **box,** *s.* boîte à ouvrage, *f.* — **day,** *s.* jour de travail, *m.*; (*not a Sunday*) jour ouvrable, jour ouvrier, *m.*; (*com. nav.*) jour de planche, *m.* — **fellow,** *s. V.* **Fellow-labourer.** — **house,** —**man,** —**manship,** &c., *See below.* — **people,** *s.* ouvriers, *m.pl.*, ouvrières, *f.pl.* — **room, shop,** *s.* atelier, *m.* — **table,** *s.* table à ouvrage, *f.* — **woman,** *s.* ouvrière, *f.* — **yard,** *s.* chantier, *m.*

Workable, *adj.* (*manageable*) maniable; praticable; (*as a speculation*) exploitable

Worker, *s.* travailleur, *m.*, -euse, *f.*; ouvrier, *m.*, -ière, *f.*; (*of*) auteur, *m.* (*V.* **Hard**)

Workhouse, *s.* asile des indigents, dépôt de mendicité, *m.*; (*fig.*) hôpital, *m.*

Working, *adj.* ouvrier; de travail; de travailleurs; — *s.* travail, *m.*; exercice, *m.*; opération, *f.*; exécution, *f.*; effet, *m.*; fermentation, *f.*; (*of sums*) calcul, *m.*; (*of manufactures,* &c.) exploitation, *f.*; (— *off, print.*) tirage, *m.*; (*of machines*) jeu, fonctionnement, *m.*; (*handling, managing, and nav.*) manœuvre, *f.* — **bee,** *s.* abeille ouvrière, *f.* — **class,** *s.*, — **classes,** *s.pl.* classe ouvrière, *f.* — **clothes,** *s.pl.* habits de travail, *m.pl.*; jaquette d'atelier, blouse, *f.* — **coat,** *s.* habit de travail, *m.*; jaquette d'atelier, *f.* — **day,** *s. V.* **Work-day.** — **drawing,** *s.* plan, *m.*; épure, *f.* — **dress,** *s. V.* — **Clothes.** — **man,** *s.* ouvrier, *m.*; travailleur, *m.* — *men's association,* association ouvrière, *f.* — **off,** *s.* (*print.*) tirage, *m.* — **order,** *s.* *To get into — order,* s'organiser. — **party,** *s. V.* **Party.** — **pay,** *s.* solde supplémentaire, *f.* — **plan,** *s.* plan, *m.*; épure, *f.* — **population,** *s.* population ouvrière, *f.* — **shaft,** *s.* puits de service, *m.* — **stock,** *s.* matériel d'exploitation, *m.* — **turner,** &c., ouvrier tourneur, &c., *m.* — **woman,** *s.* ouvrière, *f.*; travailleuse, *f.*

Workman, *s.* ouvrier, *m.*; artisan, *m.* *The — is known by his work,* à l'œuvre on connaît l'ouvrier (*or* l'artisan). — **like,** *adj.* d'ouvrier; (*clever*) habile; (*well done*) bien fait, fait artistement. —**ly,** *adv.* en ouvrier; (*cleverly*) habilement. —**ship,** *s.* travail, ouvrage, *m.*; (*as opposed to* '*materials*') main-d'œuvre, *f.*; façon, *f.*

World, *s.* monde, *m.*; multitude, infinité, *f.*; quantité énorme, masse, *f.* *A — of good,* un bien infini, un bien immense. *A — of money,* un argent fou. *A — of trouble. V.* **Trouble.** *The — to come, the next* —, *V.* **Next.** *The old* —, l'ancien monde. *The new* —, le nouveau monde. — *without end,* jusqu'à la fin des siècles. *For the —, for all the* —, pour tout au monde. *In the* —, dans le monde; du monde; au monde; possible. *In all the* —, dans le monde entier. *Nothing in the —*, rien au monde; rien du tout. *To begin the —*, entrer dans le monde, débuter dans le monde, commencer sa carrière. **—wide,** *adj.* universel, immense, répandu partout

Worldliness, *s.* mondanité, *f.*; frivolité, *f.*; prudence, *f.*; égoïsme, *m.*; amour du gain, *m.*

Worldling, *s.* mondain, *m.*, e, *f.*; homme positif, *m.*

Worldly, *adj.* du monde, de ce monde; mondain; frivole; intéressé; — *adv.* mondainement. **—minded,** *adj.* mondain. **—mindedness,** *s.* mondanité, *f.*

Worm, *s.* ver, *m.*; (*fig.*) remords, ver rongeur, *m.*; (*debased being*) ver de terre, vermisseau, *m.*; (*of fire-arms*) tire-bourre, *m.*; (*of screws*) filet taraudé, *m.*; (*spiral pipe, as of a still, &c.*) serpentin, *m.* **— bit,** *s.* mèche à vis, *f.* **— eaten,** *adj.* mangé aux vers; rongé *or* piqué des vers; véreux; vermoulu. **— eating,** *s.* vermoulure, *f.* **— fever,** *s.* fièvre rémittente, *f.* **— grass,** *s.* spigélie, *f.* **— holes,** *s.pl.* piqûres, *f.pl.*; vermoulure, *f.*; (*in the ground*) trou de ver, *m.* **— hole dust,** *s.* vermoulure, *f.* **—like,** *adj.* vermiculaire, vermiforme. **— medicine,** *s.* vermifuge, *m.* **— powder,** *s.* poudre vermifuge, *f.* **— screw,** *s.* tire-bourre, *m.* **— seed,** *s.* (*pharm.*) poudre vermifuge, *f.*; (*bot.*) santonine, *f.* **— shaped,** *adj.* vermiforme. **—wood,** *s.* absinthe, *f.*

Worm, *v.a.* miner sourdement; (*fire-arms*) débourrer; (*a dog*) éverrer; (*pierce*) tarauder; — *v.n.*, — *oneself, v.r.* se glisser, s'insinuer, s'introduire, se faufiler ('*into,*' dans); (*crawl along*) ramper. **— out,** *v.a.* traquer, dépister

Worming, *s.* (*piercing*) taraudage, *m.*

Wormy, *adj.* plein de vers; (*creeping*) rampant

Worrier, *s.* tourment, *m.*

Worry, *v.a.* tracasser, tourmenter, ennuyer; harasser; harceler; — *s.* tracas, tourment, ennui, *m.*; casse-tête, *m.*

Worse, *adj.* plus mauvais, pire; (*in temper or morals*) plus méchant; (*in health*) plus mal; — *adv.* plus mal, pis; (*less*) moins; — *s.* pis, *m.* — *and —*, de pis en pis, de mal en pis. *All the —*, d'autant plus mal (que); tant pis! *Far —, much —*, bien pire *or* pis, beaucoup *or* bien plus mauvais *or* plus mal. *For the —*, en mal, en pis. *So much the —*, tant pis. *To be —*, être plus mauvais *or* &c.; (*worse done*) être plus mal; (*less preferable, of inferior quality*) valoir moins; (*in worse health*) se porter plus mal, aller plus mal; (*not relieved*) être plus mal. *To be — than useless*, être plus qu'inutile. *To be the — for*, se trouver mal *or* plus mal de; se ressentir de, porter les traces de. (*V.* **Liquor, Drink,** *and* **Wear.**) *To be none the — for it*, ne pas s'en trouver plus mal. *To get* or *grow* or *become —*, devenir pire *or* plus mauvais *or* &c.; empirer; s'aggraver; (*in health*) aller plus mal. *To get the — of it, V.* **Worst.** *To make —*, rendre plus mauvais *or* &c.; empirer; aggraver; exaspérer. *To think the — of*, estimer moins, avoir plus mauvaise opinion de

Worship, *v.a.n.* adorer; respecter, honorer; — *s.* culte, *m.*, adoration, *f.*; (*service*) office (divin), *m.* *His —, your —*, (*title*) monsieur le maire *or* &c.; vous, monsieur. *Place of —*, lieu consacré au culte (divin), établissement du culte, *m.*, église, chapelle, *f.*, temple, *m.*, synagogue, mosquée, *f.*, &c.

Worshipful, *adj.* honorable. **—ly,** *adv.* respectueusement, avec respect

Worshipper, *s.* adorateur, *m.*, -trice, *f.*; fidèle, *m.f.*

Worshipping, *s.* adoration, *f.*

Worst, *adj.* pire, plus mauvais; (*in temper or morals*) plus méchant; (*substant., adv.*) pis, plus mal, *m.*; (*least*) moins; — *v.a.* vaincre, battre. *At the —*, au plus mal, au pis; au plus fort; au pis aller. *To be* or *get —ed*, être vaincu, être battu, avoir le dessous. *To do o.'s —*, faire du pis qu'on peut (*Do your —!* faites ce que vous voudrez). *To get* or *have the — of it*, avoir le dessous; succomber. *To put to the —*, mettre au pis, supposer le pis. *Let* (or *should*) *the — come to the —, If it comes to the —*, au pis aller

Worsted, *s.* laine filée, laine, *f.*; estame, *f.* — *stockings, socks*, bas (*m.pl.*), chaussettes (*f.pl.*) de laine. — *yarn*, fil de laine, *m.* — *stuff*, étoffe d'estame, *f.*

Wort, *s.* herbe, plante, *f.*; (*of malt*) moût, *m.*

Worth, *s.* valeur, *f.*, prix, *m.*; mérite, *m.*; (*after a sum of money*) pour ... *I have bought forty pounds — of wine*, j'ai acheté pour mille francs de vin. *Give me a penny — of it*, donnez-m'en pour dix centimes. *To have o.'s money's —*, en avoir pour son argent

Worth, *adj.* qui vaut (...); égal (à); (*said to be*) évalué à (...); (*deserving*) qui mérite (...); (*rich*) qui a (...), qui possède (...), riche de (...). *To be —*, valoir; (*— while*) mériter (de), valoir la peine (de); (*possess*) avoir, posséder, être riche de. — *reading*, qui mérite d'être lu, bon à lire. — *eating*, bon à manger. — *notice*, digne d'attention. *To be — reading* or *&c.*, mériter d'être lu *or* &c., valoir la peine d'être lu *or* &c. *To be — having*, être de quelque valeur; n'être pas à dédaigner. *Not to be — having, to be — nothing*, ne valoir rien. *To be well —*, valoir bien; mériter bien. *Not to be — much*, ne pas valoir grand' chose. *Not to be — much more than ...*, ne pas valoir beaucoup plus que ...

Worthily, *adv.* dignement; (*justly*) à juste titre

Worthiness, *s.* mérite, *m.*, valeur, *f.*

Worthless, *adj.* sans valeur, qui ne vaut rien; sans mérite; vil, bas; (*bad*) mauvais

Worthlessness, *s.* manque de valeur, *m.*; indignité, *f.*; bassesse, *f.*

Worthy, *adj.* digne (de); — *s.* personnage *or* homme illustre, grand homme, *m.*; célébrité, *f.*; sommité, *f.*; héros, *m.*; (*of the knights of old*) preux, *m.*; (*good fellow*) brave homme, *m.* — *man*, digne homme, *m.*; homme honorable, *m.*; (*fam.*) brave homme (*pl.*, braves gens), *m.*

Would, (*sign of the conditional*) *I — do it if ...*, je le ferais si ... (*When there is an ellipsis, supply it in French.*) — *you do it? Yes, I would*, le feriez-vous? oui, je le ferais. (*When 'would' is a form of the imperfect tense, use that tense in French.*) *Sometimes he — (used to) read*, quelquefois il lisait. (*When it is a distinct verb, 'would' must be rendered by* vouloir.) *I* (*thou, &c.*) *—*, (*would be willing* or *would like to*) je (tu, &c.) voudrais; (*was willing* or *determined to*) je (tu, &c.) voulais; je (tu, &c.) voulus; (*have been willing* or *determined to*) j'ai (tu as, &c.) voulu; (*after a verb, conj., &c., governing the subj. mood*) je voulusse (tu voulusses, &c.). *I told him, but he — not do it*, je lui ai dit, mais il n'a pas voulu le faire. — *you have*, voudriez-vous avoir; (*do you wish for*) voudriez-vous. *You — have it!* vous l'avez voulu! tu l'as voulu! *He — have it that ...*, il voulait absolument que ... (*For hints as to other constructions, V.* **Have.**) *I — rather, I — as soon, V.* **Rather** *and* **Soon.** — *to God! — to Heaven!* plût à Dieu! plût au ciel! *I thought I — speak to you about it*, j'ai eu l'idée de vous en parler, l'idée m'est venue de vous en parler, je me dis que je vous en parlerais; j'ai cru devoir vous en parler. *He thought he — try*, il eut l'idée d'essayer

Would-be, *adj.* soi-disant; prétendu; en espérance, en espoir, en expectative

Wound, *v.a.* blesser; — *s.* blessure, *f.*; (*sore*) plaie, *f.* **—less,** *adj.* intact, sans blessure. **— wort,** *s.* herbe vulnéraire, *f.*

Wounder, *s.* personne qui blesse, *f.*

Wounding, *s.* blessure, *f.*, blessures, *f.pl.*

Wourali. *V.* **Woorali**

Wove, *adj.* (*of paper*) vélin

Wrack, *s.* varech, *m.* **— grass,** *s. V.* **Grass.** [wrack

Wrangle, *v.n.* se disputer, se quereller; — *s.* dispute, querelle, *f.*
Wrangler, *s.* querelleur, *m.*, -euse, *f.*, chicaneur, *m.*, -euse, *f.*; (*univers.*) élève de la première série en mathématiques, *m.* *Senior* (, *second*, &c.) —, sorti le premier (, le second, &c.) en mathématiques
Wranglesome, *adj.* querelleur [querelleur
Wrangling, *s.* dispute, querelle, *f.*; — *adj.*
Wrap, *v.a.* envelopper (de); (*to wind*) entortiller, enrouler, rouler; — *s.* couverture, enveloppe, *f.* *To be —ped up in*, (*fig.*) être absorbé par; (*taken with*) être embéguiné *or* coiffé *or* engoué de
Wrapper, *s.* enveloppe, *f.*; (*of books*, &c.) couverture, *f.*; (*for manuscripts*, &c.) chemise, *f.*; (*for newspapers and book-post*) bande, *f.*; (*of tailors*, &c.) toilette, *f.*; (*outside leaf of a cigar*) robe, *f.*; (*for the legs*) couverture, *f.*; (*for the face*) cache-nez, *m.*; (*on a woman's head*) fanchon, marmotte, *f.*; (*of infants*) couche, *f.*; (*garment*) déshabillé, peignoir, *m.* *In a* —, (*book-post*, &c.) sous bande
Wrapping, *s.* couverture, *f.* — **paper,** *s.*
Wrasse, *s.* labre, *m.* [papier d'emballage, *m.*
Wrath, *s.* courroux, *m.*, colère, *f.*; indignation, *f.* —**ful,** *adj.* courroucé, irrité; indigné. —**fully,** *adv.* avec courroux, avec colère; avec indignation
Wreak, *v.a.* exécuter; infliger; assouvir, satisfaire. *To — o.'s vengeance on*, tirer vengeance sur, assouvir sa vengeance sur
Wreath, *s.* tresse, *f.*; (*garland*) guirlande, *f.*; feston, *m.*; (*of laurel*) couronne, *f.*; (*fig.*) ondulation, *f.*, tourbillon, *m.*
Wreath, Wreathe, *v.a.* (*twist*) entortiller (de); (*entwine*) entrelacer (de), tresser (de); (*with garlands*) guirlander (de), enguirlander (de); festonner (de); (*encircle*) couronner (de), ceindre (de); entourer (de); — *v.n.* s'entrelacer, s'enrouler [tonné; (*arch.*) tors
Wreathed, *adj.* entrelacé; enguirlandé; fes-
Wreathing, *s.* entrelacement, *m.*
Wreck, *s.* naufrage, *m.*; (*ship*) navire naufragé, *m.*; (*remains*) débris, *m.*, débris, *m.pl.*; (*shadow*) ombre, *f.*; (*ruin*) ruine, destruction, *f.*; (*law*) épaves, *f.pl.*; — *v.a.* jeter à la côte; (*fig.*) ruiner, détruire; — *v.n.* faire naufrage, échouer; (*fig.*) se perdre, se briser, être perdu. *To be —ed*, être naufragé; faire naufrage. *To go to* —, (*pers.*) courir à sa perte, se ruiner, se couler, s'enfoncer; (*things*) tomber en ruine; couler. —**ful,** *adj.* fécond en naufrages
Wreckage, *s.* naufrage, *m.*; (*remains*) débris,
Wrecked, *adj.* naufragé [*m.pl.*; épaves, *f.pl.*
Wrecker, *s.* (*plunderer*) vagant, *m.*
Wren, *s.* roitelet, *m.*
Wrench, *v.a.* arracher ('*from*': *things*, de; *pers.*, à); (*distort*) tordre; (*fig.*) forcer, fausser; — *s.* arrachement, *m.*; torsion, *f.*, tordage, *m.*; (*sprain*) *V.* **Sprain;** (*key*) clé anglaise, clé, *f.*; tourne-à-gauche, *m.*
Wrest, *v.a.* arracher ('*from*': *things*, de; (*pers.*, à); (*distort*) torturer, tordre, forcer, fausser; — *s.* torsion, *f.*, tordage, arrachement, *m.*; (*fig.*) violence, *f.* [combattre
Wrestle, *v.n.* lutter ('*with*' contre); (*contend*)
Wrestler, *s.* lutteur, *m.*; athlète, *m.*
Wrestling, *s.* lutte, *f.*; (*contention*) combat, *m.* —**match,** *s.* lutte, *f.*; assaut, *m.*
Wret. *V.* **Ret**
Wretch, *s.* malheureux, *m.*, -euse, *f.*, infortuné, *m.*, e, *f.*; (*in a bad sense*) misérable, *m.f.*; (*scoundrel*) scélérat, *m.*, e, *f.* *The unhappy* —, le malheureux, *m.*, la malheureuse, *f.*
Wretched, -ly. *V.* **Miserable, Miserably**
Wretchedness, *s.* misère, *f.*; (*misfortune*) malheur, *m.*, infortune, *f.*; (*paltriness*) pauvreté, *f.*; (*despicableness*) nature méprisable, *f.*; bassesse, *f.*
Wriggle, *v.n.* s'agiter, se démener, se tortiller, frétiller; (*into*) se faufiler (dans); (*out of*) se tirer (de); — *v.a.* tortiller; (*introduce*) introduire, entrer, fourrer; (*out of*) sortir (de); — *s.* *V.* **Wriggling**
Wriggling, *s.* tortillement, frétillement, *m.*
Wright, *s.* ouvrier, *m.*; constructeur (de ...), *m.*; (*jest.*) faiseur (de ...), *m.*
Wring, *v.a.* tordre; presser, serrer; tourmenter, torturer; (*distort*) fausser, forcer; (*snatch*) arracher ('*from*': *things*, de; *pers.*, à); (*the heart*) déchirer; — *v.n.* se tordre; — *s.* *V.* **Wringing.** *To — o.'s hands in despair*, se tordre les mains de désespoir. — **off,** arracher. — **out,** exprimer; (*twist*) tordre
Wringing, *s.* torsion, *f.*; tourment, remords, *m.*
Wrinkle, *v.a.* rider; (*the eyebrows*) froncer; (*stuffs*) plisser, froisser, chiffonner; — *v.n.* se rider; — *s.* ride, *f.*; (*of stuffs*) faux-pli, pli, *m.*; (*news*) (du) nouveau, *m.* *There's a — for you*, voilà du nouveau pour vous. *That's a — worth knowing*, c'est bon à savoir. *To put one up to a* —, apprendre à quelqu'un une bonne recette
Wrinkling, *s.* ridement, *m.*; (*of stuffs*) plisse-
Wrinkly, *adj.* ridé [ment, froissement, *m.*
Wrist, *s.* poignet, *m.* —**band,** *s.* manchette, *f.*; poignet, *m.*
Writ, *s.* (*Scripture*) Écriture, *f.*; (*law*) ordonnance, *f.*, ordre, mandat, *m.*; assignation, *f.*; prise de corps, *f.*; (*parl.*) lettre de convocation, *f.* — *of error*, recours pour cause d'erreur, *m.*
Write, *v.a.n.* écrire. *To — again* or *over again*, récrire. *To — oneself*, signer son nom; se qualifier, se qualifier de. *To — oneself out*, user sa réputation d'écrivain, se décaver. *To — to say that ...*, écrire que ... — **back,** répondre. — **down,** écrire; inscrire; mettre (*or* coucher) par écrit; (*disparage*) écrire contre, décrier; abîmer; (*silence*) faire taire; (*call*) appeler. — **out,** écrire d'un bout à l'autre, écrire en entier; copier, transcrire; rédiger. — **up,** faire l'éloge de, faire mousser
Writer, *s.* écrivain, *m.*; (*of a letter, article*, &c.) auteur, *m.*; (*author*) écrivain, auteur, *m.*; (*contributor or contributress to newspapers, periodicals*) rédacteur, *m.*, -trice, *f.* ('*in*' de); (*clerk*) commis aux écritures, *m.*; (*admin., and law* —) expéditionnaire, *m.*; (*attorney in Scotland*) avoué, *m.*; notaire, *m.*
Writership, *s.* charge d'avoué *or* de notaire, *f.*
Writhe, *v.a.* tordre; — *v.n.* se tordre; se débattre, se démener
Writing, *s.* (*handwriting and art*) écriture, *f.*; (*thing written*) écrit, *m.*; (*a book*) ouvrage, écrit, *m.*; (*style*) style, *m.*; (*law*) acte, contrat, *m.*; document, *m.* *In* —, par écrit. *To put in* —, *to consign* or *commit to* —, mettre *or* consigner par écrit, écrire. — **book,** *s.* cahier d'écriture, cahier, *m.* — **case,** *s.* buvard de voyage, *m.*; papeterie, *f.* — **desk,** *s.* pupitre, *m.*; secrétaire, *m.*; (*portable*) buvard de voyage, *m.* — **ink,** *s.* encre à écrire, *f.* — **master,** *s.* maître d'écriture, *m.* — **pad,** *s.* sous-main, *m.* — **paper,** *s.* papier à écrire, *m.* — **school,** *s.* classe d'écriture, *f.* — **table,** *s.* bureau, *m.*, table à écrire, *f.*
Wrong, *adj.* faux; mal; mauvais; inexact, incorrect, impropre; injuste; dérangé. *The — book* or &c., le livre *or* &c. qu'il ne faut *or* ne fallait pas, un autre livre *or* &c. *The — one*, celui (*m.*) *or* celle (*f.*) qu'il ne faut *or* ne fallait pas, un autre (*m.*), une autre (*f.*) *The — way* or *road*, le mauvais chemin, la mauvaise voie. *This is the — train* or &c., ce n'est pas le train *or* &c. *To take* or *bring the — book*, &c., se tromper de livre, &c. *To knock at the — door, to go to the — house*, &c., se tromper de porte, de maison, &c. *To be* —, être faux *or* &c.; aller mal; (*not fair*) n'être pas juste; (*improper*) n'être pas convenable, ne pas convenir; (*pers.*) avoir tort (de); (*of clocks, watches*) aller mal; n'être pas à l'heure. *To be very — (to)*, (*pers.*) avoir grand tort (de). *To set* or *make* —, déranger; égarer, faire tromper.

That is — ! c'est mal ! ce n'est pas juste ! ce n'est pas cela ! *That is all — !* c'est très mal ! ce n'est pas cela du tout ! *It is very — of you,* (*to ...*), c'est très mal à vous (de ...), c'est très mal de votre part (de ...), vous avez grand tort (de ...). **—ful, —headed,** &c., *See below*

Wrong, *adv.* mal ; à tort ; injustement ; (*incorrectly*) mal ; de travers ; à faux. *To go —*, aller mal, aller de travers ; tourner mal. *It is put on —*, c'est mal mis, c'est mis de travers

Wrong, *s.* mal, *m.* ; injustice, *f.* ; tort, dommage, préjudice, *m.* ; injure, *f.* ; erreur, *f.* ; faute, *f.* *In the —*, dans son tort. *To be in the —*, être dans son tort, avoir tort. *To do —*, faire *or* agir mal ; faire le *or* du mal ; (*prejudice*) faire du tort (à) ; porter préjudice (à). — **doer,** *s.* auteur d'un dommage *or* d'une injustice, *m.* ; (*wicked*) pervers, méchant, *m.* — **doing,** *s.* mal, *m.*, injustice, *f.*

Wrong, *v.a.* nuire à, léser ; faire tort à

Wronger, *s.* personne qui fait tort (à), *f.* ; personne injuste, *f.*

Wrongful, *adj.* injuste (envers) ; (*injurious*) nuisible (à) ; (*false*) faux, supposé. **—fully,** *adv.* injustement ; à tort ; à faux

Wrongheaded, *adj.* qui a l'esprit mal fait, qui a l'esprit de travers, obstiné, opiniâtre, entêté, têtu. **—ness,** *s.* travers d'esprit, *m.*, obstination, opiniâtreté, *f.*, entêtement, *m.*

Wrongly. *V.* **Wrongfully**

Wrongness, *s.* mal, *m.* ; défaut, *m.* ; inexactitude, *f.* ; (*error*) fausseté, *f.*

Wroth, *adj.* *V.* **Angry**

Wrought, *part. adj.* travaillé, façonné, ouvré, ouvragé, &c. (*V.* **Work,** *v.a.n.*). — **gold,** *s.* or orfévri, *m.* — **iron,** *s.* fer forgé, *m.* ; fer battu, *m.* — **iron plates,** *s.pl.* fer en feuilles, *m.*, tôle, *f.*

Wry, *adj.* de travers, tordu, tors ; (*not true*) détourné ; (*wrested*) torturé, forcé, faussé. — **face,** *s.* grimace, *f.* — **neck,** *s.* torticolis, *m.* ; (*bird*) torcol, *m.* — **necked,** *adj.* qui a le cou de travers ; qui a le torticolis

Wryness, *s.* torsion, *f.*, état tordu, *m.* ; (*slyness*) obliquité, *f.*

Wurtemberger, *s.* Wurtembergeois, *m.*, e, *f.*

Wych-elm, *s.* orme à larges feuilles, orme tilleul, *m.*

X

X, *s.* (*letter*) x, *m.*

Xanthorrhœa, *s.* xanthorrhée, *f.*

Xebec, *s.* chebec, *m.*

Xylographer, *s.* xylographe, *m.*

Xylograph-ic, al, -y. *V.* page 3, § 1

Xylolog-ic, al, -y. *V.* page 3, § 1

Xylophagan, Xylophagus, *s.* xylophage, *m.*

Xylophagous, *adj.* xylophage

Xylophagy, *s.* xylophagie, *f.*

Y

Y, *s.* (*letter*) y, *m.*

Yacht, *s.* yacht, *m.* — **club,** *s.* club des yachts, *m.* — **match, -race,** *s.* course de yachts, *f.*

Yachting, *s.* promenade en yacht, *f.*, promenades en yacht, *f.pl.* — **excursion,** *s.* promenade en yacht, *f.* — **jacket,** *s.* saute-en-barque, *m.*, vareuse, *f.* — **match, -race,** *s.* *V.* **Yacht.** **—sman,** *s.* promeneur en yacht, *m.*

Yacou, *s.* yacou, guan, *m.*

Yak, *s.* yack, *m.*

Yam, *s.* igname, *f.*

Yankee, *s. adj.* Yankee, *m.f.*

Yapock, *s.* yapock, *m.*

Yard, *s.* cour, *f.* ; (*of prisons*) cour, *f.*, préau, *m.* ; (*workyard, dockyard, timber-yard,* &c.) chantier, *m.* ; (*measure*) mètre, *m.* ; (*pace*) pas, *m.* ; (*nav.*) vergue, *f.* — **arm,** *s.* bout de vergue, *m.*

Yarn, *s.* fil, *m.* ; (*nav.*) fil de caret, *m.* *Spun —*, bitord, *m.* *To spin* (or *tell*) *a — about,* (*fig.*) débiter une longue histoire sur, (*fam.*) en dégoiser

Yarrow, *s.* mille-feuilles, *f.*

Yataghan, Yatagan, *s.* yatagan, *m.*

Yaw, *s.* (*nav.*) embardée, *f.* ; (*med.*) *V.* **Yaws ;** — *v.n.* embarder, faire une embardée. *Master or mother —*, mamapian, *m.*

Yawl, *s.* yole, *f.*

Yawn, &c. *V.* **Gape,** &c.

Yaws, *s.* (*med.*) yaws, pian, *m.*

Ycleped, Yclept, *adj.* appelé, nommé, baptisé du nom de, baptisé

Ye. *V.* **You**

Yea. *V.* **Ay**

Yean, mettre bas, agneler

Yeanling, *s.* agnelet, agneau, *m.*

Year, *s.* (*whole year, in regard to work or occupation, year's events, crop,* &c.) année, *f.* ; (*as a unit*) an, *m.*, année, *f.* ; (*mere date, and indicating age*) an, *m.* ; (*after a determinative such as 'this,' 'that,' 'these,' 'those,' 'some,' 'several,' 'a few,' 'what,'* &c., *or with 'following,' 'preceding,' 'long,' and most adjectives*) année, *f.* ; (*after the ordinal numbers 'first,' 'second,'* &c., *and after 'last'*) année, *f.* ; (*after the cardinal numbers 'one,' 'two,'* &c.) an, *m.* ; année, *f.* ; **—s,** *pl.* années, *f.pl.* ; ans, *m.pl.* ; (*age*) âge, *m.* *—s pass quickly,* les années passent vite. *Academic —*, année scolaire. *Advanced —s*, un âge avancé, *m.*, la vieillesse, *f.*, les années, *f.pl.*, les ans, *m.pl.* *All the —*, toute l'année. *Each —*, chaque année. *Every —*, tous les ans. *Every other —*, tous les deux ans. *Every third —*, tous les trois ans. *The — of ...*, l'année de ... (*except in 'the — of grace,'* l'an de grâce). *This day —*, dans un an à pareil jour. *This day last —*, *V.* **Day.** *By the —*, à l'année. *For —s*, pendant des années ; (*law*) à terme. *For a term of —s*, à terme ; à temps. *From — to —*, d'année en année. *In —s*, âgé, avancé en âge, sur l'âge. *Last —*, l'année dernière *or* passée, l'an dernier *or* passé. *Next —*, l'année prochaine. *New —*, nouvelle année, nouvel an. *New —'s Day,* jour de l'an, premier de l'an, *m.* *New —'s gift,* étrennes, *f.pl.* *One* (or *Taking one*) *— with another,* année commune (*or* bon an, mal an). *Twice a —*, deux fois par an. *Eighty pounds a —*, deux mille francs par an ; (*settled income*) deux mille francs de rente. *To be ... —s old* or *... —s of age,* avoir ... ans. *To be ... —s younger* or *older than,* avoir ... ans de moins *or* de plus que. *To wish one a happy new —*, souhaiter la bonne année à quelqu'un. — **book,** *s.* annuaire, *m.*

Yearling, *s.* animal (veau, agneau, *or* cheval, &c.) d'un an, *m.* ; — *adj.* âgé d'un an, d'un an

Yearly, *adj.* annuel ; (*by the year*) à l'année ; — *adv.* annuellement, tous les ans ; par an

Yearn, *v.n.* soupirer (après) ; ne demander (qu'à), aspirer (à), brûler (de)

Yearning, *s.* élan, *m.* ; aspiration, *f.* ; pitié, *f.*

Yeast, *s.* levure, *f.* ; levain, ferment, *m.* *German —*, levure viennoise. — **plant,** *s.* torule, *f.*

Yeasty, *adj.* écumeux, écumant

Yelk. *V.* **Yolk**

Yell, *v.n.a.* hurler, crier ; — *s.* hurlement, cri, *m.*

Yelling, *s.* hurlements, cris, *m.pl.*

Yellow, *adj. s.* jaune, *adj.m.f.*, *s.m.* ; **—s,** *pl.* jaunisse, *f.* ; — *v.a.n.* jaunir. *To make* or *turn* (or *become* or *grow*) *—*, jaunir. — **boy,** *s.* jaunet, *m.* — **fever,** *s.* fièvre jaune, *f.* — **gum,** *s.* jaunisse, *f.* **—hammer, -bunting,** *s.* bruant, *m.* **—ing,** *s.* jaunissement, jaunissage, *m.* **—ish,** *adj.* jaunâtre. **—ishness,** *s.* couleur *or* teinte jaunâtre, *f.* — **metal,** *s.* (*nav.*) cuivre jaune, *m.* — **River,** *s.* (le) Fleuve Jaune, *m.* — **Sea,** *s.* (la) Mer Jaune,

f. — **wash,** *s.* eau phagédénique, *f.* — **wort,** *s.* chlore, *f.*
Yelp, *v.n.* glapir; japper
Yelping, *s.* glapissement, *m.*; jappement, *m.*
Yeoman, *s.* fermier propriétaire, *m.*; (*volunteer*) garde national à cheval, *m.*; (— *of the guard*) garde du corps (à pied), cent-gardes, *m.* [*The French 'cent-gardes' of Napoleon III. were mounted, while the English body-guard of* 100 *yeomen are not*]
Yeomanry, *s.* corps des fermiers propriétaires, *m.*, fermiers propriétaires, *m.pl.*; (— *cavalry*) garde nationale à cheval, gendarmerie civile, *f.*
Yes, *adv.* oui; (*in answer to a question containing a negation, or in contradiction to a negative statement*) si; (*all right*) bien! (*I'm coming!*) voilà! j'y vais! on y va! — *s.* oui, *m.*; si, *m.*
Yesterday, *s. adv.* hier (*s.m.*); (*the eve*) la veille (*s.f.*). *The day before* —, avant-hier. *The day before — in the evening* or *morning*, avant-hier soir *or* matin
Yet, *conj.* cependant, toutefois, pourtant
Yet, *adv.* encore; (*already*) déjà; (*even*) même. *As* —, jusqu'à présent, jusqu'ici; encore. *Not* —, *not as* —, pas encore
Yew, — **tree,** *s.* if, *m.*
Yield, *v.a.* (*produce*) produire, rapporter, rendre; (*afford*) offrir, présenter; (*give*) donner; (*give up*) rendre; (*grant*) accorder, concéder; (*emit*) émettre, exhaler; rendre; (*resign*) céder, abandonner; (*surrender*) livrer, rendre, remettre; — *v.n.* (*submit*) se soumettre (à); céder (à), plier (sous), fléchir (sous); (*bend*) plier; (*give way*) fléchir (sous); succomber (sous; *fig.*, à); (*to temptation*) succomber (à), céder (à); (*accede*) accéder (à), se rendre (à); (*surrender*) se rendre (à); (*consent*) consentir (à); — *s.* produit, rapport, rendement, *m.*; (*crop*) récolte, *f.* —**less,** *adj.* inflexible
Yielding, *s.* soumission, *f.*; (*resignation*) abandon, *m.*; (*surrendering*) reddition, *f.*; (*produce*) *V.* **Yield,** *s.*; — *adj. V.* **Compliant.** —**ly,** *adv.* facilement; complaisamment. —**ness,** *s.* facilité, complaisance, *f.*, caractère accommodant, *m.*
Yoke, *s.* joug, *m.*; (*of two*) paire, *f.*, couple, attelage, *m.*; (*for carrying pails*) courge, palanche, *f.*; (*for swine*) carcan, tribart, *m.*; (*nav.*) barre de gouvernail, *f.*; — *v.a.* atteler, mettre au joug; (*couple*) accoupler; (*enslave*) subjuguer, asservir, assujettir; (*restrain*) enchaîner. — **elm,** *s. V.* **Wych-elm.** — **fellow, -mate,** *s.* compagnon, *m.*, compagne, *f.*, camarade, *m.f.* — **ox,** *s.* bœuf de labour, *m.*
Yolk, *s.* jaune d'œuf, jaune, *m.*; (*of sheep-skin*) suint, *m.*
Yon, Yonder, *adj.* ce, cet, cette, ces, ce ... -là, cet ... -là, cette ... -là, ces ... -là; — *adv.* là-bas [fois, jadis
Yore, *adv.* *Of* —, *in days* or *times of* —, autre-
You, *pron. pers.* vous; (*anyone*) on. *If I were* —, si j'étais de vous, si j'étais que de vous, si j'étais à votre place, à votre place
Young, *adj.* jeune; petit; naissant; novice, neuf. — *female*, — *girl*, — *lady*, jeune personne, *f.* — *man*, jeune homme, *m.* — *men*, — *people*, — *folks*, — *persons*, — *lads*, — *fellows*, jeunes gens, *m.pl.* — *one*, petit, *m.*, e, *f.*; (*in contempt*) bambin, gamin, moutard, *m.*, bambine, gamine, *f.*
Young, *s.* (*of animals*) petits, *m.pl.*; (*young people*) jeunesse, *f.* *With* —, pleine. *To bring forth* —, faire des (*or* ses) petits [cadet; jeune
Younger, *adj.* plus jeune; (*of brothers, sisters*)
Youngish, *adj.* assez jeune, encore jeune
Youngling, *s.* jeune animal, *m.*
Youngster, *s.* jeune homme, *m.*; (*in jest*) blanc-bec, *m.*; gamin, mioche, moutard, *m.*
Younker, *s.* novice, *m.*
Your, *pron. poss.* votre, *m.f. sing.*, vos, *pl.* [*When speaking of the relations of a person with whom we are not intimate, we use* monsieur, madame *or* mademoiselle, *or their plural, before* votre *or* vos; *as*, — *father*, monsieur votre père; — *sisters*, mesdemoiselles vos sœurs, &c.]. —**self,** *sing.*, —**selves,** *pl.*, *pron. pers.* vous-même, *sing.*, vous-mêmes, *pl.*; vous; (*in a reflect. verb*) vous
Yours, *pron. poss.* le vôtre, la vôtre, les vôtres; vos; (*pron. pers.*) à vous, de vous. *Is this drawing* —? (*belong to you*) ce dessin est-il à vous? (*come from you; are you the author of it?*) ce dessin est-il de vous? *A friend of* —, un de vos amis. — *truly*, — *sincerely*, — *faithfully*, *entirely* —, tout à vous, tout à vous d'amitié, votre tout dévoué. — *affectionately*, à vous de tout cœur
Youth, *s.* jeunesse, *f.*; (*lad*) jeune homme, *m.*; enfant, *m.*; (*young people*) jeunes gens, *m.pl.* *The fountain of* —, la fontaine de jouvence, *f.* —**ful,** *adj.* jeune; de jeunesse; (*fresh*) neuf, vert. —**fully,** *adv.* en jeune homme; (*of girls*) en jeune fille. —**fulness,** *s.* jeunesse, *f.*
Yucca, *s.* yucca, *m.*
Yule, — **tide,** *s.* Noël, *m.*, &c. (*V.* **Christmas**)

Z

Z *s.* (*letter*) z, *m.*
Zaffer, Zaffre, *s.* safre, *m.*
Zain, *adj. s.* zain
Zambo, Zamba. *V.* **Sambo, Samba**
Zany, *s.* zani, bouffon, *m.*
Zeal, *s.* zèle, *m.*
Zealander, *s.* Zélandais, *m.*, e, *f.*
Zealot, *s.* zélateur, *m.*, -trice, *f.*; fanatique, *m.f.*; partisan, *m.*, e, *f.*
Zealotry, *s.* zélotisme, fanatisme, *m.*
Zealous, *adj.* zélé; ardent. —**ly,** *adv.* avec zèle; ardemment. —**ness,** *s.* zèle, *m.*
Zebra, *s.* zèbre, *m.* — **striped,** *adj.* zébré. — **wood,** *s.* bois de courbaril, *m.*
Zebu, *s.* zébu, *m.*
Zechin, *s.* sequin, *m.*
Zedoary, *s.* zédoaire, *f.*
Zenith, *s.* zénith, *m.*; (*height*) comble, faîte, *m.*
Zenithal, *adj.* zénithal
Zephyr, *s.* zéphyr, *m.*
Zephyrian, *adj.* zéphyrien
Zerda, *s.* zerda, *m.*
Zero, *s.* zéro, *m.*
Zest, *s.* zeste, *m.*; (*taste*) goût, *m.*, saveur, *f.*; — *v.a.* zester; (*fig.*) assaisonner, donner du goût a. *To give a* — *to*, donner du goût à, assaisonner
Zigzag, *s.* zigzag, *m.*; — *adj. adv.* en zigzag; — *v.a.* tracer en zigzag; — *v.n.* zigzaguer, aller en zigzag, faire *or* former des zigzags
Zigzagging, *s.* direction en zigzag, *f.*, zigzag, *m.*
Zinc, Zink, *s.* zinc, *m.*; — *v.a.* zinguer. — **plates,** *s.pl.* zinc laminé, zinc en feuilles, *m.* — **plating,** *s.* zingage, *m.* — **sheets,** *s.pl. V.* — **plates.** — **trade,** *s.* zinguerie, *f.* — **white,** *s.* blanc de zinc, *m.* — **worker,** *s.* zingueur, *m.* — **works,** *s.pl.* zinguerie, *f.*
Zincic, *adj.* zincique
Zinciferous, *adj.* zincifère
Zincing, *s.* zincage, zingage, *m.*
Zincograph, *v.a.* zincographier [graphe, *m.*
Zincographer, *s.* graveur sur zinc, zinco-
Zincograph-ic, al, -y. *V.* page 3, § 1
Zincous, *adj.* zingueux
Zingari, *s.* zingari, tzingari, *m.*
Zingel, *s.* zingel, cingle, apron, *m.*
Zink, &c. *V.* **Zinc,** &c.
Zinky, *adj.* de zinc [cithare, *f.*
Zither, Zithern, Zittar, Zitter, *s.*
Zodiac, *s.* zodiaque, *m.* [zodiacale, *f.*
Zodiacal, *adj.* zodiacal. — *light*, lumière

Zoetrope, *s.* zoétrope, *m.*
Zollverein, *s.* zollverein, *m.*
Zone, *s.* zone, *f.*; (*fig.*) zone, *f.*; ceinture, *f.*; circonférence, *f.* **—less,** *adj.* sans zone
Zoned, *adj.* zoné, à zone
Zoniform, *adj.* zoniforme
Zoo, (*in compounds*) zoo ...
Zoographer, *s.* zoographe, *m.*
Zoograph-ic, al, -y. *V.* page 3, § 1
Zooks, Zookers. *V.* **Zounds**
Zoolatry, *s.* zoolâtrie, *f.*
Zoolite, *s.* zoolithe, *m.*
Zoolitic, *adj.* zoolithique
Zoolog-ic, al, -ically, -ist, -y. *V.* p. 3, § 1
Zoo-nomy, &c. *V.* page 3, § 1
Zoophagous, *adj.* zoophage
Zoophyte, *s.* zoophyte, *m.*
Zootom-ic, al, -ist, -y. *V.* page 3, § 1
Zoril, *s.* zorille, *f.m.*
Zouave, *s.* zouave, *m.*
Zounds, *int.* fichtre! diable! saprelotte! sapristi! morbleu! sacrebleu! (*in speaking to children*) sac à papier! sabre de bois!
Zymolog-ic, al, -ist, -y. *V.* page 3, § 1
Zymotic, *adj.* zymotique

PROPER NAMES OF PERSONS AND ANIMALS.

Abigail, Abigail, *f.*
Absalom, Absalon, *m.*
Achilles, Achille, *m.* —*'s tendon*, le tendon d'Achille, *m.*
Adela, Adèle, *f.*
Adelaide, Adélaïde, *f.*
Adelina, Adeline, Adeline, *f.*
Adolphus, Adolphe, *m.*
Adrian, Adrien, *m.*
Adriana, Adrienne, *f.*
Æacus, Éaque, *m.*
Æmilia, Émilie, *f.*
Æmilius, Émile, *m.*
Æmilian, Émilien, *m.*
Æneas, Énée, *m.*
Æolus, Éole, *m.*
Æschines, Eschine, *m.*
Æschylus, Eschyle, *m.*
Æsculapius, Esculape, *m.*
Æsop, Ésope, *m.*
Agatha, Agathe, *f.*
Agathocles, Agathocle, *m.*
Agesilaus, Agésilas, *m.*
Aglaia, Aglaé, *f*
Agnes, Agnès, *f.*
Agrippina, Agrippine, *f*
Ahasuerus, Assuérus, *m.*
Albano, l'Albane, *m.*
Albertina, Albertine, *f.*
Alcæus, Alcée, *m.*
Alceste, Alcestis, Alceste, *m.*
Alcibiades, Alcibiade, *m.*
Alcides, Alcide, *m.*
Alecto, Alecton, Alecto, *f.*
Alexander, Alexandre, *m.*
Alexandra, Alexandra, *f.*
Alexandrina, Alexandrine, *f.*
Allen, Alain, *m.*
Alpheus, Alphée, *m.*
Alphonso, Alphonse, *m.*
Althea, Althée, *f.*
Alwin, Aluin, *m.*
Amadeus, Amédée, *m.*
Amalthea, Amalthée, *f.*
Ambrose, Ambroise, *m.*
Amedeus, Amédée, *m.*
Amelia, Amélie, *f.*
Americus Vespucius, Améric Vespuce, *m.*
Amrus, Amrou, *m.*
Amy, Aimée, *f.*
Anacreon, Anacréon, *m.*
Anastasia, Anastasie, *f.*
Anastasius, Anastase, *m.*
Anatolius, Anatole, *m.*
Anaxagoras, Anaxagore, *m.*
Anchises, Anchise, *m.*
Andrew, André, *m.*
Andromache, Andromaque, *f.*
Andromeda, Andromède, *f.*
Angela, Angèle, *f.*
Angelica, Angélique, *f.*
Anna, Anna, *f.*; Anne, *f.*
Ann, Anne, Anne, *f.*
Annie, Annette, *f.*
Anselm, Anselmo, Anselme, [*m.*
Antæus, Antée, *m.*
Antheus, Anthée, *m.*
Anthony, Antoine, *m.*
Antigone, Antigone, *f.*
Antigonus, Antigone, *m.*
Antinous, Antinoüs, *m.*
Antonia, Antoinette, *f.*
Antonina, Antonine, *f.*
Antoninus, Antonin, *m.*
Antony, Antoine, *m.*
Apelles, Apelles, *m.*
Apollo, Apollon, *m.*
Apollodorus, Apollodore, *m.*
Appian, Appien, *m.*
Aquinas, Aquin, *m* *Thomas* —, Saint Thomas d'Aquin, *m.*
Arabella, Arabelle, *f*
Archibald, Archambaud, *m.*
Archimedes, Archimède, *m.*
Arethusa, Aréthuse, *f.*
Aretino, l'Arétin, *m.*
Ariadne, Ariane, *f.*
Ariosto, l'Arioste, *m.*
Ariovistus, Arioviste, *m.*
Aristarchus, Aristarch, Aristarque, *m.*
Aristides, Aristide, *m.*
Aristippus, Aristippe, *m.*
Aristobulus, Aristobule, *m.*
Aristodemus, Aristodème, *m.*
Aristogeiton, Aristogiton, *m.*
Aristophanes, Aristophane, *m.*
Aristotle, Aristote, *m.*
Arnold, Arnaud, Arnold, *m.*
Arrian, Arrien, *m.*
Arsenius, Arsène, *m.*
Artaxerxes, Artaxerce, *m.*
Artemisia, Artémise, *f.*
Ascanius, Ascagne, *m.*
Ashtaroth, Astaroth, *f.*
Asmodeus, Asmodée, *m.*
Aspasia, Aspasie, *f.*
Astræa, Astrée, *f.*
Atalanta, Atalante, Atalante, *f.*
Athaliah, Athalie, *f.*
Athanasius, Athanase, *m.*
Atreus, Atrée, *m.*
Augeas, Augias, Augias, *m.*
Augustina, Augustine, *f.*
Augustine, Augustin, *m.*
Augustus, Auguste, *m.*
Aulus-Gellius, Aulu-Gelle, *m.*
Aurelia, Aurélie, *f.*
Aurelian, Aurélien, *m.*
Aurelius, Aurélius, *m.*; (*Marcus* —) Marc-Aurèle, *m.*
Aurora, Aurore, *f.*
Ausonius, Ausone, *m.*
Austin, Augustin, *m.*
Baldwin, Baudouin, *m.*
Baliol, Bailleul, *m.*
Baptist, Baptiste, *m.* *Saint John the* —, Saint-Jean-Baptiste, *m.*
Barbara, Barbe, *f.*
Barbarossa, Barberousse, *m.*
Barnabas, Barnaby, Barnabé, *m.*
Bartholomew, Barthélemy, *m.* *Saint* —, Saint-Barthélemy, *m.*; (*the day*) la Saint-Barthélemy, *f.*
Basil, Basile, *m.*
Batilda, Bathilde, *f.*
Beatrice, Beatrix, Béatrice, *f.*
Beck, Becky, Rébecca, *f.*
Beelzebub, Belzébuth, *m.*
Belial, Bélial, *m.*
Belisarius, Bélisaire, *m.*
Bell, Isabelle, *f.*; Arabelle, *f.*
Bellona, Bellone, *f.*
Belshazzar, Balthazar, *m.*
Ben, Benjamin, *m.*
Benedict, Benoît, Bénédict, *m.*
Benedicta, Benoîte, Bénédicte, *f.*
Benjamin, Benjamin, *m.*
Berenice, Bérénice, *f.*
Bernardine, Bernardin, *m.*
Bertha, Berthe, *f.*
Bertram, Bertrand, *m.*
Bess, Betsy, Élisabeth, *f.*
Biddy, Brigitte, *f.*
Bill, Billy, Guillaume, Guillot, *m.*
Blanch, Blanche, Blanche, *f.*
Blase, Blaise, *m.*
Bluebeard, la Barbe-Bleue, *m.*
Boadicea, Boadicée, *f.*
Bob, Robert, *m.*
Boccaccio, Boccace, *m.*
Boethius, Boèce, *m.*
Bogie *or* **Bogy (Old),** Croquemitaine, *m.*
Boleslaus, Boleslas, *m.*
Bolognese, le Bolognèse, *m.*
Bona, Bonne, *f.*
Bonadventure, Bonaventure, *m.*
Boreas, Borée, *m.*
Briareus, Briarée, *m.*
Bridget, Brigitte, *f.*
Bruin, l'ours, *m.*
Bucephalus, Bucéphale, *m.*

Cæsar, César, *m.*
Caiaphas, Caïphe, *m.*
Cain, Caïn, *m.*
Caligula, Caligula, *m.*
Callimachus, Callimaque, *m.*
Calliope, Calliope, *f.*
Cambyses, Cambyse, *m.*
Camilla, Camille, *f.*
Camillus, Camille, *m.*
Canute, Canut, *m.*

Caracci, Carrache, *m.*
Caravaggio, Caravage, *m.*
Caroline, Cary, Caroline, *f.*
Cassander, Cassandre, *m.*
Cassandra, Cassandre, *f.*
Catharine, Catherine, Catherine, *f.*
Catiline, Catilina, *m.*
Cato, Caton, *m.*
Catullus, Catulle, *m.*
Cecilia, Cecily, Cécile, *f.*
Celestina, Célestine, *f.*
Celestine, Célestin, *m.*
Celia, Célie, *f.*
Celsus, Celse, *m.*
Cerberus, Cerbère, *m.*
Ceres, Cérès, *f.*
Chanticleer, le Réveille-matin, *m.*
Charles, Charles, *m.* — *the Fifth,* Charles V (cinq); (*of Spain and Germany*) Charles-Quint. — *the Bold,* Charles-le-Téméraire
Charly, Charlot, *m.*
Charon, Caron, *m.*
Chloe, Chloé, *f.*
Christ, le Christ, *m.* *Jesus-Christ,* Jésus-Christ
Christian, Chrétien, *m.*
Christina, Christine, *f.*
Christopher, Christophe, *m.*
Chrysostom, Chrysostome, *m.*
Cicero, Cicéron, *m.*
Cinderella, Cendrillon, *f.*
Circe, Circé, *f.*
Clara, Clara, Claire, *f.*
Clarissa, Clarisse, *f.*
Claud, Claude, *m.*
Claude Lorraine, Claude-Lorrain, *m.*
Claudia, Claude, Claudie, *f.*
Claudian, Claudien, *m.*
Claudius, Claude, *m.*
Clemence, Clementia, Clémence, *f.*
Clement, Clément, *m.*
Clementina, Clémentine, *f.*
Cleopatra, Cléopâtre, *f.*
Clotilda, Clotilde, *f.*
Clytemnestra, Clytemnestre, *f.*
Collatinus, Collatin, *m.*
Columbine, Colombine, *f.*
Columbus, Colomb, *m.*
Commodus, Commode, *m.*
Comnena, Comnène, *f.*
Comnenus, Comnène, *m.*
Constance, Constantia, Constance, *f.*
Constantine, Constantin, *m.*
Constantius, Constance, *m.*
Copernicus, Copernic, *m.*
Corinna, Corinne, *f.*
Coriolanus, Coriolan, *m.*
Cornelia, Cornélie, *f.*
Correggio, le Corrége, *m.*
Crispin, Crépin, *m.*
Crœsus, Crésus, *m.*
Crusoe, Crusoé, *m.*
Cupid, Cupidon, *m.*
Curiatii (The), les Curiaces, *m.pl.*
Cybela, Cybele, Cybèle, *f.*
Cyprian, Cyprien, *m.*
Cyril, Cyrille, *m.*

Dædalus, Dédale, *m.*
Dalilah, Dalila, *f.*
Damocles, Damoclès, *m.*
Danae, Danaé, *f.*
Dante, Dante, *m.*
Daphne, Daphné, *f.*
Deborah, Débora, *f.*
Dejanira, Déjanire, *f.*
Delia, Délie, *f.*
Delilah, Dalila, *f.*
Democritus, Démocrite, *m.*
Demosthenes, Démosthène, Démosthènes, *m.*
Denis, Dennis, Denys, Denis, Denys, *m.*
Dian, Diana, Diane, *f.*
Dick, Dicky, Richard, *m.*
Dido, Didon, *f.*
Diocletian, Dioclétien, *m.*
Diodorus, Diodore, *m.* — *Siculus,* Diodore de Sicile
Diogenes, Diogène, *m.*
Diomedes, Diomède, *m.*
Dionysia, Denise, *f.*
Dionysius, Denys, Denis, *m.*
Domenichino, le Dominiquin, *m.*
Domingo, Domingue, *m.*
Dominic, Dominique, *m.*
Domitian, Domitien, *m.*
Donatus, Donat, *m.*
Dorothea, Dorothy, Dorothée, *f.*
Draco, Dracon, *m.*
Drusilla, Drusille, *f.*
Dulcinea, Dulcinée, *f.*

Eacus, Éaque, *m.*
Edmund, Edmond, *m.*
Edward, Edouard, *m.*
Egeria, Égérie, *f.*
Eleanor, Éléonore, *f.*
Electra, Électre, *f.*
Elias, Élie, *m.*
Elijah, Élie, *m.*
Elisha, Élisée, *m.*
Eliza, Élise, Élisa, *f.*
Elizabeth, Élisabeth, *f.*
Ellen. *V.* HELEN
Eloisa, Héloïse, *f.*
Elvira, Elvire, *f.*
Emanuel, Emmanuel, *m.*
Emery, Émeri, *m.*
Emilian, Emilien, *m.*
Emilius, Émile, *m.*
Emily, Émilie, *f.*
Empedocles, Empédocle, *m.*
Enoch, Énoch, *m.*
Ephraim, Éphraim, *m.*
Epictetus, Épictète, *m.*
Epicurus, Épicure, *m.*
Epimenides, Épiménide, *m.*
Erasmus, Érasme, *m.*
Erastus, Éraste, *m.*
Erebus, Érèbe, *m.*
Esau, Ésaü, *m.*
Eteocles, Étéocle, *m.*
Euclid, Euclide, *m.*
Eudoxia, Eudoxie, *f.*
Eudoxus, Eudoxe, *m.*
Eugene, Eugène, *m.*
Eugenia, Eugénie, *f.*
Eulalia, Eulalie, *f.*
Eumæus, Eumée, *m.*
Euphemia, Euphémie, *f.*
Euphrasia, Euphrasie, *f.*
Euphrosyne, Euphrosyne, *f.*
Euripides, Euripide, *m.*
Europa, Europe, *f.*
Euryalus, Euryale, *m.*
Eurybiades, Eurybiade, *m.*
Eurydice, Eurydice, *f.*
Eusebius, Eusèbe, *m.*
Eustace, Eustachius, Eustache, *m.*
Eustathius, Eustathe, *m.*
Euterpe, Euterpe, *f.*
Eutropius, Eutrope, *m.*
Evander, Évandre, *m.*
Eve, Ève, *f.*
Ezekiel, Ézéchiel, *m.*
Ezra, Esdras, *m.*

Fabian, Fabien, *m.*
Fatima, Fatime, *f.*
Faunus, Faune, *m.*
Faustina, Faustine, *f.*
Faustus, Faust, Faust, *m.*
Felicia, Félicie, *f.*
Felician, Félicien, *m.*
Felicity, Félicité, *f.*
Felix, Félix, *m.*
Fernando, Fernand, *m.*
Flavian, Flavien, *m.*
Flora, Flore, *f.*
Fortuna, Fortune, *f.*
Frances, Françoise, *f.*
Francis, Frank, François, *m.*
Frederic, Frederick, Fred, Freddy, Frédéric, *m.*
Frederica, Frederika, Frédérique, *f.*
Fulgentius, Fulgence, *m.*
Fulvia, Fulvie, *f.*

Gabriel, Gabriel, *m.*
Gabriella, Gabrielle, *f.*
Galatea, Galatée, *f.*
Galen, Galien, *m.*
Galileo, Galilée, *m.*
Gallienus, Gallien, *m.*
Ganymedes, Ganymède, *m.*
Geoffrey, Geoffry, Geoffroy, *m.*
George, Georgy, Georges, *m.*
Georgetta, Georgey, Georgie, Georgette, *f.*
Georgiana, Georgey, Georgie, Georgienne, *f.*
Georgina, Georgey, Georgie, Georgine, *f.*
Gerald, Géralde, *m.*
Gerard, Gérard, *m.*
German, Germain, *m.*
Gervase, Gervais, *m.*
Gideon, Gédéon, *m.*
Giles, Gilles, *m.*
Godfrey, Godefroi, Godefroy, *m.*
Goodwin, Gédouin, *m.*
Gordian, Gordien, *m.*
Gorgon, Gorgone, *f.*
Gracchi (The), les Gracques, *m.pl.*
Gracchus, Gracchus, *m.*
Gratian, Gratien, *m.*
Gregory, Grégoire, *m.*
Grimalkin, Grippeminaud, Raminagrobis, *m.*
Griselda, Griselda, Grisélidis, *f.*
Grizzle, Aliboron, *m.*
Gudula, Gudule, Gudule, *f.*
Guercino, le Guerchin, *m.*
Guido, le Guide, *m.*
Gustavus, Gustave, *m.*

Habakkuk, Habacuc, *m.*
Hagar, Agar, *f.*
Haggai, Aggée, *m.*
Ham, Cham, *m.*
Haman, Aman, *m.*
Hannah, Anna, *f.*
Hannibal, Annibal, *m.*
Hardicanute, Canut-le-Hardi, *m.*
Harlequin, Arlequin, *m.*
Harpocrates, Harpocrate, *m.*
Harriet, Henriette, *f.*
Harry, Henri, *m.*
Hebe, Hébé, *f.*
Hecate, Hécate, *f.*
Hecuba, Hécube, *f.*
Hegesippus, Hégésippe, *m.*
Helen, Helena, Hélène, *f.*
Heliodorus, Héliodore, *m.*
Heliogabalus, Héliogabale, *m.*
Heloisa, Héloïse, *f.*

Henrietta, Henriette, *f.*
Henry, Henri, *m.*
Heraclides, Héraclide, *m.*
Heraclitus, Héraclite, *m.*
Hercules, Hercule, *m.*
Herod, Hérode, *m.*
Herodian, Hérodien, *m.*
Herodotus, Hérodote, *m.*
Hesiod, Hésiode, *m.*
Hezekiah, Ézéchias, *m.*
Hieronymus, Hiéronyme, *m.*; Jérôme, *m.*
Hilary, Hilaire, *m.*
Hipparchus, Hipparque, *m.*
Hippocrates, Hippocrate, *m.*
Hippolytus, Hippolyte, *m.*
Homer, Homère, *m.*
Honorius, Honoré, *m.*
Horace, Horatio, Horace, *m.*
Horatii (The), les Horaces, [*m.pl.*
Hortensia, Hortense, *f.*
Hosea, Osée, *m.*
Hubert, Hubertus, Hubert, *m.*
Hugh, Hugues, *m.*
Humphrey, Homfroi, *m.*
Hyacinthus, Hyacinthe, *m.*
Hygeia, Hygieia. *V. General Dictionary* [Hyménée, *m.*
Hymen, Hymenæus, Hymen,
Hyrcanus, Hyrcan, *m.*
Hystaspes, Hystaspe, *m.*

Iapetus, Japet, *m.*
Icarus, Icare, *m.*
Idomeneus, Idoménée, *m.*
Ignatius, Ignace, *m.*
Iphigenia, Iphigénie, *f.*
Irenæus, Irénée, *m.*
Irene, Irène, *f.*
Isabel, Isabella, Isabelle, *f.*
Isaiah, Isaïe, *m.*
Iscariot, Iscariote, *m.*
Ishmael, Ismaël, *m.*
Isidore, Isidorus, Isidore, *m.*
Isocrates, Isocrate, *m.*
Israel, Israël, *m.*
Ivanhoe, Ivanhoé, *m.*

Jack, Jacky, Jean, *m.*; Jeannot, *m.*; (*ass*) Martin, *m.* — *Ketch,* Charlot, Monsieur de Paris, *m.* — *Sheppard,* Cartouche, Mandrin, Robert Macaire, Vidocq, *m.*
James, Jacques, *m.*
Jane, Jeanne, *f.*
Janet, Jeannette, Jeanneton, *f.*
Jansen, Jansenius, Jansénius, *m.*
Januarius, Janvier, *m.*
Japhet, Japheth, Japhet, *m.*
Jasper, Jaspar, Gaspard, *m.*
Jechoniah, Jéchonias, *m.*
Jeffrey, Geoffroy, *m.*
Jehoshaphat, Josaphat, *m.*
Jehovah, Jéhovah, *m.*
Jem, Jemmy, Jacquot, Jacquet, Jacques, *m.*
Jemima, Jémima, *f.*
Jenny, Jenny, Jeannette, *f.*
Jephthah, Jephté, *m.*
Jeremiah, Jeremy, Jérémie, [*m.*
Jerome, Jérôme, *m.*
Jesus, Jésus, *m.*
Jim. *V.* JEM
Joan, Jeanne, *f.* — *of Arc,* Jeanne d'Arc, *f.*
Joanna, Jeanne, *f.*
Jocasta, Jocaste, Jocaste, *f.*
Joe, Joseph
Joel, Joël, *m.*
John, Johnny, Jean, *m.*
Jonah, Jonas, Jonas, *m.*
Jonathan, Jonathan, *m.*
Jonathan Wild, Cartouche, Mandrin, *m.*
Josaphat, Josaphat, *m.*
Joseph, Joseph, *m.*
Josephine, Joséphine, *f.*
Josephus, Josèphe, *m.*
Joseppino, le Joseppin, *m.*
Joshua, Josué, *m.*
Josiah, Josias, *m.*
Jove, Jupiter, *m.*
Jovian, Jovien, *m.*
Judah, Juda, *m.*
Judas, Judas, *m.*
Juggernaut, Jagrenat, *m.*
Julia, Julie, *f.*
Julian, Julien, *m.*
Juliana, Julienne, *f.*
Juliet, Juliette, *f.*
Julius, Jules, *m.*
Junia, Junie, *f.*
Juno, Junon, *f.*
Justina, Justine, *f.*
Justinian, Justinien, *m.*
Justus, Juste, *m.*
Juvenal, Juvénal, *m.*

Katharine, Kate, Kitty, Catherine, *f.*

Ladislaus, Ladislas, *m.*
Lælia, Lélie, *f.*
Laertes, Laërte, *m.*
Laertius, Laërce, *m.*
Laocoon, Laocoon, *m.*
Latona, Latone, *f.*
Launcelot, Lancelot, *m.*
Laura, Laure, *f.*
Laverna, Laverne, *f.*
Lavinia, Lavinie, *f.* [rent, *m.*
Lawrence, Laurence, Lau-
Lazarus, Lazare, *m.*
Leah, Lia, *f.*
Leander, Léandre, *m.*
Leda, Léda, *f.*
Leo, Léon, *m.*
Leonard, Léonard, *m.*
Leonidas, Léonidas, *m.*
Leonora, Léonore, *f.*
Leontius, Léonce, *m.*
Leopold, Léopold, *m.*
Levi, Levy, Lévi, Lévy, *m.*
Lewis, Louis, *m.*
Linnæus, Linné, Linnée, *m.*
Livia, Livie, *f.*
Livy, Tite-Live, *m.*
Lizzie, Lizzy, Lise, Lisette, *f.*
Longinus, Longin, *m.*
Longus, Longus, *m.*
Lot, Loth, *m.*
Lothario. *V. General Dictionary*
Louisa, Louise, *f.*
Lucan, Lucain, *m.*
Lucetta, Lucette, *f.*
Lucian, Lucien, *m.*
Lucilla, Lucile, *f.*
Lucina, Lucine, *f.*
Lucinda, Lucinde, *f.*
Lucretia, Lucrèce, *f.*
Lucretius, Lucrèce, *m.*
Lucy, Lucie, *f.*
Luke, Luc, *m.*
Lycurgus, Lycurgue, *m.*
Lydia, Lydie, *f.*
Lysander, Lysandre, *m.*
Lysimachus, Lysimaque, *m.*
Lysippus, Lysippe, *m.*
Maccabees (The), les Machabées, *m.pl.* [Machabée, *m.*
Maccabeus, Maccabæus,
Machiavelli, Machiavel, *m.*
Macrobius, Macrobe, *m.*
Madeline, Madeleine, *f.*
Mæcenas, Mécène, *m.*
Mag, Margot, *f.*
Magdalen, Magdalene, Madeleine, *f.* [*m.*
Malachi, Malachy, Malachie,
Manasseh, Manassé, *m.*
Manfred, Mainfroi, *m.*
Marcellina, Marcelline, *f.*
Marcellinus, Marcellin, *m.*
Marcian, Marcien, *m.*
Marcus, Marc, *m.*
Mardocheus, Mardochée, *m.*
Margaret, Margery, Marguerite, *f.*
Marget, Margot, *f.*
Mark, Marc, *m.*
Martha, Marthe, *f.*
Mary, Marie, *f.*
Mat. *V.* MATTHEW
Matilda, Mathilde, *f.* [*m.*
Matthew, Mathieu, Matthieu,
Maud, Madelon, *f.*
Mauselus, Mausole, *m.*
Maxentius, Maxence, *m.*
Maximianus, Maximian, Maximien, *m.*
Maximilian, Maximilien, *m.*
Maximinus, Maximin, *m.*
Maximus, Maxime, *m.*
Mecænas. *V.* MÆCENAS
Medea, Médée, *f.*
Medici, Médicis, *m.f.*
Medusa, Méduse, *f.*
Meg, Margot, *f.*
Megæra, Mégère, *f.*
Melania, Mélanie, *f.* [*m.*
Melchisedek, Melchisédech,
Melpomene, Melpomène, *f.*
Melusine, Mélusine, *f.*
Menander, Ménandre, *m.*
Menelaus, Ménélas, *m.*
Mephistopheles, Méphistophélès, *m.*
Mercury, Mercure, *m.*
Messalina, Messaline, *f.*
Methuselah, Mathusalem, *m.*
Micah, Michée, *m.*
Michael, Michel, *m.* — *Angelo,* (‡) Michel-Ange, *m.*
Milo, Milon, *m.*
Miltiades, Miltiade, *m.*
Minerva, Minerve, *f.*
Mithridates, Mithridate, *m.*
Mnemosyne, Mnémosyne, *f.*
Molly, Mariette, Marion, Manon, *f.*
Mordecai, Mardochée, *m.*
Morpheus, Morphée, *m.*
Morris, Maurice, *m.*
Moses, Moïse, *m.*

Nancy, Annette, Nannette, *f.*
Naomi, Noémi, *f.*
Napoleon, Napoléon, *m.*
Narcissus, Narcisse, *m.*
Nebuchadnezzar, Nabuchodonosor, *m.*
Ned, Neddy, Édouard, *m.*
Nehemiah, Néhémie, *m.*
Nell, Nellie, Nelly, Hélène, *f.*
Nemesis, Némésis, *f.*
Neoptolemus, Néoptolème, *m.*
Nereus, Nérée, *m.*
Nero, Néron, *m.* [maille, *m.*
Nibble (Squire), Ronge-

Nicephorus, Nicéphore, *m.*
Nicholas, Nick, Nicolas, *m.* *Old* —, le diable, *m.*
Nicodemus, Nicodème, *m.*
Nimrod, Nemrod, *m.*
Nina, Nino, Ninon, Ninon, *f.*
Niobe, Niobé, *f.*
Noah, Noé, *m.*
Noel, Noël, *m.*

Obadiah, Abdias, *m.*
Oceanus, Océan, *m.*
Octavia, Octavie, *f.*
Octavianus, Octavien, *m.*
Octavius, Octave, *m.*
Œdipus, Œdipe, *m.*
Oliver, Olivier, *m.*
Olivia, Olivie, *f.*
Olympia, Olympe, *f.*
Olympus, Olympe, *m.*
Onesimus, Onésime, *m.*
Ophelia, Ophélie, *f.*
Oppian, Oppien, *m.*
Orestes, Oreste, *m.*
Origen, Origène, *m.*
Orlando, Roland, *m.* — ***furioso,*** Roland le furieux
Orontes, Oronte, *m.*
Orpheus, Orphée, *m.*
Osmund, Osmond, *m.*
Othello, Otello, Othello, *m.*
Otho, Othon, *m.*
Ovid, Ovide, *m.*

Palæmon, Palémon, *m.*
Palæologus, Paléologue, *m.*
Palamedes, Palamède, *m.*
Palinurus, Palinure, *m.*
Palmyra, Palmyre, *f.*
Pandora, Pandore, *f.*
Pantaloon, Pantalon, *m.*; Cassandre, *m.*
Paracelsus, Paracelse, *m.*
Parcæ (The), les Parques, *f.pl.*
Paris, Pâris, *m.* (*pronounced Pahriss*)
Parmenides, Parménide, *m.*
Parmenio, Parménion, *m.*
Parmigiano, le Parmesan, *m.*
Pasiphae, Pasiphaé, *f.*
Patrick, Pat, Patrice, *m.*
Patroclus, Patrocle, *m.*
Paula, Paule, *f.*
Paulina, Pauline, *f.* [*m.*
Paulus Æmilius, Paul-Émile,
Peg, Peggy, Margot, *f.*
Pegasus, Pégase, *m.*
Pelagia, Pélagie, *f.*
Pelagius, Pélage, *m.*
Peleus, Pélée, *m.*
Penelope, Pénélope, *f.*
Pepin, Pépin, *m.*
Pericles, Périclès, *m.*
Perseus, Persée, *m.*
Persius, Perse, *m.*
Perugino, le Pérugin, *m.*
Peter, Pierre, *m.* [que, *m.*
Petrarca, Petrarch, Pétrar-
Petronius, Pétrone, *m.*
Phædra, Phèdre, *f.*
Phædrus, Phèdre, *m.*
Phaeton, Phaéton, *m.*
Pharaoh, Pharaon, *m.*
Philaretus, Philarète, *m.*
Philip, Philippe, *m.*
Philippa, Philippe, *f.*
Philippina, Philippine, *f.*
Philoctetes, Philoctète, *m.*
Philomela, Philomel, Philomèle, *f.*
Philoponus, Philopon, *m.*
Phineas, Phinée, Phinéas, *m.*
Phœbe, Phébé, *f.*
Phœbus, Phébus, *m.*
Pindar, Pindare, *m.*
Pisistratus, Pisistrate, *m.*
Piso, Pison, *m.*
Pius, Pie, *m.*
Pizarro, Pizarre, *m.*
Plato, Platon, *m.*
Plautus, Plaute, *m.*
Pliny, Pline, *m.*
Plutarch, Plutarque, *m.*
Pluto, Pluton, *m.*
Poll, Polly, Marie, *f.*; (*parrot*) Jacquot, *m.*
Polybius, Polybe, *m.*
Polydorus, Polydore, *m.*
Polynices, Polynice, *m.*
Polyphemus, Polyphème, *m.*
Polyxena, Polyxène, *f.*
Pomona, Pomone, *f.*
Pompey, Pompée, *m.* [*m.*
Pontius Pilate, Ponce Pilate,
Porcia, Porcie, *f.*
Porphyry, Porphyre, *m.*
Potiphar, Putiphar, *m.*
Praxiteles, Praxitèle, *m.*
Priapus, Priape, *m.*
Priscian, Priscien, *m.*
Priscilla, Priscille, *f.*
Procne, Progné, *f.*
Procopius, Procope, *m.*
Procrustes, Procuste, Procruste, *m.*
Prometheus, Prométhée, *m.*
Propertius, Properce, *m.*
Proteus, Protée, *m.*
Prudentius, Prudence, *m.*
Psyche, Psyché, *f.*
Ptolemy, Ptolémée, *m.*
Pug, (*monkey*) Bertrand, *m.*; Fagotin, *m.*
Pulcheria, Pulchérie, *f.*
Punch. *V. General Dictionary*
Puss, Pussy, (*cat*) Minet, Minon, *m.*, Minette, *f.*, Mimi, *m.f.* — ***in boots,*** le Chat botté,
Pylades, Pylade, *m.* [*m.*
Pyramus, Pyrame, *m.*
Pyrrho, Pyrrhon, *m.*
Pythagoras, Pythagore, *m.*

Quintilian, Quintilien, *m.*
Quintus Curtius, Quinte-Curce, *m.* [*m.*
Quixote (Don), Don Quichotte,

Radegund, Radegonde, *f.*
Ralph, Raoul, *m.*
Randolph, Randolphe, *m.*
Raphael, Raphaël, *m.*
Raymund, Raymond, *m.*
Rebecca, Rébecca, *f.*
Reuben, Ruben, *m.*
Reynold, Renaud, *m.*
Rhadamanthus, Rhadamanthe, *m.*
Rhea, Rhée, *f.*
Roderick, Rodrigue, *m.*
Rodolph, Rodolphe, *m.*
Romano (Giulio), Jules Romain, *m.*
Romeo, Roméo, *m.*
Rosalia, Rosalie, *f.*
Rosamund, Rosemonde, *f.*
Rosinante, Rossinante, *m.*
Rowland, Roland, *m.*
Roxana, Roxane, *f.*
Rufus. le Roux
Sabina, Sabine, *f.*
Sal, Sally, Sara, *f.*
Sallust, Salluste, *m.*
Salmasius, Saumaise, *m.*
Samson, Sampson, Samson, *m.*
Samuel, Sam, Samuel, *m.*
Sancho Panza, Sancho Pan-
Sappho, Sapho, *f.* [ça, *m.*
Sarah, Sara, *f.* [*m.*
Sardanapalus, Sardanapale,
Satan, Satan, *m.*
Saturn, Saturne, *m.*
Saturninus, Saturnin, *m.*
Saul, Saül, *m.*
Savinian, Savinien, *m.*
Savonarola, Savonarole, *m.*
Scipio, Scipion, *m.* — ***Africanus,*** Scipion l'Africain. — ***Asiaticus,*** Scipion l'Asiatique
Sebastian, Sébastien, *m.*
Sejanus, Séjan, *m.*
Selene, Sélène, *f.*
Semele, Sémélé, *f.*
Seneca, Sénèque, *m.*
Sesostris, Sésostris, *m.*
Severus, Sévère, *m.*
Shem, Sem, *m.*
Sidonius, Sidoine, *m.*
Sigismund, Sigismond, *m.*
Silenus, Silène, *m.*
Silvan, Silvain, *m.*
Silvester, Silvestre, *m.*
Silvia, Silvie, *f.*
Simeon, Siméon, *m.*
Simonides, Simonide, *m.*
Sisyphus, Sisyphe, *m.*
Sixtus, Sixte, *m.* — ***the Fifth,*** Sixte-Quint, *m.*
Socinus, Socin, *m.*
Socrates, Socrate, *m.*
Solomon, Salomon, *m.*
Sophia, Sophy, Sophie, *f.*
Sophocles, Sophocle, *m.*
Spinoza, Spinosa, *m.*
Stanislaus, Stanislas, *m.*
Statius, Stace, *m.*
Stephania, Stéphanie, *f.*
Stephen, Étienne, *m.*
Strabo, Strabon, *m.*
Suetonius, Suétone, *m.*
Sulpicius, Sulpice, *m.*
Susan, Susanna, Susannah, Susanne, Suzanne, *f.*
Suzy, Susette, Suzette, Suson, Suzon, *f.*
Sweyn, Suénon, *m.*
Sylvan, Sylvain, *m.*
Sylvester, Sylvestre, *m.*
Sylvia, Sylvie, *f.*

Tacitus, Tacite, *m.*
Tamerlane, Tamerlan, *m.*
Tancred, Tancrède, *m.*
Tantalus, Tantale, *m.*
Tasso, le Tasse, *m.*
Ted, Teddy, Édouard, *m.*
Telemachus, Télémaque, *m.*
Terence, Térence, *m.*
Tereus, Térée, *m.*
Tertullian, Tertullien, *m.*
Thales, Thalès, *m.*
Thalia, Thalie, *f.*
Themis, Thémis, *f.*
Themistocles, Thémistocle, *m.*
Theobald, Thibaut, *m.*
Theocritus, Théocrite, *m.*
Theodora, Théodore, *f.*
Theodore, Theodorus, Théodore, *m.*
Theodosia, Théodosie, *f.*
Theodosius, Théodose, *m*

Theophila, Théophile, *f.*
Theophilus, Théophile, *m.*
Theophrastus, Théophraste, [*m.*
Theresa, Thérèse, *f.*
Thersites, Thersite, *m.*
Theseus, Thésée, *m.*
Thisbe, Thisbé, *f.*
Thucydides, Thucydide, *m.*
Thyestes, Thyeste, *m.*
Tiberius, Tibère, *m.*
Tibullus, Tibulle, *m.*
Tigranes, Tigrane, *m.*
Timæus, Timée, *m.*
Timothy, Timothée, *m.*
Tintoretto, le Tintoret, *m.*
Titian, le Titien, *m.*
Tobias, Toby, Tobie, *m.*
Tom Thumb, Tom Pouce, *m.*; (*in the tale*) le Petit-Poucet, *m.*
Trajan, Trajan, *m.* *—'s column,* la colonne Trajane, *f.*
Triptolemus, Triptolème, *m.*
Trissino, Trissin, *m.*
Tubal-Cain, Tubalcaïn, *m.*
Tullia, Tullie, *f.*
Tully, Tullius Cicéron, Cicéron, [*m.*
Tyrtæus, Tyrtée, *m.*

Ulpian, Ulpien, *m.*
Ulrica, Ulrique, *f.*
Ulysses, Ulysse, *m.*
Urania, Uranie, *f.*
Uranus, Uranus, *m.*
Urban, Urbain, *m.*
Uriah, Urias, Urie, *m.*
Ursula, Ursule, *f.*

Valentine, Valentin, *m.*, Valentine, *f.*
Valentinian, Valentinien, *m.*
Valeria, Valérie, *f.*
Valerian, Valérien, *m.*
Valerius, Valère, *m.*
Varro, Varron, *m.*
Venceslaus, Venceslas, *m.*
Venus, Vénus, *f.*
Veronese, Véronèse, *m.*
Veronica, Véronique, *f.*
Vertumnus, Vertumne, *m.*
Vespasian, Vespasien, *m.*
Victoria, Victoire, Victoria, *f.*
Victorina, Victorine, *f.*
Victorinus, Victorin, *m.*
Virgil, Virgile, *m.*
Virginia, Virginie, *f.*
Vishnu, Vichnou, *m.*
Vitruvius, Vitruve, *m.*
Vivian, Vivien, *m.*
Vulcan, Vulcain, *m.*

Walter, Wat, Gautier, *m.*
Wilhelmina, Wilhelmine, *f.*
William, Will, Willy, Willie, Guillaume, *m.*

Xanthippe, Xanthippe, *f.*
Xanthippus, Xanthippe, *m.*
Xenocrates, Xénocrate, *m.*
Xenophanes, Xénophane, *m.*
Xenophon, Xénophon, *m.*
Xerxes, Xercès, Xerxès, *m.*

Zaccheus, Zachée, *m.*
Zachariah, Zachary, Zacharie, *m.*
Zedekiah, Sédécias, *m.*
Zeno, Zénon, *m.*
Zenobia, Zénobie, *f.*
Zephaniah, Sophonie, *m.*
Zephyr, Zephyrus, Zéphyre, *m.*
Zerubbabel, Zorobabel, *m.*
Zoe, Zoé, *f.*
Zoilus, Zoïle, *m.*
Zoroaster, Zoroastre, *m.*
Zosimus, Zosime, *m.*
Zwingli, Zwingle, *m.*

GEOGRAPHICAL PROPER NAMES.

Aargau, l'Argovie, *f.*
Abdera, Abdère, *f.* [*f.pl.*
Abruzzi (The), les Abruzzes,
Abruzzo, l'Abruzze, *f.*
Abyssinia, l'Abyssinie, *f.*
Acadia, l'Acadie, *f.*
Acarnania, l'Acarnanie, *f.*
Achaia, l'Achaïe, *f.*
Acre, Saint-Jean d'Acre, Acre, *m.*
Adrianople, Andrinople, *f.*
Ægean Sea (The), la Mer
Ægina, Égine, *f.* [Égée, *f.*
Æolia, l'Éolie, *f.*
Ætolia, l'Étolie, *f.*
Afghanistan, l'Afghanistan, *m.*
Africa, l'Afrique, *f.*
Agincourt, Azincourt, *m.*
Alba, Albe, *f.*
Albania, l'Albanie, *f.*
Albion, l'Albion, *f.*
Alderney, Aurigny, *m.*
Aleppo, Alep, *m.*
Alexandretta, Alexandrette, *f.*
Alexandria, Alexandrie, *f.*
Algeria, l'Algérie, *f.*
Algiers, Alger, *m.*
Alicant, Alicante, Alicante, *f.*
Alps (The), les Alpes, *f.pl.*
Alsace, Alsatia, l'Alsace, *f.*
Alva, Albe, *f.*
Amazon (The), l'Amazone, le Fleuve des Amazones, *m.*
Amboyna, Amboine, *f.*
America, l'Amérique, *f.*
Amoor (The), l'Amour, *m.*
Anatolia, l'Anatolie, *f.*
Ancona, Ancône, *f.*
Andalusia, l'Andalousie, *f.*
Andes (The), les Andes, *f.pl.*
Andorra, Andorre, *m.* *The Valley of* —, le Val d'Andorre, *m.*
Anglesea, Anglesey, *m.*
Antigua, Antigue, *f.*
Antilles (The), les Antilles, *f.pl.*
Antioch, Antioche, *f.*
Antwerp, Anvers, *m.*
Apennines (The), les Apennins, *m.pl.*
Apulia, l'Apulie, la Pouille, *f.*
Aquileia, Aquilée, *f.*
Arabia, l'Arabie, *f.* — *Deserta,* l'Arabie Déserte. — *Felix,* l'Arabie Heureuse. — *Petræa,* l'Arabie Pétrée
Aragon, l'Aragon, *m.*
Araucania, l'Araucanie, *f.*
Arbela, Arbelles, *f.*
Arcadia, l'Arcadie, *f.*
Archangel, Arkhangel, *m.*
Archipelago (The), l'Archipel,
Argovia, l'Argovie, *f.* [*m.*
Armenia, l'Arménie, *f.*
Asia, l'Asie, *f.*
Assyria, l'Assyrie
Asturias (The), les Asturies,
Athens, Athènes, *f.* [*f.pl.*
Atlas (The), l'Atlas, *m.*
Attica, l'Attique, *f.*
Augsburg, Augsbourg, *m.*
Australasia, l'Australasie, *f.*
Australia, l'Australie, *f.*
Austria, l'Autriche, *f.*
Auvergne, l'Auvergne, *f.*
Aventine (The), l'Aventin, *m.*
Averno (The), l'Averne, *m.*
Azores (The), les Açores, *f.pl.*

Babylon, Babylone, *f.*
Babylonia, la Babylonie, *f.*
Bactra, Bactres, *f.*
Bactria, Bactriana, la Bac-
Baden, Bade, *f.* [triane, *f.*
Baffin's Bay, la Baie de Baffin, *f.*
Bahama Islands (The), les Iles Bahama, les Lucayes, *f.pl.*
Balearic Isles (The), les Iles Baléares, *f.pl.* [Barbade, *f.*
Barbadoes, Barbados, la
Barbary, la Barbarie, *f.* *The — States,* les États Barbaresques, *m.pl.*
Barbuda, la Barboude, *f.*
Barcelona, Barcelone, *f.*
Basel, Basle, Bâle, *f.*
Bavaria, la Bavière, *f.*
Belgium, la Belgique, *f.*
Bearn, le Béarn, *m.*
Belt (The), le Belt, *m.*
Benevento, Bénévent, *m.*
Bengal, le Bengale, *m.* *The Bay of* —, le Golfe du Bengale,
Bergamo, Bergame, *f.* [*m.*
Bergen-op-Zoom, Berg-op-
Berlin, Berlin, *m.* [Zoom, *m.*
Bermudas (The), les Iles Bermudes, *f.pl.* [(*town*), *f.*
Berne, Berne (*canton*) *m.*,
Berry, le Berry, le Berri, *m.*
Bessarabia, la Bessarabie, *f.*
Bethlehem, Bethléem, *m.*
Bianco (Cape), le Cap Blanc, *m.*
Birmah *or* **Burmah (The Empire of), Birman Empire (The),** l'empire Birman, *m.*, la Birmanie, *f.*
Biscay, la Biscaye, *f.* *The Bay of* —, le Golfe de Gascogne, *m.*
Bœotia, la Béotie, *f.*
Bohemia, la Bohême, *f.*
Bokhara, Boukhara, *m.*
Bolivia, la Bolivie, *f.*
Bologna, Bologne, *f.*
Bona, Bone, *f.*
Bordeaux, Bordeaux, *m.*
Borysthenes (The), le Bory-
Bosnia, la Bosnie, *f.* [thène, *m.*
Bothnia, la Bothnie, *f.*
Brabant, le Brabant, *m.*
Braganza, Bragance, *f.*
Brandenburg, le Brandebourg, *m.* [sil, *m.*
Brazil, Brazils (The), le Bré-
Bremen, Brême, *f.*
Brindisi, Brindes, *m.*
Britain, Britannia, la Grande-Bretagne *or* l'Angleterre, *f.* *Great* —, la Grande-Bretagne, *f.* *New* —, la Nouvelle-Bretagne, *f.*
Brittany, la Bretagne, *f.*
Broussa, Brousse, *f.*
Brunswick (New), le Nouveau-Brunswick, *m.*
Brussels, Bruxelles, *f.*
Bucharia, la Bucharie, *f.*
Buda, Bude, *f.*
Bulgaria, la Bulgarie, *f.*
Burgundy, la Bourgogne, *f.*
Burmah. *V.* BIRMAH
Byzantium, Byzance, *f.*

Cabul, Caboul, *m.*
Cadiz, Cadix, *m.*
Cæsarea, Césarée, *f.* [frerie, *f.*
Cafferland, Caffraria, la Ca-
Cairo, le Caire, *m.*
Calabria, la Calabre, *f.*
Caledonia, la Calédonie, *f.* *New* —, la Nouvelle Calédonie,
California, la Californie, *f.* [*f.*
Campagna di Roma, la Campagne de Rome, *f.*
Campania, la Campanie, *f.*
Campeachy, Campêche, *m.*
Canaan, Chanaan, *m.*
Canada, le Canada, *m.*
Canary, Canarie, *f.* *The — Islands,* les Canaries, *f.pl.* *The Canaries,* les Canaries, *f.pl.*
Candia, l'Ile de Candie, *f.*
Canea, la Canée, *f.*
Cannæ, Cannes, *f.*
Canterbury, Cantorbéry, *m.*
Cape, Cap, *m.* — *Town,* la Ville du Cap, *f.*, le Cap, *m.* *The — of Good Hope,* le Cap de Bonne-Espérance, *m.*
Cappadocia, la Cappadoce, *f.*
Capreæ, Capri, Caprée, *f.*
Capua, Capoue, *f.*
Caria, la Carie, *f.*
Caribbean Sea (The), la Mer des Caraïbes, la Mer des Antilles, *f.* [Iles Caraïbes, *f.pl.*
Caribbee Islands (The), les
Carinthia, la Carinthie, *f.*

Carnatic, le Karnatic, *m.*
Carniola, la Carniole, *f.*
Carolina, la Caroline, *f.*
Carpathian Mountains (The), les Monts Carpathes,
Carrara, Carrare, *f.* [*m.pl.*
Carthage, Carthage, *f.*
Carthagena, Carthagène, *f.*
Cashmere, le Cachemire, *m.*; (*town*) Cachemire, *f.*
Castile, la Castille, *f.*
Catalonia, la Catalogne, *f.*
Catania, Catane, *f.* [*m.*
Cattegat (The), le Cattégat,
Caucasus, le Caucase, *m.*
Celtiberia, la Celtibérie, *f.*
Cephalonia, Céphalonie, *f.*
Ceylon, Ceylan, *m.* [ronée, *f.*
Chæronea, Chæroneia, Ché-
Chalcedon, Chalcédoine, *f.*
Chaldea, la Chaldée, *f.*
Champagne, la Champagne, *f.*
Charybdis, Charybde, *m.*
Chili, le Chili, *m.*
China, la Chine, *f.*
Chino-India, l'Indo-Chine, *f.*
Chios, Chio, *f.*
Cilicia, la Cilicie, *f.*
Circassia, la Circassie, *f.*
Coburg, Cobourg, *m.* [*f.*
Cochin-China, la Cochinchine,
Coimbra, Coïmbre, *f.*
Colombia, la Colombie, *f.*
Colonos, Colonus, Colone, *f.*
Columbia, la Colombie, *f.*
Como, Come, *f.*
Compostella, Compostelle, *f.*
Congo, le Congo, *m.*
Constantina, Constantine, *f.*
Constantinople, Constantinople, *f.*
Copenhagen, Copenhague, *f.*
Cordilleras (The), les Cordillères, *f.pl.*
Cordova, Cordoue, *f.*
Corea (The), la Corée, *f.*
Corfu, Corfou, *m.*
Corinth, Corinthe, *f.*
Cornwall, le Cornouailles, *m.*
Corsica, la Corse, *f.*
Cortona, Cortone, *f.*
Corunna, la Corogne, *f.*
Courland, la Courlande, *f.*
Cracow, Cracovie, *f.*
Cremona, Crémone, *f.*
Crete, la Crète, *f.*
Crimea (The), la Crimée, *f.*
Croatia, la Croatie, *f.*
Croton, Crotona, Crotone, *f.*
Cumæ, Cumes, *f.*
Curaçoa, Curaçao, *m.* [*f.pl.*
Cyclades (The), les Cyclades,
Cyprus, Chypre, *f.*
Cythera, Cythère, *f.*

Dacia, la Dacie, *f.*
Dalecarlia, la Dalécarlie, *f.*
Dalmatia, la Dalmatie, *f.*
Damascus, Damas, *m.*
Damietta, Damiette, *f.*
Dantzic, Dantzick, *m.*
Danube (The), le Danube, *m.*
Dardanelles (The), les Dardanelles, *f.pl.*
Dauphiny, le Dauphiné, *m.*
Deccan, le Décan, *m.*
Delphi, Delphes, *f.* [*m.*
Dendermond, Dendermonde,
Denmark, le Danemark, *m.*
Desirade, Desiderade, la Désirade, *f.*
Dnieper (The), le Dniéper, *m.*
Dniester (The), le Dniester, *m.*
Dodona, Dodone, *f.*
Dominica, la Dominique, *f.*
Don (The), le Don, *m.*
Doris, la Doride, *f.*
Dover, Douvres, *m.* *The Straits of* —, le Pas-de-Calais, *m.*
Dresden, Dresde, *f.*
Dublin, Dublin, *m.*
Duna (The), la Duna, *f.*
Dunkirk, Dunkerque, *m.*
Dwina (The), la Dwina, *f.*

Ebro (The), l'Èbre, *m.*
Ecbatana, Ecbatane, *f.*
Ecuador, la République de l'Équateur, *f.*, l'Équateur, *m.*
Edinburgh, Édimbourg, *m.*
Egina, Égine, *f.*
Egypt, l'Egypte, *f.*
Elba, l'Ile d'Elbe, *f.*
Elbe (The), l'Elbe, *m.*
Elsinore, Elseneur, *m.*
England, l'Angleterre, *f.* *New* —, la Nouvelle-Angleterre, *f.*
Eolia, l'Éolie, *f.*
Ephesus, Éphèse, *f.*
Epirus, l'Épire, *f.*
Erebus, l'Érèbe, *m.*
Erie (Lake), le lac Érié, *m.*
Esthonia, l'Esthonie, *f.* [*f.*
Estremadura, l'Estramadure,
Ethiopia, l'Éthiopie, *f.*
Etna, l'Etna, *m.*
Etolia, l'Etolie, *f.*
Etruria, l'Étrurie, *f.*
Eubœa, l'Eubée, *f.* [*m.*
Euphrates (The), l'Euphrate,
Europe, l'Europe, *f.* [*m.*
Euxine (The), le Pont-Euxin,

Falkland Islands (The), Falklands (The), les Iles Malouines, les Iles Falkland, *f.pl.* [Færoé, *f.pl.*
Faroe Islands (The), les Iles
Ferrara, Ferrare, *f.*
Finland, la Finlande, *f.*
Flanders, la Flandre, *f.*
Florence, Florence, *f.*
Florida, la Floride, *f.*
Flushing, Flessingue, *m.*
Fontarabia, Fontarabie, *f.*
Formosa, Formose, *f.*
Forth (The), le Forth, *m.* *The Frith of* —, le Golfe du Forth,
France, la France, *f.* [*m.*
Franconia, la Franconie, *f.*
Frankfort, Francfort, *m.* [*m.*
Freiburg, Friburg, Fribourg,
Friendly Islands (The), les Iles des Amis, *f.pl.*
Friesland, la Frise, *f.*
Frontignac, Frontiniac, Frontignan, *m.*

Gaboon (The), le Gabon, *m.*
Gaeta, Gaète, *f.*
Galatia, la Galatie, *f.*
Galicia, (*in Austria*) la Galicie, *f.*; (*in Spain*) la Galice, *f.*
Galilee, la Galilée, *f.*
Gallia, la Gaule, *f.*
Gambia, la Gambie, *f.*
Ganges (The), le Gange, *m.*
Garonne (The), la Garonne, *f.*
Gascony (The), la Gascogne, *f.*
Gaul, la Gaule, *f.*
Geneva, Genève, *f.*
Genoa, Gênes, *f.*
Georgia, la Géorgie, *f.*
Germany, l'Allemagne, *f.*
Ghent, Gand, *m.*
Giant's Causeway, la Chaussée des Géants, *f.*
Gironde (The), la Gironde, *f.*
Gloucester, Glocester, Gloucester, *m.*
Golconda, Golconde, *f.*
Gold Coast (The), la Côte d'Or, *f.*
Gomorrah, Gomorrhe, *f.*
Goree, Gorée, *f.*
Gothenburg, Gothenbourg, *m.*
Gothland, la Gothie, *f.*
Göttingen, Gœttingue, Gottingue, *f.*
Gottland, l'Ile Gottland, *f.*
Grain Coast (The), la Côte des Graines, *f.*
Granada, la Grenade, *f.*; (*town*) Grenade, *f.* *New* —, la Nouvelle-Grenade, *f.* [*m.*
Granicus (The), le Granique,
Greece, la Grèce, *f.*
Greenland, le Groënland, *m.*
Grenada, la Grenade, *f.*
Groningen, Groningue, *f.*
Guadaloupe, la Guadeloupe, *f.*
Guadalquivir (The), le Guadalquivir, *m.*
Guatemala, le Guatemala, *m.*
Guelderland, Guelders, la Gueldre, *f.*
Guernsey, Guernesey, *m.*
Guiana, Guyana, la Guyane, la Guiane, *f.*
Guinea, la Guinée, *f.* *New* —, la Nouvelle-Guinée, *f.*

Hague, (The), la Haye, *f.*
Hainault, le Hainaut, *m.* [*f.*
Halicarnassus, Halicarnasse,
Hamburg, Hambro, Hambourg, *m.*
Hanover, le Hanovre, *m.*
Hapsburg, Hapsbourg, *m.*
Havana, Havanna, Havannah, la Havane, *f.*
Havre, le Havre, *m.*
Hayti, Haïti, *m.* [*f.pl.*
Hebrides (The), les Hébrides,
Hebrus (The), l'Hèbre, *m.*
Helicon, l'Hélicon, *m.*
Hellespont (The), l'Hellespont, *m.*
Helvetia, l'Helvétie, *f.*
Heraclea, Heracleia, Héraclée, *f.*
Herculaneum, Herculanum, *m.*
Herzegovina, l'Herzégovine, *f.*
Hesperia, l'Hespérie, *f.*
Hesse, la Hesse, *f.*
Hibernia, l'Hibernie, *f.*
Highlands (The), la Haute Ecosse, *f.*
Hindostan, Hindustan, l'Hindoustan, l'Hindostan, *m.*
Holland, la Hollande, *f.* *New* —, la Nouvelle-Hollande, *f.*
Homburg, Hombourg, *m.*
Honduras, le Honduras, *m.*
Horn (Cape), le cap Horn, *m.*
Hudson's Bay, la Baie d'Hudson, *f.*
Hungary, la Hongrie, *f.*
Hymettus, Hymet, l'Hymette, le Mont Hymette, *m.*
Hyrcania, l'Hyrcanie, *f.*

Iberia, l'Ibérie, *f.*
Icaria, l'Icarie, *f.*
Iceland, l'Islande, *f.*
Illinois, l'Illinois, *m.*
Illyria, l'Illyrie, *f.*
India, l'Inde, *f.*; les Indes, *f.pl.* *East* —, les Indes Orientales. *The East — Company*, la Compagnie des Indes, *f.*
Indies, les Indes, *f.pl.* *The East* —, les Indes Orientales, les Grandes Indes. *The West* —, les Indes Occidentales, les Antilles, *f.pl.*
Indo-China, l'Indo-Chine, *f.*
Indus (The), (*anc.*) l'Indus, *m.*; (*modern*) le Sind, *m.*
Ingria, l'Ingrie, *f.*
Ionia, l'Ionie, *f.*
Ireland, l'Irlande, *f.*
Istria, l'Istrie, *f.*
Italia, Italy, l'Italie, *f.*
Ithaca, Ithaque, *f.*
Ivory Coast (The), la Côte d'Ivoire, *f.*

Jamaica, la Jamaïque, *f.*
Japan, le Japon, *m.*
Jerusalem, Jérusalem, *f.*
Jordan (The), le Jourdain, *m.*
Judæa, la Judée, *f.*
Juggernaut, Jagrenat, *m.*
Jutland, le Jutland, *m.*

Kabylia, la Kabylie, *f.*
Kaffrland, Kaffirland, Kaffraria. *V.* CAFFRARIA

Labrador, le Labrador, *m.*
Labuan, Labouan, *m.*
Laccadive Islands (The), les Iles Laquedives, *f.pl.*
Lacedæmon, Lacédémone, *f.*
Laconia, la Laconie, *f.*
Lancaster, Lancastre, *m.*
Land's End, le Cap Finisterre *or* Finistère, *m.*
Languedoc, le Languedoc, *m.*
Laodicea, Laodicée, *f.*
Lapland, la Laponie, *f.*
Larissa, Larisse, *f.*
Latakia, Latakieh, *m.*
Latium, le Latium, *m.*
Lebanon, le Liban, *m.* *Mount* —, le Mont Liban, *m.*
Leghorn, Livourne, *f.*
Leipsic, Leipsick, *m.*
Lepanto, Lépante, *f.*
Lerna, Lerne, *f.*
Lethe, le Léthé, *m.*
Leuctra, Leuctres, *f.*
Leyden, Leyde, *f.*
Liburnia, la Liburnie, *f.*
Libya, la Libye, *f.*
Liege, Liége, *f.*
Liguria, la Ligurie, *f.*
Limburg, Limbourg, *m.*
Lisbon, Lisbonne, *f.*
Lithuania, la Lithuanie, *f.*
Livadia, la Livadie, *f.*
Livonia, la Livonie, *f.*
Locris, la Locride, *f.*
Loir (The), le Loir, *m.*
Loire (The), la Loire, *f.*
Loiret (The), le Loiret, *m.*
Lombardo-Venetia, la Lombardo-Vénétie, *f.*
Lombardy, la Lombardie, *f.*
London, Londres, *m.*
Loretto, Lorette, *f.*
Lorraine, la Lorraine, *f.*
Louisburg, Louisbourg, *m.*
Louisiana, la Louisiane, *f.*
Low Countries (The), les Pays-Bas, *m.pl.*
Lowlands (The), la Basse Écosse, *f.*
Lucania, la Lucanie, *f.*
Lucaya Islands (The), les Lucayes, *f.pl.*
Lucca, Lucques, *f.* [(*town*), *f.*
Lucerne, Lucerne, (*canton*) *m.*,
Luneburg, Lunebourg, *m.*
Lusatia, la Lusace, *f.*
Lusitania, la Lusitanie, *f.*
Lutetia, Lutèce, *f.*
Luxemburg, (*country*) le Luxembourg, *m.*, (*town*) Luxembourg, *m.*
Luzon, Luçon, *f.*
Lydia, la Lydie, *f.*
Lyons, Lyon, *m.*

Maas (The), la Meuse, *f.*
Macedonia, Macedon, la Macédoine, *f.*
Madeira, Madère, *f.*
Mæander (The), le Méandre, *m.*
Magdeburg, Magdebourg, *m.*
Magellan (The Straits of), le Détroit de Magellan, *m.*
Main (The), (*river*) le Mein, *m.*
Maine, le Maine, *m.*
Majorca, Majorque, *f.*
Malaysia, la Malaisie, *f.*
Malta, Malte, *f.*
Malvasia, Malvoisie, *f.*
Man (The Isle of), l'Ile de Man, *f.*
Mancha (La), la Manche, *f.*
Manilla, Manille, *f.*
Mantinea, Mantinée, *f.*
Mantua, Mantoue, *f.*
Margarita, la Marguerite, *f.*
Marianne Islands (The), les Iles Mariannes, *f.pl.*
Marienburg, Marienbourg, *m.*
Marmora, Marmara, *f.*
Marne (The), la Marne, *f.*
Marquesas Isles (The), les Iles Marquises, *f.pl.*
Marseilles, Marseille, *f.* — *vinegar*, *V.* THIEF
Martinique, la Martinique, *f.*
Maryland, le Maryland, *m.*
Mauritania, la Mauritanie, *f.*
Mauritius, l'Ile Maurice, *f.*
Mecca, la Mecque, *f.*
Mechlin, Malines, *f.* [*m.*
Mecklenburg, Mecklenbourg,
Media, la Médie, *f.*
Medina, Médine, *f.*
Megara, Mégare, *f.*
Melanesia, la Mélanésie, *f.*
Mentone, Menton, Mentone, *m.*
Mentz, Mayence, *f.*
Mesopotamia, la Mésopotamie, *f.*
Messina, Messine, *f.* *The Straits of* —, le Phare de Messine, *m.*
Meuse (The), la Meuse, *f.*
Mexico, le Mexique, *m.*; (*town*) Mexico, *m.*
Middleburg, Middelbourg, *m.*
Milan, Milan, *m.*
Milanese (The), le Milanais, *m.*
Mingrelia, la Mingrélie, *f.*
Minorca, Minorque, *f.*
Minturnæ, Minturnes, *f.*
Mississippi (The), le Mississipi, *m.*
Missouri (The), le Missouri, *m.*
Modena, Modène, *f.*
Modenese (The), le Modénais, *m.*
Moldavia, la Moldavie, *f.*
Moldo-Wallachia, la Moldo-Valachie, *f.* [ques, *f.pl.*
Moluccas (The), les Molu-
Mongolia, la Mongolie, *f.*
Montenegro, le Monténégro, *m.*
Moravia, la Moravie, *f.*
Morea (The), la Morée, *f.*
Morlachia, la Morlaquie, *f.*
Morocco, le Maroc, *m.*
Moscow, Moscou, *m.*
Moselle (The), la Moselle, *f.*
Moskova (The), la Moskova, *f.*
Mosul, Mossoul, *f.*
Mozambique, le Mozambique,
Murcia, Murcie, *f.* [*m.*
Muscovy, la Moscovie, *f.*
Mysore, le Maïssour, le Mysore, *m.*

Nauplia, Nauplie, *f.*
Navarino, Navarin, *m.*
Navarre, la Navarre, *f.*
Negroland, la Nigritie, *f.*
Negropont, Négrepont, *m.*
Nepaul, le Népâl, *m.*
Netherlands (The), les Pays-Bas, *m.pl.*
Neustria, la Neustrie, *f.*
Neva (The), la Néva, *f.* [*f.*
Newfoundland, Terre-Neuve,
New-York, New-York, *m.*
Niagara (The), le Niagara, *m.*
Nicæa, Nice, Nicée, *f.*
Nice, (*in France*) Nice, *f.*
Niemen (The), le Niémen, *m.*
Niger (The), le Niger, *m.*
Nigritia, la Nigritie, *f.*
Nile (The), le Nil, *m.*
Nimeguen, Nimègue, *f.*
Nineveh, Ninive, *f.*
Normandy, la Normandie, *f.*
Norway, la Norvége, *f.*
Nova Scotia, la Nouvelle-Écosse, *f.* [Zemble, *f.*
Nova Zembla, la Nouvelle-
Novara, Novare, *f.*
Nubia, la Nubie, *f.*
Numantia, Numance, *f.*
Numidia, la Numidie, *f.*

Ocean, Océan, *m.*, Mer, *f.* *The Frozen* —, l'Océan Glacial, *m.*, la Mer Glaciale, *f.* *The German* or *Northern* —, la Mer d'Allemagne *or* du Nord. *The Indian* —, la Mer des Indes, *f.* *The* — *Sea*, la Mer Océane, *f.*
Oceania, l'Océanie, *f.*
Ohio, l'Ohio, *m.*
Oise (The), l'Oise, *f.*
Oldenburg, Oldenbourg, *m.*
Olympia, Olympie, *f.*
Olympus, l'Olympe, *m.*
Olynthus, Olynthe, *f.*
Orinoco, l'Orénoque, *m.*
Orkneys (The), les Orcades, *f.pl.*
Orleans, Orléans, *m.* *New* —, la Nouvelle-Orléans, *f.*
Osnaburg, Osnabruck, *m.*
Ostend, Ostende, *f.*
Ostia, Ostie, *f.*
Otaheite, Otahiti, Taïti, *m.*

Otranto, Otrante, *f.*
Oude, (*province*) l'Aoude, *m.*, (*town*) Aoude, *f.*
Oural. *V.* Ural

Pactolus, le Pactole, *m.*
Padua, Padoue, *f.*
Palermo, Palerme, *f.*
Palestine, la Palestine, *f.*
Palmyra, Palmyre, *f.*
Palus Mæotis (The), les Palus-Méotides, *m.pl.*
Pampeluna, Pampelune, *f.*
Pamphylia, la Pamphylie, *f.*
Pannonia, la Pannonie, *f.*
Papua, la Papouasie, *f.*
Paraguay, le Paraguay, *m.* — *tea*, thé du Paraguay, maté, *m.*
Paris, Paris, *m.* (*pronounced* [*Parree*)
Parma, Parme, *f.*
Parnassus, le Parnasse, *m.*
Parthia, la Parthie, *f.*
Patagonia, la Patagonie, *f.*
Pausilippo, le Pausilippe, *m.*
Pavia, Pavie, *f.*
Pelew Islands (The), les Iles Pelew *or* Palaos, *f.pl.*
Peloponnesus (The), le Péloponèse, le Péloponnèse, *m.*
Peneus (The), le Pénée, *m.*
Pennsylvania, la Pensylvanie, *f.* [game, *m.*
Pergamus, Pergamum, Per-
Perigord, le Périgord, *m.*
Pernambuco, Pernambouc, Fernambouc, *m.*
Persia, la Perse, *f.*
Peru, le Pérou, *m.*
Perugia, Pérouse, *f.*
Petersburg, Pétersbourg, *m.*
Phalsbourg, Phalsbourg, *m.*
Pharsalia, Pharsale, *f.*
Philadelphia, Philadelphie, *f.*
Philippi, Philippes, *f.*
Philippine Islands (The), les Iles Philippines, *f.pl.*
Philipsburg, Philippsbourg, *m.*
Phocis, la Phocide, *f.*
Phœnicia, la Phénicie, *f.*
Phrygia, la Phrygie, *f.*
Picardy, la Picardie, *f.*
Piedmont, le Piémont, *m.*
Pindus, le Pinde, *m.*
Piræus (The), le Pirée, *m.*
Pisa, Pise, *f.*
Pittsburg, Pittsbourg, *m.*
Placentia, Plaisance, *f.*; (*in Newfoundland*) Placentia, *f.*
Plate (The River), la Plata, Rio de la Plata, *m.*
Po (The), le Pô, *m.*
Podolia, la Podolie, *f.*
Poland, la Pologne, *f.*
Polynesia, la Polynésie, *f.*
Pomerania, la Poméranie, *f.*
Pompeii, Pompéi, Pompéies, *f.*
Pondicherry, Pondichéry, *m.*
Pontine Marshes (The), les Marais Pontins, *m.pl.*
Pontus, le Pont, *m.*
Portugal, le Portugal, *m.*
Potomac (The), le Potomac, *m.*
Presburg, Presbourg, *m.*
Propontis (The), la Propontide, *f.*
Provence, la Provence, *f.*
Prussia, la Prusse, *f.*
Pyrenean Mountains (The),
Pyrenees (The), les Pyrénées, *f.pl.*, les Monts Pyrénées, *m.pl.*

Quebec, Québec, *m.*

Ragusa, Raguse, *f.*
Rangoon, Rangoun, *m.*
Ratisbon, Ratisbonne, *f.*
Ravenna, Ravenne, *f.*
Rheims, Reims, Rheims, *m.*
Rhine (The), le Rhin, *m.* — *wine*, vin du Rhin, *m.*
Rhodes, Rhodes, *f.*
Rhone (The), le Rhône, *m.*
Romagna, la Romagne, *f.*
Rome, Rome, *f.* ,— *was not built in a day*, Paris ne s'est pas fait en un jour
Rosetta, Rosette, *f.*
Roumania, la Roumanie, *f.*
Roumelia, la Roumélie, *f.*
Rubicon (The), le Rubicon, *m.*
Russia, la Russie, *f.* *Asiatic* —, la Russie d'Asie. *European* —, la Russie d'Europe

Saguntum, Sagonte, *f.*
Saint Domingo, Saint-Domingue, *m.*
Saint Helena, Sainte-Hélène, *f.*
Saint Jago, Santiago, *m.*; (*in Spain*) Saint-Jacques (de Compostelle), *m.*
Saint Lawrence, Saint-Laurent, *m.*
Saint Lucia, Sainte-Lucie, *f.*
Saint Petersburg, Saint-Pétersbourg, *m.*
Salamanca, Salamanque, *f.*
Salamis, Salamine, *f.*
Salentum, Salente, *f.*
Salerno, Salernum, Salerne, *f.*
Salonica, Salonique, *f.*
Saluzzo, Saluces, *f.*
Salzburg, Salzbourg, *m.*
Samarcand, Samarkand, Samarcande, *f.*
Samaria, Samarie, *f.*
Santillana, Santillane, *f.*
Saone (The), la Saône, *f.*
Saragossa, Saragosse, *f.*
Sardinia, la Sardaigne, *f.*
Sardis, Sardes, *f.*
Sarmatia, la Sarmatie, *f.*
Savoy, la Savoie, *f.*
Saxony, la Saxe, *f.*
Scamander (The), le Scamandre, *m.*
Scandinavia, la Scandinavie, *f.*
Schaffhausen, Schaffouse, *f.*
Scheldt (The), l'Escaut, *m.*
Scilly Islands (The), les Iles Sorlingues, *f.pl.* [clavonie, *f.*
Sclavonia, la Sclavonie, l'Es-
Scotland, l'Écosse, *f.*
Scylla, Scylla, *m.*
Scythia, la Scythie, *f.*
Sea, Mer, *f.* *The Frozen* —, la Mer Glaciale. *The Irish* —, la Mer d'Irlande. *The North* —, la Mer du Nord. *The South* —, la Mer du Sud
Segovia, Ségovie, *f.*
Seine (The), la Seine, *f.*
Senegal, le Sénégal, *m.*
Senegambia, la Sénégambie, *f.*
Servia, la Servie, la Serbie, *f.*
Severn (The), la Saverne, la [Severn, *f.*
Seville, Séville, *f.*
Seychelles Islands (The), les Iles Seychelles, *f.pl.*
Shannon (The), le Shannon, *m.*
Sheba, Saba, *f.*
Siberia, la Sibérie, *f.*
Sicily, la Sicile, *f.*
Siena, Sienna, Sienne, *f.*
Silesia, la Silésie, *f.*
Silistria, Silistrie, *f.*
Siloa, Siloé, *f.*
Sinai, le Sinaï, *m.*
Sinde, (*province*) le Sindhy, *m.*, (*river*) le Sind, *m.*
Slave Coast (The), la Côte des Esclaves, *f.* [clave, *m.*
Slave Lake, le Lac de l'Es-
Slavonia, la Slavonie, *f.*
Sluys, l'Écluse, *f.*
Smyrna, Smyrne, *f.*
Society Islands (The), les Iles de la Société, *f.pl.*
Socotra, l'Ile Socotora, *f.*
Sodom, Sodome, *f.*
Soleure, Solothurn, Soleure, (*canton*) *m.*, (*town*) *f.*
Solway Frith (The), le Golfe de Solway, *m.*
Solyma, Solyme, Jérusalem, *f.*
Somme (The), la Somme, *f.*
Sound (The), le Sund, *m.*
Spain, l'Espagne, *f.*
Sparta, Sparte, *f.*
Spice Islands (The), les Iles aux Épices, les Moluques, *f.pl.*
Spitzbergen, le Spitzberg, *m.*
Sporades (The), les Sporades, [*f.pl.*
Spree (The), la Sprée, *f.*
Steenkirk, Steinkerque, *m.*
Strasburg, Strasbourg, *m.*
Styria, la Styrie, *f.*
Styx (The), le Styx, *m.*
Suabia, la Souabe, *f.*
Sunda Islands (The), les Iles de la Sonde, *f.pl.* [périeur, *m.*
Superior (Lake), le Lac Su-
Surat, Surate, *f.*
Susa, Suse, *f.*
Swabia. *V.* Suabia
Sweden, la Suède, *f.*
Switzerland, la Suisse, *f.*
Syracuse, Syracuse, *f.*
Syria, la Syrie, *f.*

Table Bay, la Baie de la Table, *f.* [le Mont de la Table, *m.*
Table Mount *or* **Mountain,**
Tagus (The), le Tage, *m.*
Tahiti, Taïti, Tahiti, *m.*
Tangier, Tanger, *m.* [*f.*
Taranto, Tarentum, Tarente,
Tarragona, Tarragone, *f.*
Tartarus, le Tartare, *m.*
Tartary, la Tartarie, *f.*
Tasmania, la Tasmanie, la Diéménie, *f.*
Taurida, Tauris, la Tauride, *f.*
Taurus (The), le Taurus, *m.*
Tempe (The vale of), la vallée de Tempé, *f.*
Terceira, Terceire, *f.*
Terra *or* **Tierra del Fuego,** la Terre de Feu, *f.*
Texas, le Texas, *m.*
Thames. *V. General Dictionary*
Thebes, Thèbes, *f.* [pyles, *f.pl.*
Thermopylæ, les Thermo-
Thessalonica, Thessalonique,
Thessaly, la Thessalie, *f.* [*f.*
Thibet, le Thibet, le Tibet, *m.*
Thrace, la Thrace, *f.* [govie, *f.*
Thurgau, Thurgovia, la Thur-
Thuringia, la Thuringe, *f.*
Tiber (The), le Tibre, *m.*
Tibet, le Tibet, le Thibet, *m.*
Ticino (The), le Tessin, *m.*

Tigris (The), le Tigre, *m.*
Timbuctoo, Tombouctou, *m.*
Tobago, Tabago, *m.*
Toledo, Tolède, *f.*
Tortona, Tortone, *f.*
Tortosa, Tortose, *f.*
Touraine, la Touraine, *f.*
Transcaucasia, la Transcaucasie, *f.*
Transylvania, la Transylvanie, *f.*
Trasimenus, Trasimène, *m.*
Trebia (The), la Trébie, *f.*
Trebizond, Trébizonde, *f.*
Trent, Trente, *f.*
Treves, Trèves, *f.*
Treviso, Trévise, *f.*
Triers, Trèves, *f.*
Trincomalee, Trincomale, *f.*
Trinidad, la Trinité, *f.*
Troas, la Troade, *f.*
Troy, Troie, *f.*
Turcomania, la Turcomanie, *f.*
Turkestan, le Turkestan, *m.*
Turkey, la Turquie, *f.* — *in Europe*, la Turquie d'Europe. — *in Asia*, la Turquie d'Asie.
Turkomania, la Turcomanie, *f.*
Turks' Islands, les Iles Turques, *f.pl.*
Tuscany, la Toscane, *f.*
Tweed (The), la Tweed, *f.*
Tyne (The), la Tyne, *f.*
Tyre, Tyr, *f.*
Tyrol (The), le Tyrol, *m.*

Ukraine (The), l'Ukraine, *f.*
Umbria, l'Ombrie, *f.*
United Kingdom (The), le Royaume-Uni, *m.*
United States (The), les États-Unis, *m.pl.*
Ural (The), l'Oural, *m.* *The — Mountains*, les Monts Ourals, *m.pl.*
Urbino, Urbin, *m.*
Uruguay, l'Uruguay, *m.*
Ushant, Ouessant, *m.*
Utica, Utique, *f.*

Valencia, Valence, *f.*
Valetta, la Valette, *f.*
Van Diemen's Land, la Terre de Van Diemen, la Diéménie, *f.*
Vendee, la Vendée, *f.*
Venetia, la Vénétie, *f.*
Venice, Venise, *f.*
Vercelli, Verceil, *m.*
Verd (Cape), le Cap Vert, *m.*
Verd-Islands (Cape), les Iles du Cap Vert, *f.pl.*
Vermilion Sea (The), la Mer Vermeille, *f.*
Verona, Vérone, *f.*
Vesuvius, le Vésuve, *m.*
Vicenza, Vicence, *f.*
Vienna, Vienne, *f.*
Virgin Islands (The), les Iles Vierges, *f.pl.*
Virginia, la Virginie, *f.*
Vistula (The), la Vistule, *f.*
Viterbo, Viterbe, *f.*
Vittoria, Vitoria, *f.*
Volga (The), le Volga, *m.*
Volhynia, la Volhynie, *f.*
Vosges (The), les Vosges, *f.pl.*

Wales, le Pays de Galles, *m.* (*Prince of* —, prince de Galles). *New South* —, la Nouvelle-Galles du Sud, *f.*
Wallachia, la Valachie, *f.*
Warsaw, Varsovie, *f.*
Waterloo, Waterloo, *m.*
Weser (The), le Weser, *m.*
Western Islands (The), les Hébrides, *f.pl.*
Westphalia, la Westphalie, *f.*
Wilna, Vilna, *f.*
Wolga. *V.* VOLGA
Wurtemberg, le Wurtemberg, *m.*
Wurzburg, Wurzbourg, *m.*

Xanthus (The), le Xanthe, *m.*
Xeres, Xérès, *f.*

Yucatan, le Yucatan, *m.*

Zealand, Zeeland, la Zélande, *f.* *New* —, la Nouvelle-Zélande, *f.*
Zollverein (The), le Zollverein, *m.*
Zuyder Zee (The), le Zuyderzée, *m.*

SUPPLEMENT.

(ENGLISH-FRENCH.)

A

Ablegate, *s.* ablégat, *m.* [porter en compte
Account, *v.n.* — *for,* (*com.*) tenir compte de,
Accountancy, *s. V.* **Accountantship**
Aconitia, Aconitine, *s.* aconitine, *f.*
Acreage, *s.* acres, *m.pl.*, nombre d'acres, *m.*
Actin-ic, -ism. *V.* page 3, § 1
Afghan, *s.adj.* Afghan, *m.*, e, *f.*, Afgan, *m.*, e, *f.*
Agonist, *s.* agoniste, *m.* [ventilation, *f.*
Air, *s* — **brick,** *s.* brique creuse, brique de
Aitch-bone, *s. V.* **Edge-bone**
All, *adj. That is* —, (*nothing else*) pas autre chose; (*I say no more*) je ne vous dis que cela. *To sell — at,* vendre le tout ensemble
Almond, *s.* — **nut,** *s.* massepain, *m.*
Altist, *s.* altiste, *m.*
Ammoniated, *adj.* ammoniacé
Andorran, *adj.* d'Andorre [ture, *f.*
Angostura *or* **Angustura bark,** *s.* angus-
Annuity, *s. Perpetual* —, rente constituée en perpétuel, *f.*
Antiliberal, *adj. s.* antilibéral, *m.*, e, *f.*
Aphis (*pl.* **Aphides**), *s.* aphis, puceron, *m.*
Argive, *s. adj.* Argien, *m.*, -ne, *f.*
Arm, *s. To order* —*s,* mettre l'arme au pied
Art, *s.* — **sale,** *s.* vente d'objets d'art, *f.*
Articles; (*of association*) statuts (d'une *or* de la société), *m.pl.*
Articulata, Articulates, *s.pl.* articulés, *m.pl.*
Arum, *s.* (*bot.*) arum, gouet, *m.*
Aspiration, *s.* rêve, *m.*; vœux, *m.pl.*; ambition, *f.*
Aspire, *v.n.* rêver; ambitionner (. . .)
Asymmetrical, *adj.* asymétrique
Asymmetry, *s.* asymétrie, *f.*
Aunt Sally, *s.* (*game*) âne salé, *m.*
Aunty, *s.* tatan, *f.*
Axolotl, *s.* (*zool.*) axolotl, *m.*

B

Baleen, *s.* baleine, *f.*
Banxring, *s.* (*zool.*) tupaïa, tupaya, *m.*
Barrowful, Barrowload, *s.* brouettée, *f.*
Bat, *s.* — *and trap,* *s.* balle à la volée, *f.*
Bear, *v.a. I can't — him,* je ne peux pas le sentir
Beggar, *v.a. To — all description,* être impossible à décrire, être indescriptible
Begonia, *s.* bégonia, *m.*, bégone, *f.*
Beheading, *s.*; (*of St. John the Baptist*) dé-
Belligerence, *s.* belligérance, *f.* [collation, *f.*
Best, *adj.* — *man,* (*at weddings*) garçon d'honneur, *m.* [(*betters*) parieurs, *m.pl.*
Betting, *s.* — **ring,** *s.* enceinte des paris, *f.*;
Biblic-ism, -ist. *V.* page 3, § 1
Bicentenary, *adj.* de deux siècles; — *s.* deuxième centenaire, *m.*
Bicyclist, *s.* bicycliste, *m.*
Bind, *s.* (*mus.*) *V.* **Tie** [pas manquer de
Bind, *v.a. To be bound to,* (*of things*) ne pouvoir
Binturong, *s.* (*zool.*) benturong, *m.*
Bloke, *s.* (*slang*) individu, particulier, *m.*
Blood, *s.* — **orange,** *s.* orange sanguine, *f.*
Blow-hole, *s.* ventilateur, *m.*
Bombastes, *s.* le capitaine Fracasse, *m.*
Book, *s. To know o.'s* —, être malin. — **packet,** *s.* (*post.*) imprimé, *m.*
Boomerang, *s.* bommerang, *m.*
Bottle, *s.* — **drainer,** *s.* égouttoir à bouteilles, *m.*
Bottom-fishing, *s. V.* **Ground-angling**
Brillantine, Brilliantine, *s.* brillantine, *f.*
Broom-handle, *s. V.* **Broom-stick**
Brush, *s.* — **tray,** *s.* boîte à brosses, *f.*
Buffer, *s.* — **stop,** *s.* (*rail.*) buttoir, *m.*

C

Cadge, *v.n.* bricoler, mendier
Calumba, *s.* colombo, *m.*
Calving, *s.* vêlage, vêlement, *m.*
Cane, *s.* (*for the ribs of an umbrella,* &c.) jonc, *m.*
Care, *s.* — **taker,** *s.* gardien, surveillant, *m.*
Carte de visite, *s.* carte de visite, *f.*
Case, *s.*; (*story*) histoire, *f.*; (*trial, pleadings,* &c.) débats, *m.pl. That is my* —, c'est mon fait, je suis dans ce cas-là
Catch, *s. The miraculous — of fishes,* la pêche miraculeuse, *f. It is no* — (or *no great* —), ce n'est pas le diable, cela n'est pas bien malin
Chair, *s.* — **caner,** *s.* canneur, (*m.*, -euse, *f.*) de chaises. — **screen,** *s.* écran de chaise, dossier, *m.* [*f.*; coulisse, *f.*
Change, *s. After-hours 'Change,* petite Bourse,
Chanticleer, *s.* Chanteclair, *m.* [gratis
Charge, *s. Free of* —, sans rien avoir à payer,
Chauvinism, *s.* chauvinisme, *m.*
Chauvinist, *s.* chauviniste, chauvin, *m.*
Chauvinistic, *adj.* chauvinique
Chromatrope, *s.* chromatrope, *m.*
Church, *s. As poor as a — mouse,* gueux comme
Clam, *s.* clovisse, *f.* [un rat d'église
Classically, *adv.* classiquement
Clean, *adj. To wash* —, *V.* **Wash** (*in this Suppl.*)
Clothes-airer, *s.* séchoir, *m.*
Cloture, Closure, *s.* (*parliam.*) clôture, *f.*
Cloud, *v.a.* (*fig.*) voiler
Coal, *s.* — **smoke,** *s.* fumée de charbon, *f.*
Cockrel, *s. V.* **Cockerel**
Collectiveness, *s.* collectivité, *f.*
Colorado-beetle, *s.* colorado, doryphore, *m.*
Columbo, *s.* colombo, *m.*
Comeatable, *adj.* accessible, abordable
Command, *s. To keep under* —, se faire obéir de
Compass-plant, *s.* silphion (à feuilles dé-
Contribute, *v.n.* collaborer (à) [coupées), *m.*
Contribution, *s.* collaboration, *f.*
Copper, *s. The hot* —*s,* le gosier sec, soif
Counter-claim, *s.* (*law*) demande reconventionnelle, *f.*
Country, *s.* — **fed,** *adj.* nourri à la campagne
Covering party, *s.* (*mil.*) corps de réserve, *m.*, réserve, *f.*; (*nav.*) réserve, *f.*
Cowage, Cowhage, Cowitch, *s.* mucuna, *m.*
Cradle, *s.* (*tree-guard*) armure (d'arbre), *f.*
Credit, *s. To take — for,* se faire un honneur *or* un mérite de, se donner les gants de
Cretonne, *s.* cretonne, *f.*
Cross, *adj. As — as two sticks,* d'une humeur de chien, comme un crin
Crown artichoke, *s.* artichaut, *m.*
Crucially, *adv.* en croix; (*fig.*) sérieusement,

gravement, principalement, excessivement; cruellement, atrocement; (*with the crucible*) à l'aide du creuset
Cucurbitaceæ, *s. pl.* cucurbitacées, *f. pl.*
Cudgel, *v.a. To — or rack o.'s brains, V.* **Brain**
Cut. *To — and thrust,* frapper d'estoc et de taille

D

Dandy-brush, *s.* brosse (à cheval) en chiendent, brosse de pansage, *f.*
Date, *s.* — **rack,** *s. V.* — **case**
Debt, *s. He has run away in my —, in everybody's —,* il a décampé sans me payer, sans payer personne
Deer-shot, *s. V.* **Buck-shot**
Deforest, &c. *V.* **Disafforest,** &c.
Desperate, *adj. — diseases require — remedies,* aux grands maux les grands remèdes
Dick Turpin, *s. V.* **Jack Sheppard**
Dictionary, *s.* —**maker,** *s.* dictionnariste, *m.f.*
Dispersal, *s. V.* **Dispersion**
District, *s.* — **school,** *s.* école communale, *f.*
Do, *v.n.* (*to last*) durer. *That will —,* c'est assez! assez comme ça!
Do, Did, &c. [*untranslated*] Ex.: *You know that as well as I do,* vous savez cela aussi bien que moi
Double, *adj.* — **fronted,** *adj.* (*of houses*) à deux façades
Down, *int. — with you!* descendez! descends!
Drag, *s.* (*hook*) croc, harpon, *m.*, gaffe, *f.*
Drain, *s.* — **trap,** *s. V.* **Stench-trap**
Draught, *s. The miraculous — of fishes,* la pêche miraculeuse, *f.*
Drawing, *s.* — **school,** *s.* école de dessin, *f.*
Drug, *s.* médicament, *m.*
Duffing, *adj.* faux
Dutch clock, *s.* coucou, *m.*

E

Edge, *s.* (*of two planes*) arête, *f.*
Electrograph, *s.* électrographe, *m.*
Encash, *v.a.* encaisser
Engage, *v.a.* (*workmen*) embaucher
Enough, *adv. — is as good as a feast,* trop est trop, rien de trop
Ensile, *v.a.* ensiler
Ensiler, *s.* ensileur, *m.*
Ephemeris (*pl.* **Ephemerides**), *s.* éphéméride, *f.*
Eucalyptus, *s.* eucalypte, *m.*
Evangelicalism, *s.* évangélisme, *m.*
Evangelistic, *adj.* évangéliste
Evangelizer, *s.* évangélisateur, *m.*
Evolutionist, *s.* évolutioniste, *m.f.*
Ewe, *s.* — **teg,** *s.* antenoise, *f.*
Extradit, *v.a.* extrader
Eye, *s. Before my —s,* devant moi

F

Fag, *v.a.* (*in schools*) brimer
Fagging, *s.* (*in schools*) brimade, *f.*
Fall, *v.n.* — **out,** (*mil.*) quitter les rangs
Fever, *s.* — **stricken,** *adj.* atteint de la fièvre, fiévreux, fébricitant
Fiction, *s. Work of —,* ouvrage d'imagination, *m.*
Fire, *s.* — **hose,** *s.* tuyau de pompe à incendie, *m.* — **implements,** *s. pl. V.* — **irons**
Fish, *s.* — **commissioner,** *s.* commissionnaire à la marée, *m.*
Fiver, *s.* billet de banque de cinq livres (sterling), *m.*
Floe, *s.* banquise flottante, *f.*
Flower-pot cover, *s.* cache-pot, *m.*
Flush lock, *s.* serrure entaillée *or* encastrée, *f.*
Foot, *s.* — **run,** *s.* pied courant, *m.*
Footer, *s.* (*swimming*) colonne, *f.*
Form, *s.* (*to fill up*) feuille imprimée, *f.*; (*law*) modèle d'acte, *m.*
Frame, *s.* (*of a chair, couch, &c.*) bois, squelette, *m.*
Fret, *v.a.* (*cut away*) découper. — **cutter,** *s.* découpeur, *m.*, -euse, *f.* — **work,** *s.* découpure, *f.*; (*of pianos*) panneau découpé, *m.*
French, *adj. The — capital,* la capitale de la France
Friend, *s. — Smith,* l'ami Smith
Frighten, *v.a. To be more —ed than hurt,* avoir plus de peur que de mal
Frog, *s.* — **spittle,** *s.* crachat de grenouille, *m.*, écume printanière, *f.*
Fruit, *s.* — **gatherer,** *s.* (*thing*) cueille-fruits, *m.*
Full, *adj. My hands are —,* j'ai les mains pleines ('*of,*' de); (*occupied*) j'ai les mains prises
Funny bone, *s.* nerf cubital, *m.*
Futilely, *adv.* futilement

G

Gadroon, *s. V.* **Godroon**
Gaff, *s. Penny —,* musico, *m.*
Garden, *s.* — **produce,** *s. V.* — **stuff**
Geodetic, *adj.* géodésique
Germanization, *s.* germanisation, *f.*
Gift, *s. At a —,* pour rien
Globe artichoke, *s.* artichaut, *m.*
Gone, *part. adj. Dead and —,* mort et enterré
Goodness, *s. All the — of* (*a thing*), tout ce qu'il y a de bon dans (une chose)
Goose, *s. The — with the golden eggs,* la poule aux œufs d'or
Grandaddy, *s.* bon papa, *m.*
Grandiloquently, *adv.* pompeusement, avec emphase
Grandiose, *adj.* grandiose
Ground, *s. To feel the —,* tâter le terrain
Growy, *adj.* (*of wheat*) humide
Guard, *s.* (*for trees*) armure, *f.*

H

Hair, *s. To take a — of the dog that bit you,* reprendre du poil de la bête
Hand, *adj.* (*by hand*) à la main. — **sewed, -sewn,** *adj.* cousu à la main. — *s.* main, *f.* *To force the — of* (or . . .'s —), forcer la main à
Handiness, *s.* maniabilité, *f.*
Handle, *s.* (*title*) titre, *m.*
Hard, *adv. It will go — with him,* il en souffrira
Head, *s. To eat o.'s — off,* (*earn nothing*) ne gagner rien; (*bring in nothing*) ne rapporter rien. — **nurse,** *s.* première bonne d'enfant, *f.*
High-class, *adj. High-class wine,* grand vin, vin fin, *m.*
High-handed, *adj.* oppressif; violent; arbitraire; à poigne
Home, *Go —!* (*to a dog*) allez coucher!
Honey, *s. — of roses,* miel rosat, *m.*
Horse, *s.* — **brush,** *s.* brosse (à cheval) en crin, limande, *f.*
Horsy, *adj.* de cheval; grossier
House, *adj.,* **Household,** *adj.* (*royal*) de la maison du roi *or* de la reine. — **hold troops,** *s. pl.* gardes du corps, *m. pl.*
Hurt, *v.n.* (*be hurt*) arriver (*imp.*) du mal à (...); (*suffer from it*) en souffrir; (*lose by it*) y perdre; (*be badly off*) être malheureux; — *v.a. He cries before he is —,* il crie avant qu'on l'écorche
Hydrotherapy, &c., hydrothérapie, *s.f.*, &c.

I

Impression, *s. To be under the —,* avoir quelque idée, penser
Increase, *v.n. To — and multiply,* croître et multiplier
Inner circle railway, *s.* chemin de fer de ceinture intérieur, *m.*
Intoxicant, *s.* substance (*or* boisson) enivrante, *f.*

K

Kerbing, *s.* bordage (de trottoir), *m.*
Kilt, *v.a.* plisser
Kilting, *s.* (*act of plaiting*) plissement, plissage, *m.*; (*plaits*) plissé, *m.* [ad patres
Kingdom, *s.* *To — come,* dans l'autre monde,
Knife, *v.a.* (*slang*) suriner
Knob, *s.* (*of a walking-stick*) pomme, *f.*
Know, *v.a.n.* *He —s better than that (would not dare do it),* il n'oserait pas

L

Lack-lustre, *adj.* terne, vitreux
Lake, *s.* **— poet,** *s.* (*Engl. liter.*) lakiste, *m.*
Lamented, *part. adj.* *The late — A. B.,* le regretté A. B.
Land, *s.* (*piece of ground*) terrain, *m.*
Lath, *s.* (*of a wooden bedstead*) goberge, *f.*; (*of an iron bedstead*) feuillard, *m.*
Lay, *v.a.* (*the fire,* &c.) préparer
Lead, *s.* (*guidance,* &c.); (*for dogs*) laisse, *f.*
Leap, *s.* *A — in the dark,* une action risquée. *To take a — in the dark,* se risquer, s'aventurer, agir en aveugle [reste plus que six
Left, *part.* *I have only six of them —,* il ne m'en
Leg, *s.* *To be carried off o.'s —s,* perdre pied
Lens, *s.* (*of the eye*) cristallin, *m.* [posable
Leviable, *adj.* percevable; perceptible; im-
Liberty, *s.* *This is — hall,* c'est ici le palais de
Life-boat man, *s.* sauveteur, *m.* [la Liberté
Light, *s.* *To see the —, (be born)* voir le jour
Linen, *s.* **— airer,** *s.* séchoir, *m.*
Lines, *s.pl.*; (*lot*) sort, *m.*
Lithia, *s.* lithine, *f.*
Love, *s.* *There is no — lost between them,* ils ne s'aiment pas de reste [commissionnaire, *m.*
Luggage, *s.* **— porter,** *s.* porteur de bagages,
Lush, *s.* boisson, *f.*, rogomme, *m.*
Lushy, *adj.* adonné à la boisson

M

Madegasy, Madegassy, Malagash, Malagasy, *s. adj.* Malgache, *m.f.*
Malconformation, *s.* *V.* **Malformation**
Man, *s.* *Best —, V.* **Best** *in this Suppl.* *Fine —,* bel homme, *m.* *Handsome —,* beau garçon, *m.*
Manageableness, *s.* maniabilité, *f.*
Mark, *s.* (*German coin*) marc, mark, *m.*
Marrying man, *s.* épouseur, *m.*
Match-board, *s.* pièces de bois rainées (*or* assemblées à rainure), *f. pl.*
Match-boarding, *s.* (*wood*) *V.* **Match-board** (*above*); (*work*) assemblage à rainure, *m.*
Matter, *s.* *What is the — with your finger?* qu'est-ce que vous avez au doigt?
Mayoral, *adj.* de *or* du maire, des maires
Meat, *s.* *One man's — is another man's poison,* (*Proverb*) ce qui guérit l'un tue l'autre
Medico-legal, *adj.* médico-légal
Medium, *s.* (*for colours*) véhicule, *m.*
Melodramatize, *v.a.* mélodramatiser
Menu, *s.* menu, *m.*
Mercuriferous, *adj.* mercurifère
Microphone, *s.* microphone, *m.*
Milk, *s.* **— roll,** *s.* petit pain au lait, *m.*
Milking, *s.* traite, *f.*
Monkey, *s.* **— puzzle,** *s.* (*bot.*) araucaria (imbricata), pehuen, pin du Chili, *m.*
Momot, Motmot, *s.* (*bird*) momot, *m.*
Mounting, *s.* *— of a* (or *the*) *play* (or *piece*), mise en scène, *f.*
Much, *adv.* (*long*) longtemps. *Too —, (too dear)* trop cher. *Very —,* énormément
Muck, *s.* (*trash*) drogue, camelote, *f.* [Crac, *m.*
Munchausen (Baron), *s.* Monsieur de
Must, *v.n.* *You — have been ten years old at that time,* vous deviez avoir dix ans à cette époque. *It — have been ten o'clock,* il devait être dix heures

N

Nail, *s.* *To pay on the —,* payer comptant
Name, *s.* *There is no — for that,* cela n'a pas de nom [Nazianze, *m.*
Nazianzene. *Gregory —,* Saint Grégoire de
Neck, *s.* (*of teeth*) collet, col, *m.*
Neptune, *s.* Neptune, *m.*
New-Caledonian, *s. adj.* Canaque, *m.f.*
Nix, *int.* nisco!
Nomadism, *s.* nomadisme, *m.*
Nomadize, *v.a.* nomadiser
Nose, *s.* *To hold o.'s —,* se boucher le nez

O

Oddment, *s.* (*com.*) article dépareillé, *m.*
On, *prep.* (*with*) avec. *He has retired — an income of £1,000,* il s'est retiré avec 25,000 francs de rente [l'agréable
Ornamental. *The useful and the —,* l'utile et
Orthophon-ic, al, -ically, -y. *V.* p. 3, § 1
Otalgia, *s.* otalgie, *f.*
Otitis, *s.* otite, *f.*
Own. *O.'s —, (o.'s property)* son bien, *m.*

P

Pain, *s.* *To put in —, to give — to,* faire souffrir
Paper, *s.* (*of exam.:*) (*set of questions*) questions *f.pl.*, (*answers*) copie, *f.*, copies, *f.pl.*
Pass, *v.a.* (*void*) évacuer, rendre
Past, *prep.* *— work,* hors d'état de travailler; hors de service
Pay, *v.a.n.* *It* or *that does not —, (in a general way)* cela ne fait pas les affaires. *This Dictionary will never — me,* ce Dictionnaire ne me rapportera jamais rien
Phalarope, *s.* phalarope, *m.*
Phonoscope, *s.* phonoscope, *m.*
Phonoscop-ic, al, -ically, -y. *V.* p. 3, § 1
Photoengraving, *s.* photogravure, *f.*
Phylloxera, *s.* phylloxéra, *m.*
Phylloxerated, *adj.* phylloxéré
Piccalilli, *s.* achars, *m.pl.*
Pie, *s.* *Raised —,* pâté en croûte, *m.*
Pieces, *s. pl.* (*butch.*) débris, *m.pl.*, rognures, *f.pl.*
Pigeon, *s.* **— shooting,** *s.* tir aux pigeons, *m.*
Pin, *s.* *—s and needles (in the legs),* picotements (dans les jambes), *m.pl.*
Pipe, *s.* **— cleaner,** *s.* (*for tobacco pipes*) ramoneur, débourre-pipe, *m.*
Plate, *s.* (*of a mirror*) glace, *f.* *— glass insurance company,* compagnie d'assurance contre le bris des glaces, *f.*
Police, *s.* **— force,** *s.* corps de police, *m.*
Politician, *s.* politicien, *m.*
Pollux, *s.* (*myth., astr.*) Pollux, *m.*
Polony, *s.* saucisson, *m.*
Polyanthus, *s.* primevère cultivée, *f.*
Post, *s.* *— office savings banks,* caisses postales d'épargne, *f.pl.*
Pot, *s.* **— cover, -screen,** *s.* cache-pot, *m.*
Pot off, *v.a.* dépoter
Pre-Raphaelism, *s.* préraphaélisme, *m.*
Pre-Raphaelite, *adj. s.* préraphaélite, *m.f.*
Preventative. *V.* **Preventive**

Prick, *s.* *To kick against the —s,* regimber contre l'éperon (*or* contre l'aiguillon)
Prison, *s.* **— breaking,** *s.* bris de prison, *m.*
Prompt, *adv.* (*of the hour*) *V.* **Sharp,** *adv.*
Proper, *adj.* (*properly so called*) proprement dit
Pyelitis, *s.* (*med.*) pyélite, *f.*

Q

Quarter-bottle, *s.* (*of wine*) carafon, *m.*

R

Rabbit, *s.* *Tame —,* lapin de clapier, lapin de choux, *m.* *Wild —,* lapin sauvage, lapin de garenne, *m.* [**Riot,** *v.n.*
Rampage, *v.n.s.* *To —, to go on the —, V.*
Reading, *s.* **— glass,** *s.* loupe à lire, *f.*
Reafforest,&c. *V.* **Reforest,** &c. (*in this Suppl.*)
Real, *adj.* *The — truth,* la vérité vraie
Recuperative, *adj.* récupératif
Refoot, *v.a.* (*stockings*) rempiéter
Reforest, *v.a.* reboiser [ment, *m.*
Reforestation, Reforesting, *s.* reboise-
Regimentals, *s. pl.* *In full —,* en grande tenue
Registered, *part. adj.* *— trade mark,* marque déposée, *f.*
Rejapan, *v.a.* relaquer, revernisser, revernir
Renumber, *v.a.* (*a street*) numéroter de nouveau, renuméroter
Reserve-man, Reservist, *s.* réserviste, *m.*
Repairing lease, *s.* bail où le locataire se
Repp. *V.* **Rep** [charge des réparations, *m.*
Resole, *v.a.* *V.* **New-sole**
Revarnish, *v.a.* revernir, revernisser
Rising, *s.* *By — and sitting,* (*of voting*) par
Rob, *s.* rob, *m.* [assis et levé
Roller, *s.* **— moth,** *s.* tordeuse, *f.* **— skate,** *s.* patin à roulettes, *m.*
Rule, *s.* *— of thumb,* routine, *f.* *To lay out by — and line,* tirer au cordeau
Running day, *s.* (*nav.*) jour de planche, *m.*

S

Sand, *s.* **— skipper,** *s.* gammare, *m.*
Saying, *s.* *—s and doings,* dits et faits, *m.pl.*
Scalp-wound, *s.* blessure à la tête, *f.*
Scholar, *s.* *Hindustani —,* hindoustaniste, *m.*
Screw, *s.* **— eye, -ring,** *s.* piton, *m.*
Seascape, *s.* marine, *f.*
Shadow, *s.* **— figure,** *s.* silhouette, *f.*
Sharp, *adj.* (*of blows*) bien appliqué, sec
Shooting, *s.* (*spouts*) gouttières, *f.pl.*
Short, *adv.* (*of drinking*) sec
Signify, *v.n.* *Nothing* (or *Not*) *to —,* rien de bien important, un rien, une bagatelle, peu de chose, pas grand' chose
Side, *s.* **— piece,** *s.* (*of a ladder*) montant, *m.*
Silo, *s.* silo, *m.*
Skeleton, *s.* **— clock,** *s.* pendule squelette, *f.*
Slipper, *s.* **— wort,** *s.* (*bot.*) calcéolaire, *f.*
Slushy, *adj.* boueux, fangeux, bourbeux
Small, *adj.* *In the — hours* (*of the morning*), (le matin) de très bonne heure
Snow, *s.* **— bound,** *adj.* retenu (*or* bloqué) par la neige
Solan goose, *s.* *V.* **Gannet**
Something, *s.* *There is — in that,* cela n'est pas mal vu; c'est assez vrai
Sort, *s.* *He is not a bad — (of man),* c'est une bonne pâte d'homme
Sough, *v.n.* bruire, murmurer, susurrer
Soughing, *s.* bruissement, murmure, susurrement, *m.*, susurration, *f.*
Spile, *s.* broche de bois, *f.*; (*of casks*) fausset, *m.*
Stack-pipe, *s.* tuyau de descente, tuyau de chute, *m.*
Stanchness, *s.* solidité, *f.*; fermeté, *f.*; zèle, *m.*
Start, *v.a.* (*a work*) mettre en train
Steen, Stein, *v.a.* (*arch.*) maçonner
Stiff, *adj.* (*fatigued*) courbaturé
Stiffness, *s.* (*fatigue*) courbature, *f.*
Straw, *s.* **— fire,** *s.* feu de paille, *m.*
String, *s.* **— band,** *s.* orchestre (*m.*) *or* musique (*f.*) d'instruments à cordes
Stuffy, *adj.* *V.* **Fusty**
Stupid, *adj.* *— ass,* âne bâté, *m.*
Stylograph, *s.* stylographe, *m.*
Suavely, *adv.* suavement
Succession, *s.* *In close —,* coup sur coup
Suck, *v.a.* *To — the monkey,* buffeter
Sue, *v.n.* *To — for a separation,* plaider en séparation
Sufficiency, *s.* (*pharm.*) quantité suffisante, *f.*
Sugar, *s.* **— peas,** *s. pl.* pois goulus, mange-tout, *m.pl.* [faire autant
Suit, *s.* *To follow —,* (*fig.*) faire de même, en
Supper, *s.* *The last —,* (*rel.*) la Cène, *f.*
Suppressed, *part. adj.* (*med.*) (*of a usual evacuation*) supprimé
Swallow, *s.* *One — does not make a summer,* (*Proverb*) une hirondelle ne fait pas le prin-
Syllabus, *s.* (*eccl.*) syllabus, *m.* [temps

T

Tangent, *s.* *To fly off at a —,* s'échapper par la tangente
Tantamount, *adj.* *This is — to saying . . .,* cela revient à dire . . .
Tapestry, *s.* **— carpet,** *s.* tapis bouclé, *m.*
Taste, *s.* *In good* or *bad —,* de bon *or* de mauvais goût
Telephone, *s.* téléphone, *m.*; — *v.a.* téléphoner
Telephonic, *adj.* téléphonique
Telephony, *s.* téléphonie, *f.*
Then, *adv.* *Before —,* avant; (*between this and then*) d'ici là [castrée, *f.*
Till, *s.* **— lock,** *s.* serrure entaillée *or* en-
Toilet, *s.* **— set, — ware,** *s.* garniture de
Torrential, *adj.* torrentiel [toilette, *f.*
Toughened glass, *s.* verre trempé, verre incassable, *m.*
Towel, *s.* *Oaken —,* huile de cotret, *f.*
Tram, *s.* tram, tramway, *m.* **— car,** *s.* voiture de tramway, *f.*
Tray, *s.* (*of a dressing-table, washstand,* &c.) retour, *m.* **— top,** *adj.* à retour
Tree, *s.* **— fence, -guard,** *s.* armure d'arbre, *f.*
Tribal, *adj.* tribal

U

Undecennial, *adj.* undécennal
Unfiltered, *adj.* non filtré [jusqu'en 1889
Until, *prep.* (*before a date*) jusqu'en. — 1889,
Unrefuted, *adj.* irréfuté
Up, *adv.* *— with you!* montez! monte!
Upholster, *v.a.* tapisser
Upper leather. *V.* **Leather**
Upset, *part. adj.* *— price,* mise à prix, *f.*

W

Walking exercise, *s.* marche, *f.*; promenade, *f.*
Wash, *v.a.* *To — clean,* bien laver, bien nettoyer; (*linen*) bien blanchir
Well, *s.* (*of a work-table*) vide-poches, *m.*

Wether, *s.* **— lamb,** *s.* agneau, *m.* **— teg,** *s.* antenois, *m.*
What, *pron. rel. adj.* *That's — it is,* voilà ce que c'est
Where, *adv.* *That's — it is,* voilà la chose, voilà ce que c'est
Whose, *pron. rel.* *The man — conscience pricks him,* l'homme que sa conscience tourmente
Will-nill, Willy-nilly, *adv.* bon gré mal gré
Wind, *s.* *In the —,* au vent
Wire, *s.* *Telegraphic —,* fil télégraphique, *m.* **— sieve,** *s.* tamis en toile métallique, *m.*
Working, *adj.* *To be in good — order,* fonctionner (*or* aller) bien
Write, *v.a.* **— off,** *v.a.* déduire, défalquer, retrancher, (*debts*) passer à profits et pertes

Y

Year, *s.* *The last —,* la dernière année
Yearling, *s.* antenois, *m.*, e, *f.*
Yokel, *s.* *V.* **Bumpkin**

Z

Zulu, *s. adj.* Zoulou, *m.*, e, *f.*